MOTOR
AUTO REPAIR MANUAL

47th Edition
First Printing

Michael J. Kromida, SAE
Editor

Warren Schildknecht, SAE
Managing Editor

Dan Irizarry, SAE
Senior Editor

Michael E. Pallien, SAE • Mark E. Flynn, SAE
Associate Editors

Daniel E. Doku • Patrick Peyton, SAE • Robert R. Savasta
Denver Steele • John R. Lypen • James M. Garripoli • John E. DeGroat
Assistant Editors

Rose-Ellen Lorber-Termaat
Production Editor

Loretta Lettner
Editorial Assistant

Published by
M O T O R

Hearst Books/Business Publishing Group,
A Division of The Hearst Corp.

Frank A. Bennack, Jr.
President

Gordon L. Jones
Vice President,
Hearst Books/Business
Publishing Group

Philip D. Shalala
General Manager,
Motor Group

Louis C. Forier, SAE
Editorial Director
Motor Publications

555 West 57th St., New York, N.Y. 10019

Printed in the U.S.A. © Copyright 1983 by The Hearst Corporation

ISBN 0-87851-570-4

DECIMAL & MILLIMETER EQUIVALENTS

INCH	INCH	MM
1/64	.015625	.397
1/32	.03125	.794
3/64	.046875	1.191
1/16	.0625	1.587
5/64	.078125	1.984
3/32	.09375	2.381
7/64	.109375	2.778
1/8	.125	3.175
9/64	.140625	3.572
5/32	.15625	3.969
11/64	.171875	4.366
3/16	.1875	4.762
13/64	.203125	5.159
7/32	.21875	5.556
15/64	.234375	5.953
1/4	.25	6.350
17/64	.265625	6.747
9/32	.28125	7.144
19/64	.296875	7.541
5/16	.3125	7.937
21/64	.328125	8.334
11/32	.34375	8.731

INCH	INCH	MM
23/64	.359375	9.128
3/8	.375	9.525
25/64	.390625	9.922
13/32	.40625	10.319
27/64	.421875	10.716
7/16	.4375	11.113
29/64	.453125	11.509
15/32	.46875	11.906
31/64	.484375	12.303
1/2	.5	12.700
33/64	.515625	13.097
17/32	.53125	13.494
35/64	.546875	13.890
9/16	.5625	14.287
37/64	.578125	14.684
19/32	.59375	15.081
39/64	.609375	15.478
5/8	.625	15.875
41/64	.640625	16.272
21/32	.65625	16.669
43/64	.671875	17.065

INCH	INCH	MM
11/16	.6875	17.462
45/64	.703125	17.859
23/32	.71875	18.265
47/64	.734375	18.653
3/4	.75	19.050
49/64	.765625	19.447
25/32	.78125	19.884
51/64	.796875	20.240
13/16	.8125	20.637
53/64	.828125	21.034
27/32	.84375	21.431
55/64	.859375	21.828
7/8	.875	22.225
57/64	.890625	22.622
29/32	.90625	23.019
59/64	.921875	23.415
15/16	.9375	23.812
61/64	.953125	24.209
31/32	.96875	24.606
63/64	.984375	25.003
1		25.400

Special Service Tools

Throughout this manual references are made and illustrations may depict the use of special tools required to perform certain jobs. These special tools can generally be ordered through the dealers of the make vehicle being serviced. It is also suggested that you check with local automotive supply firms as they also supply tools manufactured by other firms that will assist in the performance of these jobs. The vehicle manufacturers special tools are supplied by:

American Motors & General Motors . . . . Kent-Moore Tool Division
29784 Little Mack
Roseville, Michigan 48066

Chrysler Corp. . . . . Miller Special Tools
A Division of Utica Tool Co.
32615 Park Lane
Garden City, Michigan 48135

Ford Motor Co. . . . . Owatonna Tool Company
Owatonna, Minnesota 55060

INDEX

This Edition Covers Mechanical Specifications and Service Procedures on 1977–84 Models available at time of publication.

———— TROUBLE SHOOTING & AUTO CARE GUIDE SECTION—1 ————

———————— CAR INFORMATION SECTION—2* ————————

*For your convenience in locating this section, a black bar has been positioned beneath all odd page numbers.

———— GENERAL SERVICE INFORMATION SECTION—3 ————

TROUBLE SHOOTING

TABLE OF CONTENTS

Introduction

STARTING A STALLED ENGINE

When an engine fails to start the chances are that 90 per cent of the cases will involve the ignition system and seldom the fuel system or other miscellaneous reasons. If a systematic procedure is followed the trouble can almost always be found without the use of special equipment.

To begin with, turn on the ignition switch and if the ammeter shows a slight discharge (or if the telltale lamp lights) it indicates that current is flowing. A glance at the gas gauge will indicate whether or not there is fuel in the tank.

Operate the starter and if the engine turns over freely, both the battery and starter are functioning properly. On the other hand, if the starter action is sluggish it may be due to a discharged or defective battery, loose, corroded or dirty battery terminals, mechanical failure in the starter, starter switch or starter drive. If the starter circuit is okay, skip this phase of the discussion and proceed to ignition.

Starter Circuit Checkout

To determine which part of the starter circuit is at fault, turn on the light switch and again operate the starter. Should the lights go out or become dim, the trouble is either in the battery, its connections or cables. A hydrometer test of the battery should indicate better than 1.250 specific gravity, while a voltmeter, placed across the positive and negative posts, should indicate about 12 volts. If either of these tests prove okay, clean and tighten the battery connections and cable terminals or replace any cable which seems doubtful.

If the lights remain bright when the starter is operated, the trouble is between the battery and the starter, or the starter switch is at fault, since it is evident that there is no electrical connection between these points. If these connections are clean and tight, it is safe to assume that the starter or starter switch is defective.

Neutral Safety Switch

If the ammeter shows a slight discharge (or if the telltale lamp lights) when the ignition is turned on, but the system goes dead when the starting circuit is closed, the neutral safety switch may be at fault. To check, bypass the switch with a suitable jumper. If the engine now starts, adjust or replace the switch.

CAUTION: With the safety switch by-passed, the car can be started in any gear. *Be sure the transmission is in neutral or park and the parking brake is applied.*

Primary Ignition Checkout

NOTE: For troubleshooting of electronic ignition systems, refer to Electronic Ignition section.

Let's assume that the battery and starter are doing their job, and that fuel is reaching the carburetor, but the car does not start, then the trouble must be somewhere in the ignition circuit. But first, before starting your diagnosis, it is advisable to give the whole system a

visual inspection which might uncover obvious things such as broken or disconnected wires etc.

The best way to start tracing down ignition troubles is to begin with the primary circuit since this is where troubles show up most frequently. First remove the distributor cap and block the points open with a piece of cardboard, then turn on the ignition and with a test bulb or voltmeter check to see if there is current at the terminal on the distributor. If you do not get a reading at this point, the current is cut off somewhere in the connections leading back to the ignition switch or it may be that the condenser has an internal short to the ground. The latter possibility can be eliminated if you can restore current at the distributor terminal by disconnecting the condenser from the distributor plate so that its outside shell is not grounded. With the possibility of a bad condenser out of the way, work toward the ignition switch and test for current at each connection until you get to one where you get a reading. Between this connection and the distributor lies the trouble.

The foregoing steps in checking the primary circuit should include checking the ignition coil resistor for defects or loose connections. As this is done, bear in mind that while the starter cranks the engine, the resistor is by-passed by the starter switch on the American Motors 4-121 engine. This means that while the circuit through the resistor may be satisfactory, a broken connection or high resistance between the starter switch by-pass terminal and the coil would prevent starting. On the other hand, a satisfactory by-pass circuit might start the engine while the engine would stall immediately upon releasing the starter switch if there was a defect in the coil resistance circuit.

If, to begin with, the test equipment shows a current reading at the distributor terminal, it is safe to assume that the trouble is in the unit itself, most likely burned or dirty breaker points. A final positive test for defective breaker points can be made very simply by removing the cardboard from between the points, and positioning the distributor cam by turning the engine to where the points are closed. With the points closed there should be no current at the distributor terminal. If there is current, replace the points.

In an emergency, the points can be cleaned by using the sanded side of a match box, a knife blade, or the sharp edge of a screwdriver to scrape the scale from the contact faces. After cleaning the points, if a gauge is not available to set the gap, a quick adjustment can be made by using four layers of a piece of newspaper. The thickness of the paper is equivalent to about .020", which is the approximate gap setting for most distributors. Of course, at the earliest opportunity, a precise point adjustment should be made.

If the procedure outlined under "Primary Ignition Checkout" does not uncover the trouble then it will be necessary to continue the tests into the secondary ignition circuit.

Secondary Ignition Checkout

First of all, remove the wire from one of the spark plugs, turn on the ignition and operate the starter. While the engine is cranking, hold the terminal of the spark plug wire about ¼" away from the engine or spark plug base. If the spark is strong and jumps the gap, the trouble is confined to either the spark plugs or lack of fuel. Before going any further, wipe the outside of the plugs to remove any dirt or

dampness which would create an easy path for the current to flow, then try to start the engine again. If it still fails to start, remove one of the spark plugs and if it is wet around the base, it indicates that the fuel system is okay, so it naturally follows that the spark plugs are at fault. Remove all the plugs, clean them and set the gaps. An emergency adjustment of spark plug gaps can be made by folding a piece of newspaper into 6 or 7 layers. When changing the gap, always bend the side (ground) electrode and never the center one as there is danger of breaking the insulation.

Fuel System Checkout

If the spark plug that was removed showed no indication of dampness on its base, check the fuel system. A quick check can be made by simply removing the carburetor air cleaner and looking down into the carburetor. Open and close the throttle manually and if fuel is present in the carburetor, the throttle will operate the accelerating pump, causing it to push gasoline through the pump jet. If it does, check the choke valve. If the engine is cold, the choke valve should be closed. If the choke won't close, the engine can be started by covering the carburetor throat while the engine is cranking, provided, of course, that fuel is reaching the carburetor.

Check the operation of the fuel pump by disconnecting the fuel lines from the pump to the carburetor. Crank the engine and if the pump is working, fuel will pulsate out of the line. If not, either the pump isn't working or the line from the tank to the pump is clogged. Before blaming the pump, however, disconnect the line at the inlet side of the pump which leads to the tank and, while a companion listens at the tank blow through the line. If a gurgling sound is heard back in the tank, the line is open and the trouble is in the pump. Remove the sediment bowl, if so equipped and clean the screen, then replace the bowl and screen, being sure that you have an air-tight fit. If the pump still refuses to function, it should be removed and repaired.

The foregoing discussion will, in most cases, uncover the cause of why an engine won't start. However, if further diagnosis is necessary, the following list will undoubtedly provide the answer.

ENGINE NOISE TESTS

Loose Main Bearing

A loose main bearing is indicated by a powerful but dull thud or knock when the engine is pulling. If all main bearings are loose a noticeable clatter will be audible.

The thud occurs regularly every other revolution. The knock can be confirmed by shorting spark plugs on cylinders adjacent to the bearing. Knock will disappear or be less when plugs are shorted. This test should be made at a fast idle equivalent to 15 mph in high gear. If bearing is not quite loose enough to produce a knock by itself, the bearing may knock if oil is too thin or if there is no oil at the bearing.

Loose Flywheel

A loose flywheel is indicated by a thud or click which is usually irregular. To test, idle the engine at about 20 mph and shut off the ignition. If thud is heard, the flywheel may be loose.

TROUBLE SHOOTING

Loose Rod Bearing

A loose rod bearing is indicated by a metallic knock which is usually loudest at about 30 mph with throttle closed. Knock can be reduced or even eliminated by shorting spark plug. If bearing is not loose enough to produce a knock by itself, the bearing may knock if oil is too thin or if there is no oil at the bearing.

Piston Pin

Piston pin, piston and connecting rod noises are difficult to tell apart.

A loose piston pin causes a sharp double knock which is usually heard when engine is idling. Severity of knock should increase when spark plug to this cylinder is short-circuited. However, on some engines the knock becomes more noticable at 25 to 35 mph on the road.

Piston pin rubs against cylinder wall, caused by lock screw being loose or snap ring broken.

Hydraulic Lifters

The malfunctioning of a hydraulic valve lifter is almost always accompanied by a clicking or tapping noise. More or less hydraulic lifter noise may be expected when the engine is cold but if lifters are functioning properly the noise should disappear when the engine warms up.

If all or nearly all lifters are noisy, they may be stuck because of dirty or gummy oil.

If all lifters are noisy, oil pressure to them may be inadequate. Foaming oil may also cause this trouble. If oil foams there will be bubbles on the oil level dipstick. Foaming may be caused by water in the oil or by too high an oil level or by a very low oil level.

If the hydraulic plungers require an initial adjustment, they will be noisy if this adjustment is incorrect.

If one lifter is noisy the cause may be:
1. Plunger too tight in lifter body.
2. Weak or broken plunger spring.
3. Ball valve leaks.
4. Plunger worn.
5. Lock ring (if any) improperly installed or missing.
6. Lack of oil pressure to this plunger.

If ball valve leaks, clean plunger in special solvent such as acetone and reinstall. Too often, plungers are condemned as faulty when all they need is a thorough cleaning.

Gum and dirty oil are the most common causes of hydraulic valve lifter trouble. Engine oil must be free of dirt. Select a standard brand of engine oil and use no other. Mixing up one standard brand with another may cause gummy oil and sticking plungers. Do not use any special oils unless recommended by the car manufacturer and change oil filter or element at recommended intervals.

Loose Engine Mountings

Occasional thud with car in operation. Most likely to be noticed at the moment the throttle is opened or closed.

Excessive Crankshaft End Play

A rather sharp rap which occurs at idling speed but may be heard at higher speeds also. The noise should disappear when clutch is disengaged.

Fuel Pump Noise

Diagnosis of fuel pumps suspected as noisy requires that some form of sounding device be used. Judgment by ear alone is not sufficient, otherwise a fuel pump may be needlessly replaced in attempting to correct noise contributed by some other component. Use of a stethoscope, a long screwdriver, or a sounding rod is recommended to locate the area or component causing the noise. The sounding rod can easily be made from a length of copper tubing 1/4 to 3/8 inch in diameter.

If the noise has been isolated to the fuel pump, remove the pump and run the engine with the fuel remaining in the carburetor bowl. If the noise level does not change, the source of the noise is elsewhere and the original fuel pump should be reinstalled. On models using a fuel pump push rod, check for excessive wear and/or galling of the push rod.

VAPOR LOCK

The term vapor lock means the flow of fuel to the mixing chamber in the carburetor has been stopped (locked) by the formation of vaporized fuel pockets or bubbles caused by overheating the fuel by hot fuel pump, hot fuel lines or hot carburetor.

The more volatile the fuel the greater the tendency for it to vapor lock. Vapor lock is encouraged by high atmospheric temperature, hard driving, defective engine cooling and high altitude.

A mild case of vapor lock will cause missing and hard starting when engine is warm. Somewhat more severe vapor lock will stop the engine which cannot be started again until it has cooled off enough so that any vaporized fuel has condensed to a liquid.

SERVICE NOTE: Some cars have a vapor bypass system. These cars have a special fuel filter which has a metering outlet in the top. Any vapor which forms is bled off and returned to the fuel tank through a separate line alongside the fuel supply line. This system greatly reduces the possibility of vapor lock. However, if vapor lock is suspected examine the bypass valve to see if it is functioning.

PERCOLATION

Percolation means simply that gasoline in the carburetor bowl is boiling over into the intake manifold. This condition is most apt to occur immediately after a hot engine is shut off. Most carburetors have a provision for relieving the vapor pressure of overheated fuel in the carburetor bowl by means of ports. If, however, percolation should take place, the engine may be started by allowing it to cool slightly and then holding the throttle wide open while cranking to clear the intake manifold of excess fuel.

SPARK KNOCK, PING, DETONATION

All three expressions mean the same thing. It is a sharp metallic knock caused by vibration of the cylinder head and block. The vibration is due to split-second high-pressure waves resulting from almost instantaneous abnormal combustion instead of the slower normal combustion.

The ping may be mild or loud. A mild ping does no harm but a severe ping will reduce power. A very severe ping may shatter spark plugs, break valves or crack pistons.

Pinging is most likely to occur on open throttle at low or moderate engine speed. Pinging is encouraged by:
1. Overheated engine.
2. Low octane fuel.
3. Too high compression.
4. Spark advanced too far.
5. Hot mixture due to hot engine or hot weather.
6. Heavy carbon deposit which increases the compression pressure.
7. Clogged or restricted EGR passages.

Tendency to ping increases with mixture temperature including high atmospheric temperature; intake manifold heater valve "on" when engine is warm; hot cooling water; hot interior engine surfaces due to sluggish water circulation or water jackets clogged with rust or dirt especially around exhaust valves. Some of these troubles may be confined to one or two cylinders.

If an engine pings objectionably even when using the highest octane fuel available, retard the spark setting, but first be sure the EGR system is functioning, the cooling system is in good condition, the mixture is not too lean, and the combustion chambers are free of carbon deposits.

PRE-IGNITION

Pre-ignition means that the mixture is set on fire before the spark occurs, being ignited by a red hot spot in the combustion chamber such as an incandescent particle of carbon; a thin piece of protruding metal; an overheated spark plug, or a bright red hot exhaust valve. The result is reduction of power and overheating accompanied by pinging. The bright red hot exhaust valve may be due to a leak, to lack of tappet clearance, to valve sticking, or to a weak or broken spring.

Pre-ignition may not be noticed if not severe. Severe pre-ignition results in severe pinging. The most common cause of pre-ignition is a badly overheated engine.

When the engine won't stop when the ignition is shut off, the cause is often due to red hot carbon particles resting on heavy carbon deposit in a very hot engine.

AFTER-BURNING

A subdued put-putting at the exhaust tail pipe may be due to leaky exhaust valves which permit the mixture to finish combustion in the muffler. If exhaust pipe or muffler is red hot, better let it cool, as there is some danger of setting the car on fire. Most likely to occur when mixture is lean.

ENGINE CONTINUES TO RUN AFTER IGNITION IS TURNED OFF

This condition, known as "dieseling," "run on," or "after running," is caused by improper idle speed and/or high temperature. Idle speed and engine temperature are affected by:

Carburetor Adjustment: High idle speed will increase the tendency to diesel because of the inertia of the engine crankshaft and flywheel. Too low an idle speed, particularly with a lean mixture, will result in an increase in engine temperature, especially if the engine is allowed to idle for long periods of time.

Ignition Timing: Because advanced ignition timing causes a corresponding increase in idle speed and retarded timing reduces idle speed, ignition timing influences the tendency to diesel in the same manner as Carburetor Adjustment.

Fuel Mixture: Enriching the idle fuel mixture decreases the tendency to diesel by causing the engine to run cooler.

Fuel Content: High octane fuels tend to reduce dieseling. Increased fuel content of lead alkyl increases the tendency to diesel. Phosphates and nickel fuel additives help prevent dieseling.

Spark Plugs: Plugs of too high a heat range

for the engine in question can cause dieseling.

Throttle Plates: If the throttle plates are not properly aligned in the carburetor bore, a resulting leanness in fuel mixture occurs, contributing to dieseling.

Electrical System: Normally, during dieseling, ignition is self-supplied by a "hot spot," self-igniting fuel, etc. However, there is a possibility of the vehicle's electrical system supplying the necessary ignition. When the ignition switch is turned off, a small amount of current can flow from the generator into the primary of the ignition coil through the generator tell-tale light. This is particularly true when the warning light bulb has been changed for one of increased wattage.

NOTE: "Run on" is more prevalent in an engine when the ignition is turned off before the engine is allowed to return to idle. Therefore, it can be reduced by letting the engine return to idle before shutting off the ignition. "Run on" incidence can be reduced on automatic transmission units by turning off the engine when in gear.

A certain amount of "run on" can be expected from any gasoline engine regardless of make, size or configuration. (Diesel engines operate on this principle.) However, if the above suggestions are correctly employed, "Run on" will be reduced to an unnoticeable level.

ENGINE

Condition	Possible Cause	Correction
ENGINE WILL NOT START	1. Weak battery.	1. Test battery specific gravity. Recharge or replace as necessary.
	2. Corroded or loose battery connections.	2. Clean and tighten battery connections. Apply a coat of petroleum to terminals.
	3. Faulty starter.	3. Repair starter motor.
	4. Moisture on ignition wires and distributor cap.	4. Wipe wires and cap clean and dry.
	5. Faulty ignition cables.	5. Replace any cracked or shorted cables.
	6. Open or shorted primary ignition circuit.	6. Trace primary ignition circuit and repair as necessary.
	7. Malfunctioning ignition points or condensor.	7. Replace ignition points & condensor as necessary.
	8. Faulty coil.	8. Test and replace if necessary.
	9. Incorrect spark plug gap.	9. Set gap correctly.
	10. Incorrect ignition timing.	10. Reset timing.
	11. Dirt or water in fuel line or carburetor.	11. Clean lines and carburetor. Replace filter.
	12. Carburetor flooded.	12. Adjust float level—check seats.
	13. Incorrect carburetor float setting.	13. Adjust float level—check seats.
	14. Faulty fuel pump.	14. Install new fuel pump.
	15. Carburetor percolating. No fuel in the carburetor.	15. Measure float level. Adjust bowl vent. Inspect operation of manifold heat control valve.
ENGINE STALLS	1. Idle speed set too low.	1. Adjust carburetor.
	2. Incorrect choke adjustment.	2. Adjust choke.
	3. Idle mixture too lean or too rich.	3. Adjust carburetor.
	4. Incorrect carburetor float setting.	4. Adjust float setting.
	5. Leak in intake manifold.	5. Inspect intake manifold gasket and replace if necessary.
	6. Worn or burned distributor rotor.	6. Install new rotor.
	7. Incorrect ignition wiring.	7. Install correct wiring.
	8. Faulty coil.	8. Test and replace if necessary.
	9. Incorrect tappet lash.	9. Adjust to specifications.
ENGINE LOSS OF POWER	1. Incorrect ignition timing.	1. Reset timing.
	2. Worn or burned distributor rotor.	2. Install new rotor.
	3. Worn distributor shaft.	3. Remove and repair distributor.
	4. Dirty or incorrectly gapped spark plugs.	4. Clean plugs and set gap.
	5. Dirt or water in fuel line, carburetor or filter.	5. Clean lines, carburetor and replace filter.
	6. Incorrect carburetor float setting.	6. Adjust float level.
	7. Faulty fuel pump.	7. Install new pump.
	8. Incorrect valve timing.	8. Check and correct valve timing.
	9. Blown cylinder head gasket.	9. Install new head gasket.
	10. Low compression.	10. Test compression of each cylinder.
	11. Burned, warped or pitted valves.	11. Install new valves.
	12. Plugged or restricted exhaust system.	12. Install new parts as necessary.
	13. Faulty ignition cables.	13. Replace any cracked or shorted cables.
	14. Faulty coil.	14. Test and replace as necessary.
ENGINE MISSES ON ACCELERATION	1. Dirty, or gap too wide in spark plugs.	1. Clean spark plugs and set gap.
	2. Incorrect ignition timing.	2. Reset timing.
	3. Dirt in carburetor.	3. Clean carburetor and replace filter.
	4. Acceleration pump in carburetor.	4. Install new pump.
	5. Burned, warped or pitted valves.	5. Install new valves.
	6. Faulty coil.	6. Test and replace if necessary.

TROUBLE SHOOTING

ENGINE—Continued

Condition	Possible Cause	Correction
ENGINE MISSES AT HIGH SPEED	1. Dirty or gap set too wide in spark plug. 2. Worn distributor shaft. 3. Worn or burned distributor rotor. 4. Faulty coil. 5. Incorrect ignition timing. 6. Dirty jets in carburetor. 7. Dirt or water in fuel line, carburetor or filter.	1. Clean spark plugs and set gap. 2. Remove and repair distributor. 3. Install new rotor. 4. Test and replace if necessary. 5. Reset timing. 6. Clean carburetor, replace filter. 7. Clean lines, carburetor and replace filter.
NOISY VALVES	1. High or low oil level in crankcase. 2. Thin or diluted oil. 3. Low oil pressure. 4. Dirt in valve lifters. 5. Bent push rod. 6. Worn rocker arms. 7. Worn tappets. 8. Worn valve guides. 9. Excessive run-out of valve seats or valve faces. 10. Incorrect tappet lash.	1. Check for correct oil level. 2. Change oil. 3. Check engine oil level. 4. Clean lifters. 5. Install new push rods. 6. Inspect oil supply to rockers. 7. Install new tappets. 8. Ream and install new valves with O/S Stems. 9. Grind valve seats and valves. 10. Adjust to specifications.
CONNECTING ROD NOISE	1. Insufficient oil supply. 2. Low oil pressure. 3. Thin or diluted oil. 4. Excessive bearing clearance. 5. Connecting rod journals out-of-round. 6. Misaligned (bent) connecting rods.	1. Check engine oil level. 2. Check engine oil level. Inspect oil pump relief valve and spring. 3. Change oil to correct viscosity. 4. Measure bearings for correct clearance. 5. Replace crankshaft or regrind journals. 6. Replace bent connecting rods.
MAIN BEARING NOISE	1. Insufficient oil supply. 2. Low oil pressure. 3. Thin or diluted oil. 4. Excessive bearing clearance. 5. Excessive end play. 6. Crankshaft journal worn out-of-round. 7. Loose flywheel or torque converter.	1. Check engine oil level. 2. Check engine oil level. Inspect oil pump relief valve and spring. 3. Change oil to correct viscosity. 4. Measure bearings for correct clearances. 5. Check thrust bearing for wear on flanges. 6. Replace crankshaft or regrind journals. 7. Tighten to correct torque.
OIL PUMPING AT RINGS	1. Worn, scuffed, or broken rings. 2. Carbon in oil ring slot. 3. Rings fitted too tight in grooves.	1. Hone cylinder bores and install new rings. 2. Install new rings. 3. Remove the rings. Check grooves. If groove is not proper width, replace piston.
OIL PRESSURE DROP	1. Low oil level. 2. Faulty oil pressure sending unit. 3. Clogged oil filter. 4. Worn parts in oil pump. 5. Thin or diluted oil. 6. Excessive bearing clearance. 7. Oil pump relief valve stuck. 8. Oil pump suction tube loose, bent or cracked.	1. Check engine oil level. 2. Install new sending unit. 3. Install new oil filter. 4. Replace worn parts or pump. 5. Change oil to correct viscosity. 6. Measure bearings for correct clearance. 7. Remove valve and inspect, clean, and reinstall. 8. Remove oil pan and install new tube if necessary.
NO OIL PRESSURE	1. Low oil level. 2. Oil pressure gauge or sending unit inaccurate. 3. Oil pump malfunction. 4. Oil pressure relief valve sticking. 5. Oil passages on pressure side of pump obstructed. 6. Oil pickup screen or tube obstructed.	1. Add oil to correct level. 2. Replace defective unit. 3. Repair oil pump. 4. Remove and inspect oil pressure relief valve assembly. 5. Inspect oil passages for obstructions. 6. Inspect oil pickup for obstructions.
LOW OIL PRESSURE	1. Low oil level. 2. Oil excessively thin due to dilution, poor quality, or improper grade. 3. Oil pressure relief spring weak or sticking. 4. Oil pickup tube and screen assembly has restriction or air leak.	1. Add oil to correct level. 2. Drain and refill crankcase with recommended oil. 3. Remove and inspect oil pressure relief valve assembly. 4. Remove and inspect oil inlet tube and screen assembly. (Fill pickup with lacquer thinner to find leaks.)

ENGINE—Continued

Condition	Possible Cause	Correction
LOW OIL PRESSURE, Continued	5. Excessive oil pump clearance. 6. Excessive main, rod, or camshaft bearing clearance.	5. Check clearances. 6. Measure bearing clearances, repair as necessary.
HIGH OIL PRESSURE	1. Improper grade oil. 2. Oil pressure gauge or sending unit inaccurate. 3. Oil pressure relief valve sticking closed.	1. Drain and refill crankcase with correct grade oil. 2. Replace defective unit. 3. Remove and inspect oil pressure relief valve assembly.
EXTERNAL OIL LEAK	1. Fuel pump gasket broken or improperly seated. 2. Cylinder head cover gasket broken or improperly seated. 3. Oil filter gasket broken or improperly seated. 4. Oil pan side gasket broken or improperly seated. 5. Oil pan front oil seal broken or improperly seated. 6. Oil pan rear oil seal broken or improperly seated. 7. Timing chain cover oil seal broken or improperly seated. 8. Oil pan drain plug loose or has stripped threads. 9. Rear oil gallery plug loose. 10. Rear camshaft plug loose or improperly seated.	1. Replace gasket. 2. Replace gasket; check cylinder head cover gasket flange and cylinder head gasket surface for distortion. 3. Replace oil filter. 4. Replace gasket; check oil pan gasket flange for distortion. 5. Replace seal; check timing chain cover and oil pan seal flange for distortion. 6. Replace seal; check oil pan rear oil seal flange; check rear main bearing cap for cracks, plugged oil return channels, or distortion in seal groove. 7. Replace seal. 8. Repair as necessary and tighten. 9. Use appropriate sealant on gallery plug and tighten. 10. Seat camshaft plug or replace and seal, as necessary.
EXCESSIVE OIL CONSUMPTION	1. Oil level too high. 2. Oil too thin. 3. Valve stem oil seals are damaged, missing, or incorrect type. 4. Valve stems or valve guides worn. 5. Piston rings broken, missing. 6. Piston rings incorrect size. 7. Piston rings sticking or excessively loose in grooves. 8. Compression rings installed upside down. 9. Cylinder walls worn, scored, or glazed. 10. Piston ring gaps not properly staggered. 11. Excessive main or connecting rod bearing clearance.	1. Lower oil level to specifications. 2. Replace with specified oil. 3. Replace valve stem oil seals. 4. Check stem-to-guide clearance and repair as necessary. 5. Replace missing or broken rings. 6. Check ring gap, repair as necessary. 7. Check ring side clearance, repair as necessary. 8. Repair as necessary. 9. Repair as necessary. 10. Repair as necessary. 11. Check bearing clearance, repair as necessary.

OIL PRESSURE INDICATOR

LIGHT NOT LIT, IGNITION ON AND ENGINE NOT RUNNING.	1. Bulb burned out. 2. Open in light circuit. 3. Defective oil pressure switch.	1. Replace bulb. 2. Locate and correct open. 3. Replace oil pressure switch.
LIGHT ON, ENGINE RUNNING ABOVE IDLE SPEED.	1. Grounded wiring between light and switch. 2. Defective oil pressure switch. 3. Low oil pressure.	1. Locate and repair ground. 2. Replace oil pressure switch. 3. Locate cause of low oil pressure and correct.

TROUBLE SHOOTING

IGNITION, STARTER & FUEL

Condition	Possible Cause	Correction
NOTHING HAPPENS WHEN START ATTEMPT IS MADE	1. Undercharged or defective battery.	1. Check condition of battery and recharge or replace as required.
	2. Loose battery cables.	2. Clean and tighten cable connections.
	3. Burned fusible link in starting circuit.	3. Check for burned fusible link. Correct wiring problem.
	4. Incorrectly positioned or defective neutral start switch.	4. Check neutral start switch adjustment. If O.K., replace switch.
	5. Loose or defective wiring between neutral start switch and ignition switch.	5. Check for loose connections and opens between battery, horn relay, ignition switch, and solenoid "S" terminal. Check battery ground cable. Replace or repair defective item.
	6. Defective starter motor.	6. Repair or replace starter motor.
	7. Defective starter interlock system.	7. Use emergency button under hood. If car starts, repair circuit in interlock system. If car does not start, check and repair starter circuit.
SOLENOID SWITCH CLICKS BUT STARTER DOES NOT CRANK	1. Undercharged or defective battery.	1. Test battery. Recharge or replace battery.
	2. Loose battery cables.	2. Check and tighten battery connections.
	3. Loose or defective wiring at starter.	3. Tighten connections or repair wiring as required.
	4. Defective solenoid.	4. Replace solenoid.
	5. "Hot stall" condition.	5. Check engine cooling system.
	6. Excessive engine rotational torque caused by mechanical problem within engine.	6. Check engine torque for excessive friction.
	7. Defective starter motor.	7. Repair or replace starter motor.
SLOW CRANKING	1. Vehicle is overheating.	1. Check engine cooling system and repair as required.
	2. Undercharged or defective battery.	2. Recharge or replace battery.
	3. Loose or defective wiring between battery and engine block.	3. Repair or replace wiring.
	4. Loose or defective wiring between battery and solenoid "Bat" terminal.	4. Repair or replace wiring.
	5. Defective starter motor.	5. Repair or replace starter.
STARTER SPINS AND/OR MAKES LOUD GRINDING NOISE BUT DOES NOT TURN ENGINE	1. Defective starter motor.	1. Repair or replace starter motor.
	2. Defective ring gear.	2. Replace ring gear.
STARTER KEEPS RUNNING AFTER IGNITION SWITCH IS RELEASED—FROM "START" TO "RUN" POSITION	1. Defective ignition switch.	1. Replace ignition switch.
	2. Defective solenoid.	2. Replace solenoid.
STARTER ENGAGES ("Clunks") BUT ENGINE DOES NOT CRANK	1. Open circuit in solenoid armature or field coils.	1. Repair or replace solenoid or starter motor.
	2. Short or ground in field coil or armature.	2. Repair or replace starter motor.
HARD STARTING (Engine Cranks Normally)	1. Binding linkage, choke valve or choke piston.	1. Repair as necessary.
	2. Restricted choke vacuum and hot air passages.	2. Clean passages.
	3. Improper fuel level.	3. Adjust float level.
	4. Dirty, worn or faulty needle valve and seat.	4. Repair as necessary.
	5. Float sticking.	5. Repair as necessary.
	6. Exhaust manifold heat valve stuck.	6. Repair as necessary.
	7. Faulty fuel pump.	7. Replace fuel pump.
	8. Incorrect choke cover adjustment.	8. Adjust choke cover.
	9. Inadequate unloader adjustment.	9. Adjust unloader.
	10. Faulty ignition coil.	10. Test and replace as necessary.
	11. Improper spark plug gap.	11. Adjust gap.
	12. Incorrect initial timing.	12. Adjust timing.
	13. Incorrect valve timing.	13. Check valve timing; repair as necessary.
ROUGH IDLE OR STALLING	1. Incorrect curb or fast idle speed.	1. Adjust curb or fast idle speed.
	2. Incorrect initial timing.	2. Adjust timing to specifications.
	3. Improper idle mixture adjustment.	3. Adjust idle mixture.
	4. Damaged tip on idle mixture screw(s).	4. Replace mixture screw(s).
	5. Improper fast idle cam adjustment.	5. Adjust fast idle.
	6. Faulty PCV valve air flow.	6. Test PCV valve and replace as necessary.

IGNITION, STARTER & FUEL—Continued

Condition	Possible Cause	Correction
ROUGH IDLE OR STALLING, continued	7. Exhaust manifold heat valve inoperative.	7. Lubricate or replace heat valve as necessary.
	8. Choke binding.	8. Locate and eliminate binding condition.
	9. Improper choke setting.	9. Adjust choke.
	10. Vacuum leak.	10. Check manifold vacuum and repair as necessary.
	11. Improper fuel level.	11. Adjust fuel level.
	12. Faulty distributor rotor or cap.	12. Replace rotor or cap.
	13. Leaking engine valves.	13. Check cylinder leakdown rate or compression and repair as necessary.
	14. Incorrect ignition wiring.	14. Check wiring and correct as necessary.
	15. Faulty coil.	15. Test coil and replace as necessary.
	16. Clogged air bleed or idle passages.	16. Clean passages.
	17. Restricted air cleaner.	17. Clean or replace air cleaner.
	18. Faulty EGR valve operation if equipped.	18. Test EGR system and replace as necessary if equipped.
FAULTY LOW-SPEED OPERATION	1. Clogged idle transfer slots.	1. Clean transfer slots.
	2. Restricted idle air bleeds and passages.	2. Clean air bleeds and passages.
	3. Restricted air cleaner.	3. Clean or replace air cleaner.
	4. Improper fuel level.	4. Adjust fuel level.
	5. Faulty spark plugs.	5. Clean or replace spark plugs.
	6. Dirty, corroded, or loose secondary circuit connections.	6. Clean or tighten secondary circuit connections.
	7. Faulty ignition cable.	7. Replace ignition cable.
	8. Faulty distributor cap.	8. Replace cap.
FAULTY ACCELERATION	1. Improper pump stroke.	1. Adjust pump stroke.
	2. Incorrect ignition timing.	2. Adjust timing.
	3. Inoperative pump discharge check ball or needle.	3. Clean or replace as necessary.
	4. Worn or damaged pump diaphragm or piston.	4. Replace diaphragm or piston.
	5. Leaking main body cover gasket.	5. Replace gasket.
	6. Engine cold and choke too lean.	6. Adjust choke.
	7. Faulty spark plug(s).	7. Clean or replace spark plug(s).
	8. Leaking engine valves.	8. Check cylinder leakdown rate or compression, repair as necessary.
	9. Faulty coil.	9. Test coil and replace as necessary.
FAULTY HIGH-SPEED OPERATION	1. Incorrect ignition timing.	1. Adjust timing.
	2. Faulty distributor centrifugal advance.	2. Check centrifugal advance and repair as necessary.
	3. Faulty distributor vacuum advance.	3. Check vacuum advance and repair as necessary.
	4. Low fuel pump volume.	4. Replace fuel pump.
	5. Improper spark plug gap.	5. Adjust gap.
	6. Faulty choke operation.	6. Adjust choke.
	7. Partially restricted exhaust manifold, exhaust pipe, muffler, or tailpipe.	7. Eliminate restriction.
	8. Clogged vacuum passages.	8. Clean passages.
	9. Improper size or obstructed main jets.	9. Clean or replace as necessary.
	10. Restricted air cleaner.	10. Clean or replace as necessary.
	11. Faulty distributor rotor or cap.	11. Replace rotor or cap.
	12. Worn distributor shaft.	12. Replace shaft.
	13. Faulty coil.	13. Test coil and replace as necessary.
	14. Leaking engine valve(s).	14. Check cylinder leakdown or compression and repair as necessary.
	15. Faulty valve spring(s).	15. Inspect and test valve spring tension and replace as necessary.
	16. Incorrect valve timing.	16. Check valve timing and repair as necessary.
	17. Intake manifold restricted.	17. Pass chain through passages.
MISFIRE AT ALL SPEEDS	1. Faulty spark plug(s).	1. Clean or replace spark plug(s).
	2. Faulty spark plug cable(s).	2. Replace as necessary.
	3. Faulty distributor cap or rotor.	3. Replace cap or rotor.
	4. Faulty coil.	4. Test coil and replace as necessary.
	5. Primary circuit shorted or open intermittently.	5. Trace primary circuit and repair as necessary.
	6. Leaking engine valve(s).	6. Check cylinder leakdown rate or compression and repair as necessary.
	7. Faulty hydraulic tappet(s).	7. Clean or replace tappet(s).
	8. Faulty valve spring(s).	8. Inspect and test valve spring tension, repair as necessary.
	9. Worn lobes on camshaft.	9. Replace camshaft.
	10. Vacuum leak.	10. Check manifold vacuum and repair as necessary.

TROUBLE SHOOTING

IGNITION, STARTER & FUEL—Continued

Condition	Possible Cause	Correction
MISFIRE AT ALL SPEEDS, continued	11. Improper carburetor settings. 12. Fuel pump volume or pressure low. 13. Blown cylinder head gasket. 14. Intake or exhaust manifold passage(s) restricted.	11. Adjust carburetor. 12. Replace fuel pump. 13. Replace gasket. 14. Pass chain through passages.
POWER NOT UP TO NORMAL	1. Incorrect ignition timing. 2. Faulty distributor rotor. 3. Worn distributor shaft. 4. Incorrect spark plug gap. 5. Faulty fuel pump. 6. Incorrect valve timing. 7. Faulty coil. 8. Faulty ignition cables. 9. Leaking engine valves. 10. Blown cylinder head gasket. 11. Leaking piston rings.	1. Adjust timing. 2. Replace rotor. 3. Replace shaft. 4. Adjust gap. 5. Replace fuel pump. 6. Check valve timing and repair as necessary. 7. Test coil and replace as necessary. 8. Test cables and replace as necessary. 9. Check cylinder leakdown rate or compression and repair as necessary. 10. Replace gasket. 11. Check compression and repair as necessary.
INTAKE BACKFIRE	1. Improper ignition timing. 2. Faulty accelerator pump discharge. 3. Improper choke operation. 4. Lean fuel mixture.	1. Adjust timing. 2. Repair as necessary. 3. Repair as necessary. 4. Check float level or manifold vacuum for vacuum leak.
EXHAUST BACKFIRE	1. Vacuum leak. 2. Faulty A.I.R. diverter valve. 3. Faulty choke operation. 4. Exhaust leak.	1. Check manifold vacuum and repair as necessary. 2. Test diverter valve and replace as necessary. 3. Repair as necessary. 4. Locate and eliminate leak.
PING OR SPARK KNOCK	1. Incorrect ignition timing. 2. Distributor centrifugal or vacuum advance malfunction. 3. Excessive combustion chamber deposits. 4. Carburetor set too lean. 5. Vacuum leak. 6. Excessively high compression. 7. Fuel octane rating excessively low. 8. Heat riser stuck in heat on position. 9. Insufficient EGR flow.	1. Adjust timing. 2. Check advance and repair as necessary. 3. Use combustion chamber cleaner. 4. Adjust carburetor. 5. Check manifold vacuum and repair as necessary. 6. Check compression and repair as necessary. 7. Try alternate fuel source. 8. Free-up or replace heat riser. 9. Check EGR system operation.
SURGING (Cruising Speeds To Top Speeds)	1. Low fuel level. 2. Low fuel pump pressure or volume. 3. Improper PCV valve air flow. 4. Vacuum leak. 5. Dirt in carburetor. 6. Undersize main jets. 7. Clogged fuel filter screen. 8. Restricted air cleaner. 9. Excessive EGR valve flow.	1. Adjust fuel level. 2. Replace fuel pump. 3. Test PCV valve and replace as necessary. 4. Check manifold vacuum and repair as necessary. 5. Clean carburetor, replace filter. 6. Replace main jet(s). 7. Replace fuel filter. 8. Clean or replace air cleaner. 9. Check EGR system operation.

CHARGING SYSTEM

Condition	Possible Cause	Correction
ALTERNATOR FAILS TO CHARGE (No Output or Low Output)	1. Alternator drive belt loose. 2. Regulator base improperly grounded. 3. Worn brushes and/or slip rings. 4. Sticking brushes. 5. Open field circuit. 6. Open charging circuit. 7. Open circuit in stator windings.	1. Adjust drive belt to specifications. 2. Connect regulator to a good ground. 3. Install new brushes and/or slip rings. 4. Clean slip rings and brush holders. Install new brushes if necessary. 5. Test all the field circuit connections, and correct as required. 6. Inspect all connections in charging circuit, and correct as required. 7. Remove alternator and disassemble. Test stator windings. Install new stator if necessary.

CHARGING SYSTEM—Continued

Condition	Possible Cause	Correction
ALTERNATOR FAILS TO CHARGE (No Output or Low Output), continued	8. Open rectifiers.	8. Remove alternator and disassemble. Test the rectifiers. Install new rectifier assemblies if necessary.
LOW, UNSTEADY CHARGING RATE	1. High resistance in body to engine ground lead. 2. Alternator drive belt loose. 3. High resistance at battery terminals. 4. High resistance in charging circuit. 5. Open stator winding.	1. Tighten ground lead connections. Install new ground lead if necessary. 2. Adjust alternator drive belt. 3. Clean and tighten battery terminals. 4. Test charging circuit resistance. Correct as required. 5. Remove and disassemble alternator. Test stator windings. Install new stator if necessary.
LOW OUTPUT AND A LOW BATTERY	1. High resistance in charging circuit. 2. Shorted rectifier. Open rectifier. 3. Grounded stator windings. 4. Faulty voltage regulator.	1. Test charging circuit resistance and correct as required. 2. Perform current output test. Test the rectifiers and install new rectifier heat sink assembly as required. Remove and disassemble the alternator. 3. Remove and disassemble alternator. Test stator windings. Install new stator if necessary. 4. Test voltage regulator. Replace as necessary.
EXCESSIVE CHARGING RATE TO A FULLY CHARGED BATTERY	1. Faulty ignition switch. 2. Faulty voltage regulator.	1. Install new ignition switch. 2. Test voltage regulator. Replace as necessary.
NOISY ALTERNATOR	1. Alternator mounting loose. 2. Worn of frayed drive belt. 3. Worn bearings. 4. Interference between rotor fan and stator leads. 5. Rotor or rotor fan damaged. 6. Open or shorted rectifer. 7. Open or shorted winding in stator.	1. Properly install and tighten alternator mounting. 2. Install a new drive belt and adjust to specifications. 3. Remove and disassemble alternator. Install new bearings as required. 4. Remove and disassemble alternator. Correct interference as required. 5. Remove and disassemble alternator. Install new rotor. 6. Remove and disassemble alternator. Test rectifers. Install new rectifier heat sink assemble as required. 7. Remove and disassemble alternator. Test stator windings. Install new stator if necessary.
EXCESSIVE AMMETER FLUCTUATION	1. High resistance in the alternator and voltage regulator circuit.	1. Clean and tighten all connections as necessary.

CHARGING SYSTEM INDICATOR

LIGHT ON, IGNITION OFF	1. Shorted positive diode.	1. Locate and replace shorted diode.
LIGHT NOT ON, IGNITION ON AND ENGINE NOT RUNNING	1. Bulb burned out. 2. Open in light circuit. 3. Open in field.	1. Replace bulb. 2. Locate and correct open. 3. Replace rotor.
LIGHT ON, ENGINE RUNNING ABOVE IDLE SPEED	1. No generator output. 2. Shorted negative diode. 3. Loose or broken generator belt.	1. Check and correct cause of no output. 2. Locate and replace shorted diode. 3. Tighten or replace and tighten generator belt.

TROUBLE SHOOTING

COOLING SYSTEM

Condition	Possible Cause	Correction
HIGH TEMPERATURE INDICATION— OVERHEATING	1. Coolant level low. 2. Fan belt loose. 3. Radiator hose(s) collapsed. 4. Radiator blocked to airflow. 5. Faulty radiator cap. 6. Car overloaded. 7. Ignition timing incorrect. 8. Idle speed low. 9. Air trapped in cooling system. 10. Car in heavy traffic. 11. Incorrect cooling system component(s) installed. 12. Faulty thermostat. 13. Water pump shaft broken or impeller loose. 14. Radiator tubes clogged. 15. Cooling system clogged. 16. Casting flash in cooling passages. 17. Brakes dragging. 18. Excessive engine friction. 19. Car working beyond cooling system capacity. 20. Antifreeze concentration over 68%. 21. Low anti-freeze concentration.	1. Replenish coolant level. 2. Adjust fan belt. 3. Replace hose(s). 4. Remove restriction. 5. Replace cap. 6. Reduce load. 7. Adjust ignition timing. 8. Adjust idle speed. 9. Purge air. 10. Operate at fast idle intermittently to cool engine. 11. Install proper component(s). 12. Replace thermostat. 13. Replace water pump. 14. Flush radiator. 15. Flush system. 16. Repair or replace as necessary. Flash may be visible by removing cooling system components or removing core plugs. 17. Repair brakes. 18. Repair engine. 19. Install heavy-duty cooling fan and/or radiator. 20. Lower antifreeze content. 21. Add anti-freeze to provide a minimum 50% concentration.
LOW TEMPERATURE INDICATION— OVERCOOLING	1. Improper fan being used. 2. Improper radiator. 3. Thermostat stuck open. 4. Improper fan pulley (too small).	1. Install proper fan. 2. Install proper radiator. 3. Replace thermostat. 4. Install proper pulley.
COOLANT LOSS—BOILOVER **NOTE:** Immediately after shutdown, the engine enters a period known as heat soak. This is caused because the cooling system is inoperative but engine temperature is still high. If coolant temperature rises above boiling point, it may push some coolant out of the radiator overflow tube. If this does not occur frequently, it is considered normal.	Refer to Overheating Causes in addition to the following: 1. Overfilled cooling system. 2. Quick shutdown after hard (hot) run. 3. Air in system resulting in occasional "burping" of coolant. 4. Insufficient antifreeze allowing coolant boiling point to be too low. 5. Antifreeze deteriorated because of age or contamination. 6. Leaks due to loose hose clamps, loose nuts, bolts, drain plugs, faulty hoses, or defective radiator. 7. Faulty head gasket. 8. Cracked head, manifold, or block.	1. Reduce coolant level to proper specification. 2. Allow engine to run at fast idle prior to shutdown. 3. Purge system. 4. Add antifreeze to raise boiling point. 5. Replace coolant. 6. Pressure test system to locate leak then repair as necessary. 7. Replace head gasket. 8. Replace as necessary.
COOLANT ENTRY INTO CRANKCASE OR CYLINDER	1. Faulty head gasket. 2. Crack in head, manifold or block.	1. Replace head gasket. 2. Replace as necessary.
COOLANT RECOVERY SYSTEM INOPERATIVE	1. Coolant level low. 2. Leak in system. 3. Pressure cap not tight or gasket missing or leaking. 4. Pressure cap defective. 5. Overflow tube clogged or leaking. 6. Recovery bottle vent plugged.	1. Replenish coolant. 2. Pressure test to isolate leak and repair as necessary. 3. Repair as necessary. 4. Replace cap. 5. Repair as necessary. 6. Remove restriction.
NOISE	1. Fan contacting shroud. 2. Loose water pump impeller. 3. Dry fan belt. 4. Loose fan belt. 5. Rough surface on drive pulley. 6. Water pump bearing worn.	1. Reposition shroud and check engine mounts. 2. Replace pump. 3. Apply belt dressing or replace belt. 4. Adjust fan belt. 5. Replace pulley. 6. Remove belt to isolate. Replace pump.
NO COOLANT FLOW THROUGH HEATER CORE	1. Plugged return pipe in water pump. 2. Heater hose collapsed or plugged. 3. Plugged heater core. 4. Plugged outlet in thermostat housing. 5. Heater bypass hole in cylinder head plugged.	1. Remove obstruction. 2. Remove obstruction or replace hose. 3. Remove obstruction or replace core. 4. Remove flash or obstruction. 5. Remove obstruction.

COOLANT TEMPERATURE INDICATOR

Condition	Possible Cause	Correction
"HOT" INDICATOR; LIGHT NOT LIT WHEN CRANKING ENGINE	1. Bulb burned out. 2. Open in light circuit. 3. Defective ignition switch.	1. Replace bulb. 2. Locate and correct open. 3. Replace ignition switch.
LIGHT ON, ENGINE RUNNING	1. Wiring grounded between light and switch. 2. Defective temperature switch. 3. Defective ignition switch. 4. High coolant temperature.	1. Locate and correct grounded wiring. 2. Replace temperature switch. 3. Replace ignition switch. 4. Locate and correct cause of high coolant temperature.

EXHAUST SYSTEM

Condition	Possible Cause	Correction
LEAKING EXHAUST GASES	1. Leaks at pipe joints. 2. Damaged or improperly installed seals or packing. 3. Loose exhaust pipe heat tube extension connections. 4. Burned or rusted out exhaust pipe heat tube extensions.	1. Tighten U-bolt nuts at leaking joints. 2. Replace seals or packing as necessary. 3. Replace seals or packing as required. Tighten stud nuts or bolts. 4. Replace heat tube extensions as required.
EXHAUST NOISES	1. Leaks at manifold or pipe connections. 2. Burned or blown out muffler. 3. Burned or rusted out exhaust pipe. 4. Exhaust pipe leaking at manifold flange. 5. Exhaust manifold cracked or broken. 6. Leak between manifold and cylinder head.	1. Tighten clamps at leaking connections to specified torque. Replace gasket or packing as required. 2. Replace muffler assembly. 3. Replace exhaust pipe. 4. Tighten attaching bolt nuts. 5. Replace manifold. 6. Tighten manifold to cylinder head stud nuts or bolts.
LOSS OF ENGINE POWER AND/OR INTERNAL RATTLES IN MUFFLER	1. Dislodged turning tubes and or baffles in muffler.	1. Replace muffler.
LOSS OF ENGINE POWER	1. Imploding (inner wall collapse) of exhaust pipe.	1. Replace exhaust pipe.
ENGINE HARD TO WARM UP OR WILL NOT RETURN TO NORMAL IDLE	1. Heat control valve frozen in the open position.	1. Free up manifold heat control using a suitable manifold heat control solvent.
MANIFOLD HEAT CONTROL VALVE NOISE	1. Thermostat broken. 2. Broken, weak or missing anti-rattle spring.	1. Replace thermostat. 2. Replace spring.

CLUTCH & SYNCHRO-MESH TRANSMISSION

Condition	Possible Cause	Correction
CLUTCH CHATTER	1. Worn or damaged disc assembly. 2. Grease or oil on disc facings. 3. Improperly adjusted cover assembly. 4. Broken or loose engine mounts. 5. Misaligned clutch housing.	1. Replace disc assembly. 2. Replace disc assembly and correct cause of contamination. 3. Replace cover assembly. 4. Replace or tighten mounts. 5. Align clutch housing.
CLUTCH SLIPPING	1. Insufficient pedal free play. 2. Burned, worn, or oil soaked facings. 3. Weak or broken pressure springs.	1. Adjust release fork rod. 2. Replace disc assembly and correct cause of contamination. 3. Replace cover assembly.
DIFFICULT GEAR SHIFTING	1. Excessive pedal free play. 2. Excessive deflection in linkage or firewall. 3. Worn or damaged disc assembly. 4. Improperly adjusted cover assembly. 5. Clutch disc splines sticking. 6. Worn or dry pilot bushing. 7. Clutch housing misaligned.	1. Adjust release fork rod. 2. Repair or replace linkage. 3. Replace disc assembly. 4. Replace cover assembly. 5. Remove disc assembly and free up splines or replace disc. 6. Lubricate or replace bushing. 7. Align clutch housing.
CLUTCH NOISY	1. Dry clutch linkage. 2. Worn release bearing. 3. Worn disc assembly.	1. Lubricate where necessary. 2. Replace release bearing. 3. Replace disc assembly.

TROUBLE SHOOTING

CLUTCH & SYNCHRO-MESH TRANSMISSION—Continued

Condition	Possible Cause	Correction
CLUTCH NOISY, continued	4. Worn release levers. 5. Worn or dry pilot bushing. 6. Dry contact-pressure plate lugs in cover.	4. Replace cover assembly. 5. Lubricate or replace bushing. 6. Lubricate very lightly.
TRANSMISSION SHIFTS HARD	1. Incorrect clutch adjustment. 2. Clutch linkage binding. 3. Gearshift linkage incorrectly adjusted, bent, or binding. 4. Bind in steering column, or column is misaligned. 5. Incorrect lubricant. 6. Internal bind in transmissions—e.g. shift rails, interlocks, shift forks, synchronizer teeth. 7. Clutch housing misalignment.	1. Adjust clutch pedal free-play. 2. Lubricate or repair linkage as required. 3. Adjust linkage—correct any bind. Replace bent parts. 4. Disconnect shift rods at column. Check for bind/misalignment between tube and jacket by shifting lever into all positions. Correct as required. 5. Drain and refill transmission. 6. Remove transmission and inspect shift mechanism. Repair as required. 7. Check runout at rear face of clutch housing.
GEAR CLASH WHEN SHIFTING FROM ONE FORWARD GEAR TO ANOTHER	1. Incorrect clutch adjustment. 2. Clutch linkage binding. 3. Gear shift linkage incorrectly adjusted, bent, or binding. 4. Clutch housing misalignment. 5. Damaged or worn transmission components: shift forks, synchronizers, shift rails and interlocks. Excessive end play due to worn thrust washers.	1. Adjust clutch. 2. Lubricate or repair linkage as required. 3. Adjust linkage, correct binds, replace bent parts. 4. Check runout at rear face of clutch housing. 5. Inspect components. Repair or replace as required.
TRANSMISSION NOISY	1. Insufficient lubricant. 2. Incorrect lubricant. 3. Clutch housing to engine or transmission to clutch housing bolts loose. 4. Dirt, chips in lubricant. 5. Gearshift linkage incorrectly adjusted, or bent or binding. 6. Clutch housing misalignment. 7. Worn transmission components: front-rear bearings, worn gear teeth, damaged gear teeth or synchronizer components.	1. Check lubricant level and replenish as required. 2. Replace with proper lubricant. 3. Check and correct bolt torque as required. 4. Drain and flush transmission. 5. Adjust linkage, correct binds, replace bent parts. 6. Check runout at rear face of clutch housing. 7. Inspect components and repair as required.
JUMPS OUT OF GEAR	1. Gearshift linkage incorrectly adjusted. 2. Gearshift linkage bent or binding. 3. Clutch housing misaligned. 4. Worn pilot bushing. 5. Worn or damaged clutch shaft roller bearings. 6. Worn, tapered gear teeth; synchronizer parts worn. 7. Shifter forks, shift rails, or detent-interlock parts worn, missing, etc. 8. Excessive end play of output shaft gear train, countershaft gear or reverse idler gear.	1. Adjust linkage. 2. Correct bind, replace bent parts. 3. Check runout at rear face of clutch housing. 4. Replace bushing. 5. Replace bearings. 6. Inspect and replace as required. 7. Inspect and replace as required. 8. Replace thrust washers, and snap rings (output shaft gear train).
WILL NOT SHIFT INTO ONE GEAR— ALL OTHERS OK	1. Gearshift linkage not adjusted correctly. 2. Bent shift rod at transmission. 3. Transmission shifter levers reversed. 4. Worn or damaged shift rails, shift forks, detent-interlock plugs, loose setscrew in shifter fork, worn synchronizer parts.	1. Adjust linkage. 2. Replace rod. 3. Correctly position levers. 4. Inspect and repair or replace parts as required.
LOCKED IN ONE GEAR—CANNOT BE SHIFTED OUT OF THAT GEAR	1. Gearshift linkage binding or bent. 2. Transmission shifter lever attaching nuts loose or levers are worn at shifter fork shaft hole. 3. Shift rails worn or broken, shifter fork bent, setscrew loose, detent-interlock plug missing or worn. 4. Broken gear teeth on countershaft gear, clutch shaft, or reverse idler gear.	1. Correct bind, replace bent components. 2. Tighten nuts, replace worn levers. 3. Inspect and replace worn or damaged parts. 4. Inspect and replace damaged part.

BRAKES

Condition	Possible Cause	Correction
LOW BRAKE PEDAL (Excessive pedal travel required to apply brake)	1. Excessive clearance between linings and drums caused by inoperative automatic adjusters. 2. Worn brake lining. 3. Bent, distorted brakeshoes. 4. Caliper pistons corroded. 5. Power unit push rod height incorrect.	1. Make 10 to 15 firm forward and reverse brake stops to adjust brakes. If brake pedal does not come up, repair or replace adjuster parts as necessary. 2. Inspect and replace lining if worn beyond minimum thickness specification. 3. Replace brakeshoes in axle sets. 4. Repair or replace calipers. 5. Check height with gauge (only). Replace power unit if push rod height is not within specifications.
LOW BRAKE PEDAL (Pedal may go to floor under steady pressure)	1. Leak in hydraulic system. 2. Air in hydraulic system. 3. Incorrect or non-recommended brake fluid (fluid boils away at below normal temp.).	1. Fill master cylinder to within ¼-inch of rim; have helper apply brakes and check calipers, wheel cylinders combination valve, tubes, hoses and fittings for leaks. Repair or replace parts as necessary. 2. Bleed air from system. Refer to Brake Bleeding. 3. Flush hydraulic system with clean brake fluid. Refill with correct-type fluid.
LOW BRAKE PEDAL (Pedal goes to floor on first application—OK on subsequent applications)	1. Disc brakeshoe (pad) knock back; shoes push caliper piston back into bore. Caused by loose wheel bearings or excessive lateral runout of rotor (rotor wobble). 2. Calipers sticking on mounting surfaces of caliper and anchor. Caused by buildup of dirt, rust, or corrosion on abutment.	1. Adjust wheel bearings and check lateral runout of rotor(s). Refinish rotors if runout is over limits. Replace rotor if refinishing would cause rotor to fall below minimum thickness limit. 2. Clean mounting surfaces and lubricate surfaces with molydisulphide grease or equivalent.
FADING BRAKE PEDAL (Pedal falls away under steady pressure)	1. Leak in hydraulic system. 2. Master cylinder piston cups worn, or master cylinder bore is scored, worn or corroded.	1. Fill master cylinder reservoirs to within ¼-inch of rim; have helper apply brakes, check master cylinder, calipers, wheel cylinders combination valve, tubes, hoses, and fittings for leaks. Repair or replace parts as necessary. 2. Repair or replace master cylinder.

DECREASING BRAKE PEDAL TRAVEL
(Pedal travel required to apply brakes decreases, may be accompanied by hard pedal)
	1. Caliper or wheel cylinder pistons sticking or seized.
	2. Master cylinder compensator ports blocked (preventing fluid return to reservoirs) or pistons sticking or seized in master cylinder bore.
	3. Power brake unit binding internally.
	
	4. Incorrect power unit push rod height.
		1. Repair or replace calipers, or wheel cylinders.
		2. Repair or replace master cylinder.
		
		3. Test unit as follows:
		  a. Raise hood, shift transmission into neutral and start engine.
		  b. Increase engine speed to 1500 RPM, close throttle and fully depress brake pedal.
		  c. Slowly release brake pedal and stop engine.
		  d. Remove vacuum check valve and hose from power unit. Observe for backward movement of brake pedal or power unit-to-brake pedal push rod.
		  e. If pedal or push rod moves backward, power unit has internal bind—replace power brake unit.
		4. Adjust push rod height.

SPONGY BRAKE PEDAL (Pedal has abnormally soft, springy, spongy feel when depressed)	1. Air in hydraulic system. 2. Brakeshoes bent or distorted. 3. Brake lining not yet seated to drums and rotors.	1. Bleed brakes. 2. Replace brakeshoes. 3. Burnish brakes.
HARD BRAKE PEDAL (Excessive pedal pressure required to stop car. May be accompanied by brake fade)	1. Loose or leaking power brake unit vacuum hose. 2. Brake lining contaminated by grease or brake fluid. 3. Incorrect or poor quality brake lining. 4. Bent, broken, distorted brakeshoes.	1. Tighten connections or replace leaking hose. 2. Determine cause of contaminations and correct. Replace contaminated brake lining in axle sets. 3. Replace lining in axle sets. 4. Replace brakeshoes and lining.

TROUBLE SHOOTING

BRAKES—Continued

Condition	Possible Cause	Correction
HARD BRAKE PEDAL, continued	5. Calipers binding or dragging on anchor. Rear brakeshoes dragging on support plate.	5. Sand or wire brush anchors and caliper mounting surfaces and lubricate surfaces lightly. Clean rust or burrs from rear brake support plate ledges and lubricate ledges. **NOTE:** If ledges are deeply grooved or scored, do not attempt to sand or grind them smooth—replace support plate.
	6. Rear brake drum(s) bell mouthed, flared or barrel shaped (distorted).	6. Replace rear drum(s).
	7. Caliper, wheel cylinder, or master cylinder pistons sticking or seized.	7. Repair or replace parts as necessary.
	8. Power brake unit vacuum check valve malfunction.	8. Test valve as follows: a. Start engine, increase engine speed to 1500 RPM, close throttle and immediately stop engine. b. Wait at least 90 seconds then try brake action. c. If brakes are not vacuum assisted for 2 or more applications, check valve is faulty.
	9. Power brake unit has internal bind or incorrect push rod height (too long).	9. Test unit as follows: a. With engine stopped, apply brakes several times to exhaust all vacuum in system. b. Shift transmission into neutral, depress brake pedal and start engine. c. If pedal falls away under foot pressure and less pressure is required to hold pedal in applied position, power unit vacuum system is working. Test power unit as outlined in item (3) under Decreasing Brake Pedal Travel. If power unit exhibits bind condition, replace power unit. d. If power unit does not exhibit bind condition, disconnect master cylinder and check push rod height with appropriate gauge. If height is not within specifications, replace power unit.
	10. Master cylinder compensator ports (at bottom of reservoirs) blocked by dirt, scale, rust, or have small burrs (blocked ports prevent fluid return to reservoirs).	10. Repair or replace master cylinder. **CAUTION:** Do not attempt to clean blocked ports with wire, pencils, or similar implements.
	11. Brake hoses, tubes, fittings clogged or restricted.	11. Use compressed air to check or unclog parts. Replace any damaged parts.
	12. Brake fluid contaminated with improper fluids (motor oil, transmission fluid, or poor quality brake fluid) causing rubber components to swell and stick in bores.	12. Replace all rubber components and hoses. Flush entire brake system. Refill with recommended brake fluid.
GRABBING BRAKES (Severe reaction to brake pedal pressure)	1. Brake lining(s) contaminated by grease or brake fluid.	1. Determine and correct cause of contamination and replace brakeshoes and linings in axle sets.
	2. Parking brake cables incorrectly adjusted or seized.	2. Adjust cables. Free up or replace seized cables.
	3. Power brake unit binding internally or push rod height incorrect.	3. Test unit as outlined in item (3) under Decreasing Brake Pedal Travel. If o.k., check push rod height. If unit has internal bind or incorrect push rod height, replace unit.
	4. Incorrect brake lining or lining loose on brakeshoes.	4. Replace brakeshoes in axle sets.
	5. Brakeshoes bent, cracked, distorted.	5. Replace brakeshoes in axle sets.
	6. Caliper anchor plate bolts loose.	6. Tighten bolts.
	7. Rear brakeshoes binding on support plate ledges.	7. Clean and lubricate ledges. Replace support plate(s) if ledges are deeply grooved. Do not attempt to smooth ledges by grinding.
	8. Rear brake support plates loose.	8. Tighten mounting bolts.
	9. Caliper or wheel cylinder piston sticking or seized.	9. Repair or replace parts as necessary.

BRAKES—Continued

Condition	Possible Cause	Correction
GRABBING BRAKES, continued	10. Master cylinder pistons sticking or seized in bore.	10. Repair or replace master cylinder.
BRAKES GRAB, PULL, OR WON'T HOLD IN WET WEATHER	1. Brake lining water soaked.	1. Drive car with brakes lightly applied to dry out lining. If problem persists after lining has dried, replace brakeshoe lining in axle sets.
	2. Rear brake support plate bent allowing excessive amount of water to enter drum.	2. Replace support plate.
DRAGGING BRAKES (Slow or incomplete release of brakes)	1. Brake pedal binding at pivot.	1. Free up and lubricate.
	2. Power brake unit push rod height incorrect (too high) or unit has internal bind.	2. Replace unit if push rod height is incorrect. If height is o.k., check for internal bind as outlined in item (3) under Decreasing Brake Pedal Travel.
	3. Parking brake cables incorrectly adjusted or seized.	3. Adjust cables. Free up or replace seized cables.
	4. Brakeshoe return springs weak or broken.	4. Replace return springs. Replace brakeshoe if necessary in axle sets.
	5. Automatic adjusters malfunctioning.	5. Repair or replace adjuster parts as required.
	6. Caliper, wheel cylinder or master cylinder pistons sticking or seized.	6. Repair or replace parts as necessary.
	7. Master cylinder compensating ports blocked (fluid does not return to reservoirs).	7. Use compressed air to clear ports. Do not use wire, pencils, or similar objects to open blocked ports.
CAR PULLS TO ONE SIDE WHEN BRAKES ARE APPLIED	1. Incorrect front tire pressure.	1. Inflate to recommended cold (reduced load) inflation pressures.
	2. Incorrect front wheel bearing adjustment or worn—damaged wheel bearings.	2. Adjust wheel bearings. Replace worn, damaged bearings.
	3. Brakeshoe lining on one side contaminated.	3. Determine and correct cause of contamination and replace brakeshoe lining in axle sets.
	4. Brakeshoes on one side bent, distorted, or lining loose on shoe.	4. Replace brakeshoes in axle sets.
	5. Support plate bent or loose on one side.	5. Tighten or replace support plate.
	6. Brake lining not yet seated to drums and rotors.	6. Burnish brakes.
	7. Caliper anchor plate loose on one side.	7. Tighten anchor plate bolts.
	8. Caliper or wheel cylinder piston sticking or seized.	8. Repair or replace caliper or wheel cylinder.
	9. Brakeshoe linings watersoaked.	9. Drive car with brakes lightly applied to dry linings. Replace brakeshoes in axle sets if problem persists.
	10. Loose suspension component attaching or mounting bolts, incorrect front end alignment. Worn suspension parts.	10. Tighten suspension bolts. Replace worn suspension components. Check and correct alignment as necessary.
CHATTER OR SHUDDER WHEN BRAKES ARE APPLIED (Pedal pulsation and roughness may also occur)	1. Front wheel bearings loose.	1. Adjust wheel bearings.
	2. Brakeshoes distorted, bent, contaminated, or worn.	2. Replace brakeshoes in axle sets.
	3. Caliper anchor plate or support plate loose.	3. Tighten mounting bolts.
	4. Excessive thickness variation or lateral rim out of rotor.	4. Refinish or replace rotor.
	5. Rear drum(s) out of round, sharp spots.	5. Refinish or replace drum.
	6. Loose suspension component attaching or mounting bolts, incorrect front end alignment. Worn suspension parts.	6. Tighten suspension bolts. Replace worn suspension components. Check and correct alignment as necessary.
NOISY BRAKES (Squealing, clicking, scraping sound when brakes are applied)	1. Bent, broken, distorted brakeshoes.	1. Replace brakeshoes in axle sets.
	2. Brake lining worn out—shoes contacting drum or rotor.	2. Replace brakeshoes and lining in axle sets. Refinish or replace drums or rotors.
	3. Foreign material imbedded in brake lining.	3. Replace brake lining.
	4. Broken or loose hold-down or return springs.	4. Replace parts as necessary.
	5. Rough or dry drum brake support plate ledges.	5. Lubricate support plate ledges.
	6. Cracked, grooved, or scored rotor(s) or drum(s).	6. Replace rotor(s) or drum(s). Replace brakeshoes and lining in axle sets if necessary.

TROUBLE SHOOTING

BRAKES—Continued

Condition	Possible Cause	Correction
PULSATING BRAKE PEDAL	1. Out of round drums or excessive thickness variation or lateral runout in disc brake rotor(s). 2. Bent rear axle shaft.	1. Refinish or replace drums or rotors. 2. Replace axle shaft.

SUSPENSION & STEERING

Condition	Possible Cause	Correction
HARD OR ERRATIC STEERING	1. Incorrect tire pressure. 2. Insufficient or incorrect lubrication. 3. Suspension, steering or linkage parts damaged or misaligned. 4. Improper front wheel alignment. 5. Incorrect steering gear adjustment. 6. Sagging springs.	1. Inflate tires to recommended pressures. 2. Lubricate as required. 3. Repair or replace parts as necessary. 4. Adjust wheel alignment angles. 5. Adjust steering gear. 6. Replace springs.
PLAY OR LOOSENESS IN STEERING	1. Steering wheel loose. 2. Steering linkage or attaching parts loose or worn. 3. Pitman arm loose. 4. Steering gear attaching bolts loose. 5. Loose or worn wheel bearings. 6. Steering gear adjustment incorrect or parts badly worn.	1. Inspect splines and repair as necessary. Tighten steering wheel nut. 2. Tighten, adjust, or replace faulty components. 3. Inspect shaft splines and repair as necessary. Torque attaching nut and stake in place. 4. Tighten bolts. 5. Adjust or replace bearings. 6. Adjust gear or replace defective parts.
WHEEL SHIMMY OR TRAMP	1. Improper tire pressure. 2. Wheels, tires, or brake drums out-of-balance or out-of-round. 3. Inoperative, worn, or loose shock absorbers or mounting parts. 4. Loose or worn steering or suspension parts. 5. Loose or worn wheel bearings. 6. Incorrect steering gear adjustments. 7. Incorrect front wheel alignment.	1. Inflate tires to recommended pressures. 2. Inspect parts and replace unacceptable out-of-round parts. Rebalance parts. 3. Repair or replace shocks or mountings. 4. Tighten or replace as necessary. 5. Adjust or replace bearings. 6. Adjust steering gear. 7. Correct front wheel alignment.
TIRE WEAR	1. Improper tire pressure. 2. Failure to rotate tires. 3. Brakes grabbing. 4. Incorrect front wheel alignment. 5. Broken or damaged steering and suspension parts. 6. Wheel runout. 7. Excessive speed on turns.	1. Inflate tires to recommended pressures. 2. Rotate tires. 3. Adjust or repair brakes. 4. Align incorrect angles. 5. Repair or replace defective parts. 6. Replace faulty wheel. 7. Make driver aware of condition.
CAR LEADS TO ONE SIDE	1. Improper tire pressures. 2. Front tires with uneven tread depth, wear pattern, or different cord design (i.e., one bias ply and one belted tire on front wheels). 3. Incorrect front wheel alignment. 4. Brakes dragging. 5. Faulty power steering gear valve assembly. 6. Pulling due to uneven tire construction.	1. Inflate tires to recommended pressures. 2. Install tires of same cord construction and reasonably even tread depth and wear pattern. 3. Align incorrect angles. 4. Adjust or repair brakes. 5. Replace valve assembly. 6. Replace faulty tire.

HEADLAMPS

Condition	Possible Cause	Correction
ONE HEADLAMP INOPERATIVE OR INTERMITTENT	1. Loose connection. 2. Defective sealed beam.	1. Secure connections to sealed beam including ground. 2. Replace sealed beam.
ONE OR MORE HEADLIGHTS ARE DIM	1. Open ground connection at headlight. 2. Ground wire mislocated in headlight connector (type 2 sealed beam).	1. Repair ground wire connection between sealed beam and body ground. 2. Relocate ground wire in connector.
ONE OR MORE HEADLIGHTS SHORT LIFE	1. Voltage regulator maladjusted.	1. Readjust regulator to specifications.

HEADLAMPS—Continued

Condition	Possible Cause	Correction
ALL HEADLIGHTS INOPERATIVE OR INTERMITTENT	1. Loose connection.	1. Check and secure connections at dimmer switch and light switch.
	2. Defective dimmer switch.	2. Check voltage at dimmer switch with test lamp. If test lamp bulb lights only at switch "Hot" wire terminal, replace dimmer switch.
	3. Open wiring—light switch to dimmer switch.	3. Check wiring with test lamp. If bulb lights at light switch wire terminal, but not at dimmer switch, repair open wire.
	4. Open wiring—light switch to battery.	4. Check "Hot" wire terminal at light switch with test lamp. If lamp does not light, repair open wire circuit to battery (possible open fusible link).
	5. Shorted ground circuit.	5. If, after a few minutes operation, headlights flicker "ON" and "OFF" and/or a thumping noise can be heard from the light switch (circuit breaker opening and closing), repair short to ground in circuit between light switch and headlights. After repairing short, check for headlight flickering after one minute operation. If flickering occurs, the circuit breaker has been damaged and light switch must be replaced.
	6. Defective light switch.	6. Check light switch. Replace light switch, if defective.
UPPER OR LOWER BEAM WILL NOT LIGHT OR INTERMITTENT	1. Open connection or defective dimmer switch.	1. Check dimmer switch terminals with test lamp. If bulb lights at all wire terminals, repair open wiring between dimmer switch and headlights. If bulb will not light at one of these terminals, replace dimmer switch.
	2. Short circuit to ground.	2. Follow diagnosis above (all headlights inoperative or intermittent).

SIDE MARKER LAMPS

Condition	Possible Cause	Correction
ONE LAMP INOPERATIVE	1. Turn signal bulb burnt out (front lamp).	1. Switch turn signals on. If signal bulb does not light, replace bulb.
	2. Side marker bulb burnt out.	2. Replace bulb.
	3. Loose connection or open in wiring.	3. Using test lamp, check "Hot" wire terminal at bulb socket. If test lamp lights, repair open ground circuit. If lamp does not light, repair open "Hot" wire circuit.
FRONT OR REAR LAMPS INOPERATIVE	1. Loose connection or open ground connection.	1. If associated tail or park lamps do not operate, secure all connectors in "Hot" wire circuit. If park and turn lamps operate, repair open ground connections.
	2. Multiple bulbs burnt out.	2. Replace burnt out bulbs.
ALL LAMPS INOPERATIVE	1. Blown fuse.	1. If park and tail lamps do not operate, replace blown fuse. If new fuse blows, check for short to ground between fuse panel and lamps.
	2. Loose connection.	2. Secure connector to light switch.
	3. Open in wiring.	3. Check tail light fuse with test lamp. If test lamp lights, repair open wiring between fuse and light switch. If not, repair open wiring between fuse and battery (possible open fusible link).
	4. Defective light switch.	4. Check light switch. Replace light switch, if defective.

TROUBLE SHOTING

TAIL, PARK AND LICENSE LAMPS

Condition	Possible Cause	Correction
ONE SIDE INOPERATIVE	1. Bulb burnt out. 2. Open ground connection at bulb socket or ground wire terminal.	1. Replace bulb. 2. Jump bulb base socket connection to ground. If lamp lights, repair open ground circuit.
BOTH SIDES INOPERATIVE	1. Tail lamp fuse blown. 2. Loose connection. 3. Open wiring. 4. Multiple bulb burnout. 5. Defective light switch.	1. Replace fuse. If new fuse blows, repair short to ground in "Hot" wire circuit between fuse panel through light switch to lamps. 2. Secure connector at light switch. 3. Using test light, check circuit on both sides of fuse. If lamp does not light on either side, repair open circuit between fuse panel and battery (possible open fusible link). If test lamp lights at light switch terminal, repair open wiring between light switch and lamps. 4. If test lamp lights at lamp socket "Hot" wire terminal, replace bulbs. 5. Check light switch. Replace light switch, if defective.

TURN SIGNAL AND HAZARD WARNING LAMP

TURN SIGNALS INOPERATIVE ONE SIDE	1. Bulb(s) burnt out (flasher cannot be heard). 2. Open wiring or ground connection. 3. Improper bulb or defective turn signal switch. 4. Short to ground (flasher can be heard, no bulbs operate).	1. Turn hazard warning system on. If one or more bulbs are inoperative replace necessary bulbs. 2. Turn hazard warning system on. If one or more bulbs are inoperative, use test lamp and check circuit at lamp socket. If test lamp lights, repair open ground connection. If not, repair open wiring between bulb socket and turn signal switch. 3. Turn hazard warning system on. If all front and rear lamps operate, check for improper bulb. If bulbs are OK, replace defective turn signal switch. 4. Locate and repair short to ground by disconnecting front and rear circuits separately.
TURN SIGNALS INOPERATIVE	1. Blown turn signal fuse. 2. Defective flasher. 3. Loose connection.	1. Turn hazard warning system on. If all lamps operate, replace blown fuse. If new fuse blows, repair short to ground between fuse and lamps. 2. If turn signal fuse is OK and hazard warning system will operate lamps, replace defective turn signal flasher. 3. Secure steering column connector.
HAZARD WARNING LAMPS INOPERATIVE	1. Blown fuse. 2. Defective hazard warning flasher. 3. Open in wiring or defective turn signal switch.	1. Switch turn signals on. If lamps operate, replace fuse if blown. If new fuse blows, repair short to ground. (could be in stop light circuit). 2. If fuse is OK, switch turn signals on. If lamps operate, replace defective hazard flasher. 3. Using test lamp, check hazard switch feed wire in turn signal steering column connector. If lamp does not light on either side of connector, repair open circuit between flasher and connector. If lamp lights only on feed side of connector, clean connector contacts. If lamp lights on both sides of connector, replace defective turn signal switch assembly.

BACK-UP LAMP

Condition	Possible Cause	Correction
ONE LAMP INOPERATIVE OR INTERMITTENT	1. Loose or burnt out bulb. 2. Loose connection. 3. Open ground connections.	1. Secure or replace bulb. 2. Tighten connectors. 3. Repair bulb ground circuit.
BOTH LAMPS INOPERATIVE OR INTERMITTENT	1. Neutral start or back-up lamp switch maladjusted. 2. Loose connection or open circuit. 3. Blown fuse. 4. Defective neutral start or back-up lamp switch. 5. Defective ignition switch.	1. Readjust or replace bulb. 2. Secure all connectors. If OK, check continuity of circuit from fuse to lamps with test lamp. If lamp does not light on either side of fuse, correct open circuit from battery to fuse. 3. Replace fuse. If new fuse blows, repair short to ground in circuit from fuse through neutral start switch to back-up lamps. 4. Check switch. Replace neutral start or back-up lamp switch, if defective. 5. If test lamp lights at ignition switch battery terminal but not at output terminal, replace ignition switch.
LAMP WILL NOT TURN OFF	1. Neutral start or back-up switch maladjusted. 2. Defective neutral start or back-up lamp switch.	1. Readjust neutral start or back-up lamp switch. 2. Check switch. Replace neutral start or back-up lamp switch, if defective.

STOP LIGHTS

Condition	Possible Cause	Correction
ONE BULB INOPERATIVE	1. Bulb burnt out.	1. Replace bulb.
ONE SIDE INOPERATIVE	1. Loose connection, open wiring or defective bulbs. 2. Defective directional signal switch or canceling cam.	1. Turn on directional signal. If lamp does not operate, check bulbs. If bulbs are OK, secure all connections. If lamp still does not operate, use test lamp and check for open wiring. 2. If lamp will operate by turning directional signal on, the switch is not centering properly during canceling operation. Replace defective cancelling cam or directional signal switch.
ALL INOPERATIVE	1. Blown fuse. 2. Stop-switch maladjusted or defective.	1. Replace fuse. If new fuse blows, repair short to ground in circuit between fuse and lamps. 2. Check stop switch. Adjust or replace stop switch, if required.
WILL NOT TURN OFF	1. Stop switch maladjusted or defective.	1. Readjust switch. If switch still malfunctions, replace.

HORNS

Condition	Possible Cause	Correction
HORNS WILL NOT OPERATE	1. Loose connections in circuit. 2. Defective horn switch. 3. Defective horn relay. 4. Defects within horn.	1. Check and tighten connections. Be sure to check ground straps. 2. Replace defective parts. 3. Replace relay. 4. Replace horn.
HORNS HAVE POOR TONE	1. Low available voltage at horn, or defects within horn.	1. Check battery and charging circuit. Although horn should blow at any voltage above 7.0 volts, a weak or poor tone may occur at operating voltage below 11.0 volts. If horn has weak or poor tone at operating voltage of 11.0 volts or higher, remove horn and replace.
HORNS OPERATE INTERMITTENTLY	1. Loose or intermittent connections in horn relay or horn switch. 2. Defective horn switch.	1. Check and tighten connections. 2. Replace switch.

TROUBLE SHOOTING

Condition	Possible Cause	Correction
HORNS OPERATE INTERMITTENTLY, continued	3. Defective relay. 4. Defects within horn.	3. Replace relay. 4. Replace horn.
HORNS BLOW CONSTANTLY	1. Sticking horn relay. 2. Horn relay energized by grounded or shorted wiring. 3. Horn button can be grounded by sticking closed.	1. Replace relay. 2. Check and adjust wiring. 3. Adjust or replace damaged parts.

SPEEDOMETER

SPEEDOMETER NOT OPERATING PROPERLY	1. Noisy speedometer cable. 2. Pointer and odometer inoperative. Inaccurate reading. 3. Kinked cable. 4. Defective speedometer head. 5. Casing connector loose on speedometer case.	1. Loosen over-tightened casing nuts and snap-on at speedometer head. Replace housing and core. Replace broken cable. 2. Check tire size. Check for correct speedometer driven gear. 3. Replace cable. Reroute casing so that bends have no less than 6″ radius. 4. Replace speedometer. 5. Tighten connector.

NOISE, VIBRATION & HARSHNESS

Road Test

A road test and customer interview can provide much of the information needed to identify the specific condition which must be dealt with.

1. Make notes during diagnosis routine. This will ensure diagnosis is complete and systematic. Take care not to overlook details.
2. Road test vehicle and study condition by reproducing it several times during test.
3. When condition is reproduced, perform road test checks immediately. Refer to "Road Test Quick Checks" to identify proper section of diagnostic procedure. Perform checks several times to ensure valid conclusions. While the quick checks may not locate the problem, they will indicate the areas where there are no problems.
4. Do not make changes or adjustments before a road test and inspection of vehicle are performed. Any changes made can hide problems or add additional problems. Check and note tire pressures, any leaks, loose nuts or bolts, shiny spots where components may be rubbing, and if any unusually heavy items are in trunk.

Road Test Quick Checks

1. **25–50 mph**—Under light acceleration, a moaning noise can be heard possibly accompanied by a vibration in floor. Refer to "Tip-In Moan" diagnostic procedure.
2. **25–45 mph**—Under steady to heavy acceleration, a rumbling noise can be heard. Refer to "Incorrect Driveline Angle" diagnostic procedure.
3. **High Speed**—Under slow acceleration and deceleration, shaking is noticeable in steering column or wheel, seats, floor pan, trim panels, or front end sheet metal. Refer to "High Speed Shake" procedure.
4. **High Speed**—Vibration can be felt in floor pan or seats, with no visible shaking but with rumble, buzz, hum, or booming noise. Refer to "Driveline Vibration" procedure.
5. **High Speed**—Coast with clutch disengaged or with automatic transmission in neutral and engine idling. If vibration is present, refer to "Driveline Vibration" procedure. If vibration is no longer present, refer to "Engine and Accessory Vibration" or "High Speed Shake" procedures.
6. **0–High Speed**—Vibration can be felt when engine reaches particular RPM. Vibration can also be felt when vehicle is stationary. Refer to "Engine and Accessory Vibration."

Types of Conditions

High Speed Shake (35 mph)

This condition involves a visible shake and pumping feeling in steering column, seats, or floor pan. The vibration is of low frequency (about 9–15 cycles per second) and may be seen as front end sheet metal shake. The condition may or may not be intensified by lightly applying brakes.

Tip-In Moan (15–50 mph)

Acceleration between 15–50 mph is accompanied by vibration which causes moan or high frequency resonance in floor pan. This condition is usually worse at a particular engine speed and at a particular throttle opening during acceleration at that speed. A moaning sound may also be caused depending on which component is producing the noise.

Driveline Vibration (50 mph)

This condition does not involve a visible vibration, but is felt in floor pan as rumble, buzz, hum, drone, or boom. This condition is independent of engine speed and will occur at same speed in any gear, and is not sensitive to acceleration or deceleration and cannot be reduced by coasting in neutral. The condition can be duplicated by supporting vehicle on axle-type hoist and operating driveline in gear at appropriate speed.

Engine or Accessory Vibration (All Speeds)

This condition can occur at any vehicle speed but always at same engine RPM. Vibration will disappear during neutral coast and can be duplicated by operating engine at problem RPM with vehicle stationary. The condition can be caused by any component turning at engine speed when vehicle is stationary.

High Speed Shake

1. Apply brakes gently. If shake increases, proceed to step 2; if shake does not increase, proceed to step 10.
2. Lightly apply parking brake. If shake increases, proceed to step 3; if shake does not increase, proceed to step 6.
3. Check clearance between rear drum and brake shoe. Loosen cable tension if necessary. If clearance is correct, proceed to step 4; if clearance is not correct, proceed to step 7.
4. Using dial indicator, check axle flange run-out, Fig. 1. If run-out is acceptable, proceed to step 5. If run-out is unacceptable, proceed to step 8.
5. Check run-out of rear brake drum or disc. If run-out is acceptable, proceed to step 10. If run-out is unacceptable, proceed to step 9.
6. Check run-out of front brake disc. If run-out is acceptable, proceed to step 10. If run-out is unacceptable, proceed to step 9.
7. Adjust parking brake cable tension and road test vehicle. If shake is not eliminated, proceed to step 4.
8. Replace axle shaft and road test vehicle. If shake is not eliminated, proceed to step 5.
9. Replace or machine brake drums or discs and road test vehicle. If shake is not eliminated, proceed to step 10.
10. Raise and support vehicle. Turn wheels by hand and check for abnormal wear,

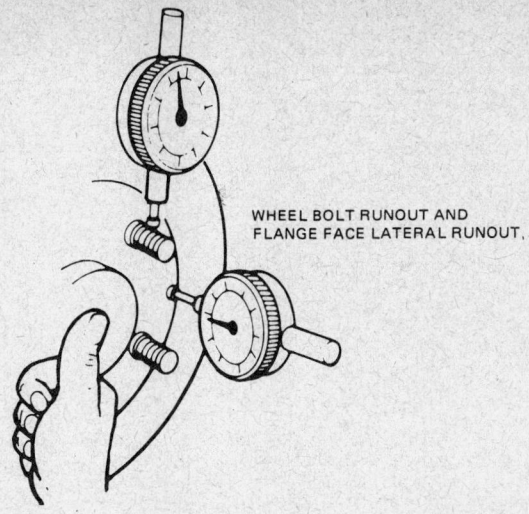

Fig. 1 Checking axle flange run-out

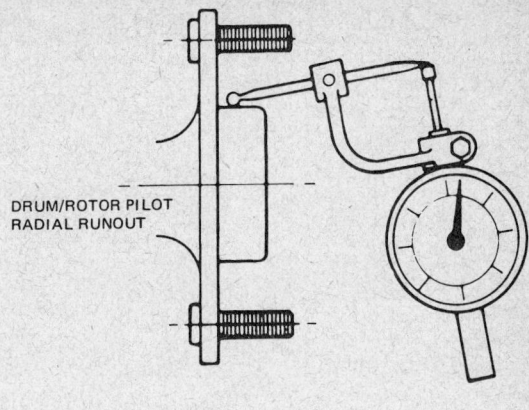

Fig. 2 Checking drum/rotor pilot radial run-out

damage, wheel bearing play or roughness. If abnormal wear or damage is found, proceed to step 12. If wheel bearing displays excessive play or roughness, proceed to step 13. If brakes drag proceed to steps 5 and 6.

11. Road test vehicle, noting carefully which area of vehicle is shaking. If front end sheet metal is shaking heavily, proceed to step 14. If shaking is felt more in floor pan, seat and steering column, proceed to step 15.

12. Replace worn or damaged tires and check for any other damaged components such as shock absorbers. Road test vehicle. If vehicle still shakes, proceed to step 15.

13. Check and adjust wheel bearings. Replace damaged wheel bearings and road test vehicle. If shake is not eliminated, proceed to step 15.

14. Check and tighten all major front end sheet metal attaching bolts and adjust hood rests. Road test vehicle. If shake is not eliminated, proceed to step 15.

15. Balance wheels on vehicle and check tires and rims for run-out. If wheel balancing is not necessary, proceed to step 16. If wheel and tire run-out are found, proceed to step 19.

16. Road test vehicle at speed at which condition was most apparent. If shake is not eliminated, proceed to step 17.

17. Install a known good set of wheels and tires on vehicle and road test. If shake is eliminated, proceed to step 18. If shake is not eliminated, proceed to step 23.

18. If one or more of the tires has a construction irregularity which causes tire to contact the road in an irregular manner, substitute known good tires until irregular tires are located.

19. Attempt to reduce run-out by mounting wheel in different position in relation to axle. If run-out is now acceptable, proceed to step 16. If run-out is still excessive, proceed to step 17. If repositioning indicates axle shaft run-out, proceed to step 22. If repositioning indicates tire and wheel run-out, proceed to step 20.

20. Attempt to correct run-out by repositioning tire on rim. If run-out is acceptable, proceed to step 15. If run-out is still excessive, proceed to step 21.

21. Replace component shown to be unserviceable and recheck run-out. If run-out is acceptable, proceed to step 15. if run-

out is excessive, proceed to step 22.

22. Measure axle shaft run-out, Fig. 2. Replace shaft if run-out is excessive and check run-out of new shaft. Install wheel and check run-out again. If run-out is acceptable, proceed to step 15. If run-out is excessive, proceed to step 20.

23. Raise and support vehicle. Remove rear wheels and tires. Check all axle and brake rotor run-out measurements if not already checked. If axle and brake run-out are acceptable, proceed to step 24. If axle run-out is excessive, proceed to step 8. If brake disc run-out is excessive, proceed to step 9.

24. Check driveshaft run-out. If run-out is acceptable, proceed to step 25. if run-out is excessive, proceed to step 27.

25. Remove driveshaft and inspect universal joints. If joints are OK, proceed to step 26. If joints are defective, replace joints.

26. Install driveshaft and check for vibration. If vibration is unacceptable, proceed to step 27.

27. Measure ring gear run-out. If run-out is excessive, proceed to step 28.

28. Install new ring and pinion. Check run-out to ensure parts are within specifications. Recheck for vibration.

Moaning Noise During Light Acceleration

1. Inspect air cleaner for correct positioning of gasket, lid and gasket, element and duct. Correct if necessary and check condition. If noise is unacceptable, proceed to step 2.

2. On vehicles where a transmission extension housing damper is specified, ensure damper is installed. Recheck condition, if noise is unacceptable, proceed to step 3.

3. Loosen engine mounts, start engine, and shift from Neutral to Drive and back to normalize engine mounts. Tighten engine mounts and check condition; if noise is unacceptable, proceed to step 4.

4. With exhaust system hot, loosen hangers, and operate engine while shifting from Neutral to Drive and back to normalize exhaust system. Tighten hangers and recheck condition; if noise is unacceptable, proceed to step 5.

5. Inspect accessory drive belts for proper tension and accessory brackets for proper

bolt torques. Adjust or tighten if necessary and check condition, if noise is unacceptable, proceed to step 6.

6. Loosen all bell housing bolts ¾ turn to test if noise is reduced. If noise is reduced, recheck step 2.

Driveline Vibration

1. Raise and support vehicle with drive wheels free. Operate driveline at problem speed. If vibration is present, proceed to step 3; if vibration is not present, proceed to step 2.

2. Retest vehicle to observe reported condition.

3. Evaluate noise and vibration by operating driveline at problem speed. If audible boom or rumble occurs above 30 mph, proceed to step 4. If buzzy feel occurs in floor pan above 30 mph, proceed to step 5. If a gravelly feel or grinding sound occurs at low speeds, proceed to step 4.

4. Install rear spring dampers if available for vehicle. If condition is still unacceptable or dampers are not available, proceed to step 5.

5. Scribe a line to index rear axle companion flange to driveshaft flange. Inspect drive shaft for dents, undercoating, proper seating of U-joint bearing caps, and tight U-joints. If driveshaft is in acceptable condition, proceed to step 6. Replace driveshaft if damaged. Replace U-joints if worn or improperly positioned.

6. Inspect wheel bearings. If bearings are OK, proceed to step 10; if wheel bearings are not in acceptable condition, proceed to step 7.

7. Replace wheel bearings and retest for vibration. If vibration is unacceptable proceed to step 10.

8. Repair or replace driveshaft. If vibration is unacceptable proceed to step 10.

9. Reposition U-joint bearing caps or replace U-joints. If vibration is unacceptable, proceed to step 10.

10. Disconnect driveshaft from rear axle companion flange and reconnect 180° from original position. Operate driveline at problem speed. If vibration is unacceptable, install rear axle pinion nose damper if available for vehicle. If pinion damper is not available or vibration is still unacceptable, proceed to step 11.

11. Disconnect driveshaft and return to orig-

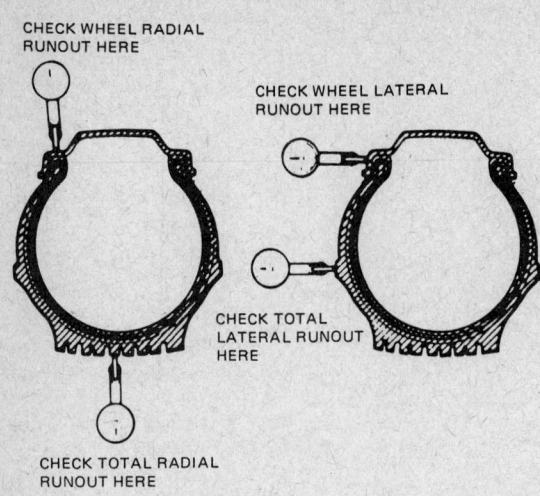

Fig. 3 Checking tire/wheel radial run-out

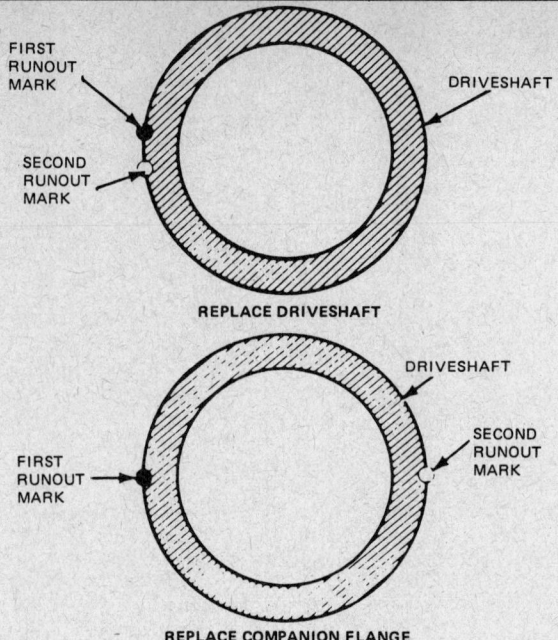

Fig. 4 Checking driveshaft run-out

inal position. Refer to "Driveshaft Run-out, Check" procedure and check run-out at front, center, and rear of driveshaft. If run-out is less than .035 inch at all positions, proceed to step 15 of "High Speed Shake" diagnosis. If run-out at front and/or center of driveshaft exceeds .035 inch while rear of shaft is acceptable, proceed to step 8. If run-out at rear of driveshaft exceeds .035 inch, proceed to "Driveshaft Run-out Check" procedure.

12. Balance driveshaft on vehicle and test vehicle at problem speed. If vibration is still unacceptable, proceed to step 17 of "High Speed Shake" diagnosis.

Incorrect Pinion Angle

1. Ensure U-joints are tight and all bearing caps are in plate. If U-joints are in good condition, proceed to step 3; if not, proceed to step 2.
2. Make an index mark on driveshaft and rear axle companion flange. Remove driveshaft and replace U-joints. Retest vehicle; if vibration is unacceptable, proceed to step 3.
3. Refer to "Driveline Pinion Angle Check" procedure to check pinion angle.
4. If pinion angle is correct, proceed to step 1 of "Driveline Vibration."

Engine or Accessory Vibration

1. With vehicle stationary, run engine at problem speed to check for condition. If vibration is present, proceed to step 2; if not, proceed to step 1 of "Driveline Vibration" diagnosis.
2. Inspect drive belts to check for wear or fraying. Ensure pulleys are not damaged or bent. Replace any damaged components and operate engine at problem speed. If vibration is present, proceed to step 3.
3. Check drive belt tension and adjust if necessary. Operate engine at problem

speed. If vibration is still present, proceed to step 4.
4. Check torque of all accessory bracket bolts and retorque as necessary. Operate engine at problem speed; if vibration is still present, proceed to step 5.
5. Check pulley alignment and run-out visually at idle. Realign or replace pulleys if necessary. Operate engine at problem speed; if condition is still present, proceed to step 6.
6. Inspect belts for severe whipping at problem speed. If whip cannot be corrected by adjusting tension, replace belts. Operate engine at problem speed; if condition is still present, proceed to step 7.
7. Check engine accessories for noise while operating engine at problem speed. If vibration is still present, proceed to step 9. If vibration is not present, proceed to step 8.
8. Repair or replace noisy accessory. Connect and tension drive belt. Operate engine at problem speed; if vibration is still present, proceed to step 9.
9. Remove accessory from bracket. Inspect all hardware and bracket. Repair or replace as necessary.

Checks & Adjustments

TIRE/WHEEL RUN-OUT

1. After road test, promptly raise car on hoist to prevent flat spots in tires. Spin front wheels by hand to check for rough wheel bearings. Ensure bearings are not loose and adjust if necessary. If bearings are OK, proceed to step 2. If bearings have rough feel, proceed to step 2.
2. Check total radial and lateral run-out of tire and wheel assembly, Fig. 3. If both run-out measurements are less than .070 inch, balance tires. If lateral run-out exceeds .070 inch, proceed to step 3. If radial run-out exceeds .070 inch, proceed to step 4.
3. Check wheel rim lateral run-out. If run-out is less than .045 inch, replace tire and

proceed to step 2. If run-out exceeds .045 inch, replace wheel and proceed to step 2.
4. Mark point of maximum run-out on tire thread. Check radial run-out of wheel. If radial run-out of wheel exceeds .045 inch, replace wheel and proceed to step 2. If radial run-out of wheel is less than .045 inch, proceed to step 5.
5. Mark point of least run-out on wheel. Remove tire from wheel and match point of maximum tire run-out with point of least run-out on wheel. Mount tire in this position and check total radial run-out of wheel and tire assembly. If total radial run-out is less than .070 inch, balance tires. If run-out exceeds .070 inch, replace tire and proceed to step 2.

DRIVESHAFT RUN-OUT

1. Raise and support vehicle. Mark position of rear wheels in relation to mounting studs to ensure reinstallation in same position.
2. Turn driveshaft by turning rear drum or disc. Measure run-out at front, center, and rear of driveshaft. Mark point of highest run-out at each location. If run-out measurement at front or center of driveshaft is greater than .035 inch, install new driveshaft and retest vehicle. If run-out measurement at all three positions is less than .035 inch, balance driveshaft. If run-out measurement is less than .035 inch at front and center of driveshaft, but greater than .045 at rear of driveshaft, proceed to step 3.
3. Make mark indexing rear axle companion flange to driveshaft. Disconnect driveshaft at flange, turn 180°, and reconnect. Check run-out at rear of driveshaft and mark high point. If run-out measures less than .035 inch and vibration is unacceptable, balance driveshaft. If run-out measures more than .035 inch, proceed to step 4.
4. Check position of run-out marks from steps 2 and 3, Fig. 4. If marks are about 1

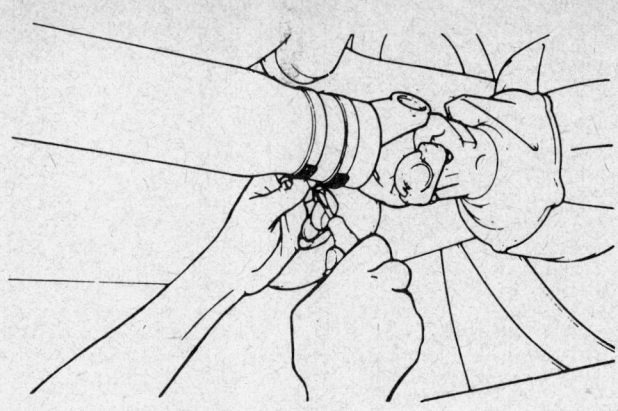

Fig. 5 Balancing driveshaft using hose clamps

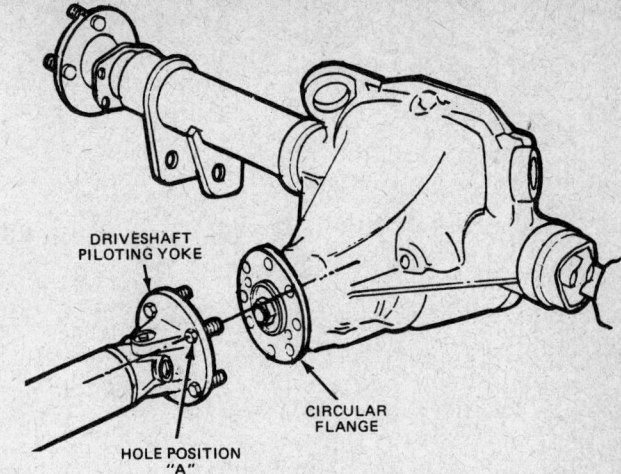

Fig. 6 Driveshaft indexing

inch apart, replace driveshaft. If marks are about 180° apart, replace rear axle companion flange and proceed to step 2.

DRIVESHAFT BALANCE

Two methods are possible depending on the method of connecting the driveshaft to the differential. Some vehicles are equipped with a drilled companion flange at the differential which allows re-indexing of the driveshaft in 45° increments. Driveshafts not equipped with this style flange can be balanced using worm-drive hose clamps, Fig. 5.

Re-indexing Method

1. Mark one hole of rear U-joint yoke flange with letter A. Number rear axle pinion flange holes 1 through 8 starting with hole opposite yoke flange hole A, Fig. 6. Position A-1 will be considered original index position.

NOTE: Check U-joints for binding while re-indexing.

2. Index driveshaft 180° to position A-5. Road test vehicle. If condition is still unsatisfactory, check condition in position A-3 and position A-7.
3. If further improvement is necessary, evaluate remaining positions that are located between best of previous positions

A-3 and A-7.
4. Coat flange bolts with suitable thread locking compound and torque to 70–95 ft. lbs.

Hose Clamp Method

1. Make a mark to index rear axle companion flange to driveshaft. Disconnect driveshaft at flange, turn 180° and reconnect. If vibration increases, return driveshaft to original position. If vibration is reduced, proceed to step 2.
2. Mark rear of driveshaft with 4 equal sections numbered 1 through 4. Install a worm-drive hose clamp with screw at position 1 on driveshaft, Fig. 7. Operate driveline at problem speed. Check with clamp in each position. If vibration is worse in each position, proceed to step 5. If vibration is reduced in any one position, proceed to step 3. If vibration is reduced in any 2 positions, turn clamp between those positions and proceed to step 3.
3. Install additional clamp with screw in same position as first clamp in its best position. Operate driveline at problem speed. If vibration is same or increased, proceed to step 4.
4. Rotate each clamp screw ½ inch away in opposite directions, Fig. 8. If vibration is reduced, continue to move clamp screws apart until vibration is minimal. If vibration is still excessive, proceed to step 5.

5. Install wheels and road test vehicle to check if vibration might be acceptable on road. If vibration is unacceptable, proceed to step 17 of "High Speed Shake" diagnosis procedure.

DRIVELINE PINION ANGLE CHECKING

1. Raise vehicle on drive-on hoist, ensuring vehicle is at proper controlled height, Fig. 9.
2. Turn driveshaft so pinion U-joint bearing cap is facing down.
3. Place Vee magnet from pinion angle measuring tool T68P-4602-A or equivalent on driveshaft. Working from left side of vehicle, position pinion angle gauge on Vee magnet with adjusting screw towards front of vehicle. Adjust screw so bubble just contacts zero line, Fig. 10.
4. Move gauge to U-joint bearing cap with tool in same relative position as it was on Vee magnet, Fig. 11.
5. Read position on left edge of bubble on scale to determine driveshaft pinion angle. If pinion angle is not correct, adjust. Recheck and proceed to step 6.
6. Position Vee magnet on front of driveshaft and position gauge on magnet. Zero bubble and move gauge to downward facing U-joint bearing cap at rear of transmission. Read driveline angle and compare with specification.

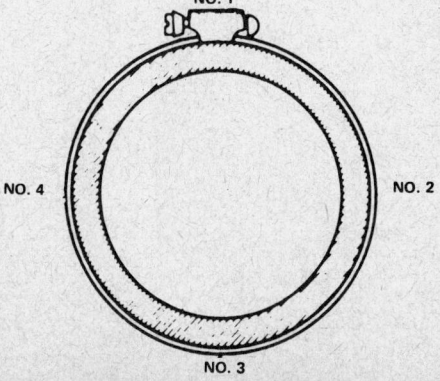

Fig. 7 Installing hose clamp

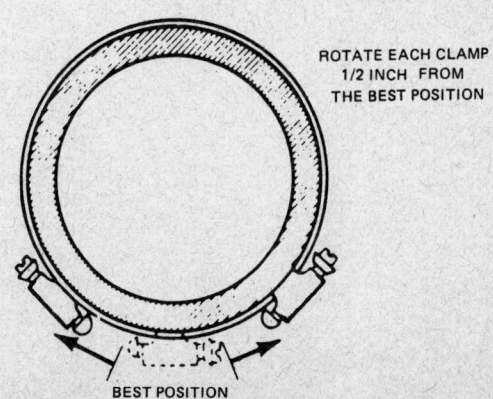

Fig. 8 Optimizing clamp location

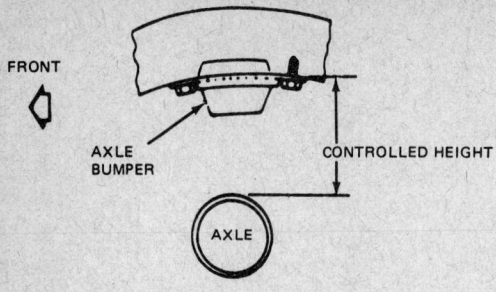

FRONT

AXLE BUMPER

CONTROLLED HEIGHT

AXLE

Fig. 9   Controlled height

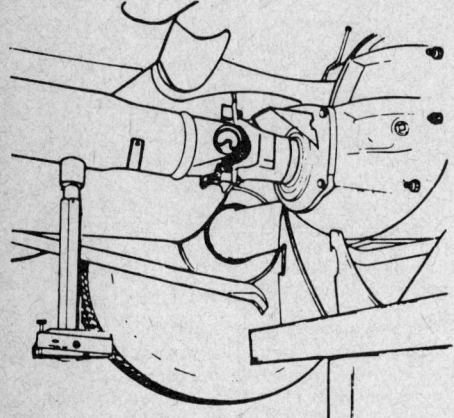

Fig. 10   Positioning driveline angle gauge on driveshaft

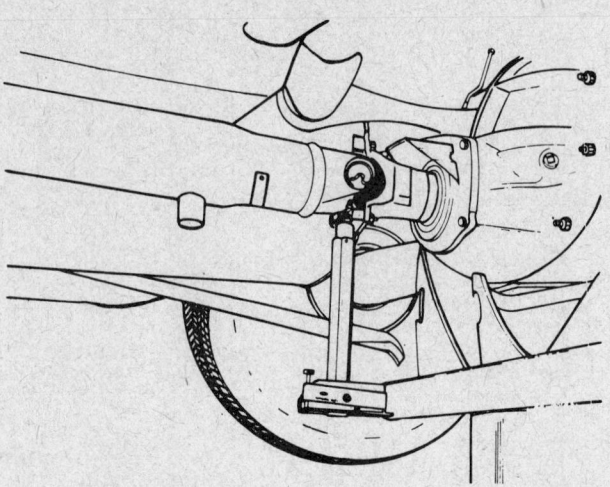

Fig. 11   Positioning driveline angle gauge on pinion U-joint cap

Electrical

CIRCUIT MALFUNCTIONS

There are three types of electrical malfunctions that cause an inoperative circuit. They are the open circuit, short circuit and grounded circuit.

Open Circuit

When there is a complete break in the normal current patch such as a broken wire, Fig. 1, it prevents the flow of electricity from the source of power to the electrical unit or from the electrical unit to the ground. In the automotive electrical circuit, the current usually flows through wires or cables, through switches and an electrical component. The component may be grounded through its mounting attachments or another wire to ground and back to the source. A break anywhere along this route results in an open circuit and a complete loss of power. A break in the circuit is an infinite high resistance. However, symptoms will appear different than the typical high resistance circuit. For example, there will be no heat created by this type of malfunction since there is no current flow. An ammeter will not produce a reading since there is no current flow. A voltmeter, depending on where it is placed in the circuit in relation to the "Open", may or may not register a reading.

A high resistance in a circuit reduces current flow and causes the unit to operate intermittently or not at all. An open or high resistance circuit may be caused by a broken wire

in the wiring harness, loose connections at terminals, broken leads or wiring within the units or poor ground connections between the unit and the ground.

Short Circuit

A short circuit, Fig. 2, is basically one that is completed the wrong way, such as two bare wires contacting each other so the current bypasses part of the circuit. When the current bypasses part of the circuit, it has found the path of least resistance and a higher current flow results. This causes blown fuses, wiring and component overheating, burned components and insulation, and inoperative components.

A short circuit causes more current flow through the conductor than the conductor can handle. This causes the conductor to overheat and, if the overload is severe or lasts long enough, will melt the wire and burn the insulation. If the wire melts through, there is no path for the current to flow and the circuit becomes an open circuit.

Grounded Circuit

A grounded circuit, Fig. 3, is similar to the short circuit since a grounded circuit also bypasses part of the normal circuit. However, the current flows directly to ground. A grounded circuit may be caused by a bare wire contacting the ground, or part of the circuit within a component contacting the frame or housing of the component. A grounded circuit

may also be caused by deposits of dirt, oil or moisture around the connections or terminals since these deposits provide a path for the current to flow to ground. The current follows the path of least resistance to complete the circuit back to ground.

CIRCUIT PROTECTION

Fuses

The most common circuit protector in the automotive electrical system is the fuse. The fuse consists of a thin wire or strip of metal enclosed in a glass tube. Some vehicles use a new type fuse where the wire is enclosed in plastic. The wire or metal strip melts when there is an overload caused by a short or grounded circuit. The fuse is designed to melt before the wiring or electrical components are damaged. The cause of the overload must be located and repaired before the new fuse is installed since the new fuse will also blow.

Fuses are rated in amperes. Since different circuits carry various amounts of current, depending upon load components and wire gauge, the properly rated fuse must be installed in the circuit. Never install a fuse with a higher amperage rating than the original.

Circuit Breakers

Circuit breakers incorporate a bimetallic strip which, when heated by an overloaded

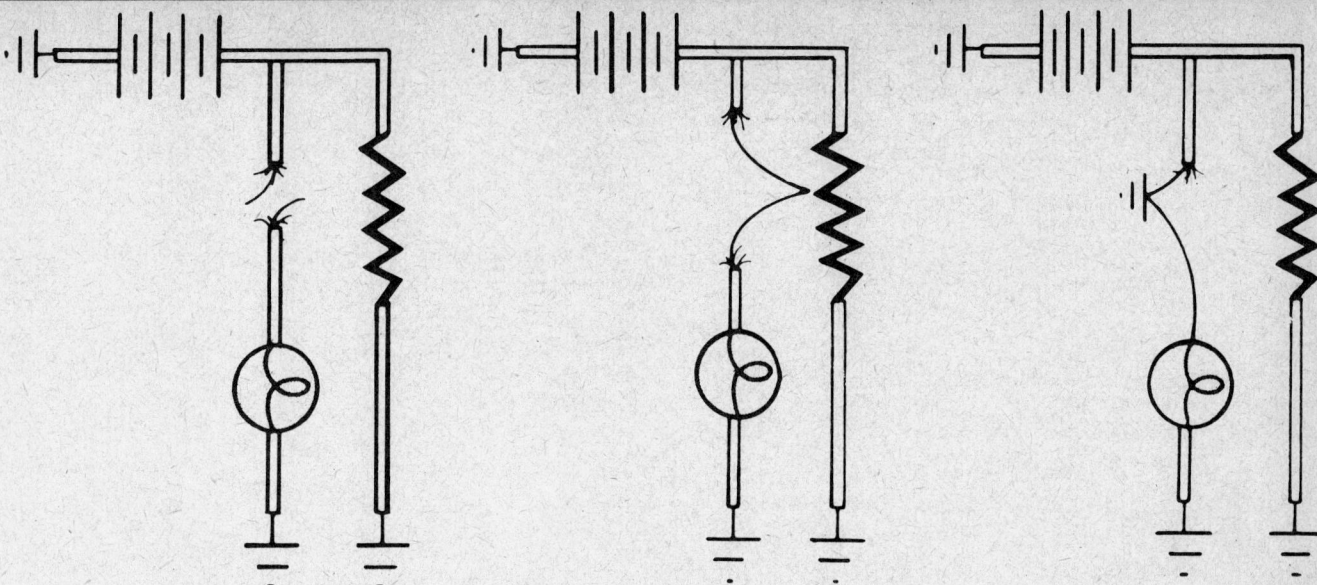

Fig. 1   Open circuit   Fig. 2   Short circuit   Fig. 3   Grounded circuit

circuit, moves and opens the contacts to break the circuit. When the bimetallic strip cools, it returns to the original position, closing the contacts and completing the circuit. The circuit breaker will open and close the circuit until the overload is located and repaired or the circuit is opened with a switch.

Fusible Link

A fusible link is a short length of wire connected into a heavy feed circuit of the wiring system. The wire is generally four gauge sizes smaller than the circuit being protected and is used when the circuit is not protected by a fuse or circuit breaker. The fusible link is designed to melt in event of an overload before damage can occur to the circuit. Fusible links are marked on the insulation with the wire gauge size since the heavy insulation causes the link to appear heavier in wire size. Engine compartment wiring harnesses incorporate fusible links. When replacing a fusible link, the overload must be located and repaired and the same size fusible link installed in the circuit.

TEST LAMP

Unpowered Type

A test light consists of a 12 volt lamp bulb fitted with a pair of convenient test leads or one lead and a probe, Fig. 4. This test light is used with the power "On."

Check for Power
1. Connect one of the leads to a good ground or the battery negative terminal, Fig. 5.
2. Use the other test lead to check for power at the suspected wires, connectors or components.
3. If the light illuminates, power exists at the location being tested.

Blown Fuse Condition Check
1. Turn off all equipment powered through the fuse.
2. Disconnect all load items powered through the fuse. If a motor is present in

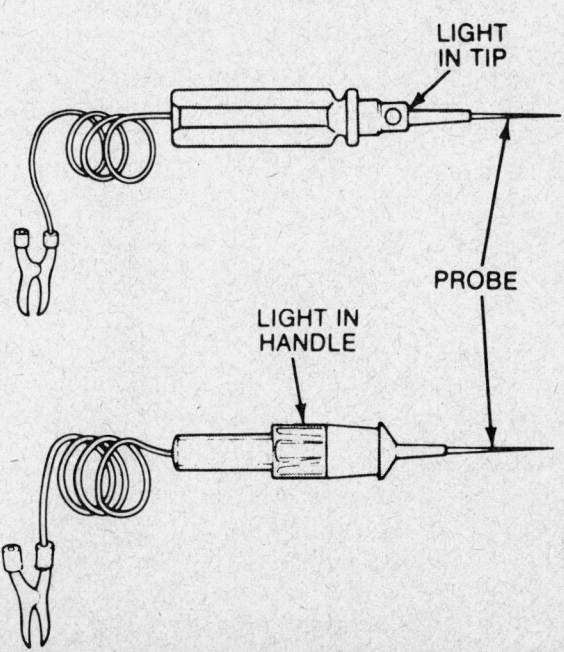

Fig. 4   12 volt test light

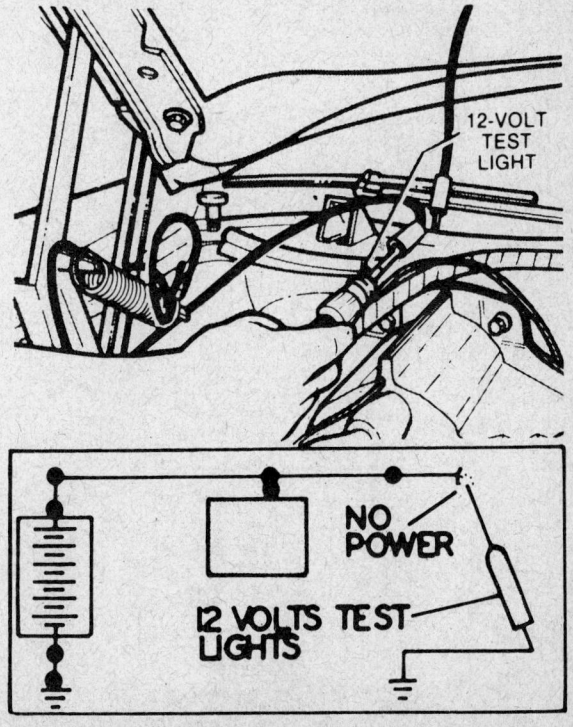

Fig. 5   Checking for power w/12 volt test light

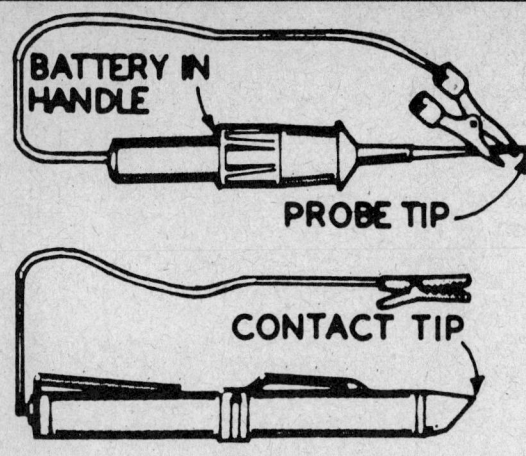

Fig. 6 Self powered test light

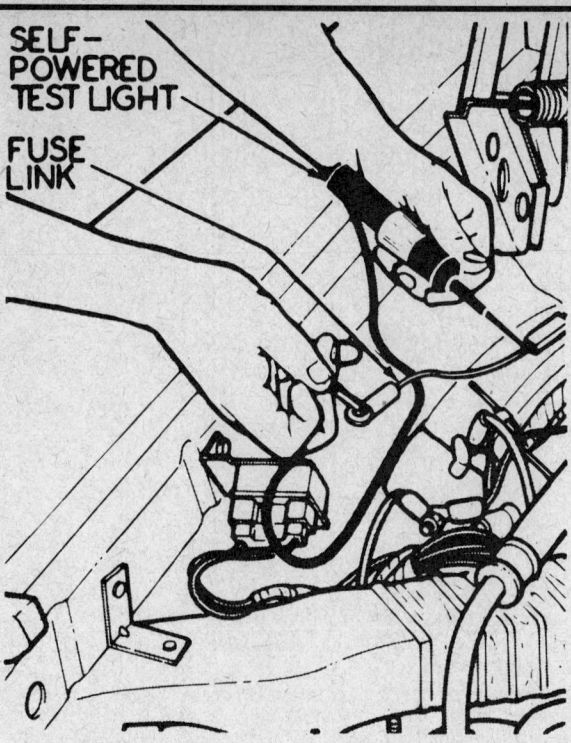

Fig. 7 Checking for continuity w/self powered test light

the circuit, disconnect the motor connector. If a light is present in the circuit, remove the lamp bulb.

3. Turn ignition switch to "Run" position if necessary to supply power to the fuse, then turn "On" the equipment switches.

4. Connect one test lead to the "Hot" end of the blown fuse and the other lead to a good ground. The light should illuminate, indicating power to the fuse.

5. Disconnect the test lead connected to ground and connect lead to the other end of the blown fuse. If the light does not illuminate, it indicates that the short circuit has been removed by disconnecting the equipment. If the light illuminates, it indicates that a ground is present in the wiring. Isolate the ground by disconnecting the connectors in the circuit one at a time. Refer to the "Power Check".

Self-Powered Type

The self-powered test light is a light and battery holder assembly fitted with test leads, or a test lead and a probe, Fig. 6. The light battery and test leads are connected in series so when the test leads are connected to two points of a continuous circuit, the light will illuminate, Fig. 7. This test light is used with the power "Off".

Continuity Check

Connect test leads to the ends of the suspected circuit. If the light illuminates, it indicates that the circuit is continuous and not broken. This test light may also be used to test a switch or other component. Connect the test leads to the switch terminals. If the light illuminates, the switch contacts are closed. At least one of the switch terminals should be disconnected from the normal switch circuit, so that only the switch is checked.

Ground Check

Connect one test lead to the suspected point and the other lead to the ground. If the light illuminates, it indicates that the point is grounded.

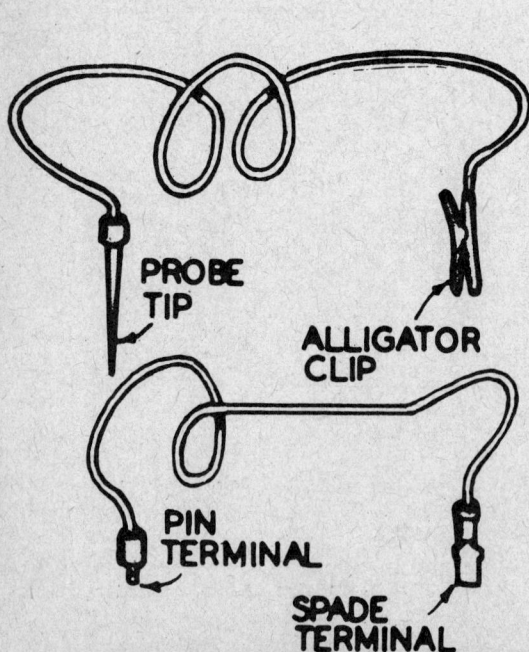

Fig. 8 Typical jumper wires

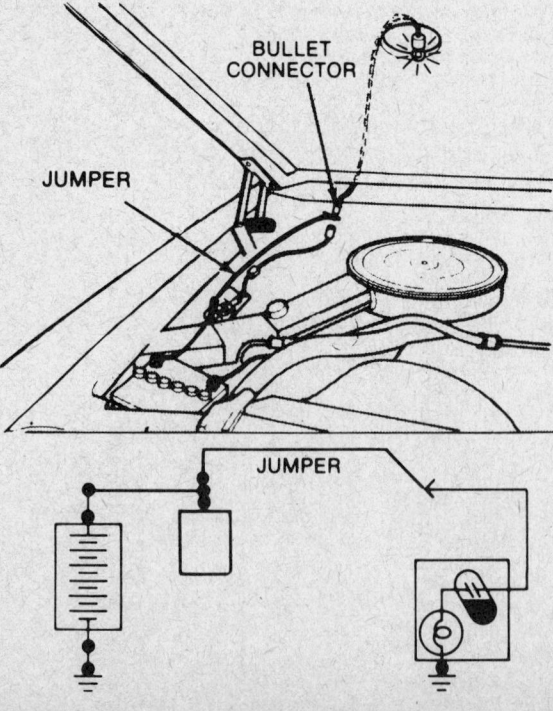

Fig. 9 Bypassing part of circuit w/jumper wire

VOLTMETER

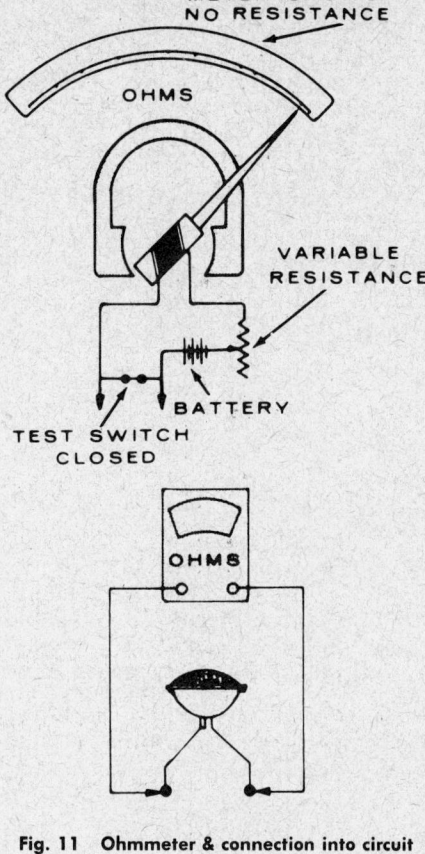

Fig. 10   Voltmeter & connection into circuit

OHMMETER

Fig. 11   Ohmmeter & connection into circuit

AMMETER

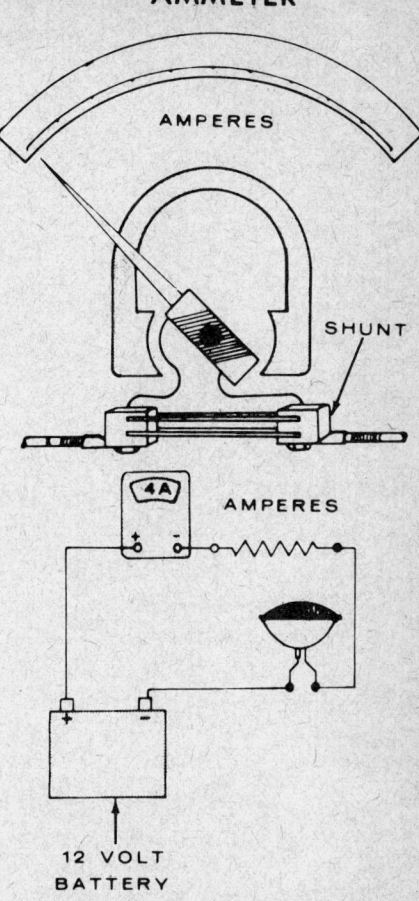

Fig. 12   Ammeter & connection into circuit

JUMPER WIRE

A jumper wire is simply a length of wire with terminals at both ends, usually alligator clips, and is used to connect two points of a circuit or component, Fig. 8. The jumper wire is used for bypassing a portion of the circuit to temporarily prevent it from causing an open circuit. The jumper wire is used with the power "On".

In an open circuit consisting of a switch in series with a light or other load component, connect the jumper wire to the switch terminals and apply power to the circuit, Fig. 9. If the connection of the jumper wire causes the circuit to operate, this indicates that the switch is open.

CAUTION: Do not use the jumper wire as a substitute for high resistance loads such as motors that are connected between the hot circuit and the ground.

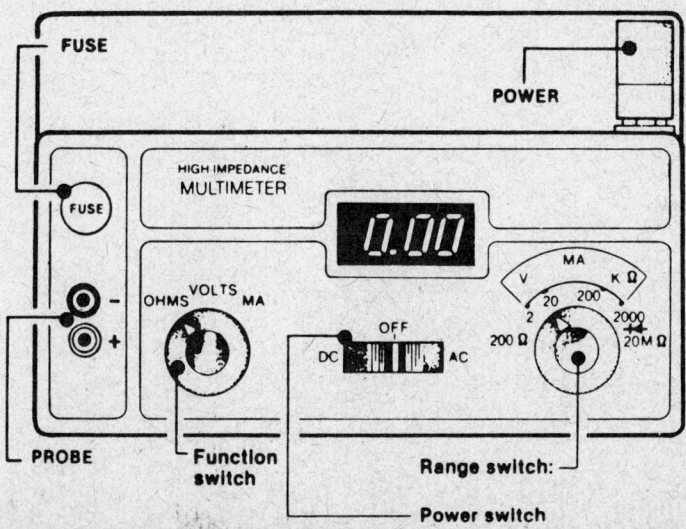

Fig. 13   Digital multimeter

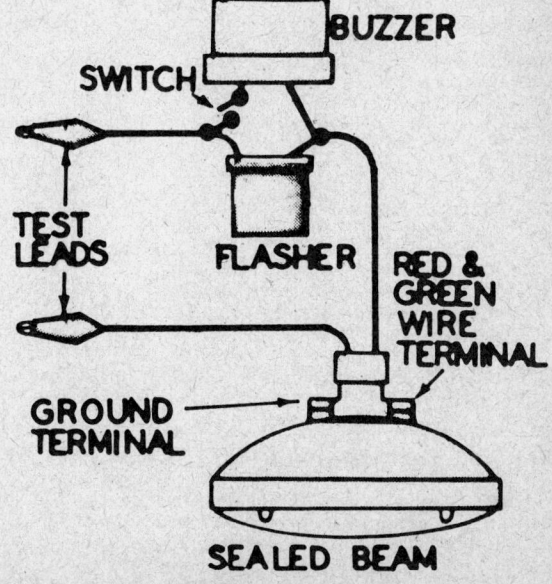

Fig. 14   Short circuit tester construction

TROUBLE SHOOTING

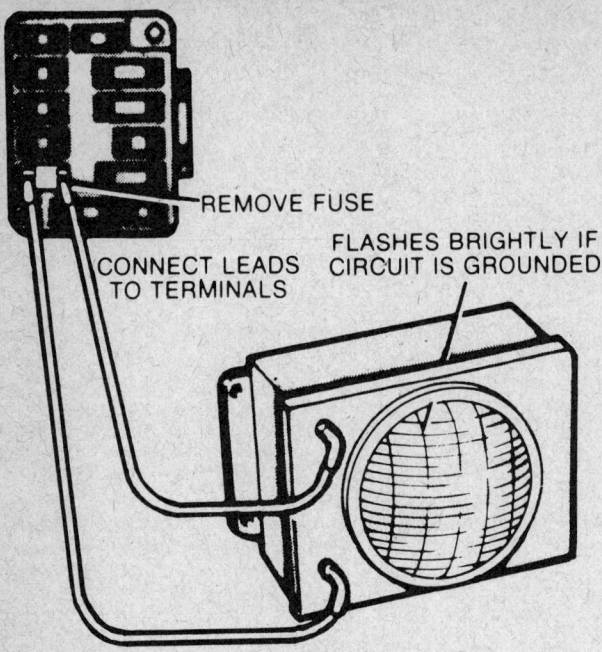

Fig. 15 Connecting a short circuit tester into circuit

REMOVE FUSE

CONNECT LEADS TO TERMINALS

FLASHES BRIGHTLY IF CIRCUIT IS GROUNDED

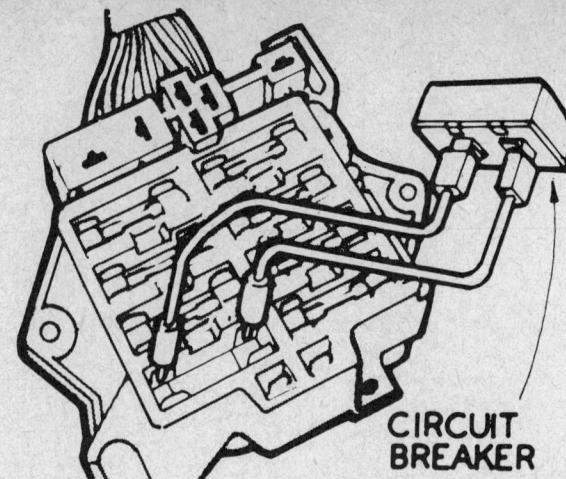

CIRCUIT BREAKER

Fig. 16 Connecting circuit breaker into circuit in place of fuse

TEST EQUIPMENT

Voltmeter

A DC voltmeter is used to measure DC voltage to ground. Connect the negative lead of the voltmeter to the ground and the positive lead to the point where voltage is to be measured, Fig. 10. This is called a parallel connection. The voltmeter is used with the power "On".

Ohmmeter

The ohmmeter is used to measure resistance between two points in a circuit. Connect one lead of the ohmmeter to one point in the circuit and the other lead to the second point in the circuit being checked, Fig. 11. The ohmmeter is also used to check continuity of a circuit. For example, if you connect the ohmmeter leads to both ends of a length of wire, the reading will indicate some resistance or simply, a reading will be obtained. Now if the same length of wire is cut in half, the circuit is broken or open and no reading will be obtained, indicating an open circuit. The ohmmeter is used with the power "Off".

Ammeter

A DC ammeter indicates current flow in amperes. The ammeter is connected into the circuit in series. Connect the positive lead of the ammeter to the power source and the negative lead into the remaining circuit so that all current must flow through the ammeter, Fig. 12. The ammeter is used with the power "On".

Some ammeters are equipped with a clamp-on probe. These ammeters are used to measure starter current.

Digital Multimeter

This test instrument, Fig. 13, combines the functions of all the above analog style instruments. The digital reading ensures more accurate voltage read out, which is especially important when testing low voltage circuits often used in microprocessor systems. When

using such a device to test voltage or current of an unknown magnitude, be sure to set the range selector to the highest range first. Reduce setting as necessary to obtain satisfactory reading.

Short Circuit Tester

A home-made short circuit tester can be made with a sealed beam, flasher or 7 amp. circuit breaker, wire and/or a buzzer as follows:

1. Connect test lead to two lengths of wire.
2. Connect one wire to the ground terminal of the sealed beam, Fig. 14.

NOTE: It is desirable that a sealed beam connector be obtained since it will be easier to replace the sealed beam when it fails.

---

3. Wire the high and low beam terminals and attach a length of wire to them.
4. Connect the flasher or circuit breaker in series with the sealed beam.
5. It is desirable but not necessary to connect a buzzer in parallel with the flasher. Also, an "On-Off" switch installed in one

of the buzzer leads will make the signal optional during testing.
6. Various adapters can be made from old wiring harnesses so the tester leads can be connected at various points of the circuit such as fuse panel, connectors, etc.

To Use the Tester

Connect the tester in series with the circuit being tested, using battery power as feed current, Fig. 15. When the circuit is closed and full power is supplied, the sealed beam will flash brightly and also, the buzzer will sound intermittently if connected in the circuit.

COMPASS

An ordinary magnetic compass may be used for locating grounded circuits. The use of the compass utilizes the principle that a current carrying conductor creates a magnetic field.

In circuits protected by a circuit breaker, a short or ground can be located quickly. Activate the circuit and follow the conductor with the compass. The compass will oscillate each time the circuit breaker closes. When the compass passes the point of the short or ground, the compass will stop oscillating, indicating the location of the malfunction.

The compass can be used without removing trim, cover plates or tape. If the circuit is protected by a fuse, the defect can be found with the compass by substituting a circuit breaker for the fuse.

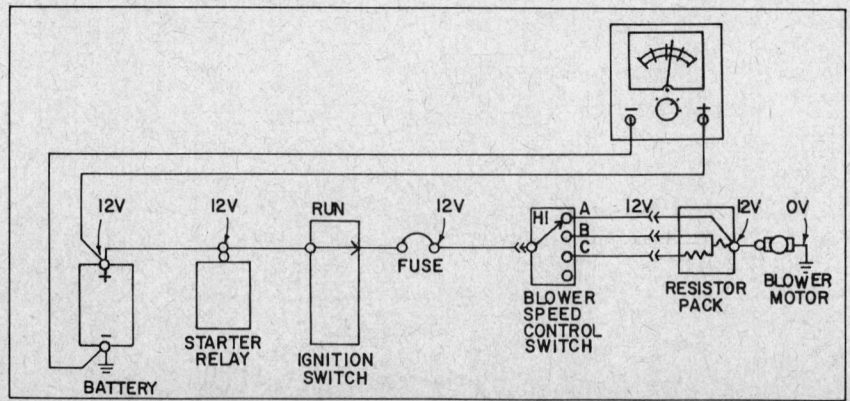

Fig. 17 Three speed blower motor circuit, typical

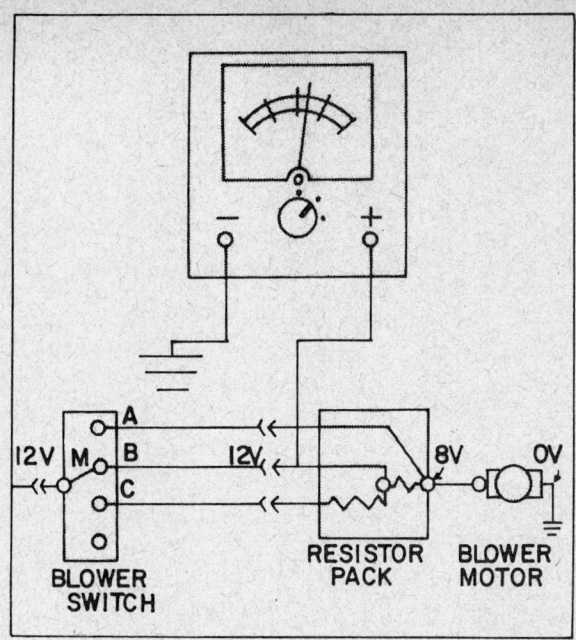

Fig. 18 Measuring voltage drop through one resistor

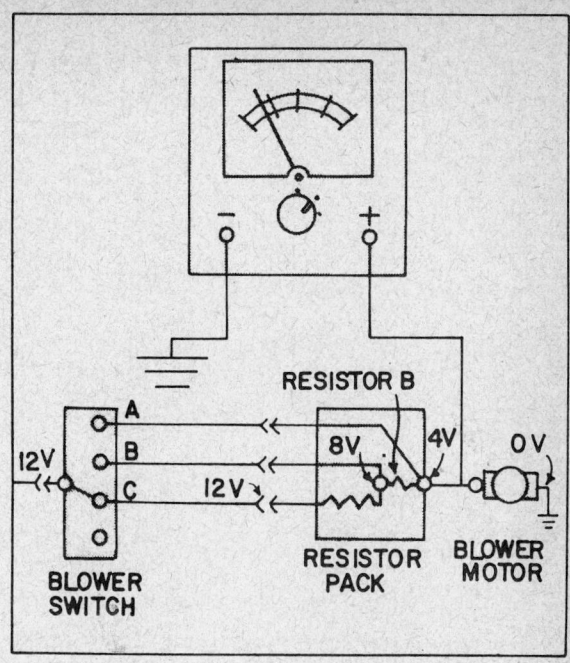

Fig. 19 Measuring voltage drop through two resistors

FUSE SUBSTITUTION

By using a circuit breaker in place of the fuse in the circuit being tested, Fig. 16, other tools can be effectively used. A turn signal flasher may be used as a circuit breaker. Solder a lead to each terminal of the flasher, solder the leads to each end cap of blown fuse. This unit may be installed in the fuse block in place of the fuse normally used. However, when attempting to locate a short or ground when using a magnetic compass, the flasher may operate too quickly to produce satisfactory needle deflection. To slow the flasher operation, insert a generator field control rheostat in series in one flasher lead. By adding additional resistance, the rate of flasher operation may be reduced to produce satisfactory compass needle deflection.

CURRENT DRAW & VOLTAGE DROP

Available Voltage & Voltage Drop

Voltage drop is the amount of voltage lost as electricity passes through a resistance (lamp bulb, blower motor, resistor) and is measured using a voltmeter. The principle of voltage drop can best be demonstrated using a heater blower circuit where resistors are used to deliberately create voltage drops. In a typical three speed blower circuit the blower motor is powered through a speed control switch. The switch has three wires leading to the resistor pack, Fig. 17. The amount of voltage available to the motor depends on which

wire is fed from the switch. Resistors in the blower circuit allow for a change in blower speed by causing a voltage drop ahead of the motor. It must be remembered that available voltage and voltage drop must be measured under load; that is, with the circuit operating a load component such as a motor, or light bulb. In Fig. 17 power to the blower is through wire A, by-passing the resistors. The blower is now operating at maximum speed. Available voltage may be measured by connecting a voltmeter negative lead to a ground and moving the positive lead various points along the blower circuit, Fig. 17. Battery voltage is available at the motor because there is little resistance in the circuit up to this point. Available voltage from the motor is zero volts because the circuit has used up the full 12 volts to operate the motor.

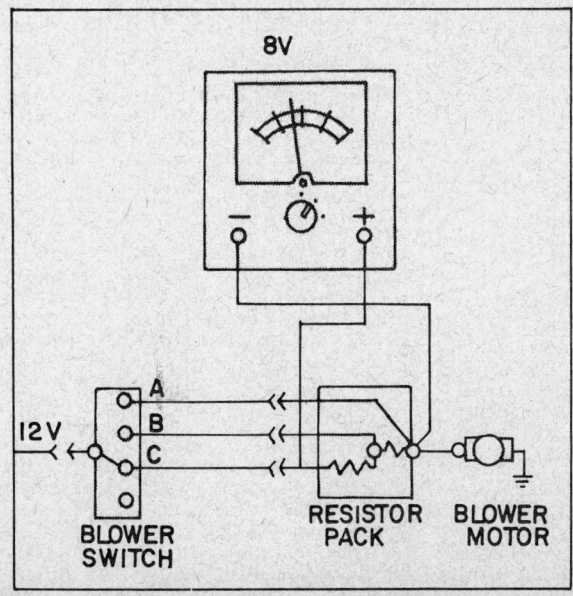

Fig. 20 Measuring voltage drop directly

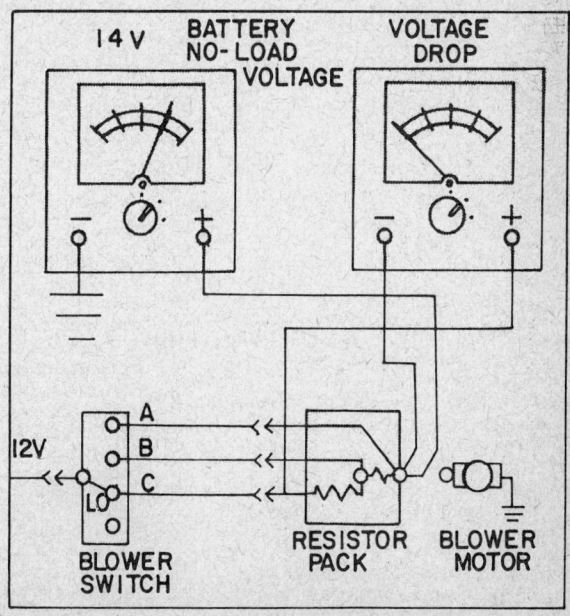

Fig. 21 Measuring no-load voltage

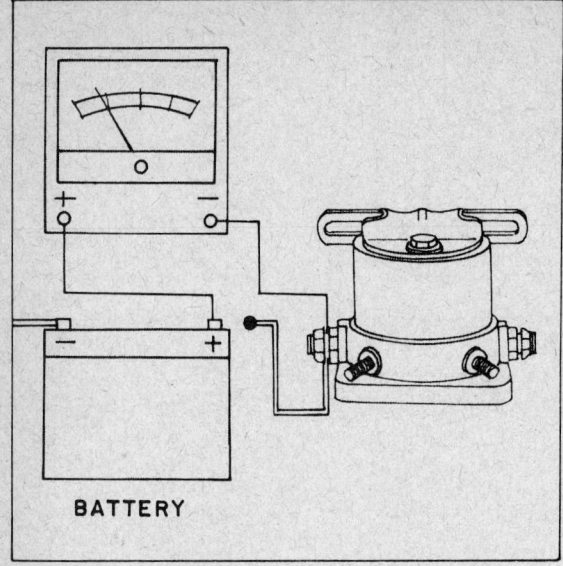

Fig. 22 Measuring current draw from battery

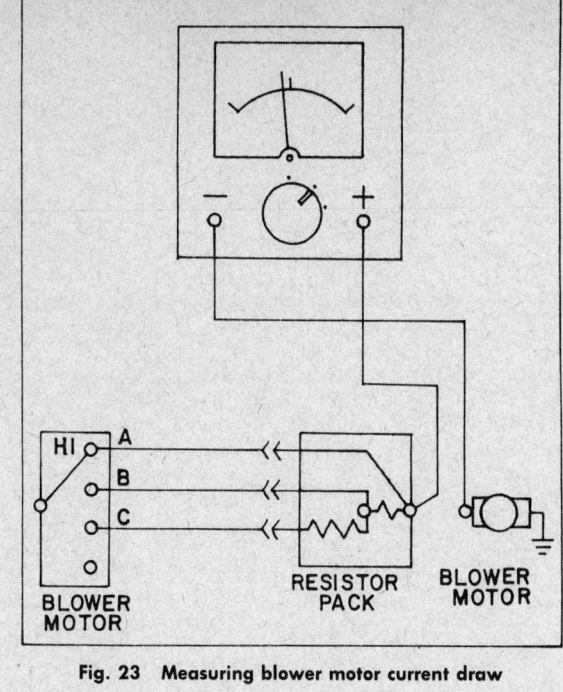

Fig. 23 Measuring blower motor current draw

Voltage Drop In A Series Circuit

If the blower switch is positioned for medium speed, power to the motor must travel through wire B and through one of the resistors in the resistor pack, Fig. 18. A resistor has now been placed in series with the motor. The voltage drop is four volts through the resistor and eight volts through the motor for a total voltage drop of 12 volts. The motor now operates slower because there are only eight volts available to operate it.

NOTE: When resistances are connected in series, the voltage drops add up to the total available voltage at the source. Each voltage drop is proportional to the resistance of component the electricity flows through.

When the blower switch is positioned for low speed, the switch feeds wire C and there are now two resistors in series with the motor, Fig. 19. The available voltages are 12 volts into the resistor block, eight volts into resistor B and 4 volts into the motor. The voltage drops are four volts at resistor A, four volts at resistor B and four volts at the motor for a total voltage drop of 12 volts. In each case zero volts are available out of the motor because the ground circuit has no resistance. If the ground circuit had resistance caused by a faulty ground connection, there would be a positive reading out of the motor. Also, each of the resistors would have proportionately lower voltage drops.

Measuring Voltage Drop Directly

Voltage drop may be read directly from the meter by connecting the meter across the component or segment of the circuit, Fig. 20. Check that the voltmeter positive lead is connected to the battery side of the circuit and the negative lead is connected to the ground side. Fig. 20 shows voltmeter connections for reading voltage drop across the resistor pack on the low blower circuit. The combined voltage drop through both resistors is eight volts.

No Load Voltage

With the blower circuit operating on low blower and the motor disconnected from the circuit, connect two voltmeters as shown in Fig. 21. Meter A is connected as if to read resistor pack voltage drop. It will read zero because there is no voltage drop in a non-operating circuit. Meter B is connected as if to read available voltage. It is actually reading battery no load voltage. The circuit must be operating, that is, under load, to read voltage drop directly and to read available voltage in order to compute voltage drop. If the circuit is not under load, there will be no voltage drop.

Current Draw

Current draw, or current, is the amount of electrical flow or volume and is measured using an ammeter. The ammeter is connected into the circuit, in series with the load, switch or resistor. It will measure current draw only when the circuit is closed and electricity is flowing. In Fig. 22, the ammeter is connected as if to read current draw from the battery. The positive battery cable is disconnected so that any current flowing must go through the meter. If the vehicle's electrical systems were turned on one at a time, the meter would measure how much current each draws. The ammeter may be connected anywhere in a circuit, even between load and ground, as long as it is connected in series and correct polarity is observed.

High Resistance Short To Ground

When a short circuit occurs and the current draw is not sufficient to cause the fuse to blow, but does cause a drain on the battery, an ammeter may be used to locate the short. If a current draw exists with everything off, then there is a short to ground.

NOTE: On some vehicles equipped with an electric clock, there will be a slight current draw at all times with all accessories off. This current draw should be taken into consideration when diagnosing a short circuit with an ammeter.

To locate the short, remove fuses one at a time until the meter reads zero. If this occurs, trouble shoot that circuit for a short to ground.

Electric Motor Current Draw

Using the previous example of a blower circuit, an ammeter connected in series between the resistor pack and blower motor with the blower switch on high, Fig. 23, will show a reading of eight amps. This is a typical current draw for this type of motor. When the blower switch is moved to the medium position, the blower is being fed through a resistor and this reduces available voltage to the motor. The motor now draws about six amps and the motor operates slower. On low blower speed, the draw would decrease to 3 or 4 amps. If the switch were turned off, the ammeter would read zero.

NOTE: Current draw is highest with no resistance and reduces as resistances are added in series.

If a second blower motor were connected in parallel and both were operated from the same switch, the electrical load would be doubled. The current draw, in the high speed position, would be 16 amps. Whenever electrical loads are added in parallel, the current draw increases. The effective resistance of the circuit decreases as parallel loads are added. If the two motors were connected in series, both would operate at reduced speed because one would act as a resistor for the other.

When an electric motor or solenoid has to work harder due to mechanical resistance, it draws more current. If the resistance is great, the motor will draw more current than that which can be safely handled by the circuit's fuse or circuit breaker. In this case the fuse blows or circuit breaker opens and interrupts the flow of current.

FUEL ECONOMY & AUTO CARE GUIDE

INDEX

INTRODUCTION

This chapter has been compiled for the absolute novice in auto care. It will enable you to perform routine chores on your car that will result in dollar savings and greater fuel economy, and will provide the satisfaction of knowing you have had a hand in keeping your car in a safe operating condition. Many of the parts required to perform these chores are available at mass merchandisers and certainly at automotive supply stores. Items such as anti-freeze and engine oil can even be found on the shelves of many supermarket food stores. Using this information, you can join the millions of car owners who are doing some of their own automotive maintenance.

Keep in mind that fuel economy is dependent upon two factors: the vehicle mechanical condition and the driver's technique. Both factors are controllable by the driver. Make sure that the vehicle is kept in optimum mechanical operating condition. Be alert to changes in power and performance. Change driving habits to achieve maximum fuel economy from the vehicle. This will result in the operation of a safer vehicle with greater fuel economy.

TUNE-UP

Spark Plug, Replace

Removal

1. Mark all ignition wires, as they must be replaced in the same sequence. This can be accomplished in the following ways:
   a. Marking tags and attaching them to the ignition wires, according to the engine firing order, front to rear on inline engines, or D1 through D4 on driver's side and P1 through P4 on the passenger side on V8 engines.
   b. Using a white magic marker or nail polish to mark each ignition wire with a white spot, one spot for the first wire, two spots for the second and so on.
2. Remove the spark plug wires from the spark plugs by twisting the boot approximately 1/4 turn and freeing it from spark plug.
3. Pull wire off by the boot only. Pulling on wires may cause internal breakage.

FUEL ECONOMY SUGGESTIONS

MECHANICAL

1. Keep engine properly tuned up. An untuned engine will waste fuel and decrease fuel economy.
2. Ensure front suspension is kept in proper alignment.
3. Check tire inflation. The tires should be inflated to recommended pressures.
4. Keep vehicle properly lubricated. Sufficiently lubricated friction surfaces will enable the vehicle to operate more efficiently.
5. Adjust dragging brakes. Make sure that service and parking brakes are properly adjusted to aid in achieving greater fuel economy.
6. Installing radial tires decreases rolling resistance, improving fuel economy.
7. Check condition of cooling system. An engine is most efficient at proper operating temperature.

DRIVER TECHNIQUE

1. Avoid jack rabbit starts. Accelerate gradually where possible.
2. Avoid sudden stops. Try to anticipate stops, as sudden stopping wastes the forward energy of the vehicle and will use more fuel to reach the previous desired speed.
3. Avoid prolonged idling, and try to avoid driving in rush hour traffic.
4. Make one long trip rather than several short ones.
5. Shift into high gear as soon as possible without damaging the engine or transmission.
6. Keep within speed limits.
7. Don't use brake or clutch pedal as a foot rest.
8. Driving with the air conditioning "On" will decrease fuel economy.
9. If equipped, use speed or cruise control wherever possible.
10. Driving with the windows closed streamlines the vehicle and improves fuel economy.
11. Avoid carrying unnecessary loads in the trunk. Additional weight adversely affects fuel economy.
12. Install a dash-mounted vacuum gauge and maintain maximum possible reading (high vacuum) during acceleration and cruise conditions, which will help in achieving greater fuel economy.
13. Select a grade of fuel which will not produce pre-ignition and detonation, or otherwise damage the engine. Don't buy unnecessary octane.

---

4. Before loosening plug, blow out loose dirt adjacent to spark plug. If a compressed air supply is not available, you can accomplish this by blowing through a straw or a rubber hose.
5. Install the proper size spark plug socket (13/16 inch or 5/8 inch) onto a spark plug. Attach ratchet wrench to socket and turn counterclockwise. Loosen all spark plugs approximately one turn, breaking loose any accumulated carbon adjacent to the spark plugs.

Inspection

Referring to Fig. 1, inspect spark plug and correct any problem causing the abnormal spark plug condition.

Installation

The spark plug should be regapped to the exact specification given by the auto manufacturer. Always use a round wire type gauge. Refer to the "Tune-Up Service" section elsewhere in this manual.

Torque spark plug to specifications as listed in the "Engine Tightening Specification" tables in the individual car chapters.

Distributor Cap, Replace

Remove the distributor cap. The distributor cap is retained either by latches, or bale clips, Fig. 2. To remove latches, depress using a flat screwdriver, then turn the latches one half turn in either direction and lift the cap off the distributor. To remove bale clips, insert a flat screwdriver between the clip and distributor cap, pry the clips to disengage them from the cap and lift the cap off the distributor. Inspect condition of cap, Fig. 3, and clean or replace as necessary.

Distributor Rotor, Replace

All distributor rotors except those used on General Motors

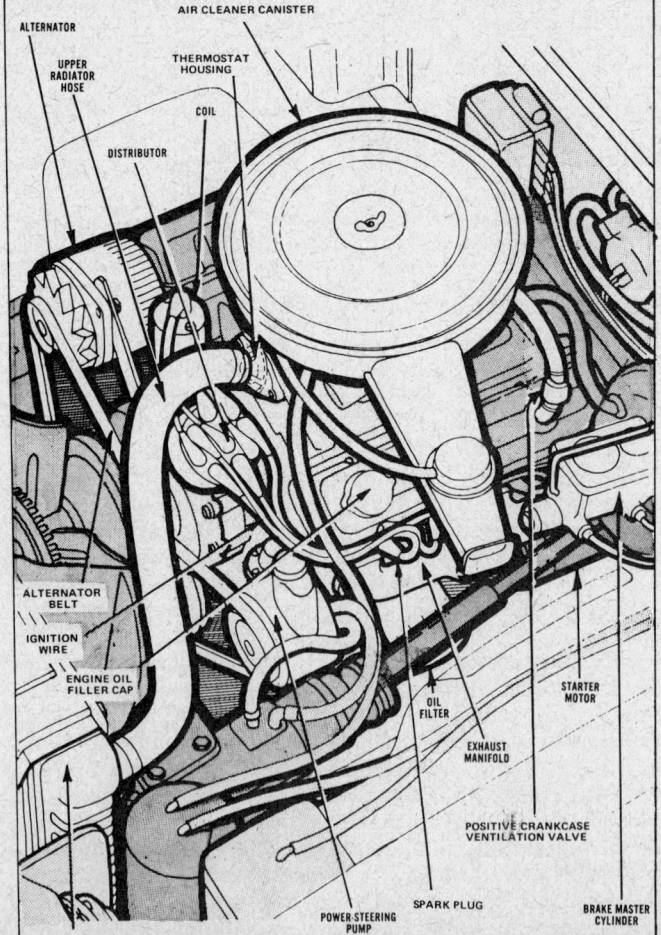

Typical engine compartment

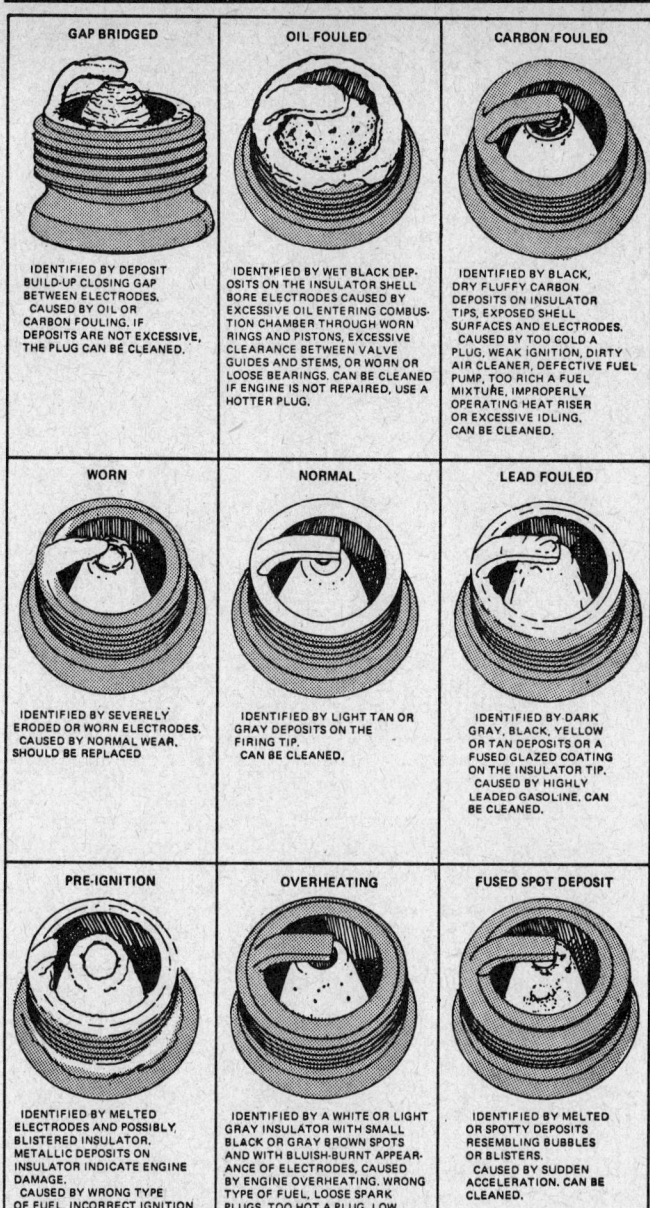

Fig. 1 Spark plug condition chart

Labels within figure:

GAP BRIDGED — IDENTIFIED BY DEPOSIT BUILD-UP CLOSING GAP BETWEEN ELECTRODES. CAUSED BY OIL OR CARBON FOULING. IF DEPOSITS ARE NOT EXCESSIVE, THE PLUG CAN BE CLEANED.

OIL FOULED — IDENTIFIED BY WET BLACK DEPOSITS ON THE INSULATOR SHELL BORE ELECTRODES CAUSED BY EXCESSIVE OIL ENTERING COMBUSTION CHAMBER THROUGH WORN RINGS AND PISTONS, EXCESSIVE CLEARANCE BETWEEN VALVE GUIDES AND STEMS, OR WORN OR LOOSE BEARINGS. CAN BE CLEANED IF ENGINE IS NOT REPAIRED, USE A HOTTER PLUG.

CARBON FOULED — IDENTIFIED BY BLACK, DRY FLUFFY CARBON DEPOSITS ON INSULATOR TIPS, EXPOSED SHELL SURFACES AND ELECTRODES. CAUSED BY TOO COLD A PLUG, WEAK IGNITION, DIRTY AIR CLEANER, DEFECTIVE FUEL PUMP, TOO RICH A FUEL MIXTURE, IMPROPERLY OPERATING HEAT RISER OR EXCESSIVE IDLING. CAN BE CLEANED.

WORN — IDENTIFIED BY SEVERELY ERODED OR WORN ELECTRODES. CAUSED BY NORMAL WEAR. SHOULD BE REPLACED

NORMAL — IDENTIFIED BY LIGHT TAN OR GRAY DEPOSITS ON THE FIRING TIP. CAN BE CLEANED.

LEAD FOULED — IDENTIFIED BY DARK GRAY, BLACK, YELLOW OR TAN DEPOSITS OR A FUSED GLAZED COATING ON THE INSULATOR TIP. CAUSED BY HIGHLY LEADED GASOLINE. CAN BE CLEANED.

PRE-IGNITION — IDENTIFIED BY MELTED ELECTRODES AND POSSIBLY BLISTERED INSULATOR. METALLIC DEPOSITS ON INSULATOR INDICATE ENGINE DAMAGE. CAUSED BY WRONG TYPE OF FUEL, INCORRECT IGNITION TIMING OR ADVANCE, TOO HOT A PLUG, BURNT VALVES OR ENGINE OVERHEATING. REPLACE THE PLUG.

OVERHEATING — IDENTIFIED BY A WHITE OR LIGHT GRAY INSULATOR WITH SMALL BLACK OR GRAY BROWN SPOTS AND WITH BLUISH-BURNT APPEARANCE OF ELECTRODES, CAUSED BY ENGINE OVERHEATING. WRONG TYPE OF FUEL, LOOSE SPARK PLUGS, TOO HOT A PLUG, LOW FUEL PUMP PRESSURE OR INCORRECT IGNITION TIMING. REPLACE THE PLUG.

FUSED SPOT DEPOSIT — IDENTIFIED BY MELTED OR SPOTTY DEPOSITS RESEMBLING BUBBLES OR BLISTERS. CAUSED BY SUDDEN ACCELERATION. CAN BE CLEANED.

Breaker Points & Condenser, Replace

American Motors 4-121 Engine

1. Remove air cleaner.
2. Remove distributor cap with ignition wires attached, and position aside.
3. Remove rotor by pulling upward with even pressure.
4. Remove dust shield.
5. Disconnect breaker point lead from connector.
6. Disconnect primary ignition lead from distributor connector. Remove retaining screw, then the connector and condenser assembly.
7. Install new connector and condenser assembly. Ensure rubber grommet is properly positioned in square hole of distributor wall. Connect primary ignition lead.
8. Remove point assembly retaining screw.
9. Remove point assembly from plate.
10. Wipe distributor cam clean and inspect.
11. Install replacement points. Ensure pivot pin is properly seated in pivot hole.
12. Install retaining screw. Do not tighten.
13. Rotate engine in direction of normal rotation until rubbing block is positioned on high point of cam lobe, Fig. 4.
14. Adjust gap to specifications. Refer to "Tune Up Service" chapter. Tighten retaining screw.
15. Apply a small bead of high temperature distributor cam lubricant to one lobe of cam.
16. Attach point assembly wire lead to connector.
17. Install dust cover and rotor. Ensure rotor seats properly on shaft.
18. Install distributor cap.
19. Install air cleaner.

Distributor Advance Check

On vehicles which use conventional advance mechanisms instead of electronic spark advance, the operation of the mechanical and vacuum advance can be checked as follows:
1. Connect timing light and check timing.
2. With vacuum hose disconnected and plugged, increase engine RPM and ensure timing mark moves in direction of advance.
3. Return engine to idle speed. Connect hand vacuum pump to distributor vacuum advance unit, or connect vacuum hose from distributor to vacuum source on engine intake manifold. Timing mark should move in direction of advance, and engine RPM will increase.
4. Reconnect distributor vacuum hose to original fittings.

LUBRICATION, OIL CHANGE, FILTERS, HEATED AIR SYSTEM CHECK, EGR & PCV VALVE SERVICE

Engine Oil & Filter Change

NOTE: Engine oil and filter should be changed at intervals recommended by the vehicle manufacturer.

1. Operate engine and allow to reach operating temperature, then turn ignition off.
2. Place drain pan under engine oil pan, then using a suitable wrench remove drain plug.
3. Allow engine oil to thoroughly drain into pan, then replace drain plug.

engines may be removed by simply pulling them upward from the shaft. On General Motors engines, it is necessary to remove the two screws securing the rotor to the top of the shaft and advance mechanism.

When installing the rotor on all distributors except those used on General Motors engines, align the notch on the shaft with the locating tab inside the open end of the rotor, then slide the rotor onto the shaft. Make sure that the rotor is firmly seated on the shaft.

Rotors used on General Motors engines have a notch on the side of the rotor. To install rotor, align this notch with extended arm of rotor support plate. Tighten the retaining screws, but not so tight as to crack the rotor.

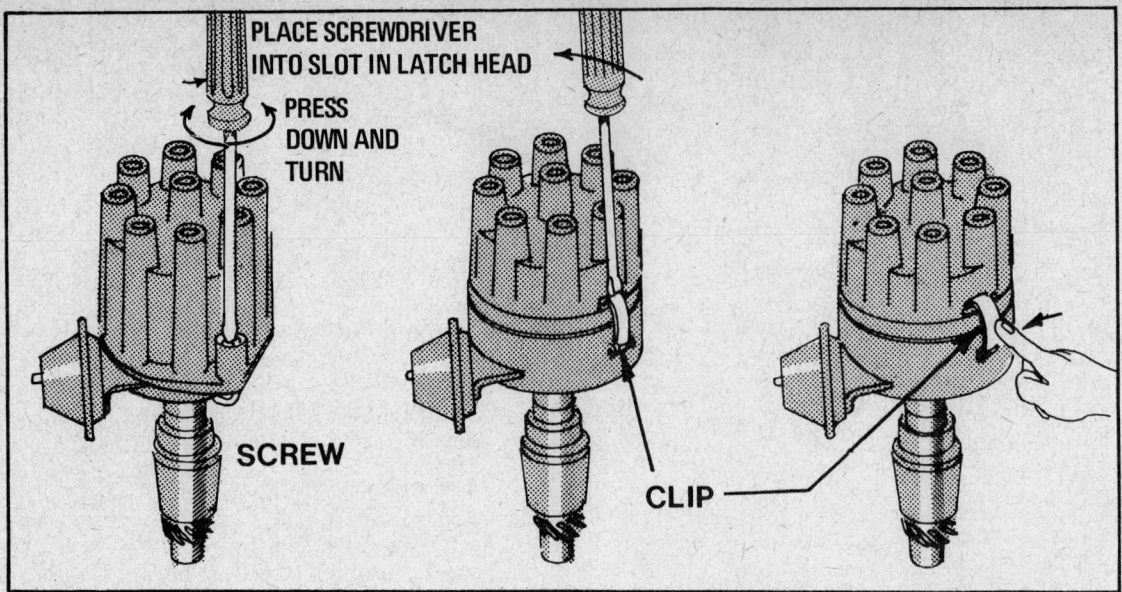

Fig. 2 Distributor cap removal

NOTE: Do not overtighten drain plug, as this can strip the threads in oil pan.

4. If oil filter is to be replaced, position drain pan under filter, then install oil filter wrench and remove filter by turning counterclockwise, Fig. 5.

NOTE: Ensure old oil filter gasket is not on the filter adapter on the engine. Clean adapter before installing new filter.

5. Coat new oil filter gasket with engine oil, then position filter on adapter, Fig. 6. Hand tighten filter until gasket contacts adapter face, then tighten filter one additional turn. Wipe filter and adapter with a clean cloth.

NOTE: Ensure gasket is in position on filter before tightening. Do not use oil filter wrench to tighten filter. Hand tighten only.

6. Remove oil filler cap and add quantity of oil specified by manufacturer, then install filler cap.

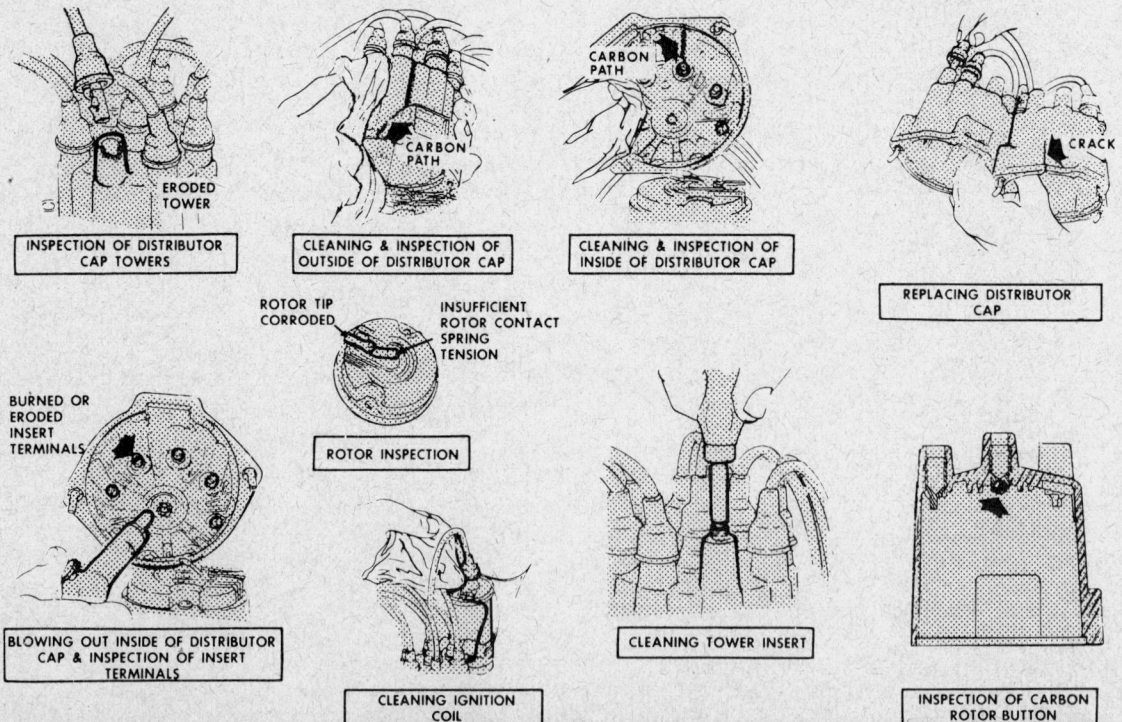

Fig. 3 Inspecting and cleaning distributor cap

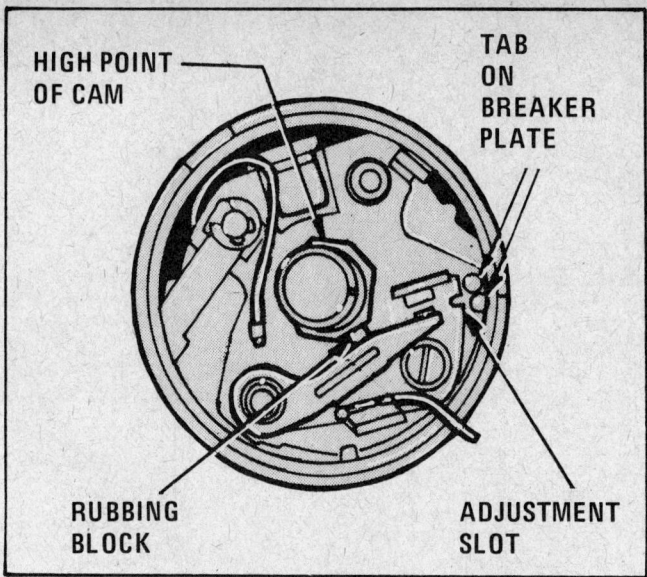

HIGH POINT OF CAM

TAB ON BREAKER PLATE

RUBBING BLOCK

ADJUSTMENT SLOT

Fig. 4 Replacing breaker points. American Motors 4-121

NOTE: Only add oil which meets the vehicle manufacturer's specifications.

7. Start engine and check to ensure oil filter and drain plug are not leaking, then turn ignition off.
8. Check oil level to ensure crankcase is full but not overfilled. Add oil as necessary.

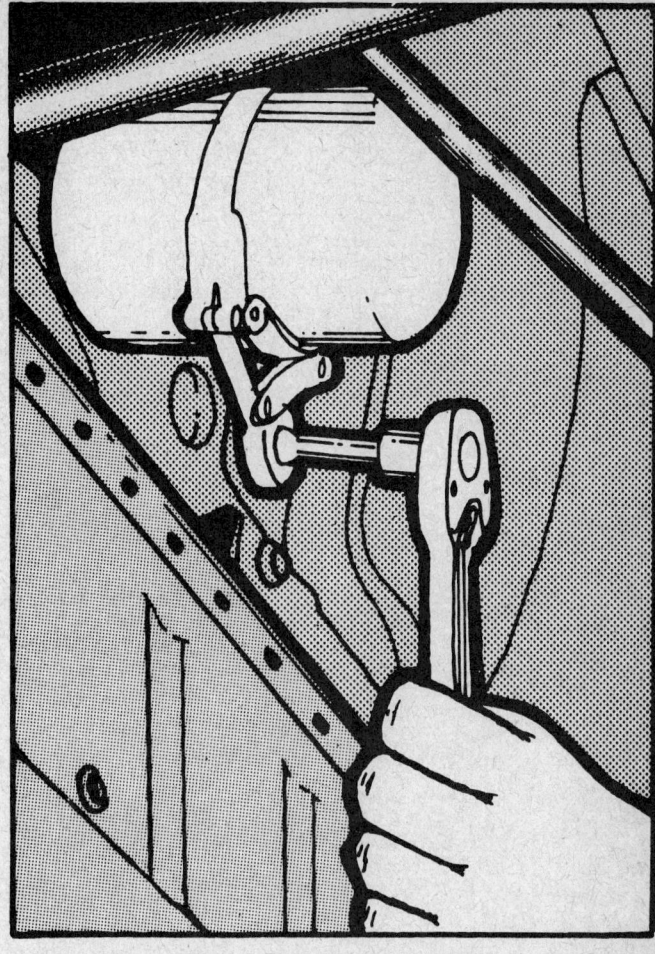

Fig. 5 Oil filter removal (typical)

Coat Gasket With Engine Oil

Fig. 6 Oil filter installation (typical)

NOTE: Do not bring oil level above "Full" mark on dipstick. Overfilling could result in damage to engine gaskets or seals causing leaks.

Air Filter, Replace

Exc. General Motors 4-140 Engine

1. Remove wing nut, hex nut or other attaching hardware securing the air cleaner lid. On some models, the air cleaner lid is also secured by clips on the sides of the housing which must be disengaged, Fig. 7.
2. Remove air cleaner lid from housing assembly and lift out air filter element.

NOTE: To check air filter condition, hold a light behind the element, Fig. 8. If no light can be seen through the element, the filter is excessively dirty and must be replaced.

3. Wipe out housing with a clean rag. Be sure to prevent dirt or other foreign material from entering the carburetor.
4. Install new air filter element, Fig. 7.
5. Install lid onto housing assembly and secure with the attaching hardware previously removed.

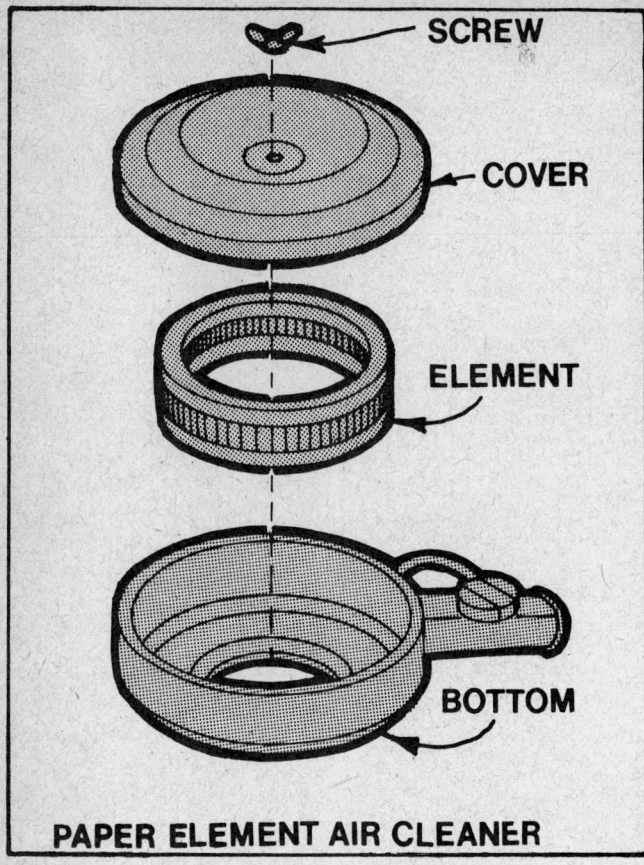

PAPER ELEMENT AIR CLEANER

Fig. 7   Replacing air filter (typical)

General Motors 4-140 Engine

1. Remove bolt or nuts securing air cleaner assembly to carburetor.
2. Pull vent pipe from air cleaner. This pipe runs between the air cleaner and the cam cover (rocker cover).
3. Remove air cleaner assembly from carburetor and discard.
4. Install new air cleaner assembly and secure with bolt or nuts previously removed.

Air Cleaner Heated Air System, Check

This system is used to improve cold engine operation by heating air entering the carburetor. On late model vehicles, the system is usually vacuum controlled. A heat sensor inside the air cleaner senses the incoming air temperature and controls vacuum to the vacuum motor on the air cleaner snorkel which opens or closes the snorkel door to exhaust

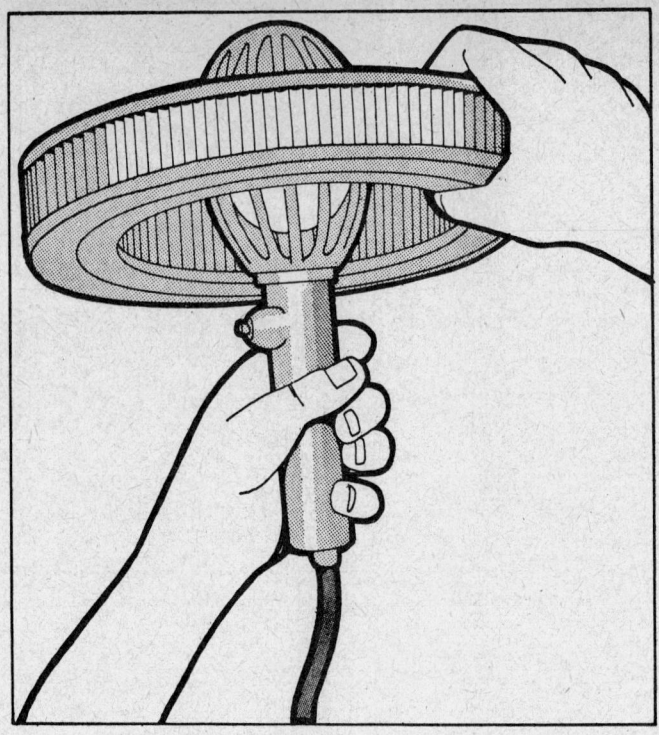

Fig. 8   Checking air filter condition

heated air. A door which remains closed during cold engine operation can result in hesitation and poor driveability until the engine warms up. A door that remains open to exhaust-heated air when the engine is warmed up can cause pinging or reduced engine power.

Some vehicles are equipped with a thermostat unit instead of a heat sensor and vacuum motor, Fig. 9. The operation of these style units can be checked by looking in the air cleaner snorkel with the aid of a mirror and light. Door should be closed when engine is cold, and open when engine is warmed up.

The operation of the vacuum motor can be checked as follows:

1. Disconnect vacuum hose at vacuum motor.
2. Connect hand vacuum pump to vacuum motor, Fig. 10.
3. Operate pump to apply 20 inches of vacuum to the actuator unit. Door in snorkel should be open to heated air (closed to outside air, Fig. 10).
4. Ensure vacuum gauge needle does not drop below 10 inches of vacuum in five minutes.

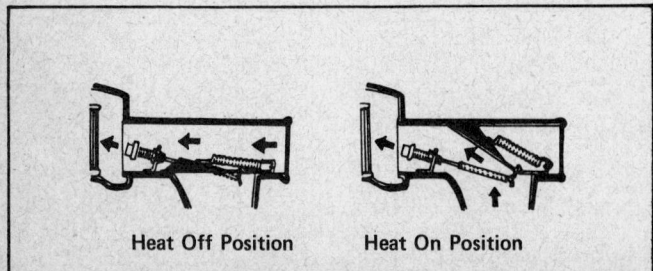

Fig. 9   Thermostatically controlled heated air system

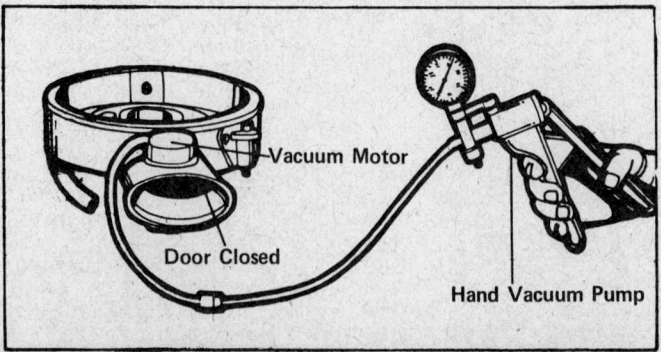

Fig. 10   Testing vacuum operated heated air system

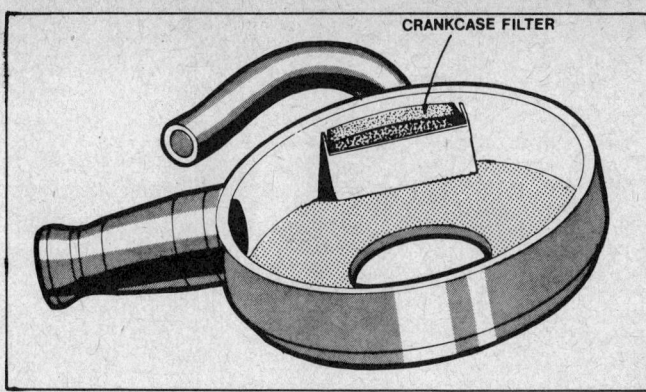

Fig. 11 Typical crankcase filter

Crankcase Emission Filter

American Motors 6 Cyl. & All Ford Motor Co., Fig. 11

1. Remove top of air cleaner housing.
2. Remove filter pack from filter retainer and clean out retainer.
3. Install new filter in retainer.
4. Install top of air cleaner.

American Motors V8

This filter is located in the sealed oil filler cap. The filter must be cleaned at mileage intervals recommended by the manufacturer by applying light air pressure in reverse direction of normal flow, then lightly oiling the filter with clean engine oil. If the filter is deteriorated, the oil filler cap must be replaced.

Chrysler Corp.

This filter must be cleaned at mileage intervals recommended by the manufacturer. Disconnect hose from filter and remove filter by pulling it out of the valve cover. Clean filter in kerosene or similar solvent, then lubricate filter by filling it with clean SAE 30 engine oil and inverting it to allow ex-

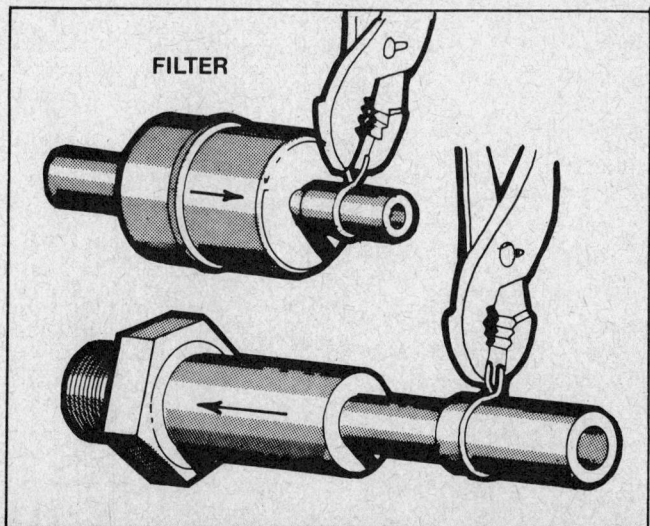

Fig. 13 Removing fuel hose from fuel filter (typical)

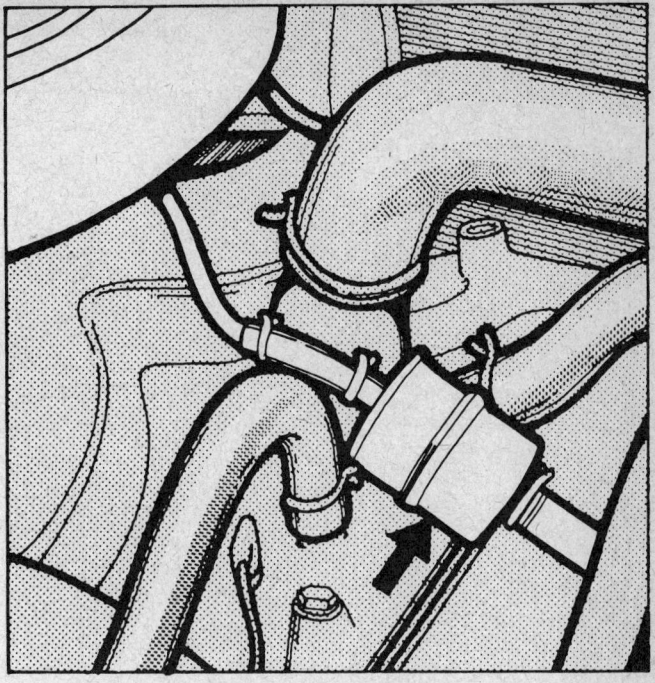

Fig. 12 Typical location of in-line fuel filter

cess oil to drain out. Reinstall filter in valve cover and reconnect hose.

General Motors, All, Fig. 11

1. Remove top of air cleaner housing.
2. Disconnect hose from filter which leads to valve cover.
3. Remove clip which retains filter to air cleaner housing and remove filter.
4. Position new filter in air cleaner housing and install retaining clip.
5. Connect hose to filter and install top of air cleaner housing.

Fuel Filter, Replace

Inline

NOTE: Inline fuel filter is located between fuel pump and carburetor, Fig. 12.

1. Remove air cleaner, if necessary.
2. Loosen fuel hose clamps, then disconnect hoses and remove fuel filter, Fig. 13.

NOTE: On some models, fuel filter may be attached to carburetor of fuel line tubing. On these models use suitable wrench to remove filter.

3. Reverse procedure to install, then start engine and check for fuel leaks.

NOTE: Before installing, refer to fuel filter body markings, which indicate the direction the fuel filter should be installed.

In-Carburetor

NOTE: The carburetor fuel filter is located in carburetor hous-

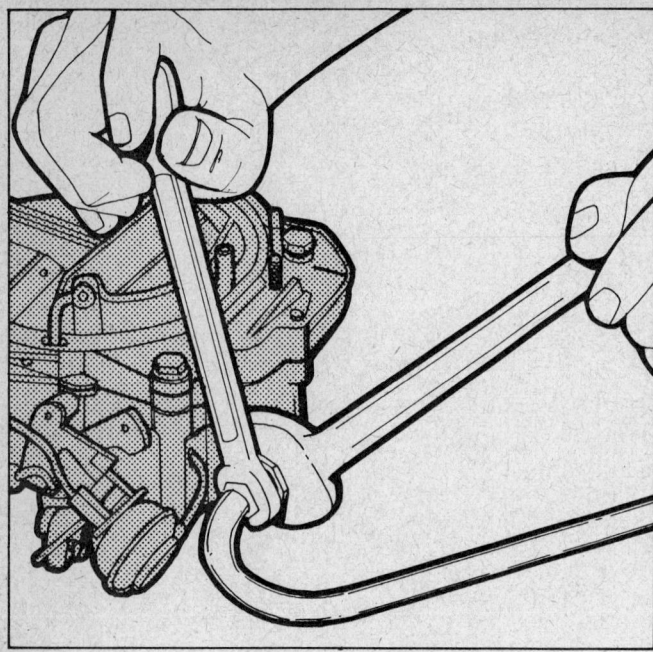

Fig. 14 Disconnecting fuel line

ing where fuel inlet line is connected to carburetor.

1. Remove air cleaner.
2. Position back up wrench on fuel filter fitting, then using a suitable wrench, disconnect fuel inlet line Fig. 14.
3. Remove fuel filter fitting, filter and spring from carburetor.
4. Position spring and filter into carburetor, then install gasket and fitting.

NOTE: Position fuel filter in carburetor with open end facing fitting.

5. With back up wrench on fuel filter fitting, carefully connect and tighten fuel inlet line using a suitable wrench Fig. 14.
6. Start engine and check for leaks, then install air cleaner.

PCV Valve, Replace

NOTE: To check PCV valve, remove valve from grommet and shake valve. A metallic clicking noise should be heard, indicating valve is free. If valve does not move freely, it should be replaced. Do not attempt to clean valve.

1. Remove PCV valve from grommet, then disconnect hose, Fig. 15.

NOTE: On American Motors models, PCV valve is located on valve cover on 6 cylinder engine and on intake manifold on V8 engine. On Chrysler Corp. models, valve is located on valve cover. On Ford Motor Co. models, valve is located in PCV valve hose on 2300cc engine, on carburetor spacer on V6 engine, on valve cover on inline 6 cylinder engine and in oil filler cap on V8 engine. On General Motors Corp. models, valve is located on valve cover on 4 cylinder and inline 6 cylinder engines, on intake manifold on V6 engines and on valve cover or intake manifold on V8 engines, depending on model.

2. Install new PCV valve on grommet and connect hose.

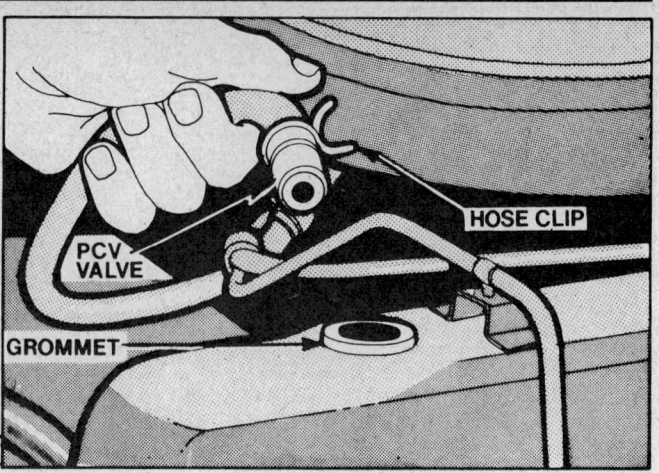

Fig. 15 PCV valve replacement (typical)

NOTE: Ensure valve is properly seated in grommet.

EGR Valve, Check

1. Start engine and allow to warm up.
2. With engine at curb idle speed, disconnect vacuum hose from EGR valve and plug hose to prevent vacuum leak.
3. Attach hand vacuum pump to EGR valve fitting.
4. Operate pump to apply at least 4 inches of vacuum to valve.
5. Observe that engine begins to misfire and run roughly. If there is no change in engine performance, EGR valve is defective or gas passages are clogged with exhaust deposits.
6. Disconnect vacuum hose from valve.
7. Remove the two bolts holding valve to manifold or spacer, and remove valve.
8. Clean old gasket off mating surface with scraper and wire brush.
9. Inspect and clean out gas passages in manifold or spacer with wire gun-bore brush or small round wire brush.
10. Exhaust deposits can be removed from EGR valve with wire brush or by tapping side of valve with soft mallet.
11. Ensure valve stem and diaphragm can move freely by pushing on diaphragm.
12. Check diaphragm for leakage by applying vacuum with hand vacuum pump.
13. Install new valve or reinstall old valve with new gasket and tighten bolts.
14. Reconnect vacuum hose and check operation. With engine warmed up, valve should be seen or felt to operate when throttle opening is increased beyond idle.

Chassis Lubricating

The first time you perform a grease job, you will spend much of the time looking for the fittings Figs. 16 and 17.

As you find a fitting, wipe it off with a clean rag. This will help you spot it later and also prevent you from injecting dirt with the grease.

The injection tip of the grease gun should be a catch fit on the fitting nipple. That is, once in place it will not slip off. Slight, straight-on pressure is all that is necessary for the gun tip to engage the fitting. Once that is done, pump the handle. Follow the recommendations below to ensure proper lubrication and also prevent damage to the seals:

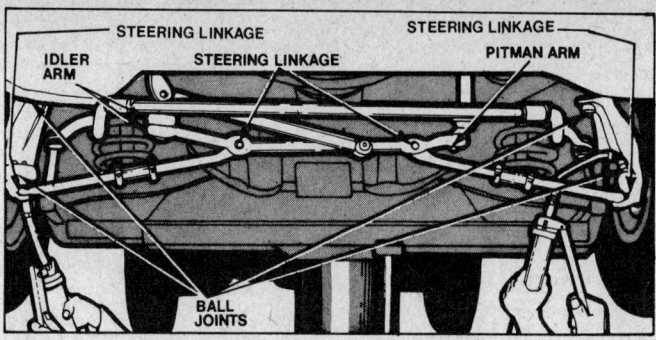

Fig. 16 Identifying grease fittings (typical). If vehicle is equipped with plugs, the plugs must be removed and a grease fitting installed prior to lubricating

American Motors and Ford:

Pump slowly until the rubber boot can be felt or seen to swell slightly.

Chrysler Corp. and General Motors:

Pump slowly until grease starts to flow from bleed holes at the base of the seals, or until the seals start to swell.

NOTE: If the fitting fails to take grease, the lubricant will ooze out between fitting and top of the gun. Do not just keep pumping, hoping some grease is getting in, or you will have a mess. It is normal for a bit of grease to seep out. However if the fitting is obviously not taking grease, it should be replaced.

Repacking Front Wheel Bearings

1. Remove inner and outer bearings as outlined in car chapters.
2. Clean old lubricant from hub and spindle.
3. Clean inner and outer bearings and bearing races with kerosene.

NOTE: Ensure all old lubricant is removed before repacking. Allow bearings and races to dry thoroughly. Do not use compressed air to clean bearings.

4. Inspect cones, rollers and races for cracks, nicks and wear, and replace as necessary.

NOTE: Bearings and race must be replaced as a unit.

5. Place a small amount of wheel bearing grease in palm of hand, then force grease into large end of roller cage until grease protrudes from small end.

NOTE: Use only wheel bearing grease which meets the vehicle manufacturer's specifications.

6. Lubricate remaining bearings in the same manner, then install and adjust bearings as outlined in car chapter.

NOTE: Apply a light film of grease to lips of grease retainer before installing.

CHECKING & MAINTAINING FLUID LEVELS

NOTE: When checking fluid levels, ensure vehicle is on a level

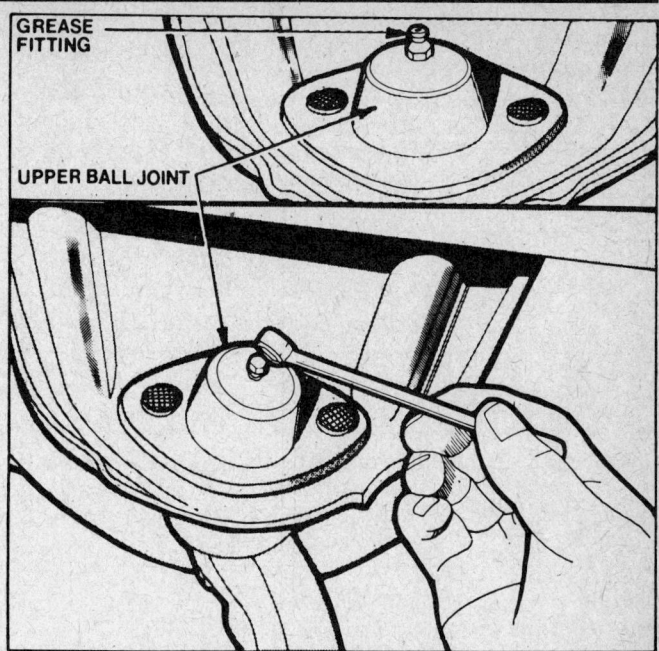

Fig. 17 Typical fitting locations

surface. If vehicle is not level, an accurate fluid level reading cannot be obtained.

Engine Oil Level

1. Warm up engine, then turn ignition off and allow a few minutes for oil to return to crankcase.
2. Remove dipstick and wipe off.
3. Replace dipstick and ensure it is seated in tube.
4. Remove dipstick and inspect to see if oil level is between "Add" and "Full" marks.

NOTE: Add oil only if level is at or below "Add" mark.

5. If oil level is at "Add" mark, one quart of oil will bring level to "Full" mark. If oil level is below "Add" mark, add sufficient amount of oil to bring level between Add & Full marks.

NOTE: Do not bring oil level above "Full" mark, as overfilling of crankcase could result in damage to engine gaskets and seals and cause leaks. Only add oil meeting the vehicle manufacturers specifications.

6. Replace dipstick.

Battery

1. Remove filler cap and check fluid level in each cell.

NOTE: Keep flame and sparks away from top of battery as combustible gases present may explode. Do not allow battery electrolyte to contact skin, eyes, fabric or painted surfaces. Flush contacted area with water immediately and thoroughly and seek medical attention if necessary. Wear eye protection when working on or near battery. Do not wear rings or other metal jewelry when working on or near battery.

2. Add water as required to bring fluid level of each cell up to split ring located at bottom of filler well.

NOTE: In areas where water is known to be hard or have a high mineral or alkali content, distilled water must be used. If water is added during freezing temperatures, the vehicle should be driven several miles afterwards to mix the water and battery electrolyte.

3. Install filler caps.

Cooling System

NOTE: Add only permanent type anti-freeze which meets the vehicle manufacturer's specifications.

CAUTION: Never add large quantities of water into radiator if car has overheated before engine has cooled off. If necessary to service at this time, start engine and add water to coolant slowly. This will avoid damage to the engine.

Less Coolant Recovery System

NOTE: Avoid checking coolant level if engine is hot. If coolant level must be checked when engine is hot, muffle radiator cap with a thick cloth, then turn cap counter clockwise until pressure starts to escape. After pressure has been completely relieved, finish removing cap.

1. With engine cold, remove radiator cap and inspect coolant level.
2. Coolant level should be approximately 1 inch below bottom of filler neck.
3. Add solution of 50% water-50% antifreeze as required.
4. Install radiator cap.

With Coolant Recovery System

NOTE: On these type systems do not remove radiator cap to check coolant level.

1. Start engine and allow to reach operating temperature.
2. Visually inspect coolant level in plastic reservoir.
3. On all models except Chrysler Corp. vehicles, coolant level should be between "Full" and "Add" marks or at "Full Hot" mark, depending on reservoir. On Chrysler Corp. vehicles, coolant level should be between the one and two quart marks with engine operating at idle speed.
4. Remove reservoir filler cap and add solution of 50% water-50% antifreeze as required.
5. Install reservoir filler cap.

Brake Master Cylinder Reservoir

1. Clean master cylinder reservoir cover, then using a screw driver, unsnap retainer(s) and remove cover.

NOTE: Do not hold cover over vehicle, as brake fluid may damage finish.

2. Brake fluid level should be ¼ inch from top of master cylinder reservoir.

NOTE: If brake fluid level is excessively low, the brake

linings should be inspected for wear and brake system checked for leaks. Fluid level in reservoirs servicing disc brakes will decrease as disc brake pads wear.

3. Add brake fluid as required.

NOTE: Only add brake fluid which meets the vehicle manufacturer's specifications. Use only brake fluid which has been in a tightly closed container to prevent contamination from dirt and moisture. Do not allow petroleum base fluids to contaminate brake fluid, as seal damage may result.

4. Install cover and snap retainer into place.

NOTE: Ensure retainer is locked into cover grooves.

Power Steering Pump Reservoir

1. Start engine and allow to reach operating temperature, then turn ignition off.
2. Clean area around filler cap or dipstick, then remove filler cap or dipstick and inspect fluid level.
3. Fluid level should be between "Full" mark and end of dipstick.

NOTE: On models without dipstick, fluid level should be half way up filler neck.

4. Add fluid as necessary, then install filler cap or dipstick.

NOTE: Only add fluid recommended by the vehicle manufacturer.

Automatic Transmission

1. Firmly apply parking brake, then start and run engine for approximately 10 minutes to bring transmission fluid to operating temperature.

NOTE: Do not run engine in unventilated area. Exhaust gases contain carbon monoxide which could be deadly in unventilated areas.

2. With engine running at idle speed, shift selector lever through all positions, then place lever in Neutral on American Motors and Chrysler Corp. vehicles, and in Park on Ford Motor Co. and General Motors Corp. vehicles.
3. Clean dipstick cap, then remove dipstick and wipe off.
4. Replace dipstick and ensure it is seated in tube.
5. Remove dipstick and inspect to see if fluid level is between "Add" and "Full" marks.

NOTE: Add fluid only if level is at or below "Add" mark.

6. If fluid level is at "Add" mark, one pint of transmission fluid will bring level to "Full" mark. If fluid level is below "Add" mark, add sufficient amount of fluid to bring level between "Add" and "Full" marks. Transmission fluid is added through the dipstick tube.

NOTE: Do not bring level above "Full" mark, as overfill-

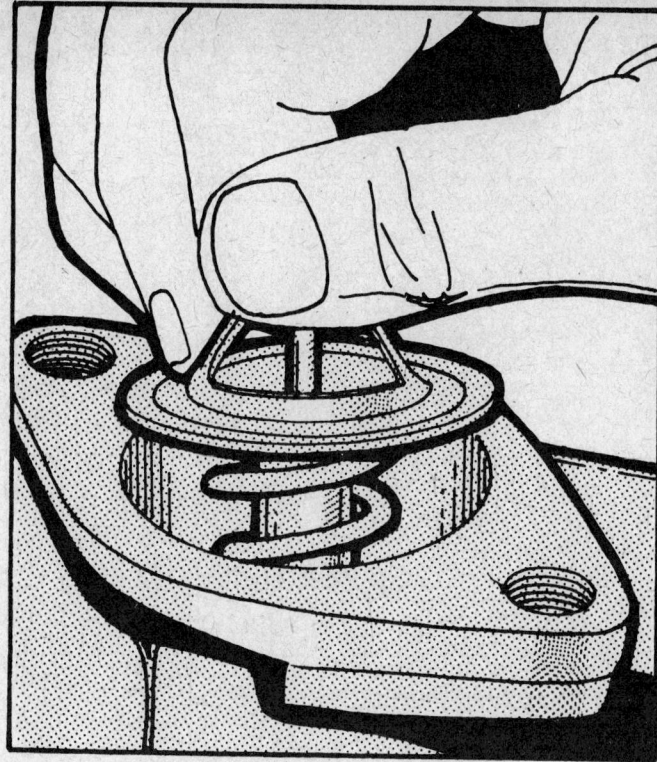

Fig. 18 Replacing thermostat (typical)

ing could result in damage to transmission. Only add automatic transmission fluid of type and specification recommended by the vehicle manufacturer.

7. Replace dipstick and ensure it is seated in tube.

Manual Transmission

1. Set parking brake and block wheels.
2. Clean area around filler plug, then using a suitable wrench or ratchet, remove filler plug.
3. Fluid should be level with bottom of filler plug hole.
4. Add fluid as required, then install filler plug.

NOTE: Only add lubricant recommended by the vehicle manufacturer.

Rear Axle

1. Set parking brake and block wheels.
2. Clean area around filler plug, then using a suitable ratchet, remove filler plug.
3. Fluid level should be approximately ½ inch below bottom of filler plug hole.
4. Add fluid as required, then install filler plug.

NOTE: Only add lubricant recommended by the vehicle manufacturer. Do not add conventional axle type lubricant to models equipped with Anti Spin, Controlled, Limited Slip, Positraction, Sure Grip, Traction Lok or Twin Grip axles. A special lubricant must be added to these type axles. Refer to vehicle manufacturer's recommendations.

COOLING SYSTEM SERVICE

CAUTION: Do not attempt to perform any system servicing when the engine is hot or the cooling system is pressurized.

Even a simple operation such as removing the radiator cap should be avoided since personal injury and loss of coolant may result.

Draining The System

Most cooling systems incorporate a radiator petcock usually located on the engine side of the radiator at either of the lower corners. Some radiator petcocks are located on the side of the radiator. Not all cooling systems are equipped with a radiator petcock.

1. Place a suitable container under radiator to catch coolant.
2. On systems equipped with a radiator petcock, turn the tangs (ears) to open the petcock. However, do not apply excessive pressure in either direction as damage to the petcock may result because some petcocks turn clockwise and others counter-clockwise to open.
3. On systems not equipped with a radiator petcock, it will be necessary to remove the lower hose from the radiator.
4. Dispose of coolant.

Flushing The System

There are two flushing methods which can be performed without the use of special equipment. One method outlined below requires the use of a garden hose only. The second method requires the use of the garden hose and a "Tee" fitting spliced into one of the heater hoses. The "Tee" fitting and other items and instructions needed to perform this type of flushing are available through aftermarket manufacturers.

1. With cooling system drained, remove thermostat as outlined below:
   a. To locate the thermostat housing on all engines except Ford V6 engines, follow the upper radiator hose from the radiator to the engine block. On Ford V6 engines, follow the lower radiator hose from the radiator to the engine block. The point at which these hoses connect is the thermostat housing.
   b. The thermostat housing is usually retained by two bolts or nuts. Remove these bolts or nuts and remove the housing.
   c. Lift the thermostat from the mounting flange, Fig. 18, noting the position in which it was installed. This is important to avoid reinstalling the thermostat upside down.
   d. Reinstall thermostat housing, however do not reinstall thermostat. Tighten retaining bolts.
2. Insert garden hose into radiator filler opening, open radiator petcock and turn on water.
3. Start engine and run engine for a few minutes. This should flush out any loose particles in the system.
4. Turn off engine and remove the garden hose.
5. Remove thermostat housing. Thoroughly clean the thermostat housing and engine surfaces of old gasket and sealer. This is necessary to prevent leakage between the housing and engine surfaces.
6. Install new thermostat housing gasket and the thermostat. Make certain the thermostat is installed exactly in the same position as it was removed.
7. Install thermostat housing and tighten retaining bolts and nuts.
8. Allow radiator to drain.
9. Close radiator petcock, if equipped.
10. Remove coolant overflow tank, if equipped. Thoroughly clean the inside of the tank and reinstall.

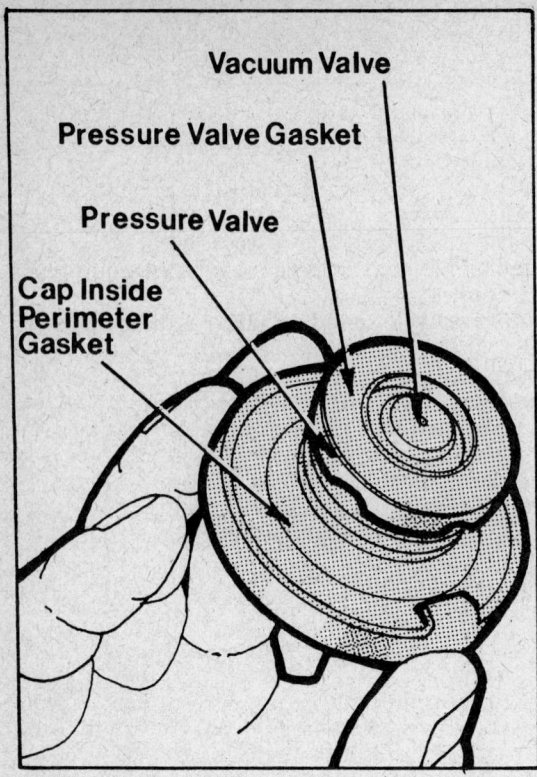

Vacuum Valve

Pressure Valve Gasket

Pressure Valve

Cap Inside Perimeter Gasket

Fig. 19 Radiator cap (typical)

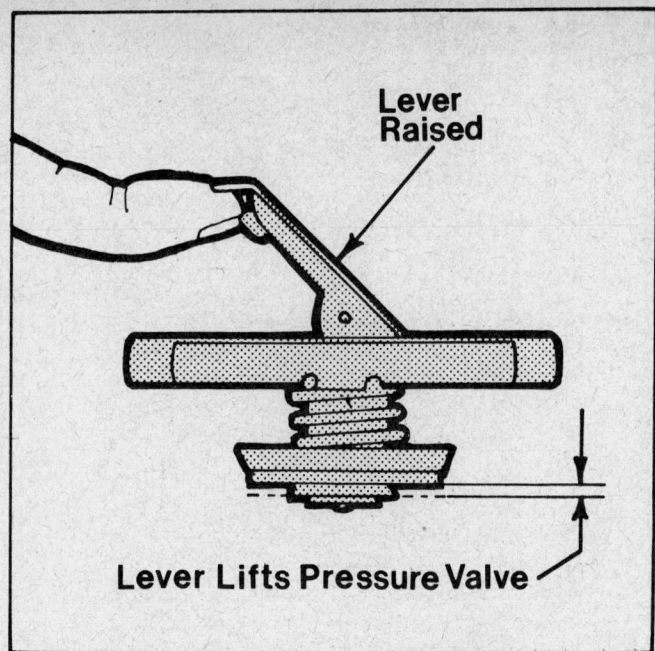

Lever Raised

Lever Lifts Pressure Valve

Fig. 20 Radiator cap with pressure release mechanism (typical)

Refilling The System

1. Determine the amount of anti-freeze required to achieve a 50/50 solution in the cooling system. Refer to the "Cooling System & Capacity Data" tables in the individual car chapters. Take the total number of quarts listed in the tables and divide by two. This number is the amount of anti-freeze, in quarts, required to achieve the 50/50 solution. This solution will generally provide protection to −35 degrees F.
2. Add the amount of anti-freeze to the radiator determined in the preceding step. If radiator fills before required amount of anti-freeze is installed, start engine and turn on heater. Add the anti-freeze as the coolant level sinks in the radiator.
3. Continue to run engine with the radiator cap removed until the upper radiator hose becomes hot to the touch.
4. Top up the coolant level in the radiator to the bottom of the filler neck with a 50/50 mixture of anti-freeze and water.
5. If equipped with an overflow tank, add a 50/50 mixture of anti-freeze and water to the cold level as marked on the side of the tank.

Radiator Cap

The radiator filler cap contains a pressure relief valve and a vacuum relief valve, Fig. 19. The pressure relief valve is held against its seat by a spring, which when compressed relieves excessive pressure out the radiator overflow. The vacuum valve is also held against its seat by a spring which when compressed opens the valve to relieve the vacuum created when the system cools.

NOTE: Some aftermarket radiator caps incorporate a pressure release mechanism to relieve cooling system pressure before rotating cap, Fig. 20.

The radiator cap should be washed with clean water and pressure checked at regular tune-up intervals. Inspect rubber seal on cap for tears or cracks. If the pressure cap will not hold pressure or does not release at the proper pressure, replace the cap.

Coolant Recovery System

The coolant recovery system supplements the standard cooling system in that additional coolant is available from a plastic reservoir, Fig. 21.

As the coolant is heated it expands within the cooling system and overflows into the plastic reservoir. As the engine cools, the coolant contracts and is drawn back into the radiator by vacuum. In this way, the radiator is filled to capacity at all times, resulting in increased cooling efficiency.

Air or vapor entering the system will be forced to the reservoir under the coolant and will exit through the reservoir cap.

A special radiator cap is designed to discourage inadvertent removal. The finger grips have been eliminated, replaced by a round configuration.

Overflow Kit

If your car does not have an overflow reservoir, it is easy to fit it with one, Fig. 22. A kit should include the following:
1. A clear plastic reservoir with quart markings to indicate fluid level.
2. A replacement radiator cap, with an air sealing gasket in the cap's inside perimeter.
3. Necessary hoses and fittings.

Hose Replacement

The radiator, heater and the coolant bypass hoses are held

Fig. 21 Factory installed coolant recovery system (typical)

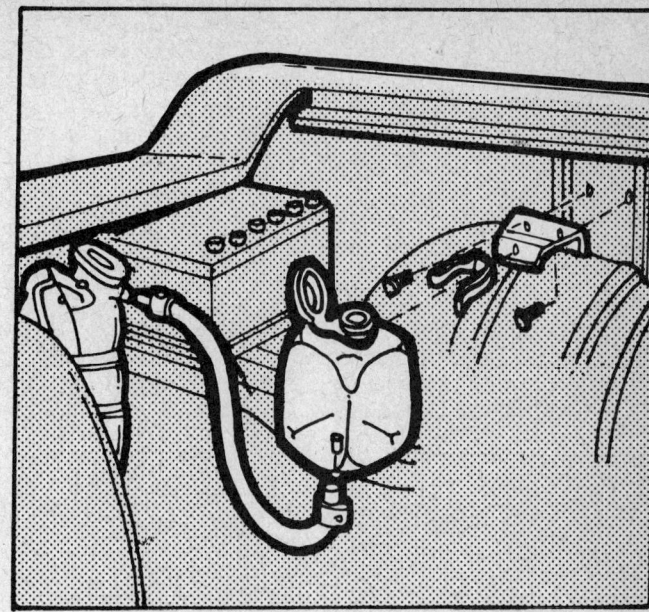

Fig. 22 Aftermarket coolant recovery system installation (typical)

at each end by a clamp. All clamps but the spring design can be loosened with a screwdriver. To save yourself time after you have removed the hose from your radiator or heater, buy the replacement hose and any necessary clamps before starting the job.

Removal

1. Drain the radiator as outlined previously. Use a clean container, large enough to hold the coolant from your cooling system to save for refilling the system after replacing the hose. If you are removing the radiator upper hose or heater hoses, you need only drain the radiator. If you are removing the lower hose, also drain the block as follows: disconnect the lower hose at the radiator, bend it down and use it as a drain spout.
2. Loosen the clamps with a screwdriver at each end of the hose to be removed. If the clamps are old and corroded, they may be stuck to the hose. Loosening the screw may not be enough on some designs, in which case you'll have to pry the clamp.

CAUTION: Be very careful when prying under the clamp. The fittings are extremely fragile and might bend or break if too much force is exerted.

If the hose is held by spring clamps, you may be in for a struggle unless you have spring clamp pliers. There are many types of pliers designed for these clamps, including ordinary slip-joint pliers with recesses cut into the jaws to grip each end of the clamp. To release the clamp you must squeeze the ends together, and if you try to use ordinary pliers, the ends may slip off. The best procedure is to discard the spring type and install a wormdrive band clamp, but if you insist on reusing the one you have, at least invest in a pair of special pliers.

3. Twist the hose back and forth to loosen it from the connector. Slide the hose off the connections. If the hose is stuck, shove in a screwdriver and try to pry loose. If the working angle is poor for the screwdriver, or if the hose is really stuck, cut the hose off the neck with a single-edge

razor blade. If the hose being removed is dried and cracked and remnants of it remain on either connection, clean the connection thoroughly with a scraper or putty knife.

Installation

1. With the old hose removed, wire brush the hose connections to remove foreign material.
2. To ease installation, coat hose neck with a soap solution.
3. Slide the hose in position so it is completely on the neck at each end, to avoid possibility of kinking and to provide room for proper positioning of the clamp. Except for the wormdrive clamp, which can be opened completely, the clamp must be loosely placed over the hose prior to fitting its end on the neck.
4. Make sure the clamps are beyond the head and placed in the center of the clamping surface of the connections.
5. Tighten the clamps.
6. Refill the cooling system as outlined previously.

Cooling System Leaks

If the coolant level must be adjusted frequently, the cooling system may be leaking either internally or externally. To determine if the system is leaking internally, special equipment must be used such as a pressure tester. To determine if the system is leaking externally, check for leakage in the following locations: radiator and its seams, hoses and their connections, heater core, water pump, coolant temperature sending unit, thermostat housing, hot water choke housing, heater water valve, coolant recovery tank and core plugs.

DRIVE BELTS

Proper belt tension is important not only to minimize noise and prolong belt life, but also to protect the accessories being driven.

Belts which are adjusted too tight may cause failure to the bearing of the accessory which it drives. Premature wear and

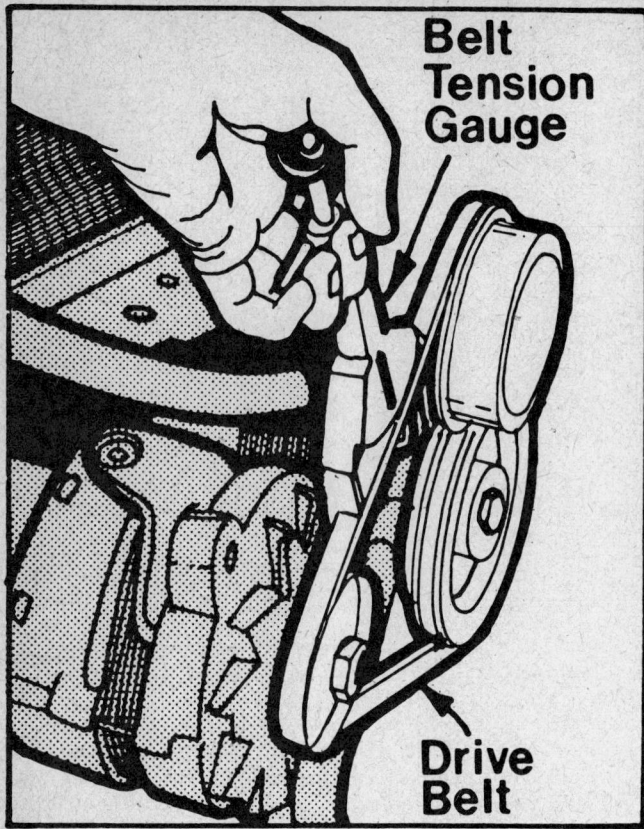

Fig. 23 Checking belt tension with a tension gauge

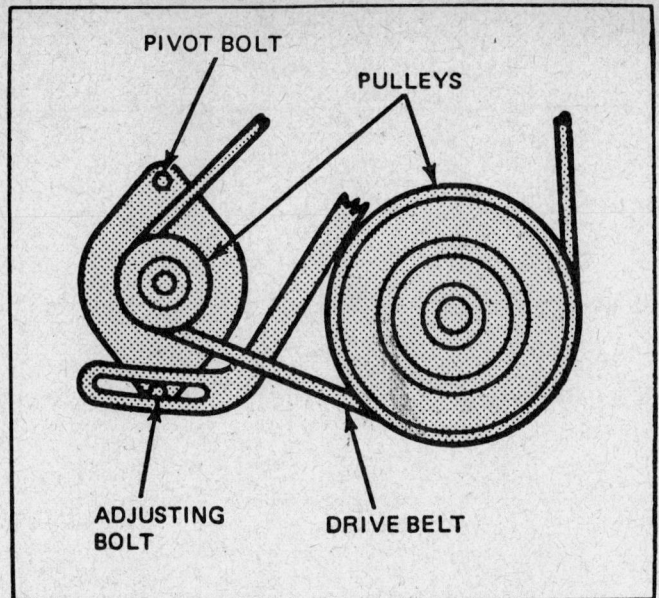

Fig. 24 Pivot bolt and adjusting bolt arrangement

breakage of the belt may also result. Belts which are too loose will slip on their pulleys and cause a screeching sound. Loose belts can also cause the battery to go dead, the engine to overheat, steering to become hard (if equipped with power steering) and air conditioner to malfunction.

Drive Belt Tension Gauge

The use of a belt tension gauge will quickly indicate whether a belt is properly adjusted or not. Low cost tension gauges give spot readings while the more expensive ones give continuous readings as the belt tension is adjusted, Fig. 23.

Drive Belt Inspection

All belts should be inspected at regular intervals for uneven wear, fraying and glazing.

CAUTION: Do not inspect belts while engine is running.

Small cracks on the underside of the belt can be enlarged for inspection by flexing the belt. Cracks expose the interior to damage, leading to breakage without warning.

Grease rots ordinary rubber belts. It also causes the belts to slip.

Glazed belts, indicated with a shiny friction surface cause the belts to slip. This can cause overheating, a low charging rate, and hard steering in the case of vehicles with power steering.

Always make sure to inspect the underside of belts. Belts that appear sound from the top, may be severely split on the sides and bottom, ready to fail.

Drive Belt Tension Adjustment

1. Run engine until it reaches normal operating temperature, then turn engine off.

CAUTION: Do not attempt to check or adjust any drive belt while engine is running. Turn engine off.

2. Using belt tension gauge following manufacturer's instructions, check tension of each belt, individually, Fig. 28. Refer to individual vehicle chapter for belt tension specifications.
3. If adjustment is necessary, proceed as follows:
   a. Pivot Bolt and Adjusting Bolt, Figs. 24 and 25: using a suitable wrench, loosen adjusting bolt and pivot bolt, then using a pry bar, move accessory toward or away from engine until tension gauge reaches specified reading. Make sure to tighten bolts before relieving force applied to pry bar.

CAUTION: Do not pry against power steering housing or air pump housing.

   b. Adjusting Bolt and Adjusting Bolt Slots, Fig. 26, loosen adjusting slot bolts, then loosen or tighten adjusting bolt until tension gauge reaches specified reading. Make sure to tighten adjusting slot bolts.
   c. Idler Pulley Pivot Bolt and Adjusting Bolt: loosen idler pulley pivot bolt and adjusting bolt, then insert a 1/2 inch flex handle into pulley arm slot and apply force on handle until tension gauge reaches specified reading. Make sure to tighten pivot and adjusting bolt before relieving force on handle.
4. To check tension on a belt without a belt tension gauge, proceed as follows:
   a. Place a straight edge along the belt from pulley to pulley, Fig. 27.
   b. Using a ruler, depress belt at midpoint between pulleys. Measure amount of deflection. For belt with a free span of less than 12 inches between pulleys, amount of deflection should be 1/4 inch. For belts with a free span of more than 12 inches between pulleys,

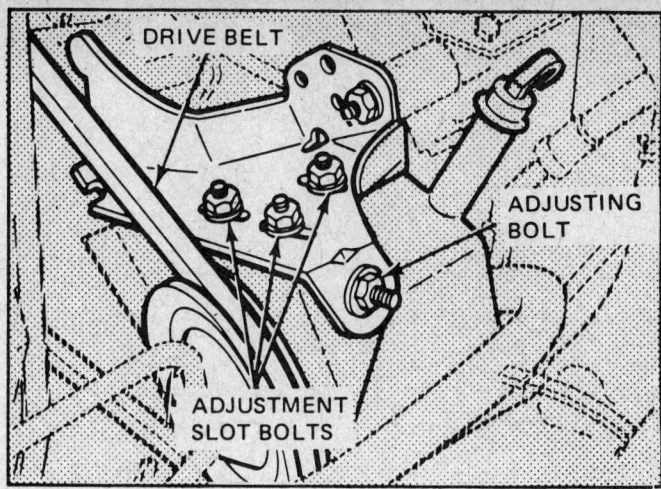

Fig. 25 Adjustment bolt and adjustment slot arrangement

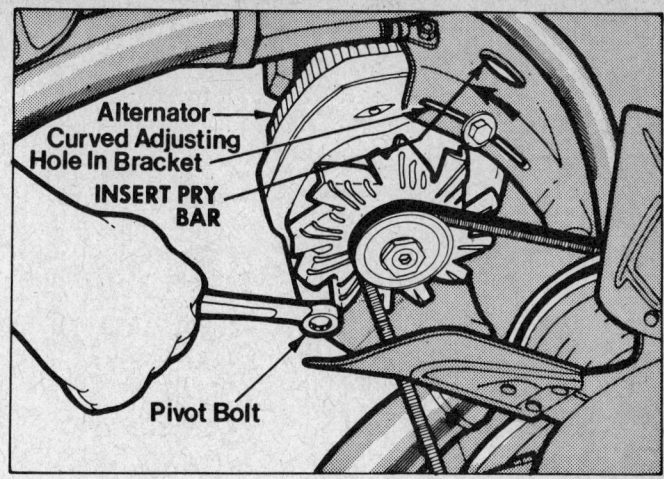

Fig. 26 Loosening adjusting bolt and pivot bolt

amount of deflection should be ½ inch.

c. Adjust belt tension, if necessary, as described previously.

5. Recheck belt tension, and readjust if necessary.

Drive Belt Replacement

To replace a belt, loosen the adjusting bolt and pivot bolt. Move accessory as required to obtain maximum slack on belt. Remove belt by lifting off the pulleys and working it around the fan or other accessories, as necessary. Occasionally on multiple belt arrangements, it will be necessary to remove one or more additional belts in order to remove the defective belt. To install belt, reverse the removal procedure and adjust belt tension as described previously.

NOTE: On accessories which are driven by dual belts, it is advisable to replace both belts even if only one needs replacement.

TIMING BELTS

Inspection

A timing belt which exhibits any of the following conditions should be replaced.

1. Hardened back surface rubber. This is indicated by a glossy non-elastic surface so hard that no mark is produced when a finger nail is forced into it.
2. Cracked back surface rubber.
3. Cracked or exfoliated canvas.
4. Badly worn teeth in their first stage indicated by worn canvas on load side tooth flank. The canvas fibers are usually fluffy, the rubber is worn away and color has changed to white. Canvas texture is unclear.
5. Badly worn teeth in their final stage indicated by worn canvas on load side tooth flank and exposed rubber. Tooth width is also greatly reduced.
6. Cracked tooth bottom.
7. Missing tooth.
8. Side of belt badly worn. A normal belt should have clean cut sides as if cut with a sharp knife.
9. Side of belt cracked.

Replacement

Refer to the individual car chapters for service procedures.

SHOCK ABSORBERS

On Vehicle Checks

Bounce Test

Check each shock absorber by bouncing each corner of vehicle. This is best accomplished by alternately lifting up and pushing down at corner of vehicle until maximum up and down movement is reached, Fig. 28. Let go of vehicle and ensure movement stops very quickly. Relative damping of

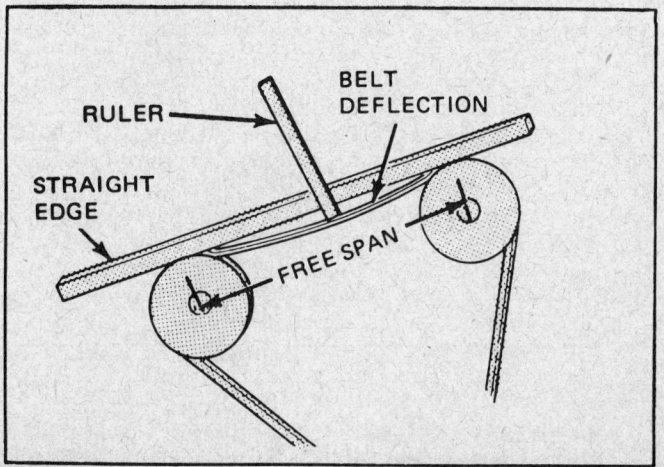

Fig. 27 Checking belt tension without belt tension gauge

Fig. 28 Bounce checking shock absorber

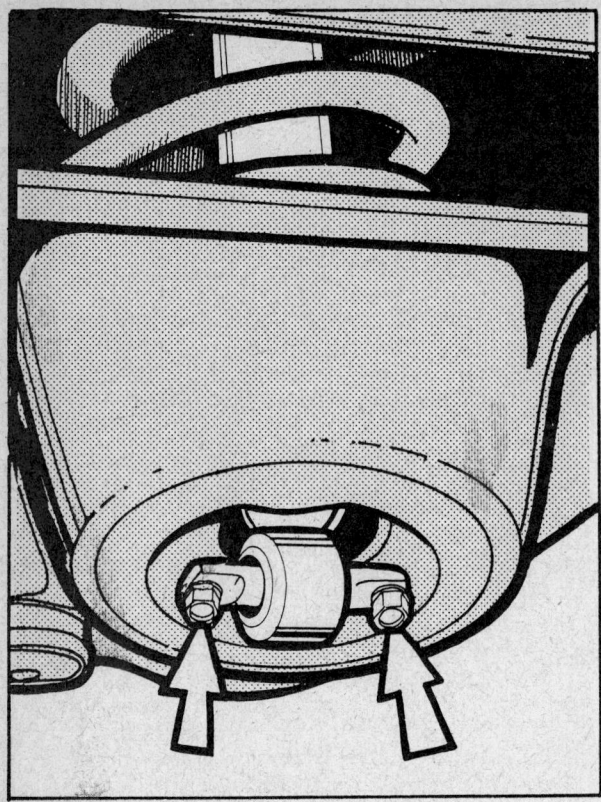

Fig. 29 Disconnecting lower shock absorber mount (typical)

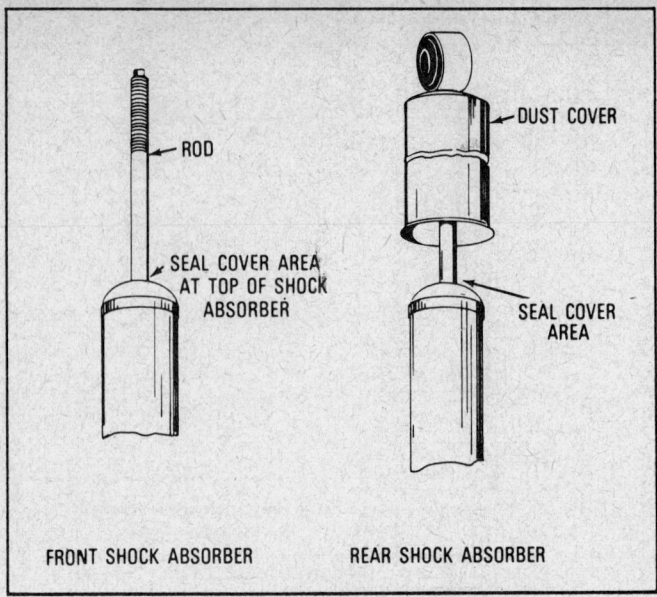

Fig. 30 Possible source of shock absorber leakage

shocks should be compared side to side but not front to rear.

Shock Mounts

If noise appears to come from shock mounts, raise vehicle on hoist that supports wheels and check mountings for the following:

1. Worn or defective grommets.
2. Loose mounting nuts or bolts.
3. Possible interference condition.
4. Missing bump stops.

If no apparent faults can be found but noise condition exists when vehicle is bounced, proceed to next check.

Leak Inspection & Manual Operation Check

1. Disconnect each shock lower mount, Fig. 29, and pull down on shock absorber until fully extended.
2. Check for leaks in seal cover area, Fig. 30. Shock absorber oil is a very thin hydraulic fluid that has a characteristic odor and dark brown color.

NOTE: Shock absorber seals are intended to allow slight seepage to lubricate rod. A trace of oil around seal cover area is not cause for shock absorber replacement since the unit has sufficient reserve fluid to compensate for this seepage.

Ensure oil spray is not from some other source. To check, wipe wet area clean and manually operate shock absorber as described in following step. Fluid will reappear if shock absorber is leaking.

NOTE: Air line must be disconnected from air adjustable shocks before they are manually operated.

3. If necessary, fabricate bracket or handle to enable a secure grip on shock absorber end, Fig. 31.
4. Check for internal binding, leakage, and improper or defective valving by pulling down and pushing up shock absorber. Upward movement will be limited by control arm. Compare rebound resistance (downward) of both shock absorbers, then compression resistance. If any noticeable difference is detected during either stroke, the weaker unit is usually at fault.
5. If shock absorber operates noisily, it should be replaced. Noise conditions that require shock absorber replacement are as follows:
   a. Grunt or squeal after full stroke in both directions.
   b. Clicking noise during fast direction reversal.
   c. Skip or lag when reversing direction in mid-stroke.

Bench Checks

If a suitable hoist is not available to perform on-vehicle shock absorber checks, or there is still doubt as to whether the units are defective, the following bench test can be performed.

Spiral Groove Reservoir Shock Absorbers

NOTE: If this style shock absorber is stored or left to lie in a horizontal position for any length of time, an air pocket will form in pressure chamber. If air pocket is not purged, shock absorber may be misdiagnosed as faulty. Purge air from pressure chamber as follows:

a. Extend shock absorber while holding it vertically and right side up, Fig. 32.
b. Invert shock absorber and fully compress unit.
c. Repeat steps a and b at least 5 times to ensure air is completely purged.

1. Obtain known good shock absorber with same part number.
2. Hold both shock absorbers in vertical position and clamp bottom mounts in vise. Do not clamp on mounting threads or on reservoir tube.
3. Operate shock absorbers by hand at different speeds and

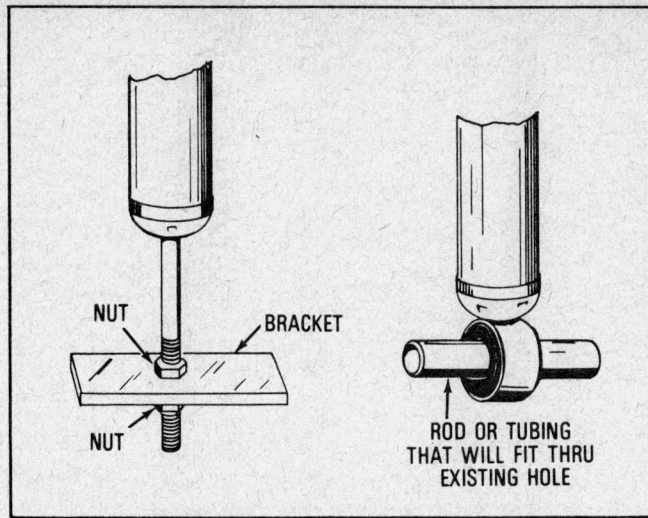

Fig. 31 Methods of gripping shock absorbers

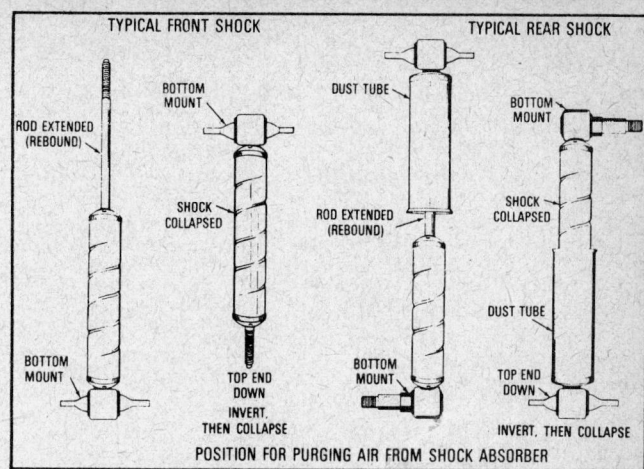

Fig. 32 Purging air from shock absorbers

compare resistance of known good shock to the other. Rebound resistance (extension) is usually greater than compression resistance (about 2:1). Resistance should be smooth and consistant for each stroke rate.

4. Check for the following conditions which indicate a defective shock absorber:
   a. Skip or lag when reversing direction in mid-stroke.
   b. Seizing or binding except at extreme end of stroke.
   c. Noises such as grunt or squeal after completing full stroke in either direction.
   d. Clicking noise at fast reversal.
   e. Fluid leakage.
5. Check for loose piston by extending shock absorber to full rebound position, then give an extra hard pull. If any give is present, piston is loose and unit must be replaced.

Gas Cell Shock Absorbers

These shock absorbers are equipped with a gas-filled cell which takes the place of air in the reservoir. Foaming of the fluid is eliminated since air and fluid cannot mix. Because of this feature, these style shock absorbers must be tested in an upside down position. If a lag is noticed when unit is stroked, gas cell has ruptured and unit must be replaced.

Air Adjustable Shock Absorbers

These shock absorbers have an air chamber similar to the

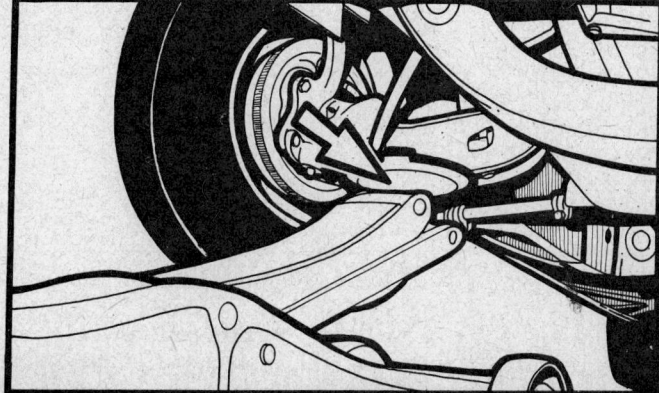

Fig. 33 Supporting control arm on vehicles with spring on lower control arm

spiral groove reservoir type which must be purged. Refer to note under "Spiral Groove Reservoir Shock Absorbers" to purge air from shock absorbers.

1. Place shock absorber in vise in vertical position with larger diameter tube at top, and clamp at lower mounting ring.
2. Operate unit manually at different speeds. A consistent degree of resistance should be felt through length of stroke. A gurgling noise is normal since unit is normally pressurized.
3. Refer to "Spiral Groove Reservoir Shock Absorbers" test procedure for remainder of bench checks.

FRONT SUSPENSION & STEERING CHECKS

To perform the following wear checks, tension must be removed from the suspension parts. Raise the vehicle and support with jack stands. Relieve load from suspension as follows: on vehicles with the spring or torsion bar on the lower control arm, place a floor jack or single piston hydraulic jack under lower control arm as close to ball joint as possible, Fig. 33, and raise control arm until vehicle chassis is about to lift off jack stand, then stop; on vehicles with spring on upper control arm, jack up lower control arm as described previously, place block of wood between upper control arm and frame, Fig. 34, and slowly lower jack from lower control arm, making sure that neither upper control nor wooden block move. Wooden block must be removed after inspection is completed.

Upper & Lower Control Arm Bushings Check

1. Have assistant sit in vehicle and apply brake to lock front wheels.
2. Grasp front wheel with both hands and vigorously attempt to rotate it forward and backward. Observe control arms for excessive front-to-rear movement.
3. Repeat procedure on other front wheel.

Upper Ball Joint Check

1. Grasp front wheel at top with one hand and at bottom with other.

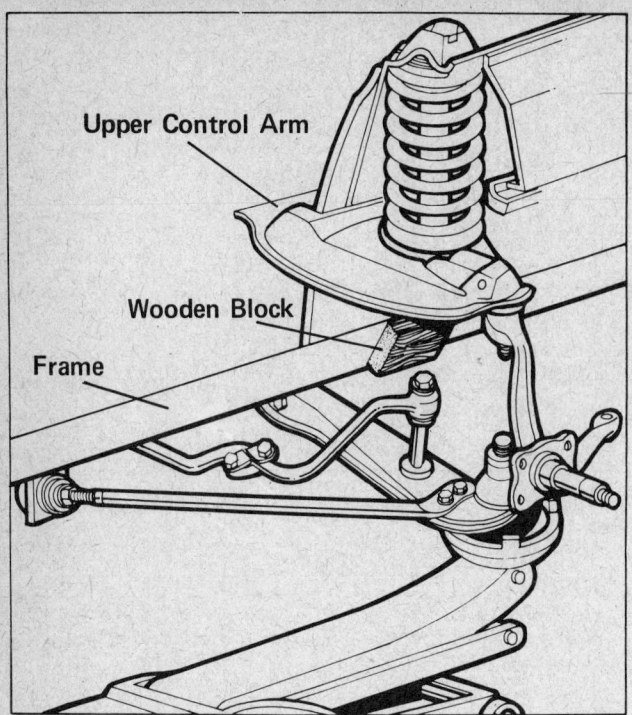

Fig. 34 Blocking upper control arm of vehicles with spring on upper control arm

2. Pull wheel out at bottom while simultaneously pushing in at top. Have assistant watch for play in upper ball joint.
3. Repeat on other front wheel.

Lower Ball Joint Check

1. Place suitable bar or pipe directly under center of tire.
2. Wedge pipe against ground and lift. Several tries may be necessary to get a good check.
3. Repeat procedure on other wheel.

Steering Linkage Check

1. Grasp wheel with both hands and vigorously shake tire from right to left. Have assistant check for wear in tie-rod ends, center link, and idler arm. Idler arm should not move up and down.
2. Repeat procedure on other wheel.

TIRE CARE

Tire Rotation

The purpose of tire rotation is to equalize normal wear. By equalizing this wear evenly over the entire tread surface, you extend tire life. Recommended rotation patterns are shown in Fig. 35.

It is wise to provide snow tires with rims of their own, so they do not have to be removed from rims in the late fall. They can be kept on rims of their own during both storage and use. In this way, you will protect tires from the bead damage which becomes a possibility when you break a tire away from a rim.

A studded snow tire should always be mounted on the same wheel of the car year after year. When storing studded snow tires, mark tire in chalk for either Right or Left, depending

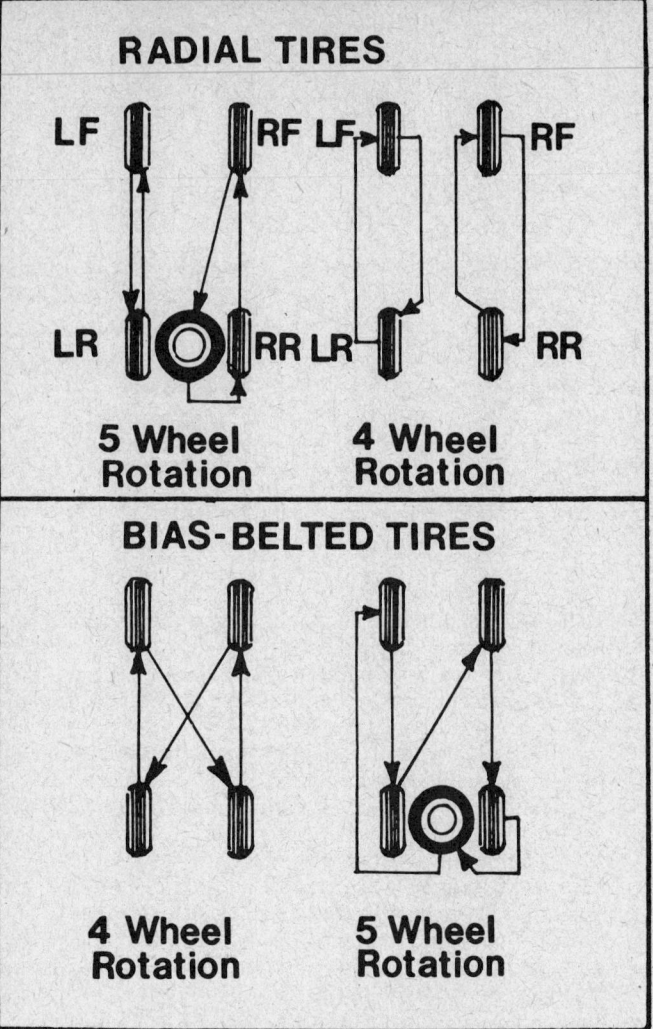

Fig. 35 Tire rotation chart

upon which side of the car the tire was mounted.

When storing tires, lay them flat, off the tread to prevent flat spots from developing. Keep tires away from electricity-producing machinery which creates ozone and can damage rubber.

Tire Maintenance

Tires should be inspected regularly for excessive or abnormal tread wear, fabric breaks, cuts or other damage, Fig. 36. A bulge or bump in the sidewall or tread is reason for discarding a tire. A bulge indicates that the tread or sidewall has separated from the tire body. The tire is a candidate for a blowout. Look also for small stones or other foreign bodies wedged in the tread. These can be removed by prying them out carefully with a screwdriver.

BATTERY SERVICE

Construction & Operation

To understand why batteries malfunction, some knowledge of batteries is important. Simply stated, the battery is constructed of two unlike materials, a positive plate and a negative plate with a porous separator between the two plates,

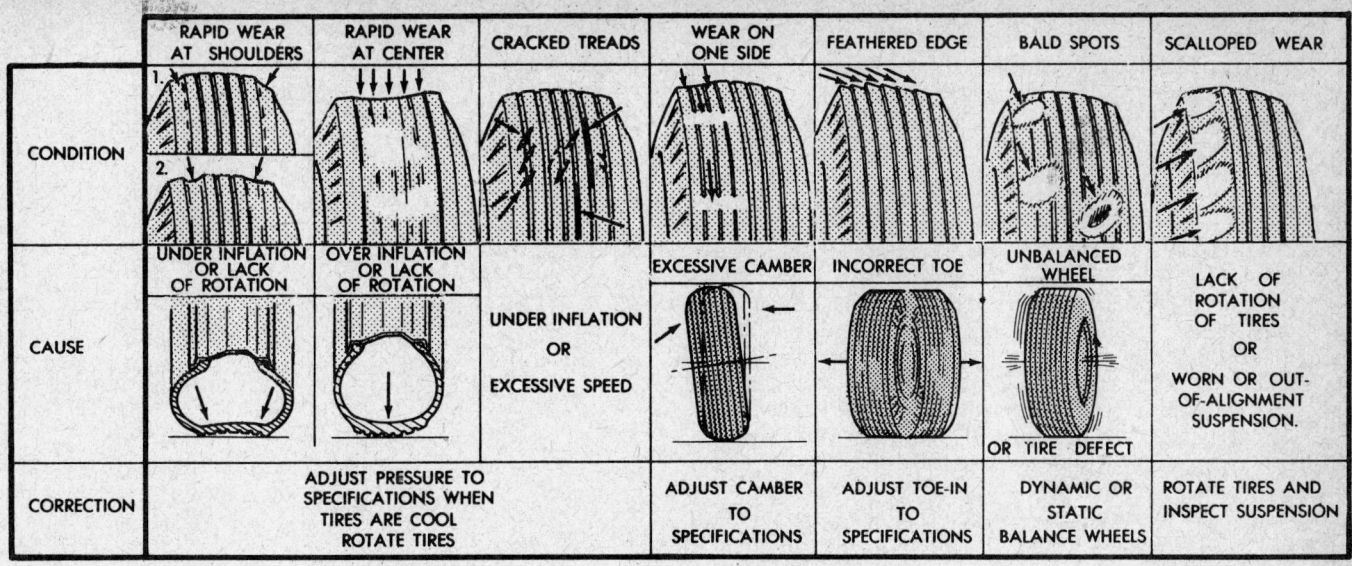

CONDITION	RAPID WEAR AT SHOULDERS	RAPID WEAR AT CENTER	CRACKED TREADS	WEAR ON ONE SIDE	FEATHERED EDGE	BALD SPOTS	SCALLOPED WEAR
CAUSE	UNDER INFLATION OR LACK OF ROTATION	OVER INFLATION OR LACK OF ROTATION	UNDER INFLATION OR EXCESSIVE SPEED	EXCESSIVE CAMBER	INCORRECT TOE	UNBALANCED WHEEL OR TIRE DEFECT	LACK OF ROTATION OF TIRES OR WORN OR OUT-OF-ALIGNMENT SUSPENSION.
CORRECTION	ADJUST PRESSURE TO SPECIFICATIONS WHEN TIRES ARE COOL ROTATE TIRES			ADJUST CAMBER TO SPECIFICATIONS	ADJUST TOE-IN TO SPECIFICATIONS	DYNAMIC OR STATIC BALANCE WHEELS	ROTATE TIRES AND INSPECT SUSPENSION

Fig. 36 Tire tread wear patterns

Fig. 37. This assembly placed in a suitable battery case and filled slightly above the top of the plates with electrolyte (sulphuric acid and distilled water) forms a cell. The 12 volt battery is composed of 6 cells interconnected by plate straps. Note that batteries have varying number of plates per cell, but each cell in any given battery has the same number of plates.

The battery performs the following four basic functions in a vehicle:
1. Supplies electrical energy to the starter motor to crank and start the engine and also to the ignition system while the engine is being started.
2. Supplies electrical energy for accessories such as radio, tape deck, heater, and lights when engine is not running and the ignition switch is in the "OFF" or the "Accessory" position.
3. Supplies additional electrical energy for accessories while the engine is running when the output of the alternator is exceeded by the various accessories.
4. Stabilizes voltage in the electrical system. Satisfactory operation of the ignition system and any other electrical device is impossible with a damaged, weak or even underpowered (low rating) battery.

Sealed Batteries

Sealed batteries, called "Maintenance Free" or "Freedom" batteries, Fig. 38, are available on some vehicles, and can also be purchased from other sources.

The sealed batteries have unique chemistry and construction methods which provide advantages.

Water never needs to be added to the battery.

The battery is completely sealed except for two small vent holes on the side. The vent holes allow what small amount of gases are produced in the battery to escape. The special chemical composition inside the battery reduces the production of gas to an extremely small amount at normal charging voltages.

The battery has a very strong ability to withstand damaging effects of overcharge, and the terminals are tightly sealed to minimize leakage. A charge indicator in the cover indicates state of charge.

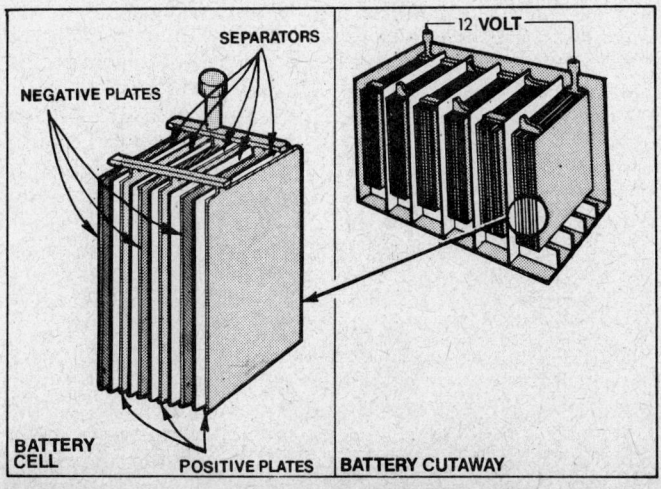

Fig. 37 Battery construction

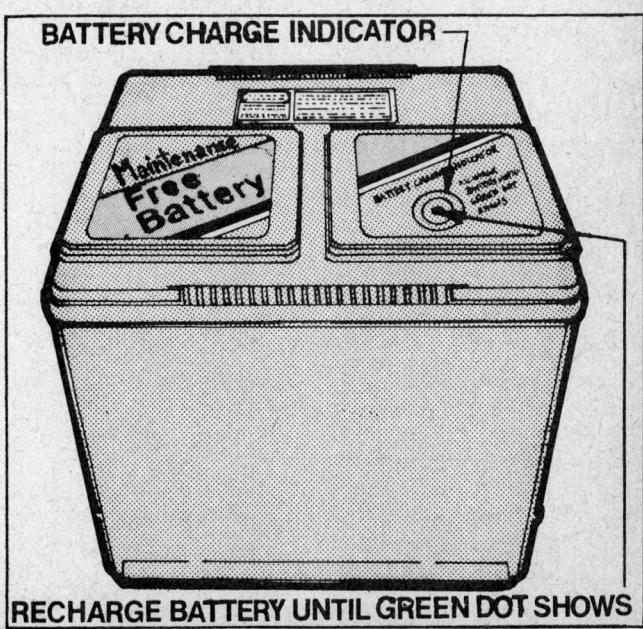

Fig. 38 Typical maintenance free battery

Compared to a conventional battery in which performance decreases steadily with age, the sealed battery delivers more available power at any time during its life. The battery has a reduced tendency to self-discharge as compared to a conventional battery.

Safety Precautions

CAUTION: Electrolyte solution in the battery is a strong and dangerous acid. It is extremely harmful to eyes, skin and clothing. If acid contacts any part of the body, flush immediately with water for a period not less than 15 minutes. If acid is accidentally swallowed, drink large quantities of milk or water, followed by milk of magnesia, a beaten raw egg or vegetable oil. Call physician immediately.

When batteries are being charged, highly explosive hydrogen and oxygen gases form in each battery cell. Some of this gas escapes through the vent holes in the plugs on top of battery case and forms an explosive atmosphere surrounding the battery. This explosive gas will remain in and/or around the battery for several hours after the battery has been charged. Sparks or flames can ignite this gas and cause a dangerous battery explosion.

The following precautions must be observed to avoid battery explosion, personal harm and damage to the vehicle's electrical system.
1. Do not smoke near batteries being charged or those which have been recently charged. It is a good practice never to smoke near a battery even though the battery is in the vehicle.
2. Always shield your eyes when working with batteries.
3. Do not disconnect live (working) circuits (lights or accessories operating) at the terminals of batteries since sparking usually occurs at a point where such a circuit is disconnected.
4. Use extreme caution when connecting or disconnecting booster leads or cable clamps from battery chargers. Make sure live (working) circuits are disconnected before connecting or disconnecting the booster leads or cable clamps. Poor booster lead connections are a common cause of electrical arcing causing battery explosions.

Causes of Discharged Batteries

There are numerous reasons that could cause a battery to discharge and appear to be defective, therefore the battery should not be targeted as the primary source of electrical and/or starting problems before it has been tested.

The following are some common conditions that could discharge a good battery:
1. Lights left "ON" or doors not closed properly, leaving dome light "ON."
2. Excessive use of accessories with the engine not running.
3. Improper installation of aftermarket accessories.
4. Alternator belt loose or damaged.
5. Dirty battery case causing a self-discharge condition.
6. Loose battery cable terminals.
7. Low alternator output.
8. High resistance in charging circuits caused by other loose electrical connections.

Battery Rating & Capacity

The two most commonly used ratings are the 20 hour

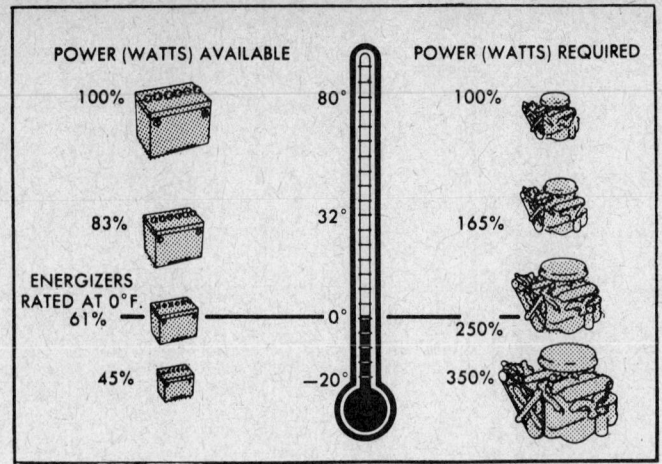

Fig. 39 Battery energy versus falling temperature comparison chart

rating at 80°F. and the cold cranking load capacity of the battery at 0°F, specified in amps. Batteries are also rated by watts in the Peak Watt Rating (PWR) which is actually the cold cranking ability of the battery at 0°F.

Another battery rating method is the reserve capacity rating in minutes. The purpose of this rating is to determine the length of time a vehicle can be operated with a faulty charging system (malfunctioning alternator or regulator). Batteries are normally marketed by the Ampere-Hour rating which is based on the 20 hour rating. The Ampere-Hour rating is also normally stamped on the battery case or on a label attached to the battery. A battery capable of furnishing 4 amps for a period of 20 hours is classified as an 80 ampere hour battery (4 amps × 20 hours = 80).

The Ampere-Hour rating should not be confused with the cranking performance of a battery at 0°F. Batteries with the same Ampere-Hour ratings can have various 0°F. cranking capacities. The higher quality battery will have a higher Ampere-Hour rating and a higher cranking capacity rating at 0°F. Note that battery capacity will increase with larger number of plates per cell, larger size of plates, and larger battery case size allowing for more electrolyte solution.

Selecting A Replacement Battery

Long and troublefree service can be better assured when the capacity or wattage rating of the replacement battery is at least equal to the wattage rating of the battery originally engineered for the application by the manufacturer.

The use of an undersized battery may result in poor performance and early failure. Fig. 39 shows how battery power shrinks while the need for engine cranking power increases with falling temperatures. Sub-zero temperatures reduce capacity of a fully charged battery to 45% of its normal power and at the same time increase cranking load to 3½ times the normal warm weather load.

Hot weather can also place excessive electrical loads on the battery. Difficulty in starting may occur when cranking is attempted shortly after a hot engine has been turned off or stalls. High compression engines can be as difficult to start under such conditions as on the coldest day. Consequently, good performance can be obtained only if the battery has ample capacity to cope with these conditions.

A battery of greater capacity should be considered if the electrical load has been increased through the addition of accessories, or if driving conditions are such that the generator cannot keep the battery charged.

Watt Rating	5 Amperes	10 Amperes	20 Amperes	30 Amperes	40 Amperes	50 Amperes
Below 2450	10 Hours	5 Hours	2½ Hours	2 Hours		
2450-2950	12 Hours	6 Hours	3 Hours	2 Hours	1½ Hours	
Above 2950	15 Hours	7½ Hours	3¼ Hours	2 Hours	1¾ Hours	1½ Hours

Fig. 40   Battery charging guide

On applications where heavy electrical loads are encountered, a higher output generator that will supply a charge during low speed operation may be required to increase battery life and improve battery performance.

Testing Battery (Specific Gravity)

NOTE: The specific gravity of a sealed battery cannot be checked.

A hydrometer can be used to measure the specific gravity of the electrolyte in each cell. There are several types of hydrometers available, the least expensive consisting of a glass tube, a rubber bulb at the end of the tube and several balls within the tube. To use this type, the specific gravity of the battery must be interpreted by the number of balls which float to the surface of the electrolyte, according to the manufacturer's instructions.

The hydrometer indicates the concentration of the electrolyte.

Boost Starting A Vehicle With A Discharged Battery

1. Be sure the ignition key is in the off position and all accessories and lights are off.
2. Shield eyes. Use goggles or similar eye protection.
3. Connect the booster cables from the positive (+) battery terminal of the discharged battery (vehicle to be started) to the positive (+) battery terminal of the vehicle used as the booster.
4. Connect one end of the other cable to negative (−) terminal of the good battery.
5. Connect the other end of the cable to engine bolthead or similar good contact spot on the vehicle being started.

CAUTION: Never connect to negative terminal of dead battery.

NOTE: To prevent damage to other electrical components on the vehicle being started, make certain engine is at idle speed before disconnecting jumper cables.

Charging The Battery

There are two separate methods of recharging batteries which differ basically in the rate of charge.

Slow Charging Method

Slow charging is the best and only method of completely recharging a battery. This method, when properly applied, may be used safely under all possible conditions providing the electrolyte is at proper level and the battery is capable of being fully charged. The normal charging rate is 5

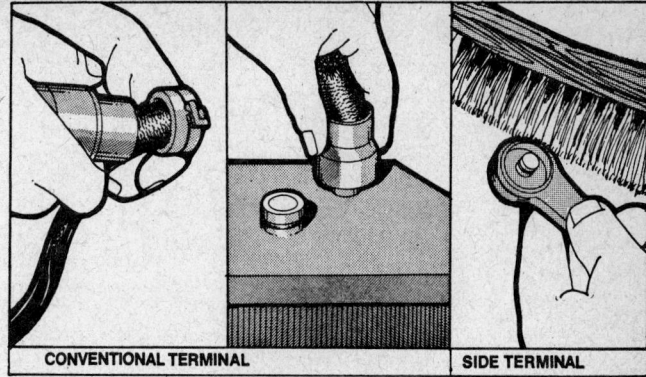

CONVENTIONAL TERMINAL | SIDE TERMINAL

Fig. 41   Cleaning battery terminals

amperes.

A fully charged battery is indicated when all cell specific gravities do not increase when checked at three one-hour intervals and all cells are gassing freely.

Charge periods of 24 hours or more may be required because of the low charging rate. See charging guide, Fig. 40.

Quick Charging Method

In order to get a car back on the road in the least amount of time, it is sometimes necessary to quick charge a battery. The battery cannot be brought up to a full charged condition by the quick charge method. It can, however, be substantially recharged or boosted but, in order to bring it to a fully charged condition, the charging cycle must be finished by charging at a low or normal rate. Some quick chargers have a provision for finishing the charging cycle at a low rate to bring the battery up to a fully charged condition.

CAUTION: Too high a current during quick charging will damage battery plates.

Battery Cable Service

NOTE: At regular intervals, perform a visual inspection of the battery.

This inspection should be performed when any of the underhood maintenance items such as engine oil, transmission fluid or radiator coolant level are checked.

1. Clean any heavy accumulation of dirt or corrosion on the battery terminals and battery tray with a wire brush, Fig. 41. Finish cleaning with a solution of baking soda and water. Diluted ammonia can also be used as a washing agent. Thoroughly flush battery with clean water.

NOTE: Baking soda and ammonia neutralize battery acid. Therefore make sure these agents are kept out of the battery by keeping the battery caps tightly in place.

2. Check for damaged cable insulation. Damaged insulation can cause the cable to short out against the body of the vehicle or other accessories. Cables in this condition should be replaced immediately.
3. Check level of electrolyte. If required, add water as described further on.
4. Make sure battery is securely held in place. A loose or broken bracket can result in battery damage (both internally and externally) from excessive vibration.

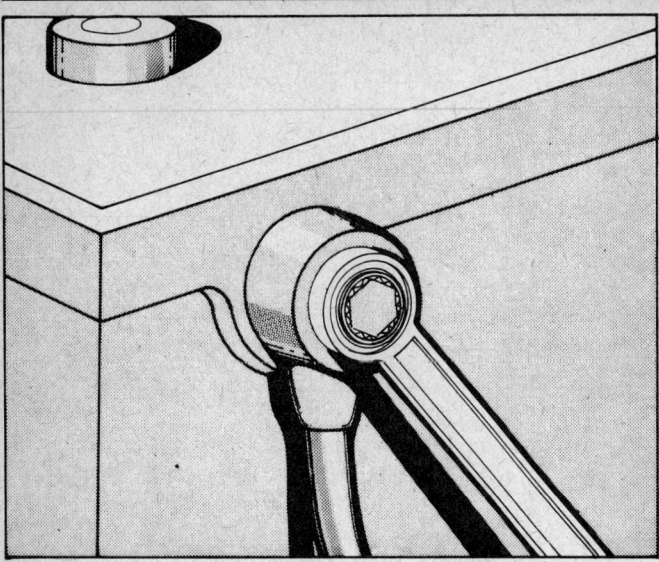

Fig. 42   Removing side type battery terminal

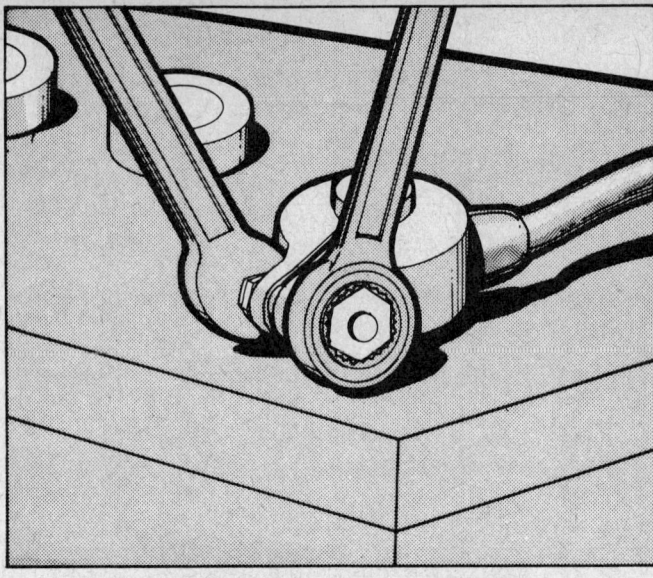

Fig. 43   Removing bolt type terminal

Battery Cable, Replace

NOTE: When disconnecting battery cables, first make sure all accessories are off, disconnect the negative battery cable and then the positive cable. Make sure to reconnect cables in the reverse order of removal.

1. On side terminal batteries, loosen the retaining bolts using a 5/16-inch wrench, and disconnect the cable from the battery, Fig. 42.
2. On all other type batteries, loosen the cable retaining bolt using a 1/2 inch or 9/16 inch box wrench, Fig. 43, and lift the cable off the battery posts. Some cables can be removed by squeezing the tabs on the cable terminal using a pair of pliers, Fig. 44, and lifting the cable off the

battery posts.
3. If the battery terminals are difficult to remove, use a terminal puller, Fig. 45. Place the legs of the puller underneath the terminal and tighten the puller screw until the terminal is removed.
4. Clean the cable terminals and battery posts using a terminal and post wire brush, Fig. 41.
5. Clean the battery top using a solution of soda and water. Ensure the battery is thoroughly cleaned and dried.

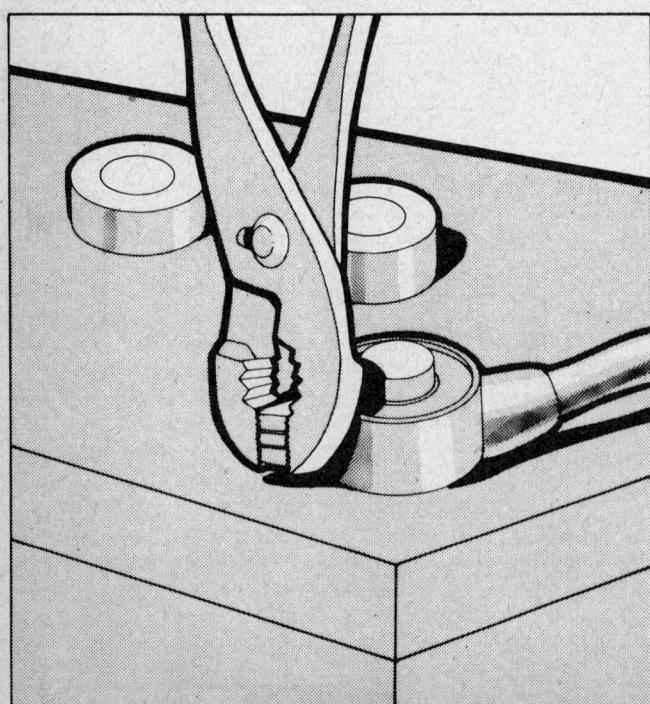

Fig. 44   Removing spread type terminal

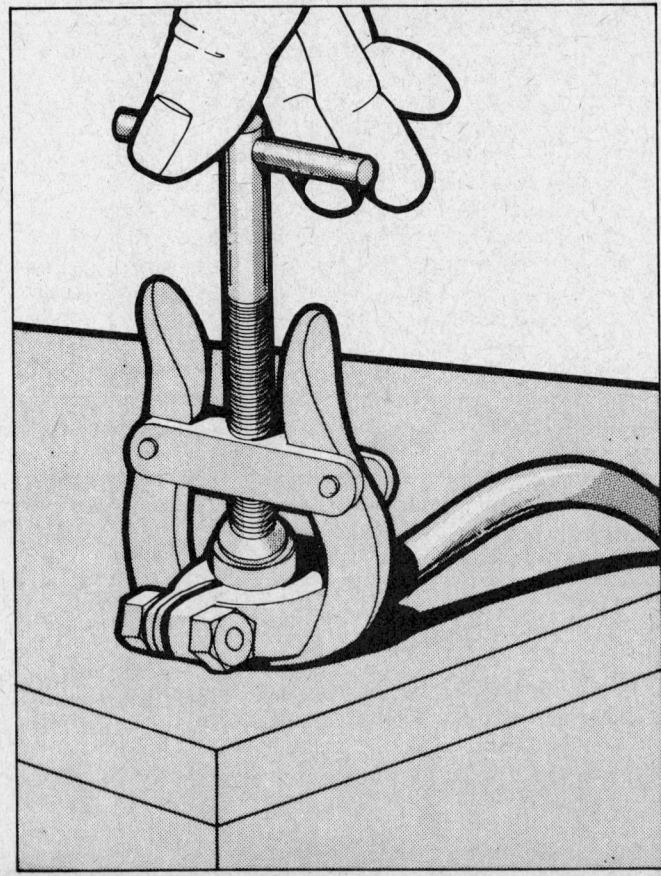

Fig. 45   Removing battery cable terminal using cable terminal puller

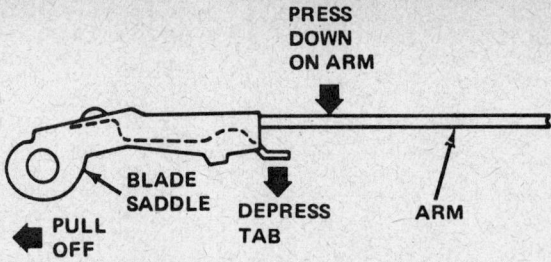

Fig. 46 Trico bayonet type wiper blade removal. American Motors & Ford Motor Co.

Make sure you cover the battery caps to avoid entry of the soda and water solution into the battery.

6. To install the cables on a side terminal battery, place the cables onto the battery and tighten the retaining screws using a 5/16 inch wrench.

7. To install the cables on all other types of batteries, place the cables on the battery post and force them all the way down. If the cable is not completely bottomed, spread the cable terminal slightly with a screwdriver, until the terminal is properly positioned.

8. Tighten the terminal bolts using a 1/2 inch or 9/16 inch box wrench.

9. Coat the outside of the terminals with petroleum jelly to prevent corrosion.

Replacing Battery

Careless installation of a new battery can ruin the battery. In removing the old battery, note the location of the positive battery post so the new battery can be installed in the same position. Always remove the negative (ground) cable first.

Use an open-end wrench to loosen the clamp. If the nut is very tight, use one wrench on the head of the bolt and the other on the nut to avoid straining and possibly cracking the battery cover. A pair of battery pliers can be used to loosen the nut, but a wrench should always be used on the head of the bolt.

If a cable terminal is corroded to the post, do not try to loosen it by hammering, or by resting a tool on the battery and prying—either method can break the battery container. Use a screw type terminal puller, Fig. 54, or spread the cable terminals slightly with a screwdriver.

Clean any corrosion from the cables, battery case, or hold-downs, and inspect them. Paint any corroded steel parts with acid-proof paint. Make sure the cable is of the correct size and that its insulation and clamp terminal are in good condition.

Put the new battery in position, making sure it sits level, and tighten the hold-downs a little at a time, alternately, to avoid distorting and breaking the battery case. The hold-downs should be snug enough to prevent bouncing, but should not be too tight.

NOTE: Before connecting the cables, check the battery terminals to be sure the battery is not reversed.

Clean the battery posts bright with sandpaper or a wire brush.

Don't hammer the terminals down on the posts, as the battery case may crack. Spread the terminals slightly if necessary. Connect the starter cable first and the negative (ground) cable last, tightening the terminal bolts after making sure the cables don't interfere with the vent plugs or rub against the hold-downs.

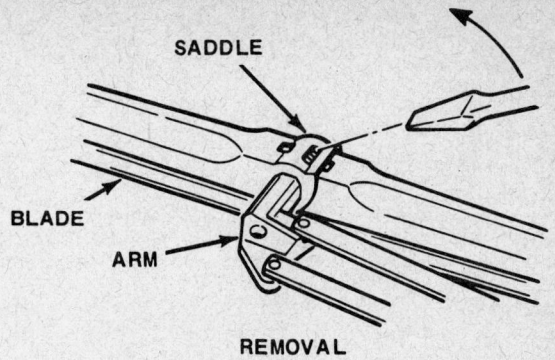

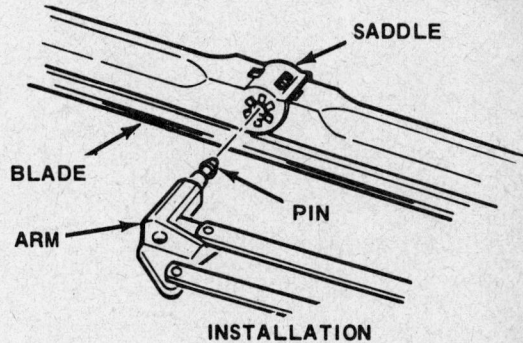

Fig. 47 Saddle pin type wiper blade removal. American Motors & Ford Motor Co.

W/S WIPER BLADE & ELEMENT, REPLACE

American Motors

WIPER BLADE

Exc. 1977—78 Matador Coupe, 1977—80 Pacer & 1977—84 Liftgate

To remove, press downward on wiper arm to disengage upper stud, then depress tab on blade saddle and pull blade assembly from arm, Fig. 46. To install, slide blade saddle over end of wiper arm until locking stud snaps into place. Check to ensure wiper blade is securely seated on wiper arm.

1977—78 Matador Coupe, 1977—79 Pacer & 1977—80 Liftgate

To remove, insert a screwdriver or other suitable tool into spring release opening of blade saddle and depress spring clip, then pull blade assembly from wiper arm, Fig. 47. Install wiper blade assembly by pushing blade saddle on wiper arm pin so clip engages pin. Check to ensure wiper blade is securely seated on wiper arm.

1980 Pacer Exc. Liftgate

NOTE: When removing the pin type plastic wiper blade, grasp ends of wiper blade frame, not wiper blade element, to avoid damaging element.

To remove, grasp both ends of wiper blade frame and reverse contour of blade assembly, then pull blade from wiper arm, Fig. 48. To install, push wiper blade assembly onto wiper arm pin so frame spring engages pin. Check to ensure blade assembly is securely seated on wiper arm.

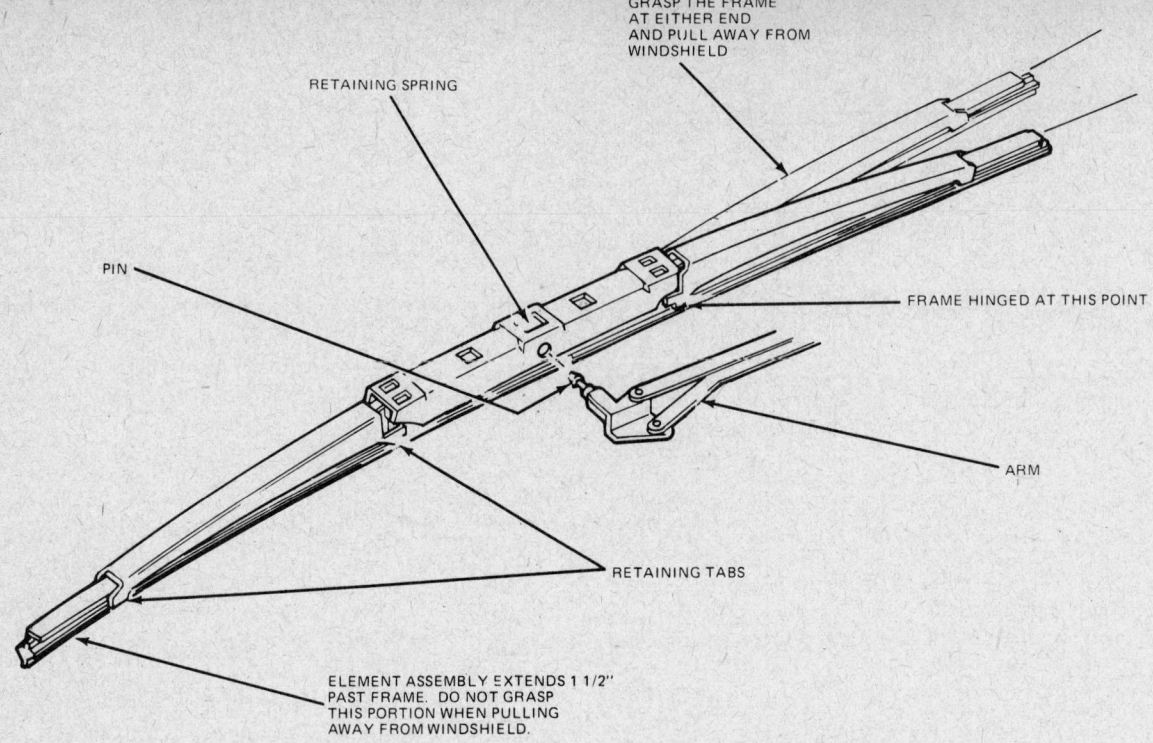

GRASP THE FRAME AT EITHER END AND PULL AWAY FROM WINDSHIELD

RETAINING SPRING

PIN

FRAME HINGED AT THIS POINT

ARM

RETAINING TABS

ELEMENT ASSEMBLY EXTENDS 1 1/2" PAST FRAME. DO NOT GRASP THIS PORTION WHEN PULLING AWAY FROM WINDSHIELD.

Fig. 48   Trico plastic pin type wiper blade removal. American Motors & Ford Motor Co.

1981–84 Liftgate

To remove, pull upward on blade spring lock, then pull blade assembly from wiper arm pin, Fig. 49. To install, push blade onto wiper arm until spring lock engages pin. Check to ensure wiper blade is securely seated on wiper arm.

WIPER BLADE ELEMENT

1977–79 All Models & 1980 Liftgate

To remove, depress wiper element latch lock release tabs and pull element from blade frame retainers, Fig. 49. To install, insert element through each of the retaining tabs and engage latch lock notches with the last retaining tab. Check to ensure element is engaged with all retainers before installing wiper blade assembly.

1980–84 Exc. Liftgate

To remove, squeeze wide area of blade element reinforcement and twist slightly to unlock element from blade frame retaining tabs. Pull element from remaining blade frame retaining tabs. To install, insert element through each of the retaining tabs and engage wide portion of element metal reinforcement with last retaining tab. Check to ensure wiper blade element is engaged with all retaining tabs before installing wiper blade assembly.

1982–84 Liftgate

To replace wiper blade element, Fig. 58, proceed as follows:

a. On wiper blade element plastic backing strip, locate a 7/16 inch notch approximately 1 inch from end of element.
b. Place wiper blade assembly on a firm surface with notched end of plastic backing strip visible, then grasp frame portion of wiper blade and push downward until blade assembly is tightly bowed.
c. With blade assembly tightly bowed, grasp tip of plastic backing strip and pull upward and twist counter clockwise at the same time to snap backing strip from blade frame tab.
d. Lift blade assembly from surface and slide backing strip down frame until notch is aligned with next retaining tab, then twist slightly to snap backing strip from tab. Continue this procedure with the remaining blade frame tabs.
e. Reverse procedure to install. Check to ensure element backing strip is engaged with all retaining tabs before installing wiper blade on wiper arm.

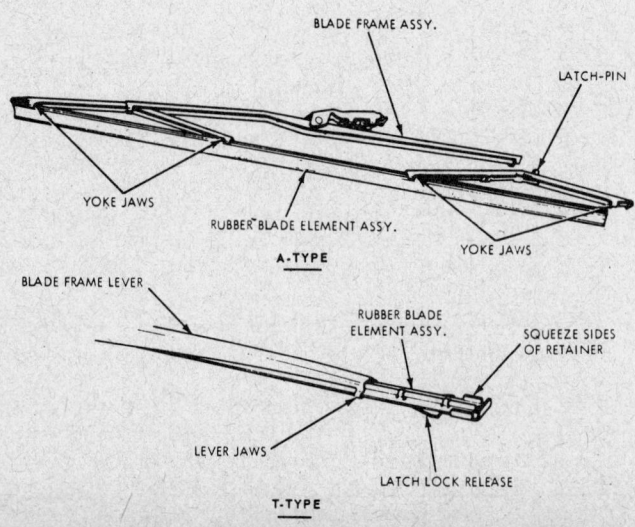

BLADE FRAME ASSY.

LATCH-PIN

YOKE JAWS

RUBBER BLADE ELEMENT ASSY.

YOKE JAWS

A-TYPE

BLADE FRAME LEVER

RUBBER BLADE ELEMENT ASSY.

SQUEEZE SIDES OF RETAINER

LEVER JAWS

LATCH LOCK RELEASE

T-TYPE

Fig. 49   Wiper blade removal. Ford Motor Co.

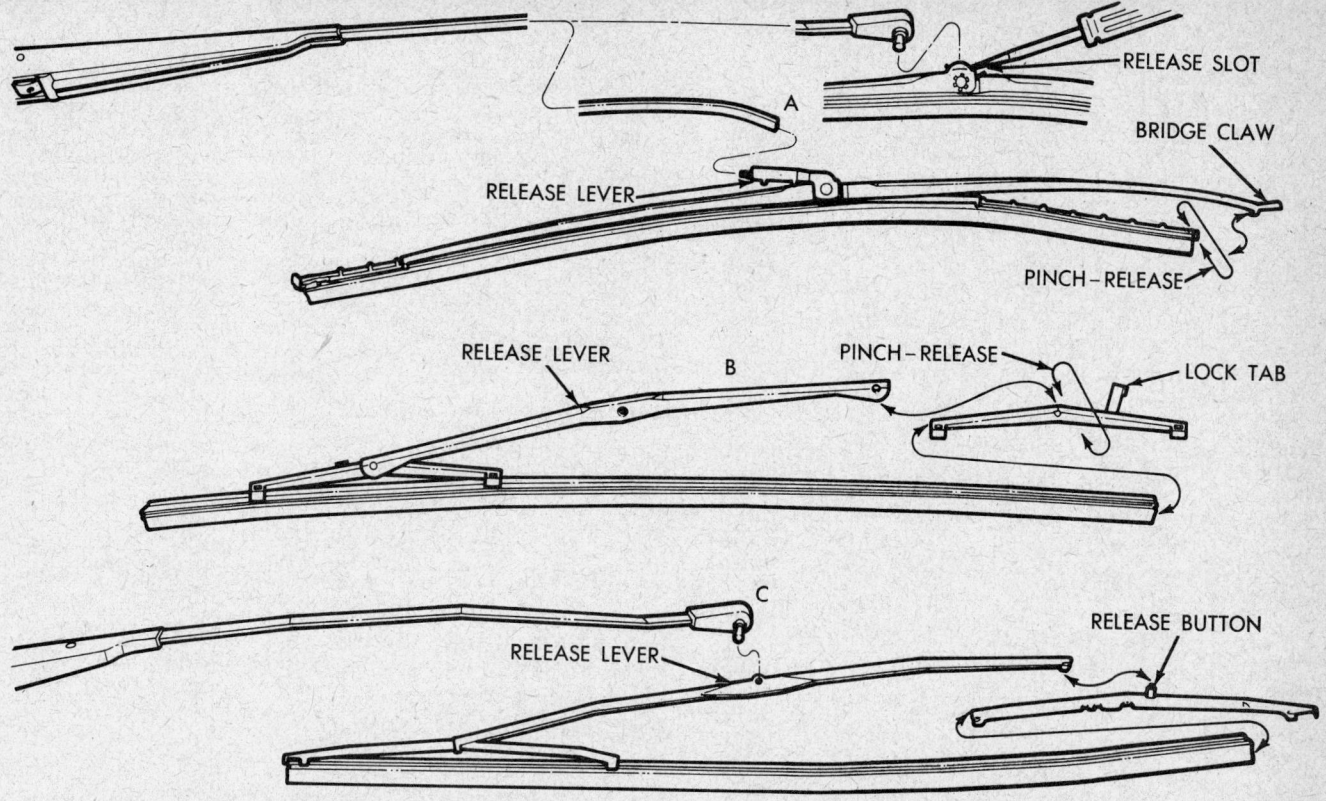

Fig. 50   Wiper blade & element removal. Chrysler Corp. 1977–79 types A, B & C 1980–84 type A except front wheel drive

Chrysler Corp.

1977–79 Exc. Front Wheel Drive

1. With wiper switch in the on position, cycle ignition switch on and off to position wiper blades for ease of removal.
2. Raise wiper arm assembly from glass, then actuate wiper blade release mechanism and remove blade from arm, Fig. 50.
3. Three different methods are used to retain wiper blade element to wiper blade. Referring to Fig. 50, replace blade element as follows:
   a. To remove type A wiper blade element, pinch lock on end of element frame, then withdraw element from blade bridge claws. Install wiper element in the same manner, ensuring wiper blade element is engaged and properly positioned in all wiper blade claws.
   b. To remove type B wiper blade element, lift tab and pinch end bridge to release from center bridge. Slide wiper blade element and end bridge from opposite end bridge. Install wiper blade element in the same manner. After installing, check to ensure end bridge tab is in the down position to lock element and end bridge to center bridge.
   c. To remove type C wiper blade element, depress button on end bridge to release from center bridge, then withdraw element. When installing wiper blade element, ensure element is engaged and properly positioned in all bridge claws.
4. Install wiper blade assembly on wiper arm. Check to ensure blade assembly is securely seated on wiper arm.

1980–84 Exc. Front Wheel Drive

1. With wiper switch in the on position, cycle ignition switch on and off to position wiper blades for ease of removal.
2. Raise wiper arm from glass.
3. Three different methods are used to retain wiper blades to wiper arms and wiper blade elements to wiper blades. Remove wiper blades and wiper blade elements as follows:
   a. To remove type A wiper blade and element, Fig. 50, pry hinge release slot to remove blade assembly from arm pin. Pinch lock on end of wiper blade element frame and withdraw element from bridge claws.
   b. To remove type B wiper blade and element, Fig. 51, lift release tab on wiper blade using a screwdriver, then remove blade from arm pin. To remove wiper blade element, hold center bridge and move end bridge into a reverse bow, then release element from end claws and slide element out through remaining bridge claws.
   c. To remove type C wiper blade and element, Fig. 52, apply a light reverse pressure to both end bridges to raise internal tension bar out of wiper arm pin lock groove, then remove blade assembly from wiper arm. To remove wiper blade element, pinch lock on end of element frame and withdraw wiper blade element from bridge claws.
4. Install wiper element in the same manner as removed. Ensure wiper blade element is locked and properly positioned in all bridge claws.
5. Install wiper blade assembly on wiper arm. Check to ensure blade assembly is securely seated on wiper arm.

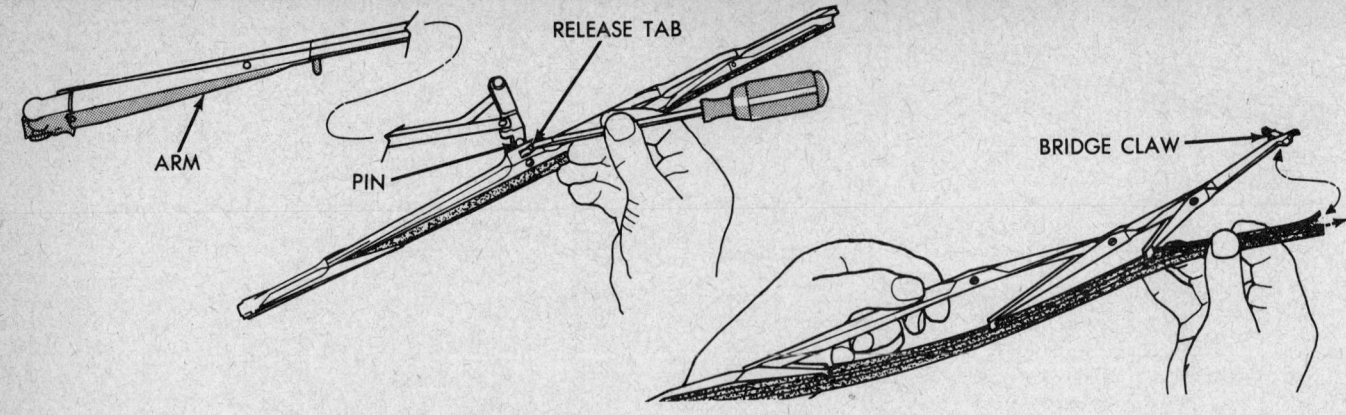

Fig. 51 Wiper blade & element removal. Chrysler Corp. 1980—84 type B

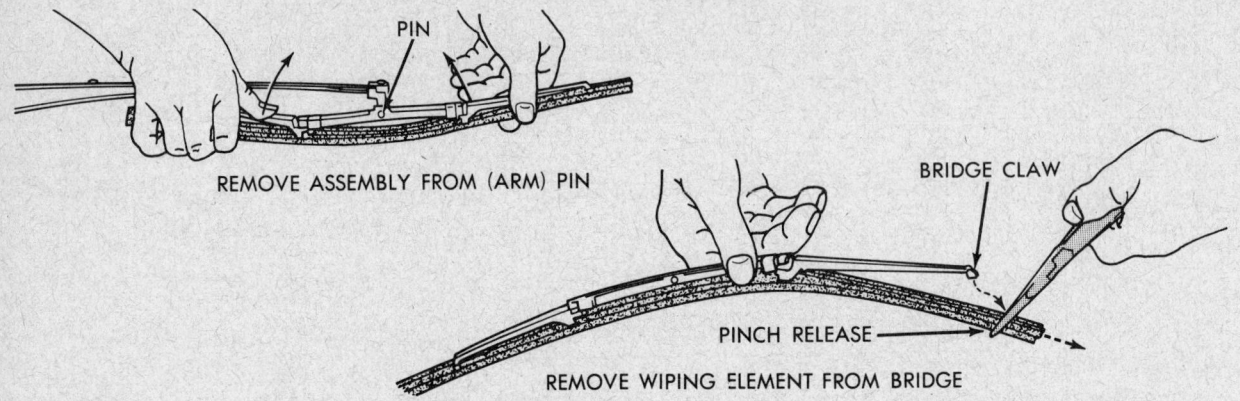

Fig. 52 Wiper blade & element removal. Chrysler Corp. 1980—84 type C

1978—84 Front Wheel Drive Exc. Liftgate

1. With wiper switch in the on position, cycle ignition switch on and off to position wiper blades for ease of removal.
2. Raise wiper arm from glass.
3. On four door models, depress release lever on wiper blade center bridge and slide blade assembly from wiper arm. To remove wiper blade element, lift tab and pinch end bridge to release from center bridge. Slide end bridge from wiper blade element, then remove element from opposite end bridge. After installing wiper blade element, check to ensure tab on end bridge is in the down position to lock element and end bridge to center bridge.
4. On two door models, lift release tab on wiper blade center bridge pivot, then remove blade assembly from wiper arm. To remove wiper blade element, move wiper blade into a slight reverse bow, then slide element out of bridge claws.
5. When installing blade assembly, check to ensure wiper blade element is locked and properly positioned in blade frame. Also ensure blade is securely seated on wiper arm.

1978—82 Front Wheel Drive Liftgate

1. With wiper switch in the on position, cycle ignition switch on and off to position wiper blade for ease of removal.
2. Lift wiper assembly from glass, then depress release lever on blade center bridge and remove blade assembly from wiper arm.
3. Depress release button on end bridge to release from center bridge, then slide wiper blade element and end

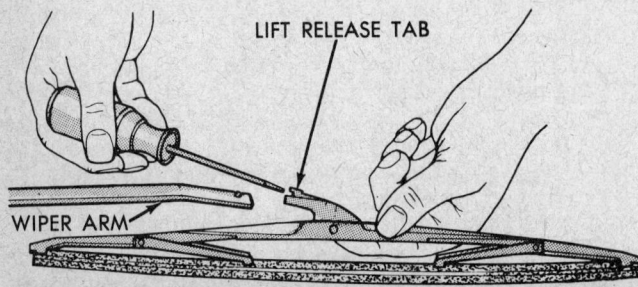

Fig. 53 Removing wiper assembly. 1981—84 Dodge Omni & Plymouth Horizon

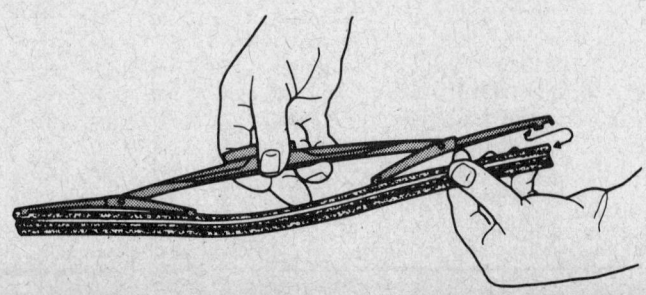

Fig. 54 Removing wiper element. 1981—84 Dodge Omni & Plymouth Horizon

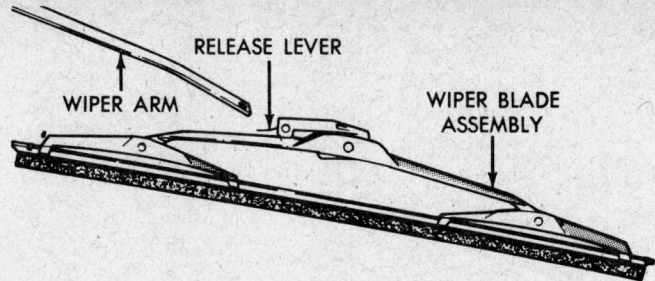

Fig. 55 Removing wiper assembly. 1981—84 Chrysler LeBaron, Dodge Aries & Plymouth Reliant

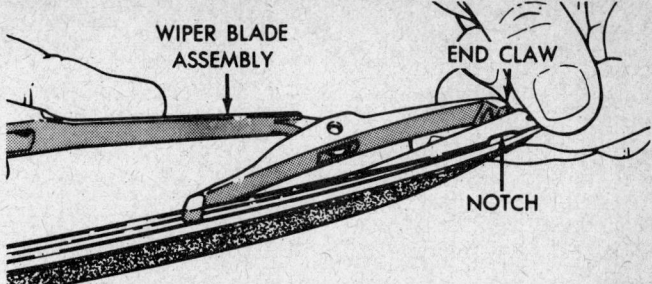

Fig. 56 Removing wiper element. 1981—84 Chrysler LeBaron, Dodge Aries & Plymouth Reliant

bridge from opposite end bridge.

4. Engage wiper blade element in all bridge claws.
5. Ensure all release points are locked with blade assembly.

1983—84 Charger, Horizon, Omni & Turismo Liftgate

1. With wiper switch on, position wipers in convenient position by turning ignition switch off.
2. Lift wiper off glass. Lift release tab on center bridge pivot and remove blade assembly, Fig. 53.
3. Bend wiper blade element into slight reverse bow and slide blade element out of end bridge claws, Fig. 54.
4. Check each release point for positive locking when installing blade element and assembly.

1983—84 Aries, LeBaron & Reliant Liftgate

1. With wiper switch on, position wipers in convenient position by turning ignition switch off.
2. Lift wiper off glass. Depress release lever on bayonet connector and remove blade from arm.
3. Bend blade forward until notch on element backing lines up with end claw, Fig. 55.
4. Twist element out of end claw and pull from bridges, Fig. 56.
5. Check each release point for proper locking during installation.

Ford Motor Co.

1977—78 Exc. Fairmont & Zephyr & 1979 Granada & Monarch

1. To replace the saddle pin type wiper blade, Fig. 47, proceed as follows:
   a. Insert a screwdriver or other suitable tool into spring release opening in blade saddle.
   b. Depress spring clip and slide blade assembly from wiper arm.
   c. To install, slide blade assembly onto wiper arm until clip engages pin.
2. To replace the bayonet type wiper blade, proceed as follows:
   a. To remove the Anco type blade, press inward on blade saddle tab, then slide blade assembly from wiper arm.
   b. To remove the Trico type blade, Fig. 46, press downward on wiper arm to detach upper stud, then depress tab and slide blade assembly from wiper arm.
   c. To install, slide blade assembly onto arm until locking stud snaps into position.

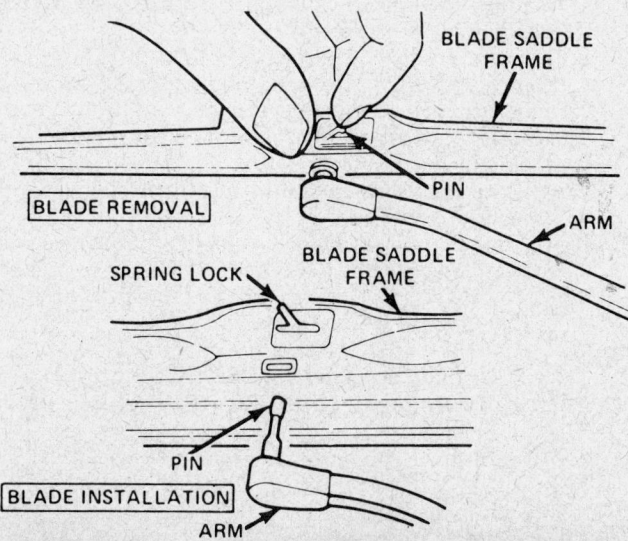

Fig. 57 Tridon wiper blade removal. American Motors & Ford Motor Co.

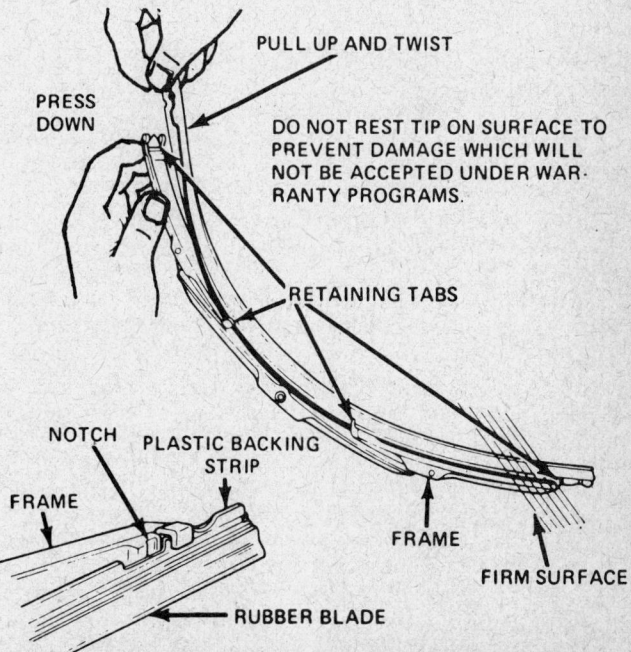

Fig. 58 Tridon wiper blade element removal. American Motors 1982—84 Liftgate; Ford Motor Co. 1978 Fairmont & Zephyr, 1979 Except Granada, Monarch & Versailles & 1980—84 All Models

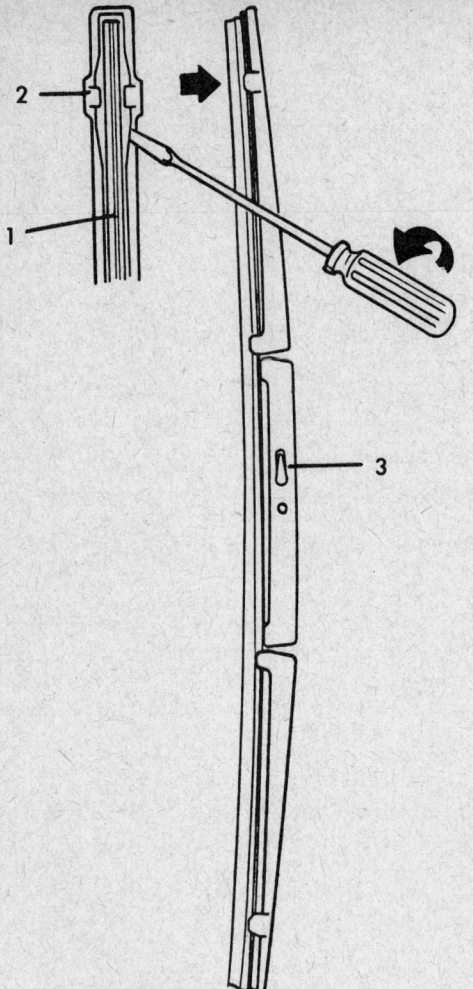

1. ELEMENT
2. HOUSING TABS
3. BLADE RELEASE LEVER

Fig. 59   Type 2 wiper assembly. General Motors

1978 Fairmont & Zephyr, 1979 Exc. Granada, Monarch & Versailles & 1980–84 All Models Exc. 1982–84 Lincoln Continental

1. With wiper switch in the on position, cycle ignition switch on and off to position wiper blades for ease of removal.
2. To replace Trico wiper blades, Fig. 48, proceed as follows:
   a. With wiper blade assembly resting on windshield, grasp either end of blade away from windshield, then remove wiper blade from wiper arm.

   NOTE: To prevent damage, be sure to grasp wiper blade frame and not end of blade element.

   ---
   b. To install, push blade assembly onto wiper arm pin until fully seated.
3. To replace Tridon wiper blades, Fig. 57, proceed as follows:
   a. Pull upward on blade spring lock, then pull blade

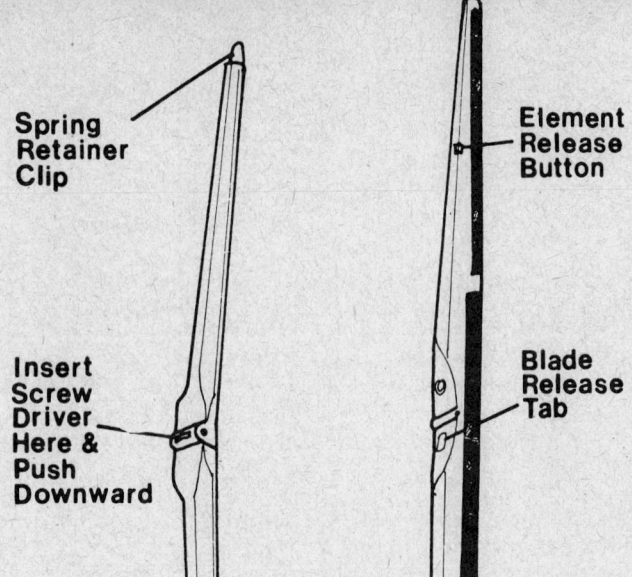

Fig. 60   Wiper blade & element removal. General Motors except Astre, Chevette, Monza, Skyhawk, Starfire, Sunbird, 1000 & Vega

assembly from wiper arm pin.
   b. To install, push blade onto wiper arm pin until spring lock engages pin.

1982–84 Lincoln Continental

Lift arm assembly and pivot lower end of blade 90° from arm, then remove blade from arm. When installing, both arm prongs must engage into blade slots.

WIPER BLADE ELEMENT

1977–78 Models Exc. Fairmont & Zephyr & 1979 Granada, Monarch & Versailles

1. To replace Anco type wiper blade element, Fig. 49, proceed as follows:
   a. Depress latch pin and slide wiper blade element from yoke jaws.
   b. To install, slide blade element through blade jaws, then install blade frame into jaw slots. Ensure element engages all yoke jaws.
2. To replace Trico type wiper blade element, Fig. 49, proceed as follows:
   a. Squeeze latch lock and pull wiper blade element from blade frame jaws.
   b. To install wiper blade element, insert element through blade frame jaws. Ensure element is engaged in all blade frame jaws and lock latch is properly seated.

1978 Fairmont & Zephyr, 1979 Exc. Granada, Monarch & Versailles & 1980–84 All Models

1. To replace Trico wiper blade element, proceed as follows:
   a. On wiper blade element, locate wide portion of metal element reinforcement.
   b. Insert a screwdriver downward and inward between blade frame and wide portion of element reinforce-

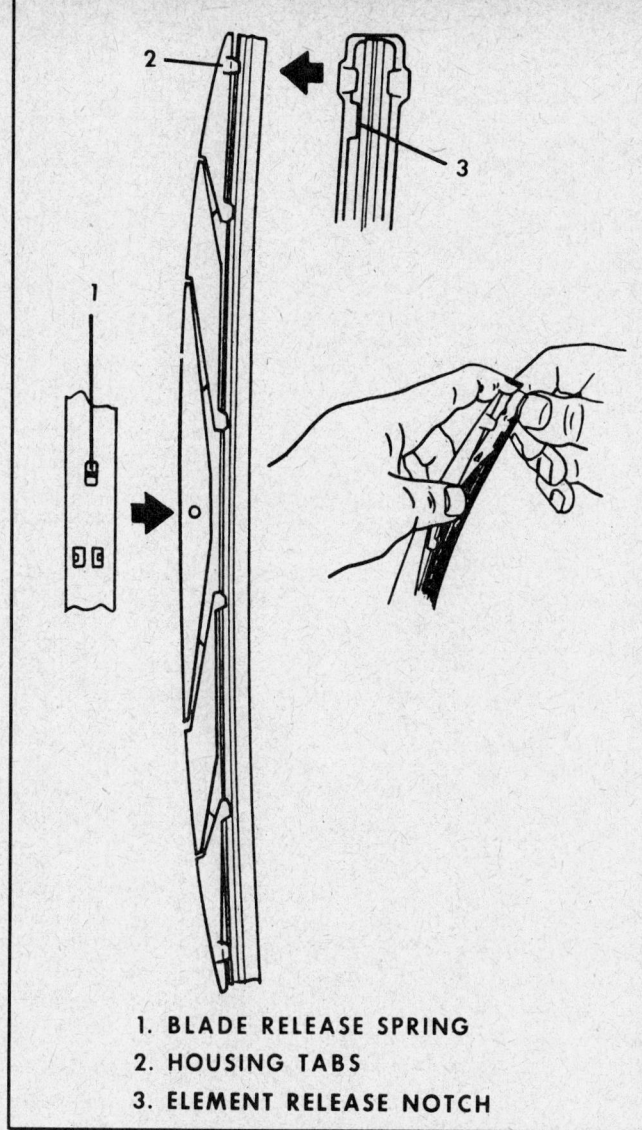

1. BLADE RELEASE SPRING
2. HOUSING TABS
3. ELEMENT RELEASE NOTCH

Fig. 61   Type 1 wiper assembly. General Motors

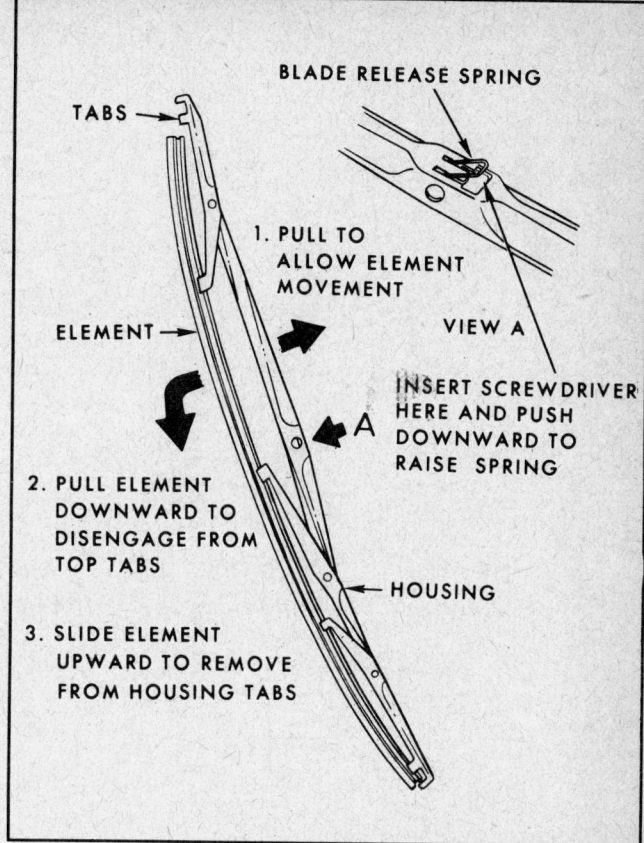

Fig. 62   Type 3 wiper assembly. General Motors

ment to release element from tab.
  c. Slide wiper blade element from the remaining blade frame jaws.
  d. To install, slide wiper blade element through blade frame jaws, ensuring element is properly locked in all tabs.
2. To replace Tridon wiper blade element, Fig. 58, proceed as follows:
  a. On wiper blade element plastic backing strip, locate a 7/16 inch notch approximately 1 inch from end of element.
  b. Place wiper blade assembly on a firm surface with notched end of plastic backing strip visible, then grasp frame portion of wiper blade and push downward until blade assembly is tightly bowed.
  c. With blade assembly tightly bowed, grasp tip of plastic backing strip and pull upward and twist counterclockwise at the same time to snap backing strip from blade frame tab.
  d. Lift blade assembly from surface and slide backing strip down frame until notch is aligned with next retaining tab, then twist slightly to snap backing strip

from tab. Continue this procedure with the remaining blade frame tabs.
  e. Reverse procedure to install. Check to ensure element backing strip is engaged with all retaining tabs before installing wiper blade on wiper arm.

General Motors

1977 Astre, Vega, 1977—80 Monza, Skyhawk, Starfire, Sunbird; 1977—82 Chevette & 1000 W/ Steel Wipers

Refer to Fig. 46 to remove wiper blade assembly and Fig. 59 to remove blade element.

1977—84 Full Size, Rear Wheel Drive Intermediate Models; 1977—81 Camaro & Firebird & 1977—82 Corvette

Refer to Fig. 60 to remove wiper blade assembly and blade element.

1980—84 Citation, Omega, Phoenix, Skylark; 1982—84 Cavalier, Cimarron, Firenza, 2000, Sunbird & Skyhawk; 1982—84 Chevette & 1000 W/ Plastic Wipers

Refer to Figs. 59, 61, and 62 to remove wiper blade assembly and blade element.

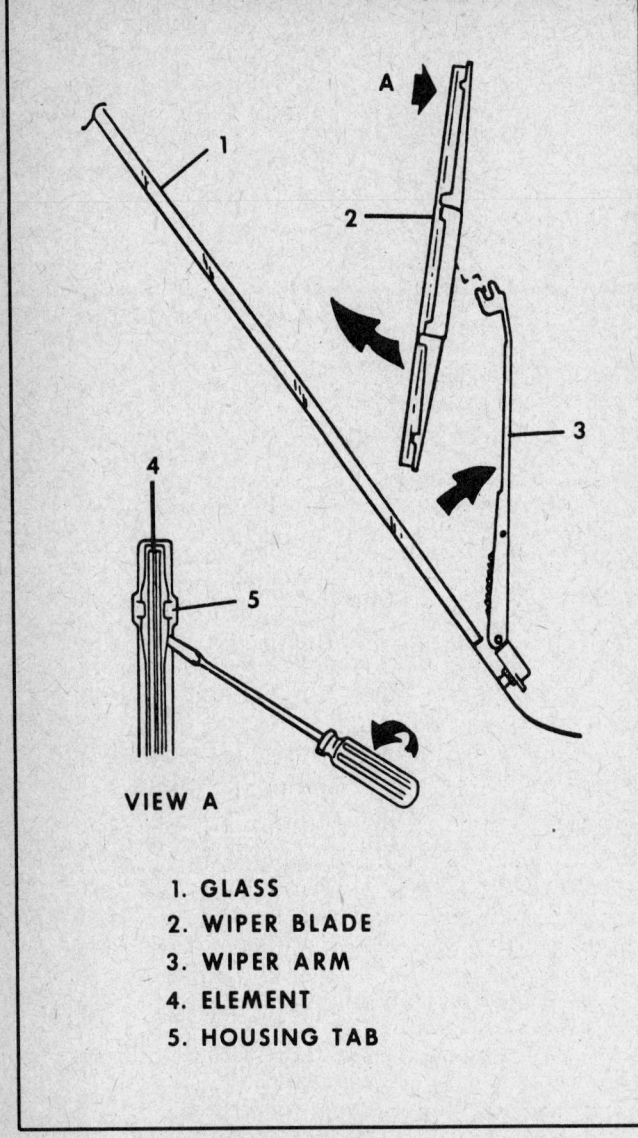

1. GLASS
2. WIPER BLADE
3. WIPER ARM
4. ELEMENT
5. HOUSING TAB

Fig. 63 Wiper assembly. 1982–84 Chevrolet Celebrity, Buick Century, Oldsmobile Cutlass Ciera & Pontiac 6000

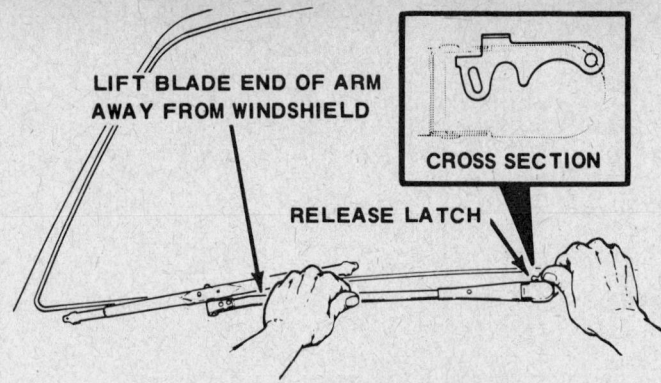

Fig. 64 Latch type wiper removal

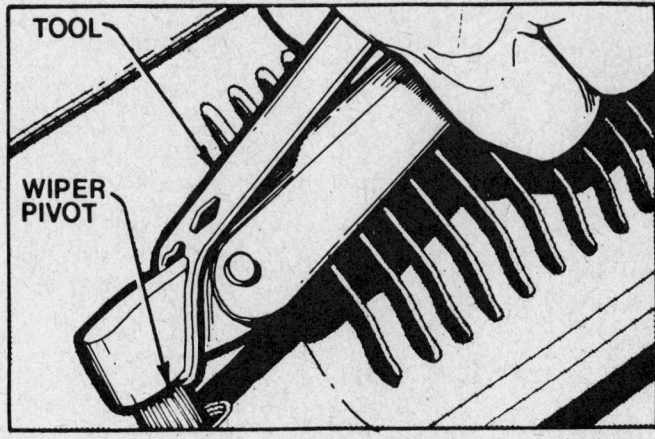

Fig. 65 Wiper arm removal (typical). Chrysler Corp. 1978–84 front wheel drive liftgate & General Motors Models w/ rectangular motor

1982–83 Camaro & Firebird

Refer to Fig. 59 to remove wiper blade assembly and blade element.

1982–84 Celebrity, Century, Ciera & 6000

Refer to Fig. 63 to remove wiper blade assembly and blade element.

WIPER ARM, REPLACE

American Motors

Exc. 1977–78 Matador Coupe & 1977–80 Pacer Exc. Liftgate

The wiper arms are set on the serrated pivot shafts and held securely by spring tension on the arm. To remove, lift arm against spring tension, then using a screwdriver, slide the cap away from the serrated pivot shaft.

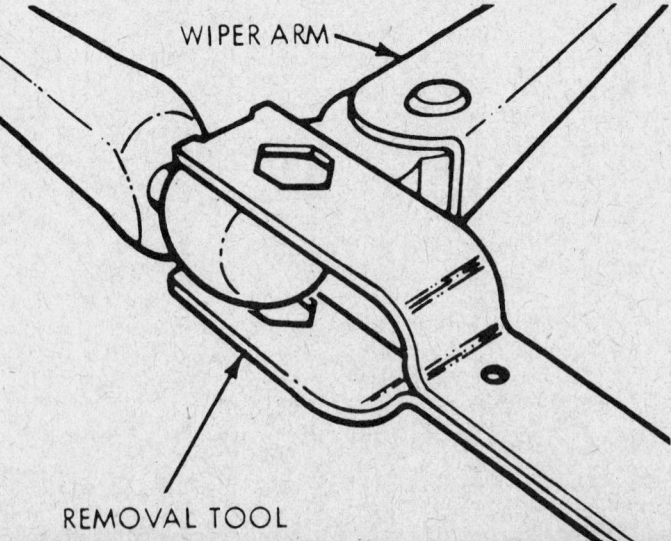

Fig. 66 Wiper arm removal. Ford Motor Co. 1977 Comet, Maverick & 1977–78 Mustang

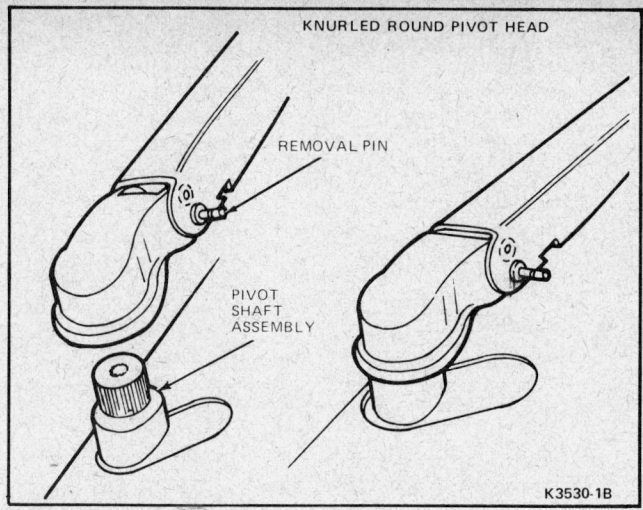

Fig. 67 Wiper arm removal. Ford Motor Co. 1977–80 Bobcat, Pinto, 1978–81 Fairmont & Zephyr Sta. Wag. tailgate, 1982 Cougar & Granada Sta. Wag. tailgate & 1983–84 LTD & Marquis Sta. Wag. tailgate

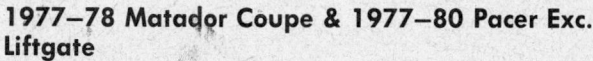

1977–78 Matador Coupe & 1977–80 Pacer Exc. Liftgate

To remove, raise blade end of arm away from windshield, then move slide latch away from pivot shaft, Fig. 64. On left hand side wiper arm, disengage auxiliary arm from pivot pin and remove arm from pivot shaft.

Chrysler Corp.

Exc. Front Wheel Drive Liftgate

1. Lift wiper arm assembly and pull latch from holding position, Fig. 64.
2. Remove arm from pivot with a rocking motion.
3. Reverse procedure to install. Install wiper arm with wiper motor in park position.

Front Wheel Drive Liftgate

Install tool No. C-3982 or equivalent on wiper arm, then lift wiper arm upward and remove from pivot shaft, Fig. 65. When installing wiper arm, wiper motor must be in the park position.

Ford Motor Co.

1977 Comet, Maverick & 1977–78 Mustang

Swing arm and blade assembly away from windshield. While holding assembly in this position, pull arm off shaft using an appropriate tool, Fig. 66. To install, hold arm in the swing out position and push arm onto pivot shaft.

1977–80 Bobcat, Pinto; 1979–81 Fairmont, Zephyr Tailgate; 1982 Cougar, Granada Tailgate & 1983–84 LTD & Marquis Tailgate

Swing arm and blade assembly away from glass, which will release spring loaded clip in arm from pivot shaft. Insert a 3/32 inch pin through pin hole to hold clip in the released position, then pull arm from pivot shaft, Fig. 67. Do not remove pin until after wiper arm has been installed on pivot shaft.

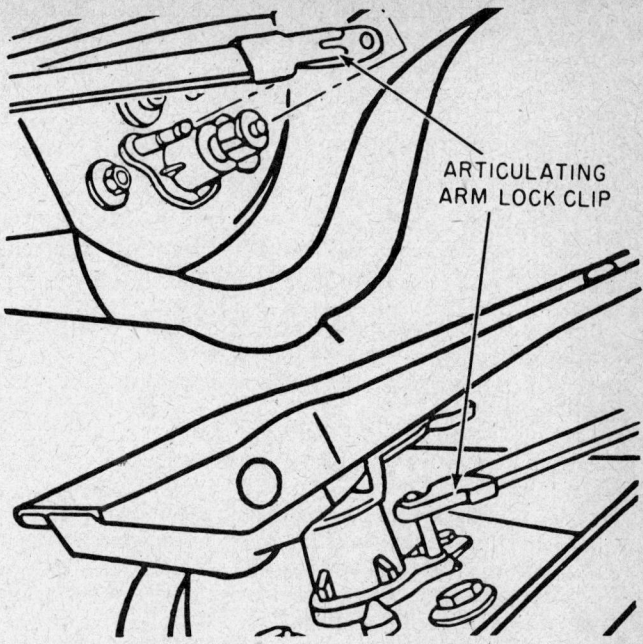

Fig. 68 Wiper articulating arm lock clip. General Motors 1977 intermediate models & 1977–78 Eldorado & Toronado

Exc. 1977 Comet, Maverick; 1977–78 Mustang; 1977–80 Bobcat, Pinto; 1978–81 Fairmont, Zephyr Tailgate; 1982 Cougar, Granada Tailgate & 1983–84 LTD & Marquis Tailgate

Raise blade end of arm off windshield and move slide latch away from pivot shaft, Fig. 64. This action will unlock the wiper arm from the pivot shaft and hold the blade end of the arm away from the windshield. The wiper arm can now be pulled from the pivot shaft without the aid of any tools. Reverse procedure to install.

General Motors

MODELS W/RECTANGULAR MOTOR

1. Wiper motor must be in "Park" position.
2. Use suitable tool to minimize the possibility of windshield or paint finish damage during arm removal.
3. Remove arm by prying up with tool to disengage arm from serrated transmission shaft, Fig. 65.
4. To install arm to transmission shaft rotate the required distance and direction so the blades rest in proper position.

MODELS W/ROUND MOTOR

Buick, Chevrolet, Oldsmobile & Pontiac

1. Wiper motor must be in the Park position. On 1979–84 Riviera and Toronado, remove cowl upper panel and screen.
2. Raise hood to gain access to wiper arms.
3. On Corvette only, remove the rubber plug from the front of the wiper door actuator then insert a screwdriver, pushing the internal piston rearward to actuate the wiper door open.
4. On 1977 Intermediate Models and 1977–78 Toronado, lift arm off transmission shaft. On left arm, slide articulating arm lock clip, Fig. 68, away from transmission

pivot pin and lift arm off pin. On Full Size and 1978–84 Intermediate Models, lift arm and slide latch clip, Fig. 64, out from under wiper arm.

5. Release the wiper arm and lift assembly off transmission shaft.
6. Reverse procedure to install.

Cadillac

1. Raise hood to gain access to wiper arms. On Seville and 1979–84 Eldorado models, remove front cowl panel and screen.
2. Lift wiper arm and slide latch clip, Fig. 64, out from under wiper arm.
3. Release wiper arm and lift wiper arm assembly off transmission shaft.
4. On 1977–78 Eldorado, at left arm, slide articulating arm lock clip away from transmission pivot pin, Fig. 68, and lift arm off pin.
5. On 1977–78 Eldorado, to install left wiper arm assembly, position the articulating arm over the transmission pivot pin until it locks in place on the pin. Install the left wiper arm assembly to the transmission shaft aligning the keyway to the shaft.
6. On 1977–78 Eldorado, align keyway in right wiper arm assembly to transmission shaft and install arm assembly to shaft.
7. On all models except 1977–79 Seville and 1977–78 Eldorado, align slot in arm and blade assembly to keyway in transmission spindle, and position wiper arm on shaft. Lift blade assembly and slide latch clip into place.

NOTE: W/S wiper blade assembly release button or clip must face toward base of arm assembly for proper matching of blade to glass contour.

8. On 1977–79 Seville, position wiper arm assembly on transmission spindle, then lift blade and slide latch clip into place.
9. On all models, release wiper arms and check wiper pattern and park position.

HEADLAMP AIMING

It is recommended that headlamps be checked for proper aim every 12 months or whenever front body work is repaired. On most vehicles, aiming can be performed without removing headlamp bezels. Vertical adjustment is usually accomplished with a screw at the top of the sealed beam retaining ring (12 o'clock position). Horizontal adjustment is provided by a screw at the right or left (3 or 9 o'clock position) of the sealed beam unit, Fig. 69. Headlamp aiming can be performed visually with a screen as follows:

1. Vehicle should be on level floor so headlamps are 25 ft. from screen or light colored wall. Fuel tank should be ½ full. Any heavy loads that are normally in trunk should remain there. Driver and passengers should not be in vehicle during aiming. Tires should be inflated to specified pressures and headlamps lenses should be cleaned.
2. Mark screen or wall with four lines as shown in Fig. 70.
3. Adjust low beam pattern only as shown in top diagram in Fig. 70.
4. On vehicles with four headlamp systems, cover low beam (outboard or upper lamps) and adjust high beam lamp pattern as shown in bottom diagram of Fig. 70.

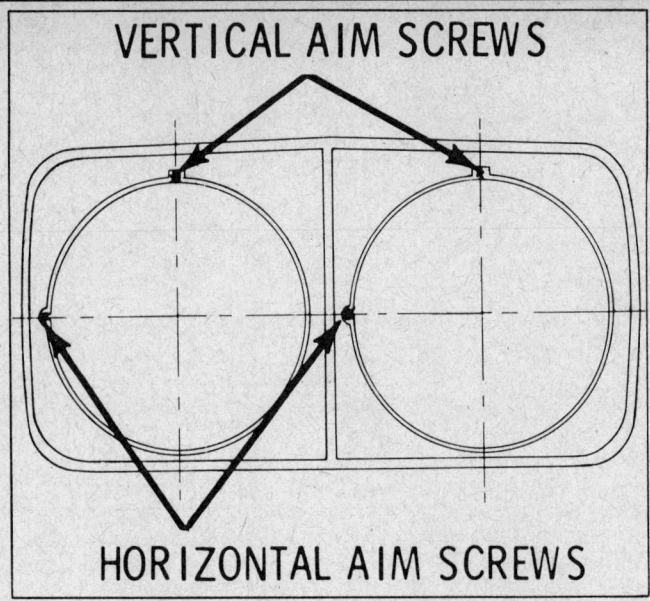

Fig. 69   Headlamp adjusting screws. Typical

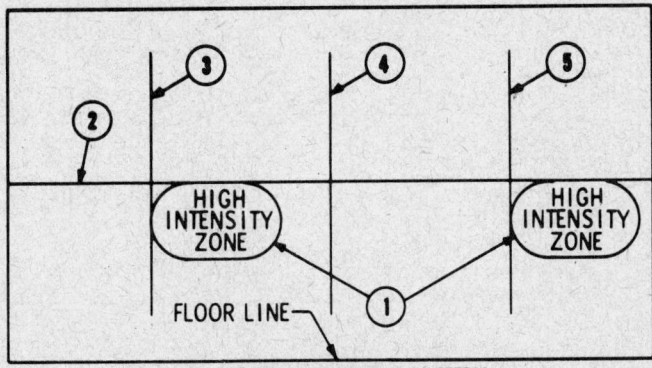

LOW BEAM ADJUSTMENT PATTERN
(VISUAL AIM AT 25 FEET)
5-3/4" TYPE 2 LAMPS (OUTBOARD ONLY) AND 7" TYPE 2 LAMPS

LINE 1   HIGH INTENSITY ZONES.
LINE 2   HORIZONTAL AND VERTICAL AT CENTER OF HEADLAMPS.
LINES 3 & 5   VERTICAL AT CENTER OF HEADLAMPS.
LINE 4   VERTICAL AT CENTER OF CAR.

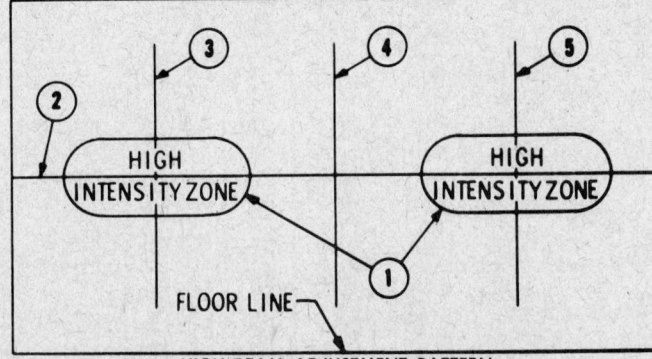

HIGH BEAM ADJUSTMENT PATTERN
(VISUAL AIM AT 25 FEET)
5-3/4" TYPE 1 LAMPS (INBOARD ONLY)

Fig. 70   Headlamp aiming

American Motors

INDEX OF SERVICE OPERATIONS

NOTE: Refer to the front of this manual for vehicle manufacturer's special service tool suppliers.

AMERICAN MOTORS

VEHICLE IDENTIFICATION NUMBER LOCATION:

1977–84: Plate is attached to top of instrument panel, on driver's side.

ENGINE IDENTIFICATION

4-121 (1977–79): The engine code is located on a machined flange at the left rear of the cylinder block adjacent to the oil dipstick. The letter "G" denotes the 4-121 engine.

4-150 (1983–84): The engine code is located on a machined surface on the right side of the cylinder block between number three and four cylinders. The letter "U" denotes the 4-150 engine.

4-151 (1980–83): The engine code is located on a pad at the right front of the cylinder block below the cylinder head. The letter B denotes the 4-151 engine.

6-232 & 6-258 (1977–84): The engine code is located on a pad between number two and three cylinders. The letter "A" denotes the 258 engine with one barrel carburetor. The letter "C" denotes the 258 engine with two barrel carburetor. The letter "E" denotes the 232 engine.

V8-304, & 360 (1977–79): The engine code is located on a tag attached to the right bank rocker cover. The letter "H" denotes the 304 engine. The letter "N" denotes the 360 engine with 2 barrel carburetor.

GRILLE IDENTIFICATION

1977 Hornet

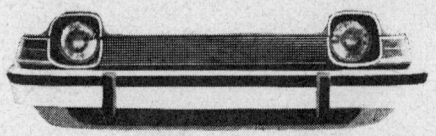

1977 Pacer

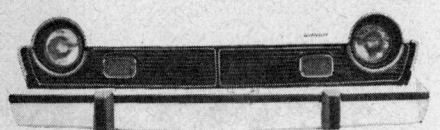

1977–78 Matador 2 Door

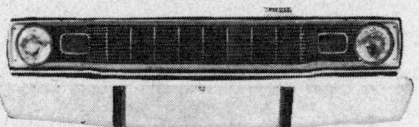

1977–78 Matador 4 Door

1977 AMX

1977–78 Gremlin

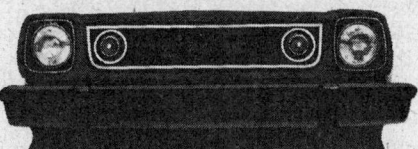

1978 AMX

1978 Concord

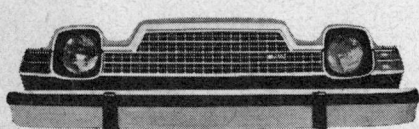

1978–80 Pacer

1979–80 AMX

1979 Concord

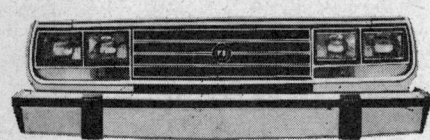

1979–80 Spirit

1980 Concord

1980 Eagle

1980 Eagle Sport

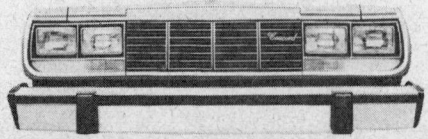

1981–83 Concord

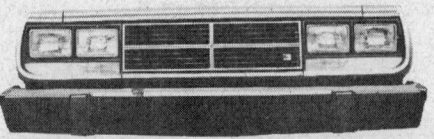

1981–83 Spirit

GRILLE IDENTIFICATION—Continued

1981–83 Eagle SX/4 Sport

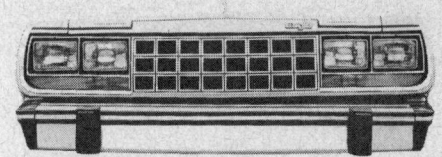

1981–84 Eagle

GENERAL ENGINE SPECIFICATIONS

Year	Engine		Carburetor	Bore and Stroke	Com- pression Ratio	Net H.P. @ R.P.M.③	Maximum Torque Ft. Lbs. @ R.P.M.	Normal Oil Pressure Pounds
	CID①/Liter	V.I.N. Code②						
1977	4-121, 2.0L	G	5210, 2 Bbl.⑩	3.41 × 3.32	8.1	80 @ 5000	105 @ 2800	28½
	6-232, 3.8L	E	YF, 1 Bbl.④⑤	3.75 × 3.50	8.0	90 @ 3050	163 @ 2200	37–75
	6-258, 4.23L	A	YF, 1 Bbl.④⑤	3.75 × 3.90	8.0	95 @ 3050	179 @ 2100	37–75
	6-258, 4.23L	C	BBD, 2 Bbl.④	3.75 × 3.90	8.0	120 @ 3600	200 @ 2000	37–75
	V8-304, 5.0L	H	2100, 2 Bbl.⑧⑨	3.75 × 3.44	8.4	120 @ 3200	220 @ 2000	37–75
	V8-360, 5.9L	N	2100, 2 Bbl.⑧⑨	4.08 × 3.44	8.25	140 @ 3300	251 @ 1600	37–75
1978	4-121, 2.0L	G	5210, 2 Bbl.⑩	3.41 × 3.32	8.2	80 @ 5000	105 @ 2800	28.5
	6-232, 3.8L	E	YF, 1 Bbl.④	3.75 × 3.50	8.0	90 @ 3400	168 @ 1600	37–75
	6-258, 4.23L	A	YF, 1 Bbl.④	3.75 × 3.90	8.0	100 @ 3400	200 @ 1600	37–75
	6-258, 4.23L	C	BBD, 2 Bbl.④	3.75 × 3.90	8.0	120 @ 3600	201 @ 1800	37–75
	V8-304, 5.0L	H	2100, 2 Bbl.⑧⑨	3.75 × 3.44	8.4	130 @ 3200	238 @ 2000	37–75
	V8-360, 5.9L	N	2100, 2 Bbl.⑧⑨	4.08 × 3.44	8.25	140 @ 3350	278 @ 2000	37–75
1979	4-121, 2.0L	G	5210, 2 Bbl.⑩	3.41 × 3.32	8.2	80 @ 5000	105 @ 2800	28.5
	6-232, 3.8L	E	YF, 1 Bbl.④	3.75 × 3.50	8.0	90 @ 3400	168 @ 1600	37–75
	6-258, 4.23L	A	YF, 1 Bbl.④	3.75 × 3.90	8.3	100 @ 3400	200 @ 1600	37–75
	6-258, 4.23L	C	BBD, 2 Bbl.④	3.75 × 3.90	8.3	110 @ 3200	210 @ 1800	37–75
	V8-304, 5.0L	H	2100, 2 Bbl.⑧	3.75 × 3.44	8.4	125 @ 3200	220 @ 2400	37–75
1980	4-151, 2.5L⑪	B	2SE, 2 Bbl.⑫	4.0 × 3.0	8.24	—	—	36–41
	6-258, 4.23L	C	BBD, 2 Bbl.④	3.75 × 3.90	8.3	—	—	37–75
1981	4-151, 2.5L⑪	B	2SE, 2 Bbl.⑫⑬	4.0 × 3.0	8.24	—	—	36–41
	6-258, 4.23L	C	BBD, 2 Bbl.④	3.75 × 3.90	8.0	—	—	37–75
1982	4-151, 2.5L⑪	B	2SE, 2 Bbl.⑫	4.0 × 3.0	8.24	—	—	36–41
	4-151, 2.5L⑪	B	E2SE, 2 Bbl.⑫⑭	4.0 × 3.0	8.24	—	—	36–41
	6-258, 4.23L	C	BBD, 2 Bbl.④	3.75 × 3.90	8.6	—	—	37–75
1983	4-151, 2.5L⑪	B	2SE, 2 Bbl.⑫⑬	4.0 × 3.0	8.2	—	—	36–41
1983–84	4-150, 2.46L	U	1 Bbl.⑮	3.88 × 3.19	9.2	—	132 @ 3200	37–75
	6-258, 4.23L	C	BBD, 2 Bbl.④	3.75 × 3.90	9.2	—	—	37–75

①—CID—cubic inch displacement.
②—On 1977–80 models, the seventh digit denotes engine code. On 1981–84 models, the fourth digit denotes engine code.
③—Ratings are net-as installed on vehicle.
④—Carter.

⑤—High altitude, YFA.
⑥—Except Matador.
⑦—Matador.
⑧—Motorcraft.
⑨—High altitude V8, 2150.
⑩—Holley.

⑪—Refer to the Chevrolet Monza, Buick Sky-hawk, Olds. Starfire, Pontiac Sunbird chapter for service procedures on this engine.
⑫—Rochester.
⑬—Calif. vehicles equipped with E2SE.
⑭—Calif. & auto. trans. only.
⑮—Electronic Feedback Carburetor.

TUNE UP SPECIFICATIONS

The following specifications are published from the latest information available. This data should be used only in the absence of a decal affixed in the engine compartment.

★ When using a timing light, disconnect vacuum hose or tube at distributor and plug opening in hose or tube so idle speed will not be affected.

● When checking compression, lowest cylinder must be within 80 percent of highest.

▲ Before removing wires from distributor cap, determine location of the No. 1 wire in cap, as distributor position may have been altered from that shown at the end of this chart.

Spark plug types shown in this chart are recommendations of the original vehicle manufacturer and not MOTOR. Check local sources for other spark plug manufacturers listings.

Year & Engine/V.I.N.	Spark Plug		Ignition Timing BTCD①★				Curb Idle Speed②		Fast Idle Speed		Fuel Pump Pressure
	Type 👉	Gap	Firing Order Fig. ▲	Man. Trans.	Auto. Trans.	Mark Fig.	Man. Trans.	Auto. Trans.	Man. Trans.	Auto. Trans.	
1977											
4-121/G ⑨	N8L	.035	F	12°	⑩	G	900	800D	1600⑪	1600⑪	4–6
6-232/E Exc. Calif.	N12Y	.035	A	⑫	10°	E	600	550D	1500④	1600④	4–5
6-232/E Calif.	N12Y	.035	A	10°	10°	E	850	700D	1500④	1600④	4–5
6-258/A 1 Barrel Exc. Calif. ⑬	N12Y	.035	A	6°	⑭	E	600	550D	1500④	1600④	4–5
6-258/A 1 Barrel Calif.	N12Y	.035	A	—	8°	E	—	700D	—	1600④	4–5
6-258/A 1 Barrel High Alt.	N12Y	.035	A	10°⑮	10°⑯	E	600	550D	1500④	1600④	4–5
6-258/C 2 Barrel	N12Y	.035	A	6°	8°	E	600	⑰	1500④	1600④	4–5
V8-304/H Exc. Calif.	RN12Y	.035	B	—	10°	C	—	600D	—	1600④	5–6½
V8-304/H Calif.	RN12Y	.035	B	—	5°	C	—	700D	—	1800④	5–6½
V8-360/N Exc. Calif. & High Alt.	RN12Y	.035	B	—	10°	C	—	600D	—	1600④	5–6½
V8-360/N Calif.	RN12Y	.035	B	—	5°	C	—	700D	—	1600④	5–6½
V8-360/N High Alt.	RN12Y	.035	B	—	10°	C	—	700D	—	1800④	5–6½
1978											
4-121/G ⑨	N8L	.035	F	12°	⑩	G	900	800D	1600⑪	1600⑪	4–6
6-232/E	N13L	.035	H	8°	10°	E	600	550D	1500④	1600④	4–5
6-258/A 1 Barrel	N13L	.035	H	6°	8°	E	850	700D	1500④	1600④	4–5
6-258/C 2 Barrel	N13L⑱	.035	H	6°	8°	E	600	600D	1500④	1600④	4–5
V8-304/H Exc. Calif. & High Alt.	N12Y	.035	I	—	10°	D	—	600D	—	1600④	5–6½
V8-304/H Calif.	N12Y	.035	I	—	5°	D	—	700D	—	—	5–6½
V8-304/H High Alt.	N12Y	.035	I	—	10°	D	—	700D	—	1600④	5–6½
V8-360/N Exc. Calif. & High Alt.	N12Y	.035	I	—	10°	D	—	600D	—	1600④	5–6½
V8-360/N Calif.	N12Y	.035	I	—	10°	D	—	650D	—	1800④	5–6½
V8-360/N High Alt.	N12Y	.035	I	—	10°⑲	D	—	700D	—	1800④	5–6½
1979											
4-121/G Exc. Calif. ⑨	N8L	.035	F	⑳	12°	G	㉑	800D	1800⑪	1800⑪	4–6
4-121/G Calif. ⑨	N8L	.035	F	—	8°	G	—	800D	—	1800⑪	4–6
6-232/E	N13L	.035	H	8°	10°㉒	E	600	550D	1500④	1600④	4–5
6-258/A 1 Barrel	N13L	.035	H	—	8°	E	—	700D	—	—	4–5
6-258/C 2 Barrel	N13L	.035	H	4°	8°	E	700	600D	1500④	1600④	4–5
V8-304/H	N12Y	.035	I	5°	8°	D	800	600D	1500④	1600④	5–6½
1980											
4-151/B Exc. Calif.	R44TSX㉓	.060	J	10°	12°	K	900	700D	2400㉔	2600㉔	6½–8
4-151/B Calif.	R44TSX㉓	.060	J	12°	10°	K	㉕	㉖	2400㉔	2600㉔	6½–8
6-258/C Exc. Eagle	N14LY⑥	.035	H	6°	⑦	E	700	600D	1700④	1850④	4–5
6-258/C Eagle Exc. Calif.	N13L⑥	.035	H	—	10°	E	—	600D	—	1850④	4–5
6-258/C Eagle Calif.	N13L⑥	.035	H	—	8°	E	—	600D	—	1850④	4–5

Continued

TUNE UP SPECIFICATIONS—Continued

The following specifications are published from the latest information available. This data should be used only in the absence of a decal affixed in the engine compartment.

★ When using a timing light, disconnect vacuum hose or tube at distributor and plug opening in hose or tube so idle speed will not be affected.

● When checking compression, lowest cylinder must be within 80 percent of highest.

▲ Before removing wires from distributor cap, determine location of the No. 1 wire in cap, as distributor position may have been altered from that shown at the end of this chart.

Spark plug types shown in this chart are recommendations of the original vehicle manufacturer and not MOTOR.

Check local sources for other spark plug manufacturers listings.

Year & Engine/V.I.N.	Spark Plug Type	Gap	Firing Order Fig. ▲	Ignition Timing BTDC[1] ★ Man. Trans.	Auto. Trans.	Mark Fig.	Curb Idle Speed[2] Man. Trans.	Auto. Trans.	Fast Idle Speed Man. Trans.	Auto. Trans.	Fuel Pump Pressure
1981											
4-151/B Concord & Spirit Exc. Calif.	R44TSX[23]	.060	J	10°	12°	K	500/900	500/700D	2400[24]	2600[24]	6½–8
4-151/B Concord & Spirit Calif.	R44TSX[23]	.060	J	10°	10°	K	500/900	500/700D	2400[24]	2600[24]	6½–8
4-151/B Eagle Exc. Calif.	R44TSX[23]	.060	J	11°	12°	K	500/900	500/700D	2400[24]	2600[24]	6½–8
4-151/B Eagle Calif.	R44TSX[23]	.060	J	10°	8°	K	500/900	500/700D	2400[24]	2600[24]	6½–8
6-258/C Concord & Spirit Exc. High Alt.	RFN14LY[6]	.035	H	6°	6°	E	650[3]	550D[8]	1700[4]	1850[4]	4–5
6-258/C Eagle Exc. Calif. & High Alt.	RFN14LY[6]	.035	H	8°	8°	E	650[3]	550D[8]	1700[4]	1850[4]	4–5
6-258/C Eagle Calif.	RFN14LY[6]		H	4°	6°	E	650[3]	550D[8]	1700[4]	1850[4]	4–5
6-258/C High Alt.	RFN14LY[6]		H	—	15°	E	—	550D[8]	—	1850[4]	4–5
1982											
4-151/B Concord & Spirit Exc. Calif. & High Alt.	R44TSX[23]	.060	J	10°	10°	K	900[28]	700D[29]	2400	2400[5]	6½–8
4-151/B Eagle Exc. Calif. & High Alt.	R44TSX[23]	.060	J	12°	12°	K	900[28]	700D[29]	2400	2500	6½–8
4-151/B Concord & Spirit Calif.	R44TSX[23]	.060	J	8°	8°	K	900[28]	700D[29]	2400	2400[5]	6½–8
4-151/B Eagle Calif.	R44TSX[23]	.060	J	8°	8°	K	900[28]	700D[29]	2500	2500	6½–8
4-151/B Concord & Spirit High Alt.	R44TSX[23]	.060	J	15°	15°	K	900[28]	700D[29]	2400	2400[5]	6½–8
4-151/B Eagle High Alt.	R44TSX[23]	.060	J	15°	15°	K	900[28]	700D[29]	2500	2500	6½–8
6-258/C Exc. High Alt.	RFN14LY[6]	.035	H	15°[27]	15°[27]	L	600[3]	500D[8]	1850	1850	4–5
6-258/C Concord & Spirit High Alt.	RFN14LY[6]	.035	H	19°[27]	19°[27]	L	600[3]	500D[8]	1850	1850	4–5
6-258/C Eagle High Alt.	RFN14LY[6]	.035	H	21°[27]	21°[27]	L	600[3]	500D[8]	1850	1850	4–5
1983											
4-150/U	RFN14LY[6]	.035	M	—	—	N	—	—	—	—	4–5
4-151/B Exc. Calif.	R44TSX[23]	.060	J	10°	10°	K	650/900	550/700D	—	—	6½–8
4-151/B Calif.	R44TSX[23]	.060	J	12°	12°	K	650/900	550/700D	—	—	6½–8
6-258/C Concord & Spirit Exc. High Alt.	RFN14LY[6]	.035	H	6°	6°	L	650[30]	550D[31]	—	—	5–6½
6-258/C Eagle Exc. Calif. & High Alt.	RFN14LY[6]	.035	H	6°	6°	L	600[30]	500D[31]	—	—	5–6½
6-258/C Eagle Calif.	RFN14LY[6]	.035	H	6°	6°	L	650[30]	550D[31]	—	—	5–6½
6-258/C High Alt.	RFN14LY[6]	.035	H	13°	13°	L	700[32]	650D[33]	—	—	5–6½

TUNE UP SPECIFICATIONS—Continued

The following specifications are published from the latest information available. This data should be used only in the absence of a decal affixed in the engine compartment.

★ When using a timing light, disconnect vacuum hose or tube at distributor and plug opening in hose or tube so idle speed will not be affected.

● When checking compression, lowest cylinder must be within 80 percent of highest.

▲ Before removing wires from distributor cap, determine location of the No. 1 wire in cap, as distributor position may have been altered from that shown at the end of this chart.

 Spark plug types shown in this chart are recommendations of the original vehicle manufacturer and not MOTOR.

Check local sources for other spark plug manufacturers listings.

Year & Engine/V.I.N.	Spark Plug		Firing Order Fig. ▲	Ignition Timing BTDC① ★			Curb Idle Speed②		Fast Idle Speed		Fuel Pump Pressure
	Type	Gap		Man. Trans.	Auto. Trans.	Mark Fig.	Man. Trans.	Auto. Trans.	Man. Trans.	Auto. Trans.	
1984											
4-150/U Exc. Calif.	RFN14LY⑥	.035	M	12°㉟	12°㉟	N	750	700D	2000㉞	2300㉞	4–5
4-150/U Calif.	RFN14LY⑥	.035	M	12°㉟	12°㉟	N	750	700D	2000㉞	2300㉞	4–5
6-258/C Exc. Calif. & High Alt.	RFN14LY⑥	.035	H	—	—	L	—	—	—	—	5–6½
6-258/C Calif.	RFN14LY⑥	.035	H	—	—	L	—	—	—	—	5–6½
6-258/C High Alt.	RFN14LY⑥	.035	H	—	—	L	—	—	—	—	5–6½

① —BTDC—Before top dead center.
② —Idle speed on man. trans. vehicles is adjusted in Neutral & on auto. trans. equipped vehicles is adjusted in Drive unless otherwise specified. When two idle speeds are listed, the higher speed is with the A/C or idle solenoid energized.
③ —With holding solenoid energized, 750 RPM; with vacuum actuator energized, 900 RPM.
④ —With stop screw on 2nd step of fast idle cam, TCS & EGR disconnected.
⑤ —Models with A/C, 2600 RPM.
⑥ —Champion.
⑦ —Concord & Spirit, 10° BTDC; Pacer, 8° BTDC.
⑧ —With holding solenoid energized, 650D RPM; with vacuum actuator energized, 800D RPM.
⑨ —Point gap, .018"; dwell angle, 44–50°.
⑩ —Except Calif., 12° BTDC; California, 8° BTDC.
⑪ —With stop screw on low step of fast idle cam against shoulder of high step & EGR disconnected.
⑫ —Except high altitude, 8° BTDC; high altitude, 10° BTDC.
⑬ —Except high altitude.

⑭ —Except Matador, 8° BTDC; Matador, 6° BTDC.
⑮ —When operating at altitudes below 4000 ft., set to 6° BTDC.
⑯ —When operating at altitudes below 4000 ft., set to 8° BTDC.
⑰ —Except Calif., 600D RPM; California, 700D RPM.
⑱ —On models with auto. trans. & 2.53 rear axle ratio, use N12Y.
⑲ —When operating at altitudes below 4000 ft., set to 5° BTDC.
⑳ —Except emission control label code EH, 12° BTDC; emission control label code EH, 16° BTDC.
㉑ —Except emission control label code EH, 900 RPM; emission control label code EH; 1000 RPM.
㉒ —On models with 2.37 rear axle ratio, set at 12° BTDC.
㉓ —AC.
㉔ —With fast idle screw on highest step of fast idle cam.
㉕ —With A/C, 900/1250 RPM; less A/C, 500/900 RPM.
㉖ —With A/C, 700/950 RPM; less A/C, 500/700 RPM.

RPM.
㉗ —With ignition module electronic retard (two wire) connector disconnected and a jumper wire connected between the two module wire connector terminals.
㉘ —On models equipped with A/C, with A/C off & solenoid disconnected, 500 RPM; with A/C on & solenoid connected, 950 RPM.
㉙ —On models equipped with A/C, with A/C off & solenoid disconnected, 500D RPM; with A/C on & solenoid connected, 1250D RPM.
㉚ —With holding solenoid energized, 750 RPM; with vacuum actuator energized, 950 RPM.
㉛ —With holding solenoid energized, 650D RPM; with vacuum actuator energized, 850D RPM.
㉜ —With holding solenoid energized, 750 RPM; with vacuum actuator energized, 1000 RPM.
㉝ —With holding solenoid energized, 750D RPM; with vacuum actuator energized, 850D RPM.
㉞ —With stop screw on 2nd step of fast idle cam and EGR disconnected.
㉟ —At altitudes above 4000 ft. set at 19° BTDC.

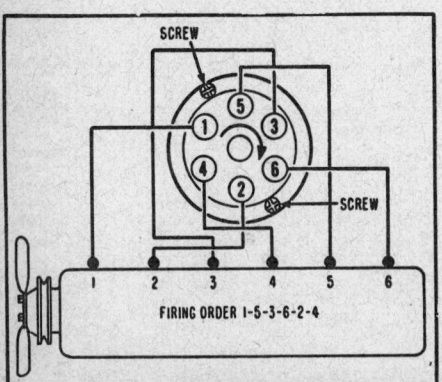

Fig. A

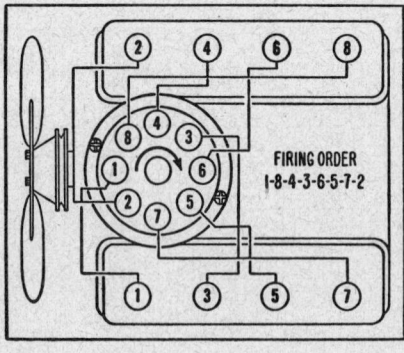

FIRING ORDER 1-8-4-3-6-5-7-2

Fig. B

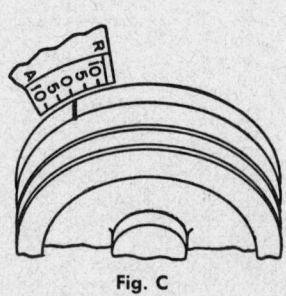

Fig. C

Continued

TUNE UP NOTES—Continued

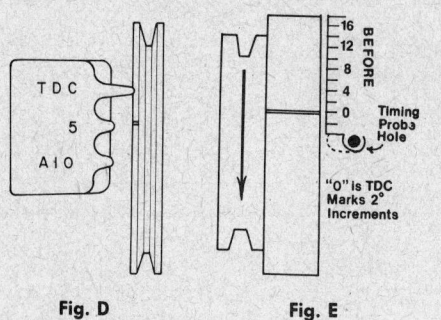

Fig. D   Fig. E

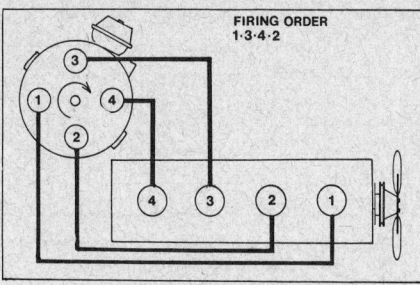

FIRING ORDER
1-3-4-2

Fig. F

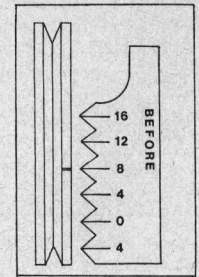

Fig. G

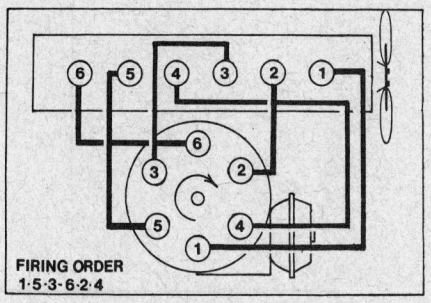

FIRING ORDER
1-5-3-6-2-4

Fig. H

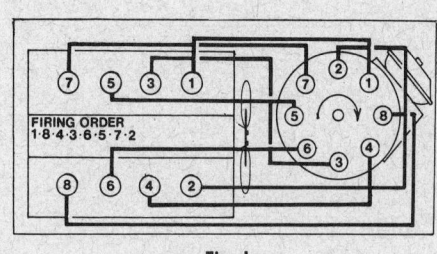

FIRING ORDER
1-8-4-3-6-5-7-2

Fig. I

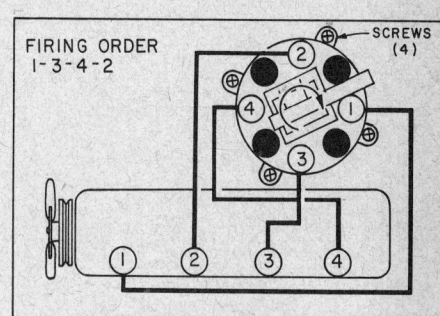

FIRING ORDER
1-3-4-2

Fig. J

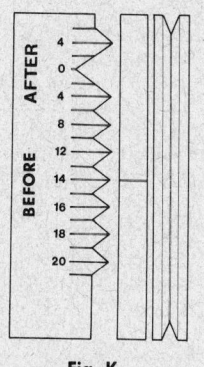

Fig. K

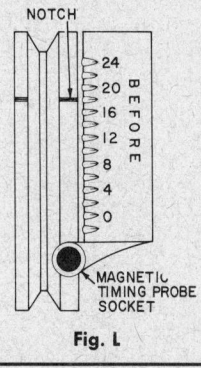

NOTCH

MAGNETIC
TIMING PROBE
SOCKET

Fig. L

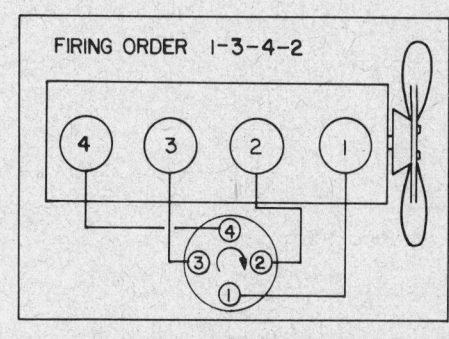

FIRING ORDER 1-3-4-2

Fig. M

Fig. N

STARTING MOTOR APPLICATIONS

Year	Engine/ V.I.N.	Starter Ident. No.
1977	6-232, 258/E,A	3229844①
	V8-304/H	3229844①
	V8-360/N	3212235①
1977–79	4-121/G	3250032①
1978	V8-360/N	3231371①
1978–79	6-232/E	3231372①
	V8-304/H	3231372①
1978–80	6-258/A,C	3231372①
1980–83	4-151/B	1109526②
	4-151/B	3236659②
1981	6-258/C	3238665①
1982–84	6-258/C	E1FF-BA①
1983–84	4-150/U	E1FF-BA①

①—Motorcraft.
②—Delco-Remy.

DRIVE AXLE SPECIFICATIONS

Year	Model	Carrier Type ②	Ring Gear & Pinion Backlash		Pinion Bearing Preload			Differential Bearing Preload		
			Method	Adjustment	Method	New Bearings Inch-Lbs.	Used Bearings Inch-Lbs.	Method	New Bearings Inch-Lbs.	Used Bearings Inch-Lbs.
1977–79	7 9/16" Dr. Gr.	Integral	Shims	.005–.009	Sleeve	15–25①	15–25①	Shims	.008	.008
	8 7/8" Dr. Gr.	Integral	Shims	.005–.009	Sleeve	17–28①	17–28①	Shims	.008	.008
1980–84	7 9/16" Dr. Gr.③	Integral	Shims	.005–.009	Sleeve	15–25①	15–25①	Shims	.008	.008
	MODEL 30④	Integral	Shims	.005–.010	Shims	20–40①	15–25①	Shims	.015	.015

①—Adjust at drive pinion flange nut with inch-pound torque wrench.
②—Rear axle shaft end play .006 inch. Eagle front axle shaft end play .003 inch.
③—Rear Axle.
④—Eagle front axle.

DISTRIBUTOR SPECIFICATIONS

★If unit is checked on vehicle, double the RPM and degrees to get crankshaft figures.

Distributor Part No. ①	Centrifugal Advance Degrees @ RPM of Distributor					Vacuum Advance	
	Advance Starts	Intermediate Advance			Full Advance	Inches of Vacuum to Start Plunger	Max. Adv. Dist. Deg. @ Vacuum
1977							
3228263	0–2.8 @ 500	2.8–4.85 @ 750	4.2–6.25 @ 1000	7.05–9.05 @ 1500	11–13 @ 2200	4–6	8½ @ 12.7
3228264	0–2.4 @ 500	3.4–6.4 @ 750	6.3–8.3 @ 1000	9.3–11.3 @ 1500	13½–15½ @ 2200	5–7	8½ @ 12.5
3228265	0–2.7 @ 500	2.4–4.4 @ 750	3.3–5.3 @ 1000	5.1–7.1 @ 1500	7½–9½ @ 2200	4–6	8½ @ 12.7
3228266	0–3¾ @ 500	4.4–6.4 @ 750	5.4–7.4 @ 1000	7.3–9.3 @ 1500	10–12 @ 2200	4–6	8½ @ 12.7
32229719	0–1.8 @ 500	1–3 @ 750	4–6 @ 1000	6–8 @ 1500	9–11 @ 2200	5–7	9 @ 13
1977–78							
3250163	0 @ 550	4 @ 800	8 @ 1000	11 @ 1500	17 @ 2200	2–4	9 @ 9.5
3230443	−¾ @ 400	4.5 @ 800	6.5 @ 1200	9.5 @ 1800	13 @ 2200	5.5–6.5	9¼ @ 12½
3231340	−¾ @ 400	5.5 @ 800	8.5 @ 1200	12 @ 1800	15.5 @ 2200	6.5–8.5	9⅛ @ 12
3231341	−¾ @ 400	3.5 @ 800	5 @ 1200	7 @ 1800	9.5 @ 2200	5.5–6.5	9¼ @ 12½
3231915	−1 @ 400	3 @ 800	5.5 @ 1200	7.5 @ 1800	10.5 @ 2200	3.5–5.5	13¼ @ 11½
3232434	−¾ @ 400	2¾ @ 800	5¼ @ 1200	7 @ 1600	10.5 @ 2200	6.5–8.5	9½ @ 13
3233173	−⅝ @ 400	4 @ 800	6¼ @ 1200	9.5 @ 1800	13 @ 2200	4–6	13⅛ @ 11¼
3233174	−¾ @ 400	3.5 @ 800	4¾ @ 1200	6⅞ @ 1800	9.5 @ 2200	4–6	13⅛ @ 11
1979							
3231915	−1 @ 400	3 @ 800	5.5 @ 1200	7.5 @ 1800	10.5 @ 2200	3.5–5.5	13¼ @ 11.5
3232434	−¾ @ 400	2¾ @ 800	5¼ @ 1200	7 @ 1600	10.5 @ 2200	6.5–8.5	9.5 @ 13
3233959	−1 @ 400	2 @ 800	5¼ @ 1200	10 @ 1800	14.5 @ 2200	1.5–3	17¼ @ 12
3234693	−¾ @ 400	3¾ @ 800	6.5 @ 1200	9 @ 1600	14.5 @ 2200	2–3.5	12¾ @ 12
3250163	0 @ 550	4 @ 800	8 @ 1000	11 @ 1500	17 @ 2200	2–4	9 @ 9.5
3250497	0 @ 500	2 @ 700	4 @ 900	7 @ 1400	10¾ @ 1800	2–4	17 @ 13
1980							
1110560	−½ to 0 @ 400	1–3 @ 800	3–5 @ 1200	4–6 @ 1600	8 @ 2200	3.5–4.5	11 @ 9.5
1110561	−½ to 0 @ 400	1–3 @ 800	3–5 @ 1200	4–6 @ 1600	8 @ 2200	2.5–3.5	8 @ 6
1110650	−½ to 0 @ 400	1–3 @ 800	3–5 @ 1200	4–6 @ 1600	8 @ 2200	3.5–4.5	10¼ @ 9.5
3235141	−½ to +½ @ 400	1–3 @ 800	2¾–5 @ 1200	3¼–5½ @ 1600	6½ @ 2200	3–5	13¼ @ 15.5
3238428	−½ to +½ @ 400	1–3¼ @ 800	3–5 @ 1200	3½–5½ @ 1600	6½ @ 2200	4.5–5.5	12½ @ 19
1981							
1110560	−½ to 0 @ 400	¾–3 @ 800	3–5 @ 1200	4¼–6¼ @ 1600	8 @ 2200	3½–4½	10½ @ 9½
1110561	−½ to 0 @ 400	¾–3 @ 800	3–5 @ 1200	4¼–6¼ @ 1600	8 @ 2200	2½–3½	8 @ 6
1110595	−½ to 0 @ 400	¾–3 @ 800	3–5 @ 1200	4¼–6¼ @ 1600	8 @ 2200	2½–3½	10½ @ 7
1111393	−½ to 0 @ 400	¼–2 @ 800	2½–4½ @ 1200	4¼–6¼ @ 1600	8¼ @ 2050	2½–3½	10½ @ 7
3235141	−½ to ½ @ 400	1½–3½ @ 800	3–5 @ 1200	3½–5½ @ 1600	6½ @ 2200	3–5	13½ @ 15½

Continued

DISTRIBUTOR SPECIFICATIONS—Continued

★If unit is checked on vehicle, double the RPM and degrees to get crankshaft figures.

Distributor Part No.①	Centrifugal Advance Degrees @ RPM of Distributor					Vacuum Advance	
	Advance Starts	Intermediate Advance			Full Advance	Inches of Vacuum to Start Plunger	Max. Adv. Dist. Deg. @ Vacuum
1981—Continued							
3239829	−3/4 to 1/2 @ 400	2–41/2 @ 800	3–51/4 @ 1200	31/4–51/2 @ 1600	61/4 @ 2200	3–5	121/2 @ 15
3239833	−1/2 to 1/2 @ 400	1–31/2 @ 800	3–5 @ 1200	31/2–51/2 @ 1600	61/2 @ 2200	3–5	121/2 @ 15
1982							
1103491	−1/2 to 0 @ 400	1/4–21/2 @ 800	21/2–43/4 @ 1200	41/4–61/4 @ 1600	8 @ 2200	31/2–5	93/4 @ 83/4
1103492	−1/2 to 0 @ 400	1–21/2 @ 800	21/2–51/2 @ 1200	41/4–61/4 @ 1600	8 @ 2200	3–41/2	101/2 @ 7
1110598	−1/2 to 0 @ 400	1/8–21/8 @ 800	21/2–41/2 @ 1200	41/8–61/8 @ 1600	81/8 @ 2200	21/4–33/4	101/2 @ 7
3241333	−1 to 3/4 @ 600	—	—	—	71/4 @ 1050	21/2–43/4	121/2 @ 18
1983							
1103527	−1/2 to 0 @ 400	1 to 21/2 @ 800	3 to 5 @ 1200	41/2 to 61/2 @ 1600	8 @ 2200	3–41/2	101/2 @ 7
1110598	−1/2 to 0 @ 400	1/8–21/8 @ 800	21/2–41/2 @ 1200	41/8–61/8 @ 1600	8 @ 2050	21/2–5	93/4 @ 83/4
3242409	−1/2 to 1/2 @ 400	2–4 @ 800	—	—	7 @ 2050	3–5	121/2 @ 18

①—Stamped on distributor housing plate.

ALTERNATOR SPECIFICATIONS

Year	Alternator							Regulator			
	Make	Model	Ground Polarity	Rated Output		Field Current ①		Model	Regulator Test @ 120°F.		
				Amperes	Volts	Amperes	Volts		Ampere Load	Altern. R.P.M.	Volts
1977	Delco	—	Negative	37	—	4.0–4.5	—	1116387④	10③	3000③	14.0–14.3③
	Delco	—	Negative	55	—	4.0–4.5	—	1116387④	10③	3000③	14.0–14.3③
	Delco	—	Negative	63	—	4.0–4.5	—	1116387④	10③	3000③	14.0–14.3③
1977–78	Motorcraft	—	Negative	40	—	2.5–3.0	—	—	—	—	13.4–14.2
	Motorcraft	—	Negative	60	—	2.5–3.0	—	—	—	—	13.4–14.2
1978–79	Delco	—	Negative	37	—	4.0–5.0	—	1116387④	—	—	13.4–14.4
	Delco	—	Negative	55	—	4.0–5.0	—	1116387④	—	—	13.4–14.4
	Delco	—	Negative	63	—	4.0–5.0	—	1116387④	—	—	13.4–14.4
1979	Bosch	—	Negative	45	—	3.5–5.0	—	④⑤	—	—	13.4–14.4
	Bosch	—	Negative	55	—	3.5–5.0	—	④⑤	—	—	13.4–14.4
1980	Delco	—	Negative	42	—	4.0–5.0	—	1116387④	—	—	13.4–14.4
	Delco	—	Negative	55	—	4.0–5.0	—	1116387④	—	—	13.4–14.4
	Bosch	—	Negative	65	14	3.5–5.0	—	②	—	—	13.4–14.4
1981–82	Delco	—	Negative	42	—	4.0–5.0	—	1116387④	—	—	13.4–14.4
	Delco	—	Negative	55	—	4.0–5.0	—	1116387④	—	—	13.4–14.4
	Delco	—	Negative	63	—	4.0–5.0	—	1116387④	—	—	13.4–14.4
	Delco	—	Negative	70	—	4.0–5.0	—	1116387④	—	—	13.4–14.4
1983–84	Delco	—	Negative	42	—	4.0–5.0	—	1116387④	—	—	13.4–14.4
	Delco	—	Negative	56	—	4.0–5.0	—	1116387④	—	—	13.4–14.4
	Delco	—	Negative	66	—	4.0–5.0	—	1116387④	—	—	13.4–14.4
	Delco	—	Negative	78	—	4.0–5.0	—	1116387④	—	—	13.4–14.4

①—Excessive current drawn indicates shorted field winding. No current draw indicates an open winding.
②—B192052193B B14V3.
③—At 80° F.
④—Integral regulator.
⑤—B 192052 193 EE 14v3.

VALVE SPECIFICATIONS

Year	Model/V.I.N.	Valve Lash Int.	Valve Lash Exh.	Valve Angles Seat	Valve Angles Face	Valve Spring Installed Height	Valve Spring Pressure Lbs. @ In.	Stem Clearance Intake	Stem Clearance Exhaust	Stem Diameter Intake	Stem Diameter Exhaust
1977	6-232, 258/⑩⑥	Hydraulic③		⑦	②	1 25/32	195 @ 1 13/32	.001–.003	.001–.003	.3715–.3725	.3715–.3725
	6-258/C⑤	Hydraulic③		⑦	②	1 25/32	205 @ 25/64	.001–.003	.001–.003	.3715–.3725	.3715–.3725
	V8-304, 360/⑩	Hydraulic③		⑦	②	1 13/16	213 @ 1 23/64	.001–.003	.001–.003	.3715–.3725	.3715–.3725
1977–79	4-121/G	⑧		45	45	①	⑨	.031	.039	.3526–.3531	.3522–.3528
1978–79	6-232, 258/⑩	Hydraulic③		⑦	②	1 25/32	195 @ 1 13/32	.001–.003	.001–.003	.3715–.3725	.3715–.3725
	V8-304, 360/⑩	Hydraulic③		⑦	②	1 25/32	④	.001–.003	.001–.003	.3715–.3725	.3715–.3725
1980–83	4-151/B	Hydraulic③		46	45	1.66	176 @ 1.254	.0010–.0027	.0010–.0027	.3418–.3425	.3418–.3425
1980–84	6-258/C	Hydraulic③		⑦	②	1.786	195 @ 1.411	.001–.003	.001–.003	.3715–.3725	.3715–.3725
1983–84	4-150/U	Hydraulic③		44 1/2	44	1.625	213 @ 1.20	.001–.003	.001–.003	.3110–.3120	.3110–.3120

①—Inner 1 1/2"; outer 1 45/64".
②—Intake 29°, exhaust 44°.
③—No adjustment.
④—1978, 211 @ 1 23/64; 1979, 195 @ 1 13/32.
⑤—2 Barrel carburetor.
⑥—1 Barrel carburetor.
⑦—Intake 30°, exhaust 44 1/2°.
⑧—Intake, .006–.009 in. H; exhaust, .016–.019 in. H.
⑨—Intake, inner 39 lbs. @ 1 3/32"; outer 166 lbs. @ 1 5/16". Exhaust, inner 37 lbs. @ 1 7/64"; outer 160 lbs. @ 1 21/64".
⑩—For V.I.N. code, refer to the "General Engine Specifications" at the front of chapter.

PISTONS, PINS, RINGS, CRANKSHAFT & BEARINGS

Year	Model/V.I.N.	Piston Clearance Top of Skirt	Ring End Gap① Comp.	Ring End Gap① Oil	Wrist-pin Diameter	Rod Bearings Shaft Diameter	Rod Bearings Bearing Clearance	Main Bearings Shaft Diameter	Main Bearings Bearing Clearance	Thrust on Bear. No.	Shaft End Play
1977	4-121/G	.0009–.0015	.010	.010	.945	1.888–1.889	.0008–.0028	2.1581–2.1587	.0008–.0031	3	.0039–.0075
	6-232, 258/④	.0009–.0017	.010	.010	.9307	2.0934–2.0955	.001–.0025	2.4986–2.5001	.001–.003	3	.0015–.0065
	V8-304/H	.0010–.0018	.010	.010	.9311	2.0934–2.0955	.001–.003	②	③	3	.003–.008
	V8-360/N	.0012–.0020	.010	.015	.9311	2.0934–2.0955	.001–.003	②	③	3	.003–.008
1978–79	4-121/G	.0007–.0017	.010	.010	.9448	1.8882–1.8888	.0007–.0029	2.1581–2.1587	.00098–.00311	3	.0039–.0075
	6-232, 258/④	.0009–.0017	.010	.010	.9307	2.0934–2.0955	.001–.0025	2.4986–2.5001	.001–.003	3	.0015–.0065
	V8-304/H	.0010–.0018	.010	.010	.9311	2.0934–2.0955	.001–.003	②	③	3	.003–.008
	V8-360/N	.0012–.0020	.010	.015	.9311	2.0934–2.0955	.001–.003	②	③	3	.003–.008
1980–83	4-151/B	.0025–.0033	.010	.015	.92725	2.000	.0005–.0026	2.2998	.0005–.0022	5	.0035–.0085
1980–84	6-258/C	.0009–.0017	.010	.010	.9307	2.0934–2.0955	.001–.003	2.4986–2.5001	.001–.003	3	.0015–.0065
1983–84	4-150/U	.0009–.0017	.010	.010	.9307	2.0934–2.0955	.001–.003	2.4986–2.5001	.001–.002	2	.0015–.0065

①—Fit rings in tapered bores for clearance listed in tightest portion of ring travel.
②—Rear main 2.7464–2.7479", others 2.7474–2.7489".
③—Rear main, .002" to .004"; all others, .001" to .003".
④—For V.I.N. code, refer to the "General Engine Specifications" at the front of chapter.

ENGINE TIGHTENING SPECIFICATIONS★

★Torque specifications are for clean and lightly lubricated threads only. Dry or dirty threads produce increased friction which prevents accurate measurement of tightness.

Year	Engine Model/V.I.N.	Spark Plugs Ft. Lbs.	Cylinder Head Bolts Ft. Lbs.	Intake Manifold Ft. Lbs.	Exhaust Manifold Ft. Lbs.	Rocker Arm Shaft Bracket Ft. Lbs.	Rocker Arm Cover Ft. Lbs.	Connecting Rod Cap Bolts Ft. Lbs.	Main Bearing Cap Bolts Ft. Lbs.	Flywheel to Crankshaft Ft. Lbs.	Vibration Damper or Pulley Ft. Lbs.
1977–79	4-121/G	22	⑥	18	18	—	①②	41	⑦	65	—
1983–84	4-150/U	27	85	23	23	19③	28①	33	80	⑩	80⑤
1980	4-151/B	11	92	37	39	20④	7	30	65	68	160
1981–82	4-151/B	11	92	37	37	20③	7	30	65	68	160
1983	4-151/B	11	92	26	37	20③	7	30	65	68	162
1977–80	6-232, 258/⑨	28	105	23	23	19③	50①	33	80	105	80⑤
1981	6-258/C	11	85	23	23	19③	28①	33	65	105	80⑤
1982–84	6-258/C	11	85	23	23	19③	28①	33	80	105	80⑤
1977–79	V8-304, 360/⑨	28	110	43	⑧	19③	50①	33	100	105	90⑤

①—Inch pounds.
②—1977–78 50 in.-lb.; 1979, 35 in.-lb.
③—Rocker arm cap screw.
④—Rocker arm stud nut.
⑤—Lubricate bolt threads lightly before assembly.
⑥—Cold, 65 ft. lbs.; warm, 80 ft. lbs.
⑦—Hex head, 58 ft. lbs.; rear main bearing socket head cap screw, 47 ft. lbs.
⑧—1977–78, 25 ft. lbs.; 1979, 3/8 inch bolts, 25 ft. lbs., 5/16 inch bolts, 15 ft. lbs.
⑨—For V.I.N. code, refer to the "General Engine Specifications" at the front of chapter.
⑩—Torque bolts to 50 ft. lbs., then tighten bolts an additional 60 degrees.

WHEEL ALIGNMENT SPECIFICATIONS

Year	Model	Caster Angle, Degrees		Camber Angle, Degrees				Toe In. Inch	Toe Out on Turns, Deg.①	
		Limits	Desired	Limits		Desired			Outer Wheel	Inner Wheel
				Left	Right	Left	Right			
1977	Hornet, Gremlin	−1/2 to +1/2	Zero	+1/8 to +5/8	0 to +1/2	+3/8	+1/4	1/16 to 3/16	③	38
	Others	+1/2 to +1 1/2	+1	+1/8 to +5/8	0 to +1/2	+3/8	+1/4	1/16 to 3/16	③	②
1978	Pacer	+1 to +3	+2	+1/8 to +5/8	0 to +1/2	+3/8	+1/4	1/16 to 3/16	③	35
	Except Pacer	0 to +2	+1	+1/8 to +5/8	0 to +1/2	+3/8	+1/4	1/16 to 3/16	③	38
1979	Pacer	+1 to +3 1/2	+2	0 to +3/4	0 to +3/4	+3/8	+3/8	1/16 to 3/16	③	35
	Except Pacer	0 to +2 1/2	+1	0 to +3/4	0 to +3/4	+3/8	+3/8	1/16 to 3/16	③	38
1980	Eagle	+3 to +5	+4	−3/8 to +3/8	−3/8 to +3/8	Zero	Zero	1/16 to 3/16	③	38
	Pacer	+1 to +3 1/2	+2	0 to +3/4	0 to +3/4	+3/8	+3/8	1/16 to 3/16	③	35
	AMX, Concord & Spirit	0 to +2 1/2	+1	+1/8 to +3/4	−1/8 to +1/2	+3/8	+1/8	1/16 to 3/16	③	38
1981	Concord & Spirit	0 to +2 1/2	+1	+1/8 to +3/4	−1/8 to +1/2	+3/8	+1/8	1/16 to 3/16	③	38
	Eagle	+2 to +3	+2 1/2	−1/8 to +5/8	−1/8 to +5/8	+3/8	+3/8	④	③	38
1982–83	Concord & Spirit	+3 1/2 to +5	+4 1/2	+1/8 to +3/4	−1/8 to +1/2	+3/8	+1/8	1/16 to 3/16	—	—
1983–84	Eagle	+3 to +5	+4	−1/8 to +5/8	−1/8 to +5/8	+3/8	+3/8	1/16 to 3/16	③	38

①—Incorrect toe-out when other adjustments are correct, indicates bent steering arms.   ②—Matador 38°; Pacer 35°.   ③—Wheels at full turn.   ④—With Select Drive System, 1/8″ toe-in; less Select Drive System 1/8″ toe-out.

COOLING SYSTEM & CAPACITY DATA

Year	Model or Engine/V.I.N.	Cooling Capacity, Qts.		Radiator Cap Relief Pressure, Lbs.	Thermo. Opening Temp.	Fuel Tank Gals.	Engine Oil Refill Qts. ①	Transmission Oil			Rear Axle Oils Pint
		Less A/C	With A/C					3 Speed Pints	4 & 5 Speed Pints	Auto. Trans. Qts. ②	
1977	4-121/G Gremlin	6 1/2	6 1/2	14	189	15	4	—	2.4	7.1	3
	6-232, 258/⑲ Gremlin	11	14	15	195	21	4	3 1/2	3 1/2	8 1/2	3
	6-232, 258/⑲ Hornet	11	11 1/2	15	195	22	4	3 1/2	3 1/2	8 1/2	3
	6-232, 258/⑲ Matador	⑪	⑪	15	195	⑫	4	—	—	8 1/2	4
	6-232, 258/⑲ Pacer	14	14	15	195	22	4	3 1/2	3 1/2	8 1/2	3
	V8-304/H Hornet	16	16	15	195	22	4	3 1/2	3 1/2	8 1/2	4
	V8-304/H Matador	⑭	⑭	15	195	⑫	4	—	—	8 1/2	4
	V8-360/N Matador	⑭	⑭	15	195	⑫	4	—	—	9 1/2	4
1978	4-121/G Gremlin	6 1/2	6 1/2	14	190	④	3 1/2 ⑤	—	2.4	7.1	3
	6-232, 258/⑲ Gremlin	11	14	14	195	⑬	4	3	3.3	8.5	3
	6-232, 258/⑲ Concord & AMX	11	14	14	195	⑬	4	3	3.3	8.5	3
	6-232, 258/⑲ Matador	⑪	⑪	14	195	⑯	4	—	—	8.5	4
	6-232, 258/⑲ Pacer	14	14	14	195	20	4	3	3.3	8.5	3
	V8-304/H Concord & AMX	18	18	14	195	22	4	3	—	8.5	4
	V8-304/H Pacer	18	18	14	195	20	4	—	—	8.5	4
	V8-360/N Matador	⑧	⑧	14	195	⑯	4	—	—	8.2	4

AMERICAN MOTORS

COOLING SYSTEM & CAPACITY DATA—Continued

Year	Model or Engine/V.I.N.	Cooling Capacity, Qts.		Radiator Cap Relief Pressure, Lbs.	Thermo. Opening Temp.	Fuel Tank Gals.	Engine Oil Refill Qts. ①	Transmission Oil			Rear Axle Oils Pint
		Less A/C	With A/C					3 Speed Pints	4 & 5 Speed Pints	Auto. Trans. Qts. ②	
1979	4-121/G AMX, Spirit	6½	6½	14	190	21	3½⑤	3	2.4	7.1	3
	4-121/G Concord	6½	6½	14	190	22	3½⑤	3	2.4	7.1	3
	6-232, 258/⑲ AMX, Spirit	11	14	14	195	21	4	3	3.3	8.5	3
	6-232, 258/⑲ Condord	11	14	14	195	22	4	3	3.3	8.5	3
	6-232, 258/⑲ Pacer	14	14	14	195	21	4	3	3.3	8.5	3
	V8-304/H AMX & Spirit	18	18	14	195	21	4	—	3.3	8.5	3
	V8-304/H Concord	18	18	14	195	22	4	—	3.3	8.5	3
	V8-304/H Pacer	18	18	14	195	21	4	—	3.3	8.5	3
1980	4-151/B Spirit & Concord	6.5	6.5	14	195	13⑦	3⑨	—	3.3	7.1	3
	6-258/C Spirit, AMX & Concord	11	14	14	195	21⑦	4	—	3.3	8.5	3
	6-258/C Pacer	14	14	14	195	21	4	—	3.3	8.5	3
	6-258/C Eagle	11	14	14	195	22	4	—	—	8.5⑥	3③
1981	4-151/B Spirit & Concord	6.5	6.5	15	195	21⑦	3⑨	—	3.3	7.1	3
	4-151/B Eagle	6.5	6.5	15	195	22⑰	3⑨	—	3.3⑥	7.1⑥	3③
	6-258/C Spirit & Concord	11⑮	14	15	195	21⑦	4	—	3.3	8.5	3
	6-258/C Eagle	14	14	15	195	22⑰	4	—	3.3⑥	8.5⑥	3③
1982	4-151/B Spirit & Concord	6.5	6.5	15	195	21⑦	3⑨	—	⑱	7.1	3
	4-151/B Eagle	6.5	6.5	15	195	22⑰	3⑨	—	⑱⑥	7.1⑥	3③
	6-258/C Spirit & Concord	11⑮	14	15	195	21⑦	4	—	⑱	8.5	3
	6-258/C Eagle	11⑮	14	15	195	22⑰	4	—	⑱⑥	8.5⑥	3③
1983	4-151/B Eagle	6.5	6.5	15	195	⑩	3⑨	—	⑱⑥	7.1⑥	3③
	6-258/C Spirit & Concord	11⑮	14	15	195	21⑦	4	—	⑳	8.5	3
	4-150/U Eagle	—	—	15	195	⑩	4	—	⑱⑥	—	3③
	6-258/C Eagle	14	14	15	195	⑩	4	—	⑱⑥	8.5⑥	3③

①—Add one quart with filter change.
②—Approximate. Make final check with dipstick.
③—Front Axle, 2.5 pts.
④—With man. trans., 13 gals.; with auto. trans., 15 gals.
⑤—Add ½ qt. with filter change.
⑥—Transfer Case, 3.0 qts.
⑦—Concord, 22 gal.
⑧—Coupe 17½ qts.; Sedan & Sta. Wag., 15½ qts.

⑨—With or without filter change.
⑩—Except SX-4, 22 gals.; SX-4, 21 gals.
⑪—Coupe, 13½ qts.; sedan & wagon 11½ qts.
⑫—Except wagon, 24½ gals.; wagon, 21 gals.
⑬—Gremlin, 21 gals.; Concord, 22 gals.
⑭—Sedan & wagon: V8-304 16½ qts. V8-360 15½ qts. Add 2 quarts with coolant recovery system; Coupe models: V8-304 18½ qts. V8-360 17½ qts.

⑮—With heavy duty cooling system, 14 qts.
⑯—Except Sta. wag., 25 gals.; sta. wag., 21 gals.
⑰—Kammback & SX-4, 21 gals.
⑱—Four speed man. trans., 3.5 pts.; five speed man. trans., 4.0 pts.
⑲—For V.I.N. code, refer to the "General Engine Specifications" at the front of chapter.
⑳—Four speed man. trans., 4 pts.; five speed man. trans., 4.5 pts.

Electrical Section

STARTER, REPLACE

1980—83 4-151

1. Disconnect battery ground cable, then remove starter motor to engine brace. On Eagle models it may be necessary to remove an additional brace to remove starter motor.
2. Remove two starter motor to engine attaching bolts, then lower starter motor and disconnect wiring from solenoid.
3. Remove starter motor from vehicle.
4. Reverse procedure to install. Reinstall any shims that were removed.

Except 1980—83 4-151

1. Disconnect battery ground cable.
2. Disconnect cable from starter motor terminal.
3. Remove attaching bolts and remove starter.
4. Reverse procedure to install.

IGNITION LOCK, REPLACE

1. Remove turn signal switch as described further on.
2. Place key lock in "Lock" position and using a small flat blade screwdriver to depress the lock cylinder retaining tab, remove the lock cylinder, Fig. 1.
3. Reverse procedure to install.

IGNITION SWITCH, REPLACE

NOTE: On Pacer models, it may be necessary to remove steering tube cover and A/C duct to gain access to ignition switch. On Concord, Eagle, Gremlin, Hornet and Spirit models, remove package tray, if equipped.

Fig. 1   Lock cylinder removal

The ignition switch, Fig. 2, is mounted on the lower section of the steering column of all models and is connected to the steering lock by a remote control rod.

Removal

1. Disconnect battery ground cable.
2. Place ignition lock in "Off-Lock" position and remove switch attaching screws.
3. Disconnect switch from control rod and wiring connectors from switch, then remove switch from steering column.

Installation

1. On standard steering columns, move slider to extreme left and on tilt steering columns, move slider to extreme right. This places the switch in the "Accessory" position.
2. Place actuator rod in slider hole and install switch on steering column without moving slider out of detent. Hold key in "Accessory" position and push switch downward to remove slack in linkage and tighten screws.
3. Connect battery ground cable and check for proper operation.

LIGHT SWITCH, REPLACE

1977—84 Concord, Eagle, Gremlin, Hornet & Spirit

1. Disconnect battery ground cable.
2. Remove package tray, if equipped, and disconnect speedometer cable.
3. Remove instrument cluster bezel attaching screws and tilt bezel away from instrument panel.
4. With switch in full "On" position, press release button on switch and remove shaft and knob assembly.
5. Remove switch mounting sleeve nut.
6. Disconnect electrical connectors from switch and remove switch from vehicle.
7. Reverse procedure to install.

1977—80 Pacer

1. Disconnect battery ground cable.
2. Remove switch overlay attaching screws and pull overlay assembly rearward.
3. With switch in full "On" position, press release button on switch and remove shaft and knob assembly.
4. Remove switch mounting sleeve nut.
5. Disconnect electrical connectors from switch and remove switch from vehicle.
6. Reverse procedure to install.

1977—78 Matador

1. Disconnect battery ground cable.
2. Remove instrument cluster bezel.
3. Remove screws attaching light switch and wiper-washer bracket to instrument panel.
4. With switch in full "On" position, press release button on switch and remove shaft and knob assembly.
5. Remove switch mounting sleeve nut.
6. Disconnect electrical connectors from switch and remove switch from vehicle.
7. Reverse procedure to install.

STOP LIGHT SWITCH, REPLACE

1. Disconnect battery ground cable.
2. On Concord, Eagle, Gremlin, Hornet and Spirit models, remove package tray, if equipped.

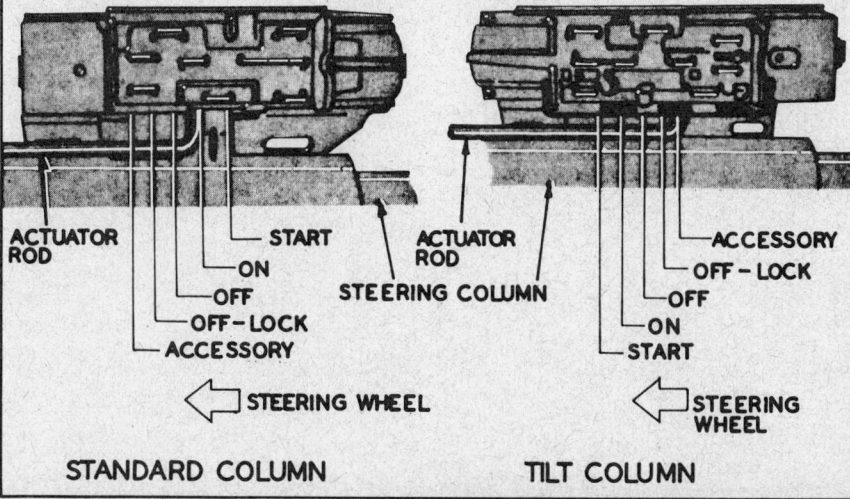

Fig. 2   Ignition switch installation (typical)

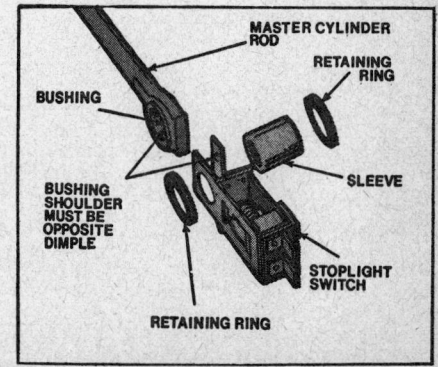

Fig. 3   Stoplight switch. (typical)

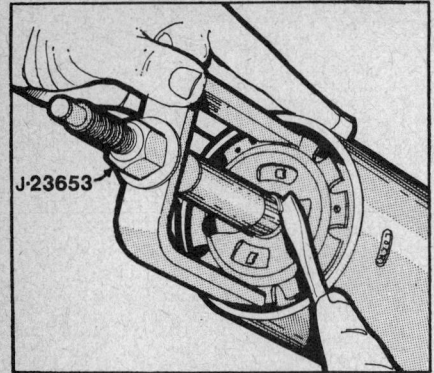

Fig. 4 Compressing lock plate & removing retaining ring

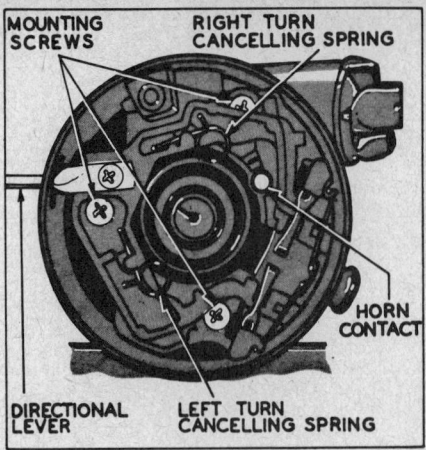

Fig. 5 Turn signal switch

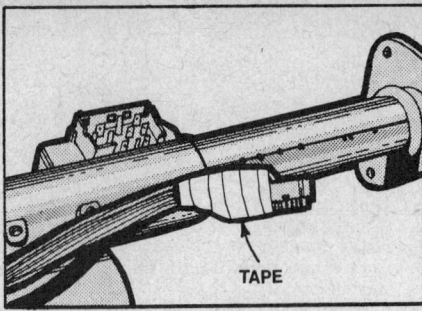

Fig. 6 Taping turn signal connector & wires

3. On Pacer models, remove steering column tube cover and intermediate duct under instrument panel, if equipped with A/C.
4. On all models, disconnect wire connector from switch.
5. Remove brake pedal pivot bolt, nylon retaining rings, sleeve, and remove switch.
6. When installing switch, be sure dimple on switch is opposite the bushing collar, Fig. 3.

NOTE: On 1977–84 models, there are two bolt holes on the brake pedal. On models equipped with power brakes, install bolt in lower hole. On models less power brakes, install bolt in upper hole.

7. Reverse procedure to install.

NEUTRAL SAFETY SWITCH, REPLACE

Except 1980–83 4-151

1. Raise and support vehicle.
2. Disconnect wiring from switch and unscrew from transmission. Allow fluid to drain into a container.
3. Move shift linkage to park and neutral positions and check switch operating fingers for proper positioning.
4. Reverse procedure to install. Correct transmission fluid level as required.

TURN SIGNAL SWITCH, REPLACE

1977–84

1. Disconnect battery ground cable, then remove steering wheel.
2. Using lock plate compressor tool No. J-23653, depress lock plate and remove and pry round wire snap ring from steering shaft groove, Fig. 4.

NOTE: On some models, the steering shaft has metric threads and is identified by a blue colored steering wheel nut and/or a groove cut into the steering shaft splines. If shaft has metric threads, replace compressor forcing screw with metric forcing screw J-23653-4 to depress lock plate.

3. Remove lock plate compressor tool, snap ring, lock plate and directional signal canceling cam from steering shaft.
4. Place directional signal lever in the right turn position, then remove lever and directional signal switch mounting screws, Fig. 5.
5. Depress hazard warning switch and remove button by turning in counter clockwise direction.
6. Remove directional signal switch wiring harness connector from mounting bracket on right side of lower column.
7. On Concord, Eagle, Gremlin, Hornet, Pacer & Spirit models, remove steering tube cover.

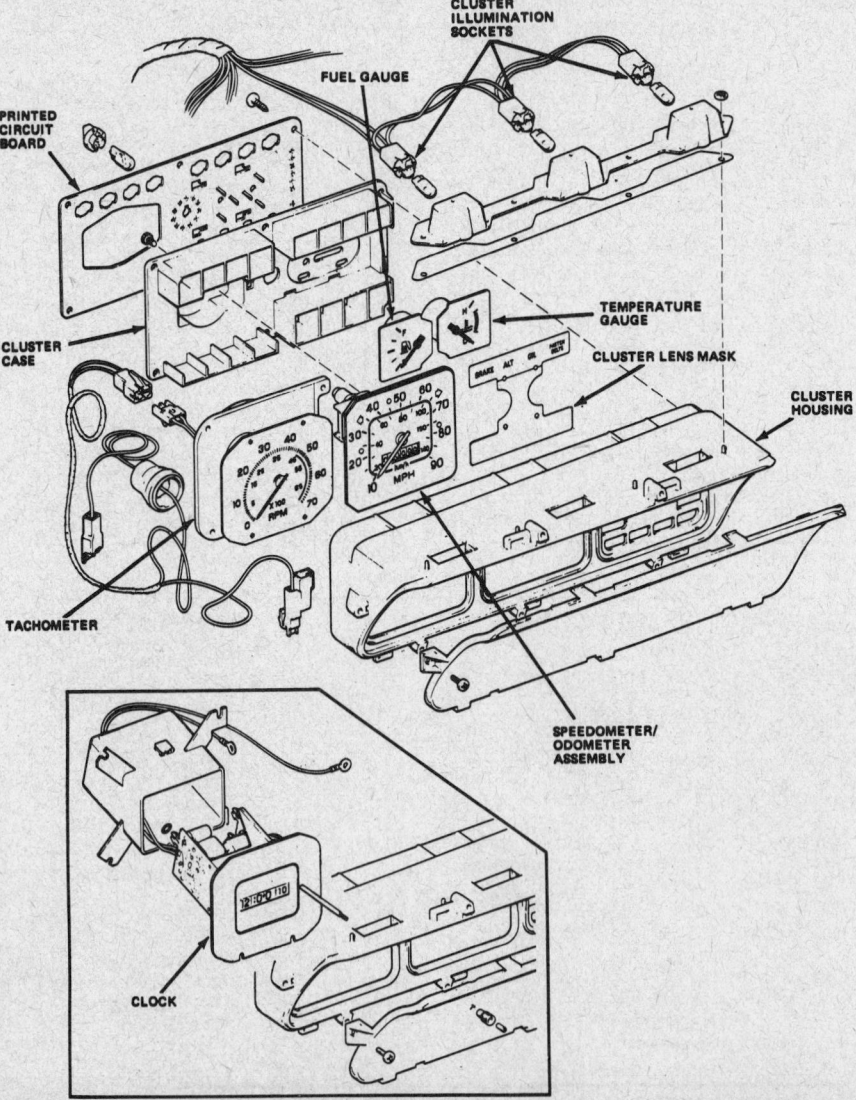

Fig. 7 Instrument cluster (typical). 1978–84 Concord, Eagle, Gremlin & Spirit

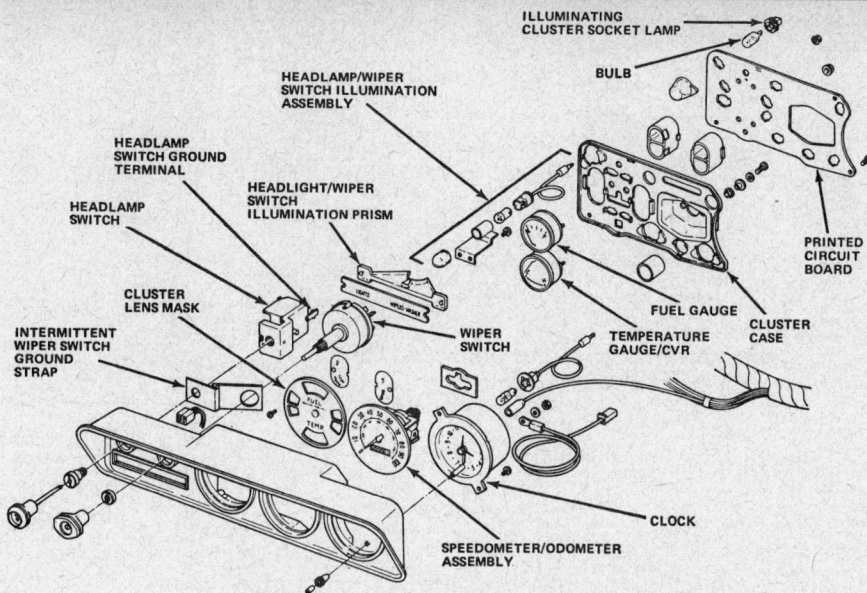

Fig. 8 Instrument cluster (typical). 1977 Gremlin & Hornet

Labels in figure:
- ILLUMINATING CLUSTER SOCKET LAMP
- BULB
- HEADLAMP/WIPER SWITCH ILLUMINATION ASSEMBLY
- HEADLAMP SWITCH GROUND TERMINAL
- HEADLIGHT/WIPER SWITCH ILLUMINATION PRISM
- HEADLAMP SWITCH
- PRINTED CIRCUIT BOARD
- CLUSTER LENS MASK
- INTERMITTENT WIPER SWITCH GROUND STRAP
- WIPER SWITCH
- TEMPERATURE GAUGE/CVR
- FUEL GAUGE
- CLUSTER CASE
- CLOCK
- SPEEDOMETER/ODOMETER ASSEMBLY

8. On Matador models, remove lower finish panel.
9. Remove steering column lower bracket bolts, then loosen steering column bracket nuts.
10. Fold connector over harness and wrap with tape to avoid snagging, Fig. 6. Raise column and pull harness out of column.

NOTE: On models with tilt column, raise column and remove plastic wiring harness protector.

11. On Concord and Hornet models, with column shift, automatic transmission, use stiff wire, such as a paper clip, to depress lock tab which retains shift quadrant light wire to wiring harness connector. The shift quadrant light wire is the grey wire connected to terminal D on wiring harness connector.
12. Reverse procedure to install.

HORN SOUNDER & STEERING WHEEL, REPLACE

1. Disconnect battery ground cable.
2. On steering wheels with horn buttons, remove button by first lifting button upward, and then pulling button out. On steering wheels equipped with horn ring or bar, remove screws from back of steering wheel, then pull wire plastic retainer out of directional signal canceling cam and remove horn ring or bar.
3. Remove steering wheel nut and washer. Note alignment marks on steering wheel and shaft for use during installation. If marks are not present, paint alignment marks on shaft and steering wheel.

NOTE: Some steering shafts have metric steering wheel nut threads. Metric steering wheel nuts are color coded blue for identification and steering shafts will have an identifying groove on shaft steering wheel splines.

4. Using a suitable puller, remove steering wheel.
5. Reverse procedure to install.

INSTRUMENT CLUSTER, REPLACE

1978–84 AMX, Concord, Eagle, Gremlin & Spirit

1. Disconnect battery ground cable.
2. On 1979–84 Concord, Eagle and Spirit models, remove lower steering column cover. On models equipped with column shift automatic transmission, remove gear selector dial actuator cable from steering column shift shroud.
3. On all models, remove instrument cluster bezel attaching screws across top of bezel, above radio and behind glove box door.
4. Tip top of bezel outward and disengage tabs along bottom edge of bezel.
5. If equipped, disconnect glove box lamp wire connector.
6. Depress speedometer cable locking tab and disconnect speedometer cable.
7. Push downward on three illumination lamp housings above bezel, until lamp housings are clear of instrument panel.
8. Disconnect headlamp switch and wiper control connectors and switch lamp.

NOTE: To disconnect headlamp switch connector, lift two locking tabs.

9. Twist and remove cluster illumination lamp sockets, then disconnect instrument cluster wire connectors.
10. Remove clock or tachometer attaching screws, if equipped. It is not necessary to remove clock adjusting knob.
11. Disconnect clock or tachometer feed wires from circuit board, if equipped.
12. Remove cluster housing and circuit board to bezel attaching screws.
13. Remove cluster housing and circuit board assembly from bezel, Fig. 7. If equipped with clock or tachometer, position aside as necessary.

14. Reverse procedure to install.

1977 Gremlin & Hornet

1. Disconnect battery ground cable.
2. Remove package tray if equipped to gain access speedometer cable.
3. Remove speedometer cable.
4. Remove top and side screws from instrument panel and tilt panel forward to gain access to headlamp and wiper control switch harness connectors.
5. Disconnect fiber-optic ashtray lamp if equipped.
6. Disconnect harness connectors and fuel economy gauge vacuum line if equipped and remove instrument cluster, Fig. 8.
7. Reverse procedure to install.

1977–80 Pacer

1. Disconnect battery ground cable.
2. Remove cluster bezel.
3. Remove radio knobs and nuts, then remove radio overlay.
4. Remove headlamp switch overlay retaining screws, then pull overlay back so that speedometer cable can be removed.
5. Remove cluster retaining screws, disconnect wiring harness and gear selector cable if equipped, then remove cluster assembly, Fig. 9.

NOTE: On models equipped with automatic transmission, remove steering tube cover.

6. Reverse procedure to install.

1977–78 Matador

1. Disconnect battery ground cable.
2. Remove radio knobs, attaching nuts and bezel retaining screws.
3. Remove right hand remote control mirror control from instrument panel, if equipped.
4. Tilt bezel forward and disconnect wiring.
5. Remove bezel, then remove clock or economy fuel gauge (if used) attaching screws, pull assembly away from cluster and disconnect bulbs and electrical leads. If equipped with fuel economy gauge, disconnect vacuum line and remove assembly.
6. Using clock opening, disconnect speedometer cable from instrument cluster, and disconnect gear selector dial cable from steering column.
7. Remove cluster mounting screws, disconnect any remaining electrical connections and remove cluster, Fig. 10.
8. Reverse procedure to install.

W/S WIPER MOTOR, REPLACE

1977–80 Pacer

1. Disconnect battery ground cable and disconnect linkage drive arm from motor crankpin.
2. Remove vacuum canister and mounting bracket assembly, if necessary.
3. On models equipped with air conditioning, remove two nuts from left side of heater housing and one nut from the right side of the housing.
4. On models not equipped with air condi-

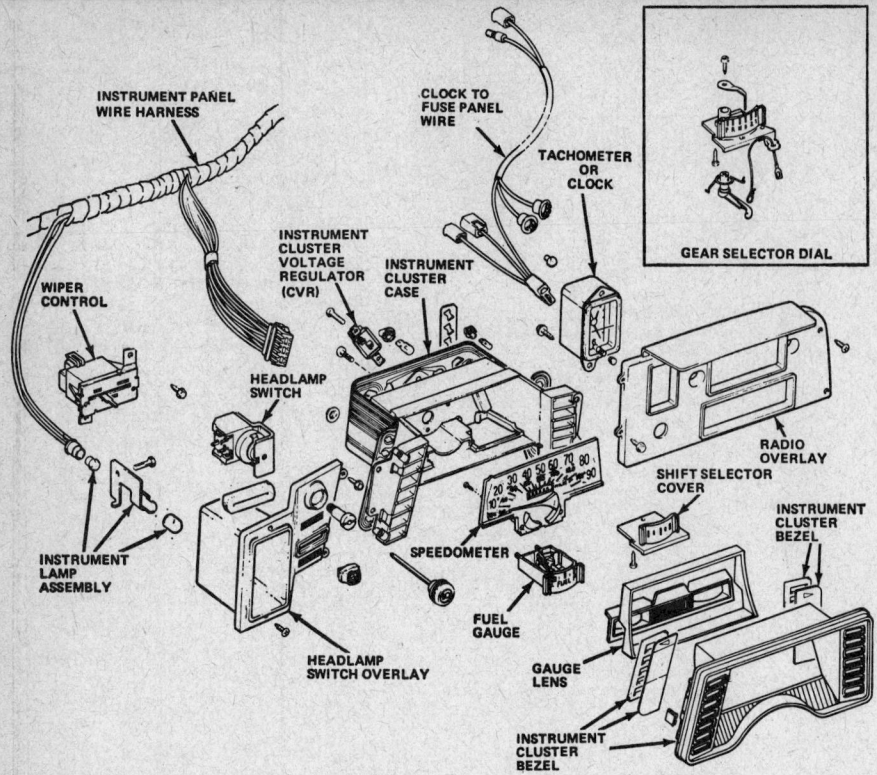

Fig. 9 Instrument cluster (typical). 1977–80 Pacer

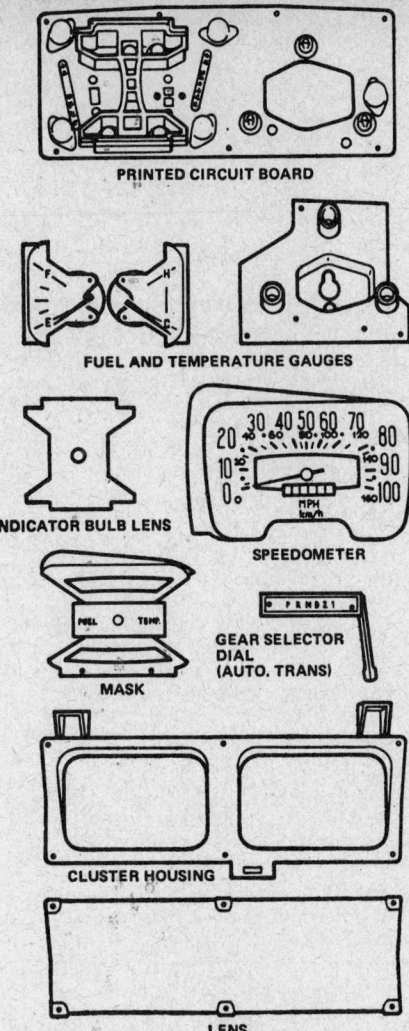

Fig. 10 Instrument cluster (typical). Matador

tioning, remove two nuts and one screw from left side of heater housing and one nut from the right side of the housing.
5. On all models, remove screw from heater housing support.
6. Pull heater housing forward.
7. Remove screws from wiper motor mounting plate and disconnect wiring harness.
8. Remove attaching screws and wiper motor.
9. Reverse procedure to install.

NOTE: Ensure output arm is in parked position before installing wiper motor.

1977–78 Matador Coupe

1. Disconnect battery ground cable. Remove wiper arms and cowl screen.
2. Remove retaining clip from linkage drive arm and disconnect electrical connectors from motor.
3. Remove wiper motor retaining screws and wiper motor.

NOTE: If output arm contacts dash panel, preventing wiper motor removal, hand turn output arm so arm clears dash opening.

4. Before installing motor, be sure output arm is in park position.
5. Reverse procedure to install.

1977–84 Exc. Matador Coupe & Pacer

1. Disconnect battery ground cable. Remove wiper arms and blades.
2. Remove four screws holding motor to dash.

3. Separate harness connector at the motor.
4. Pull motor and linkage out of opening to expose the drive link to crank stud retaining clip. Raise up the lock tab of the clip with a flat bladed screwdriver and slide clip off stud.
5. Reverse procedure to install.

LIFTGATE WIPER MOTOR, REPLACE

1. Disconnect battery ground cable. Remove wiper arm and blade.
2. Remove liftgate trim pad.
3. Disconnect wiring harness and ground wire.
4. Remove nut and pad securing wiper motor shaft to liftgate.
5. Remove screws securing wiper motor bracket, then separate bracket from motor.
6. Reverse procedure to install.

W/S WIPER TRANSMISSION, REPLACE

1977–80 Pacer

1. Disconnect battery ground cable and remove wiper arms and blades.
2. Remove pivot shaft bodies to cowl screws using tool No. J-25359-02.
3. Disconnect linkage from motor output arm, then remove pivot shaft body assembly.
4. Reverse procedure to install.

1977–78 Matador Coupe

1. Disconnect battery ground cable.
2. Remove wiper arm and blade assemblies, then remove cowl screen.
3. Remove screws attaching right and left pivot bodies to cowl using tool No. J-25359-02.
4. Disconnect linkage drive arm from motor output arm crankpin by removing retaining clip.
5. Remove pivot shaft body assembly through cowl opening.
6. Reverse procedure to install.

1977–78 Matador Exc. Coupe

1. Disconnect battery ground cable. Remove wiper arms and blades.
2. Remove cowl air intake cover.
3. Disconnect link-to-motor retainer and link from wiper arm through cowl top opening.
4. Remove screws holding each pivot shaft body to cowl top.
5. Remove both pivot body and link assemblies through cowl top opening.
6. Reverse procedure to install.

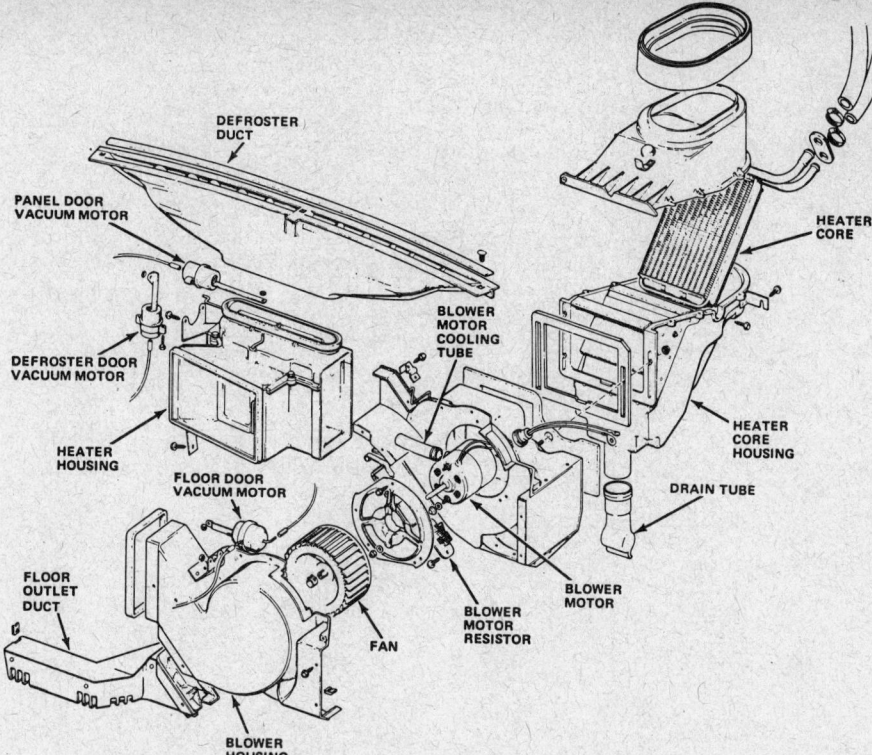

Fig. 11 Heater & blower housing assembly. Pacer (Typical)

Labels in figure:
- DEFROSTER DUCT
- PANEL DOOR VACUUM MOTOR
- DEFROSTER DOOR VACUUM MOTOR
- HEATER HOUSING
- FLOOR DOOR VACUUM MOTOR
- FLOOR OUTLET DUCT
- FAN
- BLOWER HOUSING
- BLOWER MOTOR RESISTOR
- BLOWER MOTOR
- BLOWER MOTOR COOLING TUBE
- HEATER CORE
- HEATER CORE HOUSING
- DRAIN TUBE

1977—84 AMX, Concord, Eagle, Hornet, Gremlin & Spirit

1. Disconnect battery ground cable. Remove wiper arms and blades.
2. Remove pivot shaft-to-cowl top nuts.
3. Remove wiper motor.
4. Slide pivot shaft body and link assembly to the left to clear right pivot shaft opening and move assembly to the right side of car to remove as a unit.
5. Reverse procedure to install.

NOTE: When installing pivot shafts to cowl top, flat side of pivot shaft indexes flat side of hole in cowl top when pivot shaft is in up position.

W/S WIPER SWITCH REPLACE

1978—80 Pacer

1. Disconnect battery ground cable. Using a small screwdriver, remove knob from switch by releasing tension on clip.
2. Remove bezel from instrument cluster by pulling toward rear of vehicle.
3. Remove four screws attaching headlamp switch overlay, then pull toward rear of vehicle to gain access to rear of w/s wiper switch.
4. Remove connector from rear of switch.
5. Remove two screws attaching switch to instrument panel, then remove switch.
6. Reverse procedure to install.

1977 Pacer

1. Disconnect battery ground cable.
2. Remove instrument cluster bezel, then the four screws from headlamp overlay.
3. Remove control knob, using a small screwdriver to release spring tension on clip.
4. Remove wire connector, then the two screws attaching switch to instrument panel.
5. Reverse procedure to install.

1977—84 All Exc. Pacer

1. Disconnect battery ground cable.
2. Locate small notch at base of knob and insert a small screwdriver and apply pressure to release spring and pull knob from shaft.
3. Remove slotted trim nut from front of switch.
4. Push switch through instrument panel, then disconnect wiring harness and remove switch.
5. Reverse procedure to install.

RADIO, REPLACE

NOTE: When installing radio, be sure to adjust antenna trimmer for peak performance.

1979—84 Concord, Eagle & Spirit

1. Disconnect battery ground cable.
2. Remove radio knobs and retaining nuts.

On models equipped with C.B. radio, remove radio bezel.
3. Remove instrument cluster center housing retaining screws, then remove center housing.
4. Disconnect power and speaker wiring and antenna lead, then remove radio.
5. Reverse procedure to install.

1977—80 Pacer

1. Disconnect battery ground cable.
2. Remove radio knobs, nuts and bezels, then the radio overlay.
3. Loosen radio attaching screws and lift radio from mounting bracket.
4. Disconnect antenna lead and wire connectors and remove radio.
5. Reverse procedure to install.

1977—78 Matador

1. Disconnect battery ground cable.
2. Remove radio knobs, retaining nuts and instrument cluster bezel.
3. Loosen upper radio retaining screw and lift radio disengaging bracket from screw, and pull radio slightly forward.
4. Disconnect antenna lead, electrical wiring and remove radio.
5. Reverse procedure to install.

1977—78 AMX, Concord, Gremlin & Hornet

1. Disconnect battery ground cable.
2. Remove package tray, if equipped.
3. Disconnect fiber-optic ash tray lamp from instrument cluster, if equipped.
4. Remove ash tray and bracket.
5. Remove radio knobs and shaft nuts.
6. Remove bezel retaining screws and bezel.
7. On 1977—78 models equipped with A/C, remove instrument panel center housing and attaching screws and center housing.
8. Disconnect antenna, speaker and power lead.
9. Remove radio.
10. Reverse procedure to install.

HEATER CORE, REPLACE

1977—80 Pacer, Fig. 11

1. Disconnect battery ground cable.
2. Drain approximately 2 qts. from cooling system.
3. Remove heater hoses and install plugs in hoses and core openings.
4. Position vacuum hoses away from core housing.
5. On models with A/C, disconnect outside air door vacuum hose from vacuum motor.
6. Remove core housing cover screws, disconnect overcenter spring and remove cover.
7. Remove screws attaching core to housing and remove core.
8. Reverse procedure to install.

1977—78 Matador, Fig. 12

Less Air Conditioning
1. Disconnect battery ground cable.

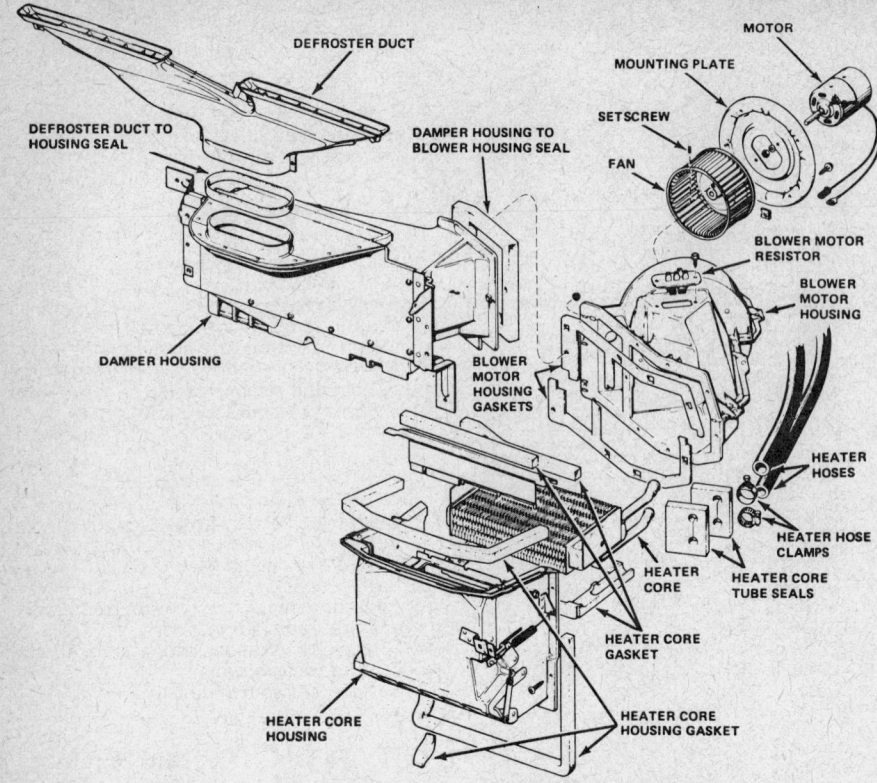

Fig. 12 Heater and blower housing assembly. Matador (Typical)

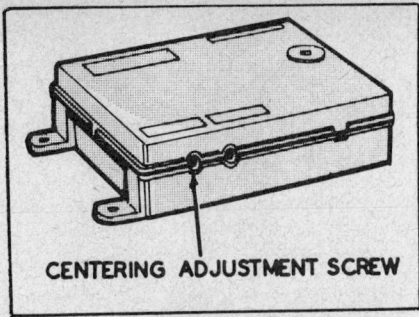

CENTERING ADJUSTMENT SCREW

Fig. 13 Centering adjusting screw location. 1978—84

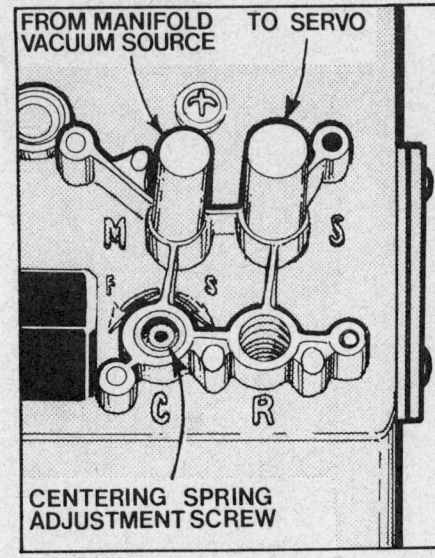

FROM MANIFOLD VACUUM SOURCE   TO SERVO

CENTERING SPRING ADJUSTMENT SCREW

Fig. 14 Centering spring adjustment. 1977

2. Drain about 2 quarts of coolant then disconnect heater houses and plug ends of hoses and core openings, Fig. 12.
3. Remove lower instrument finish panel and glove box.
4. Disconnect control cables and vacuum motor hoses.
5. On 1977–78 models, remove right side windshield reveal moulding to gain access to upper right housing attaching screw.
6. On all models, remove retaining screws and remove heater core housing assembly.
7. Remove heater core from housing.
8. Reverse procedure to install.

With Air Conditioning
1. Disconnect battery ground cable and drain cooling system.
2. Disconnect heater hoses from core and plug core tubes, Fig. 12.
3. Remove glove box and door.
4. Remove blend-air door cable from core housing and remove fuse panel.
5. Remove lower instrument finish panel.
6. Remove right windshield pillar and corner finish mouldings.
7. Remove vacuum motor hoses.
8. Remove screw attaching instrument panel to right "A" pillar.
9. Pull out right side of instrument panel and remove heater core housing assembly.
10. Remove heater core from housing.
11. Reverse procedure to install.

1977–84 AMX, Concord, Eagle, Hornet, Gremlin & Spirit

1. Disconnect battery ground cable, then drain about 2 qts. from cooling system.

2. Disconnect heater hoses and plug heater core tubes.
3. Remove blower motor and fan.
4. Remove housing attaching nut(s) from inside engine compartment.
5. Remove package tray if so equipped.
6. Disconnect wire connector at resistor.
7. On models with A/C, remove instrument panel bezel, outlet and duct.
8. Disconnect control cables from damper levers.
9. Remove right side windshield pillar moulding and the instrument panel upper attaching screws and right side cap screw at the door hinge post.
10. Remove right side kick panel and heater housing attaching screws.
11. Pull the right side of the instrument panel slightly rearward and remove the housing.
12. Remove cover and screws attaching heater core to housing, then remove heater core from housing.
13. Reverse procedure to install.

BLOWER MOTOR, REPLACE

1977–80 Pacer

Less Air Conditioning
1. Disconnect battery ground cable.
2. Remove right side windshield moulding, then the instrument panel crash pad.
3. Remove right scuff plate and cowl panel.
4. Remove lower instrument panel to pillar attaching screws, then pull instrument panel rearward and reinstall attaching screws, allowing panel to rest on screws.
5. Remove heater core housing attaching nuts and screw, position vacuum lines aside, disconnect air door, then pull hous-

ing forward and position on upper control arm.
6. Remove blower motor attaching screws, disconnect relay ground wire and resistor wiring.
7. Remove blower motor brace.
8. Loosen heater housing to instrument panel attaching nuts.
9. Pull blower motor housing rearward and downward, disconnect vacuum hoses from motors and remove blower housing.
10. Remove housing cover, disconnect wire and remove blower to housing attaching screws.
11. Remove blower from housing, then separate fan and mounting bracket from motor.
12. Reverse procedure to install.

With Air Conditioning
1. Disconnect battery ground cable.
2. Remove right scuff plate and cowl panel.
3. Remove radio overlay, then the instrument panel crash pad.
4. Remove instrument panel to right pillar attaching screws, then the upper to lower instrument panel attaching screws, located above glove box.
5. Disconnect air door cable from heater core housing and remove housing to floor pan brace screw.

6. Disconnect wires from blower motor resistor and vacuum lines from vacuum motors.
7. Remove heater core housing attaching nuts and screw, position vacuum lines aside, then pull housing forward and position on upper control arm.
8. Remove floor duct.
9. Disconnect wires from blower motor relay and remove blower motor housing attaching screw from firewall.
10. Loosen evaporator housing to dash panel attaching nuts, remove blower motor housing attaching screw from dash panel, then pull blower housing rearward and downward.
11. Pull right side of instrument panel rearward and remove blower motor.
12. Remove blower housing cover.
13. Remove blower motor from housing, the separate fan and mounting bracket from motor.
14. Reverse procedure to install.

1977–78 Matador, Fig. 12

1. Disconnect battery ground cable.
2. Disconnect blower motor wiring and cooling hose.
3. Remove blower motor attaching screws and remove blower motor.
4. Reverse procedure to install.

1977–83 AMX, Concord, Eagle, Gremlin, Hornet & Spirit

1. Disconnect battery ground cable.
2. Working in engine compartment, disconnect blower motor wire.
3. Remove three retaining nuts for blower scroll cover to which blower assembly is attached and remove blower motor and fan.
4. Reverse procedure to install.

SPEED CONTROL, ADJUST

1978–84

Centering Adjustment

This adjustment is made by turning the centering adjusting screw on the regulator, Fig. 13. If speed control engages at two or more mph higher than selected speed, turn centering adjusting screw counter clockwise a small amount. If engagement speed is two or more mph below selected speed, turn centering adjusting screw clockwise a small amount. Check for proper centering adjustment on a level road after making each adjustment.

Vacuum Dump Valve

While holding brake pedal in the depressed position, move vacuum dump valve toward pedal bracket as far as possible, then release brake pedal.

1977

Chain Linkage, Adjust

Chain linkage should never be taut. To adjust, start engine and set carburetor at hot idle with anti-stall plunger backed off so as not to affect idle speed and disconnect idle stop solenoid. Hook chain to accelerator linkage, pull taut, then loosen one ball at a time until a slight chain deflection is obtained without moving carburetor throttle or servo. After chain has been adjusted, bend servo hook tabs together and chain must be free in hook.

NOTE: Whenever adjusting chain linkage, be sure chain does not hold carburetor throttle open.

Centering Springs, Adjust

If speed control system holds speed three or more mph higher than selected speed, turn centering spring adjusting screw (C) toward (S) 1/32″ or less, Fig. 14.

If speed control system holds speed three or more mph below selected speed, turn centering spring adjusting screw (C) toward (F) 1/32″ or less. Do not move adjustment screw (R).

4-121 Engine Section

ENGINE MOUNTS, REPLACE

1. Remove nut from cushion upper stud, Fig. 1.
2. If replacing right side cushion, remove TAC flexible hose.
3. Raise engine until engine bracket clears cushion stud.
4. Remove nut from lower cushion and the cushion.
5. Reverse procedure to install.

ENGINE, REPLACE

1. Scribe hood hinge locations and remove hood.
2. Remove air cleaner and TAC flexible hose.
3. Drain coolant and disconnect battery ground cable from battery and alternator mounting bracket.
4. Remove fuel line, vapor return and canister lines.
5. Disconnect engine wiring at dash panel connectors.
6. Disconnect throttle cable and, if equipped with automatic transmission, the throttle valve linkage.
7. Disconnect upper radiator hose from radiator.
8. On models equipped with A/C, remove service valve covers and front seat valves. Loosen nuts attaching service valve to compressor head and allow compressor charge to bleed off. Remove service valves and cap compressor ports and service valves.
9. Raise vehicle and remove starter.
10. Remove exhaust pipe support backet and the bellhousing shield.
11. On automatic transmission vehicles, remove torque converter to flywheel nuts.
12. On all models, disconnect exhaust pipe from manifold.
13. Disconnect back-up light switch wire from switch and clips.
14. Disconnect the lower radiator hose and heater hose from radiator.
15. On automatic transmission vehicles, disconnect transmission oil cooler lines at flexible hose.
16. On all models, disconnect wiring harness from alternator.
17. Remove all bellhousing bolts except the top center.
18. Lower vehicle.

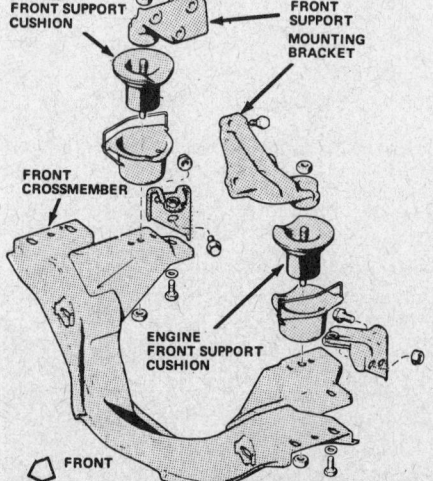

ENGINE FRONT SUPPORT CUSHION

FRONT SUPPORT MOUNTING BRACKET

FRONT CROSSMEMBER

ENGINE FRONT SUPPORT CUSHION

FRONT

Fig. 1 Engine mounts. 4-121

19. Remove screw securing cold air induction manifold to radiator.
20. Remove radiator attaching screws and move radiator approximately one inch toward the left side. Rotate radiator and remove with shroud attached.
21. Remove tie from upper heater hose, then disconnect hose from heater and secure to engine.
22. Pull back-up light harness upward and secure to engine.
23. Disconnect hoses from power steering gear, if equipped, and secure to engine.
24. On automatic transmission vehicles, remove transmission filler tube support screws.
25. On all models, remove engine mount cushion nuts on both sides.
26. Raise engine with suitable lifting equipment to clear support cushion studs.
27. Support transmission with a suitable jack and remove the top center bolt from bellhousing.

CYLINDER HEAD, REPLACE

1. Disconnect battery ground cable and drain coolant.
2. Remove air cleaner, TAC vacuum motor and valve assembly, and flexible hoses.
3. Disconnect upper radiator hose from radiator.
4. Remove bypass hose from bottom of thermostat housing.
5. Remove accessory drive belts.
6. Remove camshaft drive belt guard and the camshaft drive belt.
7. Remove fan spacer and pulley.
8. Remove air pump.
9. Remove alternator pivot screw.
10. Remove air pump front bracket.

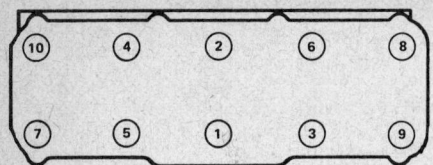

Fig. 2 Cylinder head tightening sequence

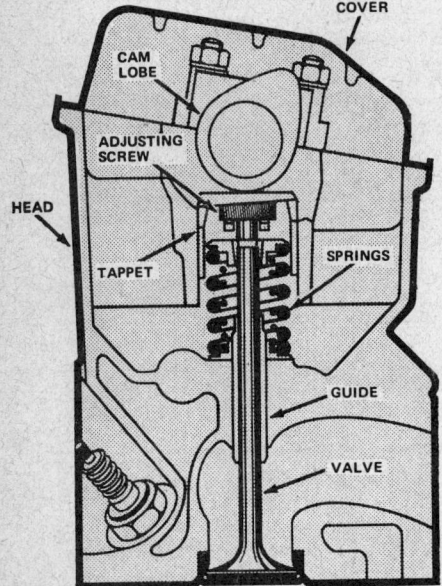

Fig. 3 Valve train

11. Disconnect exhaust pipe from manifold and the air hose from diverter valve.
12. Disconnect heater hose from rear of head.
13. Remove EGR tube to bellhousing screw.
14. Disconnect the following wiring connectors: temperature sender, oil pressure sender, electric choke, throttle solenoid, PCV valve solenoid, distributor primary and ignition secondary to coil.
15. Disconnect fuel line at bottom of intake manifold bracket, then remove screw from bottom of bracket.
16. Disconnect accelerator cable.
17. Disconnect power brake booster vacuum hose, if equipped.
18. Disconnect fuel return line from filter.
19. Disconnect intake manifold inlet and outlet hoses.
20. Disconnect canister to carburetor hoses from carburetor and the PCV hose from block.
21. Remove cylinder head cover.
22. Remove cylinder head bolts in reverse order of tightening sequence, Fig. 2.
23. Remove cylinder head from engine.
24. Reverse procedure to install. Torque cylinder head bolts in sequence, Fig. 2

VALVE ARRANGEMENT

Front to Rear
4-121 . . . . I-E-I-E-I-E-I-E

CAM LOBE LIFT SPEC.

Year	Engine	Intake	Exhaust
1977–78	4-121	.400	.380
1979	4-121	.396	.366

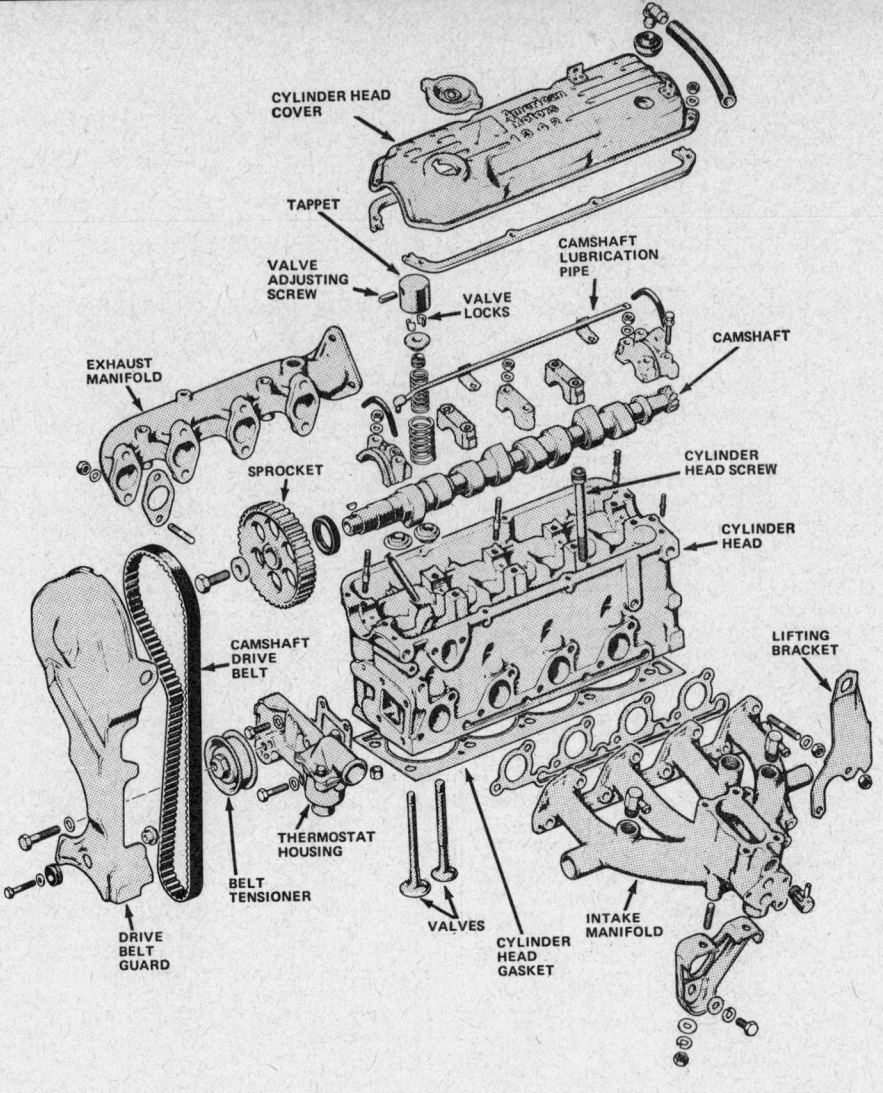

Cylinder head assembly

VALVE TIMING

Intake Opens Before TDC

Year	Engine	Degrees
1977–78	4-121	41.8
1979	4-121	25

TAPPETS, ADJUST

These mechanical tappets are provided with a clearance adjusting screw, Fig. 3. The adjusting screw is threaded into a hole drilled into the tappet at an angle of approximately 86° to the valve stem. A flat is milled onto the screw perpendicular to the valve stem. The flat is moved .002 inch relative to the valve stem each time the adjusting screw is rotated one complete turn.

1. Remove TAC flexible hose.
2. Disconnect harness clip from cylinder head cover.
3. Disconnect ignition wires from spark plugs and remove distributor cap and position aside.
4. Remove cylinder head cover.
5. Rotate crankshaft to position No. 1 piston at top dead center, compression stroke.
6. Check clearance of the following tappets,

Fig. 4: No. 1 intake and exhaust, No. 2 intake and No. 3 exhaust.
7. If tappet adjustment is required, perform the following precedure:
   a. With adjusting screw bit, J-26810, and wrench rotate adjusting screw one complete turn until it clicks, Fig. 5. Continue to rotate the adjusting screw in complete turns until clearance is within specifications.
   b. When clearance is within specifications, check position of adjusting screw in tappet with tappet adjusting screw gauge, J-26860, Fig. 6. The gauge is marked with a band. The outside edge of the tappet must be within the band. If the gauge indicated that the adjusting screw is turned too far into the tappet, the next thicker adjusting screw must be installed. Five sizes of tappet adjustings are available and are identified by grooves on the end of the screw opposite the wrench socket, Fig. 7. The tappet must be removed to replace the adjusting screw.
8. Rotate crankshaft 360° and check and adjust the clearance of the following tappets: No. 2 exhaust, No. 3 intake and No. 4 intake and exhaust. Perform step 7 if tappet adjustment is required.

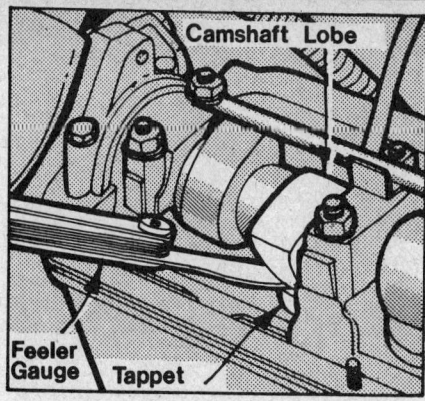

Fig. 4 Checking tappet clearance

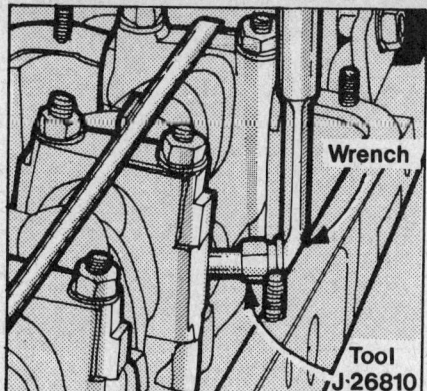

Fig. 5 Adjusting tappet clearance

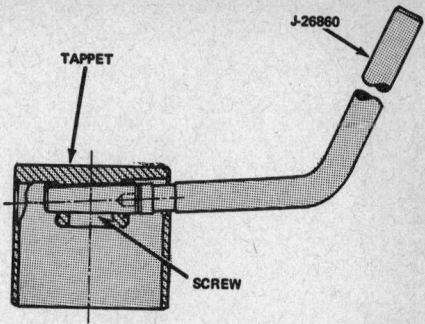

Fig. 6 Checking tappet adjusting screw position

TAPPETS, REPLACE

1. Remove camshaft as outlined under "Camshaft, Replace" procedure.
2. Remove tappets from bores by lifting upward.
3. Lubricate new tappets with AMC Engine Oil Supplement or suitable equivalent.
4. Install new tappets in bores.
5. Install camshaft.
6. Adjust tappet clearance.
7. Pour the remaining AMC Engine Oil Supplement or equivalent over the valve train.

NOTE: The engine oil supplement should remain in the engine for at least 1000 miles.

CYLINDER HEAD COVER, REPLACE

1. Remove TAC flexible hose.
2. Remove PCV valve hose from cylinder head cover.
3. Disconnect ignition wires from spark plugs, then the harness clip from the cover.
4. Remove cylinder head cover nuts and washers.
5. Clean gasket material from cylinder head and cover.
6. Install end pieces of replacement gasket in grooves of bearing caps at both ends of head, Fig. 8. Ensure the end pieces fit into

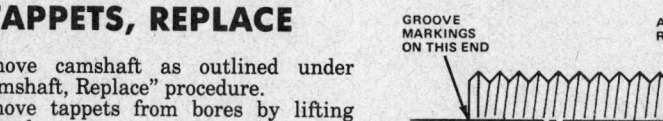

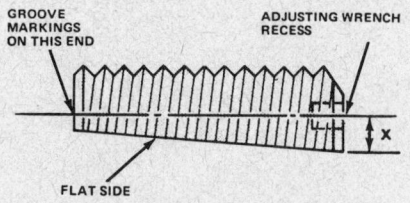

GROOVE MARKING	DIMENSION X-mm
NONE	3.00
I	3.45
II	3.57
III	3.69
IIII	3.81

Fig. 7 Tappet adjusting screw markings

the side seal slots. Also, apply silicone gasket material to all joints.
7. Install side pieces of gasket over cylinder head studs.
8. Install cylinder head cover, reinforcement strips, washers and nuts. Torque nuts to specifications.
9. Install PCV valve hose into cylinder head cover.
10. Connect ignition wires to spark plugs, then the harness clip to cover.
11. Install TAC flexible hose.

CAMSHAFT DRIVE BELT, REPLACE

1. Rotate engine to position crankshaft timing mark at "0". The camshaft sprocket timing mark should be aligned with the pointer on the cylinder head cover, Fig. 9.

NOTE: If camshaft timing mark is 180°

out of position, rotate the crankshaft 360°. The camshaft mark should then align with the pointer.

2. Loosen front pulley retaining screws.
3. Remove drive belts from alternator and power steering pump.
4. Remove cam drive belt guard.
5. Loosen tensioner retaining screw, Fig. 10.
6. Remove camshaft drive belt.
7. Install new drive belt on crankshaft sprocket.
8. Position belt in tensioner pulley and install belt on camshaft sprocket.
9. Rotate tensioner adjusting nut counterclockwise to increase tension, Fig. 10. The belt is properly tensioned when the drive side of the belt can be twisted 90° with the fingers. When checking belt tension, apply force to the crankshaft with a wrench in the counter-clockwise direction. This is done to position the belt slackness on the side of the belt being checked.
10. Maintain pressure to the tensioner pulley nut and torque the retaining screw to 29 ft. lbs. Recheck belt tension.
11. Install cam belt drive guard.
12. Install and tension alternator and power steering pump drive belts.

CAMSHAFT DRIVE SPROCKETS, REPLACE

Upper

1. Remove cam drive belt as outlined previously.

Fig. 8 Cylinder head cover gasket installation

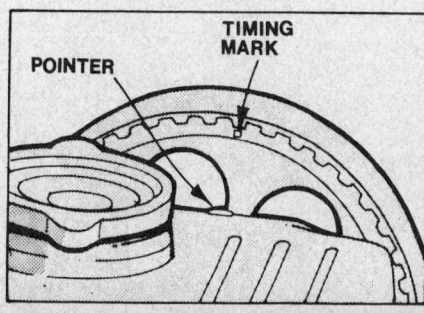

Fig. 9 Camshaft sprocket timing mark

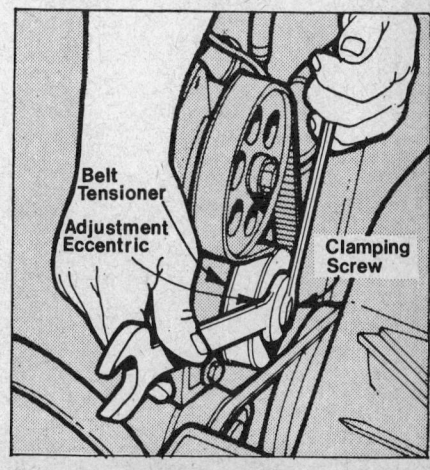

Fig. 10 Camshaft drive belt tensioner

Fig. 11   Replacing camshaft sprocket

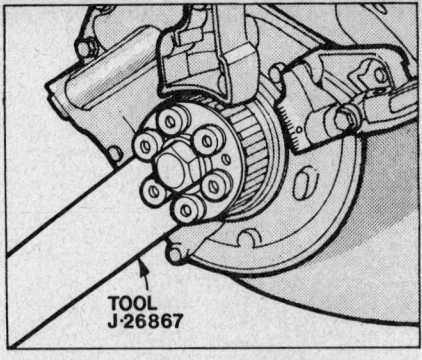

Fig. 12   Replacing crankshaft sprocket

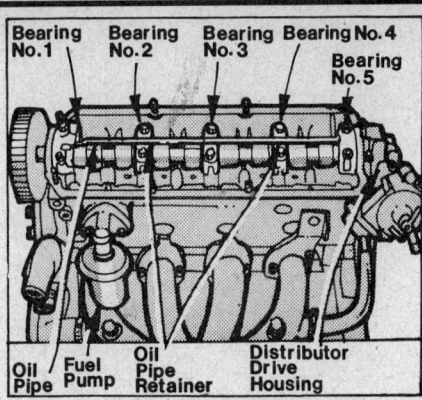

Fig. 13   Camshaft & bearings

2. Remove sprocket retaining bolt. Use a suitable tool wrapped in a shop cloth to prevent the sprocket from turning, Fig. 11.
3. Remove sprocket, key and washer.
4. Reverse procedure to install. Torque sprocket retaining bolt to 58 ft. lbs.

Lower

1. Raise vehicle and support on jack stands.
2. Loosen crankshaft pulley screws.
3. Remove accessory drive belts.
4. Remove crankshaft pulley.
5. Remove cam drive belt guard.
6. Loosen tensioner retaining screw.
7. Attach crankshaft holding tool, J-26867, Fig. 12, to crankshaft sprocket with the six pulley attaching screws. Remove crankshaft sprocket retaining bolt and the sprocket.
8. Remove tool from sprocket and attach to new sprocket, if replacing sprocket.
9. Install sprocket.

NOTE: The hole in the sprocket must index with the crankshaft locating pin.

10. Install and torque crankshaft sprocket retaining bolt to 181 ft. lbs.
11. Remove tool from sprocket and install crankshaft pulley.
12. Rotate crankshaft to position crankshaft timing mark at "0".
13. Rotate camshaft sprocket to align timing

Fig. 14   Distributor drive housing installation

mark with pointer on cylinder head cover.
14. Install and tension camshaft drive belt.
15. Remove crankshaft pulley.
16. Install cam drive belt guard.
17. Install crankshaft pulley and torque attaching bolts to 15 ft. lbs.
18. Install accessory drive belts.

CAMSHAFT, REPLACE

Removal

1. Remove TAC flexible hose.
2. Disconnect ignition wires from spark plugs, then the clip from cylinder head cover.
3. Remove distributor cap with wire attached.
4. Remove accessory drive belts.
5. Remove cam drive belt guard.
6. Loosen tensioner attaching bolt and remove camshaft drive belt.
7. Remove camshaft sprocket.

8. Disconnect the distributor primary wire and the vacuum advance hose.
9. Remove distributor housing and distributor assembly.
10. Disconnect PCV valve hose from cylinder head cover and remove the cylinder head cover.
11. Remove two 10mm screws from the No. 5 bearing cap, Fig. 13.
12. Remove nuts from bearing cap Nos. 1, 2, 3, 4 and 5.
13. Remove oil pipe, Fig. 13.
14. Remove bearing caps and the camshaft.
15. Remove distributor drive gear from camshaft with a suitable puller and install on replacement camshaft, if replacing camshaft.

Installation

1. Install camshaft.
2. Lubricate and install bearing caps.
3. Install oil pipe.
4. Install and torque nuts on cap Nos. 2 and 4 to 13 ft. lbs.
5. Install and torque nuts on cap Nos. 3 and 5 to 13 ft. lbs.
6. Install and torque the 10mm screws on cap No. 5 to 7 ft. lbs.
7. Install replacement seal on camshaft.
8. Install and torque nuts on cap No. 1 to 13 ft. lbs.
9. Install camshaft sprocket.
10. Install cylinder head cover seals and gaskets.
11. Install cylinder head cover and install

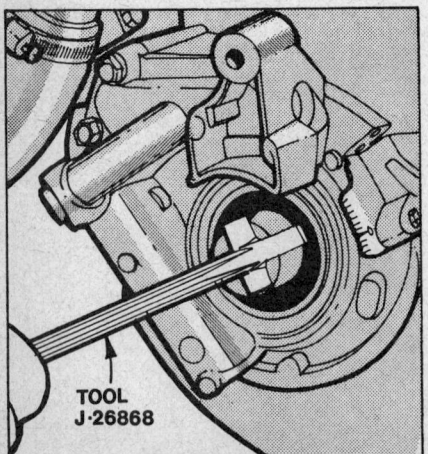

Fig. 15   Front oil seal removal

Fig. 16   Front oil seal installation

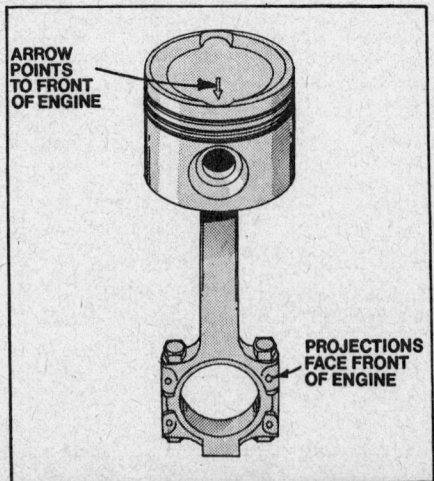

Fig. 17   Piston & rod assembly

nuts finger tight.

12. Align camshaft timing mark with pointer on cylinder head cover.
13. Install distributor housing, Fig. 14, with distributor rotor pointing to the No. 1 cylinder firing position. Install distributor cap.
14. Connect distributor primary wire and the vacuum advance hose.
15. Rotate crankshaft to position crankshaft timing mark at "0".
16. Install and tension camshaft drive belt.
17. Install cam drive belt guard.
18. Install pulley, spacer and fan.
19. Install and tension accessory drive belts.
20. Remove cylinder head cover and adjust tappets.
21. Install cylinder head cover.
22. Connect ignition wires to spark plugs and the harness clip to cylinder head cover.
23. Install TAC flexible hose and the PCV valve hose.

FRONT OIL SEAL, REPLACE

1. Remove accessory drive belts, cam drive belt guard and accessory drive pulley.
2. Loosen camshaft drive belt tensioner and remove drive belt.
3. Remove crankshaft sprocket.
4. Remove front oil seal from oil pump recess with tool J-26868, Fig. 15.
5. Lubricate seal inner lip with engine oil. Do not apply sealant to outer edge of seal.
6. Drive seal into oil pump recess with tool J-26877, Fig. 16.
7. Reverse procedure to assemble.

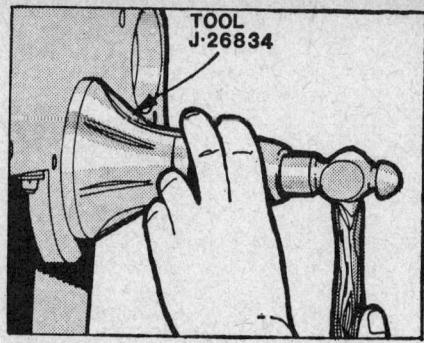

Fig. 18 Crankshaft rear oil seal installation

PISTON & ROD ASSEMBLY

Assemble piston to rod as shown in Fig. 17. Check side clearance between connecting rod and crankshaft journal. Clearance should be .002–.120 inch.

MAIN & ROD BEARINGS

Main bearings are available in undersizes of .25mm, .50mm and .75mm.
Rod bearings are available in undersizes of .25mm, .50mm and .75mm.

CRANKSHAFT REAR OIL SEAL, REPLACE

1. Remove transmission.

2. If equipped with a manual transmission, remove pressure plate and flywheel.
3. On all models, remove seal with tool J-26868.
4. Lubricate new seal lips with engine oil.
5. Drive new seal into position with tool J-26834, Fig. 18, until bottomed in bore. The seal should be positioned approximately 1/32 inch below the surface of the cylinder block.
6. Install flywheel and pressure plate, if removed.
7. Install transmission.

OIL PAN, REPLACE

1. Raise vehicle and support on jackstands.
2. Drain oil pan.
3. Install suitable engine lifting equipment.
4. Remove engine bracket to cushion nuts.
5. Loosen strut and bracket screws.
6. Raise engine approximately two inches.
7. Remove crossmember to sill attachments.
8. Remove steering gear idler bracket.
9. Pry crossmember loose and insert wooden blocks between crossmember and sill on both sides.
10. Remove oil pan attaching bolts and the oil pan.
11. Reverse procedure to install. Torque oil pan attaching bolts to 70 inch lbs. for side bolts and 90 inch lbs. for end bolts.

OIL PUMP, REPLACE

Removal

1. Remove fan shroud.
2. Raise and support vehicle on jackstands.
3. Remove accessory drive belts.
4. Remove accessory drive pulley and the cam drive belt guard.
5. Remove crankshaft sprocket and camshaft sprocket.
6. Remove oil pump screws and front oil pan screws.
7. Remove oil pump by prying in slot provided with a suitable screwdriver, Fig. 19. Remove gasket and crankshaft seal.

Installation

1. Install new gasket.
2. Rotate crankshaft to position; oil pump lugs either vertically or horizontally to ease alignment with oil pump.
3. Cut off oil pan gasket flush with front of block.
4. Apply marking material to crankshaft lugs and install pump. Then, remove

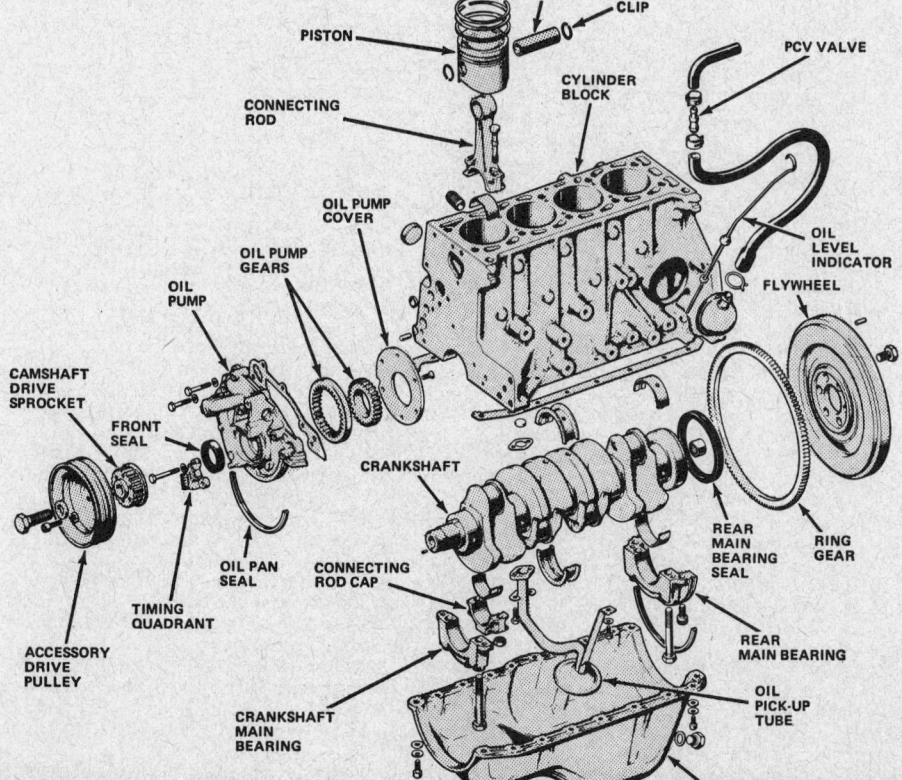

Cylinder block assembly

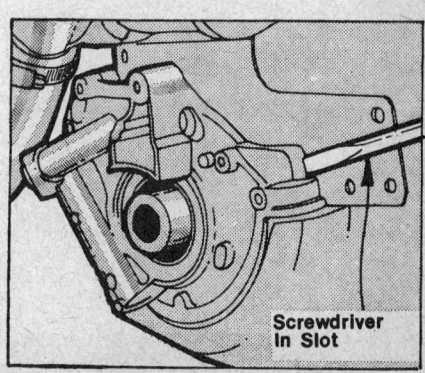

Fig. 19 Oil pump removal

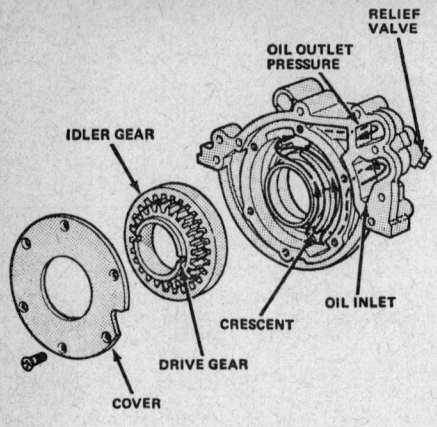

Fig. 20 Oil pump

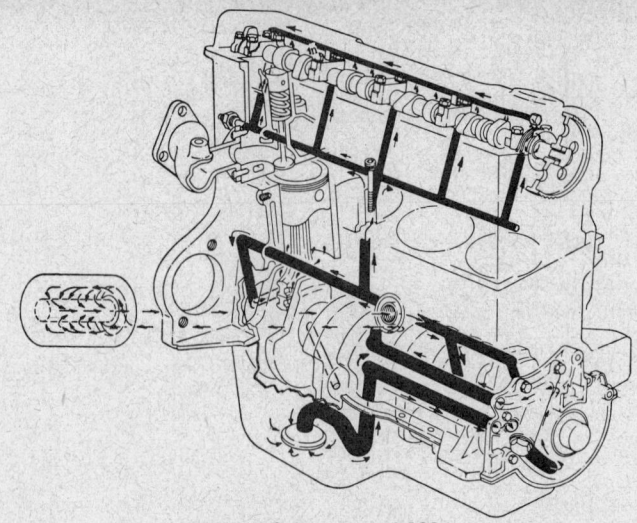

Engine oiling system. 4-121

pump and observe markings and orient gears accordingly.
5. Apply silicone material to pump sealing surface and the edges of pump and oil pan.
6. Install oil pump and torque attaching screws to 87 inch lbs.
7. Install crankshaft and camshaft sprockets and the camshaft drive belt.
8. Install cam drive belt guard and accessory drive pulley.
9. Install accessory drive belts.
10. Install fan shroud.
11. Lower vehicle.

Relief Valve Replacement
1. Remove relief valve from pump, Fig. 20.
2. Remove spring and piston from pump, if not removed with valve body.
3. Install spring and piston into valve body.
4. Install valve body into pump and torque to 35 ft. lbs.

BELT TENSION DATA

	New Lbs.	Used Lbs.
1977–79		
Air Pump	40–60	40–60
A/C, Fan & Alternator	125–155	90–115
Power Steering	125–155	90–115

WATER PUMP, REPLACE
1. Drain coolant.
2. Rotate crankshaft to place No. 1 piston at TDC, compression stroke.
3. Remove power steering drive belt, if equipped.
4. Loosen the alternator and air pump.
5. Remove fan, spacer and pulley.
6. Remove cam drive belt guard.
7. Remove air pump bracket.
8. Remove camshaft drive belt idler pulley.
9. Remove all hoses from water pump except the thermostat hose.
10. Remove water pump attaching screws and the water pump, pulling the pump from thermostat hose.
11. Reverse procedure to install.

FUEL PUMP, REPLACE
1. Disconnect fuel lines from pump.
2. Remove pump retaining screws.
3. Remove pump, spacer and gaskets.
4. Reverse procedure to install.

NOTE: Ensure the pushrod is properly positioned against the pump actuating lever. If positioned improperly, the pump may be damaged when the screws are tightened.

4-150 Engine Section

ENGINE MOUNTS, REPLACE

Removal or replacement of any cushion can be accomplished by supporting the weight of the engine or transmission at the area of the cushion to be replaced.

ENGINE, REPLACE

The engine is removed without the transmission as follows:
1. Drain cooling system.
2. Mark hood hinge locations, disconnect underhood lamp, if equipped, and remove hood.
3. Disconnect battery cables, and remove battery.
4. Disconnect alternator wiring and the ignition coil, distributor and oil pressure sender leads.
5. Remove TCS switch bracket from cylinder block, if equipped.
6. Disconnect flexible fuel line from fuel pump and plug line and pump port.
7. Disconnect engine ground strap.
8. Remove the right front engine support cushion to bracket screw.
9. If equipped with air conditioning:
   a. Remove service valve covers and front-seat valves.
   b. Loosen service valve to compressor attaching nuts.
   c. Bleed compressor refrigerant charge.
   d. Remove service valves and cap compressor ports and service valves.
   e. Disconnect clutch feed wire.
10. Remove starter.
11. Remove air cleaner and disconnect purge hose from canister and TAC vacuum hose from manifold, if equipped.
12. Disconnect throttle stop solenoid lead, if equipped.
13. Disconnect fuel return hose from fuel filter and the carburetor bowl vent hose from canister.
14. Disconnect throttle cable and remove from bracket. Disconnect throttle valve rod at carburetor and the bellcrank.
15. Disconnect heater and air conditioning system vacuum hose from intake manifold.
16. Disconnect temperature sender wire and TCS vacuum solenoid wiring harness.
17. Disconnect radiator hoses from radiator and the heater hoses from engine.
18. Disconnect transmission oil cooler lines from radiator, if equipped.
19. Remove fan shroud attaching screws, then the radiator and shroud.
20. Remove fan and spacer. Install a 5/16 × 1/2 inch capscrew through fan pulley, into water pump flange.
21. Remove power brake vacuum check valve from power brake unit, if equipped.
22. If equipped with power steering, disconnect hoses from gear and drain reservoir. Cap gear ports and hoses.
23. Remove transmission filler tube bracket screw, if equipped.
24. Raise and support vehicle on jackstands.
25. If equipped with automatic transmission:
   a. Remove converter housing spacer cover.
   b. Remove converter attaching screws.
   c. Remove exhaust pipe support from converter housing. This also supports the inner end of the transmission link-

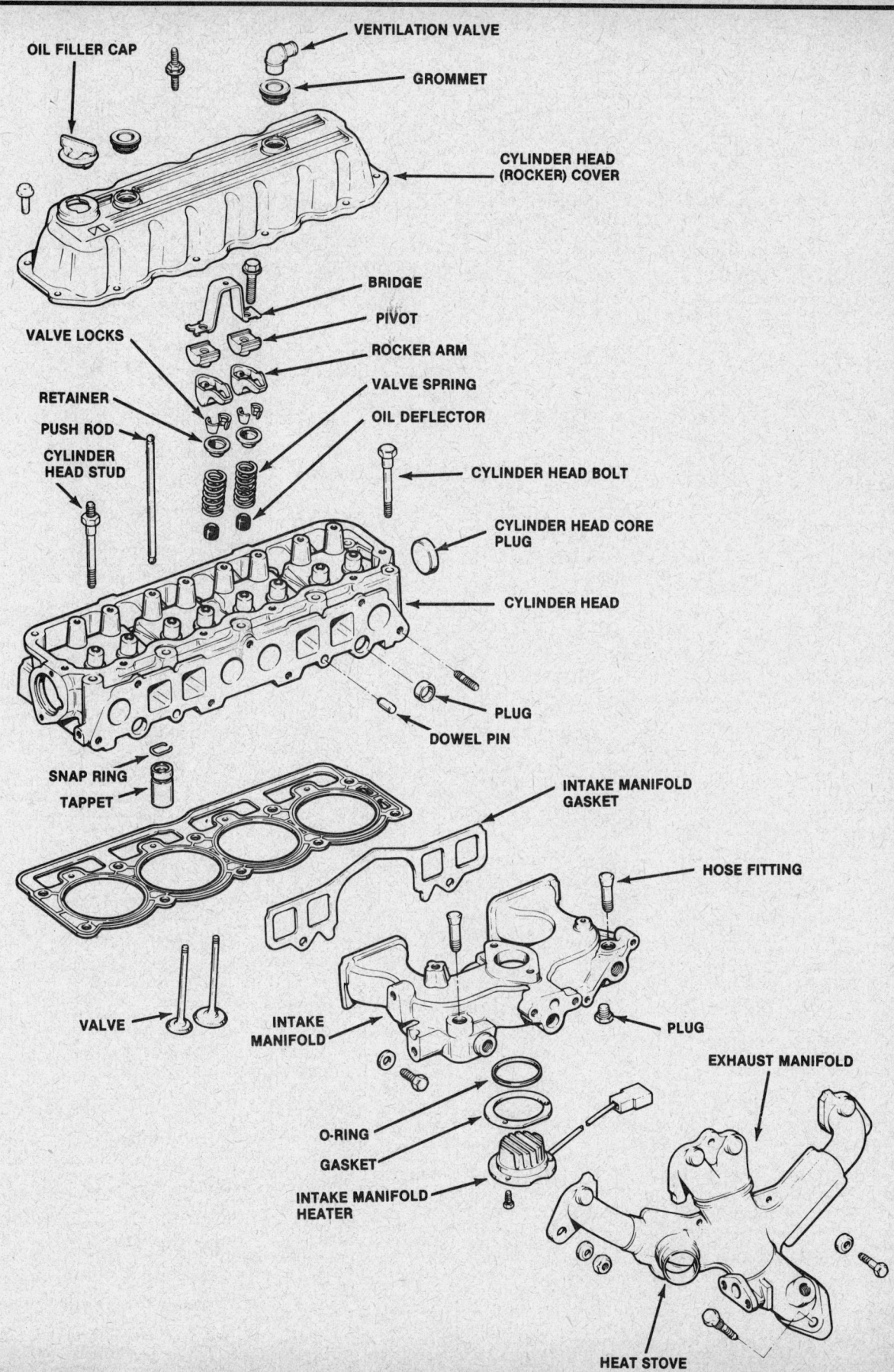

Exploded view of cylinder head, intake & exhaust manifolds. 4-150

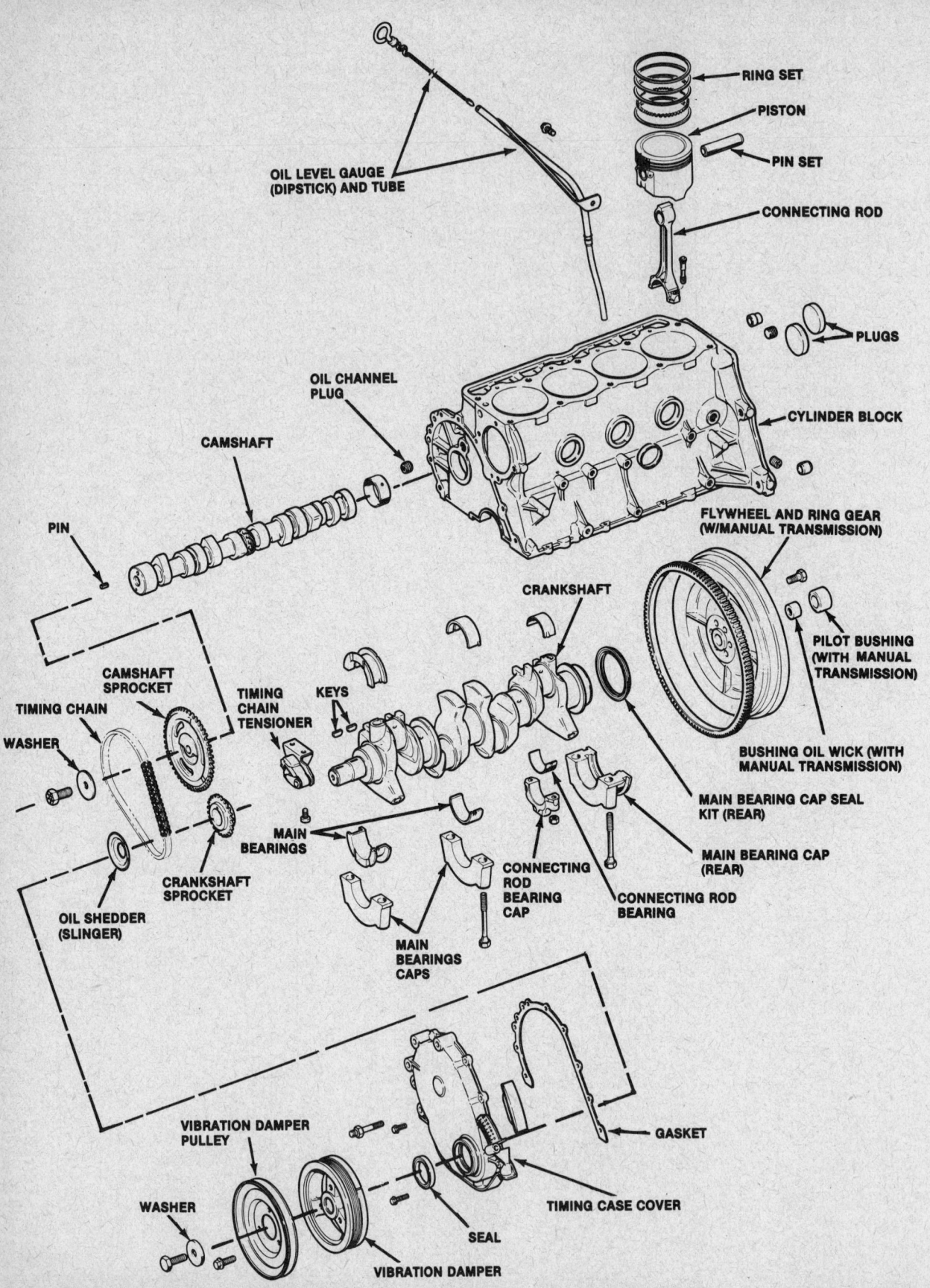

RING SET

PISTON

PIN SET

CONNECTING ROD

OIL LEVEL GAUGE
(DIPSTICK) AND TUBE

PLUGS

OIL CHANNEL
PLUG

CYLINDER BLOCK

CAMSHAFT

FLYWHEEL AND RING GEAR
(W/MANUAL TRANSMISSION)

PIN

CRANKSHAFT

PILOT BUSHING
(WITH MANUAL
TRANSMISSION)

CAMSHAFT
SPROCKET

TIMING
CHAIN
TENSIONER

KEYS

TIMING CHAIN

BUSHING OIL WICK (WITH
MANUAL TRANSMISSION)

WASHER

MAIN BEARING CAP SEAL
KIT (REAR)

MAIN
BEARINGS

MAIN BEARING CAP
(REAR)

CRANKSHAFT
SPROCKET

CONNECTING
ROD
BEARING
CAP

CONNECTING ROD
BEARING

OIL SHEDDER
(SLINGER)

MAIN
BEARINGS
CAPS

VIBRATION DAMPER
PULLEY

GASKET

WASHER

TIMING CASE COVER

SEAL

VIBRATION DAMPER

Exploded view of cylinder block & components. 4-150

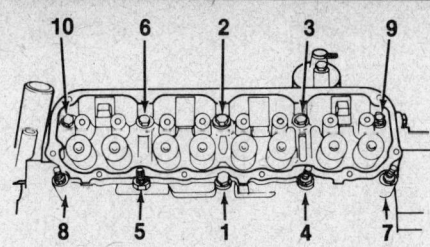

Fig. 1 Cylinder head tightening sequence. 4-150

age.

26. If equipped with manual transmission:
    a. Remove clutch housing cover and clutch bellcrank inner support screws.
    b. Disconnect springs and remove bell-crank.
    c. Remove outer bellcrank to strut rod bracket retainer.
    d. Disconnect back-up lamp switch wiring harness under hood at dash panel to gain access to clutch housing screw.
27. On all models, remove engine mount cushion to bracket screws.
28. To remove front axle assembly, proceed as follows:
    a. Support axle assembly, then remove half shaft to axle flange attaching bolts.
    b. Compress half shafts inward, toward wheels, and secure to frame side sills with wire.
    c. Remove axle bracket attaching bolts at axle tube and right hand engine mount, then remove axle bracket.
    d. Remove axle bracket attaching bolts at pinion end of axle.
    e. Remove left engine mount support to front axle bracket attaching bolts.
    f. Disconnect axle vent hose, then lower axle assembly and remove from vehicle.
29. Disconnect exhaust pipe from manifold.
30. Remove upper converter or clutch housing screws and loosen the bottom screws.
31. Raise vehicle and support on jackstands.
32. Remove air conditioning compressor drive belt idler pulley and the compressor mounting bracket, if equipped.
33. Install suitable engine lifting equipment and slightly raise engine. Support transmission with a suitable jack.
34. Remove remaining converter or clutch housing screws.
35. Remove engine from vehicle.
36. Reverse procedure to install.

CYLINDER HEAD, REPLACE

1. Disconnect battery ground cable, then drain cooling system.
2. Remove intake and exhaust manifold bolts. Remove manifolds and intake manifold gasket.
3. Remove valve cover bolts and valve cover.
4. Alternately loosen rocker arm capscrews, then remove bridges, pivots and rocker arms.
5. Remove push rods and spark plugs.
6. Remove cylinder head bolts and cylinder head.
7. Reverse procedure to install. Coat cylinder head gasket with a suitable sealer and install gasket with the word "TOP" facing upward. Install cylinder head bolts and torque to specifications in sequence, Fig. 1. Coat threads of stud No. 8 with a suitable sealer and torque nut to 75 ft. lbs. Torque intake and exhaust manifold bolts to 23 ft. lbs. in sequence, Fig. 2.

VALVE ARRANGEMENT

Front to Rear

4-150 . . . . E-I-I-E-E-I-I-E

VALVE LIFT SPECS.

Engine	Year	Intake	Exhaust
4-150	1983–84	.424	.424

VALVE TIMING SPECS.

Intake Opens Before TDC

Engine	Year	Degrees
4-150	1983–84	12

ROCKER ARMS, REPLACE

1. Remove rocker arm cover attaching screws, then remove rocker arm cover.

NOTE: RTV sealant is used between rocker arm cover and cylinder head mating surfaces. To avoid damaging rocker arm cover, do not pry cover upward until seal has been completely broken. When prying cover upward, pry only in areas marked "Pry Here," which are located near rocker arm cover bolt holes.

2. Alternately loosen the rocker arm cap screws one turn at a time to prevent damage to bridge, Fig. 3.
3. After removing rocker arm cap screws, remove bridge, pivots, rocker arms and push rods.

NOTE: Tag all components so they can be

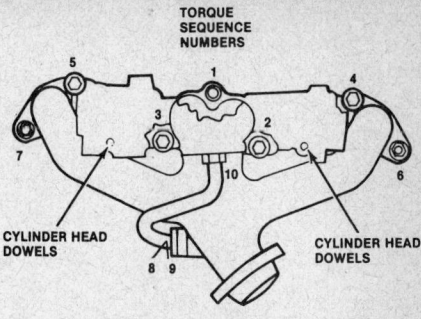

Fig. 2 Intake manifold tightening sequence. 4-150

reinstalled in the same position as removed.

4. Reverse procedure to install. When installing rocker arm cap screws, tighten each screw alternately and evenly approximately one turn at a time to prevent damage to bridge.

VALVE GUIDES

The valve guides are an integral part of the cylinder head. If valve stem to guide clearance is excessive, the guide should be reamed to the next oversize and the appropriate oversize valve installed. Valves are available in standard size and oversizes of .003 inch and .015 inch.

VALVE LIFTERS, REPLACE

Valve lifters may be removed after removing the cylinder head. Adjustable pliers with taped jaws may be used to remove lifters that are stuck due to varnish, carbon, etc. The type of lifter used on these engines is illustrated in Fig. 4.

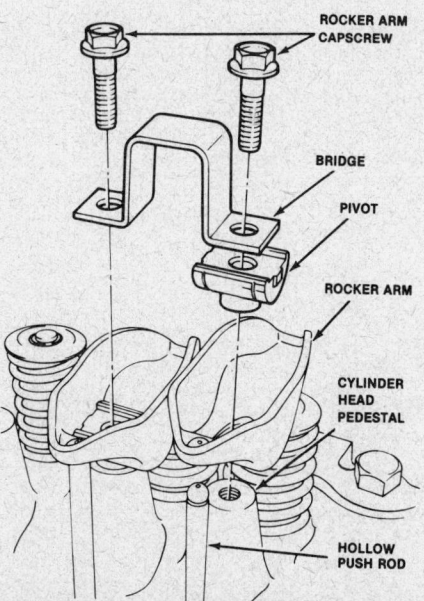

Fig. 3 Rocker arm, bridge & pivot assembly. 4-150

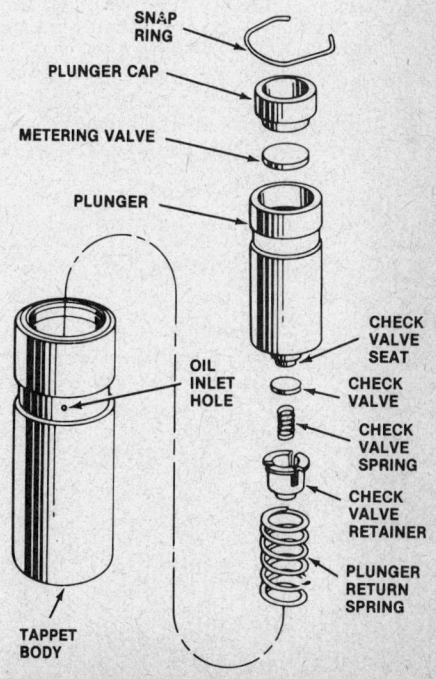

Fig. 4 Hydraulic valve lifter assembly. 4-150

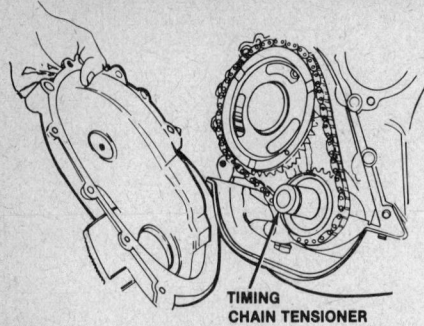

Fig. 5 Removing timing chain cover. 4-150

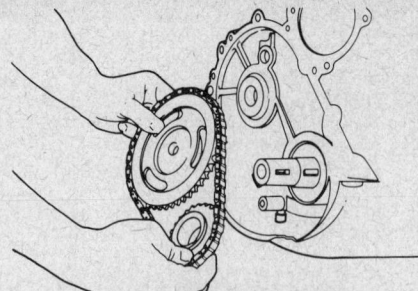

Fig. 6 Removing timing chain & gear sprockets. 4-150

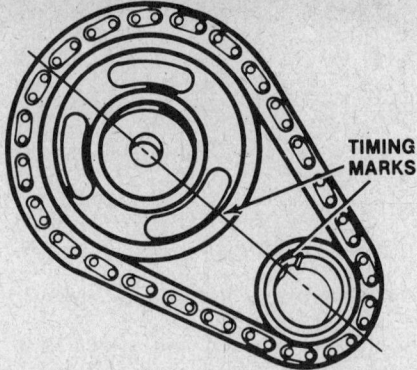

Fig. 7 Valve timing marks. 4-150

TIMING CASE COVER & TIMING CHAIN, REPLACE

Removal

1. Disconnect battery ground cable, then drain cooling system.
2. Remove bolts securing water and fuel pumps to engine, then water and fuel pumps.
3. Remove crankshaft pulley bolts and pulley.
4. Using tool No. J-9256 or equivalent, remove timing chain cover seal.
5. Remove timing chain cover bolts and cover.
6. Remove timing chain tensioner, Fig. 5.
7. Remove crankshaft oil slinger.
8. Remove camshaft sprocket retaining bolt and washer, then lift off camshaft sprocket, crankshaft sprocket and timing chain as an assembly, Fig. 6.

Installation

1. Install crankshaft sprocket, camshaft sprocket and timing chain as an assembly. Ensure crankshaft and camshaft sprocket timing marks are aligned, Fig. 7.
2. Install camshaft sprocket retaining bolt and washer. Torque camshaft sprocket retaining bolt to 50 ft. lbs.

NOTE: To verify correct installation of timing chain, rotate crankshaft to position camshaft sprocket timing mark at

one o'clock, Fig. 8. The crankshaft sprocket timing mark should now be at the three o'clock position. There should be 20 timing chain pins between the timing marks of both sprockets.

3. Install timing chain tensioner as follows:
   a. Turn tensioner lever to unlock (down) position, Fig. 9.
   b. Pull tensioner block toward tensioner lever. Hold tensioner block and turn tensioner lever to lock (up) position.
   c. Install timing chain tensioner on cylinder block and torque bolts to 14 ft. lbs.
   d. Turn timing chain lever to unlock (down) position. Ensure tensioner is released before installing timing chain cover.
4. Install oil slinger.
5. Using tool No. 22248 or equivalent for timing chain cover alignment, install timing chain cover, Fig. 10. Torque cover bolts to 5 ft. lbs.
6. Coat outside diameter of the timing chain cover seal with suitable sealer and install cover seal. With cover seal in position, coat inside diameter of seal lip with clean engine oil.
7. Insert draw screw of tool No. 9163 or equivalent into tool No. J-22248, Fig. 11. Tighten draw screw nut until tool comes in contact with timing chain cover.
8. Reverse steps 1 through 3 to complete installation procedure.

CAMSHAFT, REPLACE

1. Remove distributor, ignition wires and fuel pump.
2. Remove radiator from vehicle. If

equipped with A/C, remove condenser and receiver with refrigerant lines attached and position out of way.
3. Remove cylinder head and valve lifters.
4. Remove timing chain cover.
5. Rotate crankshaft until timing marks on sprockets are aligned, Figs. 7 and 8.
6. Remove sprockets and chain.
7. Remove front bumper or grille as required to remove camshaft.
8. Remove camshaft.
9. Reverse procedure to install.

PISTON & ROD ASSEMBLE

Pistons are marked with an arrow on the top perimeter, Fig. 12. When installing piston in engine, the arrow must face toward front of engine. Always assemble rods and caps with oil spurt holes facing camshaft. Check side clearance between connecting rod and crankshaft journal. Clearance should be .010 to .019 inch.

MAIN BEARINGS

The main bearing journal size (diameter) is identified by a color coded paint mark on adjacent cheek toward flanged (rear) end of crankshaft, except for rear main journal which is on crankshaft rear flange. Color codes used to indicate journal and corresponding bearing sizes are listed in Figs. 13 and 14.

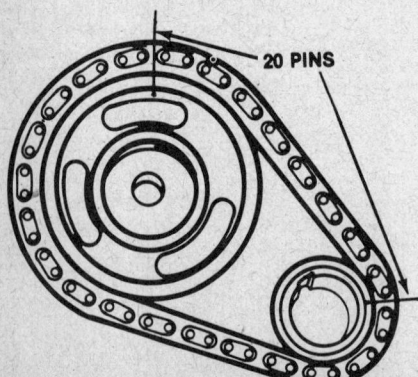

Fig. 8 Timing chain installation check. 4-150

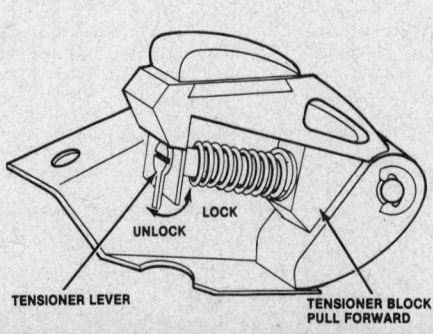

Fig. 9 Position timing chain tensioner in the unlock position. 4-150

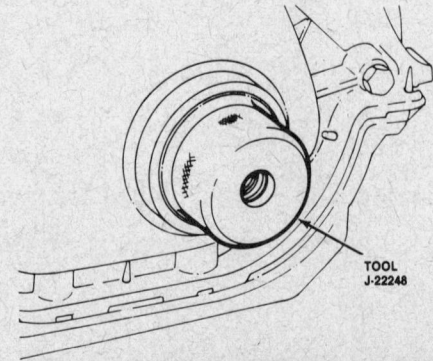

Fig. 10 Using tool No. J-22248 to align timing case cover. 4-150

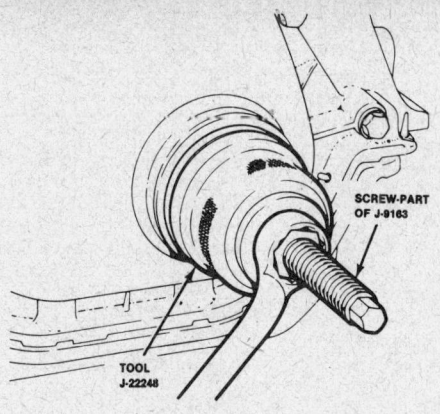

Fig. 11 Installing timing case cover front seal. 4-150

CONNECTING ROD BEARINGS

The connecting rod journal is identified by a color coded paint mark on adjacent cheek or counterweight toward flanged (rear) end of crankshaft. Color codes used to indicate journal sizes and corresponding bearing sizes are listed in Fig. 15.

OIL PAN, REPLACE

1. Disconnect battery ground cable.
2. Drain engine oil.
3. Lock steering wheel and remove air cleaner.
4. Support engine using a suitable holding fixture.
5. Raise vehicle and support on side sills.
6. Mark for assembly reference and disconnect front driveshaft.
7. Remove engine cushion bolts.

8. Remove bolts from sill-to-crossmember and position bar aside.
9. Loosen pitman arm at gear, then loosen idler arm at steering linkage.
10. Remove bolt from steering damper at crossmember.
11. Loosen sway bar bolts and lower sway bar bolts and lower sway bar.
12. Disconnect half shafts from axle.

NOTE: Compress half shafts in toward wheels, secure in compressed position with wire attached to frame sills.

13. Remove bolts from right bracket at axle tube bolt bars, then remove bolts from left upper axle bracket at upper end, and bolts from pinion end bracket at pinion.
14. Remove vent hose and remove axle assembly.
15. Support crossmembers with jack and remove crossmember nuts and bolts, then lower crossmember assembly for clearance.
16. Remove starter motor, then the torque converter housing access cover.
17. Remove oil pan screws and remove oil pan, Fig. 16.
18. Reverse procedure to install.

OIL PUMP, REPLACE

1. Drain crankcase, then remove oil pan, Fig. 16.
2. Remove bolts attaching oil pump to cylinder block, then remove oil pump and gasket.

NOTE: Do not disturb positioning of oil pump strainer and tube. If tube is moved a replacement tube and screen assembly must be installed.

3. Reverse procedure to install. Torque short attaching bolts to 10 ft. lbs. and long attaching bolts to 17 ft. lbs.

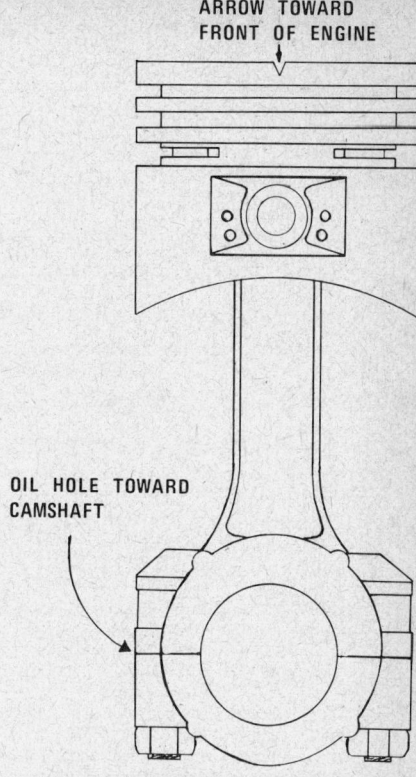

Fig. 12 Piston & rod assemble. 4-150

OIL PUMP SERVICE

1. Remove oil pump cover retaining screws, then remove cover from pump body.
2. Check gear end clearance as follows:
   a. Place straight edge across ends of gears and pump body, Fig. 17.
   b. Check clearance using a suitable feeler gauge.

Crankshaft No. 1 Main Bearing Journal Color Codes and Diameter in Inches (mm)	Cylinder Block No. 1 Main Bearing Bore Color Code and Size in Inches (mm)		Bearing Insert Color Code	
			Upper Insert Size	Lower Insert Size
Yellow — 2.5001 to 2.4996 (Standard) (63.5025 to 63.4898 mm)	Yellow —	2.6910 to 2.6915 (68.3514 to 68.3641 mm)	Yellow — Standard	Yellow — Standard
	Black —	2.6915 to 2.6920 (68.3641 to 68.3768 mm)	Yellow — Standard	Black — 0.001-inch Undersize (0.025 mm)
Orange — 2.4996 to 2.4991 (0.0005 Undersize) (63.4898 to 63.4771 mm)	Yellow —	2.6910 to 2.6915 (68.3514 to 68.3641 mm)	Yellow — Standard	Black — 0.001-inch Undersize — (0.001 mm)
	Black —	2.6915 to 2.6920 (68.3461 to 68.3768 mm)	Black — 0.001-inch Undersize (0.025 mm)	Black — 0.001-inch Undersize (0.025 mm)
Black — 2.4991 to 2.4986 (0.001 Undersize) (63.4771 to 63.4644 mm)	Yellow —	2.6910 to 2.6915 (68.3514 to 68.3641 mm)	Black — 0.001-inch Undersize — (0.025 mm)	Black — 0.001-inch Undersize — (0.025 mm)
	Black —	2.6915 to 2.6920 (68.3461 to 68.3768 mm)	Black — 0.001-inch Undersize (0.025 mm)	Green — 0.002-inch Undersize (0.051 mm)
Green — 2.4986 to 2.4981 (0.0015 Undersize) (63.4644 to 63.4517 mm)	Yellow —	2.6910 to 2.6915 (68.3514 to 68.3641 mm)	Black — 0.001-inch Undersize — (0.025 mm)	Green — 0.002-inch Undersize (0.051 mm)
Red — 2.4901 to 2.4896 (0.010 Undersize) (63.2485 to 63.2358 mm)	Yellow —	2.6910 to 2.6915 (68.3514 to 68.3641 mm)	Red — 0.010-inch Undersize (0.254 mm)	Red — 0.010-inch Undersize (0.254 mm)

Fig. 13 Main bearing selection chart. 4-150 No. 1 main bearing

Crankshaft Main Bearing Journal 2-3-4-5 Color Code and Diameter in Inches (Journal Size)	Bearing Insert Color Code	
	Upper Insert Size	Lower Insert Size
Yellow — 2.5001 to 2.4996 (Standard) (63.5025 to 63.4898 mm)	Yellow — Standard	Yellow — Standard
Orange — 2.4996 to 2.4991 (0.0005 Undersize) (63.4898 to 63.4771 mm)	Yellow — Standard	Black — 0.001-inch Undersize (0.025mm)
Black — 2.4991 to 2.4986 (0.001 Undersize) (63.4771 to 63.4644 mm)	Black — 0.001-inch Undersize (0.025 mm)	Black — 0.001-inch Undersize (0.025 mm)
Green — 2.4986 to 2.4981 (0.0015 Undersize) (63.4644 to 63.4517 mm)	Black — 0.001-inch Undersize (0.025 mm)	Green — 0.002-inch Undersize (0.051 mm)
Red — 2.4901 to 2.4896 (0.010 Undersize) (63.2485 to 63.2358 mm)	Red — 0.010-inch Undersize (0.054 mm)	Red — 0.010-inch Undersize (0.254 mm)

Fig. 14   Main bearing selection chart. 4-150 Nos. 2,3,4,5 main bearings

Crankshaft Main Bearing Journal 2-3-4-5 Color Code and Diameter in Inches (Journal Size)	Bearing Insert Color Code	
	Upper Insert Size	Lower Insert Size
Yellow — 2.0955 to 2.0948 (53.2257 - 53.2079 mm) (Standard) Orange — 2.0948 to 2.0941 (53.2079 - 53.1901 mm) (0.0007 Undersize) Black — 2.0941 to 2.0943 (53.1901 to 53.1723 mm) (0.0014 Undersize) Red — 2.0855 to 2.0848 (53.9717 to 53.9539 mm) (0.010 Undersize)	Yellow — Standard Yellow — Standard Black — 0.001-inch (0.025 mm) Undersize Red — 0.010-inch (0.254 mm) Undersize	Yellow — Standard Black — 0.001-inch (0.025 mm) Undersize Black — 0.001-inch (0.025 mm) Undersize Red — 0.010-inch (0.245 mm) Undersize

Fig. 15   Connecting rod bearing selection chart. 4-150

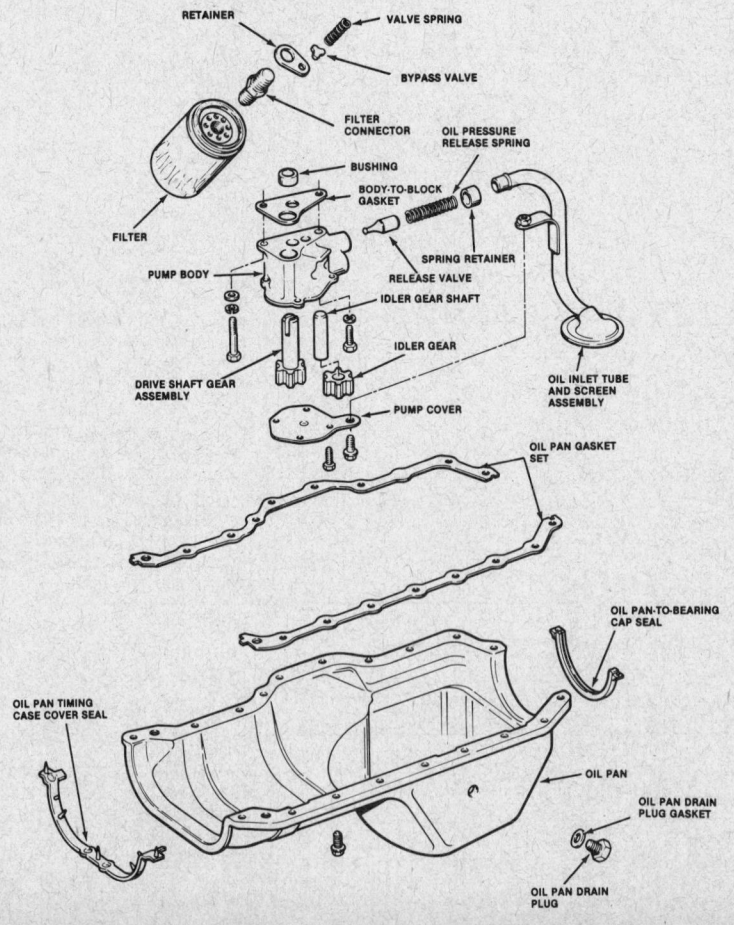

Fig. 16   Oil pan & oil pump. 4-150

c. Clearance should be .002 to .006 inch. If clearance is not within limits, replace oil pump assembly.

3. Check gear to pump body clearance as follows:
   a. Insert a suitable feeler gauge between gear tooth and pump body, Fig. 18.
   b. Clearance should be .002 to .004 inch. If clearance is not within limits, replace idler gear, idler shaft and drive gear assembly.

4. If pressure relief valve is to be checked, move pickup tube and screen assembly out of way. Remove spring retainer, spring and oil pressure relief valve plunger. Check pressure relief valve components for binding and clean or replace as necessary. After reinstalling relief valve components, install a replacement pickup tube and screen assembly.

NOTE: When replacing relief valve plunger, ensure correct size is installed. Plungers are available in standard size and .010 inch oversize.

5. If a replacement pickup tube is to be installed, apply a light coating of Permatex No. 2 sealant or equivalent to end of tube. Install pickup tube and screen using tool No. J-21882, Fig. 19.

6. Before installing pump cover, fill pump with petroleum jelly.

7. When installing pump cover, torque attaching screws to 70 inch lbs.

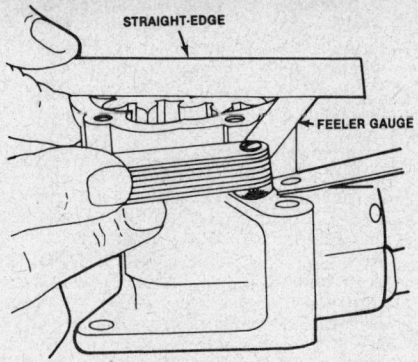

Fig. 17 Checking oil pump gear end clearance. 4-150

BELT TENSION DATA

	New Lbs.	Used Lbs.
V Type Belts		
A/C Comp.	125–155	90–115
Air Pump		
Less Power Steer.	125–155	90–115
W/Power Steer.	65–75	60–70
Alternator	125–155	90–115
Power Steer.	125–155	90–115
Serpentine Type Belt	180–200	140–160

WATER PUMP, REPLACE

1. Drain cooling system.
2. Disconnect radiator and heater hoses from water pump.
3. Remove drive belts.
4. If equipped, remove fan shroud attaching

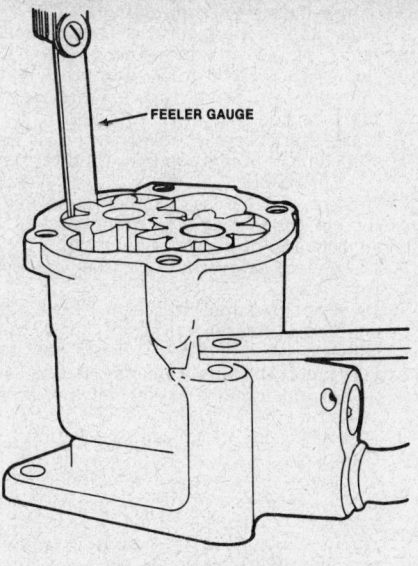

Fig. 18 Checking oil pump gear to body clearance. 4-150

screws, then remove fan and fan shroud.
5. Remove water pump attaching bolts, then remove water pump and gasket.
6. Reverse procedure to install. Torque water pump attaching bolts to 13 ft. lbs.

FUEL PUMP, REPLACE

1. Disconnect fuel lines from pump.
2. Remove retaining screws and fuel pump.

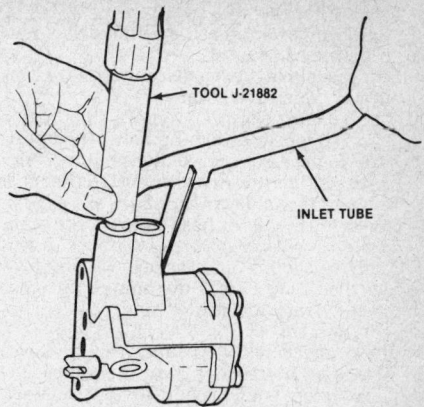

Fig. 19 Installing oil pump pickup screen & tube assembly. 4-150

3. Remove all gasket material from the pump and block gasket surfaces. Apply sealer to both sides of new gasket.
4. Position gasket on pump flange and hold pump in position against its mounting surface. Make sure rocker arm is riding on camshaft eccentric.
5. Press pump tight against its mounting. Install retaining screws and tighten them alternately.
6. Connect fuel lines. Then operate engine and check for leaks.

NOTE: When installing pump, crank engine to place camshaft eccentric in a position as to place the least amount of tension on fuel pump rocker arm. This will ease pump installation.

4-151 Engine Section

NOTE: Refer to the "1977–80 Chev. Monza • Buick Skyhawk • Olds Starfire • Pont. Sunbird chapter" for Service procedures not covered in this section.

ENGINE MOUNTS, REPLACE

NOTE: Remove fan shroud to radiator attaching screws to prevent damage to shroud.

1980–82 Concord & Spirit

Removal or replacement of any cushion can be accomplished by supporting the weight of the engine at the area of the cushion to be replaced.

1980–83 Eagle

Left Side
1. Disconnect heated air tube from air cleaner and exhaust manifold.
2. Remove bolts attaching engine cushion bracket to axle housing.
3. Remove engine mount through bolt, then

support engine using a suitable jack.
4. Remove engine cushion support bracket, then remove engine mount attaching bolts and engine mount.
5. Reverse procedure to install. Torque engine mount to engine bolts to 33 ft. lbs., cushion support bracket to engine bolts to 40 ft. lbs. and engine mount through bolt to 45 ft. lbs.

Right Side
1. Disconnect battery ground cable, then loosen left hand side engine mount through bolt.
2. Loosen bolts attaching engine cushion bracket to axle housing.
3. Remove right side engine mount through bolt, then remove engine cushion to bracket attaching bolts.
4. Disconnect axle tube at right hand side, then disconnect axle at pinion support.
5. Position a suitable jack under engine and raise engine slightly, then remove engine mount.
6. Reverse procedure to install. Torque en-

gine mount to engine bolts to 33 ft. lbs., cushion bracket bolts to 40 ft. lbs. and engine mount through bolts to 45 ft. lbs.

ENGINE, REPLACE

1980–82 Concord & Spirit

NOTE: On these models, the engine and transmission are removed as an assembly.

1. Disconnect battery ground cable, then drain cooling system.
2. Disconnect upper and lower radiator hoses at radiator.
3. Mark location of hinges on hood, then remove hood.
4. Remove air cleaner, fan and fan shroud.
5. On models equipped with automatic transmission, disconnect fluid cooler lines from radiator.
6. Remove radiator to support attaching

bolts, then remove radiator.
7. Remove power steering pump drive belt, if equipped.
8. On models less A/C, disconnect wire connector from alternator.
9. On models with A/C, remove compressor and condenser attaching bolts, then position compressor and condenser out of way with refrigerant lines connected. Remove evaporator to dryer line from sill clips.
10. Disconnect heater hose from intake manifold, then remove throttle cable clip and remove cable from bracket.
11. On models with A/C, disconnect wire connector from alternator and pull wiring through tube.
12. Disconnect pressure and return hoses from power steering gear, if equipped.
13. Disconnect module control solenoid, choke heater, idle speed solenoid and temperature sending unit wire connectors.
14. Detach dipstick tube from exhaust manifold, then remove tube and dipstick from block.
15. Remove engine mount nuts at crossmember and ground cable from left hand engine cushion bracket at engine.
16. Disconnect fuel hose from steel tube on right hand frame side rail.
17. Disconnect wiring from starter solenoid, distributor and oil pressure sending unit.
18. Loosen crossmember attaching bolts and lower crossmember slightly, then remove transmission oil cooler lines, if equipped, speedometer cable from transmission, transmission linkage, backup light switch wire connector, transmission rear mount and crossmember.
19. Disconnect exhaust pipe from exhaust manifold, then suspend exhaust pipe from strut rod bushing with wire.
20. On models equipped with manual transmission, disconnect clutch linkage.
21. Mark propeller shaft and pinion flange so they can be installed in the same position, then remove propeller shaft.
22. Using a suitable engine lifting device, remove engine and transmission from vehicle.
23. Reverse procedure to install.

1980–83 Eagle

NOTE: On these models, the engine is removed separately from the transmission.

1. Refer to the 1980–82 Concord and Spirit Engine, Replace procedure and perform steps 1 through 14.
2. Remove left front engine mount bracket

to axle housing attaching bolts.
3. Raise and support vehicle, then remove splash shield and disconnect both half shafts from front axle. Compress half shafts inward, toward wheels and secure to frame side sills with wire.
4. Mark front drive shaft so it can be installed in the same position, then remove front driveshaft.
5. Using a suitable jack, support front axle, then disconnect axle at right hand tube support and at pinion end of axle.
6. Disconnect axle vent tube, then remove front axle.
7. Remove axle support bracket from cylinder block, then remove starter motor and shims.
8. Disconnect wiring from distributor, oil pressure sending unit and backup light switch.
9. Disconnect fuel hose from steel line.
10. On models with manual transmission, disconnect clutch release cylinder from clutch housing. Position a wooden block between transfer case and skid plate, then remove clutch housing to engine attaching bolts.
11. On models with automatic transmission, disconnect manual linkage, then remove converter housing inspection cover and remove converter to flywheel attaching nuts. Remove converter housing to engine attaching bolts.
12. Disconnect exhaust pipe from exhaust manifold, then lower vehicle.
13. Remove engine mount attaching bolts, then attach a suitable engine lifting device and raise engine slightly.
14. Remove left engine mount bracket, then remove engine from vehicle.
15. Reverse procedure to install.

OIL PAN, REPLACE

1. Disconnect battery ground cable, then remove fan shroud attaching screws and slide shroud toward engine.
2. Raise vehicle and support at frame side sills, then drain crankcase.
3. On Eagle models proceed as follows:
   a. Using a suitable jack, support front axle.
   b. Mark front drive shaft so it can be installed in the same position, then remove drive shaft.
   c. Disconnect both half shafts from axle. Compress shafts inward, toward wheels, and secure to frame side sills with wire.
   d. Disconnect axle assembly at right hand axle tube, at left hand engine mount and at pinion mount.
   e. Lower axle assembly slightly and dis-

connect vent tube, then remove axle assembly.
4. Remove starter motor, then remove flywheel housing inspection cover.
5. Remove engine mount to crossmember attaching nuts.
6. Position a suitable jack under vibration damper and raise engine approximately 1 to 2 inches.
7. Remove crossmember right hand nut and screws and loosen left hand nut, then lower right side of front crossmember.
8. Remove oil pan attaching bolts, then pry crossmember downward on right side and remove oil pan.
9. Reverse procedure to install.

FUEL PUMP, REPLACE

1981–83 Eagle

1. Disconnect battery ground cable.
2. Remove alternator and harness as an assembly and position aside, then disconnect mounting bracket from cylinder block and intake manifold.
3. Loosen bottom bolt of intake manifold-to-right side engine cushion bracket and move bracket toward fender panel.
4. Disconnect carburetor vent hose and position aside.
5. Temporarily move coolant hoses to heater core to gain clearance, then disconnect vacuum hoses after tagging them.
6. Disconnect fuel inlet pipe at fuel pump, then disconnect fuel pump-to-carburetor pipe at pump.
7. Install engine holding fixture and remove right engine cushion through bolt and raise engine slightly.
8. Raise and support vehicle.
9. Disconnect right side engine cushion bracket from block and axle bracket, then lower vehicle.
10. Raise engine and position bracket to gain access clearance to fuel pump bolts, then remove fuel pump bolts and fuel pump.
11. Clean all gasket material from fuel pump-to-block mating surface, then install new gasket and fuel pump and torque to 15 ft. lbs.
12. Connect fuel pipes to fuel pump.
13. Connect engine cushion bracket to cylinder block and axle bracket, then lower engine onto cushion and remove holding fixture.
14. Install engine cushion through bolt and nut, then connect vacuum hoses and route heater hoses to original locations.
15. Install intake manifold-to-cushion bracket.
16. Install alternator mounting bracket and alternator, then install and adjust belts and reconnect battery ground cable.

Six Cylinder & V8 Engine Section

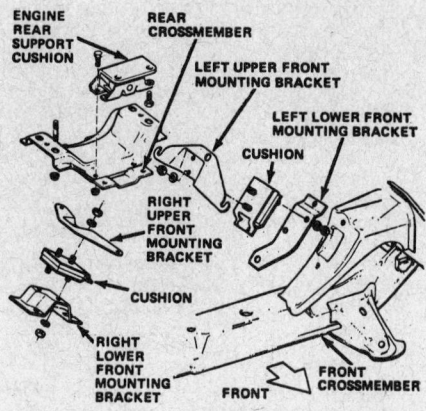

Fig. 1   Engine mounts. 1978–79 Pacer V8-304

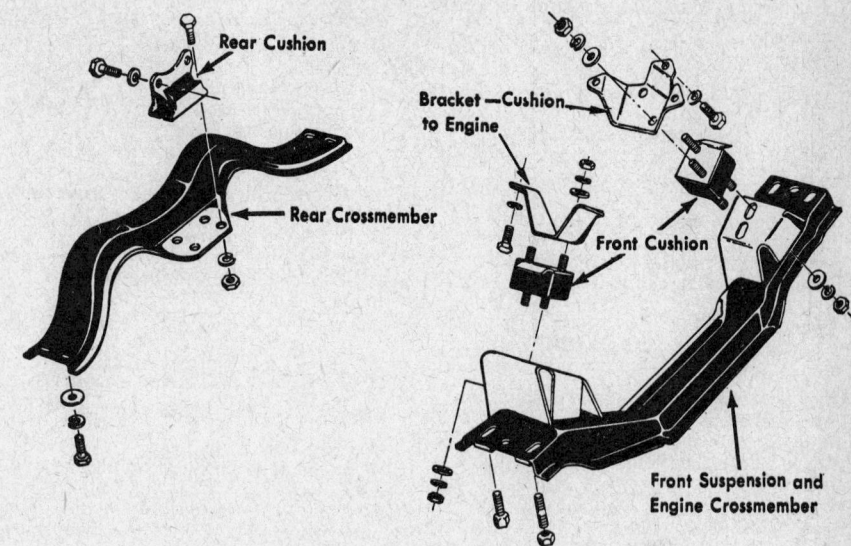

Fig. 2   Engine mounts. 1977–79 V8 except Pacer (typical)

ENGINE MARKINGS

A letter code is used to denote size of the bore, main bearings and rod bearings. On V8 engines, this code is stamped on the engine code tag. On six cylinder engines, this code is located on a boss above the oil filter. This letter code is as follows:

Letter "B"
 Cyl. bore .010″ oversize
Letter "M"
 Main bearings .010″ undersize
Letter "P"
 Rod bearings .010″ undersize
Letter "C"
 Camshaft block bore .010″ oversize
Letters "PM"
 Main and rod bearings .010″ undersize

ENGINE MOUNTS, REPLACE

1978–79 Pacer V8-304

NOTE: The right side mount must be removed before removing the left side mount.

Right Side
1. Remove air cleaner and ignition electronic control unit.
2. Attach suitable engine lifting equipment to engine and raise engine slightly.
3. Remove engine mount, Fig. 1.
4. Remove cushion from brackets.
5. Install cushion to brackets.
6. Install engine mount to engine and crossmember.

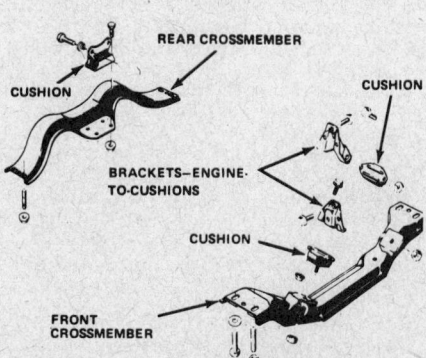

Fig. 3   Engine mounts. 1977–84 6 cyl. except Pacer (typical)

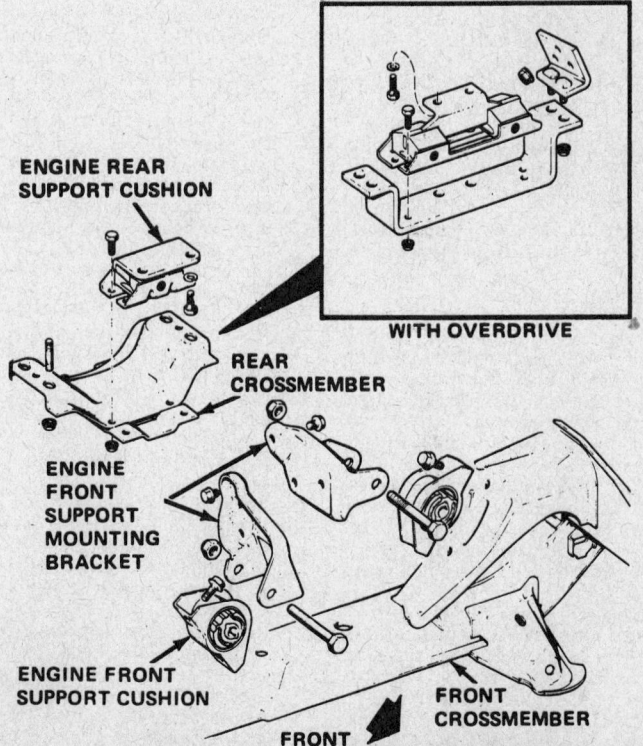

Fig. 4   Engine mounts. 1977–80 6 cyl. Pacer

7. Lower engine and remove lifting equipment.
8. Install ignition electronic control unit and air cleaner.

Left Side

1. Remove right side engine mount as outlined previously, Fig. 1.
2. Remove nuts and screw attaching upper left bracket to engine block.
3. Position engine toward right side of vehicle.
4. Remove engine mount from crossmember.
5. Remove cushion from brackets.
6. Install cusion to brackets.
7. Install engine mount to crossmember.
8. Position engine to left side of vehicle.
9. Attach upper bracket to engine block.
10. Install right side engine mount.

Exc. Pacer w/V8-304

Removal or replacement of any cushion can be accomplished by supporting the weight of the engine or transmission at the area of the cushion to be replaced, Figs. 2, 3 & 4.

ENGINE, REPLACE

1978–79 Pacer V8-304

NOTE: The engine and transmission is removed as an assembly.

1. Scribe hood hinge locations and remove hood. If equipped, disconnect underhood lamp wire.
2. Drain cooling system.
3. Remove grille, air cleaner and battery.
4. Disconnect transmission oil cooler lines from radiator, then remove the shroud and radiator assembly.
5. Remove fan attaching nuts and the fan.
6. If equipped with air conditioning, turn service valves clockwise to front seated position. Bleed refrigerant from compressor by slowly loosening the service valve fittings. Disconnect and cap the condenser and evaporator lines from compressor. Cap compressor service valve outlets. Disconnect receiver outlet at the coupling. Remove condenser and receiver assembly.
7. On all models, disconnect vacuum hoses, cable and heater hoses from heater housing.
8. Remove heater housing.
9. Disconnect the wiring at the following locations: alternator, oil pressure sending unit, ignition coil, A/C compressor, temperature sending unit, distributor, solenoid vacuum valve, TCS solenoid control switch and throttle solenoid.
10. Disconnect the hoses or lines at the following locations: fuel pump, power brake booster, fuel filter return, carburetor vapor vents, intake manifold heater vacuum hose and power steering pump.
11. Disconnect throttle cable and bracket.
12. Attach suitable engine lifting equipment to engine.
13. Raise vehicle and drain oil pan.
14. Disconnect neutral safety switch harness, starter motor wiring and speedometer cable.
15. Remove propeller shaft from vehicle.
16. Disconnect throttle valve and shift linkage.
17. Disconnect oil cooler lines from transmission.

18. Disconnect exhaust pipes from exhaust manifolds.
19. Loosen engine rear support crossmember to body retaining nuts. Do not remove the nuts.
20. Disconnect transmission linkage at shift lever.
21. On left side of engine, disconnect engine mount from engine block.
22. On right side of engine, disconnect engine mount from crossmember.
23. Disconnect steering shaft flexible coupling and position aside.
24. Support tramsmission with a suitable jack and remove the engine rear support crossmember to body nuts loosened previously.
25. Raise engine and transmission assembly from vehicle. Remove oil cooler lines when engine is moved forward.
26. Reverse procedure to install.

1977–79 V8 AMX, Concord, Gremlin, Hornet, Matador & Spirit

The engine is removed without the transmission.

1. Mark hood hinge locations, disconnect underhood lamp, if equipped, and remove hood.
2. Drain cooling system.
3. Disconnect transmission oil cooler lines, if equipped.
4. Disconnect radiator hoses from radiator.
5. Remove fan shroud screws, then the radiator and shroud.
6. Remove fan and spacer.
7. Remove air cleaner and disconnect purge hose at canister, TAC vacuum hose at manifold and TAC heat tube.
8. Install a 5/16 × 1/2 inch capscrew through the fan pulley, into the water pump flange.
9. Disconnect alternator wiring.
10. Disconnect neutral safety switch harness at cowl and the TCS harness at solenoid control switch and solenoid vacuum valve. Open clip on intake manifold and position harness on cowl.
11. Disconnect heater hoses from heater core and intake manifold.
12. Disconnect heater and A/C system vacuum hose from intake manifold.
13. Disconnect throttle cable and remove from bracket, then position aside.
14. Remove power brake vacuum check valve from power brake unit.
15. Disconnect temperature sender wire and throttle stop solenoid wire from connector near ignition coil.
16. Disconnect TCS solenoid control switch and the transmission cooler lines, if equipped.
17. Disconnect distributor leads, primary leads at coil and ground wire from coil bracket.
18. Remove fuel return hose from fuel filter.
19. Remove vapor canister and bracket.
20. Disconnect flexible fuel line from steel fuel line and plug lines.
21. If equipped with air conditioning:
    a. Remove service valve covers and front-seat valves.
    b. Loosen nuts attaching service valves to compressor head.
    c. Bleed compressor refrigerant charge.
    d. Remove service valves and cap compressor ports and service valves.
    e. Disconnect clutch feed wire.
22. If equipped with power steering, disconnect hoses from steering gear, drain res-

ervoir and cap hose fittings and gear ports.
23. On all models, raise and support vehicle on jackstands.
24. Remove starter.
25. Remove exhaust flange nuts, seals and heat valve.
26. Remove converter housing spacer cover.
27. Remove lower throttle valve bellcrank and inner manual linkage support. Disconnect throttle valve rod at lower end of bellcrank.
28. Remove converter attaching screws.
29. Remove exhaust support screws at transmission extension housing bracket, then lower the exhaust system.
30. Remove front motor mount to block attaching bolts.
31. Remove the four upper converter housing screws and loosen the lower screws.
32. Remove throttle cable housing retainer bracket.
33. Install suitable engine lifting equipment.
34. Slightly raise engine and support transmission with a suitable jack.
35. Remove the remaining converter housing screws.
36. Remove engine from vehicle.
37. Reverse procedure to install.

1977–84 Six Cyl. AMX, Concord, Eagle, Hornet, Matador & Spirit

The engine is removed without the transmission as follows:

1. Drain cooling system.
2. Mark hood hinge locations, disconnect underhood lamp, if equipped, and remove hood.
3. Disconnect battery cables and remove battery.
4. Disconnect alternator wiring and the ignition coil, distributor and oil pressure sender leads.
5. Remove TCS switch bracket from cylinder block, if equipped.
6. Disconnect flexible fuel line from fuel pump and plug line and pump port.
7. Disconnect engine ground strap.
8. Remove the right front engine support cushion to bracket screw.
9. If equipped with air conditioning:
    a. Remove service valve covers and front-seat valves.
    b. Loosen service valve to compressor attaching nuts.
    c. Bleed compressor refrigerant charge.
    d. Remove service valves and cap compressor ports and service valves.
    e. Disconnect clutch feed wire.
10. Remove starter.
11. Remove air cleaner and disconnect purge hose from canister and TAC vacuum hose from manifold, if equipped.
12. Disconnect throttle stop solenoid lead, if equipped.
13. Disconnect fuel return hose from fuel filter and the carburetor bowl vent hose from canister.
14. Disconnect throttle cable and remove from bracket. Disconnect throttle valve rod at carburetor and the bellcrank.
15. Disconnect heater and air conditioning system vacuum hose from intake manifold.
16. Disconnect temperature sender wire and TCS vacuum solenoid wiring harness.
17. Disconnect radiator hoses from radiator and the heater hoses from engine.
18. Disconnect transmission oil cooler lines from radiator, if equipped.
19. Remove fan shroud attaching screws,

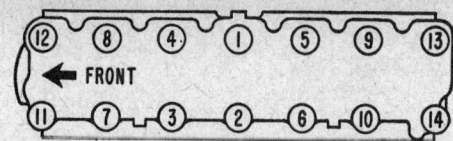

Fig. 5 Cylinder head tightening sequence 6-232, 258 engines. The No. 11 bolt must be sealed to prevent coolant leakage.

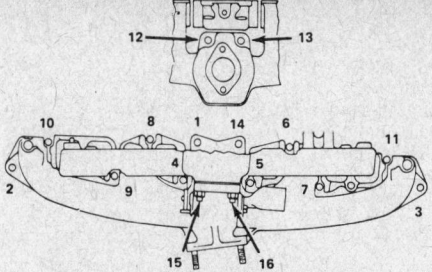

Fig. 6 Manifold tightening sequence. 1977-80 6-232 & 258

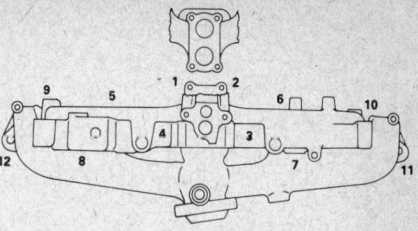

Fig. 7 Manifold tightening sequence. 1981-84 6-258

then the radiator and shroud.
20. Remove fan and spacer. Install a 5/16 × 1/2 inch capscrew through fan pulley, into water pump flange.
21. Remove power brake vacuum check valve from power brake unit, if equipped.
22. If equipped with power steering, disconnect hoses from gear and drain reservoir. Cap gear ports and hoses.
23. Remove transmission filler tube bracket screw, if equipped.
24. Raise and support vehicle on jackstands.
25. If equipped with automatic transmission:
    a. Remove converter housing spacer cover.
    b. Remove converter attaching screws.
    c. Remove exhaust pipe support from converter housing. This also supports the inner end of the transmission linkage.
26. If equipped with manual transmission:
    a. Remove clutch housing cover and clutch bellcrank inner support screws.
    b. Disconnect springs and remove bellcrank.
    c. Remove outer bellcrank to strut rod bracket retainer.
    d. Disconnect back-up lamp switch wiring harness under hood at dash panel to gain access to clutch housing screw.
27. On all models, remove engine mount cushion to bracket screws.
28. On Eagle models proceed as follows:
    a. Support axle assembly, then remove half shaft to axle flange attaching bolts.
    b. Compress half shafts inward, toward wheels, and secure to frame side sills with wire.
    c. Remove axle bracket attaching bolts at axle tube and right hand engine mount, then remove axle bracket.
    d. Remove axle bracket attaching bolts at pinion end of axle.
    e. Remove left engine mount support to front axle bracket attaching bolts.
    f. Disconnect axle vent hose, then lower axle assembly and remove from vehicle.
29. Disconnect exhaust pipe from manifold.
30. Remove upper converter or clutch housing screws and loosen the bottom screws.
31. Raise vehicle and support on jackstands.
32. Remove air conditioning compressor drive belt idler pulley and the compressor mounting bracket, if equipped.
33. Install suitable engine lifting equipment and slightly raise engine. Support transmission with a suitable jack.
34. Remove remaining converter or clutch housing screws.
35. Remove engine from vehicle.
36. Reverse procedure to install.

1977-80 Six Cyl. Pacer

The engine and transmission are removed as an assembly.
1. Mark hood hinge locations, disconnect underhood lamp, if equipped, and remove hood.
2. Drain cooling system and oil pan.
3. Disconnect heater and radiator hoses from engine.
4. Park W/S wiper at center of windshield to provide clearance for valve cover removal.
5. Remove battery.
6. Disconnect and cap transmission oil cooler lines, if equipped.
7. Remove fan shroud and radiator.
8. If equipped with air conditioning:
   a. Remove service valve covers and front-seat the valves.
   b. Bleed refrigerant charge from compressor by loosening service valve fittings.
   c. Disconnect and cap condenser and evaporator lines from compressor. Cap the service valves.
   d. Disconnect receiver outlet at coupling.
   e. Remove condenser and receiver assembly.
9. Remove air cleaner assembly.
10. Disconnect wiring at the following components, if equipped: starter, ignition coil, distributor, alternator, A/C compressor, temperature sensing unit, oil pressure sending unit, solenoid vacuum valve, TCS solenoid control switch, throttle stop solenoid and brake warning lamp switch.
11. Disconnect the following lines, if equipped: fuel pump suction, power brake vacuum supply from manifold, fuel filter return, heater and A/C system vacuum supply from manifold, carburetor pressure vent and power steering.
12. Remove carburetor and cover intake manifold opening.
13. Remove valve cover and vibration damper.
14. Disconnect accelerator cable at control cable bracket.
15. Raise and support vehicle with jackstands.
16. Disconnect exhaust pipe at manifold.
17. Disconnect transmission linkage and, if equipped, clutch linkage.
18. Disconnect speedometer cable from transmission.
19. Remove propeller shaft and cap transmission output shaft.
20. Support transmission with a suitable jack and remove rear crossmember.
21. Install suitable engine lifting equipment and support engine weight.
22. Remove engine mount bracket to front support cushion attaching bolts, then the front support cushions.
23. Lower jack from transmission.
24. Raise vehicle with a suitable positioned under front crossmember until bottom of front bumper is approximately three feet from floor, then support vehicle at that

height with jackstands.
25. Remove oil filter and starter.
26. Raise front of engine and partially remove assembly by pulling upward until rear of cylinder head clears cowl.
27. Lower the vehicle and remove engine-transmission assembly.
28. Reverse procedure to install.

CYLINDER HEAD, REPLACE

Tighten cylinder head bolts a little at a time in three steps in the sequence shown in the illustrations. Final tightening should be to the torque specifications listed in the Engine Tightening table.

6-232 & 258

NOTE: On Pacer models, park windshield wiper blades at center of windshield to aid in removal cylinder head.

1. Drain cooling system and disconnect hoses at thermostat housing.
2. Remove air cleaner and disconnect fuel line and vacuum advance line.
3. Remove valve cover and gasket.

NOTE: During removal of valve cover, use a suitable putty knife or razor blade and break silicone seal between valve cover and cylinder head. Do not pry valve cover upward until seal has been completely broken.

4. Remove rocker arms and bridged pivot assemblies. Alternately loosen each cap screw one turn at a time to prevent damage to bridge.

NOTE: Label push rods, rocker arms and bridge pivots so they can be installed in the same position.

5. Disconnect power steering pump and air pump and position pumps and brackets aside. Do not disconnect hoses from pumps.
6. Remove intake and exhaust manifold assembly from cylinder head.
7. On models equipped with A/C, remove A/C drive belt idler bracket from cylinder head. Loosen alternator drive belt, then remove alternator bracket to cylinder head mounting bolt. Remove bolts from compressor mounting bracket and position compressor aside.
8. Disconnect ignition wires and remove spark plugs.
9. Disconnect temperature sending unit wire and battery ground cable.
10. Remove ignition coil and bracket assembly.

Fig. 8 Cylinder head tightening sequence on V8-304 & 360. The No. 7 bolt indicated (second from front on left bank only) must be sealed to prevent coolant leakage.

11. Remove cylinder head bolts, cylinder head and gasket.
12. Reverse procedure to install. Torque cylinder head bolts in sequence shown in Fig. 5 and torque manifold bolts in sequence shown in Figs. 6 and 7.

V8-304 & 360

1. Drain cooling system and cylinder block.
2. Remove valve cover and gasket.
3. Remove rocker arm, bridged pivot assemblies and push rods. Alternately loosen cap screws one turn at a time to prevent damage to bridge pivots.

NOTE: Label push rods, rocker arms and bridged pivot assemblies so they can be installed in the same position.

4. Disconnect ignition wires and remove spark plugs.
5. Remove intake and exhaust manifolds, then loosen all drive belts.
6. If right hand cylinder head is to be removed, remove battery ground cable from cylinder head. Detach alternator support brace from cylinder head. On models equipped with A/C, remove compressor mounting bracket from cylinder head.
7. If left hand cylinder head is to be removed, detach air pump and power steering pump mounting bracket, if equipped, from cylinder head.
8. Remove cylinder head bolts, cylinder head and gasket.
9. Reverse procedure to install. Torque cylinder head bolts in sequence shown in Fig. 8.

VALVE ARRANGEMENT

Front to Rear

All V8s . . . . E-I-I-E-E-I-I-E
6-232, 258 . . . . E-I-I-E-I-E-E-I-E-I-I-E

VALVE LIFT SPECS.

Year	Engine	Intake	Exhaust
1977–79	6-232 & 258		
	1 Bbl. Carb.	.375	.375
1977–79	6-258		
	2 Bbl. Carb.	.400	.400
1980–84	6-258	.405	.405
1977–79	V8-304, 360	.430	.430

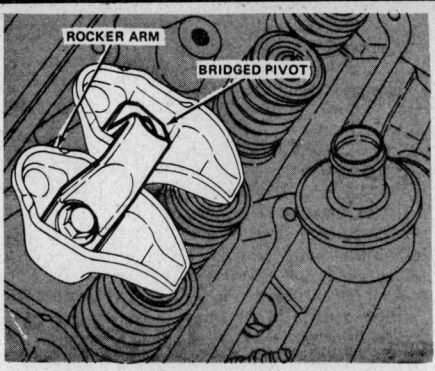

Fig. 9 Rocker arms, push rod and pivot assembly. Six cylinder & V8

VALVE TIMING

Intake Opens Before TDC

Year	Engine	Degrees
1977–80	Six①	12.12
1977–80	Six②	14.58
1981–84	Six②	9
1977–78	V8-304, 360	14¾

①—1 barrel carb.
②—2 barrel carb.

ROCKER ARMS

All engines have the intake and exhaust rocker arms pivoting on a bridged pivot assembly which is secured to the cylinder head by two cap screws, Fig. 9. When installing cap screws, turn each screw one turn at a time to avoid breaking the bridge. Torque cap screws to 19 ft. lbs.

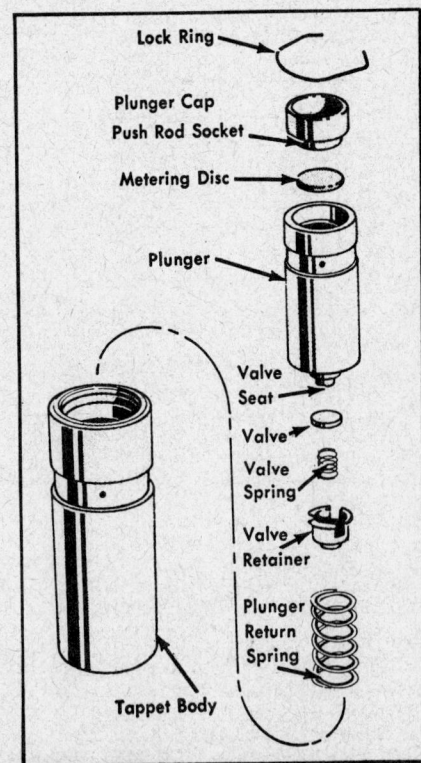

Fig. 11 Hydraulic valve lifter

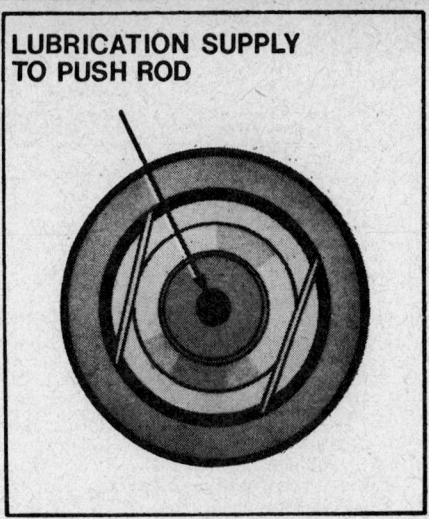

Fig. 10 Hydraulic lifter identification. Six cylinder & V8

The push rods are hollow, serving as oil galleries for lubricating each individual rocker arm assembly. Prior to installing, the push rods should be cleaned thoroughly, inspected for wear and deposits which may restrict the flow of oil to the rocker arm.

The push rods also serve as guides to maintain correct rocker arm to valve stem relationship; therefore, a contact pattern on the push rods where they contact the cylinder head is normal.

Lubrication to each rocker arm is supplied by the corresponding hydraulic valve lifter. A metering system located in each valve lifter consists of a stepped lower surface on the push rod cap that contacts a flat plate, causing a restriction, Fig. 10. The restriction meters the amount of oil flow through the push rod cap, hollow push rod, and upper valve train components. A loss of lubrication to the rocker arm could be caused by a restricted or plugged push rod or a defective hydraulic valve lifter.

CAUTION: Correct installation of push rods in these engines is critical and more than normal care must be taken upon installation. When placing the push rods through the guide hole in the cylinder head, it is important that the push rod end is inserted in the plunger cap socket. It is possible that the push rod may seat itself on the edge of the plunger cap which will restrict valve lifter rotation and lubrication to rocker arms.

It is recommended that, just prior to installation of the cylinder head covers, the engine be operated and the supply of lubrication to each rocker arm be visually inspected. If inspection reveals that an individual rocker arm is not being supplied with lubrication, the push rod and/or valve lifter must be inspected to determine the cause.

VALVE GUIDES

Excessive valve stem-to-guide clearance will cause lack of power, rough idling and noisy valves, and may cause valve breakage. Insufficient clearance will result in noisy and sticky functioning of valves and disturb engine smoothness of operation.

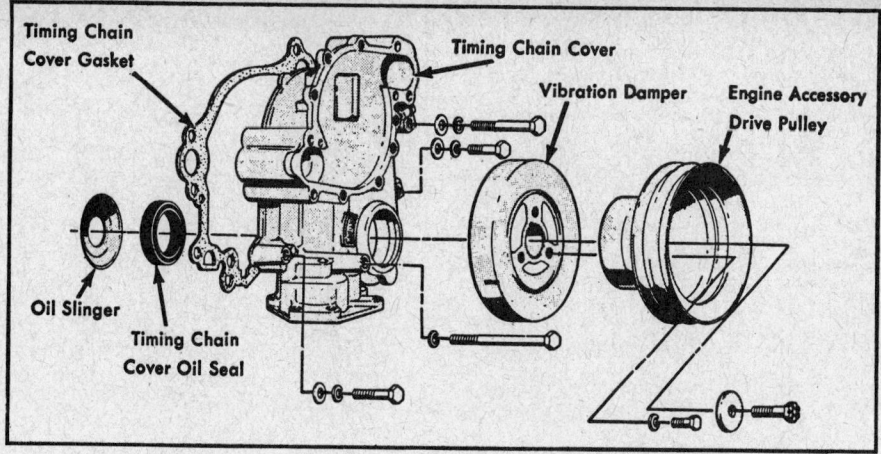

Fig. 12 Timing chain cover assembly. V8-304, 360 engines

Valve stem-to-guide clearances are listed in the Engine Valve Specifications table. By using a micrometer and a suitable telescope hole gauge, check the diameter of the valve stem in three places (top, center and bottom). Insert telescope hole gauge in valve guide bore, measuring at the center. Subtract the highest reading of valve stem diameter from valve guide bore center diameter to obtain valve-to-guide clearance. If clearance is not within specified limits, use the next oversize valve and ream bore to fit. Valves with oversize stems are available in .003", .015" and .030".

HYDRAULIC LIFTERS

Valve lifters may be removed from their bores after removing the cylinder head. Adjustable pliers with taped jaws may be used to remove lifters that are stuck due to varnish, carbon, etc. Fig. 11 illustrates the type of lifter used.

TIMING CASE COVER, REPLACE

6-232, 258

1. Remove drive belts, fan and pulley.
2. Remove vibration damper.
3. Remove oil pan-to-timing chain cover screws and cover-to-block screws.

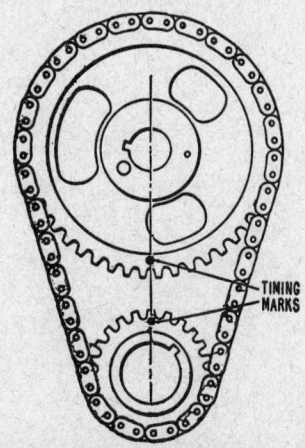

Fig. 13 Valve timing. V8 engines

4. Raise the cover and pull the oil pan front seal up enough to pull the retaining nibs from the holes in the cover.
5. Remove timing chain cover gasket from block. Cut off seal tab flush with front face of cylinder block. Clean gasket surfaces.
6. Remove oil seal.
7. Place gasket in position on cylinder block. Install new oil pan front seal, cut off protruding tab of seal to match portion of the original seal.
8. Insert suitable aligning tool in cover seal bore and on crankshaft. Install cover-to-oil pan screws and tighten lightly. Install cover screws and tighten.
9. Retighten all screws and install new cover seal.

V8-304, 360

The timing chain cover is a die casting incorporating an oil seal at the vibration damper hub, Fig. 12. On 1977 models, the crankshaft front seal is installed from the back side of the cover, therefore, it is necessary to remove the cover when replacement of the seal is required. On 1978–79 models, the oil seal may be installed from either side of the timing case cover, therefore it is not necessary to remove the cover to replace the oil seal. To remove cover, proceed as follows:

1. Drain cooling system completely.
2. Remove radiator hoses and bypass hose from cover.
3. Remove distributor, fuel pump, drive belts, fan and hub assembly, alternator, air pump and vibration damper, using a suitable puller.

NOTE: It is not necessary to disconnect power steering or discharge air conditioning system (if equipped). Remove units from their mounting brackets and place them aside.

4. Remove two front oil pan bolts and the eight hex head bolts retaining the cover to the cylinder block.

NOTE: Timing chain cover bolts are of various lengths. Note location of bolts during disassembly so they can be installed in original position.

5. Pull cover forward until free from locating dowel pins.

6. Remove used seal and clean seal bore and gasket surface of cover.
7. Apply sealing compound to outer surface of seal and a film of Lubriplate or equivalent to seal lips. Drive seal into cover bore until seal contacts outer flange of cover.

Installation of Cover
1. Prior to installation of cover, remove lower dowel pin from cylinder block.
2. Using a sharp knife or razor blade, cut oil pan gasket flush with cylinder block on both sides of oil pan.
3. Cut corresponding pieces of gasket from the replacement oil pan gasket set. Cement gasket to cover. Install replacement Neoprene oil pan seal into cover and align cork gasket tabs to the pan seal.
4. Apply a strip of sealing compound to both the cut-off oil pan gaskets at the oil pan to cylinder block location.
5. Place cover in position, install oil pan bolts in cover, tighten evenly and slowly until cover aligns with upper dowel. Then install lower dowel through cover. Drive dowel in corresponding hole in cylinder block.
6. Install cover attaching bolts and torque to 25 ft-lbs.

TIMING CHAIN

When installing a timing chain, see that the timing marks on the sprockets are in line as shown in Figs. 13, 14 and 15.

NOTE: All V8-360 heavy duty engines use a new double row roller type timing chain to improve timing chain durability. This new timing chain is available as a service replacement item and should be installed when timing chain failures occur to eliminate recurrence of the problem. Installation of the new timing chain requires the use of a new heavy duty camshaft sprocket and crankshaft sprocket.

CAMSHAFT, REPLACE

6-232, 258

1. Remove distributor and ignition wires and the fuel pump.

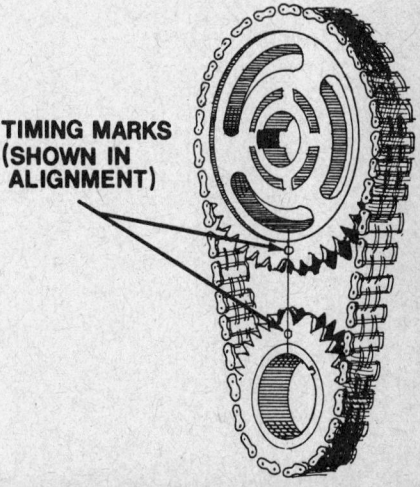

Fig. 14 Valve timing. V8-360 with double row roller timing chain

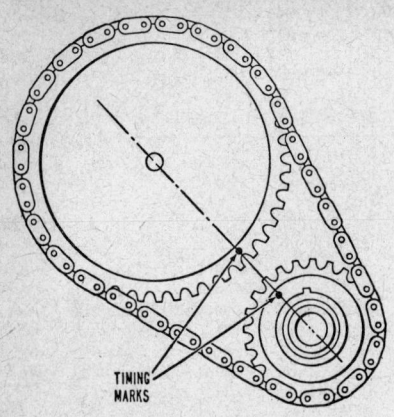

Fig. 15 Valve timing. 6-232, 258 engines

2. Remove radiator from vehicle. If equipped with A/C, remove condenser and receiver with refrigerant lines attached and position out of way.
3. Remove cylinder head and valve lifters.
4. Remove timing chain cover.
5. Rotate crankshaft until timing marks on sprockets are aligned, Fig. 15.
6. Remove sprockets and chain.
7. On all models except Pacer, remove front bumper or grille as required to remove camshaft.
8. On Pacer models, remove hood and raise engine sufficiently to permit camshaft removal.

NOTE: Mark hinge locations on hood panel for alignment during installation.

9. Remove camshaft.
10. Reverse procedure to install.

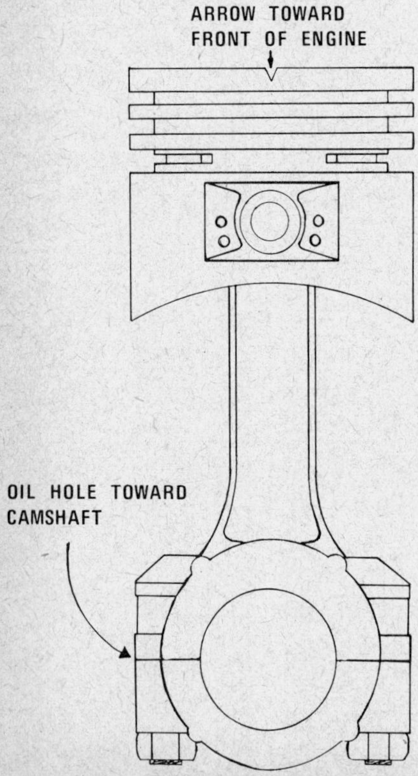

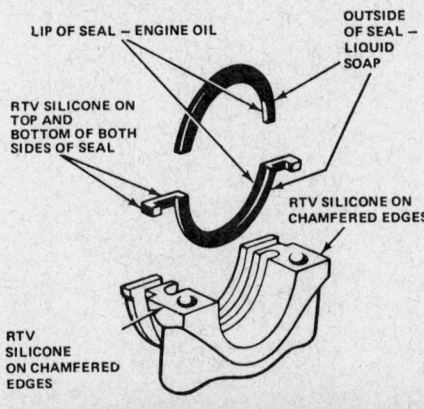

Fig. 17 Piston & rod assembly. 6-232, 258 engines

V8-304, 360

1. Disconnect battery ground cable.
2. Disconnect transmission cooler lines at radiator if so equipped.
3. Remove radiator and A/C condenser if equipped.
4. Remove distributor, wires and coil.
5. Remove intake manifold and carburetor as an assembly.
6. Remove valve covers, loosen rocker arms and remove push rods and lifters.
7. Dismount power steering pump.
8. Remove fan and hub, fuel pump and heater hose at water pump.
9. Remove alternator.
10. Remove vibration damper and pulley and lower radiator hose at water pump.
11. Remove timing chain cover, distributor-oil pump drive gear, fuel pump eccentric, sprockets and chain.

NOTE: Remove camshaft sprocket, crankshaft sprocket and timing chain as an assembly.

12. Remove hood latch support bracket upper retaining screws and move bracket as required to allow removal of camshaft.
13. Reverse procedure to install.

PISTONS & RODS, ASSEMBLE

V8 Engines

Assemble piston to connecting rod as shown in Fig. 16. Check side clearance between connecting rod and crankshaft journals. Clearance should be .006–.018 inch.

6 Cyl. Engines

Pistons are marked with a depression notch or arrow on the top perimeter, Fig. 17. When installed in the engine, this notch or arrow must be toward the front of the engine. Always assemble rods and caps with the cylinder numbers facing the camshaft side of engine. Check side clearance between connecting rod and crankshaft journals. Clearance should be .005–.014 inch on 1977–80 models and .010–.019 inch on 1981–84 models.

PISTONS, PINS & RINGS

Pistons are furnished in standard sizes and oversizes of .002, .005, .010 and .020″.
Piston pins are furnished in oversizes of .003 and .005″.
Piston rings are available in .020″ oversizes.

MAIN & ROD BEARINGS

Both main and rod bearings are supplied in undersizes of .001, .002, .010 and .012″.

CRANKSHAFT REAR OIL SEAL, REPLACE

1. To replace the seal, Fig. 18, remove oil pan and scrape oil pan surfaces clean.
2. Remove rear main bearing cap.
3. Remove and discard old seals.
4. Clean cap thoroughly.
5. Loosen all remaining main bearing cap screws.
6. With a brass drift and hammer, tap upper

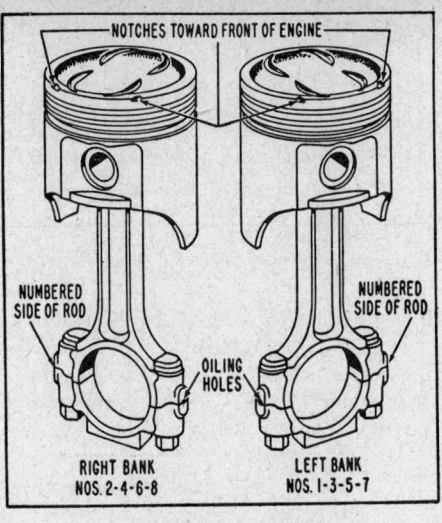

Fig. 16 Piston and rod assembly. V8-304, 360

seal until sufficient seal is protruding to permit pulling seal out completely with pliers.
7. Wipe seal surface of crankshaft clean, then oil lightly.
8. Coat back surface of upper seal with soap, and lip of seal with engine oil.
9. Install upper seal into cylinder block. Lip of seal must face to front of engine.
10. Coat cap and cylinder block mating surface portion of seal with RTV Silicone or equivalent, being careful not to apply sealer on lip of seal.
11. Coat back surface of lower seal with soap, and lip of seal with No. 40 engine oil. Place into cap, seating seal firmly into seal recess in cap.
12. Place RTV Silicone or equivalent on both chamfered edges of rear main bearing cap.
13. Install main bearings and install cap. Tighten all caps to correct torque as listed in the Engine Tightening Specifications table.
14. Cement oil pan gasket to cylinder block with tongue of gasket at each end coated with RTV Silicone or equivalent before installing into rear main bearing cap at joint of tongue and oil pan front neoprene seal.
15. Coat oil pan rear seal with soap. Place into recess of rear main bearing cap, making certain seal is firmly and evenly seated.
16. Install oil pan and tighten drain plug securely.

Fig. 18 Rear main bearing sealing

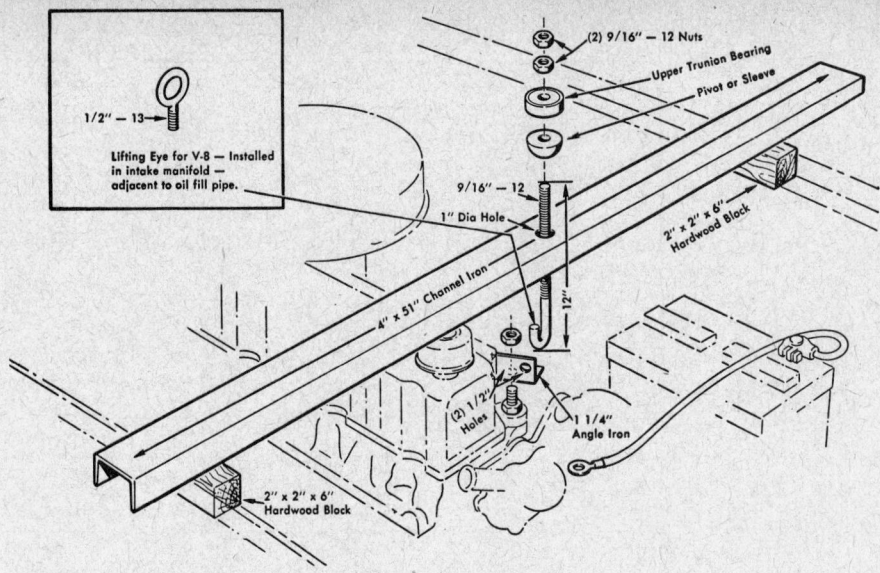

Fig. 19 Engine lifting fixture

Labels on figure:
- 1/2" – 13
- Lifting Eye for V-8 — Installed in intake manifold — adjacent to oil fill pipe.
- (2) 9/16" – 12 Nuts
- Upper Trunion Bearing
- Pivot or Sleeve
- 9/16" – 12
- 1" Dia Hole
- 2" x 2" x 6" Hardwood Block
- 4" x 51" Channel Iron
- 12"
- (2) 1/2" Holes
- 1 1/4" Angle Iron
- 2" x 2" x 6" Hardwood Block

OIL PAN, REPLACE

1977—80 Pacer 6 Cyl.

1. Drain oil, then install engine holding fixture.
2. Disconnect steering shaft flexible coupling and position out of way.
3. Raise vehicle and support on side sills.
4. Remove front engine mount through bolts.
5. Disconnect brake lines from front wheel cylinders, then disconnect upper ball joints from spindles.

NOTE: Ensure shock absorber is securely attached.

6. Remove upper control arm and position aside.
7. Support front crossmember with jack, then remove nuts from rear mounts and swing crossmember forward.
8. Remove starter.
9. Remove oil pan and front and rear oil pan seals.
10. Reverse procedure to install.

1978—79 Pacer V8-304

Removal

1. Disconnect battery ground cable.
2. Remove air cleaner and ignition control unit.
3. Attach suitable engine lifting equipment to engine and lift engine.
4. Raise and support vehicle.
5. Remove front wheels.
6. Remove brake calipers and suspend caliper with a wire.
7. Remove upper ball joint nuts, then the upper control arms.
8. Disconnect steering shaft flexible coupling and position aside.
9. On left side of engine, disconnect engine mount from engine block.
10. On right side of engine, remove engine mount.
11. Disconnect transmission oil cooler lines.

12. Remove sway bar.
13. Lower vehicle and support crossmember with a suitable jack.
14. Remove nuts from rear crossmember insulators and lower the crossmember.
15. Raise and support vehicle.
16. Drain oil pan and remove starter motor.
17. Remove torque converter inspection cover, then the oil pan.
18. Remove gaskets and seals.
19. Clean gasket surface of oil pan and cylinder block.
20. Clean oil pan sump.

Installation

1. Install oil pan front seal to timing case cover.
2. Apply an adequate amount of RTV sealer to end tabs.
3. Apply an adequate amount of RTV sealer to gasket contacting surface of seal end tabs.
4. Install seal in recess of rear main bearing cap, seating the seal fully.
5. Apply engine oil to oil pan contacting surface of front and rear oil pan seals.
6. Cement oil pan side gaskets onto cylinder block.
7. Apply an adequate amount of RTV sealer to gasket ends.
8. Install oil pan. Torque 1/4-20 screws to 7 ft. lbs. and the 5/16-18 screws to 11 ft. lbs.
9. Install and tighten oil pan drain plug.
10. Install torque converter inspection cover and starter motor.
11. Install right side engine mount.
12. Lower vehicle and install crossmember.
13. Lower engine and connect engine mounts.
14. Remove engine lifting equipment.
15. Install ignition control unit and air cleaner.
16. Raise vehicle and install upper control arms and the upper ball joint nuts.
17. Install brake calipers and front wheels.
18. Install sway bar.
19. Connect transmission oil cooler lines.
20. Connect steering shaft flexible coupling.
21. Connect battery ground cable.

1977—83 All Exc. Pacer & Eagle

6 Cyl.

1. Disconnect battery ground cable.
2. Turn steering wheel to full left lock.
3. Support engine using a suitable holding fixture, Fig. 19.
4. Raise vehicle and support on side sills.
5. Disconnect steering idler arm at side sill.
6. Disconnect engine front support cushions at engine brackets.
7. Loosen sway bar link nuts to end of threads, if equipped.
8. Remove front crossmember to side sill attaching bolts, then pull crossmember down.
9. Remove engine right support bracket from engine.
10. Loosen strut rods at lower control arms; do not remove screws.
11. Remove starter motor.
12. Drain crankcase, then remove oil pan attaching bolts and oil pan.
13. Clean gasket surfaces of oil pan and engine block. Remove all sludge and dirt from oil pan sump.
14. Reverse procedure to install.

1980—84 Eagle

6 Cyl.

1. Disconnect battery ground cable.
2. Drain engine oil.
3. Lock steering wheel and remove air cleaner.
4. Support engine using a suitable holding fixture.
5. Raise vehicle and support on side sills.
6. Mark for assembly reference and disconnect front driveshaft.
7. Remove engine cushion bolts.
8. Remove bolts from sill-to-crossmember and position bar aside.
9. Loosen pitman arm at gear, then loosen idler arm at steering linkage.
10. Remove bolt from steering damper at crossmember.
11. Loosen sway bar bolts and lower sway bar bolts and lower sway bar.
12. Disconnect half shafts from axle.

NOTE: Compress half shafts in toward wheels, secure in compressed position with wire attached to frame sills.

13. Remove bolts from right bracket at axle tube bolt bars, then remove bolts from left upper axle bracket at upper end, and bolts from pinion end bracket at pinion.
14. Remove vent hose and remove axle assembly.
15. Support crossmembers with jack and remove crossmember nuts and bolts, then lower crossmember assembly for clearance.
16. Remove starter motor, then the torque converter housing access cover.
17. Remove oil pan screws and remove oil pan.
18. Reverse procedure to install.

1977—79 All Exc. Pacer

V8-304 & 360

1. Disconnect battery ground cable.
2. Support engine using a suitable holding fixture, Fig. 19.
3. Raise vehicle and support on side sills.
4. Drain engine oil, then disconnect steering idler arm and sway bar brackets at side sills.

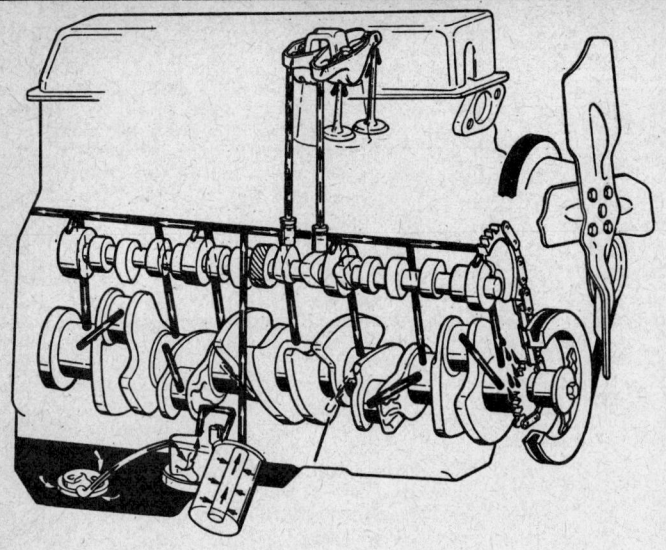

Engine oiling system. 6-232, 258

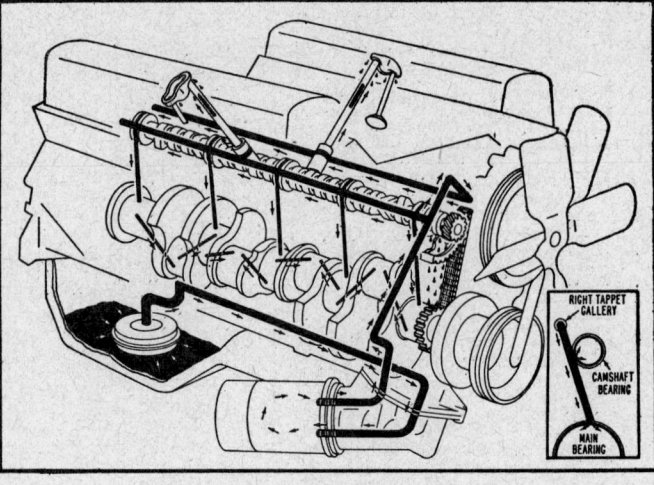

Engine oiling system. V8-304, 360 engines

5. Disconnect strut rods at lower control arms.
6. Disconnect engine to body ground cable.
7. Disconnect engine support cushions at crossmember.
8. Remove crossmember to side sill attaching bolts, then pull crossmember down.
9. Remove starter motor, then remove oil pan attaching bolts and oil pan.
10. Remove oil pan front and rear oil seals. Clean engine and pan gasket surfaces.
11. Remove all sludge and dirt from oil sump.
12. Reverse procedure to install.

OIL PUMP

6-232, 258 & V8s

NOTE: When servicing oil pump on 6 cylinder engines if inlet tube is moved out of position a new inlet tube and screen assembly must be installed.

The oil pump on six cylinder models is located in the oil pan thus necessitating removal of the pan to gain access to the pump. The pump on V8 engines is an integral part of the timing case cover and it can be serviced after removal of the oil filter adapter body.

Oil pump removal or replacement will not affect distributor timing as the distributor drive gear remains in mesh with the camshaft gear.

Upon disassembly of the oil pump, place a straightedge across gears and pump body and check clearance between straightedge and pump body which should be .004–.008 inch for 1977 engines, and 1978–80 6 cyl. engines and .004–.0065 inch for 1978–79 V8 engines and .006–.004 inch for 1981–84 6 cyl. engines. Clearance between gears and pump housing should be .0005–.0025 for 1977–79 V8 engines and all 6 cylinder engines.

NOTE: The pump cover should be installed with the pump out of the engine and pump checked for freedom of operation before installation.

The oil pressure relief valve, which is built into the pump, is not adjustable, the correct pressure being built into the relief valve spring.

BELT TENSION DATA

	New Lbs.	Used Lbs.
1977–84		
Air Condition	125–155	90–115
Air Pump—		
Except 6 cyl.	125–155	90–115
With P.S.		
6 cyl. with P.S.		
(3/8 inch belt)	65–75	60–70
Fan and Power		
Steering	125–155	90–115

WATER PUMP, REPLACE

NOTE: On 1981–84 6-258 California engines equipped with a serpentine drive belt, the water pump and fan drive assembly will operate in the reverse rotation of an engine not equipped with a serpentine drive belt. Water pumps for use on these engines can be identified by the letters "REV" cast into the pump body, while fan components can be identified by the word "REVERSE" stamped on the fan drive and on the inner side of the fan.

1. Disconnect battery ground cable.
2. Drain cooling system and disconnect radiator and heater hoses from pump.
3. Remove drive belts.

4. On V8 models, remove power steering pump, air pump and mounting bracket assembly from engine and position aside. Do not disconnect hoses.
5. On V8 models, remove A/C compressor and bracket as an assembly and position aside if equipped. Do not discharge system.

NOTE: On some models it will be necessary to remove alternator front bracket and place alternator aside, without disconnecting wires.

6. Remove fan shroud attaching bolts, then remove fan, hub and shroud.
7. Remove water pump and gasket.
8. Reverse procedure to install.

FUEL PUMP, REPLACE

1. Disconnect fuel lines from pump.
2. Remove retaining screws and fuel pump.
3. Remove all gasket material from the pump and block gasket surfaces. Apply sealer to both sides of new gasket.
4. Position gasket on pump flange and hold pump in position against its mounting surface. Make sure rocker arm is riding on camshaft eccentric.
5. Press pump tight against its mounting. Install retaining screws and tighten them alternately.
6. Connect fuel lines. Then operate engine and check for leaks.

NOTE: When installing pump, crank engine to place camshaft eccentric in a position as to place the least amount of tension on fuel pump rocker arm. This will ease pump installation.

Clutch, Transmission & Transfer Case Section

CLUTCH PEDAL, ADJUST

Pedal Free Play

1980–83 4-151 & 1983–84 4-150

These models are equipped with a hydraulic actuated clutch and no adjustment is required.

1977–79 4-121

1. Raise vehicle and remove screw attaching throwout lever boot to clutch housing, then the boot.
2. Loosen clutch cable locknut at transmission side of clutch housing, Fig. 1, View A.
3. Pull cable housing toward front of vehicle until throwout lever free play is eliminated, then rotate the adjuster nut toward rear of vehicle until adjuster nut face tabs contact housing boss, Fig. 1, View B.
4. Release cable housing and rotate adjuster nut until adjuster nut tabs engage clutch housing slots.
5. Torque clutch cable locknut to 25 ft. lbs.
6. Install throwout lever boot and attaching screw.
7. Lower vehicle.

Exc. 4-121, 150 & 151

In order to provide sufficient free movement of the clutch release bearing when the clutch is engaged and pedal fully released, free pedal play should be $7/8''$ to $1\,1/8''$ with desired free play of $1\,1/8''$ for 1977–84.

Adjustment for free pedal play is made by varying the length of the beam or link to the release lever rod. Lengthening this rod reduces pedal travel; shortening it increases pedal play, Fig. 2.

CLUTCH, REPLACE

4-121

Removal

1. Remove gearshift lever bezel and slide outer and inner boots toward top of lever.
2. Fold carpet and straighten all gearshift lever lock tabs bent downward.
3. Remove gearshift lever locknut and the gearshift lever.
4. Raise and support vehicle, then remove propeller shaft.
5. Disconnect speedometer cable and adapter from transmission.
6. Disconnect back-up lamp switch wires and disengage wire harness from clips on transmission top cover.
7. Remove starter motor.
8. Loosen clutch cable locknut and back off adjuster nut to slacken cable. Slide cable toward clutch housing until cushion and cable ball can be disengaged from throwout lever, Fig. 3.
9. Remove inspection cover at front of clutch housing.
10. Remove bolts attaching catalytic converter support bracket to transmission rear support bracket.
11. Support engine with a suitable jack.
12. Remove nuts and bolts attaching transmission support cushion to rear crossmember.
13. Remove rear crossmember.
14. Support transmission with a suitable jack and remove clutch housing to engine bolts.
15. Remove clutch housing and transmission.

16. Mark clutch cover and flywheel alignment.
17. Remove clutch cover bolts, then the cover and driven plate.

NOTE: Loosen the clutch cover-bolts evenly and alternately to prevent cover distortion.

Installation

NOTE: The clutch cover is positioned on dowel pins located on the flywheel face.

When installing the driven plate and cover, the cover must be indexed with the alignment marks and be properly engaged with the dowel pins.

1. Position clutch driven plate and cover, then install the attaching bolts finger tight.
2. Align clutch driven plate with tool J-5824-01 or equivalent.
3. Torque clutch cover bolts to 23 ft. lbs. and remove alignment tool.
4. Install transmission and clutch housing assembly and torque attaching bolts to 54 ft. lbs.
5. Install rear crossmember, then the support cushion to crossmember attaching bolts and torque to 25 ft. lbs. Torque rear crossmember stud nuts to 35 ft. lbs.
6. Connect clutch cable to throwout lever and adjust as outlined previously.
7. Connect speedometer cable and adapter to transmission.
8. Connect back-up lamp switch wires and engage harness in retaining clips at top of transmission cover.

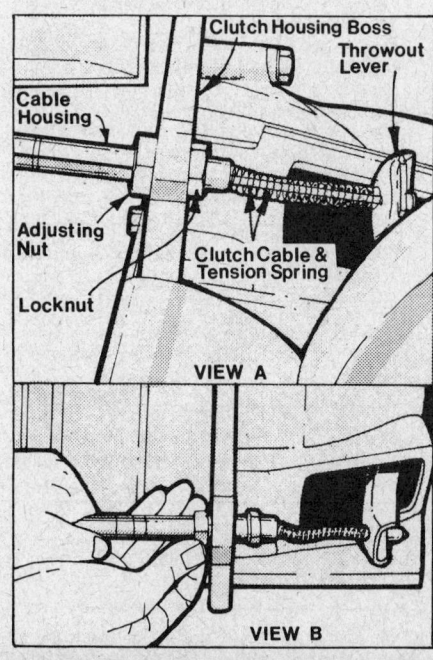

Fig. 1 Clutch adjustment. 4-121

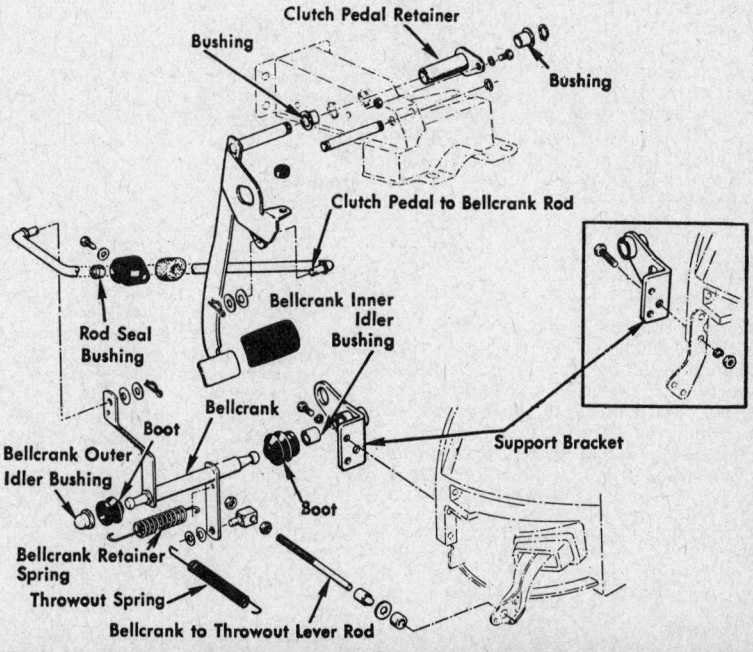

Fig. 2 Typical clutch linkage. 6 Cyl. & V8

9. Install clutch housing inspection cover.
10. Install catalytic converter support bracket bolts, then the starter.
11. Install propeller shaft.
12. Lower vehicle.
13. Install gearshift lever. Ensure shift rail insert is facing downward and that offset side of lever fork is facing right side of extension housing before lever installation. Bend at least three lock tabs down to retain lever.
14. Install inner and outer lever boots, then the bezel.

4-151, 1981—84 6-258 & 1983—84 4-150

Except Eagle
1. Remove transmission as described under Transmission, Replace.
2. Remove clutch housing to engine attaching bolts, then the clutch housing.
3. Remove throwout bearing, then mark pressure plate and flywheel for reassembly.
4. Remove pressure plate to flywheel attaching bolts, then remove pressure plate and clutch disc.

NOTE: Loosen pressure plate to flywheel bolts alternately and evenly to prevent distorting pressure plate.

5. Reverse procedure to install. Position clutch and pressure plate on flywheel and install attaching bolts finger tight. Align clutch disc using a suitable alignment tool, then tighten pressure plate attaching bolts alternately and evenly to 23 ft. lbs. Torque clutch housing to engine and transmission to clutch housing attaching bolts to 54 ft. lbs.

Eagle
1. Remove transmission as described under Transmission, Replace.
2. Remove right hand brace rod and starter motor, then disconnect clutch release cylinder spring from clutch fork.
3. Remove clutch release cylinder, with hydraulic line attached, and clutch housing inspection cover.
4. Disconnect exhaust pipe at exhaust manifold, then remove clutch housing to engine attaching bolts and remove clutch housing.
5. Mark pressure plate and flywheel for reassembly, then remove pressure plate attaching bolts and remove pressure plate and clutch disc.

NOTE: Loosen pressure plate attaching bolts alternately and evenly to prevent distorting pressure plate.

6. Reverse procedure to install. Position clutch disc and pressure plate on flywheel and install attaching bolts finger tight. Align clutch disc using a suitable alignment tool, then tighten pressure plate attaching bolts alternately and evenly to 28 ft. lbs. Torque clutch housing to engine upper attaching bolts to 27 ft. lbs. Torque clutch housing lower attaching bolts and dowel bolts to 43 ft. lbs. Torque transmission to engine attaching bolts to 55 ft. lbs.

1977—80 6 Cyl. & All V8

Removal
1. Remove transmission as described further on.

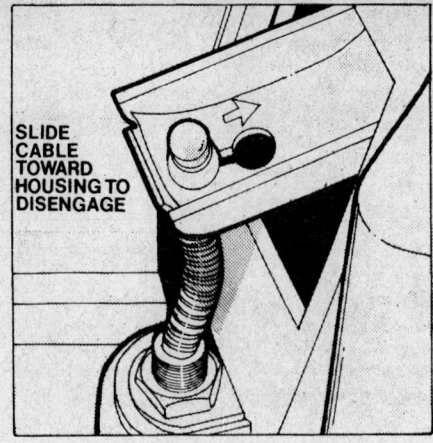

SLIDE CABLE TOWARD HOUSING TO DISENGAGE

Fig. 3 Clutch cable removal. 4-121

2. Remove starter, clutch housing, throwout lever, bearing and sleeve assembly.

NOTE: Mark clutch cover, pressure plate and flywheel to insure correct alignment during installation.

3. Remove clutch cover and pressure plate assembly.

NOTE: When removing clutch cover and pressure plate assembly from flywheel, loosen screws evenly until spring tension is released, as cover could be warped by improper removal, resulting in clutch chatter when reassembled.

4. Remove pilot bushing lubricating wick and soak in engine oil.

NOTE: Unless special clutch rebuilding equipment is available, it is recommended that the clutch assembly be exchanged for a rebuilt unit should the clutch require rebuilding. The driven disc, however, may be replaced without special equipment. If clutch rebuilding equipment is available, follow the equipment manufacturer's instructions.

Installation
1. Inspect clutch release lever height and correct as necessary. If used, lubricate pilot bushing wick with engine oil.
2. Install clutch disc and cover on flywheel and loosely install bolts. Using clutch aligning tool or transmission clutch shaft, align clutch disc.
3. Tighten cover retaining bolts several turns at a time to prevent cover distortion, then torque bolts to 28 ft. lbs.
4. Install throwout lever, bearing and sleeve assembly, clutch housing and starter.

MANUAL TRANS., REPLACE
Except Eagle

4-121
Refer to Clutch, Replace 4-121 for manual transmission removal and installation procedures.

4-151 & 1981—83 6-258
1. Remove console, if equipped, then remove gearshift lever, bezel and boot.
2. Mark propeller shaft and rear axle pinion flange so they can be installed in the same position, then remove propeller shaft.
3. Disconnect speedometer cable and back-up lamp switch wire connector.
4. Disconnect exhaust pipe, if necessary.
5. Remove starter motor, then disconnect clutch release cylinder spring at clutch fork.
6. Remove inspection cover from clutch housing, then remove bolts attaching catalytic converter support bracket to transmission rear support bracket, if equipped.
7. Place support under front of engine, then remove bolts attaching transmission mount to rear crossmember.
8. Remove nuts attaching rear crossmember to frame side sills, then remove crossmember.
9. Remove transmission to clutch housing attaching bolts, then remove transmission.
10. Reverse procedure to install. Torque transmission to clutch housing attaching bolts to 54 ft. lbs.

1977—80 6-258 & 1977—79 V8-304, 360
1. Remove knob, bezel, boot and gear shift lever.
2. Open hood and raise vehicle.
3. Mark rear universal joint and propeller shaft to ensure proper alignment at time of installation, then remove propeller shaft.
4. Disconnect speedometer cable and back-up lamp switch and TCS switch wires, if equipped.
5. If equipped with four speed transmission, release back-up lamp switch wires from clip on transmission top cover.
6. Install support stand under clutch housing to support engine when crossmember and transmission are removed.
7. On Pacer models, disconnect ground strap at support cushion bolt.
8. On all models, remove rear crossmember to frame side sill attaching nuts.
9. Remove catalytic converter support bracket, if equipped.
10. On AMX, Concord, Gremlin, Hornet and Spirit models, remove rear support cushion to crossmember attaching bolts and remove crossmember.

NOTE: On Pacer models, crossmember is removed with transmission.

11. On all models remove two lower transmission to clutch housing attaching bolts.

NOTE: On 1977—78 models, install two guide pins in place of the lower housing bolts.

12. Remove two upper transmission to clutch housing attaching bolts and remove transmission.

NOTE: Care must be taken not to damage clutch shaft, pilot bushing or clutch disc.

Eagle

4-150, 4-151 & 6-258

1. Place transmission shift lever in the neutral position, then remove console, if equipped.
2. Remove gearshift lever bezel and boot, then remove gearshift lever from mounting cover on transmission.
3. Remove skid plate, then mark position of speedometer adapter for reassembly, then disconnect speedometer cable. Plug adapter opening in transfer case to prevent lubricant spillage.
4. Mark propeller shafts and axle yokes for reassembly, then disconnect propeller shafts at transfer case.
5. Disconnect backup lamp switch wire connector, then support engine using a suitable jack.
6. Support transmission and transfer case using a suitable transmission jack, then remove rear crossmember.
7. Remove catalytic converter support bracket from transfer case.
8. Remove transmission to clutch housing attaching bolts, then remove transmission and transfer case as an assembly.
9. Remove nuts from transfer case mounting studs, then separate transfer case from transmission.
10. Reverse procedure to install. Torque transfer case to transmission adapter housing stud nuts to 33 ft. lbs. Torque transmission to clutch housing bolts to 55 ft. lbs.

TRANSFER CASE, REPLACE

1980-84 With Auto. Trans.

1. Raise and support vehicle.
2. Support engine and transmission with a suitable jack or jack stand.
3. Disconnect catalytic converter support bracket from adapter housing.
4. Remove skid plate.
5. Disconnect speedometer cable and adapter from transfer case. Discard adapter "O" ring.
6. Mark propeller shafts and transfer case yoke for assembly reference. Then, disconnect propeller shafts from yokes. Secure shafts aside.
7. Disconnect gearshift and throttle linkage from transmission.
8. Remove rear crossmember.
9. Remove transfer case to adapter housing nuts.
10. Remove transfer case from vehicle.
11. Install transfer case on adapter housing.
12. Install and torque transfer case to adapter housing nuts to 33 ft. lbs.
13. Install rear crossmember.
14. On 1981-84 models, install rear brace

rod.
15. Remove jack or jack stand, supporting engine and transmission.
16. Connect gearshift and throttle linkage to transmission.
17. Connect propeller shafts to transfer case yokes.
18. Install new "O" ring on speedometer adapter, then the adapter and speedometer cable to transfer case.
19. Install skid plate.
20. Connect catalytic converter support bracket to adapter housing.
21. Check transfer case lubricant level and adjust, if necessary. Also, check transmission linkage adjustments.

1980-84 With Manual Trans.

1. Shift transmission into neutral.
2. Remove screws attaching gear shift lever bezel to floorpan or console, (if equipped).
3. Slide bezel and boot up on gear shift lever to gain access to lever attaching bolts, then remove bolts and remove lever.
4. Remove bolts attaching gear shift lever mounting cover to transmission adapter housing and remove cover.
5. Remove nut from transfer case mounting stud from inside transmission adapter housing.
6. Raise and support vehicle.
7. Remove skid plate and stiffening brace, or rear brace rod on 1982-84 models.
8. Remove speedometer adapter retainer attaching bolt and remove retainer, adapter and cable, then plug adapter opening in transfer case to avoid excessive oil leakage.

NOTE: Before removing speedometer adapter, mark position for reference during assembly.

9. Mark propeller shafts and axle yokes for assembly reference and disconnect propeller shafts at transfer case.
10. On 1981-84 models only, remove transfer case shift motor vacuum harness.
11. Support transfer case with transmission jack, then remove nuts from transfer case mounting studs and remove transfer case.
12. Align transmission output and transfer case input shafts and install transfer case on transmission adapter housing, then install and torque transfer case mounting stud nuts to 33 ft. lbs.
13. Remove jack supporting transfer case.
14. Connect propeller shafts to axle yokes and torque clamp strap bolts to 15 ft. lbs.
15. Install new O-ring on speedometer adapter, then install adapter and cable and

retainer, torque retainer bolt to 100 inch lbs.
16. Install skid plate amd stiffening brace, or rear brace rod on 1982-84 models, and torque retaining bolts to 30 ft. lbs.
17. On 1981-84 models only, install transfer case shift motor vacuum harness.
18. Check and correct fluid levels in transmission and transfer case, then lower vehicle.
19. Install nut on transfer case mounting stud inside transmission adapter housing, torque nut to 33 ft. lbs.
20. Install gear shift lever mounting cover on transmission adapter housing, then install gear shift lever on mounting cover.
21. Position gear shift lever boot and bezel on floorpan of console (if equipped), and install bezel attaching screws.

NOTE: On 1982-84 models, steps 1 through 5 and 19 through 21 apply to SR-4 transmission only.

MANUAL TRANS. SHIFT LINKAGE, ADJUST

1977-79 Three Speed Floor Shift

1. Place transmission shift levers in neutral and loosen second-third transmission lever retaining nut and adjustment bolt.
2. Place first-reverse shift rod in neutral position, then align second-third shift rod so shift notch is exactly aligned with first-reverse shift rod notch. Tighten adjustment bolt and nut.
3. Actuate shifter lever to assure a smooth crossover between first and second speed and for proper engagement in all gears.
4. If equipped with tilt steering column on a steering column lock which is actuated by the transmission shift linkage on 1976 models, loosen steering column reverse lockup rod trunnion locknuts to allow free movement of trunnion on rod.
5. Shift transmission into reverse and lock steering column.

NOTE: It may be necessary to rotate lower column shifter lever upward until it is in locked position.

6. Tighten lower trunnion locknut until it contacts trunnion, then tighten upper locknut while holding trunnion centered in column lever.
7. Shift through all gears to check for freedom of operation. Shift into reverse and lock column. Column must lock without any binding.

Rear Axle, Propeller Shaft & Brakes

REAR AXLES

Figs. 1 and 2 illustrate the rear axle assembly used on these cars. When necessary to overhaul the unit, refer to the Rear Axle Specifications table in this chapter.

DESCRIPTION

In these rear axles, Figs. 1 and 2, the drive pinion is mounted in two tapered roller bearings. These bearings are preloaded by a washer behind the front bearing. The pinion is positioned by shims located in front of the rear bearing. The differential is supported in the carrier by two tapered roller side bearings. These bearings are preloaded by shims located between the bearings and carrier housing. The differential assembly is positioned for proper ring gear and pinion backlash by varying the position of these shims. The differential case houses two side gears in mesh with two pinions mounted on a pinion shaft which is held in place by a lock pin. The side gears and pinions are backed by thrust washers.

It is not necessary to remove the rear axle assembly. However, the underbody should be washed to prevent particles of road dirt from contaminating the parts.

REAR AXLE & PROP. SHAFT, REPLACE

1977–84

1. Remove cotter pins and remove axle shaft nuts.
2. Raise vehicle and position support stands under rear frame side sills.
3. Remove wheels and brake drum retaining screws.
4. Remove brake drums, then disconnect brake lines at wheel cylinders.
5. Using a suitable puller, remove support plates, oil seal, retainer and end play shims.

NOTE: Axle shaft end play shims are installed at left side of axle only.

6. Using a suitable puller, remove axle shafts.
7. Remove axle housing cover and drain lubricant, then reinstall cover.
8. Disconnect parking brake cables at equalizer.
9. Mark universal joint and rear axle yokes for reassembly, then disconnect propeller at rear yoke.
10. Remove stabilizer bar, if equipped.
11. Disconnect brake hose at body floor pan bracket.
12. Disconnect vent tube from axle tube.
13. Support axle assembly using a suitable jack.
14. On all except Matador models:
    a. Disconnect shock absorbers at spring plates.
    b. Remove rear spring U-bolts and spring plates.
    c. Rotate axle until it clears springs, then lower axle assembly and remove from vehicle.

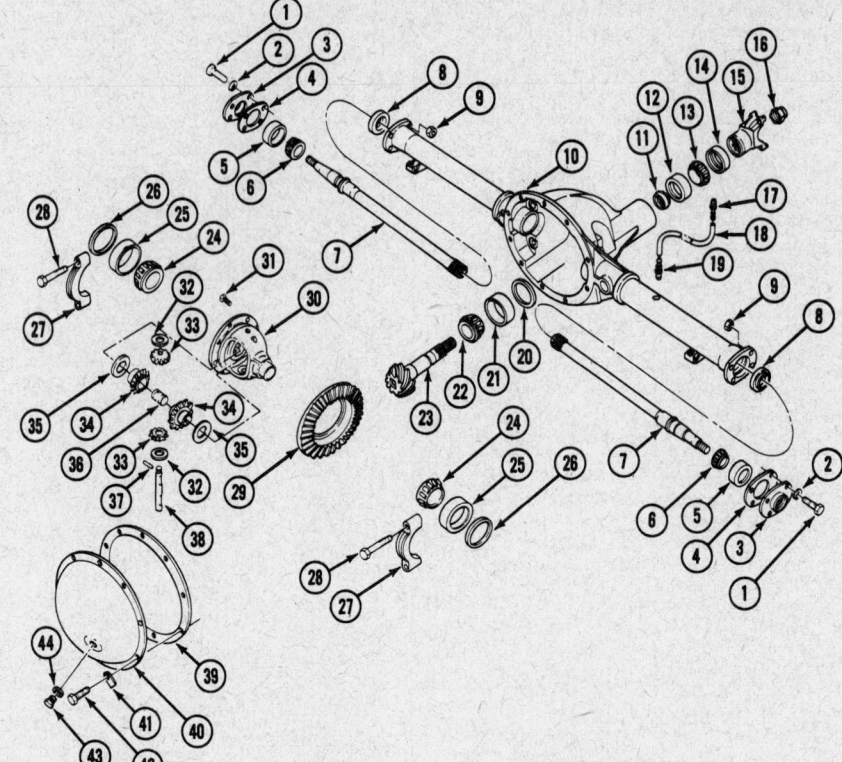

15. On Matador models:
    a. Disconnect shock absorbers from lower control arms. If equipped with air shocks, release all air pressure by opening valves before disconnecting.
    b. Lower jack and disconnect upper control arms from axle housing brackets.
    c. Pull left side axle tube downward and remove coil spring, then pull right side axle tube downward and remove coil spring.
    d. Disconnect lower control arms from axle tube brackets, then lower axle assembly and remove from vehicle.
16. On all models, reverse procedure to install.

AXLE SHAFTS, REPLACE

The hub and drum are separate units, and the hub and axle shaft are serrated to mate and fit together on the taper. Both are punch marked to insure correct assembly,

1. BOLT	16. PINION NUT	30. DIFFERENTIAL CASE
2. WASHER	17. BREATHER	31. RING GEAR BOLT
3. AXLE SHAFT OIL SEAL AND RETAINER ASSEMBLY	18. BREATHER HOSE	32. DIFFERENTIAL PINION WASHER
4. AXLE SHAFT BEARING SHIM	19. BREATHER	33. DIFFERENTIAL PINION
5. AXLE SHAFT BEARING CUP	20. PINION DEPTH ADJUSTING SHIM	34. DIFFERENTIAL SIDE GEAR
6. AXLE SHAFT BEARING	21. PINION REAR BEARING CUP	35. DIFFERENTIAL SIDE GEAR THRUST WASHER
7. AXLE SHAFT	22. PINION BEARING-REAR	36. DIFFERENTIAL PINION SHAFT THRUST BLOCK
8. AXLE SHAFT INNER OIL SEAL	23. PINION GEAR	37. DIFFERENTIAL PINION SHAFT PIN
9. NUT	24. DIFFERENTIAL BEARING	38. DIFFERENTIAL PINION SHAFT
10. AXLE HOUSING	25. DIFFERENTIAL BEARING CUP	39. AXLE HOUSING COVER GASKET
11. COLLAPSIBLE SPACER	26. DIFFERENTIAL BEARING SHIM	40. AXLE HOUSING COVER
12. PINION BEARING CUP-FRONT	27. DIFFERENTIAL BEARING CAP	41. AXLE IDENTIFICATION TAG
13. PINION BEARING-FRONT	28. DIFFERENTIAL BEARING CAP BOLT	42. BOLT
14. PINION OIL SEAL	29. RING GEAR	43. AXLE HOUSING COVER FILL PLUG
15. UNIVERSAL JOINT YOKE		44. WASHER

Fig. 1   Rear axle assembly (typical). 7⁹/₁₆ in. axle

Fig. 3. The axle shaft and bearing may be removed as follows:
1. Remove rear wheel, drum and hub, then disconnect parking brake cable at equalizer.
2. Disconnect brake tube from wheel cylinder and remove brake support plate assembly, oil seal and axle shims from axle shaft.

NOTE: Axle shaft end play shims are located on the left side only.

3. Using suitable puller, pull axle shaft and bearing from axle tube, then remove and discard inner oil seal.

NOTE: The bearing cone must be pressed off the shaft, using an arbor press.

CAUTION: On models equipped with Twin Grip differential, do not rotate differential unless both axle shafts are in place.

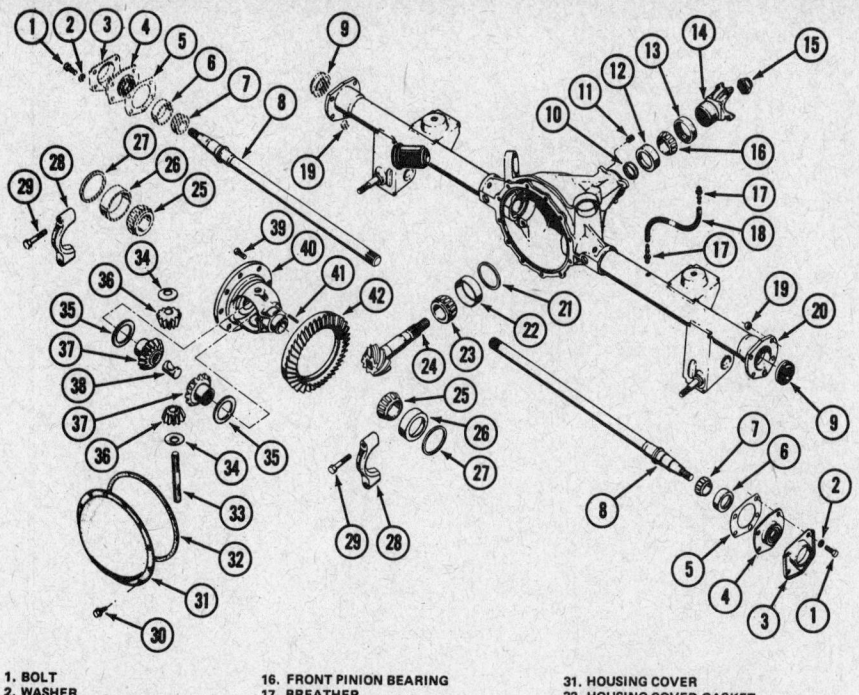

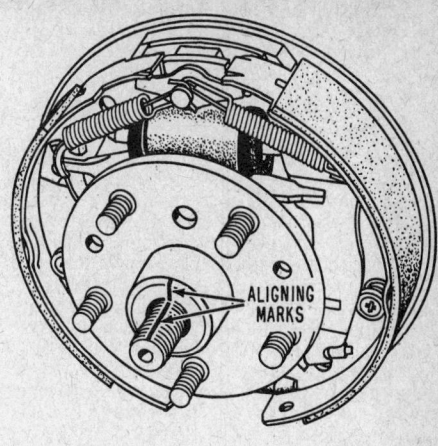

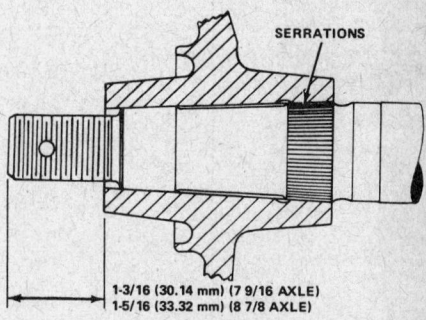

1-3/16 (30.14 mm) (7 9/16 AXLE)
1-5/16 (33.32 mm) (8 7/8 AXLE)

Fig. 3   Installing hub on axle

1. BOLT	16. FRONT PINION BEARING	31. HOUSING COVER
2. WASHER	17. BREATHER	32. HOUSING COVER GASKET
3. AXLE SHAFT OIL SEAL RETAINER	18. BREATHER HOSE	33. DIFFERENTIAL PINION SHAFT
4. AXLE SHAFT OIL SEAL	19. NUT	34. DIFFERENTIAL PINION GEAR
5. AXLE SHAFT BEARING SHIM	20. REAR AXLE HOUSING	THRUST WASHER
6. AXLE SHAFT BEARING CUP	21. DRIVE PINION DEPTH ADJUSTING SHIM	35. DIFFERENTIAL SIDE GEAR THRUST
7. AXLE BEARING	22. REAR PINION BEARING CUP	WASHER
8. AXLE SHAFT	23. REAR PINION BEARING	36. DIFFERENTIAL PINION GEAR
9. AXLE SHAFT INNER OIL SEAL	24. PINION GEAR	37. DIFFERENTIAL SIDE GEAR
10. PINION COLLAPSIBLE SPACER	25. DIFFERENTIAL BEARING	38. DIFFERENTIAL PINION SHAFT
11. FILLER PLUG	26. DIFFERENTIAL BEARING CUP	THRUST BLOCK
12. FRONT PINION BEARING CUP	27. DIFFERENTIAL BEARING SHIM	39. BOLT
13. PINION OIL SEAL	28. DIFFERENTIAL BEARING CUP	40. DIFFERENTIAL CASE
14. UNIVERSAL JOINT YOKE	29. BOLT	41. DIFFERENTIAL PINION SHAFT PIN
15. PINION NUT	30. BOLT	42. RING GEAR

Fig. 2   Rear axle assembly (typical). 8⁷/₈ in. axle

When installing hub onto axle, install two well lubricated thrust washers and axle shaft nut. Tighten axle shaft nut until hub is installed to the dimensions shown in Fig. 3. Remove axle shaft nut and one thrust washer. Reinstall axle shaft nut and tighten to 250 ft. lbs. If cotter pin hole is not aligned, tighten the nut to the next castellation and install cotter pin.

NOTE: Do not use an original hub on a replacement axle shaft; use a new hub. A new hub may be installed on an original axle shaft providing the serrations on the shaft are not worn or damaged. Be certain that the hub and axle shaft are punch marked to insure proper alignment on installation. A replacement hub, which is not serrated, can be installed and serrations will be cut in the hub when installed on the shaft due to the difference in hardness of the shaft and the hub.

Assembly

Replace the parts in the reverse order of their removal. If the old parts are replaced and the shims have not been disturbed, the axle shaft end play should be correct when the parts are assembled. However, if a new shaft, bearing, differential carrier or housing has been installed, it will be necessary to check the end play.

The end play can be checked when all parts have been replaced except the wheel and hub. To make this check, rap each axle shaft after the nuts are tight to be sure the bearing cups are seated. Then place a dial indicator so that its stem contacts the end of the shaft and work the shaft in and out to determined the amount of existing end play. If an adjustment is necessary, remove the outer oil seal and brake support and add or remove shims as required. When making this adjustment, add or subtract shims on left side of axle only.

NOTE: The application of a bead of sealing material such as "Pliobond" or "Permatex" to the outer diameter of axle tube flange and the brake support contact area is recommended. The sealing material will be used in addition to the gasket for improved sealing.

PROPELLER SHAFT VIBRATION

1. Raise and support the rear of the car at the axle and remove rear wheels.
2. Remove all undercoating and accumulated dirt from shaft.
3. With the use of an electronic wheel balancer, the propeller shaft can be balanced as follows:
   a. Place electronic pick up unit under axle housing as close as possible to pinion yoke. Use crayon or chalk to mark four equally spaced horizontal lines on the propeller shaft. To aid in identifying lines, it is suggested they be of unequal length.

NOTE: On models with an aluminum extension housing, it will be necessary to install a steel hose clamp on rear of extension housing to accommodate the magnetic pickup.

   b. Operate the car in gear at the speed of greatest vibration. Locate the heavy spot.

NOTE: Do not operate in gear for long periods as overheating may occur.

4. If electronic wheel balancer is not available, proceed as follows:
   a. Operate vehicle in gear at about 40 mph.
   b. Using a jack stand as a steady rest, slowly advance a chalk toward the spinning propeller shaft. At the instant of first contact with propeller shaft, withdraw chalk. This mark indicates the heavy spot.

NOTE: Do not operate in gear for long periods as overheating may occur.

5. Place two worm type hose clamps on propeller shaft with heads of clamps located 180° from heavy spot noted previously. Slide clamps as far to rear as possible.
6. Again operate car in gear and if vibration still exists move both clamp heads an equal distance in opposite directions to-

ward the heavy spot until vibration is at a minimum.

7. Replace rear wheels and road test car.

BRAKE ADJUSTMENTS

These brakes, Figs. 4 and 5, have self-adjusting mechanisms that assure correct lining-to-drum clearances at all times. The automatic adjusters operate only when the brakes are applied as the car is moving rearward.

Although the brakes are self-adjusting, an initial adjustment is necessary after the brake shoes have been relined or replaced, or when the length of the star wheel adjusting screw has been changed during some other serivce operation.

Frequent usage of an automatic transmission forward range to halt reverse vehicle motion may prevent the automatic adjusters from functioning, thereby inducing low pedal heights. Should low pedal heights be encountered on these models, it is recommended that numerous forward and reverse stops be made until satisfactory pedal height is obtained.

NOTE: If a low pedal condition cannot be corrected by making numerous stops (provided the hydraulic system is free of air) it indicates that the self-adjusting mechanism is not functioning. Therefore, it will be necessary to remove the brake drum, clean, free up and lubricate the adjusting mechanisms. Then adjust the brakes as follows, being sure the parking brake is fully released.

Adjustment

1. Remove access slot cover from brake support plate.
2. Using brake adjusting tool or screwdriver, rotate adjuster screw until wheel is locked.
3. Back off adjuster screw one complete turn.

NOTE: To back off adjuster screw, insert a piece of 1/8 inch rod past adjuster screw and force adjusting lever off adjuster screw.

---

4. Install rubber access slot cover.
5. Following the initial adjustment and final assembly, check the brake pedal height to insure brake operation. Then drive the car forward and reverse, making 10 to 15 brake applications prior to road testing. This action balances the adjustment of the four brake units and raises the brake pedal.

PARKING BRAKE, ADJUST

1977—80 Pacer

1. Make sure service brakes are properly adjusted.
2. Apply and release parking brake several times.
3. Place parking lever in first notch from fully released position and place transmission in neutral.
4. Raise and support vehicle at rear axle using jack stands.
5. Loosen locknut and tighten cable adjuster until there is a heavy brake drag at rear wheels.
6. Loosen adjuster until heavy drag is just eliminated and tighten locknut.

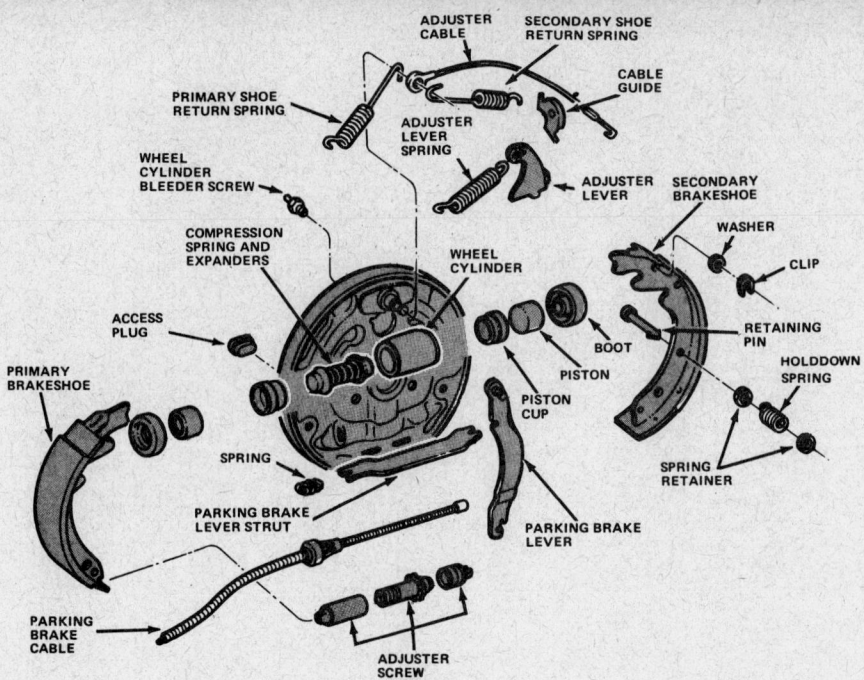

Fig. 4   9 Inch drum brake assembly

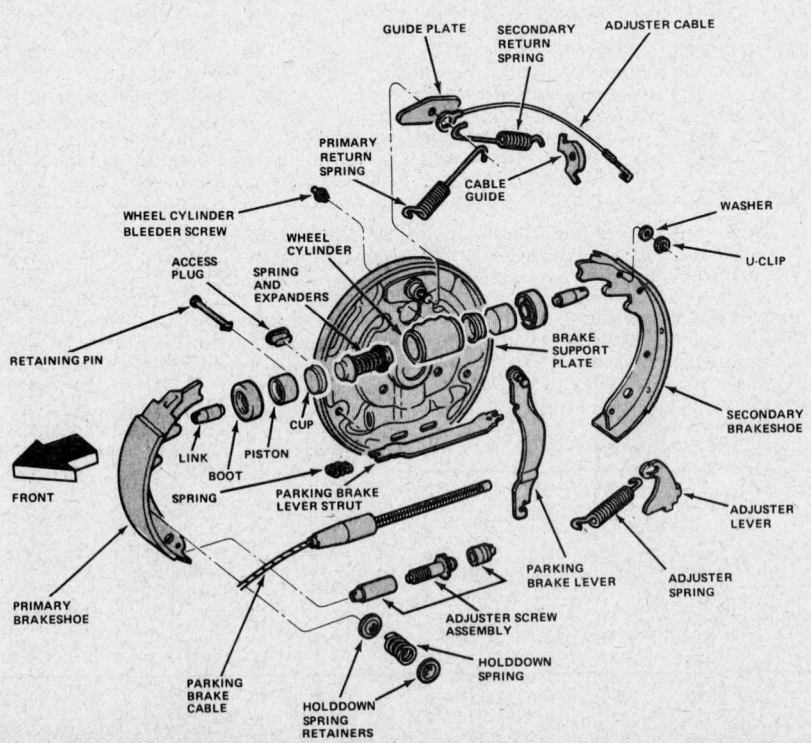

Fig. 5   10 Inch drum assembly

1977–84 Exc. Pacer

With Adjustment Gauge J-23462
1. Make sure service brakes are properly adjusted.
2. Apply and release parking brake several times.
3. Raise and support vehicle at rear axle using jack stands.
4. Place parking brake in first notch from fully released position.
5. Place an inch lb. torque wrench on Parking Brake Cable Adjustment Gauge J-23462 and place gauge on from parking brake cable, centered between cable housing ferrule and cable equalizer.
6. Apply 50 inch lbs. of torque and note indicator reading. If reading is not within the green band, adjust parking brake at equalizer until satisfactory reading is obtained.
7. Release parking brake and check for brake drag. If brake drag is evident, inspect actuating cables and equalizer for freedom of movement and proper operation. Inspect cable condition, especially at areas where cable passes near exhaust components. Correct as necessary and readjust parking brake cable.

Less Adjustment Gauge J-23462
1. With service brakes properly adjusted, set parking brake pedal on the first notch from fully released position.
2. Tighten parking brake cable at equalizer to a point where the rear wheels are locked in forward rotation.
3. Release pedal and check for rear wheel drag—wheels should rotate freely.

BRAKE MASTER CYLINDER, REPLACE

1. Disconnect brake lines from master cylinder. Cap lines and master cylinder ports.
2. On models with manual brakes, disconnect master cylinder push rod at brake pedal.
3. On all models, remove nuts or bolts attaching master cylinder to dash panel or brake booster and remove master cylinder. On Matador and Pacer models, remove mounting bracket and boot retainer plate.
4. Install in the reverse order of removal and bleed the brake system.

POWER BRAKE UNIT, REPLACE

1. Disconnect booster push rod from brake pedal.
2. Remove vacuum hose from check valve.
3. Remove nuts and washers securing master cylinder to booster unit, then separate master cylinder from booster unit.

NOTE: Do not disconnect brake lines from master cylinder.

4. Remove booster unit to firewall attaching nuts and remove booster unit.
5. Reverse procedure to install.

Rear Suspension

SHOCK ABSORBER, REPLACE

1. With the rear axle supported properly, disconnect lower end of shock absorber from stud on mounting bracket.
2. Remove upper mounting bracket from underbody.
3. Reverse procedure to install.

LEAF SPRINGS, REPLACE

1. Support rear axle, removing tension from springs.
2. Disconnect lower end of shock absorber from stud on mounting bracket.
3. Remove "U" bolts securing spring plate and spring to axle tube.
4. Disassemble rear shackle and remove eye bolt from spring forward mounting bracket.

NOTE: On Pacer, remove nuts attaching rear hanger bracket to mounting studs on side sill and remove spring.

5. Reverse procedure to install. Replace bushings as necessary.

COIL SPRINGS, REPLACE

1. Support vehicle at frame and support rear axle with a suitable jack.
2. Disconnect shock absorbers from lower mountings.
3. On 1977–78 models disconnect upper control arm at axle housing.
4. On all models, lower axle assembly until spring can be removed, Fig. 1.
5. Reverse procedure to install.

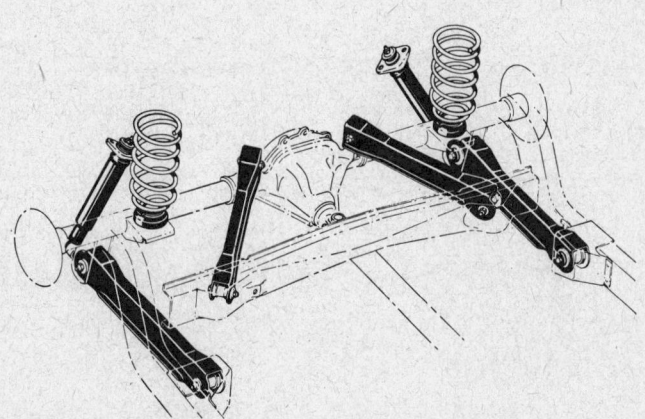

Fig. 1 Coil spring suspension (typical)

CONTROL ARMS & BUSHINGS, REPLACE

NOTE: Replace control arms one at a time to prevent axle assembly misalignment, making installation difficult.

Upper Control Arms

1. Support vehicle at frame.
2. Remove control arm bolts from frame crossmember and axle tube bracket.
3. To replace axle tube bracket bushings, refer to Figs. 2 & 3.
4. Reverse procedure to install.

Lower Control Arms

1. Support vehicle at rear axle.
2. Remove stabilizer bar, if equipped.
3. Remove control arm mount bolts from frame and axle tube brackets.
4. Reverse procedure to install.

NOTE: Lower control arm bushings are not serviceable.

STABILIZER BAR, REPLACE

Matador

1. Raise and support rear of vehicle.

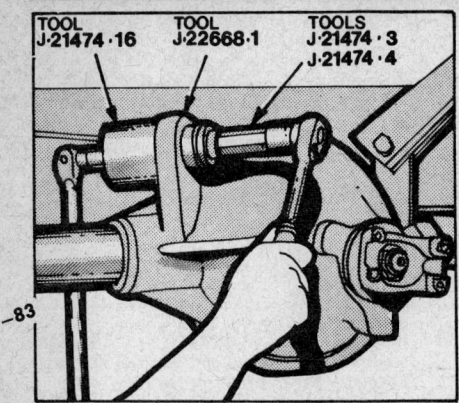

Fig. 2   Upper control arm rear bushing removal

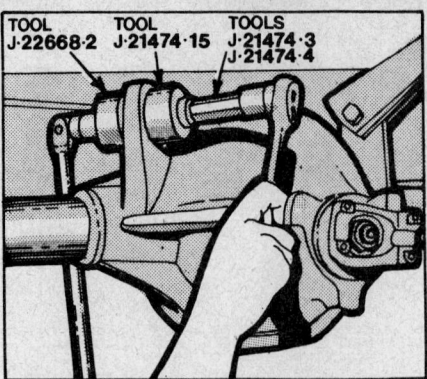

Fig. 3   Upper control arm rear bushing installation

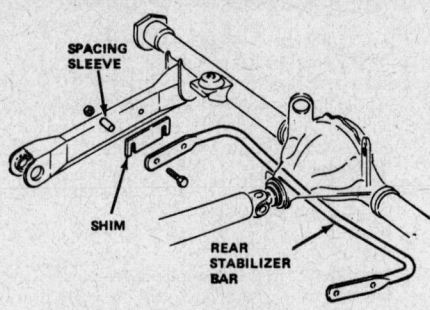

Fig. 4   Rear stabilizer bar. 1977—78 Matador

2. Remove bolts attaching stabilizer bar to lower control arms, then remove stabilizer bar, shims (if used) and spacing sleeves, Fig. 4.
3. Install spacing sleeves in lower control arms.
4. Position stabilizer bar on lower control arms, then install attaching bolts and nuts. Hand tighten bolts and nuts only.
5. Install shims, if used, then torque stabilizer bar attaching bolts to 75 ft. lbs.

1979—84 Concord, Eagle & Spirit

1. Raise and support rear of vehicle, then remove nuts and grommets attaching stabilizer to connecting links, Figs. 5 and 6.
2. Remove bolts attaching stabilizer bar mounting clamps to spring clip plates and remove stabilizer bar.
3. Reverse procedure to install. Torque link lock nuts to 7 ft. lbs. and mounting clamp bolts to 25 ft. lbs.

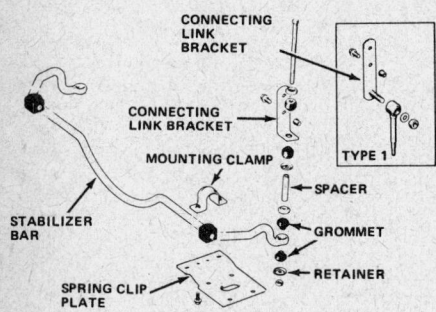

Fig. 5   Rear stabilizer bar. 1979—83 Concord & Spirit

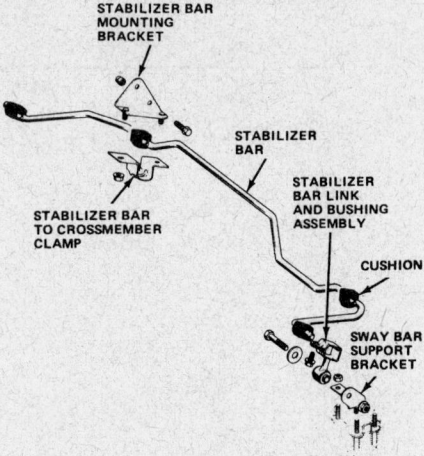

Fig. 6   Rear stabilizer bar. 1980—84 Eagle

Front End & Steering Section

DESCRIPTION

1980—84 Eagle

These models use an independent front coil spring suspension system, Fig. 1. The wheels are suspended on upper and lower control arms with a coil spring located between the upper control arm and a spring seat beneath the wheel housing panels.

Direct acting telescoping shock absorbers are located inside the coil springs. A stabilizer bar attached to each control arm with stabilizer links provides stability, and a dampener dampens steering oscillations.

1977—80 Pacer

These models have an independent front coil spring front suspension system using unequal length upper and lower control arms, Fig. 2. The coil springs are mounted between the lower control arms and the front crossmember with the lower arm functioning as the loaded member.

1977—83 Exc. Eagle & Pacer

The front suspension, Figs. 3 and 4 is an independent linked type, with the coil springs located between seats in the wheel house panels and seats attached to the upper control arms.

Directing acting telescoping shock absorbers are located inside the coil springs.

Each upper control arm assembly has two rubber bushings attached to the wheel house panel and a ball joint attached to the steering knuckle.

Each lower control arm has a rubber bushing attached to the front crossmember and a Ball joint attached to the steering knuckle.

The lower control arm strut rods are attached to the lower control arms and body side sill brackets.

WHEEL ALIGNMENT

1977—80 Pacer

Caster is adjusted by rotating the rear pivot bolt eccentric, Fig. 5. After adjustment, torque locknut to 110 ft. lbs.

Camber is adjusted by rotating both front and rear lower control arm pivot bolt eccentrics, Fig. 5. After adjustment, torque locknut to 110 ft. lbs.

1977—84 Exc. Pacer

Caster is obtained by moving the two adjusting nuts on the threaded strut rod, Fig. 6. One nut is on each side of the mounting bracket. Therefore, moving the nuts on the rod will move the lower control arm to front or rear for desired caster angle. After adjustment, torque adjusting nuts to 65 ft. lbs. Torque locknuts to 75 ft. lbs.

Camber is obtained by turning on the eccentric lower control arm bolt, Fig. 7. After adjustment, torque lock nut to 110 ft. lbs.

TOE-IN, ADJUST

To adjust toe-in, loosen the clamps at both ends of the adjustable tubes on each tie rod. Turn the tubes an equal amount until the toe-

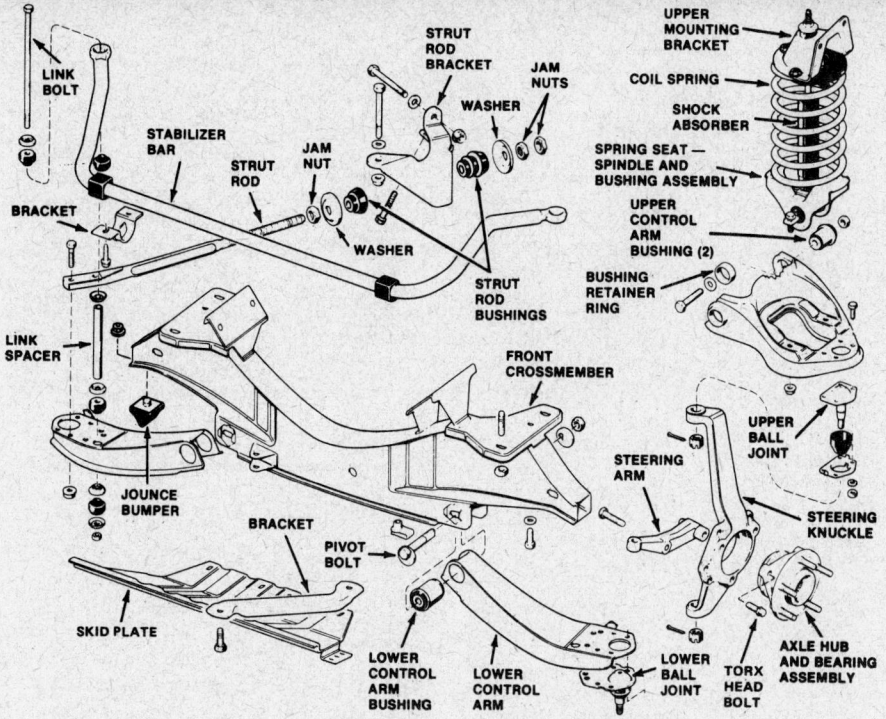

Fig. 1 Front suspension view. 1980—84 Eagle

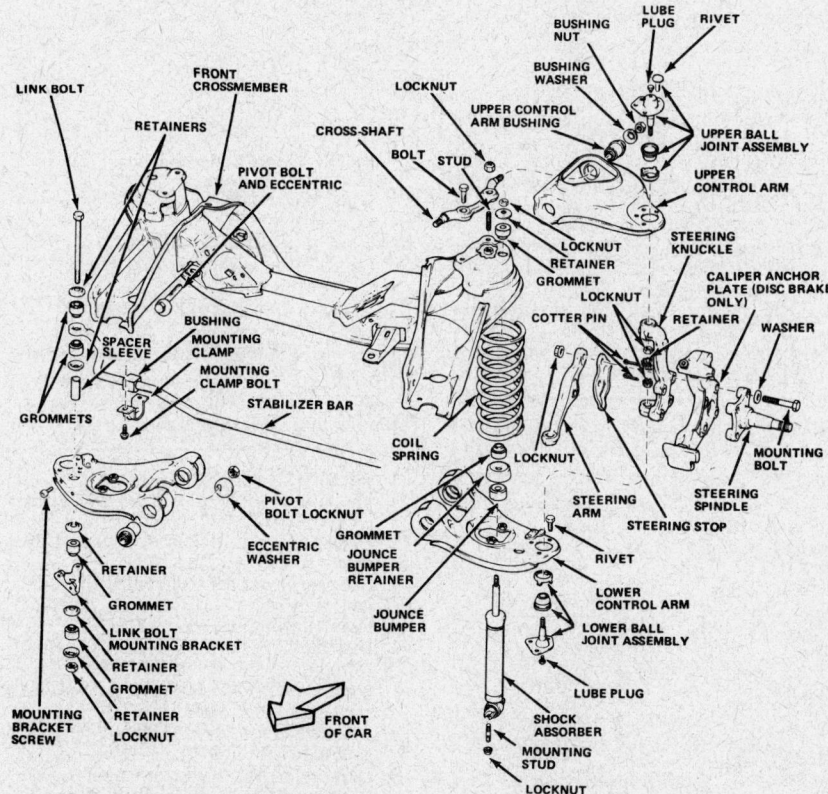

Fig. 2 Front suspension. 1977—80 Pacer (Typical)

clamp bolts.

NOTE: In performing service operations on the steering linkage or when adjusting toe-in, be sure to square the tie rod ball sockets on the studs and align the tie rod stud in the center, or slightly above center, of the cross tube opening, before tightening the steering linkage adjusting tube. This will prevent the stud from contacting the side of the cross tube opening, which would otherwise result in noise problems or damage.

WHEEL BEARINGS, ADJUST

1977—83 Exc. Eagle

1. To adjust bearings tighten spindle nut to 25 ft. lbs. while rotating the wheel to seat bearings.
2. Then loosen spindle nut 1/3 turn and with wheel rotating, retorque spindle nut to 6 inch pounds.
3. Place the nut retainer on spindle nut with the slots of the retainer aligned with the cotter pin hole on the spindle.
4. Install cotter pin and dust cap.

WHEEL BEARINGS, REPLACE

(Disc Brakes)

Exc. Eagle
1. Remove two thirds of the total fluid capacity of the master cylinder reservoir to prevent fluid overflow when the caliper pistons are pushed back on their bores.
2. Raise car and remove front wheels.
3. Disconnect hydraulic tube from mounting bracket. Do not disconnect any hydraulic fitting.
4. Holding the lower edge of the caliper, remove the lower bolt. Any shims that fall out at this point should be labeled to insure that they be replaced in their original position.
5. Holding the upper edge of the caliper, remove the upper bolt, tag these shims.
6. Hang caliper from upper suspension to prevent strain being placed on brake hose.
7. Remove spindle nut and hub and disc assembly. Grease retainer and inner bearing can now be removed.
8. Reverse procedure to install.

CHECKING BALL JOINTS FOR WEAR

1977—80 Pacer

Lower Ball Joint
1. Position vehicle on level surface and remove lower ball joint lubrication plug.
2. Insert a 2 to 3 in. pierce of stiff wire or thin rod into plug hole until it contacts ball stud, then accurately scribe mark on wire or rod at outer edge of plug hole.
3. If distance from ball stud to outer edge of plug hole is 7/16 in. or more, replace ball joint.

in is correct. Turning the right tube in the direction the wheels revolve when the car is going forward increases the toe-in and turning the left tube in the opposite direction increases toe-in. To decrease toe-in turn the right tube backward and the left tube forward. It is important that both tubes be turned an equal amount in order to maintain the correct position of the steering wheel. When adjustment is complete, tighten all clamp bolts.

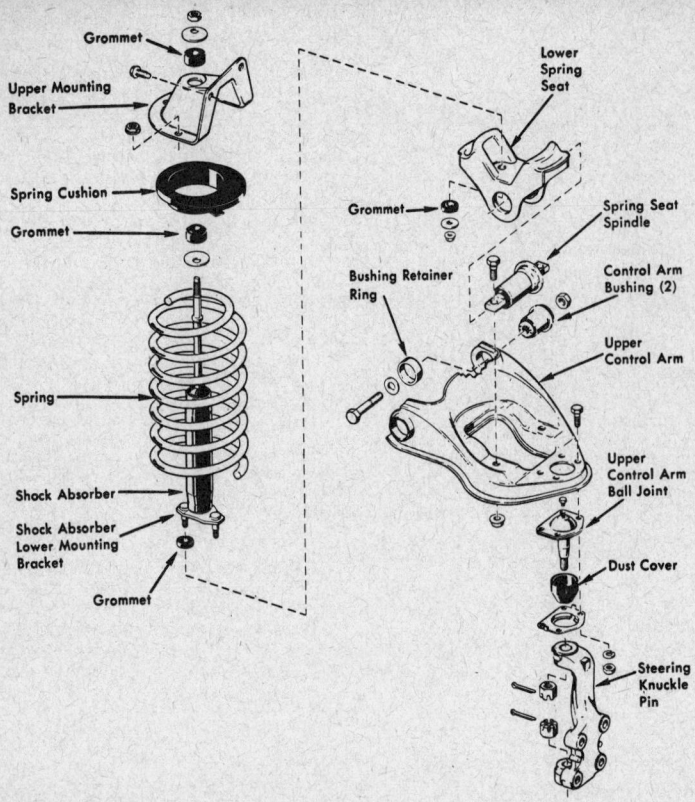

Fig. 3 Front suspension upper control arm components. Exc. Eagle & Pacer

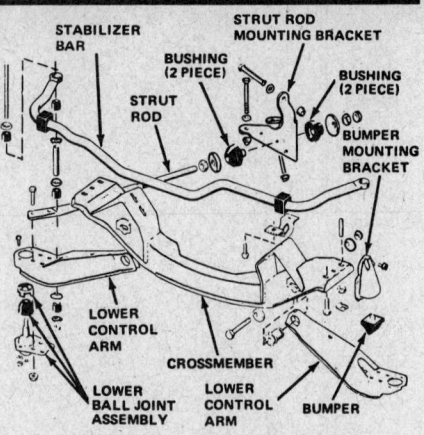

Fig. 4 Front suspension lower control arm components. Exc. Eagle & Pacer

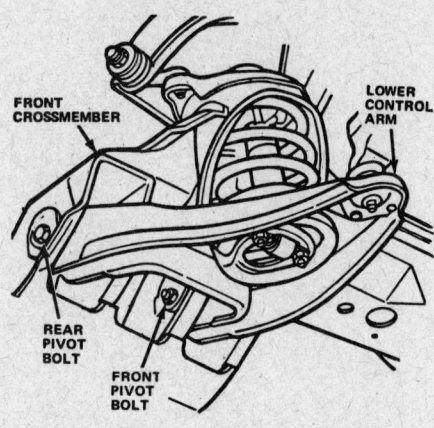

Fig. 5 Caster and camber adjustment. Pacer

Upper Ball Joint

1. Position suitable jack under lower control arm and raise vehicle until wheel is off floor.
2. Move top of wire toward and away from center of vehicle, if any looseness or play is present, replace ball joint.
3. Using a suitable tool, move uppper control arm up and down. If looseness or play is present, replace ball joint.

1977–84 Except Pacer

Before checking ball joints for wear, make sure the front wheel bearings are properly adjusted and that the control arms are tight. Referring to Fig. 8, raise wheel with a jack placed under the frame as shown. Then test by moving the wheel up and down to check axial play, and rocking it at the top and bottom to measure radial play.

The upper ball joint should be replaced if total travel when rocking and tire exceeds .160".

The lower ball joint is spring loaded and should be replaced if there is any noticeable lateral shake.

NOTE: On Eagle models, if lower ball joint is worn excessively, the lower control arm and ball joint must be replaced as an assembly.

BALL JOINTS, REPLACE

1977–80 Pacer

Upper Ball Joint
1. Raise vehicle and remove wheel and tire assembly.
2. Using suitable jack, raise lower control

arm approximately 1 in.
3. Remove cotter pin and retaining nut from upper ball joint stud.
4. Install tool J-9656 onto ball joint stud.
5. Lower jack supporting control arm slightly, then strike tool with hammer to loosen ball stud in steering knuckle.
6. Chisel heads from rivets attaching ball joint to upper control arm, then drive rivets out using a punch.
7. Remove tool from ball stud, then remove ball joint assembly.
8. Position ball joint on upper control arm and install nuts and bolts.

NOTE: Install bolts from bottom with nuts on top. Torque nuts to 25 ft. lbs.

9. Reverse procedure to assemble. Torque ball joint stud to 75 ft. lbs.

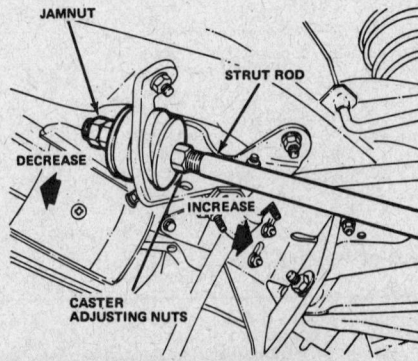

Fig. 6 Caster adjustment, Exc. Pacer

Lower Ball Joint

1. Raise vehicle and remove wheel and tire assembly.
2. Remove brake drum or caliper and rotor assembly.

NOTE: When removing caliper do not damage brake tubing or hose. Secure caliper to frame with wire.

3. Remove steering arm to steering knuckle attaching bolts and position steering arm aside.
4. Disconnect stabilizer bar link bolt at lower control arm, if equipped.
5. Support lower control arm with a suitable jack and remove cotter pin and nut from lower ball joint stud.
6. Install tool No. J-9656 on ball stud and remove jack.
7. Strike tool with hammer to loosen ball stud in steering knuckle.
8. Support lower control arm with jack and remove tool.
9. Disengage ball stud from steering knuckle and position components aside.

NOTE: Use wire to suspend components from upper control arm.

10. Chisel heads from rivets attaching ball joint to lower control arm, then drive rivets out using a punch and remove ball joint.

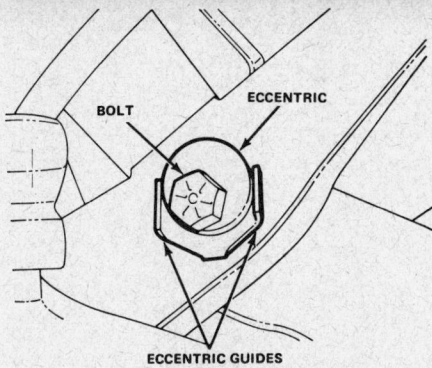

Fig. 7 Camber adjustment. Exc. Pacer

11. Position ball joint on lower control arm and install nuts and bolts.

NOTE: Install bolts from top with nuts on bottom. Torque bolts to 25 ft. lbs.

12. Reverse procedure to assemble. Torque lower ball joint stud nut to 75 ft. lbs., steering arm to knuckle bolts to 55 ft. lbs., and the stabilizer bar link bolt to 7 ft. lbs.

1977–84 Exc. Pacer

UPPER BALL JOINT
1. Position a 2x4x5 in. block of wood on side sill under upper control arm.
2. Raise vehicle and support at frame side sills.
3. Remove wheel and brake drum or caliper and rotor assembly.

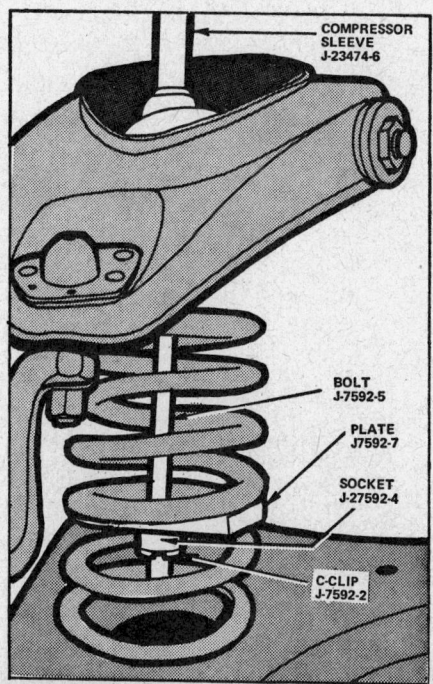

Fig. 10 Compressing spring. Pacer

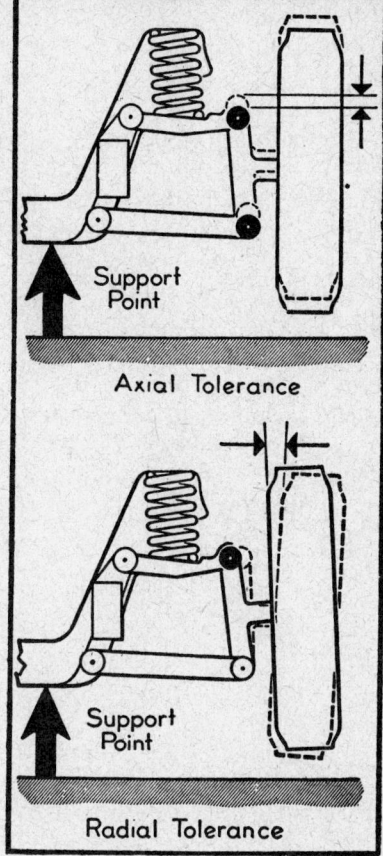

Fig. 8 Check ball joints for wear. Exc. Pacer

NOTE: When removing caliper do not damage brake tubing or hose. Secure caliper to frame with wire.

4. Remove cotter pin and retaining nut from upper ball joint stud.
5. Install tool No. J-9656 on ball stud, then using a hammer strike tool to loosen ball stud in steering knuckle.
6. Support lower control arm with a suitable jack.
7. Chisel heads from rivets attaching ball joint to upper control arm, then drive rivets out using a punch.
8. Remove tool from ball stud and ball joint from steering knuckle.
9. Position ball joint on control arm and install nuts and bolts. Torque bolts to 25 ft. lbs.
10. Reverse procedure to assemble. Torque ball joint stud nut to 75 ft. lbs.

LOWER BALL JOINT
Exc. Eagle
1. Position a 2x4x5 in. block of wood on side sill under upper control arm.
2. Raise vehicle and support at frame side sills.
3. Remove wheel and brake drum or caliper and rotor assembly.

NOTE: When removing caliper do not damage brake tubing or hose. Secure caliper to frame with wire.

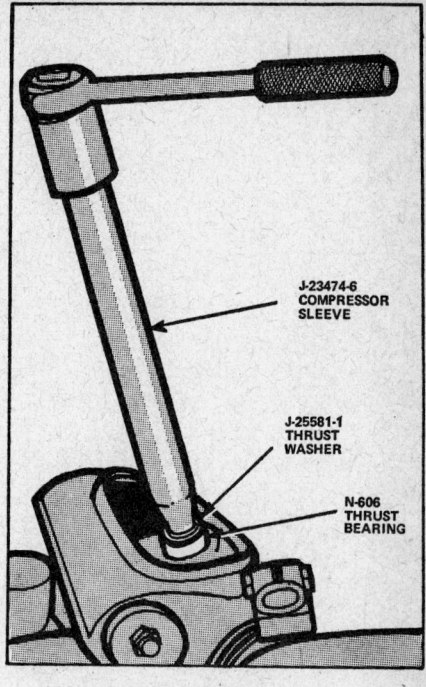

Fig. 9 Installing Spring compressor. Pacer

4. Disconnect strut rod from lower control arm and steering arm from steering knuckle.
5. Remove lower ball joint stud cotter pin and retaining nut.
6. Install tool No. 9656 on ball stud, then strike tool with hammer to loosen ball stud in steering knuckle.
7. Support lower control arm with a suitable jack.
8. Chisel heads from rivets attaching ball joint to upper control arm, then drive rivets out using a punch.
9. Remove tool from ball stud and ball joint from steering knuckle and lower control arm.
10. Position ball joint on lower control arm and install attaching bolts loosely.
11. Connect strut to lower control arm and torque bolts to 75 ft. lbs.

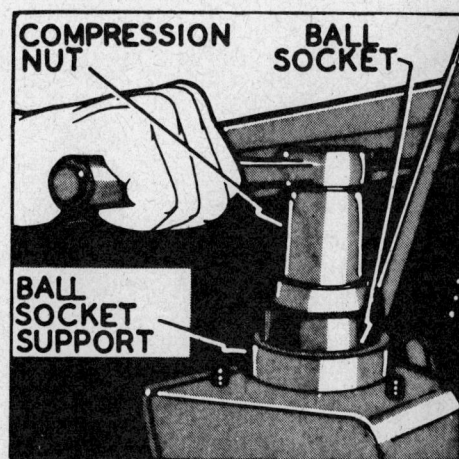

Fig. 11 Installation of spring compressor Exc. Pacer

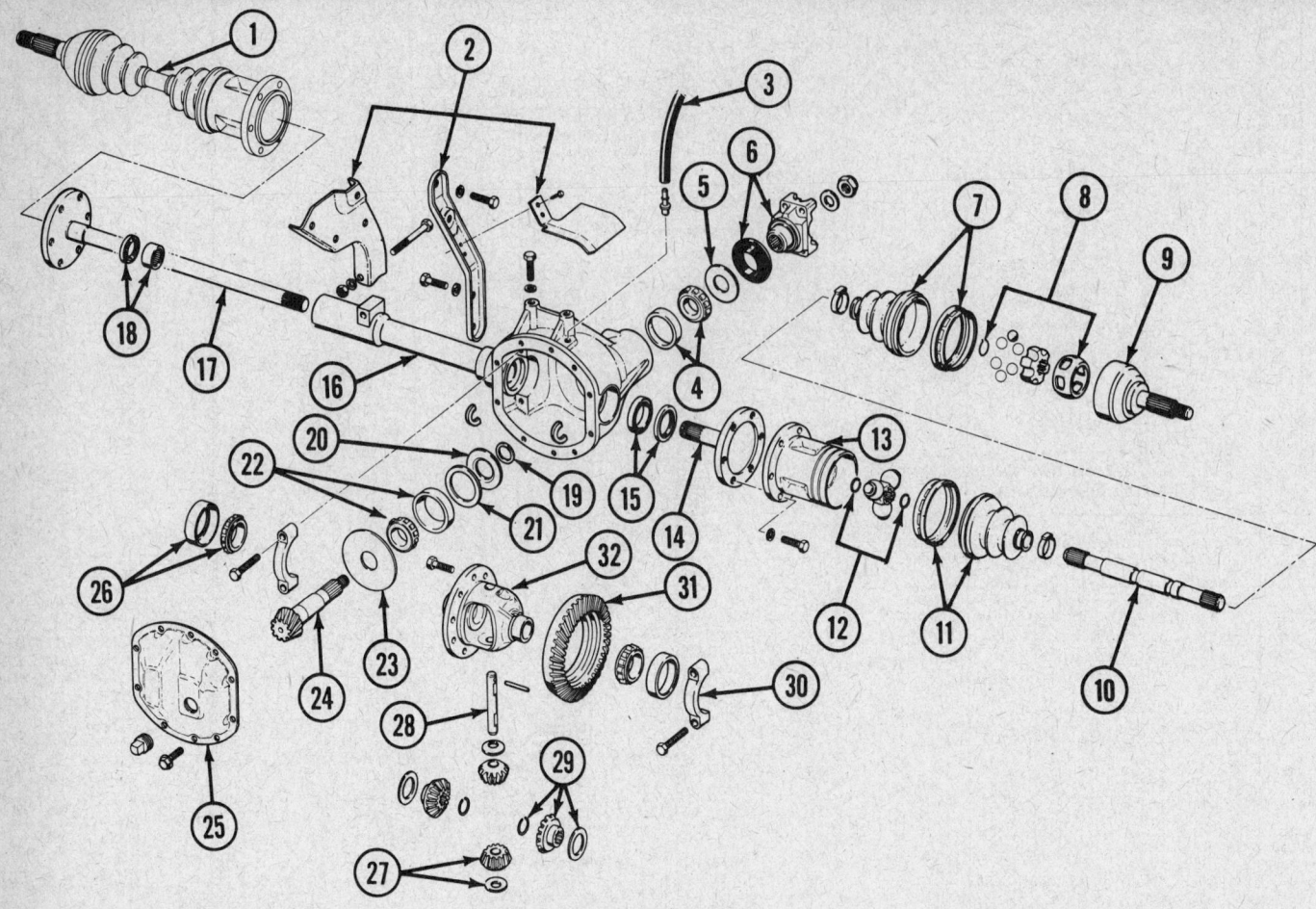

1. HALF-SHAFT ASSEMBLY
2. AXLE MOUNTING BRACKETS
3. VENT HOSE
4. PINION AND FRONT BEARING CUP
5. WASHER
6. YOKE AND SEAL
7. OUTER BOOT AND RETAINER
8. RZEPPA JOINT ASSEMBLY
9. SPINDLE
10. HALF-SHAFT
11. INNER BOOT AND RETAINER

12. TRI-POT JOINT ASSEMBLY
13. TRI-POT HOUSING
14. AXLE SHAFT (SHORT)
15. BALL BEARING AND SEAL
16. AXLE HOUSING
17. AXLE SHAFT (LONG)
18. NEEDLE BEARING AND SEAL
19. PRELOAD SHIM
20. WASHER
21. DEPTH SHIM
22. PINION REAR BEARING AND CUP

23. SLINGER
24. PINION GEAR
25. COVER
26. DIFFERENTIAL BEARING AND CUP
27. DIFFERENTIAL PINION AND THRUST WASHER
28. PINION MATE SHAFT
29. SIDE GEAR, THRUST WASHER AND LOCKRING
30. BEARING CAP
31. RING GEAR
32. DIFFERENTIAL CASE

Fig. 12 Front axle assembly. Eagle less Select Drive System

12. Torque ball joint to lower control arm attaching bolts to 25 ft. lbs.
13. Lubricate steering stop, then install ball stud on steering knuckle. Torque stud nut to 75 ft. lbs. Install cotter pin.
14. Install wheel and brake drum or caliper and rotor and lower vehicle.

Eagle

NOTE: On these models, the lower control arm and lower ball joint must be replaced as an assembly.

1. Remove cotter pin, nut lock and hub nut, then raise and support front of vehicle.

2. Remove wheel, caliper and rotor.
3. Remove lower ball joint cotter pin and retaining nut.
4. Using tool No. J-9656, disconnect lower ball joint from steering knuckle.
5. Remove half shaft flange bolts, then remove half shaft.
6. Remove bolts attaching strut rod to lower control arm, then disconnect stabilizer bar from lower control arm.
7. Remove inner pivot bolt, then remove lower control arm from crossmember.
8. Position control arm on cross member, then install inner pivot bolt. Do not tighten inner pivot bolt at this time.
9. Position lower ball joint on steering knuckle, then install ball joint stud nut.

Torque ball joint stud nut to 75 ft. lbs., then install cotter pin.
10. Connect stabilizer bar to lower control arm and torque lock nut to 7 ft. lbs.
11. Connect strut rod to lower control arm and torque attaching bolts to 75 ft. lbs.
12. Install half shaft to axle flange and torque bolts to 45 ft. lbs.
13. Position a suitable jack under control arm and raise control arm slightly to compress coil spring, then tighten inner pivot bolt to 110 ft. lbs.
14. Install rotor, caliper and hub nut. Torque hub nut to 180 ft. lbs., then install nut lock and cotter pin.
15. Install wheel and tire assembly, then lower vehicle and check wheel alignment.

SHOCK ABSORBER, REPLACE

Pacer

1. Disconnect shock absorber at upper mounting.
2. Raise and support vehicle.
3. Disconnect shock absorber at lower mounting.
4. Remove shock absorber.
5. Reverse procedure to install.

Exc. Pacer

After disconnecting shock absorber from wheelhouse panel at top and lower spring seat at the bottom, withdraw shock absorber out of top of wheelhouse.

SPRING, REPLACE

1977—80 Pacer

1. Remove shock absorber, then the stabilizer bar link bolt at lower control arm, if equipped.
2. On models with drum brakes, remove wheel, tire and drum. On disc brake models, remove wheel, tire, caliper and rotor.
3. Remove steering arm to knuckle attaching bolts and position arm aside.
4. Compress spring, Figs. 9 and 10.
5. Remove cotter pin and nut from lower ball joint, then using tool J-9656 and a hammer, disengage stud from steering knuckle and position knuckle aside.

NOTE: Use wire to support steering knuckle otherwise brake hoses may be damaged.

6. Position lower control arm aside and relieve spring tension. When all tension is relieved, remove tool and spring.
7. Reverse procedure to install.

1977—84 Exc. Pacer

1. Remove shock absorber.
2. Install spring compressor (J-23474) through upper spring seat opening, Fig. 11. Place tool lower attaching screws through shock absorber mounting holes in the lower spring seat. Install tool lower retainer.
3. Remove lower spring seat pivot retaining nuts.
4. Tighten compressor until spring is compressed approximately 1″.
5. Raise and support front of car under frame allowing control arms to fall free of lower spring seat. Remove wheel.
6. Pull lower spring seat away from car. Loosen compressor and allow lower spring seat to come out.
7. When all spring tension is released, remove tool lower retainer spring seat and spring.
8. Reverse procedure to install.

STEERING GEAR, REPLACE

1977—80 Pacer

1. Unlock steering column, then raise and support vehicle.
2. Remove reinforcement brace to crossmember and left engine support bracket attaching bolts, then remove brace.

3. On models with power steering, position a drain pan under steering gear housing and disconnect power steering hoses at gear.

NOTE: Cap hoses and connections to prevent entry of dirt.

4. Remove flexible coupling pinch bolt, then disconnect coupling from steering pinion shaft.
5. Turn wheels in direction of tie rod to be disconnected, then using a floor jack, raise lower control arm at least 2 in. Remove cotter pin and retaining nut from tie rod end and using tool J-3295, disconnect tie rod from steering arm.
6. Remove bolts attaching steering gear mounting clamp to right side of crossmember.
7. Remove steering gear housing to crossmember attaching nuts, then using a blunt punch, remove bolts, washers, sleeves and grommets from gear housing.
8. Rotate bottom of gear housing toward front of front of vehicle until pinion shaft is parallel with skid plate, then slide gear toward right side of vehicle until housing and tube clear mounting plate.
9. Reverse procedure to install.

1977—84 Except Pacer

Manual Steering
1. Remove flexible coupling bolts.
2. Remove pitman arm, using a suitable puller.
3. Remove mounting screws and lower steering gear from vehicle.
4. Reverse procedure to install.

Power Steering
1. Disconnect pressure and return hoses from gear. Raise hoses above pump level to keep oil from draining out of pump.
2. Remove flexible coupling bolt nuts, noting the different nut sizes to insure correct assembly.
3. On Eagle models, remove skid plate, if equipped, then remove left hand crossmember to sill support brace and stabilizer bar bracket from frame.
4. Remove pitman arm with a suitable puller.
5. Remove gear attaching bolts.
6. Slide lower shaft free of coupling flange, then remove gear.
7. Reverse procedure to install.

POWER STEERING PUMP, REPLACE

Models W/ 4 Cyl. Engine

1977—79
1. Remove adjuster lock nuts and washers attaching power steering pump and pivot bracket to pump mounting bracket. The lower adjuster assembly is accessible from underneath vehicle.

NOTE: To remove adjuster lock nuts, a 9/16 inch box wrench having a 45° offset must be used. All other power steering pump mounting bolts are of metric sizes.

2. Move power steering pump toward engine and remove drive belt, then loosen return hose clamp and slide clamp back along hose.

3. Pull power steering pump forward and disconnect pressure and return lines.
4. Remove bolts attaching power steering pump front mounting bracket to rear mounting bracket and engine, then remove pump, pivot bracket and front mounting bracket as an assembly.
5. Reverse procedure to install.

1980—84
1. Remove air induction hose, then remove power steering pump adjusting bracket mounting bolts.
2. Move power steering pump toward engine and remove drive belt.
3. Loosen return hose clamp and slide back along hose, then pull power steering pump forward and disconnect both pressure and return lines.
4. Remove bolts attaching power steering pump front mounting bracket to rear mounting bracket and engine.
5. Remove power steering pump, pivot bracket and front mounting bracket as an assembly.
6. Reverse procedure to install.

Models W/ 6 Cyl. Engine

Less A/C
1. Remove air pump drive belt, then remove air pump pivot stud nut.
2. Remove power steering pump adjusting stud nuts and pivot bolt, then remove pump drive belt.
3. Disconnect pressure and return lines, then remove bolts attaching power steering pump bracket to engine and remove pump.
4. Reverse procedure to install.

With A/C
1. Remove air induction hoses
2. Remove air pump adjusting bolt and pivot stud, then remove air pump drive belt.
3. Remove A/C compressor drive belt, then remove compressor pulley and pulley bracket as an assembly.
4. Remove power steering pump pivot bolt attaching lower edge of pump to engine.
5. Remove power steering pump adjusting bracket stud nuts and bolt attaching pump to rear bracket, then slide drive belt from pulley.
6. Pull power steering pump and front mounting bracket forward until bracket clears air pump pivot stud.
7. Remove air pump pivot stud and position air pump aside.
8. Disconnect power steering pump pressure and return lines, then remove pump.
9. Reverse procedure to install.

Models W/ V8 Engine

1. Remove fuel vapor charcoal canister, then disconnect pressure and return lines from power steering pump. Cap lines and fitting.
2. Remove air pump belt adjusting strap, then remove drive belt.
3. Remove two power steering pump mounting stud nuts from rear of pump mounting bracket, then remove drive belt.
4. Remove bolts attaching air pump support bracket to air pump and front of power steering pump mounting bracket.
5. Remove nut securing front of power steering pump bracket to water pump housing.
6. Remove power steering pump and front half of mounting bracket as an assembly.
7. Reverse procedure to install.

EAGLE FRONT AXLE
SERVICE, FIGS. 12 & 12A

Axle, Replace

Removal

1. Raise and support vehicle.
2. Install half shaft boot protectors J-28712 onto boots.
3. Remove half shaft to axle flange bolts and secure half shaft to vehicle underbody.
4. Insert wire through half shaft flange bolt holes, then compress half shaft and wrap wire between boots to prevent half shaft from separating.
5. Mark propeller shaft and axle yoke for reference during reassembly and remove propeller shaft.
6. Support axle assembly using suitable jack.
7. On models equipped with Select Drive System, remove brace rod and shift motor shield.
8. On all models, remove axle mounting bolts. On models less Select Drive System, the axle is secured to the engine block with five bolts. On models with Select Drive System, the axle is secured to the engine block by five bolts on the left hand side and one bolt on the right hand side.
9. On models equipped with Select Drive System, disconnect vacuum hose from axle shift motor, then partially lower axle assembly and disconnect vent hose.
10. On all models, lower axle assembly to allow access to vent hose and remove hose.
11. Remove axle assembly from vehicle.

NOTE: Do not apply any load or weight on the hub assembly whenever the half shafts are not securely attached to the axle shaft flanges.

Installation

1. Support axle assembly on suitable jack and position assembly under vehicle.
2. Raise axle assembly slightly and install vent hose.
3. Continue raising axle assembly until properly positioned and install axle mounting bolts. Torque bolts to 50 ft. lbs.
4. Connect propeller shaft to axle yoke. Ensure shaft and yoke are aligned.
5. Remove wire used to prevent half shafts from separating, then install half shaft to axle flange bolts and torque to 45 ft. lbs.
6. On models equipped with Select Drive System, connect vacuum harness on axle shift motor shield.
7. On all models, remove half shaft boot protectors.
8. On models equipped with select drive, connect brace rod to axle.

Axle Shaft Seal, Replace

1. Remove axle assembly.
2. Remove axle housing cover and drain lubricant.
3. Remove axle shaft retaining clip, then the axle shaft.
4. Remove axle shaft seal using suitable screwdriver.
5. Install replacement axle shaft seal using Installer J-29152 for right hand side axle shaft and Installer J-29154 for left hand

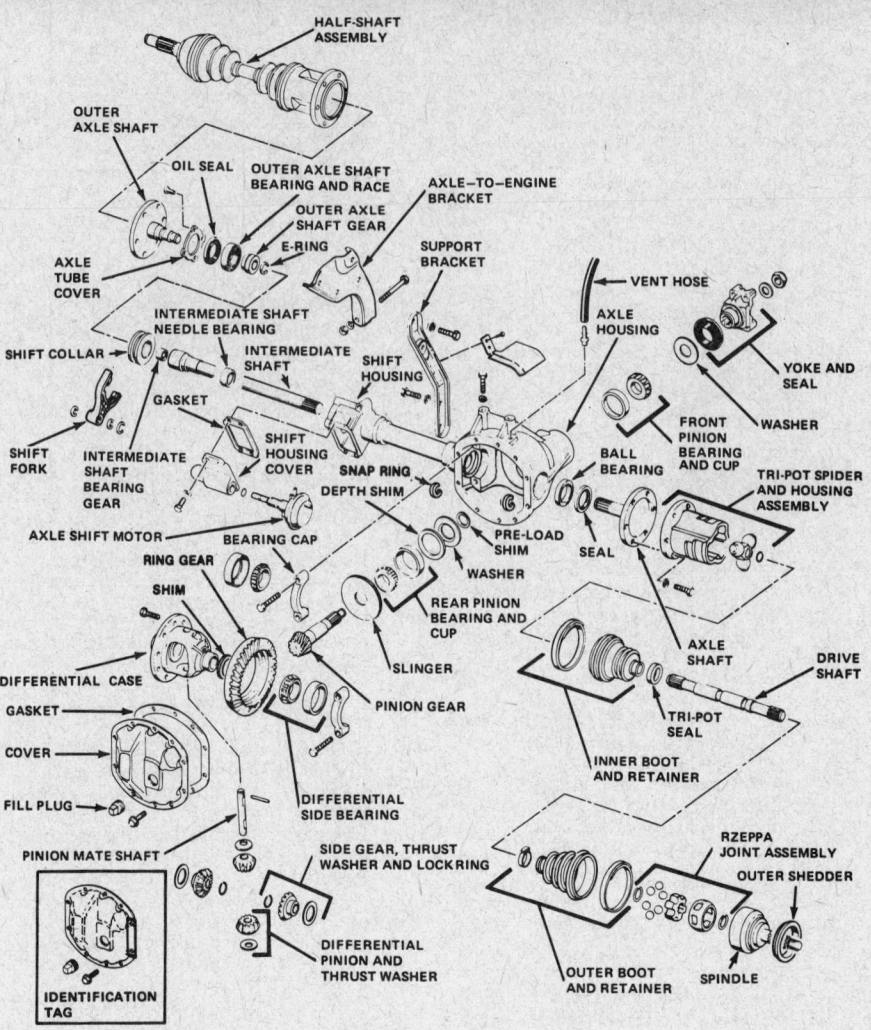

Fig. 12A Front axle assembly. Eagle models w/Select Drive System

side axle shaft.
6. Install axle shaft, then the axle shaft retaining clip.
7. Apply suitable sealant to axle housing cover and install cover. Torque cover bolts to 20 ft. lbs.
8. Fill axle with 2½ pints of SAE 85W-90 lubricant, then install assembly onto vehicle. Refer to Axle, Installation for procedures.

Axle Hub & Bearing

Removal

1. Raise and support vehicle, then remove wheel, caliper and rotor.
2. Remove bolts attaching axle shaft flange to half shaft.

NOTE: Insert wire through half shaft flange bolt holes, then compress half shaft and wrap wire between boots to prevent half shaft from separating.

3. Remove cotter pin, lock nut and axle shaft nut, then the half shaft.
4. Remove steering arm from steering knuckle.
5. Remove caliper anchor plate from steer-

ing knuckle, then the three torx head bolts retaining hub assembly using tool J-26359.
6. Remove hub assembly from steering knuckle and clean grease from steering knuckle cavity.

Disassemble

1. Press hub from bearing carrier, then remove bearings, hub spacer, steering knuckle pin seal, carrier to hub seal, carrier O-ring and bearing spacer, if equipped, Fig. 13.
2. Clean all components and inspect for wear and damage and replace as necessary.

NOTE: If hub incorporates ball bearings, the entire hub assembly must be replaced if damage to internal components is indicated. If hub incorporates tapered bearings, internal hub components may be replaced as necessary. Bearings and races must be replaced in matched sets.

3. Press bearing races from hub carrier, if necessary. Install replacement bearing races using a brass drift or suitable press.

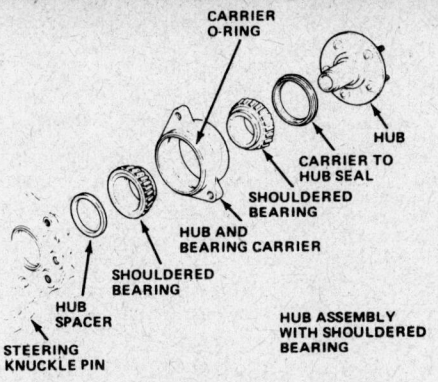

Fig. 13 Disassembled view of axle hub. 1980–84 Eagle.

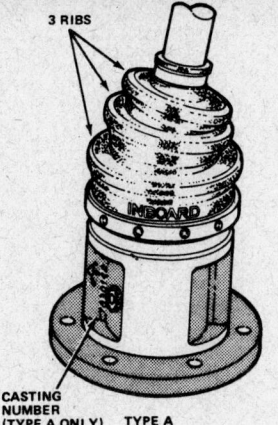
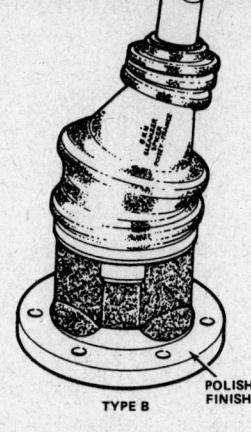

Fig. 14 Half shaft identification. 1980–84 Eagle

Assemble

1. Fill steering knuckle pin, hub, bearing carrier and lip type seal cavities with lithium base wheel bearing lubricant.
2. Pack bearings with lithium base wheel bearing lubricant, then install bearings into hub carrier, Fig. 13.
3. Install seal onto hub side of bearing carrier, then press hub into carrier and install hub spacer on end of hub shaft.

NOTE: Do not install bearing carrier O-ring at this time.

---

4. Install inner seal into steering knuckle pin.
5. Install splash shield onto hub and bearing carrier, then install bearing carrier O-ring.
6. Install splash shield and bearing carrier into steering knuckle pin, then install carrier attaching bolts and torque to 75 ft. lbs.

Installation

1. Partially fill hub cavity of steering knuckle with chassis lubricant and install hub assembly onto steering knuckle. Torque hub torx head bolts to 75 ft. lbs.
2. Install caliper anchor plate and torque plate retaining bolts to 100 ft. lbs.
3. Install steering arm onto steering knuckle and torque retaining bolts to 100 ft. lbs.
4. Install half shaft, then the axle flange to shaft bolts and hub nut. Torque half shaft to flange bolts to 45 ft. lbs and hub nut 175 ft. lbs.
5. Install lock nut, replacement cotter pin, rotor, caliper and wheel.

Axle Shaft, Replace

1. Refer to Axle Shaft Seal, Replace. Perform steps 1 through 3 for axle shaft removal and steps 6 through 8 for axle shaft installation.

Axle Shaft Bearing, Replace

NOTE: Two different style axle shaft bearings are used on the Eagle front axle. The left side axle shaft uses a ball bearing. The right side axle shaft uses a needle bearing.

---

1. Remove axle assembly. Refer to Axle, Removal for procedure.

2. Remove axle housing cover and drain lubricant.
3. Remove axle shaft retaining clip, then the axle shaft.
4. Remove axle shaft seal using suitable screwdriver.
5. Remove needle bearing using Tools J-29173 and J-2619-1. Remove ball bearing using suitable brass punch and hammer.

NOTE: If needle bearing tools are not available, then remove the differential, then the bearing using a 15/16 in. socket and three foot extension bar.

---

6. Install axle shaft bearings. Use tool J-29153 to install needle bearing and tool J-29154 to install ball bearing.
7. Install axle shaft seals using Installer J-29152 for the right hand side axle shaft and Installer J-29154 for left hand side axle shaft.
8. Install axle shafts, then the retaining clips.
9. Apply suitable sealant to axle housing cover and install cover. Torque cover bolts to 20 ft. lbs.
10. Fill axle with 2½ pints of SAE 85W-90 lubricant, then install asembly onto vehicle. Refer to Axle, Installation for procedure.

Half Shaft Service

NOTE: Three different types of half shafts are used on these models. When performing half shaft service, refer to Fig. 14 to identify type of half shaft installed in vehicle. The half shafts are identified by the different configurations of tripod housings and inner boots.

TYPE A

Disassemble

1. Using a suitable tool cut small boot clamp from outer boot.
2. Using a brass punch, separate outer boot from metal retainer. Tap evenly around retainer to remove from boot, then slide boot from constant velocity joint.
3. Using snap ring pliers, remove snap ring, then remove constant velocity joint from shaft.
4. Remove outer boot and retainer from shaft.

5. Using a brass punch, tap constant velocity joint cage until cage is tilted outward far enough to remove first ball. Remove remaining balls in the same manner.
6. Rotate constant velocity cage outward until cage is at a 90° angle from the installed position and remove cage and inner race, then rotate inner race upward and out of cage.
7. Remove small clamp from inner boot, then using a brass punch separate inner boot from metal retainer. Tap evenly around retainer to remove, then slide boot and retainer from tripod housing.
8. Remove tripod and shaft from housing, then using snap ring pliers, remove inner snap ring from groove. Slide tripod joint onto shaft to expose outer snap ring, then remove outer snap ring and tripod joint.
9. If necessary, remove inner snap ring from shaft and remove boot.

Inspection

Clean all components in a suitable solvent and dry with compressed air. Check all components for wear and damage and joints for rough operation, replace components as necessary.

NOTE: Outer constant velocity joint and inner tripod joint are replaced as an assembly.

Assemble

1. Pack spindle hub with chassis grease.
2. Install outer constant velocity joint inner race into cage, then position cage 90° from the installed position and insert cage and race into hub.
3. Using a brass punch, tilt cage outward until first ball can be installed in cage, then install remaining balls in the same manner.
4. Pack outer constant velocity joint with chassis grease, then install outer boot and retainer on half shaft.
5. Install inner race snap ring into inner race snap ring groove, then install constant velocity joint onto shaft until race snap ring seats in groove.
6. Using a brass punch, seat metal retainer on spindle, then install boot into retainer. If difficulty is encountered, support metal portion of boot on wooden blocks and press retainer into boot.
7. Using tool No. J-22610, install small outer boot clamp.
8. Pack tripod joint housing with chassis

grease, then install inner boot and retainer onto half shaft.

9. If removed, install inner snap ring onto shaft, past snap ring groove.

10. Install tripod joint onto shaft, then install outer snap ring into outer snap ring groove. Slide tripod joint toward outer snap ring, then slide inner snap ring into groove.

11. Install inner tripod joint and shaft into tripod housing, then seat inner boot retainer on tripod housing.

12. Using a brass punch, seat boot into metal retainer, then install small inner boot clamp using tool No. J-22610.

TYPES B & C

Disassemble

1. Using a suitable tool cut and remove both outer boot clamps, then roll outer boot from constant velocity joint.

2. Position a wooden block against constant velocity joint inner race and drive joint from shaft. If half shaft is to be positioned in a vise, use protective vise jaws.

3. Using a brass drift, tap constant velocity joint cage until cage is tilted outward far enough to remove first ball, then remove remaining balls in the same manner.

4. Align two outer constant velocity joint oblong holes with slots located on interior wall of spindle housing and remove cage and inner race.

5. Align shoulder between race grooves with inside of oblong cage holes, then rotate inner race out of cage using the larger of the two openings.

6. Remove two snap rings from shaft, then remove outer boot.

7. Remove rubber retaining ring from small end of inner boot, then using a brass drift, tap evenly around retainer to separate from boot. Slide boot and retainer from tripod housing.

8. Remove tripod joint and shaft assembly from housing, then remove snap ring that retains tripod joint to shaft and remove tripod joint.

9. If necessary, remove inner boot.

Inspection

Clean all components in a suitable solvent and dry with compressed air. Check all components for wear and damage and joints for rough operation, replace components as necessary.

NOTE: Outer constant velocity joint and inner tripod joint are replaced as an assembly.

Assemble

1. Pack spindle hub with chassis grease.

2. Install outer constant velocity joint inner into cage, then install cage and race assembly into spindle hub. The smaller diameter of the cage and stopping groove of race must face outward.

3. Using a brass drift, tilt cage outward until first ball can be installed into cage, then install remaining balls in the same manner.

4. Pack constant velocity joint with chassis grease, then install outer boot on half shaft.

5. Install inner and outer snap rings, then constant velocity joint onto shaft until inner race contacts inner snap ring.

6. Position boot over constant velocity joint, then install both boot clamps using tool No. J-22610.

7. Pack tripod joint housing with chassis grease, then install inner small retainer

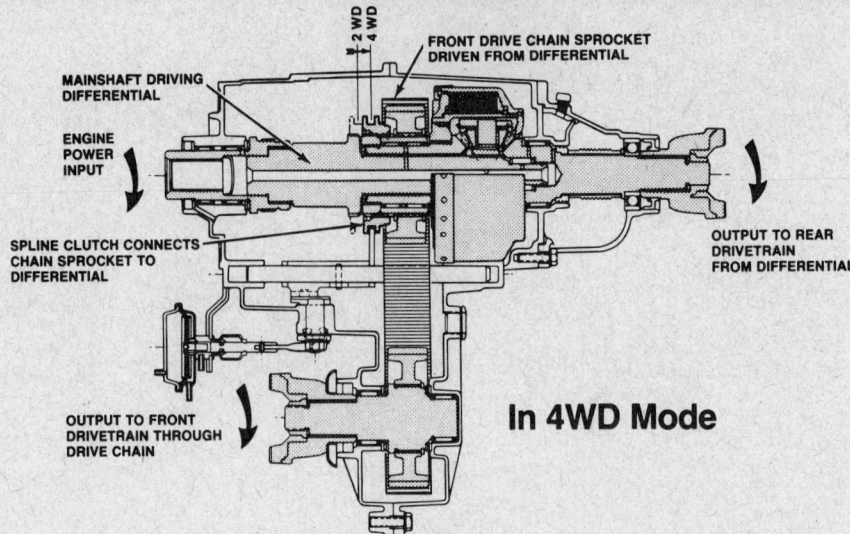

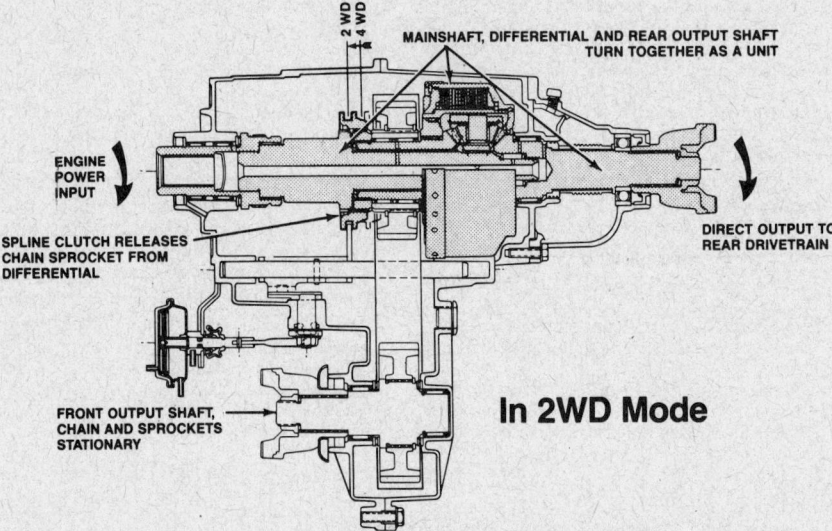

Fig. 15 Transfer case operation. 1981–84 Eagle W/ Select Drive System

ring, boot and large retainer ring onto half shaft.

8. Install tripod joint and snap ring onto shaft, then install tripod joint and shaft into housing.

9. Install boot and metal retainer over tripod housing, then using a brass drift, carefully seat boot and retainer.

10. Install rubber retaining ring over small end of boot.

Intermediate Shaft, Outer Axle Shaft & Shift Housing, Replace

Models W/Select Drive System

1. Raise and support front of vehicle.

2. Remove front axle assembly, then drain lubricant.

3. Remove bolts securing shift housing and remove shift fork, shifting housing and shift motor as an assembly, Fig. 12A.

4. Working through access hole in the outer axle shaft flange, remove screws securing axle tube cover.

5. Remove outer axle shaft assembly by tapping shaft flange with a rubber or plastic mallet.

6. Remove intermediate shaft snap ring, then remove intermediate shaft and shift collar.

7. Using a suitable puller and slide hammer, remove outer axle shaft bearing race.

8. Using adapter tool No. J-26225 and slide hammer J-6471-2, remove intermediate shaft needle bearing from axle tube end.

9. Using spreader tool No. J-29369-1 and slide hammer No. J-2619-01, remove intermediate shaft gear bearing.

NOTE: The intermediate shaft gear is retained on the axle shaft by an internal type expandable snap ring. When removing the bearing from the gear be sure to support the gear face on vise jaws to avoid pulling the gear off the shaft. The gear and shaft are serviced only as an assembly.

10. Remove outer axle shaft retaining "E" ring.

11. Make a reference mark on outer axle

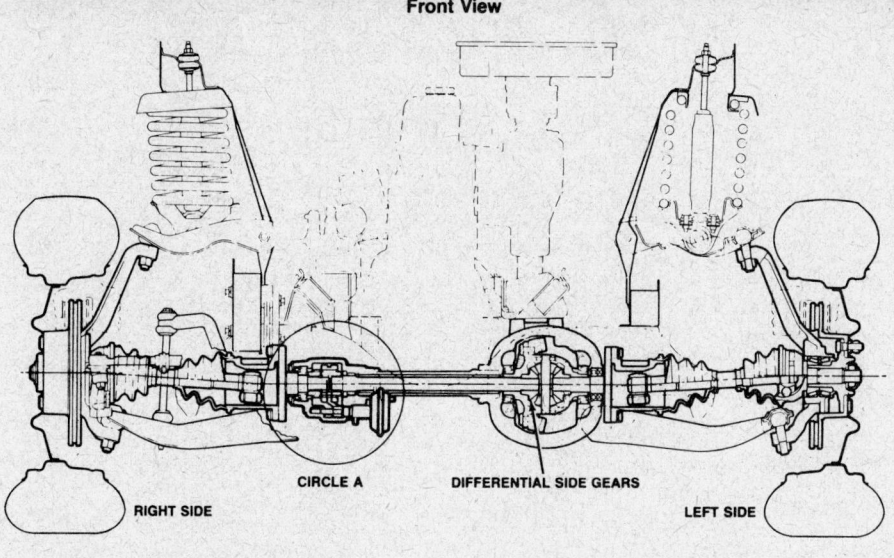

Front View

CIRCLE A

DIFFERENTIAL SIDE GEARS

RIGHT SIDE

LEFT SIDE

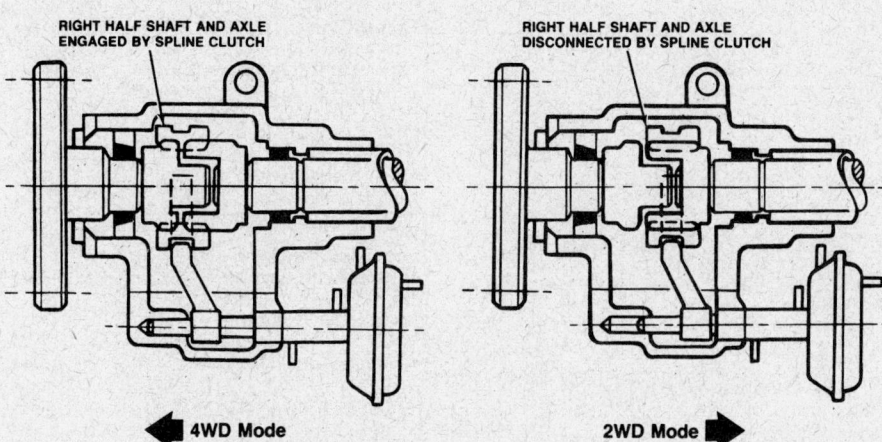

RIGHT HALF SHAFT AND AXLE ENGAGED BY SPLINE CLUTCH

RIGHT HALF SHAFT AND AXLE DISCONNECTED BY SPLINE CLUTCH

◄ 4WD Mode

2WD Mode ►

Select Drive Axle Disconnect

From Circle A Above

Fig. 16 Front drive axle assembly. 1981–84 Eagle W/ Select Drive System

shaft gear (for assembly purposes) and remove gear from shaft.
12. Remove outer axle shaft bearing using an arbor press.
13. Remove axle oil seal and tube cover.
14. Clean and carefully inspect all components for wear or damage. Replace all necessary components.
15. Install axle oil seal and tube cover on axle shaft.
16. Using an arbor press, install axle shaft bearing and race on shaft.
17. Install axle shaft gear on shaft using an arbor press. Be sure to align reference mark. Also ensure gear splines are facing outward.
18. Install axle shaft "E" ring.
19. Using tool No. J-29153, install intermediate shaft needle bearing.
20. Install intermediate shaft gear needle bearing in gear bore using an arbor press.
21. Install intermediate shaft, then install shift collar, and seat shaft in differential.
22. Install intermediate shaft lock ring.
23. Install outer axle shaft assembly, torque axle tube cover bolts evenly and in a cross sequence. Torque bolts 144 inch-pounds.
24. Install gasket on shift housing cover and install.

NOTE: Check to ensure the shift fork and tabs are aligned in the shift collar.

25. Torque shift housing cover bolts to 108 inch-pounds.
26. Install axle cover using a new gasket. Torque bolts to 20 ft. lbs.
27. Fill shift housing with five ozs. of specified lubricant, then fill axle housing.

Select Drive System

The Select Drive is a system which permits the full time four wheel drive power train to be operated in a two wheel drive mode. When the vehicle is stopped, the system can be changed from two wheel drive to four wheel or four wheel drive to two wheel drive, by pulling the instrument panel control switch pull release pin downward and moving the control switch lever to the desired position. The two major components of this system are a shifting device in the transfer case and a disconnecting mechanism in the front axle, which are controlled by the instrument panel switch through a series of vacuum actuators.

The vacuum actuated shifter mechanism located on the transfer case, Fig. 15, slides a splined clutch, located on the transfer case main shaft, rearward to engage or forward to disengage power to the front drive chain sprocket. In the two wheel drive position, the shifter mechanism also locks the transfer case differential. Also the main shaft and differential assembly will turn as a unit, transferring power to the rear driveshaft, while front output shaft, chain and sprocket remain stationary.

A vacuum actuated disconnect device, Fig. 16, is used to engage or disengage a splined clutch that connects the right hand driveshaft to the right hand half shaft. When four wheel drive is selected, the spline clutch is engaged and the front drive axle operates in a normal manner. When two wheel is selected, the vacuum actuator releases the spline clutch, which releases drive to the right hand half shaft and allows the right hand driveshaft to rotate freely. Due to the design of the differential, to equalize torque between left and right axle shafts, disconnecting the right axle shaft will allow the left axle shaft to rotate freely. The axle disconnect will not release all front drive components in the two wheel drive mode. Half shafts and different side gears will continue to rotate with the front wheels as the vehicle is driven.

AXLE SHIFT MOTOR, REPLACE

Models W/ Select Drive System
1. Make a reference mark on fork and housing for assembly purposes.
2. Rotate shift motor and remove retaining snap rings using a suitable screwdriver.
3. Remove shift motor from housing and remove O-ring from motor.
4. Reverse procedure to install.

BUICK
EXC. SKYHAWK, 1980–84 SKYLARK & 1982–84 CENTURY

INDEX OF SERVICE OPERATIONS

> NOTE: Refer to main index, "GM Front Wheel Drive," for front drive axle & drive link belt service procedures on 1979–84 Riviera. Also refer to the front of this manual for vehicle manufacturer's special service tool suppliers.

ENGINE IDENTIFICATION

Buick engines are stamped with two different sets of numbers. One is the engine production code which identifies the engine and its approximate production date. The other is the engine serial number which is the same number that is found on the vehicle identification plate. To identify an engine, look for the production code prefix letters, then refer to the following table for its identification.

Buick built engines have the distributor located at the front of the engine. On 1977–79 and 1980 V8 models, the engine production

code is located on the right front of block. On 1980–84 V6 models, the production code is located on the left rear of block. On 1977–80 vehicles, the fifth digit in the VIN denotes engine code. On 1981–84 vehicles the eighth digit in the VIN denotes engine code.

Chevrolet built V8 engines have the distributor located at rear of engine with clockwise rotor rotation; the code is stamped on the engine case pad located below the cylinder head on the right hand side of the engine.

Oldsmobile built engines have the distributor located at the rear of the engine with counter-clockwise rotor rotation and right side mounted fuel pump. The engine production code is located on the oil filler tube on early 1978 engines or the left side valve cover on late 1978 and 1979–84 engines.

Pontiac built V8 engines, have the distributor located at the rear of the engine with counter-clockwise rotor rotation and left side mounted fuel pump. The engine production code is located on the right front of the cylinder block.

ENGINE CODES

Engine	VIN	Code Prefix
1977		
V6-231⑩	C	RA, RB
V6-231⑩	C	SG, SI, SJ, SK, SL
V6-231⑩	C	SM, SN, ST, SU
V6-231⑫	A	RC, RD
V8-301①	Y	YF, YJ, YW, YX
V8-305②	U	CPA, CPY
V8-350③	H	FA, FB, FK
V8-350④	J	FC, FD, FG
V8-350④	J	FH, FL
V8-350⑤	R	QK, QL
V8-350⑤	R	QP, QQ, Q2, Q3, Q6, Q7
V8-350⑤	R	Q8, Q9, TK, TL, TN
V8-350⑤	R	TO, TQ, TX, TY
V8-350②	L	CKM, CKR
V8-403⑤	K	UA, UB, U2, U3
V8-403⑤	K	VA, VB, VJ, VK
1978		
V6-196	C	PA, PB
V6-231③⑥	A	EA, EG, OH, OK
V6-231③⑥	A	EG, EI, EJ, EK, EL
V6-231④⑦	G	EO, OL
V6-231④⑦	3	EP, ER, ES
V8-301①	Y	XA, XC
V8-305②③	U	CEK, CPZ, CRU, CRX
V8-305②③	U	CRX, CRZ, CTM, CTR
V8-305②③	U	CTW, CTX, C3P
V8-350④	X	MA, MB
V8-350④⑤	R	Q2, Q3, TO
V8-350④⑤	R	TP, TQ, TS
V8-350②④	L	CHM, CKM, CMC
V8-403⑤	K	UA, UB, U2
V8-403⑤	K	U3, VA, VB
1979		
V6-196③⑧	C	FA, FB, FE, FG, FH
V6-231③⑥	A	RA, RJ, RB, RW, NJ, RC RG, WL, RX, RY
V6-231④⑦	3	RR, RU, RV, RO, RS, RP, RT
V6-231③⑨	2	RM, RN
V8-301①③⑧	Y	XP, XR
V8-301①④⑧	W	PXL, PXN
V8-305②④	G	DNJ
V8-305②④	H	DNX, DNY, DTA
V8-350②④	L	DRJ, DRY
V8-350④⑤	R	UA, UZ, U9, VK
V8-350④⑧	X	SA, SB

Engine	VIN	Code Prefix
V8-403④⑤	K	QB, Q3, TB, GB, G3
1980		
V6-231③⑥	A	EA, EB, EC, ED, EK, EM, EP, OV, OW, OX, OY
V6-231④⑦	3	EE, EH, EJ, ER, EU, EV, EW, OS
V6-252④	4	MF
V8-301①④	W	X3, XT, XW
V8-305②④	H	CEC, CMM
V8-350②④	X	MB, MT, MU
V8-350④⑤	R	UAD, UAF, UAS, UAT
V8-350⑤⑪	N	VBM, VBN, VBS, VBT, VBU, VCD, VCH
1981		
V6-231③⑥	A	NA, NB, NC, ND, NF, NJ, NK, NL, NZ, LZ, RA, RB, RK, RL, RC, RD
V6-231④⑦	3	NE, NR, NG, RO, RR
V6-252④	4	SA, SB, SC, SD, SF, SG, SJ, SK, SL, SM, SN, SP, SQ
V8-265①③	S	AW, DB, DC, AZ, BA, DH, DJ
V8-307④⑤	Y	TKA, TKB, TKC, TKL, TKM, TKP, TKT, TKU, TKX, TKY, TKZ, TLA, TLB, TLD, TLF, TLH, TLJ, TLK, TLL, TLM, TLN, TLP, TLR, TLT, TMF, TMH, TMJ
V8-350⑤⑪	N	VKB, VKC, VKH, VKJ, VKN, VKR, VKU, VKY, VLA, VLC, VLD, VLK, VLL, VLN, VLP, VL8, VLY, VMJ, VMT, VMX, VMY, VNA, VNB, VNC, VND, VNE, VNF, VNJ, VNK, VNL, VNR, VNT, VNV, VNZ, VPA, VPK, VPL, VPR, VPS,

Engine	VIN	Code Prefix
		VPT, VPV, VPX, VPY, VPZ, VRP, VRH
1982		
V6-231③⑥	A	MA, MC, MG, MK, ML, MM
V6-231④⑦	3	MB, MF, MH
V6-252④	4	FA, FB, FC, FD, FE, FF, FG, FH, FJ, FK
V6-262⑤⑪	V	UAA, UAD, UAJ
V8-307④⑤	Y	TAA, TAB, TAC, TAD, TAF, TAK, TAM, TAW, TAX, TAY, TAZ, TBA, TBB
V8-350⑤⑪	N	VAB, VAC, VAD, VAK, VAL, VAM, VAN, VAP, VAS, VAU, VAW, VAX, VAY, VAZ, VBA, VBB, VBC, VBP, VBU, VBW
1983		
V6-231③⑥	A	ND, NG, NH, NJ, NL
V6-231④⑦	8	NB, NC, NK
V6-252④	4	SA, SB, SC, SD, SF, SG, SH
V6-262⑤⑪	V	UKA, UKB, UKC, UKJ, UKK
V8-307④⑤	Y	TKA, TKB, TKD, TKH, TKK, TKL, TKM, TKN, TKP, TKS, TKT, TKY
V8-350⑤⑪	N	VKB, VKC, VKD, VKK, VKL, VKR, VKS, VKT, VKZ, VLA, VLB, VLP, VLS, VLT, VLW

①—Pontiac built engine.
②—Chevrolet built engine.
③—Two barrel carb.
④—Four barrel carb.
⑤—Oldsmobile built engine.
⑥—Except turbocharged engine.
⑦—Turbocharged engine.
⑧—Except California.
⑨—California.
⑩—Except even fire engine.
⑪—Diesel.
⑫—Even fire engine.

GRILLE IDENTIFICATION

1977 Skylark

1977 Century Sedan

1977 Century Special Sport

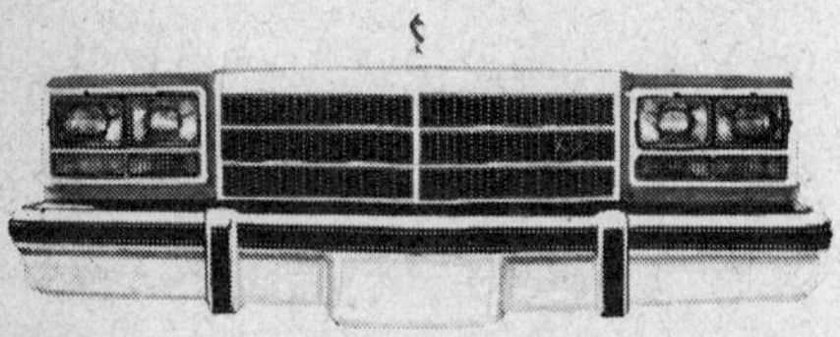

1977 Regal

1977 LeSabre & Estate Wagon

1977 Electra

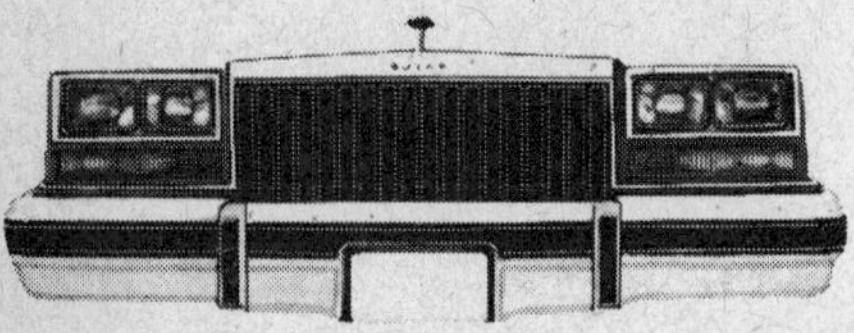

1977 Riviera

1978 Skylark SR

1978 Skylark Custom

1978 Regal

1978 Century

1978 Century Sport Coupe

1978 LeSabre

1978 Limited & Estate Wagon

1978 Riviera

1979 Skylark

1979 Century

1979 Regal

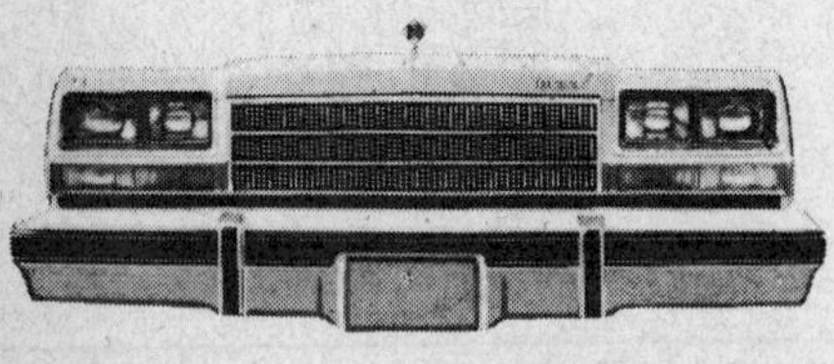

1979 LeSabre & Estate Wagon

1979 Electra

1979—80 Riviera

Continued

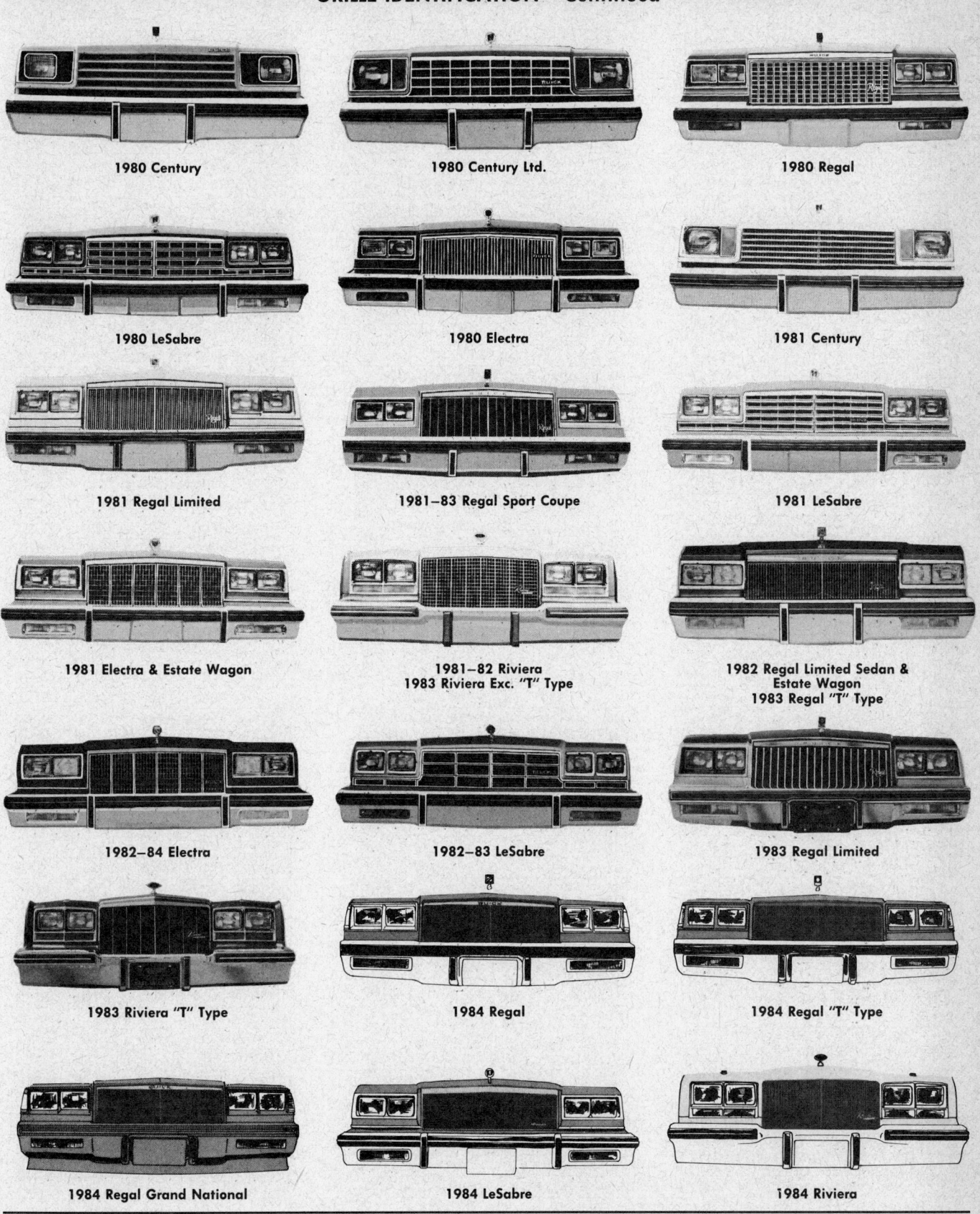

1980 Century

1980 Century Ltd.

1980 Regal

1980 LeSabre

1980 Electra

1981 Century

1981 Regal Limited

1981—83 Regal Sport Coupe

1981 LeSabre

1981 Electra & Estate Wagon

1981—82 Riviera
1983 Riviera Exc. "T" Type

1982 Regal Limited Sedan &
Estate Wagon
1983 Regal "T" Type

1982—84 Electra

1982—83 LeSabre

1983 Regal Limited

1983 Riviera "T" Type

1984 Regal

1984 Regal "T" Type

1984 Regal Grand National

1984 LeSabre

1984 Riviera

GENERAL ENGINE SPECIFICATIONS

Year	Engine CID①/Liter	V.I.N. Code②	Carburetor	Bore and Stroke	Compression Ratio	Net H.P. @ R.P.M.③	Maximum Torque Lbs. Ft. @ R.P.M.	Normal Oil Pressure Pounds
1977	V6-231, 3.8L⑰	C	2GE, 2 Bbl.④	3.80 × 3.40	8.0	105 @ 3200	185 @ 2000	37
	V6-231, 3.8L⑱	A	2GE, 2 Bbl.④	3.80 × 3.40	8.0	105 @ 3200	185 @ 2000	37
	V8-301, 4.9L⑧	Y	M2MC, 2 Bbl.④	4.00 × 3.00	8.2	135 @ 4000	250 @ 1600	38–42
	V8-305, 5.0L⑨	U	2GC, 2 Bbl.④	3.736 × 3.48	8.5	145 @ 3800	245 @ 2400	32–40
	V8-350, 5.7L	H	2GE, 2 Bbl.④	3.80 × 3.85	8.1	140 @ 3200	280 @ 1400	37
	V8-350, 5.7L	J	M4MC, 4 Bbl.④	3.80 × 3.85	8.0	155 @ 3400	275 @ 1800	37
	V8-350, 5.7L⑨	L	M4MC, 4 Bbl.④	4.00 × 3.48	8.5	170 @ 3800	270 @ 2400	32–40
	V8-350, 5.7L⑤	R	M4MC, 4 Bbl.④	4.057 × 3.385	8.5	170 @ 3800	275 @ 2400	30–45
	V8-403, 6.6L⑤	K	M4MC, 4 Bbl.④	4.351 × 3.385	8.5	185 @ 3600	315 @ 2400	30–45
1978	V6-196, 3.2L	C	2GE, 2 Bbl.④	3.50 × 3.40	8.0	90 @ 3600	165 @ 2000	37
	V6-231, 3.8L	A	2GE, 2 Bbl.④	3.80 × 3.40	8.0	105 @ 3400	185 @ 2000	37
	V6-231, 3.8L⑩	G	M2ME, 2 Bbl.④	3.80 × 3.40	8.0	150 @ 3800	245 @ 2400	37
	V6-231, 3.8L⑩	3	M4ME, 4 Bbl.④	3.80 × 3.40	8.0	165 @ 3800	265 @ 2800	37
	V8-301, 4.9L⑧	Y	M2MC, 2 Bbl.④	4.00 × 3.00	8.2	135 @ 4000	245 @ 2000	30–40
	V8-305, 5.0L⑨	U	2GC, 2 Bbl.④	4.736 × 3.48	8.5	145 @ 3800	245 @ 2400	30–40
	V8-305, 5.0L⑨	H	4GC, 4 Bbl.④	3.736 × 3.48	8.5	160 @ 4000	235 @ 2400	30–40
	V8-350, 5.7L⑤	X	M4MC, 4 Bbl.④	3.80 × 3.85	8.0	155 @ 3400	275 @ 1800	37
	V8-350, 5.7L⑤	R	M4MC, 4 Bbl.④	4.057 × 3.385	8.0	170 @ 3800	275 @ 2000	30–45
	V8-350, 5.7L⑨	L	M4MC, 4 Bbl.④	4.00 × 3.48	8.5	170 @ 3800	270 @ 2400	32–40
	V8-403, 6.6L⑤	K	M4MC, 4 Bbl.④	4.351 × 3.385	8.0	185 @ 3600	320 @ 2200	30–45
1979	V6-196, 3.2L	C	M2ME, 2 Bbl.④	3.50 × 3.40	8.0	105 @ 3800	160 @ 2000	37
	V6-231, 3.8L⑥	A	M2ME, 2 Bbl.④	3.80 × 3.40	8.0	115 @ 3800	190 @ 2000	37
	V6-231, 3.8L⑦	2	E2ME, 2 Bbl.④	3.80 × 3.40	8.0	115 @ 3800	190 @ 2000	37
	V6-231, 3.8L⑩	3	M4ME, 4 Bbl.④	3.80 × 3.40	8.0	170 @ 4000	265 @ 2400	37
	V6-231, 3.8L⑩⑪	3	M4ME, 4 Bbl.④	3.80 × 3.40	8.0	175 @ 4000	275 @ 2600	37
	V6-231, 3.8L⑩⑫	3	M4ME, 4 Bbl.④	3.80 × 3.40	8.0	185 @ 4000	280 @ 2400	37
	V8-301, 4.9L⑧	Y	M2MC, 2 Bbl.④	4.00 × 3.00	8.2	140 @ 3600	235 @ 2000	35–40
	V8-301, 4.9L⑧	W	M4MC, 4 Bbl.④	4.00 × 3.00	8.2	150 @ 4000	240 @ 2000	35–40
	V8-305, 5.0L⑨	G	M2MC, 2 Bbl.④	3.736 × 3.48	8.5	130 @ 3200	245 @ 2000	32–40
	V8-305, 5.0L⑨	H	M4MC, 4 Bbl.④	3.736 × 3.48	8.5	160 @ 4000	235 @ 2400	32–40
	V8-350, 5.7L	X	M4MC, 4 Bbl.④	3.80 × 3.85	8.0	155 @ 3400	280 @ 1800	34
	V8-350, 5.7L⑨	L	M4MC, 4 Bbl.④	4.00 × 3.48	8.5	160 @ 3800	260 @ 2400	32–40
	V8-350, 5.7L⑤⑫	R	M4MC, 4 Bbl.④	4.057 × 3.385	8.0	170 @ 3800	275 @ 2000	30–45
	V8-403, 6.6L⑤	K	M4MC, 4 Bbl.④	4.351 × 3.385	8.0	185 @ 3600	320 @ 2000	30–45
1980	V6-231, 3.8L	A	M2ME, 2 Bbl.④	3.80 × 3.40	8.0	110 @ 3800	190 @ 1600	37
	V6-231, 3.8L⑩	3	E4ME, 4 Bbl.④	3.80 × 3.40	8.0	170 @ 4000	265 @ 2400	37
	V6-252, 4.1L	4	M4ME, 4 Bbl.④	3.97 × 3.40	8.1	125 @ 4000	205 @ 2000	37
	V8-265, 4.3L⑧	S	M2ME, 2 Bbl.④	3.75 × 3.00	8.2	120 @ 3600	210 @ 1600	40
	V8-301, 4.9L⑧	W	M4ME, 4 Bbl.④	4.00 × 3.00	8.2	150 @ 4000	240 @ 2000	38–42
	V8-305, 5.0L⑨	H	E4ME, 4 Bbl.④	3.736 × 3.48	8.5	155 @ 4000	230 @ 2400	32–40
	V8-350, 5.7L	X	M4MC, 4 Bbl.④⑬	3.80 × 3.85	8.0	155 @ 3400	280 @ 1600	34
	V8-350, 5.7L⑤⑫	R	M4MC, 4 Bbl.④⑬	4.057 × 3.385	8.3	160 @ 3600	270 @ 2000	30–45
	V8-350, 5.7L⑤⑭	N	Fuel Injection	4.057 × 3.385	22.5	105 @ 3200	205 @ 1600	30–45
1981	V6-231, 3.8L	A	M2ME, 2 Bbl.④	3.80 × 3.40	8.0	110 @ 3800	190 @ 1600	37
	V6-231, 3.8L⑩	3	E4ME, 4 Bbl.④	3.80 × 3.40	8.0	⑮	⑯	37
	V6-252, 4.1L	4	E4ME, 4 Bbl.④	3.97 × 3.40	8.0	125 @ 4000	205 @ 2000	37
	V8-265, 4.3L⑧	S	M2ME, 2 Bbl.④	3.75 × 3.00	8.0	119 @ 4000	204 @ 2000	37
	V8-307, 5.0L⑤	Y	M4MC, 4 Bbl.④	3.80 × 3.385	8.0	150 @ 3600	245 @ 1600	37
	V8-350, 5.7L⑤⑭	N	Fuel Injection	4.057 × 3.385	22.5	105 @ 3200	205 @ 1600	30–45
1982	V6-231, 3.8L	A	E2ME, 2 Bbl.④	3.80 × 3.40	8.0	110 @ 3800	190 @ 1600	37
	V6-231, 3.8L⑩	3	E4ME, 4 Bbl.④	3.80 × 3.40	8.0	⑮	⑯	37
	V6-252, 4.1L	4	E4ME, 4 Bbl.④	3.97 × 3.40	8.0	125 @ 4000	205 @ 2000	37

Continued

GENERAL ENGINE SPECIFICATIONS—Continued

Year	Engine CID①/Liter	Engine V.I.N. Code②	Carburetor	Bore and Stroke	Compression Ratio	Net H.P. @ R.P.M.③	Maximum Torque Lbs. Ft. @ R.P.M.	Normal Oil Pressure Pounds
1982, Cont.	V6-262, 4.3L⑤⑭	V	Fuel Injection	4.057 × 3.385	21.6	85 @ 3600	165 @ 1600	35
	V8-307, 5.0L⑤	Y	E4ME, 4 Bbl.④	3.80 × 3.385	8.5	140 @ 3600	240 @ 1600	35
	V8-350, 5.7L⑤⑭	N	Fuel Injection	4.057 × 3.385	22.5	105 @ 3200	200 @ 1600	35
1983	V6-231, 3.8L	A	2 Bbl.④	3.80 × 3.40	8.0	110 @ 3800	190 @ 1600	37
	V6-231, 3.8L⑩	8	4 Bbl.④	3.80 × 3.40	8.0	180 @ 4000	⑲	37
	V6-252, 4.1L	4	4 Bbl.④	3.965 × 3.40	8.0	125 @ 4000	205 @ 2000	37
	V6-262, 4.3L⑤⑭	V	Fuel Injection	4.057 × 3.385	22.5	85 @ 3600	165 @ 1600	30-45
	V8-307, 5.0L⑤	Y	4 Bbl.④	3.80 × 3.385	8.0	140 @ 3600	240 @ 1600	30-45
	V8-350, 5.7L⑤⑭	N	Fuel Injection	4.057 × 3.385	22.5	105 @ 3200	200 @ 1600	30-45
1984	V6-231, 3.8L	A	2 Bbl.④	3.80 × 3.40	8.0	110 @ 3800	190 @ 1600	37
	V6-231, 3.8L⑩	9	Fuel Injection	3.80 × 3.40	8.0	190 @ 4000	300 @ 2400	37
	V6-252, 4.1L	4	4 Bbl.④	3.965 × 3.40	8.0	125 @ 4000	205 @ 2000	37
	V6-262, 4.3L⑤⑭	V	Fuel Injection	4.057 × 3.385	21.6	85 @ 3600	165 @ 1600	30-45
	V8-307, 5.0L⑤	Y	4 Bbl.④	3.800 × 3.385	8.0	140 @ 3600	240 @ 1600	30-45
	V8-350, 5.7L⑤⑭	N	Fuel Injection	4.057 × 3.385	21.6	105 @ 3200	200 @ 1600	30-45

①—CID-cubic inch displacement.
②—The fifth digit in the V.I.N. denotes engine code on 1977-80 vehicles. The eight digit in the V.I.N. denotes engine code on 1981-84 vehicles.
③—Ratings are net—as installed in the vehicle.
④—Rochester.
⑤—See Oldsmobile chapter for service procedures on this engine.
⑥—Except California.
⑦—California.
⑧—See Pontiac chapter for service procedures on this engine.
⑨—See Chevrolet chapter for service procedures on this engine.
⑩—Turbocharged engine.
⑪—Dual exhaust.
⑫—Riviera.
⑬—Vehicles equipped with C-4 system-E4ME.
⑭—Diesel.
⑮—Regal, 170 @ 4000; Riviera, 180 @ 4000.
⑯—Regal, 275 @ 2400; Riviera, 270 @ 2400.
⑰—Except even firing engine.
⑱—Even firing engine.
⑲—Regal, 280 @ 2400; Riviera, 290 @ 2400.

TUNE UP SPECIFICATIONS

The following specifications are published from the latest information available. This data should be used only in the absence of a decal affixed in the engine compartment.

★ When using a timing light, disconnect vacuum hose or tube at distributor and plug opening in tube or hose so idle speed will not be affected.

● When checking compression, lowest cylinder must be within 70 percent of highest.

▲ Before removing wires from distributor cap, determine location of the No. 1 wire in cap, as distributor position may have been altered from that shown at the end of this chart.

☞ Spark plug types shown in this chart are recommendations of the original vehicle manufacturer and not MOTOR.

Check local sources for other spark plug manufacturers listings.

Year & Engine/V.I.N.	Spark Plug Type	Spark Plug Gap	Firing Order Fig. ▲	Ignition Timing BTDC①★ Man. Trans.	Ignition Timing BTDC①★ Auto. Trans.	Mark Fig.	Curb Idle Speed② Man. Trans.	Curb Idle Speed② Auto. Trans.	Fast Idle Speed Man. Trans.	Fast Idle Speed Auto. Trans.	Fuel Pump Pressure
1977											
V6-231/C⑫	R46TS	.040	J	12°	12°	K⑬	⑭	600D	—	—	3 Min.
V6-231/A⑮	R46TSX	.060	A	—	15°	B⑬	—	600/670D	—	—	3 Min.
V8-301/Y	R46TSX	.060	N	—	12°	G	—	550/650D	—	1700⑯	7-8½
V8-305/U	R45TS	.045	E	—	8°	D	—	500/650D	—	—	7½-9
V8-350/H, 2 Barrel⑰	R46TS	.040	H	—	12°	K⑬	—	600D	—	—	3 Min.
V8-350/J, 4 Barrel⑰	R46TS	.040	H	—	12°	K⑬	—	550D	—	1800⑧	3 Min.
V8-350/L, 4 Barrel⑱	R45TS	.045	E	—	8°	D	—	⑲	—	1600⑳	7½-9
V8-350/R, 4 Barrel Exc. Calif. ㉑㉒	R46SZ	.060	L	—	20°⑦	M	—	550/650D④	—	900㉓	5½-6½
V8-350/R, 4 Barrel Calif. ㉑	R46SZ	.060	L	—	㉔	M	—	550/650D④	—	1000㉓	5½-6½
V8-350/R, 4 Barrel High Alt. ㉑	R46SZ	.060	L	—	20°⑦	M	—	600/650D④	—	1000㉓	5½-6½

TUNE UP SPECIFICATIONS—Continued

The following specifications are published from the latest information available. This data should be used only in the absence of a decal affixed in the engine compartment.

★ When using a timing light, disconnect vacuum hose or tube at distributor and plug opening in tube or hose so idle speed will not be affected.

● When checking compression, lowest cylinder must be within 70 percent of highest.

▲ Before removing wires from distributor cap, determine location of the No. 1 wire in cap, as distributor position may have been altered from that shown at the end of this chart.

☞ Spark plug types shown in this chart are recommendations of the original vehicle manufacturer and not MOTOR.
Check local sources for other spark plug manufacturers listings.

Year & Engine/V.I.N.	Spark Plug Type ☞	Gap	Ignition Timing BTDC① ★ Firing Order Fig. ▲	Man. Trans.	Auto. Trans.	Mark Fig.	Curb Idle Speed② Man. Trans.	Auto. Trans.	Fast Idle Speed Man. Trans.	Auto. Trans.	Fuel Pump Pressure
1977											
V8-403/K, Exc. Calif. & High Alt.	R46SZ	.060	L	—	24°⑦	M	—	550/650D④	—	900㉓	5½–6½
V8-403/K, Calif. & High Alt.	R46SZ	.060	L	—	20°⑦	M	—	④㉕	—	1000㉓	5½–6½
1978											
V6-196/C	R46TSX	.060	A	15°	15°	B⑬	600/800	600D	—	—	3 Min.
V6-231/A㉖	R46TSX	.060	A	15°	15°	B⑬	600/800	600/670D	—	—	3 Min.
V6-231㉗㊹	R44TSX	.060	A	—	15°	B⑬	—	650D	—	—	5
V8-301/Y	R46TSX	.060	N	—	12°	G	—	550/650D	—	2200	7–8½
V8-305/U, 2 Barrel Exc. Calif.㉒	R45TS	.045	E	—	4°	C	—	500/600D	—	—	7½–9
V8-305/U, 2 Barrel Calif.	R45TS	.045	E	—	6°	C	—	600/700D	—	—	7½–9
V8-305/U, 2 Barrel High Alt.	R45TS	.045	E	—	8°	C	—	600/700D	—	—	7½–9
V8-305/U, 4 Barrel	R45TS	.045	E	—	4°	C	—	500/600D	—	—	7½–9
V8-350/X⑰	R46TSX	.060	H	—	15°	B⑬	—	550D	—	1550	3 Min.
V8-350/L⑱	R45TS	.045	E	—	8°	C	—	㉘	—	1600	7½–9
V8-350/R㉑	R46SZ	.060	L	—	20°⑦	M	—	㉙	—	1000	5½–6½
V8-403/K, Exc. Calif. & High Alt.	R46SZ	.060	L	—	20°⑦	M	—	550/650D	—	900	5½–6½
V8-403/K, Calif. & High Alt.	R46SZ	.060	L	—	20°⑦	M	—	㉙	—	1000	5½–6½
1979											
V6-196/C	㉚	.060	A	15°	15°	B⑬	600/800	550/670D	2200	2200	3 Min.
V6-231/A, Exc. Calif.㉒㉖	㉚	.060	A	15°	15°	B⑬	600/800	550/670D	2200	2200	3 Min.
V6-231/A, Calif.㉖	㉚	.060	A	15°	15°	B⑬	600/800	㉛	2200	2200	3 Min.
V6-231/A, High Alt.㉖	㉚	.060	A	—	15°	B⑬	—	600D	—	2200	3 Min.
V6-231㉗㊺	R44TSX	.060	A	—	15°	B⑬	—	㉜	—	2500	5
V8-301/Y, 2 Barrel	R46TSX	.060	N	—	12°	G	—	500/650D	—	2000	7–8½
V8-301/W, 4 Barrel	R45TSX	.060	N	—	12°	G	—	500/650D	—	2200	7–8½
V8-305/G, 2 Barrel	R45TS	.045	E	—	4°	C	—	㉝	—	1600	7½–9
V8-305/H, 4 Barrel Calif.	R45TS	.045	E	—	4°	C	—	500/600D	—	1600	7½–9
V8-305/H, 4 Barrel High Alt.	R45TS	.045	E	—	8°	C	—	600/650D	—	1750	7½–9
V8-350/X⑰	㉚	.060	H	—	15°	B⑬	—	550D	—	1500	3 Min.
V8-350/L, Calif.⑱	R45TS	.045	E	—	8°	C	—	500/600D	—	1600	7½–9
V8-350/L, High Alt.⑱	R45TS	.045	E	—	8°	C	—	600/650D	—	1750	7½–9
V8-350/R, Exc. Calif.㉑	R46SZ	.060	L	—	20°⑦	M	—	㉙	—	900	5½–6½
V8-350/R, Calif.㉑	R46SZ	.060	L	—	20°⑦	M	—	500/600D	—	1000	5½–6½
V8-403/K, Exc. Calif. & High Alt.	R46SZ	.060	L	—	20°⑦	M	—	550/650D	—	900	5½–6½

Continued

TUNE UP SPECIFICATIONS—Continued

The following specifications are published from the latest information available. This
data should be used only in the absence of a decal affixed in the engine compartment.

★ When using a timing light, disconnect vacuum hose or tube at distributor and plug opening in tube or hose so idle speed will not be affected.

● When checking compression, lowest cylinder must be within 70 percent of highest.

▲ Before removing wires from distributor cap, determine location of the No. 1 wire in cap, as distributor position may have been altered from that shown at the end of this chart.

Spark plug types shown in this chart are recommendations of the original vehicle manufacturer and not MOTOR.

Check local sources for other spark plug manufacturers listings.

Year & Engine/V.I.N.	Spark Plug Type	Gap	Ignition Timing BTDC①★ Firing Order Fig.▲	Man. Trans.	Auto. Trans.	Mark Fig.	Curb Idle Speed② Man. Trans.	Auto. Trans.	Fast Idle Speed Man. Trans.	Auto. Trans.	Fuel Pump Pressure
1979—Continued											
V8-403/K, Calif.	R46SZ	.060	L	—	20°⑦	M	—	500/600D	—	1000	5½–6½
V8-403/K, High Alt.	R46SZ	.060	L	—	20°⑦	M	—	600/700D	—	1000	5½–6½
1980											
V6-231/A, Exc. Calif.㉒㉖	R45TSX	.060	A	15°	15°	B⑬	600/800	③	2200	2000	3 Min.
V6-231/3, Exc. Calif.㉒㉗	R45TS	.040	A	—	15°	B⑬	—	㉜	—	2200	5
V6-231/A, Calif.㉖	R45TSX	.060	A	—	15°	B⑬	—	⑥	—	2200	3 Min.
V6-231/3, Calif.㉗	R45TS	.040	A	—	15°	B⑬	—	㉜	—	⑩	5
V6-252/4, Exc. Calif.	R45TSX	.060	A	—	15°	B⑬	—	㉞	—	2000	3 Min.
V8-265/S, Exc. Calif.	R45TSX	.060	N	—	10°	G	—	㉟	—	2200	7–8½
V8-301/W, Exc. Calif.	R45TSX	.060	N	—	12°	G	—	㊱	—	2500	7–8½
V8-305/H	R45TS	.045	E	—	4°	⑤	—	㉟	—	2200	7½–9
V8-350/X, Exc. Calif.⑰	R45TSX	.060	H	—	15°	B⑬	—	③	—	1850	3 Min.
V8-350/R, Exc. Calif.㉑	R46SX	.080	L	—	18°⑦	M	—	500/600D	—	700D	5½–6½
V8-350/R, Calif.㉑	R46SX	.080	L	—	㊲	M	—	550/650D	—	700D	5½–6½
V8-350 Diesel/N㉒	—	—	—	—	4½°㊳㊴㊽	—	—	600/750D	—	750D	—
V8-350 Diesel/N㊻	—	—	—	—	5½°㊳㊴㊽	—	—	600/750D	—	750D	—
1981											
V6-231/A㉖	R45TX8	.080	A	15°	15°	B⑬	800	⑪	2200	1800	3 Min.
V6-231/3㉗	R45TS	.040	A	—	15°	B⑬	—	650D	—	2200	5
V6-252/4	R45TS8	.080	A	—	15°	B⑬	—	550/690D	—	2200	3 Min.
V8-265/S	R45TSX	.060	N	—	12°	G	—	450D	—	2300	7–8½
V8-307/Y	R46SX	.080	L	—	15°⑦	M	—	⑪	—	650D	5½–6½
V8-350 Diesel/N㉒	—	—	—	—	4°㊳㊴	—	—	600/750D	—	750D	—
V8-350 Diesel/N㊻	—	—	—	—	5°㊳㊴	—	—	600/750D	—	750D	—
1982											
V6-231/A㉖	R45TS8	.080	A	—	15°	B⑬	—	500D⑪	—	2000	5½–6½
V6-231/C㉗	R45TSX	.060	A	—	15°	B⑬	—	500D	—	2000	5½–6½
V6-252/4	R45TS8	.080	A	—	15°	B⑬	—	500D⑪	—	2000	5½–6½
V6-262 Diesel/V㉒	—	—	—	—	7°㊳㊵	—	—	650D	—	725D	—
V6-262 Diesel/V㊻	—	—	—	—	7°㊳㊶	—	—	650D	—	725D	—
V8-307/Y	R46SX	.080	L	—	20°⑦	M	—	⑪	—	650D	5½–6½
V8-350 Diesel/N㉒	—	—	—	—	4°㊳㊷	—	—	600D	—	725D	—
V8-350 Diesel/N㊻	—	—	—	—	4°㊳㊸	—	—	600D	—	725D	—
1983											
V6-231/A㉖	R45TS8	.080	A	—	15°	B⑬	—	⑪	—	2200	5½–6½
V6-231/8㉗	R45TSX	.060	A	—	15°	B⑬	—	⑪	—	2200	5½–6½
V6-252/4	R45TS8	.080	A	—	15°	B⑬	—	⑪	—	㊼	5½–6½
V6-262 Diesel/V㉒	—	—	—	—	7°㊳㊵	—	—	650D	—	725D	—
V6-262 Diesel/V㊻	—	—	—	—	7°㊳㊶	—	—	650D	—	725D	—

Continued

TUNE UP SPECIFICATIONS—Continued

The following specifications are published from the latest information available. This data should be used only in the absence of a decal affixed in the engine compartment.

★ When using a timing light, disconnect vacuum hose or tube at distributor and plug opening in tube or hose so idle speed will not be affected.

● When checking compression, lowest cylinder must be within 70 percent of highest.

▲ Before removing wires from distributor cap, determine location of the No. 1 wire in cap, as distributor position may have been altered from that shown at the end of this chart.

Spark plug types shown in this chart are recommendations of the original vehicle manufacturer and not MOTOR.

Check local sources for other spark plug manufacturers listings.

| Year & Engine/V.I.N. | Spark Plug | | Ignition Timing BTDC① ★ | | | | Curb Idle Speed② | | Fast Idle Speed | | Fuel Pump Pressure |
	Type	Gap	Firing Order Fig. ▲	Man. Trans.	Auto. Trans.	Mark Fig.	Man. Trans.	Auto. Trans.	Man. Trans.	Auto. Trans.	
1983—Continued											
V8-307/Y	R46SX	.080	L	—	20°⑦	M	—	⑪	—	900D	5½—6½
V8-350 Diesel/N㉒	—	—	—	—	4°㊳㊷	—	—	600D	—	725D	—
V8-350 Diesel/N㊻	—	—	—	—	4°㊳㊸	—	—	600D	—	725D	—
1984											
V6-231/A㉖	R45TS8	.080	A	—	15°	B⑬	—	⑪	—	2200	4¼—5¾
V6-231/9㉗	R44TSX	.060	O	—	—	—	—	—	—	—	—
V6-252/4	R45TS8	.080	A	—	15°	B⑬	—	⑪	—	㊼	5½—7
V6-262 Diesel/V	—	—	—	—	7°㊳	—	—	675D	—	775D	—
V8-307/Y	R46SX	.080	L	—	20°⑦	M	—	⑪	—	900D	6—7½
V8-350 Diesel/N	—	—	—	—	4°㊳	—	—	600D	—	750D	—

①—BTDC—Before top dead center.
②—Idle speed on man. trans. vehicles is adjusted in Neutral & on auto. trans. equipped vehicles is adjusted in Drive unless otherwise specified. Where two idle speeds are listed, the higher speed is with the A/C or idle solenoid energized.
③—Models less idle solenoid, 550D RPM; models w/idle solenoid, 550/670D RPM.
④—With A/C on & Compressor clutch wires disconnected.
⑤—Early models, Fig. C; late models, Fig. I.
⑥—Models less idle solenoid, 550D RPM; models w/idle solenoid, 550/620D RPM.
⑦—At 1100 RPM. ALDL test lead grounded.
⑧—On low step of fast idle cam with vacuum hose to EGR disconnected & plugged & A/C off.
⑨—Injection timing at 800 RPM.
⑩—Except Riviera, 2200 RPM; Riviera, 2500 RPM.
⑪—Idle speed is controlled by the idle speed control (ISC) motor or idle load compensator (ILC).
⑫—Except Even-Fire engine.
⑬—The harmonic balancer on these engines has two timing marks. The timing mark measuring 1/16 in. is used when setting timing with a hand held timing light. The mark measuring 1/8 in. is used when setting timing with magnetic timing equipment.

⑭—Except Calif., 500/800 RPM; California, 600/800 RPM.
⑮—Even fire engine.
⑯—On 2nd step against high step of fast idle cam.
⑰—Buick built engine. Distributor located at front of engine.
⑱—Chevrolet built engine. Distributor located at rear of engine, clockwise rotation.
⑲—Except high altitude, 500/650D RPM; high altitude, 600/650D RPM.
⑳—On high step of fast idle cam.
㉑—Oldsmobile built engine. Distributor located at rear of engine, counterclockwise rotation.
㉒—Except high altitude.
㉓—On low step of fast idle cam with vacuum hose to EGR disconnected & plugged & A/C off.
㉔—Except sta. wag. 18° BTDC at 1100 RPM; sta. wag., 20° BTDC at 1100 RPM.
㉕—Except high altitude, 550/650D RPM; high altitude, 600/650D RPM.
㉖—Except turbo charged engine.
㉗—Turbo charged engine.
㉘—Except high altitude, 500/600D RPM; high altitude, 600/700D RPM.
㉙—Except high altitude, 550/650D RPM; high altitude, 600/700D RPM.
㉚—R45TSX or R46TSX.
㉛—Models less idle solenoid, 600D RPM; models

with idle solenoid, 580/670D RPM.
㉜—Except Riviera, 650D RPM; Riviera, 600/650D RPM.
㉝—Less A/C, 500/600D RPM; with A/C, 550/650D RPM.
㉞—Models less idle solenoid, 550D RPM; models w/idle solenoid, 550/680D RPM.
㉟—Models less idle solenoid, 550D RPM; models w/idle solenoid, 550/650D RPM.
㊱—Models less idle solenoid, 500D RPM; models w/idle solenoid, 500/650D RPM.
㊲—Electra & LeSabre, 18° BTDC at 1100 RPM; Riviera, 16° BTDC at 1100 RPM.
㊳—ATDC—After top dead center.
㊴—At 1200 RPM.
㊵—At 1300 RPM. When operating at altitudes above 4000 ft., 8° ATDC.
㊶—At 1300 RPM. When operating at altitudes below 4000 ft., 6° ATDC.
㊷—At 1250 RPM. When operating at altitudes above 4000 ft., 8° ATDC.
㊸—At 1250 RPM. When operating at altitudes below 4000 ft., 3° ATDC.
㊹—V.I.N. code G denotes 2 Bbl. carb.; V.I.N. code 3 denotes 4 Bbl. carb.
㊺—V.I.N. code 2 denotes 2 Bbl. carb.; V.I.N. code 3 denotes 4 Bbl. carb.
㊻—High altitude.
㊼—Except Riviera, 2200 RPM; Riviera, 2100 RPM.
㊽—Using diesel timing meter J-33075.

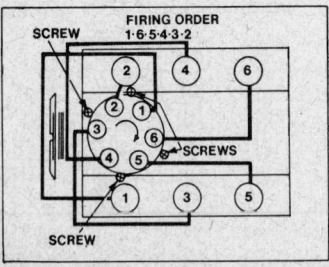

Fig. A

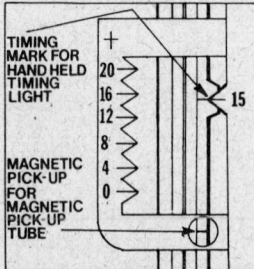

Fig. B

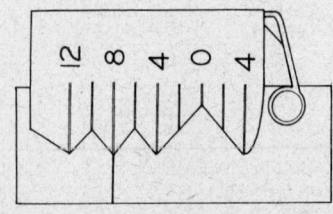

Fig. C

Continued

TUNE UP NOTES—Continued

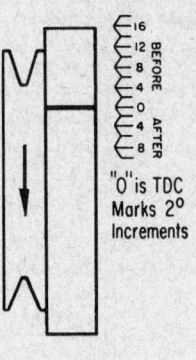

"O" is TDC
Marks 2°
Increments

Fig. D

FIRING ORDER
1·8·4·3·6·5·7·2

Fig. E

Fig. F

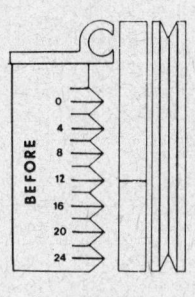

Fig. G

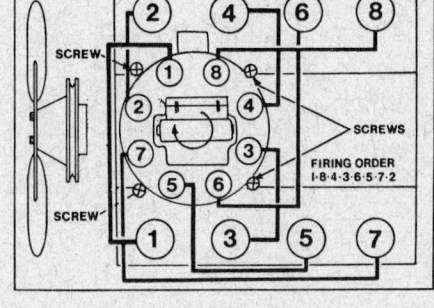

FIRING ORDER
1·8·4·3·6·5·7·2

Fig. H

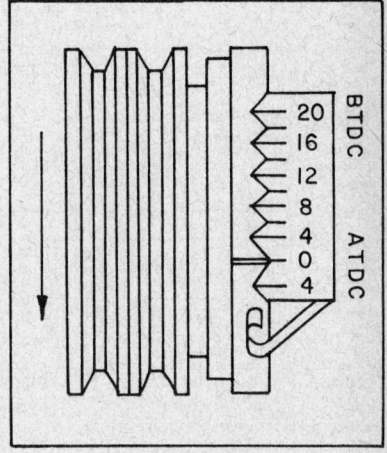

Fig. I

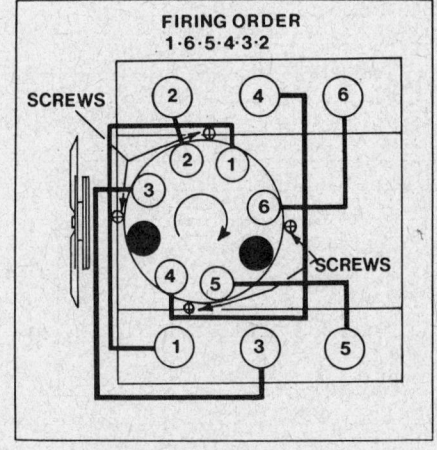

FIRING ORDER
1·6·5·4·3·2

Fig. J

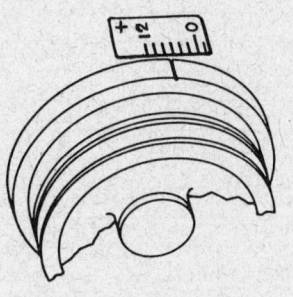

Fig. K

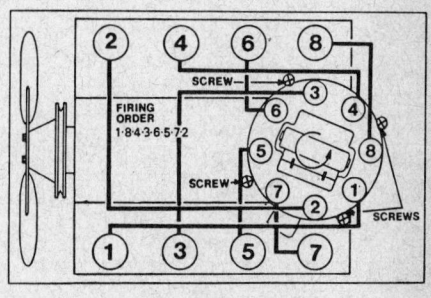

FIRING ORDER
1·8·4·3·6·5·7·2

Fig. L

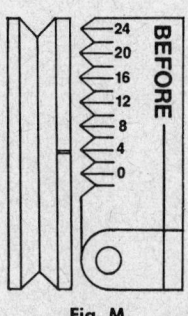

Fig. M

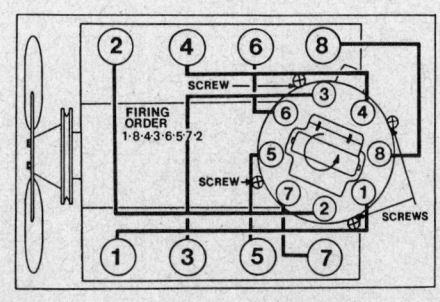

FIRING ORDER
1·8·4·3·6·5·7·2

Fig. N

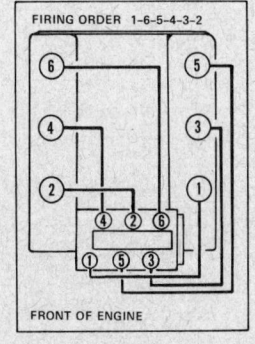

FIRING ORDER 1-6-5-4-3-2

FRONT OF ENGINE

Fig. O

DRIVE AXLE SPECIFICATIONS

Year	Model	Carrier Type	Ring Gear & Pinion Backlash		Pinion Bearing Preload			Differential Bearing Preload		
			Method	Adjustment	Method	Adjustment New Bearings Inch-Lbs.	Adjustment Used Bearings Inch-Lbs.	Method	Adjustment New Bearings Inch-Lbs.	Adjustment Used Bearings Inch-Lbs.
1977–83	Exc. Riviera	Integral	Shims	.006–.008	Spacer	20–25①	10–15①	Shims	35–40②	20–25②
1979–83	Riviera	Integral	Shims	.005–.009	Spacer	18–24	③	Shims	④	④
1984	Exc. Riviera	Integral	Shims	—	Spacer	—	—	Shims	—	—
1984	Riviera	Integral	Shims	—	Spacer	—	—	Shims	—	—

①—Measured with torque wrench at pinion flange nut.
②—Total preload measured with torque wrench
at pinion flange nut with new seal installed.
③—Pre-check reading plus 5 inch lbs.
④—Slip fit plus .006 inch clearance on each side.

DISTRIBUTOR SPECIFICATIONS

★ Note: If unit is checked on the vehicle, double the RPM and degrees to get crankshaft figures.

Distributor Part No.①	Centrifugal Advance Degrees @ RPM of Distributor				Vacuum Advance	
	Advance Starts	Intermediate Advance		Full Advance	Inches of Vacuum to Start Plunger	Max. Adv. Dist. Deg. @ Vacuum
1977						
1103275②	0 @ 725	—	—	—	10 @ 2200	5½–7½	12 @ 14
1110677②	0 @ 766	8.9–11 @ 1800	—	—	7.95–11 @ 2500	6	12.7 @ 20
1110686②	0 @ 888	3.15–5.45 @ 1300	8.8–11 @ 1800	—	8.7–11 @ 2500	6	4.7 @ 20
1110694②	0 @ 764	8.9–11 @ 1800	—	—	7.95–11 @ 2500	3.5	15.5 @ 20
1978						
1103281②	0 @ 500	5 @ 850	—	—	10 @ 1900	4	9 @ 12
1103282②	0 @ 500	5 @ 850	—	—	10 @ 1900	4	10 @ 10
1103285②	0 @ 600	6 @ 1000	—	—	11 @ 2100	4	5 @ 8
1103314②	0 @ 412	5 @ 900	—	—	10.7 @ 1700	4	12½ @ 12
1103322②	0 @ 300	5½ @ 600	—	—	14½ @ 2000	6	12 @ 13
1103323②	0 @ 500	—	—	—	9½ @ 2000	5	8 @ 11
1103324②	0 @ 300	5½ @ 600	—	—	11½ @ 1800	6	12 @ 13
1103325②	0 @ 500	—	—	—	6½ @ 1800	5	8 @ 11
1103342②	2 @ 1000	—	—	—	9½ @ 2200	7	12 @ 13
1103346②	0 @ 500	—	—	—	9½ @ 2000	6	12 @ 14
1103347②	0 @ 500	—	—	—	6½ @ 1800	6	12 @ 13
1103353②	0 @ 550	6 @ 800	—	—	8 @ 1100	4	10 @ 10
1110695②	0 @ 1000	—	—	—	9 @ 1800	3–6	12 @ 13
1110723②	—	—	—	—	6 @ 2000	4–6	4 @ 7
1110728②	—	—	—	—	9 @ 1600	1–5	10 @ 8
1110730②	—	—	—	—	11½ @ 2000	4–6	12 @ 10
1110731②	0 @ 1000	—	—	—	9 @ 1800	4–6	8 @ 9
1110732②	0 @ 1000	—	—	—	9 @ 1800	4–6	7 @ 13
1110735②	—	—	—	—	11½ @ 2000	2–4	10 @ 13
1110739②	—	—	—	—	8½ @ 1800	2–4	10 @ 13
1979						
1103281②	0 @ 500	5 @ 850	—	—	10 @ 1900	4	9 @ 12
1103314②	0 @ 412	5 @ 900	—	—	10.7 @ 1700	4	12½ @ 12
1103322②	0 @ 300	5.5 @ 600	—	—	14.5 @ 2000	6	12 @ 13
1103323②	0 @ 500	—	—	—	9½ @ 2000	5	8 @ 11
1103324②	0 @ 600	5.5 @ 600	—	—	11½ @ 1800	6	12 @ 13
1103325②	0 @ 500	—	—	—	6½ @ 1800	5	8 @ 11
1103342②	—	—	—	—	9 @ 2200	5–7	12 @ 13
1103346②	0 @ 500	—	—	—	9½ @ 2000	6	12 @ 13
1103347②	0 @ 500	—	—	—	12½ @ 1800	6	12 @ 13

Continued

DISTRIBUTOR SPECIFICATIONS—Continued

★ Note: If unit is checked on the vehicle, double the RPM and degrees to get crankshaft figures.

Distributor Part No.①	Centrifugal Advance Degrees @ RPM of Distributor					Vacuum Advance	
	Advance Starts	Intermediate Advance			Full Advance	Inches of Vacuum to Start Plunger	Max. Adv. Dist. Deg. @ Vacuum
1979—Continued							
1103368②	0 @ 500	5 @ 850	—	—	10 @ 1900	4	5 @ 8
1103379②	0 @ 500	5 @ 850	—	—	10 @ 1900	3	10 @ 7½
1103399②	1 @ 575	4 @ 700	—	—	10 @ 2200	4	12½ @ 13
1103400②	1 @ 525	4.5 @ 1000	—	—	8½ @ 2350	4	12½ @ 12
1110765②	—	—	—	—	9 @ 2200	2–4	10 @ 13
1110766②	0 @ 840	—	—	—	7½ @ 1800	4–3	12 @ 11
1110767②	0 @ 840	—	—	—	7½ @ 1800	3	10 @ 12
1110768②	0 @ 500	2½ @ 800	3 @ 1200	—	7½ @ 1800	3	10 @ 12
1110769②	0 @ 500	—	—	—	7½ @ 1800	4	12 @ 11
1110770②	0 @ 840	—	—	—	7½ @ 1800	3	10 @ 9
1110772②	—	—	—	—	9 @ 1800	2–4	12 @ 11
1110774②	—	—	—	—	6 @ 1800	2–4	10 @ 13
1110775②	—	—	—	—	9 @ 1800	3	10 @ 10
1110779②	0 @ 840	—	—	—	7½ @ 1800	3	12 @ 9½
1980							
1103379②	0 @ 600	4–6 @ 850	—	—	11 @ 1900	2–4	10 @ 9
1103384②	0 @ 500	5–8 @ 800	—	—	11 @ 2000	3–6	12 @ 13
1103386②	0 @ 600	4–6 @ 850	—	—	11 @ 1900	3–5	8 @ 8
1103398②	0 @ 550	7–10 @ 1200	—	—	14 @ 2200	—	—
1103407②	0 @ 600	7–9 @ 1300	—	—	13 @ 2200	4–5	10 @ 11
1103412②⑤	—	—	—	—	—	—	—
1103413②⑤	—	—	—	—	—	—	—
1103414②⑤	—	—	—	—	—	—	—
1103417②	0 @ 1100	—	—	—	9 @ 2200	5–6	12 @ 14
1103425②	—	—	—	—	—	—	—
1103444②	0 @ 700	—	—	—	9 @ 1000	7–8	10 @ 15
1103447②	0 @ 1100	—	—	—	9 @ 2200	—	—
1103449②	—	—	—	—	—	—	—
1103450②	0 @ 650	—	—	—	11 @ 1600	2–4	7 @ 7
1110550②	0 @ 500	4–8 @ 600	—	—	9 @ 2200	2–4	10 @ 13
1110551②	0 @ 500	—	—	—	6 @ 2200	—	—
1110554②	0 @ 1000	—	—	—	9 @ 1800	2–4	12 @ 13
1110555②	1 @ 800	2–4 @ 1200	—	—	12 @ 1800	3–5	12 @ 12
1110571②	0 @ 500	2–4 @ 600	—	—	9 @ 2200	2–4	10 @ 10
1110572②	0 @ 500	—	—	—	6 @ 2200	—	—
1110573②⑤	—	—	—	—	—	—	—
1110576②	—	—	—	—	—	—	—
1110784②⑤	—	—	—	—	—	—	—
1981							
1103443②③	—	—	—	—	—	—	—
1103451②③	—	—	—	—	—	—	—
1103453②③	—	—	—	—	—	—	—
1103466②③	—	—	—	—	—	—	—
1110567②③	—	—	—	—	—	—	—
1110573②③	—	—	—	—	—	—	—
1110579②③	—	—	—	—	—	—	—
1111381②③	—	—	—	—	—	—	—
1982–83							
1103457②③	—	—	—	—	—	—	—
1103470②③	—	—	—	—	—	—	—
1984							
—	—	—	—	—	—	—	—

DISTRIBUTOR SPECIFICATIONS NOTES

①—Stamped on distributor housing plate.
②—High Energy Ignition.
③—Equipped with EST (Electronic Spark Timing).
④—Except California.
⑤—Equipped with EMR (Electronic Module Retard) or ECM (Electronic Control Module).

ALTERNATOR SPECIFICATIONS

Year	Model	Rated Hot Output Amps.	Field Current 12 Volts @ 80 F.	Year	Model	Rated Hot Output Amps.	Field Current 12 Volts @ 80 F.	Year	Model	Rated Hot Output Amps.	Field Current 12 Volts @ 80 F.
1977	1101016	80	4.0–4.5		1102479	55	4.0–4.5		1100194	70	—
	1101024	80	4.0–4.5		1102495	55	4.0–5.0		1100198	38	—
	1102389	42	4.0–4.5		1102841	42	—		1100281	63	—
	1102391	61	4.0–4.5		1102860	63	—		1100284	85	—
	1102392	63	4.0–4.5		1102904	63	—		1101037	70	—
	1102394	37	4.0–4.5		1103033	42	—		1101045	85	—
	1102478	55	4.0–4.5		1103055	42	—		1101056	—	—
	1102479	61	4.0–4.5		1103056	63	—		1101082	70	—
	1102485	42	4.0–4.5		1103058	63	—		1101084	85	—
	1102486	61	4.0–4.5	1980	1100110	42	—		1101088	70	—
	1102491	37	4.0–4.5		1100111	63	—		1101098	70	—
	1102492	37	4.0–4.5		1101038	70	—		1103119	63	—
	1102495	55	4.0–4.5		1101044	70	—	1983	1100200	78	—
	1102841	42	4.0–4.5		1101080	80	—		1100230	42	—
	1102842	63	4.0–4.5		1101071	70	—		1100239	55	—
	1102854	63	4.0–4.5		1103088	55	—		1100240	63	—
	1102881	37	4.0–4.5		1103100	55	—		1100260	78	—
	1102882	37	4.0–4.5		1103101	37	—		1100297	42	—
	1102902	61	4.0–4.5		1103102	63	—		1100300	63	—
	1102905	55	4.0–4.5		1103103	63	—		1105022	78	—
	1102906	61	4.0–4.5		1103104	42	—		1105025	63	—
	1102913	61	4.0–4.5		1103105	42	—		1105034	63	—
1978	1101016	80	4.0–5.0		1103106	63	—		1105040	85	—
	1101024	80	4.0–5.0		1103112	63	—		1105198	85	—
	1102389	42	4.0–5.0		1103186	63	—		1105250	70	—
	1102391	61	4.0–5.0	1981	1100110	42	—	1984	1100200	78	—
	1102392	63	4.0–5.0		1100121	63	—		1100239	56	—
	1102394	37	4.0–5.0		1100156	55	—		1100260	78	—
	1102479	55	4.0–4.5		1100164	55	—		1105028	78	—
	1102485	42	4.0–5.0		1100167	63	—		1105041	78	—
	1102486	61	4.0–4.5		1101037	70	—		1105197	70	—
	1102495	55	4.0–5.0		1101045	85	—		1105250	70	—
	1102841	42	4.0–5.0		1101082	70	—		1105443	94	—
	1102842	63	4.0–5.0		1101084	85	—		1105444	94	—
	1102854	63	4.0–5.0		1101085	85	—		1105493	94	—
	1102901	61	4.0–5.0		1101437	70	—		1105547	94	—
	1102904	63	4.0–5.0		1103088	55	—		1105548	85	—
	1102906	61	4.0–5.0		1103119	63	—		1105549	108	—
	1102913	61	4.0–5.0	1982	1100110	42	—		1105561	94	—
	1103033	42	4.0–5.0		1100111	63	—		1105562	94	—
1979	1101024	80	—		1100121	63	—		1105564	66	—
	1101043	80	—		1100156	55	—		1105565	78	—
	1102389	42	—		1100164	55	—		1105566	66	—
	1102392	63	—		1100165	60	—		1105567	78	—
	1102394	37	4.0–4.5		1100190	76	—				

ENGINE TIGHTENING SPECIFICATIONS★

★ Torque specifications are for clean and lightly lubricated threads only. Dry or dirty threads produce increased friction which prevents accurate measurement of tightness.

Year	Engine/V.I.N.	Spark Plugs Ft. Lbs.	Cylinder Head Bolts Ft. Lbs.	Intake Manifold Ft. Lbs.	Exhaust Manifold Ft. Lbs.	Rocker Arm Shaft Bracket Ft. Lbs.	Rocker Arm Cover Ft. Lbs.	Connecting Rod Cap Bolts Ft. Lbs.	Main Bearing Cap Bolts Ft. Lbs.	Flywheel to Crankshaft Ft. Lbs.	Vibration Damper or Pulley Ft. Lbs.
1977-78	V6-196, 231 (19)	(12)	80	45	25	30	4	40	100	60	(13)
	V8-301/Y	15	90	40	35	20(16)	7	35	(5)	95	160
	V8-305/U	15	65	30	20	—	3¾	45	70	60	60
	V8-350 (6)(19)	(12)	80	45	25	30	4	40	100	60	(13)
	V8-350/L(7)	15	65	30	20(8)	—	3¾	45	70(9)	60	60
	V8-350/R(10)	25	130	40(15)	25	25(4)	7	42	(3)	(11)	260
	V8-403/K	25	130	40(15)	25	25(4)	7	42	(3)	(11)	260
1979-83	V6-196, 231 (19)	15	80	45	25	30	4	40	100	60	225
	V8-265, 301 (19)	15	95	40	35	20(16)	6	35	(2)	95	160
	V8-305 (19)	22	65	30	20	—	4	45	70	60	60
	V8-350/L(7)	22	65	30	20	—	4	45	70	60	60
	V8-350/X(6)	15	80	45	25	30	4	40	100	60	225
	V8-350/R(10)	25	130(15)	40(15)	25	28(4)	(17)	42	(3)	(11)	255
	V8-403/K	25	130	40(15)	25	28(4)	(17)	42	(3)	(11)	255
1980-83	V6-252/4	15	80	45	25	30	4	40	100	60	225
	V8-307/Y(10)	25	130(15)	40(15)	25	28(4)	(17)	42	(3)	60	200-310
	V8-350/N(14)	—	130(15)	40(15)	25	28(4)	(17)	42	120	60	200-310
1982-83	V6-262/V(14)	—	(18)	41	29	29(4)	(17)	42	(1)	65	160-350
1984	V6-231/A,9	15	80	45	25	30	4	40	100	60	225
	V6-252/4	15	80	45	25	30	4	40	100	60	225
	V6-262/V(14)	—	(18)	41	31	28(4)	—	42	89	57	203-350
	V8-307/Y(10)	25	125(15)	40(15)	25	28(4)	—	42	(3)	60	200-310
	V8-350/N(14)	—	130(15)	40(15)	25	28(4)	—	42	120	60	200-310

(1)—1982, 107 ft. lbs.; 1983, 89 ft. lbs.
(2)—Rear main 100 ft. lbs; all others, 70 ft. lbs.
(3)—Nos. 1, 2, 3, 4—80 ft. lbs., No. 5—120 ft. lbs.
(4)—Rocker arm pivot bolt to head.
(5)—Rear main, 100 ft. lbs.; all others 60 ft. lbs.
(6)—Buick built engine. Distributor located at front of engine.
(7)—Chevrolet built engine. Distributor located at rear of engine, clockwise rotation.
(8)—1977 only; Inside bolts; 30 ft. lbs.
(9)—Outer bolts on engines with 4 bolt caps, 65 ft. lbs.
(10)—Oldsmobile built engine. Distributor located at rear of engine, counterclockwise rotation.
(11)—Auto. trans. 60 ft. lbs.; man. trans., 90 ft. lbs.
(12)—1977; 20 ft. lbs. & 1978; 15 ft. lbs.
(13)—1977; 175 ft. lbs. & 1978; 225 ft. lbs.
(14)—Oldsmobile built diesel engine.
(15)—Clean and dip entire engine bolt in engine oil before installing and tightening.
(16)—Rocker arm to stud nut.
(17)—Fully driven, seated and not stripped.
(18)—Torque inner 8 bolts to 142 ft. lbs. Torque outer 6 bolts (bolts nearest intake & exhaust manifolds to cylinder head mating surfaces) to 59 ft. lbs.
(19)—For V.I.N. code identification refer to the "General Engine Specifications" at the beginning of the chapter.

PISTONS, PINS, RINGS, CRANKSHAFT & BEARINGS

Year	Engine/V.I.N.	Piston Clearance	Ring End Gap(1) Comp.	Ring End Gap(1) Oil	Wrist-pin Diameter	Rod Bearings Shaft Diameter	Rod Bearings Bearing Clearance	Main Bearings Shaft Diameter	Main Bearings Bearing Clearance	Thrust on Bear. No.	Shaft End Play
1977	V6-196, 231(16)	.0008-.0020	.010	.015	.9393	1.9991-2.000	.0005-.0026	2.4995	.0004-.0015	2	.004-.008
	V8-301/Y(7)	.0025-.0033	.010	.035	.927	2.25	.0005-.0025	3.00	.0004-.0020	4	.003-.009
	V8-305/U(2)	.0007-.0017	.010	.015	.9272	2.099-2.100	.0013-.0035	(11)	(12)	5	.002-.006
	V8-350(16)	.0008-.0020	.010	.015	.9393	1.9991-2.000	.0005-.0026	3.00	.0004-.0015	3	.003-.009
	V8-350/L(2)	.0007-.0017	.010	.015	.9272	2.099-2.100	.0013-.0035	(11)	(12)	5	.002-.006
	V8-350/R(4)	.001-.002	.010	.015	.9805	2.1238-2.1248	.0005-.0026	(5)	.0005-.0021(6)	3	—
	V8-403/K(4)	.001-.002	.010	.015	.9805	2.1238-2.1248	.0005-.0026	(5)	.0005-.0021(6)	3	—
1978	V6-196, 231(16)	.0008-.0020	.010	.015	.9393	2.2487-2.2495	.0005-.0026	2.4995	.0003-.0018	2	.004-.008
	V8-305/U(2)	.0007-.0017	.010	.015	.9272	2.099-2.100	.0013-.0035	(11)	(12)	5	.002-.006

PISTONS, PINS, RINGS, CRANKSHAFT & BEARINGS—Continued

Year	Engine/V.I.N.	Piston Clearance	Ring End Gap① Comp.	Oil	Wrist-pin Diameter	Rod Bearings Shaft Diameter	Bearing Clearance	Main Bearings Shaft Diameter	Bearing Clearance	Thrust on Bear. No.	Shaft End Play
	V8-350⑯	.0008–.0020	.010	.015	.9393	1.991–2.000	.0005–.0026	3.00	.0004–.0015	3	.003–.009
	V8-350/L②	.001–.002	.010	.015	.9272	2.099–2.100	.0013–.0035	⑪	⑫	5	.002–.006
	V8-350/R④	.001–.002	.010	.015	.9805	2.1238–2.1248	.0004–.0033	⑤	.0005–.0021⑥	3	.0035–.0135
	V8-403/K④	.001–.002	.010	.015	.9805	2.1238–2.1248	.0004–.0033	⑤	.0005–.0021⑥	3	.0035–.0135
1978–79	V8-301⑦⑯	.0025–.0033	.010	.035	.927	2.25	.0005–.0025	3.00	.0004–.0020	4	.006–.020
1979–80	V6-196, 231⑯	.0008–.0020	.013	.015	.9393	2.2487–2.2495	.0005–.0026	2.4995	.0003–.0018	2	.003–.009
	V8-305②⑯	.0007–.0017	.010	.015	.9272	2.099–2.100	.0013–.0035	⑪	⑫	5	.002–.006
	V8-350/X	.0008–.0020	.013	.015	.9393	1.991–2.000	.0005–.0026	3.0000	.0004–.0015	3	.003–.009
	V8-350/L②	.0007–.0017	.010	.015	.9272	2.099–2.100	.0013–.0035	⑪	⑫	5	.002–.006
	V8-350/R④	.00075–.00175	.010	.015	.9805	2.1238–2.1248	.0004–.0033	⑤	.005–.021⑥	3	.0035–.0135
	V8-403/K④	.0005–.0015	.010	.015	.9805	2.1238–2.1248	.0004–.0033	⑤	.005–.021⑥	3	.0035–.0135
1980	V8-265, 301⑦⑯	.0017–.0025	.010	.035	.940	2.00	.0005–.0025	3.00	.0002–.0018	4	.003–.009
1980–81	V6-252/4	.0008–.0020	.013	.015	.9393	2.2487–2.2495	.0005–.0026	2.4995	.0003–.0018	2	.003–.009
	V8-350/N⑧	.005–.006	.015	.015	1.0951	2.1238–2.1248	.0005–.0026	2.9998	.005–.0021⑥	3	.0035–.0135
1981	V6-231⑯	.0008–.0020	.013	.015	.9393	2.2487–2.2495	.0005–.0026	2.4995	.0003–.0018	2	.003–.009
	V8-265/S⑦	.0017–.0025	.010	.035	.940	2.00	.0005–.0025	3.00	.0002–.0018	4	.003–.009
	V8-307/Y④	.00075–.00175	.010	.015	.9805	2.1238–2.1248	.0004–.0033	⑨	⑩	3	.0035–.0135
	V8-350/N⑧	.005–.006	.015	.015	1.0951	2.1238–2.1248	.0005–.0026	2.9998	.005–.0021⑥	3	.0035–.0135
1982	V6-231/A⑬	.0008–.0020	.013	.015	.9393	2.2487–2.2495	.0005–.0026	2.4995	.0003–.0018	2	.003–.009
	V6-231/3⑭	.0022–.0034	.013	.015	.9393	2.2487–2.2495	.0005–.0026	2.4995	.0003–.0018	2	.003–.009
	V6-252/4	.0008–.0020	.013	.015	.9393	2.2487–2.2495	.0005–.0026	2.4995	.0003–.0018	2	.003–.009
	V6-262/V⑧	.003–.004	.015	.015	1.0950	2.2490–2.2510	.0003–.0035	2.9993–3.0003	⑮	3	.0035–.0135
	V8-307/Y④	.00075–.00175	.010	.015	.9805	2.1238–2.1248	.0004–.0033	⑨	⑩	3	.0035–.0135
	V8-350/N⑧	.003–.004	.015	.015	1.0951	2.1238–2.1248	.0005–.0026	2.9993–3.0003	⑲	3	.0035–.0135
1983	V6-231/A⑬	.0008–.0020	.010	.015	.9393	2.2487–2.2495	.0005–.0026	2.4995	.0003–.0018	2	.003–.009
	V6-231/8⑭	.0022–.0034	.010	.015	.9393	2.2487–2.2495	.0005–.0026	2.4995	.0003–.0018	2	.003–.009
	V6-252/4	.0008–.0020	.010	.015	.9393	2.2487–2.2495	.0005–.0026	2.4995	.0003–.0018	2	.003–.009
	V6-262/V⑧	.0035–.0045	⑰	.015	1.0950	2.2490–2.2510	.0003–.0025	2.9993–3.0003	⑮	3	.0035–.0135
	V8-307/Y④	.00075–.00175	.010	.015	.9805	2.1238–2.1248	.0004–.0033	⑨	⑩	3	.0035–.0135
	V8-350/N⑧	.003–.004	⑰	.015	1.0951	2.1238–2.1248	.0005–.0026	2.9993–3.0003	⑲	3	.0035–.0135
1984	V6-231/A⑬	.0008–.0020	.010	.015	.9392	2.2487–2.2495	.0005–.0026	2.4995	.0003–.0018	2	.003–.011
	V6-231/9⑭	.0022–.0034⑱	.010	.015	.9392	2.2487–2.2495	.0005–.0026	2.4995	.0003–.0018	2	.003–.011
	V6-252/4	.0008–.0020	.010	.015	.9392	2.2487–2.2495	.0005–.0026	2.4995	.0003–.0018	2	.003–.011
	V6-262/V⑧	.0035–.0045	⑰	.010	1.0950	2.2490–2.2510	.0005–.0025	2.9993–3.0003	⑮	3	.0035–.0135
	V8-307/Y④	.00075–.00175	.010	.015	.9805	2.1238–2.1248	.0004–.0033	⑨	⑩	3	.0035–.0135
	V8-305/N⑧	.0035–.0045	⑰	.010	1.0951	2.1238–2.1248	.0005–.0026	2.9993–3.0003	⑲	3	.0035–.0135

①—Fit rings in tapered bores for clearance given in tightest portion of ring travel. Clearances specified are minimum gaps.

②—Chevrolet built engine. Distributor located at rear of engine, clockwise rotation.

③—No. 1 .010; No. 2, .013.

④—Oldsmobile built engine. Distributor located at rear of engine, counterclockwise rotation.

⑤—No. 1: 2.4988–2.4998 inch; Nos. 2, 3, 4, 5: 2.4985–2.4995 inch.

⑥—Rear, .0015–.0031 inch.

⑦—Pontiac built engine. Distributor located at rear of engine, clockwise rotation.

⑧—Olds. built diesel engine.

⑨—No. 1, 2.4993–2.4998 inch; Nos. 2, 3, 4, 5, 2.4990–2.4995 inch.

⑩—No. 5, .0015–.0031 inch; Nos. 1, 2, 3, 4, .0005–.0021 inch.

⑪—No. 1: 2.4484–2.4493 inch; Nos. 2, 3, 4: 2.4481–2.4490 inch; No. 5: 2.4479–2.4488 inch.

⑫—No. 1: .0008–.0020 inch; Nos. 2, 3, 4: .0011–.0023 inch; No. 5: .0017–.0032 inch.

⑬—Except turbocharged engine.

⑭—Turbocharged engine.

⑮—Nos. 1, 2 & 3, .0005–.0021 inch; No. 4, .0020–.0034 inch.

⑯—For V.I.N. code, refer to the "General Engine Specifications" at the beginning of the chapter.

⑰—Top ring, .019 inch; 2nd ring, .015 inch.

⑱—At piston pin centerline.

⑲—Nos. 1, 2, 3 & 4, .0005–.0021; No. 5, .0020–.0034.

VALVE SPECIFICATIONS

Year	Model/V.I.N.	Valve Lash Int.	Valve Lash Exh.	Valve Angles Seat	Valve Angles Face	Valve Spring Installed Height ①	Valve Spring Pressure Lbs. @ In.	Stem Clearance Intake	Stem Clearance Exhaust	Stem Diameter Intake	Stem Diameter Exhaust
1977	V8-305/U④	¾ turn⑤	¾ turn⑤	46	45	③	②	.0010—.0027	.0010—.0027	.3410—.3417	.3410—.3417
	V8-350/L④	¾ turn⑤	¾ turn⑤	46	45	③	②	.0010—.0027	.0010—.0027	.3410—.3417	.3410—.3417
1977—78	V6-196, 231⑮	Hydraulic⑥		45	45	1.727	168 @ 1.327	.0015—.0032	.0015—.0032	.3405—.3412	.3405—.3412
	V8-301/Y⑩	Hydraulic⑥		46	45	1.69	170 @ 1.26	.0017—.0020	.0017—.0020	.3400	.3400
	V8-350⑪⑮	Hydraulic⑥		45	45	1.727	⑬	.0015—.0035	.0015—.0032	.3720—.3730	.3723—.3730
	V8-350/R⑦	Hydraulic⑥		⑧	⑨	1.67	187 @ 1.27	.0010—.0027	.0015—.0032	.3425—.3432	.3420—.3427
	V8-403/K⑦	Hydraulic⑥		⑧	⑨	1.67	187 @ 1.27	.0010—.0027	.0015—.0032	.3425—.3432	.3420—.3427
1978	V8-305/U④	1 Turn⑤		46	45	1.70	200 @ 1.25	.0010—.0027	.0010—.0027	.3410—.3417	.3410—.3417
	V8-350/L④	1 Turn⑤		46	45	1.70	200 @ 1.25	.0010—.0027	.0010—.0027	.3410—.3417	.3410—.3417
1979—80	V6-196, 231, 252⑮	Hydraulic⑥		45	45	1.727	⑭	.0015—.0035	.0015—.0032	.3401—.3412	.3405—.3412
	V8-265, 301⑮	Hydraulic⑥		46	45	1.69	170 @ 1.26	.0017—.0020	.0017—.0020	.3400	.3400
	V8-305④⑮	1 Turn⑤		46	45	1.70	200 @ 1.25	.0010—.0027	.0010—.0027	.3410—.3417	.3410—.3417
	V8-350/X⑪	Hydraulic⑥		45	45	1.727	⑬	.0015—.0035	.0015—.0032	.3720—.3730	.3723—.3730
	V8-350/L④	1 Turn⑤		46	45	1.70	200 @ 1.25	.0010—.0027	.0010—.0027	.3410—.3417	.3410—.3417
	V8-350/R⑦	Hydraulic⑥		⑧	⑨	1.67	187 @ 1.27	.0010—.0027	.0015—.0032	.3425—.3432	.3420—.3427
	V8-403/K⑦	Hydraulic⑥		⑧	⑨	1.67	187 @ 1.27	.0010—.0027	.0015—.0032	.3425—.3432	.3420—.3427
1980	V8-350/N⑦⑫	Hydraulic⑥		⑧	⑨	1.67	152 @ 1.30	.0010—.0027	.0015—.0032	.3425—.3432	.3420—.3427
1981	V6-231⑮	Hydraulic⑥		45	45	1.727	⑭	.0015—.0035	.0015—.0032	.3402—.3412	.3405—.3412
	V6-252/4	Hydraulic⑥		45	45	1.727	⑭	.0015—.0035	.0015—.0032	.3402—.3412	.3405—.3412
	V8-265/S⑩	Hydraulic⑥		46	45	1.66	187 @ 1.296	.0010—.0027	.0010—.0027	.3418—.3425	.3418—.3425
	V8-307/Y⑦	Hydraulic⑥		⑧	⑨	1.67	189 @ 1.27	.0010—.0027	.0015—.0032	.3425—.3432	.3420—.3427
	V8-350/N⑦⑫	Hydraulic⑥		⑧	⑨	1.67	⑭	.0010—.0027	.0015—.0032	.3425—.3432	.3420—.3427
1982—83	V6-231⑮	Hydraulic⑥		45	45	1.727	182 @ 1.34	.0015—.0035	.0015—.0032	.3401—.3412	.3405—.3412
	V6-252/4	Hydraulic⑥		45	45	1.727	182 @ 1.34	.0015—.0035	.0015—.0032	.3401—.3412	.3405—.3412
	V6-262/V	Hydraulic⑥		⑧	⑨	1.670	210 @ 1.220	.0010—.0027	.0015—.0032	.3425—.3432	.3420—.3427
	V8-307/Y	Hydraulic⑥		⑧	⑨	1.670	187 @ 1.27	.0010—.0027	.0015—.0032	.3425—.3432	.3420—.3427
	V8-350/N	Hydraulic⑥		⑧	⑨	1.670	210 @ 1.220	.0010—.0027	.0015—.0032	.3425—.3432	.3420—.3427
1984	V6-231/A	Hydraulic⑥		45	45	1.727	182 @ 1.34	.0015—.0032	.0015—.0032	.3401—.3412	.3405—.3412
	V6-231/9⑯	Hydraulic⑥		45	45	1.727	220 @ 1.34	.0015—.0032	.0015—.0032	.3401—.3412	.3405—.3412
	V6-252/4	Hydraulic⑥		45	45	1.727	182 @ 1.34	.0015—.0032	.0015—.0032	.3401—.3412	.3405—.3412
	V6-262/V	Hydraulic⑥		⑧	⑨	1.670	210 @ 1.22	.0010—.0027	.0015—.0032	.3425—.3432	.3420—.3427
	V8-307/Y	Hydraulic⑥		⑧	⑨	1.670	187 @ 1.27	.0010—.0027	.0015—.0032	.3425—.3432	.3420—.3427
	V8-350/N	Hydraulic⑥		⑧	⑨	1.670	210 @ 1.22	.0010—.0027	.0015—.0032	.3425—.3432	.3420—.3427

①—Outer spring
②—Intake 200 @ 1.25; exhaust 200 @ 1.16
③—Intake, 1.70 inch; exhaust, 1.61 inch.
④—Chevrolet built engine. Distributor located at rear of engine, clockwise rotation.
⑤—Turn rocker arm stud nut until all lash is eliminated, then tighten nut the additional turn listed.
⑥—No adjustment.
⑦—Oldsmobile built engine. Distributor located at rear of engine, counterclockwise rotation.
⑧—Intake, 45°; exhaust 31°.
⑨—Intake 44°; exhaust, 30°.
⑩—Pontiac built engine. Distributor located at rear of engine, clockwise rotation.
⑪—Buick built engine. Distributor located at front of engine.
⑫—Diesel engine.
⑬—Intake, 180 @ 1.34; exhaust, 177 @ 1.45.
⑭—Intake, 164 @ 1.34; exhaust, 182 @ 1.34.
⑮—For V.I.N. code, refer to the "General Engine Specifications" at the beginning of the chapter.
⑯—Turbocharged engine

STARTING MOTOR APPLICATIONS

Year	Engine/V.I.N.	Starter Number	Year	Engine/V.I.N.	Starter Number
1977	V6-231/C	1108797		V8-403/K	1108794
	V8-301/Y	1108758	1978	V8-350/X①	1109061
	V8-305/U, Auto. Trans.	1109056		V8-350/L②	1109065
	V8-305/U, Man. Trans.	1108799		V8-350, 403③⑨	1109072
	V8-350①⑨	1108762	1978—80	V6-196, 231⑦⑨	1109061
	V8-350/L②	1109052		V8-265, 301⑨	1109523
	V8-350/R③	1108765			

STARTING MOTOR APPLICATIONS—Continued

Year	Engine/V.I.N.	Starter Number	Year	Engine/V.I.N.	Starter Number
1979–80, cont'd.	V8-305 2 Bbl. Carb. ⑨	1109064	1982–83	V6-231/A	1998234
	V8-305/H, 4 Bbl. Carb.	1109524		V6-252/4 ⑦	1998234
1979–80	V6-231 ⑧ ⑨	1998204		V6-252/4 ⑧	1998237
	V8-350/X ①	1109062		V8-262/V	1998552
	V8-350/L ② ⑤	1109524		V8-307/Y ⑦	1109544
	V8-350/L ② ⑥	1109065		V8-307/Y ⑧	1998237
	V8-350, 403 ③ ⑦ ⑨	1109072		V8-350/N ④ ⑦	1998552
	V8-350 ⑧ ⑨	1998205		V8-350/N ④ ⑧	1109495
1980	V6-252/4	1109062	1983	V6-231/8 ⑦	1998234
	V8-350/N ④ ⑦	1100215		V6-231/8 ⑧	1998237
	V8-350/N ④ ⑧	1100214	1984	V6-231/A,9 ⑦	1998236
1981	V6-231 ⑦ ⑨	1109061		V6-231/9 ⑧	1998237
	V6-231 ⑧ ⑨	1998204		V6-252/4 ⑦	1998234
	V6-252/4 ⑦	1998227		V6-252/4 ⑧	1998237
	V6-252/4 ⑧	1998205		V6-262/V ④	1998556
	V8-265, 301 ⑨	1109523			22511854
	V8-307/Y	1998205		V8-307/Y ⑦	1109544
	V8-350/N ④ ⑦	1109216		V8-307/Y ⑧	1998237
	V8-350/N ④ ⑧	1109218		V8-350/N ④ ⑦	1998553
1982	V6-231/3 ⑦	1998234			22523207
	V6-231/3 ⑧	1998237		V8-350/N ④ ⑧	1109495

①—Distributor at front of engine.
②—Distributor at rear of engine, clockwise rotation.
③—Distributor at rear of engine, counter-clockwise rotation.
④—Diesel engine.
⑤—Exc. Skylark.
⑥—Skylark.
⑦—Exc. Riviera.
⑧—Riviera.
⑨—For V.I.N. code, refer to the "General Engine Specifications" at the beginning of the chapter.

COOLING SYSTEM & CAPACITY DATA

Year	Model or Engine/V.I.N.	Cooling Capacity, Qts.		Radiator Cap Relief Pressure, Lbs.	Thermo. Opening Temp.	Fuel Tank Gals.	Engine Oil Refill Qts. ①	Transmission Oil			Rear Axle Oil Pints
		Less A/C	With A/C					3 Speed Pints	4 Speed Pints	Auto. Trans. Qts. ②	
1977	V6-231/C ⑦	12.7	12.8	15	⑰	21	4	3½	—	⑮	3.5
	V6-231/C ⑪	12.8	12.7	15	⑰	22	4	3½	—	⑮	4¼
	V6-231/C ⑩	12.7	12.7	15	⑰	21	4	—	—	⑮	4¼
	V8-301/Y ⑦	18.6	19.2	15	195	21	4	—	—	⑮	3.5
	V8-301/Y ⑩	18.2⑳	18.1⑳	15	195	21	4	—	—	⑮	4¼
	V8-305/U ⑦	17	18	15	195	21	4	—	—	⑮	3.5
	V8-350/V ⑪㉓	14.3㉔	14.9㉔	15	195	22	4	—	—	⑮	4¼
	V8-350/V ⑥ ⑩㉓	14.2㉕	14.1㉕	15	195	㉖	4	—	—	⑮	⑳
	V8-350 ⑦ ⑱㉘㊴	15.6	15.6	15	195	21	4	—	—	⑮	3.5
	V8-350 ⑪ ⑱㉘㊴	15.3㉙	15.9㉙	15	195	22	4	—	—	⑮	4¼
	V8-350 ⑥ ⑩㉘㊴	14.6㉚	14.5㉚	15	195	㉖	4	—	—	⑮	⑳
	V8-350 ⑦㉘㊴	17	18	15	195	21	4	—	—	⑮	3.5
	V8-350 ⑪㉘㊴	14.8	15.4	15	195	22	4	—	—	⑮	4¼
	V8-403/K ⑪	16.4㉛	17㉛	15	195	22	4	—	—	⑮	4¼
	V8-403/K ⑥ ⑩	15.7㉜	15.6㉜	15	195	㉖	4	—	—	⑮	⑳

Continued

COOLING SYSTEM & CAPACITY DATA—Continued

Year	Model or Engine/V.I.N.	Cooling Capacity, Qts. Less A/C	With A/C	Radiator Cap Relief Pressure, Lbs.	Thermo. Opening Temp.	Fuel Tank Gals.	Engine Oil Refill Qts. [1]	Transmission Oil 3 Speed Pints	4 Speed Pints	Auto. Trans. Qts. [2]	Rear Axle Oil Pints
1978	V6-196/C	13.1	13.2	15	195	17.5	4	3½	—	[15]	4¼
	V6-231[7][54]	13.6	13.7	15	195	21	4	3½	—	[15]	4¼
	V6-231[11][54]	13.1	13.2	15	195	17.5	4	—	3½	[15]	4¼
	V6-231[10][54]	12.9	12.9	15	195	21	4	—	—	[15]	4¼
	V8-301/Y	20.9[5]	20.9[5]	15	195	21	4	—	—	[15]	4¼
	V8-305/U[7]	15.9[33]	16.3[33]	15	195	21	4	3½	—	[15]	4¼
	V8-305/U[11]	19.2[34]	18.9[34]	15	195	17.5	4	—	—	[15]	4¼
	V8-305/U[10]	16.6	16.7	15	195	21	4	—	—	[15]	4¼
	V8-350[7][54]	16.1	16.9	15	195	21	4	—	—	[13]	4¼
	V8-350[11][54]	19.2[34]	18.9[34]	15	195	17.5	4	—	—	[13]	4¼
	V8-350/X[6][10][23][39]	14.1[35]	14.1[35]	15	195	[19]	4	—	—	[15]	4¼
	V8-350/R[6][10][18][28][40]	14.6[30]	14.5[30]	15	195	[19]	4	—	—	[15]	4¼
	V8-350/L[6][10][28]	16.6[36]	16.7[36]	15	195	[19]	4	—	—	[15]	4¼
	V8-403/K	15.7	16.6	15	195	[19]	4	—	—	—	4¼
1979	V6-196, 231[11][54]	13.5	13.5	15	195	18.1	4	3.5	3.5	[41]	[38]
	V6-231[10][14][54]	12.9	12.9	15	195	25.3	4	—	—	[15]	[38]
	V6-231[7][54]	13.8	13.9	15	195	21	4	3.5	—	[15]	[38]
	V6-231 Turbo/3[11][37]	13.7[43]	13.8[43]	15	195	18.1	4	—	—	[41]	[38]
	V6-231 Turbo/3[13][37]	—	14[4]	15	195	20	4	—	—	[9]	3.2[8]
	V8-301[11][54]	20.3[27]	21[27]	15	195	18.1	4	3.5	3.5	[41]	[38]
	V8-301[10][14][54]	21[5]	21[5]	15	195	21[3][42]	4	—	—	[15]	[38]
	V8-305[7][54]	15.9[33]	16.3[33]	15	195	21	4	3.5	—	[15]	[38]
	V8-305[11][54]	17.6[36]	17.6[36]	15	195	18.1	4	3.5	3.5	[41]	[38]
	V8-350[11][54]	17.6[36]	18.1	15	195	18.1	4	3.5	3.5	[41]	[38]
	V8-350[7][54]	16.1[33]	16.9	15	195	21	4	3.5	—	[15]	[38]
	V8-350/X[10][14][23][39]	14.1[25]	14.1[25]	15	195	21[3][42]	4	—	—	[15]	[38]
	V8-350/R[10][14][28][40]	14.6[30]	14.5[30]	15	195	21[3][42]	4	—	—	[15]	[38]
	V8-350[13][54]	—	14.9[30]	15	195	20	4	—	—	[9]	3.2[8]
	V8-403/K[10][14]	15.7[32]	16.6	15	195	21[3][42]	4	—	—	[15]	[38]
1980	V6-231[11][54]	13.3	13.3	15	195	18.1	4	3.5	3.5	[45]	[38]
	V6-231[10][54]	13	13	15	195	25	4	3.5	—	[45]	[38]
	V6-231 Turbo/3[11]	13.7[43]	13.8[43]	15	195	18.1	4	3.5	—	[45]	[38]
	V6-231 Turbo/3[10]	13.4[44]	13.4[44]	15	195	25	4	—	—	[45]	[38]
	V6-231 Turbo/3[13]	—	13.66[47]	15	195	21	4	—	—	[9]	3.2[8]
	V6-252/4[10][14]	13	13	15	195	25	4	—	—	[45]	[38]
	V8-301/W[11]	20.3[27]	21	15	195	18.1	4[46]	3.5	—	[45]	[38]
	V8-301/W[10][14]	18.9	18.9	15	195	25[3]	4[46]	3.5	—	[45]	[38]
	V8-305/H[11]	—	17.6[36]	15	195	18.1	4	—	—	[45]	[38]
	V8-350/X[10][14][23][39]	14.3[48]	14.2[48]	15	195	25[3]	4	—	—	[45]	[38]
	V8-350/R[10][14][28][40]	—	14.5[49]	15	195	25[3]	4	—	—	[45]	[38]
	V8-350[13][54]	—	15.5	15	195	21	4	—	—	[9]	3.2[8]
	V8-350 Diesel/N[10][14]	18.3	18	15	195	27[3]	7[21]	—	—	[45]	[38]
1981	V6-231/A[11]	13	13	15	195	18.1	4	3.5	—	[12]	3½
	V6-231/A[10]	13	13	15	195	25	4	3.5	—	[12]	3½
	V6-231 Turbo/3[11]	13.4[44]	13.4[44]	15	195	18.1	4	—	—	[12]	3½
	V6-231 Turbo/3[13]	13.6[43]	13.6[43]	15	195	21	4	—	—	[12]	3.3[8]
	V6-252/4[10][14]	13	13	15	195	25	4	—	—	[12]	3½
	V6-252/4[13]	13	13	15	195	21	4	—	—	[12]	3.3[8]
	V8-265/S[11]	20.2[27]	20.2[27]	15	195	18.1	4[46]	3.5	—	[12]	3½
	V8-307/Y[10][14]	18.9	18.9	15	195	25[3]	4	—	—	[12]	3½
	V8-307/Y[13]	16.4	16.4	15	195	22	4	—	—	[12]	3.3[8]

COOLING SYSTEM & CAPACITY DATA—Continued

Year	Model or Engine/V.I.N.	Cooling Capacity, Qts. Less A/C	With A/C	Radiator Cap Relief Pressure, Lbs.	Thermo. Opening Temp.	Fuel Tank Gals.	Engine Oil Refill Qts. [1]	Transmission Oil 3 Speed Pints	4 Speed Pints	Auto. Trans. Qts. [2]	Rear Axle Oil Pints
	V8-350 Diesel/N[10][14]	17.3	17	15	195	27[3]	7[21]	—	—	[12]	3½
	V8-350 Diesel/N[13]	18.2	18.2	15	195	27	7[21]	—	—	[12]	3½
1982	V6-231/A[50]	12.98	13.02	15	195	18	4	—	—	[51]	[16]
	V6-231/A[10]	13	13	15	195	25[3]	4	—	—	[51]	[16]
	V6-231 Turbo/3[50]	13.44[44]	13.44[44]	15	195	25[3]	4	—	—	[51]	[16]
	V6-231 Turbo/3[13]	13.6[43]	13.6[43]	15	195	21	4	—	—	[51]	3.2[8]
	V6-252/4[50]	12.98	13.02	15	195	18	4	—	—	[51]	[16]
	V6-252/4[10][14]	13	13	15	195	25[3]	4	—	—	[51]	[16]
	V6-252/4[13]	13	13	15	195	21	4	—	—	[51]	3.2[8]
	V6-262 Diesel/V[50]	14.8	14.8	15	195	20	6.5[21]	—	—	[51]	[16]
	V8-307/Y[10][14]	18.9	18.9	15	195	25[3]	4	—	—	[51]	[16]
	V8-307/Y[13]	18.8	18.95	15	195	21	4	—	—	[51]	3.2[8]
	V8-350 Diesel/N[50]	17.33	17.33	15	195	20	7[21]	—	—	[51]	[16]
	V8-350 Diesel/N[10][14]	17	17	15	195	27[3]	7[21]	—	—	[51]	[16]
	V8-350 Diesel/N[13]	18.2	18.2	15	195	23	7[21]	—	—	[51]	3.2[8]
1983	V6-231/A[50]	12.9	13	15	195	[53]	4	—	—	[51]	[38]
	V6-231/A[10]	12.9	13	15	195	25[3]	4	—	—	[51]	[38]
	V6-231 Turbo/8[50]	13.4	13.4[44]	15	195	19.8	4	—	—	[51]	[38]
	V6-231 Turbo/8[13]	—	13.6[43]	15	195	21.1	4	—	—	[51]	3.2[8]
	V6-252/4[50]	12.9	13	15	195	[53]	4	—	—	[51]	[38]
	V6-252/4[10][14]	12.9	13	15	195	25[3]	4	—	—	[51]	[38]
	V6-252/4[13]	—	13	15	195	21.1	4	—	—	[51]	3.2[8]
	V6-262 Diesel/V[50]	—	14.7	18.5	195	[53]	6.5[21]	—	—	[51]	[38]
	V8-307/Y[10][14]	15.4[52]	16[52]	15	195	25[3]	4	—	—	[51]	[38]
	V8-307/Y[13]	—	16[52]	15	195	21.1	4	—	—	[51]	3.2[8]
	V8-350 Diesel/N[50]	—	17.3	15	195	[53]	6.5[21]	—	—	[51]	[38]
	V8-350 Diesel/N[10][14]	—	17.9	15	195	26[3]	6.5[21]	—	—	[51]	[38]
	V8-350 Diesel/N[13]	—	18	15	195	22.8	6.5[21]	—	—	[51]	3.2[8]
1984	V6-231/A[50]	12.9	13	15	195	19.8	4	—	—	[51]	3.5
	V6-231/A[10]	13	13	15	195	25[3]	4	—	—	[51]	[38]
	V6-231 Turbo/9[50]	13	13	15	180	19.8	5	—	—	[51]	3.5
	V6-231 Turbo/9[13]	—	12.9[44]	15	180	21.1	5	—	—	[51]	3.3[8]
	V6-252/4[50]	13	13	15	195	19.8	4	—	—	[51]	3.5
	V6-252/4[10][14]	13	13	15	195	25[3]	4	—	—	[51]	[38]
	V6-252/4[13]	—	12.6	15	195	21.1	4	—	—	[51]	3.3[8]
	V6-262 Diesel/V[50]	13.6	14.4	15	195	[53]	6[21]	—	—	[51]	3.5
	V8-307/Y[10][14]	15.4	16	15	195	25[3]	4	—	—	[51]	[38]
	V8-307/Y[13]	—	16	15	195	21.1	4	—	—	[51]	3.3[8]
	V8-350 Diesel/N[10][14]	18.3	17.9	15	195	26[3]	7[21]	—	—	[51]	[38]
	V8-350 Diesel/N[13]	18.2	18.2	15	195	22.8	7[21]	—	—	[51]	3.3[8]

[1]—Add one quart with filter change.
[2]—Approximate. Make final check with dipstick.
[3]—Estate Wagon 22 gallons.
[4]—With heavy duty cooling system, 14.5 qts.
[5]—With heavy duty cooling system, 21.6 qts.
[6]—Estate Wagon, Electra & Riviera.
[7]—Skylark.
[8]—Final drive.
[9]—Total 12 qts. Oil pan only 5 qts.
[10]—LeSabre.
[11]—Century & Regal.
[12]—THM 200C—total 9½ qts., pan only 3½ qts.; THM 325—total 12 qts., pan only 5 qts.; THM 250C—total 10¾ qts., pan only 4 qts.; THM 350C—total 10 qts., pan only 3⅛ qts.;

THM 2004R—total 11 qts., pan only 3½ qts.
[13]—Riviera.
[14]—Electra.
[15]—Total 10 qts.; pan only 3 qts.
[16]—With 7½ inch ring gear, 3.5 pints; with 8¾ inch ring gear, 5.4 pints.
[17]—Exc. Calif., 195°; Calif., 180°.
[18]—Oil filler tube located on engine front cover.
[19]—LeSabre, 21; Estate Wagon, 22.5; Electra, Riviera, 25.3.
[20]—Exc. wagon, 4¼ pts.; wagon, 5.4 pts.
[21]—Includes oil filter. For 1980 models, use recommended diesel oil, designated SE/CC. For 1981 models use recommended diesel oil

designated SF/CC, SF/CD or SE/CC. For 1982–84 models use recommended diesel oil designated SF/CC or SF/CD.
[22]—With heavy duty cooling system, 19.1 qts.
[23]—Distributor at front of engine.
[24]—With heavy duty cooling system, 16.4 qts.
[25]—With heavy duty cooling system, 15 qts.
[26]—LeSabre, 21 gal.; Electra & Riviera, 24.5 gal.; Estate wagon, 22 gal.
[27]—With heavy duty cooling system, 20.8 qts.
[28]—Distributor at rear of engine.
[29]—With heavy duty cooling system, 17.4 qts.
[30]—With heavy duty cooling system, 15.4 qts.
[31]—With heavy duty cooling system, 18.5 qts.
[32]—With heavy duty cooling system, 16.6 qts.
[33]—With heavy duty cooling system, 16.9 qts.

Continued

COOLING SYSTEM & CAPACITY DATA NOTES—Continued

㉞—With heavy duty cooling system, 19.6 qts.
㉟—With heavy duty cooling system, 14.9 qts.
㊱—With heavy duty cooling system, 18.0 qts.
㊲—4 Barrel Carb.
㊳—7 1/2 inch axle, 3.5 pts.; 8 1/2 inch axle, 4.25 pts.; 8 3/4 inch axle, 5.4 pts.
㊴—Buick built engine.
㊵—Oldsmobile built engine.
㊶—THM 200—total 9.5 qts.; oil pan only 3.5 qts. THM 350—total capacity 10 qts; oil pan only 3 qts.
㊷—Electra, 25.3 gal.
㊸—With heavy duty cooling system, 14.1 qts.
㊹—With heavy duty cooling system, 13.7 qts.
㊺—THM 200—total 9.5 qts., pan only 3.5 qts.; THM 250C—total 10 qts., pan only 4 qts.; THM 350—total 12 1/4 qts., pan only 3 1/4 qts.; THM 400—total 10 qts., pan only 3 qts.
㊻—With or without filter change.
㊼—With heavy duty cooling system, 14.17 qts.
㊽—With heavy duty cooling system, 14.8 qts.
㊾—With heavy duty cooling system, 15.2 qts.
㊿—Regal.
(51)—THM 200C—total 9.4 qts.; pan only 3.48 qts.
THM 2004R—total 11.05 qts., pan only 3.48 qts.
THM 250C—total 10.04 qts., pan only 4.0 qts.
THM 3254L—total 11.75 qts., pan only 4.86 qts.
THM 350C—total 10.04 qts.; pan only 3.17 qts.
(52)—With heavy duty cooling system, 16 qts.
(53)—Exc. wagon, 19.8 gals.; wagon, 18.2 gals.
(54)—For V.I.N. code, refer to the "General Engine Specifications" at the beginning of the chapter.

WHEEL ALIGNMENT SPECIFICATIONS

Year	Model	Caster Angle, Degrees		Camber Angle, Degrees				Toe-In. Inch	Toe Out on Turns, Deg.	
		Limits	Desired	Limits		Desired			Outer Wheel	Inner Wheel
				Left	Right	Left	Right			
1977	Skylark①	−1/2 to −1 1/2	−1	+1/4 to +1 1/4	+1/4 to +1 1/4	+3/4	+3/4	0 to 1/8	—	—
	Skylark②	+1/2 to +1 1/2	+1	+1/4 to +1 1/4	+1/4 to +1 1/4	+3/4	+3/4	0 to 1/8	—	—
	Century, Regal④	+1/2 to +1 1/2	+1	+1/2 to +1 1/2	0 to +1	+1	+1/2	0 to 1/8	—	—
	Century, Regal⑤	+1 1/2 to +2 1/2	+2	+1/2 to +1 1/2	0 to +1	+1	+1/2	0 to 1/8	—	—
	Others	+2 1/2 to +3 1/2	+3	+1/4 to +1 1/4	+1/4 to +1 1/4	+3/4	+3/4	1/16 to 3/16	—	—
1978	Skylark①	−.5 to −1.5	−1	+.3 to +1.3	+.3 to +1.3	+.8	+.8	1/16 to 3/16	—	—
	Skylark②	+.5 to +1.5	+1	+.3 to +1.3	+.3 to +1.3	+.8	+.8	1/16 to 3/16	—	—
	Century, Regal①	+.5 to +1.5	+1	0 to +1	0 to +1	+.5	+.5	1/16 to 3/16	—	—
	Century, Regal②	+2.5 to +3.5	+3	0 to +1	0 to +1	+.5	+.5	1/16 to 3/16	—	—
	Others	+2.5 to +3.5	+3	+.3 to +1.3	+.3 to +1.3	+.8	+.8	1/16 to 3/16	—	—
1979	Skylark①	−.5 to −1.5	−1	+.3 to +1.3	+.3 to +1.3	+.8	+.8	1/16 to 3/16	—	—
	Skylark②	+.5 to +1.5	+1	+.3 to +1.3	+.3 to +1.3	+.8	+.8	1/6 to 3/16	—	—
1979–80	Century, Regal①	+.5 to +1.5	+1	0 to +1	0 to +1	+.5	+.5	1/16 to 3/16	—	—
	Century, Regal②	+2.5 to +3.5	+3	0 to +1	0 to +1	+.5	+.5	1/16 to 3/16	—	—
	Riviera	+2 to +3	+2.5	−.5 to +.5	−.5 to +.5	Zero	Zero	⑥	—	—
	Others	+2.5 to +3.5	+3	+.3 to +1.3	+.3 to +1.3	+.8	+.8	1/16 to 3/16	—	—
1981	Century, Regal②	+2.5 to +3.5	+3	0 to +1	0 to +1	+.5	+.5	1/16 to 3/16	—	—
	Riviera	+2 to +3	+2.5	−.5 to +.5	−.5 to +.5	Zero	Zero	⑥	—	—
	Others	+2.5 to +3.5	+3	+.3 to +1.3	+.3 to +1.3	+.8	+.8	1/16 to 3/16	—	—
1982	Regal	+2.5 to +3.5	+3	0 to +1	0 to +1	+.5	+.5	1/16 to 3/16	—	—
	Riviera	+2 to +3	+2.5	−.5 to +.5	−.5 to +.5	Zero	Zero	⑥	—	—
	Others	+2.5 to +3.5	+3	+.3 to +1.3	+.3 to +1.3	+.8	+.8	1/16 to 3/16	—	—
1983–84	Regal	+2.5 to +3.5	+3	0 to +1	0 to +1	+.5	+.5	1/16 to 3/16	—	—
	Riviera	+2 to +3	+2.5	−.5 to +.5	−.5 to +.5	Zero	Zero	⑥	—	—
	Others	+2.5 to +3.5	+3	+.3 to +1.3	+.3 to +1.3	+.8	+.8	1/16 to 3/16	—	—

①—Manual steering.
②—Power steering.
③—Manual steering & all Sta. Wag.—right turn, 19 3/16°; left turn, 18 3/16°: power steering Exc. Sta. Wag.—right turn, 19°; left turn, 18 11/16°.
④—Equipped with bias belted tires.
⑤—Equipped with radial tires.
⑥—1/16" toe-in to 1/16" toe-out.

Electrical Section

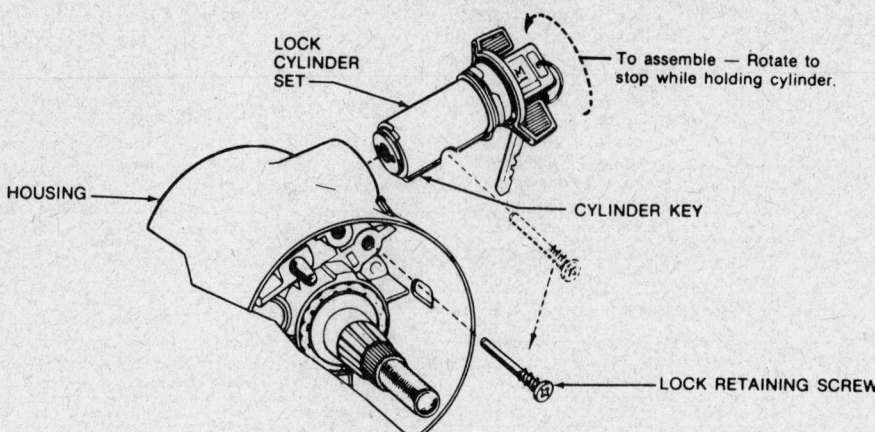

Fig. 1 Ignition lock removal. 1979–84 models

STARTER, REPLACE

To remove the starter, disconnect battery cable from battery. Disconnect cable and solenoid lead wire from solenoid switch. Remove flywheel inspection cover. Remove starter attaching bolts and remove starter.

LIGHT SWITCH, REPLACE

1977–84

1. Disconnect battery ground cable.
2. On intermediate models equipped with A/C, remove left hand duct.
3. On all models except 1978–81 Century and 1978–84 Regal, pull switch knob to full "On" position, depress latch button on rear of switch and pull knob and rod from switch. On 1978–81 Century and 1978–84 Regal, depress retainer tab behind switch knob and remove knob from stem. On all models, remove switch escutcheon or retaining nut, if used.
4. Pull switch down, disconnect electrical connector and remove switch.
5. Reverse procedure to install.

COLUMN-MOUNTED DIMMER SWITCH, REPLACE

1977–84 Full Size; 1978–81 Century; 1978–84 Regal

1. Disconnect battery ground cable.
2. Remove instrument panel lower trim and on models with A/C, remove A/C duct extension at column.
3. Disconnect shift indicator from column and remove toe-plate cover screws.
4. Remove two nuts from instrument panel support bracket studs and lower steering column, resting steering wheel on front seat.
5. Remove dimmer switch retaining screw(s) and the switch. Tape actuator rod to column and separate switch from rod.
6. Reverse procedure to install. To adjust switch, depress dimmer switch slightly and install a 3/32 inch twist drill to lock the switch to the body. Force switch upward to remove lash between switch and pivot. Torque switch retaining screw(s) to 35 inch lbs. and remove tape from actuator rod. Remove twist drill and check for proper operation.

1977 Century & Regal

1. Remove switch cover.
2. Remove three switch to column attaching screws.
3. Disconnect switch lead at lower end of column and attach a wire to lead end of harness for ease of installation.
4. Hold switch and pull harness from column.
5. Reverse procedure to install.

IGNITION LOCK, REPLACE

1979–84

1. Remove steering wheel as described under Horn Sounder and Steering Wheel, Replace.
2. Remove turn signal switch as described under Turn Signal Switch, Replace, then remove buzzer switch.
3. Place ignition switch in Run position, then remove lock cylinder retaining

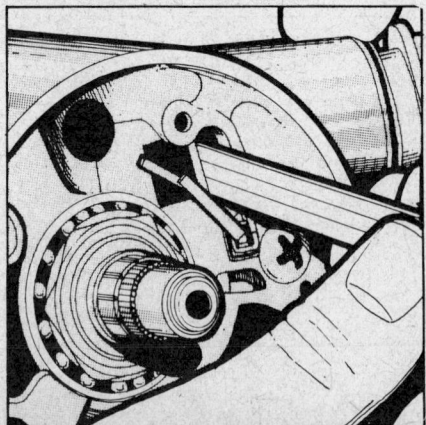

Fig. 2 Ignition lock removal. 1977–78

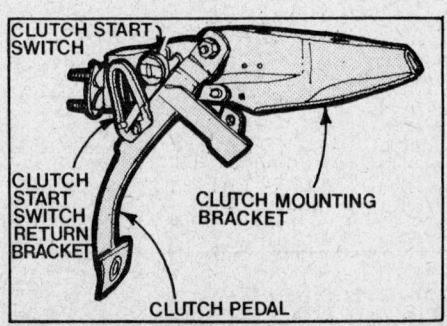

Fig. 3 Clutch start switch in start position. 1977–81

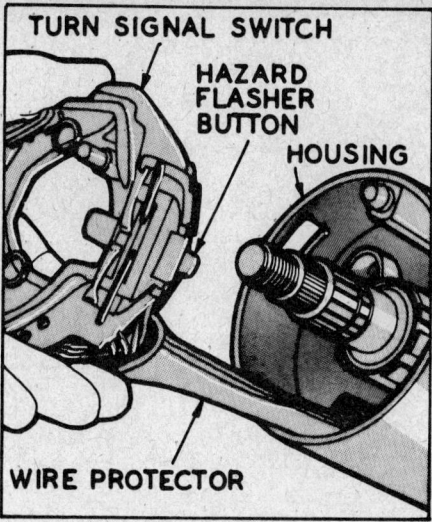

Fig. 4 Turn signal and hazard warning flasher switch assembly. 1977—84

screw and lock cylinder.
4. To install, rotate lock cylinder to stop while holding housing, Fig. 1. Align cylinder key with keyway in housing, then push lock cylinder assembly into housing until fully seated.
5. Install lock cylinder retaining screw. Torque screw to 40 in. lbs. for standard columns. On adjustable columns, torque retaining screw to 22 in. lbs.
6. Install buzzer switch, turn signal switch and steering wheel.

1977—78

1. Follow procedure to remove turn signal switch as described further on.
2. Place lock cylinder in "run" position.
3. Place a thin tool (small screw-driver or knife blade) into the slot next to the switch mounting screw boss (right hand slot) and depress spring latch at bottom of slot which releases lock Fig. 2. Remove lock.
4. To install lock, hold lock cylinder sleeve and rotate knob clockwise against stop, then insert cylinder with key on cylinder sleeve aligned with keyway in housing. Push in to abutment of cylinder and sector, then rotate knob counterclockwise, maintaining a light inward push on cylinder until drive section of cylinder mates with drive shaft.

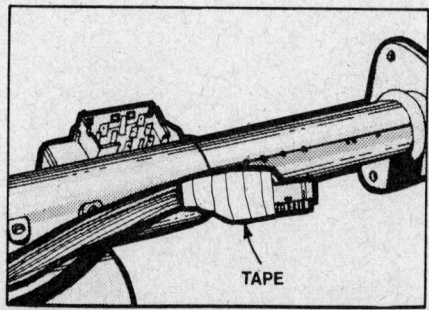

Fig. 6 Taping turn signal connector & wiring

IGNITION SWITCH, REPLACE

1977—84

The ignition switch is located on the top of the steering column under the instrument panel. To replace it the steering column must be lowered as follows:
1. Disconnect shift indicator link.
2. Remove nuts securing bracket to dash panel and carefully lower column.
3. Disconnect electrical connector from switch. On models equipped with standard column and key release feature or tilt column except key release, ensure switch is in "Accessory" position. On models equipped with standard column except key release or tilt column with key release, ensure switch is in "Off-Unlock" position.
4. Remove two screws securing switch, then remove switch.
5. On models equipped with standard column and key release feature or tilt column except key release, position switch slider and lock in the "Accessory" position. On models equipped with standard column except key release or tilt column with key release, position switch slider and lock at "Accessory" position, then move slider and lock two detents to the "Off-Unlock" position.
6. Fit actuator rod into switch and assemble to column.
7. Complete assembly in reverse of removal procedure.

STOP LIGHT SWITCH, REPLACE

1977—84

The stop lights are controlled by a mechanical switch mounted on the brake pedal bracket. This spring loaded switch makes contact whenever the brake pedal is applied. When the brake pedal is released it depresses the switch to open the contacts and turn brake lights off.

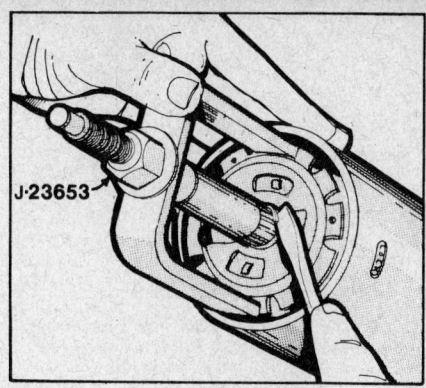

Fig. 5 Compressing lock plate & removing snap ring

CLUTCH START SWITCH

1977—81

A clutch start switch is installed on all manual transmission cars. The switch is mounted on the clutch pedal bracket and it prevents the car from being started until the clutch pedal is depressed, Fig. 3.

TURN SIGNAL SWITCH, REPLACE

1977—84

As shown in Fig. 4, the assembly is a turn signal switch and hazard warning switch. It is mounted in a housing at the upper end of the steering column mast jacket, just below the steering wheel. Therefore to get at the switch the steering wheel will have to be removed.

Also, on models equipped with tilt steering columns, it is necessary to lower the column assembly from instrument panel.
1. Disconnect battery ground cable.
2. Remove steering wheel and lock plate cover. On tilt columns, remove tilt lever.
3. With a suitable compressor, compress lock plate and spring, then remove snap ring from shaft, Fig. 5.
4. Remove lock plate cover with a suitable screwdriver.
5. Remove lock plate, cancelling cam, preload spring and thrust washer.

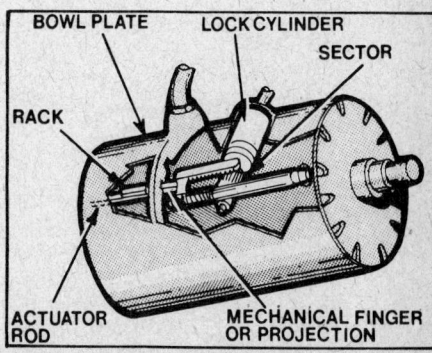

Fig. 7 Mechanical neutral start system with standard column. 1977—84 Full Size; 1978—81 Century; 1978—84 Regal

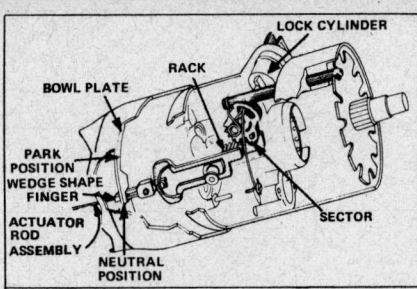

Fig. 8 Mechanical neutral start system with tilt column. 1977–84 Full Size; 1978–81 Century; 1978–84 Regal

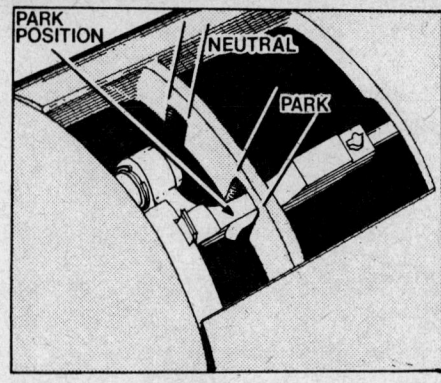

Fig. 9 Mechanical neutral start system in Park position. 1977–84 Full Size; 1978–81 Century; 1978–84 Regal

6. Remove turn signal lever and hazard warning switch knob.
7. Disconnect switch wiring connector and wrap a piece of tape around connector upper end and wiring harness, preventing snagging when removing switch, Fig. 6.
8. Remove three switch retaining screws and switch.
9. Reverse procedure to install.

NEUTRAL START SWITCH

1977–84 Full Size; 1978–81 Century; 1978–84 Regal

Actuation of the ignition switch is prevented by a mechanical lockout system, Figs. 7 and 8, which prevents the lock cylinder from rotating when the selector lever is out of Park or Neutral. When the selector lever is in Park or Neutral, the slots in the bowl plate and the finger on the actuator rod align allowing the finger to pass through the bowl plate in turn actuating the ignition switch, Fig. 9. If the selector lever is in any position other than Park or Neutral, the finger contacts the bowl plate when the lock cylinder is rotated, thereby preventing full travel of the lock cylinder.

NEUTRAL START & BACK-UP LIGHT SWITCH, REPLACE

NOTE: Some models use a combination neutral start & back-up light switch, while other models use a back-up light switch. Both type switches are serviced by the following procedures.

1977–81 Models

1. On automatic transmission equipped models, place gear selector in "Neutral" for column shift, or "Park" for console shift. On manual transmission models, place gearshift in "Reverse".
2. Remove screws attaching switch to steering column, then remove switch.
3. Disconnect wiring connectors. Connect wiring connectors to new switch.
4. Position new switch on steering column, aligning the switch carrier tang in the switch tube slot.
5. Install attaching screws and tighten.

NOTE: No adjustment is required. The switch is pinned in the proper position with a plastic shear pin.

---

6. If adjustment is required:
   a. On 1977–78 models with automatic transmission, place gear selector in "Neutral" position. On 1979–81 models with automatic transmission, place gear selector in "Neutral" for column shift, or "Park" for console shift. On all models with manual transmission, place gearshift in "Reverse".
   b. Loosen switch adjusting screws.
   c. On 1977–79 models and 1980–81 models with column shift, while rotating switch on column, insert a .096 inch gage pin in neutral gage hole a depth of 3/8 inch, Fig. 10. On 1980–81 models with console shift, while rotating switch on column, insert .096 inch gage pin in park gage hole a depth of 3/8 inch, Fig. 10.
   d. Tighten attaching screws and remove gage pin.

1982–84 Models

1. Place gear selector in "Neutral".
2. Gently rock switch out of steering column.
3. Disconnect wiring connectors. Connect wiring connectors to new switch.
4. Align switch actuator with hole in shift tube, Fig. 11.
5. Position connector side of switch into lower jacket cut out.
6. Push down front of switch, ensuring switch tangs snap into holes in steering column jacket.
7. Adjust switch by placing gear selector in "Park" position. The switch main housing and housing back should ratchet, providing proper adjustment.

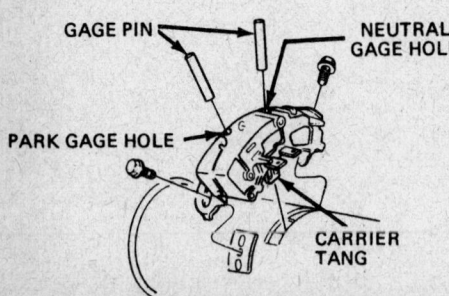

Fig. 10 Neutral start & back-up light switch adjustment. 1977–81 models

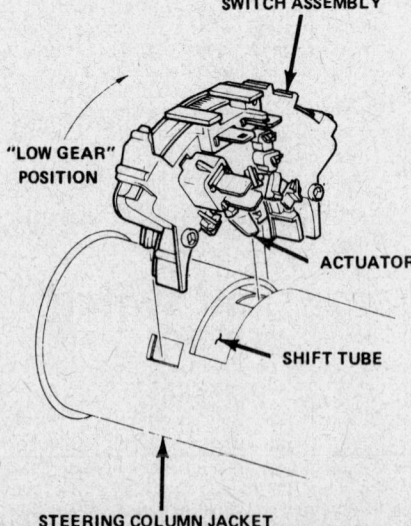

Fig. 11 Neutral start & back-up light switch installation. 1982–84 models

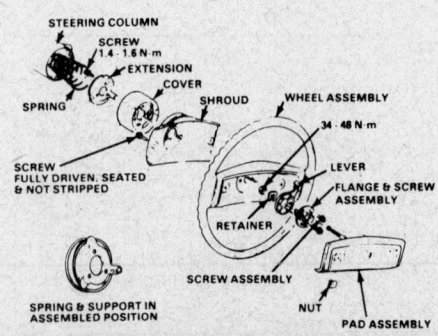

Fig. 12 Disassembled view of tilt & telescope steering wheel. 1977–84 models

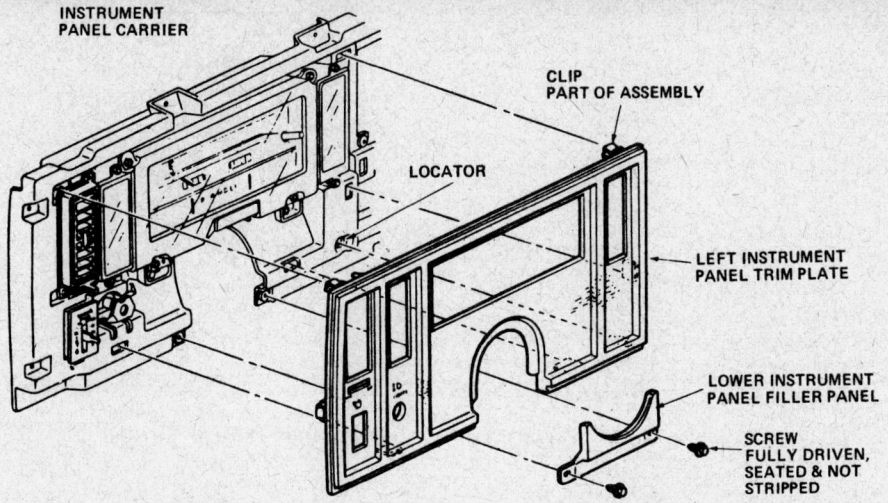

Fig. 13   Instrument cluster trim cover. 1979–84 Riviera

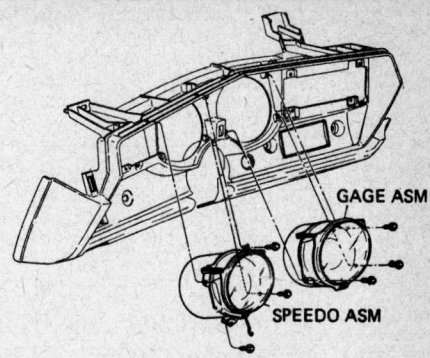

Fig. 14   Speedometer & telltale assembly. 1977 Century & Regal

STANDARD HORN SOUNDER & STEERING WHEEL, REPLACE

1977–84

1. Remove horn cap or actuator bar.
2. Remove steering wheel nut retainer, if used.
3. On all models, back off nut until flush with top of steering shaft.
4. Use a suitable puller to remove wheel.

TILT & TELESCOPE STEERING WHEEL, REPLACE

1977–84

Removal
1. Disconnect battery ground cable.
2. Remove screws, Fig. 12, and lift pad assembly up, then disconnect horn wiring electrical connector by pushing in and turning counterclockwise.
3. Push locking lever counterclockwise until full release position is obtained.
4. Scribe plate assembly where the two screws secure plate assembly to locking lever.
5. Remove screws and plate assembly.
6. Remove steering wheel nut retainer and nut.
7. Using tool No. J185903, remove steering wheel assembly.

NOTE: Use of a steering wheel puller other than the one recommended in Step 7, or a sharp blow on the end of the steering shaft or shift lever could shear or loosen the plastic fasteners which maintain steering column rigidity.

Installation
1. Install a suitable set screw into upper shaft at the full extended position and lock.
2. Align scribe mark on steering wheel hub with mark on end of shaft and install steering wheel. Ensure unsecured end of horn upper contact assembly is complete-

ly seated against top of horn contact carrier assembly.
3. Install nut onto upper steering shaft and torque to 30 ft. lbs. Install nut retainer.
4. Remove set screw and install plate assembly and screws. Tighten screws finger tight.
5. Position locking lever in vertical position and move lever counterclockwise until plate holes align with holes in lever. Install plate securing screws.
6. Align pad assembly with holes in steering wheel and install screws.
7. Connect battery ground cable. Ensure locking lever securely locks steering wheel travel and that steering wheel travel is free in the unlocked position.

INSTRUMENT CLUSTER, REPLACE

1979–84 Riviera

1. Disconnect battery ground cable.
2. Remove left hand trim cover, Fig. 13.
3. Remove headlamp and windshield wiper switches.
4. Disconnect headlamp and windshield wiper switch wire connectors from cluster carrier.
5. Disconnect speedometer cable, and wire connectors from cluster carrier.
6. Remove cluster carrier to instrument panel attaching screws, then remove cluster carrier.

1978–81 Century; 1978–84 Regal

1. Disconnect battery ground cable.
2. Remove headlamp switch knob and escutcheon.
3. Carefully pry out and remove clutch trim plate.
4. Remove five cluster lens attaching screws, then remove cluster lens.
5. To remove speedometer, remove two speedometer retaining screws. Disconnect speedometer cable and wire connector, then lift speedometer from instrument cluster.
6. To replace fuel gauge or clock, remove attaching screws, then slide gauge or clock from cluster and disconnect wire connector.

1977–84 Full Size Except 1979–84 Riviera

1. Disconnect battery ground cable.
2. Remove glove box door and glove box.
3. Remove trim plates and the steering column opening filler.
4. Disconnect electrical and vacuum connectors from gauges or controls.
5. Remove wiring harness from instrument panel carrier clips.
6. Remove instrument panel carrier attaching nuts and screws, then the carrier from vehicle.
7. Reverse procedure to install.

1977–79 Skylark

1. Disconnect battery ground cable.
2. Disconnect heater or A/C control panel from the instrument panel carrier.
3. Remove radio control knobs, bezels and nuts, leaving the radio attached to the instrument panel reinforcement.
4. Disconnect instrument panel pad from the carrier and disconnect the shift quadrant indicator cable at the shift bowl. On automatic transmission equipped vehicles remove the two nuts securing the steering column to instrument panel.
5. Remove toe plate cover and disconnect from cowl.
6. Lower steering column from instrument panel and use a protective cover (such as shop towel).
7. Disconnect the ground wire from left side of instrument panel pad followed by the speedometer cable.
8. With carrier and cluster assembly tilted rearward, disconnect printed circuit and cluster ground connectors.
9. Rest assembly on top of column and disconnect cluster from carrier assembly.
10. Reverse procedure to install.

1977 Century & Regal

Speedometer Cluster
1. Disconnect battery ground cable.
2. Place transmission selector lever in "L" position and disconnect shift indicator cable from steering column.
3. Pry trim plate from instrument panel.
4. Remove speedometer retaining screws, Fig. 14, disconnect speedometer cable and wiring connector, then remove speedometer.
5. Reverse procedure to install.

Fuel Gauge & Telltale Assembly

1. Disconnect battery ground cable.
2. Pry trim plate from instrument panel.
3. Remove retaining screws, Fig. 14, disconnect wiring connectors, then remove assembly.

NOTE: If equipped with temperature and oil pressure gauges and one gauge of the assembly is defective, all three gauges must be replaced since the cluster is serviced as an assembly.

---

4. Reverse procedure to install.

W/S WIPER MOTOR, REPLACE

1977–84

1. Disconnect battery and remove cowl screen.
2. Loosen nuts on wiper drivelink to motor cranking arm and slip drivelink off cranking arm.
3. Disconnect washer hoses and electrical connections.
4. Unfasten motor and remove.

NOTE: On models with round motor, the motor must be in "Park" position when assembling crank arm to transmission drive link.

W/S WIPER TRANSMISSION, REPLACE

1977–84

1. Disconnect battery ground cable and remove cowl vent screen or grille.
2. Disconnect wiper motor electrical connector.
3. Remove wiper arm and blade assemblies.
4. Loosen transmission drive link to motor crankarm attaching nuts, then disconnect drive link from crankarm.
5. Remove right and left transmission to body retaining screws and guide transmission and linkage through cowl opening.

NOTE: On full size models equipped with round motor, remove transmission retaining screws from transmission being removed.

6. Reverse procedure to install.

W/S WIPER SWITCH, REPLACE

1982–84 Full Size

1. Remove steering wheel as described under "Horn Sounder and Steering Wheel, Replace."
2. Remove turn signal switch as described under "Turn Signal Switch, Replace."
3. Remove ignition lock and buzzer as described under "Ignition Lock, Replace."
4. Remove and install cover and wiper switch as shown in Figs. 15 & 15A.
5. Reverse remaining procedure to install.

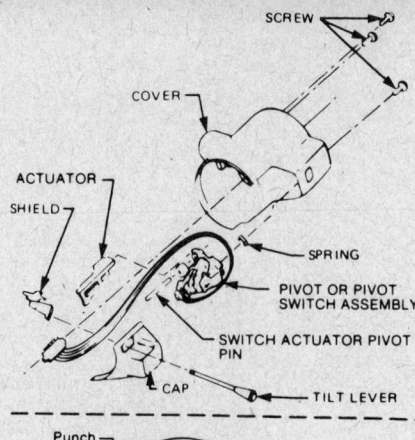

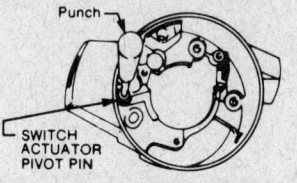

Fig. 15 Windshield wiper switch removal & installation. 1982–84 models with tilt wheel

1979–81 Riviera

1. Disconnect battery ground cable.
2. Remove left hand trim cover, Fig. 13.
3. Remove two switch to cluster attaching screws.
4. Pull switch rearward and remove.

1978–81 Century & 1978–84 Regal

1. Remove headlamp switch knob and escutcheon.
2. Remove trim plate.
3. Remove two switch attaching screws, then disconnect wire connector and remove switch.
4. Reverse procedure to install.

1977–81 Full Size Except 1979–81 Riviera

1. Remove left trim plate.
2. Remove switch attaching screws.
3. Disconnect electrical connector from switch and remove switch from vehicle.
4. Reverse procedure to install.

1977–79 Skylark

1. Remove electrical connector, three at-

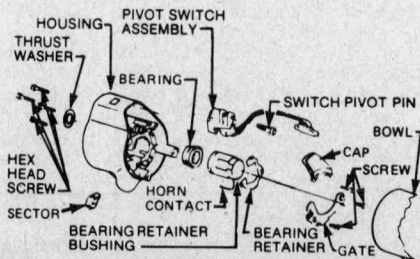

Fig. 15A Windshield wiper switch removal & installation. 1982–84 models less tilt wheel

taching screws and switch.

1977 Century & Regal

1. Insert blade of a small screwdriver into slots above knobs, bend retaining clips down and pull top of switch outward.
2. Remove electrical connector from switch.

RADIO, REPLACE

NOTE: When installing radio, be sure to adjust antenna trimmer for peak performance.

1981–84 Riviera

1. Disconnect battery ground cable.
2. Remove center trim plate by grasping firmly and pulling rearward.
3. Remove six screws from radio mounting bracket.
4. Remove six screws from instrument panel lower cover assembly, then pull cover assembly out from instrument panel enough to gain access to two screws attaching radio bracket to instrument panel lower tie bar. Remove screws.
5. Carefully pull radio assembly rearward to remove.
6. Disconnect radio harness connectors and antenna lead.
7. Reverse procedure to install.

1979–80 Riviera

1. Disconnect battery ground cable.
2. Remove center trim cover.
3. Remove four screws attaching radio mounting plate to instrument panel.
4. Disconnect radio wire connector and antenna lead.
5. Pull radio and mounting plate rearward and remove radio.

1978–81 Century & 1978–84 Regal

1. Disconnect battery ground cable.
2. Remove cigar lighter knob, radio knobs and escutcheons by pulling rearward.
3. Remove center trim plate by grasping firmly and pulling rearward.

NOTE: A flat blade screwdriver or putty knife can be used to pry up a corner of the center trim plate to aid in removal.

---

4. Remove four screws attaching radio bracket to instrument panel.
5. Open glove box door and release spring retainers, then allow door to open fully.
6. Working through glove box door, loosen holding bracket nut on right rear side of radio, then remove antenna lead.
7. Carefully pull radio assembly rearward to remove.
8. Disconnect radio harness connectors, then remove bracket.
9. Reverse procedure to install.

1981–84 Full Size Except 1981–84 Riviera

1. Disconnect battery ground cable.
2. Remove radio knobs, escutcheons and if equipped with rear defogger, rear defogger knob.

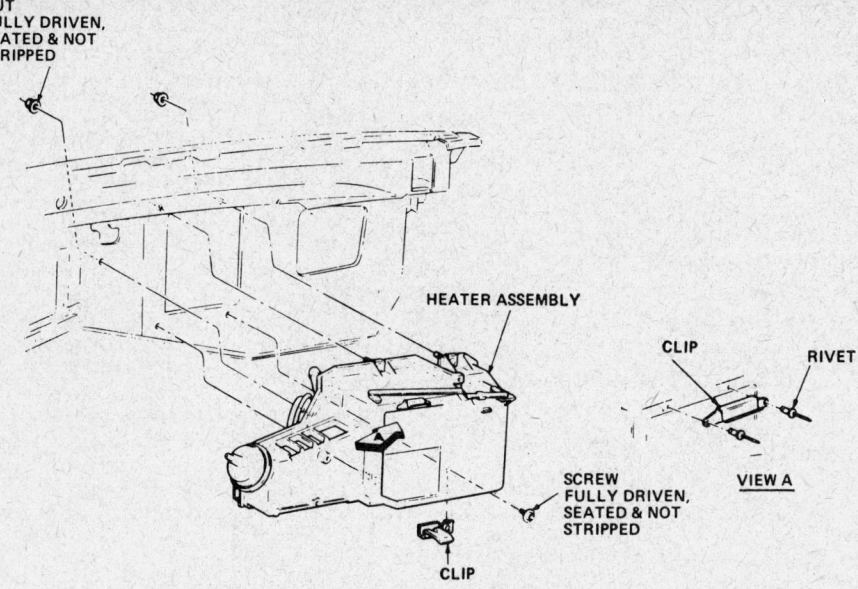

Fig. 16 Heater core. 1979–84 Riviera

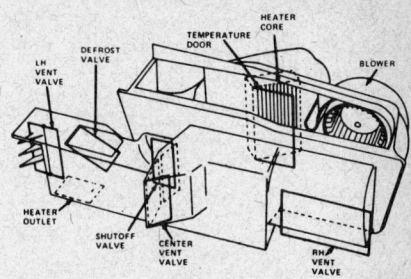

Fig. 17 Heater core & blower motor. 1977–84 Full Size Except 1979–84 Riviera without air conditioning

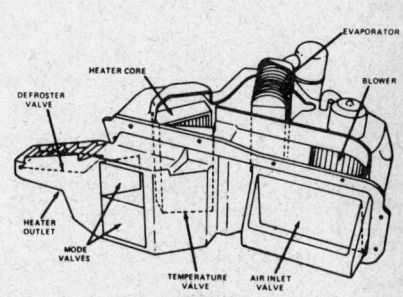

Fig. 18 Heater core & blower motor. 1977–84 Full Size Except 1979–84 Riviera with air conditioning

3. Remove left hand instrument panel trim plate by removing headlight knob, then place gear selector in low. Using a suitable flat bladed screwdriver or putty knife, remove trim plate by gently prying edge, then lifting straight out.
4. Remove center trim plate attaching screws, then trim plate.
5. Remove screws attaching radio to radio bracket, then carefully pull radio rearward out of instrument panel.
6. Disconnect radio harness connectors and antenna lead.
7. Reverse procedure to install.

1977–80 Full Size Except 1979–80 Riviera

1. Disconnect battery ground cable.
2. Remove ash tray and bracket.
3. Remove radio knobs and escutcheons from shafts.
4. Remove lower left-hand air duct.
5. Remove retaining nuts from radio control shafts.
6. Disconnect electrical connections from radio.
7. Remove rear radio attaching nut, then the radio from vehicle.
8. Reverse procedure to install.

1977–79 Skylark

1. Remove radio knobs, bezels, nuts and side brace screw.
2. Disconnect antenna and leads.
3. Remove radio from under dash.
4. Reverse procedure to install.

1977 Century & Regal

1. Remove radio knobs and escutcheons. If equipped with center air duct assembly control, remove screws.
2. Disconnect antenna and leads.
3. Remove radio support nut.

4. Remove attaching nuts and slide radio to front of car and downward.
5. Reverse procedure to install.

HEATER CORE, REPLACE
1979–84 Riviera

1. Disconnect battery ground cable and drain cooling system.
2. Disconnect heater hoses from heater core and install plugs in heater core outlets.
3. Remove instrument panel sound absorbers, then lower steering column.
4. Remove instrument cluster as described under Instrument Cluster, Replace.
5. Remove radio front speakers.
6. Remove screws attaching manifold to heater case.
7. Remove upper and lower instrument panel attaching screws.
8. Disconnect parking brake release cable.
9. Disconnect instrument panel wiring harness from dash wiring harness.
10. Disconnect right hand remote control mirror cable from instrument panel pad.
11. Disconnect speedometer cable and temperate control cable at heater case.
12. Disconnect radio, A/C wiring and vacuum lines, and all wiring necessary to remove instrument panel assembly. If equipped with pulse wiper, remove wiper switch, unlock wire connector from cluster carrier and separate pulse wiper jumper harness from wiper switch wire connector.
13. Remove instrument panel and harness assembly.
14. Remove defroster ducts, then remove blower motor resistor.
15. Remove A/C-heater housing to dash panel nuts, Fig. 16.
16. Remove housing to dash screw and clip from inside vehicle, then remove housing assembly from dash.
17. Remove heater core from housing assembly.

1978–81 Century & 1978–84 Regal

Without Air Conditioning
1. Disconnect battery ground cable and partially drain cooling system.
2. Disconnect hoses from heater core, then the electrical connectors.
3. Remove front module retaining screws and module cover.
4. Remove heater core.
5. Reverse procedure to install.

With Air Conditioning
1. Disconnect battery ground cable and partially drain cooling system.
2. Disconnect hoses from heater core, then the electrical connectors from module.
3. Remove retaining bracket, ground strap, module rubber seal and screen.
4. Remove right hand windshield wiper arm.
5. Remove retaining screws from diagnostic connector, hi-blower relay and thermostatic switch.
6. Remove module top cover, then heater core.
7. Reverse procedure to install.

1977–84 Full Size Except 1979–84 Riviera

Without Air Conditioning
1. Disconnect battery ground cable and drain radiator.
2. Disconnect heater hoses from module, then the electrical connections from module front case.
3. Remove module front case attaching screws, then the heater core, Fig. 17.

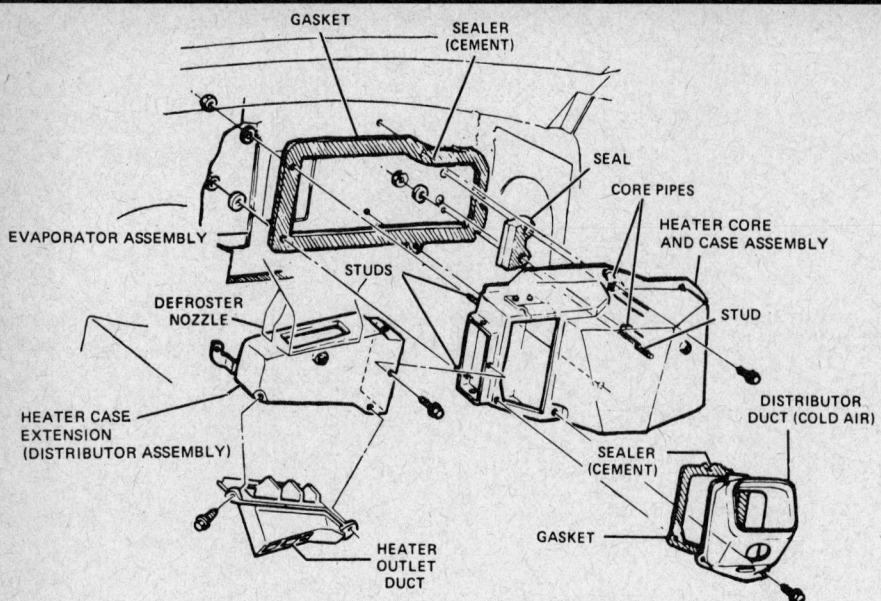

Fig. 19 Heater core. 1977–79 Skylark (Typical)

4. Reverse procedure to install.

With Air Conditioning

1. Disconnect battery ground cable and drain radiator.
2. Disconnect heater hoses from module.
3. Remove diagnostic connector and thermostatic switch from module.
4. Remove weather seal from top of module cover, then the cowl screen and windshield washer nozzle.
5. Remove module cover attaching screws.
6. Remove heater core retaining clip and the heater core from vehicle, Fig. 18.
7. Reverse procedure to install.

1977–79 Skylark

Without Air Conditioning

1. Disconnect battery ground cable and drain radiator.
2. Disconnect heater hoses from core and plug hoses and core openings to prevent coolant spillage.
3. Remove core case retaining nuts from engine side of dash, Fig. 19.
4. Remove glove compartment and door.
5. Using a ¼ inch twist drill, drill out lower right hand heater case stud from inside vehicle.
6. Pull heater core and case assembly from dash.
7. Disconnect heater cables and blower motor resistor connector from case, then remove heater core and case assembly from vehicle.
8. Remove core tube seal and retaining strips, then heater core from case.
9. Reverse procedure to install.

With Air Conditioning

1. Disconnect battery ground cable and drain radiator.

2. Disconnect upper heater hose and plug hose and core openings. Remove accessible heater core and case attaching nuts.
3. Remove right front fender skirt bolts, lower skirt and disconnect lower heater hose from core tube. Plug hose and core openings.
4. Remove lower right hand heater core and case attaching nuts, Fig. 19.
5. Remove glove compartment and door.
6. Remove right hand kick panel recirculation vacuum diaphragm.
7. Remove heater outlet from bottom of heater case, then cold air distributor duct.
8. Remove heater case extension screws, then separate extension from heater case.
9. Disconnect heater cables and electrical connectors from heater case, then remove heater core and case assembly. Separate core from case.
10. Reverse procedure to install.

1977 Century & Regal

Without Air Conditioning

1. Disconnect battery ground cable.
2. Drain cooling system and disconnect heater hoses from heater core.
3. Disconnect control cables from door levers.
4. Remove four nuts securing heater to dash, Fig. 20.
5. Remove screw securing defroster outlet to heater.
6. Work heater assembly rearward until studs clear dash.
7. Reverse procedure to install.

With Air Conditioning

1. Disconnect battery ground cable.
2. Drain cooling system and disconnect heater hoses from heater core.
3. Disconnect control cables from temperature door guides and vacuum hoses from actuator diaphragms.
4. Remove resistor assembly and reach through opening and remove one attaching nut to dash. Remove one attaching nut to dash directly over transmission and two attaching nuts to upper and lower inboard evaporator case half.
5. From inside car remove one screw in lower righthand corner on passenger side.
6. Remove lower attaching outlets and work assembly rearward until studs clear dash.
7. Reverse procedure to install.

BLOWER MOTOR, REPLACE

1979–84 Riviera

1. Disconnect battery ground cable.
2. Remove right fender skirt to provide clearance for blower motor removal.
3. Disconnect wire connector and cooling hose.
4. Remove blower motor attaching screws and blower motor.

1978–84 Regal; 1978–81 Century; 1977–84 Full Size Except 1979–84 Riviera

1. Disconnect blower motor wiring.
2. Remove blower motor attaching screws and the blower motor, Figs. 17 and 18.

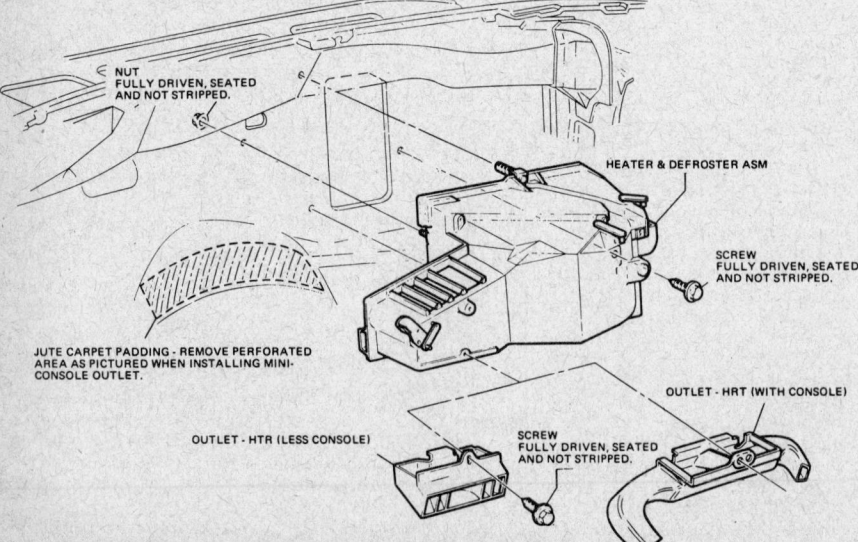

Fig. 20 Heater core. 1977 intermediate models exc. Skylark (Typical)

1977 Century & Regal
1. Disconnect blower motor wire.
2. Remove screws securing motor to air inlet and remove blower motor, Fig. 21.

1977–79 Skylark
1. Disconnect battery ground cable and raise vehicle on hoist.
2. Remove fender skirt attaching bolts except those attaching skirt to radiator support.
3. Pull skirt out and down, then place a block of wood between skirt and fender to provide clearance for motor removal.
4. Disconnect blower motor electrical connections and remove motor attaching screws and blower motor.
5. Remove blower motor retaining nut and separate impeller from motor.
6. Reverse procedure to install.

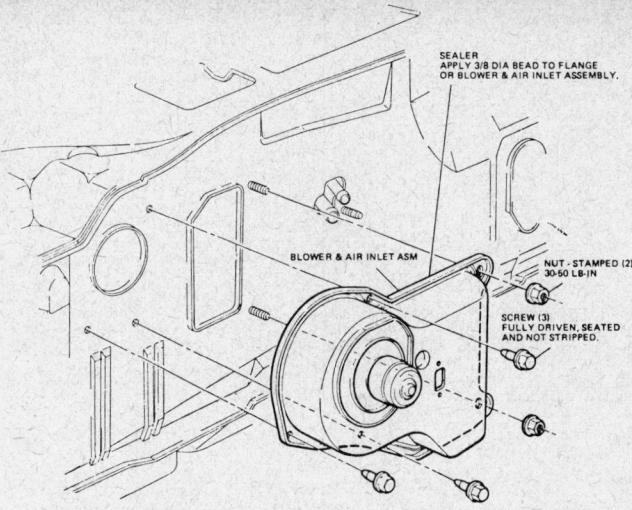

Fig. 21   Blower motor. 1977 Century & Regal (Typical)

SPEED CONTROL

Power Unit, Adjust

Units With Bead Chain
1. Make sure that engine hot idle speed is properly adjusted, then shut off engine and set carburetor choke to hot idle position.
2. Check slack in chain by disconnecting swivel from ball stud and holding chain taut at ball stud. Center of swivel should extend 1/8 inch beyond center of ball stud.
3. To adjust bead chain slack, remove retainer from swivel and chain assembly, then place chain into swivel cavities which permits chain to have slight slack.
4. Install retainer over swivel and chain assembly.

Units With Servo Rod
1. Make sure that engine hot idle speed is properly adjusted, then shut off engine and set carburetor choke to hot idle position.

2. Remove servo rod retainer, then adjust rod and install retainer in hole which provides some clearance between retainer and servo bushing. Clearance must not exceed width of one hole.

Units With Cable
1. Make sure that engine hot idle speed is properly adjusted, then shut off engine and set carburetor choke to hot idle position.
2. Remove cable pin retainer, then pull power unit end of cable toward power unit as far as it will go. If one of four holes in power unit tab aligns with cable pin, connect pin to tab with retainer.
3. If tab does not align with pin, move cable away from power unit until next closest tab hole aligns and connect pin to tab with retainer.

CAUTION: Do not force cable to make adjustment, as this will prevent engine from return-

ing to idle.

Cruise Speed Adjustment
The cruise speed adjustment can be set as follows:
1. If car cruises below engagement speed, screw orifice tube on transducer outward.
2. If car cruises above engagement speed, screw orifice tube inward.

NOTE: Each 1/4 turn of the orifice tube will change cruise speed about one mile per hour. Snug up lock nut after each adjustment.

Brake Release Switch Adjustment
Fully depress brake pedal, then push switch and valve forward to contact bracket or arm. Pull pedal rearward with approximately 15 to 20 pounds of force to adjust switch and valve properly.

Gasoline Engine Section

NOTE: For service procedures see Chevrolet Chapter for V8-305 and V8-350 with the distributor located at the rear of engine, clockwise distributor rotor rotation; Oldsmobile Chapter for V8-307, V8-350 and V8-403 with distributor located at the rear of engine, counter clockwise distributor rotor rotation; Pontiac Chapter for V8-265 and V8-301.

ENGINE MOUNTS, REPLACE

1. Raise car and provide frame support at front of car.
2. Support weight of engine at forward edge of pan.
3. Remove mount to engine block or frame bolts. Raise engine slightly and remove mount to mount bracket bolt and nut, Figs. 1, 1A and 2. Remove mount.
4. Reverse above procedure to install.

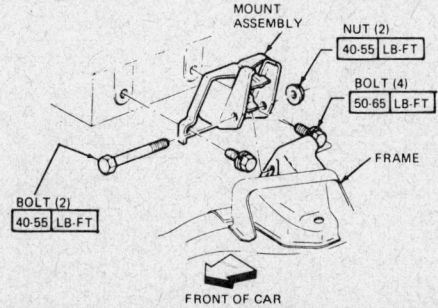

Fig. 1   Engine mounts. V6-196, 231 & 252 Exc. 1979–84 Riviera

ENGINE, REPLACE

1979–84 Riviera

1. Remove hood. Scribe alignment marks on hood around hinge areas for alignment during installation.
2. Disconnect battery ground cable and remove air cleaner.
3. Drain cooling system and disconnect heater hoses.
4. Remove fan, pulleys and belts.
5. Remove upper and lower radiator hoses

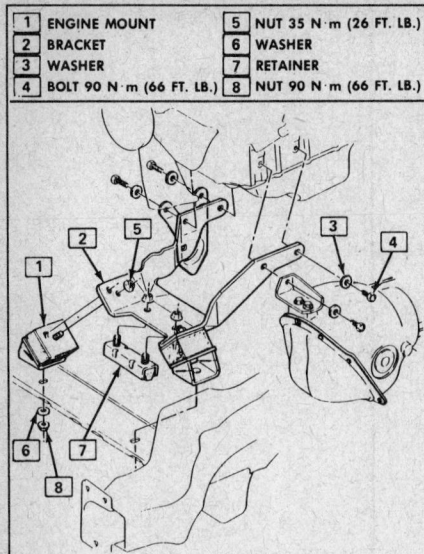

1	ENGINE MOUNT	5	NUT 35 N·m (26 FT. LB.)
2	BRACKET	6	WASHER
3	WASHER	7	RETAINER
4	BOLT 90 N·m (66 FT. LB.)	8	NUT 90 N·m (66 FT. LB.)

Fig. 1A Engine mounts. V6-231, 252. 1979–84 Riviera

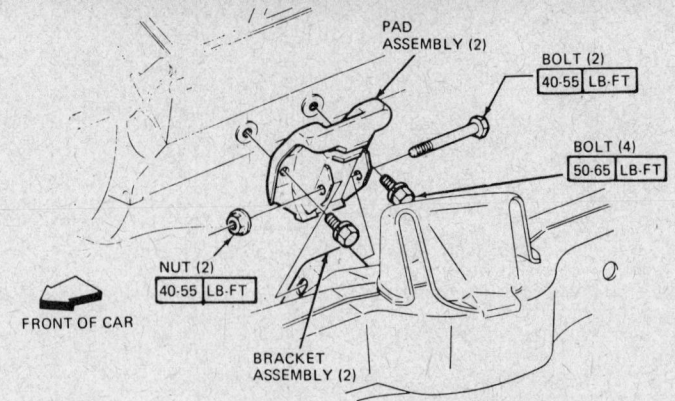

Fig. 2 Engine mounts. V8-350

and fan shroud.

6. Disconnect transmission cooler lines from radiator, then remove radiator.
7. Remove air conditioning compressor.
8. Disconnect all electrical wires and vacuum hoses.
9. On turbocharged engines:
   a. Disconnect accelerator cable at carburetor.
   b. Disconnect fuel pump lines and plug lines to prevent spilling fuel.
   c. Remove power steering pump mounting bolts and position pump assembly aside.
   d. Remove alternator, then disconnect engine to body ground straps.
   e. Disconnect turbocharger outlet exhaust pipe from turbocharger.
10. On all except turbocharged engines:
   a. Disconnect accelerator rod and throttle valve cable.
   b. Disconnect fuel lines and plug lines to prevent spilling fuel.
   c. Remove power steering pump.
   d. Remove transmission cooler line bracket.
   e. Disconnect left exhaust pipe.
11. Raise and properly support vehicle.
12. Drain engine oil, then remove starter.
13. Remove converter shield, then the flywheel to converter bolts.
14. On all except turbocharged engines, disconnect right exhaust pipe and remove

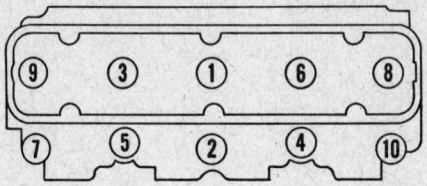

Fig. 3 Cylinder head tightening sequence V8-350

splash shield.

15. Remove the right transmission to engine bolts.
16. Remove right output shaft support bolts.
17. Remove front motor mount support bolts.
18. Support the final drive using a chain, then remove the remaining transmission to engine bolts.
19. Remove final drive to engine bracket.
20. Remove engine using a suitable hoist.
21. Reverse procedure to install.

Exc. 1979–84 Riviera

1. Remove hood and drain radiator.
2. Disconnect battery ground cable.
3. Remove fan shroud, radiator and air cleaner.
4. If equipped with A/C, disconnect compressor brackets and position out of way.
5. Remove power steering from bracket and position out of way.
6. Disconnect all hoses, linkages and electrical connections from engine.
7. Disconnect exhaust pipes and remove

converter cover.
8. Remove flywheel to converter or pressure plate bolts, engine to transmission bolts and motor mount bolts.
9. Support transmission and remove engine.

CYLINDER HEAD, REPLACE

Prior to reinstalling the cylinder head bolts on V6 engines, coat the head bolts with a suitable heavy body thread sealer. This is to prevent coolant leakage, as the head bolt holes extend into the water jacket.

An accurate torque wrench should be used when installing head bolts. Uneven tightening of the head bolts can distort the cylinder bores, causing compression loss and excessive oil consumption.

1. Drain coolant and disconnect battery.
2. Remove intake manifold.
3. When removing right cylinder head, remove Delcotron and/or A/C compressor with mounting bracket and move out of the way. *Do not disconnect hoses from A/C compressor.*
4. When removing left cylinder head, remove oil dipstick, power steering pump and move out of the way with hoses attached.
5. Disconnect exhaust manifold from head to be removed.
6. Remove rocker arm shaft and lift out push rods.
7. On 1977–79 Skylark models equipped with V6-231 and V8-350 engines, to replace left cylinder head, disconnect power

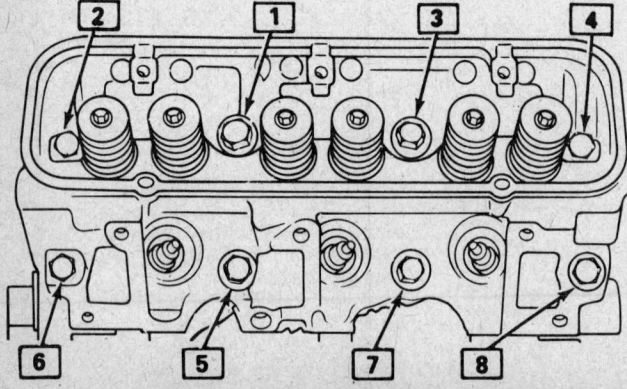

Fig. 4 Cylinder head tightening sequence. 1977–83 V6-196, 231, 252

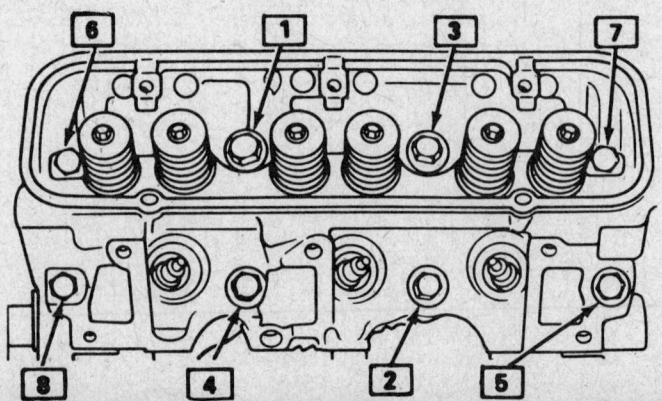

Fig. 4A Cylinder head bolt tightening sequence. 1984 V6-231, 252

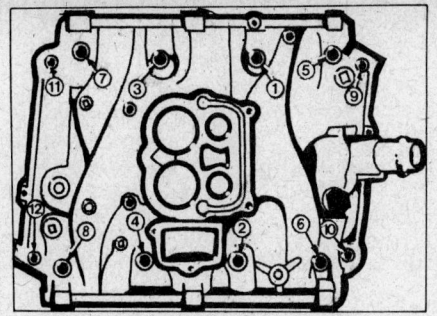

Fig. 5 Intake manifold tightening sequence. V8-350

brake unit hose at rear of cylinder head. Remove left front engine mount bolt and loosen right front engine mount bolt. Raise engine until exhaust manifold clears steering gear.
8. Remove cylinder head.
9. Reverse procedure to install and tighten bolts gradually and evenly in the sequence shown in Figs. 3, 4 and 4A.

NOTE: When installing intake manifold, refer to Figs. 5 and 6 for bolt tightening sequence.

ROCKER ARMS

V6-196, 231, 252; V8-350

A nylon retainer is used to retain the rocker arm. Break them below their heads with a chisel, or pry out with channel locks, Fig. 7. Production rocker arms can be installed in any sequence since the arms are identical.

Replacement rocker arms for all engines are identified with a stamping, right (R) and left (L), Fig. 8 and must be installed as shown in Fig. 9.

To install rocker arms, position arm on rocker shaft, centering it over the 1/4 inch hole in the rocker shaft. Install new rocker arm retainers in the provided holes using a 1/2 inch or larger drift to seat them.

VALVE ARRANGEMENT

Front to Rear

V6-196, 231, 252 .... E-I-I-E-I-E
V8-350 .... E-I-I-E-E-I-I-E

VALVE LIFT SPECS.

Engine	Year	Intake	Exhaust
V6-196	1978	.3230	.3660
V6-196	1979	.3410	.3660
V6-231	1977–78	.3830	.3660
V6-231①	1979–84	.3570	.3660
V6-231②	1979–81	.3410	.3660
V6-252	1980–84	.3570	.3660
V6-262⑧	1982	.3750	.3750
V8-265	1980–81	.3570	.3660
V8-301③	1977	.3770	.3770
V8-301④	1977–79	.3640	.3640
V8-301	1980	.3570	.3660
	1981	.3500	.3500
V8-305	1977–80	.3727	.4100
V8-307	1981–84	.4000	.4000
V8-350⑤	1977–79	.3230	.3390
V8-350⑤	1980	.3570	.3390
			.3660
V8-350⑥	1977–79	.3900	.4100
V8-350⑦	1977–79	.4000	.4000
V8-350⑧	1980–84	.3750	.3760
V8-403	1977–79	.4000	.4000

①—Exc. turbo charged engine.
②—Turbo charged engine.
③—Man. trans.
④—Auto. trans.
⑤—Distributor located at front of engine.
⑥—Distributor located at rear of engine, clockwise distributor rotor rotation.
⑦—Distributor located at rear of engine, counter distributor rotor clockwise rotation.
⑧—Diesel engine.

VALVE TIMING

Intake Opens Before TDC

Engine	Year	Degrees
V6-196	1978	18
V6-196	1979	16
V6-231	1977–78	17
V6-231	1979–84	16
V6-252	1980–84	16
V6-262⑧	1982	16
V8-265	1980	27
	1981	16
V8-301①	1977	31
V8-301②	1977–78	27
V8-301③	1979	16
V8-301①	1979	27
V8-301①⑦	1979	27
V8-301②⑦	1979	16
V8-301	1980	16
V8-305	1977–80	28

Fig. 6 Intake manifold tightening sequence. V6-196, 231, 252

V8-307	1981	20
V8-350③	1977–79	13.5
V8-350③	1980	16
V8-350④	1977–79	28
V8-350⑤	1977–79	16
V8-350⑧	1980–84	16
V8-403	1977–79	16

①—Man. trans.
②—Auto. trans.
③—Distributor located at front of engine.
④—Distributor located at rear of engine, clockwise distributor rotor rotation. Refer to Chevrolet chapter for engine service procedures.
⑤—Distributor located at rear of engine, counter clockwise distributor rotor rotation. Refer to Oldsmobile chapter for engine service procedures.
⑥—2 Bar. Carb.
⑦—4 Bar. Carb.
⑧—Diesel engine.

VALVE GUIDES

SERVICE NOTE

Abnormal oil consumption or detonation on 1980–82 V6-252 engines may be caused by intake valve seals that have lifted off the valve guide. To correct this condition, a smaller replacement seal, Part No. 25516279, should be installed onto valve guide. Since valve guide outside diameter must be reduced from .605 to .552 to accept the new seal, it will be necessary to rework the valve guides prior

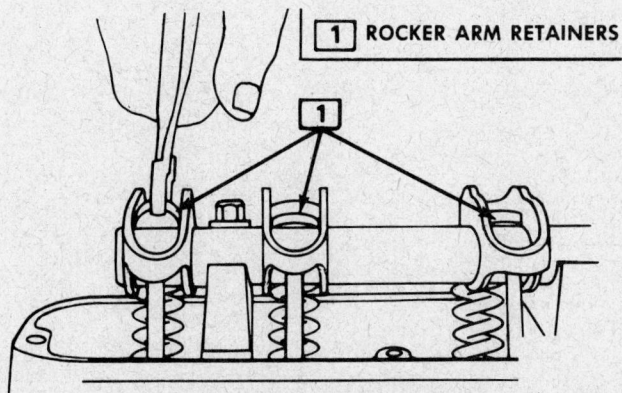

Fig. 7 Removing nylon retainer. V6-196, 231, 252 & V8-350

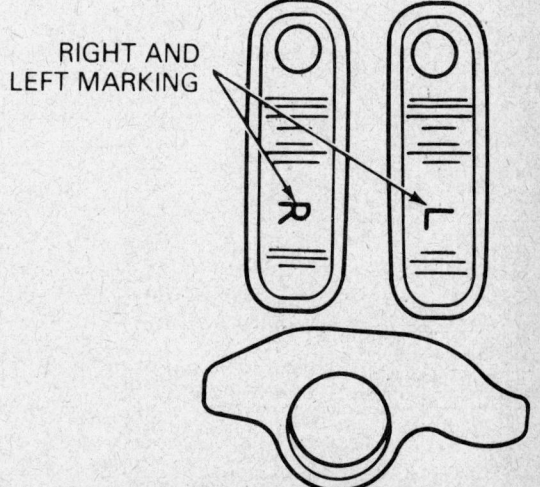

RIGHT AND LEFT MARKING

Fig. 8 Service rocker arms identification. V6-196, 231, 252 & V8-350

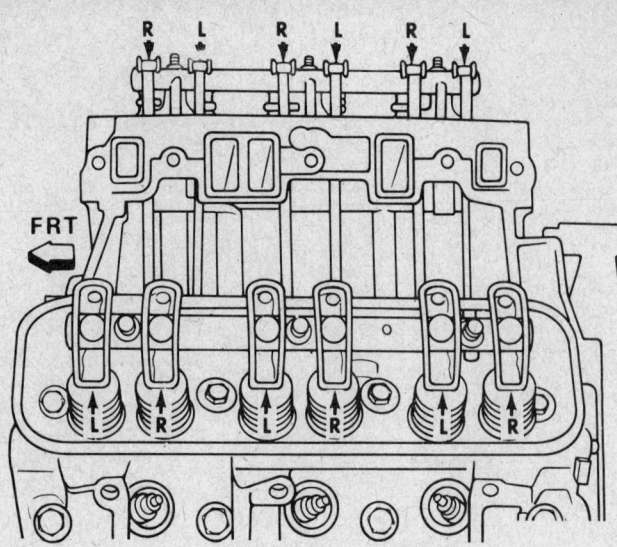

Fig. 9   Service rocker arms installation.
V6-196, 231, 252 & V8-350

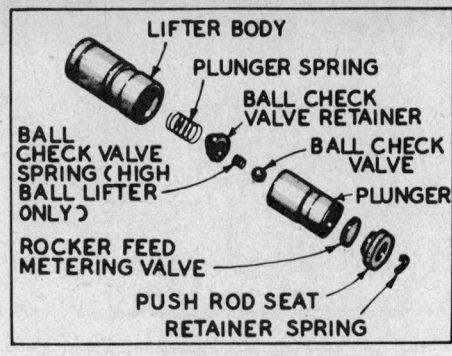

Fig. 10   Hydraulic valve lifter parts

to seal installation. Using valve guide cutting tool KL1440, or equivalent, perform the following operation.

1. Remove cylinder head as outlined in "Cylinder Head, Replace" procedure.
2. Remove all intake and exhaust valves from cylinder head to prevent metal chips from lodging in exhaust guide mechanism.
3. Insert cutting tool into chuck of low speed drill, oil tool pilot, then insert pilot into intake valve guide.
4. Applying steady pressure to cutting tool, machine valve guide until small cutter block in tool has cut chamfer on top of valve guide.
5. Thoroughly clean cylinder head and guides, then remove any burrs from valve stem and guides with a fine stone.
6. Oil valves and install them into guides.
7. Install new seals onto valve guides, then reassemble cylinder head assembly.
8. Install cylinder head.

The valve guides are an integral part of the cylinder head and cannot be replaced.

If valve stem clearance is excessive, the valve guide must be reamed and an oversize valve installed. On 1977–78 engines, valves are available in the oversizes of .010 inch for V8-350 and .006 inch for V6-196, 231, 252. On 1979–84 engines, valves are available in the oversize of .010 inch.

HYDRAULIC VALVE LIFTERS

Failure of an hydraulic valve lifter, Fig. 10, is generally caused by an inadequate oil supply or dirt. An air leak at the intake side of the oil pump or too much oil in the engine will cause air bubbles in the oil supply to the lifters, causing them to collapse. This is a probable cause of trouble if several lifters fail to function, but air in the oil is an unlikely cause of failure of a single unit.

The valve lifters may be lifted out of their bores after removing the rocker arms, push rods and intake manifold. Adjustable pliers with taped jaws may be used to remove lifters that are stuck due to varnish, carbon, etc. Fig. 10 illustrates the type of lifter used.

TIMING CASE COVER, REPLACE

V6-196, 231, 252 & V8-350

1. Drain cooling system and remove radiator and heater return hose.
2. Remove fan, pulleys and belts.
3. Remove crankshaft pulley and balancer.
4. If equipped with power steering, remove any pump bracket bolts attached to timing chain cover and loosen and remove any other bolts necessary that will allow pump and brackets to be moved out of the way.
5. Remove fuel pump.
6. Remove Delcotron and brackets.
7. Remove distributor cap and pull spark plug wire retainers off brackets on rocker arm cover. Swing distributor cap with wires attached out of the way. Disconnect distributor primary lead.
8. Remove distributor. *If chain and sprockets are not to be disturbed, note position of distributor rotor for installation in the same position.*
9. Loosen and slide clamp on thermostat bypass hose rearward.
10. Remove bolts attaching chain cover to block.
11. On V6-196, 231, 252 and V8-350 engines, remove two oil pan-to-chain cover bolts and remove cover.
12. Reverse procedure to install, noting data shown in Figs. 11 and 12.

IMPORTANT: Remove the oil pump cover and pack the space around the oil pump gears completely full of vaseline. There must be no air space left inside the pump. Reinstall the cover using a new gasket. This step is very important as the oil pump may lose its prime whenever the pump, pump cover or timing chain cover is disturbed. If the pump is not packed it may not begin to pump oil as soon as the engine is started.

TIMING CHAIN, REPLACE

V6-196, 231, 252 & V8-350

1. With the timing case cover removed as outlined above, temporarily install the vibration damper bolt and washer in end

Fig. 11   Timing chain cover installation.
V6-196, 231 & 252

Fig. 12   Timing chain cover installation.
V8-350

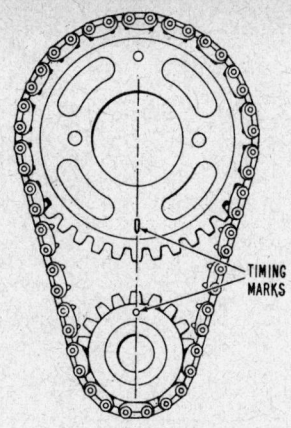

**Fig. 13 Valve timing marks.
V6-196, 231, 252 & V8-350**

of crankshaft.

2. Turn crankshaft so sprockets are positioned as shown in Fig. 13. Use a sharp rap on a wrench handle to start the vibration damper bolt out without disturbing the position of the sprockets.
3. On 1977–79 V6 engines, remove the oil pan.
4. Remove oil slinger.
5. On V6-196, 231, 252 and V8-350 remove camshaft distributor drive gear and fuel pump eccentric.
6. Use two large screwdrivers to alternately pry the camshaft sprocket then the crankshaft sprocket forward until the camshaft sprocket is free. Then remove camshaft sprocket and chain, and crankshaft sprocket off crankshaft.
7. To install, assemble chain on sprockets and slide sprockets on their respective shafts with the "O" marks on the sprockets lined up as shown.
8. Complete the installation in the reverse order of removal.

CAMSHAFT, REPLACE

NOTE: If engine is in the car, the radiator, grille and A/C components will have to be removed. If engine is out of car, proceed as follows:

1. To remove camshaft, remove intake manifold, rocker arm shaft assemblies, push

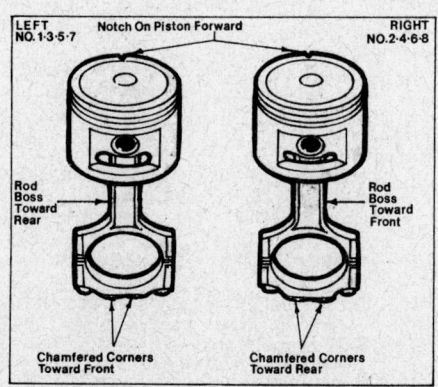

**Fig. 15 Piston and rod assembly.
V8-350**

rods and valve lifters.
2. Remove timing chain and sprockets.
3. Slide camshaft out of engine, using care not to mar the bearing surfaces.

PISTONS & RODS, ASSEMBLE

SERVICE NOTE

Some 1980–82 V6-231 (Vin A) and V6-252 engines may exhibit engine noise just above idle with transmission in gear. The noise can best be described as a light ticking sound, similar to overhead valve noise, but appears to come from the bottom portion of the engine and is most pronounced at the rear of the front wheel opening. This noise may be caused by excessive side clearance between the connecting rod and the crankshaft journal thrust surfaces on the number one, three or five cylinder. The clearance should be checked using a dial indicator or feeler gauge. If a feeler gauge is used, the gauge should be placed next to the thrust surface on the counterweight and not next to the thin wall section between two adjacent rods. Make sure the feeler gauge is fully seated on the journal and not on top of the narrow raised thrust surface. Clearance measurements should be made at several places around the journal. If rod clearance exceeds .015 inch on the above mentioned cylinders, the rod should be replaced. A new rod, Part No. 25516444, is available which is .010 inch thicker than the original. The new rod will reduce the clearance to the low side of the specified limits.

Rods and pistons should be assembled and installed as shown in Figs. 14 and 15. Measure connecting rod side clearance using a suitable feeler gauge. Clearance obtained should be .006–.027 inch for 1977–78, .006–.023 for 1979–83, .005–.026 inch for 1984.

PISTONS, PINS & RINGS

Pistons are available in standard sizes and oversizes of .005, .010 and .030 inch.
Rings are furnished in standard sizes and oversizes of .010 and .030 inch.
Piston pins are supplied in standard sizes only.

MAIN & ROD BEARINGS

Main bearings are available in standard sizes and undersizes of .001, .002, and .010 inch.
Rod bearings are furnished in standard sizes and undersizes of .001, .002 and .010", Fig. 16.

CRANKSHAFT OIL SEAL REPAIR

Since the braided fabric seal used on these engines can be replaced only when the crankshaft is removed, the following repair procedure is recommended.
1. Remove oil pan and bearing cap.
2. Drive end of old seal gently into groove, using a suitable tool, until packed tight. This may vary between 1/4 and 3/4 inch depending on amount of pack required.
3. Repeat previous step for other end of seal.

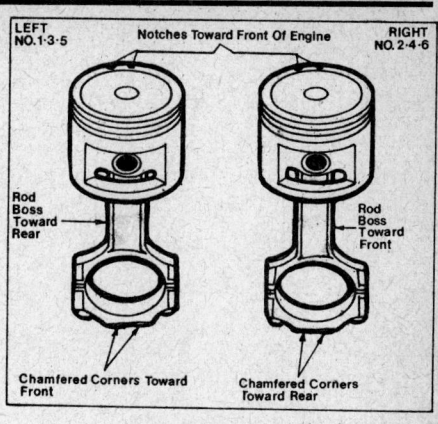

**Fig. 14 Piston and rod assembly.
V6-196, 231, 252**

4. Measure and note amount that seal was driven up on one side. Using the old seal removed from bearing cap, cut a length of seal the amount previously noted plus 1/16 inch.
5. Repeat previous step for other side of seal.
6. Pack cut lengths of seal into appropriate side of seal groove. A guide tool, J-21526-1, and packing tool, J-21526-2, may be used since these tools have been machined to provide a built-in stop.
7. Install new seal in bearing cap.

OIL PAN, REPLACE

V6-196, 231, 252

Exc. 1981–84 Riviera
1. Raise and support front of vehicle.
2. Remove flywheel cover and exhaust crossover pipe. On 1982–84 models, raise engine with a suitable lifting device to gain clearance.
3. Drain engine oil into a suitable contain-

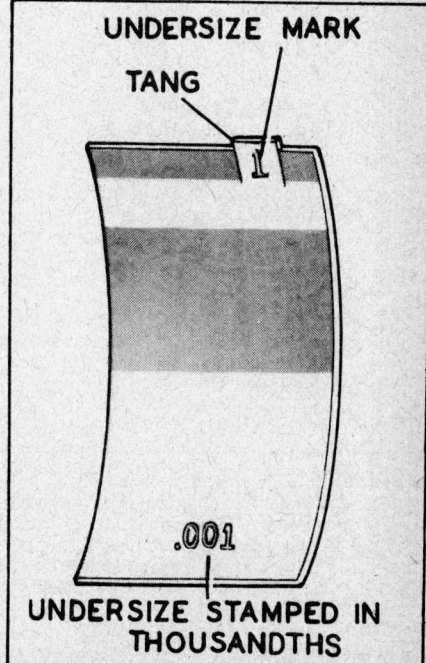

Fig. 16 Location of undersize mark on main and rod bearing shell

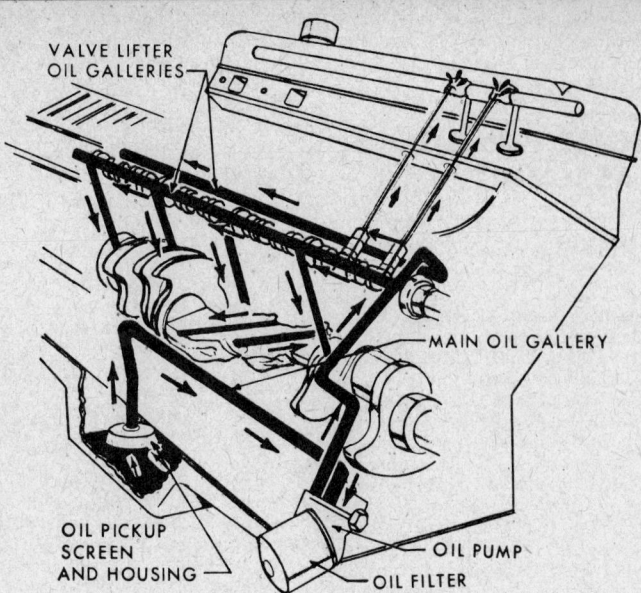

VALVE LIFTER OIL GALLERIES

MAIN OIL GALLERY

OIL PICKUP SCREEN AND HOUSING

OIL PUMP

OIL FILTER

Engine lubrication system. V8-350

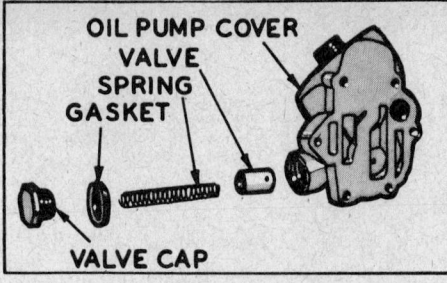

OIL PUMP COVER

VALVE

SPRING

GASKET

VALVE CAP

Fig. 17 Oil pump cover and by-pass valve. V6-196, 231, 252 & V8-350

CHECK CLEARANCE BETWEEN STRAIGHT EDGE & GASKET SURFACE SHOULD BE BETWEEN .002" & .006"

Fig. 18 Checking oil pump gear and clearance. V6-196, 231, 252 & V8-350

er.
4. Remove oil pan bolts, then pan.
5. Reverse procedure to install.

NOTE: Some 1981–84 engines use R.T.V. silicone sealer instead of a cork gasket for oil pan to crankcase sealing. When replacing the oil pan or sealing material on these engines, either R.T.V. sealer or a cork gasket can be used during reassembly. If R.T.V. sealer is used, the pan rail and block sealing surfaces should be cleaned thoroughly and a 1/4 inch bead of sealant applied evenly to the pan rail, avoiding any breaks or gaps in the sealer during application.

1981–84 Riviera

1. Disconnect battery ground cable.
2. Remove one final drive to transmission bolts.
3. Install suitable engine support fixture.
4. Raise and support vehicle.
5. Remove idler arm bracket from frame, then position steering wheel at left lock.
6. Disconnect drive axles from output shafts, then battery cable support from output shaft support.
7. Disconnect output shaft support from engine block.
8. Remove remaining final drive to transmission bolts.
9. Position suitable transmission jack under final drive, then remove final drive cover and final drive unit.
10. Remove starter, then flywheel cover.
11. Remove oil pan bolts, then oil pan.
12. Reverse procedure to install.

NOTE: Some 1981–84 engines use R.T.V. silicone sealer instead of a cork gasket for oil pan to crankcase sealing. When replacing the oil pan or sealing material on these engines, either R.T.V. sealer or a cork gasket can be used during reassembly. If R.T.V. sealer is used, the pan rail and block sealing surfaces should be cleaned thoroughly and a 1/4 inch bead of sealant applied evenly to the pan rail, avoiding any breaks or gaps in the sealer during application.

1977–80 V8-350

NOTE: On 1977–78 models except Skylark, it is no longer necessary to disconnect the idler arm. Otherwise, proceed as follows:

1. Disconnect battery and drain oil.
2. Remove fan shroud to radiator tie bar screws.
3. Remove air cleaner and disconnect linkage to throttle.
4. Raise and support car on stands.
5. With manual transmission, loosen clutch equalizer bracket to frame bolts. Disconnect crossover pipe at engine.
6. With automatic transmission, remove lower flywheel housing. Remove shift linkage attaching bolt and swing out of way. Disconnect crossover pipe at engine. Disconnect idler arm at frame and push steering linkage forward to crossmember. Remove front engine mount bolts and raise engine by placing jack under crankshaft pulley mounting.

NOTE: If car is air conditioned, at this point it will be necessary to place a support under right side of transmission prior to raising engine to prevent transmission from cocking to the right when raised.

7. Remove oil pan. It may be necessary to position crankshaft so 1 and 2 crankpin and counterweight will not interfere with front of pan.

OIL PUMP

NOTE: On some 1978–79 General Motors models with V6-196, 231 engines, the oil pressure indicator light also serves as the electric choke defect indicator. If Oil or Eng. indicator light does not light, check to ensure electric choke is not disconnected at carburetor. Also check for defect in electric choke heater,

blown gauge fuse or defect in lamp or wiring circuit. If indicator light stays on with engine running possible causes are: oil pressure is low, switch to indicator light wiring has an open circuit, oil pressure switch wire connector has disconnected or on some models, gauge or radio fuse has blown.

V6-196, 231, 252 & V8-350

1. To remove pump, take off oil filter.
2. Disconnect wire from oil pressure indicator switch in filter by-pass valve cap (if so equipped).
3. Remove screws attaching oil pump cover to timing chain cover. Remove cover and slide out pump gears. Replace any parts not serviceable.
4. Check relief valve in its bore in cover. Valve should have no more clearance than an easy slip fit. If any perceptible side shake can be felt, the valve and/or cover should be replaced.
5. The filter by-pass valve should be flat and free of nicks and scratches.

Assembly & Installation

1. Lubricate and install pressure relief valve and spring in bore of pump cover. Install cap and gasket. Torque cap to 30–35 ft-lbs.
2. Install pump gears and shaft in pump body section of timing chain cover to check gear end clearance. Check clear-

ance as shown in Fig. 18. If clearance is less than .002" for 1977–84 models, check timing chain cover for evidence of wear.

3. If gear end clearance is satisfactory, remove gears and pack gear pocket *full* of vaseline, not chassis lube.

4. Reinstall gears so vaseline is forced into every cavity of gear pocket and between teeth of gears. *Unless pump is packed with vaseline, it may not prime itself when engine is started.*

5. Install cover and tighten screws alternately and evenly. Final tightening is 10–15 ft-lbs. torque. Install filter in nipple.

BELT TENSION DATA

	New lbs.	Used lbs.
1980—84—		
5/16 in.	80	50
3/8 in. exc. cogged belt	140	70
3/8 in. cogged belt	60	
15/32 in.	165	90
1977—79—		
Alternator	130	75
Air Condition	155	90
A.I.R. Pump	70	60
Power Steering	155	90

WATER PUMP, REPLACE

Drain cooling system, being sure to drain into a clean container if antifreeze solution is to be saved. Remove the fan belt and disconnect all hoses from water pump. Remove water pump.

FUEL PUMP, REPLACE

NOTE: Before installing the pump, it is good practice to crank the engine so that the nose of the camshaft eccentric is out of the way of the fuel pump rocker arm when the pump is installed. In this way there will be the least amount of tension on the rocker arm, thereby easing the installation of the pump.

1. Disconnect fuel lines from fuel pump.
2. Remove fuel pump mounting bolts and the fuel pump.
3. Remove all gasket material from the pump and block gasket surfaces. Apply sealer to both sides of new gasket.
4. Position gasket on pump flange and hold pump in position against its mounting surface. Make sure rocker arm is riding on camshaft eccentric.
5. Press pump tight against its mounting. Install retaining screws and tighten them alternately.
6. Connect fuel lines. Then operate engine and check for leaks.

Diesel Engine Section

> REFER TO THE OLDSMOBILE CHAPTER FOR SERVICE PROCEDURES ON THE V6-262 & V8-350 DIESEL ENGINES, NOT FOUND IN THIS SECTION.

ENGINE, REPLACE

V8-350 Engine

Exc. Riviera

1. Disconnect ground cable from batteries and drain cooling system.
2. Remove air cleaner.
3. Scribe hood hinge locations and remove hood.
4. Disconnect ground wires at inner fender and the engine ground strap at right cylinder head.
5. Disconnect radiator hoses, oil cooler lines, heater hoses, vacuum hoses, power steering hoses from gear, A/C compressor with brackets and hoses attached, fuel pump hose from fuel pump and the wiring.
6. Remove hairpin clip from bellcrank.
7. Remove throttle and throttle valve cables from intake manifold brackets and position cables aside.
8. Remove upper radiator support and the radiator.
9. Raise and support vehicle.
10. Disconnect exhaust pipes from exhaust manifold.
11. Remove torque converter cover and the three bolts securing torque converter to flywheel.
12. Remove engine mount bolts or nuts.
13. Remove three engine to transmission bolts on the right side.
14. Disconnect starter wiring and remove starter.
15. Lower vehicle.
16. Attach suitable engine lifting equipment to engine. Support transmission with a suitable jack.
17. Remove the three engine to transmission bolts on the left side.
18. Remove engine from vehicle.
19. Reverse procedure to install.

Riviera

1. Disconnect battery ground cable and drain cooling system.
2. Remove radiator upper support.
3. Remove air cleaner assembly.
4. Scribe hood hinge locations and remove hood.
5. Disconnect engine ground strap.
6. Disconnect upper and lower radiator hoses from engine.
7. Disconnect transmission oil cooler lines from radiator.
8. Disconnect heater hoses from water pump and water control valve.
9. Remove radiator, fan and the shroud.
10. Disconnect power steering pump bracket from engine and position aside without disconnecting lines.
11. Disconnect A/C compressor bracket from engine and position aside without disconnecting lines.
12. Disconnect fuel lines.
13. Disconnect throttle cable, vacuum hoses and electrical connections.
14. Disconnect left hand exhaust pipe from manifold.
15. On left side of engine, remove through bolt and bracket securing final drive to engine.
16. Raise and support engine.
17. Remove flywheel shield.
18. Disconnect right hand exhaust pipe from manifold.
19. Disconnect starter motor wiring and remove starter motor.
20. Remove converter to flywheel bolts. Mark location of converter on flywheel for alignment during installation.
21. Remove splash shield.
22. Remove engine front mounting attaching nuts.
23. Remove two bolts securing right hand output shaft support brackets. Using a sharp tool, scribe a mark around the washers as far as possible. Use these scribe marks to position bracket upon installation.
24. Remove lower right hand transmission to engine attaching bolts. One bolt retains the modulator line clip.
25. Use a suitable length of chain to retain final drive in vehicle.
26. Lower vehicle and attach suitable engine lifting equipment to engine.
27. Remove the remaining transmission to engine bolts. It may be necessary to raise or lower transmission with a suitable jack to facilitate bolt removal.
28. Raise engine and remove from vehicle.
29. Reverse procedure to install.

V6-262 Engine

1. Disconnect battery ground cable and drain cooling system.
2. Scribe reference marks, then remove hood from vehicle.
3. Disconnect all hoses, lines and electrical connectors from engine.

NOTE: Do not disconnect wires from the starter.

4. Disconnect throttle cable, transmission T.V. or detent cable at injection pump and engine brackets.
5. Remove upper radiator support and radiator from vehicle.
6. Raise and support vehicle.
7. Disconnect exhaust pipes at exhaust manifold.
8. Remove torque converter flywheel cover and three torque converter to flywheel bolts.
9. Remove starter and two engine mount bolts.
10. From the right side of the vehicle, remove three engine to transmission bolts.
11. Lower vehicle and position suitable lifting equipment onto engine.
12. Using a suitable jack, raise transmission enough to gain access to the other three transmission to engine bolts. Remove bolts and lift engine from vehicle.
13. Reverse procedure to install. Torque flywheel to torque converter bolts to 35 ft. lbs. Torque two engine mount bolts to 55 ft. lbs.

Turbocharger Section

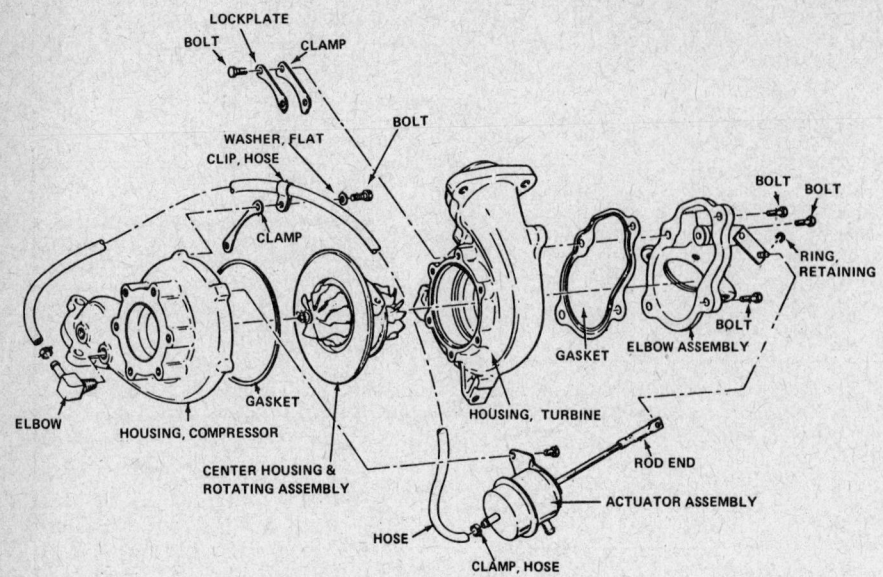

Fig. 1 Turbocharger assembly (Typical)

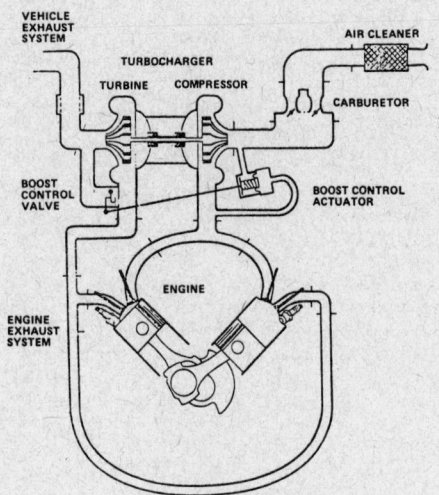

Fig. 2 Turbocharged V6 engine schematic (Typical)

The turbocharger, Fig. 1, is used to increase engine power on a demand basis, therefore allowing a smaller, more economical engine to be used. The turbocharged V6-231 is available with either two or four barrel carburetion on 1978—83 models and with sequential port fuel injection on 1984 models.

As engine load increases and the throttle opens, more air-fuel mixture is drawn into the combustion chambers. As the increased volume is burned, a larger volume of high energy exhaust gasses enters the engine exhaust system and is directed through the turbocharger turbine housing, Fig. 2. Some of the exhaust gas energy is used to increase the speed of the turbine wheel which is connected to the compressor wheel. The increased speed of the compressor wheel compresses the air-fuel mixture and delivers the compressed air-fuel mixture to the intake manifold, Fig. 2. The high pressure in the intake manifold allows a denser charge to enter the combustion chambers, in turn developing more engine power during the combustion cycle.

The intake manifold pressure (Boost) is controlled to a maximum value by an exhaust gas bypass valve (Wastegate). The wastegate allows a portion of the exhaust gas to bypass the turbine wheel, thereby not increasing turbine speed. On 1978—83 models, the wastegate is operated by a spring loaded diaphragm device sensing the pressure differential across the compressor. When intake manifold pressure reaches a set value above ambient pressure, the wastegate begins to bypass the exhaust gas. On 1984 models, an electronic wastegate is used. In this system, a pulse width modulated solenoid has been positioned between the manifold and wastegate diaphragm. Information regarding air flow, engine RPM, transmission gear and detonation is collected and analyzed by the Electronic Control Module. If the engine will tolerate

additional boost, the solenoid signals the wastegate accordingly. Inside the wastegate, the exhaust divert valve is normally closed, allowing boost pressure to rise until the mass air flow called for by the ECM is satisfied. When air flow reaches this level, the exhaust divert valve opens, allowing the exhaust gas to divert around the turbine and flow directly into the exhaust system.

An Electronic Spark Control System, Figs. 3 and 4, is used to retard ignition timing up to 20° to minimize detonation. The 1978 two barrel application uses a turbocharger vacuum bleed valve (TVBV) and the 1978 four barrel application uses a power enrichment control valve (PECV). These valves assist in proper vacuum control during boost. On 1979—80 applications, the power enrichment vacuum regulator (PEVR) is used to control vacuum flow to the carburetor power piston. On 1981—83 models, no vacuum control is required, the carburetor power enrichment circuit is controlled by the Electronic Control Module (ECM). On 1984 models, a piezo electric sensor transforms engine detonation vibrations directly into an electrical signal which is fed to the Electronic Control Module. The ECM then adjusts the spark accordingly. An electronic filter with integrated circuitry is also used to filter out vibrations not associated to pre-ignition or detonation.

NOTE: Engine oil on 1978—81 turbocharged engines must be changed every 3000 miles, otherwise, turbocharger bearing damage may occur from oil contamination. On 1982—83 turbocharged engines the recommended oil and oil filter change interval is every 7500 miles or 12 months, whichever comes first. This change is due to increased oil capacity, a higher output oil pump and a revised turbocharger oil passage.

DIAGNOSIS & TESTING

Prior to performing any diagnostic or testing procedure check all vacuum hoses and wiring for proper routing and connections, carburetor linkage for freedom of movement, wastegate linkage for damage or any problems which may occur in a non-turbocharged engine.

CAUTION: A turbocharged engine has exhaust pipes located high in the engine compartment. Care must be taken to avoid accidental contact with hot exhaust pipes since personal injury may occur.

Engine Diagnosis

1978—83

Refer to Fig. 5 for engine diagnosis.

1984

NOTE: Each turbocharged engine system has its own distinctive sound or noise level when operating. In many cases, malfunctions can be detected when this noise level changes. If the noise level changes to a higher pitch it can indicate an air leak between air cleaner and engine or an exhaust gas leak in the exhaust system between turbocharger and engine. Noise level cycling from one level to another can indicate a plugged air cleaner, restricted turbocharger air inlet or heavy dirt build up in the compressor housing and on the compressor wheel.

Engine Lacks Power
1. Restricted air outlet duct from compressor to intake manifold.

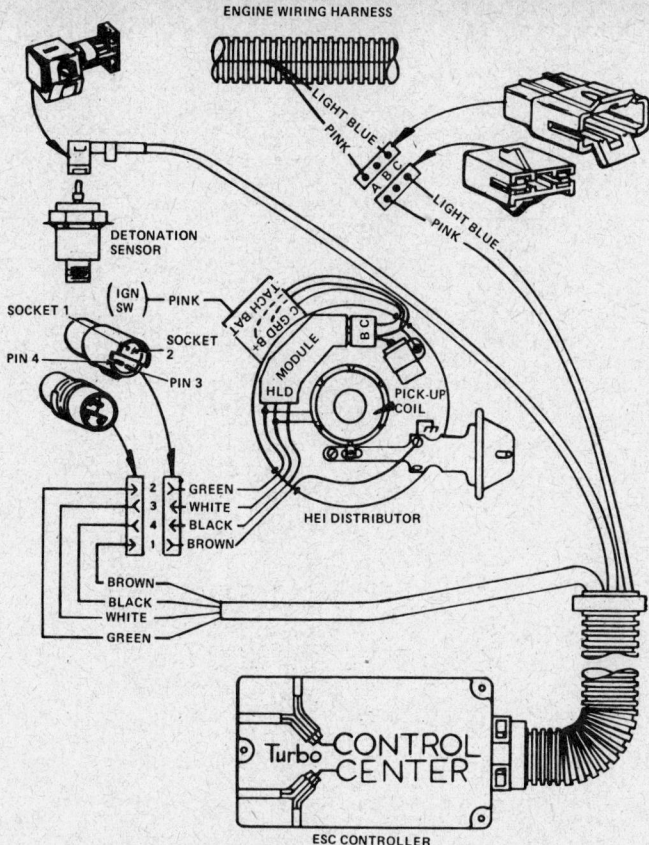

Fig. 3   Electronic spark control (ESC) system. 1978–79 models

2. Restricted intake system.
3. Air leak in duct from compressor to intake manifold.
4. Air leak at intake manifold to engine mating surface.
5. Restricted exhaust system.
6. Exhaust gas leak at exhaust manifold.
7. Exhaust gas leak in turbine inlet to exhaust manifold.
8. Incorrect camshaft timing.
9. Internal engine problem. Engine blowby, worn or damaged pistons, rings or valves.
10. Dirt on compressor wheel and or diffuser vanes.
11. Damaged turbocharger.

Black Exhaust Smoke
1. Restricted air intake duct to turbocharger compressor.
2. Restricted air outlet duct from compressor to intake manifold.
3. Restricted intake system.
4. Air leak in duct from compressor to intake manifold.
5. Air leak at intake manifold to engine mating surface.
6. Restricted exhaust system.
7. Exhaust gas leak in turbine inlet to exhaust manifold.
8. Incorrect camshaft timing.
9. Internal engine problem. Engine blowby, worn or damaged pistons, rings or valves.
10. Dirt on compressor wheel and or diffuser vanes.
11. Damaged turbocharger.

Excessive Engine Oil Consumption
1. Restricted air intake duct to turbocharger

compressor.
2. Air leak in duct from compressor to intake manifold.
3. Air leak at intake manifold to engine mating surface.
4. Restricted exhaust system.
5. Restricted turbocharger oil drain line.
6. Restricted PCV system.
7. Restricted turbocharger center housing.
8. Internal engine problem. Engine blowby, worn or damaged pistons, rings or valves.
9. Dirt on compressor wheel and or diffuser vanes.
10. Damaged turbocharger.

Blue Exhaust Smoke
1. Restricted air intake duct to turbocharger compressor.
2. Air leak in duct from compressor to intake manifold.
3. Air leak at intake manifold to engine mating surface.
4. Restricted exhaust system.
5. Restricted turbocharger oil drain line.
6. Restricted PCV system.
7. Restricted turbocharger center housing.
8. Internal engine problem. Engine blowby, worn or damaged pistons, rings or valves.
9. Dirt on compressor wheel and or diffuser vanes.
10. Damaged turbocharger.

Noisy Turbocharger
1. Restricted air intake duct to turbocharger compressor.
2. Restricted air outlet duct from compressor to intake manifold.
3. Restricted intake system.

4. Air leak in duct from compressor to intake manifold.
5. Air leak at intake manifold to engine mating surface.
6. Restricted exhaust system.
7. Exhaust gas leak in turbine inlet to exhaust manifold.
8. Exhaust gas leak in turbine outlet ducting.
9. Dirt on compressor wheel and or diffuser vanes.
10. Damaged turbocharger.

Turbocharger Noise Level Changes Constantly
1. Restricted air intake duct to turbocharger compressor.
2. Dirt on compressor wheel and or diffuser vanes.
3. Damaged turbocharger.

Oil Leak At Compressor Seal
1. Restricted air intake duct to turbocharger compressor.
2. Restricted exhaust system.
3. Exhaust gas leak at exhaust manifold.
4. Exhaust gas leak in turbine inlet to exhaust manifold.
5. Restricted turbocharger oil drain line.
6. Restricted PCV system.
7. Restricted turbocharger center housing.
8. Internal engine problem. Engine blowby, worn or damaged pistons, rings or valves.
9. Dirt on compressor wheel and or diffuser vanes.
10. Damaged turbocharger.

Oil Leak At Turbine Seal
1. Restricted turbocharger oil drain line.
2. Restricted PCV system.
3. Restricted turbocharger center housing.
4. Internal engine problem. Engine blowby, worn or damaged pistons, rings or valves.
5. Dirt on compressor wheel and or diffuser vanes.
6. Damaged turbocharger.

Wastegate-Boost Pressure Test

1. Inspect actuator linkage for damage.
2. Check tubing from compressor housing to actuator assembly and on 1978–80 models, the return tubing from the actuator to the PCV tee. Replace if necessary.
3. Remove compressor housing to actuator assembly hose, then attach vacuum-pressure pump J-23738, in series with compound gauge J-28474, to actuator assembly.
4. On 1978–80 models apply pressure to actuator assembly. At approximately 8 psi on 1978 models or 9 psi on 1979–80 models, the actuator lever should move .008 inch on 1978 models or .015 inch on 1979–80 models, actuating the wastegate. On 1981–83 models, apply vacuum to the actuator assembly. At approximately 3 in. Hg., the actuator lever should move .015 inch, actuating the wastegate. On 1984 models, apply 7½–8 psi pressure to actuator assembly. The actuator rod should move .015 inch. On all models, if the actuator did not respond properly, it should be replaced. Prior to installing actuator, test as outlined above, then crimp threads on actuator rod to maintain calibration.
5. Remove vacuum-pressure pump and reinstall hose.

Road Test
1. Tee compound gauge J-28474 into tubing between compressor housing and boost

gauge switches with a sufficient length of hose to place the gauge in the passenger compartment.

NOTE: Ensure gauge and hose are in good condition to prevent possible leakage of air/fuel mixture.

2. On 1984 models, disconnect and plug wastegate solenoid hose.
3. On all models with conditions and speed limits permitting, perform a zero to 40–50 mph, wide open throttle acceleration and maintain speed for two to three seconds. Boost pressure should reach 7–8 psi on 1978 2 barrel engines, 8–9 psi on 1978 4 barrel engines and 1981–84 engines and 9–10 psi on 1979–80 engines.
4. If boost is not satisfactory, replace actuator assembly. Prior to installation, test actuator as outlined in step 4 of Wastegate-Boost Pressure Test.

1979–80 Power Enrichment Vacuum Regulator (PEVR) Test

1. Inspect PEVR and attaching hoses for deterioration, cracking or other damage and replace as necessary.
2. Tee one hose of manometer J-23951 between yellow stripped input hose and input port. Connect other hose directly to PEVR output port.
3. Start engine and operate at idle speed. There should be no more than 14″ H_2O difference between manometer readings. If difference is greater than 14″ H_2O, replace PEVR.
4. Remove PEVR from intake manifold and install a plug in intake manifold PEVR bore. Connect input and output hoses to PEVR.
5. Tee gauge J-28474 into output hose of PEVR.
6. Start engine and operate at idle speed. The gauge reading from the output port should be 7–9″ Hg.
7. Apply 3 psi. to manifold signal port of PEVR. Vacuum reading from output port should be 1.4–2.6″ Hg. If difficulty is encountered in measuring level of vacuum, apply 5 psi. to manifold signal port of PEVR. There should be no vacuum output from PEVR.
8. If PEVR does not perform as described above, replace PEVR.

1978 Turbocharger Vacuum Bleed Valve (TVBV) Test

1. Inspect valve and attaching hoses deterioration, cracking or other damage and replace, if required.
2. Disconnect and plug the vacuum hose to the remote power enrichment port on the carburetor. Tee one hose from J-23951 manometer into the distributor vacuum hose between the carburetor and the TVBV. Tee the other hose into the hose between the TVBV and the distributor. Start and idle engine. There should be no more than a 14 inch H_2O difference on the manometer scale.
3. Repeat step 2 with the manometer teed into the vacuum hose from the Thermac sensor to the TVBV and the vacuum hose from the TVBV to the hot air door actuator.

NOTE: If the engine is at normal operating temperature, the hot air door may not

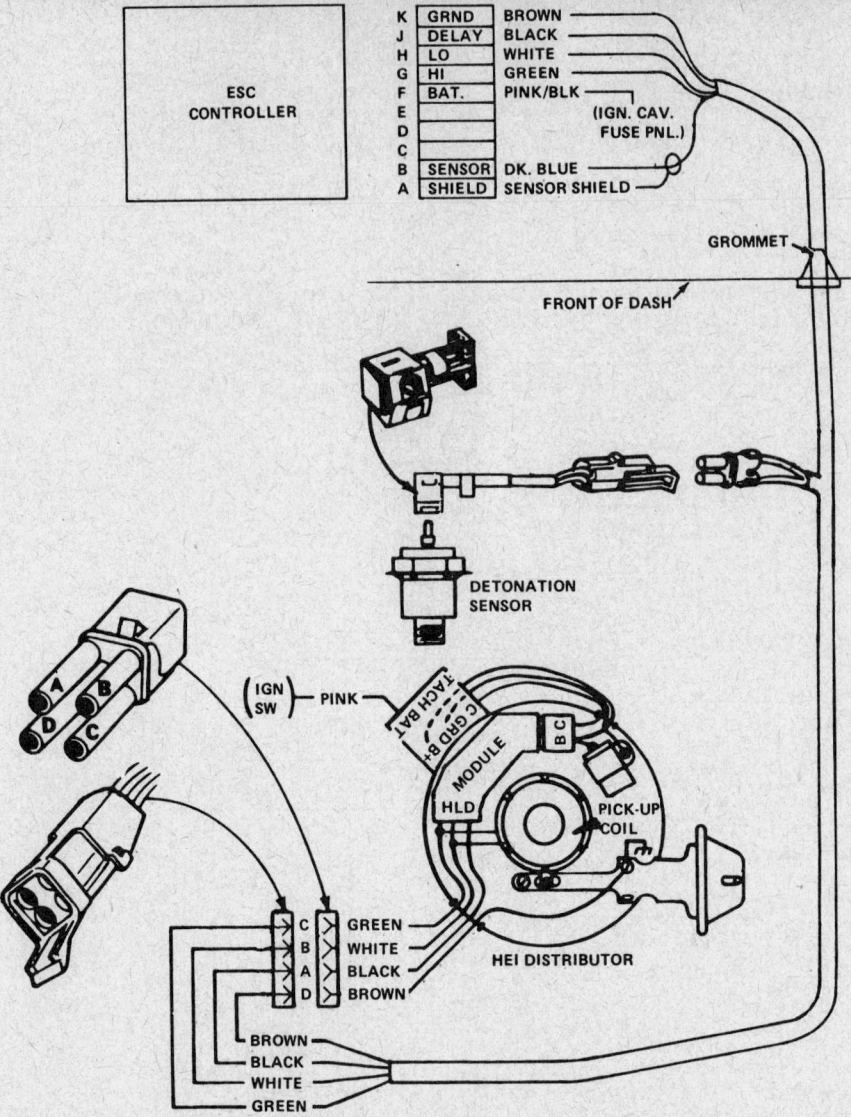

Fig. 4   Electronic Spark Control (ESC) system. 1980–83 models

have an applied vacuum signal. If so, connect manifold vacuum to port and recheck.

4. Plug the EGR hose at the EGR valve and install one hose from the manometer into the hose from the carburetor EGR signal port to the TVBV. Install the other manometer hose into the hose from the TVBV to the EGR-EFE switch. Start engine and open the throttle slightly. There should be no more than a 14 inch H_2O difference on the manometer scale.
5. Disconnect all hoses from the TVBV. Connect one side of the manometer to the center vent port and vent the other side of the manometer to the atmosphere. Start and idle engine. There should be no vacuum signal at the port.
6. If conditions in steps 2, 3, 4 and 5 are not met, replace the TVBV and install all hoses.
7. If the TVBV tests normally but is still suspect, remove the TVBV from intake manifold. Plug the intake manifold and connect all hoses to the TVBV. Using J-23738, apply at least 6 inch Hg (3 psi) to

the manifold signal port of the TVBV. Start and idle engine. Attach one side of the manometer to the output port of each pair of ports described in steps 2, 3 and 4, in turn, and vent the other side of the manometer to the atmosphere. If the manometer indicates any pressure difference, replace the TVBV.

1978 Power Enrichment Control Valve (PECV) Test

1. Inspect the valve and attaching hoses for deterioration, cracking and other damage. Replace, if necessary.
2. Tee one side of manometer J-23951 into the input port and the other side into the output port of the PECV. Start and idle engine. There should be no more than a 12 inch H_2O difference on the manometer scale.
3. Disconnect all hoses from the PECV and plug the vacuum source hose. Connect one side of the manometer to the vent port and vent the other side to the atmosphere. Start and idle engine. The manometer should not indicate any pressure differen-

Condition	Possible Cause	Correction
ENGINE DETONATION	1. Electronic Spark Control.	1. Refer to ESC Diagnosis.
	2. EGR	2. Requires Emission Control diagnostic equipment.
	3. Carburetor or Turbocharger.	3. Correct air inlet restrictions.
		a. Air cleaner duct.
		b. Thermac door operation.
		c. Air cleaner dirty.
		Eliminate actuator overboost.
		a. Mechanical linkage jammed or blocked.
		b. Hose from compressor housing to actuator assembly or return hose from actuator to PCV tee damaged or loose.
		c. Wastegate not operating-Refer to Wastegate-Boost Pressure Test.
		Service Carburetor Power System.
		a. Refer to TVBV/PECV or PEVR Test.
		b. Refer to Carburetor Chapter elsewhere in this manual.
		c. Refer to Trouble-Shooting Chapter elsewhere in this manual.
		Inspect turbocharger-Refer to Turbocharger Internal Inspection.
	4. Other causes.	4. Refer to Trouble-Shooting Chapter elsewhere in this manual.
ENGINE LACKS POWER	1. Air inlet restriction.	1. Air cleaner duct.
		Thermac door operation.
		Air cleaner element dirty.
	2. Exhaust system restriction.	2. Repair exhaust pipes if damaged.
		Repair or replace catalytic converter if damaged.
	3. Transmission.	3. Check for correct shifting.
		Refer to Automatic Transmission Chapter elsewhere in this manual.
	4. Electronic spark control.	4. Refer to ESC Diagnosis.
	5. EFE	5. Requires Emission Control diagnostic equipment.
	6. EGR	6. Requires Emission Control diagnostic equipment.
	7. Carburetion	7. Refer to Carburetor Chapter elsewhere in this manual.
		Refer to Trouble-Shooting Chapter elsewhere in this manual.
	8. Turbocharger	8. Check for exhaust leaks or restrictions.
		Refer to TVBV/PECV or PEVR test procedure. Inspect for collapsed or kinked plenum coolant hoses (if equipped).
		Check wastegate operation.
		a. Refer to Wastegate-boost pressure test.
		b. Remove exhaust pipe from elbow assembly. Using a mirror, observe movement of wastegate while manually operating actuator linkage. Replace elbow assembly if valve does not open or close.
		Refer to Turbocharger Internal Inspection.
	9. Other causes.	9. Refer to Trouble-Shooting Chapter elsewhere in this manual.
ENGINE SURGES	1. Electronic Spark Control.	1. Refer to ESC diagnosis.
	2. Carburetion.	2. Refer to TVBV/PECV or PEVR Test Procedure. Refer to Carburetor Chapter elsewhere in this manual.
		Refer to Trouble-Shooting Chapter elsewhere in this manual.
	3. EGR	3. Requires Emission Control diagnostic equipment.
	4. Turbocharger.	4. Inspect turbocharger for loose bolts on compressor side of assembly, tighten.
	5. Other causes.	5. Refer to Trouble-Shooting Chapter elsewhere in this manual.

Fig. 5 Engine Diagnosis (part 1 of 2). 1978–83

Condition	Possible Cause	Correction
EXCESSIVE OIL CONSUMPTION OR BLUE EXHAUST SMOKE	1. External turbocharger oil leaks.	1. Inspect turbocharger oil inlet for proper connection. Inspect turbocharger oil drain hose for leaks or restriction.
	2. PCV	2. Requires Emission Control diagnostic equipment.
	3. Other causes.	3. Refer to Trouble-Shooting Chapter elsewhere in this manual.
	4. Turbocharger.	4. Refer to Turbocharger Internal Inspection.
BLACK EXHAUST SMOKE	1. Carburetion.	1. Refer to TVBV/PECV or PEVR Test. Refer to Carburetor Chapter elsewhere in this manual.
	2. Other causes.	2. Refer to Trouble-Shooting Chapter elsewhere in this manual.
EXCESSIVE ENGINE NOISE	1. EFE	1. Requires Emission Control diagnostic equipment.
	2. Exhaust System.	2. Inspect for incorrect or loose mountings.
	3. AIR System.	3. Requires Emission Control diagnostic equipment.
	4. Other causes.	4. Refer to Trouble-Shooting Chapter elsewhere in this manual.
	5. Turbocharger.	5. Check for exhaust leaks. Inspect for rertriction of turbocharger oil supply. Refer to Turbocharger Internal Inspection.

Fig. 5   Engine Diagnosis (part 2 of 2). 1978–83

tial.

4. If conditions in steps 2 and 3 are not met, replace the PECV.
5. If the PECV tests normally but is still suspect, remove the PECV from intake manifold. Plug the intake manifold and connect hoses to the PECV. Tee one side of the manometer into the output port and vent the other side to the atmosphere. Apply at least 6 inch Hg (3 psi) to the manifold signal port of the PECV. Start and idle engine. If manometer indicates any pressure differential, replace the PECV.

1978–79 Electronic Spark Control (ESC) System Diagnosis

Engine Detonation Or Poor Performance

1. Check all vacuum hoses and wires for proper connections and routing.
2. With ignition switch "On," check for voltage between light blue to black wire across ESC relay. If no voltage reading is obtained, replace ESC relay.
3. If voltage reading is obtained in step 2, check initial ignition timing and correct, if necessary.
4. With engine at normal operating temperature, install a tachometer and timing meter, if available, to engine. Place air conditioner in "Off" position and the fast idle cam on high step. Run engine above 1800 RPM. Using a steel rod, tap intake manifold near detonation sensor with light to medium taps and observe tachometer or timing metering. Engine RPM should drop 300–500 RPM and timing should retard 18–22 degrees. Engine should return to original RPM and timing within 20 seconds after tapping stops.
5. If conditions are not met in step 4, check connection between ESC controller and detonation sensor, Fig. 3. Check detonation sensor for proper installation. Connect an ohmmeter between detonation sensor and the ground, Fig. 3. If resistance is not 175–375 ohms, replace deto-

nation sensor. If these checks and correction do not correct the problem, replace the ESC controller.

6. If conditions in step 4 are met, disconnect the four wire connector from ESC controller to distributor, Fig. 3. Using a jumper wire, connect socket No. 2 to pin No. 4 on the distributor side of the harness connector, Fig. 3. Test H.E.I. distributor as outlined in the "Electronic Ignition Systems" chapter. After distributor repair, remove jumper wire and connect ESC controller.

Engine Cranks But Does Not Start

1. Check all vacuum hoses and wires for proper connections and routing.
2. Check for spark at spark plug.
3. If spark is present at spark plug, refer to the "Trouble-Shooting Chapter" and the "Electronic Ignition Systems" chapter.
4. If spark is not present at spark plug, check ESC relay voltage between light blue wire and black wire while cranking. If voltage is present, replace ESC relay.
5. If no voltage was present in step 4, check voltage between the distributor "BAT" terminal and the ground with ignition "On". If voltage is under 7 volts, check for open circuit between distributor "BAT" terminal and ignition switch.
6. If voltage in step 5 is 7 volts or over, check voltage at "A" terminal, pink wire, on engine harness side of two wire connector from ESC controller to engine wiring harness, Fig. 3. If voltage is under 7 volts, check for open circuit between "A" terminal and the ignition switch.
7. If voltage in step 6 was 7 volts or over, disconnect four wire connector from ESC controller to distributor, Fig. 3. Connect a jumper wire between socket No. 2 and pin No. 4 on distributor side of harness connector, Fig. 3. Check for spark at spark plug while cranking engine. If spark is present at spark plug, replace ESC controller.
8. If spark is not present at spark plug in step 7, leave the jumper wire connected and test the H.E.I. distributor as outlined

in the "Tune-Up Chapter, Electronic Ignition Section". After distributor repair, remove the jumper wire and connect the ESC controller.

1980–83 Electronic Spark Control (ESC) System Diagnosis

Engine Detonation

1. Check all vacuum hoses and wires for proper connections and routing.
2. Check engine coolant for proper concentration and level.
3. Check initial timing.
4. With engine thoroughly warmed up, A/C off, install tachometer to engine.
5. Set throttle on high step of fast idle cam.

NOTE: Engine speed must be above 1800 RPM.

6. Using a suitable steel bar (a socket wrench breaker bar will do), tap the front area of the left exhaust manifold rapidly with medium to heavy taps.
7. Observe tachometer for RPM drop. RPM should drop 200 RPM and return to original RPM within 20 seconds. If RPM drops as indicated, problem is ignition or carburetor related. If RPM does not drop, inspect detonation sensor for any signs of physical damage.

NOTE: Detonation sensor is extremely sensitive to physical damage.

8. Check detonation sensor for proper installation and torque. Correct torque is 14 ft. lbs.
9. Disconnect detonation sensor connector at firewall. On the sensor side of the connector, connect the positive lead of a suitable ohmmeter to the connector terminal attached to the center conductor of the sensor lead. While grounding the negative ohmmeter lead to a suitable ground, measure resistance. Resistance should be

10. If sensor failed any of the above tests, replace. If sensor passed all the above tests, substitute a known good sensor and repeat steps 4 through 7. If RPM drops, replace sensor.

11. If RPM does not drop in step 10, remove ESC 10 pin connector at controller (located under dashboard), then jump pins A and B with a suitable jumper wire, Fig. 4. Disconnect detonation sensor wire connector from area of firewall, then using a suitable ohmmeter, check continuity across sensor connector. If continuity exists, replace sensor and sensor harness between firewall and sensor. If no continuity exists, repair detonation sensor wire.

12. Repeat steps 4 through 7. If RPM does not drop, replace ESC controller.

Engine Cranks But Will Not Start

1. Check for spark at cylinder number 2 spark plug.
2. If spark is present, ESC system is operating. Refer to the "Electronic Ignition Systems" chapter.
3. If spark is not present at spark plug, check ESC controller (located under dashboard) connector for proper connection, then check distributor 4 pin connector. Repair as necessary.
4. Turn ignition "On", then, using a suitable voltmeter, check voltage from pin F to pin K of the ESC controller connector, Fig. 4.
5. If voltage obtained is under 7 volts, check for and repair open circuit between pin F of ESC connector and ignition switch. If engine will not start, proceed to step 6.
6. If voltage obtained is over 7 volts, disconnect distributor 4 pin connector, then ESC 10 pin connector. Using a suitable ohmmeter, check continuity of wires at pins G, H, J & K.
7. If continuity exists, repair wire or wires causing trouble.
8. If continuity does not exist, check wiring harness for possible opens, then on distributor side of 4 pin connector, jump pins A and C together and attempt to start engine.
9. If engine does not run, check distributor. Refer to "Electronic Ignition Systems" chapter. If distributor is satisfactory, replace ESC controller.
10. If engine runs, replace ESC controller.

NOTE: When running engine with distributor 4 pin connector disconnected and pins A and C jumped, do not race engine. Run at idle only.

11. If, after completing step 10, the engine will not run, check distributor. Refer to "Electronic Ignition Systems" chapter.

Poor Engine Performance

1. Check all vacuum hoses and wires for proper connections and routing.
2. Check engine coolant for proper concentration and level.
3. Check initial timing.
4. With engine running, use a suitable voltmeter to measure voltage between pins F and K of the ESC controller 10 pin connector, Fig. 4.

NOTE: The ESC controller is located under the dashboard.

5. If voltage obtained is 11.6 volts or less, check and repair alternator and charging system. If problem still remains, proceed to step 6.
6. If voltage obtained is 11.6 volts or more, refer to "Engine Detonation" procedure and perform steps 4 through 7.
7. If RPM does not drop, perform remaining "Engine Detonation" procedure.
8. If RPM drops, disconnect distributor 4 pin connector, then jump pins A and C of the connector on the distributor side, Fig. 4.
9. Check distributor. Refer to "Electronic Ignition Systems" chapter.
10. If problem still remains, problem is ignition or carburetor related.

TURBOCHARGER INTERNAL INSPECTION

1. Remove the turbocharger assembly but do not separate the center housing rotating assembly from the turbine housing.
2. Manually operate the wastegate linkage and using a small mirror, observe wastegate movement in the elbow assembly. Replace the elbow assembly if the wastegate fails to open or close.
3. Check for loose backplate to center housing rotating assembly bolts and tighten, if necessary.
4. Spin the compressor wheel. If rotating assembly binds or drags, replace the center housing rotating assembly.
5. Inspect center rotating housing assembly for sludge in the oil drain area. Clean, if minor, or replace center housing rotating assembly if excessively sludged or caked.
6. Inspect compressor oil seal for damage or leakage on the compressor wheel side of the backplate. Replace center housing rotating assembly if oil seal damage or leakage is present.
7. If compressor wheel is damaged or severely caked, replace center housing rotating assembly.
8. If center housing rotating assembly is being replaced, pre-lubricate with engine oil.
9. Inspect compressor housing and turbine housing. If either housing is gouged, nicked or distorted, replace if necessary.
10. Remove turbine housing from center housing rotating assembly and check the journal bearing radial clearance and thrust bearing axial clearance as follows:
   a. Journal bearing radial clearance.
      (1) Attach a rack and pinion type dial indicator (Starrett model 656-517 or equivalent with a two inch long, 3/4 to 1 inch offset extension rod) to the center housing so the indicator plunger extends through the oil output port and contacts the turbine wheel assembly shaft, Fig. 6. If required, a dial indicator mounting adapter can be utilized, Fig. 6.
      (2) Manually apply pressure equally and at the same time to both the compressor wheel and turbine wheel as required to move the turbine wheel assembly shaft away from the dial indicator as far as possible.
      (3) Zero the dial indicator.
      (4) Manually apply pressure equally and at the same time to both the compressor and turbine wheels as required to move the turbine

wheel assembly shaft toward the dial indicator plunger as far as possible. Note maximum reading on dial indicator.

NOTE: To ensure that the dial indicator reading is the maximum obtainable, roll the wheels slightly in both directions while applying pressure.

   (5) Manually apply pressure equally and at the same time to both the compressor and turbine wheels as required to move the turbine wheel assembly shaft away from the dial indicator as far as possible. The dial indicator should return to zero.
   (6) Repeat steps 2 through 5 as required to ensure the maximum clearance between the center housing bores and the shaft bearing diameters, as indicated by the maximum shaft travel, has been obtained.
   (7) If the maximum bearing radial clearance is less than .003 inch or greater than .006 inch, replace the center housing rotating assembly.

NOTE: Continued operation of a turbocharger having excessive bearing radial clearance will result in severe damage to the compressor and turbine wheels and the housings.

   b. Thrust bearing axial clearance.
      (1) Mount a dial indicator (Starrett model 25-141 or equivalent) at the turbine end of the turbocharger so the dial indicator plunger contacts the end of the turbine wheel assembly, Fig. 7.
      (2) Manually move the compressor wheel and turbine wheel assembly in each direction shown on the indicator dial.
      (3) Repeat previous step to ensure the maximum clearance between the thrust bearing components, as indicated by the maximum turbine wheel assembly travel, has been obtained.
      (4) If the maximum thrust bearing axial clearance is less than .001 inch or greater than .003 inch, replace the center housing rotating assembly.

NOTE: Continued operation of a turbocharger having excessive thrust bearing axial clearance will result in severe damage to the compressor and turbine wheels and the housings.

SERVICE

Before performing turbocharger service, note the following general cautions:

1. Clean area around turbocharger assembly with a non-caustic solution before service. Cover openings of engine assembly connections to prevent entry of foreign material.
2. When removing the assembly, do not bend, nick or in any way damage the

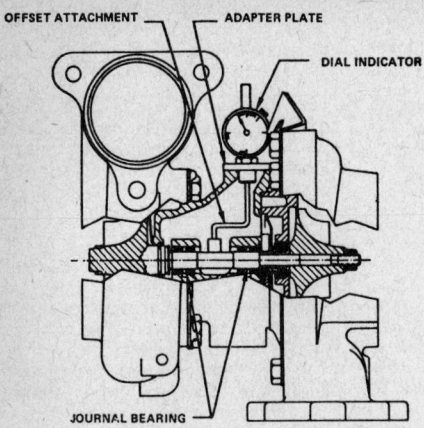

Fig. 6 Journal bearing clearance check

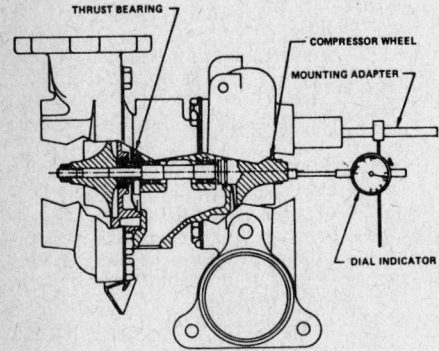

Fig. 7 Thrust bearing clearance check

compressor or turbine wheel blades. Any damage may result in rotating assembly imbalance, failure of the center housing rotating assembly, and failure of the compressor and/or turbine housings.

3. Before disconnecting center housing rotating assembly from either compressor housing or turbine housing, scribe location of components for assembly in original position.

Wastegate Actuator Assembly, Replace

1. Disconnect vacuum hose from actuator.
2. Remove clip from wastegate linkage to actuator rod, Fig. 8.
3. Remove two bolts attaching actuator and the actuator.
4. Reverse procedure to install.

Elbow Assembly, Replace

1. Raise vehicle.
2. Loosen exhaust pipe at catalytic converter.
3. Lower the vehicle.
4. Disconnect turbocharger exhaust outlet pipe from elbow, Fig. 9.
5. Disconnect actuator rod from wastegate linkage.
6. Remove elbow from turbine housing.
7. Reverse procedure to install.

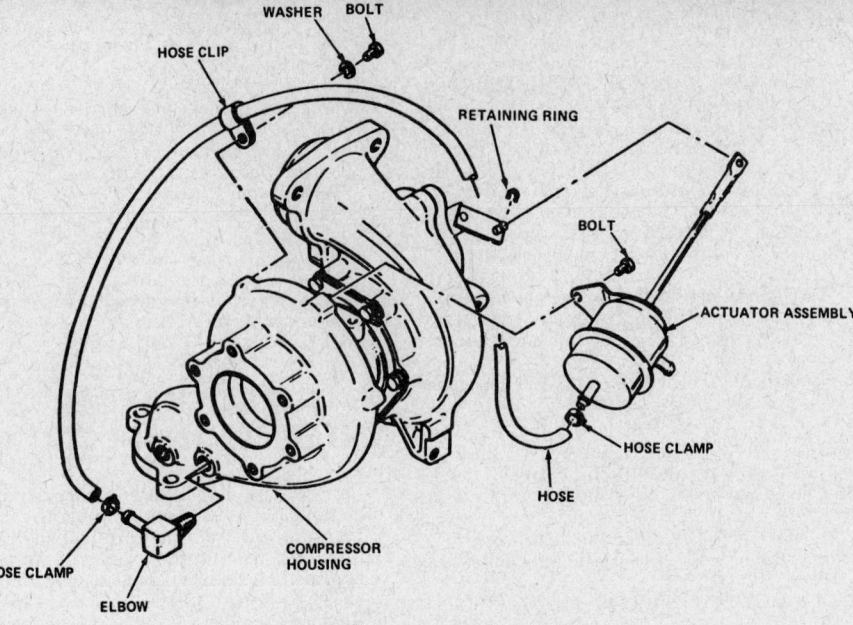

Fig. 8 Wastegate actuator assembly (Typical)

Turbine Housing & Elbow Assembly, Center Housing Rotating Assembly

1. Disconnect turbocharger exhaust outlet pipe from elbow.
2. Raise vehicle.
3. Disconnect catalytic converter from exhaust pipe and move pipe aside.
4. Lower vehicle.
5. Disconnect turbocharger exhaust inlet pipe from turbine housing, Fig. 10.
6. Disconnect turbocharger exhaust inlet pipe from right exhaust manifold, Fig.
7. Disconnect turbine housing from bracket.
8. Disconnect turbocharger oil feed pipe, Fig. 11, and oil drain hose, Figs. 12 and 13 from center housing rotating assembly.
9. Disconnect actuator rod from wastegate linkage.
10. Remove six bolts and three clamps attaching center housing rotating assembly backplate to compressor housing.
11. Remove six bolts, three lockplates and three clamps attaching turbine housing to center housing rotating assembly, Fig. 14.
12. Reverse procedure to install.

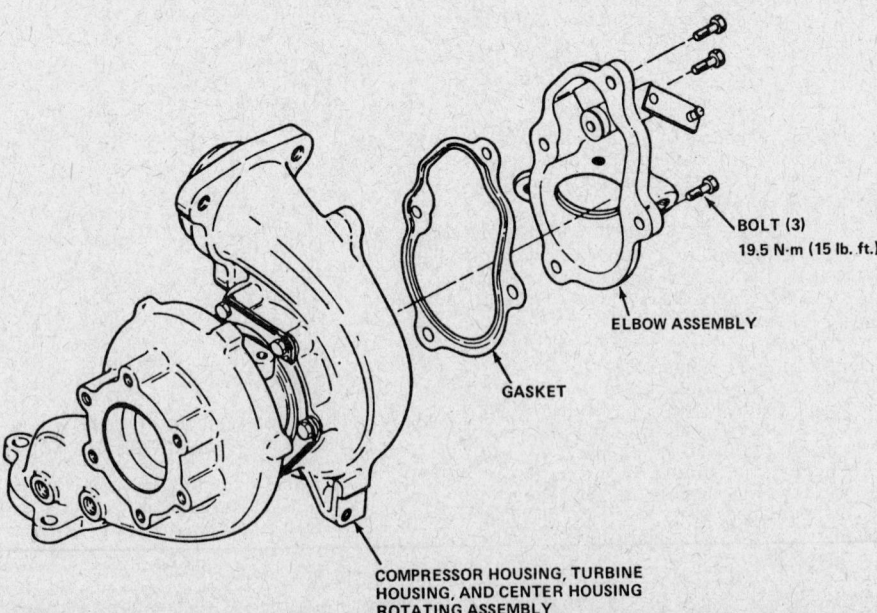

Fig. 9 Elbow assembly. 1978–83

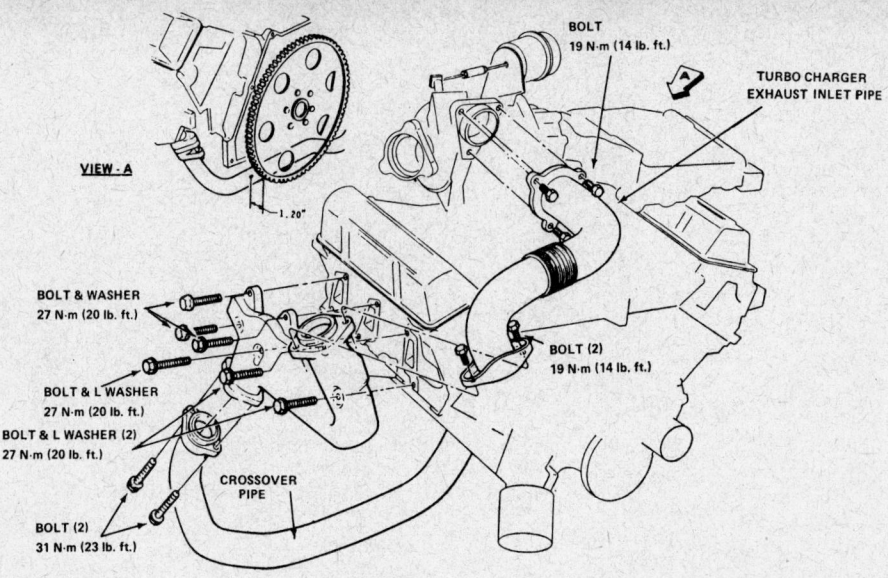

Fig. 10 Turbocharger exhaust inlet pipe. 1978—83

Compressor Housing

1. Remove turbine housing and elbow assembly/center housing rotating assembly as outlined previously, however do not separate the turbine housing from the center housing rotating assembly.
2. Remove six bolts attaching compressor housing to the plenum, Figs. 15 and 16.
3. Remove clamp attaching compressor to actuator hose, then the hose from connec-

tor.
4. Remove three bolts attaching compressor housing to intake manifold.
5. Reverse procedure to install.

Turbo Charger Assembly, Replace

1979—83 Riviera

1. Remove nut attaching air intake elbow to carburetor stud.
2. Disconnect inlet pipe from turbine housing and exhaust outlet pipe from elbow

assembly.
3. Raise vehicle and disconnect turbocharger exhaust outlet pipe at catalytic converter.
4. Lower vehicle and two bolts attaching turbocharger adjustment bracket to turbocharger support bracket on right cylinder head.
5. Disconnect oil feed line from turbocharger.
6. Disconnect choke wire connector and remove choke cover.
7. Remove five plenum chamber attaching bolts and gasket.
8. Tip turbocharger assembly upward and away from intake manifold. Disconnect vacuum line from plenum at actuator. Disconnect oil drain hose from pipe.
9. Remove turbocharger from adapter on intake manifold, Fig. 16.

1984 Riviera

1. Remove air inlet tube from throttle body.
2. Disconnect throttle body vacuum harness connector, throttle body electrical connectors, and the throttle and T.V. cable from throttle body.
3. Remove throttle body assembly to compressor housing retaining bolts, then the throttle body assembly.
4. Disconnect and plug oil pressure feed and drain lines at turbocharger.
5. Disconnect vacuum hoses from compressor housing and wastegate actuator.
6. Raise and support vehicle.
7. Disconnect exhaust crossover at turbocharger, then loosen at both exhaust manifolds.
8. Lower vehicle, then remove mounting bracket to intake manifold attaching bolts.
9. Remove support bracket to turbocharger exhaust outlet housing retaining bolts.
10. Remove turbocharger from adapter on intake manifold, Fig. 16A.

Except 1979—84 Riviera & 1984 Regal

1. Disconnect turbocharger exhaust inlet and outlet pipes at turbocharger.
2. Disconnect oil feed pipe from center housing rotating assembly.
3. Remove nut attaching air intake elbow to carburetor and remove elbow.
4. Disconnect accelerator, cruise control and detent linkages at carburetor, then remove linkage bracket from plenum.
5. Remove two bolts attaching plenum to side bracket.
6. Disconnect fuel line and necessary vacuum hoses.
7. Disconnect coolant hoses and power brake vacuum hose from plenum.

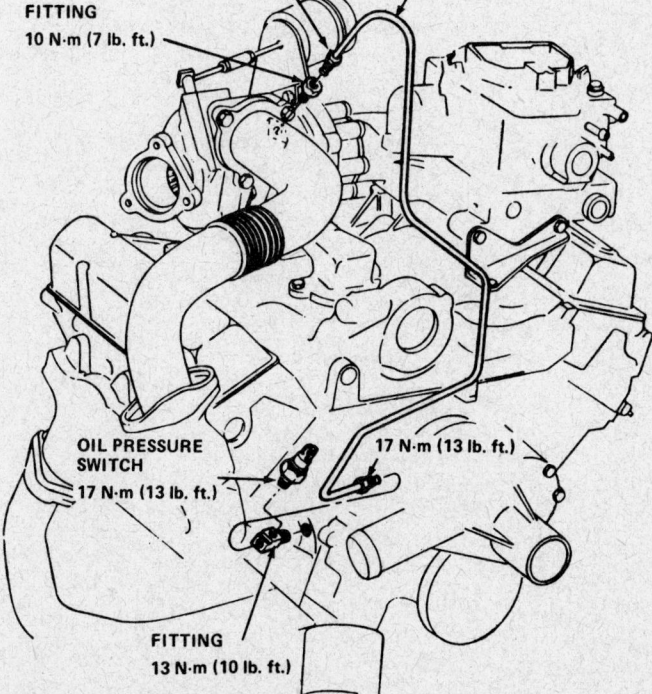

Fig. 11 Turbocharger oil feed pipe (typical)

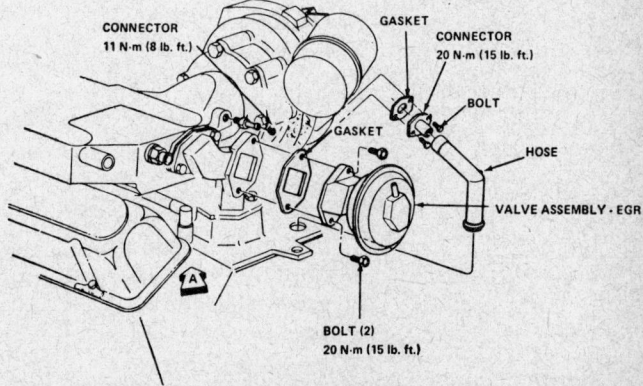

Fig. 12 EGR valve & turbocharger oil drain. Except 1979—83 Riviera & all 1984 models

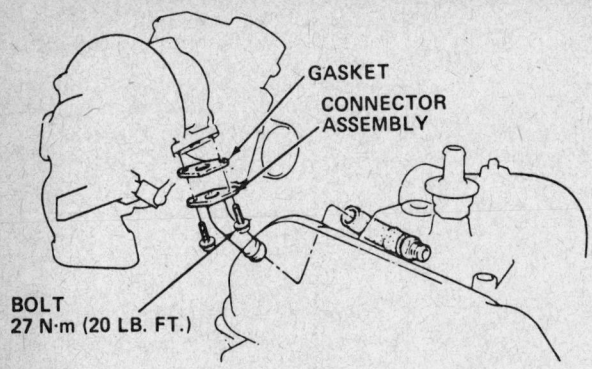

GASKET
CONNECTOR ASSEMBLY

BOLT
27 N·m (20 LB. FT.)

Fig. 13 Oil drain connector. 1979–83 Riviera

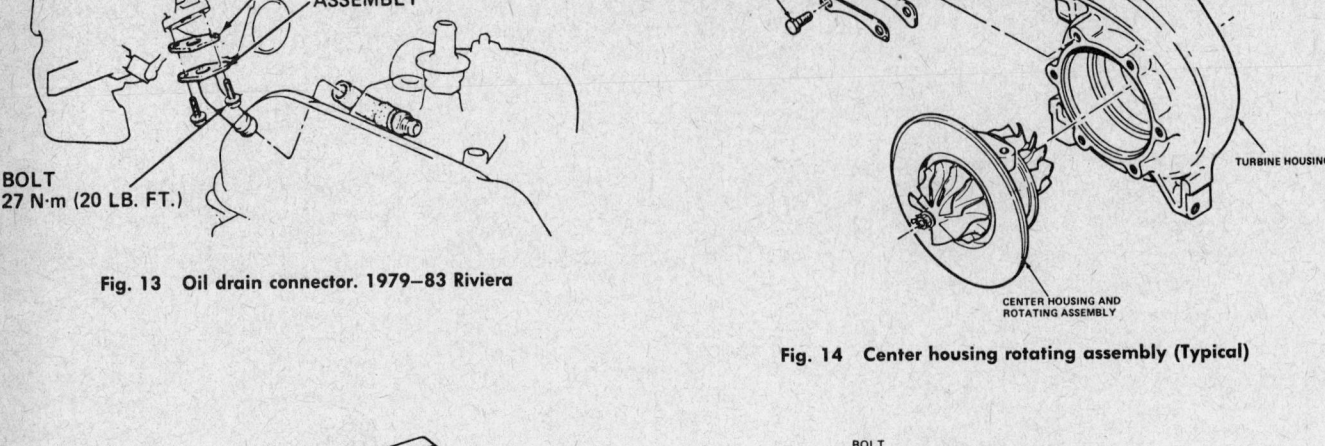

CLAMP
BOLT
19.5 N·m (15 lb. ft.)
LOCKPLATE

TURBINE HOUSING

CENTER HOUSING AND ROTATING ASSEMBLY

Fig. 14 Center housing rotating assembly (Typical)

CLAMP
BOLT
17.5 N·m (13 lb. ft.)

GASKET

COMPRESSOR HOUSING

TURBINE HOUSING AND CENTER HOUSING AND ROTATING ASSEMBLY

Fig. 15 Compressor housing (Typical)

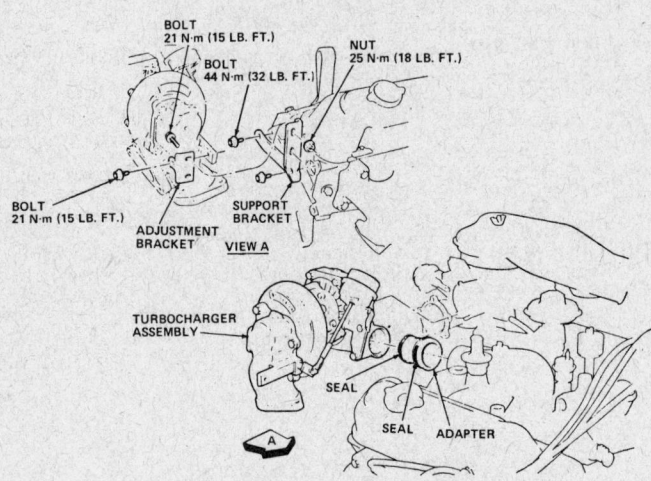

BOLT
21 N·m (15 LB. FT.)
BOLT
44 N·m (32 LB. FT.)
NUT
25 N·m (18 LB. FT.)

BOLT
21 N·m (15 LB. FT.)
ADJUSTMENT BRACKET
SUPPORT BRACKET
VIEW A

TURBOCHARGER ASSEMBLY

SEAL
SEAL ADAPTER

Fig. 16 Turbocharger assembly. 1979–83 Riviera

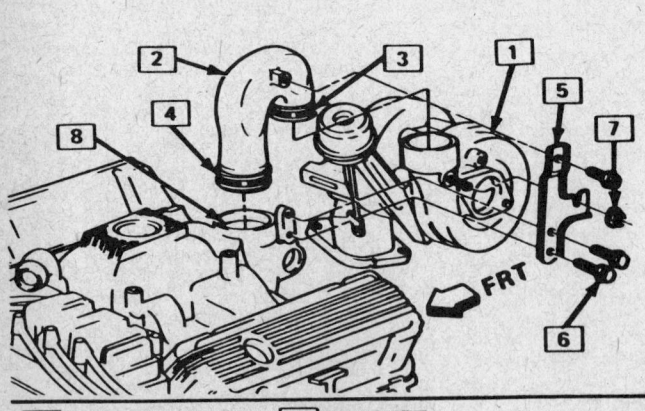

FRT

1	TURBOCHARGER ASSEMBLY	5	BRACKET
2	ADAPTER	6	BOLT 30 N·m (22 FT. LBS.)
3	SEAL	7	NUT 30 N·m (22 FT. LBS.)
4	SEAL	8	INTAKE MANIFOLD

Fig. 16A Turbocharger assembly. 1984 Riviera

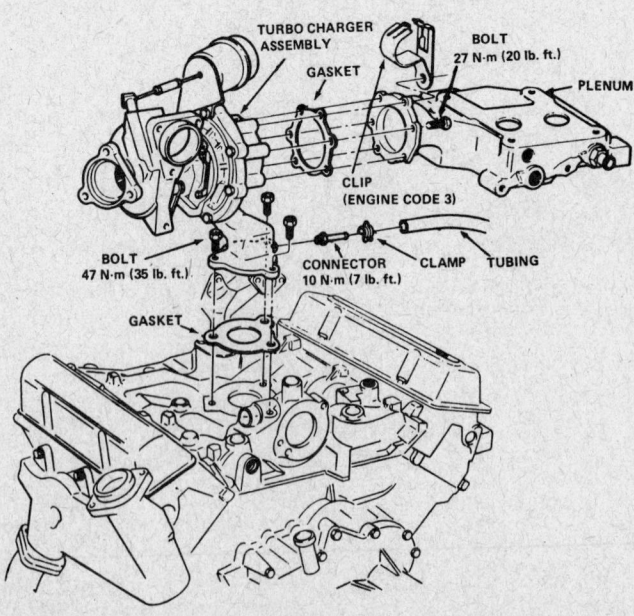

TURBO CHARGER ASSEMBLY
GASKET
BOLT
27 N·m (20 lb. ft.)
PLENUM

CLIP
(ENGINE CODE 3)

BOLT
47 N·m (35 lb. ft.)
CONNECTOR CLAMP TUBING
10 N·m (7 lb. ft.)
GASKET

Fig. 17 Plenum & turbocharger assembly. Except 1979–83 Riviera & all 1984 models

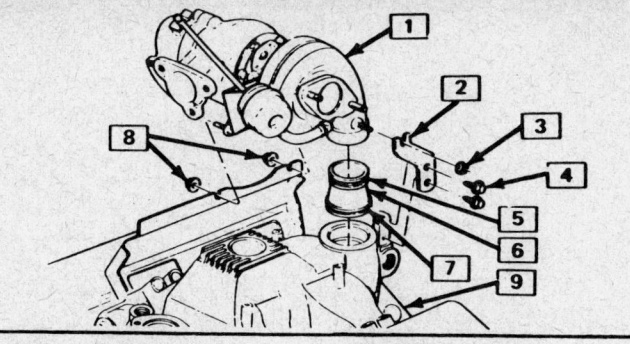

1	TURBOCHARGER ASSEMBLY	**6**	ADAPTER
2	STABILIZER BRACKET	**7**	SEAL
3	NUT 30 N·m (22 FT. LBS.)	**8**	NUT 30 N·m (22 FT. LBS.)
4	BOLT 30 N·m (22 FT. LBS.)	**9**	INTAKE MANIFOLD
5	SEAL		

Fig. 17A   Turbocharger assembly. 1984 Regal

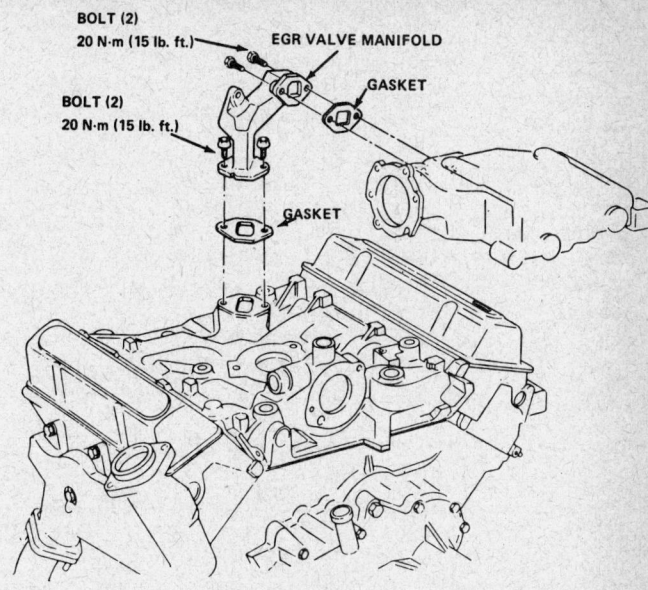

Fig. 18   EGR valve manifold. Except 1979–83 Riviera & all 1984 models

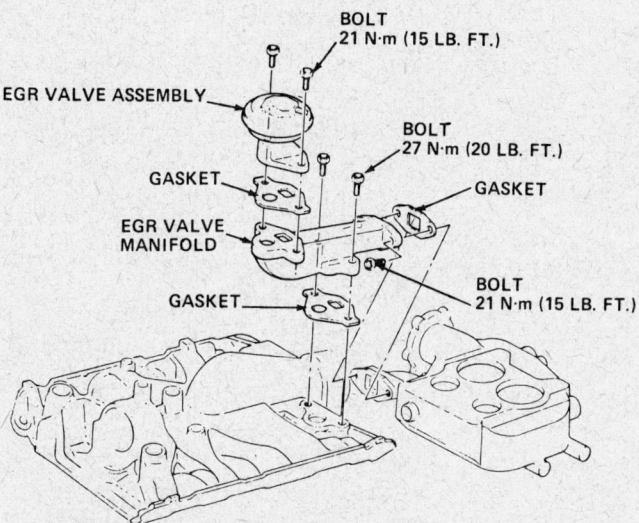

Fig. 19   EGR manifold. 1979–83 Riviera

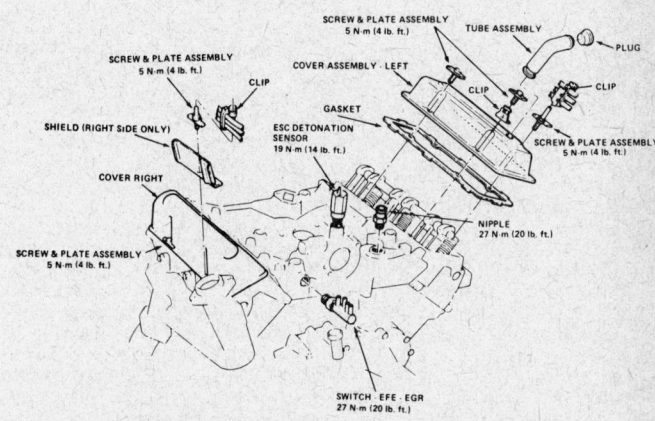

Fig. 20   ESC detonation sensor (typical). 1979–80 models

8. Disconnect plenum front bracket from intake manifold.
9. Remove two bolts attaching turbine housing to bracket on intake manifold.
10. Remove two bolts attaching EGR valve manifold to plenum, then remove AIR bypass hose from pipe.
11. Remove three bolts attaching compressor housing to intake manifold.
12. Remove turbocharger and actuator with carburetor and plenum assembly attached from engine.
13. Remove six bolts attaching turbocharger and actuator assembly to plenum assembly and carburetor Fig. 17.
14. Drain oil from center housing rotating assembly.

1984 Regal
1. Remove air inlet tube at throttle body.

2. Disconnect throttle body vacuum harness connector.
3. Disconnect and plug water and heater hoses from throttle body, then remove throttle body retaining nuts and the throttle body and position aside.
4. Disconnect and plug oil pressure feed line at turbocharger.
5. Disconnect exhaust inlet pipe from exhaust manifold and turbocharger assembly.
6. Disconnect exhaust outlet pipe at turbocharger.
7. Remove upper turbocharger mounting bracket to lower bracket retaining bolts at right side of engine.
8. Remove stabilizer bracket to compressor housing retaining bolt at left side of engine.
9. Remove turbocharger from adapter on intake manifold, Fig. 17A.

EGR Valve Manifold, Replace

1. Disconnect vacuum line.
2. Remove two bolts attaching EGR valve.
3. Remove bolts attaching EGR manifold, Figs. 18 and 19.
4. Reverse procedure to install.

ESC Detonation Sensor, Replace

1. Disconnect wire connector from sensor. Do not pull on wire.
2. Remove the sensor with a deep socket, Figs. 20, 21 & 22.
3. Reverse procedure to install. Torque ESC detonation sensor to 14 ft. lbs. on 1979–83 models and 13 ft. lbs. on 1984 models.

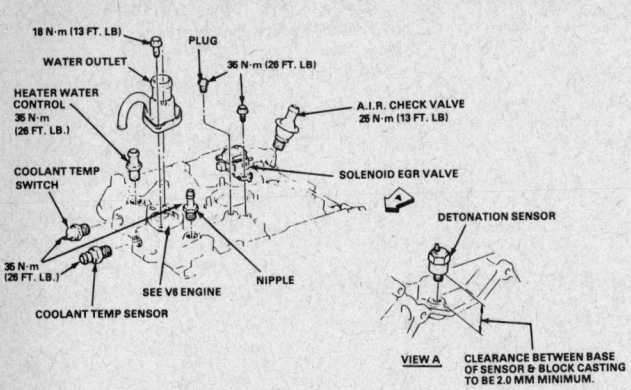

Fig. 21   ESC detonation sensor (typical). 1981–83 models

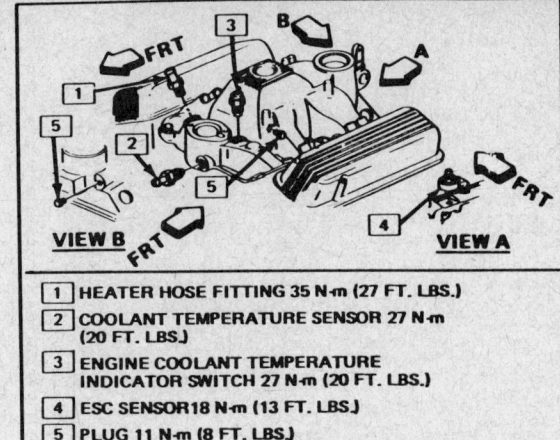

1	HEATER HOSE FITTING 35 N·m (27 FT. LBS.)
2	COOLANT TEMPERATURE SENSOR 27 N·m (20 FT. LBS.)
3	ENGINE COOLANT TEMPERATURE INDICATOR SWITCH 27 N·m (20 FT. LBS.)
4	ESC SENSOR18 N·m (13 FT. LBS.)
5	PLUG 11 N·m (8 FT. LBS.)

Fig. 22   ESC detonation sensor (typical). 1984 models

Clutch and Transmission Section

CLUTCH PEDAL, ADJUST

1. Disconnect return spring from clutch fork.
2. Rotate clutch lever and shaft assembly until pedal is against rubber bumper on dash brace.
3. Push outer end of clutch fork rearward until throwout bearing lightly contacts pressure plate fingers.
4. Install lower push rod in gauge hole and increase length until all lash is removed.
5. Install swivel or rod in hole furthest from centerline of lever and shaft assembly, then install retainer.
6. Tighten lock nut and spacer against swivel and connect clutch fork return spring.
7. Check clutch pedal free travel. Free play should be 55/64 to 129/64 for 1977 Skylark, 45/64 to 15/16 in. for 1977–81 Century and 145/64 to 25/16 in. for 1978–79 Skylark.

CLUTCH, REPLACE

1. Remove transmission.
2. Remove pedal return spring from clutch fork and *disconnect rod assembly from clutch fork.*
3. Remove flywheel housing.
4. Remove clutch throw-out bearing from clutch fork.
5. Disconnect clutch fork from ball stud by moving it toward center of flywheel housing.
6. Mark clutch cover and flywheel so it can be installed in the same position.

7. Loosen clutch cover to flywheel bolts one turn at a time to avoid bending of clutch cover flange until spring pressure is released.
8. Support pressure place and cover assembly while removing last bolts, then remove pressure plate and driven plate.
9. Reverse procedure to install being sure to line up marks made in removal.

3 SPEED TRANS. REPLACE

1. Disconnect speedometer cable from driven gear fitting.
2. Disconnect shift control rods from shifter levers at transmission.
3. Remove propeller shaft.
4. Support rear of engine and remove transmission crossmember.
5. Remove two top transmission attaching bolts and insert guide pins in these holes.
6. Remove two lower bolts and slide transmission straight back and out of vehicle.
7. Reverse procedure to install.

3 SPEED TRANS. SHIFT LINKAGE

Column Shift
1. Place column selector lever in Reverse detent, making sure the steering column selector plate engages lower most column lever (1st-reverse).
2. Loosen 1st-reverse adjusting clamp.
3. Shift transmission lever into reverse and tighten the 1st-reverse clamp.

4. Shift transmission levers into neutral and loosen 2nd-3rd clamp.
5. Install 3/16" diameter rod through 2nd-3rd lever selector plate and the 1st-reverse lever and alignment plate.
6. Tighten 2nd-3rd shift rod clamp.

Floor Shift
1. Place transmission levers in Neutral.
2. Loosen shift rod adjusting clamp bolts on shifter assembly.
3. Insert 1/4" drill rod through shift assembly and shift levers.
4. Tighten clamp bolts.

4 SPEED TRANS. REPLACE

1. Disconnect speedometer cable and remove driven gear.
2. Disconnect shift control rods from transmission.
3. Remove propeller shaft.
4. Support rear of engine and remove transmission support.
5. Remove two top transmission-to-flywheel housing bolts and insert guide pins.
6. Remove two lower bolts.
7. Slide transmission back and out.
8. Reverse procedure to install.

4 SPEED TRANS. SHIFT LINKAGE

Floor Shift
1. Place transmission in neutral.
2. Adjust all three shift rods so a 1/4" drill rod can be installed through shifter assembly and shift levers.
3. Tighten swivel nuts.

Riviera Drive Link Belt

Service procedures on Riviera drive link belt or sprockets are located in GM Front Wheel Drive Section. Refer to Main Index.

Rear Axle, Propeller Shaft & Brakes

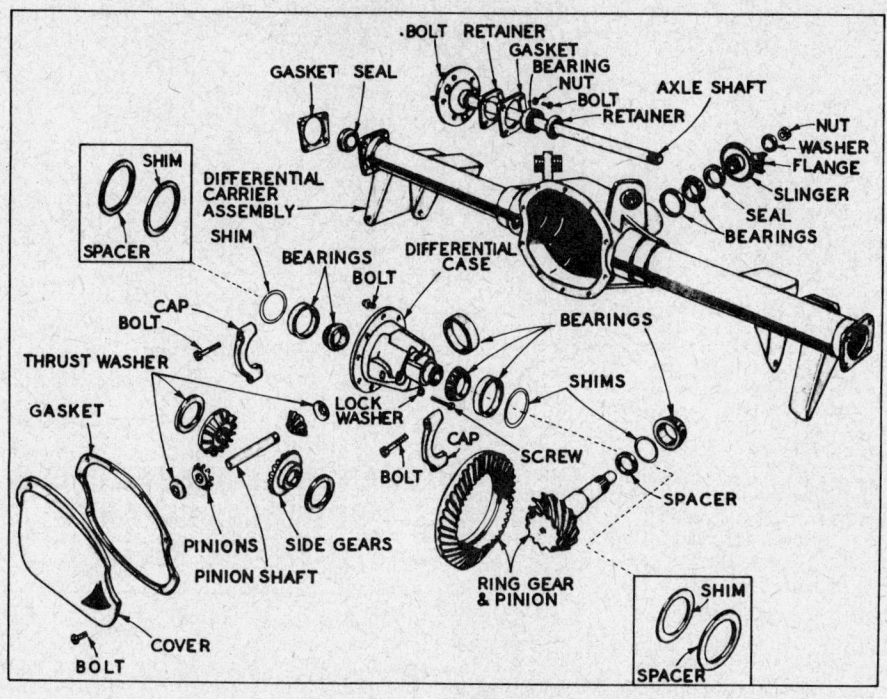

Fig. 1   Rear axle assembly (Typical). 1977–79 type "B"

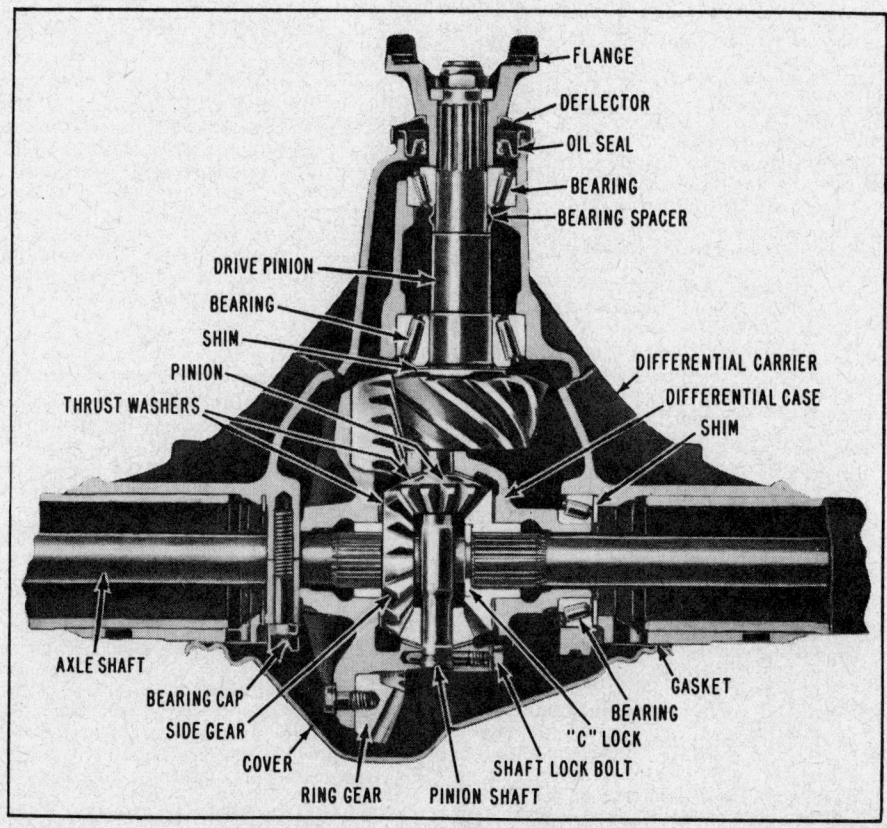

Fig. 1A   Rear axle assembly (Typical). 1977–84
type "C, G, K, O & P"

REAR AXLES

Figs. 1 and 1A illustrate the type rear axle assemblies used on Buicks. When necessary to overhaul any of these units, refer to the *Rear Axle Specifications* table in this chapter.

1977–84

In this rear axle, Figs. 1 and 1A the drive pinion is mounted in two tapered roller bearings which are preloaded by two selected spacers at assembly. The pinion is positioned by shims located between a shoulder on the drive pinion and the rear bearing. The front bearing is held in place by a large nut.

The differential is supported in the carrier by two tapered roller side bearings. These are preloaded by inserting shims between the bearings and the pedestals. The differential assembly is positioned for proper ring gear and pinion backlash by varying these shims. The ring gear is bolted to the case. The case houses two side gears in mesh with two pinions mounted on a pinion axle which is anchored in the case by a spring pin. The pinions and side gears are backed by thrust washers.

REAR AXLE ASSEMBLY, REPLACE

1977–84

It is not necessary to remove the rear axle assembly for any normal repairs but if the housing must be replaced the assembly may be removed as follows:
1. Raise vehicle and support using jack stands under both frame side rails.
2. Mark rear universal joint and flange for proper reassembly and disconnect rear joint.
3. Push propeller shaft as far forward as possible and wire up out of way.
4. Disconnect parking brake cables and rear brake hose. Cover brake hose opening to prevent entrance of dirt.
5. Support axle with jack and disconnect shock absorbers at lower ends. On 1977–79 Skylark models, remove leaf springs as outlined under "Leaf Spring, Replace" procedure in the Rear Suspension section.
6. Disconnect upper control arms at axle housing, then lower axle and remove coil springs.
7. Disconnect lower control arms and remove axle assembly.

AXLE SHAFT, REPLACE

NOTE: Design allows for axle shaft end play of .018" on 1977 "B" axle, .002 to .020" on 1978–79 "B" axles, .022" on 1977 "C", "G", "K", and "O", .025" on 1978–84 "C", "G", "K", "O" and "P" (7½") and .032" on 1977–84 "P" (except 7½"). These axles may be identified by the third letter located on the right rear tube on the forward side. This end play can be checked with the wheel and brake drum re-

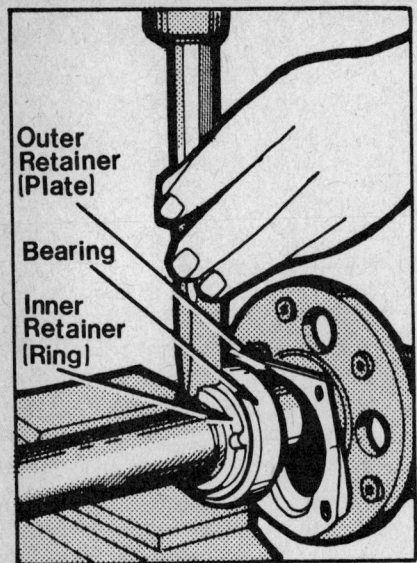

Fig. 2 Removing axle shaft bearing retainer

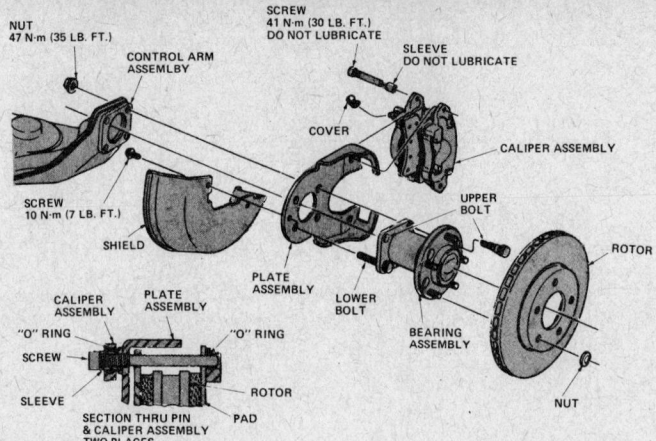

Fig. 3 Rear wheel bearing. 1979—84 Riviera with rear disc brakes

moved by measuring the difference between the end of the housing and the axle shaft flange while moving the axle shaft in and out by hand.

End play over this is excessive. Compensating for all the end play by inserting a shim inboard of the bearing in the housing is not recommended since it ignores the end play of the bearing itself, and may result in improper seating of the gasket or backing plate against the housing. If end play is excessive, the axle shaft and bearing assembly should be removed and the cause of the excessive end play determined and corrected.

Removing Axle Shaft

1977—84 C, G, K, O & P Axles
1. Remove wheels and brake drums.
2. Remove bolts and differential cover and allow lubricant to drain.
3. Remove pinion shaft lock bolt and pinion shaft then push axle shafts inward, remove C-lock and axle shaft.

1977—79 B Axles
1. Remove wheels and brake drums.
2. Remove retainer plate nuts. Pull retainers clear of bolts and reinstall two opposite nuts to hold brake backing plate in place.
3. Pull axle shaft assembly using a puller.

Replacing Axle Shaft Bearings & Seals

1977—84 C, G, K, O & P Axles
1. Using a suitable pry bar, remove seal from housing.

NOTE: Do not damage axle housing.

2. Position tool No. J-23689 behind bearing bore so tangs on tool engage bearing outer race, then using a suitable slide hammer attached to tool No. J-23689, remove bearing.
3. Using suitable gear lubricant, lubricate bearing. Then, using axle bearing installer J-23690, install bearing. Bearing is properly seated when tool bottoms

against housing shoulder.
4. Lubricate seal with suitable gear lubricant, then using seal installer J-21128, tap seal into position until seal is flush with axle tube.
5. Install axle.

1977—79 B Axle
1. Place axle shaft in a vise so that the retainer ring rests on vise jaws. Use a chisel and a hammer to crack the ring, Fig. 2.
2. Press bearing off shaft and remove seal. Inspect seal running surface for bad spots and replace if necessary.

NOTE: Before installing seal, apply grease between seal lips to avoid damaging the seal.

3. Press bearing against shoulder on shaft and retainer ring against bearing using Installer tool J-21022 for intermediate models and J-8609 for full size models.

Axle Shaft, Install

1. Apply a coat of wheel bearing grease in wheel bearing and seal recess.
2. For C, G, K, O and P axles:
   a. Install axle shaft through seal and bearing and through side gear as far in as possible.

NOTE: Do not let shaft drag across seal lip and apply grease between seal lips.

   b. Install C-lock and move axle shaft outward to bottom C-lock in recess of side gear.
   c. Install pinion shaft and torque lock bolt to 20 ft. lbs.
   d. Install gasket and cover and torque bolts to 30 ft. lbs. After 20 minutes, retorque bolts to 30 ft. lbs.
   e. Install correct type and amount of lubricant.
3. For B axle, insert axle shaft through housing and install retaining nuts. Torque retaining nuts to 55 ft. lbs. on 1977 full size models, 35 ft. lbs. on 1978—79 full size, Century and Regal models.
4. Install drum and wheel.

REAR WHEEL BEARING & SPINDLE, REPLACE 1979—84 Riviera

NOTE: The rear wheel bearing is a sealed unit. This bearing is not serviceable for repacking or adjustment. The bearing must not be subjected to heat or early bearing failure may result.

Rear Disc Brakes

Removal
1. Raise and support rear of vehicle.
2. Remove tire and wheel assembly.
3. Mark a wheel stud and a corresponding place on the rotor to assist in installation if bearing is not replaced.
4. Disconnect brake line at bracket on control arm.
5. Remove caliper and rotor assembly.
6. Remove four nuts and bolts securing the spindle to the control arm and remove bearing assembly, Fig. 3.

Installation

NOTE: Before installing bearing, remove all rust and corrosion from bearing mounting surfaces. Lack of a flat surface may result in early bearing failure. A slip fit must exist between the bearing and the control arm assembly.

1. Install rear spindle, shield and plate to lower control arm. Torque nuts to 35 ft. lbs., Fig. 3.
2. If bearing was not replaced, install rotor using reference marks made at time of removal.
3. Install brake caliper assembly.
4. Connect brake line at bracket on control arm, tighten and bleed brake system.
5. Install wheel and tire assembly.
6. Remove support and lower car.

Rear Drum Brakes

Removal
1. Raise and support rear of vehicle.

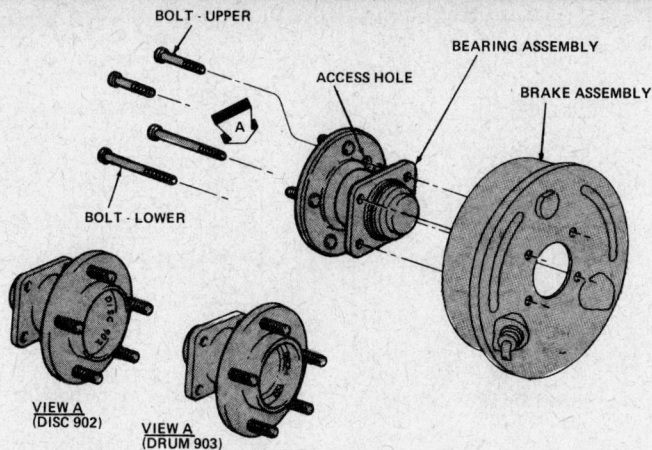

BOLT - UPPER
ACCESS HOLE
BEARING ASSEMBLY
BRAKE ASSEMBLY
BOLT - LOWER
VIEW A
(DISC 902)
VIEW A
(DRUM 903)

Fig. 4 Rear wheel bearing. 1979—84 Riviera with rear drum brakes

2. Remove tire and wheel assembly.
3. Remove brake drum.
4. Remove four nuts attaching rear wheel bearing assembly to control arm.
5. Remove wheel bearing and four attaching bolts Fig. 4.

Installation

NOTE: Before installing bearing, remove all rust and corrosion from bearing mounting surfaces. Lack of a flat surface for any reason may result in early bearing failure. A slip fit must exist between the bearing and the control arm assembly.

1. Install four nuts and bolts attaching wheel bearing to rear control arm assembly Fig. 4. Torque nuts to 35 ft. lbs.
2. Install brake drum.
3. Install wheel and tire assembly.
4. Remove supports and lower car.

PROPELLER SHAFT, REPLACE

NOTE: When service is required, the propeller shaft must be removed from the car as a complete assembly. While handling it out of the car, the assembly must be supported on a straight line as nearly as possible to avoid jamming or bending any of the parts.

1977—84

NOTE: Two attachment methods are used to secure the propeller shaft to the pinion flange or end yoke, a pair of bolted straps or a set of bolted flanges.

1. Scribe alignment marks between propeller shaft and pinion flange or end yoke to aid reassembly.
2. Remove strap or flange bolts at rear of propeller shaft. Tape bearing cups to prevent loss of needle bearings.
3. Slide shaft assembly rearward, disengaging front yoke from transmission output shaft splines and lower from vehicle.
4. Reverse procedure to install.

NOTE: Prior to installing propeller shaft, lubricate all shaft splines with engine oil. When installing propeller shaft, do not attempt to drive in place with hammer. If shaft will not slip into place, inspect for burrs on transmission output shaft splines, twisted slip yoke splines or the wrong U-joint yoke. Repair as necessary.

PROPELLER SHAFT BALANCE

A wheel balancer of the type equipped with a strobe light can be used to facilitate balancing of the driveshaft. The pick-up unit should be placed directly under the nose of the rear axle carrier and as far forward as possible.

1. Place car on twin post lift so rear of car is supported on the rear axle housing and rear wheels are free to rotate.
2. Remove both rear wheels and tire assemblies and reinstall wheel lug nuts with flat side next to drum.
3. Mark and number driveshaft at four points 90° apart at rear of shaft just forward of balance weights.
4. Place strobe light pick-up under nose of differential.
5. With car running in gear at car speed where unbalance is at its peak, allow driveline to stabilize by holding at constant speed. Point strobe light at spinning shaft and note position of one of the reference marks.
6. Shut off engine and position shaft so reference mark will be in position noted when car was running.

CAUTION: Do not run car on hoist for extended periods due to danger of overheating transmission or engine.

7. When strobe light flashed, the heaviest point of the shaft was down. To balance shaft it will be necessary to apply weight 180° away. Screw type hose clamps can be used as weights as shown in Fig. 5.

BRAKE ADJUSTMENTS

1977—84 Self-Adjusting Drum Brakes

These brakes have self-adjusting shoe mechanisms that assure correct lining-to-drum clearances at all times. The automatic adjusters operate only when the brakes are applied as the car is moving rearward.

Although the brakes are self-adjusting, an initial adjustment is necessary after the brake shoes have been relined or replaced, or when the length of the adjusting screw has been changed during some other service operation.

Frequent usage of an automatic transmission forward range to halt reverse vehicle motion may prevent the automatic adjusters from functioning, thereby inducing low pedal heights. Should low pedal heights be encountered, it is recommended that numerous forward and reverse stops be made until satisfactory pedal height is obtained.

NOTE: If a low pedal condition cannot be corrected by making numerous reverse stops (provided the hydraulic system is free of air) it indicates that the self-adjusting mechanism is not functioning. Therefore, it will be necessary to remove the brake drum, clean, free up and lubricate the adjusting mechanism. Then adjust the brakes as follows, being sure the parking brake is fully released.

Adjustment

1. Remove adjusting hole cover from backing plate. Turn brake adjusting screw to expand shoes until wheel can just be turned by hand.

HEAVY SPOT

HEAVY SPOT

HEAVY SPOT

STEP 1
DETERMINE POINT OF UNBALANCE

STEP 2
ADD HOSE CLAMPS 180° FROM POINT OF UNBALANCE UNTIL THEY BECOME HEAVY SPOT

STEP 3
ROTATE TWO CLAMPS EQUALLY AWAY FROM EACH OTHER UNTIL BEST BALANCE IS ACHIEVED

Fig. 5 Positioning hose clamps to balance shaft

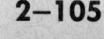

2. Using suitable tool to hold actuator away from adjuster, Fig. 6, back off adjuster 30 notches. If shoes still drag, back off one or two additional notches.

NOTE: Brakes should be free of drag when adjuster has been backed off approximately 12 notches. Heavy drag at this point indicates tight parking brake cables.

3. Install adjusting hole cover and check parking adjustment.

CAUTION: *If finger movement will not turn the screw, free it up. If this is not done, the actuator will not turn the screw during subsequent vehicle operation. Lubricate the screw with oil and coat with wheel bearing grease. Any other adjustment procedure may cause damage to the adjusting screw with consequent self-adjuster problems.*

4. Install wheel and drum, and adjusting hole cover. Adjust brakes on remaining wheels in the same manner.
5. If pedal height is not satisfactory, drive the vehicle and make sufficient reverse stops until proper pedal height is obtained.

PARKING BRAKE, ADJUST

1977–84 W/Rear Disc Brakes

1. Lubricate parking brake cables at equalizer and underbody rub points. Check all cables for freedom of operation.
2. Fully release parking brake and raise vehicle.
3. Hold cable stud from turning and tighten equalizer nut until cable slack is removed and levers are against stops on caliper housing. If levers are off stops, loosen cable until levers return to stop.
4. Operate parking brake several times to check adjustment. When properly adjusted, the parking brake pedal should move 5¼ inch to 6¾ inch when a force of approximately 125 pounds is applied on all except Riviera. On Riviera, the parking brake pedal should move 4 inch to 5½ inch when a force of approximately 125 pounds is applied.

1977–84 W/Rear Drum Brakes

Need for parking brake adjustment is indi-

BACKING PLATE
J-21281
J-6166 WRENCH
TO EXPAND SHOES MOVE END OF TOOL UPWARD

Fig. 6 Adjusting drum brakes

cated if the service brake operates with good pedal reserve but the parking brake pedal can be depressed a minimum of 9 ratchet clicks but not more than 16 on 1977–84 models, under heavy foot pressure. After making sure that the service brakes are properly adjusted, adjust the parking brake as follows:

1. Depress parking brake exactly three ratchet clicks on 1977 models except Skylark, two ratchet clicks on Skylark and all 1978–84 models.
2. Loosen jam nut, and tighten adjusting nut until rear wheels can just be turned rearward using both hands but are locked when forward motion is attempted.
3. Tighten jam nut and release parking brake. Rear wheels should turn freely in either direction with no brake drag.

MASTER CYLINDER, REPLACE

1977–84

1. Disconnect brake pipes from master cylinder and tape end of pipes to prevent entrance of dirt.
2. On manual brakes, disconnect brake pedal from master cylinder push rod.
3. Remove two nuts holding master cylinder to dash or power cylinder and remove master cylinder from car.

POWER BRAKE UNIT, REPLACE

1977–84 Exc. Hydro-Boost

1. Remove two nuts attaching master cylinder to brake unit, then position master cylinder away from brake unit with brake lines attached.

NOTE: Use care not to bend or kink brake lines.

2. Disconnect vacuum hose from check valve. Plug vacuum hose to prevent dirt from entering.
3. Remove four nuts holding power unit to dash.
4. Remove retainer and washer from brake pedal pin and disengage push rod eye or clevis.
5. Remove power unit from car.

Hydro-Boost

NOTE: Pump brake pedal several times with engine off to deplete accumulator of fluid.

1. Remove two nuts attaching master cylinder to booster, then move master cylinder away from booster with brake lines attached.
2. Remove three hydraulic lines from booster. Plug and cap all lines and outlets.
3. Remove retainer and washer securing booster push rod to brake pedal arm.
4. Remove four nuts attaching booster unit to dash panel.
5. From engine compartment, loosen booster from dash panel and move booster push rod inboard until it disconnects from brake pedal arm. Remove spring washer from brake pedal arm.
6. Remove booster unit from vehicle.
7. Reverse procedure to install. To purge system, disconnect feed wire from injection pump or ignition system. Fill power steering pump reservoir, then crank engine for several seconds and recheck power steering pump fluid level. Connect feed wheel and start engine, then cycle steering wire from stop to stop twice and stop engine. Discharge accumulator by depressing brake pedal several times, then check fluid level. Start engine, then turn steering wheel from stop to stop and turn engine off. Check fluid level and add fluid as necessary. If foaming occurs, stop engine and wait for approximately one hour for foam to dissipate, then recheck fluid level.

Rear Suspension

SHOCK ABSORBER, REPLACE

1. With the rear axle supported properly, disconnect shock absorber from lower mounting bracket. On models equipped with automatic level control, disconnect air hose from shock absorber.
2. Disconnect shock absorber upper end from underbody attachment.
3. Reverse procedure to install.

LEAF SPRINGS & BUSHINGS, REPLACE

1977–79 Skylark

1. Support vehicle at frame and rear axle, relieving tension from spring.
2. Disconnect shock absorber from lower mounting.
3. Loosen spring front mount bolt.
4. Remove spring front mounting bracket attaching screws, lower axle and remove bracket.

5. Disconnect parking brake cable from spring plate bracket.
6. Remove "U" bolts and spring plate.
7. Support spring, remove front mount bolt and disassemble rear shackle.
8. Replace rear shackle and spring eye bushings as necessary, Figs. 1 and 2.
9. Reverse procedure to install.

LEAF SPRING SERVICE

1977–79 Skylark

NOTE: The spring leaves are not serviced sep-

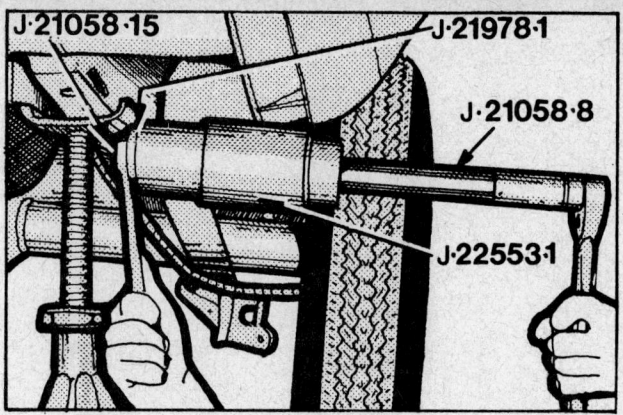

Fig. 1 Leaf spring bushings removal. 1977—79 Skylark

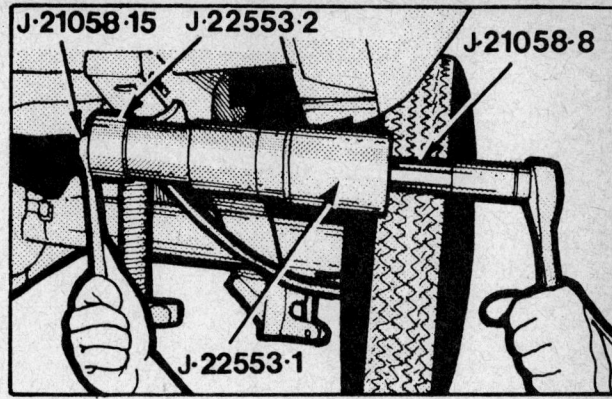

Fig. 2 Leaf spring bushings installation. 1977—79 Skylark

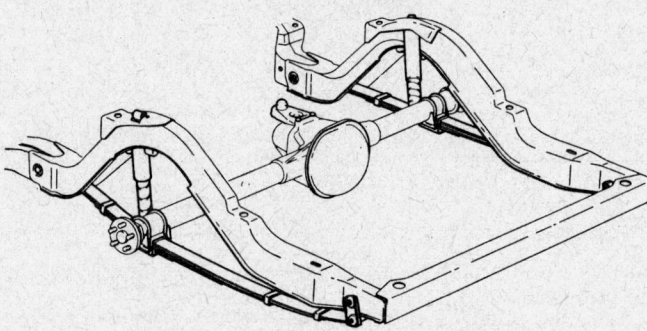

Fig. 3 Leaf spring suspension (typical)

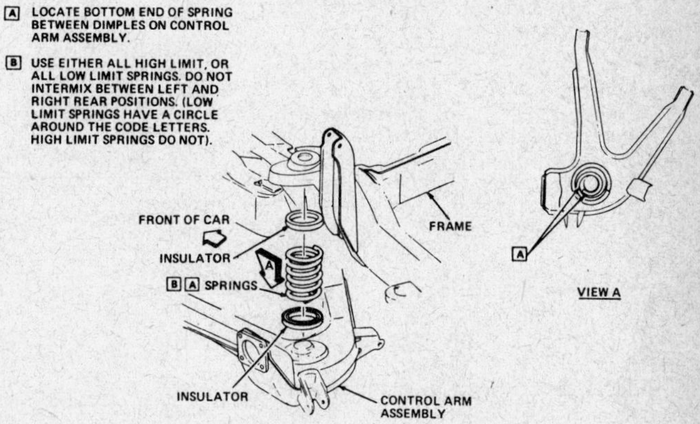

Ⓐ LOCATE BOTTOM END OF SPRING BETWEEN DIMPLES ON CONTROL ARM ASSEMBLY.

Ⓑ USE EITHER ALL HIGH LIMIT, OR ALL LOW LIMIT SPRINGS. DO NOT INTERMIX BETWEEN LEFT AND RIGHT REAR POSITIONS. (LOW LIMIT SPRINGS HAVE A CIRCLE AROUND THE CODE LETTERS. HIGH LIMIT SPRINGS DO NOT).

Fig. 4 Coil spring suspension. 1979—84 Riviera

arately, however, the spring leaf inserts may be replaced.

1. Clamp spring in a vise and remove spring clips.
2. File peened end of center bolt to permit nut removal, remove nut and open vise slowly, allowing spring to expand.
3. Replace spring leaf inserts as necessary.
4. Use a drift to align center bolt holes, compress spring in vise and install new center bolt and nut. Peen end of bolt to retain nut.
5. Align springs and bend spring clips into position.

NOTE: Overtightening of spring clips will cause spring binding.

COIL SPRINGS, REPLACE

1979—84 Riviera

1. Raise and support rear of vehicle.
2. Using a suitable jack support lower control arm.

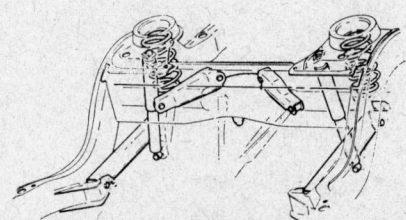

Fig. 5 Coil spring suspension.
Except 1979—84 Riviera

3. Disconnect automatic level control air hose from shock absorber. If removing spring from left hand side of vehicle, disconnect level control link from control arm.
4. Disconnect shock absorber from upper mounting.
5. Lower the control arm until all spring tension is relieved, then remove spring.
6. Reverse procedure to install. Locate spring as shown in Fig. 4.

Except 1979—84 Riviera

1. Support vehicle at frame and support rear axle with a suitable jack.
2. Disconnect shock absorbers from lower mounting brackets, Fig. 5, then the brake hose from the axle housing.
3. Disconnect upper control arms at differential.

4. Lower jack fully, extending springs, then remove springs.

NOTE: Do not allow the brake hose to become kinked or stretched.

5. Reverse procedure to install. Refer to Fig. 6, for correct coil spring staggering. After installation, bleed brakes.

CONTROL ARMS, REPLACE

NOTE: Remove and replace one control arm at a time as axle assembly may slip sideways, making installation difficult.

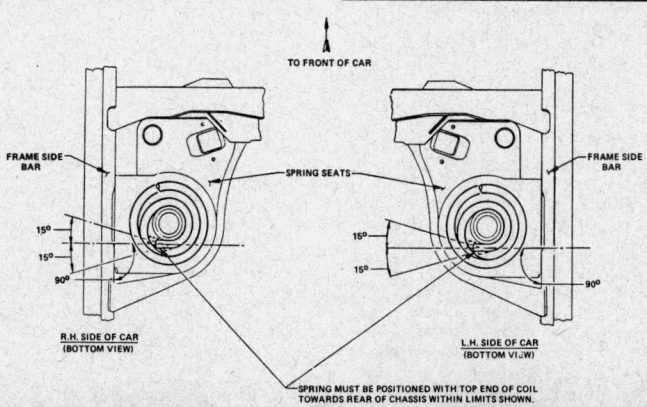

Fig. 6 Coil spring suspension. Except 1979—84 Riviera

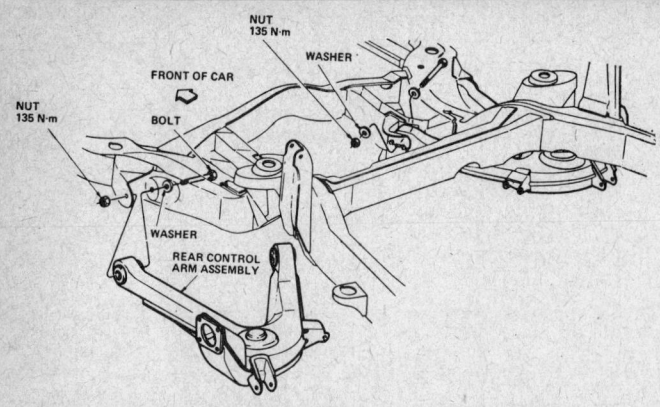

Fig. 7 Control arm assembly. 1979–84 Riviera

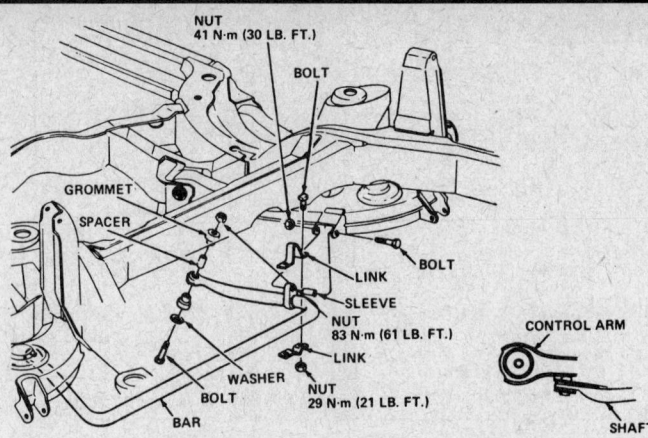

Fig. 8 Rear Stabilizer installation. 1979–84 Riviera

1979–84 Riviera

1. Raise and support rear of vehicle, then remove wheel and tire assembly.
2. Disconnect brake line at bracket on control arm.
3. Remove stabilizer bar. Refer to "Stabilizer Bar, Replace".
4. Remove rear wheel bearing and spindle. Refer to "Rear Wheel Bearing And Spindle, Replace" in Rear Axle, Propeller Shaft and Brakes Section.
5. If removing left hand control arm, disconnect automatic level control link from control arm.
6. Using a suitable jack, support control arm.
7. Disconnect air hose from shock absorber, then detach shock absorber from upper and lower mountings.
8. Lower control arm until all spring tension is relieved, then remove spring and insulators.
9. Remove two bolts attaching control arm to frame and remove control arm, Fig. 7.

Except 1979–84 Riviera

Upper Control Arms
1. Support vehicle at frame and rear axle.

2. Remove control arm mount bolts from frame and axle housing attachments, Fig. 5.
3. Reverse procedure to install.

NOTE: Control arm bolts must be tightened with vehicle at curb height.

Lower Control Arm
Lower control arms may be removed and replaced using the "Upper Control Arms" procedure. However, it may be necessary to reposition the jack farther forward under carrier to aid in removing rear mount bolt. Also, a brass drift may be needed to remove mount bolts.

STABILIZER BAR, REPLACE

1977–79 Skylark

1. Support vehicle at rear axle.
2. Disconnect stabilizer bar from spring

plate brackets, Fig. 9.
3. Disconnect stabilizer bar from body brackets.
4. Reverse procedure to install. Tighten attaching bolts with vehicle at curb height.

1979–84 Riviera

1. Raise and support rear of vehicle, Fig. 8.
2. Remove bolts attaching front of stabilizer bar to control arms.
3. Remove inside nut and bolt from each side of stabilizer bar link, then loosen nut and bolt on outside of link.
4. Rotate bottom parts of link to one side and slide stabilizer bar out of bushings.

Except 1977–79 Skylark & 1979–84 Riviera

1. Support vehicle at rear axle.
2. Remove stabilizer bar attaching bolts from brackets on lower control arms, Fig. 10.
3. Reverse procedure to install.

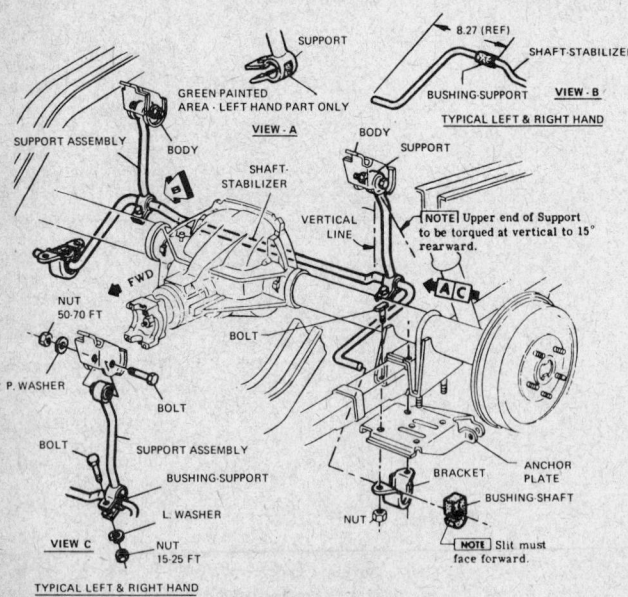

Fig. 9 Stabilizer bar installation. 1977–79 Skylark

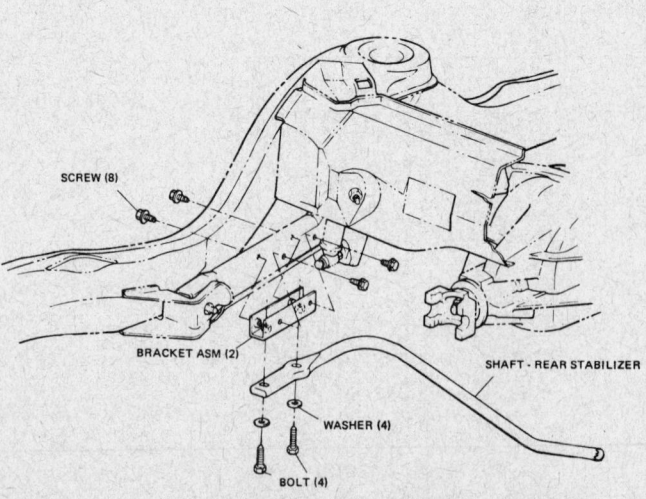

Fig. 10 Stabilizer bar installation exc. 1977–79 Skylark & 1979–84 Riviera (Typical)

Front Suspension & Steering Section

Refer to Main Index for Front Drive Axle Service.
For front suspension & steering service procedures on 1979—84 Riviera, refer to Cadillac,
"Front End & Steering Section, Eldorado & 1980—84 Seville."

FRONT SUSPENSION

On this type front suspension, Fig. 1, each wheel is connected independently to the vehicle frame by upper and lower control arms, ball joints and a steering knuckle. The upper and lower control arms are designed and positioned to allow the steering knuckles to move in a prescribed three dimensional arc. Tie rods, connected to the steering knuckles, ensure the front wheels are held in the proper relationship to each other.

A ball joint is riveted to the outer end of the upper arm and is spring loaded to insure proper alignment of the ball in the socket.

The inner end of the lower control arm has pressed-in bushings. Two bolts, passing through the bushings, attach the arm to the frame. The lower ball joint is a press fit in the arm and attaches to the steering knuckle with a castellated nut that is retained with a cotter pin.

Rubber seals are provided on upper and lower shafts and at ball socket assemblies to exclude dirt and moisture from bearing surfaces. Grease fittings are provided at all bearing locations.

WHEEL ALIGNMENT

NOTE: Prior to checking or resetting caster and camber angles, bounce the front end at least twice to allow vehicle to return to normal trim height.

Caster and camber are adjusted by shimming at the upper control arm shaft attaching points.

Adding shims at the front locations will change caster toward negative with practically no change in camber. Adding shims at the rear locations will change caster toward positive and camber toward negative. Adding equal shims at both front and rear locations will not change caster but will change camber toward negative.

To adjust, loosen both front and rear nuts to free shims for removal or addition. After installing or removing shims, torque shaft nuts to 75 ft. lbs. on all 1977 models and 1978—84 models except Century and Regal and 46 ft. lbs. for 1978—81 Century and 1978—84 Regal.

NOTE: A normal service shim pack should leave at least two threads exposed beyond the shaft nuts after final tightening. The difference between front and rear shim packs should not exceed .40 inch.

TOE-IN, ADJUST

NOTE: Prior to checking or resetting toe-in, bounce the front end at least twice to allow vehicle to return to normal trim height.

1. Ensure wheel bearings are adjusted properly. Refer to "Wheel Bearings, Adjust".
2. Using suitable alignment equipment, with steering wheel in the straight ahead position, check toe-in.
3. If toe-in is not within specifications, loosen tie rod adjustable sleeves clamp bolts.
4. Turn tie rod adjustable sleeves an equal amount of turns but in opposite directions to bring toe-in within specifications.
5. Ensure tie rod end housings are at right angles to the steering arm, then position and torque tie rod adjustable sleeves and clamps as shown in Fig. 2.

WHEEL BEARINGS, ADJUST

1. Raise and support front of vehicle.
2. Remove wheel hub dust cap.
3. Remove spindle nut cotter pin, then while rotating wheel assembly forward, torque spindle nut to 12 ft. lbs. to seat bearings.
4. Loosen spindle nut slightly to "the just loose" position.
5. Hand tighten spindle nut, then install cotter pin. If cotter pin cannot be installed, loosen spindle nut until hole in the spindle lines up with a slot in the nut. Do not loosen more then 1/2 flat of the nut.
6. With wheel bearings properly adjusted, end play should be .001 to .005 inch.

WHEEL BEARINGS, REPLACE

1. Raise and support vehicle and remove front wheels.
2. Remove brake tube support bracket bolt. Do not disconnect hydraulic tube or hose.
3. Remove caliper to mounting bracket bolts. Hang caliper from upper suspension.

NOTE: Do not place strain on brake line.

4. Remove spindle nut and hub and disc assembly. Inner wheel bearing and grease retainer can now be removed.

CHECKING BALL JOINTS FOR WEAR

If loose ball joints are suspected, first be sure front wheel bearings are properly ad-

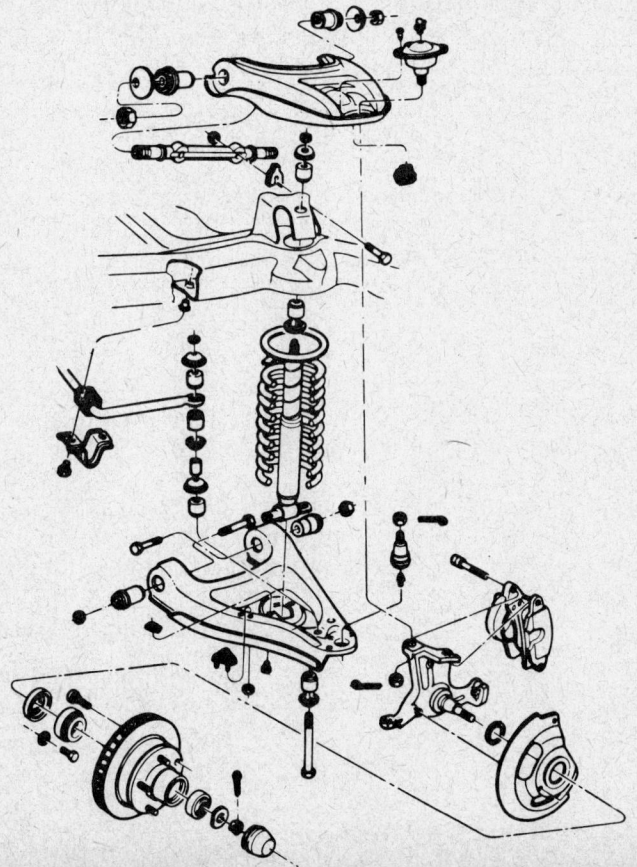

Fig. 1   Front suspension (typical). 1977—84

justed and that control arms are tight. Then check ball joints as follows:

Upper Ball Joint

1. Raise front of vehicle with jacks placed between coil spring pockets and ball joint of lower control arm.
2. On 1977–79 models, grasp wheel at top and bottom and shake top of wheel in and out. On 1980–84 models, position a suitable dial indicator at top of wheel rim, then grasp wheel top and bottom, while pulling out top, push in bottom and read dial indicator. Reverse the push-pull procedure and read dial indicator.
3. On 1977–79 models, if any looseness is detected, replace ball joint. On 1980–84 models, if dial indicator reading exceeds .125 inch, the upper ball joint should be replaced.

Lower Ball Joint

A wear indicator is built into the ball joint. Remove dirt deposits around service plug and observe position of nipple. Refer to Fig. 3 for wear tolerance.

BALL JOINTS, REPLACE

NOTE: On all models the upper ball joint is spring-loaded in its socket. If the ball stud has any perceptible shake or if it can be twisted with the fingers, the ball joint should be replaced.

On all models, the lower ball joint is not spring-loaded and depends upon car weight to load the ball. The lower ball joint should never be replaced merely because it "feels" loose when in an unloaded condition.

Upper ball joints on all models are riveted to the control arm and can be replaced.

Lower ball joints on all models are pressed into the control arm and can be replaced with a suitable ball joint tool.

CAUTION: When servicing lower ball joints, be sure to support lower control arm with a suitable jack. If lower control arm is not supported and steering knuckle is disconnected from control arm, the heavily compressed front spring will be completely released.

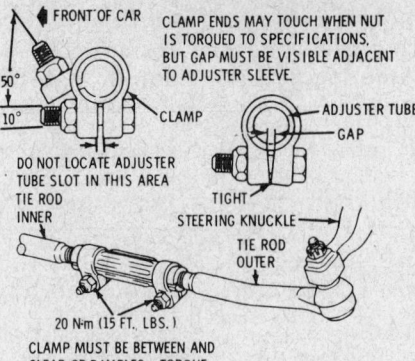

BOLTS MUST BE INSTALLED IN DIRECTION SHOWN, ROTATE BOTH INNER AND OUTER TIE ROD HOUSINGS REARWARD TO THE LIMIT OF BALL JOINT TRAVEL BEFORE TIGHTENING CLAMPS. WITH THIS SAME REARWARD ROTATION ALL BOLT CENTERLINES MUST BE BETWEEN ANGLES SHOWN AFTER TIGHTENING CLAMPS.

FRONT OF CAR

50°

10°

CLAMP

CLAMP ENDS MAY TOUCH WHEN NUT IS TORQUED TO SPECIFICATIONS, BUT GAP MUST BE VISIBLE ADJACENT TO ADJUSTER SLEEVE.

ADJUSTER TUBE

GAP

DO NOT LOCATE ADJUSTER TUBE SLOT IN THIS AREA
TIE ROD INNER

TIGHT

STEERING KNUCKLE

TIE ROD OUTER

20 N·m (15 FT. LBS.)

CLAMP MUST BE BETWEEN AND CLEAR OF DIMPLES. TORQUE NUTS TO SPECIFICATION.

Fig. 2 Tie rod adjustable sleeve & clamp installation

Upper Ball Joint

1. Support vehicle at frame and remove wheel assembly.
2. Remove cotter pin from upper ball joint stud, loosen nut approximately 2 turns, do not remove nut.
3. Position tool as shown in Fig. 4, turn threaded end of tool until stud disengages knuckle.
4. Position jack under lower control arm at spring seat, raise jack until compression is relieved from upper control arm bumper.
5. Remove stud nut, lift control arm from steering knuckle and place a block of wood between control arm and frame.
6. On all models,
   a. Center punch rivet head as close to center as possible.
   b. Using a 1/8 inch twist drill, drill through center of rivet approximately 1/2 rivet length deep.
   c. Enlarge hole using a 7/32 inch drill.
   d. Using a chisel, remove rivet heads, then drive rivets out using a suitable punch.
7. Position ball joint on upper control arm. Install bolts through bottom of control arm with nuts on top, torque to 8 ft. lbs.
8. On all models, position ball joint stud so

cotter pin hole is facing forward and remove wooden block from between control arm and frame.
9. Place wheels in straight ahead position, raise jack under lower control until ball joint stud can be installed in steering knuckle.
10. Install castellated nut on ball joint stud. Torque nut to 60 ft. lbs. on 1978 Skylark, 50 ft. lbs. on all 1977 models, 61 ft. lbs. on 1978–79 models except Skylark, 63 ft. lbs. on 1979 Skylark and 65 ft. lbs. on all 1980–84 models.

NOTE: If cotter pin holes do not align, do not loosen nut, however, tighten until cotter pin can be installed.

11. Install wheel assembly and lower vehicle.

Lower Ball Joint

1. Support vehicle under frame side rails.

NOTE: Position jack under lower control at outboard end, raise jack until it is 1/2 inch below control arm.

2. Remove cotter pin, loosen ball joint stud nut approximately 2 turns, do not remove nut.
3. Position tool as shown in Fig. 4, turn threaded end of tool until ball joint stud is disengaged from steering knuckle.
4. Position jack under lower control arm at spring seat and raise jack until compression is removed from upper control arm bumper.
5. Remove lower ball joint stud nut and position steering knuckle aside.
6. Using tool No. J-9519-10, remove ball joint from lower control arm.
7. Position ball joint on control arm with bleed vent on rubber boot facing inward.
8. Install tool J-9519-10 and turn threaded end of tool until ball joint is fully seated in lower control arm.
9. Position new ball joint stud so cotter pin hole is facing forward.
10. Place wheels in the straight ahead position and install ball joint stud on steering knuckle.
11. Install stud nut and cotter pin. Torque nut to 70 ft. lbs. on all 1977 models and 85 ft. lbs. on 1978–79 all models, except Skylark, and 81 ft. lbs. on 1979 Skylark and all 1980–84 models.

NOTE: If cotter pin holes do not align do not loosen stud nut, tighten nut until cot-

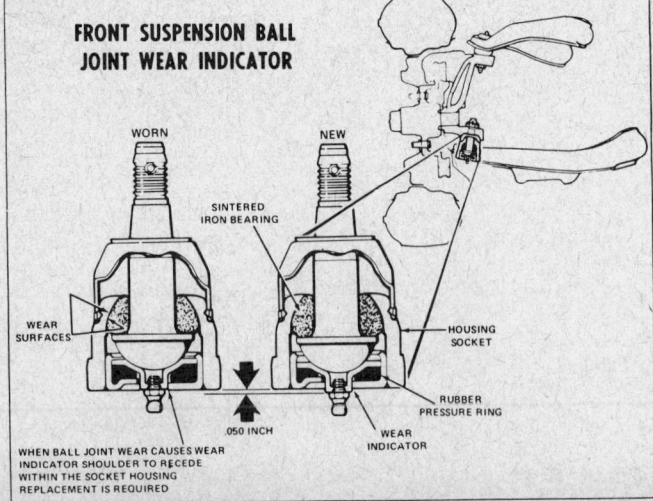

FRONT SUSPENSION BALL JOINT WEAR INDICATOR

WORN

NEW

SINTERED IRON BEARING

WEAR SURFACES

HOUSING SOCKET

RUBBER PRESSURE RING

WEAR INDICATOR

.050 INCH

WHEN BALL JOINT WEAR CAUSES WEAR INDICATOR SHOULDER TO RECEDE WITHIN THE SOCKET HOUSING REPLACEMENT IS REQUIRED

Fig. 3 Lower ball joint check

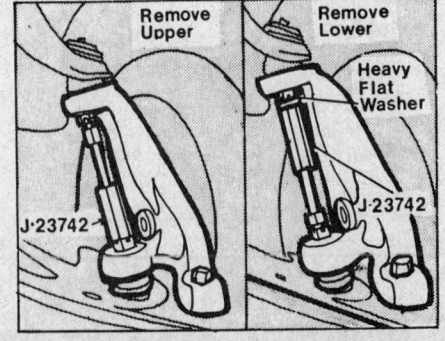

Remove Upper

Remove Lower

Heavy Flat Washer

J-23742

J-23742

Fig. 4 Removing ball joint stud from steering knuckle

ter pin can be installed.

12. Install wheel assembly.

SHOCK ABSORBER, REPLACE

Unfasten shock absorber at top and bottom and remove it through the spring seat. Check shock absorber for obvious physical damage or oil leakage. Push and pull shock absorber in an upright position. If smooth hydraulic resistance is not present in both directions, replace shock absorber.

COIL SPRING, REPLACE

1. Raise and support vehicle at frame.
2. Remove shock absorber lower mount, then push shock up through control arm and into spring.
3. Remove stabilizer bar from lower control arm. Refer to "Stabilizer Bar, Replace".
4. Position a tool No. J-23028 at lower control arm pivot bolts, Fig. 5.
5. Position a suitable jack under tool installed in step 4 and chain together, then raise jack slightly to remove tension from lower control arm pivot bolts.
6. Using a suitable chain, secure lower control arm and coil spring together.
7. Remove rear lower control arm pivot bolt, then front bolt.
8. Slowly lower jack with lower control arm and spring attached.
9. When spring compression is relieved, remove spring.
10. Reverse procedure to install. Refer to Figs. 6 and 7, for proper installation.

Fig. 5   Removing front coil spring

STABILIZER BAR, REPLACE

1. Raise and support front of vehicle.
2. Remove nut, link bolt, retainers, grommets, spacer and stabilizer linkage from lower control arms.
3. Remove bracket to frame bolts, then remove stabilizer shaft, rubber bushings and brackets. On 1978—81 Century and 1978—84 Regal models, use tool No. J-25359-20 to remove stabilizer shaft bolt.
4. Reverse procedure to install. Note the following:
   a. When installing rubber bushings, bushings should be positioned squarely in the brackets with the bushing slit facing front of vehicle.
   b. Torque stabilizer link nut to 13 ft. lbs. and bracket bolts to 25 ft. lbs.

MANUAL STEERING GEAR, REPLACE

1977—80 All Models

1. Remove two nuts or pinch bolt securing lower coupling to steering shaft flange.
2. Use a suitable puller to remove pitman arm.
3. Unfasten gear (3 bolts) from frame and remove from car.
4. Reverse procedure to install.

POWER STEERING, GEAR REPLACE

1977—84

1. Disconnect pressure and return line hoses at steering gear and elevate ends of hoses higher than pump to prevent oil from draining out of pump.
2. Remove pinch bolt securing coupling to steering gear.
3. Jack up car and remove pitman shaft nut, then use a suitable puller to remove pitman arm.
4. On full size models, remove sheet metal baffle that covers frame-to-gear attaching bolts, if equipped.
5. Loosen the three frame-to-steering gear bolts and remove steering gear.
6. Reverse procedure to install.

POWER STEERING PUMP, REPLACE

1. Disconnect battery ground cable.
2. Remove steering pump belt, alternator belt and air conditioning compressor belt, if equipped.
3. On 1977—79 models, remove steering pump bracket from engine. On 1980—81 models, remove steering pump pulley using tool J-25304 or equivalent.
4. Disconnect steering pump hoses from pump and plug all open lines and fittings to prevent entry of dirt.
5. Remove pump or pump with brackets from engine.
6. Reverse procedure to install.

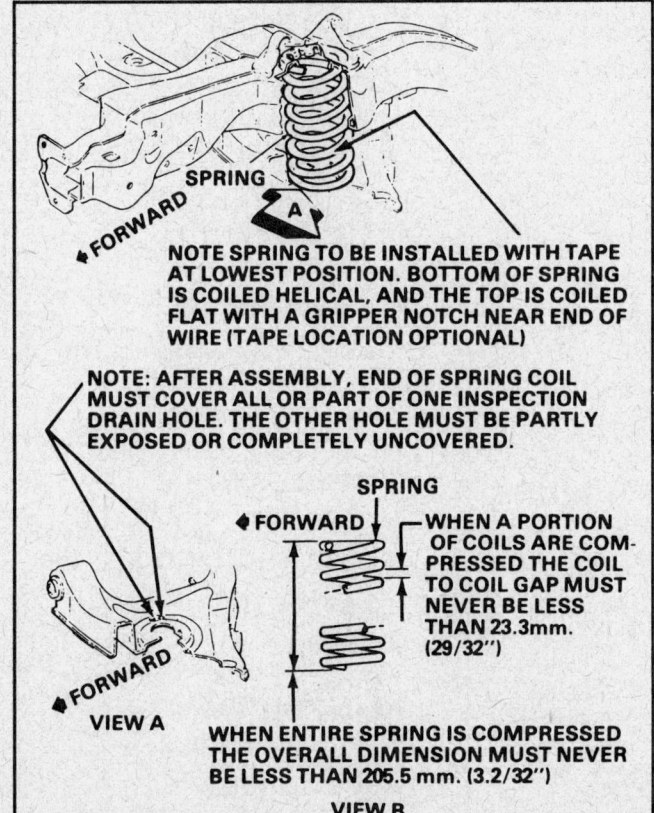

NOTE SPRING TO BE INSTALLED WITH TAPE AT LOWEST POSITION. BOTTOM OF SPRING IS COILED HELICAL, AND THE TOP IS COILED FLAT WITH A GRIPPER NOTCH NEAR END OF WIRE (TAPE LOCATION OPTIONAL)

NOTE: AFTER ASSEMBLY, END OF SPRING COIL MUST COVER ALL OR PART OF ONE INSPECTION DRAIN HOLE. THE OTHER HOLE MUST BE PARTLY EXPOSED OR COMPLETELY UNCOVERED.

WHEN A PORTION OF COILS ARE COMPRESSED THE COIL TO COIL GAP MUST NEVER BE LESS THAN 23.3mm. (29/32")

WHEN ENTIRE SPRING IS COMPRESSED THE OVERALL DIMENSION MUST NEVER BE LESS THAN 205.5 mm. (3.2/32")

VIEW A

VIEW B

Fig. 6   Coil spring installation. All exc. Full size models

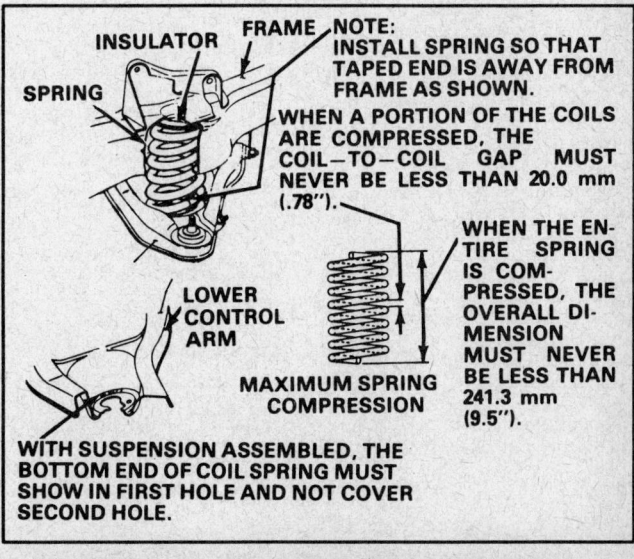

INSULATOR   FRAME   NOTE: INSTALL SPRING SO THAT TAPED END IS AWAY FROM FRAME AS SHOWN.

WHEN A PORTION OF THE COILS ARE COMPRESSED, THE COIL-TO-COIL GAP MUST NEVER BE LESS THAN 20.0 mm (.78").

WHEN THE ENTIRE SPRING IS COMPRESSED, THE OVERALL DIMENSION MUST NEVER BE LESS THAN 241.3 mm (9.5").

LOWER CONTROL ARM

MAXIMUM SPRING COMPRESSION

WITH SUSPENSION ASSEMBLED, THE BOTTOM END OF COIL SPRING MUST SHOW IN FIRST HOLE AND NOT COVER SECOND HOLE.

Fig. 7   Coil spring installation. Full size models

CADILLAC
EXC. CIMARRON
INDEX OF SERVICE OPERATIONS

> **NOTE: Refer to main index, "GM Front Wheel Drive," for front drive axle & drive link belt service procedures on 1977–84 Eldorado & 1980–84 Seville. Also refer to the front of this manual for vehicle manufacturer's special service tool suppliers.**

SERIAL NUMBER LOCATION:

On top of instrument panel, left front.

ENGINE NUMBER LOCATION:

On all engines except V6-252, V8-250 and V8-350, engine unit number is located on cylinder block behind left cylinder head. V.I.N. derivative is located on cylinder block behind intake manifold.

The engine identification number on V6-252 engines is stamped on the left rear of cylinder block.

On 1977–78 V8-350, engine identification number is located on left hand side of cylinder block at front below cylinder head. On 1979–82 V8-350, engine code label is located on top of left hand valve cover and engine unit number label is located on top of right hand valve cover. On 1983–84 V8-350, engine code label is located on front left side of crankcase below the cylinder head.

On 1982–84 V8-250 engines, the engine identification plate is located on a pad at the lower left side of the crankcase.

ENGINE IDENTIFICATION

Year/Engine	V.I.N	Engine Code
1977		
V8-350①②	R	—
V8-425③	S	—
V8-425②	T	—
1978		
V8-350①②	B	—
V8-350④	N	—
V8-425③	S	—
V8-425②	T	—
1979		
V8-350④⑤	N	C2, C3, C4, C5, C6
V8-350④⑥	N	E2, E3, E4, E5, E6
V8-350④⑦	N	K2, K3, K4, K5, K6
V8-350②⑤	B	EA, EC
V8-350②⑦	B	KA, KB
V8-425②⑤	T	JAA, JBA, JCA, JDA, JFA
V8-425③⑤	S	JHA

Year/Engine	V.I.N.	Engine Code
1980		
V6-252⑦	4	MF, MZ
V8-350④⑤	N	VCJ, VCS, VBW
V8-350④⑥⑦	N	VBK, VCK
V8-350②⑥⑦	8	HFA, VBX
V8-368③⑤	6	HAA, HBA, KA
V8-368②⑥	9	HDA
V8-368②⑦	9	HHA
1981		
V6-252⑧	4	SA, SB, SC, SD, SF, SG, SJ, SK, SL, SM, SN, SP, SQ
V8-350④	N	VKB, VKC, VKH, VKJ, VKN, VKR, VKU, VKY, VLA, VLC, VLD, VLK, VLL, VLN, VLP, VL8, VLY, VMJ, VMT, VMX, VMY, VNA, VNB, VNC, VND, VNE, VPB, VPC, VPD, VPF
V8-368②	9	AA, BA, CA, DA, FA, HA, RA, SA, TA

Year/Engine	V.I.N.	Engine Code
1982		
V6-252⑧	4	FA, FB, FC, FD, FE, FF, FG, FH, FJ, FK
V8-250②	8	AA, AB, AD, AF
V8-350④	N	VAB, VAC, VAD, VAK, VAL, VAM, VAN, VAP, VAS, VAU, VAW, VAX, VAY, VAZ, VBA, VBB, VBC, VBP, VBU, VBW
1983		
V8-250②	8	HLA, HMA, HNA, HOA, HPA, HQA, HRA
V8-350④	N	VKB, VKC, VKD, VKK, VKL, VKR, VKS, VKT, VKZ, VLA, VLB, VLP, VLS, VLT, VLW

①—Oldsmobile built engine.
②—Fuel injected engine.
③—Carbureted engine.
④—Oldsmobile built diesel engine.
⑤—Brougham & DeVille
⑥—Eldorado
⑦—Seville
⑧—Buick built engine.

GRILLE IDENTIFICATION

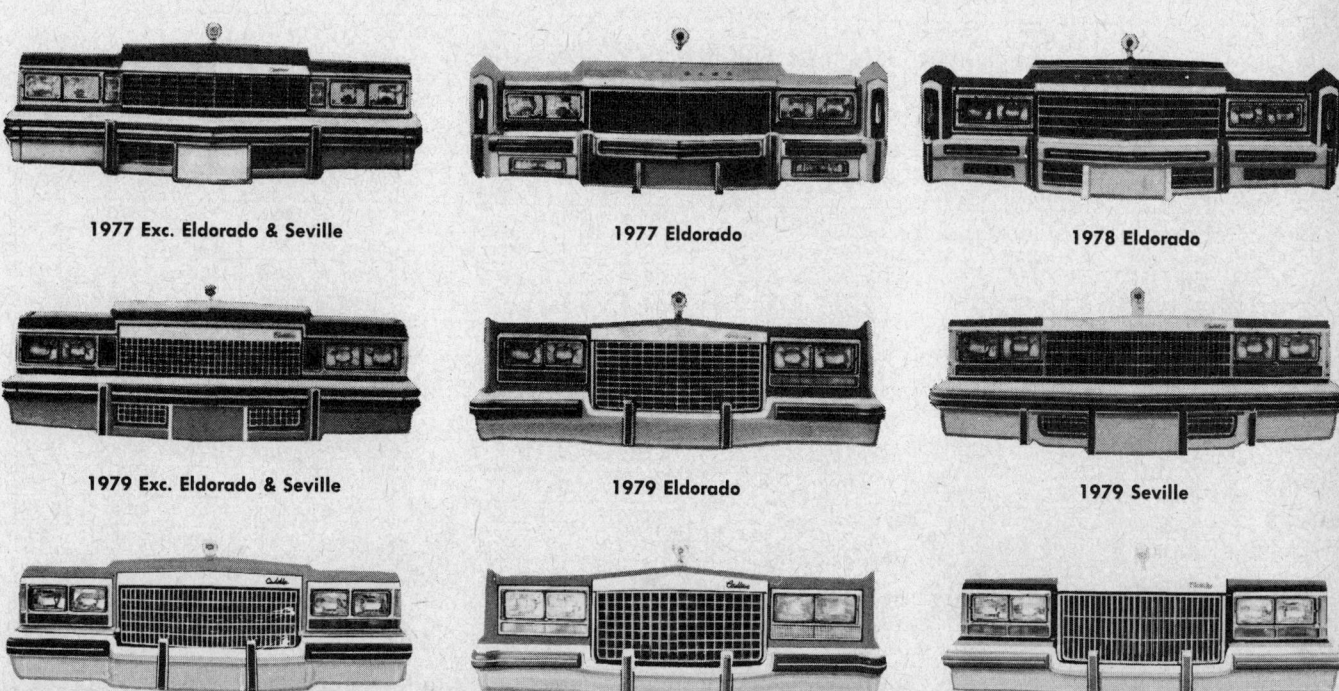

1977 Exc. Eldorado & Seville

1977 Eldorado

1978 Eldorado

1979 Exc. Eldorado & Seville

1979 Eldorado

1979 Seville

1980 Exc. Eldorado & Seville

1980 Eldorado

1980–81 Seville

GRILLE IDENTIFICATION—Continued

1981 Exc. Eldorado & Seville

1981 Eldorado

1982 Exc. Eldorado & Seville

1982 Eldorado

1982 Seville

1983 Exc. Eldorado & Seville

1983 Eldorado

1983 Seville

1984 Exc. Eldorado & Seville

1984 Eldorado

1984 Seville

GENERAL ENGINE SPECIFICATIONS

Year	Engine CID①/Liter	Engine VIN Code②	Carburetor	Bore and Stroke	Com- pression Ratio	Net H.P. @ R.P.M.③	Maximum Torque Ft. Lbs. @ R.P.M.	Normal Oil Pressure Pounds
1977	V8-350, 5.7L	R	Fuel Injection	4.057 × 3.385	8.5	180 @ 4400	275 @ 2000	30—35
	V8-425, 7.0L	S	M4ME, 4 Bbl④⑤	4.082 × 4.060	8.2	180 @ 4000	320 @ 2000	35 Min.
	V8- 425, 7.0L	T	Fuel Injection	4.082 × 4.060	8.2	195 @ 3800	320 @ 2400	35 Min.
1978	V8-350, 5.7L⑥	N	Fuel Injection	4.057 × 3.385	22.5	120 @ 3600	220 @ 1600	30—45
	V8-350, 5.7L	B	Fuel Injection	4.057 × 3.385	8.0	170 @ 4280	270 @ 2000	30—35
	V8-425, 7.0L	S	M4ME, 4 Bbl④	4.082 × 4.060	8.2	180 @ 4000	320 @ 2000	35 Min.
	V8-425, 7.0L	T	Fuel Injection	4.082 × 4.060	8.2	180 @ 4000	320 @ 2000	35 Min.
1979	V8-350. 5.7L⑥	N	Fuel Injection	4.057 × 3.385	22.5	125 @ 3600	225 @ 1600	30—45
	V8-350, 5.7L	B	Fuel Injection	4.057 × 3.385	8.0	170 @ 4200	270 @ 2000	30—45
	V8-425, 7.0L	S	M4ME, 4 Bbl④	4.082 × 4.060	8.2	180 @ 4000	320 @ 2000	35 Min.
	V8-425, 7.0L	T	Fuel Injection	4.082 × 4.060	8.2	195 @ 3800	320 @ 2400	35 Min.
1980	V6-252, 4.1L⑧	4	M4ME, 4 Bbl④	3.96 × 3.40	8.0	125 @ 4000	205 @ 2000	37
	V8-350, 5.7L⑥	N	Fuel Injection	4.057 × 3.385	22.5	105 @ 3200	205 @ 1600	30—45
	V8-350, 5.7L	8	Fuel Injection	4.057 × 3.385	8.0	160 @ 4400	265 @ 1600	30—45
	V8-368, 6.0L	9	Fuel Injection	3.800 × 4.060	8.2	145 @ 3600	270 @ 2000	30—45
	V8-368, 6.0L	6	M4ME, 4 Bbl④⑦	3.800 × 4.060	8.2	150 @ 3800	265 @ 1600	30—45

Continued

GENERAL ENGINE SPECIFICATIONS—Continued

Year	Engine CID①/Liter	Engine VIN Code②	Carburetor	Bore and Stroke	Compression Ratio	Net H.P. @ R.P.M.③	Maximum Torque Ft. Lbs. @ R.P.M.	Normal Oil Pressure Pounds
1981	V6-252, 4.1L⑧	4	E4ME, 4 Bbl④	3.96 × 3.40	8.0	125 @ 3800	210 @ 2000	37
	V8-350, 5.7L⑥	N	Fuel Injection	4.06 × 3.38	22.5	105 @ 3200	200 @ 1600	30–45
	V8-368, 6.0L	9	Fuel Injection	3.80 × 4.06	8.2	140 @ 3800	265 @ 1400	30–45
1982	V6-252, 4.1L⑧	4	E4ME, 4 Bbl④	3.96 × 3.40	8.0	125 @ 4000	205 @ 2000	37
	V8-250, 4.1L	8	Fuel Injection	3.465 × 3.307	8.5	135 @ 4600	200 @ 1600	30
	V8-350, 5.7L⑥	N	Fuel Injection	4.06 × 3.38	22.5	105 @ 3200	200 @ 1600	30–45
1983	V8-250, 4.1L	8	Fuel Injection	3.465 × 3.307	8.5	135 @ 4200	200 @ 2200	30
	V8-350, 5.7L⑥	N	Fuel Injection	4.06 × 3.38	22.5	105 @ 3200	200 @ 1600	30–45
1984	V8-250, 4.1L	—	Fuel Injection	3.465 × 3.307	8.5	135 @ 4400	200 @ 2200	30
	V8-350, 5.7L⑥	—	Fuel Injection	4.06 × 3.38	22.7	105 @ 3200	200 @ 1600	30–45

①—CID—Cubic inch displacement.
②—On 1977–80 vehicles, the fifth digit in the VIN denotes the engine code. On 1981–84 vehicles, the eighth digit in the VIN denotes the engine code.
③—Net rating—as installed in the vehicle.
④—Rochester.
⑤—On 1977 high altitude vehicles, M4MEA.
⑥—Oldsmobile built diesel engine.
⑦—DeVille and all vehicles with C-4 system, E4ME.
⑧—Buick built engine.

TUNE UP SPECIFICATIONS

The following specifications are published from the latest information available. This data should be used only in the absence of a decal affixed in the engine compartment.

★ When using a timing light, disconnect vacuum hose or tube at distributor and plug opening in hose or tube so idle speed will not be affected.

● When checking compression, lowest cylinder must be within 70 percent of highest.

▲ Before removing wires from distributor cap, determine location of No. 1 wire in cap, as distributor position may have been altered from that shown at the end of this chart.

Spark plug types shown in this chart are recommendations of the original manufacturer and not MOTOR.

Check local sources for other spark plug manufacturers listings.

Year & Engine/V.I.N.	Spark Plug Type	Spark Plug Gap	Firing Order Fig. ▲	Ignition Timing BTDC①★ Man. Trans.	Ignition Timing BTDC①★ Auto. Trans.	Mark Fig.	Curb Idle Speed Man. Trans.	Curb Idle Speed Auto Trans.②	Fast Idle Speed Man. Trans.	Fast Idle Speed Auto. Trans.③	Fuel Pump Pressure
1977											
V8-350/R, Exc. Calif.	R47SX	.060	B	—	10°	A	—	600D	—	—	—
V8-350/R, Calif.	R47SX	.060	B	—	8°	A	—	600D	—	—	—
V8-425/S, Exc. Calif. & E.F.I.	R45NSX	.060	C	—	18°⑤	D	—	⑥	—	1400⑦	5¼–6½
V8-425/S, Calif. Exc. E.F.I.	R45NSX	.060	C	—	18°⑤	D	—	⑥	—	1500⑦	5¼–6½
V8-425 E.F.I./T	R45NSX	.060	D	—	18°⑤	D	—	650D	—	—	—
1978											
V8-350 E.F.I./B, Exc. Calif.	R47SX	.060	B	—	10°	A	—	650D	—	—	—
V8-350 E.F.I./B, Calif.	R47SX	.060	B	—	8°	A	—	650D	—	—	—
V8-350 Diesel/N, Exc. High Alt.	—	—	—	—	4½°⑬⑭⑮	—	—	575D	—	650D	—
V8-350 Diesel/N, High Alt.	—	—	—	—	5½°⑬⑭⑮	—	—	575D	—	650D	—
V8-425/S, Exc. E.F.I.	R45NSX	.060	C	—	⑨	D	—	600D	—	⑦⑩	—
V8-425 E.F.I./T	R45NSX	.060	C	—	18°⑪	D	—	600D	—	—	—
1979											
V8-350 E.F.I./B	R47SX	.060	B	—	10°	A	—	600D	—	—	—
V8-350 Diesel/N, Exc. High Alt.	—	—	—	—	4½°⑬⑭⑮	—	—	575D	—	650D	—

TUNE UP SPECIFICATIONS—Continued

The following specifications are published from the latest information available. This data should be used only in the absence of a decal affixed in the engine compartment.

★ When using a timing light, disconnect vacuum hose or tube at distributor and plug opening in hose or tube so idle speed will not be affected.

● When checking compression, lowest cylinder must be within 70 percent of highest.

▲ Before removing wires from distributor cap, determine location of No. 1 wire in cap, as distributor position may have been altered from that shown at the end of this chart.

☞ Spark plug types shown in this chart are recommendations of the original manufacturer and not MOTOR.
Check local sources for other spark plug manufacturers listings.

Year & Engine/V.I.N.	Spark Plug		Ignition Timing BTDC①★				Curb Idle Speed		Fast Idle Speed		Fuel Pump Pressure
	Type ☞	Gap	Firing Order Fig. ▲	Man. Trans.	Auto. Trans.	Mark Fig.	Man. Trans.	Auto. Trans.②	Man. Trans.	Auto. Trans.③	
1979—Continued											
V8-350 Diesel/N, High Alt.	—	—	—	—	5½°⑬⑭⑮	—	—	575D	—	650D	—
V8-425/S, Exc. E.F.I.	R45NSX	.060	C	—	23°⑪	D	—	550/650D	—	⑦⑫	—
V8-425 E.F.I./T	R45NSX	.060	C	—	18°⑤	D	—	650D	—	—	—
1980											
V6-252/4, 4 Barrel	R45TSX	.060	E	—	15°	F	—	550/680D	—	2000	3 Min.
V8-350 E.F.I./8	R47SX	.060	B	—	10°	A	—	600D	—	—	—
V8-350 Diesel/N, Exc. High Alt.	—	—	—	—	4½°⑬⑭⑮	—	—	600/750D	—	750D	—
V8-350 Diesel/N, High Alt.	—	—	—	—	5½°⑬⑭⑮	—	—	600/750D	—	750D	—
V8-368/6, 4 Barrel Exc. Calif.	R45NSX	.060	C	—	18°⑤	D	—	500/650D	—	1450	5¼–6½
V8-368/6, 4 Barrel Calif.	R45NSX	.060	C	—	18°⑤	D	—	575/650D	—	1350	5¼–6½
V8-368 D.E.F.I./9	R45NSX	.060	C	—	10°④	D	—	550D	—	—	—
1981											
V6-252/4	R45TS8	.080	E	—	15°	F	—	550/690D	—	2200	3 Min.
V8-350 Diesel/N, Exc. High Alt.	—	—	—	—	4°⑬⑭⑮	—	—	600D	—	750D	—
V8-350 Diesel/N, High Alt.	—	—	—	—	5°⑬⑭⑮	—	—	600D	—	750D	—
V8-368 D.E.F.I./9	R45NSX	.060	C	—	10°	D	—	550D	—	—	—
1982											
V6-252/4	R45TS8	.080	E	—	15°	F	—	⑧	—	⑧	4¼–5¾
V8-250 D.E.F.I./8	R43NTS6	.060	G	—	10°	—	—	⑧	—	⑧	—
V8-350 Diesel/N, Exc. High Alt.	—	—	—	—	⑭⑱	—	—	600/750D	—	750D	—
V8-350 Diesel/N, High Alt.	—	—	—	—	⑭⑲	—	—	600/750D	—	750D	—
1983											
V8-250 D.E.F.I./8	R43NTS6	.060	G	—	10°	—	—	⑧	—	⑧	—
V8-350 Diesel/N	—	—	—	—	⑭⑳	—	—	600/750D	—	750D	—
1984											
V8-250 D.E.F.I./	—	—	G	—	—	—	—	—	—	—	—
V8-350 Diesel/N	—	—	—	—	⑭⑳	—	—	600/750D	—	750D	—

①—B.T.D.C.—Before top dead center.

②—Where two idle speeds are listed, the higher speed is with idle solenid energized. Curb idle speed is adjusted with A/C off, while solenoid idle speed is adjusted with A/C on. Idle speed is adjusted in Drive unless otherwise specified.

③—With transmission in Park position & parking brake fully applied.

④—Engine wiring harness test lead, green connector, must be grounded.

⑤—At 1400 RPM.

⑥—Except Eldorado, 600/675D RPM; Eldorado, 600D RPM.

⑦—With cam follower on 2nd step of fast idle cam, distributor vacuum hose & EGR vacuum hose disconnected & plugged & A/C off.

⑧—Idle speed is controlled by an idle speed control motor or idle load compensator.

⑨—Except Eldorado, except high altitude, 21° BTDC at 1600 RPM; high altitude, 23° BTDC at 1600 RPM. Eldorado, except Calif. & high altitude, 21° BTDC at 1600 RPM; California,

18° BTDC at 1600 RPM; high altitude, 23° BTDC at 1600 RPM.

⑩—Except carburetor No. 17058230, 1500 RPM; carburetor No. 17058230, 1400 RPM.

⑪—At 1600 RPM.

⑫—Except carburetor No. 17059230, 1500 RPM; carburetor No. 1705923, 1000 RPM.

⑬—ATDC—After top dead center.

⑭—The injection pump timing specifications listed are for use with Diesel Timing Meter J-33075.

Continued

TUNE UP SPECIFICATION NOTES—Continued

⑮—At 1200 RPM.
⑯—At 1250 RPM. When operating at altitudes above 4000 ft., set at 5° ATDC.
⑰—At 1250 RPM. When operating at altitudes below 4000 ft., set at 3° ATDC.
⑱—Injection timing, 4° ATDC at 1250 RPM. At altitudes above 4000 ft., set at 5° ATDC at 1250 RPM.
⑲—Injection timing, 4° ATDC at 1250 RPM. At altitudes below 4000 ft., set at 3° ATDC at 1250 RPM.
⑳—Injection timing, 4° ATDC at 1250 RPM.

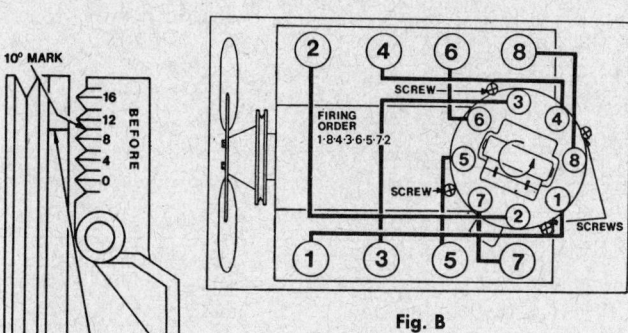

Fig. A

Fig. B

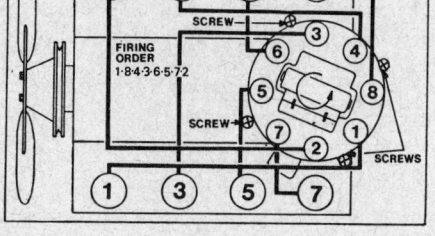

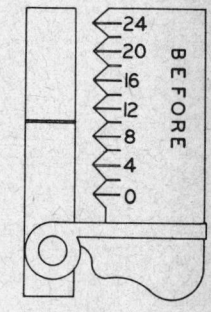

Fig. C

Fig. D

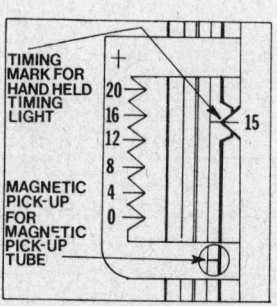

Fig. E

Fig. F

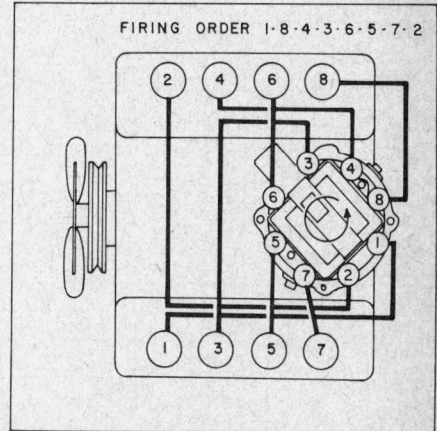

Fig. G

VALVE SPECIFICATIONS

Year	Engine/V.I.N.	Valve Lash	Valve Angles		Valve Spring Installed Height	Valve Spring Pressure Lbs. @ In.	Stem Clearance		Stem Diameter	
			Seat	Face			Intake	Exhaust	Intake	Exhaust
1977–79	V8-350/R,B	Hydraulic①	②	③	1 43/64	187 @ 19/32	.0010–.0027	.0015–.0032	.3425–.3432	.3420–.3427
1977–79	V8-425/S,T	Hydraulic①	45	44	1 61/64	160 @ 1 31/64	.0010–.0027	.0010–.0027	.3413–.3420	.3413–.3420
1978–79	V8-350/N④	Hydraulic①	②	③	1.670	151 @ 1.30	.0010–.0027	.0015–.0032	.3425–.3432	.3420–.3427
1980	V8-350/8	Hydraulic①	②	③	1.670	187 @ 1.27	.0010–.0027	.0015–.0032	.3425–.3432	.3420–.3427
1980–81	V6-252/4⑤	Hydraulic①	45	45	1.727	⑥	.0015–.0035	.0015–.0032	.3401–.3412	.3405–.3412
	V8-350/N④	Hydraulic①	②	③	1.670	210 @ 1.3	.0010–.0027	.0015–.0032	.3425–.3432	.3420–.3427
	V8-368/6,9	Hydraulic①	45	44	1.946	160 @ 1.496	.0010–.0027	.0010–.0027	.3413–.3420	.3413–.3420
1982	V8-250/8	Hydraulic①	45	44	1.73	182 @ 1.28	.001–.003	.001–.003	.3413–.3420	.3411–.3418
	V6-252/4⑤	Hydraulic①	45	45	1.727	220 @ 1.34	.0015–.0035	.0015–.0032	.3401–.3412	.3405–.3412
	V6-350/N④	Hydraulic①	②	③	1.670	210 @ 1.22	.0010–.0027	.0015–.0032	.3425–.3432	.3420–.3427
1983–84	V8-250/8	Hydraulic①	45	44	1.73	182 @ 1.28	.001–.003	.001–.003	.3413–.3420	.3411–.3418
	V8-350/N④	Hydraulic①	②	③	1.670	210 @ 1.22	.0010–.0027	.0015–.0032	.3425–.3432	.3420–.3427

①—No adjustment
②—Intake 45°; exhaust 31°.
③—Intake 44°; exhaust 30°.
④—Diesel engine.
⑤—Buick built engine.
⑥—Intake, 164 @ 1.34; Exhaust, 182 @ 1.34.

CADILLAC—Exc. Cimarron

DISTRIBUTOR SPECIFICATIONS

★ Note: If unit is checked on the vehicle, double the RPM and degrees to get crankshaft figures.

Distributor Part No.①	Centrifugal Advance Degrees @ RPM of Distributor				Full Advance	Vacuum Advance	
	Advance Starts	Intermediate Advance				Inches of Vacuum to Start Plunger	Max. Adv. Dist. Deg. @ Vacuum
1103307④	0 @ 200	−1/2 to +13/5 @ 450	41/5−73/10 @ 700	111/2−134/5 @ 1450	22 @ 2500	91/2	91/2 @ 20.7
1103307⑤	0 @ 200	−3/64 to 0 @ 400	43/4−77/8 @ 725	61/8−83/8 @ 790	22 @ 3000	9	91/2 @ 17
1103331	0 @ 200	1/2−31/2 @ 450	51/2−8 @ 700	71/2−91/2 @ 1450	91/2 @ 2500	31/2	141/2 @ 20.7
1103332④	0 @ 200	1/2−31/2 @ 450	51/2−8 @ 700	71/2−91/2 @ 1450	91/2 @ 2500	31/2	101/2 @ 20.7
1103332⑤	0 @ 200	−1/2 to +21/2 @ 400	51/4−8 @ 775	71/2−91/2 @ 1450	91/2 @ 2400	3	101/2 @ 13
1103334④	0 @ 200	1/2−31/2 @ 450	41/5−63/10 @ 700	6−8 @ 1450	91/2 @ 2500	42/5	141/2 @ 20.7
1103334⑤	0 @ 200	−1/2 to +21/2 @ 400	3−6 @ 575	4−61/8 @ 613	91/2 @ 2500	4	141/2 @ 16
1103335④	0 @ 200	−1/2 to +13/5 @ 450	11/5−33/10 @ 700	3−53/10 @ 1450	8 @ 2500	31/2	101/2 @ 20.7
1103335⑤	0 @ 200	−1/2 to +15/8 @ 463	7/8−3 @ 600	31/2−55/8 @ 1600	8 @ 2900	3	101/2 @ 13
1103345	0 @ 200	1/2−31/2 @ 450	51/2−8 @ 700	71/2−91/2 @ 1450	91/2 @ 2500	31/2	81/2 @ 20.7
1103348	0 @ 200	−1/2 to +13/5 @ 450	41/5−73/10 @ 700	111/2−134/5 @ 1450	22 @ 2500	53/5	121/2 @ 20.7
1103349	0 @ 200	−1/2 to +13/5 @ 450	41/5−74/5 @ 700	111/2−134/5 @ 1450	22 @ 2500	53/5	141/2 @ 20.7
1103352	0 @ 200	1/2−31/2 @ 450	51/2−8 @ 700	71/2−91/2 @ 1450	91/2 @ 2500	53/5	51/2 @ 20.7
1103389④	0 @ 200	1/2−31/2 @ 450	51/2−8 @ 700	71/2−91/2 @ 1450	91/2 @ 1450	4	141/2 @ 20
1103389⑤	0 @ 200	−1/2 to +21/2 @ 400	5−8 @ 675	6−81/16 @ 712	91/2 @ 2000	3	141/2 @ 16
1103392④	−1/4−0 @ 275	—	7 @ 700	—	81/2 @ 1450	6	10 @ 13.5
1103392⑤	0 @ 200	−1/2 to 21/2 @ 400	5−8 @ 725	71/2−91/2 @ 1450	91/2 @ 2400	3	101/2 @ 14
1103393④	0 @ 450	—	7 @ 750	—	21 @ 2500	5	12 @ 12
1103393⑤	0 @ 200	−1/2 to 0 @ 400	43/4−73/4 @ 725	8−10 @ 1000	22 @ 3000	4	121/2 @ 13
1103394④	0 @ 450	—	7 @ 750	—	21 @ 2500	5	14 @ 15.5
1103394⑤	0 @ 200	−1/2 to 0 @ 400	43/4−8 @ 725	77/8−10 @ 1000	22 @ 3000	4	141/2 @ 16
1103395④	0 @ 350	—	7 @ 700	—	81/2 @ 1450	8	5 @ 12
1103395⑤	0 @ 200	−1/2 to +21/2 @ 400	6−8 @ 712	71/2−91/2 @ 1000	91/2 @ 2400	7	51/2 @ 12
1103401⑥⑦	—	—	—	—	—	—	—
1103405⑥⑦	—	—	—	—	—	—	—
1103415⑥⑦	—	—	—	—	—	—	—
1103416⑥⑦	—	—	—	—	—	—	—
1103455⑦②	—	—	—	—	—	—	—
1103540⑦⑧	—	—	—	—	—	—	—
1103541⑦⑧	—	—	—	—	—	—	—
1103462⑦③	—	—	—	—	—	—	—
1103470⑦③	—	—	—	—	—	—	—
1103472⑦③	—	—	—	—	—	—	—
1110555⑦②③	—	—	—	—	—	—	—
1112891	0 @ 200	8 @ 600	—	—	9 @ 2500	41/2	141/2 @ 13
1112892	−1/4−0 @ 330	−1/2 to +21/2 @ 450	21/2−5 @ 600	5−7 @ 1400	10 @ 000	5.5	9.5−10.5 @ 14
1112954	−1/4−0 @ 330	−1/2 to +21/2 @ 450	21/2−5 @ 600	5−7 @ 1400	10 @ 3000	4.5	13.5−14.5 @ 16
1112897	0 @ 200	−1/2 to +21/2 @ 450	21/2−5 @ 600	5−7 @ 1400	10 @ 2500	51/2	91/2−101/2 @ 131/2
1112924	0 @ 200	−1 to +13/4 @ 450	11/2−3 @ 800	4−6 @ 1700	8 @ 2500	5	131/2−141/2 @ 16
1112931	0 @ 200	1/2 to 13/4 @ 450	61/4−81/2 @ 800	131/2−153/4 @ 1700	22 @ 2500	5	131/2−141/2 @ 18
1112932	0 @ 200	1/2 to 13/4 @ 450	61/4−81/2 @ 800	131/2−153/4 @ 1700	22 @ 2500	5	81/2−91/2 @ 18
1112954	−1/4−0 @ 330	−1/2 to +21/2 @ 450	21/2−5 @ 600	5−7 @ 1400	10 @ 3000	41/2	131/2−141/2 @ 16
1113202	0 @ 200	4 @ 600	—	—	9 @ 2500	41/2	101/2 @ 13

①—Stamped on distributor housing plate.
②—1981 Models.
③—1982−84 Models.
④—1978 units.
⑤—1979 units.
⑥—1980 Models.
⑦—On models equipped with E.S.S. or E.S.T. refer to Tune-up chapter for specifications.

PISTONS, PINS, RINGS, CRANKSHAFT & BEARINGS

Year	Model/ V.I.N.	Piston Clearance	Ring End Gap①		Wrist-pin Diameter	Rod Bearings		Main Bearings		Thrust on Bear. No.	Shaft End Play
			Comp.	Oil		Shaft Diameter	Bearing Clearance	Shaft Diameter	Bearing Clearance		
1977–78	V8-350/R,B	.0010–.0020	.010	.015	.9805	2.1238–2.1248	.0005–.0026	④	⑤	3	.004–.008
1977–79	V8-425/S,T	.0006–.0014	.013	.015	.9997	2.500	.0005–.0028	3.250	.0001–.0026	3	.002–.012
1978–79	V8-350/N⑥	.0050–.0060	.015	.015	1.0951	2.1238–2.1248	.0005–.0026	2.9998	⑤	3	.0035–.0135
1979	V8-350/B	.0010–.0020	.010	.015	.9805	2.1238–2.1248	.0004–.0033	④	⑤	3	.0035–.0135
1980	V8-350/8	.0010–.0020	.010	.015	.9805	2.1238–2.1248	.0004–.0033	④	⑤	3	.0035–.0135
1980–81	V6-252/4⑦	.0008–.0020	.013	.015	.9394	2.2495	.0005–.0026	2.4995	.0003–.0018	2	.003–.009
	V8-350/N⑥	.0050–.0060	.015	.015	1.0951	1.877–1.887	.0005–.0026	2.9993–3.0003	⑤	3	.0035–.0135
	V8-368/6,9	.0006–.0014	.013	.015	.9997	2.500	.0005–.0028	3.250	.0005–.0026	3	.002–.013
1982	V6-252/4⑦	.0008–.0020	.013	.015	.9393	2.2487–2.2495	③	2.4995	.0003–.0018	2	.003–.009
1982–84	V8-250/8	.0010–.0018	.009	.010	.8658	1.93	.0005–.0028	2.64	.0004–.003	—	.001–.007
	V8-350/N⑥	.0030–.0040	.015	.015	1.0951	2.1238–2.1248	.0005–.0026	2.9993–3.0003	⑤	3	.0035–.0135

①—Fit rings in tapered bores for clearance given in tightest portion of ring travel.
②—See text under "Pistons".
③—No. 1, .0005–.0025 inch; Nos. 2, 3, 4, .0005–.0035 inch.
④—Exc. No. 1, 2.4985–2.4995; No. 1, 2.4988–2.4998.
⑤—Exc. No. 5, .0005–.0021; No. 5 .0015–.0031.
⑥—Diesel engine.
⑦—Buick built engine.

ENGINE TIGHTENING SPECIFICATIONS★

★ Torque specifications are for clean and lightly lubricated threads only. Dry or dirty threads produce increased friction which prevents accurate measurement of tightness.

Year & Engine/V.I.N.	Spark Plugs Ft. Lbs.	Cylinder Head Bolts Ft. Lbs.	Intake Manifold Ft. Lbs.	Exhaust Manifold Ft. Lbs.	Rocker Arm Shaft Bracket Ft. Lbs.	Rocker Arm Cover Ft. Lbs.	Connecting Rod Cap Bolts Ft. Lbs.	Main Bearing Cap Bolts Ft. Lbs.	Flex Plate to Crankshaft Ft. Lbs.	Vibration Damper or Pulley Ft. Lbs.
1977–79 V8-425/S,T	25	95⑤	30	③	70⑥	30①	40	90	75	310
1977–80 V8-350/R,B	25	130⑤	40⑤	25⑦	25⑥	7	42	②	60	310
1978–84 V8-350/N④	—	130⑤	40⑤	25	28⑥	3	42	120	60	200–310
1980–82 V6-252/4⑧	15	80	45	25	30	4	40	100	60	225
1980–81 V8-368/6,9	25	95	30	③	⑥⑪	71①	40	90	75	17
1982–84 V8-250/8	10	⑨	⑩	20	20⑥	50①	20	85	35	20

①—Inch pounds. Retorque after engine has been run.
②—Exc. No. 5, 80 ft. lbs.; No. 5, 120 ft. lbs.
③—Long screws, 35 ft. lbs. Short screw, 12 ft. lbs.
④—Diesel engine.
⑤—Clean and dip entire bolt in engine oil before tightening.
⑥—Rocker arm pivot bolt to head.
⑦—1979 with lock tabs, 30 ft. lbs.
⑧—Buick built engine.
⑨—Torque bolts to 45 ft. lbs., then retorque to 90 ft. lbs.
⑩—Refer to text for procedure.
⑪—70 ft. lbs. on 1980 models; 22 ft. lbs. on 1981 models.

ALTERNATOR & REGULATOR SPECIFICATIONS

Year	Alternator		
	Model	Rated Hot Output Amps.	Field Current 12 Volts @ 80° F.
1977–79	1101033	80	4.0–4.5
	1102849	63	4.0–4.5
	1103061	80	4.0–4.5
1980–81	1101040	70	4.0–4.5
	1101050	100	4.0–4.5
	1101061	80	4.0–4.5
1982–84	1101044	70	—
	1101046	80	—
	1101050	100	—

WHEEL ALIGNMENT SPECIFICATIONS

| Year | Model | Caster Angle, Degrees | | Camber Angle, Degrees | | | | Toe-In. Inch | Toe-Out on Turns, Deg. | |
| | | Limits | Desired | Limits | | Desired | | | Outer Wheel | Inner Wheel |
				Left	Right	Left	Right			
1977–78	Eldorado	−1/2 to +1/2	Zero	−3/8 to +3/8	−3/8 to +3/8	Zero	Zero	−1/16 to +1/16	—	—
	Seville	+1½ to +2½	+2	−3/8 to +3/8	−3/8 to +3/8	Zero	Zero	0 to +1/8	—	—
	Others	+2½ to +3½	+3	+1/8 to +7/8	+1/8 to +7/8	+1/2	+1/2	−1/16 to +1/16	—	—
1979	Eldorado	+2 to +3	+2½	−1/2 to +1/2	−1/2 to +1/2	Zero	Zero	−1/16 to +1/16	—	—
	Seville	+1½ to +2½	+2	−3/8 to +3/8	−3/8 to +3/8	Zero	Zero	0 to +1/8	—	—
	Others	+2½ to +3½	+3	+1/8 to +7/8	+1/8 to +7/8	+1/2	+1/2	−1/16 to +1/16	—	—
1980–84	Eldorado & Seville	+2 to +3	+2½	−1/2 to +1/2	−1/2 to +1/2	Zero	Zero	−1/16 to +1/16	—	—
	Others	+2½ to +3½	+3	+.1 to +.9	+.1 to +.9	+1/2	+1/2	1/8	—	—

STARTING MOTOR APPLICATIONS

Year	Engine/V.I.N.	Starter Number	Year	Engine/V.I.N.	Starter Number
1977–78	V8-350/R,B②③	1108765		V8-350/N⑥	1109216
	V8-425/S,T④	1109038		V8-368/T②	1109062
	V8-425/S,T⑤	1109039	1982	V8-250/8②	1109531
1979	V8-350/B②③	1109072		V6-252/4①	1109062
	V8-350/B②⑤	1998205		V8-350/N⑥	1109216
	V8-350/N③⑤⑥	1109214	1983	V8-250/8②④	1109531
	V8-425/S①	1109062		V8-250/8②③⑤	1998233
	V8-425/T②	1109063		V8-350/N④⑥	1109216
1980	V8-350/N④⑥	1109216		V8-350/N③⑤⑥	1109495
	V8-350/N③⑤⑥	1109218	1984	V8-250/ ②④	—
	V8-350/8②③⑤	1998205		V8-250/ ②③⑤	—
	V8-368/5①④	1109062		V8-350/ ④⑥	—
	V8-368/T②③⑤	1998205		V8-350/ ③⑤⑥	—
1981	V6-252/4①	1109062			

①—4 Bbl.
②—Fuel injected.
③—Seville.
④—Exc. Eldorado & Seville.
⑤—Eldorado.
⑥—Diesel engine.

COOLING SYSTEM & CAPACITY DATA

| Year | Model or Engine/V.I.N. | Cooling Capacity, Qts. | | Radiator Cap Relief Pressure, Lbs. | Thermo. Opening Temp. | Fuel Tank Gals. | Engine Oil Refill Qts. ① | Transmission Oil | | | Rear Axle Oil Pints |
		Less A/C	With A/C					3 Speed Pints	4 Speed Pints	Auto. Trans. Qts. ②	
1977	Eldorado	—	25.8	15	195	27½	5	—	—	⑥	4⑧
	Seville	—	17.25	15	195	21	4	—	—	⑤	4¼
	Others	—	20.8	15	195	24½	4	—	—	⑤	4¼

Continued

COOLING SYSTEM & CAPACITY DATA—Continued

Year	Model or Engine/V.I.N.	Cooling Capacity, Qts.		Radiator Cap Relief Pressure, Lbs.	Thermo. Opening Temp.	Fuel Tank Gals.	Engine Oil Refill Qts. ①	Transmission Oil			Rear Axle Oil Pints
		Less A/C	With A/C					3 Speed Pints	4 Speed Pints	Auto. Trans. Qts. ②	
1978	Eldorado	—	24.3	15	195	27½	5	—	—	⑥	4⑧
	Seville Exc. Diesel	—	17.25	15	180	21	4	—	—	⑤	4¼
	Seville Diesel	—	18.9	15	195	21	7⑭	—	—	⑪	4¼
	Others	—	19.8	15	195	24	4	—	—	⑤	4¼
1979	Eldorado V8-350 E.F.I./B	—	14.75⑨	15	180	19.6⑬	4	—	—	⑩	3⅕⑧
	Eldorado V8-350 Diesel/N	—	18.5	15	195	19.6	7⑭	—	—	⑩	3⅕⑧
	Seville V8-350 E.F.I./B	—	17.25	15	180	21	4	—	—	⑫	4¼
	Seville V8-350 Diesel/N	—	20	15	195	21	7⑭	—	—	⑪	4¼
	Others V8-425/S,T	—	20.8	15	195	25	4	—	—	⑫	4¼
	Others V8-350 Diesel/N	—	23.8	15	195	27	7⑭	—	—	⑪	4¼
1980	Eldorado V8-350 E.F.I./8	—	15.2	15	178	20.6	4	—	—	⑩	3⅕⑧
	Eldorado V8-368 D.E.F.I./9	—	22.4	15	178	20.6	5	—	—	⑩	3⅕⑧
	Eldorado V8-350 Diesel/N	—	18.5	15	195	23	7⑭	—	—	⑩	3⅕⑧
	Seville V8-350 E.F.I./8	—	15.2	15	178	20.6	4	—	—	⑩	3⅕⑧
	Seville V8-368 D.E.F.I./9	—	22.4	15	178	20.6	5	—	—	⑩	3⅕⑧
	Seville V8-350 Diesel/N	—	18.5	15	195	23	7⑭	—	—	⑩	3⅕⑧
	Others V6-252/4	—	13	15	195	25	4	—	—	4③	4¼
	Others V8-368/6	—	21.4	15	195	20.7	4	—	—	4③	4¼
	Others V8-350 Diesel/N	—	23.7	15	195	26	7⑭	—	—	⑪	4¼
1981	Eldorado V6-252/4	—	13.1	15	195	21.1	4	—	—	⑩	3⅕⑧
	Eldorado V8-368 D.E.F.I./9	—	22.4	15	178	20.3	4	—	—	⑩	3⅕⑧
	Eldorado V8-350 Diesel/N	—	18.4	15	195	22.8	7⑮	—	—	⑩	3⅕⑧
	Seville V6-252/4	—	13.1	15	195	21.1	4	—	—	⑩	3⅕⑧
	Seville V8-368 D.E.F.I./9	—	22.4	15	178	20.3	4	—	—	⑩	3⅕⑧
	Seville V8-350 Diesel/N	—	18.4	15	195	22.8	7⑮	—	—	⑩	3⅕⑧
	Others V6-252/4	—	18.2	15	195	25	4	—	—	⑰	4¼
	Others V8-368/9	—	21.4	15	195	25	4	—	—	⑰	4¼
	Others V8-350 Diesel/N	—	23.7	15	195	27	7⑮	—	—	⑰	4¼
1982	Eldorado V6-252/4	—	13.1	15	195	21.1	4	—	—	⑦	3⅕⑧
	Seville V6-252/4	—	13.1	15	195	21.1	4	—	—	⑦	3⅕⑧
	Others V6-252/4	—	18.2	15	195	25	4	—	—	⑯	4¼
	Eldorado V8-250/8	—	11.8	15	195	20.3	5④	—	—	⑦	3⅕⑧
	Seville V8-250/8	—	11.8	15	195	20.3	5④	—	—	⑦	3⅕⑧
	Others V8-250/8	—	10.8	15	195	25	4④	—	—	⑯	4¼
	Eldorado V8-350 Diesel/N	—	18.4	15	195	22.8	7⑮	—	—	⑦	3⅕⑧
	Seville V8-350 Diesel/N	—	18.4	15	195	22.8	7⑮	—	—	⑦	3⅕⑧
	Others V8-350 Diesel/N	—	23.7	15	195	27	7⑮	—	—	⑯	4¼
1983	Eldorado V8-250/8	—	11.8	15	195	20.3	5④	—	—	⑥	3⅕⑧
	Seville V8-250/8	—	11.8	15	195	20.3	5④	—	—	⑥	3⅕⑧
	Others V8-250/8	—	11.0	15	195	24.5	4④	—	—	⑱	4¼
	Eldorado Diesel/N	—	18.4	15	195	22.8	7⑮	—	—	⑥	3⅕⑧
	Seville Diesel/N	—	18.4	15	195	22.8	7⑮	—	—	⑥	3⅕⑧
	Others Diesel/N	—	23.7	15	195	26	7⑮	—	—	⑱	4¼

Continued

COOLING SYSTEM & CAPACITY DATA—Continued

Year	Model or Engine/V.I.N.	Cooling Capacity, Qts.		Radiator Cap Relief Pressure, Lbs.	Thermo. Opening Temp.	Fuel Tank Gals.	Engine Oil Refill Qts. ①	Transmission Oil			Rear Axle Oil Pints
		Less A/C	With A/C					3 Speed Pints	4 Speed Pints	Auto. Trans. Qts. ②	
1984	Eldorado V8-250/	—	—	15	195	20.3	5④	—	—	—	3¹/₅⑧
	Seville V8-250/	—	—	15	195	20.3	5④	—	—	—	3¹/₅⑧
	Others V8-250/	—	—	15	195	24.5	4④	—	—	—	4¹/₄
	Eldorado Diesel/	—	—	15	195	22.8	7⑮	—	—	—	3¹/₅⑧
	Seville Diesel/	—	—	15	195	22.8	7⑮	—	—	—	3¹/₅⑧
	Others Diesel/	—	—	15	195	26	7⑮	—	—	—	4¹/₄

①—Add one quart with filter change.
②—Approximate. Make final check with dipstick.
③—Oil pan only.
④—Includes filter.
⑤—Oil pan 4 qts. Total capacity 12½ qts.
⑥—Oil pan 5 qts. Total capacity 13 qts.
⑦—Oil pan 5 qts. Total capacity 11¾ qts.
⑧—Front drive axle.

⑨—Heavy duty cooling system, 15½ qts.
⑩—Oil pan 5 qts. Total capacity 12 qts.
⑪—Oil pan 3 qts. Total capacity 9 qts.
⑫—Oil pan 4½ qts. Total capacity 12½ qts.
⑬—Early models, 19.6 gals.; late models, 18.1 gals.
⑭—Includes filter. Recommended diesel engine oil—1978, use oil designated SE/CD; 1979–80, use oil designated SE/CC.

⑮—Includes oil filter. Recommended diesel engine oil—use oil designated SF/CD, SF/CC or SE/CC on all except 1982–84 models or SF/CD, SF/CC on 1982–84 models.
⑯—Oil pan 3½ qts. Total capacity 11 qts.
⑰—THM 200C—oil pan 3½ qts., total capacity 11 qts.; THM 350 & 350C—oil pan 3.15 qts., total capacity 10 qts.; THM 400—oil pan 3 qts., total capacity 10 qts.
⑱—Oil pan, 5 qts. Total capacity, 11 qts.

DRIVE AXLE SPECIFICATIONS

Year	Model	Carrier Type	Ring Gear Pinion Backlash		Pinion Bearing Preload			Differential Bearing Preload		
			Method	Adjustment	Method	Adjustment New Bearings Inch-Lbs.	Adjustment Used Bearings Inch-Lbs.	Method	Adjustment New Bearings Inch-Lbs.	Adjustment Used Bearings Inch-Lbs.
1977–78	Exc. Eldorado④	Integral	Shims	.005–.008①	Shims	15–30	5–10	Shims	②	②
1979	Exc. Eldorado	Integral	Shims	.005–.009①	Shims	15–30	5–10	Shims	②	②
1979	Eldorado	Integral	Shims	.005–.009①	Shims	18–24	5	Shims	③	③
1980–82	Exc. Eldorado & Seville	Integral	Shims	.005–.009①	Shims	24–32	8–12	Shims	②	②
1980–82	Eldorado & Seville	Integral	Shims	.005–.009①	Shims	18–24	5	Shims	③	③
1983–84	Exc. Eldorado & Seville	Integral	Shims	.006–.008①	Shims	20–25	10–15	Shims	②	②
1983–84	Eldorado & Seville	Integral	Shims	.005–.009①	Shims	18–24	5	Shims	③	③

①—New gears.
②—Slip fit plus .008".
③—Slip fit plus .006".
④—Eldorado final drive units cannot be serviced internally. If defective, final drive unit should be replaced as an assembly.

Electrical Section

STARTER, REPLACE

1979–84

1. Disconnect battery ground cable (two ground cables on diesel engines).
2. Raise and support front of vehicle.
3. Remove starter braces, shields, brackets and clips that may interfere with starter removal.
4. Remove starter attaching bolts, then lower starter.
5. Disconnect wiring harness from starter and remove starter.
6. Reverse procedure to install.

1977–78

1. Disconnect battery ground cable at battery.
2. On Eldorado, disconnect starter harness at connector at right rear of engine.
3. Raise front end of car.
4. On all except Eldorado models, disconnect battery lead at starter solenoid and disconnect neutral switch wire and coil feed wire at starter solenoid terminals.
5. On Eldorado, remove spring clip securing wire to solenoid housing.
6. On Seville, remove crossover pipe.
7. Remove screw and nut securing support bracket to starter and crankcase.
8. Unfasten starter motor from crankcase and remove starter by pulling it forward, then toward RH front wheel and up over steering linkage toward rear of car.
9. Reverse procedure to install.

IGNITION LOCK, REPLACE

1979–84

1. Remove steering wheel as described under Horn Sounder and Steering Wheel.
2. Remove turn signal switch as described under Turn Signal Switch, Replace, then

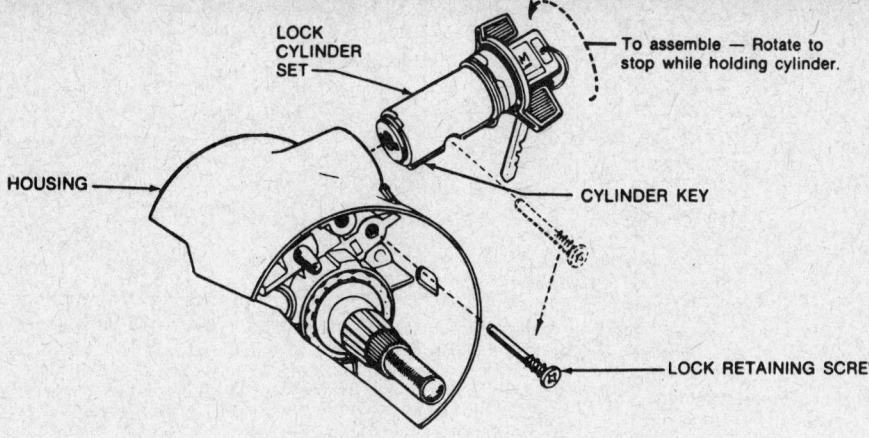

Fig. 1 Ignition lock removal. 1979—84 models

Fig. 2 Lock cylinder removal, 1977—78 models

remove buzzer switch.

3. Place ignition switch in Run position, then remove lock cylinder retaining screw and lock cylinder.
4. To install, rotate lock cylinder to stop while holding housing, Fig. 1. Align cylinder key with keyway in housing, then push lock cylinder assembly into housing until fully seated.
5. Install lock cylinder retaining screw. Torque screw to 40 in. lbs. for standard columns. On adjustable columns, torque retaining screw to 22 in. lbs.
6. Install buzzer switch, turn signal switch and steering wheel.

1977—78

1. Follow procedure to remove the turn signal switch as described further on.
2. Turn ignition switch to the "On" or "Run" position.
3. Insert a small screwdriver into slot next to the switch mounting screw boss, Fig. 2. Gently tap on screw-driver until screw-driver breaks through thin wall casting. Depress lock cylinder retaining tab with screw-driver and remove cylinder.
4. To install lock, hold lock cylinder sleeve and rotate key clockwise against stop. Making sure that buzzer switch drive tang is below outside diameter of lock cylinder, insert cylinder into cover bore with key on cylinder sleeve aligned with keyway in housing until cylinder touches lock sector shaft.

NOTE: Insert a 1/16 inch drill shank between lock cylinder knob and column

housing to avoid assembling lock cylinder too far into steering column.

5. While maintaining a light inward force, rotate lock cylinder counter-clockwise until drive section of cylinder mates with sector drive shaft. Push in until snap ring on lock snaps into groove in housing.
6. Check for freedom of operation of lock cylinder.

IGNITION SWITCH, REPLACE

1977—84

1. Disconnect battery cable and position ignition key in "Lock".
2. Remove steering column lower cover.
3. Loosen two upper column support nuts and allow column to drop as far as possible without removing the nuts.

NOTE: Do not remove nuts as column may bend under its own weight.

4. Disconnect switch connector and remove switch, Fig. 3.
5. When reassembling, make sure the ignition key is in the "Lock" position. Assemble switch on actuator rod. Hold rod stationary and move switch towards bottom of column then back off one detent on standard steering column models. On models with tilt column, move switch toward upper end of column and back off one detent.

LIGHT SWITCH, REPLACE

1979—84 Eldorado & 1980—84 Seville

1. Disconnect battery ground cable.
2. Remove instrument cluster trim panel.
3. Remove two screws attaching switch to cluster carrier, then pull switch rearward to remove.
4. Reverse procedure to install.

1977—84 Except Eldorado & Seville

1. Disconnect battery ground cable.
2. Remove left hand instrument panel insert.
3. Remove three screws attaching light switch to instrument panel.
4. On vehicles equipped with Cruise Control and Twilight Sentinel, remove two screws retaining Cruise Control switch to instrument panel.
5. Slide Cruise Control switch forward to remove headlamp switch.
6. Disconnect electrical connector from headlamp switch, then if used, disconnect Guidematic connector from under instrument panel.
7. Remove switch.
8. Reverse procedure to install.

1977—79 Seville

1. Disconnect battery ground cable.

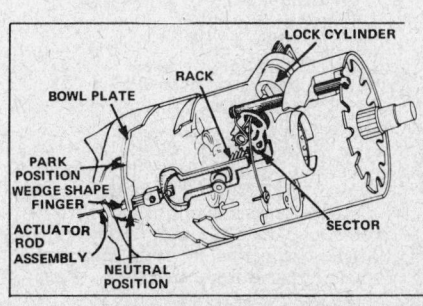

Fig. 3 Ignition switch, 1977—84

Fig. 4 Mechanical neutral switch system with Tilt-Telescope column. 1977—84

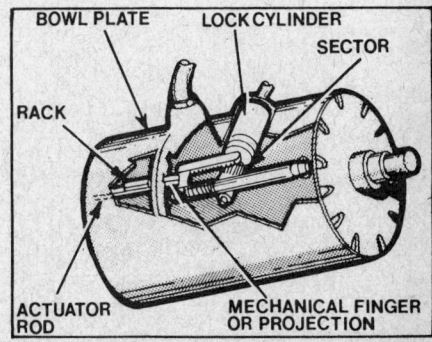

Fig. 5 Mechanical neutral start system with standard column. 1977—84 models

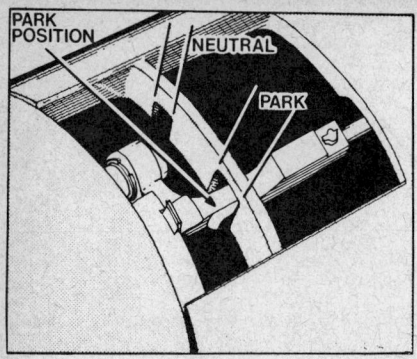

Fig. 6 Mechanical neutral start system in Park position

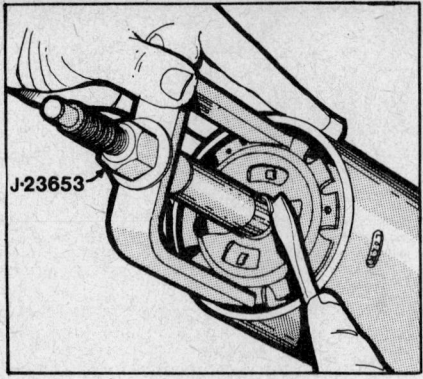

Fig. 7 Compressing lock plate & removing snap ring

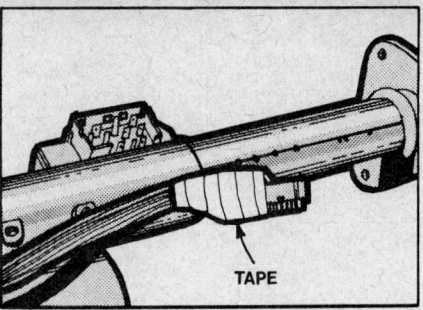

Fig. 8 Taping turn signal connector & wiring

2. Remove lower left instrument panel assembly.
3. Pull knob to "ON" position, depress button on bottom of switch and remove knob and shaft assembly.
4. Remove headlamp case to lower instrument panel attaching screws.
5. Remove sleeve attaching headlamp switch to case.
6. On vehicles without Guide-Matic and Twilight Sentinel remove sleeve retaining escutcheon, washer and lens to backplate.
7. On vehicles equipped with Guide-Matic and Twilight Sentinel, remove Guide-Matic knob, wave washer and Twilight Sentinel lever by pulling outward. Remove lens, then spanner nut and potentiometer from backplate.
8. Reverse procedure to install.

1977–78 Eldorado

1. Disconnect battery ground cable.
2. Remove steering column lower cover.
3. Disconnect headlamp electrical connector and lower bulb.
4. Pull knob to "ON" position, depress spring loaded button and remove knob and shaft, escutcheon and washer.
5. Remove case to instrument support screw.
6. Lower switch assembly, disconnect upper bulb and remove switch.
7. Reverse procedure to install.

STOP LIGHT SWITCH

1977–84

The stoplight is retained to the brake pedal bracket. To adjust, pull the brake pedal fully up to its stop. This action automatically adjusts the switch.

NEUTRAL START SWITCH

1977–84 Models

Actuation of the ignition switch is prevented by a mechanical lockout system, Figs. 4 and 5, which prevents the lock cylinder from rotating when the selector lever is out of Park or Neutral. When the selector lever is in Park or Neutral, the slots in the bowl plate and the finger on the actuator rod align allowing the finger to pass through the bowl plate in turn actuating the ignition switch, Fig. 6. If the selector lever is in any position other than Park or Neutral, the finger contacts the bowl plate when the lock cylinder is rotated, thereby preventing full travel of the lock cylinder.

NOTE: On all models incorporating an electric neutral start switch, this switch plus the back-up light switch and parking brake vacuum release valve are combined into one unit. This unit is mounted on the steering column under the instrument panel.

TURN SIGNAL SWITCH, REPLACE

1977–84

Standard Column
1. Disconnect battery ground cable, then remove steering wheel.
2. Remove lock plate cover.
3. Using a suitable spring compressor, compress lock plate and spring, then remove snap ring from groove in steering shaft, Fig. 7.
4. Remove lock plate, turn signal cancelling cam, upper bearing preload spring and thrust washer from steering shaft.

CAUTION: At this point steering shaft is free. Do not slide shaft out of steering column.

5. Remove turn signal lever attaching screw, then signal lever.
6. On vehicles equipped with cruise control, proceed as follows:
   a. Attach a long piece of piano wire to cruise control switch harness connector.
   b. Pull cruise control harness up through and out of column.
   c. Remove piano wire from harness connector. Do not remove wire from column.
7. On all models, remove turn signal switch attaching screws, then slide switch wire connector off bracket.
8. Remove mounting bracket to steering column attaching bolts, then bracket.
9. Disconnect switch connector from wire harness.
10. Wrap a piece of tape around switch connector and harness to facilitate removal, Fig. 8.
11. Pull turn signal straight up with wire protector attached, and remove switch harness and connector from column.
12. Reverse procedure to install.

Tilt & Telescope Wheel
1. Disconnect battery cable.
2. Remove steering wheel and slide rubber sleeve from steering shaft.
3. Remove plastic retainer from C-ring.
4. With a suitable compressor, thread bolt into steering shaft lock hole.
5. Compress preload spring and remove C-ring, Fig. 7.
6. Remove compressor and remove lock plate, horn contact carrier and preload spring.
7. Remove steering column lower cover and the signal lever.
8. On cars equipped with cruise control proceed as follows:
   a. Disconnect cruise control wire from harness.
   b. Remove harness protector from cruise control.
   c. Wrap wire around turn signal lever until lever is disconnected. Do not remove wire from column.
9. On all models remove bolts at upper support.
10. Remove four screws securing upper mounting bracket to column and remove bracket.
11. Disconnect turn signal harness and remove wires from plastic protector. Wrap a piece of tape around connector and harness to facilitate removal, Fig. 8.
12. Remove screw securing turn signal switch to column and pull switch out.
13. Reverse procedure to install.

HORN SOUNDER & STEERING WHEEL, REPLACE

1977–84

1. Disconnect battery ground cable.
2. Remove attaching screws from back of spokes and lift pad assembly from wheel.
3. Remove horn contact wire from plastic tower.
4. On tilt and telescope models, remove three screws securing lever assembly to adjuster, then adjuster from steering shaft.
5. On standard models, remove locking lever assembly.
6. On all models, scribe an alignment mark on wheel hub in line with slash mark on steering shaft to be used upon installation.
7. Loosen steering shaft nut, then using a suitable puller, remove nut and wheel.
8. Reverse procedure to install.

INSTRUMENT CLUSTER, REPLACE

CAUTION: On vehicles equipped with an Air

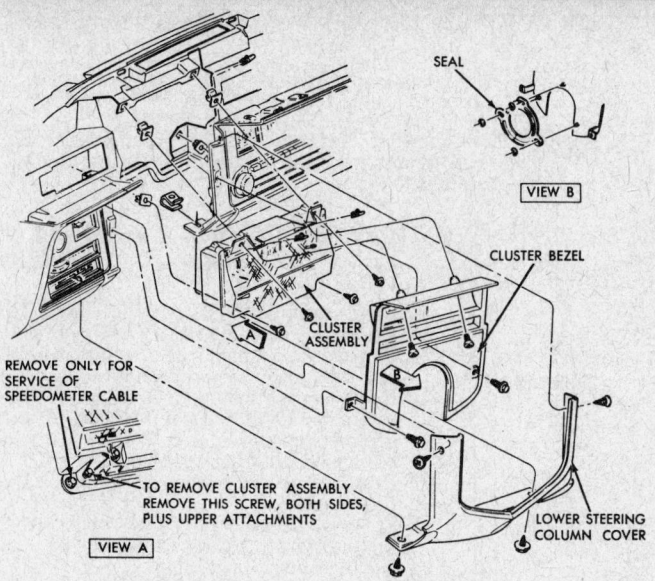

SEAL

VIEW B

CLUSTER BEZEL

CLUSTER ASSEMBLY

REMOVE ONLY FOR SERVICE OF SPEEDOMETER CABLE

TO REMOVE CLUSTER ASSEMBLY REMOVE THIS SCREW, BOTH SIDES, PLUS UPPER ATTACHMENTS

VIEW A

LOWER STEERING COLUMN COVER

Fig. 9 Instrument cluster. 1977–79 Seville

HORIZONAL SUPPORT

VIEW B

TO REMOVE CLUSTER ASSEMBLY REMOVE THIS SCREW, BOTH SIDES, PLUS UPPER TWO SCREWS.

SCREW FOR INITIAL INSTALLATION— TO BE REMOVED ONLY FOR SERVICE OF SPEEDOMETER CABLE.

STEERING COLUMN SEAL

CLUSTER BEZEL SEAL

STEERING COLUMN SEAL

VIEW A

CLUSTER BEZEL

STEERING COLUMN

Fig. 10 Instrument panel cluster. 1977–78 Eldorado

Cushion Restraint system, turn ignition switch to "Lock," disconnect battery ground cable and tape end, thereby deactivating system.

1979–84 Eldorado & 1980–84 Seville

1. Disconnect battery ground cable.
2. Remove instrument cluster trim panel.
3. Remove headlamp and windshield wiper switches.
4. Unlock headlamp, windshield wiper and cruise control wire connectors from cluster carrier.
5. Disconnect speedometer cable and instrument cluster wiring.
6. Remove instrument cluster attaching screws and remove cluster assembly.
7. Reverse procedure to install.

1977–79 Seville

1. Disconnect battery ground cable.
2. Remove steering column lower cover, 4 screws attaching cluster bezel to instrument panel, then press bezel downward, rotate top outward and carefully remove bezel.
3. Position shift lever in "Park" and remove screw attaching indicator cable to steering column.
4. Remove two screws securing top of cluster to instrument panel support and two screws securing speedometer cable retainer to cluster, Fig. 9.

NOTE: Do not remove speedometer cable retainer.

5. Pull cluster outward to disengage speedometer cable, then rotate cluster downward and disconnect wire connector. Remove cluster.
6. Reverse procedure to install.

1977–84 Except Seville & 1979–84 Eldorado

1. Disconnect battery ground cable.

2. Remove cluster bezel, then with shift lever in "Park" remove screw securing shift indicator cable to steering column.
3. Remove four screws securing cluster to instrument horizontal support, Figs. 10 and 11.
4. On 1977–78 except Eldorado models, remove screw located directly above steering column, retaining cluster to speedometer mounting plate.

NOTE: On vehicles equipped with speed control sensor, disconnect sensor from cluster before completely removing cluster assembly. This will prevent connector from damaging cluster during removal.

5. Disengage speedometer cable at neck by pulling cluster straight out and depressing retaining spring.

NOTE: To remove cluster, place shift lever in low range and on cars with tilt wheel, place wheel in lowest position.

6. Rotate cluster downward, disconnect printed circuit connector and remove cluster.
7. Reverse procedure to install.

RADIO, REPLACE

NOTE: When installing radio, be sure to adjust antenna trimmer for peak performance.

1979–84 Eldorado & 1980–84 Seville

1. Disconnect battery ground cable.
2. Remove center applique retaining screws, radio knobs, and hex nuts, then remove center applique.
3. Remove rear window defogger switch on 1979–81 Eldorado and 1980–81 Seville.
4. Remove radio mounting screws, then pull

radio rearward. Disconnect electrical connectors and antenna lead from radio, then remove radio.
5. Reverse procedure to install.

1977–84 Except Eldorado & Seville

1. Remove center instrument panel insert.
2. Remove screws retaining radio to lower instrument panel.
3. Disconnect electrical connectors and antenna leads(s) and remove radio.

1977–79 Seville

1. Remove E.F.I. Electronic Control Unit as described in "Electronic Fuel Injection Section".
2. Remove screw attaching A/C outlet to heater case.
3. Disconnect antenna lead, then remove nut securing radio to rear mounting bracket.
4. Remove control knobs, anti-rattle springs, washers and nuts.

NOTE: On models with tape player, control knobs are retained by a 5/64" allen head screw.

5. Disconnect wiring harness and remove radio.
6. Reverse procedure to install.

1977–78 Eldorado

1. Disconnect battery ground cable.
2. Remove ash tray, radio knobs, washers, control rings and nuts.
3. Remove radio to lower support brace nut from rear and rotate brace to the right.
4. Disconnect wires, antenna lead and the dial bulb from radio.
5. Lower left hand side of radio and remove radio through the ash tray opening.
6. Reverse procedure to install.

W/S WIPER MOTOR
1977–84

1. Raise hood and remove cowl screen. On 1980–84 Eldorado and Seville, remove cowl panel prior to removing cowl

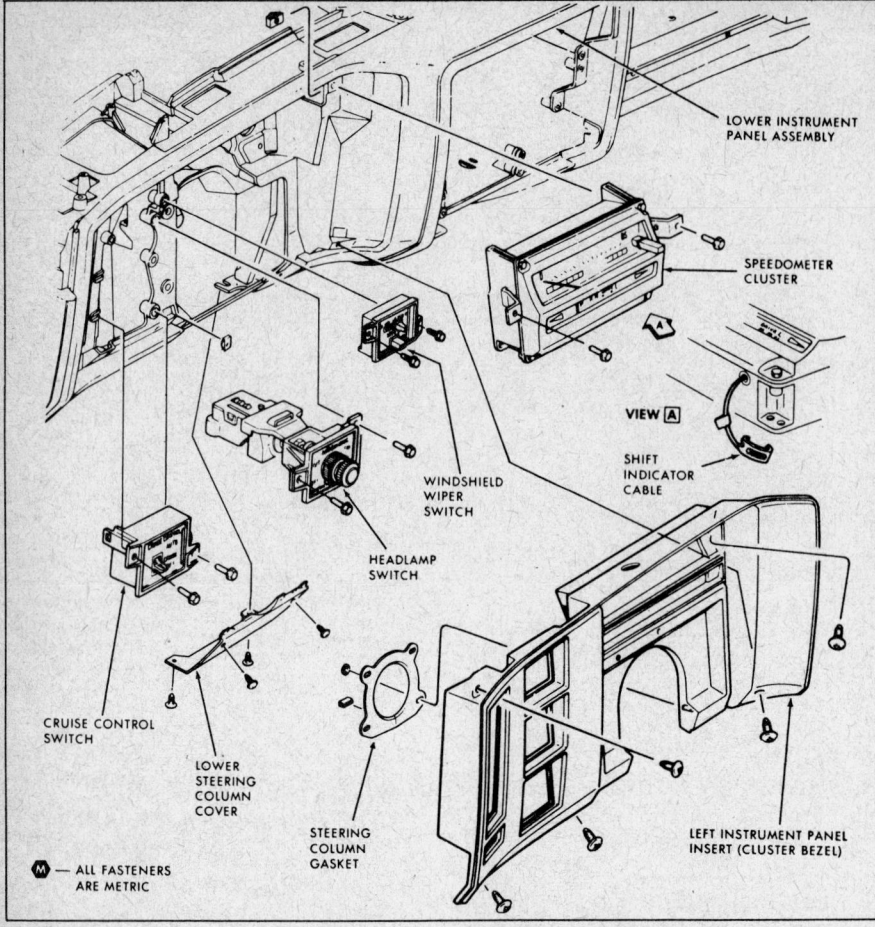

LOWER INSTRUMENT PANEL ASSEMBLY

SPEEDOMETER CLUSTER

VIEW [A]

SHIFT INDICATOR CABLE

WINDSHIELD WIPER SWITCH

HEADLAMP SWITCH

CRUISE CONTROL SWITCH

LOWER STEERING COLUMN COVER

STEERING COLUMN GASKET

LEFT INSTRUMENT PANEL INSERT (CLUSTER BEZEL)

Ⓜ — ALL FASTENERS ARE METRIC

Fig. 11   Instrument cluster. 1977–84 Except Eldorado & Seville

screen.
2. Loosen transmission drive link to crank arm attaching nuts.
3. Remove transmission drive link from motor crank arm.
4. Disconnect motor electrical connectors and hoses.
5. Remove motor attaching screws, then remove motor while guiding crank arm through hole.
6. Reverse procedure to install.

NOTE: Check to ensure wiper motor is in Park position before assembling crank arm to transmission drive link.

W/S WIPER TRANSMISSION

1977–84

1. Raise hood and remove cowl vent screen. On Seville it is first necessary to remove cowl panel.
2. On 1977–78 models except Eldorado and 1979–84 all models, remove left and right wiper arm and blade assemblies. On 1977–78 Eldorado models remove wiper arm and blade from transmission to be removed.
3. Loosen attaching nuts securing transmission drive link to motor crank arm.

NOTE: On 1977–78 Eldorado models if only left side is to be removed, it will not be necessary to loosen nuts securing right drive link to motor crank arm.

4. Disconnect transmission drive link from crank arm.
5. Remove attaching screws securing transmission to body.
6. Remove transmission and linkage assembly through plenum chamber opening.

W/S WIPER SWITCH

1979–84 Eldorado & 1980–84 Seville

1. Disconnect battery ground cable.
2. Remove instrument cluster trim panel.
3. Remove two screws attaching switch to cluster carrier, then pull switch rearward to remove.
4. Reverse procedure to install.

Except 1979–84 Eldorado & 1980–84 Seville

1. Disconnect battery ground cable.
2. Remove left hand climate control outlet grille.
3. Remove screw securing switch to instrument panel.
4. Pull control switch and electrical connec-

tor out and disconnect from panel.

HEATER CORE, REPLACE

After draining radiator and disconnecting heater hoses and battery ground cable proceed as follows:

1979–84 Eldorado & 1980–84 Seville

1. Plug heater core outlets to prevent spillage when removing heater core.
2. Remove instrument panel sound absorbers, then lower steering column.
3. Remove instrument cluster trim panel and instrument cluster as described under Instrument Cluster, Replace.
4. Remove radio front speakers.
5. Remove screws attaching manifold to heater case.
6. Remove instrument panel upper and lower attaching screws, then disconnect parkbrake release cable.
7. Disconnect instrument panel wiring harness from dash wiring assembly.
8. Disconnect right hand remote control mirror cable from instrument panel pad.
9. Disconnect speedometer cable from clip and temperature control cable from heater case.
10. Disconnect radio and A/C wiring, vacuum lines and all necessary wiring to remove instrument panel. If equipped with pulse wipers, remove wiper switch, and then disconnect wire connector from instrument cluster carrier and separate pulse wiper jumper harness from wiper switch wire connector.
11. Remove instrument panel and wiring harness assembly.
12. Remove four screws retaining defroster nozzle to cowl and one screw at heater case, then remove defroster nozzle.
13. Disconnect vacuum hoses to programmer and vacuum actuators.
14. Disconnect wire connector from programmer.
15. From engine side of dash, remove four nuts retaining heater case to cowl, Fig. 12.
16. From passenger compartment side of dash, remove one screw retaining heater case to cowl, and remove heater case.
17. Remove four screws securing heater core to case and remove heater core.
18. Reverse procedure to install.

1977–84 Except Eldorado & Seville

1. Disconnect electrical connectors from blower motor, blower resistors and thermostatic cycling switch.
2. Remove right hand windshield washer nozzle and remove right hand air inlet screen from plenum and cover plate at center of plenum opening.
3. On 1983–84 models, remove blower motor.
4. On all models, remove screws retaining thermostatic cycling switch and position switch aside.
5. Remove the 16 fasteners retaining cover and remove cover.
6. Remove one screw and retainer holding heater core to frame at top.
7. Place temperature door in the max. heat position and reach through temperature housing and push lower forward corner of heater core away from housing, then ro-

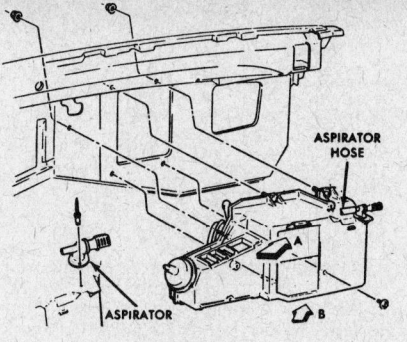

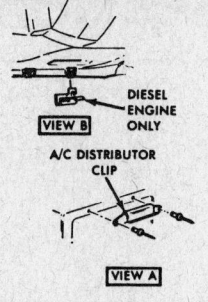

Fig. 12 Heater core. 1979–84 Eldorado & 1980–84 Seville

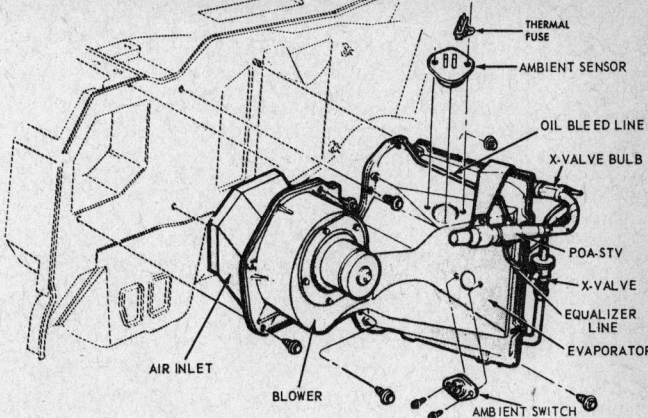

Fig. 13 Blower motor. 1977–84 (Typical)

tate core parallel to housing. This will cause core to snap out of lower clamp. Remove heater core from temperature housing.
8. Reverse procedure to install.

1977–79 Seville

1. Remove right hand wheel housing.
2. Plug heater core tubes to prevent spilling coolant into vehicle when core is removed.
3. Remove instrument panel right hand insert and applique.
4. Remove fuel injection control unit.
5. Remove radio, glove box door and glove box.
6. Remove A/C programmer.
7. Remove right hand lower instrument panel.
8. Remove screws retaining A/C distributor to heater case and remove distributor.
9. Remove clips retaining vacuum harness to heater case and disconnect vacuum hoses at heater mode door, bulkhead grommet and defroster actuator. Position vacuum harness out of way.
10. Disconnect hose from in-car sensor aspirator.
11. From under hood, remove three nuts retaining heater case to cowl, then from inside vehicle, remove two screws retaining heater case to cowl and move heater assembly from cowl.
12. Disconnect vacuum hose from A/C mode door actuator and remove heater assembly.

CAUTION: Heater core pipes are very long. Use care when removing heater assembly.

---

13. Remove rubber seal from around heater core pipes, then remove screw and clip from beneath seal.
14. Remove screws from opposite side of core and remove core.
15. Reverse procedure to install.

1977–78 Eldorado

1. Plug heater core tubes to prevent spilling coolant into vehicle when core is removed.
2. Remove instrument panel pad.
3. Remove center A/C outlet support and connector from position between cowl and horizontal support.
4. Remove left A/C outlet hose from A/C distributor, then remove center support and braces.
5. Remove A/C distributor and defroster nozzle.

6. On vehicles without Air Cushion, remove glove compartment.
7. Disconnect vacuum and electrical connectors from programmer.
8. Disconnect vacuum hoses from recirc. door actuator, defroster door actuator, mode door actuators and position hoses out of way.
9. Disconnect aspirator hose from in-car sensor.
10. Remove three nuts and one screw retaining heater case to cowl at engine side of cowl.
11. Remove heater case from under instrument panel.
12. Remove seal from around core tubes and remove screw and clip from beneath seal.
13. Remove two screws and clip from opposite side of core and remove core from case.
14. Reverse procedure to install.

BLOWER MOTOR, REPLACE

1979–80 Eldorado, 1980 Seville & 1981–84 All Models

1. Disconnect battery ground cable.
2. Disconnect wire connector and cooling hose.
3. Remove five blower motor attaching screws and remove blower motor.
4. Reverse procedure to install.

1977–80 Except 1979–80 Eldorado & 1980 Seville

1. Disconnect battery ground cable.
2. Remove cooling hose from nipple and blower.
3. Disconnect electrical connector at lead to motor.
4. Unfasten and remove motor, Fig. 13.
5. Reverse procedure to install.

SPEED CONTROL, ADJUST

Bead Chain Adjustment

On 1977–81 Eldorado, install the bead chain with second ball on the inboard slot of the throttle plate clip. This will provide the proper adjustment.

On 1977–81 Seville models, install bead

chain to throttle plate clip, and adjust chain in clip to provide a minimum of sag without holding the throttle open. Inboard to outboard slot on the clip will provide a ½ ball adjustment.

On 1977–81 models except Eldorado and Seville, a control cable is used in place of the bead chain. With cable installed in throttle bracket and throttle lever, pull power unit end of cable as far as it will go. If one of four holes in power unit tab is aligned with cable pin, connect pin to tab with retainer. If tab does not align, move cable away from tab until the next closest hole in tab aligns with cable pin and connect pin to tab with retainer.

On 1982 V6-252 models except Eldorado and Seville, a bead chain is used. Install bead chain into throttle lever clip and lock into position. With throttle lever in hot idle position and idle control solenoid de-energized, place bead chain into swivel cavity. The ball swivel must be installed on the inboard side of lever. Chain slack should not exceed one half the diameter of ball stud. Cut off excess chain.

On 1982–84 V8-250 DFI models except Eldorado and Seville, a combination cable and bead chain is used. Install cable into throttle clip and lock into position. Chain should be taut with throttle body lever in hot idle position and idle speed solenoid fully retracted. Place bead into swivel, then install retainer and lock into place. Chain slack should not exceed one half the diameter of ball stud. Cut off excess chain.

On 1982–84 Eldorado and Seville models, a rod assembly is used. Install rod into servo assembly bushing, then assemble plastic end of rod to ball stud on throttle body lever. Adjust by rotating rod assembly to obtain minimum slack with idle speed control screw fully retracted and engine stopped.

Brake Release Switch Adjustment, 1977–84

With brake pedal depressed, push cruise control/stoplight switch fully into retainer and pull brake pedal fully back to rest position. Switch will back out of retainer and adjust automatically.

Vacuum Dump Valve Adjustment

With brake pedal depressed, push vacuum valve switch all the way into the retaining clip. Pull the brake pedal to the stop to automatically adjust the valve.

Engine Section

> See Buick Exc. Skyhawk, 1980—84 Skylark & 1982—84 Century Chapter for Service Procedures on V6-252 Engine not included in this Section.
> See Oldsmobile Chapter for Service Procedures on V8-350 Diesel Engine.

1981 V8-368 MODULATED DISPLACEMENT ENGINE

Description

The 1981 V8-368 engine is of a modulated displacement design which deactivates select cylinders to reduce engine displacement from eight cylinders to six cylinders or four cylinders as necessary. Reducing the number of operating cylinders is accomplished through the use of valve selectors, Fig. 1. At low power requirements, the valve selectors deactivate both intake and exhaust valves on two or four cylinders. For full power output, normal valve operation is restored. In each of the deactivated cylinders, the piston continues to travel, but the intake and exhaust valves are closed. By closing both valves, the cylinders are not allowed to cool and there is a smooth flow of power when the valves are reactivated and the cylinders return to power operation.

Since this engine does not supply adequate vacuum, a belt-driven vacuum pump, Fig. 1A, is installed. The vacuum pump supplies vacuum for proper operation of the various vacuum operated accessories.

System Components

Certain engine operating conditions are monitored by the sensors used in the Digital Electronic Fuel Injection System's (DEFI) Electronic Control Module (ECM). This information includes engine speed, coolant temperature, throttle position and intake manifold absolute pressure. The ECM processes the input data and, based on data and programming, determines the number of operating cylinders required. The ECM then energizes the electrical solenoids in the valve selectors. Each selector controls both the intake and exhaust valve on one cylinder. Valve selectors are installed on cylinders 1, 4, 6 and 7. In the 6 cylinder mode of operation, cylinders 1 and 4 are deactivated. In the 4 cylinder mode of operation, cylinders 6 and 7 are also deactivated. Other engine system components that have been changed or modified to accommodate the Modulated Displacement engine are the ECM, rocker arm covers, rocker arm supports on modulated displacement and the necessary wiring harnesses. Also, due to the decreased engine vacuum levels during the 6 and 4 cylinder modes of operation, an auxiliary vacuum pump is used to allow normal operation of vacuum operated systems. A belt driven vacuum pump attached to the power steering pump is used.

System Operation

The operating principle of the valve selectors is to control the pivot of the rocker arm assembly, and by so doing cause the rocker arm to open the valve or allow the valve to remain closed while the remainder of the valve train operates normally. During active operation, the rocker arm pivots near the center of the rocker arm fulcrum point. As the cam lobe reaches its high point the valve is opened, allowing the air/fuel mixture to enter the cylinder. When the valve selector is activated and the engine is operating in either the 4 or 6 cylinder mode, and the cam lobe is on its highest point, the valve will not open because the rocker arm does not pivot at the center of its fulcrum point. The selector will shift the rocker arm pivot point and allow the rocker arm to slide up and down its mounting stud. This shifts the fulcrum point to the tip of the now stationary valve. With the valve held closed by its spring, the cylinder is inactive. The valve selectors are mounted on the intake and exhaust valve rocker arms above the rocker arm fulcrums. When the solenoid is not energized, view A, Fig. 1A, the selector body is prevented from moving upward by contact between the body projections and the blocking plate above it. The rocker arm pivots near its center, the valves operate normally and the cylinder is active. When the selector is energized, view B, Fig. 1A, the blocking plate is rotated by the solenoid to align the windows in the blocking plate with the body projections. As the rocker arm is lifted by the push rod, the rocker arm and body ride up the stud since the body is no longer restrained by the blocking plate. The rocker arm now pivots at the tip of the valve and the valve remains closed. The body is spring loaded downward by an internal spring. This spring provides valve train action and normal hydraulic lifter function when the valve train is deactivated by providing tension in the valve body and maintaining zero valve lash. The solenoid force is less than that required to overcome blocking plate/body friction when the valve is lifted. This prevents deactivation of the valve while it is lifted, which would cause abrupt valve seating. The valve selector, if defective, must be replaced as an assembly.

ENGINE MOUNTS, REPLACE

1982—84 V8-250

Engine Mount, Replace
1. Open hood, then remove screws securing strut support rod and position rods aside, Fig. 1B.
2. Position upper radiator shroud so that it will not be damaged when engine is raised.
3. Raise and support vehicle, then remove engine mount through bolt.
4. Raise engine slightly using suitable jack until engine mount bracket is free from mount.
5. Remove nuts securing engine mount, then remove engine mount.

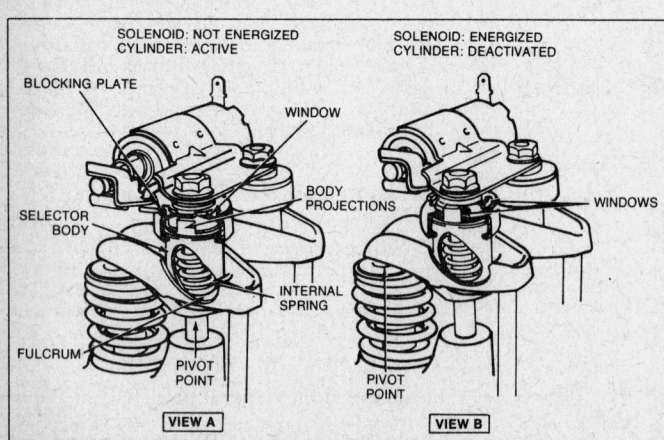

Fig. 1 Modulated displacement engine valve selector operation. 1981 V8-368

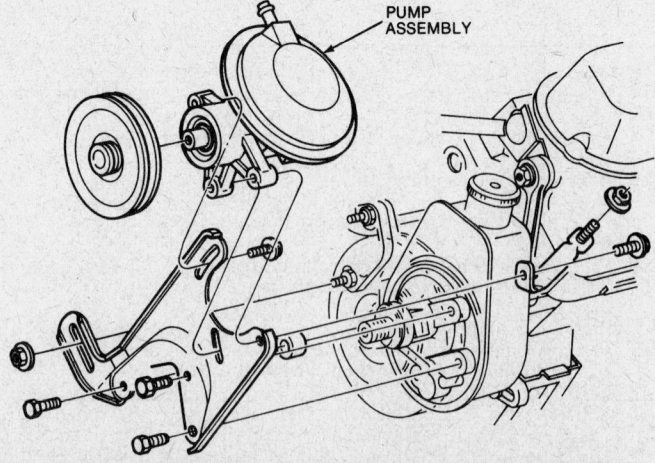

Fig. 1A Vacuum pump installation. 1981 V8-368 modulated displacement engine

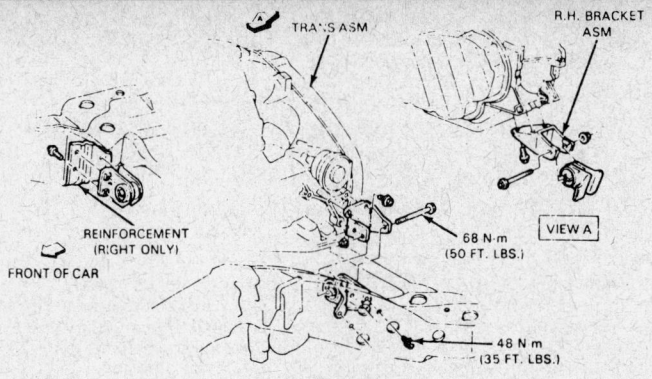

ELDORADO & SEVILLE

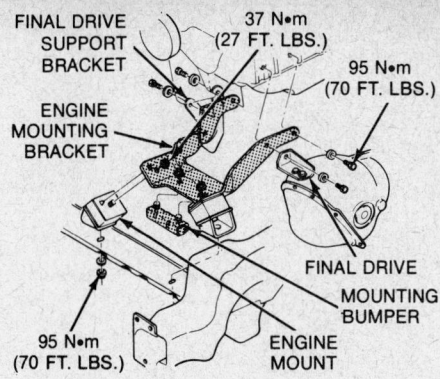

Fig. 1D Front engine mounts. 1981 Eldorado & Seville V8-368

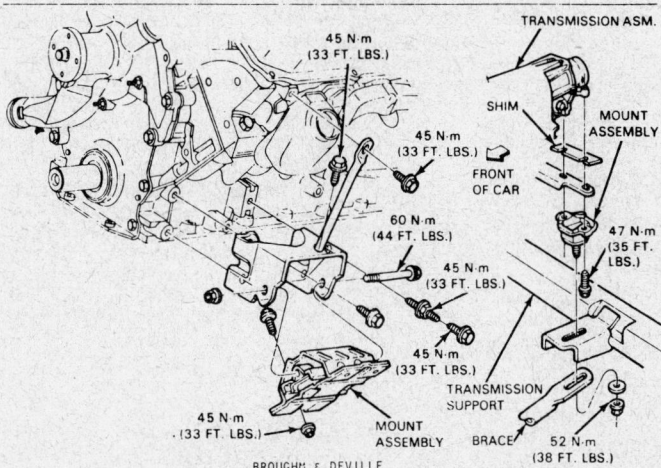

Fig. 1B Engine mounts. 1982–84 models with V8-250 engine

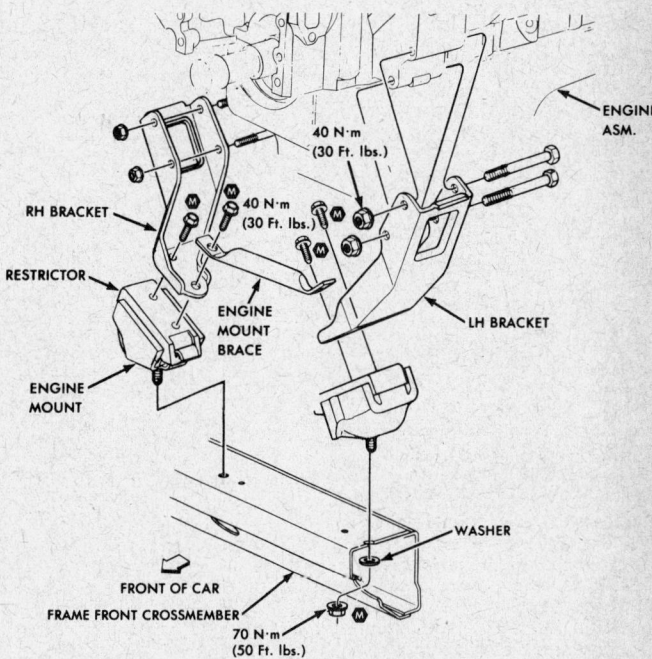

Fig. 1E Front engine mounts. 1980 Eldorado & Seville V8-368

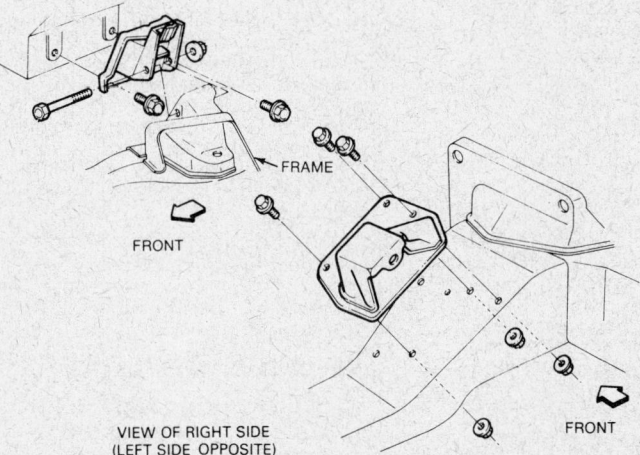

Fig. 1C Front engine mounts. 1980–82 models with V6-252 engine

1980–82 V6-252

Removal
1. Remove front engine mount to cylinder block bolts, Fig. 1C.
2. Raise and support vehicle.
3. Using a suitable jack, raise and support engine weight at front edge of oil pan.
4. Remove rear engine mount to cylinder block bolts.
5. Raise engine slightly and remove engine mount through-bolts.
6. Remove mount.

Installation
1. Install rear engine mount to cylinder block bolts and torque to 55 ft. lbs.
2. Lower engine until mounts rest on crossmember bracket.
3. Install and tighten engine mount through-bolts.
4. Lower vehicle. Install front engine mount bolts and torque to 55 ft. lbs.

1977–79 V8-425 Except Eldorado; 1980 V8-368 All

1. Open hood.
2. Remove two screws on each side securing radiator cover to strut support rods. Loosen one screw on each side and position support rods aside.
3. Remove two screws securing upper radiator shroud to radiator cover and one screw securing upper radiator hose bracket to shroud. Drill out the rivets securing upper shroud to lower shroud and remove the upper shroud.
4. Raise and support vehicle.
5. Remove through bolt from mount being replaced, Figs. 1D, 1E and 1F.
6. Loosen the through bolt on the mount on the opposite side.
7. Using a suitable jack under the oil pan, raise engine until the bracket is free from the engine mount. Remove three flanged locking nuts and bolts, then the engine mount.
8. Reverse procedure to install.

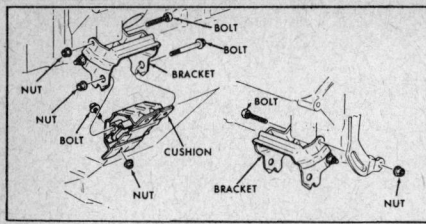

Fig. 1F Front engine mounts. 1977–81 V8 Exc. Eldorado & Seville

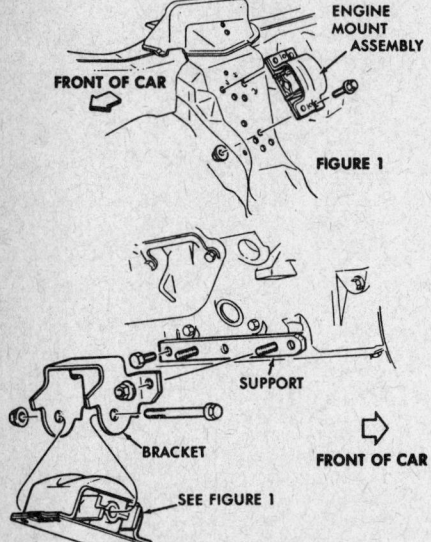

Figure 1

Fig. 2 Front engine mounts. 1977–79 Seville

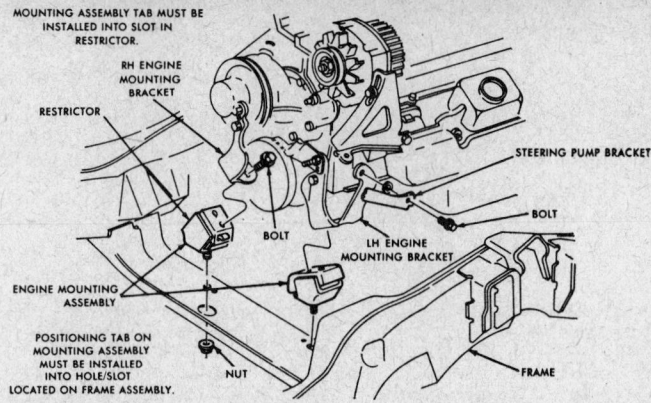

Fig. 3 Front engine mounts. 1979–80 Eldorado & 1980 Seville V8-350

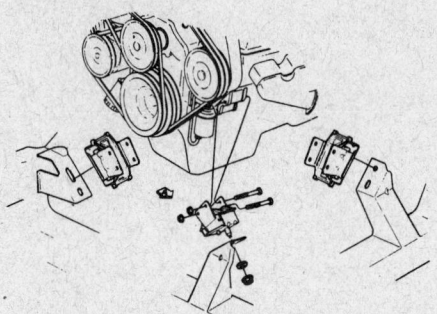

Fig. 4 Front engine mounts. 1977–78 Eldorado

1977–79 Seville

1. Remove fan shroud, then the wheel housing struts from both sides.
2. Raise vehicle, then remove crossover pipe and engine mount through bolts.
3. Support vehicle, raise engine until support can be removed from engine block.
4. Working through opening between lower control arm and frame, remove bolts attaching engine mount to frame and the mount, Fig. 2.
5. Reverse procedure to install.

1979–80 Eldorado & 1980 Seville V8-350

1. Raise and support vehicle.
2. Remove front splash shield, then two screws from engine bracket to engine mount on each side, Fig. 3.
3. Remove nut and washer from each mount.
4. Using a suitable jack and block of wood under harmonic balancer, raise engine until each mount can be removed from vehicle.
5. Reverse procedure to install.

1977–78 Eldorado V8-425

Left Front Mount

1. Remove radiator cover and disconnect battery ground cable.
2. Raise car and remove nut and washer from mount stud.
3. Remove capscrew securing transmission cooler lines to final drive bracket.
4. Remove screw securing top of steering gear flex coupling shroud to frame.
5. Remove nut from large through bolt securing top of engine mount and top of final drive bracket to engine.
6. Remove nut from lower engine mount through bolt.

NOTE: Attach box end wrench to nut, then use pry bar between wrench and engine.

7. Remove remaining screw securing flex coupling shroud to frame and remove shroud.
8. Remove cross bar bolt, nut and washers securing bottom of final drive bracket to final drive. Remove bracket by tipping back and to left of car.
9. Using block of wood and jack stand, lift engine from frame at crankshaft pulley to relieve load on engine mount bolts and remove bolts from mount.
10. Loosen, but do not remove, nut and washer from right engine mount stud.
11. Raise engine enough to remove mount, Fig. 4. Work mount down and forward between fuel pump and frame.

Right Front Mount

1. Remove radiator cover.
2. Remove nut and washer securing left engine mount to frame.
3. Raise car and remove nut and washer securing right mount to frame.
4. Reach between right mount and oil pump to attach open end wrench to nut on lower bolt securing mount to engine. Holding this wrench in place, remove lower mounting bolt from rear, using ratchet, U-joint socket and 18" extension.
5. Work end wrench up between oil pump and crankshaft pulley and position wrench in a straight vertical position to engage nut on upper mounting bolt. Holding wrench in place, use same tools as in Step 4 to remove upper mounting bolt.

NOTE: If nut is impossible to engage, an alternative is to first perform the following Step, then use a 5" extension and a 9/16" crowfoot adapter and engage tool on nut by slipping between oil pump and A.I.R. pump.

6. Place jackstand under crankshaft pulley and using wood blocks to avoid damage to pulley, either raise engine or lower chassis to remove mount.

CAUTION: When separating engine and chassis, observe relative position of frame rail and right drive axle tri-pot housing. Interference between these parts requires removal of right drive axle before mount can be removed. Furthermore, if tri-pot housing does clear the frame, vertical movement is limited by presence of fuel lines. Do not allow tri-pot housing to contact fuel lines.

7. Work mount free and pull rearward over tri-pot housing to remove, Fig. 4.
8. Reverse procedure to install.

ENGINE, REPLACE

1982–84 V8-250

1. Disconnect battery ground cable and drain cooling system.
2. Remove screws securing strut support rods and position rods aside.
3. Remove radiator shroud to radiator support screws. Remove staples securing upper and lower fan shrouds.
4. Remove radiator cover from radiator support.
5. Remove power steering reservoir from upper fan shroud, then position reservoir aside and remove fan shroud.
6. Mark hood hinge outlines on hood, then remove hood.
7. Remove air cleaner and duct assembly.
8. Disconnect upper radiator hose from thermostat housing.
9. Disconnect following electrical connec-

tors:
  a. Coolant temperature sensor.
  b. Engine metal temperature switch.
  c. MAT sensor.
  d. Idle speed control motor.
  e. Throttle position sensor.
  f. EGR solenoid.
  g. AIR management valve.
  h. Oxygen sensor.
  i. Ignition timing connector.
  j. Distributor and A/C compressor.
  k. Alternator, cruise control servo and right side cylinder head ground wires.
10. Disconnect wiring harness support clips and position harness aside.
11. Disconnect brake vacuum hose from pipe, throttle linkage, and vapor canister hose.
12. Remove clutch fan assembly, then disconnect lower radiator hose.
13. Remove A/C compresor mounting bolts and position compressor aside with all lines attached.
14. Disconnect coolant reservoir hose and remove water nipple from rear of intake manifold.
15. Disconnect fuel inlet and return lines.
16. On Brougham and DeVille models, raise and support vehicle, then proceed as follows:
  a. Disconnect oil cooler lines from filter adapter, then remove filter adapter.
  b. Remove strut rods connecting engine mounts to flywheel cover.
  c. Remove flywheel cover.
  d. Remove six engine to transmission screws, then remove motor mount through bolts.
  e. Remove screws securing flywheel to converter.
  f. Disconnect starter motor electrical connectors, then disconnect exhaust pipes from exhaust manifold.
  g. Lower vehicle to ground, then support transmission with suitable jack.
  h. Attach suitable lifting equipment to engine lift brackets, then raise engine slowly and position forward to disengage from transmission.
  i. Remove engine from vehicle.
  j. Reverse procedure to install.
7. On Eldorado and Seville models, raise and support vehicle, then proceed as follows:
  a. Disconnect oil cooler lines from junction at right hand side of engine compartment.
  b. Remove six engine to transaxle screws, then remove nuts securing engine mount brackets to transmission.
  c. Remove flywheel cover and screws securing flywheel to converter.
  d. Disconnect starter motor electrical connectors, then disconnect exhaust pipes from exhaust manifold.
  e. Lower vehicle, then support transaxle with suitable jack.
  f. Attach suitable lifting equipment to engine lift brackets, then raise engine slowly and pull forward to disengage from transmission.
  g. Remove engine from vehicle.
  h. Reverse procedure to install.

1980–82 V6-252, Except Eldorado & Seville

Removal
1. Mark hood hinge and hinge bracket for installation alignment, then remove hood.
2. Remove battery ground cable.

3. Drain engine coolant, remove air cleaner, then disconnect A/C compressor ground wire from mounting bracket.
4. Disconnect compressor clutch connector.
5. Remove compressor from mounting bracket and position out of the way.
6. Remove fan, pulley and belts.
7. Disconnect radiator and heater hoses and position aside, then remove radiator and fan shroud.
8. Remove power steering pump from bracket and position aside.
9. Disconnect and plug fuel pump hose.
10. Disconnect vacuum feed hose from carburetor, then the vacuum modulator and power brake vacuum hoses from engine.
11. Disconnect the three evaporative canister to carburetor hoses.
12. Disconnect throttle and TV cable from carburetor.
13. Disconnect Cruise Control servo cable at mounting bracket, if equipped.
14. Disconnect all sending unit switch connections from engine. Remove alternator, then disconnect engine wiring harness at engine.
15. Raise and support vehicle, then disconnect engine wiring harness at starter and remove starter.
16. Disconnect exhaust pipes from exhaust manifold.
17. Remove lower flywheel cover, then mark flywheel and converter for reassembly alignment. Remove converter to flywheel bolts.
18. Remove engine to transmission bolts and engine mount through-bolts.
19. Lower vehicle and support transmission. Using a suitable lifting device, raise engine. Ensure wiring harness, vacuum hoses and other parts are clear of engine before removal.
20. Lift engine just enough to clear engine mounts, then lift transmission support evenly and alternately until engine is separated from transmission and can be removed.

Installation
1. Lower engine into vehicle, engaging transmission. Align flywheel and converter marks, then install and torque flywheel bolts to 35 ft. lbs.
2. Install and tighten engine mount through-bolts and nuts.
3. Raise and support vehicle, then install transmission to engine bolts and torque to 35 ft. lbs.
4. Install starter, then install flywheel cover. Connect starter electrical leads.
5. Connect exhaust pipes to exhaust manifolds.
6. Lower vehicle, then connect engine wiring harness, throttle cable, vacuum and water hoses, emission control line from canister to air cleaner and the transmission cooler line clip to exhaust manifold stud.
7. Connect battery ground cable to A/C compressor bracket.
8. Connect fuel line to fuel pump.
9. Install power steering pump into bracket. Adjust power steering belt tension.
10. Install fan shroud and radiator assembly. Attach radiator hoses and transmission cooler lines.
11. Install pulley, fan and belts. Adjust belt tension.
12. Install A/C compressor into bracket and connect wiring.
13. Install alternator to bracket and connect wiring.
14. Install air cleaner.
15. Install engine coolant; ensure proper lev-

el is attained after engine reaches operating temperature.
16. Connect negative battery cable to battery.
17. Install hood, aligning marks made at removal.

1979–81 Eldorado & 1980–81 Seville

1. Mark hood hinge location on hood, then remove hood.
2. Disconnect battery cables and remove battery from vehicle.
3. Remove battery ground cable ground screw from right hand fender.
4. Drain cooling system, then remove air cleaner assembly.
5. Relieve fuel presure from E.F.I. lines by loosely installing valve depressor J-5420 on pressure fitting. Position shop towels or a suitable container under fitting, then slowly tighten valve depressor until pressure is relieved.
6. Raise vehicle and remove crossover pipe from vehicle.
7. Disconnect shift linkage from transmission.
8. Remove clamp and disconnect fuel hose from fuel pipe.
9. Remove left and right drive axle to output shaft attaching screws.
10. Remove nuts from left and right hand engine mounts and nut and washer from left and right hand transmission mounts.
11. Remove two fan shroud lower attaching screws and disconnect lower radiator hose from radiator, then lower vehicle.
12. Disconnect upper radiator hose and transmission cooler lines from radiator, then remove radiator upper cover and slide radiator out of vehicle.
13. Remove clutch fan and radiator shroud.
14. Disconnect power steering hoses at steering gear and cap hoses and fittings.
15. Remove clamp and disconnect fuel return hose from presure regulator fuel return pipe.
16. Disconnect M.A.P. hose at throttle body, then pull hose out of tie straps and position aside.
17. If equipped with cruise control, disconnect vacuum hose from power unit, then pull hose out of tie strap and position on top of cowl.
18. Disconnect canister hose, vacuum supply hose and throttle cable from throttle body and position out of way.
19. Disconnect heater hoses at water valve and water pump.
20. Disconnect power brake unit vacuum hose.
21. Disconnect speedometer cable from transmission.
22. Disconnect engine wiring harness from bulkhead connector, E.S.S. connector from distributor, heater wire from water valve, wiring from wiper motor and washer bottle and ground strap from cowl.
23. Remove coolant reservoir and disconnect wiring from A/C compressor clutch.
24. Remove A/C compressor and A.I.R. pump drive belts.
25. Remove compressor to mounting bracket attaching bolts and position compressor on right hand fender skirt. Use care not to damage refrigerant hoses.
26. Install a suitable engine lifting fixture.
27. Carefully raise engine and pull forward until transmission clears front of dash.
28. Remove engine, transmission and drive as an assembly.
29. Reverse procedure to install.

CADILLAC—Exc. Cimarron

1977–79 Seville

1. Disconnect battery ground cable.
2. Drain cooling system and remove air cleaner.
3. Remove hood and wheel housing struts from both sides.

NOTE: Scribe outline of hinge on underside of hood before removing to aid alignment at installation.

4. Remove fan shroud and disconnect power brake vacuum hose at steel line.
5. Disconnect wiring harness left side branch at fuel injectors, coolant sensor, oil pressure switch, HEI feed, heater turn-on switch, speed sensor and generator. Position harness aside.
6. Remove heater hose at rear of intake manifold.
7. Remove radiator hoses.
8. Remove fan and clutch assembly.
9. Remove distributor cap and secondary wiring.
10. Disconnect wiring harness right side branch at fuel injectors, throttle switch, EGR solenoid, fast idle valve, air temperature sensor, A/C compressor, MAP sensor, economy lite hose and two compressor ground wires.
11. Disconnect throttle linkage and position aside, remove vapor canister hose from throttle body.
12. Remove fuel inlet line from fuel rail.

NOTE: Use backup wrench on fuel rail to prevent damage to fitting. Ensure fuel pressure is relieved before loosening fitting.

13. Disconnect power steering hoses at steering gear and cap hoses and connections.
14. Disconnect fuel return line from pressure regulator outlet.
15. Remove compressor from engine and position aside.

NOTE: Do not disconnect refrigerant hoses from compressor.

16. Raise vehicle and remove exhaust pipe from right bank manifold.
17. Remove torque converter cover, then remove starter.
18. Remove clip securing transmission oil cooler lines to oil pan.
19. Remove bolts securing flex plate to converter.
20. Remove engine mount through bolts, then the crossover pipe.
21. Remove engine to transmission attaching bolts.
22. Remove screws attaching heater water valve to evaporator and position valve aside.
23. Support transmission, then raise engine off mounts and reposition transmission mount. Raise engine, then pull forward to disengage transmission and remove engine.
24. Reverse procedure to install.

1977–78 Eldorado

1. Disconnect battery ground cable.
2. Scribe hood hinge locations and remove hood.

---

3. Drain cooling system.
4. Remove air cleaner, inlet duct, vacuum hoses and hot air ducts.
5. Disconnect upper radiator hose from thermostat housing and remove at cradle.
6. Remove radiator cover.
7. Remove fan assembly.
8. Disconnect alternator wiring, right bank spark plug wires and heater turn-on switch wiring and position harness aside.
9. Disconnect water control valve hose at rear of cylinder block.
10. Disconnect starter motor wiring harness at multiple connector.
11. Remove power steering pump and position aside with hoses attached.
12. Remove all drive belts.
13. Remove A/C compressor mounts and position aside with refrigerant hoses attached.
14. Disconnect throttle and Cruise Control linkage from carburetor or throttle body and bracket, then position cables aside.
15. Disconnect wiring on left branch of engine harness and position harness aside.
16. On vehicles equipped with Electronic Fuel Injection, disconnect manifold harness and position aside.
17. On all models, disconnect vacuum lines from carburetor or throttle body and position aside.
18. Remove left exhaust manifold flange nuts.
19. Remove transmission cooler line bracket screw, then the filler pipe nut from exhaust manifold.
20. Remove upper screw securing steering gear flex coupling shroud to frame.
21. Raise and support vehicle.
22. Remove remaining screw securing steering gear flex coupling shroud to frame.
23. Remove bolt and nut securing final drive bracket to engine mount.
24. Disconnect fuel pump fuel lines and plug lines and pump ports.
25. Remove lower radiator hose.
26. Remove right exhaust manifold flange nuts.
27. Remove starter motor and position aside with wiring attached.
28. Remove flywheel inspection cover.
29. Remove converter to flywheel retaining screws.
30. Remove the two lower transmission to engine screws.
31. Remove right output shaft screws.
32. Remove two output shaft bracket to cylinder block screws and one screw securing bracket to final drive.
33. Loosen right shock absorber mounting nut and position shock absorber outboard.
34. Move drive axle rearward as far as possible and remove output shaft.
35. Lower vehicle.
36. Remove four screws securing transmission to engine, two screws at the top and two screws at the left side.
37. Attach suitable engine lifting equipment to engine.
38. Support transmission with a suitable jack.
39. Remove engine from vehicle.
40. Reverse procedure to install.

1977–81 Brougham & DeVille Except V6-252

1. Disconnect battery ground cable.

---

2. Drain cooling system.
3. Remove self-tapping screw and washer securing each wheelhouse strut to radiator cover and position struts aside.
4. Remove two screws securing top radiator shroud to cradle and one screw securing upper radiator hose to shroud. Drill out nine rivets securing upper shroud to lower shroud. Remove two screws securing radiator cover to cradle and the cover.
5. On all models, scribe hood hinge locations and remove hood.
6. Remove air cleaner and inlet duct.
7. Disconnect upper radiator hose from thermostat housing.
8. Disconnect wiring at the following locations: coolant temperature sender, ignition coil or H.E.I. distributor, downshift switch, engine metal temperature switch, anti-dieseling solenoid, oil pressure switch, heater turn-on switch and A/C compressor.
9. On vehicles equipped with Electronic Fuel Injection, disconnect EFI wiring harness and position aside.
10. On all models, bend back clips on rocker cover and position harness aside.
11. Disconnect brake hose from brake pipe.
12. Remove Cruise Control servo and disconnect bead chain at carburetor.
13. Disconnect throttle linkage from carburetor and position aside.
14. Disconnect vapor canister hose.
15. Disconnect power steering pump and position aside with hoses attached.
16. Remove fan and spacer.
17. Remove right side spark plug wires and position aside.
18. Remove A/C compressor and position aside with refrigerant line attached.
19. Disconnect alternator wiring and bend back clips securing harness to right valve cover and position harness aside.
20. Disconnect PCV vacuum line and the automatic level control vacuum line, if equipped.
21. Disconnect modulator line from carburetor.
22. Remove hot water valve hose from rear of right cylinder head.
23. Remove two nuts securing each cowl to wheelhouse tie strut to wheelhousing. Loosen nuts securing each strut to cowl and swing the struts outboard.
24. Remove two top screws securing engine to transmission.
25. Raise and support vehicle.
26. Remove nut and washer securing each engine mount to frame.
27. Remove starter motor.
28. Remove flywheel inspection cover.
29. Remove screws securing converter to flywheel.
30. Support the exhaust system and disconnect exhaust pipes from exhaust manifolds.
31. Disconnect fuel line and vapor return line from fuel pump.
32. Support transmission with a suitable jack. Remove remaining engine to transmission bolts.
33. Attach suitable engine lifting equipment to engine.
34. Remove engine from vehicle.
35. Reverse procedure to install.

INTAKE MANIFOLD, REPLACE

With E.F.I.

V8-250

1. Drain coolant from radiator, then discon-

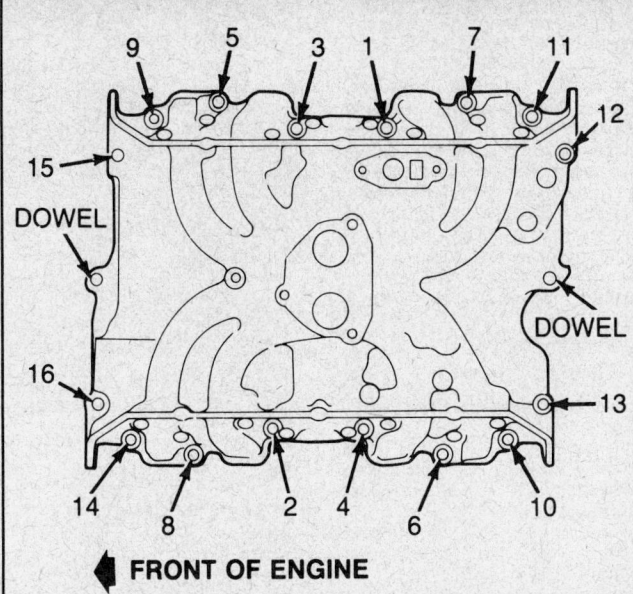

FRONT OF ENGINE

BOLT TIGHTENING
SEQUENCE

1. TIGHTEN BOLTS 1, 2, 3,
   & 4 IN SEQUENCE TO
   15.0-20.0 N•m
   (11-15 FT-LBS).

2. TIGHTEN BOLTS 5
   THRU 16 IN SEQUENCE
   TO 24.5-30.0 N•m
   (18-22 FT-LBS).

3. RETIGHTEN ALL BOLTS
   IN SEQUENCE TO
   24.5-30.0 N•m
   (18-22 FT-LBS).

Fig. 4A Intake manifold bolt tightening sequence. V8-250

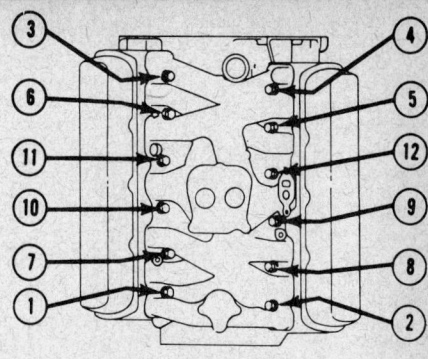

Fig. 5 Intake manifold tightening sequence.
V8-350

nect radiator hose from thermostat housing.

2. Disconnect electrical connectors from coolant sensor, MAT sensor, throttle position sensor, distributor, ISC motor and fuel injectors.
3. Disconnect heater hoses from manifold.
4. Disconnect fuel lines from throttle body and distributor.
5. Remove both rocker arm covers.
6. Remove rocker arm support and rocker arms as an assembly.
7. Remove bolts securing A/C compressor, then position compressor aside with all hoses and lines attached.
8. Remove vacuum harness connectors from rear of manifold.
9. Remove intake manifold bolts and lower thermostat housing to front cover bolts.

NOTE: Engine lift brackets must be bent or positioned aside for intake manifold removal.

10. Remove intake manifold by lifting straight up off dowels.
11. Reverse procedure to install. Refer to Fig. 4A for intake manifold bolt tightening sequence and torque procedure.

SERVICE NOTE

The V8-250 engine uses three different intake manifolds, all using different intake manifold to cylinder head bolts. To determine which manifold and bolts are used, an identification mark is located next to the manifold air temperature sensor.

The first type manifold has no identification mark. Bolt location, Fig. 4A, and size are as follows: locations 1, 2, 3, 4, 12, 13 and 16, 1.57 inch (40 mm) bolts; locations 5, 6, 7, 8, 9, 10, 11 and 14, 1.18 inch (30 mm) bolts; and location 15, 2.36 inch (60 mm) bolt.

The second type manifold is identified by an X. Bolt location, Fig. 4A, and sizes are as follows: locations 1, 2, 3 and 4, 2.16 inch (55 mm) bolts; locations 5, 6, 7, 8, 9, 10, 11 and 14, 1.18 inch (30 mm) bolts; locations 12, 13 and 16, 1.57 inch (40 mm) bolts; and location 15, 2.36 inch (60 mm) bolt.

The third type manifold is identified by an Ⓧ. This manifold uses the same bolts in the same location as the manifold with the X identification mark, with the exception of bolt 12. In this manifold a 2.16 inch (55 mm) bolt is used, Fig. 4A.

V8-350
1. Disconnect battery ground cable and drain cooling system.
2. Remove air cleaner and crankcase filter.
3. Disconnect throttle and Cruise Control linkage from throttle body. Remove cable from bracket and position aside.
4. Disconnect coolant temperature tell-tale switch, H.E.I. lead wire, speed sensor connector and injector valve wiring.
5. Disconnect EGR solenoid leads, throttle position switch, fast idle valve, air temperature sensor connector and MAP sensor hose.
6. Disconnect the two ground wires from A/C compressor bracket.
7. Disconnect the two vacuum hoses from throttle body to TVS switch.
8. Disconnect vacuum hoses and power brake pipe from rear of throttle body.
9. Disconnect fuel line from fuel rail.
10. Remove PCV valve from rocker cover.
11. Disconnect spark plug leads and position aside.
12. Disconnect upper radiator hose, by-pass hose and the heater hose, located at the rear of the manifold.
13. Remove A/C compressor and position aside with refrigerant hoses attached.
14. Remove fuel return hose from pressure regulator.
15. On 1978–82 models, remove oil pressure switch and oil fill tube.
16. Remove intake manifold bolts and the intake manifold.
17. Reverse procedure to install. Torque intake manifold bolts in sequence, Fig. 5, to 40 ft. lbs.

V8-368 & 425
1. Disconnect battery ground cable and remove air cleaner and crankcase filter.
2. Disconnect throttle cable and cruise control linkage, if equipped, from throttle body. Remove cable from bracket and position aside.
3. Working on engine left side, disconnect coolant temperature tell-tale switch wire, HEI lead wire, speed sensor connector,

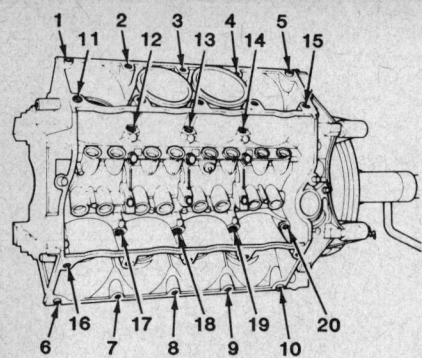

Fig. 6   Cylinder head bolt hole locations. V8-250

downshift switch and injector wires. Disconnect harness from fuel rail brackets and position aside.

4. Disconnect two vacuum hoses from throttle body to TVS switch.
5. Disconnect vacuum hoses and power brake pipe from throttle body.

NOTE: Use a back-up wrench when removing power brake pipe to prevent damage to fitting.

6. Disconnect fuel line from fuel rail.

NOTE: Use a back-up wrench on fuel rail to prevent damage to fitting.

7. Working on engine right side, disconnect injector wires, EGR solenoid leads, air temperature sensor connector and MAP sensor hose. Disconnect harness from fuel rail brackets and position aside.
8. Remove PCV valve from rocker cover and position aside.
9. Remove spark plug leads and distributor cap.
10. Remove front fuel rail.
11. Position A/C compressor aside, do not disconnect refrigerant lines.
12. Remove fuel return hose from pressure regulator.
13. Remove manifold bolts and lift manifold from engine. Do not pry or lift manifold by the fuel rails or the mounting brackets.
14. Reverse procedure to install. Torque manifold bolts to 30 ft. lbs.

Less E.F.I.

Except V6-252

1. Disconnect battery ground cable and remove air cleaner.
2. Disconnect throttle linkage and Cruise Control linkage, if equipped.
3. Disconnect coil wires at H.E.I. connector, then remove distributor cap and disconnect right hand spark plug wires at spark plugs and place aside.
4. Disconnect wire connectors from temperature sender, down shift switch and antidieseling solenoid.
5. Remove coil, anti-dieseling solenoid and solenoid bracket.
6. Disconnect vacuum lines from carburetor, remove Cruise Control servo top mounting bolt and position brake hose aside, if equipped.
7. Disconnect wiring connector from A/C

compressor, if equipped.
8. Disconnect fuel line at carburetor and remove vacuum lines from intake manifold.
9. Loosen power steering mounting bolts and pivot pump toward engine. Remove A/C compressor drive belt, then the screws attaching compressor rear mounting to engine and the screws attaching compressor mounting flange to front mounting bracket. Position compressor aside.
10. Remove PCV valve from rocker cover.
11. Remove manifold to cylinder head bolts, intake manifold, manifold shield and gaskets.
12. Reverse procedure to install.

V6-252

1. Disconnect battery ground cable, then drain cooling system.
2. Remove air cleaner.
3. Disconnect the following:
   a. Upper radiator hose and heater hose at manifold.
   b. Accelerator linkage at carburetor, linkage bracket at manifold and cruise control chain if equipped.
   c. Booster vacuum pipe at manifold.
   d. Fuel line at carburetor.
   e. Transmission vacuum modulator line.
   f. Idle stop solenoid wire, if equipped.
   g. Distributor wires and temperature sending unit wire.
   h. Vacuum hoses from, distributor TVS and EFE valve pipe, from carburetor to vacuum manifold.
   i. Fuel economy and load leveler hose, if equipped.
   j. Coolant by-pass hose at manifold.
4. Remove distributor cap and rotor to gain access to left intake manifold torx head bolt. Use Tool J-24394 or equivalent to remove torx head bolt.
5. Remove accelerator linkage springs.
6. Remove compressor upper bracket, if equipped.
7. Remove intake manifold.
8. Reverse procedure to install.

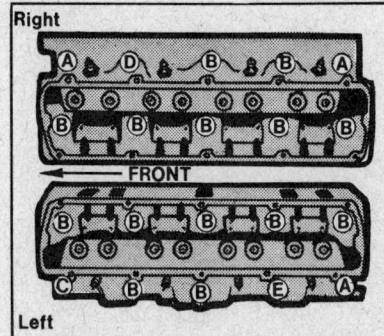

Bolt Location	Length
A (Bolt)	2.96 (Short)
B (Bolt)	4.16 (Long)
C (Bolt/Stud Head)	2.96 (Short)
D (Bolt/Stud Head)	4.16 (Long)
E (Bolt-Special)*	4.16 (Long)*

*This special bolt has an extra thick hex head which is drilled and tapped to accept the temperature switch.

Fig. 7   Location and length of cylinder head bolts. V8-350

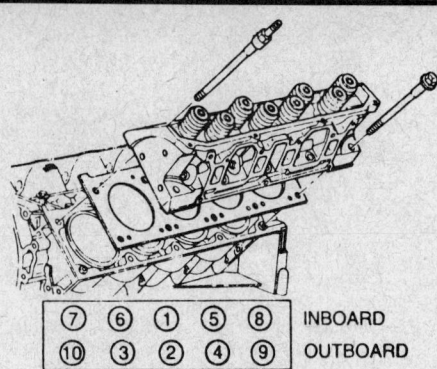

					INBOARD
7	6	1	5	8	
10	3	2	4	9	OUTBOARD

Fig. 6A   Cylinder head bolt tightening sequence. V8-250

CYLINDER HEAD, REPLACE

V8-250

NOTE: Some V8-250 engine blocks may exhibit casting porosity, indicated by oil leakage around the threads of cylinder head bolts. This leakage is caused by porosity between a pressurized oil passage and the threaded bolt hole. This condition occurs between an oil gallery and holes #11, 12, 13, 14, 17, 18, 19 or 20, Fig. 6. An internal oil leak will occur around these bolts and will rarely be detected. However, when this condition is experienced at bolt holes #1, 2, 3, 4, 5, 6, 7, 8, 9, 10, 15, or 16, Fig. 6, an external oil leak may result. To provide a permanent repair for this condition, remove the bolt and clean both the bolt and hole with a suitable cleaner. With compressed air, blow out the bolt hole and apply a suitable two-part epoxy to the lower 5 or 6 threads of the bolt. Install the bolt and torque to 90 ft. lbs.

1. Remove valve covers, then remove intake manifold as described under "Intake Manifold, Replace".
2. On right hand side cylinder head removal, remove alternator and AIR pump.
3. For left hand side cylinder head removal, remove vacuum pump and bracket. Remove bolts and position power steering pump aside.
4. Remove exhaust manifold from cylinder head, then bolt securing AIR pipe to cylinder head.
5. Remove cylinder head bolts, then remove cylinder head.
6. Reverse procedure to install. refer to Fig. 6A for cylinder head bolt tightening sequence.

V8-350

1. Drain cooling system and remove intake manifold as described under "Intake Manifold Replace".
2. Remove exhaust manifolds.
3. Remove rocker cover, rocker arm bolts, pivots, rocker arms and push rods.

NOTE: Note location of rocker arms and pivots to ensure installation in original position.

4. Remove cylinder head bolts and the cylinder head.
5. When installing cylinder head it is impor-

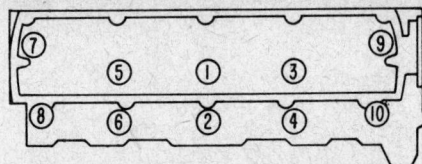

Fig. 7A   Cylinder head tightening sequence. V8-350

tant that cylinder head bolts are installed in the correct position, refer to Fig. 7. Torque cylinder head bolts in sequence, Fig. 7A. Torque intake manifold bolts in sequence shown in Fig. 5.

V8-368 & 425

NOTE: Engine rocker arm covers on 1980–81 V8-368 engines are made of a nylon material and are sealed to the cylinder head with RTV sealer. Use caution when removing covers. Do not pry the cover off. If cover removal is difficult, use a rubber mallet and tap gently in an upward direction on lower surface and only at ribbed areas of the cover. When installing covers, clean off all old sealant thoroughly, including sealing groove in cover face. Apply a new bead of sealer, P/N 1051435 or equivalent and torque attaching screws to 30 inch pounds.

1. Drain coolant from radiator.
2. Remove intake manifold.
3. Disconnect ground strap at rear of cylinder heads from cowl where used.
4. Disconnect wiring connector for high engine temperature warning system from sending unit at rear of left cylinder head.
5. Remove alternator if working on right cylinder head, or partially remove power steering pump if working on left cylinder head.
6. Remove A.I.R. manifold from both cylinder heads if equipped.
7. Disconnect wiring harness from cylinder head and and position out of the way.
8. Remove exhaust manifold from cylinder head.

NOTE: On early production V8-368 D.E.F.I. engine, with non-locking bolts and lock tabs, exhaust manifold leaks may be corrected by replacing lock tabs and bolts with prevailing torque bolts. The prevailing torque bolts should be torqued to 15 ft. lbs. Later production V8-368 D.E.F.I. engines are equipped with prevailing torque bolts.

9. Remove rocker arm cover.
10. Remove rocker arm asemblies and lift out push rods.
11. Remove cylinder head bolts, remove head.
12. After carefully removing all gasket material from mating surfaces of head and block, position new gasket over dowels and install cylinder head in reverse order of removal, being sure to install the bolts as indicated in Fig. 8.

NOTE: When installing cylinder head bolts no torque sequence is required, start at center and work from side to side outwards and towards the ends.

VALVE ARRANGEMENT
Front to Rear

V6-252	E-I-I-E-I-E
V8-368, 425	
Left	E-I-E-I-E-I-E-I
Right	I-E-I-E-I-E-I-E
V8-250, 350	I-E-I-E-E-I-E-I

VALVE LIFT SPECS

Engine	Year	Intake	Exhaust
V8-350	1977–80	.400	.400
V8-368	1980–81	.457	.473
V8-425	1977–79	.457	.473
V6-252①	1980–82	.357	.366
V8-250	1982–84	.384	.396

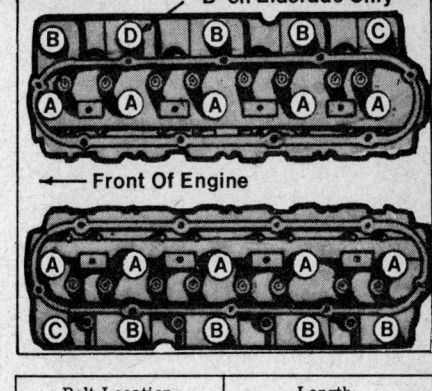

"B" on Eldorado Only

← Front Of Engine

Bolt Location	Length
A (Bolt)	4.36" (Medium)
B (Bolt)	4.77" (Long)
C (Bolt)	3.02" (Short)
D (Bolt/stud)	4.77" (Long)

Fig. 8   Location and length of cylinder head screws. V8-368 & 425

①—Refer to Buick Chapter for service procedures.

VALVE TIMING
Intake Opens Before TDC

Engine	Year	Degrees
V6-252①	1980–82	16
V8-250	1982–84	37
V8-350	1977–80	22
V8-368	1980–81	11
V8-425	1977–79	21

①—Refer to Buick Chapter for service procedures.

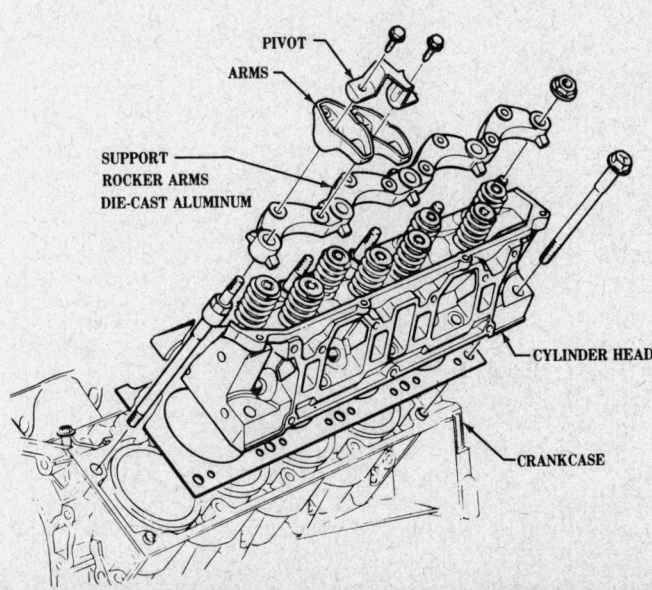

Fig. 8A   Rocker arm assembly exploded view. V8-250

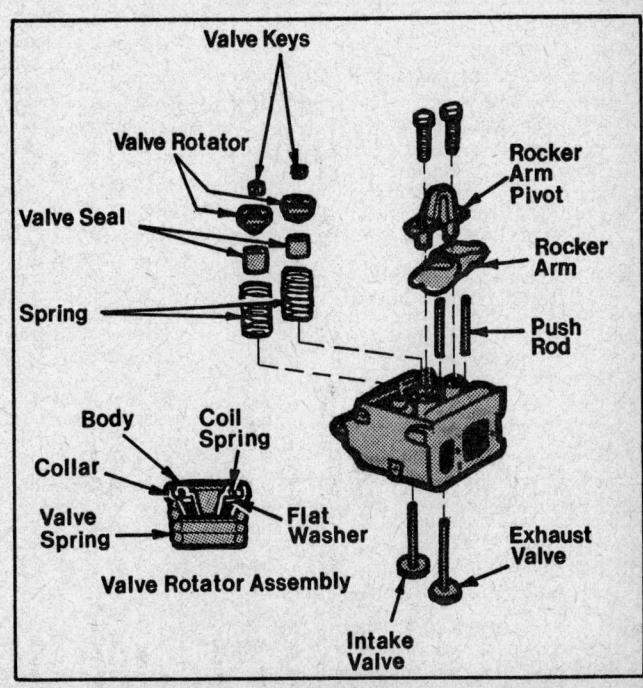

Fig. 9   Rocker arm components disassembled. V8-350

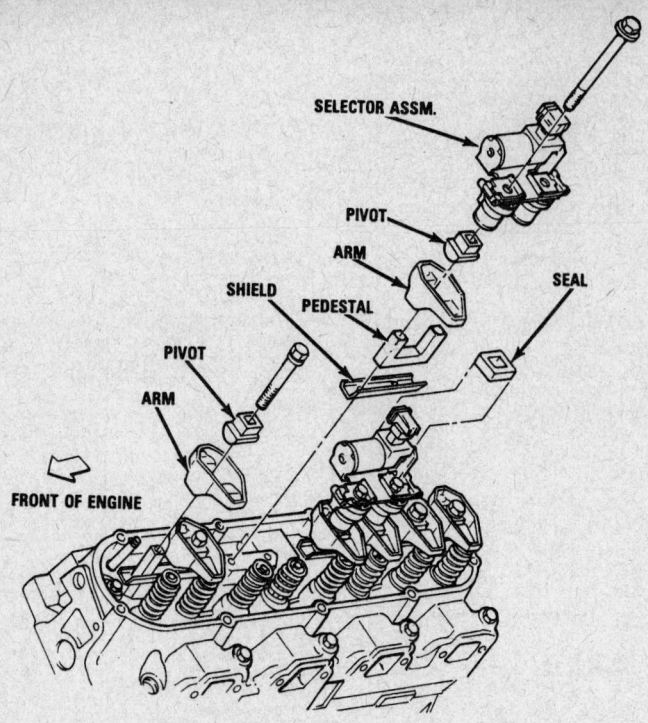

Fig. 9A   Rocker arm assembly. V8-368 modulated displacement engine.

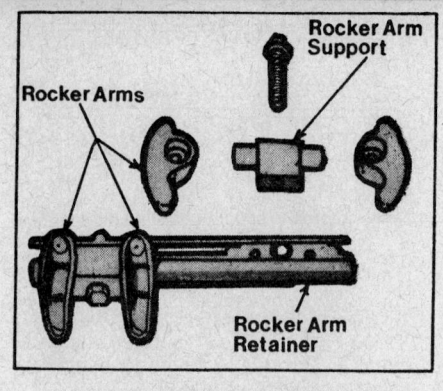

Fig. 10   Rocker arm components

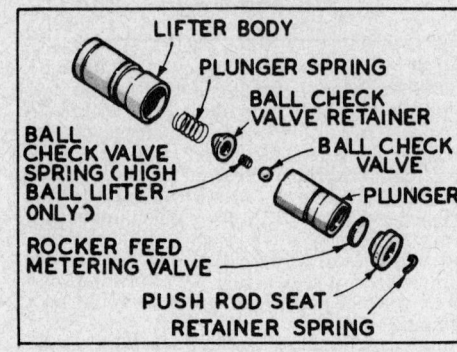

Fig. 11   Hydraulic valve lifter

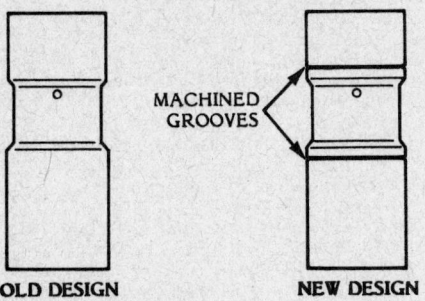

Fig. 11A   New design valve lifter. V8-250

ROCKER ARMS, REPLACE

V8-250

1. Remove valve cover.
2. Remove nuts from stud headed cylinder head bolts, then remove valve train support with rocker arms and pivots as an assembly, Fig. 8A.

NOTE: Pivot assemblies may be damaged unless rocker arms and pivots are removed as an assembly.

3. Position rocker arm support in suitable vise and remove rocker arms and pivots.
4. Install rocker arms and pivots into valve train support and tighten pivot bolts.
5. Position valve train support over mounting studs and snug tighten retaining nuts.
6. Check push rods for correct positioning, then tighten nuts alternately and evenly.

V8-350

1. Remove rocker cover, rocker arm bolts, pivot and rocker arms.

NOTE: Remove each set as a unit.

2. Position rocker arms on cylinder head, apply lubricant 1050169 or equivalent to wear points on pivot, then install pivot.
3. Install rocker arm bolts, tighten alternately, torque to 25 ft. lbs., Fig. 9.

1981 V8-368

On V8-368 modulated displacement engines, refer to Fig. 9A for rocker arm replacement.

1977–79 V8-425 & 1980 V8-368

When disassembling the rocker arm assembly, be sure to keep the supports and rocker arms in order so they can be installed in the exact same position.

Install rocker arms on supports and place supports in retainers as shown in Fig. 10.

Place capscrews through the reinforcements, supports and retainers and position assemblies on cylinder head. Make sure that push rods are properly seated in the lifter seats and in the rocker arms. Lubricate rocker arm bearing surfaces before assembling in order to prevent wear. Torque rocker arm support bolts to 70 ft. lbs.

VALVE GUIDES

V8-350

Valve stem to guide clearance should be .001-.003 inch. Service valves are available in standard (.343 inch) and .003, .005, .010, .013 inch oversizes. If stem to guide clearance is excessive, ream valve guide bore to the next oversize using appropriate reamer. Install proper oversize valve and valve seal. Valve seals can be identified as follows:

Intake
Std.-.005 O.S........ Gray Colored
.010-.013 O.S..... Orange Colored

Exhaust
Std.-005 O.S. .... Ivory Colored
.010-.013 O.S....... Blue Colored

On occasion an engine will be manufactured with an oversize valve and valve guide bore. A number stamped on the inboard side of the head will indicate which valve and valve guide bore are oversize. The number 10 would indicate that a .010 inch oversize valve is installed in the adjacent valve guide bore.

V8-250, 368, 425

Check valve stem to valve guide clearance, clearance should be no more than .005 inch. Service valves are available in standard (.343 inch) and .003, .006 and .013 inch oversizes. If clearance is found to be excessive, valve guide should be reamed out to next oversize using appropriate reamer, and a corresponding oversize valve installed. On some engines, valves with a .003 inch oversize diameter and .003 inch oversize valve guides are installed at the factory. Engines so fitted will be identified by a "3" stamped on the cylinder head gasket surface inline with the oversize valve.

HYDRAULIC VALVE LIFTERS, REPLACE

The valve lifters may be lifted out of their bores after removing the rocker arms, push rods and intake manifold. Adjustable pliers with taped jaws may be used to remove lifters that are stuck due to varnish, carbon, etc. Fig. 11 illustrates the type of lifter used.

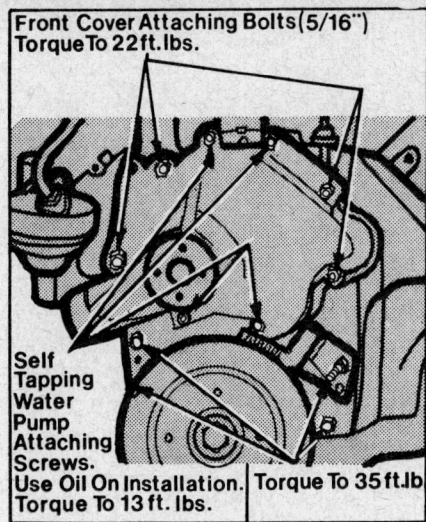

Front Cover Attaching Bolts (5/16")
Torque To 22 ft. lbs.

Self Tapping Water Pump Attaching Screws. Use Oil On Installation. Torque To 13 ft. lbs. Torque To 35 ft.lb

Fig. 12 Engine front cover attaching screws V8-350

SERVICE NOTE

On 1982–83 V8-250 engines, if valve lifter replacement is required, replacement should be made with the new design type. The new design type lifter foot is more convex in shape and is identified by two machined grooves on the lifter body, Fig. 11A. If camshaft replacement is necessary, all 16 lifters should be replaced with the new design type.

TIMING CASE COVER, REPLACE

V8-250

1. Disconnect battery ground cable and drain cooling system.
2. On Brougham and DeVille models, position support rods aside.
3. Disconnect wiring harness from upper fan shroud clamps.
4. Remove power steering pump reservoir from upper fan shroud, then remove upper fan shroud.
5. Remove clutch fan, then loosen alternator and AIR pump mounting bolts and remove drive belts.

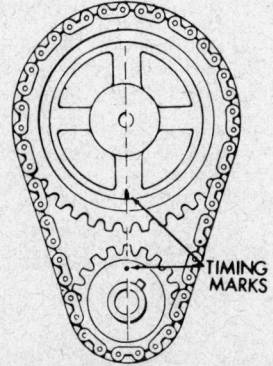

Fig. 15 Timing gear locating marks. V8-350

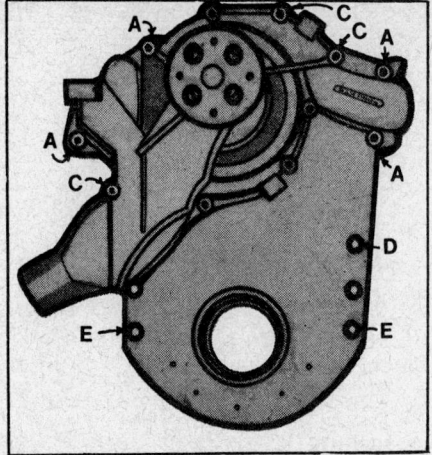

Key	No.	Size	Torque
V8-368			
A	4	3/8–16 × 1–3/8	22 ft. lbs.
C	3	5/16–18 × 1–1/4	10 ft. lbs.
D	1	5/16–18 × 5/8	10 ft. lbs.
E	2	3/8–16 × 5/8	22 ft. lbs.
V8-425			
A	4	3/8–16 × 1–3/8	25 ft. lbs.
C	3	5/16–18 × 1–1/4	15 ft. lbs.
D	1	5/16–18 × 5/8	15 ft. lbs.
E	2	3/8–16 × 5/8	25 ft. lbs.

Fig. 13 Engine front cover attaching screws. V8-368, 425

6. Loosen power steering pump retaining bolts and remove vacuum pump drive belts.
7. Remove A/C compressor mounting bolts, then remove drive belt and position compressor aside with all hoses and lines attached.
8. Remove alternator and support bracket, then disconnect coolant reservoir hose at water pump.
9. Disconnect hoses from water pump.
10. Remove water pump and crankshaft pulleys.
11. Remove A/C compressor bracket from engine.
12. Remove timing mark tab from front cover, then remove crankshaft vibration damper.
13. Remove bolts securing front cover to cylinder block, then remove cover, water pump and lower thermostat housing as an assembly.
14. Reverse procedure to install. Coat oil pan front lip with suitable sealer.

V8-350

1. Drain cooling system, disconnect radiator hoses, heater hose and bypass hose.
2. Remove radiator upper support and radiator.
3. Remove belts, fan, fan pulley, crankshaft pulley and harmonic balancer.
4. Remove oil pan, front cover attaching bolts, front cover and water pump.
5. Reverse procedure to install, refer to Fig. 12.

V8-368, 425

1. Remove harmonic balancer.
2. Loosen starter sufficiently to gain access

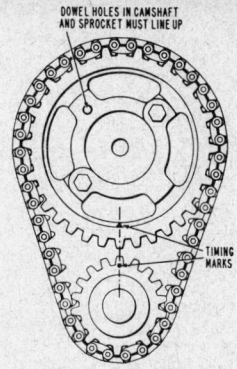

DOWEL HOLES IN CAMSHAFT AND SPROCKET MUST LINE UP

TIMING MARKS

Fig. 14 Timing gear locating marks. V8-368, 425

to oil pan screws and lower front of oil pan until it clears front studs.
3. Drain radiator and remove lower hose from water pump.
4. Remove the 10 screws securing front cover to the cylinder block and remove cover with water pump as an assembly.
5. Reverse removal procedure, to install, referring to Fig. 13

TIMING CASE COVER OIL SEAL, REPLACE

V8-250

1. Remove crankshaft pulley and vibration damper.
2. Remove front cover oil seal using tools J-1859-03 and J-23129 or equivalents.
3. Lubricate new seal with engine oil, then install using tool J-29662 or equivalent.
4. Install vibration damper and crankshaft pulley.

V8-350

1. Remove drive belts, crankshaft pulley and harmonic balancer.
2. Using tool J-1859-03 or a suitable puller, remove front cover oil seal.
3. Apply sealer to outside diameter of seal.
4. Position seal on front cover, then using tools No. J-25264 and J-21150, drive seal into place.
5. Install harmonic balancer and crankshaft pulley, install and adjust drive belts.

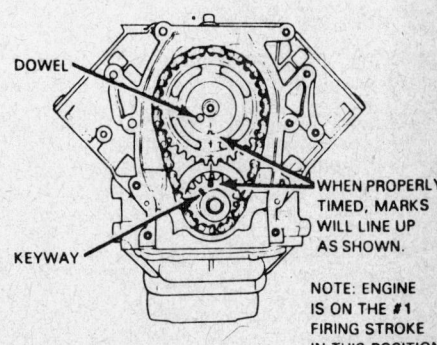

DOWEL

WHEN PROPERLY TIMED, MARKS WILL LINE UP AS SHOWN.

KEYWAY

NOTE: ENGINE IS ON THE #1 FIRING STROKE IN THIS POSITION.

Fig. 15A Timing gear location marks. V8-250

NOTCH TOWARD
FRONT OF ENGINE

Fig. 16   Piston & rod assembly. V8-250

V8-368, 425, 500

1. Remove vibration damper.
2. With a thin blade screw driver or similar tool, pry out front cover oil seal.
3. Lubricate new seal and fill cavity with wheel bearing grease. Position seal on end of crankshaft with garter spring side toward engine.
4. Using a suitable installer, drive seal into cover until it bottoms against cover.

TIMING CHAIN, REPLACE

V8-368 & 425

1. Remove engine timing case cover as described under "Timing Case Cover, Replace".
2. Remove distributor, oil pump and crankshaft oil slinger.
3. On models less fuel injection, remove fuel pump, then remove fuel pump slinger from camshaft.
4. Rotate crankshaft to align camshaft and crankshaft sprocket timing marks, Fig. 14.
5. Remove two screws attaching camshaft sprocket to camshaft, then remove camshaft sprocket and timing chain.
6. If necessary, remove crankshaft sprocket using a suitable puller.
7. Reverse procedure to install. Ensure that timing marks are aligned as shown in Fig. 14.

NOTE: The valve timing marks, Fig. 14, do not indicate TDC compression stroke for No. 1 cylinder, which is used during distributor installation. Rotate engine until No. 1 cylinder is on compression stroke and camshaft timing mark is 180° from the valve timing position shown in Fig. 14, then install distributor.

V8-350

1. Remove engine timing case cover as described under "Timing Case Cover, Replace".
2. Remove oil slinger from crankshaft.
3. Rotate crankshaft to align camshaft and crankshaft sprocket timing marks, Fig. 15.
4. Remove screw attaching camshaft sprocket to camshaft, then remove camshaft sprocket and timing chain.
5. If necessary, remove crankshaft sprocket using a suitable puller.
6. Reverse procedure to install. Ensure that timing marks are aligned as shown in Fig. 15.

NOTE: The valve timing marks, Fig. 15, do

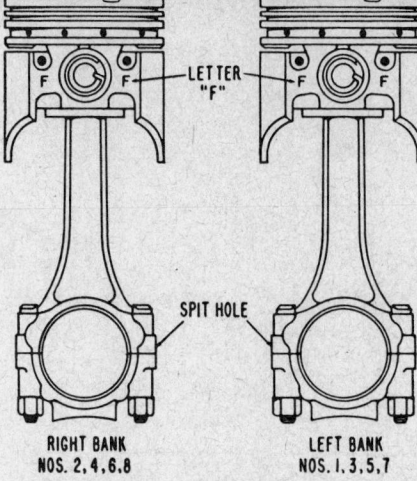

LETTER "F"

SPIT HOLE

RIGHT BANK
NOS. 2, 4, 6, 8

LEFT BANK
NOS. 1, 3, 5, 7

Fig. 16A   Piston & rod assembly. V8-350

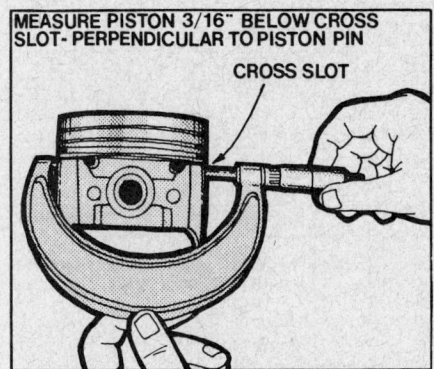

MEASURE PISTON 3/16" BELOW CROSS SLOT- PERPENDICULAR TO PISTON PIN

CROSS SLOT

Fig. 18   Measuring piston diameter

not indicate TDC compression stroke for No. 1 cylinder, which is used during distributor installation. If distributor was removed, rotate engine until No. 1 cylinder is on compression stroke and camshaft timing mark is 180° from the valve timing position shown in Fig. 15, then install distributor.

V8-250

1. Remove engine timing case cover as described under "Timing Case Cover, Replace".
2. Remove oil slinger from crankshaft.
3. Rotate crankshaft to align camshaft and crankshaft sprocket timing marks, Fig. 15A.
4. Remove screw attaching camshaft sprocket to camshaft, then remove camshaft and crankshaft sprockets with timing chain attached.
5. Reverse procedure to install. Ensure that timing marks are aligned as shown in Fig. 15A.

CAMSHAFT, REPLACE

V8-250

1. Remove timing chain as described previously.
2. Remove valve lifters as described under "Valve Lifters, Replace".
3. Remove radiator, then remove camshaft from engine. Use caution not to damage

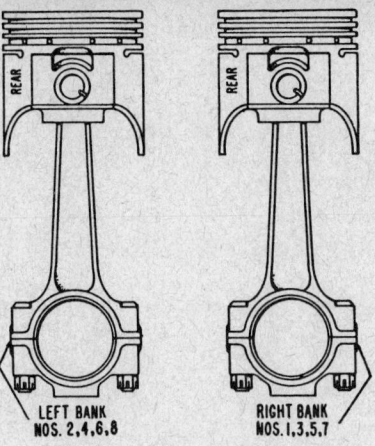

REAR

LEFT BANK
NOS. 2, 4, 6, 8

RIGHT BANK
NOS. 1, 3, 5, 7

Fig. 17   Piston & rod assembly. V8-368, 425

camshaft bearings when removing camshaft.
4. Reverse procedure to install.

V8-350

1. Disconnect battery, then remove air cleaner.
2. Drain cooling system and remove radiator, four bolts attaching A/C condenser to radiator and position condenser aside.
3. Remove crankshaft pulley and balancer, then the front cover.
4. Remove A/C compressor from engine and position aside.

NOTE: Do not disconnect refrigerant hoses from compressor.

5. Remove intake manifold as described under "Intake Manifold Replace".
6. Remove rocker covers, rocker arms, push rods and lifters.

NOTE: Note position of rocker arms, pivots, push rods and lifers to ensure installation in original position.

7. Remove camshaft.
8. Reverse procedure to install.

V8-368, 425

1. Remove engine front cover.
2. Remove distributor and oil pump.
3. Remove oil slinger from crankshaft.
4. Remove fuel pump and fuel pump eccentric.
5. Unfasten and remove camshaft sprocket with chain attached.
6. Remove valve lifters as previously outlined.
7. Remove radiator.
8. Carefully slide camshaft forward until it is out of engine.
9. Reverse procedure to install.

PISTONS & RODS ASSEMBLE

On all engines, assemble and install the piston and rod assemblies as shown in Figs. 16, 16A and 17.
Measure connecting rod side clearance us-

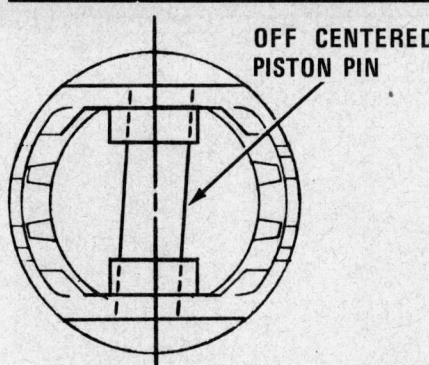

OFF CENTERED PISTON PIN

Fig. 18A   Off centered piston pin. V8-250

Letter	Cylinder Size (Diameter in inches)	Piston Size (Diameter in inches)
A	4.0560-4.0565	4.05475-4.05525
B	4.0565-4.0570	4.05525-4.05575
C	4.0570-4.0575	4.05575-4.05625
D	4.0575-4.0580	4.05625-4.05675
J	4.0660-4.0665	4.06475-4.06525
K	4.0665-4.0670	4.06525-4.06575
L	4.0670-4.0675	4.06575-4.06625
M	4.0675-4.0680	4.06625-4.06675

Fig. 19   Cylinder and piston sizes. V8-350

LETTER	CYLINDER SIZE (DIAMETER IN INCHES)	PISTON SIZE (DIAMETER IN INCHES)
A	3.8000 - 3.8004	3.7990 - 3.7994
B	3.8004 - 3.8008	3.7994 - 3.7998
C	3.8008 - 38012	3.7998 - 3.8002
D	3.8012 - 3.8016	3.8002 - 3.8006
E	3.8016 - 3.8020	3.8006 - 3.8010

Fig. 20   Cylinder & piston sizes. V8-368

Letter	Cylinder Size (Diameter in Inches)	Piston Size (Diameter in Inches)
A	4.0820-4.0824	4.0810-4.0814
B	4.0824-4.0828	4.0814-4.0818
C	4.0828-4.0832	4.0818-4.0822
D	4.0832-4.0836	4.0822-4.0826
E	4.0836-4.0840	4.0826-4.0830
AA	4.0920-4.0924	4.0910-4.0914
BB	4.0924-4.0928	4.0914-4.0918
CC	4.0928-4.0932	4.0918-4.0922
DD	4.0932-4.0936	4.0922-4.0926
EE	4.0936-4.0940	4.0926-4.0930

Fig. 21   Cylinder & piston sizes. V8-425

ing a suitable feeler gauge. Clearances should be .008–.020 inch on Cadillac built engines, .006–.020 inch on Oldsmobile built engines and .006–.023 inch on Buick built engines.

PISTONS

V8-250

When measuring piston diameter, place micrometer 3/16 inch below cross slot or 3/8 inch below oil ring groove, Fig. 18. Cylinder liner diameter is measured by placing a micrometer two inches down from top of liner and perpendicular to cylinder centerline. The difference between the two readings should be .0010–.0018 inch. Cylinder bore out-of-round should not exceed .0008 inch and piston bore taper should not exceed .0005–.002 inch. If any reading is not as specified, piston and cylinder liner assembly must be replaced. No attempt should be made to rebore or hone cylinder liners. Refer to "Cylinder Liner, Replace" for procedure.

SERVICE NOTE On some 1982 V8-250 engines a minor to severe internal metallic knock may be encountered. This may be caused by close piston to counterbalance tolerance on cylinder Nos. 1, 2, 3, 6, 7 and 8 and is usually heard when engine is at operating temperature between 800–1400 RPM.
The following procedure should be used to correct this problem:
1. Remove engine oil pan and cylinder heads as previously described.
2. Inspect all pistons for correct installation.

3. Using a wax pencil, mark right and left sides of outboard piston skirts which rotate next to crankshaft counterbalance weights on piston Nos. 1, 2, 3, 6, 7 and 8.
4. Remove and inspect all pistons for off-centered piston wrist pins, Fig. 18A. If off-centered piston pins are encountered, replace piston and liner assembly.
5. Using a suitable file, remove a small amount of material from piston skirt edges marked in step 3. All surfaces must be smooth and free of all file marks after reworking. If interference marks are evident in the piston skirts and filing does not remove marks, replace piston and liner assembly.
6. Reinstall pistons into block.
7. Check piston skirt to crankshaft counterweight clearance by placing an index card between skirts and counterweights while rotating crankshaft. No drag should be felt on card. If drag is felt, crankshaft should be replaced.
8. Reinstall cylinder heads and oil pan.

V8-350

Measure pistons for size, Fig. 18. Measure cylinder bore, piston to cylinder bore clearance should be .00075–.00175 inch. Measure piston for taper, the largest reading must be at the bottom of the skirt. Allowable taper is .000–.0001 inch.
Cylinder and piston sizes are indicated by a letter stamped on the cylinder gasket surface of the block. The letters that denote cylinder and piston sizes are listed in Fig. 19.

V8-368, 425

Pistons should be measured for size as shown in Fig. 18. Cylinders should be measured 1⅛" from the top, crosswise to the cylinder block. The clearance should be .0006–.0014 for V8-368, 425 engines in this position at room temperature (70°F). Subtract .0001" from measurement for every 6° above 70°.
On V8-368, 425 engines an identification letter is stamped on the cylinder head face of cylinder block located directly below cylinder bore. The letters are in groups of two for adjacent cylinders (such as "A" "B") midway between the two cylinders. This letter denotes the cylinder size as shown in Figs. 20 and 21. The table indicates piston sizes to match corresponding bore sizes. This makes it possible to maintain the proper clearance between block and piston.
If double letters (such a "AA" "BB") appear, it indicates that the cylinder has been bored .010" over the diameter indicated by the single letter in the chart.
Cylinder bores must not be reconditioned to more than .0100 inch oversize, as pistons are not available over this range.

PISTON RINGS

NOTE: On 1979–80 V8-350 engines except

TOP & SECOND

PERFECT CIRCLE

TOP & SECOND

SEALED POWER

TOP & SECOND

MUSKEGON

Fig. 22   Piston ring identification. 1979–80 V8-350 gasoline engine

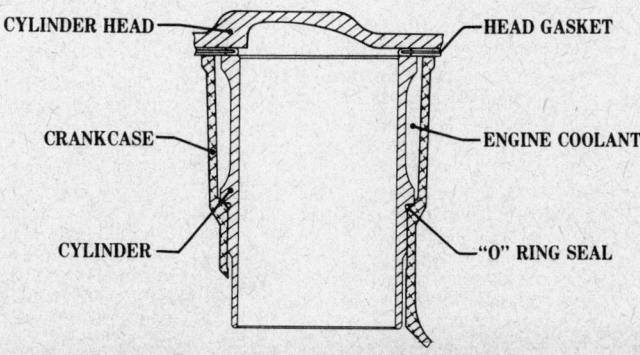

CYLINDER HEAD — HEAD GASKET

CRANKCASE — ENGINE COOLANT

CYLINDER — "O" RING SEAL

Fig. 22A   Cylinder liner assembly. V8-250

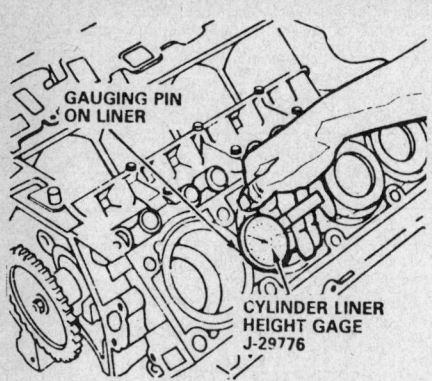

Fig. 22B Measuring liner to liner height. V8-250

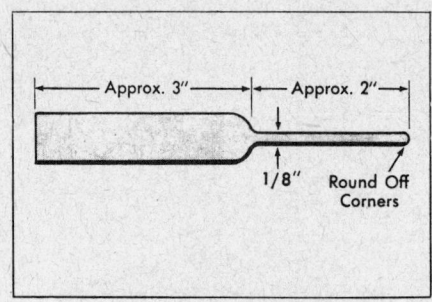

NO.LETTER · STD
LETTER 'A' · .0005
LETTER 'B' · .0010
LETTER 'C' · .0015

Fig. 23 Main bearing identification. V8-350

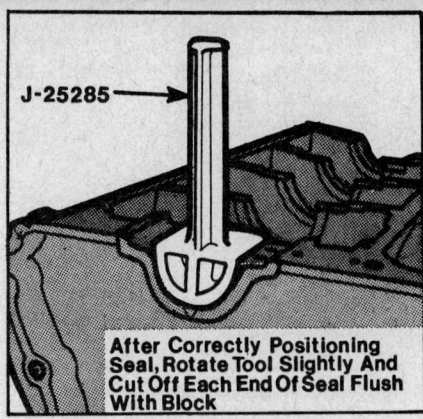

After Correctly Positioning Seal, Rotate Tool Slightly And Cut Off Each End Of Seal Flush With Block

Fig. 24 Rear main bearing oil seal installation. V8-350

diesel, when measuring compression ring gap clearance, refer to Fig. 22 for piston ring identification. For Muskegon and Perfect Circle piston rings, ring gap should be .013 to .023 in. For Sealed Power piston rings, ring gap should be .010 to .020 in.

Replacement rings are available on all except V8-250 engines in standard size and .010 inch oversize. On V8-250 engine, replacement rings are available in standard size only. If piston ring clearance is excessive on this engine, new piston and cylinder liner must be installed. Refer to "Cylinder Liner, Replace".

PISTON PINS

V8-350

Piston pin to piston clearance should be .0003–.0005 inch. If clearance is more than .0005 inch, a new piston pin should be installed. Piston pin to connecting rod is a press fit and clearance should be .0008–.0018 inch tight fit.

V8-250, 368, 425

Piston pins are a matched fit with the piston and are not available separately. Piston pins are pressed in the connecting rods and will not become loose enough to cause a knock or tapping until after very high mileages. In such cases a new piston and pin assembly should be installed.

CYLINDER LINER, REPLACE

V8-250

NOTE: The cylinder heads, pistons, connecting rods, bearings and crankshaft must be removed from engine before replacing cylinder liners.

1. If original liners, Fig. 22A, are to be reinstalled, mark position of liner in cylinder block and keep piston with original liner for reference during installation.
2. Use tool J-29775 or equivalent to remove liners from cylinder block. Discard O ring from bottom of cylinder liner.
3. Check cylinder liner and block mating surfaces to ensure they are free of nicks and burrs.

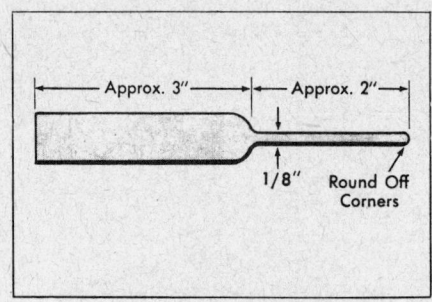

Fig. 25 Main bearing oil seal tool. V8-250, 368, 425

Approx. 3"   Approx. 2"
1/8"   Round Off Corners

4. If original liners are to be installed into original block, it is not necessary to gauge their height. Install new O ring seal onto liner, align reference marks made during removal, then install liner into block using tool J-29775 or equivalent.
5. If new liner and piston assembly is to be installed, or if original block experienced overheating, then cylinder liner height must be gauged.
6. Position new liner into block without O ring.
7. Position gauge J-29776 or equivalent onto cylinder liner. Check to ensure that spring loaded guide pins fit into liner with machined pads resting on edge of liner and dial indicator contacting block deck face. Apply moderate pressure to gauge until dial indicator stops moving.
8. Record this reading. If reading is on + side of dial indicator, cylinder liner is higher than block face by indicated amount. If reading is on − side, cylinder liner is below block face.
9. Repeat steps 7 and 8 at two other locations. Take average of three readings as actual liner height.
10. Specified liner height is .01–.08 mm above block deck face. If specified height cannot be obtained, replace liner with new one. Liners may be rotated in block to obtain specified height.
11. If liner height is satisfactory, then liner-to-liner height must be checked. Install adjacent liners into cylinder block without O ring. Using gauge J-29766 or equivalent, measure height between liners while second liner is held firmly in place, Fig. 22B. Liner-to-liner height should be ±.05 mm. Mark liners in this position.
12. When installing liners into block, check to ensure that liners are installed in marked position. Install O ring onto liner,

then install liner into block using tool J-29775 or equivalent.

MAIN & ROD BEARINGS

V8-350

Main bearing clearance should not exceed .0035 inch. If clearance is more than .0035 inch replace both bearing shells. Main bearings are available in undersizes, Fig. 23. Rod bearing clearance should not exceed .0035 inch. If clearance is more than .0035 inch replace both bearing shells and recheck clearance.

V8-250, 368, 425

Main and rod bearings are supplied by Cadillac in standard sizes only.

CRANKSHAFT OIL SEAL, REPLACE

V8-350

To replace upper rear main bearing seal, the crankshaft must be removed. After removing crankshaft use tool No. J-25285 to install seal, Fig. 24.

Lower rear main bearing seal can be installed with crankshaft in place and engine in vehicle. Remove oil pan, then the rear main bearing cap. Remove bearing and seal from cap. Position new seal in groove in bearing cap. Using tool J-25285, hammer seal into groove. Rotate tool slightly, then cut seal ends flush with bearing cap surface. Pack seal end fibers away from edges, using a screw driver. Install bearing in cap, then install cap, lubricate bolt threads and torque to 120 ft. lbs. Install oil pan and lower flywheel cover.

V8-250, 368, 425

Rear main bearing installation tool can be made from shim stock or a metal banding strap using dimensions in Fig. 25.

The two seal halves are identical and can be used in either the lower or upper location. However, both seal halves are pre-lubricated with a film of wax for break-in. Do not remove or damage this film.

To install the lower half of the seal into the bearing cap, slide either end of seal into position at one end of bearing cap and place tool on seal land at other end of bearing. Make sure seal is positioned over bearing ridge and lip of seal is facing forward (car position).

Hold thumb over end of seal that is flush

with split line to prevent it from slipping upward, and push seal into seated position by applying pressure to the other end. Make sure seal is pressed down firmly and is flush on each side to avoid possibility of a leak at seal split line. Avoid pressing on lip as damage to sealing edge could result.

To install upper half of seal in cylinder block (with crankshaft in car), position "shoehorn" tool on land of block, Fig. 26. Start seal into groove in block with lip facing forward and rotate seal into position. Do not press on lip or sealing edge may be damaged. Both ends of seal must be flush at seal split line to avoid leaks. If necessary, Lubriplate or its equivalent may be used to facilitate installation of both upper and lower seal halves. Do not use silicone or a leak may result.

OIL PAN, REPLACE

NOTE: Some 1981 V8 engines might exhibit an oil leak at the second oil pan bolt from front of the engine, on the left hand side. The hole for the bolt in the block may have been drilled through into the crankcase. A leak can be corrected by removing and cleaning the bolt and hole. Coat the bolt with a suitable sealer and reinstall.

1982–84 V8-250 Except Eldorado & Seville

1. Disconnect battery ground cable, then raise and support vehicle.
2. Drain engine oil and remove oil filter.
3. Remove flywheel cover and support struts.
4. Disconnect exhaust pipe from manifold and remove catalytic converter bracket bolt.
5. Remove oil pan nuts and bolts, then lower exhaust pipe and remove oil pan from vehicle.
6. Reverse procedure to install. Use suitable RTV sealer in sufficient quantities when installing pan. Torque pan attaching bolts and nuts to 11 ft. lbs. on 1982 models and 15 ft. lbs. on 1983–84 models.

1982–84 V8-250 Eldorado & Seville

1. Raise and support vehicle and drain engine oil. Remove oil filter.
2. Remove flywheel cover, then remove final drive assembly.
3. Disconnect exhaust pipe from manifold, then remove front suspension stone shield.
4. Remove bolts securing engine mount to frame crossmember.
5. Remove oil pan bolts and nuts, then lower exhaust pipe and remove oil pan from vehicle.

NOTE: To facilitate oil pan removal, place suitable jack under cylinder head ledge of crankcase or against cylinder head, and raise engine just enough to remove oil pan.

6. Reverse procedure to install. Use suitable RTV sealer in sufficient quantities when installing pan. Torque pan attaching bolts to 10 to 11 ft. lbs.

1980–82 V6-252 Except 1982 Eldorado & Seville

Removal
1. Raise and support vehicle. Drain oil.

Fig. 26 Installing rear main bearing oil seal. V8-250, 368 & 425

2. Remove flywheel cover.
3. Remove exhaust crossover pipe.
4. Remove oil pan attaching bolts and the oil pan.

Installation
1. Reverse procedure to install. Ensure oil pan and cylinder block mating surfaces are clean.

NOTE: 1981–82 V6-252 engines use RTV silicone sealer in place of a cork gasket for oil pan to crankcase sealing. If replacement of the oil pan or gasket is necessary, either RTV sealer or a cork gasket may be used for reassembly. If RTV sealer is used, the pan rail and block mating surfaces should be thoroughly cleaned and a ¼ inch bead of sealant applied evenly to the pan rail. Use caution to avoid any breaks or gaps in the sealer during application.

2. Torque oil pan bolts to 14 ft. lbs.
3. Torque flywheel cover bolts to 4 ft. lbs.
4. Lower vehicle and add oil.

1982 V6-252 Eldorado & Seville

1. Disconnect battery ground cable.
2. Remove one final drive to transmission bolt.
3. Install engine support and hoist car, then install jack stands and lower hoist.
4. Disconnect idler arm bracket at frame.
5. Lock steering wheel in full left position.
6. Disconnect drive axles from output shafts and disconnect battery cable bracket from output shaft support, then disconnect shaft support from engine block.
7. Remove remaining final drive to transmission bolts and place transmission jack under final drive.
8. Remove final drive cover and final drive unit.
9. Remove splash shield, then disconnect starter wires and remove starter.
10. Remove flywheel cover and drain oil pan.
11. Remove oil pan attaching bolts and remove oil pan.
12. Reverse procedure to install. Apply suitable RTV sealer when installing pan.

1977–82 Except V6-252 & Eldorado & Seville

1. Disconnect battery ground cable.
2. Remove two screws on each side securing radiator cover to strut rods, support rods and loosen two screws at strut. Position support rods aside.

3. Remove two screws securing upper radiator shroud to radiator and one screw securing upper radiator hose clamp to shroud.
4. Drill out the six rivets securing the upper shroud to the lower shroud and remove shroud.
5. Loosen drive belts and remove crankshaft pulleys.
6. Raise vehicle and drain oil pan.
7. Remove exhaust "Y" pipe at exhaust manifold and converter.
8. Remove through bolts from engine mounts.
9. Remove starter motor.
10. Remove transmission lower cover.
11. Using a suitable jack, raise engine to gain clearance for oil pan removal.
12. Remove nuts and screws securing oil pan to cylinder block.
13. Reverse procedure to install.

1977–80 V8-350 Seville

1. Remove wheel housing struts from both fenders.
2. Remove fan shroud.
3. Remove front motor mount through bolts, disconnect crossover pipe at manifold.
4. Remove starter, then remove converter cover.
5. Remove oil pan attaching bolts, raise engine until pan can be removed.
6. Reverse procedure to install.

1977–78 Eldorado

To remove the oil pan it is necessary to remove the engine as described previously.

1979–80 Eldorado V8-350

1. Remove final drive assembly with output shafts attached. Refer to "Final Drive" section for procedure.
2. Disconnect starter motor electrical connectors, then remove starter.
3. Drain oil from crankcase, then remove oil pan attaching screws and the oil pan.
4. Reverse procedure to install.

OIL PUMP, REPLACE

1982–84 V8-250

1. Remove oil pan as described previously.
2. Remove bolts securing oil pump to engine, then remove pump.
3. Reverse procedure to install.

V8-350

1. Remove oil pan, then remove pump to rear main bearing attaching screws, remove pump.

V8-368, 425

1. Raise car and remove oil filter.
2. Remove five screws securing pump to engine. *The screw nearest the pressure regulator should be removed last, allowing the pump to come down with the screw.*
3. Remove pump drive shaft.
4. Reverse procedure to install, being sure to pack the pump with petrolatum.

OIL PUMP, SERVICE

V8-250

1. Remove screws securing pump cover to

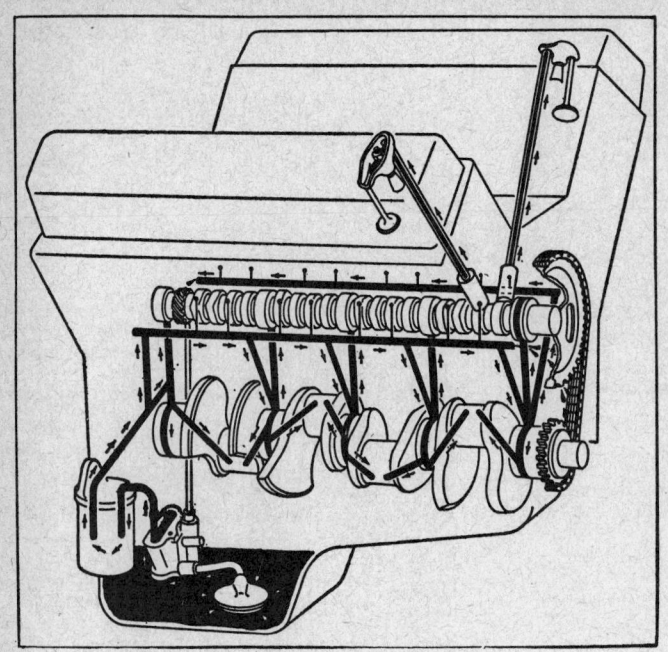

Engine oiling system. V8-350

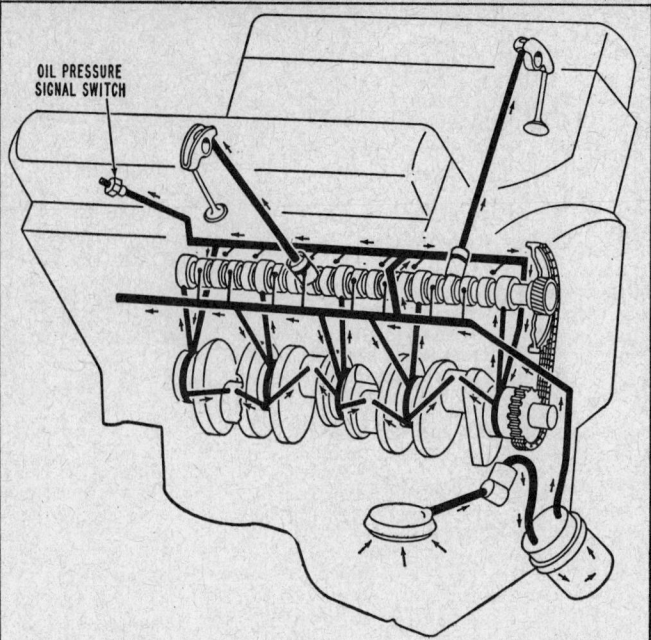

OIL PRESSURE SIGNAL SWITCH

Engine oiling system. V8-368, 425

housing.
2. Remove drive shaft, drive gear and driven gear from pump housing.
3. Remove oil pressure regulator valve and spring from bore in housing assembly. Inspect oil pressure regulator for nicks and burrs.
4. Check for free length of 2.57 inches on regulator spring. Check that spring can be compressed to 1.46 inches under 9.3–10.5 lbs. load.
5. Inspect drive gear and driven gear for nicks and burrs.
6. Inspect pump housing for excessive wear.
7. Check pump cover interior surface for scoring. Check pump housing cover surface for wear.
8. Check drive shaft for damage and wear.
9. To assemble, install pump drive gear over drive shaft so that retaining ring is inside gear. Position drive gear over pump housing shaft closest to pressure regulator bore.
10. Position driven gear over remaining shaft in pump housing, meshing driven gear with drive gear.
11. Install oil pressure regulator spring and valve in bore of housing.
12. install pump cover over drive shaft and install retaining screws. Torque to 5 ft. lbs.

V8-350

1. Remove oil pump as described previously.
2. Remove oil pump driveshaft extension.

NOTE: Do not attempt to remove washers from drive shaft extension. The drive shaft extension and washers must be serviced as an assembly if washers are not $1^{11}/_{32}$ inch from end of shaft.

3. Remove cotter pin, spring and pressure regulator valve.

NOTE: Place finger over pressure regula-

tor bore before removing cotter pin, as the spring is under pressure.

4. Remove oil pump cover screws, then remove cover and washer.
5. Remove drive gear and idler gear from pump housing.
6. Check gears for scoring or other damage. If damaged, install new gears.
7. Check pressure regulator valve, valve spring and bore for damage. Check valve to bore clearance which should be .0025–.0050 inch.
8. Install gears and shaft in pump body and check gear end clearance by placing a straight edge over the gears and measure the clearance between the straight edge and gasket surface. The end clearance should be .0015–.0025 inch. If end clearance is near the excessive clearance, check for scores in the cover that would bring the clearance over the specified limit.
9. Reverse procedure to assemble.

V8-368, 425

1. Remove oil pump as described previously.
2. Slide drive shaft, drive gear and driven gear out of pump housing.
3. Using a $5/_{16}$ inch hex head wrench, remove plug from pump housing assembly and remove oil pressure regulator valve and spring from bore in housing assembly.
4. Inspect oil pressure regulator valve for nicks and burrs that might cause a leak or binding condition in bore of pump housing.
5. Check free length of regulator valve spring. It should be about 2.57 inches to 2.69 inches. A force of 9.3 to 10.5 pounds should be required to compress spring to a length of 1.46 inches.
6. Inspect drive gear and driven gear for nicks and burrs.
7. Inspect pump housing for wear and score marks.

8. Check pump mating surfaces on engine block for wear and score marks.
9. Reverse procedure to assemble.

BELT TENSION DATA

	New Lbs.	Used Lbs.
1977–80		
All	110–140	60–120
1981–82 Brougham & DeVille, Exc. V8-250		
Air Conditioning	168	67
A.I.R. Pump	78	45
Generator	145	90
Power Steering	168	67
1981–82 Eldorado & Seville, Exc. V8-250		
Air Conditioning	168	67
A.I.R. Pump	78	45
Generator	145	90
Power Steering	145	67
1982 V8-250		
Air Conditioning/Steering Pump	202	90
A.I.R. Pump	180	67
Generator	147	56
Vacuum Pump	49	25
1983–84 V8-250		
Air Conditioning/Steering Pump	191	146
A.I.R. Pump	169	135
Generator	135	90
Vacuum Pump	45	34

WATER PUMP, REPLACE

1977–80

1. Disconnect battery ground cable, then drain cooling system.
2. On DeVille models, remove two screws, one from each side at radiator end of support rods. Loosen screws at strut end of support rods and move support rods aside.
3. Remove screws from upper fan shroud and remove screw securing upper radiator hose brace.

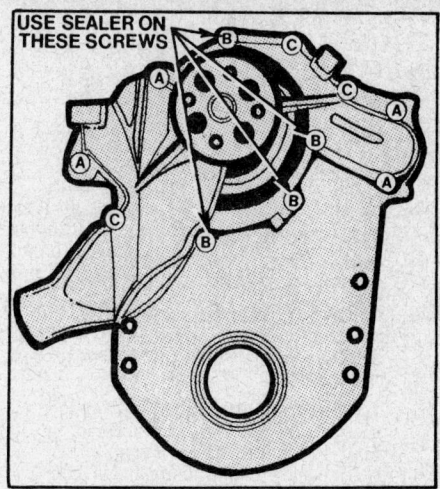

USE SEALER ON THESE SCREWS

Fig. 27 Water pump attaching screws. V8-368, 425

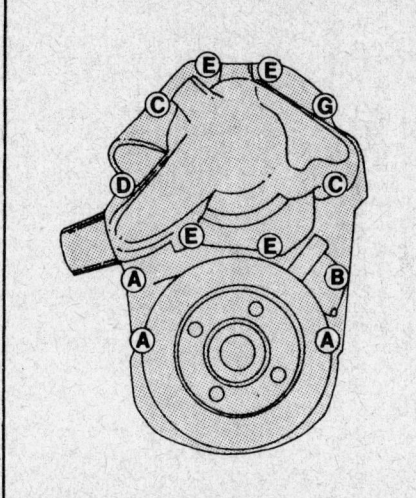

Key	No.	Size	Torque
C	(2)	5/16·18× 1·1/2	22 foot/ lbs.
D	(1)	5/16·18× 2·1/2	22 foot/ lbs.
E	(4)	1/4·20× 1·1/4	13 foot/ lbs.
G	(1)	5/16·18× 1·1/2 (Stud On Head)	22 foot/ lbs.

Fig. 28 Water pump attaching screws. V8-350

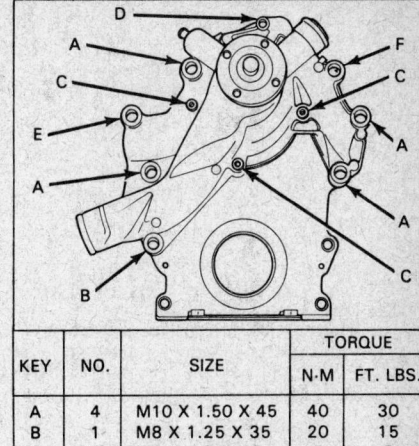

KEY	NO.	SIZE	TORQUE N·M	FT. LBS.
A	4	M10 X 1.50 X 45	40	30
B	1	M8 X 1.25 X 35	20	15
C	3	M6 X 1.0 (NUT)	7	5
D	1	(1620262)	10	7
E	1	M10 X 1.50 (NUT)	40	30
F	1	M10 X 1.50 X 50 (STUD HEAD)	40	30

Fig. 29 Water pump attaching screws. V8-250

4. Drill out seven rivets securing upper fan shroud to lower fan shroud, then remove upper shroud.
5. Remove fan assembly.
6. Loosen generator mounting screws and remove drive belt.
7. Loosen power steering pump mounting screws and remove power steering pump belt.
8. Remove water pump pulley from shaft.
9. Disconnect water inlet hose from water pump.
10. Disconnect fuel line at carburetor inlet and fuel pump. Remove fuel line.
11. Loosen screws securing crankshaft pulley to hub approximately half way and move pulley out slightly.
12. Remove screws securing water pump to engine front cover, then remove pump, Figs. 27 and 28. Discard gasket and clean gasket surfaces.
13. Remove studs from pump flange, if equipped.
14. Reverse procedure to install.

1981–84

1. Disconnect battery ground cable, then drain cooling system.
2. On DeVille and Brougham models, remove two screws, one from each side at radiator end of support rods. Loosen screws at strut end of support rods and move support rods aside.
3. Remove screws from upper fan shroud, then remove wiring harness from upper fan shroud clamps.
4. Remove screws securing power steering pump reservoir to upper fan shroud, then remove reservoir.
5. Remove staples securing upper fan shroud to lower shroud and remove upper shroud.
6. Remove fan assembly.
7. Loosen generator mounting screws and remove drive belt.
8. Loosen A.I.R. pump mounting screws and remove drive belt.
9. Remove lower power steering pump mounting bolt and loosen the remaining bolt. Remove the vacuum pump drive belt.
10. Loosen A/C compressor mounting bolts and remove drive belt.

11. Remove air conditioning compressor from engine mounting brackets and position aside. Do not remove high and low pressure lines from compressor.
12. Remove generator and support bracket from engine.
13. Loosen clamp and disconnect coolant reservoir to water pump hose at pump.
14. Loosen clamps and disconnect water pump inlet and outlet hoses at pump.
15. Remove water pump and crankshaft pulleys.
16. Remove A/C compressor bracket at water pump.
17. Remove timing mark tab from front cover.
18. Remove screws and nuts securing water pump, Fig. 29, to engine front cover and remove pump. Discard gasket and clean gasket surfaces.
19. Reverse procedure to install.

FUEL PUMP, REPLACE

With Fuel Injection

NOTE: On 1977–80 models with EFI, two fuel pumps are used; one in-tank unit and a chassis mounted unit. All other models use an in-tank fuel pump.

In-Tank Fuel Pump
1. Drain and remove fuel tank.
2. Remove locknut(s) securing wiring to fuel gauge pump unit, then fuel pump feed and gauge wires to tank unit.
3. Using tool J-24187, disengage lock ring from fuel tank. Remove tool, then lift gauge pump unit from tank and separate components.

4. On 1980 Eldorado and Seville models, proceed as follows:
   a. Remove filter screen from pump.
   b. Cut off rubber coupler, then remove fuel pump from bracket.
   c. Disconnect electrical wiring from pump.
   d. Lubricate fuel tube and fuel pump outlet tube with suitable lubricant. Slide new rubber coupler into fuel tube.
   e. Connect wiring to fuel pump, then install new rubber isolator and pump on to mounting bracket. Align fuel pump outlet with fuel tube and slide rubber coupler into position.

NOTE: Support pump bracket to prevent it from bending during coupler installation.

   f. Position new in-tank filter in same position as old filter.
5. Reverse procedure to install.

Chassis Mounted Fuel Pump
1. Remove fuel inlet and outlet hoses.
2. Pull back rubber boot and remove nuts from electrical terminals, then electrical leads.
3. Remove fuel pump to mounting bracket screws, then fuel pump assembly.
4. Reverse procedure to install. Torque fuel pump mounting screws to 25 inch lbs. Connect 14 dark green wire to positive terminal and 14 black wire to negative terminal.

1977–82 Less Fuel Injection
1. Raise vehicle and disconnect fuel inlet line at pump and plug line.
2. Disconnect fuel outlet pipe at pump.
3. Disconnect vapor return hoses, if equipped.
4. Remove upper pump flange mounting screws.
5. Remove nut from mounting stud at lower pump flange.
6. Tipping pump upward, pull pump straight out from engine and remove.
7. Reverse procedure to install.

Rear Axle, Propeller Shaft & Brakes

REAR AXLE

1979–84 Eldorado & 1980–84 Seville

The spindle and wheel bearing is a unitized assembly which eliminates the need for periodic maintenance and adjustments. The spindle and wheel bearing assembly is bolted to the rear suspension control arm, Fig. 1.

Wheel Bearing Inspection

1. Raise and support rear of vehicle, then remove wheel and tire assembly.
2. Free disc brake shoes from disc or remove calipers, then reinstall two wheel nuts to secure disc to bearing.
3. Mount dial indicator as shown in Fig. 2, then grasp rotor and check inward and outward movement of spindle assembly. Movement should be less than .020 in.
4. Remove dial indicator and rotate spindle by hand to check for roughness or grinding within the spindle.
5. Replace spindle and bearing assembly if out of specifications or roughness or grinding is present.

Spindle & Bearing Assembly, Replace

1. Raise vehicle and remove wheel and tire assembly.
2. Remove brake caliper assembly.
3. Mark wheel stud and corresponding place on rotor for use during installation, then remove rotor.
4. Remove four nuts and bolts attaching spindle and bearing assembly to control arm, Fig. 1.
5. Reverse procedure to install. Torque spindle to lower control arm attaching bolts to 34 ft. lbs.

1977–78 Eldorado

On these axles the rear wheel spindles are a press fit and bolted to the rear axle, Fig. 3. As shown, tapered roller bearings are used in the rear wheels. These bearings do not require regularly scheduled repacking. When major brake service work is to be performed, however, it is recommended that the bearings be cleaned and repacked.

Wheel Bearing Adjustment

Adjustment of the rear wheel bearings should be made while revolving the wheel at least three times the speed of the nut rotation when taking torque readings.

1. Check to make sure that hub is completely seated on wheel spindle.
2. While rotating wheel, tighten spindle nut to 30 ft-lbs. Make certain all parts are properly seated and that threads are free.
3. Back nut off ½ turn, then retighten nut to 2 ft. lbs. and install cotter pin.
4. If cotter pin cannot be installed in either of the two holes in the spindle, with the nut at 2 ft. lbs., back nut off until cotter pin can be installed.
5. The rear hub must be rotated at least three revolutions during tightening of spindle nut. The final adjustment to be 2 ft. lbs. to provide .004″ bearing end play.
6. Peen end of cotter pin snug against side of nut. If it can be moved with a finger, vibration may cause it to wear and break.

Wheel Spindle, Replace

1. Raise and support rear of vehicle.
2. Remove tire and wheel assembly.
3. Remove rear brake drum or caliper and disc assembly.
4. Remove dust cap, cotter pin, spindle nut, washer and outer cone and roller bearing assembly.
5. Carefully pull hub off spindle.
6. On vehicles with rear drum brakes:
   a. If equipped with Track Master, loosen sensor mounting screw, and pull sensor downward, part way out of

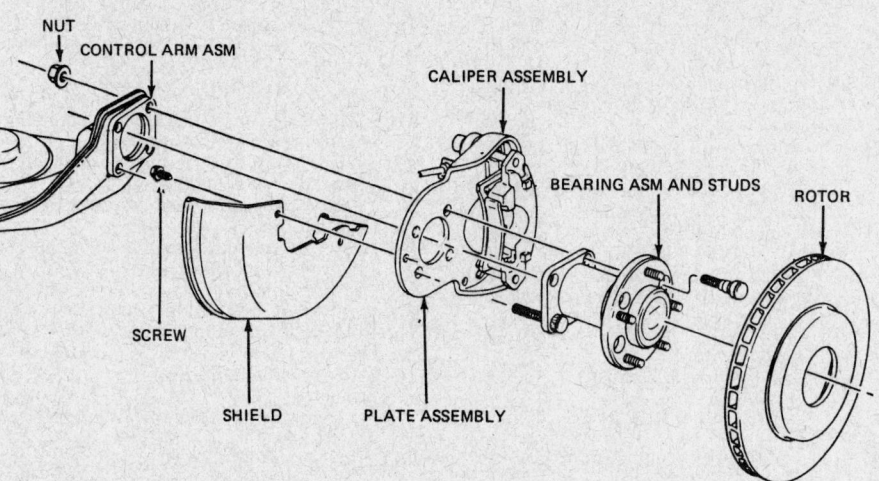

Fig. 1 Rear wheel spindle disassembled. 1979–84 Eldorado & 1980–84 Seville

Fig. 2 Checking wheel bearing for looseness. 1979–84 Eldorado & 1980–84 Seville

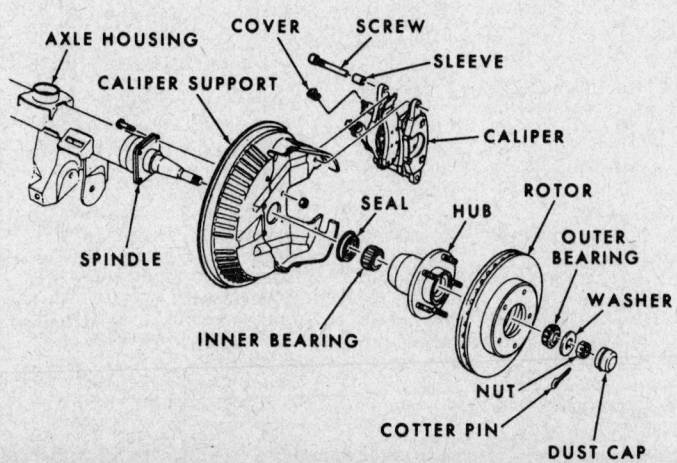

Fig. 3 Rear wheel spindle disassembled. 1977–78 Eldorado

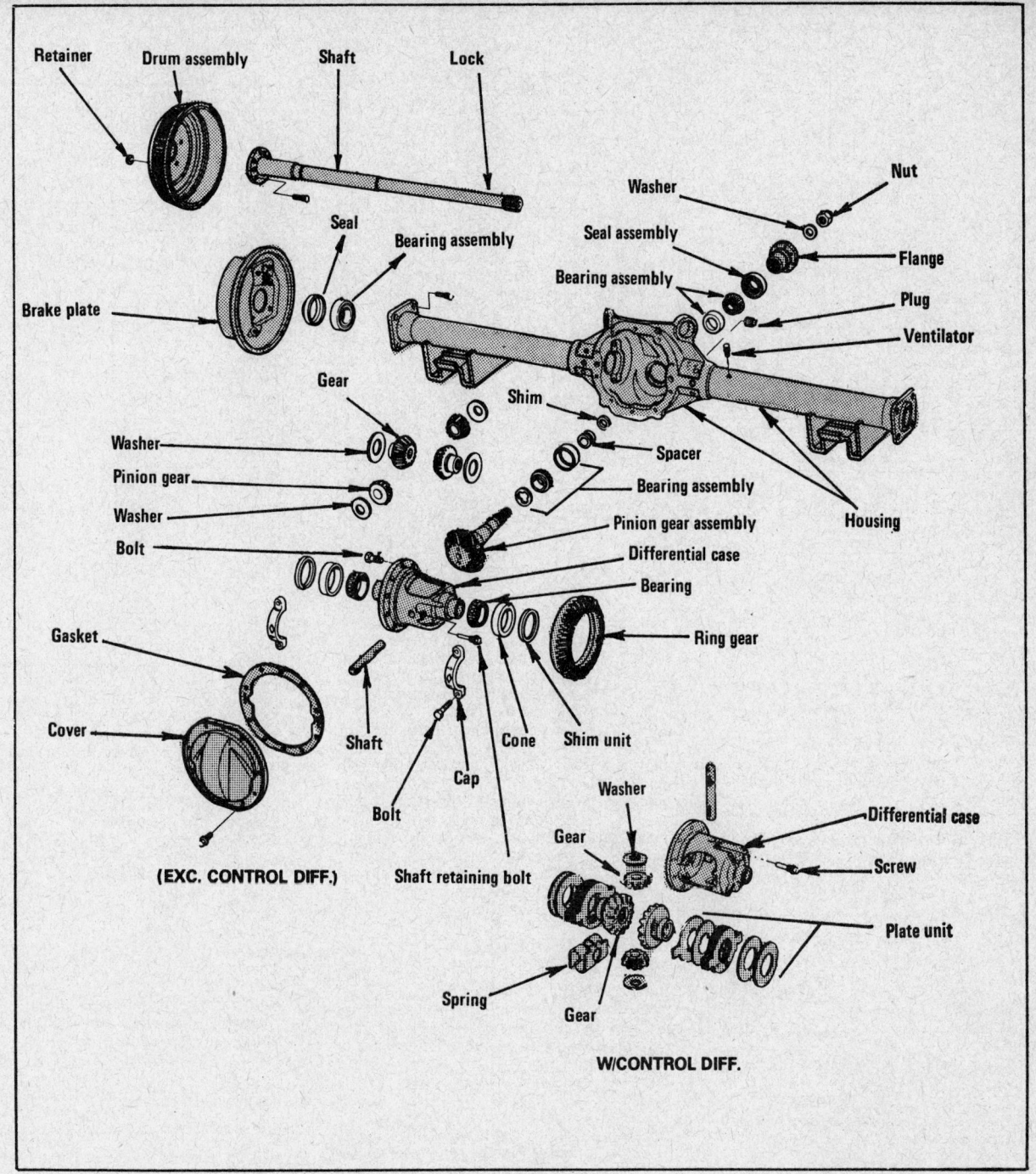

Fig. 4 Rear axle assembly. 1977–79 Seville & 1977–84 Deville & Brougham (Typical)

installed position. This will avoid possible damage to sensor when hub is reinstalled.

b. Disconnect brake line from brake cylinder, then remove backing plate retaining nuts and position backing plate out of the way.

CAUTION: Do not allow backing plate to hang unsupported, as parking brake cable or sensor wiring harness can be damaged.

7. On vehicles with rear disc brakes, remove the four nuts retaining spindle to axle housing.
8. Install one axle housing to spindle nut just far enough to engage threads, then using a slide hammer puller, pull spindle from axle housing.
9. Remove the remaining nut and bolt and remove spindle.

NOTE: If spindle threads were damaged during removal, use a ³⁄₄"-20 thread chaser to

repair threads.

10. To install, use a slide hammer puller and drive spindle into axle until spindle is fully seated.
11. Install a new gasket on wheel spindle.
12. On vehicles with rear drum brakes, reinstall backing plate and torque retaining nuts to 40 ft. lbs., then reconnect brake line and torque fitting to 14 ft. lbs.
13. On vehicles with rear disc brakes, install spindle to axle housing retaining nuts and bolts and torque nuts to 40 ft. lbs.

14. Install hub, outer cone and roller bearing assembly, washer and nut. Adjust rear bearing as described previously.
15. Install brake drum or disc and caliper assembly.
16. If brake line was disconnected, bleed brake system.

Rear Axle, Replace

1. Raise and support vehicle with jack stands placed underneath frame side rails.
2. Using a suitable jack, support weight of axle by raising it about 3/8 inch.
3. Remove brake drums or disc and caliper assembly.
4. Remove hubs.
5. If equipped with Track Master, disconnect wiring connectors from sensor harness and brake pipe and position harness out of the way.
6. On vehicles with rear drum brakes, disconnect brake lines at wheel cylinders and remove the four brake backing plate nuts.

CAUTION: Do not allow backing plate to hang unsupported, as parking brake cable can be damaged.

7. Disconnect rubber brake hose and plug hose to minimize fluid leakage.
8. Disconnect overtravel link from bracket and deflate shock absorbers.
9. On vehicles with rear drum brakes, remove screw retaining rear brake pipe distributor to axle and disconnect brake pipes from the four retaining clips.
10. Disconnect shock absorbers at lower mounts, then raise axle to relieve tension on upper control arms and remove bolt and nut retaining each upper control arm to axle brackets.

CAUTION: Stand clear of axle assembly before performing next step, as springs can snap from their seats, resulting in personal injury or damage.

11. Carefully lower axle assembly until spring tension is relieved, then remove springs.
12. Remove bolt and nut retaining each lower control arm to axle brackets.

NOTE: It may be necessary to rotate axle slightly to remove bolts.

13. Remove rubber bumpers from top of axle housing, then lower axle assembly and remove from vehicle.
14. Reverse procedure to install.
15. Torque upper control arm bolts at frame end to 145 ft. lbs. and at axle end to 110 ft. lbs. Torque lower control arm bolts to 145 ft. lbs. Torque shock absorber lower mounting nuts to 50 ft. lbs. Torque spindle or brake backing retaining nuts to 40 ft. lbs.
16. On vehicles with Track Master, adjust sensor as described under "Anti-Skid Brake Systems" located elsewhere in this manual.

1977–79 Seville, 1977–84 DeVille & Brougham

In this axle, Fig. 4, the rear axle housing and differential carrier are cast into an inte-

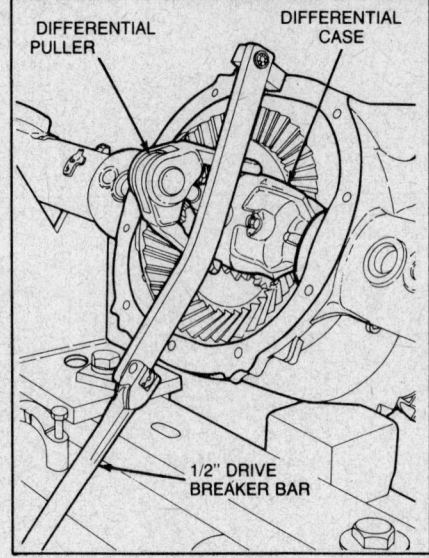

Fig. 5 Removing differential. 1977–79 Seville & 1977–84 DeVille & Brougham

gral assembly. The drive pinion assembly is mounted in two opposed tapered roller bearings. The pinion bearings are preloaded by a spacer behind the front bearing. The pinion is positioned by a washer between the head of the pinion and the rear bearing.

The differential is supported in the carrier by two tapered roller side bearings. These bearings are preloaded by spacers located between the bearings and carrier housing. The differential assembly is positioned for proper ring gear and pinion backlash by varying these spacers. The differential case houses two side gears in mesh with two pinions mounted on a pinion shaft which is held in place by a lock pin. The side gears and pinions are backed by thrust washers.

REAR AXLE, REPLACE

Exc. 1977–79 Seville

1. Raise vehicle and support rear axle and frame, then remove rear wheels and drums.
2. Disconnect overtravel lever from link, if equipped.
3. Remove shock absorbers from lower mount.
4. Place jack under front differential to relieve tension on lower control arm.
5. Remove upper and lower control arms as outlined under "Control Arms and Bushings, Replace" procedure in Rear Suspension Section.

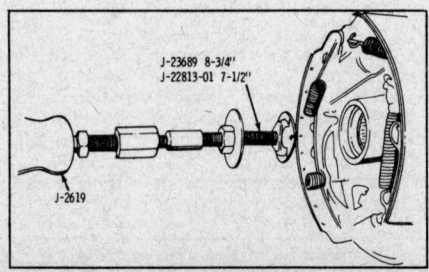

Fig. 6 Removing axle bearing

6. Remove propeller shaft and support with wire.
7. Remove brake hose at differential housing and plug.

CAUTION: If axle is allowed to wind up as it is lowered, springs may snap from their seats and could cause injury or damage. Use extreme caution to prevent wind-up condition.

8. Lower axle shaft and remove springs from vehicle.
9. Reverse procedure to install.

1977–79 Seville

1. Remove rear springs as outlined under "Leaf Spring, Replace" procedure in Rear Suspension Secion.
2. Remove clip securing brake hose to underbody and disconnect hose from brake line.
3. Remove stabilizer bar.
4. Mark propeller shaft flange and pinion flange to insure installation in original position. Then, disconnect prop shaft from pinion flange and secure with wire to underbody.
5. Lower axle and remove from vehicle.
6. Reverse procedure to install.

DIFFERENTIAL, REMOVE

1. Raise vehicle and support so axle can be raised and lowered.
2. Disconnect leveling control lever from link and hold lever down until shock absorbers are deflated.
3. Remove shock absorber lower mounting bolts and position shock aside.
4. Mark propeller shaft flange and pinion flange to ensure installation in original position. Remove attaching screws and position propeller shaft aside.
5. Remove stabilizer bar link nuts, retainer and bushings.
6. Remove nut from parking brake equalizer, then disconnect cables at connectors.
7. Remove clips securing brake tubing to axle, then lower axle slightly.
8. Position drain pan under axle, loosen rear cover bolts and allow axle to drain, then remove cover.
9. Remove wheel and brake drum.
10. Remove differential cross shaft through bolt, then the shaft. Push in on axle shafts, then remove "C" locks and pull axle shafts out about 1 inch.
11. Install cross shaft and bolt, then remove side bearing cap and bearing.

NOTE: Mark bearing caps to ensure installation in original position

12. Remove one ring gear attaching bolt, position tools, Fig. 5, and pull differential case from housing until side shims can be removed, then remove differential.

NOTE: Mark shims to ensure installation in original position.

13. Reverse procedure to install.

AXLE SHAFT, REPLACE

1. Raise vehicle and remove wheel and brake drum.
2. Place drain pan under differential and remove cover.
3. Remove differential cross shaft.

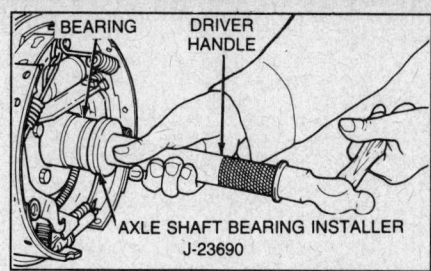

Fig. 7 Installing axle bearing

4. Push axle shaft toward center of vehicle and remove "C" lock from butt end of axle shaft.
5. Remove axle shaft from housing.
6. Reverse procedure to install.

BEARING REPLACE

1. Remove axle shaft.
2. Position tool J-22813-01 or J-23689 on bearing, attach slide hammer J-2619, then remove bearing and seal, Fig. 6.
3. Lubricate bearing and seal with bearing lubricant.
4. Position bearing on tool J-23690 and drive bearing in until tool bottoms against tube, Fig. 7.
5. Using suitable tool, tap seal in until flush with axle tube.

PROPELLER SHAFT, REPLACE

1. Raise vehicle on hoist with transmission in neutral.

NOTE: Mark propeller shaft relationship to axle pinion flange to maintain balance.

2. Remove propeller shaft flange retaining bolts.

CAUTION: Do not allow propeller shaft to be supported by front or center universal joint, as damage to universal joint may result. Rear of propeller shaft must be supported to underbody of vehicle.

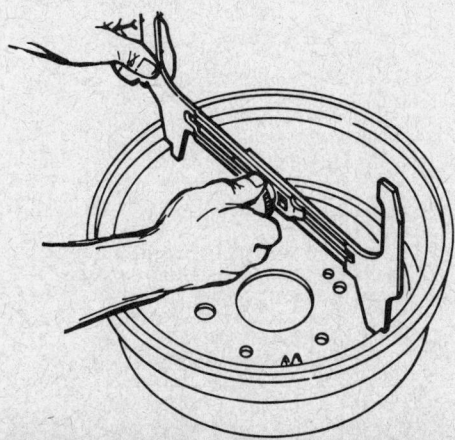

Fig. 9 Measuring brake drum inner diameter

3. Pull propeller shaft forward to clear pinion flange and support rear end of shaft.

NOTE: Place a suitable container under transmission, to catch any fluid which may leak when slip joint is removed.

4. On two piece type propeller shafts, remove the two center bearing supports to frame bolts and nuts.
5. On all types, slide propeller shaft rearward until slip yoke comes off transmission output shaft.

NOTE: Place a protective device such as a cardboard shipping cover, over yoke. This will prevent damage to yoke when shaft is removed.

6. Remove shaft and install a spare yoke into transmission extension housing to prevent loss of oil.
7. Reverse procedure to install. Torque flange attaching bolts to 70 ft. lbs.
8. Check transmission oil.

DRUM BRAKE ADJUSTMENTS
Self-Adjusting Brakes

These brakes, Fig. 8, have self-adjusting shoe mechanisms that assure correct lining-to-drum clearances at all times. The automatic adjusters operate only when the brakes are applied as the car is moving rearward.

Although the brakes are self-adjusting, an initial adjustment is necessary after the brake shoes have been relined or replaced, or when the length of the star wheel adjuster has been changed during some other service operation.

Frequent usage of an automatic transmission forward range to halt reverse vehicle motion may prevent the automatic adjusters from functioning, thereby inducing low pedal heights. Should low pedal heights be encountered, it is recommended that numerous forward and reverse stops be made with a moderate pedal effort until satisfactory pedal height is obtained.

NOTE: If a low pedal height condition cannot be corrected by making numerous reverse stops (provided the hydraulic system is free of air) it indicates that the self-adjusting mechanism is not functioning. Therefore, it will be necessary to remove the brake drum, clean, free up and lubricate the adjusting mechanism. Then adjust the brakes, being sure the parking brake is fully released.

The recommended method of adjusting the brakes is by using the Drum-to-Brake Shoe Clearance Gauge to check the diameter of the brake drum inner surface, Fig. 9. Turn the tool to the opposite side and fit over the brake shoes by turning the star wheel until the gauge just slides over the linings, Fig. 10. Rotate the gauge around the brake shoe lining surface to assure proper clearance.

PARKING BRAKE, ADJUST
1977–84 W/Rear Disc Brakes

1. Lubricate parking brake cables at equal-

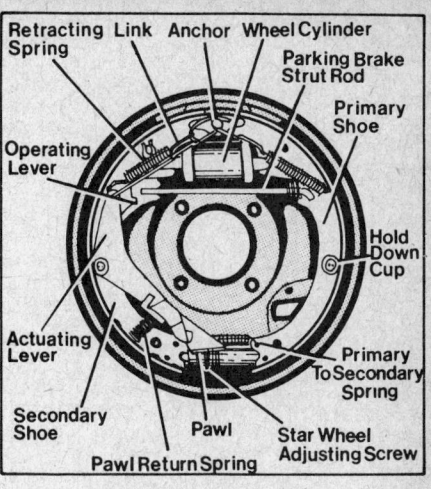

Fig. 8 Rear drum brake.

izer and underbody rub points. Check all cables for freedom of operation.
2. Fully release parking brake and raise vehicle.
3. Hold cable stud from turning and tighten equalizer nut until cable slack is removed and levers are against stops on caliper housing. If levers are off stops, loosen cable until levers return to stop.
4. Operate parking brake several times to check adjustment. When properly adjusted, the parking brake pedal should move 6¼–7¼ inches on 1977–78 Seville, 5¼–6¾ inches on 1977–82 all except Seville and 1980–83 Eldorado, 4–5½ inches on 1979–84 Eldorado and 1980–84 Seville and 6¾–7¾ inches on 1979 Seville.

1977–84 W/Rear Drum Brakes

1. With service brakes properly adjusted, lubricate parking brake linkage at equalizer and cable stud with heat-resistant lubricant, and check for free movement of cables.
2. Depress parking brake pedal about 1½" from full released position.
3. Raise rear wheels off floor.
4. Hold brake cable and stud from turning and tighten equalizer nut until a slight drag is felt on either wheel (going forward). After each turn of equalizer nut, check to see if either wheel begins to drag.

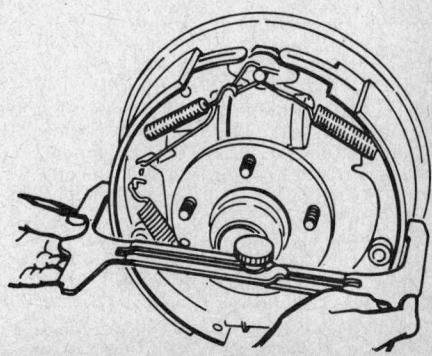

Fig. 10 Checking brake shoe lining clearance

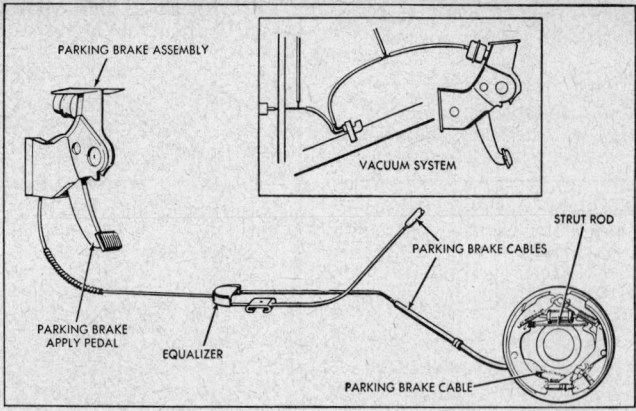

Fig. 11 Parking brake linkage. 1977–84 drum brake (typical)

5. Release parking brake. No brake drag should be felt at either rear wheel. Operate several times to check adjustment. When properly adjusted, the parking brake pedal should move 5¼ to 6¾ inches.

VACUUM RELEASE PARKING BRAKE

1977–84

The foot-operated parking brake is mounted on the cowl to the left of the steering column. It incorporates a vacuum release, Fig. 11, operated by a vacuum diaphragm that is connected to the parking brake mechanism. When the transmission selector is moved into any Drive position, a vacuum valve in the neutral safety switch opens, allowing diaphragm to be actuated by engine vacuum.

The diaphragm is connected by a link to a release mechanism on the parking brake. Vacuum acting on the diaphragm unlocks the parking brake pedal, permitting it to return to the release position by spring action. Any abnormal leaks in the vacuum release system will prevent proper brake release. A manual release is provided and may be used if the automatic release is inoperative or if manual release is desired at any time.

NOTE: Under some conditions, aided by cold weather, the parking brake vacuum release valve (integral with the back-up light switch on steering column) may not release the parking brake automatically. Although when the brake is applied, the "Brake" indicator light will go on, brake can be released manually. If this condition is present the back-up light switch must be replaced.

Testing Vacuum Release

1. If the mechanism is inoperative, first check for damaged or kinked vacuum hoses and for loose hose connections at the diaphragm, vacuum release valve at neutral safety switch, and at engine manifold connection.
2. Check adjustment of neutral safety switch and operation of vacuum release valve.

3. Check diaphragm piston travel by running engine and moving transmission selector lever from drive to neutral. The manual release lever should move up and down as vacuum is applied and released. If no movement is observed, or if movement is slow (more than 1 or 2 seconds to complete the full stroke) diaphragm is leaking and should be replaced.
4. Check brake release with vacuum applied. If diaphragm piston completes full stroke but does not release brake, a malfunction of the pedal assembly is indicated, and the complete parking brake assembly should be replaced.
5. Check operation of parking brake with engine off. Parking brake should remain engaged regardless of transmission selector lever position. If not, replace parking brake assembly.

MASTER CYLINDER, REPLACE

1. Remove brake lines from master cylinder. Plug lines and ports.
2. Remove booster to master cylinder attaching nuts, then remove master cylinder.
3. Reverse procedure to install. On 1977–80 models, torque master cylinder attaching nuts to 20 ft. lbs., 1981 models to 22–30 ft. lbs. and 1982–84 models to 28 ft. lbs. On 1977–78 models, torque brake line to master cylinder nuts to 15 ft. lbs., on 1979–80 models to 20 ft. lbs., on 1981 models to 10–15 ft. lbs. and on 1982–84 models to 18 ft. lbs.

POWER BRAKE UNIT, REPLACE

Service Bulletin

A sign of brake fluid dampness below the master cylinder at the power brake unit or on wheel cylinders at the bottom of the boot, does not necessarily indicate that these cylinders are leaking.

A small amount of fluid leakage at these areas can occur due to the creeping action of a very light film of fluid on the cylinder bores

around the seals. This action provides proper seal lubrication. In addition, normal brake heat will produce a slight escape of lubricant from the impregnated, porous-metal wheel cylinder pistons.

Normal dampness at the master cylinder or wheel cylinders is not easily distinguishable from a definite leak. Therefore, this condition must be checked carefully.

If there is sufficient dampness to form a "teardrop" of fluid at the bottom of the master cylinder or on the bottom of the wheel cylinders at the boot area, the rate of fluid seepage is too high and the cause should be determined and corrected.

Hydro-Boost

1977–84
1. With engine off pump brake pedal several times to empty accumulator of fluid.
2. Remove master cylinder to booster attaching nuts, then move master cylinder away from booster with brakes lines attached.
3. Remove three hydraulic lines from booster, cap all ports and lines to prevent entry of dirt and loss of fluid.
4. Remove retainer and washer securing booster pedal rod to brake pedal arm.
5. Remove four booster to firewall attaching nuts.
6. Loosen booster from firewall and move booster pedal rod inboard until it disconnects from brake arm.
7. Remove spring washer from brake pedal arm and remove booster.
8. Reverse procedure to install. To purge system, disconnect feed wire from injection pump. Fill power steering pump reservoir, then crank engine for several seconds without starting and recheck power steering pump fluid level. Connect injection pump feed wire and start engine, then cycle steering gear wheel from stop to stop twice and turn off engine. Discharge accumulator by depressing brake pedal several times, then check fluid level. Start engine, then turn steering wheel from stop to stop and turn off engine. Check fluid level and add fluid if necessary. If foaming occurs, turn off engine and wait for approximately one hour for foam to dissipate, then recheck fluid level.

Vacuum Booster

1. Remove master cylinder to booster attaching nuts, then move master cylinder away from booster with brake lines attached.

NOTE: On some models, it may be necessary to remove brake lines from master cylinder. If lines must be removed, cover exposed ends of brake lines to prevent contamination.

2. Remove vacuum hose from check valve on booster.
3. Remove nuts attaching brake unit to cowl and pedal support bracket.
4. From inside of vehicle, disconnect power brake push rod from brake pedal and remove vacuum booster.
5. Reverse procedure to install.

Rear Suspension

SHOCK ABSORBER, REPLACE

1977—84

1. If equipped with Automatic Level Control, disconnect air lines from shock absorber fittings.
2. With the rear axle supported properly disconnect shock absorber at upper and lower mountings.

NOTE: Use care not to damage brake hoses or lines when removing shock absorber.

3. Reverse procedure to install, noting the following:
   a. When installing shocks equipped with automatic level control, air ports should face front of vehicle.
   b. Extend shocks completely before installation.

COIL SPRINGS, REPLACE

1979—84 Eldorado & 1980—84 Seville

1. Raise and support rear of vehicle, then remove wheel and tire assembly.
2. Remove stabilizer bar as described under Stabilizer Bar, Replace.
3. Using a suitable jack support lower control arm.
4. Disconnect automatic level air line at shock absorber. If removing left hand spring from vehicle, disconnect automatic level control link from ball pivot at control arm.
5. Disconnect shock absorber from upper and lower mountings and remove shock absorber.
6. Carefully lower control arm until spring

tension is relieved, then remove spring and insulator, Fig. 1.
7. Reverse procedure to install. Locate bottom end of spring between dimples on lower control arm assembly, Fig. 2.

1977—84 Except Eldorado & Seville

1. Support vehicle at frame and support rear

axle using a suitable jack.
2. Remove shock absorbers.
3. If equipped with Automatic Level Control, remove bolts attaching stabilizer bar to lower control arms and remove stabilizer bar.
4. Remove bolt attaching brake line junction block to rear axle housing, then disconnect brake lines from clips on rear axle housing.

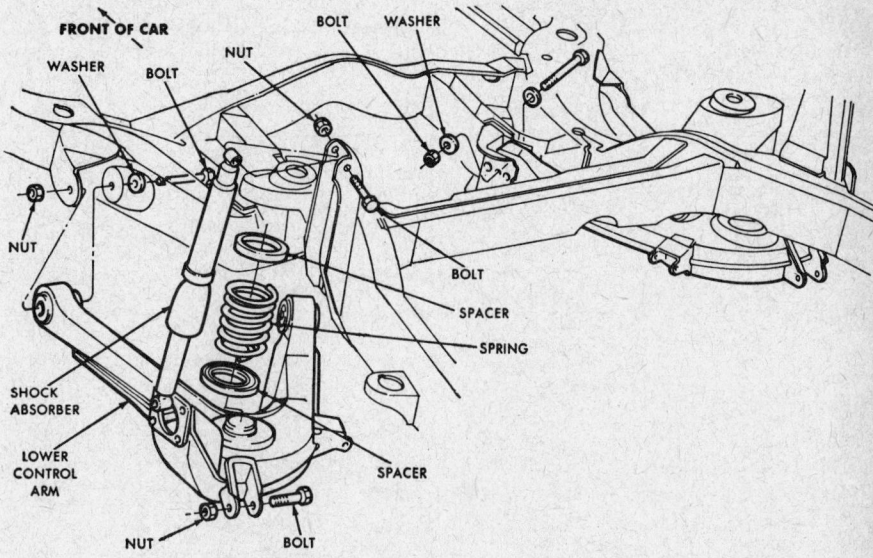

Fig. 1   1979—84 Eldorado & 1980—84 Seville rear suspension

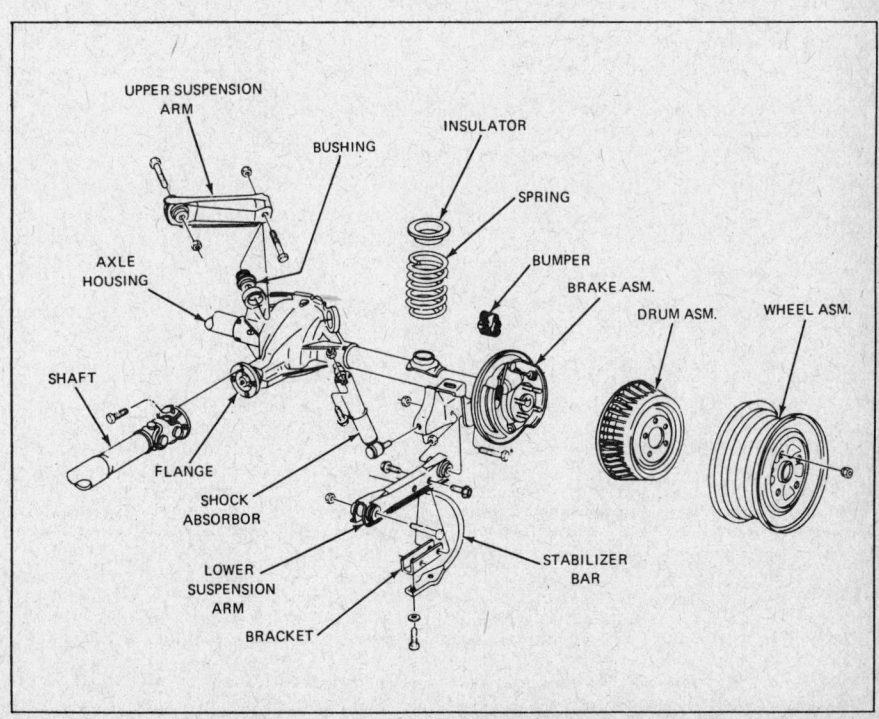

Fig. 3   1977—84 rear suspension (typical). Except Eldorado & Seville

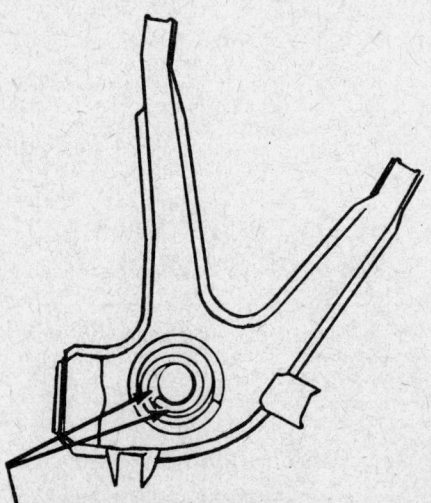

POSITIONING DIMPLES

Fig. 2   Coil spring installation. 1979—84 Eldorado & 1980—84 Seville

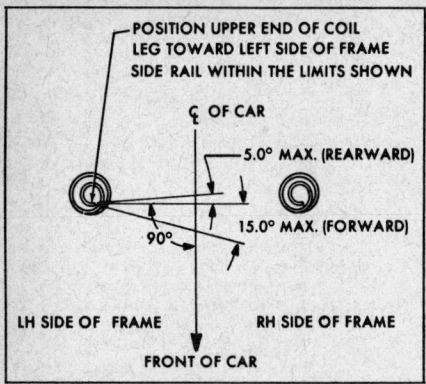

Fig. 4 Coil spring installation. 1977—78 Except Eldorado & Seville

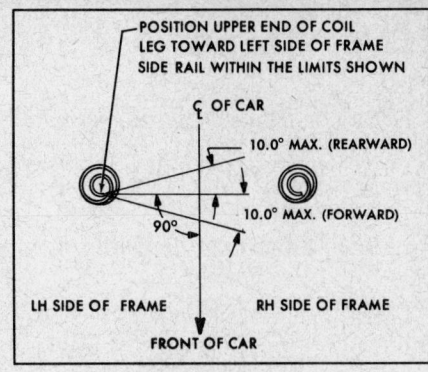

Fig. 5 Coil spring installation. 1979—84 Except Eldorado & Seville

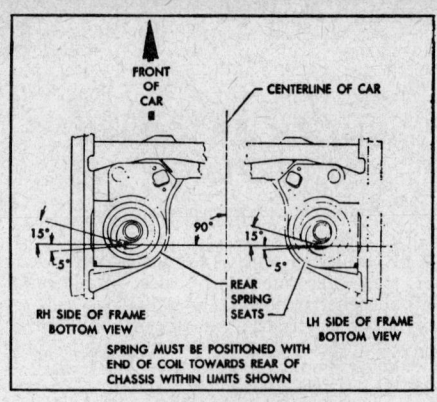

Fig. 7 Coil spring installation. 1977—78 Eldorado

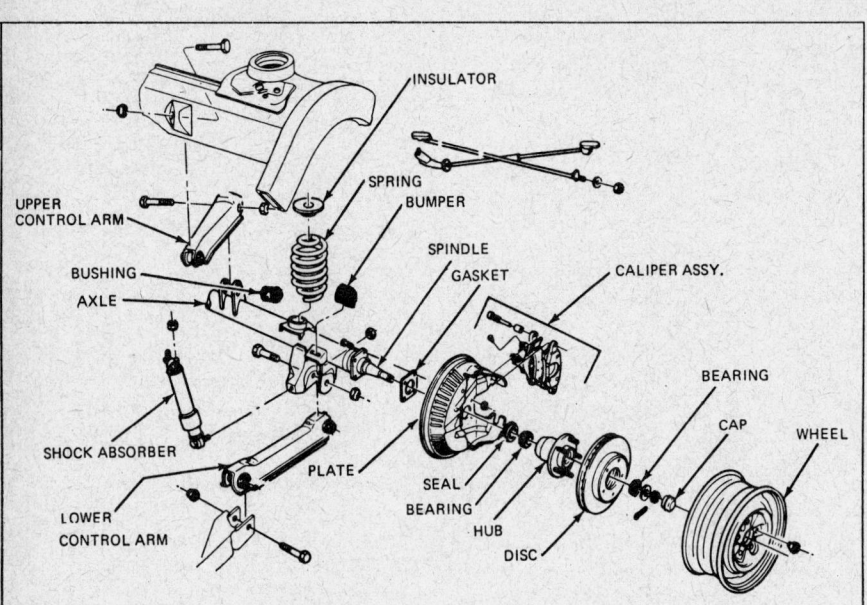

Fig. 6 1977—78 Eldorado rear suspension (typical)

5. If equipped with Automatic Level Control, disconnect link from leveling valve arm.
6. Position a jack stand under nose of differential carrier to relieve tension on lower control arm to axle housing bolts, then remove bolts, Fig. 3.
7. Disconnect drive shaft from pinion flange and support from frame with wire.
8. Remove jack stand from under nose of differential carrier, then remove upper control arm pivot bolts at rear axle housing.
9. Disconnect left hand parking brake cable at equalizer and cable at frame by removing clip.
10. Disconnect parking brake cable from clip at center of rear cross member and cable at "C" connector located at left hand side of frame.
11. Lower axle assembly to a point where springs can be pryed out, using care not to stretch brake lines or parking brake cables.

NOTE: When lowering axle and prying

out springs, use care to prevent axle assembly from rotating, as springs may snap from seats.

12. Reverse procedure to install. Note spring positions, Figs. 4 and 5.

1977—78 Eldorado

1. Support vehicle at frame and support rear axle with a suitable jack.
2. If equipped with Automatic Level Control, disconnect overtravel lever link and place lever in center position.
3. Disconnect shock absorbers from lower mountings and rear brake hose from brake line.
4. On standard cars, disconnect propeller shaft from differential pinion flange.
5. Remove upper control arm rear mount bolt and lift arm from axle bracket, Fig. 6.
6. Lower axle assembly slowly until springs are free.

NOTE: When lowering axle assembly, use

care to prevent axle from rotating, as springs may snap from the seats. If necessary, compress springs by hand to remove.

7. Reverse procedure to install. Note spring positions, Fig. 7. Tighten control arm bolt with vehicle at curb height.

LEAF SPRING, REPLACE

1977—79 Seville

1. Raise vehicle on hoist.
2. Using a suitable jack, raise axle until spring tension is relieved, Fig. 8.
3. Disconnect Automatic Level Control overtravel lever from link.
4. Push overtravel lever down to deflate shock absorbers, then remove shock lower mounting nut and bolt and position shock absorber aside.
5. Back off parking brake adjustment at equalizer and remove cable clip from spring front retaining bracket and cable clamps from bottom of spring.
6. Loosen spring front eye to retaining bracket bolt.
7. Remove spring front bracket to underbody attaching screws.
8. Lower axle until bolt can be removed from spring front eye and remove bracket from spring.
9. Remove nuts securing lower spring plate to axle and stabilizer bar brackets.
10. Remove upper and lower spring pads and spring plate, support spring, then remove both nuts from rear shackle.
11. Separate spring and shackle and remove spring.

CONTROL ARMS & BUSHINGS, REPLACE

NOTE: Replace one control arm at a time as axle assembly may slip sideways, making installation difficult.

Upper Control Arms

1977—84 Except Eldorado & Seville
1. Support vehicle at frame and support rear axle using a suitable jack.
2. If vehicle is equipped with Automatic Level Control, remove bolt attaching

height control link to right upper control arm. Position overtravel lever in center position.

3. Position a jack stand under differential pinion retainer.
4. Remove both control arm pivot bolts and control arm.
5. Reverse procedure to install. Tighten control arm pivot bolts with vehicle curb weight applied to axle.

1977–78 Eldorado
1. Perform steps 1 and 2 as outlined under "Coil Springs, Replace" 1977–78 Eldorado. On Eldorado disconnect shock absorbers from lower mountings.
2. Remove control arm front and rear mount bolts.
3. On Eldorado, replace axle bracket bushing as required, Figs. 9 and 10. New bushing is installed with flanged side outboard of bracket.
4. Reverse procedure to install. Tighten control arm bolts with vehicle at curb height.

Lower Control Arms

1979–84 Eldorado & 1980–84 Seville
1. Raise and support rear of vehicle, then remove wheel and tire assembly.
2. Remove stabilizer bar as described under Stabilizer Bar, Replace.
3. Disconnect brake line bracket from control arm, then remove caliper assembly.
4. Mark a wheel stud and a corresponding point on the rotor for alignment, then remove rotor.
5. If left hand control arm is to be removed, disconnect automatic level control link from ball pivot on control arm.
6. Using a suitable jack support control arm.
7. Disconnect air line from shock absorber, then disconnect shock absorber from upper and lower mountings and remove shock absorber.
8. Carefully lower the control arm until spring tension is relieved, then remove spring and insulator.
9. Remove two bolts mounting control arm to frame and remove control arm, Fig. 1.
10. Reverse procedure to install. Torque control arm to frame mounting bolts to 75 ft. lbs.

1977–84 Except Eldorado & Seville
1. Support vehicle at frame and support rear axle using a suitable jack.
2. If equipped with Automatic Level Control, remove two bolts securing stabilizer bar to control arm being removed.
3. Remove front and rear lower control arm nuts.
4. Position a suitable jack under front of differential carrier to relieve tension on lower control arms.
5. Remove front and rear lower control arm bolts and lower control arm.

NOTE: Lower control arm bushings are not serviceable.

6. Reverse procedure to install. Tighten control arm bolts with vehicle at curb height.

1977–78 Eldorado

Follow "Upper Control Arms" 1977–78 Eldorado procedure for replacement of lower control arms.

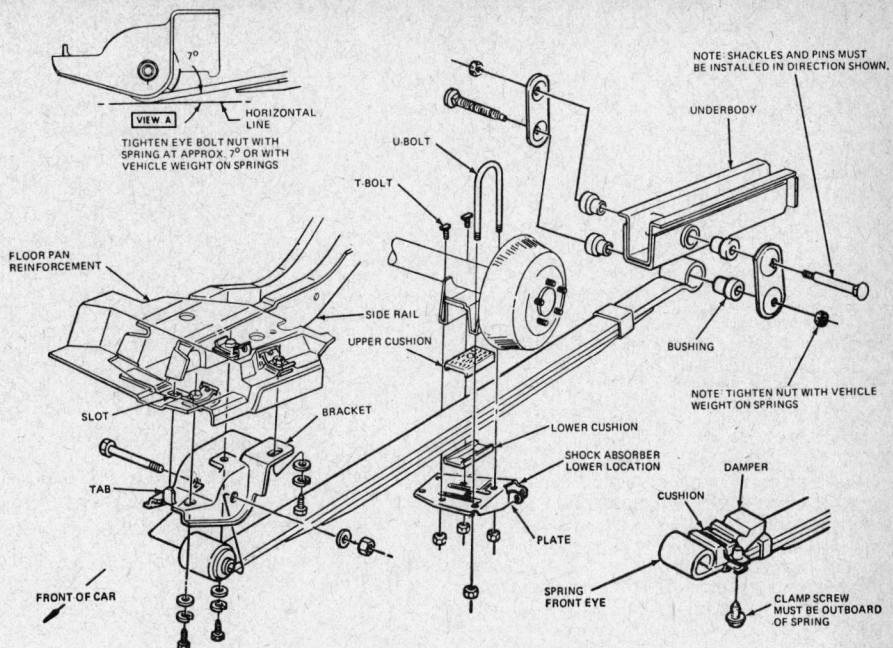

Fig. 8   Rear suspension. 1977–79 Seville

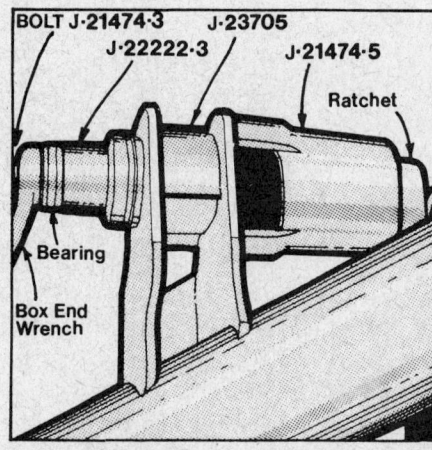

Fig. 9   Upper control arm axle bracket bushing removal, 1977–78 Eldorado

NOTE: Lower control arm bushings are not serviceable.

STABILIZER BAR, REPLACE

1979–84 Eldorado & 1980–84 Seville
1. Raise and support rear of vehicle.
2. Remove nuts and bolts securing front of stabilizer bar to control arms.
3. Remove inside nut and bolt from each side of stabilizer bar link, then loosen outside nut and bolt on the stabilizer link.
4. Rotate bottom parts of link to one side

Fig. 10   Upper control arm axle bracket bushing installation, 1977–78 Eldorado

and slip stabilizer out of bushings.

1977–84 Except Eldorado & Seville
1. Raise and support rear of vehicle.
2. Remove bolts securing stabilizer bar to lower control arms, then remove stabilizer bar from vehicle.

1977–79 Seville
1. Raise and support rear of vehicle.
2. Remove nuts and bolts securing stabilizer bushings and brackets to lower spring plates.
3. Remove nuts from link bolts, then remove washers and grommets.
4. Remove stabilizer bar from vehicle, then remove bushings and brackets from bar.

Front End & Steering Section

Refer to Main Index for Front Drive Axle Service

1977—79 SEVILLE & 1977—84 BROUGHAM & DEVILLE FRONT SUSPENSION

The front suspension consist of two upper and lower control arm assemblies, steel coil springs, shock absorbers, stabilizer bar, two integral steering arms, and knuckles, Fig. 1.

Ball joints are used at outer ends of upper and lower control arms. The upper ball joints is riveted to the upper control arm. The lower ball joint is pressed into the lower control arm.

A stabilizer bar is mounted in rubber bushings to the front frame side rails and is attached to the lower control arms by means of steel links.

Wheel Alignment

Caster and camber are adjusted by adding or removing shims from between the upper control arm and frame bracket, Fig. 2. Caster is adjusted by transfering shims from front to rear and rear to front. Transfering shims from front bolt to rear bolt will increase positive caster, from rear bolt to front bolt will increase negative caster.

Camber is adjusted by adding or removing an equal number of shims from the front and rear bolts. To increase positive camber remove an equal amount of shims from front and rear bolts, to increase negative camber add an equal amount of shims to front and rear bolts.

After adjusting caster and camber torque nut to 70—80 ft. lbs. Tighten bolt with the least amount of shims first. After adjusting caster and camber toe-in must be adjusted.

NOTE: The difference in thickness between front and rear shim packs should not exceed .40 inch. If difference is greater than .40 inch check arms, frame and related parts for damage.

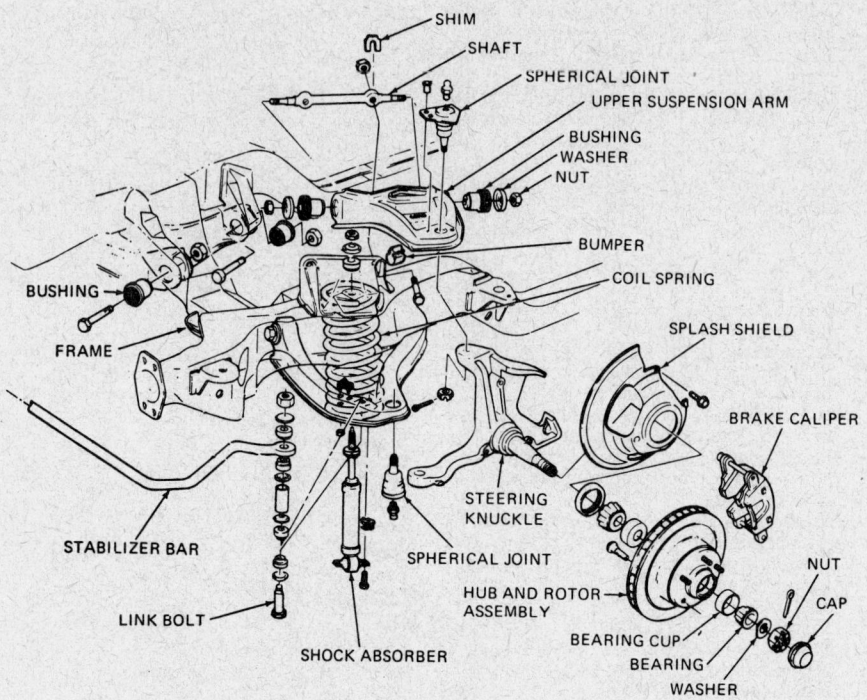

Fig. 1 Front suspension disassembled. 1977—79 Seville & 1977—84 Brougham & DeVille

front wheels of all standard Cadillacs should not be preloaded and normally can have up to .004" end play.

1. While rotating wheel and tire assembly, tighten spindle nut to 15 ft. lbs. for 1977 vehicles and 12 ft. lbs. for 1978—84 vehicles making certain that hub is fully seated on spindle.

2. Back off spindle nut until free, and tighten nut finger tight.

3. Install new cotter pin. If pin cannot be installed, back off nut to next hole and install pin.

NOTE: Cotter pin must be tight after installation, as vibration can break pin.

Toe-In, Adjust

Toe-in can be adjusted by loosening the clamp bolts at each end of each tie rod and turning each tie rod to increase or decrease its length as necessary until proper toe-in is secured and the steering gear is on the high point for straight-ahead driving.

Wheel Bearings, Adjust

Service Bulletin

Looseness at a front wheel does not necessarily indicate worn bearings or a loose spindle nut, since the tapered roller bearings used on

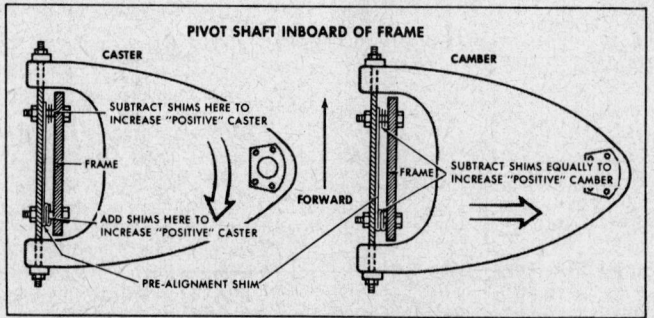

Fig. 2 Caster and camber adjustment. 1977—79 Seville & 1977—84 Brougham & DeVille

FRONT SUSPENSION BALL JOINT WEAR INDICATOR

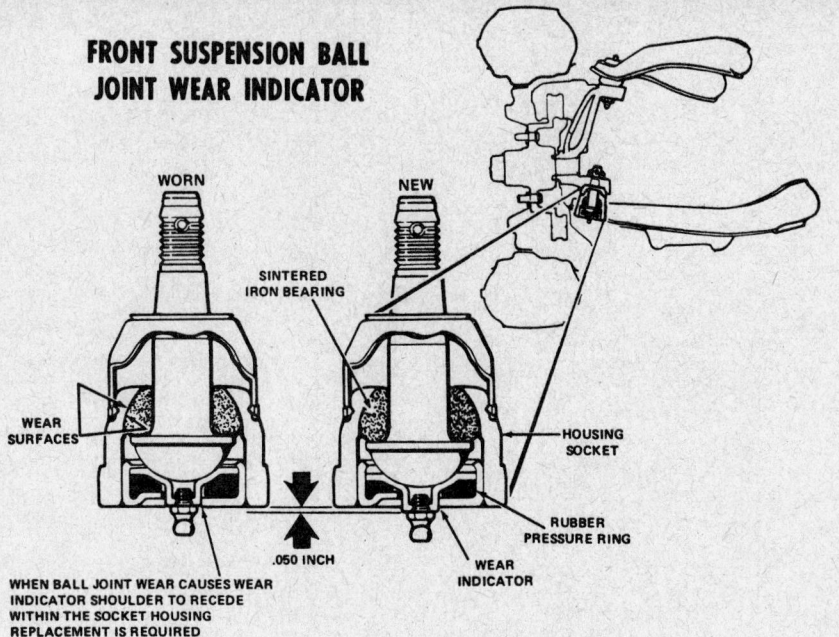

WORN

NEW

SINTERED IRON BEARING

WEAR SURFACES

HOUSING SOCKET

.050 INCH

RUBBER PRESSURE RING

WEAR INDICATOR

WHEN BALL JOINT WEAR CAUSES WEAR INDICATOR SHOULDER TO RECEDE WITHIN THE SOCKET HOUSING REPLACEMENT IS REQUIRED

Fig. 3 Ball joint wear indicator.

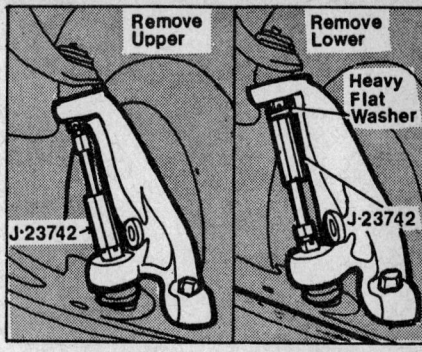

Fig. 4 Removing ball joint studs from steering knuckle. 1977—79 Seville & 1977—84 Brougham & DeVille

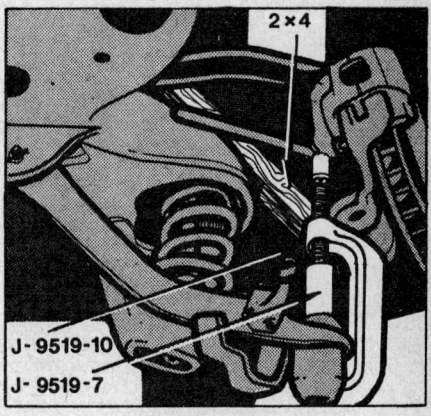

Fig. 5 Removing ball joint from lower control arm. 1977—79 Seville & 1977—84 DeVille

Wheel Bearings, Replace

1. Remove caliper retaining bolts, then slide caliper off disc and using a length of wire, attach caliper to upper control arm.

NOTE: Never allow caliper to hang from brake hose.

2. Remove dust cap, cotter pin, spindle nut, washer and outer bearing assembly.
3. Remove hub and disc assembly, being careful to avoid damage to spindle threads or grease seal.
4. Remove inner bearing grease seal and bearing assembly.

NOTE: Inner and outer bearing cups are press fit in hub and can be driven out from the opposite side using a brass drift. Tap alternately on opposite sides to prevent cocking cup and damaging hub.

Checking Ball Joints For Wear

Upper Ball Joint
If ball joint has any noticeable lateral movement or can be twisted within its socket using finger pressure, the joint must be replaced.

Lower Ball Joint
A wear indicator is built in the ball joint. Remove dirt deposits around service plug and observe position of nipple. Refer to Fig. 3, for wear tolerance.

Upper Ball Joint, Replace

1. Raise vehicle and remove wheel.
2. Remove cotter pin from upper ball joint stud.
3. Remove caliper and position aside.

NOTE: When removing caliper use care not to damage brake tubing or hose. Secure caliper to frame with wire.

4. Loosen stud nut, however, not more than one turn.
5. Using tool No. J-23742, free ball joint stud from steering knuckle, Fig. 4.

NOTE: The lower control arm must be supported so spring can not force arm down.

6. Remove upper ball joint stud nut, allow steering knuckle to swing out of way and place block of wood between frame and upper control arm.
7. To remove rivets securing ball joint to upper control arm, grind rivet heads off, then, using a punch, drive rivets out.

NOTE: Use care not to damage ball joint seat or upper control arm when removing rivets.

8. Remove ball joint.
9. Install new ball joint in control arm and attach with bolt and nut assembly provided with new joint. Install bolts from bottom and torque nuts to 25 ft. lbs. on 1977–81 models, and 20 ft. lbs. on 1982–84 models.
10. Remove block of wood from between frame and upper control arm, position upper ball stud to steering knuckle, install and torque nut to 60 to 61 ft. lbs. Install cotter pin.

NOTE: If cotter pin hole is not aligned do not back nut off. Nut may be torqued to a maximum of 100 ft. lbs. (1/6 additional turn) to align cotter pin hole.

11. Install caliper, lubricate ball joint and install wheel.
12. Check wheel alignment.

Lower Ball Joint, Replace

1. Raise vehicle and remove wheel.
2. Remove cotter pin from lower ball joint stud and loosen nut one turn.
3. Using tool No. J-23742, free ball joint stud from steering knuckle, Fig. 4.

NOTE: Lower control arm must be supported so spring cannot force arm down.

4. Remove lower stud nut and pull upward and outward on bottom of brake disc to free ball joint stud from steering knuckle.
5. Lift upper control arm up with steering knuckle and hub attached and place a block of wood between frame and upper control arm.

NOTE: It may be necessary to remove tie rod from steering knuckle.

6. Using tools J-9519-10 and J-9519-7 or equivalent, remove ball joint from lower control arm, Fig. 5.
7. Install ball joint in lower control arm using tools J-9519-9 and J-9519-10 or equivalent.

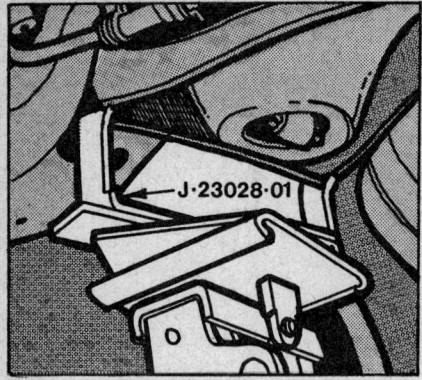

Fig. 6 Removing and installing front spring. 1977–79 Seville & 1977–84 Brougham & DeVille

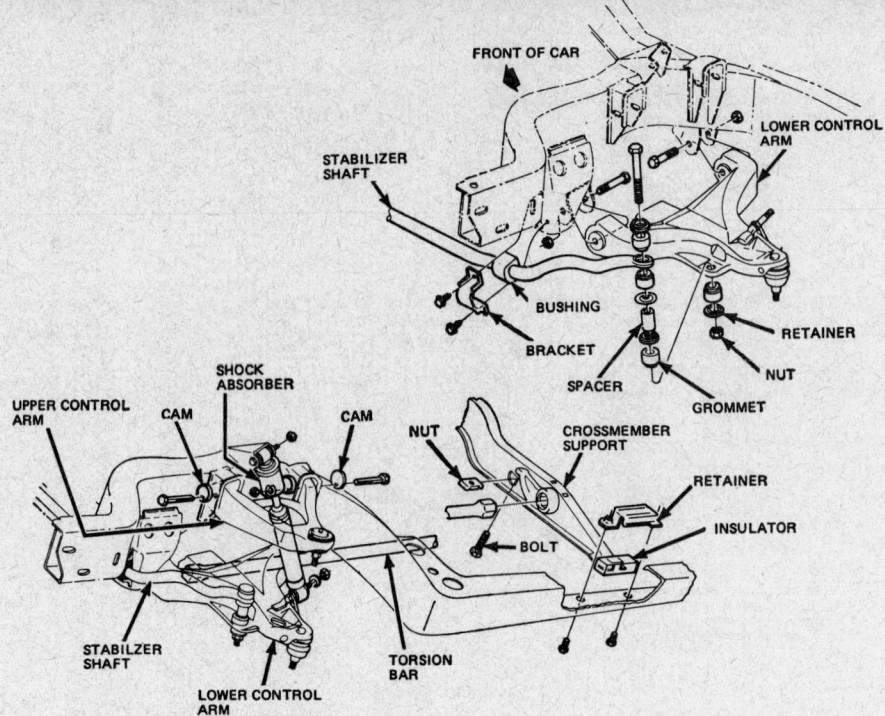

Fig. 7 Front suspension disassembled. 1979–84 Eldorado & 1980–84 Seville

NOTE: Position bleed vent in ball joint rubber boot to face inward and the stud cotter pin hole to face forward.

8. Remove block of wood from between frame and upper control arm, then install lower ball joint stud in steering knuckle. Install and torque nut to 80 to 83 ft. lbs. and install cotter pin.

NOTE: Some models are equipped with prevailing torque fasteners, and therefore no cotter pins are used. On models with fasteners that use cotter pins as locking devices, nut may be torqued to a maximum of 125 ft. lbs. on 1977–81 models or a maximum of 92 ft. lbs. on 1982–84 models to align cotter pin holes.

9. Lubricate ball joint and install tie rod, if removed. Torque tie rod nut to 35 ft. lbs. for 1977–79 and 1981 models, 40 ft. lbs. for 1980 and 1982 models, and 30 ft. lbs. for 1983–84 models.

NOTE: Some models are equipped with prevailing torque fasteners, and therefore no cotter pins are used.

10. Install wheel and check wheel alignment.

Shock Absorber, Replace

The shock absorbers are removed through the bottom of the lower control arm after unfastening it at the top and bottom.

To install, place the retainer and rubber grommet on the upper stem and fully extend the shock absorber rod. Insert the shock absorber up into the coil spring and guide the stem through the tower in the crossmember. Then place the lower end in position on the lower control arm. Install bolts and torque to 20 to 22 ft. lbs. on all except Seville or 19 ft. lbs. on Seville. On all models, install shock stud retaining nut and tighten to end of threads on stud (about 1⅛ inch).

Coil Spring, Replace

1. Raise vehicle on hoist, remove shock absorber lower mounting bolts and push shock through control arm up into spring.

2. Support vehicle so control arms hang free and disconnect stabilizer bar from lower control arm.
3. Secure tool No. J-23028-01 to a suitable jack, position tool so lower control arm is supported by inner bushings, Fig. 6.
4. Raise jack to relieve spring tension from lower control arm pivot and install a safety chain around spring and through lower control arm.
5. Remove bolt from rear of lower control arm, then remove other bolt and slowly lower control arm until all spring tension is relieved.
6. Remove safety chain, spring and spring insulator.
7. Reverse procedure to install.

NOTE: When installing spring, bottom coil must cover all or part of one inspection hole on the lower control arm. The other inspection hole must be fully or partially uncovered.

1977–84 ELDORADO & 1980–84 SEVILLE FRONT SUSPENSION

The front suspension consists of two upper and two lower control arms, a stabilizer bar, shock absorbers and a right and left torsion bar, Figs. 7 and 8. Torsion bars are used instead of the conventional coil springs. The front end of the torsion bar is attached to the lower control arm. The rear of the torsion bar is mounted into an adjustable arm in the torsion bar crossmember. The standing height of the car is controlled by this adjustment.

Standing Height, Adjust

NOTE: Before standing height adjustment is performed, vehicle should be on a flat, level surface, with front seat all the way back, fuel tank full and tires inflated to proper pressure. Air lines must be loosened at shock absorbers, if equipped with electronic level control, and system must be depressurized.

The standing height must be checked and adjusted if necessary before checking and adjusting front wheel alignment. The standing height is controlled by the adjustment setting of the torsion bar adjusting bolt, Figs. 7 and 8. Clockwise rotation of the bolt increases standing height; counterclockwise rotation decreases standing height.

To check vehicle height, measure from lower edge of front shock absorber dust tube (A) to centerline of lower attachment (B), Fig. 9. This dimension between (A) and (B) should be 8³⁄₁₆–8⁷⁄₁₆ inch on 1977–78 vehicles and 5½–6″ on 1979–84 vehicles.

Wheel Alignment, Adjust

1979–84 Eldorado & 1980–84 Seville
Caster
Record camber reading, then hold front cam bolt and loosen nut, Fig. 10. Turn front cam bolt to obtain ¼ of the desired caster change. At front cam bolt a positive camber change produces a positive caster change and a negative camber change produces a negative caster change. Hold cam bolt in position and tighten nut. Loosen rear cam bolt nut and rotate cam bolt to return camber to setting recorded previously, Fig. 10. When adjustment has been completed hold rear cam bolt

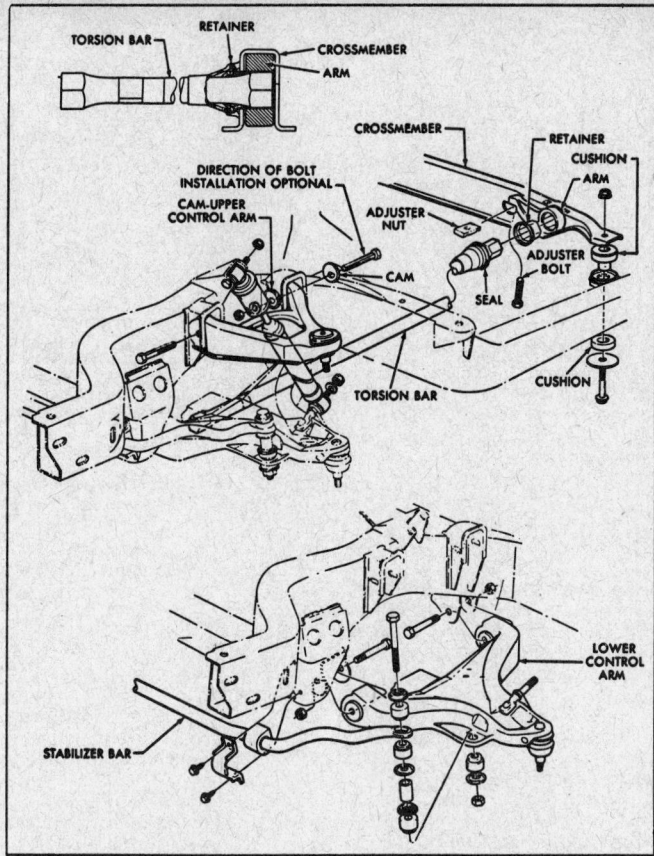

Fig. 8 Front suspension disassembled. 1977–78 Eldorado

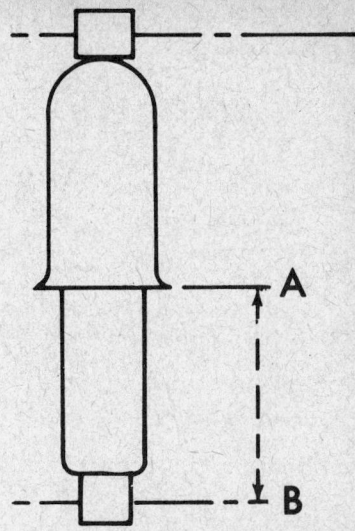

Fig. 9 Checking standing height
1977–84 Eldorado & 1980–84 Seville

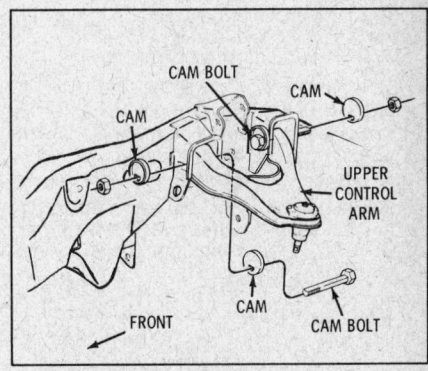

Fig. 10 Caster-camber cam locations.
1977–84 Eldorado & 1980–84 Seville

and torque nut to 90 ft. lbs. on 1977–81 models and 70 ft. lbs. on 1982–84 models.

Camber

While holding cam bolt in position, loosen cam bolt nut, Fig. 10. Rotate cam bolt to obtain a change in camber equal to ½ the needed correction. Hold cam bolt in position and tighten cam bolt nut. To obtain the remaining ½ of needed correction apply the above procedue to the other cam bolt.

1977–78 Eldorado

Caster and camber can be adjusted from under hood or under car. If under hood method is used, adjustments must be rechecked due to the change in weight distribution. After checking vehicle standing height adjust caster and camber as follows:
1. Loosen front and rear adjusting cam nuts, Fig. 10.
2. Rotate front cam to correct for ½ of incorrect camber reading.
3. Rotate rear cam to bring camber reading to 0°.
4. Tighten front and rear cam nuts, then check caster.

NOTE: If caster is within specifications, procede to step 7.

5. If caster is to be adjusted, loosen front and rear cam nuts.
6. Rotate front cam bolt so that camber will change ¼ of desired caster change.

NOTE: A change of 1° in camber reading will change caster reading about 2°. To correct for excessive negative caster ro-

tate front cam bolt to increase positive camber. To correct for excessive positive caster rotate front cam bolt to increase negative camber.

7. Set camber to specifications by rotating rear cam bolt.
8. Torque front and rear cam nuts to 95 ft. lbs.

NOTE: When tightening cam nuts ensure cam bolt does not move, any movement of cam bolt will affect wheel alignment.

Toe-In, Adjust

Toe-in is adjusted by turning the tie rod adjusting tubes at outer ends of each tie rod after loosening clamp bolts. Readings should be taken only when front wheels are straight ahead and steering gear is on its high spot.

1979–84 Eldorado & 1980–84 Seville
1. Loosen clamp bolts at each end of tie rod adjusting sleeve.
2. Turn tie rod adjusting sleeve to obtain the proper toe-in adjustment.
3. After completing adjustment, check to ensure that the number of threads at each end of sleeve are equal and tie rod end housings and clamps are properly positioned, Fig. 11. Torque clamp bolt to 14 to 15 ft. lbs.

1977–78 Eldorado
1. Center steering wheel, raise car and

check wheel run-out.
2. Loosen tie rod adjuster nuts and adjust tie rods to obtain the specified toe-in.
3. Tighten tie rod adjuster nuts to 20–22 ft. lbs.
4. Position adjuster clamps so that opening of clamps are facing up. Interference with front suspension components could occur while turning if clamps are facing down.

Wheel Bearing Inspection

1979–84 Eldorado & 1980–84 Seville

The front wheel bearing is a sealed unit bearing. The bearing can not be adjusted or repacked. There are darkened areas on the bearing assembly. These darkened areas are from a heat treatment process and do not indicate need for bearing replacement, Fig. 12.

To check wheel bearing assembly for looseness, free brake pads from disc or remove calipers. Install two lug nuts to secure disc to bearing. Mount dial indicator as shown in Fig. 13, then rock disc and note indicator reading. If looseness exceeds .005 in. replace hub and bearing assembly.

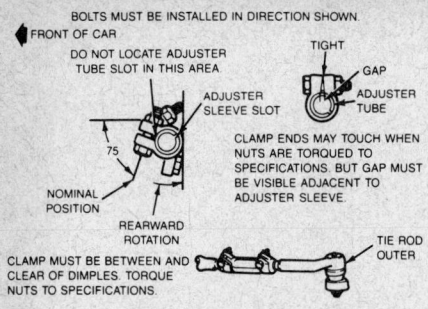

Fig. 11   Tie rod clamp and sleeve positioning

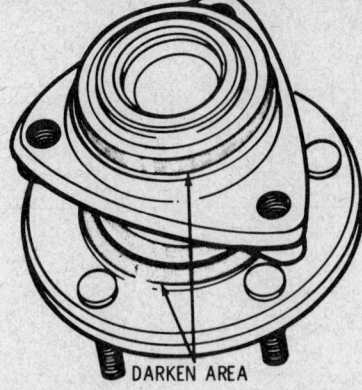

Fig. 12   Sealed wheel bearing assembly. 1979–84 Eldorado & 1980–84 Seville

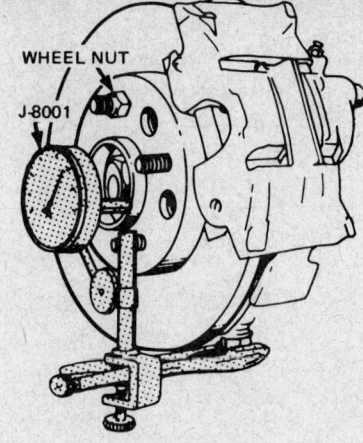

Fig. 13   Checking wheel bearing for looseness. 1979–84 Eldorado & 1980–84 Seville

Wheel Bearing & Steering Knuckle, Replace

1977–84 Eldorado & 1980–84 Seville

1. Raise and support vehicle under lower control arms.
2. Remove drive axle nut and washer and remove wheel and tire assembly.
3. Remove brake hose clip from ball joint and replace nut, then remove brake caliper off disc, and using a length of wire support caliper on suspension.

NOTE: Do not allow caliper to hang from brake hose as this could cause damage and premature failure of hose.

4. Mark hub and disc assembly for alignment during assembly and remove disc, then strike steering knuckle in area of upper ball joint until upper ball joint is loose.

CAUTION: Use extreme care to prevent striking and damaging brake hose or ball joint seal.

5. Place a short length of rubber hose over lower control arm torsion bar connector to avoid damage to inboard tri-pot joint seal when hub and knuckle are removed.
6. Using appropriate puller, disconnect tie rod end, upper and lower ball joints and remove steering knuckle and hub assembly, Figs. 14 and 15.
7. Reverse procedure to install, noting the following torque values: drive axle nut to hub and bearing, 110 ft. lbs. on 1977–78 Eldorado or 175 ft. lbs. on 1979–84 models; lower ball joint nut, 80 ft. lbs. on 1977–78 Eldorado, 65 ft. lbs. on 1979–81 models or 83 ft. lbs. on 1982–84 models; upper ball joint nut, 60 ft. lbs. on 1977–78 Eldorado, 90 ft. lbs. on 1979–81 models or 61 ft. lbs. on 1982–84 models; tie rod to steering knuckle nut, 40 ft. lbs. on 1977–78 Eldorado, 35 ft. lbs. on 1979–81 models or 40 ft. lbs. on 1982–84 models; hub and bearing to knuckle bolts, 30 ft. lbs. on 1977–78 Eldorado, 75 ft. lbs. on 1979–84 models.

Checking Ball Joints For Wear

1. Raise car and position jack stands under lower control arms as near as possible to each ball joint.
2. Clamp vise grips on end of drive axle and

position a dial indicator so that dial indicator ball rests on vise grip, Fig. 16.
3. Place a pry bar between lower control arm and outer race and pry down on bar. Reading must not exceed 1/8".

Upper Ball Joint, Replace

1979–84 Eldorado & 1980–84 Seville

1. Raise vehicle and support under lower control arms.
2. Remove wheel and tire assembly.
3. Remove cotter pin and nut from upper ball joint stud, then disconnect brake hose clip from stud.
4. Using a hammer and brass drift, disengage ball joint stud from steering knuckle.
5. Place a block of wood between control arm and frame, then drill rivets with a 1/8 in. drill bit 1/4 in. deep from top side of control arm.
6. Drill rivet heads off using a 1/2 inch drill bit. Do not drill into control arm.
7. Using a hammer and punch, drive rivets out and remove ball joint.
8. Install ball joint into control arm and torque nuts and bolts to 8 ft. lbs. for 1979–81 models, or 3 ft. lbs. for 1982–84 models.

1977–78 Eldorado

1. Remove upper control arm and grind head off three rivets. Using a hammer and punch, drive out rivets.
2. Install new ball joint, securing it in place with three bolts and nuts contained in the kit.
3. Install upper control arm and lubricate ball joint fitting until grease escapes between seal and steering knuckle, Fig. 17.

Lower Ball Joint, Replace

1979–84 Eldorado & 1980–84 Seville

1. Remove knuckle.
2. Using 1/8 in. drill bit, drill center of rivets 1/4 in. deep, then using 1/2 in. drill bit, drill deep enough to remove rivet heads.
3. Using a hammer and punch, drive rivets out and remove ball joint.
4. Install ball joint into control arm and torque nuts and bolts to 8 ft. lbs. for 1979–81 models, or 3 ft. lbs. for 1982–84 models.

1977–78 Eldorado

1. Remove lower control arm and cut off two rivet heads from sides of control arm. Grind off head of rivet at bottom of control arm, then drive rivet out of arm.
2. Install service ball joint, securing it to control arm with bolts and nuts contained in kit.

Torsion Bar, Replace

1977–78 ELDORADO

Removal

1. Support vehicle so front suspension hangs at full rebound position.
2. Remove adjusting bolts from torsion bar adjuster nuts.
3. Install tool J-22517-01 on torsion bar crossmember, Fig. 18. It may be necessary to pry the crossmember downward to install the tool "U"-bolt.
4. Tighten tool center bolt until torsion bar adjusting arm is raised enough to permit removal of adjuster nut, then remove nut.
5. Loosen tool center bolt until clear of adjusting arm.
6. Repeat steps 3 through 5 on other end of crossmember.
7. Remove parking brake cable from guide at right side of vehicle.
8. Remove torsion bar crossmember bolts, nuts, shim and retainer from both ends of crossmember. Move crossmember as far as possible toward the side opposite torsion bar being removed. One end of crossmember should be clear of frame.
9. Lower end of crossmember and drive rearward until torsion bar is free from crossmember.

NOTE: Use caution not to damage parking brake cable when lowering crossmember. It may be necessary to loosen parking brake cable at equalizer to provide additional slack.

10. Remove torsion bar from lower control arm connector.

NOTE: It is possible to remove both torsion bars at one time, however, installation is easier with one torsion mounted at all times.

Inspection

1. Check torsion bar for nicks, scratches or dents. If any of these conditions exist the torsion bar must be replaced.

Installation

1. Lubricate approximately three inches of each end of torsion bar with suitable lubricant, P/N 9985092 or equivalent.
2. Install torsion bar into lower control arm connector.

NOTE: Torsion bars are stamped with letters "R" for right hand and "L" for left hand. The stamped end of torsion bar is installed in lower control chamber.

3. Position torsion bar adjusting arm in crossmember, hold arm in place and slide torsion bar rearward until seated in adjusting arm.

NOTE: The tape on torsion bar, located near lower control arm connector, should be fully visible but within 1/4 inch of connector.

4. Position crossmember on frame and install shim between crossmember and frame on each side. Install retainer over crossmember insulator.
5. Ensure torsion bar adjusting arms are properly positioned and install and torque crossmember nuts and bolts to 120 inch lbs.
6. Install parking brake cable through guide on vehicle right side and adjust cable if loosened.
7. Install tool J-22517 or J-22517-01 and tighten tool center bolt until torsion bar adjusting arm is raised enough to install adjuster nut and install nut. Remove tool.
8. Lubricate threads on new torsion bar adjusting bolts and install bolts into adjuster nuts.
9. Check vehicle standing height and wheel alignment. Adjust if necessary.

1979–84 ELDORADO & 1980–84 SEVILLE

1. Raise and support vehicle, then remove

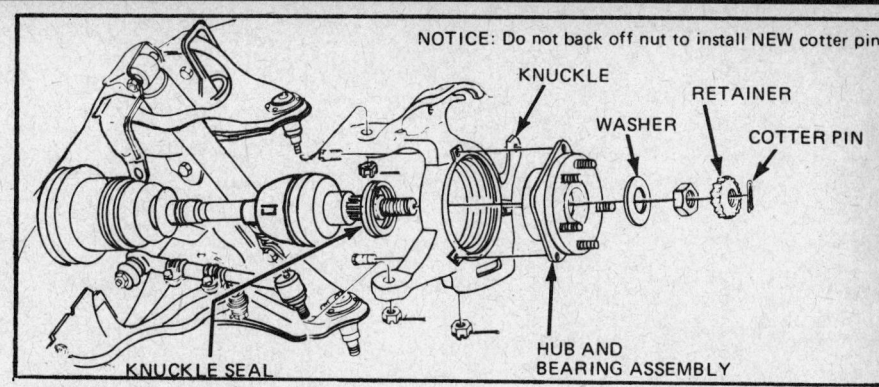

Fig. 14   Wheel bearing & steering knuckle assembly. 1979–84 Eldorado & 1980–84 Seville

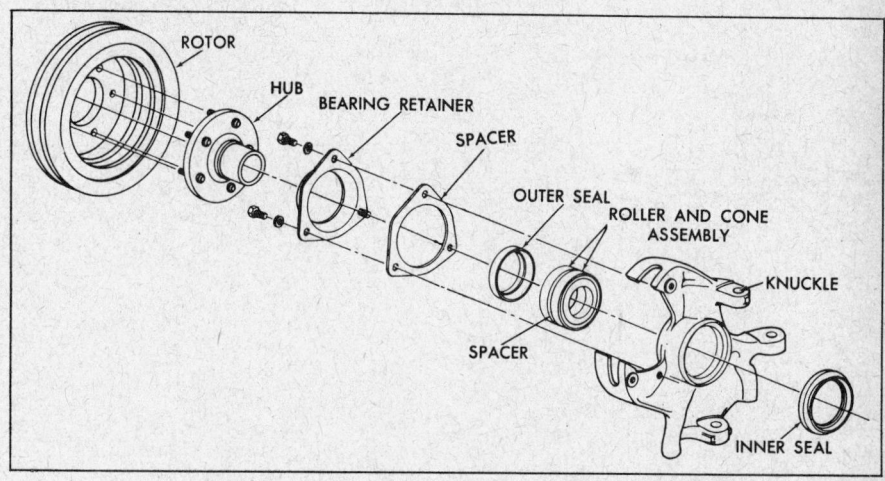

Fig. 15   Wheel bearing & steering knuckle assembly. 1977–78 Eldorado

parts as shown in Fig. 19.
2. Remove torsion bar adjusting screw as shown in Fig. 19.

NOTE: Count number of turns when removing screw. When installing, turn screw in the same number of turns to

return vehicle to proper height.

3. Slide torsion bar forward in lower control arm until torsion bar clears support, then pull down on bar and remove from control arm.
4. Reverse procedure to install. Torque tor-

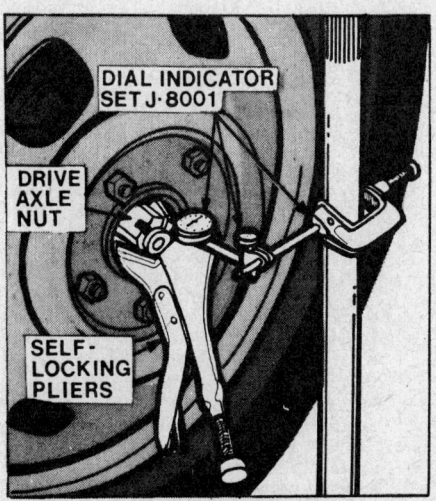

Fig. 16   Checking ball joints for wear. 1977–84 Eldorado & 1980–84 Seville

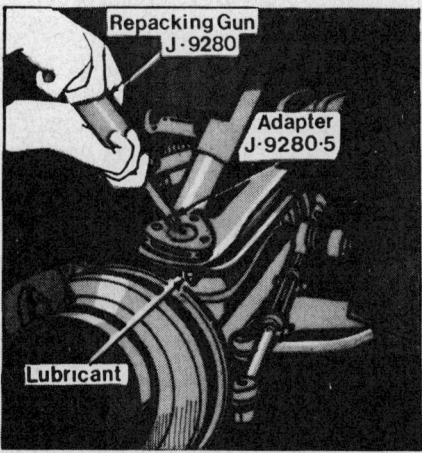

Fig. 17   Repacking upper ball joint. 1977–78 Eldorado

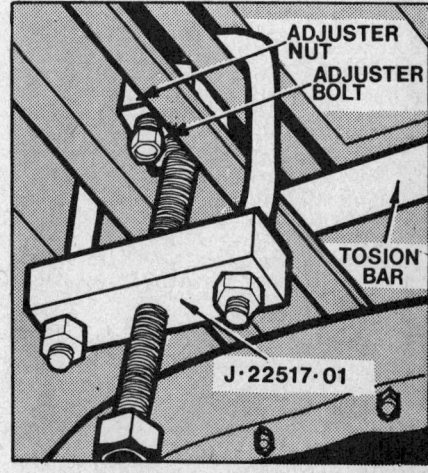

Fig. 18   Torsion bar removal tool installation 1977–78 Eldorado

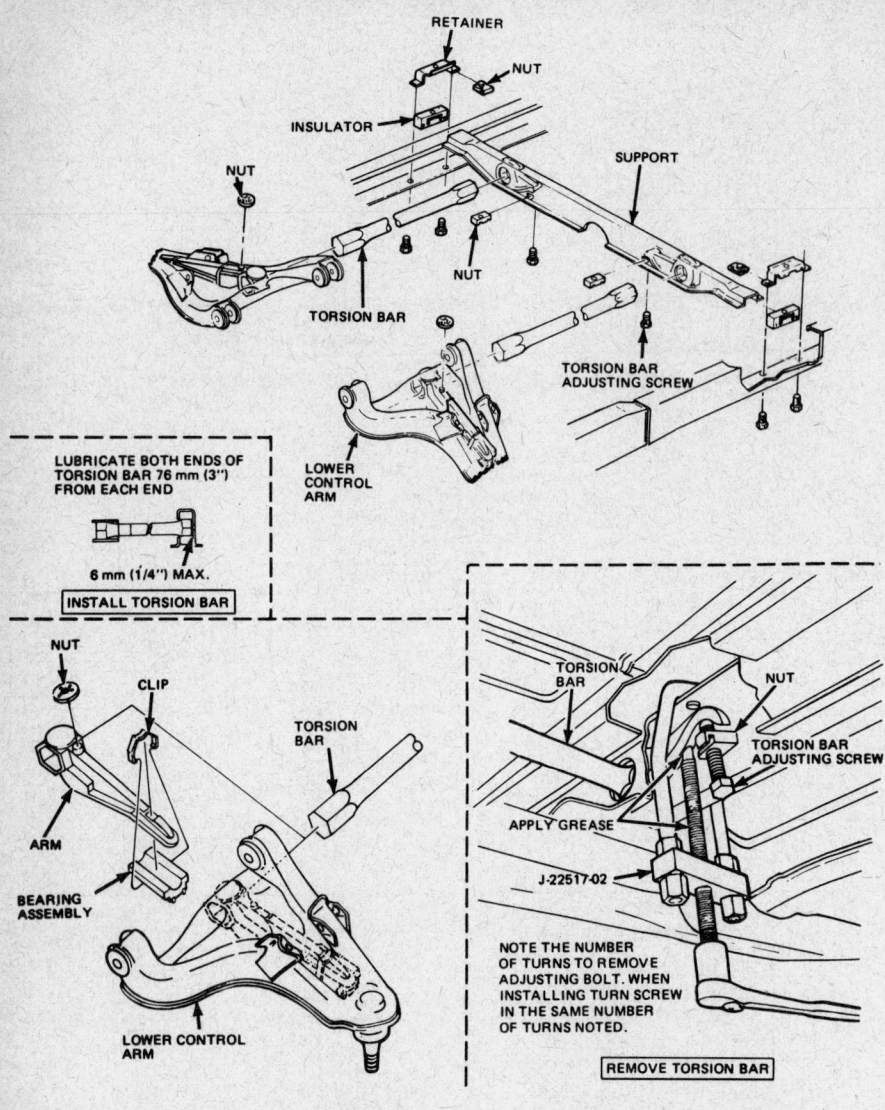

Fig. 19 Torsion bar removal. 1979–84 Eldorado & 1980–84 Seville

sion bar support retainer bolts to 35 ft. lbs. for 1979–81 models or 20 ft. lbs. for 1982–84 models.

POWER STEERING GEAR, REPLACE

1. Disconnect pressure and return lines from gear and plug all lines and openings.
2. Remove stone shield, if equipped. On 1977 Eldorado remove plastic retainers from frame coupling shield, then shield.
3. Remove pinch bolt, then flex coupling from gear.
4. Raise and support vehicle.
5. On all models except 1983–84 Eldorado and Seville, remove pitman arm nut and lock washer, then using a suitable puller remove pitman arm from steering gear.
6. Remove steering gear to side rail retaining bolts, then steering gear.
7. On 1983–84 Eldorado and Seville, remove pitman arm from steering shaft.
8. Reverse procedure to install, noting the following torque values: steering gear to side rail retaining bolts, 70 ft. lbs.; pitman arm to pitman shaft nut, 185 ft. lbs.; flex coupling pinch bolt, 30 ft. lbs.; steering gear pressure lines, 30 ft. lbs. on 1977–80 models or 20 ft. lbs. on 1981–84 models.

POWER STEERING PUMP, REPLACE

1977–80

Except Seville

1. Disconnect pressure and return lines from pump and filter inlet.
2. Remove nut securing pump mounting bracket to cylinder head stud.
3. Remove adjusting screw securing mount-

ing bracket to front of cylinder block.
4. Remove drive belts from pulley.
5. Remove bottom pivot screw and steering pump with bracket and filter attached.
6. Reverse procedure to install.

Seville

1. Remove alternator and alternator adjusting bracket.
2. Disconnect pressure and return lines at pump.
3. Loosen pump adjusting bolt, pivot bolt and pivot nut. Remove belt from pulley.
4. Remove nuts and spacer securing pump mounting bracket to water pump and timing chain cover.
5. Remove bracket connecting bolt, then remove pump and bracket as an assembly.

1981–84

V6-252

1. Disconnect pressure and return lines from pump.
2. Loosen adjusting screws on front and rear bracket, then remove drive belt.
3. Remove adjusting screws securing front of mounting bracket.
4. Remove adjusting nut securing pump to rear mounting bracket.
5. Remove pivot screw, then remove steering pump and bracket as an assembly.
6. Reverse procedure to install.

V8-250

1. Loosen A/C mounting bracket and vacuum pump bracket, then remove belts from pulley.
2. Disconnect pressure and return lines from pump and plug all openings.
3. Remove two bolts holding pump to engine block through access holes in pulley, then remove pump.
4. Reverse procedure to install.

V8-350

1. Remove cruise control servo as necessary, if equipped.
2. Loosen generator adjusting bolt, then remove alternator belt. Pivot alternator aside with wiring attached.
3. Remove alternator adjusting bracket, then disconnect pressure and return hoses from pump.
4. Loosen pump adjusting bolt, pivot bolt and pivot nut. Remove belt from pulley.
5. Remove nuts and spacer securing pump mounting bracket to water pump and timing chain cover. Remove bracket connecting bolt, then remove steering pump and bracket as an assembly.
6. Reverse procedure to install.

V8-368

1. Disconnect pressure and return lines from steering pump.
2. Loosen vacuum pump adjusting screw, then remove drive belt.
3. Remove nut securing pump mounting bracket to cylinder head stud.
4. Remove adjusting screw and nuts securing mounting bracket.
5. Remove drive belts from pulley.
6. Remove nut and bolt securing vacuum pump brace, then remove brace.
7. Remove pivot bolt, then remove pump and bracket as an assembly.
8. Reverse procedure to install.

CAMARO • CHEVROLET • CORVETTE
MALIBU • MONTE CARLO • NOVA

INDEX OF SERVICE OPERATIONS

NOTE: Refer to the front of this manual for vehicle manufacturer's special service tool suppliers.

SERIAL NUMBER LOCATION

Plate on left front door pillar or top of left side instrument panel

ENGINE NUMBER LOCATION

Buick built engines have the distributor located at the front of the engine. On 1979–84 models, the engine production code is located on front of right hand valve cover and top of left hand valve cover. On 1978 models, the engine production code is located on the right front of block.

On Chevrolet built 6-250 engines, the code is located on the cylinder block next to the distributor. Chevrolet built V8 engines have the distributor located at the rear of the engine with clockwise rotor rotation. On 1979–84 engines, the engine production code is located front of right hand valve cover. On 1977–78 V8 engines, the code is stamped on the right hand side of engine.

Pontiac built 4-151 engine, stamped on engine flange at left rear of engine above drive end of starter motor.

ENGINE IDENTIFICATION CODE

Engines are identified in the following table by the code letter or letters immediately following the engine serial number.

ENGINE V.I.N. CODE

On 1977–80 vehicles, the fifth digit in the V.I.N. denotes engine code. On 1981–84 vehicles, the eighth digit in the V.I.N. denotes engine code.

CAMARO

CODE		V.I.N. CODE	YEAR	CODE		V.I.N. CODE	YEAR	CODE		V.I.N. CODE	YEAR
CCD	6-250	D	1977	C8X	8-267	J	1980	CFD	V8-305	H	1982
CCF	6-250	D	1977	CPD	8-267	J	1980	CFF	V8-305	H	1982
CCW	6-250	D	1977	D9B	8-305	H	1980	CFH	V8-305	H	1982
CKH	6-250	D	1977	CEJ	8-305	H	1980	CFR	V8-305	H	1982
CKM	8-350	L	1977	CEL	8-305	H	1980	CFT	V8-305	H	1982
CKR	8-350	L	1977	CEM	8-305	H	1980	CFW	V8-305	H	1982
CKS	8-350	L	1977	CET	8-305	H	1980	CFY	V8-305	H	1982
CPA	8-305	U	1977	CML	8-305	H	1980	CFZ	V8-305	H	1982
CPC	8-305	U	1977	CHA	8-350	L	1980	CRA	V8-305	H	1982
CPY	8-305	U	1977	CEU	8-350	L	1980	C2R	V8-305	H	1982
C2K	8-305	U	1977	DAH	V6-229	K	1981	C2S	V8-305	H	1982
C2L	8-305	U	1977	DAJ	V6-229	K	1981	C2T	V8-305	H	1982
C8Y	6-250	D	1977	RA	V6-231①	A	1981	C2U	V8-305	H	1982
CCC	6-250	D	1977	DFH	V8-267	J	1981	C2W	V8-305	H	1982
CCH	6-250	D	1978	D8H	V8-267	J	1981	C2X	V8-305	H	1982
CCJ	6-250	D	1978	DHJ	V8-305	H	1981	CFJ	V8-305	7	1982
CCK	6-250	D	1978	DHK	V8-305	H	1981	CFK	V8-305	7	1982
C3Y	6-250	D	1978	DHZ	V8-305	H	1981	CFM	V8-305	7	1982
CTH	8-305	U	1978	DKB	V8-305	H	1981	CFN	V8-305	7	1982
CTJ	8-305	U	1978	DMA	V8-350	L	1981	YMM	4-151	2	1983
CTK	8-305	U	1978	D5A	V8-350	L	1981	YMT	4-151	2	1983
C3N	8-305	U	1978	D5B	V8-350	L	1981	DAF	V6-173	1	1983
CHF	8-350	L	1978	5A	4-151③	9	1982	DAJ	V6-173	1	1983
CHJ	8-350	L	1978	5F	4-151③	9	1982	DAK	V6-173	1	1983
CHL	8-350	L	1978	5H	4-151③	9	1982	DAA	V6-173	1	1983
CHR	8-350	L	1978	X3A	4-151③	2	1982	DAB	V6-173	1	1983
CHS	8-350	L	1978	X3C	4-151③	2	1982	DAC	V6-173	1	1983
CHT	8-350	L	1978	X3F	4-151③	2	1982	DAD	V6-173	1	1983
CHU	8-350	L	1978	X3H	4-151③	2	1982	D6A	V6-173	1	1983
C3T	8-350	L	1978	X5A	4-151③	2	1982	D6B	V6-173	1	1983
DKA	6-250	D	1979	X5F	4-151③	2	1982	D6C	V6-173	1	1983
DKB	6-250	D	1979	X5H	4-151③	2	1982	D6D	V6-173	1	1983
DKD	6-250	D	1979	CBT	V6-173	1	1982	D5B	V8-305	H	1983
DNH	8-305	G	1979	CBU	V6-173	1	1982	DDB	V8-305	H	1983
DNK	8-305	G	1979	CBW	V6-173	1	1982	DDD	V8-305	H	1983
DRC	8-350	L	1979	CBX	V6-173	1	1982	DDF	V8-305	H	1983
DRD	8-350	L	1979	CBZ	V6-173	1	1982	DDH	V8-305	H	1983
DRF	8-350	L	1979	CJB	V6-173	1	1982	DDJ	V8-305	H	1983
DRH	8-350	L	1979	CKA	V6-173	1	1982	DDK	V8-305	H	1983
DRL	8-350	L	1979	CKB	V6-173	1	1982	D5C	V8-305	H	1983
DRY	8-350	L	1979	C7A	V6-173	1	1982	DDN	V8-305	H	1983
DTM	8-305	G	1979	C7B	V6-173	1	1982	D5F	V8-305	H	1983
C8B	8-305	G	1979	C7C	V6-173	1	1982	D5H	V8-305	H	1983
C8C	8-350	L	1979	C7D	V6-173	1	1982	DGN	V8-305	H	1983
CRA	V6-229	K	1980	CFA	V8-305	H	1982	DDA	V8-305	S	1983
CRC	V6-229	K	1980	CFB	V8-305	H	1982	DUA	V8-305	S	1983
OM	V6-231①	A	1980	CFC	V8-305	H	1982				
ON	V6-231①	A	1980								

Continued

CHEVROLET

CODE		V.I.N. CODE	YEAR	CODE		V.I.N. CODE	YEAR	CODE		V.I.N. CODE	YEAR
CCC	6-250	D	1977	CMJ	8-305	H	1980	CRA	V8-305	H	1982
CCF	6-250	D	1977	CMR	8-305	H	1980	C2R	V8-305	H	1982
CCR	6-250	D	1977	CMS	8-305	H	1980	C2S	V8-305	H	1982
CCS	6-250	D	1977	CMT	8-305	H	1980	C2T	V8-305	H	1982
CKA	8-350	L	1977	CHC	8-350	L	1980	C2U	V8-305	H	1982
CKB	8-350	L	1977	VBS	8-350 Diesel [2]	N	1980	C2W	V8-305	H	1982
CKC	8-350	L	1977	VBT	8-350 Diesel [2]	N	1980	C2X	V8-305	H	1982
CLL	8-350	L	1977	DAD	V6-229	K	1981	VAB	V8-350 [2]	N	1982
CMM	8-350	L	1977	NL	V6-231 [1]	A	1981	VAC	V8-350 [2]	N	1982
CPM	8-305	U	1977	RL	V6-231 [1]	A	1981	VAD	V8-350 [2]	N	1982
CPR	8-305	U	1977	RK	V6-231 [1]	A	1981	VAK	V8-350 [2]	N	1982
CUB	8-350	L	1977	DFD	V8-267	J	1981	VAL	V8-350 [2]	N	1982
CUC	8-350	L	1977	DFF	V8-267	J	1981	VAM	V8-350 [2]	N	1982
CUD	8-350	L	1977	D8D	V8-267	J	1981	VAN	V8-350 [2]	N	1982
CCA	6-250	D	1977	D8F	V8-267	J	1981	VAP	V8-350 [2]	N	1982
CJA	6-250	D	1977	DHD	V8-305	H	1981	VAS	V8-350 [2]	N	1982
CJB	6-250	D	1977	DHF	V8-305	H	1981	VAU	V8-350 [2]	N	1982
CJF	6-250	D	1977	DHH	V8-305	H	1981	VAW	V8-350 [2]	N	1982
CCH	6-250	D	1978	DHR	V8-305	H	1981	VAX	V8-350 [2]	N	1982
CCK	6-250	D	1978	DHS	V8-305	H	1981	VAY	V8-350 [2]	N	1982
CCL	6-250	D	1978	DHT	V8-305	H	1981	VAZ	V8-350 [2]	N	1982
CCM	6-250	D	1978	D6B	V8-305	H	1981	VBA	V8-350 [2]	N	1982
CEJ	8-305	U	1978	D6C	V8-305	H	1981	VBL	V8-350 [2]	N	1982
CEK	8-305	U	1978	DMD	V8-350	L	1981	VBP	V8-350 [2]	N	1982
CTL	8-305	U	1978	VKH	V8-350 [2]	N	1981	VBW	V8-350 [2]	N	1982
CHF	8-350	L	1978	VKJ	V8-350 [2]	N	1981	VB4	V8-350 [2]	N	1982
CHH	8-350	L	1978	VKK	V8-350 [2]	N	1981	DBA	V6-229	9	1983
CHJ	8-350	L	1978	VKN	V8-350 [2]	N	1981	DBB	V6-229	9	1983
CHK	8-350	L	1978	VKP	V8-350 [2]	N	1981	DBC	V6-229	9	1983
CHL	8-350	L	1978	CCA	V6-229	K	1982	NJ	V6-231	A	1983
CHM	8-350	L	1978	CCC	V6-229	K	1982	ND	V6-231	A	1983
CNT	8-350	L	1978	CCF	V6-229	K	1982	NG	V6-231	A	1983
DCA	6-250	D	1979	CCH	V6-229	K	1982	NH	V6-231	A	1983
DCB	6-250	D	1979	CCK	V6-229	K	1982	NL	V6-231	A	1983
DCC	6-250	D	1979	CCM	V6-229	K	1982	D5B	V8-305	H	1983
DCD	6-250	D	1979	CCN	V6-229	K	1982	DDB	V8-305	H	1983
DKB	6-250	D	1979	CCR	V6-229	K	1982	DDC	V8-305	H	1983
DKC	6-250	D	1979	CCS	V6-229	K	1982	DDD	V8-305	H	1983
DKD	6-250	D	1979	MA	V6-231 [1]	A	1982	DDF	V8-305	H	1983
DKF	6-250	D	1979	MC	V6-231 [1]	A	1982	DDH	V8-305	H	1983
DNL	8-305	G	1979	MG	V6-231 [1]	A	1982	DDJ	V8-305	H	1983
DNM	8-305	G	1979	MK	V6-231 [1]	A	1982	DDK	V8-305	H	1983
DNR	8-305	G	1979	ML	V6-231 [1]	A	1982	D5C	V8-305	H	1983
DRA	8-350	L	1979	MM	V6-231 [1]	A	1982	DDN	V8-305	H	1983
DRB	8-350	L	1979	CDB	V8-267	J	1982	D5F	V8-305	H	1983
DRH	8-350	L	1979	CDC	V8-267	J	1982	D5H	V8-305	H	1983
DRJ	8-350	L	1979	CDD	V8-267	J	1982	DGN	V8-305	H	1983
DRK	8-350	L	1979	CDJ	V8-267	J	1982	D5N	V8-350	6	1983
DRL	8-350	L	1979	C4N	V8-267	J	1982	DUC	V8-350	6	1983
DRY	8-350	L	1979	C4R	V8-267	J	1982	VKB	V8-350	N	1983
DRZ	8-350	L	1979	C4S	V8-267	J	1982	VKC	V8-350	N	1983
DTY	V8-305	G	1979	C4T	V8-267	J	1982	VKD	V8-350	N	1983
DTZ	V8-305	G	1979	C4U	V8-267	J	1982	VKK	V8-350	N	1983
DXA	V8-305	G	1979	C4W	V8-267	J	1982	VKL	V8-350	N	1983
DUB	8-350	L	1979	CFA	V8-305	H	1982	VKR	V8-350	N	1983
DUC	8-350	L	1979	CFB	V8-305	H	1982	VKS	V8-350	N	1983
DUD	8-350	L	1979	CFC	V8-305	H	1982	VKT	V8-350	N	1983
CLC	V6-229	K	1980	CFD	V8-305	H	1982	VKZ	V8-350	N	1983
ES	V6-231 [1]	A	1980	CFF	V8-305	H	1982	VLA	V8-350	N	1983
ET	V6-231 [1]	A	1980	CFH	V8-305	H	1982	VLB	V8-350	N	1983
CPC	8-267	J	1980	CFR	V8-305	H	1982	VLP	V8-350	N	1983
CPH	8-267	J	1980	CFT	V8-305	H	1982	VLS	V8-350	N	1983
CED	8-305	H	1980	CFW	V8-305	H	1982	VLT	V8-350	N	1983
CEH	8-305	H	1980	CFY	V8-305	H	1982	VLW	V8-350	N	1983
CMH	8-305	H	1980	CFZ	V8-305	H	1982				

Continued

MALIBU & MONTE CARLO

CODE		V.I.N. CODE	YEAR	CODE		V.I.N. CODE	YEAR	CODE		V.I.N. CODE	YEAR
CCC	6-250	D	1977	CRC	V6-229	K	1980	C4S	V8-267	J	1982
CCD	6-250	D	1977	ED	V6-231①	A	1980	C4T	V8-267	J	1982
CCF	6-250	D	1977	EF	V6-231①	A	1980	C4U	V8-267	J	1982
CKH	8-350	L	1977	EG	V6-231①	A	1980	C4W	V8-267	J	1982
CKJ	8-350	L	1977	EH	V6-231①	3	1980	CFA	V8-305	H	1982
CKK	8-350	L	1977	OP	V6-231①	A	1980	CFB	V8-305	H	1982
CKM	8-350	L	1977	OR	V6-231①	A	1980	CFC	V8-305	H	1982
CKR	8-350	L	1977	CPA	8-267	J	1980	CFD	V8-305	H	1982
CPY	8-305	U	1977	CPB	8-267	J	1980	CFF	V8-305	H	1982
EA	6-231①	A	1978	CEA	8-305	H	1980	CFH	V8-305	H	1982
OH	6-231①	A	1978	CEC	8-305	H	1980	CFR	V8-305	H	1982
OK	6-231①	A	1978	CER	8-305	H	1980	CFT	V8-305	H	1982
CWA	6-250	D	1978	CMC	8-305	H	1980	CFW	V8-305	H	1982
CWB	6-250	D	1978	CMD	8-305	H	1980	CFY	V8-305	H	1982
CWC	6-250	D	1978	CMF	8-305	H	1980	CFZ	V8-305	H	1982
CWD	6-250	D	1978	CMM	8-305	H	1980	CRA	V8-305	H	1982
CER	8-305	U	1978	CHB	8-350	L	1980	C2R	V8-305	H	1982
CPZ	8-305	U	1978	DAA	V6-229	K	1981	C2S	V8-305	H	1982
CRU	8-305	U	1978	DAB	V6-229	K	1981	C2T	V8-305	H	1982
CRW	8-305	U	1978	DAC	V6-229	K	1981	C2U	V8-305	H	1982
CRX	8-305	U	1978	D7A	V6-229	K	1981	C2W	V8-305	H	1982
CRY	8-305	U	1978	D7B	V6-229	K	1981	C2X	V8-305	H	1982
CRZ	8-305	U	1978	DAK	V6-229	K	1981	DBA	V6-229	9	1983
CMA	8-350	U	1978	NB	V6-231①	A	1981	DBB	V6-229	9	1983
CMB	8-350	L	1978	NE	V6-231①	3	1981	DBC	V6-229	9	1983
CMC	8-350	L	1978	RO	V6-231①	3	1981	NJ	V6-231	A	1983
CMD	8-350	L	1978	DFA	V8-267	J	1981	ND	V6-231	A	1983
NJ	V6-231①	A	1979	DFB	V8-267	J	1981	NG	V6-231	A	1983
RA	V6-231①	A	1979	DFC	V8-267	J	1981	NH	V6-231	A	1983
RB	V6-231①	A	1979	D8A	V8-267	J	1981	NL	V6-231	A	1983
RJ	V6-231①	A	1979	D8B	V8-267	J	1981	UKA	V6-260	V	1983
RM	V6-231①	A	1979	D8C	V8-267	J	1981	UKB	V6-260	V	1983
SJ	V6-231①	A	1979	DHA	V8-305	H	1981	UKC	V6-260	V	1983
SO	V6-231①	A	1979	DHB	V8-305	H	1981	UKJ	V6-260	V	1983
DHA	V6-200	M	1979	DHC	V8-305	H	1981	UKK	V6-260	V	1983
DHB	V6-200	M	1979	DHM	V8-305	H	1981	D5B	V8-305	H	1983
DHC	V6-200	M	1979	DHN	V8-305	H	1981	DDB	V8-305	H	1983
DMA	8-267	J	1979	D6A	V8-305	H	1981	DDC	V8-305	H	1983
DMB	8-267	J	1979	DMC	V8-350	L	1981	DDD	V8-305	H	1983
DMC	8-267	J	1979	CCA	V6-229	K	1982	DDF	V8-305	H	1983
DMD	8-267	J	1979	CCC	V6-229	K	1982	DDH	V8-305	H	1983
DMF	8-267	J	1979	CCF	V6-229	K	1982	DDJ	V8-305	H	1983
DMH	8-267	J	1979	CCH	V6-229	K	1982	DDK	V8-305	H	1983
DNS	8-305	H	1979	CCK	V6-229	K	1982	D5C	V8-305	H	1983
DNT	8-305	H	1979	CCM	V6-229	K	1982	DDN	V8-305	H	1983
DNU	8-305	H	1979	CCN	V6-229	K	1982	D5F	V8-305	H	1983
DNW	8-305	H	1979	CCR	V6-229	K	1982	D5H	V8-305	H	1983
DNX	8-305	H	1979	CCS	V6-229	K	1982	DGN	V8-305	H	1983
DNY	8-305	H	1979	MA	V6-231①	A	1982	VKB	V8-350	N	1983
DRX	8-350	L	1979	MC	V6-231①	A	1982	VKC	V8-350	N	1983
DTA	8-305	H	1979	MG	V6-231①	A	1982	VKD	V8-350	N	1983
DTB	8-305	H	1979	MK	V6-231①	A	1982	VKK	V8-350	N	1983
DTF	8-305	H	1979	ML	V6-231①	A	1982	VKL	V8-350	N	1983
DTH	8-305	H	1979	MM	V6-231①	A	1982	VKR	V8-350	N	1983
DTJ	8-305	H	1979	UAA	V6-262②	V	1982	VKS	V8-350	N	1983
DTS	8-305	H	1979	UAD	V6-262②	V	1982	VKT	V8-350	N	1983
DTU	8-305	H	1979	UAJ	V6-262②	V	1982	VKZ	V8-350	N	1983
DTW	8-305	H	1979	CDB	V8-267	J	1982	VLA	V8-350	N	1983
DTX	8-305	H	1979	CDC	V8-267	J	1982	VLB	V8-350	N	1983
DUF	8-350	L	1979	CDD	V8-267	J	1982	VLP	V8-350	N	1983
DUH	8-350	L	1979	CDJ	V8-267	J	1982	VLS	V8-350	N	1983
DUJ	8-350	L	1979	C4N	V8-267	J	1982	VLT	V8-350	N	1983
CLA	V6-229	K	1980	C4R	V8-267	J	1982	VLW	V8-350	N	1983
CLB	V6-229	K	1980								

Continued

CHEVY NOVA

CODE		V.I.N. CODE	YEAR	CODE		V.I.N. CODE	YEAR	CODE		V.I.N. CODE	YEAR
CCD	6-250	D	1977	C2D	6-250	D	1977	CHJ	8-350	L	1978
CCF	6-250	D	1977	C2K	8-305	U	1977	CHL	8-350	L	1978
CCT	6-250	D	1977	C2L	8-305	U	1977	DKA	6-250	D	1979
CCU	6-250	D	1977	C8Y	6-250	D	1977	DKB	6-250	D	1979
CCW	6-250	D	1977	CCH	6-250	D	1978	DKD	6-250	D	1979
CKH	8-350	L	1977	CCK	6-250	D	1978	DNF	8-305	G	1979
CKM	8-350	L	1977	CCJ	6-250	D	1978	DNJ	8-305	G	1979
CKR	8-350	L	1977	C2D	6-250	D	1978	DNK	8-305	G	1979
CKS	8-350	L	1977	CTH	8-305	U	1978	DRJ	8-350	L	1979
CPA	8-305	U	1977	CTJ	8-305	U	1978	DRY	8-350	L	1979
CPC	8-305	U	1977	CTK	8-305	U	1978	DTM	8-305	G	1979
CPY	8-305	U	1977	C2K	8-305	U	1978	C8D	8-305	G	1979

CORVETTE

CODE		V.I.N. CODE	YEAR	CODE		V.I.N. CODE	YEAR	CODE		V.I.N. CODE	YEAR
CKZ	8-350	L	1977	CLS	8-350	L	1978	ZAK	8-350	8	1980
CLA	8-350	L	1977	CUT	8-350	L	1978	ZBC	8-350	6	1980
CLB	8-350	L	1977	CMR	8-350	H	1978	ZAM	8-350	8	1980
CLC	8-350	L	1977	CMS	8-350	H	1978	ZBD	8-350	6	1980
CLD	8-350	X	1977	ZAA	8-350	8	1979	ZDA	V8-350	6	1981
CLF	8-350	X	1977	ZAB	8-350	8	1979	ZDB	V8-350	6	1981
CLH	8-350	L	1977	ZAC	8-350	8	1979	ZDC		6	1981
CHD	8-350	L	1977	ZAD	8-350	8	1979	ZDD		6	1981
CKD	8-350	L	1977	ZAF	8-350	8	1979	ZBA		8	1982
CHW	8-350	L	1978	ZBA	8-350	4	1979	ZBC		8	1982
CLM	8-350	L	1978	ZBB	8-350	4	1979	ZFN		8	1982
CLR	8-350	L	1978	ZCA	8-305	H	1980	—		8	1984

①—Buick built engine.　②—Oldsmobile built engine.　③—Pontiac built engine.

GRILLE IDENTIFICATION

1977 Nova

1977 Nova Concours

1977 Malibu Classic

1977 Monte Carlo

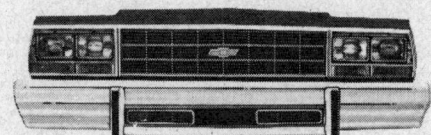

1977 Impala

1977 Caprice & Estate Wagon

1977–78 Corvette

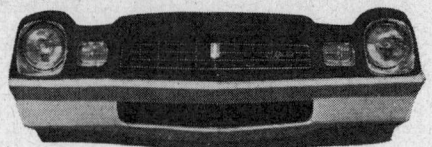

1978 Camaro

1978 Camaro Z28

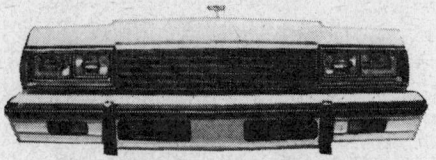

1978 Caprice & Estate Wagon

1978 Chevy Nova

1978 Impala

1978 Malibu

1978 Malibu Classic

1978–79 Monte Carlo

1979 Corvette

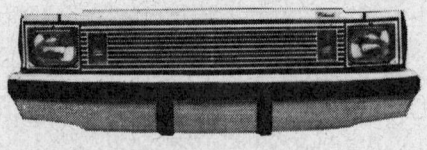

1979 Chevy Nova

1979 Caprice

Continued

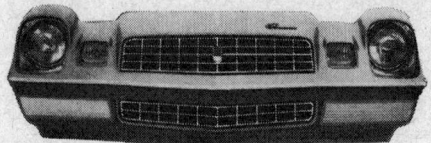

1979 Camaro

1979 Camaro Z28

1979 Malibu

1980 Malibu Classic

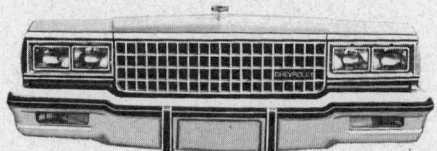

1980 Caprice Classic

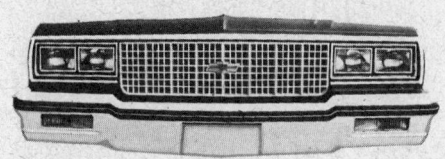

1980 Impala

1980 Monte Carlo

1980—81 Camaro Sport Coupe

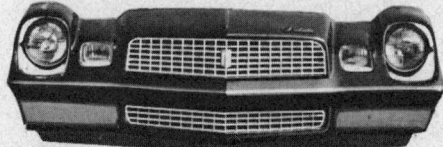

1980—81 Camaro Berlinetta

1980—81 Camaro Z28

1980—82 Corvette

1981 Malibu

GRILLE IDENTIFICATION—Continued

1981 Monte Carlo

1981—84 Caprice

1982 Malibu

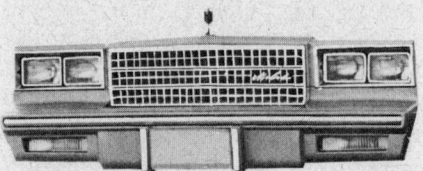

1982 Monte Carlo

1982—84 Camaro Exc. Z28

1982—84 Camaro Z28

1983 Malibu

1983—84 Monte Carlo
1984 Monte Carlo Exc. SS

1984 Corvette

1984 Monte Carlo SS

GENERAL ENGINE SPECIFICATIONS

Year	Engine CID①/Liter	V.I.N. Code ②	Carburetor	Bore and Stroke	Compression Ratio	Net Brake H.P. @ R.P.M.③	Maximum Torque Ft. Lbs. @ R.P.M.	Normal Oil Pressure Pounds
1977	6-250, 4.1L	D	1ME, 1 Bbl. ④	3.875 × 3.53	8.25	110 @ 3800	195 @ 1600	36–41
	V8-305, 5.0L	U	2GC, 2 Bbl.④	3.736 × 3.48	8.5	145 @ 3800	245 @ 2400	32–40
	V8-350, 5.7L	L	M4MC, 4 Bbl.④	4.00 × 3.48	8.5	170 @ 3800	270 @ 2400	32–40
	V8-350, 5.7L	L	M4MC, 4 Bbl.④	4.00 × 3.48	8.5	180 @ 4000	270 @ 2400	32–40
	V8-350, 5.7L	X	M4MC, 4 Bbl.④	4.00 × 3.48	9.0	210 @ 5200	255 @ 3600	32–40
1978	V6-200, 3.3L	M	M2ME, 2 Bbl.④	3.50 × 3.48	8.2	95 @ 3800	160 @ 2000	34–39
	V6-231, 3.8L⑤	A	2GE, 2 Bbl.④	3.80 × 3.40	8.0	103 @ 3800	180 @ 2000	37
	6-250, 4.1L	D	1 ME, 1 Bbl.④	3.875 × 3.53	8.2	90 @ 3600	180 @ 1600	36–41
	6-250, 4.1L	D	1ME, 1 Bbl.④	3.875 × 3.53	8.2	110 @ 3800	195 @ 1600	36–41
	V8-305, 5.0L	U	2GC, 2 Bbl.④	3.736 × 3.48	8.5	135 @ 3800	240 @ 2000	45
	V8-305, 5.0L	U	2GC, 2 Bbl.④	3.736 × 3.48	8.5	145 @ 3800	245 @ 2000	45
	V8-350, 5.7L	L	M4MC, 4 Bbl.④	4.00 × 3.48	8.2	160 @ 3800	260 @ 2400	32–40
	V8-350, 5.7L	L	M4MC, 4 Bbl.④	4.00 × 3.48	8.2	170 @ 3800	270 @ 2400	32–40
	V8-350, 5.7L	L	M4MC, 4 Bbl.④	4.00 × 3.48	8.2	175 @ 3800	265 @ 2400	32–40
	V8-350, 5.7L	L	M4MC, 4 Bbl.④	4.00 × 3.48	8.2	185 @ 4000	280 @ 2400	32–40
1979	V6-200, 3.3L	M	M2ME, 2 Bbl.④	3.50 × 3.48	8.2	95 @ 3800	160 @ 2000	45
	V6-231, 3.8L③	A	M2ME, 2 Bbl.④	3.80 × 3.40	8.0	115 @ 3800	190 @ 2000	37
	6-250, 4.1L	D	1ME, 1 Bbl.④	3.876 × 3.53	8.1	90 @ 3600	175 @ 1600	40
	6-250, 4.1L	D	1ME, 1 Bbl.④	3.876 × 3.53	8.0	115 @ 3800	200 @ 1600	40
	V8-267, 4.4L	J	M2MC, 2 Bbl.④	3.50 × 3.48	8.2	125 @ 3800	215 @ 2400	45
	V8-305, 5.0L	G	M2MC, 2 Bbl.④	3.736 × 3.48	8.4	125 @ 3200	235 @ 2000	45
	V8-305, 5.0L	G	M2MC, 2 Bbl.④	3.736 × 3.48	8.4	130 @ 3200	245 @ 2000	45
	V8-305, 5.0L	H	M4MC, 4 Bbl.④	3.736 × 3.48	8.4	155 @ 4000	225 @ 2400	45
	V8-305, 5.0L	H	M4MC, 4 Bbl.④	3.736 × 3.48	8.4	160 @ 4000	235 @ 2000	45
	V8-350, 5.7L	L	M4MC, 4 Bbl.④	4.00 × 3.48	8.2	165 @ 3800	260 @ 2400	45
	V8-350, 5.7L	L	M4MC, 4 Bbl.④	4.00 × 3.48	8.2	170 @ 4000	265 @ 2400	45
	V8-350, 5.7L	L	M4MC, 4 Bbl.④	4.00 × 3.48	8.2	170 @ 3800	270 @ 2400	45
	V8-350, 5.7L	L	M4MC, 4 Bbl.④	4.00 × 3.48	8.2	175 @ 4000	270 @ 2400	45
	V8-350, 5.7L	L	M4MC, 4 Bbl.④	4.00 × 3.48	8.9	195 @ 4000	280 @ 2400	45
	V8-350, 5.7L	L	M4MC, 4 Bbl.④	4.00 × 3.48	8.2	195 @ 4000	285 @ 3200	45
	V8-350, 5.7L	L	M4MC, 4 Bbl.④	4.00 × 3.48	8.9	225 @ 5200	270 @ 3600	45
1980	V6-229, 3.8L	K	M2ME, 2 Bbl.④	3.736 × 3.48	8.6	115 @ 4000	175 @ 2000	45
	V6-231, 3.8L⑤	A	M2ME, 2 Bbl.⑥④	3.80 × 3.40	8.0	110 @ 3800	190 @ 1600	45
	V6-231, 3.8L⑤⑦	3	M4ME, 4 Bbl.④⑧	3.80 × 3.40	8.0	170 @ 4000	265 @ 2400	37
	V8-267, 4.4L	J	M2ME, 2 Bbl.④	3.50 × 3.48	8.5	120 @ 3600	215 @ 2000	45
	V8-305, 5.0L	8	M4ME, 4 Bbl.④⑧	3.736 × 3.48	8.6	155 @ 4000	240 @ 1600	45
	V8-305⑫	H	M4ME④	3.736 × 3.48	8.5	180 @ 4200	255 @ 2000	45
	V8-350, 5.7L⑬	L	M4ME, 4 Bbl.④	4.00 × 3.48	8.5	190 @ 4200	280 @ 2400	45
	V8-350, 5.7L⑫	6	M4ME, 4 Bbl.④	4.00 × 3.48	9.0	230 @ 5200	275 @ 3600	45
	V8-350, 5.7L⑫	8	M4ME, 4 Bbl.④	4.00 × 3.48	8.5	190 @ 4400	280 @ 2400	45
	V8-350, 5.7L⑨⑩	N	Fuel Injected	4.057 × 3.385	22.5	105 @ 3200	205 @ 1600	30–45
1981	V6-229, 3.8L⑪	K	E2ME, 2 Bbl.④	3.736 × 3.48	8.6	110 @ 4200	170 @ 2000	45
	V6-231, 3.8L⑤	A	E2ME, 2 Bbl.④	3.80 × 3.40	8.0	110 @ 3800	190 @ 1600	45
	V6-231, 3.8L⑤⑦	3	E4ME, 4 Bbl.④	3.80 × 3.40	8.0	170 @ 4000	275 @ 2400	45
	V8-267, 4.4L⑪	J	E2ME, 2 Bbl.④	3.50 × 3.48	8.3	115 @ 4000	200 @ 2400	45
	V8-305, 5.0L	H	E4ME, 4 Bbl.④	3.736 × 3.48	8.6	150 @ 3800	240 @ 2400	45
	V8-305⑬	H	M4ME④	3.736 × 3.48	8.6	165 @ 4000	180 @ 4200	45
	V8-350, 5.7L	L	E4ME, 4 Bbl.④	4.00 × 3.48	8.2	175 @ 4000	275 @ 2400	45
	V8-350, 5.7L⑫	6	E4ME, 4 Bbl.④	4.00 × 3.48	8.2	190 @ 4200	280 @ 1600	45
	V8-350, 5.7L⑨⑩	N	Fuel Injection	4.057 × 3.385	22.5	105 @ 3200	200 @ 1600	45
1982	4-151, 2.5L⑭	2	Fuel Injection	4.00 × 3.00	8.2	90 @ 4000	132 @ 2800	37.5
	V6-173, 2.8L	1	E2SE, 2 Bbl.④	3.50 × 2.99	8.5	102 @ 4800	142 @ 2400	50–65
	V6-229, 3.8L⑪	K	E2ME, 2 Bbl.④	3.736 × 3.480	8.6	110 @ 4200	170 @ 2000	50–65

Continued

GENERAL ENGINE SPECIFICATIONS—Continued

Year	Engine CID①/Liter	V.I.N. Code ②	Carburetor	Bore and Stroke	Compression Ratio	Net Brake H.P. @ R.P.M.③	Maximum Torque Ft. Lbs. @ R.P.M.	Normal Oil Pressure Pounds
	V6-231, 3.8L⑤	A	E2ME, 2 Bbl.④	3.80 × 3.40	8.0	110 @ 3800	190 @ 1600	50—65
	V6-262, 4.3L⑨⑩	V	Fuel Injection	4.057 × 3.385	22.5	85 @ 3600	165 @ 1600	30—45
	V8-267, 4.4L⑪	J	E2ME, 2 Bbl.④	3.50 × 3.48	8.3	115 @ 4000	205 @ 2400	45
	V8-305, 5.0L	H	E4ME, 4 Bbl.④	3.736 × 3.480	8.6	145 @ 4000	240 @ 2000	50—65
	V8-305, 5.0L	7	Fuel Injection	3.736 × 3.480	9.5	165 @ 4200	240 @ 2400	50—65
	V8-350, 5.7L	6	Fuel Injection	4.00 × 3.48	9.0	200 @ 4200	285 @ 2800	45
	V8-350, 5.7L⑨⑩	N	Fuel Injection	4.057 × 3.385	22.5	105 @ 3200	200 @ 1600	30—45
1983	4-151, 2.5L⑭	2	Fuel Injection	4.00 × 3.00	8.2	92 @ 4000	134 @ 2800	37.5
	V6-173, 2.8L	1	E2SE, 2 Bbl.④	3.50 × 2.99	8.5	107 @ 4800	145 @ 2100	50—65
	V6-229, 3.8L	9	E2ME, 2 Bbl.④	3.736 × 3.480	8.6	110 @ 4200	170 @ 2000	50—65
	V6-231, 3.8L⑤	A	E2ME, 2 Bbl.④	3.80 × 3.40	8.0	110 @ 3800	190 @ 1600	45
	V6-262, 4.3L⑨⑩	V	Fuel Injection	4.057 × 3.385	21.6	85 @ 3600	165 @ 1600	30—45
	V8-305, 5.0L	H	E4ME, 4 Bbl.④	3.736 × 3.480	8.6	150 @ 3800	240 @ 2400	50—65
	V8-305, 5.0L	S	Fuel Injection	3.736 × 3.480	9.5	175 @ 4200	250 @ 2800	45
	V8-350, 5.7L⑨⑩	N	Fuel Injection	4.057 × 3.385	21.6	105 @ 3200	200 @ 1600	30—45
1984	4-151, 2.5L⑭	2	Fuel Injection	4.00 × 3.00	8.2	90 @ 4000	132 @ 2800	37.5
	V6-173, 2.8L	1	E2SE, 2 Bbl.④	3.50 × 2.99	8.5	112 @ 5100	148 @ 2400	50—65
	V6-229, 3.8L	9	E2ME, 2 Bbl.④	3.736 × 3.480	8.6	110 @ 4200	170 @ 2000	50—65
	V6-231, 3.8L⑤	A	E2ME, 2 Bbl.④	3.80 × 3.40	8.0	110 @ 3800	190 @ 1600	45
	V6-262, 4.3L⑨⑩	V	Fuel Injection	4.057 × 3.385	21.6	85 @ 3600	165 @ 1600	30—45
	V8-305, 5.0L	H	E4ME, 4 Bbl.④	3.736 × 3.480	8.6	150 @ 3800	240 @ 2400	50—65
	V8-305, 5.0L	S	Fuel Injection	3.736 × 3.480	9.5	175 @ 4200	250 @ 2800	50—65
	V8-350, 5.7L	8	Fuel Injection	4.00 × 3.48	9.0	205 @ 4300	290 @ 2800	50—65
	V8-350, 5.7L⑨⑩	N	Fuel Injection	4.057 × 3.385	21.6	105 @ 4200	200 @ 1600	30—45

①—C.I.D.—Cubic inch displacement.
②—V.I.N.—On 1977–80 vehicles, the fifth digit in the V.I.N. denotes engine code. On 1981–84 vehicles, the 8th digit in the V.I.N. denotes engine code.
③—Ratings are net—As installed in the vehicle.
④—Rochester.
⑤—For service procedures on this engine, see Buick chapter.
⑥—Calif. V6-231 with Electronic Fuel Control E2ME.
⑦—Turbocharged.
⑧—Calif. V8 with Electronic Fuel Control, E4ME.
⑨—For service procedures on this engine, see Oldsmobile chapter.
⑩—Diesel.
⑪—Exc. Calif.
⑫—Corvette.
⑬—Camaro Z28.
⑭—For service procedures on this engine, refer to Pontiac chapter.

TUNE UP SPECIFICATIONS

The following specifications are published from the latest information available. This data should be used only in the absence of a decal affixed in the engine compartment.

★ When using a timing light, disconnect vacuum hose or tube at distributor and plug opening in hose or tube so idle speed will not be affected.

● When checking compression, lowest cylinder must be within 70 percent of highest.

▲ Before removing wires from distributor cap, determine location of the No. 1 wire in cap, as distributor position may have been altered from that shown at the end of this chart.

☞ Spark plug types shown in this chart are recommendations of the original vehicle manufacturer and not MOTOR.

Check local sources for other spark plug manufacturers listings.

Year & Engine/V.I.N.	Spark Plug Type ☞	Gap	Ignition Timing BTDC①★ Firing Order Fig. ▲	Man. Trans.	Auto. Trans.	Mark Fig.	Curb Idle Speed② Man. Trans.	Auto. Trans.	Fast Idle Speed Man. Trans.	Auto. Trans.	Fuel Pump Pressure
CAMARO **1977**											
6-250/D Exc. Calif. & High Alt.	R46TS	.035	H	6°	8°	B	⑥	⑦	2000	2000	4—5

Continued

TUNE UP SPECIFICATIONS—Continued

The following specifications are published from the latest information available. This data should be used only in the absence of a decal affixed in the engine compartment.

★ When using a timing light, disconnect vacuum hose or tube at distributor and plug opening in hose or tube so idle speed will not be affected.

● When checking compression, lowest cylinder must be within 70 percent of highest.

▲ Before removing wires from distributor cap, determine location of the No. 1 wire in cap, as distributor position may have been altered from that shown at the end of this chart.

☞ Spark plug types shown in this chart are recommendations of the original vehicle manufacturer and not MOTOR.

Check local sources for other spark plug manufacturers listings.

Year & Engine/V.I.N.	Spark Plug Type ☞	Gap	Firing Order Fig. ▲	Ignition Timing BTDC① ★ Man. Trans.	Auto. Trans.	Mark Fig.	Curb Idle Speed② Man. Trans.	Auto. Trans.	Fast Idle Speed Man. Trans.	Auto. Trans.	Fuel Pump Pressure
CAMARO—Continued											
1977											
6-250/D Calif.	R46TS	.035	H	—	⑧	B	—	⑦	—	1800	4–5
6-250/D High Alt.	R46TS	.035	H	—	10°	B	—	425/600D	—	2000	4–5
V8-305/U Exc. Calif.	R45TS	.045	C	8°	8°	B	600/700	500/650D	—	—	7½–9
V8-305/U Calif.	R45TS	.045	C	—	6°	B	—	500/650D	—	—	7½–9
V8-350/L Exc. High Alt.	R45TS	.045	C	8°	8°	B	700	500/650D	1300⑤	1600⑤	7½–9
V8-350/L High Alt.	R45TS	.045	C	—	8°	B	—	600/650D	—	1600⑤	7½–9
1978											
6-250/D Exc. Calif.	R46TS	.035	H	6°	10°	B	425/800	425/550D	2000	2100	4–5
6-250/D Calif.	R46TS	.035	H	—	6°	B	—	400/600D	—	2000	4–5
V8-305/U Exc. Calif.	R45TS	.045	C	4°	4°	B	600	500D	—	—	7½–9
V8-305/U Calif.	R45TS	.045	C	—	8°	B	—	500/600D	—	—	7½–9
V8-350/L Exc. Calif. & High Alt.	R45TS	.045	C	6°	6°	B	700	500/600D	1300	1600	7½–9
V8-350/L Calif.	R45TS	.045	C	—	8°	B	—	500/600D	—	1600	7½–9
V8-350/L High Alt.	R45TS	.045	C	—	⑨	B	—	500/650D	—	1600	7½–9
1979											
6-250/D Exc. Calif.	R46TS	.035	H	12°	8°	B	800	675D	1800	2000	4–5
6-250/D Calif.	R46TS	.035	H	—	6°	B	—	600D	—	2000	4–5
V8-305/G Exc. Calif.	R45TS	.045	C	4°	4°	G	600/700	500/600D	1300	1600	7½–9
V8-305/G Calif.	R45TS	.045	C	—	4°	G	—	600/650D	—	1950	7½–9
V8-350/G Exc. Calif. & High Alt.	R45TS	.045	C	6°	6°	G	700	500/600D	1300	1600	7½–9
V8-350/L Calif.	R45TS	.045	C	—	8°	G	—	500/600D	—	1600	7½–9
V8-350/L High Alt.	R45TS	.045	C	—	8°	G	—	600/650D	—	1750	7½–9
1980											
V6-229/K	R45TS	.045	F	8°	12°	G	700/800	600/675D	1300	1750	4½–6
V6-231/A	R45TSX	.060	D	—	15°	E⑪	—	600D	—	2200	4¼–5¾
V8-267/J	R45TS	.045	C	—	4°	④	—	500/600D	—	1850	7½–9
V8-305/H Exc. Calif.	R45TS	.045	C	4°	4°	④	700	500/600D	1500	1850	7½–9
V8-305/H Calif. Exc. Z28	R45TS	.045	C	—	4°	④	—	550/650D	—	2200	7½–9
V8-305/H Calif. Z28	R45TS	.045	C	—	—	④	—	550/650D	—	—	7½–9
V8-350/L	R45TS	.045	C	6°	6°	④	700	500/600D	1500	1850	7½–9
1981											
V6-229/K	R45TS	.045	F	6°	6°	G	③	③	2200	2200	4½–6
V6-231/A	R45TS8	.080	D	—	15°	E⑪	—	③	—	1800	3 Min.
V8-267/J	R45TS	.045	C	—	6°	A	—	500	—	2200	4½–6
V8-305/H	R45TS	.045	C	6°	6°	A	700/800	500/600D	2200	2200	7½–9
V8-350/L	R45TS	.045	C	—	6°	A	—	500/600D	—	2200	7½–9

TUNE UP SPECIFICATIONS—Continued

The following specifications are published from the latest information available. This data should be used only in the absence of a decal affixed in the engine compartment.

★ When using a timing light, disconnect vacuum hose or tube at distributor and plug opening in hose or tube so idle speed will not be affected.

● When checking compression, lowest cylinder must be within 70 percent of highest.

▲ Before removing wires from distributor cap, determine location of the No. 1 wire in cap, as distributor position may have been altered from that shown at the end of this chart.

Spark plug types shown in this chart are recommendations of the original vehicle manufacturer and not MOTOR.

Check local sources for other spark plug manufacturers listings.

Year & Engine/V.I.N.	Spark Plug Type	Gap	Firing Order Fig.▲	Ignition Timing BTDC①★ Man. Trans.	Auto. Trans.	Mark Fig.	Curb Idle Speed② Man. Trans.	Auto. Trans.	Fast Idle Speed Man. Trans.	Auto. Trans.	Fuel Pump Pressure
CAMARO—Continued											
1982											
4-151 E.F.I./2	R44TSX	.060	I	8°⑳	8°⑳	J	⑲	⑲	⑲	⑲	—
V6-173/1	R43TS	.045	K	10°	10°	L	850㉑	600D㉒	2600	2500	6—7½
V8-305/H	R45TS	.045	C	6°	6°	A	700/800	500/600D	1800	2200	7½—9
V8-305 E.F.I./7	R45TS	.045	C		6°㉓	A	—	⑲	⑲	⑲	—
1983											
4-151 E.F.I./2	R44TSX	.060	I	—	—	J	775N⑲	500D⑲	⑲	⑲	—
V6-173/1	R43CTS	.045	K	10°	10°	L	775/1100N	600/750D	2500	2500	5½—6½
V8-305/H	R45TS	.045	C	6°	6°	A	700/800N	500/650D	1800	2200	5½—6½
V8-305 E.F.I./7S	R45TS	.045	C	6°	6°	A	—	⑲	⑲	⑲	—
1984											
4-151 E.F.I./2	R44TSX	.060	I	—	—	J	775N⑲	500D⑲	⑲	⑲	—
V6-173/1	RV12YC4	.045	K	—	—	L	775/1100N	600/750D	2500	2500	5½—6½
V8-305/H	R45TS	.045	C	—	—	A	700/800N	500/650D	1800	2200	5½—6½
V8-305 E.F.I./S	R45TS	.045	C	—	—	A	—	⑲	⑲	⑲	—
MALIBU & MONTE CARLO											
1977											
6-250/D Exc. Calif. & High Alt.	R46TS	.035	H	6°	8°	B	⑥	⑦	2000	2000	4—5
6-250/D Calif.	R46TS	.035	H	—	6°	B	—	425/550D	—	1800	4—5
6-250/D High Alt.	R46TS	.035	H	—	10°	B	—	425/600D	—	2000	4—5
V8-305/U	R45TS	.045	C	—	8°	B	—	500/650D	—	—	7½—9
V8-350/L Exc. High Alt.	R45TS	.045	C	—	8°	B	—	500/650D	—	1600⑤	7½—9
V8-350/L High Alt.	R45TS	.045	C	—	8°	B	—	500/650D	—	1600⑤	7½—9
1978											
V6-200/M	R45TS	.045	F	8°	8°	G	700	600D	1300	1600	4½—6
V6-231/A	R46TSX	.060	D	15°	15°	E⑪	600/800	600/670D	—	—	3 Min.
V8-305/U Exc. Calif. & High Alt.	R45TS	.045	C	4°	4°	G	600	500D	—	—	7½—9
V8-305/U Calif.	R45TS	.045	C	—	6°	G	—	500/600	—	—	7½—9
V8-305/U High Alt.	R45TS	.045	C	—	8°	G	—	600/700D	—	—	7½—9
V8-350/L Exc. Calif. & High Alt.	R45TS	.045	C	—	6°	G	—	500/600D	—	1600	7½—9
V8-350/L Calif.	R45TS	.045	C	—	8°	G	—	500/600D	—	1600	7½—9
V8-350/L High Alt.	R45TS	.045	C	—	8°	G	—	500/650D	—	1600	7½—9
1979											
V6-200/M	R45TS	.045	F	8°	12°	G	700/800	600/700D	1300	1600	4½—6
V6-231/A Exc. Calif. & High Alt.	R45TSX	.060	D	—	15°	E⑪	—	⑫	—	2200	3 Min.

Continued

TUNE UP SPECIFICATIONS—Continued

The following specifications are published from the latest information available. This data should be used only in the absence of a decal affixed in the engine compartment.

★ When using a timing light, disconnect vacuum hose or tube at distributor and plug opening in hose or tube so idle speed will not be affected.

● When checking compression, lowest cylinder must be within 70 percent of highest.

▲ Before removing wires from distributor cap, determine location of the No. 1 wire in cap, as distributor position may have been altered from that shown at the end of this chart.

☞ Spark plug types shown in this chart are recommendations of the original vehicle manufacturer and not MOTOR.

Check local sources for other spark plug manufacturers listings.

Year & Engine/V.I.N.	Spark Plug		Firing Order Fig. ▲	Ignition Timing BTDC[1] ★			Curb Idle Speed[2]		Fast Idle Speed		Fuel Pump Pressure
	Type ☞	Gap		Man. Trans.	Auto. Trans.	Mark Fig.	Man. Trans.	Auto. Trans.	Man. Trans.	Auto. Trans.	
MALIBU & MONTE CARLO—Continued											
1979											
V6-231/A Calif. & High Alt.	R45TSX	.060	D	—	15°	E[11]	—	600D	—	2200	3 Min.
V8-267/J	R45TS	.045	C	4°	8°	G	600/700	500/600D	1300	1600	7½–9
V8-305/H Exc. High Alt.	R45TS	.045	C	4°	4°	G	700	500/600D	1300	1600	7½–9
V8-305/H High Alt.	R45TS	.045	C	—	8°	G	—	600/650D	—	1750	7½–9
V8-350/L	R45TS	.045	C	—	8°	G	—	600/650	—	1750	7½–9
1980											
V6-229/K	R45TS	.045	F	8°	12°	G	700/800	600/675D	1300	1750	4½–6
V6-231/A Exc. Calif.[20]	R45TSX	.060	D	—	15°	E[11]	—	560/670D	—	2200	4¼–5¾
V6-231/A Calif.[13]	R45TSX	.060	D	—	15°	E[11]	—	600D	—	2200	4¼–5¾
V6-231/3 Exc. Calif.[14]	R45TS	.040	D	—	15°	E[11]	—	550D	—	2200	5
V6-231/3 Calif.[14]	R45TS	.040	D	—	15°	E[11]	—	600D	—	2200	5
V8-267/J	R45TS	.045	C	—	4°	[4]	—	500/600D	—	1850	7½–9
V8-305/H Exc. Calif.	R45TS	.045	C	4°	4°	[4]	700	500/600D	1500	1850	7½–9
V8-305/H Calif.	R45TS	.045	C	—	4°	[4]	—	550/650D	—	2200	7½–9
1981											
V6-229/K	R45TS	.045	F	6°	6°	G	[3]	[3]	2200	2200	4½–6
V6-231/A[20]	R45TS8	.080	D	—	15°	E[11]	—	[3]	—	1800	3 Min.
V6-231/3[21]	R45TS	.040	D	—	15°	E[11]	—	650D	—	2200	5
V8-267/J	R45TS	.045	C	—	6°	A	—	500/600D	—	2200	7½–9
V8-305/H	R45TS	.045	C	6°	6°	A	700/800	500/600D	2200	2200	7½–9
V8-350/L	R45TS	.045	C	—	6°	A	—	500/600D	—	2200	7½–9
1982											
V6-229/K	R45TS	.045	F	—	TDC	G	—	[3]	—	2200	4½–6
V6-231/A	R45TS8	.080	D	—	15°	E[11]	—	[3]	—	1800	3 Min.
V6-262 Diesel/V Exc. High Alt.	—	—	—	—	7°[25][26][27]	—	—	650D	—	725D	—
V6-262 Diesel/V High Alt.	—	—	—	—	7°[25][26][28]	—	—	650D	—	725D	—
V8-267/J	R45TS	.045	C	—	2°	A	—	500/600D	—	2200	7½–9
V8-305/H	R45TS	.045	C	—	6°	A	—	500/600D	—	2200	7½–9
V8-350 Diesel/N Exc. High Alt.	—	—	—	—	4°[25][26][29]	—	—	600D	—	750D	—
V8-350 Diesel/N High Alt.	—	—	—	—	4°[25][26][30]	—	—	600D	—	750D	—
1983											
V6-229/9	R45TS	.045	F	—	TDC	G	—	—	—	—	4½–6
V6-231/A	R45TS8	.080	D	—	15°	E[11]	—	[3]	—	2200	4¼–5¾
V6-262 Diesel/V	—	—	—	—	[15][33]	—	—	660/775D	—	775D	—
V8-305/H	R45TS	.045	C	—	6°	A	—	500/650D	—	2200	7½–9
V8-350 Diesel/N	—	—	—	—	[25][32]	—	—	600/750D	—	750D	—

Continued

TUNE UP SPECIFICATIONS—Continued

The following specifications are published from the latest information available. This data should be used only in the absence of a decal affixed in the engine compartment.

★ When using a timing light, disconnect vacuum hose or tube at distributor and plug opening in hose or tube so idle speed will not be affected.

● When checking compression, lowest cylinder must be within 70 percent of highest.

▲ Before removing wires from distributor cap, determine location of the No. 1 wire in cap, as distributor position may have been altered from that shown at the end of this chart.

☞ Spark plug types shown in this chart are recommendations of the original vehicle manufacturer and not MOTOR.

Check local sources for other spark plug manufacturers listings.

Year & Engine/V.I.N.	Spark Plug ☞ Type	Gap	Ignition Timing BTDC① ★ Firing Order Fig. ▲	Man. Trans.	Auto. Trans.	Mark Fig.	Curb Idle Speed② Man. Trans.	Auto. Trans.	Fast Idle Speed Man. Trans.	Auto. Trans.	Fuel Pump Pressure
MALIBU & MONTE CARLO—Continued											
1984											
V6-229/9	R45TS	.045	F	—	TDC	G	—	—	—	—	4½-6
V6-231/A	R45TS8	.080	D	—	15°	E⑪	—	③	—	2200	4¼-5¾
V8-305/H	R45TS	.045	C	—	6°	A	—	500/650D	—	2200	7½-9
V8-350 Diesel/N	—	—	—	—	㉕㉜	—	—	600/750D	—	750D	7½-9
CHEVY NOVA											
1977											
6-250/D Exc. Calif. & High Alt.	R46TS	.035	H	6°	8°	B	⑥	⑦	2000	2000	4½-6
6-250/D Calif.	R46TS	.035	H	—	6°	B	—	⑦	—	1800	4¼-5¾
6-250/D High Alt.	R46TS	.035	H	—	10°	B	—	425/600D	—	2000	4-5
V8-305/U Exc. Calif.	R45TS	.045	C	8°	8°	B	600/700	500/650D	—	—	7½-9
V8-305/U Calif.	R45TS	.045	C	—	6°	B	—	500/650D	—	—	7½-9
V8-350/L Exc. High Alt.	R45TS	.045	C	8°	8°	B	700	500/650D	1300⑤	1600⑤	7½-9
V8-350/L High Alt.	R45TS	.045	C	—	8°	B	—	600/650D	—	1600⑤	7½-9
1978											
6-250/D Exc. Calif.	R46TS	.035	H	6°	10°⑮	B	425/800	425/550D	2000	2100	4-5
6-250/D Calif.	R46TS	.035	H	—	6°	B	—	400/600D	—	2000	4-5
V8-305/U Exc. Calif.	R45TS	.045	C	4°	4°	G	600	500D	—	—	7½-9
V8-305/U Calif.	R45TS	.045	C	—	6°	G	—	500/600D	—	—	7½-9
V8-350/L	R45TS	.045	C	—	8°	G	—	⑯	—	1600	7½-9
1979											
6-250/D Exc. Calif.	R46TS	.035	H	12°	8°	B	800	675D	1800	2000	4-5
6-250/D Calif.	R46TS	.035	H	—	6°	B	—	600D	—	2000	4-5
V8-305/G Exc. Calif.	R45TS	.045	C	4°	4°	G	600/700	500/600D	1300	1600	7½-9
V8-305/G Calif.	R45TS	.045	C	—	4°	G	—	600/650D	—	1950	7½-9
V8-350/L Calif.	R45TS	.045	C	—	8°	G	—	500/600D	—	1600	7½-9
V8-350/L High Alt.	R45TS	.045	C	—	8°	G	—	600/650D	—	1750	7½-9
CHEVROLET											
1977											
6-250/D Exc. Calif. & High Alt.	R46TS	.035	H	—	8°	B	—	⑦	—	2000	4-5
6-250/D Calif.	R46TS	.035	H	—	6°	B	—	⑦	—	1800	4-5
6-250/D High Alt.	R46TS	.035	H	—	10°	B	—	425/600D	—	2000	4-5
V8-305/U Exc. Calif.	R45TS	.045	C	—	8°	B	—	500/650D	—	—	7½-9
V8-305/U Calif.	R45TS	.045	C	—	6°	B	—	500/650D	—	—	7½-9
V8-350/L Exc. High Alt.	R45TS	.045	C	—	8°	B	—	500/650D	—	1600⑤	7½-9
V8-350/L High Alt.	R45TS	.045	C	—	8°	B	—	600/650D	—	1600⑤	7½-9

Continued

TUNE UP SPECIFICATIONS—Continued
The following specifications are published from the latest information available. This
data should be used only in the absence of a decal affixed in the engine compartment.

★ When using a timing light, disconnect vacuum hose or tube at distributor and plug opening in hose or tube so idle speed will not be affected.

● When checking compression, lowest cylinder must be within 70 percent of highest.

▲ Before removing wires from distributor cap, determine location of the No. 1 wire in cap, as distributor position may have been altered from that shown at the end of this chart.

Spark plug types shown in this chart are recommendations of the original vehicle manufacturer and not MOTOR.
Check local sources for other spark plug manufacturers listings.

Year & Engine/V.I.N.	Spark Plug		Ignition Timing BTDC①★				Curb Idle Speed②		Fast Idle Speed		Fuel Pump Pressure
	Type	Gap	Firing Order Fig. ▲	Man. Trans.	Auto. Trans.	Mark Fig.	Man. Trans.	Auto. Trans.	Man. Trans.	Auto. Trans.	
CHEVROLET—Continued											
1978											
6-250/D Exc. Calif.	R46TS	.035	H	—	⑰	B	—	425/550D	—	2100	4–5
6-250/D Calif.	R46TS	.035	H	—	6°	B	—	400/600D	—	2000	4–5
V8-305/U Exc. Calif.	R45TS	.045	C	—	4°	G	—	500D	—	—	7½–9
V8-305/U Calif.	R45TS	.045	C	—	6°	G	—	500/600D	—	—	7½–9
V8-350/L Exc. Calif. & High Alt.	R45TS	.045	C	—	6°	G	—	500/600D	—	1600	7½–9
V8-350/L Calif.	R45TS	.045	C	—	8°	G	—	500/600D	—	1600	7½–9
V8-350/L High Alt.	R45TS	.045	C	—	8°	G	—	500/650D	—	1600	7½–9
1979											
6-250/D Exc. Calif.	R46TS	.035	H	—	8°	B	—	675D	—	2000	4–5
6-250/D Calif.	R46TS	.035	H	—	6°	B	—	600D	—	2000	4–5
V8-305/G Exc. Calif.	R45TS	.045	C	—	4°	G	—	500/600D	—	1600	7½–9
V8-305/G Calif.	R45TS	.045	C	—	4°	G	—	600/650D	—	1950	7½–9
V8-350/L Exc. Calif. & High Alt.	R45TS	.045	C	—	6°	G	—	500/600D	—	1600	7½–9
V8-350/L Calif.	R45TS	.045	C	—	8°	G	—	600/650D	—	1750	7½–9
V8-350/L High Alt.	R45TS	.045	C	—	8°	G	—	500/600D	—	1600	7½–9
1980											
V6-229/K	R45TS	.045	F	—	12°	G	—	600/675D	—	1750	4½–6
V6-231/A	R45TSX	.060	D	—	15°	E⑪	—	600D	—	2200	4¼–5¾
V8-267/J	R46TS	.035	C	—	6°	④	—	500/600D	—	1850	7½–9
V8-305/H Exc. Calif.	R45TS	.045	C	—	4°	④	—	500/600D	—	1850	7½–9
V8-305/H Calif.	R45TS	.045	C	—	4°	④	—	550/650D	—	2200	7½–9
V8-350/L	R45TS	.045	C	—	6°	④	—	500/600D	—	1850	7½–9
V8-350 Diesel/N Exc. High Alt.	—	—	—	—	4½°㉕㉖㉛	—	—	600/750D	—	750D	—
V8-350 Diesel/N High Alt.	—	—	—	—	5½°㉕㉖㉛	—	—	600/750D	—	750D	—
1981											
V6-229/K	R45TS	.045	F	—	6°	G	—	㉒	—	2200	4½–6
V6-231/A	R45TS8	.080	D	—	15°	E⑪	—	㉒	—	1800	3 Min.
V8-267/J	R45TS	.045	C	—	6°	A	—	500/600D	—	2200	7½–9
V8-305/H	R45TS	.045	C	—	6°	A	—	500/600D	—	2200	7½–9
V8-350/L	R45TS	.045	C	—	6°	A	—	500/600D	—	2200	7½–9
V8-350 Diesel/N Exc. High Alt.	—	—	—	—	4°㉕㉖㉛	—	—	600/750D	—	750D	—
V8-350 Diesel/N High Alt.	—	—	—	—	5°㉕㉖㉛	—	—	600/750D	—	750D	—
1982											
V6-229/K	R45TS	.045	F	—	TDC	G	—	③	—	2200	4½–6
V6-231/A	R45TS8	.080	D	—	15°	E⑪	—	③	—	1800	3 Min.
V8-267/J	R45TS	.045	C	—	2°	A	—	500/700D	—	2200	7½–9
V8-305/H	R45TS	.045	C	—	6°	A	—	500/600D	—	2200	7½–9
V8-350 Diesel/N Less High Alt. Package	—	—	—	—	4°㉕㉖㉙	—	—	600D	—	750D	7½–9

Continued

TUNE UP SPECIFICATIONS—Continued

The following specifications are published from the latest information available. This
data should be used only in the absence of a decal affixed in the engine compartment.

★ When using a timing light, disconnect vacuum hose or tube at distributor and plug opening in hose or tube so idle speed will not be affected.

● When checking compression, lowest cylinder must be within 70 percent of highest.

▲ Before removing wires from distributor cap, determine location of the No. 1 wire in cap, as distributor position may have been altered from that shown at the end of this chart.

☞ Spark plug types shown in this chart are recommendations of the original vehicle manufacturer and not MOTOR.

Check local sources for other spark plug manufacturers listings.

| Year & Engine/V.I.N. | Spark Plug | | Ignition Timing BTDC①★ | | | | Curb Idle Speed② | | Fast Idle Speed | | Fuel Pump Pressure |
	Type ☞	Gap	Firing Order Fig. ▲	Man. Trans.	Auto. Trans.	Mark Fig.	Man. Trans.	Auto. Trans.	Man. Trans.	Auto. Trans.	
CHEVROLET—Continued											
1982											
V8-350 Diesel/N With High Alt. Package	—	—	—	—	4°㉕㉖㉚	—	—	600D	—	750D	7½–9
1983											
V6-229/9	R45TS	.045	F	—	TDC	G	—	—	—	—	4½–6
V6-231/A	R45TS8	.080	D	—	15°	E⑪	—	③	—	2000	4¼–4¾
V8-305/H	R45TS	.045	C	—	6°	A	—	500/650D	—	2200	7½–9
V8-350 Diesel/N	—	—	—	—	㉕㉜	—	—	600/750D	—	750D	—
1984											
V6-229/9	R45TS	.045	F	—	TDC	G	—	—	—	—	4½–6
V6-231/A	R45TS8	.080	D	—	15°	E⑪	—	③	—	2000	4¼–4¾
V8-305/H	R45TS	.045	C	—	6°	A	—	500/650D	—	2200	7½–9
V8-350 Diesel/N	—	—	—	—	㉕㉜	—	—	600/750D	—	750D	—
CORVETTE											
1977											
V8-350/L Exc. High Alt. & High Perf.	R45TS	.045	C	8°	8°	B	700	500/650D	1300⑤	1600⑤	7½–9
V8-350/L High Alt. Exc. High Perf.	R45TS	.045	C	—	8°	B	—	600/650D	—	1600⑤	7½–9
V8-350/X High Perf.	R45TS	.045	C	12°	12°	B	800	700/800D	1300⑤	1600⑤	7½–9
1978											
V8-350/L Exc. Calif. & High Perf.	R45TS	.045	C	6°	6°	B	700	⑲	1300	1600	7½–9
V8-350/L Calif. Exc. High Perf.	R45TS	.045	C	—	8°	B	—	500/600D	—	1600	7½–9
V8-350/H High Perf.	R45TS	.045	C	12°	12°	B	900	700/800D	1600	1600	7½–9
1979											
V8-350/8 Exc. High Alt. & High Perf.	R45TS	.045	C	6°	6°	B	700	500/600D	1300	1600	7½–9
V8-350/8 High Alt. & High Perf.	R45TS	.045	C	—	8°	B	—	600/650D	—	1750	7½–9
V8-350/4 High Perf.	R45TS	.045	C	12°	12°	B	900	700/800D	1300	1600	7½–9
1980											
V8-305/H	R45TS	.045	C	—	4°	④	—	650D	—	—	7½–9
V8-350/8 Exc. High Alt. & High Perf.	R45TS	.045	C	6°	6°	B	700	500/600D	1300	1600	7½–9
V8-350/8 High Alt. & High Perf.	R45TS	.045	C	—	8°	B	—	600/650D	—	1750	7½–9
V8-350/6 High Perf.	R45TS	.045	C	12°	12°	B	900	500/600D	1300	1600	7½–9
1981											
V8-350/6	R45TS	.045	C	6°	6°	B	700/800	500/600D	2200	2200	7½–9

Continued

TUNE UP SPECIFICATIONS—Continued

The following specifications are published from the latest information available. This data should be used only in the absence of a decal affixed in the engine compartment.

★ When using a timing light, disconnect vacuum hose or tube at distributor and plug opening in hose or tube so idle speed will not be affected.

● When checking compression, lowest cylinder must be within 70 percent of highest.

▲ Before removing wires from distributor cap, determine location of the No. 1 wire in cap, as distributor position may have been altered from that shown at the end of this chart.

🖑 Spark plug types shown in this chart are recommendations of the original vehicle manufacturer and not MOTOR.

Check local sources for other spark plug manufacturers listings.

| Year & Engine/V.I.N. | Spark Plug | | Ignition Timing BTDC①★ | | | | Curb Idle Speed② | | Fast Idle Speed | | Fuel Pump Pressure |
	Type 🖑	Gap	Firing Order Fig. ▲	Man. Trans.	Auto. Trans.	Mark Fig.	Man. Trans.	Auto. Trans.	Man. Trans.	Auto. Trans.	
CORVETTE—Continued											
1982											
V8-350/6	R45TS	.045	C	—	6°㉒	A	—	⑲	—	⑲	—
1984											
V8-350 E.F.I./8	R45TS	.045	C	—	—	M	—	⑲	—	⑲	—

① —BTDC—Before top dead center.
② —Idle speed on man. trans. vehicles is adjusted in Neutral and on auto. trans. equipped vehicles is adjusted in Drive unless otherwise specified. Where two idle speeds are listed, the higher speed is with A/C or idle solenoid energized.
③ —Equipped with idle speed control motor.
④ —Early models, Fig. G; late models, Fig. A.
⑤ —With cam follower tang on high step of fast idle cam, EGR vacuum hose disconnected & plugged & A/C off.
⑥ —Less A/C, 425/750 RPM; with A/C, 425/800 RPM.
⑦ —Less A/C, 425/550D RPM; with A/C, 425/600D RPM.
⑧ —Except distributor No. 1110725, 6° BTDC; distributor No. 1110725, 8° BTDC.
⑨ —Except engine code CHU, 8° BTDC; engine code CHU, 6° BTDC.
⑩ —Injection timing to 800 RPM.

⑪ —The harmonic balancer on these engines has two timing marks. The timing mark measuring 1/16 in. is used when setting timing with a hand held timing light. The mark measuring 1/8 in. is used when setting timing with magnetic timing equipment.
⑫ —Less idle solenoid, 500D RPM; with idle solenoid, 560/670D RPM.
⑬ —Except turbocharged engine.
⑭ —Turbocharged engine.
⑮ —Nova 4 dr. sedan with A/C, set at 8° BTDC.
⑯ —Except high altitude, 500/600D RPM; high altitude, 500/650D RPM.
⑰ —Less A/C, 10° BTDC; with A/C, 8° BTDC.
⑱ —Except high altitude, 500/600D RPM; high altitude, 600/650D RPM.
⑲ —Automatically controlled by Electronic Fuel Injection.
⑳ —Ground diagnostic terminal for base timing.

㉑ —1100N with A/C.
㉒ —700D with A/C.
㉓ —Disconnect single near HEI distributor.
㉔ —Less A/C, 850 RPM; with A/C, 900 RPM.
㉕ —Using diesel timing meter J-33075.
㉖ —ATDC—After top dead center.
㉗ —Injection timing at 1300 RPM. When operating at altitudes above 4000 ft., set at 8° ATDC.
㉘ —Injection timing at 1300 RPM. When operating at altitudes below 4000 ft., set at 6° ATDC.
㉙ —Injection timing at 1250 RPM. When operating at altitudes above 4000 ft., set at 5° ATDC.
㉚ —Injection timing at 1250 RPM. When operating at altitudes below 4000 ft., set at 3° ATDC.
㉛ —Injection timing at 1200 RPM.
㉜ —Injection timing, 4° ATDC at 1250 RPM.

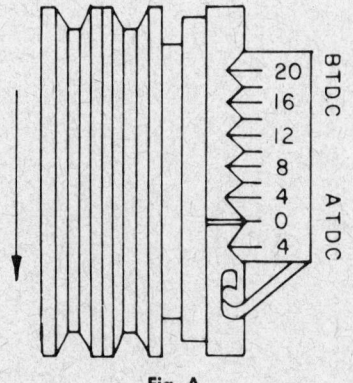

Fig. A

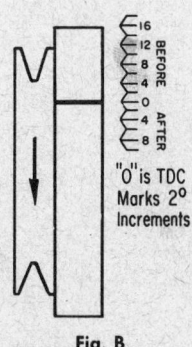

Fig. B

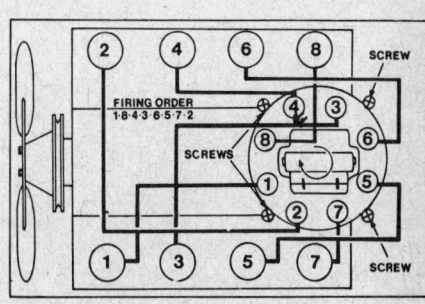

Fig. C

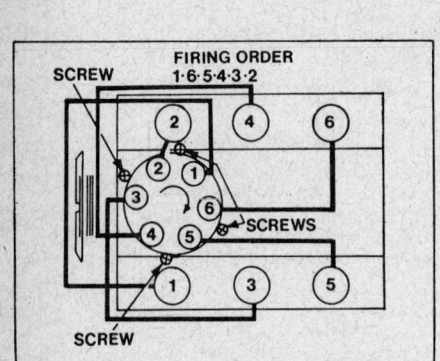

Fig. D

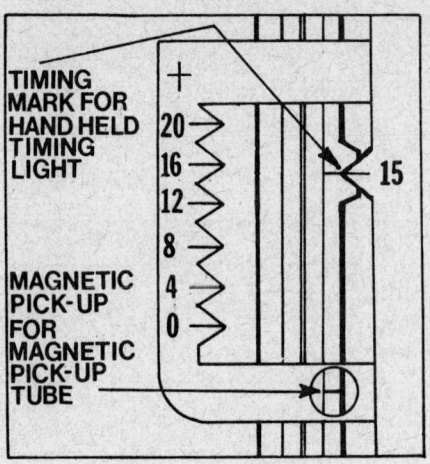

Fig. E

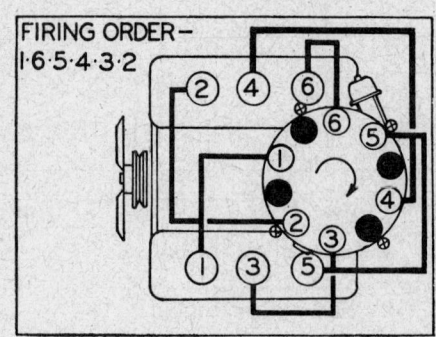

Fig. F

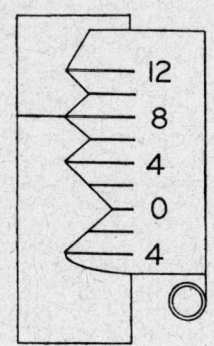

Fig. G

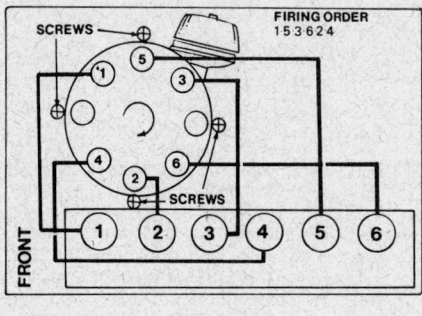

Fig. H

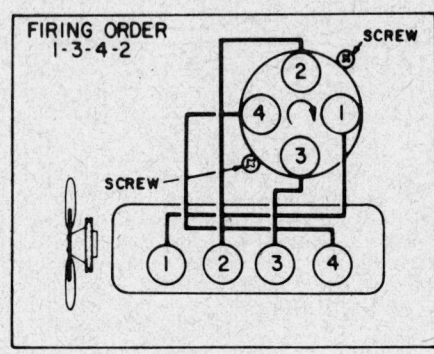

Fig. I

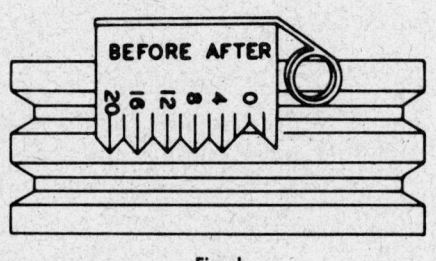

Fig. J

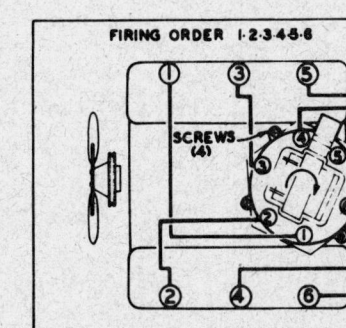

Fig. K

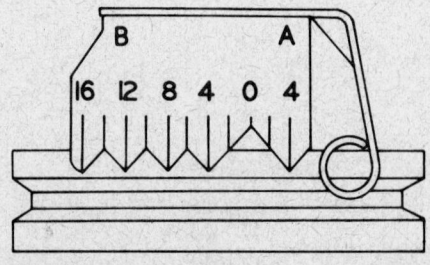

Fig. L

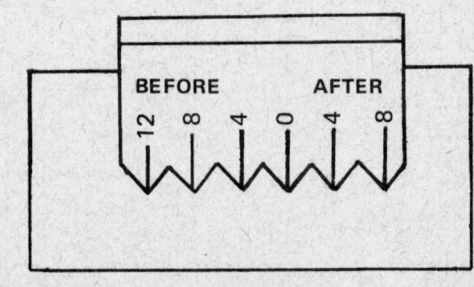

Fig. M

DISTRIBUTOR SPECIFICATIONS

★Note: If unit is checked on vehicle, double the RPM and degrees to get crankshaft figures.

Distributor Part No. ①	Centrifugal Advance Degrees @ RPM of Distributor					Vacuum Advance	
	Advance Starts	Intermediate Advance			Full Advance	Inches of Vacuum to Start Plunger	Max. Adv. Dist. Deg. @ Vacuum
1977							
1103239	—	—	—	—	—	—	—
1103244	—	—	—	—	—	—	—
1103246	—	—	—	—	—	—	—
1103248	—	—	—	—	—	—	—
1103256	—	—	—	—	—	—	—
1110678	0 @ 500	3½ @ 800	—	—	10 @ 2050	4	12 @ 15
1110681	0 @ 500	3½ @ 800	—	—	10 @ 2100	4	7½ @ 12
1978							
1103281	0 @ 500	5 @ 850	—	—	10 @ 1900	—	—
1103282	0 @ 500	5 @ 850	—	—	10 @ 1900	4	10 @ 10
1103285	0 @ 600	6 @ 1000	—	—	11 @ 2200	4	5 @ 8
1103286	0 @ 550	6 @ 800	8 @ 1200	—	11 @ 2300	—	—
1103291	0 @ 600	6½ @ 800	—	—	8 @ 1000	—	—
1103337	0 @ 550	6 @ 800	—	—	8 @ 1200	4	12 @ 10
1103353	0 @ 550	6 @ 800	—	—	8 @ 1200	4	10 @ 10
1110695	0–3 @ 1000	—	—	—	6–9 @ 1800	7	12 @ 13
1110696	0 @ 500	5 @ 850	—	—	10 @ 1900	3	8 @ 6½
1110697	0 @ 500	5 @ 850	—	—	10 @ 1900	3	8 @ 6½
1110715	0 @ 500	3½ @ 800	—	—	10 @ 2100	4	12 @ 15
1110716	0 @ 500	3½ @ 800	—	—	10 @ 2100	4	7½ @ 12
1110718	0 @ 500	3½ @ 800	—	—	10 @ 2100	4	9 @ 12
1110731	0–2 @ 1000	—	—	—	6–9 @ 1800	4	8 @ 9
1979							
1103281	0 @ 500	5 @ 850	—	—	10 @ 1900	4	9 @ 12
1103282	0 @ 500	5 @ 850	—	—	10 @ 1900	4	10 @ 11
1103285	0 @ 600	6 @ 1000	—	—	11 @ 2100	4	5 @ 8
1103291	0 @ 600	6½ @ 800	—	—	8 @ 1000	4	5 @ 8
1103337	0 @ 550	6 @ 800	8 @ 1200	—	11 @ 2300	4	12 @ 11
1103353	0 @ 550	6 @ 800	8 @ 1200	—	11 @ 2300	4	10 @ 10
1103368	0 @ 500	5 @ 850	—	—	10 @ 1900	4	10 @ 11
1103370	0 @ 650	—	—	—	8 @ 2100	3	12 @ 10
1103371	0 @ 500	4 @ 850	—	—	11 @ 2200	3	12 @ 10
1103379	0 @ 500	5 @ 850	—	—	10 @ 1900	3	10 @ 8½
1110696	0 @ 500	5 @ 850	—	—	10 @ 1900	2	8 @ 7½
1110716	0 @ 500	3½ @ 800	—	—	10 @ 2100	4	7½ @ 12
1110748	0 @ 500	3½ @ 800	—	—	10 @ 2100	4	10 @ 11
1110766	0–2 @ 1000	—	—	—	8½ @ 1800	4	12 @ 12
1110767	0–2 @ 1000	—	—	—	8½ @ 1800	3	10 @ 12
1980							
1103282	0 @ 500	5 @ 850	—	—	10 @ 1900	4	10 @ 11
1103337	0 @ 550	6 @ 800	8 @ 1200	—	11 @ 2300	4	12 @ 11
1103353	0 @ 550	6 @ 800	8 @ 1200	—	11 @ 2300	4	10 @ 10
1103368	0 @ 500	5 @ 850	—	—	10 @ 1900	4	5 @ 8
1103370	0 @ 650	—	—	—	8 @ 2100	3	12 @ 10
1103371	0 @ 500	4 @ 850	—	—	11 @ 2200	3	12 @ 10
1103379	0 @ 500	5 @ 850	—	—	10 @ 1900	3	10 @ 8.5
1110696	0 @ 500	5 @ 850	—	—	10 @ 1900	2	8 @ 7.5
1110716	0 @ 500	3½ @ 800	—	—	10 @ 2100	4	7½ @ 12
1110756	0 @ 700	2 @ 850	—	—	7 @ 1900	2	12 @ 10
1110766	0 @ 1000	—	—	—	6½–8½ @ 1800	4	12 @ 12
1110767	0 @ 2000	—	—	—	6½–8½ @ 1800	4	10 @ 12

Continued

DISTRIBUTOR SPECIFICATIONS—Continued

★Note: If unit is checked on vehicle, double the RPM and degrees to get crankshaft figures.

Distributor Part No.①	Advance Starts	Centrifugal Advance Degrees @ RPM of Distributor			Full Advance	Vacuum Advance	
		Intermediate Advance				Inches of Vacuum to Start Plunger	Max. Adv. Dist. Deg. @ Vacuum
1981							
1103434②	—	—	—	—	—	—	—
1103443②	—	—	—	—	—	—	—
1110754②	—	—	—	—	—	—	—
1111386②	—	—	—	—	—	—	—
1982							
1103494②							
1110597②							
1983							
1103470②	—	—	—	—	—	—	—
1103519②	—	—	—	—	—	—	—
1103539②	—	—	—	—	—	—	—
1110584②	—	—	—	—	—	—	—
1984							
1103539②	—	—	—	—	—	—	—
1110584②	—	—	—	—	—	—	—
1103523②	—	—	—	—	—	—	—

①—Stamped on distributor housing cover.　②—Equipped w/ EST (Electronic Spark Timing).

PISTONS, PINS, RINGS, CRANKSHAFT & BEARINGS

Year	Engine Model/V.I.N. Code	Piston Clearance	Ring End Gap①		Wristpin Diameter	Rod Bearings		Main Bearings		Thrust on Bear. No.	Shaft End Play
			Comp. ②	Oil ②		Shaft Diameter	Bearing Clearance	Shaft Diameter	Bearing Clearance		
1982–84	4-151/F⑭	.0017–.0041	.010	.015	.9400	2.0000	.0005–.0026	2.3000	.0005–.0022	5	.0035–.0085
1982	V6-173/1	.0016–.0027	.010	.020	.9054	1.9983–1.9993	.0014–.0035	2.4936–2.4946	.0017–.0029	3	.002–.007
1983–84	V6-173/1	.0006–.0016	.010	.020	.9054	1.9983–1.9993	.0014–.0037	⑮	.0016–.0032	3	.002–.007
1978–79	V6-200/M	.0007–.0017	.010	.015	.9272	2.0986–2.0998	.0013–.0035	③	④	4	.002–.006
1980–82	V6-229/K	.0007–.0017	.010	.015	.9272	2.0986–2.0998	.0013–.0035	③	④	4	.002–.006
1983–84	V6-229/9	.007–.017	.010	.015	.9393	2.2487–2.2495	.0005–.0026	2.4995	.0003–.0018	4	.003–.011
1978	V6-231/A⑨	.0008–.0020	.010	.015	.9392	2.2487–2.2495	.0005–.0026	2.4995	.0004–.0015	2	.004–.008
1979	V6-231/A⑨	.0008–.0020	.013	.015	.9392	2.2487–2.2495	.0005–.0026	2.4995	.0004–.0015	2	.003–.009
1980–82	V6-231/A⑨	.0008–.0020	.013	.015	.9392	2.2487–2.2495	.0005–.0026	2.4995	.0003–.0018	2	.003–.009
1983–84	V6-231/A⑨	.007–.017	.010	.015	.9393	2.2487–2.2495	.0005–.0026	2.4995	.0003–.0018	2	.006–.015
1977	6-250/D	.0010–.0020	.010	.015	.9272	1.9928–2.000	.0007–.0027	2.2983–2.2993	.0003–.0029	7	.002–.006
1978–79	6-250/D	.0010–.0020	.010	.015	.9272	1.998–2.000	.0010–.0026	2.2979–2.2994	⑩	7	.002–.006
1982	V6-262/V⑤⑪	.0030–.0040	.015	.015	1.0952	2.3742–2.3750	.0003–.0025	2.9993–3.0003	⑫	3	.0035–.0135
1983	V6-262/V⑤⑪	.0035–.0045	.013	.015	1.0951	2.3742–2.3750	.0003–.0025	2.9993–3.0003	⑫	3	.0035–.0135
1979–82	V8-267/J	.0007–.0017	.010	.015	.9272	2.0986–2.0998	.0013–.0035	③	④	5	.002–.006
1977	8-305/U	.0007–.0017	.010	.015	.9272	2.099–2.100	.0013–.0035	③	④	5	.002–.006
1978–83	8-305⑬	.0007–.0017	.010	.015	.9272	2.0986–2.0998	.0013–.0035	③	④	5	.002–.006
1983–84	V8-305/H	.0007–.0017	.010	.015	.9272	2.0986–2.0998	.0018–.0039	③	④	5	.002–.006
1977	8-350/L⑥	.0007–.0017	.010	.015	.9272	2.099–2.100	.0013–.0035	③	④	5	.002–.006
	8-350/L⑦	.0046–.0056	.010	.015	.9272	2.099–2.100	.0013–.0035	③	④	5	.002–.006
1978–80	8-350/L⑥	.0007–.0017	.010	.015	.9272	2.0986–2.0998	.0013–.0035	③	④	5	.002–.006
	8-350/L⑦	.0046–.0056	.010	.015	.9272	2.0986–2.0998	.0013–.0035	③	④	5	.002–.006
1981–82	V8-350/L⑥	.0007–.0017	.015	.020	.9272	2.099–2.100	.0013–.0035	③	④	5	.002–.007
	V8-350/L⑦	.0046–.0056	.010	.015	.9272	2.0986–2.0998	.0013–.0035	③	④	5	.002–.006
	V8-350/6⑦	.0025–.0035	.010	.015	.9272	2.0988–2.0998	.0013–.0035	③	④	5	.002–.006
1984	V8-350/8	.0025–.0045	.010	.015	.9272	2.0988–2.0998	.0013–.0035	③	④	5	.002–.006
1980–82	8-350/N⑤⑪	.0050–.0060	.015	.015	1.0951	2.1238–2.1248	.0005–.0026	2.9993–3.0003	⑧	3	.0035–.0135
1983–84	V8-350/N⑤⑪	.0035–.0045	.013	.015	1.0951	2.2495–2.2500	.0005–.0026	2.9993–3.0003	⑧	3	.0035–.0135

Continued

PISTONS, PINS, RINGS, CRANKSHAFT & BEARINGS NOTES

① —Fit rings tapered bores to the clearance listed in tightest portion of ring travel.

② —Clearances specified are minimum gaps.

③ —Front: 2.4484–2.4493; intermediate: 2.4481–2.4490; rear: 2.4479–2.4488.

④ —Front: .0008–.0020; intermediate: .0011–.0023; rear: .0017–.0032.

⑤ —Refer to Oldsmobile Chapter for service procedures on this engine.

⑥ —Except Corvette High Performance engine.

⑦ —Corvette High Performance engine.

⑧ —No. 1, 2, 3, 4: .0005–.0021; 1980–82 No. 5: .0015–.0031; 1983–84 No. 5: .0020–.0034.

⑨ —Refer to Buick Chapter for service procedures on this engine.

⑩ —Nos. 1–6; .0010–.0024. Nos. 7; .0016–0035.

⑪ —Diesel engine.

⑫ —No. 1, 2, 3: .0005–.0021; No. 4: .0020–.0034.

⑬ —For V.I.N. code, refer to the "General Engine Specifications" at the beginning of the chapter.

⑭ —Refer to the Pontiac chapter for service procedures on this engine.

⑮ —Nos. 1, 2, 4, 2.4937–2.4946 inch; No. 3, 2.4932–2.4941 inch.

REAR AXLE SPECIFICATIONS

Year	Model	Carrier Type	Ring Gear & Pinion Backlash		Pinion Bearing Preload			Differential Bearing Preload		
			Method	Adjustment	Method	New Bearings Inch-Lbs.	Used Bearings Inch-Lbs.	Method	New Bearings	Used Bearings
1977–79	Corvette	Integral	Shims	.005–.008	Spacer	20–25①	5–10①	Shims	.008	.008
1977–79	Exc. Corvette	Integral	Shims	.005–.008	Spacer	15–30①	5–10①	Shims	.008	.008
1980–81	Exc. Corvette	Integral	Shims	.005–.008	Spacer	15–30①	10–15①	Shims	.008	.008
1982	Exc. Corvette	Integral	Shims	.005–.008	Spacer	20–25①	10–15①	Shims	.008②	.006②
1980–82	Corvette	Integral	Shims	.005–.009	Shims	15–35①	—	Shims	.008	.008
1983–84	Exc. Corvette	Integral	Shims	.005–.008	Spacer	24–32①	8–12①	Shims	.008	.008
1984	Corvette	Integral	Shims	.005–.008	Shims	15–35	—	Shims	.008	.008

① —Use inch-pound torque wrench on pinion shaft nut.

② —Total preload measured with torque wrench at pinion flange nut with new seal installed. 35–40 inch lbs., new bearings; 20–25 inch lbs., used bearings.

ALTERNATOR SPECIFICATIONS

Year	Model	Rated Hot Output Amps	Field Current 12 Volts @ 80°F.	Year	Model	Rated Hot Output Amps	Field Current 12 Volts @ 80°F.	Year	Model	Rated Hot Output Amps	Field Current 12 Volts @ 80°F.
1977–79	1102394	37	4–4.5		1103162	37	4–4.5	1983	1105360	42	4–4.5
	1102474	61	4–4.5	1981	1101044	70	4–4.5		1100250	63	4–4.5
	1102478	55	4–4.5		1101066	70	4–4.5		1101040	70	4–4.5
	1102479	55	4–4.5		1101071	70	4–4.5		1105360	37	4–4.5
	1102480	61	4–4.5		1103043	42	4–4.5		1103061	42	4–4.5
	1102484	42	4–4.5		1103044	63	4–4.5		1105357	63	4–4.5
	1102486	61	4–4.5		1103085	55	—	1984	1100200	78	4–4.5
	1102491	37	4–4.5		1103088	55	4–4.5		1100226	37	4–4.5
1980	1101044	70	4–4.5		1103091	63	4–4.5		1100228	37	4–4.5
	1101066	70	4–4.5		1103092	55	4–4.5		1100230	40	4–4.5
	1101071	70	4–4.5		1103100	55	4–4.5		1100237	55	4–4.5
	1102474	61	4–4.5		1103102	63	4–4.5		1100239	55	4–4.5
	1102484	42	4–4.5		1103103	63	4–4.5		1100246	63	4–4.5
	1103043	42	4–4.5		1103118	37	4–4.5		1100247	63	4–4.5
	1103044	63	4–4.5		1103122	—	4–4.5		1100260	78	4–4.5
	1103085	55	4–4.5		1103161	37	4–4.5		1100263	78	4–4.5
	1103088	55	4–4.5		1103162	37	4–4.5		1100264	78	4–4.5
	1103091	63	4–4.5		1103169	63	4–4.5		1100270	78	4–4.5
	1103092	55	4–4.5	1982	1103060	42	4–4.5		1100297	42	4–4.5
	1103100	55	4–4.5		1101040	70	4–4.5		1100300	63	4–4.5
	1103102	63	4–4.5		1100195	70	4–4.5		1105022	78	4–4.5
	1103118	37	4–4.5		1100294	63	4–4.5		1105025	63	4–4.5
	1103122	63	4–4.5		1101097	85	4–4.5		1105041	78	4–4.5
	1103161	37	4–4.5		1100285	85	4–4.5		1105513	97	4–4.5

STARTING MOTOR APPLICATIONS

Year	Model/V.I.N.	Starter Number	Year	Model/V.I.N.	Starter Number	Year	Model/V.I.N.	Starter Number
1977–78	6-250/D	1108774		V8-305/H④⑤	1109074		V8-267/J⑩	1109534
	V8-305/U③	1109056		V8-305/H①	1998217		V8-305/H⑨	1109064
	V8-305/U④	1108799		V8-350⑫①③	1109052		V8-305/H⑩	1109534
	V8-350/L④	1109059		V8-350⑫①④	1109059		V8-350/8①	1998241
	V8-350/L③	1109052		V8-350/L③	1109067		V8-350 Diesel/N	1998552
1978	V6-200/M	1109524		V8-350/L④	1109065	1983	4-151/2⑯	1109556
	V6-231/A	1108797	1980–81	V8-350 Diesel/N	1109213		V6-173/1	1109535
1979	V6-200/M	1109056	1981	V6-229/K	1109524		V6-229/9	1998236
	V6-231/A	1109061		V6-231/A⑦	1109061		V6-231/A	1998236
	6-250/D	1108774		V8-267/J②	1109064		V6-262 Diesel/V	1998554
	V8-267/J	1109524		V8-267/J⑦	1109524		V8-305/H	1109534
	V8-305/G②	1108774		V8-305/L③	1109064		V8-305/S	1109534
	V8-305/G⑦	1109056		V8-305/L④⑤	1109074		V8-350 Diesel/N	1998554
	V8-350/L③	1109052		V8-350/L⑤	1109065	1984	4-151/2⑬	1109556
	V8-350/L④	1109059		V8-350 Diesel/N	1109213		V6-173/1	1109535
1980	V6-229/K	1109524	1982	4-151/F⑬	1109533		V6-229/9	1998236
	V6-231/A	1109061		V6-173/1	1109535		V6-231/A	1981109
	V8-267/J⑧	1109524		V6-229/K⑨	1109524		V6-262 Diesel/V	1981104
	V8-267/J⑤	1109064		V6-229/K⑩	1109534		V8-305/H⑧	1981102
	V8-305/H⑥	1109524		V6-231/A	1109524		V8-305/S & H⑤	1109534
	V8-305/H③⑤	1109064		V6-262 Diesel/V	1998552		V8-350/8①	1998435
	V8-305/H④⑤	1109067		V8-267/J⑨	1109064		V8-350 Diesel/N⑧	1981104⑭

①—Corvette.
②—Exc. Malibu & Malibu Classic.
③—With auto. trans.
④—With manual trans.
⑤—Camaro.
⑥—Except Camaro & Corvette.
⑦—Malibu & Malibu Classic.
⑧—Exc. Camaro.
⑨—Malibu & Monte Carlo.
⑩—Exc. Malibu & Monte Carlo.
⑪—Exc. Corvette.
⑫—1980 V.I.N. code is 8 or 6 (high performance).
⑬—Refer to Pontiac chapter for service procedures.
⑭—With heavy duty battery, 1981106.

ENGINE TIGHTENING SPECIFICATIONS

★Torque specifications are for clean and lightly lubricated threads only. Dry or dirty threads produce increased friction which prevents accurate measurement of tightness.

Year	Engine Model/V.I.N.	Spark Plugs Ft. Lbs.	Cylinder Head Bolts Ft. Lbs.	Intake Manifold Ft. Lbs.	Exhaust Manifold Ft. Lbs.	Rocker Arm Stud Ft. Lbs.	Rocker Arm Cover Ft. Lbs.	Connecting Rod Cap Bolts Ft. Lbs.	Main Bearing Cap Bolts Ft. Lbs.	Flywheel to Crankshaft Ft. Lbs.	Vibration Damper or Pulley Ft. Lbs.
1982–84	4-151/⑱⑲	7–15	85	29	44	20⑳	6	32	70	44	160
1982–84	V6-173⑱	7–15	70	23	25	46	8	37	69	50	75
1978–79	V6-200/M	⑨	65	30	20	—	45③	45	70	60	60
1980–84	V6-229⑱	22	65	30	20	—	45③	45	70	60	60
1978–84	V6-231/A⑩	15	80	45	25	30④	4	40	100	60	225
1982–83	V6-262/V⑭⑮	15㉒	⑯⑰	41⑯	29	28⑦	㉑	42	107	48	160–350
1977–79	6-250/D	15	95⑧	⑥	30	—	45③	35	65	60	60
1979–82	8-267/J	22	65	30	20	—	45③	45	70	60	60
1977–84	8-305⑱	②	65	30	20	—	45③	45	70	60	60
1977–84	V8-350⑱⑫	②	65	30	20①	⑪	45③	45	70	60	60
1980–84	V8-350/N⑭⑮	12㉒	130⑯	40⑯	25	28⑦	—	42	120	60	200–310

①—Inside bolts 30 ft. lbs.
②—1977-78, 15 ft. lbs. 1979-84, 22 ft. lbs.
③—Inch lbs.
④—Rocker arm shaft to cylinder head bolts.
⑤—Outer bolts on engines with 4 bolt caps 65 ft. lbs.
⑥—Integral Intake Manifold.
⑦—Rocker arm pivot bolt.
⑧—Left hand front head bolt 85 ft. lbs.
⑨—1978, 20 ft. lbs.; 1979, 22 ft. lbs.
⑩—Refer to Buick Chapter for service procedures on this engine.
⑪—Corvette, 50 ft. lbs.
⑫—Gasoline engine.
⑬—Outer bolts on engines with 4 bolt caps 70 ft. lbs.
⑭—Diesel engine.
⑮—Refer to Oldsmobile Section for service procedures on this engine.
⑯—Clean & dip bolt in engine oil before tightening to obtain correct torque reading.
⑰—Bolts 5, 6, 11, 12, 13 & 14, 59 ft. lbs.; All others, 142 ft. lbs.
⑱—For V.I.N. code, refer to the "General Engine Specifications" at the beginning of the chapter.
⑲—Refer to Pontiac chapter for service procedures.
⑳—Rocker arm bolts.
㉑—Fully driven seated, not stripped.
㉒—Glow plug torque.

VALVE SPECIFICATIONS

Year	Engine Model/V.I.N.	Valve Lash Int. Exh.	Valve Angles Seat	Face	Valve Spring Installed Height	Valve Spring Pressure Lbs. @ In.	Stem Clearance Intake	Exhaust	Stem Diameter Intake	Exhaust
1977	6-250/D	¾ Turn⑤	46	45	1²¹/₃₂	175 @ 1.26	.0010–.0027	.0010–.0027	.3410–.3417	.3410–.3417
	8-305/U	¾ Turn⑤	46	45	②	①	.0010–.0027	.0010–.0027	.3410–.3417	.3410–.3417
	8-350/L	¾ Turn⑤	46	45	②	①	.0010–.0027	.0010–.0027	.3410–.3417	.3410–.3417
1978	V6-200/M	1 Turn⑤	46	45	1²³/₃₂	200 @ 1.25	.0010–.0027	.0010–.0027	.3410–.3417	.3410–.3417
	V6-231/A④	Hydraulic③	45	45	1.727	168 @ 1.327	.0015–.0032	.0015–.0032	.3402–.3412	.3405–.3412
	6-250/D	1 Turn⑤	46	45	1²¹/₃₂	175 @ 1.26	.0010–.0027	.0010–.0027	.3410–.3417	.3410–.3417
	V8-305/U	1 Turn⑤	46	45	1²³/₃₂	200 @ 1.25	.0010–.0027	.0010–.0027	.3410–.3417	.3410–.3417
	V8-350/L⑦	1 Turn⑤	46	45	1²³/₃₂	200 @ 1.25	.0010–.0027	.0010–.0027	.3410–.3417	.3410–.3417
	V8-350/L⑥	1 Turn⑤	46	45	②	①	.0010–.0027	.0010–.0027	.3410–.3417	.3410–.3417
1979	V6-200/M	1 Turn⑤	46	45	1²³/₃₂	200 @ 1.25	.0010–.0027	.0010–.0027	.3410–.3417	.3410–.3417
	V6-231/A④	Hydraulic③	45	45	1.727	168 @ 1.327	.0015–.0032	.0015–.0032	.3402–.3412	.3405–.3412
	6-250/D	1 Turn⑤	46	45	1²¹/₃₂	175 @ 1.26	.0010–.0027	.0015–.0032	.3410–.3417	.3410–.3417
	V8-267/J	1 Turn⑤	46	45	1²³/₃₂	200 @ 1.25	.0010–.0027	.0010–.0027	.3410–.3417	.3410–.3417
	V8-305/G	1 Turn⑤	46	45	1²³/₃₂	200 @ 1.25	.0010–.0027	.0010–.0027	.3410–.3417	.3410–.3417
	V8-350/L⑦	1 Turn⑤	46	45	1²³/₃₂	200 @ 1.25	.0010–.0027	.0010–.0027	.3410–.3417	.3410–.3417
	V8-350/L⑥	1 Turn⑤	46	45	②	①	.0010–.0027	.0010–.0027	.3410–.3417	.3410–.3417
1980	V6-229/K	1 Turn⑤	46	45	1²³/₃₂	200 @ 1.25	.0010–.0027	.0010–.0027	.3410–.3417	.3410–.3417
	V6-231/A④	Hydraulic③	45	45	1.727	182 @ 1.34	.0015–.0035	.0015–.0032	.3402–.3412	.3405–.3412
	V8-267/J	1 Turn⑤	46	45	1²³/₃₂	200 @ 1.25	.0010–.0027	.0010–.0027	.3410–.3417	.3410–.3417
	V8-305/H	1 Turn⑤	46	45	1²³/₃₂	200 @ 1.25	.0010–.0027	.0010–.0027	.3410–.3417	.3410–.3417
	V8-350/L⑦	1 Turn⑤	46	45	1²³/₃₂	200 @ 1.25	.0010–.0027	.0010–.0027	.3410–.3417	.3410–.3412
	V8-350/L⑥	1 Turn⑤	46	45	②	①	.0010–.0027	.0010–.0027	.3410–.3417	.3410–.3412
	V8-350 Diesel/N⑧	Hydraulic③	⑨	⑩	1.67	151 @ 1.30	.0010–.0027	.0015–.0032	.3425–.3432	.3420–.3427
1981	V6-229/K	1 Turn⑤	46	45	1.70	175 @ 1.25	.0010–.0027	.0010–.0027	.3410–.3417	.3410–.3417
	V6-231/A④	Hydraulic③	45	45	1.727	182 @ 1.34	.0015–.0035	.0015–.0032	.3402–.3412	.3405–.3412
	V8-267/J	1 Turn⑤	46	45	1.70	175 @ 1.25	.0010–.0027	.0010–.0027	.3410–.3417	.3410–.3417
	V8-305/H	1 Turn⑤	46	45	1.70	175 @ 1.25	.0010–.0027	.0010–.0027	.3410–.3417	.3410–.3417
	V8-350/L⑦	1 Turn⑤	46	45	1.70	⑪	.0010–.0027	.0010–.0027	.3410–.3417	.3410–.3417
	V8-350/L⑥	1 Turn⑤	46	45	②	①	.0010–.0027	.0010–.0027	.3410–.3417	.3410–.3417
	V8-350 Diesel/N⑧	Hydraulic③	⑨	⑩	1.67	155 @ 1.30	.0010–.0027	.0015–.0032	.3425–3432	.3420–.3427
1982	4-151/F⑫	Hydraulic③	46	45	1.66	151 @ 1.254	.0010–.0027	.0010–.0027	.3418–.3425	.3418–.3425
	V6-173/1	1½ Turn⑤	46	45	1.57	195 @ 1.1811	.0010–.0027	.0010–.0027	.3410–.3420	.3410–.3420
	V6-229/K	1 Turn⑤	46	45	1²³/₃₂	200 @ 1.25	.0010–.0027	.0010–.0027	.3410–.3417	.3410–.3417
	V6-231/A④	Hydraulic③	45	45	1.727	220 @ 1.34	.0015–.0035	.0015–.0032	.3401–.3412	.3405–.3412
	V6-262 Diesel/V⑧	Hydraulic③	⑨	⑩	1.67	210 @ 1.22	.0010–.0027	.0015–.0032	.3425–.3432	.3420–.3427
	V8-267/J	1 Turn⑤	46	45	1²³/₃₂	200 @ 1.25	.0010–.0027	.0010–.0027	.3410–.3417	.3410–.3417
	V8-305/H & 7	1 Turn⑤	46	45	1²³/₃₂	200 @ 1.25	.0010–.0027	.0010–.0027	.3410–.3417	.3410–.3417
	V8-350/6⑥	1 Turn⑤	46	45	②	①	.0010–.0027	.0010–.0027	.3410–.3417	.3410–.3417
	V8-350 Diesel/N⑧	Hydraulic③	⑨	⑩	1.67	210 @ 1.22	.0010–.0027	.0015–.0032	.3425–3432	.3420–.3427
1983	4-151/2⑫	Hydraulic③	46	45	1.69	151 @ 1.254	.0010–.0027	.0010–.0027	.3425–.3418	.3425–.3418
	V6-173/1	1½ Turns⑤	46	45	1.57	195 @ 1.1811	.0010–.0027	.0010–.0027	.3410–.3420	.3410–.3420
	V6-229/9	1 Turn⑤	46	45	1²³/₃₂	200 @ 1.25	.0010–.0027	.0010–.0027	.3410–.3417	.3410–.3420
	V6-231/A④	Hydraulic③	45	45	1.727	182 @ 1.340	.0015–.0035	.0015–.0032	.3401–.3412	.3405–.3412
	V6-262 Diesel/V⑧	Hydraulic③	⑨	⑩	1.67	210 @ 1.22	.0010–.0027	.0015–.0032	.3425–.3432	.3420–.3427
	V8-305/H & S	1 Turn⑤	46	45	1²³/₃₂	200 @ 1.25	.0010–.0027	.0010–.0027	.3410–.3417	.3410–.3420
	V8-350 Diesel/N⑧	Hydraulic③	⑨	⑩	1.67	210 @ 1.22	.0010–.0027	.0015–.0032	.3425–3432	.3420–.3427
1984	4-151/2⑫	Hydraulic③	46	45	1.66	151 @ 1.254	.0010–.0027	.0010–.0027	.3425–.3418	.3425–.3418
	V6-173/1	1½ Turns⑤	46	45	1.57	195 @ 1.1811	.0010–.0027	.0010–.0027	.3410–.3420	.3410–.3420
	V6-229/9	1 Turn⑤	46	45	1²³/₃₂	200 @ 1.25	.0010–.0027	.0010–.0027	.3410–.3417	.3410–.3420
	V6-231/A④	Hydraulic③	45	45	1.727	182 @ 1.340	.0015–.0035	.0015–.0032	.3401–.3412	.3405–.3412
	V8-305/H & S	1 Turn⑤	46	45	1²³/₃₂	200 @ 1.25	.0010–.0027	.0010–.0027	.3410–.3417	.3410–.3420
	V8-350/8⑥	1 Turn⑤	46	45	②	①	.0010–.0027	.0010–.0027	.3410–.3417	.3410–.3417
	V8-350/N⑧	Hydraulic③	⑨	⑩	1.67	210 @ 1.22	.0010–.0027	.0015–.0032	.3425–3432	.3420–.3427

VALVE SPECIFICATIONS NOTES

①—Intake 200 @ 1.25; Exhaust 200 @ 1.16.
②—Intake, 1²³/₃₂. Exhaust 1¹⁹/₃₂.
③—No Adjustment.
④—Refer to Buick Chapter for service procedures on this engine.
⑤—Turn rocker arm stud nut until all lash is

eliminated, then tighten nut the additional turn listed.
⑥—Corvette.
⑦—Except Corvette.
⑧—Refer to Oldsmobile Chapter for service procedures on this engine.

⑨—Intake, 45°; Exhaust, 31°.
⑩—Intake, 44°; Exhaust, 30°.
⑪—Intake, 184 @ 1.70; Exhaust, 190 @ 1.16.
⑫—Refer to Pontiac chapter for service procedures.

WHEEL ALIGNMENT SPECIFICATIONS

Year	Model	Caster Angle, Degrees		Camber Angle, Degrees				Toe-In. Inch	Toe-Out on Turns, Deg.①	
		Limits	Desired	Limits		Desired			Outer Wheel	Inner Wheel
				Left	Right	Left	Right			
CAMARO										
1977	All	+½ to +1½	+1	+½ to +1½	+½ to +1½	+1	+1	0 to ⅛	—	—
1978–81	All	+½ to +1½	+1	+½ to +1½	+½ to +1½	+1	+1	1/16 to 3/16	—	—
1982–84	All	+2½ to +3½	+3	+½ to +1½	+½ to +1½	+1	+1	⑤	—	—
CHEVELLE, MALIBU & MONTE CARLO										
1977	Chevelle③	+½ to +1½	+1	+½ to +1½	0 to +1	+1	+½	0 to ⅛	—	—
	Chevelle④	②	①	+½ to +1½	0 to +1	+1	+½	0 to ⅛	—	—
	Monte Carlo	+4½ to +5½	+5	+½ to +1½	0 to +1	+1	+½	0 to ⅛	—	—
1978–84	All③	+½ to +1½	+1	0 to +1	0 to +1	+½	+½	1/16 to 3/16	—	—
	All④	+2½ to +3½	+3	0 to +1	0 to +1	+½	+½	1/16 to 3/16	—	—
CHEVY NOVA										
1977	All③	−1½ to −½	−1	+.3 to +1.3	+.3 to +1.3	+.8	+.8	0 to ⅛	—	—
	All④	+½ to +1½	+1	+.3 to +1.3	+.3 to +1.3	+.8	+.8	0 to ⅛	—	—
1978–79	All③	−1½ to −½	−1	+.3 to +1.3	+.3 to +1.3	+.8	+.8	1/16 to 3/16	—	—
	All④	+½ to +1½	+1	+.3 to +1.3	+.3 to +1.3	+.8	+.8	1/16 to 3/16	—	—
CHEVROLET										
1977	All	+2½ to +3½	+3	+.3 to +1.3	+.3 to +1.3	+.8	+.8	+1/16 to ⅛	—	—
1978–84	All	+2½ to +3½	+3	+.3 to +1.3	+.3 to +1.3	+.8	+.8	1/16 to 3/16	—	—
CORVETTE										
1977–78	Front Whl. Align.	+2 to +2½	+2¼	+¼ to +1¼	+¼ to +1¼	+¾	+¾	3/16 to 5/16	—	—
	Rear Whl. Align.	—	—	+⅝ to +1⅛	+⅝ to +1⅛	+⅞	+⅞	−1/32 to +1/32	—	—
1979	Front Whl. Align.	+2 to +2½	+2¼	+¼ to +1¼	+¼ to +1¼	+¾	+¾	3/16 to 5/16	—	—
	Rear Whl. Align.	—	—	−1 to 0	−1 to 0	−½	−½	1/16 to ⅛	—	—
1980	Front Whl. Align.	+2 to +2½	+2¼	+¼ to +1¼	+¼ to +1¼	+¾	+¾	3/16 to 5/16	—	—
	Rear Whl. Align.	—	—	+.2 to +1.2	+.2 to +1.2	+.7	+.7	−1/16 to +1/16	—	—
1981–82	Front Whl. Align.	+1¾ to +2¾	+2¼	+¼ to +1¼	+¼ to +1¼	+¾	+¾	3/16 to 5/16	—	—
	Rear Whl. Align.	—	—	−½ to +½	−½ to +½	Zero	Zero	0 to ⅛	—	—
1984	Front Whl. Align.	+2½ to +3½	+3	−½ to +½	−½ to +½	0	0	⑥	—	—
	Rear Whl. Align.	—	—	−½ to +½	−½ to +½	0	0	⑦	—	—

①—Equipped with radial tires, +2°; equipped with bias belted tires, +1°.
②—Equipped with radial tires, +1½° to +2½°; equipped with bias belted tires, +½° to

1½°.
③—Manual steering.
④—Power steering.
⑤—Z-28, +.15°; except Z-28, +.2°.

⑥—Toe-in .05° to .25° per wheel, with steering wheel in straight ahead position.
⑦—Toe-in .10° to .20° per wheel.

COOLING SYSTEM & CAPACITY DATA

Year	Model or Engine/V.I.N.	Cooling Capacity, Qts.		Radiator Cap Relief Pressure, Lbs.	Thermo. Opening Temp.	Fuel Tank Gals.	Engine Oil Refill Qts. ①	Transmission Oil			Rear Axle Oil Pints
		Less A/C	With A/C					3 Speed Pints	4 & 5 Speed Pints	Auto. Trans. Qts. ②	
CAMARO											
1977	6-250/D	14.6	14.7	15	195	21	4	3	—	⑤	4¼
	V8-305/U	17.2	17.9	15	195	21	4	3	—	⑤	4¼
	V8-350/L	17.3	18.0	15	195	21	4	—	3	⑤	4¼

Continued

COOLING SYSTEM & CAPACITY DATA—Continued

Year	Model or Engine/V.I.N.	Cooling Capacity, Qts.		Radiator Cap Relief Pressure, Lbs.	Thermo. Opening Temp.	Fuel Tank Gals.	Engine Oil Refill Qts. ①	Transmission Oil			Rear Axle Oil Pints
		Less A/C	With A/C					3 Speed Pints	4 & 5 Speed Pints	Auto. Trans. Qts. ②	
CAMARO—Continued											
1978	6-250/M	15	16	15	195	21	4	3	—	⑪	4¼
	V8-305/U	17.5	18.5	15	195	21	4	—	3	⑪	4¼
	V8-350/L	17.5	18.5	15	195	21	4	—	3	⑪	4¼
1979	6-250/D	14.5	14.5	15	195	21	4	3	—	⑪	4¼
	V8-305/G	17⑬	18	15	195	21	4	—	3	⑪	4¼
	V8-350/L	17⑬	18	15	195	21	4	—	3	⑪	4¼
1980	V6-229/K	14.5	14.5	15	195	21	4⑯	3	—	⑳	4¼
	V6-231/A	12	12	15	195	21	4	—	—	⑳	4¼
	V8-267/J	15	15	15	195	21	4	—	—	⑳	4¼
	V8-305/H	15	15	15	195	21	4	—	3	⑳	4¼
	V8-350/L	16	16	15	195	21	4	—	3	⑳	4¼
1981	V6-229/K	14½	14½	15	195	20.8	4⑯	3½	—	⑪	③
	V6-231/A	12	12	15	195	20.8	4	—	—	⑪	③
	V8-267/J	15	15	15	195	20.8	4	—	—	⑪	③
	V8-305/H	15	15	15	195	20.8	4	—	3½	⑪	③
	V8-350/L	16	16	15	195	20.8	4	—	—	⑪	③
1982	4-151/F⑯	8.8	9.1	15	195	16	3⑯	—	3½	㉗	3½
	V6-173/I	12½	12½	15	195	16	4⑯	—	3½	㉗	3½
	V8-305/H,7	15	15	15	195	16	4	—	3½	㉗	3½
1983	4-151/F㉖	8.8	9.1	15	195	16	3⑯	—	㉚	㉘	3½
	V6-173/I	12½	12½	15	195	16	4⑯	—	㉚	㉘	3½
	V8-305/H	15	15	15	195	16	4	—	㉚	㉘	3½
	V8-305 E.F.I./7	15	15	15	195	16	4	—	㉚	㉘	3½
1984	4-151/F㉖	8.8	9.1	15	195	16	3⑯	—	㉚	㉙	3½
	V6-173/1	12.5	12.5	15	195	16	4⑯	—	㉚	㉙	3½
	V8-305/H	15	15	15	195	16	4	—	㉚	㉙	3½
	V8-305 E.F.I./7	15	15	15	195	16	4	—	㉚	㉙	3½
MALIBU & MONTE CARLO											
1977	6-250/D	15	17	15	195	22	4	3	—	⑤	4
	V8-305/U	17½	18½	15	195	22	4	—	—	⑤	4
	V8-350/L	17½	18½	15	195	22	4	—	—	⑤	4
1978	V6-200/M	15	17	15	195	17.5	4	3	3	⑪	3¼
	V6-231/A	15	17	15	195	17.5	4	3	3	⑪	3¼
	V8-305/U	18	20	15	195	17.5	4	—	3	⑪	3¼
	V8-350/L	18	20	15	195	17.5	4	—	—	⑪	3¼
1979	V6-200/M	18.5	18.5	15	195	18.1	4	3	—	⑪	3¼
	V6-231/A	15.5	15.5	15	195	18.1	4	—	—	⑪	3¼
	V8-267/J	21	21	15	195	18.1	4	—	3	⑪	3¼
	V8-305/G	19	19	15	195	18.1	4	—	3	⑪	③
	V8-350/L	19.5	19.5	15	195	18.1	4	—	—	⑪	③
1980	V6-229/K	18.5	18.5	15	195	18.1	4⑯	3	—	⑳	③
	V6-231/A	15.5	15.5	15	195	18.1	4	—	—	⑳	③
	V8-267/J	21.0	21.0	15	195	18.1	4	—	—	⑳	③
	V8-305/H	19.0	19.0	15	195	18.1	4	—	3	⑳	③
1981	V6-229/K	18½	18½	15	195	18.1	4⑯	3½	—	⑪	③
	V6-231/A	15½	15½	15	195	18.1	4	—	—	⑪	③
	V8-267/J	21	21	15	195	18.1	4	—	—	⑪	③
	V8-305/H	19	19	15	195	18.1	4	—	3½	⑪	③
1982	V6-229/K	18½	18½	15	195	18.1	4⑯	—	—	⑪	③
	V6-231/A	15½	15½	15	195	18.1	4⑯	—	—	⑪	③

Continued

COOLING SYSTEM & CAPACITY DATA—Continued

Year	Model or Engine/V.I.N.	Cooling Capacity, Qts. Less A/C	With A/C	Radiator Cap Relief Pressure, Lbs.	Thermo. Opening Temp.	Fuel Tank Gals.	Engine Oil Refill Qts. ①	3 Speed Pints	4 & 5 Speed Pints	Auto. Trans. Qts. ②	Rear Axle Oil Pints
MALIBU & MONTE CARLO—Continued											
	V8-267/J	21	21	15	195	18.1	4	—	—	(11)	(3)
	V8-305/H	19	19	15	195	18.1	4	—	—	(11)	(3)
1983	V6-229/9	18½	18½	15	195	18.1	4(16)	—	—	(11)	3½
	V6-231/A	15½	15½	15	195	18.1	4(16)	—	—	(11)	3½
	V6-262/V	13.4	13.4	15	195	19.8	6(12)	—	—	(11)	3½
	V8-305/H	19	19	15	195	18.1	4	—	—	(11)	3½
	V8-350/N(18)	18.3	18.4	15	195	19.8	7(12)	—	—	(11)	3½
1984	V6-229/9	14¼	14¼	15	195	25(15)	4(16)	—	—	(31)	(3)
	V6-231/A	11¾	11¾	15	195	25(15)	4(16)	—	—	(31)	(3)
	V8-305/H	(17)	(17)	15	195	25(15)	4	—	—	(31)	(3)
	V8-350/N(18)	18.3	18.3	15	195	27(15)	7(12)	—	—	(31)	(3)
CHEVY NOVA											
1977	6-250/D	14	15	15	195	21	4	3	—	(9)	(10)
	V8-305/U	17	18	15	195	21	4	3	—	(9)	(10)
	V8-350/L	17	18	15	195	21	4	—	3	(9)	(10)
1978–79	6-250/D	14	15	15	195	21	4	3	—	(11)	(10)
	V8-305(21)	16	17	15	195	21	4	—	3	(11)	(10)
	V8-350/L	16	17	15	195	21	4	—	—	(11)	(10)
CHEVROLET											
1977	6-250/D	15	16	15	195	21(15)	—	—	—	4(8)	(10)
	V8-305/U	18	20	15	195	21(15)	4	—	—	4(8)	(10)
	V8-350/L	18	20	15	195	21(15)	4	—	—	4(8)	(10)
1978–79	6-250/D	14	15	15	195	21(15)	4	—	—	(11)	(10)
	V8-305(21)	16½(13)	17½	15	195	21(15)	4	—	—	(11)	(10)
	V8-350/L	16½(13)	17½	15	195	21(15)	4	—	—	(11)	(10)
1980	V6-229/K	14.25	14.25	15	195	25(15)	4(16)	—	—	(20)	(3)
	V6-231/A	11.75	11.75	15	195	25(15)	4	—	—	(20)	(3)
	V8-267/J	(17)	(17)	15	195	25(15)	4	—	—	(20)	(3)
	V8-305/H	15.5	15.5	15	195	25(15)	4	—	—	(20)	(3)
	V8-350/L	16.25	16.25	15	195	25(15)	4	—	—	(20)	(3)
	V8-350/N(18)	18.3	18	15	195	25(15)	7(4)	—	—	(20)	(3)
1981	V6-229/K	14¼	14¼	15	195	25(15)	4(16)	—	—	(11)	(3)
	V6-231/A	11¾	11¾	15	195	25(15)	4(16)	—	—	(11)	(3)
	V8-267/J	(17)	(17)	15	195	25(15)	4	—	—	(11)	(3)
	V8-305/H	15½	15½	15	195	25(15)	4	—	—	(11)	(3)
	V8-350/N(18)	18.3	18	15	195	25(15)	7(4)	—	—	(11)	(3)
1982	V6-229/K	14¼	14¼	15	195	25(15)	4(16)	—	—	(11)	(3)
	V6-231/A	11¾	11¾	15	195	25(15)	4(16)	—	—	(11)	(3)
	V8-267/J	(17)	(17)	15	195	25(15)	4	—	—	(11)	(3)
	V8-305/H	15½	15½	15	195	25(15)	4	—	—	(11)	(3)
	V8-350/N(18)	18.3	18.3	15	195	27(15)	7(12)	—	—	(11)	(3)
1983	V6-229/K	14¼	14¼	15	195	25(15)	4(16)	—	—	(31)	(3)
	V6-231/A	11¾	11¾	15	195	25(15)	4(16)	—	—	(31)	(3)
	V8-305/H	15½	15½	15	195	25(15)	4	—	—	(31)	(3)
	V8-350/N(18)	18.3	18.3	15	195	27(15)	7(12)	—	—	(31)	(3)
1984	V6-229/K	18½	18½	15	195	18.1	4(16)	—	—	(31)	(3)
	V6-231/A	15½	15½	15	195	18.1	4(16)	—	—	(31)	(3)
	V8-305/H	19	19	15	195	18.1	4	—	—	(31)	(3)

Continued

COOLING SYSTEM & CAPACITY DATA—Continued

Year	Model or Engine/V.I.N.	Cooling Capacity, Qts.		Radiator Cap Relief Pressure, Lbs.	Thermo. Opening Temp.	Fuel Tank Gals.	Engine Oil Refill Qts. ①	Transmission Oil			Rear Axle Oil Pints
		Less A/C	With A/C					3 Speed Pints	4 & 5 Speed Pints	Auto. Trans. Qts. ②	

CORVETTE

Year	Model or Engine/V.I.N.	Less A/C	With A/C	Radiator Cap Relief Pressure, Lbs.	Thermo. Opening Temp.	Fuel Tank Gals.	Engine Oil Refill Qts. ①	3 Speed Pints	4 & 5 Speed Pints	Auto. Trans. Qts. ②	Rear Axle Oil Pints
1977	V8-350㉒	21	21	15	195	17	4	—	3	⑥	3¾
1978	V8-350㉓	21	21	15	195	23.7	4	—	3	10	3¾
1979	V8-350㉔	21	21⑭	15	195	24	4	—	3	⑦	3¾
1980	V8-305/H	17½	18½	15	195	20	3¼	—	—	⑦	3¾
	V8-350㉕	17½	18½	15	195	20	3¼	—	3½	⑦	3¾
1981	V8-350/6	21	22	15	195	23.7	4	—	3.4	4⑧	3¾
1982	V8-350/6	21	21	15	195	23.7	4	—	3	10	4
1984	V8-350/8	14.5	14.5	15	195	20	4	—	⑲	10	4

①—Add one quart with filter change.
②—Approximate. Make final check with dipstick.
③—7½" ring gear, 3½ pts.; 8½" ring gear, 4¼ pts.; 8¾" ring gear, 5.4 pts.
④—Includes filter. Use recommended diesel engine oil, designated SF/CC, SF/CD or SE/CC.
⑤—THM 200, 250 & 350 total capacity 10 qts. THM 400 total capacity 11 qts.
⑥—THM 350, 10 qts.; THM 400, 11 qts.
⑦—Oil pan only, 3 qts. Total capacity, 10 qts.
⑧—Oil pan only.
⑨—Refill capacities: THM 200, 8¼ qts. THM 350, 6¾ qts.
⑩—3¼ pts. for 7½" ring gear. 4 pts. for 8½" and 8¾" ring gears.
⑪—THM 200 oil pan only, 3½ qts. Total capacity, 5 qts., CBC 350 oil pan only, 3 qts. Total capacity, 10 qts.
⑫—Includes filter. Use recommended diesel engine oil, designated SF/CC or SF/CD.
⑬—With heavy duty cooling system, add 1 qt.
⑭—With auto. trans., add 1 qt.
⑮—Sta. Wag., 22 gals.
⑯—With or without filter change.
⑰—Exc. Sta. Wag. Standard cooling, 16.75 qts.; Sta. Wag. with standard cooling, 15.5 qts.
⑱—Diesel.
⑲—4 spd., 2 pts.; over drive, 4 pts.
⑳—THM 200, oil pan only 3½ qts., total capacity 5 qts. THM 250, oil pan 4 qts., total capacity 10¾ qts. THM 350, oil pan only 3 qts., total capacity 10 qts.
㉑—1978 V.I.N. code is V, 1979 V.I.N. code is G.
㉒—1977 V.I.N. code is L or X (high performance).
㉓—1978 V.I.N. code is L or H (high performance).
㉔—1979 V.I.N. code is 8 or 4 (high performance).
㉕—1980 V.I.N. code is 8 or 6 (high performance).
㉖—Refer to Pontiac chapter for service procedures.
㉗—Oil pan only, 3½ qts.; total capacity, 5 qts.
㉘—T.H.M. 200c, oil pan only, 3½ qts.; total capacity 5 qts. T.H.M. 700-R4, oil pan only, 4.95 qts.; total capacity, 11½ qts.
㉙—Oil pan only, 4.95 qts.; total capacity, 11½ qts.
㉚—4 spd. trans., 4.3 pts.; 5 spd. trans., 5.3 pts.
㉛—T.H.M. 200C, oil pan only 4½ qts.; total capacity, 10½ qts.; T.H.M. 200-4R, oil pan only, 3.48 qts.; total capacity, 11.05 qts. T.H.M. 250C & 350C, oil pan only, 3.15 qts.; total capacity, 10 qts. T.H.M. 700-R4, oil pan only, 4.95 qts.; total capacity, 11½ qts.

Electrical Section

STARTER, REPLACE

NOTE: If shims are used between starter and engine block, they should be placed in their original location during installation. If starter is noisy during cranking, remove one .015 inch double shim or add one .015 single shim to the outer bolt. If starter makes a high pitched whine after firing, add .015 inch double shims until noise ceases.

1. Disconnect battery ground cable.
2. Raise and support vehicle.
3. Remove starter to engine brace and starter heat shields, if equipped.
4. Remove starter mounting bolts and lower starter. Note position of shims, if used.
5. Disconnect solenoid wires and the battery ground cable.
6. Remove starter from vehicle.
7. Reverse procedure to install.

IGNITION LOCK, REPLACE

1979–84

1. Remove steering wheel as described under Horn Sounder and Steering Wheel.
2. Remove turn signal switch as described under Turn Signal Switch, Replace, then remove buzzer switch.
3. Place ignition switch in "Run" position, then remove lock cylinder retaining screw and lock cylinder.
4. To install, rotate lock cylinder to stop while holding housing, Fig. 1. Align cylinder key with keyway in housing, then push lock cylinder assembly into housing until fully seated.
5. Install lock cylinder retaining screw. Torque screw to 35 in. lbs. for standard columns. On adjustable columns, torque retaining screw to 35 in. lbs.
6. Install buzzer switch, turn signal switch and steering wheel.

1977–78

1. Follow the procedure to remove the turn signal switch as described further on.
2. The lock cylinder should be removed in the "Run" position only.

NOTE: On all models except Corvette, do not remove buzzer switch since damage to the lock cylinder will result.

3. Place a thin tool (small screwdriver or knife blade) into the slot, Fig. 2, next to the switch mounting screw boss (right hand slot) and depress spring latch at bottom of slot which releases lock. Remove lock.

IGNITION SWITCH, REPLACE

1977–84

The ignition switch is mounted on top of the mast jacket inside the brake pedal support and is actuated by a rod and rack assembly.
1. Disconnect battery cable.
2. Disconnect and lower steering column.

NOTE: It may be necessary, on some models, to remove the upper column mounting bracket if it hinders servicing of switch.

CAUTION: Use extreme care when lowering steering column to prevent damage to column assembly. Only lower steering column a sufficient distance to perform ignition switch service.

3. Rotate ignition lock to "Off" unlocked position.
4. If lock cylinder has been removed, pull switch actuator rod up to stop, then push rod down to second detent to place switch in "Off" unlocked position, Fig. 3.
5. Remove column mounted dimmer switch, if equipped, then remove switch retaining screws and switch.
6. Reverse procedure to install, noting the following:
   a. Place gear shift lever in neutral.
   b. Place lock cylinder and switch in "Off" unlocked position, Fig. 3.
   c. Fit actuator rod into hole in switch slider and secure switch with retaining screws, ensuring switch does not move out of detent.
   d. Install and adjust dimmer switch, if removed, as outlined in "Dimmer Switch, Replace."
   e. Torque retaining screws to 35 inch lbs., then check switch operation.

LIGHT SWITCH, REPLACE

1978–83 Malibu & 1978–84 Monte Carlo

1. Disconnect battery ground cable.
2. Remove instrument panel bezel.
3. Pull switch knob to "On" position.
4. Remove three screws attaching windshield wiper/light switch mounting plate to cluster and pull assembly rearward.
5. Depress shaft retainer button on switch and pull knob and shaft assembly from switch, Fig. 4.
6. Remove ferrule nut and switch assembly from mounting plate.
7. Reverse procedure to install.

1978–82 Corvette

1. Disconnect battery ground cable.
2. Remove left air distribution duct.
3. Remove instrument cluster to instrument panel attaching screws and pull cluster rearward.
4. Disconnect speedometer cable and electrical connectors and remove cluster.
5. Remove two instrument panel to left door pillar attaching screws and pull left side of instrument panel slightly rearward.
6. Pull switch knob to "On" position, depress release button on switch and remove shaft and knob assembly, Fig. 4. Remove bezel nut securing switch to instrument panel.
7. Disconnect vacuum hoses from switch and the electrical connector.
8. Remove light switch from vehicle.
9. Reverse procedure to install.

1984 Corvette

1. Disconnect battery ground cable.

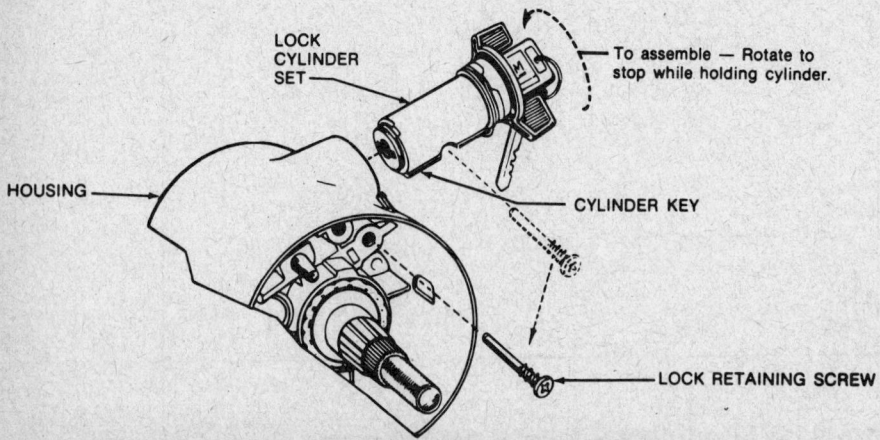

Fig. 1   Ignition lock installation. 1979–84

Fig. 2   Ignition lock removal. 1977–78

LOCK CYLINDER SET

To assemble — Rotate to stop while holding cylinder.

HOUSING

CYLINDER KEY

LOCK RETAINING SCREW

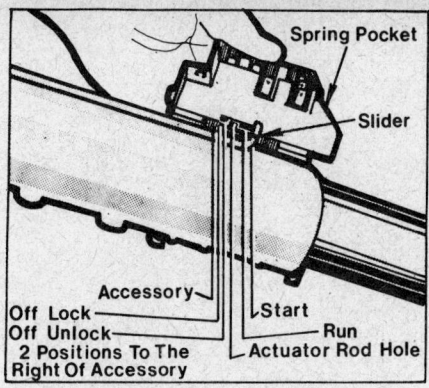

Fig. 3 Ignition switch

2. Remove hush panel from under left side of instrument panel.
3. Pull switch knob to "On" position, reach up under dash and depress release button on switch, and remove shaft and knob assembly, Fig. 4.
4. Remove bezel nut securing switch to instrument panel and lower switch.
5. Disconnect electrical connectors and remove switch.
6. Reverse procedure to install.

1977–84 Chevrolet

1. Disconnect battery ground cable.
2. Pull switch knob to "On" position and reach up under instrument panel and depress switch shaft retainer, then pull knob and shaft assembly from switch, Fig. 4.
3. Remove windshield wiper switch.
4. Remove light switch ferrule nut and remove switch from panel.
5. Disconnect electrical connector from switch and remove switch from vehicle.
6. Reverse procedure to install.

1977 Chevelle & Monte Carlo

1. Disconnect battery ground cable.
2. Remove instrument panel pad.
3. Remove left radio speaker to one side.
4. Pull headlamp control knob to "ON" position and while standing outside vehicle on left side, reach in and behind instrument panel and depress switch shaft retainer and pull knob and shaft assembly out, Fig. 4.
5. Remove ferrule nut and switch from panel.

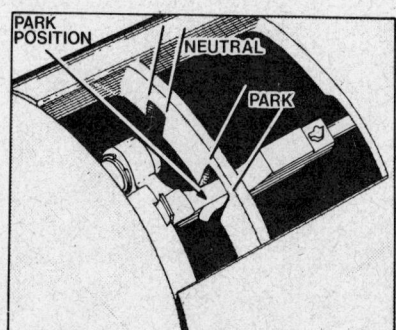

Fig. 5 Mechanical neutral start system, shown in park position. 1977–84 Chevrolet, 1978–83 Malibu & 1978–84 Monte Carlo

1977 Corvette

1. Disconnect battery cable.
2. Remove screws securing mast jacket trim covers and remove covers.
3. Remove left side console forward trim panel.
4. Lower steering column.
5. Remove screws securing left instrument panel to door opening, top of dash and left side of center instrument panel.
6. Pull cluster down and tip forward for access.
7. Pull switch knob to "On" position, depress release button on switch and remove shaft and knob assembly, Fig. 4. Remove bezel nut securing switch to instrument panel.
8. Disconnect vacuum hoses from switch, tagging them for assembly. Pry the connector from the switch and remove the switch.

1977–81 Camaro

1. Disconnect battery ground cable.
2. Remove steering column lower cover.
3. Pull switch knob to "On" position, depress release button on switch and remove shaft and knob assembly, Fig. 4.
4. Remove nut securing switch to carrier.
5. Remove cluster carrier screws and tilt right side of cluster out.
6. Unplug connector and remove switch.

1982–84 Camaro
Exc. 1984 Berlinetta

1. Disconnect battery ground cable.
2. Remove 4 screws securing defroster ducts to instrument panel pad and screws under lip of pad, then remove pad. On models with A/C, remove instrument cluster.
3. Pull switch knob to "On" position, depress release button on switch, and remove shaft and knob assembly, Fig. 4.
4. Remove bezel nut securing switch, disconnect electrical connectors and remove switch.
5. Reverse procedure to install.

1977–79 Nova

1. Disconnect battery ground cable.
2. Pull switch knob to "ON" position.
3. Reach up under instrument panel and depress switch shaft retainer, then remove knob and shaft assembly, Fig. 4.
4. Remove ferrule nut and switch from panel.
5. Disconnect multi-contact connector from light switch.
6. Reverse procedure to install.

STOP LIGHT SWITCH, REPLACE

1977–84 Except Corvette

NOTE: On 1982–84 Camaro, remove hush panel.

1. Disconnect wiring connector at switch.
2. Remove retaining nut, if so equipped, and unscrew switch from bracket.
3. To install: Depress brake pedal and push new switch into clip until shoulder bottoms out.
4. Plug connector onto switch and check operation. Electrical contact should be made when pedal is depressed 3/8 to 5/8 from fully released position.

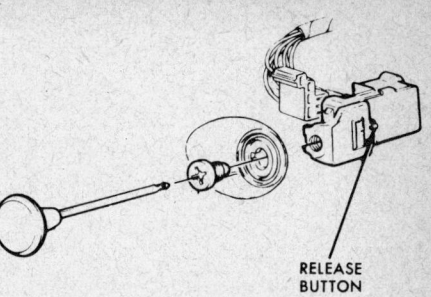

Fig. 4 Headlamp switch knob removal

1977–82 Corvette

1. Disconnect wiring connector at switch.
2. Remove retaining nut and unscrew switch from bracket.
3. Upon installation, check for proper operation. Electrical contact should be made when pedal is depressed 1/4 to 5/8. Switch bracket has a slotted screw hole for adjustment.

1984 Corvette

1. Remove hush panel from under left side of instrument panel.
2. Disconnect electrical connectors from switch and pull switch out of retaining clip on brake pedal support.
3. Depress brake pedal and push replacement switch into retainer until switch shoulder is bottomed against bracket.
4. Adjust switch by pulling brake pedal back against stop.
5. Ensure switch has continuity when pedal is depressed .53 inch from normal rest position, and pedal fully returns to rest position.
6. Reconnect electrical connectors and install hush panel.

CLUTCH START SWITCH, REPLACE

1982–84 Camaro

1. Disconnect wire connector at switch.
2. Remove retaining nut, if so equipped and unscrew switch from bracket.
3. To install: depress clutch pedal, then insert and push switch into clip until shoulder bottoms out.
4. Plug connector on switch and check for proper operation.

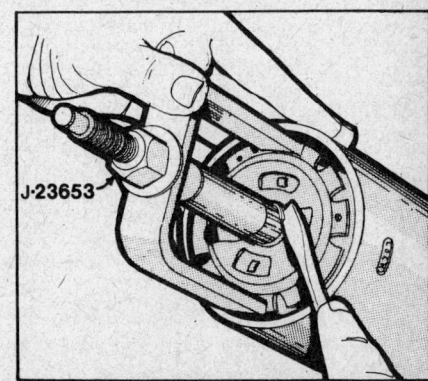

Fig. 6 Lock plate retaining ring removal

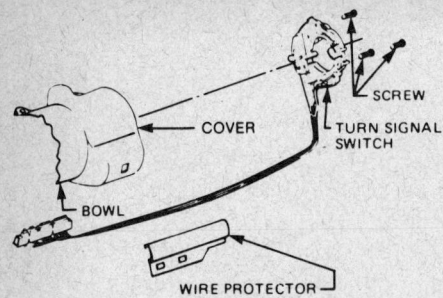

Fig. 7 Turn signal switch assembly

1977–82 Corvette

1. Disconnect wiring connector from switch.
2. Remove retainer from pins or link on clutch pedal arm.
3. Remove retaining screw and switch.

1984 Corvette

1. Disconnect battery ground cable and set parking brake.
2. Remove retaining screw and switch from clutch pedal bracket, rotate switch slightly, and pull switch actuating lever from hole in pedal arm.
3. Disconnect electrical connector and remove switch.
4. Position replacement switch with actuating lever installed in hole in pedal arm, then secure switch to bracket with retaining screw.
5. Connect electrical connector to switch and adjust by fully depressing clutch pedal.

NOTE: If readjustment is necessary, depress detent on switch adjusting block and slide block fully forward on switch rod. Fully depress clutch pedal to complete adjustment.

Except Corvette & 1982–84 Camaro

1. Disconnect wiring connector from switch.
2. Compress switch actuating shaft retainer and remove shaft with switch attached from switch bracket.

NEUTRAL SAFETY SWITCH, REPLACE

1977–84 Chevrolet; 1978–83 Malibu & 1978–84 Monte Carlo

Actuation of the ignition switch is prevented by a mechanical lockout system, Fig. 5, which prevents the lock cylinder from rotating when the selector lever is out of Park or Neutral. When the selector lever is in Park or Neutral, the slots in the bowl plate and the finger on the actuator rod align allowing the finger to pass through the bowl plate in turn actuating the ignition switch, Fig. 5. If the selector lever is in any position other than Park or Neutral, the finger contacts the bowl plate when the lock cylinder is rotated, thereby preventing full travel of the lock cylinder.

1977 Malibu & Monte Carlo, 1977–79 Nova & 1977–81 Camaro

1. Disconnect wiring connector at switch

terminals.
2. Unfasten and remove switch from mast jacket.
3. To install: position shift lever against "Park" gate on models with floor shift, or "Neutral" gate on models with column shift, by rotating lower lever counterclockwise as viewed from drivers seat.
4. Assemble switch to column by inserting actuating tang in shifter tube slot.
5. Tighten screws, connect wiring connector and move selector lever out of "Park" on models with floor shift or "Neutral" on models with column shift to shear pin which is part of new switch.

1977–82 Corvette

1. Disconnect shift control lever arm from transmission control rod.
2. Remove shift control knob.
3. Remove trim plate.
4. Remove control assembly from seal and disconnect switch wiring.
5. Remove switch from control assembly.
6. To install, position gearshift in Drive position, align hole in contact support with hole in switch and insert a pin (3/32") to hold support in place.
7. Place contact support drive slot over drive tang and tighten switch mounting screws.
8. Connect wiring harness to switch wiring.
9. Install trim plate control knob and connect shift lever arm to transmission control rod.

1982–84 Camaro & 1984 Corvette

1. Remove floor console cover, then disconnect electrical connectors from switch.
2. Place shift lever in "Neutral" position of detent plate, then remove switch attaching screws and switch.
3. To install, ensure that the shift lever is in "Neutral", then position switch on shift lever making sure pin on shaft is in slot of switch.
4. Install attaching screws and torque to 16 inch lbs.
5. Move shift lever out of "Neutral" to shear pin which is part of new switch.
6. Reconnect electrical connectors to switch, then apply parking brake and start engine. Check backup lights and seat belt warning system for proper operation and ensure that engine will start only in "Park" or "Neutral".
7. Turn ignition off and install floor console.

TURN SIGNAL SWITCH, REPLACE

1. Disconnect battery cable, then remove steering wheel and column to instrument panel trim cover.
2. On models with telescoping column, remove bumper spacer and snap ring retainer. On all other models, remove cover from lockplate.
3. Using a suitable tool, compress lock plate (horn contact carrier on tilt models) and remove snap ring ("C" ring on tilt models), Fig. 6.

NOTE: On 1977–82 Corvette models with tilt-telescopic column, place a 5/16 inch nut under each leg of puller.

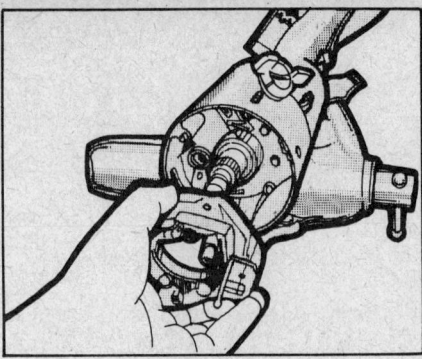

Fig. 8 Turn signal switch removal

4. Remove lock plate, cancelling cam, upper bearing preload spring, thrust washer and signal lever.
5. Remove turn signal lever or actuating arm screw, if equipped, or on models with column mounted wiper switch, pull lever straight out of detent. Depress hazard warning button, then unscrew button.
6. Pull connector from bracket and wrap upper part of connector with tape to prevent snagging the wires during removal. On Tilt models, position shifter housing in "Low" position. Remove harness cover.
7. Remove retaining screws and remove switch, Figs. 7 and 8.
8. Reverse procedure to install.

COLUMN-MOUNTED DIMMER SWITCH, REPLACE

1. Disconnect battery ground cable.
2. Remove instrument panel lower trim and on models with A/C, remove A/C duct extension at column.
3. Disconnect shift indicator from column and remove toe-plate cover screws.
4. Remove two nuts from instrument panel support bracket studs and lower steering column, resting steering wheel on front seat.
5. Remove dimmer switch retaining screws and the switch. Tape actuator rod to column and separate switch from rod.
6. Reverse procedure to install. To adjust switch, depress dimmer switch slightly and install a 3/32 inch twist drill to lock the switch to the body, Fig. 9. Force switch upward to remove lash between switch and pivot. Torque switch retaining screw to 35 inch lbs. and remove tape from actuator rod. Remove twist drill and check for proper operation.

HORN SOUNDER & STEERING WHEEL, REPLACE

NOTE: Mark position of steering wheel in relation to shaft prior to removal to ensure correct installation.

1977–84 Cushioned Rim Wheel

1. Disconnect battery ground cable.
2. Pry off horn button cap.

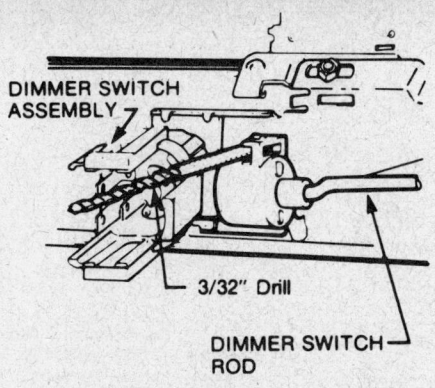

Fig. 9 Column mounted dimmer switch installation

3. Remove three spacer screws, spacer, plate and belleville spring.
4. Remove steering wheel nut, washer and snap ring.
5. Using a suitable puller, remove steering wheel.
6. Reverse procedure to install.

1977–83 Standard Wheel

1. Disconnect battery ground cable.
2. Remove attaching screws on underside of the steering wheel, Fig. 10.
3. Lift steering wheel shroud and pull horn wires from cancelling cam tower.
4. Remove steering wheel nut, washer and snap ring.
5. Using a suitable puller, remove steering wheel.
6. Reverse procedure to install.

1977–82 Corvette

1. Disconnect battery ground cable.
2. Remove horn button cap, 3 screws securing upper horn contact, and upper contact.
3. Remove shim, if used, then the screw securing the center star screw and the star screw and lever.
4. Remove snap ring and nut from shaft.
5. Using a suitable puller, remove steering wheel assembly.
6. To disassemble the steering wheel assembly, remove three screws securing wheel

and separate, then remove four screws retaining extension to wheel and separate.
7. Reverse procedure to install.

1984 Corvette

1. Disconnect battery ground cable.
2. Pry up horn button cap, disconnect contact from steering wheel, and remove cap.
3. Remove screws securing center star screw, star screw, and adjusting lever.
4. Remove snap ring and nut from steering shaft.
5. Remove steering wheel using a suitable puller.
6. Reverse procedure to install.

INSTRUMENT CLUSTER, REPLACE

NOTE: On some 1980 models, a yellow flag with the word "emissions" will rotate into the odometer window at 30,000 mile intervals indicating either a catalyst or oxygen sensor change is required. After performing the required maintenance, the emissions flag can be reset after removing the instrument cluster lens. Using a pointed tool inserted at an angle to engage flag wheel detents, rotate flag wheel downward. When flag wheel is reset, the alignment mark will be in center of odometer window.

1978–81 Malibu Standard Cluster

1. Disconnect battery ground cable.
2. Remove clock set stem knob, if equipped.
3. Remove instrument bezel retaining screws, Fig. 11.
4. Pull bezel from panel slightly and disconnect rear defogger switch, if equipped.
5. Remove bezel, Fig. 11.
6. Remove two screws at transmission selector indicator and lower indicator assembly to disconnect cable.
7. Remove three screws at windshield wiper/light switch mounting plate and pull assembly rearward for access to lower left

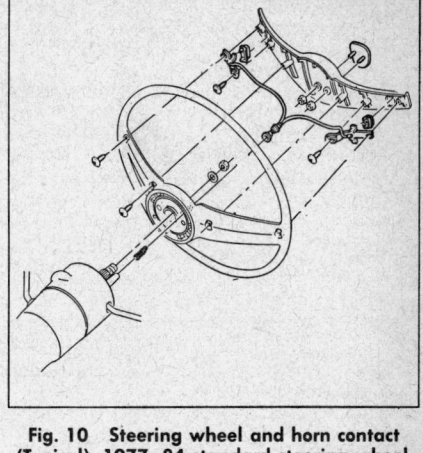

Fig. 10 Steering wheel and horn contact (Typical). 1977–84 standard steering wheel

cluster attaching bolt and nut.
8. Remove nuts attaching cluster to instrument panel.
9. Pull cluster rearward and disconnect the speedometer cable and all wiring and cables.
10. Remove cluster from vehicle, Fig. 12.
11. Reverse procedure to install.

1978–81 Malibu Optional Cluster & 1978–84 Monte Carlo & 1982–83 Malibu

1. Disconnect battery ground cable.
2. Remove radio knobs and clock set stem knob.
3. Remove instrument bezel retaining screws, Fig. 11.
4. Pull bezel rearward slightly and disconnect the rear defogger switch and remote control mirror control, if equipped.
5. Remove bezel, Fig. 11.
6. Remove speedometer retaining screws, pull speedometer from cluster slightly, disconnect speedometer cable and remove speedometer.
7. Remove fuel gauge or tachometer retaining screws, disconnect electrical connectors and remove fuel gauge or tachometer.
8. Remove clock or voltmeter retaining screws, disconnect electrical connectors and remove clock or voltmeter.
9. Disconnect transmission shift indicator cable from steering column.
10. Disconnect all wiring connectors and remove cluster case, Fig. 12.
11. Reverse procedure to install.

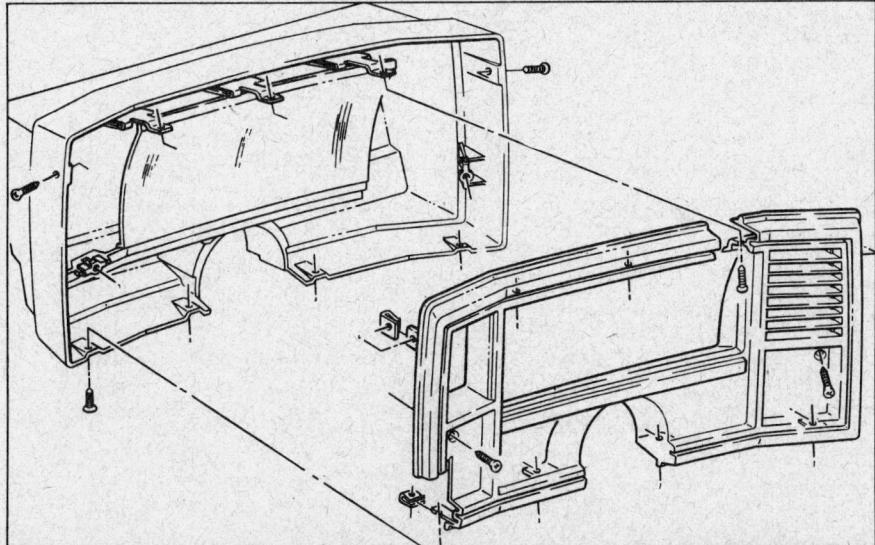

Fig. 11 Instrument cluster bezel removal (Typical). 1978–83 Malibu & 1978–84 Monte Carlo

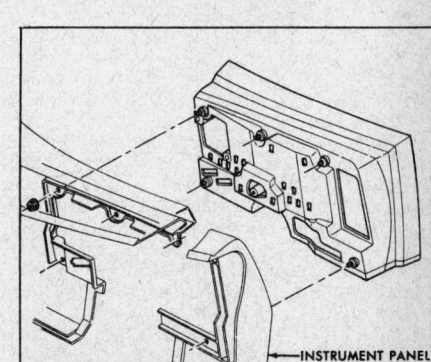

Fig. 12 Instrument cluster removal (Typical). 1978–83 Malibu & 1978–84 Monte Carlo

1977–84 Chevrolet

1. Disconnect battery ground cable.
2. Remove four steering column lower cover screws and the cover.
3. If equipped with automatic transmission, disconnect shift indicator cable from steering column.
4. Remove two steering column to instrument panel screws and lower steering column.

CAUTION: Use extreme care when lowering steering to prevent damage to column assembly.

5. Remove six screws and the three snap-in fasteners from perimeter of instrument cluster lens, Fig. 13.
6. Remove two screws from upper surface of grey sheet metal trim plate.
7. Remove two stud nuts from lower corner of cluster.
8. Disconnect speedometer cable and pull cluster from instrument panel.
9. Disconnect electrical connectors from cluster and remove from vehicle.
10. Reverse procedure to install.

1977 Chevelle & Monte Carlo

1. Disconnect battery ground cable.
2. Remove radio knobs and clock stem set knob, if equipped.
3. Remove instrument bezel retaining screws, Figs. 14 and 15.
4. Pull bezel out to disconnect tail gate release or rear defogger switch, if equipped.
5. Remove instrument bezel.
6. Reverse procedure to install.

1982–84 Camaro
Exc. 1984 Berlinetta

1. Disconnect battery ground cable.
2. Remove instrument cluster bezel, Fig. 16.
3. Remove 6 cluster retaining screws, then pull cluster back and disconnect speedometer cable and electrical connectors.
4. Reverse procedure to install.

1977–81 Camaro

1. Disconnect battery ground cable.
2. Remove 6 screws securing trim cover beneath steering column. Two of these screws are located above the ash tray.
3. Remove headlamp switch retaining nut.
4. From behind panel, disconnect cigar lighter and unscrew retainer. Note grounding ring.
5. From under lower edge of cluster, remove screw on either side of column, Fig. 16A.
6. Remove 4 screws visible on front of carrier.
7. Remove screw retaining ground wire for wiper switch. Screw is fastened under top left corner of switch.
8. Carefully tilt carrier out of access to the connectors on headlamp and wiper switches.
9. Remove lens screws then cluster screws.
10. Disconnect shift indicator from steering column.
11. Disconnect speedometer cable and tilt cluster forward and remove remaining connectors.
12. Lift cluster out.
13. Reverse procedure to install.

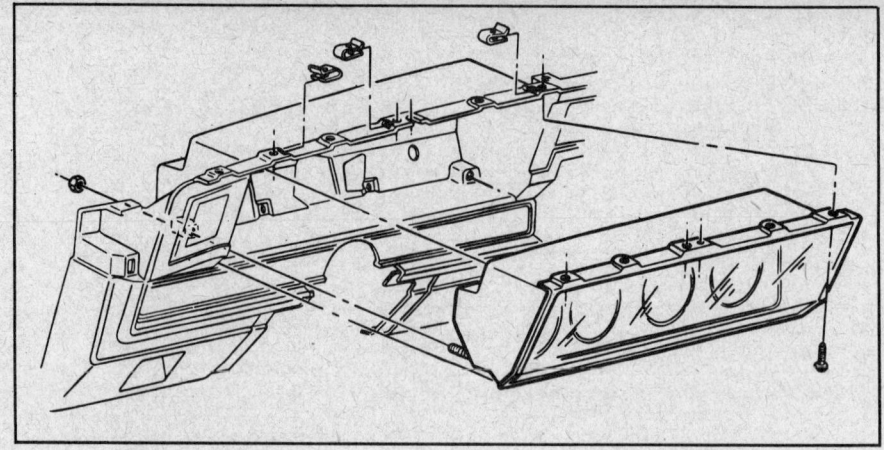

Fig. 13 Instrument cluster, exploded view. 1977–84 Chevrolet full size

1977–79 Nova

1. Disconnect battery ground cable.
2. Lower steering column and apply protective covering to mast jacket to protect paint.
3. Remove three screws above front of heater control securing it to instrument cluster, Fig. 17.
4. Remove radio control knobs, washers, bezel nuts and front support at lower edge of cluster. This will allow radio to remain in panel.
5. Remove screws at top, bottom and sides of cluster securing it to panel.
6. Tilt cluster forward and reach behind to disconnect speedometer cable and all other connections and lift instrument panel out of carrier after removing screws.
7. Reverse procedure to install.

1977–82 Corvette

Left Hand Side 1978–82

1. Disconnect battery ground cable.
2. Remove left air distribution duct.
3. Remove lens to bezel attaching screws and the lens.
4. Remove cluster to instrument panel attaching screws.
5. Pull cluster rearward slightly, then disconnect speedometer cable and electrical connectors.
6. Remove cluster from vehicle.
7. Reverse procedure to install.

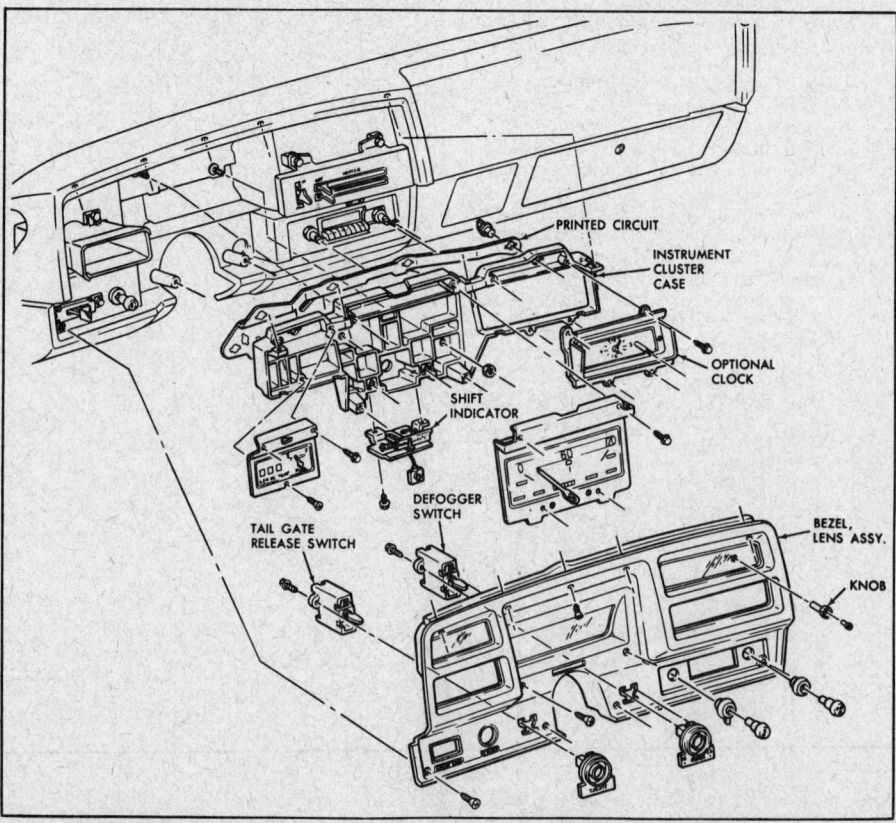

Fig. 14 Instrument cluster, exploded view. 1977 Chevelle w/ standard cluster

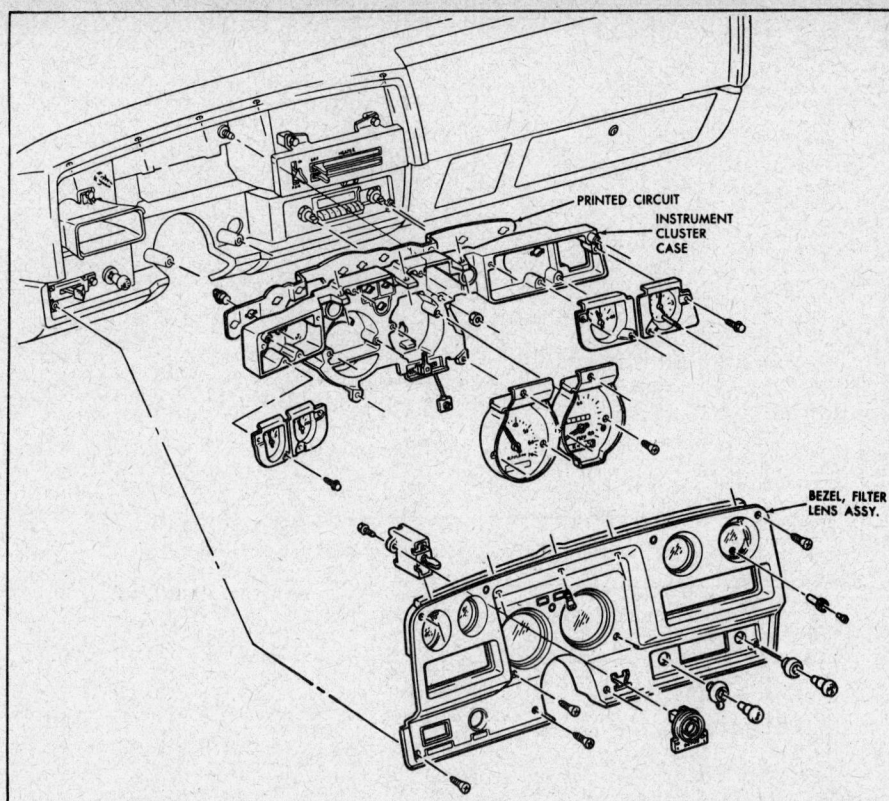

Fig. 15 Instrument cluster, exploded view. 1977 Monte Carlo & 1977 Chevelle with optional cluster

Left Hand Side 1977
1. Disconnect battery ground cable.
2. Lower steering column.
3. Remove screws and washers securing left instrument panel to door opening, top of dash and left side of center instrument panel, Fig. 18.
4. Unclip and remove floor console trim panel.
5. Pull cluster slightly forward to obtain clearance for removal of speedometer cable housing nut, tachometer cable housing nut, headlamp and ignition switch connectors and panel illuminating lamps.
6. Reverse procedure to install.

Center Cluster 1977–82 Models
1. Disconnect battery ground cable.
2. Remove console tunnel side panels.
3. Remove radio knobs.
4. Remove two screws securing console trim plate to instrument cluster, Fig. 18A.
5. Remove rear window defogger switch, if equipped, from console trim plate.
6. Remove five screws from upper perimeter of instrument cluster.
7. Pull instrument cluster outward slightly and disconnect electrical connectors.
8. Remove cluster from vehicle.
9. Reverse procedure to install.

1984 Corvette
1. Disconnect battery ground cable.
2. Remove left hush panel, lower instrument panel pad, and steering column cover.

3. Remove light switch knob and shaft, and bezel nut securing switch
4. Remove nuts securing steering column to instrument panel brace and lower column.
5. Remove cluster bezel retaining screws and bezel.
6. Remove cluster retaining screws and pull cluster away from dash.
7. Release metal retainers securing electrical connectors, disconnect electrical connectors from cluster, and remove cluster assembly.

FRONT WIPER MOTOR, REPLACE

1977–84 Except Corvette

1. Raise hood and remove cowl screen or grille.
2. Disconnect wiring and washer hoses.
3. Reaching through cowl opening, loosen transmission drive link attaching nuts to motor crankarm.
4. Disconnect drive link from motor crankarm.
5. Remove motor attaching screws.
6. Remove motor while guiding crankarm through hole.
7. Reverse procedure to install.

1977–82 Corvette

1. Make sure wiper motor is in "Park" position.
2. Disconnect washer hoses and electrical connectors from assembly.
3. Remove the air intake screen.
4. Remove the nut which retains the crank arm to the motor.
5. Remove the ignition shield and distributor cap to gain access to the motor retaining screws or nuts.

NOTE: *Remove left bank spark plug wires from the cap and mark both cap and wires for aid in reinstallation.*

6. Remove three motor retaining screws or nuts and remove motor.

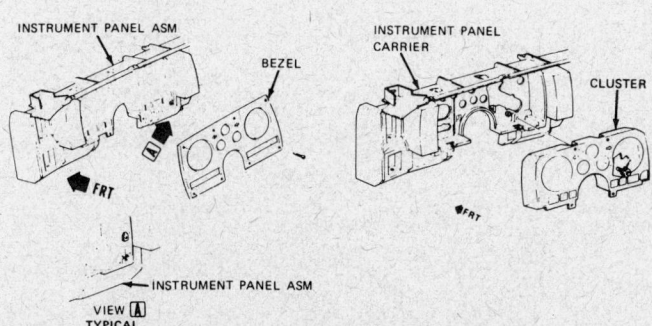

Fig. 16 Instrument cluster, exploded view. 1982–84 Camaro exc. 1984 Berlinetta

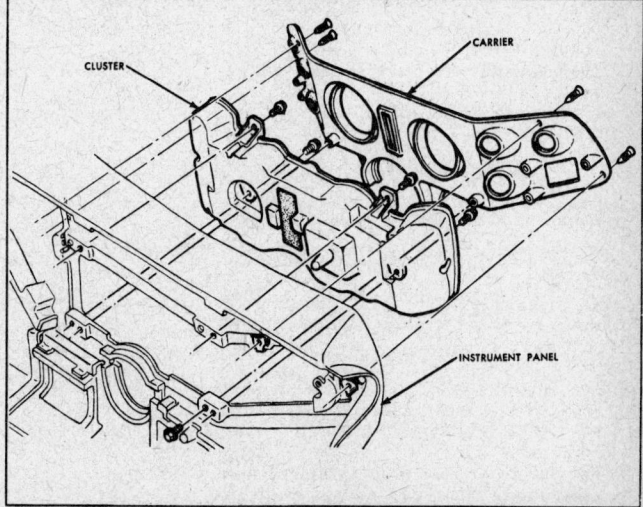

Fig. 16A Instrument cluster, exploded view. 1977–81 Camaro

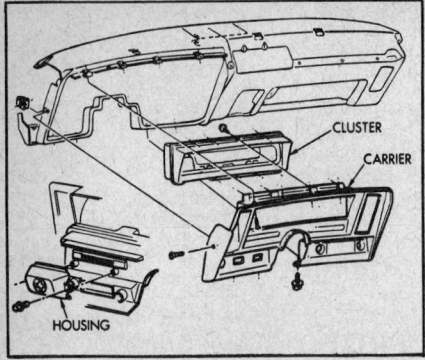

Fig. 17 Instrument cluster (Typical). 1977–79 Nova

CAUTION: Wiper motor must be in the "Park" position prior to installation on the cowl. Do not install a motor that was dropped or hung by the drive link.

1984 Corvette

1. Open hood, then remove wiper arms and air inlet screen.
2. Turn ignition on and operate motor. Stop motor with crank arm pointing to a position between 4 and 5 o'clock (viewed from passenger compartment) by turning ignition off.
3. Disconnect battery ground cable.
4. Disconnect upper electrical connector from wiper motor.
5. Remove motor retaining bolts, and remove motor after disconnecting lower electrical connector and linkage.
6. Reverse procedure to install.

REAR WIPER MOTOR, REPLACE

1982–84 Camaro

1. Remove wiper arm using tool No. J-8966 or equivalent.
2. Remove nut and spacer from wiper motor shaft, then raise lid and remove lift window trim panel.
3. Disconnect wire connectors from motor, then remove rivets securing motor support to trim panel and remove assembly from vehicle.
4. Remove motor attaching screws and motor.
5. Reverse procedure to install.

FRONT WIPER TRANSMISSION, REPLACE

1977–80 W/Rectangular Motor

1. Remove wiper arms and blades.
2. Raise hood and remove cowl vent screen or grille.
3. Disconnect wiring from motor.
4. Loosen, but do not remove, transmission drive link to motor crankarm attaching nuts and disconnect drive link from crankarm.
5. Remove right and left transmission to body attaching screws and guide transmission and linkage through cowl opening.

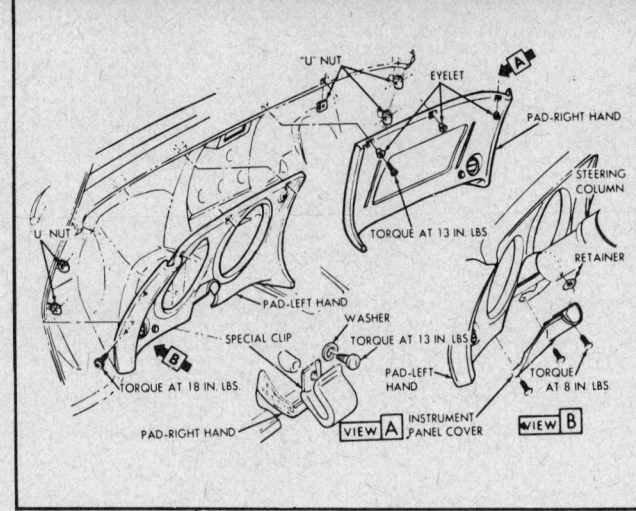

Fig. 18 Instrument panel, exploded view. 1977 Corvette

NOTE: When installing, motor must be in "Park" position.

6. Reverse procedure to install.

1977–84 W/Round Motor

1. Raise hood and remove cowl vent screen.
2. On Chevelle, Monte Carlo, Camaro and 1977–80 Chevrolet models, remove right and left wiper arm and blades.
3. Loosen, do not remove, attaching nuts securing drive link to motor crankarm.
4. Disconnect transmission drive link from motor crankarm.
5. On Chevelle, Monte Carlo, Camaro and 1977–80 Chevrolet models, remove right and left transmission to body screws.
6. Remove transmission and linkage through cowl opening.

NOTE: When installing, motor must be in "Park" position.

7. Reverse procedure to install.

1977–82 Corvette

1. Make sure motor is in "Park" position.
2. Disconnect battery ground cable.
3. Open hood and remove chamber screen.
4. Loosen nuts retaining ball sockets to crankarm and detach drive rod from crankarm.
5. Remove transmission nuts, then lift rod

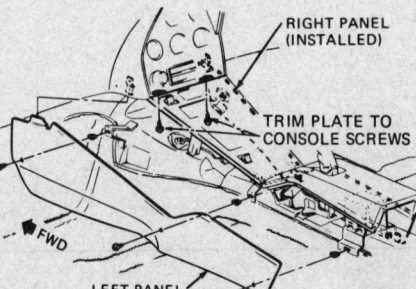

Fig. 18A Center cluster bezel removal. 1977–82 Corvette

assemblies from chamber.
6. Remove transmission linkage from chamber.
7. Reverse procedure to install.

REAR WIPER TRANSMISSION, REPLACE

1982–84 Camaro

1. Remove three mounting grommets from transmission housing cover and cover.
2. Remove drive link retainer, then disengage drive link from cam drive pin and position so that cam retainer is accessible.

NOTE: When reassembling drive link to cam, a new retainer must be used.

3. Remove cam retainer and washer, then cam from shaft.

NOTE: During assembly, if cam does not seat fully when pushed onto drive shaft, rotate cam 180 degrees.

4. Drill out three rivets attaching housing to wiper gearbox, and remove transmission.
5. Reverse procedure to install.

NOTE: A service kit is available for installation of the transmission. The kit includes screw, nuts and washers to replace the rivets.

WINDSHIELD WIPER SWITCH, REPLACE

1978–82 Corvette

1. Disconnect battery ground cable.
2. Remove left air distribution duct.
3. Remove instrument cluster attaching screws and pull cluster rearward.
4. Disconnect speedometer cable and all electrical connectors, then remove cluster.
5. Remove two instrument panel to left door

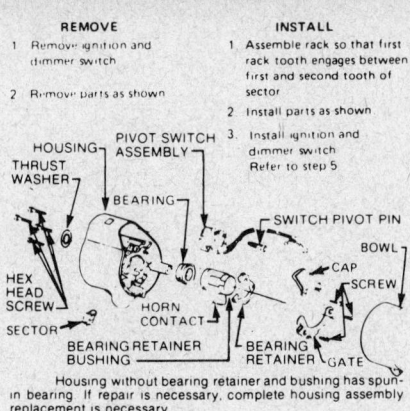

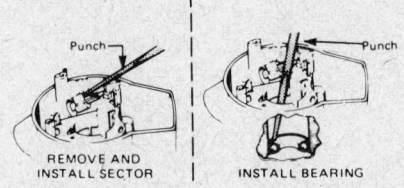

Fig. 19 Column mounted wiper switch removal. 1982–84 w/ standard column

pillar attaching screws and pull left side of instrument panel rearward for access.
6. Remove wiper switch to mounting plate screws, disconnect electrical connector and remove switch.
7. Reverse procedure to install.

1984 Corvette

1. Disconnect battery ground cable.
2. Remove 2 screws securing left armrest, push inward to release armrest from door trim and remove armrest.
3. Remove screws securing accessory trim plate to door panel, including screw behind handle, and remove lock button.
4. Pull accessory plate away from door panel and disconnect electrical connectors to panel switches.
5. Remove wiper switch from trim plate.
6. Reverse procedure to install.

1978–82 Malibu & Monte Carlo

1. Disconnect battery ground cable.
2. Remove instrument panel bezel.
3. Remove screws securing wiper switch mounting plate to cluster and pull assembly rearward.
4. Disconnect electrical connector and remove wiper switch.
5. Reverse procedure to install.

1978–83 Chevrolet

1. Disconnect battery ground cable.
2. Remove screws securing control shroud on instrument panel. (One screw is hidden above headlight switch shaft and one is hidden above cigarette lighter knob.)
3. Lift off shroud and remove remaining screws.
4. Unplug wiper switch and remove.
5. Reverse procedure to install.

1977 Corvette

1. Disconnect battery ground cable.

2. Remove steering wheel, turn signal switch and ignition lock as outlined previously.
3. Remove tilt release lever.
4. Remove three turn signal housing attaching screws, then remove housing while guiding the w/s wiper switch wire connector up through column shroud.
5. Turn housing over, then remove 7/16 in. pivot bolt and lift switch from housing.
6. Reverse procedure to install.

1977–79 Nova

1. Disconnect battery ground cable.
2. Disconnect wire connector from rear of wiper switch.
3. Remove three attaching screws from rear of switch.
4. Lift switch out from rear of instrument panel.
5. Reverse procedure to install.

1977 Chevrolet

1. Disconnect battery ground cable.
2. Pull light switch to "On" position and reach under instrument panel and depress shaft release button, then pull shaft from switch.
3. With a suitable tool, pry out wiper switch assembly and disconnect electrical connector.
4. Remove switch from vehicle.
5. Reverse procedure to install.

1977 Chevelle & Monte Carlo

1. Disconnect battery ground cable.
2. Remove instrument cluster.
3. Pull electric connector off rear of wiper switch.
4. Remove screws from front of switch and lift switch out front of panel.
5. Reverse procedure to install.

1977–81 Camaro

1. Disconnect battery ground cable.
2. Remove trim plate and A/C outlet from below steering column if so equipped.
3. Remove light switch.
4. Remove 6 screws securing instrument carrier. Two of these are behind the cluster on either side of steering column.

NOTE: Cigar lighter grounding ring may have to be removed with lighter housing to gain access to left side of carrier.

---

5. Disconnect wiper switch wiring.
6. Tilting carrier forward, reach behind and remove 3 switch retaining screws and lift out switch.
7. Reverse procedure to install.

1982–84 Camaro, 1983 Malibu, 1983–84 Monte Carlo & 1984 Chevrolet

1. Disconnect battery ground cable and remove turn signal switch as outlined.
2. Remove ignition lock, ignition switch and dimmer switch as outlined.
3. Remove ignition lock housing retaining screws and housing, Figs. 19 and 19A.
4. Remove pivot bolt and wiper switch from lock housing, Fig. 19B.
5. Reverse procedure to install.

Fig. 19A Column mounted wiper switch removal. 1982–84 w/ tilt column

---

RADIO, REPLACE

NOTE: When installing radio, be sure to adjust antenna trimmer for peak reception. Also, be sure to connect speaker before applying power to radio.

1978–83 Malibu & 1978–84 Monte Carlo

1. Disconnect battery ground cable.
2. Remove control knobs from control shafts.
3. Remove trim plate attaching screws and trim plate.
4. Disconnect antenna lead and wire connector from radio.
5. Remove stud nut at right side of bracket attachment.
6. Remove control shaft nuts and washers.
7. Remove instrument panel bracket screws and bracket.
8. Remove radio through opening in instrument panel.
9. Reverse procedure to install.

1977–84 Chevrolet

1. Disconnect battery ground cable.
2. Remove control knobs from control shafts.
3. Remove three radio trim plate attaching screws.
4. Remove two screws and bottom nut attaching radio bracket to instrument panel.
5. Disconnect antenna lead and wire connector from radio.
6. Remove radio with mounting bracket attached from instrument panel.
7. Remove bracket from radio.
8. Reverse procedure to install.

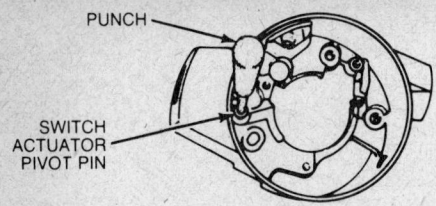

Fig. 19B Wiper switch pivot removal. 1982-84 w/ column mounted wiper switch

1977-82 Corvette

1. Disconnect battery ground cable.
2. Remove control knobs from control shafts.
3. Remove instrument cluster as described under Instrument Cluster, Replace.
4. Remove screw attaching radio mounting bracket to reinforcement on floor pan.
5. Pull radio outward and disconnect antenna lead and wire connector from rear of radio.
6. Remove mounting bracket from radio.
7. Reverse procedure to install.

1984 Corvette

1. Disconnect battery ground cable and remove instrument cluster as outlined.
2. Remove accessory trim plate retaining screws and trim plate.
3. Remove screws securing radio and bracket, and pull radio away from dash.
4. Disconnect electrical connectors and antenna lead, then remove radio.
5. Reverse procedure to install, ensuring A/C center outlet seal is properly positioned.

1977 Chevelle & Monte Carlo

1. Disconnect battery ground cable.
2. On A/C vehicles, remove left lap cooler duct.
3. Pull off radio knobs and bezels.
4. Remove control shaft nuts and washers.
5. Disconnect antenna, speaker and power wires.
6. Remove radio to support bracket stud nut.
7. Push radio forward until shafts clear instrument panel and then lower from car.
8. Reverse procedure to install.

1977-81 Camaro & 1977-79 Nova

1. Disconnect battery ground cable.
2. Pull off radio control knobs and bezels.
3. Remove control shaft nuts and washers.
4. Remove screws or nuts from radio brackets.
5. Push radio forward until shafts clear instrument panel and lower unit enough to remove electrical connections.
6. Disconnect antenna, speaker and power leads and remove radio.
7. Reverse procedure to install.

1982-84 Camaro Exc. 1984 Berlinetta

1. Disconnect battery ground cable.
2. Remove three console bezel and four radio to console attaching screws.
3. Pull radio outward and disconnect electrical connector, then remove radio.
4. Reverse procedure to install.

HEATER MODULE
R&R GLOVE BOX
R&R HEATER AIR DISTRIBUTOR OUTLET
& UPPER LEVEL VENT DUCT
R&R DEFROSTER OUTLET ATTACH.
SCREW
D&C ELECTRICAL HARNESS AT MODULE
D&C PASS. COMPT. CABLES & GROUND
AT MODULE
D&C BLOWER MOTOR & RESISTOR
CONNECTORS
D-R RADIATOR COOLANT
R&R R.H. W/SHLD. WIPER ARM
R&R MODULE LEAF SCREEN & SEAL
D&C HEATER HOSES
R&R MODULE TO COWL SCREWS
TRANSFER PARTS
APPLY NEW STRIP-CAULK TYPE
SEALING MATERIAL

SEAL
PULL OFF

MODULE LEAF SCREEN
R&R SCREWS

BLOWER MOTOR
D&C ELECTRICAL CONNECTORS
R&R MOTOR SCREWS

HEATER CORE
R&R HEATER HOSES
D&C ELECTRICAL CONNECTORS
R&R FRONT MODULE COVER
SCREWS
R&R CORE

APPLY TO TOP AND SIDES ONLY
EXTEND COVERAGE BELOW LOWER
SCREW ON BOTH VERTICAL FLANGES.
*SCREW ATTACHING SEQUENCE
AS FOLLOWS: ①,②, THEN CLOCKWISE
AROUND MODULE.

SECTION SHOWING SCREEN
IN RELATION TO REVEAL MOULDING

Fig. 20 Blower motor & heater core. 1978-83 Malibu & 1978-84 Monte Carlo less A/C

BLOWER MOTOR, REPLACE

1977-83 Malibu, 1977-84 Monte Carlo & Chevrolet & 1978-81 Camaro

1. Disconnect battery ground cable.
2. Disconnect blower motor lead wire. On models with A/C, disconnect cooling tube.
3. Remove blower motor to case attaching screws, then remove blower motor, Figs. 20 through 23.
4. Reverse procedure to install.

1982-84 Camaro

1. Disconnect battery ground cable.
2. Disconnect blower motor and resistor wires.
3. On models equipped with A/C, disconnect cooling tube.
4. Remove blower motor retaining screws and motor/cage assembly from case.
5. While holding blower motor cage, remove cage retaining screw and slide cage from motor shaft.
6. Reverse procedure to install.

1984 Corvette

1. Disconnect battery ground cable.
2. Remove right front wheel housing rear panel, and push housing aside.
3. Remove motor cooling tube and screws securing relay, and set relay aside.
4. Remove motor retaining screws, motor and impeller.
5. Reverse procedure to install.

1980-82 Corvette

1. Disconnect battery ground cable.
2. Remove A/C compressor mounting bolts and position compressor aside with refrigerant lines attached.
3. Remove air cleaner from front and right side inlet ducts, then position air cleaner out of way.
4. Remove engine coolant recovery bottle.
5. Disconnect hose and electrical connections from blower motor.
6. Remove blower motor mounting flange attaching screws, then remove blower with impeller from vehicle.

1977-79 Corvette

1. Disconnect battery ground cable.
2. Remove radiator supply tank, if so equipped.
3. Disconnect blower motor wires.
4. Remove blower motor to case mounting screws and remove motor, Fig. 23.
5. Reverse procedure to install.

1977 Camaro & 1977-79 Nova

1. Disconnect battery ground cable.
2. Disconnect blower lead and remove all hoses and wires connected to fender skirt then raise vehicle.
3. On all except Nova, remove all fender skirt retaining bolts except those retaining skirt to radiator support. On Nova, remove the eight rearmost fender skirt to fender retaining screws.
4. Pull out and down on fender skirt and wedge a 2 × 4 inch block of wood between skirt and fender to allow room for blower motor removal.
5. Remove blower to case retaining screws

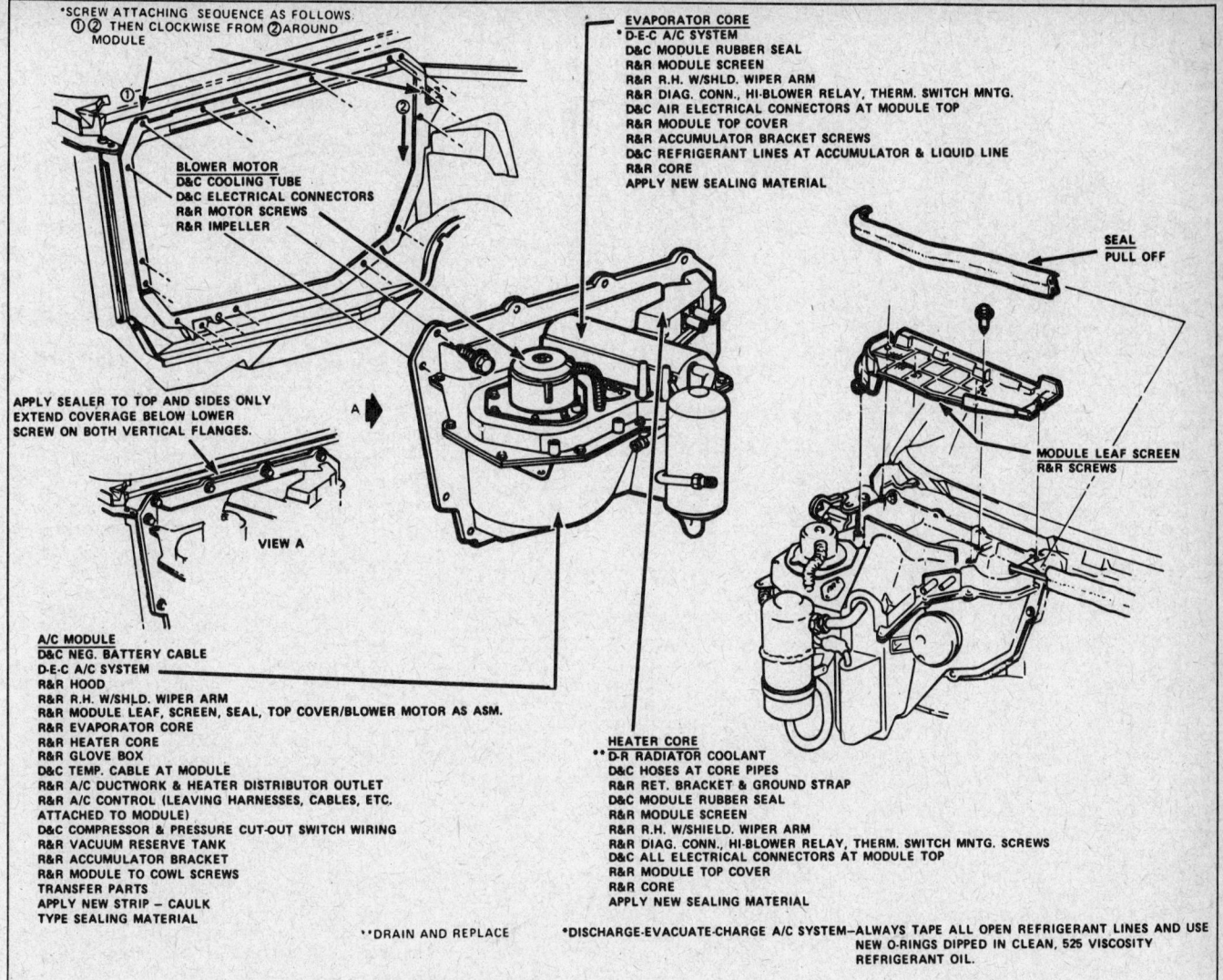

Fig. 20A   Blower motor & heater core. 1978–83 Malibu & 1978–84 Monte Carlo with A/C

and remove blower assembly. Gently pry flange, since sealer will act as an adhesive, Fig. 23.

NOTE: On Nova, remove blower retaining nut and separate wheel and motor before removing through fender and skirt.

6. Reverse procedure to install.

HEATER CORE, REPLACE

Less Air Cond.

1982–84 Camaro
1. Disconnect battery ground cable and drain cooling system.
2. Remove right lower hush panel and instrument panel trim panel.
3. On models equipped with V8-305 fuel injected engine, remove ESC module.
4. Remove lower right instrument panel carrier to cowl screw.
5. Remove heater case cover attaching screws and cover.

NOTE: To gain access to the upper left

screw, position a long 3/8 inch socket extension through the opening exposed by removal of the trim panel. Carefully lift lower right corner of instrument panel to align socket extension.

6. Remove support plate and baffle screws, then heater core, support plate and baffle from case.

1978–83 Malibu & 1978–84 Monte Carlo
1. Disconnect battery ground cable and drain cooling system.
2. Disconnect heater hoses from heater core. Plug core outlets to prevent coolant spillage.
3. Disconnect wire connectors, then remove front module cover attaching screws and cover.
4. Remove heater core from module, Fig. 20.
5. Reverse procedure to install.

1977–84 Chevrolet
1. Disconnect battery ground cable and drain cooling system.
2. Disconnect heater hoses from heater core. Plug core outlets to prevent coolant spillage.

3. Remove attaching screws from around perimeter of heater core cover on engine side of dash panel.
4. Pull heater core cover from dash panel mounting.
5. Remove heater core from module assembly, Fig. 21.
6. Reverse procedure to install.

1977–84 Exc. 1977–84 Chevrolet & 1978–83 Malibu & 1978–84 Monte Carlo & 1982–84 Camaro
1. Disconnect battery ground cable.
2. Drain radiator, disconnect heater hoses at core and plug openings to prevent spillage of water.
3. Remove nuts from air distributor duct studs on engine side of firewall, Figs. 24 through 27.
4. On 1977 Chevelle and Monte Carlo, remove distributor duct retaining screw.
5. On Nova, remove glove box and door and drill out lower right hand distributor stud with a 1/4″ drill.
6. On Camaro, remove glove box, radio, and defroster duct to distributor duct screw.
7. On Corvette, remove right instrument panel pad, right hand dash braces, center dash console duct and floor outlet duct, radio and center dash console.

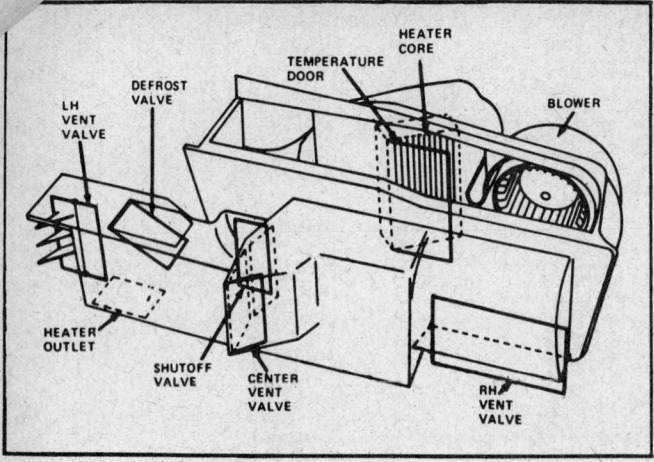

Fig. 21   Blower motor & heater core. 1977–84 Chevrolet less A/C

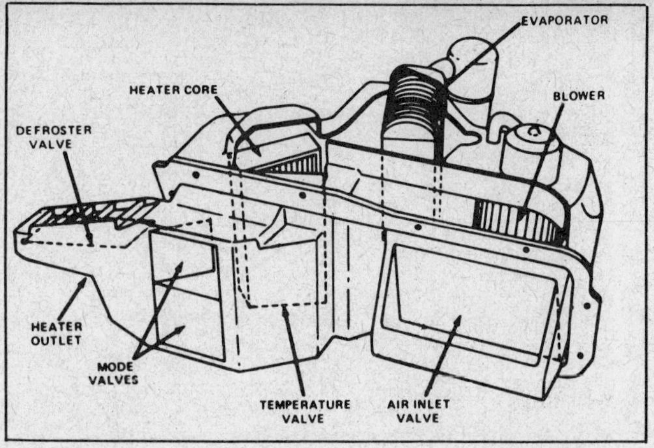

Fig. 22   Blower motor & heater core. 1977–84 Chevrolet with A/C

8. On all models, pull distributor duct from firewall being careful not to bend cable.
9. On Camaro, disconnect cable and resistor wires and remove distributor and core.
10. On all other models, remove core assembly from duct.
11. Reverse procedure to install.

With Air Cond.

1982–84 Camaro
For removal procedure, refer to "Heater Core, Replace" less air conditioning.

1978–83 Malibu & 1978–84 Monte Carlo
1. Disconnect battery ground cable and drain cooling system.
2. Disconnect heater hoses at heater core.
3. Remove retaining bracket and ground strap.
4. Remove module rubber seal and module screen, Fig. 20A.
5. Remove right hand w/s wiper arm.
6. Remove high blower relay and thermostatic switch mounting screws.
7. Disconnect wire connector at top of module, then remove module top cover.
8. Remove heater core from module.
9. Reverse procedure to install.

1977–84 Chevrolet
1. Disconnect battery ground cable and drain cooling system.
2. Disconnect heater hoses at heater core. Cap core outlets to prevent coolant spillage.
3. Remove diagnosis connector to upper case attaching screws.
4. Disconnect wire connectors from blower motor, resistor, blower relay and thermostatic switch.
5. Remove wiring harness retainer from blower case shroud.

6. Remove module screen to cowl attaching screws and remove screen.
7. Remove upper case to lower case attaching screws.

NOTE: Two screws are located inside air intake area at case separation point.

8. Disconnect wire connector from thermostatic switch, then remove screws attaching switch to evaporator case. Carefully remove insulation and loosen two clamps enough to pull formed end of switch capillary tube from under clamps attaching tube to evaporator inlet pipe for installation.
9. Remove evaporator inlet pipe support bracket to case attaching screws and remove bracket.
10. Remove heater-evaporator core case cover, using care not to damage sealer.
11. Remove heater core to case attaching screws at top of heater core, then remove heater core, Fig. 22.

NOTE: The heater core is held in position at bottom by a spring clip. Pull up firmly on heater core to disengage from clip. When installing, position core base in alignment with clip before lowering core into case. Upper retaining bracket will line up with hole at top of core when core is properly seated.

12. Reverse procedure to install.

1977 Chevelle & Monte Carlo
1. Disconnect battery ground cable and drain radiator.
2. Disconnect heater hoses from core and plug hoses and core openings.
3. Remove distributor case stud nuts projecting through firewall, Fig. 24. On 1977, remove resistor assembly and the last stud nut through its opening.
4. Remove glove box door and glove box.
5. On all models, remove right hand lap cooler and kick pad cover.
6. On all models, disconnect center duct hoses and remove center duct to selector duct screws, then remove center duct.
7. Remove floor distributor duct.
8. Remove lower right hand distributor duct to dash panel screw.
9. On all models, remove air selector retaining screws, then lower selector assembly. Disconnect all wiring, vacuum lines and

cables.
10. On all models, remove core and housing from selector assembly, then core from housing.
11. Reverse procedure to install.

1977–79 Nova
1. Disconnect battery ground cable and drain radiator.
2. Disconnect heater hoses and plug hoses and core openings to prevent coolant spillage.
3. Remove accessible stud nut from air selector duct, Fig. 25.
4. Remove right hand fender skirt to fender and skirt reinforcing screws. Lower skirt to wheel and remove remaining stud nut.
5. Remove glove box door, glove box and right hand kick pad recirculating air valve.
6. Remove center and floor ducts. Remove screws securing selector duct halves together, then separate.
7. Remove selector duct right half to firewall screws and remove duct.
8. Disconnect all wiring and cables. Scribe location of temperature camming plate on selector duct and remove plate and core.
9. Reverse procedure to install.

1977–81 Camaro
1. Disconnect battery ground cable.
2. Drain radiator and disconnect heater hoses from core. Plug openings to prevent spillage of coolant.
3. Remove nuts from distributor studs on engine side of firewall, Fig. 26.
4. Remove glove box and radio.
5. Remove defroster duct to distributor duct screw. With radio removed, the defroster duct can be pulled rearward to gain clearance for distributor duct removal.

Fig. 23   Blower motor installation (Typical). 1977–84 exc. Chevrolet, 1978–83 Malibu & 1978–84 Monte Carlo

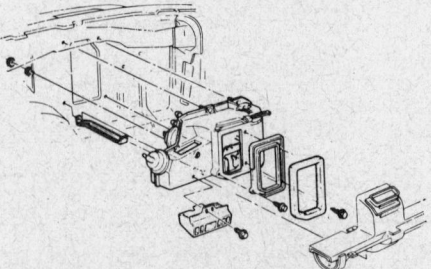

Fig. 24   Heater core installation. 1977 Chevelle & Monte Carlo

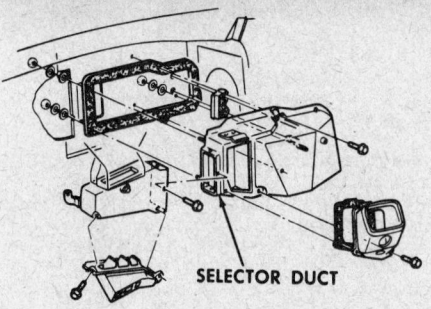

SELECTOR DUCT

**Fig. 25 Heater core installation.
1977–79 Nova**

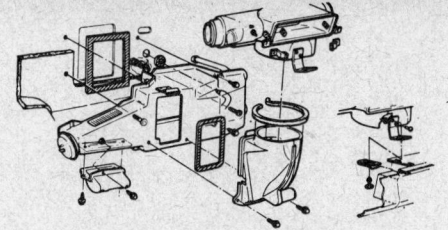

**Fig. 26 Heater core installation.
1977–81 Camaro**

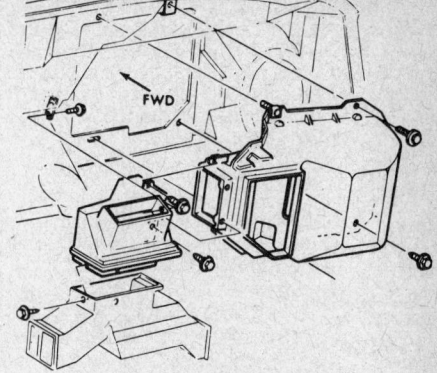

FWD

**Fig. 27 Heater core installation.
1977–82 Corvette**

6. Carefully pull distributor from firewall and disconnect wiring and cables. Remove duct and core from vehicle.
7. Reverse procedure to install.

1984 Corvette
1. Disconnect battery ground cable, place heater control in warm position, and drain cooling system.
2. Remove instrument cluster bezel and tilt wheel control lever.
3. Remove instrument panel upper trim pad retaining screws and trim pad, then remove A/C distribution ducts and disconnect flex hoses.
4. Remove right lower hush panel and side defroster flex hose.
5. Remove screws securing side defroster outlet to heater cover, and disconnect extension.
6. Remove temperature control cable and bracket from heater cover and disconnect heater door control shaft.
7. Remove electronic control module and disconnect electrical connectors to module.
8. Remove support brace between door pillar and instrument panel reinforcement brace.
9. Remove screws securing heater core cover, heater pipe bracket and water control valve bracket.
10. Cut heater hoses at core pipes and remove heater core.

NOTE: Measure and install replacement heater hose links during reassembly.

11. Reverse procedure to install. Refill cooling system and check for leaks.

1981–82 Corvette
1. Disconnect battery ground cable and drain radiator.

2. Disconnect heater hoses from core and plug hoses and core openings.
3. Remove heater case retaining nut from top of blower case.
4. Remove glove box.
5. Remove console side panels retaining screw and swing both sides out.
6. Remove center gauge cluster assembly and radio.
7. Remove right windshield pillar trim panel.
8. Remove right side dash panel retaining screws and pull panel rearward to release upper retaining clip.
9. Remove right side vent, main vent distribution, and lower heater deflector ducts.
10. Remove heater-defroster distribution duct assembly, then disconnect temperature cable and vacuum hose from heater housing.
11. Remove heater housing assembly from vehicle and heater core from housing.
12. Reverse procedure to install.

1977–80 Corvette
1. Disconnect battery ground cable. Drain radiator and disconnect heater hoses from core. Plug openings to prevent spillage of coolant.
2. Remove nuts from engine side distributor duct, Fig. 27.
3. Remove right hand dash pad and center instrument cluster. Remove dash braces.
4. Disconnect right dash outlet duct from center duct. Remove screws attaching center duct to selector duct and remove center duct.
5. Remove screws attaching selector duct to firewall and pull selector rearward and to the right. Disconnect cables and wiring.
6. Remove selector duct from car. Remove temperature door camming plate from duct and remove core and housing.
7. Reverse procedure to install.

SPEED CONTROLS
1977–83 Cruise Master

Servo Unit Adjustment

Adjust the bead chain cable or rod so that it is as tight as possible without holding the throttle open when the carburetor is set at its lowest idle throttle position. The cable is adjusted by turning the hex portion of servo. The bead chain or cable is adjusted so there is 1/16 inch of lost motion in servo cable. The rod is adjusted by turning link onto rod. With rod hooked through tab, on power unit, turn link onto rod until dimension in Fig. 28 is obtained, then install link and retainer. This adjustment should be made with ignition off and fast idle cam in off position with throttle completely closed.

When connecting the bead chain or cable (engine stopped) manually set the fast idle cam at its lowest step and connect the chain so that it does not hold the idle screw off the cam. If the chain needs to be cut, cut it three beads beyond the bead that pulls the linkage.

Regulator Unit Adjustment

To remove any difference between engagement and cruising speed, one adjustment is possible. However, no adjustment should be made until the following items have been checked or serviced.
1. Bead chain or cable properly adjusted.
2. All hoses in good condition, properly attached, not leaking, pinched or cracked.
3. Regulator air filter cleaned and properly oiled.
4. Electric and vacuum switches properly adjusted.

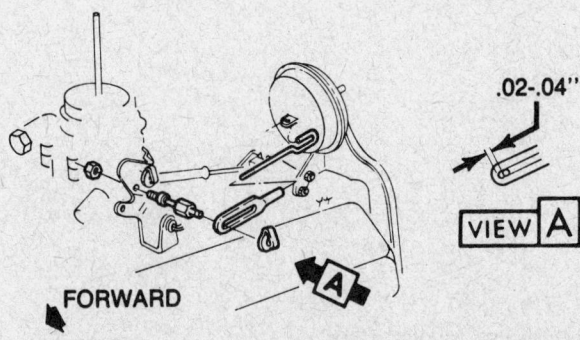

.02-.04"

VIEW A

FORWARD

Fig. 28 Servo unit rod adjustment. 1977–83

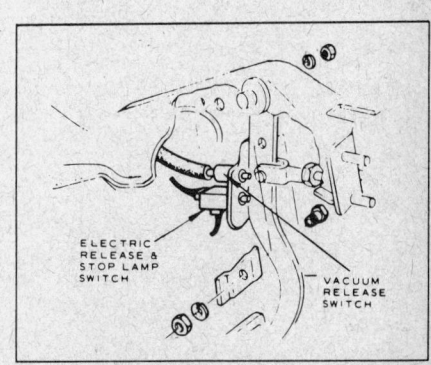

ELECTRIC RELEASE & STOP LAMP SWITCH

VACUUM RELEASE SWITCH

**Fig. 29 Release switches and brackets.
1977–83**

Engagement—Cruising Speed Zeroing

If the cruising speed is lower than the engagement speed, loosen the orifice tube locknut and turn the tube outward; if higher turn the tube inward. Each 1/4 turn will alter the engagement-cruising speed difference one mph. Tighten locknut after adjustment and check the system operation at 50 mph.

Brake Release Switch

The electric brake switch is actuated when the brake pedal is depressed .38–.64 inch, Fig. 29. The vacuum release switch is actuated when brake pedal is moved 5/16 inch on all units.

1984

Cruise Set Speed Too High Or Low

1. Check vacuum hoses for restrictions, leaks and proper routing, and repair as needed.
2. Check servo linkage, and adjust or repair as needed.
3. If all other components are satisfactory, replace electronic controller assembly.

Servo Adjustment

1. With servo cable installed on bracket, place second ball of cable chain on cable end.
2. With throttle completely closed (ignition and fast idle control off), adjust cable housing jam nuts until cable is tight, but not holding throttle open.
3. Tighten jam nuts and check system operation.

Gasoline Engine Section

Refer to Pontiac Chapter for service procedures on 4-151 engines.
Refer to Buick Chapter for service procedures on V6-231 engines & turbocharger service.

ENGINE MOUNTS, REPLACE

1982–84 V6-173

1. Disconnect battery ground cable.
2. Remove upper half of fan shroud.
3. Raise and support vehicle.
4. Remove engine mount through bolt, then raise front of engine to release weight from mount.
5. Remove mount to engine bolts and mount.

NOTE: Raise engine only enough to provide sufficient clearance for mount removal. Check for interference between rear of engine and cowl panel which could result in distributor damage.

6. Reverse procedure to install.

1978–79 V6-200

1. Remove mount retaining bolt from below frame mounting bracket, Fig. 1.
2. Raise front of engine and remove mount to engine bolts and remove mount.

NOTE: Right hand mount may be removed by loosening through bolt. It is not necessary to remove it. Raise engine only enough to provide sufficient clearance for mount removal. Check for interference between rear of engine and cowl panel.

3. Reverse procedure to install.

1977–79 6-250

1. Remove nut, washer and engine mount through-bolt.
2. Raise engine to release weight from mount.
3. Remove bracket-to-mount bolt, then remove mount.
4. Install new mount on bracket.
5. Lower engine, install through-bolt and tighten all mount bolts, Figs. 2, 3 and 4.

1977–84 All V-8 Exc. 1984 Corvette & 1980–84 V6-229

1. Remove mount retaining bolt from below frame mounting bracket, Figs. 5 and 6.
2. Raise front of engine and remove mount to engine bolts and mount. On models equipped with V6-229 engine, the right hand mount may be removed by loosening the through bolt.

NOTE: Raise engine only enough to provide sufficient clearance for mount removal. Check for interference between rear of engine and cowl panel which could result in distributor damage.

3. Reverse procedure to install.

1984 Corvette

1. Disconnect battery ground cable, then raise and support vehicle.
2. Support engine and remove mount through bolt, Fig. 6A.
3. Disconnect AIR injection pipe at manifold, exhaust pipe and catalytic converter.
4. Raise engine sufficiently to provide clearance for mount bolt removal.
5. Remove bolts securing engine mount to block and the mount.
6. Position replacement mount on engine, lower engine into position and install retaining bolts.
7. Reverse procedure to install.

ENGINE, REPLACE

1977–84 Exc. 1982–84 Camaro & 1984 Corvette

1. Disconnect battery ground cable and remove air cleaner.
2. Mark position of hinges for reassembly, then remove hood.
3. Drain cooling system, remove radiator hoses, and disconnect heater hoses from engine.
4. On models with A/C, disconnect electrical connector from compressor clutch and ground wire from bracket, remove compressor and secure aside.
5. On V6-231 engines, remove fan blade,

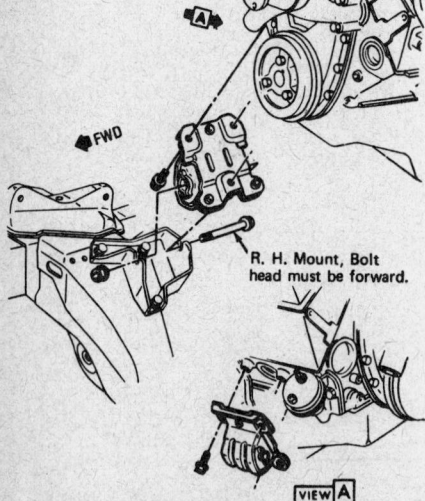

Fig. 1 Engine mounts (Typical). All w/ V6-200 engine

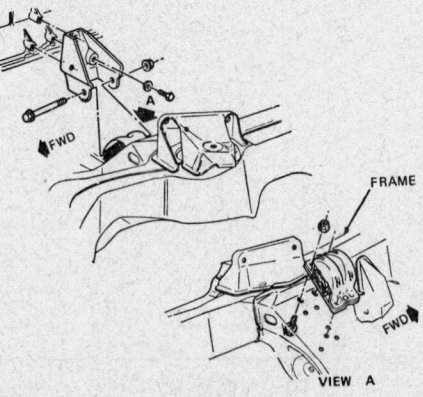

Fig. 2 Engine mounts (Typical). Chevrolet, Malibu & Monte Carlo w/ 6-250 engine

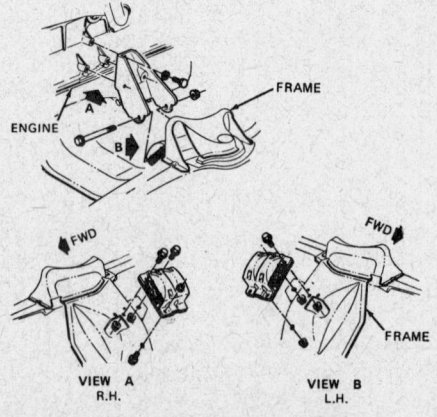

Fig. 3 Engine mounts (Typical). Nova w/ 6-250 engine

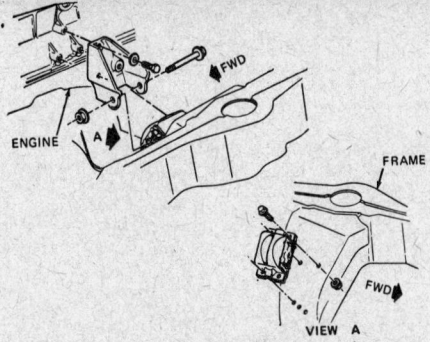

**Fig. 4 Engine mounts (Typical).
1977–79 Camaro w/6-250 engine**

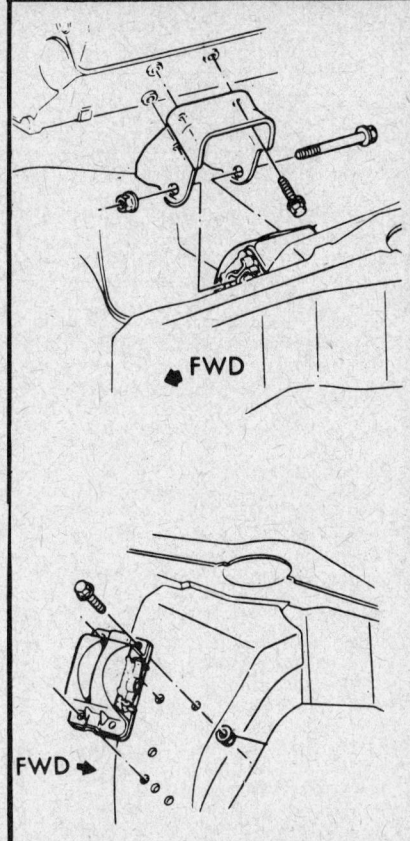

**Fig. 5 Engine mounts (Typical).
1977–84 w/ V8 engine exc. Corvette**

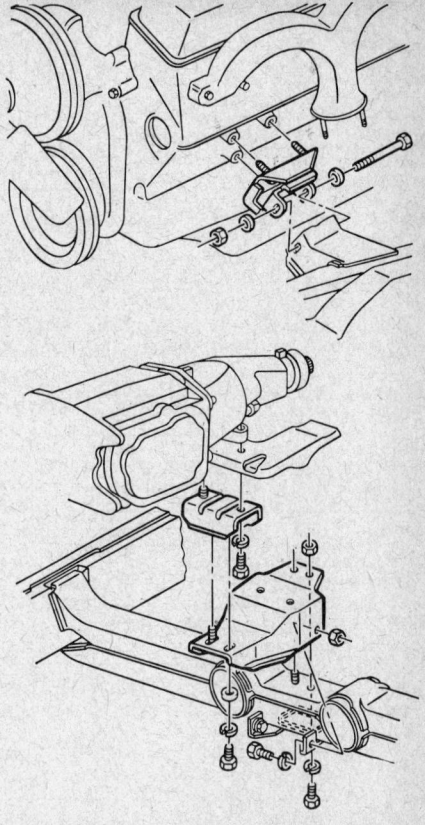

**Fig. 6 Engine mounts (Typical).
1977–82 Corvette**

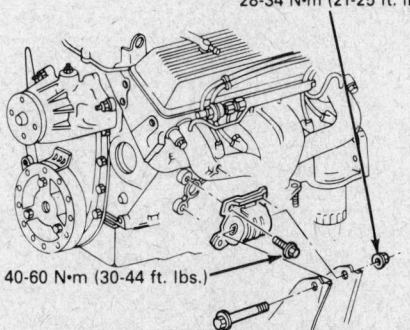

**Fig. 6A Engine mounts (typical).
1984 Corvette**

pulleys and shroud. On all other engines, remove fan shroud and radiator.

NOTE: On models with automatic transmission, disconnect and plug cooler lines.

6. Remove power steering pump retaining bolts, if equipped, and secure pump aside.
7. Disconnect accelerator linkage at throttle lever and bracket. Disconnect vacuum hoses to body mounted accessories and fuel hoses at fuel pump, then plug fuel hoses.
8. Disconnect battery and chassis ground straps from engine.
9. Disconnect electrical connectors from alternator, distributor or remote mounted coil and all engine mounted switches and accessories.
10. Remove engine harness from retaining clips and secure aside.
11. Raise and support vehicle and drain crankcase.
12. Disconnect exhaust pipes and AIR pipe from manifolds, and remove front exhaust and cruise control brackets, if equipped.
13. Disconnect electrical connectors and battery cable from starter, or remove starter.
14. Remove flywheel shield and remove bolts securing torque converter to flex plate, if equipped.

NOTE: Mark position of converter in relation to flex plate for reassembly.

15. Remove motor mount through bolts and bolts securing bell housing to engine.
16. Lower vehicle and support transmission with suitable floor jack.
17. Attach suitable lifting equipment to engine lifting brackets, raise engine and transmission, and remove motor mount to engine brackets.
18. Separate engine and transmission while supporting transmission with jack.

NOTE: On automatic transmission models, ensure converter remains with transmission during engine removal and is properly seated prior to engine installation.

19. Lift and remove engine after disconnecting any remaining harness connectors.
20. Reverse procedure to install.

1982–84 Camaro

1. Disconnect battery ground cable and remove air cleaner and fresh air hoses.

2. Disconnect electrical connectors from hood lamp or air door, if equipped, mark position of hood hinges for reassembly, and remove hood.
3. Drain cooling system, remove radiator hoses, and disconnect heater hoses from engine.
4. If equipped with A/C, disconnect electrical connector from compressor clutch and ground wire from bracket, remove compressor and secure aside.
5. Disconnect and plug transmission cooler lines at radiator, if equipped, then remove fan blade, shroud and radiator.

NOTE: On 4-151 engines with manual transmission, only fan blade and upper shroud should be removed.

6. On V6 and V8 engines, remove power

steering pump retaining bolts and secure pump aside. On 4-151 engines, disconnect and plug power steering hoses at pump.
7. Disconnect accelerator and cruise control linkage at throttle and brackets, then the vacuum hoses from all body mounted accessories, and secure cables and hoses.
8. Disconnect and plug fuel supply and return hoses.

NOTE: On models with EFI, relieve fuel system pressure before disconnecting hoses.

9. On V6 and V8 engines, proceed as follows:
   a. Remove distributor cap and lay wiring aside.
   b. Disconnect electrical connectors to alternator, distributor and all other engine mounted switches and accessories.
   c. Release engine harness from retaining clips and secure aside.
10. On 4-151 engines, proceed as follows:
    a. Disconnect engine electrical harness at bulkhead connector.
    b. From inside vehicle, lower right hush panel and remove ECM harness from main ECM connector.
    c. Remove splash shield from right inner fender and carefully pull ECM harness into engine compartment.
    d. Secure harnesses to engine.
11. Disconnect battery and chassis ground straps from engine, then raise and support vehicle.
12. Disconnect exhaust pipes from manifolds, and on 4-151 engines, remove exhaust pipe assembly.
13. On V6 and V8 engines, disconnect electri-

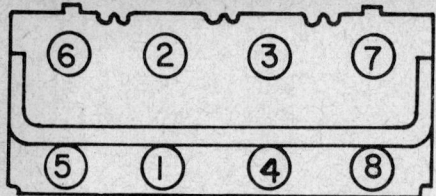

Fig. 7 Cylinder head tightening sequence. V6-173

cal connectors and battery cable from starter and remove wiring shields. On 4-151 engines, disconnect electrical connectors from transmission and remove starter.

14. Remove flywheel shield and bolts securing converter to flex plate, if equipped.

NOTE: Mark position of converter in relation to flex plate for reassembly.

15. On models with manual transmission, remove clutch linkage.
16. Remove motor mount through bolts and bolts securing bell housing to engine.
17. Lower vehicle and support transmission with suitable floor jack.
18. Attach suitable lifting equipment to engine lifting brackets, remove bracket securing AIR injection pipe, then raise engine and transmission assembly.
19. Separate engine and transmission, and lift engine from vehicle after removing bracket from rear of left cylinder head (V6 and V8).

NOTE: On automatic transmission models, ensure that converter remains with transmission during engine removal, and that it is properly seated prior to engine installation.

20. Reverse procedure to install.

1984 Corvette

1. Disconnect battery ground cable, remove air cleaner and fresh air ducts, and drain cooling system.
2. Disconnect AIR pump inlet and outlet hoses at check valves.
3. Rotate belt tensioner counterclockwise to release tension, then remove drive belt.
4. Remove A/C compressor rear brackets and disconnect electrical connectors to compressor.
5. Remove pulley and air management valves from AIR pump, then remove pump.
6. Remove upper radiator hose and bolt securing power steering reservoir brace to thermostat housing.
7. Disconnect electrical connectors to alternator, then remove alternator and brace.
8. Remove bolt securing AIR pipe and steering reservoir bracket to intake manifold.
9. Remove power steering pump lower

Fig. 8 Cylinder head tightening sequence. V8 engines

bracket, then secure pump, reservoir and A/C harness toward front of vehicle.
10. Disconnect and plug fuel supply and return lines.

NOTE: Relieve fuel system pressure before disconnecting hoses.

11. Remove nuts securing A/C bracket to water pump and lower compressor mounting bolt, move bracket forward and remove upper mounting bolt, then secure compressor aside.
12. Remove fuel line and idler pulley brackets, disconnect hoses from water pump and secure hoses and fuel lines aside.
13. Disconnect accelerator, cruise control and downshift cables from TBI and brackets.
14. Disconnect brake booster and PCV hoses from intake cover and vacuum hoses between engine and body mounted components.
15. Disconnect electrical connectors from TBI, front ground stud, coolant sensor and EGR solenoid.
16. Release clips securing wiring to valve cover, then move harness, AIR pipe and air management valves toward rear of engine.
17. Remove tach filter and ground wire from intake stud, and disconnect electrical connectors to distributor.
18. Remove distributor cap and spark plug wires after removing shields, then disconnect heater hose from manifold.
19. Mark and remove distributor, then remove oil pressure sensor and bolt securing ground strap to engine.
20. Remove crankshaft damper, raise and support vehicle.
21. Disconnect crossover pipe and AIR pipe from manifolds and converter, and remove crossover pipe brace.
22. Disconnect electrical connectors from block, coolant, oil, and oxygen sensors and starter, remove wiring shields and release harness clips, and secure harness aside.
23. Disconnect battery and chassis ground straps from above oil filter.
24. Remove flywheel shield and bolts securing converter to flex plate, if equipped.

NOTE: Mark position of converter in relation to flex plate for reassembly.

25. Remove right lower and upper bell housing bolts, then remove right center and left side bolts.
26. Support engine and remove bolts securing right and left motor mounts to block.
27. Lower vehicle and support transmission with suitable floor jack.
28. Attach suitable lifting equipment to engine lifting brackets, then separate engine and transmission.
29. Lift and remove engine assembly after disconnecting wiring from rear of left cylinder head.

NOTE: On automatic transmission models, ensure that converter remains with transmission during engine removal, and that it is properly seated prior to engine installation.

30. Reverse procedure to install.

CYLINDER HEAD, REPLACE
V6-173

1. Remove intake manifold.

Fig. 7A Intake manifold tightening sequence. V6-173

2. Raise and support vehicle.
3. Disconnect exhaust pipe from manifold, then drain engine block.
4. If left hand cylinder head is to be removed, remove dipstick tube attachment.
5. Lower vehicle.
6. Loosen rocker arms until push rods can be removed.
7. If right hand cylinder head is to be removed, remove alternator bracket.
8. Remove cylinder head bolts and cylinder head.
9. Reverse procedure to install. Coat cylinder head bolts with sealer. Torque cylinder bolts in sequence shown in Fig. 7 and intake manifold bolts in sequence shown in Fig. 7A.

V6-200, 229 & All V8s Exc. 1984 Corvette

1. Drain cooling system and engine block.
2. Remove intake and exhaust manifolds.
3. Remove alternator lower mounting bolt and position alternator aside.
4. If equipped with A/C, remove compressor and forward mounting bracket and position aside.
5. Remove rocker arm cover, rocker arms and push rods.

NOTE: Keep rocker arm, rocker arm balls and push rods in order so they can be installed in the same position.

6. On all 1981–84 models, except Corvette, remove diverter valve.
9. Remove cylinder head bolts and cylinder head.
8. Reverse procedure to install. Tighten cylinder head and intake manifold bolts in sequence shown in Figs. 8 through 10A.

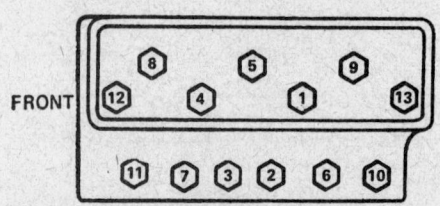

Fig. 9 Cylinder head tightening sequence. V6-200, 229

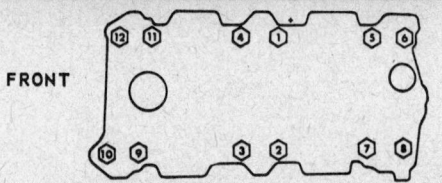

FRONT

Fig. 10 Intake manifold tightening sequence. V6-200, 299 & V8 engines exc. 1982 & 1984 Corvette

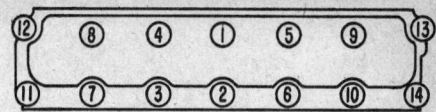

Fig. 11 Cylinder head tightening sequence. 6-250 engines

1984 Corvette

1. Disconnect battery ground cable and remove air cleaner.
2. Drain cooling system and remove intake manifold as follows:
   a. Disconnect and plug fuel supply and return lines.

   NOTE: Relieve fuel system pressure before disconnecting fuel hoses.

   b. Disconnect electrical connectors and vacuum hoses as needed, and secure wiring and hoses aside.
   c. Disconnect accelerator, cruise control and downshift cables from TBI unit and brackets.
   d. Rotate belt tensioner counterclockwise to release tension, and remove drive belt.
   e. Remove AIR pump pulley, air management valve adapter and AIR pump.
   f. Disconnect upper radiator and heater hoses, and remove bolts securing accessory mounting brackets to manifold.
   g. Disconnect spark plug wires from cylinder head to be removed, remove distributor cap, and lay cap and wire assembly aside.
   h. Mark position of distributor rotor and remove distributor.
   i. Remove intake cover and TBI assembly.
   j. Remove intake manifold bolts and manifold.
3. Disconnect AIR hose from exhaust manifold check valve, and if right cylinder head is to be removed, disconnect AIR hose from converter pipe.
4. If right cylinder head is to be removed, remove A/C compressor as follows:
   a. Remove lower compressor mounting bolt and nuts securing bracket to water pump.
   b. Move compressor assembly forward, remove upper mounting bolt and disconnect electrical connector, and secure compressor aside.
5. If left cylinder head is to be removed, remove alternator and brace.
6. Remove valve cover retaining bolts, bend plug wire bracket away from cover for clearance, and remove cover.
7. Remove spark plugs and temperature sending unit from cylinder head.
8. Raise and support vehicle, and disconnect exhaust pipe from manifold. If right cylinder head is to be replaced, remove 2 rear manifold bolts and dipstick tube bolt.
9. Lower vehicle and remove exhaust manifold.
10. If left cylinder head is to be removed, remove AIR pump upper bracket and power steering reservoir, and set aside.
11. Remove spark plug wire bracket and bolts securing ground straps to cylinder head.

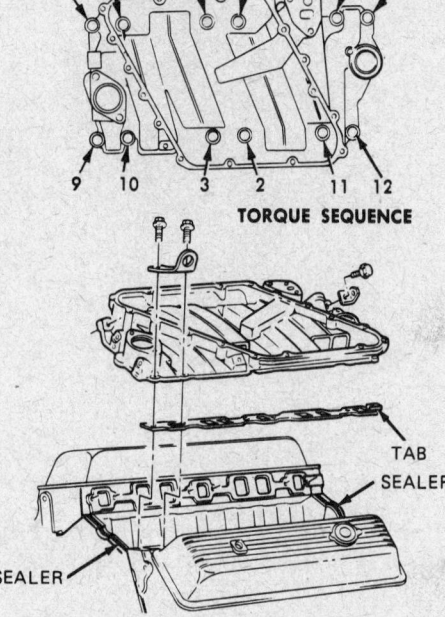

TORQUE SEQUENCE

TAB SEALER

SEALER

Fig. 10A Intake manifold installation. 1982 & 1984 Corvette

12. Loosen rocker arm nuts and remove pushrods.
13. Remove head bolts and cylinder head.
14. Reverse procedure to install, noting the following:
    a. Ensure gasket surfaces are clean and free of nicks or deep scratches, and bolt and block threads are clean.
    b. Coat both sides of head gasket with a thin even coat of sealer, and ensure gasket is properly positioned over dowel pins.
    c. Coat cylinder head bolt threads with GM sealer No. 1052080 or equivalent, then install all bolts finger tight.
    d. Torque cylinder head bolts to specifications in sequence shown in Fig. 8.
    e. Install intake manifold gaskets on head with blocked openings toward rear, bend gasket tabs flush with rear face of cylinder head, and apply a 3/16 inch bead of RTV sealer on front and rear cylinder block ridges, Fig. 10A.
    f. Install manifold, apply Locktite No. 1052624 or equivalent to manifold bolts, and torque bolts to 30 ft. lbs. in sequence shown in Fig. 10A.

1977-79 6-250

Exc. Integral Intake Manifold

1. Drain cooling system and remove air cleaner.
2. Disconnect choke rod, accelerator pedal rod at bellcrank on manifold, and fuel and vacuum lines at carburetor.
3. Disconnect exhaust pipe at manifold flange, then unfasten and remove manifolds and carburetor as an assembly.
4. Remove fuel and vacuum line retaining clip from water outlet and disconnect wire harness from temperature sending unit and coil, leaving harness clear of clips on rocker arm cover.
5. Disconnect radiator hose at water outlet housing and battery ground strap at cylinder head.
6. Remove spark plugs and coil.
7. Remove rocker arm cover. Back off rocker arm nuts, pivot rocker arms to clear push rods and lift out push rods.

8. Unfasten and remove cylinder head.
9. Reverse procedure to install and tighten head bolts in the sequence shown in Fig. 11.

With Integral Intake Manifold

1. Disconnect battery ground cable and remove air cleaner.
2. Remove power steering pump and A.I.R. pump brackets, if equipped.
3. Raise vehicle and disconnect exhaust pipe at manifold and converter bracket at transmission mount. If equipped with manifold converter, disconnect exhaust pipe from converter and remove converter.
4. Lower vehicle and remove rear heat shield and accelerator cable bracket.
5. Remove exhaust manifold attaching bolts and exhaust manifold.
6. Remove rocker arm covers, rocker arms and push rods.

   NOTE: Keep rocker arms, rocker arm balls and push rod in order so they can be installed in the same position.

7. Drain cooling system and engine block.
8. Remove fuel and vacuum line from retaining clip at water outlet, then disconnect wires at temperature sending unit.
9. Disconnect air injection hose at check valve, if equipped.
10. Disconnect radiator hose at water outlet housing and battery ground cable at cylinder head.
11. Remove cylinder attaching bolts and cylinder head.
12. Reverse procedure to install. Tighten cylinder head bolts in sequence shown in Fig. 11.

VALVES, ADJUST

NOTE: After the engine has been thoroughly warmed up the valves may be adjusted with the engine shut off as follows: With engine in position to fire No. 1 cylinder the following valves may be adjusted: V6-173, Exhaust 1-2-3, intake 1-5-6. V6-200 and 229, Exhaust 1-5-6, intake 1-2-3. 6-250, Exhaust 1-3-5, intake 1-2-4. V8's, Exhaust 1-3-4-8, intake 1-2-5-7. Then crank the engine one more complete revolution which will bring No. 4 cylinder on V6-173, V6-200 and 229, engine and No. 6 cylinder on 6-250 and V8 engines, to the firing position at which time the following valves may be adjusted: V6-173, Exhaust 4-5-6, intake 2-3-4. V6-200 and 229, Exhaust 2-3-4, intake 4-5-6. 6-250, Exhaust 2-4-6, intake 3-5-6. V8's, Exhaust 2-5-6-7, intake 3-4-6-8.

The following procedure, performed with the engine running should be done only in case readjustment is required.

1. After engine has been warmed up to operating temperature, remove valve cover and install a new valve cover gasket.
2. With engine running at idle speed, back off valve rocker arm nut until rocker arm starts to clatter.
3. Turn rocker arm nut down slowly until the clatter just stops. This is the zero lash position.

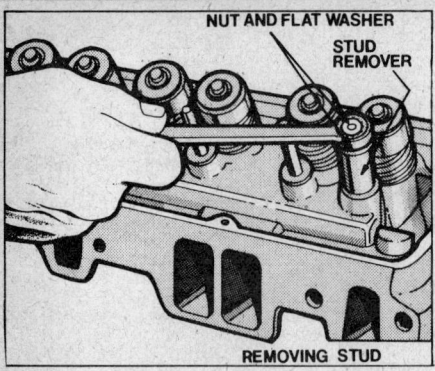

Fig. 12 Rocker arm stud removal. Press type studs

4. Turn nut down 1/4 additional turn and pause 10 seconds until engine runs smoothly. Repeat additional 1/4 turns, pausing 10 seconds each time, until nut has been turned down the number of turns listed in the *Valve Specifications Chart* from the zero lash position.

NOTE: This preload adjustment must be done slowly to allow the lifter to adjust itself to prevent the possibility of interference between the intake valve head and top of piston, which might result in internal damage and/or bent push rods. Noisy lifters should be replaced.

ROCKER ARM STUDS, REPLACE

Damaged rocker arm studs can be replaced using the following procedure. If studs are loose in cylinder head, .003 inch or .013 inch oversize studs may be installed on all engines with pressed-in type studs, after reaming holes with a proper size reamer. On engines with threaded rocker studs, looseness can be corrected by installing the proper size Heli-Coil insert, or by replacing cylinder head.
1. Remove the old stud by placing a suitable spacer, Fig. 12, over stud. Install nut and flat washer and remove stud by turning nut.
2. Ream hole for oversize stud.
3. Coat press-fit area of stud with rear axle lube. Then install new stud, Fig. 13. If tool shown is used, it should bottom on the head.

VALVE ARRANGEMENT

Front to Rear

6-250 . . . . E-I-I-E-E-I-I-E-E-I-I-E
Small V8 . . . . E-I-I-E-E-I-I-E

VALVE LIFT SPECS

Engine	Year	Intake	Exhaust
V6-173	1982–84	.3466	.3938
V6-200	1978–79	.3730	.4200
V6-229	1980–82	.5355	.5355
V6-229	1983–84	.3510	.3855
6-250	1977–79	.3879	.4051
V8-267	1979	.3730	.4100
V8-267	1980–82	.3570	.3900
V8-305	1977–81	.3726	.4000
V8-305①	1982	.3726	.4000
V8-305②③	1982	.3570	.3900
V8-305④	1982	.3900	.4095

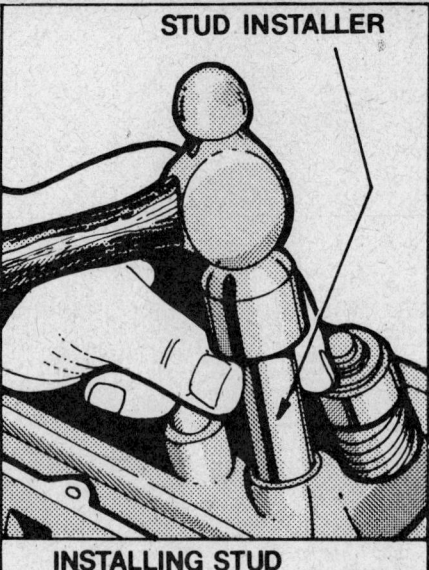

Fig. 13 Rocker arm stud installation. Press type studs

Engine	Year	Intake	Exhaust
V8-305③	1983–84	.3510	.3855
V8-305④	1983–84	.3855	.4035
V8-350⑤	1977–82	.3900	.4100
V8-350⑥	1977–81	.4500	.4600
V8-350⑦	1982 & 84	.4100	.4230
V8-350⑧	1983–84	.3855	.4035

①—Exc. Camaro.
②—Camaro.
③—Exc. EFI.
④—EFI.
⑤—Exc. Corvette high performance.
⑥—Corvette high performance.
⑦—Corvette.
⑧—Exc. Corvette.

VALVE TIMING

Intake Opens Before TDC

Engine	Year	Degrees
4-151⑥	1982	33
V6-173	1982	25
V6-200	1978–79	34
V6-229	1980–82	42
V6-231①	1979–82	16
	1978	17
6-250	1977–79	16
V6-262④⑤	1982	16
V8-267	1981–82	44
V8-267	1979–80	28
V8-305⑦	1982	38
V8-305	1981–82	44
V8-305	1977–80	28
V8-350	1981	38
V8-350②	1977–80	28
V8-350③	1977–80	52
	1982	32
V8-350④⑤	1980–82	16

①—Refer to Buick Chapter for service procedures on this engine.
②—Except Corvette high performance engine.
③—Corvette high performance engine.
④—Diesel engine.
⑤—Refer to Oldsmobile Chapter for service procedures on this engine.
⑥—Refer to Pontiac Chapter for service procedures on this engine.
⑦—Fuel injected engine.

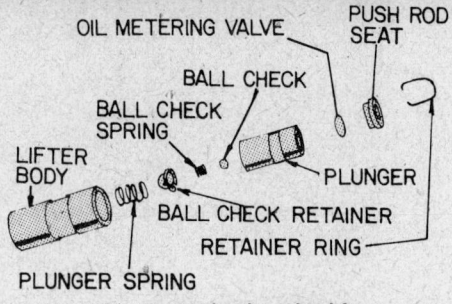

Fig. 14 Hydraulic valve lifter

PUSH RODS

On engines that use push rods with a hardened insert at one end, the hardened end is identified by a color stripe and should always be installed toward the rocker arm during assembly.

Service Bulletin

On 6-250 engines with air conditioning, it is not necessary to remove the distributor wires, etc. to replace the valve push rod cover and/or gasket.
1. Remove coil and bracket from block.
2. Remove distributor hold-down clamp.
3. Lift distributor up for clearance (do not disengage from cam gear), then remove push rod cover.
4. Use new gasket and reverse procedure to install.

VALVE GUIDES

On all engines valves operate in guide holes bored in the head. If clearance becomes excessive, use the next oversize valve and ream the bore to fit. Valves with oversize stems are available in .003, .015 and .030 inch.

HYDRAULIC LIFTERS, REPLACE

Valve lifters can be lifted from their bores after removing rocker arms and push rods. On V6 and V8 engines, intake manifold must be removed, and on L-4 and L-6 engines, engine side covers must be removed in order to gain accesss to lifers. Adjustable pliers with protected jaws may be used to remove lifters which are stuck due to carbon or varnish deposits. Fig. 14 illustrates the type of valve lifter used.

TIMING CASE COVER, REPLACE

NOTE: On all engines the cover oil seal may be replaced without taking off the timing gear cover. After removing the vibration damper, pry out the old seal with a screwdriver. Install the new seal with the lip or open end toward inside of cover and drive it into position.

V6-173

1. Remove water pump, then, on vehicles

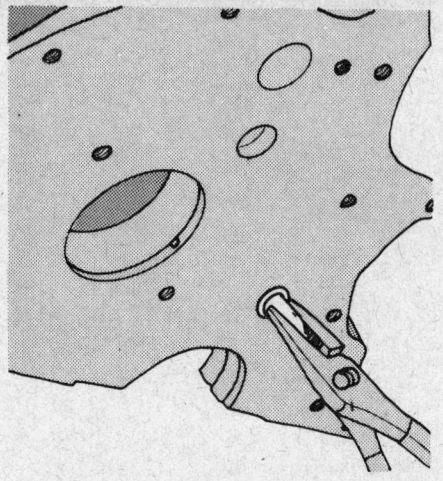

Fig. 15   Timing gear oiler removal. 6-250

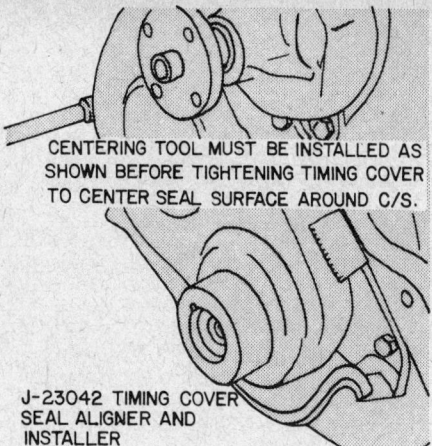

CENTERING TOOL MUST BE INSTALLED AS SHOWN BEFORE TIGHTENING TIMING COVER TO CENTER SEAL SURFACE AROUND C/S.

J-23042 TIMING COVER SEAL ALIGNER AND INSTALLER

Fig. 16   Timing cover installation. 6-250

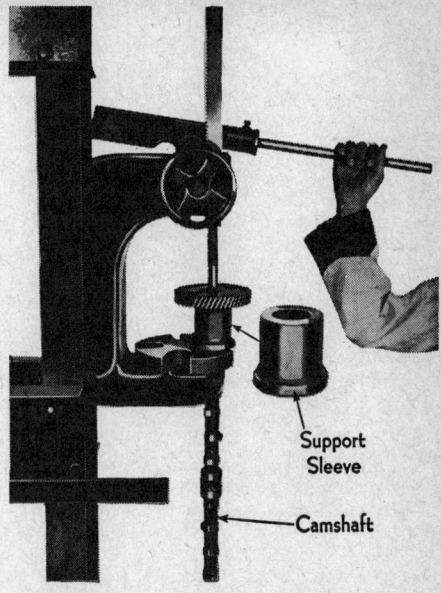

Support Sleeve

Camshaft

Fig. 17   Camshaft gear removal. 6-250

equipped with A/C, remove compressor and mounting bracket and position aside.

2. Remove vibration damper, then disconnect lower radiator hose from cover and heater hose from water pump.
3. Remove cover retaining bolts and cover.
4. Thoroughly clean sealing surfaces of front cover and engine block, then apply a continuous thin bead of anaerobic sealant #1052357 or equivalent to front cover sealing surface.
5. Install front cover and water pump on engine, then install retaining bolts and nut and torque to specifications.

NOTE: Final torquing of bolts must be completed within five minutes of installing the cover.

6. Reconnect hoses and install vibration damper.
7. Install A/C compressor and mounting bracket.
8. Service cooling system as required.

6-250

1. To remove cover, remove radiator.
2. Remove vibration damper.
3. Remove the two oil pan to front cover attaching screws.
4. Remove front cover to cylinder block attaching screws.
5. Pull cover slightly forward; then, using a

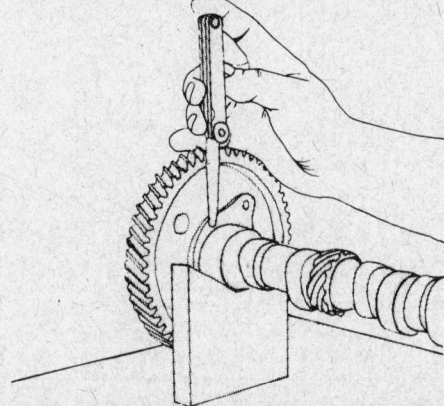

Fig. 18   Checking camshaft end play. 6-250

sharp knife, cut oil pan front seal flush with cylinder block at both sides of cover.

6. Remove cover and attached portion of oil pan front seal.
7. Pry oil seal out of cover with a large screwdriver. Install new seal with open side of seal inside of cover and drive or press seal into place.
8. If oil nozzle is to be replaced, remove it with pliers as shown in Fig. 15. Drive new nozzle in place, using a suitable light plastic or rubber hammer.
9. Clean gasket surfaces.
10. Cut tabs from new oil pan front seal, then install seal on cover, pressing tips into cover holes.
11. Install a suitable centering tool over end of crankshaft.
12. Coat gasket with light grease and stick it in position on cover.
13. Apply a 1/8 inch bead of RTV sealer at joint of oil pan and cover.
14. Install cover over centering tool, Fig. 16, and install cover screws, tightening them to 6 to 8 ft. lbs. *It is important that the centering tool be used to align the cover so the vibration damper installation will not damage the seal and position seal evenly around damper hub surface.*

V6 & V8 Engines Exc. V6-173

1. Remove vibration damper and water pump.
2. Remove cover retaining screws and cover.
3. Clean gasket surface of block and timing case cover.
4. Remove any excess oil pan gasket material that may be protruding at the oil pan to engine block junction.
5. Apply a thin bead of RTV #1052366 sealer or equivalent to the joint formed at oil pan and block.
6. Coat new gasket with sealer and position it on cover, then install cover to oil pan seal on cover and coat bottom of seal with engine oil.
7. Position cover on engine and loosely install the upper bolts.
8. Tighten screws alternately and evenly while pressing downward on cover so that dowels are aligned with holes in cover. Do not force cover over dowels as cover can be distorted.
9. Install remaining cover screws, vibration damper and water pump.

TIMING GEARS, REPLACE

6-250

When necessary to install a new camshaft gear, the camshaft will have to be removed as the gear is a pressed fit on the shaft. The camshaft is held in position by a thrust plate which is fastened to the crankcase by two capscrews which are accessible through two holes in the gear web.

Use an arbor press to remove the gear and when doing so, a suitable sleeve, Fig. 17, should be employed to support the gear properly on its steel hub.

Before installing a new gear, assemble a new thrust plate on the shaft and press the gear on just far enough so that the thrust plate has practically no clearance, yet is free to turn. The correct clearance is from .001" to .005", Fig. 18.

The crankshaft gear can be removed by utilizing the two tapped holes in conjunction with a gear puller.

When the timing gears are installed, be sure the punch-marks on both gears are in mesh, Fig. 19. Backlash between the gears should be from .004" to .006", Fig. 20. Check the run-out of the gears, and if the camshaft gear run-out exceeds .004" or the crank gear run-out is in excess of .003", remove the gear (or gears) and examine for burrs, dirt or some other fault which may cause the run-out. If these conditions are not the cause, replace the gear (or gears).

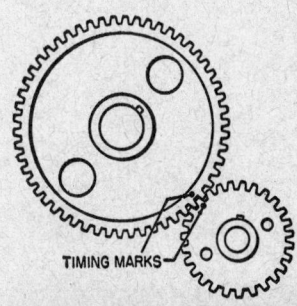

TIMING MARKS

Fig. 19   Timing gear locating marks. 6-250

Fig. 20 Checking timing gear backlash. Lash should be .004—.006" on 6-250 engines

TIMING CHAIN, REPLACE

V6 & V8 Engines

1. Remove timing chain cover as outlined previously.
2. Remove crankshaft oil slinger.
3. Crank engine until timing marks on sprockets are in alignment, Fig. 21.
4. Remove three camshaft-to-sprocket bolts.
5. Remove camshaft sprocket and timing chain together. Sprocket is a light press fit on camshaft for approximately 1/8". If sprocket does not come off easily, a light blow with a plastic hammer on the lower edge of the sprocket should dislodge it.
6. If crankshaft sprocket is to be replaced, remove it with a suitable gear puller. Install new sprocket, aligning key and keyway.
7. Install chain on camshaft sprocket. Hold sprocket vertical with chain hanging below and shift around to align the timing marks on sprockets.
8. Align dowel in camshaft with dowel hole in sprocket and install sprocket on camshaft. *Do not attempt to drive sprocket on camshaft as welch plug at rear of engine can be dislodged.*

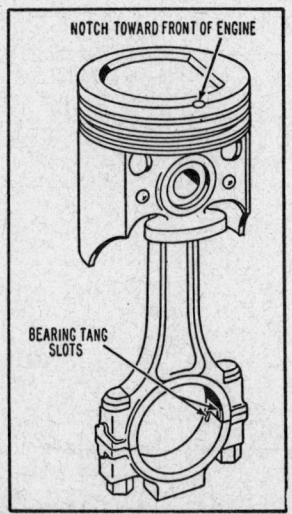

Fig. 22 Piston & rod assembly. 6-250

9. Draw sprocket onto camshaft, using the three mounting bolts. Tighten to 20 ft. lb. torque.
10. Lubricate timing chain and install cover.

CAMSHAFT, REPLACE

6-250 Engines

It is recommended that the engine be removed from the vehicle for camshaft removal. Remove valve train components, engine front cover, fuel pump and distributor. Remove camshaft thrust plate screws and pull camshaft from cylinder block.

V6 & V8 Engines

1. Remove valve lifters and engine front cover.
2. Remove grille, radiator and condenser.
3. On all models, remove fuel pump and the push rod.
4. Remove timing chain as outlined previously.
5. On all except V6-173, install two 5/16-18×4 bolts in camshaft bolt holes, then remove camshaft.
6. Reverse procedure to install.

PISTONS & RODS, ASSEMBLE

1977—83

Assemble pistons to connecting rods as shown in Figs. 22 to 25A.

Upon installation, measure the connecting rod side clearance using a suitable feeler gauge. Clearance should be as follows:

Engine	Year	Clearance
4-151	1982—84	.006—.022
V6-173	1982—84	.006—.017
V6-200	1978—79	.006—.014
V6-229	1980—84	.006—.014
V6-231	1978—82	.006—.027
V6-231	1983—84	.005—.015
6-250	1977—79	.007—.016
V6-262①	1982—83	.0062—.021
V8-267	1979—82	.006—.016
V8-305	1977—78	.008—.014
V8-305	1979—84	.006—.014
V8-350	1977—78	.008—.014
V8-350②	1979—84	.006—.014
V8-350③	1977—82 & 1984	.008—.014
V8-350①	1980—84	.006—.020

①—Diesel.
②—Exc. Corvette & Diesel.
③—Corvette.

PISTONS, PINS & RINGS

Pistons are available in standard and oversizes of .010 and .030 inch on all except V6-200 and .030 inch on V6-200.

Piston rings are available in standard and oversizes of .030 inch.

MAIN & ROD BEARINGS

Connecting rod bearings are available in standard and undersizes of .001, .002, .010 and .020 inch.

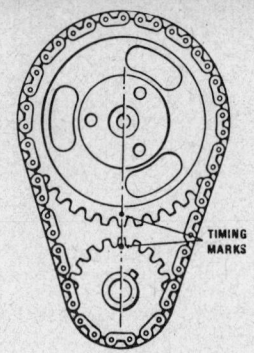

Fig. 21 Timing gear locating marks. V6 & V8 engines

Main bearings are available in standard and undersizes of .001, .002, .009, .010 and .020 inch.

NOTE: 6-250 Engines

The rear main bearing journal has no oil hole drilling. To remove the upper bearing half (bearing half with oil hole) proceed as follows after cap is removed:

1. Use a small drift punch and hammer to start the bearing rotating out of the block.
2. Use a pair of pliers (tape jaws) to hold the bearing thrust surface to the oil slinger and rotate the crankshaft to pull the bearing out.
3. To install, start the bearing (side not notched) into side of block by hand, then use pliers as before to turn bearing half into place.
4. The last 1/4 inch movement may be done by holding just the slinger with the pliers or tap in place with a drift punch.

CRANKSHAFT REAR OIL SEAL, REPLACE

Exc. V6-173

NOTE: These engines are equipped with helix

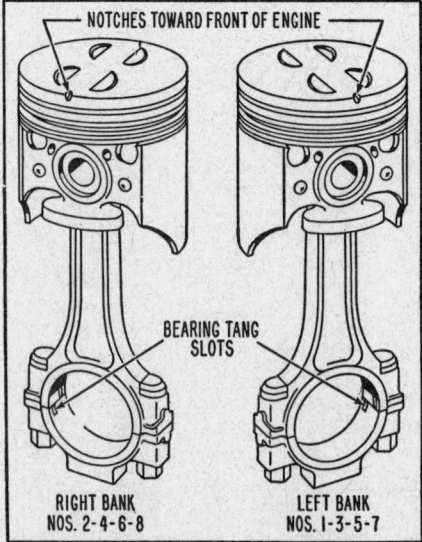

Fig. 23 Piston & rod assembly. V8 engines exc. V8-350 high performance

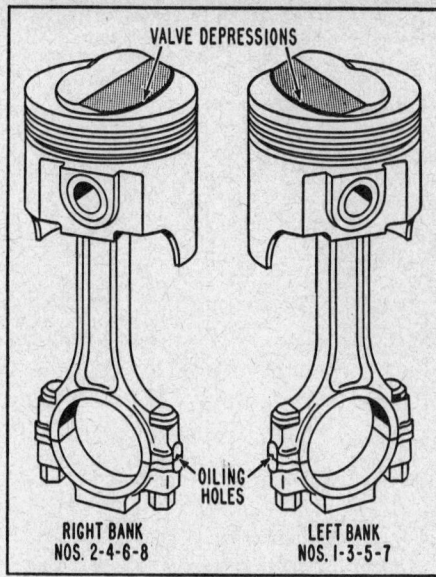

Fig. 24   Piston & rod assembly. V8-350 high performance

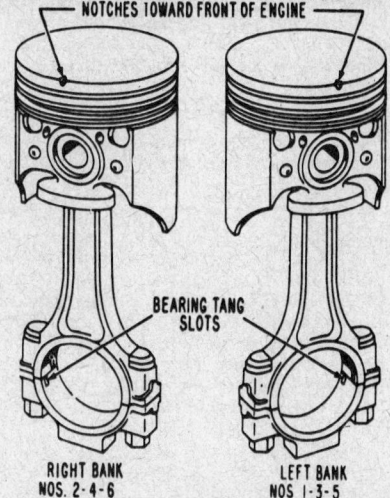

Fig. 25   Piston & rod assembly. V6-200 & 229

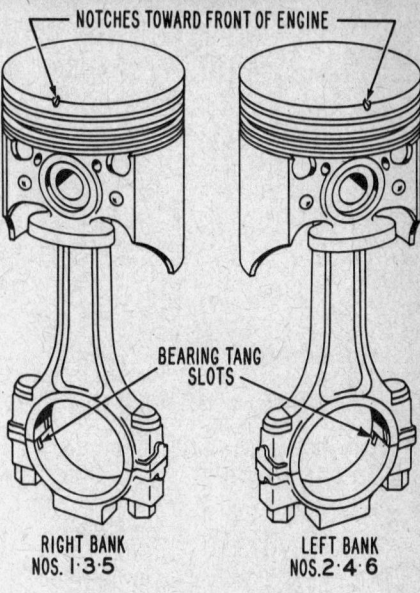

Fig. 25A   Piston & rod assembly. V6-173

type rear seal. A seal starting tool, Fig. 26, must be used to prevent the upper seal half from coming into contact with the sharp edge of the block.

When necessary to correct an oil leak due to a defective seal, always replace the upper and lower seal halves as a unit, Fig. 27. *When installing either half, lubricate the lip portion only with engine oil, keeping oil off the parting line surface as this is treated with glue.* Always clean crankshaft surface before installing a new seal.

1. To replace the lower seal, remove seal from groove in bearing cap, using a small screwdriver to pry it out.
2. Insert new seal and roll it in place with finger and thumb.
3. To replace the upper seal (with engine in car) use a small hammer and tap a brass pin punch on one end of the seal until it protrudes far enough to be removed with pliers.
4. Position tip of tool, Fig. 26, between crankshaft and seal seat in cylinder block.
5. Position seal between crankshaft and tip of tool with seal bead contacting tip of tool. Ensure oil seal lip is facing toward front of engine.
6. Roll seal around crankshaft, using tool as a "Shoehorn" to protect seal bead from sharp corner of seal seat surface in cylinder block.

NOTE: Tool must remain in position until

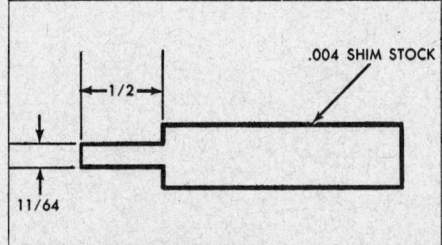

Fig. 26   Helix type rear main seal installation tool

seal is properly seated with both ends flush with block.

7. Remove tool, using care not to dislodge seal.
8. Install new seal into bearing cap with tool as outlined previously.
9. Install bearing cap with sealant applied to the cap to case interface. Do not apply sealant to seal ends. Torque rear main bearing cap bolts to specifications as listed in the "Engine Tightening Specification Chart".

V6-173

1. Remove oil pan and oil pump as described further on.
2. Remove rear main bearing cap.
3. Using tool No. J-29114-2, gently drive upper seal into groove approximately ¼ in.
4. Repeat step 3 for other end of seal.
5. Measure the amount that was driven in on one side and add 1/16 in. Using a suitable cutting tool, cut this length from the oil rear main bearing cap lower seal using the main bearing cap as a guide. Repeat this step for the other end of seal.
6. Place piece of cut seal into groove of seal installer tool guide No. J-29114-1 and install tool guide onto engine block.
7. Using seal packing tool No. J29114-2, drive piece of seal into block. Drive seal in until packing tool contacts machined stop.
8. Remove tool guide and repeat steps 6 and 7 for other end of seal.
9. Install new seal in bearing cap.
10. Install rear main bearing cap. Apply a thin film of sealant No. 1052357 or equivalent to rear main bearing cap and case interface. Use care not to allow sealant to contact crankshaft journal or main bearing.

OIL PAN, REPLACE

1982–84 Camaro V6-173 & V8-305

1. Disconnect battery ground cable, then remove fan shroud.
2. Raise and support vehicle, then drain crankcase.
3. Remove A.I.R. pipe and hanger bolts from

catalytic converter.
4. Remove starter motor attaching bolts and position starter motor aside.
5. Remove engine mount through bolts, then raise engine.
6. Remove oil pan attaching bolts and oil pan.

NOTE: If oil pan removal is hampered by the forward crankshaft throw and/or counterweight extending downward, turn crankshaft as needed to put throw in a horizontal position.

7. Reverse procedure to install. Apply a ⅛ inch wide bead of RTV sealant #1052366 or equivalent on oil pan sealing flange.

NOTE: If M6 x 1.0 bolts are used, torque to 8 ft. lbs. If M8 x 1.25 bolts are used, torque to 18 ft. lbs.

1980–84 V6-229

1. Disconnect battery ground cable, then remove upper half of fan shroud.
2. On 1981–83 models equipped with cruise control, remove cruise control servo bracket.
3. Raise vehicle and drain crankcase.
4. Disconnect exhaust crossover pipe from exhaust manifold.
5. Remove torque converter cover, if equipped.

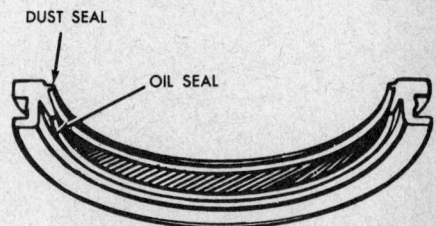

Fig. 27   Crankshaft rear main oil seal (Typical)

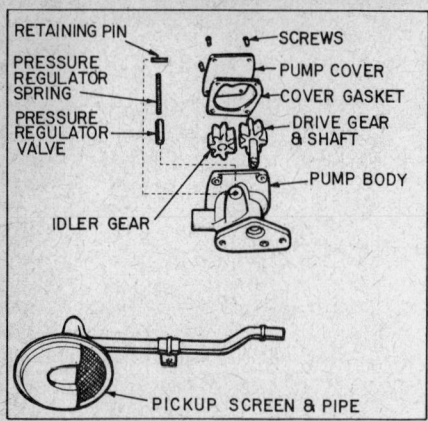

Fig. 28   Oil pump, exploded view. 6-250 engine

6. Remove starter motor attaching bolts and position starter motor aside.
7. Remove left hand engine mount through bolt, then lossen right hand engine mount through bolt.
8. Raise engine and reinstall through bolt. Do not tighten through bolt.
9. Remove oil pan attaching bolts and remove oil pan.
10. Reverse procedure to install. Torque oil pan attaching bolts to 80 inch lbs. Torque engine mount attaching bolts to 50 ft. lbs.

1978–84 V8 Exc. Corvette & 1982–84 Camaro

1. Disconnect battery ground cable.
2. Remove air cleaner and snorkle.
3. Remove upper half of fan shroud.

NOTE: On 1978–80 Camaro and 1978–79 Nova equipped with heavy duty cooling system, and all 1981–84 except Chevrolet, remove fan shroud since it is of one piece construction.

4. On 1978–79 Malibu and Monte Carlo, remove engine oil dipstick and tube.
5. On 1978–79 Chevrolet, remove vacuum reservoir, if equipped.
6. On 1978–80 Camaro and 1978–79 Nova, remove distributor cap and position aside.
7. On 1981–84 models equipped with cruise control, remove cruise control servo bracket.
8. On all models, raise and support vehicle, then drain oil pan.

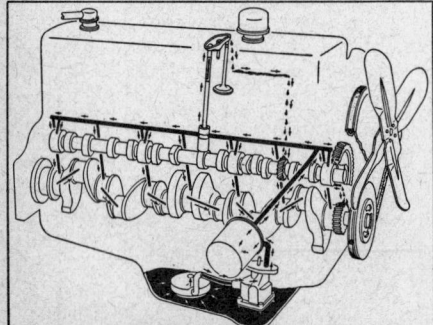

Engine oiling system. 6-250

9. Disconnect exhaust crossover pipe at exhaust manifold and catalytic converter.
10. Remove flywheel cover or torque converter cover.

NOTE: If equipped with manual transmission, remove starter motor before the flywheel cover.

11 Support engine with a suitable jack and remove engine mount through bolts.
12. Remove oil pan bolts and lower oil pan. Check that the forward crankshaft throw and/or counterweight is not extending downward as to block removal of oil pan. Rotate crankshaft as necessary to position crankshaft to permit pan removal.
13. Raise engine and install engine mount through bolts.
14. Remove oil pan.
15. Reverse procedure to install. Torque oil pan bolts to 80 inch lbs.

1977–79 6-250

1. Disconnect battery ground cable.
2. Raise vehicle on hoist, then drain engine oil.
3. Remove starter, then remove flywheel housing cover, or torque converter housing cover.
4. Remove engine mount through bolts, then raise engine, reinstall through bolts to engine mounts and lower the engine.
5. Remove oil pan bolts and oil pan.
6. Reverse procedure to install.

1978–79 V6-200 & 1977 V8 Exc. Corvette

1. Disconnect battery ground cable.
2. Remove oil dipstick and tube.
3. Remove exhaust crossover pipe.
4. If equipped with automatic transmission, remove converter housing cover.
5. Remove starter bolt and inboard brace, then swing starter aside.
6. Remove oil pan retaining bolts and oil pan.
7. Reverse procedure to install.

1977–82 Corvette

1. Disconnect battery ground cable.
2. Raise and support vehicle, then drain oil pan.
3. Remove engine oil dipstick and tube.
4. Disconnect idler arm and lower steering linkage.
5. Remove flywheel splash shield.
6. On 1977–80 models, disconnect exhaust pipe from exhaust manifold and catalytic converter.
7. Remove oil pan bolts and oil pan.
8. Reverse procedure to install. Torque oil pan bolts to 80 inch lbs.

1984 Corvette

1. Disconnect battery ground cable.
2. Raise and support vehicle, then drain crankcase.
3. Remove starter brace and retaining bolts, and secure starter aside.
4. Remove flywheel cover.
5. Remove oil pan bolts and oil pan.
6. Reverse procedure to install. Torque oil pan retaining bolts to 80 inch lbs.

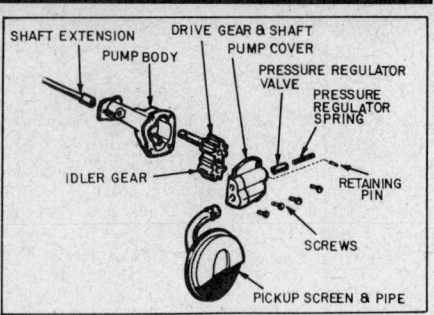

Fig. 29   Oil pump, exploded view (Typical). V6 & V8 engines

OIL PUMP

Oil Pump, Replace

1. Remove oil pan as described previously.
2. On 6-250 engines, remove the two flange mounting bolts, pickup pipe bolt and then remove pump.
3. On all except 6-250 engines, remove pump to rear main bearing cap bolt and remove pump and extension shaft.
4. Reverse procedure to install. Make sure that installed position of oil pump screen is with bottom edge parallel to oil pan rails on all except 6-250 engines.

Oil Pump Service

1. Remove oil pump as described previously.
2. Remove pump cover screws and pump cover. On 6-250 engine oil pump, remove gasket, Figs. 28 & 29.
3. Mark gear teeth so they can be reassembled with same teeth indexing, then remove drive gear, idler gear and shaft.
4. Remove pressure regulator valve retaining pin, pressure regulator valve and related parts.
5. If pickup screen and pipe require replacement, mount pump in a soft-jawed vise and extract pipe from pump.
6. Wash all parts in cleaning solvent and dry with compressed air.
7. Inspect pump body and cover for cracks and excessive wear.
8. Inspect pump gears for damage or excessive wear.
9. Check drive gear shaft for looseness in pump body.
10. Inspect inside of pump cover for wear that would allow oil to leak past the ends of the gears.
11. Inspect pickup screen and pipe assembly for damage to screen, pipe or relief grommet.

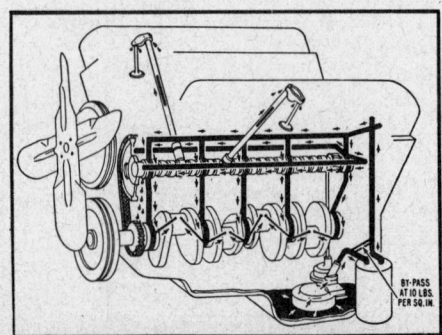

Engine oiling system. V8 engines

12. Check pressure regulator valve for fit in pump housing.
13. Reverse procedure to assemble. Turn drive shaft by hand to check for smooth operation.

NOTE: The pump gears and body are not serviced separately. If the pump gears or body are damaged or worn, the pump assembly should be replaced. Also, if the pick-up screen and pump assembly was removed, it should be replaced with a new one as loss of the press fit condition could result in an air leak and loss of oil pressure.

BELT TENSION DATA

1977–79	New Lbs.	Used Lbs.
A/C Compressor	135–145	90–100
A.I.R Pump, Alternator & P/S Pump	120–130	70–80
1980–82		
A/C Compressor		
V6-229	135–145	90–100
V6-231	165	100
V8-350 Diesel	135–165	85–95
1980–82		
A.I.R. Pump, Alternator & P/S Pump		
V6-229	120–130	70–80
V6-231	145	80
V8-350 Diesel	110–140	70–80
1983–84 Exc. 1984 Corvette		
A/C Compressor		
V6-229	145	65–95
V6-231	165	100
V8-350 Diesel	135–165	85–95
A.I.R. Pump, Alternator & P/S Pump		
V6-229	138	65–80
V6-231	145	80
V8-350 Diesel	110–140	70–80
1984 Corvette		
Serpentine Drive Belt	120–140①	120–140①

① —Checked between alternator & AIR Pump.

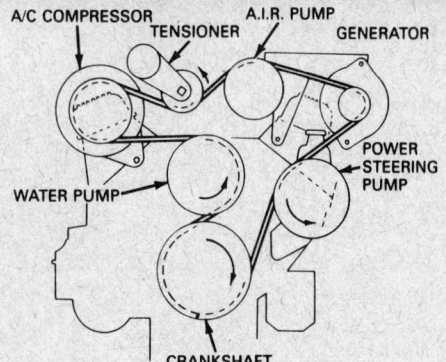

Fig. 30 Serpentine drive belt installation. 1984 Corvette

WATER PUMP, REPLACE

Exc. 1984 Corvette

1. Disconnect battery ground cable and drain cooling system.
2. Remove fan shroud or upper radiator support, as applicable, then remove accessory drive belts.
3. Remove fan and pulley from water pump hub.
4. Remove upper and lower alternator brackets. On 1982–84 Camaro, remove AIR brace and bracket.
5. If equipped with power steering, remove power steering lower bracket from water pump and position aside.
6. Remove radiator lower hose and heater hose from water pump.
7. Remove water pump attaching bolts and pump, noting position of bolts for assembly.

NOTE: On 6-250 engines, pull pump straight out of block first to prevent damage to the impeller.

8. Reverse procedure to install.

1984 Corvette

1. Disconnect battery ground cable, and drain cooling system.
2. Rotate belt tensioner counterclockwise to release tension, and remove drive belt, Fig. 30.
3. Remove water pump and AIR pump pulleys, and disconnect air management valve adapter from AIR pump.
4. Remove AIR pump, then disconnect fuel supply and return lines.

NOTE: Relieve fuel system pressure before disconnecting fuel hoses.

5. Remove A/C compressor rear braces and lower mounting bolt.
6. Remove nuts securing A/C compressor and idler pulley bracket to water pump and disconnect electrical connector from compressor.
7. Move compressor bracket forward, remove upper mounting bolt and compressor, and secure aside.
8. Disconnect AIR hoses at check valves and AIR pipe at intake manifold and power steering bracket.
9. Remove power steering reservoir bracket and upper alternator mounting bolt.
10. Remove lower AIR pump bracket, then disconnect hoses from water pump.
11. Remove mounting bolts and water pump.
12. Reverse procedure to install.

FUEL PUMP, REPLACE

Carbureted Engines

1. Disconnect fuel lines from pump.
2. Disconnect vapor return line, if so equipped.
3. Remove fuel pump attaching bolts and pump.
4. Reverse procedure to install.

Diesel Engine Section

Refer to the Oldsmobile Chapter for service procedures on the V6-262 and V8-350 Diesel engines.

Clutch & Transmission Section

CLUTCH PEDAL, ADJUST

1977–83 Except Corvette

1. Disconnect return spring at clutch fork.
2. Rotate clutch lever and shaft assembly until pedal is against rubber bumper on dash brace.
3. Push outer end of clutch fork rearward until throwout bearing lightly contacts pressure plate fingers.
4. Install push rod in gauge hole and increase length until all lash is removed, Figs. 1 and 2.
5. Remove swivel or rod from gauge hole and insert into lower hole on lever. Install retainer and tighten lock nut being careful not to change rod length.
6. Reinstall return spring and check pedal free travel:
   1982–83 Camaro .... ½ to 1 inch
   1978–81 Camaro ...... ⅞ to 1⁷⁄₁₆ inches
   1978–81 Malibu .. 1¹⁄₁₆ to 1¼ inches
   1978–79 Monte Carlo 1¹⁄₁₆ to 1¼ inches
   1978–79 Nova .... ⅞ to 1⁷⁄₁₆ inches
   1977 All .... 1 to 1½ inches

1984 Camaro

The hydraulic clutch release mechanism on these models consists of a clutch master cylinder, slave cylinder and connecting hose which is serviced as a complete assembly. The hydraulic system is supplied filled with fluid, and no adjustment or bleeding is required. Before removig release mechanism for service, verify that a malfunction exists as follows:

1. Remove clutch housing dust shield and note position of slave cylinder plunger.
2. Depress clutch pedal fully and measure slave cylinder plunger travel.
3. If plunger moves release lever a minimum of .57 inch, check clutch disc, pressure plate, release fork and bearing for damage and repair as needed.

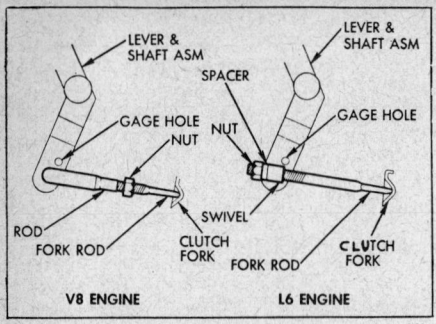

Fig. 1 Clutch linkage adjustment. 1977–81 Exc. Corvette

4. If plunger does not move lever at least .57 inches, check fluid level in clutch master cylinder with pedal depressed, and fill to step in reservoir.

NOTE: Do not overfill. Upper portion of reservoir must be open to accept fluid displaced in slave cylinder due to clutch wear.

5. Recheck plunger travel and check hydraulic components for leaks.
6. If plunger travel is still less than .57 inch, or if excessive leakage is noted, replace hydraulic system as an assembly.

1977–81 Corvette

1. Disconnect return spring between toe pan brace and cross shaft lever, Fig. 3.
2. Rotate clutch lever and shaft assembly until pedal is against dash brace rubber bumper.
3. Install swivel (C) into clutch lever hole and install retainer.
4. Loosen nuts (A) and (B), then apply a 5 pound load in direction of arrow (F) until bearing lightly contacts plate fingers.
5. Rotate nut (B) toward swivel until dimension "X" is approximately 3/8 to 7/16 inch, then tighten nut (A) to lock swivel against nut (B).
6. Reinstall return spring and adjust clutch pedal free travel which should be 1 to 1½ inch.

CLUTCH, REPLACE

1977–84

1. Support engine and remove transmission as outlined further on.
2. On all except 1984 Camaro, disconnect clutch fork push rod and return spring. On 1984 Camaro, remove slave cylinder heat shield and cylinder from flywheel housing.
3. Remove flywheel housing.
4. Slide clutch fork from ball stud and remove fork from dust boot.

NOTE: Look for "X" mark on flywheel and on clutch cover. If "X" mark is not evident, prick punch marks on flywheel and clutch cover for indexing purposes during installation.

5. Loosen clutch-to-flywheel attaching bolts evenly one turn at a time until spring pressure is released. Then remove bolts and clutch assembly.
6. Reverse procedure to install, using suitable pilot tool to center clutch disc. Tighten clutch cover bolts evenly and gradually to avoid distorting cover.

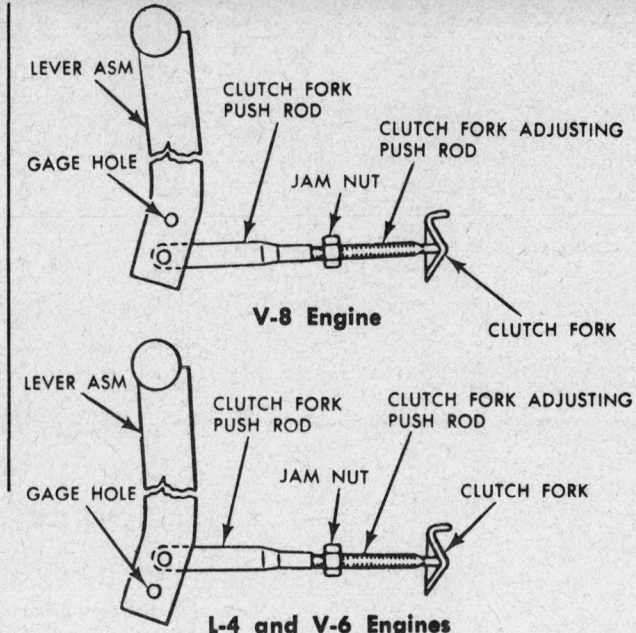

Fig. 2 Clutch linkage adjustment. 1982–83 Camaro

MANUAL TRANSMISSION, REPLACE

NOTE: It may be necessary to remove the catalytic converter and its support bracket to facilitate transmission removal.

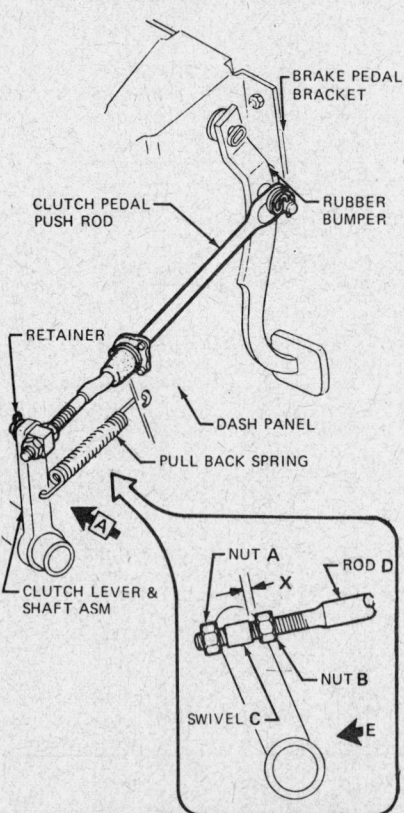

Fig. 3 Clutch linkage adjustment (Typical). 1978–81 Corvette

1982–84 Camaro

Four Speed

1. Raise and support vehicle, then drain transmission fluid.
2. Remove torque arm and propeller shaft.
3. Disconnect speedometer cable and all electrical connectors at transmission, then remove exhaust brace.
4. Remove shifter support attaching bolts from transmission and disconnect shift linkage from shifter.
5. Support transmission with a suitable jack, then remove crossmember and transmission mount attaching bolts and the crossmember and mount.
6. Remove transmission attaching bolts and the transmission.
7. Reverse procedure to install.

Five Speed

1. Disconnect battery ground cable, remove shifter boot retaining screws and slide boot up lever.
2. Remove shift lever retaining bolts and lever, then raise and support vehicle.
3. Remove torque arm and propeller shaft, and on 1983 models disconnect clutch cable.
4. Disconnect speedometer cable and electrical connectors from transmission.
5. Support transmission and remove transmission mount retaining bolts and catalytic converter bracket.
6. Remove crossmember retaining bolts, crossmember and bolts securing flywheel cover.
7. Remove bolts securing transmission to engine, transmission and flywheel cover.
8. Reverse procedure to install.

1977–81 Exc. Corvette

1. Disconnect battery ground cable.
2. Remove shift lever knob and, on four speed models, the spring and "T" handle.
3. Raise and support vehicle.
4. Disconnect speedometer cable and TCS wiring at transmission.
5. Remove propeller shaft.

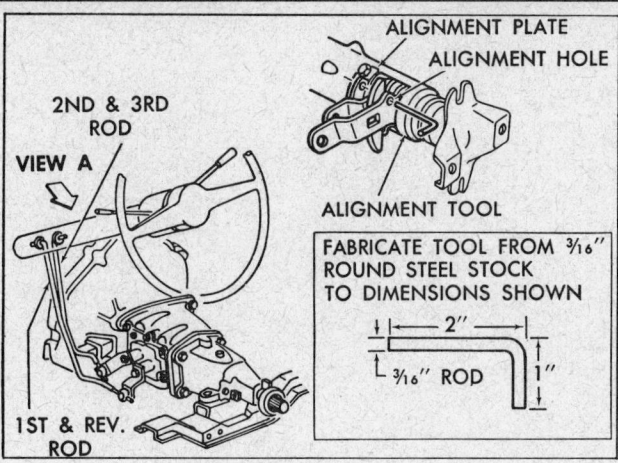

Fig. 4 Three-speed column shift linkage adjustment.

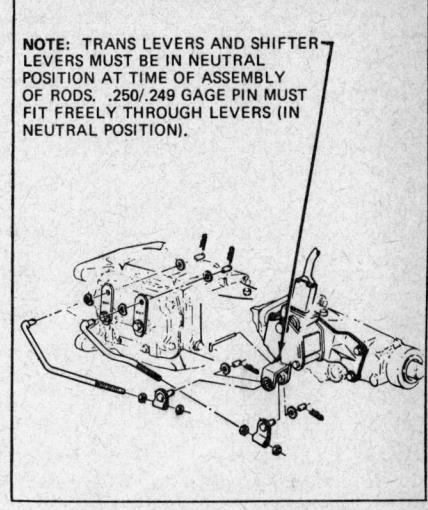

Fig. 5 Three-speed floor shift linkage adjustment. 1978–81 Malibu & Monte Carlo

6. Remove transmission mount to crossmember bolts and the crossmember to frame bolts.
7. Remove shift lever attaching bolts and shift levers from transmission. Disconnect back drive rod at bell housing crank on floor shift models.
8. On floor shift models, remove bolts attaching shift control assembly to support on transmission. Carefully pull unit downward until shift lever clears rubber boot and remove assembly from vehicle.
9. On all models, remove transmission to clutch housing upper retaining bolts and install guide pins in holes and remove the lower retaining bolts.
10. Slide transmission rearward until clutch drive gear clears the clutch assembly and remove transmission from vehicle.
11. Reverse procedure to install.

1977–81 Corvette

1. Disconnect battery ground cable.
2. Remove shifter ball spring and "T" handle.
3. Remove console trim plate.
4. Raise and support vehicle.
5. Remove right and left exhaust pipes from vehicle.
6. Disconnect propeller shaft from transmission slip yoke. Lower the propeller shaft and remove slip yoke from transmission.
7. Remove transmission rear mount to rear mount bracket.
8. With a suitable jack, raise engine slightly to lift transmission off rear mount bracket.
9. Remove bolts retaining transmission linkage mounting bracket to frame.
10. Disconnect shifter rods from levers at transmission cover.
11. Remove bolts attaching shift control to mounting bracket, then the mounting bracket. Remove shifter mechanism with rods and levers attached.
12. Remove shift levers from transmission and disconnect the speedometer cable and TCS switch wiring.
13. Remove transmission mount bracket to crossmember bolts, then the mount bracket. Remove bolts retaining rear mount cushion and exhaust pipe yoke.
14. Remove transmission to clutch housing bolts and the lower left extension bolt.
15. Pull transmission rearward until clear of clutch housing, rotating transmission clockwise while pulling rearward. To

allow clearance for transmission removal, slowly lower rear of engine until tachometer drive cable at distributor clears horizontal ledge across front of dash.
16. Remove transmission from vehicle.
17. Reverse procedure to install.

THREE SPEED SHIFT LINKAGE, ADJUST

1977–81

Column Shift
1. Place shift lever in "Reverse" position and ignition switch in "Lock".
2. Raise vehicle on a hoist.
3. Loosen shift control rod swivel lock nuts. Pull down slightly on 1/R rod attached to column lever to remove any slack and then tighten clevis lock nut at transmission lever, Fig. 4.
4. Unlock ignition switch and shift column lever to "Neutral". Position column lower levers in "Neutral", align gauge holes in levers and insert gauge pin.

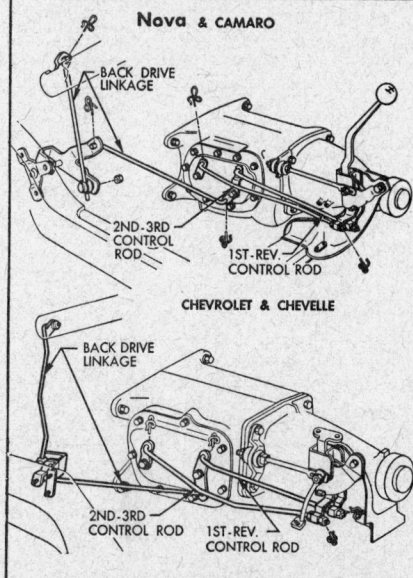

Fig. 6 Three-speed floor shift linkage adjustment. Exc. 1978–81 Malibu & Monte Carlo

5. Support rod and swivel to prevent movement and tighten 2/3 shift control rod lock nut.
6. Remove alignment tool from column lower levers and check operation. Then place column lever in "Reverse" and check interlock control.

Floor Shift
1. Place ignition switch in "Off" position and raise vehicle.
2. Loosen lock nuts at shift rod swivels, Figs. 5 and 6. The rods should pass freely through the swivels.
3. Place transmission shift levers in neutral position.
4. Move shift control lever into the neutral detent position, align control assembly levers and insert locating pin into lever alignment slot.
5. Tighten lock nuts at shift rod swivels and remove locating pin.
6. Place transmission control lever in reverse position and the ignition switch in "Lock" position. Loosen lock nut at backdrive control rod swivel, then pull rod downward slightly to remove slack in the column mechanism, then tighten the lock nut.
7. Check interlock control. The ignition switch should move freely to and from the "Lock" position.
8. Check transmission shift operation and if satisfactory, lower vehicle.

FOUR SPEED SHIFT LINKAGE, ADJUST

1982–84 Camaro

1. Place levers (L), (M) and (N) in neutral position, Fig. 7. To obtain neutral position, move levers counter-clockwise to foward detent, then clockwise one detent.
2. Move lever (F) to neutral position. Align holes of levers (E), (H) and (J) with notch in lever and bracket assembly, then insert Gauge J-33195 or equivalent to secure levers in neutral position.
3. Attach rod (C) to lever (N) with washer (A) and retainer (B).
4. Loosely assemble nuts (R) and (T) and

swivel (S) on rod (C).

5. Insert swivel (S) into lever (E), then attach washer (Q) and secure with retainer (P). Apply a load on lever (N) in direction of arrow (Z). At the same time, finger tighten nuts (T) and (R) against swivel, then torque nuts to 25 ft. lbs.
6. Repeat steps 3, 4 and 5 for rod (D) and levers (J) and (M).
7. Repeat steps 3, 4 and 5 for rod (K) and levers (H) and (L).
8. Remove gauge and check that centerlines of shift levers are aligned to provide free crossover motion.

1977–81

Exc. Corvette

The procedure, Figs. 8 and 9, is the same as that for Three Speed transmissions described previously.

1978–81 Corvette

1. Place levers (K), (M), and (P) in neutral position, Fig. 10. To obtain neutral position, move levers counter-clockwise to forward detent, then clockwise one detent.
2. Move lever (E) to neutral position. Align

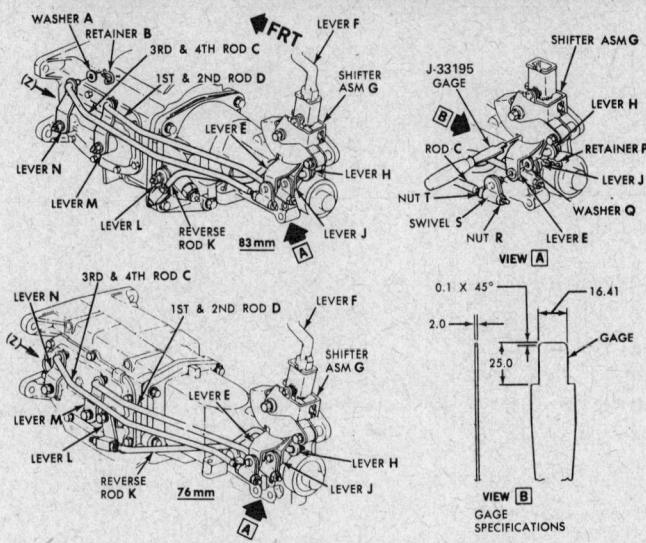

Fig. 7 Four-speed shift linkage adjustment. 1982–84 Camaro

levers (C), (D) and (F) with notch in lever and bracket assembly, then insert a suitable tool to secure levers in neutral position.
3. Attach rod (N) to lever (C) with retainer (G).
4. Loosen assembly nuts (Q) and (S) and swivel (R) on rod (N).
5. Insert swivel (R) into lever (P), attach washer (B) and secure retaining (A). Apply a load on lever (P) in direction of arrow (Z). Tighten nut (S) against swivel, then nut (Q) against swivel.
6. Repeat steps 3, 4 and 5 for rod (J) and levers (F) and (K).
7. Repeat steps 3, 4 and 5 for rod (L) and levers (D) and (M).
8. Remove alignment tool from levers. The centerlines of shift levers must be aligned to provide free crossover motion.
9. Check for proper operation. Be sure all cables have adequate clearance around control rods.

1977 Corvette

1. Place ignition switch in "Lock" position

and raise vehicle.
2. Loosen swivel and clevis lock nuts from both shift rods, Fig. 11. The rods should pass freely through the swivels. Disconnect backdrive cable from column lock tube lever.
3. Place shift control lever in neutral position and insert a locking pin, .644 inch diameter, in notch of lever and bracket assembly.
4. Place transmission levers in neutral position.
5. Hold reverse rod and lever rearward against locating pin, tighten rear lock nut against swivel and tighten the front lock nut.
6. Hold 1st–2nd rod against locating pin and adjust clevis so clevis pin passes freely through clevis and lever. Tighten lock nut against clevis and install washer and lock pin.
7. Hold 3rd–4th rod and lever rearward

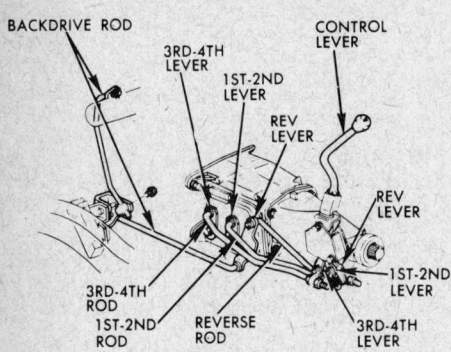

CHEVELLE

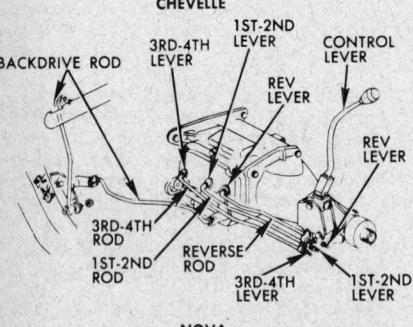

NOVA

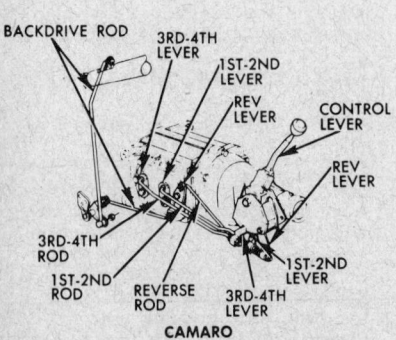

CAMARO

Fig. 8 Four-speed shift linkage adjustment. 1977 Chevelle & Monte Carlo & 1977–81 Camaro

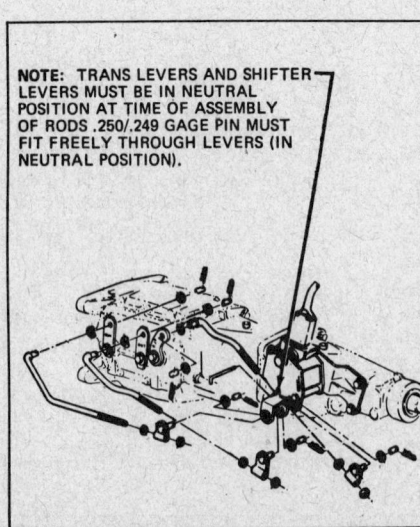

NOTE: TRANS LEVERS AND SHIFTER LEVERS MUST BE IN NEUTRAL POSITION AT TIME OF ASSEMBLY OF RODS .250/.249 GAGE PIN MUST FIT FREELY THROUGH LEVERS (IN NEUTRAL POSITION).

Fig. 9 Four-speed shift linkage adjustment. 1978–81 Malibu & Monte Carlo

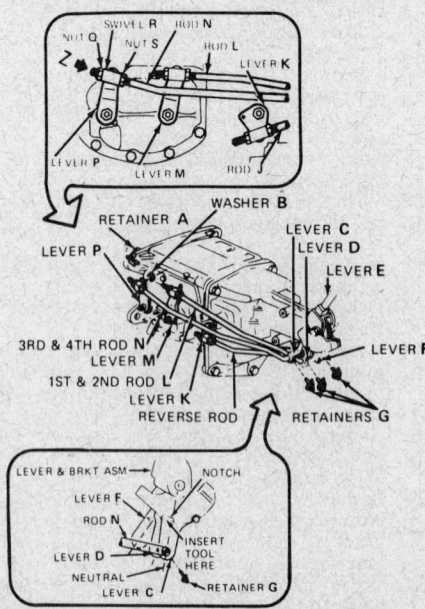

Fig. 10 Four-speed shift linkage adjustment. 1978–81 Corvette

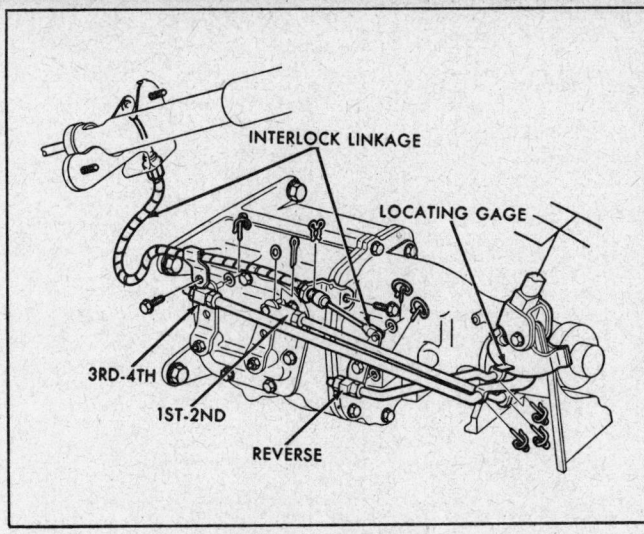

Fig. 11 Four-speed shift linkage adjustment. 1977 Corvette

against locating pin and adjust swivel so swivel pin freely passes through lever. Tighten forward nut against lever, then the rear nut. Remove locating pin.
8. Check for proper operation.
9. Loosen two nuts at steering column to dash panel bracket.
10. Place transmission shift lever in reverse and the ignition switch in "Lock" position, if not previously done.
11. Rotate lock tube lever counter-clockwise to remove any free play. Reposition cable bracket until cable eye passes over retaining pin on lever.
12. Hold the bracket in position and have an assistant tighten the steering column to dash panel bracket retaining nuts.
13. Install cotter pin and washer retaining backdrive cable to lever pin.
14. Check interlock. The ignition switch must move freely to and from "Lock" position with transmission shift lever in reverse.
15. Lower vehicle.

Rear Axle, Propeller Shaft & Brakes

REAR AXLE

Figs. 1 and 2 illustrate the rear axle assemblies used. When necessary to overhaul any of these units, refer to the *Rear Axle Specifications* table in this chapter.

Corvette

NOTE: These models are equipped with Positraction differentials.

In this axle, the drive pinion is mounted in two tapered roller bearings that are preloaded by a spacer. The pinion is positioned by a shim located between the head of the drive pinion and the rear pinion bearing. The front bearing is held in place by a large washer and a locking pinion nut.

The differential is supported in the carrier by two tapered roller side bearings.

The differential side bearings are preloaded by shims between the bearings and carrier housing, Fig. 2. The differential assembly is positioned for proper ring gear and pinion backlash by varying the position and thickness of these shims.

The ring gear is bolted to the case. The case houses two side gears in mesh with two pinions mounted on a pinion shaft which is held in place by a lock screw. The side gears are backed by thrust washers.

The differential side gears drive two splined yokes which are retained by snap rings located on the yoke splined end. The yokes are supported on caged needle bearings pressed into the carrier, adjacent to the differential bearings. A lip seal, pressed into the carrier outboard of the bearing, prevents oil leakage and dirt entry.

REMOVE & REPLACE

1984 Corvette
1. Remove air cleaner and distributor shields, then disconnect cap from distributor.
2. Raise and support vehicle, and remove spare and tire cover.
3. Remove exhaust system assembly as follows:
   a. Disconnect AIR pipe at converter and AIR pipe clamps at manifold.
   b. Disconnect electrical connector from oxygen sensor.
   c. Support exhaust system, remove bolts securing mufflers to hangers, and remove converter bracket.
   d. Disconnect exhaust pipes at manifolds and remove exhaust system.
4. Disconnect leaf spring from spindle support knuckles, then remove bolts securing spring to differential carrier and spring as outlined in "Rear Suspension Sec-

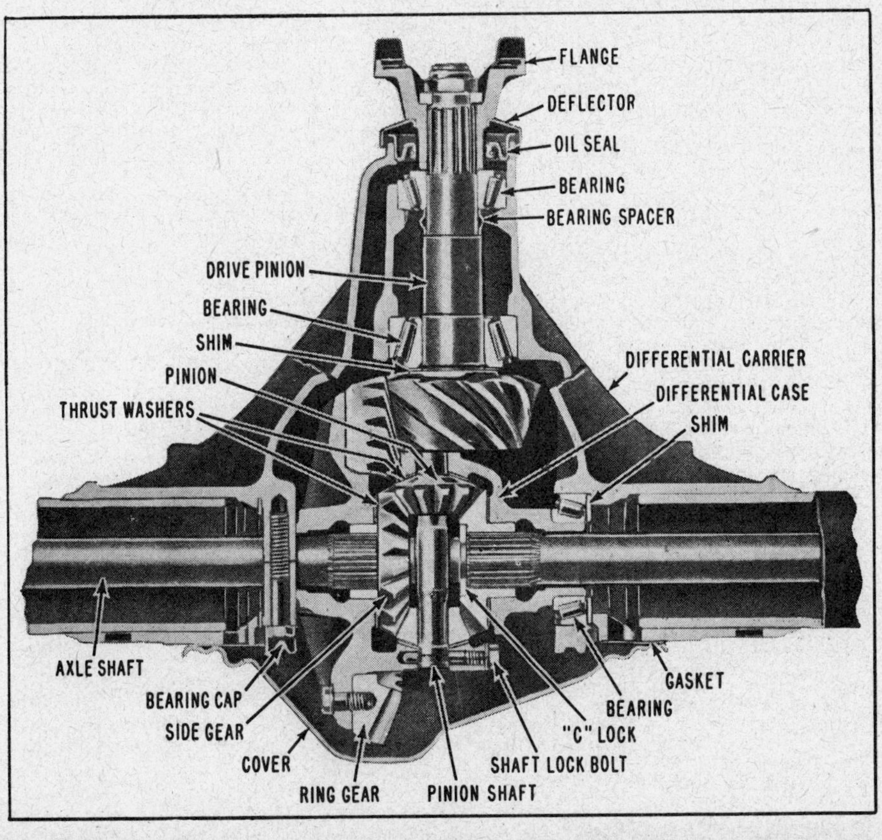

Fig. 1 Rear axle, cutaway view (Typical of C, G, K, M & P types; similar to B & O types). 1977–84 Exc. Corvette

tion."

5. Scribe mark between cam bolts and brackets, then remove cam bolts and mounting bracket from carrier.
6. Disconnect tie rods from left and right spindle support knuckles.
7. Remove straps securing driveshaft universal joints to differential side yokes, push wheel and tire assemblies outward, and disconnect drive shafts from side yokes.

NOTE: Tape bearing cups to universal joint yokes to prevent loss of needle bearings.

8. Remove straps securing propeller shaft universal joint to pinion flange, push propeller shaft forward into transmission and tie shaft to support beam.
9. Support transmission and remove bolts securing differential carrier beam to frame brackets, Fig. 3.
10. Remove mounting bolts at front of differential carrier and carrier assembly.
11. Reverse procedure to install, then check rear suspension alignment.

1980–82 Corvette
1. Raise vehicle and remove spare tire.
2. Remove spare tire cover by removing support hooks attached to carrier cover.
3. Remove exhaust system, then position jack stands under front control arms to support vehicle.
4. Remove heat shield.
5. Using a suitable jack and C-clamp, raise spring to relieve tension, then disconnect spring from spindle support.
6. Remove rear spring cover plate.
7. Place alignment marks on cam bolt for reassembly, then remove cam bolt from bracket.
8. Remove bolts attaching strut bracket to carrier, then lower strut rods by pushing outward on wheel and tire assembly.
9. Mark propeller shaft and pinion flange, then disconnect propeller shaft
10. Remove differential carrier to frame crossmember mount bolt, Fig. 3A.
11. Position jack stand under carrier, then remove carrier to body attaching bolts, Fig. 3A.
12. Lower differential to gain access to cover bolts.
13. Drain differential and remove cover.
14. Disconnect drive shaft at spindle at companion flange.
15. Lower and remove differential assembly.
16. Remove drive shafts from side yokes.
17. Reverse procedure to install.

1977–79 Corvette
1. Raise and support vehicle.
2. Remove exhaust system components located behind front crossmember for clearance.
3. Disconnect driveshaft at carrier yokes.
4. Remove carrier front mounting bracket bolt.
5. Remove driveshaft shaft.
6. Disconnect strut rod bracket from carrier and lower bracket with strut rods attached.
7. Loosen the four spring to carrier bolts.
8. Remove eight carrier cover bolts, allowing lubricant to drain from carrier.
9. Position drive yokes in a position to facilitate carrier removal.
10. Remove carrier from vehicle.
11. Reverse procedure to install.

Exc. Corvette

In these rear axles, Fig. 1, the rear axle housing and differential carrier are cast into an integral assembly. The drive pinion assembly is mounted in two opposed tapered roller bearings. The pinion bearings are preloaded by a spacer behind the front bearing. The pinion is positioned by a washer between the head of the pinion and the rear bearing.

The differential is supported in the carrier by two tapered roller side bearings. These bearings are preloaded by spacers located between the bearings and carrier housing.

The differential assembly is positioned for proper ring gear and pinion backlash by varying these spacers. The differential case houses two side gears in mesh with two pinions mounted on a pinion shaft which is held in place by a lock pin. The side gears and pinions are backed by thrust washers.

A limited slip rear axle, available on most models, uses disc or cone type clutches which are splined to the side gears to "lock" the axle shafts to the case, or in effect to each other. Therefore, if one drive wheel is on a slippery surface, the other wheel must develop more torque than on a standard type differential before the differential case will allow wheel spin. However, axle shaft torques produced during cornering are sufficient to overcome the clutch action, allowing axles to rotate at different speeds.

Remove & Replace

Construction of the axle assembly is such that service operations may be performed with the housing installed in the vehicle or

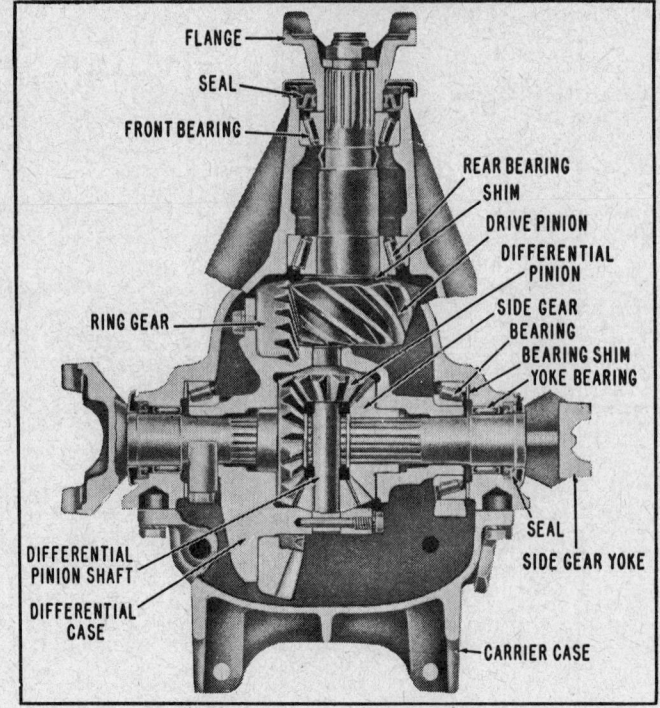

Fig. 2   Rear axle, cutaway view. Corvette

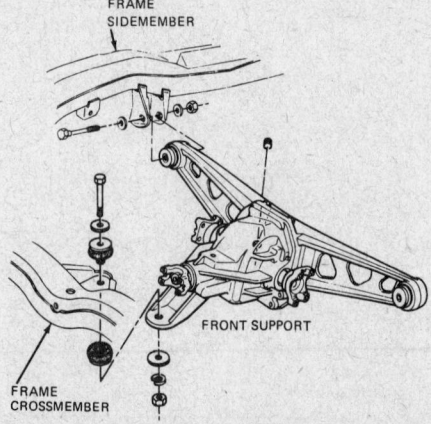

Fig. 3A   Rear axle assembly mounting. 1977–82 Corvette

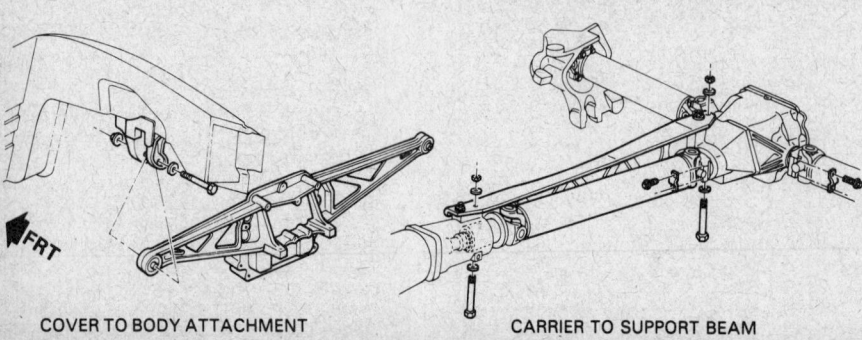

COVER TO BODY ATTACHMENT   CARRIER TO SUPPORT BEAM

Fig. 3   Rear axle assembly mounting. 1984 Corvette

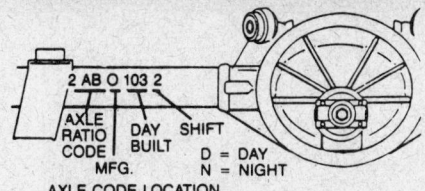

Fig. 4 Rear axle identification. 1977–84 exc. Corvette

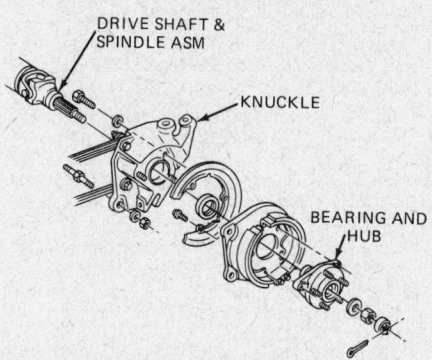

Fig. 5 Rear hub & spindle assembly, exploded view. 1984 Corvette

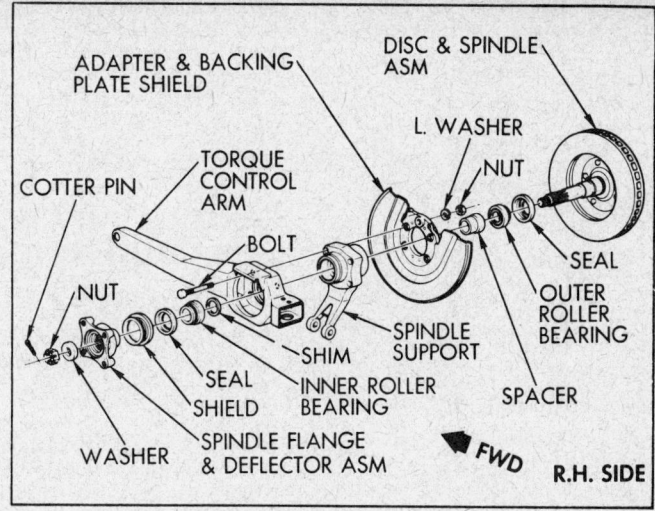

Fig. 6 Rear hub & spindle assembly, exploded view. 1977–82 Corvette

with the housing removed and installed in a holding fixture. The following procedure is necessary only when the housing requires replacement.

1. Raise and support vehicle, then support rear axle with a suitable jack.
2. Disconnect shock absorbers from lower mountings.
3. Remove propeller shaft.
4. Disconnect upper control arms from axle housing attachments, if equipped with coil springs.
5. Disconnect brake line from axle housing junction block and the parking brake cable.
6. Disconnect lower control arms from axle housing attachments, if equipped with coil springs.
7. On models equipped with coil springs, lower axle slowly until springs can be moved. Roll axle assembly out from under vehicle.
8. On models equipped with leaf springs, remove leaf springs as outlined under "Leaf Springs & Bushings, Replace" in Rear Suspension Section. Roll axle assembly out from under vehicle.
9. Reverse procedure to install.

AXLE SHAFT, REPLACE

NOTE: Refer to manufacturer's code to determine rear axle service procedures. Codes are stamped on the left or right axle tube, Fig. 4, or on a tag attached to the housing.

1977–84 C, G, K, M, & P Type

1. Raise vehicle and remove wheel and brake drum.
2. Drain lube from carrier and remove cover.
3. Remove differential pinion shaft lock screw and remove differential pinion shaft.
4. Pull flanged end of axle shaft toward center of vehicle and remove "C" lock from button end of shaft.
5. Remove axle shaft from housing, being careful not to damage seal.
6. Reverse foregoing procedure to install the axle shaft.

1977–79 "B" & "O" Type

1. Raise vehicle and remove wheel and brake drum.
2. Remove bolts attaching axle shaft retainer plate to backing plate.
3. Using a slide hammer/puller, the axle shaft can now be removed.

NOTE: You may find the wheel bearing will come out in pieces as you remove the shaft. The inner race with bearing and one retainer plate will come out with the shaft. The outer race and inner retainer plate will remain in the axle housing. These pieces can easily be removed. Even though the bearing is not in one piece it is no indication that the bearing has failed.

1977–82 Corvette

1. Raise and support vehicle.
2. Disconnect inboard driveshaft trunnion from side gear yoke.
3. On 1982 models, remove plastic splash shields attaching screws and the shields.
4. On 1977–79 models, bend bolt lock tabs downward.
5. Remove bolts securing shaft flange to spindle drive flange.
6. Scribe a mark on the camber adjusting cam and mounting bracket for alignment during assembly.
7. Loosen camber adjusting nut and rotate cam so the high point of the cam faces inboard. This pushes the control arm outboard providing spindle-driveshaft clearance.
8. Remove driveshaft by withdrawing outboard end first.
9. Reverse procedure to install, then check rear suspension alignment.

1984 Corvette

1. Remove center cap from wheel.
2. Remove cotter pin, spindle nut and washer from spindle, Fig. 5.
3. Raise and support vehicle, and remove wheel and tire.
4. Disconnect tie rod and spring from spindle support knuckle as outlined in "Rear Suspension Section."
5. Scribe a reference mark between cam bolt and bracket, remove cam bolt and sepa-

rate spindle support rod from bracket.
6. Remove straps securing inner universal joint to drive yoke, pull knuckle assembly outward, and disconnect driveshaft from yoke.

NOTE: Tape bearing cups to universal joint yoke to prevent loss of needle bearings.

7. Pull spindle out of hub and remove driveshaft.
8. Reverse procedure to install, torquing cam bolt to 158–213 ft. lbs. and spindle nut to 151–177 ft. lbs., then check rear suspension alignment.

REAR SPINDLE & BEARINGS, REPLACE

1977–82 Corvette

1. Raise and support vehicle, and remove wheel and tire.
2. Remove axle driveshaft as outlined in "Drive Axle, Replace."
3. Set parking brake to prevent spindle from turning, and remove cotter pin and nut from spindle, Fig. 6.
4. Release parking brake and remove spindle flange and deflector.
5. Remove 2 brake caliper mounting bolts and secure caliper assembly aside.
6. Disconnect shock absorber and strut rod from spindle support.
7. Install thread protector over end of spindle, and puller J-22602 or equivalent on strut rod stud, Fig. 7.

NOTE: Ensure puller is installed vertically on spindle support before tightening puller screw.

8. Tighten puller screw and remove spindle and outer bearing.
9. Remove outer bearing from spindle using a suitable puller, then the outer seal.
10. Remove spacer tube, end play shim, inner bearing, race, seal and outer bearing race from spindle support.
11. Clean and inspect all components, and replace as needed.
12. Install bearing races in spindle support

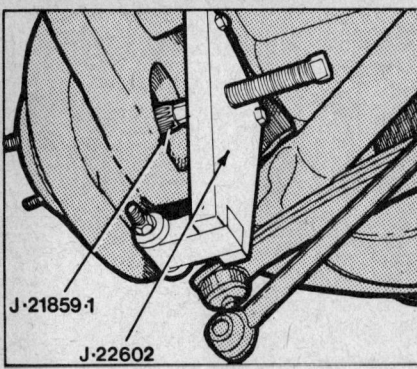

Fig. 7   Spindle removal. 1977–82 Corvette

using driver J-7827 or equivalent, and pack bearings with EPB-2 bearing lube or equivalent.

13. CHeck end play prior to spindle installation as follows:
    a. Mount outer bearing, spacer and end play shim on gauging tool J-24626, and insert assembly into spindle support.
    b. Install inner bearing, washer and nut on gauging tool, ensure bearings are properly seated in races, and torque nut to 100 ft. lbs.
    c. Mount dial indicator on control arm with pointer bearing on outer end of gauging tool.
    d. Move gauging tool in and out while observing end play on indicator.
    e. End play should be .001 to .008 inch. If end play is not within specifications, replace shim as needed to provide proper clearance.

NOTE: If gauging tool is not available, install spindle and bearings as outlined, then check end play at spindle flange. If end play is not within specifications, note dial indicator reading, press out spindle, and replace shim with one which will provide .001 to .008 inch clearance.

14. Remove gauging tool, bearings, spacer and shim.
15. Install outer bearing in race, then seat outer seal in bore of spindle support using a suitable driver.
16. Insert spindle through outer seal and bearing, taking care not to damage seal.
17. Install spacer, shim and inner bearing over end of spindle.
18. Install threaded shaft J-24490-1 on end of spindle.
19. Install sleeve J-24490-2, washer and nut on threaded shaft, then tighten nut to draw spindle into final installed position.
20. Remove installation tool, install inner seal and reverse remaining procedure to complete installation. Torque spindle nut to 100 ft. lbs., and check rear suspension alignment.

NOTE: If specified nut does not allow insertion of cotter pin, tighten spindle flange nut to next flat, then install pin.

1984 Corvette

1. Remove drive shaft assembly as outlined in "Drive Axle, Replace."
2. Remove 2 bolts securing brake caliper bracket to support knuckle, secure caliper aside, then remove brake rotor.
3. Remove hub and bearing retaining bolts using a No. 45 Torx driver, Fig. 5.
4. Remove hub and bearing assembly.
5. Reverse procedure to install, torquing hub retaining bolts to 59–73 ft. lbs., then check rear suspension alignment.

PROPELLER SHAFT, REPLACE

Exc. 1984 Corvette

1. With transmission in neutral and parking brake released, raise and support vehicle.
2. Mark position of shaft in relation to pinion flange for reassembly.
3. Remove straps securing universal joint to pinion flange, then disconnect shaft from flange.

NOTE: Tape bearing cups to universal joint to prevent loss of needle bearings.

4. Slide yoke out of transmission and remove propeller shaft. Insert suitable plug in transmission to prevent fluid loss.
5. Reverse procedure to install.

1984 Corvette

1. With transmission in neutral and parking brake released, raise and support vehicle.
2. Remove exhaust system as follows:
    a. Disconnect AIR pipe from catalytic converter and exhaust pipe.
    b. Disconnect electrical connector to oxygen sensor.
    c. Remove bolts securing muffler to hangers, disconnect exhaust pipes from manifolds and remove exhaust system as an assembly.
3. Remove support beam retaining bolts and support beam.
4. Mark position of shaft in relation to pinion flange for installation.
5. Remove straps securing universal joint to pinion flange, then disconnect shaft from flange.

NOTE: Tape bearing cups to universal joint to prevent loss of needle bearings.

6. Slide yoke out of transmission and remove propeller shaft. Insert suitable plug in transmission to prevent fluid loss.
7. Reverse procedure to install.

BRAKE ADJUSTMENTS

1977–84 Self-Adjusting Brakes

These brakes, have self-adjusting shoe mechanisms that assure correct lining-to-drum clearances at all times. The automatic adjusters operate only when the brakes are applied as the car is moving rearward or when the car comes to an uphill stop.

Although the brakes are self-adjusting, an initial adjustment is necessary after the brake shoes have been relined or replaced, or when the length of the adjusting screw has been changed during some other service operation.

Frequent usage of an automatic transmission forward range to halt reverse vehicle

Fig. 8   Parking Brake Shoe adjustment (Typical). Corvette

motion may prevent the automatic adjusters from functioning, thereby inducing low pedal heights. Should low pedal heights be encountered, it is recommended that numerous forward and reverse stops be made until satisfactory pedal height is obtained.

NOTE: If a low pedal condition cannot be corrected by making numerous reverse stops (provided the hydraulic system is free of air) it indicates that the self-adjusting mechanism is not functioning. Therefore it will be necessary to remove the brake drum, clean, free up and lubricate the adjusting mechanism. Then adjust the brakes, being sure the parking brake is fully released.

Adjustment

1. Using a suitable punch, knock out lanced area in backing plate or drum. If drum is installed on vehicle when this is done, remove drum and clean brake compartment of all metal.

NOTE: When adjustment is completed, a new hole cover must be installed in the backing plate.

2. Using Tool J-6166 or equivalent, turn brake adjusting screw to expand brake shoes at each wheel until wheel can just be turned by hand. Drag should be equal on all wheels.
3. On all except 1982–84 Camaro, back off adjusting screw at each wheel 30 notches.
4. On 1982–84 Camaro, back off screw 12 notches.
5. If shoe still drags slightly on drum, back off adjusting screw an additional one or two notches.
6. When adjusting screw has been backed off approximately 12 notches, brakes should be free of drag. Heavy drag at this point indicates tight parking brake cables.
7. Install adjusting hole cover in brake backing plate.
8. Check parking brake for proper adjustment.

PARKING BRAKE, ADJUST

1977–84 Except Corvette & 1982–84 Camaro With Rear Disc Brakes

1. Jack up both rear wheels.
2. Apply parking brake exactly two notches on all except 1977 Chevelle and Monte Carlo and 1977–81 Chevrolet, 3 notches on 1977 Chevelle and Monte Carlo, and 1 notch on 1977–81 Chevrolet.

3. Tighten adjusting nut until left rear wheel can just be rotated rearward but is locked when forward rotation is attempted.
4. Release parking brake and check to ensure that rear wheels rotate freely in either direction with no brake drag.

1982—84 Camaro With Rear Disc Brakes

1. Lubricate parking brake cables at underbody rub points and at equalizer hooks and ensure free movement of all cables.
2. With parking brake fully released, jack up both rear wheels.
3. Remove slack from cable by holding brake cable stud and tightening equalizer nut.

NOTE: After tightening nut, check that caliper levers are against stops on caliper housing. If not, loosen cable until levers return to stops.

---

4. Actuate parking brake several times to check adjustment.

1977—82 Corvette

1. Release parking brake lever, then raise and support vehicle.
2. Loosen parking brake cable adjusting nut at equalizer until brake shoe actuating levers move freely to the released position with slack in cables.
3. Remove rear wheels and turn each brake rotor until parking brake shoe star adjuster is visible through hole in rotor hub.
4. Insert a suitable adjusting tool through hole in rotor, and tighten adjusters by moving hand away from floor, Fig. 8.
5. Adjust one side at a time, tightening adjuster until rotor cannot be turned by hand, then backing star wheel off 6 to 8 notches.
6. Install rear wheels and pull parking brake lever up 13 notches to the applied position.
7. Tighten cable adjusting nut at equalizer until 80 lbs. pull is required to lift parking brake lever to the 14th notch, then secure adjustment with lock nut.
8. Release parking brake lever and check adjustment. Rear wheels should turn freely in both directions with no brake drag.

1984 Corvette

1. Release parking brake lever, then raise and support vehicle.
2. Remove rear wheels, then install lug nuts on 2 opposite wheel studs to hold brake rotor in position.
3. Back caliper pistons into bores.
4. Loosen parking brake cable adjusting nut until there is no tension on parking brake shoes.
5. Turn each brake rotor until parking brake shoe star adjuster is visible through hole in rotor.
6. Adjusting one side at a time, tighten adjuster until rotor cannot be turned by hand, then back star wheel off 5 to 7 notches.

NOTE: Adjust parking brake shoes by inserting a suitable tool through hole in rotor. On driver's side, tighten adjuster by moving handle of tool upwards. On passenger side, tighten adjuster by moving handle of tool downwards.

---

7. Install rear wheels and pull parking brake lever up 2 notches.
8. Tighten cable adjusting nut at equalizer until there is drag on wheels.
9. Release parking brake lever and check adjustment. No drag should be felt when rotating wheels.

MASTER CYLINDER, REPLACE

1977—84

1. Disconnect brake pipes from master cylinder. Plug lines and master cylinder ports to prevent entry of foreign material.
2. Disconnect brake pedal from master cylinder push rod, if equipped with manual brakes.
3. Remove master cylinder attaching nuts and the master cylinder.
4. Reverse procedure to install.

POWER BRAKE UNIT

1980—84 Hydro-Boost

NOTE: Pump brake pedal several times with engine off to deplete accumulator of fluid.

1. Remove two nuts attaching master cylinder to booster, then move master cylinder away from booster with brake lines attached.
2. Remove three hydraulic lines from booster. Plug and cap all lines and outlets.
3. Remove retainer and washer securing booster push rod to brake pedal arm.
4. Remove four nuts attaching booster unit to dash panel.
5. From engine compartment, loosen booster from dash panel and move booster push rod inboard until it disconnects from brake pedal arm. Remove spring washer from brake pedal arm.
6. Remove booster unit from vehicle.
7. Reverse procedure to install. To purge system, disconnect feed wire from injection pump. Fill power steering pump reservoir, then crank engine for several seconds and recheck power steering pump fluid level. Connect injection pump feed wire and start engine, then cycle steering wheel from stop to stop twice and stop engine. Discharge accumulator by depressing brake pedal several times, then check fluid level. Start engine, then turn steering wheel from stop to stop and turn engine off. Check fluid level and add fluid as necessary. If foaming occurs, stop engine and wait for approximately one hour for foam to dissipate, then recheck fluid level.

1977—84 Except Hydro-Boost

1. Remove vacuum hose from check valve and master cylinder retaining nuts.
2. Pull master cylinder forward so it clears mounting studs and move to one side. Support cylinder to avoid stress on hydraulic lines.
3. Remove power unit to dash nuts. On 1977 Chevelle and Monte Carlo, remove brake line clip from power unit.
4. Remove brake pedal push rod retainer and disconnect push rod from pin.

NOTE: On 1977 Chevelle and Monte Carlo, push brake pedal to floor. This pushes power unit away from dash, providing clearance to remove push rod.

---

5. Remove power unit from vehicle.
6. Reverse procedure to install.

Rear Suspension

SHOCK ABSORBER, REPLACE

1977—84 All

1. If equipped with Superlift shock absorbers, disconnect air lines from shock absorber fittings.
2. With rear axle properly supported, disconnect shock absorber from upper and lower mountings, Figs. 1 through 3A.
3. Reverse procedure to install.

COIL SPRINGS, REPLACE

1977—84 Chevrolet, Chevelle, Malibu & Monte Carlo

1. Support vehicle at frame and rear axle.
2. Disconnect shock absorbers at lower mountings.
3. Disconnect upper control arms from axle housing.
4. If equipped with a stabilizer bar, disconnect bar from either right or left hand side of control arm.
5. If necessary on 1977 models, disconnect brake line at junction block on axle housing. On all models, remove brake hose support bolt and support without disconnecting the brake lines.
6. Lower axle until it reaches end of its travel and using a suitable tool, pry lower pigtail over retainer on axle bracket. Remove spring and insulator.
7. Reverse procedure to install. Springs must be installed with an insulator between upper seat and spring and posi-

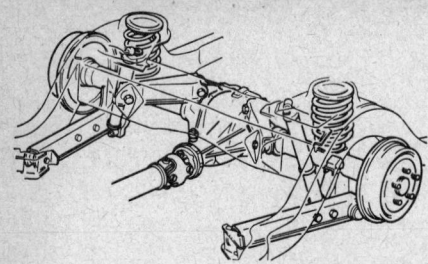

Fig. 1   Rear suspension (Typical). Exc. Camaro, Corvette & Nova

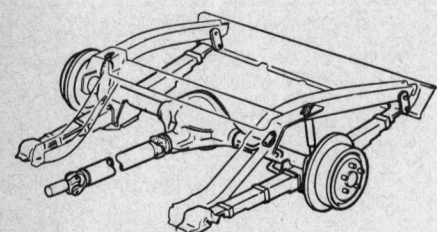

Fig. 2   Rear suspension. 1977–81 Camaro & 1977–79 Nova

tioned properly, Fig. 4.

1982–84 Camaro

1. Raise and support vehicle and support rear axle with a suitable adjustable jack.
2. Remove track bar mounting bolt from axle and loosen track bar bolt at body brace.
3. Disconnect rear brake hose clip at underbody, then disconnect shock absorbers at lower mountings.
4. On models equipped with 4-151 engine, remove propeller shaft.
5. Lower rear axle and remove springs and insulators.
6. Reverse procedure to install.

LEAF SPRINGS & BUSHINGS, REPLACE

1977–81 Camaro & 1977–79 Nova

1. Support vehicle at frame and rear axle, removing tension from spring.
2. Disconnect shock absorber from lower mounting.
3. Loosen spring front mount bolt.
4. Remove spring front mounting bracket attaching screws, lower axle and remove bracket.
5. Disconnect parking brake cable from spring plate bracket.
6. Remove spring plate by removing axle bracket nuts on single leaf models and the "U" bolts on multi-leaf models.
7. Support spring, remove front mount bolt and disassemble rear shackle.
8. Replace rear shackle and spring eye bushings as necessary, Figs. 5 and 6.
9. Reverse procedure to install.

1977–82 Corvette

1. Support vehicle at frame and remove rear wheels.
2. Install a "C" clamp approximately 9

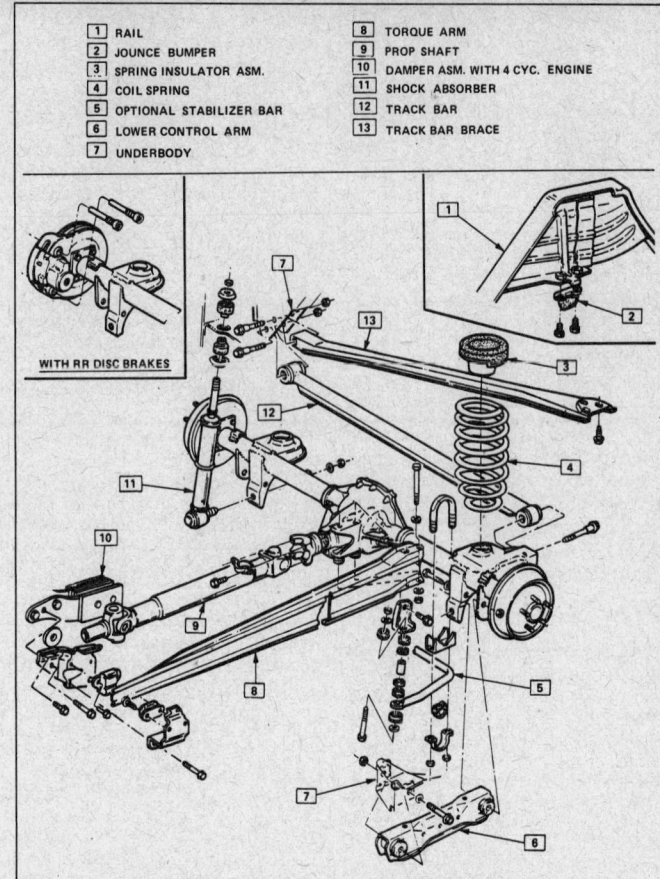

1	RAIL	8	TORQUE ARM
2	JOUNCE BUMPER	9	PROP SHAFT
3	SPRING INSULATOR ASM.	10	DAMPER ASM. WITH 4 CYC. ENGINE
4	COIL SPRING	11	SHOCK ABSORBER
5	OPTIONAL STABILIZER BAR	12	TRACK BAR
6	LOWER CONTROL ARM	13	TRACK BAR BRACE
7	UNDERBODY		

Fig. 2A   Rear suspension. 1982–84 Camaro

inches from end of spring.
3. Place a suitable jack under spring, Fig. 7, and place a wooden block between "C" clamp and jack pad.
4. Raise jack until load is off spring link, then remove cotter pin, link nut and spring cushion, Figs. 8 and 8A. Lower jack, removing tension from spring.
5. Repeat steps 2, 3 and 4 on opposite side of spring.
6. Remove bolts from spring center clamp plate, then remove clamp plate.

7. Remove spring from vehicle.
8. Reverse procedure to install.

1984 Corvette

1. Raise and support vehicle and remove one wheel and tire assembly.
2. Remove cotter pin, retaining nuts, bushings and link bolts securing spring to spindle support knuckles, Fig. 9.
3. Remove bolts securing spring to cover beam, spacers, insulators and spring, Fig.

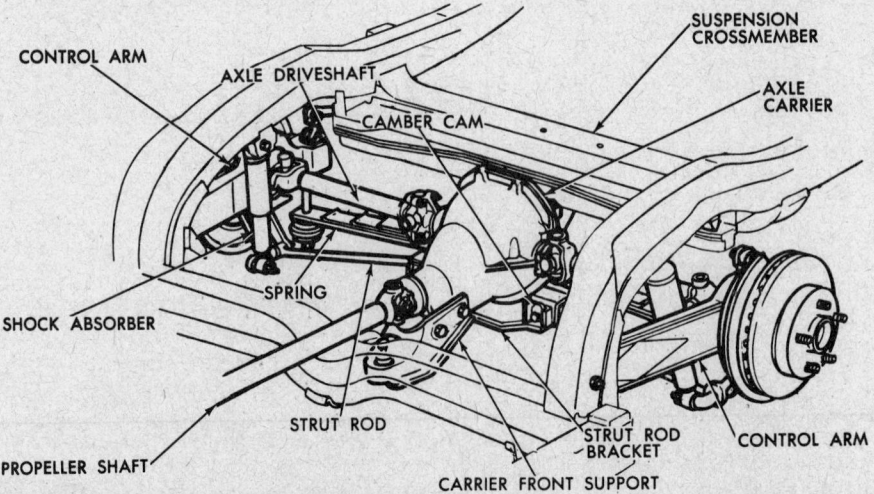

Fig. 3   Rear suspension (Typical). 1977–82 Corvette

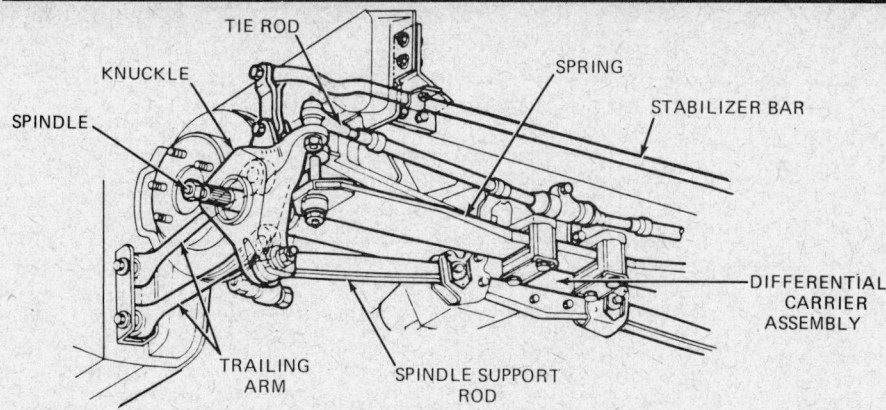

Fig. 3A   Rear suspension. 1984 Corvette

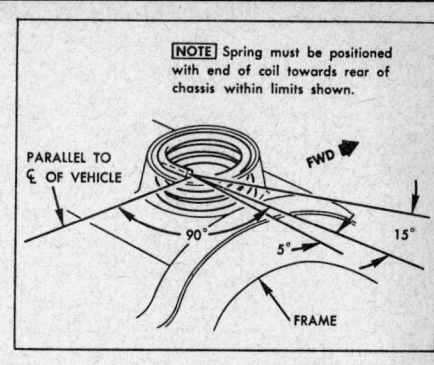

Fig. 4   Coil spring installation

9A.
4. Reverse procedure to install. Torque bolts securing spring to cover beam to 29–44 ft. lbs.

LEAF SPRING SERVICE

NOTE: The spring leaves are not serviced separately, however, the spring leaf inserts may be replaced.

1. Clamp spring in a vise and remove spring clips.
2. File peened end of center bolt to permit nut removal, remove nut and open vise slowly, allowing spring to expand.
3. Replace spring leaves or leaf inserts.
4. On 1977–81 Corvette, to replace main leaf cushion retainers, chisel flared portion until retainer can be removed from leaf. Install new retainers and flare over with a hammer.
5. On all models use a drift to align center bolt holes, compress spring in vise and install new center bolt and nut. Peen end of bolt to retain nut.

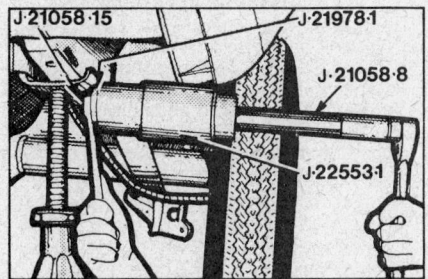

Fig. 5   Leaf spring bushing removal. 1977–79 Nova & 1977–81 Camaro

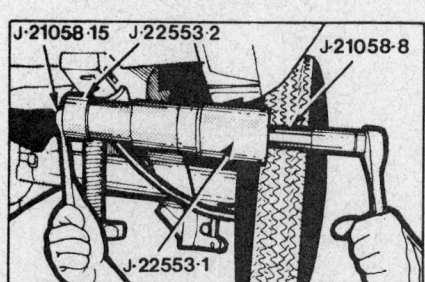

Fig. 6   Leaf spring bushing installation. 1977–79 Nova & 1977–81 Camaro

6. Align springs and bend spring clips into position.

NOTE: Overtightening of spring clips will cause spring binding.

CONTROL ARMS & BUSHINGS, REPLACE
1977–84 Exc. Corvette

NOTE: If more than one control arm is being replaced, remove and install one arm at a time to prevent axle assembly from slipping or twisting out of position.

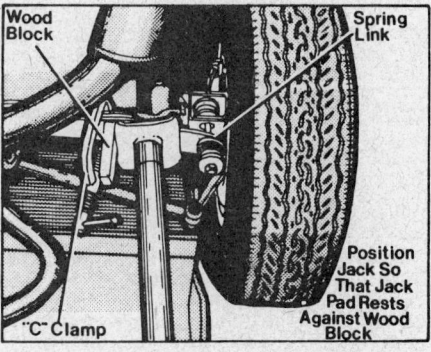

Fig. 7   Supporting leaf spring. 1977–82 Corvette

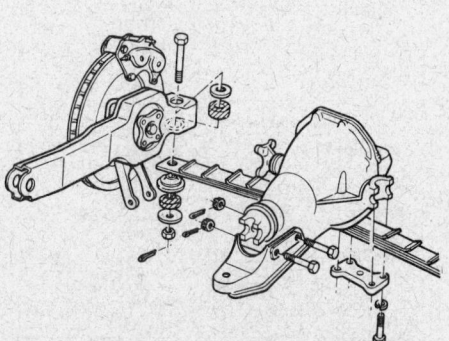

Fig. 8   Transverse leaf spring mounting. 1977–80 Corvette

CONTROL ARMS, REPLACE

1. Raise vehicle and support at frame pads. Support nose of axle housing to prevent assembly from twisting when control arm is removed.
2. If lower control arm is being replaced, remove bolts securing stabilizer bar to control arm, if equipped.
3. Remove bolts securing control arm to chassis and rear axle, and the control arm.
4. Reverse procedure to install, lower vehicle and torque control arm bolts to specifications, Fig. 10, with vehicle at normal ride height.

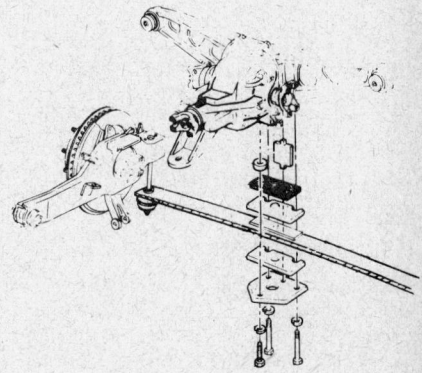

Fig. 8A   Transverse leaf spring mounting. 1981–82 Corvette

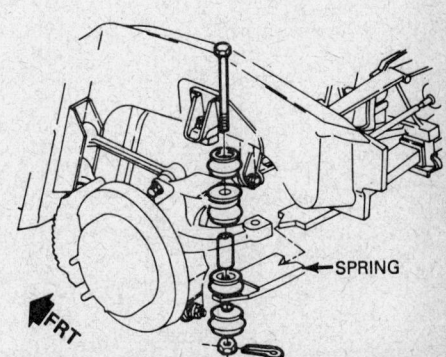

Fig. 9   Transverse leaf spring link assembly. 1984 Corvette

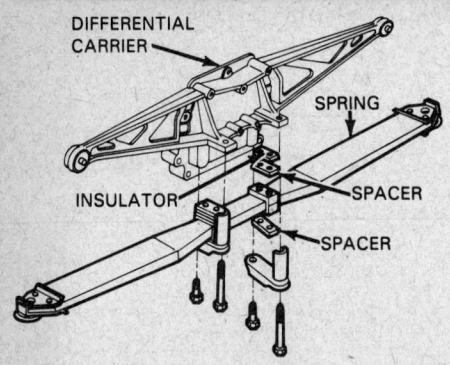

Fig. 9A Transverse leaf spring mounting. 1984 Corvette

Year	Model	Upper		Lower	
		F	R	F	R
1977	Chevrolet	115	80	115	115
	Chevelle & Monte Carlo	80	80	80	80
1978–83	Malibu & Monte Carlo	70	73	70	73①
1978–84	Chevrolet	92	70	92	92
1982–84	Camaro	—	—	68	68
1984	Monte Carlo	70	73	70	73①
①—Bolt torque.					

Fig. 10 Control arm retaining nut torque specifications

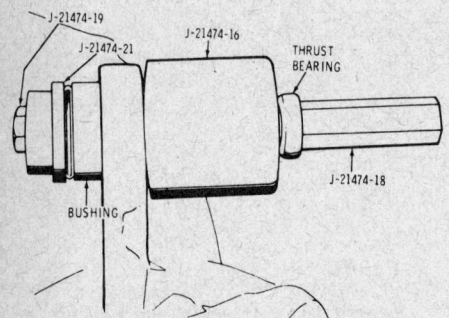

Fig. 11 Upper control arm rear bushing (differential carrier bushing) removal

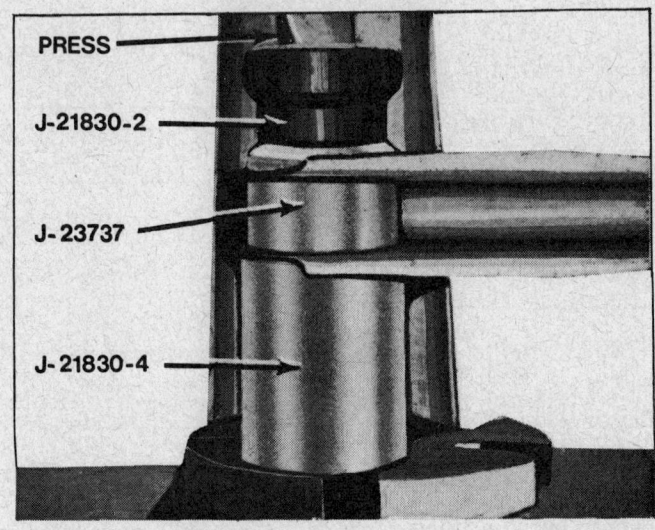

Fig. 13 Control arm bushing removal. 1977

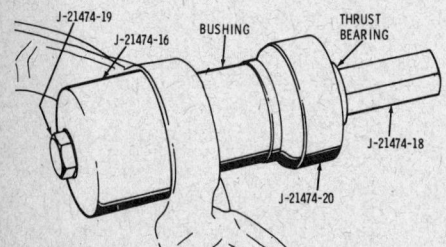

Fig. 12 Upper control arm bushing (differential carrier bushing) installation

NOTE: All torque prevailing type fasteners must be torqued at the nut, not at the bolt, to ensure proper clamping force.

BUSHING REPLACEMENT

Differential Carrier Bushings (Upper Control Arm Rear Bushing)

The upper control arm rear bushing, which is pressed into the differential carrier, can be replaced using the following procedure:
1. Raise vehicle and support at frame pads, and support nose of axle housing to prevent assembly from twisting.
2. Lower rear axle to obtain clearance, disconnect upper control arm from axle and position aside.
3. Install suitable bushing removal tool as shown in Fig. 11, tighten puller screw and press bushing out of housing.
4. To install replacement bushing, reverse position of removal tool and pull bushing into position by tightening screw.

Control Arm Bushings
1. Raise and support vehicle and remove control arm as outlined previously.
2. Press bushings out of control arm using suitable tools as shown in Figs. 12 through 18.
3. Reverse procedure to install, ensuring

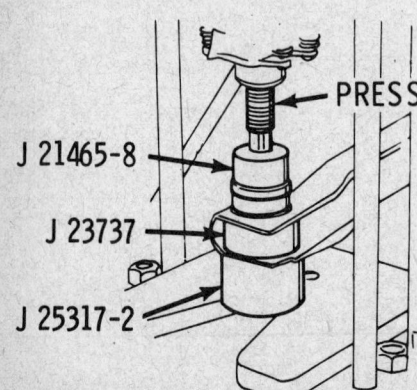

Fig. 14 Control arm bushing removal. 1978–84

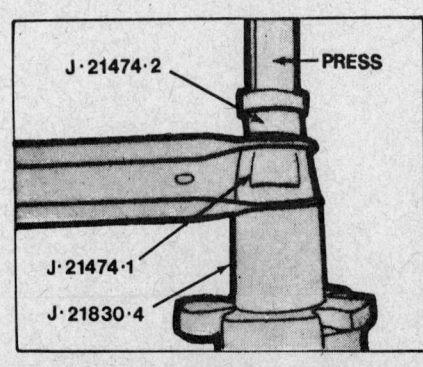

Fig. 15 Control arm bushing installation. 1977 Chevelle & Monte Carlo

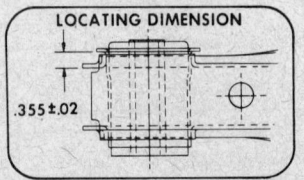

Fig. 16 Control arm bushing locating dimension. 1977 Chevelle & Monte Carlo

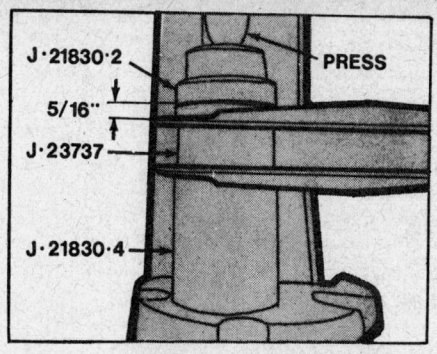

Fig. 17   Control arm bushing installation.
1977 Chevrolet full size

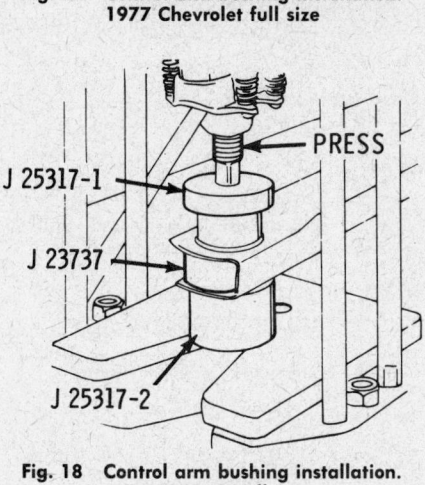

Fig. 18   Control arm bushing installation.
1978—84 all

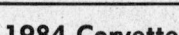

bushing is properly seated in control
arm.

NOTE: If replacement bushing fits loosely in
control arm, or if mounting areas are damaged or deformed, control arm must be
replaced.

1984 Corvette

Control Arms, Replace
1. Raise and support vehicle, and remove
wheel and tire assembly.
2. Remove shock absorber. Use a back-up
wrench on lower mounting stud when
removing retaining nut.
3. Remove bolts securing control arm to
spindle support knuckle.
4. Remove control arm bolt at mounting
bracket and control arm.
5. Reverse procedure to install. Torque control arm to bracket bolt to 55–70 ft. lbs.,
and control arm to knuckle bolt to
125–154 ft. lbs.

STABILIZER BAR,
REPLACE

Chevrolet, Malibu & Monte Carlo
1. Support vehicle at rear axle.
2. Remove bolts securing stabilizer bar to
lower control arms, Fig. 14.
3. Reverse procedure to install. Use spacer
shims, if needed, placed equally on each
side of stabilizer bar. Tighten attaching
bolts with vehicle at curb height.

1977–81 Camaro & 1977–79
Nova
1. Support vehicle at rear axle.

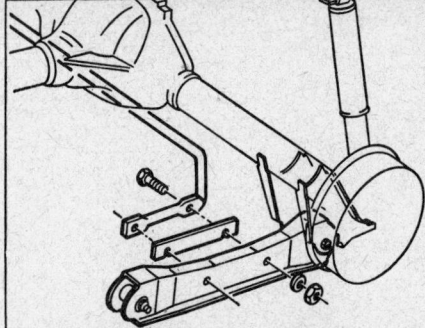

Fig. 19   Stabilizer bar installation.
Chevrolet, Malibu & Monte Carlo

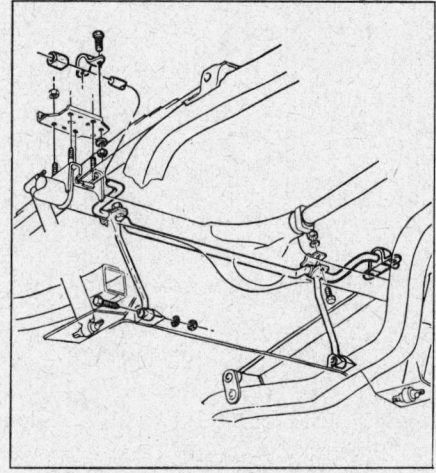

Fig. 20   Stabilizer bar installation
(Typical). 1977–79 Nova & 1977–81 Camaro

2. Disconnect stabilizer bar from spring
plate brackets, Fig. 20.
3. Disconnect stabilizer bar from body
brackets.
4. Reverse procedure to install. Tighten
attaching bolts with vehicle at curb
height.

1982–84 Camaro

1. Raise and support vehicle.
2. Remove link bolt nuts, washers, bushings, spacers and link bolts securing stabilizer to chassis, Fig. 21.
3. Remove clamps securing stabilizer shaft
to rear axle and stabilizer shaft.

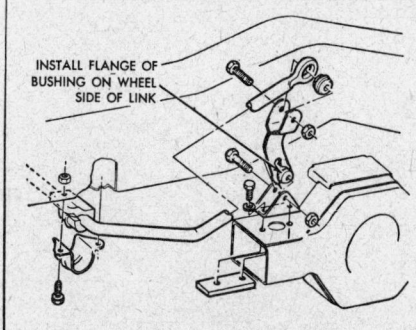

Fig. 22   Stabilizer bar installation.
1977–82 Corvette

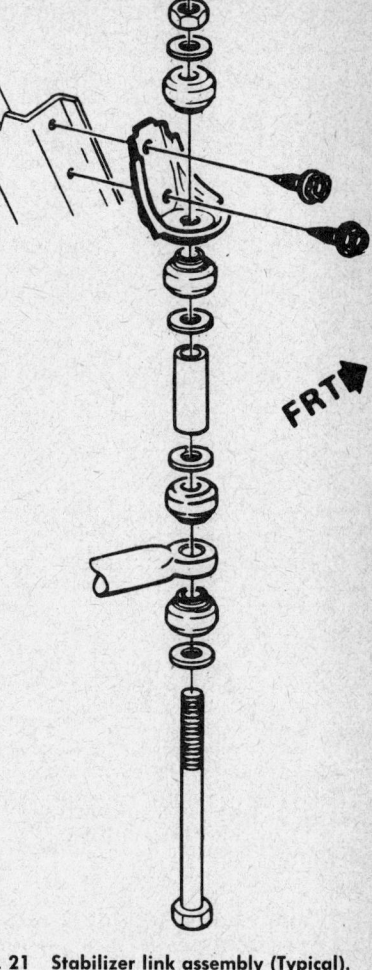

Fig. 21   Stabilizer link assembly (Typical).
1982–84 Camaro

4. Reverse procedure to install. Torque link
bolts to 12 ft. lbs., and U-bolt nuts to 20 ft.
lbs.

1977–82 Corvette

1. Disconnect stabilizer bar from torque control arms and remove stabilizer bar frame
brackets, Fig. 22.
2. Replace bushings as necessary, Fig. 22.
3. Reverse procedure to install.

1984 Corvette

1. Raise and support vehicle.
2. Remove spare tire and carrier.
3. Disconnect stabilizer links from spindle
support knuckles.
4. Remove retainers securing shaft bushings to crossmember, bushings and stabilizer shaft.
5. Reverse procedure to install. Torque
bushing retaining nuts and bolts securing
stabilizer links to knuckles to 14–22 ft.
lbs., and bolts securing links to stabilizer
bar to 25–35 ft. lbs.

TRACK BAR & BRACE,
REPLACE

1982–84 Camaro

1. Raise vehicle and support rear axle at

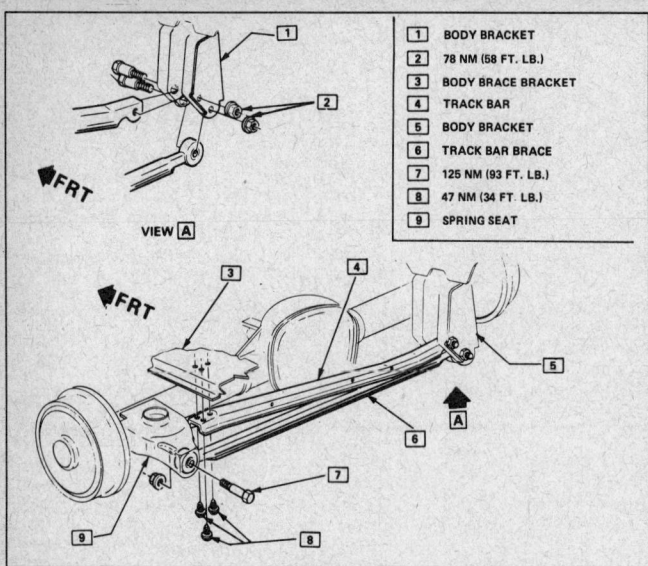

1	BODY BRACKET
2	78 NM (58 FT. LB.)
3	BODY BRACE BRACKET
4	TRACK BAR
5	BODY BRACKET
6	TRACK BAR BRACE
7	125 NM (93 FT. LB.)
8	47 NM (34 FT. LB.)
9	SPRING SEAT

VIEW A

FRT

FRT

A

Fig. 23   Track bar and brace installation. 1982–84 Camaro

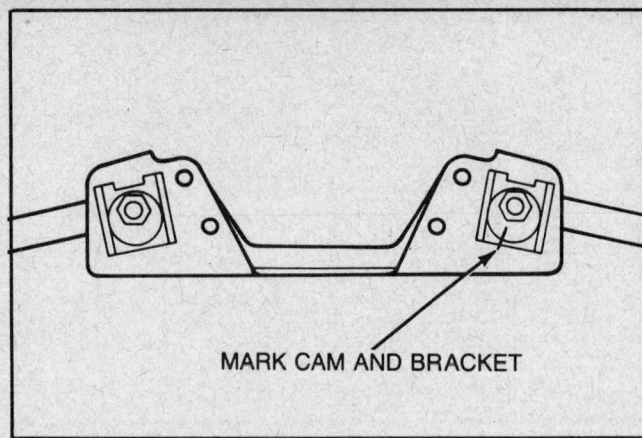

MARK CAM AND BRACKET

Fig. 24   Indexing adjustment cam bolt and bracket (Typical). Corvette

curb height.
2. Remove track bar mounting bolt and nut from rear axle and from body bracket, then remove track bar, Fig. 23.
3. Remove heat shield attaching screws from track bar brace.
4. Remove three track bar brace to body brace screws.
5. Remove nut and bolt from body bracket, then remove track bar brace.
6. Reverse procedure to install.

STRUT ROD, SPINDLE SUPPORT ROD & TIE ROD, REPLACE

1977–82 Corvette

Strut Rod
1. Support vehicle at frame.
2. Disconnect shock frame from lower mounting.
3. Remove cotter pin and nut from strut rod shaft. Pull shaft toward front of vehicle and remove from bracket.
4. Mark position of camber adjusting cam to ensure proper installation, Fig. 24 and loosen camber bolt nut.
5. Remove bolts securing strut rod bracket

to carrier.
6. Remove camber bolt and nut, pull strut rod out of bracket and remove bushing caps.
7. Replace bushings as necessary, Fig. 25.
8. Reverse procedure to install.

1984 Corvette

Spindle Support Rod
1. Raise and support vehicle, and remove wheel and tire.
2. Scribe mark between cam bolt and bracket for reassembly, Fig. 24.
3. Remove cam bolt and disconnect support rod from bracket.
4. Remove bolt securing spindle support rod to knuckle and rod.
5. Reverse procedure to install, then check rear suspension alignment. Torque retaining bolt at knuckle to 95–118 ft. lbs., and cam bolt to 158–213 ft. lbs.

Tie Rod
1. Raise and support vehicle, and remove wheel and tire.
2. Remove cotter pin and nut securing tie rod to spindle support knuckle.
3. Press tie rod from knuckle using tool J-24319-01 or equivalent.
4. Remove tie rod from adjusting sleeve,

counting number of turns necessary.
5. Reverse procedure to install, then check rear suspension alignment. Torque tie rod nut 29–36 ft. lbs., and locking nut to 39–53 ft. lbs.

SPINDLE SUPPORT KNUCKLE, REPLACE

1984 Corvette

1. Remove center cap from wheel, cotter pin and spindle nut.
2. Raise and support vehicle, and remove wheel and tire.
3. Remove 2 bolts securing brake caliper to knuckle, brake caliper assembly and brake rotor.
4. Disconnect tie rod, leaf spring and stabilizer shaft from knuckle as outlined previously.
5. Disconnect parking brake cable from backing plate and bracket.
6. Disconnect shock absorber and support rod from knuckle, using a back-up wrench on shock mounting stud.
7. Remove bolts securing control arms to knuckle, lower knuckle assembly and slide spindle out of hub and bearing.
8. Remove hub and bearing and parking brake assembly from knuckle, using a No. 45 Torx bit to remove hub retaining bolts, then remove splash shield.
9. Reverse procedure to install, then check rear suspension alignment. Torque all

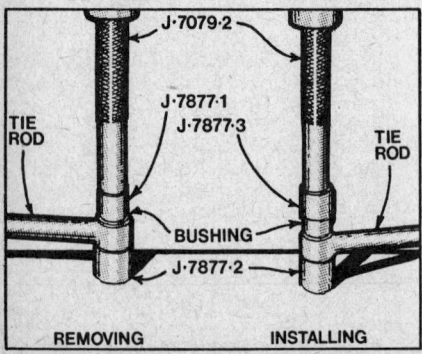

J-7079-2

J-7877-1
J-7877-3

TIE ROD

TIE ROD

BUSHING

J-7877-2

REMOVING   INSTALLING

Fig. 25   Strut rod bushing replacement. 1977–82 Corvette

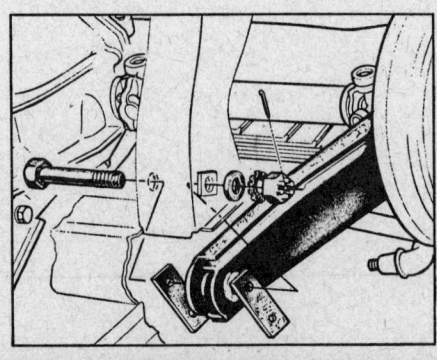

Fig. 26   Torque control arm installation. 1977–82 Corvette

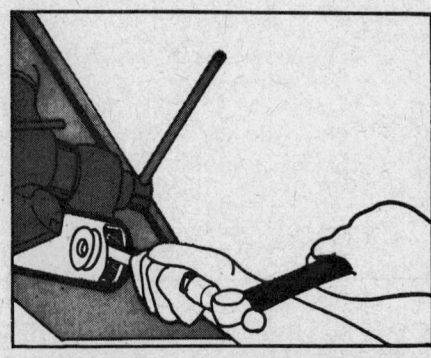

Fig. 27   Torque control arm bushing removal. 1977–82 Corvette

Fig. 28 Torque control arm bushing installation. 1977–82 Corvette

bolts to specifications given in individual component replacement procedures.

TORQUE CONTROL ARMS & BUSHINGS, REPLACE

1977–82 Corvette

1. Perform steps 1 thru 4 as outlined under "Leaf Spring Replace" 1977–82 Corvette procedure.
2. If equipped with a stabilizer shaft, disconnect shaft at torque arms.
3. Disconnect shock absorber at lower mounting.
4. Disconnect and lower strut rod shaft.
5. Disconnect axle drive shaft from spindle flange by removing attaching bolts.

NOTE: It may be necessary to force torque arm outboard providing clearance to lower axle drive shaft.

6. Disconnect brake line from caliper and from torque arm. Disconnect parking brake cable.
7. Remove torque arm forward mounting bolt and toe-in shims, Fig. 26, and pull torque arm out of frame attachment.

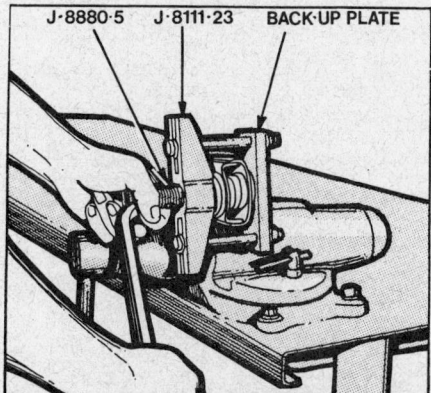

Fig. 30 Flaring torque control arm bushing retainer. 1977–82 Corvette

8. Replace bushings if necessary as described under "Torque Control Arm Bushing Service."
9. Reverse procedure to install.

Torque Control Arm Bushing Service

1. Using an $11/16$ inch twist drill, drill out flared end of bushing retainer, remove retainer plate and retainer from bushing.
2. Spread bushing with a chisel, Fig. 27, and tap bushing from arm.

NOTE: If bushing is rusted in torque arm, torque arm may spread during bushing removal. Install a "C" clamp torque arm, preventing torque arm spreading.

3. Oil steel portion of new bushing and press bushing into arm, Fig. 28.
4. Place retainer plate over flared portion of bushing retainer and insert retainer into bushing.
5. Make a flaring tool back-up plate, Fig. 29, with $1/2$ inch bolt holes.
6. Place back-up plate on flared end of bushing retainer and assemble tool to plate, Fig. 30, with $1/2 \times 5$ inch bolts. Center threaded hole in tool # J-8111-23 over unflared end of bushing retainer. Also center chamfered retainer plate over retainer tube.
7. Lubricate end of tool # J-8880-5 and thread screw into tool, flaring retainer.

CROSSMEMBER & ISOLATION MOUNT, REPLACE

1977–79 Corvette

1. Remove leaf spring as outlined under "Leaf Spring Replace" 1977–82 Corvette procedure.
2. Remove differential carrier and cover as outlined in "Rear Axle, Propeller Shaft & Brakes" section 1977–82 Corvette procedure.
3. Support crossmember and remove bolts securing isolation mounts to frame and lower the crossmember.
4. To replace isolation mount, straighten isolation mount tabs and using a suitable ram, press on outer steel shell or inner steel insert, removing mount from crossmember. Install new mount into position, compress outer sleeve, press mount into crossmember and bend over locking tabs, Fig. 32.
5. Reverse procedure to install crossmember.

REAR WHEEL ALIGNMENT

Corvette

Rear wheel alignment should be checked and adjusted periodically, when rear tires indicate abnormal wear, or when suspension components are replaced. Prior to rear wheel alignment, check suspension components for

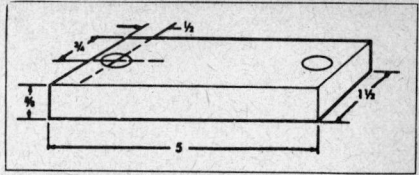

Fig. 29 Flaring tool back-up plate

damage or excessive wear and repair as needed. Also ensure tires are properly inflated, and wheel bearing end play is within specifications.

Camber, Adjust

Wheel camber is adjusted by rotating the eccentric cam and bolt located at the inboard end of the strut rod or spindle support rod, Figs. 3 and 3A. To check and adjust camber, proceed as follows:

1. Place rear wheels of vehicle on suitable alignment equipment following manufacturer's instructions, then check camber reading.
2. If wheel camber is not within specifications, loosen cam bolt retaining nut.
3. Rotate cam bolt until camber reading is within specifications listed at the front of this chapter.
4. Torque cam bolt nut to specifications while holding position of bolt, then recheck camber reading.

Toe-In Adjust

1977–82

Rear wheel toe-in is adjusted by inserting slotted shims of varying thickness inside the frame side member on both sides of the torque control arm pivot bushing. Shims are available in thicknesses of $1/64''$, $1/32''$, $1/8''$ and $1/4''$.

To adjust, loosen torque arm pivot bolts until shims are free enough to remove. Position torque arm assembly until toe-in is within specifications listed in the front of this chapter. Shim gap toward vehicle centerline between end of control arm bushing and frame side inner wall.

1984

Toe-in is adjusted by loosening lock nuts on tie rod ends and rotating adjuster sleeves until desired setting is obtained. Refer to front of this chapter for toe-in specifications.

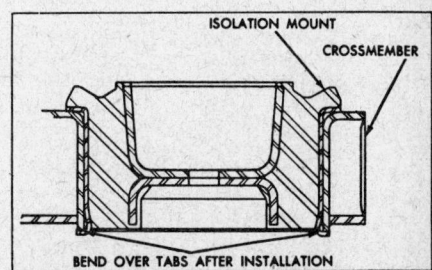

Fig. 31 Crossmember isolation mount installation. 1977–82 Corvette

Front Suspension & Steering Section

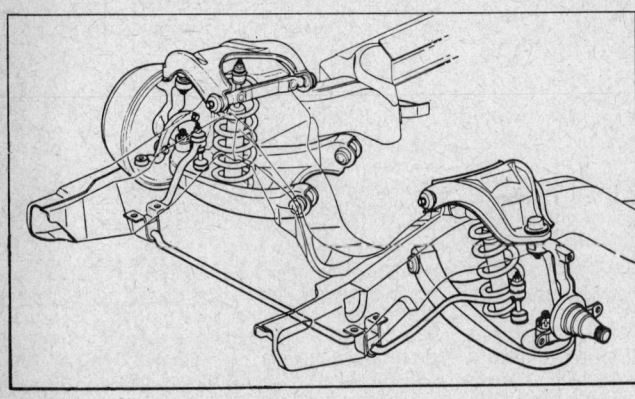

Fig. 1   Front suspension (Typical). Exc. 1982–84 Camaro & 1984 Corvette

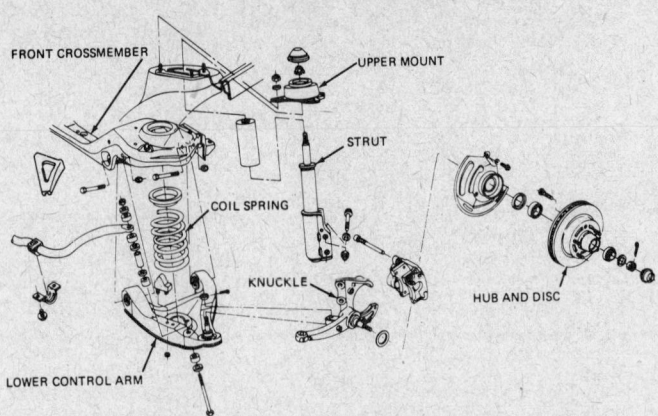

Fig. 2   Front suspension, exploded view. 1982–84 Camaro

FRONT SUSPENSION

All models except 1982–84 Camaro and 1984 Corvette use a Short-Long Arm (SLA) type front suspension with independent coil springs riding on lower control arms, Fig. 1. Ball joints link upper and lower control arms to a spindle assembly, and tubular shock absorbers are used to dampen spring action. On some models, a spring steel stabilizer shaft is connected between the chassis and lower control arms to control side roll.

A modified strut type suspension is used on 1982–84 Camaro, Fig. 2. Each wheel is independently connected to the chassis by a lower control arm, spindle and a strut assembly which locates the spindle and controls ride by dampening spring action. Coil springs are mounted between the lower control arm and crossmember, and a stabilizer shaft is connected between the chassis and control arms to control side roll.

The front suspension used on 1984 Corvette consists of forged aluminum upper and lower control arms and steering knuckle, a fiberglass mono-leaf spring, shock absorbers and stabilizer bar, Fig. 3. The front spring is transverse mounted on the crossmember and bears against lower control arms. The stabilizer bar and shock absorbers are connected between the chassis and lower control arms, and control side roll and dampen spring action respectively. Upper and lower control arms are connected through the knuckle, which is specially designed to move the wheel centerline rearward of the conventional ball joint centerline.

WHEEL ALIGNMENT

NOTE: Prior to checking or adjusting front suspension alignment, inspect suspension components for damage or excessive wear, and replace as needed. Ensure tire pressures and wheel bearings are properly adjusted, then raise and release front bumper several times to allow vehicle to assume normal ride height.

1977–84 All Exc. 1982–84 Camaro

Caster and camber adjustments are made by means of shims between the upper control arm inner support shaft and the support bracket attached to the frame. Shims may be added, subtracted or transferred to change the readings as follows:

Caster, Adjust

Transfer shims from front to rear or rear to front. The transfer of one shim to the front bolt from the rear bolt will decrease positive caster. On shim (1/32") transferred from the rear bolt to the front bolt will change caster about 1/2 degree.

Camber, Adjust

Change shims at both the front and rear of the shaft. Adding an equal number of shims at both front and rear of the support shaft will decrease positive camber. One shim (1/32") at each location will move camber approximately 1/5 degree on 1977–81 Camaro, Chevelle and Nova, on Chevrolet and Corvette the change will be about 1/6 degree.

1982–84 Camaro

Caster and camber adjustments are made by moving the position of the upper strut mount assembly. To make adjustment, remove dust cap and fender bolt and attach tool J-29724 to original fender bolt, Fig. 4. Tighten the turnbuckle and loosen the three strut mount attaching nuts.

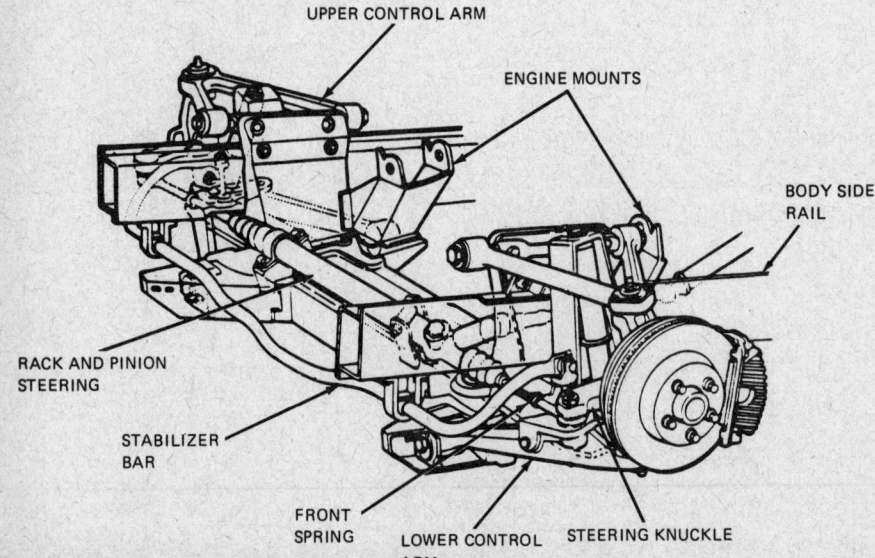

Fig. 3   Front suspension. 1984 Corvette

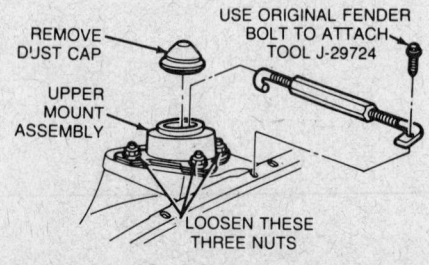

Fig. 4   Camber and caster adjustment. 1982–84 Camaro

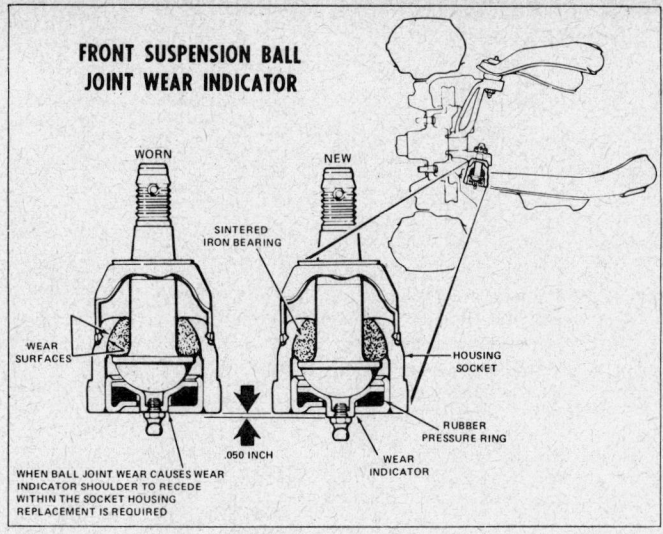

Fig. 5 Lower ball joint wear indicator.

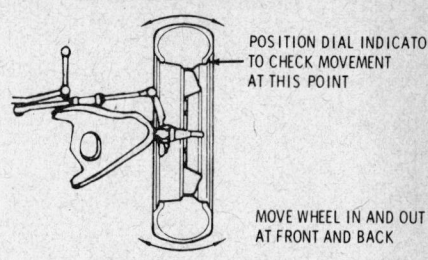

Fig. 6 Suspension & steering linkage check

Adjust camber by rotating the turnbuckle to move mount assembly inward or outward. Move mount inboard to decrease camber, or outboard to increase camber.

Adjust caster by lightly tapping the mount assembly foward or rearward. Move mount foward to decrease caster, or rearward to increase caster.

When adjustments are completed, torque the three strut mount attaching nuts to 20 ft. lbs.

TOE-IN, ADJUST

Toe-in can be adjusted by loosening the clamp bolts at each end of each tie rod and turning each tie rod to increase or decrease its length as necessary until proper toe-in is secured and the steering gear is on the high point for straight-ahead driving.

WHEEL BEARINGS, ADJUST

Exc. 1984 Corvette

1. While rotating wheel forward, torque spindle nut to 12 ft. lbs.
2. Back off nut until "just loose" then hand tighten nut and back it off again until either hole in spindle lines up with hole in nut.

NOTE: Do not back off nut more than 1/2 flat.

3. Install new cotter pin. With wheel bearing properly adjusted, there will be .001–.005 inch end play.

WHEEL BEARINGS, REPLACE

Exc. 1984 Corvette

1. Raise car and remove front wheels.
2. Remove bolts holding brake caliper to its mounting and insert a fabricated block (1 1/16 × 1 1/16 × 2 inches in length) be-

tween the brake pads as the caliper is being removed. Once removed, the caliper can be wired or secured in some manner away from the disc.
3. Remove spindle nut and hub and disc assembly. Grease retainer and inner wheel bearing can now be removed.
4. Reverse procedure to install.

1984 Corvette

NOTE: The wheel bearing and hub assembly is a sealed unit. If end play exceeds .005 inch, or if noise or roughness is detected, unit must be replaced as an assembly.

1. Raise and support vehicle, and remove wheel and tire.
2. Remove 2 bolts securing brake caliper bracket to steering knuckle, and secure caliper assembly aside.
3. Remove brake rotor, bolts securing hub to knuckle and hub assembly.
4. Reverse procedure to install.

CHECKING BALL JOINTS FOR WEAR

Upper Ball Joint
1. Raise front of vehicle with jacks placed between the coil spring pocket and ball joint of lower control arm.
2. Shake top of wheel in and out. Observe steering knuckle for any movement relative to the control arm.
3. Replace upper ball joint if looseness is indicated.

Lower Ball Joint
Raise car and support lower control arm so spring is compressed in the same manner as if the wheels were on the ground and check axial (up and down) play at ball joint. If play exceeds 1/8", replace the joint.

Another indication of lower ball joint excessive wear is when difficulty is experienced when lubricating the joint. If the liner has worn to the point where the lubrication grooves in the liner have been worn away, then abnormal pressure is required to force lubricant through the joint. Should this condi-

tion be evident, replace both lower ball joints.

NOTE: All models except 1977–82 Corvette and 1982–84 Camaro have a wear indicator built into the lower ball joint, Fig. 5. When inspecting wear indicator, vehicle must be supported normally on wheels to properly load ball joint.

SUSPENSION & STEERING LINKAGE CHECK

1. Raise vehicle with jack placed under frame torque box behind front wheel.
2. Lock steering wheel with wheels in straight ahead position, then mount dial indicator on a suitable stand with pointer bearing against outer rim of wheel, Fig. 6.
3. Move wheel in and out at front and rear, without moving steering wheel, while observing gauge.
4. If gauge reading exceeds .108 inches, check steering linkage and suspension for excessive wear or damage.

UPPER BALL JOINT, REPLACE

1977–84 Exc. 1977–82 Corvette

1. Raise vehicle and support with stands at outer ends of lower control arms.
2. Remove wheel and tire.
3. Remove cotter pin and retaining nut, then separate ball joint stud from knuckle using a suitable tool, Fig. 7.
4. Support upper control arm in a raised position.
5. Remove heads of rivets securing joint to arm, then drive out rivets to remove joint.
6. Position replacement joint on top of control arm, insert retaining bolts supplied with joint from under arm, install nuts and torque to 13 ft. lbs.
7. Remove upper control arm support, assemble ball joint to steering knuckle, install washer, if equipped, and retaining nut.

NOTE: On 1980–82 models, seat ball joint stud in knuckle before installing nut. Install tool J-29293 on stud, torque tool to 40 ft. lbs., then remove tool and install nut.

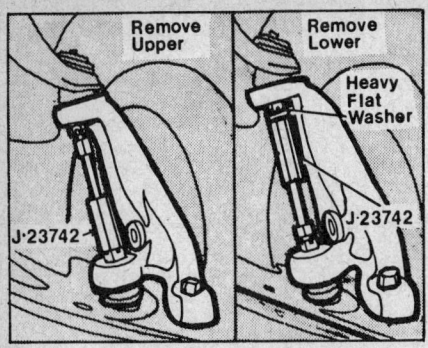

Fig. 7 Removing ball joint studs from steering knuckle (Typical). Exc. 1977–82 Corvette & 1982–84 Camaro

8. Torque retaining nut to 60 ft. lbs. on 1977–82 models, 65 ft. lbs. on 1983–84 models except Corvette, and 32 ft. lbs. on 1984 Corvette.
9. Tighten retaining nut up to an additional 1/16 turn, if necessary, to align hole in ball stud with nut, then install cotter pin.

NOTE: On 1978–82 Malibu and Monte Carlo, install cotter pin from rear.

1977–82 Corvette

1. Raise and support vehicle, and remove wheel and tire.
2. Remove cotter pin and loosen but do not remove ball joint retaining nut.

NOTE: Nut should not be loosened more than one full turn.

3. To release ball stud from knuckle, tap on boss of knuckle with hammer using another heavy hammer or similar tool as a drift.
4. Support lower control arm at outer end to release spring tension on upper control arm, remove retaining nut and support upper control arm in raised position.
5. Remove heads of rivets securing joint to arm, then drive out rivets to remove joint.
6. Position replacement joint on top of control arm, insert retaining bolts supplied with joint from under arm, install nuts and torque to 25 ft. lbs.
7. Remove upper control arm support, assemble ball joint to steering knuckle, install retaining nut and torque to 50 ft. lbs.
8. Tighten nut up to an additional 1/16 of a turn, if necessary, to align hole in ball stud with nut, then install cotter pin.

Fig. 9 Coil spring removal (Typical)

LOWER BALL JOINT, REPLACE

1977–84 Exc. 1977–82 Corvette

1. Raise vehicle and support at frame, and remove wheel and tire.
2. Position a suitable jack under lower control arm spring seat, and raise jack to compress coil spring.

NOTE: Jack must remain in place during ball joint replacement to hold spring and lower control arm in position.

3. Remove cotter pin and nut securing ball joint stud to steering knuckle, then disconnect joint from knuckle using a suitable tool, Fig. 7.
4. Lift knuckle assembly from ball stud, guiding control arm out of splash shield, then support knuckle aside to allow clearance for joint removal.
5. Remove grease fitting, then press ball joint assembly out of lower control arm using a suitable tool, Fig. 8.
6. Press replacement joint into arm by reversing removal tools, fit spindle over ball stud, install washer, if equipped, and retaining nut.

NOTE: On 1980–82 models except 1982 Camaro, seat ball stud in steering knuckle before installing nut. Install tool J-29194 over stud, torque tool to 40 ft. lbs., then remove tool and install nut.

7. Torque retaining nut to 93 ft. lbs. on 1977 Chevrolet; 83 ft. lbs. on 1977–79 models except 1977 Chevrolet, 90 ft. lbs. on 1980–84 models except Corvette and 48 ft. lbs. on 1984 Corvette.
8. Tighten nut up to an additional 1/16 turn, if necessary, to align hole in ball stud with nut, then install cotter pin.

NOTE: On 1978–82 Malibu and Monte Carlo, install cotter pin from rear.

1977–82 Corvette

1. Raise vehicle and support at frame, and remove wheel and tire.
2. Remove cotter pins from upper and lower joints and loosen but do not remove

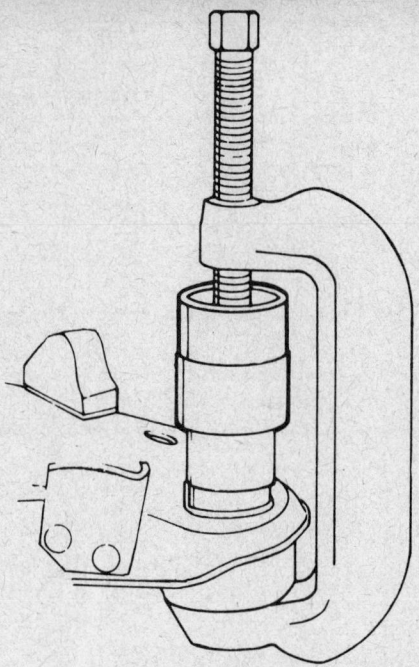

Fig. 8 Pressing ball joint from lower control arm (Typical)

retaining nuts.

NOTE: Do not loosen nuts more than one full turn.

3. To release ball studs from knuckle, tap on boss of knuckle with a hammer, using another heavy hammer or similar tool as a drift.
4. Place a suitable floor jack under lower control arm, and raise jack to compress coil spring. Position jack as close to outer end of arm as possible, while leaving clearance for ball joint removal.
5. Remove ball joint retaining nuts and secure spindle assembly aside, taking care not to stretch brake hose.
6. Remove rivets securing ball joint to control arm and ball joint.
7. Position replacement joint on control arm, install retaining bolts and nuts, and torque to 25 ft. lbs.

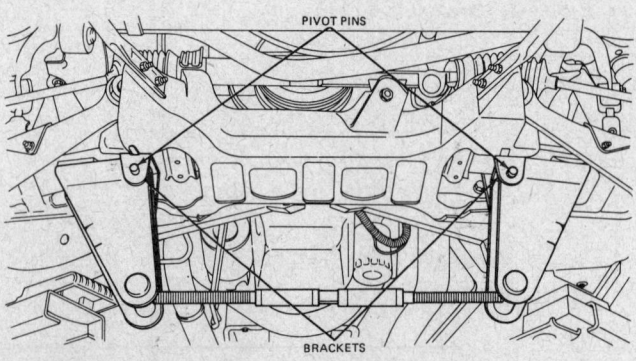

Fig. 10 Leaf spring removal. 1984 Corvette

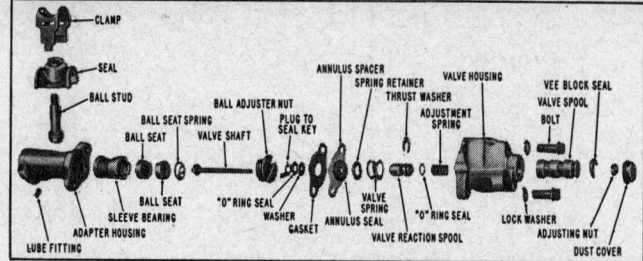

Fig. 11 Power steering control valve and adapter, exploded view. 1977–82 Corvette

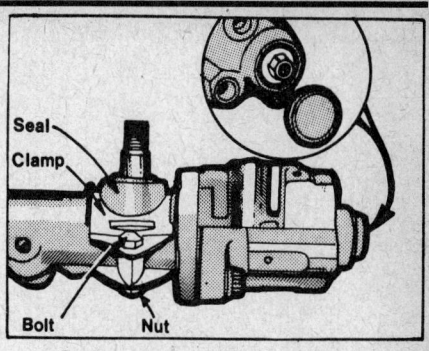

Fig. 12 Control valve ball stud seal replacement. 1977–82 Corvette

8. Install spindle assembly and ball joint retaining nuts, then torque upper nut to 50 ft. lbs. and lower nut to 80 ft. lbs.
9. Tighten nuts up to an additional 1/16 turn, if necessary, to align holes in ball studs with nuts, then install cotter pins.

SHOCK ABSORBER, REPLACE

NOTE: On 1982–84 Camaro, refer to "Strut, Replace" procedure.

1. Raise and support vehicle as needed, and remove wheel and tire.
2. Hold shock absorber shaft with a suitable wrench and remove upper retaining nut, washer and bushing.
3. Remove lower retaining bolts and shock absorber. On 1984 Corvette, remove shock mounting bracket, if necessary, to provide clearance for shock absorber removal.
4. Reverse procedure to install. Torque upper retaining nut to 90 inch lbs. on all 1977–79 Models and 1980–82 Corvette; 8 ft. lbs. on all 1980–84 models except Corvette, and 19 ft. lbs. on 1984 Corvette. Torque lower mounting bolts to 20 ft. lbs. on all models except Corvette; 150 inch lbs. on 1977–82 Corvette, and 22 ft. lbs. on 1984 Corvette.

STRUT, REPLACE

1982–84 Camaro

1. Raise and support vehicle.
2. Remove wheel and support lower control arm with a suitable jack.
3. Remove brake hose bracket and two strut to knuckle bolts, Fig. 2.
4. Remove upper mounting assembly cover.
5. Remove nut from upper end of strut, then the strut and shield.
6. Reverse procedure to install. Tighten strut to knuckle bolts to 195 ft. lbs., and strut to upper mount nut to 50 ft. lbs.

COIL SPRING, REPLACE

1977–84 All, Exc. 1982–84 Camaro

1. Disconnect shock absorber from lower mounting, push shock absorber through hole in lower control arm and compress into spring.
2. Support vehicle by frame so control arms hang free.
3. Install a safety chain through spring and lower control arm.
4. Install tool J-23028 onto a suitable jack and position jack so control arm is sup-

ported by bushings seated in grooves of tool, Fig. 9.
5. Remove stabilizer to lower control arm attachment.
6. Raise jack to relieve tension on control arm bolts and remove bolts.
7. Lower jack until tension is removed from spring, remove chain and spring from vehicle.
8. Reverse procedure to install, installing front pivot bolt first.

NOTE: To ensure adequate suspension clearance, install front pivot bolt from front, with nut toward rear of vehicle. Rear bolt can be installed from either direction.

9. Torque pivot bolts to specifications:
1977 Exc. Corvette . . . . 100 ft. lbs.
1977–82 Corvette front . . . . 70 ft. lbs.
              rear . . . . . . 95 ft. lbs.
1978–79 Chevrolet . . . . 92 ft. lbs.
1978–79 Exc. Chevrolet &
  Corvette . . . . 62 ft. lbs.
1980–81 Camaro . . . . 90 ft. lbs.
1980–83 Malibu . . . . 65 ft. lbs.
1980–84 Chevrolet . . . . 90 ft. lbs.
1980–84 Monte Carlo . . . . 65 ft. lbs.

1982–84 Camaro

1. Raise and support vehicle and remove wheel.
2. Remove stabilizer link and bushings from lower control arm.
3. Remove pivot bolt nuts, leaving the bolts installed.
4. Install tool J-23028 onto a suitable jack and position so that tool supports bushings, Fig. 7.
5. Raise jack to relieve tension on pivot bolts and remove bolts.
6. Carefully lower jack until tension is removed from spring and remove spring from vehicle.
7. Reverse procedure to install. Torque pivot bolt nuts to 65 ft. lbs. and stabilizer link nut to 20 ft. lbs.

CAUTION: The spring force under compression is very great. Exercise every safety precaution when performing this operation to see that individuals and materials subject to damage are removed from the path of the spring when the control arm is being lowered. Also, the compressed spring should be relaxed immediately after lowering the control arm to reduce the time of exposure to the great compressive force.

LEAF SPRING, REPLACE

1984 Corvette

1. Raise and support vehicle, and remove front wheels.

2. Remove both spring protectors.
3. Install spring compressor J-33432 or equivalent, Fig. 10.
4. Disconnect lower ball joints from steering knuckles.
5. Compress spring by rotating turnbuckle on spring compressor.
6. Remove bolts securing shock brackets to lower control arms and spring mounting bolts.
7. Release tension on spring compressor and remove compressor.
8. Remove spring.
9. Reverse procedure to install. Torque spring mounting bolts to 46 ft. lbs. with vehicle on ground.

MANUAL STEERING GEAR, REPLACE

1977–84 All Models

NOTE: On models where shield is installed, remove shield from coupling.

1. Remove nuts, washers and bolts at steering coupling.
2. Remove pitman arm nut and washer from sector shaft and mark relation of arm position to shaft.
3. Use a suitable puller to remove pitman arm.
4. Unfasten gear from frame and remove assembly.
5. Reverse procedure to install. Torque the steering gear to frame attaching bolts to 30 ft. lbs. on 1977–82 Corvette, 70 ft. lbs. on all 1977–81 and 1983–84 except Corvette, or 80 ft. lbs. on all 1982 except Corvette. Torque coupling flange bolts to 30 ft. lbs. on all models. Torque coupling flange nuts to 20 ft. lbs. on all except 1977–78 Nova. On 1977–78 Nova, torque to 18 ft. lbs. Torque sector shaft to pitman arm nut to 185 ft. lbs. on all 1977–84 except 1980–81 Camaro, Chevrolet, Malibu and Monte Carlo. On these models, torque to 180 ft. lbs.

INTEGRAL POWER STEERING, REPLACE

1977–84 Exc. Corvette

To remove gear assembly, disconnect pressure and return hoses from gear housing and cap both hoses and steering gear outlets to prevent foreign material from entering system, then follow procedure as outlined under *Steering Gear, Replace.*

LINKAGE TYPE POWER STEERING

1977–82 Corvette

Power steering equipment consists of a recirculating ball type steering gear and linkage to which a hydraulic power mechanism has been added as part of the steering linkage. The hydraulic mechanism furnishes additional power to *assist* the manual operation so that the turning effort at the steering wheel is greatly reduced. The hydraulic mechanism consists of three basic units: a hydraulic pump and reservoir, a control valve, and a power cylinder.

Control Valve, Adjust
1. Disconnect cylinder rod from frame bracket.
2. With car on a hoist, start the engine. One of the following two conditions will exist:
   a. If piston rod remains retracted, turn the adjusting nut clockwise until the rod begins to move out. Then turn the nut counterclockwise until the rod just begins to move in. Now turn the nut clockwise to exactly one half the rotation needed to change the direction of shaft movement.
   b. If the rod extends upon starting the pump, move the nut counter-clockwise until the rod begins to retract, then clockwise until the rod begins to move out again. Now turn the rod to exactly one half the rotation needed to change the direction of shaft movement.

NOTE: *Do not turn the nut back and forth more than is absolutely necessary to balance the valve.*

---

3. Restart engine. Front wheels should not turn from center if valve has been properly balanced.

Power Cylinder Repairs

Removal
1. Disconnect two hydraulic lines at power cylinder.
2. Unfasten power cylinder rod from brace at frame.
3. Unfasten power cylinder from relay rod bracket.
4. Remove power cylinder from car.

Inspection
1. Inspect seals for leaks around cylinder rod and if leaks are present, replace seals as follows:
2. Use a hook tool to remove retaining ring. Remove wiper ring, back-up washer, back-up ring and seal. *Piston rod seal*

should not be removed unless there are signs of leakage along the piston shaft at shaft seal.
3. Examine brass fitting hose connection seats for cracks or damage and replace if necessary.
4. For service other than seat or seal replacement, replace the power cylinder.

Installation
1. Install power cylinder on car by reversing removal procedure. Torque the frame bracket to rod nut to 23 ft lbs. and the relay rod bracket nut to 45 ft. lbs. Additional torque may be applied to align castellation with hole in stud, not to exceed 30 ft. lbs. on frame bracket to rod nut and 50 ft. lbs. on relay rod bracket nut.
2. Reconnect two hoses, fill system with fluid and bleed system as outlined below.

Filling & Bleeding System
1. Fill reservoir to proper level with Automatic Transmission Fluid and let fluid remain undisturbed for about two minutes.
2. Raise front wheels off floor.
3. Run engine at idle for two minutes.
4. Increase engine speed to about 1500 rpm.
5. Turn wheels from one extreme to the other, lightly contacting stops.
6. Lower wheels to floor and turn wheels right and left.
7. Recheck for leaks.
8. Check oil level and refill as required. Pump pressure should be 870 lbs.

Control Valve Repairs

Replace, Fig. 11
1. Loosen relay rod-to-control valve clamp.
2. Disconnect hose connections at control valve.
3. Disconnect control valve from pitman arm.
4. Unscrew control valve from relay rod.
5. Remove control valve from car.
6. Reverse procedure to install. Torque relay rod clamp bolt to 25 ft. lbs. Torque pitman arm nut to 45 ft. lbs. plus additional torque required to align castellation with hole in stud not to exceed 50 ft. lbs.

Ball Stud Seal, Replace
In servicing the control valve, refer to Fig. 11. To replace the ball stud seal, refer to Fig. 12 and proceed as follows:
1. Remove pitman arm with a suitable puller.
2. Remove clamp by removing nut, bolt and spacer. If crimped type clamp is used, straighten clamp end and pull clamp and seal off end of stud.
3. Install new seal and clamp over stud so lips on seal mate with clamp. (A nut and bolt attachment type clamp replaces the

crimped type for service, Fig. 11).
4. Center the ball stud, seal and clamp in opening in adapter housing, then install spacer, bolt and nut.

RACK & PINION STEERING GEAR, REPLACE

1984 Corvette

1. Raise and support vehicle, and remove left wheel and tire.
2. Disconnect hoses at steering gear, and plug lines and open ports.
3. Disconnect outer tie rods from steering knuckles.
4. Remove upper and lower mounting bolts on right side and single mounting bolt on left side.
5. Disconnect intermediate shaft universal joint from steering gear.
6. Remove stabilizer shaft and electric fan to provide clearance.
7. Remove steering gear.
8. Reverse procedure to install. Torque bolts securing right bracket to 18 ft. lbs., and bolt securing gear to crossmember to 25 ft. lbs.
9. Top off fluid reservoir, bleed system and check for leaks.

POWER STEERING PUMP, REPLACE

1977–84

Exc. 1984 Corvette
1. Disconnect hoses at power steering pump, then plug pump parts and hoses.
2. Loosen pump adjusting bolt and remove pump drive belt.
3. Remove pump to support bracket attaching bolts and the pump.
4. Reverse procedure to install. Torque attaching bolts to the following specifications: 1977–82 Corvette, 25 ft. lbs., 1977–78 with V8 engine, all except Corvette, 25 ft. lbs., 1977–78 with six cylinder engine, all except Corvette, 18 ft. lbs., 1979–84 all except Corvette, 35 ft. lbs.

1984 Corvette
1. Rotate belt tensioner counterclockwise, and remove serpentine drive belt.
2. Remove AIR pump pulley.
3. Remove bolts securing power steering reservoir bracket and bolts securing reservoir brace to intake manifold.
4. Disconnect power steering hoses between pump and steering gear, then plug hoses and open fittings.
5. Remove pump mounting bolts, pump and reservoir.
6. Reverse procedure to install, torquing pump and bracket bolts to 18 ft. lbs.

CHEVROLET CHEVETTE • PONTIAC 1000

INDEX OF SERVICE OPERATIONS

NOTE: Refer to the front of this manual for vehicle manufacturer's special service tool suppliers.

CHEVROLET CHEVETTE • PONTIAC 1000

VEHICLE IDENTIFICATION NUMBER LOCATION

On top of instrument panel, left front.

ENGINE NUMBER LOCATION

On right side of cylinder block, below No. 1 spark plug on gasoline models; at left rear of engine on diesel models.

ENGINE V.I.N. CODE

On 1977–80 vehicles, the fifth digit in the V.I.N. denotes engine code. On 1981–84 vehicles, the eighth digit in the V.I.N. denotes engine code.

ENGINE IDENTIFICATION CODE

Engines are identified in the following table by the code letter or letters immediately following the engine serial number.

Year	Engine	V.I.N. Code	Code	Year	Engine	V.I.N. Code	Code	Year	Engine	V.I.N. Code	Code
1977	4-85	I	CDS, CVA, CVB		4-97	E	DBT, DBU, DBW		4-110①②⑤	D	CWA
	4-97	E	CNA, CNB, CNC		4-97	E	DBX, DBY, DBZ		4-110①③⑤	D	CWB
	4-97	E	CND, CNF, CNH	1980	4-97	9	CKA, CKB, CKC	1983	4-97①②	C	DWC, DWF, DWZ
	4-97	E	CNR, CNS, CNT		4-97	9	CKD, CKF, CKH		4-97①③	C	DWB, DWD, DWH, DWU
	4-97	E	CNU		4-97	9	CKJ, CKK				
	4-97	E	CYC, CYD, CYF		4-97	O	CKL, CKM, CKR, CKS		4-97②④	C	DWA, DWC
	4-97	E	CYH, CYY, CYZ	1981	4-97	9	DCA, DCB, DCC		4-97③④	C	DWB, DWU
1978	4-97	E	CYA, CYB, CYJ		4-97	9	DCD, DCF, DCH		4-110①②⑤	D	DJB, DJD
	4-97	E	CYK, CYL, CYM		4-97	9	DCJ, DCU, DCW		4-110①③⑤	D	DJA, DJC, DMR, DMT
	4-97	E	CYR, CYS, CYT		4-97	9	DCX, DCY, DCZ				
	4-97	E	CYU, CYW, CYX		4-110	D			4-110②④⑤	D	DJC
	4-97	J	ZTT, ZTU, ZTW	1982	4-97①②	C	CHA, CHF, CHR		4-110③④⑤	D	DJD
		J	ZTX		4-97①③	C	CHT, CHW, CHX				
1979	4-97	E	DBA, DBB, DBC		4-97②④	C	CUA, CUB				
	4-97	E	DBD, DBF, DBH		4-97③④	C	CUC, CUD, CUF				
	4-97	E	DBJ, DBK, DBL								
	4-97	E	DBM, DBR, DBS								

①—Except Calif.
②—Manual Trans.
③—Auto. Trans.
④—California.
⑤—Diesel engine.

GRILLE IDENTIFICATION

1977 Chevette

1978 Chevette

1979–80 Chevette

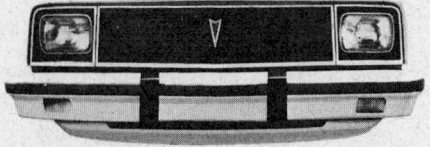

1981 1000

1981–82 Chevette

1982–84 1000

1983–84 Chevette

GENERAL ENGINE SPECIFICATIONS

Year	Engine CID①/Liter	Engine VIN Code	Carburetor	Bore and Stroke	Compression Ratio	Net H.P. @ R.P.M.②	Maximum Torque Lbs. Ft. @ R.P.M.	Normal Oil Pressure Pounds
1977	4-85, 1.4 Liter⑨	I③	IME, 1 Bbl④	3.228 × 2.606 82.0 × 66.2 mm.	8.5	52 @ 5300	67 @ 3400 97 Joules @ 3400	36—46
	4-97, 1.6 Liter⑤	E③	IME, 1 Bbl④	3.228 × 2.980 82.0 × 75.7 mm.	8.5	60 @ 5300	77 @ 3200 104 Joules @ 3200	36—46
1978	4-97, 1.6 Liter⑤	E③	IME, 1 Bbl④	3.228 × 2.980 82.0 × 75.7 mm.	8.5	63 @ 4800	82 @ 3200	34—42
	4-97, 1.6 Liter⑤⑥	J③	IME, 1 Bbl④	3.228 × 2.980 82.0 × 75.7 mm.	8.5	68 @ 5000	84 @ 3200	34—42
1979	4-97, 1.6 Liter⑤	E③	5210C, 2 Bbl⑦	3.228 × 2.980 82.0 × 75.3 mm.	8.5	70 @ 5200	82 @ 2400	55
	4-97, 1.6 Liter⑤⑥	O③	5210C, 2 Bbl⑦	3.228 × 2.980 82.0 × 75.7 mm.	8.5	74 @ 5200	88 @ 2800	55
1980	4-97, 1.6 Liter⑤	9③	6510C, 2 Bbl⑦	3.228 × 2.980 82.0 × 75.7 mm.	8.5	70 @ 5200	82 @ 2400	55
	4-97, 1.6 Liter⑤⑥	O③	5210C, 2 Bbl⑦	3.228 × 2.980 82.0 × 75.7 mm.	8.6	74 @ 5200	88 @ 2800	55
1981	4-97, 1.6 Liter⑤	9⑧	5210C, 2 Bbl⑦	3.228 × 2.980 82.0 × 75.7 mm.	8.6	70 @ 5200	82 @ 2400	55
	4-110, 1.8 Liter⑩	D⑧	Fuel Injection	3.310 × 3.230 84.0 × 82.0 mm.	22.1	51 @ 5000	72 @ 2000	64
1982	4-97, 1.6 Liter⑤	C⑧	6510C, 2Bbl.⑦	3.228 × 2.980 82.0 × 75.7 mm.	9.2	65 @ 5200	80 @ 3200	55
	4-110, 1.8 Liter⑩	D⑧	Fuel Injection	3.310 × 3.230 84.0 × 82.0 mm.	22.1	51 @ 5000	72 @ 2000	64
1983–84	4-97, 1.6 Liter⑤	C⑧	6510C, 2 Bbl.⑦	3.228 × 2.980 82.0 × 75.7 mm.	9.0	65 @ 5200	80 @ 3200	57
	4-110, 1.8 Liter⑩	D⑧	Fuel Injection	3.310 × 3.230 84.0 × 82.0 mm.	22	51 @ 5000	72 @ 2000	64

①—CID—Cubic inch displacement.
②—Ratings are net as installed in vehicle.
③—Fifth digit in the VIN denotes engine code.
④—Rochester
⑤—1600 cc engine.
⑥—High output engine.
⑦—Holley.
⑧—Eighth digit in the VIN denotes engine code.
⑨—1400 cc engine.
⑩—Diesel engine

TUNE UP SPECIFICATIONS

The following specifications are published from the latest information available. This data should be used only in the absence of a decal affixed in the engine compartment.

★ When using a timing light, disconnect vacuum hose or tube at distributor and plug opening in hose or tube so idle speed will not be affected.

● When checking compression, lowest cylinder must be within 70 percent of highest.

▲ Before removing wires from distributor cap, determine location of the No. 1 wire in cap, as distributor position may have been altered from that shown at the end of this chart.

☞ Spark plug types shown in this chart are recommendations of the original vehicle manufacturer and not MOTOR.

Check local sources for other spark plug manufacturers listings.

Year & Engine/V.I.N.	Spark Plug Type ☞	Spark Plug Gap	Firing Order Fig. ▲	Ignition Timing BTDC① ★ Man. Trans.	Ignition Timing BTDC① ★ Auto. Trans.	Mark Fig.	Curb Idle Speed② Man. Trans.	Curb Idle Speed② Auto. Trans.	Fast Idle Speed Man. Trans.	Fast Idle Speed Auto. Trans.	Fuel Pump Pressure
1977											
4-85/I	R43TS	.035	A	12°	12°	B	600/800	600/800D	2300④	2400④	5—6½
4-97.6/E, Exc. Calif. & High Alt.	R43TS	.035	A	8°	8°	B	600/800	⑦	2300④	2400④	5—6½
4-97.6/E, Calif. & High Alt.	R43TS	.035	A	8°	8°	B	800	⑦	—	2400④	5—6½
1978											
4-97.6 Exc. Calif. & High Alt.⑭	R43TS	.035	A	8°	8°	B	600/800	⑦⑧	④⑨	2400④	5—6½
4-97.6 Calif. & High Alt.⑭	R43TS	.035	A	8°	8°	B	800	⑦⑧	—	2400④	5—6½

Continued

TUNE UP SPECIFICATIONS—Continued

The following specifications are published from the latest information available. This
data should be used only in the absence of a decal affixed in the engine compartment.

★ When using a timing light, disconnect vacuum hose or tube at distributor and plug opening in hose or tube so idle speed will not be affected.

● When checking compression, lowest cylinder must be within 70 percent of highest.

▲ Before removing wires from distributor cap, determine location of the No. 1 wire in cap, as distributor position may have been altered from that shown at the end of this chart.

Spark plug types shown in this chart are recommendations of the original vehicle manufacturer and not MOTOR.

Check local sources for other spark plug manufacturers listings.

Year & Engine/V.I.N.	Spark Plug Type	Gap	Firing Order Fig. ▲	Ignition Timing BTDC①★ Man. Trans.	Auto. Trans.	Mark Fig.	Curb Idle Speed② Man. Trans.	Auto. Trans.	Fast Idle Speed Man. Trans.	Auto. Trans.	Fuel Pump Pressure
1979											
4-97.6/E, Exc. Calif.	R42TS	.035	A	12°	18°	③	800/1150	750/1150	2500⑤	2500⑤	2½–6½
4-97.6/E, Calif.⑩	R42TS	.035	A	12°	16°	③	800/1150	750/1150	2500⑤	2500⑤	2½–6½
4-97.6/O, Calif.⑪	R42TS	.035	A	12°	12°	③	800/1150	750/1150	2500⑤	2500⑤	2½–6½
1980											
4-97.6 Exc. Calif.⑮	R42TS	.035	A	12°	18°	C	800/1150	750/1150	2500	2500	2½–6½
4-97.6 Calif.⑮	R42TS	.035	A	12°	18°	C	800/1150	800/1150	2600	2500	2½–6½
1981											
4-97.6/9	R42TS	.035	A	18°	18°	C	800/1150⑥	700D⑫	2500	2500	2½–6½
4-110 Diesel/D	—	—	—	18°⑬	18°⑬	—	625	725D	950	950	—
1982											
4-97.6/C	R42TS	.035	A	4°	4°	C	700	700D	2500	2500	2½–6½
4-110 Diesel/D	—	—	—	18°⑬	18°⑬	—	625	725D	950	950	—
1983											
4-97.6/C	R42TS	.035	A	6°	6°	C	800/1150	700/875D	2500	2500	2½–6½
4-110 Diesel/D	—	—	—	18°⑬	18°⑬	—	625	725N	950	950N	—
1984											
4-97.6/C	R42CTS	.035	A	—	—	C	800⑯	700D	—	—	5–6½
4-110 Diesel/D	—	—	—	11°⑬	11°⑬	—	620	720N	—	—	—

①—BTDC—Before top dead center.
②—Idle speed on man. trans. vehicles is adjusted in Neutral & on auto, trans. equipped vehicles is adjusted in Drive unless otherwise specified. Where two idle speeds are listed, the higher speed is with the A/C or idle solenoid energized.
③—Early production, Fig. B; late production, Fig. C.

④—With stop screw on high step of fast idle cam & A/C off.
⑤—With stop screw on high step of fast idle cam, EGR vacuum line disconnected & plugged & A/C off.
⑥—Models with carburetor No. 14023777, set at 700 RPM.
⑦—Less A/C, 600/800D RPM; with A/C, 800/950D RPM.
⑧—With A/C on, compressor clutch wires disconnected.
⑨—Except high output engine, 2300 RPM; high output engine, 2400 RPM.
⑩—Exc. high output engine.
⑪—High output engine.
⑫—With solenoid energized, 1400 RPM with

transmission in Park.
⑬—Injection timing static.
⑭—On 4-97.6 C.I.D. engine, V.I.N. code is E; 4-97.6 H.O. engine, V.I.N. code is J.
⑮—On 4-97.6 C.I.D. engine, V.I.N. code is 9; 4-97.6 H.O. engine, V.I.N. code is O.
⑯—700 RPM with 3.36:1 axle.

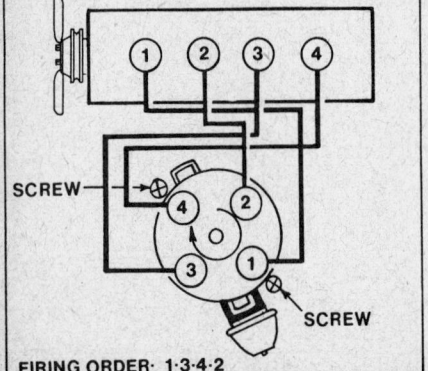

FIRING ORDER· 1·3·4·2

Fig. A

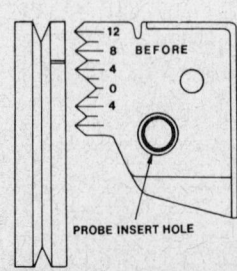

12
8
4
0
4
BEFORE

PROBE INSERT HOLE

Fig. B

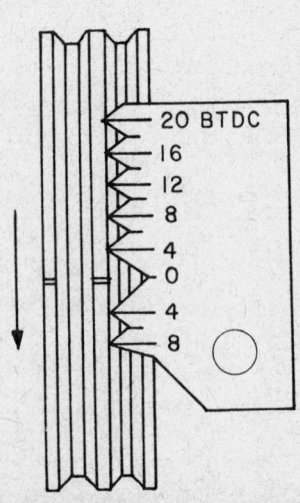

20 BTDC
16
12
8
4
0
4
8

Fig. C

VALVE SPECIFICATIONS

Year	Engine/V.I.N.	Valve Lash Int.	Valve Lash Exh.	Valve Angles Seat	Valve Angles Face	Valve Spring Installed Height	Valve Spring Pressure Lbs. @ In.	Stem Clearance Intake	Stem Clearance Exhaust	Stem Diameter Intake	Stem Diameter Exhaust
1977–79	All	Hydraulic		①	②	1.26 32 mm.	173 @ .886 770N @ 22.5 mm.	.0006–.0017 .015–.045 mm.	.0014–.0025 .035–.065 mm.	.3138–.3144 7.970–7.986 mm.	.3130–.3136 7.950–7.965 mm.
1980–81	4-97.6/9	Hydraulic		45	46	1.26 32 mm.	173 @ .886 770N @ 22.5 mm.	.0006–.0017 .015–.045 mm.	.0014–.0025 .035–.065 mm.	.3138–.3144 7.970–7.986 mm.	.3130–.3136 7.950–7.965 mm.
1981–82	4-110/D③	.010④ .25 mm.	.014④ .35 mm.	45	45	⑤	⑥	.0015–.0028 .039–.071 mm.	.0018–.0030 .045–.077 mm.	.3128–.3124 7.946–7.961 mm.	.3126–.3132 7.940–7.955 mm.
1982–84	4-97.6/C	Hydraulic		45	46	1.30 33.1 mm.	170 @ .917 756N @ 23.3 mm.	.0006–.0017 .015–.045 mm.	.0014–.0025 .035–.065 mm.	.3138–.3144 7.970–7.986 mm.	.3130–.3136 7.950–7.965 mm.
1983–84	4-110/D③	.010④ .25 mm.	.014④ .35 mm.	45	45	⑤	⑥	.0015–.0028 .039–.071 mm.	.0018–.0030 .045–.077 mm.	.310–.314 7.88–8.0 mm.	.310–.314 7.88–8.0 mm.

①—46° on 1977 models; 45° on 1978–79 models
②—45° on 1977 models; 46° on 1978–79 models
③—Diesel Engine
④—Hot or Cold
⑤—Free length, inner 1.783 inch; outer 1.846 inch.
⑥—Inner, 19–22 lbs. @ 1.516 inch; outer, 32–37 lbs. @ 1.614 inch.

DISTRIBUTOR SPECIFICATIONS

★ Note: If unit is checked on vehicle, double the RPM and degrees to get crankshaft figures.

Distributor Part No.①	Advance Starts	Centrifugal Advance Degrees @ RPM of Distributor Intermediate Advance			Full Advance	Vacuum Advance Inches of Vacuum to Start Plunger	Max. Adv. Dist. Deg. @ Vacuum
1977							
1110687	0 @ 600	4 @ 1200	—	—	12 @ 2400	4② (14kPa③)	13 @ 12② (41 kPa③)
1110693	0 @ 600	4 @ 1200	—	—	12 @ 2400	4② (14 kPa③)	17 @ 18② (27 kPa③)
1110702	0 @ 600	4 @ 1200	—	—	12 @ 2400	4② (14 kPa③)	15 @ 12② (41 kPa③)
1110703	0 @ 600	4 @ 1200	—	—	12 @ 2850	4② (14 kPa③)	15 @ 12② (41 kPa③)
1978							
1110705	0 @ 600	4 @ 1000	—	—	10 @ 2400	4② (14 kPa③)	15 @ 12② (41 kPa③)
1110707	0 @ 600	4 @ 1000	—	—	10 @ 2400	4② (14 kPa③)	7 @ 8② (27 kPa③)
1110712	0 @ 600	4 @ 1000	—	—	10 @ 2400	4② (14 kPa③)	13 @ 12② (41 kPa③)
1110713④	0 @ 600	4 @ 1000	—	—	11 @ 2625	4② (14 kPa③)	15 @ 12② (41 kPa③)
1979							
1110740	0 @ 760	1.5 @ 1100	—	—	8 @ 1625	4	15 @ 10②
1110741	0 @ 760	1 @ 850	1.5 @ 1100	—	8 @ 2625	4	7 @ 8②
1110742	0 @ 600	4 @ 1000	—	—	10 @ 2400	5	8 @ 11.5②
1110743	0 @ 600	4 @ 1000	—	—	12 @ 2850	4	15 @ 10②
1110744	0 @ 600	4 @ 1000	—	—	10 @ 2400	4	15 @ 10②
1110759	0 @ 600	4 @ 1000	—	—	12 @ 2850	4	9 @ 7.5②
1110760	0 @ 760	1 @ 850	1.5 @ 1100	—	8 @ 2625	5	8 @ 11.5②
1110778	0 @ 600	4 @ 1000	—	—	12 @ 2850	5	12 @ 12②
1980							
1110788	—	—	—	—	—	—	—
1110789	—	—	—	—	—	—	—
1110792	—	—	—	—	—	—	—
1110793	—	—	—	—	—	—	—
1110794	0 @ 760	1.5 @ 1100	—	—	8 @ 2625	2.9	10 @ 5.9②
1110795	0 @ 600	4 @ 1000	—	—	12 @ 2850	2.9	12.5 @ 7.4②
1981							
1110580	—	—	—	—	—	—	—

Continued

DISTRIBUTOR SPECIFICATIONS—Continued

★ Note: If unit is checked on vehicle, double the RPM and degrees to get crankshaft figures.

Distributor Part No.①	Centrifugal Advance Degrees @ RPM of Distributor				Vacuum Advance	
	Advance Starts	Intermediate Advance		Full Advance	Inches of Vacuum to Start Plunger	Max. Adv. Dist. Deg. @ Vacuum
1982						
1103440	—	—	—	—	—	—	—
1103501	—	—	—	—	—	—	—
1110575	—	—	—	—	—	—	—
1110585	—	—	—	—	—	—	—
1983						
1103506						
1984						
1103506	—	—	—	—	—	—	—

①—Stamped on distributor housing.
②—Inches Hg.
③—kPa—kilopascals.
④—High output engine.

WHEEL ALIGNMENT SPECIFICATIONS

Year	Model	Caster Angle, Degrees		Camber Angle, Degrees				Toe-In. Inch	Toe-Out on Turns, Deg.	
		Limits	Desired	Limits		Desired			Outer Wheel	Inner Wheel
				Left	Right	Left	Right			
1977–81	All	+3½° to 5½°	+4½°	−.2° to +.6°	−.2° to +.6°	+.2°	+.2°	①	—	—
1982–84	All	+4° to +6°	+5°	−.2° to +.6°	−.2° to +.6°	+.2°	+.2°	②	—	—

①—1977 & 1981, 1/64 to 7/64 inch (.5 to 2.5 mm); ②—+.06° ± .04° (+1.5 mm ± 1.0 mm)
1978–80, 1/8 to 9/64 inch (1.3 to 3.7 mm).

PISTONS, PINS, RINGS, CRANKSHAFT & BEARINGS

Year	Engine/ V.I.N.	Piston Clearance Top of Skirt	Ring End Gap①		Wrist-pin Diameter	Rod Bearings		Main Bearings		Thrust on Bear. No.	Shaft End Play
			Comp.	Oil		Shaft Diameter	Bearing Clearance	Shaft Diameter	Bearing Clearance		
1977–80	All	.0008–.0016 .020–.040 mm	⑤	.015 .381 mm	.9052 22.992 mm	1.8093– 1.8103 45.958– 45.984 mm	.0014–.0031 .036– .078 mm	2.0078–2.0088 51.0– 51.024 mm	②	5	.004–.008 .100– .202 mm
1981–83	4-97④	.0007–.0015 .020–.040 mm	⑤	.015 .381 mm	.9052 22.994 mm	1.8093–1.8103 45.958– 45.984 mm	.0014–.0031 .036–.078 mm	2.0078–2.0088 51.0–51.024 mm	②	5	.004–.008 .100– .202 mm
1984	4-97④	.0007–.0015 .020–.040 mm	⑤	.015 .381 mm	.9052 22.994 mm	1.8093–1.8103 45.958– 45.984 mm	.0014–.0031 .036– .078 mm	⑥	②	5	.004–.008 .100– .202 mm
1981–82	4-110/D ③	.0060–.0070 .143–.167 mm	.0078 .200 mm	.0078 .200 mm	.984 25.0 mm	1.925–1.926 48.895– 48.920 mm	.0016–.0032 .040–.081 mm	2.201–2.202 55.920–55.935 mm	.0015–.0027 .039–.080 mm	3	.002–.009 .06–.24 mm
1983–84	4-110/D ③	.0060–.0070 .143–.167 mm	.0078 .200 mm	.0078 .200 mm	.984 25.0 mm	1.925–1.926 48.895– 48.920 mm	.0016–.0027 .040–.070 mm	2.201–2.202 55.920–55.935 mm	.0015–.0027 .039–.080 mm	3	.002–.009 .06–.24 mm

①—Fit ring in tapered bore for clearance listed in tightest portion of ring travel.
②—No. 1, 2, 3 & 4, .0006–.0018 (.014–046 mm); No. 5, .0009–.0026 (.024–.066 mm).
③—Diesel Engine.
④—For V.I.N. code, refer to the "General Engine Specifications" at the front of the chapter.
⑤—Top ring, .011 inch (.229 mm); 2nd ring, .008 inch (.203 mm).
⑥—Nos. 1, 2, 3, 4—2.0078–2.0088 inch (51.0–51.025 mm); No. 5, 2.0395–2.0405 inch (50.987–51.013 mm).

REAR AXLE SPECIFICATIONS

Year	Model	Carrier Type	Ring Gear & Pinion Backlash		Pinion Bearing Preload			Differential Bearing Preload		
			Method	Adjustment	Method	New Bearings Inch-Lbs.	Used Bearings Inch-Lbs.	Method	New Bearings Inch-Lbs.	Used Bearings Inch-Lbs.
1977–79	All	Integral	Shims	—	Spacer	15–25 1.7–2.82 N-m	5–10 .056–1.13 N-m	Shims	—	—
1980–81	All	Integral	Shims	—	Spacer	15–25 1.7–2.82 N-m	5–10 .056–1.13 N-m	Shims	—	—
1982–84	All	Integral	Shims	—	Spacer	①	5–10 .056–1.13 mm	Shims	—	—

①—With NDH bearings, 10–20 inch lbs; with Timken bearings, 5–15 inch lbs.

ALTERNATOR SPECIFICATIONS

Year	Alternator		
	Model	Rated Hot Output Amps.	Field Current 12 Volts @ 80° F.
1977	1102845	32	4.0–4.5
	1102846	55	4.0–4.5
1978–80	1102845	32	4.0–4.5
1980	1103080	32	—
1981–82	1100138②	42	—
	LR155-12B③	55	—
1983–84	1100234②	42	—
	1100253②	63	—
	1100261②	78	—
	— ③	50	—

①—At 85° F.
②—Exc. diesel engine
③—Diesel engine

STARTING MOTOR APPLICATIONS

Year	Model	Starter Number
1977	All	1109414
1978	All	1110941
1979–80	All	1109522
1981–84	4-97/9, C	1109532
	4-110 Diesel/D	94238758

ENGINE TIGHTENING SPECIFICATIONS

★ Torque specifications are for clean and lightly lubricated threads only. Dry or dirty threads produce increased friction which prevents accurate measurement of tightness.

Year	Engine/ V.I.N.	Spark Plugs Ft. Lbs.	Camshaft Carrier Bolts Ft. Lbs.	Intake Manifold Ft. Lbs.	Exhaust Manifold Ft. Lbs.	Camshaft Sprocket Bolt Ft. Lbs.	Cam Cover In. Lbs.	Connecting Rod Cap Bolts Ft. Lbs.	Main Bearing Cap Bolts Ft. Lbs.	Flywheel to Crankshaft Ft. Lbs.	Vibration Damper or Pulley Ft. Lbs.
1977–78	All	15 20.3 N-m	75 102 N-m	16 22 N-m	①	75 102 N-m	14 1.6 N-m	37 50N-m	46 63 N-m	46 63 N-m	75 102 N-m
1979	All	18.4 25 N-m	71 97 N-m	16 22 N-m	①	75 102 N-m	14 1.6 N-m	37 50 N-m	46 63 N-m	46 63 N-m	75 102 N-m

Continued

CHEVROLET CHEVETTE • PONTIAC 1000

ENGINE TIGHTENING SPECIFICATIONS—Continued

★ Torque specifications are for clean and lightly lubricated threads only. Dry or dirty threads produce increased friction which prevents accurate measurement of tightness.

Year	Engine/ V.I.N.	Spark Plugs Ft. Lbs.	Camshaft Carrier Bolts Ft. Lbs.	Intake Manifold Ft. Lbs.	Exhaust Manifold Ft. Lbs.	Camshaft Sprocket Bolt Ft. Lbs.	Cam Cover In. Lbs.	Connecting Rod Cap Bolts Ft. Lbs.	Main Bearing Cap Bolts Ft. Lbs.	Flywheel to Crankshaft Ft. Lbs.	Vibration Damper or Pulley Ft. Lbs.
1980–82	4-97⑧	18.4 25 N-m	75 100 N-m	15 20 N-m	①	75 100 N-m	14 1.6 N-m	40 54 N-m	50 68 N-m	50 68 N-m	75 100 N-m
1981	4-110/D②	③	④	28 40 N-m	15 20 N-m	47 64 N-m	⑤	65 88 N-m	75 100 N-m	40⑥ 54 N-m	110 149 N-m
1982	4-110/D②	③	⑦	30	—	45	⑤	65	65–72	40⑥	110
1983–84	4-97⑧	18.4 25 N-m	75	18	25	75	14	40	50	50	100
1983–84	4-110②	③	⑦	30	—	55	⑤	65	65–72	40⑥	110

①—Center bolts, 15 ft. lbs. (22 Newton-meters); end legs, 22 ft. lbs. (30 Newton-meters).
②—Diesel engine
③—Glow Plugs–54 ft. lbs., 73 N-m
④—Cylinder head bolts–105 ft. lbs., 142 N-m
⑤—Rocker arm cover–7 ft. lbs., 10 N-m
⑥—Apply loctite to threads, do not lubricate bolts
⑦—Cylinder head bolts; new, 83–98 ft. lbs.; used, 90–105 ft. lbs.
⑧—For V.I.N. code, refer to the "General Engine Specifications" at the beginning of the chapter.

COOLING SYSTEM & CAPACITY DATA

Year	Model or Engine/ V.I.N.	Cooling Capacity, Qts. Less A/C	Cooling Capacity, Qts. With A/C	Radiator Cap Relief Pressure, Lbs.	Thermo. Opening Temp.	Fuel Tank Gals.	Engine Oil Refill Qts.	Transmission Oil 4 Speed Pints	5 Speed Pints	Auto. Trans. Qts. ①	Rear Axle Oils Pints
1977	All	8½ 8 ltr.	9 8.5 ltr.	15 —	190 —	13 49.2 ltr.	4 3.8 ltr.	3 1.5 ltr.	—	⑤	2 .9 ltr.
1978	All	8.5 8 ltr.	9.0 8.5 ltr.	15 —	190 —	12.5 47.3 ltr.	4 3.8 ltr.	3 1.5 ltr.	—	5 4.6 ltr.	2 .92 ltr.
1979	All	9 8.5 ltr.	9.25 8.8 ltr.	15	190	12.5 47.3 ltr.	4 3.8 ltr.	3 1.5 ltr.	—	5 4.6 ltr.	1.75 .83 ltr.
1980	All	9 8.5 ltr.	9.25 8.8 ltr.	15 —	190 —	12.5 47.3 ltr.	4 3.8 ltr.	3.4 1.6 ltr.	—	③	1.75 .83 ltr.
1981	All	9 8.5 ltr.	9.25 8.8 ltr.	15 —	190 —	12.5 47.3 ltr.	4 3.8 ltr.	3.4 1.6 ltr.	—	③	1.75 .83 ltr.
1981–82	4-110/D④	9 8.5 ltr.	—	15	180	12.5 47.3 ltr.	6⑤ 5.8 ltr.	3.25 1.5 ltr.	4 1.9 ltr.	⑥	1.75 .81 ltr.
1982	4-97/C	9 8.5 ltr.	9.25 8.6 ltr.	15	190	12.5 47.3 ltr.	4⑤ 3.8 ltr.	3.5	4 1.9 ltr.	②	1.75 .81 ltr.
1983–84	4-97/C	9 8.5 ltr.	9.25 8.6 ltr.	15	190	12.5 47.3 ltr.	4⑤ 3.8 ltr.	3.4 1.6 ltr.	4 1.9 ltr.	⑥	1.75 .81 ltr.
	4-110/D④	9 8.5 ltr.	—	15	180	12.5 47.3 ltr.	6⑤ 5.8 ltr.	3.3 1.55 ltr.	4 1.9 ltr.	⑥	1.75 .81 ltr.

①—Approximate. Make final check with dipstick.
②—After overhaul, 4.9 qts.; oil pan only, 3 qts.
③—Drain and refill, 3 qts. (2.7 ltrs.)
④—Diesel engine.
⑤—Includes filter.
⑥—After overhaul, 5 qts.; oil pan only, 3.5 qts.

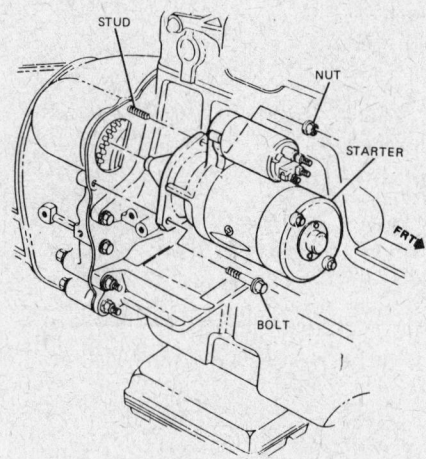

Fig. 1 Starter removal & installation. 1981—84 Diesel engine models

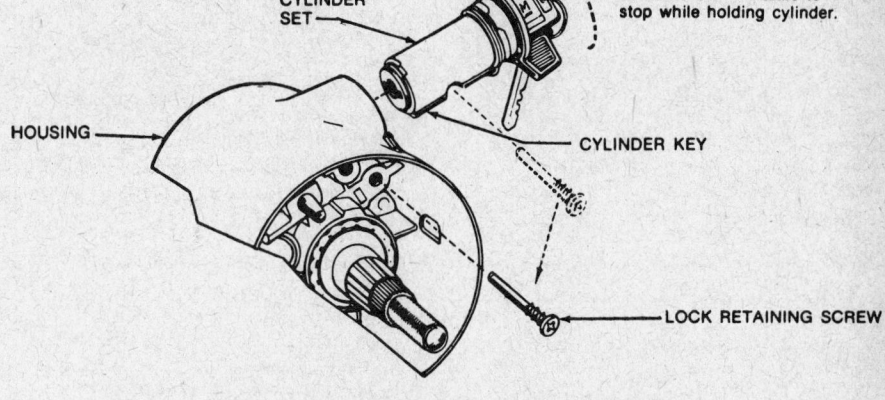

Fig. 1A Ignition lock removal & installation. 1979—84

STARTER REPLACE

Diesel Engine

Refer to Fig. 1 for starter removal and installation.

Gasoline Engine

1980—84 Less Power Brakes

1. Disconnect battery ground cable, then remove air cleaner.
2. Disconnect fuel line at carburetor and position aside.
3. Disconnect vacuum hoses at carburetor.
4. Remove splash shield from distributor coil and position aside.
5. Remove upper and lower starter retaining bolts.
6. Disconnect electrical leads from starter and position starter aside for access.
7. Remove master cylinder mounting nuts to gain access for removing starter. It will be necessary to move the master cylinder aside to remove the starter.
8. Remove starter.
9. Reverse procedure to install.

1980—84 With Power Brakes

1. Disconnect battery ground cable, then remove air cleaner.
2. Disconnect fuel line at carburetor and position aside.
3. Remove splash shield from distributor coil and position aside.
4. Remove upper starter retaining bolt.

NOTE: To remove the upper starter retaining bolt on models equipped with A/C, use a 15mm short socket with short extension, universal 12 inch extension and a ratchet or speed handle. Access to the bolt is gained through the intake manifold 3rd and 4th runners. After completely loosening the bolt, remove it with a magnet.

5. Remove steering column cover screws and cover.

6. Remove steering column upper mounting nuts and toe pan screw.
7. Raise and support front of vehicle.
8. Remove steering shaft from steering coupling. Lower vehicle and move steering column from inside vehicle for access to starter.
9. Disconnect electrical leads from starter.
10. Remove lower starter retaining bolt and remove starter.
11. Reverse procedure to install.

1977—79 Less A/C

1. Disconnect battery ground cable and remove air cleaner.
2. Remove distributor cap and position aside.
3. Remove the fuel line from fuel pump and carburetor.
4. Disconnect electrical connectors from ignition coil, remove coil bracket retaining screws and the coil and bracket assembly.
5. Disconnect vacuum hose from vacuum advance unit and the electrical connector from the oil pressure sender, then remove the sender.

Fig. 2 Ignition lock removal. 1977—78

6. Disconnect electrical leads from starter and remove the brace screw from bottom of starter housing.
7. Remove starter retaining screws and the starter from vehicle.
8. Reverse procedure to install.

1977—79 With A/C

1. Disconnect battery ground cable and remove air cleaner.
2. Remove starter upper retaining screw.
3. Remove steering column lever cover attaching screws.
4. Remove mast jacket lower bracket screw and the steering column upper mounting bracket.
5. Disconnect the four electrical connectors from steering column, then raise vehicle.
6. Disconnect steering column flexible coupling and position aside.
7. Disconnect electrical leads from starter and remove brace screw from bottom of starter.
8. Remove starter lower mounting screw.
9. With a suitable jack, raise engine approximately 1/2 inch to provide clearance for starter removal.
10. Lower starter and remove from vehicle.
11. Reverse procedure to install.

IGNITION LOCK, REPLACE

1979—84

1. Remove steering wheel as described under Horn Sounder and Steering Wheel.
2. Remove turn signal switch as described under Turn Signal Switch, Replace, then remove buzzer switch.
3. Place ignition switch in Run position, then remove lock cylinder retaining screw and lock cylinder.
4. To install, rotate lock cylinder to stop while holding housing, Fig. 1A. Align cylinder key with keyway in housing, then push lock cylinder assembly into housing until fully seated.
5. Install lock cylinder retaining screw. Torque screw to 40 in. lbs. for standard columns. On adjustable columns, torque retaining screw to 22 in. lbs.

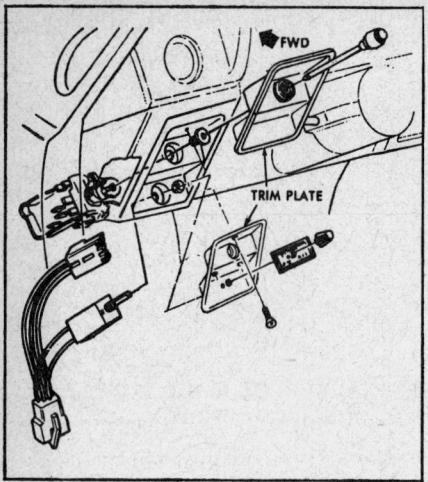

Fig. 3 Light switch replacement

6. Install buzzer switch, turn signal switch and steering wheel.

1977–78

1. Remove steering wheel as outlined under "Horn Sounder & Steering Wheel".
2. Remove turn signal switch as outlined under "Turn Signal Switch, Replace".

NOTE: Do not remove buzzer switch or damage to lock cylinder may result.

3. With ignition lock in run position, insert a small screw driver or similar tool into turn signal housing slot, Fig. 2. Keep tool to right side of housing slot and depress retainer at bottom of slot.
4. Remove lock cylinder from housing.

LIGHT SWITCH, REPLACE

1. Disconnect battery ground cable.
2. Pull headlamp switch knob to "ON" position, Fig. 3.
3. Reach under instrument panel and depress switch shaft retainer button while pulling on the switch control shaft knob.
4. With a large bladed screwdriver, remove the light switch ferrule nut from front of instrument panel.

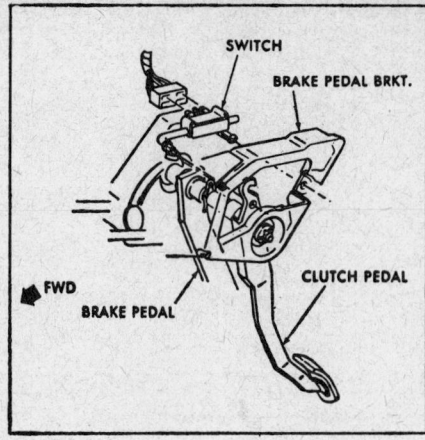

Fig. 4 Clutch start switch replacement

5. Disconnect the multi-contact connector from side of switch and remove switch.
6. Reverse procedure to install.

STOP LIGHT SWITCH, REPLACE

1. Reach under right side of instrument panel at brake pedal support and release wiring harness connector at switch.
2. Pull switch from mounting bracket.
3. When installing switch, adjust by bringing brake pedal to normal position. Electrical contact should be made when pedal is depressed .53 inch (13.5 mm). To adjust, the switch may be rotated or pulled in the clip.

CLUTCH START SWITCH, REPLACE

NOTE: The clutch pedal must be fully depressed and the ignition switch in START position for the vehicle to start.

The clutch switch assembly mounts with two tangs to the clutch pedal brace switch pivot bracket and the clutch pedal arm, Fig. 4.
1. Under the instrument panel on the clutch pedal support remove the multi-contact connector from switch.

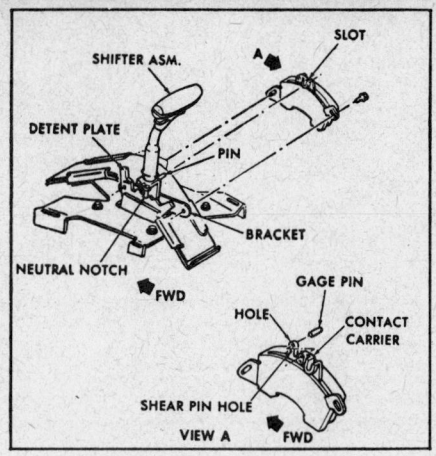

Fig. 5 Neutral start switch replacement

2. Compress switch assembly actuating shaft barb retainer and push out of clutch pedal.
3. Compress switch assembly pivot bracket barb and lift off switch.
4. When installing new switch, no adjustments are necessary as the switch is self aligning.

NEUTRAL SAFETY SWITCH, REPLACE

1. Remove floor console cover.
2. Disconnect electrical plugs on backup contacts, seat belt warning contacts and neutral start contacts of switch assembly, Fig. 5.
3. Place shift lever in Neutral.
4. Remove two screws securing switch to lever assembly.
5. When installing switch, make sure it is in Neutral position. When switch is installed, shifting out of Neutral will shear the switch plastic locating pin.

A/C COMPRESSOR CUT-OUT SWITCH

Vehicles equipped with automatic transmission and air conditioning utilize a full throttle A/C compressor cut-out switch, Fig. 6, which de-energizes the A-C compressor clutch

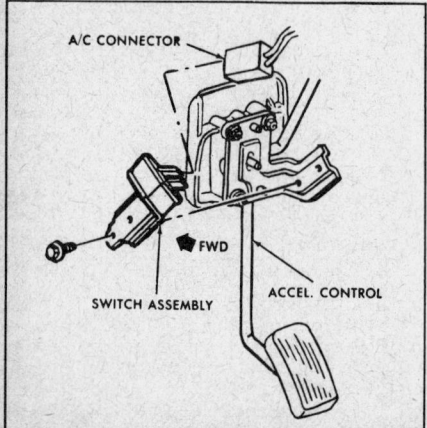

Fig. 6 A/C compressor cut-out switch

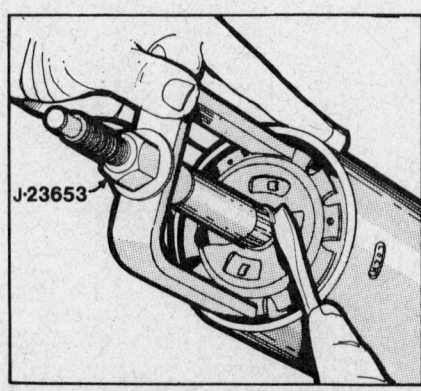

Fig. 8 Compressing lock plate and removing retaining ring

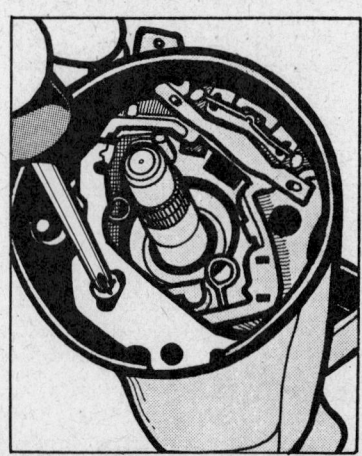

Fig. 9 Removing pivot arm

Key No.	Part Name
1	NUT, HEXAGON JAM
2	COVER ASSEMBLY, SHAFT LOCK
3	RING, RETAINING
4	LOCK, STEERING SHAFT
5	CAM ASSEMBLY, TURN SIGNAL CANCELLING
6	SPRING, UPPER BEARING
7	SCREW, PAN HEAD CROSS RECESS
8	SCREW, FLAT HEAD CROSS RECESS
9	SCREW, ROUND HEAD CROSS RECESS
10	ARM, PIVOT
11	SPACER, TURN SIGNAL SCREW
12	SWITCH ASSEMBLY, TURN SIGNAL
13	SWITCH ASEMBLY, PIVOT &
14	SCREW HEX WASHER HEAD TAPPING
15	WASHER, THRUST
16	SWITCH ASSEMBLY, BUZZER

Key No.	Part Name
17	CLIP, BUZZER SWITCH RETAINING
18	HOUSING, STEERING COLUMN
19	BEARING ASSEMBLY
20	RETAINER, BEARING
21	SECTOR, SWITCH ACTUATOR
22	SPRING, RACK PRELOAD
23	RACK, SWITCH ACTUATOR
24	BOLT ASSEMBLY, SPRING &
25	WASHER, SPRING THRUST
26	WASHER, WAVE
27	LEVER, KEY RELEASE

Key No.	Part Name
28	SPRING, LOCK INHIBITER
29	HOUSING ASSEMBLY, SHROUD &
30	SCREW, PAN HEAD CROSS RECESS
31	ROD, SWITCH ACTUATOR

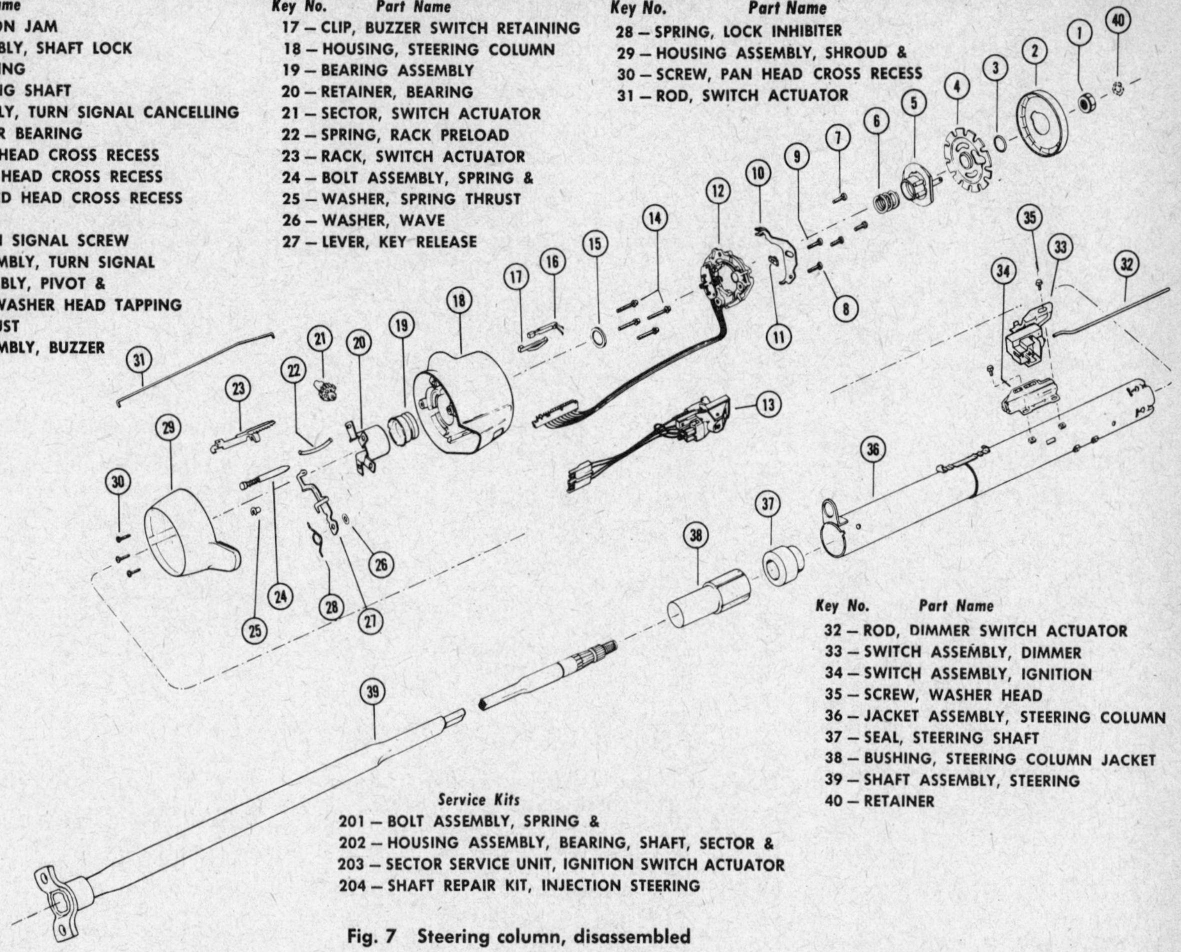

Key No.	Part Name
32	ROD, DIMMER SWITCH ACTUATOR
33	SWITCH ASSEMBLY, DIMMER
34	SWITCH ASSEMBLY, IGNITION
35	SCREW, WASHER HEAD
36	JACKET ASSEMBLY, STEERING COLUMN
37	SEAL, STEERING SHAFT
38	BUSHING, STEERING COLUMN JACKET
39	SHAFT ASSEMBLY, STEERING
40	RETAINER

Service Kits

201 — BOLT ASSEMBLY, SPRING &
202 — HOUSING ASSEMBLY, BEARING, SHAFT, SECTOR &
203 — SECTOR SERVICE UNIT, IGNITION SWITCH ACTUATOR
204 — SHAFT REPAIR KIT, INJECTION STEERING

Fig. 7 Steering column, disassembled

during full throttle acceleration. A pressure sensitive switch, located in the transmission, overrides the cut-out switch when the transmission is in third gear during full throttle acceleration.

TURN SIGNAL SWITCH, REPLACE

1. Remove steering wheel as described under "Horn Sounder & Steering Wheel" procedure.
2. Using a screw driver pry up and out to free cover from lock, Fig. 7.
3. Position lock plate compressing tool No. J-23653 on end of steering shaft and compress lock plate, Fig. 8.
4. Pry snap ring out of groove and discard, then remove tool J-23653 and lift lock plate off end of shaft.
5. Slide canceling cam, upper bearing preload spring and thrust washer off end of shaft.
6. Rotate multi-function lever to off position, then pull lever straight out to disengage.
7. Depress hazard warning knob and unscrew knob.
8. Remove two screws, pivot arm and spacer, Fig. 9.
9. Wrap upper part of connector with tape to prevent snagging of wires during switch removal, Fig. 10.
10. Remove three switch attaching screws and pull switch straight up guiding wires through column housing.

HORN SOUNDER & STEERING WHEEL, REPLACE

1. Disconnect battery ground cable.
2. Pry off horn button cap and retainer.
3. Remove steering wheel nut retainer and nut.

NOTE: Do not over expand retainer.

4. Using a suitable puller remove steering wheel.

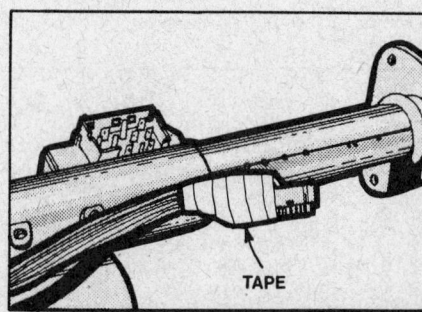

Fig. 10 Taping turn signal switch and wires

W/S WIPER, DIMMER OR IGNITION SWITCHES

Removal

1. Disconnect battery ground cable.
2. Remove steering column mounting bracket and unsnap switch connector from jacket.
3. Remove steering wheel.
4. Remove lock plate cover with a suitable screwdriver, Fig. 7.
5. Remove ring and lock plate. Use caution to prevent shaft from sliding out bottom of column. Slide upper bearing preload spring and turn signal cancelling cam off upper steering shaft, then the thrust washer off shaft.
6. Rotate turn signal lever-W/S switch assembly counter-clockwise to stop (Off position) and pull straight out to disengage.
7. Remove two screws, pivot arm and spacer, Fig. 9. Note that pivot arm retains spacer.
8. Lower steering column, then remove turn signal switch mounting screws and the switch.
9. Pull actuator rod to the stop to place ignition switch in "Off-Unlock". Remove upper attaching screw, releasing dimmer switch and actuator. The switches may now be removed, Figs. 11 and 12.
10. Remove remaining ignition switch retaining screw and the ignition switch.

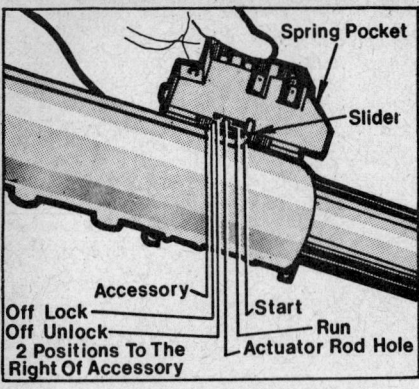

Fig. 11 Ignition switch

Installation

1. Assemble windshield wiper switch and pivot assembly onto housing.
2. Assemble buzzer switch and lock cylinder, then turn lock cylinder clockwise to stop and then counter-clockwise to other stop (OFF-UNLOCK) position. Position ignition switch, Fig. 13, then move slider to extreme left (ACC) and slide back two positions to the right to OFF-UNLOCK position. Install actuator rod into slider and install the bottom screw only, to retain the ignition switch. Do not move switch out of detent.
3. Install washer, spring and cancelling cam on steering shaft. Position cancelling cam lobes in relation to signal switch springs and assemble shaft lock and install new retaining ring, Fig. 7.
4. Install cover and snap ring, then install multi-function switch lever. Align lever pin with switch slot and push lever until it seats.
5. Install pinched end of dimmer switch actuator rod into dimmer switch, then install other end of rod into pivot switch. Install but do not tighten upper ignition switch screw. Depress dimmer switch and insert a 3/32 inch drill to lock switch body, Fig. 13.
6. Move dimmer switch up, removing lash between both switches and rod, then install and tighten upper ignition switch screw. Remove drill and check dimmer switch for proper operation.
7. Snap electrical connector into place and raise steering column, then install mounting nuts and torque to 22 ft. lbs. (30 Nm) and install steering wheel.

Fig. 13 Dimmer switch alignment

INSTRUMENT CLUSTER, REPLACE

1. Disconnect battery ground cable.
2. Remove clock stem knob.
3. Remove cluster bezel and lens retaining screws, then the bezel and lens, Fig. 14.
4. Remove instrument cluster to instrument panel retaining nuts and pull cluster toward vehicle rear.
5. Disconnect all electrical connectors and speedometer cable from cluster, then remove cluster.
6. Reverse procedure to install.

RADIO, REPLACE

1. Disconnect battery ground cable.
2. Remove mounting stud nut from bottom of radio, and the control knobs from shafts.
3. Remove screws from center trim panel and pull panel and radio toward the rear of the vehicle.
4. Disconnect all electrical connectors from radio.
5. Remove radio retaining nuts from radio control shafts.
6. Remove radio from vehicle.
7. Reverse procedure to install.

HEATER CORE, REPLACE

1. Disconnect battery ground cable and drain cooling system.
2. Disconnect heater hoses from core and plug openings in core.
3. Remove heater core housing to dash panel attaching screws, then the housing.
4. Remove core from housing.

BLOWER MOTOR, REPLACE

1. Disconnect battery ground cable.
2. Disconnect blower lead wire.
3. Remove blower motor to case attaching screws then the blower and wheel as an assembly.

NOTE: Scribe mark on blower motor and case so motor is installed in original position.

4. Remove nut and separate motor from wheel.
5. Reverse procedure to install.

NOTE: At assembly position open end of blower wheel away from blower motor. Replace sealer at blower motor flange if necessary.

W/S WIPER MOTOR, REPLACE

1. Reach under instrument panel above steering column and loosen transmission drive link to motor crank arm attaching nuts.
2. Disengage transmission drive link from motor crank arm.

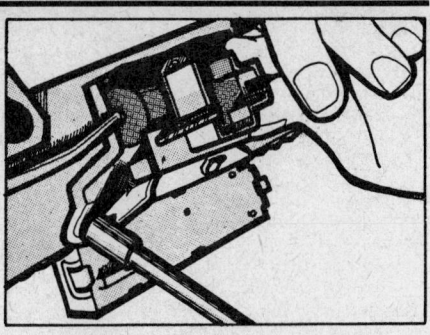

Fig. 12 Dimmer & ignition switch replacement

3. Raise hood and disconnect electrical connectors.
4. Remove motor attaching bolts.
5. Remove motor while guiding crank arm through hole.
6. To install, align sealing gasket to base of motor assembly and reverse remaining removal procedure.

NOTE: If the wiper motor to dash panel sealing gasket is damaged during removal, it should be replaced to prevent possible water leaks.

W/S WIPER TRANSMISSION, REPLACE

1. Remove instrument panel pad and cluster housing.
2. On models with A/C, remove left A/C duct attaching screws and position duct aside.
3. On all models, remove left side air duct.
4. Remove speedometer cable shield and left side instrument brace.
5. From under instrument panel, loosen transmission drive link to motor crank arm attaching nuts and disengage drive link.
6. Remove wiper arms and blades, then remove transmission to dash panel attaching bolts.
7. Move transmission assembly to left, then while rotating assembly, work out through instrument panel access hole at right upper center of instrument panel.

NOTE: When installing, ensure motor is in park position.

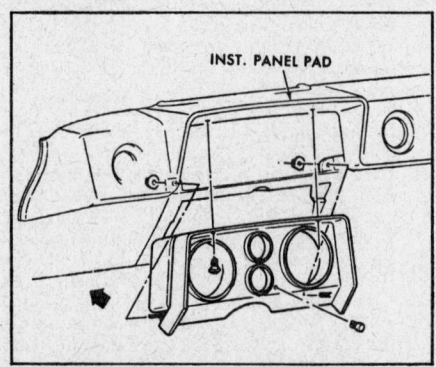

Fig. 14 Instrument cluster

Gasoline Engine Section

ENGINE MOUNT, REPLACE

Front

1. Remove heater assembly and position on top of engine.
2. Remove radiator upper support.
3. Remove engine mount nuts and the restraint cable.
4. Raise vehicle, install engine lifting device and raise engine to relieve weight from mounts.
5. Remove mount to engine bracket, then using tool J-25510, remove mount.

Rear

1. Raise vehicle and remove crossmember to mount bolts.
2. Raise transmission at extension housing to relieve weight from mount.
3. Remove mount to transmission bolts and the mount.

ENGINE, REPLACE

1. Remove hood.
2. Disconnect battery cables and remove clips securing battery cable to right side frame rail.
3. Drain cooling system and disconnect radiator and heater hoses.
4. Disconnect engine wiring harness.
5. Remove radiator upper support, radiator and fan.
6. Remove air cleaner.
7. Disconnect fuel line at rubber hose located along left side frame rail.
8. Disconnect accelerator and automatic transmission throttle valve linkage, if equipped.
9. Remove A/C compressor from mounting bracket and position aside, if equipped.
10. Raise vehicle and disconnect exhaust pipe at manifold.
11. Remove flywheel dust cover.
12. On models with automatic transmission, remove converter to flywheel bolts.
13. Remove converter housing to engine bolts on automatic transmission models or flywheel housing to engine bolt on manual transmission models, then lower vehicle.
14. Support transmission using a suitable jack.
15. Remove safety straps from engine mounts, then remove engine mount bolts.
16. Install engine lifting device, raise engine

slowly, pull engine forward to clear transmission and remove engine from vehicle.

INTAKE MANIFOLD, REPLACE

1. Disconnect battery ground cable and drain cooling system.
2. Remove air cleaner and disconnect upper radiator hose and heater hoses from intake manifold.
3. Remove EGR valve.
4. Disconnect fuel line, wiring, vacuum hoses and linkage from carburetor.
5. If equipped with A/C, perform the following:
   a. Remove radiator upper support, alternator and A/C drive belts.
   b. Remove fan, pulley and timing belt cover.
   c. Position A/C compressor aside.
   d. Raise vehicle and remove the lower A/C compressor bracket.
   e. Lower vehicle and remove the upper A/C compressor bracket.
6. On all models, remove ignition coil and position aside.
7. Remove intake manifold attaching bolts and the intake manifold.
8. Reverse procedure to install.

CYLINDER HEAD, REPLACE

1. Remove timing belt.
2. Drain cooling system, remove upper radiator hose and heater hose at intake manifold.
3. Remove air cleaner, then remove accelerator support bracket.
4. Disconnect spark plug wires.
5. Disconnect wiring harnesses at idle solenoid, choke, temperature sending switch and alternator.
6. Raise vehicle and disconnect exhaust pipe at manifold.
7. Lower vehicle and remove bolt retaining dipstick bracket to manifold.
8. Disconnect fuel line at carburetor.
9. Remove coil bracket bolts and position coil aside.
10. Remove camshaft covers, then remove camshaft cover to housing attaching studs.
11. Remove rocker arms, guides and lash adjusters.

NOTE: Rocker arms, guides and lash adjusters must be installed in original location during assembly.

12. Remove camshaft carrier from cylinder head.

NOTE: It may be necessary to use a wedge to separate camshaft carrier from cylinder head.

13. Remove cylinder head and manifold as an assembly.
14. Reverse procedure to install, tighten cylinder bolts in the sequence, Fig. 1.

HYDRAULIC VALVE LASH ADJUSTERS

Failure of an hydraulic valve lash adjuster is generally caused by an inadequate oil supply or dirt. An air leak at the intake side of the oil pump or too much oil in the engine will cause air bubbles in the oil supply to the lash adjusters, causing them to collapse. This is a probable cause of trouble if several lash adjusters fail to function, but air in the oil is an unlikely cause of failure of a single unit.

ROCKER ARMS, REPLACE

1. Remove camshaft covers.
2. On 1980–84 models, remove carburetor.
3. Using tool J-25477, depress valve spring and remove rocker arm, guide and lash adjuster, Fig. 2.

NOTE: Rocker arms, guides and lash adjusters must be installed in the same location during assembly.

VALVE GUIDES

Valve guides are an integral part of the cylinder head. If stem to guide clearance is excessive, the guide should be reamed to the next oversize and the appropriate oversize valve installed. Valves are available in standard size and oversizes of .003 in. (.075mm), .006 in. (.150mm), and .012 in. (.300mm).

CAMSHAFT COVER, REPLACE

1. Raise hood to fully open position.
2. Disconnect battery ground cable.
3. Remove air cleaner, PCV valve, air cleaner snorkle and heat tube assembly.
4. Remove spark plug wires from retainer on camshaft cover.
5. Remove accelerator cable support and position aside.
6. Remove nut and gasket from stud and the camshaft cover.

Fig. 2 Depressing valve spring

```
FRONT   7   3   2   6   10
        O   O   O   O   O

        O   O   O   O   O
        8   4   1   5   9
```

Fig. 1 Cylinder tighening sequence

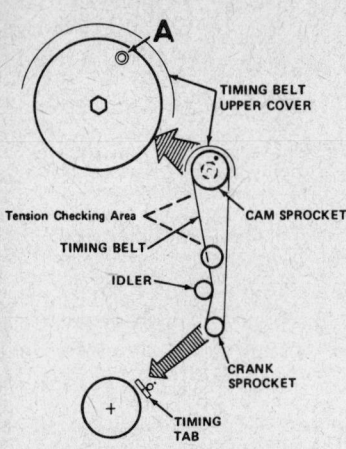

Quick Check Hole (In Sprocket) should align with hole in Timing Belt Upper Cover (A) when #1 Cyl. is at T.D.C.

TIMING BELT UPPER COVER

CAM SPROCKET

Tension Checking Area

TIMING BELT

IDLER

CRANK SPROCKET

TIMING TAB

Pulley timing mark should align with 0° mark on timing tab.

Fig. 3   Camshaft & crankshaft sprocket alignment marks

CAMSHAFT SPROCKET, REPLACE

1. Remove drive belts, then the fan and pulley.
2. Remove timing belt front cover.
3. Loosen idler pulley and remove timing belt from camshaft sprocket.
4. Remove camshaft sprocket bolt and washer, remove camshaft sprocket.

CAMSHAFT, REPLACE

1. Remove camshaft sprocket as described under "Camshaft Sprocket" procedure.
2. Remove rocker arms.
3. Remove heater assembly and position aside.
4. Remove camshaft carrier rear cover.
5. Remove camshaft thrust plate bolts, slide camshaft rearward and remove thrust plate.
6. Raise engine, then carefully slide camshaft from carrier.

IDLER ARM

Fig. 5   Timing belt idler arm and pulley

CAM LOBE LIFT SPECS.

Year	Intake	Exhaust
All 1977	.232 (5.893mm)	.232 (5.893mm)
All 1978–84	.2407 (6.1163mm)	.2407 (6.1163mm)

VALVE TIMING

Intake Open Before TDC

Engine	Year	Degrees
All	1976	32
All	1977	29
Exc. Hi Output	1978	28
Hi Output	1978–80	31
All	1981–84	28

TIMING BELT FRONT COVER, REPLACE

Upper Cover

1. Raise hood and disconnect battery ground cable.
2. Remove fan.
3. Remove upper cover retaining screw and the upper cover.

Lower Cover

1. Remove crankshaft pulley.
2. Remove upper front cover.
3. Remove lower cover attaching nut and the lower cover.

UPPER REAR TIMING BELT COVER, REPLACE

1. Remove timing belt front cover, timing belt and camshaft sprocket.
2. Remove three upper rear timing belt cover to camshaft carrier attaching screws.
3. Inspect camshaft seal and replace, if necessary.

TIMING BELT, REPLACE

NOTE: To verify camshaft timing, position crankshaft so that No. 1 cylinder is at top dead center compression stroke. With No. 1 cylinder at top dead center compression stroke, a 1/8 inch drill bit can be inserted through a hole in rear cover and hole in camshaft sprocket, if timing is correct, Fig. 3.

1. Remove timing belt front upper and lower covers and crankshaft pulley.
2. Loosen idler pulley bolt and remove timing belt from camshaft and crankshaft sprockets.
3. Position timing belt over crankshaft sprocket, then install crankshaft pulley.
4. Position crankshaft at TDC number 1 cylinder.
5. Align timing mark on camshaft sprocket with hole in upper rear cover, Fig. 3.
6. Install timing belt on crankshaft and camshaft sprockets, then adjust belt tension.

TIMING BELT TENSION, ADJUST

1. Remove fan, drive belt, pulley and upper timing belt cover.
2. Rotate crankshaft at least one revolution and position No. 1 piston at top dead cen-

Fig. 4   Adjusting timing belt tension

ter.
3. Install belt tension gauge, Tool J-26486, Fig. 4, on timing belt midway between the cam sprocket and idler pulley. Ensure the gauge center finger engages in a notch on the belt.
4. Correct belt tension is 70 ft. lbs. To adjust, loosen idler pulley attaching bolt, Fig. 5. Then, using a 1/4 inch allen wrench, rotate the pulley counterclockwise on the attaching bolt until correct belt tension is obtained and torque attaching bolt to 13–18 ft. lbs. (18–24 N-m).
5. Remove gauge and install upper timing belt cover, pulley, drive belt and fan.

CRANKSHAFT SPROCKET, REPLACE

1. Remove timing belt front cover, crankshaft pulley and timing belt.
2. Remove crankshaft sprocket.

PISTON & ROD ASSEMBLE

Assemble pistons and rods as indicated in Fig. 6. Measure connecting rod side clearance with a feeler gauge. Side clearance should be .004–.012 inch.

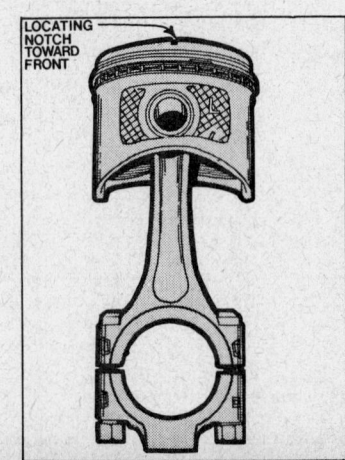

LOCATING NOTCH TOWARD FRONT

Fig. 6   Piston and rod assembly

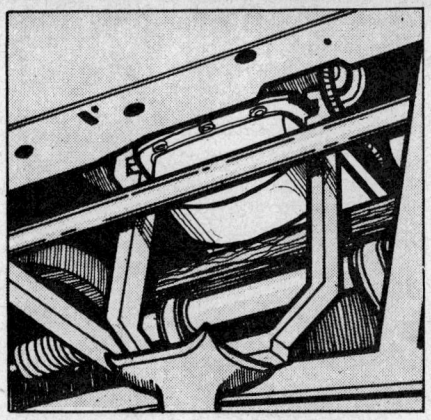

Fig. 7 Installing engine lifting device to facilitate oil pan removal

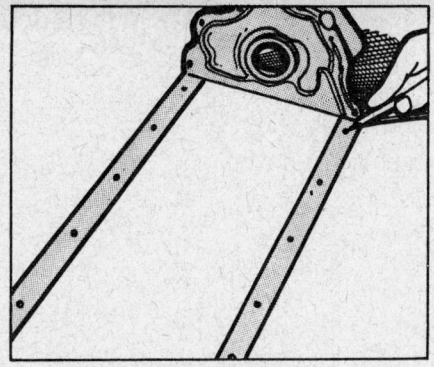

Fig. 8 Fabricating crankcase front cover to oil pan seal

Fig. 9 Installing crankcase front cover

PISTONS, & RINGS

Pistons and rings are available in standard size, .001 and .030 in. (.750mm) oversize.

MAIN & ROD BEARINGS

Main bearings are available in standard size and undersizes of .001 in. (.026mm), .002 in. (.050mm), .010 in. (.250mm) and .020 in. (.500mm).

Rod bearings are available in standard size and undersizes of .001 in. (.026mm), .010 in. (.250mm) and .020 in. (.500mm).

OIL PAN, REPLACE

1977

1. Remove heater housing from dash and position on top of engine.
2. Remove motor mount nuts, then pull back motor mount restraint cables.
3. Remove radiator upper support, on models with A/C remove upper fan shroud.
4. Remove flywheel splash shield.
5. On models with manual transmission, remove rack and pinion to front crossmember attaching bolts and position aside.
6. On all models, loosen converter to exhaust pipe clamp bolts.
7. Remove oil pan bolts.
8. Install engine lifting device and raise engine until oil pan can be removed, Fig. 7.

1978 All & 1979–84 Less Turbo Hydra-Matic 200 Automatic Transmission

NOTE: This procedure applies only to 1978–84 models equipped with manual transmission or Turbo Hydra-Matic 180 automatic transmission. The Turbo Hydra-Matic 180 automatic transmission is equipped with a full converter housing, while the Turbo Hydra-Matic 200 automatic transmission has a partial converter housing and splash shield.

1. Disconnect battery ground cable, then drain cooling system.
2. Remove upper radiator support. On models equipped with A/C, remove upper half of fan shroud.

3. On models equipped with automatic transmission, disconnect transmission oil cooler lines from radiator.
4. On all models, disconnect radiator hoses, then remove radiator from vehicle.
5. If equipped with A/C, remove condenser to radiator support attaching nuts and position on top of engine.
6. Remove heater core housing and position on top of engine.
7. Remove engine mount retaining nuts and clips.
8. Raise and support front of vehicle, then drain crankcase.
9. Disconnect exhaust pipe at exhaust manifold, then remove body to crossmember braces.
10. Remove rack and pinion steering gear unit from cross member and steering shaft, then pull unit down and out of way.
11. Remove stabilizer bar from body.
12. Install a suitable engine lifting device and raise engine sufficiently to permit oil pan removal.
13. Remove oil pan attaching screws, then pull pan down and remove oil pump pick-up tube and screen assembly.
14. Remove oil pan through from of vehicle.
15. Reverse procedure to install. When installing oil pump pick-up tube and screen assembly, use a new seal. Torque oil pan attaching screws to 55 inch lbs.

1979–84 With Turbo Hydra-Matic 200 Automatic Transmission

NOTE: This procedure applies only to 1979–84 models equipped with Turbo Hydra-Matic 200 automatic transmission. The Turbo Hydra-Matic 200 automatic transmission is equipped with a partial converter housing and splash shield, while the Turbo Hydra-Matic 180 automatic transmission has a full converter housing.

1. Disconnect battery ground cable, then remove air cleaner.
2. Remove heater housing assembly from front of dash panel and position on top of engine.
3. Pull back on motor mount wire restraints and remove mount nuts.
4. Remove radiator upper support or fan shroud, as necessary.
5. Raise and support front of vehicle, then drain crankcase.

6. Remove converter housing splash shield.
7. Remove rack and pinion steering gear unit from front crossmember.
8. Loosen catalytic converter to rear exhaust pipe clamp bolts.
9. Install a suitable engine lifting device and raise engine sufficiently to permit oil pan removal.
10. Remove oil pan attaching screws, then remove oil pan.
11. Reverse procedure to install. Torque oil pan attaching screws to 55 inch lbs.

OIL PUMP, REPLACE

1. Remove coil bracket attaching bolts and position coil aside.
2. Remove fuel pump and push rod.
3. Remove distributor.
4. Remove oil pan.
5. Remove oil pump screen and pipe assembly.
6. Remove oil pump.
7. Reverse procedure to install.

CRANKSHAFT REAR OIL SEAL, REPLACE

1. Disconnect battery ground cable.
2. Remove transmission, as described under "TRANSMISSION, REPLACE".
3. Remove flywheel.
4. Remove rack and pinion bracket bolts.
5. Remove left side strut assembly.
6. Disconnect flex coupling and pull steering gear down.
7. Drain engine oil, then remove oil pan mounting bolts.
8. With oil pan pulled down away from engine block, remove oil pump suction pipe and screen.
9. With engine mounts attached, raise engine slightly with suitable jack and block of wood and remove oil pan from vehicle.
10. Remove rear main bearing cap and oil seal.
11. Clean bearing cap, case and crankshaft seal surface, then inspect crankshaft seal surface for excessive wear and knicks. If excessive wear or knicks exist, replace crankshaft.
12. Install new seal in case, then install bearing cap, but do not tighten bolts.

NOTE: When installing seal in case, ensure seal is seated against rear main bearing bulkhead.

13. Torque main bearing cap bolts to 11 ft. lbs., then using suitable soft-faced hammer, tap end of crankshaft rearward, then forward. Retorque main bearing cap to specifications.
14. Using 2 part RTV sealer or equivalent, pack sealer into vertical grooves until excess flows from slots adjacent to rear seal. Clean excess sealer.
15. Reverse steps 1 through 9 to install.

CRANKCASE FRONT COVER, REPLACE

1. Remove timing belt upper and lower front covers, crankshaft pulley, timing belt and crankshaft sprocket.
2. Remove three crankcase front cover to oil pan attaching bolts, then the crankcase cover to engine attaching bolts.
3. Remove crankcase front cover, cover gasket and front portion of oil pan gasket.

NOTE: To fabricate a replacement crankcase front cover to oil pan gasket, position crankcase cover over a new oil pan gasket as shown in Fig. 8. When installing gasket apply sealer to cut off portion of gasket.

4. Inspect crankshaft oil seal, replace if necessary.
5. Install crankcase front cover using tool J-26434, Fig. 9.

BELT TENSION DATA

	New Lbs.	Used Lbs.
1977–81		
A/C Compressor	135–145	90–100
Timing Belt		
15 mm	55	—
19 mm	70	—
All other belts	120–130	70–80
1982–84		
A/C Compressor	168	90
Timing Belt	70	—
All other belts	146	70

FUEL PUMP, REPLACE

1979–84

1. Disconnect battery ground cable.
2. Remove distributor cap.
3. Remove spark plug wire retaining clips.
4. Remove coil wire and coil assembly.
5. Remove air cleaner assembly.
6. Disconnect fuel pump inlet and outlet hoses.
7. Remove fuel pump and gasket.
8. Reverse procedure to install.

1977–78

1. Raise vehicle and remove ignition coil.
2. Remove A/C compressor rear bracket, if equipped.
3. Remove fuel pump attaching bolts and fuel pump.
4. Reverse procedure to install.

WATER PUMP, REPLACE

1. Position No. 1 cylinder at top dead center.

NOTE: When No. 1 cylinder is at top dead center, a 1/8 in. drill rod may be inserted through the hole in the rear timing belt cover into the hole located on camshaft sprocket.

2. Disconnect battery ground cable, then drain cooling system.
3. Loosen alternator and A/C drive belts, then remove crankshaft pulley.
4. On models equipped with A/C, remove upper portion of fan shroud, if equipped.
5. On models less A/C, remove radiator upper mounting panel, if equipped.
6. On all models, remove engine fan.
7. Remove timing belt cover attaching bolts and nuts, then remove timing belt cover.
8. Loosen idler pulley mounting bolts and allow pulley to rotate clockwise.
9. Remove timing belt from camshaft and crankshaft pulleys.
10. Disconnect lower radiator hose and heater hose from water pump.
11. Remove water pump to cylinder block attaching bolts, then remove water pump.
12. Reverse procedure to install. Before installing timing belt cover, adjust timing belt tension as described under "Timing Belt Tension Adjust."

Diesel Engine Section

DIESEL ENGINE TROUBLESHOOTING

Hard Starting

1. Check fuel level, replenish if necessary.
2. Check notched line on injection pump flange, reset timing as necessary.
3. Check to ensure fuel is reaching injection nozzles. If fuel is reaching injectors:
   a. Check connections of fuse, glow plugs, Q.S.S.I. controller and glow plug relays.
   b. Check fuel spray pattern, and ensure injection starting pressure is 1707 p.s.i.
   c. Check to ensure valve clearances are satisfactory. Refer to specifications.
   d. Check compression pressure in each cylinder. Standard value should be 441 psi.
   e. Check to ensure proper installation of timing belt and camshaft.
   If fuel is not reaching injectors:
   a. Check for air in fuel filter.
   b. Check if air is being drawn into fuel line through leakage in the pipe joints.
   c. Check operation of fuel cut out solenoid.
   d. Check fuel filter for restrictions.
   e. Check fuel pipes for restrictions.
   f. Check delivery valve for possible sticking.
4. Replace or readjust setting of injection pump.

Engine Idling Rough

1. Check if idle speed is within specifica-

tions.
2. Check to ensure accelerator control cable is not binding or twisting.
3. Check accelerator lever setting for looseness.
4. Check for air or water in fuel filter.
5. Check for proper alignment on injection pump flange.
6. Check engine mounting for cracks or looseness.
7. Check fuel spray pattern, and ensure injection starting pressure is 1707 p.s.i.
8. Check to ensure intake clearances are satisfactory. Refer to specifications.
9. Check compression pressure in each cylinder. Standard value should be 441 p.s.i.
10. Check to ensure proper installation of timing belt and camshaft.
11. Check delivery valve for sticking.
12. Replace or readjust setting of injection pump.

Engine Lacks Power

1. Check air cleaner for restrictions.
2. Check to ensure accelerator control cable is not binding or twisting.
3. Check seals on full load adjustment bolt and maximum speed stop bolt.
4. Check to ensure accelerator control lever is in full contact with maximum speed stop bolt.
5. Check exhaust system for restrictions.
6. Check for air in fuel filter.
7. Check notched line on injection pump flange, repair as necessary.
8. Check engine mounting for cracks or looseness.

9. Check fuel spray pattern, and ensure injection starting pressure is 1707 p.s.i.
10. Check to ensure valve clearances are satisfactory. Refer to specifications.
11. Check compression pressure in each cylinder. Standard value should be 441 p.s.i.
12. Check to ensure proper installation of timing belt and camshaft.
13. Check delivery valve for sticking.
14. Replace or readjust setting of injection pump.

Engine Overheating

1. Check coolant level in radiator.
2. Check condition of coolant for contamination, ratio of anti-freeze to water, and leakage of oil into coolant.
3. Check for leakage in hoses, and clamps.
4. Check water pump and thermostat housing for leakage.
5. Check for damaged cylinder head gasket.
6. Check fan belt tension. Deflection of fan belt should be no more than .4 inch.
7. Check operation of fan clutch.
8. Check for proper operation of radiator cap.
9. Check thermostat operation. Thermostat opening temperature is 180° F.
10. Check injection timing.
11. Check condition of water pump impeller.
12. Check to ensure proper level of engine oil.
13. Replace or readjust setting of injection pump.

CONTROLLER

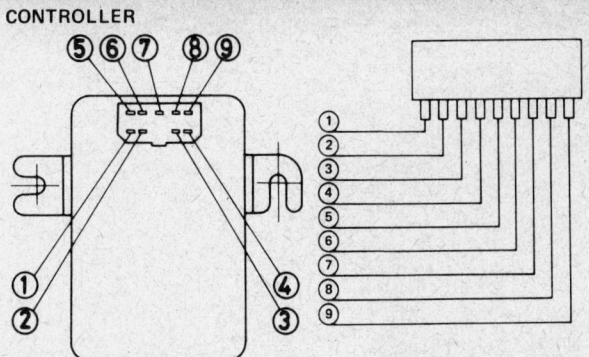

Position to which connector terminal is connected

1. Starter switch (ON position)
2. Sensing resistor
3. Thermo switch
4. Starter switch (ST position)
5. Sensing resistor
6. Glow plug relay No. 1
7. Ground
8. Glow indicator lamp
9. Not used

Fig. 1   Controller wiring connections

Engine Knocking

1. Check if engine has been thoroughly warmed up.
2. Check injection timing.
3. Check fuel spray pattern, and ensure injection starting pressure is 1707 p.s.i.
4. Check compression pressure in each cylinder. Standard value should be 441 p.s.i.
5. Check to ensure proper quality of fuel.
6. Replace or readjust setting of injection pump.

Noise Indicating Abnormal Leakage

1. Check exhaust system for loose connections or leakage.
2. Check to ensure proper installation of nozzles and glow plugs.
3. Check for damaged cylinder head gasket.
4. Check to ensure valve clearances are satisfactory. Refer to specifications.
5. Check compression pressure in each cylinder. Standard value should be 441 p.s.i.

Continuous Noise

1. Check fan belt tension. Deflection of fan belt should be no more than .4 inch.
2. Check to ensure cooling fan is secure.
3. Check water pump bearing for wear and damage.
4. Check operation of generator and vacuum pump.
5. Check to ensure valve clearances are satisfactory. Refer to specifications.

Slapping Noise

1. Check valve retainers for damage.
2. Check to ensure valve clearances are satisfactory. Refer to specifications.
3. Check rocker arms for damage.
4. Check camshaft for seizure.
5. Check to ensure flywheel bolts are secure.
6. Check crankshaft and thrust bearing for wear and damage.
7. Check main bearing oil clearances.
8. Check connecting rod bearing and bushing oil clearances.
9. Check to ensure clearance between pistons and cylinder walls is satisfactory. Refer to specifications.

Excessive Oil Consumption

1. If oil is leaking:

a. Check engine oil level.
b. Check to ensure drain plug is secure.
c. Check oil pipes for leakage.
d. Check cooler seat gasket, oil filter and oil seal retainer for leakage.
e. Check cylinder head cover, oil pan and oil pump gaskets for leakage.
f. Check cylinder head gasket for leakage.
g. Check oil seals for leakage.
h. Check function of P.C.V.
i. Check to ensure flywheel bolts are secure.

2. If oil is burning:

a. Check to ensure quality of oil.
b. Check valve stem oil seals.
c. Check valve guides and valve stems for wear and damage.
d. Check for damaged cylinder head gasket.
e. Check to ensure proper setting of piston rings.
f. Check piston rings for wear and damage.
g. Check cylinder walls for wear and damage.

Excessive Fuel Consumption

1. Check air cleaner for restrictions.
2. Check fuel lead adjustment bolt seal for leakage.
3. Check fuel pipes for leakage.
4. Check exhaust system for restrictions.
5. Check if idle speed is within specifications.
6. Check to ensure proper quality of fuel.
7. Check injection timing.
8. Check fuel spray pattern, and ensure injection starting pressure is 1707 p.s.i.
9. Check to ensure valve clearances are satisfactory. Refer to specifications.
10. Check compression pressure in each cylinder. Standard valve should be 441 p.s.i.
11. Check delivery valve for sticking.
12. Replace or readjust setting of injection pump.

DIESEL ENGINE ELECTRICAL TROUBLESHOOTING

NOTE: In a normally operating quick start system, when coolant temperature is below 122° F. and the key is in the "On" position, the glow plug indicator turns on for about 3.5 seconds and No. 1 Relay turns on for a few seconds.

Relay No. 1 And Glow Indicator Are Both Inoperative

1. Starter circuit fuse is burnt out or fusible link wire is open.
2. Starter wire circuit is open or not properly connected.
3. Controller defective or not properly connected.
4. Starter switch is inoperative.

Relay No. 1 Inoperative

1. Relay No. 1 is open.
2. Relay coil in relay No. 1 is open.
3. Controller to No. 1 relay circuitry is open or not properly connected.
4. Grounding circuit for No. 1 relay is open or not properly connected.
5. Controller is inoperative.
6. Circuit from controller to signal feed wire of sensing resistor is open or not properly connected.
7. Terminals of sensing resistor are not connected.
8. Main terminal of No. 1 relay not connected.
9. Main contact open in No. 1 relay.
10. Terminals in quick preheat circuit not connected.
11. Engine harness ground not properly connected.
12. Quick preheating wiring not properly connected or circuit open.

Glow Indicator Light Inoperative

1. Controller damaged.
2. Indicator circuit not properly connected or open.
3. Light bulb burnt out.

Relay No. 1 Turns Off Within 2 Seconds

1. Controller damaged.
2. One or more glow plugs defective.
3. Wiring at connector poorly connected.

Relay No. 1 Will Not Turn Off After A Few Seconds

1. Controller damaged.

Relay No. 1 Operates When Coolant Temperature Is Above 122° F.

1. Thermostat switch is inoperative.
2. Short in circuit.

NOTE: In a normally operating quick start system, when coolant temperature is below 122° F. and, the key held in the "Start" position, the glow plug indicator and the No. 2 relay will remain on until key is moved to "On" position.

Relay No. 2 And Glow Indicator Inoperative

1. Starter switch "R" circuit not properly connected or open.

Relay No. 2 Inoperative

1. Relay No. 2 terminals not connected.
2. Circuit between R terminal and No. 2

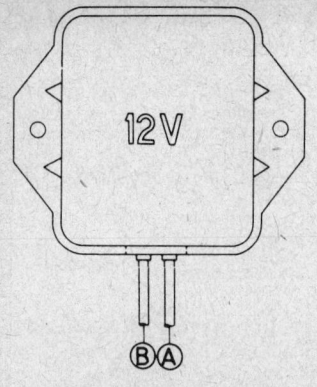

Fig. 2   Dropping resistor test connections

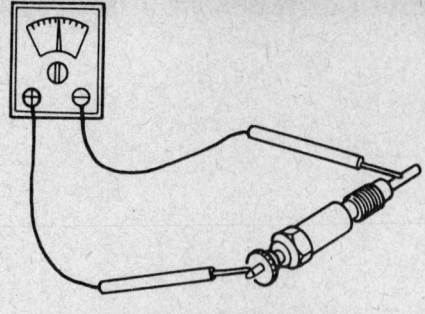

Fig. 3   Testing glow plug

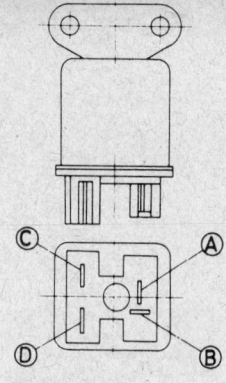

Fig. 4   Glow plug relay test connections

relay not properly connected or open.

3. No. 2 relay coil is open.

Glow Indicator Light Inoperative

1. Controller damaged.

NOTE: In a normally operating quick start system, when coolant temperature is above 122° F. and the key is in the "On" position the glow plug indicator light will turn on for about 0.3 seconds.

Glow Plug Light Remains On For 3.5 Seconds And Causes Relay No. 1 To Turn On

1. Thermo-switch circuit not properly connected or open.
2. Thermostat switch is inoperative.

DIESEL ENGINE ELECTRICAL DIAGNOSIS & TESTING

Controller

Controller in this system has four functions. As engine coolant temperature changes, it controls the glow plug relay. For determining glow plug heating requirements, it monitors differences between sensing resistance and glow plug resistance. It controls rapid preheat circuit to 1,908° F. of glow plug temperature and, during pre-heat cycle, controls glow plug pre-heat indicator lamp (3.5 sec.). Refer to Fig. 1 for wiring connections.

Dropping Resistor

During stabilized heating, this fixed value resistor is used to lower voltage of glow plugs. Check dropping resistor by performing continuity check across the terminals. Replace resistor if no continuity is found. Refer to Fig. 2.

Glow Plugs

The glow plugs used in this system are the fast warm up type. Check glow plugs by performing continuity test across plug terminals and body. If no continuity is found, heater wire is damaged and glow plug should be replaced. Refer to Fig. 3.

Glow Plug Relay

This relay is main relay for stabilized heating circuit and rapid pre-heat cycle. Check glow relay by performing continuity test across terminals C and D while battery voltage is applied to terminals A and B. If no continuity is found, replace glow plug relay. Refer to Fig. 4.

Glow Plug Relay 2

During starting, this relay is used to provide stabilized heating. To check this relay, use same procedure as for glow plug relay 1.

Fusible Links

These two in-line fusible links are used to protect the glow plug electrical wiring. To check fusible links, perform continuity check across terminals. If no continuity is found, fusible link should be replaced. Refer to Fig. 5.

Sensing Resistor

Used in series with the glow plugs, this shunt type sensing resistor causes a small voltage drop which is monitored by the controller.

Thermo Switch

This thermo switch is used to provide a ground circuit to controller circuitry when engine temperature is above 122° F. To check thermo switch, perform continuity check across terminal and body while end of thermal switch is submerged in water. Gradually bring temperature of water to 122° F. Replace thermal switch if continuity is not found at this temperature. Refer to Fig. 6.

ENGINE, REPLACE

1. Remove hood.
2. Disconnect battery ground cable and drain cooling system.
3. Disconnect radiator hoses and remove radiator.
4. Disconnect engine wiring harnesses.
5. Remove air cleaner.
6. Disconnect accelerator and automatic transmission throttle valve linkage, if equipped.
7. Disconnect fuel lines and heater hoses.
8. Remove A/C compressor from mounting bracket and position aside, if equipped.
9. Remove power steering pump and bracket and position aside, if equipped.
10. Disconnect vacuum hose to master cylinder.
11. Remove engine mount nuts.
12. Raise vehicle and disconnect exhaust pipe at manifold.
13. Remove engine strut (shock type).
14. Remove flywheel dust cover.
15. On models with automatic transmission, remove converter to flywheel bolts.
16. Remove transmission rear crossmember to body bolts and bellhousing bolts.
17. Reinstall crossmember bolts.
18. Lower vehicle.
19. Remove oil filter.
20. Install engine lifting device, raise and remove engine.
21. Reverse procedure to install.

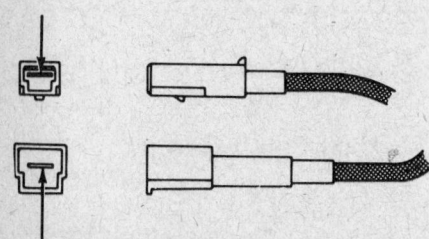

Fig. 5   Fusible link test connections

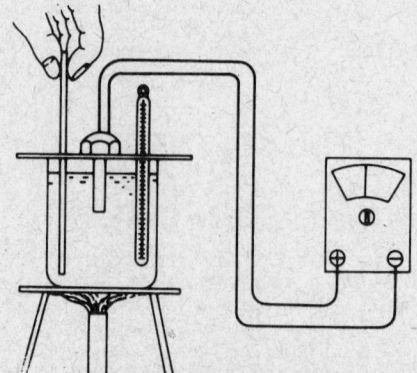

Fig. 6   Testing thermo switch

LUBRICATE WITH ENGINE OIL

Fig. 7   Cylinder head tightening sequence

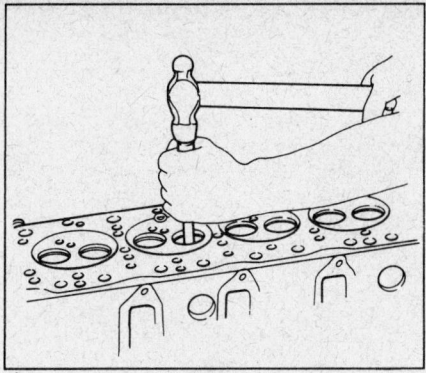

Fig. 8 Removing valve guides

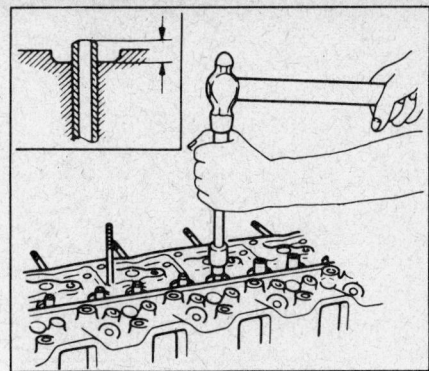

Fig. 9 Installing valve guides

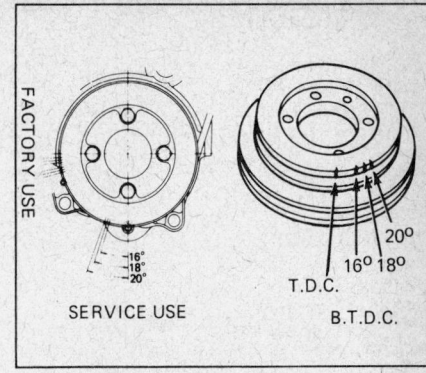

Fig. 10 Timing mark locations on damper pulley

CYLINDER HEAD, REPLACE

1. Disconnect battery ground cable and drain cooling system.
2. Remove cam cover.
3. Remove timing belt. It will not be necessary to remove lower cover and damper.
4. Remove camshaft.
5. Remove glow plug resistor wires and injector lines.
6. Remove fuel return line hose.
7. Raise vehicle and disconnect exhaust pipe at manifold.
8. Lower vehicle and remove oil feed pipe at rear of cylinder head.
9. Disconnect upper radiator hose.
10. Remove cylinder head bolts. Remove cylinder head and gasket.
11. Reverse procedure to install, tighten cylinder head bolts in sequence shown in Fig. 7.

VALVE TIMING

Intake Opens Before TDC

Engine	Year	Degrees
4-110.8	1981–84	32°

VALVES, ADJUST

1. Remove cam cover.
2. Inspect the rocker arm shaft bracket bolts for looseness, retorque as necessary.
3. Bring No. 1 cylinder to TDC on compression stroke.
4. Adjust valve clearances of cylinder No. 1, intake valve of No. 2 and exhaust valve of No. 3. Turn crankshaft one full revolution to bring cylinder No. 4 TDC on compression stroke. Adjust clearances of cylinder No. 4, exhaust valve of No. 2 and intake valve of No. 3.
5. Reinstall cam cover.

VALVE GUIDE, REPLACE

1. Using tool No. J-26512 drive out the valve guide from the lower face of the cylinder head, Fig. 8.
2. Apply engine oil to outer circumference of valve guide, using tool No. J-26512 drive the guide into position from the upper face of the cylinder head, Fig. 9.

NOTE: Always replace valve guide and valve as a set.

TIMING BELT, REPLACE

1. Disconnect battery ground cable.
2. Remove undercover and drain coolant.
3. Remove fan shroud, alternator belt, cooling fan and water pump pulley.
4. Remove ten bolts securing upper dust cover, remove dust cover.
5. Remove bypass hose.
6. Bring cylinder No. 1 to TDC, Fig 10, ensure that setting mark on injection pump pulley is in alignment with front plate, then fix the pulley with 8 mm 1.25 pitch bolt, Fig. 11 and Fig. 12.
7. Remove cam cover and loosen valve adjustment screws so rocker arms are in a free state. Fix the camshaft by installing fixing plate, tool No. J-29761 into the slit in rear end of the camshaft, Fig. 13.
8. Remove crankshaft damper pulley, lower dust cover and timing belt holder, Fig. 14.

NOTE: Under no circumstances should the crankshaft be disturbed from TDC.

9. Remove tension pulley spring then loosen tension pulley and plate bolts, remove timing belt.
10. Remove camshaft pulley bolt, using a suitable puller remove camshaft pulley, then reinstall pulley and bolt. Tighten bolt just enough to allow the pulley to be turned smoothly by hand.
11. Install new timing belt using sequence shown in Fig. 15. Ensure that belt cogs are properly installed in pulleys. Do not disturb crankshaft setting.
12. Concentrate belt looseness on tension pulley, depress tension pulley with finger and install tension spring. Semi-tighten bolts in numerical sequence 1 and 2 to prevent movement of tension pulley, Fig. 16.
13. Tighten camshaft pulley bolt.
14. Remove injection pump pulley lock bolt and camshaft fixing plate.
15. Install crankshaft damper pulley, ensure No. 1 cylinder is at TDC.
16. Ensure injection pump pulley mark is in alignment with mark on plate and fixing plate should fit smoothly into the rear slit of the camshaft. Remove plate.
17. Loosen tensioner plate bolts and pulley. Concentrate looseness of belt on tensioner, then tighten the bolts in numerical sequence 1, 2, and 3. Fig. 17. Torque bolts 1 and 2, 11 to 18 ft. lbs. Bolt 3, 47 to 61 ft. lbs.

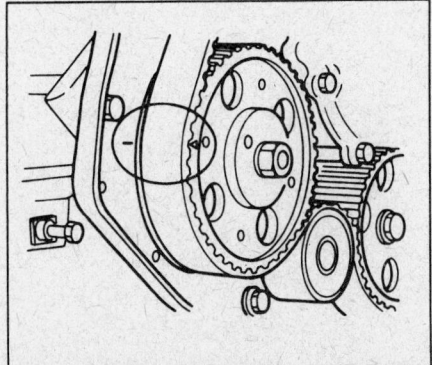

Fig. 11 Injection pump pulley alignment

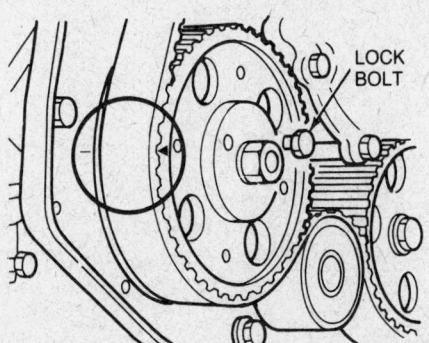

Fig. 12 Fixing injection pump pulley with lock bolt

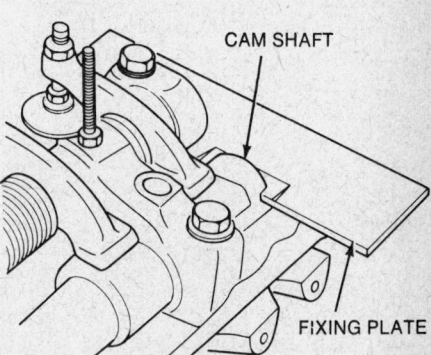

Fig. 13 Fixing camshaft in place with tool No. J-29761

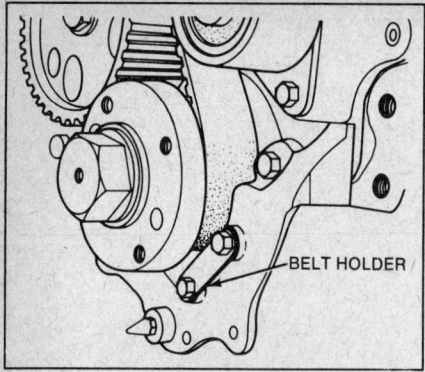

Fig. 14   Timing belt holder

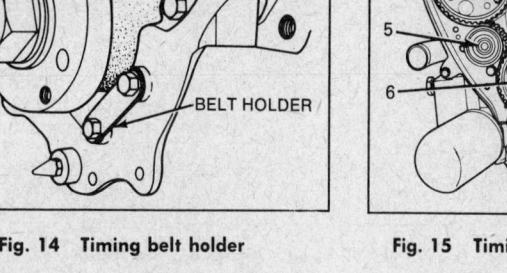

Fig. 15   Timing belt installation sequence

Fig. 16   Semi-tightening sequence of tension pulley

18. Using a belt tension gauge, check tension between camshaft pulley and injection pump pulley. Tension should be 47 to 64 lbs.
19. Remove crankshaft damper and install timing belt holder.
20. Adjust valves. Refer to "Valves, Adjust" for procedure.
21. Reverse steps 1 through 8 to reassemble.

INJECTION TIMING, ADJUST

1. Check that alignment mark on injection pump flange is aligned with alignment mark on front plate.
2. Bring cylinder No. 1 to TDC on compression stroke by turning crankshaft until timing mark on pulley aligns with pointer, Fig. 10.

NOTE: The damper pulley has eleven notched lines as shown in Fig. 10. Four lines on one side, seven elsewhere. The four lines are intended for service use while the other seven are for factory use only.

3. Remove upper dust cover, ensure the injection pump belt is properly tensioned and the timing marks are aligned. See "Timing Belt, Replace".
4. Remove the cam cover and rear plug, ensure that the fixing plate fits smoothly into the camshaft rear slit, then remove the fixing plate. See "Timing Belt, Replace".
5. Disconnect the injection pipe from the injection pump, remove distributor head screw and gasket, install static timing gauge J-29763, Fig. 18. Set the lift approximately .040 inch (1 mm) from the plunger.
6. Bring No. 1 piston to a point 45–60 degrees BTDC by turning the crankshaft, set dial indicator to zero. Turn crankshaft slightly in both directions, ensuring gauge indication is stable.
7. Turn crankshaft in normal direction of rotation until the 18 degree mark on the damper is aligned with the timing pointer, Fig. 10. Note reading of dial indicator, if reading is not .020 inch (.5 mm), hold crankshaft at 18 degrees and loosen the two nuts on injection pump flange, Fig. 19. Move pump until reading on dial indicator is .020 inch (.5 mm), then tighten nuts.

INJECTION PUMP, REPLACE

1. Remove timing belt. See "Timing Belt, Replace".
2. To prevent rotation of injection pump pulley during disassembly, thread a 8 mm 1.25 pitch bolt through the pulley into the housing, Fig. 12.
3. Remove injection pump pulley bolt.
4. Remove bolt installed in step two, then using a suitable puller remove injection pump pulley.
5. Disconnect fuel cut solenoid valve switch wiring and tachometer pick up sensor wiring at connector.
6. Disconnect accelerator cable from pump lever. If equipped with automatic transmission, remove throttle valve control cable.
7. Disconnect vacuum hose from fast idle actuator.
8. Disconnect fuel hoses from injection pump.
9. Remove six screws attaching injection pipe clips and remove.
10. Remove injection pipes.
11. Remove injection pump rear bracket then control lever spring.
12. Remove attaching nuts and pump with fast idle device installed.
13. Install injection pump with fast idle device installed by aligning notched line on pump flange with the line on the front plate.
14. Install rear bracket bolts following sequence in Fig. 20.
15. Install the injection pump pulley by aligning it with key groove, torque nut to 43 to 50 ft. lbs. Hold pulley from rotating by installing a bolt as described in step 2.
16. Refer to "Timing Belt, Replace" for reassembly procedures.

ROCKER ARM SHAFT ASSEMBLY, REPLACE

1. Remove cam cover.
2. Remove rocker arm shaft bracket bolts and nuts, then remove rocker arm shaft and rocker arm assembly.

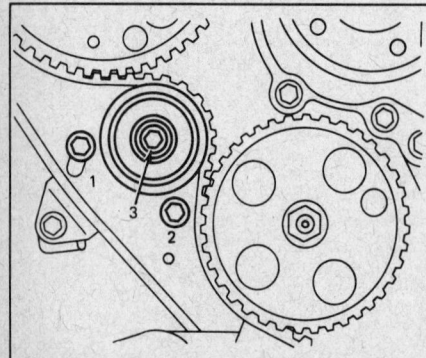

Fig. 17   Torquing tension pulley bolt sequence

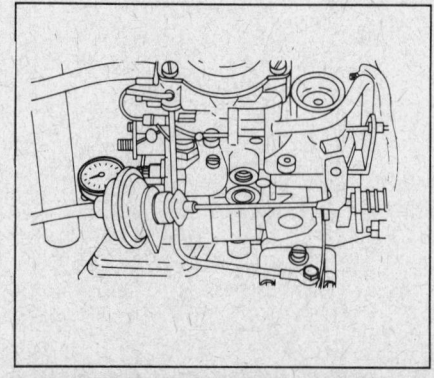

Fig. 18   Static timing gauge, J-29763 installed

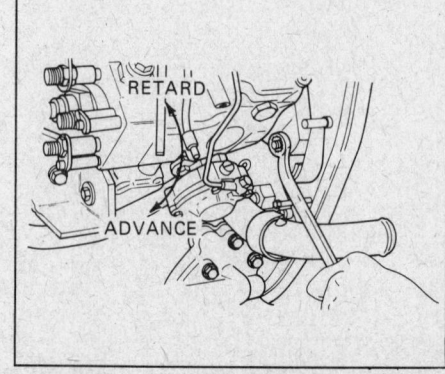

Fig. 19   Injection pump flange nuts

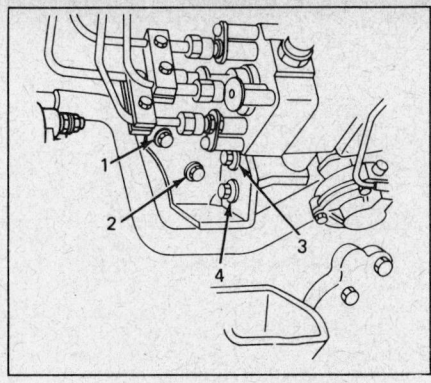

Fig. 20 Injection pump rear bracket tightening sequence

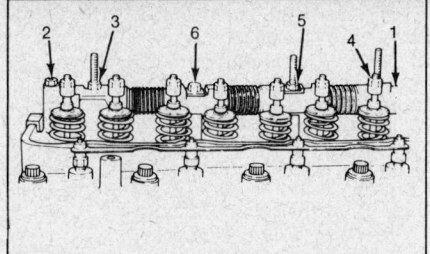

Fig. 21 Rocker arm bracket bolt tightening sequence

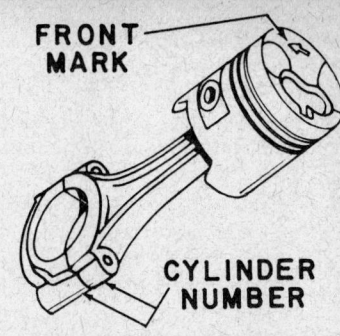

Fig. 22 Piston & connecting rod assembly

3. Prior to installation, apply a generous amount of engine oil to the rocker arm shaft, rocker arms and valve stem end caps.
4. Install rocker arm shaft assembly and tighten bolts in sequence as shown in Fig. 21.
5. Adjust valves. Refer to "Valves, Adjust" for procedure.

CAMSHAFT, REPLACE

1. Remove cam cover.
2. Remove timing belt as described in "Timing Belt, Replace".
3. Remove camshaft gear as described in "Timing Belt, Replace".
4. Remove rocker arm shaft assembly as described in "Rocker Arm Shaft Assembly, Replace".
5. Remove bolts attaching front head plate and remove.
6. Remove the camshaft bearing cap bolts, then remove bearing caps with cap side bearing.
7. Remove camshaft oil seal followed by the camshaft.
8. Install camshaft oil seal, camshaft and rocker arm shaft assembly. Loosen rocker arm adjustment screws so the rocker arms are in a free state. Reverse procedure from step five to reinstall.

CRANKSHAFT FRONT OIL SEAL, REPLACE

1. Remove timing belt. Refer to 'Timing Belt, Replace".

2. Remove crankshaft hub center bolt and washer.
3. Using a suitable puller, remove hub from crankshaft.
4. Using puller No. J-29752, remove crankshaft timing belt pulley.
5. Pry out front oil seal using a suitable screwdriver.
6. Apply clean engine oil to inner and outer surfaces of new seal, using a suitable seal installer, install the oil seal.
7. Postion crankshaft timing belt pulley flange into seal, align pulley groove with crankshaft key. Drive pulley onto crankshaft using installer tool No. J-26587.
8. Align crankshaft hub keyway with crankshaft key, install center bolt. Torque to 98 to 119 ft. lbs.
9. Reinstall timing belt. Refer to 'Timing Belt, Replace".

CRANKSHAFT REAR OIL SEAL, REPLACE

1. Remove the clutch pressure plate assembly.
2. Remove the six flywheel attaching bolts, then the flywheel.
3. Using a suitable screwdriver, pry out the rear seal.
4. Apply clean engine oil to all sides of new seal.
5. Install the oil seal in the oil seal retainer using tool No. J-29818.
6. Position flywheel on crankshaft hub. Using new bolts, apply loctite to threads and install flywheel. Torque bolts 36 to 43 ft. lbs.
7. Reverse procedure to install remaining parts.

PISTON & CONNECTING ROD

Install the piston on the connecting rod, so that the combustion chamber on piston head is on the same side with the cylinder mark side (side with bearing stopper) of the connecting rod big end. The front of the piston should be on same side as the "Isuzu" mark on the connecting rod, Fig. 22. Pistons are available in oversizes of .010 and .030 in.

Check connecting rod side clearance with a feeler gauge. Clearance should be .003–.024 inch.

OIL PAN, REPLACE

1. Remove engine assembly. Refer to "Engine, Replace" for procedure.
2. Remove fourteen bolts and four nuts attaching oil pan and remove.
3. Discard old gasket, clean mounting surfaces. Install new gasket using a suitable sealing compound on oil pan, and install.
4. Torque bolts 4 to 6 ft. lbs.

OIL PUMP, REPLACE

1. Remove timing belt. Refer to "Timing Belt, Replace".

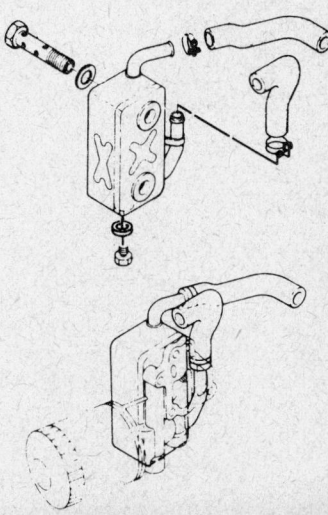

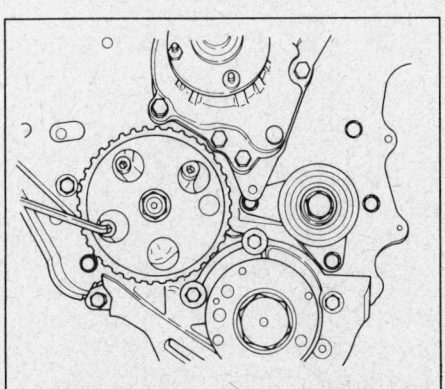

Fig. 23 Removing oil pump

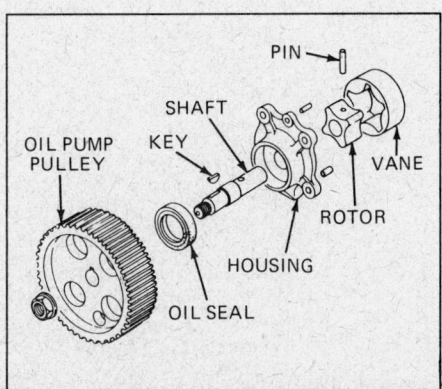

Fig. 24 Oil pump, disassembled

Fig. 25 Oil cooler assembly

four allen bolts securing oil ~~~ remove oil pump and pulley as an ~~~mbly, see Fig. 23.

~~~ fer to "Oil Pump, Inspection & Service".

4. Prior to installation apply a generous amount of clean engine oil to vane, install with taper side towards the cylinder body.
5. Install new pump O-ring, lubricate with motor oil and install in the housing groove. Lubricate oil pump rotor and install pump body together with pulley.
6. Reverse procedure to install.

OIL PUMP, INSPECTION & SERVICE

Disassembly, Fig. 24.

1. Inspect all parts for any signs of abnormal wear, or damage.

2. Measure outside diameter of pulley flange. Diameter should be 1.1–1.1035 inch (27.94–28.03 mm).
3. Using a straightedge and feeler gauge, check clearance between vane and cylinder body in direction of thrust. Clearance should be .0011–.0027 inch (.03–.07 mm).
4. Check clearance between vane and cylinder body. Clearance should be .0094–.0141 inch (.24–.36 mm).
5. Check clearance between vane and rotor. Clearance should be .0051–.0059 (.13–.15).
6. Reassemble as shown in Fig. 24.

OIL COOLER, REPLACE

1. Disconnect battery ground cable.

2. Remove oil cooler drain plug, allow cooler to drain.
3. Remove rubber hoses.
4. Remove two joint bolts securing cooler, Fig. 25.
5. Install new joint bolt gaskets and install cooler.
6. Reverse steps 1 to 3 to install.

WATER PUMP, REPLACE

1. Disconnect battery ground cable.
2. Drain cooling system.
3. Remove four nuts securing cooling fan and pulley assembly and remove. Remove fan belt.
4. Remove crankshaft damper pulley.
5. Remove front engine dust covers.
6. Remove by-pass hose.
7. Remove five water pump attaching bolts and remove pump.
8. Reverse procedure to install.

Clutch & Transmission Section

CLUTCH, ADJUST

Initial Ball Stud Adjustment

1. Place gage, J-23644 for 1977 models, J-28449 for 1978–84 models, with flat end against clutch housing front face and the hooked end positioned in the bottom depression of the clutch fork, Fig. 1.
2. Turn ball inward until clutch release bearing contacts clutch spring.
3. Install and torque lock nut to 25 ft. lbs. (33 N-m).
4. Remove gage.

Clutch Cable
Attachment & Adjustment

Late 1977 & 1978–84
1. Install clutch cable through hole in clutch fork and seat, then install return spring.
2. From engine compartment, pull cable until clutch pedal is firmly against pedal stop and hold in position, Fig. 2.
3. Install snap ring in first fully visble groove in cable from sleeve, then release cable.
4. Clutch pedal lash should be .58 to 1.08 in. (15–27 mm), if not, adjust clutch pedal as described under Clutch Pedal Adjustment.

Early 1977
1. Install cable through clutch fork hole and pull until clutch pedal firmly contacts bumper. Hold cable in position.
2. Push clutch fork forward until throwout bearing contacts clutch spring fingers. Then, thread nut on cable until bottomed against spherical surface of clutch fork.
3. To adjust clutch pedal free play, follow either of the two methods outlined below Fig. 3.
4. Attach return spring.
5. Clutch pedal free travel should be .812 inch (20.6mm).

Method 1—Place a .171 inch (4.35 mm) shim stock against surface D of nut B. Thread locknut onto cable until it contacts shim stock. Remove shim stock and back off nut B until it contacts lock nut. Torque lock nut to 4 ft. lbs. (6 N-m).

Method 2—Rotate nut B 4.35 turns counter-clockwise. Thread lock nut on cable until it contacts nut B. Torque lock nut to 4 ft. lbs. (6 N-m).

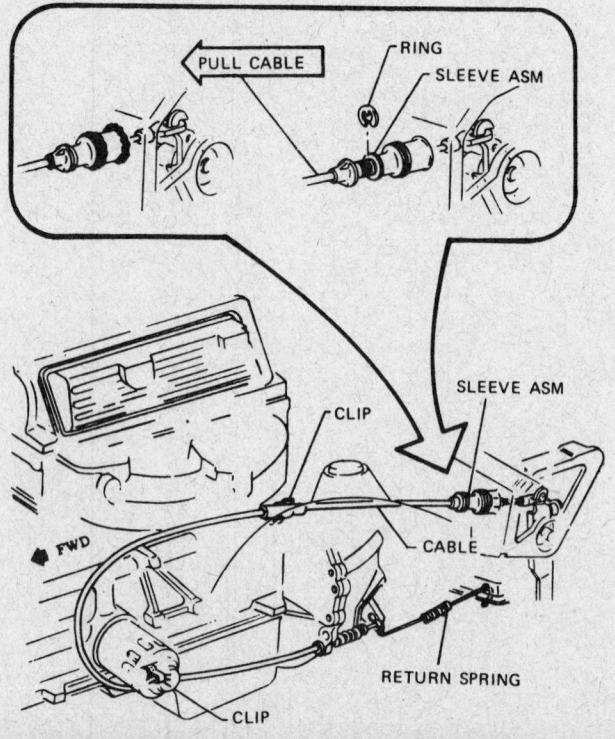

Fig. 2 Clutch cable adjustment. Late 1977 & 1978–84

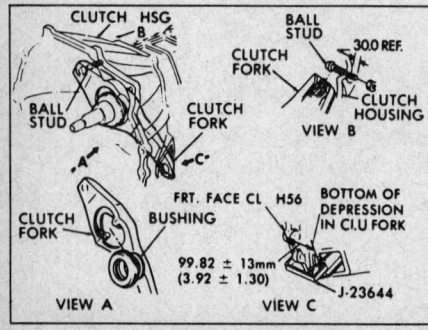

Fig. 1 Ball stud adjustment

Clutch Pedal Adjustment

Later 1977 & 1978–84

1. If clutch pedal lash is insufficient, remove snap ring from cable and allow cable to move into dash by one cable notch, then reinstall snap ring, Fig. 2.
2. If clutch pedal lash is excessive, remove snap ring from cable, and pull cable out of dash by one cable notch, then reinstall snap ring, Fig. 2.
3. Check to ensure clutch pedal lash is .58 to 1.08 in. (15–27 mm).

Early 1977

1. Loosen cable ball stud lock nut, located on the clutch housing right side.
2. Adjust ball stud to obtain .812 inch (20.6mm) clutch pedal free travel.
3. Torque lock nut to 25 ft. lbs. (33 N-m).
4. Check adjustment.

CLUTCH, REPLACE

1. Raise vehicle and remove transmission as outlined under "Manual Transmission, Replace" procedure.
2. Remove release bearing from the clutch fork and sleeve by sliding lever off ball stud and against spring force. If ball stud is to be replaced, remove cap, lock nut and stud from housing.
3. Make sure alignment marks on clutch assembly and flywheel are distinguishable.

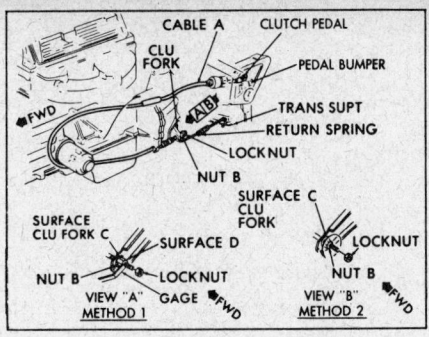

Fig. 3   Clutch cable adjustment. Early 1977

4. Loosen clutch cover to flywheel bolts one turn at a time until spring pressure is released, to avoid bending the clutch cover flange.
5. Support the pressure plate and cover assembly while removing bolts and clutch assembly.

NOTE: Do not disassemble the clutch cover, spring and pressure plate for repairs. If defective replace complete assembly.

6. Reverse procedure to install making sure to index alignment marks.

CAUTION: Check position of engine in front mounts and realign as necessary.

MANUAL TRANSMISSION, REPLACE

1. Remove shifter assembly.
2. Raise vehicle and drain transmission lubricant.
3. Remove propeller shaft.
4. Disconnect speedometer cable and the back-up lamp switch.
5. Disconnect return spring and clutch cable from clutch fork.
6. Remove transmission to crossmember bolts.
7. Remove exhaust manifold nuts and the catalytic converter to transmission bracket bolts.
8. Remove crossmember to frame bolts, then the crossmember from vehicle.
9. Remove dust cover.
10. Remove clutch housing to engine retaining bolts, slide transmission rearward and remove from vehicle.
11. Reverse procedure to install.

Rear Axle, Propeller Shaft & Brakes

REAR AXLE

Description

The rear axle, Fig. 1, is a semi-floating type consisting of a cast carrier and large bosses on each end into which two welded steel tubes are fitted. The carrier contains an overhung hypoid pinion and ring gear. The differential is a two pinion arrangment.

The overhung hypoid drive pinion, is supported by two preloaded tapered roller bearings. The pinion shaft is sealed by means of a molded, spring loaded, rubber seal. The seal is mounted on the pinion shaft flange which is splined and bolts to the hypoid pinion shaft.

The ring gear is bolted to a one piece differential case and is supported by two preloaded tapered roller bearings.

A rear axle extension housing is bolted to the axle housing and is attached to the underbody by a center bearing support. An extension shaft inside the housing is splined to the drive pinion at the rear end and to the companion flange at the forward end.

Removal

1. Raise vehicle on a hoist.
2. Place adjustable lifting device under axle.
3. Disconnect rear shock absorbers from axle and remove propeller shaft and extension housing, Fig. 2.
4. Remove both rear wheels.
5. Retract shoes and remove right and left brake drums, Fig. 3.
6. Disconnect brake lines from clips on axle tubes.

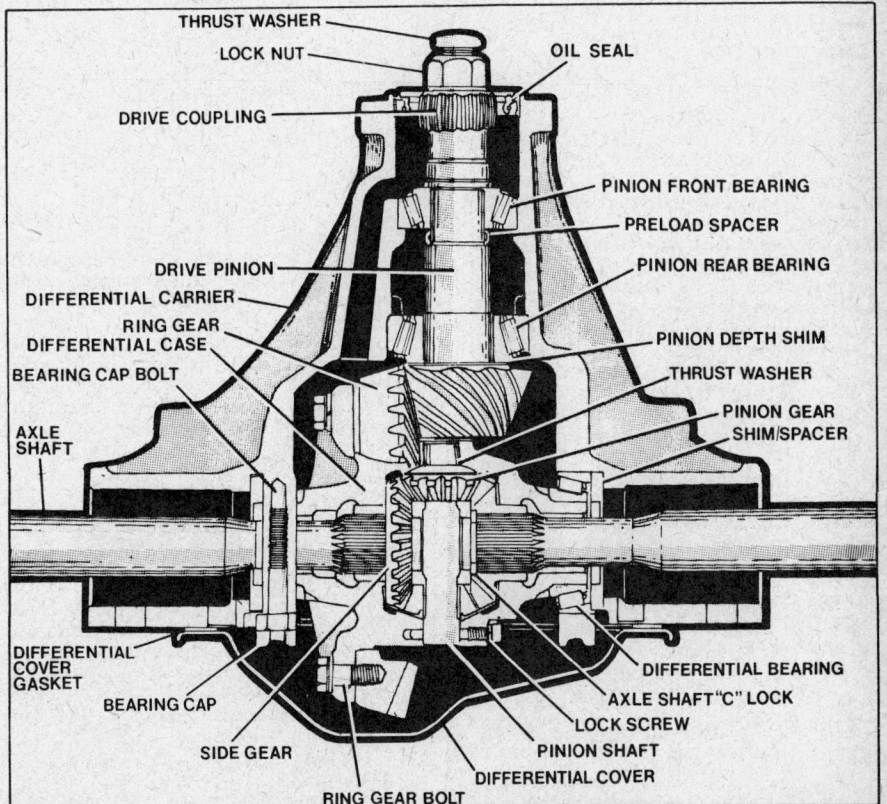

Fig. 1   Rear axle cross section

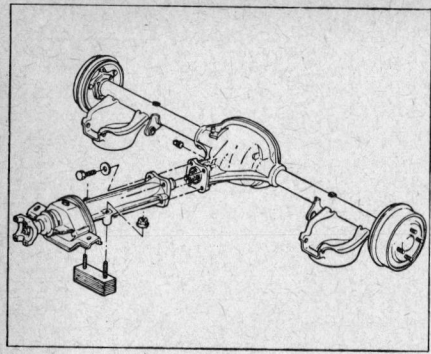

Fig. 2   Rear axle assembly

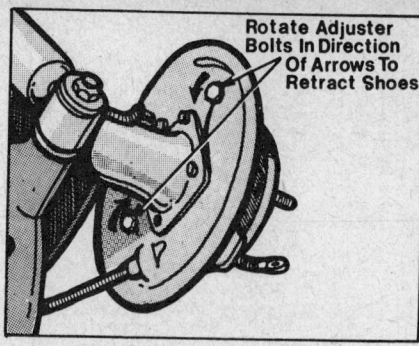

Rotate Adjuster Bolts In Direction Of Arrows To Retract Shoes

Fig. 3   Retracting brake shoes

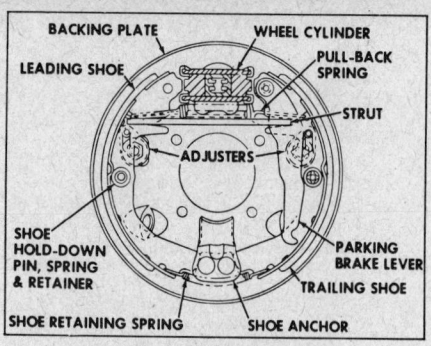

BACKING PLATE — WHEEL CYLINDER
LEADING SHOE — PULL-BACK SPRING
— STRUT
ADJUSTERS
SHOE HOLD-DOWN PIN, SPRING & RETAINER — PARKING BRAKE LEVER
TRAILING SHOE
SHOE RETAINING SPRING — SHOE ANCHOR

Fig. 4   Rear drum brake

7. Disconnect track and stabilizer bars from axle tube.
8. Remove differential cover and drain lubricant.
9. Unscrew differential lock screw, remove pinion shaft and axle shaft "C" locks. Reinstall pinion shaft and tighten lock screw to retain differential gears.
10. Remove both axle shafts.
11. Remove brake backing plate retaining nuts and remove backing plates, with shoes and brake lines attached, and wire to frame.
12. Remove right and left lower control arm pivot bolts at axle.
13. Lower axle assembly slowly until coil spring tension is released, then remove axle.

AXLE SHAFT, REPLACE

1. Raise vehicle on a hoist and remove wheel and tire assembly and brake drum.
2. Drain lubricant from axle by removing carrier cover.
3. Unscrew pinion shaft lock screw and remove pinion shaft.
4. Push flanged end of axle shaft toward center of car and remove "C" lock from button end of shaft.
5. Remove axle shaft from housing being careful not to damage seal.

Oil Seal &/or Bearing Replacement

1. If replacing seal only, remove the seal by using the button end of axle shaft. Insert the button end of shaft behind the steel case of the seal and pry seal out of bore being careful not to damage housing.
2. If replacing bearings, insert tool J-25593 into bore so tool head grasps behind bearing. Slide washer against seal, or bearing, and turn nut against washer. Attach slide hammer J-2619 and remove bearing.
3. Lubricate bearing with rear axle lubricant, then install bearing into housing bore with tool J-25594 and slide hammer J-8092. Make sure tool contacts end of axle housing to insure proper bearing depth.
4. Pack cavity between seal lips with a high melting point wheel bearing lubricant. Position seal on tool J-22922 and position seal in axle housing bore, tap seal in bore until flush with end of axle housing.

REAR AXLE EXTENSION

Replace

1. Raise vehicle and support rear axle.
2. Disconnect propeller shaft from the rear

yoke and remove from transmission, Fig. 2.
3. Support front end of rear axle carrier housing. Ensure the rear axle extension is also supported.
4. Disconnect center support bracket from underbody and the extension housing flange from axle housing.
5. Remove axle extension housing from vehicle. Pry extension housing from axle housing with a suitable screwdriver, if necessary.
6. Reverse procedure to install.

Service

1. Remove bolt securing extension housing to center support bracket.
2. Mount companion flange in a vise and loosen lock nut.
3. Drive splined companion flange off shaft by tapping on lock nut end of shaft.
4. Remove lock nut, companion flange and thrust washer, then pull shaft from housing. If centering bearing, located in the rubber cushion, remains on extension shaft, drive off shaft with a suitable drift.
5. Note position of bearing in rubber cushion and the cusion in center support. Then, using a suitable screwdriver, separate rubber cushion from center support bracket and remove bearing from cushion.
6. Clean, inspect and replace components, if necessary.
7. Install rubber cushion into center support bracket and place center support assembly over extension housing.
8. Press bearing onto extension shaft and insert shaft into housing through rubber cushion. Install thrust washer with circular cavity facing toward bearing, then the companion flange, using the lock nut to press flange onto shaft splines.
9. Install bolts retaining bracket to housing.

PROPELLER SHAFT, REPLACE

1. Raise vehicle on a hoist. Mark relationship of shaft to companion flange and disconnect the rear universal joint by removing trunnion bearing "U" bolts. Tape bearing cups to trunnion to prevent dropping and loss of bearing rollers.
2. Withdraw propeller shaft front yoke from transmission.
3. When installing, be sure to align marks made in removal to prevent driveline vibration.

BRAKE ADJUSTMENTS

Disc brakes are used on front wheels and drum brakes are use on rear wheels. Rear brake adjustment is automatic. Adjustment takes place whenever brakes are applied. An adjuster is attached to each brake shoe by means of a pin, Fig. 4. This pin is smaller than the slot in the brake shoe. When brakes are applied and brake shoes move outward the automatic adjuster follows. When brakes are released the brake shoe moves inward until it contacts the automatic adjuster pin. The space between adjuster pin and slot in brake shoe provides shoe to drum clearance.

NOTE: If manual adjustment or shoe retraction is necessary refer to Fig. 3.

PARKING BRAKE, ADJUST

1. Raise vehicle.
2. Apply parking brake three notches from fully released position.
3. Tighten equalizer adjusting nut until a light drag is felt when rear wheels are rotated in a forward direction.
4. Release parking brake and rotate rear wheels. No drag should be felt.

MASTER CYLINDER, REPLACE

1. Disconnect push rod from brake pedal and remove push rod boot.
2. Remove air cleaner.
3. Disconnect brake lines from master cylinder. Cap ends of lines to prevent entry of dirt.
4. Remove master cylinder to dash attaching nuts and the master cylinder.

POWER BRAKE UNIT, REPLACE

1. Remove air cleaner, then disconnect vacuum hose from check valve.
2. Remove master cylinder brace rod.

3. Remove remaining master cylinder to brake unit attaching nuts, then pull master forward until it clears brake unit mounting studs. Carefully move master cylinder aside with brake lines attached.

NOTE: Support master cylinder to avoid stress on brake lines. Move master cylinder only enough to provide clearance for brake unit removal.

4. Remove nuts attaching brake unit to dash panel.
5. Remove push rod to pedal retainer and slide push rod off pedal pin.
6. Remove power brake unit from vehicle.

Rear Suspension Section

DESCRIPTION

This suspension system, Fig. 1, incorporates two tubular lower control arms, a straight track rod, two shock absorbers, two coil springs and a stabilizer bar.

SHOCK ABSORBER, REPLACE

1. Raise vehicle and support rear axle with a suitable jack.
2. Disconnect shock absorber from upper and lower mounting.
3. Reverse procedure to install.

COIL SPRING, REPLACE

1. Raise vehicle and support rear axle with a suitable jack.
2. Disconnect both shock absorbers from lower brackets.
3. Disconnect rear axle extension bracket.

NOTE: Ensure axle is properly supported before disconnecting extension bracket.

4. Slowly lower axle until springs and insulators can be removed.

NOTE: When lower axle ensure that brake hoses do not stretch or become damaged.

5. Reverse procedure to install.

TRACK ROD, REPLACE

1. Raise vehicle and support rear axle with a suitable jack.
2. Disconnect stabilizer bar, if equipped, Fig. 2.
3. Remove control arm front and rear attaching bolts and control arm, Fig. 3.
4. Remove attaching bolts and track rod.
5. Reverse procedure to install.

NOTE: Vehicle must be at curb height when tightening pivot bolts.

LOWER CONTROL ARMS, REPLACE

1. Raise vehicle and support rear axle.
2. Disconnect stabilizer bar, if equipped, Fig. 2.
3. Disconnect the front and rear control arm attaching bolts and remove control arm from vehicle, Fig. 3.

NOTE: Replace one control arm at a time to prevent axle from rolling or slipping sideways.

4. Reverse procedure to install.

STABILIZER BAR, REPLACE

1. Raise vehicle and support rear axle.
2. Disconnect stabilizer bar from underbody and axle tube connections, Fig. 2, then remove stabilizer bar from vehicle.
3. Reverse procedure to install.

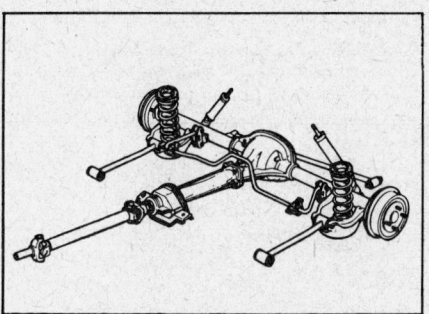

Fig. 1   Rear suspension

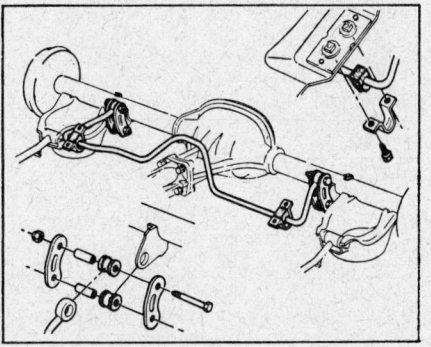

Fig. 2   Stabilizer bar installation

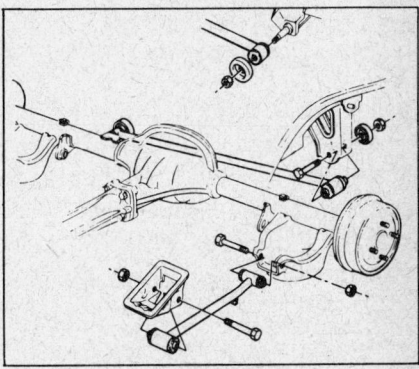

Fig. 3   Track rod and lower control arm

Front Suspension & Steering Section

DESCRIPTION

This front suspension system, Fig. 1, uses long and short control arms with coil springs mounted between the lower control arms and front suspension crossmember.

WHEEL ALIGNMENT

Caster
Caster angle is adjusted by rearranging washers located at both ends of the upper control arm, Fig. 2. A kit consisting of two washers, one of 3 mm thickness and one of 9mm thickness, must be used when adjusting caster angle.

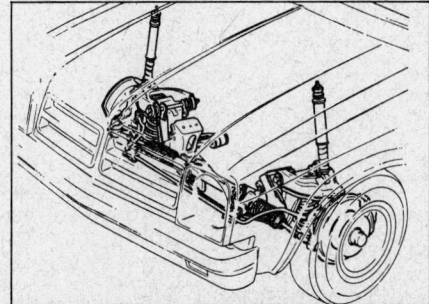

Fig. 1   Front suspension

Camber
Camber is adjusted by removing the upper ball joint, rotating it ½ turn and reinstalling it with flat of upper flange on inboard side of control arm, Fig. 3. This will increase positive camber by approximately 1°.

TOE-IN ADJUST

To adjust toe-in, loosen tie rod jam nuts at tie rod ends and loosen clamp at rubber bellows. Turn each tie rod to increase or decrease its length until proper toe-in is obtained. Torque jam nut to 50 ft. lbs.

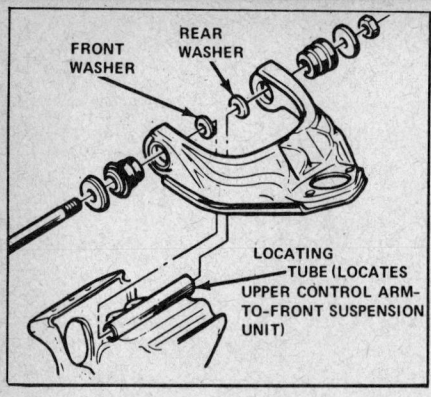

Fig. 2   Caster adjustment

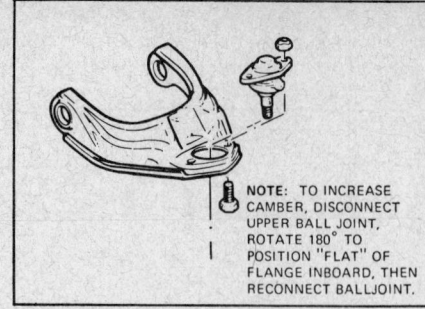

Fig. 3   Camber adjustment

Fig. 4   Separating ball joint studs from steering knuckle

WHEEL BEARINGS, ADJUST

1. While rotating wheel in the forward direction, torque spindle nut to 12 ft. lbs.
2. Back spindle nut off to the just loose position.
3. Hand tighten spindle nut, then loosen until cotter holes are aligned, install cotter pin.

NOTE: Do not loosen nut more than 1/2 flat to align cotter pin holes.

4. With bearings properly adjusted, end play must be .001–.005 inch.

WHEEL BEARINGS, REPLACE

1. Raise vehicle, remove wheel and tire assembly.
2. Remove two caliper mounting bracket to steering knuckle attaching bolts, remove caliper.
3. Remove hub dust cap, cotter pin, spindle nut, washer, outer wheel bearing and hub.
4. Pry out grease seal, then remove inner bearing from hub.

SHOCK ABSORBER, REPLACE

1. Hold upper stem of shock absorber, and remove nut, retainer and grommet.
2. Raise vehicle and remove lower shock absorber retaining bolts.
3. Lower shock absorber from vehicle.
4. Reverse procedure to install. Torque shock absorber lower retaining bolts to 35–50 ft. lbs. and the upper retaining nut to 60–120 in. lbs.

BALL JOINTS, REPLACE

Upper Ball Joint

1. Raise vehicle and remove wheel and tire assembly.
2. Support lower control arm using a suitable jack.
3. Loosen upper ball joint stud nut, however, do not remove nut.

4. Position tool J-26407 with cupped end over lower ball joint stud and turn threaded end of tool until upper ball joint stud is free of steering knuckle, Fig. 4.
5. Remove tool, then the upper stud nut.

NOTE: Discard the stud nut. The stud nut is of special design and must be replaced whenever removed or loosened.

6. Remove two nuts securing ball joint to upper control arm and the ball joint.

NOTE: Inspect tapered hole in steering knuckle. If out of round or damaged, the knuckle must be replaced.

7. Install ball joint on upper control arm and torque bolts to 29 ft. lbs.
8. Position upper ball joint stud on steering knuckle, then install a standard nut to draw ball joint into position on knuckle. Torque standard nut to 35 ft. lbs., then remove standard nut. Install special nut for final assembly and torque to 29–36 ft. lbs.
9. Install wheel and tire assembly and lower vehicle.

Lower Ball Joint

1. Raise vehicle and remove wheel and tire assembly.
2. Support lower control arm using a suitable jack.
3. Loosen lower ball joint stud nut, however, do not remove nut.
4. Position tool J-26407 with cupped end of tool over upper ball joint stud and turn threaded end of tool until lower ball joint stud is free of steering knuckle, Fig. 4.
5. Remove tool, then the lower ball joint stud nut.

NOTE: Discard the stud nut. The stud nut is of special design and must be replaced whenever removed or loosened.

6. Remove ball joint from lower control arm.

NOTE: Inspect tapered hole in steering knuckle, if out of round or damaged, the knuckle must be replaced.

7. Insert ball joint through lower control arm and into steering knuckle.
8. Install a standard nut to draw ball joint

into position on knuckle. Torque standard nut to 35 ft. lbs., then remove standard nut. Install special nut for final assembly and torque to 41–54 ft. lbs.
9. Install wheel and tire assembly and lower vehicle.

COIL SPRING, REPLACE

1. Support vehicle by frame, remove wheel and tire assembly.
2. Disconnect stabilizer bar from lower control arm and tie rod from steering knuckle.
3. Support lower control arm using a suitable jack.
4. Loosen lower ball joint stud nut, then use tool J-26407 to free stud from steering knuckle, position knuckle and hub out of way. Remove stud nut.

NOTE: Discard stud nut. The stud nut is of special design and must be replaced whenever removed or loosened.

5. Loosen lower control arm pivot bolts.
6. Install a safety chain around spring and through lower control arm.
7. Slowly lower control arm until spring is extended as far as possible, then use pry bar to carefully lift spring over lower control arm spring seat.

LOWER CONTROL ARM, REPLACE

1. Remove coil spring as described in "Coil Spring, Replace".
2. Remove control arm pivot bolts, and then remove arm.
3. Reverse procedure to install. Torque lower control arm pivot bolts to 49 ft. lbs.

UPPER CONTROL ARM, REPLACE

1. Support vehicle by frame, remove tire and wheel assembly.
2. Position jack to support lower control arm.
3. Disconnect upper ball joint as described in "Ball Joints, Replace".
4. Remove upper control arm pivot bolts, then remove control arm from vehicle.
5. Reverse procedure to install. Torque upper control arm pivot bolts to 47 ft. lbs.

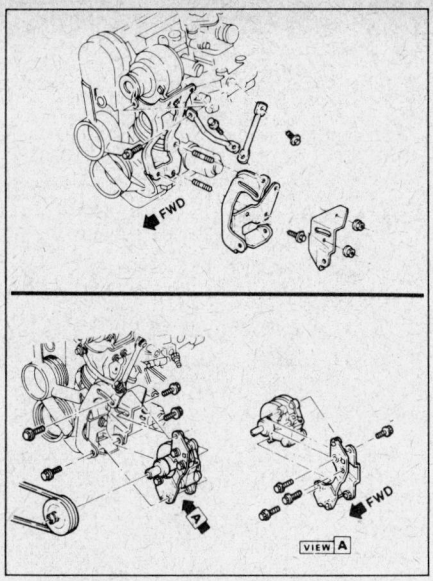

Fig. 5   Power steering pump installation (Typical)

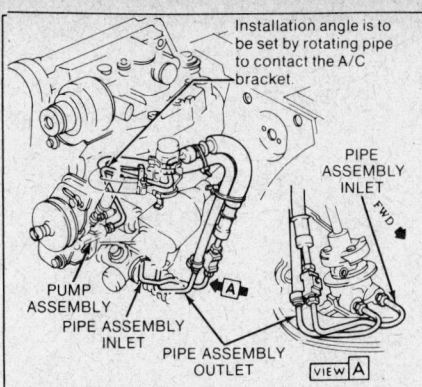

Fig. 6   Power steering reservoir installation

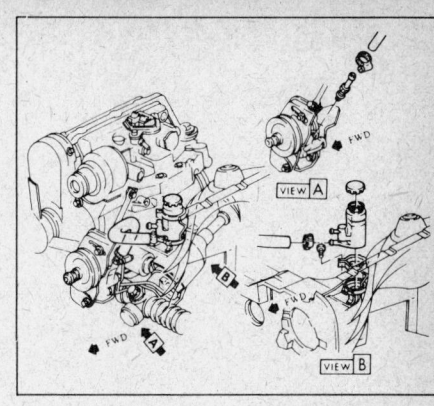

Fig. 7   Power steering hoses installation

MANUAL STEERING GEAR, REPLACE

1. Raise vehicle and remove bolts and shield.
2. Remove tie rod cotter pins and nuts from tie rod ends and separate tie rods from steering knuckles.
3. Remove flexible coupling pinch bolt.

4. Remove steering gear clamp bolts, then the steering gear assembly from vehicle.
5. Reverse procedure to install. Torque steering knuckle to tie rod nut to 30 ft. lbs., flex coupling pinch bolt to 30 ft. lbs. and steering gear clamp bolt to 14 ft. lbs.

POWER STEERING GEAR, REPLACE

1981—84

The procedure for power steering gear replacement is identical to manual type gear replacement. In addition, it is necessary to disconnect and connect the two hydraulic lines at the steering gear.

POWER STEERING PUMP, REPLACE

1981—84

1. Remove pump adjusting bolt.
2. Remove lower brace to pump bracket attaching bolt.
3. Remove crossmember to frame support brace, then disconnect hydraulic lines at pump.
4. Remove rear pump adjusting bracket, then the front pivot bolt.
5. Remove front pump bracket to engine attaching bolt, then the pump and bracket.
6. Reverse procedure to install.

NOTE: Refer to Figs. 6 and 7 for installation of power steering reservoir and hoses.

1982–84 CHEV. CAVALIER · BUICK SKYHAWK · CAD. CIMARRON · OLDS. FIRENZA · PONT. SUNBIRD & 2000

INDEX OF SERVICE OPERATIONS

NOTE: Refer to the front of this manual for vehicle manufacturer's special service tool suppliers.

VEHICLE IDENTIFICATION NUMBER LOCATION

On top of instrument panel, left front.

ENGINE NUMBER LOCATION

On pad on left front of engine block below cylinder head.

ENGINE IDENTIFICATION CODE

Year	Engine	V.I.N. Code	Engine Code
1982	4-112①	G	CXA, CXC, CXD
	4-112①	G	CYA, CYB, CYC
	4-112①	G	CYD, CYF, CYH
	4-112①	G	CYJ, CYK, CYM
	4-112①	G	CYN, CYR, CYS
	4-112①	G	CYT, CYU, CYW
	4-112①	G	CYX, CYY, CYZ
	4-112①	G	CZF, CZJ, CZK
	4-112①	G	CZY, CZZ
	4-112①	G	C8A, C8B, C8C
	4-112①	G	C8D, C8F, C8H
	4-112①	G	C8J, C8K, C8M

Year	Engine	V.I.N. Code	Engine Code
	4-112②	O	UHJ, UHK, UHL
	4-112②	O	UHP, UHS, UHT
	4-112②	O	UHY, UHZ
1983	4-112②	O	YLL, YLM, YCP, YDD
	4-121	B	CSA, CSB, CSC
	4-121	P	DJN, DJR, DJS
	4-121	P	DJT, DJU, DJW
	4-121	P	DJX, DJY, DJM
	4-121	P	DMN, DMR, DMS
	4-121	P	DMT, DMU, DMW
	4-121	P	DMX, DMY, DMZ
	4-121	P	DSA, DSB, DSC

Year	Engine	V.I.N. Code	Engine Code
	4-121	P	DSD, DSF, DSH
	4-121	P	DSJ, DSK, DSM
	4-121	P	DSN, DSR, DSS
	4-121	P	DST, DSU, DSW
	4-121	P	DSX, DSY, DSZ
1984	4-112	O	
	4-112③	J	
	4-121	P	

①—Overhead valve engine.
②—Overhead cam engine.
③—Turbocharged engine.

GRILLE IDENTIFICATION

1982–84 Buick Skyhawk Exc. "T" Type

1982 Cadillac Cimarron

1982–83 Chevrolet Cavalier Except Hatchback

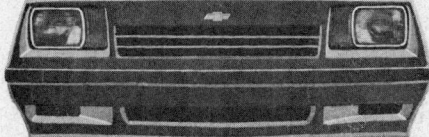

1982–83 Chevrolet Cavalier Hatchback

1982–83 Olds Firenza

1982–83 Pontiac 2000

1983–84 Buick "T" Type

1983 Cadillac Cimarron

1984 Cadillac Cimarron

1984 Chevrolet Cavalier Exc. Convertible

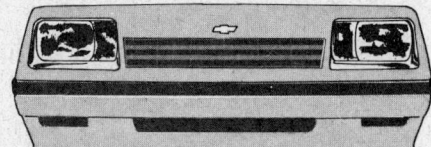

1984 Chevrolet Cavalier Convertible

1984 Olds Firenza

1984 Pontiac 2000 Sunbird Exc. LE, SE & Convertible Less Driving Lamps

1984 Pontiac 2000 Sunbird LE, SE & Convertible Less Driving Lamps

1984 Pontiac 2000 Sunbird w/Driving Lamps

GENERAL ENGINE SPECIFICATIONS

Year	Engine CID①/Liter	Engine V.I.N. Code②	Carburetor	Bore and Stroke	Compression Ratio	Net H.P. @ R.P.M.③	Maximum Torque Ft. Lbs. @ R.P.M.	Normal Oil Pressure Pounds
1982	4-112/1.8L⑤	G	E2SE, 2 Bbl.④	3.50 × 2.90	9.0	85 @ 5100	100 @ 2800	45
	4-112/1.8L⑥	O	E.F.I.⑦	3.34 × 3.12	9.0	84 @ 5200	102 @ 2800	65
	4-121/2.0L	B	E2SE, 2 Bbl.④	3.50 × 3.14	9.0	90 @ 5100	111 @ 2700	45
1983	4-112/1.8L⑥	O	E.F.I.⑦	3.34 × 3.12	9.0	84 @ 5200	102 @ 2800	45
	4-121/2.0L	P	E.F.I.⑦	3.50 × 3.15	9.3	86 @ 4900	110 @ 3000	63–77
1984	4-112/1.8L⑥	O	E.F.I.⑦	3.34 × 3.12	9.0	84 @ 5200	102 @ 2800	65
	4-112/1.8L⑥⑧	J	E.F.I.⑦	3.34 × 3.12	8.0	150 @ 5600	150 @ 2800	65
	4-121/2.0L	P	E.F.I.⑦	3.50 × 3.15	9.3	86 @ 4900	110 @ 2400	63–77

① —CID—cubic inch displacement.
② —On 1982–84 vehicles the eighth digit denotes engine code.
③ —Ratings are net as installed in vehicle.
④ —Rochester.
⑤ —Overhead valve engine.
⑥ —Overhead cam engine.
⑦ —Electronic Fuel Injection.
⑧ —Turbocharged engine.

TUNE UP SPECIFICATIONS

The following specifications are published from the latest information available. This data should be used only in the absence of a decal affixed in the engine compartment.

★ When using a timing light, disconnect vacuum hose or tube at distributor and plug opening in hose or tube so idle speed will not be affected.

● When checking compression, lowest cylinder must be within 70 percent of highest.

▲ Before removing wires from distributor cap, determine location of the No. 1 wire in cap, as distributor position may have been altered from that shown at the end of this chart.

☞ Spark plug types shown in this chart are recommendations of the original vehicle manufacturer and not MOTOR.

Check local sources for other spark plug manufacturers listings.

Year & Engine/V.I.N.	Spark Plug Type ☞	Spark Plug Gap	Ignition Timing BTDC① ★ Firing Order Fig. ▲	Ignition Timing BTDC① ★ Man. Trans.	Ignition Timing BTDC① ★ Auto. Trans.	Ignition Timing BTDC① ★ Mark Fig.	Curb Idle Speed② Man. Trans.	Curb Idle Speed② Auto. Trans.	Fast Idle Speed Man. Trans.	Fast Idle Speed Auto. Trans.	Fuel Pump Pressure
1982											
4-112/G 2 Barrel③	④	.035	A	12°⑤	12°⑤	B⑥	⑦	⑦	2400	2300	4½⑧
4-112 E.F.I./O⑨	R42XLS6	.060	C	—	8°⑩	D	—	800D⑪	—	⑪	—
4-121/B	④	.035	A	—	12°	B⑥	—	⑦	—	2300	4½⑧
1983											
4-112 E.F.I./O⑨	R44XLS	.035	C	8°	8°	D	⑪	⑪	⑪	⑪	—
4-121 E.F.I./P③	R42CTS	.035	A	TDC	TDC	B⑥	⑪	⑪	⑪	⑪	—
1984											
4-112 E.F.I./O⑨	R44XLS	.035	C	—	—	D	—	—	—	—	—
4-112 Turbo/J⑨	R44XLS	.035	C	—	—	D	—	—	—	—	—
4-121 E.F.I./P③	R42CTS	.035	A	—	—	B	—	—	—	—	—

① —BTDC—Before top dead center.
② —Idle speed on man. trans. vehicles is adjusted in Neutral & on auto. trans. equipped vehicles is adjusted in Drive unless otherwise specified.
③ —Overhead valve engine.
④ —Original equipment spark plugs, R42TS or R42CTS. When replacing spark plugs, use R42CTS.
⑤ —Disconnect 4 terminal Electronic Spark Timing (EST) wire connector to place system in ignition timing bypass mode. Connect a suitable inductive pickup timing light to igni-

tion coil high tension lead near distributor. The pulley notch will appear to move slightly as each cylinder is fired during the ignition timing check. This slight pulley notch movement should be centered at the proper timing degree mark on the timing tab, see note 6. After completing adjustment, reconnect EST wire connector.
⑥ —The crankshaft pulley has two ignition timing notches located 180° apart. The notch for No. 1 cylinder is scribed across the three pulley sheave surfaces, while the second notch is scribed across the center sheave

only.
⑦ —Idle speeds are controlled by the idle speed control motor.
⑧ —Minimum.
⑨ —Overhead cam engine.
⑩ —Ground diagnostic connector located under dash panel. The check engine light should begin flashing. Check average timing of cylinder Nos. 1 & 4. After completing adjustment, remove ground from diagnostic connector.
⑪ —Idle speed is controlled by the idle air control assembly.

Continued

TUNE UP NOTES—Continued

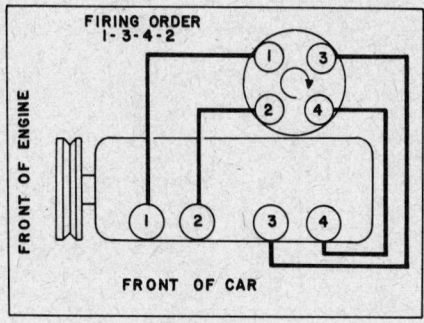

Fig. A

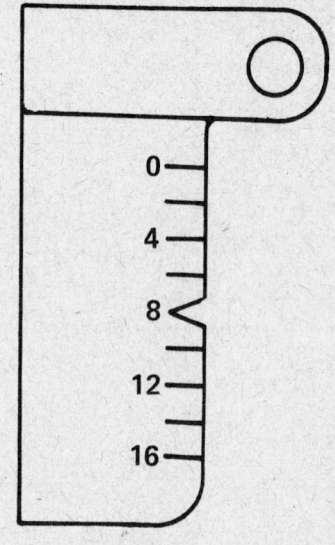

Fig. C

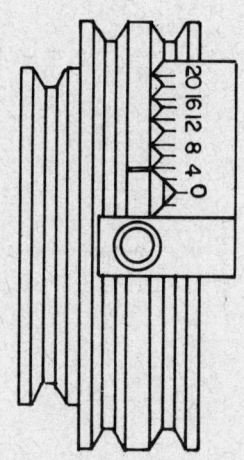

Fig. B

Fig. D

DISTRIBUTOR SPECIFICATIONS

| Distributor Ident. No.① | Centrifugal Advanced Degrees @ RPM of Distributor | | | | Vacuum Advance | |
	Advance Starts	Intermediate Advance		Full Advance	Inches of Vacuum to Start Plunger	Max. Adv. Dist. Deg. @ Vacuum
1982						
1103440②	—	—	—	—	—	—
1103500②	—	—	—	—	—	—
1103575②	—	—	—	—	—	—
1110599②	—	—	—	—	—	—
1983						
1103455②	—	—	—	—	—	—
1103514②	—	—	—	—	—	—
1103515②	—	—	—	—	—	—
1984						
1103514②	—	—	—	—	—	—
1103515②	—	—	—	—	—	—

①—Stamped on distributor housing plate.　②—Electronic Spark Timing.

ALTERNATOR SPECIFICATIONS

Year	Model	Rated Hot Output Amps.	Year	Model	Rated Hot Output Amps.	Year	Model	Rated Hot Output Amps.
1982	1100169①	63		1105091③	63		1100291	56
	1100220①	63		1105092③	63		1105091	66
	1101438②	70		1105249②	85		1105092	66
1983	1100258③	78		1105331②	85		1105446	94
	1100288③	78		1105335③	63		1105447	94
	1100289③	78	1984	1100288	78		1105508	78
	1100290③	55		1100289	78		1105541	94
	1100291③	55		1100290	56			

①—10 SI. ②—15 SI. ③—12 SI.

STARTING MOTOR APPLICATIONS

Year	Engine/V.I.N.	Starter Ident. No.	Year	Engine/V.I.N.	Starter Ident. No.
1982	4-112/G①	1109537		4-121/P	1109562
	4-112/O②	—	1984	4-112/O②	1998447
	4-121/B	1109562		4-112 Turbo/J②	1998447
1983	4-112/O②	1109551		4-121/P	1998429

①—Overhead valve engine. ②—Overhead cam engine.

VALVE SPECIFICATIONS

Year	Engine/V.I.N.	Valve Lash Int.	Valve Lash Exh.	Valve Angles Seat	Valve Angles Face	Valve Spring Installed Height	Valve Spring Pressure Lbs. @ In.	Stem Clearance Intake	Stem Clearance Exhaust	Stem Diameter Intake	Stem Diameter Exhaust
1982	4-112/G②	1½ Turn①		46	45	1.598	182 @ 1.33	.0011–.0026	.0014–.0031	.3139–.3144	.3129–.3136
1982-83	4-112/O③	Hydraulic④		45	46	—	—	.0006–.0016	.0012–.0024	—	—
	4-121/B,P	1½ Turn①		46	45	1.598	182 @ 1.33	.0011–.0026	.0014–.0031	.3139–.3144	.3129–.3136
1984	4-112/O③	Hydraulic④		45	46	—	—	.0006–.0020	.0010–.0024	—	—
	4-112 Turbo/J③	Hydraulic④		45	46	—	—	.0006–.0020	.0010–.0024	—	—
	4-121/P	1½ Turn①		46	45	1.62	180 @ 1.33	.0010–.0027	.0010–.0030	—	—

①—Turn rocker arm adjusting nut until all lash is eliminated, then tighten nut an additional one and one-half turn to center plunger.
②—Overhead valve engine.
③—Overhead cam engine.
④—Hydraulic valve compensator, no adjustment.

PISTONS, PINS, RINGS, CRANKSHAFT & BEARINGS

Year	Engine Model/V.I.N.	Piston Clearance	Ring Gap① Comp.	Ring Gap① Oil	Wristpin Diameter ②	Rod Bearings Shaft Diameter	Rod Bearings Bearing Clearance	Main Bearings Shaft Diameter	Main Bearings Bearing Clearance	Thrust on Bear. No.	Shaft End Play
1982	4-112/G③	.0008–.0018	.010	—	.9054	1.9983–1.9993	.0010–.0031	④	⑤	4	.002–.007
1982-83	4-112/O⑥	.0008⑧	.012	.016	—	1.9280–1.9286	.0007–.0024	⑦	.0006–.0016	3	.002–.012
	4-121/B,P	.0008–.0018	.010	—	.9054	1.9983–1.9993	.0010–.0031	④	⑤	4	.002–.007
1984	4-112/O⑥	.0008⑧	.012	.015	—	1.9278–1.9286	.0007–.0025	⑦	.0006–.0016	3	.003–.012
	4-112 Turbo/J⑥	.0004–.0012	.012	.015	—	1.9278–1.9286	.0007–.0025	⑦	.0006–.0016	3	.003–.012
	4-121/P	.0008–.0019	.010	.020	.9385	1.9983–1.9994	.0010–.0031	④	⑤	4	.002–.007

①—Fit rings in tapered bores for clearance given in tightest portion of ring travel. Clearances specified are minimum gaps.
②—Minimum diameter.
③—Overhead valve engine.
④—Nos. 1, 2, 3, 4, 2.4945–2.4954 inch; No. 5, 2.4937–2.4946 inch.
⑤—Nos. 1, 2, 3, 4, .0006–.0018 inch; No. 5, .0014–.0026 inch.
⑥—Overhead cam engine.
⑦—Brown color code, 2.2830–2.2832 inch; green color code, 2.2827–2.2830 inch.
⑧—Maximum.

ENGINE TIGHTENING SPECIFICATIONS ★

★ Torque specifications are for clean and lightly lubricated threads only. Dry or dirty threads produce increased friction which prevents accurate measurement of tightness.

Year	Engine Model/V.I.N.	Spark Plugs Ft. Lbs.	Cylinder Head Bolts Ft. Lbs.	Intake Manifold Ft. Lbs.	Exhaust Manifold Ft. Lbs.	Rocker Arm Stud Ft. Lbs.	Rocker Arm Cover Ft. Lbs.	Connecting Rod Cap Bolts Ft. Lbs.	Main Bearing Cap Bolts Ft. Lbs.	Flywheel to Crankshaft Ft. Lbs.	Vibration Damper or Pulley Ft. Lbs.
1982	4-112/G①	7–15	65–75	20–25	22–28	43–49	6–9	34–40	63–74	45–55	66–84
1982–83	4-112/O②	15	③	16	19	—	5	39	57	45	20
	4-121/B,P	7–15	65–75	20–25	22–28	43–49	6–9	34–40	63–74	45–55	66–84
1984	4-112/O②	15	③	25	16	—	5	39	57	45	20
	4-112 Turbo/J②	15	③	25	16	—	5	39	57	45	20
	4-121/P	7–15	65–75	20–25	22–28	43–49	6–9	34–40	63–74	45–55	66–84

①—Overhead valve engine.
②—Overhead cam engine.
③—Torque cylinder head & camshaft carrier bolts to 18 ft. lbs., then tighten bolts an additional 180° in 60° increments. Start engine & allow to reach operating temperature, then tighten bolts an additional 30° to 50°.

WHEEL ALIGNMENT SPECIFICATIONS

Year	Model	Caster Angle, Degrees		Camber Angle Degrees				Toe-Out Inch	Toe-Out on Turns, Deg.	
		Limits	Desired	Limits		Desired			Outer Wheel	Inner Wheel
				Left	Right	Left	Right			
1982	All	—	—	+.1 to +1.1	+.1 to +1.1	+.6	+.6	①	—	—
1983–84	All	+.7 to +2.7	+1.7	+.2 to +1.2	+.2 to +1.2	+.7	+.7	②	—	—

①—.25° toe-out.   ②—.13° toe-out.

COOLING SYSTEM & CAPACITY DATA

Year	Model or Engine/V.I.N.	Cooling Capacity, Qts.		Radiator Cap Relief Pressure, Lbs.	Thermo. Opening Temp.	Fuel Tank Gals.	Engine Oil Refill Qts.	Transaxle Oil	
		Less A/C	With A/C					Manual Transaxle Pts.	Auto. Transaxle Qts. ①
1982	Cavalier 4-112/G	9.0	9.3	15	195	14	4②	6	③
	Cimarron 4-112/G	—	8.28	15	195	14	4②	6	③
	Firenza 4-112/G	8.0	8.0	15	195	14	4②	6	③
	J2000 4-112/G	8.3	8.3	15	195	14	4②	6	③
	Skyhawk 4-112/G	—	—	15	195	14	4②	6	③
	Firenza 4-112/O	7.8	7.9	15	195	14	3②	6	③
	J2000 4-112/O	—	—	15	195	14	3②	6	③
	Skyhawk 4-112/O	—	—	15	195	14	3②	6	③
	Firenza 4-121/B	—	—	15	195	14	4②	6	③
	Skyhawk 4-121/B	—	—	15	195	14	4②	6	③
1983	Cavalier 4-112/O	7.8	7.8	15	195	13.6	3②	5.4	③
	Firenza 4-112/O	8.0	8.0	15	195	13.6	3②	5.4	③
	2000 4-112/O	7.8	7.9	15	195	13.6	3②	⑤	③
	Skyhawk 4-112/O	7.8	7.8	15	195	13.6	3②	5.4	③
	Cavalier 4-121/P	9.6	9.7	15	195	13.6	4②	5.4	③
	Cimarron 4-121/P	④	④	15	195	13.6	4②	5.4	③
	Firenza 4-121/P	8.0	8.0	15	195	13.6	4②	5.4	③
	2000 4-121/P	7.8	7.9	15	195	13.6	4②	⑤	③
	Skyhawk 4-121/P	9.7	9.75	15	195	13.6	4②	5.4	③
1984	Cavalier 4-121/P	9.5	9.6	15	195	13.6	4②	⑤	③
	Cimarron 4-121/P	④	④	15	195	13.6	4②	5.4	③
	Firenza 4-112/O	7.8	7.9	15	195	13.6	4②	5.8	③
	Firenza 4-121/P	7.8	7.9	15	195	13.6	4②	5.8	③
	Skyhawk 4-112/O	7.4	7.4	15	195	13.6	4②	5.8	③
	Skyhawk 4-112 Turbo/J	7.8	7.9	15	—	13.6	4②	5.8	③
	Skyhawk 4-121/P	9.5	9.6	15	195	13.6	4②	5.8	③
	Sunbird 4-112/O	7.8	7.9	15	195	13.6	4②	⑤	③
	Sunbird 4-112 Turbo/J	7.8	7.9	15	—	13.6	4②	⑤	③
	Sunbird 4-121/P	7.8	7.9	195	195	13.6	4②	⑤	③

COOLING SYSTEM & CAPACITY DATA—NOTES

①—Approximate, make final check with dipstick.

②—With or without filter change.

③—Oil pan only, 4 qts. After overhaul, less torque converter drain, 6 qts.; with torque converter drain, 9 qts.

④—Man. trans., 8.7 qts.; auto. trans., 9.3 qts.

⑤—4 spd., 5.9 pts.; 5 spd., 5.3 pts.

Electrical Section

STARTER, REPLACE

4-112 & 4-121 Overhead Valve Engine

1. Disconnect battery ground cable.
2. Raise and support front of vehicle.
3. Disconnect solenoid wires and battery cable at starter.
4. Remove rear engine mount support bracket, then the A/C compressor support rod (if equipped).
5. Remove starter to engine mounting bolts and lower starter. Note position of shims if used.
6. Reverse procedure to install.

4-112 Overhead Cam Engine Except Turbocharged

Models W/ Manual Transaxle
1. Disconnect battery ground cable.
2. Remove upper starter to engine block bolt.
3. Raise and support front of vehicle.
4. Remove rear starter brace attaching bolt from engine block and nut from starter, then the brace.
5. Remove lower starter to engine mounting bolt.
6. Disconnect battery positive cable and solenoid leads from starter motor, then lower starter from engine.
7. Reverse procedure to install.

Models W/ Automatic Transaxle
1. Disconnect battery ground cable.
2. Remove air cleaner from engine.
3. Remove lower starter to engine block bolt.

4. Remove rear starter brace attaching bolt from engine block and nut from starter, then the brace.
5. Disconnect battery positive cable and solenoid leads from starter motor.
6. Remove starter to engine block bolt, then raise and support front of vehicle.
7. Disconnect speedometer cable.
8. While pushing upward on shift cable, lower armature end of starter motor down between stabilizer bar and engine, then remove starter motor from engine.

NOTE: It may be necessary to pry engine block forward to provide clearance for starter motor removal.

9. Reverse procedure to install.

4-112 Overhead Cam Turbocharged Engine

1. Disconnect battery ground cable.
2. Remove intake manifold support brace.
3. Disconnect lead at coil and MAT electrical connector at intake manifold.
4. Remove upper starter to engine block bolt.
5. Remove engine harness bracket to intake manifold bolt.
6. Raise and support front of vehicle, then remove transmission strut.
7. Remove fuel line to support bracket bolt, then loosen fuel lines ½ turn to gain access to the starter motor.
8. Remove fuel line support bracket.
9. Remove rear starter support bracket. Do not bend turbocharger oil supply line.
10. Disconnect battery positive cable and solenoid leads from starter motor.

11. Remove lower starter bolt, then starter from engine.
12. Reverse procedure to install.

IGNITION LOCK, REPLACE

1. Remove steering wheel as outlined under "Steering Wheel, Replace" procedure.
2. Remove turn signal switch as outlined under "Turn Signal Switch, Replace" procedure.
3. Remove buzzer switch.
4. Turn lock cylinder to "Run" position, then remove the lock cylinder retaining screw and lock cylinder, Fig. 1.
5. To install, rotate lock cylinder to stop while holding housing. Align cylinder key with keyway in housing, then push cylinder into housing until fully seated.
6. Install lock cylinder retaining screw.
7. Install buzzer switch, turn signal switch and steering wheel.

IGNITION & DIMMER SWITCHES, REPLACE

1. Remove steering wheel as outlined under "Steering Wheel, Replace" procedure, then the turn signal switch and lock cylinder as previously described.
2. Refer to Figs. 2 and 3 to remove ignition and dimmer switches.
3. When installing dimmer switch, depress switch slightly and install a 3/32 drill into switch. Force switch upward to remove lash and tighten retaining screw.

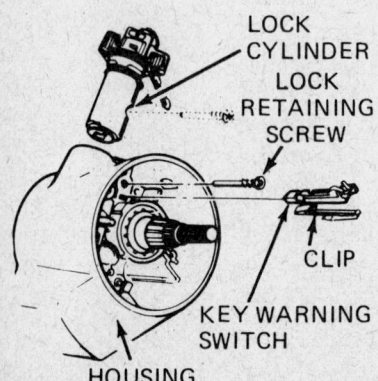

Fig. 1 Lock cylinder removal

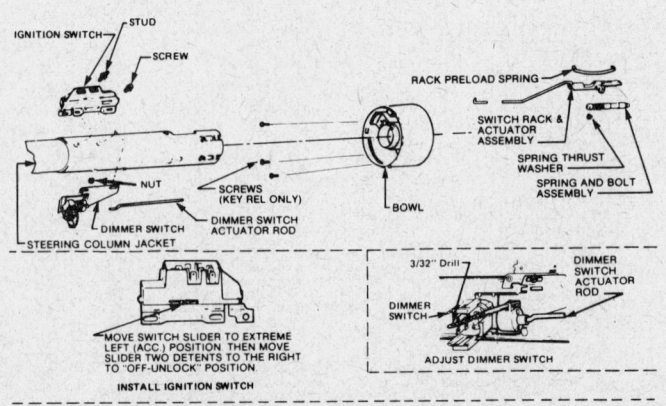

Fig. 2 Ignition & dimmer switch removal. Models less tilt column

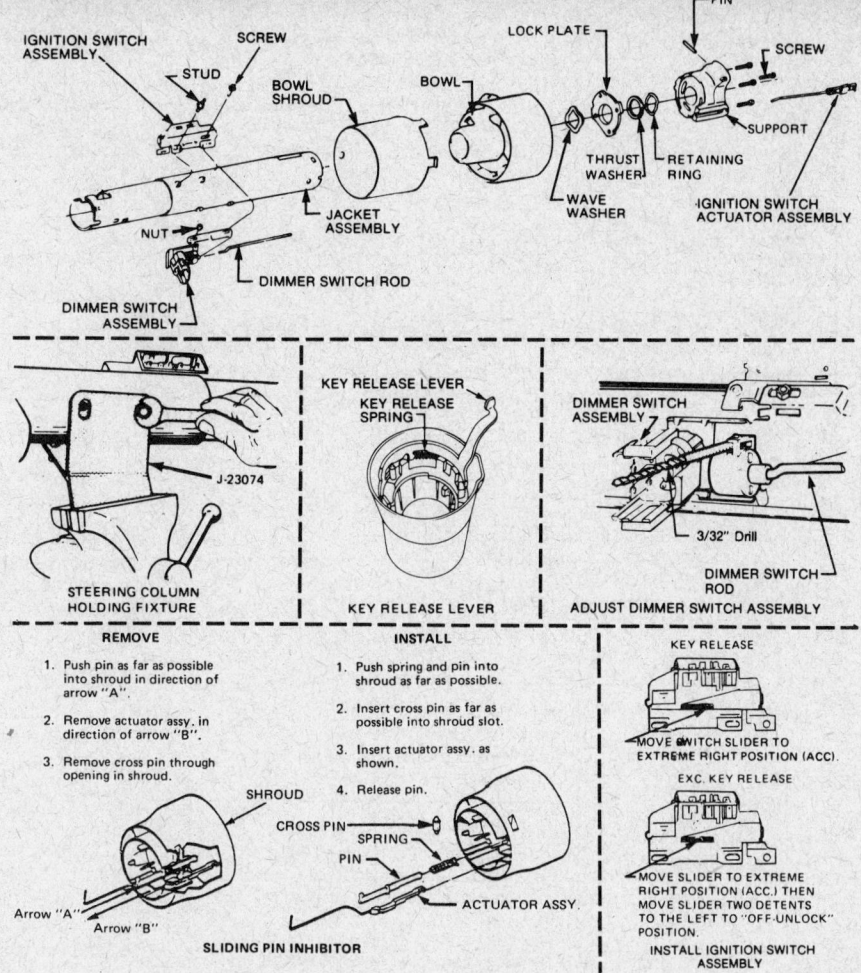

Fig. 3   Ignition & dimmer switch removal. Models with tilt column

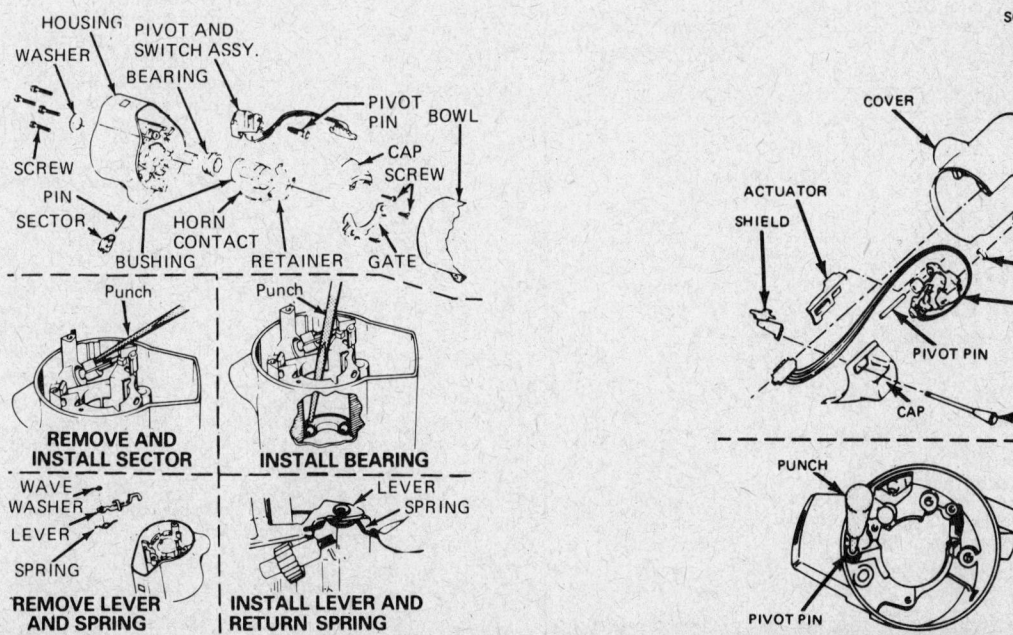

Fig. 4   W/S wiper switch removal. Models less tilt column

Fig. 5   W/S wiper switch removal. Models with tilt column

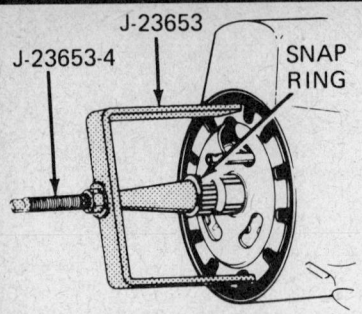

Fig. 6 Compressing lock plate

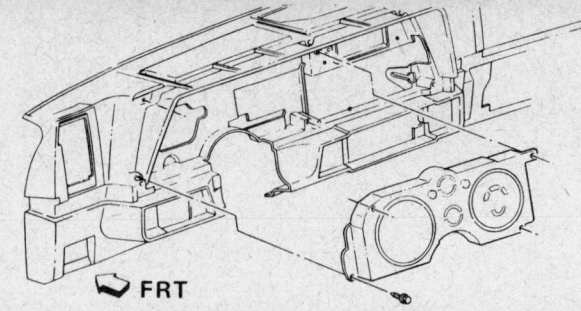

Fig. 7 Instrument cluster. 1982–83 2000, 1982–84 Cavalier, Cimarron & 1984 Sunbird

W/S WIPER SWITCH, REPLACE

1. Remove turn signal switch as outlined under "Turn Signal Switch, Replace" procedure.
2. Refer to Figs. 4 and 5 for wiper switch replacement.

PULSE W/S WIPER MODULE, REPLACE

1982–83 2000; 1982–84 Cavalier, Cimarron & 1984 Sunbird

1. Disconnect battery ground cable.
2. Remove headlamp switch knob by depressing retaining clip behind knob and pulling knob from shaft.
3. Remove left hand trimplate attaching screws and the trimplate.
4. Remove screws retaining module to adapter assembly.
5. Disconnect wire connectors from module.
6. Remove module from instrument panel.
7. Reverse procedure to install.

1982–84 Firenza & Skyhawk

1. Disconnect battery ground cable.
2. Remove six screws attaching steering column trim cover to instrument panel and two screws attaching cover to left hand instrument panel insulator, then remove trim cover.
3. Disengage retaining clip and remove pulse wiper module from cover.
4. Remove screw attaching module ground wire to instrument panel lower brace, then disconnect wire connector and remove module.
5. Reverse procedure to install.

REAR WINDOW DEFROSTER OR WASHER/WIPER SWITCH, REPLACE

1. Disconnect battery ground cable.
2. Remove lower trimplate and disconnect switch wiring connector.
3. Depress switch retaining tabs and remove switch from dash.
4. Reverse procedure to install.

STOPLIGHT SWITCH, ADJUST

Insert stoplight switch into tubular clip until switch body seats fully into clip. Pull brake pedal rearward against internal pedal stop. The switch will be properly positioned in the tubular clip automatically.

NOTE: Rotate switch ½ turn counterclockwise to be sure that switch does not hold brake pedal down after adjustment.

BACKUP LIGHT/NEUTRAL START SWITCH, REPLACE

NOTE: On vehicles equipped with automatic transmission, the neutral start and backup light switches are combined into one unit and must be replaced as an assembly.

Man. Trans.
1. Disconnect battery ground cable.
2. Apply parking brake and block wheels, then place gear shift lever in Neutral position.
3. Remove front ash tray, then remove two console attaching screws through ash tray opening.
4. Remove retaining screw, then remove gear shift knob.
5. On 1982–83 2000, 1982–84 Cavalier, Cimarron and 1984 Sunbird, proceed as follows:
   a. Remove console attaching screw located under parking brake handle.
   b. Toward rear of console, remove one screw from each side, retaining console to rear bracket.
6. On 1982–84 Firenza and Skyhawk, proceed as follows:
   a. Pull upward on front of console trim cover, then lift cover from console and disconnect wire connector.
   b. Remove three screws attaching console to front mounting bracket.
   c. Remove rear ash tray, then remove screw attaching console to rear mounting bracket.
7. On all models, remove console assembly.

NOTE: On models equipped with arm rest, it may be necessary to remove arm rest assembly to provide clearance for console removal.

8. Disconnect wire connector from backup light switch.
9. Remove retaining clip, then remove backup light switch from side of shifter.
10. Reverse procedure to install.

Auto. Trans.
1. Disconnect battery ground cable.
2. Apply parking brake and block wheels,
then place gear shift lever in Neutral position.
3. Remove front ash tray, then remove two console attaching screws through ash tray opening.
4. Carefully pry button from center of shift lever knob, then remove snap ring retaining knob.
5. Pull front of console trim cover upward, then lift trim cover from console and disconnect wire connector.
6. Remove three screws attaching front of console to mounting bracket.
7. Remove rear ash tray, then remove screw attaching console to rear support.
8. Remove console assembly.

NOTE: On models equipped with arm rest, it may be necessary to remove arm rest assembly to provide clearance for console removal.

9. Disconnect wire connector from Neutral Safety/Backup light switch.
10. Remove screws attaching switch to shifter lever, then remove switch.
11. If the same switch is to be reinstalled, proceed as follows:
    a. Place shift lever in Neutral position.
    b. Position switch to shift lever and loosely install attaching screws.
    c. Rotate switch on shifter to align adjustment hole with carrier tang, then insert a 2.34 mm diameter pin into hole to a depth of 5 mm.
    d. Torque switch attaching screws to 20 inch lbs., then remove gauge pin.
12. If a new replacement switch is to be installed, proceed as follows:
    a. Position shift lever in the Neutral position.
    b. Insert switch carrier tang into hole on shift lever, then install switch and torque attaching screws to 20 inch lbs.

NOTE: Replacement switches are held in the Neutral position by an internal plastic pin.

    c. Move shift lever out of Neutral position to shear switch internal plastic pin.
13. Install console and connect battery ground cable.
14. Check to ensure that vehicle will not start in any shift lever position except Neutral and Park.

CLUTCH START SWITCH, REPLACE

1. Remove lower left hush panel.

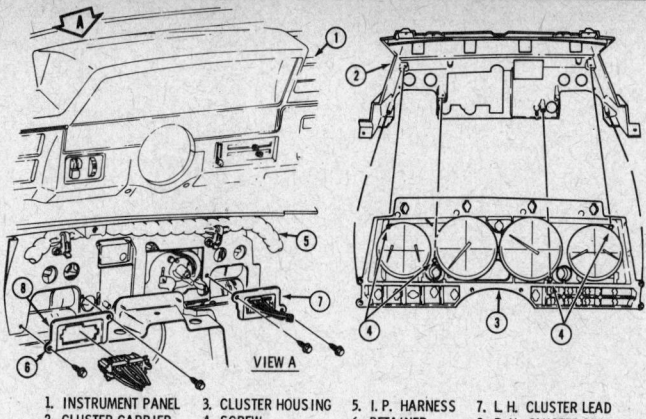

1. INSTRUMENT PANEL	3. CLUSTER HOUSING	5. I. P. HARNESS	7. L. H. CLUSTER LEAD
2. CLUSTER CARRIER	4. SCREW	6. RETAINER	8. R. H. CLUSTER LEAD

VIEW A

Fig. 7A   Instrument cluster. 1982–84 Firenza & Skyhawk

2. Disconnect wiring connector from switch.
3. Disconnect switch link from pedal, then remove switch retaining screw and switch.
4. Reverse procedure to install.

TURN SIGNAL SWITCH, REPLACE

1. Disconnect battery ground cable.
2. Remove steering wheel as outlined under "Steering Wheel, Replace" procedure.
3. Using a suitable screwdriver, pry cover from housing.
4. Using lock plate compressing tool J-23653-4, compress lock plate and pry snap ring from groove on steering shaft, Fig. 6. Slowly release compressing tool, then remove tool and lock plate from shaft.
5. Slide canceling cam and bearing preload spring from steering shaft.
6. Remove turn signal (multi-function) lever.
7. Remove hazard warning knob retaining screw, button, spring and knob.
8. Remove actuator arm screw and actuator arm.
9. Remove switch retaining screws and pull switch upward from column, guiding wire harness through column.
10. Reverse procedure to install.

STEERING WHEEL, REPLACE

1. Disconnect battery ground cable.
2. Remove steering wheel center pad.
3. Remove steering wheel retaining nut and retainer.
4. Scribe alignment marks on steering wheel and shaft to aid installation.
5. Using tool J-1859-03 or equivalent, remove steering wheel from shaft.
6. Reverse procedure to install.

INSTRUMENT CLUSTER, REPLACE

1982–83 2000, 1982–84 Cavalier, Cimarron & 1984 Sunbird

1. Disconnect battery ground cable.
2. Remove six screws attaching instrument panel trimplate to instrument panel.
3. Pull top of trimplate outward and remove trimplate from instrument panel.
4. Remove four screws securing instrument

cluster to instrument panel, Fig. 7.
5. Remove screws attaching steering column cover to instrument panel, then the lower column cover.
6. Remove two steering column retaining bolts and lower steering column to floor.
7. Pull instrument cluster out slightly and disconnect speedometer cable.
8. On automatic transmission equipped vehicles, disconnect vehicle speed sensor (VSS) connector from rear of cluster.
9. Remove cluster and disconnect instrument panel harness connector from printed circuit located at rear of cluster.
10. Reverse procedure to install.

1982–84 Firenza & Skyhawk

1. Disconnect battery ground cable.
2. Remove six screws attaching steering column trim cover to instrument panel and two screws attaching trim cover to left hand instrument panel trim cover, then remove trim cover.
3. Remove screw attaching right end of left hand trim cover to instrument panel, then pull trim cover rearward to disengage retaining clips and remove cover.
4. Remove screw attaching left end of right hand trim cover to instrument panel, then remove two screws from under center trim cover and four screws from front of glove compartment. Pull right hand trim cover rearward to disengage retaining clips, then disconnect wire connectors and remove trim cover.
5. Remove seven screws attaching cluster trim cover to instrument cluster pad, then remove trim cover.
6. Remove five screws attaching bezel and lens to instrument cluster carrier, then remove bezel and lens.
7. Loosen two upper steering column mounting bolts, then lower steering column slightly to provide clearance for cluster removal.
8. Remove four screws attaching cluster housing to cluster carrier, then pull housing slightly outward and disconnect speedometer cable and remove cluster housing, Fig. 7A.
9. Reverse procedure to install.

HEADLIGHT SWITCH, REPLACE

1982–83 2000, 1982–84 Cavalier, Cimarron & 1984 Sunbird

1. Disconnect battery ground cable.

2. Remove headlight switch knob by pulling knob to full "ON" position, depressing retaining clip behind knob and pulling knob from shaft.
3. Gently pry left hand side trimplate out of instrument panel.
4. Remove switch retaining nut, rotate and tilt switch forward and pull switch instrument panel.
5. Disconnect wiring connector and remove switch.
6. Reverse procedure to install.

1982–84 Firenza & Skyhawk

1. Disconnect battery ground cable.
2. Remove six screws attaching steering column lower cover to instrument panel, then remove lower cover.
3. Remove one screw attaching right end of left hand trim cover to instrument panel, then pull cover rearward to detach retaining clips.
4. Remove four screws attaching headlamp switch to instrument panel, then pull switch rearward and disconnect wire connector.
5. Reverse procedure to install.

RADIO, REPLACE

1982–83 2000, 1982–84 Cavalier, Cimarron & 1984 Sunbird

1. Disconnect battery ground cable.
2. Loosen six instrument panel trimplate to instrument panel attaching screws and remove trimplate.

NOTE: Determine whether right side of radio is retained with nut or rubber stud.

3. On vehicles equipped with radio side retainer nut:
   a. Without A/C, remove right lower hush panel then loosen side retainer nut. Disconnect wire and antenna connections and remove radio from instrument panel.
   b. With A/C, remove right lower hush panel, A/C duct and A/C control head, then loosen side retainer nut. Disconnect wiring and antenna connections and remove radio from instrument panel.
4. On vehicles equipped with radio side retainer rubber stud, remove two radio bracket to instrument panel attaching screws, then pull radio forward and disconnect wiring and antenna connections. Remove radio from instrument panel.
5. Reverse procedures to install.

1982–84 Firenza & Skyhawk

1. Disconnect battery ground cable.
2. Remove six screws attaching steering column trim cover to instrument panel, then lower trim cover.
3. Remove screw attaching left end of right hand trim cover to instrument panel.
4. Remove two screws from under center trim cover and four screws from front of glove compartment, then pull trim cover rearward to disengage retaining clips and disconnect wire connectors.
5. Remove four screws attaching upper and lower radio mounting brackets to instrument panel.
6. Pull radio out just enough to disconnect wire connector and antenna lead, then re-

move radio.
7. Reverse procedure to install.

W/S WIPER MOTOR, REPLACE

1. Disconnect battery ground cable.
2. Remove wiper arms from transmission spindle shafts.
3. Remove shroud top vent grille panel and screen.
4. Loosen, but do not remove, transmission drive link to motor crank arm attaching nuts, then pull drive link out of motor crank arm.
5. Disconnect wiper motor electrical connections and remove wiper motor attaching bolts.
6. Rotate wiper motor upward and outward, and remove from vehicle.
7. Reverse procedure to install.

W/S WIPER TRANSMISSION ASSEMBLY, REPLACE

1. Remove wiper arms from transmission spindle shafts.
2. Remove shroud top vent grille panel and screen.
3. Loosen, but do not remove, transmission drive link to motor crank arm attaching nuts then pull drive link from motor crankarm.
4. Remove transmission to cowl panel attaching screws and the transmission assembly.
5. Reverse procedure to install.

BLOWER MOTOR, REPLACE

1. Disconnect battery ground cable.
2. Disconnect blower motor electrical connections.
3. Remove plastic water shield from right side of cowl.
4. Remove blower motor retaining screws and blower motor.
5. Reverse procedure to install.

HEATER CORE, REPLACE

Less Air Conditioning

1. Disconnect battery ground cable and drain cooling system.
2. Disconnect heater hoses from heater core.
3. Remove heater outlet deflector.
4. Remove heater core module cover retaining screws and module cover, Fig. 8.
5. Remove heater core retaining straps and heater core.
6. Reverse procedure to install.

With Air Conditioning

1. Disconnect battery ground cable and drain cooling system.
2. Raise and support vehicle and disconnect drain tube from heater and evaporator assembly.
3. Lower vehicle and remove right and left hush panels, steering column trim cover and glovebox.
4. Remove heater duct retaining screw and heater duct.

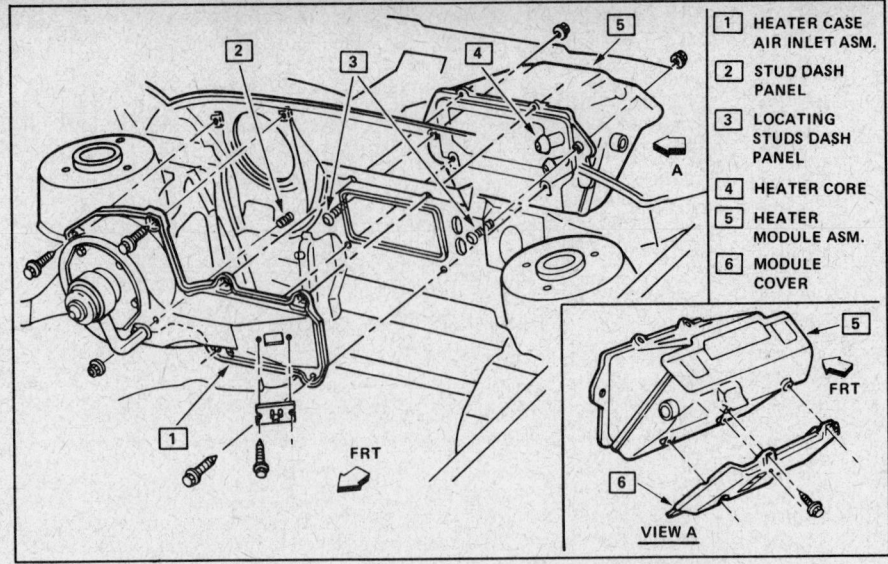

1	HEATER CASE AIR INLET ASM.
2	STUD DASH PANEL
3	LOCATING STUDS DASH PANEL
4	HEATER CORE
5	HEATER MODULE ASM.
6	MODULE COVER

Fig. 8 Heater core & blower motor. (Typical) Models less A/C

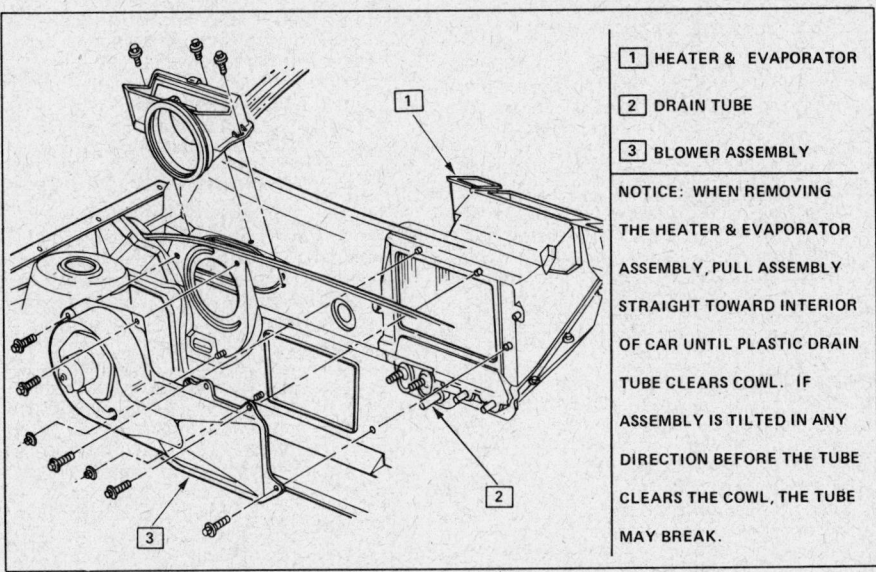

1	HEATER & EVAPORATOR
2	DRAIN TUBE
3	BLOWER ASSEMBLY

NOTICE: WHEN REMOVING THE HEATER & EVAPORATOR ASSEMBLY, PULL ASSEMBLY STRAIGHT TOWARD INTERIOR OF CAR UNTIL PLASTIC DRAIN TUBE CLEARS COWL. IF ASSEMBLY IS TILTED IN ANY DIRECTION BEFORE THE TUBE CLEARS THE COWL, THE TUBE MAY BREAK.

Fig. 9 Heater core & blower motor. (Typical) Models with A/C

5. Remove heater core cover attaching screws, then gently pull cover rearward and out of vehicle, Fig. 9.

CAUTION: When removing heater core assembly, pull assembly straight toward interior of vehicle until plastic drain tube clears cowl. If assembly is tilted in any direction before tube clears cowl, the drain tube may break.

6. Remove heater core retaining clamps and heater core from case.
7. Reverse procedure to install.

CRUISE CONTROL

Release Switches

Automatic Transmission
Both the electrical and vacuum release switches are located at the brake pedal. To adjust, depress brake pedal and insert switch fully into tubular clip. Pull pedal rearward until clicking sounds are no longer audible. The switch is now automatically adjusted.

Manual Transmission
On manual transmission equipped vehicles, the electrical release switch is located at the clutch pedal, while the vacuum release switch is found at the brake pedal. Adjustment procedures for these switches are the same as for those under automatic transmission equipped vehicles.

Servo, Adjust

With engine off and carburetor in slow idle position, connect cable swivel to third ball on servo chain. Adjust cable nuts until chain has a slight amount of slack, then tighten lock nut securely.

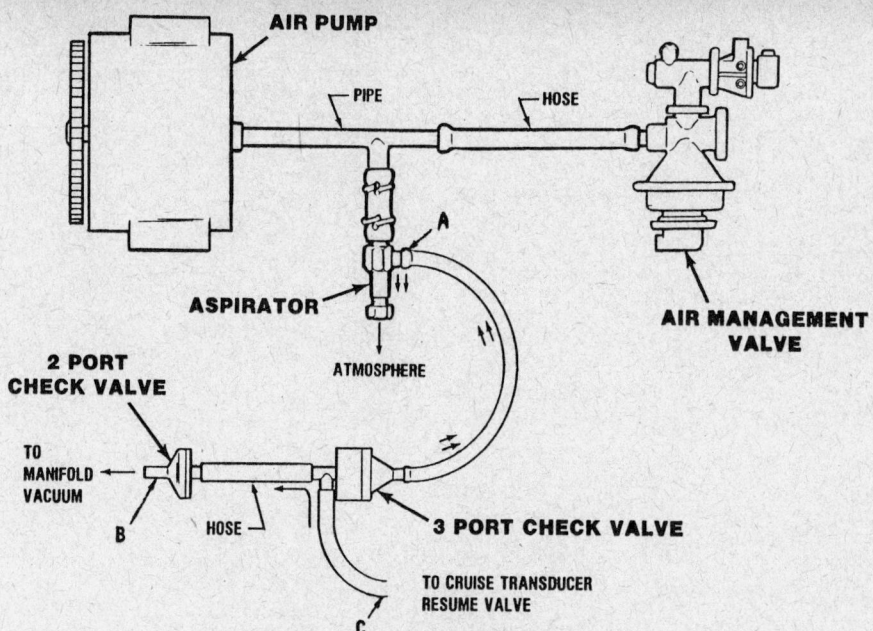

Fig. 10 Aspirated assisted vacuum system schematic

Cruise Speed, Adjust

The cruise speed adjustment can be set as follows:
1. If cruise speed is lower than engagement speed, loosen orifice tube locknut and turn orifice tube counterclockwise.
2. If cruise speed is higher than engagement speed, loosen orifice tube locknut and turn orifice tube clockwise.

NOTE: Each 1/4 turn of orifice tube will change cruise speed approximately one mile per hour. Tighten locknut after adjustment is completed.

ASPIRATOR ASSISTED VACUUM SYSTEM

The aspirator assisted vacuum system supplements engine vacuum when engine vacuum is low. The system, Fig. 10, consists of an aspirator, 3-port check valve, 2-port check valve and related components such as the air pump and air management valve. The air for the aspirator is tapped off the air line that connects the air pump to the air management valve. Aspirator vacuum and manifold vacuum (after passing through the 2-port check valve) supply the two upper ports of the 3-port check valve. The lower of the 3-port check valve supplies air to the cruise control transducer. The aspirator assisted vacuum system operates as follows:
a. Under normal vacuum conditions, air is bled into the system from the transducer resume valve to the lower "T" of the 3-port check valve, then to the 2-port check valve and finally into the intake manifold, Fig. 10.
b. Also during normal operation, as the air pump is pumping air into the air management valve, a small amount of air is diverted through the aspirator to the atmosphere. As air passes through the aspirator, a venturi action inside the aspirator assembly develops a vacuum. This vacuum is used to provide the vacuum assist needed under high cruise conditions.

c. Should manifold vacuum fall below aspirator vacuum, the 2-port check valve is designed to close while the 3-port check valve is designed to open. Opening of the 3-port check valve exposes the higher vacuum at the aspirator, providing the needed vacuum for proper cruise operation.
To check the aspirator system for correct operation, note the following information:
a. Ensure all hoses and connections are secure and check valves are correctly installed.

NOTE: The check valves are arrowhead shaped in the direction of air flow.

b. Connect a suitable vacuum gauge to the aspirator output at point A, Fig. 10.
c. Start and operate engine at 2500 RPM.

NOTE: Engine should be thoroughly warmed up to ensure that the computer command control system (CCC) is operating in closed loop.

d. Check vacuum gauge. A minimum of 6 inches should be indicated. If vacuum reading is not within specified amount, clean aspirator using a suitable solvent and recheck. Also check air pump for air output. If there is no air output from the air pump, check air pump for air output. If there is no air output from the air pump, check air pump for damage. If air pump is not damaged, proceed to step e.
e. Disconnect vacuum gauge at port A, Fig. 10. Disconnect and plug 2-port check valve at port B. Blow air into the resume valve hose at port C. Air should flow through and exit at port A.
f. Remove plug from 2-port check valve at port B and plug hose at port A. Blow air into cruise resume valve at port C. Air should flow and exit at port B.

NOTE: Steps e & f determine if the hoses and check valves are operating in one direction. To check for operation in the opposite direction, proceed to step g.

g. Blow air into hose at port A while port B is plugged, then into port B while hose at port A is plugged.

NOTE: No air should exist at port C in either case.

4-112 & 121 Overhead Valve Engine Section

ENGINE MOUNTS, REPLACE

Front Engine Mount

1. Disconnect battery ground cable.
2. Remove engine mount nuts, then raise and support vehicle.
3. Remove inner fender shield attaching bolts, then the shield.

4. Support engine and remove and discard engine mount attaching bolts, Fig. 1.
5. Remove engine mount from vehicle.

CAUTION: Whenever engine mount is removed, alignment bolt M6X1X65 must be used during installation to prevent power train misalignment.

6. Reverse procedure to install, using new engine mount bolts. Remove alignment

bolt and torque engine mount to side frame bolts to 35–45 ft. lbs. Torque all other nuts and bolts to 25–35 ft. lbs.

NOTE: If excessive effort is required to remove alignment bolt, loosen transaxle adjusting bolts to align powertrain components.

Rear Engine Mount

1. Disconnect battery ground cable.

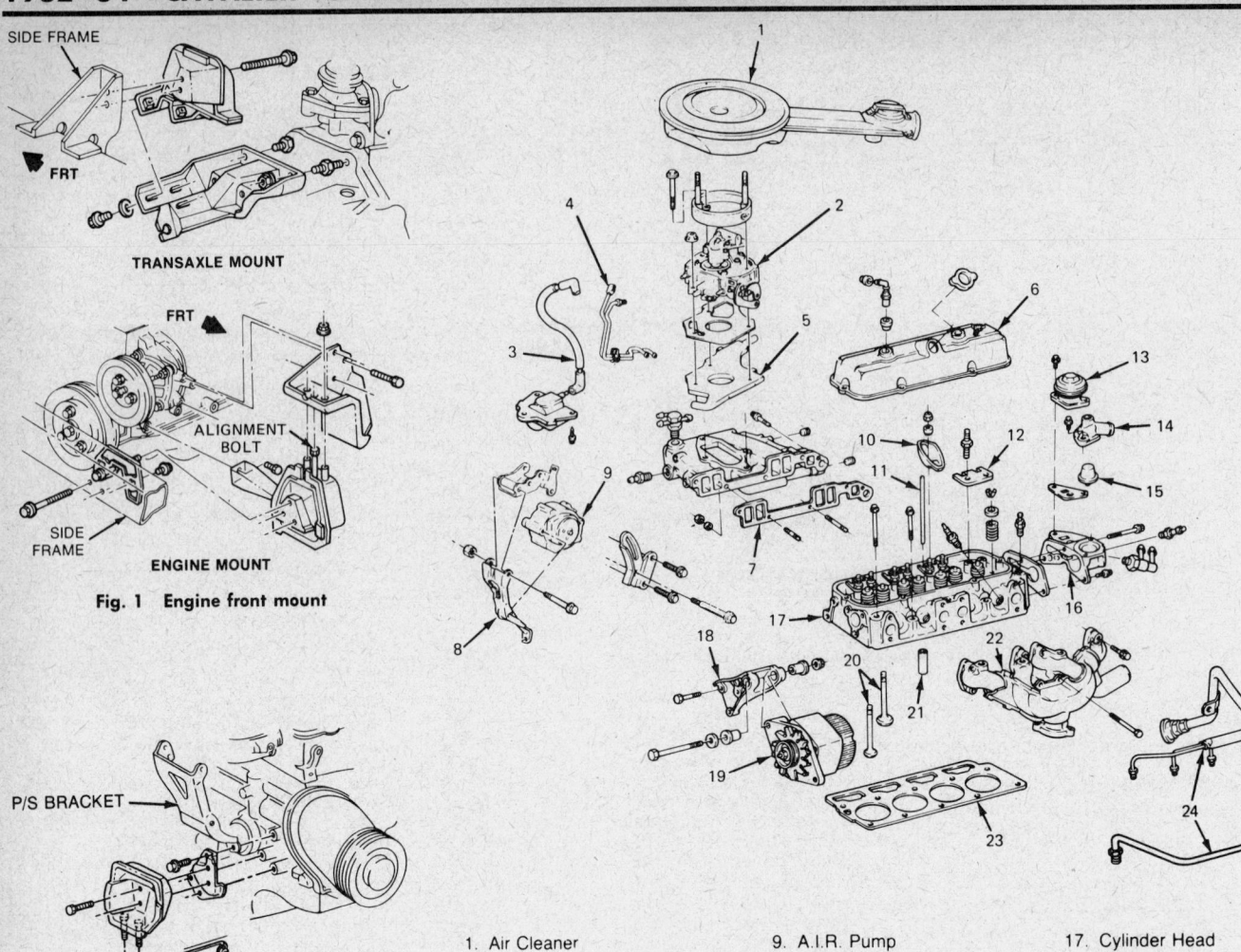

SIDE FRAME

FRT

TRANSAXLE MOUNT

FRT

ALIGNMENT BOLT

SIDE FRAME

ENGINE MOUNT

Fig. 1 Engine front mount

P/S BRACKET

Fig. 2 Engine rear mount

Cylinder head assembly & related components

1. Air Cleaner	9. A.I.R. Pump	17. Cylinder Head
2. TBI Unit or Carb.	10. Rocker Arm	18. Generator Bracket
3. Coil and Coil Wire	11. Push Rod	19. Generator
4. Fuel Line	12. Push Rod Guide	20. Valves
5. E.F.E. Grid	13. E.G.R. Valve	21. Lifter
6. Rocker Arm Cover	14. Thermostat Outlet	22. Exhaust Manifold
7. Intake Manifold & Gasket	15. Thermostat	23. Cylinder Head Gasket
8. A.I.R. Mounting Bracket	16. Adapter	24. A.I.R. or Pulsair Pipe

2. Raise and support vehicle.
3. If equipped with manual transaxle, remove oil filter.
4. Support engine and remove engine mount nuts, Fig. 2.
5. Remove and discard engine mount to engine attaching bolts.
6. Remove engine mount from vehicle.
7. Reverse procedure to install. Check oil level and torque nuts to 15–20 ft. lbs. and bolts to 25–35 ft. lbs.

ENGINE, REPLACE

1. Disconnect battery ground cable, then drain cooling system.
2. Remove air cleaner.
3. Remove power steering pump, if equipped, and position aside.
4. Disconnect window washer bottle and position aside.
5. If equipped with A/C, remove A/C relay bracket at bulkhead.
6. Disconnect bulkhead wire harness con-

nections.
7. If equipped with cruise control, disconnect servo bracket and position aside.
8. Disconnect and tag all vacuum hoses and electrical wires that will interfere with engine removal.
9. Remove master cylinder attaching nuts, disconnect master cylinder from vacuum booster and position aside.
10. Disconnect heater hose at engine hot water pipe, then remove upper radiator hose.
11. Remove fan assembly, horn and carburetor or TBI unit linkage.
12. Raise and support vehicle, then disconnect fuel line at fuel pump and heater hose at intake manifold. Remove lower radiator hose.
13. If equipped with A/C, remove A/C support brace retaining bolts and the support brace.
14. Remove exhaust manifold shield, starter to engine retaining bolts and starter.
15. Disconnect exhaust pipe from exhaust manifold.
16. Remove front tires, then disconnect front

stabilizer bar from lower control arms.
17. Separate ball joints from steering knuckles using tool J-29330, or equivalent.
18. Disengage, then remove drive axles from transaxle.
19. Remove transaxle strut to transaxle bracket attaching bolts, then disconnect strut at bracket and crossmember.
20. If equipped with A/C, remove inner fender shield attaching bolts and inner fender shield.
21. If equipped with A/C, remove A/C compressor drive belt, then disconnect A/C compressor from mounting bracket and position compressor aside. Do not disconnect hoses from compressor.
22. Remove rear engine mount attaching nuts and plate.
23. If equipped with automatic transaxle, remove oil filter.
24. Disconnect speedometer cable at transaxle or, if equipped with cruise control, at transducer.
25. Lower vehicle and, if equipped with automatic transaxle, disconnect oil coolant lines at transaxle.

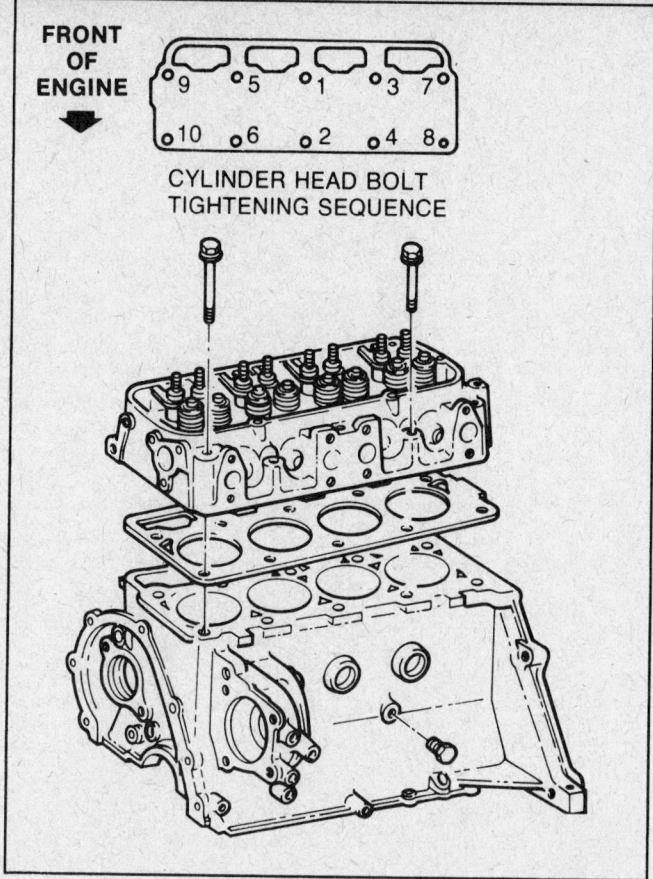

Fig. 3 Cylinder head bolt tightening sequence

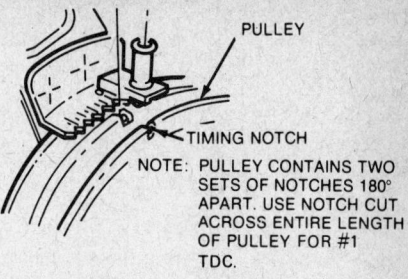

NOTE: PULLEY CONTAINS TWO SETS OF NOTCHES 180° APART. USE NOTCH CUT ACROSS ENTIRE LENGTH OF PULLEY FOR #1 TDC.

Fig. 4 Aligning crankshaft pulley timing marks

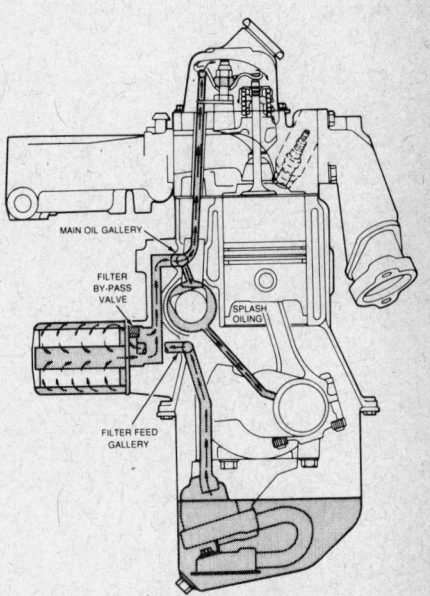

Engine Oiling System

26. Remove front engine mount nuts.
27. Disconnect clutch, shift and/or detent cables from transaxle.
28. Install suitable lifting device, then remove transaxle mount attaching bolts, transaxle mount and bracket.
29. Remove engine and transaxle as an assembly.
30. Install engine/transaxle assembly using engine mount alignment bolt M6X1X65 to ensure proper power train alignment.
31. Lower engine/transaxle assembly into vehicle then install transaxle mount and bracket, using new bolts, Fig. 1.
32. Tighten transaxle mount and front engine mount nuts.
33. Remove engine/transaxle assembly lifting device and raise vehicle.
34. Reverse procedures to complete installation.

CYLINDER HEAD, REPLACE

NOTE: The cylinder head, carburetor or TBI (Throttle Body Injection) unit and the intake and exhaust manifolds are removed as an assembly.

1. Disconnect battery ground cable, drain cooling system and remove air cleaner.
2. Raise and support vehicle, then remove exhaust manifold shield.
3. Disconnect exhaust pipe at exhaust manifold and heater hose at intake manifold.
4. Lower vehicle, then remove engine lift bracket and distributor.
5. Disconnect vacuum manifold from alternator bracket.
6. Disconnect and tag all vacuum lines that will interfere with cylinder head removal, then disconnect AIR pipe at exhaust check valve.
7. Disconnect accelerator linkage at carburetor or TBI unit, then remove accelerator linkage bracket bolt and the bracket.
8. Disconnect all electrical wires that will interfere with cylinder head removal, then remove upper radiator hose from cylinder head.
9. Remove dipstick tube bracket bolt and the hot water tube bracket.
10. Remove idler pulley assembly and AIR/power steering belt.
11. Remove power steering pump, if equipped, and position aside.
12. Remove AIR bracket to intake manifold bolt.
13. On power steering equipped vehicles, remove AIR pump pulley, AIR pump through bolt and power steering pump adjusting bracket.
14. Loosen AIR bracket lower bolt and rotate bracket aside.
15. Disconnect fuel line from carburetor or TBI unit.
16. Remove alternator and position aside. Do not remove wires.
17. Remove alternator upper support bracket and brace.
18. Remove rocker arm cover and rocker arms, then the push rods.
19. Remove cylinder head bolts and the cylinder head assembly.
20. Reverse procedure to install. Coat cylinder head and cylinder head bolts with sealer and install bolts finger tight. Torque cylinder head bolts to specification in sequence shown in Fig. 3.

ROCKER ARM STUDS

Rocker arm studs that have stress cracks or damaged threads can be replaced. If threads in cylinder head are damaged or stripped, the head can be retapped and a helical type insert added. When installing a new rocker arm stud, torque stud to 43–49 ft. lbs.

VALVES, ADJUST

1. Crank engine until mark on crankshaft pulley is aligned with TDC mark on timing tab. Check to ensure engine is in the No. 1 cylinder firing position by placing fingers on No. 1 cylinder rocker arms as mark on pulley comes near TDC mark on timing tab. If valves are not moving, the engine is in the No. 1 firing position. If valves move as pulley nears TDC mark on timing tab, engine is in No. 4 cylinder firing position and should be rotated one revolution to reach the No. 1 cylinder firing position.

NOTE: The crankshaft pulley contains

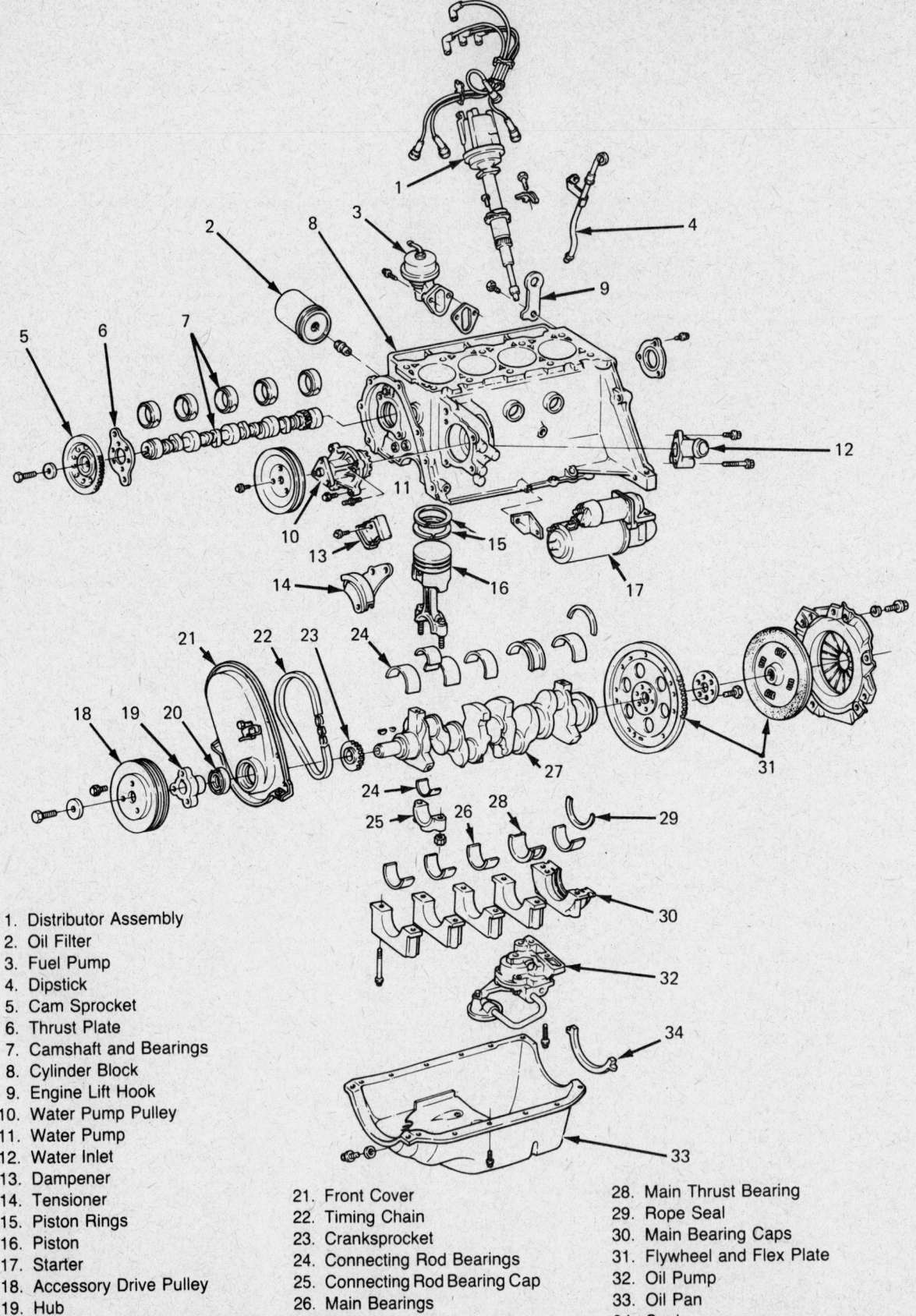

1. Distributor Assembly
2. Oil Filter
3. Fuel Pump
4. Dipstick
5. Cam Sprocket
6. Thrust Plate
7. Camshaft and Bearings
8. Cylinder Block
9. Engine Lift Hook
10. Water Pump Pulley
11. Water Pump
12. Water Inlet
13. Dampener
14. Tensioner
15. Piston Rings
16. Piston
17. Starter
18. Accessory Drive Pulley
19. Hub
20. Seal

21. Front Cover
22. Timing Chain
23. Cranksprocket
24. Connecting Rod Bearings
25. Connecting Rod Bearing Cap
26. Main Bearings
27. Crankshaft

28. Main Thrust Bearing
29. Rope Seal
30. Main Bearing Caps
31. Flywheel and Flex Plate
32. Oil Pump
33. Oil Pan
34. Seal

Cylinder block assembly & components

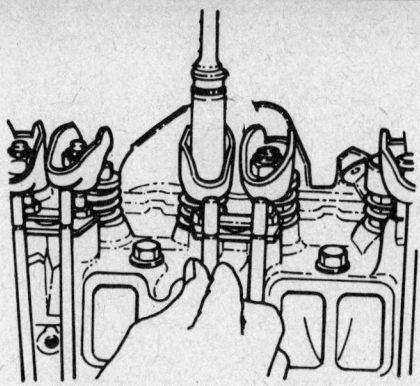

Fig. 5 Valve adjustment

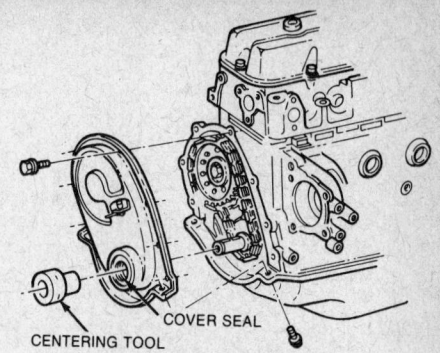

1. Lifter Body	6. Push Rod Seat
2. Push Rod Seat	Retainer
3. Metering Valve	7. Plunger
4. Check Ball	8. Check Ball Spring
5. Check Ball Retainer	9. Plunger Spring

Fig. 7 Sectional view of hydraulic valve lifter

Fig. 9 Installing front cover

NOTE: AT TIME OF INSTALLATION, FLANGES MUST BE FREE OF OIL. A 2.0-3.0 BEAD OF SEALANT MUST BE APPLIED TO FLANGES AND SEALANT MUST BE WET TO TOUCH WHEN BOLTS ARE TORQUED.

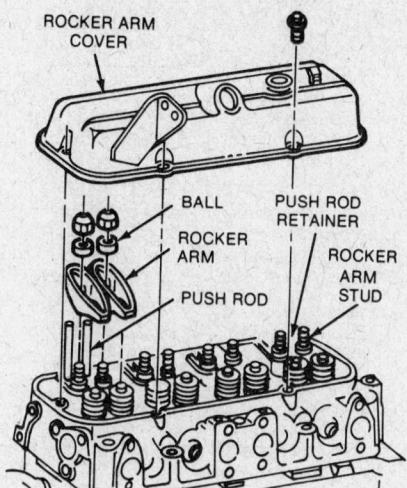

Fig. 6 Rocker arms & rocker arm cover

Fig. 8 Removing crankshaft pulley & hub

VALVE ARRANGEMENT

Front to Rear

4-112 & 121 .... E-I-I-E-I-I-E

VALVE LIFT SPECS.

Engine	Year	Intake	Exhaust
4-112 & 121	1982	.393	.393
4-121	1983–84	.393	.393

VALVE TIMING

Intake Opens Before TDC

Year	Engine	Degrees
1982	4-112 & 121	32

VALVE GUIDES

Valve guides are an integral part of the cylinder head and are not removable. If valve stem clearance becomes excessive, the valve guide should be reamed to the next oversize and the appropriate oversize valves installed. Valves are available in .003, .006, and .012 inch oversizes.

VALVE LIFTERS, REPLACE

1. Remove rocker arm cover attaching bolts and rocker arm cover, Fig. 6.
2. Loosen rocker arm stud nut and rotate rocker arm so that pushrod can be removed. Remove pushrod.
3. Using tool J-29834, remove valve lifter from lifter bore.

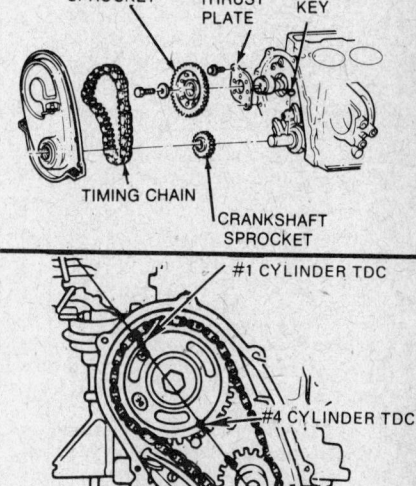

Fig. 10 Valve timing marks

4. Coat base of new lifter, Fig. 7, with "Molykote", or equivalent, and install lifter into lifter bore.
5. Reverse procedure to install and adjust valves as outlined under "VALVES, ADJUST" procedure.

ENGINE FRONT COVER, REPLACE

1. Disconnect battery ground cable.
2. Remove accessory drive belts, then raise and support vehicle.
3. Remove right front wheel and tire.
4. Remove right inner fender splash shield attaching bolts and the shield.
5. Remove A/C drive belt, if equipped.
6. Remove crankshaft pulley retaining bolts and crankshaft pulley, Fig. 8.
7. Using tool J-24420, remove crankshaft hub from crankshaft.
8. Remove engine front cover retaining bolts and front cover.
9. Clean sealing surface of front cover and engine block. Apply a 2 mm bead of RTV sealant to front cover sealing surface.
10. Position front cover to engine block. Using centering tool J-23042, install

two sets of marks 180° apart. Use those marks which cut across entire length of pulley to find No. 1 cylinder firing position, Fig. 4.

2. With engine in No. 1 cylinder firing position, adjust the following valves: Exhaust: 1, 3; Intake: 1, 2. To adjust valves, back off adjusting nut until lash is felt at push rod, then tighten adjusting nut until all lash is removed, Fig. 5. This can be determined by rotating the push rod while tightening the adjusting nut. When all lash has been eliminated, the push rod will no longer rotate, Fig. 5. Turn the adjusting nut the additional number of turns listed in the Valve Specifications Chart.
3. Crank engine one full revolution until mark on crankshaft pulley and TDC mark are again aligned. This is the No. 4 cylinder firing position. With engine in this position, the following valves can be adjusted: Exhaust 2, 4; Intake 3, 4.
4. Install rocker arm cover, then start engine and check timing and idle speed.

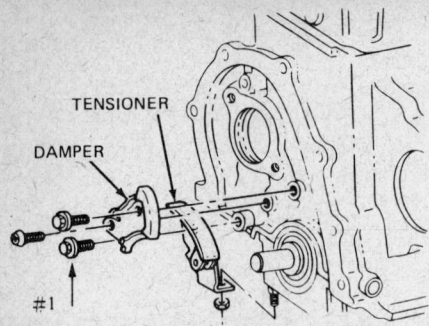

Fig. 11   Timing chain tensioner. 1982 4-112 & 4-121

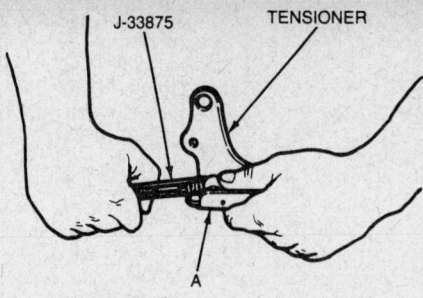

Fig. 12   Compressing timing chain tensioner spring. 1983–84 4-121

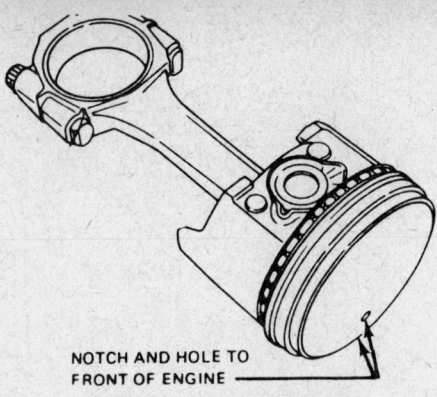

NOTCH AND HOLE TO FRONT OF ENGINE

Fig. 13   Piston & rod assembly

front retaining bolts and torque bolts to 6–9 ft. lbs. Remove centering tool, Fig. 9.

11. Reverse procedure to install.

TIMING CHAIN, REPLACE

1. Remove engine front cover as previously described.
2. Place No. 1 cylinder at TDC and align timing marks on crankshaft and camshaft sprockets, Fig. 10.
3. On 1982 models, remove timing chain upper attaching bolts, then loosen nut as far as possible without removing. On 1983–84 models, remove timing chain tensioner as described under Timing Chain Tensioner, Replace.
4. Remove camshaft sprocket retaining bolt. Tap lower edge of sprocket with plastic mallet and remove sprocket and timing chain.
5. If crankshaft sprocket is to be replaced, remove sprocket using a suitable puller.
6. To install crankshaft sprocket, align keyway on sprocket with key on crankshaft.
7. Align timing marks, Fig. 10, and install timing chain on sprockets.
8. Align dowel on camshaft with dowel hole on camshaft sprocket, then install sprocket to camshaft, using retaining bolt to draw sprocket fully to camshaft. Torque bolt to 66–85 ft. lbs.
9. Lubricate timing chain with engine oil, then install timing chain tensioner.
10. Install engine front cover as outlined previously.

TIMING CHAIN TENSIONER, REPLACE

1982 4-112 & 121

1. Remove engine front cover as described under Engine Front Cover, Replace.
2. Remove attaching bolt (1), Fig. 11, and lower nut.

NOTE: Use a suitable tool, such as a loop of wire, to prevent nut from falling into oil pan.

3. Remove timing chain tensioner.
4. Position timing chain tensioner to engine.
5. Using a suitable tool, such as a wire loop around nut, position nut on stud.
6. Install bolt (1), Fig. 11, finger tight.

7. Torque nut to 15 to 22 ft. lbs. and bolt to 13 to 18 ft. lbs.

1983–84 4-121

1. Remove engine front cover as described under Engine Front Cover, Replace.
2. Remove tensioner attaching bolts, then remove tensioner.
3. Position tangs of tool No. J33875 under tensioner sliding blocks, then pull tool to compress tensioner spring.
4. While compressing tensioner spring, insert a cotter pin or other suitable tool into hole (A), Fig. 12, to hold spring in the compressed position, then remove tool No. J33875.
5. Position tensioner to engine, then install attaching bolts and remove cotter pin holding tensioner spring in the compressed position.

CAMSHAFT, REPLACE

1. Remove engine from vehicle as previously described.
2. Remove valve lifters and engine front cover as described previously.
3. Mark position of rotor to distributor body, then remove distributor from engine.
4. Remove fuel pump and fuel pump push rod from engine block.
5. Remove timing chain and camshaft sprocket as previously described.
6. Remove camshaft thrust plate to engine block retaining bolts and the thrust plate, Fig. 10.
7. Remove camshaft from engine block.
8. Reverse removal procedure to install. When installing camshaft, align crankshaft and camshaft sprocket timing marks, Fig. 10.

PISTON & ROD ASSEMBLE

Install piston to rod with notch and hole on piston facing toward front of engine and rod bearing tang slot opposite camshaft, Fig. 13. Upon installation, measure the connecting rod side clearance using a suitable feeler gauge. Measurement taken should be as follows:

Engine	Year	Clearance in Inch
4-112	1982	.004–.024
4-121	1982–84	.004–.024

PISTONS, PINS, & RODS

Pistons and rings are available in standard

and oversizes of .020 and .040 inch. Oversize piston pins are not available due to the press fit design.

MAIN & ROD BEARINGS

NOTE: When removing No. 1 main bearing cap, it will be necessary to remove the timing chain tensioner, refer to Timing Chain Tensioner, Replace.

Main bearings are available in standard size and undersizes of .0013 inch, and connecting rod bearings are available in standard size and undersizes of .0010 inch.

OIL PAN, REPLACE

1. Disconnect battery ground cable, then remove exhaust pipe shield.
2. Raise and support front of vehicle, then drain crankcase.
3. Disconnect exhaust pipe at exhaust manifold.
4. Detach A/C compressor brace at starter motor and A/C compressor bracket.
5. Remove flywheel cover and starter motor bracket, then remove starter motor and position aside.
6. Remove A/C compressor mounting bracket.
7. Remove four right hand suspension support bolts, then lower suspension support slightly to provide clearance for oil pan removal.
8. On models equipped with auto. transaxle, remove oil filter adapter.
9. Remove oil pan attaching bolts and oil pan.
10. Reverse procedure to install. Before installing oil pan, apply a thin coat of RTV sealer to both ends of oil pan rear seal, then seat seal firmly into rear main bearing cap. Do not allow sealer to extend beyond oil pan rear seal tabs. Apply a continuous 2 mm bead of RTV sealer along oil pan side rails in line with bolt holes, circling inward around each bolt hole location. Also apply RTV sealer to oil pan surface which contacts engine front cover. This bead of sealer must meet the bead at each oil pan side rail. Do not apply any RTV sealer to oil pan rear seal mating surface. Carefully install oil pan and torque attaching bolts alternately and evenly to 6 to 9 ft. lbs., then to a final torque of 13 to 18 ft. lbs. Torque attaching

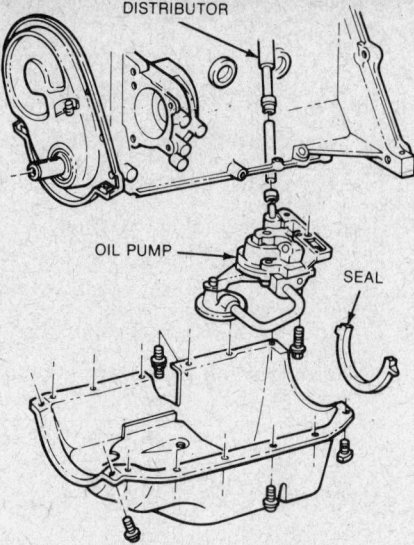

Fig. 14 Removing oil pan & pump

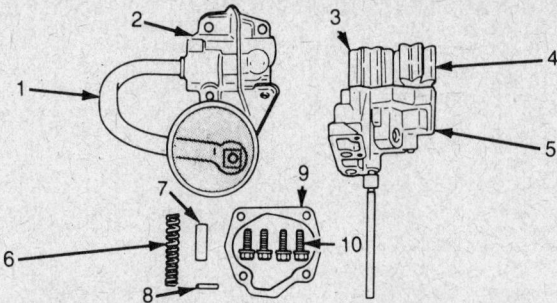

1. PICK UP TUBE AND SCREEN.
2. PUMP COVER.
3. DRIVE GEAR AND SHAFT.
4. IDLER GEAR.
5. PUMP BODY.
6. PRESSURE REGULATOR SPRING.
7. PRESSURE REGULATOR VALVE.
8. RETAINING PIN.
9. GASKET.
10. ATTACHING BOLTS.

Fig. 15 Sectional view of oil pump assembly

bolts while RTV sealer is still wet to touch.

OIL PUMP SERVICE

Removal

1. Drain crankcase, then remove oil pan as previously described.
2. Remove pump to rear main bearing attaching bolt, then remove pump, extension shaft and retainer, Fig. 14.

Disassemble

1. Remove four pump cover to body attaching bolts, then remove cover, idler and drive gears and shaft, Fig. 15.

NOTE: Place align mark on oil pump drive and idler gear teeth so they can be installed in the same position.

2. Remove pressure regulator valve retaining pin, spring and the valve from pump body.

Inspection

Inspect pump components and should any of the following conditions exist, the oil pump assembly should be replaced.
1. Inspect pump body, gears and cover for

cracks or excessive wear.
2. Check drive gear shaft for looseness in housing.
3. Check inside of pump cover for wear that would allow oil to leak past ends of gears.
4. Check oil pickup screen assembly for damage to screen or pickup tube.
5. Check pressure regulator valve for fit in pump body.

Assemble

1. Install a replacement pickup screen and tube assembly, if removed. Position pump in a soft jawed vise, then apply sealer to end of tube and tap into position using tool No. J8369 and a plastic hammer. Use care not to damage inlet screen and tube assembly when installing on pump housing.
2. Place pressure regulator valve, spring and retaining pin into pump body, then install drive gear and shaft.
3. Install idler gear into pump body, then the pump cover gasket. Fig. 15.
4. Install pump cover and cover retaining bolts, then torque bolts to 6–9 ft. lbs.

Installation

1. Align oil pump extension shaft to distributor drive gear socket and pump housing with dowels on cap, then install shaft retainer and pump assembly.
2. Install oil pump assembly retaining bolt to rear main bearing cap and torque bolt to 26–35 ft. lbs.
3. Install oil pan as previously described.

REAR MAIN BEARING OIL SEAL, REPLACE

SERVICE NOTE

All 1982 4-112 engines use a rope type rear main bearing seal. When service replacement of seal is indicated, a new rubber split seal, Part No. 14069889, should be used. Refer to procedure below when replacing rope type seal with rubber split design.

1. Remove oil pan and oil pump as described previously.
2. Remove rear main bearing cap.
3. Remove upper and lower seal, then clean seal channel of oil.

NOTE: Loosening No. 2, 3 & 4 main bearing caps may be helpful when removing and replacing upper seal.

4. Apply a thin coat of sealing compound 1050026, or equivalent, to outer diameter of upper seal. Roll seal into position in block, turning crankshaft to ease installation.
5. Apply sealer to lower seal as described above, and position into main bearing cap.
6. Position a piece of Plastigage onto main journal or bearing, install main bearing cap and torque to specifications.
7. Remove bearing cap and measure Plastigage for proper bearing clearance. If clearance is not within specifications, correct as necessary.
8. Clean Plastigage from journal and bearing, then lubricate bearing lightly.
9. Apply a 1 mm bead of sealant 1052357 or equivalent to the bearing cap between the rear main seal end and the oil pan rear seal groove as shown, Fig. 16. Keep sealant off main seal and out of drain slot in bearing cap.
10. Apply light coat of engine oil to crank-

COATED AREA INDICATED WITH #1052357 SEALER OR EQUIVALENT.

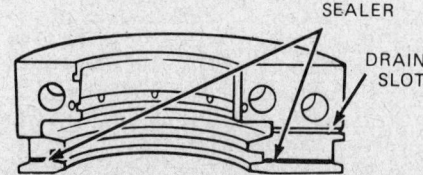

Fig. 16 Replacing crankshaft rear main bearing oil seal

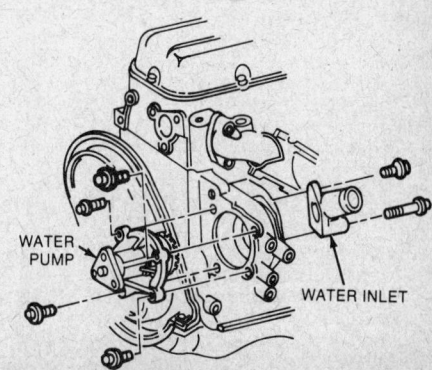

Fig. 17 Replacing water pump assembly

shaft to seal contact surface.

11. Install rear main bearing cap, then torque all bolts to specifications.

12. Install oil pump and oil pan, then start engine and check for leaks.

WATER PUMP, REPLACE

1. Disconnect battery ground cable and drain cooling system.
2. Remove accessory drive belts.
3. Remove alternator to alternator bracket retaining bolts and position alternator aside.
4. Remove water pump pulley to water pump attaching bolts, then the pulley from water pump.
5. Remove four water pump to block attach-

ing bolts and the water pump, Fig. 17.

6. Clean sealing surfaces of pump and engine block and place a 1/8 inch bead of sealant 1052289, or equivalent, to sealing surfaces. Install pump. Coat threaded area of pump bolts with sealant 1052080, install torque bolts to 13–18 ft. lbs.

7. Reverse removal procedures to complete installation.

BELT TENSION DATA

	New Lbs.	Used Lbs.
Air Cond.	168②	90①
Alternator	145②	70①
Power Steer.	145②	70①
Air Pump	145②	70①

①—Minimum
②—Maximum

FUEL PUMP, REPLACE

1. Disconnect battery ground cable.
2. Raise and support vehicle.
3. Disconnect inlet hose and outlet pipe from fuel pump.
4. Remove two fuel pump retaining nuts and rotate pump upward to clear studs in block. Remove fuel pump from vehicle.
5. Clean block to pump mating surface and install new gasket over studs in block.
6. Install pump and pump retaining nuts and torque nuts to 15–22 ft. lbs.
7. Reverse procedure to complete installation.

4-112 Overhead Cam Engine Section

ENGINE MOUNTS, REPLACE

Front Engine Mount

1. Disconnect battery ground cable.
2. Remove engine mount nuts, then raise and support vehicle.
3. Remove inner fender shield attaching bolts, then the shield.
4. Support engine and remove and discard engine mount attaching bolts, Figs. 1 and 2.
5. Remove engine mount from vehicle.

CAUTION: Whenever engine mount is removed, alignment bolt M6X1X65 must be used during installation to prevent power train misalignment.

6. Reverse procedure to install, using new engine mount bolts. Remove alignment bolt.

NOTE: If excessive effort is required to remove alignment bolt, loosen transaxle adjusting bolts to align powertrain components.

Rear Engine Mount

1. Disconnect battery ground cable.
2. Raise and support vehicle.
3. If equipped with manual transaxle, remove oil filter.
4. Support engine and remove engine mount nuts, Fig. 3.
5. Remove and discard engine mount to engine attaching bolts.
6. Remove engine mount from vehicle.
7. Reverse procedure to install.

ENGINE, REPLACE

1. Disconnect battery ground cable, then drain cooling system.
2. Remove air cleaner, then disconnect engine electrical harness connector at bulkhead and electrical connector at brake cylinder.
3. Disconnect throttle cable from bracket and E.F.I. assembly.

1 TORQUE 50 N·m (38 LB. FT.)
2 ENGINE MOUNTING BRACKET
3 ALIGNMENT BOLT MUST BE REMOVED AFTER ENGINE INSTALLATION
4 TORQUE 7 N·m (5 LB. FT.)
5 TORQUE 31 N·m (23 LB. FT.)
6 TORQUE 27 N·m (20 LB. FT.)

Fig. 1   Front engine mounts

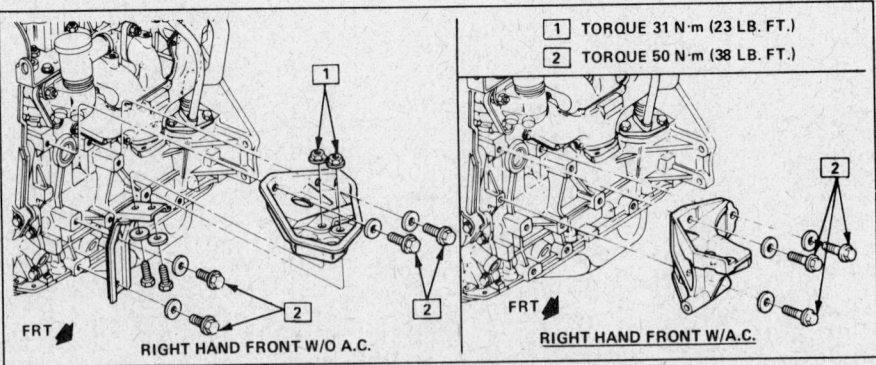

1 TORQUE 31 N·m (23 LB. FT.)
2 TORQUE 50 N·m (38 LB. FT.)

RIGHT HAND FRONT W/O A.C.

RIGHT HAND FRONT W/A.C.

Fig. 2   Right hand front engine mount brackets

4. Disconnect vacuum hoses from E.F.I. assembly, then disconnect power steering high pressure hose at cut-off switch.
5. Disconnect vacuum hoses at map sensor and canister, then disconnect air conditioning relay cluster switches.

6. Disconnect power steering return hose at power steering pump.
7. Disconnect ECM electrical connectors, then pull harness through bulkhead and position harness over engine.
8. Disconnect upper and lower radiator hos-

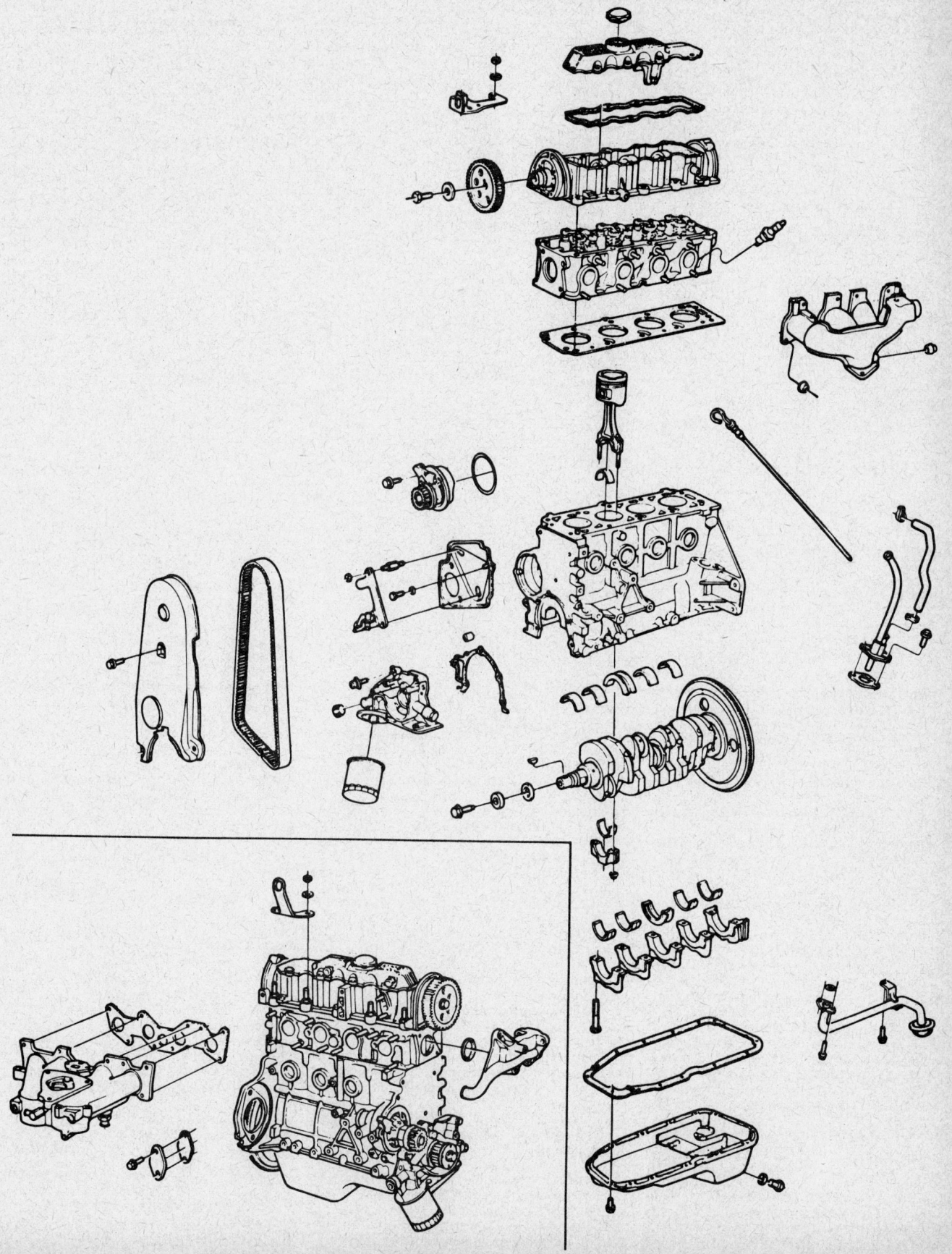

Disassembled view of engine

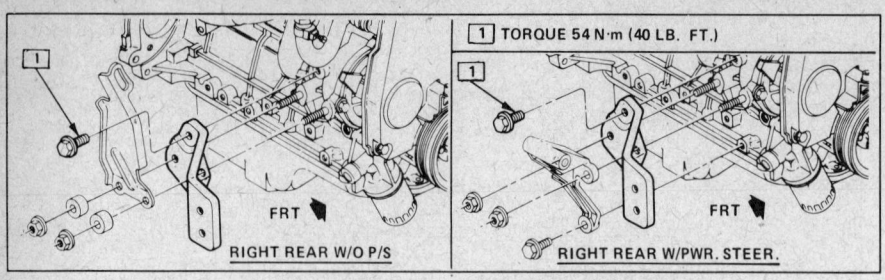

Fig. 3   Right hand rear engine mount brackets

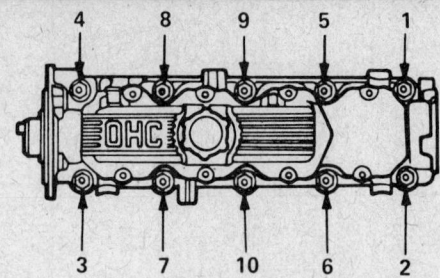

Fig. 4   Cylinder head & camshaft carrier bolt loosening sequence

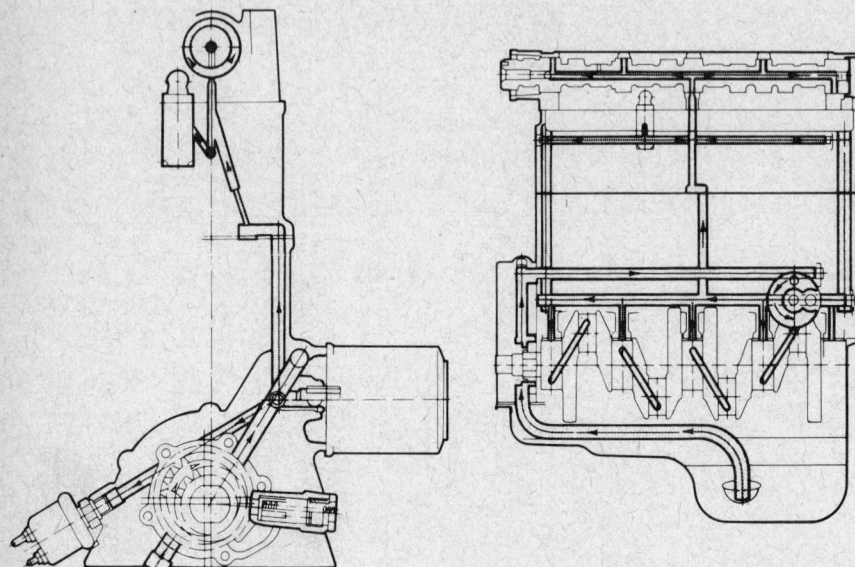

Engine oiling system. 4-112 overhead cam engine

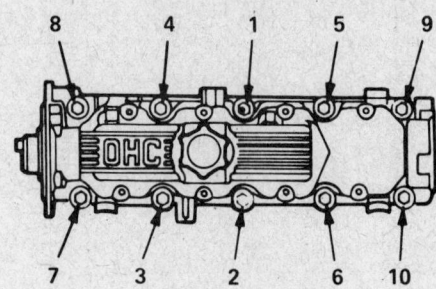

Fig. 5   Cylinder head & camshaft carrier bolt tightening sequence

tion.

CYLINDER HEAD, REPLACE

1. Disconnect battery ground cable, remove air cleaner and drain cooling system.
2. Remove alternator and pivot bracket from camshaft carrier housing.
3. Remove power steering pump and bracket and position aside.
4. Disconnect ignition coil electrical connectors, then remove coil.
5. Disconnect spark plug wires from distributor cap.
6. Remove throttle cable from bracket on intake manifold.
7. Disconnect accelerator cable, downshift cable and throttle valve cable from E.F.I. assembly.
8. Disconnect ECM connectors from E.F.I. assembly.
9. Disconnect vacuum brake hose from filter, then disconnect inlet and return fuel lines from flex joints.
10. Remove water pump bypass hose from intake manifold and water pump.
11. Disconnect ECM harness connectors and heater hose from intake manifold.
12. Disconnect exhaust pipe from exhaust manifold and breather hose from camshaft carrier.
13. Disconnect upper radiator hose, then disconnect engine electrical harness and wires from thermostat housing.
14. Remove timing cover and timing probe holder.
15. Loosen water pump bolts and remove timing belt.
16. Loosen camshaft carrier and cylinder head bolts a little at a time in sequence shown in Fig. 4.

NOTE: Camshaft carrier and cylinder head bolts should only be removed when engine is cold.

es from engine, then disconnect wire connector at temperature switch on thermostat housing.
9. Disconnect transmission shift cable at transmission, then raise and support vehicle.
10. Disconnect speedometer cable at transmission and bracket.
11. Disconnect exhaust pipe at exhaust manifold and remove exhaust pipe from converter.
12. Remove heater hoses from heater core, fuel lines at flex hoses and transmission cooler lines at flex hoses.
13. Remove front wheels, right hand spoiler section and splash shield.
14. Remove and support right and left brake calipers.
15. Using tool No. J-24319-1 or equivalent, remove right and left tie rod ends.
16. Disconnect electrical connectors at A/C compressor, then remove A/C compressor and mounting brackets. Using a piece of wire, support compressor in wheel opening.
17. Remove six front suspension support attachment bolts.
18. Lower vehicle and support front end by placing jack stands under core support.
19. Using a suitable hoist, position front post of hoist to rear of cowl.
20. Using a suitable piece of wood (4″ × 4″ × 6′), position onto front post of hoist.
21. Raise vehicle slightly and remove jack stands from front end.
22. Position a suitable dolly under engine and transaxle assembly.

23. Position three pieces of wood (4″ × 4″ × 12″) under engine and transaxle assembly only, allowing support rails to hang free.
24. Slightly lower vehicle onto dolly and remove two rear transaxle mount attaching bolts.
25. Remove three left front engine mount attaching bolts and two engine support to body attaching bolts behind right hand inner axle U-joint.
26. Remove one bolt and nut from right hand chassis side rail to engine mount bracket.
27. Remove six strut attaching nuts, then raise vehicle, allowing engine, transaxle and suspension assemblies to rest onto dolly.
28. Remove engine and transaxle as an assembly.
29. Position engine and transaxle assembly into vehicle.
30. Loosely install transaxle and left front mounts to side rail bolts.
31. To prevent powertrain misalignment, install bolt No. M6X1X65 into left front mount.
32. Torque transaxle mount bolts to 42 ft. lbs. and left front mount to 18 ft. lbs.
33. Install right rear mount to body bolts and torque to 38 ft. lbs.
34. Position a suitable jack under control arms and raise struts into position, then install retaining nuts.
35. Raise vehicle, then using suitable lifting equipment, raise control arms and install tie rod ends.
36. Reverse procedure to complete installa-

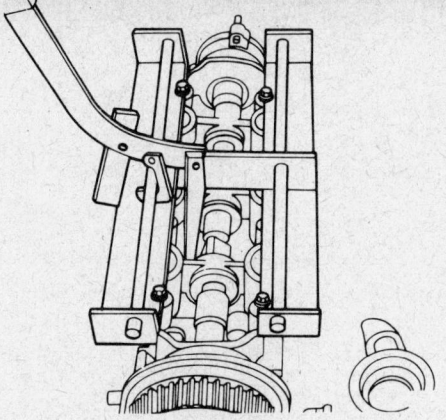

Fig. 6 Using tool No. 33302 to compress valve spring

17. Remove camshaft carrier assembly.
18. Remove cylinder head, intake manifold and exhaust manifold as an assembly.
19. Remove all carbon deposits from combustion chambers and valve ports. Check cylinder head for cracks in the exhaust ports and combustion chambers. Remove water jacket plugs and clean, if necessary.
20. Reverse procedure to install. Torque cylinder head bolts a little at a time in sequence shown in Fig. 5 to 18 ft. lbs. Tighten each bolt in the proper sequence an additional 180° in 60° increments.
21. After installation is completed (with the exception of brackets that install onto carrier), start engine and let engine idle until thermostat opens. Turn engine off and torque all bolts an additional 30 to 50° in the proper sequence.

ROCKER ARM & HYDRAULIC VALVE LASH COMPENSATORS, REPLACE

1. Disconnect battery ground cable.
2. Remove camshaft carrier cover.
3. Using tool No. J-33302 or equivalent, Fig. 6, compress valve springs and remove rocker arms. Place rocker arms in a suitable rack so they can be installed in the same location.
4. Remove hydraulic lash compensators and place them in a rack so they can be installed in the same location.
5. Reverse procedure to install.

NOTE: No adjustment of valve lash is required. The preload of the hydraulic valve lash compensator is automatic and servicing of the compensator requires only care and cleanliness be exercised in the handling of these components.

VALVE SPRING & VALVE STEM OIL SEAL, REPLACE

Removal

1. Disconnect battery ground cable.
2. Remove rocker arms and spark plugs.
3. Install air line adapter tool No. J-23590 or equivalent, into spark plug port and apply compressed air to hold valves in place.
4. Using tool No. J-33302 or equivalent, Fig.

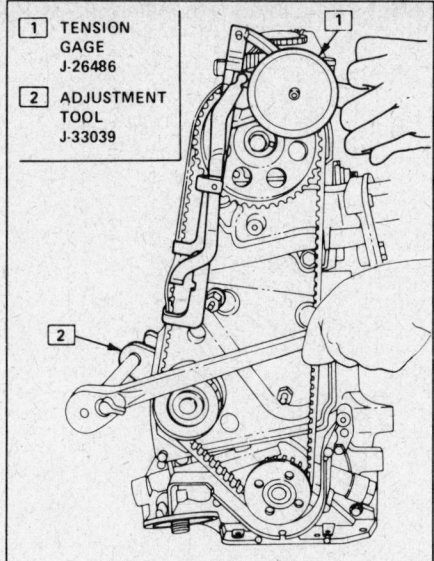

```
┌─┐ TENSION
│1│ GAGE
└─┘ J-26486

┌─┐ ADJUSTMENT
│2│ TOOL
└─┘ J-33039
```

Fig. 7 Timing belt tension adjustment

6, compress valve spring and remove rocker guides, valve locks, caps and valve spring.
5. Remove valve stem oil seal.

Installation

1. Using clean engine oil, lubricate valve stem and install new valve stem oil seal over valve stem and seat onto valve guide.
2. Position valve spring and cap over valve stem. Using tool No. J-33302 or equivalent, compress valve spring and install valve locks.
3. Install rocker guides and rocker arms, then remove tool No. J-33302.
4. Remove air line adapter tool and install spark plugs.
5. Install camshaft carrier cover. Torque bolts to 5 ft. lbs.

VALVE SEAT SERVICE

Using a suitable dial indicator measure valve seat concentricity. Valve seat should be concentric to within .002 inch of total indicator reading. Ensure valve guide bores are free from carbon or dirt to allow proper seating of the pilot in the valve guide. When reconditioning the valve seats, use a 45° stone to rough the valve seat and another stone with the same angle to finish the valve seat. Narrow down the valve seats to the proper width, .051–.055 inch for intake valves and .067–.071 for exhaust valves.

VALVE GUIDES

Valve guides are an integral part of the cylinder head. If valve stem to guide clearance is excessive, the guide should be reamed to the next oversize and the appropriate oversize valve installed. Valves are available in standard size and oversize of .010 inch (.25 mm).

CRANKSHAFT PULLEY

Removal

1. Disconnect battery ground cable.
2. Loosen alternator and power steering bracket bolt, then remove drive belt.
3. Remove inner fender splash shield, then

Fig. 8 Camshaft sprocket removal

remove crankshaft pulley bolts and pulley.

Installation

1. Position pulley onto crankshaft sprocket. Using a suitable sealer, coat threads of pulley bolts and install onto pulley. Torque bolts to 15 ft. lbs.
2. Install splash shield.
3. Install alternator and power steering belt, then connect battery ground cable.

TIMING BELT, REPLACE

1. Disconnect battery ground cable.
2. Remove timing belt front cover, then rotate crankshaft until timing mark on crankshaft pulley aligns with 10° BTDC mark on indicator tab. The mark on the camshaft sprocket must align with mark on camshaft carrier.
3. Remove crankshaft pulley as previously described.
4. Remove timing probe holder.
5. Loosen water pump bolts, then rotate water pump to loosen and remove timing belt.
6. Reverse procedure to install. Note the following information:
   a. Ensure mark on camshaft sprocket aligns with mark on camshaft carrier. The timing mark on the crankshaft pulley should align with the 10° BTDC mark on the indicator tab.
   b. Using tool No. J-33039 or equivalent, Fig. 7, rotate water pump clockwise until all slack is removed from timing belt. Install tool No. J-26486 or equivalent, Fig. 1, between water pump and camshaft sprockets so pointer is midway between sprockets.
7. To adjust timing belt tension, refer to Fig. 7 and note the following information:

Belt Size .... 748 inch

Initial Adjustment

New Belt .... 74 ft. lbs.
Used Belt .... 59 ft. lbs.

Checking Valve

New Belt .... 59–88 ft. lbs.
Used Belt .... 44–74 ft. lbs.

NOTE: These values are for a cold engine.

a. If timing belt tension is incorrect, loosen and using tool No. J-33039 or equivalent, rotate water pump until proper tension is obtained.
b. Torque water pump bolts to 19 ft. lbs. Ensure water pump does not shift when torquing bolts.

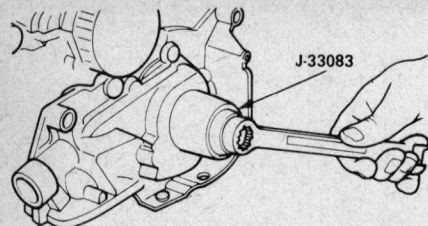

Fig. 9 Crankshaft front oil seal installation

TIMING BELT REAR COVER, REPLACE

1. Disconnect battery ground cable.
2. Remove timing belt as described under "TIMING BELT, REPLACE".
3. Remove timing belt rear cover bolts and cover.
4. Reverse procedure to install. Torque cover bolts to 19 ft. lbs.

CAMSHAFT CARRIER COVER, REPLACE

1. Remove air cleaner and disconnect breather hoses.
2. Remove cover bolts and cover.
3. Reverse procedure to install. Torque camshaft carrier cover bolts to 5 ft. lbs.

CAMSHAFT SPROCKET, REPLACE

1. Disconnect battery ground cable.
2. Remove timing belt front cover and align mark on camshaft sprocket with mark on camshaft carrier cover.
3. Remove timing probe holder.
4. Loosen water pump bolts and remove timing belt from camshaft sprocket.
5. Remove camshaft carrier cover.
6. Using a suitable tool, secure camshaft and remove camshaft sprocket bolt, washer and sprocket, Fig. 8.
7. Reverse procedure to install. Torque camshaft sprocket bolt to 34 ft. lbs, timing probe holder to 19 ft. lbs and camshaft carrier cover bolts to 5 ft. lbs.

CAMSHAFT

Removal

1. Disconnect battery ground cable.
2. Remove camshaft carrier cover.
3. Using tool No. J-33302 or equivalent, Fig. 6, compress valve springs and remove rocker arms.
4. Remove timing belt front cover and timing belt as described under "TIMING BELT, REPLACE".
5. Remove camshaft sprocket as described under "CAMSHAFT SPROCKET, REPLACE".
6. Disconnect spark plug wires from spark plugs, then remove distributor from engine.
7. Remove camshaft thrust plate from rear of camshaft carrier.
8. Slide camshaft rearward and remove camshaft from carrier.

Installation

1. Using tool No. J-33085 or equivalent, in-

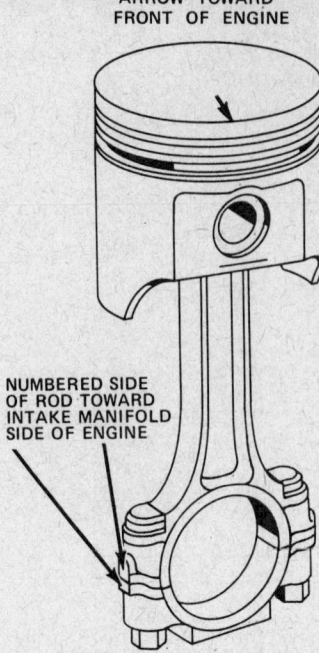

ARROW TOWARD FRONT OF ENGINE

NUMBERED SIDE OF ROD TOWARD INTAKE MANIFOLD SIDE OF ENGINE

Fig. 10 Piston & rod assembly

stall new front oil seal onto camshaft carrier.
2. Position camshaft into carrier.

NOTE: Ensure not to damage front oil seal when installing camshaft.

3. Install camshaft thrust plate and bolts. Torque bolts to 70 inch lbs.
4. Check camshaft end play. End play should be within .016 to .064 inch.
5. Install distributor, camshaft sprocket, timing belt and timing belt front cover.
6. Using tool No. J-33302 or equivalent, Fig. 6, compress valve springs and install rocker arms.
7. Install camshaft carrier cover. Torque bolts to 5 ft. lbs.

CRANKSHAFT SPROCKET, REPLACE

1. Disconnect battery ground cable.
2. Remove timing belt as described under "TIMING BELT, REPLACE".
3. Remove crankshaft sprocket bolt, washer and sprocket.
4. Reverse procedure to install. Refer to step 7 under "TIMING BELT, REPLACE" and adjust belt tension. Torque crankshaft sprocket bolt to 115 ft. lbs.

CRANKSHAFT FRONT OIL SEAL, REPLACE

1. Disconnect battery ground cable.
2. Remove crankshaft sprocket as described under "CRANKSHAFT SPROCKET, REPLACE".
3. Remove key and rear thrust washer from end of crankshaft.
4. Using a suitable tool, remove crankshaft front oil seal.
5. During installation of crankshaft front oil seal, position tool No. J-33083 or equiva-

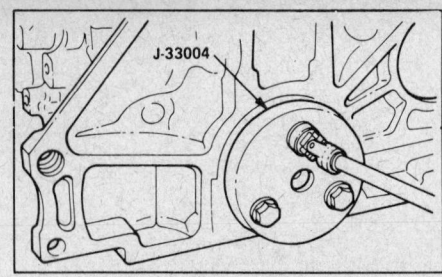

Fig. 11 Rear main bearing oil seal installation

lent, Fig. 9, onto crankshaft. Lubricate front oil seal lip and install onto crankshaft.
6. Reverse procedure to complete installation.

PISTON & ROD ASSEMBLE

Assemble piston to rod, with arrow on piston facing toward front of engine and numbered side toward intake manifold side of engine, Fig. 10. Upon installation, measure connecting rod side clearance using a suitable feeler gauge. Side clearance should be .0027 to .0095 inch.

PISTONS, PINS & RINGS

Pistons and rings are available in standard size and oversize of .020 inch (.5 mm). Piston pins are available in standard size only.

MAIN & ROD BEARINGS

Main and rod bearings are available in standard sizes and undersizes of .010 inch (.25 mm) and .020 inch (.5 mm).

REAR MAIN BEARING OIL SEAL, REPLACE

1. Remove engine from vehicle as described under "ENGINE, REPLACE".
2. On vehicles equipped with automatic transaxle, remove flywheel dust cover and flex plate to torque converter bolts.
3. Remove bell housing bolts and separate engine from transaxle assembly.
4. On vehicles equipped with automatic transaxle, remove flex plate.
5. On vehicles equipped with manual transaxle, remove pressure plate, clutch disc and flywheel.
6. Using a suitable tool, remove rear main bearing oil seal.
7. Reverse procedure to install. During installation of seal, position seal over seal pilot tool No. J-33004 or equivalent, Fig. 11. Using clean engine oil, lubricate new rear oil seal and position onto crankshaft by turning starter bolts on tool No. J-33004 in rotational sequence until rear oil seal bottoms in engine block.

OIL PAN, REPLACE

1. Disconnect battery ground cable.
2. Raise and support vehicle.
3. Remove right front wheel and right hand splash shield.
4. Remove lower A/C bracket strut rod bolt and swing aside.
5. Remove flywheel dust cover.
6. Disconnect exhaust pipe from exhaust

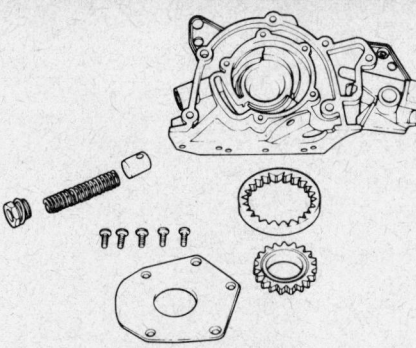

Fig. 12 Disassembled view of oil pump

manifold.
7. Drain engine oil, remove oil pan bolts and oil pan.
8. Reverse procedure to install. Using a suitable sealer, coat threads of oil pan bolts. Torque bolts to 4 ft. lbs.

OIL PUMP SCREEN & PICK-UP TUBE, REPLACE

1. Disconnect battery ground cable.
2. Remove oil pan as described under "OIL PAN, REPLACE".
3. Remove pick-up tube support bolts, pick-up tube to oil pump bolts, pick-up tube and "O" ring.
4. Reverse procedure to install. Torque pick-up tube to oil pump bolts to 5 ft. lbs. Torque pick-up tube support bolts to 5 ft. lbs.

OIL PUMP

Removal

1. Disconnect battery ground cable.
2. Remove crankshaft sprocket and timing belt rear cover.
3. Disconnect engine oil pressure switch electrical connector from the switch.
4. Remove oil pan and oil filter.
5. Remove pick-up tube to engine block bolts, pick-up tube and oil pump.

Disassemble

1. Remove five screws and rear cover from oil pump, Fig. 12.

2. Remove gears, plug, pressure regulator valve plunger and spring.
3. If necessary, remove pick-up tube and "O" ring from oil pump body.

Inspection

NOTE: After disassembling the oil pump, thoroughly clean all oil pump components and check them for excessive wear and damage.

1. Using a suitable straight edge and feeler gauge, Fig. 13, check oil pump clearances.
2. Check clearances for the following oil pump components:
   a. Clearance between idler gear and oil pump body should be .004–.007 inch.
   b. Clearance between drive gear and oil pump body should be .014–.018 inch.
   c. Clearance between gears and oil pump cover should be .002–.004 inch.
3. If clearances obtained are not within specified limits, replace worn or damaged oil pump components.

Assemble

1. Install valve plunger and spring.
2. Using a suitable sealer, coat threads of pressure regulator valve plunger plug and install. Torque plug to 15 ft. lbs.
3. Install oil pump gears into oil pump body.

Installation

1. Install gasket and oil pump onto engine. Torque oil pump bolts to 5 ft. lbs.
2. Install pick-up tube and bolts. Torque bolts to 5 ft. lbs.
3. Install oil pan and oil filter.
4. Connect engine oil pressure switch electrical connector to switch.
5. Install timing belt rear covers and crankshaft sprocket.

WATER PUMP, REPLACE

1. Disconnect battery ground cable.
2. Remove hose from water pump.
3. Remove water pump bolts, water pump, and "O" ring.
4. Reverse procedure to install.

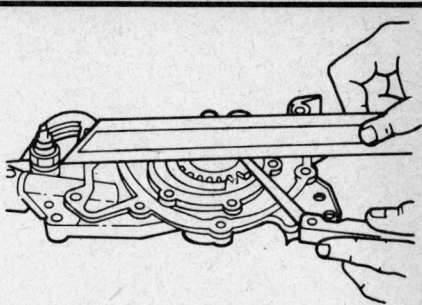

Fig. 13 Checking drive gear to oil pump housing clearance

ELECTRIC FUEL PUMP, REPLACE

1. Depressurize fuel system as follows:
   a. Remove fuel pump fuse from fuse panel.
   b. Start engine and operate until fuel supply remaining in fuel lines is consumed. Engage starter for approximately 3 seconds to ensure fuel pressure has been relieved.
   c. With ignition switch in the "OFF" position, install fuel pump fuse.

NOTE: Unless this procedure is followed before servicing fuel system, fuel spray could occur.

2. Disconnect battery ground cable.
3. Raise and support vehicle.
4. Remove fuel tank.
5. Remove fuel meter pump assembly by turning cam lock ring counterclockwise.
6. Remove fuel meter pump assembly from fuel tank and fuel pump from fuel meter.
7. Pull fuel pump upward into fuel hose while pulling outward away from bottom support.

NOTE: Do not damage rubber insulator and strainer during fuel pump removal.

8. After fuel pump assembly is clear of bottom support, pull pump assembly out of rubber connector and from vehicle.
9. Reverse procedure to install.

Turbocharger Section

DESCRIPTION

The turbocharger is used to increase power on a demand basis. As engine load increases and the throttle is opened, more air/fuel mixture is drawn into the combustion chambers. As this increased volume is burned, a larger volume of high energy exhaust gasses enters the engine exhaust system and is directed through the turbocharger turbine housing, Fig. 1. Some of the exhaust gas energy is used to increase the speed of the turbine wheel which is connected to the compressor wheel. The increased speed of the compressor wheel compresses the air/fuel mixture and delivers it to the intake manifold. The high pressure in the intake manifold allows a denser charge to enter the combustion chambers, in turn developing more engine power during the combus-

tion cycle. The intake manifold pressure (boost) is controlled to a maximum value by an exhaust gas bypass valve (wastegate). The wastegate allows a portion of the exhaust gas to bypass the turbine wheel, thereby not increasing turbine speed. The wastegate is operated by a spring-loaded diaphragm device sensing the pressure differential across the compressor. When intake manifold pressure reaches a predetermined value above ambient pressure, the wastegate begins to bypass the exhaust gas.

TROUBLESHOOTING

NOTE: Each turbocharged engine system has a distinctive sound or noise level when oper-

ating. In many cases, malfunctions can be detected when this noise level changes. If the noise changes to a higher pitch, this can indicate an air leak between air cleaner and engine or an exhaust gas leak in the exhaust system between turbocharger and engine. Noise level cycling from one level to another can indicate a plugged air cleaner, restricted turbocharger air inlet or heavy dirt build up in the compressor housing and on the compressor wheel.

Engine Lacks Power

1. Restricted air outlet duct from compressor to intake manifold.
2. Restricted intake system.

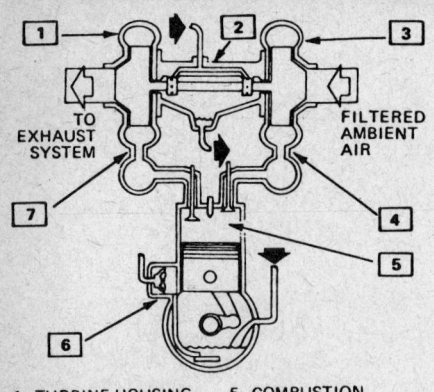

1—TURBINE HOUSING
2—CENTER HOUSING
3—COMPRESSOR HOUSING
4—INTAKE MANIFOLD
5—COMBUSTION CHAMBER
6—LUBE OIL PUMP
7—EXHAUST MANIFOLD

Fig. 1 Turbocharger operation

3. Air leak in duct from compressor to intake manifold.
4. Air leak at intake manifold to engine mating surface.
5. Restricted exhaust system.
6. Exhaust gas leak at exhaust manifold.
7. Exhaust gas leak in turbine inlet to exhaust manifold.
8. Incorrect camshaft timing.
9. Internal engine problem; engine blowby, worn or damaged pistons, rings or valves.
10. Dirt on compressor wheel and/or diffuser vanes.
11. Damaged turbocharger.

Black Exhaust Smoke

1. Restricted air intake duct to turbocharger compressor.
2. Restricted air outlet duct from compressor to intake manifold.
3. Restricted intake system.
4. Air leak in duct from compressor to intake manifold.
5. Air leak at intake manifold to engine mating surface.
6. Restricted exhaust system.
7. Exhaust gas leak in turbine inlet to exhaust manifold.
8. Incorrect camshaft timing.
9. Internal engine problem. Engine blowby, worn or damaged pistons, rings or valves.
10. Dirt on compressor wheel and/or diffuser vanes.
11. Damaged turbocharger.

Excessive Engine Oil Consumption

1. Restricted air intake duct to turbocharger compressor.
2. Air leak in duct from compressor to intake manifold.
3. Air leak in intake manifold to engine mating surface.
4. Restricted exhaust system.
5. Restricted turbocharger oil drain line.
6. Restricted PCV system.
7. Restricted turbocharger center housing.
8. Internal engine problem; engine blowby, worn or damaged pistons, rings or valves.
9. Dirt on compressor wheel and or diffuser vanes.
10. Damaged turbocharger.

Blue Exhaust Smoke

1. Restricted air intake duct to turbocharger compressor.
2. Air leak in duct from compressor to intake manifold.
3. Air leak at intake manifold to engine mating surface.
4. Restricted exhaust system.
5. Restricted turbocharger oil drain line.
6. Restricted PCV system.
7. Restricted turbocharger center housing.
8. Internal engine problem; engine blowby, worn or damaged pistons, rings or valves.
9. Dirt on compressor wheel and or diffuser vanes.
10. Damaged turbocharger.

Noisy Turbocharger

1. Restricted air intake duct to turbocharger compressor.
2. Restricted air outlet duct from compressor to intake manifold.
3. Restricted intake system.
4. Air leak in duct from compressor to intake manifold.
5. Air leak in intake manifold to engine mating surface.
6. Restricted exhaust system.
7. Exhaust gas leak in turbine inlet to exhaust manifold.
8. Exhaust gas leak in turbine outlet ducting.
9. Dirt on compressor wheel and or diffuser vanes.
10. Damaged turbocharger.

Turbocharger Noise Level Changes Constantly

1. Restricted air intake duct to turbocharger compressor.
2. Dirt on compressor wheel and or diffuser vanes.
3. Damaged turbocharger.

Oil Leak At Compressor Seal

1. Restricted air intake duct to turbocharger compressor.
2. Restricted exhaust system.
3. Exhaust gas leak at exhaust manifold.
4. Exhaust gas leak in turbine inlet to exhaust manifold.
5. Restricted turbocharger oil drain line.
6. Restricted PCV system.
7. Restricted turbocharger center housing.
8. Internal engine problem; engine blowby, worn or damaged pistons, rings or valves.
9. Dirt on compressor wheel and or diffuser vanes.
10. Damaged turbocharger.

Oil Leak At Turbine Seal

1. Restricted turbocharger oil drain line.
2. Restricted PCV system.
3. Restricted turbocharger center housing.
4. Internal engine problem; engine blowby, worn or damaged pistons, rings or valves.
5. Dirt on compressor wheel and or diffuser vanes.
6. Damaged turbocharger.

DIAGNOSIS & TESTING

Prior to performing any diagnostic or testing procedure, check all vacuum hoses and wiring for proper routing and connections, actuator linkage for freedom of movement,

1 CRACKED BLADE 2 BROKEN BLADE

Fig. 2 Checking turbocharger for cracked or broken compressor & turbine blades

wastegate linkage for damage, or any problems which may occur in a non-turbocharged engine.

CAUTION: A turbocharged engine has exhaust pipes located high in the engine compartment. Care must be taken to avoid accidental contact with hot exhaust pipes since personal injury may occur.

Wastegate Boost Pressure Test

1. Inspect actuator linkage for damage.
2. Check throttle body to wastegate hose and wastegate solenoid to actuator assembly hose for damage.
3. Tee the hand operated vacuum/pressure pump J-23738 in series with gauge J-28474 to actuator assembly, replacing wastegate solenoid to actuator assembly hose.
4. Apply pressure to the actuator assembly. At approximately 4 psi the actuator rod should move .015 inch, actuating the wastegate linkage. If not as specified, replace actuator assembly and calibrate assembly to open at 4 psi. Crimp adjustment barrel on actuator rod to maintain correct calibration.

TURBOCHARGER INTERNAL INSPECTION

1. Remove inlet and exhaust tubing from turbocharger.
2. Inspect compressor and turbine wheel for blade damage, Figs. 2 through 5.

NOTE: The compressor wheel can be inspected by looking through the compressor housing inlet opening while holding the throttle plate open. The turbine wheel can be inspected by looking between the turbine wheel blades from the exhaust outlet end of the turbine housing. Use a suitable light to check turbine blade tip condition.

3. Inspect compressor and turbine wheel outer blade tip edges for wheel rub.
4. Rotate shaft wheel assembly and check for wheel binding or drag. Push shaft to one side and rotate. Shaft should rotate smoothly.
5. Simultaneously push both ends of shaft up and down, and check for excessive journal bearing clearance. Bearing clearance will be normal when very little movement is detected. If a shaft having normal bearing clearance of .003–.006 inch is pushed up and down from one side only, the movement at shaft end could be indicated at .015–.020 inch.
6. If the shaft assembly rotates freely and no

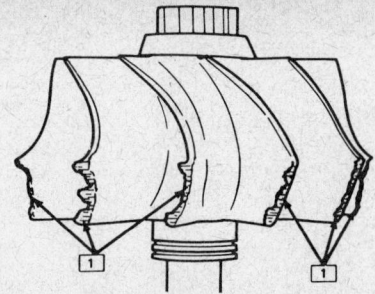

1 BLADE DAMAGE FROM FOREIGN MATERIAL

Fig. 3 Checking turbocharger blades for foreign material damage

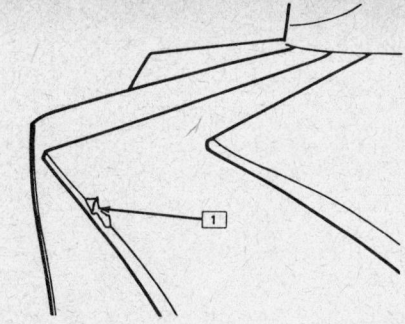

1 NICK IN BLADE

Fig. 4 Checking turbocharger blades for nicks

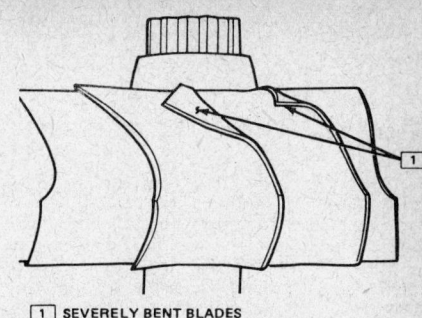

1 SEVERELY BENT BLADES

Fig. 5 Checking turbocharger for bent blades

wheel damage, binding or rub has been detected, the turbocharger is operating properly.

TURBOCHARGER FAILURE ANALYSIS & CORRECTIVE PROCEDURES

NOTE: Major causes of turbocharger failure are lack of lubrication and/or oil lag, oil contamination, oil oxidation or breakdown and foreign material in either the exhaust or intake systems.

Lack Of Lubrication & Or Oil Lag

Turbocharger failure due to lack of lubrication and/or oil lag occurs when oil pressure and flow is insufficient to lubricate the journal and thrust bearings before the turbocharger is accelerated to high speeds. The turbocharger bearings' need for oil increases as turbocharger speed and engine load increases.

Corrective Procedure
1. During first engine start-up after oil and/or oil filter change, crank engine without starting until oil filter and system are filled and engine oil pressure is obtained, or start and run engine at low idle speed until normal engine oil pressure is obtained.
2. After installation of a turbocharger, note the following:
   a. Ensure oil inlet and drain line are clean.

   NOTE: If rubber hoses are used, ensure hoses are not hardened or deteriorated. If metal lines are used, ensure lines are not restricted or collapsed.

   b. Ensure engine oil is clean and at operating level.
   c. Disconnect oil drain line at turbocharger and crank engine without starting until oil flows out of turbocharger center housing.

NOTE: A steady flow of oil indicates that any air pockets have been purged from oil system.

Oil Contamination

Under certain engine operating conditions

the oil bypasses the oil filter, which may allow contaminated oil to enter the turbocharger. Under the following conditions the oil filter may be bypassed: during cold weather when the engine oil is congealed (thickened), when oil filter is restricted, when filter bypass valve is sticking open, when filter element is ruptured, and when filter element is incorrectly installed. Contaminated or dirty oil will wear and fail turbocharger bearings faster than engine bearings due to the high rotational speed of the turbocharger shaft.

Corrective Procedure
Oil and oil filter change periods should never be extended beyond the specified oil and oil filter change intervals.

Oil Oxidation & Or Oil Breakdown

Primary causes of oil oxidation and/or oil breakdown are engine overheating, piston blowby, engine coolant leaking into oil system, wrong grade of oil used and lack of proper oil change intervals. Oil oxidation and or oil breakdown will cause sludge accumulation in the oil.

The spinning action of the turbocharger shaft throws the oil against the internal walls of the turbocharger center housing where sludge particles stick and accumulate, affecting oil drainage from the turbine and journal bearings. This will cause turbine seal leakage. The deposited sludge at the turbine end may become hardened due to high turbine temperature, wearing the turbine end journal bearing and bearing bore.

Corrective Procedure
1. When oil leakage at the turbine end of the turbocharger is found, check turbocharger oil drain tube and engine crankcase breathers for restriction. Replace oil drain tube and/or crankcase breathers as required.
2. When an engine oil sludge condition has been found, change oil and oil filter as necessary. Inspect oil drain opening and turbine shaft.

Foreign Material In Exhaust Or Intake Systems

Foreign material such as sand, dirt, and dust will damage the turbocharger compressor and turbine wheels due to their high rotational speeds. When servicing the turbocharger, ensure exhaust and intake systems are clean and turbocharger tubing connections are secure.

SERVICE

Before performing turbocharger service,

note the following general cautions:
1. Clean area around turbocharger assembly with a non-caustic solution before service. Cover opening of engine assembly connections to prevent entry of foreign material.
2. During removal of turbocharger assembly, do not bend, nick or in any way damage compressor or turbine wheel blades. Any damage may result in rotating assembly imbalance, and failure of the center housing rotating assembly and the compressor and/or turbine housing.
3. Before disconnecting center housing rotating assembly from either compressor housing or turbine housing, mark location of components for assembly in original position.

NOTE: Do not use a sharp tool to mark positions of turbocharger components. Use a piece of chalk.

Wastegate Actuator, Replace

1. Disconnect air induction tube from intake manifold and turbocharger.
2. Remove actuator rod to wastegate clip, then disconnect vacuum hose from wastegate.
3. Remove screws retaining actuator to turbocharger.
4. Remove actuator assembly.
5. Reverse procedure to install.

Turbocharger, Replace

1. Disconnect battery ground cable.
2. Raise and support vehicle.
3. Remove lower fan retaining screw, then disconnect exhaust pipe from exhaust manifold.
4. Remove rear A/C support bracket bolt, then loosen remaining bolts.
5. Remove turbocharger support bracket to engine bolt and oil drain hose from turbocharger.
6. Lower vehicle.
7. Disconnect coolant recovery line from engine and position aside.
8. Disconnect air induction tube from intake manifold and turbocharger.
9. Remove coolant fan from vehicle.
10. Remove oxygen sensor from exhaust manifold.
11. Disconnect oil feed pipe from engine.
12. Remove air intake duct from turbocharger, then disconnect vacuum hose from actuator.
13. Remove exhaust manifold retaining nuts, exhaust manifold and turbocharger assembly from engine.
14. Reverse procedure to install.

Clutch & Transaxle Section

CLUTCH PEDAL, ADJUST

The clutch is automatically adjusted by a self-adjusting mechanism, Fig. 1, mounted to the clutch pedal and bracket assembly. The clutch cable is a fixed length and cannot be shortened or lengthened, however, the position of the cable can be changed by adjusting the position of the detent in relation to the clutch pedal. This is accomplished by pulling the clutch pedal upward to the rubber bumper. This action forces the pawl against the stop and causes the pawl to be out of mesh with the detent teeth, allowing the cable to play out until the detent spring load is balanced against the load applied by the release bearing.

Inspection

1. With engine running and parking brake applied, depress clutch pedal to approximately 1/2 inch from floor mat.
2. Move shift lever between "First" and "Reverse" gears several times. If no gear clashing occurs when shifting into "Reverse", the clutch is releasing fully.
3. If the shifting in Step 2 is not smooth, the clutch is not releasing fully and the linkage should be inspected.
4. Check clutch pedal bushings for sticking or excessive wear.
5. Have an assistant depress the clutch pedal to the floor and observe clutch fork lever travel at transaxle. The end of the clutch fork lever should have a total travel of approximately 1.5 to 1.7 inches.
6. To check the self-adjusting mechanism, depress the clutch pedal and observe if the pawl firmly engages the teeth of the detent.

CLUTCH, REPLACE

1. Remove transaxle as outlined under "MANUAL TRANSAXLE, REPLACE" procedure.
2. Mark position of pressure plate to flywheel to aid reassembly.
3. Gradually loosen pressure plate to flywheel attaching bolts until spring tension is relieved.
4. Support pressure plate and remove attaching bolts, pressure plate and driven disc, Fig. 2.

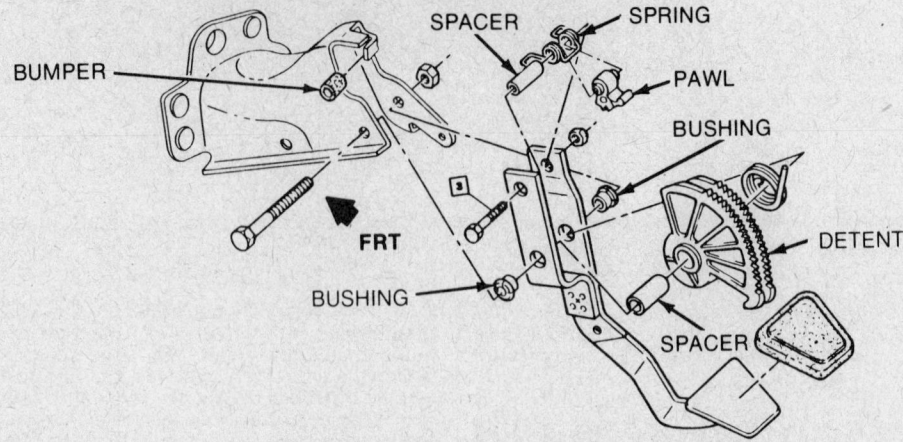

Fig. 1 Clutch self-adjusting mechanism

5. Clean pressure plate and flywheel mounting surfaces. Inspect bearing retainer outer surface of the transaxle.
6. Place pressure plate and driven disc in position and support with tool No. J-29074, Fig. 3.

NOTE: The driven disc is installed with the damper springs offset toward the transaxle. Stamped letters found on the driven disc identify the "Flywheel Side".

7. Install and gradually torque the pressure plate to flywheel attaching bolts to 15 ft. lbs. Remove support tool.
8. Lubricate the release bearing outside diameter groove and inside diameter recess.
9. Install transaxle.

MANUAL TRANSAXLE SHIFT CABLE, ADJUST

4 Speed Manual Transaxle

Shift Cable Adjustment
1. Disconnect battery ground cable.
2. Place shift lever into first gear position, then loosen shift cable nuts at levers (D) and (F), Fig. 4.
3. Remove console trim plate, then slide shift lever boot upward on shift lever.
4. Remove console assembly.
5. With shift lever in the first gear position and held against stop, insert a suitable yoke type clip to hold lever in position, Fig. 4.
6. Insert a 5/32 inch drill bit into alignment hole on side of shifter assembly, Fig. 4.
7. Rotate lever (D), Fig. 4, in direction of arrow while tightening cable retaining nut.
8. Tighten cable retaining nut at lever (F), Fig. 4.
9. Remove drill bit and yoke clip, then install console and connect battery ground cable.
10. Check shift lever for proper operation and readjust as necessary.

Shifter Shaft Washer Selection
When shift cables are properly adjusted, but improper first and second gear shifts are encountered, it may be necessary to check the shifter shaft selective thrust washer. This washer helps position the shifter shaft for proper shifter operation. Proceed as follows to determine the correct selective thrust washer thickness:

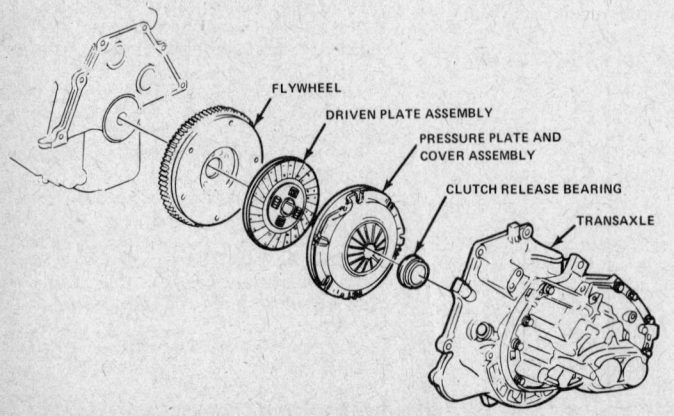

Fig. 2 Clutch assembly

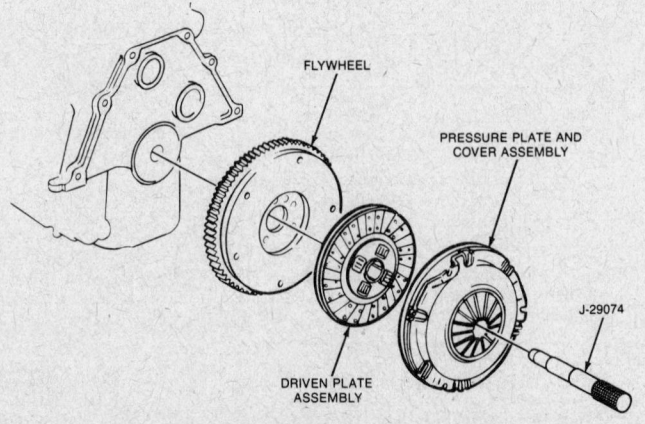

Fig. 3 Aligning clutch disc & pressure plate

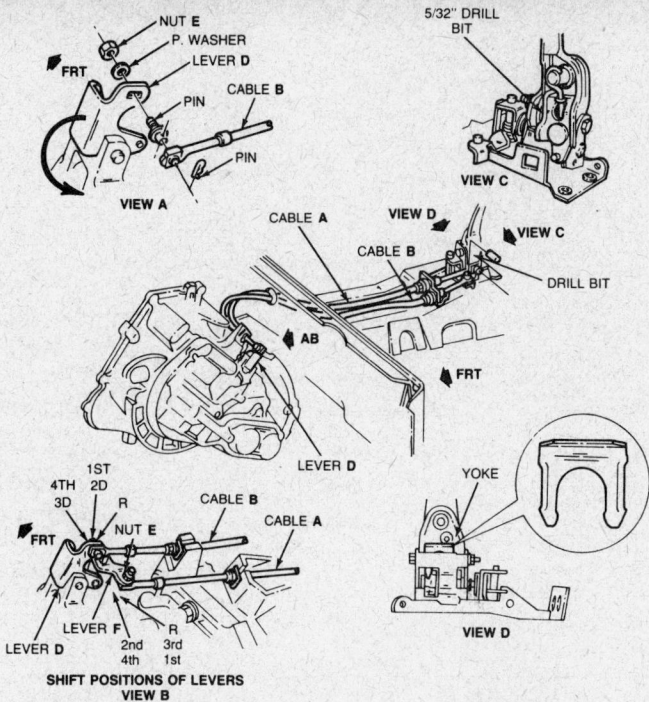

Fig. 4   Four speed manual transaxle shift cable adjustment

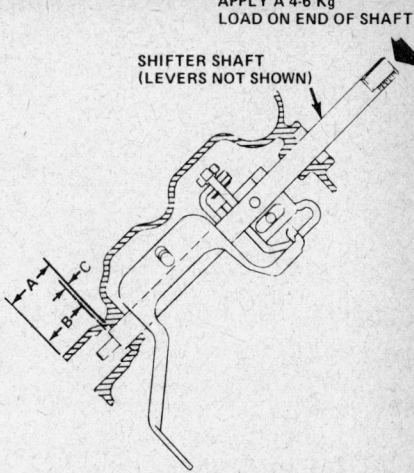

Fig. 5   Four speed manual transaxle shifter shaft selective washer measurement

Dimension "C" Fig. 5 Inch (mm)	Ident. Color & No. of Stripes	Shim Part No.
.0708 (1.8)	3 White	14008235
.0827 (2.1)	1 Orange	476709
.0945 (2.4)	2 Orange	476710
.1063 (2.7)	3 Orange	476711
.1181 (3.0)	1 Blue	476712
.1299 (3.3)	2 Blue	476713
.1417 (3.6)	3 Blue	476714
.1535 (3.9)	1 White	476715
.1654	2 White	476716

Fig. 5A   Shifter shaft selective thrust washer identification chart. Four speed manual transaxle

1. Remove reverse inhibitor fitting, spring and washer from end housing, then position shifter shaft into second gear.
2. Measure distance from end of housing to shifter shaft shoulder, dimension A, Fig. 5.
3. Apply a load of 9 to 13 lbs. to opposite end of shifter shaft, then measure distance from end of housing to shifter shaft shoulder, dimension B, Fig. 5.
4. Subtract measurement obtained in step 2 from measurement obtained in step 3, which will equal the thickness of the selective thrust washer to be installed, dimension C, Fig. 5. When selecting a thrust washer, refer to Fig. 5A.

5 Speed Manual Transaxle

1. Disconnect battery ground cable.
2. Place shift lever in third gear position, then remove lock pin (H), Fig. 6, and reinstall with tapered end of pin facing downward to lock transaxle in third gear.
3. Loosen shift cable retaining nuts at levers (G) and (F), Fig. 6.
4. Remove console trim plate and pull shifter boot upward on shift lever.
5. Remove console assembly from vehicle.
6. Insert a 5/32 inch drill bit into align hole on side of shifter assembly, Fig. 6.

7. Align shifter lever slot with slot in shifter plate, then insert a 13/16 inch drill bit.
8. Tighten nuts at levers (G) and (F), Fig. 6, then remove drill bits from alignment holes.
9. Remove lock pin (H), Fig. 6, and reinstall with tapered end facing upward.
10. Install console assembly and connect battery ground cable.
11. Check shifter for proper operation and readjust as necessary.

MANUAL TRANSAXLE, REPLACE

4 Speed Manual Transaxle

1. Disconnect battery ground cable.
2. Install engine support fixture so that one end is supported on cowl tray over the wiper motor and the other end rests on the radiator support. Connect fixture hook to engine lift ring and raise engine to relieve weight from engine mounts, Fig. 7.

CAUTION: The engine support fixture must be positioned in the center of the cowl and the attaching parts properly tightened before supporting engine. This

fixture is not intended to support entire weight of engine and transaxle. Personal injury may result from improper use of support fixture.

3. Remove heater hose clamp at transaxle mount bracket, then disconnect horn wires and remove horn assembly.

NOTE: Whenever the transaxle mount is removed, alignment bolt M6X1X65 must be installed in right front engine mount to prevent powertrain misalignment.

4. Remove transaxle mount attaching bolts. Discard mount to sideframe attaching bolts.
5. Disconnect clutch cable at clutch release lever, then remove transaxle mount bracket attaching bolts and nuts.
6. Disconnect shift cables and remove retaining clips at transaxle.
7. Disconnect ground cable at transaxle mounting stud, then remove air management valve attaching bolts to provide clearance for removal of upper right hand transaxle to engine attaching bolt. Remove four upper transaxle to engine mounting bolts.
8. Raise and support vehicle, then remove left front wheel.
9. Remove left front inner splash shield retaining screws and the splash shield.
10. Remove transaxle strut to transaxle bracket and crossmember attaching bolts and remove strut from vehicle.
11. Remove transaxle strut bracket attaching bolts and the strut bracket.
12. Remove clutch housing cover attaching bolts, then disconnect speedometer cable at transaxle.
13. Disconnect stabilizer bar at the left suspension support and control arm.
14. Using tool J-29330, separate left ball joint from steering knuckle.
15. Remove left suspension support to chassis attaching bolts, then remove the support and lower control arm as an assembly.
16. Install boot protectors at drive axles, then disengage both drive axles at transaxle. Remove left drive axle from transaxle housing bore.
17. Attach the transaxle case to a suitable jack, then remove two lower transaxle to engine mounting bolts.
18. Slide transaxle away from engine, lower

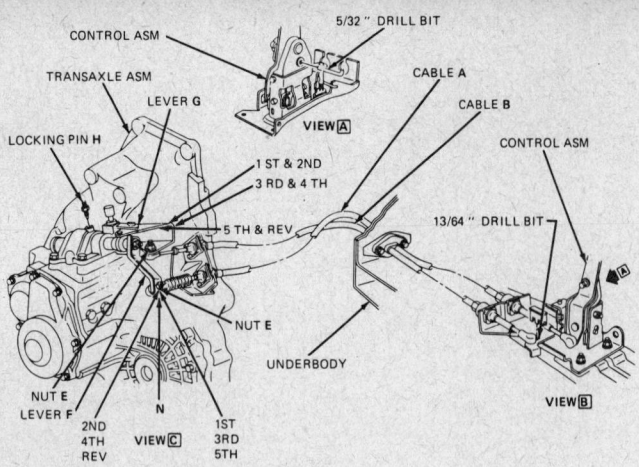

Fig. 6 Five speed manual transaxle shift cable adjustment

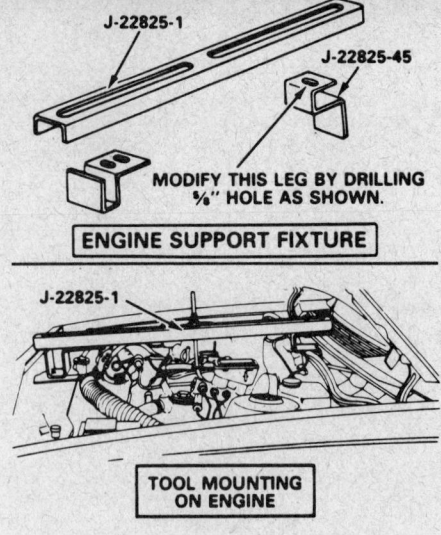

Fig. 7 Engine support fixture installation

jack and guide right drive axle from transaxle housing bore. Remove transaxle from vehicle.
19. Reverse removal procedure to install.

NOTE: When installing transaxle, guide the right drive axle into transaxle bore as transaxle is being raised. The right drive axle cannot be installed after the transaxle is connected to engine.

5 Speed Manual Transaxle

1. Disconnect battery ground cable.
2. Support engine using engine holding fixture J22825-1. Position holding fixture so that one end is supported by the cowl tray and the other end is resting on the radiator support, Fig. 7. Attach holding fixture hook to engine lifting bracket and raise engine just enough to relieve weight from engine mounts.

NOTE: The engine holding fixture must be located in center of cowl and fixture attachments properly tightened before supporting engine. This support is not designed to support the entire weight of the engine and transaxle assembly.

3. Remove transaxle mount attaching bolts.

NOTE: When removing transaxle mount, alignment bolt M6X1X65 must be installed in right front engine mount to ensure proper powertrain alignment.

4. Disconnect clutch cable at clutch fork, then remove transaxle mount bracket retaining bolts and nuts.
5. Disconnect shift cables and remove retaining clips at transaxle.
6. Disconnect ground cables at transaxle mounting stud, then remove air management valve attaching bolts to provide clearance for upper right hand transaxle to engine attaching bolt.
7. Raise and support front of vehicle, then drain transaxle fluid.
8. Remove left hand front wheel and tire assembly, then remove front inner splash shield.
9. Remove transaxle strut and strut bracket.
10. Remove clutch cover attaching bolts, then disconnect speedometer cable at trans-

axle.
11. Disconnect stabilizer bar at left hand suspension support and control arm.
12. Detach ball joint from steering knuckle.
13. Remove left hand front suspension support attaching bolts, then remove support and control arm as an assembly.
14. Install boot protectors, then disengage drive axle shafts at transaxle using tool Nos. J28468, J29794 and a suitable screwdriver. Remove left hand drive axle shaft from transaxle.
15. Secure transaxle to a suitable transaxle jack, then remove transaxle to engine attaching bolts.
16. Remove transaxle by sliding toward drivers side of vehicle (away from engine), then carefully lower jack while guiding right hand drive axle shaft out of transaxle.
17. Reverse procedure to install. When installing transaxle, carefully guide right hand drive axle shaft into transaxle bore as transaxle is being raised. The right hand drive axle shaft cannot be installed once the transaxle has been connected to the engine.

Rear Axle, Rear Suspension & Brakes Section

DESCRIPTION

The rear suspension, Fig. 1, is a semi-independent type suspension consisting of an axle assembly with trailing arms and twisting cross beam, coil springs and double action shock absorbers. A stabilizer bar is available and is attached to the inside of the axle beam and to the lower end of the control arms. A single unit hub and bearing assembly is bolted to each end of the axle assembly. The hub and bearing assembly is a sealed, non-serviceable unit and must be replaced as an assembly.

REAR AXLE, REPLACE

1. Raise vehicle and support vehicle. Support rear suspension with suitable jack.
2. Disconnect stabilizer bar at axle assembly, if equipped, Fig. 2.
3. Remove rear wheel assembly and brake drum. Do not hammer on brake drum since damage to bearings may result.
4. Remove shock absorber to lower mounting bracket attaching bolts, then disconnect shock absorbers from axle assembly, Fig. 2.
5. Disconnect parking brake cable and brake lines at axle brackets.
6. Carefully lower rear axle assembly and remove coil springs and insulators.
7. Remove control arm to underbody bracket bolts, then lower the axle assembly and remove from vehicle.
8. Remove hub to rear axle attaching bolts,

then the hubs, bearings and backing plates from rear axle assembly.
9. Reverse procedure to install and bleed brake system.

HUB & BEARING ASSEMBLY, REPLACE

1. Raise and support vehicle, then remove wheel and tire assembly and brake drum.

NOTE: Do not hammer brake drum since damage to bearing may result.

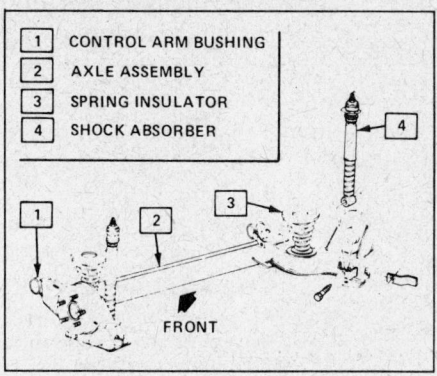

Fig. 1   Rear suspension

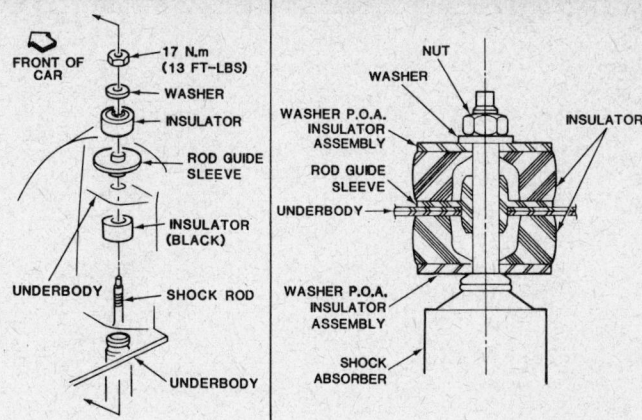

Fig. 2A   Rear shock absorber upper attachment components.

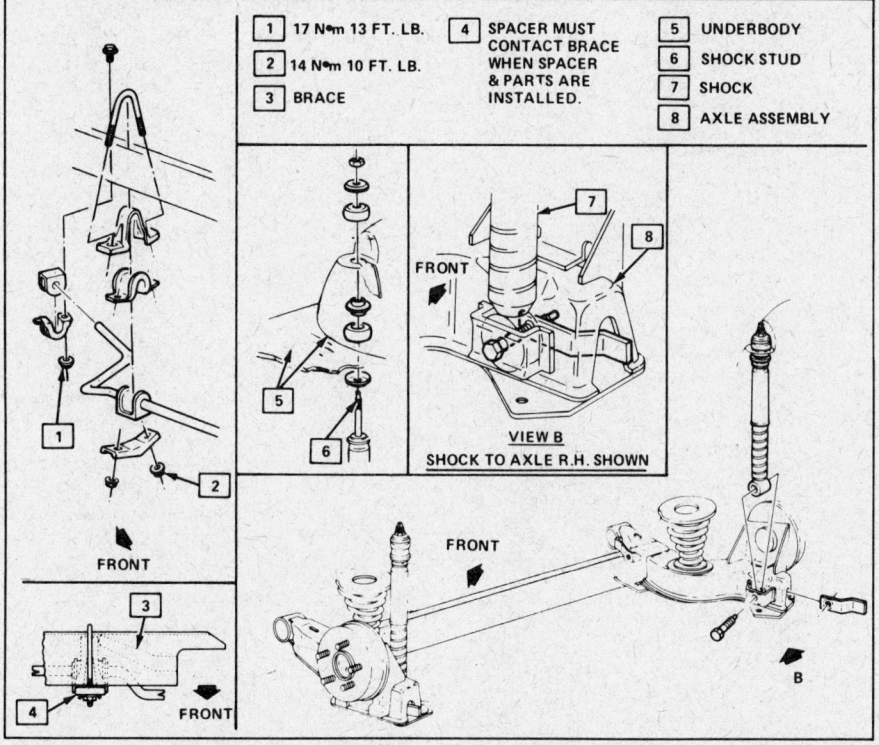

Fig. 2   Stabilizer bar & shock absorber removal

2. Remove four hub/bearing assembly to rear axle attaching bolts, then the hub/bearing assembly from axle.

NOTE: The upper rear hub attaching bolt may not clear brake shoe when removing hub and bearing assembly. Partially remove hub and bearing assembly prior to removing this bolt.

3. Reverse procedure to install. Torque hub to axle attaching bolts to 37 ft. lbs.

CAUTION: Use care not to drop hub/bearing assembly since damage to bearing may result.

SHOCK ABSORBER, REPLACE

1. Open deck lid, then remove trim cover

and shock absorber upper retaining nut.
2. Raise rear of vehicle and support rear axle using a suitable jack.
3. Remove shock absorber lower attaching bolt, then disconnect shock absorber from mounting bracket, Fig. 2. Remove shock absorber from vehicle.
4. Reverse procedure to install. Torque lower attaching bolt to 41 ft. lbs. and upper attaching nut to 13 ft. lbs.

NOTE: When installing upper shock absorber attachment components, refer to Fig. 2A, for proper installation order.

COIL SPRING, REPLACE

1. Raise and support rear of vehicle. Support rear axle using a suitable jack.
2. Remove wheel and tire assemblies.
3. Remove brake line bracket attaching-

bolts from frame, Fig. 2, and allow brake lines to hang freely.
4. Remove shock absorber to lower mounting bracket bolts, then disconnect shock absorbers from axle assembly.

CAUTION: Do not suspend rear axle by brake hoses since damage to hoses may result.

5. Carefully lower rear axle assembly and remove springs and insulators.
6. Reverse procedure to install. Position ends of upper coil in seat of body and within limits shown in Fig. 3.

CONTROL ARM BUSHING, REPLACE

1. Raise rear of vehicle and support rear axle under front side of spring seat using a suitable jack.
2. Remove wheel and tire assembly.
3. If right hand side bushing is to be replaced, disconnect brake line bracket from body. If left hand side bushing is to be replaced, disconnect brake line bracket from frame and parking brake cable at hook guide.
4. Remove control arm to mounting bracket attaching nut, bolt and washer, then allow control arm to rotate downward.
5. The bushing can now be replaced using tools shown in Figs. 4 and 5. When installing bushing, the arrow on the installer must align with arrow on the receiver, Fig. 4.
6. Reverse procedure to complete installation.

NOTE: The control arm attaching bolt must be torqued after vehicle is lowered to floor and is in its standing height position. Torque attaching bolt to 67 ft. lbs.

DRUM BRAKE ADJUSTMENTS

The rear drum brakes, have self-adjusting shoe mechanisms that assure correct lining-to-drum clearances at all times. The automatic adjusters operate only when the brakes are applied as the vehicle is moving rearward.

Although the brakes are self-adjusting, an initial adjustment is necessary after the brake

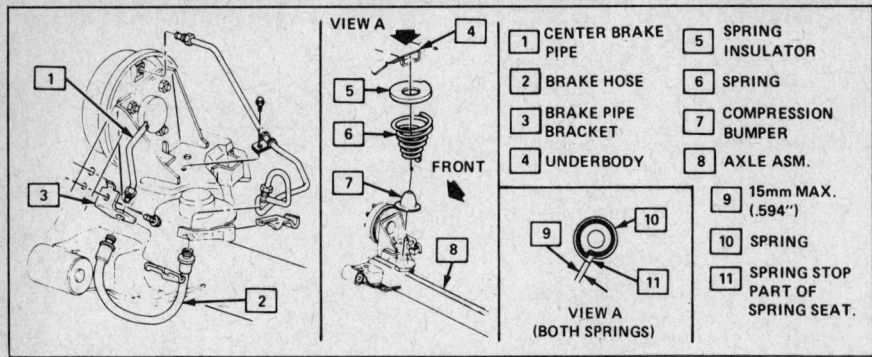

1	CENTER BRAKE PIPE	5	SPRING INSULATOR
2	BRAKE HOSE	6	SPRING
3	BRAKE PIPE BRACKET	7	COMPRESSION BUMPER
4	UNDERBODY	8	AXLE ASM.
		9	15mm MAX. (.594")
		10	SPRING
		11	SPRING STOP PART OF SPRING SEAT.

Fig. 3 Coil spring installation

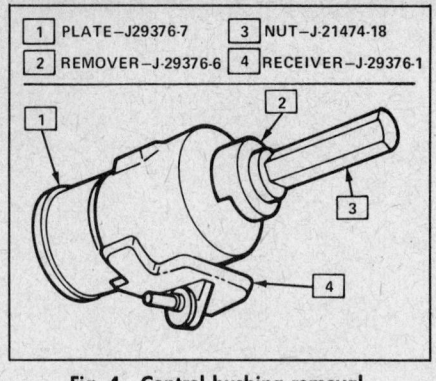

1	PLATE–J29376-7	3	NUT–J-21474-18
2	REMOVER–J-29376-6	4	RECEIVER–J-29376-1

Fig. 4 Control bushing removal

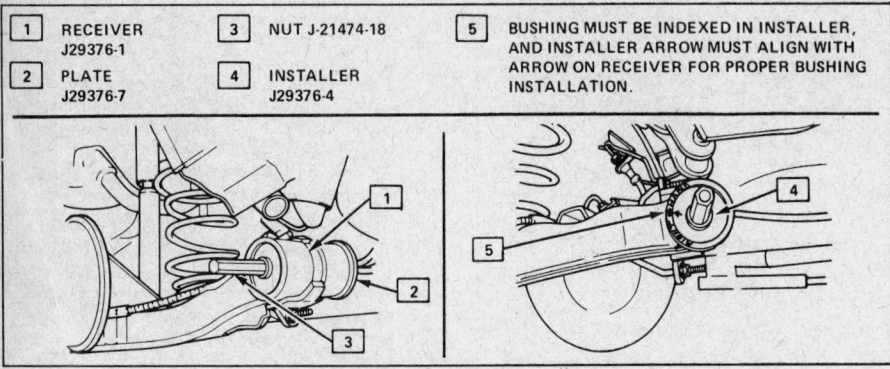

1	RECEIVER J29376-1	3	NUT J-21474-18
2	PLATE J29376-7	4	INSTALLER J29376-4

5 BUSHING MUST BE INDEXED IN INSTALLER, AND INSTALLER ARROW MUST ALIGN WITH ARROW ON RECEIVER FOR PROPER BUSHING INSTALLATION.

Fig. 5 Control arm bushing installation

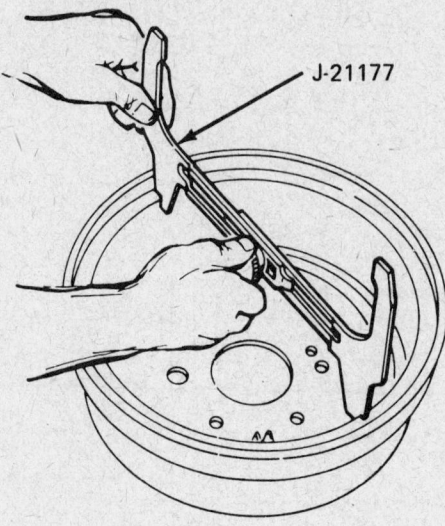

J-21177

Fig. 6 Measuring brake drum inside diameter

shoes have been replaced, or when the length of the star wheel adjuster has been changed during some other service operation.

Adjustment

1. Raise and support vehicle, then remove rear wheels and brake drums.
2. Check to make sure that parking brake cable linkage and levers on secondary brake shoe are in "free" position.
3. Using tool J-21177, measure brake drum inside diameter, Fig. 6.
4. Turn brake adjusting screw to expand shoes to diameter obtained on outside caliper portion of tool J-21177, Fig. 7.
5. Adjust parking brake.

NOTE: Whenever rear drum brakes are serviced, the parking brake linkage cable at the equalizer must always be readjusted to prevent possible damage to brake shoes.

6. Install brake drums, wheels and tires and lower vehicle to floor.
7. Drive vehicle alternately forward and backward, applying brakes moderately, to obtain satisfactory pedal height.

PARKING BRAKE, ADJUST

1. Lift parking brake lever five ratchet

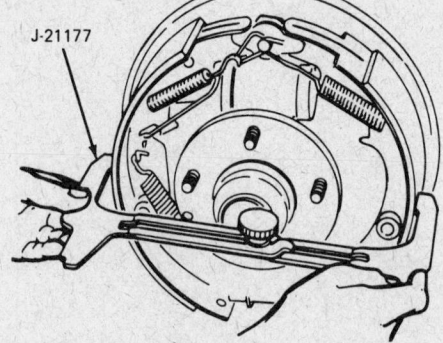

J-21177

Fig. 7 Adjusting brake shoe clearance

clicks, then raise and support rear of vehicle.
2. Tighten adjusting nut until right rear wheel can be rotated backward, but is locked when forward rotation is attempted.
3. Release parking brake lever. Both wheels should rotate freely with no brake drag.

MASTER CYLINDER, REPLACE

1. Disconnect electrical connector and four

brake lines at master cylinder.
2. Remove two master cylinder to brake booster attaching nuts, then the master cylinder from vehicle.
3. Reverse procedure to install. Bleed brake system.

POWER BRAKE UNIT, REPLACE

1. Remove master cylinder as previously described.
2. Disconnect power brake unit pushrod at brake pedal.
3. Disconnect vacuum hose from vacuum check valve. Plug vacuum hose to prevent entry of dirt.
4. Remove four power brake unit to dash panel attaching nuts, then the power brake unit from vehicle.
5. Reverse procedure to install. Torque attaching bolts to 22–33 ft. lbs.

Front Suspension & Steering Section

Refer to the Main Index for drive axle service

DESCRIPTION

The front suspension, Fig. 1, on these vehicles is of the MacPherson strut design. The lower control arms pivot from the lower side rails through rubber bushings. The upper end of the strut is isolated by a rubber mount incorporating a non-serviceable bearing for wheel turning. The tie rods connect to the steering arm on the strut, below the spring seat. The lower end of the steering knuckle pivots on a ball stud which is retained to the lower control arm by rivets and is secured to the steering knuckle with a nut and cotter pin. The sealed wheel bearings are integral with the hub and are serviced as an assembly.

WHEEL ALIGNMENT

NOTE: Toe setting is the only adjustment normally required. However, in special circumstances, such as damage due to road hazard or collision, camber may be adjusted by modifying the strut assembly.

Camber Adjustment

1. Secure bottom of strut assembly in a suit-able vise.
2. Enlarge bottom holes in outer flanges with a round file until holes in outer flanges match slots in inner flanges, Fig. 2.
3. Connect strut to steering knuckle and install bolts finger tight.
4. Grasp top of tire firmly, then move tire inboard or outboard until correct camber reading is obtained. Tighten retaining bolts enough to secure camber setting.
5. Remove wheel and tire and torque strut to steering knuckle retaining bolts to 140 ft. lbs.

Toe-Out

Toe-Out is controlled by tie rod position. Adjustment is made by loosening the clamp bolts at the steering knuckle end of the tie rods and rotating the rods to obtain proper toe setting. After correct toe setting is obtained, torque clamp bolts to 14 ft. lbs.

WHEEL BEARING, REPLACE

Removal

1. Loosen hub nut with vehicle on ground.
2. Raise and support vehicle, then remove front wheel.
3. Install drive axle protective boot cover J-28712.
4. Remove hub nut.
5. Remove brake caliper from support and suspend caliper from flame with a length of wire. Do not suspend caliper by brake hose.
6. Remove three hub and bearing attaching bolts. If the old bearing is being reinstalled, mark attaching bolts and corresponding holes for reinstallation, Fig. 3.
7. Using tool J-28733 or equivalent, remove bearing from steering knuckle, Fig. 4.

NOTE: If excessive corrosion is present, ensure that bearing is loose in the knuckle before using puller tool.

8. If installing new bearing, replace steering knuckle seal.

NOTE: Do not move drive axle until hub nut is installed and torqued to specifications.

Installation

1. Clean and inspect bearing mating sur-

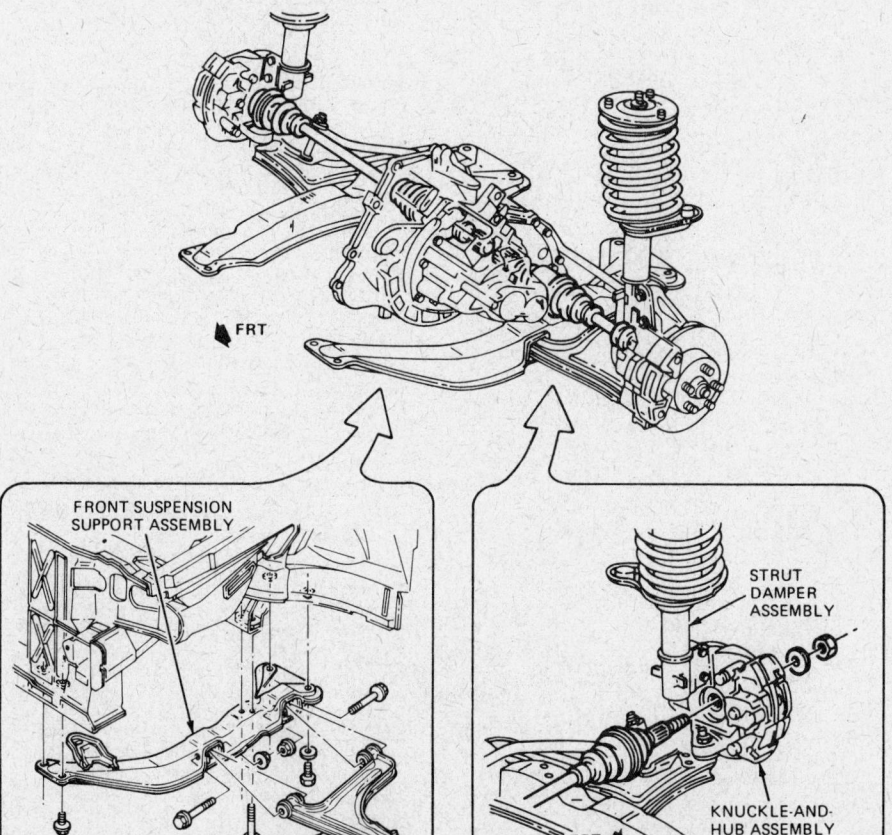

Fig. 1 Front suspension

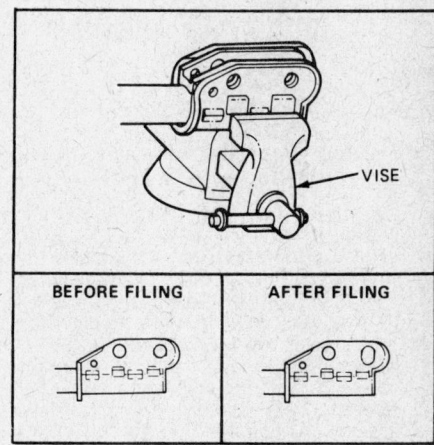

Fig. 2 Modifying strut bracket to adjust camber

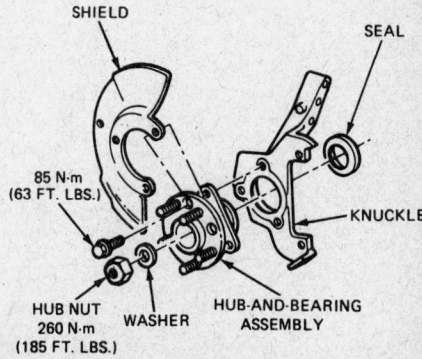

Fig. 3 Front hub & wheel bearing assembly

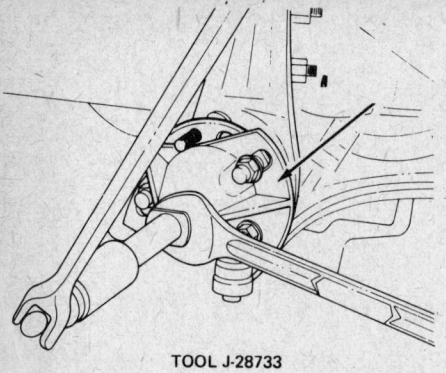

Fig. 4 Front hub & bearing assembly removal

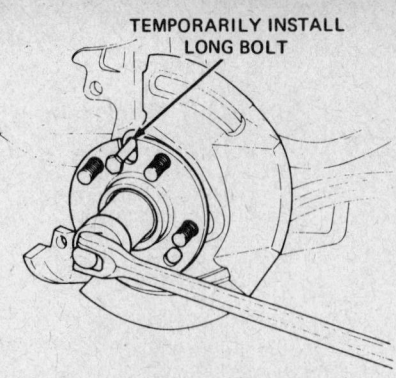

Fig. 5 Hub nut installation

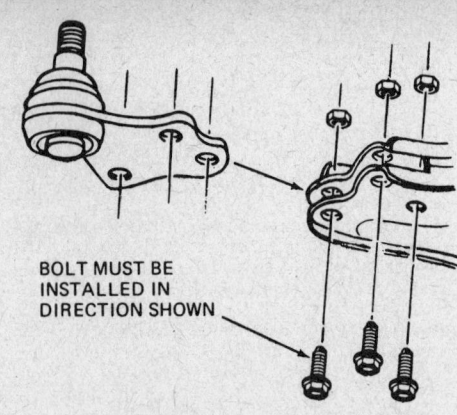

Fig. 6 Assembling lower ball joint to lower control arm

faces and steering knuckle bore for dirt, nicks and burrs.

2. If installing new steering knuckle seal, apply grease to seal and knuckle bore, then press seal into steering knuckle.
3. Push bearing onto axle shaft and install two hub to steering knuckle attaching bolts. Install a longer bolt into third mounting hole and through hub cutout. Install hub to axle retaining nut and torque to 70 ft. lbs., Fig. 5.
4. Remove long bolt and replace with original bolt. Torque hub to steering knuckle attaching bolts to 63 ft. lbs.
5. Install brake caliper and wheel assembly.
6. Lower vehicle and torque hub to axle nut to 185 ft. lbs.

LOWER BALL JOINT, REPLACE

1. Raise and support vehicle, then remove wheel and tire.
2. Locate center of rivet body and mark with a center punch.
3. Using a 1/8 inch drill, drill pilot holes completely through the rivets. Using a 1/2 inch drill, drill final holes through rivets to ensure fitting of new ball joint.
4. Remove ball joint stud retaining nut, then, using tool J-29330, separate ball joint from steering knuckle. Remove ball joint from lower control arm.
5. Assemble new ball joint to lower control arm with bolts provided in service package, Fig. 6. Torque bolts to 50 ft. lbs.
6. Insert ball joint stud into steering knuckle and torque nut to 55 ft. lbs.
7. Install wheel and tire, check toe setting and adjust as required.

LOWER CONTROL ARM & BUSHING, REPLACE

1. Raise and support vehicle, then remove wheel and tire.
2. Disconnect stabilizer bar at lower control arm and control arm support.
3. Using tool J-29330, separate ball joint from steering knuckle.
4. Remove control arm support to chassis retaining bolts and remove control arm support and control arm as an assembly.
5. Separate control arm from support, then using tools shown in Fig. 7, remove bushings from control arm.
6. Lubricate new bushings and install into control arm using tools in Fig. 7.
7. Attach lower control arm to control arm support and torque pivot bolts to 67 ft. lbs.
8. Install control arm support to chassis, using attaching bolt tightening sequence shown in Fig. 8. Torque bolts to 63 ft. lbs.
9. Reverse procedure to complete installation. Check toe setting and adjust as required.

STEERING KNUCKLE, REPLACE

1. Raise and support vehicle, then remove wheel and tire.
2. Remove front hub and bearing as outlined under "WHEEL BEARING, REPLACE" procedure.
3. Using tool J-29330, separate ball joint from steering knuckle.

4. Remove strut to steering knuckle attaching bolts, then disconnect strut from steering knuckle.
5. Assemble strut to new steering knuckle and install attaching bolts finger tight.
6. Insert ball joint stud into steering knuckle and torque stud nut to 55 ft. lbs.
7. Torque strut to steering knuckle attaching bolts to 140 ft. lbs.
8. Reverse removal procedure to complete installation.

STABILIZER BAR & BUSHINGS, REPLACE

1. Raise and support vehicle, allowing control arms to hang freely.
2. Remove left front wheel and tire.
3. Disconnect stabilizer bar at control arms and control arm supports.
4. Remove rear and center control arm support bolts, lower support assembly and remove stabilizer bar through left side of vehicle.
5. Install stabilizer bar bushing with slit facing toward front of vehicle, Fig. 9.
6. Holding stabilizer bar approximately 2 1/4 inches above support assembly, torque stabilizer bar to control arm support attaching bolts to 20 ft. lbs, Fig. 9.
7. Install stabilizer bar to lower control arm and torque attaching bolts to 15 ft. lbs, Fig. 9.

STRUT ASSEMBLY, REPLACE

1. Raise hood and remove strut protective

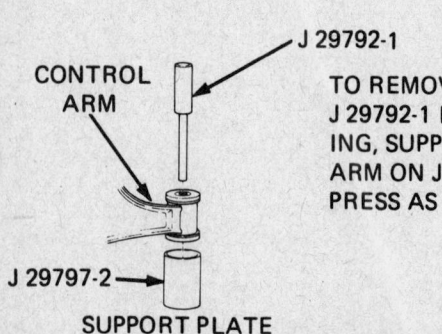

CONTROL ARM

J 29792-1

TO REMOVE, INSERT J 29792-1 INTO BUSHING, SUPPORT CONTROL ARM ON J 29792-2, AND PRESS AS SHOWN.

J 29797-2

SUPPORT PLATE

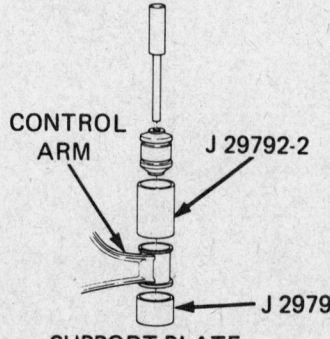

CONTROL ARM

J 29792-2

J 29792-3

SUPPORT PLATE

TO INSTALL, SUPPORT CONTROL ARM ON J 29792-3, PLACE BUSHING INTO J 29792-2, AND PRESS BUSING INTO CONTROL ARM USING J 29792-1. LUBRICATE BUSHING.

Fig. 7 Replacing lower control arm bushing

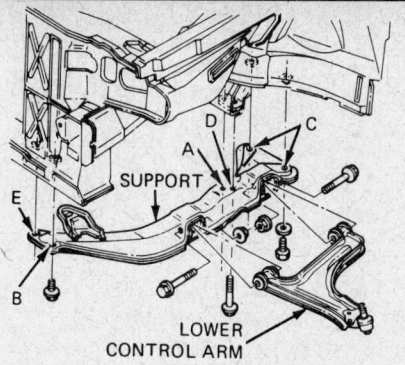

1. LOOSELY INSTALL CENTER BOLT INTO HOLE (A).
2. LOOSELY INSTALL TIE BAR BOLT INTO OUTBOARD HOLE (B).
3. INSTALL BOTH REAR BOLTS INTO HOLES (C) TORQUE REAR BOLTS.
4. INSTALL BOLT INTO CENTER HOLE(D), THEN TORQUE.
5. TORQUE BOLT IN HOLE (A).
6. INSTALL BOLT INTO FRONT HOLE (E), THEN TORQUE.
7. TORQUE BOLT IN HOLE (B).

Fig. 8   Replacing lower control arm

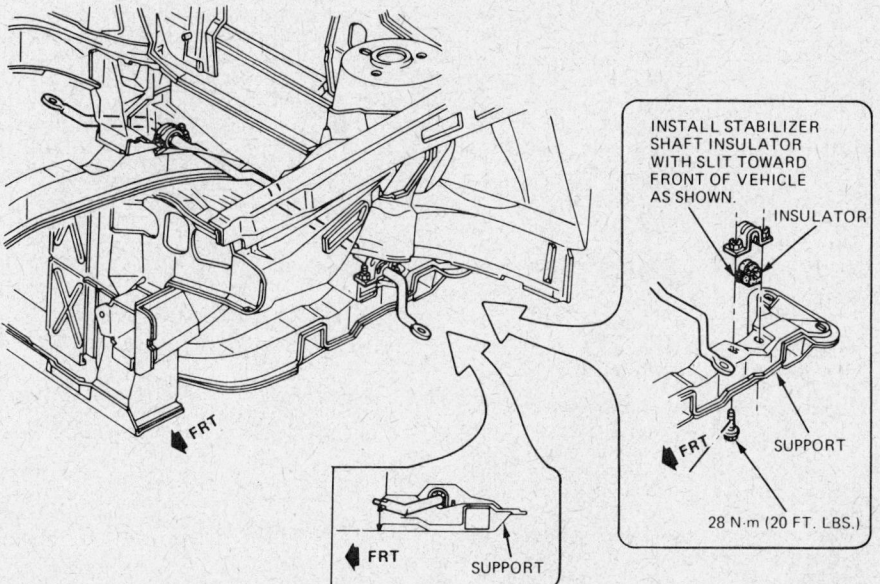

Fig. 9   Stabilizer bar installation

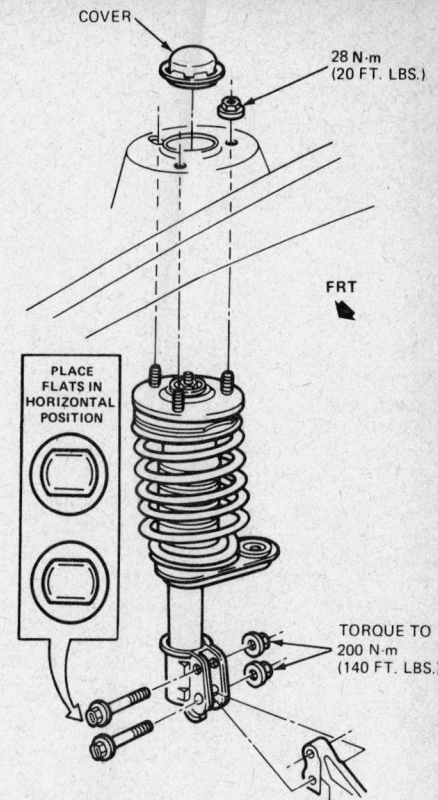

Fig. 10   Installing strut assembly

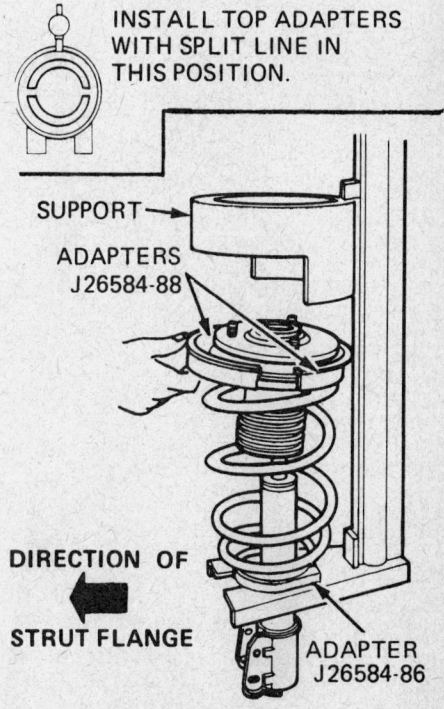

Fig. 11   Removing damper & coil spring from strut

cap and three strut to body attaching nuts.
2. Raise and support vehicle, allowing suspension to hang freely.
3. Remove wheel and tire, then install drive axle protective cover, J-28712.
4. Using tool J-24319, disconnect tie rod from strut assembly.
5. Remove strut to steering knuckle attaching bolts, then remove strut from vehicle.
6. Reverse procedure to install. Position flats of strut mounting bolts as shown in Fig. 10. Torque all nuts and bolts to specifications.

STRUT ASSEMBLY SERVICE

Disassembly

1. Clamp strut compressor tool J-26584 in a suitable vise.
2. Place strut assembly in compressor tool and install bottom adapter J-26584-86, making sure that adapter captures strut and locating pins are fully engaged, Fig. 11.
3. Rotate strut assembly to align top mounting assembly lip with strut compressor support notch.

4. Insert J-26584-88 top adapters between top mounting assembly and top spring seat. Position top adapters so that split line is perpendicular to spring compressor, Fig. 11.
5. Rotate compressor forcing screw clockwise until top support flange contacts top adapters. Continue rotating forcing screws until strut spring is compressed approximately ½ inch.

CAUTION: Do not bottom the spring or strut damper rod.

6. Remove damper top nut, then remove strut mounting assembly from damper shaft.
7. Rotate forcing screw counterclockwise to relieve spring tension, then remove spring from strut assembly.

Strut Cartridge Replacement

1. Clamp strut assembly firmly in a suitable vise. Do not overtighten.
2. Install pipe cutter at cut line groove located at top of strut damper. Cut around groove until reservoir tube is cut completely through, Fig. 12.
3. Remove and discard end cap, cylinder and piston rod assembly.

4. Place flaring cup tool, provided in service package, onto open end of reservoir tube and strike with hammer until cup flat outer surface rests on reservoir tube.

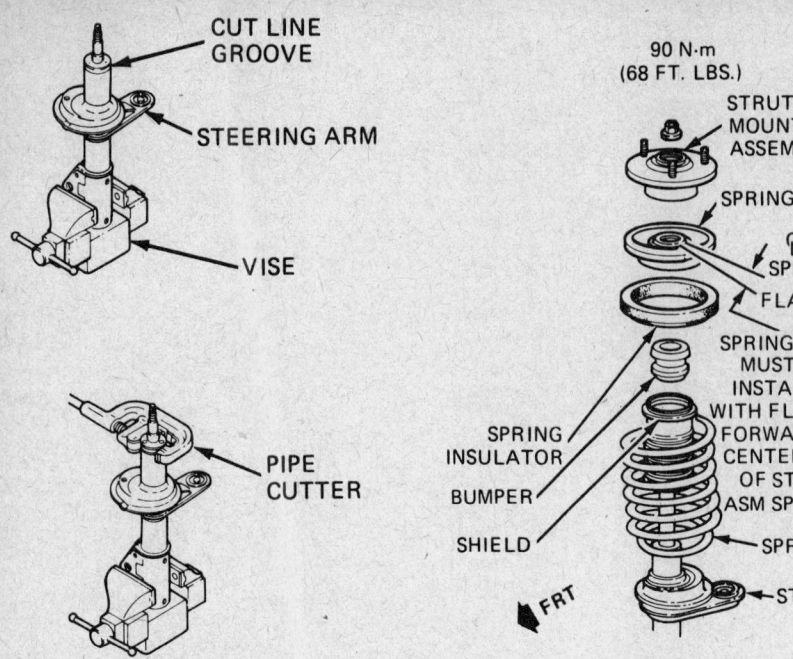

Fig. 12   Strut reservoir tube removal

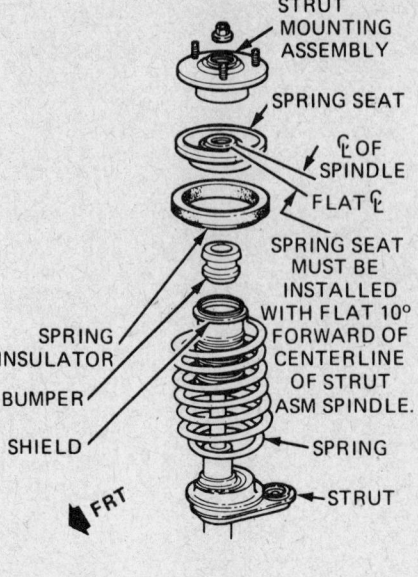

Fig. 13   Strut coil spring & upper mounting installation

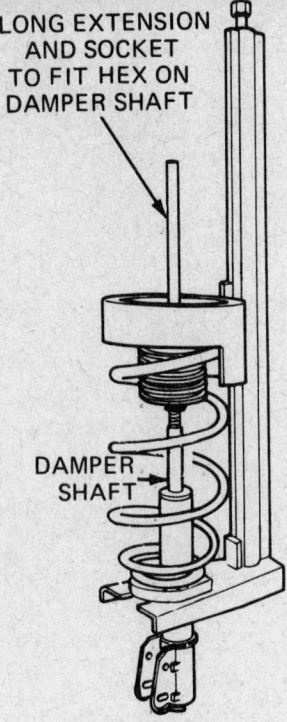

Fig. 14   Aligning strut assembly

5. Install strut carriage into reservoir tube and align grooves on cartridge base with pads at bottom of reservoir tube.
6. Using tool J-29778, torque cartridge retaining hex nut to 140–170 ft. lbs.

Assembly

1. Perform Steps 1 & 2 as outlined in the "Disassembly" procedure.
2. Rotate strut assembly until mounting flange is facing outward, opposite compressor forcing screw.
3. Position spring on strut, making sure spring is properly seated on bottom spring plate, Fig. 13.
4. Install strut spring seat assembly and J26584-88 top adapters over strut spring.
5. Turn compressor forcing screw until compressor top support contacts top adapters.
6. Install a long extension and socket onto hex on damper shaft to align components during installation, Fig. 14.
7. Compress spring until approximately 1½" of damper shaft extends through spring plate.
8. Remove extension and socket, then position top mounting assembly over damper shaft and install retaining nut. Torque

retaining nut to 68 ft. lbs.
9. Turn forcing screw counterclockwise and remove strut assembly from compressor.

MANUAL STEERING GEAR, REPLACE

1. Disconnect battery ground cable.
2. Remove left hand sound insulator.
3. From under instrument panel, pull downward on steering column seal, then remove upper pinch bolt from flexible coupling.
4. Remove air cleaner, then remove wind-

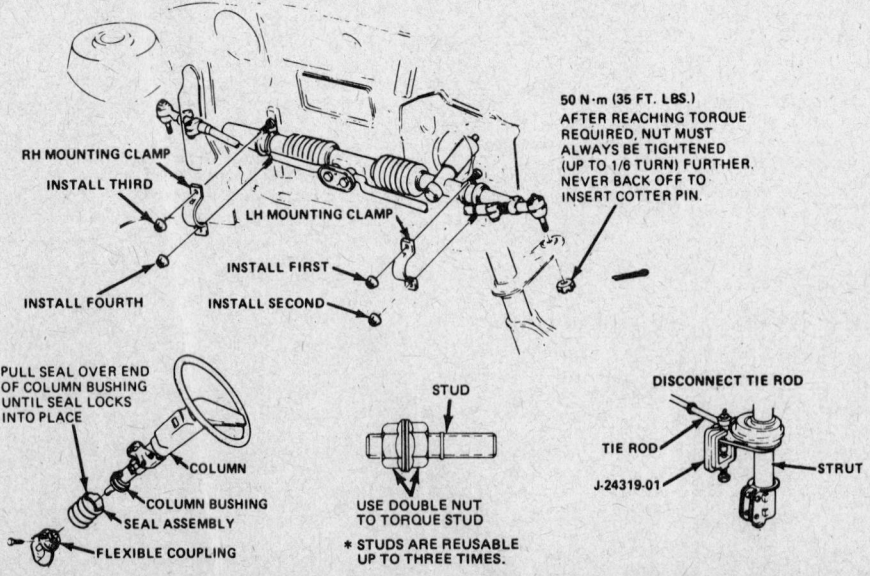

Fig. 15   Power rack & pinion steering gear removal

shield washer reservoir attaching screws and position reservoir aside.

5. Raise and support front of vehicle, then remove both front wheel and tire assemblies.
6. Disconnect tie rods from struts using tool No. J24319-01, then lower vehicle.
7. Remove steering gear mounting clamps, Fig. 15.
8. Move steering gear assembly slightly forward, then remove lower pinch bolt from flexible coupling and detach coupling from steering gear stub shaft.
9. Remove dash panel seal from steering gear.
10. Raise and support front of vehicle, then remove splash shield from left inner fender.
11. Place left hand knuckle and hub assembly in the full left turn position, then remove steering gear through access hole in left hand inner fender.
12. Reverse procedure to install. If steering gear mounting clamp studs have backed out during removal, install double nuts on stud and torque stud to 15 ft. lbs. Torque coupling to stub shaft pinch bolt to 29 ft. lbs. and coupling to steering column shaft pinch bolt to 30 ft. lbs. Torque steering gear mounting clamp attaching nuts to 28 ft. lbs. Torque tie rod to strut attaching nuts to 35 ft. lbs. The tie rod to strut attaching nuts can be tightened up to an additional 1/6 turn to allow installation of cotter pin.

POWER STEERING GEAR, REPLACE

1. Disconnect battery ground cable.
2. Remove left hand sound insulator.
3. From under instrument panel, pull downward on steering column seal, then remove upper pinch bolt from flexible coupling.
4. Remove air cleaner, then remove windshield washer reservoir attaching screws and position reservoir aside.

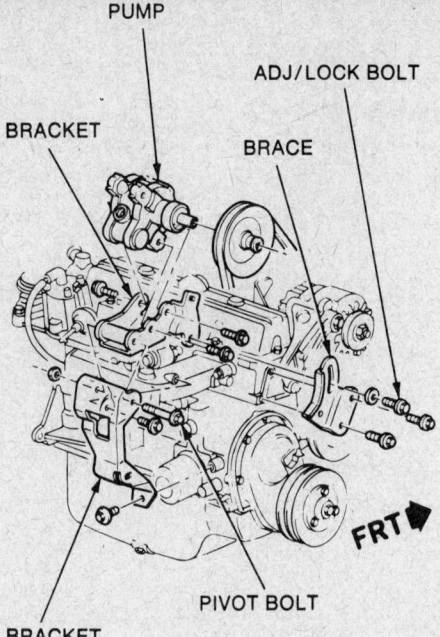

Fig. 16   Power steering pump removal

5. Disconnect pressure line from steering gear and remove screw attaching line bracket to cowl.
6. Raise and support front of vehicle, then remove both front wheel and tire assemblies.
7. Disconnect tie rods from struts using tool No. J24319-01, then lower vehicle.
8. Remove steering gear mounting clamps, Fig. 15.
9. Move steering gear slightly forward, then disconnect return line from gear and drain power steering fluid.
10. Remove lower pinch bolt from flexible coupling, then detach coupling from steering gear stub shaft and remove dash seal.
11. Raise and support front of vehicle, then remove splash shield from left inner fender.
12. Place steering knuckle and hub assembly into the full left turn position, then remove steering gear through access hole in left hand inner fender.
13. Reverse procedure to install. If steering gear mounting clamps have backed out during removal, install double nuts on stud and torque to 15 ft. lbs. Torque coupling to stub shaft pinch bolt to 37 ft. lbs. and coupling to steering column shaft pinch bolts to 30 ft. lbs. Torque steering gear mounting clamp attaching nuts to 28 ft. lbs. Torque pressure and return line fittings to 20 ft. lbs. Torque tie rod to strut attaching nuts to 35 ft. lbs. The tie rod to strut attaching nuts can be tightened up to an additional 1/6 turn to allow installation of cotter pin.

POWER STEERING PUMP, REPLACE

1. Remove air cleaner assembly.
2. Disconnect reservoir to pump hose and pressure line from pump.
3. Remove clip attaching pressure line to pump.
4. Loosen pump pivot and adjusting bolts, then remove pump drive belt.
5. Remove three pump to bracket attaching bolts, Fig. 16.

NOTE: On some models, the pump may be attached to bracket by special bolts. To remove these special bolts, use tool No. T-45 or equivalent.

6. Remove pump from mounting bracket.
7. Reverse procedure to install.

1980–84
CHEVROLET CITATION · BUICK SKYLARK
OLDSMOBILE OMEGA · PONTIAC
PHOENIX

INDEX OF SERVICE OPERATIONS

NOTE: Refer to the front of this manual for vehicle manufacturer's special service tool suppliers.

SERIAL NUMBER LOCATION

On top of instrument panel, left front.

ENGINE NUMBER LOCATION

On 4-151 engine, the engine code stamping is located on pad at left front of cylinder block below cylinder head. On V6-173, the engine code label is located at front and rear of left rocker arm cover.

ENGINE V.I.N. CODE

On 1980 vehicles, the fifth digit in the V.I.N. denotes engine code. On 1981–84 vehicles, the eighth digit in the V.I.N. denotes engine code.

ENGINE IDENTIFICATION CODE

4-151 engine are identified by code letters on pad. V6-173 are identified by code letters immediately following the engine number.

Year	Engine	V.I.N. Code	Code
1980	4-151①②	5	WA, WB
	4-151①③	5	XA, XB
	4-151②④	5	AC, AU
	4-151③	5	Z4, Z6, Z9
	V6-173①②	7	CNF, CNH
	V6-173①③	7	CNJ, CNK
	V6-173②④	7	CNL, CNM

Year	Engine	V.I.N. Code	Code
	V6-173③④	7	CNR, CNS
	V6-173	7	DDB, DCZ
1981	4-151③	5	WAN, WAO
	4-151②	5	WAL, WAM
	V6-173③	X	DBB, DBD
	V6-173③	X	DBA, DBC
	V6-173③	X	DBN, DBS
	V6-173③	Z	DJD, DJF
	V6-173③	Z	DBU, DBX
1982	4-151②	R	3L, 3M
	4-151③	R	3P, 3S
	4-151③	R	X3K, X33
	V6-173①②	X	CAY, CBC
	V6-173③	X	CBJ, CBK
	V6-173①②	X	CBT, CBE
	V6-173①③	X	CBU, CBX

Year	Engine	V.I.N. Code	Code
	V6-173②④	X	CBA, CBF
	V6-173①②	Z	CAM, CJJ
	V6-173③	Z	CJK, CJS
	V6-173③	Z	CAN, CAU
	V6-173②④	Z	CAR, CJM
1983	4-151②	R	YAL
	4-151③	R	YAA, YAP
	V6-173②	X	DCB, DCF
	V6-173③	X	DCD, DCH
	V6-173②	Z	DFA, DTB
	V6-173③	Z	DFB, DFC
	V6-173③	Z	DTA, DTC

①—Except Calif.
②—Man. trans.
③—Auto. trans.
④—California.

GRILLE IDENTIFICATION

1980 Buick Skylark

1980 Buick Skylark Sport Coupe

1980 Chevrolet Citation

1980 Oldsmobile Omega

1980 Pontiac Phoenix

1981 Buick Skylark

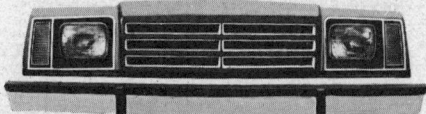

1981 Buick Skylark Sport Coupe

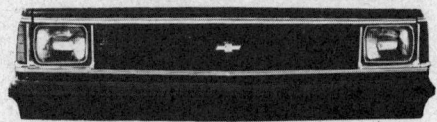

1981–84 Chevrolet Citation "X-11"

1981–83 Oldsmobile Omega "ES"

1981 Pontiac Phoenix

1981–83 Chevrolet Citation Exc. "X-11"

1982 Oldsmobile Omega Exc. "ES"

Continued

GRILLE IDENTIFICATION—Continued

1982–83 Buick Skylark
Exc. "T" Type

1983 Buick Skylark "T" Type

1983 Oldsmobile Omega
Exc. "ES"

1983 Pontiac Phoenix

1984 Buick Skylark Exc. "T" Type

1984 Buick Skylark "T" Type

1984 Chevrolet Citation Exc. "X-11"

1984 Oldsmobile Omega Exc. "ES"

1984 Oldsmobile Omega "ES"

1984 Pontiac Phoenix "LE"

GENERAL ENGINE SPECIFICATIONS

Year	Engine CID①/Liter	Engine V.I.N. Code②	Carburetor	Bore and Stroke	Compression Ratio	Net H.P. @ R.P.M.③	Maximum Torque Lbs. Ft. @ R.P.M.	Normal Oil Pressure Pounds
1980	4-151, 2.5L	5	2SE, 2 Bbl.④⑤	4.0 × 3.0	8.3	90 @ 4000	134 @ 2400	36–41
	V6-173, 2.8L	7	2SE, 2 Bbl.④⑤	3.5 × 3.0	8.6	115 @ 4800	150 @ 2000	30–45
1981	4-151, 2.5L	5	2 Bbl.④	4.0 × 3.0	8.2	84 @ 3600	125 @ 2400	30–45
	V6-173, 2.8L	X	2 Bbl.④	3.5 × 3.0	8.5	110 @ 4800	145 @ 2400	30–45
	V6-173, 2.8L	Z	2 Bbl.④	3.5 × 3.0	8.9	135 @ 5400	142 @ 2400	30–45
1982	4-151, 2.5L	R	T.B.I.⑥	4.0 × 3.0	8.2	90 @ 4000	134 @ 2400	37.5
	V6-173, 2.8L	X	E2SE, 2 Bbl.④	3.5 × 3.0	8.5	112 @ 5100	148 @ 2400	50–65
	V6-173, 2.8L H.O.	Z	E2SE, 2 Bbl.④	3.5 × 3.0	8.9	135 @ 5400	142 @ 2400	50–65
1983	4-151, 2.5L	R	T.B.I.⑥	4.0 × 3.0	8.2	90 @ 4000	134 @ 2800	37.5
	V6-173, 2.8L	X	E2SE, 2 Bbl.④	3.5 × 3.0	8.5	112 @ 4800	145 @ 2100	50–65
	V6-173, 2.8L H.O.	Z	E2SE, 2 Bbl.④	3.5 × 3.0	8.9	130 @ 5400	145 @ 2400	50–65
1984	4-151, 2.5L	R	T.B.I.⑥	4.0 × 3.0	8.2	92 @ 4400	132 @ 2800	37.5
	V6-173, 2.8L	X	E2SE, 2 Bbl.④	3.5 × 3.0	8.5	112 @ 4800	145 @ 2100	50–65
	V6-173, 2.8L H.O.	Z	E2SE, 2 Bbl.④	3.5 × 3.0	8.9	130 @ 5400	145 @ 2400	50–65

①—CID—cubic inch displacement.
②—On 1980 vehicles the fifth digit in the VIN denotes engine code. On 1981–82 vehicles the eighth digit denotes engine code.
③—Ratings are net—as installed in vehicle.
④—Rochester.
⑤—Model E2SE used on vehicles equipped with C-4 system.
⑥—Throttle body injection.

TUNE UP SPECIFICATIONS

The following specifications are published from the latest information available. This data should be used only in the absence of a decal affixed in the engine compartment.

★ When using a timing light, disconnect vacuum hose or tube at distributor and plug opening in hose or tube so idle speed will not be affected.

● When checking compression, lowest cylinder must be within 70 percent of highest.

▲ Before removing wires from distributor cap, determine location of the No. 1 wire in cap, as distributor position may have been altered from that shown at the end of this chart.

Spark plug types shown in this chart are recommendations of the original vehicle manufacturer and not MOTOR. Check local sources for other spark plug manufacturers listings.

Year & Engine/V.I.N.	Spark Plug Type	Gap	Firing Order Fig. ▲	Ignition Timing BTDC①★ Man. Trans.	Auto. Trans.	Mark Fig.	Curb Idle Speed② Man. Trans.	Auto. Trans.	Fast Idle Speed Man. Trans.	Auto. Trans.	Fuel Pump Pressure
1980											
4-151/5 Exc. Calif.	R43TSX	.060	A	10°	10°	B	1000/1300	650/900D	2200	2600	6½–8
4-151/5 Calif.	R43TSX	.060	A	10°	10°	B	1000/1200	650/900D	2200	2600	6½–8
V6-173/7 Exc. Calif.	R44TS	.045	C	2°	6°	D	750/1200	③	1900	2000	6–7½
V6-173/7 Calif.	R44TS	.045	C	6°	10°	D	750	④	2000	2000	6–7½
1981											
4-151/5	R44TSX	.060	E	4°	4°	B	800/1000	550/675D	2600	2600	6½–8
V6-173/X⑤	R43TS⑥	.045	C	6°	10°	D	850/1100	600/850D	⑦	2600	6–7½
V6-173/Z H.O.⑧	R43TS⑥	.045	C	—	10°	D	—	650/850D	—	2400	6–7½
1982											
4-151/R	R44TSX	.060	E	8°⑨⑩	8°⑨⑩	B	⑪	⑪	⑪	⑪	—
V6-173/X Exc. H.O.	R43TS⑥	.045	C	10°	10°	D	800/1050	600/800D	⑦	2600	6–7½
V6-173/Z H.O.⑧	R42TS	.045	C	6°	10°	D	850/1100	750/900D	2600	2800	6–7½
1983											
4-151/R	R44TSX	.060	E	8°⑨⑩	8°⑨⑩	B	⑪	⑪	⑪	⑪	—
V6-173/X Exc. H.O.	R43CTS	.045	C	10°	10°	D	775	600D	2500N	2500N	6–7½
V6-173/Z H.O.⑧	R42CTS	.045	C	10°	10°	D	800	725D	2600N	2700N	6–7½
1984											
4-151/R	R44TSX	.060	E	—	—	B	—	—	—	—	—
V6-173/X Exc. H.O.	R43CTS	.045	C	—	—	D	—	—	—	—	6–7½
V6-173/Z H.O.⑧	R42CTS	.045	C	—	—	D	—	—	—	—	6–7½

①—BTDC—Before top dead center.
②—Idle speed on man. trans. vehicles is adjusted in Neutral & on auto. trans. equipped vehicles is adjusted in Drive unless otherwise specified. Where two idle speeds are listed, the higher speed is with the A/C or idle solenoid energized.
③—Less A/C, 700D RPM; with A/C, 700/850D RPM.
④—Less A/C, 700D RPM; with A/C, 700/800D RPM.
⑤—Except Citation X-11 models
⑥—R42TS recommended for heavy duty operation.
⑦—Models less A/C, 2400 RPM; models with A/C 2600 RPM.
⑧—High output engine.
⑨—At 1050 RPM.
⑩—Ground diagnostic connector located under dash. The check engine light should flash on and off when in diagnostic mode. Check average ignition timing of cylinder Nos. 1 and 4, and reset as necessary. After completing ignition timing check, remove ground from diagnostic connector and ensure that check engine light is off.
⑪—Idle speed controlled by an electronic control module.

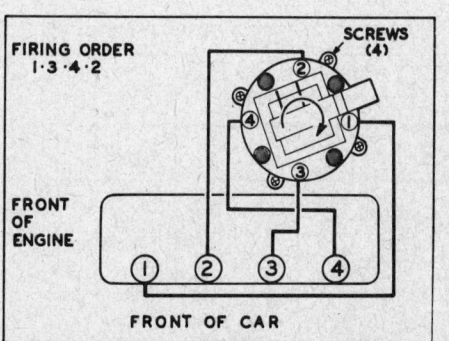

FIRING ORDER 1·3·4·2
SCREWS (4)
FRONT OF ENGINE
FRONT OF CAR

Fig. A

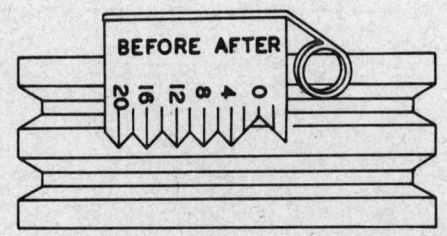

BEFORE AFTER

Fig. B

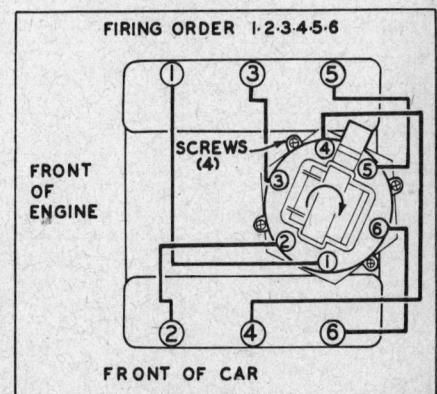

FIRING ORDER 1·2·3·4·5·6
SCREWS (4)
FRONT OF ENGINE
FRONT OF CAR

Fig. C

Continued

TUNE UP SPECIFICATION NOTES—Continued

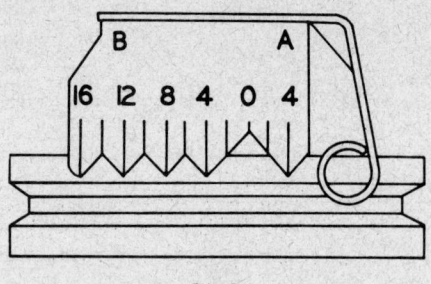

Fig. D

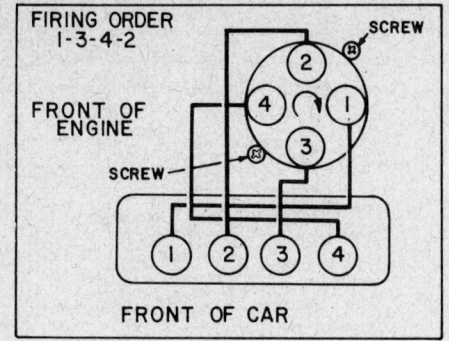

Fig. E

DISTRIBUTOR SPECIFICATIONS

★If unit is checked on the vehicle, double the RPM and degrees to get crankshaft figures.

| Distributor Ident. No.① | Centrifugal Advanced Degrees @ RPM of Distributor | | | | | Vacuum Advance | |
	Advance Starts	Intermediate Advance			Full Advance	Inches of Vacuum to Start Plunger	Max. Adv. Dist. Deg. @ Vacuum
1980							
1103361	0–2¼ @ 550	5¾–8 @ 1100	—	—	12 @ 2400	3½	5¾ @ 20
1103362	0–2¼ @ 550	8¼–10½ @ 1250	—	—	14 @ 2400	3½	5¾ @ 20
1110782	0–2 @ 525	1¼–4½ @ 650	—	—	11½ @ 2000	3½	10½ @ 8
1110783	0–1½ @ 700	2–4½ @ 850	—	—	11½ @ 2000	4	10 @ 10½
1110786	0–1½ @ 525	1¼–3½ @ 650	—	—	11½ @ 2000	3½	10½ @ 9
1110787	0 @ 525	3½ @ 850	—	—	10½ @ 2000	3½	10 @ 9
1981							
1110567	—	—	—	—	—	—	—
1110579	—	—	—	—	—	—	—
1982							
1110593	—	—	—	—	—	—	—
1110597	—	—	—	—	—	—	—
1983							
1103519	—	—	—	—	—	—	—
1984							
1103569	—	—	—	—	—	—	—

①—Stamped on distributor housing plate.

Continued

ALTERNATOR SPECIFICATONS

Year	Model	Rated Hot Output Amps.	Year	Model	Rated Hot Output Amps.	Year	Model	Rated Hot Output Amps.
1980	1103043	42		1100235	42		1100235	42
	1103078	42		1100208	63		1100208	66
	—	63		1100252	63		1100252	66
	—	70		1100254	63		1100254	66
1981–82	11100115	42		1100217	78		1100217	78
	1103187	42		1100260	78		1100268	78
	1103197	63		1100272	78		1100272	78
	1101067	70		1105199	85		1105441	94
1983	1100231	42	1984	1100231	42		1105443	94
	1100233	42		1100233	42		1105542	94

STARTING MOTOR APPLICATIONS

Year	Engine/V.I.N.	Starter Ident. No.
1980	4-151/5, V6-173/7	1109526
1981	4-151/5, V6-173/X,Z	1109530
1982	4-151/R, V6-173/X,Z	1109530
1983	4-151/R	1109556
	4-151/R	1998556
	V6-173/X,Z	1109533
	V6-173/X,Z	1109564
1984	4-151/R	1998450
	V6-173/X,Z	1109564

VALVE SPECIFICATIONS

Year	Engine/V.I.N.	Valve Lash		Valve Angles		Valve Spring Installed Height	Valve Spring Pressure Lbs. @ In.	Stem Clearance		Stem Diameter	
		Int.	Exh.	Seat	Face			Intake	Exhaust	Intake	Exhaust
1980	4-151/5	Hydraulic①		46	45	1.69	151 @ 1.254	.0010–.0027	.0010–.0027	.3418–.3425	.3418–.3425
	V6-173/7	1½ Turn②		46	45	1.57	195 @ 1.181	.0010–.0027	.0010–.0027	.3409–.3417	.3409–.3417
1981	4-151/5	Hydraulic①		46	45	1.69	151 @ 1.254	.0010–.0027	.0010–.0027	.3418–.3425	.3418–.3425
	V6-173/X,Z	1½ Turn②		46	45	1.57	195 @ 1.181	.0010–.0027	.0010–.0027	.3410–.3417	.3410–.3417
1982–84	4-151/R	Hydraulic①		46	45	1.69	151 @ 1.254	.0010–.0027	.0010–.0027	.3418–.3425	.3418–.3425
	V6-173/X,Z	1½ Turn②		46	45	1.57	195 @ 1.181	.0010–.0027	.0010–.0027	.3410–.3417	.3410–.3417

①—No adjustment.

②—Turn rocker arm stud nut until all lash is eliminated, then tighten nut the additional turn listed.

PISTONS, PINS, RINGS, CRANKSHAFT & BEARINGS

| Year | Engine Model/V.I.N. | Piston Clearance | Ring Gap① | | Wristpin Diameter | Rod Bearings | | Main Bearings | | | |
			Comp.	Oil		Shaft Diameter	Bearing Clearance	Shaft Diamater	Bearing Clearance	Thrust on Bear. No.	Shaft End Play
1980	4-151/5	.0017–.0041	②	.015	.9400	2.000	.0005–.0026	2.300	.0005–.0022	5	.0035–.0085
	V6-173/7	.0017–.0027	.010	.020	.9054	1.9983–1.9994	.0014–.0035	2.4937–2.4946	.0017–.0030	3	.0020–.0079
1981	4-151/5	.0017–.0041	.010	.015	.9400	2.000	.0005–.0026	2.300	.0005–.0022	5	.0035–.0085
	V6-173/X,Z	.0017–.0027	.010	.020	.9054	1.9983–1.9994	.0014–.0035	2.4937–2.4946	.0017–.0030	3	.0020–.0067
1982	4-151/R	.0017–.0041	.010	.015	.9400	2.000	.0005–.0026	2.300	.0005–.0022	5	.0035–.0085
	V6-173/X,Z	.0017–.0027	.010	.020	.9054	1.9983–1.9994	.0014–.0035	2.4937–2.4946	.0017–.0030	3	.0020–.0067
1983	4-151/R	.0017–.0041	.010	.015	.9400	2.000	.0005–.0026	2.300	.0005–.0022	5	.0035–.0085
	V6-173/X,Z	.0017–.0027	.010	.020	.9054	1.9983–1.9994	.0014–.0037	③	.0016–.0032	3	.0024–.0083
1984	4-151/R	.0015–.0040	.010	.020	.9400	2.000	.0005–.0026	2.300	.0005–.0022	5	.0035–.0085
	V6-173/X,Z	.0017–.0030	.010	.020	.9054	2.0713–2.0715	.0014–.0037	③	.0016–.0032	3	.0024–.0083

①—Fit rings in tapered bores for clearance given in tightest portion of ring travel. Clearances specified are minimum gaps.
②—Upper, .015"; lower, .009".
③—Nos. 1, 2, & 4, 2.5336–2.5345 inch; No. 3, 2.5328–2.5340 inch.

ENGINE TIGHTENING SPECIFICATIONS★

★ Torque specifications are for clean and lightly lubricated threads only. Dry or dirty threads produce increased friction which prevents accurate measurement of tightness.

Year	Engine Model/V.I.N.	Spark Plugs Ft. Lbs.	Cylinder Head Bolts Ft. Lbs.	Intake Manifold Ft. Lbs.	Exhaust Manifold Ft. Lbs.	Rocker Arm Stud Ft. Lbs.	Rocker Arm Cover Ft. Lbs.	Connecting Rod Cap Bolts Ft. Lbs.	Main Bearing Cap Bolts Ft. Lbs.	Flywheel to Crankshaft Ft. Lbs.	Vibration Damper or Pulley Ft. Lbs.
1980	4-151/5	7–15	75	29	44	75①	6	32	70	44	200
	V6-173/7	7–15	65–75	20–25	22–28	43–49	6–9	34–40	63–74	45–55	66–84
1981	4-151/5	7–15	75	29	44	20②	6	32	70	44	200
	V6-173/X,Z	7–15	65–75	20–25	22–28	43–49	6–9	34–40	63–74	45–55	66–84
1982–83	4-151/R	7–15	85③	29	44	20②	6	32	70	44	200
	V6-173/X,Z	7–15	65–75	20–25	22–28	43–49	6–9	34–40	63–74	45–55	66–84
1984	4-151/R	7–15	92③	29	44	20②	6	32	70	44	200
	V6-173/X,Z	7–15	65–75	20–25	22–28	43–49	6–9	34–40	63–74	45–55	66–84

①—Rocker arm nut, 20 ft. lbs.
②—Rocker arm bolt.
③—Requires thread sealer.

WHEEL ALIGNMENT SPECIFICATIONS

| Year | Model | Caster Angle, Degrees | | Camber Angle Degrees | | | | Toe-In Inch | Toe-Out on Turns, Deg. | |
| | | Limits | Desired | Limits | | Desired | | | Outer Wheel | Inner Wheel |
				Left	Right	Left	Right			
1980–81	All	−2° to +2°	Zero	+½° to +1½°	+½° to +1½°	+1°	+1°	①	—	—
1982–84	All	—	—	−½° to +½°	−½° to +½°	Zero	Zero	Zero	—	—

①—2.5 mm.

COOLING SYSTEM & CAPACITY DATA

Year	Model or Engine/V.I.N.	Cooling Capacity, Qts. Less A/C	With A/C	Radiator Cap Relief Pressure, Lbs.	Thermo. Opening Temp.	Fuel Tank Gals.	Engine Oil Refill Qts.	Transaxle Oil Manual Transaxle Pts.	Auto. Transaxle Qts. ①
1980	Citation 4-151/5	9½	9¾	15	195	14	3②	6	③
	Omega 4-151/5	8½	8¾	15	195	14	3②	6	③
	Phoenix 4-151/5	8.3④	8.6④	15	195	14	3②	6	③
	Skylark 4-151/5	8.3⑤	8.6⑤	15	195	14	3②	6	③
	Citation V6-173/7	11½	11¾	15	195	15	4②	6	③
	Omega V6-173/7	10¼⑥	10¾⑥	15	195	14	4②	6	③
	Phoenix V6-173/7⑦	10.2⑧	10.6⑧	15	195	14	4②	6	③
	Phoenix V6-173/7⑨	10.5⑧	10.8	15	195	14	4②	6	③
	Skylark V6-173/7	10.2⑧	10.6⑧	15	195	14	4②	6	③
1981	Citation 4-151/5	9½	9¾	15	195	14	3②	6	③
	Omega 4-151/5	8.4⑩	8.6⑩	15	195	14	3②	6	③
	Phoenix 4-151/5	8.3④	8.6④	15	195	14	3②	6	③
	Skylark 4-151/5	8.3⑤	8.6⑤	15	195	14	3②	6	③
	Citation V6-173/X,Z	11½	11¾	15	195	14	4②	6	③
	Omega V6-173/X	10	10.1	15	195	14	4②	6	③
	Phoenix V6-173/X⑦	10.2⑧	10.6⑧	15	195	14	4②	6	③
	Phoenix V6-173/X⑨	10.5⑧	10.8	15	195	14	4②	6	③
	Skylark V6-173/X	10.2	10.6	15	195	14	4②	6	③
1982	Citation 4-151/R	9.5	9.75	15	195	14	3②	5.9	⑪
	Omega 4-151/R	9.5	9.75	15	195	14	3②	5.9	⑪
	Phoenix 4-151/R	8.3④	8.6④	15	195	14	3②	5.9	⑪
	Skylark 4-151/R	9.4⑬	9.8⑬	15	195	14	3②	5.9	⑪
	Citation V6-173/X,Z	11.5	11.75	15	195	14	4②	5.9	⑪
	Omega V6-173/X,Z	11.5	11.75	15	195	14	4②	5.9	⑪
	Phoenix V6-173/X,Z⑦	10.2⑧	10.6⑧	15	195	14	4②	5.9	⑪
	Phoenix V6-173/X,Z⑨	10.5⑧	10.8	15	195	14	4②	5.9	⑪
	Skylark V6-173/X,Z	11.4	11.8	15	195	14	4②	5.9	⑪
1983	Citation 4-151/R	8.5	9	15	195	14.6	3②	5.9	⑪
	Omega 4-151/R	9.5⑬	9.75⑬	15	195	14.6	3②	5.9	⑪
	Phoenix 4-151/R	9.5⑭	9.8⑭	15	195	14.6	3②	5.9	⑪
	Skylark 4-151/R	9.5	9.7	15	195	14.6	3②	5.9	⑪
	Citation V6-173/X,Z	10.5	11	15	195	15.1	4②	5.9	⑪
	Omega V6-173/X,Z	10.25⑧	10.5⑧	15	195	15.1	4②	5.9	⑪
	Phoenix V6-173/X,Z	11.4⑫	11.8⑫	15	195	15.1	4②	5.9	⑪
	Skylark V6-173/X,Z	11.4⑫	11.8⑫	15	195	15.1	4②	5.9	⑪
1984	Citation 4-151/R	8.7⑬	9	15	195	14.6	3②	5.9	⑪
	Omega 4-151/R	9.3⑬	9.6⑬	15	195	14.2	3②	5.9	⑪
	Phoenix 4-151/R	9.5	10.4	15	195	14.6	3②	5.9	⑪
	Skylark 4-151/R	9.5⑫	9.7⑫	15	195	14.6	3②	5.9	⑪
	Citation V6-173/X,Z	10.7⑥	11	15	195	15.1	4②	5.9	⑪
	Omega V6-173/X,Z	⑯⑧	10.5⑧	15	195	15.1	4②	5.9	⑪
	Phoenix V6-173/X,Z	11.1	11.8	15	195	15.1	4②	5.9	⑪
	Skylark V6-173/X,Z	11.4	11.8	15	195	15.1	4②	5.9	⑪

①—Approximate make final check with dip-stick.
②—Additional oil may be required when changing filter.
③—Oil pan capacity, 4 qts.; total capacity, 9 qts.
④—With heavy duty cooling system, man. trans. 8.7 qts., auto. trans., 9.3 qts.
⑤—With heavy duty cooling system, man. trans., 8.7 qts.; auto. trans., 10.8 qts.
⑥—With heavy duty cooling system, 11 qts.
⑦—Exc. Calif.
⑧—Heavy duty cooling system, 10.8 qts.
⑨—California.
⑩—With heavy duty cooling system, 8.9 qts.
⑪—Oil pan capacity, 4 qts.; total capacity, 6 qts.
⑫—Heavy duty cooling system, 12 qts.
⑬—Heavy duty cooling system, 10 qts.
⑭—Heavy duty cooling system, 10.4 qts.
⑮—Heavy duty cooling system, 9 qts.
⑯—Auto. trans., 9.9 qts.; man. trans., 10.5 qts.

Electrical Section

STARTER, REPLACE

Exc. 1983—84 Phoenix

1. Disconnect battery ground cable.
2. Raise and support vehicle.
3. Remove the starter to engine brace, if equipped.
4. Remove starter mounting bolts and lower starter. Note position of shims, if used.
5. Disconnect solenoid wires and the battery cable.
6. Remove starter from vehicle.
7. Reverse procedure to install.

1983—84 Phoenix

1. Disconnect battery ground cable.
2. Raise and support vehicle.
3. Remove three dust cover attaching bolts.
4. Pull dust cover back to gain access to front starter attaching bolt, then remove bolt.
5. Pull rear of dust cover backward and remove rear starter attaching bolt.

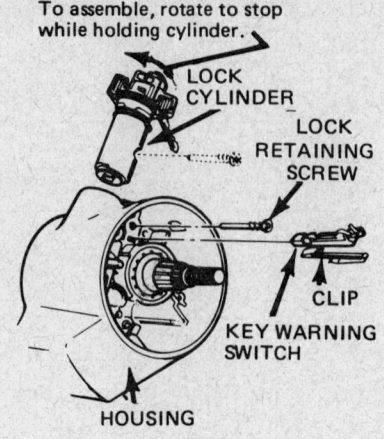

Fig. 1   Lock cylinder removal

6. Push dust cover back into position, then pull starter back and out.
7. Disconnect solenoid wires and battery cable, then remove starter from vehicle.
8. Reverse procedure to install. Replace any shims that were removed.

IGNITION LOCK, REPLACE

1. Remove steering wheel as outlined under "Steering Wheel, Replace" procedure.
2. Remove turn signal switch as outlined under "Turn Signal Switch, Replace" procedure.
3. Remove the buzzer switch.
4. Turn lock cylinder to "Run" position, then remove the lock cylinder retaining screw and the lock cylinder, Fig. 1.
5. To install, rotate lock cylinder to the stop while holding housing. Align cylinder key with keyway in housing, then push lock cylinder into housing until fully seated.

REMOVE

1. Remove parts as shown.

INSTALL

1. Install parts as shown.
2. Position rod in slider hole and install ignition switch. Install lower stud and tighten to 3.9 N•m (35 in. lbs.)
3. Install dimmer switch and depress switch slightly to insert 3/32" drill. Force switch up to remove lash, then tighten screw, and nut to 3.9 N•m (35 in. lbs.).
4. Place shifter in neutral and install shift lever.

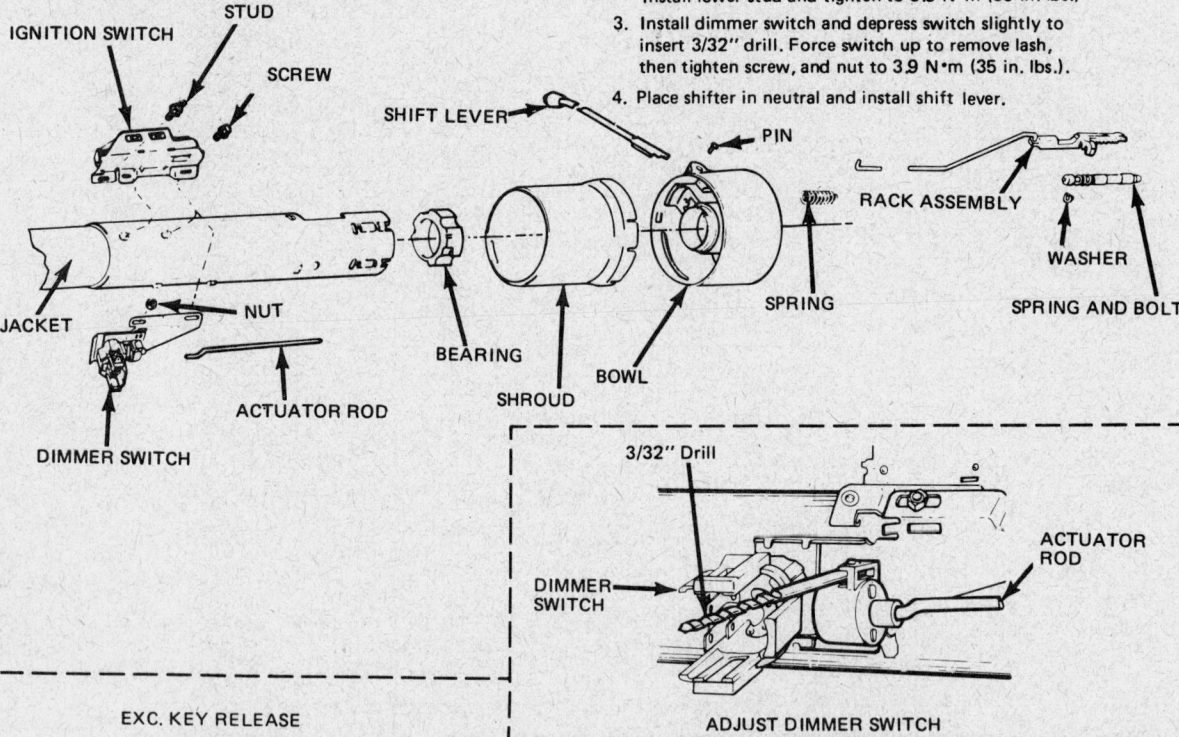

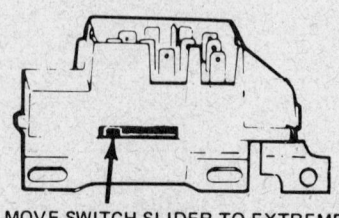

Fig. 2   Ignition & dimmer switch removal & installation. Except tilt column

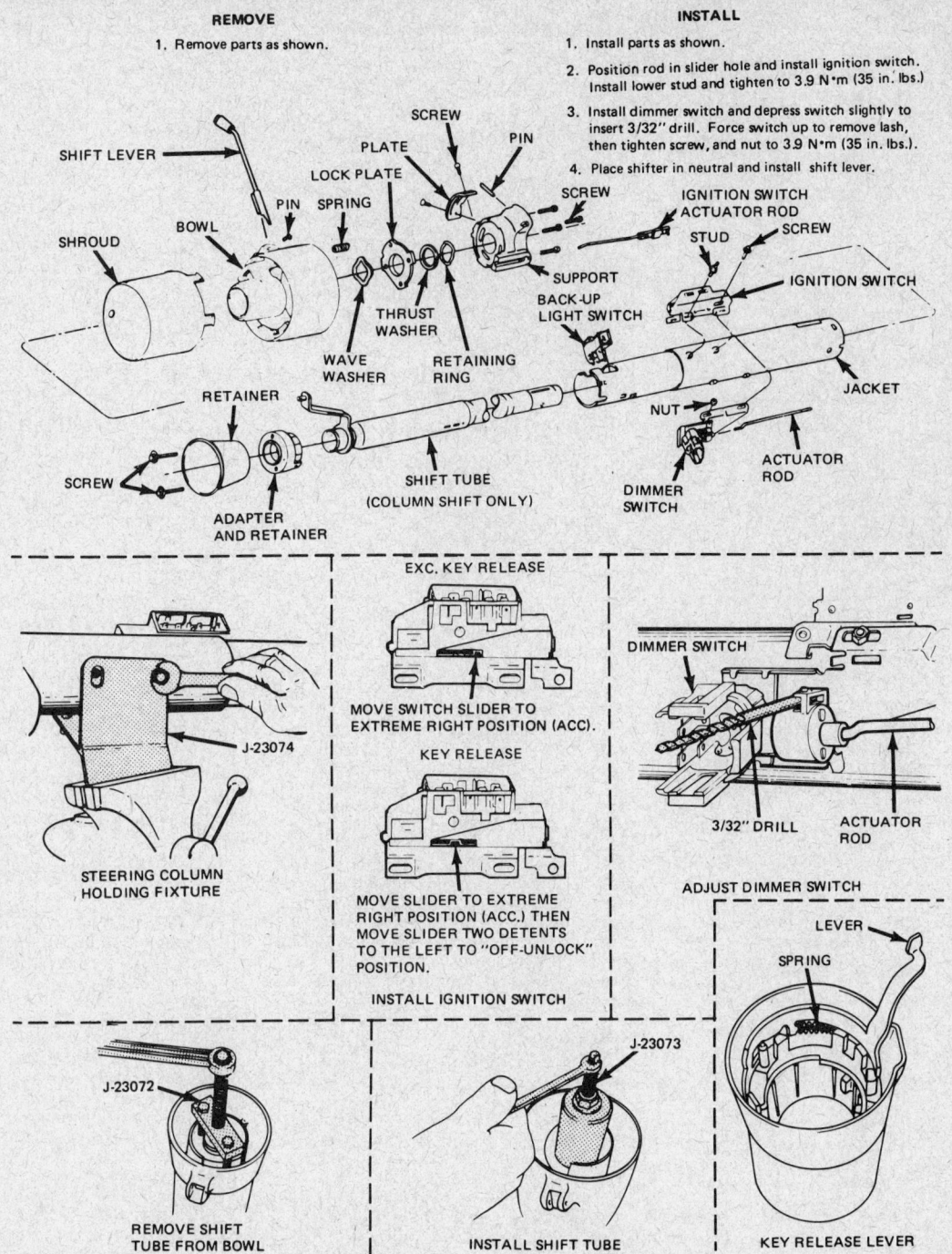

REMOVE

1. Remove parts as shown.

INSTALL

1. Install parts as shown.
2. Position rod in slider hole and install ignition switch. Install lower stud and tighten to 3.9 N·m (35 in. lbs.)
3. Install dimmer switch and depress switch slightly to insert 3/32″ drill. Force switch up to remove lash, then tighten screw, and nut to 3.9 N·m (35 in. lbs.).
4. Place shifter in neutral and install shift lever.

Fig. 3 Ignition & dimmer switch removal & installation. Tilt column

6. Install lock cylinder retaining screw.
7. Install buzzer switch, turn signal switch and steering wheel.

IGNITION & DIMMER SWITCHES, REPLACE

1. Remove turn signal switch as outlined under "Turn Signal Switch, Replace" procedure.
2. Refer to Figs. 2 and 3 to remove ignition and dimmer switches.

3. When installing dimmer switch, depress switch slightly to install a 3/32 inch twist drill. Force switch upward to remove lash and tighten retaining screw.

W/S WIPER SWITCH, REPLACE

1. Remove turn signal switch as outlined under "Turn Signal Switch, Replace" procedure.
2. Refer to Figs. 4 and 5 for wiper switch replacement.

PULSE W/S WIPER SWITCH, REPLACE

NOTE: On models where pulse wipers are controlled at turn signal lever, a malfunction may be caused by a faulty pulse wiper module. The module is located behind left hand side of instrument panel and must be replaced as an assembly.

Citation

1. Disconnect battery ground cable.

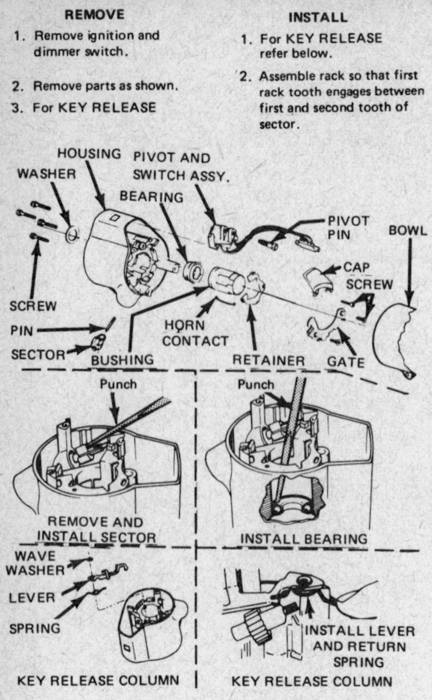

REMOVE

1. Remove ignition and dimmer switch.

2. Remove parts as shown.

3. For KEY RELEASE

INSTALL

1. For KEY RELEASE refer below.

2. Assemble rack so that first rack tooth engages between first and second tooth of sector.

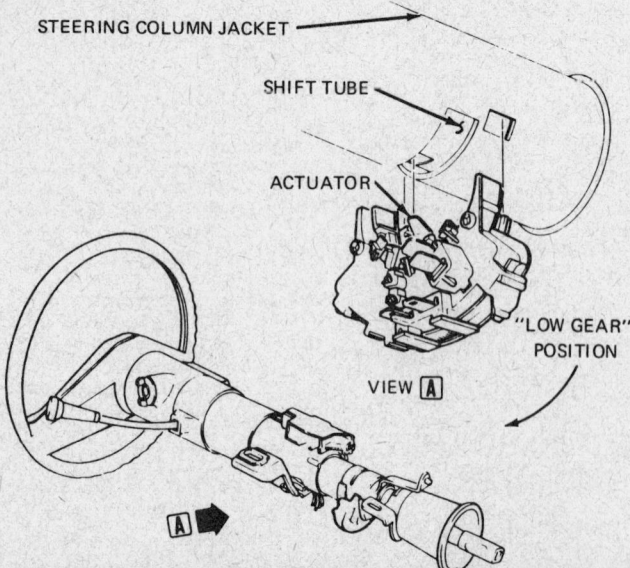

WASHER HOUSING PIVOT AND SWITCH ASSY. BEARING PIVOT PIN BOWL CAP SCREW SCREW PIN SECTOR HORN CONTACT BUSHING RETAINER GATE

Punch — REMOVE AND INSTALL SECTOR

Punch — INSTALL BEARING

WAVE WASHER LEVER SPRING — KEY RELEASE COLUMN

INSTALL LEVER AND RETURN SPRING — KEY RELEASE COLUMN

Fig. 4 Windshield wiper switch removal & installation. Except tilt column

2. Remove radio knobs and nuts and the clock knob.

3. Remove instrument cluster bezel to instrument panel carrier retaining screws and pull bezel rearward.

4. Depress headlamp switch shaft retaining button and pull knob and shaft assembly from switch.

5. Disconnect accessory switch wiring connectors.

6. Remove controller knob and ferrule nut attaching controller to bezel.

7. Disconnect wiring connector at steering column.

8. Remove switch from vehicle.

9. Reverse procedure to install.

1981–84 Omega

Refer to "W/S Wiper Switch, Replace" for pulse wiper switch replacement procedure on these models.

1980 Omega

1. Disconnect battery ground cable.
2. Remove headlamp switch knob by depressing retaining clip behind knob and pulling knob from shaft.
3. Remove left hand trim cover attaching screws and the trim cover.
4. Remove two screws retaining controller switch to adapter assembly.
5. Disconnect wiring connector at steering column.
6. Remove switch from instrument panel.
7. Reverse procedure to install.

1981–84 Phoenix

Refer to "W/S Wiper Switch, Replace" for pulse wiper switch replacement procedure on these models.

1980 Phoenix

1. Disconnect battery ground cable.
2. Remove the switch knob and the four screws securing the trim plate.
3. Pull trim plate rearward and rotate for clearance for switch.
4. Remove light guide and the switch retaining screws.
5. Remove screws securing steering column trim cover to instrument panel and the trim cover.
6. Disconnect switch harness connector.
7. Cut both ends of pulse wiring harness as close to the steering column as possible. Remove the switch end and wiring harness end.
8. Install new switch in instrument panel and make electrical connection at instrument panel wiring harness. Route the new controller wiring under steering column and secure wiring so as not to fall in the driver's foot area.
9. Reverse Steps 1 through 5 to complete installation.

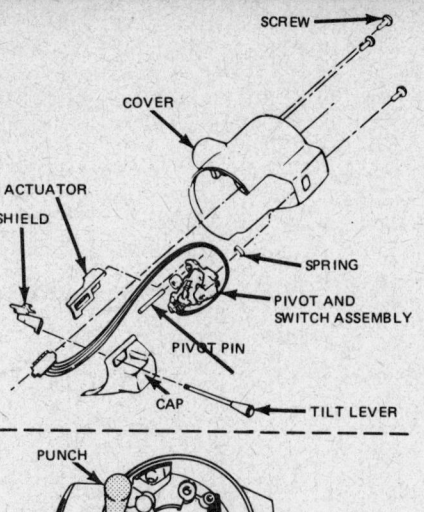

SCREW COVER ACTUATOR SHIELD SPRING PIVOT AND SWITCH ASSEMBLY PIVOT PIN CAP TILT LEVER

PUNCH PIVOT PIN

REMOVE AND INSTALL PIVOT ASSEMBLY

Fig. 5 Windshield wiper switch removal & installation. Tilt column

1981–84 Skylark

Refer to "W/S Wiper Switch, Replace" for pulse wiper switch replacement procedure on these models.

1980 Skylark

1. Disconnect battery ground cable.
2. Remove the knobs from the following: W/S wiper switch, rear window defogger switch and radio.
3. Remove headlamp switch knob by depressing retaining clip behind knob and pulling knob from shaft.
4. Remove radio retaining nuts.
5. Remove three screws at bottom of instrument panel trim plate.
6. Place transmission shift lever in "Low" and remove instrument panel trim plate.
7. Remove switch retaining screws.
8. Pull switch rearward and cut the five wire harness at rear of switch.
9. Feed new wiring harness through switch cavity and pull through bottom of instrument panel.
10. Connect wiring harness between column mounted switch and related junction block.
11. Reverse Steps 1 through 7 to complete installation.

STOPLAMP SWITCH, ADJUST

Insert switch into tubular clip until the switch body seats on the tube clip. Pull the brake pedal rearward against internal pedal stop. The switch will be properly positioned in the tubular clip.

STEERING COLUMN JACKET

SHIFT TUBE

ACTUATOR

"LOW GEAR" POSITION

VIEW A

A

Fig. 6 Neutral safety switch removal. 1981–82 models with auto. trans. & console shift & all 1983–84 models with auto. trans.

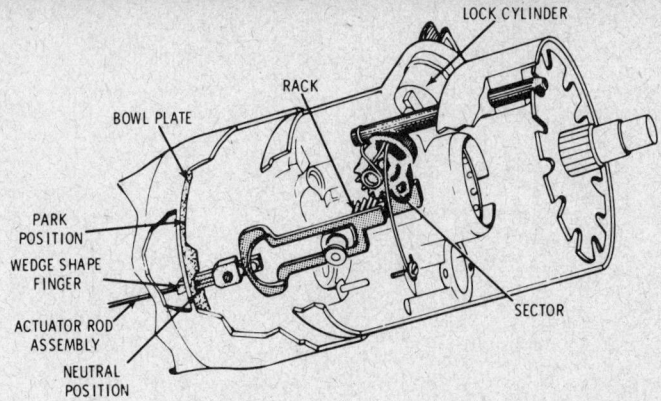

Fig. 7 Mechanical neutral start system. All 1980 models with auto. trans. & 1981–82 models with auto. trans. & column shift

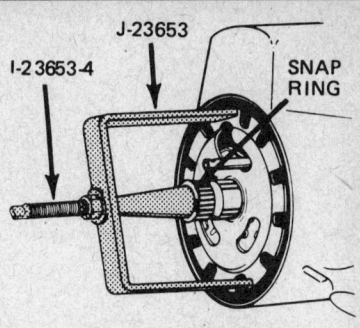

Tighten nut until tool slightly depresses lock plate

Fig. 8 Compressing lock plate

NEUTRAL SAFETY SWITCH, REPLACE

1981–82 Models w/ Auto. Trans. & Console Shift & All 1983–84 Models w/ Auto. Trans.

1. Disconnect battery ground cable.
2. Place gear selector in Neutral.
3. Gently rock switch out of steering column, Fig. 6.
4. Disconnect electrical connectors, then remove switch from vehicle.
5. Connect electrical connectors to new switch.
6. Align switch actuator with hole in shift tube.
7. Position connector side of switch into lower jacket cutout.
8. Push down front of switch, ensuring switch tangs snap into holes in steering column jacket.
9. Adjust switch by replacing gear selector in Park position. The switch main housing and housing back should ratchet, providing proper adjustment.
10. If readjustment is needed, move housing as far as possible toward Low gear position, then repeat step 9.

All 1980 Models w/ Auto. Trans. & 1981–82 Models w/ Auto. Trans. & Column Shift

These vehicles do not use a neutral safety switch. A mechanical block on the transmission gear selector, Fig. 7, prevents starting the engine when the transmission is in any gear other than Park or Neutral.

TURN SIGNAL SWITCH, REPLACE

1. Disconnect battery ground cable.
2. Remove steering wheel as outlined under "Steering Wheel, Replace" procedure.
3. Using a screwdriver, pry cover from housing.
4. Using lock plate compressing tool J-23653, compress lock plate and pry snap ring from groove on shaft, Fig. 8. Slowly release lock plate compressing tool, remove tool and lock plate from shaft end.
5. Slide canceling cam and upper bearing preload spring from end of shaft.

6. Remove turn signal (multi-function) lever.
7. Remove hazard warning knob retaining screw, button, spring and knob.
8. Remove pivot arm.
9. Wrap upper part of electrical connector with tape to prevent snagging of wires during switch removal.
10. Remove switch retaining screws and pull switch up from column, guiding wire harness through column.
11. Reverse procedure to install.

STEERING WHEEL, REPLACE

1. Disconnect battery ground cable.
2. Remove horn button or pad.
3. Remove retainer and steering wheel retaining nut.
4. Remove steering wheel with a suitable puller (tool No. J-1859-03 or BT-61-9).
5. Reverse procedure to install.

HEADLAMP SWITCH, REPLACE

Citation

1. Disconnect battery ground cable.
2. Pull switch knob to full "On" position.
3. On 1980 models, proceed as follows:
   a. Remove instrument panel bezel-to-panel carrier attaching screws.
   b. Remove radio knobs and nuts and the clock knob.
   c. Pull bezel rearward, then depress headlamp switch shaft release button and pull knob and shaft assembly from switch.
4. On 1981–84 models, remove spring clip retainer from knob shaft, then slide shaft out of switch housing.
5. On all models, disconnect accessory switch electrical connectors.
6. Remove switch ferrule nut, then push switch forward out from mounting hole.
7. Lift switch up and out through opening above switch mounting, then disconnect electrical connector.
8. Remove switch from instrument panel.
9. Reverse procedure to install.

Omega

1. On 1980–82 models disconnect battery ground cable.
2. Remove headlamp switch knob by depressing retaining clip behind knob and

pulling knob from shaft.
3. On all models, remove left hand trim cover attaching screws and the trim cover.
4. Remove switch attaching screws and pull switch from panel.

NOTE: The switch plugs directly into a terminal plug in the switch mounting cavity.

5. Reverse procedure to install.

Phoenix

1. Disconnect battery ground cable.
2. Remove steering column trim cover attaching screws and the trim cover.
3. Pull headlamp switch to full "On" position, depress knob release button on switch and remove rod and knob assembly.
4. Remove left hand trim plate attaching screws and the trim plate.
5. Remove switch escutcheon, disconnect electrical connector from switch and remove switch from instrument panel.
6. Reverse procedure to install.

1983–84 Skylark

1. Disconnect battery ground cable.
2. Remove headlamp switch knob by using a small screwdriver through slot to depress retainer while pulling knob out.
3. Remove switch bezel.
4. Remove rear window defogger switch knob, if equipped, by pulling straight off.
5. Remove 3 attaching screws from lower edge of left hand trim panel.
6. Pull left hand trim panel straight forward and remove from vehicle.
7. Remove 2 headlamp switch attaching screws and the switch.

NOTE: Pulling switch straight out of dash will also disconnect the electrical connector.

8. Reverse procedure to install.

1980–82 Skylark

1. Disconnect battery ground cable.
2. Remove headlamp switch knob by depressing retaining clip behind knob and pulling knob from shaft.
3. Remove escutcheon from switch and shaft.

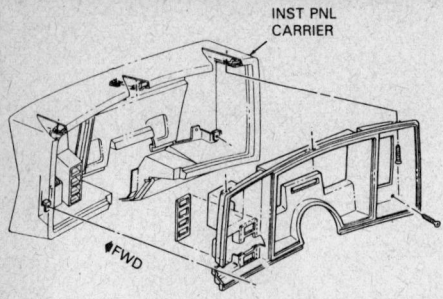

Fig. 9   Instrument cluster trim cover. 1980—84 Citation

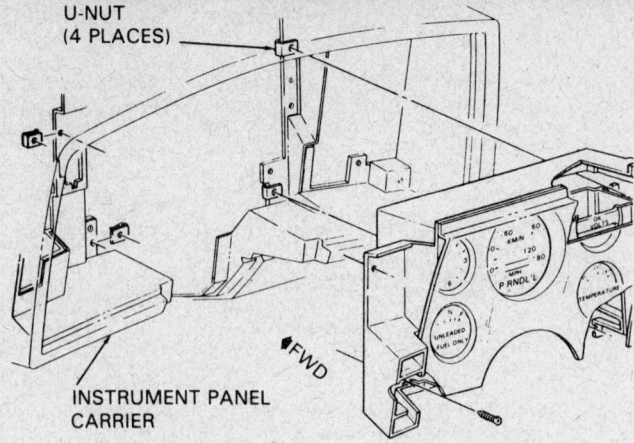

Fig. 10   Instrument cluster. 1980—84 Citation

4. Remove the knobs from the following: W/S wiper switch, rear window defogger switch and radio.
5. Remove radio retaining nuts.
6. Remove three screws from bottom of instrument panel trim plate.
7. Place transmission shift lever in "Low", then remove instrument panel trim plate.
8. Remove headlamp switch retaining screws and pull switch from panel.

NOTE: The switch plugs directly into a terminal plug in the switch mounting cavity.

---

9. Reverse procedure to install.

INSTRUMENT CLUSTER, REPLACE

Citation

1. Disconnect battery ground cable.
2. Remove radio knobs and nuts and the clock knob.
3. Remove instrument cluster bezel to panel carrier attaching screws, then pull bezel rearward for access, Fig. 9.
4. On 1980 models, depress headlamp switch shaft release button and pull knob and shaft assembly from switch.

5. On 1980—81 models, remove spring clip retainer from knob shaft, then slide shaft out of switch housing.
6. On all models, pull bezel rearward and disconnect accessory switch electrical connectors.
7. Remove instrument cluster bezel.
8. Remove four screws securing cluster assembly to instrument panel pad.
9. Disconnect shift indicator cable from steering column shift bowl.
10. Pull cluster rearward and disconnect speedometer cable and electrical connectors.
11. Remove instrument cluster from vehicle, Fig. 10.
12. Reverse procedure to install.

1983—84 Omega

1. Disconnect battery ground cable.
2. Remove 4 steering column lower trim pad attaching screws and the pad.
3. Remove 6 center instrument panel trim cover attaching screws and the cover.
4. Disconnect shift indicator from steering column shift bowl.
5. Remove 4 instrument cluster-to-instrument panel attaching screws.

6. Disconnect speedometer cable from transaxle, or from transducer on models equipped with cruise control.
7. Pull cluster rearward and disconnect speedometer cable.
8. Remove vehicle speed sensor L.E.D./photo cell attaching screw from rear of speedometer head.
9. Remove instrument cluster from vehicle, Fig. 11.
10. Reverse procedure to install.

1980—82 Omega

1. Disconnect battery ground cable.
2. Remove the 2 screws attaching assembly line communication link connector bracket to steering column trim cover if so equipped. Remove the 2 screws attaching steering column trim cover to instrument panel and remove trim cover.
3. Mark location of shift indicator clip on steering column shift bowl for proper reassembly. Remove shift indicator clip. Remove the 2 bolts holding steering column to support and lower steering column, resting steering wheel on front seat.
4. Remove four screws attaching center instrument panel trim cover to instrument panel pad.
5. Pull trim cover rearward and disconnect accessory switch wiring and remote control mirror cable, if equipped. Remove trim cover.
6. Remove four screws attaching instrument cluster assembly to instrument panel pad.
7. Disconnect shift indicator cable from steering column shift bowl.
8. Pull cluster rearward and disconnect speedometer cable and electrical connections.
9. Remove instrument cluster from vehicle, Fig. 11.
10. Reverse procedure to install.

Phoenix

1. Disconnect battery ground cable.
2. Remove four speedometer cluster trim plate attaching screws and the trim plate.
3. Remove steering column trim cover attaching screws and the trim cover.
4. Remove speedometer cluster attaching screws.
5. Disconnect shift indicator detent cable, marking the cable location on steering

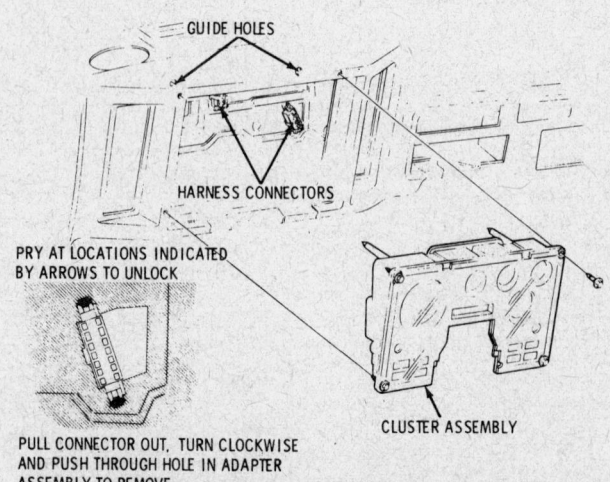

Fig. 11   Instrument cluster. 1980—84 Omega

6. Disconnect speedometer cable and pull cluster from panel.
7. Disconnect wiring harness from cluster and remove cluster from vehicle, Fig. 12.
8. Reverse procedure to install.

Skylark

1. Disconnect battery ground cable.
2. Disconnect speedometer cable at cruise control transducer, if equipped, or at upper and lower cable connections.
3. Remove trip meter reset knob retaining screw and pull knob from meter.
4. Remove knobs from the following: W/S wiper switch, rear window defogger switch and radio.
5. Remove headlamp switch knob by depressing retaining clip behind knob and pulling knob from shaft. Remove switch escutcheon.
6. Remove radio retaining nuts.
7. Remove three screws from bottom of instrument panel trim plate, Fig. 13.
8. Place transmission shift lever in "Low" and remove instrument panel trim plate.
9. Remove four instrument cluster lens plate screws and the lens plate.
10. Remove four instrument cluster cover plate screws and the cover plate.
11. Disconnect shift indicator spring below speedometer and slide indicator needle toward the right side and out from cluster housing.
12. Pull instrument cluster rearward and disconnect speedometer cable and electrical connections.
13. Remove instrument cluster from vehicle, Fig. 14.
14. Reverse procedure to install.

RADIO, REPLACE

Citation

1. Disconnect battery ground cable.
2. Remove radio knob and nuts and the clock knob.
3. Remove instrument cluster bezel to panel carrier attaching screws, then pull bezel rearward.

4. On 1980 models, depress headlamp switch shaft release button and pull knob and shaft assembly from switch.
5. On 1981–84 models, remove spring clip retainer from knob shaft, then slide shaft out of switch housing.
6. On all models, pull bezel rearward and disconnect accessory switch wiring connectors.
7. Remove instrument cluster bezel.
8. Remove two screws securing radio bracket to instrument panel.
9. Pull radio rearward while twisting slightly toward left side and disconnect electrical connections. Remove lamp socket.
10. Remove radio from instrument panel.
11. Reverse procedure to install.

1983–84 Omega

1. Disconnect battery ground cable.
2. Remove 4 steering column lower trim pad attaching screws and the pad.
3. Remove 6 center instrument panel attaching screws and the cover.
4. Remove 4 radio-to-instrument panel attaching screws.
5. Pull radio rearward, then disconnect all electrical connections from radio.
6. Remove radio from vehicle.
7. Reverse procedure to install.

1980–82 Omega

1. Disconnect battery ground cable.
2. Remove radio knobs.
3. Pull out glove box switches and disconnect the wiring connectors.
4. Remove two screws securing glove box stop arm to door.
5. Remove two screws from instrument panel molding and pull molding rearward to remove. Note that the molding is retained by five clips.
6. Remove ash tray assembly, then the lamp and socket assembly from lamp housing.
7. Pull radio and ash tray retainer out from panel and disconnect all electrical connections.
8. Remove radio from panel.
9. Reverse procedure to install.

Phoenix

1. Disconnect battery ground cable.
2. Remove eight screws attaching center instrument panel trim plate and the trim plate.
3. Remove two radio attaching screws and pull radio from panel, then disconnect all electrical connectors from radio. Remove radio from panel.
4. Remove radio knobs and separate face plate from radio.
5. Reverse procedure to install.

1983–84 Skylark

1. Disconnect battery ground cable.
2. Remove steering column opening cover plate.
3. Remove headlamp switch knob by using a small screwdriver through slot to depress retainer while pulling knob out.
4. Remove headlamp switch bezel.
5. Remove rear window defogger switch knob, if equipped, by pulling straight off.

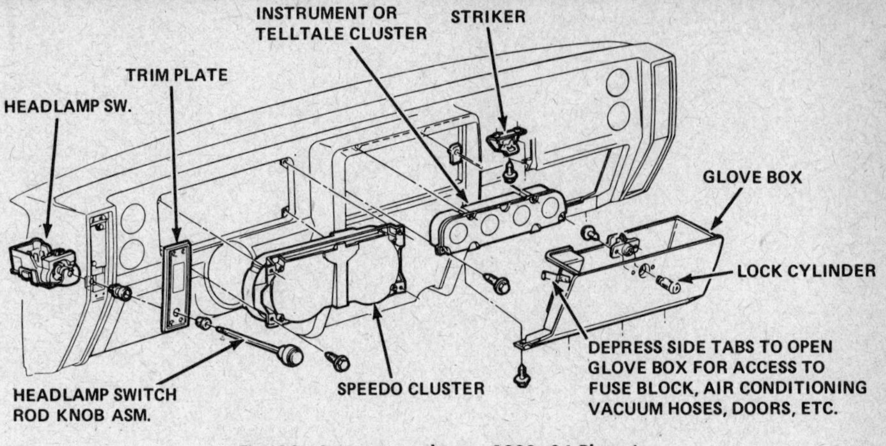

Fig. 12   Instrument cluster. 1980–84 Phoenix

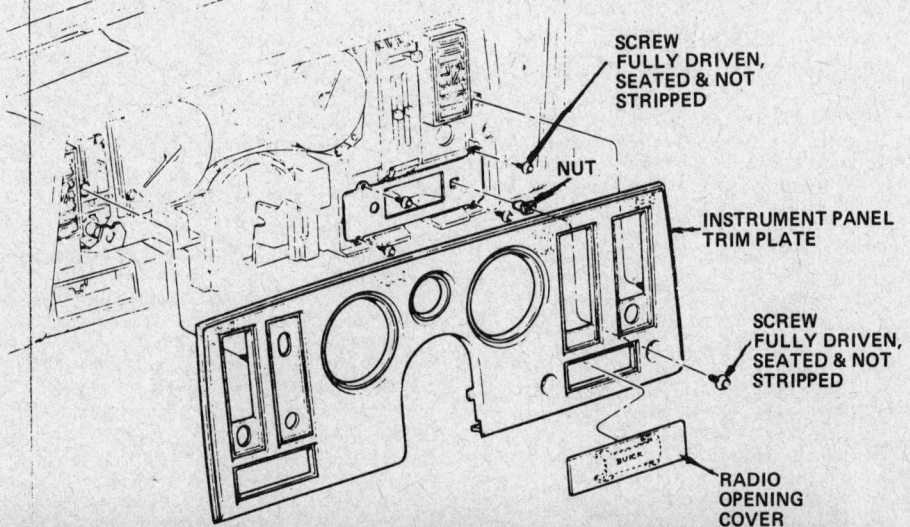
Fig. 13   Instrument cluster trim cover. 1980–84 Skylark

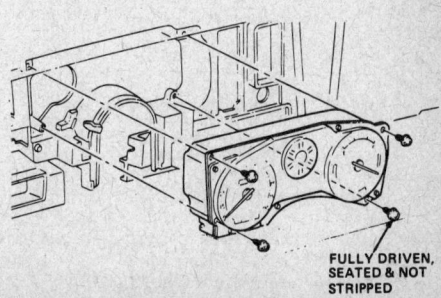
Fig. 14   Instrument cluster. 1980–84 Skylark

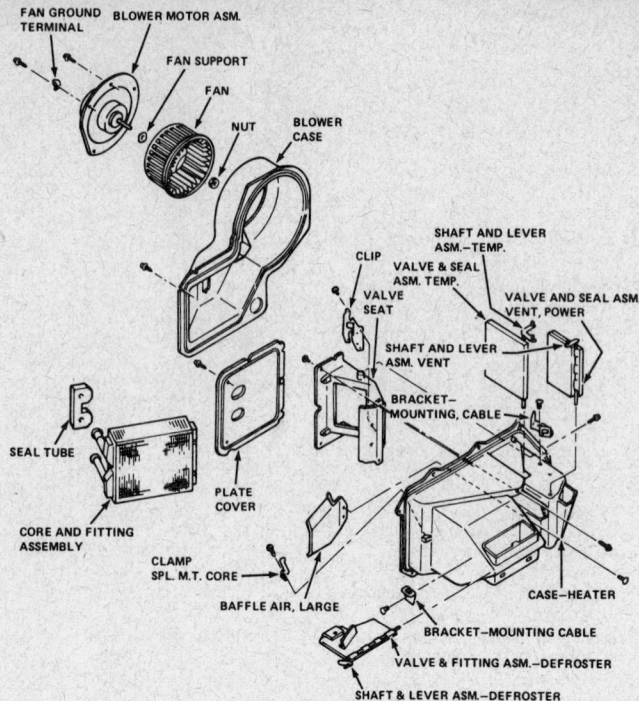

FAN GROUND TERMINAL BLOWER MOTOR ASM.
FAN SUPPORT
FAN
NUT BLOWER CASE
CLIP
VALVE SEAT
VALVE
SEAT
SHAFT AND LEVER ASM.–TEMP.
VALVE & SEAL ASM. TEMP.
VALVE AND SEAL ASM. VENT, POWER
SHAFT AND LEVER ASM. VENT
BRACKET–MOUNTING, CABLE
SEAL TUBE
CORE AND FITTING ASSEMBLY
PLATE COVER
CLAMP SPL. M.T. CORE
BAFFLE AIR, LARGE
BRACKET–MOUNTING CABLE
CASE–HEATER
VALVE & FITTING ASM.–DEFROSTER
SHAFT & LEVER ASM.–DEFROSTER

Fig. 15 Heater core & blower motor, less A/C

HEATER CORE, REPLACE

Less Air Conditioning

1. Disconnect battery ground cable and drain cooling system.
2. Disconnect the heater hoses from heater core.
3. Remove radio noise supression strap.
4. Remove heater core cover retaining screws and the cover, Fig. 15.
5. Remove heater core from vehicle.
6. Reverse procedure to install.

With Air Conditioning

1. Disconnect battery ground cable and drain cooling system.
2. Disconnect heater hoses from heater core.
3. Remove right side hush panel and open the glove box.
4. Remove heater duct retaining screw and the duct.
5. Remove instrument panel support bracket.
6. Remove heater case side cover retaining screws and the cover.
7. Remove heater core retaining clamps and the inlet and outlet tube support clamps.
8. Remove heater core from case.
9. Reverse procedure to install.

---

6. Remove 3 attaching screws from lower edge of left hand trim panel.
7. Pull left hand trim straight forward and remove from vehicle.
8. Remove 2 attaching screws from left side of radio and 1 nut from lower right side of radio.
9. Pull radio out through instrument panel opening and disconnect all electrical connectors.
10. Remove radio from vehicle.
11. Reverse procedure to install.

1980–82 Skylark

1. Disconnect battery ground cable.
2. Remove the knobs from the following: W/S wiper switch, rear window defogger switch and radio.
3. Remove headlamp switch knob by depressing retaining clip behind knob and pulling knob from shaft. Remove the switch escutcheon.
4. Remove radio retaining nuts.
5. Remove three screws at bottom of instrument panel trim plate.
6. Place transmission shift lever in "Low" and remove instrument panel trim plate.
7. Remove radio mounting plate screws.
8. Disconnect all electrical connection from radio.
9. Pull radio out through instrument panel opening.
10. Reverse procedure to install.

W/S WIPER MOTOR, REPLACE

1. Remove wiper arms as outlined previously.
2. Remove the lower windshield reveal molding, front cowl panel and cowl screen. Disconnect washer hose.

NOTE: Prior to removing the front cowl screen, mask the corners of the hood to prevent damage to paint.

---

3. Loosen but do not remove transmission drive link to motor crank arm attaching nuts. Then, disconnect drive link from motor crank arm.
4. Disconnect wiper motor electrical connections.
5. Remove wiper motor attaching bolts.
6. On models equipped with A/C, support motor assembly and remove motor crank arm. Use a suitable pair of locking pliers and wrench, remove crank arm nut and the crank arm.
7. On all models, rotate motor assembly upward and outward to remove.
8. Reverse procedure to install.

W/S WIPER TRANSMISSION, REPLACE

1. Remove lower windshield reveal molding, wiper arms and front cowl panel.
2. Loosen but do not remove drive link to motor crank arm attaching nuts.
3. Remove transmission to cowl panel attaching screws and the transmission.
4. Reverse procedure to install.

BLOWER MOTOR, REPLACE

1. Disconnect battery ground cable.
2. Disconnect blower motor electrical connections.
3. Remove blower motor attaching screws and the blower motor, Fig. 15.
4. Reverse procedure to install.

CRUISE CONTROL, ADJUST

Brake Release Switches

Electrical & Vacuum Switches
Push the switch fully into the retaining clip, then pull the brake pedal upward to adjust switch position. The electrical switch should break the electrical circuit when the brake pedal is depressed approximately .23–.51 inch.

Servo, Adjust

Models With Rod
Install the pin retainer to provide minimum slack with carburetor in slow idle position.

Models With Bead Chain
Assemble the chain into swivel and install retainer so that slack in the chain is not greater than one-half the diameter of the ball stud with the engine at operating temperature and the idle solenoid de-energized.

Cruise Speed, Adjust

The cruise speed adjustment can be set as follows:
1. If car cruises below engagement speed, screw orifice tube on transducer outward.
2. If car cruises above engagement speed, screw orifice tube inward.

NOTE: Each 1/4 turn of the orifice tube will change cruise speed about one mile per hour. Snug up lock nut after each adjustment.

Engine Section

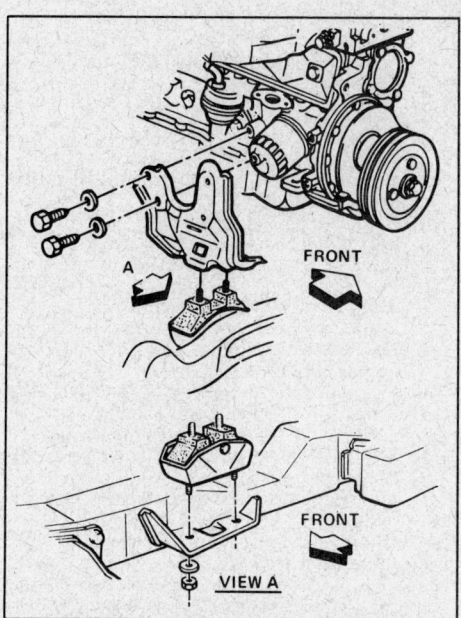

Fig. 1 Engine mounts. 1980–81 4-151

ENGINE MOUNTS, REPLACE

4-151

1. Raise and support front of vehicle, then remove chassis to mount attaching nuts, Figs. 1 and 1A.
2. On models equipped with A/C, remove forward torque rod attaching bolts at radiator support panel.
3. Raise engine slightly using a suitable engine lifting device. Raise engine only enough to provide clearance for mount removal.
4. Remove two upper mount to engine support bracket attaching nuts and remove engine mount.
5. Reverse procedure to install.

V6-173

1. Remove mount retaining nuts from below cradle mounting bracket.
2. Raise engine and remove mount to engine attaching nuts, then remove mount, Figs. 2 and 2A. Raise engine only enough to provide clearance for mount removal.
3. Reverse procedure to install, then lower engine into position. Install retaining nuts and torque to 35 ft. lbs.

NOTE: After engine mount is properly installed, check both transaxle mounts for proper alignment. If window "A" is not properly located, Fig. 3, loosen mount to cradle retaining nuts and allow mount to reposition itself. If transaxle mount is allowed to remain out of position, damage to drive train components may result. Torque retaining nuts to 18 ft. lbs.

ENGINE, REPLACE

1980 4-151

1. Disconnect battery ground cable.

2. Drain cooling system, then remove air cleaner.
3. Disconnect distributor, starter, alternator, oil pressure and engine temperature sender wiring and all other electrical connections that will interfere with engine removal. Also disconnect engine to body ground cable.
4. Disconnect and tag all vacuum hose connections that will interfere with engine removal.
5. Disconnect throttle and transaxle linkage at carburetor, then remove upper radiator hose.
6. On models equipped with A/C, remove A/C compressor from mounting bracket and position aside. Do not disconnect hoses.
7. Remove front engine strut assembly.
8. Disconnect heater hose at intake manifold.

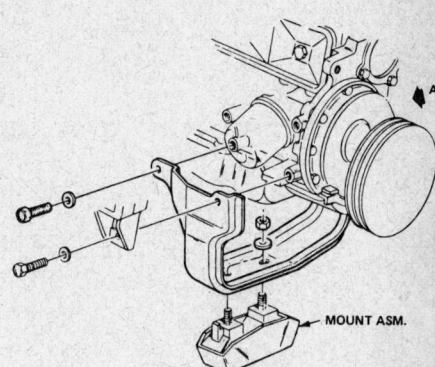

Fig. 1A Engine mounts. 1982–84 4-151

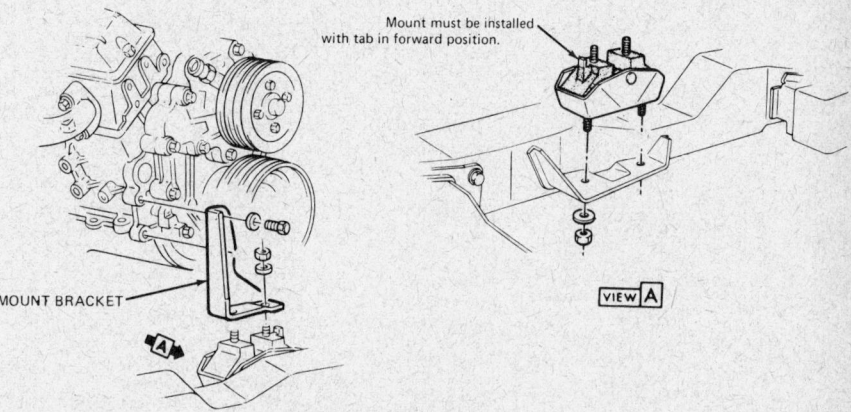

FRONT ENGINE MOUNT

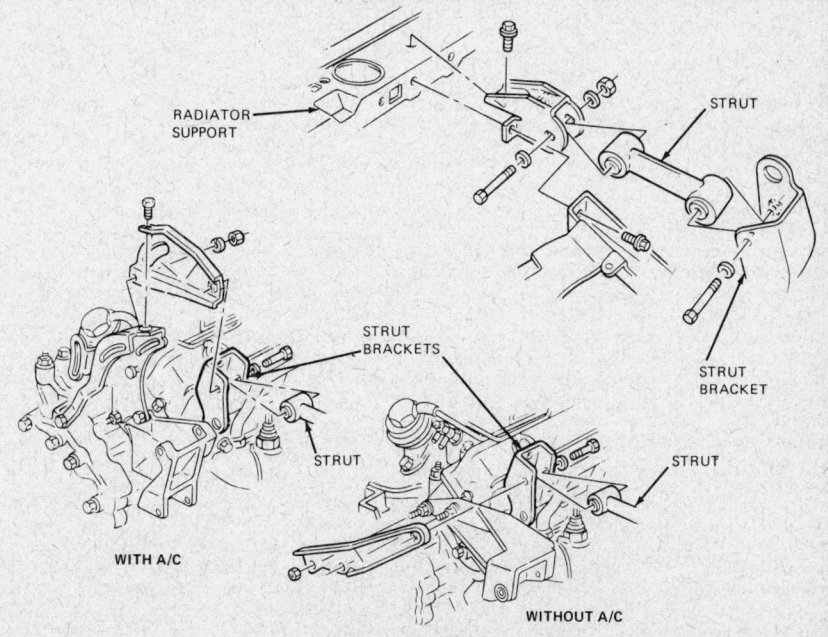

ENGINE STRUT

Fig. 2 Engine mounts. 1980–81 V6-173

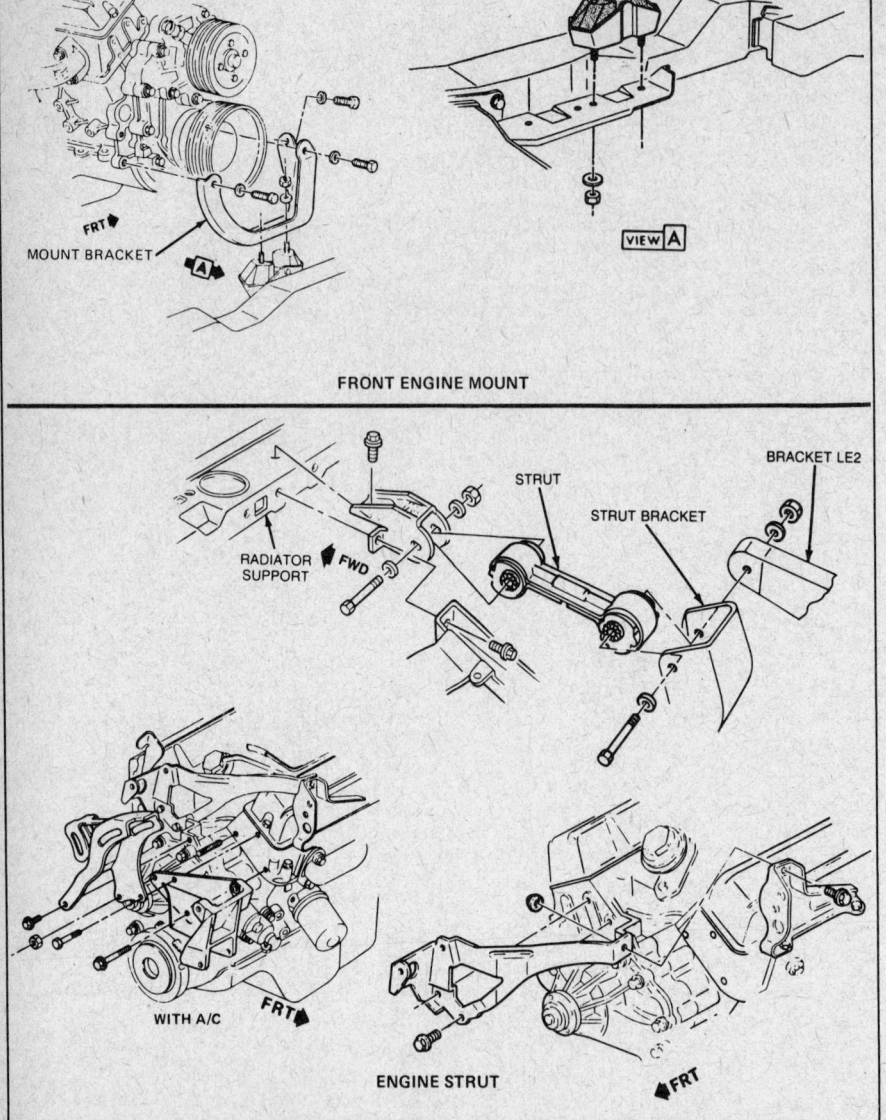

DRAIN HOLE MUST POINT REARWARD.

VIEW A

FRONT ENGINE MOUNT

RADIATOR SUPPORT — FWD — STRUT — STRUT BRACKET — BRACKET LE2

WITH A/C — FRT

ENGINE STRUT — FRT

Fig. 2A Engine mounts. 1982–84 V6-173

9. Remove transaxle to engine attaching bolts, leaving the upper two bolts in place.
10. Remove front mount to cradle bracket attaching nuts.
11. Remove forward exhaust pipe, then remove flywheel inspection cover and starter motor.
12. On models equipped with automatic transmission, remove torque converter to flywheel attaching bolts.
13. Remove power steering pump and bracket and position aside, if equipped.
14. Remove heater hose and lower radiator hose.
15. Remove two rear transaxle support bracket bolts.
16. Disconnect fuel line at fuel pump.
17. Using a suitable jack and a block of wood placed under the transaxle, raise engine and transaxle until engine front mount studs clear cradle bracket.
18. Using suitable engine lifting equipment,

put tension on engine, then remove the two remaining transaxle bolts.
19. Slide engine forward and lift engine from vehicle.
20. Install engine using suitable engine lifting equipment. Align engine with transaxle bell housing.

NOTE: Do not completely lower engine into chassis while jack is supporting transaxle.

21. With engine lifting equipment supporting engine, install two upper bell housing to engine attaching bolts.
22. Remove jack supporting transaxle, then lower engine onto chassis mounts and remove engine lifting equipment.
23. Raise and support front of vehicle, then install front mount to chassis attaching nuts.

24. To complete installation, reverse procedure following steps 1 through 16.

1981–84 4-151

Manual Transaxle
1. Disconnect cables from battery.
2. Raise and support vehicle.
3. Remove front engine mount-to-cradle attaching nuts.
4. Remove front exhaust pipe, then disconnect starter motor and position aside.
5. Remove flywheel inspection cover, then lower vehicle.
6. Remove air cleaner assembly.
7. Remove all bell housing attaching bolts.
8. Remove front torque reaction rod from engine and core support.
9. On models equipped with A/C, remove compressor drive belt, then disconnect compressor and position aside. Do not disconnect refrigerant lines from compressor.
10. Disconnect vacuum hoses from vapor canister.
11. On models equipped with power steering, disconnect power steering hose.
12. Disconnect all vacuum hoses and electrical connections needed for engine removal.
13. Remove heater blower motor as described under "Blower Motor, Replace" in the electrical section of this chapter.
14. Disconnect throttle cable.
15. Drain cooling system.
16. Disconnect heater hoses from engine and radiator hoses from radiator.
17. Disconnect engine electrical harness at bulkhead connector.
18. Install suitable engine lifting equipment and raise engine. Disconnect fuel line and the heater hose from intake manifold, then remove engine from vehicle.
19. Reverse procedure to install.

Automatic Transaxle
1. Disconnect cables from battery, then drain cooling system.
2. Remove air cleaner assembly and preheat tube.
3. Disconnect engine electrical harness connector.
4. Disconnect all external vacuum hose connections.
5. Remove throttle and transaxle linkages at the throttle body assembly and intake manifold.
6. On models equipped with A/C, disconnect compressor and position aside. Do not disconnect refrigerant lines from compressor.
7. Remove front engine strut assembly.
8. Disconnect heater hose from intake manifold.
9. Remove all transaxle-to-engine attaching bolts except the top two bolts.
10. Remove front engine mount-to-cradle nuts.
11. Remove front exhaust pipe, then the flywheel inspection cover.
12. Remove starter motor.
13. Remove torque converter-to-flywheel attaching bolts.
14. On models equipped with power steering, remove power steering pump and bracket and position aside.
15. Disconnect heater hose and lower radiator hose.
16. Remove 2 rear transaxle support bracket bolts.
17. Disconnect fuel feed line at fuel filter.

18. Using a suitable jack and a block of wood placed under transaxle, raise engine and transaxle until engine front mount studs clear cradle bracket.
19. Attaching suitable lifting equipment to engine. Put tension on engine and remove 2 remaining transaxle-to-engine attaching bolts.
20. Slide engine assembly forward and lift from vehicle.
21. Reverse procedure to install.

1980—81 V6-173

Manual Transaxle
1. Disconnect battery cables from battery, then remove air cleaner.
2. Drain cooling system, then disconnect and tag all vacuum hoses that will interfere with engine removal.
3. Disconnect throttle linkage from carburetor.
4. Disconnect engine wiring harness connector.
5. Disconnect radiator hoses from radiator and heater hoses from engine.
6. Remove power steering pump and bracket from engine, if equipped.
7. Disconnect clutch cable from transaxle and shift linkage from transaxle shift levers. Remove cables from transaxle bosses.
8. Disconnect speedometer cable from transaxle, then lower vehicle.
9. Install engine support fixture J-22825 between cowl and radiator support, locate support hook into engine rear lifting eye, Fig. 4. Raise engine until weight is relieved from mount assemblies.
10. Remove all but one transaxle to engine attaching bolts.
11. Unlock steering column and raise vehicle.
12. Remove stabilizer bar to lower control arm attaching nuts.
13. Remove side and crossmember plate to side and crossmember assembly attaching bolts and remove plate assembly on lefthand side. Loosen plate bolts on right side.
14. Remove crossover pipe, then remove front, rear and side powertrain mount to cradle attaching bolts.
15. Remove left front wheel and tire assembly.
16. Remove front crossmember to right side member attaching bolts.
17. Using tool No. J-28468, pull both driveshafts from transaxle assembly.
18. Remove lefthand side cradle to body mount attaching bolts.
19. Swing side and crossmember assembly to left and secure to fender well.
20. Lower left side of engine by loosening engine support fixture J-22825, then position a suitable jack under transaxle.
21. Remove the one remaining transaxle to engine attaching bolt, then separate transaxle from engine and lower transaxle from vehicle.
22. Install suitable engine lifting equipment.
23. If equipped with A/C, remove A/C compressor from mounting bracket and position aside. Do not disconnect hoses.
24. Disconnect forward strut bracket from radiator support and position out of way.
25. Raise engine and remove from vehicle.
26. Reverse procedure to install.

Automatic Transaxle
1. Disconnect battery ground cable and remove air cleaner.

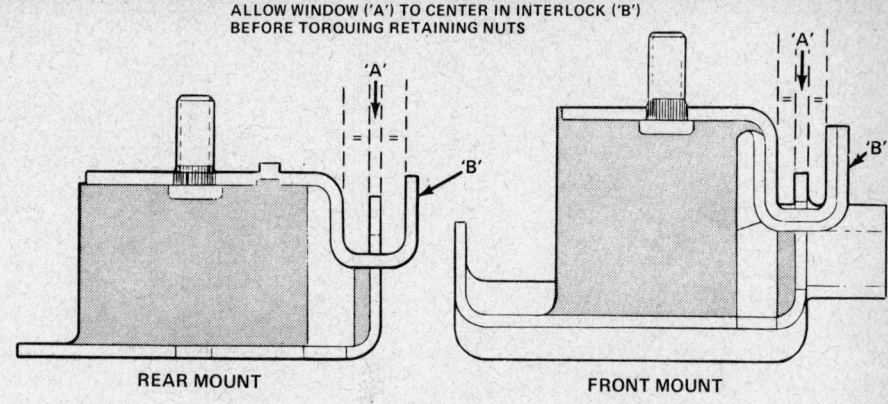

ALLOW WINDOW ('A') TO CENTER IN INTERLOCK ('B') BEFORE TORQUING RETAINING NUTS

REAR MOUNT FRONT MOUNT

Fig. 3 Transaxle mount alignment. V6-173

2. Drain cooling system, then disconnect all vacuum hoses that will interfere with engine removal.
3. Disconnect detent cable and throttle cable from carburetor.
4. Disconnect engine wiring harness connector and engine to body ground strap at engine forward strut.
5. Disconnect radiator hoses from radiator and heater hoses from engine.
6. Remove power steering pump and bracket from engine and position aside.
7. Raise vehicle and remove crossover pipe.
8. Disconnect fuel lines at hose connects on right hand side of engine.
9. Remove engine front mount to cradle attaching nuts.
10. Disconnect battery cables from starter motor and transaxle case.
11. Remove torque converter housing cover and disconnect torque converter from flex plate.
12. Remove transaxle to engine block support bracket bolts.
13. Lower vehicle and support transaxle by positioning a suitable jack under transaxle rear extension.
14. Remove engine strut bracket from radiator support and position out of way.
15. Remove transaxle to engine retaining bolts. Note location of ground stud.
16. If equipped with A/C, remove A/C compressor from mounting bracket and position aside.
17. Install suitable engine lifting equipment, then raise engine and remove from vehicle.
18. Reverse procedure to install.

1982—84 V6-173

1. Disconnect battery cables from battery and remove air cleaner.
2. Drain cooling system.
3. Remove engine strut bracket from radiator support and swing rearward.
4. Remove AIR pump and bracket, then remove A/C compressor from mounting bracket and place aside, if so equipped.
5. Disconnect vacuum hosing to all non-engine mounted components.
6. Disconnect accelerator cable and detent cable if so equipped.
7. Disconnect engine harness from ECM and pull connector through front of dash.
8. Disconnect engine harness from junction block at left side of dash panel.
9. Disconnect radiator and heater hoses from engine.
10. Remove power steering pump and bracket assembly from engine, if so equipped.

11. Disconnect fuel lines rubber hose connections at left side of engine compartment.
12. Raise vehicle, remove engine front mount-to-cradle and mount-to-engine bracket retaining nuts at right side of vehicle.
13. Disconnect battery cables from starter motor and transaxle case and remove starter.
14. Remove transaxle inspection cover and on automatic transaxle models, disconnect torque converter flex plate.
15. Remove crankshaft lower pulley and remove all bolts.
16. Disconnect exhaust pipe.
17. Remove lower transaxle-to-engine bolt, located at back side of engine.
18. Disconnect power steering cut-off switch, if so equipped.
19. Remove exhaust cross over pipe, then lower vehicle.
20. Remove remaining transaxle-to-engine bolts. Make note of ground stud location.
21. Place a support under transaxle rear extension. Install suitable lifting device and remove engine.
22. Reverse procedure to install.

CYLINDER HEAD, REPLACE

4-151

1. Raise and support front of vehicle, then drain cooling system and disconnect exhaust pipe from exhaust manifold.
2. Lower vehicle and remove oil dipstick tube and air cleaner.
3. Disconnect wire connectors and vacuum hoses from carburetor.
4. Remove EGR valve base plate from intake manifold.
5. Disconnect heater hose from intake manifold, then remove AIR system discharge tube attaching bolt from intake manifold.
6. Remove ignition coil lower attaching bolt, then disconnect wiring from coil.
7. Disconnect all wiring from cylinder head and intake manifold, then remove engine upper support attaching bolt from engine strut.
8. Remove A/C compressor and position aside with refrigerant lines attached.
9. Remove alternator drive belt, then remove AIR pump bracket bolt from engine block.
10. Disconnect throttle and throttle valve cables from carburetor and intake mani-

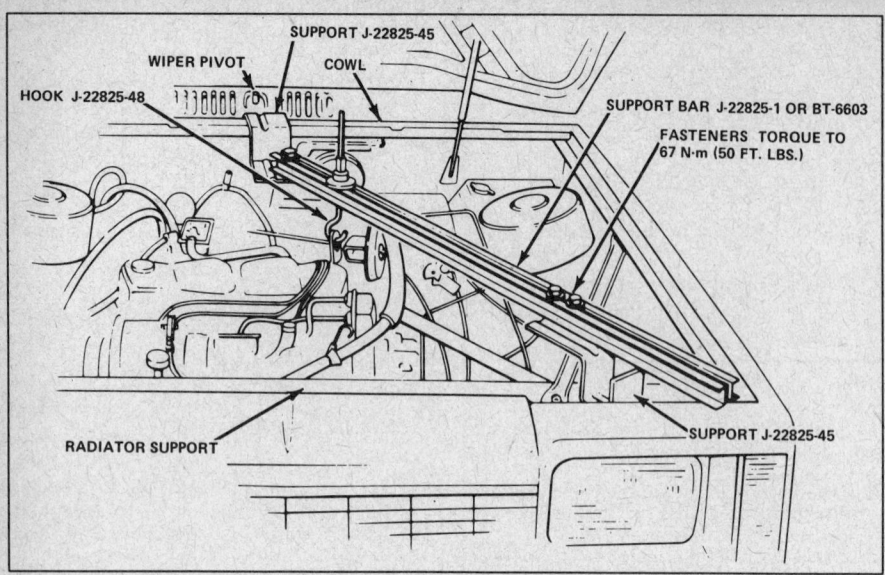

Fig. 4   Engine support fixture

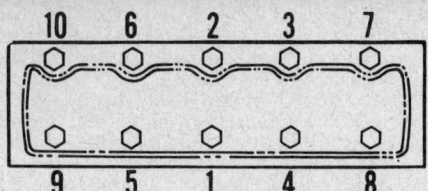

Fig. 5   Cylinder head tightening sequence. 1980 4-151

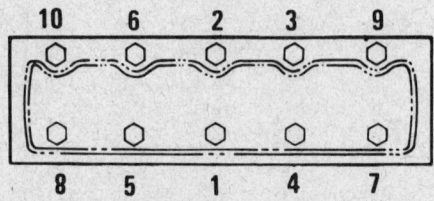

Fig. 5A   Cylinder head bolt tightening sequence. 1981—84 4-151

fold.

11. Disconnect upper radiator hose from cylinder head, then disconnect AIR hose from tube assembly.
12. Remove rocker arm cover, then remove rocker arms and push rods.
13. Remove cylinder head attaching bolts, then lift cylinder head and intake and exhaust manifolds as an assembly from cylinder block.
14. Reverse procedure to install. Coat heads and threads of cylinder bolts with a suitable sealing compound, then install bolts finger tight. Tighten cylinder head bolts in sequence shown in Figs. 5 and 5A. Tighten intake manifold bolts in sequence shown in Fig. 6, if necessary.

1982—84 V6-173

Right
1. Raise and support vehicle.
2. Drain cooling system.
3. Disconnect exhaust pipe, then lower vehicle.
4. On models equipped with cruise control, remove servo bracket.
5. Remove air management valve and hose.
6. Remove intake manifold, then disconnect exhaust crossover pipe.
7. Loosen rocker arm stud nuts until push rods can be removed.
8. Remove cylinder head attaching bolts and the cylinder head.
9. Reverse procedure to install. Coat cylinder head bolt threads with a suitable sealing compound. Torque cylinder head attaching bolts to specifications in

sequence shown in Fig. 7 and intake manifold attaching bolts in sequence shown in Fig. 8.

Left
1. Raise and support vehicle.
2. Drain cooling system.
3. Lower vehicle, then remove intake manifold and exhaust crossover pipe.
4. Remove alternator bracket, then the air injection pump and brackets.
5. Remove dipstick tube, then loosen rocker arm stud nuts until push rods can be removed.
6. Remove cylinder head attaching bolts and the cylinder head.
7. Reverse procedure to install. Coat cylinder head bolt threads with suitable sealing compound. Torque cylinder head attaching bolts to specifications in sequence shown in Fig. 7, and intake manifold attaching bolts in sequence shown in Fig. 8.

1980—81 V6-173

1. Remove intake manifold, then disconnect exhaust pipe from exhaust manifold.
2. If left hand cylinder head is to be removed, remove alternator bracket and stud, heat stove pipe, P.A.I.R. pipe and dipstick tube pipe bracket from cylinder head.
3. Loosen rocker arm stud nuts until push rods can be removed.
4. Remove cylinder head attaching bolts, then remove cylinder head.
5. Reverse procedure to install. Coat cylin-

der head bolt threads with sealer and install bolts finger tight. Torque cylinder bolts in sequence shown in Fig. 7 and intake manifold bolts in sequence shown in Fig. 8.

ROCKER ARM STUDS

4-151

Rocker arm studs that are cracked or have damaged threads can be removed from the cylinder head using a deep well socket. Install and torque new rocker arm stud to 75 ft. lbs.

V6-173

Rocker arm studs that are cracked or have damaged threads can be replaced. If threads

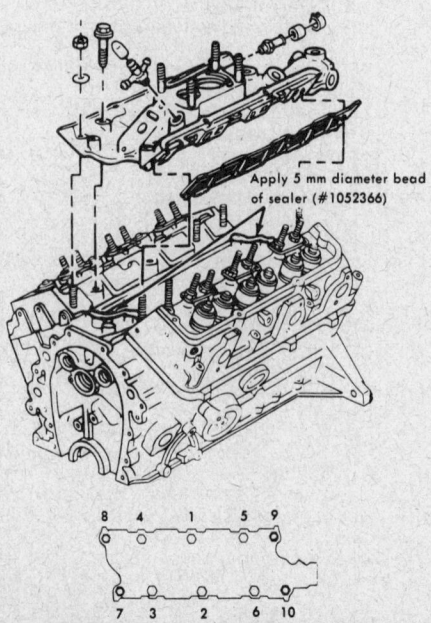

Apply 5 mm diameter bead of sealer (#1052366)

Fig. 8   Intake manifold tightening sequence. V6-173

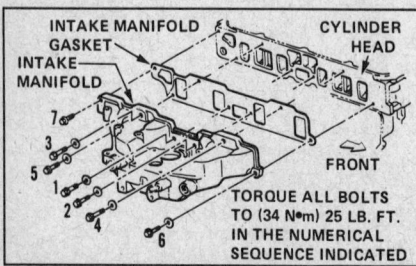

Fig. 6   Intake manifold tightening sequence. 4-151

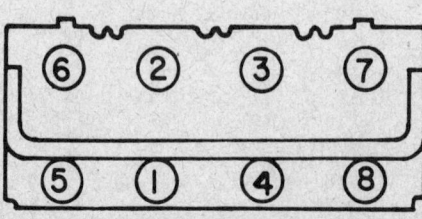

Fig. 7   Cylinder head tightening sequence. V6-173

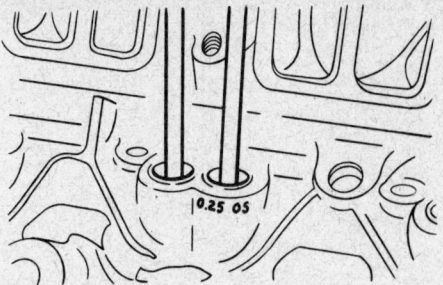

Fig. 9 Oversize valve lifter marking. V6-17′

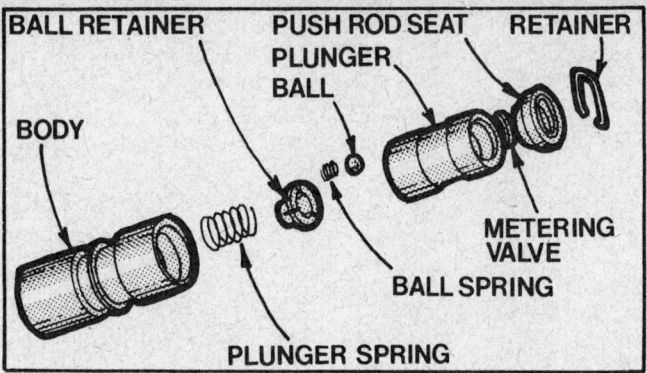

Fig. 10 Hydraulic valve lifter components

in cylinder head are damaged or stripped, the head can be retapped and a helical type insert added. When installing a new rocker arm stud, torque stud to 43 to 49 ft. lbs.

VALVES, ADJUST

V6-173

1. Crank engine until mark on torsional damper is aligned with TDC mark on timing tab. Check to ensure engine is in the No. 1 cylinder firing position by placing fingers on No. 1 cylinder rocker arms as mark on damper comes near TDC mark on timing tab. If valves are not moving, the engine is in the No. 1 firing position. If valves move as damper mark nears TDC mark on timing tab, engine is in the No. 4 cylinder firing position and should be rotated one revolution to reach the No. 1 cylinder firing position.
2. With engine in the No. 1 cylinder firing position, adjust the following valves: Exhaust- 1, 2, 3; Intake- 1, 5, 6. To adjust valves, back off adjusting nut until lash is felt at push rod, then tighten adjusting nut until all lash is removed. This can be determined by rotating the push rod while tightening the adjusting nut. When all lash has been eliminated, turn adjusting nut the additional number of turns listed in the Valve Specifications.
3. Crank engine one revolution until mark on torsional damper and TDC mark are again aligned. This is the No. 4 cylinder firing position. With engine in this position, the following valves can be adjusted: Exhaust- 4, 5 & 6; Intake- 2, 3 & 4.
4. Install rocker arm covers, then start engine and check timing and idle speed.

VALVE ARRANGEMENT

Front to Rear

4-151	I-E-I-E-E-I-E-I
V6-173 Right	E-I-E-I-I-E
V6-173 Left	E-I-I-E-I-E

VALVE LIFT SPECS.

Engine	Year	Intake	Exhaust
4-151	1980	.406	.406
	1981–84	.398	.398
V6-173	1980–84	.347	.394
V6-173 H.O.	1981	.393	.410
	1982–84	.394	.410

VALVE TIMING

Intake Opens Before TDC

Engine	Year	Degrees
4-151	1980–84	33
V6-173	1980–84	25
V6-173 H.O.	1981–84	31

VALVE GUIDES

Valve guides are an integral part of the cylinder head and are not removable. If valve stem clearance becomes excessive, the valve guide should be reamed to the next oversize and the appropriate oversize valves installed. Valves are available in .003 and .005 inch oversizes for 4-151 engine and .0035, .0155 and .0305 inch for V6-173 engines.

VALVE LIFTERS

NOTE: Some V6-173 engines will be equipped with both standard and .25 mm. oversize valve lifters. The cylinder case will be marked where the oversize valve lifters are installed with a daub of white paint and .25 mm. O.S. will be stamped on the valve lifter boss, Fig. 9.

Failure of a hydraulic valve lifter, Fig. 10, is generally caused by an inadequate oil supply or dirt. An air leak at the intake side of the oil pump or too much oil in the engine will cause air bubbles in the oil supply to the lifters causing them to collapse. This is a probable cause of trouble if several lifters fail to function, but air in oil is an unlikely cause of failure of a single unit.

On 4-151 engines, valve lifters can be removed after removing rocker arm cover, intake manifold and push rod cover. Loosen rocker arm stud nut and rotate rocker arm so that push rod can be removed, then remove valve lifter. It may be necessary to use tool No. J-3049 to facilitate lifter removal.

On V6-173 engines, valve lifters can be removed after removing rocker arm covers, intake manifold, rocker stud nuts, rocker arm balls, rocker arms and push rods.

ENGINE FRONT COVER, REPLACE

4-151

1. Remove drive belts, then remove right

front inner fender splash shield.
2. Remove crankshaft pulley attaching bolt, then remove pulley and hub from shaft.
3. Remove alternator lower bracket.
4. Remove front engine mount to cradle nuts, then install suitable engine lifting equipment and raise engine.
5. Remove engine mount bracket to cylinder block bolts, then remove mount and bracket as an assembly.
6. Remove oil pan to front cover attaching screws. Pull front cover slightly forward to permit cutting of oil pan front seal.
7. Using a suitable cutting tool, cut oil pan front seal flush with cylinder block at both sides of cover.
8. Remove front cover and attached portion of oil pan front seal, then remove front cover gasket.
9. Clean gasket surfaces on cylinder block and front cover.
10. Cut tabs from a new oil pan front seal using a suitable cutting tool, then install seal to front cover, pressing tabs into holes provided on front cover.
11. Coat front cover gasket with gasket sealer, then position gasket on front cover.
12. Apply a ⅛ inch bead of RTV sealer to joint formed at oil pan and cylinder block.
13. Install centering tool No. J-23042 into front cover seal bore. It is important that the centering tool be used to align front cover, otherwise damage to seal may result when hub is installed.
14. Install front cover to block, then install and partially tighten the two oil pan to front cover screws.
15. Install front cover to cylinder block attaching screws. Torque all cover attaching screws to 90 inch lbs., then remove centering tool J-23042.
16. Install front mount bracket assembly and alternator lower mounting bracket.
17. Lower engine and remove engine lifting equipment.
18. Install lower mount to cradle nuts, crankshaft pulley and hub, right front fender inner splash shield and drive belts.

NOTE: Apply Drylock No. 299 or equivalent to threaded area of crankshaft pulley to hub bolts before installing bolts.

V6-173

1. Disconnect battery ground cable.
2. Remove accessory drive belts.
3. On 1983–84 models equipped with A/C, remove air injection pump and pump bracket.

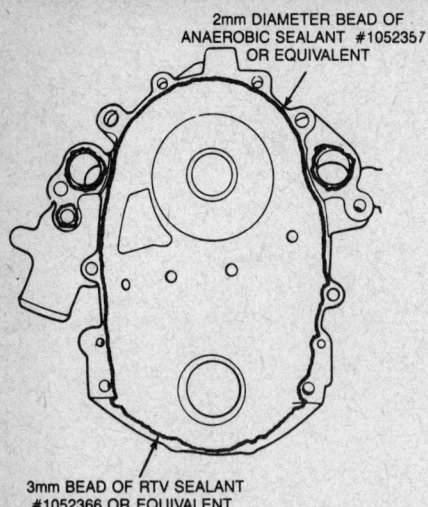

2mm DIAMETER BEAD OF ANAEROBIC SEALANT #1052357 OR EQUIVALENT

3mm BEAD OF RTV SEALANT #1052366 OR EQUIVALENT

Fig. 11   Engine front cover installation. V6-173

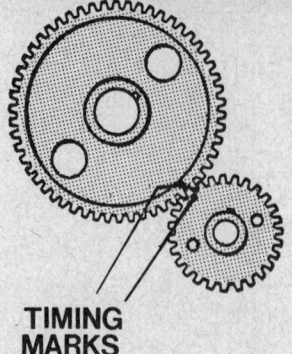

TIMING MARKS

Fig. 12   Valve timing marks. 4-151

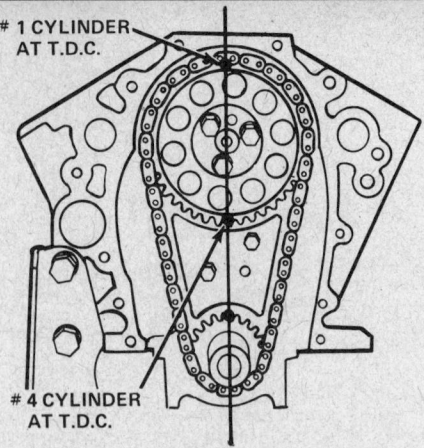

1 CYLINDER AT T.D.C.

4 CYLINDER AT T.D.C.

Fig. 13   Valve timing marks. V6-173

4. On all models, remove water pump as described under "Water Pump, Replace."
5. On 1980–82 models equipped with A/C, remove compressor from mounting bracket and position compressor aside, then remove bracket.
6. On all models, raise and support vehicle.
7. Remove inner fender splash shield, then the accessory drive pulley and damper retaining bolt.
8. Remove damper using tool No. J-23523, or equivalent.
9. On 1980–82 models, disconnect lower radiator hose from front cover and heater hose from water pump.
10. On 1983–84 models, remove oil pan-to-cover attaching bolts, then lower vehicle.
11. On all models, remove remaining front cover attaching bolts and the cover.
12. Reverse procedure to install. Apply sealant to mating surfaces as shown in Fig. 11.

TIMING GEARS

4-151 Engine

When necessary to install a new camshaft gear, the camshaft will have to be removed as the gear is a pressed fit on the camshaft. The camshaft is held in place by a thrust plate which is retained to the engine by two capscrews which are accessible through the two holes in the gear web.

To remove gear, use an arbor press and a suitable sleeve to properly support gear on its steel hub.

Before installing gear, assemble thrust plate and gear spacer ring, then press gear onto shaft until it bottoms against spacer ring. The thrust plate end clearance should be .0015–.0050 inch. If clearance is less than .0015 inch, the spacer ring should be replaced. If clearance is greater than .0050 inch, the thrust plate should be replaced.

The crankshaft gear can be removed using a puller and two bolts in the tapped holes of the gear.

When installing timing gears, make sure that the marks on the gears are properly aligned, Fig. 12.

NOTE: The valve timing marks, Fig. 12, do

not indicate TDC, compression stroke for No. 1 cylinder for use during distributor installation. When installing the distributor, rotate engine until No. 1 cylinder is on compression stroke and the camshaft timing mark is 180° from the valve timing position shown in Fig. 12.

TIMING CHAIN, REPLACE

V6-173

1. Remove front cover as described under "Front Cover, Replace."
2. Place No. 1 piston at top dead center with marks on camshaft and crankshaft sprockets aligned, Fig. 13.
3. Remove camshaft sprocket bolts, then remove sprocket and timing chain. If sprocket does not come off easily, tap lower edge of sprocket with a plastic mallet.
4. If crankshaft sprocket is to be replaced, remove sprocket using a suitable puller. Install new sprocket, aligning key and keyway.
5. Install timing chain on camshaft sprocket. Hold sprocket vertically with chain hanging down and align marks on camshaft and crankshaft sprockets.
6. Align dowel pin hole in sprocket with dowl pin on camshaft, then install sprocket on camshaft.
7. Using camshaft sprocket attaching bolts, draw sprocket on camshaft. Torque bolts to 15 to 20 ft. lbs.
8. Lubricate timing chain with engine oil, then install front cover as outlined previously.

CAMSHAFT, REPLACE

4-151

1. Remove engine from vehicle as described under "Engine, Replace."
2. Remove rocker arm cover, then loosen rocker arm stud nuts and pivot rocker arms clear of push rods.
3. Remove distributor and fuel pump or vacuum pump, if equipped.
4. Remove push rod cover, push rods and valve lifters.
5. Remove alternator, alternator lower mounting bracket and engine front mount bracket assembly.
6. Remove oil pump driveshaft and gear assembly.
7. Remove front pulley hub and front cover

assembly.
8. Working through holes in camshaft sprocket, remove two camshaft thrust plate retaining screws.
9. Pull camshaft and gear assembly from engine block. Use care not to damage camshaft bearings.
10. Reverse procedure to install. When installing camshaft, align crankshaft and camshaft valve timing marks on gear teeth, Fig. 12.

NOTE: The valve timing marks, Fig. 12, does not indicate TDC compression stroke for No. 1 cylinder for use during distributor installation. When installing the distributor, rotate engine until No. 1 cylinder is on compression stroke and the camshaft timing mark is 180 degrees from valve timing position shown in Fig. 12.

V6-173

1. Remove engine from vehicle as described under "Engine, Replace."
2. Remove valve lifters and engine front cover as described previously.
3. Remove fuel pump and push rod.
4. Remove timing chain and sprocket as described under "Timing Chain, Replace."
5. Withdraw camshaft from engine, using care not to damage camshaft bearings.
6. Reverse procedure to install. When installing timing chain, align valve timing marks as shown in Fig. 13.

NOTE: The valve timing marks, Fig. 13, does not indicate TDC compression stroke for No. 1 cylinder for use during distributor installation. When installing the distributor, rotate engine until No. 1 cylinder is on compression stroke and the camshaft timing mark is 180 degrees from valve timing position shown in Fig. 13.

PISTONS & RODS, ASSEMBLE

4-151

Assemble piston to rod with notch on piston facing toward front of engine and the raised notch side of rod at bearing end facing toward rear of engine, Fig. 14.

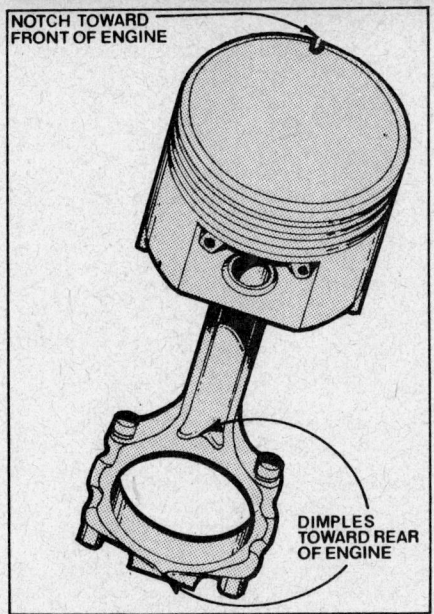

Fig. 14   Piston & rod assembly. 4-151

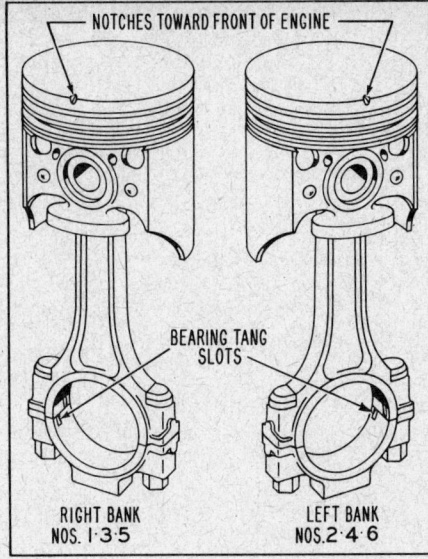

Fig. 15   Piston & rod assembly. V6-173

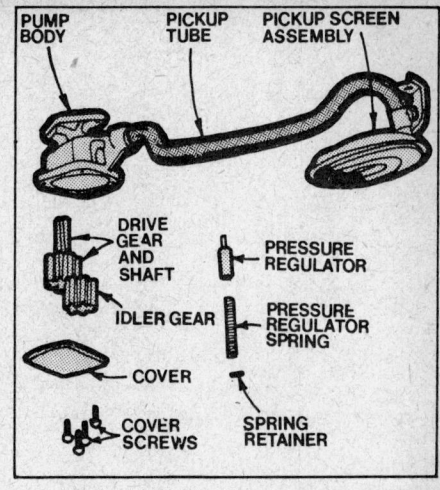

Fig. 16   Oil pump disassembled. 4-151

Upon installation, measure the connecting rod side clearance using a suitable feeler gauge. Clearance should be .006 to .022 inch.

V6-173

Assemble pistons to connecting rods as shown in Fig. 15.

Upon installation, measure the connecting rod side clearance using a suitable feeler gauge. Clearance should be .006 to .017 inch.

PISTONS, PINS & RINGS

4-151

Pistons and rings are available in standard and oversizes of .010, .020 and .030 inch. Piston pins are available in oversizes of .001 and .003 inch.

V6-173

Pistons and rings are available in standard size and oversizes of .05 and 1 mm.

MAIN & ROD BEARINGS

Main and rod bearings are available in standard size and undersizes of .001, .002 and .010 inch for the 4-151 engine. Main bearings are available in standard size and undersizes of .013 and .026 mm and connecting rod bearings are available in standard size and undersizes of .016 and .032 mm. for the V6-173 engine.

OIL PAN, REPLACE

4-151

1. Raise vehicle and drain crankcase.
2. Remove engine front mount to cradle attaching nuts.
3. Disconnect exhaust pipe at manifold and rear transaxle mount.
4. Remove starter motor and flywheel housing cover.

5. Remove alternator upper mounting bracket.
6. Install a suitable engine lifting device and raise engine.
7. Remove lower alternator mounting bracket and engine support bracket.
8. Remove oil pan attaching bolts and oil pan.
9. Clean engine block and oil pan gasket surfaces.
10. Reverse procedure to install. Apply a 1/8 in. by 1/4 in. long bead of RTV sealer at split lines of front and side oil pan gaskets. Also apply a small amount of RTV sealer in depressions where rear oil pan gasket engages engine block.

NOTE: When installing oil pan attaching bolts, the bolts attaching the oil pan to the front cover should be installed last. These bolts are installed at an angle and the bolt holes will only be aligned after the other oil pan bolts have been installed.

V6-173

1. Disconnect battery ground cable.
2. Raise and support vehicle.
3. Drain engine oil from crankcase.
4. On 1980–81 models, disconnect crossover pipe from exhaust manifold.
5. On all models, remove flywheel housing shield or clutch housing cover as applicable.
6. Remove starter motor.
7. On 1980–81 models with manual transmission and all 1982–84 models, attach suitable lifting equipment to engine. Remove engine mount bracket-to-engine attaching bolts and raise engine slightly.
8. On all models, remove oil pan attaching bolts and the oil pan.
9. Reverse procedure to install. Apply a 1/8 inch bead of RTV sealer to oil pan sealing flange.

OIL PUMP SERVICE

4-151

Removal
1. Drain crankcase, then remove oil pan as

described under "Oil Pan, Replace."
2. Remove two oil pump mounting bolts and nuts from main cap bolt and remove oil pump and screen as an assembly.

Disassemble
1. Remove four pump cover to body attaching screws, then remove cover, idler and drive gears and shaft, Fig. 16.
2. Remove pin, retainer, spring and pressure regulator valve.

Inspection
Inspect pump components and should any of the following conditions be found, the oil pump assembly should be replaced.
a. Inspect pump body for cracks and excessive wear.
b. Inspect oil pump gears for damage, cracks or excessive wear.
c. Check shaft for looseness in housing.
d. Check cover for wear that would allow oil to leak past ends of gears.
e. Check oil pick screen for damage to screen or relief grommet. Also remove any debris from screen surface.
f. Check pressure regulator valve for fit in body.

Assemble
1. Place drive gear and shaft in pump body, then install idler gear with smooth side of gear facing pump cover, Fig. 16.
2. Install and torque pump cover attaching screws to 105 inch lbs. Check to ensure that pump rotates freely.
3. Install pressure regulator valve, spring, retainer and pin.

Installation
1. Align oil pump shaft with tang on oil pump drive shaft, then install pump on block, positioning pump flange over oil pump drive shaft lower bushing.
2. Install oil pump mounting bolts and torque bolts to 20 ft. lbs., then install oil pan as described under "Oil Pan, Replace."

V6-173

Removal
1. Remove oil pan as described under "Oil Pan, Replace."
2. Remove pump to rear main bearing cap bolt and remove pump and extension shaft.

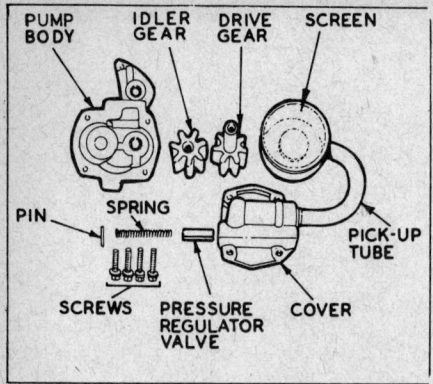

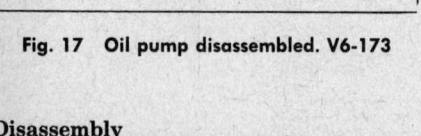

Fig. 17 Oil pump disassembled. V6-173

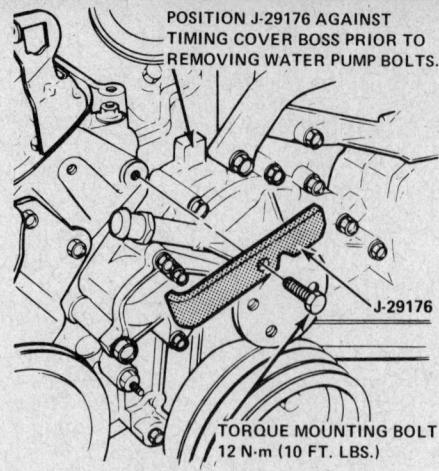

Fig. 18 Positioning tool J-29176 against timing cover boss. V6-173

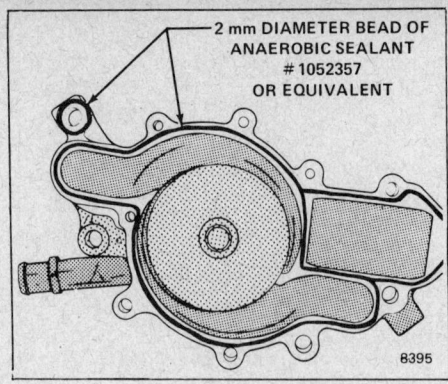

Fig. 19 Applying sealer to water pump mating surfaces. V6-173

Disassembly

1. Remove pump cover attaching bolts and pump cover, Fig. 17.
2. Mark drive and idler gear teeth so they can be installed in the same position, then remove idler and drive gear and shaft from pump body.
3. Remove pin, spring and pressure regulator valve from pump cover.
4. If pick-up tube and screen assembly are to be replaced, mount pump cover in a soft jawed vise and remove pick-up tube from cover. Do not remove screen from pick-up tube, these components are serviced as an assembly.

Inspection

1. Inspect pump body and cover for excessive wear and cracks.
2. Inspect pump gear for damage or excessive wear. If pump gears are damaged or worn, the entire pump assembly must be replaced.
3. Check drive gear shaft for looseness in pump body.
4. Inspect pump cover for wear that would allow oil to leak past gear teeth.
5. Inspect pick-up tube and screen assembly for damage.
6. Check pressure regulator valve for fit in pump cover.

Assembly

1. If pick-up tube and screen were removed, apply sealer to end of pick-up tube, then mount pump cover in a soft jawed vise and using tool No. J-8369, tap pick-up tube into position using a plastic mallet.

NOTE: Whenever the pick-up tube and screen assembly has been removed, a new pick-up tube and screen assembly should be installed. Use care when installing pick-up tube and screen assembly so that tube does not twist, shear or collapse. Loss of a press fit condition could result in an air leak and a loss of oil pressure.

2. Install pressure regulator valve, spring and pin, Fig. 17.
3. Install drive gear and shaft in pump body.
4. Align marks made during disassembly, then install idler gear.
5. Install pump cover gasket, cover and attaching bolts. Torque bolts to 6 to 9 ft. lbs.
6. Rotate pump drive shaft by hand and check pump for smooth operation.

Installation

1. Assemble pump and extension shaft with retainer to rear main bearing cap, aligning top end of hexagon extension shaft with hexagon socket on lower end of distributor shaft.
2. Install pump to rear main bearing cap bolt.
3. Install oil pan as described under Oil Pan, Replace.

CRANKSHAFT REAR OIL SEAL, REPLACE

4-151

NOTE: The rear main oil seal is a one piece unit and is replaced without removing the oil pan or crankshaft.

1. Remove transaxle and flywheel.
2. Using a suitable screwdriver, remove rear main bearing oil seal. Use care not to scratch crankshaft.
3. Lubricate inside and outside diameters of replacement seal with engine oil. Install seal by hand onto rear crankshaft flange with helical lip side facing toward engine. Ensure seal is firmly and evenly seated.
4. Install flywheel and transaxle.

REAR MAIN BEARING OIL SEAL REPAIR

V6-173

1. Remove oil pan and oil pump as described previously.
2. Remove rear main bearing cap.
3. Using tool No. J-29114-2, gently drive upper seal into groove approximately 1/4 in.
4. Repeat step 3 for other end of seal.
5. Measure the amount that was driven in on one side and add 1/16 in. Using a suitable cutting tool, cut this length from the oil rear main bearing cap lower seal using the main bearing cap as a guide. Repeat this step for the other end of seal.
6. Place piece of cut seal into groove of seal installer tool guide No. J-29114-1 and install tool guide onto engine block.
7. Using seal packing tool No. J29114-2, drive piece of seal into block. Drive seal in until packing tool contacts machined stop.

8. Remove tool guide and repeat steps 6 and 7 for other end of seal.
9. Install new seal in bearing cap.
10. Install rear main bearing cap. Apply a thin film of sealant No. 1052357 or equivalent to rear main bearing cap and case interface. Use care not to allow sealant to contact crankshaft journal or main bearing.

BELT TENSION DATA

	New Lbs.	Used Lbs.
Air Cond.		
4-151	135—165	65①
V6-173	145	65—80
A.I.R. Pump		
V6-173	100	45①
Alternator		
4-151	120—150	55①
V6-173	145	65—80
Power Steer.		
4-151	120—150	55①
V6-173	135	65—80

①—Minimum.

WATER PUMP, REPLACE

4-151

Removal

1. Disconnect battery negative cable.
2. Remove accessory drive belts.
3. Using tool J 25034, remove pulley.
4. Remove water pump attaching bolts and remove pump.

Installation

1. With sealing surfaces cleaned, place a 1/8 inch bead of sealant, part number 1052289 or equivalent, on water pump sealing surface.
2. With sealing surfaces still wet, install pump and attaching bolts. Coat threaded area of bolts with part number 1052080 sealer or equivalent and torque bolts to 6 ft. lbs.
3. Using tool J-25033, install pulley on pump.
4. Install accessory drive belts and adjust to specifications.
5. Connect battery negative cable.

V6-173

1. Disconnect battery ground cable, then drain cooling system.
2. Disconnect heater hose at water pump, then remove drive belts and water pump pulley.

3. Using the existing tapped hole in the cylinder head, install tool No. J-29167 and torque mounting bolt to 10 ft. lbs., Fig. 18.
4. Remove water pump attaching bolts, then remove pump assembly from engine.
5. Clean mating surfaces of water pump and cylinder block, then apply a bead of sealant 1052375 or equivalent to water pump mating surface, Fig. 19.
6. Apply sealant 1052080 or equivalent to pump attaching bolt threads, then install water pump assembly. Torque M6x1.0 bolts to 8 ft. lbs., M8x1.25 bolts to 16 ft. lbs. and M10x1.5 bolts to 25 ft. lbs.
7. Remove tool J-29176, then install water pump pulley and drive belts and connect heater hose to pump.
8. Fill cooling system and connect battery ground cable, then start engine and check for leaks.

FUEL PUMP, REPLACE

1982—84 V6-173

1. Disconnect fuel inlet and outlet lines

from pump.
2. Disconnect vapor return hose if equipped.
3. Remove fuel pump attaching nuts and the fuel pump.
4. Reverse procedure to install, using a new gasket.
5. Start engine and check for leaks.

1980—81 All

1. Disconnect battery ground cable, then raise and support vehicle.
2. On V6-173 models, remove shields and oil filter.
3. On all models, disconnect fuel inlet hose from pump, then disconnect vapor return hose if equipped.
4. Loosen fuel line at carburetor, then disconnect fuel outlet line from fuel pump.
5. Remove two fuel pump attaching bolts, then remove fuel pump.
6. Position fuel pump and gasket on block,

then install attaching bolts. Tighten fuel pump attaching bolts evenly and alternately.

NOTE: Before installing fuel pump, it is a good practice to crank the engine so that the fuel pump eccentric is out of the way of the fuel pump rocker arm when pump is installed. In this way there will be less tension on the rocker arm, thereby easing installation of pump.

7. Connect fuel outlet line to fuel pump. If difficulty is encountered in starting fitting, disconnect upper end of fuel line from carburetor and connect fuel line to fuel pump, then tighten fittings at carburetor and fuel pump.
8. Install fuel inlet hose and vapor return hose, if equipped.
9. On V6-173 models, install oil filter and shields, then check oil level.
10. On all models, lower vehicle and connect battery ground cable. Start engine and check for leaks.

Clutch & Transaxle Section

CLUTCH PEDAL, ADJUST

The clutch is automatically adjusted by a self-adjusting mechanism, Fig. 1, mounted to the clutch pedal and bracket assembly. The cable is a fixed length cable and cannot be shortened or lengthened, however, the position of the cable can be changed by adjusting the position of the quadrant in relation to the clutch pedal. The self-adjusting mechanism monitors clutch cable tension and adjusts the quadrant position, changing the effective cable length.

Inspection

1. With engine running and service and parking brakes applied, depress clutch pedal to approximately 1/2 inch from floor mat.
2. Move shift lever between "First" and "Reverse" gears several times. If no clashing of the gears occur when going into "Reverse," the clutch is releasing fully.
3. If the shifting in Step 2 is not smooth, the clutch is not releasing fully and the linkage should be inspected and corrected as necessary.
4. Check clutch pedal bushings for sticking or excessive wear.
5. Have an assistant depress the clutch pedal to the floor and observe clutch fork lever travel at transaxle. The end of the clutch fork lever should have a total travel of approximately 1.6–1.8 inches on 1980–81 models, or 1.5–1.7 inches on 1982–84 models.
6. To check the self-adjusting mechanism, proceed as follows:
   a. Depress the clutch pedal and observe if the pawl firmly engages the teeth of the quadrant.
   b. Release the clutch pedal and observe if the pawl is lifted off the quadrant teeth by the stop on the bracket.

CLUTCH, REPLACE

1. On 1982–84 models, disconnect clutch cable from clutch release lever and trans-

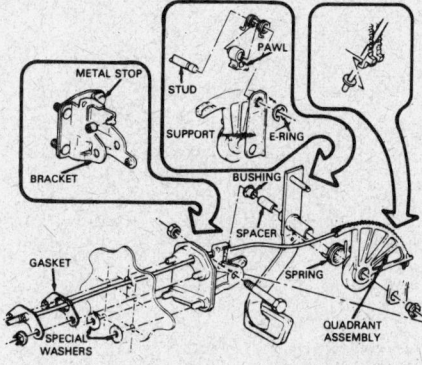

Fig. 1 Clutch self-adjusting mechanism

axle as follows:
   a. Support clutch pedal upward against bumper stop to release pawl from quadrant.
   b. Disconnect cable from clutch release lever on transaxle. Use care to avoid cable from snapping toward rear of vehicle.
   c. Disconnect cable from quadrant. Lift the locking pawl away from quadrant, then slide cable out on right side.
2. On all models, remove transaxle as described under "Manual Transaxle, Replace."
3. Mark position of pressure plate to flywheel to aid reassembly.
4. Gradually loosen pressure plate attaching bolts until spring pressure is relieved.
5. Support pressure plate and remove mounting bolts, pressure plate and driven disc, Fig. 2.
6. Clean pressure and flywheel mounting surfaces. Inspect bearing retainer outer surface of transaxle.
7. Place driven disc in relative installed position and support with a dummy shaft.

NOTE: The driven disc is installed with

the damper springs offset toward the transaxle. Stamped letters found on the driven disc identify the "Flywheel Side."

8. Install and gradually tighten the pressure plate to flywheel bolts. Remove dummy shaft.
9. Lubricate the release bearing outside diameter groove and the inside diameter recess.
10. Install transaxle.

MANUAL TRANSAXLE SHIFT CABLE, ADJUST

1982—84

1. Disconnect battery ground cable.
2. Shift transaxle into first gear.
3. Loosen shift cable attaching nuts "E" on transaxle lever "D" and "F," Fig. 3.
4. Remove console trim plate, then slide shifter boot up shifter handle and remove console.
5. Insert a yoke clip to hold lever as shown in view "D," Fig. 3.
6. Insert 5/32 inch or No. 22 drill bit into alignment hole on side of shifter assembly, view "C," Fig. 3.
7. Rotate lever "D" in direction of arrow while tightening nut "E," Fig. 3, to remove lash from transaxle.
8. Tighten nut "E" on lever "F," Fig. 3.
9. Remove drill bit and yoke from shifter assembly.
10. Reconnect battery ground cable.
11. Check for proper operation. If "hang-up" is encountered when shifting in the 1–2 gear range and shift cables are adjusted properly, it may be necessary to change shifter shaft selective washer. To determine correct washer thickness, refer to step 8 under "Manual Transaxle Shift Cable, Adjust," "1980–81."

1980—81

1. Remove shifter boot and retainer.
2. Install two 5/32 inch diameter pins or No. 22 twist drills into the alignment holes in

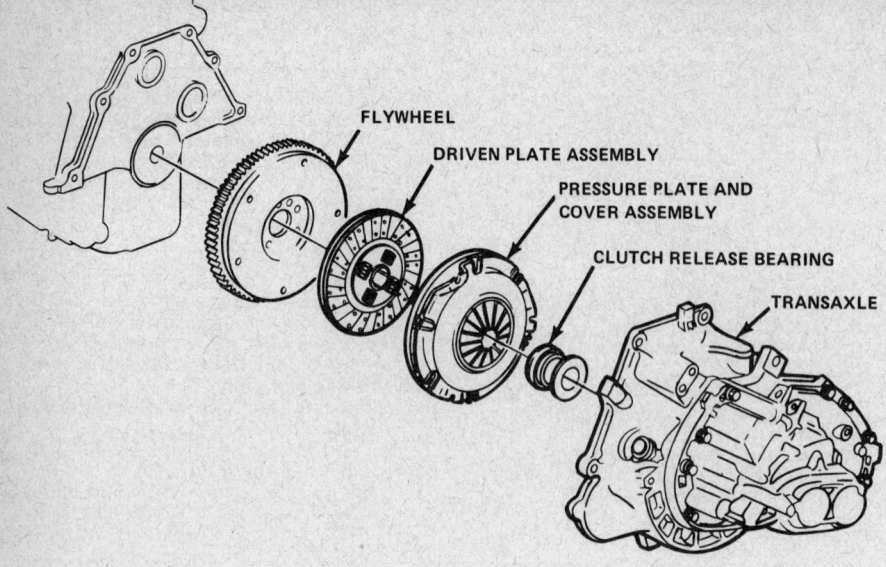

Fig. 2 Clutch assembly

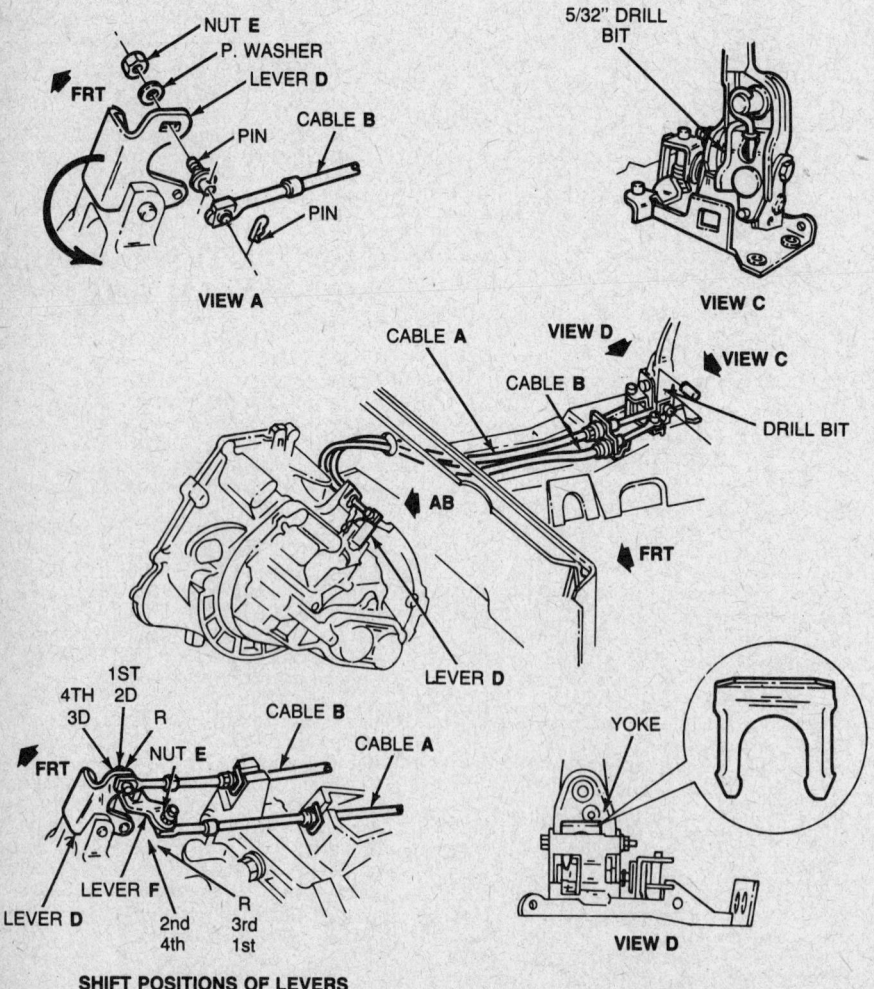

SHIFT POSITIONS OF LEVERS
VIEW B

Fig. 3 Manual transaxle shift cable adjustment. 1982–84

the control assembly.

3. Connect the two shift cables to the control assembly using the studs and pin retainers. The cables must be routed properly and operate freely.

4. Place transaxle into "First" gear by pushing the rail selector shaft inward (Downward) just to the point of resistance of the inhibitor spring. Then, rotate shift lever fully counter-clockwise.

5. Install stud with cable "A" attached, Fig. 4, into slotted area in shift lever "F".

6. Install stud with cable "B" attached, Fig. 4, into slotted area of select lever "D" while gently pulling on lever "D" to remove lash.

7. Remove the two pins or twist drills from control assembly.

8. Check for proper operation. If "Hang-up" is encountered when shifting in the 1–2 gear range and the shift cables are adjusted properly, it may be necessary to change the shifter shaft selective washer. Perform the following procedure to obtain correct washer thickness:

   a. Remove reverse inhibitor fitting spring and washer from end of housing.

   b. Place shifter shaft in "Second" gear.

   c. Measure dimension "A", Fig. 5, which is distance between end of housing and the shoulder just behind end of shaft.

   d. Apply a 9–13 pound load on opposite end of shaft, then measure dimension "B", Fig. 5, which is distance between end of housing and end of shifter shaft major diameter.

   e. Subtract dimension "B" from dimension "A" to obtain dimension "C".

   f. Refer to the following chart to obtain correct thickness shim:

Dimension "C" Inch	Shim Part No.
.07	14008235
.08	476709
.09	476710
.11	476711
.12	476712
.13	476713
.14	476714
.15	476715
.16	476716

MANUAL TRANSAXLE, REPLACE

1980–81

1. Disconnect battery ground cable from transaxle case and secure to upper radiator hose.

2. If equipped, remove transaxle strut bracket bolts at transaxle on left side of vehicle.

3. Remove the upper four engine to transaxle bolts and the bolt toward the rear of the vehicle near the cowl, Fig. 6. This bolt is installed from the engine side.

4. Loosen but do not remove the engine to transaxle bolt near the starter at front of vehicle.

5. Disconnect speedometer cable from transaxle. If equipped with Cruise Control, remove transaxle speedometer cable at cruise control transducer.

6. Remove retaining clip and washer from transaxle shift linkage at transaxle.

7. Remove clips securing shift cable to mounting bosses on transaxle case.

8. Install engine support fixture, Fig. 7, so that one end is supported on cowl tray over wiper motor and the other end rests

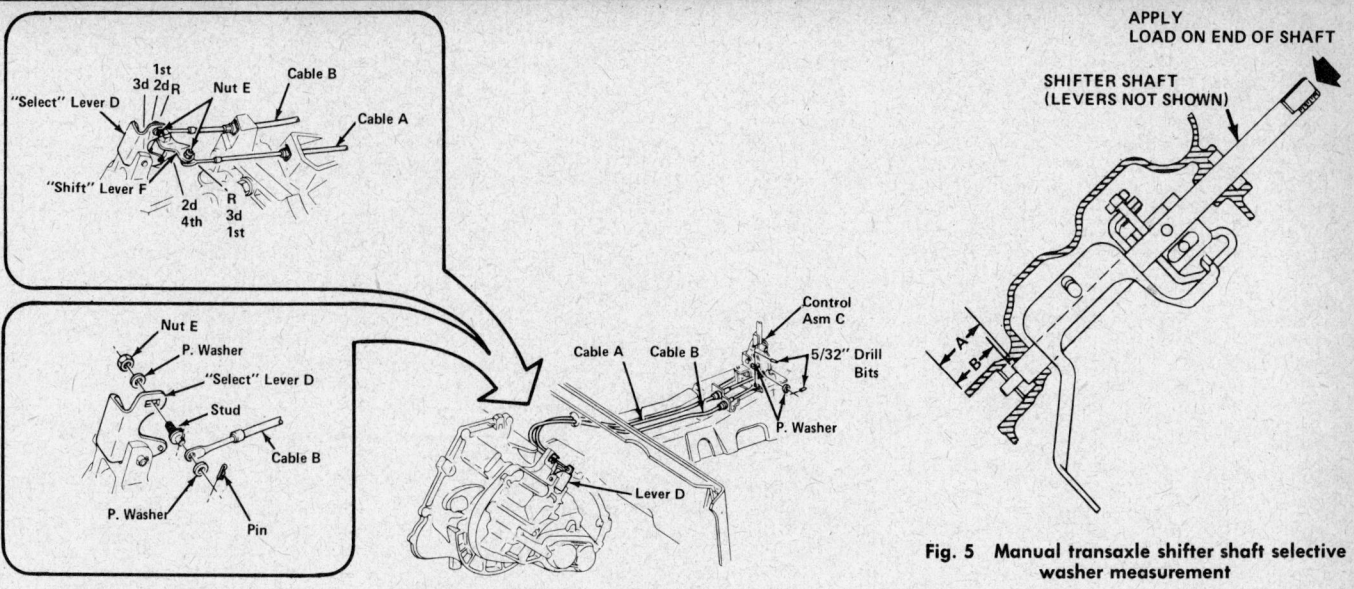

Fig. 4 Manual transaxle shift cable adjustment. 1980—81

Fig. 5 Manual transaxle shifter shaft selective washer measurement

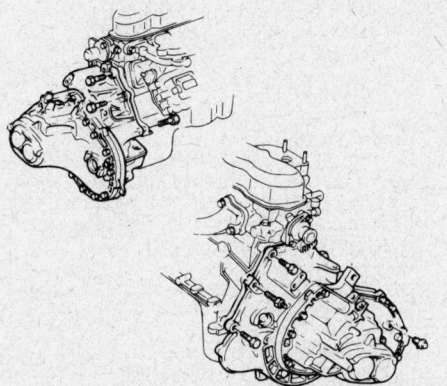

Fig. 6 Transaxle to engine attachment

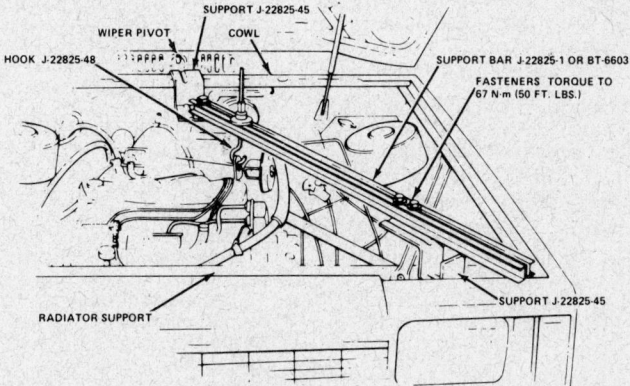

Fig. 7 Engine support tool installation

on the radiator support. Connect fixture hook to engine lift ring and raise engine to relieve weight from engine mounts.

CAUTION: The engine support fixture must be positioned in the center of the cowl and the attaching parts properly torqued before supporting engine. This fixture is not intended to support entire weight of engine and transaxle. Personal injury could result from improper use of the support fixture.

9. Unlock steering column and raise and support vehicle.
10. Drain fluid from transaxle case.
11. Remove two nuts securing stabilizer bar to vehicle left side lower control arm, Fig. 8.
12. Remove four bolts securing vehicle left side stabilizer bar retaining plate to cradle, Fig. 8.
13. Loosen four bolts securing stabilizer bracket on vehicle right side, Fig. 8.
14. If necessary, disconnect and remove exhaust pipe.
15. Pull stabilizer bar downward on vehicle left side.
16. Remove four nuts and disconnect the front and rear transaxle mounts at cradle, Fig. 8.
17. Remove two rear center crossmember bolts, Fig. 8.
18. Remove three front cradle attaching bolts

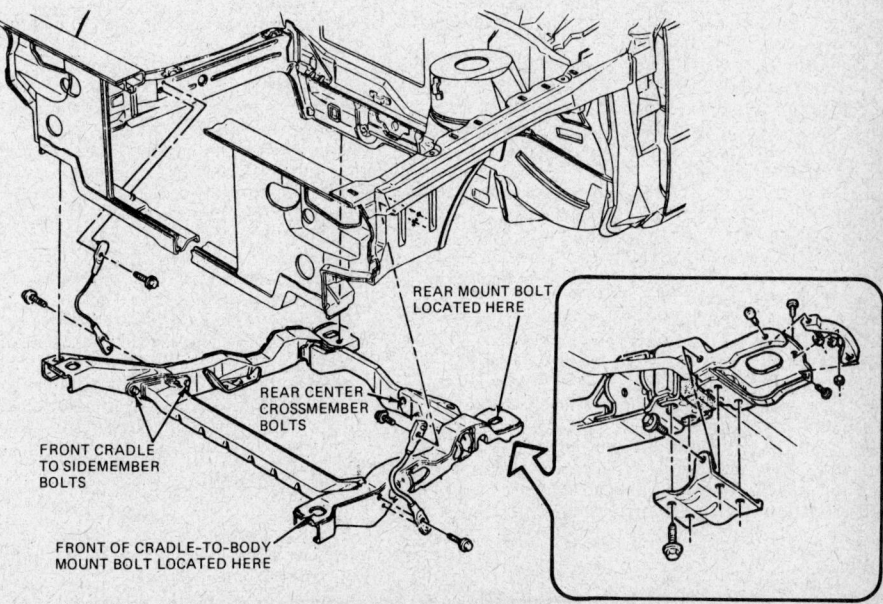

Fig. 8 Cradle attachments

at vehicle right side, Fig. 8. The nuts are accessible by pulling back the splash shield next to the frame rail.

19. If equipped, remove top bolt from lower front transaxle damper "Shock Absorber".
20. Remove left front wheel.
21. Remove the front cradle to body attaching bolts on left side of vehicle, then the rear cradle to body attaching bolts, Fig. 8.
22. Using tool J-28468 or equivalent, pull left side driveshaft from transaxle assembly. The right side driveshaft may be disconnected from the case. When the transaxle assembly is removed, the right side driveshaft may be swung aside. Use the boot protector when disconnecting the driveshafts.
23. Swing the partial cradle toward the vehicle left side and secure outboard of the fender well.
24. Remove the flywheel and starter shield bolts and the shields.
25. If equipped, remove two transaxle extension bolts from engine to transaxle bracket.
26. Securely attach the transaxle case to a suitable jack.
27. Remove the last transaxle to engine bolt.
28. Remove transaxle by sliding toward vehicle left side, away from engine. Lower transaxle from vehicle.
29. Reverse procedure to install and note the following:
   a. When installing the transaxle, position the right side drive axle shaft into its bore as transaxle is being installed. The right hand driveshaft cannot be readily installed after the transaxle is attached to the engine.
   b. After the transaxle is attached to the engine, swing the cradle into position and immediately install the cradle to body bolts. When swinging the cradle into the installed position, guide the left side driveshaft into the case bore.

1982

1. Disconnect battery ground cable from transaxle case and attach to upper radiator hose with wire or tape.
2. Remove two transaxle strut bracket bolts at transaxle, on left side of engine compartment, if so equipped.
3. Remove exhaust crossover pipe, if equipped.
4. Remove top four engine to transaxle bolts and one to rear of vehicle near cowl. The bolt nearer cowl is installed from engine side, Fig. 9.
5. Loosen but do not remove transaxle bolt near starter, at front of vehicle.
6. Disconnect speedometer cable at transaxle. On vehicles equipped with cruise control, remove transaxle speedometer cable at cruise control transducer.
6. Remove retaining clip and washer from transaxle shift linkage at transaxle.
7. Remove clips securing shift cables to mounting bosses on transaxle case.
8. Disconnect clutch cable. Install engine support fixture.
9. Remove left hand side and crossmember assembly using following procedures:
   a. Rotate steering wheel so that intermediate shaft to steering gear stub shaft attaching bolt is in up position and remove bolt.
   b. Raise vehicle.

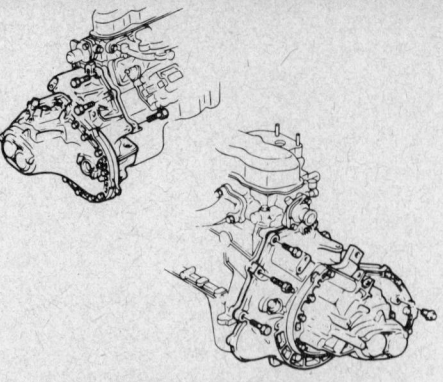

Fig. 9 Transaxle to engine attachment

   c. Position jack under engine to act as a support during removal and installation.
   d. Remove left front tire and wheel assembly.
   e. Remove power steering pressure and return line brackets.
   f. Disconnect drive line vibration absorber and disconnect front stabilizer bar from left hand lower control arm.
   g. Disconnect left lower ball joint at knuckle then remove both front stabilizer bar reinforcement.
   h. Using a 1/2 inch drill bit, drill through spot weld located between rear holes of left hand front stabilizer bar mounting.
   i. Disconnect engine and transaxle mounts from cradle.
   j. Remove side to crossmember bolts also bolts from left side body mounts.
   k. Remove left side and front crossmember assembly. It may be necessary to pull or gently pry crossmember loose.
10. Drain fluid from transaxle.
11. Install drive axle boot seal protectors. Disconnect drive axles from transaxle then swing left side drive axle outward from transaxle. Right side drive axle can be removed as transaxle is being removed from vehicle.
12. Remove flywheel and starter shield bolts. Remove shields.
13. Securely attach transaxle case to jack for removal.
14. Remove last transaxle to engine bolt.
15. Remove transaxle by sliding to left side, away from engine. Carefully lower jack, and move transaxle to bench.
16. Reverse procedure to install and note the following:
   a. When installing the transaxle, position the right side drive axle shaft into its bore as transaxle is being installed. The right hand driveshaft cannot be readily installed after the transaxle is attached to the engine.
   b. After the transaxle is attached to the engine, swing the cradle into position and immediately install the cradle to body bolts. When swinging the cradle into the installed position, guide the left side driveshaft into the case bore.

1983—84

1. Disconnect battery ground cable from transaxle and attach to upper radiator hose with wire or tape.

2. Disconnect electrical connector from horn, then remove horn attaching bolt.
3. Remove air cleaner assembly.
4. Disconnect clutch cable as follows:
   a. Support clutch pedal upward against bumper stop to release pawl from quadrant.
   b. Disconnect cable from clutch release lever on transaxle. Use care to prevent cable from snapping toward rear of vehicle.
   c. Disconnect cable from quadrant. Lift locking pawl away from quadrant, then slide cable out on right side.
   d. Disconnect 2 upper nuts on engine side of cowl, holding cable retainer to upper studs.
   e. Disconnect cable from bracket on transaxle.
5. On models with V6-173 engine, disconnect fuel lines and fuel line clamps from clutch cable bracket.
6. On all models, remove clutch cable bracket from transaxle.
7. On models with V6-173 engine, remove exhaust crossover pipe.
8. On all models, remove retaining clips and washers from transaxle shift linkage at transaxle.
9. Remove shift cable to mounting boss retaining clips from transaxle case.
10. Remove speedometer cable from transaxle.
11. Remove 5 upper engine-to-transaxle attaching bolts.
12. Install engine support fixture.
13. Raise and support vehicle.
14. Drain fluid from transaxle.
15. Install suitable drive axle boot seal protectors on both inner and outer seals.
16. Remove left front wheel assembly.
17. Remove left side cradle and crossmember assembly as follows:
   a. Position jack under engine to act as a support during removal and installation.
   b. Disconnect front ball joint.
   c. Disconnect front stabilizer bar from control arm.
   d. Remove front stabilizer bar plate and bushing from sidemember.
   e. Disconnect engine and transaxle mount from left sidemember.
   f. Remove sidemember-to-crossmember attaching bolts.
   g. Remove 2 left side body mount bolts.
   h. Remove left side and crossmember assembly.
18. Disconnect drive axles from transaxle, then swing left side drive axle outward from transaxle. Right side drive axle can be removed as transaxle is being removed from vehicle.
19. Remove flywheel and starter motor shield attaching bolts.
20. Securely attach transaxle case to jack for removal.
21. Remove remaining transaxle-to-engine attaching bolts.
22. Remove transaxle by sliding to left side away from engine and carefully lowering assembly from vehicle.
23. Reverse procedure to install, noting the following:
   a. When installing transaxle, position right side drive axle shaft into it's bore, as driveshaft cannot be installed after transaxle is attached to engine.
   b. After transaxle is attached to engine, swing cradle into position and immediately install cradle-to-body attaching bolts.

Rear Axle, Rear Suspension & Brakes

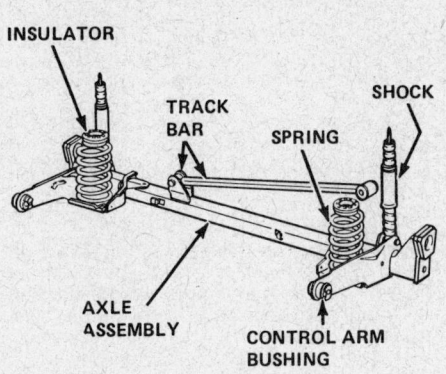

Fig. 1 Rear axle and suspension

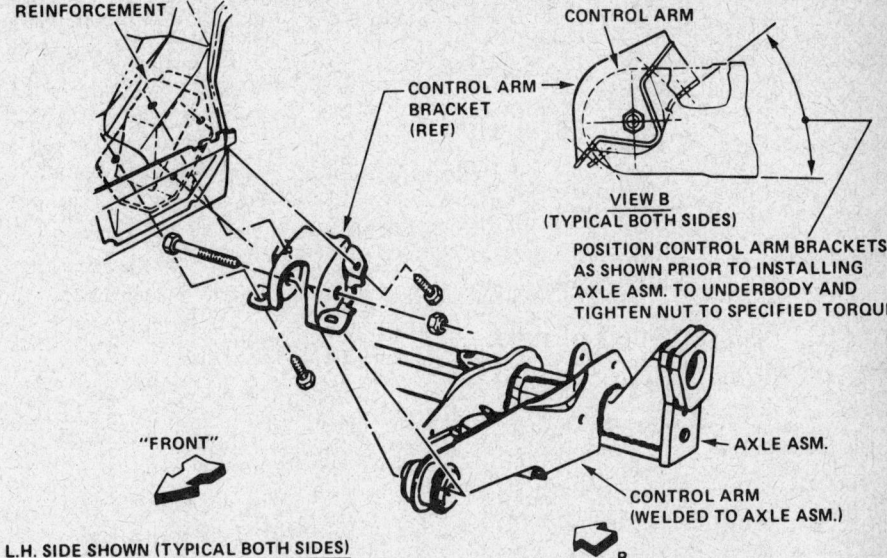

VIEW B
(TYPICAL BOTH SIDES)

POSITION CONTROL ARM BRACKETS AS SHOWN PRIOR TO INSTALLING AXLE ASM. TO UNDERBODY AND TIGHTEN NUT TO SPECIFIED TORQUE

L.H. SIDE SHOWN (TYPICAL BOTH SIDES)

Fig. 2 Control arm bracket installation

DESCRIPTION

The rear suspension. Fig. 1, consists of a rear axle assembly, control arms, coil springs, shock absorbers and a track bar. The rear axle is trailing arm type design. A stabilizer bar is welded to the inside of the axle housing and is an integral part of the axle assembly. A single unit hub and bearing assembly is bolted to each end of the axle assembly. The hub and bearing assembly is a sealed unit and must be replaced as an assembly.

REAR AXLE, REPLACE

1. Raise rear of vehicle and support rear axle using a suitable jack.
2. Remove rear wheel assembly and brake drum. Do not hammer on brake drum since damage to bearings may result.
3. Disconnect parking brake cable at equalizer, then remove brake line brackets from frame.
4. Disconnect shock absorber from lower mountings on axle housing.
5. Remove track bar attaching nut and bolt and disconnect track bar from axle housing.

NOTE: Do not suspend rear axle by brake hoses, otherwise damage to hoses may result.

6. Carefully lower rear axle assembly and remove coil spring and insulators.
7. Disconnect brake lines from control arm attachments.
8. Remove parking brake cable from rear axle attachments.
9. Remove hub attaching bolts, then the hub and bearing assembly and position backing plate out of way.
10. Remove control arm bracket to underbody attaching bolts, then lower axle assembly and remove from vehicle.
11. Reverse procedure to install, noting the following:
    a. If control arm brackets were removed from control arms, torque attaching nuts to 34 ft. lbs. on 1980–81 models, or 78 ft. lbs. on 1982–84 models.
    b. Install control arm bracket at a 45°

angle on 1980–81 models, or a 40.5–44.5° angle on 1982–84 models as shown in Fig. 2.
    c. Torque control arm-to-underbody attaching bolts to 20 ft. lbs. on 1980 models, or 28 ft. lbs. on 1981–84 models.
    d. Torque track bar attaching nut to 33 ft. lbs. on 1980–81 models, or 35 ft. lbs. on 1982–84 models.

HUB & BEARING ASSEMBLY, REPLACE

1. Raise and support rear of vehicle, then remove wheel and tire assembly and brake drum.

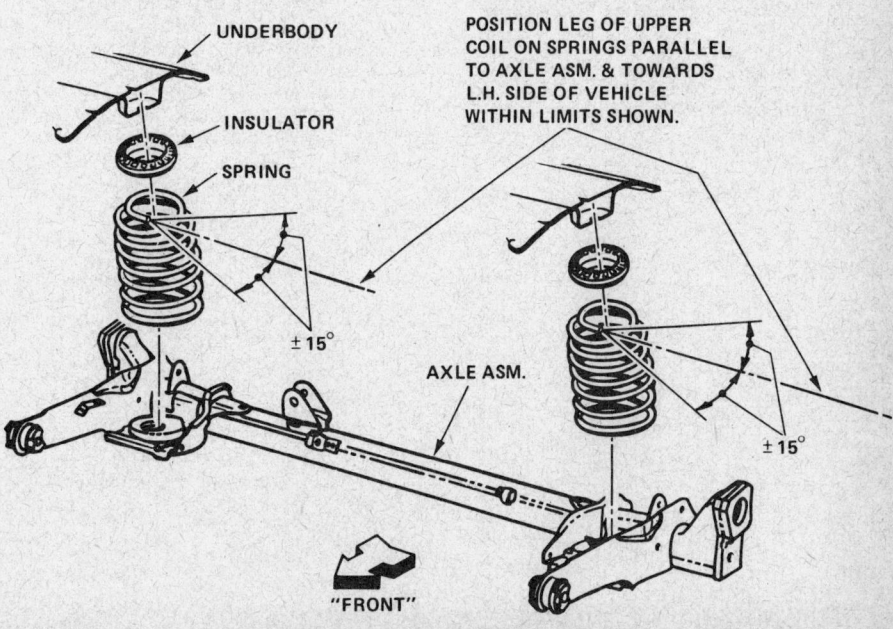

POSITION LEG OF UPPER COIL ON SPRINGS PARALLEL TO AXLE ASM. & TOWARDS L.H. SIDE OF VEHICLE WITHIN LIMITS SHOWN.

Fig. 3 Coil spring & insulator installation

NOTE: Do not hammer on brake drum since damage to bearing may result.

2. Remove four hub and bearing assembly to rear axle attaching bolts, then the hub and bearing assembly from axle.
3. Reverse procedure to install. Torque hub and bearing assembly to rear axle attaching bolts to 35 ft. lbs on 1980–81 models, or 45 ft. lbs. on 1982–84 models.

NOTE: Use care not to drop hub and bearing assembly since damage to bearing may result.

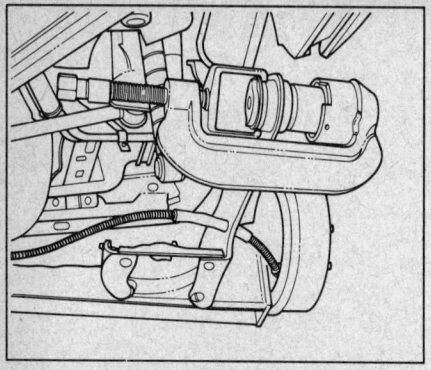

Fig. 4 Control arm bushing removal

COIL SPRING, REPLACE

1. Raise rear of vehicle and support rear axle using a suitable jack.
2. Remove right and left brake line bracket attaching bolts from frame and allow brake lines to hang freely.
3. Remove track bar attaching nut and bolt, then disconnect track bar from axle housing.
4. Disconnect shock absorbers at lower mountings.

NOTE: Do not suspend rear axle by brake hoses since damage to hoses may result.

5. Carefully lower rear axle assembly and remove springs and insulators.
6. Reverse procedure to install, Fig. 3.

CONTROL ARM BUSHING, REPLACE

1. Raise rear of vehicle and support rear axle under front side of spring seat using a suitable jack.
2. If right hand side bushing is to be replaced, disconnect parking brake cable from equalizer.
3. Remove parking brake cables from bracket attachment and position out of way.
4. Disconnect brake line bracket from frame.
5. Disconnect shock absorber from lower mounting, then pull spring out of way.
6. Remove four control arm to underbody attaching bolts and allow control arm to rotate downward.

7. Remove nut and bolt from bracket attachment and remove bracket.
8. The bushing can now be replaced using tools shown in Figs. 4 and 5. When installing bushing, press bushing in until end of bushing is aligned with scribed line on tool J-28685-2, Fig. 5.
9. Reverse procedure to install control arm. Install bracket to control arm as shown in Fig. 2.

TRACK BAR, REPLACE

1. Raise rear of vehicle and support rear axle using a suitable jack.
2. Remove nut and bolt attaching track bar at axle housing and underbody and remove track bar, Fig. 6.
3. Reverse procedure to install, Fig. 6. Open side of track bar must face rear of vehicle. Also nut must be at rear of attachments at both axle and underbody attachments. Torque attaching nut at axle bracket to 33 ft. lbs. Torque attaching nut at underbody reinforcement to 34 ft. lbs.

SHOCK ABSORBER, REPLACE

1. Open deck lid and remove trim cover, then remove shock absorber upper attaching nut.
2. Raise rear of vehicle and support rear axle using a suitable jack.
3. Disconnect shock absorber at lower attachment and remove shock absorber from vehicle.
4. Reverse procedure to install. Torque shock absorber lower attaching nut to 34 ft. lbs. on 1980–81 models, or 43 ft. lbs. on 1982–84 models. Torque shock absorber upper attaching nut to 7 ft. lbs. on 1980–81 models, or 13 ft. lbs. on 1982–84 models.

DRUM BRAKE ADJUSTMENTS

These brakes have self adjusting shoe mechanisms that assure correct lining-to-drum clearances at all times. The automatic adjusters operate only when the brakes are applied as the car is moving rearward.

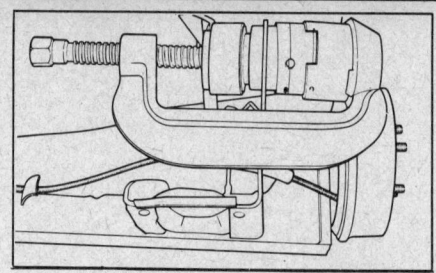

Fig. 5 Control arm bushing installation

Although the brakes are self-adjusting, an initial adjustment is necessary after the brake shoes have been relined or replaced, or when the length of the star wheel adjuster has been changed during some other service operation.

Frequent usage of an automatic transmission forward range to halt reverse vehicle motion may prevent the automatic adjusters from functioning, thereby inducing low pedal heights. Should low pedal heights be encountered, it is recommended that numerous forward and reverse stops be made until satisfactory pedal height is obtained.

NOTE: If a low pedal height condition cannot be corrected by making numerous reverse stops (provided the hydraulic system is free of air) it indicates that the self-adjusting mechanism is not functioning. Therefore, it will be necessary to remove the brake drum, clean, free up and lubricate the adjusting mechanism. Then adjust the brakes as follows, being sure the parking brake is fully released.

Adjustment

A lanced "knock out" area is provided in the web of the brake drum for servicing purposes on some models. When adjustment is required on models that do not have a lanced area on the brake drum, carefully drill a ½ in. hole into the round flat area on the backing plate opposite the parking brake cable. If lanced area of brake drum has been knocked out or if a hole was drilled in backing plate, ensure that all metal particles are removed from the brake compartment.

1. Turn brake adjusting screw to expand shoes until wheel can just be turned by hand.
2. Using a suitable tool to hold actuator from adjuster, back off adjuster 30 notches. If shoes still drag, back off one or two additional notches.

NOTE: Brakes should be free of drag when adjuster has been backed off approximately 12 notches. Heavy drag at this point indicates tight parking brake cables.

3. Install adjusting hole cover on brake drum or backing plate.
4. Check parking brake adjustment.

PARKING BRAKE, ADJUST

Need for parking brake adjustment is indicated if the service brake operates with sufficient pedal reserve, but the parking brake pedal travel is less than 9 ratchet clicks or more than 16 ratchet clicks.

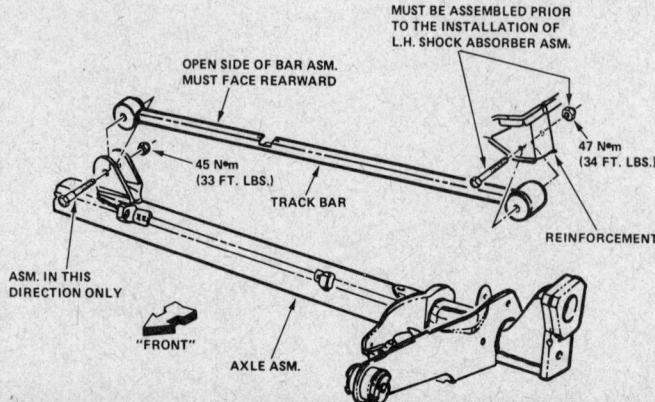

OPEN SIDE OF BAR ASM. MUST FACE REARWARD

MUST BE ASSEMBLED PRIOR TO THE INSTALLATION OF L.H. SHOCK ABSORBER ASM.

45 N•m (33 FT. LBS.)

47 N•m (34 FT. LBS.)

TRACK BAR

REINFORCEMENT

ASM. IN THIS DIRECTION ONLY

"FRONT"

AXLE ASM.

Fig. 6 Track bar installation

1. Depress parking brake pedal three ratchet clicks, then raise and support rear of vehicle.
2. Check to ensure that equalizer nut groove is sufficiently lubricated with grease, then tighten adjusting nut until right rear wheel can just be rotated rearward, but is locked when forward rotation is attempted.
3. Release parking brake lever. Both wheels should rotate freely in either direction with no brake drag.

MASTER CYLINDER, REPLACE

1. Disconnect master cylinder push rod from brake pedal.
2. Disconnect wire connector at brake warning pressure switch.
3. Disconnect brake lines from master cylinder, then remove two master cylinder mounting nuts and remove master cylinder.
4. Reverse procedure to install, then bleed brake system.

POWER BRAKE UNIT, REPLACE

1. Disconnect brake unit push rod from brake pedal.
2. Remove two master cylinder to power brake unit mounting nuts, then position master cylinder away from brake unit with brake lines attached.

NOTE: Use care not to bend or kink brake lines.

3. Disconnect vacuum hose from vacuum check valve. Plug vacuum hose to prevent entry of dirt.
4. Remove power brake unit to dash panel attaching nuts, then remove brake unit.
5. Reverse procedures to install.

Front Suspension & Steering Section

Refer to the Main Index for drive axle service.

DESCRIPTION

The front suspension, Fig. 1, on these vehicles is a MacPhereson strut design. The lower control arms pivot from the engine cradle. This engine cradle has isolation mounts to the body and conventional rubber bushings are used for the lower control arm pivots. The upper end of the strut is isolated by a rubber mount incorporating a bearing for wheel turning. The lower end of the steering knuckle pivots on a ball stud which is retained in the lower control arm with rivets and is clamped to the steering knuckle. Sealed wheel bearings are used and are bolted to the steering knuckle.

WHEEL ALIGNMENT

NOTE: Camber and toe-in are the only adjustments that can be performed on these vehicles.

Camber

The camber angle is adjusted by loosening the strut cam bolt and the through bolt and rotating the cam bolt to move the upper portion of the steering knuckle inboard or outboard. When correct camber angle is obtained, torque cam and through bolts to 140 ft. lbs.

NOTE: When performing this adjustment, the top through bolt must be loosened to prevent damage to the outer cam guide.

Toe-In

Toe-in is controlled by tie-rod position. Adjustment is made by loosening the nuts at the steering knuckle end of the tie-rods and rotating the rods to obtain proper toe-in setting. When adjusting toe-in, the tie-rod boot clamps

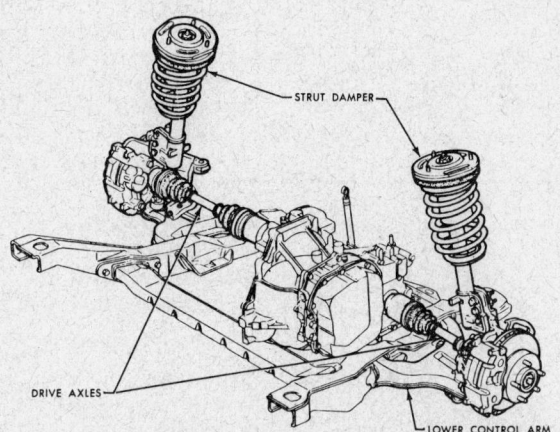

Fig. 1 Front suspension

must be removed. After correct toe-in setting is obtained, torque tie-rod nuts to 45 ft. lbs.

WHEEL BEARING, REPLACE

Removal

1. Loosen hub nut with vehicle on ground.
2. Raise and support vehicle and remove front wheel.
3. Install drive axle boot cover, tool J-28712.
4. Remove and discard hub nut.
5. Remove brake caliper from support and suspend caliper from frame with a length of wire. Do not suspend caliper by the brake hose.
6. Remove three hub and bearing attaching bolts. If the old bearing is being re-installed, mark attaching bolts and holes for re-installation, Fig. 2.
7. Using tool J-28733 or equivalent, remove bearing, Fig. 3.

NOTE: If excessive corrosion is present, ensure that the bearing is loose in the knuckle before using puller tool.

8. If installing new bearing, replace steering knuckle seal.

Installation

1. Clean and inspect bearing mating surfaces and steering knuckle bore for dirt, nicks and burrs.
2. If installing steering knuckle seal, use tool J-28671 or equivalent to install seal, Fig. 4. Apply grease to seal and knuckle bore.
3. Push bearing onto axle shaft.
4. Tighten hub nut to fully seat bearing.
5. Install bearing attaching bolts and torque to 63 ft. lbs, Fig. 2.
6. Install caliper assembly and the wheel.
7. Lower vehicle and torque hub nut to 225 ft. lbs. on 1980—82 models, or 185 ft. lbs. on 1983—84 models.

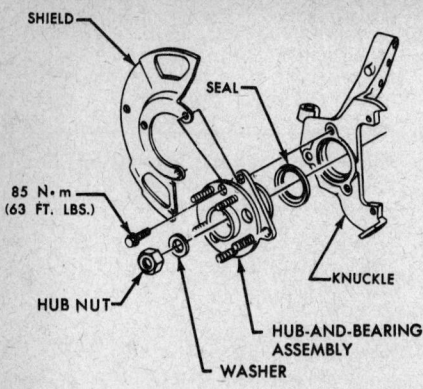

SHIELD

SEAL

85 N·m
(63 FT. LBS.)

HUB NUT

KNUCKLE

HUB-AND-BEARING
ASSEMBLY

WASHER

Fig. 2   Front wheel bearing assembly & seal

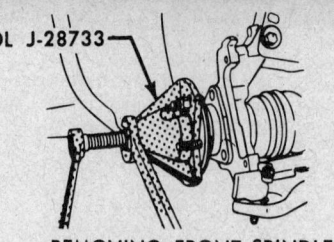

TOOL J-28733

REMOVING FRONT SPINDLE

Fig. 3   Removing front wheel bearing assembly

J-28671

STEERING KNUCKLE

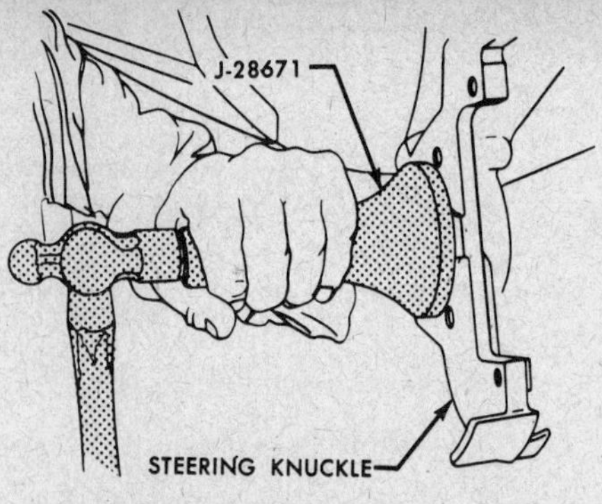

Fig. 4   Installing front wheel bearing seal

LOWER BALL JOINT, REPLACE

For removal and installation procedures, refer to Fig. 5.

LOWER CONTROL ARM & BUSHINGS, REPLACE

For removal and installation procedures, refer to Fig. 6. Torque ball joint clamping bolt to 45 ft. lbs. on 1980 models, or 40 ft. lbs. on 1981–84 models. Torque control arm attaching bolts to 48 ft. lbs. on 1980 models, 50 ft. lbs. on 1981 models, or 66 ft. lbs. on 1982–84 models.

STEERING KNUCKLE, REPLACE

For removal and installation procedures, refer to Fig. 7.

STABILIZER BAR & BUSHINGS, REPLACE

For removal and installation procedures, refer to Fig. 8.

STRUT ASSEMBLY, REPLACE

For removal and installation procedures, refer to Fig. 9.

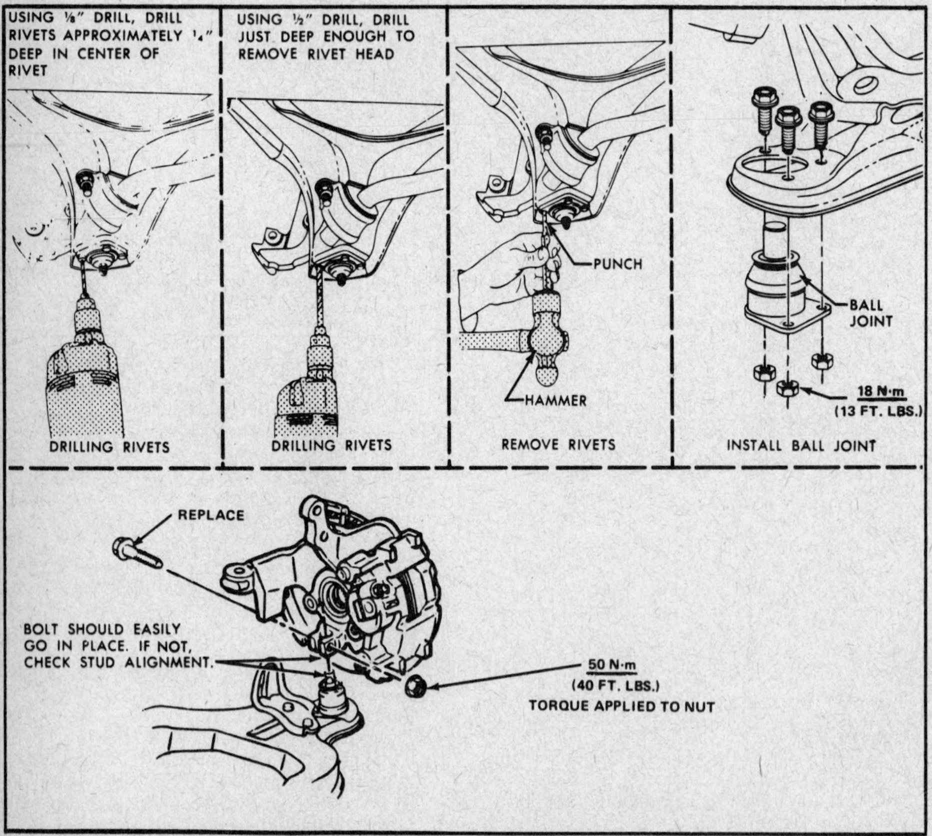

STRUT ASSEMBLY SERVICE

Disassembly

1. Clamp strut compressor, tool No. J-26584, in a suitable vise.
2. On 1980–81 models, open hinged front section of tool No. J-26584-4 bottom adapter, Fig. 10. Place strut assembly into bottom adapter of compressor, then close front section of adapter. Ensure adapter is closed and locating pin is fully engaged.
3. On 1982–84 models, position strut assembly in bottom adapter of compressor and install tool No. J-26584-89. Ensure adapter is closed and locating pin is fully engaged.
4. On all models, rotate strut assembly to align top mounting assembly lip with strut compressor support notch.
5. Insert both top adapters, tool No. J-26584-40, between top mounting assembly and top spring seat.
6. Rotate compressor forcing screw clockwise until top support flange contacts top adapters. Continue rotating forcing screw, compressing strut spring approximately ½ inch or 4 complete turns. Use extreme care to avoid bottoming spring or strut damper rod.
7. Remove top nut from strut damper shaft and top mounting assembly from strut assembly.
8. Rotate compressor forcing screw counterclockwise until spring tension is relieved, then remove adapters and the strut, Fig. 11.

Assembly

1. Perform steps 1 through 3 as outlined in the "Disassembly" procedure.
2. Rotate strut assembly until mounting flange is facing outward opposite compressor forcing screw.
3. Install spring and related components on strut. Ensure spring is properly seated on bottom spring plate.
4. Install strut spring seat assembly on top of spring. Ensure flat faces in same direction as lower flange.
5. Position both top adapters over spring seat assembly.
6. Rotate compressor forcing screw until compressor top support makes contact with top adapters. Do not compress spring at this time.
7. Install strut alignment rod, tool No. J-26584-27, through top spring seat. Thread rod onto damper shaft hand tight, Fig. 12.

USING ⅛" DRILL, DRILL RIVETS APPROXIMATELY ¼" DEEP IN CENTER OF RIVET

DRILLING RIVETS

USING ½" DRILL, DRILL JUST DEEP ENOUGH TO REMOVE RIVET HEAD

DRILLING RIVETS

PUNCH

HAMMER

REMOVE RIVETS

BALL JOINT

18 N·m
(13 FT. LBS.)

INSTALL BALL JOINT

REPLACE

BOLT SHOULD EASILY GO IN PLACE. IF NOT, CHECK STUD ALIGNMENT.

50 N·m
(40 FT. LBS.)
TORQUE APPLIED TO NUT

Fig. 5   Lower ball joint removal & installation

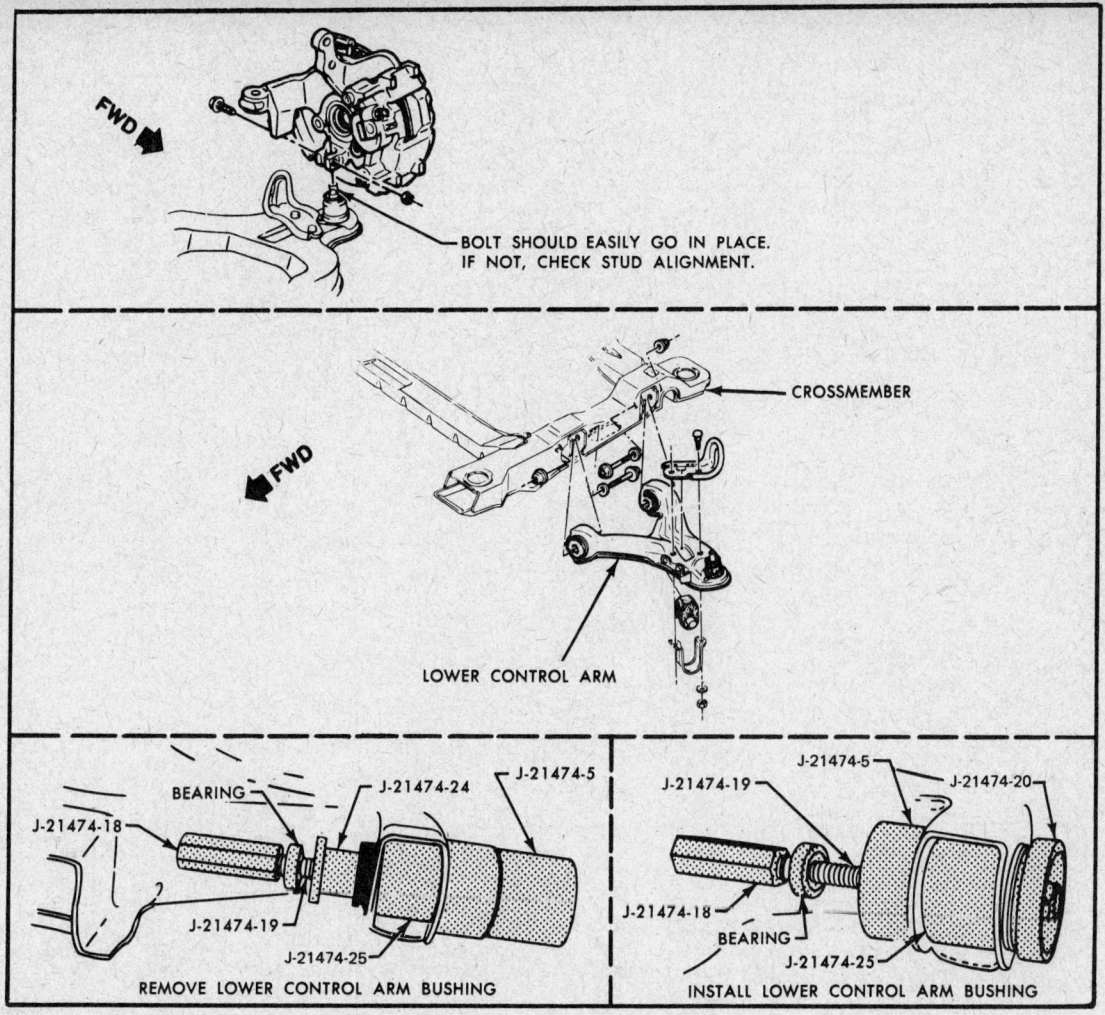

BOLT SHOULD EASILY GO IN PLACE. IF NOT, CHECK STUD ALIGNMENT.

Fig. 6 Lower control arm & bushing removal & installation

NOTE: Install shims between lower spring seat and bottom adapter to keep alignment rod centered in upper spring seat opening.

8. Compress spring by slowly rotating forcing screw. While rotating screw, observe position of damper shaft, as it must pass directly through center of opening in upper spring seat to provide proper operation. If spring is off-center, back off screw and proceed as follows:
   a. Reposition both top adapters in support fixture to provide proper spring seat-to-damper position.
   b. Install thin shim stock between lower spring seat and bottom adapter to tilt strut assembly into proper position.
   c. When damper shaft can be held in proper position, rotate screw until approximately 1½ inch of shaft can be pulled through upper spring seat. Do not compress spring beyond this point.
9. Remove alignment rod, place strut mounting assembly over damper shaft and install nut. Torque nut to 68 ft. lbs. on 1980–81 models, or 65 ft. lbs. on 1982–84 models.
10. Rotate forcing screw counterclockwise and remove strut assembly from compressor.

STEERING GEAR, REPLACE

1982–84

Removal

1. On models equipped with power steering, remove air cleaner, then disconnect and cap hydraulic lines from steering gear.
2. Pull intermediate shaft seal upward, then remove intermediate shaft to steering gear stub shaft pinch bolt, Fig. 13.
3. Raise and support vehicle, then remove both front wheel and tire assemblies.
4. Using tool J6627 or equivalent, disconnect tie rod ends from steering knuckles.
5. Remove AIR pipe bracket to crossmember attaching bolt, if equipped.
6. Remove two rear frame cradle mounting bolts and lower rear of cradle 4 to 5 inches.

CAUTION: Do not lower cradle more than specified, as damage to engine components may result.

7. Remove steering gear heat shield from crossmember.
8. Remove steering gear assembly mounting bolts, then the steering gear assembly

through the left wheel opening.

Installation

1. Place steering gear assembly into mounts on crossmember, then install and torque mounting bolts to 70 ft. lbs.
2. Install heat shield.
3. Raise frame cradle and install mounting bolts. Torque bolts to specification.
4. Install AIR pipe bracket to crossmember, then connect tie rod ends to steering knuckles. Torque ball studs to 30 ft. lbs.
5. Install wheel and tire assemblies and lower vehicle.
6. Connect intermediate shaft to steering gear stub shaft, install pinch bolt and torque to 45 ft. lbs.
7. Check and adjust toe-in as required.

1980–81

Removal

1. On models equipped with power steering, remove line clip to bracket attaching bolt, then disconnect and cap pressure and return lines at steering gear.
2. On all models, remove bolt attaching speedometer cable retainer clip to transmission, then position cable aside to provide clearance for gear removal.
3. Remove upper left hand steering gear housing bracket nut, then raise and sup-

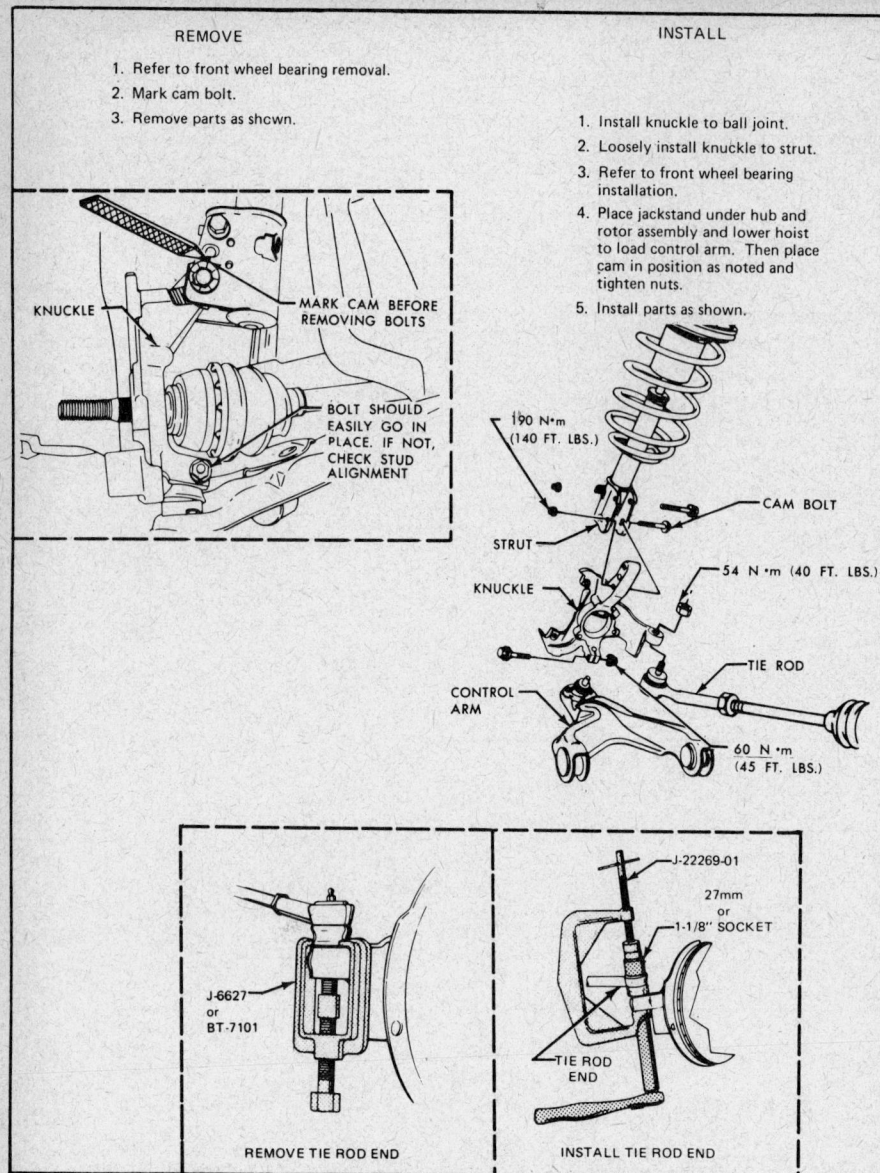

REMOVE

1. Refer to front wheel bearing removal.
2. Mark cam bolt.
3. Remove parts as shown.

INSTALL

1. Install knuckle to ball joint.
2. Loosely install knuckle to strut.
3. Refer to front wheel bearing installation.
4. Place jackstand under hub and rotor assembly and lower hoist to load control arm. Then place cam in position as noted and tighten nuts.
5. Install parts as shown.

KNUCKLE

MARK CAM BEFORE REMOVING BOLTS

BOLT SHOULD EASILY GO IN PLACE. IF NOT, CHECK STUD ALIGNMENT

190 N•m (140 FT. LBS.)

CAM BOLT

STRUT

54 N•m (40 FT. LBS.)

KNUCKLE

TIE ROD

CONTROL ARM

60 N•m (45 FT. LBS.)

J-6627 or BT-7101

REMOVE TIE ROD END

J-22269-01

27mm or 1-1/8" SOCKET

TIE ROD END

INSTALL TIE ROD END

Fig. 7 Steering knuckle removal & installation

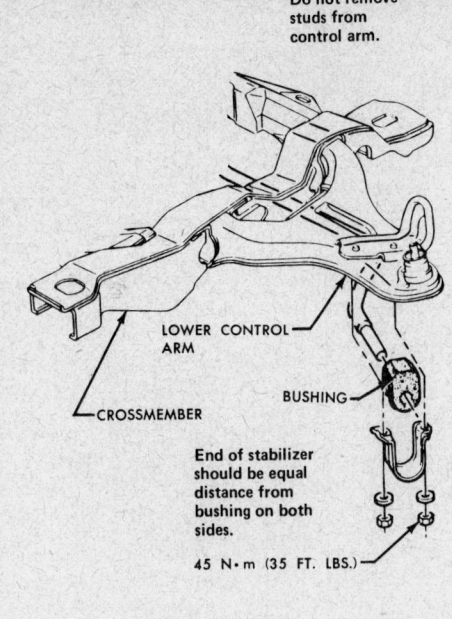

Do not remove studs from control arm.

LOWER CONTROL ARM

BUSHING

CROSSMEMBER

End of stabilizer should be equal distance from bushing on both sides.

45 N•m (35 FT. LBS.)

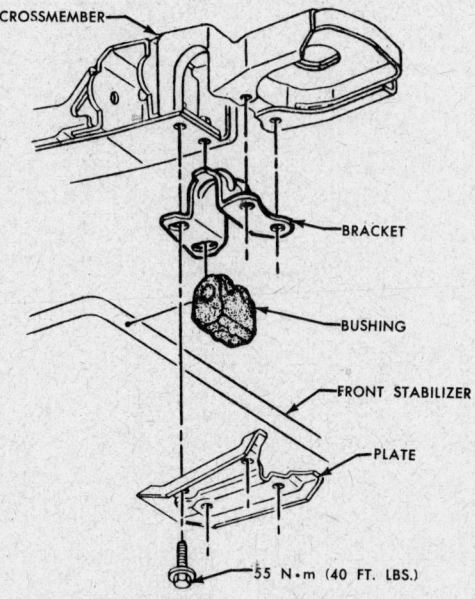

CROSSMEMBER

BRACKET

BUSHING

FRONT STABILIZER

PLATE

55 N•m (40 FT. LBS.)

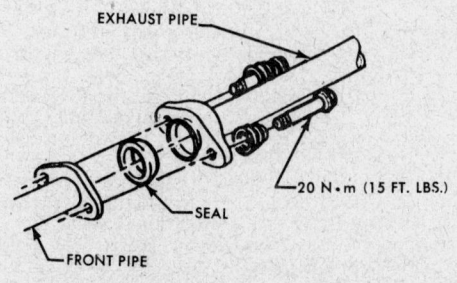

EXHAUST PIPE

20 N•m (15 FT. LBS.)

SEAL

FRONT PIPE

Fig. 8 Stabilizer bar & bushing removal & installation

port front of vehicle at body.
4. Remove both wheel and tire assemblies.
5. Remove cotter pins and nuts from both tie rod ends, then disconnect tie rod ends from steering knuckles using tool No. J-6627 or BT-7101, Fig. 14.
6. Remove AIR hose shield.
7. Remove rear frame cradle mounting bolts, then lower rear of frame cradle approximately 3 to 4 inches.
8. Remove remaining steering gear housing bracket nuts, then remove reinforcement and brackets.
9. Disconnect intermediate shaft from steering gear stub shaft, then remove steering gear through left wheel opening, Fig. 14.

Installation
1. Install supports, then position steering gear in vehicle.
2. Connect intermediate shaft to steering gear stub shaft, then torque clamp bolt to 45 ft. lbs.

3. Install steering gear housing brackets, reinforcement and attaching nuts. Torque right hand upper and lower and left hand lower bracket nuts to 24 ft. lbs.
4. Raise frame cradle, then install and torque rear mounting bolts to 80 ft lbs.
5. Install A.I.R. hose shield, then connect tie rod ends to steering knuckles. Torque tie rod end nuts to 40 ft. lbs. on 1980 models, 35 ft. lbs. on 1981 models, then install cotter pins. If cotter pins cannot be inserted, tighten nut up to an additional 1/16 turn to align cotter pin holes.
6. Install wheel and tire assemblies, then lower vehicle.
7. Torque upper left hand steering gear housing bracket bolt to 24 ft. lbs.
8. Install speedometer cable retainer clip.
9. On models with power steering, connect pressure and return lines to steering gear, then install line clip. Check power steering fluid level and bleed system.
10. On all models, check and adjust toe-in as necessary.

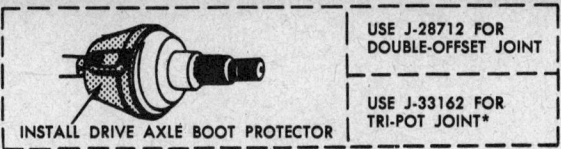

INSTALL DRIVE AXLE BOOT PROTECTOR

USE J-28712 FOR DOUBLE-OFFSET JOINT

USE J-33162 FOR TRI-POT JOINT*

REMOVE

1. Remove (3) top attaching nuts.
2. Loosen wheel lug nuts.
3. Raise car and support on frame.
4. Remove wheel-and-tire; remove brake line clip.
5. Install boot protectors as shown in upper panel.
   *Whenever a tri-pot design joint is used on a drive axle shaft, it is necessary to disconnect the axle shaft from the trans-axle BEFORE separating the knuckle from the strut. Use J-33008.
6. Scribe the parts
7. Remove (2) bolts; separate the strut from the knuckle.
8. Remove the strut.

INSTALL

1. Install parts in reverse order of removal.
2. Place jack stand under hub and rotor assembly. Lower hoist and place car in position as noted in removal.
3. Raise hoist.
4. Install brake line clip.
5. Remove boot protectors.
6. Install wheel and lower car.

24 N•m (18 FT. LBS)

190 N•m (140 FT. LBS)

FWD

Fig. 9 Strut assembly removal & installation

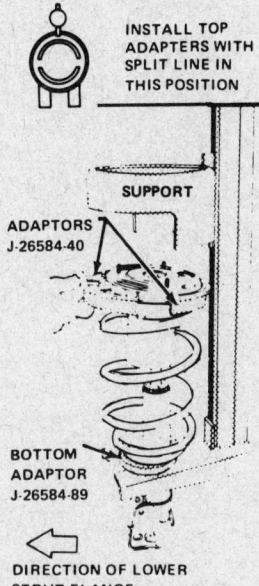

INSTALL TOP ADAPTERS WITH SPLIT LINE IN THIS POSITION

SUPPORT

ADAPTORS J-26584-40

BOTTOM ADAPTOR J-26584-89

DIRECTION OF LOWER STRUT FLANGE

Fig. 10 Strut damper & coil spring removal. 1982-84 shown (Typical of 1980-81)

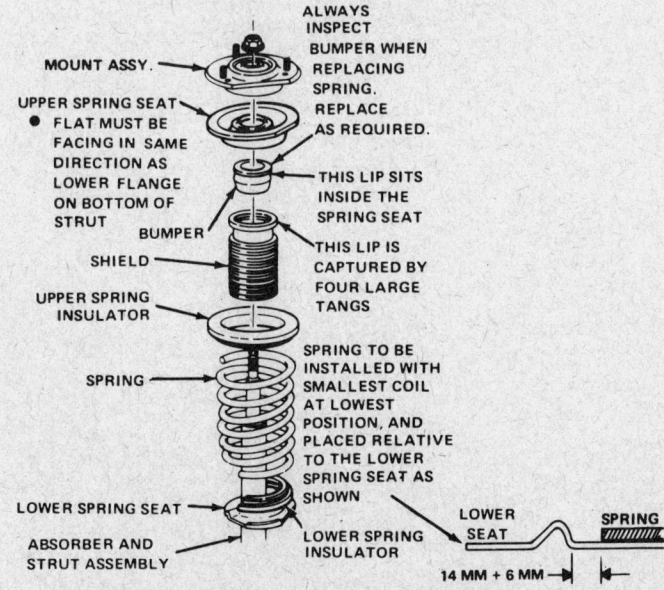

MOUNT ASSY.

UPPER SPRING SEAT
• FLAT MUST BE FACING IN SAME DIRECTION AS LOWER FLANGE ON BOTTOM OF STRUT

BUMPER

SHIELD

UPPER SPRING INSULATOR

SPRING

LOWER SPRING SEAT

ABSORBER AND STRUT ASSEMBLY

ALWAYS INSPECT BUMPER WHEN REPLACING SPRING. REPLACE AS REQUIRED.

THIS LIP SITS INSIDE THE SPRING SEAT

THIS LIP IS CAPTURED BY FOUR LARGE TANGS

SPRING TO BE INSTALLED WITH SMALLEST COIL AT LOWEST POSITION, AND PLACED RELATIVE TO THE LOWER SPRING SEAT AS SHOWN

LOWER SPRING INSULATOR

LOWER SEAT   SPRING

14 MM + 6 MM

Fig. 11 Strut assembly components. 1982-84 shown (Typical of 1980-81)

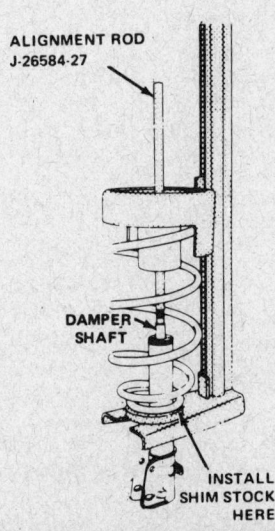

ALIGNMENT ROD J-26584-27

DAMPER SHAFT

INSTALL SHIM STOCK HERE

Fig. 12 Installing strut alignment rod

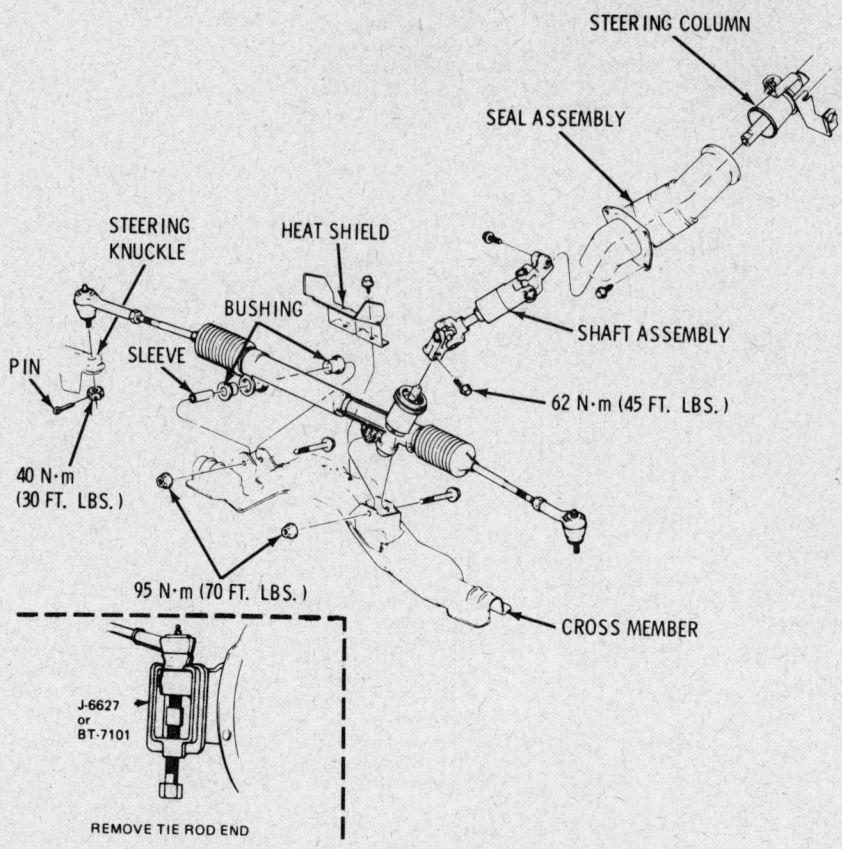

Fig. 13 Steering gear Replacement. 1982—84

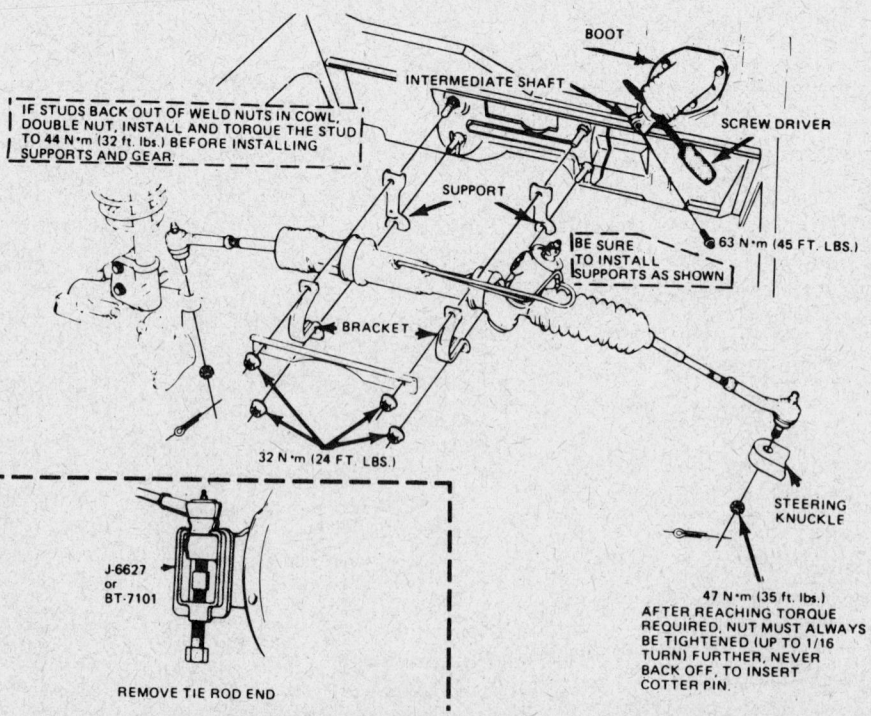

Fig. 14 Steering gear replacement. 1980—81

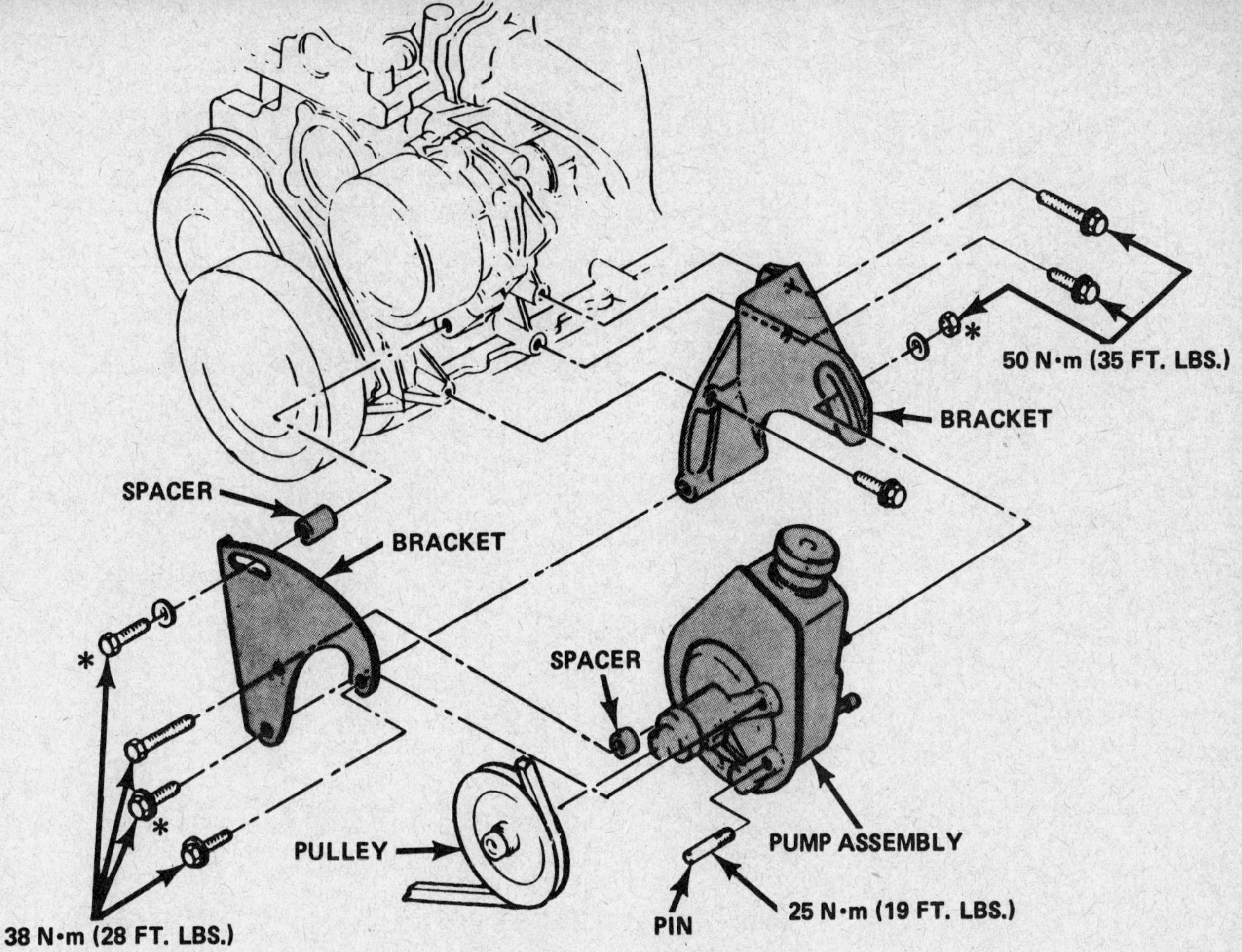

SPACER

BRACKET

50 N•m (35 FT. LBS.)

BRACKET

SPACER

PULLEY

PUMP ASSEMBLY

PIN

25 N•m (19 FT. LBS.)

38 N•m (28 FT. LBS.)

Fig. 15 Power steering pump replacement. 4-151

POWER STEERING PUMP, REPLACE

4-151

1. Raise and support vehicle, then remove radiator hose clamp bolt.
2. Disconnect and cap hydraulic lines at power steering pump.
3. Remove power steering pump to rear bracket attaching nut.
4. Remove front pump bracket to engine and front pump bracket to rear pump bracket attaching bolts, Fig. 15.
5. Remove pump and bracket assembly from vehicle.
6. Reverse procedure to install.

6-173

1. Disconnect battery ground cable.
2. Disconnect electrical connector at blower motor, then remove blower motor from vehicle.
3. Disconnect heater hose from water pump and hydraulic lines from power steering pump. Cap lines to avoid fluid leakage.
4. Remove rear pump bracket to engine bracket attaching nut and front pump bracket to cylinder head attaching bolts, Fig. 16.
5. Remove pump and bracket assembly from vehicle.
6. Reverse procedure to install.

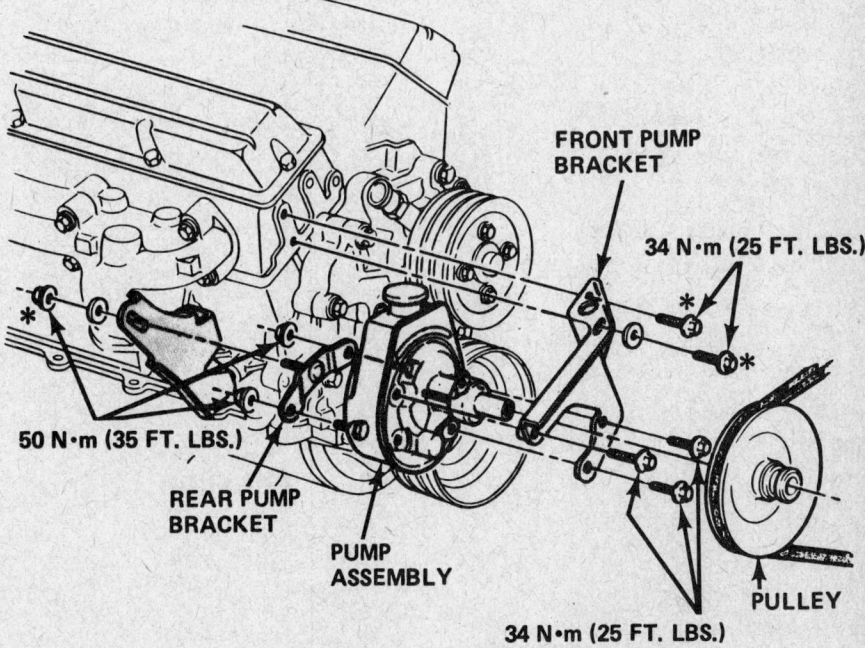

FRONT PUMP BRACKET

34 N•m (25 FT. LBS.)

50 N•m (35 FT. LBS.)

REAR PUMP BRACKET

PUMP ASSEMBLY

PULLEY

34 N•m (25 FT. LBS.)

Fig. 16 Power steering pump replacement. V6-173

Refer to the 1980–84 Citation, Omega, Phoenix and Skylark Chapter for service procedures not covered in this chapter.

INDEX OF SERVICE OPERATIONS

NOTE: Refer to the front of this manual for vehicle manufacturer's special service tool suppliers.

VEHICLE IDENTIFICATION NUMBER LOCATION

On top of instrument panel, left front.

ENGINE NUMBER LOCATION

On 4-151, V6-173, V6-181, V6-231 engines, the engine code stamping is located on vertical pad on engine to transmission mounting flange located on forward side of block. On V6-262 diesel engines, the engine code stamping is located on vertical pad located on right side of engine front cover.

ENGINE V.I.N. CODE

The eighth digit of the seventeen digit V.I.N. code denotes engine code.

ENGINE IDENTIFICATION CODES

Year	Engine	V.I.N. Code	Code
1982	4-151①	R	3M, 3S, 3J
	4-151①	R	3K, 3L, 3P
	V6-173②	X	CAY, CAZ, CBA
	V6-173②	X	CBC, CBD, CBF
	V6-173②	X	CBH, CBJ, CBK
	V6-173②	X	CMC, CMF, CMH
	V6-173②	X	CMJ, CMM, CMS
	V6-173②	X	C7N, C7R, C7S
	V6-173②	X	C7T, C7U, C7W
	V6-173②	X	D2A, D2B, D2C
	V6-173②	X	D2D, D2F, D2H
	V6-181③	E	EA, EB
	V6-262④	T	UAC, UAH, UAL
1983	4-151①	R	YAA, YAL, YAP

Year	Engine	V.I.N. Code	Code
	V6-173②	X	D2J, D2K, D2M
	V6-173②	X	D2N, D2R, D2S
	V6-173②	X	DCA, DCB, DCC
	V6-173②	X	DCD, DCF, DCH
	V6-173②	X	DCJ, DCK, DCM
	V6-173②	X	DCN, DCR, DCS
	V6-173②	X	DCT, DCV
	V6-173②	X	DCW, DCX
	V6-173 HO②⑤	Z	DFA, DFB, DFC
	V6-173 HO②⑤	Z	DFD, DFF, DFH
	V6-173 HO②⑤	Z	DTA, DTB, DTC
	V6-173 HO②⑤	Z	DTJ, DTK
	V6-181③	E	RA, RB, RC
	V6-262④	T	ULJ, ULK, ULL

Year	Engine	V.I.N. Code	Code
	V6-262④	T	ULM, ULN, ULP
1984	4-151①	R	
	V6-173②	X	
	V6-173 HO②⑤	Z	
	V6-181③	E	
	V6-231 MFI③	3	
	V6-262④	T	

①—Pontiac built engine.
②—Chevrolet built engine.
③—Buick built engine.
④—Oldsmobile built diesel engine.
⑤—High output engine.

GRILL IDENTIFICATION

1982–83 Buick Century Exc. "T" Type

1982–83 Chevrolet Celebrity

1982–83 Olds. Cutlass Ciera Exc. Brougham, ES & LS

1982–83 Olds. Cutlass Ciera Brougham & LS

1982–83 Pontiac 6000 Exc. "STE"

1983 Buick Century "T" Type

1983 Pontiac 6000 "STE"

1984 Buick Century Exc. "T" Type

1984 Buick Century "T" Type

1984 Chevrolet Celebrity

1984 Pontiac 6000 LF 4 Door & Station Wagon

GENERAL ENGINE SPECIFICATIONS

Year	Engine CID①/Liter	V.I.N. Code②	Carburetor	Bore and Stroke	Compression Ratio	Net H.P. @ R.P.M.③	Maximum Torque Ft. Lbs. @ R.P.M.	Normal Oil Pressure Pounds
1982	4-151, 2.5L	R	T.B.I	4.00 × 3.00	8.2	90 @ 4000	132 @ 2800	36–41
	V6-173, 2.8L	X	E2SE, 2 Bbl④	3.50 × 2.99	8.5	112 @ 5100	145 @ 2400	50–65
	V6-181, 3.0L	E	E2ME, 2 Bbl④	3.80 × 2.66	8.45	110 @ 4800	145 @ 2600	37
	V6-262, 4.3L⑤	T	Fuel Injection	4.05 × 3.385	21.6	85 @ 3600	165 @ 1600	30–45
1983	4-151, 2.5L	R	T.B.I	4.00 × 3.00	8.2	90 @ 4000	135 @ 2800	36–41
	V6-173, 2.8L	X	E2SE, 2 Bbl④	3.50 × 2.99	8.5	112 @ 4800	145 @ 2400	50–65
	V6-173 H.O., 2.8L⑥	Z	E2SE, 2 Bbl④	3.50 × 2.99	8.9	130 @ 5400	145 @ 2400	50–65
	V6-181, 3.0L	E	E2ME, 2 Bbl④	3.80 × 2.66	8.45	110 @ 4800	145 @ 2600	37
	V6-262, 4.3L⑤	T	Fuel Injection	4.05 × 3.385	21.6	85 @ 3600	165 @ 1600	30–45
1984	4-151, 2.5L	R	T.B.I	4.00 × 3.00	8.2	90 @ 4000	134 @ 2400	36–41
	V6-173, 2.8L	X	E2SE, 2 Bbl④	3.50 × 2.99	8.5	112 @ 5100	148 @ 2400	50–65
	V6-173 H.O., 2.8L⑥	Z	E2SE, 2 Bbl④	3.50 × 2.99	8.9	130 @ 5400	145 @ 2400	50–65
	V6-181, 3.0L	E	E2ME, 2 Bbl④	3.80 × 2.666	8.45	110 @ 4800	145 @ 2600	37
	V6-231 MFI, 3.8L	3	Fuel Injection	3.80 × 3.40	8.0	125 @ 4400	195 @ 2000	37
	V6-262, 4.3L⑤	T	Fuel Injection	4.05 × 3.385	21.6	85 @ 3600	165 @ 1600	30–45

①—CID—cubic inch displacement.   ③—Ratings are net—as installed in vehicle.   ⑤—Diesel engine.
②—The eighth digit denotes engine code.   ④—Rochester.   ⑥—High output engine.

TUNE UP SPECIFICATIONS

The following specifications are published from the latest information available. This
data should be used only in the absence of a decal affixed in the engine compartment.

★ When using a timing light, disconnect vacuum hose or tube at distributor and plug opening in hose or tube so idle speed will not be affected.

● When checking compression, lowest cylinder must be within 70 percent of highest.

▲ Before removing wires from distributor cap, determine location of the No. 1 wire in cap, as distributor position may have been altered from that shown at the end of this chart.

Spark plug types shown in this chart are recommendations of the original vehicle manufacturer and not MOTOR.

Check local sources for other spark plug manufacturers listings.

Year & Engine/V.I.N.	Spark Plug Type	Gap	Firing Order Fig. ▲	Ignition Timing BTDC① ★ Man. Trans.	Auto. Trans.	Mark Fig.	Curb Idle Speed② Man. Trans.	Auto Trans.	Fast Idle Speed Man. Trans.	Auto. Trans.	Fuel Pump Pressure
1982											
4-151/R	R44TXS	.060	A	—	8°③⑦	B	—	⑩	—	⑩	9–13
V6-173/X	R43TS	.045	C	—	10°⑤	D	—	600D	—	2600N	6–7½
V6-181/E	R44TS8	.080	E	—	15°	F	—	⑩	—	2300P	6–7½
V6-262/T Diesel	—	—	—	—	5°⑥⑧⑨	—	—	650/725D	—	725D	—
1983											
4-151/R	R44TSX	.060	A	—	8°⑦⑪	B	—	⑩	—	⑩	—
V6-173/X	R43CTS	.045	C	—	10°	D	—	600/750D	—	2500	5½–6½
V6-173 H.O./Z④	R42CTS	.045	C	—	10°	D	—	725/850D	—	2700	5½–6½
V6-181/E Exc. Calif.	R44TSX	.060	E	—	15°	F	—	⑩	—	2400	4–6½
V6-181/E Calif.	R44TSX	.060	E	—	15°	F	—	⑩	—	2300	4–6½
V6-262/T Diesel	—	—	—	—	6°⑥⑧⑨	—	—	675/775D	—	775D	—
1984											
4-151/R	R44TSX	.060	A	—	—	B	—	—	—	—	—
V6-173/X	R43CTS	.045	C	—	—	D	—	—	—	—	6–7½
V6-173 H.O./Z④	R42CTS	.045	C	—	—	D	—	—	—	—	6–7½
V6-181/E	R44TS8	.080	E	—	—	F	—	—	—	—	3.9–6.5
V6-231 MFI/3	R44TS8	.080	—	—	—	—	—	—	—	—	—
V6-262/T Diesel	—	—	—	—	6°⑥⑧⑨	—	—	675/775D	—	775D	—

Continued

TUNE UP SPECIFICATIONS NOTES

①—BTDC—Before top dead center.
②—Idle speed on auto. trans. equipped vehicles is adjusted in Drive unless otherwise specified. Where two idle speeds are listed, the higher speed is with the A/C or idle solenoid energized.
③—At 1050N RPM.
④—High output engine.

⑤—At 600D RPM.
⑥—At 1300P RPM.
⑦—Ground diagnostic connector located under dash. The check engine light should flash on & off when in diagnostic mode. Check average ignition timing of cylinder Nos. 1 & 4, reset as necessary. After completing ignition

timing check, remove ground from diagnostic connector & ensure that check engine light is off.
⑧—ATDC—After top dead center.
⑨—Using diesel engine timing meter J-33073.
⑩—Idle speed controlled by electronic control module.

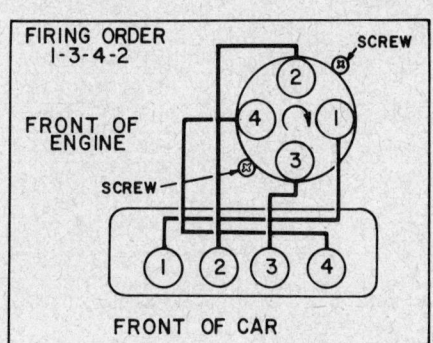

Fig. A

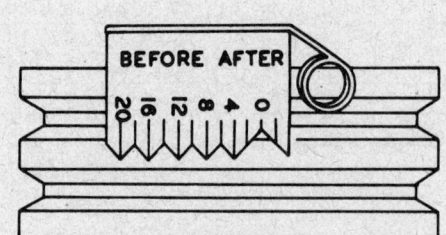

Fig. B

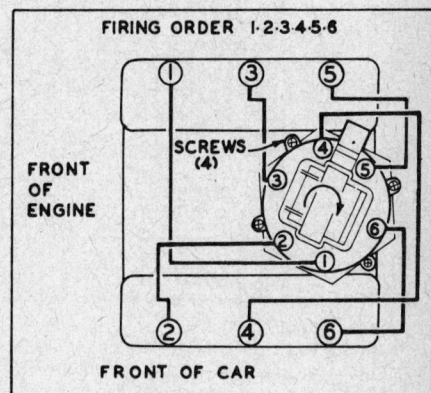

Fig. C

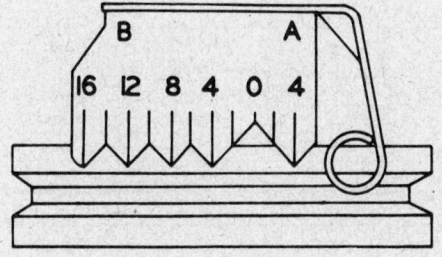

Fig. D

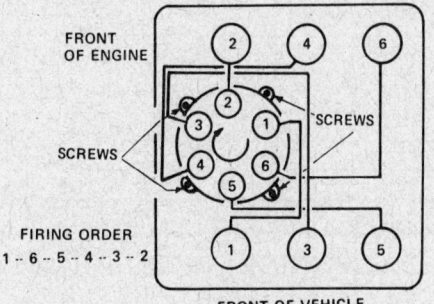

Fig. E

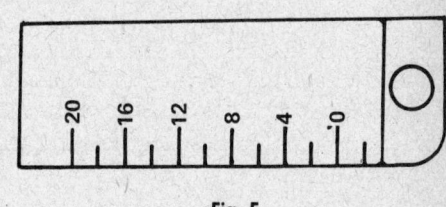

Fig. F

DISTRIBUTOR SPECIFICATIONS

★If unit is checked on the vehicle, double the RPM and degrees to get crankshaft figures.

| Distributor Ident. No.① | Centrifugal Advanced Degrees @ RPM of Distributor | | | Vacuum Advance | |
	Advance Starts	Intermediate Advance	Full Advance	Inches of Vacuum to Start Plunger	Max. Adv. Dist. Deg. @ Vacuum
1982					
1110593③	—	—	—	—	—
1110597②	—	—	—	—	—
1103470④	—	—	—	—	—
1983					
1103513②	—	—	—	—	—
1103519③	—	—	—	—	—
1103470④	—	—	—	—	—

①—Stamped on distributor housing plate.
②—4-151.
③—V6-173.
④—V6-181.

ENGINE TIGHTENING SPECIFICATIONS★

★Torque specifications are for clean and lightly lubricated threads only. Dry or dirty threads produce increased friction which prevents accurate measurement of tightness.

Year	Engine Model/ V.I.N.	Spark Plugs Ft. Lbs.	Cylinder Head Bolts Ft. Lbs.	Intake Manifold Ft. Lbs.	Exhaust Manifold Ft. Lbs.	Rocker Arm Stud Ft. Lbs.	Rocker Arm Cover Ft. Lbs.	Connecting Rod Cap Bolts Ft. Lbs.	Main Bearing Cap Bolts Ft. Lbs.	Flywheel to Crankshaft Ft. Lbs.	Vibration Damper or Pulley Ft. Lbs.
1982	4-151/R	15	85	29	44	20⑥	6	32	70	44	200
	V6-173/X	7–15	65–75	20–25	22–28	43–49	6–9	34–40	63–74	45–55	66–84
	V6-181/E	15	80	45	25	30⑦	4	40	100	60	225
	V6-262/T①	—	②③	41	29	④	⑤	42	107	76	160–350
1983	4-151/R	15	85	29	44	20⑥	6	32	70	63	200
	V6-173/X,Z	7–15	65–75	20–25	22–28	43–49	6–9	34–40	63–74	45–55	66–84
	V6-181/E	15	80	45	25	30⑦	4	40	100	60	225
	V6-262/T①	—	②③	41	29	④	⑤	42	89	76	160–350
1984	4-151/R	15	92	29	44	20⑥	6	32	70	44	200
	V6-173/X,Z	7–15	65–75	20–25	22–28	43–49	6–9	34–40	63–74	45–55	66–84
	V6-181/E	15	80	45	25	30⑦	4	40	100	60	225
	V6-231/3	15	80	45	25	30⑦	4	40	100	60	225
	V6-262/T①	—	②③	41	31	④	⑤	42	89	76	203–350

①—Diesel engine.
②—Clean & dip entire bolt in engine oil before tightening to obtain a correct torque reading.
③—Torque inner 8 bolts to 142 ft. lbs. Torque outer 6 bolts (bolts nearest intake & exhaust manifold to cylinder block mating surfaces) to 59 ft. lbs.
④—Rocker arm pivot studs, 11 ft. lbs.; rocker arm nuts, 28 ft. lbs.
⑤—Fully driven, seated & not stripped.
⑥—Rocker arm bolt.
⑦—Rocker arm shaft.

WHEEL ALIGNMENT SPECIFICATIONS

Year	Model	Caster Angle, Degrees		Camber Angle, Degrees				Toe-In Inch	Toe-Out on Turns Deg.	
		Limits	Desired	Limits		Desired			Outer Wheel	Inner Wheel
				Left	Right	Left	Right			
1982–83	All	0°–+4°	+2°	−1/2° to +1/2°	−1/2° to +1/2°	0°	0°	0	—	—
1984	All	.9° to 2.9°	1.9°	−1/2° to +1/2°	−1/2° to +1/2°	0°	0°	0	—	—

ALTERNATOR SPECIFICATIONS

Year	Model	Rated Hot Output Amps.	Year	Model	Rated Hot Output Amps.	Year	Model	Rated Hot Output Amps.
1982	1100113	63		1100233	42		1100217	78
	1100164	55		1100235	42		1100233	42
	1100166	63		1100239	55		1100235	42
	1100174	55		1100240	63		1100239	56
	1100192	85		1100243	63		1100243	66
	1100193	85		1100252	63		1100247	66
	1100196	63		1100254	63		1100252	66
	1101037	70		1100260	78		1100254	66
	1101039	70		1100272	78		1100268	78
	1101044	70		1105023	63		1100272	78
	1101067	70		1105189	85		1105425	94
	1101084	85		1105190	85		1105428	94
	1101086	85		1105196	85		1105441	94
	1101448	80		1105199	85		1105443	94
	1103197	63		1105200	85		1105444	94
1983	1100200	78		1105244	42		1105509	108
	1100208	63		1105245	78		1105542	94
	1100217	78	1984	1100200	78		1105552	85
	1100231	42		1100206	56		1105553	97
	1100232	42		1100208	66			

STARTING MOTOR APPLICATIONS

Year	Engine/V.I.N.	Starter Ident. No.	Year	Engine/V.I.N.	Starter Ident. No.
1982	4-151, V6-173, V6-181①	1109530②		V6-181	1109560①
	V6-262 Diesel/T	1998553②		V6-262 Diesel/T	22515863②
	V6-262 Diesel/T	22515863③	1984	4-151/R	1109556①
1983	4-151/R	1109556①		V6-173/X,Z	1109564①
	V6-173/X,Z	1109533①		V6-181/E	1998448①
	V6-173/X,Z	1109564①		V6-231 MFI/3	1998445①
				V6-262 Diesel/T	22515863②

①—For V.I.N. code, Refer to the "General Engine Specifications" at the beginning of chapter.
②—Delco-Remy.
③—Mitsubishi.

PISTONS, PINS, RINGS, CRANKSHAFT & BEARINGS

Year	Engine Model/V.I.N.	Piston Clearance	Ring Gap ①		Wristpin Diameter	Rod Bearings		Main Bearings			Shaft End Play
			Comp.	Oil		Shaft Diameter	Bearing Clearance	Shaft Diameter	Bearing Clearance	Thrust on Bear. No.	
1982	4-151/R	.0025–.0033	.010	.015	.9400	2.000	.0005–.0026	2.300	.0005–.0022	5	.0035–.0085
	V6-173/X	.0017–.0027	.010	.020	.9199	2.0303–2.0314	.0014–.0036	2.5336–2.5346	.0018–.0030	3	.0020–.0068
	V6-181/E	.0008–.0020	.013	.015	.9392	2.2487–2.2495	.0005–.0026	2.4995	.0003–.0018	3	.0030–.0090
	V6-262/T②	.0030–.0040	.015	.015	1.095	2.2490–2.2510	.0003–.0025	2.9993–3.0003	③	3	.0035–.0135
1983	4-151/R	.0025–.0033	.010	.015	.9400	2.000	.0005–.0026	2.300	.0005–.0022	5	.0035–.0085
	V6-173/X,Z	.0007–.0017	.010	.020	.9199	2.0303–2.0314	.0014–.0038	④	.0016–.0032	3	.0020–.0068
	V6-181/E	.0008–.0020	.010	.015	.9392	2.2487–2.2495	.0005–.0026	2.4995	.0003–.0018	3	.0030–.0110
	V6-262/T②	.0035–.0045	⑤	.015	1.095	2.2490–2.2510	.0003–.0025	2.9993–3.0003	③	3	.0035–.0135
1984	4-151/R	.0025–.0030	.010	.020	.9400	2.000	.0005–.0026	2.300	.0005–.0022	5	.0035–.0085
	V6-173/X,Z	.0007–.0017	.010	.020	.9199	2.0303–2.0314	.0014–.0038	④	.0016–.0032	3	.0024–.0084
	V6-181/E	.0008–.0020	.010	.015	.9392	2.2487–2.2495	.0005–.0026	2.4995	.0003–.0018	3	.0030–.0110
	V6-231/3	.0008–.0020	.010	.015	.9392	2.2487–2.2495	.0005–.0026	2.4995	.0003–.0018	3	.0030–.0110
	V6-262/T②	.0035–.0045	⑤	.015	1.095	2.2490–2.2510	.0003–.0025	2.9993–3.0003	③	3	.0035–.0135

①—Fit rings in tapered bores for clearances given in tightest portion of ring travel. Clearances specified are minimum gaps.
②—Diesel engine.
③—Nos. 1, 2 & 3, .005–.0021 inch; No. 4, .0020–.0034 inch.
④—Nos. 1, 2 & 4, 2.5336–2.5346 inch; No. 3, 2.5331–2.5340 inch.
⑤—Top ring, .019 inch; 2nd ring, .013 inch.

VALVE SPECIFICATIONS

Year	Engine/V.I.N.	Valve Lash		Valve Angles		Valve Spring Installed Height	Valve Spring Pressure Lbs. @ In.	Stem Clearance		Stem Diameter	
		Int.	Exh.	Seat	Face			Intake	Exhaust	Intake	Exhaust
1982–84	4-151/R	Hydraulic①		46	45	1.66	151 @ 1.254	.0010–.0027	.0010–.0032	.3418–.3425	.3418–.3425
	V6-173/X	1½ Turns②		46	45	1.57	195 @ 1.180	.0010–.0027	.0010–.0027	.3410–.3417	.3410–.3417
	V6-181/E	Hydraulic①		45	45	1.727	220 @ 1.340	.0015–.0035	.0015–.0032	.3401–.3412	.3405–.3412
	V6-262 Diesel/T	Hydraulic①		③	④	1.67	210 @ 1.220	.0010–.0027	.0015–.0032	.3425–.3432	.3420–.3427
1984	V6-231/3	Hydraulic①		45	45	1.727	210 @ 1.340	.0015–.0035	.0015–.0032	.3401–.3412	.3405–.3412

①—No adjustment.
②—Turn rocker arm stud nut until all lash is eliminated, then tighten nut the additional turns listed.
③—Intake, 45°; Exhaust, 31°.
④—Intake, 44°; Exhaust, 30°.

COOLING SYSTEM & CAPACITY DATA

Year	Model & Engine/V.I.N.	Cooling Capacity Qts.		Radiator Cap Relief Pressure, Lbs.	Thermo. Opening Temp.	Fuel Tank Gals.	Engine Oil Refill Qts.	Transaxle Oil	
		Less A/C	With A/C					Manual Trans. Pts.	Auto. Transaxle Qts.①
1982	4-151/R	9.4	9.7	15	195	16	3②	—	5
	V6-173/X	11.4	11.7	15	195	16	4②	—	5
	V6-181/E	13.5	14.25	15	195	16	4③	—	5
	V6-262/T⑤	13.2	13.7	15	195	16	6④	—	5
1983	4-151/R	9.4⑥	9.7⑥	15	195	16	3②	—	⑦
	V6-173/X,Z	11.9⑧	12.4⑧	15	195	16	4②	—	⑦
	V6-181/E	13.5⑨	14.4	15	195	16	4③	—	⑦
	V6-262/T⑤	13⑩	13.9	16–18.5	195	16	6④	—	⑦
1984	4-151/R	9.4⑥	9.7⑥	15	195	15.7	3②	6	⑦
	V6-173/X,Z	12.5⑬	12.6⑬	15	195	15.7	4②	6	⑦
	V6-181/E	12.8⑪	13.1⑪	15	195	15.7	4③	6	⑦
	V6-231 MFI/3	12.1	12.6	15	195	15.7	4③	6	⑦
	V6-262/T⑤	12.4⑫	12.6	16–18.5	185	16.4	6④	6	⑦

①—Approximate, make final check with dipstick.
②—With or without filter change.
③—Add 1 qt. with filter change.
④—Includes filter. Use recommended diesel engine oil, designated SF/CC or SF/CD.
⑤—Diesel Engine.
⑥—W/heavy duty cooling system, 12 qts.
⑦—Oil pan only, 4 qts.; total capacity, 6 qts.
⑧—W/heavy duty cooling system, 12.7 qts.
⑨—W/heavy duty cooling system, 14 qts.
⑩—W/heavy duty cooling system, 13.9 qts.
⑪—Heavy duty, 13.3 qts.
⑫—Heavy duty, 12.6 qts.
⑬—Heavy duty, 12.8 qts.

Electrical Section

Refer to the 1980–84 Citation, Omega, Phoenix and Skylark, "Electrical Section" for service procedures not covered in this section.

STARTER, REPLACE

NOTE: Upon removal of starter, note if any shims are used. If shims are used, they should be reinstalled in their original location during installation.

If starter is noisy during cranking, remove one .015 inch double shim or add one .015 inch single shim to the outer bolt. If starter makes a high pitched whine after firing, add .015 inch double shims until noise ceases.

Except V6-262 Diesel

1. Disconnect battery ground cable.
2. Raise and support vehicle.
3. From beneath vehicle, remove two starter motor to engine bolts and lower starter. On 4-151 engine remove nut securing starter bracket to rear of starter.
4. Disconnect solenoid wires and battery cable then, remove starter.
5. Reverse procedure to install.

V6-262 Diesel

1. Disconnect battery ground cable. On engines with heavy duty option there will be two batteries. Install a suitable engine holding device.
2. Raise and support vehicle. Remove left and center engine mount stud nuts, then 2 front cradle mount bolts and lower cradle. Remove flywheel cover.
3. Remove starter lower shield nut and starter flex shield for removal accessibility.
4. Disconnect wires from starter noting position of wires for installation.
5. Remove starter attaching bolts, then remove starter.

STEERING WHEEL, REPLACE

1. Disconnect battery ground cable.
2. Remove horn button or pad.
3. Remove retainer and steering wheel retaining nut.
4. Remove steering wheel with a suitable puller (tool No. J-1859-03 or BT-61-9).

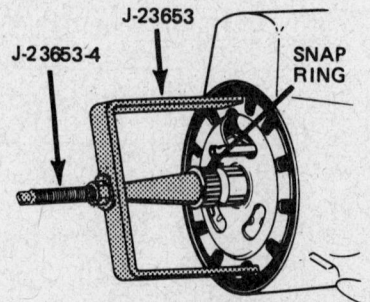

Tighten nut until tool slightly depresses lock plate

Fig. 1   Compressing lock plate

5. Reverse procedure to install.

TURN SIGNAL SWITCH, REPLACE

1. Disconnect battery ground cable.
2. Remove steering wheel as outlined under "Steering Wheel, Replace" procedure.
3. Using a screwdriver, pry cover from housing.
4. Using lock plate compressing tool J-23653, compress lock plate, and pry snap ring from groove on shaft, Fig. 1. Slowly release lock plate compressing tool, then remove tool and lock plate from shaft end.
5. Slide canceling cam and upper bearing preload spring from end of shaft.
6. Remove turn signal (multi-function) lever.
7. Remove hazard warning knob retaining screw, button, spring and knob.
8. Remove pivot arm.
9. Wrap upper part of electrical connector with tape to prevent snagging of wires during switch removal.
10. Remove switch retaining screws and pull switch up from column, guiding wire harness through column.
11. Reverse procedure to install.

WIPER SWITCH, REPLACE

Windshield

1. Remove turn signal switch as outlined

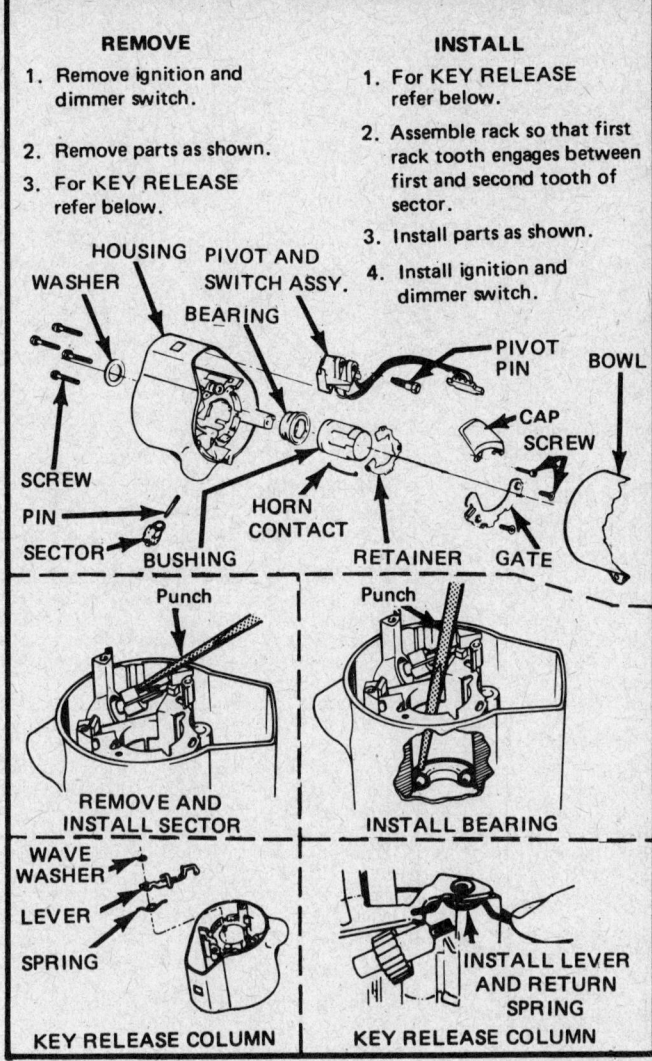

REMOVE

1. Remove ignition and dimmer switch.
2. Remove parts as shown.
3. For KEY RELEASE refer below.

INSTALL

1. For KEY RELEASE refer below.
2. Assemble rack so that first rack tooth engages between first and second tooth of sector.
3. Install parts as shown.
4. Install ignition and dimmer switch.

Fig. 2   Housing and wiper switch removal & installation. Standard steering column

Fig. 3   Cover and wiper switch removal & installation. Tilt steering column

under "Turn Signal Switch, Replace" procedure.
2. Refer to Figs. 2 and 3 for wiper switch replacement.

Rear Window

1. Disconnect battery ground cable.
2. Remove left hand trim panel, then right side switch trim cover.
3. Remove switch attaching screws, then switch.
4. Reverse procedure to install.

HEADLAMP SWITCH, REPLACE

Celebrity

1. Disconnect battery ground cable.
2. Remove headlamp switch knob.
3. Remove instrument cluster trim cover.
4. Remove screws attaching headlamp switch mounting plate to instrument cluster carrier.
5. Disconnect headlamp switch connector.
6. Remove headlamp switch from mounting

plate.
7. Reverse procedure to install.

Century

1. Disconnect battery ground cable.
2. Remove instrument cluster trim cover.
3. Remove left side instrument cluster switch trim panel by removing three screws and gently rocking panel out.
4. Remove the headlamp rocker switch or rheostat by removing three screws and pulling switch assembly straight out (one screw is common to both switch assemblies).
5. Reverse procedure to install.

Cutlass Ciera

1. Remove left hand trim pad.
2. Remove screws attaching switch to instrument panel.
3. Pull switch rearward to remove.
4. Reverse procedure to install.

6000

1. Disconnect battery ground cable.

2. Remove steering column trim cover, headlight rod and knob assembly.
3. Remove left trim plate.
4. Remove three screws attaching switch and bracket assembly to instrument panel, disconnect electrical connector and remove switch/bracket assembly.
5. Loosen bezel and remove switch from bracket.
6. Reverse procedure to install.

INSTRUMENT CLUSTER, REPLACE

Celebrity,

1. Disconnect battery ground cable.
2. Remove headlamp switch knob, then remove ten screws attaching trim plate to carrier and remove trim plate, Fig. 4.
3. Remove three screws at underside of trim pad, then remove upper screw at right of trim pad opening and two screws at right end of trim pad. Remove trim pad, Fig. 5.
4. Remove six cluster lens to carrier attaching screws, Fig. 6.

5. Tilt cluster rearward slightly and disconnect all electrical connectors and speedometer cable. Remove cluster.
6. Reverse procedure to install.

Century

1982
1. Disconnect battery ground cable.
2. Disconnect speedometer cable at cruise control transducer (if equipped). If not equipped with cruise control, disconnect cable at upper and lower cable connections.
3. Remove nine screws retaining trim plate to cluster, then put gear shift lever in low and gently pull on trim plate to remove.
4. Remove shift indicator cable clip from shift bowl.
5. Remove lap vent trim cover by removing two attaching screws.
6. Lower steering column by removing front two retaining bolts.
7. Pull instrument cluster outward three inches, and disconnect speedometer cable from cluster by pushing retaining clip toward cluster and pulling cable away from speedometer.
8. Pull cluster out remainder of the way, then remove one screw retaining electrical connector, Fig. 7.
9. Reverse procedure to install.

1983–84 Mechanical Cluster
1. Disconnect battery ground cable.
2. Remove 4 screws attaching cluster assembly to instrument panel.
3. Disconnect speedometer cable from transmission. If two piece cable is used, disconnect in engine compartment to ensure there is cable slack.
4. Remove shift indicator clip and position gear selector in low.
5. Pull cluster assembly out far enough to reach behind and disconnect speedometer cable.
6. To ease removal of cluster on vehicles equipped with tilt wheel, lower wheel, then unscrew tilt lever.
7. On all models, tilt top side of cluster assembly downward and remove cluster.
8. Reverse procedure to install.

1983–84 Digital Cluster
1. Disconnect battery ground cable.

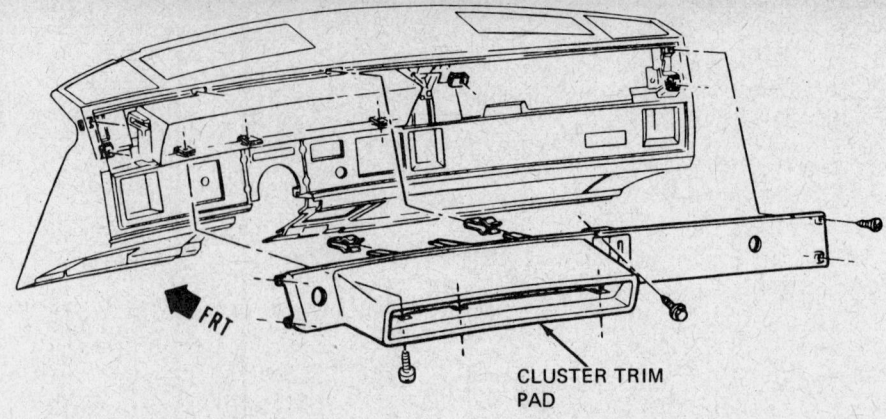

Fig. 4   Trim plate removal. 1982–84 Celebrity

2. Remove 4 screws attaching cluster assembly to instrument panel.
3. Disconnect speedometer cable from transmission. If two piece cable is used, disconnect in engine compartment to ensure there is cable slack.
4. Pull cluster assembly out far enough to disconnect optics head from vehicle speed sensor, then remove cluster assembly.
5. Disconnect 2 electrical connectors on printed circuit from the tube and circuit board assembly.
6. Remove cluster push buttons by pulling straight out.
7. Remove lens and bezel attaching screws, then lens and bezel.
8. Remove tube and circuit board to cluster attaching screws, then tube and circuit board.
9. Remove mechanical odometer from tube and circuit board.
10. Remove 2 telltale lenses and pads from face plate.

NOTE: Shift indicator needle, spring and cable stay with tube and circuit board.

11. Reverse procedure to install.

Cutlass Ciera
1. Carefully insert a clean putty knife blade

between the trim panel and left trim pad, then gently pry trim panel outward. Using same procedure, remove center trim cover.
2. Remove three screws in steering column trim collar and remove collar, then remove ash tray.
3. Remove six screws attaching trim pad to instrument panel, Fig. 8. Remove trim pad.
4. Remove 8 screws attaching cluster trim cover to instrument panel, then remove cover.
5. Disconnect speedometer cable at transmission or cruise control transducer (if equipped).
6. Remove steering column trim cover.
7. Disconnect shift indicator clip from steering column shift bowl.
8. Remove 4 screws attaching cluster assembly to instrument panel.
9. Pull assembly out far enough to reach behind cluster and disconnect speedometer cable.
10. Remove cluster assembly.
11. Reverse procedure to install.

6000
1. Remove headlight rod knob assembly.
2. Using thin, flat tool carefully pry left side trim plate away from instrument panel.

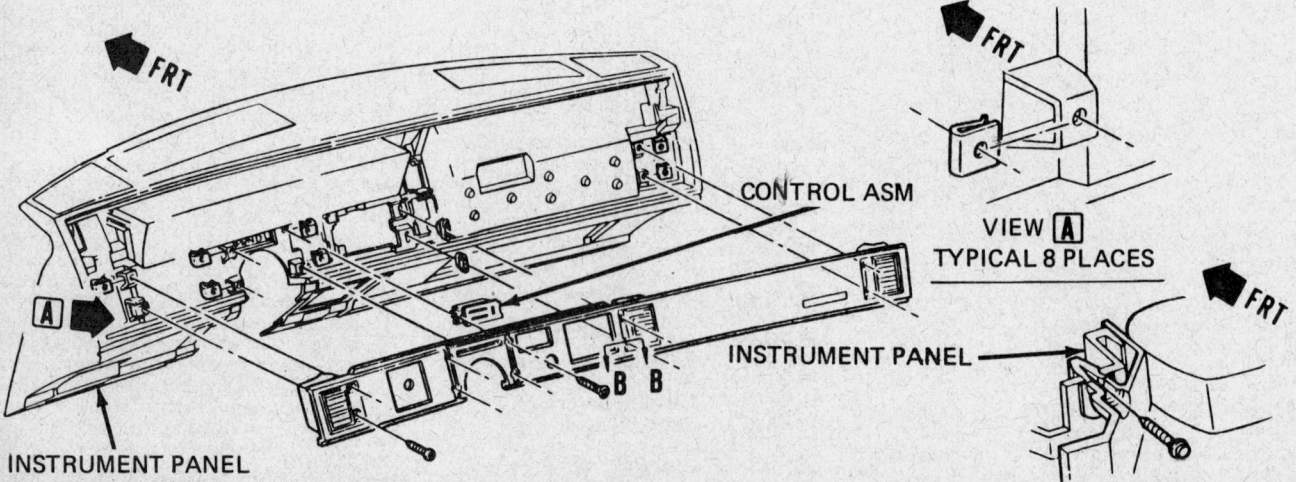

Fig. 5   Trim pad removal. 1982–84 Celebrity

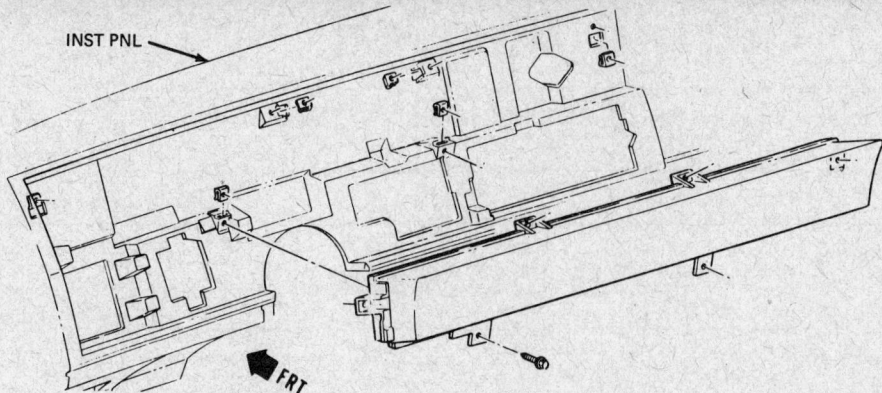

Fig. 6 Instrument cluster. 1982–84 Celebrity

3. Remove six screws attaching instrument cluster to instrument panel carrier.
4. Remove instrument panel cluster.
5. Reverse procedure to install.

RADIO, REPLACE

Century

1. Disconnect battery ground cable.
2. Remove instrument panel trim plate.
3. Remove right side instrument panel switch trim panel by removing three screws and gently rocking panel out.
4. Remove four radio assembly attaching screws.
5. Disconnect antenna cable, power and speaker electrical connections.
6. Pull radio outward through instrument panel carrier housing.
7. Reverse procedure to install.

Except Century

1. Disconnect battery ground cable.
2. Remove instrument panel trim plate, except Cutlass Ciera, on Cutlass Ciera left side trim pad.
3. Remove three screws at radio bracket, except Cutlass Ciera, on Cutlass Ciera four screws.
4. Pull radio rearward and disconnect electrical connectors and antenna lead.
5. Remove radio.
6. Reverse procedure to install.

W/S WIPER MOTOR, REPLACE

1. Raise hood, then remove right and left wiper arm and blade assemblies.
2. Remove shroud grille to body attaching screws, then shroud grille.
3. Loosen, but do not remove nuts securing transmission drive link to motor crank arm, then disconnect drive link.
4. Disconnect wiring connectors and washer hoses.
5. Remove 3 screws attaching wiper motor to firewall.
6. Remove motor while guiding crank arm through hole.
7. Reverse procedure to install. Motor must be in "Park" position before assembling transmission drive link to crank arm. Torque transmission drive link to 53–75 in. lbs.

W/S WIPER TRANSMISSION, REPLACE

1. Raise hood, then remove right and left wiper arm and blade assemblies.
2. Remove shroud grille to body attaching screws, then shroud grille.
3. Loosen, but do not remove nuts securing transmission drive link to motor crank arm, then disconnect drive link, Fig. 9.
4. Remove 6 screws attaching wiper transmission to body, Fig. 9.
5. Carefully guide transmission assembly through access hole in upper shroud panel to remove.
6. Reverse procedure to install. Torque transmission drive link nuts to 53–75 in. lbs.

HEATER CORE, REPLACE

Less A/C

Exc. 1983–84 Century & Cutlass Ciera

NOTE: For service procedures on 1983–84 Century and Cutlass Ciera, refer to models with A/C.

1. Drain cooling system.
2. Remove heater inlet and outlet hoses.
3. Remove radio noise supression strap.
4. Remove cover retaining screws and cover.
5. Remove heater core.
6. Reverse procedure to install.

With A/C

1. Drain cooling system.
2. On all except diesel engine models, disconnect heater inlet and outlet hoses. On diesel engine models, raise vehicle and disconnect heater inlet and outlet hoses, then lower vehicle.
3. On diesel engine models, remove instrument panel lower sound absorber. On all models, working inside vehicle, remove the heater ducts, then the heater case side cover.
4. Remove heater lower outlet.
5. Remove 2 housing cover to air valve housing clips, then the housing cover.
6. Remove heater core retaining straps, core tubing retainers, then the core.
7. Reverse procedure to install.

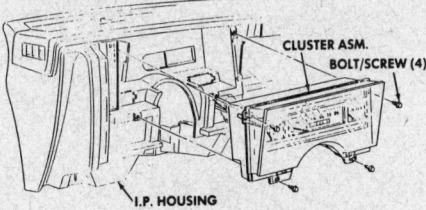

Fig. 7 Instrument cluster removal. 1982–84 Century

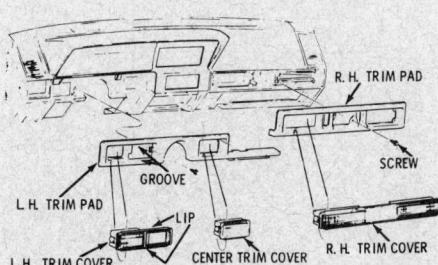

Fig. 8 Trim pad removal. 1982–84 Cutlass Ciera

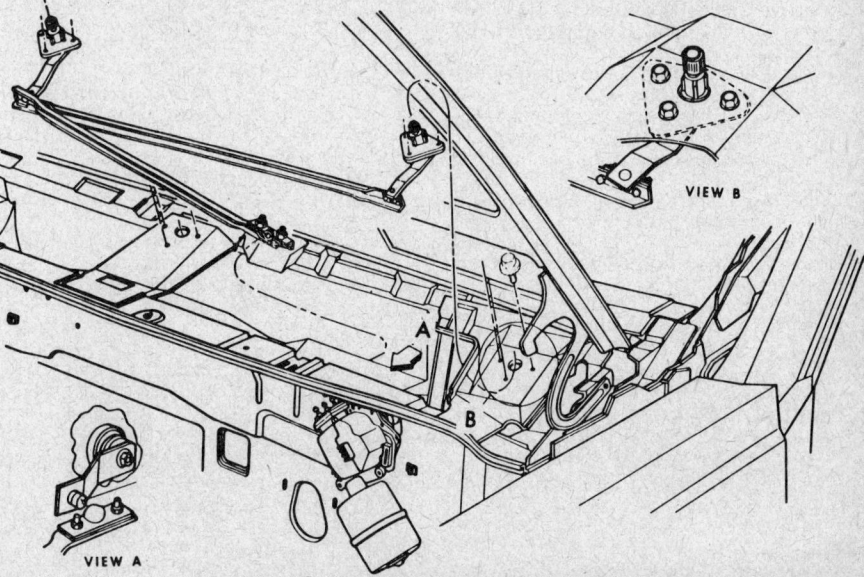

Fig. 9 Windshield wiper transmission removal (typical)

4-151 Engine Section

> Refer to 1980–84 Citation, Omega, Phoenix and Skylark "ENGINE SECTION" for service procedures on this engine.

V6-173 Engine Section

> Refer to 1980–84 Citation, Omega, Phoenix and Skylark "ENGINE SECTION" for service procedures on this engine.

V6-181 & V6-231 MFI Engine Section

ENGINE MOUNTS, REPLACE

1. Raise and support front of vehicle.
2. Attach suitable engine lifting fixture to engine.
3. Remove mount to engine mount bracket nuts. Raise engine slightly and remove mount to frame nuts. Remove mount, Fig. 1.
4. Reverse procedure to install.

ENGINE, REPLACE

1. Disconnect battery cables from battery and remove air cleaner.
2. Drain cooling system.
3. Disconnect vacuum hosing to all non-engine mounted components.
4. Disconnect detent cable from carburetor lever.
5. Disconnect accelerator linkage.
6. Disconnect engine harness connector.
7. Remove alternator attaching bolts, then alternator.
8. Remove fan blower motor, then AIR pump and mounting bracket, if equipped.
9. Disconnect radiator hoses from radiator and heater hose from engine.
10. Remove power steering pump and bracket assembly from engine, if equipped.
11. Disconnect fuel lines at rubber hose connections.
12. Remove gas spring cylinder from hood, if equipped, then place hood in full open position.
13. Raise vehicle and disconnect exhaust pipe at manifold.

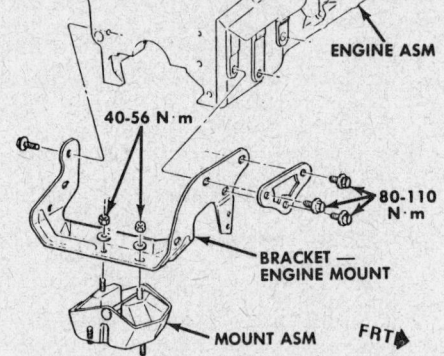

Fig. 1   Engine mount removal

14. Remove engine front mount to cradle retaining nuts, located at right side of vehicle.
15. Disconnect battery cables from starter motor and transaxle case.
16. Remove flex plate cover, then disconnect torque converter form flex plate.
17. Remove transaxle case to cylinder case support bracket bolts, Fig. 2.
18. Lower vehicle. Place a support under transaxle rear extension.
19. Disconnect ground strap from engine at engine forward strut. Remove engine strut bracket from radiator support and swing rearward.
20. Remove transaxle to cylinder case retaining bolts. Make note of ground stud location.
21. If equipped with A/C, remove compressor and lay aside.
22. Using a suitable lifting device, remove engine.
23. Reverse procedure to install.

CYLINDER HEAD, REPLACE

1. Disconnect battery ground cable.
2. Remove intake manifold, then loosen and remove belts.
3. If left cylinder head is to be removed, remove dipstick, also remove air and vacuum pumps with mounting bracket if equipped, and position aside with hoses attached.
4. If right cylinder head is to be removed, remove alternator, also disconnect power steering gear pump and brackets attaching to cylinder head.
5. Disconnect wires from spark plugs, then remove spark plug wire clips from rocker arm cover studs.
6. Remove exhaust manifold bolts from head being removed.
7. With air hose and cloths, clean dirt off cylinder head and adjacent area.
8. Remove rocker arm cover, then rocker arm and shaft assembly from cylinder head. Lift out push rods, keeping them in order to ensure proper installation.
9. Loosen all cylinder head bolts, then remove bolts and lift off cylinder head.
10. Reverse procedure to install. Torque cylinder head bolts in sequence shown in Figs. 3 and 4 to specifications.

ROCKER ARMS

A nylon retainer is used to retain the rocker arm. Break them below their heads with a

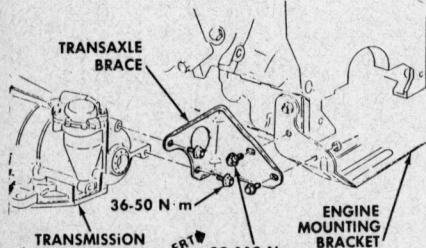

Fig. 2   Transaxle to engine case support bracket removal

Fig. 3   Cylinder head bolt tightening sequence. 1982–83 models

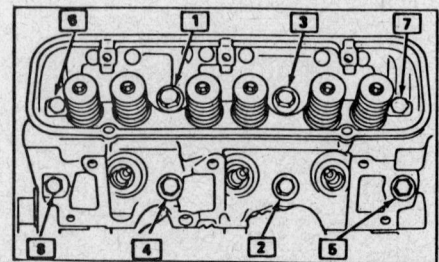

Fig. 4   Cylinder head bolt tightening sequence. 1984 models

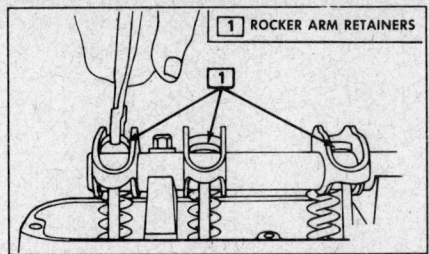

Fig. 5 Removing nylon retainer

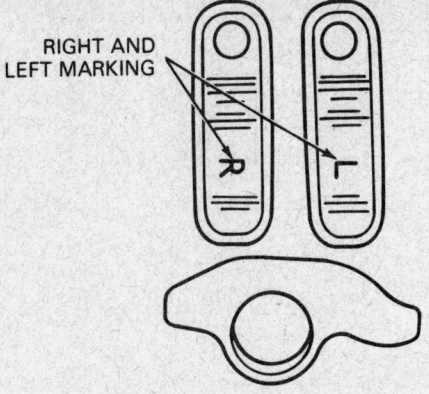

RIGHT AND LEFT MARKING

Fig. 6 Service rocker arm identification

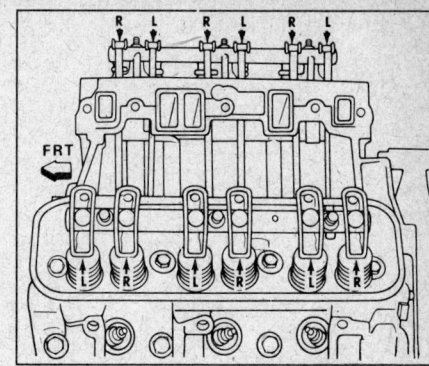

FRT

Fig. 7 Service rocker arm installation

chisel, or pry out with channel locks Fig. 5. Production rocker arms can be installed in any sequence since the arms are identical.

Replacement rocker arms for all engines are identified with a stamping, right (R) and left (L), Fig. 6 and must be installed as shown in Fig. 7.

To install rocker arms, position arm on rocker shaft, centering it over the 1/4 inch hole in the rocker shaft. Then, install new rocker arm retainers in the holes using a 1/2 inch drift to seat them.

VALVE ARRANGEMENT

Front to Rear

V6-181	E-I-I-E-I-E
V6-231 MFI	E-I-I-E-I-E

VALVE LIFT SPEC.

Engine	Year	Intake	Exhaust
V6-181	1982–84	—	—
V6-231 MFI	1984	—	—

VALVE TIMING

Engine	Year		Degrees
V6-181	1982–84		—
V6-231	1984		—

VALVE GUIDES

The valve guides are an integral part of the cylinder head and cannot be replaced.

If valve stem clearance is excessive, the valve guide must be reamed and an oversize valve installed. On 1982–84 V6-181 and 1984 V6-231 MFI engines, valves are available in oversize of .010 inch.

VALVE LIFTERS

Failure of an hydraulic valve lifter, Fig. 8, is generally caused by dirt or an inadequate

oil supply. An air leak at the intake side of the oil pump or too much oil in the engine will cause air bubbles in the oil supply to the lifters, causing them to collapse. This is a probable cause of trouble if several lifters fail to function, but air in the oil is an unlikely cause of failure of a single unit.

The valve lifters may be lifted out of their bores after removing the rocker arms, push rods and intake manifold. Adjustable pliers with taped jaws may be used to remove lifters that are stuck due to varnish, carbon, etc. Fig. 7 illustrates the type of lifter used.

ENGINE FRONT COVER, REPLACE

1. Drain engine coolant.
2. Disconnect upper and lower radiator hoses and heater return hose at water pump.
3. Remove water pump pulley and belts.
4. Remove alternator bracket and alternator.
5. Remove distributor. If timing chain and sprockets are not going to be disturbed, note position of distributor rotor for reinstallation in same position.
6. Remove balancer bolt and washer, then remove balancer assembly.
7. Remove bolts attaching engine front cover to cylinder block, Fig. 9, also remove

two oil pan to engine front cover bolts.
8. Remove engine front cover assembly and gasket, Fig. 9.
9. Reverse procedure to install.

NOTE: Prior to reinstalling the engine front cover, remove the oil pump cover and pack the space around the oil pump drive gears completely full of petroleum jelly. Failure to do this may result in the pump losing its prime, causing a "dry" engine start.

When reinstalling engine front cover bolts, apply a suitable sealer to the threads to prevent leakage.

TIMING CHAIN, REPLACE

1. With front cover removed, as outlined in "ENGINE FRONT COVER, REPLACE", temporarily install balancer bolt and washer in end of crankshaft. Turn crankshaft so timing marks on sprockets are as close together as possible. Remove balancer bolt and washer using a sharp blow on wrench handle, so bolt can be removed without changing position of sprockets.
2. Remove crankshaft oil slinger and camshaft sprocket bolts.
3. Using two large screwdrivers, alternately pry off sprockets and chain.
4. Thoroughly clean all parts that are to be

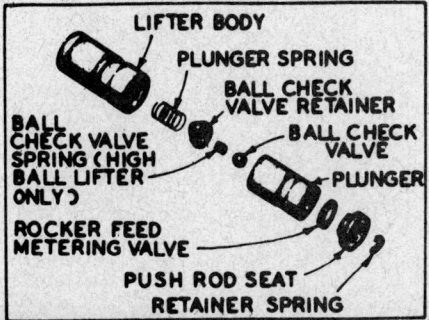

LIFTER BODY
PLUNGER SPRING
BALL CHECK VALVE RETAINER
BALL CHECK VALVE SPRING (HIGH BALL LIFTER ONLY)
BALL CHECK VALVE
PLUNGER
ROCKER FEED METERING VALVE
PUSH ROD SEAT RETAINER SPRING

Fig. 8 Exploded view of hydraulic valve lifter

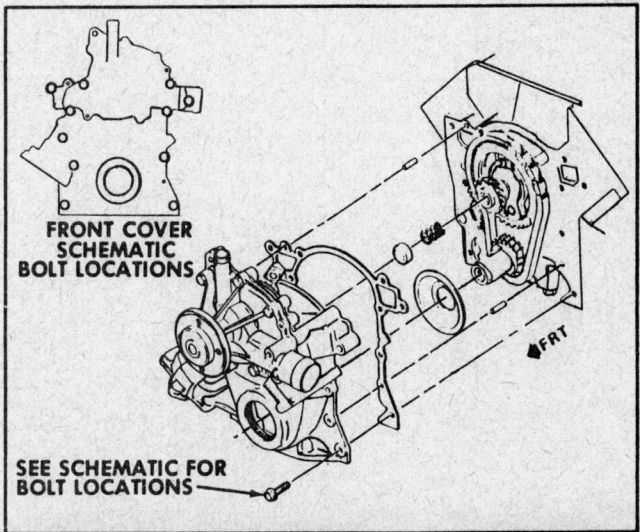

FRONT COVER SCHEMATIC BOLT LOCATIONS

SEE SCHEMATIC FOR BOLT LOCATIONS

FRT

Fig. 9 Engine front cover removal & installation

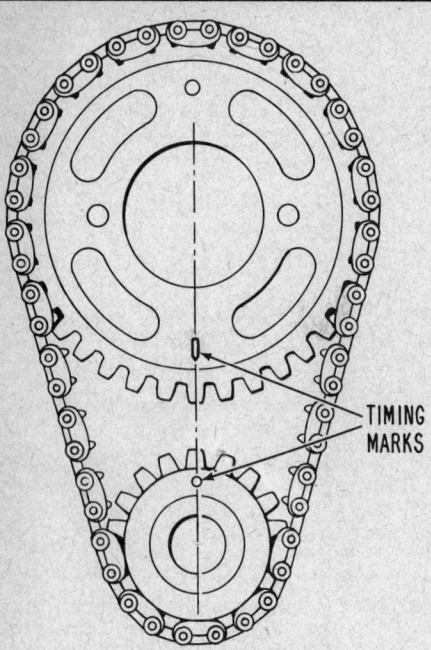

Fig. 10   Valve timing marks

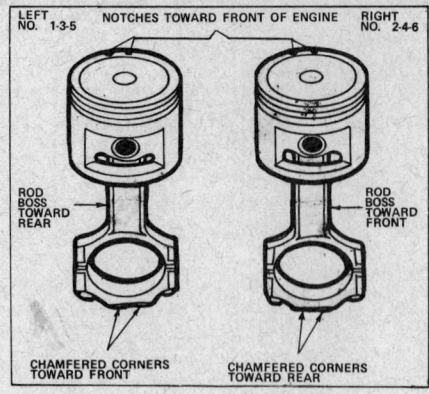

Fig. 11   Piston and rod assembly

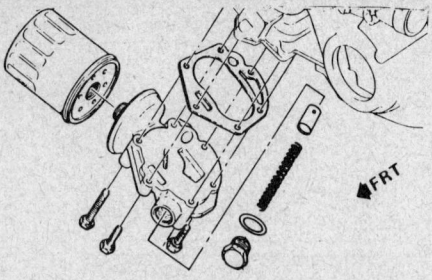

Fig. 12   Oil pump cover and relief valve and spring installation

reused.

5. Assemble timing chain on sprockets and slide sprockets and chain assembly onto camshaft and crankshaft with timing marks aligned as shown in Fig. 10.
6. Install sprocket bolts and torque to 20 ft. lbs.
7. Install oil slinger, camshaft thrust button and engine front cover.

CAMSHAFT, REPLACE

1. Remove engine as outlined in "ENGINE, REPLACE".
2. Remove intake manifold.
3. Remove rocker arm covers.
4. Remove rocker arm and shaft assemblies, push rods and valve lifters.
5. Remove timing chain cover.
6. Align timing marks of camshaft and crankshaft sprocket. This avoids burring of camshaft journals by crankshaft during removal. Remove timing chain and sprocket.

7. Slide camshaft forward out of bearing bores, using care so as not to damage bearing surfaces.
8. Reverse procedure to install. When installing camshaft, align crankshaft and camshaft timing marks as shown in Fig. 10.

PISTON & ROD, ASSEMBLE

Rods and pistons should be assembled and installed as shown in Fig. 11.

Measure connecting rod side clearance using a suitable feeler gauge. Clearance should be .0005–.0026 inch.

PISTONS, PINS & RINGS

Pistons are available in standard sizes and oversizes of .010 and .030 inch. Rings are available in standard sizes and oversizes of .010 and .030 inch. Piston pins are supplied with piston and available only in standard sizes.

MAIN & ROD BEARINGS

Main bearings are available in standard sizes and undersizes of .001 and .002 inch. Rod bearings are available in standard sizes and in undersize of .008.

OIL PAN, REPLACE

1. Disconnect battery ground cable.

2. Raise and support vehicle.
3. Drain oil and remove flywheel cover.
4. Remove oil pan.
5. Reverse procedure to install. Apply RTV sealer to oil pan flange and torque oil pan bolts to 14 ft. lbs.

OIL PUMP SERVICE

Removal & Inspection

1. Remove oil filter.
2. Remove screws attaching oil pump cover assembly to timing chain cover. Remove cover assembly and slide out oil pump gears.
3. Wash off gears and inspect for wear or scoring. Replace any gears not found serviceable.
4. Remove oil pressure relief valve cap, spring and valve, Fig. 12. Oil filter by-pass valve and spring are staked in place and should not be removed.
5. Wash parts thoroughly, inspect relief valve for wear or scoring. Check relief valve spring to see that it is not worn on its side or collapsed. Replace any relief valve spring that is questionable.
6. Check relief valve in its bore in cover. The valve should have no more clearance than an easy slip fit. If any excessive clearance can be felt, valve and/or cover should be replaced.
7. Check relief by-pass valve for cracks, or warping. Valve should be free of nicks or scratches.

Assembly & Installation

1. Lubricate and install pressure relief valve and spring in bore of oil pump cover, Fig. 12.
2. Install cap and gasket. Torque cap to 35 ft. lbs.

Fig. 13   Checking oil pump gear end clearance

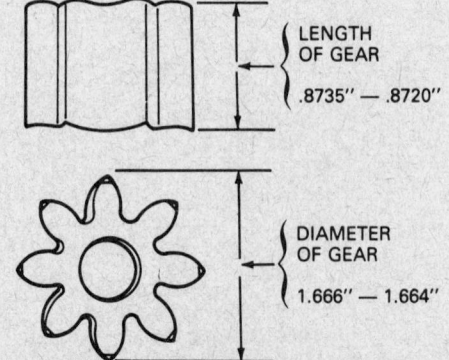

Fig. 14   Checking length and diameter of pump gear

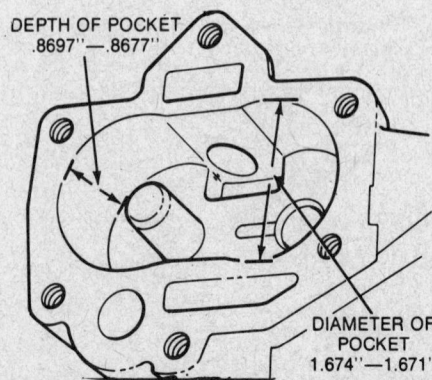

Fig. 15   Checking depth and diameter of gear pocket

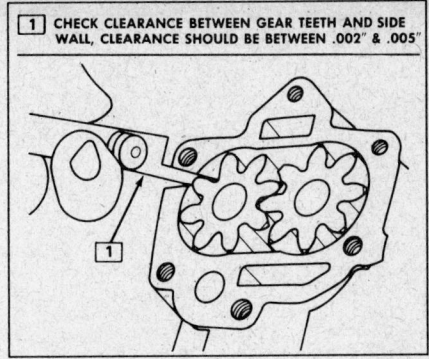

1 CHECK CLEARANCE BETWEEN GEAR TEETH AND SIDE WALL, CLEARANCE SHOULD BE BETWEEN .002" & .005"

Fig. 16 Checking oil pump gear side clearance

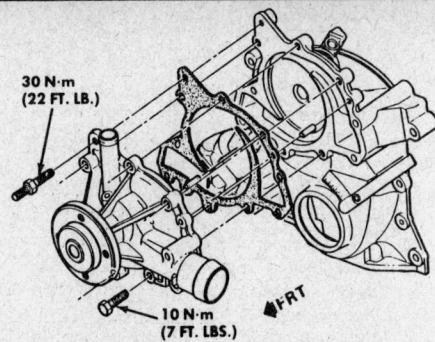

30 N·m
(22 FT. LB.)

10 N·m
(7 FT. LBS.)

FRT

Fig. 17 Water pump removal & installation

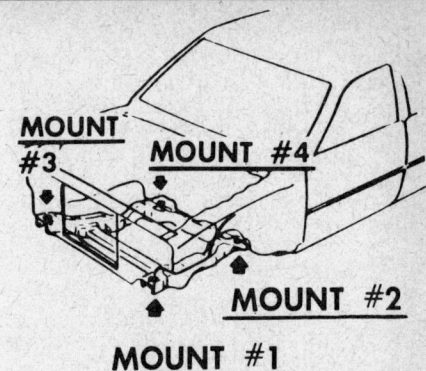

MOUNT #3
MOUNT #4
MOUNT #2
MOUNT #1

Fig. 18 Removing front body mounts

3. Install oil pump gears and shaft in oil pump body section of timing chain cover to check gear end clearance and side clearance.
4. Check oil pump end clearance by placing a straight edge over gears and measure clearance between straight edge and gasket surface, Fig. 13. Clearance should be between .002 and .006 inch. If clearance is less than .002 inch, measure gears and pocket to determine which is out of specification, Figs. 14 and 15.
5. Check oil pump side clearance, Fig. 16. Clearance should be between .002 and .005 inch. If clearance is greater than .0050 inch, measure gears and pocket to determine which is out of specification, Figs. 14 and 15.
6. Check oil pump cover flatness by placing a straight edge across cover face, using feeler gauge between straight edge and pump cover. If clearance is .001 or more pump cover must be replaced.
7. If gear clearance and oil pump cover is flat and side clearance is satisfactory remove gears and pack gear pocket full of petroleum jelly.

NOTE: Never use chassis lube when reinstalling oil pump gears.

8. Reinstall gears so petroleum jelly fills entire gear pocket and between teeth of gears. Place gasket in position.

NOTE: Unless the pump is packed with petroleum jelly it may fail to prime itself when engine is started and damage to engine may result.

9. Install cover assembly screws. To ensure proper seal of gasket, torque screws alternately and evenly to 10 ft. lbs.
10. Install filter on nipple.

REAR MAIN BEARING OIL SEAL REPAIR

1. Remove oil pan and oil pump as described

previously.
2. Remove rear main bearing cap.
3. Using tool No. J-21526-2, gently drive upper seal into groove approximately 1/4 in.
4. Repeat step 3 for other end of seal.
5. Measure the amount that was driven in on one side and add 1/16 in. Using a suitable cutting tool, cut this length from the oil rear main bearing cap lower seal using the main bearing cap as a guide. Repeat this step for the other end of seal.
6. Place piece of cut seal into groove of seal installer tool guide No. J-21526-1 and install tool guide onto engine block.
7. Using seal packing tool No. J-21526-2, drive piece of seal into block. Drive seal in until packing tool contacts machined stop.
8. Remove tool guide and repeat steps 6 and 7 for other end of seal.
9. Install new seal in bearing cap.
10. Install rear main bearing cap. Apply a thin film of sealant No. 1052357 or equivalent to rear main bearing cap and case interface. Use care not to allow sealant to contact crankshaft journal or main bearing.

ELECTRIC FUEL PUMP, REPLACE

1. Disconnect battery ground cable, then drain fuel tank.
2. Disconnect tank unit wire from connector in rear compartment.
3. Remove ground wire retaining screw from under body.
4. Disconnect hoses from tank unit.
5. Support fuel tank and disconnect the two fuel tank retaining straps.
6. Remove fuel tank from vehicle.
7. Remove fuel gage retaining cam, using tool J-24187, or other suitable tool.
8. Remove sending unit from tank.
9. Electric fuel pump can be unbolted from tank sending unit after sending unit has been removed.
10. Reverse procedure to install.

WATER PUMP, REPLACE

1. Disconnect battery ground cable, then drain cooling system.
2. Remove accessory drive belts.
3. Remove water pump attaching bolts, Fig. 17.
4. Remove engine support strut.
5. Place jack under front crossmember and raise jack until vehicle just starts to raise.
6. Remove front two body mount bolts, (#1 and #3), Fig. 18, also remove lower cushions and retainers.
7. Thread body mount bolts with retainers a minimum of three turns into cage nuts so bolts restrain cradle movement.
8. Release floor jack slowly until crossmember contacts body mount bolt retainers. As jack is being lowered watch and correct any interference with hose, lines, pipes and cables.

NOTE: Do not lower the cradle without it being restrained as possible damage can occur to the body and underhood items.

9. Remove water pump from engine.
10. Reverse procedure to install.

BELT TENSION DATA

	New Lbs.	Used Lbs.
1982		
Air Cond.	145	65–80
Alternator	145	65–80
Power Steer.	135	65–80
Air Pump	100	45
1983–84		
Air Cond.	165	90
Alternator	145	70
Power Steer.	165	90
AIR or Vacuum Pump	75	45

V6-262 Diesel Engine Section

DIESEL ENGINE DIAGNOSIS

For engine diagnosis, refer to "Diesel Engine Section" of Oldsmobile 88, 98, Toronado, 1977–79 Omega, Cutlass except Ciera and 1984 Cruiser Chapter.

DIESEL ENGINE ELECTRICAL TROUBLESHOOTING

1982–83

Engine Runs Rough On Cold Start

1. With ignition switch in Run position and engine off, disconnect electrical connector from engine temperature switch, Fig. 1.
2. Connect jumper wire between terminals on engine temperature switch electrical connector, and note if fast idle solenoid extends.
3. If solenoid extends, proceed to step 4. If solenoid does not extend, check throttle linkage or solenoid plunger for binding. If linkage is satisfactory, replace solenoid.
4. Connect tachometer J-26925 or equivalent to engine, then start engine and leave jumper wire attached to the engine temperature switch.
5. Disconnect electrical connector from cold advance solenoid. Engine speed should vary 30 RPM when connector is removed.
6. If there is no change in RPM, check solenoid and pump for proper operation and repair or replace as necessary.
7. Turn engine off, then check continuity of engine temperature switch using suitable self-powered test lamp.
8. Test lamp should not light above 120° F. If not satisfactory, replace switch.
9. Using suitable test lamp, ground one lead and connect other lead to dark green wire terminal at diode module A. If test lamp lights and engine is cold, replace coolant temperature switch.
10. Turn ignition OFF, then disconnect all glow plug wire connectors. Connect suitable self-powered test lamp between rear post of glow plug relay and ground.
11. At each glow plug, momentarily connect glow plug wire connector to plug spade terminal. Observe test light.
12. If test lamp lights, glow plug and wire connector are satisfactory. If test lamp does not light, touch wire connector to engine block or other ground. If test lamp lights, replace glow plug. If lamp does not light, replace wire to glow plug.

Engine Stays On Fast Idle

1. With ignition switch in Run position and engine not running, disconnect electrical connector from engine temperature switch, Fig. 1.
2. Connect jumper wire between terminals on engine temperature switch and note if fast idle solenoid extends.
3. If solenoid extends, proceed to step 4. If solenoid does not extend, check throttle linkage or solenoid plunger for binding. If linkage is satisfactory, replace solenoid.
4. Check continuity of engine temperature switch with suitable self-powered test lamp.
5. Lamp should light below 120° F and shut off above 120° F. If not satisfactory, replace switch.

place switch.

Engine Continues To Run With Ignition Off

1. With ignition turned off and engine running, disconnect electrical connector from diode module, Fig. 1.
2. If engine stops, diode "C" is shorted. Replace diode module.
3. If engine continues to run, disconnect fuel solenoid pink wire connector.
4. If engine stops, repair or replace fuel solenoid.
5. If engine continues to run, stop engine by crimping flexible fuel return line near fuel supply pump, then repair or replace fuel solenoid.

No Fast Idle W/ Cold Engine

1. With ignition switch in Run position and engine off, disconnect electrical connector from engine temperature switch, Fig. 1.
2. Connect jumper wire to both terminals on engine temperature switch connector.
3. Momentarily disconnect and connect fast idle solenoid electrical connector while noting if fast idle solenoid extends.
4. If solenoid does not extend, refer to step 5. If solenoid extends, readjust for correct fast idle operation.
5. Connect one end of suitable test lamp to ground and the other end to white/green lead on models without A/C, or black/pink lead at fast idle solenoid on models with A/C.
6. If test lamp lights, proceed as follows:
   a. Disconnect electrical connector from fast idle solenoid.
   b. Check continuity of fast idle solenoid using suitable self-powered test lamp.
   c. If lamp does not light, replace solenoid.
7. If test lamp does not light, proceed as follows:
   a. Momentarily connect test light lead to pink/black terminal of engine temperature switch.
   b. If test lamp lights, remove connector from switch and check switch for continuity using suitable self-powered test lamp.
   c. If test light shuts off below 120° F, replace engine temperature switch.

No Wait Lamp On Cold Engine

1. With ignition switch in Run position and engine off, observe "Charge" light, which should illuminate.
2. If "Charge" light is not lit, check condition of GAUGES fuse and replace if necessary.
3. If GAUGES fuse is satisfactory, confirm glow plug operation by listening for clicking noise from relay.
4. If relay operates, check pink/black wire between fuse block and splice S204 for a short or open and repair as necessary, Fig. 1. If wire is satisfactory, proceed to step 6.
5. If relay does not operate, check pink wires between ignition switch and fuse block for a short or open and repair as necessary. If wires are satisfactory, proceed to step 6.
6. Disconnect electrical connector from "Wait" lamp control relay. Connect jumper wire between ground and dark blue wire at connector, and observe "Wait" light, which should illuminate.
7. If "Wait" light is not lit, check condition of lamp bulb and replace if necessary.

8. If lamp bulb is satisfactory, check dark blue wire between "Wait" lamp control relay electrical connector and "Wait" lamp, and the pink/blue wire between "Wait" lamp and splice S204 for a short or open, and repair as necessary. If wires are satisfactory, proceed to step 9.
9. Using suitable test lamp, check ground connection at G104. Attach one end of test lamp to red wire terminal of Glow Plug Relay and the other end to the black wire lead of "Wait" lamp control relay.
10. If lamp does not light, circuit is satisfactory. If lamp lights, replace "Wait" lamp control relay.

Wait Lamp Pulses Slowly On & Off

1. With "Wait" lamp pulsing, connect suitable test lamp between white and yellow wires of wait lamp control relay, Fig. 1.
2. If test light is on when "Wait" lamp is off, and off when "Wait" lamp is on, replace "Wait" lamp control relay.
3. If test light does not turn on, connect test lamp between orange and orange or orange/black wires at thermal controller. With "Wait" lamp pulsing, confirm test light pulses on and off with "Wait" lamp.
4. If test lamp does not light, connect test lamp to front red wire and rear dark blue/black wire terminals of glow plug relay. Defect may be in red wire between battery and glow plug relay, or in black, dark blue, dark green, and orange or orange/black wires between relay and thermal controller or glow plug relay. Repair as necessary.
5. If test light flashes on and off with "Wait" lamp when connected to orange or orange/black wires at thermal controller, then connect test light between black wire at controller and ground.
6. If test lamp flashes on and off, repair black wire between controller and ground.
7. If test lamp does not light, replace controller.

Wait Lamp Stays On Longer Than 10 Seconds

1. Check glow plug relay operation. Disconnect connector at diesel diode module, Fig. 1. Connect one end of test lamp to ground and other end of test lamp to red (front) post of glow plug relay. Then touch test lamp to rear post (dark blue and black wires) of glow plug relay. Test lamp should light, indicating glow plug relay is operating properly.
2. If test lamp remains OFF, proceed as follows:
   a. Check ECM fuse and ground connection G104.
   b. Disconnect connector from thermal controller. Connect a suitable test lamp between pin 3 (pink/black wire) and pin 6 (yellow wire) of harness connector. If test lamp lights with ignition ON, check continuity between pins 3 and 6 of thermal controller. If test lamp remains ON, replace thermal controller.
   c. If test lamp remains OFF, connect a suitable ohmmeter to glow plug relay coil, and check resistance of coil. If ohmmeter indicates a high glow plug relay coil resistance, replace coil. Check continuity of pink/black, yellow and black wires.
3. If test lamp lights (glow plug relay is operating properly), proceed as follows:

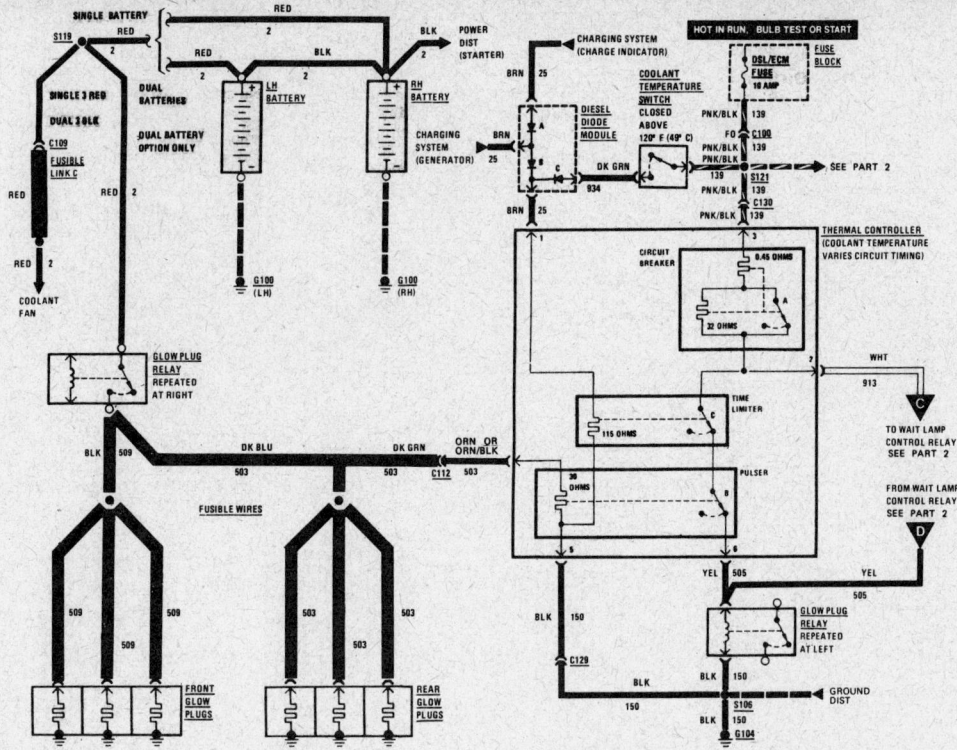

Fig. 1 Glow plug wiring schematic (part 1 of 2). 1982–83 models

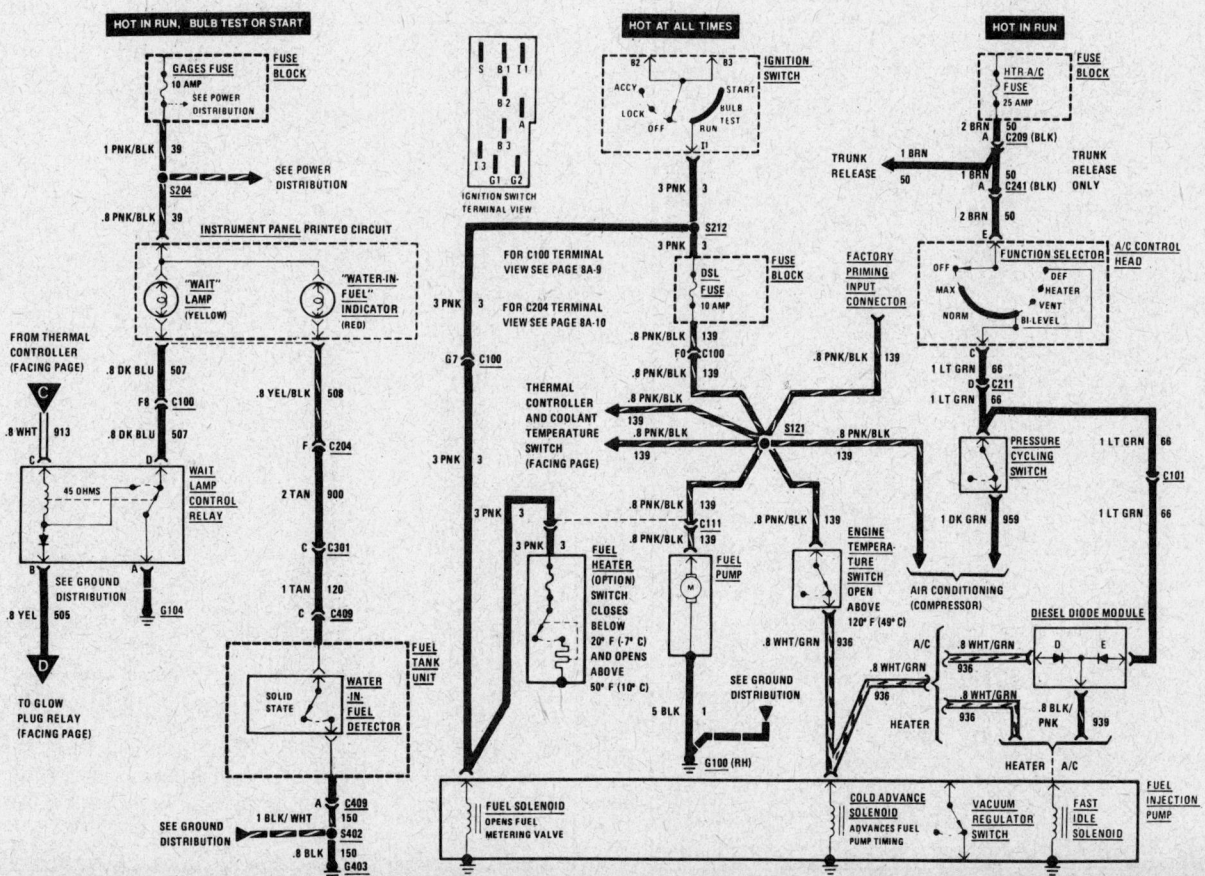

Fig. 1 Glow plug wiring schematic (part 2 of 2). 1982–83 models

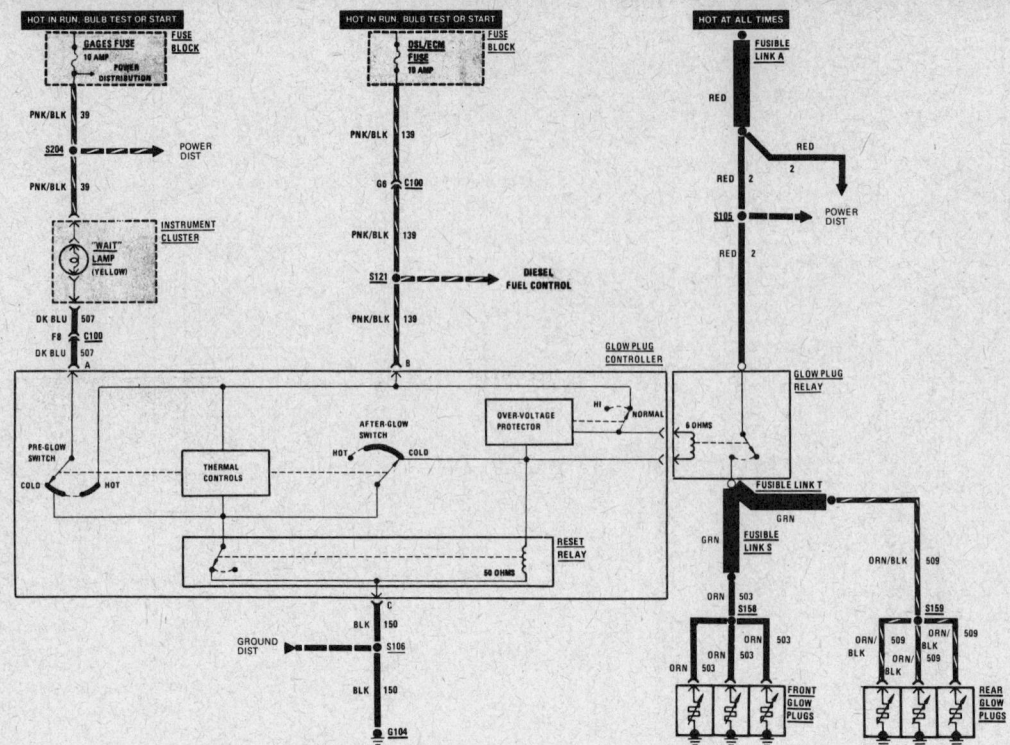

Fig. 1A   Glow plug wiring schematic. 1984 models

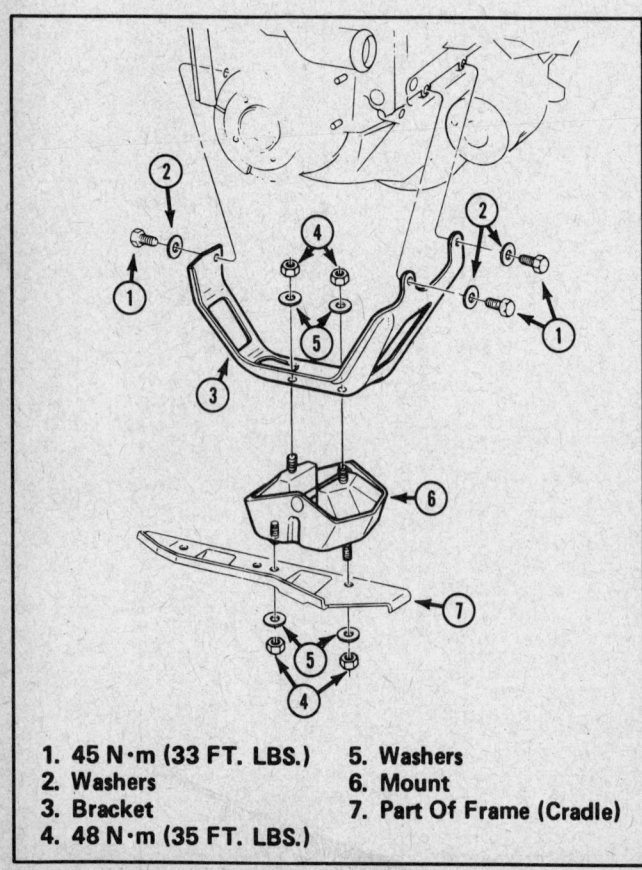

1. 45 N·m (33 FT. LBS.)   5. Washers
2. Washers   6. Mount
3. Bracket   7. Part Of Frame (Cradle)
4. 48 N·m (35 FT. LBS.)

1. 41 N·m (30 FT. LBS.)
2. Bracket
3. Washers
4. 57 N·m (42 FT. LBS.)
5. Spacer
6. Strut
7. Nut (Torque No. 4)
8. Bracket
9. 23 N·m (17 FT. LBS.)
10. Brace
11. 48 N·m (35 FT. LBS.)

Fig. 1B   Front engine mount removal and installation

Fig. 2   Engine mount strut & bracket removal and installation

a. Disconnect "Wait" lamp control relay connector. "Wait" lamp should go OFF. Connect test lamp between white and yellow wires of connector. If test lamp lights, replace "Wait" lamp control relay.

b. If test lamp remains OFF, turn ignition OFF. Connect a suitable ohmmeter to pins 4 and 5 of thermal controller, and check for 30 ohms resistance. If ohmmeter indicates more than 30 ohms, replace thermal controller. Check continuity of black, dark green, dark blue, orange or orange/black, white, yellow and black wires.

Engine Does Not Start When Cold (Wait Lamp OK-Goes On, Then Off)

1. If engine cranking speed is slow, turn ignition OFF, then, using a suitable voltmeter, check battery voltage. Voltmeter should indicate approximately 12.4 volts.
2. Using a suitable test lamp and with ignition in RUN position, check voltage at pink wire at fuel injection pump solenoid, Fig. 1. If test lamp remains OFF, repair pink wire. If test lamp lights, turn ignition OFF and check for continuity through fuel solenoid to ground using test lamp KD-125 or equivalent. If there is no continuity, replace fuel injection pump solenoid.
3. With ignition switch in RUN position and engine not operating, check glow plug relay operation. Glow plug should click ON and OFF.
4. If glow plug relay operates as described in step 3, proceed as follows:
   a. Turn ignition OFF.
   b. Disconnect all glow plug harness connectors from glow plugs.
   c. Connect test lamp KD-125 or equivalent between rear post (dark blue and black wires) of glow plug relay and ground.
   d. At each glow plug, touch harness connector to glow plug spade terminal. If test lamp lights, glow plug and harness are operating properly. Connect harness connector to glow plugs.

   NOTE: Disconnect harness connector after testing each glow plug.

   e. If test lamp does not light, touch harness connector to engine block. If test lamp lights, replace glow plug. If test lamp remains OFF, replace wire(s) to glow plug(s).
   f. If test lamp remains OFF for each glow plug tested after replacement of wires, replace glow plugs and thermal controller, as required.
5. If glow plug relay does not operate as described in step 3, proceed as follows:
   a. If glow plug relay does not click ON and OFF, and "Wait" lamp comes ON then OFF, check thermal controller and glow plug relay circuit.
   b. Disconnect connector at thermal controller. Connect one end of suitable test lamp to ground and turn ignition to RUN position. Connect other end of test lamp to brown wire and check for voltage. If test lamp lights, check coolant temperature switch. If coolant temperature switch is closed, replace switch.
   c. With one end of test lamp grounded, connect other end of test lamp to orange or orange/black wire. If test lamp lights, check for shorted glow plug relay wires (red to dark blue and black wires). Replace damaged wires.

as required. If test lamp remains OFF after replacement of wires, replace glow plugs and thermal controller as required.
   d. Connect one end of test lamp to battery. With other end of test lamp touch yellow wire between thermal controller and glow plug relay. If test lamp remains OFF, repair yellow wire between thermal controller and glow plug relay. If test lamp lights, replace thermal controller.

1984

Refer to Fig. 1A for troubleshooting.

GLOW PLUG RESISTANCE TEST

1. In 1982–83 models, use a high impedence digital multimeter tool No. J-29125. On 1984 models, use high impedence digital multimeter tool No. J-29125A.
2. Position multimeter lefthand switch to "OHMS," turn righthand switch counterclockwise to "200 OHMS" and slide center switch to the left "D.C. LO."
3. Start engine, turn heater ON and allow engine to reach normal operating temperature. Remove all feed wires from glow plugs.
4. On 1983–84 models, disconnect electrical connector from alternator.
5. Using magnetic tachometer No. J-26925, turn idle speed screw located on the side of injection pump until the roughest engine idle is obtained. Do not exceed 900 rpm.
6. Allow engine to operate at its roughest idle speed for at least 1 minute. Thermostat must be open and upper radiator hose hot.
7. Connect a suitable clip to the black test lead of multimeter. The clip must be grounded to the fast idle solenoid and must remain grounded until all tests are completed.
8. With engine idling, probe each glow plug terminal and note resistance values on each cylinder in firing order. On 1982–83 models, reading will be between 1.8 and 3.4 ohms. If these readings are not obtained, turn engine OFF and check glow plugs. Resistance should be .7 or .8 ohms. If reading is not obtained, check multimeter for correct settings and for low or incorrect battery in multimeter. Check multimeter ground wire to engine. On 1984 models equipped with an electric cooling fan, note resistance values with cooling fan OFF. Do not disconnect electrical connector from fan.

   NOTE: The resistance values are dependent on the temperature in each cylinder, and indicate the output of each cylinder.

9. If an ohm reading on any cylinder is approximately 1.2 or 1.3 ohms on 1982–83 models, or 1.3 or 1.4 ohms on 1984 models, check for engine mechanical problem. Check compression of the low reading cylinder and the cylinder which fires before and after the low cylinder reading.

   NOTE: Correct the cause of the low compression cylinder before proceeding to the fuel system.

10. Compare glow plug resistance readings, checking for differences between cylinders. Rough idle engines will normally vary .3 ohms on 1982–83 models, and on

1984 models, .4 ohms or more between cylinders in firing order. To compensate, it will be necessary to raise or lower the reading on one or more cylinders by selecting nozzles.
11. Remove nozzles from cylinders with the high or low ohm reading. Determine nozzle pop off pressure and check nozzle for leakage and spray pattern.
12. Install nozzles with a higher pop off pressure to lower ohm reading and nozzles with a lower pop off pressure to raise ohm readings.

NOTE: A change of approximately 30 psi in pressure will change reading by .1 ohm.

13. During cleaning or replacement of nozzle and before installation of injection pipe, crank engine and check for air bubbles at nozzle inlet. If bubbles are present, clean or replace nozzles as required.
14. Install injection tube, start engine and check idle speed. If engine idle is rough, check and note glow plug resistance values of each cylinder firing order.
15. Compare glow plug resistance readings, noting differences of .3 ohms on 1982–83 models, and on 1984 models, .4 ohms between cylinders.

NOTE: It will be necessary to raise or lower resistance reading on one or more cylinders as described previously.

16. After additional nozzle changes have been performed, check engine idle.

NOTE: After completing two resistance checks and nozzle changes, correct engine idle can now be obtained.

17. Injection pump replacement may be necessary if the following occurs:
   a. Problem cylinder moves from cylinder as nozzle changes are made.
   b. Cylinder ohm readings do not change when nozzles are changed (replaced).

NOTE: Always check cylinders at the same engine rpm. A nozzle with a tip leak can allow more fuel into the cylinder, which will raise glow plug ohm reading. This will rob fuel from the next nozzle in firing order, and will result in glow plug having a low ohm reading. Remove and check nozzle with a high reading. If nozzle is leaking, this could cause a rough engine idle. If a low glow plug resistance value is noted and it does not change with nozzle replacement, switch glow plugs between a known good cylinder and a bad cylinder. If resistance reading of each cylinder is not the same as before the switch, the glow plug cannot be used for rough engine idle diagnosis.

ENGINE MOUNTS, REPLACE

Refer to Figs. 1B and 2 for service procedures.

ENGINE, REPLACE

1. Drain cooling system. Remove serpentine drive belt, also remove vacuum pump drive belt if equipped.
2. Remove air cleaner and install a suitable cover.
3. Disconnect battery ground cable at battery (on vehicles equipped with heavy

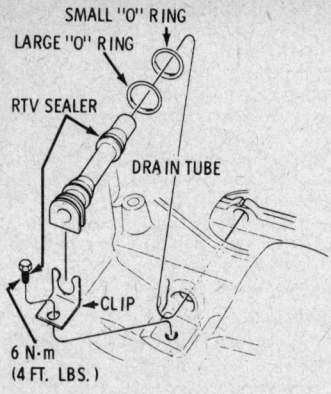

Fig. 3 Intake manifold drain tube removal & installation

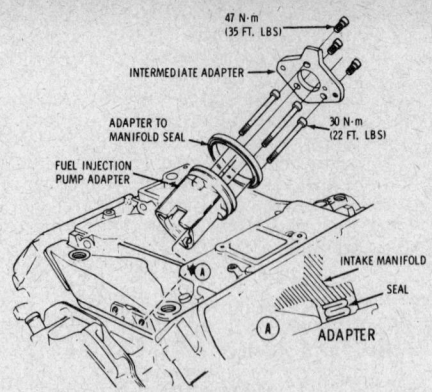

Fig. 4 Removal & installation of intermediate adapter, pump adapter & seal

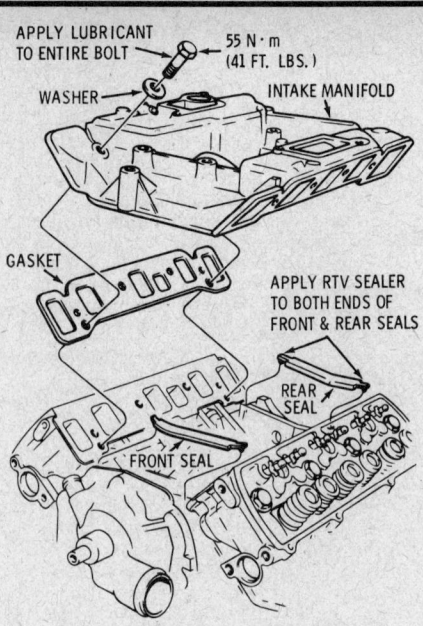

Fig. 5 Intake manifold installation

duty system there will be two batteries), ground wires at inner fender and engine ground strap.

4. Raise vehicle. Remove flywheel cover.
5. Remove flywheel to torque converter attaching bolts.
6. Disconnect exhaust pipe from rear exhaust manifold.
7. Remove engine to transaxle brace.
8. Remove engine mount to cradle retaining nuts and washers.
9. Disconnect leads to starter motor, No. 2 cylinder glow plug and battery ground cable at transaxle to engine bolt.
10. Disconnect lower oil cooler hose and plug openings.
11. Remove accessible power steering pump bracket fasteners and lower vehicle.
12. Remove remaining power steering pump bracket/brace.
13. Remove heater outlet pipe.
14. Disconnect all remaining glow plug leads at glow plugs.
15. Disconnect all other leads at engine, disconnect engine harness at cowl connector and body mounted relays and position engine harness aside.
16. If equipped with A/C, disconnect compressor with brackets and lines attached and position aside.
17. Disconnect fuel and vacuum hoses, plug all fuel line openings.
18. Disconnect throttle and T.V. cables at injection pump and cable bracket. Position cables aside.
19. Disconnect upper oil cooler hose and plug openings. Remove exhaust crossover pipe heat shield.
20. Disconnect and position aside transaxle filler tube.
21. Remove exhaust crossover pipe.
22. Remove engine mounting strut and strut brackets.
23. Install a suitable engine lifting device.

NOTE: When installing lifting chains to cylinder heads, ensure that washers are used under the chains and bolt heads and the bolts are torqued to 20 ft. lbs.

24. Position a suitable support under transaxle rear extension. As engine is being removed it may be necessary to raise support. Remove engine to transaxle bolts, then engine.
25. Reverse procedure to install.

NOTE: Before installing the flex plate to converter bolts, ensure the weld nuts on the converter are flush with the flex plate and converter rotates freely by hand in this position. Hand start the three bolts and finger tighten, then torque converter bolts to 35 ft. lbs. This ensures proper alignment of converter.

INTAKE MANIFOLD, REPLACE

Removal

1. Disconnect battery ground cable(s), then remove air cleaner.
2. Drain radiator coolant, then disconnect upper radiator hose from water outlet, and heater hoses from intake manifold.
3. Remove fuel injection pump. Refer to "Injection Pump, Replace".
4. Disconnect wiring from engine accessories.
5. If equipped with cruise control, remove servo.
6. If equipped with A/C, remove compressor and braces. Position aside.
7. Remove alternator assembly.
8. Disconnect engine mounting strut.
9. Remove fuel lines, filter and brackets. Plug all openings.
10. Disconnect glow plug controller and sending units wire connectors.
11. Disconnect heat shield from exhaust pipe crossover.
12. Using a suitable back-up wrench, remove left (forward) injection lines and plug all openings.
13. Disconnect T.V. and throttle cables from bracket.
14. Remove intake manifold drain tube, Fig. 3.
15. Remove injection pump intermediate adapter, pump adapter and seal, Fig. 4.
16. Remove intake manifold.

Installation

1. Thoroughly clean machined surfaces of cylinder head and intake manifold, ensuring neither surface becomes gouged or scratched. Clean all bolts and bolt holes.
2. Using a suitable sealer, coat both sides of the manifold to head sealing gasket surface, and place in position, Fig. 5.
3. Install end seals, ensure ends are positioned under cylinder heads. Apply RTV sealer to each end of seal, Fig. 5.

NOTE: The end seals and mating surfaces must be dry to prevent gasket slippage.

4. Carefully position intake manifold on engine.
5. Lubricate intake manifold bolts entire length with lubricant 1052080 or equivalent.
6. Install bolts. Torque to specifications following sequence shown in Fig. 6, to 15 ft. lbs. Then retorque to specifications.
7. Reverse steps 1 through 15 of removal procedure to complete installation.

CYLINDER HEAD, REPLACE

1. Remove intake manifold and valve cov-

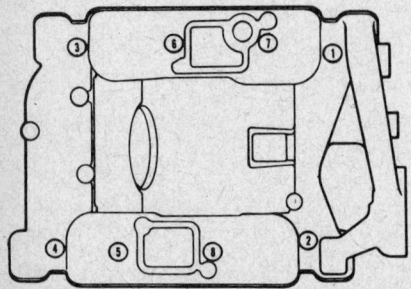

Fig. 6 Intake manifold torquing sequence

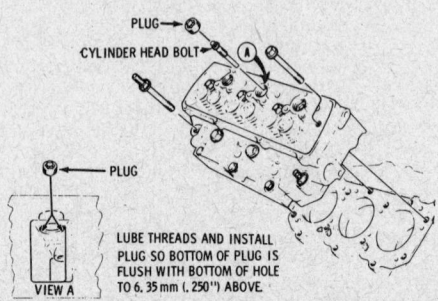

Fig. 7 Cylinder head pipe plug removal

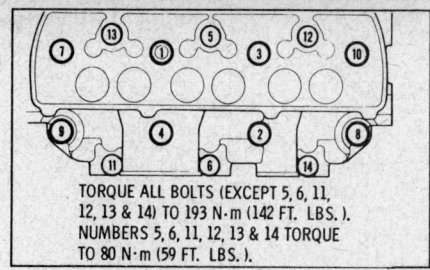

TORQUE ALL BOLTS (EXCEPT 5, 6, 11, 12, 13 & 14) TO 193 N·m (142 FT. LBS.). NUMBERS 5, 6, 11, 12, 13 & 14 TORQUE TO 80 N·m (59 FT. LBS.).

Fig. 8 Cylinder head bolt tightening sequence

er.

2. Remove or loosen any accessory bracket or pipe that interferes with removal of cylinder head.
3. Disconnect glow plug wiring and block heater lead (if equipped).
4. Remove ground strap from right cylinder head.
5. Remove rocker arm nuts, pivots, rocker arms and push rods. Scribe mark on pivots and separate so they may be easily identified and replaced in their original location.
6. Disconnect exhaust crossover pipe from exhaust manifold on side being removed and loosen it on opposite side.
7. Remove pipe plugs covering upper cylinder head bolts, Fig. 7.
8. Remove engine block drain plug, from side that is to be worked on.
9. Remove cylinder head bolts and cylinder head. If necessary to remove pre-chamber, remove glow plug and nozzle, then tap out with a small blunt 1/8 inch drift. Do not use tapered drift.
10. Reverse procedure to install. Refer to Fig. 8 for correct torque sequence. Torque cylinder head bolts except bolts 5, 6, 11, 12, 13 and 14 to 142 ft. lbs. Torque bolts 5, 6, 11, 12, 13 and 14 to 59 ft. lbs.

NOTE: The head gaskets used on this engine are composition type, and not to be used with a sealer of any kind. Any sealer applied may result in head gasket leakage.

ROCKER ARMS

NOTE: This engine uses valve rotators, Fig. 9. The rotator operates on a sprag clutch principle utilizing the collapsing action of a coil spring to give rotation to the rotor body which turns the valve.

1. Remove valve cover.
2. Remove flanged bolts, rocker arm pivot and rocker arms, Fig. 10.
3. When installing rocker arm assemblies,

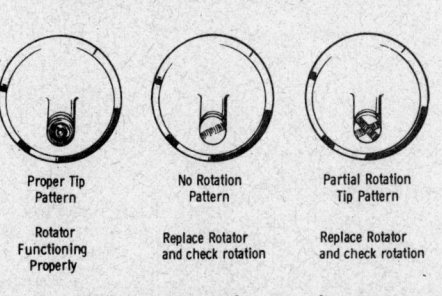

Proper Tip Pattern	No Rotation Pattern	Partial Rotation Tip Pattern
Rotator Functioning Properly	Replace Rotator and check rotation	Replace Rotator and check rotation

Fig. 11 Inspecting valve stem for rotator malfunction

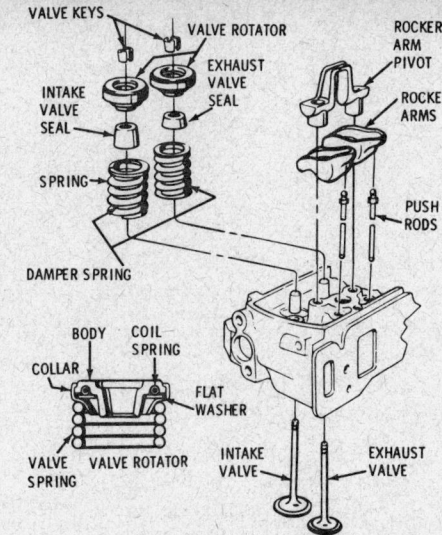

Fig. 9 Exploded view of cylinder head

lubricate wear surfaces with suitable lubricant. Torque flanged bolts to 28 ft. lbs.

VALVE ROTATORS

The rotator operates on a Sprag clutch principle utilizing the collapsing action of coil spring to give rotation to the rotor body which turns the valve, Fig. 9.

To check rotator action, draw a line across rotator body and down the collar. Operate engine at 1500 rpm, rotator body should move around collar. Rotator action can be in either direction. Replace rotator if no movement is noted.

When servicing valves, valve stem tips should be checked for improper wear pattern which could indicate a defective valve rotator, Fig. 11.

VALVE LIFT SPECS.

Engine	Year	Intake	Exhaust
V6-262 Diesel	1982–84	.375	.375

VALVE ARRANGEMENT

V6-262 Diesel . . . . I-E-E-I-E-I

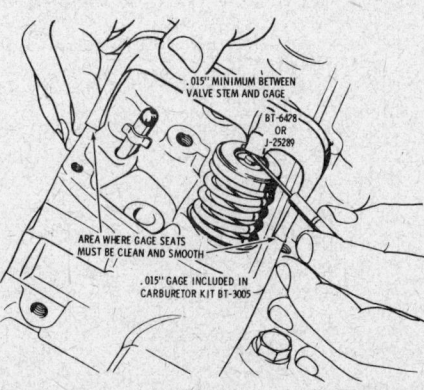

Fig. 12 Measuring valve stem height

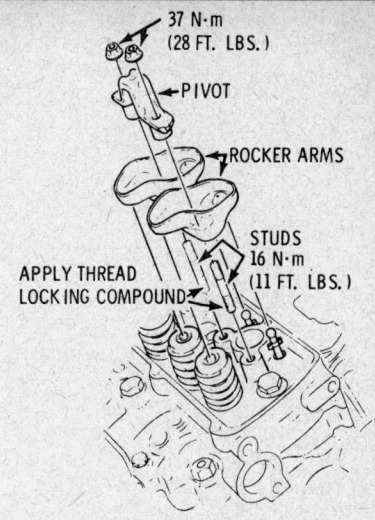

Fig. 10 Rocker arm assembly

VALVE TIMING

Intake Opens Before TDC

Engine	Year	Degrees
V6-262 Diesel	1982–84	16

VALVES

Whenever a new valve is installed or after grinding valves, it is necessary to measure the valve stem height with the special tool as shown in Fig. 12.

There should be at least .015 inch clearance between the gauge and end of valve stem. If clearance is less than .015 inch, remove valve and grind end of valve stem as required.

Check valve rotator height, Fig. 13. If valve stem end is less than .005 inch above rotator, the valve is too short and a new valve must be installed.

VALVE GUIDES

Valve stem guides are not replaceable, due to being cast in place. If valve guide bores are worn excessively, they can be reamed oversize.

If a standard valve guide bore is being reamed, use a .003″ or .005″ oversize reamer. For the .010″ oversize valve guide bore, use a .013″ oversize reamer. If too large a reamer is

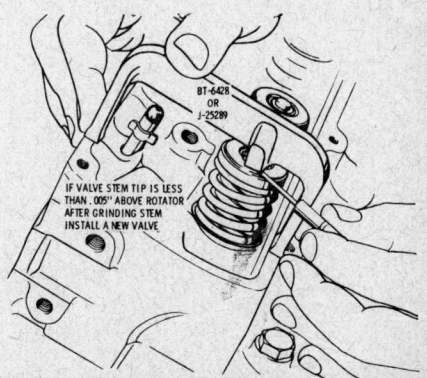

Fig. 13 Measuring valve rotator height

Fig. 14   Oversize valve lifter marking

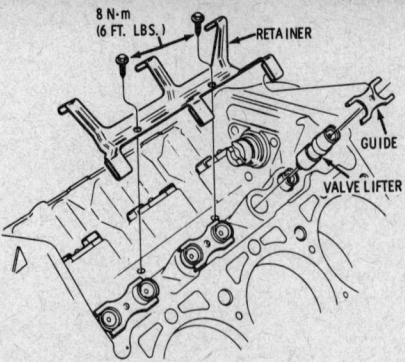

Fig. 15   Hydraulic roller lifter retainer and guide

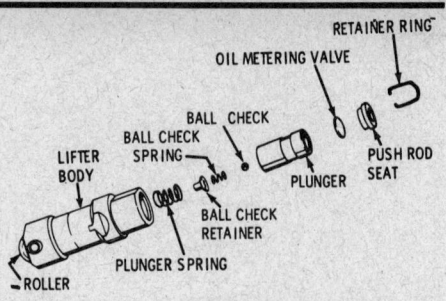

Fig. 16   Exploded view of hydraulic roller lifter

used and the spiraling is removed, it is possible that the valve will not receive the proper lubrication.

NOTE: Occasionally a valve guide will be oversize as manufactured. These are marked on the cylinder head. If no markings are present, the guide bores are standard. If oversize markings are present, any valve replacement will require an oversize valve. Service valves are available in standard diameters as well as .003″, .005″, .010″ and .013″ oversize.

VALVE LIFTER, REPLACE

NOTE: Some engines have both standard and .010 inch oversize valve lifters. The .010 inch oversize valve lifters are etched with a "O" on the side of the lifter. Also, the cylinder block will be marked if an oversize lifter is used, Fig. 14.

1. Remove intake manifold as outlined previously.
2. Remove valve covers, rocker arm assemblies and push rods. Note location of valve train components so they can be installed in original position.
3. Remove hydraulic lifter retainer bolts, then retainer, Fig. 15.
4. Remove valve lifters, then disassemble, Fig. 16.
5. If plunger and body appear satisfactory, blow off air to remove all particles of dirt. Install the plunger in the body without other parts and check for free movement. A simple test is to be sure that the plunger will drop of its own weight in the body, Fig. 16.
6. Reverse procedure to install.

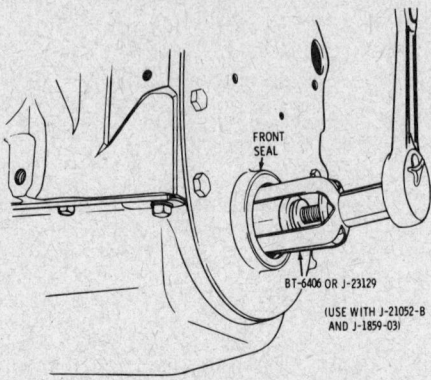

Fig. 17   Front oil seal removal

NOTE: Before installation, prime new or reassembled lifters by working lifter plunger while submerged in kerosene or diesel fuel. Lifter could be damaged if installed dry when starting engine. When assembling lifters, do not interchange plungers, as they are specifically fitted to the bodies during manufacture.

FRONT OIL SEAL, REPLACE

1. Disconnect battery ground cables.
2. Remove accessory drive belts.
3. Remove crankshaft pulley and harmonic balancer.
4. Using tool BT-6406 or equivalent, remove front oil seal, Fig. 17.
5. Apply suitable sealant to outside diameter of new oil seal.
6. Using tool J-29659 or equivalent, install new oil seal, Fig. 18.
7. Install harmonic balancer and crankshaft pulley.
8. Install and tension accessory drive belts.

ENGINE FRONT COVER, REPLACE

1. Disconnect battery ground cables.
2. Drain cooling system and disconnect lower radiator and heater hoses.
3. Remove drive belts, crankshaft pulley, harmonic balancer and accessory brackets.
4. Remove timing indicator.
5. Remove front cover attaching bolts, then the front cover. Also, remove the dowel pins. It may be necessary to grind a flat on the dowel pin to provide a rough surface for gripping.
6. Grind a chamber on one end of each dowel pin, Fig. 19.
7. Cut excess material from front end of oil pan gasket on each side of cylinder block.
8. Trim approximately 1/8 inch from each end of new front pan seal, Fig. 20.
9. Install new front cover gasket and apply suitable sealer to gasket around coolant holes.
10. Apply RTV sealer to mating surfaces of cylinder block, oil pan and front cover.
11. Place front cover on cylinder block and press downward to compress seal. Rotate cover right and left and guide oil pan seal into cavity with a small screwdriver.
12. Apply engine oil to bolts.
13. Install two bolts finger tight to retain cover.
14. Install the two dowel pins, chamfered end first.
15. Install timing indicator and remaining bolts, Fig. 21. Torque bolts as follows: water pump bolts, 21 ft. lbs.; timing cover bolts, 41–42 ft. lbs.
16. Install harmonic balancer and crankshaft pulley, Fig. 21. Torque crankshaft bolt to 160–350 ft. lbs. and pulley bolts to 30 ft. lbs.
17. Install accessory brackets.
18. Install drive belts.
19. Connect lower radiator and heater hoses.
20. Connect ground cables to batteries.

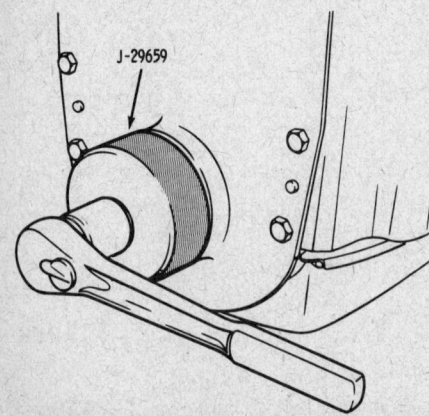

Fig. 18   Front oil seal installation

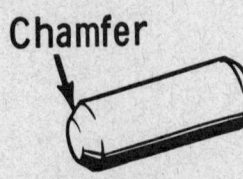

Fig 19   Dowel pin chamfer

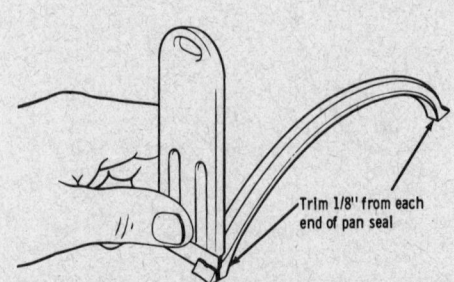

Fig. 20   Trimming oil pan seal

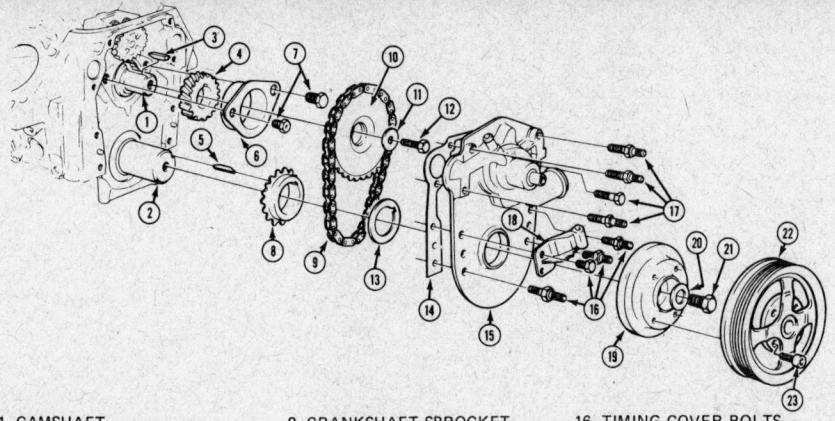

1. CAMSHAFT
2. CRANKSHAFT
3. CAMSHAFT SPROCKET KEY
4. INJECTION PUMP DRIVE GEAR
5. CRANKSHAFT SPROCKET KEY
6. FRONT CAMSHAFT BEARING RETAINER
7. RETAINER BOLT
8. CRANKSHAFT SPROCKET
9. TIMING CHAIN
10. CAMSHAFT SPROCKET
11. WASHER
12. CAMSHAFT SPROCKET BOLT
13. SLINGER
14. GASKET
15. FRONT COVER
16. TIMING COVER BOLTS
17. WATER PUMP BOLTS
18. PROBE HOLDER (RPM COUNTER)
19. CRANKSHAFT BALANCER
20. WASHER
21. CRANKSHAFT BOLT
22. PULLEY ASSEMBLY
23. PULLEY BOLTS

Fig. 21   Engine front cover installation

Fig. 22   Valve timing marks

TIMING CHAIN & GEARS, REPLACE

1. Remove front cover as outlined previously. Loosen rocker arm pivot bolts evenly so that some lash is present between rocker arms and valves.
2. Remove oil slinger, cam gear, crank gear and timing chain.
3. Install key in crankshaft, if removed.
4. Install cam gear, crank gear and timing chain with timing marks aligned, Fig. 22. Torque cam gear bolt to 64 ft. lbs. on 1982 models, or 70 ft. lbs. on 1983–84 models.
5. Install oil slinger.
6. Install front cover.

CAMSHAFT & INJECTION PUMP DRIVE & DRIVEN GEARS, REPLACE

1. Remove engine assembly as previously outlined.
2. Remove intake manifold and gasket.
3. Remove oil pump drive assembly.
4. Remove front cover, then rotate crankshaft so that timing marks are in alignment.
5. Remove all rocker arms, pivots, push rods, and lifters. Note valve train component location for proper location upon installation.
6. Remove bolt securing camshaft sprocket, then remove both cam and crank sprocket. If crank sprocket is tight on shaft, remove with a suitable puller.
7. Remove bolts retaining front camshaft bearing retainer, then remove retainer.
8. Remove cam sprocket key.
9. Remove injection pump drive gear.
10. Remove intake manifold, intermediate pump adapter and pump adapter. Remove snap ring, selective washer, driven gear and spring, Fig. 23.
11. Install a long bolt into camshaft to act as a handle and carefully slide camshaft out of block.

NOTE: Do not force the camshaft out of the block. Damage to the bearings and or the camshaft can result.

If the bearings are to be replaced, it will be necessary to remove the oil pan before removing the bearings.

12. Reverse procedure to install. Check injection pump driven gear end play. If end play is not .002–.006 inch, replace selective washer, Fig. 23. Selective washers are available from .080 to .115 inch in increments of .003 inch.

PISTON & ROD, ASSEMBLE

The pistons must be installed with the notch in the top facing the front of the engine.

Measure the connecting rod side clearance using a suitable feeler gauge. Clearance should be .008–.021 inch.

PISTON & RINGS

Pistons are available in standard sizes and .010 oversizes. Rings are available in standard and oversizes of .010 and .030.

MAIN & ROD BEARINGS

Main bearings are available in standard sizes and undersizes of .0005, .0010 and .0015 inch. The amount of undersize is stamped on the bearing shell, Fig. 24.

Rod bearings are available in standard sizes and an undersize of .010 inch.

REAR CRANKSHAFT SEAL SERVICE

Since the braided fabric seal used on these engines can be replaced only when the crankshaft is removed, the following repair procedure is recommended.

1. Remove oil pan and bearing cap.
2. Drive end of old seal gently into groove, using a suitable tool, until packed tight. This may vary between ¼ and ¾ inch depending on amount of pack required.
3. Repeat previous step for other end of seal.
4. Measure and note amount that seal was driven up on one side. Using the old seal removed from bearing cap, cut a length of seal the amount previously noted plus ¹⁄₁₆ inch.
5. Repeat previous step for other side of seal.
6. Pack cut lengths of seal into appropriate side of seal groove. A packing tool, BT-6433, Fig. 25, may be used since the tool has been machined to provide a built-in

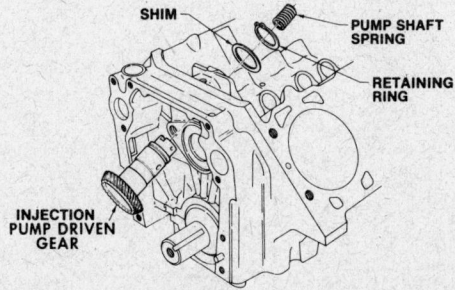

Fig. 23   Fuel injection pump driven gear removal and installation

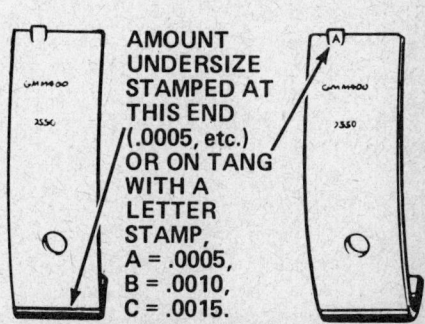

AMOUNT UNDERSIZE STAMPED AT THIS END (.0005, etc.) OR ON TANG WITH A LETTER STAMP,
A = .0005,
B = .0010,
C = .0015.

Fig. 24   Main bearing identification

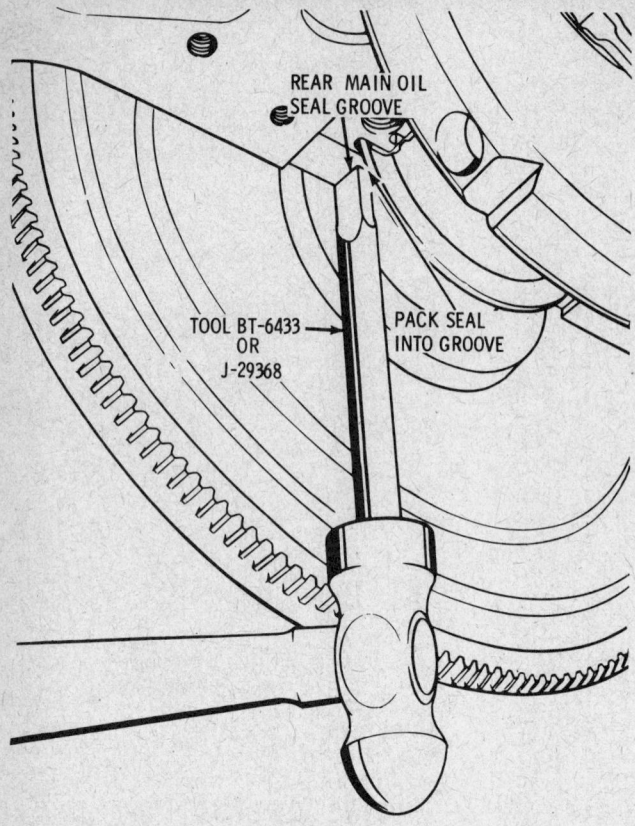

Fig. 25   Packing upper rear main bearing seal

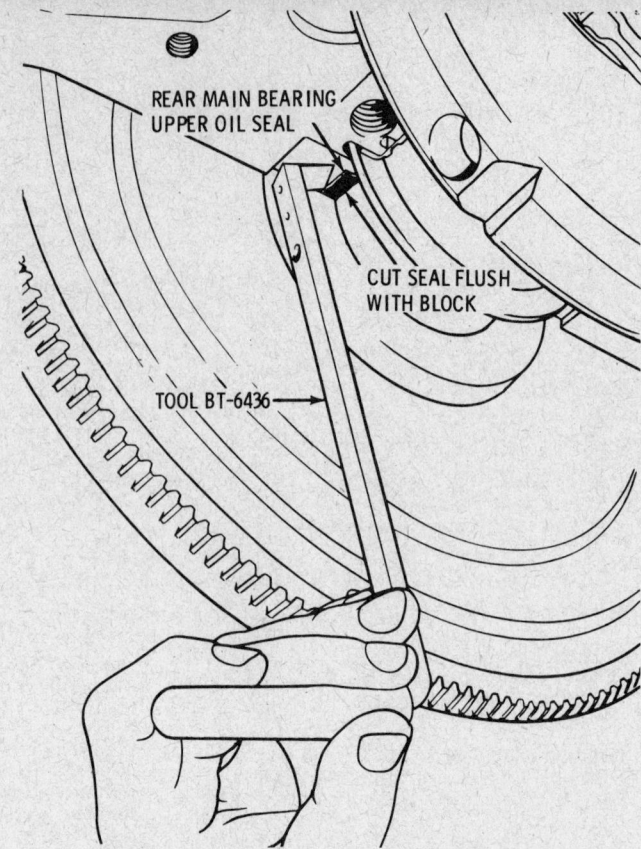

Fig. 26   Trimming upper rear main bearing seal

stop. Use tool BT-6436 to trim the seal flush with block, Fig. 26.

7. Install new seal in lower bearing cap.

OIL PAN, REPLACE

1. Install suitable engine lifting fixture.
2. Raise vehicle but keep rear slightly lower than front.
3. Install suitable supports at front of body at forward lift points.
4. Drain engine oil.
5. Remove left side steering gear to cradle bolt, then loosen right side steering gear to cradle bolt.
6. Remove front stabilizer bar.
7. Using ½ inch drill bit, drill through spot weld located between rear holes at left

hand front stabilizer bar mounting.
8. Remove engine and transaxle to cradle mount nuts.
9. Disconnect left lower ball joint from knuckle.
10. Position suitable support and block of wood under transaxle oil pan, then raise transaxle until mount stud clears cradle.
11. Remove bolts securing front crossmember to right side of cradle.
12. Remove left side body mount bolts.
13. Remove left side and front crossmember assembly, then lower rear crossmember below left side by careful use of a pry bar.
14. Remove flywheel cover, starter assembly and engine mount bracket.
15. Remove oil pan attaching bolts and oil pan.
16. Reverse procedure to install.

OIL PUMP, REPLACE & SERVICE

Replacement

1. Remove oil pan as outlined previously.
2. Remove oil pump to rear main bearing cap attaching bolts, Fig. 27.
3. Remove oil pump and drive shaft extension.
4. Reverse procedure to install. Torque attaching bolts to 18 ft. lbs.

Service
Disassembly
1. Remove oil pump drive shaft extension, Fig. 28. Do not attempt to remove wash-

ers from drive shaft extension. The drive shaft extension and washers are serviced as an assembly.
2. Remove cotter pin, spring and pressure regulator valve, Fig. 28.

NOTE: Apply pressure on pressure regulator bore before removing cotter pin since the spring is under pressure.

3. Remove oil pump cover attaching screws, then oil pump cover and gasket.
4. Remove drive gear and idler gear from pump body.

Inspection
1. Check gears for scoring or other damage, replace if necessary.
2. Proper end clearance is .0005–.0075 inch.

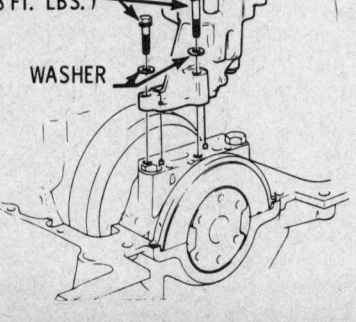

Fig. 27   Oil pump removal

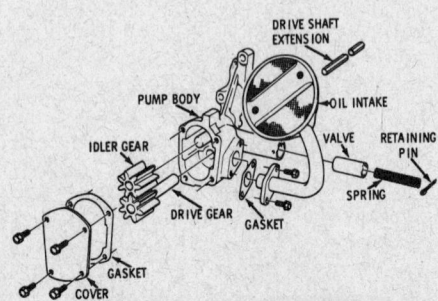

Fig. 28   Oil pump disassembled

3. Check pressure regulator valve, valve spring and bore for damage. Proper bore to valve clearance is .0025–.0050 inch.
4. Check extension shaft ends for wear.

Assembly

1. Install gears and shaft in oil pump body.
2. Check gear end clearance by placing a straight edge over the gears and measure the clearance between the straight edge and gasket surface. If end clearance is excessive, check for scores in cover that would bring the clearance over specified limits.
3. Install cover and torque attaching screws to 7 ft. lbs.
4. Install pressure regulator valve, closed end first, into bore, then the valve spring and cotter pin.

WATER PUMP, REPLACE

1. Disconnect battery ground cable.
2. Drain radiator.
3. Disconnect heater return hose at water pump, then remove bolt retaining heater water return pipe to intake manifold and position aside.
4. Remove vacuum pump drive belt, if equipped with A/C.
5. Remove serpentine drive belt.
6. Remove alternator. Then, remove A/C compressor or vacuum pump brackets (if equipped).
7. Remove water pump attaching bolts and water pump assembly.
8. Remove water pump pulley, Fig. 29.
9. Reverse procedure to install.

FUEL PUMP, REPLACE

1. Ensure ignition switch is in "off" position.
2. Remove air cleaner and disconnect 12 volt lead wire from pump.
3. Use ¾ inch wrench to support the inlet fitting firmly, then with ⅝ inch wrench disconnect inlet tube and plug openings.
4. Repeat step three to disconnect outlet fitting. Place a suitable rag under pump outlet side to collect fuel since this line is slightly pressurized.

NOTE: Do not overtwist pump outlet fit-

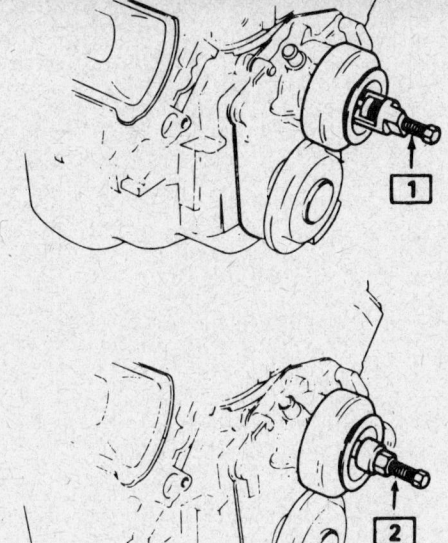

1 J-29785 REMOVAL

2 J-29786 INSTALL UNTIL FLUSH

Fig. 29 Water pump pully removal & installation

ting; otherwise cover crimp may be loosened.

5. Remove pump mounting bracket nut and pump.
6. Remove dust plugs from openings on new pump, then install pump and bracket assembly on engine. Torque pump mounting bracket nut to 18 ft. lbs. Torque inlet and outlet fuel line fittings to 19 ft. lbs.

NOTE: In some instances, it may be necessary to adjust pump location by loosening the bracket screw and turning the pump to get the exact alignment between pump fittings and fuel lines. Be sure to torque bracket screw after the adjustment.

7. After pump is installed, disconnect fuel line at fuel filter and turn ignition switch "On" in order to prime and bleed lines. Use a suitable container to catch fuel. If pump runs with a clicking sound or there are air bubbles in fuel, check for leaks in line. Check all connections to see that they are dry and that no fuel is leaking. When clicking sound disappears, tighten fuel line at filter.

BELT TENSION DATA

NOTE: This engine is equipped with a serpentine drive belt that is self adjusting

DIESEL FUEL INJECTION SYSTEM DESCRIPTION

The V6-262 diesel engine may be equipped with one of two fuel injection pumps: the Roosa Master which can be identified by a looped fuel inlet pipe, and CAV pump which can be identified by a straight fuel inlet pipe.

Injection timing is controlled by two pressure regulators. One regulator is the Housing Pressure Cold Advance (HPCA), located in the pump. The other pressure regulator, used on 1984 except California models, is the Housing Pressure Altitude Advance (HPAA), located in the fuel return line. The HPCA is designed to advance injection timing about 4° during cold operation. The HPAA will regulate housing pressure according to altitude.

The Metering Valve Sensor (MVS), used on 1984 California models with Diesel Electronic Control System, is a variable resistor which electronically signals the diesel ECM as to the position of the metering valve.

The injection pump is mounted on top of the engine. It is gear driven off the camshaft and turns at camshaft speed. It is a high pressure rotary pump that injects a metered amount of fuel to each cylinder at the proper time. The six high pressure delivery pipes from the pump to the injection nozzle in each cylinder are the same length to prevent any difference in timing, cylinder-to-cylinder. The fuel injection pump provides the required timing advance under all operating conditions.

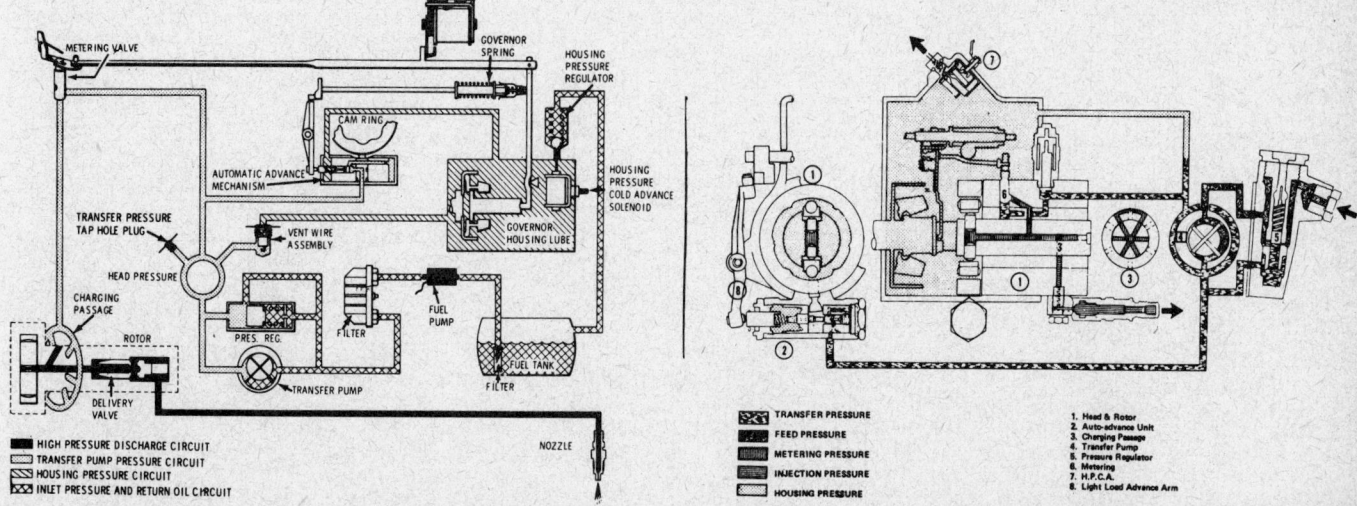

Fig. 30 Roosa-Master pump fuel flow schematic

Fig. 31 CAV pump fuel flow schematic

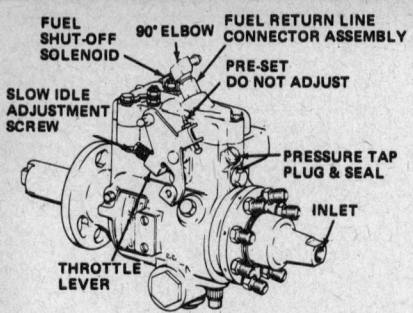

Fig. 32 Roosa-Master pump pressure tap plug location

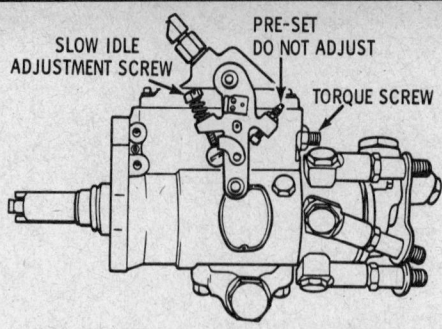

Fig. 33 CAV pump torque screw location

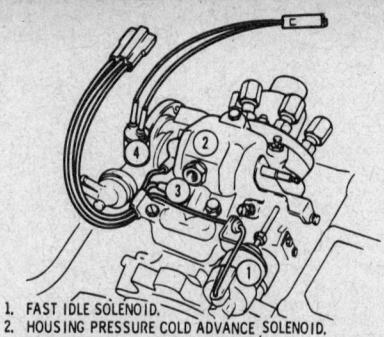

1. FAST IDLE SOLENOID.
2. HOUSING PRESSURE COLD ADVANCE SOLENOID.
3. FUEL SHUT OFF (SHUT DOWN) SOLENOID.
4. TORQUE CONVERTER CLUTCH SWITCH (PART OF VACUUM REGULATOR VALVE).

Fig. 34 Roosa Master pump solenoids and connectors location

Engine RPM is controlled by a rotary fuel metering valve. Pushing down on the accelerator pedal moves the throttle cable to open the metering valve and allow more fuel to be delivered. The injection pump also has a low pressure transfer pump to deliver fuel from the fuel line to the high pressure pump.

The fuel filter is located between the electric fuel pump and the injection pump.

The fuel tank is at the rear of the vehicle, connected by fuel pipes and hoses to the fuel pump. Excess fuel returns from the fuel injection pump to the fuel tank through pipes and hoses.

The fuel flow schematics, Figs. 30 and 31, show the major components and their relationships and also provides a means of determining the differences in the two systems.

INJECTION PUMP TIMING

Using Timing Meter J-33075

Checking
1. Block drive wheels and apply parking brake.
2. Start engine, allow to reach normal operating temperature, then shut off.
3. Remove air cleaner, then place suitable screen over intake manifold inlets. EGR valve hose must be disconnected.
4. Clean any dirt or oil from engine probe holder, crankshaft balancer rim, glow plug probe lens and lens in photo-electric pickup.

NOTE: Retarded reading will result if probe of injection pump timing meter is

not clean.

5. Install RPM probe into crankshaft RPM counter.
6. Remove glow plug from number 1 cylinder, then install glow plug probe in glow plug opening. Torque probe to 8 ft. lbs.
7. Set timing meter selector to A (20), then connect meter battery leads.
8. Disconnect alternator electrical connector, then start engine and adjust engine RPM to specifications.
9. Observe timing reading at 2 minute intervals. When readings stabilize, compare to reading under "Tune-Up Specifications" at beginning of chapter.
10. Disconnect timing meter, then apply suitable thread lubricant to glow plug.
11. Install glow plug and torque to 12 ft. lbs.
12. Connect alternator and install air cleaner.

Adjust
1. Loosen injection pump retaining nuts with tool J-25304.
2. Rotate pump to left to advance timing, and to right to retard timing.
3. Torque injection pump retaining nut to 35 ft. lbs.
4. Start engine and recheck timing as previously described. Reset as needed.

Without Timing Meter J-33075

NOTE: Alignment of timing marks may be used in situations where timing meter

J-33075 is not available. However for optimum engine operation, the timing should be adjusted with the meter. For adjustment of timing marks use following procedure.

---

1. The mark on the injection pump adapter must be aligned with the mark on the injection pump flange.
2. To adjust:
   a. Loosen the injection pump retaining nuts with tool J-25304.
   b. Align the mark on the injection pump flange with the mark on the injection pump adapter.
   c. Torque injection pump retaining nuts to 35 ft. lbs.

FUEL INJECTION PUMP HOUSING FUEL PRESSURE CHECK

1. Remove air crossover and install screen covers J-29657 or other suitable covers.
2. On Roosa-Master pumps, remove pressure tap plug or metering valve sensor on 1984 California models. On CAV pumps, remove torque screw, Figs. 32 and 33. If equipped with torque screw, to avoid disturbing adjustment add a second nut to lock nut, then back out screw with nuts attached.
3. Attach low pressure gage to adapters.
4. Connect magnetic pick-up tachometer.
5. With gear shift lever in park position and parking brake on, check pressure with engine running at 1000 RPM. Pressure should be between 8–12 psi with no more than 2 psi fluctuation for 1982–83 models, and between 9–11 psi with no more than 1 psi fluctuation for 1984 models.
6. If pressure is at 0, check operation of housing pressure cold advance as follows:
   a. Remove electrical connector from housing pressure cold advance terminal, Figs. 34 and 35. If pressure

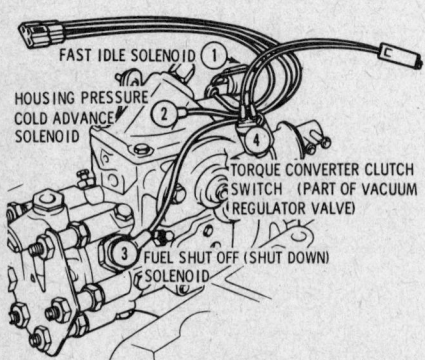

Fig. 35 CAV pump solenoids and connectors location

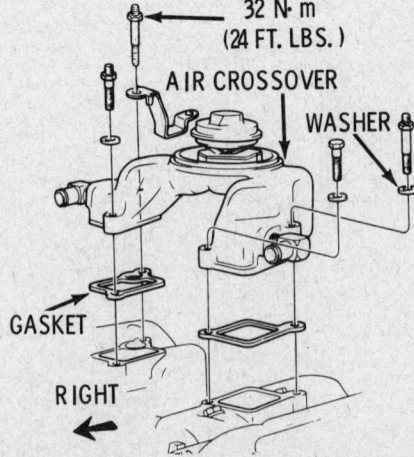

Fig. 36 Air crossover removal & installation

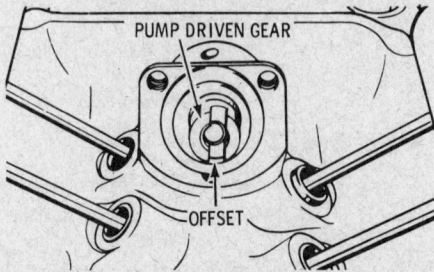

Fig. 37 Offset on fuel injection pump

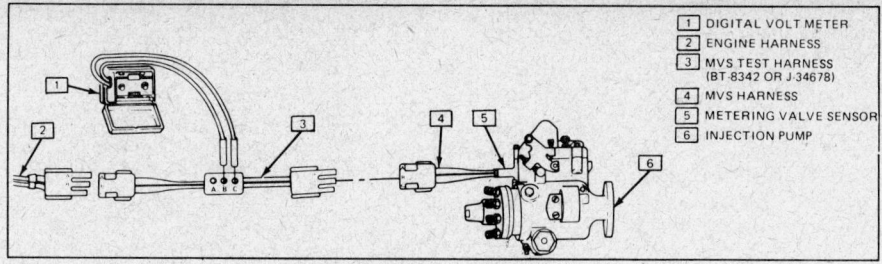

1	DIGITAL VOLT METER
2	ENGINE HARNESS
3	MVS TEST HARNESS (BT-8342 OR J-34678)
4	MVS HARNESS
5	METERING VALVE SENSOR
6	INJECTION PUMP

Fig. 38   MVS voltage

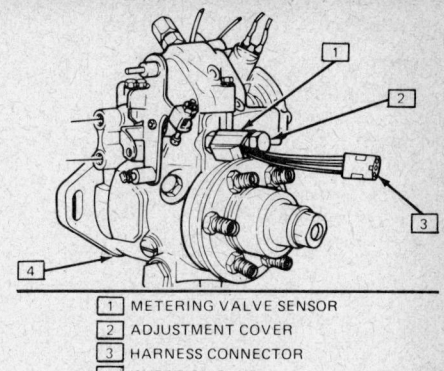

1	METERING VALVE SENSOR
2	ADJUSTMENT COVER
3	HARNESS CONNECTOR
4	INJECTION PUMP

Fig. 40   MVS assembly

remains at 0, remove injection pump cover and check operation of advance solenoid. If it is binding, repair or replace parts as necessary.

b. If pressure is as specified with housing cold pressure advance electrical connector disconnected, check operation of temperature switch located in cylinder head bolt.

7. If pressure is not within specifications, replace fuel return line connector assembly or check for restricted HPAA, if equipped.

8. Remove tachometer, pressure gauge and adapter.

9. Install a new pressure tap plug seal on pressure tap plug and install plug into pump housing.

10. Remove screened covers and install air crossover.

INJECTION PUMP, REPLACE

Removal

1. Remove air cleaner assembly.
2. Remove crankcase ventilation filter and pipes from valve cover and air crossover.
3. Remove air crossover, Fig. 36, and install suitable intake screen covers.
4. Remove fuel lines, filter and fuel pump as an assembly. Plug all openings.
5. Remove throttle and T.V. cables from intake manifold brackets and position aside.
6. Disconnect fuel return line from injection pump.
7. Disconnect injection line clamps that are closest to the pump.
8. Disconnect injection lines from pump and plug all openings. Then carefully reposition lines to gain enough clearance to remove pump.
9. Remove two bolts retaining injection pump.
10. Remove pump and discard pump to adapter "O"-ring.

Installation

1. Position No. 1 cylinder at firing position by aligning mark on balance with zero mark on indicator located at front of engine.
2. Align offset tang on pump drive shaft with pump driven gear, Fig. 37.
3. Install new pump to adapter "O"-ring, then install pump.
4. If a new intermediate adapter is installed, set injection pump at center of slots in pump mounting flange. If original intermediate adapter is being used, align pump timing mark with mark on intermediate adapter. Install two bolts and washers retaining pump and torque bolts to 35–37 ft. lbs.
5. Reverse steps 1 through 8 of removal procedure for remainder of installation. If necessary adjust T.V. cable, pump timing, vacuum regulator valve or idle speed.

METERING VALVE SENSOR (MVS)

Checking

1. Block drive wheels and apply parking brake.
2. Start engine, allow it to reach normal operating temperature, then shut off.
3. Remove air cleaner and air crossover assembly, then place suitable screens over intake manifold openings, Fig. 36.
4. Disconnect MVS harness connector and install tool BT-8342 or T-34678 as shown, Fig. 38.
5. Install suitable tachometer.
6. Torque MVS assembly attaching bolts to 30 inch lbs. before attempting to check or adjust voltage.
7. Start engine in park, then raise engine speed to 1500 RPM for 10–20 seconds to stabilize fuel flow.
8. Return engine to idle and shift transmission to drive.
9. Set engine speed to 650 RPM.
10. Using suitable multi-meter set at 20 volt scale, measure V-REF voltage between terminals A and C, Fig. 38.

11. Measure MVS voltage between terminals B and C for given engine load.
12. Shift transmission into park, then compare voltage recorded in steps 10 and 11 with chart in Fig. 39.
13. Measure the voltage between terminals B and C as the throttle is moved from idle to wide open position. Voltage should range from zero to over 4 volts.
14. If MVS voltage is within specifications in steps 12 and 13, sensor is operating correctly. If not as specified, refer to "Adjust" procedure.
15. Connect MVS connectors, then start engine and adjust idle speed to specifications.
16. Remove screens from intake manifold openings, then install air crossover and air cleaner assembly, Fig. 36.

Adjust

1. With engine shut off, remove MVS hole plug, Fig. 40.
2. Using a file, resize metering valve sensor adjuster tool J-24182-2 so it enters into the MVS.
3. Turn the MVS adjustment screw clockwise to increase the voltage reading and counterclockwise to decrease voltage reading.
4. Install MVS hole plug finger tight, then proceed to steps 7 through 12 in MVS "Checking."
5. If voltage reading is not within chart specifications, readjust the MVS as necessary.
6. When the MVS voltage reading is within specifications, install MVS hole plug using new "O" ring. Torque plug to 30 inch lbs.

INJECTION NOZZLES, REPLACE

1. Remove fuel lines, using a backup wrench

MVS VOLTAGE TABLE

V-REF →	4.5	4.6	4.7	4.8	4.9	5.0	5.1	5.2	5.3	5.4	5.5
MVS VOLTAGE → (IN "0" 650 RPM)	.53–.55	.54–.56	.55–.57	.57–.59	.58–.60	.59–.61	.60–.62	.61–.63	.63–.65	.64–.66	.65–.67

Fig. 39   MVS voltage chart

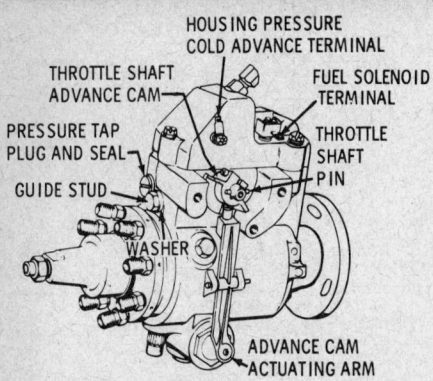

Fig. 41 Roosa-Master pump right side view

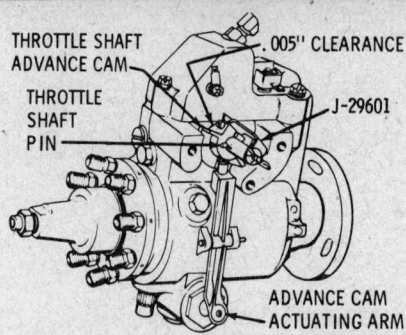

Fig. 42 Installation of tool J-29601 on injection pump. Roosa-Master pump

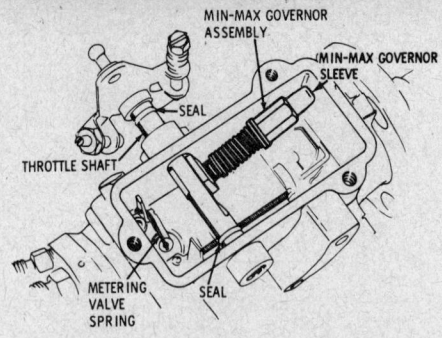

Fig. 43 Roosa-Master pump with cover removed

on upper injection nozzle hex.

2. Plug nozzle and lines to prevent damage or contamination, then remove nozzles by applying torque to largest nozzle hex.

3. When working on rear bank, it may be necessary to perform the following procedures:

   a. Rotate the intermediate steering shaft so steering gear stub shaft clamp bolt is in up position, then remove clamp bolt.

   b. Disconnect intermediate shaft from stub shaft.

   c. Remove engine support strut.

   d. Place a floor jack under front crossmember of cradle and raise jack until it just starts to raise vehicle.

   e. Remove front two body mount bolts with lower cushions and retainers. Remove cushions from bolts.

   f. Thread body mount bolts with retainers a minimum of three turns into cage nuts so that the bolts restrain cradle movement.

   g. Release floor jack slowly until crossmember contacts body mount bolt retainers. As jack is being lowered watch and correct any interference with hose, lines, pipes and cables.

NOTE: Do not lower cradle without it being restrained as possible damage may occur to the body and underhood items.

4. Remove copper nozzle gasket from cylinder head if gasket did not remain on nozzle.

5. Reverse procedure to install. Apply suitable lubricant to nozzle threads, then torque nozzles to 25 ft. lbs. When tightening nozzle, torque must be applied to largest nozzle hex. Torque fuel line to 25 ft. lbs. using a backup wrench on upper injection nozzle hex.

NOTE: Failure to apply the correct lubricant can cause engine damage. Use lubricant No. 9985462 or equivalent.

VACUUM REGULATOR VALVE, REPLACE

1. Note location of valve vacuum hoses, then disconnect vacuum hoses.

2. Remove two valve attaching bolts, then valve.

3. Reverse procedure to install.

ROOSA-MASTER PUMP ON VEHICLE SERVICE

Throttle Shaft Seal, Replace

1. Disconnect battery ground cable.

2. Remove air cleaner and air crossover, Fig. 36, then install air screens J-29657.

3. Disconnect injection pump fuel solenoid, housing pressure cold advance wires and fuel return pipe, Fig. 41.

4. Remove throttle rod, vacuum regulator valve, return spring and throttle cable bracket.

5. Place tool J-29601 over throttle shaft and pin, then position spring clip of tool over throttle shaft advance cam and tighten wing nut. Without loosening wing nut, pull tool off shaft. This will provide proper alignment during reassembly, Fig. 42.

6. Drive pin from throttle shaft and remove shaft advance cam and fiber washer. Remove any burrs from shaft which may have resulted from pin removal.

7. Clean injection pump cover, upper portion of pump, throttle shaft and guide stud area. Position several shop cloths in engine valley area to absorb fuel.

8. On 1984 California models only, remove MVS.

9. On all models, remove injection pump cover screws, then cover.

CAUTION: Use care to avoid any foreign matter from entering pump when cover is removed. If any object or foreign matter enter pump, it must be removed before engine is started as injection pump damage or engine damage may occur.

10. Note position of metering valve spring before removal as its position must be duplicated exactly during reassembly, Fig. 43.

11. Remove guide stud and washer, noting parts before removal.

12. Rotate min-max governor assembly up for clearance then remove it, Fig. 43. If idle governor spring becomes disengaged from throttle block, it must be reinstalled with tightly wound coils toward throttle block.

13. Remove throttle shaft assembly and inspect shaft for unusual wear or damage, replace if necessary. It may be necessary to loosen nuts at injection pump mounting flange and rotate pump slightly to allow throttle shaft to clear intake manifold.

14. Inspect throttle shaft bushings in pump housing for damage or unusual wear. If replacement of bushings is necessary, it must be performed by a qualified repair facility.

15. Remove throttle shaft seals. Do not cut seals to remove, as any nicks in the seal seat will cause leakage.

16. Install new shaft seals, lubricated with chassis grease. Use care to avoid cutting seals on sharp edges of shaft.

17. Carefully slide throttle shaft into pump to point where min-max governor assembly will slide back onto throttle shaft, Fig. 43.

18. Rotate min-max governor assembly downward, then hold in position and slide throttle shaft and governor into position.

19. Install new fiber washer, throttle shaft advance cam (do not tighten screw at this time) and a new throttle shaft drive pin, Fig. 41.

20. Align throttle shaft advance cam so tool J-20601 can be installed over throttle shaft, pins in slots and spring clip over advance cam.

21. Insert a .005 inch feeler gauge between cam and fiber washer, then tighten cam screw and remove tool J-29601.

22. Install guide stud with new washer, assuring that upper extension of metering valve spring slides on top of guide stud. Torque guide studs to 85 inch lbs.

CAUTION: Over torquing may strip the aluminum threads in the housing.

23. Hold throttle in idle position and install new pump cover seal. Making sure that screws are not in cover, position cover above 1/4 inch forward toward shaft end and about 1/8 inch above pump, Fig. 44. More cover rearward and downward into position, using care to avoid cutting seal, then reinstall cover screws. Each screw must have a flat washer and internal lock washer, with flat washer against pump cover. Torque screws to 33 inch lbs. and install vacuum regulator.

24. On 1984 California models only, install the MVS using a new "O" ring. Coat the threads using a suitable sealer and torque to 30 inch lbs.

25. On all models, reconnect both battery ground cables, then turn ignition switch to run position and touch pink solenoid wire to solenoid.

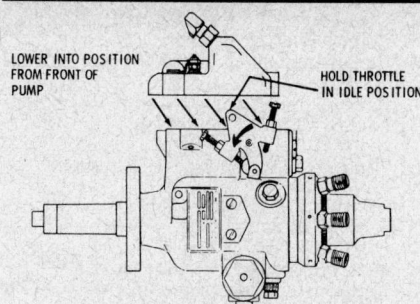

Fig. 44 Installation of pump cover. Roosa-Master pump

1. **FUEL RETURN PIPE**
2. **CLIP**
3. **FULLY DRIVEN, SEATED & NOT STRIPPED**
4. **HOUSING PRESSURE ALTITUDE ADVANCE SOLENOID**
5. **13 N·m (9.5 LBS. FT.)**

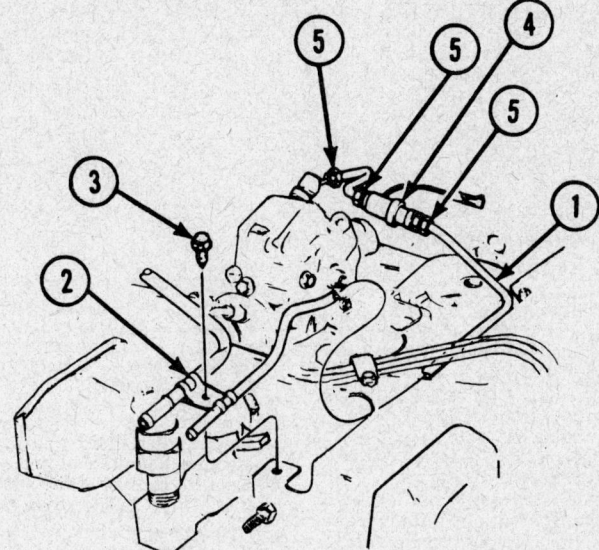

Fig. 44A HPAA removal & installation

A clicking noise should be heard as the wire is connected and disconnected. If not, the linkage may be jammed in the wide open position and the engine must not be started. Proceed to step 26. If clicking is heard, connect pump solenoid and housing pressure cold advance wires and proceed to step 27.

26. Remove cover, then ground solenoid lead (opposite hot lead) and connect pink wire. With ignition switch in run position, the solenoid in the cover should move the linkage. If not, the solenoid must be replaced. Minimum voltage across solenoid terminals must be 12 volts. Reinstall cover and repeat step 25.

27. Install throttle cable bracket, throttle rod, throttle cable and return springs. Make sure timing marks on pump and adapter are aligned and make sure nuts retaining pump are tight. Install fuel return pipe.

28. Start engine and check for fuel leaks.

NOTE: Rough idle may be due to air in the pump. Allow sufficient time for air to purge by allowing engine to idle. It may be necessary to turn engine off to allow air bubbles to rise to top of pump where they will be purged.

29. Adjust Vacuum Regulator Valve or MVS if equipped, then remove intake manifold screens and install air crossover and air cleaner, Fig. 36.

Pump Cover Seal And/Or Guide Stud, Replace

1. Disconnect battery ground cable.

2. Remove air cleaner and air crossover, Fig. 36, and install air screen J-29657.
3. Disconnect injection pump fuel solenoid, housing pressure cold advance wires and fuel return pipe.
4. Clean injection pump cover, upper portion of pump and guide stud area. Position shop cloths to absorb fuel.
5. Remove injection pump cover screws, then cover.

CAUTION: Use care to avoid any foreign matter from entering pump when cover is

removed. If any object or foreign matter enter pump, it must be removed before starting engine as injection pump damage or engine damage may occur.

6. Note position of metering valve spring before removal as its position must be duplicated exactly during reassembly, Fig. 43.
7. Remove guide stud and washer, noting location of parts before removal.
8. Refer to steps 21 thru 27 under "Throttle Shaft Seal, Replace" procedure for reas-

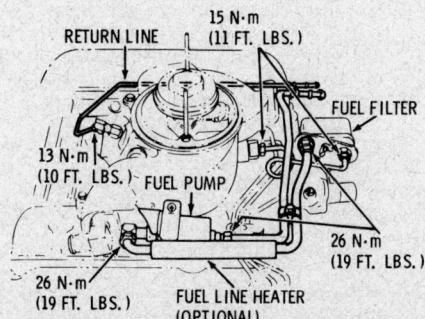

Fig. 45 CAV pump fuel inlet pipe removal

RETURN LINE
15 N·m (11 FT. LBS.)
FUEL FILTER
13 N·m (10 FT. LBS.) FUEL PUMP
26 N·m (19 FT. LBS.)
26 N·m (19 FT. LBS.)
FUEL LINE HEATER (OPTIONAL)

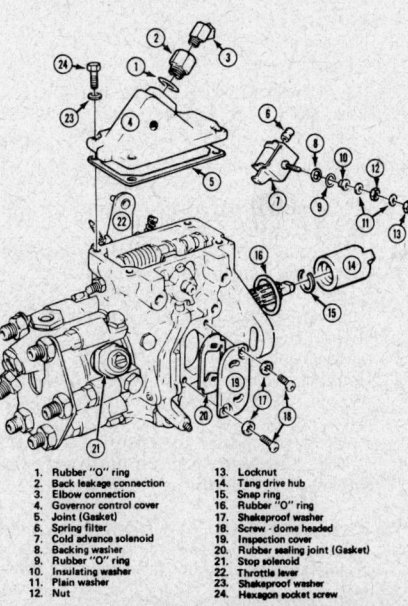

Fig. 46 Exploded view of CAV pump

1. Rubber "O" ring
2. Back leakage connection
3. Elbow connection
4. Governor control cover
5. Joint (Gasket)
6. Spring filter
7. Cold advance solenoid
8. Backing washer
9. Rubber "O" ring
10. Insulating washer
11. Plain washer
12. Nut
13. Locknut
14. Tang drive hub
15. Snap ring
16. Rubber "O" ring
17. Shakeproof washer
18. Screw - dome headed
19. Inspection cover
20. Rubber sealing joint (Gasket)
21. Stop solenoid
22. Thrust lever
23. Shakeproof washer
24. Hexagon socket screw

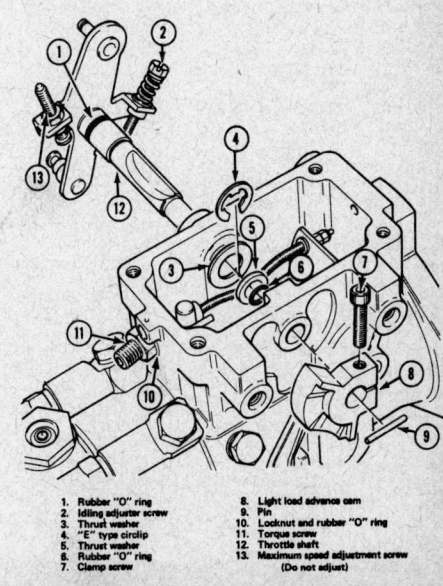

Fig. 47 Throttle shaft and seals. CAV pump

1. Rubber "O" ring
2. Idling adjuster screw
3. Thrust washer
4. "E" type circlip
5. Thrust washer
6. Rubber "O" ring
7. Clamp screw
8. Light load advance cam
9. Pin
10. Locknut and rubber "O" ring
11. Torque screw
12. Throttle shaft
13. Maximum speed adjustment screw (Do not adjust)

sembly of "Pump Cover Seal And/Or Guide Stud".

Metering Valve Sensor (MVS), Replace

1. Remove air cleaner and air crossover, Fig. 36, then install cover J-29657.
2. Disconnect sensor electrical connector, then remove sensor from pump, Fig. 40.
3. Install new "O" ring on sensor, then coat threads with suitable sealer. Torque sensor to 30 inch lbs.
4. Remove cover J-29657, then install air cleaner and air crossover.

Housing Pressure Cold Advance (HPCA) & Shutdown Solenoid, Replace

1. Remove pump cover.
2. Remove terminal contact nuts, then remove solenoid from cover noting position of any insulating washers.
3. Place solenoid in cover ensuring that shut-off solenoid linkage is free. Also, check that housing pressure cold advance solenoid plunger is centered so that it will contact fitting check ball, Fig. 34.
4. Place insulator washers on terminal studs and install terminal nuts. Torque nuts to 10–15 inch lbs. and replace pump cover.

Housing Pressure Altitude Advance (HPAA), Replace

Refer to Fig. 44A for removal and installation procedures.

CAV PUMP ON VEHICLE SERVICE

End Plate Access Plug Or Stop Plug Washer, Replace

1. Remove air cleaner and install cover J-26996-1 or equivalent.
2. Clean any dirt from area.
3. Remove stop plug and/or end plate plug and discard washers.
4. Reverse procedure to install. Torque stop plug to 80 inch lbs. and end plate to 43 ft. lbs.

Fuel Inlet Connection Washer, Replace

1. Remove air cleaner and install cover J-26996-1 or equivalent.
2. Clean any dirt from area.
3. Remove fuel inlet pipe, Fig. 45.
4. Remove inlet connection and discard washer.
5. Reverse procedure to install. Using new washer, install inlet to pump and torque to 33 ft. lbs.

Governor Control Cover Gasket, Replace, Fig. 46

1. Remove air crossover, Fig. 36, and install cover J-29657.
2. Clean any dirt from injection pump cover and upper area of pump.
3. Place several rags in engine valley to

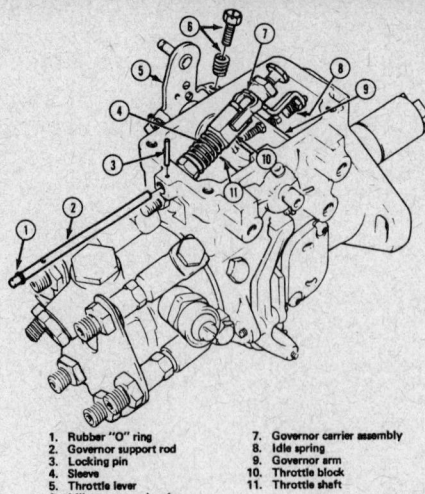

1. Rubber "O" ring
2. Governor support rod
3. Locking pin
4. Sleeve
5. Throttle lever
6. Idling screw and spring
7. Governor carrier assembly
8. Idle spring
9. Governor arm
10. Throttle block
11. Throttle shaft

Fig. 48   Governor assembly. CAV pump

catch spilled fuel.
4. Remove fuel return pipe.
5. Remove control cover screws and cover, discarding washers and gasket.

NOTE: Extreme care must be exercised to keep foreign material out of the pump when the cover is off. If any objects are dropped into the pump, they must be removed before the engine is started or injection pump or engine damage may occur.

---

6. Reverse procedure to install. Torque screws to 25 inch lbs.

Housing Pressure Cold Advance Solenoid, Replace, Fig. 46

1. Remove governor control cover, see "Governor Control Cover Gasket, Replace".
2. Remove solenoid terminal nut, spring filter, insulating washers and solenoid. Discard gasket.
3. Reverse procedure to install. Torque terminal nut to 20 in. lbs. and ensure solenoid is centered in cover.

Inspection Cover Plate Gasket, Replace

1. Remove air cleaner and install cover J-26996-1.
2. Place several shop rags in engine valley to catch spilled fuel.
3. Scribe a line on the vacuum regulator valve and pump body so valve can be reinstalled without readjusting.
4. Remove vacuum regulator valve from pump, then clean dirt from inspection plate area.
5. Remove inspection plate retaining screws, then inspection plate and gasket.
6. Reverse procedure to install. Using new gasket, torque inspection plate retaining screws to 20 inch lbs.

Stop Solenoid, Replace, Fig. 46

1. Remove air cleaner and install cover J-26996-1

2. Clean dirt from area around solenoid.
3. Remove electrical lead.
4. Remove solenoid and "O"-ring. Discard "O"-ring.
5. Reverse procedure to install. Torque solenoid to 130 inch lbs.

Throttle Shaft Seal, Replace

1. Remove air crossover and install cover J-29657 or equivalent.
2. Disconnect fuel return pipe, then remove governor control cover screws and cover.
3. Remove fast idle solenoid and vacuum regulator valve.
4. Disconnect throttle cable and T.V. cable.
5. Disconnect throttle return spring.
6. Install tool J-29601 or equivalent over throttle shaft with slots of tool engaging vacuum regulator valve lock pin. Place spring clip of tool over throttle shaft advance cam and tighten wing nut. Without loosening wing nut, pull tool off of shaft.
7. Remove lock pin from throttle shaft, Fig. 47.
8. Remove rollpin from pump housing and remove governor support rod.
9. Tilt governor carrier assembly by lifting end nearest drive end of pump and remove carrier from pump housing.
10. Remove clamping screw from light load cam, then remove cam.
11. Remove "E" clip from throttle shaft, then remove throttle shaft from pump.
12. Remove and discard "O" rings.
13. Check throttle shaft assembly and governor housing bores for damage and wear and replace as necessary.
14. Lubricate shaft and "O" rings with oil and assemble larger "O" rings onto shaft.
15. Install throttle shaft into housing until thrust washers can be installed onto shaft in original positions. Install smaller "O" ring onto shaft.
16. Assemble light load advance cam onto shaft and install but do not tighten clamping screw.
17. Install "E" clip into throttle shaft recess. If new throttle shaft is installed, shaft end play must be checked and adjusted by selective fitting of thrust washers. Throttle shaft end play should be .006–.012 inch.
18. Install new pin onto head of shaft. Align throttle shaft advance cam until tool J-29601 or equivalent can be installed over throttle shaft. Tighten cam screw, then remove tool J-29601.
19. Rotate throttle lever forwards to the drive end of pump. Install governor carrier assembly onto pump housing and engage lug on underside of throttle block with cut away notch in throttle shaft.
20. Lubricate governor support rod and new "O" ring, then install "O" ring onto support rod using tool J-33096 or equivalent.
21. Insert plain end of rod through rear of governor housing and into carrier assembly sleeve.
22. Install support rod into housing and install new locking pin, Fig. 48.
23. Install governor cover and fuel return pipe.
24. Install throttle return springs and connect throttle cable.
25. Connect TV detent cable.
26. Install vacuum regulator valve and fast idle solenoid.
27. Start engine and check for leaks. Install air crossover and air cleaner.

Clutch & Transaxle Section

> Refer to the 1980–84 Citation, Omega, Phoenix and Skylark, "CLUTCH & TRANSAXLE SECTION" for service procedures.

Rear Axle, Rear Suspension & Brakes

> Refer to the 1980–84 Citation, Omega, Phoenix and Skylark, "REAR AXLE, REAR SUSPENSION & BRAKES" section for service procedures.

Front Suspension & Steering Section

> Refer to the 1980–84 Citation, Omega, Phoenix and Skylark, "FRONT SUSPENSION & STEERING SECTION" for service procedures not covered in this section

POWER STEERING PUMP, REPLACE

V6-262 Diesel

1982

1. Remove drive belt, then drain power steering fluid from power steering pump reservoir.
2. Raise and support vehicle and disconnect pressure and return lines from power steering pump.
3. Working through access holes in pump pulley, remove three bolts from front of pump.
4. Remove two nuts holding lower brace to engine and remove bracket.
5. Remove pump and pulley assembly from vehicle.
6. Reverse procedure to install, Fig. 1.

1983–84

1. Remove drive belt, then drain power steering fluid from power steering pump reservoir.
2. Disconnect pressure and return lines from power steering pump.
3. Remove pulley using puller J-25034 or equivalent.
4. Remove two pump attaching bolts, then pump from vehicle.
5. Reverse procedure to install, Fig. 2.

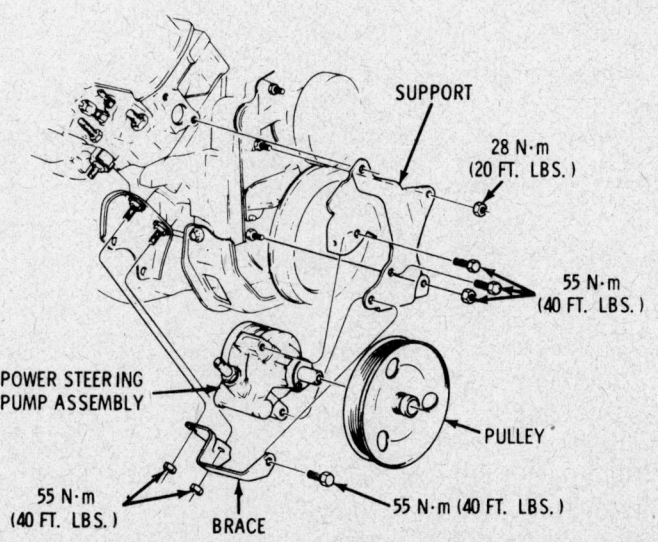

Fig. 1 Power steering pump removal & installation. 1982 V6-262 Diesel

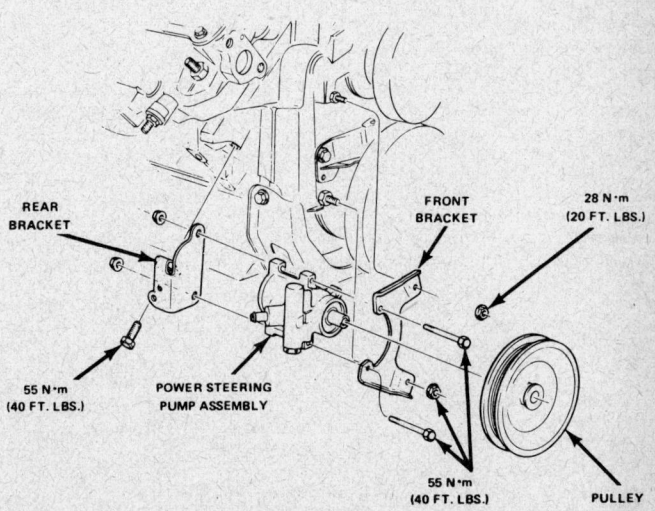

Fig. 2 Power steering pump removal & installation. 1983–84 V6-262 Diesel

CHEV. MONZA & VEGA • 1977–80
BUICK SKYHAWK • OLDS STARFIRE
PONT. ASTRE & 1977–80 SUNBIRD

INDEX OF SERVICE OPERATIONS

NOTE: Refer to the front of this manual for vehicle manufacturer's special service tool suppliers.

VEHICLE IDENTIFICATION LOCATION

On top of instrument panel, left front.

ENGINE NUMBER LOCATION

4-140 Cyl: On pad at right side of cylinder block, above starter.

4-151 Exc. Crossflow Engine: On pad at right front side by distributor shaft hole.

4-151 Crossflow Engine: On pad at left front corner of engine above water pump.

V6 & V8: On pad at front right hand side of cylinder block.

ENGINE IDENTIFICATION CODE

4-140 & Chevrolet V8 engines are identified by the code letters immediately following the engine number. 4-151 engines are identified by the code letters on the pad. V6 engines are identified by the code letters immediately preceding the engine number.

Astre & Vega

Year/Engine	V.I.N. Code⑤	Engine Code
1977		
4-140	B	CAA
4-140	B	CAB
4-140	B	CAC
4-140	B	CAY
4-140	B	CAZ
4-140	B	CBK
4-140	B	CBL
4-140	B	CBS
4-140	B	CBT
4-140	B	CBU
4-140	B	CBV
4-140	B	CBW
4-140	B	CBX
4-140	B	CBY
4-140	B	CBZ
4-151	V	WC
4-151	V	WD
4-151	V	YL
4-151	V	YM
4-151	V	ZH
4-151	V	ZJ

Monza

Year/Engine	V.I.N. Code	Engine Code
1977		
4-140	B	CAY, CAZ, CBK, CBL
4-140	B	CBS, CBT, CBU, CBW
4-140	B	CBX, CBY, CBZ
V8-305	U	CPK, CPL, CPU, CPX
V8-305	U	CRC, CRD
1978		
4-151	V	WB, WD, WH
4-151	V	XL, XN
4-151	V	AC, AD
4-151	V	ZA, ZB, ZC, ZD, ZF
4-151	V	ZH, ZJ, ZK, ZL, ZN
V6-196	C	PC, PD
V6-231	—	OC, OD, OE, OF
V8-305	U	CTA, CTB, CTC, CTD, CTF
1979		
4-151	I, V	AB, AC, AD, AF, AM
4-151	I, V	WD, WJ, XJ, XK
4-151	I, V	ZA, ZB, ZP, ZR
V6-196	C	FC, FD
V6-231A	A	NA, NB, NC, NF
V8-305	G	DNA, DNB, DNC, DND
V8-305	G	DTK, DTL
1980		
4-151	V	A7, A9
4-151	V	XC, XD
4-151	V	WD, WJ
4-151	V	XC, XD
V6-231	A	EX, EY, EZ
V6-231	A	OA, OB, OC

Skyhawk

Year/Engine	V.I.N. Code⑤	Engine Code
1977		
V6-231	C	SA, SB, SD
V6-231	C	SO, SX, SY
1978		
V6-231	A, G, 2	OA, OB, OC
V6-231	A, G, 2	OD, OE, OF
V6-231	A, G, 2	OG
1979		
V6-231	A, C, 2	NA, NB, NC
V6-231	A, C, 2	N3, NG, NH
V6-231	A, C, 2	NM
1980		
V6-231	A	EL, EN, EX, EY, EZ
V6-231	A	OA, OB, OC

Starfire

Year/Engine	V.I.N. Code	Engine Code
1977		
4-140 Std. Tr.①	B	CAY, CBS
4-140 Std. Tr.②	B	CAZ, CBK
4-140 Auto. Tr.①	B	CBT
4-140 Auto. Tr.②	B	CBL
4-140 Std. Tr.③	B	CBS
4-140 Auto. Tr.③	B	CBT
V6-231 Std. Tr.①	C	SA
V6-231 Std. Tr.②	C	SB
V6-231 Auto. Tr.①	C	SD, SW
V6-231 Auto. Tr.②	C	SE, SY
V6-231 Auto. Tr.③	C	SF
V6-231 Std. Tr.①	C	FH
V6-231 Std. Tr.②	C	FO
V6-231 Auto. Tr.①	C	FI
V6-231 Auto. Tr.②	C	FJ
V6-231	C	SQ, SR
V8-305 Auto. Trans.①	U	CRL
V8-305 Auto. Trans.②	U	CRM, CRS
V8-305 Auto. Trans.③	U	CRT
V8-305	U	CPX, CPY
1978		
4-151 Auto. Trans.①	V	XL, XN
4-151 Man. Trans.①	V	WB, WD, WH
4-151 Auto. Trans.②	1	ZK, ZJ
V6-231 Man. Trans.①	A	OA
V6-231 Man. Trans.②	A	ED, OB
V6-231 Man. Trans.②	A	OD
V6-231 Auto. Trans.②	A	OE
V6-231 Man. Trans.③	A	OF
V6-231 Auto. Trans.③	A	OC
V6-231	A	OH
V8-305 Man. Trans.①	U	CTA
V8-305 Auto. Trans.①	U	CTB
V8-305 Auto. Trans.②	U	CTF
V8-305 Auto. Trans.③	U	CTD
1979		
4-151 Auto. Trans.④	V	XJ, XK
4-151 Man. Trans.④	V	WJ, WM
4-151 Auto. Trans.②	1	ZP, ZR
4-151 Man. Trans.①	1	AF, AH
V6-231 Auto. Trans.④	A	NB, NM
V6-231 Auto. Trans.②	AL	NH
V6-231 Man. Trans.①	A	NA
V6-231 Man. Trans.②	A	NC
V6-231 Auto. Trans.②	A	NE
V6-231 Auto. Trans.③	A	SM, SS
V8-305 Auto. Trans.④	G	DTL

Starfire—cont'd.

Year/Engine	V.I.N. Code⑤	Engine Code
V8-305 Man. Trans.④	G	DTK
V8-305 Auto. Trans.②	G	DND
1980		
4-151 Auto. Trans.①	V	XC, XD
4-151 Man. Trans.①	V	WD, WJ
4-151 Man. Trans.②	V	ZA, ZB
4-151 Man. Trans.②	V	A7, A9
V6-231 Auto. Trans.①	A	EZ, OA
V6-231 Man. Trans.①	A	EX
V6-231 Auto. Trans.②	A	OB, OC
V6-231 Man. Trans.②	A	EY

Sunbird

Year/Engine	V.I.N. Code⑤	Engine Code
1977		
4-140 Std. Tr.①	B	CAY, CBS, CBZ
4-140 Std. Tr.②	B	CAZ, CBK, CBV
4-140 Std. Tr.③	B	CBS, CBZ
4-140 Auto. Tr.①③	B	CBT
4-140	B	CAK, CBL, CBU
4-140	B	CBW, CBX, CBY
4-151 Std. Tr.①	V	WC, WD
4-151 Auto. Tr.①	VV	YL, YM
4-151 Auto. Tr.②	V	ZH, ZJ
4-151	V	ZD, ZF, ZN, ZP
V6-231 Std. Tr.①	C	SA
V6-231 Std. Tr.②	C	SB
V6-231 Auto. Tr.①	C	SD
V6-231 Auto. Tr.②	C	SY
V6-231 Auto. Tr.③	C	SX
V6-231	C	SO
1978		
4-151 Man. Trans.①	V, 1	WB, WD, WH
4-151 Auto. Trans.①	V, 1	XN, XL
4-151 Auto. Trans.②	V, 1	ZJ, ZK
4-151	V, 1	AC, AD
4-151	V, 1	ZA, ZB, ZC, ZD
4-151	V, 1	ZH, ZF, ZL, ZN
V6-231 Auto. Trans.①	A	ED
V6-231 Man. Trans.①	A	OA
V6-231 Man. Trans.①	A	EK, EL, EE, OE, EG
V6-231 Man. Trans.②	A	OD
V6-231 Man. Trans.③	A	OC
V6-231 Man. Trans.③	A	OF
V6-231	A	OE, OB
1979		
4-151 Man. Trans.②	V, 1	AF, AH
4-151 Man. Trans.④	V, 1	WJ, WM
4-151 Auto. Trans.②	V, 1	XJ, XK
4-151 Auto. Trans.④	V, 1	ZP, ZR
V6-231 Man. Trans.④	A	NA, NG, RA
V6-231 Man. Trans.③	A	NC
V6-231 Man. Trans.③	A	NE
V6-231 Auto. Trans.④	A	NK, NL, NM
V6-231 Auto. Trans.②	A	RG, RH, RW, RY
V8-305 Auto. Trans.②	G	DND
V8-305 Auto. Trans.④	G	DNJ, DTL
V8-305 Man. Trans.④	G	DTK, DTM
4-151 Auto. Trans.①	V, 1	XC, XD
4-151 Man. Trans.①	V, 1	WD, WJ
4-151 Man. Trans.②	V, 1	ZA, ZB
4-151 Man. Trans.②	V, 1	A7, A9
V6-231 Auto. Trans.①	A	EB, EC, EO, EP

Continued

ENGINE IDENTIFICATION CODE—Continued

Sunbird—cont'd.

Year/Engine	V.I.N. Code⑤	Engine Code
V6-231 Auto. Trans.①	A	EZ, OA, OK, OL
V6-231 Man. Trans.①	A	EA, EJ, OX
V6-231 Auto. Trans.②	A	EF, EG, ES, ET

Sunbird—cont'd.

Year/Engine	V.I.N. Code⑤	Engine Code
V6-231 Auto. Trans.②	A	OB, OC, OM, ON
V6-231 Man. Trans.②	A	EY
1980		
4-151	V	A7, A9

Sunbird—cont'd.

Year/Engine	V.I.N. Code⑤	Engine Code
4-151	V	WD, WJ
4-151	V	XC, XD
4-151	V	ZA, ZB
V6-231	A	EX, EY, EZ
V6-231	A	OA, OB, OC

①—Except California.
②—California.
③—High altitude.
④—Exc. High altitude & Calif.
⑤—Fifth digit of the V.I.N. denotes the engine code.

GRILLE IDENTIFICATION

1977–78 Buick Skyhawk

1977 Chevrolet Monza Towne Coupe Less Sport Option

1977 Chevrolet Monza & Towne Coupe with Sport Option

1977 Chevrolet Vega

1977–78 Oldsmobile Starfire

1977 Pontiac Astre

1977 Pontiac Sunbird

1977 Pontiac Formula Sunbird

1978–79 Chevrolet Monza 2+2
1980 Chevrolet Monza Spyder

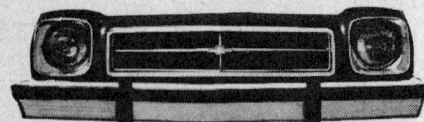

1978–80 Chevrolet Monza

1978 Pontiac Sunbird

1979–80 Buick Skyhawk

1979 Oldsmobile Starfire

1979 Pontiac Sunbird Sport Safari

1979 Pontiac Sunbird Coupe & Hatchback

1980 Oldsmobile Starfire

1980 Pontiac Sunbird

GENERAL ENGINE SPECIFICATIONS

Year	Engine CID①/Liter	Engine V.I.N. Code②	Carburetor	Bore and Stroke	Compression Ratio	Net H.P. @ R.P.M.③	Maximum Torque Lbs. Ft. @ R.P.M.	Normal Oil Pressure Pounds
1977	4-140, 2.3L	B	5210C, 2Bbl⑤	3.501 × 3.625	8.0	84 @ 4400	117 @ 2400	36–45
	4-151, 2.5L	V	5210C, 2Bbl⑤	4.00 × 3.00	8.3	87 @ 4400	128 @ 2400	36–41
	V6-231, 3.8L	C	2GC, 2Bbl④	3.80 × 3.40	8.0	105 @ 3200	185 @ 2000	37
	V8-305, 5.0L	U	2GC, 2Bbl④	3.736 × 3.48	8.5	145 @ 3800	245 @ 2400	32–40
1978	4-151, 2.5L	V	5210C, 2Bbl⑤⑥	4.00 × 3.00	8.3	85 @ 4400	123 @ 2800	36–41
	V6-196, 3.2L	C	2GE, 2Bbl④	3.50 × 3.40	8.0	86 @ 3600	160 @ 2000	37
	V6-231, 3.8L	A	2GE, 2Bbl④	3.80 × 3.40	8.0	103 @ 3800	180 @ 2000	37
	V8-305, 5.0L	U	2GC, 2Bbl④	3.736 × 3.48	8.5	135 @ 3800	240 @ 2000	32–40
	V8-305, 5.0L	G	2GC, 2Bbl④	3.736 × 3.48	8.5	145 @ 3800	245 @ 2400	32–40
1979	4-151, 2.5L	V	2SE, 2Bbl④	4.00 × 3.00	8.3	85 @ 4400	123 @ 2800	36–41
	4-151, 2.5L	9	6510, 2Bbl⑤	4.00 × 3.00	8.3	90 @ 4400	128 @ 2400	36–41
	V6-196, 3.2L	C	M2ME, 2Bbl④	3.50 × 3.40	8.0	105 @ 4000	160 @ 2000	37
	V6-231, 3.8L	A	M2ME, 2Bbl④	3.80 × 3.40	8.0	115 @ 3800	190 @ 2000	37
	V8-305, 5.0L	G	M2MC, 2Bbl④	3.736 × 3.48	8.4	130 @ 3200	245 @ 2000	32–40
1980	4-151, 2.5L	9	2SE, 2Bbl④	4.00 × 3.00	8.2	90 @ 4000	134 @ 2400	36–41
	4-151, 2.5L	5	E2SE, 2Bbl④	4.00 × 3.00	8.2	90 @ 4000	130 @ 2400	36–41
	V6-231, 3.8L	A	M2ME, 2Bbl④	3.80 × 3.40	8.0	115 @ 3800	188 @ 2000	37

①—CID—cubic inch displacement.
②—The fifth digit in the V.I.N. denotes engine code.
③—Ratings are net—As installed in vehicle.
④—Rochester.
⑤—Holley.
⑥—Calif. only.

WHEEL ALIGNMENT SPECIFICATIONS

Year	Model	Caster Angle, Degrees Limits	Caster Angle, Degrees Desired	Camber Angle, Degrees Limits Left	Camber Angle, Degrees Limits Right	Camber Angle, Degrees Desired Left	Camber Angle, Degrees Desired Right	Toe-In Inch	Toe-Out on Turns, Deg.① Outer Wheel	Toe-Out on Turns, Deg.① Inner Wheel
1977	Exc. Astre & Vega	−1.25 to −.25	−.75	−.25 to +.75	−.25 to +.75	+.25	+.25	0 to 1/8②	—	—
	Astre & Vega	−1.3 to .3	−.8	−.3 to +.7	−.3 to +.7	+.2	+.2	0 to 1/8②	—	—
1978–79	All	−1.3 to −.3	−.8	−.3 to +.7	−.3 to +.7	+.2	+.2	0 to 1/8②	—	—
1980	Monza	−1.3 to −.3	−.8	−.6 to +1	−.6 to +1	+.4	+.4	−2/5 to +1/20	—	—
	Skyhawk	−.8 to −.7	−.75	−.3 to −.2	−.3 to −.2	+1/4	+1/4	0 to +1/8	—	—
	Starfire③	0 to −2	−1	0 to +1½	0 to +1½	+3/4	+3/4	1/16	—	—
	Starfire④	0 to +2	+1	0 to +1½	0 to +1½	+3/4	+3/4	1/16	—	—
	Sunbird	−1/4 to −1¼	−3/4	−3/4 to +1/4	−3/4 to +1/4	+1/4	+1/4	1/16②	—	—

①—Incorrect toe out when other adjustments are correct indicates bent steering arms.
②—Toe-out.
③—Manual steering.
④—Power steering.

REAR AXLE SPECIFICATIONS

Year	Model	Carrier Type	Ring Gear & Pinion Backlash Method	Ring Gear & Pinion Backlash Adjustment	Pinion Bearing Preload Method	Pinion Bearing Preload New Bearings Inch-Lbs.	Pinion Bearing Preload Used Bearings Inch-Lbs.	Differential Bearing Preload Method	Differential Bearing Preload New Bearings Inch-Lbs.	Differential Bearing Preload Used Bearings Inch-Lbs.
1977–80	Exc. Skyhawk & Sunbird	Integral	Shim	.005–.008	Spacer	10–25	8–12	Shim	—	—
	Skyhawk & Sunbird	Integral	Shim	.006–.008	Spacer	10–25	8–12	Shim	35–40	20–25

TUNE UP SPECIFICATIONS

The following specifications are published from the latest information available. This data should be used only in the absence of a decal affixed in the engine compartment.

★ When using a timing light, disconnect vacuum hose or tube at distributor and plug opening in hose or tube so idle speed will not be affected.

● When checking compression, lowest cylinder must be within 70 percent of highest.

▲ Before removing wires from distributor cap, determine location of No. 1 wire in cap, as distributor position may have been altered from that shown at the end of this chart.

☞ Spark plug types shown in this chart are recommendations of the original vehicle manufacturer and not MOTOR. Check local sources for other spark plug manufacturers listings.

Year & Engine	Spark Plug		Firing Order Fig. ▲	Ignition Timing BTDC①★			Curb Idle Speed②		Fast Idle Speed		Fuel Pump Pressure
	Type ☞	Gap		Man. Trans.	Auto. Trans.	Mark Fig.	Man. Trans.	Auto. Trans.	Man. Trans.	Auto. Trans.	
1977											
4-140 Exc. Calif. & High Alt.	R43TS	.035	A	TDC	2°	B	700/1250	650/850D	2500③	2500③	3–4½
4-140 Calif.	R43TS	.035	A	⑧	TDC	B	800/1250	650/850D	2500③	2500③	3–4½
4-140 High Alt.	R43TS	.035	A	TDC	2°	B	800/1250	700/850D	2500③	2500③	3–4½
4-151 Exc. Calif.	R44TSX	.060	E	14⑨	14°⑨	F	⑩	⑪	2200③	2400③	4–5½
4-151 Calif.	R44TSX	.060	E	—	12°⑨	F	—	⑪	—	2400③	4–5½
V6-231⑫	⑬	⑬	G	12°	12°	H⑭	600/800	600D	—	—	3–4½
V6-231⑮	R46TSX	.060	J	—	15°	I⑭	—	600/670D	—	—	3–4½
V8-305 Exc. Calif. & High Alt.	R45TS	.045	C	8°	8°	D	600/700	500/700D	—	—	7½–9
V8-305 Calif.	R45TS	.045	C	—	6°	D	—	500/700D	—	—	7½–9
V8-305 High Alt.	R45TS	.045	C	—	⑯	D	—	600/700D	—	—	7½–9
1978											
4-151 Exc. Calif.	R43TSX	.060	E	14°⑨	12°⑨	F	⑦	⑪	2200③	2200③	4–5½
4-151 Calif.	R43TSX	.060	E	—	14°⑨	F	—	⑪	—	2400③	4–5½
V6-196	R46TSX	.060	J	15°	15°	I⑭	600/800	600D	—	—	3–4½
V6-231	R46TSX	.060	J	15°	15°	I⑭	600/800	600/670D	—	—	3–4½
V8-305 Exc. Calif. & High Alt.	R45TS	.045	C	4°	4°	K	600	500D	—	—	7½–9
V8-305 Calif.	R45TS	.045	C	—	6°	K	—	500D	—	—	7½–9
V8-305 High Alt.	R45TS	.045	C	—	8°	K	—	600D	—	—	7½–9
1979											
4-151 Exc. Calif.	R43TSX	.060	E	12°	12°	F	④	⑪	2200	2400	4–5½
4-151 Calif.	R43TSX	.060	E	14°⑨	14°⑨	F	⑦	⑪	2000	2400	4–5½
V6-196	⑤	.060	J	15°	15°	I⑭	600/800	550/670D	2200	2200	3–4½
V6-231	⑤	.060	J	15°	15°	I⑭	600/800	⑥	2200	2200	3–4½
V8-305 Exc. Calif.	R45TS	.045	C	4°	4°	K	600	500/600D	1300	1600	7½–9
V8-305 Calif.	R45TS	.045	C	—	2°	K	—	600/650D	—	1600	7½–9
1980											
4-151 Exc. Calif.	R44TSX	.060	E	12°	12°	F	1000	650D	—	—	6½–8
4-151 Calif.	R44TSX	.060	E	14°	14°	F	1000	650D	—	—	6½–8
V6-231	⑤	.060	J	15°	15°	I⑭	800	600D	—	—	3–4½

①—BTDC— Before top dead center.
②—Idle speed on man. trans. vehicles is adjusted in Neutral & on auto. trans. equipped vehicles is adjusted in Drive unless otherwise specified. Where two idle speeds are listed, the higher speed is with the A/C or idle solenoid energized.
③—On high step of fast idle cam with A/C off.
④—Less A/C, 500/900 RPM; with A/C, 900/1250 RPM.
⑤—R45TSX or R46TSX.
⑥—Less idle solenoid, 600D RPM; with idle solenoid, 550/670D RPM.
⑦—Less A/C, 500/1000 RPM; with A/C, 900/1200 RPM.
⑧—2°ATDC, after top dead center.
⑨—At 1000 RPM.
⑩—Less A/C, 500/1000 RPM; with A/C, 500/1200 RPM.
⑪—Less A/C, 500/650D RPM; with A/C, 650/850D RPM.
⑫—Except even fire engine.
⑬—On early models, use R46TS gapped at .040"; on late models, use R46TSX gapped at .060".
⑭—The harmonic balancer on these engines has two timing marks. The mark measuring 1/16 inch is used when setting timing with a conventional timing light. The mark measuring 1/8 inch is used when setting timing with magnetic timing equipment.
⑮—Even fire engine.
⑯—Except engine code CPU, 8°BTDC; engine code CPU, 6°BTDC.

Continued

TUNE UP NOTES—Continued

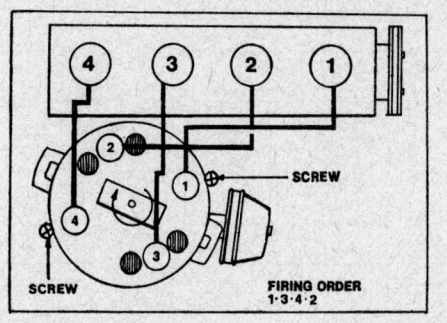

Fig. A

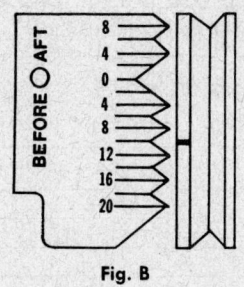

Fig. B

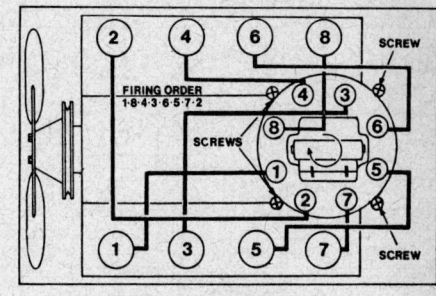

Fig. C

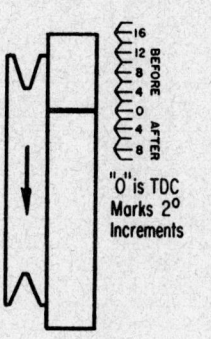

Fig. D

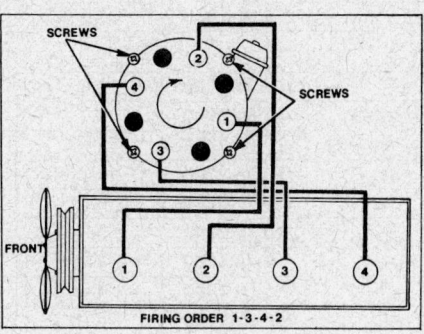

Fig. E

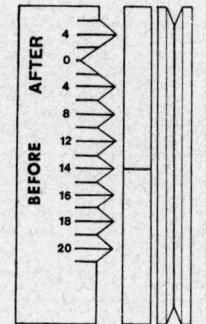

Fig. F

FIRING ORDER 1·6·5·4·3·2

Fig. G

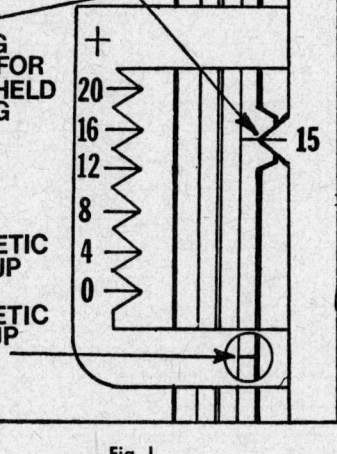

Fig. I

Fig. H

FIRING ORDER 1·6·5·4·3·2

Fig. J

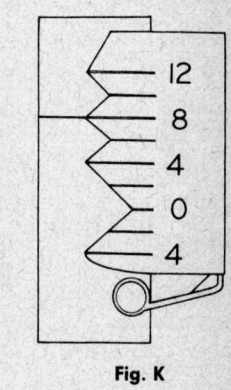

Fig. K

DISTRIBUTOR SPECIFICATIONS

★ If unit is checked on vehicle double the RPM and degrees to get crankshaft figures.

Distributor Part No.①	Centrifugal Advance Degrees @ RPM of Distributor					Vacuum Advance		Distributor Retard
	Advance Starts	Intermediate Advance			Full Advance	Inches if Vacuum To Start Plunger	Max. Adv. Dist. Deg. @ Vacuum	Max. Ret. Dist. Deg. @ Vacuum
1977								
1103229	0 @ 600	3 @ 800	—	—	10 @ 2200	3½	10 @ 12	—
1103230	0 @ 600	3 @ 800	—	—	10 @ 2200	3½	10 @ 9	—
1103231	0 @ 600	—	—	—	10 @ 2200	3½	10 @ 12	—
1103239	—	—	—	—	—	—	—	—
1103244	—	—	—	—	—	—	—	—
1103252	—	—	—	—	—	—	—	—

Continued

DISTRIBUTOR SPECIFICATIONS—Continued

★ If unit is checked on vehicle double the RPM and degrees to get crankshaft figures.

Distributor Part No.①	Centrifugal Advance Degrees @ RPM of Distributor					Vacuum Advance		Distributor Retard
	Advance Starts	Intermediate Advance			Full Advance	Inches if Vacuum To Start Plunger	Max. Adv. Dist. Deg. @ Vacuum	Max. Ret. Dist. Deg. @ Vacuum
1977—Continued								
1103303	0 @ 600	—	—	—	10 @ 2200	9	10 @ 16	—
1110538	0 @ 425	4 @ 600	—	—	8½ @ 1000	5	12 @ 10	—
1110539	0 @ 425	4 @ 600	—	—	8½ @ 1000	5	12 @ 10	—
1110677	0–2.2 @ 760	8.9–11 @ 1800	—	—	11 @ 2500	6	12¾ @ 20	—
1110686	0–2.15 @ 890	3.15–5.5 @ 1300	8.8–11 @ 1800	—	11 @ 2500	6	4¾ @ 20	—
1110695	1 @ 900	—	—	—	7½ @ 1800	5	12 @ 12	—
1978								
1103281	0 @ 500	5 @ 850	—	—	10 @ 1900	4	9 @ 12	—
1103282	0 @ 500	5 @ 850	—	—	10 @ 1900	4	10 @ 10	—
1103312	0 @ 600	—	—	—	10 @ 2200	5	8 @ 11	—
1103328	0 @ 600	—	—	—	10 @ 2200	3½	10 @ 9③	—
1103329	0 @ 600	—	—	—	10 @ 2200	3½	10 @ 12	—
1103365	0 @ 600	—	—	—	10 @ 2200	5	8 @ 11	—
1110695	0–3 @ 1000	—	—	—	9 @ 1800	3–6	12 @ 13②	—
1110731	0–2 @ 1000	—	—	—	7½ @ 1800	4–6	8 @ 9	—
1110732	0–2 @ 1000	—	—	—	7½ @ 1800	4–6	7 @ 13	—
1979								
1103281	1 @ 575	5 @ 850	—	—	10 @ 1900	4	10 @ 13	—
1103285	1 @ 675	6 @ 1000	—	—	11 @ 2100	4	12 @ 7	—
1103365	0 @ 1000	—	—	—	10 @ 2350	5	11 @ 11½	—
1103379	1 @ 575	5 @ 850	—	—	10 @ 1900	2½	11 @ 8½	—
1110677	0 @ 638	—	—	—	10 @ 1800	5	12 @ 9½	—
1110695	0 @ 840	—	—	—	7½ @ 1800	4	12 @ 11	—
1110726	0 @ 600	5 @ 1200	—	—	9 @ 2000	3½	10½ @ 8	—
1110757	0 @ 600	5 @ 1200	—	—	9 @ 2000	3½	10½ @ 8	—
1110766	1 @ 975	—	—	—	7½ @ 1800	4	12½ @ 11½	—
1110767	1 @ 975	—	—	—	7½ @ 1800	3½	10½ @ 12½	—
1110768	1 @ 625	3 @ 1200	—	—	7½ @ 1800	3½	10½ @ 12½	—
1110770	1 @ 975	—	—	—	7½ @ 1800	3	10½ @ 9½	—
1980								
1110554	0 @ 840	—	—	—	7½ @ 1800	3	12 @ 11.9	—
1110555	0 @ 425	3 @ 1200	—	—	7½ @ 1800	4	12 @ 11	—
1110558	0 @ 500	4½ @ 1200	—	—	7 @ 2000	3	7½ @ 5	—
1110559	0 @ 600	4½ @ 1200	—	—	7 @ 2000	3	7½ @ 5	—
1110560	0 @ 500	3½ @ 1000	—	—	7 @ 2325	4	10 @ 10	—

①—Located on distributor housing plate.　②—High altitude, 8° @ 9″.　③—Manual trans., 10° @ 12″.

STARTING MOTOR APPLICATIONS

Year	Engine	Starter Number	Year	Engine	Starter Number
1977	4-140 Std. Trans.	1108771		V6-231	1108797
	4-140 Auto. Trans.	1108772		V6-231	1109061
	4-151	1109412		V8-305	1108415
	V6-231	1108797		V8-305	1108790
	V8-305	1108790		V8-305	1109064
1978–79	4-151	1109521		V8-305	1109524
	4-151	1108771	1979	V8-305	1109062
	4-151	1108772	1980	4-151	1109521
	V6-196	1108797		V6-231	1109061

ALTERNATOR SPECIFICATIONS

Year	Model	Rated Hot Output Amps	Year	Model	Rated Hot Output Amps	Year	Model	Rated Hot Output Amps
1977	1102881	37		1102851	55		1102881	37
	1102854	63		1102854	63		1102910	63
	1102851	55		110258	37		1102911	55
	1102891	55		1102891	55		1103033	37
	1102893	63		1102893	63		1103059	63
1977–78	1102394	37		1102910	63	1980	1103084	55
	1102479	55		1102911	55		1103085	55
	1102495	55		1102913	61		1103086	63
	1102858	37	1979	1102394	37		1103100	55
1978	1102394	37		1102478	55		1103101	37
	1102478	55		1102479	55		1103102	63
	1102479	55		1102495	55		1103118	37
	1102495	55		1102844	63		1103120	63
	1102844	63		1102854	63		1103121	63

VALVE SPECIFICATIONS

Year	Engine Model	Valve Lash Int.	Valve Lash Exh.	Valve Angles Seat	Valve Angles Face	Valve Spring Installed Height	Valve Spring Pressure Lbs. @ In.	Stem Clearance Intake	Stem Clearance Exhaust	Stem Diameter Intake	Stem Diameter Exhaust
1977	4-140	Hydraulic④		46	45	1.746	190 @ 1.31	.0010–.0027	.0010–.0027	.3410–.3417	.3410–.3417
	4-151	Hydraulic④		46	45	1.69	82 @ 1.66	.0017–.0030	.0017–.0030	.340	.340
	V6-231	Hydraulic④		45	45	1.727	168 @ 1.327	.0015–.0032	.0015–.0032	.3402–.3412	.3405–.3412
	V8-305	¾ Turn③		46	45	②	⑤	.0010–.0027	.0010–.0027	.3410–.3417	.3410–.3417
1978	4-151	Hydraulic④		46	45	1.69	176 @ 1.254	.0010–.0027	.0010–.0027	.340	.340
	V6-196	Hydraulic④		45	45	1.727	168 @ 1.327	.0015–.0035	.0015–.0032	.3402–.3412	.3405–.3412
	V6-231	Hydraulic④		45	45	1.727	168 @ 1.327	.0015–.0035	.0015–.0032	.3402–.3412	.3405–.3412
	V8-305	1 Turn③		46	45	②	⑤	.0010–.0027	.0010–.0027	.3410–.3417	.3410–.3417
1979	4-151	Hydraulic④		46	45	1.66	151 @ 1.254	.0010–.0027	.0010–.0027	.3418–.3425	.3418–.3425
	V6-196	Hydraulic④		45	45	1.727	168 @ 1.34	.0015–.0035	.0015–.0032	.3402–.3412	.3405–.3412
	V6-231	Hydraulic④		45	45	1.727	①	.0015–.0035	.0015–.0032	.3402–.3412	.3405–.3412
	V8-305	1 Turn③		46	45	②	⑥	.0010–.0027	.0010–.0027	.3410–.3417	.3410–.3417
1980	4-151	Hydraulic④		46	45	1.66	176 @ 1.254	.0010–.0027	.0010–.0027	.3418–.3425	.3418–.3425
	V6-231	Hydraulic④		45	45	1.727	①	.0015–.0035	.0015–.0032	.3402–.3412	.3405–.3412

①—Intake 164 @ 1.34, Exhaust 182 @ 1.34.
②—Intake 1.70, Exhaust 1.61.
③—Turn rocker arm stud nut until all lash is eliminated, then tighten nut the additional turn listed.
④—No adjustment.
⑤—Intake 200 @ 1.25; Exhaust 200 @ 1.16.
⑥—Intake, 180 @ 1.25; exhaust 190 @ 1.16.

COOLING SYSTEM & CAPACITY DATA

Year	Model or Engine	Cooling Capacity, Qts. Less A/C	Cooling Capacity, Qts. With A/C	Radiator Cap Relief Pressure, Lbs.	Thermo. Opening Temp.	Fuel Tank Gals.	Engine Oil Refill Qts. ①	Transmission Oil 3 Speed Pints	Transmission Oil 4 Speed Pints	Transmission Oil 5 Speed Pints	Transmission Oil Auto. Trans. Qts. ②	Rear Axle Oil Pints
1977	4-140 Astre	8.8	8.8	15	195	16	3½⑫	—	2.4	3½	⑪	2¾
	4-140 Vega	8	8	15	195	16	3½⑫	—	3	3½	⑪	2¾
	4-140 Exc. Astre & Vega	8	8	15	195	18½	3½⑫	—	2.4	3½	④	3½
	4-151 Astre	11.2	11.2	15	195	16	3	—	3	3½	⑪	2¾
	4-151 Exc. Astre	12	12	15	195	18½	3	—	2.4	3½	④	3½
	V6-231	⑦	⑦	15	195	18½	4	—	2.4	3½	④	3½
	V8-305	18	18	15	195	18½	4	—	2.4	3½	④	3½

Continued

COOLING SYSTEM & CAPACITY DATA—Continued

Year	Model or Engine	Cooling Capacity, Qts.		Radiator Cap Relief Pressure, Lbs.	Thermo. Opening Temp.	Fuel Tank Gals.	Engine Oil Refill Qts. ①	Transmission Oil				Rear Axle Oil Pints
		Less A/C	With A/C					3 Speed Pints	4 Speed Pints	5 Speed Pints	Auto. Trans. Qts. ②	
1978–79	4-151	10.7	10.7	15	195	⑤	3	—	3	3½	④	3½③
	V6-196	12	12	15	195	⑤	4	—	3	3½	④	3½③
	V6-231	12	12	15	195	⑤	4	—	3	3½	④	3½③
	V8-305	16.6	18.0	15	195	⑤	4	—	3	3½	④	3½③
1980	Monza 4-151	11¾	11¾	15	195	18½	3⑧	—	3.4	—	⑨	3½
	Starfire 4-151	11	11.5	15	195	18½	3⑧	—	3.12	—	⑨	3½
	Sunbird 4-151	10.9	—	15	195	18½	3⑧	—	3	—	⑨	3½
	Monza V6-231	12	12	15	195	18½	4	—	3.4	—	⑩	3½
	Skyhawk V6-231	12.35	12.72	15	195	18½	4	—	—	—	⑩	3½
	Starfire V6-231	12	12.5	15	195	18½	4	—	3.12	—	⑩	3½
	Sunbird V6-231	12.3	12.3	15	195	18½	4	—	3	—	⑩	3½

①—Add 1 qt. with filter change.
②—Approximate. Make final check with dip stick.
③—3¾ qts. on Skyhawk.
④—Refill 3 qts., total capacity 10 qts.
⑤—Exc. Sunbird Station Wagon, Monza "S" Coupe & Station Wagon 18½; Sunbird Sta-

tion Wagon 16; Monza "S" Coupe & Station Wagon 15.
⑥—Skyhawk; 2.8. Sunbird; 3.5.
⑦—Exc. Sunbird, 12 qts.; Sunbird 13 qts.
⑧—With or without filter change.
⑨—T.H.M. 200, refill, 3½ qts.; total capacity, 9½ qts.

⑩—T.H.M. 350, refill, 3¼ qts.; total capacity, 12¼ qts.
⑪—T.H.M. 200, refill, 3 qts.; total capacity, 9.6 qts. T.H.M. 250, refill, 2½ qts.; total capacity, 10 qts.
⑫—Add ½ qt. with filter change.

PISTONS, PINS, RINGS, CRANKSHAFT & BEARINGS

Year	Engine Model	Piston Clearance	Ring End Gap①		Wrist-pin-Diameter	Rod Bearings		Main Bearings			
			Comp.	Oil		Shaft Diameter	Bearing Clearance	Shaft Diameter	Bearing Clearance	Thrust on Bear. No.	Shaft End Play
1977	4-140	.0018–.0028	②	.010	.9272	1.999–2.000	.0007–.0027	2.3004	.0003–.0029	4	.002–.008
	4-151	.0025–.0033	.010	.010	.9272	1.999–2.000	.0006–.0026	2.2983–2.2993	.0003–.0022	5	.0015–.0085
	V6-231	.0008–.0020	.013	.015	.9393	1.9991–2.000	.0005–.0026	2.4995	.0004–.0015	2	.004–.008
	V8-305	.0007–.0027	.010	.015	.9272	2.099–2.100	.0013–.0035	2.4502	③	5	.002–.007
1978	4-151	.0025–.0033	.010	.010	.9400	2.000	.0005–.0026	2.2983–2.2993	.0002–.0022	5	.0015–.0085
	V6-196	.0008–.0020	.010	.015	.9393	2.2487–2.2495	.0005–.0026	2.4995	.0004–.0017	2	.0004–.0008
	V6-231	.0008–.0020	.010	.015	.9393	2.2487–2.2495	.0005–.0026	2.4995	.0003–.0017	2	.003–.009
	V8-305	.0007–.0027	.010	.015	.9272	2.099–2.100	.0013–.0035	④	③	5	.002–.006
1979	4-151	.0025–.0033	②	.015	.940	2.000	.0005–.0026	2.300	.0005–.0022	5	.0035–.0085
	V6-196	.0008–.0020	.010	.010	.9393	2.2487–2.2495	.0005–.0026	2.4995	.0003–.0018	2	.003–.009
	V6-231	.0008–.0020	.013	.015	.9393	2.2487–2.2495	.0005–.0026	2.4995	.0003–.0018	2	.003–.009
	V8-305	.0007–.0017	.010	.015	.9272	2.099–2.100	.0013–.0035	④	③	5	.002–.006
1980	4-151	.0025–.0033	.010	.015	.940	2.000	.0005–.0026	2.300	.0005–.0022	5	.0035–.0085
	V6-231	.0008–.0020	.013	.015	.9393	2.2487–2.2495	.0005–.0026	2.4995	.0003–.0018	2	.003–.009

①—Fit rings in tapered bore for clearance listed in tightest portion of ring travel.
②—#1—.015", #2—.009".

③—#1—.0008—.0020, #2, 3 & 4—.0011—.0023, #5—.0017—.0032.
④—#1—2.4484—2.4493, #2, 3 & 4—

2.4481–2.4490, #5—2.4479–2.4488.

ENGINE TIGHTENING SPECIFICATIONS★

★ Torque specifications are for clean and lightly lubricated threads only. Dry or dirty
threads produce increased friction which prevents accurate measurement of tightness.

Year	Engine Model	Spark Plugs Ft. Lbs.	Cylinder Head Bolts Ft. Lbs.	Intake Manifold Ft. Lbs.	Exhaust Manifold Ft. Lbs.	Rocker Arm Stud Ft. Lbs.	Cam Cover Ft. Lbs.	Connecting Rod Cap Bolts Ft. Lbs.	Main Bearing Cap Bolts Ft. Lbs.	Flywheel to Crankshaft Ft. Lbs.	Vibration Damper or Pulley Ft. Lbs.
1977	4-140	20	60	30	30	—	80②	35	65	65	80
	V6-231	20	80	45	25	30③	4①	40	100	60	175
	V8-305	15	65	30	20④	—	45②	45	70	60	60
1977	4-151	15	95	⑤	⑤	—	—	32	65	55	160
1978	4-151	15	95	⑤	⑤	20	85②	30	65	55	160
1978–79	V6-196	20	80	45	25	30③	4①	40	100	60	225
	V6-231	20	80	45	25	30③	4①	40	100	60	225
	V8-305	22	65	30	20④	—	①⑦	45	80	60	60
1979–80	4-151	15	90	29	44	75	6①	32	70	⑥	200
1980	V6-231	20	80	45	25	30③	4①	40	100	60	225

①—Rocker arm cover ft. lbs.　　　　　④—Inside bolts 30 ft. lbs.　　　　　⑥—1979, 50 ft. lbs.; 1980, 44 ft. lbs.
②—In. lbs.　　　　　　　　　　　　⑤—Bolts, 40; Nuts, 30.　　　　　　　⑦—1978, 45 in. lbs.; 1979, 50 in. lbs.
③—Rocker arm shaft to cylinder head.

Electrical Section

STARTER, REPLACE

Exc. V6-196, 231

1. Disconnect battery ground cable and disconnect all wires at solenoid terminals.

NOTE: Reinstall the nuts on the terminals as each wire is removed, as thread size is different and if mixed, stripping of threads may occur.

---

2. Loosen starter front bracket and remove the two mounting bolts, Fig. 1.
3. Remove from bracket bolt or nut and rotate brace clear of work area, then remove starter from vehicle by lowering front end of starter first.
4. Reverse procedure to install.

V6-196, 231

1. Disconnect battery ground cable.
2. On models with manual transmission loosen engine crossmember attaching bolts.
3. On models with automatic transmission, remove crossover pipe and flywheel inspection cover.

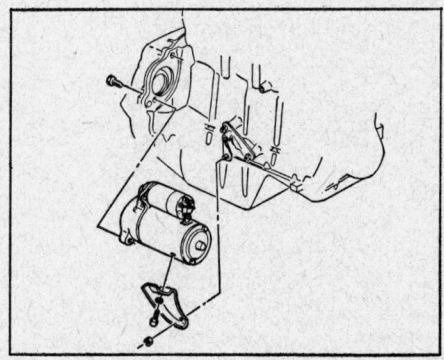

Fig. 1 Starter motor installation

4. On all models, remove starter attaching bolts, then lower starter and disconnect wiring.

NOTE: On models with manual transmission, it may be necessary to pull down on engine crossmember to gain clearance when removing starter assembly.

---

5. Reverse procedure to install.

IGNITION LOCK, REPLACE

Late 1978 & 1979–80

1. Remove steering wheel as described under Horn Sounder and Steering Wheel.
2. Remove turn signal switch as described under Turn Signal Switch, Replace, then remove buzzer switch.
3. Place ignition switch in Run position, then remove lock cylinder retaining screw and lock cylinder.
4. To install, rotate lock cylinder to stop while holding housing, Fig. 1A. Align cylinder key with keyway in housing, then push lock cylinder assembly into housing until fully seated.
5. Install lock cylinder retaining screw. Torque screw to 40 in. lbs. for standard columns. On adjustable columns, torque retaining screw to 22 in. lbs.
6. Install buzzer switch, turn signal switch and steering wheel.

1977 & Early 1978

1. Remove steering wheel as described under "Horn Sounder & Steering Wheel" procedure.
2. On Astre, Vega, 1978 Coupe, S Coupe and

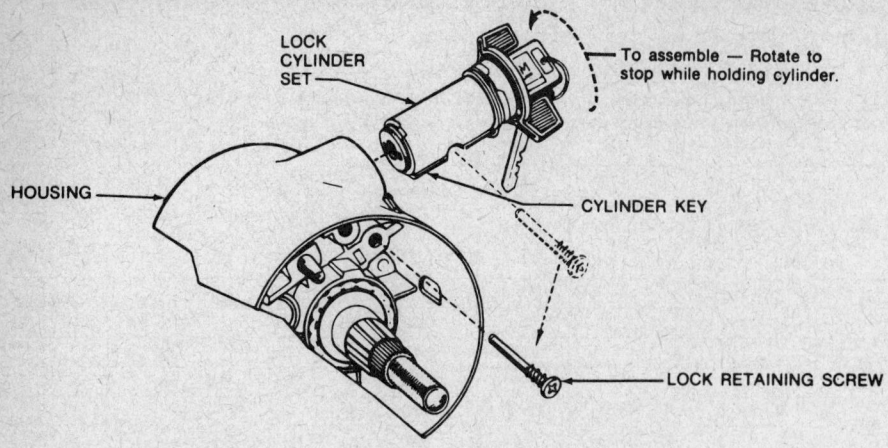

Fig. 1A   Ignition lock removal. Late 1978 & 1979—80

Fig. 1B   Ignition lock removal 1977 & early 1978

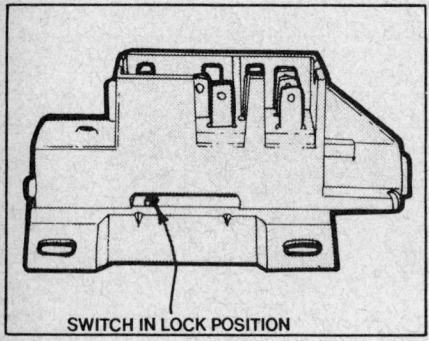

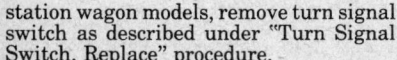

Fig. 2   Ignition switch assembly

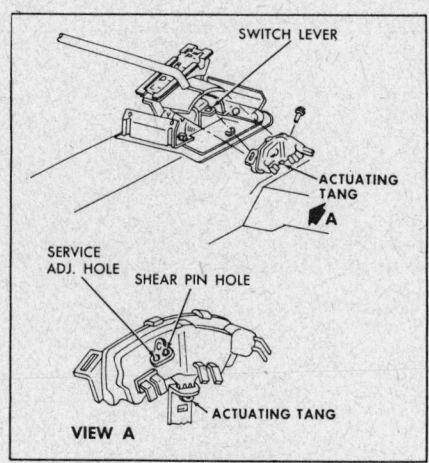

Fig. 3   Neutral safety switch installation. Astre, Vega & 1978—79 Station Wagon

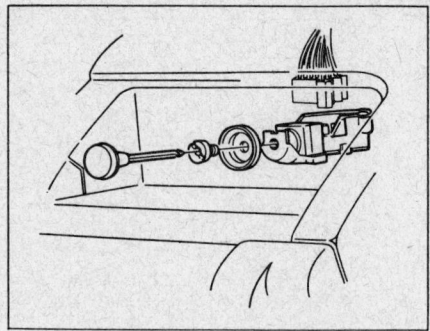

Fig. 4   Light switch replacement. Astre, Vega & 1978—79 Station Wagon

station wagon models, remove turn signal switch as described under "Turn Signal Switch, Replace" procedure.
3. On all models except Astre, Vega, 1978 Coupe, S Coupe and station wagon, pull directional switch rearward far enough to slip it over end of shaft. Do not pull harness out of column.
4. With ignition switch in "Run" position, insert a small screwdriver or similar tool into turn signal housing slot, Fig. 1B. Keeping tool to right side of slot, break housing flash loose and at same time depress spring latch at lower end of lock cylinder.
5. Remove lock cylinder from housing.

IGNITION SWITCH, REPLACE

Exc. Astre, Vega & 1978—79 Station Wagon

1. Disconnect battery ground cable.
2. Remove left A/C outlet duct.
3. Remove steering column to support retaining nuts and allow column to lower.

4. Disconnect connector from switch, then remove switch retaining screws and remove switch.
5. Reverse procedure to install with ignition switch in "lock" position, Fig. 2.

Astre, Vega & 1978—79 Station Wagon

The ignition switch is mounted on the top of the steering column jacket near the front of the dash. It is located inside the channel section of the brake pedal support and is completely inaccessible without first lowering the steering column.
1. Lower the steering column and be sure it is properly supported before proceeding.
2. The switch should be positioned in Lock position before removing, Fig. 2.
3. Unfasten and remove the switch, detaching it from the actuating rod.
4. When installing, make sure the lock and the switch are in the Lock position. Then install the activating rod into the switch and fasten the switch.

NEUTRAL SAFETY SWITCH, REPLACE

Exc. Astre, Vega & 1978—79 Station Wagon

1. Disconnect battery ground cable.
2. Remove console cover.
3. Disconnect connector from switch, then remove switch retaining screws and remove switch.
4. Reverse procedure to install and make certain that switch is correctly adjusted.

Astre, Vega & 1978—79 Station Wagon

1. Remove screws securing floor console, Fig. 3.
2. Disconnect electrical plugs on backup contacts and neutral start contacts of switch assembly.
3. Place shift lever in Neutral.
4. Remove two screws securing shift indicator plate.
5. Remove two screws securing shift lever curved cover.
6. Remove two screws securing switch to lever assembly.

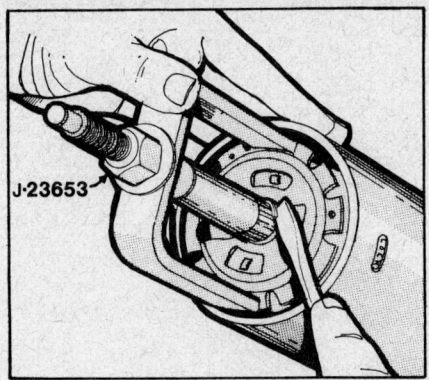

Fig. 5 Compressing lock plate and removing retaining ring

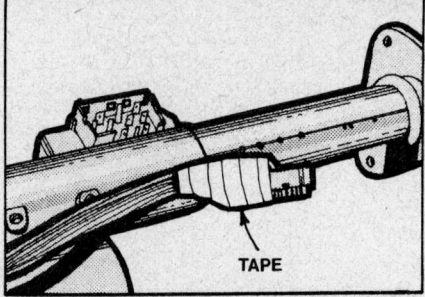

Fig. 6 Taping turn signal connector and wires

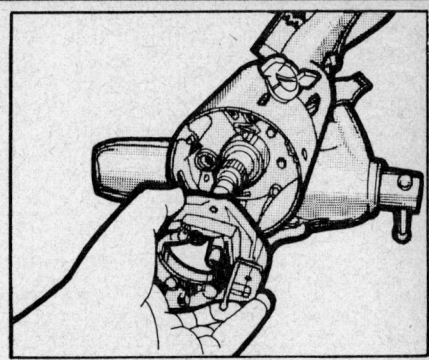

Fig. 7 Removing turn signal switch

NOTE: Screws are hidden beneath lever cover.

---

7. Tilt switch to right as you lift switch out of lever hole.
8. When installing switch, make sure it is in Neutral position. When switch is installed shifting out of Neutral will shear the switch plastic locating pin.

LIGHT SWITCH, REPLACE

Exc. Astre, Vega & 1978—79 Station Wagon

1. Disconnect battery ground cable.
2. Remove left A/C duct if equipped.
3. Reaching under instrument panel, release and pull switch knob and shaft assembly out of switch.
4. Remove switch bezel retaining nut, then

disconnect switch connector and remove switch.
5. Reverse procedure to install.

Astre, Vega & 1978—79 Station Wagon

1. Disconnect ground cable at battery.
2. Pull headlamp switch knob to "ON" position.
3. Reach under instrument panel and depress switch shaft retainer button while pulling on the switch control shaft knob.
4. With a large bladed screwdriver, remove the light switch ferrule nut from front of instrument panel, Fig. 4.
5. Disconnect the multi-contact connector from side of switch and remove switch.

STOP LIGHT SWITCH, REPLACE

1. Reach under right side of instrument panel at brake pedal support and disconnect wiring harness connector at switch.
2. Pull switch from mounting bracket.
3. When installing switch, adjust by bring-

ing brake pedal to normal position. Electrical contact should be make when pedal is depressed 3/8 to 5/8 inch. To adjust, the switch may be rotated or pulled in the clip.

CLUTCH START SWITCH, REPLACE

NOTE: The clutch pedal must be fully depressed and the ignition switch in START position for the vehicle to start.

The clutch switch assembly mounts with two tangs to the clutch pedal brace switch pivot bracket and the clutch pedal arm.

1. Under the instrument panel on the clutch pedal support, remove the multi-contact connector from switch.
2. Compress switch assembly actuating shaft barb retainer and push out of clutch pedal.
3. Compress switch assembly pivot bracket barb and lift off switch.
4. When installing new switch, no adjustments are necessary as the switch is self aligning.

TURN SIGNAL SWITCH, REPLACE

1. Remove steering wheel with suitable puller.
2. Remove three cover screws and lift cover off the shaft.

NOTE: These screws have plastic retainers on the back of the cover so it is not necessary to completely remove these screws.

---

3. Place Lock Plate Compressing Tool J23653, Fig. 5, on end of steering shaft and compress the lock plate as far as possible using the shaft nut as shown. Pry the round wire shap ring out of the shaft grove and discard the ring. Remove tool and lift lock plate and cover off end of shaft.
4. Slide the signal cancelling cam, upper bearing preload spring and thrust washer off the end of the shaft.
5. Remove turn signal lever screw and remove the lever.
6. Push hazard warning knot in and unscrew the knob.

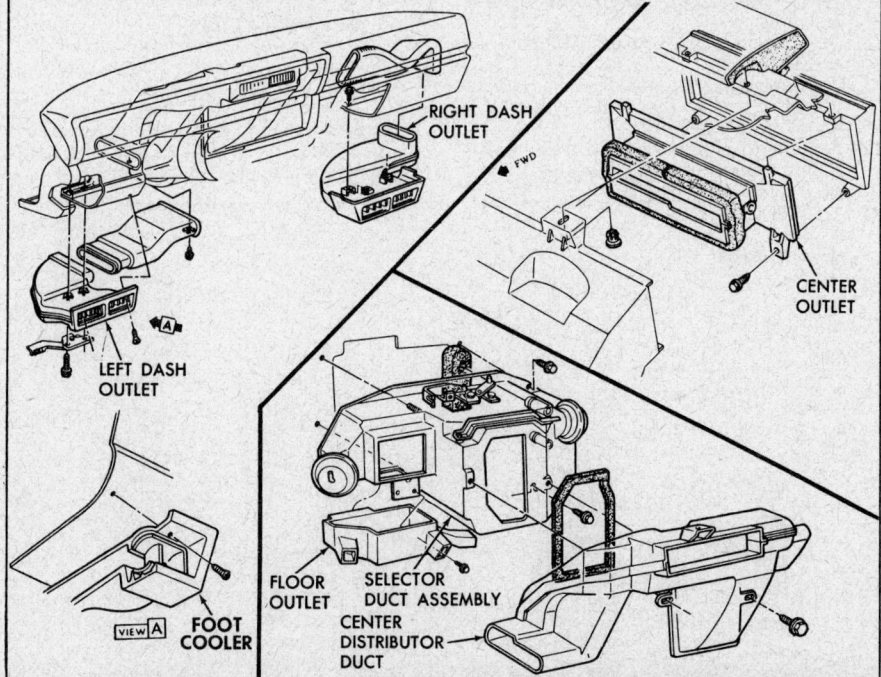

Fig. 8 Air distribution ducts and outlets on air conditioned models. Astre, Vega & 1978—79 Station Wagon

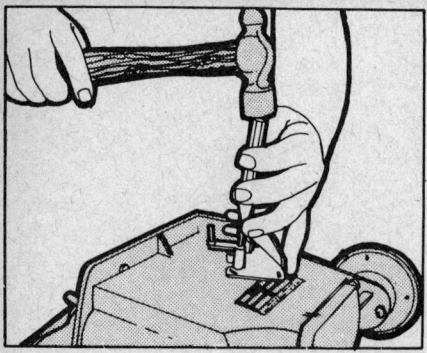

Fig. 9 Removing temperature door bell crank on air conditioned vehicles. Astre, Vega & 1978—79 Station Wagon

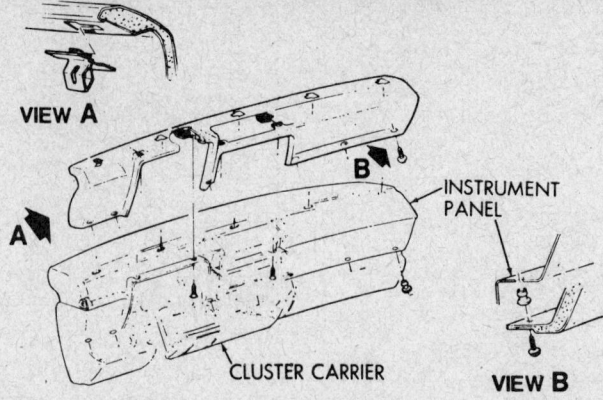

Fig. 10 Instrument panel pad. Exc. Astre, Vega & Station Wagon

7. Wrap upper part of connector with tape, Fig. 6, to prevent snagging of wires during switch removal.
8. Remove three screws on switch and pull switch straight up through housing, Fig. 7.

HORN SOUNDER & STEERING WHEEL, REPLACE

1. Disconnect battery ground cable.
2. On regular production steering wheel models, remove the two screws securing the steering wheel shroud from beneath the wheel and remove the shroud. On optional wheels models, pry off horn button cap.
3. Remove steering wheel nut and use a suitable puller to remove the steering wheel.

RADIO, REPLACE

1. Disconnect battery ground cable.
2. Remove radio control knobs and bezels, then the shaft nuts and washers.
3. Disconnect antenna lead from radio rear and remove screws securing radio to instrument panel reinforcement.
4. Lower radio from instrument panel and disconnect electrical connectors from radio.
5. Remove mounts from radio.
6. Reverse procedure to install.

HEATER CORE, REPLACE

Exc. Astre, Vega & 1978—79 Station Wagon

Less Air Conditioning
1. Disconnect battery ground cable and disconnect blower motor electrical lead.
2. Place a pan under vehicle, then disconnect heater hoses from core and secure hoses in a raised position.
3. Remove blower inlet to dash panel screws and nuts, then remove blower inlet and blower motor and wheel assembly.
4. Remove core retaining strap screws and remove core.
5. Reverse procedure to install making certain that blower inlet sealer is intact, replace as necessary.

1977—80 With Air Conditioning

NOTE: The heater core can be removed without purging the A/C refrigerant system or removing the evaporator case half of the assembly by using the following procedure.

1. Disconnect battery ground cable.
2. Remove floor outlet duct, then remove glove box and door as an assembly.
3. Remove left and right hand dash outlets using a suitable tool.
4. Remove instrument panel pad.
5. Disconnect vacuum hoses at valves on left end of heater and evaporator unit.
6. Remove insulation tray located below instrument cluster, then loosen console and slide console rearward.
7. Remove instrument panel to dash attaching screws. Place a protective covering over steering column, then lower instrument panel to steering column. Disconnect speedometer cable, radio leads and control head connectors.
8. Remove right hand instrument panel and lap cooler as an assembly.
9. Remove modular duct to heater and evaporator case screw, then remove duct assembly.
10. Disconnect temperature door cable and wiring harness.
11. Disconnect heater hoses from heater core. Plug core tubes to prevent spillage when removing heater core.
12. Remove three heater case stud nuts located in engine compartment.

13. Remove heater core case to evaporator core case attaching screws.
14. Drive on studs to break case loose from dash panel.
15. Remove heater core case assembly.
16. Remove heater core to case attaching screws, then remove heater core.

Astre, Vega & 1978—79 Station Wagon

Less Air Conditioning
1. Disconnect battery ground cable.
2. Disconnect blower motor lead wire.
3. Place a pan under vehicle and disconnect heater hoses at core connections and secure ends of hoses in a raised position.
4. Remove the coil bracket to dash panel stud nut and move coil out of way.
5. Remove the blower inlet to dash panel screws and nuts and remove the blower inlet, blower motor and wheel as an assembly.
6. Remove the core retainer strap screws and remove the core.
7. When replacing core, be sure the blower inlet sealer is intact.

With Air Conditioning
1. Disconnect battery ground cable.
2. Position a pan under heater core tubes, then disconnect heater hoses and secure in a raised position. Cap core tubes to prevent coolant spillage during removal.
3. From engine side of dash panel remove nuts from selector duct studs, Fig. 8.

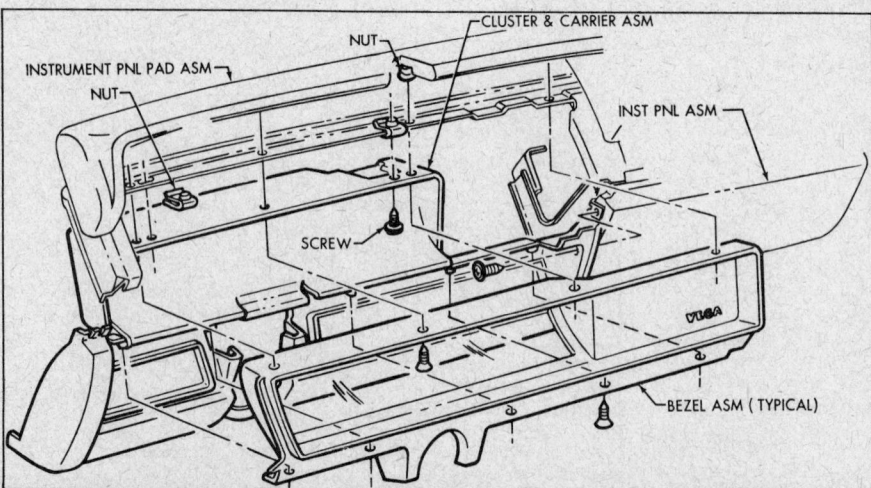

Fig. 11 Standard instrument panel cluster. Astre, Vega & 1978—79 Station Wagon

4. Remove glove box and door as an assembly.
5. Remove right hand outlet to instrument panel attaching screws, then remove outlet and flexible hose.
6. Remove intermediate duct to left hand outlet.
7. Remove steering column to toe pan plastic retainer, insulation and attaching screws.
8. Remove steering column to dash panel attaching nuts, then lower column and support on driver's seat.

NOTE: Place protective tape over steering column to prevent damage to finish when lowering instrument cluster assembly.

9. Remove instrument panel bezel, then remove ash tray and retainer.
10. Remove A/C control to instrument panel attaching screws.
11. Disconnect wire connector and antenna lead from radio.
12. Remove instrument cluster to dash panel attaching screws and allow cluster assembly to rest on steering column.
13. Disconnect speedometer cable, then push A/C control forward and allow control to rest on floor, using care not to kink cable.
14. Remove center duct to selector duct attaching screws and duct to upper instrument panel retainer.
15. Slide center duct to left to clear lower instrument panel to cluster tab, then slide to right to remove.
16. Remove defroster duct to selector duct attaching screws.
17. Remove remaining selector duct to dash panel attaching screws, then pull duct rearward and disconnect all electrical leads and vacuum lines.
18. Disconnect temperature door cable and remove selector duct assembly.

NOTE: Ensure all electrical leads and vacuum lines are disconnected before removing duct assembly.

19. Pry off or punch out temperature door bell crank, then remove temperature door Fig. 9.
20. Remove backing plate attaching screws and temperature door cable retainer.
21. Remove heater core and backing plate as an assembly.
22. Remove core straps, then remove heater core.

BLOWER MOTOR, REPLACE

1. Disconnect battery ground cable and disconnect blower motor electrical leads. On some models, it may be necessary to remove coolant recovery tank attaching screws and position tank aside. Do not disconnect hoses from tank.
2. Scribe blower motor flange to case position.
3. Remove blower motor retaining screws and remove blower motor and wheel assembly. Pry flange gently, if sealer acts as an adhesive.
4. Reverse removal procedure to install, aligning scribe marks made during removal.

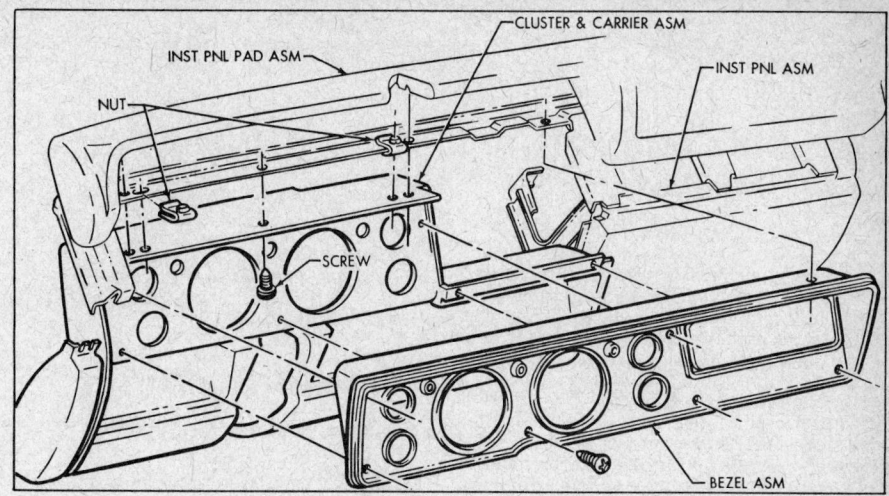

Fig. 12 Optional instrument panel cluster. Astre, Vega, 1978—79 Coupe, S Coupe & Station Wagon

INSTRUMENT PANEL PAD, REPLACE

Exc. Astre, Vega & Station Wagon

1. Remove eleven screws from around edge of pad, Fig. 10.
2. On models equipped with A/C, disconnect left hand duct.
3. Pry upward on pad to disengage clips located rear of pad, then remove pad assembly.

Astre, Vega & 1978—79 Station Wagon

1. Remove clock stem knob, then remove instrument cluster bezel, Figs. 11 and 12.
2. Remove one screw at lower left edge of pad and three screws located along lower right hand side of pad.
3. Sharply rap lower right edge of pad upward to disengage retaining clips at top right of pad, then remove pad assembly.

INSTRUMENT CLUSTER, REPLACE

Astre, Vega & 1978—79 Station Wagon

Standard Cluster
The instrument cluster bezel is retained by nine screws, Fig. 11. After removal of bezel, remove cluster lens-light shield combination (2 screws at top of lens and 2 screws at bottom of light shield). The lens tips out at the top and then lifts off. Instruments are then easily removed.

GT Cluster
The cluster bezel is retained by six screws, Fig. 12. After removal of bezel, remove the lens light shield (6 screws). Then lift lens and light shield straight out. Instruments are then accessible for replacement.

Exc. Astre, Vega & Station Wagon

Standard Cluster
Remove four screws securing bezel and lens to instrument panel. Remove bezel and lens. Instruments are then accessible for replacement.

GT Cluster
Disconnect battery ground cable. Remove knob from clock stem, then remove six screws attaching cluster bezel to instrument panel. Remove six lens and light shield attaching screws, then remove lens and light shield. Instruments are then accessible for replacement.

W/S WIPER SWITCH, REPLACE

Exc. Astre, Vega & Station Wagon

1. Disconnect battery ground cable.
2. Remove screws securing light shield to wiper switch and position light shield aside.

NOTE: The light shield retaining screws also retain the upper portions of the wiper switch to the mounting bosses.

3. Remove lower switch mounting screw, lower switch from panel and disconnect electrical connector, then remove switch.
4. Reverse procedure to install.

Astre, Vega & 1978—79 Station Wagon

1. Beneath instrument panel, unplug the headlamp switch multi-connector for clearance to wiper switch screw.
2. Unplug connector on bottom of wiper switch.
3. Remove two mounting screws from switch and lower switch from instrument panel.

W/S WIPER MOTOR, REPLACE

1. Raise hood, remove cowl screen.
2. Reaching through cowl opening, loosen the two transmission drive link attaching nuts to motor crankarm.
3. Remove transmission drive link from motor crankarm.
4. Disconnect wiring and unfasten motor and remove.

Engine Section

ENGINE MOUNTS, REPLACE

4-140

1. Raise vehicle on hoist and support front of engine to take weight off front mounts.
2. If only one mount is being replaced, remove the mount-to-engine bracket nut on the mount not being replaced.
3. Remove the stud nut and two bolts securing mount to housing support.
4. Remove the three stud nuts securing the bracket to the engine. On the right side remove the starter brace at starter and on air conditioned equipped vehicles, remove the compressor rear lower brace at the compressor.
5. Raise front of engine to provide maximum clearance without imposing stress on other engine components.
6. Reverse procedure to install.

4-151

1. Remove bracket to engine bolts and the chassis to engine mount attaching nut, Fig. 1.
2. Raise engine to release weight from mount.
3. Remove mount and separate from engine bracket.
4. Reverse procedure to install.

V6-196, 231

1. Raise car and provide frame support at front of car.
2. Support weight of engine at forward edge of pan.
3. Remove mount to engine block bolts. Raise engine slightly and remove mount to mount bracket bolt and nut. Remove mount.
4. Reverse above procedure to install and torque to specifications as shown in Fig. 2.

V8-305

1. Remove lower mount bolts from frame bracket, Fig. 3, and raise engine to relieve weight from mount.
2. Remove mount from engine.
3. Install new mount on engine, lower engine and install lower mount bolts to frame bracket.

ENGINE, REPLACE

4-140 & V8-305

1. Scribe relationship between hood hinges and the hood, then remove hood from hinges.
2. Disconnect battery positive cable at battery and negative cable at engine block (except on air conditioned vehicles).
3. Drain cooling system and disconnect hoses at radiator. Disconnect heater hoses at water pump and at heater inlet (bottom hose).
4. Disconnect emission system hoses: PCV at cam cover; cannister vacuum hose at carburetor; PCV vacuum at inlet manifold and bowl vent at carburetor.
5. Remove radiator panel or shroud and remove radiator, fan and spacer.
6. Remove air cleaner, disconnecting vent tube at base of cleaner.
7. Disconnect electrical leads at: Delcotron, ignition coil, starter solenoid, oil pressure switch, engine temperature switch, transmission controlled spark switch at transmission, transmission controlled spark solenoid and engine ground strap at cowl.
8. Disconnect: Fuel line at rubber hose to rear of carburetor, transmission vacuum modulator and air conditioning vacuum line at inlet manifold, accelerator cable at manifold bellcrank.
9. On air conditioned cars, disconnect compressor at front support, rear support,

rear lower bracket and remove drive belt from compressor.
10. Move compressor slightly forward and allow front of compressor to rest on frame forward brace, then secure rear of compressor to engine compartment so it is out of way.
11. Disconnect power steering pump, if equipped, and position it out of way.
12. Raise car on a hoist and disconnect exhaust pipe at manifold.
13. Remove engine flywheel dust cover or converter underpan.
14. On automatic transmission cars, remove converter-to-flywheel retaining bolts and nuts and install coverter safety strap.
15. Remove converter housing or flywheel housing-to-engine retaining bolts.
16. Loosen engine front mount retaining bolts at frame attachment and lower vehicle.
17. Install floor jack under transmission.
18. Install suitable engine lifting equipment and raise engine slightly to take weight from engine mounts and remove engine front mount retaining bolts.
19. Remove engine and pull forward to clear transmission while slowly lifting engine from car.

4-151

1. Disconnect battery cables and drain cooling system.
2. Scribe relationship between hood hinges and the hood, then remove hood from hinges.
3. Disconnect distributor, starter and alternator wiring, engine to body ground strap, oil pressure and engine temperature sender wires, and all external vacuum hoses.
4. Remove air cleaner.
5. Remove radiator shroud assembly and fan, then disconnect coolant hoses from engine.
6. Disconnect accelerator linkage.

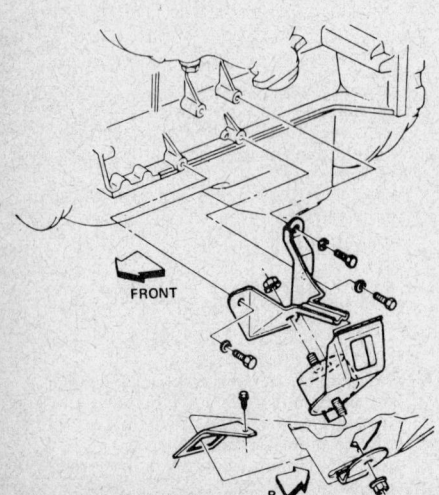

Fig. 1 Engine mounts. 4-151

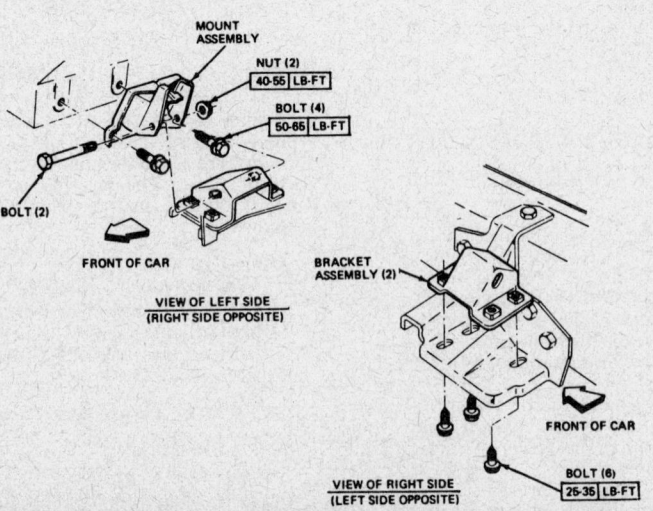

Fig. 2 Engine mounts. V6-196, 231

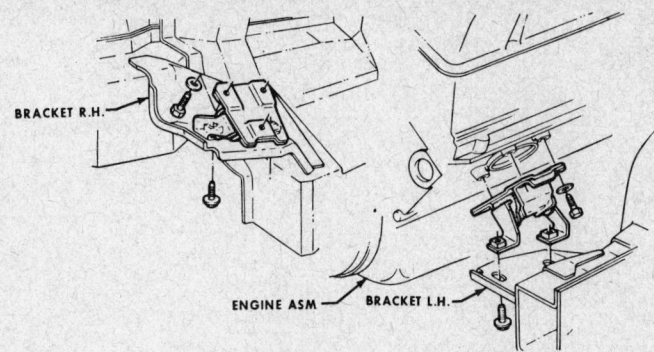

Fig. 3 Engine mounts, V8-305, 350

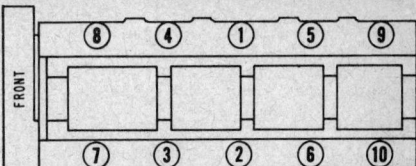

Fig. 4 Cylinder head tightening sequence. 4-140

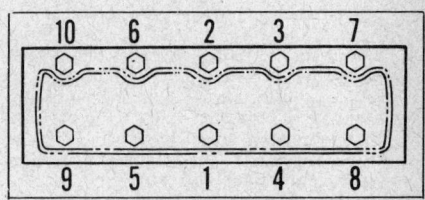

Fig. 5 Cylinder head tightening sequence. 4-151

7. If equipped with power steering or A/C, remove pump or compressor from mounting brackets and position aside. Do not disconnect hoses or lines.
8. Disconnect fuel lines.
9. Raise vehicle and drain oil pan.
10. Disconnect exhaust pipe from manifold.
11. If equipped with automatic transmission, remove converter cover and the converter retaining bolts, then slide converter rearward.
12. If equipped with manual transmission, disconnect clutch linkage and remove clutch cross shaft.
13. On all models, remove four lower bell housing bolts.
14. Disconnect transmission filler tube support and the starter wiring harness.
15. Remove front engine mount bolts.
16. Lower vehicle and, using a suitable jack and block of wood, support transmission.
17. Install suitable engine lifting equipment and support engine.
18. Remove the two remaining bell housing bolts.
19. Raise transmission slightly.
20. Move engine forward to separate from transmission, tilt front of engine upward and remove from vehicle.

V6-196, 231

NOTE: On models with manual transmission, engine and transmission are removed as an assembly.

1. Scribe alignment marks at hood hinge and hinge bracket, then remove hood.

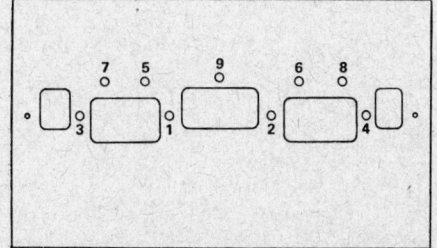

Fig. 6 Intake manifold tightening sequence. 1977—80 4-151 except cross flow engine

2. Disconnect battery ground cable, then drain cooling system.
3. Remove air cleaner.
4. On models equipped with A/C, disconnect compressor ground wire and wire connector, then remove compressor mounting bracket bolts and position compressor aside.
5. Remove drive belts, fan and pulley.
6. Disconnect radiator and heater hoses from engine and position out of way.
7. Remove fan shroud assembly.
8. Remove power steering pump bracket bolts and position pump aside, if equipped.
9. Disconnect fuel pump hoses and install plugs.
10. Disconnect battery ground cable from engine.
11. Disconnect vacuum hose from carburetor to manifold and vacuum hoses to vacuum modulator and power brake unit, if equipped.
12. Disconnect throttle cable from carburetor.
13. Disconnect wire connectors from alternator, oil and coolant sending units.
14. Disconnect engine to body ground straps at engine.
15. Raise vehicle and disconnect starter cables and cable shields, if equipped.
16. Disconnect exhaust pipe from exhaust manifold.
17. Remove lower flywheel cover.
18. On models with automatic transmission, remove flywheel to converter attaching bolts. Mark converter and flywheel so they can be installed in the same position. Remove transmission to engine attaching bolts.
19. On models with manual transmission, disconnect driveshaft, shift linkage, clutch equalizer shaft and transmission.
20. Remove motor mount through bolts and cruise control bracket, if equipped, then lower vehicle.
21. On models with automatic transmission, support transmission.
22. Attach a suitable lifting device to engine and raise engine so that mounting through bolts can be removed. Ensure all wiring harness, vacuum lines and other components are clear before removing engine from vehicle.
23. On models with automatic transmission, raise engine clear of mounts and raise transmission support accordingly and alternately until transmission can be disengaged from engine. On all models carefully raise engine and remove from vehicle.

CYLINDER HEADS, REPLACE

Some cylinder head gaskets are coated with a special lacquer to provide a good seal once the parts have warmed up. Do not use any additional sealer on such gaskets. If the gasket does not have this lacquer coating, apply suitable sealer to both sides.

4-140

1. Remove engine front cover and camshaft cover as outlined further on.
2. Remove timing belt and camshaft sprocket.
3. Remove intake and exhaust manifolds.
4. Disconnect hose at thermostat housing.
5. Remove cylinder head bolts and with the aid of an assistant lift head and gasket from engine. Place head on two blocks of wood to prevent damage to valves.
6. Reverse procedure to install and tighten head bolts in sequence shown in Fig. 4.

4-151

1979—80 Cross Flow Engine
1. Drain cooling system and remove air cleaner.
2. Remove alternator, power steering pump and A/C compressor brackets from cylinder head and engine block.
3. Remove intake and exhaust manifolds.
4. Disconnect all electrical connectors from cylinder head.

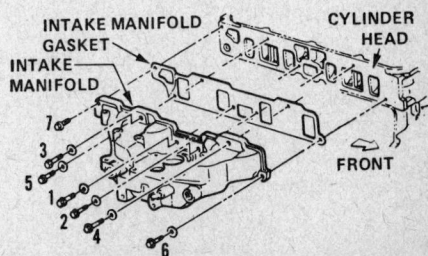

Fig. 7 Intake manifold tightening sequence. 1979—80 4-151 cross flow engine

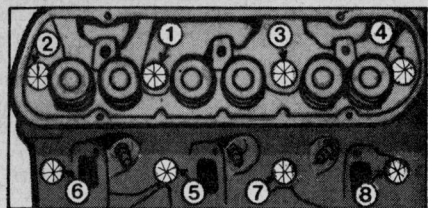

Fig. 8 Cylinder head tightening sequence. V6-196, 231

Fig. 9 Intake manifold tightening sequence. V6-196, 231

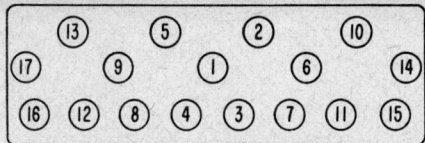

Fig. 10 Cylinder head tightening sequence. V8-305

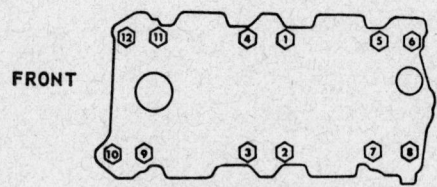

Fig. 11 Intake manifold tightening sequence. V8-305

5. Disconnect ignition wire from spark plugs, then remove spark plugs.
6. Disconnect fuel line at rear engine lifting bracket.
7. Remove rocker arm cover and back off rocker arm nuts. Pivot rocker arm and remove push rods.
8. Remove cylinder head attaching bolts, cylinder head and gasket.
9. Reverse procedure to install. Torque cylinder head bolt in sequence shown in Fig. 5 and intake manifold bolts in sequence shown, Fig. 7.

1977–80 Except Cross Flow Engine
1. Disconnect battery ground cable.
2. Drain cooling system and remove air cleaner.
3. Disconnect accelerator cable from bellcrank at manifold, then the fuel and vacuum lines at carburetor.
4. Remove intake and exhaust manifolds.
5. Remove alternator to cylinder head bracket bolts.

NOTE: If equipped with power steering or A/C, remove right side front bracket to facilitate cylinder head removal.

6. Disconnect wiring harness from temperature sender and remove from clips on rocker arm cover.
7. Disconnect coolant hoses at water outlet housing and the ground strap at cylinder head.
8. Remove spark plugs and rocker arm cover. Loosen rocker arm nuts, pivot rocker arms aside and remove push rods.
9. Remove cylinder head bolts and the cylinder head.
10. Reverse procedure to install. Torque cylinder head and intake manifold bolts in sequence shown in Figs. 5 and 6.

V6-196, 231

1. Drain coolant and disconnect battery.
2. Remove intake manifold.
3. When removing right cylinder head, remove Delcotron and/or A/C compressor with mounting bracket and move out of the way. *Do not disconnect hoses from A/C compressor.*
4. When removing left cylinder head, remove oil dipstick, power steering pump and move out of the way with hoses attached.
5. Disconnect exhaust manifold from head to be removed.
6. Remove rocker arm shaft and lift out push rods.
7. Remove cylinder head.
8. Reverse procedure to install. Torque cylinder head and intake manifold bolts in sequence shown in Figs. 8 and 9.

V8-305

1. Remove intake and exhaust manifolds.
2. Remove rocker arm covers.
3. Remove rocker arm nuts, rocker arm balls and rocker arms.

NOTE: Rocker arms, rocker arm balls and push rods must be installed in the original position.

4. Drain coolant from cylinder block, then remove cylinder head bolts and cylinder head.
5. Reverse procedure to install. Torque cylinder head and intake manifold bolts on sequence shown in Figs. 10 and 11.

ROCKER ARMS, REPLACE

V6-196, 231

A nylon retainer is used to retain the rocker arms. Break them below their heads with a chisel, Fig. 12, or pry out with channel locks. Production rocker arms can be installed in any sequence since the arms are identical, however, replacement arms are identified with a stamping right (R) and left (L).

ROCKER ARM STUDS, REPLACE

4-151

Rocker arm studs that are cracked or have damaged heads, can be removed from the cylinder head using a deep socket. Install and torque replacement rocker arm stud to 60 ft. lbs. on 1977–80 except cross flow engine and 75 ft. lbs. on 1979–80 cross flow engine.

V8-305

Rocker arm studs that have damaged threads may be replaced with standard studs. If studs are loose in the head, oversize studs (.003″ or .013″) may be installed after reaming

Fig. 12 Removing nylon rocker arm retainer. V6-196, 231

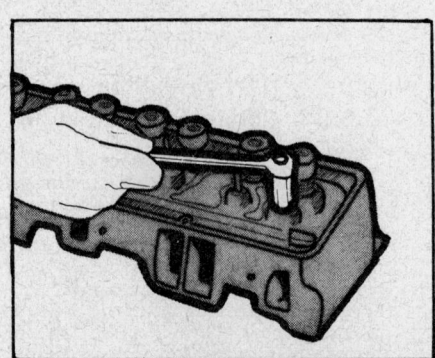

Fig. 13 Removing rocker arm stud. V8-305

Fig. 14 Installing rocker arm stud. V8-305

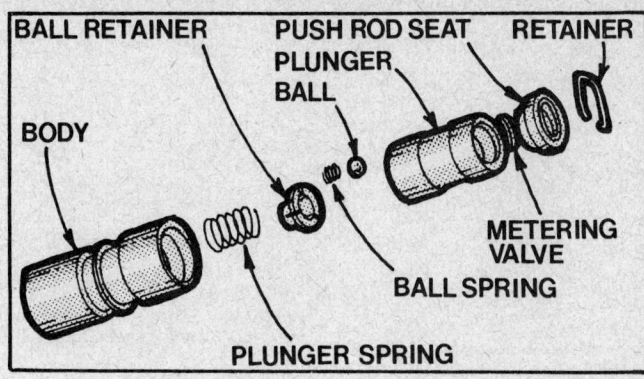

Fig.15   Hydraulic valve lifter. 4-151, V6-196, 231 and V8-305

the holes with a proper size reamer.
1. Remove old stud by placing a suitable spacer, Fig. 13 over stud. Install nut and flat washer and remove stud by turning nut.
2. Ream hole for oversize stud.
3. Coat press-fit area of stud with rear axle lube. Then install new stud, Fig. 14. If tool J-6880 shown is used, it should bottom on the head.

VALVES, ADJUST

4-140

These engines use hydraulic valve lifters are used and no valve lash adjustment is required. These lifters are not interchangeable with the type previously used since the cylinder head has been re-designed to facilitate installation of the new type lifter.

V8-305

NOTE: *After the engine has been thoroughly warmed up the valves may be adjusted with the engine shut off as follows: With engine in position to fire No. 1 cylinder the following valves may be adjusted: Exhaust 1-3-4-8, intake 1-2-5-7. Then crank the engine one more complete revolution which will bring No. 6 cylinder to the firing position at which time the following valves may be adjusted: Exhaust 2-5-6-7, intake 3-4-6-8.*

The following procedure, performed with the engine running should be done only in case readjustment is required.
1. After engine has been warmed up to operating temperature, remove valve cover and install a new valve cover gasket on cylinder head to prevent oil from running out.
2. With engine running at idle speed, back off valve rocker arm nut until rocker arm starts to clatter.
3. Turn rocker arm nut down slowly until the clatter just stops. This is the zero lash position.
4. Turn nut down 1/4 additional turn and pause 10 seconds until engine runs smoothly. Repeat additional 1/4 turns, pausing 10 seconds each time, until nut has been turned down the number of turns listed in the *Valve Specifications*

Chart from the zero-lash position.

NOTE: This preload adjustment must be done slowly to allow the lifter to adjust itself to prevent the possibility of interference between the intake valve head and top of piston, which might result in internal damage and/or bent push rods. Noisy lifters should be replaced.

VALVE ARRANGEMENT

Front to Rear

Engine	Arrangement
4-140	I-E-I-E-I-E-I-E
4-151	E-I-I-E-E-I-I-E
V6-196, 231	E-I-E-I-I-E
V8-305	E-I-I-E-E-I-I-E

CAM LOBE LIFT SPECS.

	Year	Intake	Exhaust
4-140	1977	.4000	.4150

VALVE LIFT SPECS.

Engine	Year	Intake	Exhaust
4-151	1977–80	.406	.406
V6-196	1978	.323	.366
V6-196	1979	.341	.366
V6-231	1977–78	.3830	.3660
V6-231	1979–80	.3570	.3660
V8-305	1977–79	.3727	.4100

VALVE TIMING

Intake Opens Before TDC

Engine	Year	Degrees
4-140	1977	34
4-151	1977–80	33
V6-196	1978	18
V6-196	1979	16
V6-231	1977–78	17
V6-231	1979–80	16
V8-305	1977–79	28

VALVE GUIDES

Valve guides are an integral part of the cylinder head and are not removable. If valve stem clearance is excessive, the valve guide should be reamed to the next oversize and the appropriate oversize valves installed. Valves are available in .003, .015 and .030 inch oversize for the 4-140 and V8-305, .003 and .005 for the 4-151 and .010 and .006 inch for the V6-196, 231.

VALVE LIFTERS, REPLACE

4-151, V6-196, 231 & V8-305

Failure of an hydraulic valve lifter is generally caused by an inadequate oil supply or dirt. An air leak at the intake side of the oil pump or too much oil in the engine will cause air bubbles in the oil supply to the lifters, causing them to collapse. This is a probable cause of trouble if several lifters fail to function, but air in the oil is an unlikely cause of failure of a single unit.

On 4-151 engines, valve lifters may be lifted out of their bores after loosening and rotating rocker arm for clearance and removing push rod and push rod cover. On V6 and V8 models, valve lifters may be lifted out of their bores after removing the rocker arms, push rods and intake manifold. Adjustable pliers with taped jaws may be used to remove lifters that are stuck due to varnish, carbon, etc. Fig. 15 illustrates the type of lifter used.

CAMSHAFT COVER, REPLACE

4-140

1. Raise hood to fully open position and install bolt through the hood hold-open link.
2. Disconnect battery negative cable at battery.
3. Remove air cleaner wing nut. Disconnect ventilation tube at camshaft cover or at air cleaner; then remove air cleaner.
4. Remove PCV valve from grommet at front of cover.
5. Remove cover-to-cylinder head screws and withdraw cover from head.

ENGINE FRONT COVER, REPLACE

4-140

1. Raise hood to fully open position and install hood hold-open bolt.
2. Disconnect battery ground cable at battery.
3. Remove fan and spacer.
4. Loosen, but do not remove, the two cover lower screws. Cover is slotted to permit easy removal.
5. Remove the two cover upper retaining screws and remove cover.

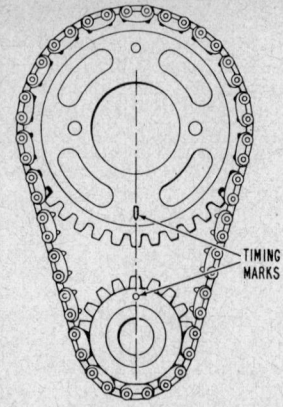

Fig. 16   Valve timing marks aligned for correct valve timing. V6-196, 231

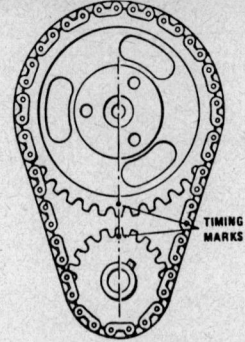

Fig. 17   Valve timing marks aligned for correct valve timing. V8-305, 350

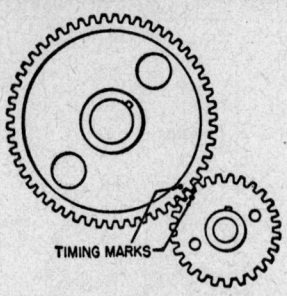

Fig. 18   Valve timing marks aligned for correct valve timing. 4-151

4-151

1. Disconnect battery ground cable.
2. Remove torsional damper and the two oil pan to front cover screws, then front cover bolts.
3. Pull cover forward slightly and cut oil pan front seal flush with cylinder block at both sides of cover.
4. Remove front cover.

V6-196, 231

1. Drain cooling system and remove radiator.
2. Remove fan, pulleys and belts.
3. Remove crankshaft pulley and reinforcement.
4. If equipped with power steering, remove any pump bracket bolts attached to timing chain cover and loosen and remove any other bolts necessary that will allow pump and brackets to be moved out of the way.
5. Remove fuel pump.
6. Remove Delcotron and brackets.
7. Remove distributor cap and pull spark plug wire retainers off brackets on rocker arm cover. Swing distributor cap with wires attached out of the way.
8. Remove distributor. *If chain and sprockets are not to be disturbed, note position of distributor rotor for installation in the same position.*
9. Loosen and slide clamp on thermostat bypass hose rearward.
10. Remove bolts attaching chain cover to block.
11. Remove two oil pan-to-chain cover bolts and remove cover.
12. If seal replacement is required, drive seal from cover using a suitable punch.
13. Position packing around opening with ends of packing facing upward. Drive shedder into position using a suitable punch and stake in three locations.
14. Rotate a hammer handle around packing until balancer hub can be inserted through opening.

V8-305

1. Drain cooling system.
2. Remove alternator and A.I.R. pump, if necessary.
3. Remove fan, fan shroud and radiator.
4. Remove crankshaft damper.
5. Remove front cover attaching bolts and front cover.
6. If seal replacement is required, pry seal

from cover using a screw driver.
7. Position seal so open end faces toward inside of cover.
8. Drive seal into position using tool No. J-23042.

TIMING CHAIN, REPLACE

V6-196, 231 & V8-305

1. Remove timing chain cover.
2. Turn crankshaft so that sprockets are aligned as shown in Figs. 16 and 17.
3. Remove oil slinger.
4. On V6-196, 231, remove camshaft distributor drive gear and fuel pump eccentric, then using two large screwdrivers, alternately pry camshaft sprocket and crankshaft sprocket until camshaft is free. Remove camshaft sprocket and chain, then slide crankshaft sprocket off crankshaft.
5. On V8-305 remove three camshaft to sprocket bolts, then remove camshaft sprocket and timing chain together. Sprocket is a light press fit on camshaft, if sprocket does not come off easily, a light blow with a plastic hammer should dislodge it. If crankshaft sprocket is to be replaced, remove it with a suitable puller.
6. To install, assemble chain on sprockets with timing marks aligned as shown in Figs. 16 and 17.
7. Complete installation in reverse order of removal.

TIMING GEARS

4-151 Engine

When necessary to install a new camshaft gear, the camshaft will have to be removed as the gear is a pressed fit on the camshaft. The camshaft is held in place by a thrust plate which is retained to the engine by two capscrews which are accessible through the two holes in the gear web.

To remove gear, use an arbor press and a suitable sleeve to properly support gear on its steel hub.

Before installing gear, assemble thrust plate and gear spacer ring, then press gear onto shaft until it bottoms against spacer ring. The thrust plate end clearance should be .0015–.0050 inch. If clearance is less than .0015 inch, the spacer ring should be replaced. If clearance is greater than .0050 inch, the thrust plate should be replaced.

The crankshaft gear can be removed using a puller and two bolts in the tapped holes of the gear.

When installing timing gears, make sure that the marks on the gears are properly aligned, Fig. 18

NOTE: The valve timing marks, Fig. 18, does not indicate TDC, compression stroke for No. 1 cylinder for use during distributor installation. When installing the distributor, rotate engine until No. 1 cylinder is on compression stroke and the camshaft timing mark is 180° from the valve timing position shown in Fig. 18.

CAMSHAFT, REPLACE

4-140

1. Remove hood.
2. Remove camshaft timing sprocket.
3. Remove timing belt upper cover and cam retainer and seal assembly.
4. Remove camshaft cover.
5. Disconnect fuel line at carburetor and remove idle solenoid from bracket.
6. Remove carburetor choke coil, cover and rod assembly.
7. Remove distributor.
8. Raise vehicle on a hoist, disconnect engine front mounts at body attachment, raise front of engine and install wood blocks, about 1½" thick, between engine mounts and body. Lower vehicle.
9. Install camshaft removal tool as shown in Fig. 19, to cylinder head as follows:
   a. Position tool to cylinder head so attaching holes align with cam cover lower attaching holes.
   b. Align tappet depressing levers on tool so each lever will depress both intake and exhaust valve for their respective cylinder. Lever should fit squarely in notches adjacent to valve tappets.
   c. With tool aligned, make sure screws in bottom of tool are backed off so they do not make contact with bosses beneath tool.
   d. Install hardened screws supplied with tool, to attach tool to head. Torque screws securely.
   e. Turn screws in bottom of tool downward until they just seat against corresponding bosses on head.
   f. Apply a heavy body lubricant to ball end of lever depressing screws and proceed to tighten screws to depress

Fig. 19 Camshaft removal tool installed. 4-140

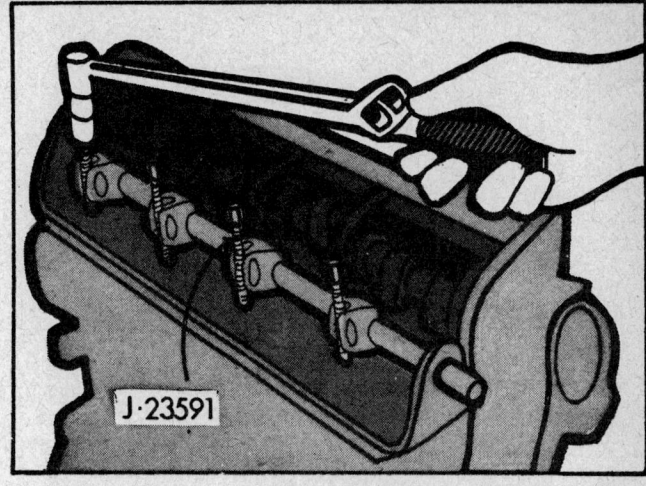

Fig. 20 Depressing valve tappets. 4-140

tappets, Fig. 20.

NOTE: Use a torque wrench to tighten screws the final few turns. About 10 ft. lbs. is required to depress tappets.

10. At this point the camshaft can be removed by sliding it forward from the head.

4-151

1979–80 Cross Flow Engine
1. Disconnect battery ground cable, then drain crankcase and cooling system.
2. Remove radiator, fan, water pump pulley and grille assembly.
3. Remove rocker arm cover, then loosen, remove rocker arm stud nuts and pivot rocker arms so that push rod can be removed.
4. Remove push rod cover, then remove push rods and valve lifters.
5. Remove oil pump driveshaft and gear assembly.
6. Remove front pulley hub and timing gear cover, then remove spark plugs.
7. Remove two camshaft thrust plate screws through holes in camshaft gear.
8. Pull camshaft and gear assembly from block. Use care not to damage camshaft bearings.

1977–80 Except Cross Flow Engine
1. Disconnect battery ground cable.
2. Drain oil pan and cooling system.
3. Remove fan, water pump pulley, radiator and the grille.
4. Remove distributor, fuel pump and spark plugs.
5. Remove valve train components.
6. Remove engine front cover.
7. Remove two camshaft thrust plate screws.
8. Remove camshaft and gear assembly from engine. Use care not to damage camshaft bearing surfaces.

V6-196, 231 & V8-305

NOTE: If engine is in the car, the radiator, grille and A/C components will have to be removed. If engine is out of car, proceed as follows:

1. To remove camshaft, remove rocker arm assemblies, push rods and valve lifters.
2. Remove timing chain and sprockets.
3. On V8-305 engines install two ⁵⁄₁₆″ (18×4″) bolts in camshaft bolt holes.
4. On all engines, slide camshaft out of engine using care not to damage the bearing surfaces.

TIMING BELT, REPLACE

4-140

1. Remove engine front cover as previously described.

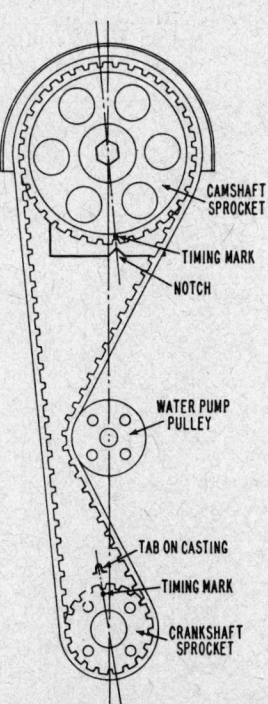

Fig. 21 Sprocket alignment marks. 4-140

2. Remove accessory drive pulley or damper.
3. Drain coolant and loosen water pump bolts to relieve tension on belt.
4. Remove timing belt lower cover, then remove belt from sprockets.

CAMSHAFT SPROCKET, REPLACE

4-140

After removal of timing belt, the camshaft sprocket can be removed as follows:
1. Align one hole in sprocket with bolt head behind sprocket, then using a socket on bolt head to prevent cam from turning, remove sprocket retaining bolt and withdraw sprocket from camshaft.
2. When installing, be sure timing marks are aligned as in Fig. 21.

NOTE: A simplified method is provided for checking camshaft and crankshaft alignment. Proper alignment is assured by making sure hole in left rear of the timing belt upper cover is in line with the corresponding hole in the camshaft sprocket. Check alignment by inserting a pencil or other similar tool through hole in cover. If alignment is correct, the tool will enter small hole in cam gear, Fig. 22.

CRANKSHAFT SPROCKET, REPLACE

4-140

1. Remove engine front cover, accessory drive pulley, timing belt and timing belt lower cover.
2. Install suitable puller to crankshaft sprocket and remove sprocket.

OIL PUMP (CRANKCASE FRONT COVER) SEAL, REPLACE

4-140

1. Remove engine front cover, accessory

Fig. 22   Checking sprocket alignment. 4-140

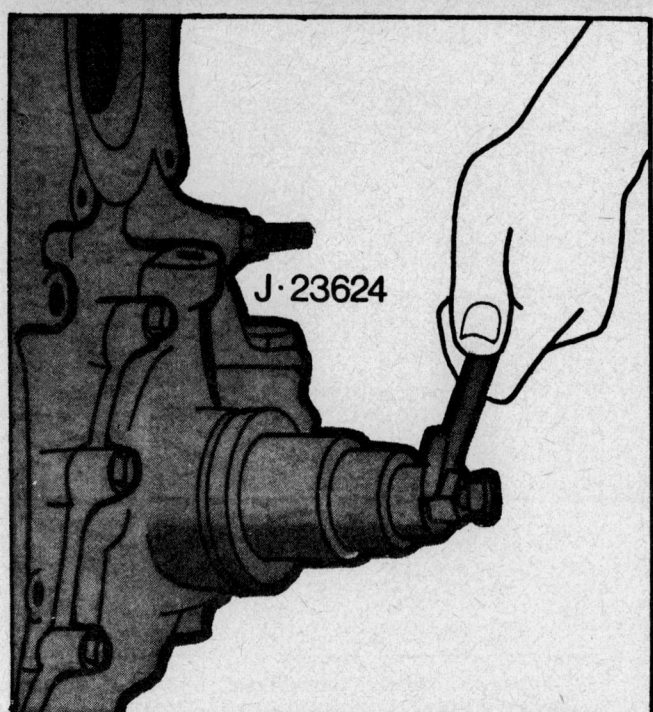

J·23624

Fig. 23   Installing crankcase front oil seal. 4-140

drive pulley, timing belt and timing belt lower cover and crankshaft sprocket.
2. Pry old seal from front cover being careful not to damage seal housing or seal lip contact surfaces.
3. Coat seal with light engine oil and apply an approved sealing compound to outside diameter of seal.
4. Position seal, closed end outward, onto crankshaft. Then install seal into bore using tool J-23624, Fig. 23.

PISTONS & RODS, ASSEMBLE

When installing connecting rod to crankshaft check side clearance. On all engines except V8-305 side clearance should be between .006–.022 inch, on V8-305 clearance should be between .006–.017 inch.

4-140

The "F" on the front of the piston must face the front of the engine when the piston and rod assembly is installed in its proper cylinder, Fig. 24.

4-151

Assemble piston to rod with the notch on piston facing toward front of engine and the raised notch side of rod at bearing end facing toward rear of engine, Fig. 25.

V6-196, 231 & V8-305

Rods and pistons should be assembled and installed as shown in Figs. 26 and 27.

PISTONS, PINS & RINGS

4-140

Pistons and rings are avilable in standard sizes and oversizes of .010, .020 and .030 inch.

4-151

Pistons and rings are available in standard

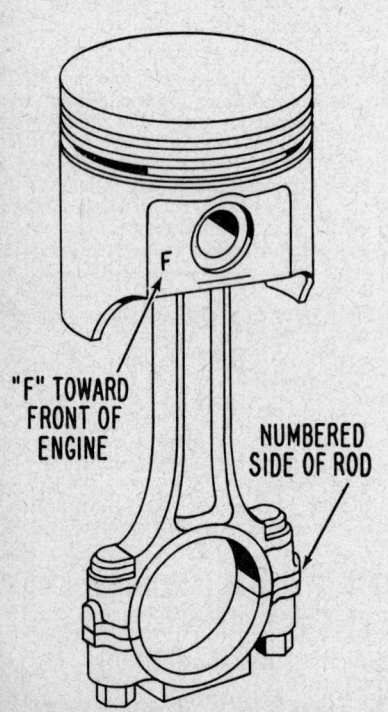

"F" TOWARD FRONT OF ENGINE

NUMBERED SIDE OF ROD

Fig. 24   Piston and rod assembly. 4-140

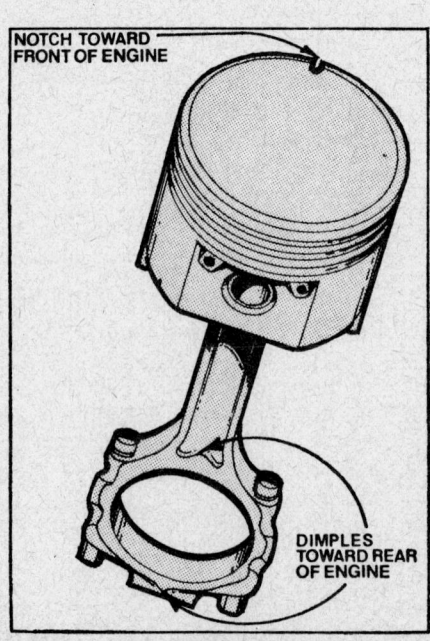

NOTCH TOWARD FRONT OF ENGINE

DIMPLES TOWARD REAR OF ENGINE

Fig. 25   Piston and rod assembly. 4-151

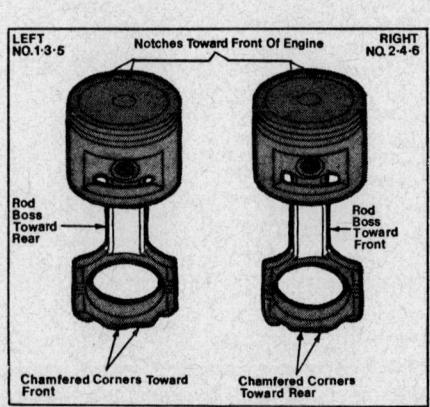

LEFT NO. 1·3·5   Notches Toward Front Of Engine   RIGHT NO. 2·4·6

Rod Boss Toward Rear

Rod Boss Toward Front

Chamfered Corners Toward Front

Chamfered Corners Toward Rear

Fig. 26   Piston and rod assembly. V6-196, 231

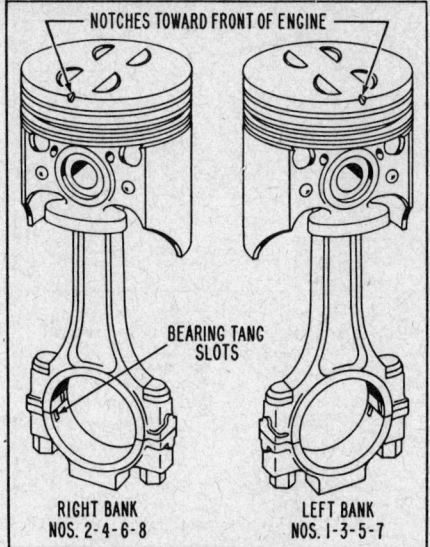

Fig. 27 Piston and rod assembly. V8-305

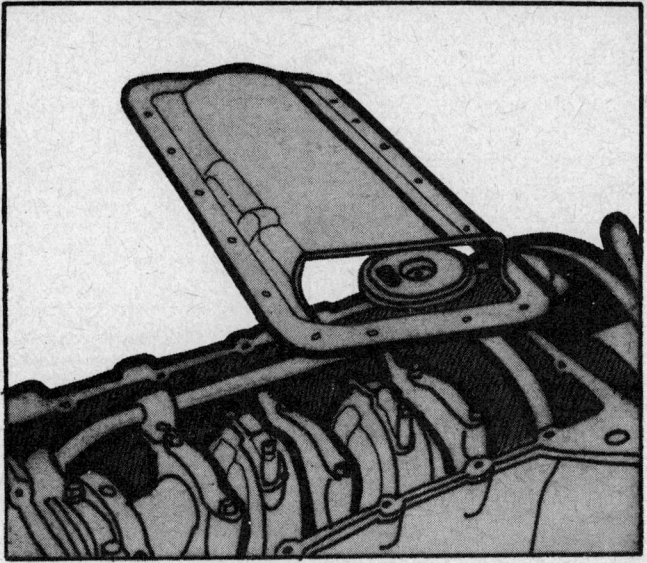

Fig. 28 Removing oil pan baffle. 4-140

sizes and oversizes of .010 and .030 inch. Piston pins are avilable in oversizes of .001 and .003 inch.

V6-196, 231 & V8-305

Pistons are available in standard sizes and oversizes of .001, .005, .010, .020 and .030 inch for the V6-196, 231 & .001, .020 and .030 for the V8-305.

Rings are furnished in standard sizes and oversizes of .010, .020 and .030 inch for the V6-196, 231 and .020 and .030 for the V8-305.

Piston pins are furnished in standard sizes and oversizes of .003 and .005 inch for the V6-196, 231.

MAIN & ROD BEARINGS

Main and rod bearings are available in standard sizes and undersizes of .001, .002, .020 and .030 inch for the 4-140, .001, .002 and .010 inch for the 4-151, .001, .002, .003 and .010 inch for the V6-196, 231 and .001, .002, .009, .010 and .020 inch for the V8-305.

NOTE: If for any reason the bearing caps are replaced on the 4-140, shimming may be necessary. Laminated shims for each cap are available for service. Shim requirements will be determined by bearing clearance.

OIL PAN, REPLACE

4-140

1. Raise vehicle on a hoist and drain engine oil.
2. Support front of engine so weight is off front mounts, and remove frame crossmember and both front crossmember braces.
3. Disconnect idler arm at frame side rail.

NOTE: On air conditioned vehicles, disconnect idler arm at relay rod.

4. Mark relationship of steering linkage pitman arm to steering gear pitman shaft and remove pitman arm.

NOTE: Do not rotate steering gear pitman shaft while arm is disconnected as this will change steering wheel alignment.

5. Remove flywheel cover or converter underpan.
6. Remove oil pan to cylinder case screws, tap pan lightly to brake sealing bond and remove oil pan.
7. Remove pick up screen to baffle support bolts, then remove support from baffle.
8. Remove bolt securing oil pan drain back tube to baffle. Then rotate baffle 90 degrees towards left side of car and remove baffle from pick up screen, Fig. 28.

4-151

1. Disconnect battery ground cable.
2. Raise vehicle and drain oil pan.
3. Remove rear section of frame crossmember.
4. Disconnect exhaust pipe from manifold and loosen hanger bracket.
5. Remove starter and position aside.
6. Remove flywheel housing inspection cover.
7. Disconnect steering linkage at steering gear and idler arm support.
8. Remove oil pan bolts and the oil pan.

V6-196, 231

1. Support vehicle on hoist and drain oil.
2. Remove transmission dust cover and exhaust crossover pipe.
3. Remove oil pan bolts and allow pan to drop.
4. Reverse removal procedure to install.

V8-305

1. Disconnect battery ground cable.
2. Raise vehicle, drain oil pan and discon-

nect crossover pipe.
3. Remove underpan and splash shield from converter housing.
4. On 1976 models, support engine, then remove crossmember and braces.

NOTE: Scribe reference marks on each side of brace to ensure crossmember installation in original position.

5. On 1976 models, disconnect idler arm at frame side rail.
6. On all models, remove starter, then the oil pan.

OIL PUMP, REPLACE

4-140

1. Remove engine front cover, accessory drive pulley, timing belt, timing belt lower cover and crankshaft sprocket.
2. Raise vehicle on a hoist and remove oil pan and baffle.
3. Remove bolts and stud securing oil pump to cylinder case.

Inspection

1. Clean gasket surfaces, then wash parts in approved solvent and blow out all passages.
2. Check pressure regulator for free operation, Fig. 29.
3. Inspect pump gears for nicks, broken parts and other damage.
4. Check clearance between outside diameter, of driven gear and pump. Clearance should be .0038–.0068″, Fig. 30.
5. Check clearance between outside diameter of drive gear and crescent. Clearance should be .0023–.0093″, Fig. 31.
6. Check clearance between inside diameter of driven gear and pump crescent. Clearance should be .0068–.0148″, Fig. 32.
7. Check gear end clearance. It should be .0009–.0023″, Fig. 33.

NOTE: The pump gears and body are not serviced separately. If pump gears or body are worn, replacement of the entire oil pump is necessary.

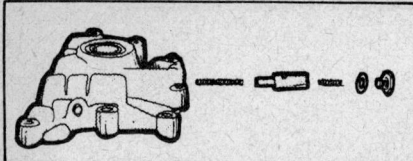

Fig. 29   Oil pump pressure regulator. 4-140

Fig. 32   Checking driven gear to crescent clearance. 4-140

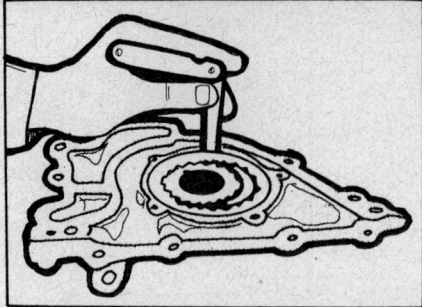

Fig. 30   Checking driven gear to housing clearance. 4-140

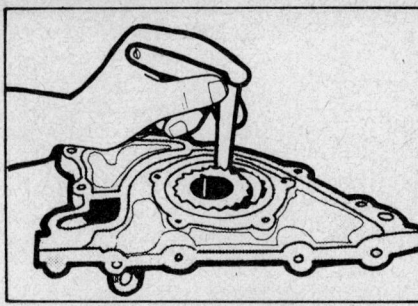

Fig. 31   Checking drive gear to crescent clearance. 4-140

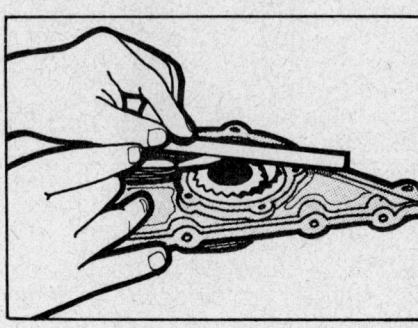

Fig. 33   Checking gear end clearance. 4-140

4-151

1. Remove oil pan as outlined previously.
2. Remove two flange mounting bolts and nut from main bearing cap bolt, then the oil pump and screen assembly.
3. Should any of the following conditions be found, it is advisable to replace the pump assembly:
   a. Inspect pump body for cracks or wear.
   b. Inspect gears for wear or damage.
   c. Check shaft for looseness in housing.
   d. Check inside of cover for wear that would permit oil to leak past ends of gear.
   e. Check oil pick-up screen for damage.
   f. Check pressure regulator valve plunger for proper fit in body.

V6-196, 231

1. To remove pump, take off oil filter.
2. Disconnect wire from oil pressure indicator switch in filter by-pass valve cap (if so equipped).
3. Remove screws attaching oil pump cover to timing chain cover. Remove cover and slide out pump gears. Replace any parts not serviceable.
4. Remove oil pressure relief valve cap, spring and valve, Fig. 34. Remove oil filter by-pass valve cap, spring and valve. Replace any parts of valve not serviceable.
5. Check relief valve in its bore in cover. Valve should have no more clearance than an easy slip fit. If any perceptible side shake can be felt, the valve and/or cover should be replaced.
6. The filter by-pass valve should be flat and free of nicks and scratches.

Assembly & Installation

1. Lubricate and install pressure relief valve and spring in bore of pump cover. Install cap and gasket. Torque cap to 30–35 lbs.
2. Install filter by-pass valve flat in its seat in cover. Install spring, cap and gasket. Torque cap to 30–35 ft-lbs.
3. Install pump gears and shaft in pump body section of timing chain cover to check gear end clearance. Check clearance as shown in Fig. 35. If clearance is less than .0018″ check timing chain cover for evidence of wear.
4. If gear end clearance is satisfactory, remove gears and pack gear pocket *full* of vaseline, not Chassis lube.
5. Reinstall gears so vaseline is forced into every cavity of gear pocket and between teeth of gears. *Unless pump is packed with vaseline, it may not prime itself when engine is started.*
6. Install cover and tighten screws alternately and evenly. Final tightening is 10–15 ft-lbs. torque. Install filter on nipple.

V8-305

After removing the oil pan, remove pump from rear main bearing cap. Disconnect pump

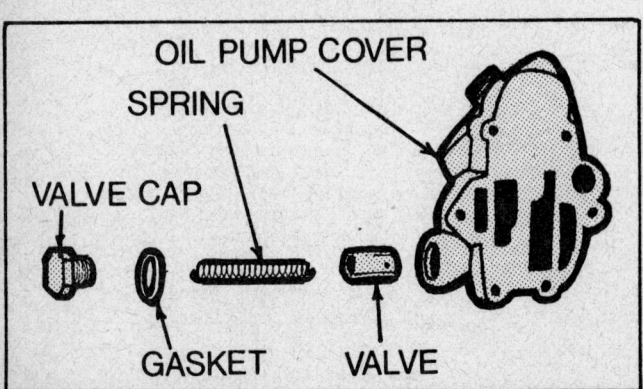

Fig. 34   Oil pump cover and pressure relief valve. V6-196, 231

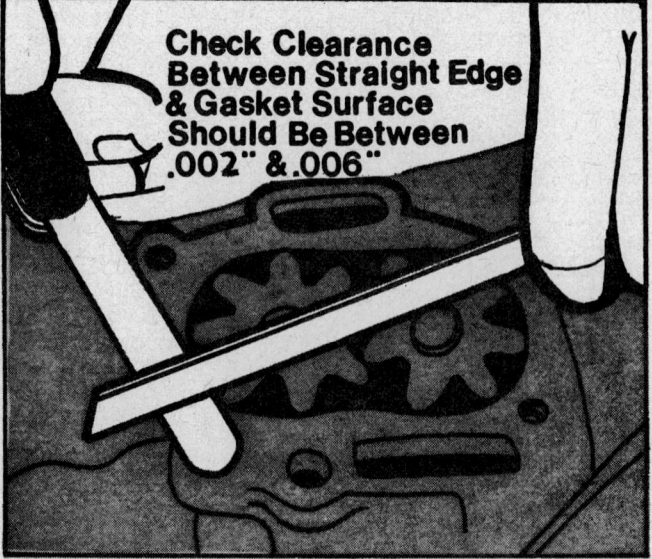

Check Clearance Between Straight Edge & Gasket Surface Should Be Between .002″ & .006″

Fig. 35   Checking oil pump gear end clearance. V6-196, 231

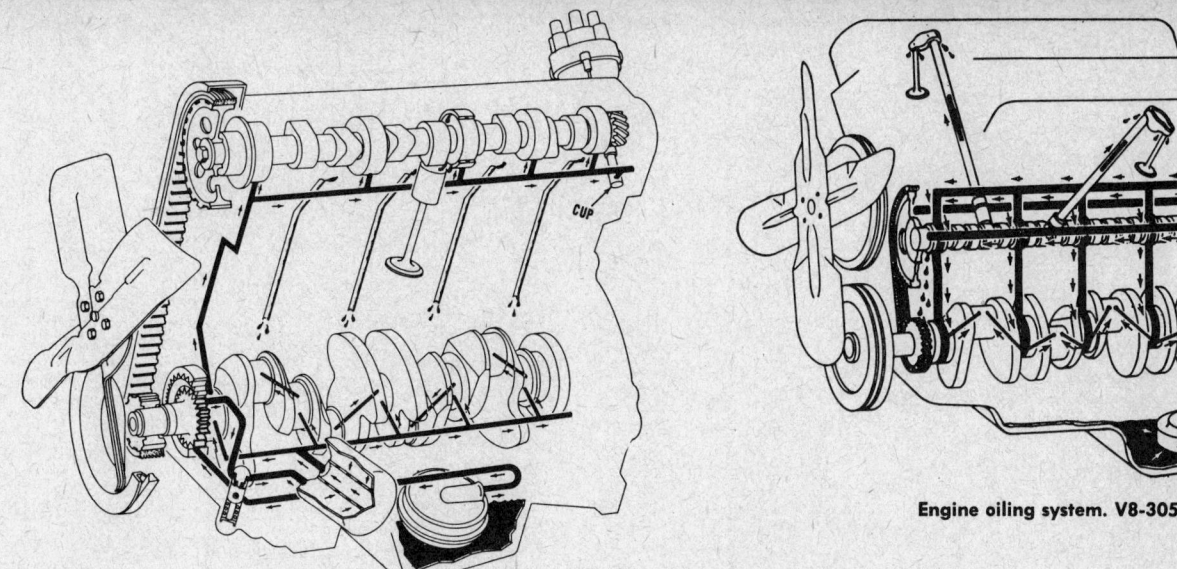

Engine oiling system. 4-140

Engine oiling system. V8-305

shaft from extension by removing clip from collar. Remove pump cover and take out idler gear, drive gear and shaft.

Should any of the following conditions be found it is advisable to replace the pump assembly.

1. Inspect pump body for cracks or wear.
2. Inspect gears for wear or damage.
3. Check shaft for looseness in housing.
4. Check inside of cover for wear that would permit oil to leak past the ends of gear.
5. Check oil pick-up screen for damage to screen, by-pass valve or body.
6. Check for oil in air chamber.

CRANKSHAFT REAR OIL SEAL, REPLACE

When necessary to correct an oil leak due to a defective seal, always replace the upper and lower halves as a unit. *When installing either half, lubricate the lip portion only with engine oil, keeping oil off the parting line surface as this is treated with glue.* Always clean crankshaft surface before installing a new seal. Be careful of seal retainer tang while inserting a new seal so that it doesn't cut the seal.

4-151

1979–80 Cross Flow Engine

The rear main bearing oil seal is a one piece unit and is replaced without removing the oil pan or crankshaft.

1. Remove transmission, flywheel housing and flywheel.
2. Using a suitable screwdriver, remove rear main bearing oil seal. Use care not to scratch crankshaft.
3. Lubricate inside and outside diameters of replacement seal with engine oil. Install seal by hand onto rear crankshaft flange with helical lip side facing toward engine. Ensure seal is firmly and evenly seated.
4. Install flywheel, flywheel housing and transmission.

1977–80 Except Cross Flow Engine

The rear main bearing oil seal can be

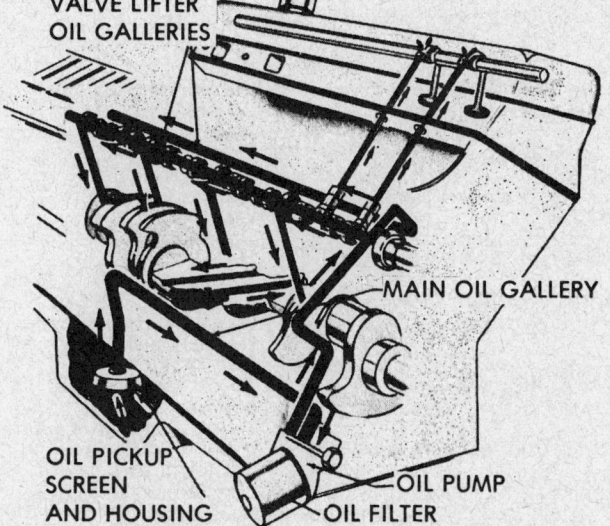

Engine oiling system (typical). V6-196, 231

replaced without removing the crankshaft.

1. Remove oil pan and rear main bearing cap.
2. To replace the lower seal, remove seal from groove in bearing cap, using a small screwdriver to pry it out.
3. Insert new seal and roll it in place with finger and thumb.

Fig. 36   Fabricated seal starting tool for helix type seal. V8-305

4. To replace the upper seal (with engine in car) use a small hammer and tap a brass pin punch on one end of the seal until it protrudes far enough to be removed with pliers.
5. Insert the new seal, gradually pushing with a hammer handle until seal is rolled into place.
6. Install bearing cap with new seal and tighten bearing cap bolts.

V8-305

NOTE: V8-305 engines are equipped with helix type rear seal. A seal starting tool, Fig. 36, must be used to prevent the upper seal half from coming into contact with the sharp edge of the block. Place the tip of the tool into the seal channel and "shoehorn" the seal into the upper seal channel.

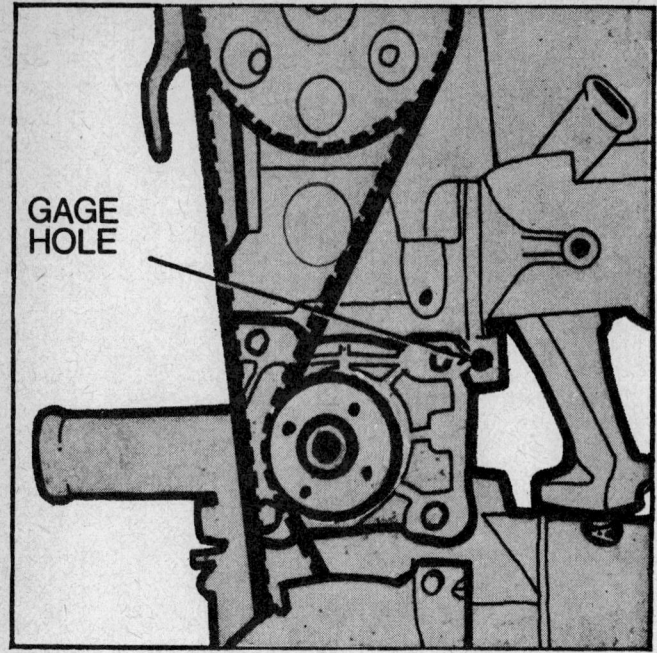

GAGE HOLE

Fig. 37   Tensioning adaptor locating hole

J-23654

Fig. 38   Adjusting timing belt

1. To replace the lower seal, remove seal from groove in bearing cap, using a small screwdriver to pry it out.
2. Insert new seal and roll it in place with finger and thumb.
3. To replace the upper seal (with engine in car) use a small hammer and tap a brass pin punch on one end of the seal until it protrudes far enough to be removed with pliers.
4. Position tip of tool, Fig. 36, between crankshaft and seal seat in cylinder block.
5. Position seal between crankshaft and tip of tool with seal bead contacting tip of tool. Ensure oil seal lip is facing toward front of engine.
6. Roll seal around crankshaft, using tool as a "Shoehorn" to protect seal bead from sharp corner of seal seat surface in cylinder block.

NOTE: Tool must remain in position until seal is properly seated with both ends flush with block.

7. Remove tool, using care not to dislodge seal.
8. Install new seal into bearing cap with tool as outlined previously.
9. Install bearing cap with sealant applied to the cap to case interface. Do not apply sealant to seal ends. Torque rear main bearing cap bolts to specifications as listed in the "Engine Tightening Specification Chart".

CRANKSHAFT REAR OIL SEAL, REPAIR

V6-196, 231

Since the braided fabric seal used on these engines can be replaced only when the crank-shaft is removed, the following repair procedure is recommended.

1. Remove oil pan and bearing cap.
2. Drive end of old seal gently into groove, using a suitable tool, until packed tight. This may vary between 1/4 and 3/4 inch depending on amount of pack required.
3. Repeat previous step for other end of seal.
4. Measure and note amount that seal was driven up on one side. Using the old seal removed from bearing cap, cut a length of seal the amount previously noted plus 1/16 inch.
5. Repeat previous step for other side of seal.
6. Pack cut lengths of seal into appropriate side of seal groove. A guide tool, J-21526-1, and packing tool, J-21526-2, may be used since these tools have been machined to provide a built-in stop.
7. Install new seal in bearing cap.

TIMING BELT TENSION, ADJUST

4-140

1. Drain coolant at engine block and remove fan and extension.
2. Remove engine front cover.
3. Remove water pump retaining bolts, clean gasket surfaces on block and pump. Install new gasket and loosely install water pump bolts.

NOTE: Apply an approved anti-seize compound to the water pump bolts before installation.

4. Position tool J-23564 in gauge hole adjacent to left side of pump, Fig. 37.
5. Apply 15 ft. lbs. of torque to water pump as shown in Fig. 38. Tighten water pump bolts while maintaining torque on side of pump.
6. Reinstall front cover, fan, extension and fill cooling system.

BELT TENSION DATA

	New lbs.	Used lbs.
Alternator		
4-140	120–130	75
4-151		
1977	110–140	70
1978–79	120–130	75
1980		
5/16 in.	80	50
3/8 in. exc. cogged belt	140	70
3/8 in. cogged belt	—	60
15/32 in.	165	90
V6-196, 231		
1977–78	120–140	75
1979	146	67
1980		
5/16 in.	80	50
3/8 in. exc. cogged belt	140	70
3/8 in. cogged belt	—	60
15/32 in.	165	90
V8-305	120–130	75
Air Conditioning		
4-140	135–145	95
4-151		
1977	110–140	70
1978–79	120–130	75
1980		
5/16 in.	80	50
3/8 in. exc. cogged belt	140	70
3/8 in. cogged belt	—	60
15/32 in.	165	90
V6-196, 231		
1977–78	145–165	90
1979	168	90
1980		
5/16 in.	80	50
3/8 in. exc. cogged belt	140	70

	New lbs.	Used lbs.
Alternator		
3/8 in. cogged belt	—	60
15/32 in.	165	90
V8-305	135–145	95
Air Pump		
4-140	120–130	75
V6-196, 231		
1977–78	60–80	60
1979	79	45
1980		
5/16 in.	80	50
3/8 in. exc. cogged belt	140	70
3/8 in. cogged belt	—	60
15/32 in.	165	90
V8-305	120–130	75
Power Steering		
4-140	120–130	75
4-151		
1977	110–140	70
1978–79	120–130	75
1980		
5/16 in.	80	50
3/8 in. exc. cogged belt	140	70
3/8 in. cogged belt	—	60
15/32 in.	165	90
V6-196, 231		
1977–78	145–165	90
1979	168	90
1980		
5/16 in.	80	50
3/8 in. exc. cogged belt	140	70
3/8 in. cogged belt	—	60
15/32 in.	165	90
V8-305	120–130	75
Timing belt		
4-140	100–140	

WATER PUMP, REPLACE

4-140

1. Raise hood to fully open position and install hold-open bolt.
2. Disconnect battery ground cable at battery.
3. Remove engine fan and spacer.
4. Loosen, but do not remove, the two cover lower screws. Cover is slotted to permit easy removal.
5. Remove the two cover upper retaining screws and remove cover.
6. Drain coolant and loosen water pump bolts to relieve tension in timing belt.

Fig. 39 Removing fuel pump and gauge unit

7. Remove radiator lower hose and heater hose at water pump.
8. Remove water pump bolts and water pump.

4-151, V6-196, 231 & V8-305

1. Drain cooling system and loosen fan pulley bolts.
2. On V8-262, 305 engines, remove alternator and A.I.R. pump, if necessary.
3. On all engines, disconnect radiator and heater hoses from water pump.
4. Remove fan and pulley, then remove water pump.

FUEL PUMP, REPLACE

4-151

NOTE: Before installing the pump, it is good practice to crank the engine so that the nose of the camshaft eccentric is out of the way of the fuel pump rocker arm when the pump is installed. In this way there will be the least amount of tension on the rocker arm, thereby easing the installation of the pump.

1. Disconnect fuel line from pump.
2. Remove pump attaching bolts and pump.
3. Remove all gasket material from the pump and block gasket surfaces. Apply sealer to both sides of new gasket.
4. Position gasket on pump flange and hold pump in position against its mounting surface. Make sure rocker arm is riding on camshaft eccentric.
5. Press pump tight against its mounting. Install retaining screws and tighten them alternately.
6. Connect fuel lines. Then operate engine and check for leaks.

Except 4-151

Removal
1. Disconnect battery ground cable.
2. Disconnect meter and pump wires at rear wiring harness connector.
3. Raise vehicle on hoist and drain fuel tank.
4. Disconnect fuel line hose at gauge unit pick up line.
5. Disconnect tank vent lines to vapor separator.
6. Remove gauge ground wire screw at underbody floorpan.
7. Remove tank straps bolts and lower tank carefully.
8. Unscrew retaining ring using spanner wrench J-22554, Fig. 39, and remove pump-tank unit assembly.

Installation
1. Remove flat wire conductor from plastic lip on fuel tube.
2. Squeeze clamp and pull pump straight back about 1/2 inch.
3. Remove two nuts and lockwasher and conductor wires from pump terminals.
4. Squeeze clamp and pull pump straight back to remove it from tank unit. Take care to prevent bending of circular support bracket.
5. Slide replacement pump through circular support bracket until it rests against rubber coupling. Make sure pump has rubber isolator and saran strainer attached.
6. Attach two conductor wires to pump terminals using lockwashers and nuts being certain flat conductor is attached to terminal located on side away from float arm.
7. Squeeze clamp and push pump into rubber coupling.
8. Replace flat wire conductor in plastic clip on fuel pick up tube.
9. Install unit into tank and replace fuel tank.

Clutch & Transmission Section

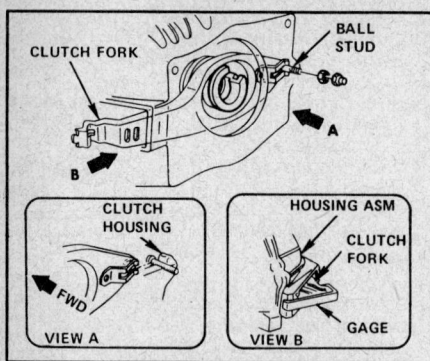

Fig. 1 Ball stud adjustment

CLUTCH PEDAL, ADJUST

Ball Stud Adjustment

1. Before attaching clutch cable, place gauge J-23644 with flat end against face of clutch housing and locate hooked end of gauge at point of cable attachment for fork, Fig. 1.
2. Turn ball stud inward until clutch release bearing contacts clutch spring fingers.
3. Install lock nut and torque to 25 ft. lbs., use care not to change ball stud adjustment.
4. Install ball stud cap, then remove gauge by pulling outward at housing end.

Clutch Cable Adjustment

NOTE: Ball stud adjustment must be correct before adjusting clutch cable.

1. With return spring disconnected, place cable through hole in clutch fork, Fig. 2.

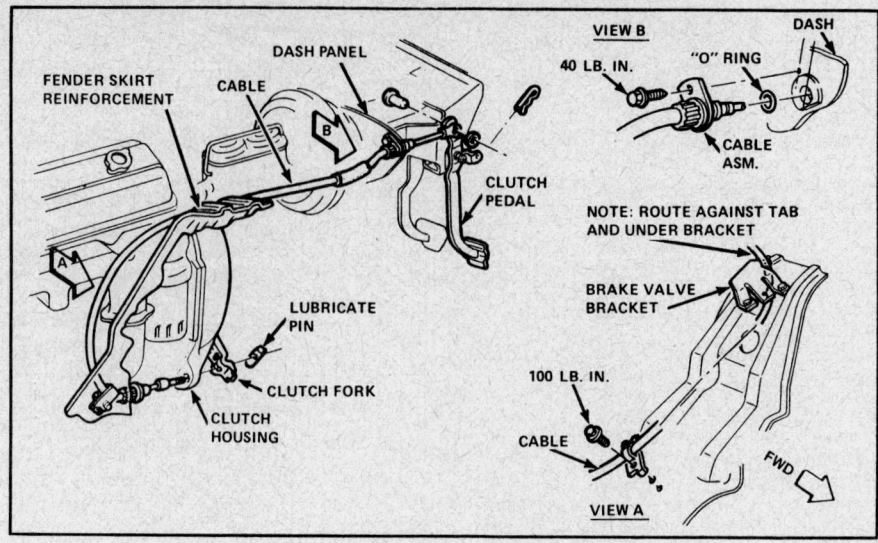

Fig. 2 Clutch cable adjustment

2. Pull cable until clutch pedal is firmly against clutch pedal stop.
3. Push clutch fork forward until release bearing contacts clutch spring fingers.
4. Tighten adjusting pin on cable until it contacts fork surface.
5. Rotate cable pin an additional 1/4 turn clockwise and position pin into groove on fork.
6. Attach return spring, then cycle clutch pedal approximately 3 times. Lash at clutch pedal should be .65 to 1.15 in. for 1978-80 Skyhawk, 1977-80 Monza and Sunbird, 5/8 to 1 1/8 in. for 1977 Skyhawk and 11/16 to 1 1/8 in. for 1977-80 Starfire.

CLUTCH, REPLACE

1. Remove transmission.
2. Remove clutch fork cover then disconnect clutch return spring and control cable from clutch fork.
3. Remove flywheel housing lower cover and flywheel housing.
4. Remove release bearing from the clutch fork and sleeve by sliding lever off ball stud and against spring pressure. If ball stud is to be replaced, remove cap, lock nut and stud from housing.
5. Make sure alignment marks on clutch assembly and flywheel are distinguishable.
6. Loosen clutch cover to flywheel bolts one turn at a time until spring pressure is released to avoid bending clutch cover flange, Fig. 3.
7. Support the pressure plate and cover assembly while removing bolts and clutch assembly.

NOTE: Do not disassemble the clutch cover, spring and pressure plate for repairs. If defective, replace complete assembly.

8. Reverse procedure to install making sure to index alignment marks.
9. After installing crossmember, loosely install retaining bolts, then the crossmember to transmission mount bolts. Tighten all bolts to specifications and remove the engine support.

CAUTION: Check position of engine in front mounts and realign as necessary.

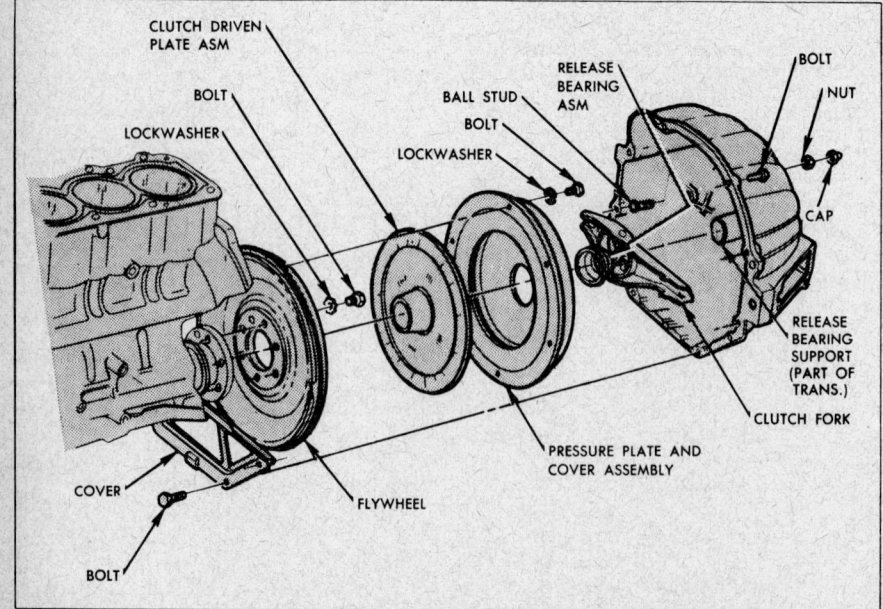

Fig. 3 Clutch & components (typical)

FOUR SPEED TRANSMISSION, REPLACE

1977–80

1. Raise vehicle on a hoist and drain lubricant.
2. Place shift lever in neutral, then disconnect transmission control rod and lever assemblies from shifter shafts. Tie rods up and out of way.
3. Remove propeller shaft and torque arm bracket.
4. Remove catalytic converter bracket from transmission and disconnect exhaust pipe and converter.
5. Disconnect speedometer cable, TCS switch and back-up lamp switch.
6. Remove crossmember to transmission mount bolts.
7. Support engine with an appropriate jack stand and remove crossmember to frame bolts and remove crossmember.
8. Remove transmission to clutch housing upper retaining bolts and install guide pins in holes.
9. Remove lower bolts, then slide transmission rearward and remove from vehicle.

NOTE: Inspect throwout bearing support gasket located beneath lip of support. If necessary, replace gasket before installing transmission.

LINKAGE, ADJUST

1977–80 4 Speed Except 70mm (Brazil)
1. Place ignition switch in off position.
2. Raise vehicle, then loosen lock nuts at swivels on shift rods, Fig. 4. Rods should pass freely through swivels.
3. Place transmission shift levers in neutral position.
4. Place shift control lever in neutral position, then align control levers and install gauge pin into levers and bracket.
5. Tighten 1st-2nd shift rod nut against swivel, then tighten 3rd-4th shift rod nut against swivel. Torque nuts to 120 in. lbs.
6. Torque reverse shift rod control nut to 120 in. lbs.
7. Remove gauge pin from shifter assembly and check linkage adjustment.

FIVE SPEED TRANS., REPLACE

1. Remove shifter assembly and raise vehicle.
2. Remove propeller shaft and torque arm bracket, then disconnect speedometer cable from transmission.
3. Remove crossmember to transmission bolts and the catalytic converter support bracket.
4. Support engine and remove crossmember.
5. Remove transmission to clutch housing upper retaining bolts and install guide pins.
6. Remove lower transmission to clutch housing bolts, slide transmission rearward and lower from vehicle.
7. Remove back-up lamp switch and fill plug, then drain transmission.

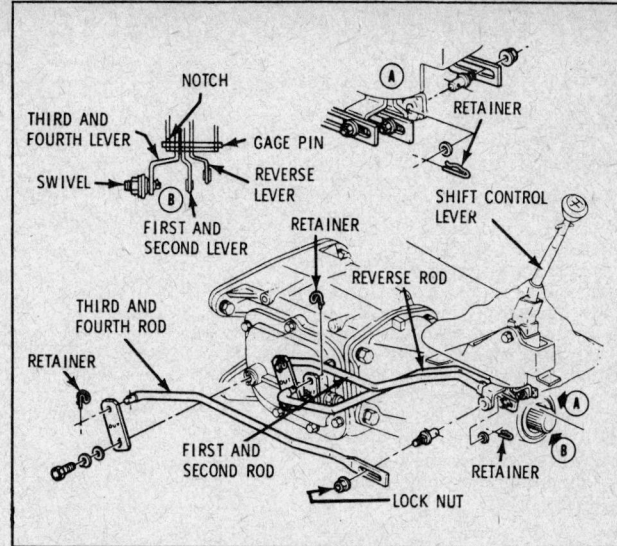

Fig. 4   Shift linkage adjustment. 4 speed transmission

Rear Axle, Propeller Shaft & Brakes

REAR AXLE

Description

The rear axle, Fig. 1, is a semi-floating type consisting of a cast carrier and large bosses on each end into which two welded steel tubes are fitted. The carrier contains an overhung hypoid pinion and ring gear. The differential is a two pinion arrangement.

The overhung hypoid drive pinion is supported by two preloaded tapered roller bearings. The pinion shaft is sealed by means of a molded, spring loaded, rubber seal. The seal is mounted on the pinion shaft flange which is splined and bolts to the hypoid pinion shaft.

The ring gear is bolted to a one piece differential case and is supported by two preloaded tapered roller bearings.

Removal

1. Support vehicle at frame and using a suitable jack support axle housing.
2. Remove wheels, brake drums and axle shafts.
3. Disconnect brake lines from axle tube clips and remove bolt securing brake line junction block to rear axle housing.

NOTE: Do not disconnect brake lines from wheel cylinders or junction block.

4. Remove brake backing plates and secure backing plates to frame.
5. Remove parking brake cable adjusting nuts at equalizer, pull center cable rearward and disconnect two rear cables from body connectors.
6. Disconnect rear brake hose at floor pan and cap ends of hose and line.
7. Disconnect shock absorber from rear axle.
8. Disconnect track rod, then slowly lower axle until all spring tension is relieved and pry springs from axle housing pads.
9. Disconnect propeller shaft and torque arm and position aside.

NOTE: Support axle at companion flange to prevent housing from rotating.

10. Remove lower control arm attaching bolts from axle housing.
11. Remove support at companion flange, then the axle assembly.

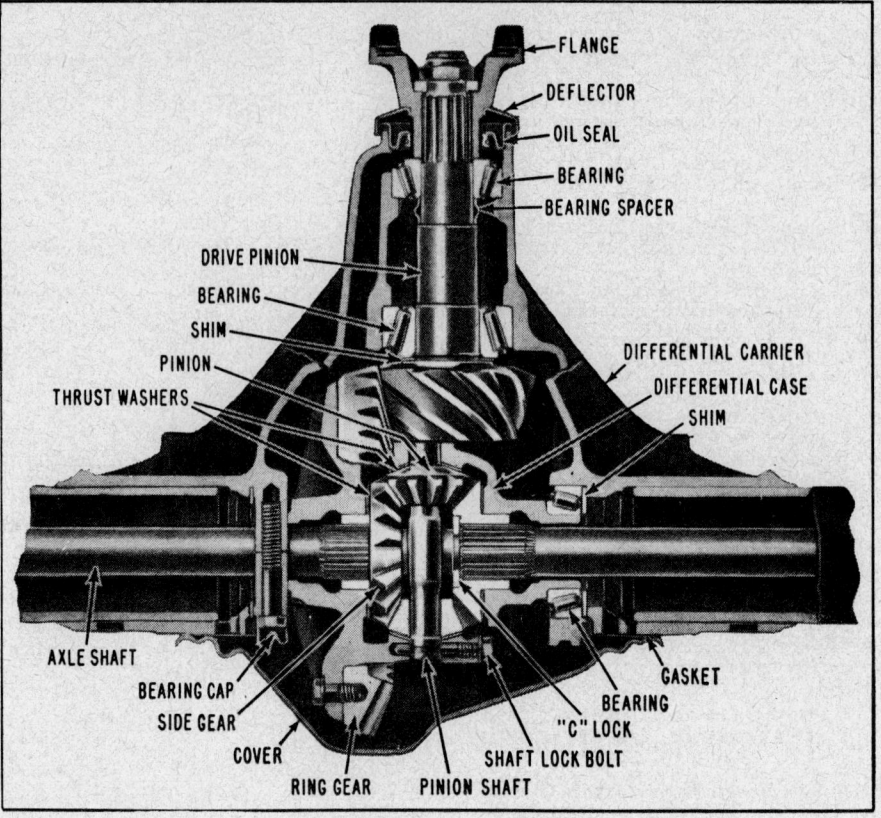

Fig. 1   Rear axle cross section

AXLE SHAFT, REPLACE

1. Raise vehicle on a hoist and remove wheel and tire assembly and brake drum.
2. Drain lubricant from axle by removing carrier cover.
3. Unscrew pinion shaft lock screw and remove pinion shaft, Fig. 2.
4. Push flanged end of axle shaft toward center of car and remove "C" lock from button end of shaft.
5. Remove axle shaft from housing being careful not to damage seal.

Oil Seal &/ or Bearing Replacement

1. If replacing seal only, remove the seal by using the button end of axle shaft. Insert the button end of shaft behind the steel case of the seal and pry seal out of bore being careful not to damage housing.
2. If replacing bearings, insert tool J-22813 into bore so tool head grasps behind bearing, Fig. 3. Slide washer against seal, or bearing, and turn nut against washer. Attach slide hammer J-2619 and remove bearing.
3. Pack cavity between seal lips with a high melting point wheel bearing lubricant. Position seal on tool J-21491 and position seal in axle housing bore, tap seal in bore just below end of housing, Fig. 4.

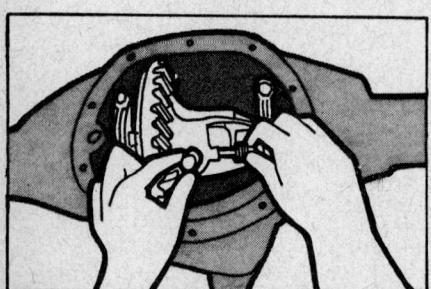

Fig. 2   Differential pinion shaft removal

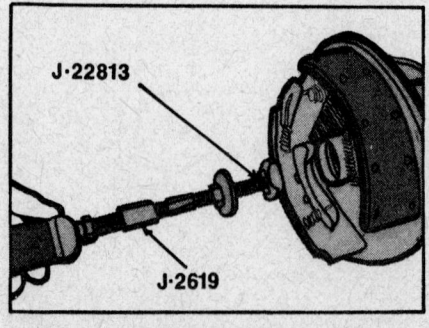

Fig. 3   Removing wheel bearing and seal

Fig. 4   Installing seal and wheel bearing

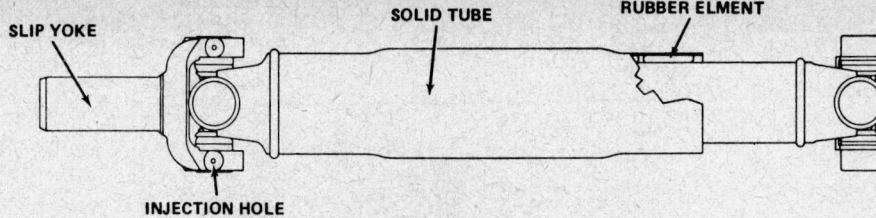

Fig. 5 Propeller shaft cross section (typical)

PROPELLER SHAFT

The propeller shaft used is made up of concentric steel tubes with rubber elements between, Fig. 5.

Propeller Shaft, Replace

1. Raise vehicle on a hoist.
2. Disconnect torque arm at rear axle, then referring to the "Rear Suspension" section, loosen attaching bolt at transmission and swing torque arm away from shaft. Mark relationship of shaft to companion flange and disconnect the rear universal joint by removing trunnion bearing "U" bolts. Tape bearing cups to trunnion to prevent dropping and loss of bearing rollers.
3. Withdraw propeller shaft front yoke from transmission.
4. When installing, be sure to align marks made in removal to prevent driveline vibration.

BRAKE ADJUSTMENTS

These rear wheel brakes, have self-adjusting shoe mechanisms that assure correct lining-to-drum clearances at all times. The automatic adjusters operate only when the brakes are applied as the car is moving rearward.

Although the brakes are self-adjusting, an initial adjustment is necessary after the brake shoes have been relined or replaced, or when the length of the adjusting screw has been changed during some other service operation.

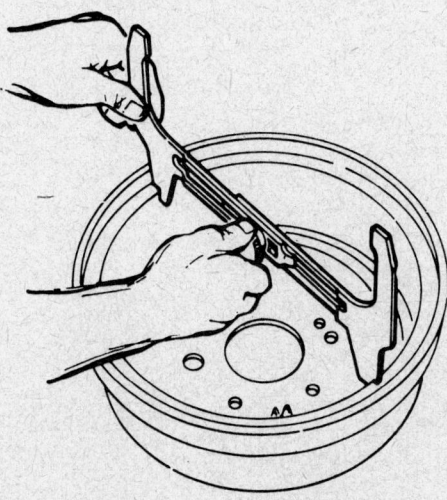

Fig. 6 Measuring brake drum inner diameter

Frequent usage of an automatic transmission forward range to halt reverse vehicle motion may prevent the automatic adjusters from functioning, thereby inducing low pedal heights. Should low pedal heights be encountered, it is recommended that numerous forward and reverse stops be made until satisfactory pedal height is obtained.

NOTE: If a low pedal condition cannot be corrected by making numerous reverse stops (provided the hydraulic system is free of air) it indicates that the self-adjusting mechanism is not functioning. Therefore it will be necessary to remove the brake drum, clean, free up and lubricate the adjusting mechanism. Then adjust the brakes, being sure the parking brake is fully released.

Adjustment

A lanced "knock out" area is provided in the web of the brake drum for servicing purposes in the event retracting of the brake shoes is required in order to remove the drum.

1. With brake drum off, disengage the actuator from the star wheel and rotate the star wheel by spinning or turning with a screwdriver.
2. Using the brake drum as an adjustment fixture, turn the star wheel until the drum slides over the brake shoes with a slide drag.
3. Turn the star wheel 1¼ turns to retract the brake shoes. This will allow sufficient lining-to-drum clearance so final adjustment may be made.
4. Install drum and wheel.

NOTE: *If lanced area in brake drum was knocked out, be sure all metal has been removed from brake compartment. Install new hole cover in drum to prevent contamination of brakes. Make certain that drums are installed in the same position as when removed with the drum locating tang in line with the locating hole in the wheel hub.*

5. Make final adjustment by driving and stopping in forward and reverse until satisfactory pedal height is obtained.

NOTE: The recommended method of adjusting the brakes is by using the Drum-to-Brake Shoe Clearance Gauge to check the diameter of the brake drum inner surface, Fig. 6. Turn the tool to the opposite side and fit over the brake shoes by turning the star wheel until the gauge just slides over the linings, Fig. 7. Rotate the gauge around the brake shoe lining surface to assure proper clearance.

PARKING BRAKE, ADJUST

1. Raise vehicle and remove propeller shaft.
2. Apply parking brake one notch from fully released position and raise hoist.
3. Loosen equalizer check nut and tighten the adjusting nut until a slight drag is felt when rear wheels are rotated.

NOTE: It may be necessary to remove drive shaft to gain access to parking brake equalizer.

4. Tighten check nut securely.
5. Release parking brake and rotate rear wheels. No drag should be present.

MASTER CYLINDER, REPLACE

1. Disconnect cylinder push rod from brake pedal.
2. Disconnect brake lines from two outlets on cylinder and cover ends of lines to prevent entry of dirt.
3. Unfasten and remove cylinder from brake booster.

POWER BRAKE UNIT, REPLACE

1. Remove the vacuum hose from check valve and then remove the master cylinder retaining nuts.
2. Remove the bolt securing the brake pipe distributor and switch assembly to fender skirt.
3. Pull master cylinder forward until it just clears mounting studs and move aside. Support cylinder to avoid stress on hydraulic lines.
4. Remove power unit to dash nuts.
5. Remove brake pedal pushrod retainer and disconnect push rod from pin.
6. Remove power unit from vehicle.

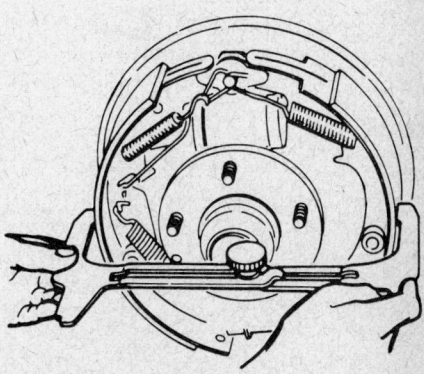

Fig. 7 Checking brake shoe lining clearance

Rear Suspension

DESCRIPTION

This rear suspension system does not use upper control arms, instead, it uses a torque arm mounted rigidly to the differential housing at the rear and to the transmission through a rubber bushing at the front. This torque arm prevents axle housing rotation caused by starting and stopping. Along with the torque arm a track rod is used to connect the axle housing to the body to control side sway and a rear stabilizer shaft is used for improved handling, Fig. 1.

SHOCK ABSORBER, REPLACE

1. With the rear axle supported properly disconnect shock absorber from upper and lower mounting, Fig. 1.

NOTE: Use a wrench to hold lower mounting stud from turning.

---

2. Reverse procedure to install.

COIL SPRING, REPLACE

1. Support vehicle at frame and rear axle with a suitable jack.
2. Disconnect shock absorbers from lower mountings.
3. Lower rear axle until springs can be

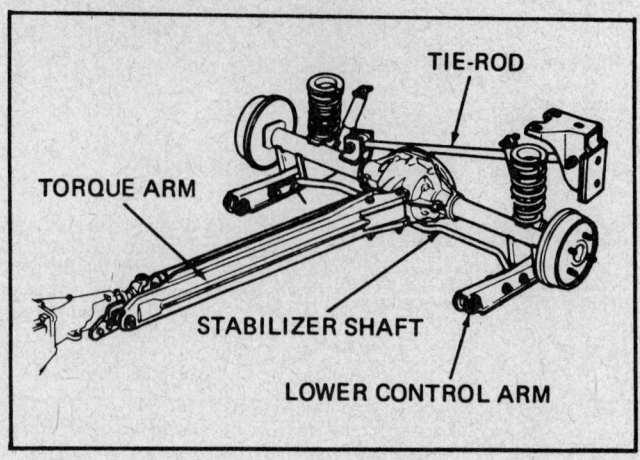

Fig. 1   Rear suspension.

removed.
4. Reverse procedure to install.

STABILIZER BAR, REPLACE

1. Remove bolts securing stabilizer bar to lower control arms. Fig. 2.
2. Reverse procedure to install and torque bolts to specifications.

TRACK ROD, REPLACE

1. Raise vehicle and support axle assembly.
2. Remove bolts at underbody end of rod, Figs. 2 and 3.
3. Remove bolts at axle bracket and remove track rod.
4. Reverse removal procedure to install and torque bolts to specifications.

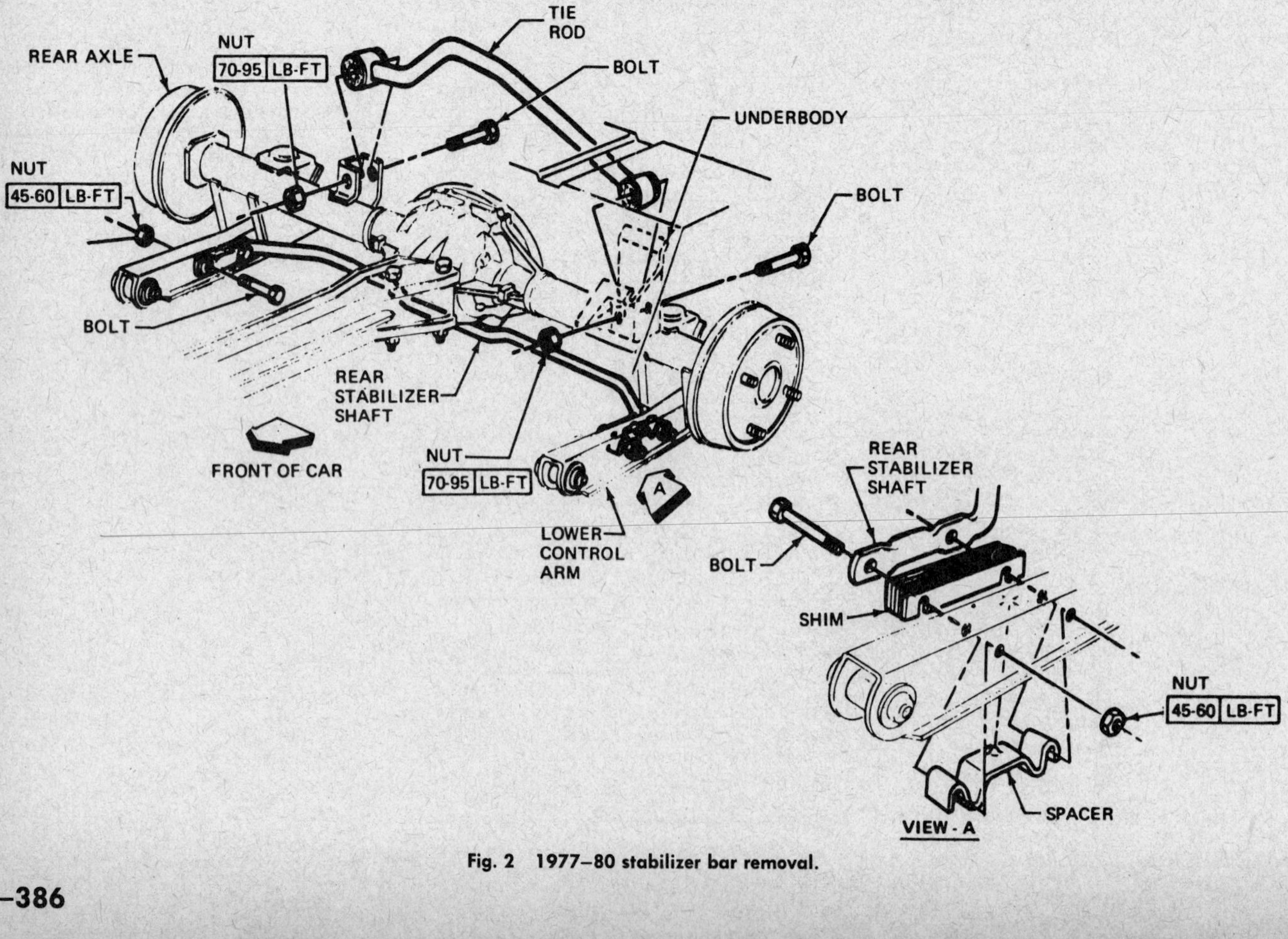

Fig. 2   1977–80 stabilizer bar removal.

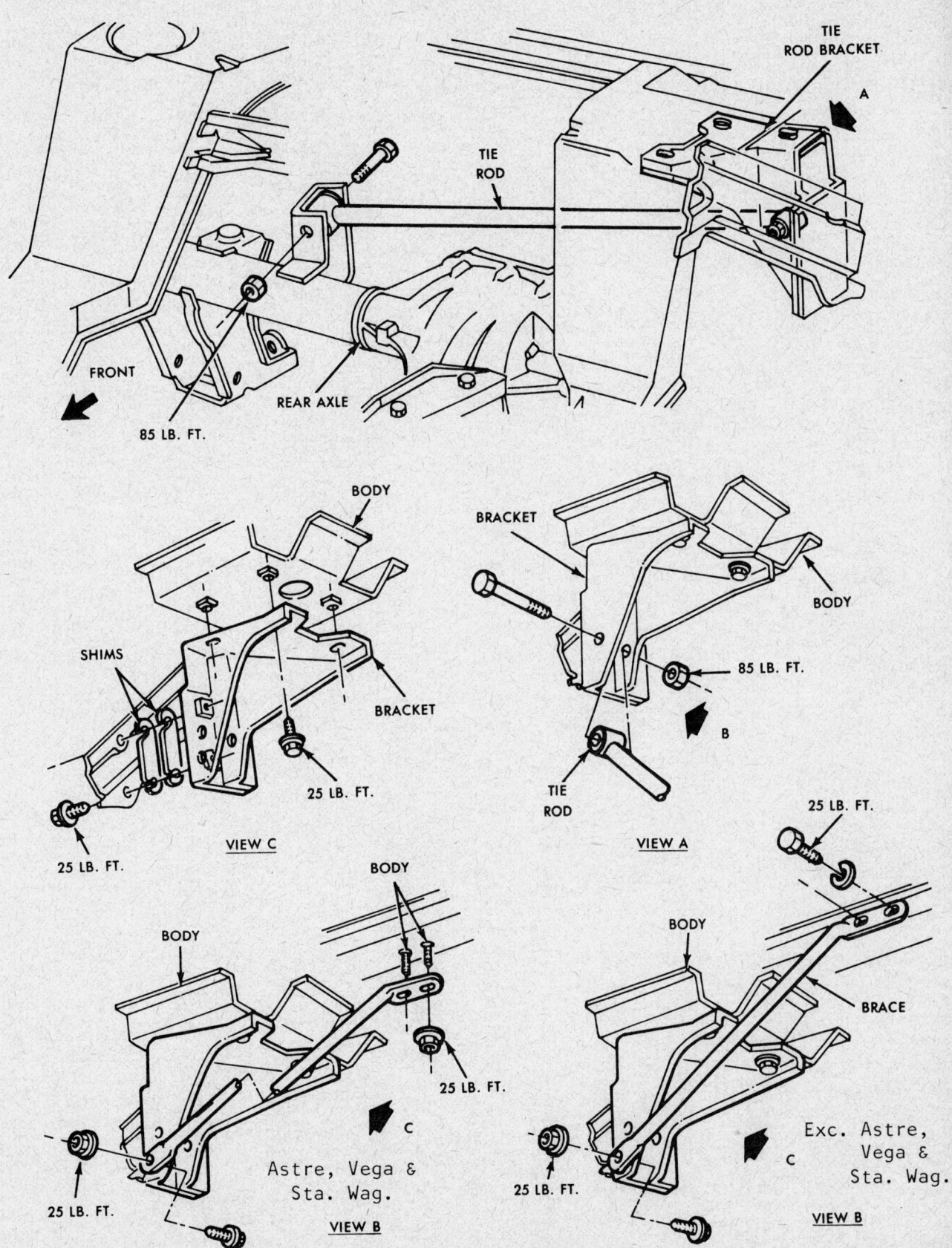

Fig. 3 Track rod removal. 1977—80

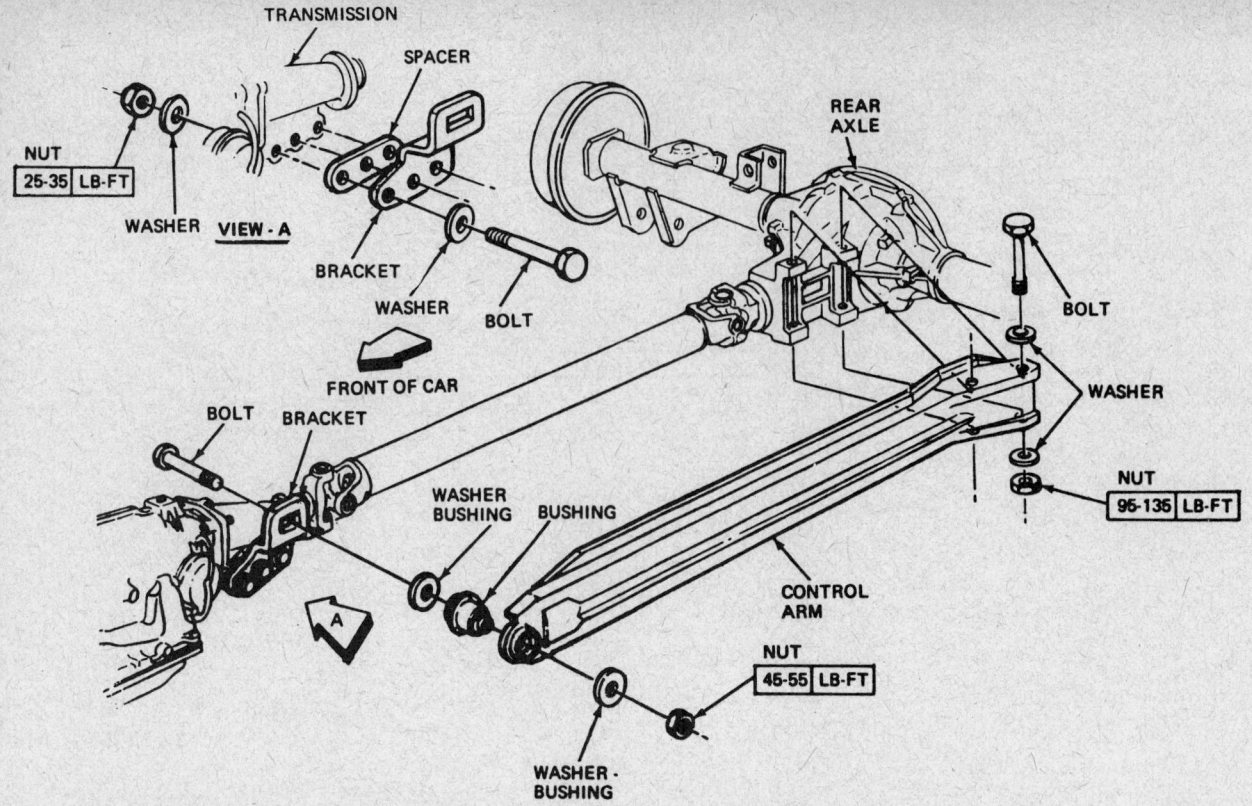

Fig. 4 Torque arm removal. Manual transmission. Except models w/4-151 engine

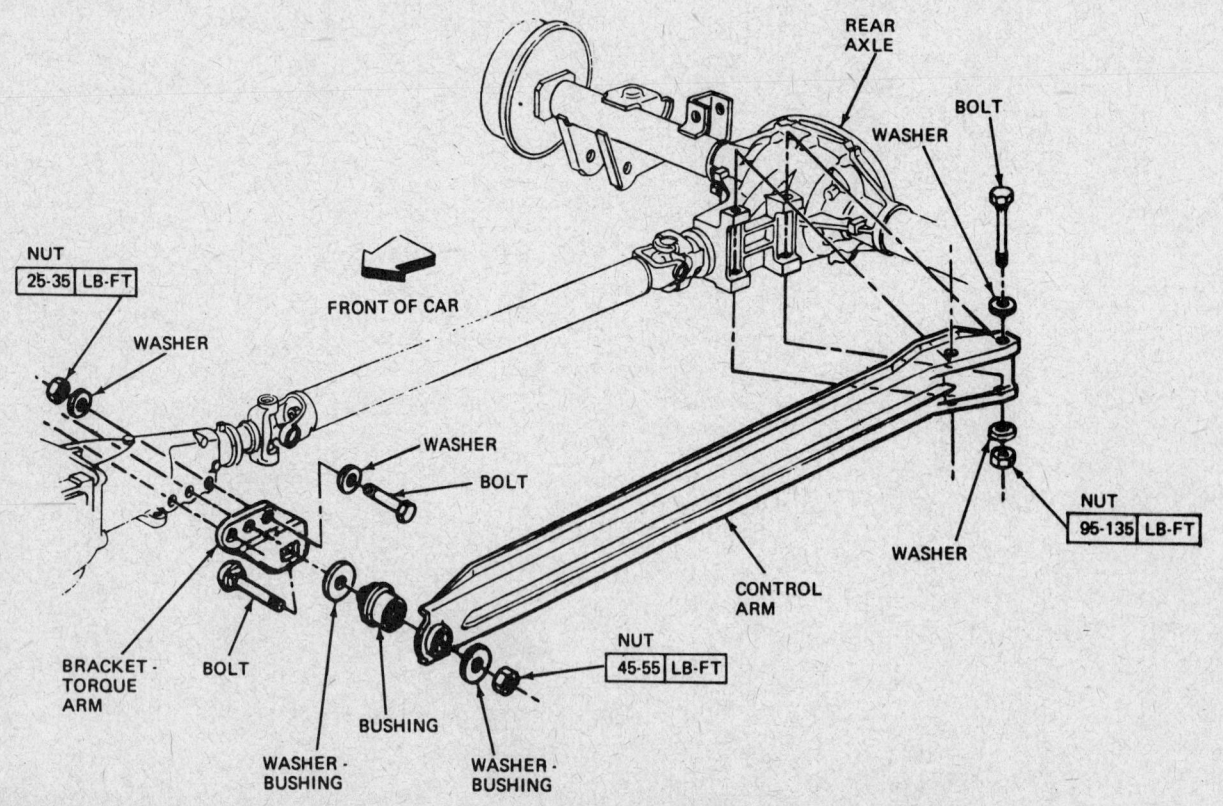

Fig. 5 Torque arm removal. Automatic transmission. Except models w/4-151 engine

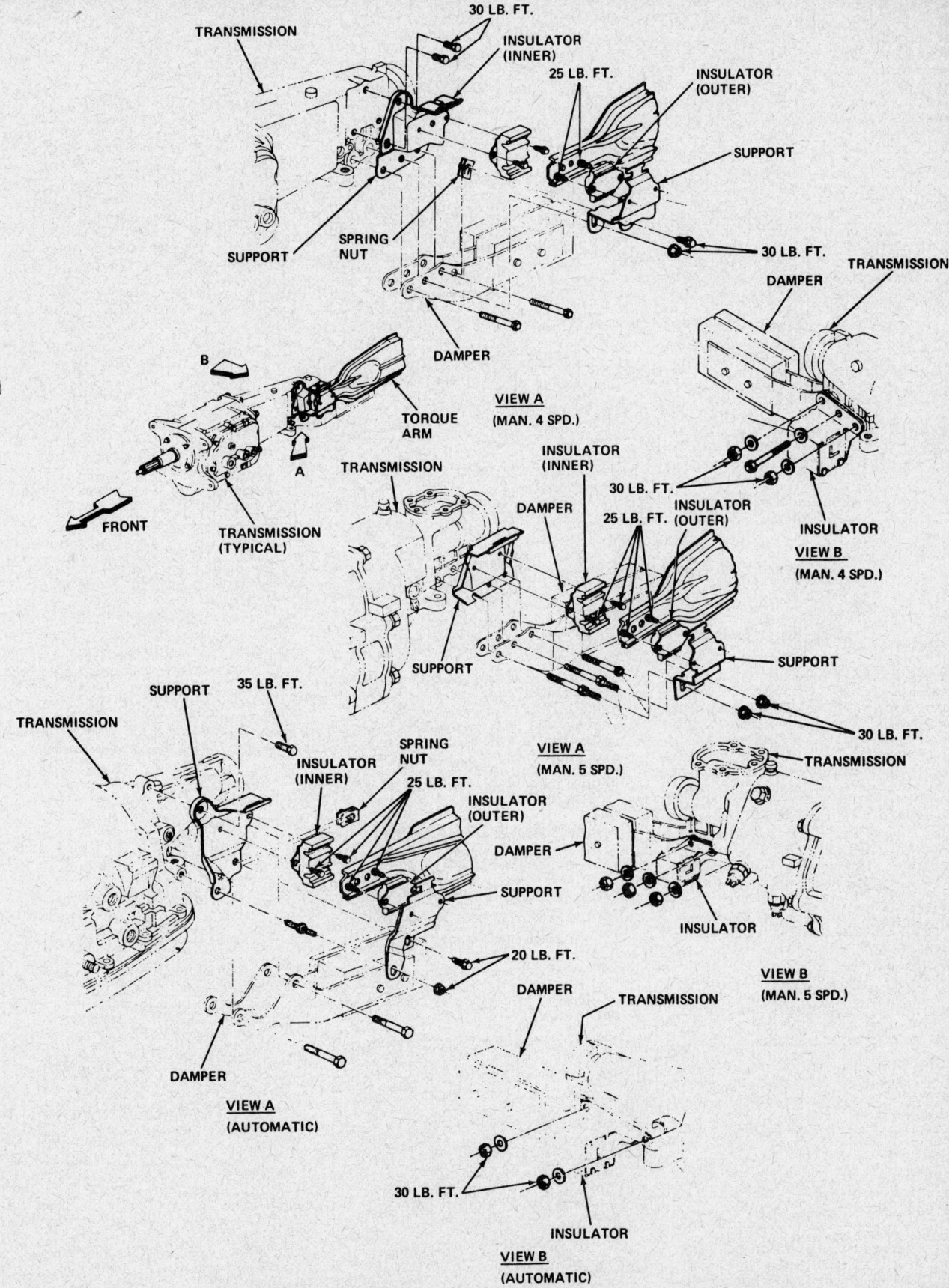

Fig. 6   Torque arm removal. 1977–80 models w/4-151 engine (typical)

TORQUE ARM, REPLACE

1. Raise vehicle by axle assembly and support underbody with jackstands.
2. Lower axle assembly slightly and remove torque arm to differential bolts.
3. Disconnect mounting bracket from transmission and then remove through bolt from bracket and remove torque arm, Figs. 4 and 5.

NOTE: On 1977—80 models with 4-151 engine, refer to Fig. 6 for torque arm to transmission removal and installation.

4. To replace bushing, use an arbor press and tool J-25317-2 as a receiver and press bushing out of arm, then position new bushing in torque arm with bushing sleeve aligned with the length of the torque arm. Press bushing into place using tool J-25317-1 over bushing to properly locate bushing in arm.
5. Reverse removal procedure to install and torque nuts and bolts to specifications.

LOWER CONTROL ARM, REPLACE

1. Raise and support vehicle at rear axle.
2. Disconnect stabilizer bar from lower control arms.
3. Remove control arm front and rear mount bolts and remove control arm, Fig. 7.
4. Reverse removal procedure to install and torque bolts to specifications.

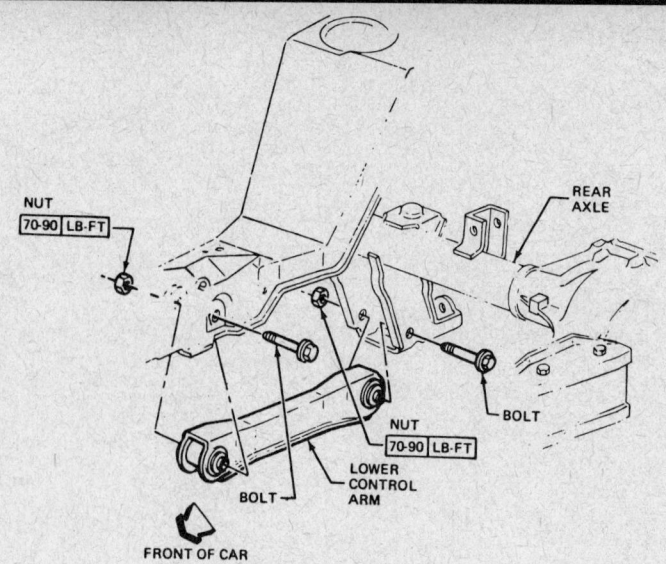

Fig. 7   Lower control arm

Front End & Steering Section

FRONT SUSPENSION

The front suspension, Fig. 1, is of the A frame type with short and long control arms. The upper control arm is bolted to the front end sheet metal at each inner pivot point. Rubber bushings are used for mounting.

The lower control arms attach to the front end sheet metal with cam type bolts through rubber bushings. The cam bolts adjust caster and camber.

The upper ball joint is riveted in the upper arm and the lower ball joint is pressed into the lower arm.

Coil springs are mounted between the lower control arms and the shock absorber tower.

WHEEL ALIGNMENT

Caster
Caster angle is adjusted by loosening the rear lower control arm pivot nut and rotating the cam until proper setting is reached, Fig. 2.

NOTE: This eccentric cam action will tend to move the lower control arm fore or aft thereby varying the caster. Hold the cam bolt while tightening the nut.

Camber
Camber angle is adjusted by loosening the front lower control arm pivot nut and rotating the cam until setting is reached, Fig. 2.

NOTE: This eccentric cam action will move the lower arm in or out thereby varying the setting. Hold the cam bolt head while tightening the nut.

TOE-IN, ADJUST

1. Loosen clamp bolt nut at each end of each tie rod and rotate the sleeve until proper toe-in is reached.
2. Position tie rod ball stud assembly straight on a center line through their attaching points.
3. Position clamp as shown in Fig. 3 and tighten clamp nuts.

WHEEL BEARINGS, ADJUST

1977 Astre & Vega, 1977—80 Monza, Skyhawk, Sunbird & 1978—80 Starfire

1. While rotating wheel, tighten spindle nut

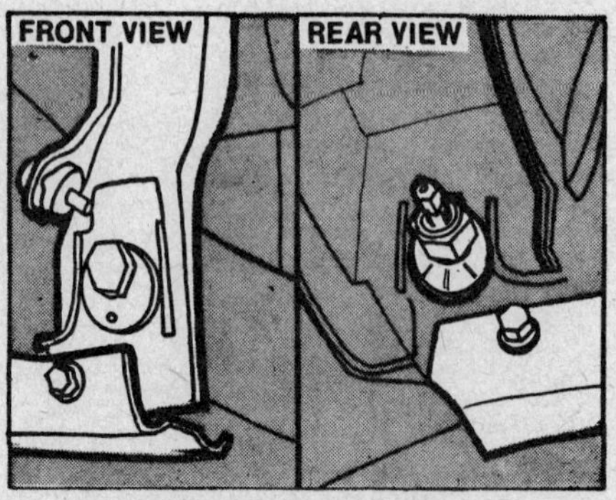

Fig. 2   Caster and camber adjustment

to 12 ft. lbs.
2. Backoff adjusting nut to the just loose position, then retighten nut hand tight.
3. Loosen until either hole in spindle is aligned with slot in nut, then install cotter pin.
4. Spin wheel to check that it rolls freely and then lock the cotter pin.

NOTE: Wheel bearings should have zero preload and the allowable end play is .001–.005 inch.

1977 Starfire

1. While rotating wheel, torque spindle nut to 30 ft. lbs.
2. Back off nut ½ turn.
3. Tighten spindle nut finger tight and insert cotter pin. If cotter pin cannot be installed, back off nut not more than 1/24 turn to align slot and pin hole.
4. With bearings properly adjusted, end play should be .001–.008 inch.

WHEEL BEARINGS, REPLACE

1. Raise vehicle on a hoist and remove the wheel and tire assembly.
2. Remove the brake caliper from the disc by removing the mounting pins and stamped nuts, Figs. 4 & 5.
3. Remove hub grease cap, cotter pin, spindle nut and washer and remove hub and bearings.
4. Remove inner bearing by prying out the grease seal.

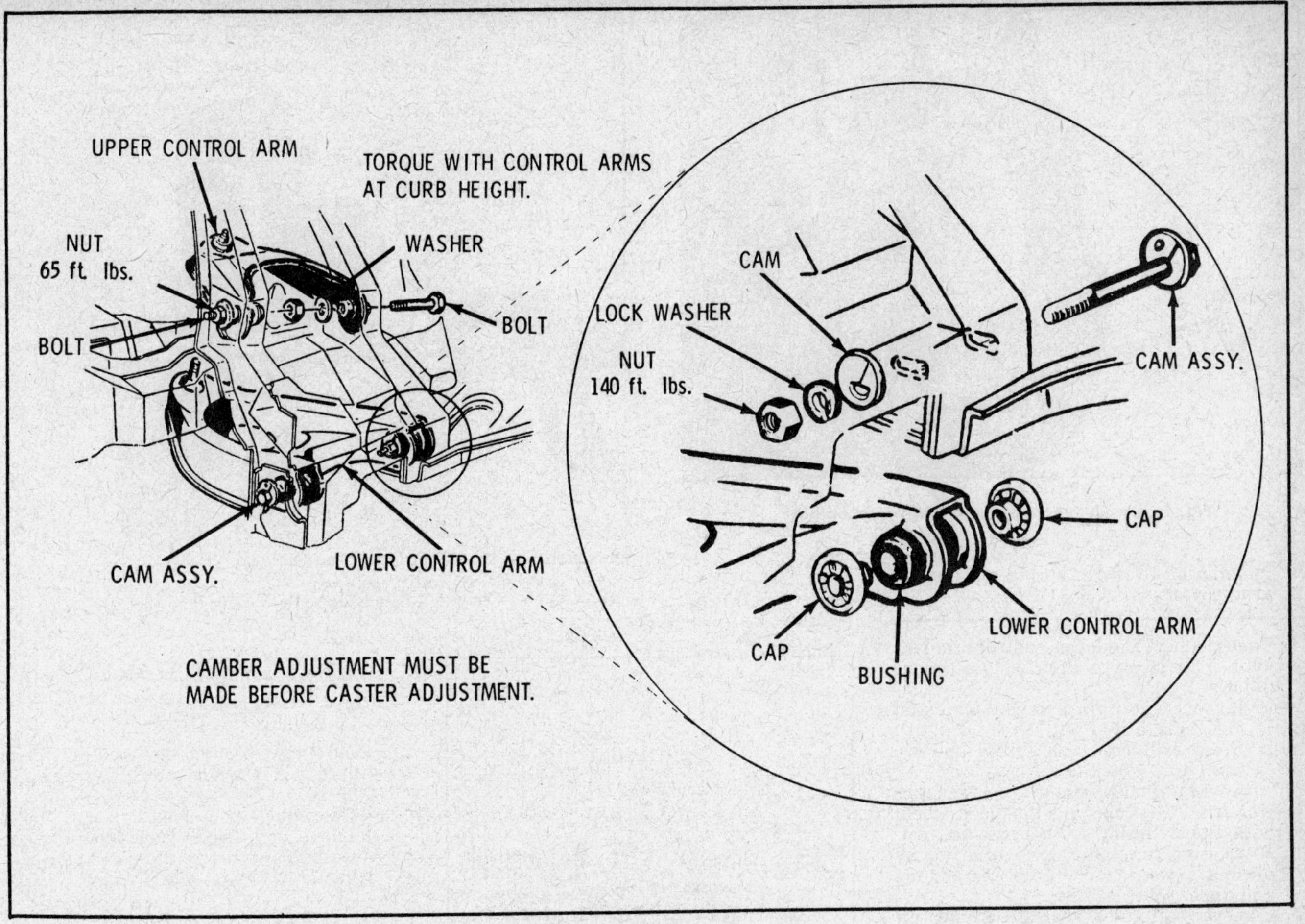

UPPER CONTROL ARM

TORQUE WITH CONTROL ARMS AT CURB HEIGHT.

NUT 65 ft. lbs.

WASHER

BOLT

BOLT

CAM ASSY.

LOWER CONTROL ARM

CAMBER ADJUSTMENT MUST BE MADE BEFORE CASTER ADJUSTMENT.

CAM

LOCK WASHER

NUT 140 ft. lbs.

CAM ASSY.

CAP

CAP

BUSHING

LOWER CONTROL ARM

Fig. 1   Front suspension (typical)

CHECKING BALL JOINTS FOR WEAR

Upper Ball Joint

The upper ball joint is checked for wear by checking the torque required to rotate the ball joint stud in the assembly. This is done after first dislodging the ball joint from the steering knuckle.

1. Install the stud nut to the ball stud in the seat.
2. Check the torque required to turn the ball stud.

NOTE: Specified torque for a new joint is 2 to 4 ft. lbs. rotating torque. If readings are excessively high or low, replace the joint.

Lower Ball Joint

The lower ball joints incorporate wear indicators for visual inspection, Fig. 6.

UPPER BALL JOINT, REPLACE

1. Raise vehicle on hoist and support lower control arm with a suitable jack stand.

NOTE: Floor jack or stand must remain under control arm spring seat during removal and installation to retain spring and control arm in position. Since the weight of the vehicle is used to relieve spring tension to the upper control arm, the floor stands must be positioned between the spring seats and ball joints of the lower control arms for maximum leverage.

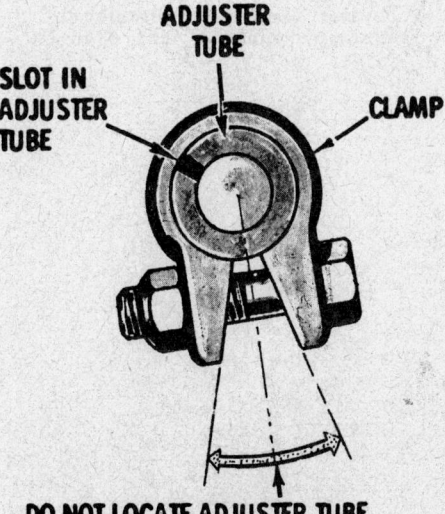

ADJUSTER TUBE

SLOT IN ADJUSTER TUBE

CLAMP

DO NOT LOCATE ADJUSTER TUBE SLOT IN THIS AREA

Fig. 3   Adjuster sleeve and clamp location

2. Remove wheel, then loosen upper ball joint from steering knuckle as follows:
   a. Remove cotter pin from upper ball joint stud and clean threads.
   b. Remove upper ball joint nut and install tool J-8806, Fig. 7.
   c. Apply pressure on stud by expanding tool until stud breaks loose.
   d. Remove tool and upper ball joint nut, then pull stud free from knuckle. Support knuckle assembly to prevent weight of assembly from damaging brake hose.
3. With control arm in raised position, drill four rivets 1/4 inch deep using a 1/8 inch diameter drill bit. Using 1/2 inch diameter drill bit, drill off rivet heads.
4. Using a suitable punch, punch out rivets then remove ball joint.
5. Using four bolts and nuts provided in kit install new ball joint, torque to 8 ft. lbs. Torque upper ball joint nut to 65 ft. lbs.

LOWER BALL JOINT, REPLACE

1. Raise vehicle and support with suitable stands positioned under frame.
2. Remove tire and wheel assembly.
3. Place floor jack under control arm spring seat.

NOTE: Floor jack must remain under control arm spring seat during removal and

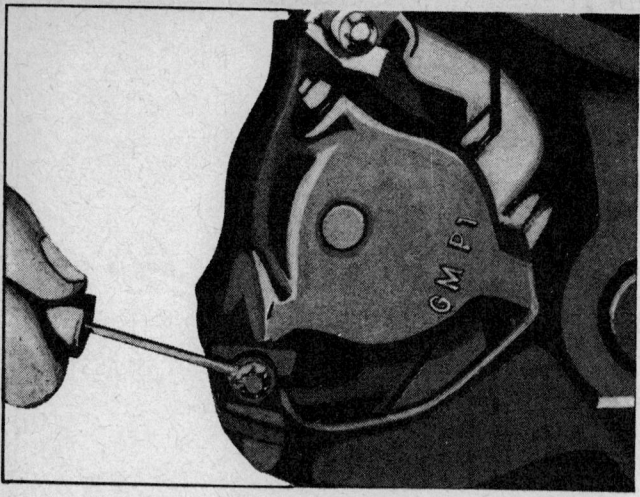

Fig. 4 Removing caliper retaining stamped nuts

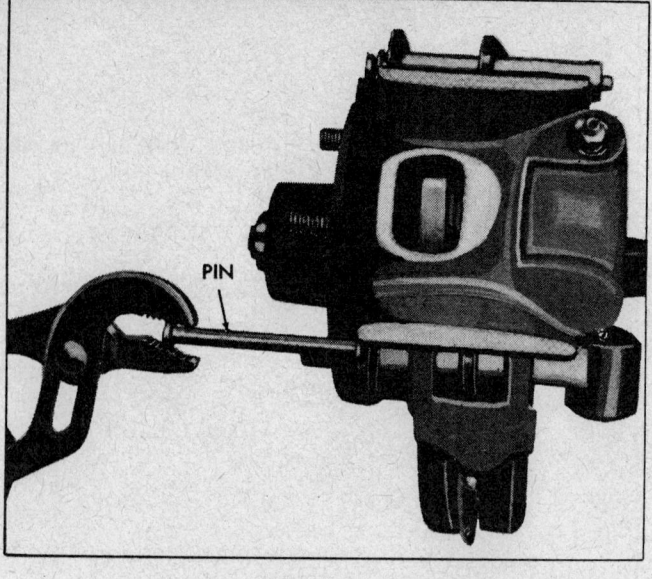

Fig. 5 Removing caliper mounting pins

installation to retain spring and control arm in position.

4. To disconnect the lower control arm ball joint from steering knuckle proceed as follows:
   a. Remove cotter pin from ball joint stud and remove stud nut.
   b. Break ball joint loose from knuckle using tool J-8806, Fig. 7A.
5. After stud breaks loose guide lower control arm out of opening in splash shield with a putty knife or other suitable tool.
6. Block knuckle assembly out of the way by placing a wooden block between frame and upper control arm.
7. Remove ball joint seal by prying off retainer with a screwdriver or driving off with a chisel.
8. Remove grease fitting and install tools, Fig. 8, and remove lower ball joint from lower control arm.

NOTE: When installing new ball joint

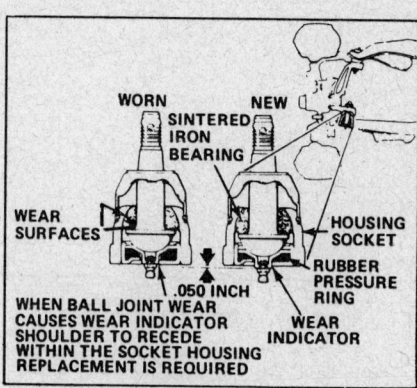

Fig. 6 Lower ball joint wear indicator

position the grease fitting so it faces inboard.

9. Reverse procedure to install, Fig. 9. Torque ball joint stud nut to 60 ft. lbs.

SHOCK ABSORBER, REPLACE

1. Hold shock absorber stem and remove the nut, upper retainer and rubber grommet, Fig. 10.
2. Raise vehicle on a hoist.
3. Remove bolts from lower end of shock absorber and lower the shock from the vehicle.

COIL SPRING, REPLACE

Exc. Starfire

1. With shock absorber removed and stabilizer bar removed, raise the vehicle and place jackstands under front braces.
2. Remove the wheel and tire assembly.
3. Place a floor jack under the lower arm and support the arm. Use a block of wood between the control arm and the jack, Fig. 11.
4. Remove the lower ball stud from the knuckle.

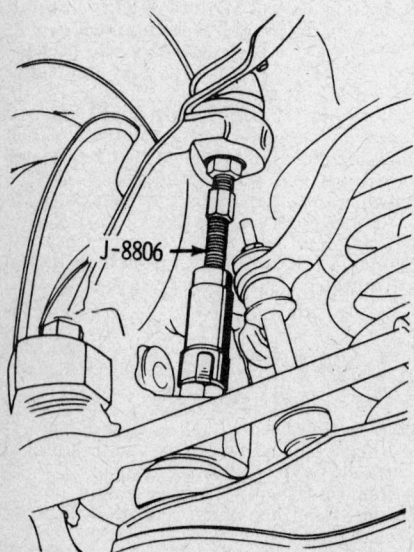

Fig. 7 Removing upper ball joint from steering knuckle

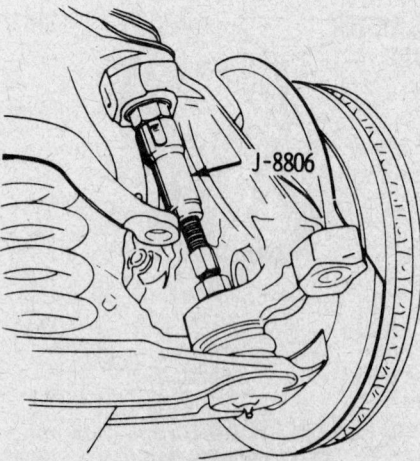

Fig. 7A Removing lower ball joint from steering knuckle

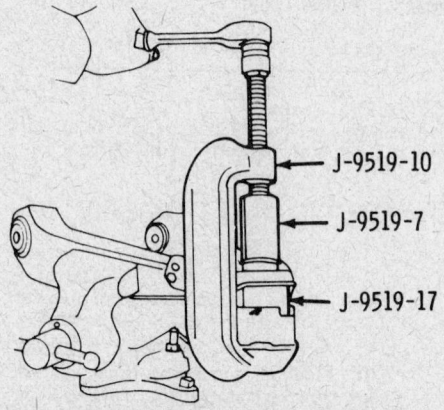

Fig. 8 Removing lower ball joint

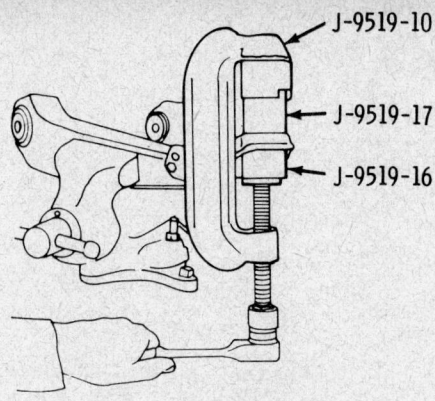

Fig. 9   Installing lower ball joint

5. Remove the tie rod end from the knuckle.
6. Lower the control arm by slowly lowering the jack until the spring can be removed.
7. Reverse procedure to install. Torque steering knuckle stud nut to 60 ft. lbs. and install cotter pin.

NOTE: Do not back off nut to insert cotter pin. Advance nut to the next slot that lines up with the hole in the stud.

Starfire

1. Place transmission in Neutral.
2. Disconnect shock absorber from upper mounting.
3. Raise vehicle, support at frame and remove wheel.
4. Remove stabilizer link nut, grommets, washers and bolt.
5. Remove shock absorber.
6. Install lower plate BT-7522, Fig. 12, with pivot ball seat facing downward into spring coils. Rotate plate to fully seat it in lower control arm spring seat.
7. Install upper plate BT-7522, Fig. 12, with pivot ball seat facing upward into spring coils. Insert ball nut BT-7408-4 through spring coils and onto upper plate.
8. Install rod BT-7408-5 through shock absorber opening in lower control arm and through the lower and upper plates. Depress lock pin on shaft and thread shaft into upper ball nut BT-7408-4. Ensure lock pin is fully extended above ball nut upper surface.
9. With ball nut tang engaged in upper plate slot, rotate upper plate until it contacts upper spring seat.
10. Install lower pivot ball, thrust bearing

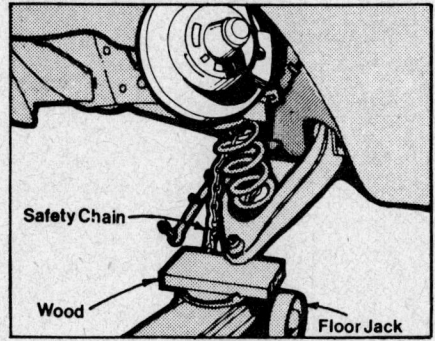

Fig. 11   Removing front coil spring. Exc. Starfire

and nut on rod, then rotate nut until coil spring is compressed to be free in the seat.
11. Mark location of lower control arm pivot bolt cams and remove the pivot bolts. Move control arm forward and remove coil spring.
12. Reverse procedure to install.

MANUAL STEERING GEAR, REPLACE

1. Remove the pot joint coupling clamp bolt at the steering gear wormshaft.
2. Remove pitman arm nut and washer from pitman shaft and mark relation of arm position to shaft.
3. Remove pitman arm with suitable puller.
4. Remove bolts securing gear to frame and remove gear assembly.

POWER STEERING GEAR, REPLACE

Exc. Astre, Vega & 1978—79 Station Wagon

Replacement procedures for removing the gear assembly are the same as for the manual type gear with the following additions:
1. Remove left front crossmember brace.
2. Disconnect both pressure and return hoses from the gear housing and cap both hoses and steering gear outlets to prevent entry of dirt.

Astre, Vega & 1978—79 Station Wagon

1. If necessary, remove battery to gain access to steering gear.
2. Remove clamp securing intermediate shaft to steering shaft.
3. Disconnect both hydraulic lines from steering gear and allow to drain. Position lines out of way to provide clearance for gear removal.
4. Raise vehicle and remove clamps at stabilizer bar.
5. Remove left front crossmember.
6. Remove pitman shaft nut, then using tool No. J-6632, remove pitman arm from pitman shaft.
7. Remove three steering mounting bolts and lock washers.
8. Lift steering gear and remove pitman arm, then position gear to provide clearance for removal.
9. Remove steering gear and intermediate shaft as an assembly, the steering gear spacer is also removed.
10. Remove plastic shield.
11. Remove pot joint clamp and separate steering gear from pot joint.
12. Remove pot joint from intermediate shaft.

POWER STEERING PUMP, REPLACE

Removal

1. Disconnect hoses at pump or steering gear. Plug hose ends and ports to prevent fluid loss and entrance of dirt.
2. Loosen pump attaching bolts and remove drive belt. On some models with air conditioning, it will be necessary to remove the compressor belt first.
3. Remove attaching bolts and the pump from vehicle.

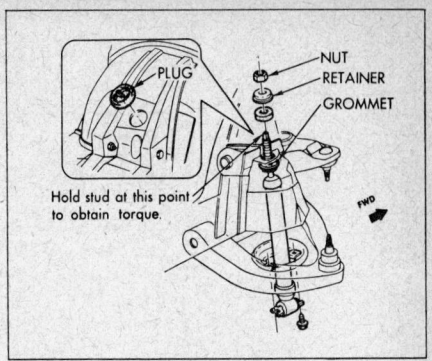

Fig. 10   Front shock absorber mountings

Installation

1. Position pump assembly on mounting brackets and loosely install attaching bolts.
2. Connect and tighten the hoses at the pump and steering gear.
3. Fill the reservoir. Bleed the pump by turning the pulley backwards (counterclockwise as viewed from the front) until air bubbles cease to appear.
4. Reinstall the pump belt over the pulley. Adjust to proper tension given in the belt tension chart and tighten the attaching bolts. Reinstall the compressor belt, if removed.
5. Bleed the system.
   a. Start the engine and run for a few seconds. Add fluid if necessary. Repeat this procedure until the fluid level remains constant after running the engine.
   b. Raise the front wheels off the ground and support the vehicle.
   c. Run engine at high idle (approximately 1500 rpm) and turn the wheels right and left, lightly contacting the wheel stops.
   d. Lower vehicle and turn the wheels right and left on the ground. Check the fluid level and fill as required.
   e. If fluid is extremely foamy, allow vehicle to stand a few minutes and repeat bleeding procedure.

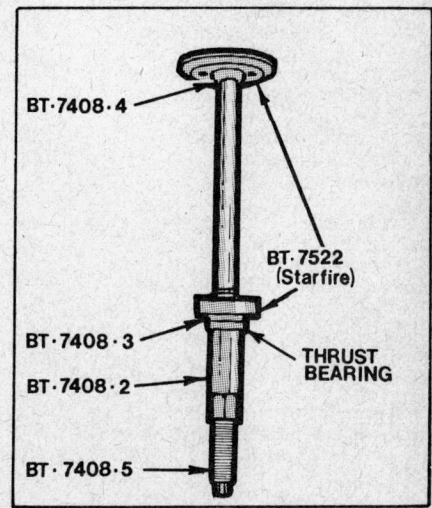

Fig. 12   Coil spring replacement tool. Starfire

CHRYSLER CORP.
REAR WHEEL DRIVE

> **NOTE:** This chapter includes service procedures for all models except 1978–84 Dodge Omni & Plymouth Horizon; 1981–84 Dodge Aries & Plymouth Reliant; 1982–83 Dodge 400; 1982–84 Chrysler LeBaron; 1983–84 Chrysler E Class & New Yorker, Dodge 600 & Charger 2.2 & Plymouth Turismo; 1984 Chrysler Laser & Dodge Daytona.

INDEX OF SERVICE OPERATIONS

NOTE: Refer to the front of this manual for vehicle manufacturer's special service tool suppliers.

VEHICLE NUMBER LOCATION

1977—84: On plate attached to dash pad and visible through windshield.

ENGINE NUMBER LOCATION

1977—83 Six: Right front of block below cylinder head.

1977—84 318, 360: Left front of block below cylinder head.

1977—80 V8-400: Upper right front of cylinder block.

1977—78 V8-440: Top of block left bank next to front tappet rail.

ENGINE IDENTIFICATION CODE

1977—84 engines are identified by the cubic inch displacement found within the engine number stamped on the pad.

CHRYSLER & IMPERIAL GRILLE IDENTIFICATION

1977 New Yorker

1977 Cordoba

1977—78 LeBaron
1978 Town & Country

1978 Cordoba

1978 New Yorker

1979 Cordoba

1979 300 Limited Edition

1979 LeBaron & Town & Country

1979—80 Newport

1979—80 New Yorker

1980 Cordoba

1980 LeBaron

1981 LeBaron

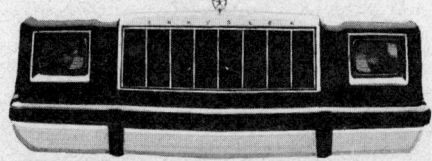
1981—83 Cordoba

1981 Newport

1981 New Yorker

1981—83 Imperial

CHRYSLER & IMPERIAL GRILLE IDENTIFICATION—Continued

1981 "300" & 1982 Cordoba LS

1982 New Yorker & 1983 New Yorker Fifth Avenue

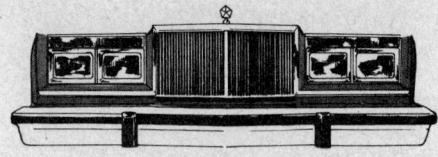

1984 Fifth Aveue

DODGE GRILLE IDENTIFICATION

1977 Aspen

1977 Aspen R/T

1977–78 Monaco

1977 Charger Daytona

1977–78 Charger SE

1977–78 Diplomat

1978–79 Aspen

1978–79 Magnum

1979 Diplomat

1979–81 St. Regis

1980 Aspen

1980–82 Diplomat

1980–83 Mirada

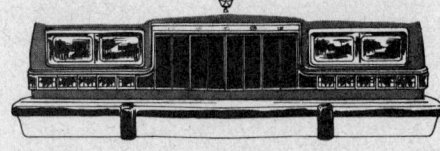

1983–84 Diplomat

PLYMOUTH GRILLE IDENTIFICATION

1977 Volaré & Road Runner

1977–78 Fury

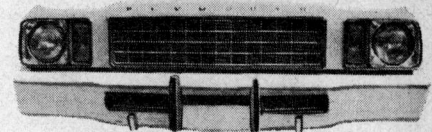

1977 Gran Fury

1978 Volaré & Road Runner

1979 Volaré & Road Runner

1980 Volaré

1980–81 Gran Fury

1982–84 Gran Fury

GENERAL ENGINE SPECIFICATIONS

Year	Engine CID①/Liter	V.I.N. Code②	Carburetor	Bore and Stroke	Compression Ratio	Net H.P. @ R.P.M.③	Maximum Torque Ft. Lbs. @ R.P.M.	Normal Oil Pressure Pounds
CHRYSLER & IMPERIAL								
1977	V8-318, 5.2L④	G	BBD, 2 Bbl.⑤	3.91 × 3.31	8.6	135 @ 3600	235 @ 1600	30–80
	V8-318, 5.2L	G	BBD, 2 Bbl.⑤	3.91 × 3.31	8.6	145 @ 4000	245 @ 1600	30–80
	V8-360, 5.9L⑥	K	2245, 2 Bbl.⑦	4.00 × 3.58	8.4	155 @ 3600	275 @ 2000	30–80
	V8-360, 5.9L④	J	TQ, 4 Bbl.⑤	4.00 × 3.58	8.4	170 @ 4000	270 @ 1600	30–80
	V8-400, 6.6L	N	TQ, 4 Bbl.⑤	4.34 × 3.38	8.2	190 @ 3600	305 @ 3200	30–80
	V8-440, 7.2L	T	TQ, 4 Bbl.⑤	4.32 × 3.75	8.2	185 @ 3600	310 @ 2400	30–80
1978	6-225, 3.7L	C	1945, 1 Bbl.⑦	3.40 × 4.12	8.4	100 @ 3600	170 @ 1600	30–70
	6-225, 3.7L	D	BBD, 2 Bbl.⑤	3.40 × 4.12	8.4	110 @ 3600	180 @ 2000	30–70
	V8-318, 5.2L⑨⑲	G	BBD, 2 Bbl.⑤	3.91 × 3.31	8.5	140 @ 4000	245 @ 1600	30–80
	V8-318, 5.2L⑩	G	2280, 2 Bbl.⑦	3.91 × 3.31	8.5	145 @ 4000	245 @ 1600	30–80
	V8-318, 5.2L⑧⑨	H	TQ, 4 Bbl.⑤	3.91 × 3.31	8.5	155 @ 4000	245 @ 1600	30–80
	V8-360, 5.9L⑲	K	2245, 2 Bbl.⑦	4.00 × 3.58	8.4	155 @ 3600	270 @ 2400	30–80
	V8-360, 5.9L⑧	J	TQ, 4 Bbl.⑤	4.00 × 3.58	8.4	170 @ 4000	270 @ 1600	30–80
	V8-400, 6.6L	N	TQ, 4 Bbl.⑤	4.34 × 3.38	8.2	190 @ 3600	305 @ 3200	30–80
	V8-440, 7.2L	T	TQ, 4 Bbl.⑤	4.32 × 3.75	8.2	185 @ 3600	310 @ 2400	30–80
1979	6-225, 3.7L	C	1945, 1 Bbl.⑦	3.40 × 4.12	8.4	100 @ 3600	165 @ 1600	30–70
	6-225, 3.7L	D	BBD, 2 Bbl.⑤	3.40 × 4.12	8.4	110 @ 2000	180 @ 2000	30–70
	V8-318, 5.2L⑥	G	2280, 2 Bbl.⑦	3.91 × 3.31	8.5	135 @ 4000	250 @ 1600	30–80
	V8-318, 5.2L④	H	TQ, 4 Bbl.⑤	3.91 × 3.31	8.5	155 @ 4000	245 @ 1600	30–80
	V8-360, 5.9L⑲	K	2245, 2 Bbl.⑦	4.00 × 3.58	8.4	150 @ 3600	265 @ 2400	30–80
	V8-360, 5.9L⑧	J	TQ, 4 Bbl.⑤	4.00 × 3.58	8.4	170 @ 4000	270 @ 1600	30–80
	V8-360, 5.9L	L	TQ, 4 Bbl.⑤	4.00 × 3.58	8.0	195 @ 4000	280 @ 2400	30–80
1980	6-225, 3.7L	C	1945, 1 Bbl.⑦	3.40 × 4.12	8.4	90 @ 3600	160 @ 1600	30–70
	V8-318, 5.2L	G	BBD, 2 Bbl.⑤	3.91 × 3.31	8.5	120 @ 3600	245 @ 1600	30–80
	V8-318, 5.2L	H	TQ, 4 Bbl.⑤	3.91 × 3.31	8.5	155 @ 4000	240 @ 2000	30–80
	V8-360, 5.9L	K	BBD, 2 Bbl.⑤	4.00 × 3.58	8.4	130 @ 3200	—	30–80

Continued

GENERAL ENGINE SPECIFICATIONS—Continued

Year	Engine CID①/Liter	V.I.N. Code②	Carburetor	Bore and Stroke	Compression Ratio	Net H.P. @ R.P.M.③	Maximum Torque Ft. Lbs. @ R.P.M.	Normal Oil Pressure Pounds
CHRYSLER & IMPERIAL—Continued								
	V8-360, 5.9L⑪	L	TQ, 4 Bbl.⑤	4.00 × 3.58	8.0	185 @ 4000	275 @ 2000	30–80
1981	6-225, 3.7L⑥	E	1945, 1 Bbl.⑦	3.40 × 4.12	8.4	85 @ 3600	165 @ 1600	30–70
	6-225, 3.7L④	E	6145, 1 Bbl.⑦	3.40 × 4.12	8.4	85 @ 3600	165 @ 1600	30–70
	V8-318, 5.2L⑥	K	BBD, 2 Bbl.⑤	3.91 × 3.31	8.6	130 @ 4000	230 @ 2000	30–80
	V8-318, 5.2L④	M	TQ, 4 Bbl.⑤	3.91 × 3.31	8.6	165 @ 4000	240 @ 2000	30–80
	V8-318, 5.2L	J	E.F.I.⑱	3.91 × 3.31	8.4	140 @ 4000	240 @ 2000	30–80
1982	6-225, 3.7L⑥	E	1945, 1 Bbl.⑦	3.40 × 4.12	8.4	90 @ 3600	160 @ 1600	30–70
	6-225, 3.7L④	E	6145, 1 Bbl.⑦	3.40 × 4.12	8.4	90 @ 3600	160 @ 1600	30–70
	V8-318, 5.2L⑥	K	BBD, 2 Bbl.⑤	3.91 × 3.31	8.5	130 @ 4000	230 @ 2000	30–80
	V8-318, 5.2L④	M	TQ, 4 Bbl.⑤	3.91 × 3.31	8.5	165 @ 4000	240 @ 2000	30–80
	V8-318, 5.2L	J	E.F.I.⑱	3.91 × 3.31	8.5	140 @ 4000	245 @ 2000	30–80
1983	6-225, 3.7L	H	6145, 1 Bbl.⑦	3.40 × 4.12	8.4	90 @ 3600	165 @ 1600	30–70
	V8-318, 5.2L	P	BBD, 2 Bbl.⑤	3.91 × 3.31	8.5	130 @ 4000	230 @ 1600	30–80
	V8-318, 5.2L	N	E.F.I.⑱	3.91 × 3.31	8.5	140 @ 4000	245 @ 2000	30–80
1984	V8-318, 5.2L		BBD, 2 Bbl.⑤	3.91 × 3.31	8.6	130 @ 4000	235 @ 1600	30–80
DODGE								
1977	6-225, 3.7L④	C	1945, 1 Bbl.⑦	3.40 × 4.12	8.4	90 @ 3600	170 @ 1600	30–70
	6-225, 3.7L⑥	C	1945, 1 Bbl.⑦	3.40 × 4.12	8.4	100 @ 3600	170 @ 1600	30–70
	6-225, 3.7L	D	BBD 2 Bbl.⑤	3.40 × 4.12	8.4	110 @ 3600	180 @ 2000	30–70
	V8-318, 5.2L④	G	BBD, 2 Bbl.⑤	3.91 × 3.31	8.6	135 @ 3600	235 @ 1600	30–80
	V8-318, 5.2L	G	BBD, 2 Bbl.⑤	3.91 × 3.31	8.6	145 @ 4000	245 @ 1600	30–80
	V8-360, 5.9L⑥	K	2245, 2 Bbl.⑦	4.00 × 3.58	8.4	155 @ 3600	275 @ 2000	30–80
	V8-360, 5.9L④	J	TQ, 4 Bbl.⑤	4.00 × 3.58	8.4	170 @ 4000	270 @ 1600	30–80
	V8-360, 5.9L⑫	L	TQ, 4 Bbl.⑤	4.00 × 3.58	8.0	175 @ 4000	275 @ 2000	30–80
	V8-400, 6.6L	N	TQ, 4 Bbl.⑤	4.34 × 3.38	8.2	190 @ 3600	305 @ 3200	30–80
	V8-440, 7.2L⑧	T	TQ, 4 Bbl.⑤	4.32 × 3.75	8.2	185 @ 3600	310 @ 2400	30–80
	V8-440, 7.2L⑲	T	TQ, 4 Bbl.⑤	4.32 × 3.75	8.2	195 @ 3600	320 @ 2000	30–80
	V8-440, 7.2L④⑫	U	TQ, 4 Bbl.⑤	4.32 × 3.75	7.8	230 @ 4000	330 @ 3200	30–80
	V8-440, 7.2L⑥⑫	U	TQ, 4 Bbl.⑤	4.32 × 3.75	7.8	245 @ 4000	350 @ 3200	30–80
1978	6-225, 3.7L⑬	C	1945, 1 Bbl.⑦	3.40 × 4.12	8.4	90 @ 3600	160 @ 1600	30–70
	6-225, 3.7L⑥	C	1945, 1 Bbl.⑦	3.40 × 4.12	8.4	100 @ 3600	170 @ 1600	30–70
	6-225, 3.7	D	BBD, 2 Bbl.⑤	3.40 × 4.12	8.4	110 @ 3600	180 @ 2000	30–70
	V8-318, 5.2L	G	BBD, 2 Bbl.⑤	3.91 × 3.31	8.5	140 @ 4000	245 @ 1600	30–80
	V8-318, 5.2L④	H	TQ, 4 Bbl.⑤	3.91 × 3.31	8.5	155 @ 4000	245 @ 1600	30–80
	V8-360, 5.9L	K	2245, 2 Bbl.⑦	4.00 × 3.58	8.4	155 @ 3600	270 @ 2400	30–80
	V8-360, 5.9L⑧⑬	J	TQ, 4 Bbl.⑤	4.00 × 3.58	8.0	160 @ 3600	265 @ 1600	30–80
	V8-360, 5.9L⑧⑭	L	TQ, 4 Bbl.⑤	4.00 × 3.58	8.4	170 @ 4000	270 @ 1600	30–80
	V8-360, 5.9L⑬⑲	L	TQ, 4 Bbl.⑤	4.00 × 3.58	8.0	175 @ 4000	260 @ 2400	30–80
	V8-400, 6.6L	N	TQ, 4 Bbl.⑤	4.34 × 3.38	8.2	190 @ 3600	305 @ 3200	30–80
1979	6-225, 3.7L④	C	1945, 1 Bbl.⑦	3.40 × 4.12	8.4	90 @ 3600	170 @ 1600	30–70
	6-225, 3.7L⑥	C	1945, 1 Bbl.⑦	3.40 × 4.12	8.4	100 @ 3600	160 @ 1600	30–70
	6-225, 3.7L⑥	D	BBD, 2 Bbl.⑤	3.40 × 4.12	8.4	110 @ 3600	180 @ 2000	30–70
	V8-318, 5.2L⑥	G	2280, 2 Bbl.⑦	3.91 × 3.31	8.5	135 @ 4000	250 @ 1600	30–80
	V8-318, 5.2L④	H	TQ, 4 Bbl.⑤	3.91 × 3.31	8.5	155 @ 4000	245 @ 1600	30–80
	V8-360, 5.9L⑥	K	2245, 2 Bbl.⑦	4.00 × 3.58	8.4	150 @ 3600	265 @ 2400	30–80
	V8-360, 5.9L④	J	TQ, 4 Bbl.⑤	4.00 × 3.58	8.4	170 @ 4000	270 @ 1600	30–80
	V8-360, 5.9L④	L	TQ, 4 Bbl.⑤	4.00 × 3.58	8.0	190 @ 3600	275 @ 1600	30–80
	V8-360, 5.9L⑥	L	TQ, 4 Bbl.⑤	4.00 × 3.58	8.0	195 @ 4000	280 @ 2400	30–80
1980	6-225, 3.7L	C	1945, 1 Bbl.⑦	3.40 × 4.12	8.4	90 @ 3600	160 @ 1600	30–70
	V8-318, 5.2L	G	BBD, 2 Bbl.⑤	3.91 × 3.31	8.5	120 @ 3600	245 @ 1600	30–80

Continued

GENERAL ENGINE SPECIFICATIONS—Continued

Year	Engine CID①/Liter	V.I.N. Code②	Carburetor	Bore and Stroke	Compression Ratio	Net H.P. @ R.P.M.③	Maximum Torque Ft. Lbs. @ R.P.M.	Normal Oil Pressure Pounds
DODGE—Continued								
	V8-318, 5.2L	H	TQ, 4 Bbl.⑤	3.91 × 3.31	8.5	155 @ 4000	240 @ 2000	30—80
	V8-360, 5.9L	K	BBD, 2 Bbl.⑤	4.00 × 3.58	8.4	130 @ 3200	—	30—80
	V8-360, 5.9L	L	TQ, 4 Bbl.⑤	4.00 × 3.58	8.4	185 @ 4000	275 @ 2000	30—80
	V8-360, 5.9L⑪	L	TQ, 4 Bbl.⑤	4.00 × 3.58	8.0	185 @ 4000	275 @ 2000	30—80
1981	6-225, 3.7L⑥	E	1945, 1 Bbl.⑦	3.40 × 4.12	8.4	85 @ 3600	83 @ 2400	35—65
	6-225, 3.7L④	E	6145, 1 Bbl.⑦	3.40 × 4.12	8.4	85 @ 3600	165 @ 1600	30—70
	V8-318, 5.2L⑥	K	BBD, 2 Bbl.⑤	3.91 × 3.31	8.6	130 @ 4000	230 @ 2000	35—65
	V8-318, 5.2L	M	TQ, 4 Bbl.⑤	3.91 × 3.31	8.6	165 @ 4000	240 @ 2000	35—65
1982	6-225, 3.7L⑥	E	1945, 1 Bbl.⑦	3.40 × 4.12	8.4	90 @ 3600	160 @ 1600	30—70
	6-225, 3.7L④	E	6145, 1 Bbl.⑦	3.40 × 4.12	8.4	90 @ 3600	160 @ 1600	30—70
	V8-318, 5.2L⑥	K	BBD, 2 Bbl.⑤	3.91 × 3.31	8.5	130 @ 4000	230 @ 2000	30—80
	V8-318, 5.2L④	M	TQ, 4 Bbl.⑤	3.91 × 3.31	8.5	165 @ 4000	240 @ 2000	30—80
1983	6-225, 3.7L	H	6145, 1 Bbl.⑦	3.40 × 4.12	8.4	90 @ 3600	165 @ 1600	30—70
	V8-318, 5.2L	P	BBD, 2 Bbl.⑤	3.91 × 3.31	8.5	130 @ 4000	230 @ 1600	30—70
1984	V8-318, 5.2L		BBD, 2 Bbl.⑤	3.91 × 3.31	8.6	130 @ 4000	235 @ 1600	30—80
PLYMOUTH								
1977	6-225, 3.7L④	C	1945, 1 Bbl.⑦	3.40 × 4.12	8.4	90 @ 3600	170 @ 1600	30—70
	6-225, 3.7L⑥	C	1945, 1 Bbl.⑦	3.40 × 4.12	8.4	100 @ 3600	170 @ 1600	30—70
	6-225, 3.7L	D	BBD, 2 Bbl.⑤	3.40 × 4.12	8.4	110 @ 3600	180 @ 2000	30—70
	V8-318, 5.2L④	G	2245, 2 Bbl.⑦	3.91 × 3.31	8.6	135 @ 3600	235 @ 1600	30—80
	V8-318, 5.2L⑥	G	2245, 2 Bbl.⑦	3.91 × 3.31	8.6	145 @ 4000	245 @ 1600	30—80
	V8-360, 5.9L	K	2245, 2 Bbl.⑦	4.00 × 3.58	8.4	155 @ 3600	275 @ 2000	30—80
	V8-360, 5.9L	J	TQ, 4 Bbl.⑤	4.00 × 3.58	8.4	170 @ 4000	270 @ 1600	30—80
	V8-360, 5.9L⑫	L	TQ, 4 Bbl.⑤	4.00 × 3.58	8.0	175 @ 4000	275 @ 2000	30—80
	V8-400, 6.6L	N	TQ, 4 Bbl.⑤	4.34 × 3.38	8.2	190 @ 3600	305 @ 3200	30—80
	V8-440, 7.2L⑧	T	TQ, 4 Bbl.⑤	4.32 × 3.75	8.2	185 @ 3600	310 @ 2400	30—80
	V8-440, 7.2L⑲	T	TQ, 4 Bbl.⑤	4.32 × 3.75	8.2	195 @ 3600	320 @ 2000	30—80
	V8-440, 7.2L④⑫	U	TQ, 4 Bbl.⑤	4.32 × 3.75	7.8	230 @ 4000	330 @ 3200	30—80
	V8-440, 7.2L⑥⑫	U	TQ, 4 Bbl.⑤	4.32 × 3.75	7.8	245 @ 4000	350 @ 3200	30—80
1978	6-225, 3.7L⑬	C	1945, 1 Bbl.⑦	3.40 × 4.12	8.4	90 @ 3600	160 @ 1600	30—70
	6-225, 3.7L	C	1945, 1 Bbl.⑦	3.40 × 4.12	8.4	100 @ 3600	170 @ 1600	30—70
	6-225, 3.7L	D	BBD, 2 Bbl.⑤	3.40 × 4.12	8.4	110 @ 3600	180 @ 2000	30—70
	V8-318, 5.2L⑥⑯	G	BBD, 2 Bbl.⑤	3.91 × 3.31	8.5	140 @ 4000	245 @ 1600	30—80
	V8-318, 5.2L⑥⑰	G	BBD, 2 Bbl.⑤	3.91 × 3.31	8.5	145 @ 4000	245 @ 1600	30—80
	V8-318, 5.2L⑧	H	TQ, 4 Bbl.⑤	3.91 × 3.31	8.5	155 @ 4000	245 @ 1600	30—80
	V8-360, 5.9L	K	2245, 2 Bbl.⑦	4.00 × 3.58	8.4	155 @ 3600	270 @ 2400	30—80
	V8-360, 5.9L	L	TQ, 4 Bbl.⑤	4.00 × 3.58	8.4	175 @ 4000	260 @ 2400	30—80
	V8-400, 6.0L	N	TQ, 4 Bbl.⑤	4.34 × 3.38	8.2	190 @ 3600	305 @ 3200	30—80
1979	6-225, 3.7L	C	1945, 1 Bbl.⑦	3.40 × 4.12	8.4	100 @ 3600	165 @ 1600	30—70
	6-225, 3.7L⑥	C	BBD, 2 Bbl.⑤	3.40 × 4.12	8.4	110 @ 3600	180 @ 2000	30—70
	V8-318, 5.2L⑥	G	2280, 2 Bbl.⑦	3.91 × 3.31	8.5	135 @ 4000	250 @ 1600	30—80
	V8-318, 5.2L④	H	TQ, 4 Bbl.⑤	3.91 × 3.31	8.5	155 @ 4000	245 @ 1600	30—80
	V8-360, 5.9L	J	TQ, 4 Bbl.⑤	4.00 × 3.58	8.0	195 @ 4000	280 @ 2400	30—80
1980	6-225, 3.7L	C	1945, 1 Bbl.⑦	3.40 × 4.12	8.4	90 @ 3600	160 @ 1600	30—70
	V8-318, 5.2L	G	BBD, 2 Bbl.⑤	3.91 × 3.31	8.5	120 @ 3600	245 @ 1600	30—80
	V8-318, 5.2L	H	TQ, 4 Bbl.⑤	3.91 × 3.31	8.5	155 @ 4000	240 @ 2000	30—80
	V8-360, 5.9L	K	BBD, 2 Bbl.⑤	4.00 × 3.58	8.4	130 @ 3200	—	30—80
	V8-360, 5.9L	L	TQ, 4 Bbl.⑤	4.00 × 3.58	8.4	185 @ 4000	275 @ 2000	30—80
1981	6-225, 3.7L⑥	E	1945, 1 Bbl.⑦	3.40 × 4.12	8.4	85 @ 3600	165 @ 1600	30—70
	6-225, 3.7L④	E	6145, 1 Bbl.⑦	3.40 × 4.12	8.4	85 @ 3600	165 @ 1600	30—70
	V8-318, 5.2L⑥	K	BBD, 2 Bbl.⑤	3.91 × 3.31	8.6	130 @ 4000	230 @ 2000	35—65
	V8-318, 5.2L	M	TQ, 4 Bbl.⑤	3.91 × 3.31	8.6	165 @ 4000	240 @ 2000	35—65

Continued

GENERAL ENGINE SPECIFICATIONS—Continued

Year	Engine CID①/Liter	V.I.N. Code②	Carburetor	Bore and Stroke	Compression Ratio	Net H.P. @ R.P.M.③	Maximum Torque Ft. Lbs. @ R.P.M.	Normal Oil Pressure Pounds
PLYMOUTH—Continued								
1982	6-225, 3.7L⑥	E	1945, 1 Bbl.⑦	3.40 × 4.12	8.4	90 @ 3600	160 @ 1600	30-70
	6-225, 3.7L④	E	6145, 1 Bbl.⑦	3.40 × 4.12	8.4	90 @ 3600	160 @ 1600	30-70
	V8-318, 5.2L⑥	K	BBD, 2 Bbl.⑤	3.91 × 3.31	8.5	130 @ 4000	230 @ 2000	30-80
	V8-318, 5.2L④	M	TQ, 4 Bbl.⑤	3.91 × 3.31	8.5	165 @ 4000	240 @ 2000	30-80
1983	6-225, 3.7L	H	6145, 1 Bbl.⑦	3.40 × 4.12	8.4	90 @ 3600	165 @ 1600	30-70
	V8-318, 5.2L	P	BBD, 2 Bbl.⑤	3.91 × 3.31	8.5	130 @ 4000	230 @ 1600	30-80
1984	V8-318, 5.2L	—	BBD, 2 Bbl.⑤	3.91 × 3.31	8.6	130 @ 4000	235 @ 1600	30-80

①—CID—Cubic Inch Displacement.
②—On 1977-80 vehicles, the fifth digit in the VIN denotes engine code. On 1981-83 vehicles, the eighth digit in the VIN denotes engine code.
③—Ratings are net—as installed in vehicle.
④—California.
⑤—Carter.
⑥—Exc. California.
⑦—Holley.
⑧—California & high altitude.
⑨—LeBaron.
⑩—Cordoba.
⑪—With dual exhaust.
⑫—High performance.
⑬—High altitude.
⑭—Exc. Aspen Coupe & Sedan.
⑮—Aspen Coupe & Sedan.
⑯—Fury.
⑰—Volare.
⑱—Electronic Fuel Injection.
⑲—Except Calif. & high altitude.

TUNE UP SPECIFICATIONS

The following specifications are published from the latest information available. This data should be used only in the absence of a decal affixed in the engine compartment.

★ When using a timing light, disconnect vacuum hose or tube at distributor and plug opening in hose or tube so idle speed will not be affected.

● When checking compression, lowest cylinder must be within 80 percent of highest.

▲ Before removing wires from distributor cap, determine location of the No. 1 wire in cap, as distributor position may have been altered from that shown at the end of this chart.

☞ Spark plug types shown in this chart are recommendations of the original vehicle manufacturer and not MOTOR.

Check local sources for other spark plug manufacturers listings.

Year & Engine/V.I.N.	Spark Plug Type ☞	Gap	Firing Order Fig. ▲	Ignition Timing BTDC① ★ Man. Trans.	Auto. Trans.	Mark Fig.	Curb Idle Speed Man. Trans.	Auto. Trans.②	Fast Idle Speed Man. Trans.	Auto. Trans.	Fuel Pump Pressure
CHRYSLER & IMPERIAL											
1977											
V8-318/G Exc. Calif. & High Alt.⑬	RN12Y④	.035	H	—	8°	B	—	700N	—	1400⑦	5-7
V8-318/G Calif. & High Alt.⑬	RN12Y④	.035	H	—	TDC	B	—	850N	—	1500⑦	5-7
V8-318/G Exc. Calif.⑭	RN12Y④	.035	H	—	6°	B	—	700N	—	1300⑦	5-7
V8-318/G Calif.⑭	RN12Y④	.035	H	—	8°	B	—	750N	—	1500⑦	5-7
V8-360/K 2 Barrel	RN12Y④	.035	H	—	10°	B	—	700N	—	1700⑦	5-7
V8-360/J 4 Barrel⑬	RN12Y④	.035	H	—	6°	B	—	750N	—	1700⑦	5-7
V8-360/J 4 Barrel⑭	RN12Y④	.035	H	—	10°	B	—	750N	—	1500⑦	5-7
V8-400/N⑭	④⑮	.035	I	—	10°	F	—	750N	—	1400⑦	5-7
V8-440/T⑬	RJ13Y④	.035	I	—	8°	D	—	750N	—	1200⑦	5-7
V8-440/T Exc. Calif. & High Alt.⑭	RJ13Y④	.035	I	—	12°	D	—	750N	—	1400⑦	5-7
V8-440/T Calif. & High Alt.⑭	RJ13Y④	.035	I	—	8°	D	—	750N	—	1600⑦	5-7
1978											
6-225/C,D Exc. Calif. & High Alt.	RBL16Y④	.035	G	12°	12°	J	750	750N	1500	1600⑦	3½-5
6-225/C Calif. & High Alt.	RBL16Y④	.035	G	—	8°	J	—	750N	—	⑦⑯	3½-5

Continued

TUNE UP SPECIFICATIONS—Continued

The following specifications are published from the latest information available. This
data should be used only in the absence of a decal affixed in the engine compartment.

★ When using a timing light, disconnect vacuum hose or tube at distributor and plug opening in hose or tube so idle speed will not be affected.
● When checking compression, lowest cylinder must be within 80 percent of highest.
▲ Before removing wires from distributor cap, determine location of the No. 1 wire in cap, as distributor position may have been altered from that shown at the end of this chart.

☞ Spark plug types shown in this chart are recommendations of the original vehicle manufacturer and not MOTOR.
Check local sources for other spark plug manufacturers listings.

Year & Engine/V.I.N.	Spark Plug Type ☞ ▲	Gap	Firing Order Fig. ▲	Ignition Timing BTDC①★ Man. Trans.	Ignition Timing BTDC①★ Auto. Trans.	Mark Fig.	Curb Idle Speed Man. Trans.	Curb Idle Speed Auto. Trans.②	Fast Idle Speed Man. Trans.	Fast Idle Speed Auto. Trans.	Fuel Pump Pressure
CHRYSLER & IMPERIAL											
1978—Continued											
V8-318/G 2 Barrel	RN12Y④	.035	H	16°	16°	C	700	750N	1400	⑦⑰	5–7
V8-318/H 4 Barrel	RN12Y④	.035	H	—	10°	C	—	750N	—	1600⑦	5–7
V8-360/K 2 Barrel	RN12Y④	.035	H	—	20°	C	—	750N	—	1600⑦	5–7
V8-360/J 4 Barrel Exc. Calif.⑭⑱	RN12Y④	.035	H	—	16°	C	—	750N	—	1500⑦	5–7
V8-360/J 4 Barrel Calif.⑩⑬	RN12Y④	.035	H	—	⑲	C	—	750N	—	1500⑦	5–7
V8-400/N	④⑳	.035	J	—	㉑	E	—	750N	—	1500⑦	5–7
V8-440/T Exc. Calif. & High Alt.	OJ13Y④	.035	J	—	12°	C	—	750N	—	1400⑦	5–7
V8-440/T Calif. & High Alt.	OJ13Y④	.035	J	—	8°	C	—	750N	—	1600⑦	5–7
1979											
6-225/C 1 Barrel Exc. Calif.	RBL16Y④	.035	G	12°	12°	J	675	675N	1400⑦	1600⑦	3½–5
6-225/C 1 Barrel Calif.	RBL16Y④	.035	G	—	8°	J	—	750N	—	1500⑦	3½–5
6-225/D 2 Barrel	RBL16Y④	.035	G	—	12°	J	—	725N	—	1600⑦	3½–5
V8-318/G 2 Barrel	RN12Y④	.035	H	—	16°	C	—	730N	—	1600⑦	5–7
V8-318/H 4 Barrel⑱	RN12Y④	.035	H	—	16°	C	—	750N	—	1600⑦	5–7
V8-318/H 4 Barrel⑩	RN12Y④	.035	H	—	16°	C	—	850N	—	1600⑦	5–7
V8-360/K 2 Barrel	RN12Y④	.035	H	—	12°	C	—	750N	—	1600⑦	5–7
V8-360/J 4 Barrel	RN12Y④	.035	H	—	16°	C	—	750N	—	1600⑦	5–7
1980											
6-225/C Exc. Calif.	RBL16Y④	.035	G	—	12°	J	—	725N	—	1600⑦	3½–5
6-225/C Calif.	RBL16Y④	.035	G	—	12°	J	—	750N	—	—	3½–5
V8-318/G 2 Barrel	RN12Y④	.035	H	—	12°	C	—	700N	—	1500⑦	5–7
V8-318/H 4 Barrel	RN12Y④	.035	H	—	16°	C	—	700N	—	—	5–7
V8-360/K 2 Barrel	RN12Y④	.035	H	—	12°	C	—	700N	—	1500⑦	5–7
V8-360/L 4 Barrel	RN12Y④	.035	H	—	16°	C	—	750N	—	—	5–7
1981											
6-225/E Exc. Calif.	560PR4⑥	.048	G	—	12°	J	—	650N	—	1600	4–5½
6-225/E Calif.	560PR4⑥	.048	G	—	16°	J	—	750N	—	2000	4–5½
V8-318/K, M Less E.F.I.	65PR4③⑥	.048③	H	—	16°	C	—	700N	—	1400	5¾–7¼
V8-318/J E.F.I.	68ER⑥	.035	H	—	12°	C	—	580N	—	—	7½–11½ ⑨
1982											
6-225/E Exc. Calif.	560PR⑥	.035	G	—	12°	J	—	625N	—	1600	4–5½
6-225/E Calif.	560PR⑥	.035	G	—	12°	J	—	725N	—	1950	4–5½
V8-318/K 2 Barrel	65PR⑥	.035	H	—	16°	C	—	600N	—	1400	5¾–7¼
V8-318/M 4 Barrel	65PR⑥	.035	H	—	16°	C	—	650N	—	1400	5¾–7¼
V8-318/J E.F.I.	68ER⑥	.035	H	—	12°	C	—	580N	—	—	7½–11½ ⑨

Continued

TUNE UP SPECIFICATIONS—Continued

The following specifications are published from the latest information available. This
data should be used only in the absence of a decal affixed in the engine compartment.

★ When using a timing light, disconnect vacuum hose or tube at distributor and plug opening in hose or tube so idle speed will not be affected.

● When checking compression, lowest cylinder must be within 80 percent of highest.

▲ Before removing wires from distributor cap, determine location of the No. 1 wire in cap, as distributor position may have been altered from that shown at
the end of this chart.

Spark plug types shown in this chart are recommendations of the original vehicle manufacturer and not MOTOR.
Check local sources for other spark plug manufacturers listings.

Year & Engine/V.I.N.	Spark Plug		Ignition Timing BTDC①★				Curb Idle Speed		Fast Idle Speed		Fuel Pump Pressure
	Type	Gap	Firing Order Fig. ▲	Man. Trans.	Auto. Trans.	Mark Fig.	Man. Trans.	Auto. Trans.②	Man. Trans.	Auto. Trans.	
CHRYSLER & IMPERIAL—Continued											
1983											
6-225/H	RBL16Y④	.035	G	—	16°	K	—	750N	—	2000	4–5½
V8-318/P Less E.F.I.	RN12YC④⑤	.035	H	—	16°	C	—	700N	—	1400	5¾–7½
V8-318/N E.F.I.	RN12YC④⑤	.035	H	—	12°	C	—	580D	—	—	7½–11½ ⑨
1984											
V8-318/2 Barrel Exc. Calif.	RN12YC④	.035	H	—	16°	C	—	700N	—	—	5¾–7¼
V8-318/2 Barrel Calif.	RN12YC④	.035	H	—	16°	C	—	730N	—	—	5¾–7¼
DODGE											
1977											
6-225/C 1 Barrel⑧	RBL15Y④	.035	G	12°	12°	A	700	700N	1700⑦	1700⑦	3½–5
6-225/C 1 Barrel Exc. Calif.⑱㉒	RBL15Y④	.035	G	6°	2°	A	700	700N	1400⑦	1700⑦	3½–5
6-225/C 1 Barrel Calif.⑩㉒	RBL15Y④	.035	G	8°	8°	A	750	750N	1600⑦	1700⑦	3½–5
6-225/D 2 Barrel Exc. Calif.	RBL15Y④	.035	G	12°	12°	A	750	750N	1500⑦	1600⑦	3½–5
6-225/D 2 Barrel Calif.	RBL15Y④	.035	G	4°	4°	A	850	850N	1600⑦	1700⑦	3½–5
V8-318/G Exc. Calif. & High Alt.⑬	RN12Y④	.035	H	8°	8°	B	700	700N	1400⑦	1400⑦	5–7
V8-318/G Calif. & High Alt.⑬	RN12Y④	.035	H	—	TDC	B	—	850N	—	1500⑦	5–7
V8-318/G Exc. Calif.⑭	RN12Y④	.035	H	—	6°	B	—	700N	—	1300⑦	5–7
V8-318/G Calif.⑭	RN12Y④	.035	H	—	8°	B	—	750N	—	1500⑦	5–7
V8-360/K 2 Barrel	RN12Y④	.035	H	—	10°	B	—	700N	—	1700⑦	5–7
V8-360/J,L 4 Barrel⑬	RN12Y④	.035	H	—	6°	B	—	750N	—	1700⑦	5–7
V8-360/J,L 4 Barrel⑭	RN12Y④	.035	H	—	10°	B	—	750N	—	1500⑦	5–7
V8-400/N⑭	④⑮	.035	I	—	10°	F	—	750N	—	1400⑦	5–7
V8-440/T⑬	RJ13Y④	.035	I	—	8°	D	—	750N	—	1200⑦	5–7
V8-440/T Exc. Calif. & High Alt.⑭	RJ13Y④	.035	I	—	12°	D	—	750N	—	1400⑦	5–7
V8-440/T Calif. & High Alt.⑭	RJ13Y④	.035	I	—	8°	D	—	750N	—	1200⑦	5–7
V8-440/U High Perf.⑭	RJ11Y④	.035	I	—	8°	D	—	750N	—	1600⑦	6–7½
1978											
6-225/C 1 Barrel Exc. Calif.⑱	RBL16Y④	.035	G	12°	12°	J	700	700N	1400⑦	1600⑦	3½–5
6-225/C 1 Barrel Calif.⑩	RBL16Y④	.035	G	—	8°	J	—	750N	—	⑦⑯	3½–5
6-225/D 2 Barrel	RBL16Y④	.035	G	12°	12°	J	750	750N	1500⑦	1600⑦	3½–5

Continued

TUNE UP SPECIFICATIONS—Continued

The following specifications are published from the latest information available. This
data should be used only in the absence of a decal affixed in the engine compartment.

★ When using a timing light, disconnect vacuum hose or tube at distributor and plug opening in hose or tube so idle speed will not be affected.

● When checking compression, lowest cylinder must be within 80 percent of highest.

▲ Before removing wires from distributor cap, determine location of the No. 1 wire in cap, as distributor position may have been altered from that shown at the end of this chart.

☞ Spark plug types shown in this chart are recommendations of the original vehicle manufacturer and not MOTOR.
Check local sources for other spark plug manufacturers listings.

Year & Engine/V.I.N.	Spark Plug Type ☞	Gap	Firing Order Fig. ▲	Ignition Timing BTDC① ★ Man. Trans.	Auto. Trans.	Mark Fig.	Curb Idle Speed Man. Trans.	Auto. Trans.②	Fast Idle Speed Man. Trans.	Auto. Trans.	Fuel Pump Pressure
DODGE											
1978—Continued											
V8-318/G 2 Barrel	RN12Y④	.035	H	—	16°	C	—	750N	—	⑦⑰	5—7
V8-318/H 4 Barrel⑱	RN12Y④	.035	H	—	10°	C	—	750N	—	1600⑦	5—7
V8-318/H 4 Barrel⑩	RN12Y④	.035	H	—	16°	C	—	850N	—	1600⑦	5—7
V8-360/K 2 Barrel	RN12Y④	.035	H	—	20°	C	—	750N	—	1600⑦	5—7
V8-360/J,L 4 Barrel Exc. Calif.⑭⑱	RN12Y④	.035	H	—	16°	C	—	750N	—	1500⑦	5—7
V8-360/J,L 4 Barrel Calif.⑩⑬	RN12Y④	.035	H	—	⑲	C	—	750N	—	1500⑦	5—7
V8-400/N	④⑳	.035	I	—	㉑	E	—	750N	—	1500⑦	5—7
1979											
6-225/C 1 Barrel Exc. Calif.	RBL16Y④	.035	G	12°	12°	J	675	675N	1400⑦	1600⑦	3½—5
6-225/C 1 Barrel Calif.	RBL16Y④	.035	G	—	8°	J	—	750N	—	1500⑦	3½—5
6-225/D 2 Barrel	RBL16Y④	.035	G	—	12°	J	—	725N	—	1600⑦	3½—5
V8-318/G 2 Barrel	RN12Y④	.035	H	—	16°	C	—	730N	—	1600⑦	5—7
V8-318/H 4 Barrel	RN12Y④	.035	H	—	16°	C	—	750N	—	1600⑦	5—7
V8-360/K 2 Barrel	RN12Y④	.035	H	—	12°	C	—	750N	—	1600⑦	5—7
V8-360/J,L 4 Barrel	RN12Y④	.035	H	—	16°	C	—	750N	—	1600⑦	5—7
1980											
6-225/C Exc. Calif.	RBL16Y④	.035	G	12°	12°	J	725	725N	—	1600⑦	3½—5
6-225/C Calif.	RBL16Y④	.035	G	—	12°	J	—	750N	—	—	3½—5
V8-318/G 2 Barrel	RN12Y④	.035	H	—	12°	C	—	700N	—	1500⑦	5—7
V8-318/H 4 Barrel	RN12Y④	.035	H	—	16°	C	—	700N	—	—	5—7
V8-360/K 2 Barrel	RN12Y④	.035	H	—	12°	C	—	700N	—	1500⑦	5—7
V8-360/L 4 Barrel	RN12Y④	.035	H	—	16°	C	—	750N	—	—	5—7
1981											
6-225/E Exc. Calif.	560PR4⑥	.048	G	—	12°	J	—	650N	—	1600	4—5½
6-225/E Calif.	560PR4⑥	.048	G	—	16°	J	—	750N	—	2000	4—5½
V8-318/K,M	65PR4③⑥	.048③	H	—	16°	C	—	700N	—	1400	5¾—7¼
1982											
6-225/E Exc. Calif.	560PR⑥	.035	G	—	12°	J	—	625N	—	1600	4—5½
6-225/E Calif.	560PR⑥	.035	G	—	12°	J	—	725N	—	1950	4—5½
V8-318/K 2 Barrel	65PR⑥	.035	H	—	16°	C	—	600N	—	1400	5¾—7¼
V8-318/M 4 Barrel	65PR⑥	.035	H	—	16°	C	—	650N	—	1400	5¾—7¼

TUNE UP SPECIFICATIONS—Continued

The following specifications are published from the latest information available. This
data should be used only in the absence of a decal affixed in the engine compartment.

★ When using a timing light, disconnect vacuum hose or tube at distributor and plug opening in hose or tube so idle speed will not be affected.

● When checking compression, lowest cylinder must be within 80 percent of highest.

▲ Before removing wires from distributor cap, determine location of the No. 1 wire in cap, as distributor position may have been altered from that shown at
the end of this chart.

☞ Spark plug types shown in this chart are recommendations of the original vehicle manufacturer and not MOTOR.
Check local sources for other spark plug manufacturers listings.

| Year & Engine/V.I.N. | Spark Plug | | Firing Order Fig. ▲ | Ignition Timing BTDC①★ | | | Curb Idle Speed | | Fast Idle Speed | | Fuel Pump Pressure |
	Type ☞	Gap		Man. Trans.	Auto. Trans.	Mark Fig.	Man. Trans.	Auto. Trans.②	Man. Trans.	Auto. Trans.	
DODGE—Continued											
1983											
6-225/H 1 Barrel	RBL16Y④	.035	G	—	16°	K	—	750N	—	2000	4–5½
V8-318/P 2 Barrel	RN12YC④⑤	.035	H	—	16°	C	—	700N	—	1400	5¾–7½
1984											
V8-318/2 Barrel Exc. Calif.	RN12YC④	.035	H	—	16°	C	—	700N	—	—	5¾–7¼
V8-318/2 Barrel Calif.	RN12YC④	.035	H	—	16°	C	—	730N	—	—	5¾–7¼
PLYMOUTH											
1977											
6-225/C 1 Barrel⑫	RBL15Y④	.035	G	12°	12°	A	700	700N	1700⑦	1700⑦	3½–5
6-225/C 1 Barrel Exc. Calif.⑱⑳	RBL15Y④	.035	G	6°	2°	A	700	700N	1400⑦	1700⑦	3½–5
6-225/C 1 Barrel Calif.⑩㉓	RBL15Y④	.035	G	8°	8°	A	750	750N	1600⑦	1700⑦	3½–5
6-225/D 2 Barrel Exc. Calif.	RBL15Y④	.035	G	12°	12°	A	750	750N	1500⑦	1600⑦	3½–5
6-225/D 2 Barrel Calif.	RBL15Y④	.035	G	4°	4°	A	850	850N	1600⑦	1700⑦	3½–5
V8-318/G Exc. Calif. & High Alt.	RN12Y④	.035	H	8°	8°	B	700	700N	1400⑦	1400⑦	5–7
V8-318/G Calif. & High Alt.	RN12Y④	.035	H	—	TDC	B	—	850N	—	1500⑦	5–7
V8-360/J 2 Barrel	RN12Y④	.035	H	—	10°	B	—	700N	—	1700⑦	5–7
V8-360/J,L 4 Barrel⑬	RN12Y④	.035	H	—	6°	B	—	750N	—	1700⑦	5–7
V8-360/J,L 4 Barrel⑭	RN12Y④	.035	H	—	10°	B	—	750N	—	1500⑦	5–7
V8-400/N⑭	④⑮	.035	I	—	10°	F	—	750N	—	1400⑦	5–7
V8-440⑬	RJ13Y④	.035	I	—	8°	D	—	750N	—	1200⑦	5–6
V8-440/T Exc. Calif. & High Alt.⑭	RJ13Y④	.035	I	—	12°	D	—	750N	—	1400⑦	5–7
V8-440/T Calif. & High Alt.⑭	RJ13Y④	.035	I	—	8°	D	—	750N	—	1200⑦	5–7
V8-440/U High Perf.⑭	RJ11Y④	.035	I	—	8°	D	—	750N	—	1600⑦	6–7½
1978											
6-225/C 1 Barrel Exc. Calif.⑱	RBL16Y④	.035	G	12°	12°	J	700	700N	1400⑦	1600⑦	3½–5
6-225/C 1 Barrel Calif.⑩	RBL16Y④	.035	G	—	8°	J	—	750N	—	⑦⑯	3½–5
6-225/D 2 Barrel	RBL16Y④	.035	G	12°	12°	J	750	750N	1500⑦	1600⑦	3½–5

Continued

TUNE UP SPECIFICATIONS—Continued

The following specifications are published from the latest information available. This
data should be used only in the absence of a decal affixed in the engine compartment.

★ When using a timing light, disconnect vacuum hose or tube at distributor and plug opening in hose or tube so idle speed will not be affected.

● When checking compression, lowest cylinder must be within 80 percent of highest.

▲ Before removing wires from distributor cap, determine location of the No. 1 wire in cap, as distributor position may have been altered from that shown at the end of this chart.

☞ Spark plug types shown in this chart are recommendations of the original vehicle manufacturer and not MOTOR.
Check local sources for other spark plug manufacturers listings.

Year & Engine/V.I.N.	Spark Plug Type ☞	Gap	Firing Order Fig. ▲	Ignition Timing BTDC① ★ Man. Trans.	Auto. Trans.	Mark Fig.	Curb Idle Speed Man. Trans.	Auto. Trans.②	Fast Idle Speed Man. Trans.	Auto. Trans.	Fuel Pump Pressure
PLYMOUTH											
1978—Continued											
V8-318/G 2 Barrel	RN12Y④	.035	H	—	16°	C	—	750N	—	⑦⑰	5–7
V8-318/H 4 Barrel	RN12Y④	.035	H	—	10°	C	—	750N	—	1600⑦	5–7
V8-360/K 2 Barrel	RN12Y④	.035	H	—	20°	C	—	750N	—	1600⑦	5–7
V8-360/L 4 Barrel Exc. Calif.⑭⑱	RN12Y④	.035	H	—	16°	C	—	750N	—	1500⑦	5–7
V8-360/L 4 Barrel Calif.⑩⑬	RN12Y④	.035	H	—	⑲	C	—	750N	—	1500⑦	5–7
V8-400/N⑭	④⑳	.035	I	—	㉑	E	—	750N	—	1500⑦	5–7
1979											
6-225/C 1 Barrel Exc. Calif.	RBL16Y④	.035	G	12°	12°	J	675	675N	1400⑦	1600⑦	3½–5
6-225/C 1 Barrel Calif.	RBL16Y④	.035	G	—	8°	J	—	750N	—	1500⑦	3½–5
6-225/D 2 Barrel	RBL16Y④	.035	G	—	12°	J	—	725N	—	1600⑦	3½–5
V8-318/G 2 Barrel	RN12Y④	.035	H	—	16°	C	—	730N	—	1600⑦	5–7
V8-318/H 4 Barrel⑱	RN12Y④	.035	H	—	16°	C	—	750N	—	1600⑦	5–7
V8-318/H 4 Barrel⑩	RN12Y④	.035	H	—	16°	C	—	850N	—	1600⑦	5–7
V8-360/K 2 Barrel	RN12Y④	.035	H	—	12°	C	—	750N	—	1600⑦	5–7
V8-360/J 4 Barrel	RN12Y④	.035	H	—	16°	C	—	750N	—	1600⑦	5–7
1980											
6-225/C Exc. Calif.	RBL16Y④	.035	G	12°	12°	J	725	725N	—	1600⑦	3½–5
6-225/C Calif.	RBL16Y④	.035	G	—	12°	J	—	750N	—	—	3½–5
V8-318/G 2 Barrel	RN12Y④	.035	H	—	12°	C	—	700N	—	1500⑦	5–7
V8-318/H 4 Barrel	RN12Y④	.035	H	—	16°	C	—	700N	—	—	5–7
V8-360/K 2 Barrel	RN12Y④	.035	H	—	12°	C	—	700N	—	1500⑦	5–7
V8-360/L 4 Barrel	RN12Y④	.035	H	—	16°	C	—	750N	—	—	5–7
1981											
6-225/E Exc. Calif.	560PR4⑥	.048	G	—	12°	J	—	650N	—	1600	4–5½
6-255/E Calif.	560PR4⑥	.048	G	—	16°	J	—	750N	—	2000	4–5½
V8-318/K,M	65PR4③⑥	.048③	H	—	16°	C	—	700N	—	1400	5¾–7¼
1982											
6-225/E Exc. Calif.	560PR⑥	.035	G	—	12°	J	—	625N	—	1600	4–5½
6-255/E Calif.	560PR⑥	.035	G	—	12°	J	—	725N	—	1950	4–5½
V8-318/K 2 Barrel	65PR⑥	.035	H	—	16°	C	—	600N	—	1400	5¾–7¼
V8-318/M 4 Barrel	65PR⑥	.035	H	—	16°	C	—	650N	—	1400	5¾–7¼
1983											
6-225/H 1 Barrel	RBL16Y④	.035	G	—	16°	J	—	750N	—	2000	4–5½
V8-318/P 2 Barrel	RN12YC④⑤	.035	G	—	16°	C	—	700N	—	1400	5¾–7½

Continued

TUNE UP SPECIFICATIONS—Continued

The following specifications are published from the latest information available. This data should be used only in the absence of a decal affixed in the engine compartment.

★ When using a timing light, disconnect vacuum hose or tube at distributor and plug opening in hose or tube so idle speed will not be affected.

● When checking compression, lowest cylinder must be within 80 percent of highest.

▲ Before removing wires from distributor cap, determine location of the No. 1 wire in cap, as distributor position may have been altered from that shown at the end of this chart.

Spark plug types shown in this chart are recommendations of the original vehicle manufacturer and not MOTOR.
Check local sources for other spark plug manufacturers listings.

| Year & Engine/V.I.N. | Spark Plug | | Firing Order Fig. ▲ | Ignition Timing BTDC①★ | | | | Curb Idle Speed | | Fast Idle Speed | | Fuel Pump Pressure |
	Type	Gap		Man. Trans.	Auto. Trans.	Mark Fig.		Man. Trans.	Auto. Trans.②	Man. Trans.	Auto. Trans.	
PLYMOUTH—Continued **1984**												
V8-318/2 Barrel Exc. Calif.	RN12YC④	.035	H	—	16°	C		—	700N	—	—	5¾—7¼
V8-318/2 Barrel Calif.	RN12YC④	.035	H	—	16°	C		—	730N	—	—	5¾—7¼

①—BTDC—Before top dead center.

②—N: Neutral. D: Drive.

③—If poor driveability condition is encountered during engine warmup on 1981 V8-318 2 Barrel engines built prior to Feb. 1, 1981, the spark plugs should be removed & regapped to .035 inch. These engines are equipped with spark plug type 65PR4 gapped at .048 inch. When replacing spark plugs, type 65PR gapped at .035 inch should be used.

④—Champion.

⑤—Original equipment spark plug. When replacing spark plugs use RN12Y.

⑥—Mopar.

⑦—With stop screw on second highest step of fast idle cam.

⑧—Aspen.

⑨—In tank electric fuel pump.

⑩—High altitude.

⑪—Carburetor No. 9109S, 1400 RPM; carburetor No. 9112S, 1200 RPM.

⑫—Volare.

⑬—Except Electronic Lean Burn engines.

⑭—Electronic Lean Burn engines.

⑮—Except high perform, engine, RJ13Y; high perf. engine, RJ11Y.

⑯—Except high altitude, 1500 RPM; high altitude, 1700 RPM.

⑰—Except high altitude, 1600 RPM; high altitude, 1700 RPM.

⑱—Except high altitude.

⑲—Distributor No. 3874115, 6° BTDC; distributor No. 3874858, 8° BTDC.

⑳—Except high perf., OJ13Y; high perf., OJ11Y.

㉑—Engine code E-64, 4500 lbs. vehicle curb weight, 24° BTDC; all other 20° BTDC.

㉒—Monaco.

㉓—Fury.

㉔—Except high perf., 5—7 psi.; high perf., 6—7½ psi.

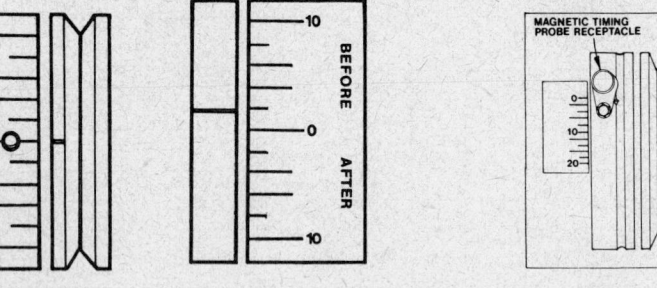

Fig. A   Fig. B   Fig. C   Fig. D   Fig. E

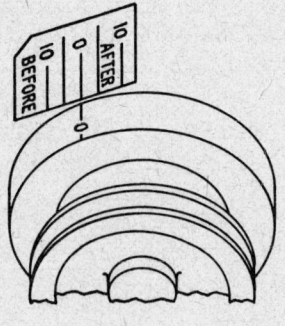

Fig. F

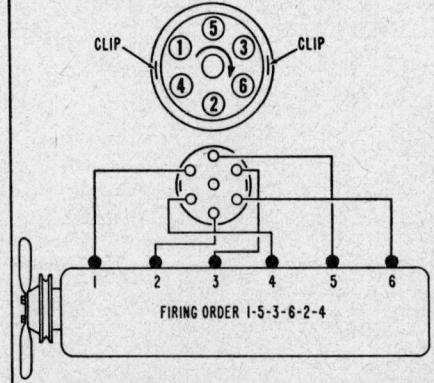

FIRING ORDER 1-5-3-6-2-4

Fig. G

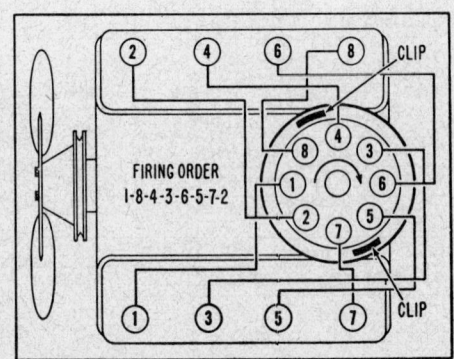

FIRING ORDER 1-8-4-3-6-5-7-2

Fig. H

Continued

TUNE UP NOTES—Continued

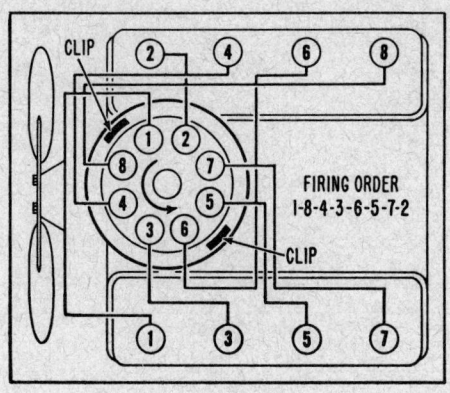

FIRING ORDER
1-8-4-3-6-5-7-2

Fig. I

MAGNETIC TIMING
PROBE RECEPTACLE

Fig. J

DISTRIBUTOR SPECIFICATIONS

★ Note: If unit is checked on vehicle, double the RPM and degrees to get crankshaft figures.

Distributor Part No.①	Centrifugal Advance Degrees @ RPM of Distributor				Vacuum Advance		Distributor Retard
	Advance Starts	Intermediate Advance		Full Advance	Inches of Vacuum to Start Plunger	Max. Adv. Dist. Deg. @ Vacuum	Max. Retard Dist. Deg. @ Vacuum
CHRYSLER & IMPERIAL							
1977							
3874115	1.3–3.1 @ 600	5.8–7.5 @ 800	—	12 @ 2000	7	12 @ 12.5	—
3874173	1.3–3.1 @ 600	3.5–5.5 @ 700	—	10 @ 2000	8	11 @ 14	—
3874858	1.4–3.4 @ 600	6–8 @ 800	—	8.5 @ 2400	7	12.5 @ 12.5	—
3874909	.2–2.2 @ 600	1.5–3.5 @ 650	—	9.6 @ 2300	8	12 @ 13.5	—
3874913	1.7–4.1 @ 600	4.8–7 @ 700	—	13.6 @ 2350	8	12 @ 13.5	—
3874917	.6–2 @ 500	3.7–5.4 @ 700	—	10 @ 2000	7	12.5 @ 12.5	—
4091015②	—	—	—	—	—	—	—
4091017②	—	—	—	—	—	—	—
4091019②	—	—	—	—	—	—	—
4091140②	—	—	—	—	—	—	—
1978							
3874115	1.3–3.1 @ 600	5.8–7.5 @ 800	—	12 @ 2000	7	12 @ 12.5	—
3874173	1.3–3.1 @ 600	3.5–5.5 @ 700	—	10 @ 2000	8	11 @ 14.0	—
3874858	1.4–3.4 @ 600	6–8 @ 800	—	8.5 @ 2400	7	12.5 @ 12.5	—
3874876	.2–2.2 @ 600	1.5–3.5 @ 650	—	5.7 @ 2500	7	9.8 @ 11.5	—
3874929	1.4–3.4 @ 600	5.6–7.6 @ 800	—	11.7 @ 2300	7	9.8 @ 11.5	—
4091101	1–1.2 @ 600	1.7–3.7 @ 800	—	5.8–7.8 @ 2060	9	9.5 @ 12.5	—
4091140②	—	—	—	—	—	—	—
4091709②	—	—	—	—	—	—	—
4091711②	—	—	—	—	—	—	—
1979							
3874876	.2–2.2 @ 600	1.5–3.5 @ 650	—	3.7–5.7 @ 2500	7	9.8 @ 11.5	—
4091101	1.0–1.2 @ 600	1.7–3.7 @ 800	—	5.8–7.8 @ 2060	9	9.5 @ 12.5	—
4091140②	—	—	—	—	—	—	—
1980							
3874876	.2 @ 600	1.5–3.5 @ 650	—	5.7 @ 2500	7	9.8 @ 11.5	—
4091490②	—	—	—	—	—	—	—
4111501	1.5 @ 700	1.5–3.5 @ 900	—	10 @ 2200	6	12 @ 15	—
4111784②	—	—	—	—	—	—	—

Continued

DISTRIBUTOR SPECIFICATIONS—Continued

★ Note: If unit is checked on vehicle, double the RPM and degrees to get crankshaft figures.

| Distributor Part No.① | Centrifugal Advance Degrees @ RPM of Distributor | | | | | Vacuum Advance | | Distributor Retard |
	Advance Starts	Intermediate Advance			Full Advance	Inches of Vacuum to Start Plunger	Max. Adv. Dist. Deg. @ Vacuum	Max. Retard Dist. Deg. @ Vacuum
CHRYSLER & IMPERIAL—Continued								
1981								
4091140②	—	—	—	—	—	—	—	—
4145717	.2–2.2 @ 600	1.5–3.5 @ 650	—	—	5.7 @ 2500	7	12 @ 15	—
4145751②	—	—	—	—	—	—	—	—
4145753②	—	—	—	—	—	—	—	—
4145848	.2–2.2 @ 600	1.5–3.5 @ 650	—	—	5.7 @ 2500	7	12 @ 15	—
1982								
4145954	0–1.6 @ 600	0–2 @ 900	—	—	4.5 @ 2500	4	12 @ 11	—
1982–83								
4091140②	—	—	—	—	—	—	—	—
4145751②	—	—	—	—	—	—	—	—
4145753②	—	—	—	—	—	—	—	—
1984								
4145753②	—	—	—	—	—	—	—	—

①—Stamped on distributor housing. ②—Electronic Spark Control distributor cannot be checked on vehicle.

Distributor Part No.	Advance Starts	Intermediate Advance			Full Advance	Inches of Vacuum	Max. Adv.	Max. Retard
DODGE & PLYMOUTH								
1977								
3874115	1.3–3.1 @ 600	5.8–7.5 @ 800	—	—	12 @ 2000	7	12 @ 12.5	—
3874173	1.3–3.1 @ 600	3.5–5.5 @ 700	—	—	10 @ 2000	8	11 @ 14	—
3874714	.3–2.4 @ 500	4.2–6.2 @ 650	—	—	8.9 @ 2500	7	9.8 @ 11.5	—
3874858	1.4–3.4 @ 600	6–8 @ 800	—	—	8.5 @ 2400	7	12.5 @ 12.5	—
3874876	.2–2.2 @ 600	1.5–3.5 @ 650	—	—	5.7 @ 2500	7	9.8 @ 11.5	—
3874909	.2–2.2 @ 600	1.5–3.5 @ 650	—	—	9.6 @ 2300	8	12 @ 13.5	—
3874913	1.7–4.1 @ 600	4.8–7.0 @ 700	—	—	13.6 @ 2350	8	12 @ 13.5	—
3874917	.6–2 @ 500	3.7–5.4 @ 700	—	—	10 @ 2000	7	12.5 @ 12.5	—
3874929	1.4–3.4 @ 600	5.6–7.6 @ 800	—	—	11.7 @ 2300	7	9.8 @ 11.5	—
4091015②	—	—	—	—	—	—	—	—
4091017②	—	—	—	—	—	—	—	—
4091019②	—	—	—	—	—	—	—	—
4091039	.2–2.2 @ 600	1.5–3.5 @ 650	—	—	5.7 @ 2500	7	9.8 @ 11.5	—
4091101	1.0–1.2 @ 600	1.7–3.7 @ 800	—	—	7.8 @ 2060	9	9.5 @ 12.5	—
4091140②	—	—	—	—	—	—	—	—
1978								
3874115	1.3–3.1 @ 600	5.8–7.5 @ 800	—	—	12 @ 2000	7	12 @ 12.5	—
3874173	1.3–3.1 @ 600	3.5–5.5 @ 700	—	—	10 @ 2000	8	11 @ 14.0	—
3874858	1.4–3.4 @ 600	6–8 @ 800	—	—	8.5 @ 2400	7	12.5 @ 12.5	—
3874876	.2–2.2 @ 600	1.5–3.5 @ 650	—	—	5.7 @ 2500	7	9.8 @ 11.5	—
4091101	1–1.2 @ 600	1.7–3.7 @ 800	—	—	5.8–7.8 @ 2060	9	9.5 @ 12.5	—
4091140②	—	—	—	—	—	—	—	—
4091709②	—	—	—	—	—	—	—	—
4091711②	—	—	—	—	—	—	—	—
1979								
3874876	.2–2.2 @ 600	1.5–3.5 @ 650	—	—	3.7–5.7 @ 2500	7	9.8 @ 11.5	—
4091101	1–1.2 @ 600	1.7–3.7 @ 800	—	—	5.8–7.8 @ 2060	9	9.5 @ 12.5	—

Continued

DISTRIBUTOR SPECIFICATIONS—Continued

★ Note: If unit is checked on vehicle, double the RPM and degrees to get crankshaft figures.

Distributor Part No.①	Centrifugal Advance Degrees @ RPM of Distributor				Vacuum Advance		Distributor Retard
	Advance Starts	Intermediate Advance		Full Advance	Inches of Vacuum to Start Plunger	Max. Adv. Dist. Deg. @ Vacuum	Max. Retard Dist. Deg. @ Vacuum
DODGE & PLYMOUTH							
1979—Continued							
4091140②	—	—	—	—	—	—	—
1980							
3874876	.2 @ 600	1.5–3.5 @ 650	—	5.7 @ 2500	7	9.8 @ 11.5	—
4091490②	—	—	—	—	—	—	—
4111501	0 @ 675	1.5–3.5 @ 900	—	10 @ 2200	6	12 @ 15	—
4111784②	—	—	—	—	—	—	—
1981							
4145717	.2–2.2 @ 600	1.5–3.5 @ 650	—	5.7 @ 2500	7	12 @ 15	—
4145751②	—	—	—	—	—	—	—
4145753②	—	—	—	—	—	—	—
4145848	.2–2.2 @ 600	1.5–3.5 @ 650	—	5.7 @ 2500	7	12 @ 15	—
1982							
4145954	0–1.6 @ 600	0–2 @ 900	—	4.5 @ 2500	4	12 @ 11	—
1982–83							
4145751②	—	—	—	—	—	—	—
4145753②	—	—	—	—	—	—	—
1984							
4145753②	—	—	—	—	—	—	—

①—Stamped on distributor housing.   ②—Electronic Spark Control system distributor, cannot be checked on vehicle.

VALVE SPECIFICATIONS

Year	Engine/V.I.N.	Valve Lash		Valve Angles		Valve Spring Installed Height	Valve Spring Pressure Lbs. @ In.	Stem Clearance		Stem Diameter	
		Int.	Exh.	Seat	Face			Intake	Exhaust	Intake	Exhaust
CHRYSLER & IMPERIAL											
1977	V8-318/G	Hydraulic①		45	②	1¹¹⁄₁₆	177 @ 1⁵⁄₁₆	.001–.003	.002–.004	.372–.373	.371–.372
	V8-360/K,J	Hydraulic①		45	②	1²¹⁄₃₂	193 @ 1¹⁄₄	.001–.003	.002–.004	.372–.373	.371–.372
	V8-400/N, 440/T	Hydraulic①		45	45	1⁵⁵⁄₆₄	200 @ 1⁷⁄₁₆	.0011–.0028	④	.3723–.3730	⑥
1978	6-225/C,D	.010H	.020H	45	②	1²¹⁄₃₂	144 @ 1⁵⁄₁₆	.001–.003	.002–.004	.372–.373	.371–.372
	V8-318/G,H	Hydraulic①		45	②	1²¹⁄₃₂	177 @ 1⁵⁄₁₆	.001–.003	.002–.004	.372–.373	.371–.372
	V8-360/K,J	Hydraulic①		45	②	1²¹⁄₃₂	177 @ 1⁵⁄₁₆	.001–.003	.002–.004	.372–.373	.371–.372
	V8-360/L③	Hydraulic①		45	②	1²¹⁄₃₂	193 @ 1¹⁄₄	.0015–.0035	.0025–.0045	.3715–.3725	.3705–.3715
	V8-400/N, 440/T	Hydraulic①		45	45	1⁵⁵⁄₆₄	200 @ 1⁷⁄₁₆	.0011–.0028	④	.3723–.3730	⑥
1979–80	6-225/C,D	.010H	.020H	45	②	1¹¹⁄₁₆	144 @ 1⁵⁄₁₆	.001–.003	.002–.004	.372–.373	.371–.372
	V8-318/G,H	Hydraulic①		45	45	1¹¹⁄₁₆	177 @ 1⁵⁄₁₆	.001–.003	.002–.004	.372–.373	.371–.372
	V8-360/K,J	Hydraulic①		45	45	1¹¹⁄₁₆	177 @ 1⁵⁄₁₆	.001–.003	.002–.004	.372–.373	.371–.372
	V8-360/L③	Hydraulic①		45	45	1²¹⁄₃₂	193 @ 1¹⁄₄	.0015–.0035	.0025–.0045	.3715–.3725	.3705–.3715
1981–83	6-225/E,H,P	Hydraulic①		45	②	1¹¹⁄₁₆	144 @ 1⁵⁄₁₆	.001–.003	.002–.004	.372–.373	.371–.372

VALVE SPECIFICATIONS—Continued

Year	Engine/V.I.N.	Valve Lash Int.	Valve Lash Exh.	Valve Angles Seat	Valve Angles Face	Valve Spring Installed Height	Valve Spring Pressure Lbs. @ In.	Stem Clearance Intake	Stem Clearance Exhaust	Stem Diameter Intake	Stem Diameter Exhaust
CHRYSLER & IMPERIAL—Continued											
	V8-318⑩⑪	Hydraulic①		45–45½	44½–45	1¹¹⁄₁₆	177 @ 1⁵⁄₁₆	.001–.003	.002–.004	.372–.373	.371–.372
	V8-318⑧⑪	Hydraulic①		45–45½	44½–45	1²¹⁄₃₂	193 @ 1¼	.0015–.0035	.0025–.0045	.3715–.3725	.3705–.3715
1984	V8-318	Hydraulic①		45–45½	44½–45	1¹¹⁄₁₆	177 @ 1⁵⁄₁₆	.001–.003	.002–.004	.372–.373	.371–.372
DODGE & PLYMOUTH											
1977	6-225/C,D	.010H	.020H	45	②	1¹¹⁄₁₆	144 @ 1⁵⁄₁₆	.001–.003	.002–.004	.372–.373	.371–.372
	V8-318/G	Hydraulic①		45	②	1¹¹⁄₁₆	177 @ 1⁵⁄₁₆	.001–.003	.002–.004	.372–.373	.371–.372
	V8-360/K,J	Hydraulic①		45	②	1²¹⁄₃₂	193 @ 1¼	.001–.003	.002–.004	.372–.373	.371–.372
	V8-360/L③	Hydraulic①		45	②	1²¹⁄₃₂	193 @ 1¼	.0015–.0035	.0025–.0045	.3715–.3725	.3705–.3715
	V8-400/N, 440/T	Hydraulic①		45	45	1⁵⁵⁄₆₄	200 @ 1⁷⁄₁₆	.0011–.0028	④	.3723–.373	⑥
	V8-400/N, 440/U③	Hydraulic①		45	45	1⁵⁵⁄₆₄	246 @ 1²³⁄₆₄	.0016–.0033	⑤	.3718–.3725	⑦
1978	6-225/C,D⑨	.010H	.020H	45	②	1²¹⁄₃₂	144 @ 1⁵⁄₁₆	.001–.003	.002–.004	.372–.373	.371–.372
	V8-318/G,H	Hydraulic①		45	②	1²¹⁄₃₂	177 @ 1⁵⁄₁₆	.001–.003	.002–.004	.372–.373	.371–.372
	V8-360/K,J	Hydraulic①		45	②	1²¹⁄₃₂	177 @ 1⁵⁄₁₆	.001–.003	.002–.004	.372–.373	.371–.372
	V8-360/L③	Hydraulic①		45	②	1²¹⁄₃₂	193 @ 1¼	.0015–.0035	.0025–.0045	.3715–.3725	.3705–.3715
	V8-400/N, 440/T	Hydraulic①		45	45	1⁵⁵⁄₆₄	200 @ 1⁷⁄₁₆	.0011–.0028	④	.3723–.3730	⑥
	V8-400/N, 440/U③	Hydraulic①		45	45	1⁵⁵⁄₆₄	246 @ 1²³⁄₆₄	.0016–.0033	⑤	.3718–.3725	⑦
1979–80	6-225/C,D	.010H	.020H	45	②	1¹¹⁄₁₆	144 @ 1⁵⁄₁₆	.001–.003	.002–.004	.372–.373	.371–.372
	V8-318/G,H	Hydraulic①		45	45	1¹¹⁄₁₆	177 @ 1⁵⁄₁₆	.001–.003	.002–.004	.372–.373	.371–.372
	V8-360/K,J	Hydraulic①		45	45	1¹¹⁄₁₆	177 @ 1⁵⁄₁₆	.001–.003	.002–.004	.372–.373	.371–.372
	V8-360/L③	Hydraulic①		45	45	1²¹⁄₃₂	193 @ 1¼	.0015–.0035	.0025–.0045	.3715–.3725	.3705–.3715
1981–83	6-225/E,H	Hydraulic①		45	②	1¹¹⁄₁₆	144 @ 1⁵⁄₁₆	.001–.003	.002–.004	.372–.373	.371–.372
	V8-318/K,M,P	Hydraulic①		45–45½	44½–45	1¹¹⁄₁₆	177 @ 1⁵⁄₁₆	.001–.003	.002–.004	.372–.373	.371–.372
1984	V8-318	Hydraulic①		45–45½	44½–45	1¹¹⁄₁₆	177 @ 1⁵⁄₁₆	.001–.003	.002–.004	.372–.373	.371–.372

①—No adjustment.
②—Intake 45°, exhaust 43°.
③—High Performance.
④—Hot end .0021–.0038, Cold end .0011–.0028.
⑤—Hot end .0026–.0043, Cold end .0016–.0033.
⑥—Hot end 3713–.372, Cold end .3723–.373.
⑦—Hot end .3708–.3715, Cold end .3718–.3725.
⑧—With Electronic Fuel Injection.
⑨—Some Aspen & Volaré models w/6-225 2 bar.
carb. will be equipped w/hydraulic lifters which cannot be adjusted.
⑩—Less Electronic Fuel Injection.
⑪—Refer to General Engine Specifications for V.I.N. code.

PISTONS, PINS, RINGS, CRANKSHAFT & BEARINGS

Year	Engine/V.I.N.	Piston Clearance Top of Skirt	Ring End Gap① Comp.	Ring End Gap① Oil	Wristpin Diameter	Rod Bearings Shaft Diameter	Rod Bearings Bearing Clearance	Main Bearings Shaft Diameter	Main Bearings Bearing Clearance	Thrust on Bear. No.	Shaft End Play
CHRYSLER & IMPERIAL											
1977	V8-318/G	.0005–.0015	.010	.015	.9842	2.124–2.125	.0005–.0025	2.4995–2.5005	.0005–.0020	3	.002–.009
	V8-360/J,K	.0005–.0015	.010	.015	.9842	2.124–2.125	.0005–.0025	2.4995–2.5005	.0005–.0020	3	.002–.009
	V8-400/N	.0003–.0013	.013	.015	1.0936	2.375–2.376	.0005–.0025	2.6245–2.6255	.0005–.0020	3	.002–.009
	V8-440/T	.0003–.0013	.013	.015	1.0936	2.375–2.376	.0005–.0025	2.7495–2.7505	.0005–.0020	3	.002–.009
1978	6-225/C,D	.0005–.0015	.010	.015	.9008	2.1865–2.1875	.0005–.0025	2.7495–2.7505	.0005–.0020	3	.002–.009
	V8-318/G,H	.0005–.0015	.010	.015	.9842	2.1240–2.1250	.0005–.0025	2.4995–2.5005	.0005–.0020	3	.002–.009
	V8-360/J,K	④	.010	.015	.9842	2.1240–2.1250	.0005–.0025	2.8095–2.8105	.0005–.0020	3	.002–.009
	V8-400/N	.0003–.0013	.013	.015	1.0936	2.375–2.376	③	2.6245–2.6255	.0005–.0020	3	.002–.009
	V8-440/T	.0003–.0013	.013	.015	1.0936	2.375–2.376	③	2.7495–2.7505	.0005–.0020	3	.002–.009
1979	6-225/C,D	.0005–.0015	.010	.015	.9008	2.1865–2.1875	.0005–.0025	2.7495–2.7505	.0005–.0020	3	.002–.009

Continued

PISTONS, PINS, RINGS, CRANKSHAFT & BEARINGS—Continued

| Year | Engine/V.I.N. | Piston Clearance Top of Skirt | Ring End Gap① | | Wristpin Diameter | Rod Bearings | | Main Bearings | | | |
			Comp.	Oil		Shaft Diameter	Bearing Clearance	Shaft Diameter	Bearing Clearance	Thrust on Bear. No.	Shaft End Play
CHRYSLER & IMPERIAL—Continued											
	V8-318/G,H	.0005–.0015	.010	.015	.9842	2.1240–2.1250	.0005–.0025	2.4995–2.5005	.0005–.0020	3	.002–.009
	V8-360/J,K,L	④	.010	.015	.9842	2.1240–2.1250	.0005–.0025	2.8095–2.8105	.0005–.0020	3	.002–.009
1980	6-225/C	.0005–.0015	.010	.015	.9008	2.1865–2.1875	.0005–.0025	2.7495–2.7505	.0005–.0020	3	.002–.009
	V8-318/G,H	.0005–.0015	.010	.015	.9842	2.1240–2.1250	.0005–.0025	2.4995–2.5005	②	3	.002–.009
	V8-360/J,K,L	④	.010	.015	.9842	2.1240–2.1250	.0005–.0025	2.8095–2.8105	②	3	.002–.009
1981–83	6-225/E,H	.0005–.0015	.010	.015	.9008	2.1865–2.1875	.0010–.0025	2.7495–2.7505	.0010–.0025	3	.0035–.0095
	V8-318⑤	.0005–.0015	.010	.015	.9842	2.124–2.125	.0005–.0025	2.4995–2.5005	②	3	.002–.009
1984	V8-318/	.0005–.0015	.010	.015	.9482	2.124–2.125	.0005–.0025	2.4995–2.5005	②	3	—
DODGE & PLYMOUTH											
1977	6-225/C,D	.0005–.0015	.010	.015	.9008	2.1865–2.1875	.0005–.0025	2.7495–2.7505	.0005–.0020	3	.002–.009
	V8-318/G	.0005–.0015	.010	.015	.9842	2.124–2.125	.0005–.0025	2.4995–2.5005	.0005–.0020	3	.002–.009
	V8-360/J,K,L	.0005–.0015	.010	.015	.9842	2.125–2.125	.0005–.0025	2.4995–2.5005	.0005–.0020	3	.002–.009
	V8-400/N	.0003–.0013	.013	.015	1.0936	2.375–2.376	.0005–.0025	2.6245–2.6255	.0005–.0020	3	.002–.009
	V8-440/T,U	.0003–.0013	.013	.015	1.0936	2.375–2.376	.0005–.0025	2.7495–2.7505	.0005–.0020	3	.002–.009
1978	6-225/C,D	.0005–.0015	.010	.015	.9008	2.1865–2.1875	.0005–.0025	2.7495–2.7505	.0005–.0020	3	.002–.009
	V8-318/G,H	.0005–.0015	.010	.015	.9842	2.1240–2.1250	.0005–.0025	2.4995–2.5005	.0005–.0020	3	.002–.009
	V8-360/J,K,L	④	.010	.015	.9842	2.1240–2.1250	.0005–.0025	2.8095–2.8105	.0005–.0020	3	.002–.009
	V8-400/N	.0003–.0013	.013	.015	1.0936	2.375–2.376	③	2.6245–2.6255	.0005–.0020	3	.002–.009
	V8-440/T	.0003–.0013	.013	.015	1.0936	2.375–2.376	③	2.7495–2.7505	.0005–.0020	3	.002–.009
1979	6-225/C,D	.0005–.0015	.010	.015	.9008	2.1865–2.1875	.0005–.0025	2.7495–2.7505	.0005–.0020	3	.002–.009
	V8-318/G,H	.0005–.0015	.010	.015	.9842	2.1240–2.1250	.0005–.0025	2.4995–2.5005	.0005–.0020	3	.002–.009
	V8-360/J,K,L	④	.010	.015	.9842	2.1240–2.1250	.0005–.0025	2.8095–2.8105	.0005–.0020	3	.002–.009
1980	6-225/C	.0005–.0015	.010	.015	.9008	2.1865–2.1875	.0005–.0025	2.7495–2.7505	.0005–.0020	3	.002–.009
	V8-318/G,H	.0005–.0015	.010	.015	.9842	2.1240–2.1250	.0005–.0025	2.4995–2.5005	②	3	.002–.009
	V8-360/J,K,L	④	.010	.015	.9842	2.1240–2.1250	.0005–.0025	2.8095–2.8105	②	3	.002–.009
1981–83	6-225/E,H	.0005–.0015	.010	.015	.9008	2.1865–2.1875	.0010–.0025	2.7495–2.7505	.0010–.0025	3	.0035–.0095
	V8-318⑤	.0005–.0015	.010	.015	.9842	2.124–2.125	.0005–.0025	2.4995–2.5005	②	3	.002–.009
1984	V8-318/	.0005–.0015	.010	.015	.9842	2.124–2.125	.0005–.0025	2.4995–2.5005	②	3	—

①—Fit rings in tapered bores for clearance listed in tightest portion of ring travel.
②—No. 1, .0005–.0015"; No. 2, 3, 4 & 5, .0005–.0020".
③—Exc. High perf. engine, .0005"–.0025"; High perf. engine, .0005"–.0030".
④—With 2 bbl. carb., .0005"–.0015"; With 4 bbl. carb., .001"–.002".
⑤—Refer to General Engine Specifications for V.I.N. code.

ALTERNATOR & REGULATOR SPECIFICATIONS

| Year | Unit Number | Ground Polarity | Field Coil Draw Amperes | Current Output | | | Operating Voltage | | | Voltage Regulator Point Gap | Regulator Armature Air Gap |
				Engine R.P.M.	Amperes	Volts	Engine R.P.M.	Volts	Voltage @ 80°F ①		
1977–80	Bronze Tag	Negative	4.5–6.5②	1250	40⑤	15	1250	15	13.9–14.6	—	—
	Natural Tag	Negative	4.5–6.5②	1250	47⑤	15	1250	15	13.9–14.6	—	—
1977–81	Yellow Tag③	Negative	4.5–6.5②	1250	57⑤	15	1250	15	13.9–14.6	—	—
	Brown Tag	Negative	4.5–6.5②	1250	62⑤	15	1250	15	13.9–14.6	—	—
	Yellow Tag④	Negative	4.75–6.0②	900	72⑤	13	900	13	13.9–14.6	—	—
1978–80	Violet Tag	Negative	4.5–6.5②	1250	40⑤	15	1250	15	13.9–14.6	—	—
1982–83	Yellow Tag③	Negative	4.5–6.5②	1250	47⑤	15	1250	15	13.9–14.6	—	—
	Brown Tag	Negative	4.5–6.5②	1250	58⑤	15	1250	15	13.9–14.6	—	—
	Yellow Tag⑥	Negative	4.75–6.0②	900	97⑤	13	900	13	13.9–14.6	—	—
1984	Yellow Tag③	Negative	2.5–5.0②	1250	47⑤	15	1250	15	13.9–14.6	—	—
	Brown Tag	Negative	2.5–5.0②	1250	58⑤	15	1250	15	13.9–14.6	—	—
	Yellow Tag⑥	Negative	2.5–5.0②	900	97⑤	13	900	13	13.9–14.6	—	—

Continued

ALTERNATOR & REGULATOR SPECIFICATION NOTES

①—For each 10 degree rise in temperature subtract .04 volt. Temperature is checked with thermometer two inches from installed voltage regulator cover.

②—Current draw at 12 volts while turning rotor shaft by hand.

③—60 amp rating.

④—100 amp rating.

⑤—Minimum output.

⑥—114 amp rating.

STARTING MOTOR APPLICATIONS

Year	Engine	Starter Ident. No.
1977–79	6-225, V8-318	3755900
	V8-360, 400, 440	3755250
1980	6-225①, V8-318	4118855
	6-225②, V8-360	4111860
1981–83	6-225, V8-318	4111860
1984	6-225	4111860

①—Except Diplomat & LeBaron.
②—Diplomat & LeBaron.

ENGINE TIGHTENING SPECIFICATIONS★

★ Torque specifications are for clean and lightly lubricated threads only. Dry or dirty threads produce increased friction which prevents accurate measurement of tightness.

Year	Engine/V.I.N	Spark Plugs Ft. Lbs.	Cylinder Head Bolts Ft. Lbs.	Intake Manifold Ft. Lbs.	Exhaust Manifold Ft. Lbs.	Rocker Arm Shaft Bracket Ft. Lbs.	Rocker Arm Cover In. Lbs.	Connecting Rod Cap Bolts Ft. Lbs.	Main Bearing Cap Bolts Ft. Lbs.	Flywheel to Crankshaft Ft. Lbs.	Vibration Damper to Crankshaft Ft. Lbs.
1977	6-225/C,D	10	70	240①	120①	24	40	45	85	55	②
	V8-318/G, 360/J,K,L	30	95	45	20	200①	40	45	85	55	100
	V8-400, 440	30	70	45	40	24	40	45	85	55	135
1978	6-225/C,D	10	70	④	120①	24	40	45	85	55	②
	V8-318/G,H, 360/J,K,L	30	105	45	③	200①	40	45	85	55	100
	V8-400/N, 440/T	30	70	45	30	25	40	45	85	55	135
1979–80	6-225/C,D	10	70	④	120①	24	40	45	85	55	②
1979	V8-318/G,H, 360/J,K,L	30	⑤	45	③	200①	40	45	85	55	100
1980	V8-318/G,H, 360/J,K,L	30	95	40	③	200①	40	45	85	55	100
1981–83	6-225/E,H	10	70	④	120①	24	80	45	85	55	②
	V8-318⑥	30	95	45	③	200①	80	45	85	55	100
1984	V8-318	30	95	45	③	200①	95	45	85	—	100

①—Inch pounds.
②—Press fit.
③—Screw, 20 ft. lbs.; Nut, 15 ft. lbs.
④—Intake to exhaust manifold stud nut 240 in. lbs., Intake to exhaust manifold bolts 200 in. lbs.
⑤—V8-360, 105 ft. lbs. Some V8-318 engine blocks have cylinder head bolt holes drilled through the block into the water jacket. Insert a screwdriver into block head bolt holes. If it goes in at least 2 inches, head bolt must be sealed with suitable sealer and torqued to 95 ft. lbs.; all other V8-318 head bolts, 105 ft. lbs.
⑥—Refer to General Engine Specifications for V.I.N. code.

WHEEL ALIGNMENT SPECIFICATIONS

NOTE: See that riding height is correct before checking wheel alignment

Year	Model	Caster Angle, Degrees		Camber Angle, Degrees				Toe In. Inch.	Toe Out on Turns, Deg.	
		Limits	Desired	Limits		Desired			Outer Wheel	Inner Wheel
				Left	Right	Left	Right			
CHRYSLER & IMPERIAL										
1977–78	Chrysler	−1/2 to +2	+3/4	0 to +1	−1/4 to +3/4	+1/2	+1/4	1/8	18.3	20
1977–79	Cordoba	−1/2 to +2	+3/4	0 to +1	−1/4 to +3/4	+1/2	+1/4	1/8	18	20
	LeBaron	+1 1/2 to +3 3/4	+2 1/2	0 to +1	−1/4 to +3/4	+1/2	+1/4	1/8	18	20
1979	Chrysler	−1/2 to +2	+3/4	0 to +1	−1/4 to +3/4	+1/2	+1/4	1/8	18	20
1980–81	Cordoba, LeBaron	+1 1/4 to +3 3/4	+2 1/2	−1/4 to +1 1/4	−1/4 to +1 1/4	+1/2	+1/2	1/16 to 3/16	18	20
	Newport, New Yorker	−1/4 to +2 1/4	+1	−1/4 to +1 1/4	−1/4 to +1 1/4	+1/2	+1/2	1/16 to 3/16	18	20
1981	Imperial	+1 1/4 to +3 3/4	+2 1/2	−1/4 to +1 1/4	−1/4 to +1 1/4	+1/2	+1/2	1/16 to 3/16	18	20
1982–84	All	+1 1/4 to +3 3/4	+2 1/2	−1/4 to +1 1/4	−1/4 to +1 1/4	+1/2	+1/2	1/16 to 3/16	18	20
DODGE										
1977	Man. Steer.②	−1 3/4 to +3/4	−1/2	0 to +1	−1/4 to +3/4	+1/2	+1/4	1/16 to 1/4	①	20
	Power Steer.②	−1/2 to +2	+3/4	0 to +1	−1/4 to +3/4	+1/2	+1/4	1/16 to 1/4	①	20
	Aspen	+1 1/2 to +3 3/4	+2 1/2	0 to +1	−1/4 to +3/4	+1/2	+1/2	1/16 to 1/4	18.0	20
	Diplomat	+1 1/2 to +3 3/4	+2 1/2	0 to +1	−1/4 to +3/4	+1/2	+1/4	1/8	18.0	20
1978–79	Man. Steer.②	−1 3/4 to +3/4	−1/2	0 to +1	−1/4 to +3/4	+1/2	+1/4	1/8	18.0	20
	Power Steer.②	−1/2 to +2	+3/4	0 to +1	−1/4 to +3/4	+1/2	+1/4	1/8	18.0	20
	Aspen	+1 1/2 to +3 3/4	+2 1/2	0 to +1	−1/4 to +3/4	+1/2	+1/4	1/8	18.0	20
	Diplomat	+1 1/2 to +3 3/4	+2 1/2	0 to +1	−1/4 to +3/4	+1/2	+1/4	1/8	18.0	20
1980–81	Aspen, Diplomat & Mirada	+1 1/4 to +3 3/4	+2 1/2	−1/4 to +1 1/4	−1/4 to +1 1/4	+1/2	+1/2	1/16 to 3/16	18	20
	St. Regis	−1/4 to +2 1/4	+1	−1/4 to +1 1/4	−1/4 to +1 1/4	+1/2	+1/2	1/16 to 3/16	18	20
1982–84	All	+1 1/4 to +3 3/4	+2 1/2	−1/4 to +1 1/4	−1/4 to +1 1/4	+1/2	+1/2	1/16 to 3/16	18.	20

①—Charger SE & Monaco, 18°; Royal Monaco, 18.3°. ②—Except Aspen & Diplomat.

PLYMOUTH

Year	Model	Caster Angle, Degrees		Camber Angle, Degrees				Toe In. Inch.	Toe Out on Turns, Deg.	
1977	Man. Steer.②	−1 3/4 to +3/4	−1/2	0 to +1	−1/4 to +3/4	+1/2	+1/4	1/16 to 1/4	①	20
	Power Steer.②	−1/2 to +2	+3/4	0 to +1	−1/4 to +3/4	+1/2	+1/4	1/16 to 1/4	①	20
	Volaré	+1 1/2 to +3 3/4	+2 1/2	0 to +1	−1/4 to +3/4	+1/2	+1/2	1/16 to 1/4	18.0	20
1978	Man. Steer.②	−1 3/4 to +3/4	−1/2	0 to +1	−1/4 to +3/4	+1/2	+1/4	1/8	18.0	20
	Power. Steer.②	−1/2 to +2	+3/4	0 to +1	−1/4 to +3/4	+1/2	+1/4	1/8	18.0	20
	Volaré	+1 1/2 to 3 3/4	+2 1/2	0 to +1	−1/4 to +3/4	+1/2	+1/4	1/8	18.0	20
1979	Volaré	+1 1/2 to +3 3/4	+2 1/2	0 to +1	−1/4 to +3/4	+1/2	+1/4	1/8	18.0	20
1980	Gran Fury	−1/4 to +2 1/4	+1	−1/4 to +1 1/4	−1/4 to +1 1/4	+1/2	+1/2	1/16 to 3/16	18	20
	Volaré	+1 1/4 to +3 3/4	+2 1/2	−1/4 to +1 1/4	−1/4 to +1 1/4	+1/2	+1/2	1/16 to 3/16	18	20
1981	Gran Fury	−1/4 to +2 1/4	+1	−1/4 to +1 1/4	−1/4 to +1 1/4	+1/2	+1/2	1/16 to 3/16	18	20
1982–84	All	+1 1/4 to +3 3/4	+2 1/2	−1/4 to +1 1/4	−1/4 to +1 1/4	+1/2	+1/2	1/16 to 3/16	18	20

①—Fury, 18.8° ②—Except Volaré.

COOLING SYSTEM & CAPACITY DATA

Year	Model or Engine/V.I.N.	Cooling Capacity, Qts,		Radiator Cap Relief Pressure, Lbs.	Thermo. Opening Temp.	Fuel Tank Gals.	Engine Oil Refill Qts. ①	Transmission Oil			Rear Axle Oil Pints
		Less A/C	With A/C					3 Speed Pints	4 Speed Pints	Auto. Trans. Qts. ②	
CHRYSLER											
1977	V8-318/G	16 1/2	18	16	195	⑤	4	—	—	8 1/2	4 1/2
	V8-360/JK	16	16	16	195	⑤	4	—	—	8 1/2 ③	4 1/2

Continued

COOLING SYSTEM & CAPACITY DATA—Continued

Year	Model or Engine/V.I.N.	Cooling Capacity, Qts, Less A/C	With A/C	Radiator Cap Relief Pressure, Lbs.	Thermo. Opening Temp.	Fuel Tank Gals.	Engine Oil Refill Qts. ①	3 Speed Pints	4 Speed Pints	Auto. Trans. Qts. ②	Rear Axle Oil Pints
CHRYSLER—Continued											
	V8-400/N	16½	16½	16	195	⑤	4	—	—	8¼	4¼
	V8-440/T	16	16	16	195	⑤	4	—	—	8¼	4½
1978	6-225/C,D	12	14	16	195	19½	4	—	—	8½	2
	V8-318/G,H	16	17½	16	195	⑪	4	—	—	8½	4½
	V8-360/J,K	16	16	16	195	⑪	4	—	—	8¼	4½
	V8-400/N	16½	16½	16	195	⑪	4	—	—	8¼	4½
	V8-440/T	16½	16½	16	195	⑪	4	—	—	8¼	4½
1979	6-225/C,D	11.5	⑯	16	195	⑫	4	—	7	8½	⑮
	V8-318/G,H	15	⑧	16	195	⑭	4	—	7	8½	⑮
	V8-360/J,K,L	⑨	⑨	16	195	⑭	4	—	7	8½	⑮
1980	LeBaron 6-225/C	11½	12½	16	195	18	4	—	—	8.15	④
	LeBaron V8-318/G,H	15	15½	16	195	18	4	—	—	8.15	④
	Cordoba 6-225/C	11½	12½	16	195	21	4	—	—	8.15	4½
	Cordoba V8-318/G,H	15	15½	16	195	21	4	—	—	8.15	4½
	Cordoba V8-360/K,L	14	14	16	195	21	4	—	—	8.15	4½
	Newport, New Yorker 6-225/C	11½	14½	16	195	21	4	—	—	8.15	4½
	Newport, New Yorker V8-318/G,H	15	17½	16	195	21	4	—	—	8.15	4½
	Newport, New Yorker V8-360/K,L	16	16	16	195	21	4	—	—	8.15	4½
1981	LeBaron 6-225/E	11½	12½	16	195	18	4	—	—	8.15	⑥
	LeBaron V8-318/K,M	15	15½	16	195	18	4	—	—	8.15	⑥
	Cordoba 6-225/E	11½	14½	16	195	18	4	—	—	8.15	⑥
	Cordoba V8-318/K,M	15	17½	16	195	18	4	—	—	8.15	⑥
	Newport, New Yorker 6-225/E	11½	14½	16	195	21	4	—	—	8.15	⑥
	Newport, New Yorker V8-318/K,M	15	17½	16	195	21	4	—	—	8.15	⑥
1982–83	Cordoba 6-225/E,H	11½	15	16	195	18	4	—	—	8½	⑥
	Cordoba V8-318 ㉕	15	15½	16	195	18	4	—	—	8½	⑥
	New Yorker 6-225/E,H	11½	12½	16	195	18	4	—	—	8½	⑥
	New Yorker V8-318 ㉕	15	15½	16	195	18	4	—	—	8½	⑥
1984	Fifth Avenue V8-318/	15½ ㉑	15½ ㉑	16	195	18	4	—	—	㉒㉓	㉔
IMPERIAL											
1981	All	15	17.5	16	195	18	4	—	—	8.15	4.4
1982–83	All	15½	16½	16	195	18	4	—	—	8½	4.4
DODGE											
1977	Aspen 6-225/C,D	12	14	16	195	18⑦	4	4¾	7	8½	2
	Aspen 8-318/G	16	17½	16	195	20	4	4¾	7	8½	4½
	Aspen 8-360/J,K,L	16	17½	16	195	20	4	—	—	8½	4½
	Charger 8-318/G	16½	18	16	195	25½	4	—	—	8½	4½
	Charger 8-360/J,K,L	16	16	16	195	25½	4	—	—	8½③	4½
	Charger 8-400/N	16½	16½	16	195	25½	4	—	—	8¼	4½
	Monaco 6-225/C,D	13	14½	16	195	25½⑦	4	4¾	—	8½	4½
	Monaco 8-318/G	16½	18	16	195	25½⑦	4	4¾	—	8½	4½
	Monaco 8-360/J,K,L	16	16	16	195	25½⑦	4	—	—	8½③	4½

Continued

COOLING SYSTEM & CAPACITY DATA—Continued

Year	Model or Engine/V.I.N.	Cooling Capacity, Qts,		Radiator Cap Relief Pressure, Lbs.	Thermo. Opening Temp.	Fuel Tank Gals.	Engine Oil Refill Qts. ①	Transmission Oil			Rear Axle Oil Pints
		Less A/C	With A/C					3 Speed Pints	4 Speed Pints	Auto. Trans. Qts. ②	
DODGE—Continued											
	Monaco 8-400/N	16½	16½	16	195	25½⑦	4	—	—	8¼	4½
	Monaco 8-440/T,U	16	16	16	195	20½	4	—	—	8½	4½
	Royal Monaco 8-318/G	17½	17½	16	195	20½	4	—	—	8½③	4½
	Royal Monaco 8-360/J,K,L	16	16	16	195	26½⑬	4	—	—	8½③	4½
	Royal Monaco 8-400/N	16½	16½	16	195	26½⑬	4	—	—	8½③	4½
	Royal Monaco 8-440K/T,U	16	16	16	195	20½	4	—	—	8½③	4½
1978	Diplomat	16	17½	16	195	19½	4	—	—	8½	4½
	Aspen 6-225/C,D	12	14	16	195	⑩	4	4¾	7	8½	2
	Aspen V8-318/G,H	16	17½	16	195	⑩	4	4¾	7	8½	2
	Aspen V8-360/J,K,L	16	16	16	195	⑩	4	4¾	7	8½	4½
	Charger V8-318/G,H	16½	18	16	195	25½	4	—	—	8½	4½
	Charger V8-360/J,K,L	16	16	16	195	25½	4	—	—	8¼	4½
	Charger V8-400/N	16½	16½	16	195	25½	4	—	—	8¼	4½
	Diplomat 6-225/C,D	12	14	16	195	19½	4	—	7	8½	2
	Diplomat V8-318/G,H	16	17½	16	195	19½	4	—	7	8½	2
	Diplomat V8-360/J,K,L	16	16	16	195	19½	4	—	7	8½	4½
	Monaco 6-225/C,D	13	14½	16	195	20½	4	4¾	—	8½	4½
	Monaco V8-318/G,H	16½	18	16	195	25½⑦	4	4¾	—	8½	4½
	Monaco V8-360/J,K,L	16	16	16	195	25½⑦	4	4¾	—	8½	4½
	Monaco V8-400/N	16½	16½	16	195	25½⑦	4	4¾	—	8¼	4½
1979	Aspen 6-225/C,D	11.5	12.5	16	195	⑩	4	4.8	7	8½	④
	Aspen V8-318/G,H	15	16.5	16	195	19.5	4	4.8	7	8½	④
	Aspen V8-360/J,K,L	15	15	16	195	19.5	4	4.8	7	8½	④
	Diplomat 6-225/C,D	12.5	12.5	16	195	⑩	4	—	7	8½	④
	Diplomat V8-318/G,H	15	16.5	16	195	19.5	4	—	7	8½	④
	Diplomat V8-360/J,K,L	15	15	16	195	19.5	4	—	7	8½	④
	Magnum XE V8-318/G,H	15	17.5	16	195	21	4	—	—	8½	4.5
	Magnum XE V8-360J,K,L	16	16	16	195	21	4	—	—	8½	4.5
	St. Regis 6-225/C,D	11.5	14.5	16	195	21	4	—	—	8½	4.5
	St. Regis V8-318/G,H	15	17.5	16	195	21	4	—	—	8½	4.5
	St. Regis V8-360/J,K,L	16	16	16	195	21	4	—	—	8½	4.5
1980	Aspen, Diplomat 6-225/C	11½	12½	16	195	18	4	4¾	—	8.15	④
	Aspen, Diplomat V8-318/G,H	15	15½	16	195	18	4	—	—	8.15	④
	Aspen V8-360/K,L	14	14	16	195	18	4	—	—	8.15	④
	Mirada 6-225/C	11½	12½	16	195	21	4	—	—	8.15	4½
	Mirada V8-318/G,H	15	15½	16	195	21	4	—	—	8.15	4½
	Mirada V8-360/K,L	14	14	16	195	21	4	—	—	8.15	4½
	St. Regis 6-225/C	11½	14½	16	195	21	4	—	—	8.15	4½

Continued

COOLING SYSTEM & CAPACITY DATA—Continued

Year	Model or Engine/V.I.N.	Cooling Capacity, Qts,		Radiator Cap Relief Pressure, Lbs.	Thermo. Opening Temp.	Fuel Tank Gals.	Engine Oil Refill Qts. ①	Transmission Oil			Rear Axle Oil Pints
		Less A/C	With A/C					3 Speed Pints	4 Speed Pints	Auto. Trans. Qts. ②	
DODGE—Continued											
	St. Regis V8-318/G,H	15	17½	16	195	21	4	—	—	8.15	4½
	St. Regis V8-360/K,L	16	16	16	195	21	4	—	—	8.15	4½
1981	All 6-225/E	11.5	⑰	16	195	⑱	4	—	—	8.15	⑥
	All V8-318/KM	15	⑲	16	195	⑱	4	—	—	8.15	⑥
1982–83	Diplomat 6-225/E,H	11½	⑳	16	195	18	4	—	—	8½	⑥
	Diplomat V8-318 ㉕	15	15½	16	195	18	4	—	—	8½	⑥
	Mirada 6-225/E,H	11½	12½	16	195	18	4	—	—	8½	⑥
	Mirada V8-318 ㉕	15	15½	16	195	18	4	—	—	8½	⑥
1984	Diplomat V8-318/	15½ ㉑	15½ ㉑	16	195	18	4	—	—	㉒ ㉓	㉔
PLYMOUTH											
1977	Fury 6-225/C,D	13	14½	16	195	25½ ⑦	4	4¾	—	8½	4½
	Fury 8-318/G	16½	18	16	195	25½ ⑦	4	4¾	—	8½	4½
	Fury 8-360/J,K,L	16	16	16	195	25½ ⑦	4	—	—	8½	4½
	Fury 8-400/N	16½	16½	16	195	25½ ⑦	4	—	—	8¼	4½
	Fury 8-440/T,U	16	16	16	195	20½	4	—	—	8½	4½
	Gran Fury 8-318/G	17½	17½	16	195	20½	4	—	—	8½ ③	4½
	Gran Fury 8-360/J,K,L	16	16	16	195	26½ ⑬	4	—	—	8½ ③	4½
	Gran Fury 8-400/N	16½	16½	16	195	26½ ⑬	4	—	—	8½ ③	4½
	Gran Fury 8-440/T,U	16	16	16	195	26½ ⑬	4	—	—	8½ ③	4½
1978	Fury 6-225/C,D	13	14½	16	195	25½ ⑦	4	4¾	—	8½	4½
	Fury V8-318/G,H	16½	18	16	195	25½ ⑦	4	4¾	—	8½	4½
	Fury V8-360/J,K,L	16	16	16	195	25½ ⑦	4	4¾	—	8½	4½
	Fury V8-400/N	16½	16½	16	195	25½ ⑦	4	4¾	—	8¼	4½
1980	Gran Fury 6-225/C	11½	14½	16	195	21	4	—	—	8.15	4½
	Gran Fury V8-318/G,H	15	17½	16	195	21	4	—	—	8.15	4½
	Gran Fury V8-360/K,L	16	16	16	195	21	4	—	—	8.15	4½
1981	Gran Fury 6-225/E	11½	14½	16	195	21	4	—	—	8.15	⑥
	Gran Fury V8-318/K,M	15	17½	16	195	21	4	—	—	8.15	⑥
1982–83	Gran Fury 6-225/E,H	11½	12½	16	195	18	4	—	—	8½	⑥
	Gran Fury V8-318 ㉕	15	15½	16	195	18	4	—	—	8½	⑥
1984	Gran Fury V8-318/	15½ ㉑	15½ ㉑	16	195	18	4	—	—	㉒ ㉓	㉔
VOLARÉ											
1977	Volaré 6-225/C,D	12	14	16	195	18 ⑦	4	4¾	7	8½	2
	Volaré 8-318/G	16	17½	16	195	20	4	4¾	7	8½	4½
	Volaré 8-360/J,K,L	16	17½	16	195	20	4	—	—	8½	4½
1978	Volaré 6-225/C,D	12	14	16	195	⑩	4	4¾	7	8½	2
	Volaré V8-318/G,H	16	17½	16	195	⑩	4	4¾	7	8½	2
	Volaré V8-360/J,K,L	16	16	16	195	⑩	4	4¾	7	8½	4½
1979	Volaré 6-225/C,D	12.5	12.5	16	195	⑩	4	4.8	7	8½	④
	Volaré V8-318/G,H	15	16.5	16	195	19.5	4	—	—	8½	④
	Volaré V8-360/J,K,L	15	15	16	195	19.5	4	—	—	8½	④
1980	Volaré 6-225/C	11½	12½	16	195	18	4	4¾	—	8.15	④
	Volaré V8-318/G,H	15	15½	16	195	18	4	—	—	8.15	④
	Volaré V8-360/K,L	14	14	16	195	18	4	—	—	8.15	④

Continued

COOLING SYSTEM & CAPACITY DATA—NOTES

①—Add 1 qt. with filter change.
②—Approximate. Make final check with dipstick.
③—With A-727 transmission (heavy duty), 8¼ qts.
④—With 7¼ inch ring gear, 2 pts.; 8¼ inch ring gear, 4½ pts.
⑤—Cordoba 25½ gals.; Chrysler 26½ gals.; Wagon 24 gals.
⑥—With 7¼" ring gear, 2½ pts.; with 8¼" ring gear, 4.4 pts.; with 9¼" ring gear, 4½ pts.
⑦—Wagons, 20 gals.
⑧—Exc. LeBaron, 17.5 qts.; LeBaron 16.5 qts.

⑨—Exc. LeBaron, 16 qts.; LeBaron 15 qts.
⑩—6 cyl. exc. Station Wag. 18 gal.; 8 cyl. & Station Wag., 19½ gals.
⑪—LeBaron, 19½ gals.; Cordoba, 25½ gals.; Chrysler, 26½ gal.
⑫—Exc. LeBaron, 21 gal.; LeBaron exc. Wag, 18 gal.; LeBaron Wagon, 19½ gals.
⑬—Wagons, 24 gals.
⑭—Exc. LeBaron, 21 gals.; LeBaron, 19.5 gals.
⑮—Exc. LeBaron, 4½ pts.; LeBaron, 7¼ inch ring gear, 2 pts.; 8¼ & 9¼ inch ring gear, 4½ pts.
⑯—Exc. LeBaron, 14.5 qts.; LeBaron, 12.5 qts.
⑰—Except Diplomat, 14½ qts.; Diplomat, 12½ qts.

⑱—Diplomat & Mirada, 18 gals.; St. Regis, 21 gals.
⑲—Except Diplomat, 17½ qts.; Diplomat, 15½ qts.
⑳—1982, 15 qts.; 1983, 12½ qts.
㉑—Heavy duty cooling system, 16½ qts.
㉒—A904 trans., 8.15 qts., A727 trans., 8 qts.
㉓—Add an additional ¼ qt. with auxiliary cooler.
㉔—7¼ inch axle, 2.5 pts.; 8¼ inch axle, 4.4 pts.
㉕—Refer to General Engine Specifications for V.I.N. code.

REAR AXLE SPECIFICATIONS

Year	Model	Carrier Type	Ring Gear & Pinion Backlash		Pinion Bearing Preload			Differential Bearing Preload		
			Method	Adjustment	Method	New Bearings Inch-Lbs.	Used Bearings Inch-Lbs.	Method	New Bearings Inch-Lbs.	Used Bearings Inch-Lbs.
1977–83	8¼"⑤	Integral	②	.006–.008	①	20–35④	10–25④	②	③	③
	9¼"⑤	Integral	②	.006–.008	①	20–35④	10–25④	②	③	③
	7¼"⑤	Integral	②	.004–.006	①	15–25	—	②	③	③
1984	7¼"	Integral	—	—	①	—	—	—	—	—
	8¼"	Integral	—	—	①	—	—	—	—	—

①—Collapsible spacer.
②—Threaded adjusters.
③—Preload is correct when ring gear and pinion backlash is properly adjusted.
④—Adjust by turning pinion shaft nut with an inch-pound torque wrench with seal removed.
⑤—"C" lock type.

Electrical Section

STARTER, REPLACE

1. Disconnect ground cable at battery.
2. Remove cable at starter.
3. Disconnect wires at solenoid.
4. Remove one stud nut and one bolt attaching starter motor to flywheel housing.
5. Slide transmission oil cooler bracket off stud (if so equipped).
6. Remove starter motor and removeable seal.
7. Reverse above procedure to install.

NOTE: When tightening attaching bolt and nut be sure to hold starter away from engine to insure proper alignment.

CLUTCH SWITCH

1977-80

A clutch switch is used which necessitates depressing the clutch pedal before the engine can be started.

IGNITION SWITCH & LOCK, REPLACE

1977-84

1. Disconnect battery ground cable and remove turn signal switch as outlined elsewhere in this chapter.
2. Remove ignition key lamp assembly retaining screw and the assembly.
3. Remove snap ring from upper end of steering shaft.
4. Remove bearing housing to lock housing retaining screws, then the bearing housing from shaft.
5. Remove bearing lower snap ring from shaft.
6. Pry sleeve from steering shaft lock plate hub, then, using a suitable punch, drive lock plate groove pin from lock plate.

NOTE: Drive pin from end without grooves.

7. Remove lock plate from shaft, then the shaft through lower end of column.
8. Remove shift indicator pointer screw, if equipped.
9. Remove buzzer switch retaining screw and the switch.
10. Remove lock lever guide plate retaining screws and the guide plate.
11. Place lock cylinder in the "Lock" position and remove key. With a suitable tool, depress spring loaded lock retainer and pull lock cylinder from housing bore, Fig. 1.
12. Remove ignition switch retaining screws and the ignition switch.
13. Reverse procedure to install.

IGNITION SWITCH, ADJUST

1979-84 Except Cordoba, Mirada & 1979-80 Magnum

1. Disconnect battery ground cable.
2. Place transmission in Park and ignition lock in the lock position.
3. If switch was not removed from column, loosen two mounting bolts and insert a lock pin into hole on switch marked lock. If switch was removed from column, pin switch in the lock position, then place switch into rod and rotate 90 degrees over mounting holes. Loosely install mounting bolts. Replacement switches are supplied with locking pins.
4. Apply light upward pressure to align rod and switch and hold switch in this position while tightening retaining bolts. Remove locking pin.
5. Remove lock pin from switch.
6. Reverse procedure to install.

COLUMN MOUNTED DIMMER SWITCH, ADJUST

1979-81 Newport, New Yorker & St. Regis; 1980-81 Gran Fury; 1980-83 Cordoba & Mirada; 1981-83 Imperial

1. Loosen two switch mounting screws, then depress switch plunger slightly and insert locking pin.
2. Apply light upward pressure to remove free play between switch and rod.
3. While holding switch with slight upward pressure tighten the two mounting screws.
4. Remove locking pin and check switch for proper operation.

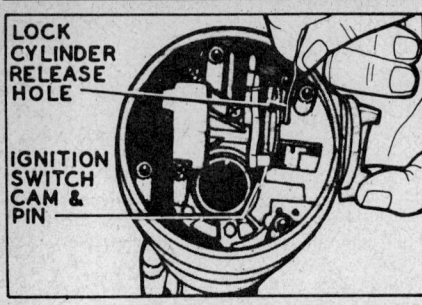

Fig. 1 Lock cylinder removal. 1977—83

LIGHT SWITCH, REPLACE

1979—81 Newport, New Yorker & St. Regis; 1980—81 Gran Fury; 1980—83 Cordoba & Mirada; 1981—83 Imperial

1. If equipped, remove intermittent wipe and power antenna module assembly.
2. Disconnect battery ground cable.
3. Depress switch stem release button and pull knob and stem from switch.
4. Using a small screwdriver, snap out switch trim bezel, then remove mounting nut.
5. Pull switch from cluster and disconnect wire connector.
6. Reverse procedure to install.

1977—80 Aspen, Volaré, 1977—81 LeBaron, 1977—84 Diplomat, 1982 New Yorker, 1982—84 Gran Fury, 1983 New Yorker Fifth Avenue & 1984 Fifth Avenue

1. Disconnect battery ground cable.
2. Remove cluster bezel.
3. Remove switch mounting plate attaching screws and pull switch and plate assembly outward.
4. Depress headlight switch stem, then depress release button and pull knob and stem from switch.
5. Remove switch mounting nut, then disconnect electrical connector and remove switch.
6. Reverse procedure to install.

1977—78 Fury, 1977—79 Charger, Cordoba, 1977—78 Monaco & 1978—79 Magnum

1. Disconnect battery ground cable and fusible link.
2. Remove instrument cluster upper bezel and escutcheon mounting screw.
3. Remove switch mounting plate to cluster housing screws, pull switch from housing and disconnect electrical connector.
4. Depress release button on rear of switch and pull knob and stem from switch.
5. Remove switch escutcheon and mounting nut.
6. Reverse procedure to install.

1977—78 Chrysler Newport & New Yorker

1. Disconnect battery ground cable.
2. Remove headlight switch lens.
3. Remove headlight switch to mounting

plate retaining nut.
4. Remove switch.
5. Reverse procedure to install.

1977 Gran Fury & Royal Monaco

1. Disconnect battery ground cable.
2. Remove instrument cluster bezel.
3. Remove windshield wiper switch mounting screws and headlight switch mounting screws.
4. Pull switch outwards and disconnect electrical leads, then pull switch to the "ON" position and depress release button on side of switch. Remove knob and stem from switch.
5. Remove escutcheon and mounting plate retaining nut and remove switch.
6. Reverse procedure to install.

STOP LIGHT SWITCH, REPLACE

1977—84

1. Disconnect battery ground cable.
2. Disconnect wiring from switch and remove switch from brake pedal bracket.
3. Reverse procedure to install.

NEUTRAL SAFETY & BACK-UP SWITCH, REPLACE

1977—84

1. Unscrew switch from transmission case, allowing fluid to drain into a container, Fig. 2.
2. Move shift lever to "Park" and then to "Neutral" positions and inspect to see that switch operating lever is centered in switch opening in case.
3. Screw switch into transmission case and torque to 24 ft. lbs.
4. Add fluid to proper level.
5. Check to see that switch operates only in "Park" and "Neutral".

HORN SOUNDER & STEERING WHEEL, REPLACE

1977—84

1. Disconnect ground cable at battery.
2. On steering wheels with center horn button, remove button by pulling outwards. On steering wheels with pressure sensitive switch pad, remove mounting screws from underside of wheel, then disconnect horn wire when removing pad.
3. On models with center horn button, disconnect horn switch wire and remove switch and ring.
4. On all models, remove steering wheel nut and use a suitable puller to remove steering wheel.

CAUTION: Do not bump or hammer on steering shaft to remove wheel as damage to shaft may result.

5. Reverse procedure to install.

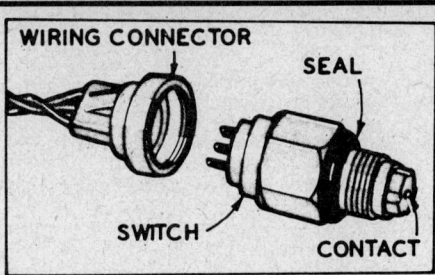

Fig. 2 Neutral safety switch.

TURN SIGNAL SWITCH, REPLACE

1981—84

1. Disconnect battery ground cable.
2. Remove steering wheel as described under "Steering Wheel, Replace".
3. On models equipped with tilt column, remove lock plate cover and lock plate.
4. On all models, remove lower instrument panel bezel.
5. On 1981 LeBaron, 1981—84 Diplomat, 1982 New Yorker, 1982—84 Gran Fury, and 1983 New Yorker Fifth Avenue and 1984 Fifth Avenue models equipped with tilt column, remove gear shift indicator, then the two steering column to lower instrument panel reinforcement retaining screws. Remove mounting bracket from steering column.
6. On all models, unsnap four plastic retainers and remove wiring through steering column.
7. Disconnect light blue wire connector, then remove turn signal lever attaching screw and allow lever assembly to hang loosely from column.
8. Remove turn signal/hazard warning switch attaching screws, then pull switch from steering column, while carefully guiding wires up through column opening.
9. Reverse procedure to install.

1977—80

1. Disconnect battery ground cable and remove steering wheel.
2. Remove steering column cover. On Charger, Cordoba, Coronet, Fury, Magnum and 1977—78 Monaco, it is necessary to remove the lower instrument panel bezel.
3. On models with tilt column proceed as follows:
   a. On all models except Charger, Cordoba, Coronet, Fury, Magnum and 1977—78 Monaco, remove gearshift indicator.
   b. On all models, remove steering column to lower panel reinforcement nuts.
   c. Remove mounting bracket attaching bolts and the mounting bracket from steering column.
   d. Remove wiring trough screws and the wiring trough.
4. On all models except models with Tilt columns, unsnap retainer clips attaching wiring trough to steering column and remove wiring trough.
5. Position shift lever at the full clockwise position except on Tilt columns. On Tilt columns, position shift lever at the mid-

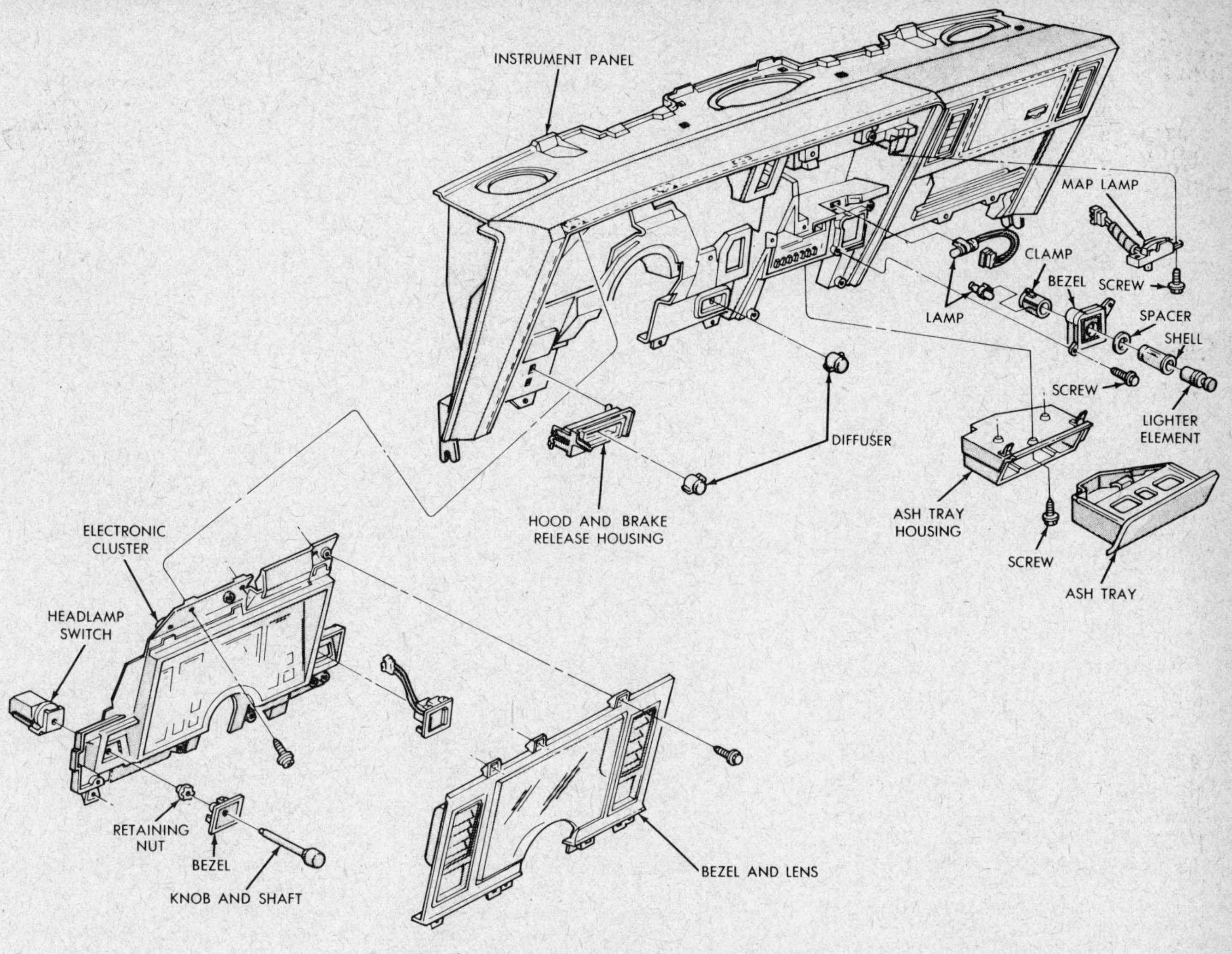

INSTRUMENT PANEL

MAP LAMP

CLAMP

BEZEL SCREW

LAMP

SPACER

SHELL

SCREW

LIGHTER ELEMENT

DIFFUSER

HOOD AND BRAKE RELEASE HOUSING

ASH TRAY HOUSING

SCREW

ASH TRAY

ELECTRONIC CLUSTER

HEADLAMP SWITCH

RETAINING NUT

BEZEL

KNOB AND SHAFT

BEZEL AND LENS

Fig. 2A   Electronic instrument cluster. 1981–83 Imperial

point.

6. Disconnect turn signal switch wiring harness connector.
7. Remove turn signal lever attaching screw and the lever.

NOTE: On models equipped with speed control, it is not necessary to remove lever but allow lever to hang.

8. Remove hazard warning switch and upper bearing retainer mounting screws.
9. Carefully pull switch from column, guiding wires through column opening.
10. Reverse procedure to install.

INSTRUMENT CLUSTER, REPLACE

1981–83 Imperial

1. Disconnect battery ground cable.
2. Remove cigar lighter and ash tray from instrument panel.
3. Remove instrument panel cluster overlay attaching screws, then remove overlay.
4. Remove lower instrument panel cluster bezel attaching screws, then remove bezel.

5. Remove instrument cluster bezel attaching screws and bezel then remove plastic pins retaining cluster mask to cluster and remove mask.
6. Remove instrument cluster to panel attaching screws, then pull cluster forward and disconnect wire connectors from cluster.

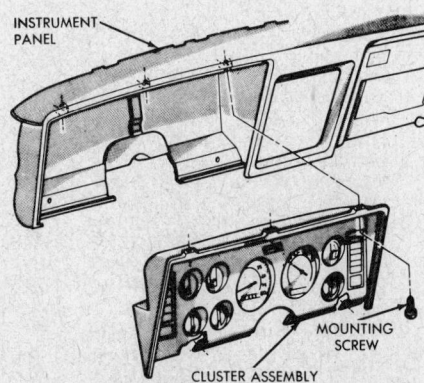

INSTRUMENT PANEL

MOUNTING SCREW

CLUSTER ASSEMBLY

Fig. 3   Instrument cluster removal. 1979–81 Newport, New Yorker & St. Regis & 1980–81 Gran Fury & 1980–83 Cordoba & Mirada

7. Remove cluster assembly.
8. Reverse procedure to install.

1979–81 Newport, New Yorker & St. Regis, 1980–81 Gran Fury & 1980–83 Cordoba & Mirada

1. Disconnect battery ground cable.
2. Remove five hood and brake release beel screws, then the bezel.
3. Remove four accessory switch bezel screws, then the bezel.
4. Pull gearshift pointer cable from steering column.
5. Remove the lower left and right hand bezels and the gearshift pointer cable.
6. Remove three steering column toe plate bolts at firewall, then the nuts and washers attaching steering column bracket to instrument panel steering column support bracket. Lower the steering column, allowing steering wheel to rest on seat.
7. Disconnect speedometer cable and the right hand mirror control cable.
8. Remove five screws securing instrument cluster to panel, Fig. 3.
9. Roll cluster downward and disconnect headlamp switch electrical connector and instrument cluster wiring.

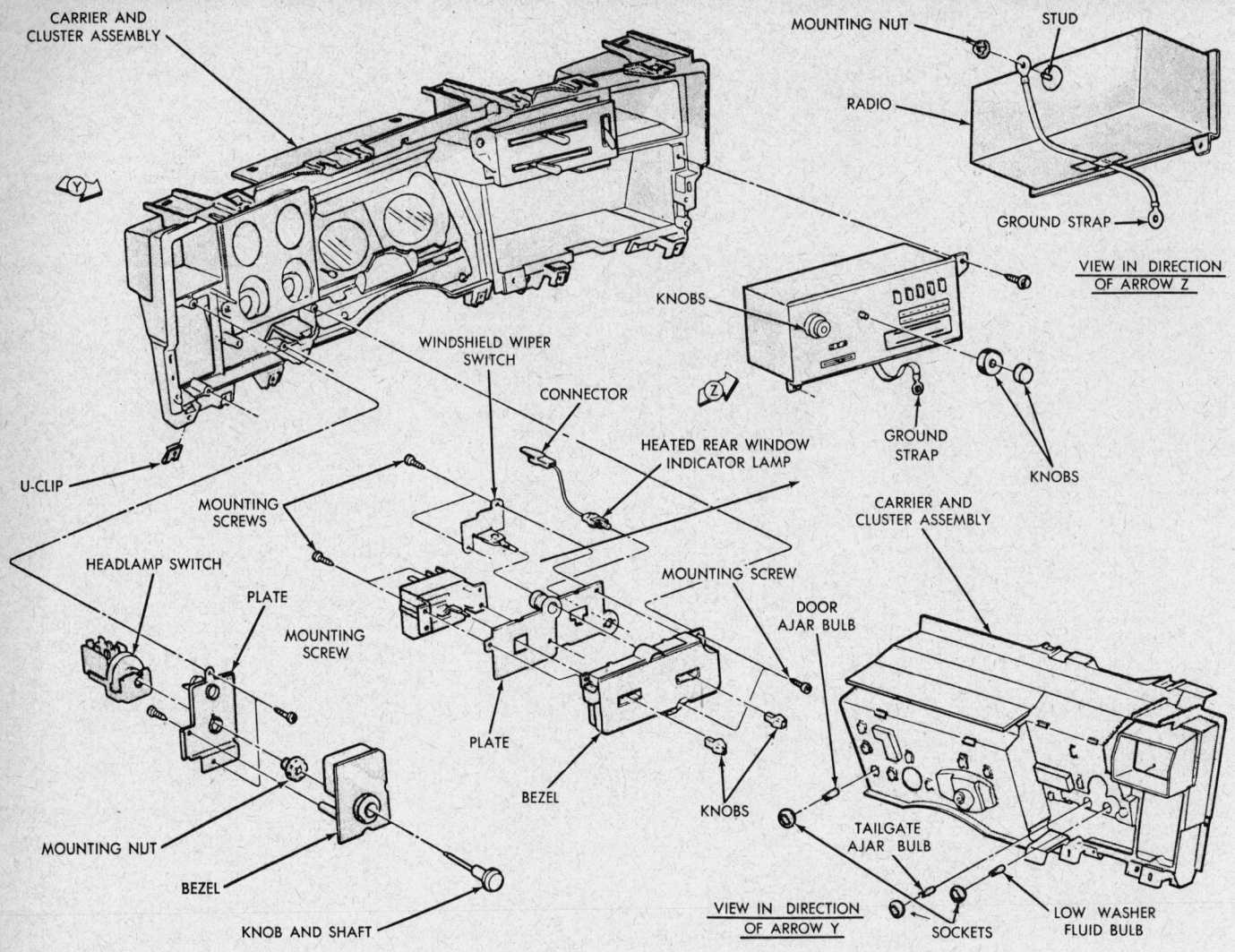

Fig. 4 Instrument cluster. (Typical) 1977–81 LeBaron, 1977–84 Diplomat, 1982 New Yorker, 1982–84 Gran Fury, 1983 New Yorker Fifth Avenue & 1984 Fifth Avenue

10. Remove instrument cluster from vehicle.
11. Reverse procedure to install.

1977–81 LeBaron, 1977–84 Diplomat, 1982 New Yorker, 1982–84 Gran Fury, 1983 New Yorker Fifth Avenue & 1984 Fifth Avenue

1. Disconnect battery ground cable.
2. Remove lower panel assembly.
3. Remove left lower reinforcement by removing two screws located at left end.
4. Remove gear shift indicator.
5. Remove steering column toe plate mounting bolts and upper steering column mounting nuts, then lower steering column.
6. Disconnect speedometer cable.
7. Remove two mounting screws and detach fuse block from mid reinforcement.
8. Remove one screw attaching radio to mid reinforcement.
9. Remove four upper and four lower cluster mounting screws, Fig. 4.

10. Pull cluster out from instrument panel and disconnect wire connectors, control cables and vacuum harness, then remove cluster assembly.
11. Reverse procedure to install.

1977–80 Aspen & Volaré

1. Disconnect battery ground cable.
2. Remove steering column cover and instrument panel end cap.
3. Remove lower left reinforcement and remove gearshift indicator.
4. Remove steering column toe plate bolts, then remove the two upper mounting nuts and lower steering column.
5. Remove left side cowl mouldings, then disconnect speedometer cable.
6. Remove two mounting screws, then detach fuse block from mid reinforcement.
7. Remove 1 screw attaching radio to mid-reinforcement, 4 screws at bottom of cluster and 3 screws at top of cluster, Fig. 5.
8. Pull cluster from panel, then disconnect all electrical connectors, control cables and vacuum hoses and remove cluster.
9. Reverse procedure to install.

1977–78 Fury, 1977–79 Charger, Cordoba, 1977–78 Monaco & 1978–79 Magnum

1. Disconnect battery ground cable.
2. Remove trim pad, radio and heater or A/C controls, Fig. 6.
3. Remove cluster housing reinforcement bracket.
4. Disconnect speedo cable, all electrical connectors and three wiring through clips from cluster.
5. Remove upper cluster bezel and instrument panel and cap.
6. Remove steering column to support bracket nuts.
7. Remove cluster housing to instrument panel retaining screws, then remove cluster.
8. Reverse procedure to install.

1977 Gran Fury, Royal Monaco & 1977–78 Chrysler Newport & New Yorker

1. Disconnect battery ground cable.

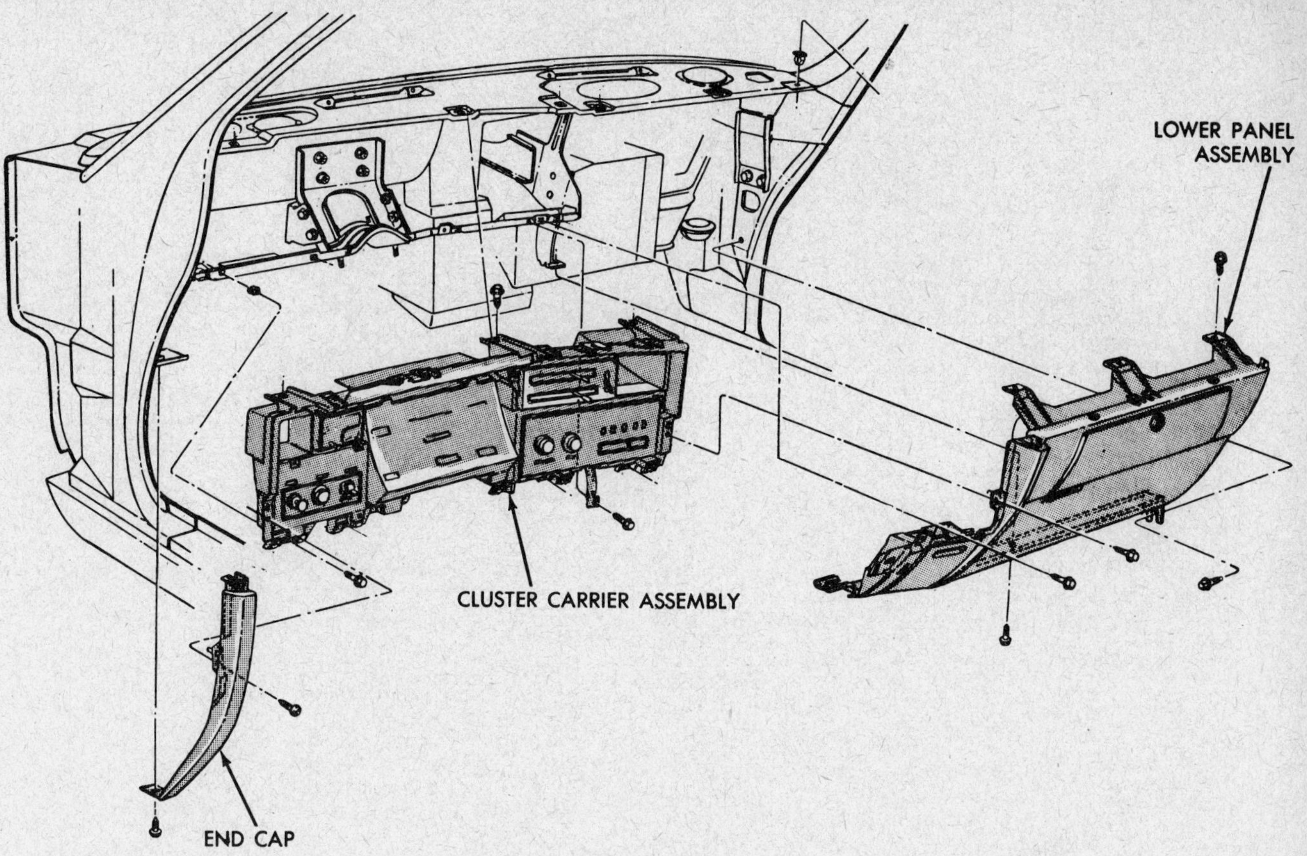

LOWER PANEL ASSEMBLY

CLUSTER CARRIER ASSEMBLY

END CAP

Fig. 5 Instrument cluster. 1977–80 Aspen & Volaré

2. Remove instrument panel upper cover, then working through top of panel, disconnect speedometer cable and printed circuit multiple connector.
3. Remove instrument cluster bezel, Figs. 7 & 8.
4. On Chrysler, remove gear selector and warning lamp bezel.
5. On all models disconnect instrument cluster lens and cluster housing from carrier.
6. Pull cluster out and disconnect two illumination and warning light modules.
7. Disconnect remaining electrical leads and remove cluster assembly.
8. Reverse procedure to install.

W/S WIPER MOTOR, REPLACE

1977–84

1. Disconnect battery ground cable.

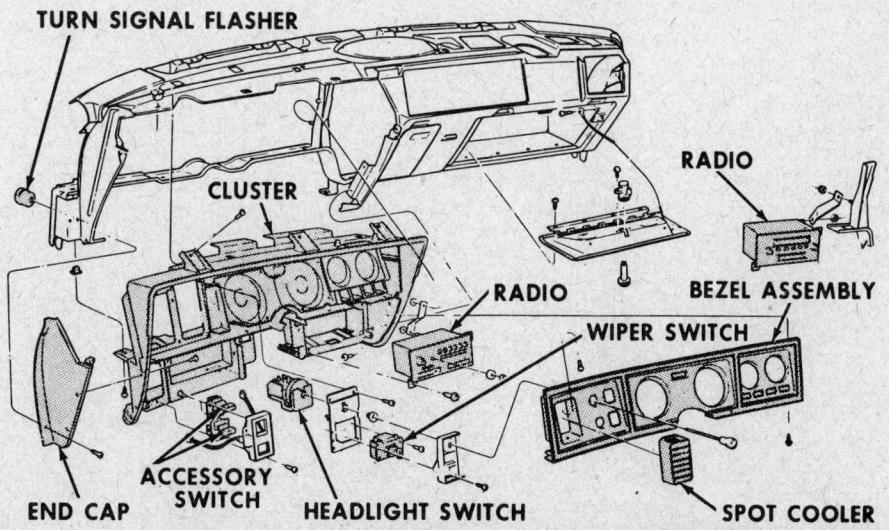

TURN SIGNAL FLASHER

CLUSTER

RADIO

RADIO

BEZEL ASSEMBLY

WIPER SWITCH

ACCESSORY SWITCH

HEADLIGHT SWITCH

END CAP

SPOT COOLER

Fig. 6 Instrument cluster. 1977–78 Fury, 1977–79 Charger, Cordoba, 1977–78 Monaco & 1978–79 Magnum

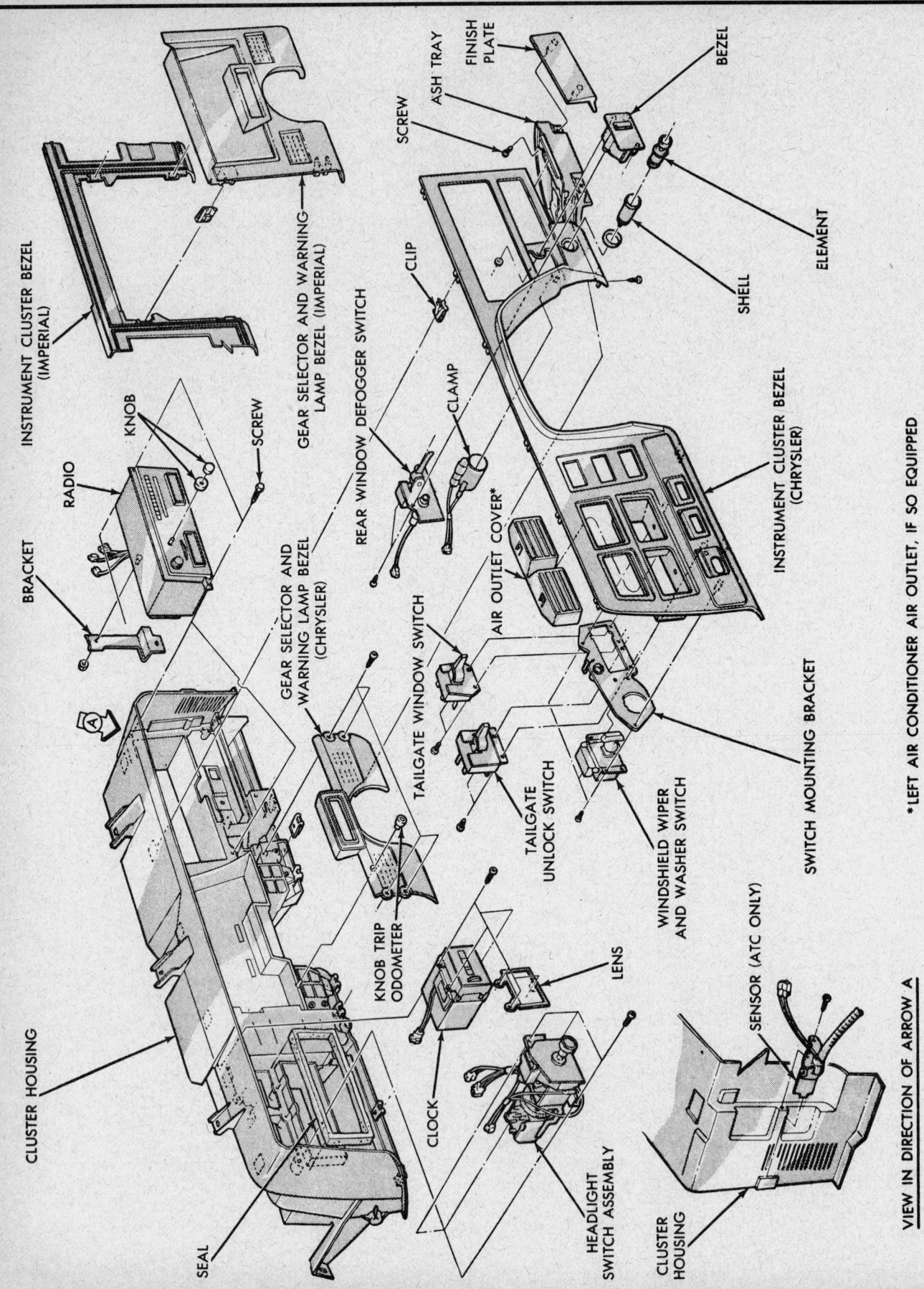

INSTRUMENT CLUSTER BEZEL (IMPERIAL)

GEAR SELECTOR AND WARNING LAMP BEZEL (IMPERIAL)

KNOB

RADIO

BRACKET

SCREW

GEAR SELECTOR AND WARNING LAMP BEZEL (CHRYSLER)

KNOB TRIP ODOMETER

CLUSTER HOUSING

SEAL

REAR WINDOW DEFOGGER SWITCH

CLIP

CLAMP

TAILGATE WINDOW SWITCH

AIR OUTLET COVER*

TAILGATE UNLOCK SWITCH

CLOCK

LENS

HEADLIGHT SWITCH ASSEMBLY

WINDSHIELD WIPER AND WASHER SWITCH

SWITCH MOUNTING BRACKET

INSTRUMENT CLUSTER BEZEL (CHRYSLER)

SCREW

ASH TRAY

FINISH PLATE

BEZEL

ELEMENT

SHELL

SENSOR (ATC ONLY)

CLUSTER HOUSING

VIEW IN DIRECTION OF ARROW A

*LEFT AIR CONDITIONER AIR OUTLET, IF SO EQUIPPED

Fig. 7 Instrument cluster. 1977-78 Chrysler Newport & New Yorker

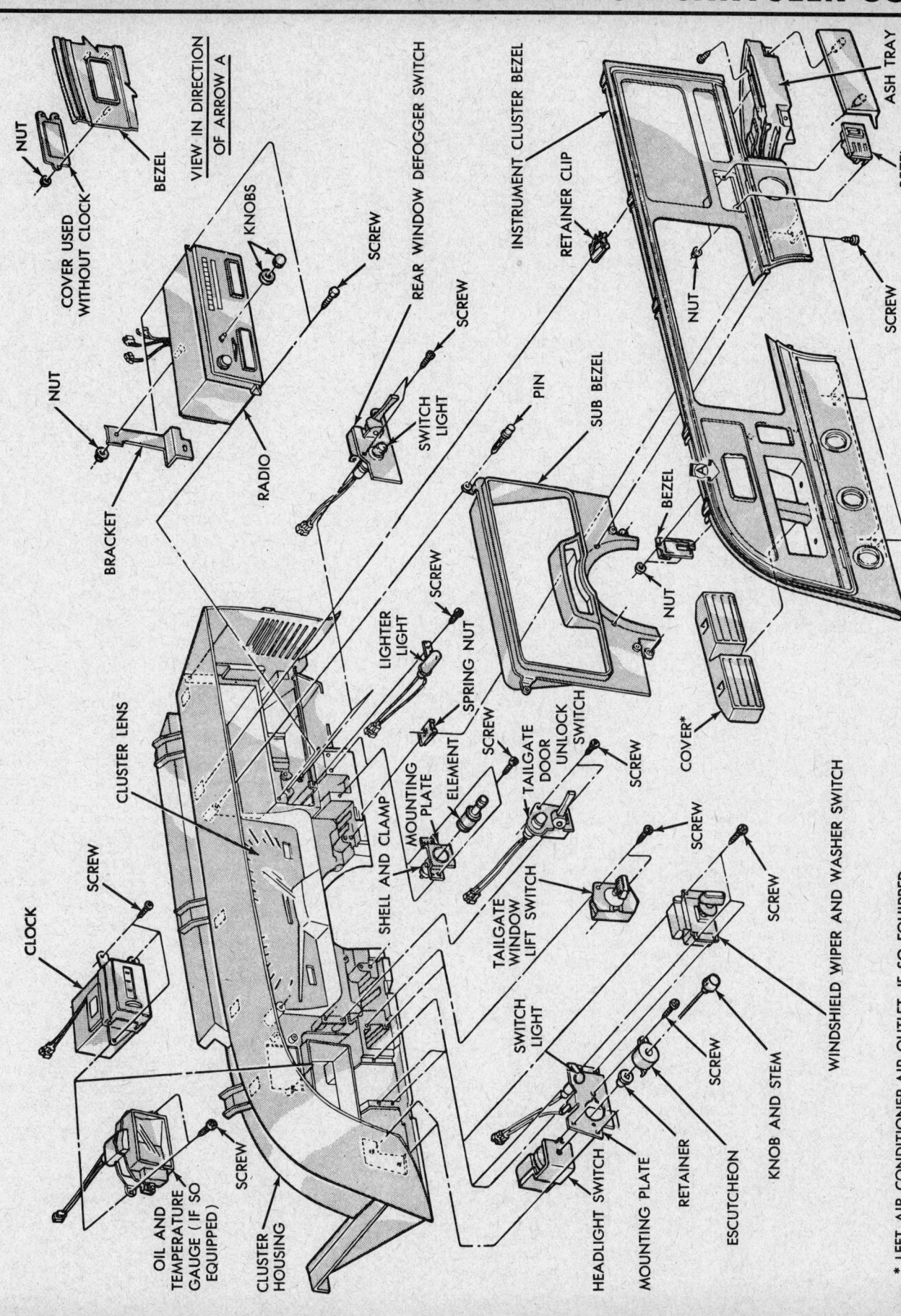

NUT

BEZEL

VIEW IN DIRECTION OF ARROW A

COVER USED WITHOUT CLOCK

KNOBS

SCREW

REAR WINDOW DEFOGGER SWITCH

SCREW

INSTRUMENT CLUSTER BEZEL

RETAINER CLIP

ASH TRAY PH139

BEZEL

NUT

SCREW

NUT

SWITCH LIGHT

PIN

SUB BEZEL

BRACKET

RADIO

BEZEL

NUT

SCREW

LIGHTER LIGHT

SPRING NUT

CLUSTER LENS

ELEMENT

MOUNTING PLATE

SCREW

TAILGATE DOOR UNLOCK SWITCH

SCREW

COVER*

SCREW

SHELL AND CLAMP

TAILGATE WINDOW LIFT SWITCH

CLOCK

SCREW

SWITCH LIGHT

SCREW

OIL AND TEMPERATURE GAUGE (IF SO EQUIPPED)

SCREW

CLUSTER HOUSING

HEADLIGHT SWITCH

MOUNTING PLATE

RETAINER

ESCUTCHEON

SCREW

KNOB AND STEM

WINDSHIELD WIPER AND WASHER SWITCH

SCREW

* LEFT AIR CONDITIONER AIR OUTLET, IF SO EQUIPPED

Fig. 8 Instrument cluster. 1977 Gran Fury & Royal Monaco

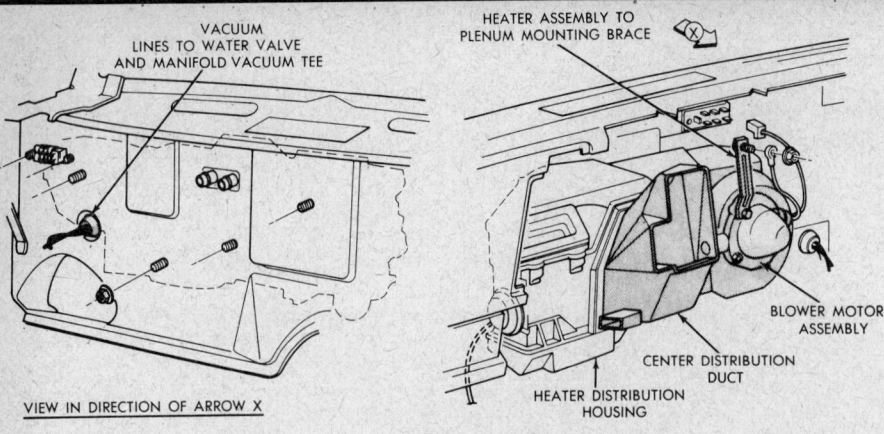

VIEW IN DIRECTION OF ARROW X

Fig. 9 Heater core & blower motor assembly (less A/C). 1979 Magnum, 1979–81 Newport, New Yorker, St. Regis & Cordoba & 1980–81 Gran Fury & Mirada

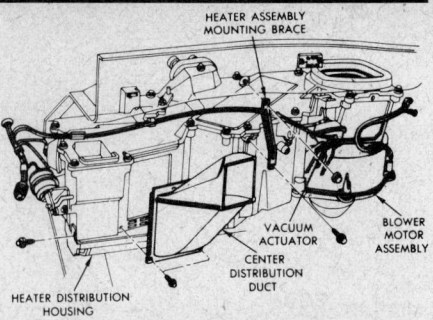

Fig. 9A Heater core & blower motor assembly (less A/C). 1982–83 Cordoba & Mirada

2. Remove wiper arm and blades.
3. Remove cowl screen.
4. Remove drive crank arm retaining nut and drive crank. Disconnect wiring to motor.
5. Unfasten and remove wiper motor.
6. Reverse procedure to install.

W/S WIPER TRANSMISSION REPLACE

1977–84

1. Disconnect battery ground cable.
2. On all models except Aspen & Volaré, remove top plastic screen. On Aspen and Volaré, disconnect washer hose to gain access to drive crank.
3. On all models, remove the arm and blade assemblies.
4. Remove the drive crank from the wiper motor by removing the attaching nut.
5. On all models except Aspen, Diplomat, LeBaron, Volare, 1982 New Yorker, 1982–84 Gran Fury, 1983 New Yorker Fifth Avenue and 1984 Fifth Avenue, remove six pivot mounting screws.
6. On Aspen, Diplomat, LeBaron, Volare, 1982 New Yorker, 1982–84 Gran Fury, 1983 New Yorker Fifth Avenue and 1984 Fifth Avenue, remove pivot mounting nut and washer.
7. Reverse procedure to install.

W/S WIPER SWITCH, REPLACE

1979–81 Newport, 1979–82 New Yorker & St. Regis; 1980–84 Gran Fury; 1980–83 Cordoba & Mirada; 1981–83 Imperial; 1983 New Yorker Fifth Avenue; 1982–84 Diplomat & 1984 Fifth Avenue

Refer to 1977–84 procedure for turn signal switch removal.

1977–80 Aspen, Volaré, 1977–81 LeBaron & Diplomat

1. Disconnect battery ground cable.

2. Remove instrument cluster bezel.
3. Remove switch module assembly attaching screws, then pull assembly out and let hang in order to gain access to switch.
4. Remove switch knob from stem, then remove switch mounting screws.
5. Disconnect switch wire connector and remove switch.
6. Reverse procedure to install.

1977 Aspen, Volaré, Diplomat & LeBaron

1. Disconnect battery ground cable.
2. Remove cluster bezel.
3. Remove switch mounting plate attaching screws and pull switch and plate assembly outward.
4. Pull knob off switch and remove switch retaining nut.
5. Disconnect electrical connector and remove switch.
6. Reverse procedure to install.

1977–79 Charger, Cordoba & Fury, 1977–78 Monaco & 1978–79 Magnum

1. Disconnect battery ground cable.
2. Remove instrument cluster upper bezel and the switch escutcheon mounting screw.
3. Remove switch to cluster housing retaining screws and pull headlamp switch to the "On" position.
4. Slide escutcheon on shaft toward rear of vehicle and rotate upward, thereby gaining clearance for switch removal.
5. Pull switch from cluster housing, disconnect electrical connector and remove switch.
6. Reverse procedure to install.

1977 Gran Fury, Royal Monaco, 1977–78 Chrysler Newport & New Yorker

1. Disconnect battery ground cable.
2. Remove instrument cluster bezel.
3. Remove switch mounting screws.
4. Disconnect electrical connector and remove switch from bezel.
5. Reverse procedure to install.

RADIO, REPLACE

NOTE: When installing radio, be sure to adjust antenna trimmer for peak performance.

1979–81 Newport, New Yorker & St. Regis; 1980–81 Gran Fury; 1980–83 Cordoba & Mirada; 1981–83 Imperial

1. Disconnect battery ground cable.
2. Remove center bezel, then remove radio to panel attaching screws.
3. Pull radio from instrument panel, then disconnect antenna and electrical leads.
4. Reverse procedure to install.

1977–80 Aspen, Volare; 1977–81 LeBaron; 1977–84 Diplomat; 1982 New Yorker; 1982–84 Gran Fury; 1983 New Yorker Fifth Avenue & 1984 Fifth Avenue

1. Disconnect battery ground cable.
2. Remove instrument cluster bezel, then the radio mounting screws.
3. Pull radio from panel and disconnect all wiring, then remove radio from vehicle.
4. Reverse procedure to install.

1977–78 Fury, 1977–79 Charger, Cordoba, 1977–78 Monaco & 1978–79 Magnum

1. Disconnect battery ground cable.
2. Remove instrument cluster lower bezel.
3. From under panel, disconnect electrical leads and support bracket from radio.
4. From front of panel, remove radio attaching screws and remove radio from front of panel.
5. Reverse procedure to install.

1977 Gran Fury, Royal Monaco, 1977–78 Chrysler Newport & New Yorker

1. Disconnect battery ground cable.
2. Remove bezel. On Fury and Monaco, also remove sub bezel.
3. Remove lamp assembly from radio (monaural only).

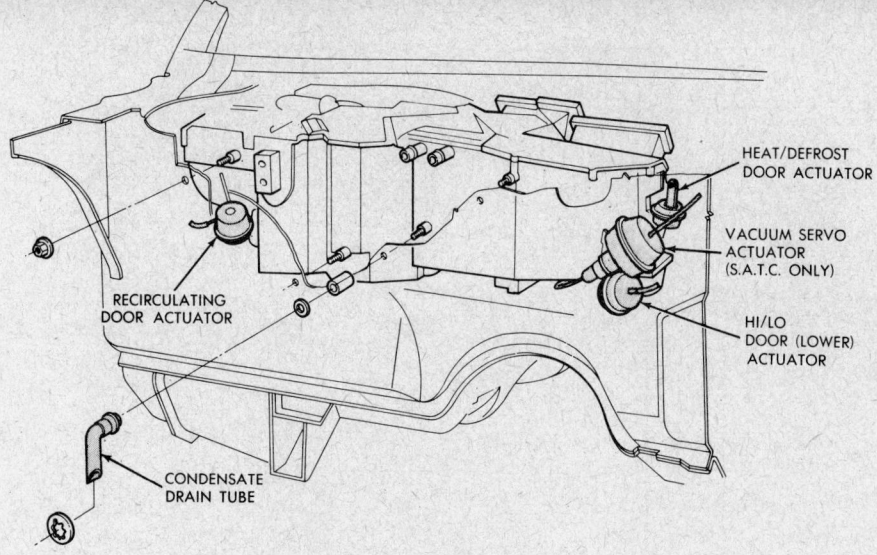

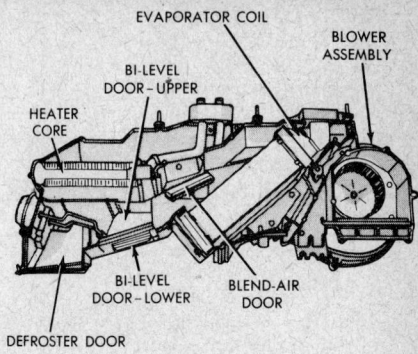

Fig. 10A   Heater core & blower motor assembly (with A/C). 1982—83 Cordoba, Imperial & Mirada

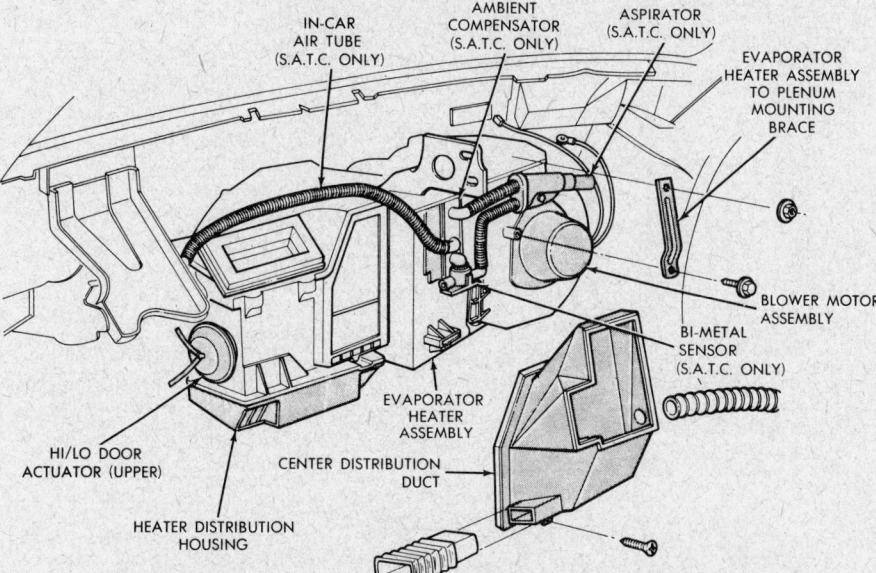

Fig. 10   Heater core & blower motor assembly (with A/C). 1979 Magnum, 1979—81 Newport, New Yorker, St. Regis & Cordoba & 1980—81 Gran Fury, Mirada & 1981 Imperial

4. Remove radio to panel retaining screws and instrument panel upper cover.
5. Working through top of panel, disconnect antenna lead and remove radio mounting bracket nut.
6. On monaural radio, disconnect speaker lead from speaker. On stereo radio, disconnect speaker lead from radio.
7. Pull radio out from panel and disconnect electrical lead.
8. Reverse procedure to install.

HEATER CORE, REPLACE

Before attempting to remove a heater core, disconnect the battery ground cable, drain the radiator and remove inlet and outlet hoses from heater assembly in engine compartment.

1979 Magnum; 1979—81 Newport, New Yorker & St. Regis; 1979—83 Cordoba; 1980—81 Gran Fury; 1980—83 Mirada; 1981—83 Imperial

Less Air Conditioning
1. Disconnect battery ground cable and drain cooling system.
2. Disconnect heater hoses from heater core.
3. Disconnect vacuum hoses from water valve and manifold tee, then push hoses and grommet through dash panel.
4. Remove four nuts securing heater assembly to dash panel.
5. Move front seat rearward and remove console, if equipped.
6. On models except Cordoba, Imperial, Magnum and Mirada, remove heater control and disconnect vacuum harness from extension harness.

7. On all models, remove glove box, ash tray and housing, right hand lap cooler duct, lower right hand trim panel or bezel, and the right hand cowl trim pad.
8. Disconnect blower motor electrical connections.
9. Disconnect temperature control cable from heater housing, then remove heater distribution housing, Figs. 9 and 9A.
10. Support heater housing and remove the heater housing to plenum mounting brace. Pull housing rearward and move toward right side to remove.
11. Remove heater housing top cover, then the heater core retaining screw.
12. Lift heater core from housing.
13. Reverse procedure to install.

With Air Conditioning
1. Disconnect battery ground cable and drain cooling system.
2. Discharge air conditioning refrigerant system.
3. Disconnect heater hoses from heater core.
4. Remove "H" valve and cap refrigerant lines. Remove condensate drain tube.
5. Disconnect vacuum lines from engine compartment and push grommet and vacuum lines through dash panel.

NOTE: On manual air conditioning systems, the vacuum lines are connected to the manifold vacuum tee and water valve. On semi-automatic air conditioning systems, the vacuum lines are connected to the vacuum reservoir and water valve.

6. Remove four nuts attaching evaporator heater assembly to dash panel.
7. Move front seat rearward and remove console, if equipped.
8. On models except Cordoba, Imperial, Magnum and Mirada, remove air conditioning switch control from dash panel and disconnect vacuum harness from harness extension.
9. On all models, remove ash tray and housing and the glove box assembly.
10. Disconnect right hand lap cooler tube from lap cooler and remove the right hand trim panel or bezel.
11. Remove right hand cowl trim pad and disconnect blower motor electrical connections.
12. On Cordoba, Imperial, Magnum and Mirada, disconnect vacuum harness from harness extension, then remove heater distribution duct.

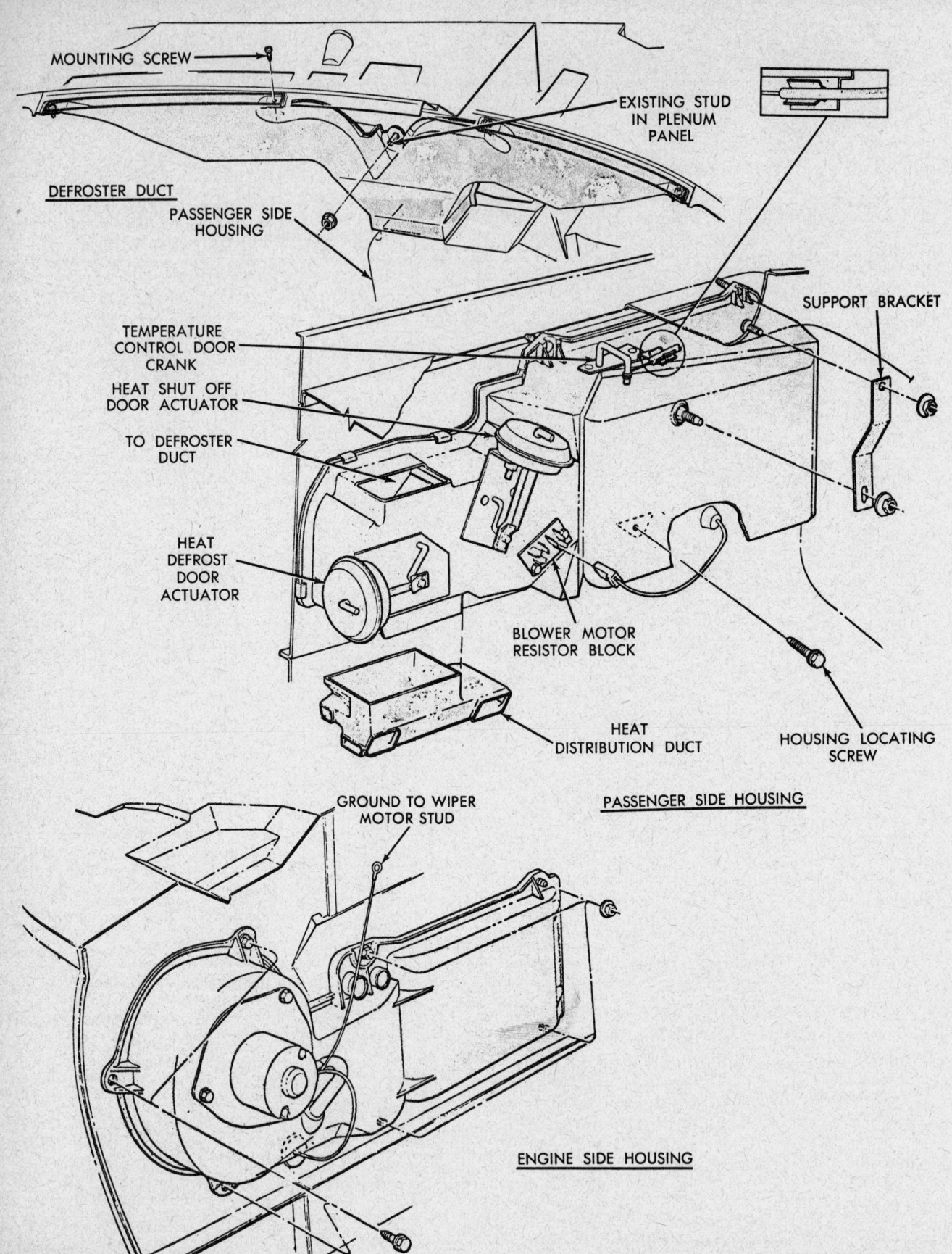

MOUNTING SCREW

EXISTING STUD IN PLENUM PANEL

DEFROSTER DUCT

PASSENGER SIDE HOUSING

SUPPORT BRACKET

TEMPERATURE CONTROL DOOR CRANK

HEAT SHUT OFF DOOR ACTUATOR

TO DEFROSTER DUCT

HEAT DEFROST DOOR ACTUATOR

BLOWER MOTOR RESISTOR BLOCK

HEAT DISTRIBUTION DUCT

HOUSING LOCATING SCREW

PASSENGER SIDE HOUSING

GROUND TO WIPER MOTOR STUD

ENGINE SIDE HOUSING

Fig. 11 Heater core & blower motor. 1977–78 less air conditioning (Typical)

13. On all models, disconnect temperature control cable from evaporator heater housing.
14. On models except Cordoba, Imperial, Magnum and Mirada, remove heater distribution housing and the center distribution duct.
15. On all models, remove the hi/lo door actuator, Figs. 10 and 10A.
16. On models with semi-automatic air conditioning system, remove vacuum servo actuator from housing and the in-car air hose from compensator.
17. On all models, support housing and remove brace between housing and plenum. Then, pull housing rearward and move toward right aide to remove.
18. Remove housing top cover and the heater core retaining screw.
19. Lift heater core from housing.
20. Reverse procedure to install.

1977–80 Aspen, Volare; 1977–81 LeBaron; 1977–84 Diplomat; 1982 New Yorker; 1982–84 Gran Fury; 1983 New Yorker Fifth Avenue & 1984 Fifth Avenue

Less Air Conditioning
1. Disconnect battery ground cable and drain cooling system.
2. Disconnect and plug heater hoses from dash panel.
3. Remove heater core tube dash panel seals and retainer.
4. Remove instrument cluster bezel assembly, upper cover, steering column cover, right intermediate side cowl trim panel and the lower instrument panel.
5. Remove instrument panel center to lower reinforcement.
6. Remove right vent control cable from unit.
7. Disconnect temperature and mode door control cables from unit, then the blower motor resistor block wiring.
8. Remove heater assembly mounting nuts in engine compartment.
9. Remove heater support to plenum bracket and pull heater unit from dash panel.
10. Separate heater housing by removing retainer clips.
11. Remove heater core tube support clamp and slide heater core from housing.
12. Reverse procedure to install.

With Air Conditioning
1. Disconnect battery ground cable and drain cooling system.
2. Discharge refrigerant system.
3. Remove air cleaner, then disconnect heater hoses from heater core. Install plugs in heater core tubes to prevent coolant from spilling when removing unit.
4. Remove "H" valve, then cap refrigerant lines to prevent dirt and moisture from entering.
5. Remove instrument cluster bezel assembly.
6. Remove instrument panel upper cover, steering column cover and right intermediate side cowl trim panel.
7. Remove lower instrument panel.
8. Remove instrument center to lower reinforcement.
9. Remove floor console, if equipped.
10. Remove right center air distribution duct.
11. Disconnect locking tab on defroster distribution duct.
12. Disconnect temperature control cable from evaporator housing.

13. Disconnect blower motor resistor block wire connector.
14. Disconnect vacuum lines from water valve and vacuum source tee.
15. Remove wiring from evaporator housing and vacuum lines from inlet air housing, then disconnect vacuum harness coupling.
16. Remove drain tube from engine compartment.
17. Remove nuts from evaporator housing mounting studs on engine side of dash panel.
18. Remove hanger strap from plenum stud above evaporator housing, then tilt evaporator housing back to clear dash panel and remove housing from vehicle.
19. Remove blend air door lever from shaft.
20. Remove top cover screws and the cover.
21. Remove heater core from housing.
22. Reverse procedure to install.

1977–78 Fury, Charger, Cordoba, Monaco & 1978 Magnum

Less Air Conditioning
1. Disconnect fusible link and drain coolant.
2. Disconnect heater hoses from core tubes and plug tubes to prevent coolant from spilling into interior of vehicle.
3. Remove nuts from around blower motor and one from center of dash panel, then remove lower instrument panel bezel, glove box and door.
4. Disconnect antenna lead from radio, then remove screw from housing to plenum support rod on right side of housing above outside air opening.
5. Disconnect air door control cables and wire from blower motor resistor.
6. Tip heater assembly down and out from under instrument panel.
7. Remove screws retaining front cover to heater assembly, then cut rubber seal in two places where front cover separates cover from housing.
8. Remove core tube retaining screw located behind housing and between core tubes.
9. Remove sponge rubber gaskets from core tubes and remove heater core from housing.
10. Reverse procedure to install.

With Air Conditioning
1. Disconnect fusible link and drain coolant.
2. Disconnect heater hoses from core tubes and plug tubes to prevent coolant from spilling into interior of vehicle.
3. Discharge A/C refrigerant and disconnect line from H-valve and cover tubing sealing plate. Remove expansion valve from evaporator and cover evaporator sealing plate and both sealing surfaces of expansion valve.
4. Disconnect blower motor wires and remove blower motor cooling tube.
5. Remove glove box, ash tray and housing bezel, right lap cooler, right side cowl panel and air distribution duct.
6. Remove A/C mode door vacuum actuator from bracket and shift actuator forward on top of unit.
7. Disconnect connector from seat belt interlock control module and disconnect wires from blower motor resistor.
8. Disconnect antenna lead from radio and remove radio.
9. Remove housing retaining nuts through

engine compartment, then remove rubber drain tube.
10. Remove support bracket from rear of unit to plenum.
11. Pull unit back so that tubes clear dash panel, then rotate so that right end of unit comes out first from under the instrument panel.
12. Carefully remove plenum air seal, then disconnect vacuum hose from inlet air door actuator.
13. On 1977–78 models, remove 18 clamps holding front and rear covers separate housings.
14. On all models, carefully lift left half of housing seal from rear cover. Do not remove entire seal as the lower portion is a water seal.
15. Remove two retaining screws from mounting plate and one from between heater core tubes and lift heater core from housing.
16. Reverse procedure to install.

1977 Gran Fury, Royal Monaco, 1977–78 Chrysler Newport & New Yorker

Less Air Conditioning
1. Disconnect battery ground cable and drain radiator.
2. Disconnect heater hoses and plug hose fittings on heater core.
3. Move front seat rearward and remove instrument panel lower cover. Unplug antenna lead from radio and disconnect upper level vent vacuum line.
4. Disconnect the upper level vent from heater housing and the mounting bracket from dash, then swing duct back.
5. Disconnect electrical connectors from blower motor resistor and control cable from clip and crank.
6. Disconnect support bracket and swing bracket out of way.
7. From engine compartment, remove five retaining nuts from studs.
8. Roll or tip housing out from under instrument panel and disconnect control cable from clip and the blend air door crank.
9. Remove core tube locating screw from between core tubes, remove housing retaining nuts, separate housing and remove core.
10. Reverse procedure to install.

With Air Conditioning
1. Discharge refrigerant system.
2. Disconnect fusible link, drain cooling system, remove air cleaner and disconnect heater hoses at heater core. Install plugs in heater core tube to prevent coolant spillage when removing heater core.
3. Remove "H" valve, then cap refrigerant lines to prevent entry of dirt and moisture.
4. Move front seat rearward to provide room to remove unit.
5. Remove lap cooler and instrument panel lower cover.
6. Remove A/C distribution duct.
7. Disconnect antenna lead from radio and wires and vacuum lines from unit.
8. Remove drain tube. On models with ATC, disconnect wire connectors and vacuum connector from servo, amplifier and master and compressor switches. Disconnect aspirator tube.
9. On all models, remove temperature control cable from clip on unit.
10. Remove retaining nut from support bracket.

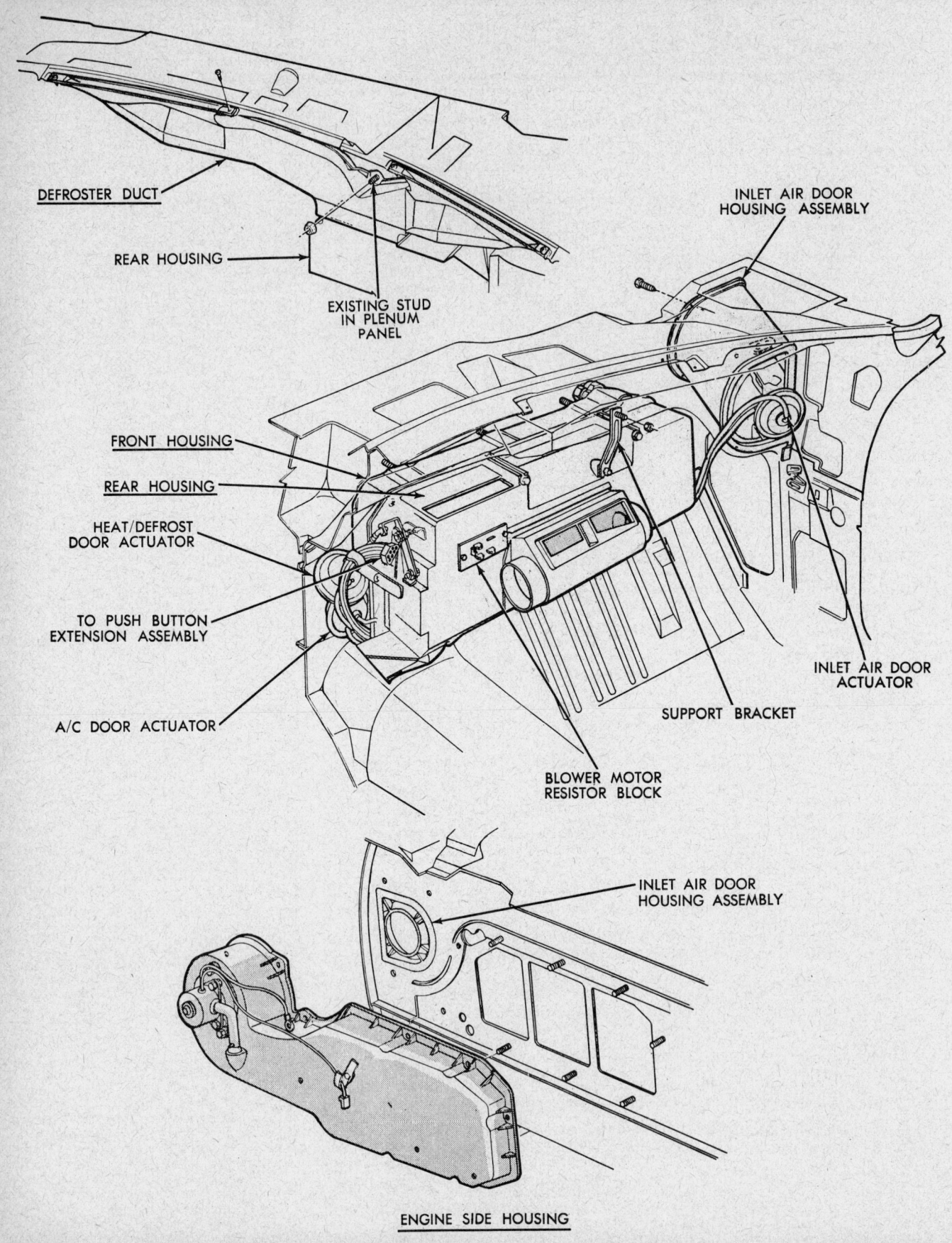

DEFROSTER DUCT

REAR HOUSING

EXISTING STUD
IN PLENUM
PANEL

INLET AIR DOOR
HOUSING ASSEMBLY

FRONT HOUSING

REAR HOUSING

HEAT/DEFROST
DOOR ACTUATOR

TO PUSH BUTTON
EXTENSION ASSEMBLY

A/C DOOR ACTUATOR

INLET AIR DOOR
ACTUATOR

SUPPORT BRACKET

BLOWER MOTOR
RESISTOR BLOCK

INLET AIR DOOR
HOUSING ASSEMBLY

ENGINE SIDE HOUSING

Fig. 12 Heater core & blower motor. 1977–78 with air conditioning (Typical)

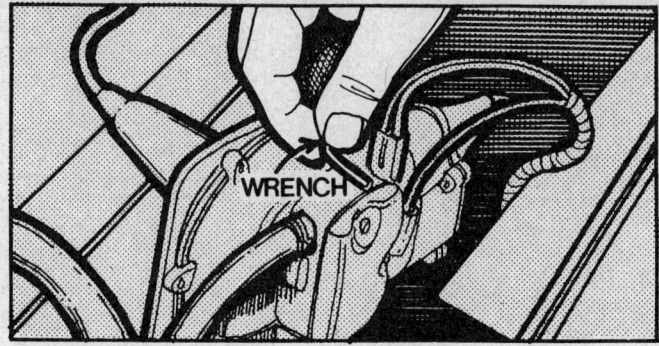

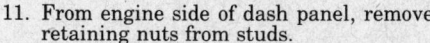

Fig. 13   Speed Control lock-in screw adjustment. 1977–84

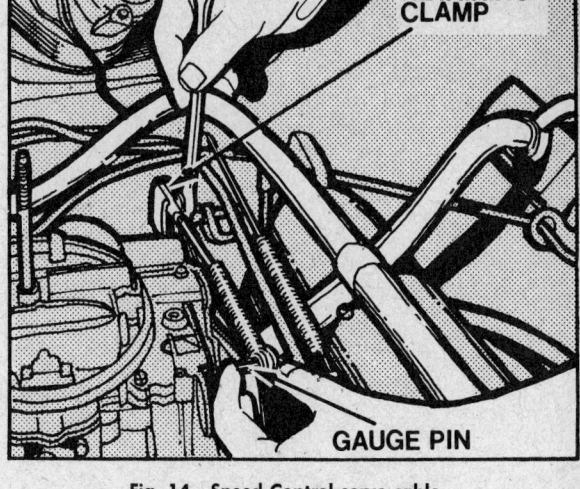

Fig. 14   Speed Control servo cable throttle adjustment. 1977–84

11. From engine side of dash panel, remove retaining nuts from studs.
12. Tilt housing and remove from under instrument panel.
13. Remove mode door and blend air door levers.
14. Remove attaching screws and lift off top cover.
15. Remove four heater core retaining screws and three screws from core tube seal, then lift heater core from housing.
16. Reverse procedure to install.

BLOWER MOTOR, REPLACE

1982 New Yorker; 1982–84 Diplomat, Gran Fury; 1983 New Yorker Fifth Avenue & 1984 Fifth Avenue

NOTE: The blower motor is accessible from under right side of instrument panel.

Less A/C
1. Disconnect battery ground cable.
2. Disconnect blower motor ground and feed wires.
3. Remove blower motor to heater housing attaching screws, then remove blower motor.
4. Reverse procedure to install.

With A/C
1. Disconnect battery ground cable.
2. Disconnect blower motor feed wire, then remove blower motor housing to recirculation housing attaching nuts and separate blower motor housing from upper housing.
3. Remove blower motor plate attaching screws, then remove wire grommet, mounting plate and blower motor and wheel as an assembly.
4. Reverse procedure to install.

1979 Magnum; 1979–81 Newport, New Yorker & St. Regis; 1979–83 Cordoba; 1980–81 Gran Fury; 1980–83 Mirada & 1981–83 Imperial

NOTE: The blower motor is accessible from under right side of instrument panel.

1. Disconnect battery ground cable.
2. Remove glove box assembly.

3. Disconnect blower motor electrical connections.
4. Remove heater housing or evaporator-heater housing to plenum brace.
5. Remove blower motor mounting screws and the blower motor, Figs. 9, 9A, 10, and 10A.
6. Reverse procedure to install.

1977–80 Aspen, Volaré, 1977–81 LeBaron & Diplomat

Less Air Conditioning
1. Remove heater assembly and heater core as outlined under "Heater Core, Replace".
2. Remove blower motor vent tube.
3. Remove blower motor mounting nuts and the blower motor.
4. Reverse procedure to install.

With Air Conditioning

NOTE: All service to the blower motor is performed under the right side of the instrument panel.

1. Disconnect battery ground cable and the blower motor feed wire.
2. Remove blower motor mounting nuts from bottom of recirculation housing.
3. Separate upper and lower blower motor housing, then remove blower motor mounting plate screws.
4. Remove wire grommet, mounting plate and blower motor.
5. Reverse procedure to install.

1977 Gran Fury & Royal Monaco, 1977–78 Chrysler Newport & New Yorker

The blower motor is mounted to the engine side housing under the right front fender between the inner fender shield and the fender, Figs. 11 and 12. The inner fender shield must be removed to service the blower motor.

1977–78 Charger, Fury, Cordoba, Monaco; 1978 Magnum

Less Air Conditioning
The heater assembly must be removed to service the blower motor. See procedure for

Heater Core Removal to remove assembly, then proceed to *Remove Blower Motor* as follows:
1. Disconnect blower motor lead from resistor block. Disconnect the ground wire from the mounting plate.
2. Remove six screws and retaining clips holding blower motor mounting plate to housing. Separate the blower motor and mounting plate from the housing, Fig. 12.
3. Remove the blower wheel from the motor shaft.
4. Remove the two retaining nuts and separate the motor from the mounting plate. Remove the motor, Fig. 11.
5. Reverse procedure to install.

With Air Conditioning

NOTE: All service to the blower motor is made from the engine compartment side.

1. Disconnect battery ground cable. Disconnect the feed wire at the connector and the ground wire. Remove the air tube.
2. Remove three screws located on the outer surface of the mounting plate.
3. Remove the mounting plate and blower motor as an assembly, Fig. 12.

SPEED CONTROLS, ADJUST

Lock-in Screw Adjustment, Fig. 13
Lock-in accuracy will be affected by poor engine performance (need for tune-up), loaded gross weight of car (trailering), improper slack in control cable. After the foregoing items have been considered and the speed sags or drops more than 2 to 3 mph when the speed control is activated, the lock-in adjusting screw should be turned counter-clockwise approximately 1/4 turn per one mph correction required.

If a speed increase of more than 2 to 3 mph occurs, the lock-in adjusting screw should be turned clockwise 1/4 turn per one mph correction required.

CAUTION: This adjustment must not exceed

two turns in either direction or damage to the unit may occur.

Throttle Cable Adjustment, Fig. 14

Optimum servo performance is obtained with a given amount of free play in the throttle control cable. To obtain proper free play, insert a 1/16″ diameter pin between forward end of slot in cable end of carburetor linkage pin (hair pin clip removed from linkage pin). With choke in full open position and carbure-tor at curb idle, pull cable back toward dash panel without moving carburetor linkage until all free play is removed. Tighten cable clamp bolt to 45 inch-pounds, remove 1/16″ pin and install hair pin clip.

Brake Switch Adjustment

1. Loosen switch bracket.
2. Insert proper spacer gauge between brake push rod and switch with pedal in free position. On 1977–78 models, the spacer must be .120 in. for 1977–78 full size models and .140 in. for 1977–78 inter-mediates. On all 1979 models a .140 inch spacer is used. On 1980–81 Gran Fury, Newport, New Yorker and St. Regis mod-els, a .150 inch spacer is used. On 1980–81 models except Gran Fury, New-port, New Yorker and St. Regis and all 1982–84 models, a .130 inch spacer is used.
3. Push switch bracket assembly toward brake push rod until plunger is fully depressed and switch contacts spacer.
4. Tighten bracket bolt to 75 in-lbs. and remove spacer.

Engine Section

ENGINE MOUNTS, REPLACE

1. Disconnect throttle linkage at transmis-sion and at carburetor.
2. Raise hood and position fan to clear radi-ator hose and radiator top tank.
3. Remove torque nuts from insulator studs.
4. Raise engine just enough to remove front engine mount.
5. Reverse above to install.

ENGINE, REPLACE

All V8 Engines

1. Scribe a line on hinge brackets on hood to assure proper adjustments when install-ing. Then remove hood.
2. Remove battery, drain cooling system, remove all hoses, fan shroud, disconnect oil cooler lines and remove radiator.
3. On models with A/C, remove compressor from mounting bracket and position on right fender.

NOTE: Do not tilt compressor when re-moved from mounting bracket. Before installing compressor turn pulley several revolutions by hand to ensure all oil is back in compressor oil sump.

4. On all models, remove distributor cap, vacuum lines and wiring.
5. Remove carburetor, linkage, starter wires and oil pressure wire.
6. Disconnect power steering hoses, if equipped.
7. Remove starter, alternator, charcoal can-ister and horns.
8. Disconnect exhaust pipe at manifold.
9. On vehicles with automatic transmis-sion:
   a. Mark converter and drive plate to aid in installation.
   b. Remove torque converter drive plate bolts.
   c. Install a C-clamp on bottom front of torque converter, to assure that con-verter remains properly positioned in transmission housing.
   d. Remove converter housing to engine bolts.
   e. Support transmission in its normal position to assure ease of installa-tion.
10. On vehicles with manual transmission, remove transmission.
11. Attach engine lifting fixture.
12. Remove engine front mounting bolts, then raise and work engine out of chas-sis.
13. Reverse procedure to install.

6-225

1. Scribe hood hinge outlines on hood and remove hood.
2. Drain cooling system and remove battery and carburetor air cleaner.
3. Disconnect transmission cooler lines at radiator (if equipped).
4. Remove radiator and hoses.
5. On models with A/C, remove compressor from mounting bracket and position on right fender.

NOTE: Do not tilt compressor when re-moved from mounting bracket. Before installing compressor turn pulley several revolutions by hand to ensure all oil is back in compressor sump.

6. On all models, remove closed ventilation system and evaporative control system from cylinder head cover.
7. Disconnect fuel lines, vacuum lines, car-buretor linkage and wiring to engine.
8. Disconnect power steering hoses, if equipped.
9. Remove starter, alternator and horns.
10. Disconnect exhaust pipe at manifold.
11. Remove converter cover plate.
12. On manual transmission equipped vehi-cles disconnect propeller shaft, tie out of the way and disconnect wires and linkage at transmission.
13. On manual transmission equipped vehi-cles attach engine support fixture, re-move engine rear crossmember and re-move transmission.
14. On automatic transmission equipped ve-hicles disconnect torque converter drive plate from engine. Mark converter and drive plate to aid in installation. Support transmission in its normal position in relation to the vehicle, to insure ease of installation.
15. Attach lifting fixture to cylinder head and attach chain hoist.
16. Remove engine support and front engine mounting bolts and lift engine from chas-sis.
17. Reverse procedure to install.

CYLINDER HEAD, REPLACE

6-225

1. Drain cooling system.
2. Remove carburetor air cleaner and fuel line.
3. Disconnect accelerator linkage.
4. Remove vacuum control tube at carbure-tor and distributor.
5. Disconnect spark plug wires, heater hose and clamp holding by-pass hose.
6. Disconnect heat indicator sending unit wire.

NOTE: On models equipped with air pump, disconnect diverter valve vacuum line from intake manifold and remove air tubes from cylinder head.

7. Disconnect exhaust pipe at manifold.
8. On 1977 models, remove intake and ex-haust manifold and carburetor as a unit.
9. On all models, remove closed vent system and rocker arm cover.
10. Remove rocker shaft assembly and push rods.

NOTE: During disassembly note location of push rods so they can be installed in the same position.

11. On 1977 models, remove cylinder head bolts and lift off cylinder head. On 1978–83 models, remove cylinder head bolts, then remove cylinder head and intake and exhaust manifold as an as-sembly.

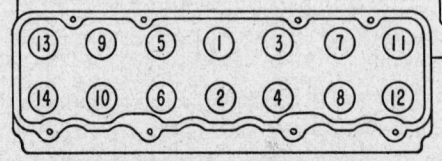

Fig. 1 Cylinder head tightening sequence. 6-225

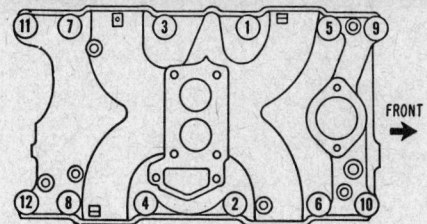

Fig. 2 Intake manifold tightening sequence. V8-318, 360

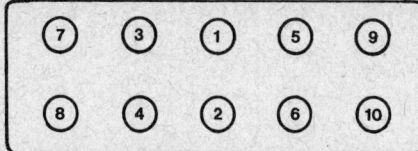

Fig. 3 Cylinder head tightening sequence. V8-318, 360

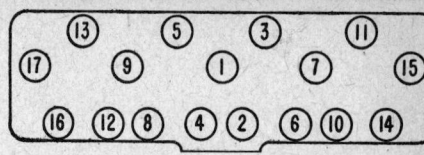

Fig. 4 Cylinder head tightening sequence. V8-400, 440

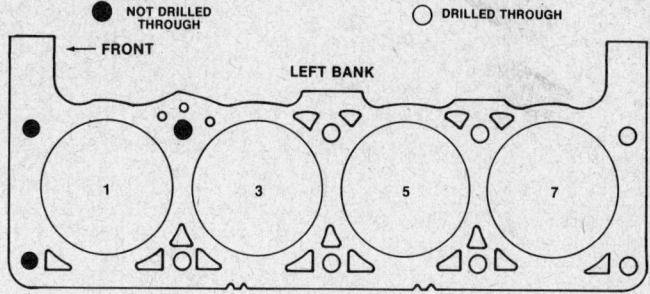

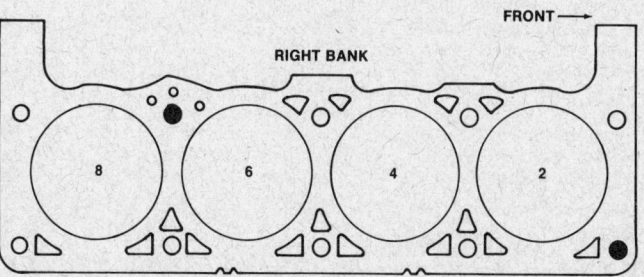

Fig. 3A Cylinder head bolt hole identification. Some 1979 and all 1980–84 Chrysler Corp. V8-318 engines.

12. Install the head in the reverse order of removal, and tighten the bolts in the sequence shown in Fig. 1.
13. *When installing the manifolds, loosen the three bolts holding the intake and exhaust manifolds together. This is required to maintain proper alignment.* Install intake and exhaust manifolds with cup side of the conical washers against the manifolds.

V8-318, 360

NOTE: The intake manifold attaching bolts on some engines are tilted upward about 30 degrees at an angle to the manifold-to-cylinder head gasket face. The purpose of this design is to provide more effective sealing at the cylinder block end gaskets. If the intake manifold is removed the installation should be such that the bolt tightening is done evenly and in the sequence shown in Fig. 2.

With gaskets in place start all bolts, leaving them loose. Run bolts 1 through 4 down so the heads just touch manifold. Then tighten these four bolts to 25 foot-pounds torque. After checking to see that gaskets are properly seated at all surfaces, tighten remaining bolts to 25 foot-pounds. Finally tighten all bolts in the sequence shown to specifications.

1. Drain cooling system and disconnect battery ground cable.
2. Remove alternator, carburetor air cleaner and fuel line. Disconnect accelerator linkage.
3. Remove vacuum advance hose and distributor cap and wires.
4. Disconnect coil wires, heat indicator wire, heater and by-pass hoses.
5. Remove closed ventilation system and rocker arm covers.
6. Remove intake manifold, coil and carburetor as an assembly.
7. Remove exhaust manifolds.
8. Remove rocker arm and shaft assemblies. Remove push rods.

NOTE: During disassembly note location of push rods so they can be installed in the same position.

9. Remove head bolts and cylinder heads.
10. Reverse procedure to install heads and tighten bolts in sequence, Fig. 3.

Service Note

Some 1979 and all 1980–84 V8-318 engines have cylinder head bolt holes drilled through the block into the water jacket in certain locations, Fig. 3A. On 1979 models, this type cylinder block is identified by engine numbers beginning with 9M3180702 or 4104230-318. If engine number cannot be determined, refer to Fig. 3A and insert a screwdriver into the head bolt holes. If the screwdriver can be inserted at least two inches into a hole, that hole is open to the water jacket. Cylinder head bolts in these locations must have sealer 4057989 or equivalent applied to the threads to prevent engine coolant leakage. Ensure old sealer is cleaned from the threads before applying new sealer. Cylinder head bolt torque on these engines has been reduced to 95 ft. lbs.

V8-400, 440

1. Drain cooling system, remove air cleaner, fuel line from pump and carburetor, distributor vacuum tube and alternator.

NOTE: On models equipped with high mount air pump, disconnect diverter

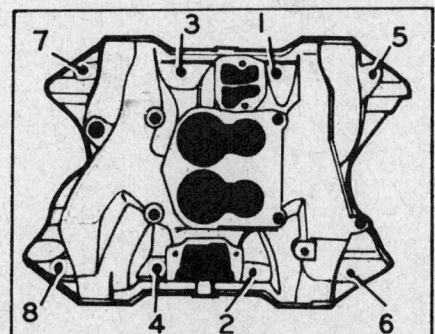

Fig. 5 Intake manifold tightening sequence. V8-400 & 440

valve vacuum line from intake manifold and air pump line from exhaust manifolds.

2. Disconnect throttle linkage at carburetor, distributor cap, coil wires, heat indicator sending unit wire and heater hoses at engine.
3. Remove spark plugs and cables, and closed vent system.
4. Remove intake manifold, carburetor and coil as an assembly.
5. Remove exhaust manifolds.
6. Remove cylinder head covers and spark plug cable support brackets.
7. Remove rocker shaft assemblies. *Do not remove bolts from end brackets.*
8. Remove push rods and valve lifter chamber cover.

NOTE: During disassembly note location of push rods so they can be installed in the same position.

9. Remove attaching bolts and lift off heads.
10. Reverse the foregoing procedure to install the heads. Tighten bolts in the sequence shown in Fig. 4. Tighten intake manifold bolts in sequence shown in Fig. 5.

VALVES, ADJUST

6-225

NOTE: Some 1978 Aspen and Volare models

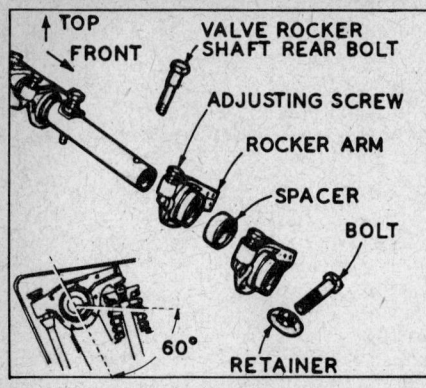

Fig. 6 Rocker arm and shaft assembly. 6-225

VALVE TIMING SPECS.

Intake Opens Before TDC

Engine	Year	Degrees
6-225	1977–80	16
	1981–83	6
8-318	1977–84	10
8-360	1977–80	18
8-400	1977 All	20
	1978 All	18
8-440	1977 All	20
	1978 Exc. Hi. Perf.	18
	1978 Hi. Perf.	21

```
ROCKER ARMS "RIGHT"
```

```
ROCKER ARMS "LEFT"
```

Fig. 7 Rocker arm and shaft assembly installed. 8-318, 360, 400, 440

with 6-225 2 barrel carb engines, and all 1981–83 vehicles are equipped with hydraulic lifters which cannot be adjusted.

Before the final valve lash adjustment is made, operate the engine for 5 minutes at a fast idle to stabilize engine temperatures.

Before starting the adjustment procedure, make two chalk marks on the vibration damper. Space the marks approximately 120° apart (⅓ of circumference) so that with the timing mark the damper is divided into three equal parts. Adjust the valves for No. 1 cylinder. Repeat the procedure for the remaining valves, turning the crankshaft ⅓ turn while adjusting the valves in the firing order sequence of 153624.

VALVE ARRANGEMENT

Front to Rear

8-318, 360	E-I-I-E-E-I-I-E
8-400, 440	E-I-I-E-E-I-I-E
6-225	E-I-E-I-E-I-I-E-I-E

VALVE LIFT SPECS.

Engine	Year	Intake	Exhaust
6-225	1977–80	.406	.414
	1981–83	.378	.378
8-318	1977	.373	.399
	1978–84	.373	.400
8-360	1977–80	.410	.410
8-400	1977②	.434	.464
	1977①	.434	.430
	1978 All	.434	.430
8-440	1977①	.434	.430
	1977–78②	.449	.464

①—Exc. Hi. Perf.
②—Hi. Perf.

ROCKER ARMS, REPLACE

6-225

1. Remove closed ventilation and evaporation control systems.
2. Remove rocker arm cover.
3. Remove rocker shaft bolts and retainers.
4. Lift off rocker arms and shaft.

Inspection

Clean all parts with a suitable solvent. Be sure the inside of the shaft is clean and the oil holes are open. The drilled oil hole in the bore of the rocker arm must be open to the trough and valve end of the arms. The trough also feeds oil to the adjusting screw and push rod.

The shaft should be free from excessive wear in arm contact areas. The shaft should be smooth in retainer contact areas. The adjusting screws in the rocker arms should have a uniform round end. The drag torque should be smooth and uniform. The retainers should be smooth and undamaged in the shaft contact area.

Assemble and Install

1. Referring to Fig. 6, note position of oil hole on forward end of shaft which denotes the upper side of shaft. Rocker arms must be put on the shaft with the adjusting screw to the right side of the engine. Place one of the small retainers on the one long bolt and install the bolt in the rear hole in the shaft from the top side.
2. Install one rocker arm and one spacer; then two rocker arms and a spacer. Continue in same sequence until all rocker arms and spacers are on the shaft.
3. Place a bolt and small retainer in front

hole in shaft.
4. Place a bolt and the one *wide* retainer through the center hole in the shaft with six rocker arms on each side of center.
5. Install remaining bolts and retainers.
6. Locate the assembly on the cylinder head and position rocker arm adjusting screws in push rods.
7. Tighten bolts finger tight, bringing retainers in contact with the shaft *between rocker arms.*
8. Tighten bolts to specified torque.
9. After running engine to normal operating temperature, adjust valve lash to specifications.
10. Complete the job by installing the remaining parts removed.

V8-318, 360

To provide correct lubrication for the rocker arms on these engines, the rocker shafts have a small notch machined at one end and these notches must always face inward toward the center of the engine when installed. In other words, the notched end must be toward the rear of the engine on the right bank, and to the front of the engine on the left bank.

Rocker arms must be correctly positioned on the shaft prior to installation on cylinder head, Fig. 7.

It is also important when installing the rocker shaft assembly on the cylinder head to position the short retainers at each end and in the center, and to place long retainers in the two remaining positions.

V8-400, 440

1. Install rocker shafts so that the ³⁄₁₆" diameter rocker arm lubrication holes point downward into rocker arm, and so that the 15 degree angle of these holes point outward toward valve end of rocker arm, Fig. 8. The 15 degree angle is determined from the center line of the bolt holes through the shaft which are used to attach the shaft assembly to the cylinder head.
2. On all engines, install rocker arms and shaft assembly, making sure to install long stamped steel retainers in No. 2 and 4 positions.

NOTE: Use extreme care in tightening the bolts so that valve lifters have time to bleed down to their operating length. Bulged lifter bodies, bent push rods and permanent noisy operation may result if lifters are forced down too rapidly.

3. Installation should be as shown in Fig. 7.

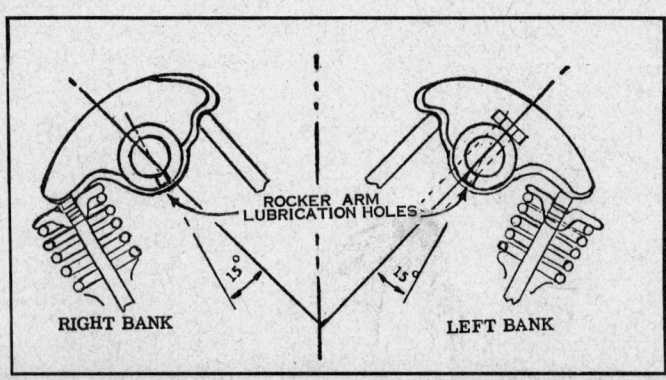

Fig. 8 Rocker arm shaft installation. V8-400, 440

Fig. 9 Removing valve lifter

VALVE GUIDES

Valves operate in guide holes bored directly in the cylinder head. When valve stem-to-guide clearance becomes excessive, valves with oversize stems of .005, .015 and .030 inch are available for service replacement. When necessary to install valves with oversize stems the valve bores should be reamed to provide the proper operating clearance.

VALVE LIFTERS, REPLACE

1977–83 6-225 & 1980–84 V8-318

After taking off rocker arm and shaft assembly, lift out push rods. The valve lifters may then be removed with a suitably long magnet rod. If the lifters cannot be removed with the magnet rod, a special tool (C-4129) may be used, Fig. 9. Insert the tool through the push rod opening in the cylinder head and into lifter. Turn the handle to expand the tool in the lifter, then with a twisting motion remove the lifter from its bore.

1978–79 V8-318, 360

1. Drain cooling system and remove air cleaner.
2. Remove valve covers, rocker shaft assemblies and push rods.

NOTE: Keep push rods in order so they can be installed in the same position.

3. Remove upper radiator hose, heater hose and bypass hose from intake manifold.
4. Remove distributor and intake manifold assembly, then remove lifters.

NOTE: Keep lifters in order so they can be installed in the same position.

5. Reverse procedure to install.

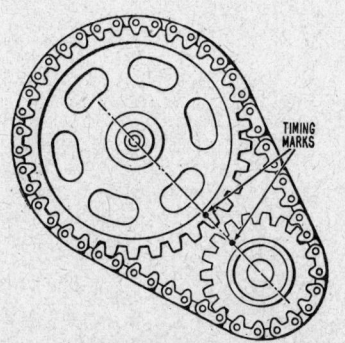

Fig. 11 Valve timing marks aligned for correct valve timing. All Sixes

1977 V8-318, 360 & 1977–78 V8-400, 440

Chrysler Tool is available for this operation. To remove the lifter, insert the tool in the lifter body. (This portion of the tool can be used to remove lifters without a varnish build-up around the bottom of the body.) Lift the lifter out of the bore, Fig. 10. If they are stuck, proceed as follows:

Slide the puller portion of the tool through the cylinder head push rod holes and seat it firmly in the top of the lifter. Insert the puller pin through the body and tool shaft in the holes provided, Fig. 9. Grasp the tool handle and pull the lifter out of the bore as shown.

TIMING CHAIN COVER, REPLACE

6-225

1. To remove cover, drain cooling system and remove radiator and fan.
2. Remove vibration damper with a puller.
3. Loosen oil pan bolts to allow clearance and remove chain case cover.
4. Reverse above procedure to install cover.

V8-400, 440

1. Drain cooling system.
2. Remove radiator, fan and belt.
3. Remove power steering pump and alternator attaching bolts and position pump and alternator aside.
4. If equipped with A/C, position compressor aside.
5. Remove water pump and housing as an assembly.
6. Remove crankshaft bolt and pulley from vibration damper and remove damper with a puller.
7. Remove key from crankshaft.
8. Remove chain case cover and gasket, *Use extreme caution to avoid damaging the oil pan gasket; if damaged it will be necessary to remove the oil pan in order to install a new pan gasket.*
9. Reverse procedure to install.

V8-318, 360

1. Remove radiator, fan and belt.
2. Remove water pump and housing as a unit.
3. Remove power steering pump, if necessary.
4. Remove crankshaft pulley.
5. Remove key from crankshaft.
6. Remove fuel pump.
7. Loosen oil pan bolts and remove front bolt at each side.
8. Remove chain case cover and gasket, *using extreme caution to avoid damaging oil pan gasket otherwise oil pan will have to be removed. It is normal to find particles of neoprene collected between crankshaft seal retainer and oil slinger.*
9. Reverse procedure to install.

TIMING CHAIN, REPLACE

6-225

1. After removing chain case cover as outlined above, take off camshaft sprocket attaching bolt.
2. Remove chain with camshaft sprocket.

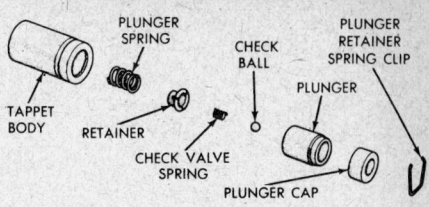

Fig. 10 Hydraulic valve lifter

3. Clean all parts and dry with compressed air.
4. Inspect timing chain for broken or damaged links. Inspect sprockets for cracks and chipped, worn or damaged teeth.

Installation

1. Turn crankshaft so sprocket timing mark is toward and directly in line with centerline of camshaft.
2. Temporarily install camshaft sprocket. Rotate camshaft to position sprocket timing mark toward and directly in line with centerline of crankshaft; then remove camshaft sprocket.
3. Place chain on crankshaft sprocket and position camshaft sprocket in chain so sprocket can be installed with timing marks aligned without moving camshaft, Fig. 11.
4. Install parts removed in reverse order of removal.

V8 Engines

To install chain and sprockets, lay both the camshaft and crankshaft sprockets on the bench. Position the sprockets so that the timing marks are next to each other. Place the chain on both sprockets, then push the gears apart as far as the chain will permit. Use a straightedge to form a line through the exact centers of both gears. The timing marks must be on this line, Fig. 12.

Slide the chain with both sprockets on the camshaft and crankshaft at the same time; then recheck the alignment.

NOTE: On V8 engines, use tool No. C-3509 to prevent camshaft from contacting welch plug in rear of engine block. Remove distributor

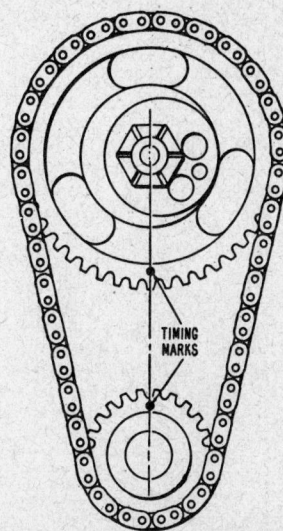

Fig. 12 Valve timing marks aligned for correct valve timing. All V8s

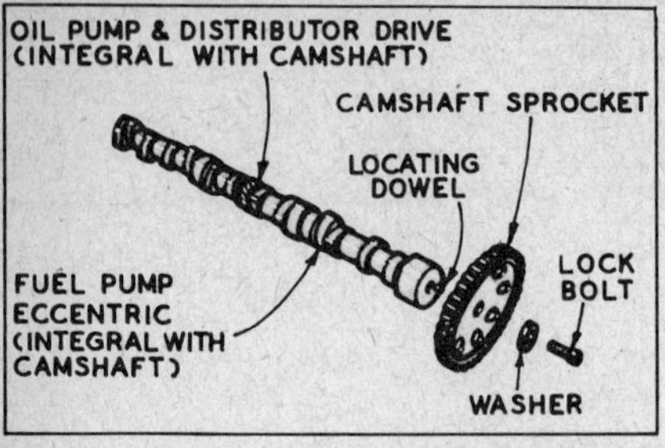

Fig. 13 Camshaft and related parts. 6-225

and oil pump-distributor drive gear. Position tool against rear side of cam gear and attach tool with distributor retainer plate bolt.

CAMSHAFT & BEARINGS, REPLACE

6-225

The camshaft is supported by four precision type, steel backed, babbitt-lined bearings. Rearward thrust is taken by the rear face of the sprocket hub contacting the front of the engine block.

The camshaft, Fig. 13, can be removed after removing the grille, radiator and timing chain. To remove the camshaft bearings, the engine must be removed from the vehicle.

1. Remove valve lifters, oil pump, fuel pump and distributor.
2. Install a long bolt into front of camshaft to aid removal. Remove camshaft using care not to damage bearings.
3. Remove welch plug back of rear camshaft bearing.
4. Remove bearings with suitable puller equipment.
5. Install new bearings, being sure the oil holes in bearings line up with the corresponding oil holes in the crankcase.

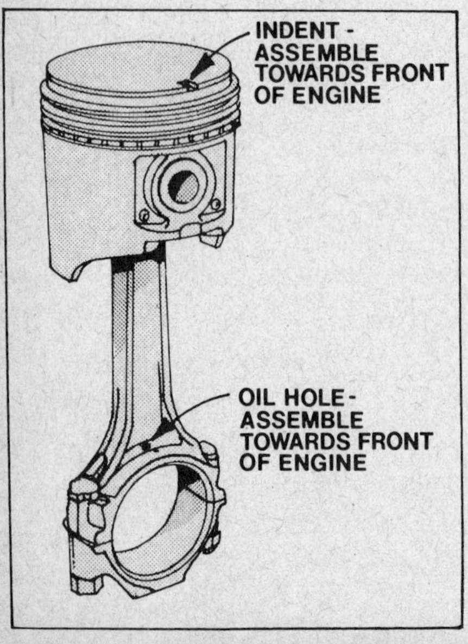

Fig. 15 Piston and rod assembly. 1978–83 6-225

NOTE: Install No. 1 camshaft bearing 3/32 in. inward from front face of cylinder block.

6. Apply sealer to welch plug and plug bore, then install plug at rear of camshaft.

V8 Engines

To remove the camshaft, remove all valve lifters, timing chain and sprockets. Remove distributor and oil pump-distributor drive gear. Remove fuel pump and see that push rod has moved away from eccentric drive cam. On V8-318 & 360 engine, remove thrust plate, 1977–84 engines incorporate a timing chain oil tab, before removing, note position of tab so it can be installed in the same manner. On all engines withdraw camshaft from engine, using care to see that camshaft lobes do not damage the camshaft bearings.

If camshaft bearings are to be replaced, it is recommended that the engine be removed from the chassis and the crankshaft taken out in order that any chips or foreign material may be removed from the oil passages.

NOTE: On V8-400 & 440 engines, install No. 1 camshaft bearing 1/32 in. inward from front face of cylinder block.

Apply sealer to welch plug and plug bore, then install plug at rear of camshaft.

PISTON & ROD, ASSEMBLE

6-225

Piston and rod assemblies must be installed as shown in Figs. 14 and 15.

V8 Engines

When installing piston and rod assemblies in the cylinders, the compression ring gaps should be diametrically opposite one another and not in line with the oil ring gap. The oil ring expander gap should be toward the outside of the "V" of the engine. The oil ring gap should be turned toward the inside of the engine "V".

Immerse the piston head and rings in clean engine oil and, with a suitable piston ring compressor, insert the piston and rod assembly into the bore. Tap the piston down into the bore, using the handle of a hammer.

Assemble the pistons to the rods as shown in Fig. 16.

PISTONS, PINS & RINGS

Pistons are available in standard sizes and the following oversizes: 1977 .005, .020; 1978–84 .020.

Pins are available in the following oversizes: V8-318 & 360, .003, .008 inch. Not furnished on all other engines.

Rings are available in the following oversizes: std. to .009, .020–.029, .040–.049 inch.

MAIN & ROD BEARINGS

Main bearings are furnished in standard sizes and the following undersizes: .001, .002, .003, .010, .012".

Rod bearings are furnished in standard sizes and the following undersizes: .001, .002, .003, .010, .012".

V8-400 and 440 use either forged or cast

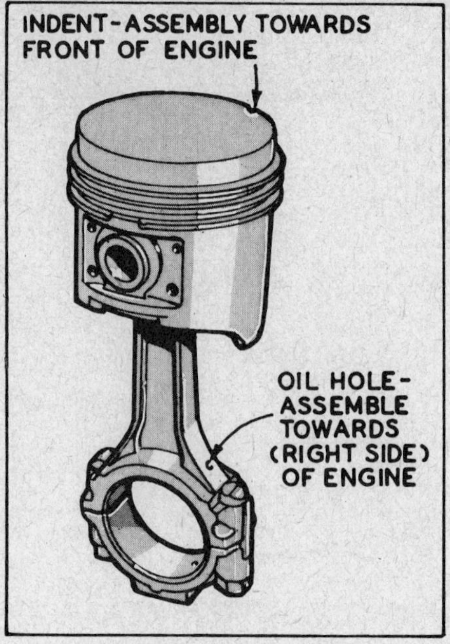

Fig. 14 Piston and rod assembly. 1977 6-225, engines

crankshafts. These engines require that a matching torque converter, short block, damper and connecting rods be used.

If replacement of the crankshaft, torque converter, crankshaft damper or short engine is required, it is important that matching parts are used otherwise severe engine vibration will result, (Consult Chrysler Parts Dept.).

The cast crankshaft engine can be easily identified since it has the letter "E" stamped on the engine numbering pad following the built date.

Also, V8-440 engines built starting January 1976, will have external balance weights at the front damper and torque converter and a clock face will appear on the number 1 counterweight of the cast crankshaft.

6-225 engines built after June 1, 1976 may be equipped with either a cast or forged

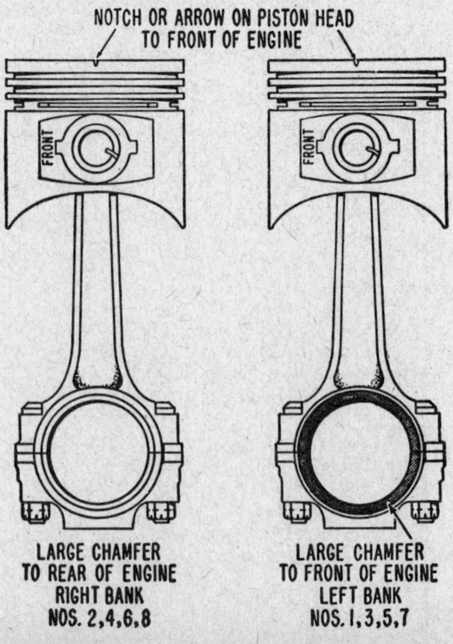

Fig. 16 Piston and rod assembly, V8 engines

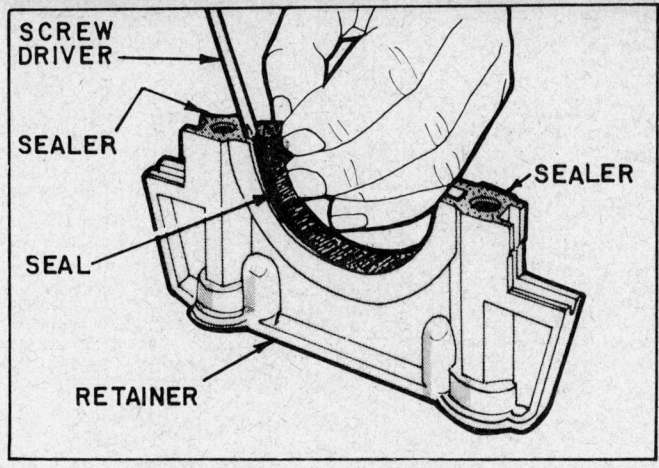

Fig. 17 Lower oil seal & retainer. 6-225

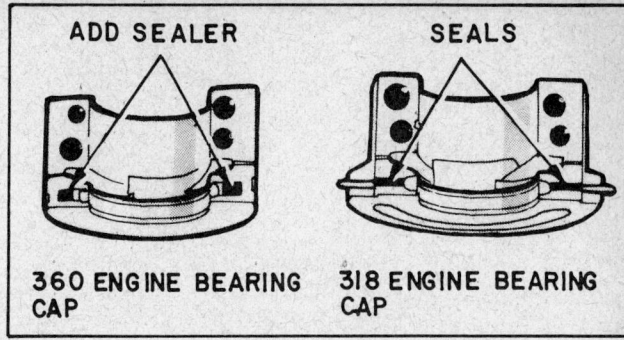

Fig. 18 Rear main bearing caps. V8-318 & 360

crankshaft. The following parts are not interchangeable between cast and forged crankshaft engines, crankshaft, crankshaft bearings, connecting rods and bearings and cylinder block. On models equipped with manual transmission, cast crankshaft engine vibration damper is not interchangeable with forged crankshaft engine and requires that a crankshaft screw and washer be used and torqued to 135 ft. lbs. On models equipped with automatic transmission, vibration damper and torque converter are interchangeable between cast and forged crankshaft engines.

CRANKSHAFT REAR OIL SEAL, REPLACE

6-225

SERVICE BULLETIN

Crankshaft oil seal leaks on 1981–83 6-225 engines can sometimes be difficult to locate and repair without proper diagnosis. When a seal leak is suspected, always perform an air test to verify the condition and location before you begin disassembly. Test for oil leaks as follows:

NOTE: Only regulated air adjusted to 4 psi should be used to air test engine.

1. Remove crankcase vent valve and cap and plug valve cover holes.
2. Remove dipstick, then install rubber hose connected to air source into dipstick tube.
3. Raise and support vehicle, then remove torque convertor or clutch housing cover.
4. Visually inspect rear of engine block for leakage. Leakage between rear seal and crankshaft will cause oil spray in a circular pattern. Leakage from retainer side seals, retainer joint face or back side of rear seal will tend to run straight down. Other possible leak paths are a pourous block and rear cam and gallery plugs.
5. Apply air pressure to crankcase and check seal area for leaks. If leakage is evident, check seal or seal retainer. If no leakage is detected, rotate crankshaft and watch for leakage. If a leak is detected while crankshaft is being rotated, check crankcase seal surface for damage or

scratches. If no leakage is detected, pressurize lubrication system and check for leaking oil passage.
6. Remove rear seal retainer. Inspect retainer and seal sides for proper sealing and half round seal for correct positioning. If leak is evident only when crankshaft is rotated, inspect crankshaft for nicks, scratches or cuts in seal area. Polish nicks or scratches with emery cloth.
7. Clean old sealer from seal retainer and block, and remove upper seal half. Ensure seal was not installed backwards, since this can cause leakage. Check outside diameter of seal for cuts or peeled rubber.

Replacement seals are of two piece rubber type composition which make possible the replacement of upper rear seal without removing crankshaft. Both halves must be used. After removing oil pan, rear main bearing cap and seal retainer, pry lower rope seal from retainer with small screwdriver. Screw a special tool into upper rope seal and carefully pull to remove seal while rotating crankshaft. Install upper half of new seal into block, making sure stripe on seal faces rear of engine. Shim stock or equivalent may be used to protect back side of seal against sharp side of block. Rotate crankshaft to ease installation. Apply a 1/8 inch bead of RTV sealant into groove in retainer, starting and ending 1/2 inch from ends of groove. Install other half of seal into retainer, ensuring stripe on seal faces rearward, then install rear main bearing cap and torque to specifications. Install side seals onto retainer using bonder part #4057988 or equivalent. Apply a small amount of RTV sealer to retainer in areas shown in Fig. 17. Install retainer and torque to 30 ft. lbs.

NOTE: Do not apply sealer to seal lip surface, as leakage may result.

V8-318 & 360

Replacement of rear main bearing oil seals is similar to procedure given above for 6 cylinder engines. A seal retainer is not found on these engines; lower half of seal is installed into groove in rear main bearing cap.

The 318 engine has capseals in addition to lower seal secured by rear main bearing cap. Cap seal with yellow paint is installed, narrow sealing edge up, into right side with bearing cap in engine position. Cap seals must be

flush with shoulder of bearing cap to prevent oil leakage.

The 360 engine requires sealer to be applied adjacent to rear main bearing oil seal as cap seals are not used, Fig. 18. After applying sealer, quickly assemble rear main bearing cap to block and torque to specifications.

V8-400, 440

Replacement seals are of two piece rubber type composition which make possible the replacement of upper rear seal without removing crankshaft. Both halves must be used. After removing oil pan, seal retainer and rear main bearing cap, pry lower rope seal and side seals from lower seal retainer with small screwdriver. Thoroughly clean seal retainer grooves. Screw a special tool into upper rope seal and carefully pull to remove seal while rotating crankshaft. Wipe crankshaft surface clean, then oil lightly before installing new upper seal. After oiling seal lip, hold seal with paint stripe to rear tightly against crankshaft with thumb. Carefully slide seal into groove in block making sure sharp edge does not shave or nick seal. Crankshaft may be rotated to ease seal into groove but sealing lip must not be damaged. Install other half of seal with paint stripe to rear into seal retainer. Install rear main bearing cap and torque to specifications. The side seals used with the rear seal retainer should be installed in the retainer and then into the engine as quickly as possible. These seals are made from a material that expands rapidly when oiled. Apply sealer to mating face of seal retainer but not to side seals or main bearing seal ends, then oil side seals with mineral spirits or diesel fuel. Install seals in seal retainer grooves then quickly install retainer and torque to 30 ft. lbs. Failure to pre-oil seals will result in an oil leak.

OIL PAN, REPLACE

CAUTION: *Engine oil pan bolts on V8-440 engines are 13/16" long with the exception of two bolts at the rear center of the oil pan. The two rear center bolts are 9/16" long and thread into the aluminum seal retainer. Do not use longer bolts than 9/16" at this location as they will bottom in the aluminum seal retainer and, if forced in may strip the threads and damage the seal retainer, causing an oil leak.*

6-225

1. Drain radiator, disconnect battery ground cable and radiator hoses and remove oil dipstick.

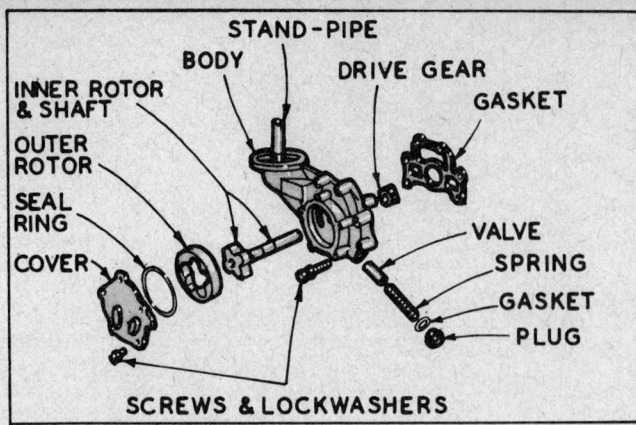

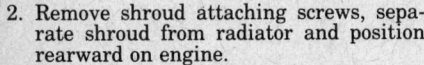

Fig. 19 Oil pump. 6-225

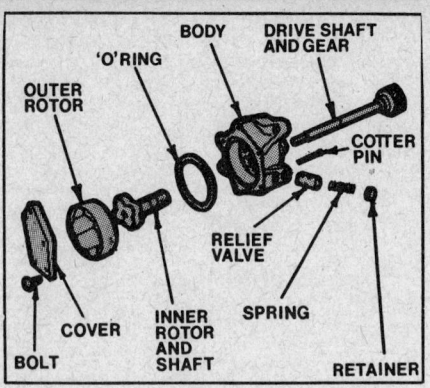

Fig. 20 Oil pump. V8-318 & 360

2. Remove shroud attaching screws, separate shroud from radiator and position rearward on engine.
3. Raise vehicle and drain oil pan.
4. Remove engine to transmission support bracket.
5. Disconnect exhaust pipe, then torque converter inspection shield.
6. Remove center link from steering arm and idler arm ball joints.
7. Support front of engine with a jack stand placed under the right front corner of oil pan.
8. Remove engine front mount bolts. Raise engine approx. 1½ to 2".
9. Remove oil pan attaching screws, rotate engine crankshaft to clear counterweights and remove oil pan.
10. Reverse procedure to install.

V8-400, 440

1. Disconnect battery ground cable and drain crankcase.
2. Raise car on hoist and disconnect steering linkage from idler arm and pitman arm.
3. Remove outlet vent pipe and disconnect exhaust pipe branches from manifolds.
4. Remove clamp attaching exhaust pipe to extension and remove exhaust pipe.
5. Remove converter dust shield.
6. Remove oil pan bolts and turn flywheel until counterweight and connecting rods at the front end of crankshaft are at their highest position to provide clearance, and lower the pan. Turn the pan to clear oil screen and suction pipe.
7. On some models, it may be necessary to release motor mounts and raise engine approximately 1½ to 2 inches.
8. Reverse procedure to install.

V8-318, 360

1977 Royal Monaco, Gran Fury; 1977–78 Charger, Fury & Monaco; 1977–79 Cordoba; 1979 Magnum; 1979–81 Newport, New Yorker & St. Regis
1. Disconnect battery ground cable and remove oil level dipstick.
2. Raise vehicle and drain crankcase, then remove engine to torque converter left housing strut.
3. Remove steering idler arm ball joints from center link.
4. Disconnect exhaust pipes from exhaust manifolds.
5. Remove oil pan attaching bolts.
6. Position a suitable jack under transmis-

sion remove rear engine mount to transmission extension attaching bolts.
7. Raise transmission until rear of oil pan can be lowered to clear transmission.
8. Reverse procedure to install.

1977–80 Aspen & Volare; 1977–81 LeBaron; 1977–84 Diplomat; 1978 Chrysler; 1980–83 Cordoba & Mirada; 1981–83 Imperial; 1982 New Yorker; 1982–84 Gran Fury; 1983 New Yorker Fifth Avenue & 1984 Fifth Avenue
1. Disconnect battery ground cable and remove engine oil level dipstick.
2. Raise vehicle and drain crankcase.
3. Remove exhaust crossover pipe, then disconnect and lower center link.
4. Remove starter and starter mounting stud.
5. Remove torque converter inspection cover.
6. Remove oil pan attaching bolts and oil pan.
7. Reverse procedure to install.

1977–80 V8-360 4 Bar. Carb.
1. Disconnect battery ground cable and remove oil dipstick.
2. Remove fan shroud attaching bolts and place shroud over fan.
3. Raise vehicle and disconnect steering linkage center link.
4. Remove oil pan bolts.
5. Raise transmission slightly with a suitable jack and remove rear engine mount to transmission bolts.
6. Lower rear of oil pan until clear of transmission.

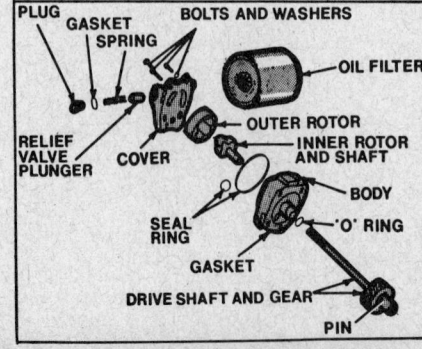

Fig. 21 Oil pump. V8-400 & 440

7. Lower transmission and loosely install the rear engine mount bolts.
8. Loosen front engine mounts from frame.
9. Raise engine with a suitable jack approximately one inch and remove oil pan.
10. Reverse procedure to install.

OIL PUMP, REPLACE

Six Cylinder

1. Drain radiator and disconnect upper and lower hoses.
2. Remove fan shroud (if equipped).
3. Raise vehicle on a hoist, support front of engine with a jack stand place under right front corner of engine oil pan. *Do not support engine at crankshaft pulley or vibration damper.*
4. Remove front engine mounts.
5. Raise engine 1½ to 2 inches.
6. Remove oil filter, pump attaching bolts and remove pump assembly.
7. Reverse procedure to install.

V8 Engines

SERVICE BULLETIN

1978–80 V8-318, 360 Low Oil Pressure: An incorrectly installed oil line plug, part number 3462871, may cause low or dropping oil pressure. To check plug for proper position:
1. Remove oil pressure sending unit from rear of cylinder block.
2. Insert a 1/8 inch wire into sensing unit hole to measure distance between plug and top of machined surface of oil pressure sending unit hole.
3. The distance should be 7½ to 7 11/16 inches.
4. If measurement is less than 7½ inches, use a suitable dowel drift to drive plug into proper position.
5. If measurement is greater than 7 11/16 inches, remove oil pan and the No. 5 main bearing cap. Drive plug upward to properly position.

On 318, 360 engines, remove oil pump from rear main bearing cap.
On V8-400 and 440 engines, unfasten oil pump from engine and remove pump and filter assembly from bottom of engine.

OIL PUMP SERVICE
6-225

To disassemble, remove the pump cover seal

ring, Fig. 19. Press off the drive gear, supporting the gear to keep load off aluminum body. Remove rotor and shaft and lift out outer pump rotor. Remove oil pressure relief valve plug and lift out spring and plunger. Remove oil pressure sending unit.

Inspection

1. The rotor contact area and the bores for the shaft and valve in the pump body should be smooth, free from scratches, scoring or excessive wear.
2. The pump cover should be smooth, flat and free from scoring or ridges. Lay a straightedge across the cover. If a .0015" feeler gauge can be inserted under the straightedge, the cover should be replaced.
3. All surfaces of the outer rotor should be smooth and uniform, free from ridges, scratches or uneven wear. Discard a rotor less than .649 inch thick for 1977–80 or .825 inch thick for 1981–83 and/or less than 2.469 inch in diameter.
4. The inner rotor and shaft assembly should be smooth, free from scoring and uneven wear. Discard rotors less than .649 inch thick for 1977–80 or .825 inch thick for 1981–83.
5. Place outer rotor in pump body and measure clearance between rotor and body. Discard pump body if clearance is more than .014".
6. Install inner rotor and shaft in pump body. Shaft should turn freely but without side play. If clearance between rotor teeth is more than .010 inch, replace both rotors.
7. Measure rotor end clearance. If feeler gauge of more than .004 inch can be inserted between straightedge and rotors, install a new pump body.
8. The oil pressure relief valve should be smooth, free from scratches or scoring, and should be a free fit in its bore.
9. The relief valve spring has a free length of 2¼ inches and should test between 22.3 and 23.3 pounds when compressed to 1 19/32 inch. If not, replace the spring.

Assemble and Install

1. With pump rotors in body, press drive gear on shaft, flush with end of shaft.
2. Install seal ring in groove in body and install cover. Tighten bolts to 95 inch lbs. Test pump for free turning.
3. Install oil pressure relief valve spring. Use new washer (gasket) and tighten plug securely.
4. If pump shaft turns freely, remove pump cover and outer rotor before installation of pump on engine.
5. Install oil pressure sending unit and tighten to 60 inch lbs. (5 ft. lbs.)
6. Using a new gasket, install pump on engine and tighten bolts to 200 inch lbs. (16 ft. lbs.)
7. Install oil filter reservoir on pump. Install filter element and tighten cover nuts to 25 ft. lbs.
8. Connect oil pressure sending unit wire.
9. Complete the installation by reversing steps as given under Oil Pump, Replace.

V8-318, 360

After removing the pump from the engine, it should be disassembled, cleaned and inspected for wear, Fig. 20.

1. To remove the relief valve, remove the cotter pin and drill a 1/8 inch hole into the relief valve retainer cap and install a self-threading sheet metal screw.
2. Clamp screw into vise and tap on housing lightly with a soft hammer to remove the retaining cap, then remove the relief valve spring and valve.
3. Remove the oil pump cover and discard the oil seal ring.
4. Remove pump rotor, shaft and lift out outer rotor.
5. Mating surface of the pump cover should be smooth. If scratched or grooved, replace the pump.
6. Lay a straight edge across the cover. If a .0015 inch feeler gauge can be inserted between the cover and the straight edge, replace the pump.
7. Measure thickness and diameter of outer rotor. If rotor thickness is .825 inch or less on V8-318 engines, or .943 inch or less on V8-360 engines or if the diameter of the rotor is 2.429 inches or less, replace the outer rotor.
8. If the inner rotor is .825 inch or less on V8-318 engines, or .943 inch or less on V8-360 engines, replace the inner rotor and shaft assembly.
9. Install the outer rotor into the housing. Press rotor to one side with the fingers and measure the clearance between the rotor and body with a feeler gauge. If the measurement is .014 inch or greater, replace the pump.
10. Place the inner rotor and shaft into the pump. If clearance between the rotors is .010 inch or greater, replace the shaft and

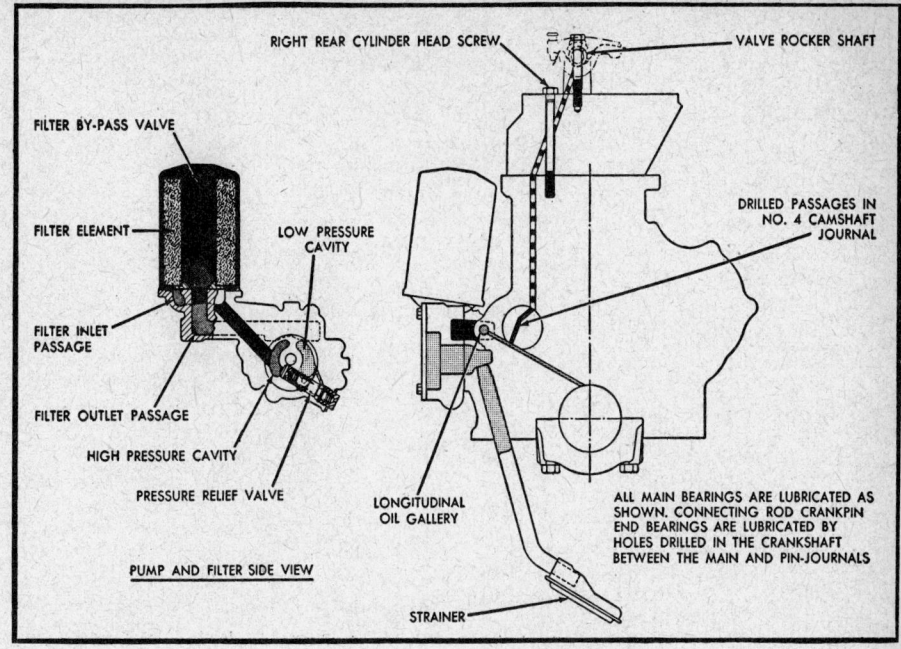

Engine oiling system. 6-225

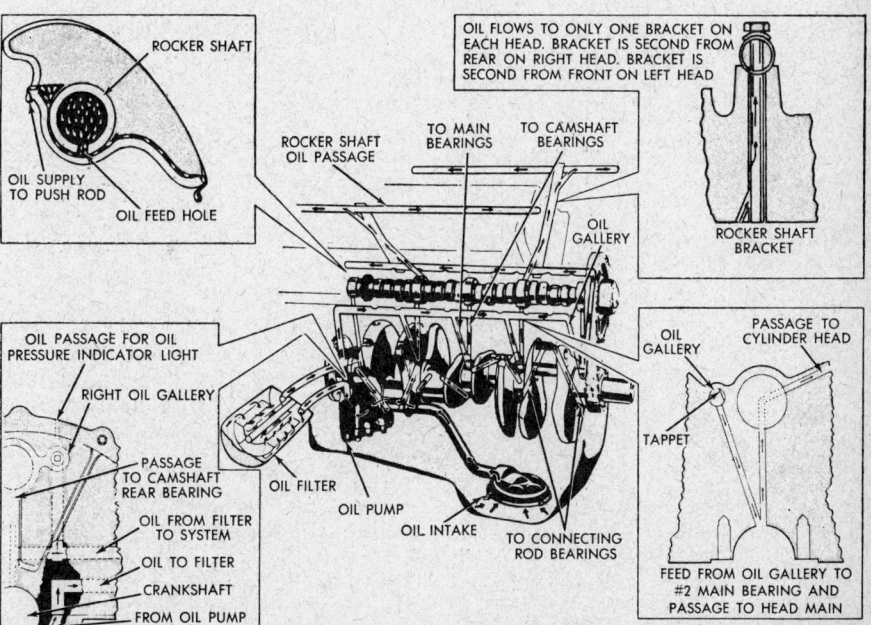

Engine oiling system, 1977 V8-318, 360

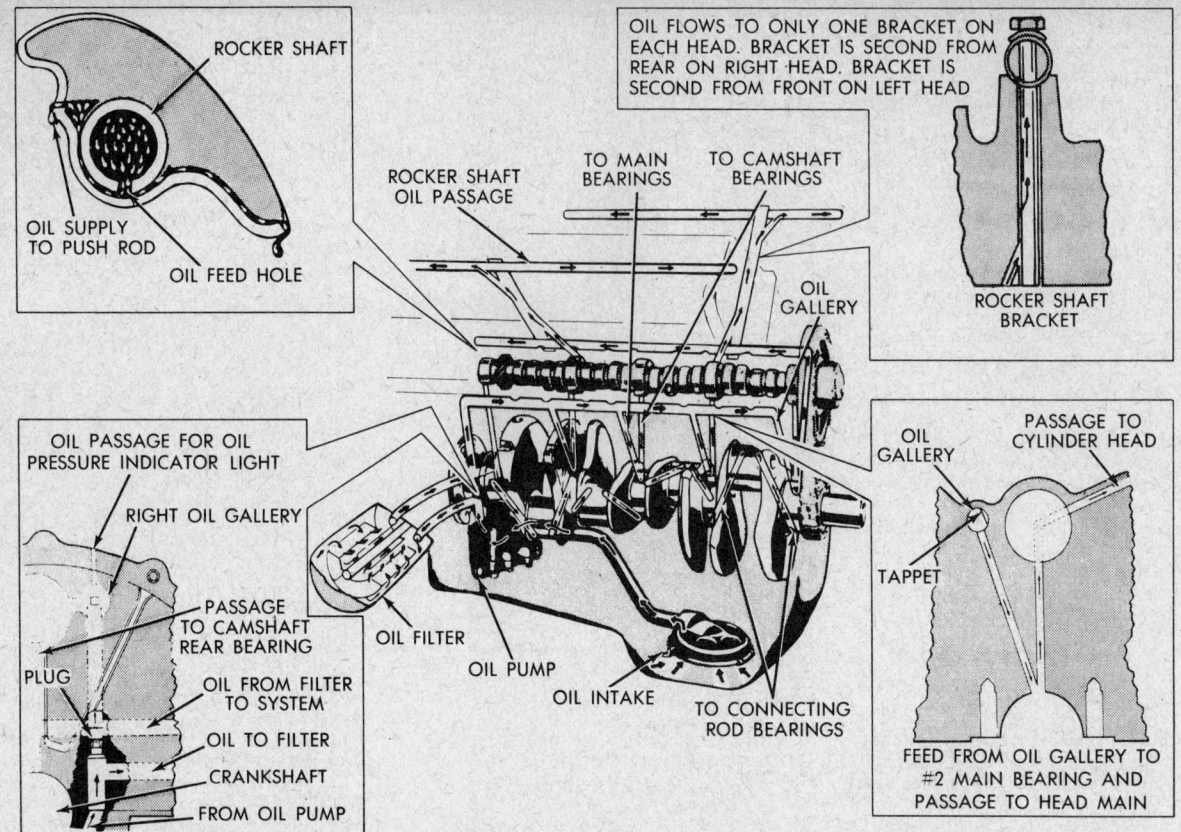

Engine Oiling System, 1978–80 V8-360 & 1978–84 V8-318

both rotors.

11. Place a straightedge across the face of the pump between bolt holes. If a feeler gauge of .004 inch or greater can be inserted, replace the pump.

12. Check the oil pump relief valve plunger for scoring and free operation in the bore. Small marks may be removed with 400-grit sand paper.

13. The relief valve spring should have a free length of 2-1/32 to 2-3/64 inch and should

test between 16.2 and 17.2 pounds when compressed to 1-11/32 inch. If not, replace the spring.

V8-400, 440

After removing the pump from the engine it should be disassembled, cleaned and inspected for wear, Fig. 21.

1. The mating surface of the filter base (oil pump cover) should be smooth. Replace

the filter base if scratched or grooved.

2. Lay a straightedge on the filter base surface. If a .0015 inch feeler gauge can be inserted between the pump cover and straightedge, replace the filter base.

3. If the outer rotor thickness is .943 inch or less and diameter 2.469 inches or less, replace shaft and both rotors.

4. If inner rotor length is .943 inch or less, replace both rotors and shaft.

5. Install outer rotor into pump body, press to one side with fingers and measure clearance between pump body and rotor. If measurement is .014 inch or greater, replace the pump body.

6. Install inner rotor into pump body and place a straightedge across the face between two bolt holes. If a feeler gauge of .004 inch or greater can be inserted between the rotors and the straightedge, replace the pump body.

7. If the tip clearance between the rotors is .010 inch or greater, replace shaft and both rotors.

8. The relief valve spring has a free length of 2 1/4 inches and should test between 22.3 and 23.3 pounds when compressed to 1 19/32 inch. If not, replace the spring.

9. Check the oil pump relief valve plunger for scoring and free operation in its bore. Small marks may be removed with 400-grit sand paper.

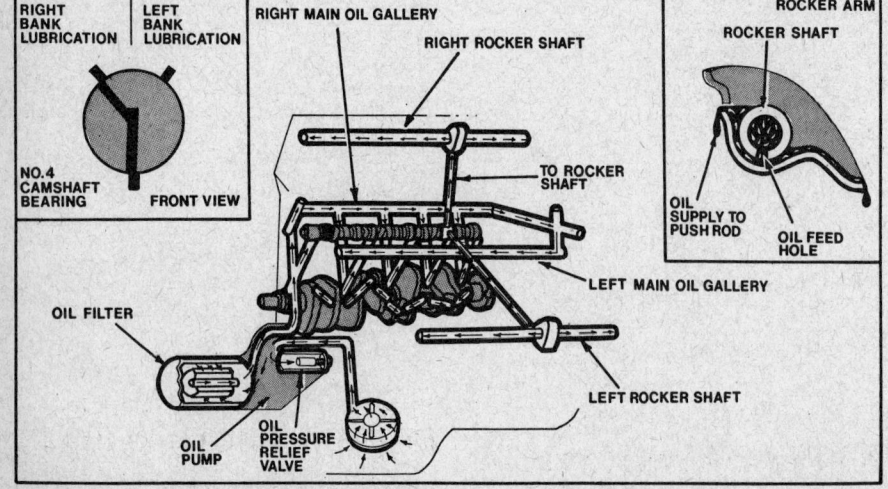

Engine oiling system. V8-400, 440 engines

BELT TENSION DATA

1977–84 All	New①	Used①
	120	70

①—Belt tension in lbs.

WATER PUMP, REPLACE

CAUTION: When it becomes necessary to remove a fan clutch of the silicone type, the assembly must be supported in the vertical position to prevent leaks of silicone fluid from the clutch mechanism. This loss of fluid will render the fan clutch inoperative.

6-225

1. Drain cooling system, then remove battery, upper and lower radiator hoses and fan shroud.
2. Remove all drive belts, then remove fan attaching bolts, fan, spacer and pulley.
3. Remove A/C compressor and air pump bracket to water pump attaching bolts, then position compressor and air pump aside. Keep compressor in upright position.
4. Disconnect by-pass and heater hoses from water pump.
5. Remove water pump attaching bolts and remove pump assembly.
6. Reverse procedure to install.

V8-318, 360

1. Drain cooling system and disconnect battery ground cable.
2. Remove all drive belts, then remove radiator shroud and position over fan.
3. Remove fan assembly, pulley and fan shroud.
4. Remove alternator adjusting strap and mounting bolts and position alternator aside.
5. Remove A/C compressor with mounting brackets and position aside, if equipped. Keep compressor in upright position.
6. Remove power steering pump mounting bolts and position pump aside, if equipped.
7. Remove air pump and mounting brackets, if equipped. Disconnect air hose at pump fittings.
8. Disconnect by-pass and heater hoses at water pump.
9. Disconnect lower radiator hose from pump.
10. Remove remaining water pump attaching bolts and remove pump assembly.
11. Reverse procedure to install.

V8-400, 440

1. Drain cooling system and disconnect battery ground cable.
2. Remove upper radiator hose and fan shroud. Position shroud back on engine.
3. Remove all drive belts, then remove fan attaching bolts, fan, spacer and pulley.
4. Remove water pump attaching bolts and remove pump assembly.
5. Reverse procedure to install.

SERVICE BULLETIN

CORE HOLE PLUG SIZES: When replacing a cup-type core hole plug in an engine, the size of the hole in the cylinder head, water jacket or rear bearing bore for the camshaft should be checked. At these locations a $1/16''$ oversize hole is sometimes bored in production and an oversize core plug installed.

Core plugs $1/16''$ oversize are available for replacement should they be required at these locations.

FUEL PUMP, REPLACE

SERVICE NOTE

Before installing the pump, it is good practice to crank the engine so that the nose of the camshaft eccentric is out of the way of the fuel pump rocker arm when the pump is installed. In this way there will be the least amount of tension on the rocker arm, thereby easing the installation of the pump.

1. Disconnect fuel lines from fuel pump.
2. Remove fuel pump attaching bolts and fuel pump.
3. Remove all gasket material from the pump and block gasket surfaces. Apply sealer to both sides of new gasket.
4. Position gasket on pump flange and hold pump in position against its mounting surface. Make sure rocker arm is riding on camshaft eccentric.
5. Press pump tight against its mounting. Install retaining screws and tighten them alternately.
6. Connect fuel lines. Then operate engine and check for leaks.

Clutch & Transmission Section

CLUTCH PEDAL, ADJUST

1. Inspect condition of clutch pedal rubber stop, if stop is damaged install a new one.
2. Where necessary, disconnect interlock clutch rod at transmission end.
3. Adjust linkage by turning self-locking adjusting nut to provide $5/32''$ free movement at outer end of fork. This movement will provide the prescribed one-inch free play at pedal.
4. Assemble interlock clutch rod (if used) to transmission pawl.

CLUTCH, REPLACE

Removal

1. Remove transmission and clutch housing pan.
2. Remove return spring from clutch release fork and clutch housing or torque shaft lever.
3. Remove spring washer securing fork rod to torque shaft lever and remove rod from torque shaft and release fork.
4. Remove clutch release bearing assembly, release fork and boot from clutch housing.
5. Mark clutch cover and flywheel so that they may be assembled in their original position to maintain balance.
6. Loosen clutch cover retaining screws one or two turns at a time in succession until cover is loose and remove screws.
7. Remove clutch assembly and disc from clutch housing using care to avoid contaminating the friction surfaces.

Installation

1. Lubricate pilot bushing in crankshaft with Multi-Purpose Grease number 2932524 or equivalent.
2. Clean surfaces of flywheel and pressure plate, making certain no oil or grease remains on these parts.
3. Hold cover plate and disc in place and insert a special clutch aligning tool or a spare clutch shaft through the hub of the disc and into the crankshaft pilot bearing.
4. Bolt clutch cover loosely to flywheel, being sure marks previously made are lined up.
5. To avoid distortion of clutch cover, tighten cover bolts a few turns each in progression until all are tight. The final tightening should be 200 inch lbs.

THREE SPEED TRANSMISSION, REPLACE

1. Disconnect shift rods from transmission levers.

NOTE: If shift rods are retained by plastic grommets, disconnect the shift levers from the transmission to avoid replacing the grommets.

2. Drain lubricant from transmission and disconnect propeller shaft.
3. Disconnect speedometer cable and backup light switch connector.
4. If necessary, disconnect exhaust pipes from exhaust manifolds.
5. Raise engine slightly using a suitable support fixture or jack and disconnect extension housing from center crossmember.
6. Support transmission with a suitable jack and remove center crossmember.
7. Remove transmission to clutch housing retaining bolts, then slide transmission rearward until input shaft clears clutch disc and remove transmission.
8. Reverse procedure to install.

FOUR SPEED & OVERDRIVE TRANSMISSION, REPLACE

1. Remove console and shift components.
2. Drain fluid from transmission.

Fig. 1 Gearshift lever adjustment. 1977–80 three speed transmission

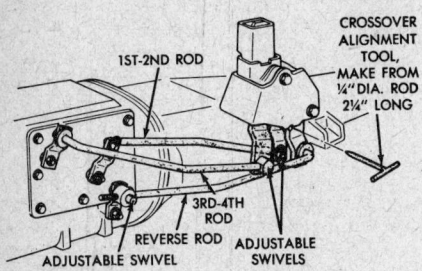

Fig. 3 Gearshift linkage adjustment. 1977–79 four speed transmission

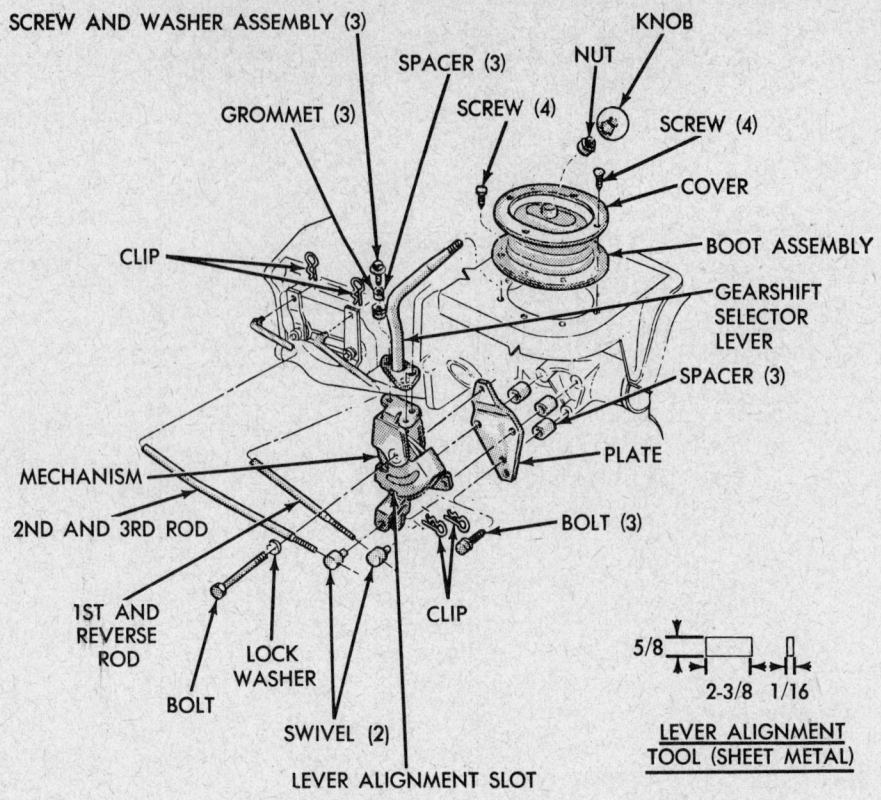

Fig. 2 Gearshift linkage adjustment. 1977–80 three speed floor shift transmission

3. Disconnect propeller shaft at rear universal joint and carefully pull yoke out of extension housing. *Be careful not to scratch or nick ground surface on sliding spline yoke during removal and installation of shaft.*
4. Disconnect speedometer cable and stop light switch leads.
5. Disconnect left-hand exhaust pipe (dual exhaust) from manifold.
6. Disconnect parking cable where necessary.
7. Support rear of engine with a jack.
8. Raise engine slightly and disconnect extension housing from removable center crossmember.
9. Support transmission with a suitable jack and remove center crossmember.
10. Remove transmission-to-clutch housing bolts.
11. Slide transmission rearward and out of vehicle.
12. Reverse procedure to install.

SHIFT LINKAGE, ADJUST THREE SPEED TRANS.

Column Shift

1. Loosen both shift rod swivels.

2. With transmission shift levers in neutral (middle detent), move shift lever to align locating slots in bottom of steering column shift housing and bearing housing. Install suitable tool in slot to maintain alignment.
3. Place screwdriver or other suitable tool between crossover blade and 2nd-3rd lever at steering column so that both lever pins are engaged by crossover blade, Fig. 1.
4. Torque both shift rod swivel bolts to 125 inch lbs.
5. Remove gearshift housing locating tool and remove tool from crossover blade at steering column.
6. Shift through all gears to check adjustment and crossover smoothness. Check for operation of steering column lock in reverse and other gear positions. If properly adjusted, ignition should lock in reverse position only without having to force shift lever.

Floor Shift

1. Place shift lever in neutral position and disconnect shift rods from levers.
2. Fabricate alignment tool from 1/16 in. thick sheet metal as shown in Fig. 2.

3. Insert alignment tool into slots in levers and frame to hold levers in neutral position, Fig. 2.
4. Place transmission levers in neutral position and adjust shift rod swivels so that rods will install freely into levers.
5. Secure rods with washers and clips, then remove alignment tool and check shifter operation.

SHIFT LINKAGE, ADJUST FOUR SPEED TRANS.

1977–79

1. Install floor shift lever aligning tool, Fig. 3, to hold levers in neutral position. Crossover alignment tool shown in Fig. 3, will have to be fabricated.
2. With all rods disconnected from transmission shift levers, place levers in neutral position.
3. Starting with 1-2 shift rod, rotate shift rods until ends of rods enter shift levers. It may be necessary to remove clip at shifter end to rotate rods.
4. Replace washers and clips, then remove aligning tool and check shifting action.

Rear Axle, Propeller Shaft & Brakes

NOTE: Figs. 1, 1A and 2 illustrate the various rear axle assemblies used on these cars. When necessary to overhaul any of these units, refer to the *Rear Axle Specifications* table in this chapter.

INTEGRAL TYPE REAR AXLE

NOTE: The following changes have been made in the design of the 7¼ inch rear axle during the 1982 model year for all models except Imperial.

1. The inboard ends of the 8¼ inch axle shaft tubes are swadged down in size and pressed into the 7¼ inch carrier, Fig. 1A.
2. The 7¼ inch axle shafts ball bearings are replaced with the 8¼ inch axle shaft roller bearings.
3. The axle shafts are retained with the standard 8¼ inch axle "C" lock washer, Fig. 1A.
4. The 7¼ inch differential side gears now have a counterbore to incorporate the "C" lock washers. These side gears can be used on the early design 7¼ inch axles, but the early design side gears cannot be used on the later design 7¼ inch axle.
5. The late design carrier has two cast holes to allow lube to flow into the tubes to lubricate the axle shaft roller bearings, Fig. 1A.

Servicing the late design 7¼ inch rear axle is the same as the early design 7¼ differential, except for the axle shaft and axle shaft bearing. When replacing axle shaft or axle shaft bearing refer to "Axle Shaft, Replace (Fig. 2 Type)" for service procedures.

Two types of integral carrier axles are used. In both types, the drive pinion is mounted in two opposing tapered roller bearings which are preloaded by a spacer positioned between them.

In the unit shown in Fig. 1, the differential is supported by two tapered roller side bearings. These bearings are preloaded by spacers located between the bearings and carrier housing. The differential assembly is positioned for ring and pinion backlash by varying these spacers.

Axle shafts in this unit are held in place by retainers at the outer ends of the shafts. These retainers are bolted through the brake backing plates to the rear axle tubes.

In the unit shown in Fig. 2, the differential is also supported by two tapered roller bearings. A threaded differential bearing adjuster is located in each bearing pedestal cap to eliminate differential side play, adjust and maintain ring and pinion backlash and provide a means of obtaining differential bearing preload.

Axles are retained by means of a "C" washer which is installed into a groove in the inner end of the axle shaft inside the differential unit.

On both these units, a removable stamped steel cover, bolted to the rear of the carrier, permits inspection and service of the differential without removal of the complete axle assembly from the vehicle.

NOTE: 7¼ and 8¼ in. axle differentials have balanced side and pinion gears. Any attempt to mix these side or pinion gears with previously manufactured ones will result in lock up or excessive differential backlash. Side and pinion gears must be replaced as a set.

REAR AXLE, REPLACE

1. Raise rear of vehicle and position safety stands at front of rear springs.
2. Remove rear wheels, then disconnect brake lines at wheel cylinders. Cap brake line fittings to prevent loss of fluid.
3. Disconnect parking brake cables.
4. Mark drive shaft and pinion flanges for reassembly, then remove drive shaft.
5. Disconnect shock absorbers from spring plate studs, then loosen rear spring U-bolt nuts and remove U-bolts.
6. Remove axle assembly from vehicle.

Axle Shaft, Replace (Fig. 1 Type)

1. With wheel removed, remove clips holding brake drum on wheel studs and re-

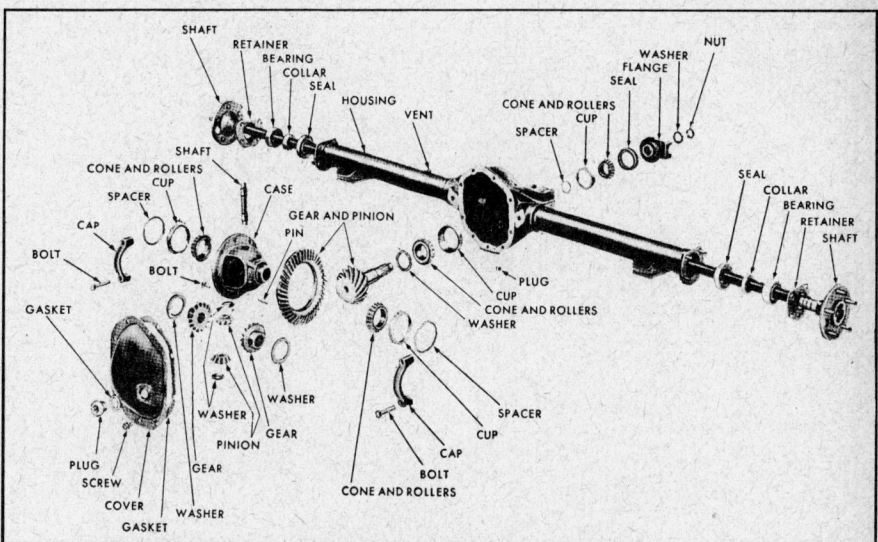

Fig. 1 Integral rear axle (typical). 1977–84

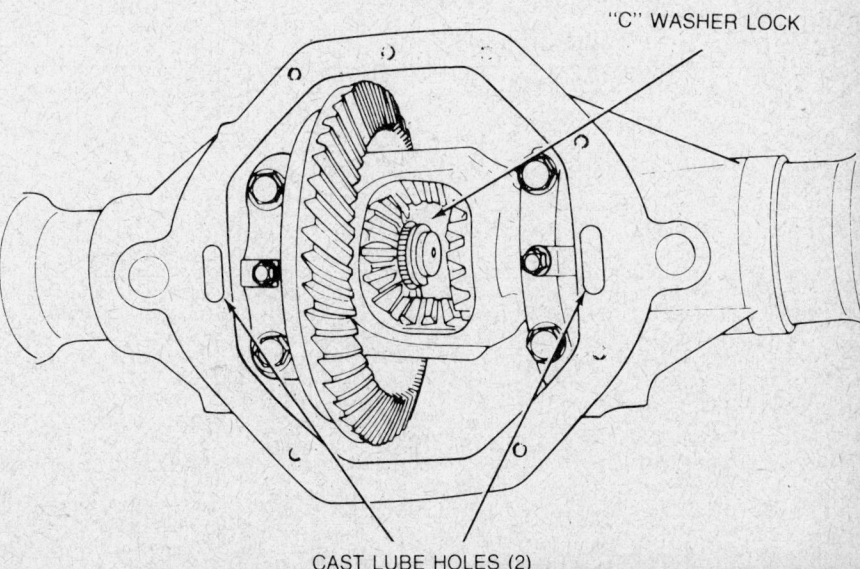

Fig. 1A Late design 7¼ inch "C" lock type rear axle. 1982–84

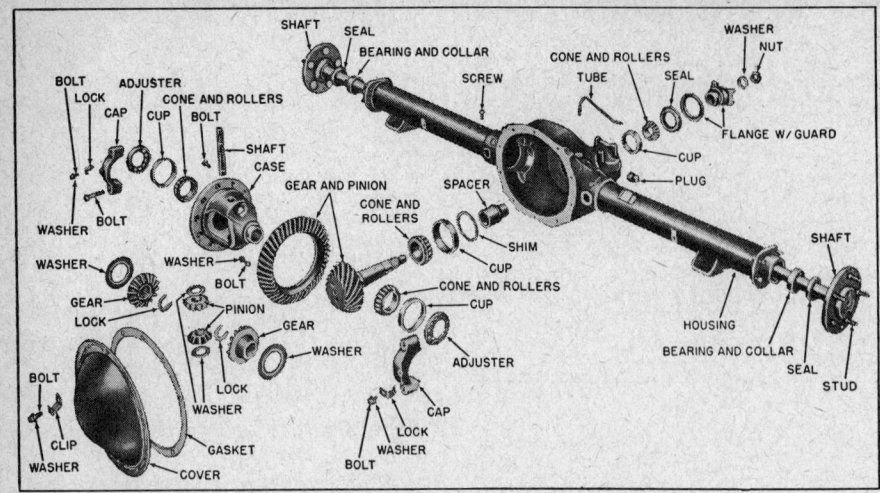

Fig. 2 Integral "C" washer type rear axle (typical). 1977–84

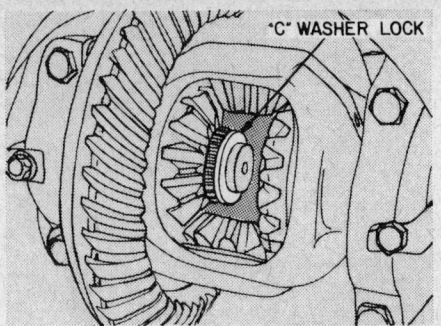

Fig. 3 Location of "C" washer locks

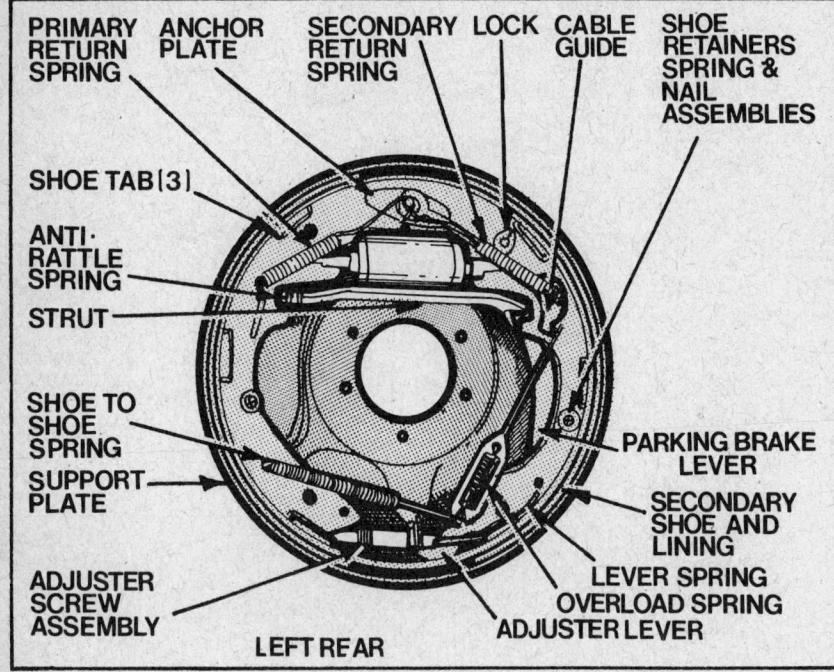

Fig. 4 Left rear brake (10–11 inch). 1977–84

move drum.

2. Disconnect brake lines at wheel cylinders.
3. Using access hole in axle flange, remove retainer nuts from end of housing.
4. Remove axle shaft and brake assembly, using a slide hammer-type puller.
5. Remove brake assembly from axle shaft with care to avoid damaging shaft in seal contact area.
6. Remove oil seal from axle housing.
7. *Remove axle shaft bearings only when necessary. Removal of bearings makes them unfit for further use.*
8. *Axle shaft end play is pre-set and not adjustable. End play is accomplished by the amount of end play built into the bearings. The two axle housing brake support plate gaskets on each side are used for sealing purposes only. Always replace the gaskets once they have been removed.*
9. Press bearing and collar on shaft firmly against shoulders on shaft.
10. Install new oil seal in housing.
11. Install brake assembly on axle housing and carefully slide axle shaft through oil seal and into side gear splines.
12. Tap end of axle shaft lightly to position axle shaft bearing into bearing bore and attach retainer plate to housing.
13. Install brake drums and wheels.

Axle Shaft, Replace (Fig. 2 Type)

1. With wheel and brake drum removed, or caliper and rotor assembly removed, loosen differential housing cover and drain lubricant. Remove cover.
2. Turn differential case to make pinion shaft lock screw accessible and remove

lock screw and shaft.
3. Push axle shaft inward toward center of car and remove "C" washer from groove in axle shaft, Fig. 3.
4. Remove axle shaft from housing, being careful not to damage the axle bearing, which will remain in the housing.
5. The axle bearing and/or seal can now be removed if necessary.
6. Reverse procedure to install.

PROPELLER SHAFT, REPLACE

1. Remove both rear universal joint roller and bushing assembly clamps from pinion yoke. Do not disturb retaining strap holding roller assemblies on cross.
2. Lower front of vehicle slightly to prevent loss of transmission oil and pull drive shaft out as an assembly.
3. To install, carefully slide yoke into splines on transmission output shaft.
4. Align rear of propeller shaft with pinion yoke and position roller and bushing assemblies into seats of pinion yoke.
5. Install bushing clamps and tighten clamp bolts to 170 inch lbs.

BRAKE ADJUSTMENTS

1977–84 Self Adjusting Brakes

These brakes, Fig. 4, have self-adjusting shoe mechanisms that assure correct lining-to-drum clearances at all times. The automatic adjusters operate only when the brakes are applied as the car is moving rearward.

Although the brakes are self-adjusting, an initial adjustment is necessary when the brake shoes have been relined or replaced, or when the length of the star wheel adjuster has been changed during some other service operation.

Frequent usage of an automatic transmission forward range to halt reverse vehicle motion may prevent the automatic adjusters from functioning, thereby inducing low pedal heights. Should low pedal heights be encountered, it is recommended that numerous forward and reverse stops be made until satisfactory pedal height is obtained.

SERVICE NOTE

If a low pedal height condition cannot be corrected by making numerous reverse stops (provided the hydraulic system is free of air) it indicates that the self-adjusting mechanism is not functioning. Therefore, it will be necessary to remove the drum, clean, free up and

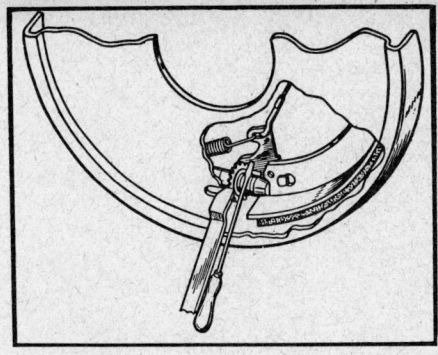

Fig. 5 Releasing brake lever with screwdriver while adjusting star wheel

lubricate the adjusting mechanism. Then adjust the brakes, being sure the parking brake is fully released.

Adjustment

1. Each backing plate has two adjusting hole covers; remove the rear cover and turn the adjusting screw upward with a screwdriver or other suitable tool to expand the shoes until a slight drag is felt when the drum is rotated.
2. While holding the adjusting lever out of engagement with the adjusting screw, Fig. 5, back off the adjusting screw until wheel rotates freely with no drag.
3. Install wheel and adjusting hole cover. Adjust brakes on remaining wheels in the same manner.
4. If pedal height is not satisfactory, drive the vehicle and make sufficient reverse stops until proper pedal height is obtained.

PARKING BRAKE, ADJUST

1. Release parking brake lever and loosen cable adjusting nut to be sure cable is slack.
2. With rear wheel brakes properly adjusted tighten cable adjusting nut until a slight drag is felt when the rear wheels are rotated. Then loosen the cable adjusting nut until both rear wheels can be rotated freely.
3. To complete the operation, back off an additional two turns of the cable adjusting nut.
4. Apply and release parking brake several times to be sure rear wheels are not dragging when cable is in released position.

VACUUM RELEASE PARKING BRAKE

The parking brake is pedal applied and released by a vacuum chamber. When the engine is started and vacuum is developed, energy is then available to release the parking brake. This is controlled by the transmission shift linkage. When the transmission is in "Neutral", vacuum is cut off from the release chamber and there is no action of the parking brake pedal.

When the transmission is shifted into a drive gear (forward or reverse), the vacuum control valve is opened, actuating the vacuum release chamber mounted on the parking brake assembly.

NOTE: *In the event of engine failure and no vacuum, the brake may be released by a manual release lever mounted on the left side of the parking brake pedal assembly. This assembly prevents the vehicle from being driven with the parking brake in the applied position.*

Testing Vacuum Release

1. If the mechanism is inoperative, first check for damaged or kinked vacuum hoses and for loose hose connections at the vacuum chamber, vacuum release valve at neutral safety switch, and at engine manifold connection.
2. Check adjustment of neutral safety switch and operation of vacuum release valve.
3. Check vacuum chamber piston travel by running engine and shifting transmission selector from drive to neutral. The manual release lever should move up and down as vacuum is applied and released. If no movement is observed or if movement is slow (more than 1 or 2 seconds to complete full stroke), the vacuum chamber is leaking and should be replaced.
4. Check brake release with vacuum applied. If vacuum chamber piston completes full stroke but does not release brake, a malfunction of the pedal assembly is indicated.
5. Check operation of parking brake with engine off. Parking brake should remain engaged regardless of transmission selector position.

Parking Brake Vacuum Valve, Replace

1. With engine off, place shift lever in drive, remove vacuum hoses and retaining screws and remove valve from steering column.
2. To install, move actuating arm on valve against spring to extreme position or until locating holes line up and install a #42 drill in hole, Fig. 6.
3. Place shift lever in park and install valve but do not tighten screws. Rotate valve clockwise until actuating arm contacts tab in steering column then tighten screws.
4. Remove drill and install vacuum hoses making sure that hose from engine manifold is attached to center fitting on valve.
5. Start engine and check that parking brake can be set in neutral and park and will release in reverse and drive positions.

BRAKE MASTER CYLINDER, REPLACE

Exc. 1978-84 With Aluminum Master Cylinder

1. Disconnect brake lines from master cylinder. Install plugs in outlets to prevent fluid leakage.
2. Remove nuts that attach master cylinder to cowl panel or power brake unit.
3. Disconnect pedal push rod (manual brakes) from brake pedal.
4. Slide master cylinder straight out from cowl panel and/or power brake unit.
5. Reverse procedure to install.

Fig. 6 Parking brake vacuum release valve. 1977-78 (typical)

1978-84 With Aluminum Master Cylinder

Manual Brakes
1. Disconnect brake lines from master cylinder. Install plugs in outlets to prevent fluid leakage.
2. From under instrument panel, disconnect stop lamp switch mounting bracket and position aside.
3. Grasp brake pedal and pull backward to disengage push rod from master cylinder piston.

NOTE: This will require a pull of about 50 pounds. Also, the retention grommet will be destroyed.

4. Remove master cylinder to cowl retaining nuts and remove master cylinder by pulling straight out.

CAUTION: Make sure to remove all traces of old grommet from push rod groove and master cylinder piston.

5. Reverse procedure to install. Install new grommet on push rod, then lubricate grommet with water and align push rod with master cylinder piston. Using brake pedal, apply pressure to fully seat push rod into piston.

Power Brakes
1. Disconnect primary and secondary brake tubes from master cylinder, then cap lines and master cylinder fitting.
2. Remove nuts attaching master cylinder to power brake unit, then slide master cylinder from power brake unit.
3. Reverse procedure to install.

POWER BRAKE UNIT, REPLACE

1977-84

1. Remove master cylinder retaining nuts, then carefully slide out master cylinder from power brake and allow it to rest on fender shield.
2. Disconnect vacuum hose from power brake.
3. From under instrument panel, disconnect push rod from brake pedal. On linkage type power brake unit, also remove lower pivot retaining bolt.
4. Remove power brake retaining nuts and remove power brake unit.
5. Reverse procedure to install.

Rear Suspension

SHOCK ABSORBER, REPLACE

To replace shock absorber, support rear axle properly and disconnect shock absorber at upper and lower mountings.

LEAF SPRINGS & BUSHINGS, REPLACE

1. Support rear axle, relieving tension from spring.

NOTE: 1977–78 Full Size Models are equipped with preloaded "tension" type springs and a spring stretcher (C-4211) must be used during spring removal.

2. Disconnect shock absorber from lower mounting.
3. Remove "U" bolts and spring plate, Figs.

1 and 2, or lower spring seat isolator retainer and isolator, Figs. 1 and 2.
4. Remove spring front hanger to body mount bracket nuts, Fig. 3.
5. Remove rear shackle bolts, lower spring, thus pulling spring front hanger bolts out of holes.
6. Remove front hanger and rear shackle from spring. To replace pivot bushings, refer to Fig. 4. Bushing replacement is accomplished in one operation.
7. Reverse procedure to install.

Leaf Spring Service

To replace interliners, remove spring alignment clips and on all models except Imperial, discard alignment clips. Separate spring leaves with a screwdriver or other suitable tool and remove interliners. Thoroughly clean

spring surfaces before installation of new interliners.
To replace zinc interleaves, clamp spring in a vise and remove center bolt. Open vise carefully, allowing spring to expand. Interleaves can now be serviced. Install a drift through spring center bolt holes and clamp spring in a vise. Remove drift and install center bolt.

SWAY BAR, REPLACE

1. Remove nuts, retainers and rubber insulators from sway bar upper links, Figs. 5 and 6.
2. Disconnect sway bar brackets from frame.
3. Remove link from support assembly and replace insulators. Reverse procedure to install.

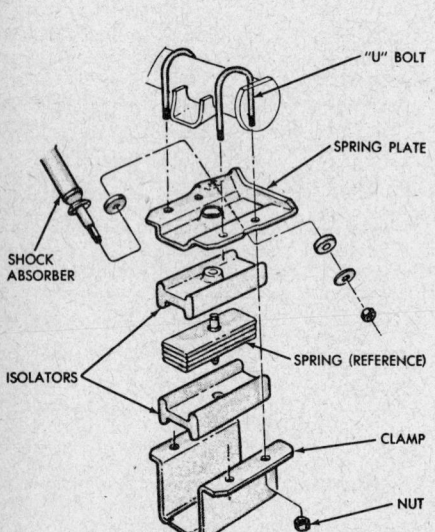

Fig. 1 Rear spring isolator. 1977 All & 1978 Chrysler

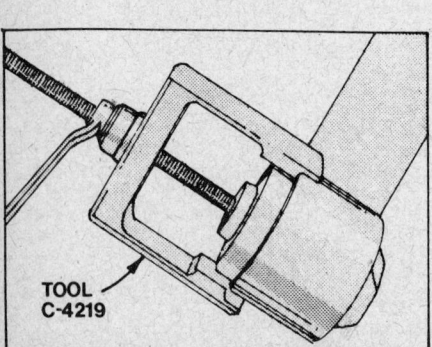

Fig. 4 Spring pivot bushing replacement

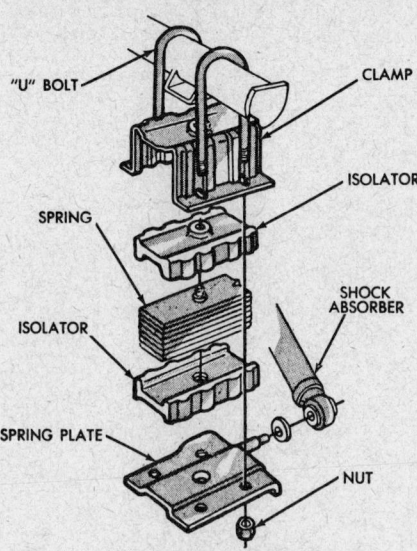

Fig. 2 Rear spring isolator. 1978 except Chrysler & 1979–84 All

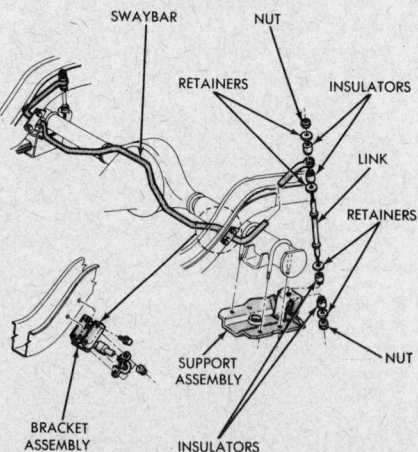

Fig. 5 Sway bar installation. 1977–80 Aspen, Volare, 1977–81 LeBaron, 1977–84 Diplomat, 1980–83 Cordoba, Mirada, 1981–83 Imperial, 1982 New Yorker, 1982–84 Gran Fury, 1983 New Yorker Fifth Avenue & 1984 Fifth Avenue

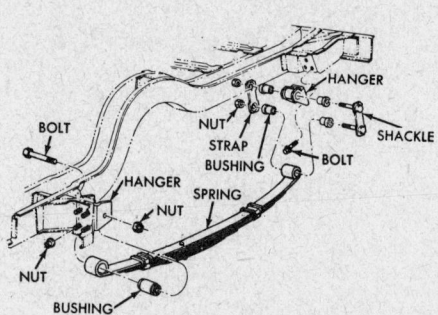

Fig. 3 Rear spring (typical)

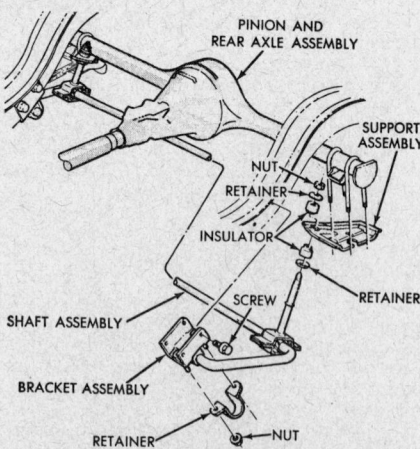

Fig. 6 Sway bar installation. Except 1977–80 Aspen, Volare, 1977–81 LeBaron, 1977–84 Diplomat, 1980–83 Cordoba, Mirada, 1981–83 Imperial, 1982 New Yorker, 1982–84 Gran Fury, 1983 New Yorker Fifth Avenue & 1984 Fifth Avenue

Front Suspension & Steering Section

FRONT SUSPENSION

Models with Transverse Torsion Bar Front Suspension

This front suspension, Fig. 1, incorporates two transverse torsion bars which react on the outboard end of the lower control arms. The torsion bars are anchored in the front crossmember opposite the affected wheel. The torsion bars are mounted parallel to the front crossmember through a "Pivot Cushion Bushing", attached to the crossmember, and turns and extends rearward to the lower control arm. The torsion bar ends are provided with an isolated bushing, bolted to the lower control arm and sway bar, which acts as the lower control arm strut.

Riding height is controlled by the torsion bar adjusting bolts on the anchor end of the torsion bar. The right torsion bar is adjusted from the left side and the left torsion bar is adjusted from the right side.

The torsion bar assembly incorporates the "Pivot Cushion Bushing" and "Bushing to Lower Control Arm". The lower control arm inner ends are bolted to the crossmember and pivots through bushings.

Caster and camber settings are made by loosening the upper control arm pivot bar bolt nuts and adjusting as necessary.

Models with Longitudinal Torsion Bar Front Suspension

This suspension, Figs. 2 and 3, consists of two torsion bar springs (right and left), two sets of upper and lower control arms, four ball joints and two struts.

The front ends of the torsion bar springs engage the lower control arms at the inner pivot points. The rear end of the torsion bars engage adjustable anchor and cam assemblies that are supported by brackets welded to the frame side rails and a removable crossmember.

The upper control arms are mounted on removable brackets that are bolted to the frame side rails. The lower control arms are attached to the frame front crossmember by a pivot shaft and bushing assembly. The pivot shafts are mounted in replaceable rubber bushings.

The steering knuckles are connected to the upper and lower control arms by means of ball joints. To prevent the possibility of fore and aft movement of the lower control arms, a strut is attached to the front crossmember and to the lower control arm.

1977–78 Chrysler Exc. Cordoba, 1977 Gran Fury, Royal Monaco

This suspension has new lower control arms with pressed in ball joints and more serviceable struts. Caster and camber settings are made by loosening the upper control arm pivot bar bolt nuts and adjusting as necessary.

1977–78 Charger, Fury & Monaco; 1977–79 Cordoba; 1978–79 Magnum; 1979–81 Newport, New Yorker & St. Regis; 1980–81 Gran Fury

This suspension has a rubber mounted crossmember, a torsion bar crossmember, more serviceable struts and a lower control arm with pressed in ball joints. Caster and camber settings are made by loosening the upper control arm pivot bar bolt nuts and adjusting as necessary.

WHEEL ALIGNMENT

NOTE: Front suspension height must be checked and corrected as necessary before performing wheel alignment.

1. Remove all foreign material from exposed threads of cam adjusting bolt nuts or pivot bar adjusting bolt nuts.
2. Record initial camber and caster readings before loosening cam bolt nuts or pivot bar bolt nuts.
3. On vehicles using cam bolts, the camber and caster is adjusted by loosening the cam bolt nuts and turning the cam bolts as necessary until the desired setting is obtained. On vehicles using pivot bars, tool C-4576 is required to adjust caster and camber. When performing adjustments, the camber settings should be held as close as possible to the "desired" setting, and the caster setting should be held as nearly equal as possible on both wheels.

SERVICE NOTE:

There may be cases when the vehicle may not have sufficient positive camber adjustment. Upper control arm plate spacers are available that will allow more positive camber adjustment, if required. If this condition is encountered, use spacer 1-4014352 for front suspension upper control arm front pivot support and spacer 1-4014353 for the rear pivot support. To install spacers, proceed as follows:

1. Loosen but do not remove caster/camber adjustment nut.
2. Raise vehicle and remove wheel and tire assembly.
3. Loosen but do not remove shock absorber upper mounting nut.
4. Remove two support plate bolts at front end of plate, then loosen two rear bolts enough to slide front spacer between support plate and frame.
5. Align holes in spacer with holes in support plate and frame.
6. Insert two front bolts and start threads. Do not tighten.
7. Repeat steps 4 through 6 for rear spacer.
8. Torque the four support plate bolts to 65 ft. lbs. and the shock absorber upper nut to 25 ft. lbs.
9. Lower vehicle and adjust alignment on side that spacers were installed.

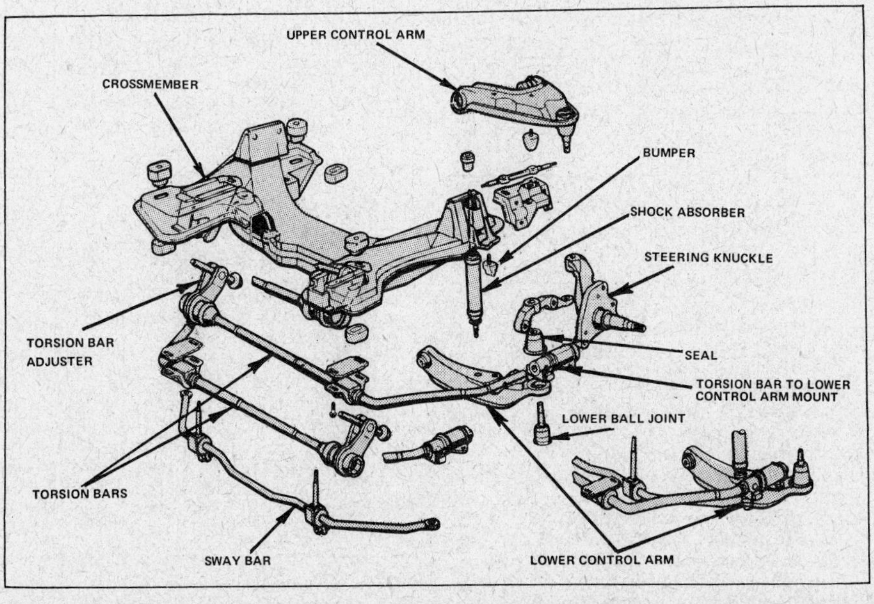

Fig. 1   Transverse torsion bar front suspension.

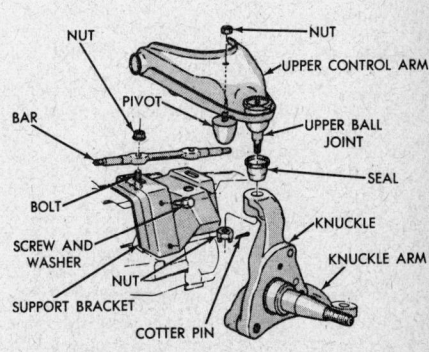

Fig. 2   Upper control arm & steering knuckle (Typical).

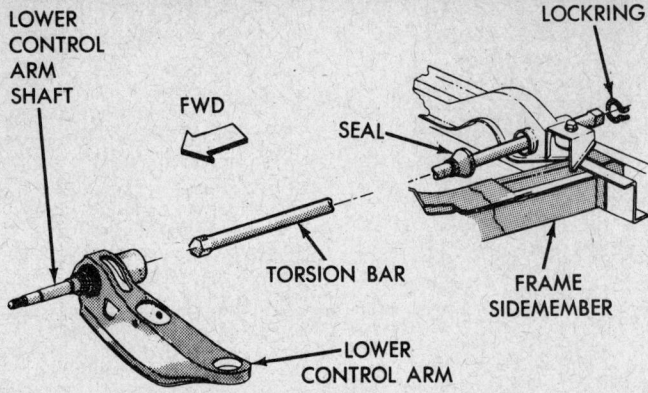

Fig. 3 Longitudinal torsion bar & lower control arm (Typical).

Fig. 4 Checking lower ball joint for wear

TOE-IN, ADJUST

1977–84

With the front wheels in straight ahead position, loosen the clamps at each end of both adjusting tubes. Adjust toe-in by turning the tie rod sleeve which will "center" the steering wheel spokes. If the steering wheel was centered, make the toe-in adjustment by turning both sleeves an equal amount. Position the clamps so they are on the bottom and tighten bolts to 15 ft. lbs.

WHEEL BEARINGS, ADJUST

1. Tighten adjusting nut to 20–25 ft. lbs. while rotating wheel.
2. On 1977–80 models, back off adjusting nut to completely release bearing. On 1981–84 models, back off adjusting nut ¼ turn.
3. Finger tighten adjusting nut while rotating wheel, then align nut lock with cotter pin slot and install cotter pin.
4. The resulting adjustment should be .0001–.003 end play.

WHEEL BEARINGS, REPLACE

(Disc Brakes)

1. Raise car and remove front wheels.
2. Remove grease cap, cotter pin, lock nut and bearing adjusting nut.
3. Remove bolts that attach caliper to steering knuckle.
4. Slowly slide caliper up and away from disc and support caliper on steering knuckle arm.

NOTE: Do not allow caliper to hang by brake hose.

5. Remove thrust washer and outer bearing cone. Remove hub and disc assembly. Grease retainer and inner bearing can now be removed.
6. Reverse procedure to install.

CHECKING BALL JOINTS FOR WEAR

Upper Ball Joint

1. Position a suitable jack under lower control arm and raise wheel and tire assembly clear of floor, then remove wheel cover and wheel bearing dust cover and cotter pin.
2. Tighten wheel bearing adjusting nut just enough to remove all play between hub, bearings and spindle.
3. Lower jack positioned under lower control arm to allow tire to lightly contact floor.
4. Grasp top of tire and move wheel and tire assembly inward and outward. While moving tire inward and outward, check for movement at ball joints between steering knuckle and upper control arm.
5. If any lateral movement is present, the upper ball joint should be replaced.
6. After completing upper ball joint check, readjust wheel bearing as described under "Wheel Bearings, Adjust".

Lower Ball Joint

NOTE: If loose ball joints are suspected, first make sure the front wheel bearings are properly adjusted and that the control arms are tight.

1. Raise front of vehicle and place jack stands underneath each lower control arm as far out as possible.

NOTE: The upper control arms must not contact the rubber rebound bumpers.

2. With weight of vehicle on lower control arms, attach dial indicator onto lower control arm, Fig. 4.
3. Place dial indicator plunger tip against ball joint housing and zero dial indicator.
4. Using a pry bar under the center of the tire, raise and lower the tire and measure the axial travel of the ball joint housing with respect to the ball joint. If the axial travel is .030 inch or more than specified, the ball joint should be replaced.

BALL JOINTS, REPLACE

Upper Ball Joint

1. Place ignition switch in the "Off" position.
2. Using a suitable jack raise front of vehicle and position a jack stand under lower control arm as close to wheel and tire assembly as possible. Check to ensure that jack stand is not in contact with brake splash shield. Also check to ensure that rubber rebound bumper is not in contact with frame.

NOTE: The torsion bar will remain in the loaded position.

3. Remove wheel and tire assembly.
4. Remove cotter pin and nut from lower ball joint stud. Position tool No. C3564-A over lower ball joint stud, allowing tool to rest on knuckle arm, then set tool securely against upper ball joint stud.
5. Tighten tool to apply pressure against upper ball joint stud, then strike knuckle with hammer to loosen stud.
6. Remove tool, then detach upper ball joint from knuckle.

NOTE: Support knuckle and brake assembly to prevent damage to lower ball joint and brake hoses.

7. Remove upper ball joint from upper control arm, using tool No. C3561 for 1977 Gran Fury, Royal Monaco and 1977–78 Newport and New Yorker. On all models except 1977 Gran Fury, Royal Monaco and 1977–78 Newport and New Yorker, use tool No. C3560 to remove ball joint from upper control arm.
8. Reverse procedure to install. Thread upper ball joint into control arm as far as possible by hand. On 1977 Gran Fury, Royal Monaco and 1977–78 Newport and New Yorker, torque upper ball joint into control to 150 ft. lbs. using tool No. C3561. On all models except 1977 Gran Fury, Royal Monaco and 1977–78 Newport and New Yorker, torque upper ball joint into control arm to 125 ft. lbs. using tool No. C3560. Torque upper and lower ball joint stud nuts to 135 ft. lbs. on 1977 Gran Fury, Royal Monaco and Newport and New Yorker, 100 ft. lbs. on all models except 1977 Gran Fury, Royal Monaco and 1977–78 Newport and New Yorker. After tightening lower ball joint stud nut, install cotter pin.

NOTE: Ball joint seals should be replaced whenever they have been removed.

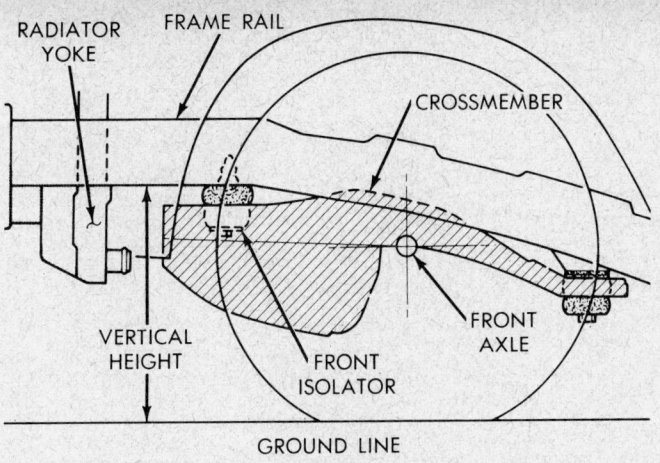

Fig. 5   Measuring front suspension height. 1981 Newport, New Yorker & St. Regis

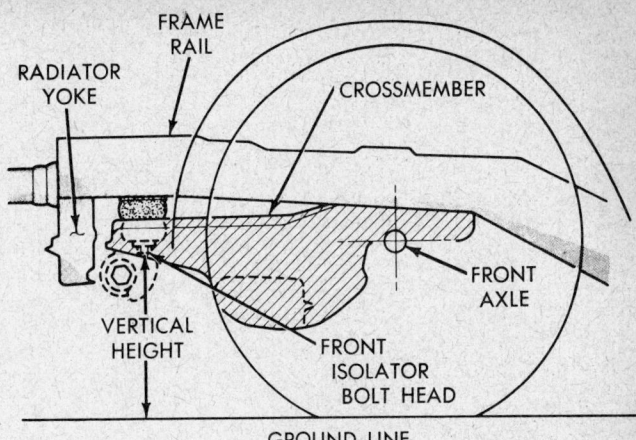

Fig. 6   Measuring front suspension height. 1981 LeBaron, 1981–83 Cordoba, Imperial, Mirada, 1981–84 Diplomat, 1982 New Yorker, 1982–84 Gran Fury, 1983 New Yorker Fifth Avenue & 1984 Fifth Avenue

Lower Ball Joint

1. Place ignition switch in the "Off" position.
2. Raise vehicle and support so front suspension is in the full rebound position. Position jack stands under front frame for additional support.
3. Remove wheel and tire assembly, then remove disc brake caliper and support with wire hook to prevent brake hose from becoming damaged.
4. Remove disc brake hub and rotor assembly and splash shield, then disconnect shock absorber at lower mounting.
5. Release load on torsion bar by rotating adjusting bolt counter-clockwise.
6. Remove upper and lower ball joint stud nuts and cotter pin, then position tool No. C3564-A over upper ball joint stud so that tool is resting on steering knuckle.
7. Rotate threaded portion of tool to lock it against lower ball joint stud. Tighten tool to place pressure on lower ball joint stud, then strike steering knuckle with a hammer to loosen stud. Remove tool and disconnect lower ball joint.
8. Use tool No. C4212 to press ball joint from lower control arm.
9. Position replacement ball joint on lower control arm, then press into control arm using tool No. C4212.
10. Install seal over lower ball joint. On 1977 Gran Fury, Royal Monaco and 1977–78 Newport and New Yorker, use tool No. C4034 to press retainer portion of seal until it is locked in position. On all models except 1977 Gran Fury, Royal Monaco and 1977–78 Newport and New Yorker, use tool No. C4039 to press retainer portion of seal until it is locked in position.
11. Position lower ball joint to steering knuckle, then install upper and lower stud nuts and torque to 135 ft. lbs. on 1977 Gran Fury, Royal Monaco and 1977–78 Newport and New Yorker, 100 ft. lbs. on all models except 1977 Gran Fury, Royal Monaco and 1977–78 Newport and New Yorker. After tightening stud nuts, install cotter pin.
12. Place tension on torsion bar by rotating adjusting bolt clockwise.
13. Install disc brake assembly and wheel and tire assembly, then adjust front wheel bearing as described under "Wheel Bearings, Adjust".
14. Lubricate ball joint, then lower vehicle and adjust vehicle riding height.

TORSION BAR, REPLACE
1977–80 Aspen, Volare, 1977–81 LeBaron, 1977–84 Diplomat, 1980–83 Cordoba, Imperial, Mirada, 1982 New Yorker, 1982–84 Gran Fury, 1983 New Yorker Fifth Avenue & 1984 Fifth Avenue

Removal

1. Raise vehicle and support so front suspension is in full rebound position.
2. Rotate anchor adjusting bolts located in frame crossmember, counter-clockwise to release load on both torsion bars. Then, remove anchor adjusting bolt from torsion bar to be removed.
3. Raise lower control arms until 2⅞ inch clearance is obtained between crossmember ledge at jounce bumper and the torsion bar end bushing and support lower arms at this height.

NOTE: This procedure will align the sway bar and the lower control arm attaching points for disassembly and component realignment and attachment during assembly.

4. Remove sway bar to control arm attaching bolt and retainers, then the two bolts securing torsion bar end bushing to lower control arm.
5. Remove two bolts securing torsion bar pivot cushion bushing to crossmember, then the torsion bar and anchor assembly from crossmember.
6. Separate anchor from torsion bar.

Inspection

1. Inspect seal for damage and replace, if necessary.
2. Inspect bushing to lower control arm and pivot cushion bushing. Inspect seals on cushion bushing for cuts, tears or severe deterioration that may allow moisture to enter under cushion. If corrosion is evident, replace torsion bar assembly.
3. Inspect torsion bars for paint damage and touch up, if necessary.
4. Clean anchor hex openings and torsion bar hex ends.
5. Inspect torsion bar adjusting bolt and swivel for damage or corrosion and replace, if necessary.

Installation

1. Slide balloon seal over torsion bar end with cupped end facing toward hex.
2. Lubricate torsion bar hex end with lubricant, P/N 2525035, and install hex end into anchor bracket. With the torsion bar in horizontal position, the anchor bracket ears should be positioned nearly straight upward. Position swivel into anchor bracket ears.
3. Install torsion bar anchor bracket assembly into crossmember anchor retainer, then the anchor adjusting bolt and bearing.
4. Install two bolt and washer assemblies securing pivot cushion bushing to crossmember. Leave assemblies loose enough to install friction plates.
5. With lower control arms supported as outlined in step 3 under "Removal", install the two bolt and nut assemblies securing torsion bar bushing to lower control arm and torque nuts to 70 ft. lbs.
6. Ensure that torsion bar anchor bracket is fully seated in crossmember. Then install friction plates between crossmember and pivot cushion bushing with open end of slot to rear and bottomed out on mounting bolt. Tighten cushion bushing bolts to 85 ft. lbs. Place balloon seal over anchor bracket.
7. Install new bolt through sway bar, retainer cushions and sleeve and attach to lower control arm end bushing, then torque bolt to 50 ft. lbs.
8. Rotate anchor adjusting bolt clockwise to load torsion bar.
9. Lower vehicle and adjust riding height.

Except 1977–80 Aspen, Volaré, 1977–81 LeBaron, 1977–84 Diplomat, 1980–83 Cordoba, Imperial, Mirada, 1982 New Yorker, 1982–84 Gran Fury, 1983 New Yorker Fifth Avenue & 1984 Fifth Avenue

The torsion bars are not interchangeable side for side. The bars are marked either right or left by an "R" or an "L" stamped on one end of the bar. The general procedure for replacing a torsion bar is as follows:

Removal

1. Remove upper control arm rebound bumper.

2. If vehicle is to be raised on a hoist, make sure it is lifted on the body only so suspension is in full rebound position (no load).
3. Release all load from torsion bar by turning anchor adjusting bolt counterclockwise.
4. Slide rear anchor balloon seal off of rear anchor and remove lock ring from anchor.
5. Remove torsion bar, by sliding bar out through rear of rear anchor. Use care not to damage balloon seal when it is removed from torsion bar.

NOTE: On some models, it may be necessary to remove transmission torque shaft to provide clearance.

Inspection

1. Inspect balloon seal for damage and replace if necessary.
2. Inspect torsion bar for scores or nicks. Dress down all scratches and nicks to remove sharp edges, then paint repaired areas with a rust preventive.
3. Remove all foreign material from hex openings in anchors and from hex ends of torsion bars.
4. Inspect adjusting bolt and swivel and replace if there is any sign of corrosion or other damage. Lubricate for easy operation.

Installation

1. Insert torsion bar through rear anchor.
2. Slide balloon seal over torsion bar with cupped end toward rear of bar.
3. Coat both ends of torsion bar with a long mileage lubricant.
4. Slide torsion bar in hex opening of lower control arm.
5. Install lock ring, making sure it is seated in groove.
6. Pack annular opening in rear anchor completely full of a long mileage lubricant.
7. Position lip of balloon seal in groove of anchor.
8. Turn adjusting bolt clockwise to place a load on torsion bar.
9. Lower vehicle to floor and adjust front suspension height.
10. Install upper control arm rebound bumper.

SWAY BAR, REPLACE

1977–80 Aspen & Volare; 1977–81 Diplomat & LeBaron; 1980–81 Cordoba & Mirada; 1981 Imperial & 1982–84 All Models

1. Raise and support front of vehicle

NOTE: Sway bar to lower control arm attaching points are aligned only when lower control arms are at design height. If frame contact or twin post hoist is used, release load on torsion bar by turning adjuster bolts counter-clockwise, then raise lower control arms until clearance between crossmember ledge and torsion bar to lower control arm bushing is 27/8 inches. Support lower control arms with jack stand during sway bar removal and installation.

2. With lower control arms properly supported, remove sway bar to torsion bar bushing attaching bolts, retainers, cush-

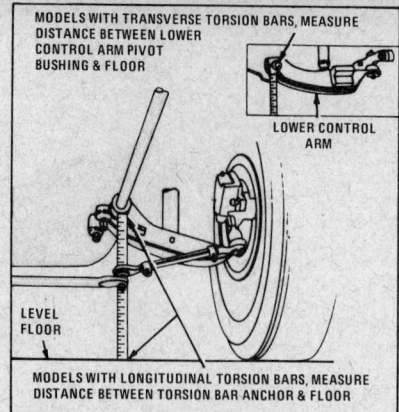

Fig. 7 Measuring front suspension height. 1977–80 models

ions and sleeves.
3. Remove retainer assembly strap bolts and retainer straps, then remove sway bar.
4. Reverse procedure to install. Inspect cushions and bushings for excessive wear or deterioration and replace as necessary.

1977 Gran Fury & Royal Monaco; 1977–78 Chrysler Station Wagon

1. Place ignition switch in off or unlocked position.
2. Raise vehicle on suitable hoist to place front suspension in rebound position.
3. Turn front wheel to extreme right or left.
4. Remove upper bolts, retainers and insulators from both sides of bar. Link sleeve will remain in position as secured through lower control arm.
5. Remove two screws and washers securing retainers to bar bushings at frame and remove retainers.
6. Remove bar by moving in direction that wheels are turned until opposite end clears lower control arm strut, lower that end below strut and move in opposite directions until other end clears strut, then move bar clear of frame in direction wheels are turned.
7. Reverse procedure to install. Inspect cushions and bushing for excessive wear or deterioration and replace as necessary.

Except 1977 Gran Fury & Royal Monaco; 1977–78 Chrysler Station Wagon; 1977–80 Aspen & Volare; Diplomat & LeBaron; 1980–81 Cordoba & Mirada; 1981 Imperial & 1982–84 All Models

1. Place ignition switch in off or unlocked position.
2. Raise vehicle on hoist to place front suspension in rebound position.
3. Remove wheel cover and wheel and tire assembly.
4. Remove nut and bolt on each end of bar attaching sway bar to strut clamp. Remove nut and bolt from both sway bar link straps to free sway bar from links.
5. Remove sway bar by pulling unit out through frame crossmember openings in direction of area where wheel has been removed.

6. Reverse procedure to install. Inspect cushions and bushing for excessive wear or deterioration and replace as necessary.

RIDING HEIGHT, ADJUST

Before taking measurements, grasp the bumpers at the center (rear bumper first) and jounce the car up and down several times. Jounce the car at the front bumper the same number of times and release the bumper at the same point in the cycle each time.

1981–84 Models

1. On 1981 Newport, New Yorker and St. Regis models, the height is measured from the bottom of the frame side rail, between radiator yoke and forward edge of crossmember, to ground, Fig. 5.
2. On 1981 LeBaron, 1981–83 Cordoba, Imperial & Mirada, 1981–84 Diplomat, 1982 New Yorker, 1982–84 Gran Fury, 1983 New Yorker Fifth Avenue & 1984 Fifth Avenue, the height is measured from the head of the front suspension front crossmember insulator bolt to ground, Fig. 6.
3. If necessary, turn torsion bar adjusting bolt clockwise to increase height and counterclockwise to decrease height.
4. After completing adjustment, jounce vehicle and recheck riding height. Both sides must be measured even though only one side may have been adjusted. Front vehicle height should not vary more than 1/4 inch from the specified riding height. Riding height should also be within 1/4 inch side to side.

1977–80 Models

1. On 1977–80 models except Aspen, Volaré and Diplomat and LeBaron, measure distance from a point 1 inch forward of rear face of torsion bar anchor to the floor (Measurement A), Fig. 7. The distance should be as listed below.
2. On 1977–80 Aspen, Volaré and Diplomat and LeBaron, measure distance from lowest point of lower control arm inner pivot bushing to the floor, Fig. 7. The distance should be as listed below.
3. Measure the other side in the same manner.
4. Adjust by turning the torsion bar anchor adjusting nut *clockwise to increase* the height and *counterclockwise to decrease* the height. The difference from side-to-side should not exceed 1/8 inch.
5. After adjusting, jounce the car and recheck the measurements on both sides, even if only one side may have been adjusted.

Chrysler & Imperial

1977–78	Newport, New Yorker	10-1/8"
1977–79	Cordoba	10-3/4"
1977–80	LeBaron	10-1/4"
1979–80	Newport, New Yorker	10-3/4"
1980	Cordoba	10-1/4"
1981	Newport, New Yorker	16-3/4"
1981–83	Cordoba, LeBaron	12-1/2"
1981–83	Imperial	12-1/2"
1982	New Yorker	12-1/2"
1983	New Yorker Fifth Ave.	12-1/2"
1984	Fifth Avenue	12-1/2"

Dodge

1977–79	Charger, Magnum	10-3/4"
	Dart	10-15/16"
	Monaco	10-1/8"
1977–80	Aspen	10-1/4"

1977	Royal Monaco	10-1/8"
1977–78	Monaco Exc. Sta. Wag.	10-3/4"
	Monaco Sta. Wag.	11-1/4"
1977–80	Diplomat	10-1/4"
1979–80	St. Regis	10-3/4"
1980	Mirada	10-1/4"
1981	St. Regis	16-3/4"
1981–83	Diplomat, Mirada	12-1/2"
1984	Diplomat	12-1/2"

Plymouth

1977	Gran Fury	10-1/8"
1977–78	Fury Exc. Sta. Wag.	10-3/4"
	Fury Sta. Wag.	11-1/4"
1977–80	Volare	10-1/4"
1980–80	Gran Fury	10-3/4"
1981	Gran Fury	16-3/4"
1982–84	Gran Fury	12-1/2"

MANUAL STEERING GEAR, REPLACE

CAUTION: To avoid damage to the energy absorbing steering column, it is recommended that the steering column be completely detached from floor and instrument panel before steering gear is removed.

1. Use a suitable puller to remove steering arm from under vehicle.
2. Remove gear to frame retaining bolts and remove gear.
3. Reverse procedure to install.

POWER STEERING GEAR, REPLACE

1. Disconnect battery ground cable.
2. Remove steering column.
3. Disconnect fluid hoses from steering gear and support free ends above pump to avoid loss of fluid. Plug fittings on gear.
4. Disconnect steering arm from gear with suitable puller.
5. Remove gear to frame retaining bolts or nuts and remove gear.
6. Reverse procedure to install.

POWER STEERING PUMP, REPLACE

1. Loosen power steering pump mounting and locking bolts, then remove drive belt.
2. Disconnect pressure and return lines at power steering pump.
3. Remove pump mounting bolts, then remove pump and mounting bracket.
4. Reverse procedure to install.

> **NOTE:** The following models are covered in this chapter: 1978–84 Dodge Omni & Plymouth Horizon; 1981–84 Dodge Aries & Plymouth Reliant; 1982–83 Dodge 400; 1982–84 Chrysler LeBaron & Town & Country; 1983–84 Chrysler E Class, Executive, New Yorker, Dodge Charger, Shelby Charger, 600 & Plymouth Turismo; 1984 Chrysler Laser & Dodge Daytona.

INDEX OF SERVICE OPERATIONS

NOTE: Refer to the front of this manual for vehicle manufacturer's special service tool suppliers.

Front Wheel Drive—CHRYSLER CORP.

GRILLE IDENTIFICATION

1978—80 Omni (4 Door)

1978—80 Horizon (4 Door)

1979—80 Omni 024 (2 Door)

1979—81 Horizon TC3 (2 Door)

1981 Omni (4 Door)

1981 Horizon (4 Door)

1981—82 Omni 024 (2 Door)

1981—82 Reliant

1981—83 Aries

1982 Horizon TC3 (2 Door)

1982—83 400

1982—83 Horizon (4 Door)

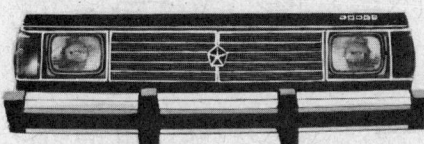
1982—83 Omni (4 Door)

1982—84 LeBaron, Town & Country

1983 Charger 2.2

1983 Reliant

1983 Turismo

1983—84 E Class, Executive & New Yorker

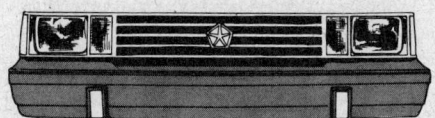
1984 Aries

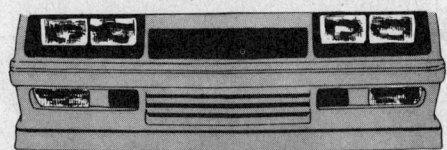
1984 Daytona

1984 Horizon

GRILL IDENTIFICATION—Continued

1984 Laser

1984 Omni

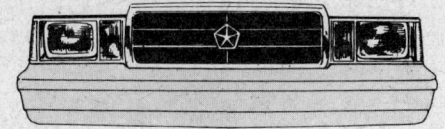

1984 Reliant

1983-84 600

1984 Turismo

GENERAL ENGINE SPECIFICATIONS

Year	CID①/Liter	VIN Code②	Carburetor	Bore and Stroke Inch (Millimeters)	Compression Ratio	Net H.P. @ R.P.M.③	Maximum Torque Ft. Lbs. @ R.P.M.	Normal Oil Pressure Pounds @ 2000 RPM
1978	4-105, 1.7L④⑥	A	5220, 2 Bbl.⑦	3.13 × 3.40 (79.5 × 86.4)	8.2	70 @ 5600	85 @ 3200	60–90
	4-105, 1.7L⑤⑥	A	5220, 2 Bbl.⑦	3.13 × 3.40 (79.5 × 86.4)	8.2	75 @ 5600	90 @ 3200	60–90
1979	4-105, 1.7L④⑥	A	5220, 2 Bbl.⑦	3.13 × 3.40 (79.5 × 86.4)	8.2	65 @ 5200	85 @ 2800	60–90
	4-105, 1.7L⑤⑥	A	5220, 2 Bbl.⑦	3.13 × 3.40 (79.5 × 86.4)	8.2	70 @ 5200	85 @ 2800	60–90
1980	4-105, 1.7L④⑥	A	5220, 2 Bbl.⑦	3.13 × 3.40 (79.5 × 86.4)	8.2	65 @ 5200	85 @ 2400	60–90
	4-105, 1.7L⑤⑥	A	5220, 2 Bbl.⑦	3.13 × 3.40 (79.5 × 86.4)	8.2	65 @ 5200	85 @ 2400	60–90
1981	4-105, 1.7L⑥	A	6520, 2 Bbl.⑦	3.13 × 3.40 (79.5 × 86.4)	8.2	63 @ 5200	83 @ 2400	60–90
	4-135, 2.2L⑧	B	6520, 2 Bbl.⑦	3.44 × 3.62 (87.5 × 92)	8.5	84 @ 4800	111 @ 2500	50
	4-156, 2.6L⑨	D	Mikuni, 2 Bbl.	3.59 × 3.86 (91.1 × 98)	8.2	92 @ 4800	131 @ 2500	57
1982	4-105, 1.7L⑥	A	6520, 2 Bbl.⑦	3.13 × 3.40 (79.5 × 86.4)	8.2	63 @ 4800	83 @ 2400	60–90
	4-135, 2.2L⑧	B	6520, 2 Bbl.⑦	3.44 × 3.62 (87.5 × 92)	8.5	84 @ 4800	111 @ 2400	50
	4-156, 2.6L⑨	D	Mikuni, 2 Bbl.	3.59 × 3.86 (91.1 × 98)	8.2	92 @ 4500	131 @ 2500	57
1983	4-97, 1.6L⑩	A	6520, 2 Bbl.⑦	3.17 × 3.07 (80.6 × 78)	8.8	62 @ 4800	86 @ 3200	58–87⑪
	4-105, 1.7L⑥	B	6520, 2 Bbl.⑦	3.13 × 3.40 (79.5 × 86.4)	8.2	63 @ 4800	83 @ 2400	60–90
	4-135, 2.2L⑧	C	6520, 2 Bbl.⑦	3.44 × 3.62 (87.5 × 92.0)	9.0	94 @ 5200	117 @ 3200	50
	4-135, 2.2L⑧⑫	F	6520, 2 Bbl.⑦	3.44 × 3.62 (87.5 × 92)	9.6	107 @ 5600	126 @ 3600	50
	4-135, 2.2L⑧	D	E.F.I.⑬	3.44 × 3.62 (87.5 × 92)	9.0	94 @ 5200	120 @ 3200	50
	4-156, 2.6L⑨	G	Mikuni, 2 Bbl.	3.59 × 3.86 (91.1 × 98.0)	8.2	93 @ 4500	131 @ 2500	57
1984	4-97, 1.6L⑩	A	6520, 2 Bbl.⑦	3.17 × 3.07 (80.6 × 78)	8.8	64 @ 4800	87 @ 2800	58–87

Continued

GENERAL ENGINE SPECIFICATIONS—Continued

Year	Engine		Carburetor	Bore and Stroke Inch (Millimeters)	Com-pression Ratio	Net H.P. @ R.P.M.③	Maximum Torque Ft. Lbs. @ R.P.M.	Normal Oil Pressure Pounds @ 2000 RPM
	CID①/Liter	VIN Code②						
	4-135, 2.2L⑧	C	6520, 2 Bbl.⑦	3.44 × 3.62 (87.5 × 92)	9.0	96 @ 5200	119 @ 3200	50
	4-135, 2.2L⑧⑫	F	6520, 2 Bbl.⑦	3.44 × 3.62 (87.5 × 92)	10.0	110 @ 5600	129 @ 3600	50
	4-135, 2.2L⑧	D	E.F.I.⑬	3.44 × 3.62 (87.5 × 92)	9.0	99 @ 5600	121 @ 3200	50
	4-135, 2.2L⑧⑭	E	E.F.I.⑬	3.44 × 3.62 (87.5 × 92)	8.5	142 @ 5600	160 @ 3600	50
	4-156, 2.6L⑨	G	Mikuni, 2 Bbl.	3.59 × 3.86 (91.1 × 98)	8.7	101 @ 4800	140 @ 2800	85⑮

①—CID—cubic inch displacement.
②—On 1978–80 models, the 5th digit of the V.I.N. denotes engine code. On 1981–84 models, the 8th digit of the V.I.N. denotes engine code.
③—Ratings are net—as installed in vehicle.
④—Calif. & high altitude.
⑤—Exc. Calif. & high altitude.
⑥—1700 cc.
⑦—Holley.
⑧—2200 cc.
⑨—2600 cc.
⑩—1600cc.
⑪—At 3000 RPM.
⑫—High output engine.
⑬—Electronic fuel injection.
⑭—Turbocharged engine.
⑮—At 2500 RPM.

TUNE UP SPECIFICATIONS

The following specifications are published from the latest information available. This data should be used only in the absence of a decal affixed in the engine compartment.

▲Before removing wires from distributor cap, determine location of the No. 1 wire in cap, as distributor position may have been altered from that shown at the end of this chart.

●When checking compression, lowest cylinder must be within 25 PSI of the highest.

☞ Spark plug types shown in this chart are recommendations of the original vehicle manufacturer and not MOTOR.
Check local sources for other spark plug manufacturers listings.

Year & Engine/VIN Code	Spark Plug		Ignition Timing BTDC①★				Curb Idle Speed		Fast Idle Speed		Fuel Pump Pressure
	Type ☞	Gap	Firing Order Fig. ▲	Man. Trans.	Auto. Trans.	Mark Fig.	Man. Trans.	Auto. Trans.	Man. Trans.	Auto. Trans.	
1978											
4-105/A Man. Trans.	RN12Y⑤	.035	A	15°	—	B	900	—	1100⑥	—	4–6
4-105/A Auto. Trans.	RN12Y⑤	.035	A	—	15°	C	—	900N	—	1100⑥	4–6
1979											
4-105/A Man. Trans.	RN12Y⑤	.035	A	15°	—	B	900	—	1400⑥	—	4–6
4-105/A Auto. Trans.	RN12Y⑤	.035	A	—	15°	C	—	900N	—	1700⑥	4–6
1980											
4-105/A Man. Trans.③	RN12Y⑤	.035	A	12°	—	B	900	—	1400⑦	—	4–6
4-105/A Man. Trans.④	RN12Y⑤	.035	A	10°	—	B	900	—	1400⑦	—	4–6
4-105/A Auto. Trans.③	RN12Y⑤	.035	A	—	12°	C	—	900N	—	1700⑦	4–6
4-105/A Auto. Trans.④	RN12Y⑤	.035	A	—	10°	C	—	900N	—	1700⑦	4–6
1981											
4-105/A Man. Trans.	65PR4⑧	.048	A	12°	—	B	900	—	1400⑨	—	4½–6
4-105/A Auto. Trans.	65PR4⑧	.048	A	—	10°	C	—	900N	—	1400⑨	4½–6
4-135/B Man. Trans.③	65PR⑧	.035	D	10°	—	C	900	—	1100⑨	—	4½–6
4-135/B Auto. Trans.③	65PR⑧	.035	D	—	10°	C	—	900N	—	1500⑩	4½–6
4-135/B Man. Trans.④	65PR⑧	.035	D	10°	—	C	900	—	1100⑨	—	4½–6
4-135/B Auto. Trans.④	65PR⑧	.035	D	—	10°	C	—	900N	—	1600⑩	4½–6
4-156/D	65PR⑧	.041	F	—	7°	G	—	800N⑪	—	—	4½–6
1982											
4-105/A Man. Trans.	⑬	.035	A	20°⑫	—	B	850	—	1400	—	4½–6
4-105/A Auto. Trans.	⑬	.035	A	—	12°	C	—	900N	—	1400	4½–6
4-135/B Man. Trans.	⑬	.035	D	12°	—	C	850	—	1300	—	4½–6
4-135/B Auto. Trans.	⑬	.035	D	—	12°	C	—	900N	—	1600	4½–6
4-156/D	⑬	.041	F	—	7°	G	—	800N⑪	—	—	4½–6

Continued

TUNE UP SPECIFICATIONS—Continued

The following specifications are published from the latest information available. This
data should be used only in the absence of a decal affixed in the engine compartment.

▲ Before removing wires from distributor cap, determine location of the No. 1 wire in cap, as distributor position may have been altered from that shown at
the end of this chart.

● When checking compression, lowest cylinder must be within 25 PSI of the highest.

✍ Spark plug types shown in this chart are recommendations of the original vehicle manufacturer and not MOTOR.

Check local sources for other spark plug manufacturers listings.

Year & Engine/VIN Code	Spark Plug		Ignition Timing BTDC① ★				Curb Idle Speed		Fast Idle Speed		Fuel Pump Pressure
	Type ✍	Gap	Firing Order Fig. ▲	Man. Trans.	Auto. Trans.	Mark Fig.	Man. Trans.	Auto. Trans.	Man. Trans.	Auto. Trans.	
1983											
4-97/A	⑬	.035	E	12°	—	H	⑭	—	1400	—	4½–6
4-105/B	⑬	.035	A	20°⑫	12°	⑮	850	900N	1400	1350	4½–6
4-135/C⑯	⑬	.035	D	10°	10°	C	775	900N	1400	1500	4½–6
4-135/C⑰	⑬	.035	D	6°	6°	C	900	850N	1350	1375	4½–6
4-135/F	②⑬	.035	D	15°	—	C	850	—	1500	—	4½–6
4-135/D	⑬	.035	D	—	—	⑮	—	⑱	—	—	—
4-156/G	⑬	.040	F	—	7°	G	—	800N	—	—	4½–6
1984											
4-97/A	⑬	.035	E	12°	12°	H	850	1000N	—	—	4½–6
4-135/C	⑬	.035	D	10°	10°⑧	⑮	800	900N	1500	1600	4½–6
4-135/F	②⑬	.035	D	15°	—	C	850	—	1500	—	4½–6
4-135/D	⑬	.035	D	6°	6°	⑮	⑲	⑳	—	—	4½–6
4-135/E	⑬	.035	D	12°	12°	C	㉑	㉑	—	—	4½–6
4-156/G	⑬	.040	F	—	7°	G	—	800	—	950	4½–6

① —BTDC—Before top dead center.
② —For extended high speed operation, RN9Y.
③ —Exc. California
④ —California
⑤ —Champion.
⑥ —On lowest step of fast idle cam, w/radiator fan operating, EGR disconnected & plugged, idle stop switch grounded & A/C off.
⑦ —On lowest step of fast idle cam, w/radiator fan operating, EGR & dist. vacuum advance disconnected & plugged & A/C off.
⑧ —Mopar.
⑨ —On 3rd step of fast idle cam (next to lowest), w/radiator fan operating, carb. switch grounded & EGR disconnected & plugged.
⑩ —On 3rd step of fast idle cam (next to lowest), w/radiator fan operating, carb. switch grounded, EGR disconnected & plugged & green duty cycle solenoid wire disconnected.
⑪ —If mileage on vehicle is less than 300 mi., set at 750 RPM.
⑫ —If an adjustable timing light is unavailable,

use following procedure to mark flywheel for standard timing light:
a. On models with A-412 manual transaxle, align 12° BTDC mark on flywheel with pointer on housing, cover flywheel timing marks with tape, then mark tape at 12° and 16° BTDC positions. Remove tape and reposition so that 12° BTDC mark on tape is aligned with 16° BTDC mark on flywheel. Permanently mark flywheel at 16° BTDC mark on tape; a position which should correspond to 20° BTDC.
b. On models with A-460 manual transaxle, align flywheel timing mark with 16° BTDC mark on housing, then scribe a line on flywheel aligned with 12° BTDC mark on housing. When checking or adjusting ignition timing, 20° BTDC will be indicated when scribed line is aligned with 16° BTDC mark on housing.
⑬ —Early production 1982, Mopar 65PR. From late production 1982 original equipment, RN12YC; replacement RN12Y.

⑭ —Exc. high altitude, 900 RPM; high altitude, 850 RPM.
⑮ —Exc. A-412 manual transaxle, Fig. C; A-412 manual transaxle, Fig. B.
⑯ —Exc. high altitude.
⑰ —High altitude.
⑱ —Idle speed controlled by Automatic Idle Speed (AIS) motor. Basic adjustment (AIS disconnected and closed), 650–675 RPM; normal curb idle speed, 700±100 RPM.
⑲ —Idle speed controlled by Automatic Idle Speed (AIS) motor. Basic adjustment (AIS disconnected and closed), 725 RPM; normal curb idle speed, 800 RPM.
⑳ —Idle speed controlled by Automatic Idle Speed (AIS) motor. Basic adjustment (AIS disconnected and closed), 800 RPM; normal curb idle speed, 900N RPM.
㉑ —Idle speed controlled by Automatic Idle Speed (AIS) motor. Basic adjustment (AIS disconnected and closed), 570–800 RPM; normal curb idle speed, 950 RPM.

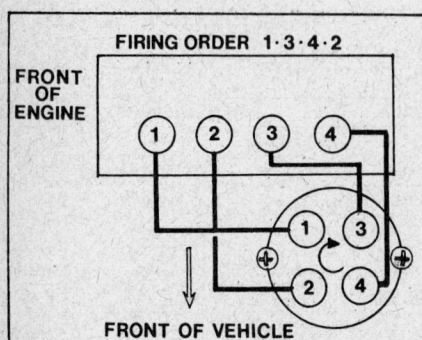

Fig. A

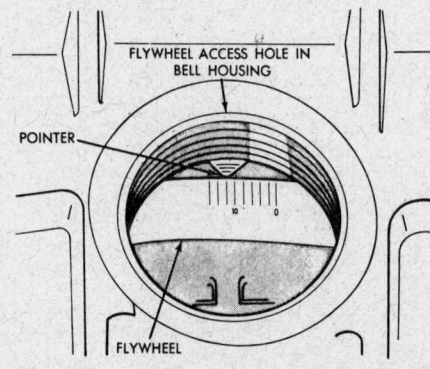

Fig. B

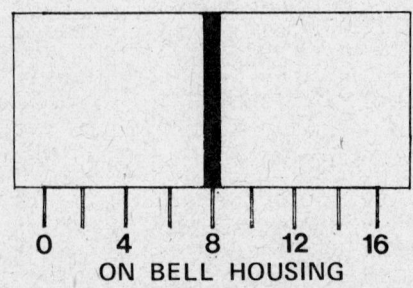

Fig. C

Continued

TUNE UP NOTES—Continued

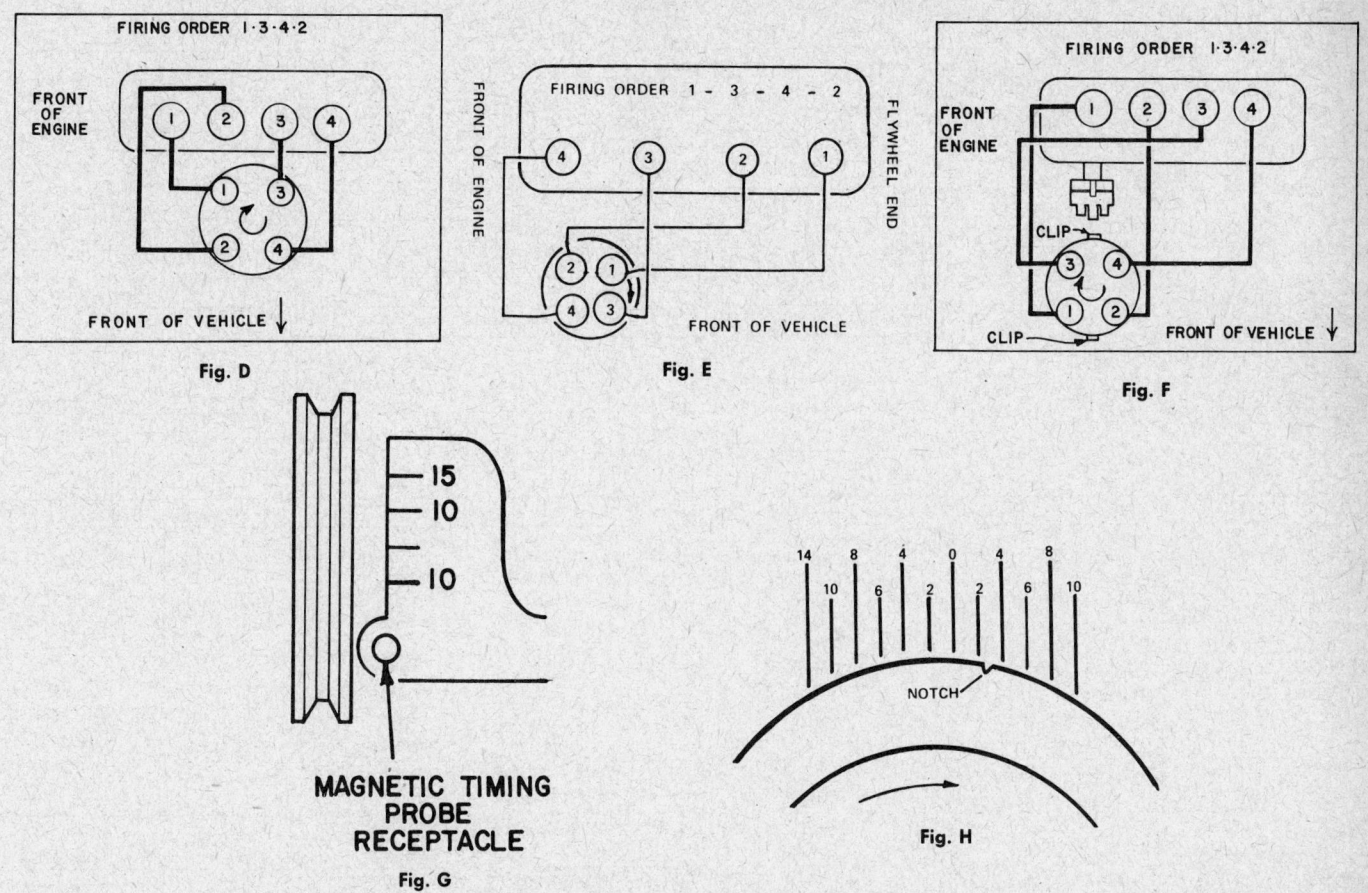

Fig. D   Fig. E   Fig. F

MAGNETIC TIMING PROBE RECEPTACLE

Fig. G   Fig. H

DISTRIBUTOR SPECIFICATIONS

★Note: If unit is checked on vehicle, double the RPM and degrees to get crankshaft figures.

| Distributor Part No.① | Centrifugal Advance Degrees @ RPM of Distributor | | | Vacuum Advance | |
	Advance Starts	Intermediate Advance	Full Advance	Start Dist. Degrees @ Inches of Vacuum	Maximum Dist. Degrees
1978–79					
5206275④	—	—	—	—	—
1980					
5206935②	.2 @ 600	1.5–3.5 @ 650	3.7–5.7 @ 2500	.8–2.5 @ 7"	11.5
5206925②	0 @ 575	6 @ 800	11 @ 2800	2 @ 11"	12.5
5206945③④	—	—	—	—	—
1981–82					
4243694③	0 @ 600	6 @ 1400	10 @ 3000	0 @ 5.1	7.5
4243707②	0 @ 600	6 @ 1400	10 @ 3000	0 @ 3.1	10
5206945	—	—	—	—	—
5206975	—	—	—	—	—
1983					
5213366	—	—	—	—	—
5206945	—	—	—	—	—
5206975	—	—	—	—	—
4243694③	0 @ 600	6 @ 1400	10 @ 3000	0 @ 5.1	7.5
4243707②	0 @ 600	6 @ 1400	10 @ 3000	0 @ 3.1	10

DISTRIBUTOR SPECIFICATIONS—Continued

★Note: If unit is checked on vehicle, double the RPM and degrees to get crankshaft figures.

Distributor Part No. ①	Centrifugal Advance Degrees @ RPM of Distributor			Vacuum Advance	
	Advance Starts	Intermediate Advance	Full Advance	Start Dist. Degrees @ Inches of Vacuum	Maximum Dist. Degrees
1984					
4243134	—	—	—	—	—
4243251	—	—	—	—	—
5206525	—	—	—	—	—
5206975	—	—	—	—	—
5213366	—	—	—	—	—

①—Stamped on distributor housing
②—Exc. Calif.
③—Calif.
④—Electronic spark control (Lean Burn) system.

VALVE SPECIFICATIONS

Year	Model/ VIN	Valve Lash		Valve Angles		Valve Spring Installed Height Inch (Milli-meters)	Valve Spring Pressure Lbs. @ In.	Stem Clearance		Stem Diameter	
		Int. in. (MM)	Exh. in. (MM)	Seat	Face			Intake Inch (Milli-meters) ①	Exhaust Inch (Milli-meters) ①	Intake Inch (Milli-meters)	Exhaust Inch (Milli-meters)
1978–80	4–105/A (1700 cc)	.008C (.20C)	.016C (.30C)	45°	45°	③	④	.020 (.5)	.027 (.7)	.314 (7.97)	.313 (7.95)
1981–83	4–105/A (1700 cc)	.010H (.25H)	.018H (.45H)	45°	45°	③	④	.020 (.5)	.027 (.7)	.314 (7.97)	.313 (7.95)
1981–84	4–135/⑤ (2200 cc)	Hydraulic		45°	45°	1.65 (41.9)	⑦	.0009–.0026 (.022–.065)	⑥	.312–.313 (7.935–7.953)	.311–.312 (7.906–7.924)
	4–156/⑤ (2600 cc)	.006H② (.15H)	.010H (.25H)	43°	45°	1.59 (40.4)	61 @ 1.59	.0012–.0024 (.03–.06)	.0020–.0035 (.05–.09)	.300 (8)	.300 (8)
1983–84	4–97/A (1600 cc)	.010C (.25C)	.012C (.35C)	46°	45°	—	—	.0015–.00275 (.037–.070)	.00225–.0035 (.057–.090)	.3137 (7.970)	.3129 (7.950)

①—Refer to text.
②—Jet valve clearance, .006H.
③—Inner valve spring, 1.13 inch (28.6 mm); outer valve spring, 1.28 inch (32.6 mm).
④—Inner valve spring, 48 @ .720; outer valve spring, 100 @ .878.
⑤—For V.I.N. code, refer to the "General Engine Specifications" at the front of the chapter.
⑥—On 1981–82 stem clearance is .0028–.0044 (.070–.113) & on 1983–84 stem clearance is .0030–.0047 (.076–.119).
⑦—Exc. 1984 VIN codes C & D, 175 lbs. @ 1.22 in.; 1984 VIN codes C & D, 135 lbs. @ 1.22 in.

ENGINE TIGHTENING SPECIFICATIONS★

★Torque specifications are for clean and lightly lubricated threads only. Dry or dirty threads produce increased friction which prevents accurate measurement of tightness.

Year	Engine Model/ VIN	Spark Plugs Ft. Lbs.	Cylinder Head Bolts Ft. Lbs.	Intake Manifold Inch Lbs.	Exhaust Manifold Inch Lbs.	Camshaft Cover Inch Lbs.	Connecting Rod Cap Bolts Ft. Lbs.	Main Bearing Cap Bolts Ft. Lbs.	Flywheel to Crankshaft Ft. Lbs.	Crankshaft Pulley Ft. Lbs.
1978–80	4-105/A 1700 cc	20	60①	200②	150	48	35	47	52	58
1981–83	4-105/④ 1700 cc	20	60①	200②	200	48	35	47	⑤	58
1981–84	4-135/④ 2200 cc	20	45①	200	200	105	40①	30①	65	20.8
	4-156/④ 2600 cc	20	③	150	150	53	34	58	100	87
1983–84	4-97/A 1600 cc	20	52	133	180	44⑥	28	48	—	110

①—Turn torque wrench an additional 90 degrees after the specified torque has been achieved.
②—Intake to exhaust manifold inboard nut, 150 inch lbs. Intake to exhaust manifold out-board nut, 200 inch lbs.
③—Cold engine, 69 ft. lbs.; warm engine, 76 ft. lbs.
④—For V.I.N. code, refer to the "General Engine Specifications" at the front of the chapter.
⑤—Man. trans., 60 ft. lbs.; auto. trans., 40 ft. lbs.
⑥—Rocker arm covers.

PISTONS, PINS, RINGS, CRANKSHAFT & BEARINGS

Year	Engine Model/ VIN	Piston Clearance Top of Skirt Inch (Millimeter)	Ring End Gap① Comp. Inch (Milli- meter)	Ring End Gap① Oil Inch (Milli- meter)	Wristpin Diameter Inch (Millimeter)	Rod Bearings Shaft Diameter Inch (Millimeter)	Rod Bearings Bearing Clearance Inch (Millimeter)	Main Bearings Shaft Diameter Inch (Millimeter)	Main Bearings Bearing Clearance Inch (Millimeter)	Thrust on Bear. No.	Shaft End Play Inch (Millimeter)
1978–80	4-105/A 1700 cc	.0004–.0015 (.011–.039)	.012 (.3)	.012 (.3)	.866 (21.997– 22.001)	1.81 (46)	.0004–.0025 (.010–.064)	2.12 (54)	.0008–.0030 (.020–.080)	3	.003–.007 (.07–.18)
1981–83	4-105/A 1700 cc	.0004–.0015 (.011–.039)	.012 (.3)	.016 (.41)	.866 (21.997– 22.001)	1.8087–1.8094 (45.94–45.96)	.0011–.0034 (.028–.088)	2.1236–2.1244 (53.94–53.96)	.0008–.0030 (.020–.080)	3	.003–.007 (.07–.18)
1981	4-135/B 2200 cc	.0005–.0015 (.013–.038)	.011 (.28)	.015 (.38)	.9008 (22.88)	1.968–1.969 (49.987–50.013)	.0004–.0026 (.011–.067)	2.362–2.363 (59.987–60.013)	.0004–.0026 (.011–.067)	3	.002–.007 (.05–.18)
1981–84	4-156/② 2600 cc	.0008–.0016 (.02–.04)	.010 (.25)	.0078 (.2)	.866 (22)	2.0866 (53)	.0008–.0028 (.02–.07)	2.3622 (60)	.0008–.0028 (.02–.07)	3	.002–.007 (.05–.18)
1983–84	4-97/A 1600 cc	.0016–.0020 (.041–.051)	.012 (.3)	.010 (.25)	.866 (21.991– 21.995)	1.6124–1.6127 (40.957–40.965)	.001–.0025 (.025–.064)	2.046–2.047 (51.975–51.985)	.0009–.0031 (.04–.078)	3	.0035–.011 (.09–.27)

①—Minimum.   ②—For V.I.N. code, refer to the "General Engine   Specifications" at the front of the chapter.

ALTERNATOR & REGULATOR SPECIFICATIONS

Year	Alternator Part Number	Alternator Rated Hot Output Amps.	Alternator Field Current 12 Volts @ 80° F.	Alternator Output @ 15 Volts 1250 R.P.M.	Regulator Part Number	Field Relay Air Gap In.	Field Relay Point Gap In.	Field Relay Closing Voltage	Voltage Regulator Air Gap In.	Voltage Regulator Point Gap In.	Voltage Regulator Voltage @ 80° F.
1978–81	Yellow①	60	5	57	4091050	—	—	—	—	—	13.9–14.6
	Brown①	65	5	62	—	—	—	—	—	—	13.9–14.6
1981–84	A4T25191②	75	—	63–70③	Integral	—	—	—	—	—	14.1–14.7④
1982–83	Yellow①	60	4.5–6.5	45	4111990	—	—	—	—	—	13.9–14.6
	Brown①	78	4.5–6.5	56	4111990	—	—	—	—	—	13.9–14.6
1983–84	K1⑤	65	4.5–6.5	50	—	—	—	—	—	—	—
1984	Yellow	60	2.5–5.0	45	—	—	—	—	—	—	13.9–14.6
	Brown	78	2.5–5.0	56	—	—	—	—	—	—	13.9–14.6
	B120 427 850MP⑤	90	—	78–85③	Integral	—	—	—	—	—	13.8–14.2⑥

①—Chrysler alternator.　③—At 13.5 volts & 1000 RPM.　⑤—Bosch alternator.
②—Mitsubishi alternator.　④—At 68° F.　⑥—At 77° F.

STARTING MOTOR APPLICATIONS

Year	Engine/VIN	Model	Ident. Number	Year	Engine/VIN	Model	Ident. Number
1978–80	4-105/A (1700 cc)①	Bosch	5206260	1982–83	4-105 (1700 cc)①③	Bosch	5213395
	4-105/A (1700 cc)①	Nippondenso	5206270		4-105 (1700 cc)①③	Nippondenso	5213295
1978–83	4-105 (1700 cc)②③	Bosch	5206255		4-135 (2200 cc)①③	Bosch	5213045
	4-105 (1700 cc)②③	Nippondenso	5206265		4-135 (2200 cc)②③	Bosch	5213395
1981	4-105/A (1700 cc)①	Bosch	5213080		4-135 (2200 cc)③	Nippondenso	5213645
	4-105/A (1700 cc)①	Nippondenso	5213085	1983–84	4-97/A (1600 cc)	Mitsubishi	5213301
	4-135/B (2200 cc)	Bosch	5213045	1984	4-135 (2200 cc)④	Bosch	5213045
	4-135/B (2200 cc)	Nippondenso	5213190		4-135 (2200 cc)④	Nippondenso	5213645
1981–84	4-156/D (2600 cc)	Nippondenso	5213235		4-135/E (2200 cc)	Bosch	5213450

①—Automatic Transmission.　③—For V.I.N. code, refer to the "General Engine　④—VIN codes C, D & F
②—Manual Transmission.　Specifications" at the front of the chapter.

WHEEL ALIGNMENT SPECIFICATIONS

Year	Model	Caster Angle, Degrees		Camber Angle, Degrees					Toe In. Inch	Toe Out on Turns, Deg.	
		Limits	Desired	Limits			Desired			Outer Wheel	Inner Wheel
				Left	Right		Left	Right			
1978–83	Horizon & Omni①	—	—	−1/4 to +3/4	−1/4 to +3/4		+5/16	+5/16	②	—	—
	Horizon & Omni③	—	—	⑦	⑦		⑦	⑦	④	—	—
1981	Aries & Reliant①	—	—	−1/4 to +3/4	−1/4 to +3/4		+5/16	+5/16	⑤	—	—
	Aries & Reliant③	—	—	−1 to 0	−1 to 0		−1/2	−1/2	⑥	—	—
1982–83	Aries & Reliant①	—	—	−1/4 to +3/4	−1/4 to +3/4		+5/16	+5/16	⑤	—	—
	Aries & Reliant③	—	—	−1 to 0	−1 to 0		−1/2	−1/2	⑥	—	—
	LeBaron & 400①	—	—	−1/4 to +3/4	−1/4 to +3/4		+5/16	+5/16	⑤	—	—
	LeBaron & 400③	—	—	−1 to 0	−1 to 0		−1/2	−1/2	⑥	—	—
1983	Charger & Turismo①	—	—	−1/4 to +3/4	−1/4 to +3/4		+5/16	+5/16	⑤	—	—
	Charger & Turismo③	—	—	−1/4 to −1 1/4	−1/4 to −1 1/4		−3/4	−3/4	④	—	—
	New Yorker, E Class & 600①	—	—	−1/4 to +3/4	−1/4 to +3/4		+5/16	+5/16	⑤	—	—
	New Yorker, E Class & 600③	—	—	−1 to 0	−1 to 0		−1/2	−1/2	⑥	—	—
1984	All①	—	—	−1/4 to +3/4	−1/4 to +3/4		+5/16	+5/16	⑤	—	—
	Charger, Horizon, Omni & Turismo③	—	—	−1 1/4 to −1/4	−1 1/4 to −1/4		−3/4	−3/4	④	—	—
	Exc. Charger, Horizon, Omni & Turismo③	—	—	−1 to 0	−1 to 0		−1/2	−1/2	⑥	—	—

①—Front wheel alignment.
②—1978–80, 5/32" out to 1/8" in (.3° out to .2° in); 1981–83, 7/32" out to 1/8" in (.4° out to .2° in).
③—Rear wheel alignment.
④—5/32" out to 11/32" in (.3° out to .7° in).
⑤—7/32" out to 1/8" in (.4° out to .2° in).
⑥—3/16" out to 3/16" in (.38° out to .38° in).
⑦—1978–81 Limits, −1 1/4° to −1/2°; Desired, −1°. 1982–83 Limits, −1 1/4° to −1/4°; Desired, −3/4°.

COOLING SYSTEM & CAPACITY DATA

Year	Model or Engine/VIN	Cooling Capacity		Radiator Cap Relief Pressure, Lbs.	Thermo. Opening Temp. Degrees F. (Centigrade)	Fuel Tank Gals. (Litres)	Engine Oil Refill Qts. (Litres)	Transmission Oil		Final Drive Pints (Litres) ②
		Less A/C Qts. (Litres)	With A/C Qts. (Litres)					4 & 5 Speed Pints (Litres)	Auto. Trans. Qts. (Litres) ①	
1978–80	All/⑧	⑨	⑨	16	195 (90.6)	13 (49)	4④ (3.8)	2.8 (1.25)	7.3③ (6.9)	2.4 (1.1)
1981–82	4-105/A (1.7L)	6 (5.7)	6 (5.7)	16	195 (90.6)	13 (49)	4④ (3.8)	3 (1.4)	7.3⑤ (6.9)	2.4 (1.1)
	4-135/B (2.2L)	7 (6.6)	7 (6.6)	16	195 (90.6)	13 (49)	4④ (3.8)	4 (1.8)	7.5⑤ (7.1)	2.4 (1.1)
	4-156/D (2.6L)	8.5 (8.1)	8.5 (8.1)	16	190 (88)	13 (49)	5⑥ (5)	4 (1.8)	8.5⑤ (8.1)	2.4 (1.1)
1983	4-97 (1.6L)/A	7 (6.6)	7 (6.6)	16	195 (90.6)	13 (49)	3.5⑥ (3.3)	⑪	—	—
	4-105 (1.7L)/B	6 (5.7)	6 (5.7)	16	195 (90.6)	13 (49)	4④ (3.8)	⑪	8.4⑦ (7.9)	2.4 (1.1)
	4-135 (2.2L)/⑧	9 (8.5)	9 (8.5)	16	195 (90.6)	13⑩ (49)	4④ (3.8)	⑪	8.9⑦⑫ (8.4)	2.4 (1.1)
	4-156 (2.6L)/G	9 (8.5)	9 (8.5)	16	190 (88)	13 (49)	4④ (3.8)	⑪	8.9⑦⑫ (8.4)	2.4 (1.1)
1984	4-97 (1.6L)/A	6.8 (6.4)	6.8 (6.4)	16	195 (90.6)	13 (49)	3.5⑥ (3.3)	3.8⑬ (1.7)	8.9⑦ (8.4)	2.4 (1.1)
	4-135 (2.2L)/⑧	9 (8.5)	9 (8.5)	16	195 (90.6)	⑭	4.0④ (3.8)	4.0⑬ (1.8)	8.9⑦⑫ (8.4)	2.4 (1.1)
	4-156 (2.6L)/G	9 (8.5)	9 (8.5)	16	190 (88)	14 (53)	5.0⑥ (4.8)	—	8.9⑦⑫ (8.4)	2.4 (1.1)

①—Approximate. Make final check with dipstick.
②—Automatic trans. only.
③—Drain & refill, 2.5 qts.
④—With or without filter change.
⑤—Drain & refill, 3 qts.
⑥—Includes 1/2 qt. for filter change.
⑦—Drain & refill, 4 qts.
⑧—For V.I.N. code, refer to "General Engine Specifications" at the front of the chapter.
⑨—Exc. 1978, 6.0 qts. (5.7L); 1978, 6.5 qts. (6.2L).
⑩—EFI models, 14.0 gals.
⑪—A-412, 3.0 pts.; A-460, 4.0 pts.; A-465 (5 spd.), 4.6 pts.
⑫—Vehicles with fleet option package, 9.2 qts.
⑬—5 spd. transaxle, 4.6 pts.
⑭—Exc. Charger, Horizon, Omni & Turismo—14.0 gals.; Charger, Horizon, Omni & Turismo—13.0 gals.

Electrical Section

STARTER, REPLACE

4-97, 4-135 & 1981—83 4-105

1. Disconnect battery ground cable.
2. Remove starter to flywheel housing and rear bracket to engine or transaxle attaching bolts.
3. On models equipped with 4-135 engine, loosen air pump tube at exhaust manifold, then position tube bracket away from starter motor.
4. If equipped, remove heat shield clamp and heat shield.
5. Disconnect starter cable at starter motor and solenoid leads at solenoid, then remove starter motor.
6. Reverse procedure to install.

4-156 & 1978—80 4-105

1. Disconnect battery ground cable.
2. Disconnect starter cable at starter.
3. Disconnect solenoid lead wire from solenoid.
4. Remove starter attaching bolts and the starter.
5. Reverse procedure to install.

IGNITION LOCK, REPLACE

Exc. 1978—84 Horizon & Omni; 1983—84 Charger & Turismo

Models Less Tilt Column
1. Disconnect battery ground cable.
2. Remove turn signal switch as described under Turn Signal Switch, Replace.
3. Disconnect horn and ignition key lamp ground wires, then remove ignition key lamp attaching screw and lamp.
4. Remove four screws attaching upper bearing housing to lock housing, then remove snap ring from upper end of steering shaft and remove upper bearing housing.
5. Remove lock plate spring and lock plate from steering shaft.
6. Position lock cylinder in Lock position and remove ignition key.
7. Remove key waring buzzer attaching screws, then remove buzzer.
8. Remove two screws attaching ignition switch to steering column, then remove switch by rotating switch 90° and sliding from rod.

9. Remove two screws attaching dimmer switch, then disengage dimmer switch from actuator rod.
10. Remove two bellcrank attaching screws, then slide bellcrank up into lock housing until it can be disconnected from ignition switch actuator rod.
11. With lock cylinder in Lock position, insert a small diameter screwdriver into lock cylinder release holes and push inward until spring loaded lock cylinder retainers release, Fig. 1.
12. Grasp lock cylinder and pull from lock housing bore.
13. Reverse procedure to install. The lock cylinder and ignition switch must be in the Lock position.

Models W/Tilt Column
1. Disconnect battery ground cable.
2. Remove turn signal switch as described under Turn Signal Switch, Replace.
3. Remove ignition key lamp.
4. Position ignition lock cylinder in the Lock position, then remove ignition key.
5. Insert a thin screwdriver into lock cylinder release slot and depress spring latch which release lock cylinder, then grasp lock cylinder and remove from column, Fig. 2.
6. Reverse procedure to install.

1978—84 Horizon & Omni; 1983—84 Charger & Turismo

1. Remove steering wheel, column covers and turn signal switch.
2. With a hack saw blade, cut the upper 1/4 inch from the retainer pin boss, Fig. 3.
3. Using a suitable drift, drive roll pin from housing and remove lock cylinder.
4. Insert new cylinder into housing, ensuring that it engages the lug or ignition switch driver.
5. Install roll pin.
6. Check for proper operation.

IGNITION SWITCH, REPLACE

Exc. 1978—84 Horizon & Omni; 1983—84 Charger & Turismo

1. Disconnect battery ground cable.
2. Remove under panel sound deadener.
3. Disconnect speed control switch.
4. Remove two screws attaching switch to column.
5. Rotate switch 90° and pull-up to disen-

gage from ignition switch rod, Fig. 4.
6. Reverse procedure to install. When installing new switch push up gently on switch to take up slack in rod system.

1978—84 Horizon & Omni; 1983—84 Charger & Turismo

1. Disconnect battery ground cable.
2. Remove connector from ignition switch.
3. Place ignition lock in "Lock" position and remove key.
4. Remove the two ignition switch mounting screws and permit the switch and push rod to drop below the column jacket, Fig. 5.
5. Rotate the switch 90° for removal of switch from push rod.
6. Position ignition switch in "Lock" position, the second detent from the top of the switch.
7. Place switch at right angle to column and insert push rod.
8. Align switch on bracket and loosely install screws.
9. With a light rearward load on the switch, tighten attaching screws.
10. Connect ignition switch wiring connector and battery ground cable.
11. Check for proper operation.

LIGHT SWITCH, REPLACE

Exc. 1978—84 Horizon & Omni; 1983—84 Charger & Turismo

1. Disconnect battery ground cable, then place gearshift lever in "1" position.
2. Remove left upper and lower instrument cluster bezel attaching screws, then detach bezel from five retaining clips and remove bezel.
3. Remove three screws attaching headlamp switch retainer plate to instrument panel.
4. Pull headlamp switch and retainer plate rearward and disconnect wire connector, then depress button on switch and remove switch knob and stem.
5. Remove switch retainer plate escutcheon, then remove nut attaching switch to plate.
6. Reverse procedure to install.

1978—84 Horizon & Omni; 1983—84 Charger & Turismo

1. Disconnect battery ground cable.
2. Reach under instrument panel and depress light switch knob release button, then pull light switch knob and shaft from switch.
3. Remove four bezel attaching screws and the bezel.

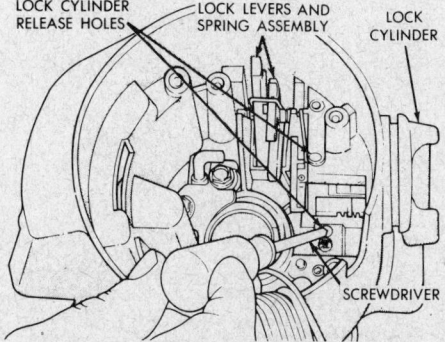

Fig. 1 Ignition lock cylinder removal. Models with standard column exc. 1978—84 Horizon & Omni; 1983—84 Charger & Turismo

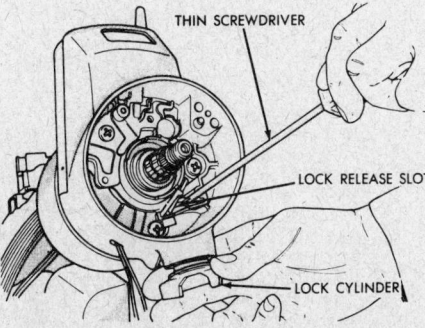

Fig. 2 Ignition lock cylinder removal. Models with tilt column exc. 1978—84 Horizon & Omni; 1983—84 Charger & Turismo

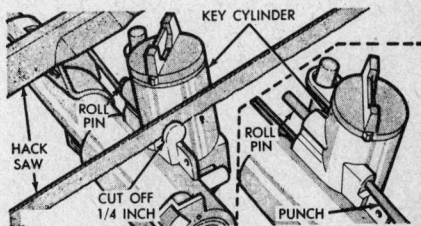

Fig. 3 Ignition lock cylinder retaining pin removal. 1978—84 Horizon & Omni; 1983—84 Charger & Turismo

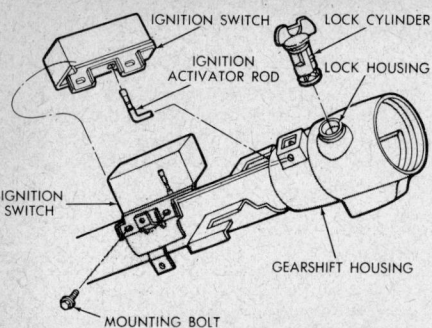

Fig. 4 Ignition switch replacement. Exc. 1978–84 Horizon & Omni; 1983–84 Charger & Turismo

4. Remove switch attaching screws and disconnect electrical connector from switch, Fig. 6.
5. Remove switch from panel.
6. Reverse procedure to install.

DIMMER SWITCH, REPLACE

Exc. 1978–84 Horizon & Omni; 1983–84 Charger & Turismo

1. Disconnect battery ground cable, then disconnect electrical connector from switch.
2. Remove two screws attaching switch to column, Fig. 7.
3. Reverse procedure to install. During installation, gently push up on switch to take up slack on rod.

1978–84 Horizon & Omni; 1983–84 Charger & Turismo

1. Disconnect battery ground cable, then disconnect connector from switch.
2. Remove the two switch mounting screws and disengage switch from push rod, Figs. 7 and 8.
3. To install switch, firmly seat push rod into switch, then compress switch until two .093 inch drill shanks can be inserted into alignment holes. Position upper end of push rod in pocket of wash/wipe switch.

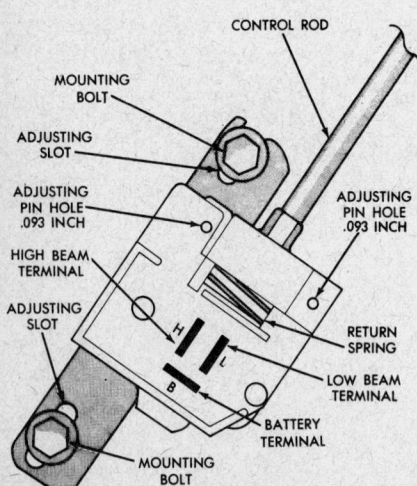

Fig. 8 Dimmer switch installation. 1978–84 Horizon & Omni; 1983–84 Charger & Turismo

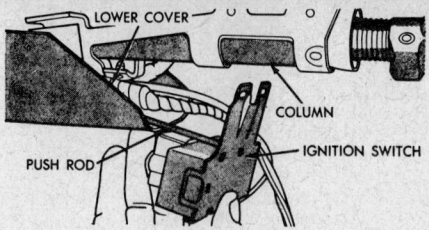

Fig. 5 Ignition switch replacement. 1978–84 Omni & Horizon; 1983–84 Charger & Turismo

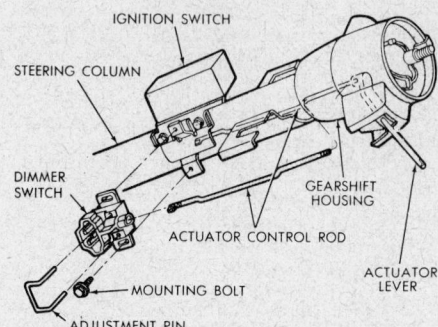

Fig. 7 Dimmer switch replacement. Exc. 1978–84 Horizon & Omni; 1983–84 Charger & Turismo

---

NOTE: This can be done by feel, or if necessary, by removing lower column cover.

---

4. Apply a light rearward pressure on switch, then install screws and remove drills.

NOTE: The switch should click when lever is lifted, and again as lever returns, just before it reaches its stop in the down position.

---

5. Reconnect wiring connector to switch and connect battery ground cable.

TURN SIGNAL SWITCH, REPLACE

Exc. 1978–84 Horizon & Omni; 1983–84 Charger & Turismo

1. Disconnect battery ground cable.

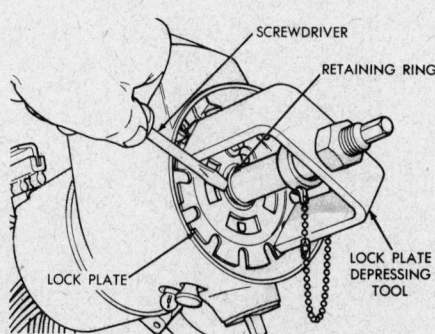

Fig. 9 Lock plate removal. Models with tilt column exc. 1978–84 Horizon & Omni; 1983–84 Charger & Turismo

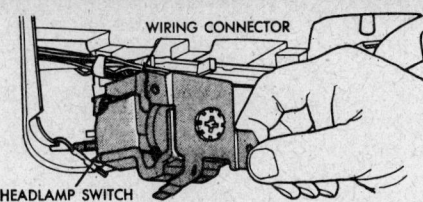

Fig. 6 Light switch replacement (Typical)

2. Remove horn button and switch and steering wheel nut, then remove steering wheel using a suitable puller.
3. Remove instrument panel lower bezel and steering column cover.
4. On models with tilt steering column, remove transmission gearshift indicator, then remove two nuts attaching steering column to lower panel. Remove four attaching bolts, then remove bracket from column.
5. On models less tilt column, position gearshift lever into its full clockwise position. On models with tilt column, place gearshift lever to its midway position.
6. On models with tilt column, carefully remove plastic cover from lock plate, then depress lock plate with tool No. C-4156 and remove snap ring, Fig. 9. Remove lock plate, canceling cam and upper bearing spring from steering shaft.
7. Remove turn signal lever attaching screws, then remove lever. On models with speed control allow lever to hang from column.
8. Remove turn signal switch and upper bearing attaching screws, then carefully remove turn signal switch, while guiding wire up through column opening, Fig. 10.
9. Reverse procedure to install.

1978–84 Horizon & Omni; 1983–84 Charger & Turismo

Removal

1. Disconnect battery ground cable.
2. Remove horn button or horn pad, three screws and the horn switch.
3. Remove steering wheel nut and the steering wheel with a suitable puller.
4. Remove four screws from the lower steering column cover and the cover.

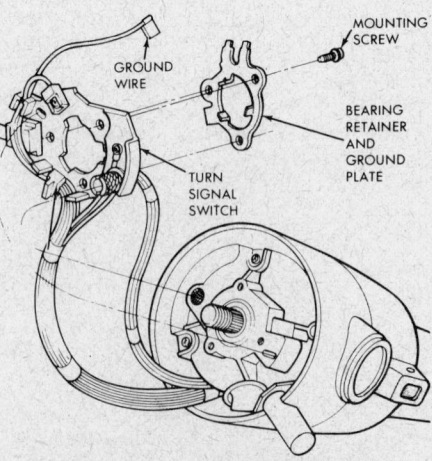

Fig. 10 Turn signal switch replacement. Exc. 1978–84 Horizon & Omni; 1983–84 Charger & Turismo

5. Remove screw securing washer-wiper switch and position switch aside.
6. Disconnect turn signal and hazard warning wiring connector, disengage wiring harness from support bracket and remove vinyl tape securing key in buzzer wires to turn signal harness.
7. Remove three turn signal switch retainer screws, Fig. 11.
8. Remove turn signal and hazard warning switch while guiding wiring harness out from column.

Installation
1. Guide wiring harness downward through column until the switch is properly seated.
2. Install switch retainer and the three screws.
3. Snap plastic harness retainer into support bracket, connect harness connector and tape key in buzzer wires to harness.
4. Install washer-wiper switch and retaining screw.
5. Install lower steering column cover.
6. Install steering wheel, horn switch and horn button.
7. Connect battery ground cable.

INSTRUMENT CLUSTER, REPLACE

1981–84 Aries, Reliant; 1982–83 LeBaron, 400; 1983 E Class, Executive, New Yorker & 600

1. Disconnect battery ground cable.

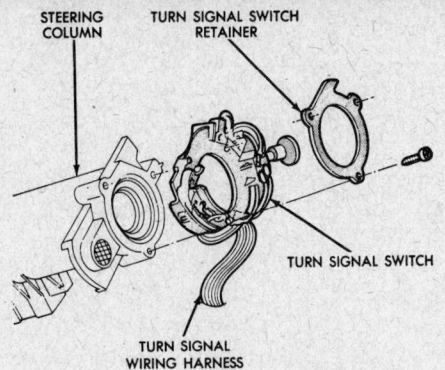

Fig. 11 Turn signal switch replacement. 1978–84 Horizon & Omni; 1983–84 Charger & Turismo

2. Remove screws securing instrument cluster bezel and pull bezel from retaining clips, Fig. 12.
3. Remove screws securing upper right bezel and bezel.
4. Remove screws securing instrument panel pad, as needed, and raise pad slightly to allow cluster removal.
5. Remove 4 screws securing instrument cluster and pull cluster away from dash.
6. Disconnect electrical connectors and speedometer cable, then remove cluster.
7. Reverse procedure to install.

1984 E Class, Executive, LeBaron, New Yorker & 600

1. Disconnect battery ground cable.
2. Remove screws securing instrument cluster bezel, Fig. 12A, and the bezel.
3. Remove screws securing instrument panel pad, Fig. 12B, and raise pad slightly to allow cluster removal.
4. Remove 4 screws securing cluster and pull cluster from dash.
5. Disconnect electrical connectors and speedometer cable, if equipped, then remove cluster.
6. Reverse procedure to install.

1984 Daytona & Laser

1. Disconnect battery ground cable.
2. Remove screws securing cluster bezel and the bezel.
3. Remove 4 screws securing cluster and pull cluster away from dash.
4. Disconnect electrical connectors and speedometer cable, if equipped, then remove cluster.
5. Reverse procedure to install.

1978–83 Horizon, Omni; 1983 Charger & Turismo

1. Disconnect battery ground cable.
2. Remove two mask-lens assembly lower attaching spring pins by pulling rearward with suitable pliers.
3. Pull mask-lens rearward, lower slightly and remove from cluster.
4. Disconnect speedometer cable.
5. Remove two speedometer attaching

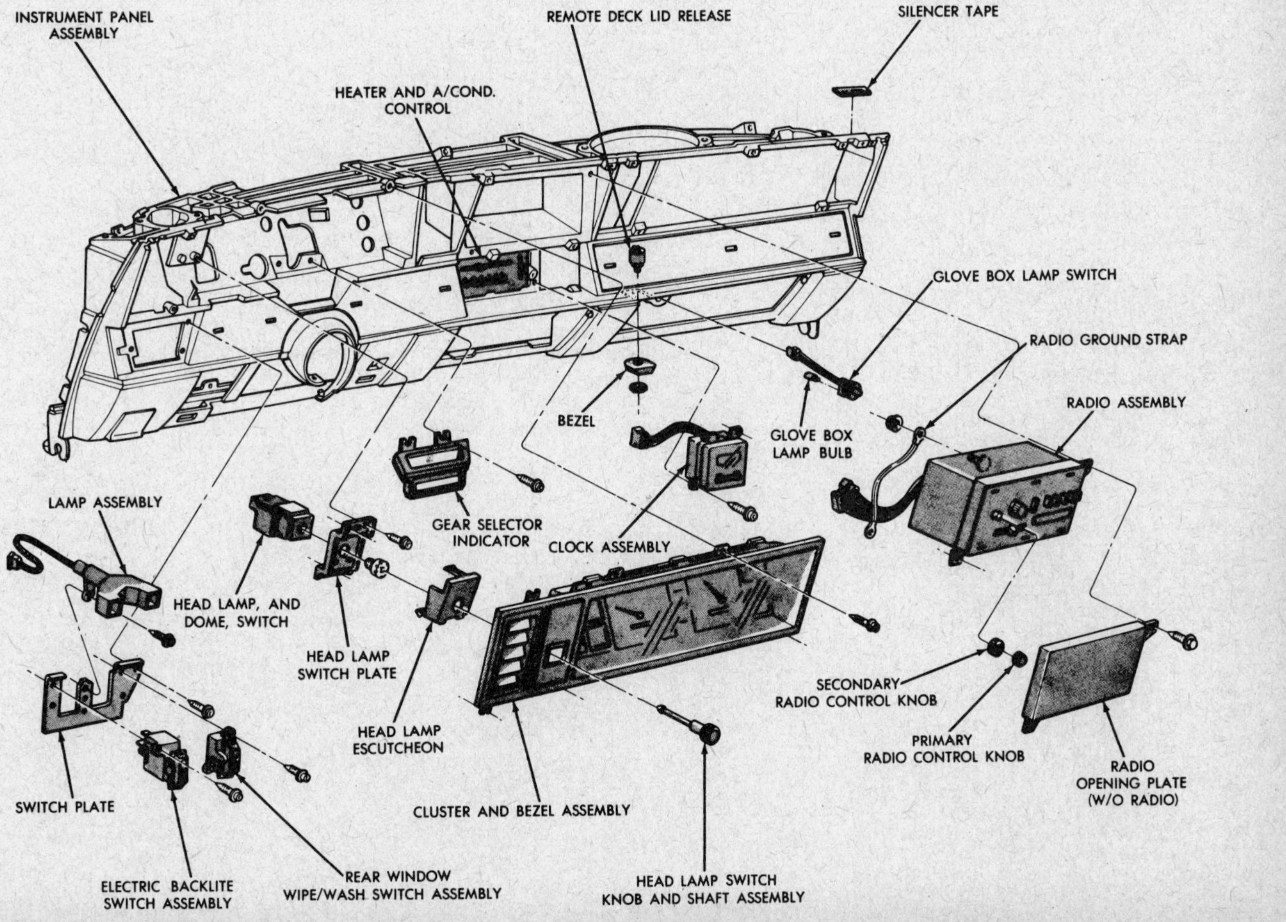

Fig. 12 Instrument panel, exploded view (Typical). 1981–84 Aries & Reliant; 1982–83 LeBaron & 400; 1983 E Class, Executive, New Yorker & 600

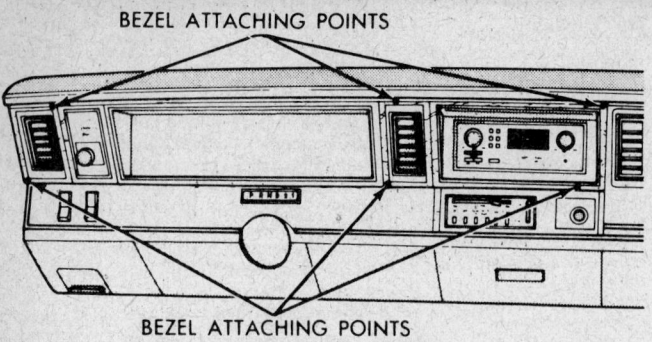

Fig 12A Instrument cluster removal. 1984 E Class, Executive Sedan, LeBaron, New Yorker & 600

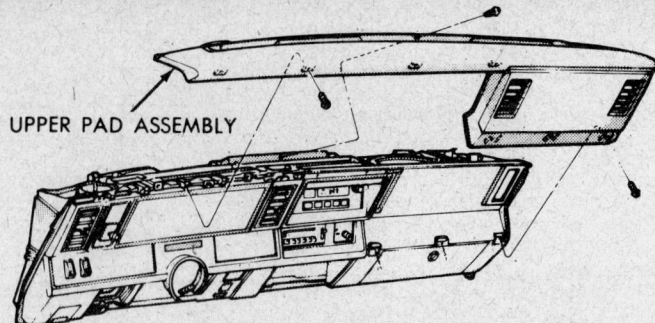

Fig 12B Instrument panel pad removal. 1984 E Class, Executive Sedan, LeBaron, New Yorker & 600

screws and the speedometer.

6. Disengage two wiring harness connectors. On Rallye cluster disconnect three harness connectors.
7. Remove two cluster attaching screws, Fig. 13. On Rallye cluster remove four screws.
8. Remove cluster upper attaching spring pins and pull cluster from panel.
9. Disconnect clock wiring, if equipped.
10. Remove cluster from vehicle.
11. Reverse procedure to install.

1984 Charger, Horizon, Omni & Turismo

1. Disconnect battery ground cable.
2. Remove 2 lower cluster bezel retaining screws, Fig. 13A.
3. Allow bezel to drop slightly, then remove bezel.
4. Remove 4 screws securing instrument cluster and pull cluster away from dash.
5. Disconnect electrical connectors and speedometer cable, then remove cluster.
6. Reverse procedure to install.

WIPER SWITCH, REPLACE

Exc. 1978—84 Horizon & Omni; 1983—84 Charger and Turismo

1. Disconnect battery ground cable and remove steering wheel, using a suitable puller.
2. On models equipped with intermittent wiper system, remove two screws attaching turn signal lever cover to lock housing and remove turn signal lever cover.
3. Remove screw attaching W/S wiper switch and the switch, Fig. 14.
4. Reverse procedure to install.

1978—84 Horizon & Omni; 1983—84 Charger & Turismo

1. Disconnect battery ground cable.
2. Disconnect wiper switch and turn signal switch wiring harness connectors.
3. Remove lower column cover.
4. Remove horn button.
5. Place ignition lock in "Off" position and turn steering wheel so the access hole in the hub area is at the 9 o'clock position on 1978 and 1983—84 models, and in the 3 o'clock position on 1979–82 models.

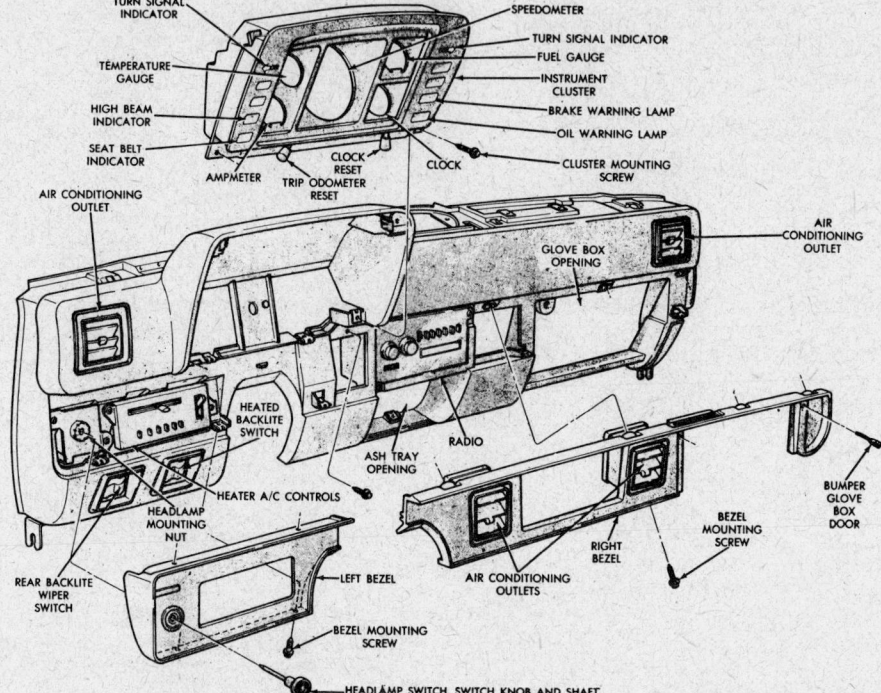

Fig. 13 Instrument panel, exploded view (Typical). 1978–83 Horizon & Omni; 1983 Charger & Turismo

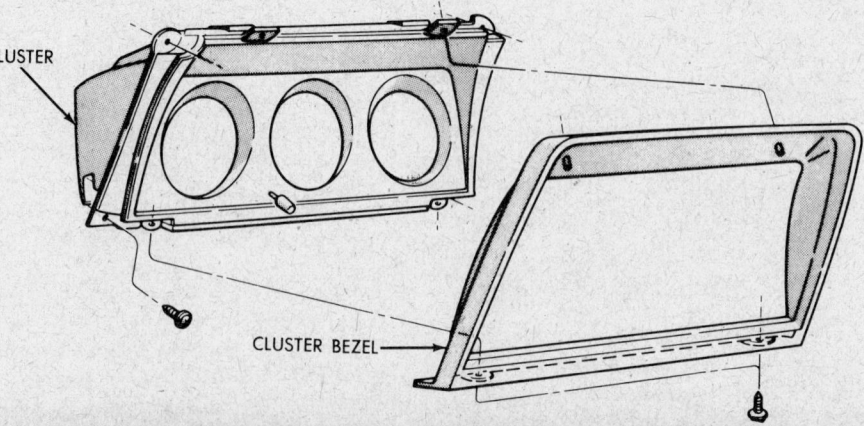

Fig. 13A Instrument cluster & bezel. 1984 Charger, Horizon, Omni & Turismo

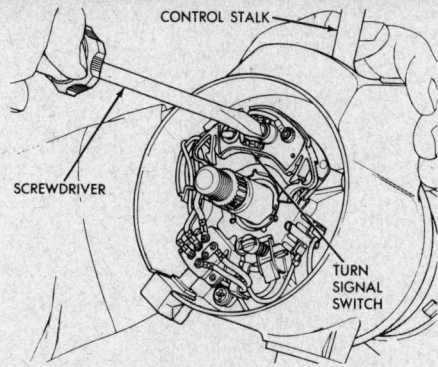

Fig. 14 W/S wiper switch removal. Exc. 1978–84 Horizon & Omni; 1983–84 Charger & Turismo

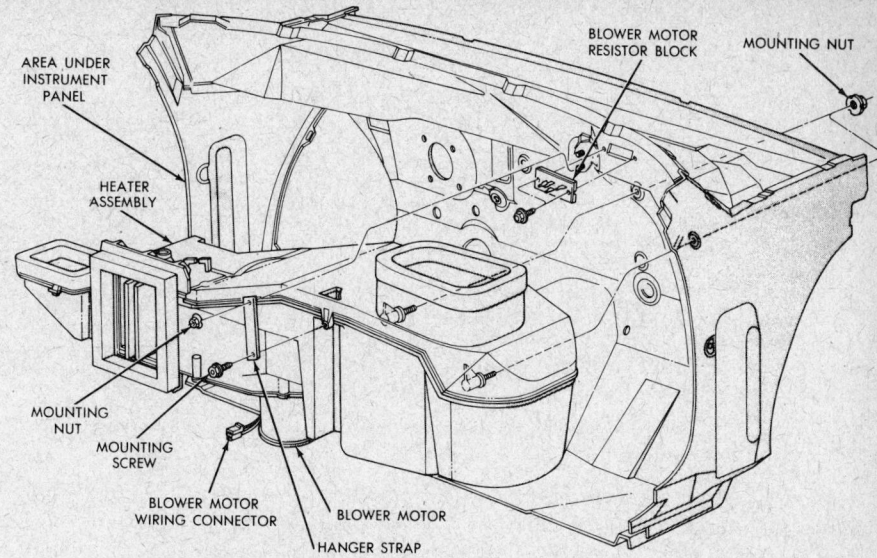

Fig. 15 Heater assembly. Models less A/C exc. 1978–84 Horizon & Omni; 1983–84 Charger & Turismo

6. With a suitable screwdriver, loosen turn signal lever screw through access hole.
7. Disengage dimmer push rod from wiper switch.
8. Unsnap wiring clip and remove wiper switch.
9. Reverse procedure to install.

WINDSHIELD WIPER MOTOR, REPLACE

Front

Exc. 1978–84 Horizon & Omni; 1983–84 Charger & Turismo
1. Disconnect battery ground cable, then remove wiper arms and pivot attaching nuts.
2. Remove plastic screen covering cowl, if equipped, and disconnect reservoir hose from "T" connector on Daytona and Laser.
3. Remove wiper motor cover and disconnect electrical connectors to motor.
4. Push pivots downward into plenum chamber, then pull motor outward to clear mounting stud. Move wiper motor toward driver's side of vehicle as far as possible and pull right hand pivot and link assembly through opening, then move motor toward passenger side of vehicle and remove wiper motor, and left hand pivot and link assembly.
5. Remove nut from end of motor shaft and remove motor crank.
6. Reverse procedure to install.

1978–84 Horizon & Omni; 1983–84 Charger & Turismo
1. Remove wiper arm assemblies.
2. Remove the nuts from the left and right pivots.
3. Remove wiper motor plastic cover.
4. Disconnect wiper motor wiring harness.
5. Remove three bolts from wiper motor mounting bracket.
6. Disengage the pivots from cowl top mounting positions.
7. Remove wiper motor, cranks, pivots and drive link assembly from cowl plenum chamber.

8. Remove wiper motor from drive crank linkage.
9. Reverse procedure to install.

Rear

1981–84 Aries, Reliant & 1982–84 LeBaron, W/ Liftgate
1. Disconnect battery ground cable.
2. Remove wiper arm and blade assembly.
3. Remove wiper motor cover, then disconnect wire connector from motor.
4. Remove four screws attaching wiper motor bracket to liftgate, then remove wiper motor.
5. Reverse procedure to install.

1984 Daytona and Laser
1. Disconnect battery ground cable.
2. Raise wiper arm, release latch and remove arm assembly.
3. Remove inner trim panel and disconnect electrical connector to motor.
4. Remove grommet from liftgate glass.
5. Remove 2 screws securing motor and the motor.
6. Reverse procedure to install.

1978–84 Horizon & Omni; 1983–84 Charger & Turismo
1. Disconnect battery ground cable and remove wiper arm assembly.
2. Remove pivot shaft nut, bezel and seal.
3. Remove wiper motor cover and disconnect electrical connector to motor.
4. Remove screws securing wiper motor and the motor.
5. Reverse procedure to install.

RADIO, REPLACE

1981–84 Aries, Reliant; 1982–83 LeBaron, 400; 1983 E Class, Executive, New Yorker & 600

1. Disconnect battery ground cable, then remove center bezel.
2. On vehicles equipped with mono-speaker, remove speaker, then disconnect from radio.
3. Remove two screws attaching radio to base panel, then pull radio through front face of base panel.

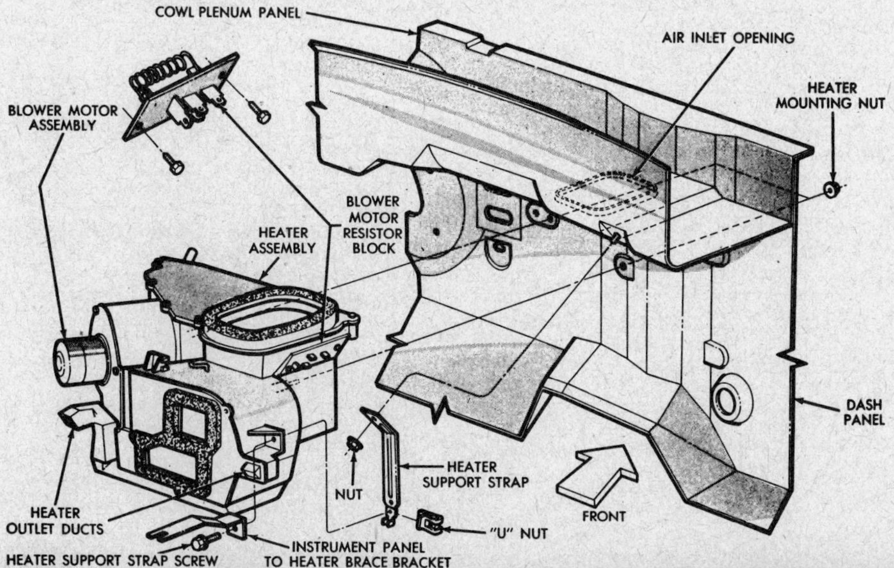

Fig. 16 Heater assembly. 1978–84 Horizon & Omni; 1983–84 Charger & Turismo less A/C

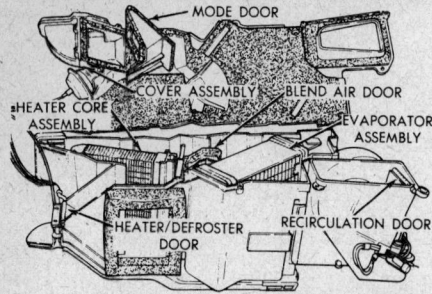

Fig. 17 Heater assembly. Models with A/C exc. 1978–84 Horizon & Omni; 1983–84 Charger & Turismo

4. Disconnect wiring harness, antenna lead and ground strap.
5. Reverse procedure to install.

1984 E Class, Executive Sedan, LeBaron, New Yorker & 600

1. Disconnect battery ground cable.
2. Remove screws securing instrument cluster bezel, Fig. 12A, and the bezel.
3. Remove screws securing radio and pull radio away from dash panel.
4. Disconnect electrical connectors and antenna lead, then remove radio.
5. Reverse procedure to install.

1984 Daytona & Laser

1. Disconnect battery ground cable.
2. Remove 2 screws securing bottom of console bezel, then lift bezel from console.
3. Remove 2 screws securing radio and pull radio away from console.
4. Disconnect electrical connectors and antenna lead, then remove radio.
5. Reverse procedure to install.

1978–84 Horizon & Omni; 1983–84 Charger & Turismo

1. Disconnect battery ground cable.
2. Remove right bezel attaching screws and open the glove box.
3. Remove bezel, guiding the right end around glove box. as needed.
4. Remove radio mounting screws.
5. Pull radio from panel and disconnect wiring, ground strap and antenna lead from radio.
6. Remove radio from vehicle.
7. Reverse procedure to install.

HEATER CORE, REPLACE

Less A/C

Exc. 1978–84 Horizon & Omni; 1983–84 Charger & Turismo
1. Disconnect battery ground cable, then drain cooling system.
2. Disconnect wire connector from blower motor, then disconnect control cable from mode door.
3. Disconnect heater hoses from heater core, then cap heater core tube openings to prevent coolant spillage.
4. Remove glove box, then remove nut attaching hanger bracket to heater assembly through glove box opening.

NOTE: On Daytona and Laser, remove 2 screws and disconnect demister adapter from top of heater case.

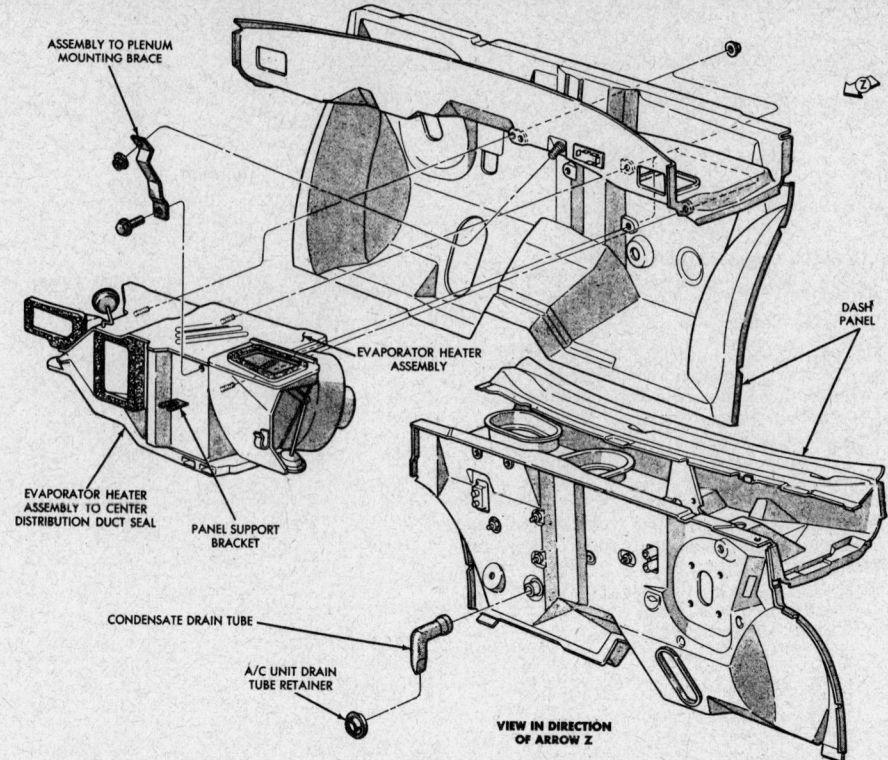

Fig. 18 Heater assembly. 1978–84 Horizon & Omni; 1983–84 Charger & Turismo with A/C

5. From engine compartment of dash panel, remove two nuts attaching heater assembly.
6. Carefully slide heater assembly out from under instrument panel, Fig. 15.
7. Remove insulation from around heater core tubes, then remove upper core mounting screw.
8. Using a screwdriver, pry retainer tabs from outer edges of heater housing cover, then remove cover.
9. Remove lower heater core to housing attaching screws, then slide heater core from housing.
10. Reverse procedure to install.

1978–84 Horizon & Omni; 1983–84 Charger & Turismo
1. Disconnect battery ground cable and drain cooling system.
2. Remove center outside air floor vent housing.
3. Remove ash tray.
4. Remove two screws retaining defroster duct adapter to heater unit.

NOTE: The left hand screw is accessible through the ash tray housing access hole.

5. Remove the adapter and push the flexible connector upward and position aside.
6. Disconnect temperature control cable.
7. Remove glove box and door assembly.
8. Disconnect electrical connectors to blower motor and blower resistor.
9. Disconnect heater hoses and plug heater core tube openings.
10. Remove two nuts retaining heater unit to dash panel, Fig. 16.
11. Remove screw attaching heater brace bracket to instrument panel.
12. Remove heater unit support strap nut. Disconnect strap from plenum stud and

lower heater unit from panel.
13. Disconnect mode control cable and remove heater unit from vehicle.
14. Remove left heater outlet duct.
15. Remove four screws from blower motor mounting plate, then the blower motor from heater unit.
16. Remove defroster duct adapter.
17. Remove outside air and defroster door cover.
18. Remove screw from center of defroster door, then the door, screw and screw retaining plate.
19. Remove defroster door control rod from heater unit.
20. Remove heater core cover.
21. Slide heater core from heater unit.
22. Reverse procedure to install.

With A/C

Exc. 1978–84 Horizon & Omni; 1983–84 Charger & Turismo
1. Disconnect battery ground cable, drain cooling system and discharge A/C system.
2. Disconnect heater hoses and refrigerant lines and remove "H" valve. Plug lines, hoses and open fittings.
3. Disconnect vacuum hoses at intake manifold and water valve.
4. Remove two screws attaching heater control bezel to instrument panel, then remove bezel.
5. Remove two screws attaching A/C and heater control to instrument panel, then remove control.
6. Remove right hand scuff plate and cowl trim panels, then remove glove box.
7. If equipped, remove console, then remove forward console mounting bracket.
8. Remove two center duct retaining screws from bottom of lower panel, then disconnect center duct to right hand duct retain-

Fig. 19 Blower motor replacement. 1978–84 Horizon & Omni; 1983–84 Charger & Turismo less A/C

ing tabs through glove box opening.

9. Disconnect over column duct, then slide center duct downward from instrument panel.
10. Remove defroster duct from under panel, then disconnect condensation drain tube from engine side of dash panel.
11. Disconnect wire connectors and control cables from A/C and heater housing.
12. Remove right hand cowl to plenum brace, then pull carpet rearward from under unit.
13. Remove A/C and heater housing hanger bracket attaching screw, then remove four nut attaching unit to dash panel from engine compartment.
14. Pull unit rearward so that mounting studs clear dash panel, then carefully remove unit from under instrument panel.
15. Remove nut from mode door actuator arm, then remove two retaining clips from front edge of cover.
16. Remove two attaching screws, then remove mode door actuator from housing.
17. Remove fifteen cover to housing attaching screws, then remove cover and lift out mode door, Fig. 17.
18. Remove screw from heater core retaining bracket, then remove heater core.
19. Reverse procedure to install.

1978–84 Horizon & Omni; 1983–84 Charger & Turismo

1. Disconnect ground cable, drain radiator and discharge refrigerant system.
2. Disconnect temperature door cable from evaporator heater assembly.
3. Remove glove box.
4. Disconnect vacuum harness from control panel and the blower motor feed wire and anti-diesel relay wires.
5. On 1978–83 models, remove right instrument panel bezel. On 1984 models, remove center bezel.
6. Remove central air duct cover from central air distribution duct.
7. Remove three screws retaining central air distribution duct, then the duct.
8. Remove defroster duct adapter.
9. Remove "H" valve and disconnect heater hoses. Plug heater core tube openings.
10. Remove condensate drain tube from evap-

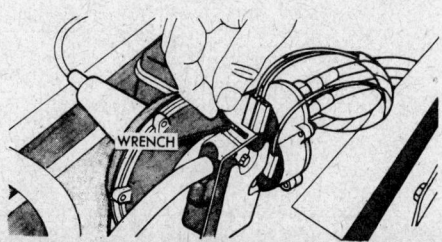

Fig. 21 Speed control lock-in screw adjustment

orator heater unit.
11. Disconnect vacuum lines at intake manifold and water valve.
12. Remove evaporator heater unit to dash panel retaining nuts, Fig. 18.
13. Remove panel support bracket.
14. Remove right side cowl lower panel.
15. Remove right instrument panel pivot bracket screw and screws securing lower panel at steering column.
16. On 1984 models, remove instrument panel top cover and all screws securing panel below windshield except farthest left screw.
17. Pull back carpet from under evaporator heater assembly as far as possible.
18. Remove nut from A/C to plenum mounting brace and blower motor ground cable.
19. Support unit and remove brace from stud.
20. Lift evaporator heater unit and pull rearward to clear dash panel and liner. Also, the lower instrument panel will have to be pulled rearward to provide adequate clearance for unit removal. Slowly lower the evaporator heater unit, slide rearward and remove from vehicle.
21. Remove 1/4-20 nut from mode door actuator arm on top cover and two retaining clips from front edge of cover.
22. Remove mode door actuator attaching screws and the actuator.
23. Remove fifteen screws securing cover to evaporator heater assembly and the cover.
24. Remove mode door from unit.
25. Remove screw from heater core tube retaining bracket, then the heater core from evaporator heater assembly.
26. Reverse procedure to install.

BLOWER MOTOR, REPLACE

Less A/C

Exc. 1978–84 Horizon & Omni; 1983–84 Charger & Turismo

1. Perform steps 1 through 14 as described under Heater Core, Replace.
2. Remove blower motor to heater housing attaching screws, then remove blower motor.
3. Remove clamp retaining blower motor wheel to shaft, then remove two nuts attaching retainer plate to blower motor and remove plate.
4. Reverse procedure to install.

1978–84 Horizon & Omni; 1983–84 Charger & Turismo

1. Disconnect battery ground cable.
2. Disconnect blower motor wiring connector.
3. Remove left heater outlet duct.
4. Remove screws retaining blower motor mounting plate to heater unit.
5. Remove blower motor assembly, Fig. 19.
6. Reverse procedure to install.

With A/C

1. Disconnect battery ground cable.
2. Remove three screws securing glove box to instrument panel and the glove box.
3. Disconnect blower motor feed and ground wires. Remove wires from retaining clip on recirculating housing.
4. Disconnect blower motor vent tube from A/C unit.
5. Loosen recirculation door actuator from bracket and remove actuator from housing. Do not disconnect vacuum lines.
6. Remove seven screws securing recirculat-

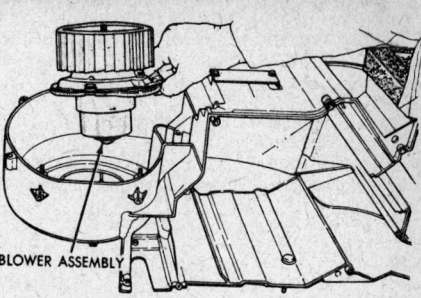

Fig. 20 Blower motor replacement. Models with A/C

ing housing to A/C unit, then the housing.
7. Remove three blower motor mounting flange nuts and the blower motor, Fig. 20.
8. Reverse procedure to install.

SPEED CONTROL

Lock-in Screw Adjustment

Lock-in accuracy will be affected by poor engine performance (need for tune-up), loaded gross weight of car (trailering), improper slack in control cable. After the foregoing items have been considered and the speed sags or drops more than 2 to 3 mph when the speed control is activated, the lock-in adjusting screw should be turned counter-clockwise approximately 1/4 turn per one mph correction required, Fig. 21.

If a speed increase of more than 2 to 3 mph occurs, the lock-in adjusting screw should be turned clockwise 1/4 turn per one mph correction required.

CAUTION: This adjustment must not exceed two turns in either direction or damage to the unit may occur.

Throttle Cable Adjustment

Optimum servo performance is obtained with a given amount of free play in the throttle control cable. To obtain proper free play, insert a 1/16" diameter pin, Fig. 22, between forward end of slot in cable end of carburetor linkage pin (hair pin clip removed from linkage pin). With choke in full open position and carburetor at curb idle, pull cable back toward dash panel without moving carburetor link-

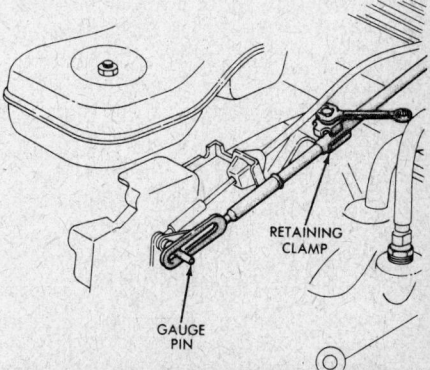

Fig. 22 Speed control servo throttle cable adjustment (Typical)

age until all free play is removed. Tighten cable clamp bolt to 45 inch-pounds, remove 1/16" pin and install hair pin clip.

Brake Switch Adjustment

Exc. 1978–84 Horizon & Omni; 1983–84 Charger & Turismo

Position stop light switch to retaining bracket, then with brake pedal depressed, push switch forward into retaining bracket until it is fully seated. Slowly release brake pedal and allow pedal striker to rachet switch rearward in bracket to the correct position. No further adjustment is necessary.

1980–84 Horizon & Omni; 1983–84 Charger & Turismo

1. Loosen switch bracket.

2. Insert .130 spacer gauge between brake push rod and switch with pedal in free position.
3. Push switch bracket assembly toward brake push rod until plunger is fully depressed and switch contacts spacer.
4. Tighten bracket bolt to 75 in-lbs. and remove spacer.

4-97 Engine Section

ENGINE MOUNTS, REPLACE

NOTE: When positioning the engine on 1983–84 models, check driveshaft's length as outlined in the "Front Suspension & Steering Section" under "Driveshaft Length, Adjust." The engine mounts incorporate slotted bolt holes to permit side-to-side positioning of the engine thereby affecting the length of the driveshaft. Failure to properly position engine may result in extensive damage to the engine.

Refer to Figs. 1 and 2 when replacing engine mounts.

ENGINE, REPLACE

Manual Trans.

NOTE: The engine and transmission are removed as an assembly.

1. Disconnect battery cables and drain cooling system.
2. Scribe hood hinge locations and remove hood.
3. Remove radiator hoses, then the radiator and shroud assembly.
4. Remove air cleaner.
5. Remove A/C compressor mounting bolts and position compressor aside, if equipped.
6. Disconnect all wiring, hoses, lines and cables from engine.
7. Remove air diverter valve and lines from air pump.
8. Remove alternator belt and alternator.
9. Disconnect clutch and speedometer cables.
10. Raise and support vehicle.
11. Disconnect drive shafts from transmission and secure aside with wire.
12. Disconnect exhaust pipe from manifold.
13. Remove air pump hoses and lines, then the air pump belt and the air pump.
14. Disconnect transmission linkage.
15. Lower vehicle.
16. Attach suitable engine lifting equipment to engine.
17. Raise engine slightly and remove front engine mount bolt.
18. Remove right and left engine mount bolts.
19. Remove engine and transmission assembly from vehicle.
20. Reverse procedure to install.

Auto. Trans.

NOTE: The engine is removed without the transmission.

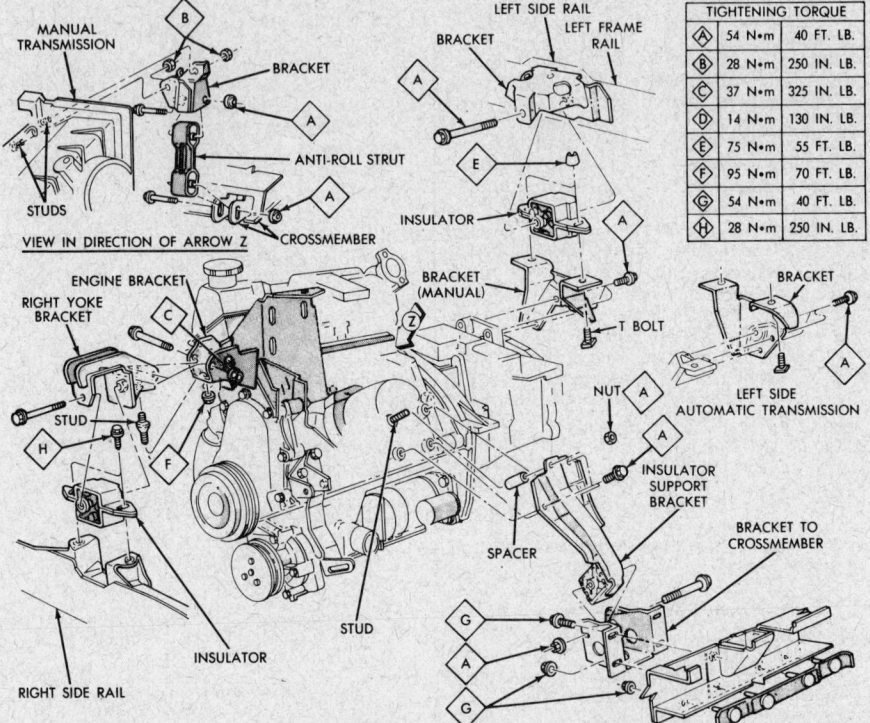

Fig. 1 Engine mount replacement. 1983

TIGHTENING TORQUE		
Ⓐ	54 N•m	40 FT. LB.
Ⓑ	28 N•m	250 IN. LB.
Ⓒ	37 N•m	325 IN. LB.
Ⓓ	14 N•m	130 IN. LB.
Ⓔ	75 N•m	55 FT. LB.
Ⓕ	95 N•m	70 FT. LB.
Ⓖ	54 N•m	40 FT. LB.
Ⓗ	28 N•m	250 IN. LB.

1. Disconnect battery cables and drain cooling system.
2. Scribe hood hinge locations and remove hood.
3. Remove radiator hoses and the air cleaner.
4. Remove A/C compressor mounting bolts and position compressor aside, if equipped.
5. Disconnect all wiring, hoses, lines and cables from engine.
6. Remove air diverter valve and lines from air pump, if equipped.
7. Remove alternator belt and the alternator.
8. Remove upper bellhousing bolts.
9. Raise and support vehicle and remove front wheels.
10. Remove left and right splash shields.
11. Remove power steering pump belt and pump mounting bolts. Position pump aside.
12. Remove water pump and crankshaft pulleys.
13. Remove front engine mounting bolt.
14. Remove transmission inspection cover, then the flex plate bolts.
15. Remove starter motor.

16. Remove lower bellhousing bolts.
17. Lower vehicle and support transmission with a suitable jack.
18. Attach suitable engine lifting equipment to engine.
19. Remove engine oil filter and the right engine mount.
20. Lift and remove engine from vehicle.
21. Reverse procedure to install.

CYLINDER HEAD, REPLACE

NOTE: Cylinder head must be cool prior to removal to avoid cylinder head distortion.

1. Drain cooling system.
2. Remove intake and exhaust manifolds from cylinder head.
3. Remove rocker arm cover.
4. Remove cylinder head bolts evenly in sequence, Fig. 3.

NOTE: Rocker arm supporting brackets are located on dowels and are retained by

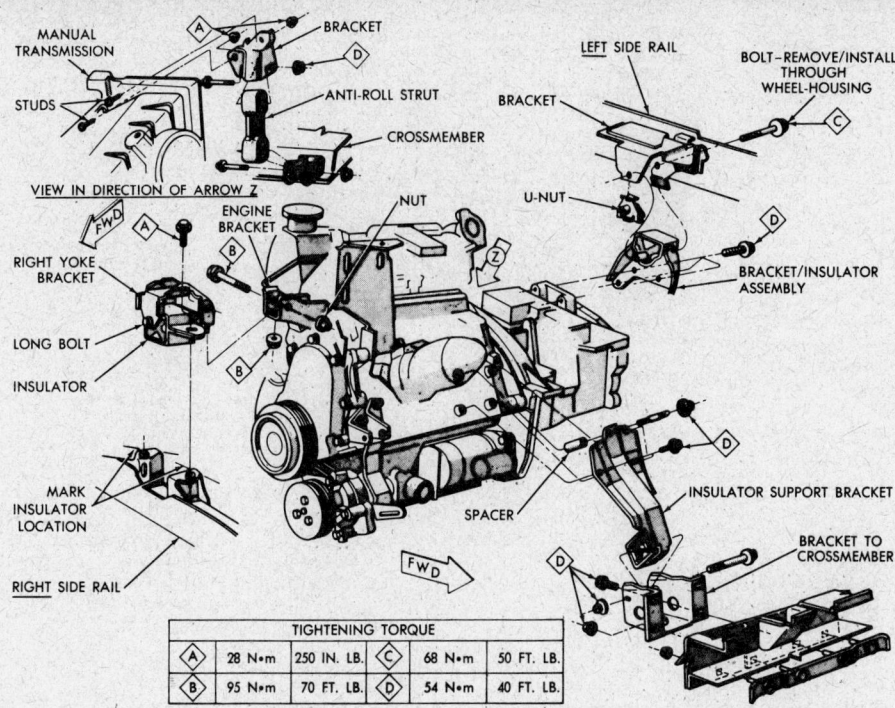

VIEW IN DIRECTION OF ARROW Z

TIGHTENING TORQUE					
A	28 N·m	250 IN. LB.	C	68 N·m	50 FT. LB.
B	95 N·m	70 FT. LB.	D	54 N·m	40 FT. LB.

Fig. 2 Engine mount replacement. 1984

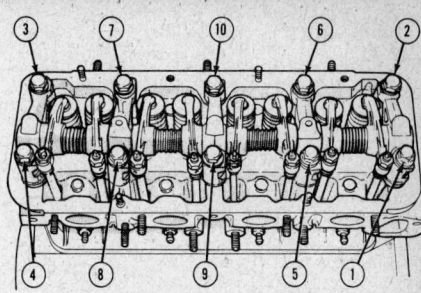

Fig. 3 Cylinder head bolt removal sequence

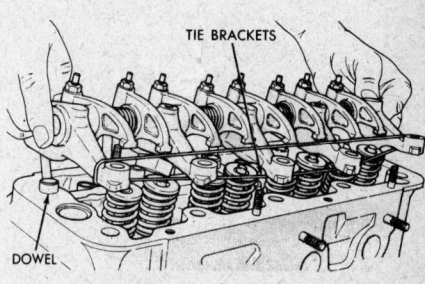

Fig. 4 Rocker arm assembly removal

head bolts. Only brackets 2 and 4 are pinned to rocker arm shaft.

5. Tie rocker arm assembly together with suitable wire, then remove, Fig. 4.
6. Remove push rods, noting location of each to facilitate installation, then remove cylinder head.
7. Reverse procedure to install.

NOTE: Refer to Fig. 5 for cylinder head bolt tightening sequence. Bolts are to be torqued progressively to 52 ft. lbs.

VALVE ARRANGEMENT

Front to Rear

4-97........................I-E-I-E-E-I-E-I

VALVE TIMING

Intake Opens Before TDC

Engine 4-97	Year 1983–84	Degrees 13

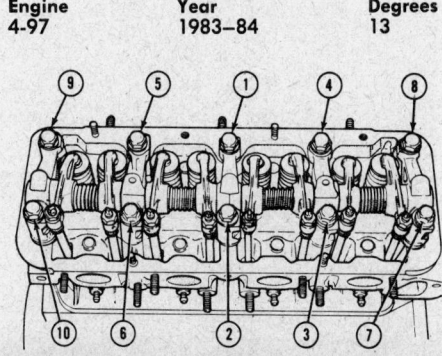

Fig. 5 Cylinder head bolt tightening sequence

VALVES, ADJUST

NOTE: For proper clearance, valve adjustment must be set with piston at TDC on the compression stroke with engine cold.

1. Rotate crankshaft noting exhaust valve movement. When one valve begins to close continue turning slowly until intake valve on same cylinder just starts to open. This is the "Valve Rocking" position. In this position, the clearance in the opposite cylinder can be adjusted.
2. After checking both clearances, Fig. 6, rotate crankshaft one half turn to bring the next cylinder in firing order to the "Valve Rocking" position and the paired cylinder can be adjusted. Valve rocking cylinders are paired to valve adjust cylinders as follows: 4–1, 2–3, 1–4, 3–2.
3. Adjust valve clearance by loosening locknut and turning screw until a sliding fit is obtained between valve stem and rocker, Fig. 6.

VALVE GUIDE, SERVICE

NOTE: Remove varnish and carbon deposits from valve guide interior with a suitable guide cleaner.

Valve Guide Wear

1. Insert valve into guide leaving .400 inch above cylinder gasket surface.
2. Firmly attach a dial indicator to cylinder head so indicator needle is in contact with valve margin.
3. Move valve to and from indicator and note total indicator reading, Fig. 7.
4. Total indicator reading shows valve guide wear. Wear must not exceed .020 inch for intake valves, or .027 inch for exhaust valves.

CAMSHAFT, REPLACE

1. Remove oil filter, then the 7 oil pump attaching screws and pull assembly from block.
2. Remove distributor and drive housing and mark crankcase in relation to drive slot, Fig. 8.
3. Remove distributor drive from drive shaft spindle using a suitable magnet, Fig. 9.
4. Remove shaft drive gear circlip.

NOTE: Insert a shop towel into cavity around gear to prevent circlip from falling into crankcase during removal or installation.

5. Remove driveshaft toward pump side of crankcase with a tapping motion until gear is free of spline, and remove gear.
6. Remove fuel pump and tappets, noting location of tappets to facilitate proper installation.
7. Remove camshaft thrust plate and camshaft.
8. Reverse procedure to install.

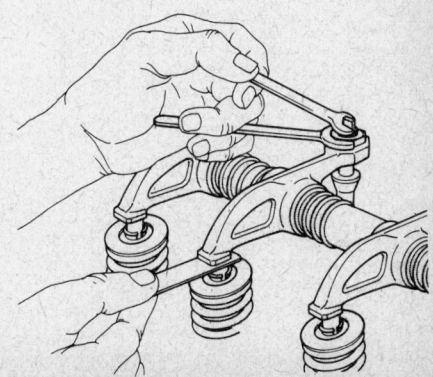

Fig. 6 Checking valve clearance

Fig. 7 Checking valve guide wear

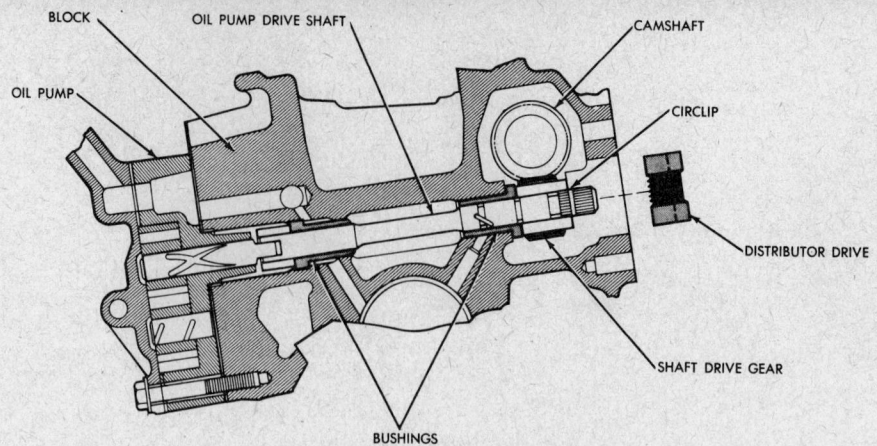

Fig. 9 Oil pump driveshaft assembly

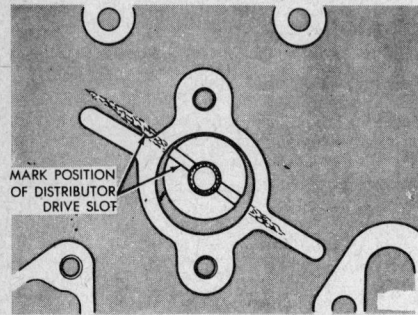

Fig. 8 Distributor drive slot marking

PISTON & ROD ASSEMBLY

When installing piston and connecting rod assembly, the notches on pistons 1 and 3 must face toward flywheel end of engine and the notches on pistons 2 and 4 must be facing timing chain, Fig. 10.

TIMING CHAIN COVER, REPLACE

1. Disconnect battery ground cable.
2. Loosen AIR pump adjusting screw and bracket and remove belt.
3. Raise vehicle and remove right inner splash shield.
4. Loosen alternator adjusting screw, then move alternator inward and remove alternator/water pump drive belt.

5. Remove crankshaft pulley belt, washer and pulley.
6. Drain cooling system and remove water pump to timing cover hose.
7. Slightly raise and support engine at the timing cover end and remove engine mount bracket to timing cover and block attaching bolts.
8. Remove crankcase extension to cover screws, then the cover to block attaching screws.

NOTE: Two cover to block screws extend through tubular locating dowels, Fig. 11. During removal, ensure dowels do not fall into crankcase extension.

9. Remove timing cover.
10. Reverse procedures to install.

TIMING COVER, REPLACE

1. Perform steps 1 through 5 under "Timing Chain Cover, Replace".
2. Using tool No. C-4762-1 on 1983 models, or C-748 on 1984 models, and a suitable wrench, insert tool over crankshaft nose and turn tool firmly into seal.
3. Tighten thrust screw to remove seal, then tap side of thrust screw to remove seal.
4. Using tool No. C-4761 and a new seal

drive seal into timing cover with the lips of seal toward engine until tool stops aginst cover.
5. Examine pulley hub for dirt and defects and polish with 400 grit sandpaper as necessary.
6. Lubricate pully hub and seal lip using a suitable lubricant, then align keyway and install crankshaft pulley, washer and bolt.
7. Torque retaining bolt to 110 ft. lbs.
8. Reverse steps 1 through 4 to assemble.

TIMING CHAIN, REPLACE

1. Remove timing chain cover as described under "Timing Chain Cover, Replace."
2. Before removing timing chain, check timing chain stretch as follows:
   a. Rotate crankshaft until one of the three camshaft sprocket bolts is located at top of crankshaft and camshaft centerlines.
   b. Using a suitable size socket and torque wrench, apply torque in direction of crankshaft rotation to the camshaft sprocket bolt, Fig. 12. Apply 30 ft. lbs. of torque if cylinder head is installed on engine and 15 ft. lbs. of torque if cylinder head is removed from engine.

NOTE: Do not allow engine to turn

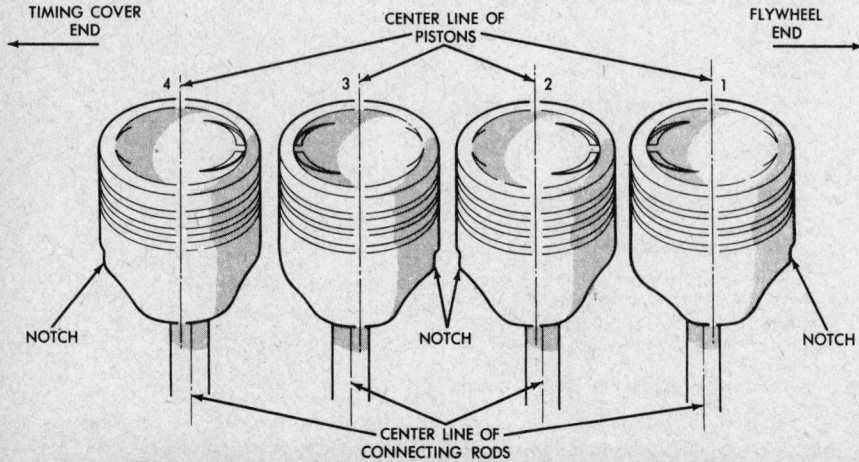

Fig. 10 Piston installation

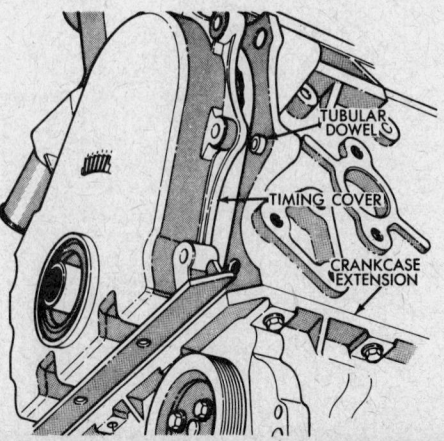

Fig. 11 Tubular dowel location

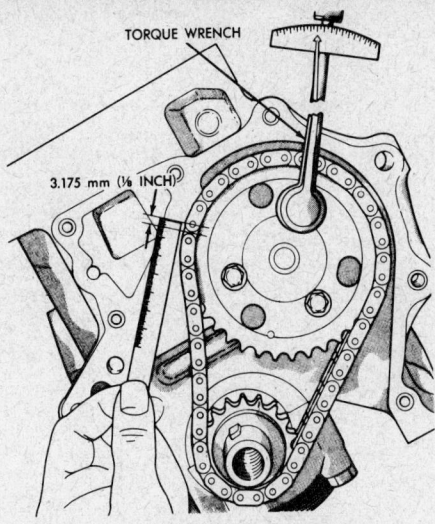

Fig. 12 Measuring timing chain stretch

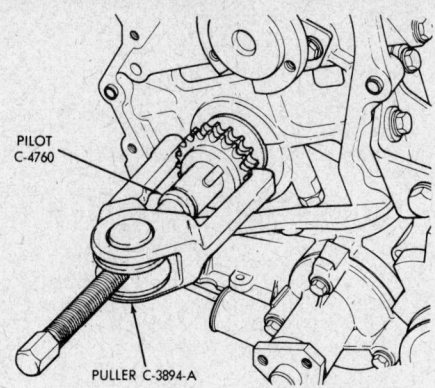

Fig. 13 Crankshaft sprocket removal

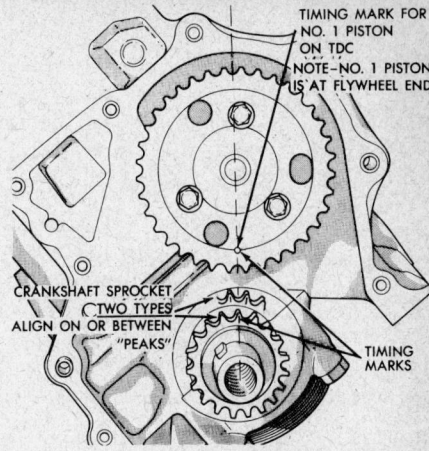

Fig. 14 Timing mark alignment

while applying torque.

c. Hold a ruler alongside a link in the chain and apply same torque as described previously in opposite direction and note amount of chain movement, Fig. 12. If movement exceeds 1/8 inch, timing chain must be replaced.
3. Remove camshaft sprocket attaching bolts, sprocket and chain.
4. Remove crankshaft sprocket using tools C-4760 (adapter) and C-3894-A (puller) or equivalent, Fig. 13.
5. Align crankshaft sprocket with key and drive firmly onto crankshaft.
6. Loosely install camshaft sprocket onto camshaft.
7. Rotate crankshaft and camshaft until timing marks on both sprockets are on a line passing through crankshaft and camshaft centerlines, Fig. 14.
8. Remove camshaft sprocket without disturbing timing marks, then reinstall sprocket and timing chain making sure marks are aligned as described previously.
9. Install camshaft sprocket bolts and

torque to 113 inch lbs.
10. Reverse remainder of procedure to assemble.

REAR CRANKSHAFT OIL SEAL SERVICE

1. Place inner surface of seal housing on spacers to allow clearance for seal removal.
2. Install tool No. C-4759 or equivalent and drive seal from housing, Fig. 15.

NOTE: Tool No. C-4759 with universal driver C-4171 is used as both a seal remover and, when reversed, a seal installer, Figs. 15 and 16.

3. Place outer seal housing on a flat surface, Fig. 16.
4. Using tool No. C-4759 with tool No. C-4171 (driver) tap seal into housing to full depth.

OIL PAN, REPLACE

1. Drain engine oil.
2. Remove 16 oil pan attaching screws.
3. Remove pan and gasket.
4. Clean pan and gasket surfaces.
5. Install new gasket and reinstall pan.
6. Torque oil pan attaching screws to 9.4 ft. lbs (111 inch lbs.)
7. Refill engine oil.

OIL PUMP, REPLACE

Removal

1. Remove oil filter.
2. Remove the seven oil pump mounting bolts while holding pump together as an assembly, Fig. 17.
3. Pull assembly from block.

Replace

1. Install new housing to block and housing to cover gaskets.
2. Place cover on housing and insert two bolts to maintain alignment.
3. Install housing into block, then rotate assembly as necessary to engage drive gear shaft with slot in driveshaft.
4. Align bolt pattern, install remaining bolts and torque bolts to 9.4 ft. lbs. (111 inch lbs.)

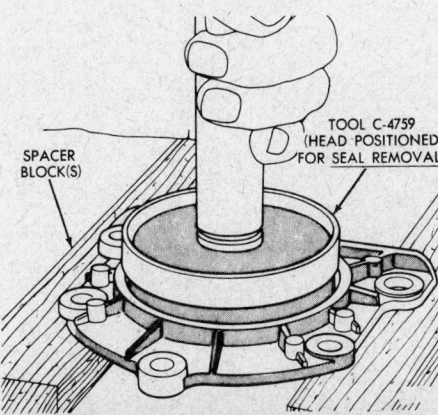

Fig. 15 Crankshaft rear oil seal removal

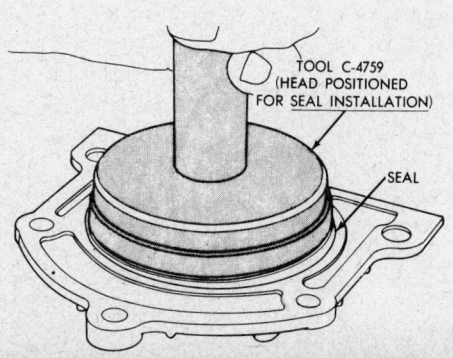

Fig. 16 Crankshaft rear oil seal installation

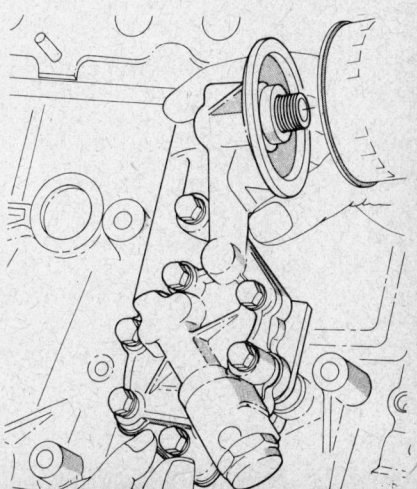

Fig. 17 Oil pump replacement

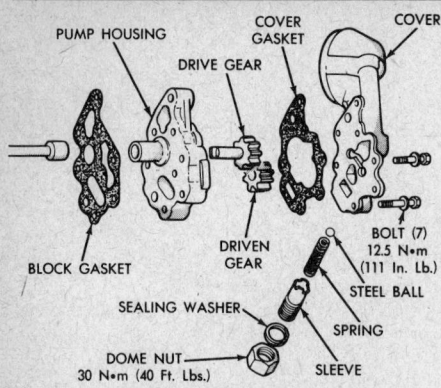

Fig. 18 Exploded view of oil pump

OIL PUMP SERVICE

Disassembly

1. For oil pump disassembly, refer to Fig. 18.
2. Disassemble oil pressure relief valve by unscrewing dome nut and removing sealing washer, Fig. 19.
3. Remove relief valve sleeve using a suitable allen wrench.
4. Remove spring and ball.

NOTE: Examine the ball for defects such as grooves or scuffing. Check ball for roundness using a micrometer and replace if defective.

Assembly

1. Place ball on its seat in relief valve cover,

then using a soft rod, tap ball into place with a small hammer.
2. Insert spring into sleeve and screw sleeve into cover and torque to 62 inch lbs, Fig. 19.
3. Install sealing washer and dome nut and torque to 30 ft. lbs, Fig. 19.
4. Refer to Fig. 18 to reassemble oil pump.

FUEL PUMP, REPLACE

1. Disconnect battery ground cable.
2. Disconnect fuel lines from fuel pump.
3. Remove fuel pump mounting bolts.
4. Remove fuel pump from vehicle.
5. Reverse procedure to install.

WATER PUMP

Removal

1. Disconnect battery ground cable.
2. Remove radiator cap and drain cooling system from water pump drain plug.
3. Remove pump to block coolant hose at water pump.
4. Loosen alternator/water pump drive belt, then remove pump pulley.
5. Remove 4 pump to crankcase extension screws and pull assembly from crankcase.

Installation

1. Position water pump on crankcase extension with new gasket.
2. Install 4 pump to crankcase extension screws and torque to 9 ft. lbs.
3. Install pump to block hose and torque clamp to 35 inch lbs.
4. Install drain plug and torque to 13 ft. lbs.
5. Install pump pulley and adjust belt tension to specifications, then refill cooling system.

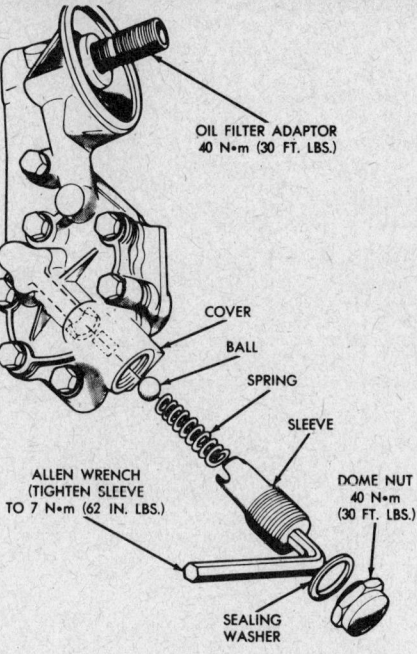

Fig. 19 Exploded view of oil pressure relief valve

BELT TENSION DATA

		New	Used
1983	AIR Pump	95	70
	Alternator/Water Pump	115	95
	Power Steering	95	70
1984	AIR Pump	95	70
	Alternator/Water Pump	115	80
	Power Steering	95	70

4-105 Engine Section

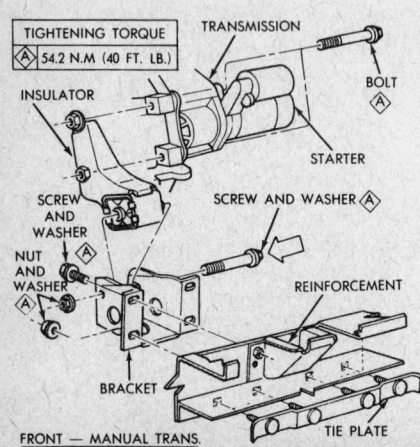

Fig. 1 Front engine mount

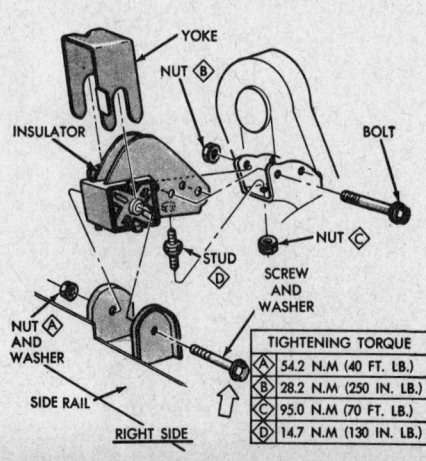

Fig. 2 Right side engine mount. 1978–80

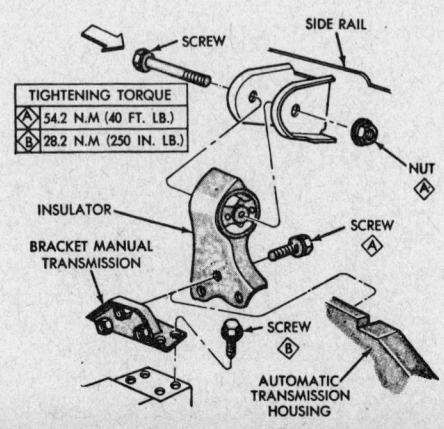

Fig. 3 Left engine mount. 1978–80

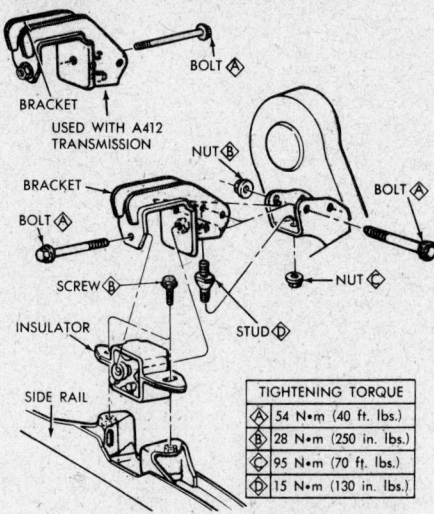

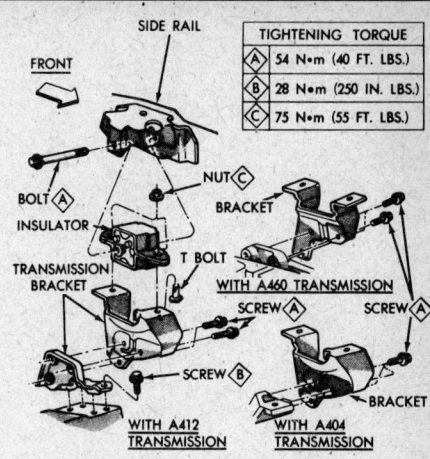

TIGHTENING TORQUE	
Ⓐ	54 N•m (40 FT. LBS.)
Ⓑ	28 N•m (250 IN. LBS.)
Ⓒ	75 N•m (55 FT. LBS.)

Fig. 6   Left engine mount. 1983

TIGHTENING TORQUE	
Ⓐ	54 N•m (40 ft. lbs.)
Ⓑ	28 N•m (250 in. lbs.)
Ⓒ	95 N•m (70 ft. lbs.)
Ⓓ	15 N•m (130 in. lbs.)

Fig. 4   Right engine mount. 1981–83

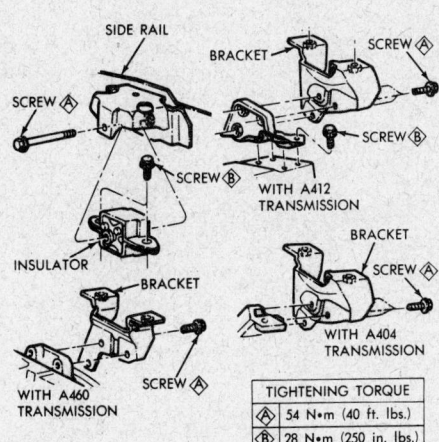

TIGHTENING TORQUE	
Ⓐ	54 N•m (40 ft. lbs.)
Ⓑ	28 N•m (250 in. lbs.)

Fig. 5   Left engine mount. 1981–82

ENGINE MOUNTS

NOTE: When positioning the engine on 1981–83 models, check driveshaft length as outlined in the "Front Suspension & Steering Section" under "Driveshaft Length, Adjust." The engine mounts incorporate slotted bolt holes to permit side-to-side positioning of the engine thereby affecting the length of the driveshaft. Failure to properly position engine may result in extensive damage to the engine.

Refer to Figs. 1 through 7 when replacing the engine mounts.

NOTE: The left engine mount is attached with two types of mounting screws. Two of the three are of the pilot type with extended tips. Extended tip screws must be installed in the proper position, Fig. 7. Damage to the shift cover or difficult shifting may occur if the screws are incorrectly installed.

ENGINE, REPLACE

Manual Trans.

NOTE: The engine and transmission are removed as an assembly.

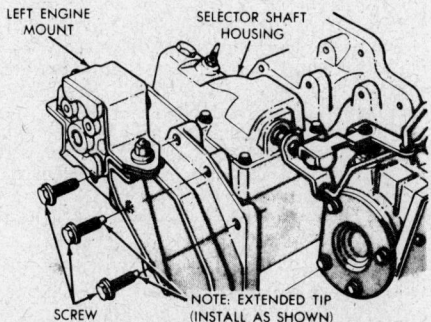

Fig. 7   Correct positioning of extended tip mount bolts

1. Disconnect battery cables and drain cooling system.
2. Scribe hood hinge locations and remove hood.
3. Remove radiator hoses, then the radiator and shroud assembly.
4. Remove air cleaner.
5. Remove A/C compressor mounting bolts and position compressor aside, if equipped.
6. Disconnect all wiring, hoses, lines and cables from engine.
7. Remove air diverter valve and lines from air pump.
8. Remove alternator belt and alternator.
9. Disconnect clutch and speedometer cables.
10. Raise and support vehicle.
11. On models with A-412 transaxle, disconnect drive shaft from transaxle and secure aside. On models with A-460 transaxle, remove driveshafts as outlined in "Front Suspension and Steering."
12. Disconnect exhaust pipe from manifold.
13. Remove air pump hoses and lines, then the air pump belt and the air pump.
14. Disconnect transmission linkage.
15. Lower vehicle.
16. Attach suitable engine lifting equipment to engine.
17. Raise engine slightly and remove front engine mount bolt.
18. Remove right and left engine mount bolts.
19. Remove engine and transmission assembly from vehicle.
20. Reverse procedure to install. Align engine as outlined in "Front Suspension And Steering," to ensure proper driveshaft length.

Auto. Trans.

NOTE: The engine is removed without the transmission.

1. Disconnect battery cables and drain cooling system.
2. Scribe hood hinge locations and remove hood.
3. Disconnect transmission cooler lines and radiator hoses, then remove radiator,

hoses and cooling fan.
4. Remove air cleaner assembly, then remove A/C compressor, if equipped, and position aside.
5. Disconnect all wiring, hoses, lines and cables from engine.
6. Remove air diverter valve and lines from air pump, if equipped.
7. Remove alternator belt and the alternator.
8. Remove upper bellhousing bolts.
9. Raise and support vehicle and remove front wheels.
10. Remove left and right splash shields.
11. Remove power steering pump belt and pump mounting bolts. Position pump aside.
12. Remove water pump and crankshaft pulleys.
13. Remove front engine mounting bolt.
14. Remove transmission inspection cover, then the flex plate bolts.
15. Remove starter motor.
16. Remove lower bellhousing bolts.
17. Lower vehicle and support transmission with a suitable jack.
18. Attach suitable engine lifting equipment to engine.
19. Remove engine oil filter and the right engine mount.
20. Lift and remove engine from vehicle.
21. Reverse procedure to install. Align engine as outlined in "Front Suspension And Steering," to ensure proper driveshaft length.

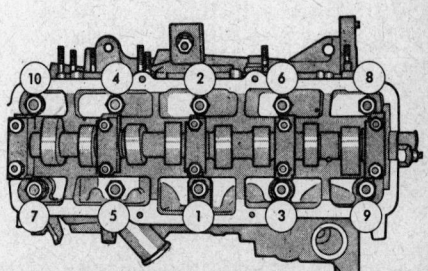

Fig. 8   Cylinder head tightening sequence

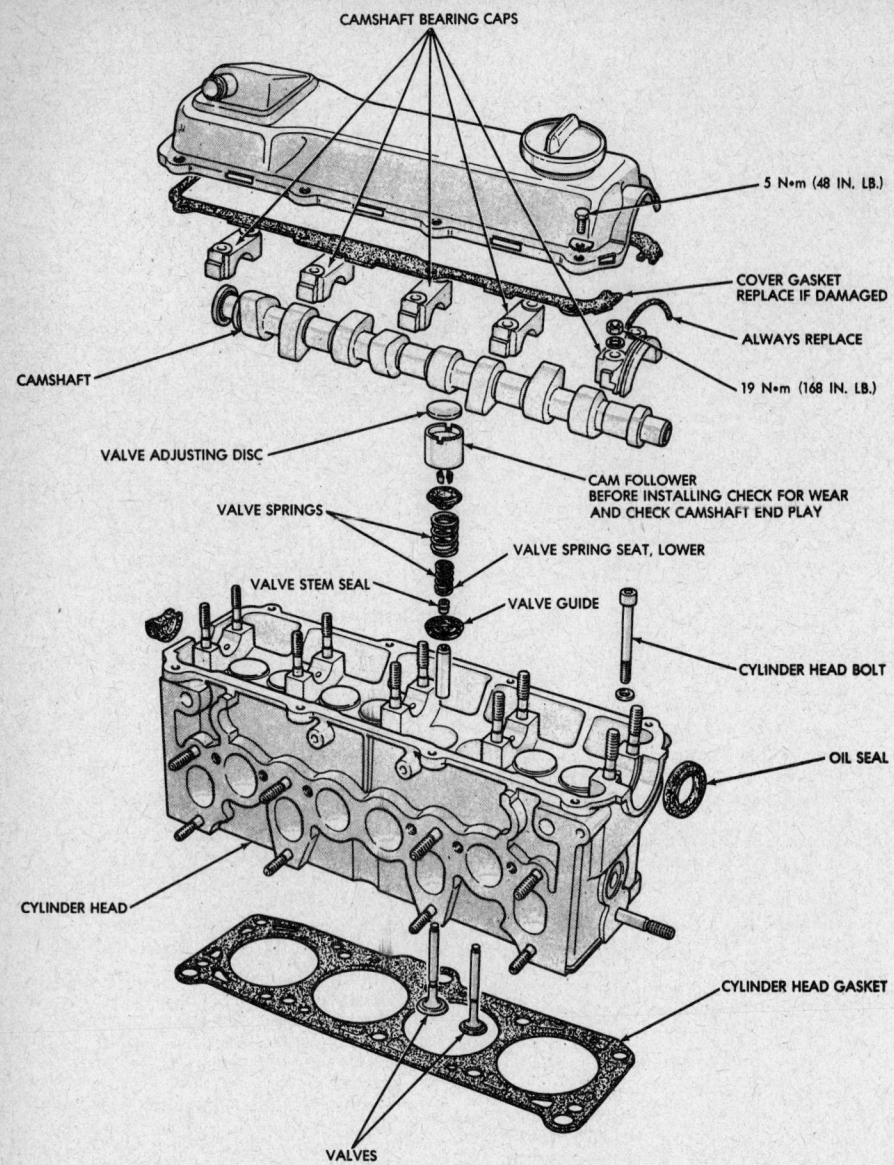

Fig. 9 Cylinder head assembly, exploded view

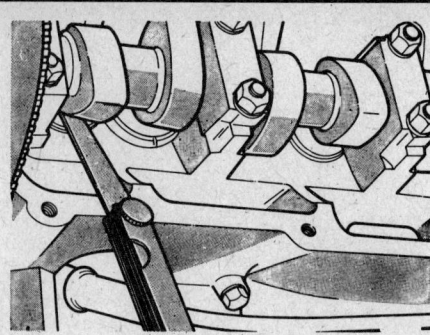

Fig. 10 Checking valve clearance

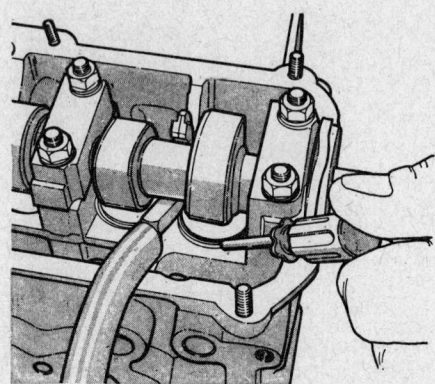

Fig. 11 Valve adjusting disc replacement

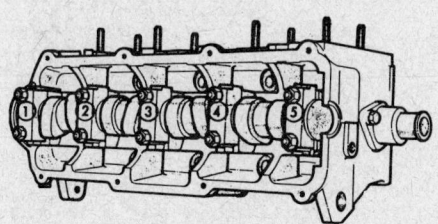

Fig. 12 Camshaft bearing cap identification

CYLINDER HEAD, REPLACE

1. Drain cooling system and perform Steps 1 through 15 as outlined under "Timing Belt, Replace" procedure.
2. Remove intake and exhaust manifolds from cylinder head.
3. Disconnect all wiring, hoses and cables attached to cylinder head.
4. Remove cam cover bolts and the cam cover.
5. Loosen cylinder head attaching bolts in reverse sequence found in Fig. 8.
6. Remove cylinder head from engine, Fig. 9.
7. Reverse procedure to install. Insert bolts No. 8 and 10 first, to center the cylinder head on engine block. Torque bolts to specifications in sequence, Fig. 8. To properly tension the timing belt, perform Steps 16 through 22 as outlined under "Timing Belt, Replace" procedure.

VALVE ARRANGEMENT

Front to Rear

4-105 .... E-I-E-I-I-E-I-E

VALVE LIFT SPECS.

Engine	Year	Intake	Exhaust
4-105	1978–83	.406	.406

VALVE TIMING

Intake Opens Before TDC

Engine	Year	Degrees
4-105	1978	23
	1979–82	14

VALVES, ADJUST

1. Using feeler gauges, check valve clearance with cam lobe in position shown in Fig. 10.

NOTE: Engine should be at normal operating temperature, with thermostat open and coolant temperature approximately 195°F. If necessary to check valve clearance with cylinder head cold, use following specifications: Intake, .006–.010 inch; Exhaust, .014–.018 inch, then recheck after engine has reached normal operating temperature.

2. If valve clearance is greater than specified, remove valve adjusting disc and insert a thicker disc to obtain proper clearance.
3. If valve clearance is less than specified, remove valve adjusting disc and insert a thinner disc to obtain proper clearance.

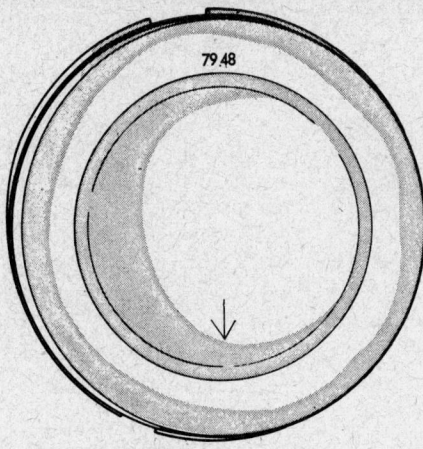

Fig. 13 Piston identification markings

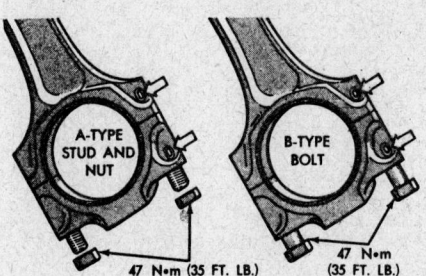

Fig. 14 Connecting rod assemblies

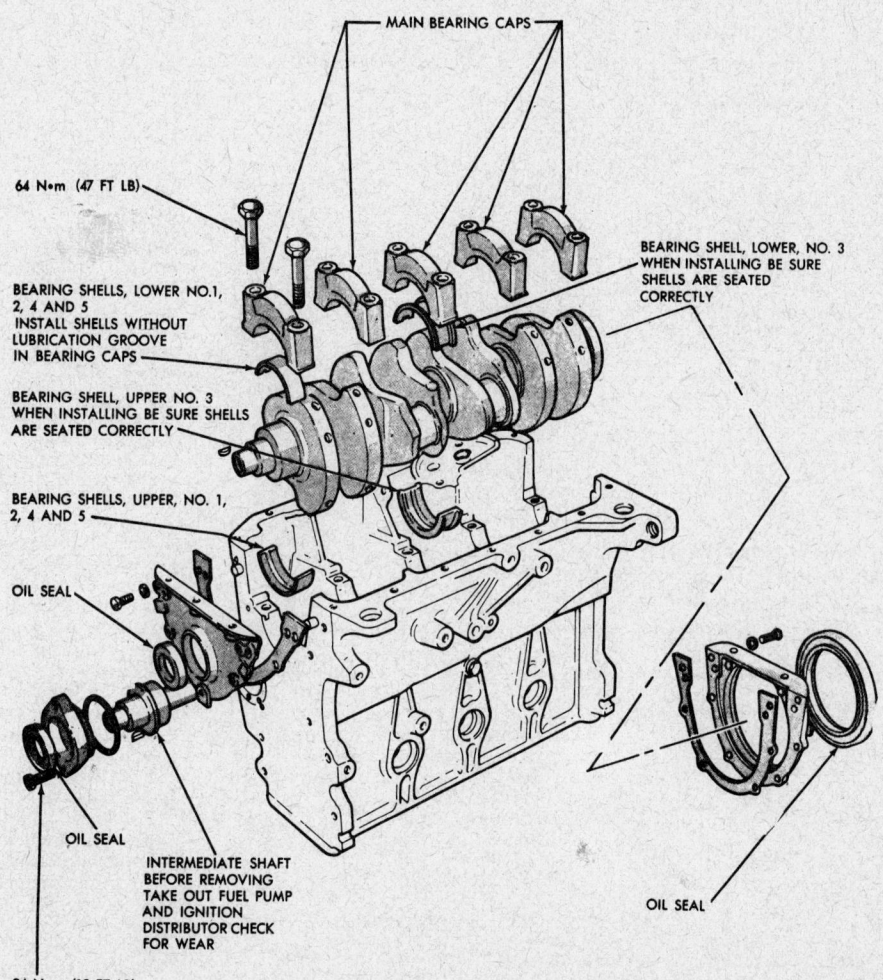

Fig. 15 Crankshaft and bearing assembly, exploded view

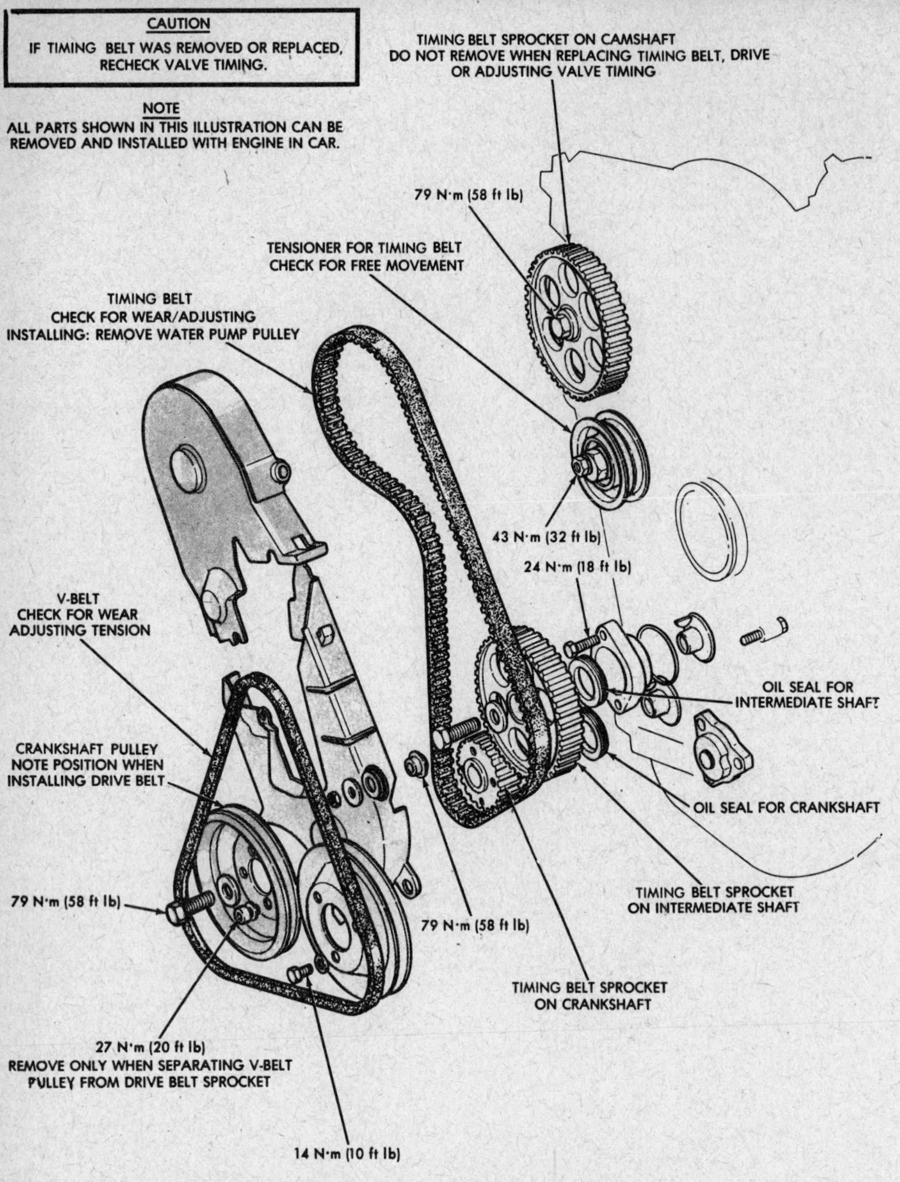

NOTE
ALL PARTS SHOWN IN THIS ILLUSTRATION CAN BE REMOVED AND INSTALLED WITH ENGINE IN CAR.

TIMING BELT SPROCKET ON CAMSHAFT
DO NOT REMOVE WHEN REPLACING TIMING BELT, DRIVE OR ADJUSTING VALVE TIMING

79 N·m (58 ft lb)

TENSIONER FOR TIMING BELT
CHECK FOR FREE MOVEMENT

TIMING BELT
CHECK FOR WEAR/ADJUSTING
INSTALLING: REMOVE WATER PUMP PULLEY

43 N·m (32 ft lb)

24 N·m (18 ft lb)

V-BELT
CHECK FOR WEAR
ADJUSTING TENSION

OIL SEAL FOR
INTERMEDIATE SHAFT

CRANKSHAFT PULLEY
NOTE POSITION WHEN
INSTALLING DRIVE BELT

OIL SEAL FOR CRANKSHAFT

79 N·m (58 ft lb)

TIMING BELT SPROCKET
ON INTERMEDIATE SHAFT

79 N·m (58 ft lb)

TIMING BELT SPROCKET
ON CRANKSHAFT

27 N·m (20 ft lb)
REMOVE ONLY WHEN SEPARATING V-BELT
PULLEY FROM DRIVE BELT SPROCKET

14 N·m (10 ft lb)

Fig. 16 Timing belt & sprocket assembly, exploded view

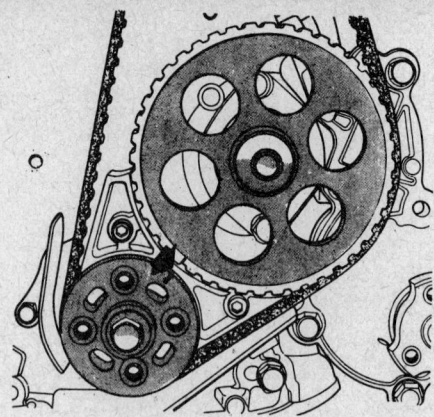

Fig. 17 Aligning timing marks on crankshaft & intermediate shaft sprockets

assemblies. One uses a stud and nut to retain the bearing cap and the other uses a bolt to retain the bearing cap, Fig. 14.

PISTONS, RINGS & PINS

Pistons are available in standard sizes and oversizes of 0.25, 0.50 and 1.0 mm.

Rings are available in standard sizes and oversizes of 0.25, 0.50 and 1.0 mm.

MAIN & ROD BEARINGS

Main bearings are available in standard sizes and undersizes of 0.25, 0.50 and 0.75 mm. Refer to Fig. 15 for bearing installation.

Rod bearings are available in standard sizes and undersizes of 0.25, 0.50 and 0.75 mm.

TIMING BELT, REPLACE

1. Disconnect battery ground cable.
2. Remove A/C compressor adjusting strap screws and the drive belt, if equipped. Remove screws from compressor mount and stabilizer brackets, then position compressor aside. Remove compressor bracket from alternator and the compressor mount bracket.
3. Loosen alternator adjusting strap and remove drive belt.
4. Remove alternator mount bolts and position alternator aside.
5. Remove alternator and compressor mounting bracket from retainer bracket.
6. Loosen power steering pump drive belt, if equipped.
7. Raise and support vehicle.
8. Remove inner fender shield.
9. Remove air compressor, water pump and air pump drive belts, if equipped.
10. Remove idler pulley assembly.
11. Remove crankshaft pulley, Fig. 16, and power steering belt, if equipped.
12. Remove lower plastic timing belt cover.
13. Lower vehicle and support engine with a suitable jack.
14. Remove right engine mounting bolt and raise engine slightly.
15. Loosen timing belt tensioner and remove timing belt.
16. Rotate crankshaft and intermediate sprockets until markings are aligned on sprockets, Fig. 17.

4. To replace valve adjusting disc, depress cam follower with tool L-4417 or equivalent and remove with a narrow screwdriver, Fig. 11, and a magnet. Install new disc and recheck clearance.
5. Valve adjusting discs are available in thicknesses of 3.00 mm to 4.25 mm in increments of .05 mm.

VALVE GUIDES

The valve guides may be removed by pressing out from the combustion chamber side. Coat the new valve guide with oil and press into cold cylinder head until the shoulder is seated. The replacement valve guides have a shoulder. Do not exert a pressure greater than one ton after the valve guide shoulder is seated since the shoulder may break. Ream valve guide to .315–.316 inch.

CAMSHAFT, REPLACE

1. Remove timing belt as outlined under "Timing Belt, Replace".

2. Remove camshaft sprocket.
3. Remove bearing caps 5, 1 and 3, Fig. 12.
4. Diagonally loosen and remove bearing caps 2 and 4, Fig. 12.
5. Remove camshaft from cylinder head.
6. Lubricate bearing shells, journals and contact faces of bearing caps.
7. Install caps in proper order, observing off center bearing position.
8. Reverse Steps 1 through 5 to complete installation.

PISTON & ROD ASSEMBLY

When installing the piston and connecting rod assembly the arrow on top of the piston must face toward the front of engine, Fig. 13, and the forged mark on the connecting rod must face toward the intermediate shaft, Fig. 14.

Connecting rod side clearance should be .015 inch maximum.

NOTE: There are two types of connecting rod

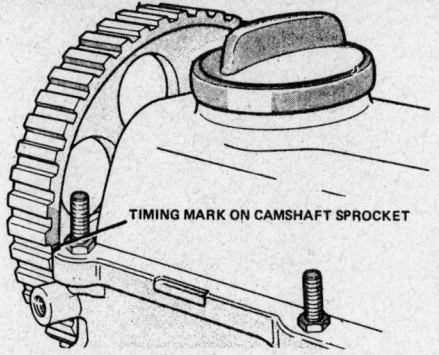

Fig. 18 Aligning timing mark on camshaft sprocket

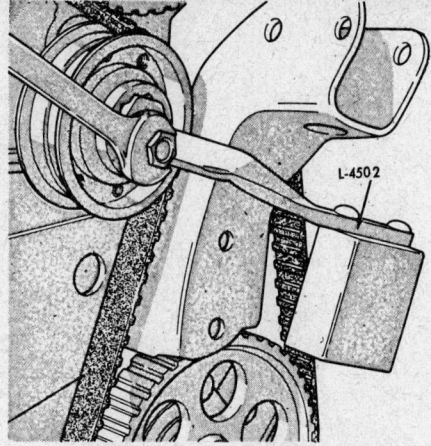

Fig. 19 Timing belt tensioner tool installation

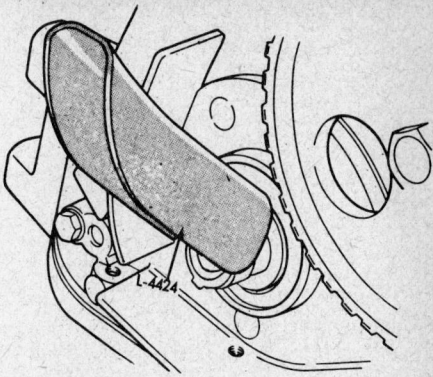

Fig. 20 Front engine oil seal removal

17. Rotate camshaft sprocket until marking on sprocket is aligned with cylinder head cover, Fig. 18.
18. Install timing belt.
19. Install belt tensioning tool L-4502 on large belt tensioner nut in horizontal position, Fig. 19.
20. Reset tool index, as needed, to maintain axis within 15° of horizontal with tensioner bearing against belt.
21. Rotate engine clockwise, 2 full revolutions, then tighten tensioner lock nut.

NOTE: Ensure that timing marks are properly aligned with No. 1 cylinder at TDC of compression stroke.

22. Remove tensioning tool, then reverse remaining procedure to complete installation.

FRONT ENGINE OIL SEAL SERVICE

Refer to Figs. 20 and 21 to replace the crankshaft, intermediate shaft or camshaft seal.

REAR CRANKSHAFT OIL SEAL SERVICE

1. Using a suitable screwdriver, pry oil seal out. Use caution not to nick or damage crankshaft flange seal surface.
2. Place tool L-4455-1 over crankshaft, Fig. 22.
3. Place replacement oil seal over tool and tap seal into position with a mallet.

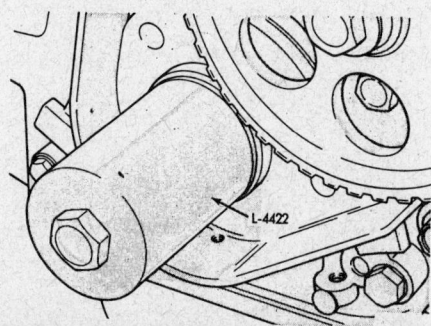

Fig. 21 Front engine oil seal installation

OIL PUMP, REPLACE

Removal

1. Remove oil pan and gasket.
2. Remove oil pump mounting screws, then the oil pump from engine block, Fig. 23.

Installation

1. Install oil pump with shaft in bore until pump mounting face contacts engine block. It may be necessary to rotate pump body to engage pump shaft tongue in distributor shaft groove.
2. Install oil pump mounting screws.
3. Install oil pan gasket and oil pan.

OIL PUMP SERVICE

Disassembly

1. Lightly clamp oil pump in a vise with shaft facing downward.
2. Remove two screws from cover.
3. Push shaft upward and remove shaft and drive gear assembly.
4. Pry deflector plate from assembly and remove strainer.

NOTE: The relief valve is staked in place and is not serviceable.

Inspection

1. Check end play, Fig. 24. End play should be .001–.006 inch.
2. Check gear backlash, Fig. 25. Backlash should be .002–.008 inch. If not, replace pump gears.
3. Check cover for flatness with a .002 inch feeler gauge, Fig. 26.
4. Use compressed air to check relief valve for proper movement, Fig. 27.

Assembly

1. Lightly lubricate all parts.
2. Install driven gear and the drive gear/shaft assembly.
3. Place cover on pump body and install cover screws.
4. Rotate shaft in each direction. If any binding is detected, disassemble pump and inspect for nicks on gears and/or foreign material.

FUEL PUMP, REPLACE

1. Disconnect fuel lines from fuel pump.
2. Remove fuel pump mounting bolts.
3. Remove fuel pump from vehicle.
4. Reverse procedure to install.

WATER PUMP, REPLACE

1. Disconnect battery ground cable.
2. Drain cooling system.
3. Disconnect radiator hoses and bypass hose from water pump.
4. Remove A/C compressor from mounting brackets and position aside with refrigerant lines attached, if equipped.
5. Remove alternator.
6. Disconnect diverter valve hose at valve, then remove the rear air pump bracket and front air pump bracket, if equipped.
7. Remove alternator bracket from water pump.
8. Remove timing belt cover bolt and two top water pump attaching bolts.
9. Remove water pump from vehicle.
10. Reverse procedure to install.

BELT TENSION DATA

		New	Used
1978–80	Air Cond.	55	40
	Air Pump	65	45
	Alternator	75	55
	Power Steer.	40	25
1981–83	Air Cond.	90	45
	Air Pump	70	40
	Alternator	65	40
	Power Steer.	80	50

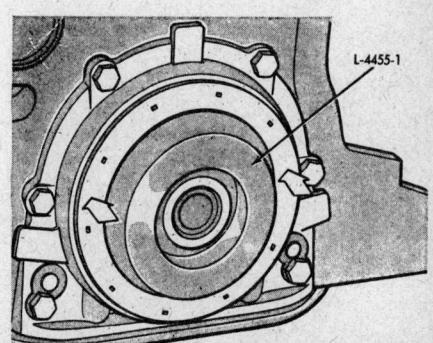

Fig. 22 Rear crankshaft seal installation

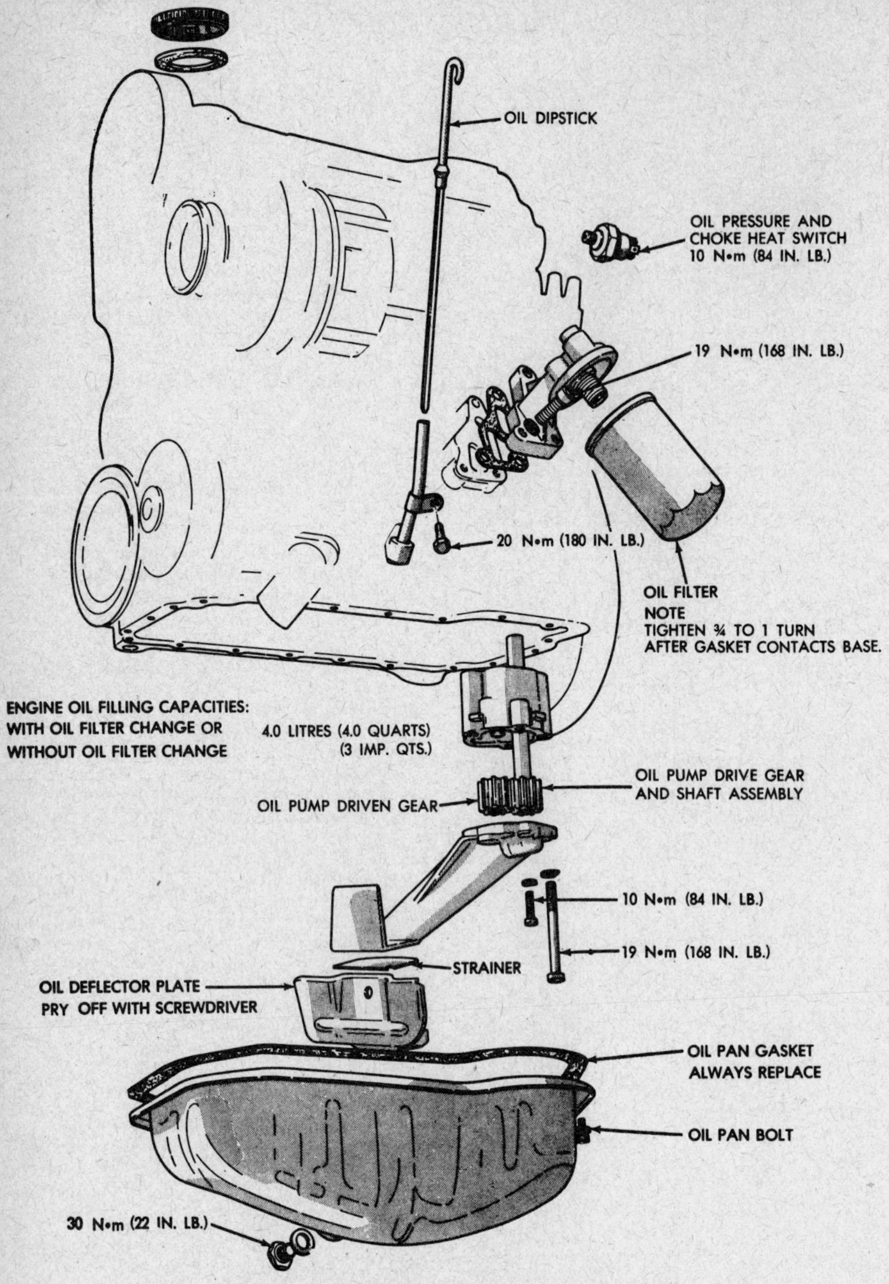

OIL DIPSTICK

OIL PRESSURE AND
CHOKE HEAT SWITCH
10 N•m (84 IN. LB.)

19 N•m (168 IN. LB.)

20 N•m (180 IN. LB.)

OIL FILTER
NOTE
TIGHTEN ¾ TO 1 TURN
AFTER GASKET CONTACTS BASE.

ENGINE OIL FILLING CAPACITIES:
WITH OIL FILTER CHANGE OR
WITHOUT OIL FILTER CHANGE

4.0 LITRES (4.0 QUARTS)
(3 IMP. QTS.)

OIL PUMP DRIVE GEAR
AND SHAFT ASSEMBLY

OIL PUMP DRIVEN GEAR

10 N•m (84 IN. LB.)

19 N•m (168 IN. LB.)

STRAINER

OIL DEFLECTOR PLATE
PRY OFF WITH SCREWDRIVER

OIL PAN GASKET
ALWAYS REPLACE

OIL PAN BOLT

30 N•m (22 IN. LB.)

Fig. 23 Engine lubrication system, exploded view

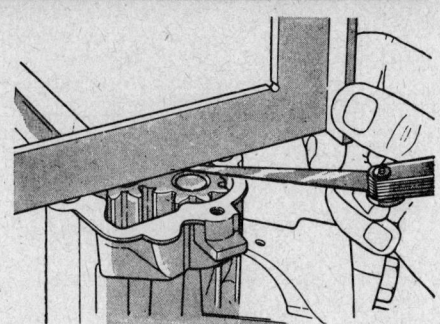

Fig. 24 Checking oil pump gear end play

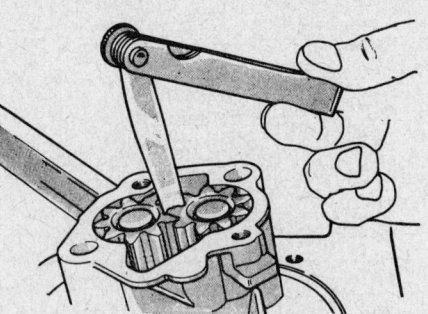

Fig. 25 Checking oil pump gear backlash

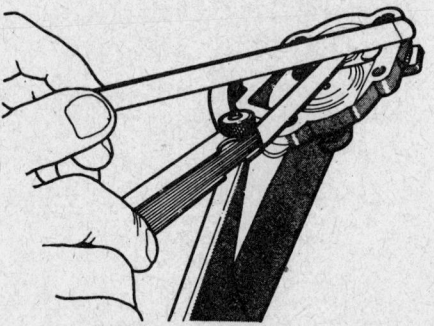

Fig. 26 Checking oil pump gear cover flatness

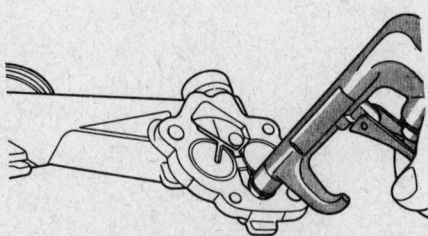

**Fig. 27 Checking oil pump relief valve with
compressed air**

ENGINE MOUNTS

NOTE: When positioning the engine on 1981–84 models, check driveshaft length as outlined in the "Front Suspension & Steering Section" under "Driveshaft Length, Adjust." The engine mounts incorporate slotted bolt holes to permit side-to-side positioning of the engine thereby affecting the length of the driveshaft. Failure to properly position engine may result in extensive damage to the engine.

Refer to Figs. 1 through 8 when replacing the engine mounts.

NOTE: On 1981–83 vehicles, the left engine mount is attached with two types of mounting screws. Two of the three are of the pilot type with extended tips. Extended tip screws must be installed in the proper position, Fig. 8. Damage to the shift cover or difficult shifting may occur if the screws are incorrectly installed.

ENGINE, REPLACE

1981–83

1. Disconnect battery ground cable.
2. Scribe alignment marks on hood and hood hinge, then remove hood.
3. Drain cooling system, then disconnect radiator hoses at radiator and engine.
4. Remove radiator and fan shroud, then remove air cleaner.
5. Remove A/C compressor from mounting bracket and position aside with hoses attached, if equipped.
6. Remove power steering pump from mounting bracket and position aside with hoses attached, if equipped.
7. Drain crankcase and remove oil filter.
8. Disconnect wire connectors at alternator, carburetor and engine.
9. Disconnect fuel line, heater hose and accelerator cable.
10. Remove alternator from mounting bracket and position aside.
11. On models equipped with manual transmission, disconnect clutch cable, then remove transmission lower cover.
12. On all models, disconnect exhaust pipe from exhaust manifold, then remove starter motor.
13. On models equipped with automatic transmission, remove transmission case

lower cover and place alignment marks on flex plate and torque converter, then remove converter to flex plate attaching screws. Attach a C-clamp to front lower portion of converter housing to retain torque converter in housing when engine is being removed.
14. On all models, install a suitable transmission holding fixture and attach a suitable engine lifting device.
15. Remove right hand inner splash shield, then disconnect ground strap.
16. Remove right hand engine mount to insulator through bolt.
17. Remove transmission case to engine block attaching bolts.
18. Remove front engine mount to bracket bolt, then carefully lift engine from vehicle.
19. Reverse procedure to install.

1984

1. Perform steps 1 through 15 for 1981–83 models.
2. Remove long bolt through yoke bracket and insulator.

CAUTION: If insulator screws are to be removed, mark position on side rail for exact reinstallation.

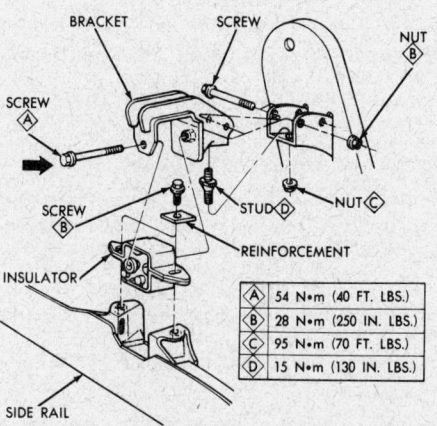

Fig. 1   Engine mount. 1981–83 right side

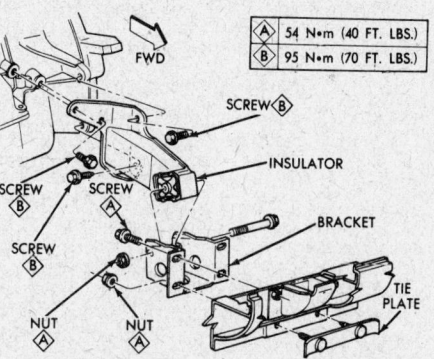

Fig. 2   Front engine mount. 1981–83

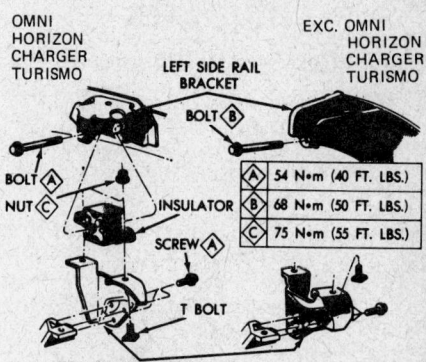

Fig. 3   Engine mount. 1981–83 left side Automatic Transaxle

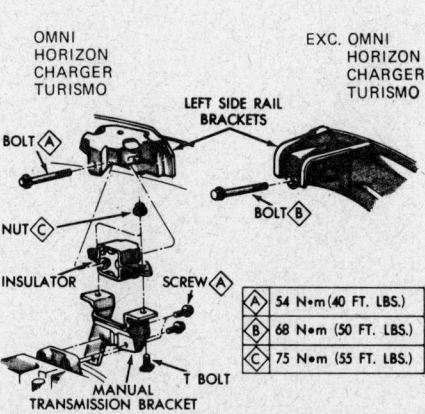

Fig. 4   Engine mount. 1981–83 left side Manual Transaxle

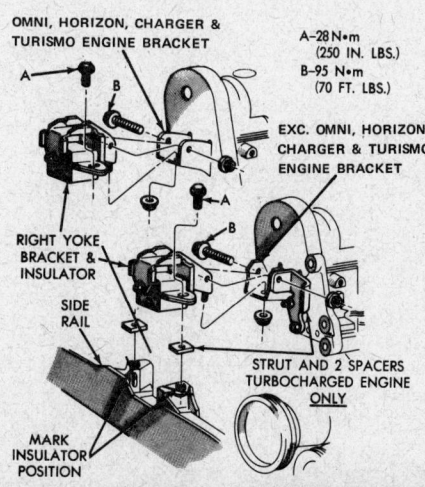

Fig. 5   Engine mount. 1984 right side

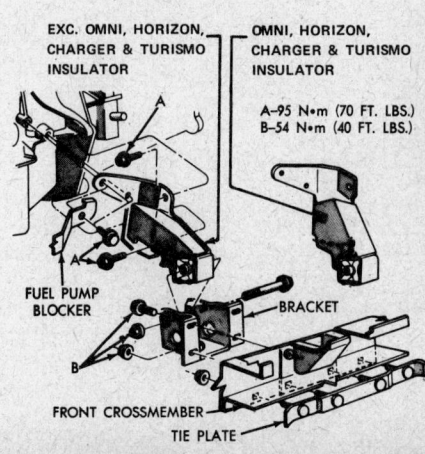

Fig. 6   Front engine mount. 1984

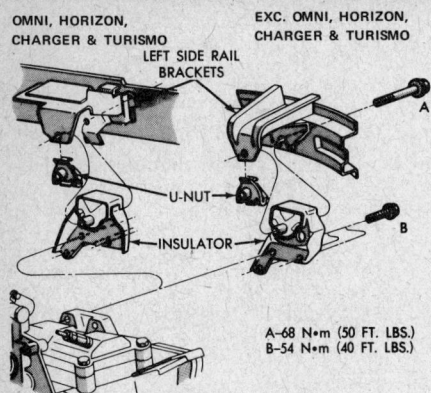

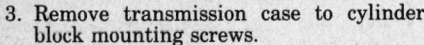

Fig. 7   Engine mount. 1984 left side

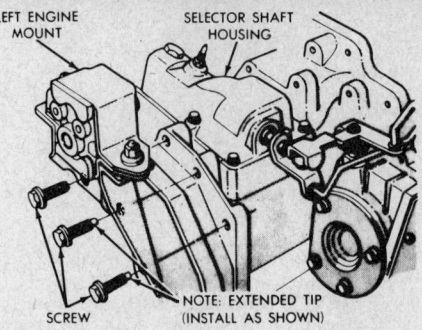

Fig. 8   Correct positioning of extended tip screws

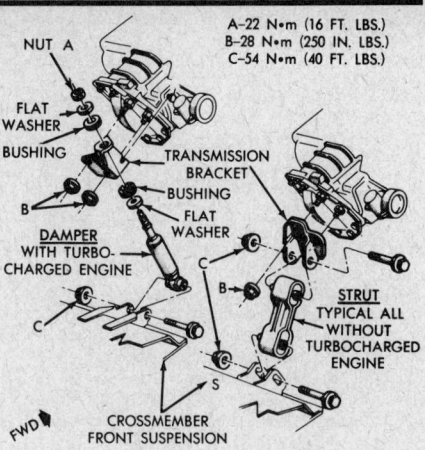

Fig. 9   Anti roll strut & damper

3. Remove transmission case to cylinder block mounting screws.
4. Remove front engine mount screw and nut.
5. On vehicles with manual transmission, remove anti roll strut or damper, Fig. 9.
6. On vehicles with manual transmission, remove insulator through bolt from inside wheel house, or the insulator bracket to transmission screws.
7. On all vehicles, carefully lift engine from vehicle.
8. Reverse procedure to install.

TIMING SPROCKETS & OIL SEALS

Alternator Belt Removal

1. Disconnect battery ground cable.
2. Loosen alternator locking screw, then loosen adjusting screw and remove belt.
3. Reverse procedure to install.

Alternator & Compressor Mounting Bracket

For replacement of alternator and compressor mounting bracket refer to Fig. 10.

Power Steering Pump Mounting Bracket

1. Remove pump locking screw, Fig. 11.
2. Remove pivot bolt and pivot nut, then the drive belt.
3. Remove power steering pump and lay aside.
4. Remove mounting bracket bolts, then the bracket.
5. Reverse procedure to install.

Crankshaft Pulley & Water Pump Pulley

1. Remove screws retaining water pump pulley to pump shaft.
2. Remove bolts retaining crankshaft pulley.
3. Raise and support front of vehicle, then remove right inner splash shield and remove crankshaft pulley.
4. Reverse procedure to install

Timing Belt Cover

1. Remove nuts securing cover to cylinder head, Fig. 12.
2. Remove screws securing cover to cylinder head, then remove both halves of timing belt cover.
3. Position a suitable jack under engine, then remove right hand engine mount bolt and raise engine slightly.
4. Loosen timing belt tensioner, then remove timing belt.
5. Reverse procedure to install.

Crankshaft Sprocket

1. With timing belt removed from engine, remove the crankshaft sprocket bolt.
2. Remove crankshaft sprocket using a suitable puller.

Crankshaft, Intermediate Shaft & Camshaft Oil Seal Service

Refer to Figs. 13 and 14 for removal and installation of crankshaft, intermediate shaft or camshaft seals.

NOTE: On late model 1981 2.2L engines, the camshaft oil seals were changed from steel backed to uni-directional rubber backed type seals. This change made necessary an increase in the cylinder rear seal bore to prevent accidental mixing of the uni-directional front and rear seals.

The replacement seal for early built 2.2L engines will also be rubber backed with arrows indicating the direction of rotation and location in the head marked on the seal. The seals must be installed as indicated.

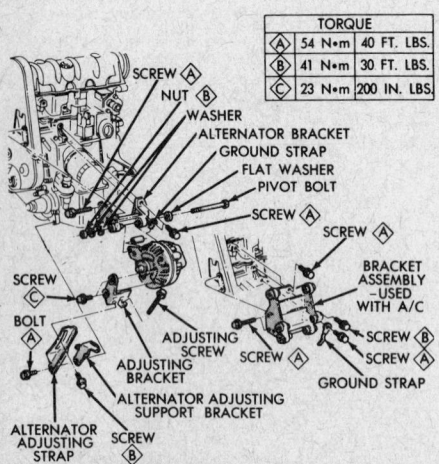

Fig. 10.   Alternator & compressor mounting bracket, replacement

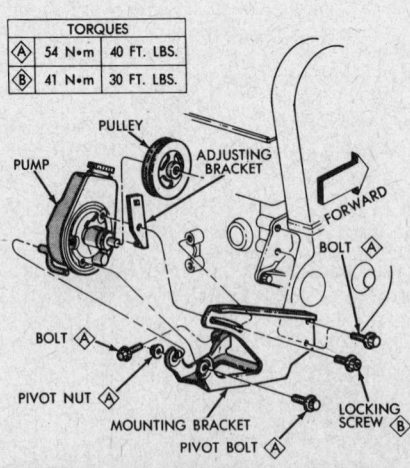

Fig. 11   Power steering pump & mounting bracket, replacement

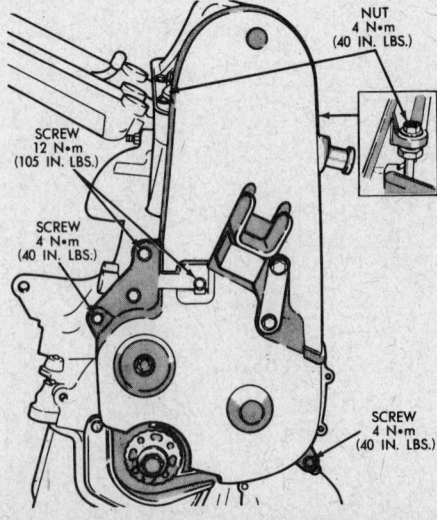

Fig. 12   Timing belt cover removal

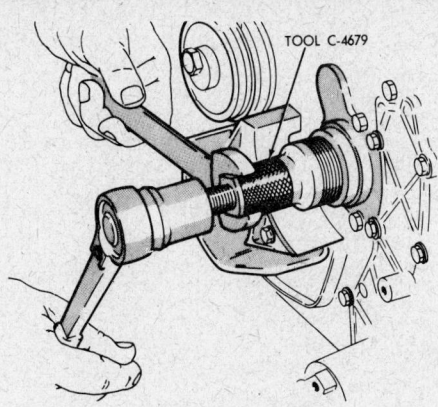

Fig. 13 Crankshaft, intermediate shaft & camshaft oil seal removal

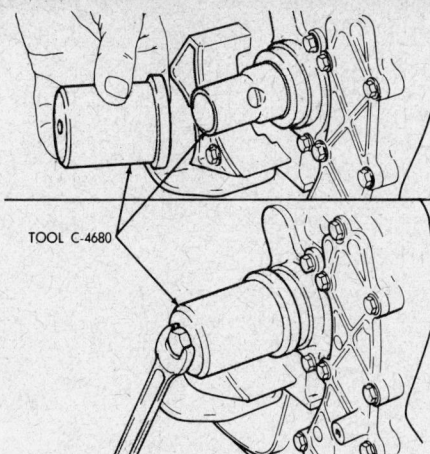

Fig. 14 Cranskhaft, intermediate shaft & camshaft oil seal installation

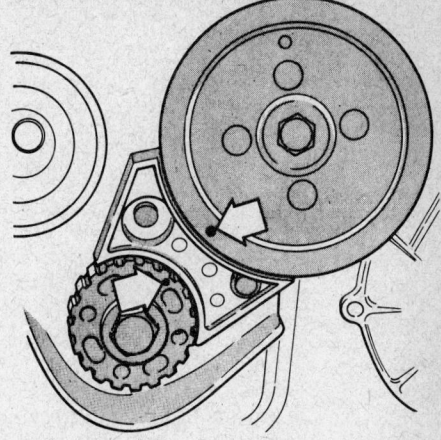

Fig. 15 Aligning crankshaft & intermediate shaft timing marks

Crankshaft & Intermediate Shaft Timing

1. Rotate crankshaft and intermediate shaft until markings on sprockets are aligned, Fig. 15.

Camshaft Timing

1. Rotate camshaft until arrows on hub are aligned with No. 1 camshaft cap to cylinder head line, Fig. 16. Small hole must be located along vertical center line.
2. Install timing belt. Refer to "Adjusting Drive Belt Tension" described elsewhere for proper drive belt adjustment.
3. Rotate crankshaft two full revolutions and recheck timing.

NOTE: Do not allow oil or solvents to contact the timing belt since they will deteriorate the rubber and cause tooth skippage.

Camshaft & Intermediate Shaft Removal & Installation

Refer to Fig. 17 for removal and installation of camshaft and intermediate shaft sprocket.

Adjusting Drive Belt Tension

1. Remove spark plugs then rotate crankshaft to TDC position.
2. Using a suitable tool, loosen tensioner lock nut, Fig. 18.
3. Reset belt tension so that belt tensioning tool axis is within 15° of horizontal.
4. Rotate crankshaft two revolutions in clockwise direction and position at TDC, then tighten tensioner lock nut.

INTAKE & EXHAUST MANIFOLD

Except Turbo

1. Disconnect battery ground cable and drain coolant system.
2. Remove air cleaner and disconnect all vacuum and fuel lines and electrical connectors from carburetor.
3. Disconnect throttle linkage, then remove power steering pump drive belt.
4. Disconnect power brake vacuum hose from manifold, if equipped.
5. Disconnect hoses from water crossover, then raise and support vehicle and disconnect exhaust pipe from exhaust manifold.
6. Remove power steering pump and position aside, then remove intake manifold support bracket.
7. Remove EGR tube, then the intake manifold retaining screws.
8. Lower vehicle and remove intake manifold.
9. Remove exhaust manifold retaining nuts, then the exhaust manifold.
10. Reverse procedure to install.

Turbo

1. Disconnect battery ground cable and drain cooling system.
2. Raise and support vehicle.
3. Disconnect exhaust pipe at articulated joint and disconnect oxygen sensor at electrical connectors.
4. Remove turbocharger to block support bracket.
5. Loosen oil drain bvack tube connector hose clamps and move tube down on block fitting.
6. Disconnect turbocharger coolant inlet tube at cylinder block and disconnect tube support bracket.
7. Lower vehicle.
8. Remove air cleaner assembly including throttle body adaptor, hose, and air cleaner box with support bracket, Fig. 19.
9. Disconnect accelerator linkage, throttle body electrical connector, and vacuum hoses, Fig. 20.

Fig. 16 Aligning camshaft timing marks

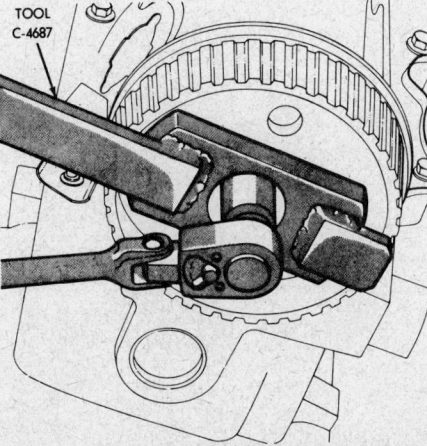

Fig. 17 Camshaft & intermediate shaft sprocket replacement

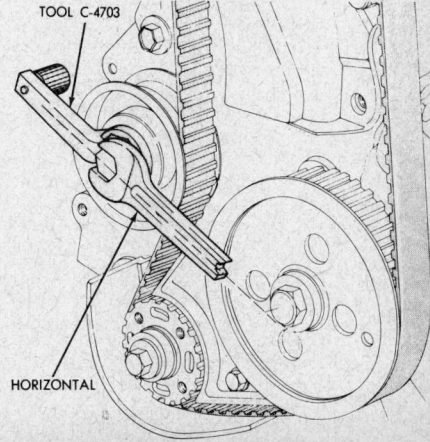

Fig. 18 Adjusting drive belt tension

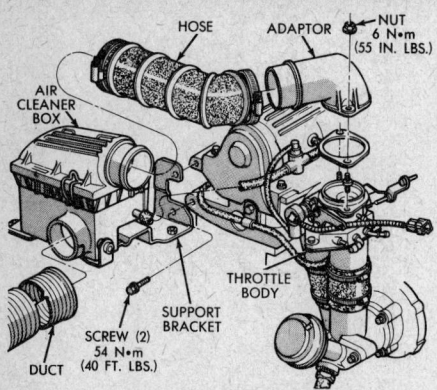

Fig. 19 Air cleaner box & support, hoses, & throttle body adaptor

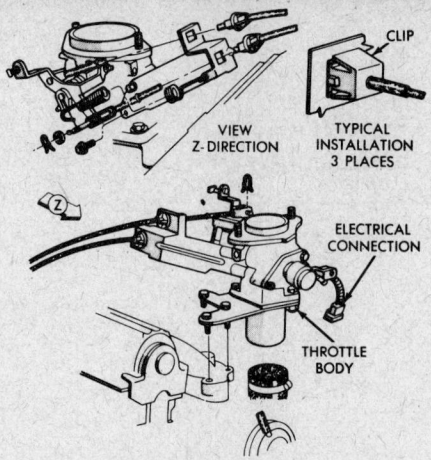

Fig. 20 Accelerator linkage & throttle body

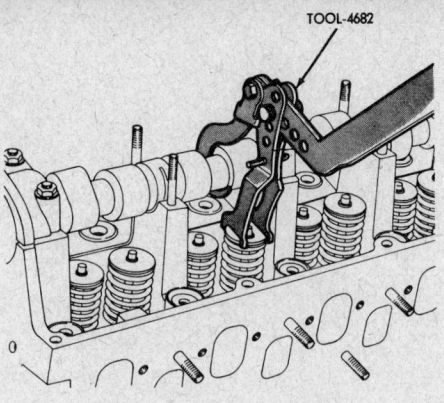

Fig. 21 Valve spring, replace

10. Remove four bracket to intake manifold screws and two bracket to heat shield retaining clips, then lift and secure fuel rail, with injectors, wiring harness, and fuel lines intact, up out of way.
11. Disconnect turbocharger oil feed line at oil sending unit tee.
12. Disconnect upper radiator hose at thermostat housing.
13. Remove cylinder head with manifolds and turbocharger as an assembly as described under "Cylinder Head & Valve Assembly".
14. Reverse procedure to install.

CYLINDER HEAD & VALVE ASSEMBLY

Removing & Installing Valve Springs

Cylinder Head Off Engine
1. Using suitable tool to hold valves in head, compress valve spring enough to remove and install valve bead locks, Fig. 21.

Cylinder Head On Engine
1. Rotate crankshaft until piston is at TDC on compression stroke.
2. Apply 90–100 psi. of compressed air into spark plug hole of valve being removed.
3. Using suitable tool, compress valve spring enough to remove valve stem locks.
4. Remove valve spring and spring seat.
5. Remove valve seal.

Cylinder Head Bolt Remove Sequence

When removing cylinder head, remove cylinder head bolts in proper sequence, Fig. 22.

Cylinder Head Bolt Tightening Sequence

1. Referring to bolt tightening sequence, Fig. 23, tighten cylinder head bolts in

three steps as follows:
a. Torque bolts to 30 ft. lbs.
b. Torque bolts to 45 ft. lbs.
c. Advance each bolt an additional ¼ turn (90 degrees).

Camshaft Bearing Caps

1. With caps removed from engine, check oil holes for obstructions.
2. With caps aligned in proper sequence, ensure arrow on caps 1, 2, 3 and 4 point toward timing belt, Fig. 24.
3. Apply suitable sealant to No. 5 bearing cap.
4. Install caps before installing camshaft seals, then torque cap bolts to 160 inch lbs.

NOTE: Some 1983–84 engines may be equipped with oversize camshaft bearings. Engines with oversize camshaft bearings can be identified by green markings on cylinder head and camshaft at AIR pump side of engine.

VALVE LIFT SPECS.

Engine	Year	Intake	Exhaust
4-135	1981–84	.430	.430

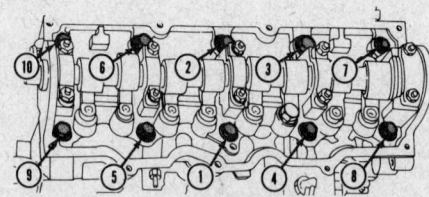

Fig. 23 Cylinder head bolt tightening sequence

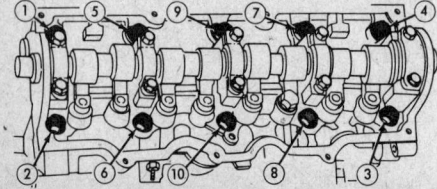

Fig. 22 Cylinder head bolt removal sequence

Fig. 24 Camshaft bearing cap installation

VALVE TIMING

Intake Opens Before TDC

Engine	Year	Degrees
4-135	1981–84	12
	1983	16
	1984 exc. Shelby Opt. & Turbocharged	16
	Shelby	10.5
	Turbocharged	10

PISTON & ROD ASSEMBLY

When installing the piston and rod assembly, indentation on top of piston must face towards timing belt side of engine, Fig. 25. The oil hole on the connecting rod must face timing belt side of engine and be on the same side as the indented mark on the piston.

Connecting rod clearance should be .005–.013 inch.

ENGINE LUBRICATION SYSTEM

Oil Pump Assembly

1. With oil pan removed, remove screw securing oil pump to cylinder block, Fig. 26.
2. Reverse procedure to install. Torque oil pump attaching screws to 200 inch lbs.

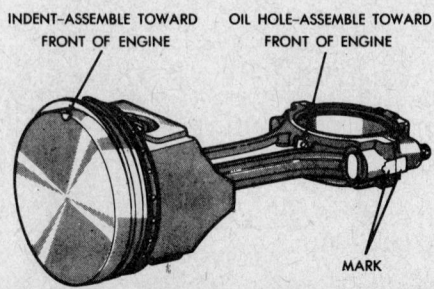

Fig. 25 Piston & connecting rod assembly

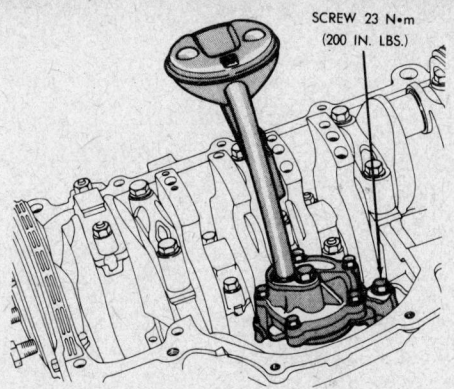

Fig. 26 Oil pump replacement

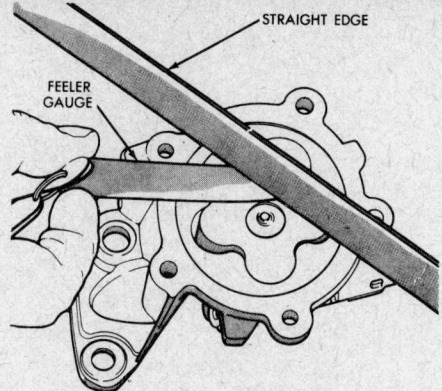

Fig. 27 Measuring oil pump end play

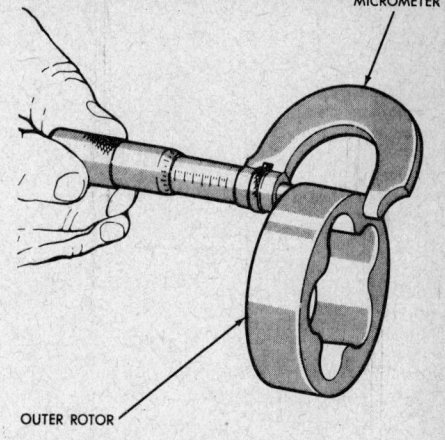

Fig. 28 Measuring oil pump outer rotor thickness

NOTE: The oil pump must fully seat on the cylinder block before the mounting bolts are tightened. Check for proper seating by rotating the pump body on the block. The pump body should move a few degrees in both directions with no further movement into the block. If not, the mating surfaces should be cleaned of any foreign material preventing proper seating, otherwise damage to the oil pump, pump driveshaft and gear, or distributor drive may result.

Oil Pump Service

1. Measure the following oil pump clearances:
   a. End play, Fig. 27. End play should be .001–.006 in on 1981–82 models or .001–.004 in. on 1983–84 models.
   b. Outer rotor thickness, Fig. 28. Thickness should be .825 in. minimum. Install outer rotor with chamfered edge in pump body.
   c. Clearance between rotors, Fig. 29, should be .010 in. maximum.
   d. Outer rotor clearance, Fig. 30. Clearance should be .014 in. maximum.
   e. Oil pump cover, Fig. 31. Clearance should be .015 in. maximum on 1981–82 models or .003 in. maximum on 1983–84 models.
   f. Oil pressure relief valve spring length should be 1.95 in.

WATER PUMP, REPLACE

1. Disconnect battery ground cable.
2. Drain cooling system, and remove upper radiator hose.
3. Remove A/C compressor from mounting brackets and position aside with refrigerant lines attached, if equipped.
4. Remove alternator.
5. Disconnect lower radiator hose, bypass hose and four water pump to engine attaching screws, then remove water pump.
6. Reverse procedure to install.

BELT TENSION DATA

1981–84		New	Used
	Air Cond.	40	30
	Air Pump	45	35
	Alternator	110	80
	Power Steer.	75	55

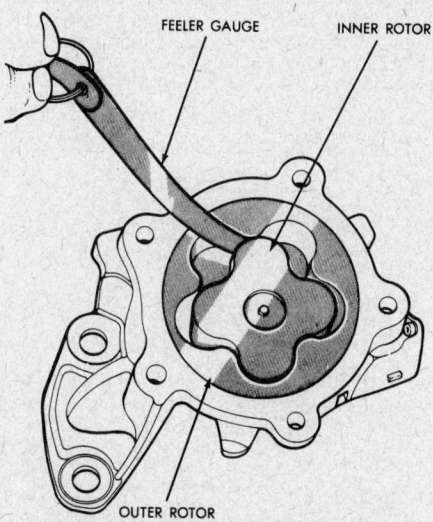

Fig. 29 Measuring clearance between oil pump rotors

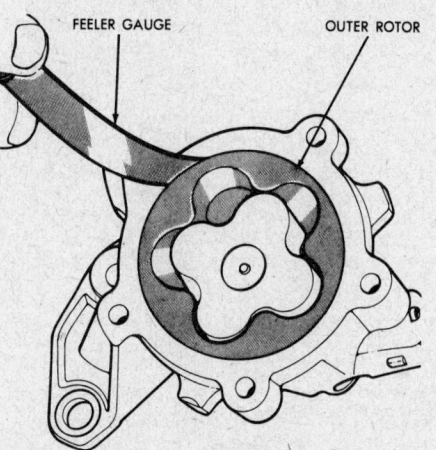

Fig. 30 Measuring oil pump outer rotor clearance

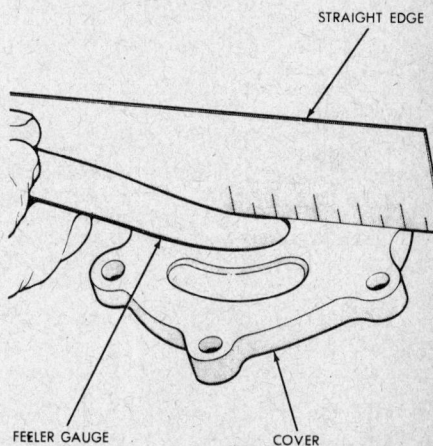

Fig. 31 Measuring oil pump cover clearance

4-156 Engine Section

ENGINE MOUNTS

NOTE: When positioning the engine on 1981–84 models, check driveshaft length as outlined in the "Front Suspension & Steering Section" under "Driveshaft Length, Adjust." The engine mounts incorporate slotted bolt holes to permit side-to-side positioning of the engine thereby affecting the length of the driveshaft. Failure to properly position engine may result in extensive damage to the engine.

Refer to Figs. 1 through 3 when replacing the engine mounts.

NOTE: The left engine mount is attached with two types of mounting screws. Two of the three are of the pilot type with extended tips. Extended tip screws must be installed in the proper position, Fig. 4. Damage to the shift cover or difficult shifting may occur if the screws are incorrectly installed.

ENGINE, REPLACE

1. Disconnect battery ground cable.
2. Scribe alignment marks on hood and hood hinge, then remove hood.
3. Drain cooling system, then disconnect radiator hoses at radiator and engine.
4. Remove radiator and fan shroud, then remove air cleaner.
5. Remove A/C compressor from mounting bracket and position aside with hoses attached, if equipped.
6. Remove power steering pump from mounting bracket and position aside with hoses attached, if equipped.
7. Drain crankcase and remove oil filter.
8. Disconnect wire connectors at alternator, carburetor and engine.
9. Disconnect fuel line, heater hose and accelerator cable.
10. Remove alternator from mounting bracket and position aside.
11. Disconnect exhaust pipe from exhaust manifold, then remove starter motor.
12. Remove transmission case lower cover and place alignment marks on flex plate and torque converter, then remove converter to flex plate attaching screws. Attach a C-clamp to front lower portion of converter housing to retain torque converter in housing when engine is being removed.
13. Install a suitable transmission holding fixture and attach a suitable engine lifting device.
14. Remove right hand inner splash shield, then disconnect ground strap.
15. Remove right hand engine mount to insulator through bolt.
16. Remove transmission case to engine block attaching bolts.
17. Remove front engine mount to bracket bolt, then carefully lift engine from vehicle.
18. Reverse procedure to install.

TIMING GEARS & OIL SEALS

Timing Chain Case Cover, Removal

1. Disconnect battery ground cable.
2. Remove alternator locking screw, then loosen jam nut and adjusting screw. Remove drive belt.
3. Remove distributor retaining nut, then remove distributor from cylinder head and position aside.

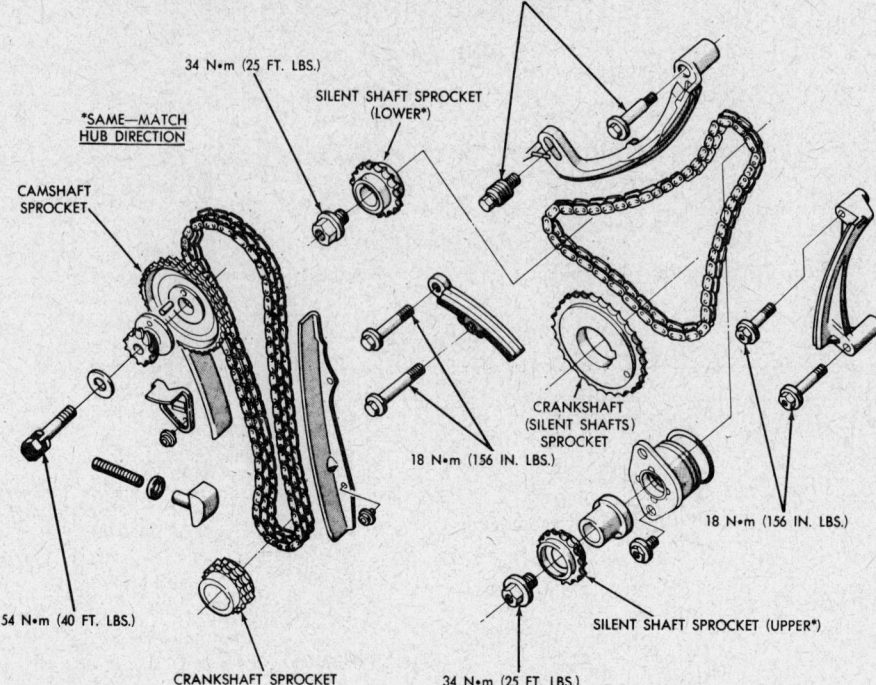

Timing gears & chain assembly

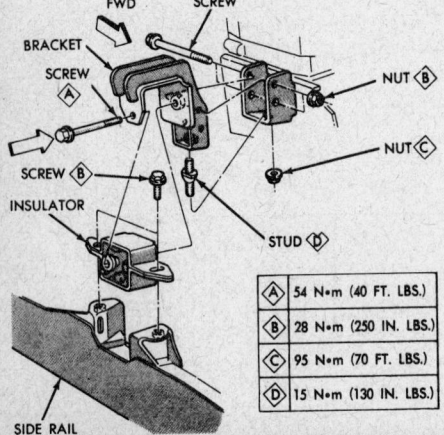

Fig. 1 Engine mount. Right side

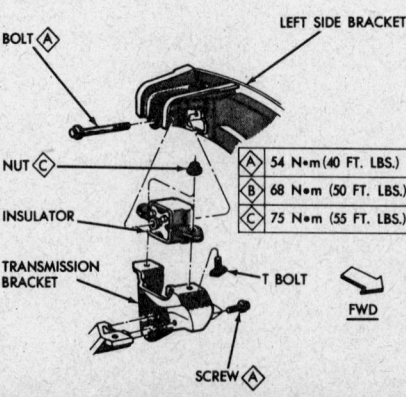

Fig. 2 Front engine mount

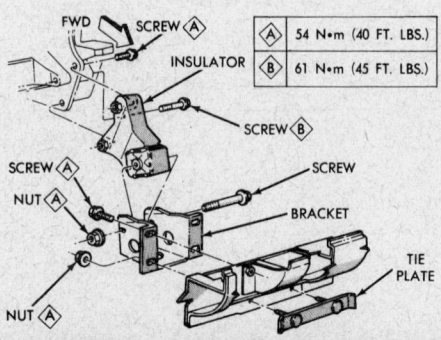

Fig. 3 Engine mount. Left side

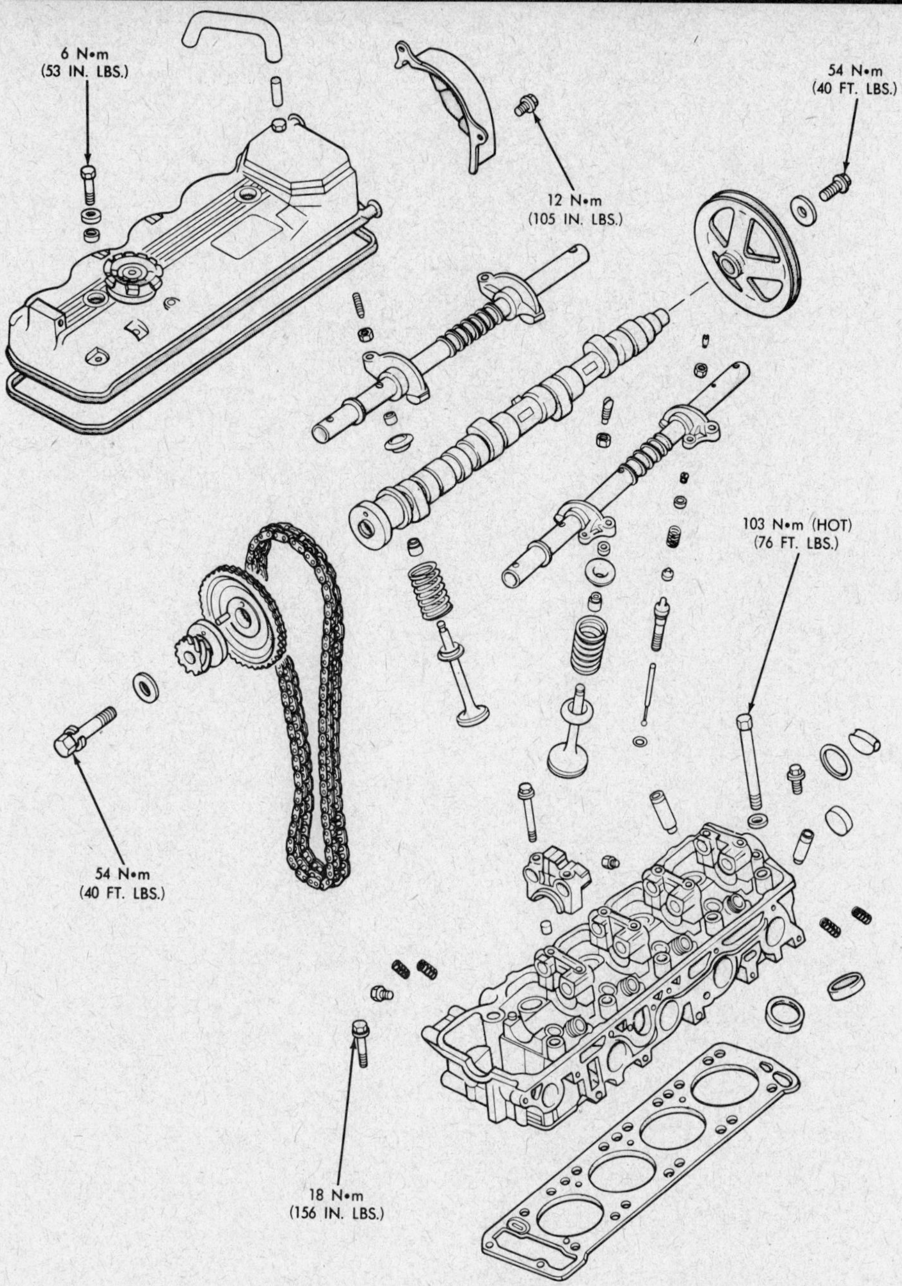

6 N•m
(53 IN. LBS.)

12 N•m
(105 IN. LBS.)

54 N•m
(40 FT. LBS.)

103 N•m (HOT)
(76 FT. LBS.)

54 N•m
(40 FT. LBS.)

18 N•m
(156 IN. LBS.)

Cylinder head & valve assembly

4. Remove front and rear A/C compressor to bracket attaching screws, then remove A/C compressor and position aside.
5. Remove power steering pump pivot and lock screws, then remove drive belt.
6. Remove power steering pump mounting screw and nut, then position power steering pump aside.
7. Remove power steering pump bracket to engine attaching screws, then remove bracket.
8. Raise vehicle and remove right inner splash shield.
9. Drain crankcase, then remove crankshaft drive pulley.
10. Lower vehicle and position a suitable jack under engine.
11. Remove engine mount to frame side rail through bolt, then remove engine oil dipstick.
12. Remove air cleaner assembly.
13. Disconnect battery ground cable, then the spark plug wires.
14. Disconnect vacuum hoses from cylinder head cover.
15. Remove cylinder head cover screws, then the cylinder head cover.
16. Remove oil pan attaching screws, then remove oil pan.
17. Remove timing indicator plate from timing chain case cover.
18. Remove engine mounting plate from timing chain case cover.
19. Remove cylinder head cover as previously described.
20. Remove two front cylinder head screws. Do not disturb any other cylinder head bolts.
21. Refer to Fig. 5 and remove remaining screws securing chain case cover to engine.

Silent Shaft Drive Chain, Removal

1. Remove chain case cover as previously described.
2. Remove sprocket screws, then the drive chain, crankshaft sprocket and silent shaft sprocket, Fig. 6.

Camshaft Drive Chain, Removal

1. Remove chain case cover as previously described.
2. Remove camshaft sprocket holder, then the left and right timing chain guides, Fig. 7.
3. Depress tensioner to remove drive chain.
4. Remove crankshaft and camshaft sprockets.

Camshaft Installation

1. With camshaft bearing caps installed,

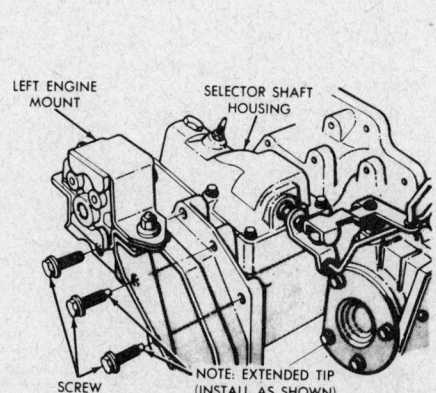

LEFT ENGINE MOUNT

SELECTOR SHAFT HOUSING

NOTE: EXTENDED TIP (INSTALL AS SHOWN)

SCREW

Fig. 4 Correct positioning of extended tip screws

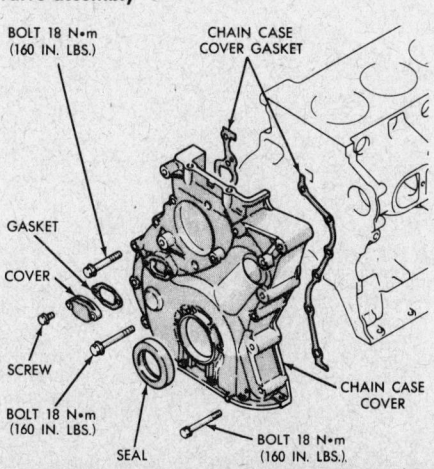

BOLT 18 N•m (160 IN. LBS.)

CHAIN CASE COVER GASKET

GASKET

COVER

SCREW

BOLT 18 N•m (160 IN. LBS.)

SEAL

BOLT 18 N•m (160 IN. LBS.)

CHAIN CASE COVER

Fig. 5 Chain case cover removal

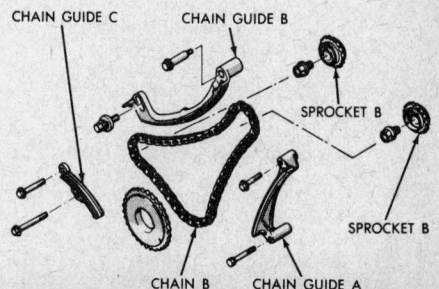

CHAIN GUIDE C

CHAIN GUIDE B

SPROCKET B

SPROCKET B

CHAIN B

CHAIN GUIDE A

Fig. 6 Silent shaft drive chain, replace

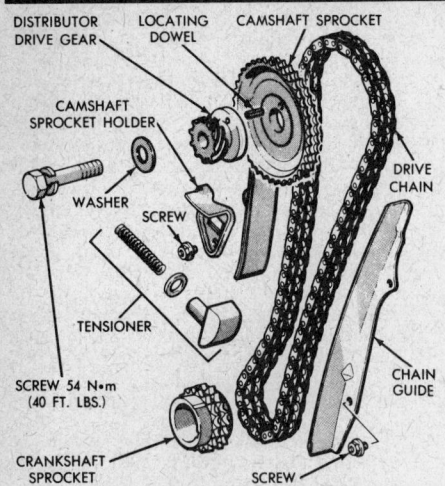

Fig. 7 Camshaft drive chain, replace

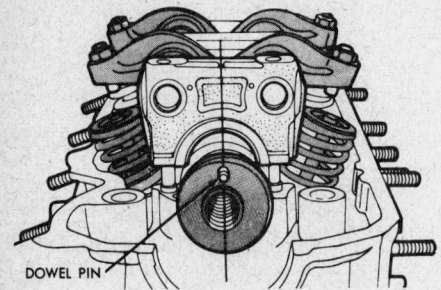

Fig. 8 Camshaft timing mark alignment

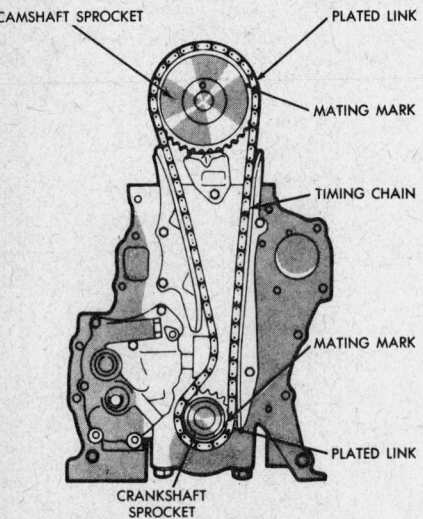

Fig. 9 Timing chain installation

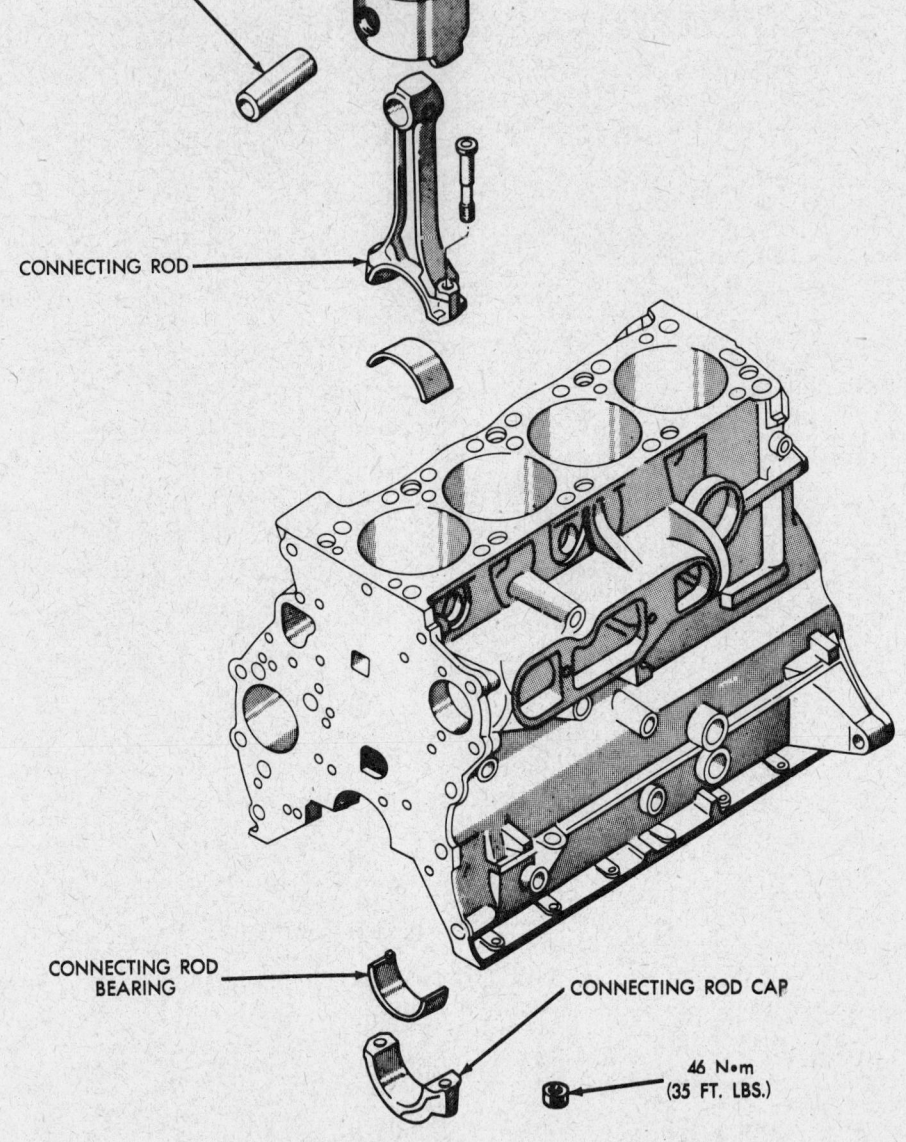

Cylinder block, piston & connecting rod assembly

rotate camshaft until timing marks are aligned as shown in Fig. 8.

Timing Chain Installation

1. Install sprocket holder, then left and right chain guides, Fig. 6.
2. Rotate crankshaft until No. 1 piston is at TDC on compression stroke.
3. Install tensioner spring assembly onto oil pump body, Fig. 7.
4. Install timing chain on camshaft sprocket and crankshaft sprocket. Ensure timing marks are aligned, Fig. 9. Timing marks on sprockets are punch marks on the teeth while timing marks on chain are plated links.
5. Align crankshaft sprocket to the crankshaft keyway and slide into place. Align camshaft sprocket dowel hole to camshaft dowel hole.
6. Install dowel pin, then the distributor drive gear. Install sprocket screw onto camshaft and torque to 40 ft. lbs.

Silent Shaft Chain Installation & Adjustment

1. Install silent shaft chain drive pulley onto crankshaft.
2. Install silent shaft chain onto oil pump sprocket and silent shaft sprocket, Fig. 10.
3. Ensure timing marks are aligned. Timing marks on the sprockets are punch marks on the teeth, while timing marks on the

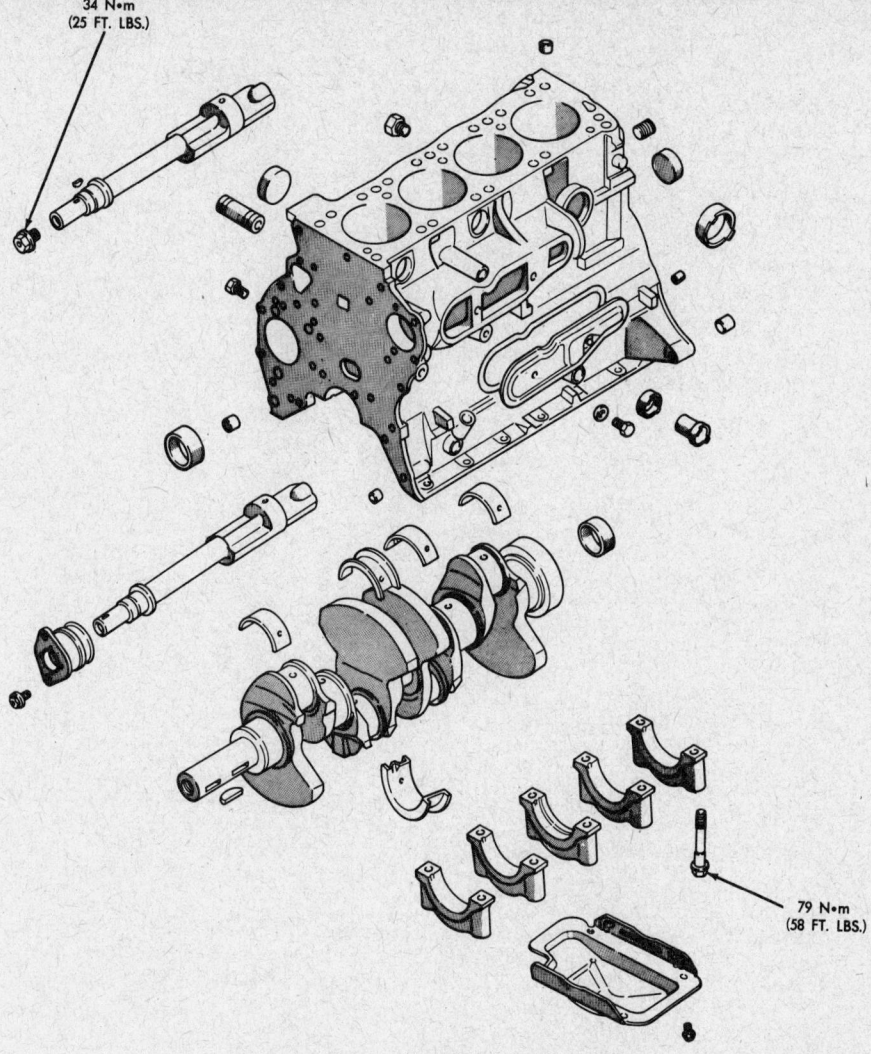

Crankshaft, bearings & silent shaft assembly

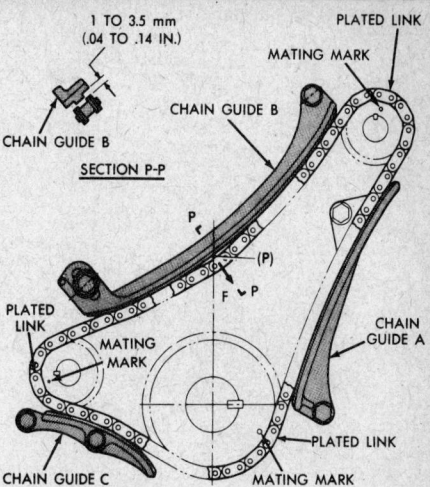

Fig. 10 Silent Shaft chain adjustment & installation with engine removed

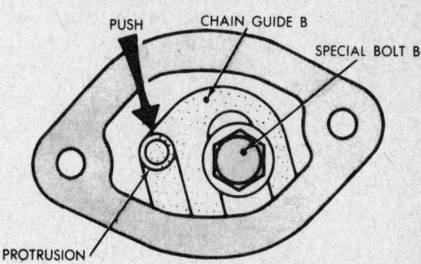

Fig. 11 Silent Shaft chain adjustment with engine installed

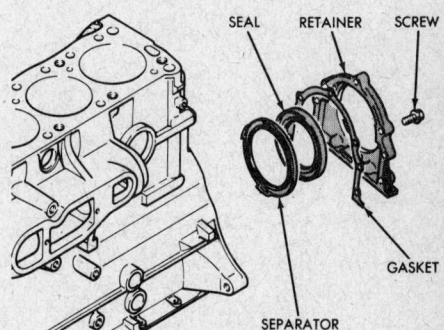

Fig. 12 Rear oil seal, replace

chain are plated links.

4. Align crankshaft sprocket plated link with punch mark on sprocket.
5. Position chain on crankshaft sprocket, then install oil pump sprocket and silent shaft sprockets on their respective shafts.
6. Install oil pump and silent shaft sprocket screws and torque to 25 ft. lbs.
7. Install three chain guides. Snug tighten retaining bolts.
8. Refer to Fig. 10 and adjust silent shaft chain tension as follows:
   a. Tighten chain guide "A" mounting screws.
   b. Tighten chain guide "C" mounting screws.
   c. Shake oil pump and silent shaft sprockets to collect slack at point "P".
   d. Adjust position of chain guide "B" so that when the chain is pulled in direction of arrow "F", clearance between chain guide "B" and chain links will be .4–.14 in. Tighten chain guide "B" mounting screws.
9. Install new gasket on chain case, coat gasket with suitable sealant, then install chain case to block and torque attaching screws to 156 in. lbs.

Tension Adjustment With Engine Installed

1. Remove cover over access hole in chain case cover, Fig. 11.
2. Loosen bolt "B", Fig. 11.
3. Apply pressure by hand on boss indicated in Fig. 11, then torque bolt "B" to 160 in. lbs.

CRANKSHAFT, BEARINGS & SILENT SHAFT

Rear Oil Seal, Replace

1. Remove screws attaching crankshaft rear oil seal retainer, then the retainer, Fig. 12.
2. Remove separator from retainer, then the oil seal.
3. Install new seal into retainer, then the separator. Ensure oil hole is positioned at separator bottom.

Main Bearing Caps

1. Install main bearing caps in sequence and ensure arrows on caps are pointed in direction of timing chain, Fig. 13.

Oil Pump & Silent Shaft

1. Refer to Fig. 14 and remove silent shaft screw, then the silent shaft.
2. Remove oil pump to cylinder block screw, then the oil pump.

Silent Shaft Clearances

Before installing silent shaft, measure outer diameter to outer bearing clearance. Clearance should be .0008–.0024 in. (.02–.06mm). Measure inner diameter to inner bearing clearance. Clearance should be .0020–.0035 in. (.05–.09mm).

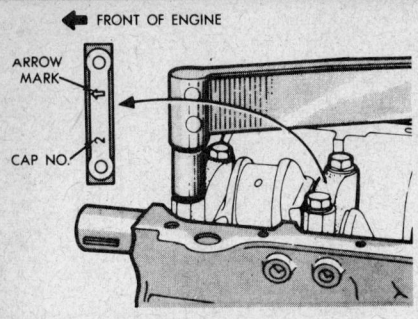

Fig. 13 Main bearing cap installation

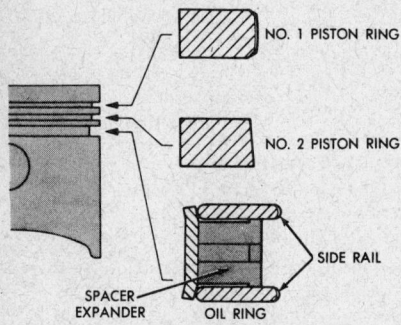

Fig. 16 Piston ring installation

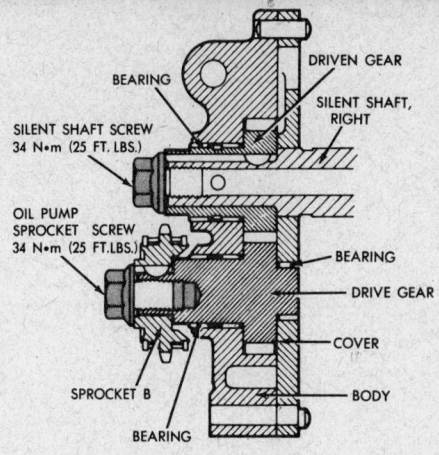

Fig. 14 Oil pump & Silent Shaft, removal

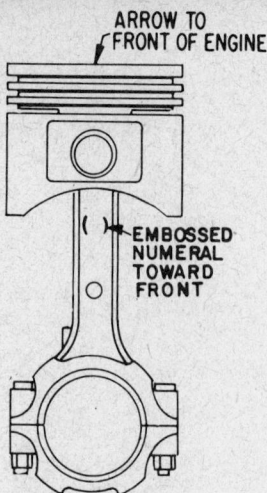

NOTE: NUMBERED SIDE OF CAP SHOULD FACE NUMBERED SIDE OF ROD

Fig. 15 Piston & Rod assembly

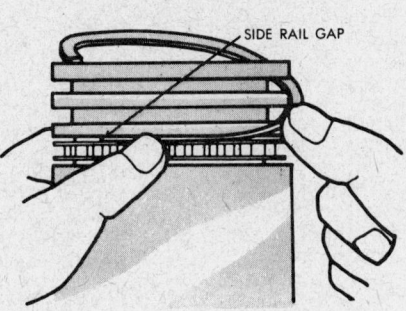

Fig. 17 Installing oil ring side rail

PISTON & ROD ASSEMBLY

During installation of piston and rod assembly, arrow at top of piston must face toward front of engine (timing chain), Fig. 15. Refer to Fig. 16 for correct piston ring installation and note the following groove clearances:

1. No. 1 upper: .0024–.0039 in. (.06–.10 mm). wear limit: .004 in. (.1 mm).
2. No. 2 intermediate: .0008–.0024 in. (.02–.06 mm). Wear limit: .004 in. (.1 mm).
3. Oil ring upper: .010–.018 in. (.25–.45 mm). Wear limit: .039 in. (.1 mm).
4. Oil ring intermediate: .010–.018 in. (.25–.45 mm). Wear limit: .039 in. (.1 mm).
5. Oil ring side rail: .008–.035 in. (.2–.4 mm) Wear limit: .059 in. (.15 mm). Con-

necting rod side clearance should be .004–.010 inch.

Installing Piston Ring Side Rail

1. Place one end of side rail between piston ring groove and spacer expander, Fig. 17.
2. Hold end of ring firmly and press downward on portion to be installed until side rail is in position. Do not use a piston ring expander.
3. Install upper side rail first, then the lower side rail.

Piston Ring End Gap Location

1. Position piston ring end gaps as shown in Fig. 18.
2. Position oil ring expander gap at least 45° from side rail gaps but not on piston pin center line or in thrust direction.

CYLINDER HEAD & VALVE ASSEMBLY

Cylinder Head, Replace

1. Disconnect battery ground cable, then drain cooling system. Disconnect upper radiator hose and heater hoses.
2. Disconnect spark plug wires from spark plugs, then remove distributor.
3. Remove carburetor to valve cover bracket.
4. Disconnect fuel lines from fuel pump, then remove fuel pump.
5. Remove cylinder head cover bolts, then the cylinder head cover.
6. Disconnect all electrical connectors and vacuum lines from cylinder head.
7. Disconnect throttle linkage from carburetor.
8. Remove water pump belt and pulley.
9. Rotate crankshaft until No. 1 piston is at TDC.

10. Paint a white reference mark on the timing chain in line with the timing mark on camshaft sprocket.
11. Remove camshaft sprocket bolt, sprocket and distributor drive gear.
12. Raise and support vehicle.
13. Disconnect air feed lines.
14. Remove power steering pump and position aside.
15. Disconnect ground strap and remove dipstick tube.
16. Remove exhaust manifold heat shield, then disconnect exhaust pipe from catalytic converter. Lower vehicle.
17. Remove cylinder head bolts in sequence shown in Fig. 19.
18. Reverse procedure to install. Refer to cylinder head bolt tightening sequence, Fig. 20, tighten cylinder head bolts in three steps as follows:

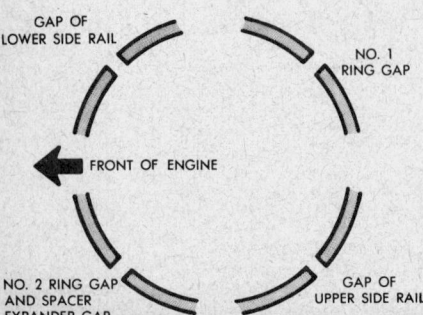

Fig. 18 Piston ring end gap location

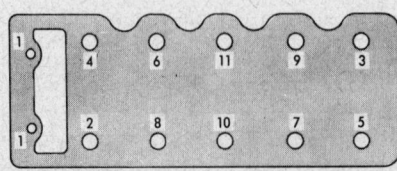

Fig. 19 Cylinder head bolt removal sequence

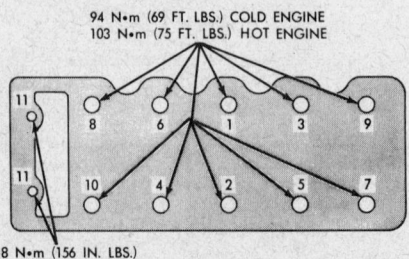

94 N•m (69 FT. LBS.) COLD ENGINE
103 N•m (75 FT. LBS.) HOT ENGINE

18 N•m (156 IN. LBS.)

Fig. 20 Cylinder head bolt tightening sequence

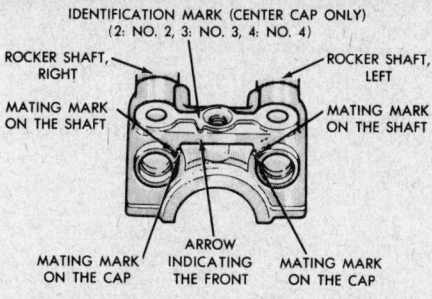

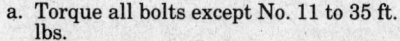

Fig. 21 Camshaft bearing cap installation

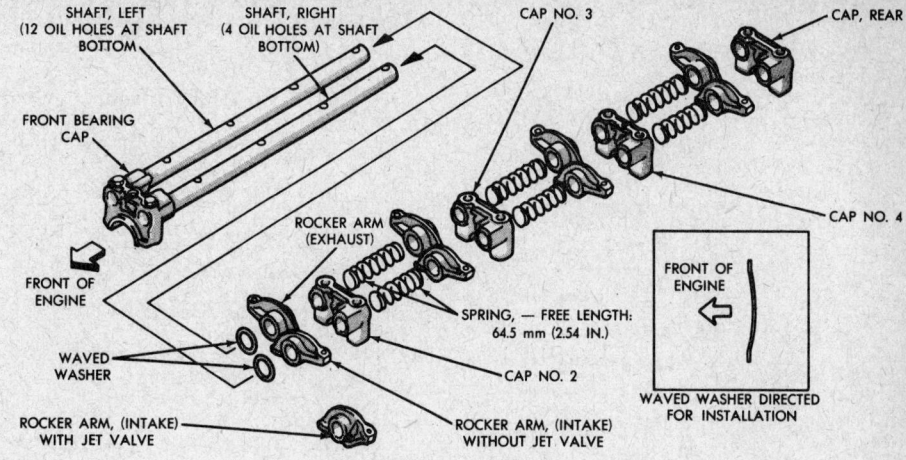

Fig. 22 Rocker arm shaft assembly

a. Torque all bolts except No. 11 to 35 ft. lbs.
b. Torque all bolts except No. 11 to 69 ft. lbs. on a cold engine or 75 ft. lbs. on a hot engine.
c. Torque cylinder head to chain case cover bolts (No. 11) to 156 in. lbs.

Camshaft Bearing Cap

1. Align camshaft bearing caps with arrows pointing toward timing chain, Fig. 21. Install caps in numerical order.

Rocker Arm Shaft Assembly

1. Refer to Fig. 22 and install bolts into front bearing caps.
2. Install wave washers, rocker arms, bearing caps and springs in order shown, Fig. 22.
3. Place rocker shaft assembly into position, then rotate camshaft until dowel pin hole is at vertical centerline, Fig. 8.
4. Tighten camshaft bearing cap bolts in the following order:
   a. No. 3 cap bolts to 85 inch. lbs.
   b. No. 2 cap bolts to 85 inch. lbs.
   c. No. 4 cap bolts to 85 inch. lbs.
   d. Front cap bolts to 85 inch. lbs.
   e. Rear cap bolts to 85 inch. lbs.
5. Repeat step 4, increasing torque to 175 inch lbs.

Installed Valve Spring Height

1. Measure installed height of valve spring between spring seat and spring retainer, Fig. 23. Installed height should be 1.590 in. If height is greater than 1.629 in., replace spring.

Valve Clearance Adjustment

NOTE: Check hot torque on cylinder head bolts before performing valve adjustments.

1. With engine at operating temperature, position piston at TDC on compression stroke.
2. Loosen valve adjuster lock nut, then adjust valve clearance by rotating adjusting screw while measuring with a feeler gauge, Fig. 24.
3. Valve clearance should be as follows: Intake—.006 in; Exhaust—.010 in.
4. Tighten lock nut securely while holding adjusting screw with screwdriver.

Jet Valve Service

1. Install jet valve assembly into cylinder

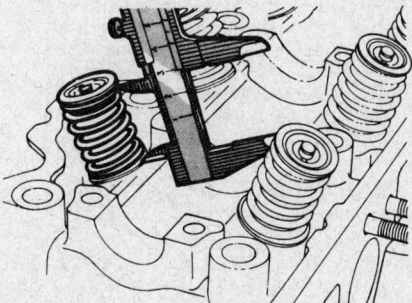

Fig. 23 Measuring installed valve spring height

head.
2. Using suitable socket, torque jet valve to 168 inch lbs., (14 ft. lbs.).

NOTE: Ensure that socket wrench is not tilted with respect to centerline of jet valve as damage to the valve stem may result. Check hot torque on cylinder head bolts before performing jet valve adjustments.

3. With engine at operating temperature, position piston at TDC of compression stroke.
4. Loosen jet valve adjuster lock nut, Fig. 25.
5. Proper valve clearance is obtained by rotating adjusting screw while measuring clearance with feeler gauge.
6. Valve clearance should be .006 in.
7. Tighten lock nut securely while holding adjusting screw with screwdriver.

Intake Manifold, Replace

1. Disconnect battery ground cable and drain coolant system.
2. Disconnect hose between water pump and intake manifold.
3. Disconnect carburetor air horn and position aside.
4. Disconnect carburetor and intake mani-

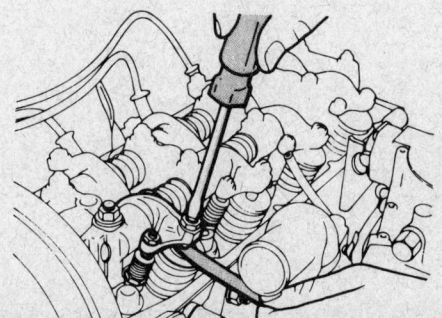

Fig. 24 Adjusting valve clearance

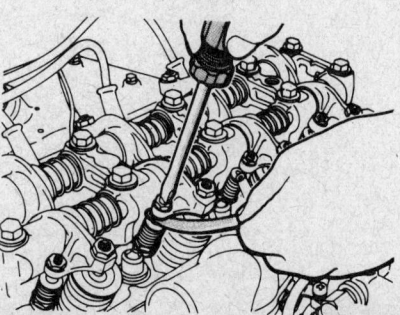

Fig. 25 Adjusting jet valve clearance

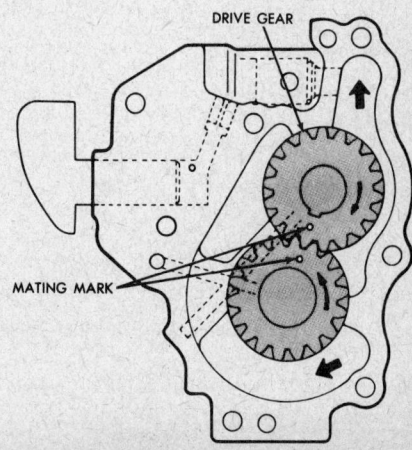

Fig. 26 Oil pump gear alignment

fold vacuum hoses, throttle linkage, and fuel line.
5. Remove fuel filter and fuel pump and position aside.
6. Remove mounting nuts and washers securing intake manifold, then the intake manifold.

VALVE LIFT SPECS.

Engine	Year	Intake	Exhaust
4-156	1981–84	.410	.410

VALVE TIMING

Intake Opens Before TDC

Engine	Year	Degrees
4-156	1981–84	25

ENGINE LUBRICATION SYSTEM

Oil Pump Clearances

Refer to Fig. 14 and measure the following clearances:
1. Drive gear to body—.0043–.0059 in. (.11–.15 mm).
2. Driven gear to bearing—.0008–.0020 in. (.02–.05 mm).
3. Driven gear end play—.0024–.0047 in. (.06–.12 mm).
4. Drive gear end play—.0016–.0028 in. (.04–.07 mm).
5. Drive gear to body clearance—.0043–.0059 in. (.11–.15 in).
6. Drive gear to bearing—.0008–.0020 in (.02–.05 mm).
7. Relief valve spring length—1.850 in. (47 mm).
8. Relief valve spring load—9.5 lbs. at 1.575 in. (40 mm).
Refer to Fig. 26 and align mating marks of drive and driven gears, then prime pump with clean oil and install onto engine.

WATER PUMP, REPLACE

1. Disconnect battery ground cable.
2. Drain cooling system.
3. Disconnect radiator hose, bypass hose, and heater hose from water pump.
4. Remove drive pulley shield.
5. Remove locking screw and pivot screws.
6. Remove drive belt and remove water pump from engine.
7. Reverse procedure to install.

BELT TENSION DATA

	New	Used
1981–84		
Power Steer.	110	75
Exc. Power Steer.	120	80

Clutch & Transaxle Section

CLUTCH, ADJUST

1981–84 Models W/ 4-135 Engine & 1983–84 Models W/ 4-97 Engine

The clutch release cable, Fig. 1, on these models cannot be adjusted. When the cable is properly routed, the spring between the clutch pedal and positioner adjuster will hold the clutch cable in the proper position. An adjuster pivot is used to hold release cable in place to ensure complete clutch release when the clutch pedal is depressed.

1978–83 Models W/ 4-105 Engine

1. Pull upward on clutch cable at housing attachment, Fig. 2.
2. Rotate sleeve downward until sleeve snugly contacts grommet.
3. Rotate sleeve so end of sleeve seats into rectangular groove in grommet.
4. Check for proper operation.

CLUTCH, REPLACE

1981–84 Models W/ 4-135 Engine & 1983–84 Models W/ 4-97 Engine

1. Remove transaxle as outlined under "Manual Transaxle, Replace" procedure.
2. Mark relationship between clutch cover and flywheel for reference during reassembly, then insert suitable clutch disc aligning tool through clutch disc hub.
3. Gradually loosen clutch cover attaching bolts, then remove pressure plate and cover assembly and disc from flywheel.
4. Remove clutch release shaft and slide release bearing assembly off input shaft seal retainer. Remove fork from release bearing thrust plate.
5. Reverse procedure to install. Align reference marks made during disassembly, then using a clutch disc alignment tool, install disc, plate and cover to flywheel. Refer to Figs. 3 and 4 for torque specifications.

1978–83 Models W/ 4-105 Engine

Removal

1. Remove transaxle as outlined under "Manual Transaxle, Replace" procedure.
2. Gradually loosen and remove bolts attaching flywheel to pressure plate.
3. Remove flywheel and clutch disc, Fig. 5.
4. Remove retaining ring and release plate.
5. Mark position of pressure plate on crankshaft.
6. Gradually loosen and remove bolts attaching pressure plate to flywheel.
7. Remove spacer and pressure plate.

Installation

1. Thoroughly clean surfaces of flywheel and pressure plate with fine sandpaper or crocus cloth. Also, ensure that all oil or grease has been removed.
2. Align marks on pressure plate and crankshaft and install pressure plate and spacer on crankshaft. Install and torque attaching bolts to 55 ft. lbs. (75 Nm).
3. Install release plate and retaining ring.
4. Using tool L-4533 to center clutch disc, Fig. 6, install disc and flywheel onto pressure plate. Ensure the drilled mark on flywheel is at the top so the two dowels in the flywheel align the proper holes in the pressure plate.
5. Install and torque flywheel to pressure plate attaching bolts to 15 ft. lbs. (20 Nm).
6. Remove centering tool.
7. Install transaxle and adjust clutch.
8. Check for proper operation.

GEARSHIFT LINKAGE, ADJUST

1981–84 Models W/ 4-135 Engine & 1983–84 Models W/ 4-97 Engine

Rod Linkage

1. Remove lock pin from transaxle selector shaft housing (Fig. 5).
2. Reverse lock pin so long end is facing downward, and insert pin into same threaded hole while pushing selector shaft into selector housing.
3. Raise and support vehicle then loosen clamp bolt that secures gearshift tube to gearshift rod.
4. Check that gearshift connector slides and

Fig. 1 Clutch cable routing. 1981–84 models w/ 4-135 engine & 1983–84 models w/ 4-97 engine

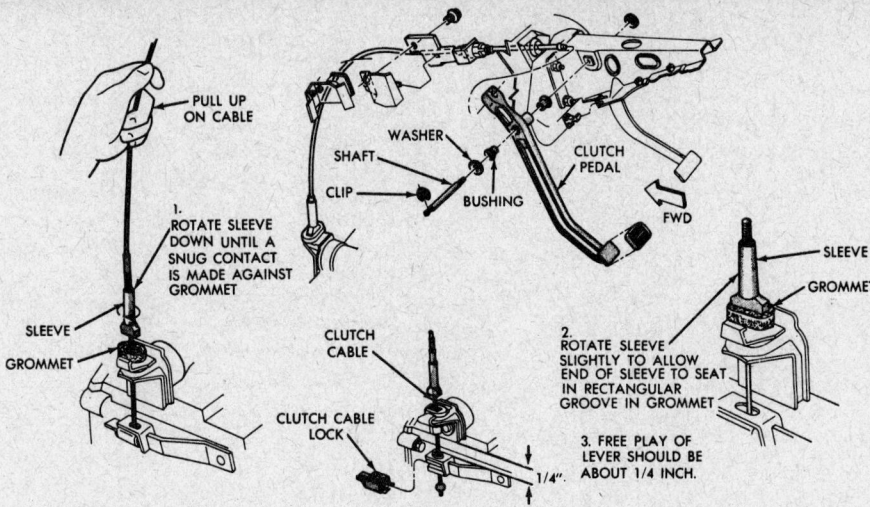

Fig. 2 Clutch pedal free play adjustment. 1978–83 models w/ 4-105 engine

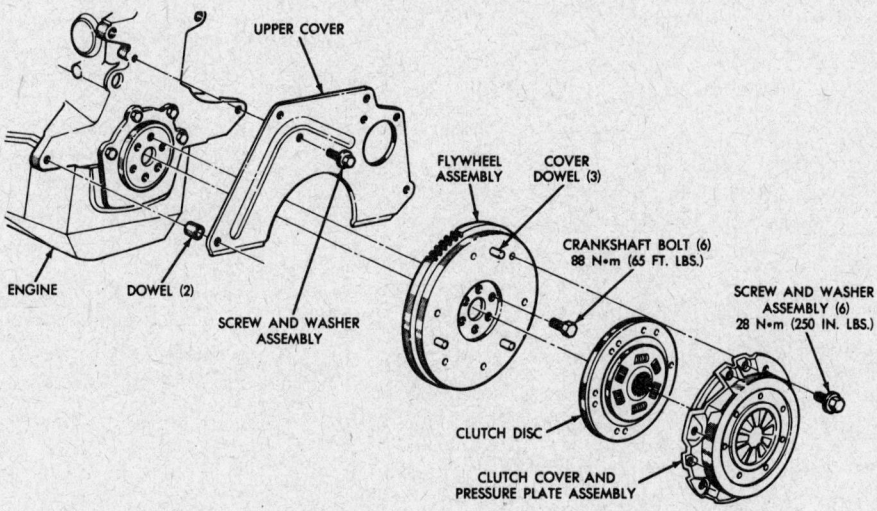

Fig. 3 Clutch assembly. 1981–84 models w/ 4-135 engine

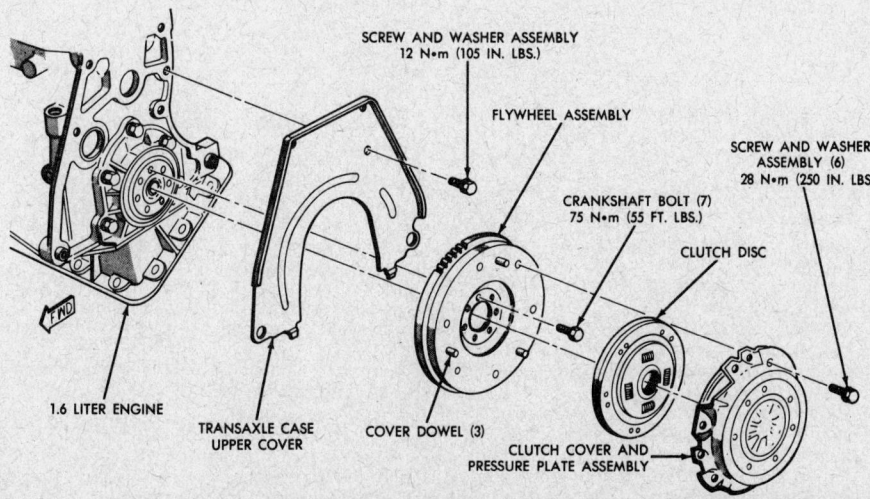

Fig. 4 Clutch assembly. 1983–84 models w/ 4-97 engine

rotates freely in gearshift tube.

5. Position shifter mechanism connector assembly so that isolator is spaced .050 inch away from upstanding flange, while rib on isolator is aligned fore and aft with hole in blocker bracket. Hold connector isolator in this position and torque clamp bolt on gearshift tube to 170 inch lbs. No significant force should be placed on linkage during this procedure, Fig. 8.
6. Lower vehicle, remove lock pin from selector shaft housing and reinstall lock pin in reversed position. Torque pin to 105 in. lbs.
7. Check for proper operation.

1981–84 Models W/ 4-135 Engine

Cable Linkage, Figs. 9 & 10
1. Remove lock pin from transaxle selector shaft housing, Fig. 7.
2. Reverse lock pin so long end is down, and insert lock pin into same threaded hole while pushing selector shaft in 1–2 neutral position.
3. Remove gearshift knob, retaining nut and pull-up ring.
4. On all models except 1984 Daytona and Laser, remove console attaching screws and the console.
5. On 1984 Daytona and Laser models, remove console as follows:
   a. Remove front seat assemblies.
   b. Remove 2 forward console bezel attaching screws and the bezel.
   c. Remove carpet retaining clips from console.
   d. Remove console attaching bolts and screws.
   e. Disconnect electrical connectors from console, then remove console from vehicle.
6. On all models, fabricate 2 cable adjusting pins as shown in Fig. 11.
7. Adjust selector cable and torque adjusting screw to 60 inch lbs. (7 Nm) on 1981–83 models, or 55 inch lbs. (6 Nm) on 1984 models, Fig. 12.

NOTE: The selector cable adjusting screw must be properly torqued.

8. Adjust crossover cable and torque adjusting screw to 60 inch lbs. (7 Nm) on 1981–83 models, or 55 inch lbs. (6 Nm) on 1984 models, Fig. 13.

NOTE: The crossover cable adjusting screw must be properly torqued.

9. Remove lock pin from selector shaft housing and reinstall lock pin so long end is up in selector shaft housing, Fig. 7.
10. Check for proper operation and reinstall console, pull-up ring, retaining nut and gearshift knob.

1978–83 Models W/ 4-105 Engine

1. Place shift lever in neutral at 3–4 position.
2. Loosen shift tube clamp.
3. Align tab on slider with hole in blocker bracket, Fig. 14.
4. Install a 1/2 inch spacer, Fig. 15, to set gearshift unit lock-out.

NOTE: If the blocker bracket has a 5/8 stamp imprint at the forward vertical face of the reinforcement strap, Fig. 16, it indicates that a 5/8 inch spacer must be used in place of the 1/2 inch spacer.

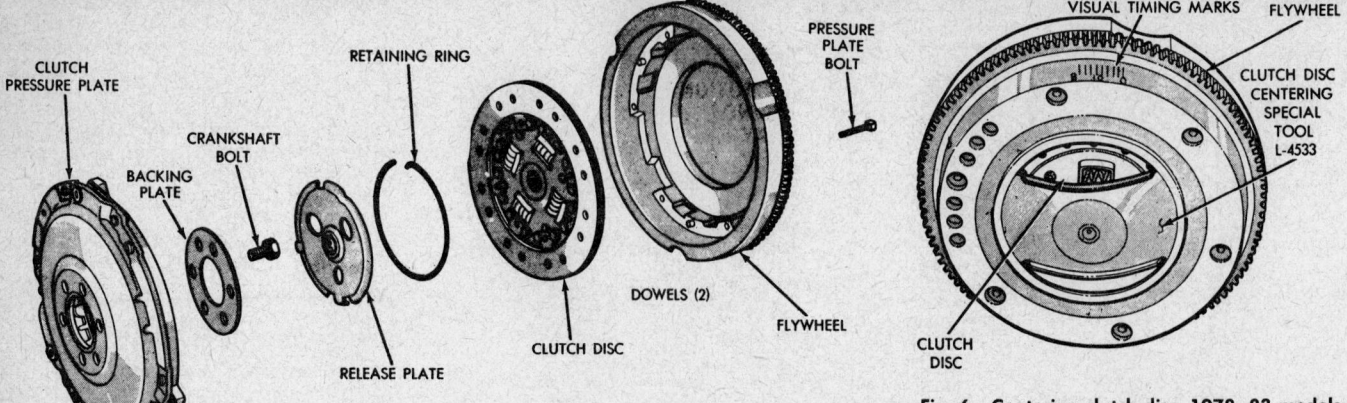

Fig. 5 Clutch assembly. 1978—83 models w/ 4-105 engine

Fig. 6 Centering clutch disc. 1978—83 models w/ 4-105 engine

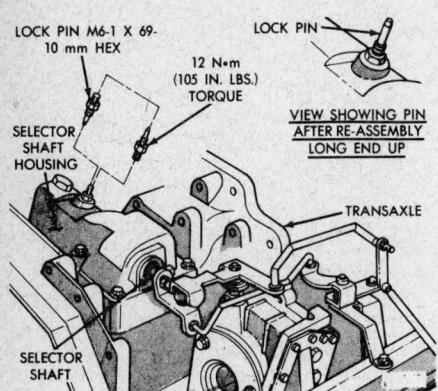

Fig. 7 Lock pin removal & installation. 1981—84 models w/ 4-135 engine & 1983—84 models w/ 4-97 engine

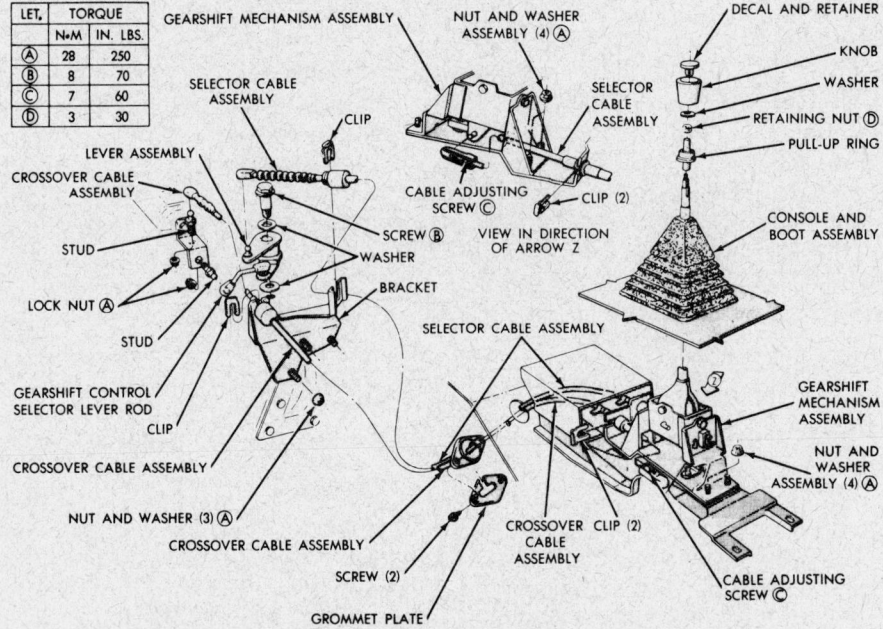

LET.	TORQUE	
	N·M	IN. LBS.
Ⓐ	28	250
Ⓑ	8	70
Ⓒ	7	60
Ⓓ	3	30

Fig. 9 Cable operated gearshift linkage. 1981—83 models w/ 4-135 engine

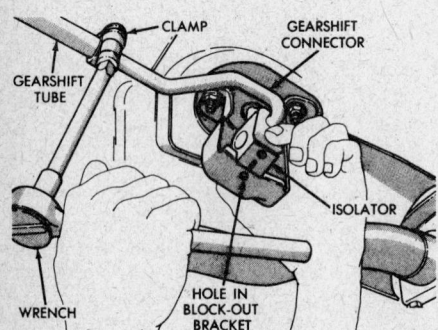

Fig. 8 Adjusting rod-type gear shift linkage. 1981—84 models w/ 4-135 engine & 1983—84 models w/ 4-97 engine

5. Tighten shift tube clamp and remove spacer.
6. Check for proper operation.

MANUAL TRANSAXLE, REPLACE

1981—84 Models W/ 4-135 Engine & 1983—84 Models W/ 4-97 Engine

1. Disconnect battery ground cable.

2. Raise and support vehicle and install suitable engine support fixture.
3. Disconnect gearshift linkage and clutch cable from transaxle.
4. Remove front wheel and tire assemblies.
5. Remove left front splash shield, then the impact bracket from transaxle if so equipped.
6. Refer to "Driveshafts, Replace" to disconnect driveshafts.
7. Support transaxle and remove upper clutch housing bolts.
8. Remove left engine mount from transaxle noting location of bolts.
9. Remove anti-rotational link, Fig. 17.
10. Remove engine to transaxle toward left side of vehicle until mainshaft clears clutch and lower and remove transaxle.
12. Reverse procedure to install. When installing left engine mount, refer to "Engine mounts" section.

1978—83 Models W/ 4-105 Engine

1. Remove engine timing access hole plug, then rotate engine to align drilled mark on flywheel with pointer on clutch housing on 1978 early production models only.
2. Disconnect battery ground cable.
3. Disconnect shift linkage rods, starter wiring and backup lamp switch wiring.
4. Remove starter and disconnect clutch cable.
5. Remove bolt attaching speedometer adapter to transaxle.
6. With speedometer cable housing connected, pull adapter and pinion from transaxle.
7. Raise and support vehicle. Also, support engine with suitable equipment.
8. Disconnect right hand drive shaft and position aside.

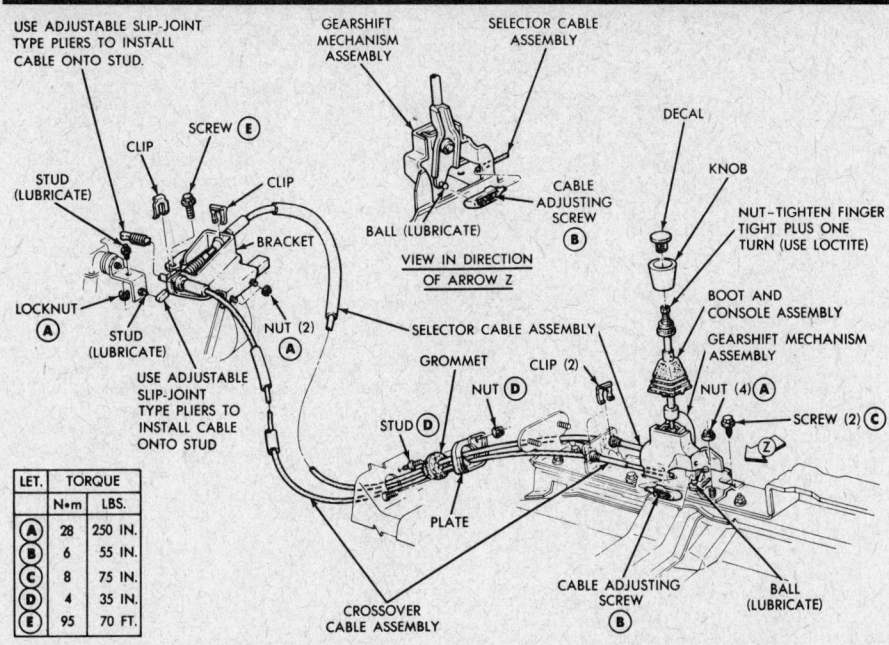

LET.	TORQUE	
	N•m	LBS.
Ⓐ	28	250 IN.
Ⓑ	6	55 IN.
Ⓒ	8	75 IN.
Ⓓ	4	35 IN.
Ⓔ	95	70 FT.

Fig. 10 Cable operated gearshift linkage. 1984 models w/ 4-135 engine

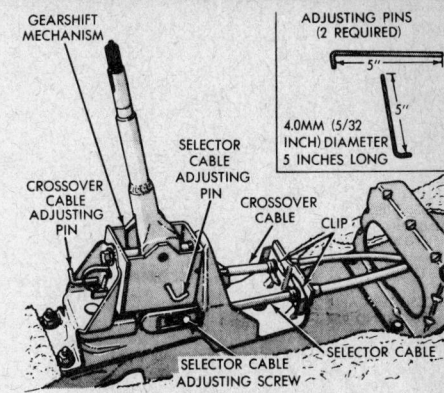

Fig. 11 Cable adjusting pins

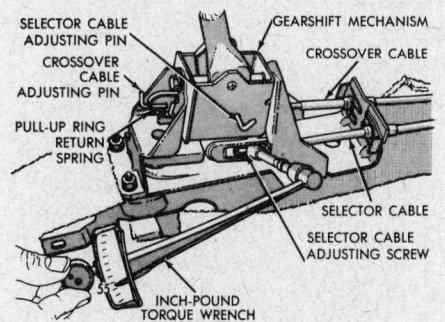

Fig. 12 Adjusting selector cable

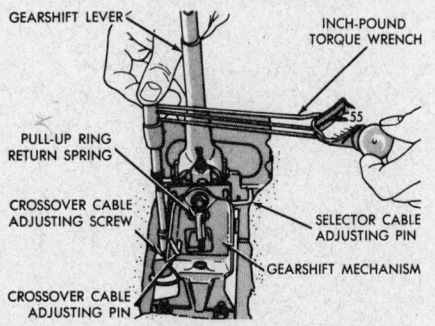

Fig. 13 Adjusting crossover cable

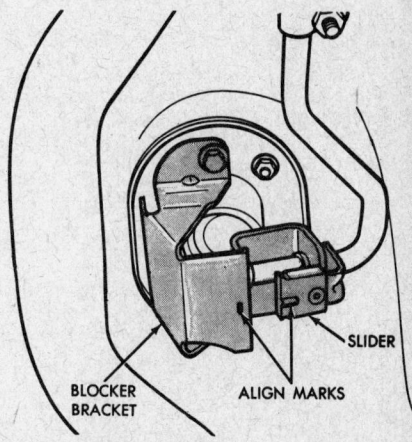

Fig. 14 Aligning slider & block bracket marks. 1978-83 models w/ 4-105 engine

9. Remove left hand drive shaft.
10. Remove left splash shield.
11. Drain transaxle fluid.
12. Remove bolts from left engine mount.

13. Remove transaxle to engine attaching nuts and bolts.
14. Slide transaxle toward left side of vehicle until mainshaft clears clutch.

15. Lower and remove transaxle from vehicle.
16. Reverse procedure to install.

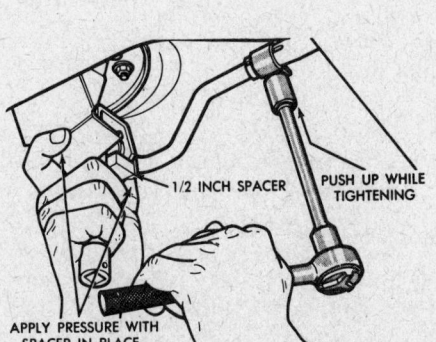

Fig. 15 Installing spacer. 1978-83 models w/ 4-105 engine

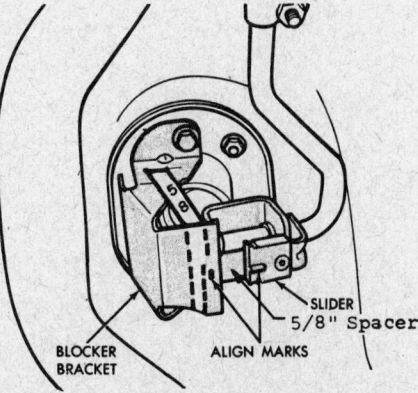

Fig. 16 Revised gearshift blocker bracket. 1978-83 models w/ 4-105 engine

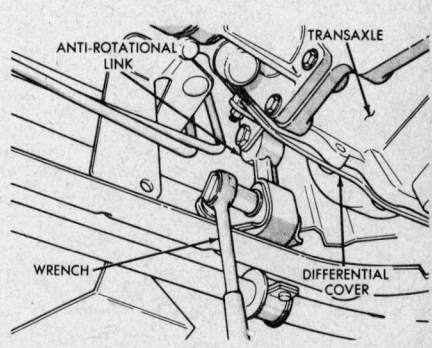

Fig. 17 Removing anti-rotational link

Rear Axle, Rear Suspension & Brakes Section

REAR AXLE, REPLACE

Exc. 1978—84 Horizon, Omni, 1983—84 Charger & Turismo

1. Raise and support vehicle, support rear axle, and remove rear wheels.
2. Disconnect parking brake cable at connector and cable housing at floor pan bracket, Fig. 1.
3. Disconnect brake tube assembly from brake line on trailing arm support bracket, and remove lock.
4. Disconnect shock absorbers and track bar at rear axle. Support track bar end.
5. Lower axle until spring and isolator assemblies, Figs. 2 and 3, come free and can be removed.
6. Support pivot ends of trailing arms and remove pivot bracket bolts. Lower and remove axle from vehicle.
7. Reverse procedure to install. Torque brake tube assembly to hose fitting to 140 inch lbs. Torque other components as shown in Figs. 2 and 3.

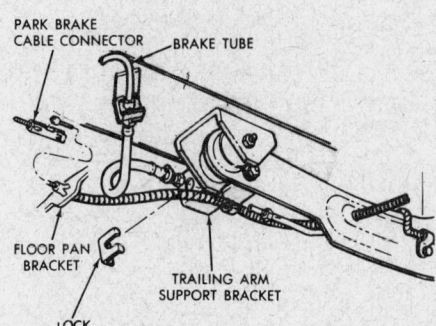

FLOOR PAN BRACKET

PARK BRAKE CABLE CONNECTOR — BRAKE TUBE

TRAILING ARM SUPPORT BRACKET

LOCK

Fig. 1 Parking brake cable & brake tube assemblies. 1981—84 Aries & Reliant; 1982—83 400; 1982—84 LeBaron; 1983—84 New Yorker, E Class, Executive & 600; 1984 Daytona & Laser

1978—84 Horizon & Omni & 1983—84 Charger & Turismo

1. Raise and support vehicle.
2. Remove wheels.

3. Removing brake fitting and retaining clips securing flexible brake line.
4. Remove parking brake cable adjusting connection nut.
5. Release parking brake cables from bracket by slipping ball-end of cables through brake connectors.
6. Pull parking brake cable through bracket.
7. Remove brake drums.
8. Remove brake assembly and spindle retaining bolts.
9. Position spindle aside using a piece of wire.
10. Support axle and suspension with a suitable jack.
11. Remove shock absorber mounting bolts.
12. Remove trailing arm to hanger bracket mounting bolt.
13. Lower rear axle from vehicle.
14. Reverse procedure to install.

SHOCK ABSORBER & COIL SPRING, REPLACE

Exc. 1978—84 Horizon, Omni, 1983—84 Charger & Turismo

1. Raise and support vehicle.
2. Support axle assembly and remove both upper and lower shock absorber attaching bolts and the shock absorbers.
3. Lower axle assembly until spring and spring upper isolater can be removed, Figs. 2 and 3.

Installation
1. Position jounce bumper to rail, install and torque attaching screws to 70 in. lbs. (7Nm).
2. Install isolator over jounce bumper and install spring.
3. Raise axle and install shock absorber. Loosely assemble lower shock absorber attaching bolts and torque upper attaching bolts to 40 ft. lbs.
4. With suspension supporting vehicle, torque shock absorber attaching screws to 40 ft. lbs. (54 Nm.).

1978—84 Horizon & Omni; 1983—84 Charger & Turismo

Replacement
1. Remove upper shock absorber mounting protective cap, located inside vehicle at upper rear wheel well area.

NOTE: On 024, TC3, Charger and Turismo models, it is necessary to remove the lower rear quarter trim panel for access.

2. Remove upper shock absorber mounting nut, isolator retainer and upper isolator, Fig. 3.

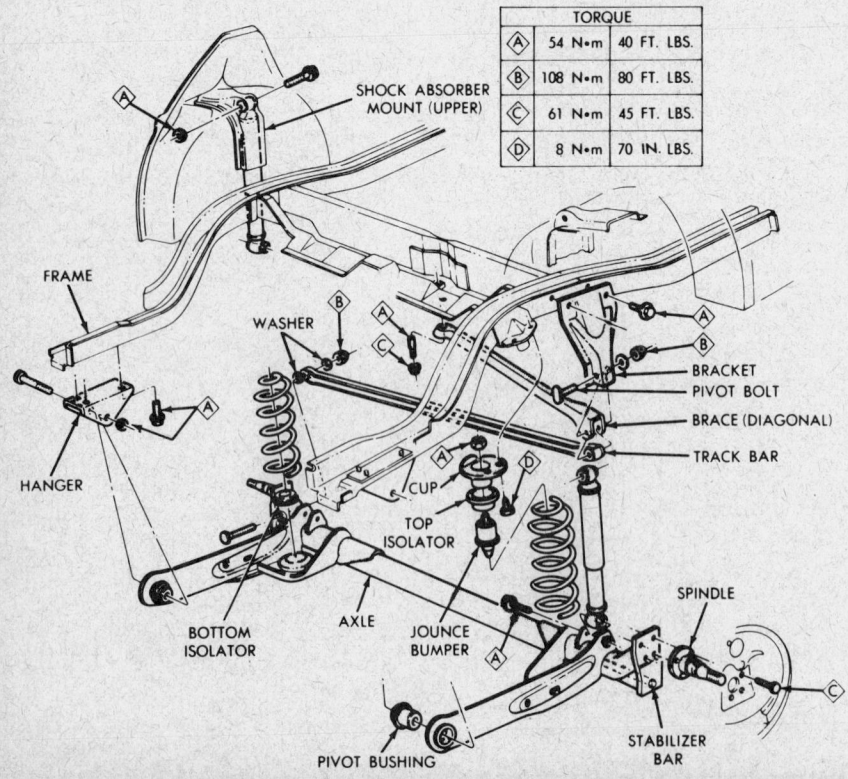

	TORQUE	
A	54 N•m	40 FT. LBS.
B	108 N•m	80 FT. LBS.
C	61 N•m	45 FT. LBS.
D	8 N•m	70 IN. LBS.

SHOCK ABSORBER MOUNT (UPPER)

FRAME

WASHER

HANGER

BOTTOM ISOLATOR

CUP

TOP ISOLATOR

AXLE

JOUNCE BUMPER

PIVOT BUSHING

BRACKET

PIVOT BOLT

BRACE (DIAGONAL)

TRACK BAR

SPINDLE

STABILIZER BAR

Fig. 2 Rear axle & suspension assembly. 1981—83 Aries & Reliant; 1982—83 LeBaron & 400; 1983 New Yorker, E Class, Executive & 600

TORQUE		
Ⓐ	40 FT. LBS.	54 N•m
Ⓑ	50 FT. LBS.	68 N•m
Ⓒ	55 FT. LBS.	75 N•m
Ⓓ	70 IN. LBS.	8 N•m

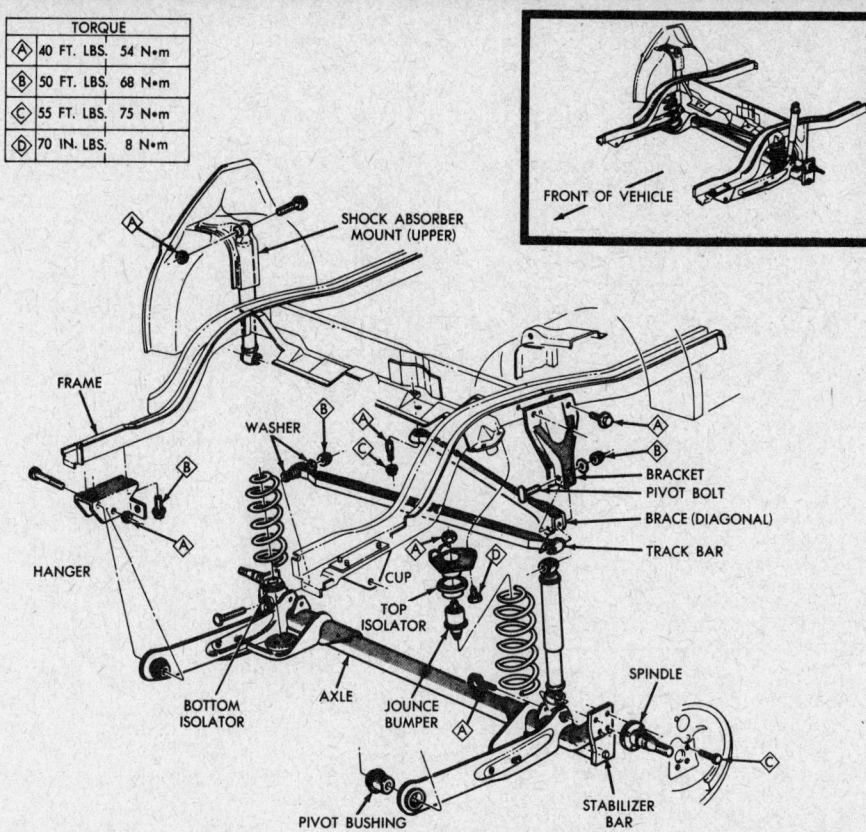

FRONT OF VEHICLE

Fig. 3 Rear axle & suspension assembly. 1984 Aries, Reliant, Daytona, Laser, New Yorker, E Class, Executive, LeBaron & 600

3. Raise and support vehicle.
4. Remove shock absorber lower mounting bolt.
5. Remove shock absorber and coil spring assembly from vehicle.
6. Reverse procedure to install.

Service

1. Install coil spring retractors, tool L-4514, on coil spring and support in a vise, Fig. 5. Grip 4 or 5 coils of the spring in the retractors. Also, do not extend retractors more than 9¼ inches.

2. Tighten retractors evenly until spring pressure is released from upper spring seat.
3. Hold flat end of push rod and loosen retaining nut.

CAUTION: Ensure that spring is properly compressed before loosening retaining nut since personal injury may result.

4. Remove lower isolator, push rod sleeve and upper spring seat.
5. Remove shock absorber from coil spring.
6. Remove jounce bumper and dust shield from push rod, Fig. 6.
7. Remove lower spring seat. Fig. 6.
8. Reverse procedure to assemble.

REAR WHEEL ALIGNMENT

Due to the design of the rear suspension and the incorporation of stub axles or wheel spindles, it is possible to adjust the camber and toe of the rear wheels on these vehicles. Adjustment is controlled by adding shims approximately .010 inch thick between the spindle mounting surface and spindle mounting plate. The amount of adjustment is approximately 0° 18′ per shim. Refer to Figs. 7 through 10 for proper placement of the shims.

REAR WHEEL BEARING, ADJUST

1. Torque adjusting nut to 270 inch lbs. (30 Nm) while rotating wheel.
2. Stop wheel and loosen adjusting nut, Fig. 11.
3. Tighten adjusting nut finger tight. End play should be .001–.003 inch on 1978–80 models, or .001–.002 inch on 1981–84 models.
4. Install castle lock with slots aligned with cotter pin hole.
5. Install cotter pin and grease cap.

SERVICE BRAKES, ADJUST

The rear brakes on 1983–84 models are self-adjusting and no adjustment is necessary. On 1978–82 models, the rear brakes are not self-adjusting and periodic adjustment is required as follows:

LET	TORQUE	
Ⓐ	20 FT LBS	27 N•m
Ⓑ	40 FT LBS	54 N•m
Ⓒ	45 FT LBS	61 N•m
Ⓓ	80 FT LBS	108 N•m

Fig. 4 Rear axle & suspension assembly. 1978–83 Horizon & Omni; 1983 Charger & Turismo

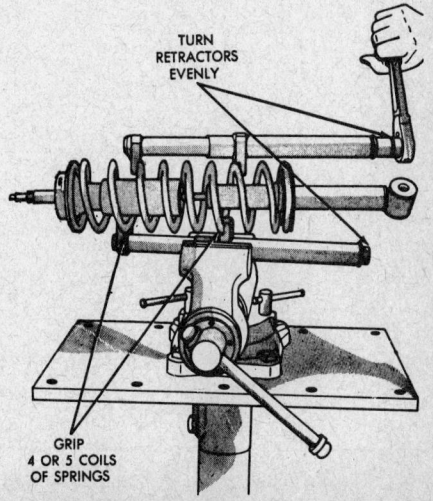

TURN RETRACTORS EVENLY

GRIP 4 OR 5 COILS OF SPRINGS

Fig. 5 Retracting coil spring

1. Raise and support vehicle.
2. Remove adjusting hole covers from brake supports.
3. Release parking brake and back off cable adjustment to slacken cable.
4. Insert a narrow screwdriver into adjusting nut hole. Move screwdriver handle downward on left side or upward on right side until wheels are locked, Fig. 12.
5. Back off nut 10 clicks.
6. Adjust parking brake.

PARKING BRAKE, ADJUST

1. Raise and support vehicle.
2. Release parking brake and back off adjustment to slacken cable.
3. Tighten cable adjusting nut until a slight drag is obtained while rotating wheels.
4. Loosen cable adjusting nut until the wheels rotate freely, then an additional two turns.
5. Apply and release parking brake to check for proper operation. The rear wheels should rotate without dragging.

MASTER CYLINDER, REPLACE

Manual Brakes

1. Disconnect and plug brake tubes from

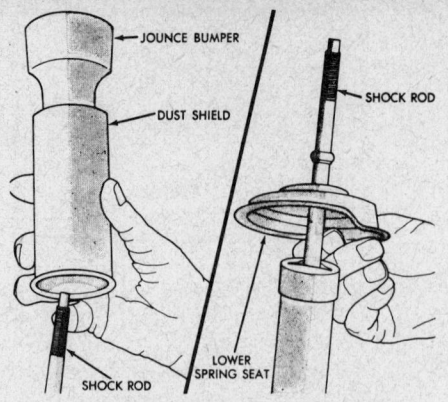

Fig. 6   Jounce bumper, dust shield & lower spring seat replacement

master cylinder. Cap master cylinder ports.
2. Disconnect stop lamp switch mounting bracket from beneath instrument panel.
3. Pull brake pedal rearward to disengage push rod from master cylinder.

NOTE: Pulling the brake pedal rearward will destroy the grommet. Install a new grommet when installing the push rod.

4. Remove master cylinder attaching nuts.

5. Remove master cylinder from vehicle.
6. Reverse procedure to install.

Power Brakes

1. Disconnect and plug brake tubes from master cylinder. Cap master cylinder ports.
2. Remove master cylinder attaching nuts.
3. Remove master cylinder from power brake unit.
4. Reverse procedure to install.

POWER BRAKE UNIT, REPLACE

1. Remove master cylinder attaching nuts, slide master cylinder from mounting studs and support on fender shield. Do not disconnect brake tubes from master cylinder.
2. Disconnect vacuum hose from power brake unit.
3. From beneath instrument panel, install a suitable screwdriver between the center tang on retainer clip and the brake pedal pin. Rotate the screwdriver so the retainer center tang will pass over brake pedal pin. Pull retainer clip from pin.
4. Remove power brake unit attaching nuts and the power brake unit from vehicle.
5. Reverse procedure to install.

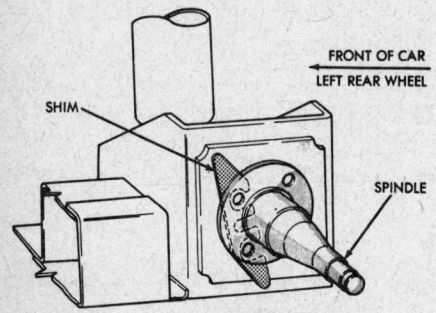

Fig. 7   Shim installation for toe-out

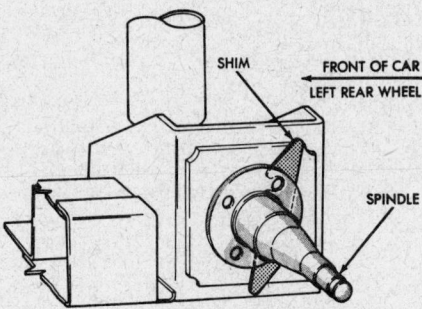

Fig. 8   Shim installation for toe-in

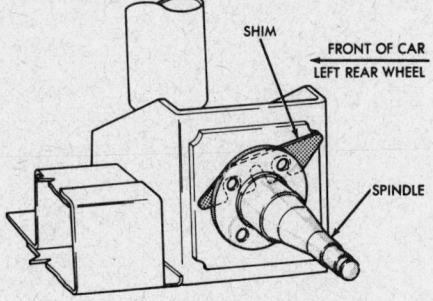

Fig. 9   Shim installation for positive camber

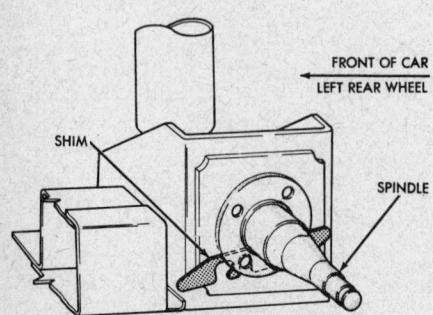

Fig. 10   Shim installation for negative camber

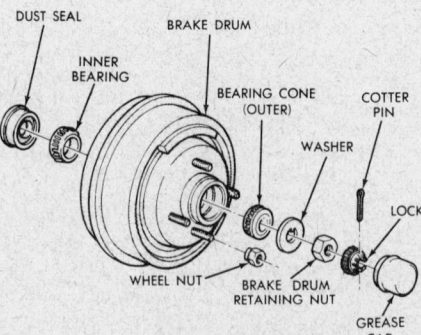

Fig. 11   Wheel bearing assembly

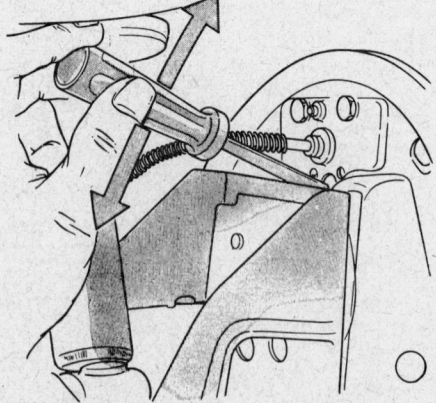

Fig. 12   Adjusting service brakes

Front Suspension & Steering Section

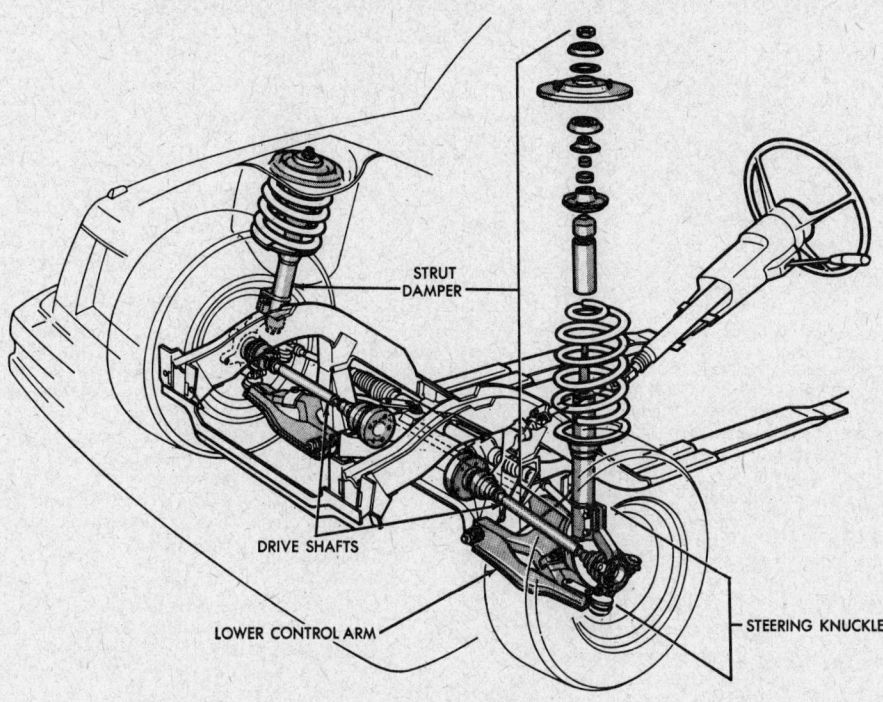

Toe-In

To adjust toe-in, center the steering wheel and hold in position with a suitable tool. Loosen the tie rod lock nuts and rotate the rod, Fig. 4, to adjust toe-in to specifications. Use care not to twist the steering gear rubber boots. Torque the tie rod lock nuts to 55 ft. lbs. (75 Nm). Adjust position of steering gear rubber boots. Remove steering wheel holding tool.

STRUT DAMPER ASSEMBLY, REPLACE

Removal

1. Raise and support vehicle, then remove front wheels.
2. Mark position of camber adjusting cam, then remove the camber adjusting bolt and through bolt and the brake hose to damper bracket retaining screw, Fig. 5.
3. Remove strut damper to fender shield mounting nut and washer assemblies.
4. Remove strut damper from vehicle.

Installation

1. Position strut assembly into fender reinforcement, then install retaining nuts and washers and torque to 20 ft. lbs.
2. Position steering knuckle and washer plate to strut, then install upper cam and lower through bolts.
3. Install brake hose retainer on damper, then index cam bolt to alignment mark made during removal.
4. Position a 4 inch or larger C-clamp on steering knuckle and strut, Fig. 6, then tighten clamp just enough to eliminate any looseness between strut and knuckle. Check alignment of marks made during removal. Torque cam bolts to 85 ft. lbs. on 1978 models, or 90 ft. lbs. on 1979 models. On all 1980–83 models and 1984 Charger, Horizon, Omni and Turismo, torque cam bolt nuts to 45 ft. lbs., then advance nuts an additional 1/4 turn. On 1984 models except Charger, Horizon, Omni and Turismo, torque nuts to 75 ft. lbs., then advance an additional 1/4 turn.
5. Remove C-clamp, then install wheel and tire assembly.

Fig. 1 Front suspension

DESCRIPTION

These vehicles use a MacPherson type front suspension with the vertical shock absorber struts attached to the upper fender reinforcement and the steering knuckle, Fig. 1. The lower control arms are attached inboard to a crossmember and outboard to the steering knuckle through a ball joint to provide lower steering knuckle position. During steering maneuvers, the strut and steering knuckle rotate as an assembly.

The drive shafts are attached inboard to the transaxle output drive flanges and outboard to the driven wheel hub.

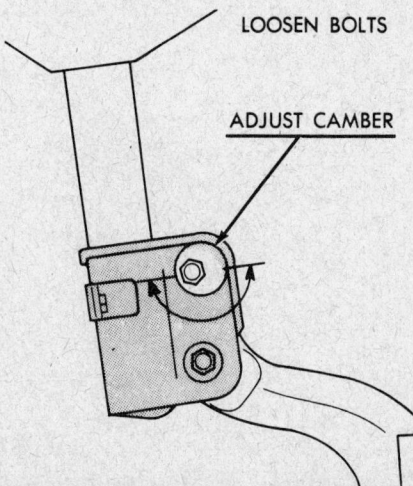

WHEEL ALIGNMENT

NOTE: Prior to wheel alignment ensure tires are at recommended pressure, are of equal size and have approximately the same wear pattern. Check front wheel and tire assembly for radial runout and inspect lower ball joints and steering linkage for looseness. Check front and rear springs for sagging or damage. Front suspension inspections should be performed on a level floor or alignment rack with fuel tank at capacity and vehicle free of luggage and passenger compartment load.

Prior to each alignment reading the vehicle should be bounced an equal number of times from the center of the bumper alternately, first from the rear, then the front, releasing at bottom of down cycle.

Caster

The caster angle on these vehicles cannot be adjusted.

Camber

To adjust camber, loosen the cam and through bolts, Figs. 2 and 3. Rotate the upper cam bolt to move the top of the wheel in or out to achieve the specified camber angle. Torque cam bolts to 85 ft. lbs. on 1978 models, or 90 ft. lbs. on 1979 models. On all 1980–83 models and 1984 Charger, Horizon, Omni and Turismo, torque cam bolt nuts to 45 ft. lbs., then advance nuts an additional 1/4 turn. On 1984 models except Charger, Horizon, Omni and Turismo, torque nuts to 75 ft. lbs., then advance an additional 1/4 turn.

Fig. 2 Camber adjustment. 1978–83 All & 1984 Charger, Horizon, Omni & Turismo

Fig. 3 Camber adjustment. 1984 exc. Charger, Horizon, Omni & Turismo

COIL SPRING, REPLACE

1. Remove strut damper assembly as outlined previously.
2. Using a suitable tool, compress coil spring.
3. Remove strut rod nut while holding strut rod to prevent rotation.
4. Remove the mount assembly, Fig. 7.
5. Remove coil spring from strut damper.
6. Inspect mount assembly for deterioration of rubber isolator, retainers for cracks and distortion and bearings for binding.
7. Install the bumper dust shield assembly.
8. Install spring and seat, upper spring retainer, bearing and spacer, mount assembly and the rebound bumper, retainer and rod nut upper.

NOTE: Position the spring retainer alignment notch parallel to the damper lower attaching brackets.

---

9. Torque strut rod nut to 60 ft. lbs. (81 Nm). Do not release spring compressor before torquing nut.
10. Remove spring compressor.

BALL JOINTS

The lower control arm ball joints operate with no free play. On early 1978 models, the ball joints are riveted to the lower control arm. On these models the ball joint and lower control arm are replaced as an assembly. On late 1978 and 1979–80 models, the ball joints are bolted to the lower control arm. On these

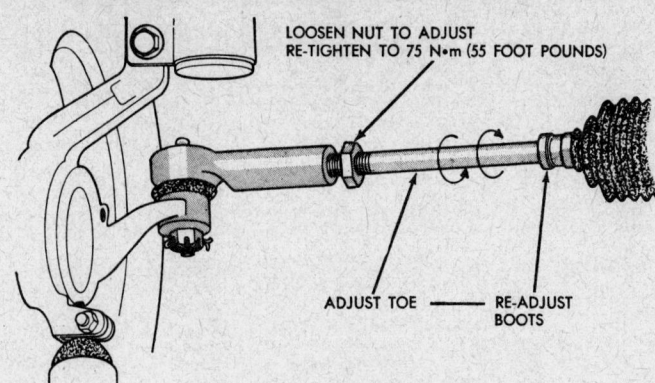

Fig. 4 Toe-in adjustment

LOOSEN NUT TO ADJUST
RE-TIGHTEN TO 75 N•m (55 FOOT POUNDS)

ADJUST TOE — RE-ADJUST BOOTS

models, the ball joint can be replaced without replacing the entire lower control arm. When installing ball joint to lower control arm, tighten attaching bolt to 60 ft. lbs. On 1981–84 models, the ball joint is pressed into the lower control arm. On these models, the ball joint can be pressed from the lower control arm using a 1¹¹⁄₁₆ inch deep socket and tool No. C-4699-2. When pressing ball joint into lower control arm, use tool Nos. C-4699-1 and C-4699-2. Install ball joint seal using a 1½ socket and tool No. C-4699-2.

NOTE: On some models the ball joint is welded to the lower control arm. On these models the ball joint and lower control arm must be replaced as an assembly.

Checking Ball Joints

1981–84

With weight of vehicle resting on wheel and tire assembly, attempt to move grease fitting with fingers, Fig. 8. Do not use a tool or added force to attempt to move grease fitting. If grease fitting moves freely, then ball joint is worn and should be replaced.

1978–80

1. Raise and support vehicle.
2. With suspension in full rebound position, attach a dial indicator to lower control arm with the plunger resting against steering knuckle leg, Fig. 9.
3. Place a pry bar on top of the ball joint housing to lower control arm bolt with tip of bar under the steering knuckle leg.
4. With the pry bar, raise and lower the steering knuckle to measure the axial travel.
5. If measurement is .050 inch or greater, thd ball joint should be replaced.

LOWER CONTROL ARM, REPLACE

Removal

1. Raise and support vehicle.
2. Remove the front inner pivot through bolt, the rear stub strut nut, retainer and bushing and the ball joint to steering knuckle clamp bolt, Fig. 10.
3. Separate the ball joint from the steering knuckle by prying between the ball stud

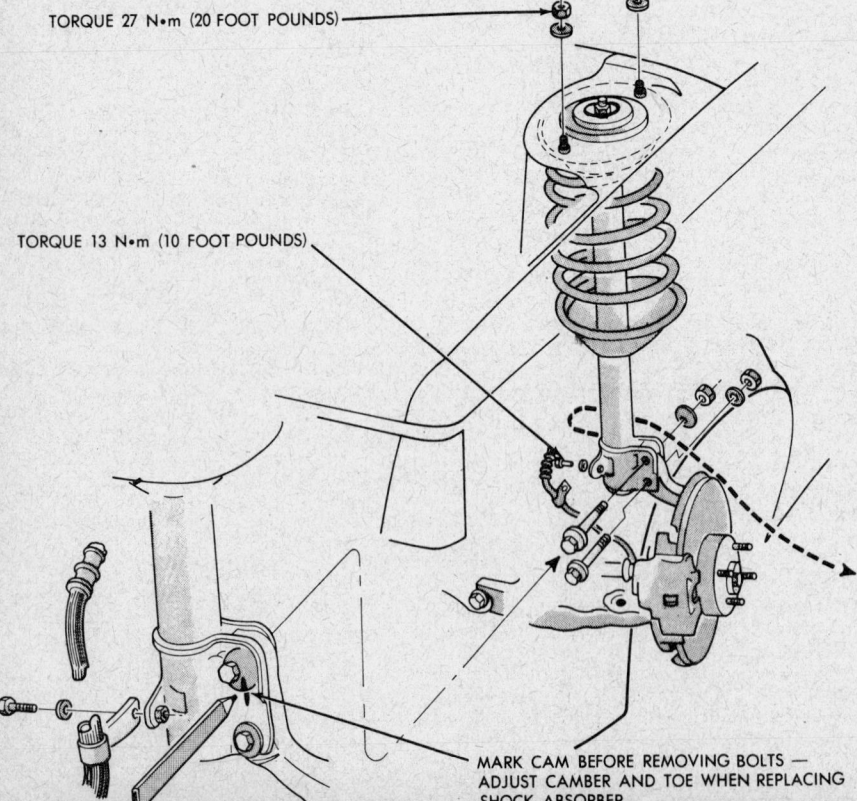

TORQUE 27 N•m (20 FOOT POUNDS)

TORQUE 13 N•m (10 FOOT POUNDS)

MARK CAM BEFORE REMOVING BOLTS — ADJUST CAMBER AND TOE WHEN REPLACING SHOCK ABSORBER

Fig. 5 Strut damper replacement. 1978–83 (Typical of 1984)

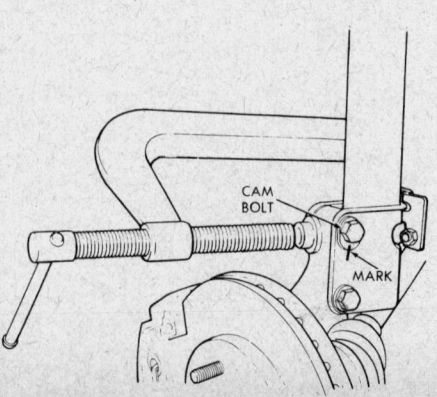

CAM BOLT

MARK

Fig. 6 Strut damper installation

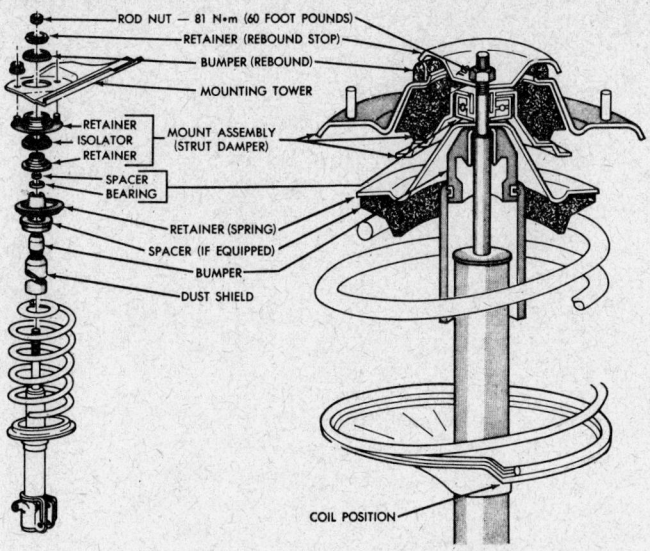

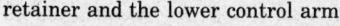

Fig. 7 Strut damper assembly. 1978-83 (Typical of 1984)

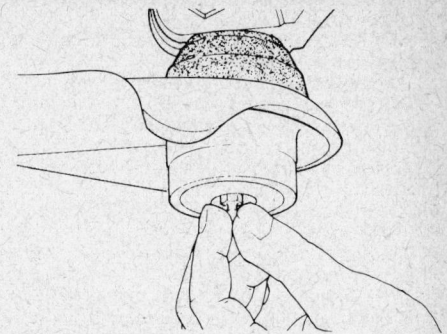

Fig. 8 Checking ball joint for wear. 1981-84

STEERING KNUCKLE, REPLACE

Removal

1. On 1979-84 models, remove cotter pin and nut lock.
2. Loosen hub nut with brakes applied, Figs. 12 and 13.

NOTE: The nub and driveshaft are splined together through the knuckle (Bearing) and retained by the hub nut.

3. Raise and support vehicle, then remove front wheel.
4. Remove hub nut. Ensure that the splined driveshaft is free to separate from spline in hub during knuckle removal. A pulling force on the shaft can separate the inner C/V joint. Tap lightly with a brass drift, if required.

---

retainer and the lower control arm.

NOTE: Pulling the steering knuckle "Out" from vehicle after releasing from ball joint can separate inner C/V joint.

4. Remove sway bar to control arm nut and reinforcement and rotate control arm over sway bar. Remove rear stub strut bushing, sleeve and retainer.

Installation

1. Install retainer, bushing and sleeve on stub strut.
2. Position control arm over sway bar and install rear stub strut and front pivot into crossmember.
3. Install front pivot bolt and loosely assemble nut, Figs. 10 and 11.
4. Install stub strut bushing and retainer and loosely assemble nut.
5. Place sway bar bracket stud through control arm and install retainer and nut. Torque nut to 70 ft. lbs. (94 Nm) on 1978-80 vehicles, 22 ft. lbs. (30 Nm) on 1981-83 vehicles, or 25 ft. lbs. (34 Nm) on 1984 vehicles.

6. Install ball joint stud into steering knuckle, then the clamp bolt. Torque bolt to 50 ft. lbs. (68 Nm) on all 1978-83 vehicles and 1984 Charger, Horizon, Omni and Turismo, or 70 ft. lbs. (94 Nm) on all 1984 models except Charger, Horizon, Omni and Turismo.
7. Lower vehicle and with suspension support vehicle torque front pivot bolt to 105 ft. lbs. (142 Nm) and the stub strut nut to 70 ft. lbs. (94 Nm).

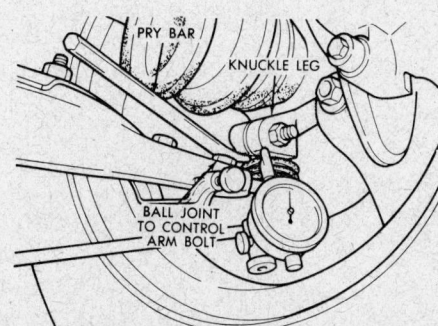

Fig. 9 Checking lower ball joint. 1978-80

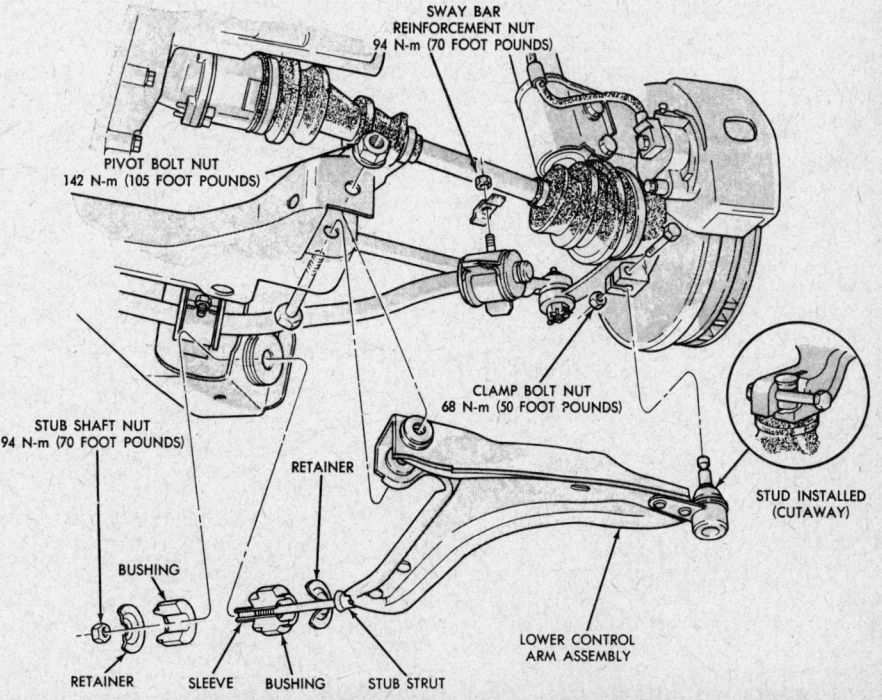

Fig. 10 Lower control arm assembly. 1978-80

5. Disconnect the tie rod end from steering arm with a suitable puller.
6. Disconnect brake hose retainer from strut damper.
7. Remove clamp bolt securing ball joint stud into steering knuckle and brake caliper adapter screw and washer assemblies.
8. Support caliper with a piece of wire. Do not hang by brake hose.
9. Remove rotor.
10. Mark position of camber cam upper adjusting bolt and loosen both bolts.
11. Support steering knuckle and remove cam adjusting and through bolts. Move upper knuckle "Leg" from strut damper bracket and lift knuckle from ball joint stud.

NOTE: Support driveshaft during knuckle removal. Do not permit driveshaft to hang after separating steering knuckle from vehicle.

Installation

1. Place steering knuckle on lower ball joint stud and the driveshaft through hub.
2. Position upper "Leg" of knuckle into strut damper bracket and install cam and through bolts. Place cam in original position. Place a 4 inch or larger C-clamp on strut and steering knuckle, then tighten clamp just enough to eliminate looseness between knuckle and strut. Ensure cam alignment marks are aligned. Torque bolts to 85 ft. lbs. (115 Nm) on 1978 models, or 90 ft. lbs. (122 Nm) on 1979 models. On all 1980–83 models and 1984 Charger, Horizon, Omni and Turismo, torque cam bolt nuts to 45 ft. lbs. (61 Nm), then advance nuts an additional 1/4 turn. On 1984 models except Charger, Horizon, Omni and Turismo, torque nuts to 75 ft. lbs. (100 Nm), then advance an additional 1/4 turn.
3. Install and torque ball joint to steering knuckle clamp bolt to 50 ft. lbs. (68 Nm) on all 1978–83 models and 1984 Charger, Horizon, Omni and Turismo, or 70 ft. lbs. (95 Nm) on 1984 models except Charger, Horizon, Omni and Turismo.
4. Install tie rod end into steering arm and torque nut to 25 ft. lbs. (33 Nm) on 1978 models, or 35 ft. lbs. (47 Nm) on 1979–83 models. Install cotter pin.
5. Install rotor.
6. Install caliper over rotor and position adapter to steering knuckle. Install adapter to knuckle bolts and torque to 85 ft. lbs. (115 Nm) on 1978–82 models, or 160 ft. lbs (216 Nm) on 1983–84 models.
7. Attach brake hose retainer to strut damper and torque screw to 10 ft. lbs. (13 Nm).
8. On 1978 models, proceed as follows:
   a. Install washer and new hub nut after cleaning chips from thread lock groove. Do not reuse hub nuts.
   b. Torque hub nut to 200 ft. lbs. (271 Nm) with brakes applied.
   c. Stake the hub nut as shown in Fig. 14.
9. On 1979–84 models, proceed as follows:
   a. Install washer and hub nut.
   b. Torque hub nut to 180 ft. lbs. (245 Nm) with brakes applied.
   c. Install nut lock and new cotter pin, Fig. 13.

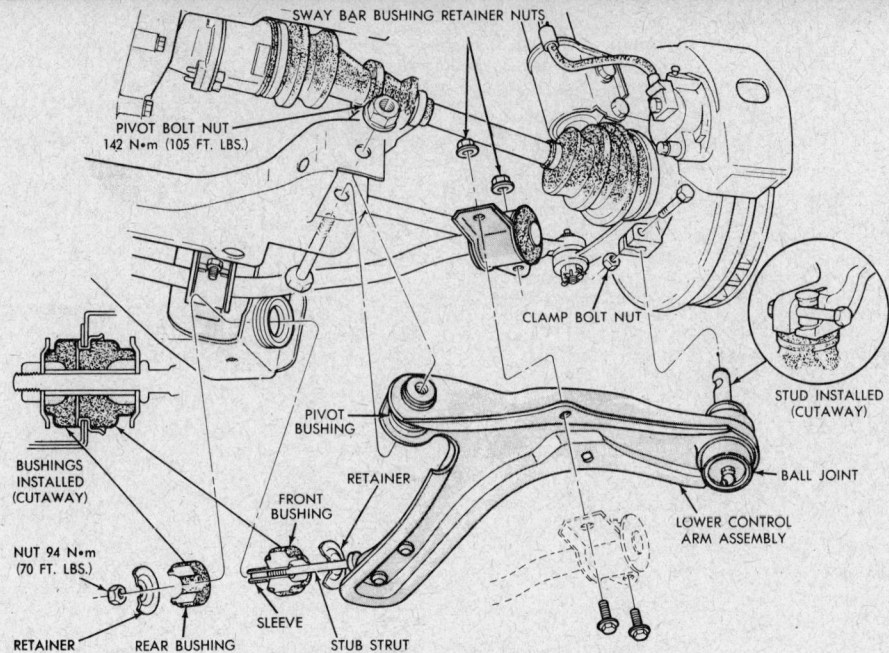

Fig. 11 Lower control assembly. 1981–84

HUB & BEARING, REPLACE

NOTE: If 1978–80 Horizon and Omni models show premature wheel bearing failures, an improperly grounded engine may be the cause. When this problem is encountered, a high pitch whining noise will be emitted from the bearing and the bearing outer race and bearing balls will appear black due to arcing across the race. Also a wear pattern will be indicated on the outer surface of the bearing race. Check for the following proper ground conditions: battery ground cable to transmission mounting bolt, battery ground cable to body ground, braided strap from right hand motor mount to frame side rail and braided strap from right rear of engine to firewall. If all ground cables and straps are properly installed, check for a broken or separated battery ground cable or body ground cable and replace as necessary. After correcting the improper engine ground condition, replace wheel bearing and race.

Removal

1. Remove steering knuckle as described under "Steering Knuckle, Replace."
2. Remove hub using tool No. L-4539 on 1979–83 models, or tool No. C-4811 on 1984 models, Figs. 15 and 15A.

NOTE: On 1978–83 models, the bearing inner races will separate and the outer race will remain in the hub.

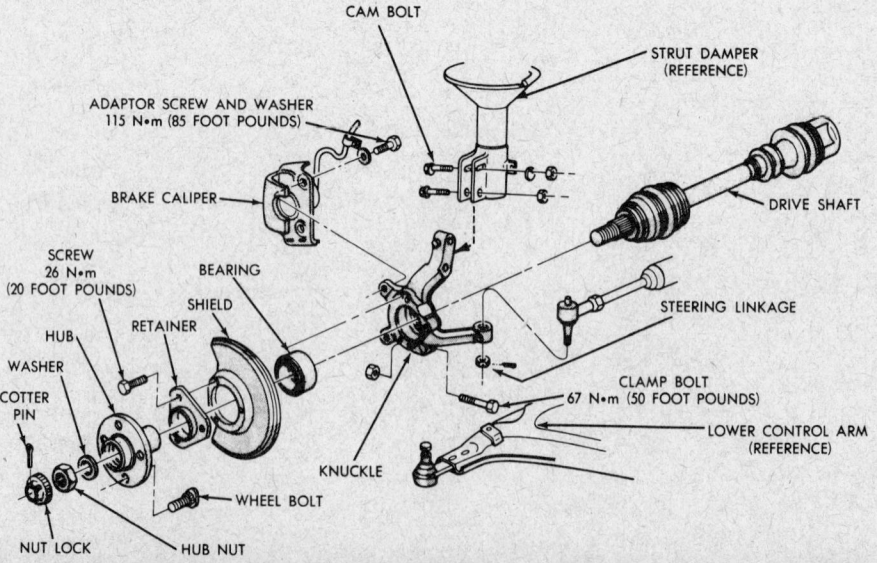

Fig. 12 Steering knuckle assembly. 1978–79

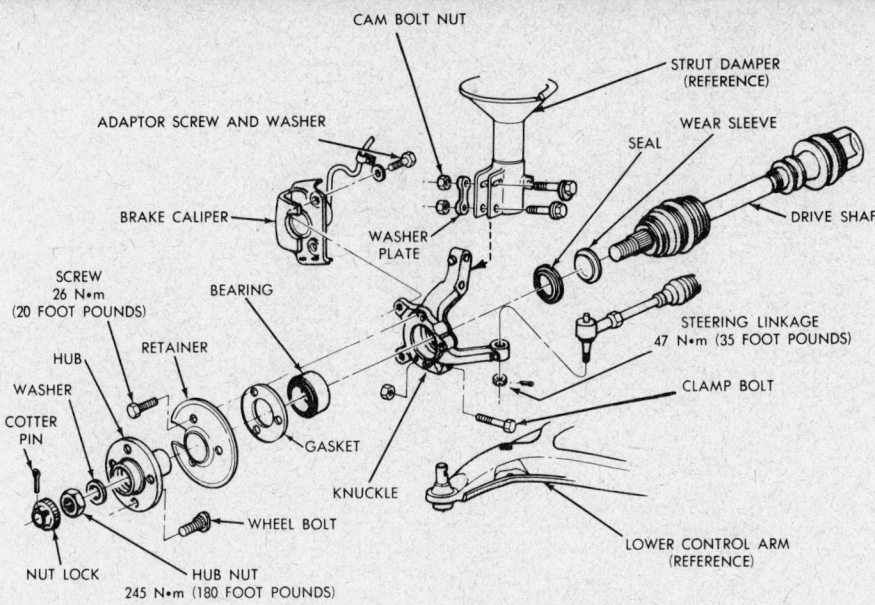

Fig. 13   Steering knuckle assembly. 1980—84

be thoroughly cleaned. The seal and knuckle contact surfaces must be packed with Mopar Multi Mileage Grease or equivalent.

SWAY BAR, REPLACE

Removal, Figs. 20 & 21

1. Raise and support front of vehicle.
2. On 1978–81 models, remove end bushing to control arm nut and reinforcement plate. On 1982–84 models, remove nuts, bolts and retainer at control arm.
3. On 1978–81 models, remove sway bar to crossmember linkage (nut, retainer and insulators at top of crossmember). Bushing are permanently installed on sway bars. On 1982–84 models, remove bolts at crossmember clamps, then remove clamps.
4. Remove sway bar.

NOTE: On 1978–81 models it may be necessary to disassemble the intermediate linkage.

Installation

NOTE: 1982–84 vehicles have a linkless sway bar in the front suspension. The new sway bar is nearly symmetric looking and it is possible to install the sway bar improperly in the vehicle when it is removed for service. Always mark the sway bar prior to removal to assure proper installation. Sway bars used for pro-

---

3. On 1978–83 models, remove bearing outer race from hub using a suitable puller, Fig. 16, then remove brake dust shield.
4. On all models, remove bearing retainer attaching screws and the retainer.
5. Remove bearing from knuckle using a suitable press and socket, Fig. 17.

Installation

1. Press new bearing into knuckle using a suitable press and installer tool, Fig. 18.
2. On 1978–83 models, install brake dust shield.
3. On all models, install bearing retainer

and torque retainer attaching screws to 20 ft. lbs. (27 Nm).
4. Press hub into bearing using a suitable press and a socket, Fig. 19.
5. Install steering knuckle as described under "Steering Knuckle, Replace."

SERVICE NOTE

A new front wheel bearing seal is available for 1978–80 Omni and Horizon that replaces the original slinger assembly. The new seal assembly should be installed in place of the original slinger any time a bearing or outer CV joint is serviced. The sealing surface must

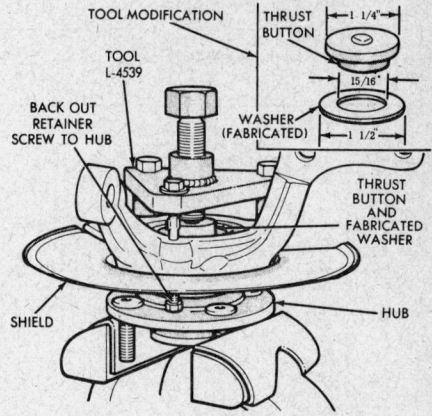

Fig. 15   Hub removal. 1978–83

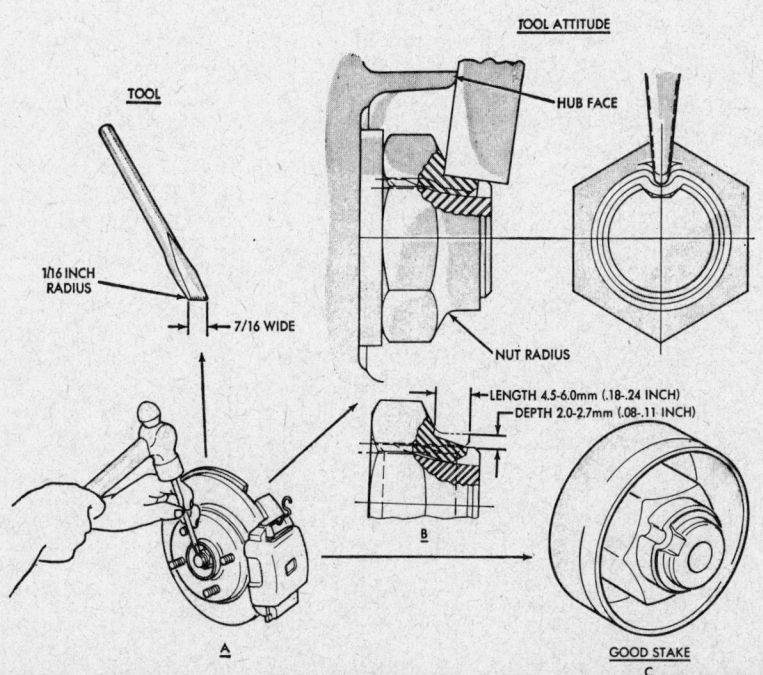

Fig. 14   Staking hub nut. 1978

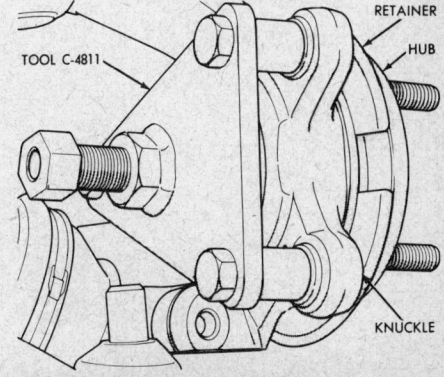

Fig. 15A   Hub removal. 1984

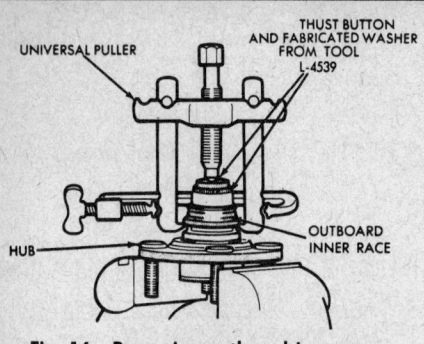

Fig. 16 Removing outboard inner race. 1978—83

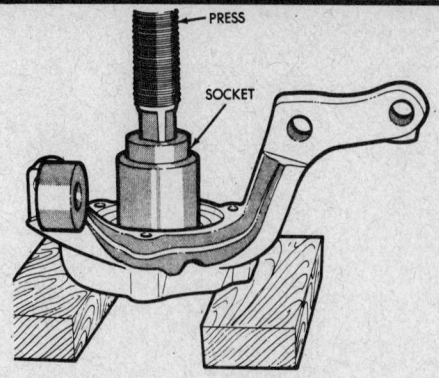

Fig. 17 Removing bearing from knuckle

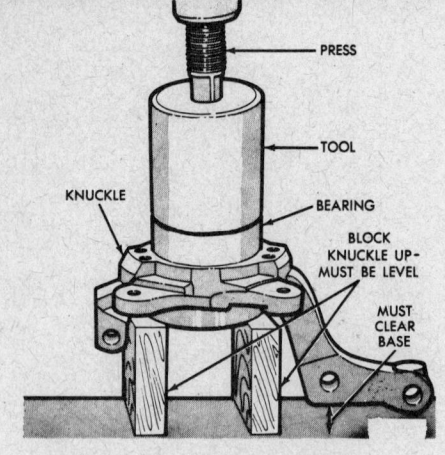

Fig. 18 Installing bearing into knuckle

duction and service replacement are marked on the left (driver side) by a daub or stripe of paint.

1. On 1978—1981 models, loosely assemble intermediate links and straps to sway bar, and sleeve, retainer and isolators to links. On 1982—84 models, position crossmember bushings on bar with curved surface up and split to front of vehicle. Set upper clamps onto crossmember bushings, lift bar assembly into crossmember and install lower clamps and bolts.
2. On 1978—81 models, position link ends through crossmember and install upper isolators, retainers and nut. On 1982—84 models, position retainers at control arms, then insert bolts and install nuts.
3. With lower control arms raised to design height, tighten bolts, Figs. 20 and 21. Refer to Fig. 20 for bolt torques on 1978—81 models. Torque bolts to 22 ft. lbs. (30 Nm) on 1982—83 models, or 25 ft. lbs. (34 Nm) on 1984 models.

NOTE: A bushing retainer is not used on 1984 models.

DRIVESHAFTS, REPLACE

1978—83 Models W/ 4-105 Engine & Manual Transaxle

Removal
1. Remove hub nut as outlined under

"Steering Knuckle, Replace" procedure.
2. Remove clamp bolt securing ball joint stud into steering knuckle.
3. Separate ball joint stud from steering knuckle.
4. Separate outer C/V joint splined shaft from hub while moving knuckle/hub assembly away from C/V joint, Figs. 22 and 23.

NOTE: The separated outer joint and shaft must be supported during inner joint separation from transaxle drive flange. Secure assembly to control arm during next step. Also, the grease slonger must not be bent or damaged during service procedures. Do not attempt to remove, repair or replace.

5. Using a suitable tool or tool L-4550, remove six 8mm allen head screws attaching inner C/V joint to transaxle drive flange. Clean foreign material from C/V joint and drive flange.

NOTE: On 1979—83 models, remove plastic caps installed over allen head screws.

6. Release outer assembly from control arm.
7. To remove driveshaft assembly, hold both inner and outer housings parallel and rotate outer assembly downward and the inner assembly upward at drive flange.
8. Remove driveshaft from vehicle.

Installation
1. If lubricant was lost during handling, fill C/V joint housing with lubricant, P/N 4131389 or equivalent.
2. Clean grease from joint housing, face, screw holes and transaxle drive flange prior to installation.
3. Support assembly vertically with inner housing upward.

NOTE: Do not move inner joint in or out during reassembly to drive flange since this movement can force the lubricant from the joint.

4. Position inner housing to drive flange and rotate assembly upward. Locate inner housing in drive flange. Support

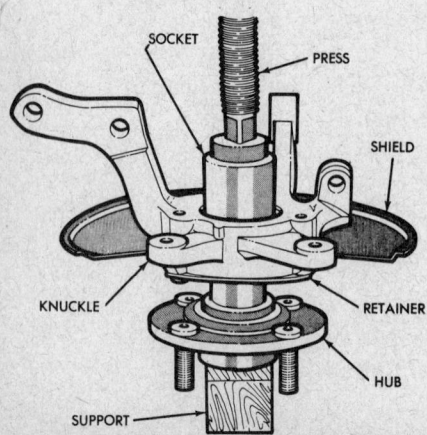

Fig. 19 Installing hub into knuckle

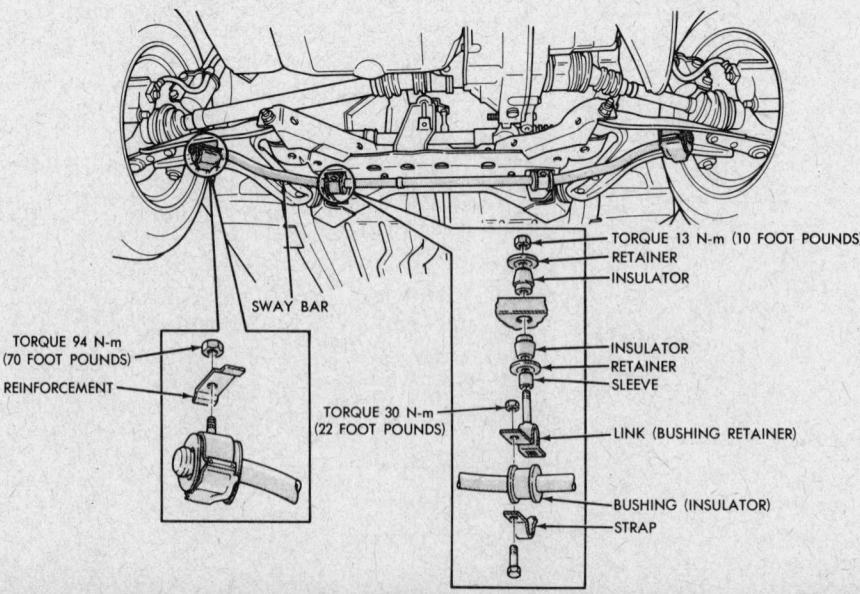

Fig. 20 Sway bar assembly. 1978—81

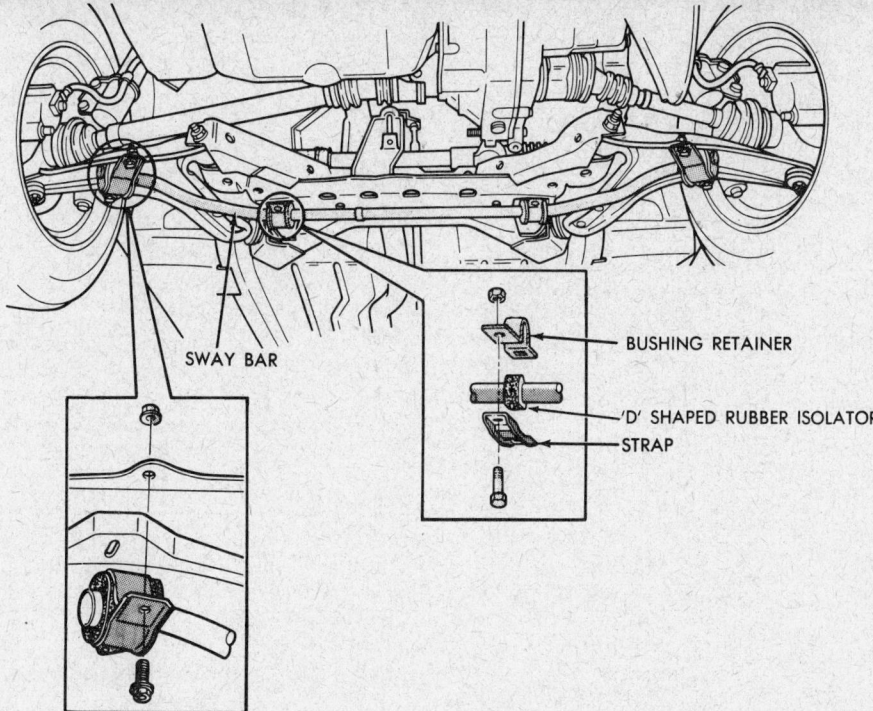

SWAY BAR

BUSHING RETAINER

'D' SHAPED RUBBER ISOLATOR

STRAP

Fig. 21 Sway bar assembly. 1982–83. (Typical of 1984)

the outer end of driveshaft, Fig. 22. Do not permit assembly to hang.

5. Secure inner C/V joint to drive flange with new allen head screws. Then, using tool L-4550 or equivalent, torque the six screws to 440 inch lbs. (50 Nm). On 1979–83 models, install plastic caps over allen head screws.

NOTE: Failure to properly torque screws may result in failure during vehicle operation.

---

6. Push knuckle/hub assembly out and install splined outer C/V joint shaft into hub.
7. Install knuckle assembly on ball joint stud. Install and torque clamp bolt to 50 ft. lbs. (68 Nm).
8. On 1978 models, install and torque hub nut to 200 ft. lbs. (271 Nm). Stake hub nut as shown in Fig. 14.
9. On 1979–83 models, install washer and hub nut. Torque nut to 180 ft. lbs. (245 Nm). Install nut lock and cotter pin.
10. If, after attaching driveshaft assembly in the vehicle the inboard boot appears col-

lapsed or deformed, vent the inner boot by inserting a round tipped, small diameter rod between the boot and shaft. As venting occurs, the boot will return to the normal shape.

NOTE: After installation of driveshaft, check the driveshaft length as outlined in "Driveshaft Length, Adjust."

Except 1978–83 Models W/ 4–105 Engine & Manual Transaxle

Removal

NOTE: On 1978–81 and early 1982 models, the inboard C/V joints have stub shafts splined into the differential side gears and are retained with circlips, Figs. 22 and 23. The circlip "Tangs" are located on a machined surface on the inner end of the stub shafts and are removed and installed with the shaft. On late 1982 & 1983–84 models, the driveshafts are spring loaded and are retained to the side gears by constant spring pressure provided by the spring contained in the C/V joints, Fig. 24.

1. On 1978–81 and early 1982 models, drain transaxle differential unit and remove cover.
2. If removing the right hand driveshaft, the speedometer pinion must be removed prior to driveshaft removal, Fig. 25.
3. On 1978–81 and early 1982 models, rotate driveshaft to expose circlip tangs, Fig. 26. Using needle nose pliers, compress circlip tangs while prying shaft into side gear splined cavity, Fig. 27. The circlip will be compressed in the cavity with the shaft.
4. Remove clamp bolt securing ball joint clamp bolt to steering knuckle. Then, separate ball joint stud from steering knuckle. Do not damage ball joint or C/V joint boots.
5. Separate outer C/V joint splined shaft from hub by holding C/V housing while moving knuckle/hub assembly away from C/V joint.

NOTE: Do not damage slinger on outer C/V joint. Do not attempt to remove, repair or replace.

---

6. Support assembly at C/V joint housings and remove by pulling outward on the inner C/V joint housing. Do not pull on the shaft.

NOTE: If removing left hand driveshaft assembly, the removal may be aided by inserting a screwdriver blade between the differential pinion shaft and carefully prying against the end face of stub.

---

7. Remove driveshaft assembly from vehicle.

Installation

NOTE: On 1978–81 and early 1982 units, install new circlips on inner joint shaft before installation, Fig. 28.

1. On 1978–81 and early 1982 units, ensure tang on circlips are aligned with flattened end of shaft before inserting shaft into

SHAFT RETAINER

SIDE GEAR

TRIPOD JOINT

DIFFERENTIAL UNIT

STRUT DAMPER

KNUCKLE

AUTOMATIC

HUB

MANUAL

RZEPPA JOINT

BEARING

HUB NUT

TRIPOD JOINT

CONNECTING SHAFT (LEFT)

WASHER

Fig. 22 Driveshaft assemblies. 1978–80

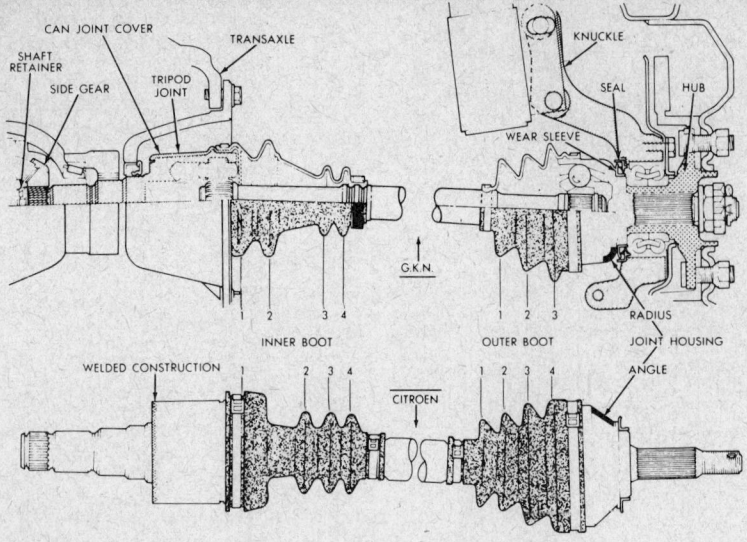

Fig. 23 Driveshaft assemblies. 1981 & early 1982

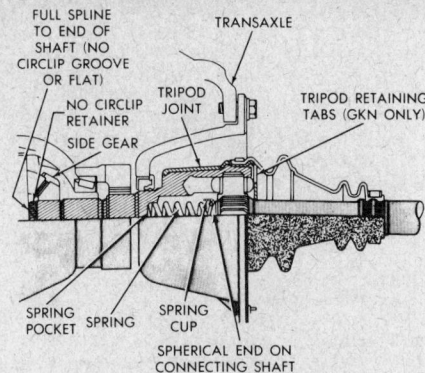

Fig. 24 Drive shaft assembly.
Late 1982 & 1983–84 except models w/ 4-105
engine & manual transaxle

NOTE: After installation of driveshaft, check the driveshaft length as outlined in "Driveshaft Length, Adjust."

transaxle. If not, this can cause jamming or component damage.

2. Hold inner joint assembly at housing while aligning and guiding the inner joint spline into transaxle.

3. On 1978–81 and early 1982 units, while holding the inner joint housing, quickly thrust the shaft into the differential. This will complete the lock-up of the driveshaft to the axle side gear.

NOTE: On 1978–81 and early 1982 models, inspect circlip positioning in side gears to verify lock-up.

4. Push knuckle/hub assembly out and install splined outer C/V joint shaft into hub.

5. Install knuckle assembly on ball joint stud.

6. Install clamp bolt. Torque to 50 ft. lbs. (68 Nm) on all 1978–83 models and 1984 Charger, Horizon, Omni and Turismo, or 70 ft. lbs. (95 Nm) on all 1984 models except Charger, Horizon, Omni and Turismo.

7. Install speedometer pinion, Fig. 25.

8. On 1978–81 and early 1982 models, apply a 1/16 inch bead of silicone sealant, part number 4026070, to differential cover sealing surface and mating surface of transaxle case after both have been properly cleaned and inspected.

9. On 1978–81 and early 1982 models, install differential cover and torque retaining screws to 250 inch lbs. (28 Nm).

10. Fill differential to bottom of filler plug hole with Dexron automatic transmission fluid.

11. On 1978 models, install and torque hub nut to 200 ft. lbs. (271 Nm). Stake nut as shown in Fig. 14.

12. On 1979–84 models, install washer and hub nut. Torque hub nut to 180 ft. lbs. (245 Nm). Install nut lock and cotter pin.

13. If, after attaching driveshaft assembly in vehicle the inboard boot appears collapsed or deformed, vent the inner boot by inserting a round tipped, small diameter rod between the boot and shaft. As venting occurs, the boot will return to the normal shape.

DRIVESHAFT LENGTH, ADJUST

If the vertical bolts on both engine mounts have been loosened, or the vehicle has experienced front structural damage, driveshaft length must be checked.

The engine mounts incorporate slotted bolt holes to permit side-to-side positioning of the engine, thereby affecting the length of the driveshaft. To check driveshaft length proceed as follows.

1981–82

NOTE: Measuring of the right driveshaft (passenger side) will indicate proper positioning of both sides.

1. Position the vehicle so that the weight of the body is on all four wheels.

2. Using a tape measure or other suitable measuring device, measure direct distance from inner edge of outboard boot to inner edge of inboard boot, Fig. 29.

3. If measurement matches length shown in

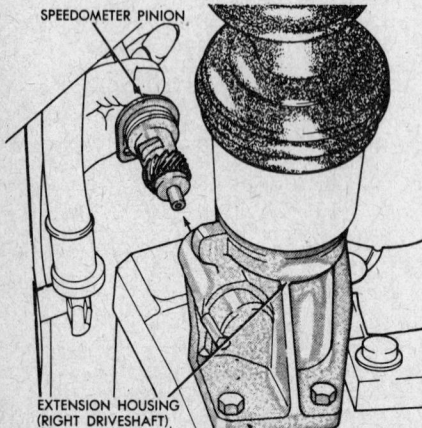

Fig. 25 Speed pinion replacement.
Except 1978–83 models w/4-105 engine & manual transaxle

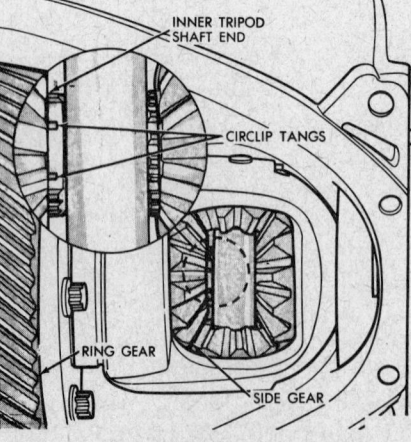

Fig. 26 Circlips exposed. 1978–81 & early 1982 models less 4-105 engine & manual transaxle

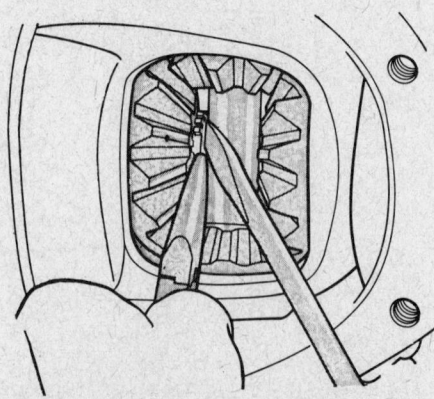

Fig. 27 Compressing circlip. 1978–81 & early 1982 models less 4-105 engine & manual transaxle

Fig. 29, no further action is required. If measurement is not within given range, engine position must be corrected as follows:

a. Remove load on engine motor mounts by carefully supporting engine and transmission assembly with a floor jack.

b. Loosen right and left engine mount vertical fasteners and front engine mount bracket to front crossmember bolts.

NOTE: The right and left engine mount rubber bushings should be positioned to provide approximately .06–.14 inch clearance between the bushing and the supporting bracket, Fig. 30. When bracket movement is required, it will be necessary to obtain proper bushing to bracket clearance as well as proper driveshaft length.

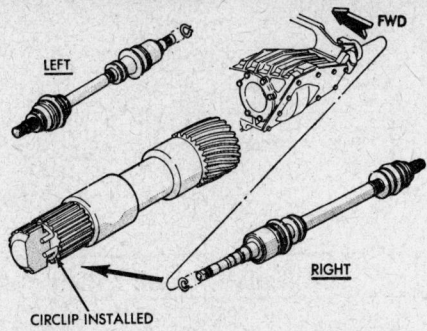

Fig. 28 Circlip installation. 1978–81 & early 1982 models less 4-105 engine & manual transaxle

c. Pry engine right or left as required to achieve proper driveshaft assembly length. A total of .47 inch is available for driveshaft length adjustment. Insert 3mm thick spacers adjacent to isolator snubber on each side. These spacers must be in place when engine mount fasteners are tightened, Fig. 30.

d. Torque right and left engine mount vertical bolts to 250 inch lbs. and torque front engine mount bolts to 40 ft. lbs.

1983–84

1. Position vehicle with wheels straight ahead and body weight distributed on all 4 tires.
2. Measure direct distance between inner edge of outboard boot to inner edge of inboard boot on both driveshafts.

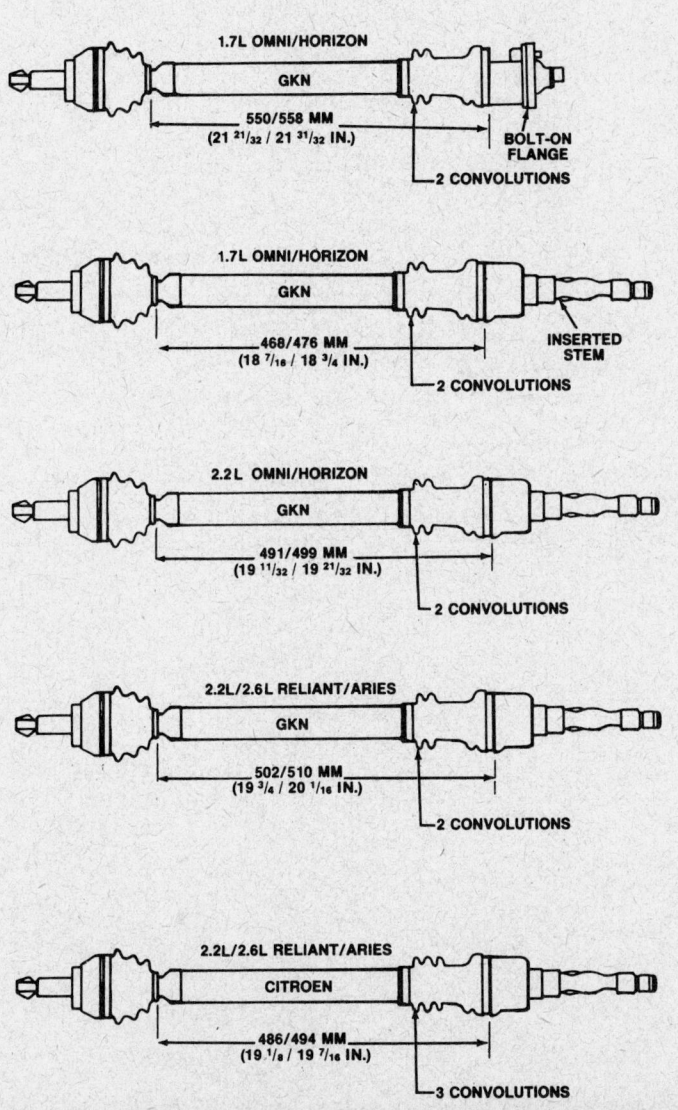

Fig. 29 Right side driveshaft length. 1981

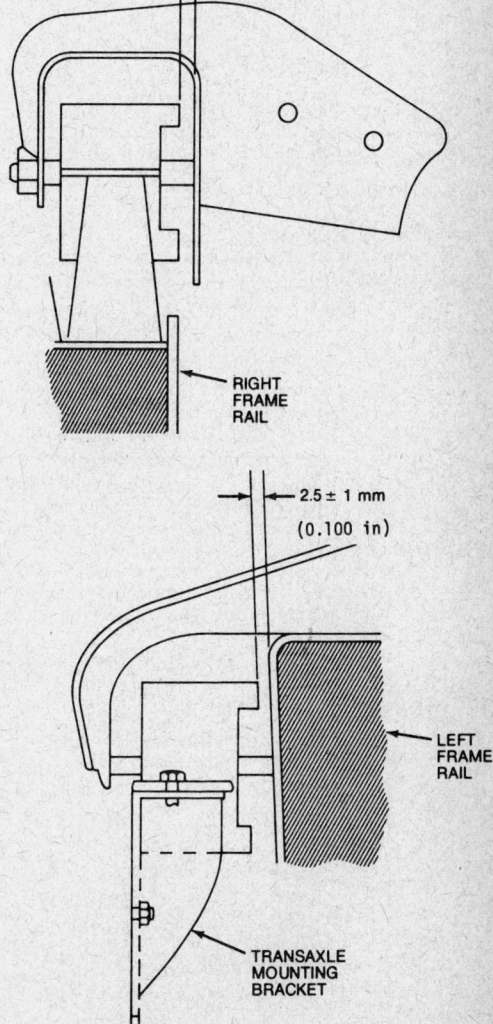

Fig. 30 Measuring clearance between bushing and support bracket. 1981

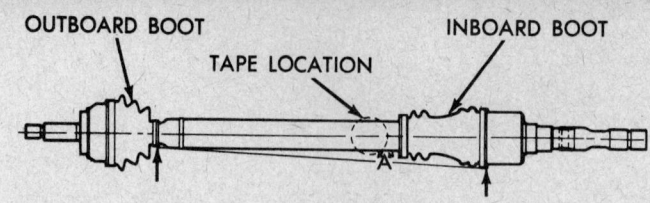

| Body | Engine | Driveshaft Identification | | | "A" Dimension | |
		Type	Side	Tape Color	mm	Inch
CHARGER, HORIZON, OMNI & TURISMO	1.6L/2.2L	G.K.N.	Right	Yellow	498-509	19.6-20.0
			Left	Yellow	240-253	9.5-10.0
		A.C.I.	Right	Red	469-478	18.5-19.0
			Left	Red	208-218	8.2- 8.6
EXC. CHARGER, DAYTONA, HORIZON, LASER, OMNI & TURISMO	2.2L	G.K.N.	Right	Blue	505-515	19.9-20.3
			Left	Blue	259-277	10.2-10.9
		A.C.I.	Right	Green	477-485	18.8-19.1
			Left	Green	229-244	9.0- 9.6
		G.K.N./A.C.I.	Right	Orange	492-500	19.4-19.7
			Left	Orange	243-258	9.6-10.2
		Citroen	Right	White	480-492	18.9-19.4
			Left	White	238-255	9.4-10.0
	2.6L	G.K.N.	Right	Silver	501-510	19.7-20.1
			Left	Silver	254-269	10.0-10.6
		Citroen	Right	Yellow	480-492	18.9-19.4
			Left	Yellow	238-255	9.4-10.0
EXC. CHARGER, HORIZON, OMNI & TURISMO	2.2L Turbo	G.K.N.	Right	Tan	257-265	10.1-10.4
			Left	Silver	254-269	10.0-10.6
		Citroen	Right	Red	241-251	9.5- 9.9
			Left	Yellow	238-255	9.4-10.0

Fig. 30A Driveshaft length specifications. 1984

NOTE: On 1983 models equipped with 4-105 engine and manual transaxle, measure from outer edge of inboard flange.

3. Driveshaft length must be within specifications in chart, Fig. 30A. If measurement is not within specifications, engine position must be corrected as follows:
   a. Remove load from engine mounts by carefully supporting engine and transmission assembly with a suitable jack.
   b. Loosen right and left engine mount vertical bolts (1984 models, right only) and the front engine mount bracket-to-crossmember attaching bolts.
   c. Pry engine to the right or left as necessary to bring driveshaft length within specifications.

NOTE: On 1984 models, the left engine mount is sleeved over long support bolt and shaft, Fig. 30B, to provide lateral adjustment whether or not engine weight is removed.

   d. Torque engine mount vertical bolts to 250 inch lbs. and front engine mount bolts to 40 ft. lbs.
   e. On 1984 models, center left engine mount.

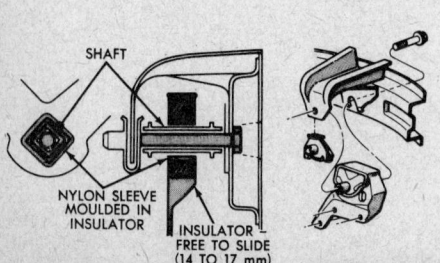

Fig. 30B Left engine mount adjustment. 1984

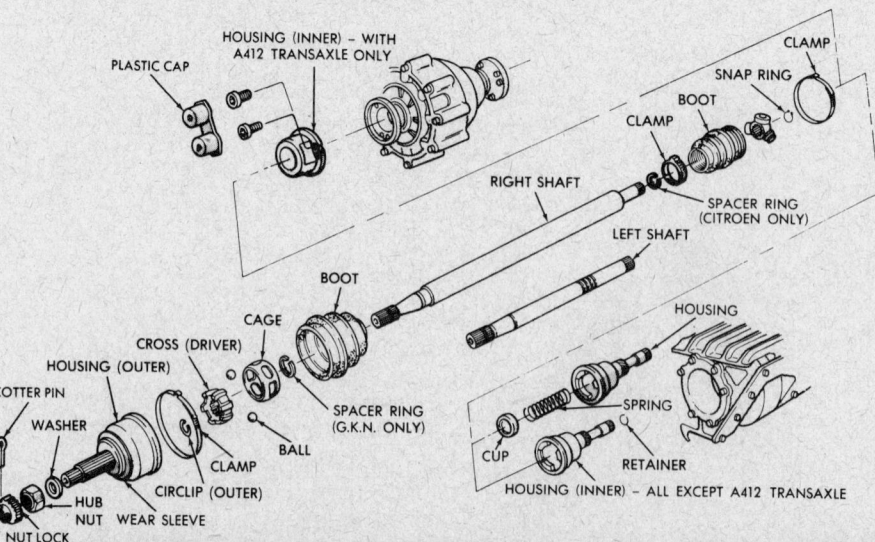

Fig. 31 Driveshaft components. 1981–84

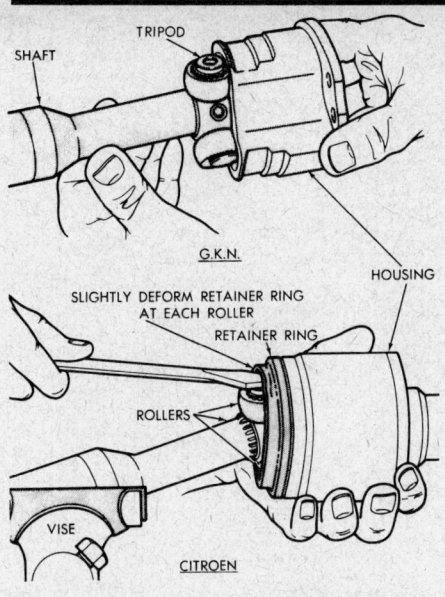

Fig. 32 Removing 3 ball tripod housing. 1981–84 inner C/V joint

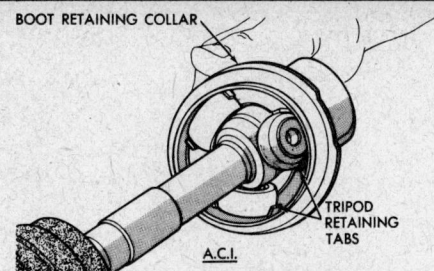

Fig. 32A Removing 3 ball tripod housing. 1984 A.C.I. inner C/V joint

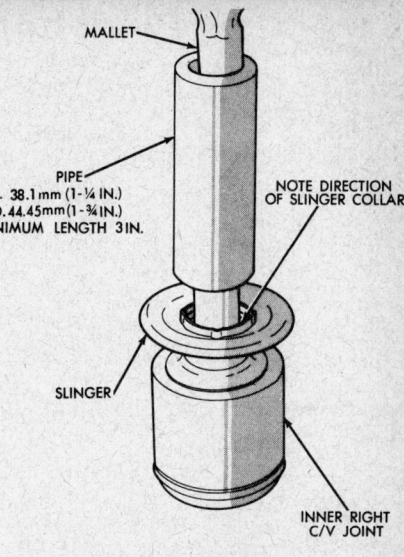

Fig. 32B Slinger installation. 1984 w/ turbocharged engine

INNER CONSTANT VELOCITY JOINT SERVICE
1981–84

Disassemble, Fig. 31

1. Remove clamp and boot from joint and discard.
2. On Citroen units, separate tripod from housing by slightly deforming retaining ring at three locations, Fig. 32. If necessary, cut retaining ring from housing and install replacement retaining ring with inner flange rolled, then stake into machined groove with a suitable punch.

NOTE: When removing tripod from housing, secure rollers. After tripod has been removed, secure assembly with tape.

3. On 1981 and early 1982 G.K.N. non-spring loaded units, slide tripod from housing, Fig. 32. On late 1982–84 G.K.N. spring loaded units, bend tabs on joint cover using needle nose pliers, then remove tripod from housing.
4. On A.C.I. units, position housing so all 3 rollers are flush with retaining tabs. Pull housing out by hand at a slight angle to pop one roller at a time out of the retaining tabs, Fig. 32A. Do not hold joint at too severe an angle, as the rollers may be damaged.

NOTE: The retaining tabs must not be bent during removal or installation of the housing.

5. Remove snap ring from end of shaft, then remove tripod using brass punch.

Inspection

Remove grease from assembly and inspect bearing race and tripod components for wear and damage and replace as necessary. On late 1982–84 spring loaded joints inspect spring, spring cup and sperical end of connecting shaft for wear and damage and replace as necessary.

NOTE: Components of spring loaded and non-spring loaded inner C/V joints cannot be interchanged.

Assemble

1. On models equipped with turbocharged

engine, install a new slinger, Fig. 32B. Tap slinger down until collar is flush with journal, then slide rubber seal over stub shaft and into groove.
2. On all models, Slide small end of boot over shaft. On Tubular type shafts, align boot lip with mark on shaft outer diameter. On solid type shafts, position small end of boot in groove on shaft.
3. Place rubber clamp over groove on boot.
4. Install tripod on shaft with non-chamfered face of tripod body facing shaft retainer groove.
5. Lock tripod assembly on shaft by installing retaining ring in shaft groove.
6. Distribute two packets of grease provided with boot and clamp kit into boot assembly on G.K.N. units, one packet on A.C.I. units, or 2/3 packet on Citroen units.
7. On 1981–83 models with 4-105 engine and manual transaxle, install joint housing over tripod, then position large end of boot in groove in housing. Add two additional packets of grease after boot has been secured to housing.
8. On 1981 and early 1982 models less 4-105 engine with manual transaxle, distribute one packet of grease in housing before positioning housing over tripod. On Citroen units, reform retainer ring. On all units, secure boot to housing with boot clamp.
9. On late 1982 & 1983–84 models less 4-105 engine and manual transaxle, distribute remaining grease supplied into housing. Position spring, with spring cup attached to exposed end, into spring pocket. Place a small amount of grease on spring cup, then position housing over tripod. On Citroen units, reform or replace retainer ring. On G.K.N. units, bend retaining tabs. On A.C.I. units, align rollers with retaining tabs and housing tracks and pop one roller at a time through the retaining tabs. On all units, position boot over boot groove in housing, then install clamp.

NOTE: When installing housing, check to insure that spring remains in pocket and centered in housing. Also ensure that spring cup contacts spherical end of connecting shaft.

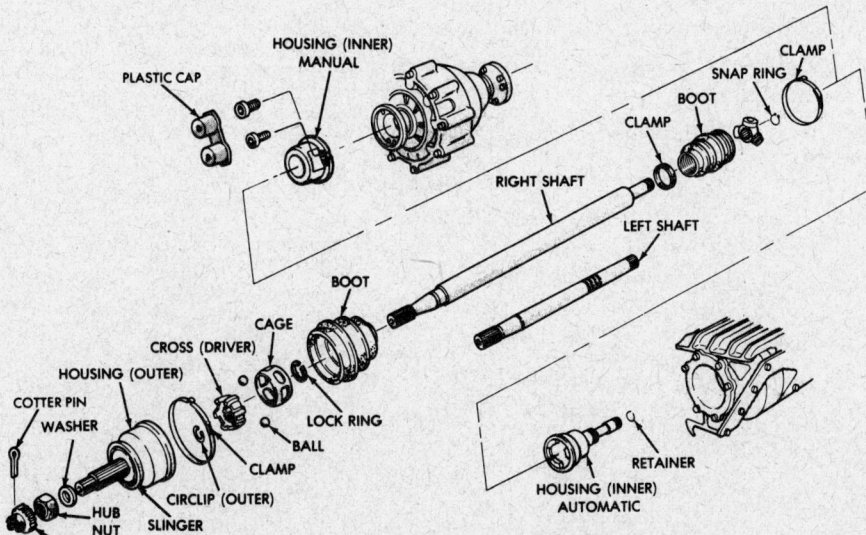

Fig. 33 Driveshaft components. 1979–80

1978–80

Disassembly, Figs. 33 & 34

1. Cut the metal clamps from the boot and discard boot.
2. Remove grease from inside of joint housing and 3-ball and trunion assembly, Fig. 35.
3. Remove retaining rings from shaft-end groove, then the tripod with a brass drift, Fig. 36.

Inspection

Inspect the joint housing ball raceway and tripod components for excessive wear. Replace if necessary.

Assembly, Figs. 33 & 34

1. To install new boot, slide small rubber clamp onto shaft, then the small end of boot over the shaft.

NOTE: On tubular shafts, position the boot lip face in line with the mark on the shaft outside diameter. On solid shafts, position the small boot end in the machined groove.

2. Clamp the small boot end by placing the rubber clamp over the boot groove.
3. Install the tripod on the shaft with the non-chamfered face of the tripod body facing the shaft retainer groove.
4. Install the retaining ring in the groove to lock the tripod assembly on the shaft.
5. Distribute two packets of grease in the boot. The packets of proper lubricant are provided in the boot joint kits.
6. On manual driveshafts, install the joint housing over the tripod and position the large end of boot in the groove on the housing. Two additional packets of grease are to be added after the boot is secured to the housing.
7. On automatic driveshafts, position housing over tripod and position boot over housing groove. One additional packet of grease is to be added after securing boot to housing.
8. On all driveshafts, install large metal clamp on boot, ensuring that the boot is properly located on the shaft and is not twisted.
9. Install the clamp tags in the slots and tighten clamp by hand.
10. Clamp bridge with tool C-4124 and squeeze to complete tightening the clamp. Do not cut through the clamp bridge and/or damage the boot.
11. On manual driveshafts, distribute two additional packets of grease in the joint housing. First push forward gently on the

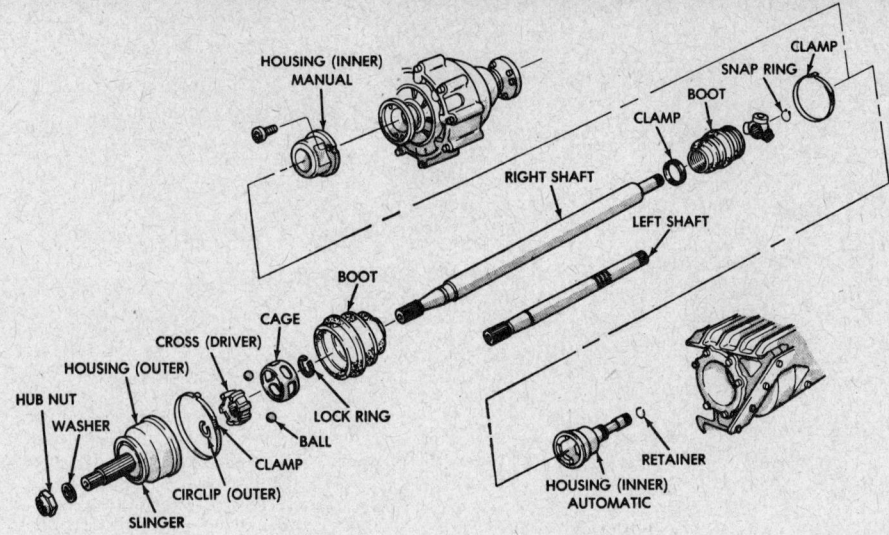

Fig. 34   Driveshaft components. 1978

housing to provide space to accommodate volume of grease required.

OUTER CONSTANT VELOCITY JOINT SERVICE

Disassembly

Figs. 32, 33, 34, 37 & 38

1. Cut boot clamps from boot and discard boot and clamps.
2. Clean grease from joint.
3. Support shaft in a soft jawed vise, support the outer joint and tap with a mallet to dislodge joint from internal circlip installed in a groove at the outer end of the shaft, Fig. 39. Do not remove slinger from housing.
4. Remove circlip from shaft groove and discard, Fig. 40.
5. Unless the shaft requires replacement, do not remove the heavy lock ring from the shaft, Fig. 40.
6. If the constant velocity joint was operating satisfactorily and the grease does not appear contaminated, proceed to "Assembly" procedure, Step 7.
7. If the constant velocity joint is noisy or badly worn, replace entire unit. The repair kit will include boot, clamps, circlip and lubricant. Clean and inspect the joint outlined in the following steps.
8. Clean surplus grease and mark relative

position of inner cross, cage and housing with a dab of paint.
9. Hold joint vertically in a soft jawed vise.
10. Press downward on one side of the inner race to tilt cage and remove ball from opposite side, Fig. 41. If joint is tight, use a hammer and a brass drift to tap inner race. Do not strike the cage. Repeat this step until all six balls are removed. A screwdriver may be used to pry the balls loose.
11. Tilt the cage assembly vertically and position the two opposing, elongated cage windows in area between ball grooves. Remove cage and inner race assembly by pulling upward from the housing, Fig. 42.
12. Rotate inner cross 90 degrees to cage and align one of the race spherical lands with an elongated cage window. Raise land into cage window and remove inner race by swinging outward, Fig. 43.

Inspection

1. Check housing ball races for excessive wear.
2. Check splined shaft and nut threads for damage.
3. Inspect the balls for pitting, cracks, scouring and wear. Dulling of the surface is normal.
4. Inspect cage for excessive wear on inner and outer spherical surfaces, heavy brinelling of cage, window cracks and chip-

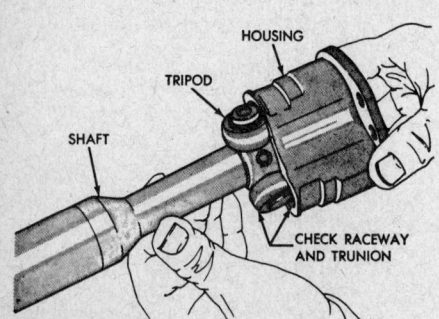

Fig. 35   Removing 3-ball tripod, housing & shaft assembly. 1978–80 inner C/V joints

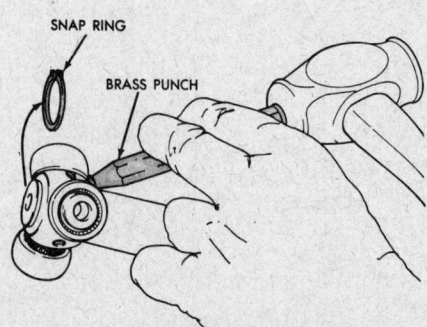

Fig. 36   Remove snap ring & tripod. Inner C/V joints

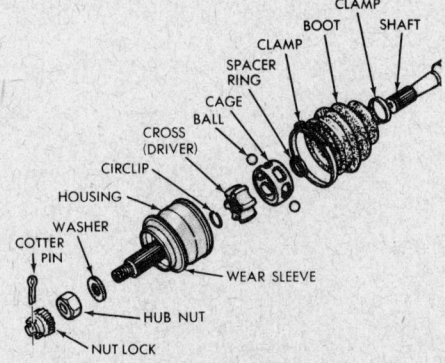

Fig. 37   Outer C/V joint disassembled. 1981–84

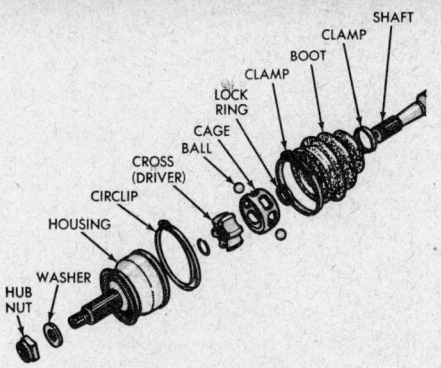

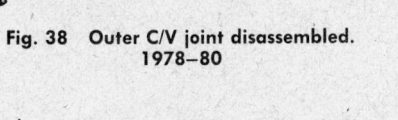

Fig. 38   Outer C/V joint disassembled. 1978–80

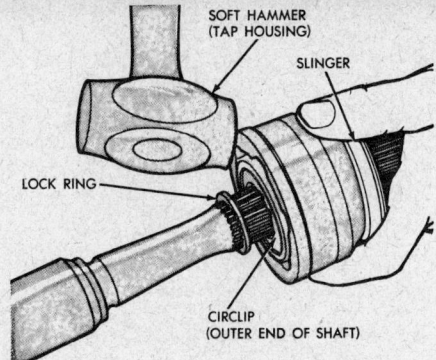

Fig. 39   Removing joint from shaft. Outer C/V joints

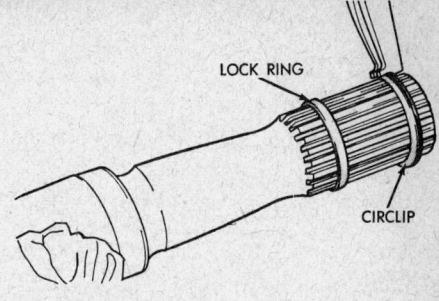

Fig. 40   Circlip removal. Outer C/V joints

ping.

5. Inspect inner race (Cross) for excessive wear or scouring of ball races.
6. If any of the defects listed in Steps 1 through 5, are found, replace the C/V assembly as a unit.

NOTE: Polished areas in races (Cross and housing) and on cage spheres are normal and does not indicate a need for joint replacement unless they are suspected of causing noise and vibration.

Assembly

1981–84 Units, Figs. 31 & 37

1. If removed, position wear sleeve on joint housing, then tap sleeve onto housing using tool No. C-4698.
2. Lightly oil components, then align marks made during disassembly.
3. Align one of the inner race lands with elongated window of cage, then insert race into cage and pivot 90°.
4. Align elongated cage windows with housing land, then pivot cage 90°. The curved side of the elongated cage windows and inner race counterbore should face outward from joint.
5. Lubricate ball races with one packet of grease from kit.
6. Tilt cage and inner race assembly and insert balls.
7. With shaft supported in a soft jawed vise, install boot. On G.K.N. and A.C.I. units, slip small clamp over spacer ring and

shaft.
8. Slide small end of boot over spacer ring and shaft, then position boot end in machined groove.

NOTE: On Citroen units, position vent sleeve under boot at clamp area.

9. Install snap ring on shaft. When installing use care not to overexpand snap ring.
10. Position joint housing on shaft, then engage by tapping sharply with a soft faced mallet.
11. Check to ensure that snap ring is properly seated, by attempting to pull joint from shaft.
12. Locate large end of boot over housing.
13. On G.K.N. and A.C.I. units, secure boot clamps using tool No. C-4124. On Citroen units, secure boot clamps using tool C-4653.

NOTE: G.K.N. and A.C.I. units use steel clamps, while Citroen units use a strap type clamp.

1978–80 Units, Figs. 33, 34 & 38

1. Lightly lubricate all components before assembling joint.
2. Align parts according to paint markings.
3. Insert one inner race (Cross) lands into an elongated cage window and feed race into cage. Pivot cross 90 degrees to complete cage assembly.

4. Align opposite elongated cage windows with housing land and insert cage assembly into housing. Pivot cage 90 degrees to complete installation.

NOTE: When properly assembled, the curved side of the elongated cage windows and the inner cross counterbore should face outward from the joint, Fig. 44.

5. Apply lubricant to ball races between all sides of ball grooves.
6. Insert balls into raceway by tilting cage and inner race assembly. Ensure that locking ring is seated in the groove.
7. To install new boot, slide small metal clamp over lock ring and shaft.
8. Slide end of boot over lock ring and shaft, then position in machined groove.
9. Place small metal clamp over boot groove. Locate clamp tags in slots and hand tighten. Clamp bridge with tool C-4124 and squeeze to complete tightening.
10. Insert new circlip in shaft groove. Do not expand or twist circlip during assembly.
11. Position tool L-4538 on shaft splines with the tapered end outboard and compress circlip, Fig. 45. Ensure that sufficient spline area is left ahead of the tool to provide entry of outer joint onto shaft, Fig. 46.
12. Place outer joint on splined end, engage splines and rap with a mallet, allowing tool to slide along with the joint.
13. Remove tool and check that circlip is properly seated by attempting to pull joint from shaft.
14. Place large end of boot over joint housing, ensuring that boot is not twisted.
15. Place large metal clamp over boot and

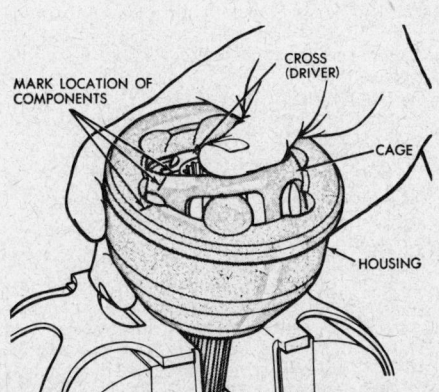

Fig. 41   Ball removal. Outer C/V joints

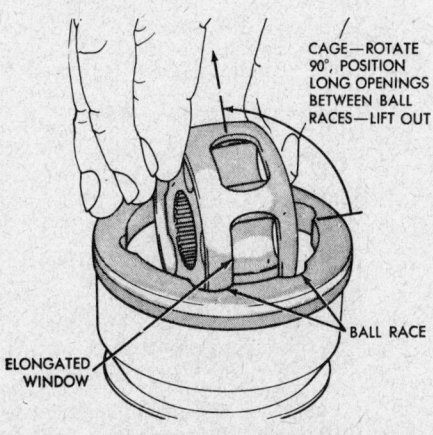

Fig. 42   Cage & cross assembly removal. Outer C/V joints

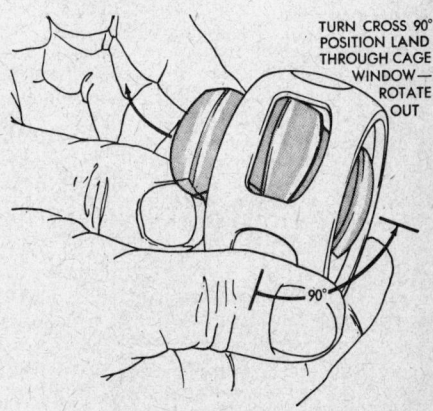

Fig. 43   Removing cross from cage. Outer C/V joints

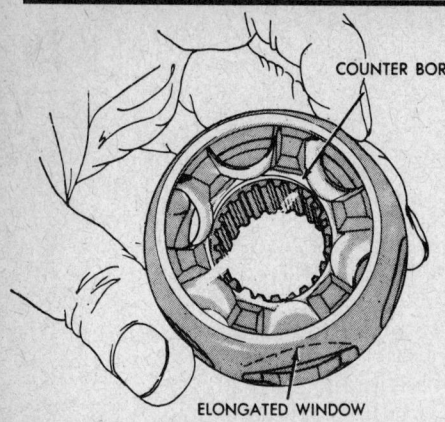

COUNTER BORE

ELONGATED WINDOW

**Fig. 44 Cage & cross assembly.
Outer C/V joints**

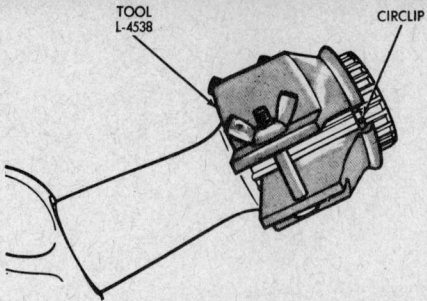

TOOL L-4538   CIRCLIP

Fig. 45 Compressing circlip. Outer C/V joints

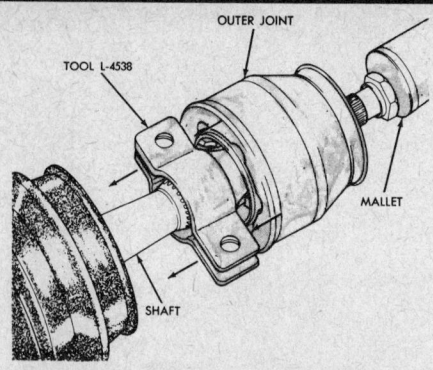

OUTER JOINT

TOOL L-4538

MALLET

SHAFT

**Fig. 46 Positioning joint into shaft splined.
Outer C/V joints**

locate clamp tags in slots, hand tightening the clamp.
16. Clamp bridge with tool L-4124 and squeeze to complete tightening. Do not cut through clamp bridge and/or damage boot.

RACK & PINION STEERING GEAR, REPLACE

NOTE: These vehicles are equipped with manual steering gears supplied by two manufacturers, Burman and Cam Gears. The replacement rubber boots for these gears are not interchangeable.

The Burman gear can be identified by the name "Burman" cast on the housing, and is visible from under the hood.

The Cam Gear steering gear has no identification markings.

1. Raise and support vehicle, then remove front wheels.
2. Remove tie rod ends with a suitable puller.
3. On all models except Omni, Horizon, Charger and Turismo, remove steering column as follows:
   a. Disconnect battery ground cable.
   b. On column shift vehicles, disconnect cable rod by prying rod out of grommet in shift lever.
   c. Disconnect all wiring connectors at steering column jacket and remove steering wheel center pad.
   d. Disconnect horn wires and horn switch, then pull steering wheel from column.
   e. Expose steering column bracket, remove instrument panel steering column cover and lower reinforcement. Remove bezel.
   f. Remove indicator set screw and shaft indicator pointer from shift housing.
   g. Remove nuts attaching steering column bracket to instrument panel support, then lower the bracket support to the floor.

CAUTION: Do not remove roll pin to remove steering column assembly.

   h. Pull steering column rearward, and disconnect lower shaft from coupling.
   i. Reinstall anti-rattle clips into lower coupling tube slot.
   j. Remove column assembly out through passenger compartment, being careful not to damage paint or trim.
   k. Cut plastic grommets from shift levers and install new grommets from rod side of lever using pliers and a backup washer. Apply grease to grommets.
4. On Omni, Horizon, Charger and Turismo, drive out lower roll pin attaching pinion shaft to lower universal joint.
5. On all models except Omni, Horizon, Charger and Turismo, support the front suspension crossmember with a suitable jack, then remove bolts attaching steering gear to front crossmember. Lower crossmember from vehicle frame.
6. On Omni, Horizon, Charger and Turismo, remove 2 rear crossmember nuts and loosen 2 front bolts, then lower crossmember slightly to gain access to boot seal shields.
7. Remove splash shields and boot seal shields.
8. On power steering units, disconnect hoses from steering gear.
9. Disconnect tie rod ends from steering knuckles.
10. Remove gear to front suspension crossmember attaching bolts, then remove gear from left side of vehicle.
11. Reverse procedure to install. On all models except Omni, Horizon, Charger and Turismo, reinstall steering column as follows:
    a. Align and insert lower stub shaft into coupling, raise column into position and loosely install bracket nuts. Pull column assembly rearward and torque nuts to 105 inch lbs.
    b. With needle nose pliers, pull coupling spring upward until it touches the universal flange.
    c. Snap gearshift rods into grommets.
    d. Readjust gearshift linkage as necessary.
    e. Install steering wheel and torque nut to 60 ft. lbs. except on 1982–84 models. On 1982–84 models, torque nut to 45 ft. lbs.
    f. Install horn switch and horn switch wire.
    g. Connect all wiring connectors at steering column jacket and install steering wheel pad.
    h. Connect battery ground cable and test operation of lights and horn.
    i. On column shift vehicles, connect gearshift indicator pointer to its approximate original location. Slowly move gear shift lever from 1 (low) to park, pausing briefly at each position. The indicator pointer must align with each selector position. If necessary, loosen and readjust pointer correctly.
    j. Install instrument panel steering column cover.

POWER STEERING PUMP, REPLACE

4-97 Engine

1. Loosen pressure hose connector at pump.
2. Remove drive belt adjustment nut from top rubber isolator stud, then loosen 3 lock nuts on rear studs.
3. Place a suitable container on top of radiator yoke to catch any spilled fluid.
4. Remove drive belt and 3 lock nuts, then lift pump and bracket assembly from vehicle.
5. Remove pump reservoir cap and drain fluid, then disconnect hoses from pump. Plug pump ports and hose ends to prevent contamination.
6. Reverse procedure to install.

4-105 & 135 Engines

1. Remove power steering pump drive belt adjusting bolt and nut, then remove nut attaching pump end hose bracket, if equipped.
2. Raise and support vehicle, then remove nut attaching pump pressure hose locating bracket to crossmember.
3. Disconnect pressure hose from steering gear and allow fluid to drain into a suitable container.
4. Remove drive belt splash shield, then disconnect both pressure and return hoses at power steering pump. Cap hoses and fitting to prevent entry of dirt.
5. Remove lower stud nut and pivot bolt from power steering pump, then lower vehicle.
6. Remove drive belt pulley from pump, then move pump rearward to clear mounting bracket and remove adjusting bracket.
7. Rotate pump so that pulley faces rear of vehicle, then lift pump assembly from vehicle.
8. Reverse procedure to install.

4-156 Engine

1. Disconnect pressure and return lines from pump. Cap all lines and fittings.
2. Remove belt adjustment and pivot bolts, then remove drive belt from pulley.
3. Remove power steering pump and mounting bracket as an assembly from vehicle.
4. Reverse procedure to install.

FORD & MERCURY
Full Size Models

> **NOTE:** This chapter includes service procedures for the 1977–82 LTD, Marquis & 1983–84 LTD Crown Victoria & Grand Marquis.
>   For service procedures on the 1983–84 LTD & Marquis models, refer to the "Ford & Mercury—Compact Intermediate Models Chapter."
>   Refer to the front of this manual for vehicle manufacturer's special service tool suppliers.

INDEX OF SERVICE OPERATIONS

FORD & MERCURY—Full Size Models

ENGINE & SERIAL NUMBER LOCATION

Engine code is fifth digit of serial number on 1977—80 models, or eighth digit of serial number on 1981—84 models. The serial number is stamped on a metal tag located on top left side dash and visible through windshield.

GRILLE IDENTIFICATION

1977—78 Ford "LTD" & Custom

1977—78 Ford "LTD" Landau

1977—78 Mercury

1979—82 Mercury Marquis

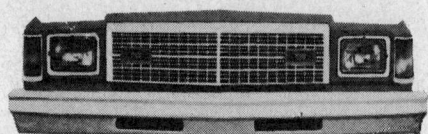

1979—82 LTD

1979—82 Ford LTD Landau & Country Squire

1983—84 Ford LTD Crown Victoria & Country Squire

GENERAL ENGINE SPECIFICATIONS

Year	Engine CID①/Liter	V.I.N. Code②	Carburetor	Bore and Stroke	Com-pression Ratio	Net H.P. @ R.P.M.③	Maximum Torque Ft. Lbs. @ R.P.M.	Normal Oil Pressure Pounds
FORD								
1977	V8-302, 5.0L	F	2150, 2 Bbl.⑤	4.00 × 3.00	8.4	—	—	40–65
	V8-351M, 5.8L④⑥	Q	2150, 2 Bbl.⑤	4.00 × 3.50	8.0	161 @ 3600	285 @ 1800	50–75
	V8-351W, 5.8L⑥⑦	H	2150, 2 Bbl.⑤	4.00 × 3.50	8.3	149 @ 3200	291 @ 1600	40–65
	V8-400, 6.6L⑥	S	2150, 2 Bbl.⑤	4.00 × 4.00	8.0	173 @ 3800	326 @ 1600	50–75
	V8-400, 6.6L⑧	S	2150, 2 Bbl.⑤	4.00 × 4.00	8.0	168 @ 3800	323 @ 1600	50–75
	V8-460, 7.5L	A	4350, 4 Bbl.⑤	4.36 × 3.85	8.0	197 @ 4000	353 @ 2000	35–65
1978	V8-302, 5.0L	F	2150, 2 Bbl.⑤	4.00 × 3.00	8.4	134 @ 3400	248 @ 1600	40–65
	V8-351M, 5.8L④	Q	2150, 2 Bbl.⑤	4.00 × 3.50	8.3	145 @ 3400	273 @ 1800	50–75
	V8-351W, 5.8L⑦	H	2150, 2 Bbl.⑤	4.00 × 3.50	8.0	144 @ 3200	277 @ 1600	40–65
	V8-400, 6.6L	S	2150, 2 Bbl.⑤	4.00 × 4.00	8.0	160 @ 3800	314 @ 1800	50–75
	V8-460, 7.5L⑨	A	4350, 4 Bbl.⑤	4.36 × 3.85	8.0	—	—	40–65
	V8-460, 7.5L⑩	A	4350, 4 Bbl.⑤	4.36 × 3.85	8.0	202 @ 4000	348 @ 2000	40–65
1979	V8-302, 5.0L⑥	F	2700VV, 2 Bbl.⑤	4.00 × 3.00	8.4	129 @ 3600	223 @ 2600	40–65
	V8-302, 5.0L⑧	F	2700VV, 2 Bbl.⑤	4.00 × 3.00	8.4	130 @ 3600	226 @ 2200	40–65
	V8-351W, 5.8L⑥⑦	H	7200VV, 2 Bbl.⑤	4.00 × 3.50	8.3	142 @ 3200	286 @ 1400	40–65
	V8-351W, 5.8L⑦⑧	H	2150, 2 Bbl.⑤	4.00 × 3.50	8.3	138 @ 3200	260 @ 2200	40–65
1980	V8-302, 5.0L	F	2700VV, 2 Bbl.⑤	4.00 × 3.00	8.4	130 @ 3600	230 @ 1600	40–60
	V8-351W, 5.8L⑦	G	7200VV, 2 Bbl.⑤	4.00 × 3.50	8.3	140 @ 3400	265 @ 2000	40–60
	V8-351W, 5.8L H.O.⑦⑪	G	7200VV, 2 Bbl.⑤	4.00 × 3.50	8.3	—	—	40–60

Continued

GENERAL ENGINE SPECIFICATIONS—Continued

Year	Engine CID①/Liter	V.I.N. Code②	Carburetor	Bore and Stroke	Com-pression Ratio	Net H.P. @ R.P.M.③	Maximum Torque Ft. Lbs. @ R.P.M.	Normal Oil Pressure Pounds
FORD—Continued								
1981	V8-255, 4.2L	D	7200VV, 2 Bbl.⑤	3.68 × 3.00	8.2	120 @ 3400	205 @ 2600	40–60
	V8-302, 5.0L⑧	F	7200VV, 2 Bbl.⑤	4.00 × 3.00	8.4	130 @ 3400	230 @ 2200	40–60
	V8-302, 5.0L⑥	F	7200VV, 2 Bbl.⑤	4.00 × 3.00	8.4	130 @ 3400	235 @ 1800	40–60
	V8-351W, 5.8L⑦	G	7200VV, 2 Bbl.⑤	4.00 × 3.50	8.3	145 @ 3200	270 @ 1800	40–60
	V8-351W, 5.8L H.O.⑦⑪	G	7200VV, 2 Bbl.⑤	4.00 × 3.50	8.3	165 @ 3600	285 @ 2200	40–60
1982	V8-255, 4.2L	D	7200VV, 2 Bbl.⑤	3.68 × 3.00	8.2	122 @ 3400	209 @ 2400	40–60
	V8-302, 5.0L	F	7200VV, 2 Bbl.⑤	4.00 × 3.00	8.4	132 @ 3400	236 @ 1800	40–60
1983–84	V8-302, 5.0L	F	E.F.I.⑫	4.00 × 3.00	—	—	—	40–60
MERCURY								
1977	V8-400, 6.6L⑥	S	2150, 2 Bbl.⑤	4.00 × 4.00	8.0	173 @ 3800	326 @ 1600	50–75
	V8-400, 6.6L⑧	S	2150, 2 Bbl.⑤	4.00 × 4.00	8.0	168 @ 3800	323 @ 1600	50–75
	V8-460, 7.5L	A	4350, 4 Bbl.⑤	4.36 × 3.85	8.0	197 @ 4000	353 @ 2000	35–65
1978	V8-351M, 5.8L④	Q	2150, 2 Bbl.⑤	4.00 × 3.50	8.0	145 @ 3400	273 @ 1800	50–75
	V8-400, 6.6L	S	2150, 2 Bbl.⑤	4.00 × 4.00	8.0	160 @ 3800	314 @ 1800	45–75
	V8-460, 7.5L⑨	A	4350, 4 Bbl.⑤	4.36 × 3.85	8.0	—	—	35–65
	V8-460, 7.5L⑩	A	4350, 4 Bbl.⑤	4.36 × 3.85	8.0	202 @ 4000	348 @ 2000	35–65
1979	V8-302, 5.0L⑥	F	2700VV, 2 Bbl.⑤	4.00 × 3.00	8.4	129 @ 3600	223 @ 2600	40–65
	V8-302, 5.0L⑧	F	2700VV, 2 Bbl.⑤	4.00 × 3.00	8.4	130 @ 3600	226 @ 2200	40–65
	V8-351W, 5.8L⑦	H	7200VV, 2 Bbl.⑤	4.00 × 3.50	8.3	138 @ 3200	260 @ 2200	40–65
1980	V8-302, 5.0L	F	2700VV, 2 Bbl.⑤	4.00 × 3.00	8.4	130 @ 3600	230 @ 1600	40–60
	V8-351W, 5.8L⑦	G	7200VV, 2 Bbl.⑤	4.00 × 3.50	8.3	140 @ 3400	265 @ 2000	40–60
	V8-351W, 5.8L H.O.⑦⑪	G	7200VV, 2 Bbl.⑤	4.00 × 3.50	8.3	—	—	40–60
1981	V8-255, 4.2L	D	7200VV, 2 Bbl.⑤	3.68 × 3.00	8.2	120 @ 3400	205 @ 2600	40–60
	V8-302, 5.0L⑧	F	7200VV, 2 Bbl.⑤	4.00 × 3.00	8.4	130 @ 3400	230 @ 2200	40–60
	V8-302, 5.0L⑥	F	7200VV, 2 Bbl.⑤	4.00 × 3.00	8.4	130 @ 3400	235 @ 1800	40–60
	V8-351W, 5.8L⑦	G	7200VV, 2 Bbl.⑤	4.00 × 3.50	8.3	145 @ 3200	270 @ 1800	40–60
	V8-351W, 5.8L H.O.⑦⑪	G	7200VV, 2 Bbl.⑤	4.00 × 3.50	8.3	165 @ 3600	285 @ 2200	40–60
1982	V8-255, 4.2L	D	7200VV, 2 Bbl.⑤	3.68 × 3.00	8.2	122 @ 3400	209 @ 2400	40–60
	V8-302, 5.0L	F	7200VV, 2 Bbl.⑤	4.00 × 3.00	8.4	132 @ 3400	236 @ 1800	40–60
1983–84	V8-302, 5.0L	F	E.F.I.⑫	4.00 × 3.00	—	—	—	40–60

①—C.I.D.—cubic inch displacement.
②—On 1977–80 models the fifth digit of V.I.N. denotes engine code. On 1980–83 models, the eighth digit of V.I.N. denotes engine code.
③—Ratings are net—as installed in vehicle.
④—Modified engine.
⑤—Motorcraft.
⑥—Exc. Calif.
⑦—Windsor engine.
⑧—Calif. only.
⑨—Police Interceptor.
⑩—Exc. Police Interceptor.
⑪—High Output engine.
⑫—E.F.I.—electronic fuel injection.

TUNE UP SPECIFICATIONS

The following specifications are published from the latest information available. This data should be used only in the absence of a decal affixed in the engine compartment.

★ When using a timing light, disconnect vacuum hose or tube at distributor and plug opening in tube or hose so idle speed will not be affected.

● When checking compression, lowest cylinder must be within 75% of the highest.

▲ Before removing wires from distributor cap, determine location of the No. 1 wire in cap, as distributor position may have been altered from that shown at the end of this chart.

☞ Spark plug types shown in this chart are recommendations of the original vehicle manufacturer and not MOTOR.

Check local sources for other spark plug manufacturers listings.

Year & Engine/V.I.N.	Spark Plug Type ☞	Gap	Ignition Timing BTDC① ★ Firing Order Fig. ▲	Man. Trans.	Auto. Trans.	Mark Fig.	Curb Idle Speed② Man. Trans.	Auto. Trans.	Fast Idle Speed Man. Trans.	Auto. Trans.	Fuel Pump Pressure
1977											
V8-302/F	ARF-52	.050	A	—	8°	C	—	650D	—	2000⑤	6-8
V8-351W/H⑥	ARF-52	.050	B	—	4°	C	—	625D	—	2100⑤	6-8
V8-351M/Q③⑦⑧	ARF-52	.050	B	—	10°	C	—	650D	—	1350④	6-8
V8-351M/Q③⑦⑨	ARF-52	.050	B	—	9°	C	—	650D	—	1350④	6-8
V8-351M/Q③⑦⑩	ASF-52	.050	B	—	8°	C	—	500/600D	—	1350④	6-8
V8-400/S Exc. Calif.⑦⑪	ARF-52	.050	B	—	8°	C	—	⑫	—	1350④	6-8
V8-400/S Exc. Calif.⑦⑬	ARF-52	.050	B	—	12°	C	—	600D	—	1350④	6-8
V8-400/S Exc. Calif.⑦⑭	ARF-52	.050	B	—	10°	C	—	600D	—	1350④	6-8
V8-400/S Exc. Calif.⑦⑮	ARF-52	.050	B	—	6°	C	—	600D	—	1350④	6-8
V8-400/S Calif.	ARF-52-6	.060	B	—	6°	C	—	500/600D	—	1350④	6-8
V8-460/A Exc. High Alt.⑦⑯	ARF-52	.050	A	—	16°	C	—	525/650D	—	1350④	5.7-6.7
V8-460/A Exc. High Alt.⑦⑰	ARF-52	.050	A	—	10°	C	—	⑱	—	1350④	5.7-6.7
V8-460/A High Alt.	ARF-52	.050	A	—	18°	C	—	500/600D	—	1350④	5.7-6.7
1978											
V8-302/F	ARF-52	.050	A	—	14°	C	—	500/600D	—	2100⑤	6-8
V8-351W/H⑥	ARF-52	.050	B	—	14°	C	—	600/675D⑲	—	2100⑤	6-8
V8-351M/Q③⑦⑳	ASF-52	.050	B	—	9°	C	—	600/675D⑲	—	1350④	6-8
V8-351M/Q③⑦㉑	ASF-52	.050	B	—	12°	C	—	600/675D⑲	—	1350④	6-8
V8-400/S Exc. Calif. & High Alt.	ASF-52	.050	B	—	13°	C	—	575/650D⑲	—	1350④	6-8
V8-400/S Calif.	ASF-52	.050	B	—	16°	C	—	600/650D⑲	—	1350④	6-8
V8-400/S High Alt.	ASF-52	.050	B	—	8°	C	—	650D	—	2100⑤	6-8
V8-460/A⑦㉒	ARF-52	.050	A	—	16°	C	—	580/650D⑲	—	1350④	5.7-7.7
V8-460/A⑦㉓	ARF-52	.050	A	—	10°	C	—	580/650D⑲	—	1350④	5.7-7.7
1979											
V8-302/F Exc. Calif.⑦㉔	㉕	.050	A	—	8°	C	—	600/675D⑲	—	2100⑤	6-8
V8-302/F Exc. Calif.⑦㉖	㉕	.050	A	—	6°	C	—	550/625D⑲	—	1750⑤	6-8
V8-302/F Calif.⑦㉗	㉘	.060	A	—	12°	C	—	600/675D⑲	—	1800⑤	6-8
V8-302/F Calif.⑦㉙	㉘	.060	A	—	6°	C	—	550/625D⑲	—	1800⑤	6-8
V8-351W/H Exc. Calif.⑥㉚㉛	㉕	.050	B	—	15°	C	—	600/650D⑲	—	2100⑤	6-8
V8-351W/H Exc. Calif.⑥㉚㉜	㉕	.050	B	—	10°	C	—	600/650D⑲	—	2200⑤	6-8
V8-351W/H Exc. Calif.⑥㉝	㉕	.050	㉞	—	㉟	C	—	550/640D⑲	—	2000⑤	6-8
V8-351W/H Calif.⑥㉝	㉕	.050	㉞	—	㉟	C	—	620D	—	2100⑤	6-8
1980											
V8-302/F Sedan Exc. Calif.⑦㉚㊳㊴	ASF-52	.050	A	—	6°	C	—	500D	—	1850④	6-8
V8-302/F Sedan Exc. Calif.⑦㉚㊳㊵	ASF-52	.050	A	—	8°	C	—	500D	—	1850④	6-8
V8-302/F Sta. Wag. Exc. Calif.㉚㊳	ASF-52	.050	A	—	6°	C	—	500D	—	④⑦㊶	6-8
V8-302/F Calif. & High Alt.㉝	ASF-52	.050	㊱	—	㉟	C	—	500/650D	—	2000㊲	6-8
V8-351W/G Exc. High Output⑥㉝	ASF-52	.050	㉞	—	㉟	C	—	550/640D	—	1650㊲	6-8
V8-351W/G High Output⑥㉝	ASF-42	.044	㉞	—	㉟	C	—	550/700D	—	1500㊲	6-8

Continued

TUNE UP SPECIFICATIONS—Continued

The following specifications are published from the latest information available. This data should be used only in the absence of a decal affixed in the engine compartment.

★ When using a timing light, disconnect vacuum hose or tube at distributor and plug opening in tube or hose so idle speed will not be affected.
● When checking compression, lowest cylinder must be within 75% of the highest.
▲ Before removing wires from distributor cap, determine location of the No. 1 wire in cap, as distributor position may have been altered from that shown at the end of this chart.

☞ Spark plug types shown in this chart are recommendations of the original vehicle manufacturer and not MOTOR.

Check local sources for other spark plug manufacturers listings.

| Year & Engine/V.I.N. | Spark Plug | | Ignition Timing BTDC① ★ | | | | Curb Idle Speed② | | Fast Idle Speed | | Fuel Pump Pressure |
	Type ☞	Gap	Firing Order Fig. ▲	Man. Trans.	Auto. Trans.	Mark Fig.	Man. Trans.	Auto. Trans.	Man. Trans.	Auto. Trans.	
1981											
V8-255/D Exc. Calif.	ASF-52	.050	A	—	7°	C	—	500/650D	—	1800④	6–8
V8-255/D Calif.	ASF-52	.050	A	—	5°	C	—	500/650D	—	1800④	6–8
V8-302/F	ASF-52	.050	A	—	8°	C	—	500D	—	1800④	6–8
V8-351W/G⑥㉝	ASF-52	.050	㉞	—	—	C	—	550/640D	—	1650㊲	6–8
1982											
V8-255/D	ASF-52	.050	A	—	7°	C	—	500/650D	—	1800④	6–8
V8-302/F Exc. High Alt.	ASF-52	.050	A	—	8°	C	—	500D	—	1800④	6–8
V8-302/F High Alt.	ASF-52	.050	A	—	14°	C	—	500D	—	1800④	6–8
1983–84											
V8-302/F Exc. Calif.	ASF-52	.050	A	—	—	C	—	500D	—	2200④	6–8
V8-302/F Calif.	ASF-52	.050	A	—	—	C	—	550D	—	2400④	6–8

①—B.T.D.C.—Before top dead center.
②—Idle speed on manual trans. vehicles is adjusted in Neutral & on auto. trans. equipped vehicles is adjusted in Drive unless otherwise specified. Where two idle speeds are listed, the higher speed is with the A/C or throttle solenoid energized. On models equipped with vacuum release brake, whenever adjusting ignition timing or idle speed, vacuum line to brake release mechanism must be disconnected & plugged to prevent parking brake from releasing when selector lever is moved to Drive.
③—Modified engine.
④—On kickdown step of cam.
⑤—On high step of fast idle cam.
⑥—Windsor engine.
⑦—Refer to engine calibration code on engine identification label located at rear of left valve cover. The calibration code is located on the label after the engine code number and preceded by the letter C and the revision code is located below the calibration code and is preceded by the letter R.
⑧—Calibration code 7-14B-R1.
⑨—Calibration codes 7-14B-R10 & 7-14C-R11.
⑩—Calibration code 7-34B-R0.
⑪—Calibration codes 7-17B-R1 & 7-37A-R0.
⑫—Calibration code 7-17B-R1, 600D RPM;

7-37A-R0, 500/650D RPM.
⑬—Calibration code 7-17B-R15.
⑭—Calibration code 7-17B-R16.
⑮—Calibration codes 7-17C-R1 & 7-17C-R11.
⑯—Calibration codes 7-19A-R1 & 7-19A-R17.
⑰—Calibration codes 7-19A-R2 & 7-19A-R3.
⑱—Calibration codes 7-19A-R2, 525/650D RPM; 7-19A-R3, 550/650D RPM.
⑲—With throttle solenoid energized. Higher idle speed is with A/C on, compressor clutch de-energized, if equipped.
⑳—Calibration code 8-14B-R0.
㉑—Calibration codes 8-14B-R13 & 8-14B-R22.
㉒—Calibration code 8-19A-R1.
㉓—Calibration codes 8-19C-R11 & 8-19C-R14.
㉔—Calibration codes 9-11B-R0, 9-11C-R1A, 9-11C-R1N & 9-11J-R0.
㉕—ASF-52 or ARF-52.
㉖—Calibration codes 9-11E-R1 & 9-11F-R1.

㉗—Calibration codes 9-11N-R0, 9-11R-R0, 9-11S-R0 & 9-11V.
㉘—ASF-52-6 or ARF-52-6.
㉙—Calibration code 9-11Q-R0.
㉚—Models less Electronic Engine Control (EEC) System.
㉛—Models less variable venturi carburetor.
㉜—Models with variable venturi carburetor.
㉝—Models with Electronic Engine Control (EEC) System.
㉞—Firing order, 1-3-7-2-6-5-4-8. Cylinder numbering (front to rear): Right bank 1-2-3-4, left bank 5-6-7-8. Refer to Fig. D for spark plug wire connections at distributor.
㉟—Engine cranking reference timing 10° BTDC. Ignition timing is not adjustable.
㊱—Firing order, 1-5-4-2-6-3-7-8. Cylinder numbering (front to rear): Right bank 1-2-3-4, left bank 5-6-7-8. Refer to Fig. D for spark plug wire connections at distrubutor.
㊲—On 2nd highest step of fast idle cam.
㊳—Except high altitude.
㊴—Calibration codes, 0-13A-R0, R11, R14 & 0-13F-R11.
㊵—Calibration codes, 0-13D-R0, R10, & R11.
㊶—Except calibration code 0-13A-R11, 1850 RPM; calibration code 0-13A-R11, 1700 RPM.

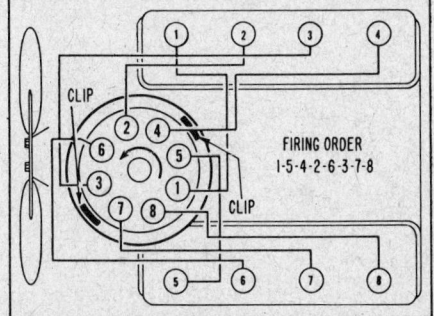

Fig. A

FIRING ORDER
1-5-4-2-6-3-7-8

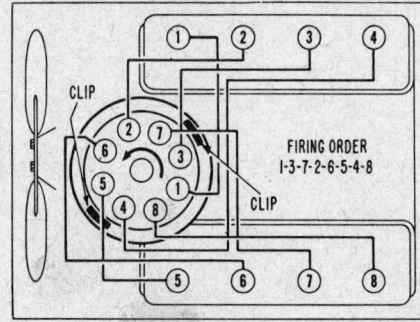

FIRING ORDER
1-3-7-2-6-5-4-8

Fig. B

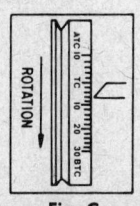

Fig. C

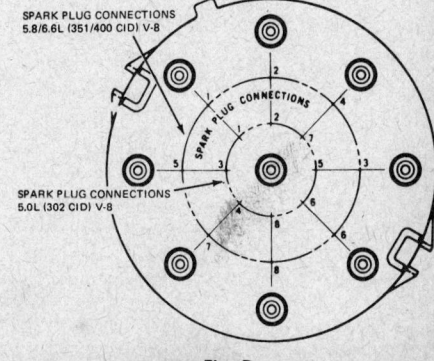

SPARK PLUG CONNECTIONS
5.8/6.6L (351/400 CID) V-8

SPARK PLUG CONNECTIONS
5.0L (302 CID) V-8

Fig. D

STARTING MOTOR APPLICATIONS

Year	Model/V.I.N.	Ident. No.	Year	Model/V.I.N.	Ident. No.
1977	V8-302/F	D8OF-AA		V8-351W/H①	D8OF-AA
	V8-351W/H①②	D6OF-AA		V8-400/S	D8AF-AA
	V8-351W/H①③	D8OF-AA		V8-460/A	D8AF-BA
	V8-351M/Q④⑤	D5AF-EA	1979	V8-302/F	D8OF-AA
	V8-351M/Q④⑥	D8AF-AA		V8-351W/H①	D8OF-AA
	V8-400/S⑤	D5AF-EA	1980	V8-255/D, 302/F⑨	D8OF-AA
	V8-400/S⑥	D8AF-AA		V8-351W/G①⑨	D8OF-AA
	V8-460/A⑦	D6AF-AA		V8-255/D, 302F⑩	E1AF-BA
	V8-460/A⑧	D8AF-BA		V8-351/W/G①⑩	E1AF-BA
1978	V8-302/F	D8OF-AA	1981–82	V8-255/D, 302/F	E1AF-BA
	V8-351M/Q④	D8AF-AA	1983–84	V8-302/F	E3AF-AA

①—Windsor engine.
②—Models built prior to February 1, 1977.
③—Models built from February 1, 1977.
④—Modified engine.
⑤—Models built prior to December 13, 1976.
⑥—Models built from December 13, 1976.
⑦—Models built prior to April 15, 1977.
⑧—Models built from April 15, 1977.
⑨—Models built prior to March 2, 1981.
⑩—Models built from March 2, 1981.

ALTERNATOR & REGULATOR SPECIFICATIONS

Year	Make or Model ①	Current Rating		Field Current @ 75°F.		Voltage Regulator	
		Amperes	Volts	Amperes	Volts	Part No. (10316)	Voltage @ 75°F.
1977	Orange②	40	15	2.9	12	D4AF-AA	13.5–15.3
	Green②	60	15	2.9	12	D4AF-AA	13.5–15.3
	All③	70	15	2.9	12	D4TF-AA	13.5–15.3
	All③	90	15	2.9	12	D4TF-AA	13.5–15.3
1978	Orange②	40	15	2.9	12	D4AF-AA	13.5–15.3
	Green②	60	15	2.9	12	D4AF-AA	13.5–15.3
	Green②④	60	15	4.0	12	D8BF-AA⑤	
	Black③	70	15	2.9	12	D4TF-AA	13.5–15.3
	Red③	90	15	2.9	12	D4TF-AA	13.5–15.3
	Red③④	90	15	4.0	12	D8BF-AA⑤	—
1979	Orange②④	40	15	4.0	12	D8BF-AA⑤	13.8–14.6
	Black②④	65	15	4.0	12	D8BF-AA⑤	13.8–14.6
	Green②④	60	15	4.0	12	D8BF-AA⑤	13.8–14.6
	Black③④	70	15	4.0	12	D8BF-AA⑤	13.8–14.6
	Red③④	90	15	4.0	12	D8BF-AA⑤	13.8–14.6
1980–81	Orange②④	40	15	4.0	12	D9BF-AB⑤	13.8–14.6
	Black②④	65	15	4.0	12	D9BF-AB⑤	13.8–14.6
	Green②④	60	15	4.0	12	D9BF-AB⑤	13.8–14.6
	Black③④	70	15	4.0	12	D9BF-AB⑤	13.8–14.6
	Red③④	100	15	4.0	12	D9BF-AB⑤	13.8–14.6
1982	Orange②④	40	15	4.0	12	E1AF-BA⑤	13.8–14.6
	Black②④	65	15	4.0	12	E1AF-BA⑤	13.8–14.6
	Green②④	60	15	4.0	12	E1AF-BA⑤	13.8–14.6
	Black③④	70	15	4.0	12	E1AF-BA⑤	13.8–14.6
	Red③④	100	15	4.0	12	E1AF-BA⑤	13.8–14.6
1983–84	Orange②④	40	15	4.25	12	E2AF-AA⑤	—
	Black②④	65	15	4.25	12	E2AF-AA⑤	—
	Green②④	60	15	4.25	12	E2AF-AA⑤	—
	Black③④	70	15	4.25	12	E2AF-AA⑤	—
	Red③④	100	15	4.25	12	E2AF-AA⑤	—

①—Stamp color code.
②—Rear terminal alternator.
③—Side terminal alternator.
④—Solid state alternator.
⑤—Electronic voltage regulator. These units are color coded black for systems w/warning indicator lamp & blue for systems w/ammeter.

REAR AXLE SPECIFICATIONS

Year	Carrier Type	Ring Gear & Pinion Backlash Inch	Nominal Pinion Locating Shim, Inch	Pinion Bearing Preload				Differential Bearing Preload	Pinion Nut Torque Ft.-Lbs.①
				New Bearings With Seal Inch-Lbs.	Used Bearings With Seal Inch-Lbs.	New Bearings Less Seal Inch-Lbs.	Used Bearings Less Seal Inch-Lbs.		
1977–78	Integral	.008–.012	.030	17–27	8–14	—	—	.008–.012⑤	140
	Removable	.008–.012	.015	17–27④	8–14	—	—	.008–.012③	②
1979	Integral	.008–.012	.030	17–27	8–14	—	—	.008–.012	140
	Removable	.008–.012	.015	17–27	8–14	—	—	.008–.012	170①
1980	Integral	.008–.015	.030	17–27	8–14	—	—	.008–.012	140
1981–84	Integral	.008–.015	.030	16–29	8–14	—	—	.016⑥	⑦

①—If torque cannot be obtained, install new spacer.
②—Collapsible spacer 170 ft. lbs.; solid spacer 200 ft. lbs.
③—Case spread with new bearings; with used bearings .005–.008".
④—Solid spacer 13–33 inch-lbs.
⑤—Case spread with new bearing; with used bearings .006–.010".
⑥—Differential case spread.
⑦—With 7.5 inch ring gear, 170 ft.-lbs.; with 8.5 inch ring gear, 140 ft.-lbs.

DISTRIBUTOR SPECIFICATIONS

★Note: If unit is checked on vehicle, double the RPM and degrees to get crankshaft figures.

Distributor Part No.①	Centrifugal Advance Degrees @ RPM of Distributor				Vacuum Advance		Distributor Retard
	Advance Starts	Intermediate Advance		Full Advance	Inches of Vacuum to Start Plunger	Max. Adv. Dist. Deg. @ Vacuum	Max. Retard Dist. Deg. @ Vacuum
1977							
D6AE-AA	0–2 @ 500	4–6 @ 700	—	14 @ 2500	3	15¼ @ 11½	—
D6VE-CA	0–1 @ 450	7½–9½ @ 725	—	14 @ 2500	3½	13¼ @ 15	—
D7AE-BA	0–1 @ 425	2¾–4¾ @ 625	—	13½ @ 2250	3½	15¼ @ 12	—
D7AE-CA	0–1 @ 700	3½–6 @ 1600	—	10¾ @ 2500	3	15¼ @ 11	—
D7AE-DA	0–1 @ 450	3¾–5¾ @ 675	—	14 @ 2500	3.2	15¼ @ 14.5	—
D7DE-CA	0–1 @ 450	4¾–6¾ @ 700	—	15½ @ 2500	3	15¼ @ 11	—
D70E-CA	0–1 @ 450	2¾–4¾ @ 575	—	16 @ 2500	3½	15¼ @ 14.5	—
1978							
D8AE-CA	0 @ 1100	3.5–6 @ 1600	—	9.5 @ 2500	3	17.5 @ 14	—
D8AE-GA	0 @ 450	3.5–5.5 @ 700	—	8.25 @ 2500	5.5	15.25 @ 16.5	—
1979–80							
D9AE-AAA	0–2.75 @ 500	.9–2.9 @ 530	—	10.6–13.25 @ 2500	2.3	12.75–15.25 @ 25	—
D9AE-ABA	0–2 @ 580	4.25–6.25 @ 950	—	9.25–12.25 @ 2500	2.8	6.75–9.25 @ 25	2–4 @ 9.3
D9AE-DA	②	—	—	—	—	—	—
D9AE-TA	0–3 @ 490	2.9–4.9 @ 600	—	10–13 @ 2500	2.2	12.75–15.25 @ 25	—
D9AE-ZA	0–3 @ 500	4.9–6.9 @ 660	—	12.25–14.75 @ 2500	1.8	14.75–17.25 @ 25	—
D9SE-AA	0–2 @ 500	2–4 @ 600	—	3.6–6.1 @ 2500	2.8	14.75–17.25 @ 25	—
D94E-AA	②	—	—	—	—	—	—
1981							
D9AE-DA	—	—	—	—	—	—	—
E1AE-EA	—	—	—	—	—	—	—
E1AE-JA	—	—	—	—	—	—	—
E1AE-KA	—	—	—	—	—	—	—
E1SE-BA	—	—	—	—	—	—	—
1982							
E1SE-BA	—	9.5–12 @ 1250	—	—	—	—	—
E2AE-FA	—	9.5–12 @ 1250	—	—	—	—	—
E1AE-KA	—	7–9 @ 1250	—	—	—	—	—
1983							
E1AE-MA	—	—	—	—	—	—	—
E1AE-GA	—	—	—	—	—	—	—
E2VE-BA	—	—	—	—	—	—	—

①—Basic part No. 12127.
②—EEC system distributor.

VALVE SPECIFICATIONS

Year	Engine Model/V.I.N.	Valve Lash Int.	Valve Lash Exh.	Valve Angles Seat	Valve Angles Face	Valve Spring Installed Height	Valve Spring Pressure Lbs. @ In.	Stem Clearance Intake	Stem Clearance Exhaust	Stem Diameter Intake	Stem Diameter Exhaust
1977	V8-302/F	.096–.168[4]		45	44	[7]	[9]	.0010–.0027	.0015–.0032	.3416–.3423	.3411–.3418
	V8-351W/H[3]	.096–.168[4]		45	44	[8]	[10]	.0010–.0027	.0015–.0032	.3416–.3423	.3411–.3418
	V8-351M/Q[2]	.125–.175[4]		45	44	1 53/64	226 @ 1.39	.0010–.0027	.0015–.0032	.3416–.3423	.3411–.3418
	V8-400/S	.125–.175[4]		45	44	1 53/64	226 @ 1.39	.0010–.0027	.0015–.0032	.3416–.3423	.3411–.3418
	V8-460/A	.100–.150[4]		45	44	1 13/16	229 @ 1.33[11]	.0010–.0027	.0010–.0027	.3416–.3423	.3416–.3423
1978	V8-302/F	.071–.193[4]		45	44	[7]	[9]	.0010–.0027	.0015–.0037	.3416–.3423	.3411–.3418
	V8-351M/Q[2]	.100–.200[4]		45	44	1 13/16	226 @ 1.39	.0010–.0027	.0015–.0037	.3416–.3423	.3411–.3418
	V8-351W/H[3]	.071–.193[4]		45	44	[1]	[5]	.0010–.0027	.0015–.0037	.3416–.3423	.3411–.3418
	V8-400/S	.100–.200[4]		45	44	1 13/16	226 @ 1.39	.0010–.0027	.0015–.0037	.3416–.3423	.3411–.3418
	V8-460/A	.075–.175[4]		45	44	1 13/16	229 @ 1.33	.0010–.0027	.0010–.0027	.3416–.3423	.3416–.3423
1979	V8-302/F	.096–.165[4]		45	44	[7]	[5]	.0010–.0027	.0015–.0032	.3416–.3423	.3411–.3418
	V8-351W/H[3]	.123–.173[4]		45	44	[6]	[12]	.0010–.0027	.0015–.0032	.3416–.3423	.3411–.3418
1980	V8-302/F	.096–.163		45	44	[8]	[13]	.0010–.0027	.0015–.0032	.3416–.3423	.3411–.3418
	V8-351W/G[3]	.096–.163[4]		45	44	[8]	[13]	.0010–.0027	.0015–.0032	.3416–.3423	.3411–.3418
1980–81	V8-351W H.O./G[3][15]	.096–.146[4]		45	44	[8]	[16]	.0010–.0027	.0015–.0032	.3416–.3423	.3411–.3418
1981	V8-351W/G[3]	.096–.146[4]		45	44	[8]	[13]	.0010–.0027	.0015–.0032	.3416–.3423	.3411–.3418
	V8-255, 302[18]	.096–.146[4]		45	44	[14]	[13]	.0010–.0027	.0015–.0032	.3416–.3423	.3411–.3418
1982	V8-255/D, 302/F	.096–.146[4]		45	44	[14]	[17]	.0010–.0027	.0015–.0032	.3416–.3423	.3411–.3418
1983–84	V8-302/F	.096–.146[4]		45	44	[14]	[18]	.0010–.0027	.0015–.0032	.3416–.3423	.3411–.3418

[1]—Intake, 1 51/64; exhaust, 1 39/64.
[2]—Modified engine.
[3]—Windsor engine.
[4]—Clearance specified is obtainable at valve stem tip with lifter collapsed. See "Valves, Adjust" text.
[5]—Intake, 200 @ 1.34; exhaust, 200 @ 1.20.
[6]—Intake, 1 25/32; exhaust 1 11/16.
[7]—Intake, 1 11/16; exhaust, 1 39/64.
[8]—Intake, 1 25/32; exhaust, 1 39/64.
[9]—Intake, 200 @ 1.31; exhaust, 200 @ 1.20.
[10]—Intake, 200 exhaust, 200 @ 1.20.
[11]—Police, 315 @ 1.32.
[12]—Intake, 226 @ 1.39; exhaust, 200 @ 1.20.
[13]—Intake, 205 @ 1.36; exhaust, 200 @ 1.20.
[14]—Intake, 1 11/16; exhaust, 1 19/32.
[15]—High output engine.
[16]—Intake, 204 @ 1.33; exhaust, 205 @ 1.15.
[17]—Intake, 205 @ 1.36; exhaust, 205 @ 1.15.
[18]—Intake, 205 @ 1.36; exhaust, 205 @ 1.05.

PISTONS, PINS, RINGS, CRANKSHAFT & BEARINGS

Year	Engine Model/V.I.N.	Piston Clearance	Ring End Gap[1] Comp.	Ring End Gap[1] Oil	Wristpin Diameter	Rod Bearings Shaft Diameter	Rod Bearings Bearing Clearance	Main Bearings Shaft Diameter	Main Bearings Bearing Clearance	Thrust on Bear. No.	Shaft End Play
1977	V8-302/F	.0018–.0026	.010	.015	.9122	2.1228–2.1236	.0008–.0015	2.2482–2.2490	[2]	3	.004–.008
	V8-351W/H[3]	.0018–.0026	.010	.015	.9122	2.3103–2.3111	.0008–.0015	2.9994–3.0002	.0008–.0015	3	.004–.008
	V8-351M/Q[5]	.0014–.0022	.010	.015	.9752	2.3103–2.3111	.0008–.0015	2.9994–3.0002	.0008–.0015	3	.004–.008
	V8-400/S	.0014–.0022	.010	.015	.9752	2.3103–2.3111	.0008–.0015	2.9994–3.0002	.0008–.0015	3	.004–.008
	V8-460/A	.0014–.0022	.010	.015	1.0401	2.4992–2.5000	.0008–.0015	2.9994–3.0002	.0008–.0015	3	.004–.008
	V8-460/A[4]	.0022–.0032	.010	.015	1.0401	2.4992–2.5000	.0008–.0015	2.9994–3.0002	.0008–.0015	3	.004–.008
1978	V8-302/F	.0018–.0026	.010	.015	.9122	2.1228–2.1236	.0008–.0015	2.2482–2.2490	[2]	3	.004–.008
	V8-351W/H[3]	.0018–.0026	.010	.015	.9122	2.3103–2.3111	.0008–.0015	2.9994–3.0002	.0008–.0015	3	.004–.008
	V8-351M/Q[5]	.0014–.0022	.010	.015	.9752	2.3103–2.3111	.0008–.0015	2.9994–3.0002	.0008–.0015	3	.004–.008
	V8-400/S	.0014–.0022	.010	.015	.9752	2.3103–2.3111	.0008–.0015	2.9994–3.0002	.0008–.0015	3	.004–.008
	V8-460/A	.0014–.0022	.010	.015	1.0401	2.4992–2.5000	.0008–.0015	2.9994–3.0002	.0008–.0015	3	.004–.008
1979	V8-302/F	.0018–.0026	.010	.015	.9122	2.1228–2.1236	.0008–.0015	2.2482–2.2490	[2]	3	.004–.008
	V8-351W/H[3]	.0018–.0026	.010	.015	.9122	2.3103–2.3111	.0008–.0015	2.9994–3.0002	.0008–.0015	3	.004–.008
1980	V8-302/F	.0018–.0026	.010	.015	.9122	2.1228–2.1236	.0008–.0026	2.2486	[2]	3	.004–.008
	V8-351W/G[3]	.0018–.0026	.010	.015	.9122	2.1228–2.1236	.0008–.0026	2.9998	.0008–.0015	3	.004–.008

Continued

PISTONS, PINS, RINGS, CRANKSHAFT & BEARINGS—Continued

Year	Engine Model/V.I.N.	Piston Clearance	Ring End Gap①		Wristpin Diameter	Rod Bearings		Main Bearings			
			Comp.	Oil		Shaft Diameter	Bearing Clearance	Shaft Diameter	Bearing Clearance	Thrust on Bear. No.	Shaft End Play
1981	V8-255/D	.0014–.0024	.010	.015	.9122	2.1228–2.1236	.0008–.0024	2.2482–2.2490	②	3	.004–.008
	V8-302/F	.0018–.0026	.010	.015	.9122	2.1228–2.1236	.0008–.0024	2.2482–2.2490	②	3	.004–.008
	V8-351W/G③	.0018–.0026	.010	.015	.9122	2.3103–2.3111	.0007–.0025	2.9994–3.0002	.0008–.0015	3	.004–.008
1982	V8-255/D	.0014–.0024	.010	.015	.9122	2.1228–2.1236	.0008–.0015	2.2482–2.2490	.0005–.0015	3	.004–.008
1982–83	V8-302/F	.0018–.0026	.010	.015	.9122	2.1228–2.1236	.0008–.0015	2.2482–2.2490	.0005–.0015	3	.004–.008
1984	V8-302/F	.0018–.0026	.010	.015	.9122	2.1228–2.1236	.0008–.0015	2.2482–2.2490	⑥	3	.004–.008

①—Fit rings in tapered bores for clearance listed in tightest portion of ring travel.
②—No. 1, .0001–.0015; all others, .0004–.0015.
③—Windsor engine.
④—Police.
⑤—Modified engine.
⑥—No. 1, .0004–.0025; all others, .0004–.0015.

WHEEL ALIGNMENT SPECIFICATIONS

Year	Model	Caster Angle, Degrees		Camber Angle, Degrees				Toe-In. Inch	Toe-Out on Turns, Deg.	
		Limits	Desired	Limits		Desired			Outer Wheel	Inner Wheel
				Left	Right	Left	Right			
1977–78	All	+1¼ to +2¾	+2	−¼ to +1¼	−½ to +1	+½	+½	3/16	18.72	20
1979–82	All	+2¼ to +3¾	+3	−¼ to +1¼	−¼ to +1¼	+½	+½	3/16①	18.51	20
1983–84	All	+2¼ to +4	+3	−¼ to +1¼	−¼ to +1¼	+½	+½	1/16	18.51	20

①—1980–82, 1/16 inch.

ENGINE TIGHTENING SPECIFICATIONS★

★Torque specifications are for clean and lightly lubricated threads only. Dry or dirty threads produce increased friction which prevents accurate measurement of tightness.

Year	Engine Model/V.I.N.	Spark Plugs Ft. Lbs.	Cylinder Head Bolts Ft. Lbs.	Intake Manifold Ft. Lbs.	Exhaust Manifold Ft. Lbs.	Rocker Arm Stud Nut or Bolt Ft. Lbs.	Rocker Arm Cover Ft. Lbs.	Connecting Rod Cap Bolts Ft. Lbs.	Main Bearing Cap Bolts Ft. Lbs.	Flywheel to Crankshaft Ft. Lbs.	Vibration Damper or Pulley Ft. Lbs.
1977–80	V8-302/F	10–15	65–72	23–25	18–24	④	3–5	19–24	60–70	75–85	70–90
	V8-351W/H,G①	10–15	105–112	23–25	18–24	④	3–5	40–45	95–105	75–85	70–90
	V8-351M/Q②	10–15	95–105	③	18–24	18–25	3–5	40–45	95–105	75–85	70–90
	V8-400/S	10–15	95–105	③	18–24	18–25	3–5	40–45	95–105	75–85	70–90
	V8-460/A	10–15	130–140	22–32	28–33	18–25	5–6	40–45	95–105	75–85	70–90
1981	V8-351W/G①	10–15	105–112	23–25	18–24	18–25	3–5	40–45	95–105	75–85	70–90
1981–82	V8-255/D	10–15	65–72	18–20	18–24	18–25	3–5	19–24	60–70	75–85	70–90
1981–84	V8-302/F	10–15	65–72	23–25	18–24	18–25	3–5	19–24	60–70	75–85	70–90

①—Windsor engine.
②—Modified engine.
③—1977–78: 5/16" bolts 19–25 ft. lbs., 3/8" bolts 22–32 ft. lbs.
④—1977 & early 1978 rocker arm stud nut, 17–23 ft. lbs.; late 1978 & 1979–80 fulcrum bolt to cylinder head, 18–25 ft. lbs.

FORD & MERCURY—Full Size Models

COOLING SYSTEM & CAPACITY DATA

Year	Model or Engine/V.I.N.	Cooling Capacity, Qts. Less A/C	With A/C	Radiator Cap Relief Pressure, Lbs.	Thermo. Opening Temp.	Fuel Tank Gals.	Engine Oil Refill Qts. [1]	3 Speed Pints	4 Speed Pints	Auto. Trans. Qts. [2]	Rear Axle Oil Pints
FORD											
1977	V8-351/Q[10]	17.1	17.5	13–19	191	24.2[4]	4	—	—	[13]	[5]
	V8-400/S	17.1	17.2	13–19	191	24.2[4]	4	—	—	[13]	[5]
	V8-460/A[7]	18.5	18.5	13–19	191	24.2[4]	4	—	—	[13]	[5]
	V8-460/A[3]	19.0	19.0	13–19	191	24.2[4]	6	—	—	[13]	[5]
1978	V8-302/F	14.7	15.2	14–18	191	24.2[14]	4	—	—	10	[6]
	V8-351/H[9]	15.9	16.3	14–18	191	24.2[14]	4	—	—	11	[6]
	V8-351/Q[10]	17.0	17.0	14–18	191	24.2[14]	4	—	—	11	[6]
	V8-400/S	17.0	17.0	14–18	191	24.2[14]	4	—	—	11	[6]
	V8-460/A[3]	19.7	19.7	14–18	191	24.2[14]	6	—	—	12½	[6]
	V8-460/A[7]	18.6	18.6	14–18	191	24.2[14]	4	—	—	12½	[6]
1979	V8-302/F	13.3[8]	13.8[8]	16	196	19[16]	4	—	—	11.8	[17]
	V8-351W/H[9]	14.6[11]	15.2[11]	16	196	19[16]	4	—	—	11.0	[17]
1980	V8-302/F	13	13.3	16	196	19[16]	4[12]	—	—	[20]	[19]
	V8-351W/G[9]	13.9	14	16	196	19[16]	4[12]	—	—	[18]	[19]
1981	V8-255/D	13.8	13.8	16	191	20	4[12]	—	—	12	[19]
	V8-302/F	13	13.4	16	196	20	4[12]	—	—	12	[19]
	V8-351W/G[9]	13.8	13.8[15]	16	196	20	4[12]	—	—	12	[19]
1982	V8-255/D	14.7	15	16	191	20	4[12]	—	—	12	3¾
1982-84	V8-302/F	13	13.4	16	196	20	4[12]	—	—	12	3¾
MERCURY											
1977	V8-400/S	17.1	17.2	13–19	191	24.2[6]	4	—	—	[13]	[5]
	V8-460/A	18.5	18.5	13–19	191	24.2[4]	4	—	—	[13]	[5]
	V8-460/A	19.0	19.0	13–19	191	24.2[4]	6	—	—	[13]	[5]
1978	V8-351/H[9]	16.3	16.3	14–18	191	24.2[14]	4	—	—	[13]	[6]
	V8-400/S	17.0	17.5	14–18	191	24.2[14]	4	—	—	11	[6]
	V8-460/A[3]	19.7	19.7	14–18	191	24.2[14]	6	—	—	12½	[6]
	V8-460/A[7]	18.6	18.6	14–18	191	24.2[14]	4	—	—	12½	[6]
1979	V8-302/F	13.3[8]	13.8[8]	16	196	19[16]	4	—	—	11.8	[17]
	V8-351W/H[9]	14.6[11]	15.2[11]	16	196	19[16]	4	—	—	11.0	[17]
1980	V8-302/F	13	13.3	16	196	19[16]	4[12]	—	—	[20]	[19]
	V8-351W/G[9]	13.9	14	16	196	19[16]	4[12]	—	—	[18]	[19]
1981	V8-255/D	13.8	13.8	16	191	20	4[12]	—	—	12	[19]
	V8-302/F	13	13.4	16	196	20	4[12]	—	—	12	[19]
	V8-351W/G[9]	13.8	13.8[15]	16	196	20	4[12]	—	—	12	[19]
1982	V8-255/D	14.7	15	16	191	20	4[12]	—	—	12	3¾
1982-84	V8-302/F	13	13.4	16	196	20	4[12]	—	—	12	3¾

[1]—Add one quart with filter change.
[2]—Approximate. Make final check with dipstick.
[3]—Police models.
[4]—Station wagons 21 gals. Add 8 gals. with auxiliary tank.
[5]—WER axles 4 pts.; all others 5 pts.
[6]—Exc. models with 460 engine, locking or optional axles, 4 pts.; Models with 460 engine, locking or optional axles, 5 pts.
[7]—Exc. police models.
[8]—Police, 14.2 qts.
[9]—Windsor engine.
[10]—Modified engine.
[11]—Police, Trailer tow, 15.6 qts.
[12]—When changing engine oil on these models, both drain plugs must be removed to fully drain crankcase. One drain plug is located at the front of the oil pan, while the other drain plug is located at rear left side of the oil pan.
[13]—FMX 11 qts., C6 12¼ qts. C4, 10¼ qts.
[14]—Station wagons, 21 gals.
[15]—Trailer tow, 15 qts.
[16]—Station wagon, 20 gal.
[17]—Axle code WGZ, 4 pts.; Axle code WGY, 3.5 pts.
[18]—C4, 10 qts.; FMX, 11 qts.; F10D Overdrive auto. trans., 12 qts.
[19]—7½" ring gear, 3½ pts.; 8½" ring gear, 4 pts.
[20]—C4, 10 qts.; FMX, 11 qts.; C6, 11.8 qts.; Overdrive auto. trans., 12 qts.

Electrical Section

STARTER, REPLACE

SERVICE BULLETIN

STARTER PROBLEMS: If the starter is noisy or if it locks up, before condemning the starter, loosen the three mounting bolts enough to hand fit the starter properly into the pilot plate. Then tighten the mounting bolts, starting with the top bolt.

1. Disconnect battery ground cable.
2. Raise and support vehicle.
3. Disconnect starter cable from motor.
4. Remove mounting bolts and starter.

NOTE: On some models it may be necessary to turn the wheels right or left to remove starter.

5. Reverse procedure to install. Torque bolts to 15–20 ft. lbs.

IGNITION LOCK, REPLACE

1979–84

1. Disconnect battery ground cable.
2. Remove steering column trim shroud.
3. Disconnect key warning switch electrical connector.
4. Turn ignition lock to "On" position.
5. Using a 1/8" pin or punch located in the 4 o'clock hole and 1¼ inch from outer edge of lock cylinder housing, depress retaining pin while pulling the lock cylinder from housing.
6. Turn lock cylinder to "On" position and insert cylinder into housing. Ensure that the lock cylinder is fully seated and aligned into the interlocking washer before turning key to "Off" position. This will permit the retaining pin to extend into the lock cylinder housing hole.

7. Rotate key to check for proper mechanical operation.
8. Connect key warning switch electrical connector.
9. Connect battery ground cable.
10. Check for proper operation.

1977–78

1. Disconnect battery ground cable.
2. *Units with Fixed Steering Columns:* Remove steering wheel and trim pad. Insert a wire pin in the hole located inside the column halfway down the lock cylinder housing, Fig. 1, *Units with Tilt Steering Columns:* Insert wire pin in the hole located on the outside of the flange casting next to the emergency flasher button, Fig. 1.
3. Place the gear shift lever in "Park" position, and turn the lock cylinder with the ignition key to "Run" position.
4. Depress the wire pin while pulling up on the lock cylinder to remove. Remove the wire pin.
5. To install insert the lock cylinder into housing in the flange casting, and turn the key to "Off" position. Be certain that the cylinder is fully inserted before turning to the "Off" position. This action will extend the cylinder retaining pin into the cylinder housing.
6. Turn the key to check for correct operation in all positions.
7. Install the steering wheel and trim pad on fixed column units.
8. Connect the battery ground cable.

IGNITION SWITCH, REPLACE

1979–84

1. Disconnect battery ground cable.
2. Remove upper column shroud.
3. Disconnect ignition switch electrical connector.
4. With a 1/8 inch twist drill, drill out the switch retaining bolt heads. Then, remove the bolts with a "Easy Out" or

equivalent.
5. Disengage ignition switch from actuator and remove from vehicle, Fig. 2.
6. On 1979–81 models, adjust ignition switch to "Lock" position. On 1982–84 models, adjust ignition switch to "Run" position. Insert a .050 inch drill or equivalent through the switch housing and into the carrier to prevent movement.

NOTE: A replacement ignition switch includes an installed adjusting pin.

7. On 1979–81 models, rotate ignition key to "Lock" position. On 1982–84 models, place lock cylinder in the "Run" position, which is approximately 90° from the "Lock" position.
8. Install ignition switch on actuator pin.
9. Install switch break-off head mounting bolts and tighten until the bolt heads shear.
10. Remove adjusting pin or drill.
11. Connect ignition switch electrical connector.
12. Connect battery ground cable and check for proper operation.
13. Install column shroud.

1977–78

1. Disconnect battery cable.
2. Remove steering column shroud and lower steering column from brake support bracket.
3. Disconnect switch wiring and remove two switch retaining nuts. Disconnect switch from actuator and remove switch, Fig. 3.
4. Move shift lever to Park position. Place ignition key in Lock position and remove the key.

NOTE: New replacement switches are pinned in the Lock position by a plastic shipping pin inserted in a locking hole in the switch. For an existing switch, pull plunger out as far as it will go then back one detent to Lock position and insert a 3/32" drill in locking hole to retain switch in Lock position.

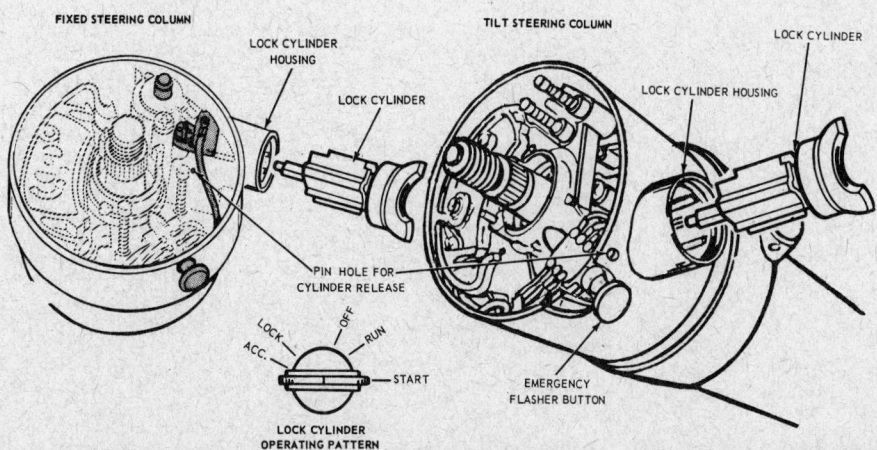

Fig. 1   Ignition Lock

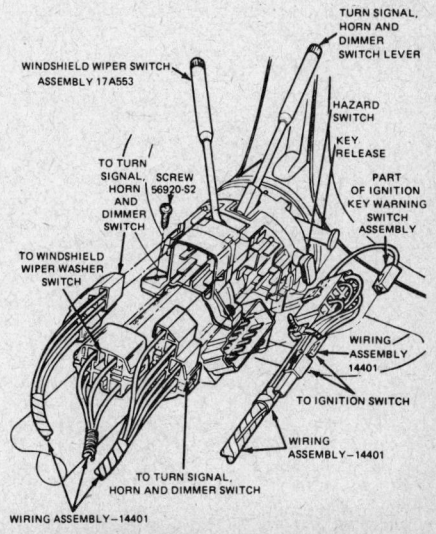

Fig. 2   Ignition switch. 1979–84

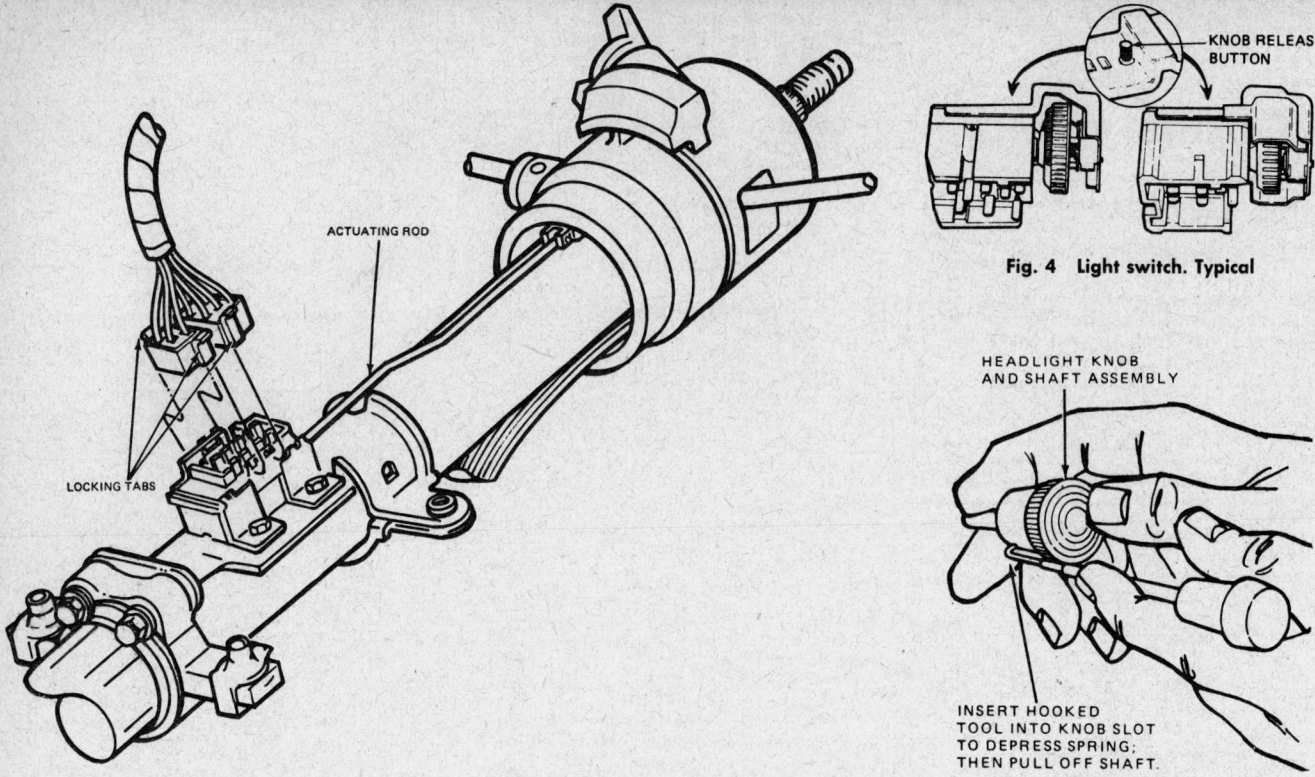

ACTUATING ROD

LOCKING TABS

Fig. 3   Ignition switch. 1977–78

KNOB RELEASE BUTTON

Fig. 4   Light switch. Typical

HEADLIGHT KNOB AND SHAFT ASSEMBLY

INSERT HOOKED TOOL INTO KNOB SLOT TO DEPRESS SPRING; THEN PULL OFF SHAFT.

Fig. 5   Light switch knob removal

5. With locking pin in place, install switch on steering column, determine mid position of actuator lash and tighten retaining bolts.
6. Remove locking pin.

LIGHT SWITCH, REPLACE

1979–84

1. Disconnect battery ground cable.
2. From instrument panel, depress light switch knob and shaft retainer button on side of switch and, while holding button in, pull knob and shaft assembly from switch, Fig. 4.
3. Unscrew trim bezel and remove lock nut.
4. From under instrument panel, pull switch from panel while tilting downward, disconnect electrical connector and remove switch.
5. Reverse procedure to install.

1977–78

1. Disconnect battery ground cable.
2. Remove wiper switch knob.
3. Remove shaft knob by inserting hooked wire, Fig. 5, into knob slot and depressing spring.
4. With headlight switch "On" on all models, depress release button on switch housing and remove knob and shaft, Fig. 4.
5. On all models remove bezel nut from light switch, then remove lower finish panel.
6. Remove three mounting plate screws.
7. Disconnect electrical connector. If equipped with concealed headlamps, disconnect vacuum hoses from switch and remove switch.

8. Reverse procedure to install.

STOP LIGHT SWITCH, REPLACE

1. Referring to Fig. 6, disconnect wires at connector.
2. Remove hairpin retainer and slide switch, push rod and nylon washers and bushing away from pedal, and remove switch.
3. Position the new switch, push rod, bushing and washers on brake pedal pin and secure with hairpin retainer.
4. Connect wires at connector and install wires in retaining clip.

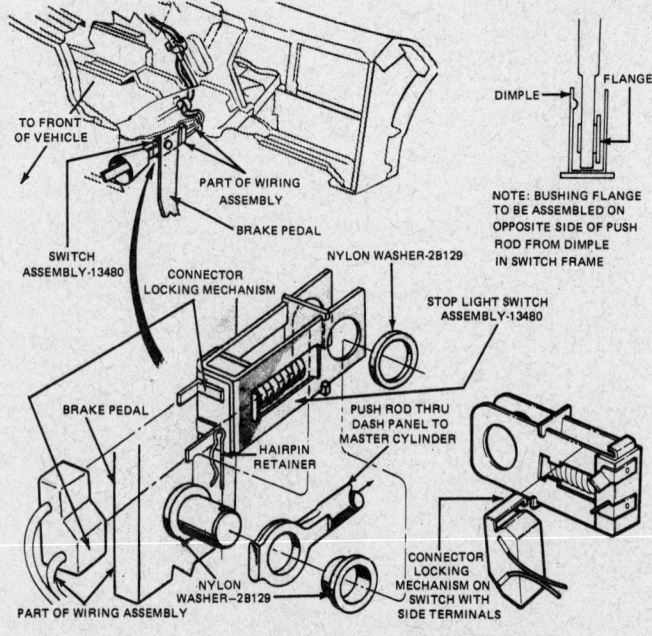

TO FRONT OF VEHICLE

PART OF WIRING ASSEMBLY

BRAKE PEDAL

SWITCH ASSEMBLY–13480

CONNECTOR LOCKING MECHANISM

NYLON WASHER–2B129

STOP LIGHT SWITCH ASSEMBLY–13480

BRAKE PEDAL

HAIRPIN RETAINER

PUSH ROD THRU DASH PANEL TO MASTER CYLINDER

NYLON WASHER–2B129

PART OF WIRING ASSEMBLY

CONNECTOR LOCKING MECHANISM ON SWITCH WITH SIDE TERMINALS

DIMPLE

FLANGE

NOTE: BUSHING FLANGE TO BE ASSEMBLED ON OPPOSITE SIDE OF PUSH ROD FROM DIMPLE IN SWITCH FRAME

Fig. 6   Mechanical stop light switch.

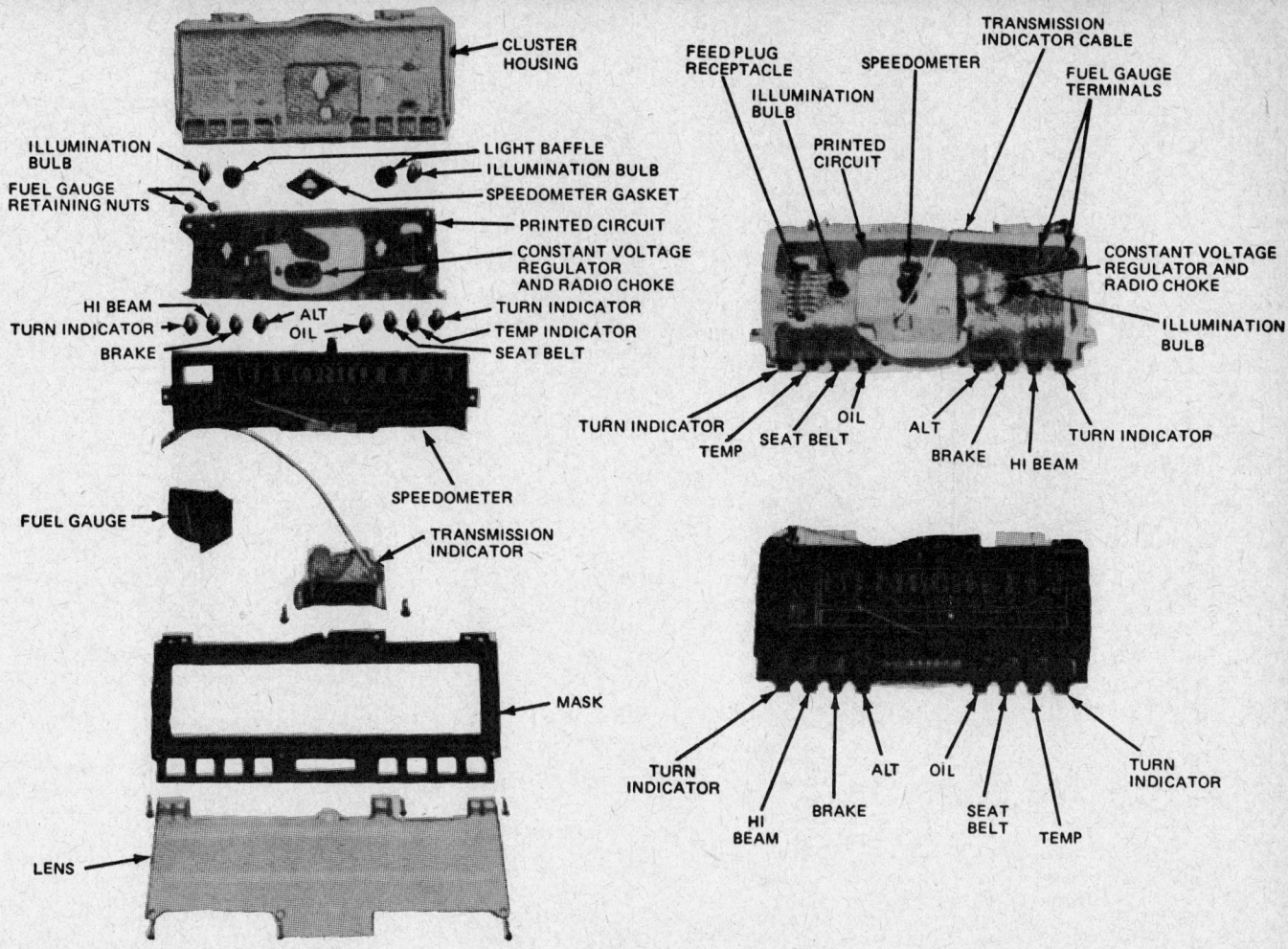

Fig. 7 Instrument cluster. 1977–78

TURN SIGNAL SWITCH, REPLACE

1979–84

1. Disconnect battery ground cable.
2. On models with tilt column, unsnap extension shroud, located below steering wheel, from retaining clip. On all models, remove five attaching screws, then remove steering column trim shroud.
3. Remove turn signal switch lever by grasping lever and using a pulling twisting motion of the hand, while pulling lever straight out of switch.
4. Peel foam sight shield from switch, then disconnect two turn signal switch wire connectors.
5. Remove two screws attaching turn signal switch to lock cylinder housing, then disengage switch from housing.
6. Reverse procedure to install.

1977–78

1. Remove retaining screw from underside of steering wheel spoke and lift off the pad horn switch/trim cover and medallion as an assembly.
2. Disconnect horn switch wires from terminals.
3. Remove steering wheel retaining nut and remove steering wheel with a suitable puller.
4. Remove turn signal switch lever by un-

screwing it from column.
5. Remove shroud from steering column.
6. Disconnect column wiring connector plug and remove screws that secure switch to column.
7. On tilt column models, remove wires and terminals from column wiring plug.

NOTE: *Record the color code and position of each wire before removing it from plug. A hole provided in the flange casting on fixed column models makes it unnecessary to separate wires from plug. The plug with wires installed can be guided through the hole.*

8. Remove plastic cover sleeve from wiring harness and remove the switch from top of column. On vehicles equipped with speed control, transfer the ground brush located in the turn signal cancelling cam to the new switch assembly.
9. Reverse procedure to install.

NEUTRAL SAFETY SWITCH

Exc. Models W/Automatic Overdrive Transmission

The neutral safety switch has been eliminated and is replaced by a series of steps incorporated into the steering column selector lever hub casting.

Models W/Automatic Overdrive Transmission

1. Disconnect battery ground cable.
2. Remove air cleaner assembly.
3. Place transmission selector lever in manual low position, then disconnect neutral safety switch electrical connector from switch. Lift connector straight off without any side-to-side motion.
4. Remove switch and "O" ring using a 24 inch extension, universal adapter and socket No. T74P-77247-A.

NOTE: Use of any tools other than those specified may result in damage to the vehicle.

5. Reverse procedure to install. Torque switch to 7–10 ft. lbs.

HORN SOUNDER, REPLACE

1979–84

Refer to "TURN SIGNAL SWITCH, REPLACE" for horn switch replacement.

1977–78

Rim-Blow Type
The rubber insert and copper strip assembly is not replaceable on vehicles with speed control. If a new insert assembly is required the entire steering wheel must be replaced.

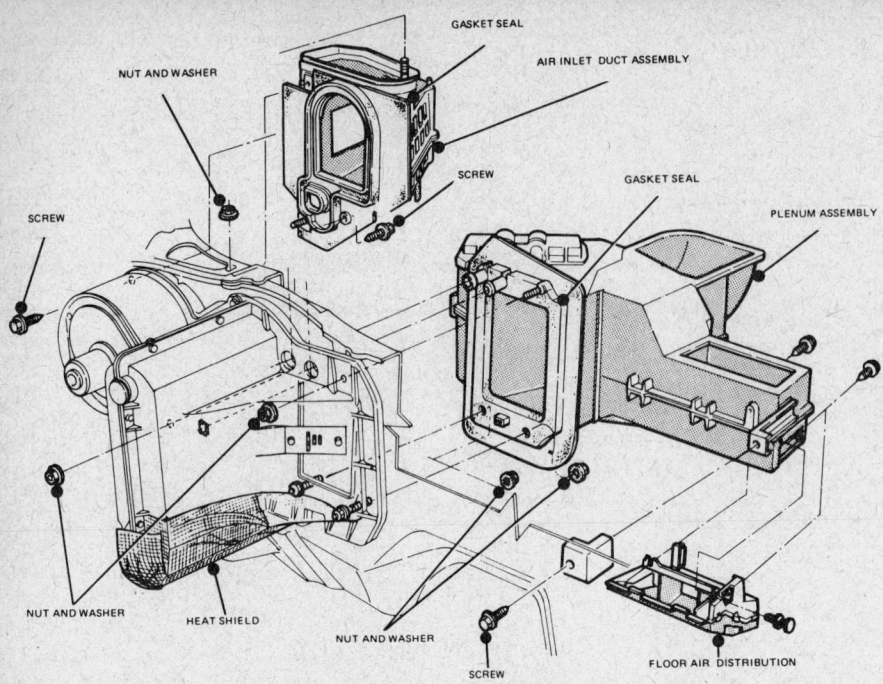

Fig. 8   Plenum assembly removal (Typical). 1979–84

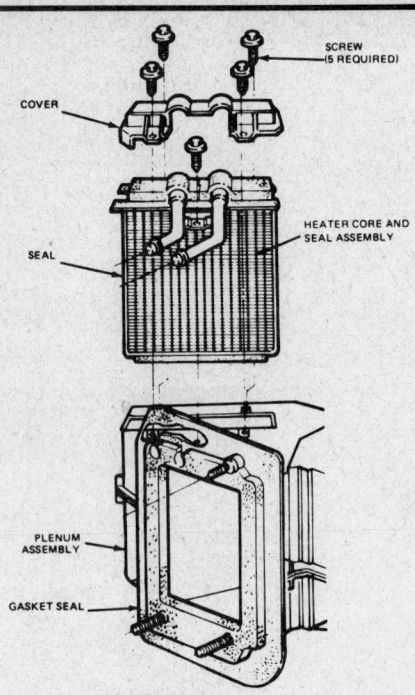

Fig. 9   Heater core removal (Typical). 1979–84

1. Remove the pad from the steering wheel (three screws).
2. Remove medallion from the pad.
3. After removing the steering wheel nut the wheel can be removed from the shaft with a wheel puller.
4. Reverse procedure to install.

Except Rim-Blow Type
1. Disconnect battery ground cable.
2. Remove steering column pad (2 screws).
3. Push down and turn horn ring and remove ring and spring.
4. Reverse procedure to install.

INSTRUMENT CLUSTER, REPLACE

1979–84

1. Disconnect battery ground cable.
2. Disconnect speedometer cable.
3. Remove instrument cluster trim cover attaching screws and the trim cover.
4. Remove the two lower steering column cover attaching screws and the cover.
5. Remove steering column shroud lower half.
6. Remove screws securing transmission indicator column bracket to steering column. Detach cable loop from pin on shift lever and remove bracket from column.
7. Remove four instrument cluster attaching screws.
8. Disconnect cluster feed plug and remove cluster assembly from vehicle.
9. Reverse procedure to install.

1977–78

1. Disconnect the battery ground cable.
2. Remove two steering column cover screws and remove the cover.
3. Remove two instrument cluster trim cover attaching screws and remove cover, Fig. 7.
4. Reach behind the cluster and disconnect the cluster feed plug from its receptacle.

5. Disconnect the speedometer cable.
6. Remove steering column cover shroud, then remove the screw attaching the transmission indicator cable to the steering column.
7. Remove the four cluster attaching screws and remove the cluster assembly.
8. Reverse procedure to install.

W/S WIPER MOTOR, REPLACE

1979–84

1. Disconnect battery ground cable.
2. On 1979 and 1982–84 models, disconnect right side washer nozzle hose and remove right side wiper arm and blade assembly from pivot shaft.
3. Remove wiper motor and linkage cover.
4. Disconnect linkage drive arm from the motor output arm crankpin by removing retaining clip.
5. Disconnect the wiring connectors from the motor.
6. Remove three bolts retaining the motor to the dash panel extension and the motor.
7. Reverse procedure to install.

1977–78

1. Disconnect battery ground cable.
2. Remove wiper arm and blade assemblies from pivot shafts.
3. Remove left cowl screen (four screws) for access.
4. Disconnect linkage drive arm from the motor output crankpin by removing retaining clip.
5. From engine side of dash, remove two wire connectors from motor.
6. Remove three bolts that retain motor to dash and remove motor. If output arm catches on dash during removal, hand-turn the arm clockwise so it will clear opening in the dash. Before installing motor, be sure output arm is in park position.
7. Reverse procedure to install.

W/S WIPER SWITCH, REPLACE

1979–84

1. Disconnect battery ground cable.
2. Remove the steering column cover screws and separate the two halves.
3. Remove wiper switch retaining screws, disconnect wiring connector and remove switch.
4. Reverse procedure to install.

1977–78

1. Disconnect battery ground cable.
2. Remove wiper and headlight switch knobs.
3. Remove headlight switch bezel, trim panel retaining screw and trim panel.
4. Remove wiper switch retaining screws, pull switch rearward, disconnect connector and remove switch.
5. Reverse procedure to install.

W/S WIPER TRANSMISSION, REPLACE

1979–84

1. Disconnect battery ground cable.
2. Remove wiper arm and blade assemblies from the pivot shafts. Remove rear hood seal.
3. Remove wiper motor and linkage cover for access to linkage.
4. Disconnect the linkage drive arm from the motor crank pin by removing the retaining clip.
5. Remove the six bolts retaining the left and right pivot shafts to the cowl, and remove the complete linkage assembly.
6. Reverse procedure to install.

1977–78

1. Disconnect battery and remove wiper arm and blade assemblies from pivot Shafts.

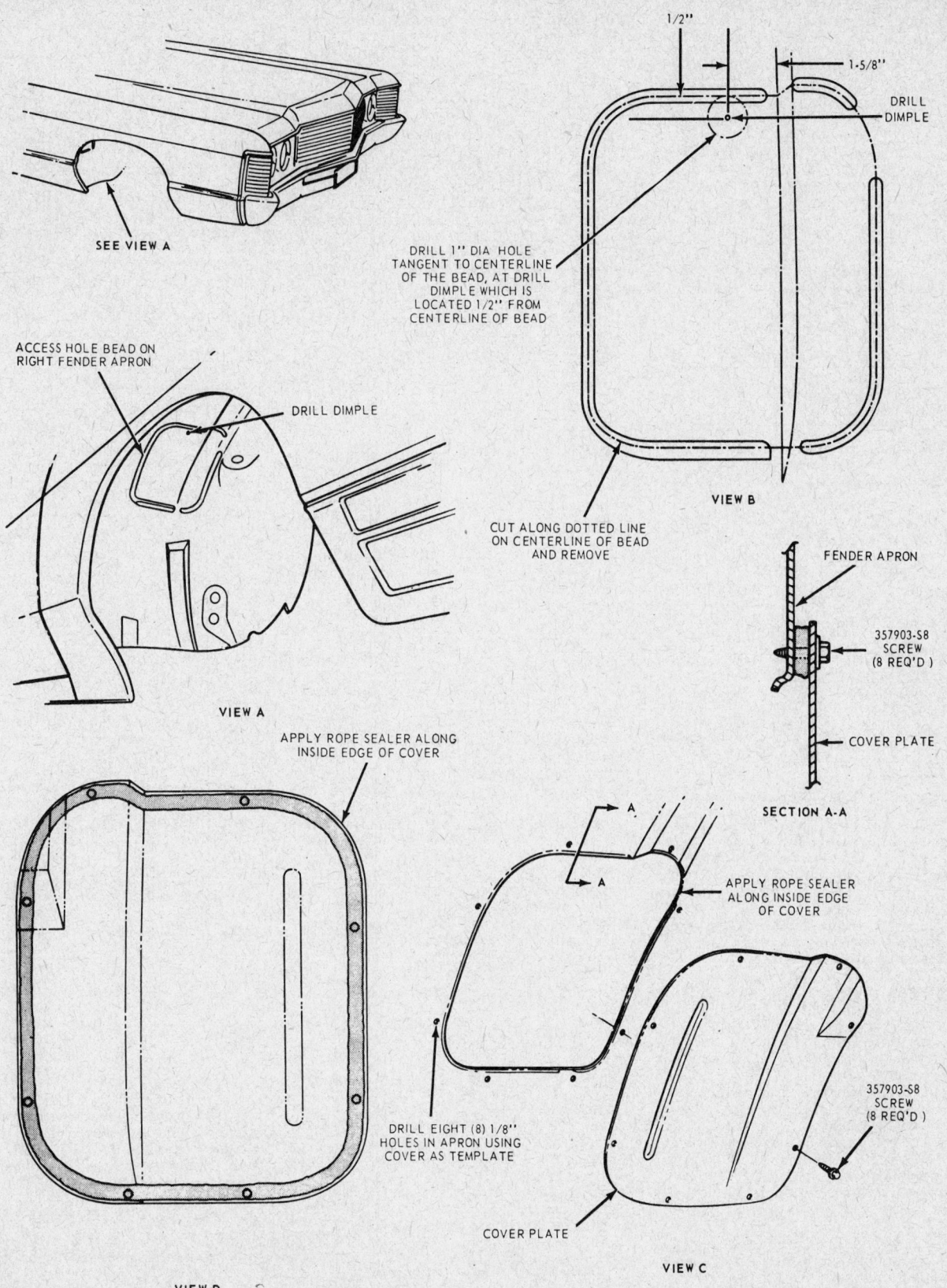

SEE VIEW A

1/2"

1-5/8"

DRILL
DIMPLE

DRILL 1" DIA HOLE
TANGENT TO CENTERLINE
OF THE BEAD, AT DRILL
DIMPLE WHICH IS
LOCATED 1/2" FROM
CENTERLINE OF BEAD

VIEW B

ACCESS HOLE BEAD ON
RIGHT FENDER APRON

DRILL DIMPLE

CUT ALONG DOTTED LINE
ON CENTERLINE OF BEAD
AND REMOVE

FENDER APRON

357903-S8
SCREW
(8 REQ'D)

COVER PLATE

SECTION A-A

VIEW A

APPLY ROPE SEALER ALONG
INSIDE EDGE OF COVER

A

A

APPLY ROPE SEALER
ALONG INSIDE EDGE
OF COVER

357903-S8
SCREW
(8 REQ'D)

DRILL EIGHT (8) 1/8"
HOLES IN APRON USING
COVER AS TEMPLATE

COVER PLATE

VIEW D

VIEW C

Fig. 10 Blower motor access. 1977—78

2. Remove cowl screens for access to linkage.
3. Disconnect the left linkage arm from the drive arm by removing the clip.
4. Remove the three bolts retaining the left pivot shaft assembly to the cowl.
5. Remove the left arm and pivot shaft assembly through the cowl opening.
6. Disconnect linkage drive arm from motor crankpin by removing the clip.
7. Remove three bolts that connect drive arm pivot shaft assembly to the cowl and remove the pivot shaft drive arm and right arm as an assembly.
8. Reverse procedure to install.

RADIO, REPLACE

NOTE: When installing radio, be sure to adjust antenna trimmer for peak performance.

1979–84

NOTE: For an all-electronic radio, perform stem 6 first.

1. Disconnect battery ground cable.
2. Remove radio knobs and screws attaching the bezel to instrument panel.
3. Remove the radio mounting plate attaching screws.
4. Pull radio to disengage it from the lower rear support bracket.
5. Disconnect radio wiring and remove radio.
6. Remove the radio to mounting plate retaining nuts and washers and remove the mounting plate.
7. Remove the rear upper support retaining nut and remove the support.
8. Reverse procedure to install. Perform step 6 first if equipped with all-electronic radio.

1977–78

1. Disconnect battery ground cable.
2. Remove radio knobs and instrument panel bezel.
3. Remove mounting plate retaining screws and pull radio disengaging it from rear bracket.
4. Disconnect antenna and electrical wires and remove radio.
5. Reverse procedure to install.

HEATER CORE, REPLACE

1979–84

1. Disconnect battery ground cable, then drain cooling system.
2. Disconnect heater hoses from heater core. Plug heater hoses and core fittings to prevent coolant spillage.
3. Remove bolt located below w/s wiper motor, attaching left end of plenum to dash panel.
4. Remove nut attaching upper left hand corner of evaporator or heater case to dash panel.
5. Disconnect vacuum control system supply hose from vacuum source, then push grommet and hose into pasenger compartment.
6. Remove glove box, then loosen right hand door sill plate and remove side cowl trim panel.
7. Remove bolt attaching right hand side of instrument panel to side cowl.

8. Remove instrument panel pad as follows:
   a. Remove two screws from each defroster nozzle opening in pad.
   b. From front lower edge of panel pad, remove five attaching screws.
   c. From each end of pad, remove one attaching screw.
   d. On 1979–81 Ford models, remove screw from lower end of pad through glove box door opening.
   e. Lift pad assembly from instrument panel.
9. On models less ATC, disconnect temperature control cable from plenum bracket and blend air door crank.
10. On models equipped with ATC, disconnect temperature control cable and vacuum harness connector from ATC sensor. Disconnect ATC sensor tube from sensor and evaporator case connector, then disconnect wire connector from EV relay.
11. Remove push clip attaching center duct bracket to plenum, then rotate bracket upward and to the right.
12. Disconnect vacuum harness at vacuum connector near floor air distribution duct.
13. Disconnect the white vacuum hose from the outside recirculating air door vacuum motor.
14. Remove two screws from rear side of floor air distribution duct to plenum, Fig. 8. To remove the right hand screw, it may be necessary to remove the two screws attaching the lower panel door vacuum motor to the mounting bracket.
15. Remove push fastener attaching floor air distribution duct to left end of plenum, then remove floor air distribution duct.
16. Remove two nuts located along lower flange of plenum.
17. Carefully move plenum rearward, so that heater core tubes and plenum case upper stud clear openings in dash panel, then remove plenum from vehicle by rotating upper portion of the plenum forward, down and out from under instrument panel. It may be necessary to carefully pull the lower edge of the instrument panel rearward while the plenum is being removed from behind the instrument panel.
18. Remove retaining screws from heater core cover, then the cover from the plenum assembly, Fig. 9.
19. Remove retaining screw from heater core inlet and outlet tube bracket.
20. Pull heater core and seal assembly from plenum assembly.
21. Reverse procedure to install.

1977–78 with Air Cond.

1. Drain cooling system.
2. Disconnect heater hoses from core tubes.
3. Remove heater core cover plate and gasket.
4. Pull heater core and mounting gasket up out of case.
5. Remove core mounting gasket. Remove heater core.
6. Reverse procedure to install.

1977–78 less Air Cond.

1. Drain cooling system and disconnect heater hoses from the core.
2. Remove the core cover and gasket and remove the heater core.
3. Reverse procedure to install.

BLOWER MOTOR, REPLACE

1979–84

1. Disconnect battery ground cable.
2. Disconnect blower motor ground wire and the engine ground wire and position wiring aside.
3. Disconnect blower motor lead connector from wiring harness hard shell connector.
4. Remove blower motor cooling tube from blower motor.
5. Remove blower motor retaining screws.
6. Rotate blower motor slightly to the right so the bottom edge of the mounting plate follows the contour of the wheelwell splash panel. Then, lift blower motor up and out of housing assembly.
7. Reverse procedure to install.

1977–78

NOTE: The blower motor is located in the right side of the case to the right of the hood hinge under the right front fender. It is necessary to cut an opening in the right front fender apron to gain access to the blower motor assembly.

1. Disconnect the blower motor lead wire (orange) at the rear of the right hood hinge.
2. Remove the ground wire (black) from the upper cowl.
3. Remove the right front tire and wheel assembly.
4. Locate and cut opening in fender apron, Fig. 10. Care must be taken to avoid damage to the heater case by drill push-through or over-travel.
5. Remove the four blower motor mounting screws and disconnect the cooler tube from the motor.
6. Carefully move the motor and wheel assembly forward out of the heater case through the access hole.
7. A replacement cover plate is available from Ford, part no. #18A475.
8. Reverse procedure to install.

SPEED CONTROLS

1979–84

Actuator Cable Adjustment
1. Remove cable retaining clip.
2. Deactivate the throttle positioner.
3. Set carburetor at hot idle.
4. Pull the actuator cable to remove slack.
5. While maintaining light tension on the actuator cable, insert the cable retaining clip.

Vacuum Dump Valve
The vacuum dump valve is mounted on a moveable mounting bracket. The valve should be adjusted so that it is closed when the brake pedal is not depressed and opens when the brake pedal is depressed.

1977–78

Adjust bead chain to obtain .06–.25″ actuator arm free travel when engine is at hot idle. The adjustment should be made to take as much slack as possible out of the chain without restricting the carburetor lever from returning to idle.

On vehicles with a solenoid anti-diesel valve, perform adjustment with ignition switch in the "On" position.

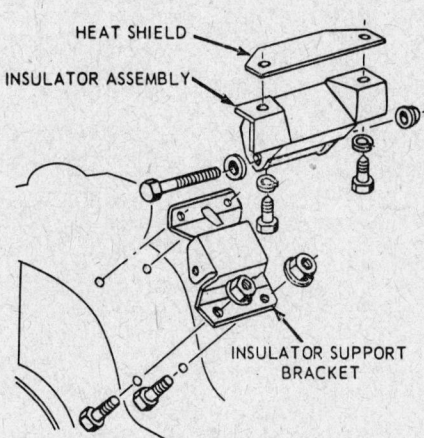

Fig. 1 Engine mount (typical). 1977–78 V8-302, 351W

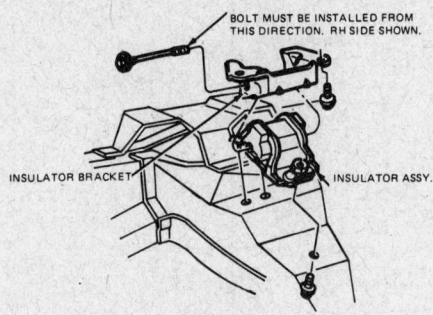

Fig. 2 Engine mount. 1979–84 V8-255, 302 & 351W

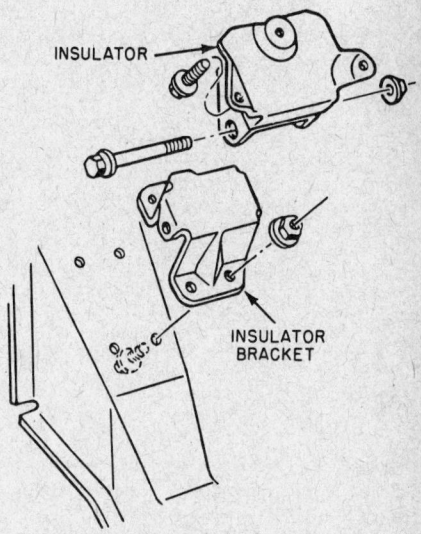

Fig. 3 Engine mount. 1977–78 V8-351 M, 400

ENGINE MOUNTS, REPLACE

CAUTION: Whenever self-locking mounting bolts and nuts are removed, they must be replaced with new self-locking bolts and nuts.

1977–84 V8-255, 302, 351W

1. On 1982–84 models, remove fan shroud attaching screw.
2. On all models, remove nut and through bolt attaching insulator to support bracket, Figs. 1 and 2.
3. Raise the engine slightly with a jack and a wood block placed under the oil pan.
4. Remove the engine insulator assembly to cylinder block attaching bolts. Remove the engine insulator assembly and the heat shield, if so equipped.
5. Reverse procedure to install.

1977–78 V8-351M, 400

1. Remove the fan shroud attaching bolts. Remove the transmission oil cooler lines from the retaining bracket on the block.
2. Remove the through bolt and lock nut attaching the insulator support bracket, Fig. 3. Remove the bolt and nut on the opposite mount to prevent distortion of the insulator.
3. Raise the engine slightly with a jack and a wood block placed under the oil pan.
4. Remove the engine insulator assembly to cylinder block attaching bolts and lockwashers.
5. Remove the engine insulator assembly and heat shield, if equipped.
6. Reverse procedure to install.

1977–78 V8-460

1. Block rear wheels and set parking brake. Raise front of vehicle with floor jack and install safety stands.
2. Position jack under the front area of the oil pan. Place a wood block between the jack and oil pan. Raise the jack just

enough to support the engine.
3. Remove the nut through bolt that attaches the front support insulator to the lower support bracket, Fig. 4.
4. Remove the bolts attaching the support insulator and heat shield to the cylinder block. Replace the insulator on one side before proceding to the other insulator.
5. Reverse procedure to install.

ENGINE, REPLACE

NOTE: Because of engine compartment tolerances, the engine should not be removed and installed with the transmission attached.

1979–84

1. Disconnect battery and alternator ground cables.
2. Drain cooling system and oil pan.
3. Remove hood.
4. Remove air cleaner and intake duct assembly.
5. Disconnect radiator hoses from engine.
6. Disconnect transmission oil cooler lines from radiator.

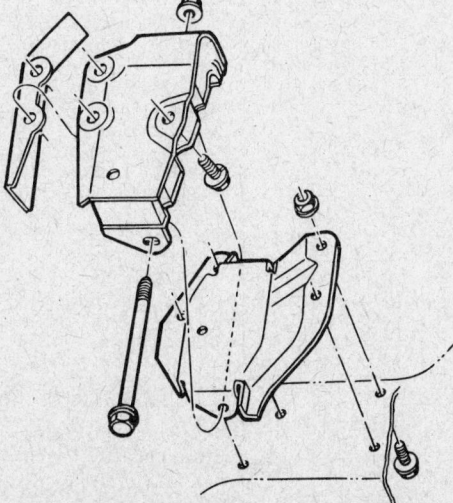

Fig. 4 Engine mount (typical). 1977–78 V8-460

7. Remove fan shroud attaching bolts, then the radiator, fan, spacer, pulley and shroud.
8. Remove alternator mounting bolts and position alternator aside.
9. Disconnect oil pressure sending unit electrical connector.
10. Disconnect fuel tank line at fuel pump and plug line.
11. Disconnect accelerator cable and speed control cable, if equipped, from carburetor.
12. Disconnect throttle valve vacuum line from intake manifold.
13. Disconnect manual shift rod and retracting spring at shift rod stud.
14. Disconnect transmission filler tube bracket from engine block.
15. Isolate and remove A/C compressor from vehicle, if equipped.
16. Disconnect power steering pump bracket from cylinder head and water pump and position aside, if equipped.
17. Disconnect power brake vacuum line from intake manifold, if equipped.
18. Disconnect heater hoses from engine.
19. Disconnect coolant temperature sending unit electrical connector.
20. Remove upper converter housing to engine attaching bolts.
21. Disconnect ignition coil and distributor wiring. Remove harness from left hand rocker arm cover and position aside. Disconnect ground strap from engine block.
22. Raise and support front of vehicle.
23. Disconnect starter motor wiring and remove starter motor.
24. Disconnect exhaust pipes from manifold.
25. Disconnect engine mounts from frame brackets.
26. Disconnect secondary air line to catalytic converter, if equipped.
27. Disconnect transmission oil cooler lines from retainer.
28. Remove converter housing inspection cover.
29. Disconnect converter from flywheel. Secure converter in housing.
30. Remove remaining converter housing to

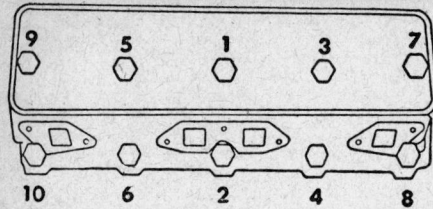

Fig. 5 Cylinder head tightening sequence.

engine bolts.

31. Lower vehicle and support transmission. Attach suitable engine lifting equipment to engine.
32. Raise engine slight and pull forward to disengage from transmission.
33. Remove engine from vehicle.
34. Reverse procedure to install.

1977–78

1. Disconnect battery ground cable, drain cooling system and crankcase and remove hood and air cleaner assembly.
2. Disconnect or remove all Thermactor components that may interfere with engine removal.
3. Disconnect hoses and oil cooler lines from radiator, then remove radiator, fan shroud and fan.
4. Remove all drive belts.
5. Disconnect power steering pump and alternator and position units out of the way.
6. If equipped with air conditioning, isolate and remove compressor.
7. Disconnect all hoses, lines and wiring from engine. Make certain to remove ground wires from block and right cylinder head.
8. Disconnect fuel line from pump and plug line.
9. Disconnect accelerator cable or linkage, then disconnect downshift linkage (if used).
10. Raise and properly support vehicle, then disconnect exhaust system from engine and remove starter. On six cylinder engines, remove transmission oil filler tube bracket.
11. Remove engine front support through bolts.
12. If equipped with automatic transmission, remove converter cover, converter to flywheel bolts, and downshift rod.
13. If equipped with manual transmission, remove clutch linkage from engine block.
14. Remove the four lower engine to clutch housing or converter housing bolts, then lower vehicle and remove the two upper engine to clutch housing or converter housing bolts.
15. Position jack under transmission, then using a suitable hoist, carefully remove engine from vehicle.
16. Reverse procedure to install.

CYLINDER HEAD, REPLACE

Tighten cylinder head bolts a little at a time in three steps in the sequence shown in Fig. 5. Final tightening should be to the torque specifications listed in the *Engine Tightening* table. After bolts have been tightened to specifications, *they should not be disturbed.*

FRONT

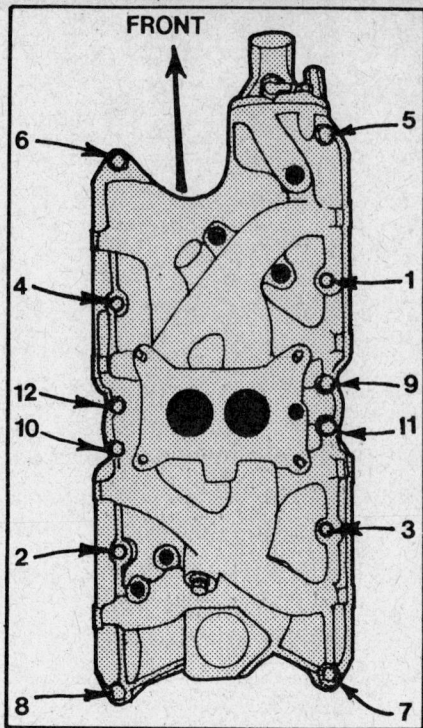

Fig. 6 Intake manifold tightening sequence. V8-225, 302, 351W

1979–84 V8-255, 302 & 351W

1. Disconnect battery ground cable.
2. Remove intake manifold and carburetor as an assembly.
3. Remove rocker arm cover.
4. If left cylinder head is being removed, isolate and remove A/C compressor, if equipped.
5. Remove EGR cooler, if equipped with V8-351W and EEC system.
6. If left cylinder head is being removed, disconnect power steering pump bracket from cylinder head and engine block and position assembly aside.
7. Remove Thermactor crossover tube from rear of cylinder heads.
8. If right cylinder head is being removed, remove alternator bracket bolt and spacer and, if equipped, the A/C compressor mounting bracket.
9. Loosen rocker arm stud nuts or bolts so that rocker arms can be rotated to the side.
10. Remove push rods, keeping them in sequence so they may be returned to their original locations. Remove exhaust valve stem caps.
11. Disconnect exhaust pipes from exhaust manifold.
12. Unfasten and remove cylinder head.
13. Reverse removal procedure to install the head. Tighten cylinder head down in the sequence shown in Fig. 5. When installing intake manifold refer to Fig. 6 for bolt tightening sequence.

NOTE: On V8-255 engines, when installing intake manifold, a 1/8 in. bead of RTV sealer should be applied at mating surfaces of intake manifold, cylinder head and cylinder block, Fig. 7. After intake manifold seals and gaskets have been positioned, apply a 1/16 in. bead of RTV sealer to the outer end of each intake

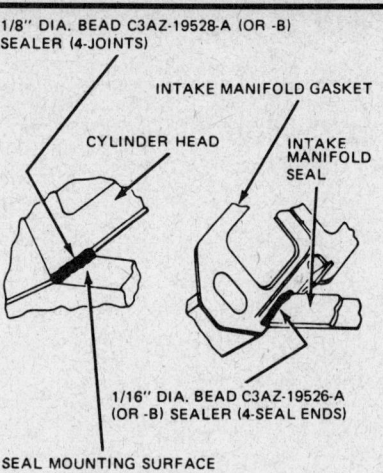

1/8" DIA. BEAD C3AZ-19528-A (OR -B) SEALER (4-JOINTS)

INTAKE MANIFOLD GASKET

CYLINDER HEAD

INTAKE MANIFOLD SEAL

1/16" DIA. BEAD C3AZ-19526-A (OR -B) SEALER (4-SEAL ENDS)

SEAL MOUNTING SURFACE OF CYLINDER BLOCK

Fig. 7 Applying RTV sealer for intake manifold installation. V8-255

manifold seal for the entire width of the seal, Fig. 7.

SERVICE NOTE: On V8-302 engines equipped with cork intake manifold seals, both the front and rear seals should be replaced with RTV sealer. Apply a 1/4 inch bead of sealer to front and rear sealing surfaces of engine block.

1977–78 V8-302, 351, 400

1. Remove intake manifold and carburetor as an assembly. Remove EGR cooler if equipped.
2. Disconnect battery ground cable at cylinder head.
3. Remove rocker arm cover.
4. On air conditioned cars, remove compressor.
5. On car with power steering, disconnect pump bracket from left cylinder head and remove drive belt. Wire power steering pump out of the way and in position that will prevent oil from draining out.

NOTE: If left cylinder head is being removed on an engine equipped with Thermactor Exhaust Emission Control System, disconnect hose from air manifold on left head. If a right head is to be removed, remove air pump and bracket and disconnect hose on right head.

6. Remove generator or alternator.
7. Disconnect exhaust manifold at exhaust pipes.
8. Loosen rocker arm stud nuts or bolts so that rocker arms can be rotated to the side.
9. Remove push rods, keeping them in sequence so they may be returned to their original locations.
10. Unfasten and remove cylinder head.
11. Reverse removal procedure to install the head. Tighten cylinder head down in the sequence shown in Fig. 5. When installing intake manifold refer to Figs. 6, 7 and 8 for bolt tightening sequence.

1977–78 V8-460

1. Remove intake manifold and carburetor

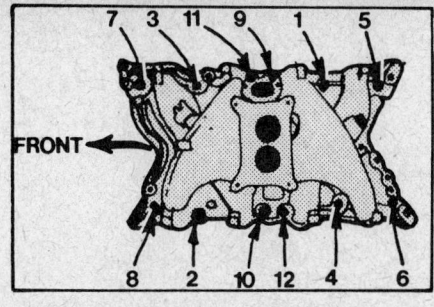

Fig. 8   Intake manifold tightening sequence. V8-351M, 400

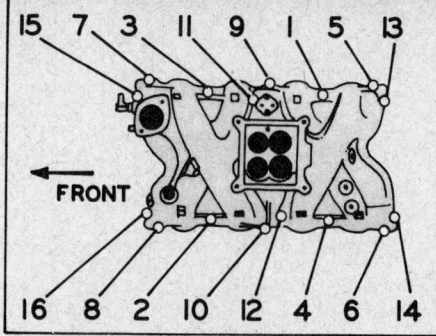

Fig. 9   Intake manifold tightening sequence. V8-460

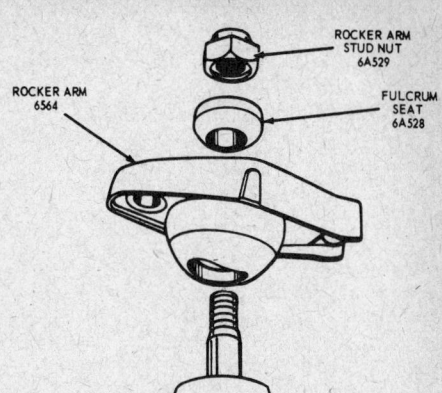

Fig. 10   Valve rocker arm parts. 1977 & early 1978 V8-302, 351W

as an assembly.

2. Disconnect muffler inlet pipe at exhaust manifold.
3. Loosen air conditioner compressor belt if so equipped.
4. Loosen alternator retaining bolts and remove bolt retaining alternator bracket to right head.
5. If air conditioned, isolate compressor at service valves and hoses from compressor. Remove nuts retaining compressor bracket to water pump. Remove bolts retaining compressor to upper mounting bracket and lay compressor out of way. Remove compressor upper bracket from head.
6. If not air conditioned, remove bolts retaining power steering reservoir bracket to left head and position reservoir out of way.
7. Remove rocker arm covers and rocker arms. Remove push rods in sequence so they can be installed in their positions.
8. Remove head retaining bolts and lift head with exhaust manifold.

NOTE: If necessary to break gasket seal, pry at forward corners of cylinder heads against casting bosses provided on cylinder block. Avoid damaging machine surfaces on head and gasket.

9. Install cylinder heads in reverse order of removal and torque bolts in sequence shown in Fig. 5. When installing intake manifold refer to Fig. 9 for bolt tightening sequence.

VALVE ARRANGEMENT
Front to Rear

Right . . . . I-E-I-E-I-E-I-E
Left . . . . E-I-E-I-E-I-E-I

VALVE LIFT SPECS.

Engine	Year	Intake	Exhaust
V8-255	1982	.375	.375
V8-302	1977–79	.382	.398
	1980–84	.375	.391
V8-351	1977–78②	.406	.406
	1978–79①	.419	.419
	1980–81①	.411	.411
V8-351 H.O.	1980–81①③	.442	.450
V8-400	1977	.427	.433
	1978	.428	.432
V8-460	1977–78	.437	.481

①—Windsor engine.
②—Modified engine.
③—High output engine.

VALVE TIMING
Intake Opens Before TDC

Engine	Year	Degrees
V8-255	1981–82	16
V8-302	1977–84	16
V8-351	1977–78②	19½
	1978–80①	23
V8-400	1977–78	17
V8-460	1977–78	8

①—Windsor engine.
②—Modified engine.

VALVES, ADJUST

To eliminate the need of adjusting valve

lash, a positive stop rocker arm stud and nut is used on 1977 and early 1978 V8-302 and 351W engines, Fig. 10, and a positive stop fulcrum bolt and seat is used on V8-351M, 400 and 460 and late 1978 and 1979–84 V8-255, 302 and 351W engines, Figs. 12 and 16.

It is very important that the correct push rod be used and all components be installed and torqued as follows:

1. Position the piston of the cylinder being worked on at TDC of its compression stroke.
2. On 1977 and early 1978 V8-302 and 351W engines, lubricate and install rocker arm and fulcrum seat on the stud. Thread nut onto the stud until it contracts the shoulder and torque to 17–23 ft. lbs.

NOTE: Each rocker arm stud nut should be inspected when adjusting valve clearance, Fig. 11.

3. On V8-351M, 400, 460 and late 1978 and 1979–84 V8-255, 302 and 351W engines, install rocker arm, fulcrum seat and oil deflector. Install fulcrum bolt and torque to 18–25 ft. lbs.

A .060" shorter push rod or a .060" longer rod are available for service to provide a means of compensating for dimensional changes in the valve mechanism. Valve stem-to-rocker arm clearance should be as listed in

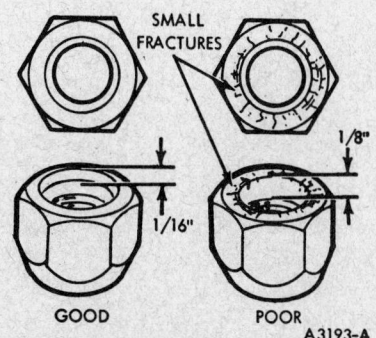

Fig. 11   Inspection of rocker arm stud nut. 1977 & early 1978 V8-302, 351W

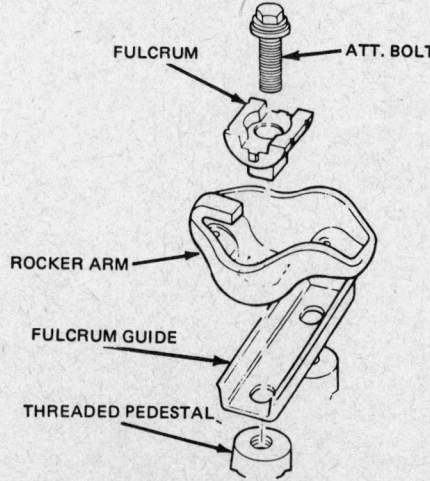

Fig. 12   Rocker arm. Late 1978 & 1979–84 V8-255, 302 & 351W

Fig. 13   Checking valve clearance on models with hydraulic lifters

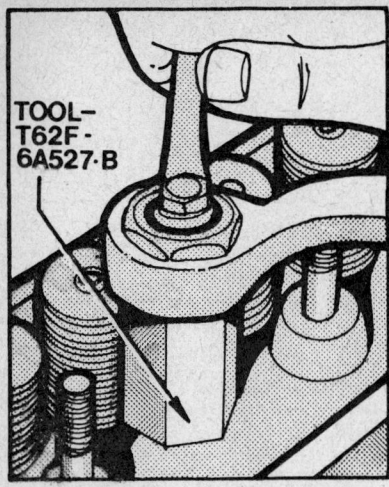

Fig. 14 Rocker arm stud removal. 1977 & early 1978 V8-302, 351W

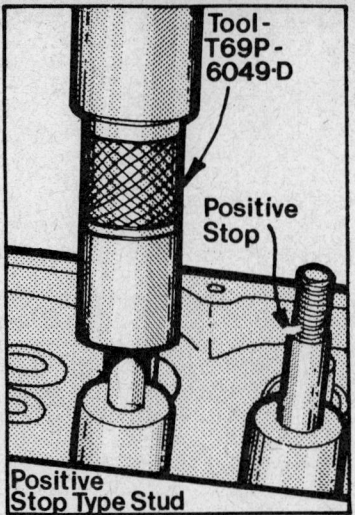

Fig. 15 Positive stop type rocker arm stud installation. 1977 & early 1978 V8-302, 351W

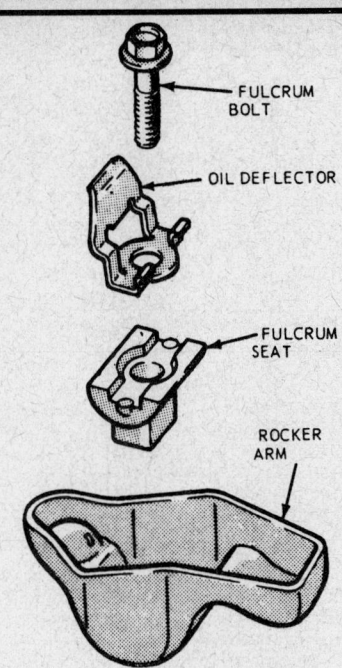

Fig. 16 Rocker arm and related parts. V8-351M, 400, 460

the *Valve Specifications* table, with the hydraulic lifter completely collapsed, Fig. 13. Repeated valve grind jobs will decrease this clearance to the point that if not compensated for the lifters will cease to function.

When checking valve clearance, if the clearance is less than the minimum, the .060″ shorter push rod should be used. If clearance is more than the maximum, the .060″ longer push rod should be used. (See *Valve Specifications* table.) To check valve clearance, proceed as follows:

1. Mark crankshaft pulley at three locations, with number 1 location at TDC timing mark (end of compression stroke), number 2 location one half turn (180°) clockwise from TDC and number 3 location three quarter turn clockwise (270°) from number 2 location.
2. Turn the crankshaft to the number 1 location and check the clearance on the following valves:

V8-255, 302 & 460

No. 1 Intake	No. 1 Exhaust
No. 7 Intake	No. 5 Exhaust
No. 8 Intake	No. 4 Exhaust

V8-351W, 351M & 400

No. 1 Intake	No. 1 Exhaust
No. 4 Intake	No. 3 Exhaust
No. 8 Intake	No. 7 Exhaust

3. Turn the crankshaft to the number 2 location and check the clearance on the following valves:

V8-255, 302 & 460

No. 5 Intake	No. 2 Exhaust
No. 4 Intake	No. 6 Exhaust

V8-351W, 351M & 400

No. 3 Intake	No. 2 Exhaust
No. 7 Intake	No. 6 Exhaust

4. Turn the crankshaft to the number 3 location and check the clearance on the following valves:

V8-255, 302 & 460

No. 2 Intake	No. 7 Exhaust
No. 3 Intake	No. 3 Exhaust
No. 6 Intake	No. 8 Exhaust

V8-351W, 351M & 400

No. 2 Intake	No. 4 Exhaust
No. 5 Intake	No. 5 Exhaust
No. 6 Intake	No. 8 Exhaust

VALVE GUIDES

Valve guides in these engines are an inte-

gral part of the head and, therefore, cannot be removed. For service, guides can be reamed oversize to accommodate one of three service valves with oversize stems (.003″, .015″ and .030″).

Check the valve stem clearance of each valve (after cleaning) in its respective valve guide. If the clearance exceeds the service limits of .0055″, ream the valve guides to accommodate the next oversize diameter valve.

ROCKER ARM & STUD SERVICE

1977 & Early 1978 V8-302 & 351W

If necessary to replace a rocker arm stud, a kit is available which contains a stud remover, Fig. 14, a stud installer, Fig. 15, and two reamers, one .006″ and the other .015″. For .010″ oversize studs, use reamer No. T66P-6A527-B.

Rocker arm studs that are broken or have damaged threads may be replaced with standard studs. Loose studs in the head may be replaced with .006″, .010″ or .015″ oversize studs which are available for service.

When going from a standard size stud to a .010 or .015″ oversize stud, always use a .006″ reamer before finish reaming with a .010 or .015″ reamer.

If a stud is broken off flush with the stud boss, use an easy-out to remove the broken stud, following the instructions of the tool manufacturer.

ROCKER ARMS

Late 1978 & 1979—84 V8-255, 302, 351W

These engines use a bolt and fulcrum attachment, Fig. 12. To remove, remove attaching bolt, then the fulcrum, rocker arm and fulcrum guide, if the other rocker arm is being removed.

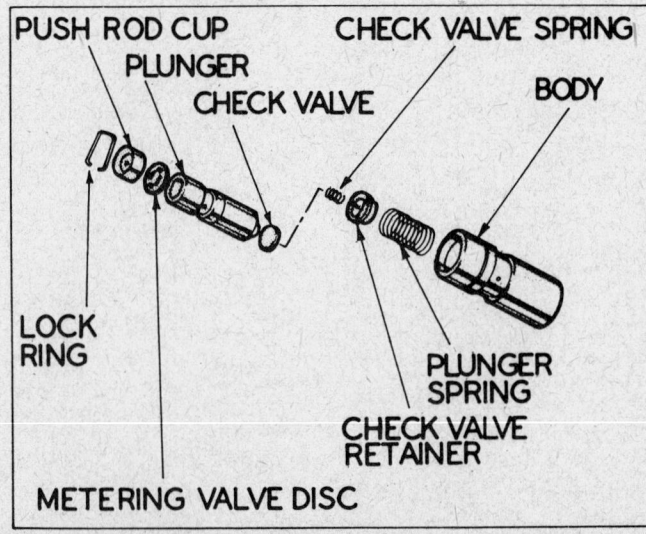

Fig. 17 Hydraulic valve lifter disassembled (typical)

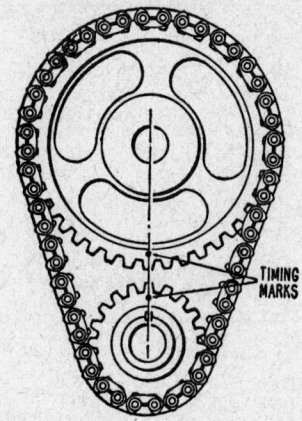

Fig. 18 Timing marks aligned for correct valve timing

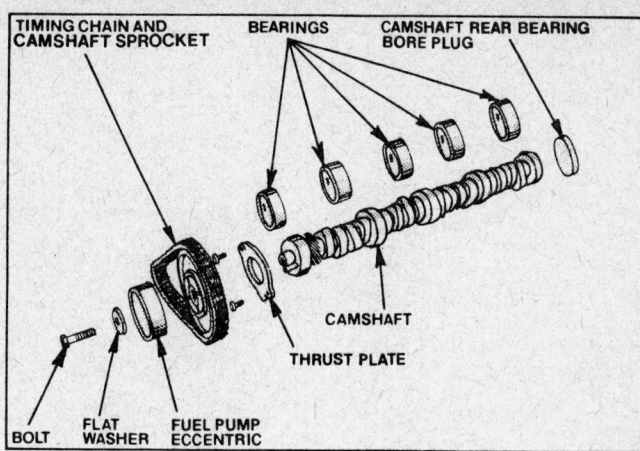

Fig. 19 Camshaft and related parts

SERVICE NOTE: Some 1981–82 models equipped with low profile rocker arm fulcrums (part No. E1TZ-6A528-A) may experience excessive oil displacement when engine is operated for extended periods during high ambient temperatures. This problem may be corrected by replacing original rocker arm fulcrums with part No. D7AZ-6A528-A.

1977 & Early 1978 V8-302, 351W

A positive stop rocker arm stud and nut eliminates the need for adjusting valve lash, Fig. 10.

Installation
1. Position the piston of the cylinder to be worked on at TDC compression stroke.
2. Locate stud properly with tool T69P-6049D. Make sure tool bottoms on the head.
3. Lubricate rocker arm components and place rocker arm and fulcrum on the stud.
4. Thread nut onto the stud until it contacts the shoulder then tighten nut to 18–22 ft. lbs.

V8-351M, 400, 460

The rocker arm is supported by a fulcrum bolt which fits through the fulcrum seat and threads into the cylinder head. To disassemble, remove the bolt, oil deflector, fulcrum seat and rocker arm, Fig. 16.

VALVE LIFTERS, REPLACE

NOTE: The internal parts of each hydraulic valve lifter assembly are a matched set. If these are mixed, improper valve operation may result. Therefore, disassemble, inspect and test each assembly separately to prevent mixing the parts.

Fig. 17 illustrates the type of hydraulic lifter used. See the *Trouble Shooting Chapter* under the heading *Engine Noises* for causes of hydraulic valve lifter noise.

1. Remove intake manifold and related parts.
2. Remove rocker arm covers.
3. Loosen rocker arm stud nuts or bolts and rotate rocker arms to the side.
4. Lift out push rods, keeping them in sequence in a rack so they may be installed in their original location.
5. Using a magnet rod, remove valve lifters

and place them in sequence in a rack so they may be installed in their original location.
6. Reverse procedure to install.

TIMING CASE COVER, REPLACE

NOTE: To replace the seal in the timing gear cover, it is necessary to remove the cover as outlined below.

V8-255, 302, 351, 400
1. Drain cooling system and oil pan.
2. Disconnect lower radiator hose from water pump.
3. Disconnect heater hose from water pump and slide water pump bypass hose clamp toward pump.
4. Unfasten and position alternator and bracket out of way.
5. If equipped with power steering or air conditioning, remove the drive belts.
6. Remove the fan, spacer, pulley and drive belt.
7. Remove crankshaft pulley and vibration damper.

NOTE: If equipped with EEC II system, disconnect crankshaft position sensor electrical connector.

8. Disconnect fuel pump outlet line from pump and remove pump retaining bolts and lay pump to one side with flex line attached.
9. Remove oil dipstick and the oil pan to front cover attaching bolts.
10. Unfasten and remove the front cover and water pump as an assembly.
11. Reverse procedure to install.

V8-460
1. Drain cooling system and crankcase.
2. Remove bolts attaching fan to water pump and remove screws attaching radiator shroud to radiator.
3. Remove fan assembly and radiator shroud.
4. Disconnect radiator hoses at engine and cooler lines at radiator and remove radiator upper support and radiator assembly.
5. Loosen alternator and air pump, then remove drive belt with water pump pul-

ley.
6. If air conditioned, loosen idler pulley and remove compressor support.
7. Remove vibration damper from crankshaft.
8. Disconnect power steering lines at pump and unfasten and remove the pump.
9. Loosen bypass hose at pump and disconnect heater return tube at pump.
10. Disconnect and plug fuel inlet line at pump and disconnect fuel outlet line from pump. Unfasten and remove fuel pump.
11. Unfasten and remove cylinder front cover.
12. Reverse procedure to install.

TIMING CHAIN, REPLACE
V8-255, 302, 351, 400

After removing the cover as outlined above, crank the engine until the timing marks are aligned as shown in Fig. 18. Remove camshaft sprocket retaining bolt, washer and fuel pump eccentric and, on 1981–84 models with electronic fuel injection, remove spacer. Slide both sprockets and chain forward and remove them as an assembly.

Reverse procedure to install the chain and sprockets, being sure the timing marks are aligned.

V8-460
1. To remove the chain, first take off the front cover as outlined previously.
2. Crank engine until timing marks on camshaft sprocket is adjacent to timing mark on crankshaft sprocket, Fig. 18.
3. Remove camshaft sprocket cap screw and fuel pump eccentric.
4. Slide both sprockets and chain forward and remove as an assembly.
5. Reverse procedure to install the chain, being sure to align the timing marks as shown, Fig. 18.

CAMSHAFT, REPLACE

NOTE: It may be necessary to remove or reposition radiator, A/C compressor and grille components to provide adequate clearance.

1. To remove camshaft, remove cylinder front cover and timing chain.
2. Remove distributor cap and spark plug wires, then remove distributor.
3. Disconnect automatic transmission oil cooler lines from radiator and remove radiator.

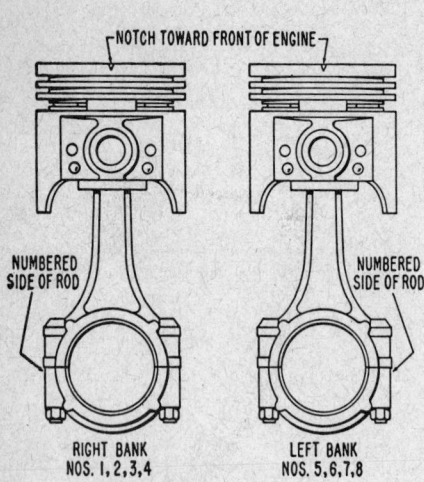

Fig. 20 Piston and rod assembly

4. Remove intake manifold and carburetor as an assembly.
5. Remove rocker arm covers.
6. Loosen rocker arm stud nuts or bolts and rotate rocker arms to one side.
7. Remove push rods, keeping them in sequence in a rack so they may be installed in their original location.
8. Using a magnet, remove valve lifters and place them in a rack in sequence so they may be installed in their original location.
9. Remove camshaft thrust plate, Fig. 19 and carefully pull camshaft from engine, using care to avoid damaging camshaft bearings.
10. Reverse procedure to install.

CAMSHAFT BEARINGS

When necessary to replace camshaft bearings, the engine will have to be removed from the vehicle and the plug at the rear of the cylinder block will have to be removed in order to utilize the special camshaft bearing removing and installing tools required to do this job. If properly installed, camshaft bearings require no reaming—nor should this type bearing be reamed or altered in any manner in an attempt to fit bearings.

PISTON & ROD, ASSEMBLE

Assemble the pistons to the rods so the notch or arrow faces toward the front of engine and the numbered side of rod faces away from center of engine, Fig. 20. After installation, check side clearance between connecting rods at each crankshaft journal. Clearance should be .010–.020 in.

PISTONS, PINS & RINGS

Pistons and rings are available in standard sizes and oversizes of .003, .020, .030 and .040 inch.
Oversize piston pins of .001 and .002" are available.

MAIN & ROD BEARINGS

Main and rod bearings are available in standard sizes and the following undersizes: .001, .002, .010, .020, .030, .040".

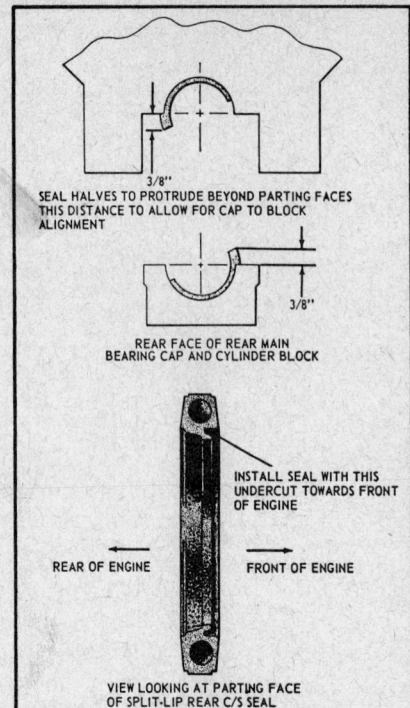

Fig. 21 Split-lip rear crankshaft seal installation

CRANKSHAFT OIL SEAL, REPLACE

A rubber split-lip rear crankshaft oil seal is available for service. This seal can be installed without removal of the crankshaft and also eliminates the necessity of seal installation tools.

1. Remove oil pan and, if necessary, the oil pump.
2. Remove rear main bearing cap.
3. Loosen remaining bearing caps, allowing crankshaft to drop down about 1/32".
4. Remove old seals from both cylinder block and rear main bearing cap. Use a brass rod to drift upper half of seal from cylinder block groove. Rotate crankshaft while drifting to facilitate removal.
5. Carefully clean seal groove in block with a brush and solvent. Also clean seal groove in bearing cap. Remove the oil seal retaining pin from the bearing cap if so equipped. *The pin is not used with the split-lip seal.*
6. Dip seal halves in clean engine oil.
7. Carefully install upper seal half in its groove with undercut side of seal toward front of engine, Fig. 21, by rotating it on shaft journal of crankshaft until approximately 3/8" protrudes below the parting surface. *Be sure no rubber has been shaved from outside diameter of seal by bottom edge of groove.*
8. Retighten main bearing caps and torque to specifications.
9. Install lower seal in main bearing cap with undercut side of seal toward front of engine, and allow seal to protrude about 3/8" above parting surface to mate with upper seal upon cap installation.
10. Apply suitable sealer to parting faces of cap and block. Install cap and torque to specifications.

NOTE: If difficulty is encountered in installing the upper half of the seal in position, lightly lap (sandpaper) the side of the seal opposite

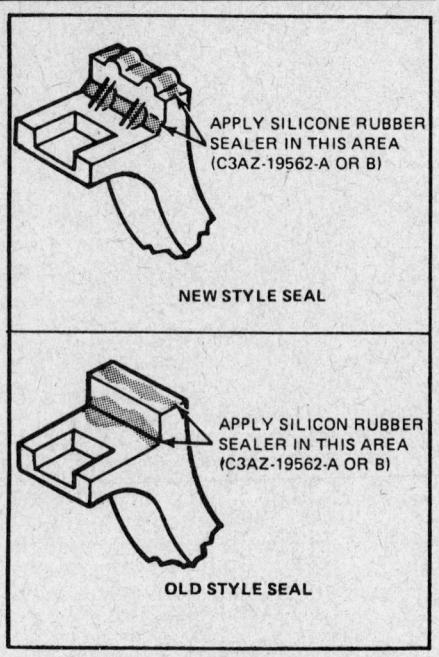

Fig. 22 Crankshaft rear oil seals

the lip side using a medium grit paper. After sanding, the seal must be washed in solvent, then dipped in clean engine oil prior to installation.

SERVICE BULLETIN

A revised crankshaft rear oil seal has been released for service. This new seal may be received when ordering an oil pan gasket kit and is installed in the same manner as described previously, Fig. 22.

OIL PAN, REPLACE
1979–84 V8-255, 302 & 351W

1. Disconnect battery ground cable and remove air cleaner assembly.
2. Disconnect accelerator cable and kickdown rod from carburetor.
3. Remove accelerator mounting bracket bolts and bracket.
4. Remove fan shroud attaching screws and position shroud over fan.
5. Disconnect wiper motor electrical connector and remove wiper motor.
6. Disconnect windshield washer hose.
7. Remove wiper motor mounting cover.
8. Remove oil level dipstick, then the dipstick tube retaining bolt from exhaust manifold.
9. If equipped with EGR cooler or EEC, remove Thermactor air dump tube retaining clamp, then the Thermactor crossover tube at rear of engine.
10. On all models, raise and support vehicle.
11. Drain oil pan.
12. On vehicles equipped with EGR cooler or EEC, remove filler tube from transmission oil pan and drain transmission, then remove starter motor.
13. Disconnect fuel line at fuel pump and plug line.

NOTE: Vehicles equipped with electronic fuel injection use a high pressure electric fuel pump. Prior to disconnecting fuel lines from the pump, pressure must be released at the Schrader valve on the fuel charging assembly.

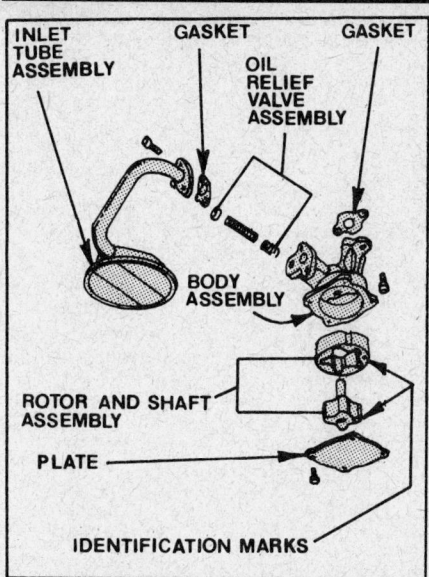

Fig. 23   Oil pump. V8-255, 302, 351W & 460

14. Disconnect exhaust pipes from manifolds.
15. If equipped with EGR cooler or EEC, remove exhaust gas sensor from exhaust manifold, then the Thermactor secondary air tube to converter housing clamps.
16. On all models, remove dipstick tube from oil pan.
17. Loosen rear engine mount attaching nuts.
18. Remove engine mount through bolts.
19. Remove shift crossover bolts at transmission.
20. If equipped with EGR cooler or EEC, disconnect exhaust pipes from catalytic converter outlet, then the catalytic converter

secondary air tube and inlet pipes to exhaust manifold.
21. On all models, disconnect transmission kickdown rod.
22. Remove torque converter housing cover.
23. Remove brake line retainer from front crossmember.
24. With a suitable jack, raise engine as far as possible.
25. Place a block of wood between each engine mount and chassis bracket. When engine is secured in this position, remove jack.
26. Remove oil pan attaching bolts and lower the oil pan.
27. Remove oil pick-up tube bolts and lower tube in oil pan.
28. Remove oil pan from vehicle.
29. Reverse procedure to install.

1977–78 V8-302, 351, 400

1. Drain oil pan and remove dip stick.
2. Remove fan shroud bolts and place shroud over fan.
3. On V8-351M, 400 engines, remove starter.
4. On all engines, remove engine front mount to chassis bolts, raise engine and install wood blocks between mounts and chassis, then lower engine onto the wood blocks.
5. On V8-302, 351W engines, disconnect stabilizer bar from lower control arms and position stabilizer bar and control arms to permit oil pan removal. Also, on all models with automatic transmission, position oil cooler lines aside for pan removal.
6. Remove oil pan bolts and oil pan.
7. Reverse procedure to install.

V8-460

1. Drain oil pan, then remove starter.
2. Disconnect sway bar and pull forward on struts.

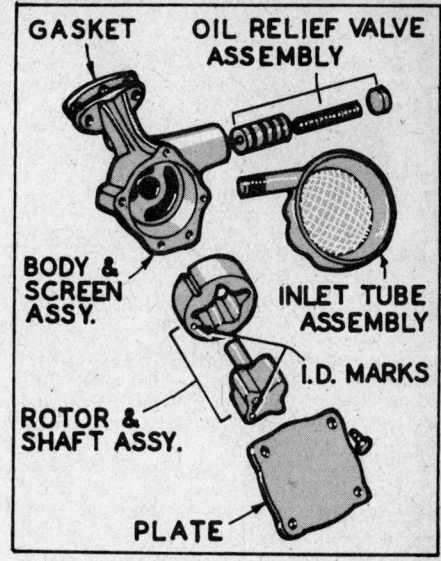

Fig. 24   Oil pump assembly. V8-351M & 400

3. Remove fan shroud bolts, place shroud on fan and remove oil filter.

NOTE: *To allow clearance for removal of oil pan, remove the front engine mount nuts. Then position floor jack under front leading edge of oil pan (use wood block between pan and jack). Raise engine about 1¼" and insert a 1" block of wood between insulators and frame crossmember. Then remove floor jack.*

4. Remove oil pan screws and lower pan to crossmember.
5. Crank engine to obtain necessary clearance between crankshaft counterweight and rear of oil pan. Then remove pan.
6. Reverse procedure to install.

OIL PUMP, REPLACE

1. Remove oil pan as described under Oil Pan, Replace.
2. On V8-255, 302 and 351W engine, remove oil inlet pickup tube and screen assembly.
3. On all engines, remove oil pump attaching bolts and remove oil pump and intermediate drive shaft.
4. Reverse procedure to install. Prime oil pump with engine oil before installing. Position intermediate drive shaft into distributor sprocket. With intermediate drive shaft firmly seated, the stop on the shaft should contact crankcase surface. Remove shaft and adjust as necessary. Position pump with intermediate drive shaft insert to cylinder block, then install and torque attaching bolts to 22 to 32 ft. lbs.

NOTE: Do not force oil pump into position on cylinder block. If pump drive shaft is misaligned with distributor shaft, rotate drive shaft to a new position.

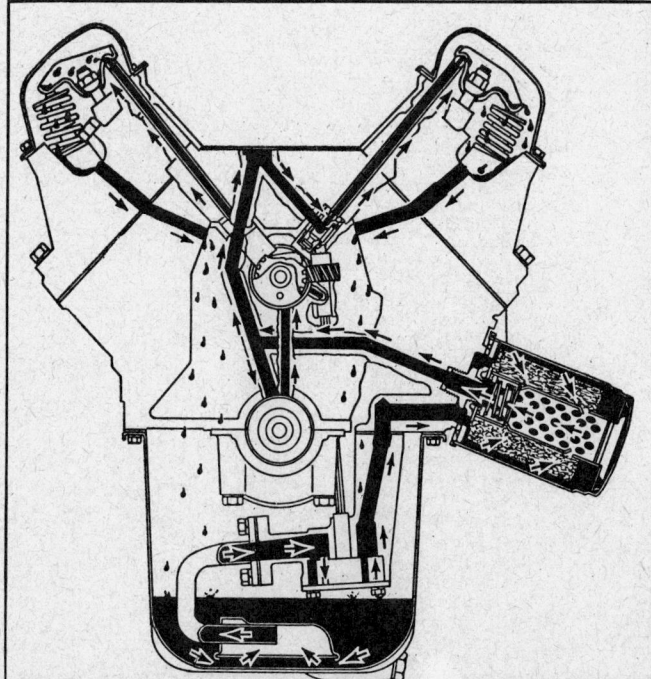

Engine oiling system (typical)

OIL PUMP, SERVICE

Figs. 23 & 24

1. With all parts clean and dry, check the

inside of the pump housing and the outer race and rotor for damage or excessive wear.

2. Check the mating surface of the pump cover for wear. If this surface is worn, scored or grooved, replace the pump.

3. Measure the clearance between the outer race and housing. This clearance should be .001–.013 inch.

4. With the rotor assembly installed in the housing, place a straight edge over the rotor assembly and housing. Measure the clearance between the straight edge and the rotor and outer race. Maximum recommended limits is .004". *The outer race, shaft and rotor are furnished only as an assembly.*

5. Check the drive shaft-to-housing bearing clearance by measuring the O.D. of the shaft and the I.D. of the housing bearing. The recommended clearance limits are .0015–.0030".

6. Inspect the relief valve spring for a collapsed or worn condition.

7. Check the relief valve piston for scores and free operation in the bore. The specified piston clearance is .0015–.0030".

BELT TENSION DATA

	New Lbs.	Used Lbs.
1977–80 Exc. ¼"	140	110
¼" inch	65	50

		New Lbs.	Used Lbs.
1980	Ribbed belt		
	w/o tensioner	155	150
	Ribbed belt		
	with tensioner	130	130
	¼" V Belt	65	50
1981	All other V Belts	140	105
	V Ribbed Belts		
	4K①	110	100
	5K②	125	120
	5K③	108	108
	6K④	165	150
	6K⑤	113	113
1982–84	¼" V Belt	65	50
	All other V Belts	140	105
	V Ribbed Belt		
	4K Exc. Air Pump①	130	115
	4K Air Pump①	110	105
	5K②	150	135
	6K⑤	113	110
	6K⑥	160	145

①—4 grooves.
②—5 grooves fixed.
③—5 grooves with absorber.
④—6 grooves with absorber.
⑤—6 grooves with tensioner.
⑥—6 grooves fixed.

WATER PUMP, REPLACE

1. Drain cooling system, then remove carburetor air inlet tube.
2. On models equipped with a fan shroud, remove shroud attaching bolts and place shroud over fan and spacer. Remove fan and spacer from water pump shaft, then remove fan shroud.
3. Remove alternator drive belt, A/C drive belt and idler pulley bracket, if so equipped. Remove power steering drive belt and power steering pump, if so equipped. Remove all brackets from water pump, then remove water pump.
4. Disconnect radiator lower hose and heater hose at water pump.
5. Remove drive belt, fan, spacer or fan drive clutch and pulley.
6. Reverse procedure to install.

FUEL PUMP, REPLACE

1. Loosen, then retighten fuel line connection(s) using a suitable wrench. Do not disconnect lines at this time.
2. Loosen fuel pump attaching bolts one or two turns. Apply hand force to pump to loosen gasket.
3. Rotate engine until fuel pump cam lobe is near low position to reduce pressure on pump.
4. Disconnect fuel lines and, if equipped, the vapor return line from pump.
5. Remove fuel pump attaching bolts and pump. Remove and discard gasket.
6. Clean all gasket material from engine and fuel pump.
7. Install attaching bolts into fuel pump. Then install new gasket over bolts.
8. Install pump and tighten attaching bolts alternately and evenly.
9. Connect fuel lines and vapor return line, if equipped, then operate engine and check for leaks.

Rear Axle, Propeller Shaft & Brakes

REAR AXLES

Figs. 1 and 2 illustrate the rear axle assemblies used on these cars. When necessary to overhaul either of these units, refer to the *Rear Axle Specifications* table in this chapter.

Integral Carrier Type

The gear set consists of a ring gear and an overhung drive pinion which is supported by two opposed tapered roller bearings, Fig. 1. The differential case is a one-piece design with openings allowing assembly of the internal parts and lubricant flow. The differential pinion shaft is retained with a threaded bolt (lock) assembled to the case.

The roller type wheel bearings have no inner race, and the rollers directly contact the bearing journals of the axle shafts. The axle shafts do not use an inner and outer bearing retainer. Rather, they are held in the axle by means of C-locks, Fig. 3. These C-locks also fit into a machined recess in the differential side gears within the differential case. There is no retainer bolt access hole in the axle shaft flange.

Rear Axle, Replace

1. Raise vehicle and support using jack stands under both frame side rails.
2. Mark drive shaft and pinion flange for reassembly, then disconnect drive shaft at pinion flange and remove drive shaft from transmission extension housing. Install seal replacer tool in extension housing to prevent leakage.
3. Disconnect parking brake cable and brake lines. Cover brake lines to prevent contamination.

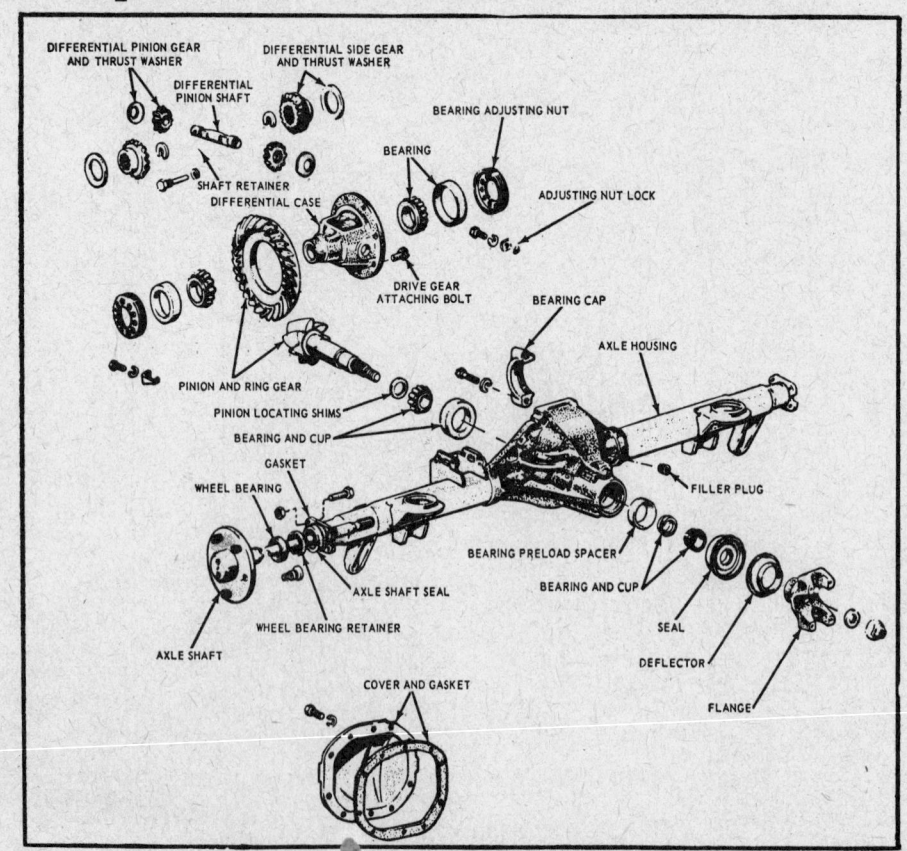

Fig. 1 Integral type rear axle assembly (typical)

Fig. 3 Axle shaft C locks. Integral type axle

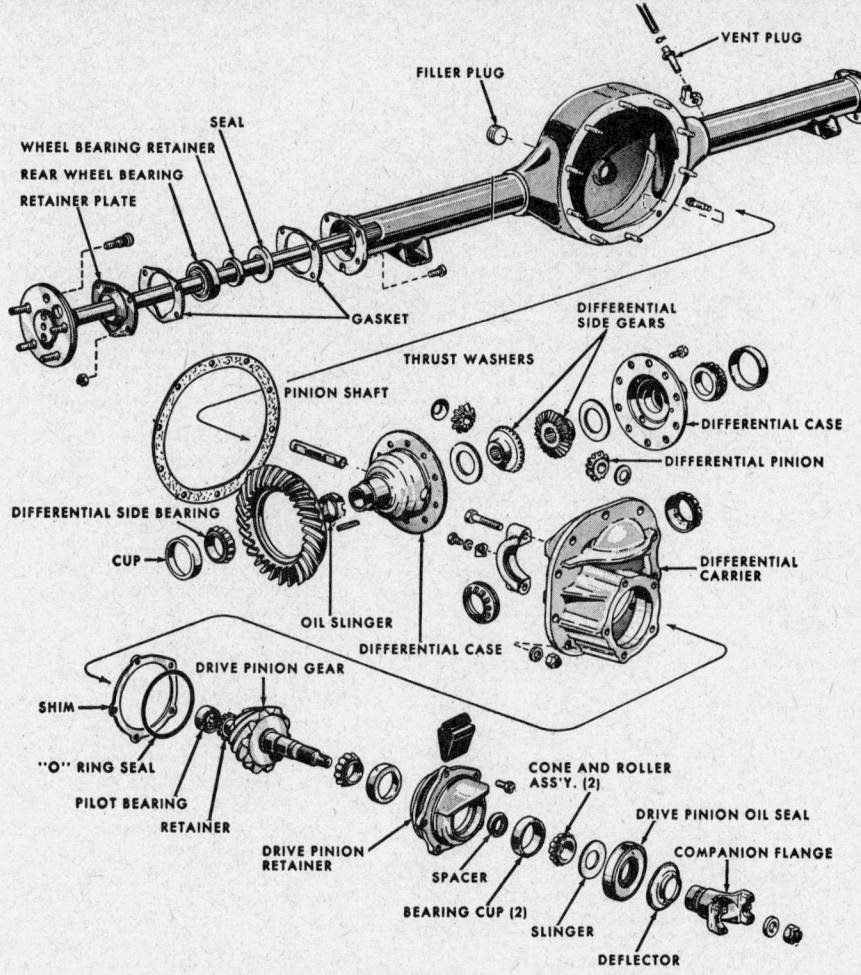

Fig. 2 Removable carrier type of rear axle assembly (typical)

Fig. 4 Using hook-type tool to remove oil seal

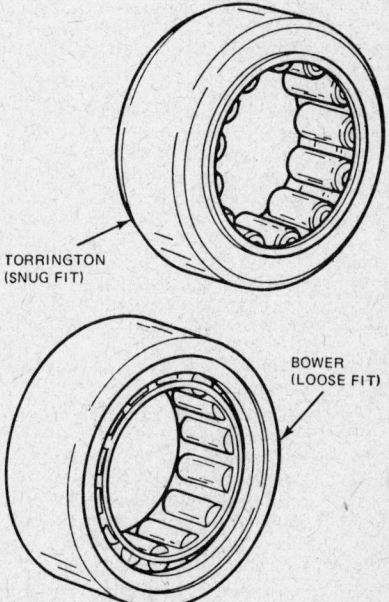

TORRINGTON (SNUG FIT)

BOWER (LOOSE FIT)

Fig. 5 Axle shaft bearing identification 1977–79 models w/integral type axle

4. Support axle with jack, then lower axle far enough to relieve spring tension.
5. Disconnect shock absorbers at lower mounting brackets.
6. If equipped, disconnect track bar from axle housing stud.
7. Remove nuts, washers and pivot bolts connecting lower suspension arms to axle housing, then disconnect both arms from housing.
8. Remove nuts, bolts, washers and two eccentric washers, then disconnect upper suspension arm from axle housing.
9. Lower rear axle and remove from vehicle.

Axle Shaft, Bearing & Seal, Replace
1. Raise car on hoist and remove wheels.
2. Drain differential lubricant.
3. Remove brake drums.
4. Remove differential housing cover.
5. Position safety stands under rear frame member and lower hoist to allow axle to lower as far as possible.
6. Working through differential case opening, remove pinion shaft lock bolt and pinion shaft.
7. Push axle shaft(s) inward toward center of axle housing and remove C-lock(s) from housing, Fig. 3.
8. Remove axle shaft, using extreme care to avoid contact of shaft seal lip with any portion of axle shaft except seal journal.
9. Use a hook-type puller to remove seal and bearing, Fig. 4.

NOTE: On 1977–79 models, two types of bearings are used, one requires a snug press fit in the axle housing flanges and the other has a ground race and a loose fit is acceptable, Fig. 5. Therefore, when removing bearings, if a loose fit is encountered it does not indicate excessive wear or damage.

10. Reverse procedure to install, using suitable driving tools, Fig. 6, to install seal and bearing. New seals are pre-packed with lubricant and do not require oil soaking before installation.

Removable Carrier Type

In these axles, Fig. 2, the drive pinion is straddle-mounted by two opposed tapered roller bearings which support the pinion shaft in front of the drive pinion gear, and straight roller bearing that supports the pinion shaft at the rear of the pinion gear. The drive pinion is assembled in a pinion retainer that is bolted to the differential carrier. The tapered roller bearings are preloaded by a collapsible spacer between the bearings. The pinion is positioned by a shim or shims located between the drive pinion retainer and the differential carrier.

The differential is supported in the carrier by two tapered roller side bearings. These bearings are preloaded by two threaded ring nuts or sleeves between the bearings and pedestals. The differential assembly is positioned for proper ring gear and pinion backlash by varying the adjustment of these ring nuts. The differential case houses two side gears in mesh with two pinions mounted on a pinion shaft which is held in place by a pin. The side gears and pinions are backed by

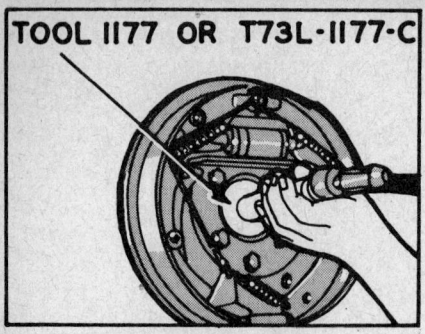

Fig. 6 Using special driver to install oil seal

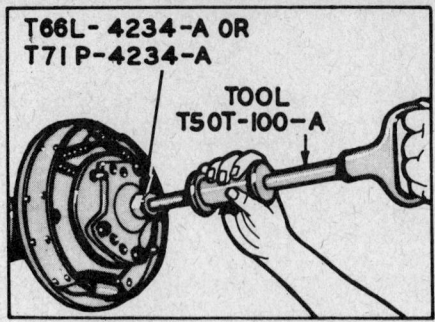

Fig. 7 Removing axle shaft with slide hammer-type puller

Fig. 8 Splitting bearing inner retainer for bearing removal

thrust washers. With high performance engines, an optional rear axle having a four-pinion differential is also used.

The axle shafts are of unequal length, the left shaft being shorter than the right. The axle shafts are mounted on sealed ball bearings or tapered roller bearings which are pressed on the shafts.

SERVICE BULLETIN

All Ford Built Rear Axles: Recent manufacturing changes have eliminated the need for marking rear axle drive pinions for individual variations from nominal shim thicknesses. In the past, these pinion markings, with the aid of a shim selection table, were used as a guide to select correct shim thicknesses when a gear set or carrier assembly replacement was performed.

With the elimination of pinion markings, use of the shim selection table is no longer possible and the methods outlined below must be used.
1. Measure the thickness of the original pinion depth shim removed from the axle. Use the same thickness upon installation of the replacement carrier or drive pinion. If any further shim change is necessary, it will be indicated in the tooth pattern check.
2. If the original shim is lost, substitute a nominal shim for the original and use the tooth pattern check to determine if further shim changes are required.

Rear Axle, Replace
1. Raise rear of vehicle and remove wheel and tire assembly.
2. On models equipped with rear drum brakes, remove brake drums.
3. On models equipped with rear disc brakes, remove calipers from anchor plates, then remove two retaining nuts and slide rotors off axle shafts.

NOTE: Secure calipers to frame with wire.

4. Make marks on drive shaft yoke and pinion flange for reassembly, then disconnect drive shaft at rear axle U-joint and remove drive shaft from transmission extension housing. Install seal replacer tool in extension housing to prevent leakage.
5. Disconnect anti-skid sensor, if equipped.
6. Position safety stands under frame rear members, then support axle housing using a suitable jack.
7. Disconnect brake hydraulic lines from axle housing retaining clips.

8. Disconnect vent tube from rear housing.
9. Disconnect shock absorbers from lower mounting brackets.
10. Disconnect track bar from mounting stud on rear axle housing bracket.

NOTE: The axle housing mounting bracket has two holes, the track bar should be attached to the lower hole.

11. Lower rear axle housing until coil springs are released, then remove springs and insulators.
12. Disconnect suspension lower arms from axle housing, then disconnect suspension upper arms from housing.
13. Lower axle housing and remove from vehicle.

Axle Shaft, Bearing & Seal, Replace
1. Remove rear wheel assembly, then the brake drum or caliper and rotor assembly.
2. Remove axle shaft retainer nuts and bolts.
3. Pull axle shaft assembly from housing. It may be necessary to use a suitable slide hammer type puller, Fig. 7.
4. To replace wheel bearing on models equipped with tapered roller bearings:
   a. Drill a ¼ inch hole in inner bearing retainer approximately ¾ of the thickness of the bearing retainer deep.

NOTE: Do not drill completely through the bearing retainer since damage to the axle shaft may result.

   b. Place a cold chisel across the drilled hole and strike with a hammer to break retainer, then discard retainer, Fig. 8.
   c. Using suitable press and plates, press bearing from axle shaft. Do not apply heat since the heat will weaken the axle shaft bearing journal area.
   d. Install lubricated seal and bearing on axle shaft, ensuring the cup rib ring faces toward the axle flange.

NOTE: The lubricated seal of the bearing assembly used with drum brake installations is of a different length than the seal used on disc brake installations and are not interchangeable. For identification, the seal used on drum brake installations has a grey color outer rim and on disc brake installations, the seal has a black oxide appearance.

   e. Press new bearing into place, then the bearing retainer firmly against the

bearing.
   f. Remove old bearing cup from axle housing with a suitable puller. Place new bearing cup on bearing and apply lubricant to outside diameter of seal and bearing cup and install in axle housing.
5. To replace wheel bearing on models equipped with ball bearings:
   a. Remove oil seal from axle housing, Fig. 4.
   b. Loosen bearing inner retainer by striking retainer ring in several places with a cold chisel and slide off shaft, Fig. 8.

NOTE: On some models, it may be necessary to drill a ¼ inch hole in inner bearing retainer approximately ¾ of the thickness of the bearing retainer deep before using the cold chisel.

   c. Using suitable press and plates, press bearing from shaft. Do not heat axle shaft since the heat will damage the shaft.
   d. Install outer retainer on shaft and press bearing into place. Press inner retainer onto shaft until firmly seated against bearing.
   e. Install oil seal into axle housing, Fig. 6.
6. On all units, slide axle shaft assembly into housing, engaging axle shaft splines in the side gear.
7. Install and torque axle shaft retainer nuts and bolts to 50–75 ft. lbs. on 1977 models, 50–70 ft. lbs. on 1978 models.

SERVICE NOTE: If replacing an axle shaft and bearing assembly of the sealed ball bearing design, the replacement assembly will have a tapered roller bearing. This tapered roller bearing is interchangeable with the ball bearing as an assembly only, however the inner oil seal must be removed before the tapered bearing shaft can be installed into the housing bore. The housing wheel bearing bore should be sanded with emery cloth before installing the bearing to provide a good sealing surface for the seal.

When removing a tapered roller bearing axle shaft, the outer bearing race may separate from the retainer ring and remain in the housing bore. If this occurs, the bearing must be removed and reinstalled on the shaft to prevent damage to the seal.

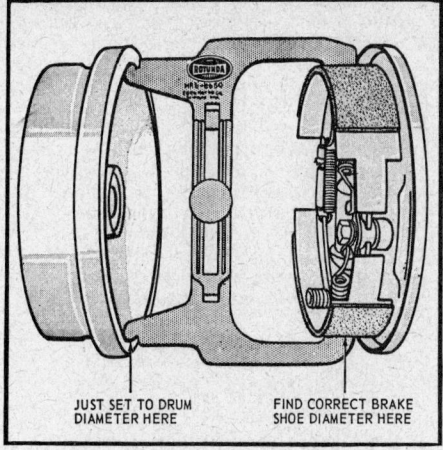

Fig. 9 Brake adjustment gauge

JUST SET TO DRUM DIAMETER HERE   FIND CORRECT BRAKE SHOE DIAMETER HERE

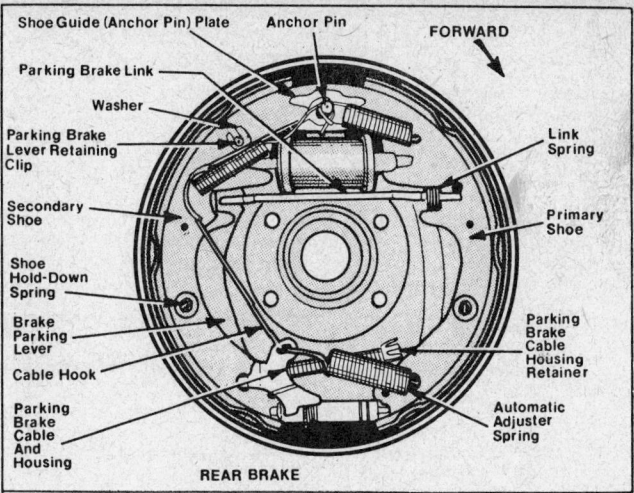

Shoe Guide (Anchor Pin) Plate   Anchor Pin   FORWARD

Parking Brake Link

Washer

Parking Brake Lever Retaining Clip

Secondary Shoe

Shoe Hold-Down Spring

Brake Parking Lever

Cable Hook

Parking Brake Cable And Housing

Link Spring

Primary Shoe

Parking Brake Cable Housing Retainer

Automatic Adjuster Spring

REAR BRAKE

Fig. 10 Rear drum type brakes

PROPELLER SHAFT, REPLACE

1. Mark the relationship of the driveshaft to pinion flange, then disconnect rear U-joint or companion flange from drive pinion flange.
2. Pull drive shaft toward rear of car until front U-joint yoke clears transmission extension housing and output shaft.
3. Install a suitable tool, such as a seal driver, in seal to prevent lube from leaking from transmission.
4. Before installing, check U-joints for freedom of movement. If a bind has resulted from misalignment after overhauling the U-joints, tap the ears of the drive shaft sharply to relieve the bind.
5. If rubber seal installed on end of transmission extension housing is damaged, install a new seal.
6. Lubricate yoke spline with special spline lubricant. *This spline is sealed so that transmission fluid does not "wash" away spline lubricant.*
7. Install yoke on transmission output shaft.
8. Align marks on driveshaft and pinion flange, then install U-bolts and nuts which attach U-joint to pinion flange. Tighten U-bolts evenly to prevent binding U-joint bearings.

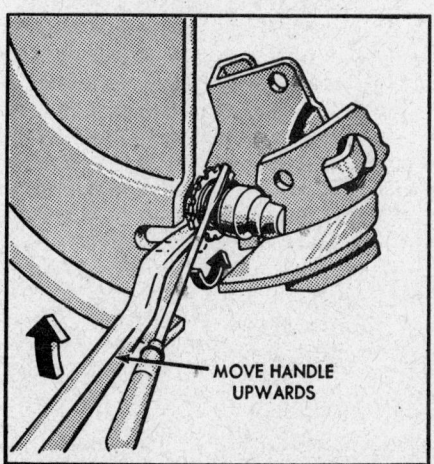

MOVE HANDLE UPWARDS

Fig. 11 Backing off brake adjustment by disengaging adjusting lever with screwdriver

BRAKE ADJUSTMENTS

1. Use the brake shoe adjustment gauge shown in Fig. 9 to obtain the drum inside diameter as shown. Tighten the adjusting knob on the gauge to hold this setting.
2. Place the opposite side of the gauge over the brake shoes and adjust the shoes by turning the adjuster screw until the gauge just slides over the linings. Rotate the gauge around the lining surface to assure proper lining diameter adjustment and clearance.
3. Install brake drum and wheel. Final adjustment is accomplished by making several firm reverse stops, using the brake pedal.

Self-Adjusting Brakes

These brakes, Fig. 10, have self-adjusting shoe mechanisms that assure correct lining-to-drum clearances at all times. The automatic adjusters operate only when the brakes are applied as the car is moving rearward.

Although the brakes are self-adjusting, an initial adjustment is necessary after the brake shoes have been relined or replaced, or when the length of the star wheel adjuster has been changed during some other service operation.

Frequent usage of an automatic transmission forward range to halt reverse vehicle motion may prevent the automatic adjusters from functioning, thereby inducing low pedal heights. Should low pedal heights be encountered, it is recommended that numerous forward and reverse stops be performed with a firm pedal effort until satisfactory pedal height is obtained.

NOTE: If a low pedal height condition cannot be corrected by making numerous reverse stops (provided the hydraulic system is free of air), it indicates that the self-adjusting mechanism is not functioning. Therefore, it will be necessary to remove the brake drums, clean, free up and lubricate the adjusting mechanism. Then adjust the brakes, being sure the parking brake is fully released.

Initial Adjustment

1. Remove adjusting hole cover from brake backing plate and, from the backing plate side, turn the adjusting screw upward

with a screwdriver or other suitable tool to expand the shoes until a slight drag is felt when the drums are rotated.
2. Remove the drum.
3. While holding the adjusting lever out of engagement with the adjusting screw, Fig. 11, back off the adjusting screw about one full turn with the fingers.

NOTE: *If finger movement will not turn the screw, free it up. If this is not done, the adjusting lever will not turn the screw during vehicle operation. Lubricate the screw with oil and coat with wheel bearing grease. Any other adjustment procedure may cause damage to the adjusting screw with consequent self-adjuster problems.*

4. Install wheel and drum, and adjusting hole cover. Adjust brakes on remaining wheels in the same manner.
5. If pedal height is not satisfactory, drive the vehicle and make sufficient reverse stops with a firm pedal effort until proper pedal height is obtained.

PARKING BRAKE, ADJUST

Check parking brake cables when brakes

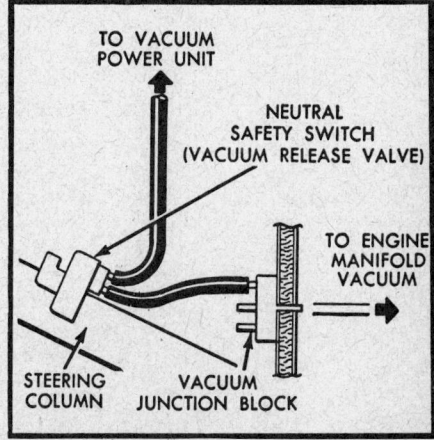

TO VACUUM POWER UNIT

NEUTRAL SAFETY SWITCH (VACUUM RELEASE VALVE)

TO ENGINE MANIFOLD VACUUM

STEERING COLUMN

VACUUM JUNCTION BLOCK

Fig. 12 Connections for automatic parking brake release. Typical

are fully released. If cables are loose, adjust as follows:

1977–84 Rear Drum Brakes
1. Make sure parking brake is released.
2. Place transmission in neutral and raise the vehicle.
3. Tighten the adjusting nut against the cable equalizer to cause rear brakes to drag.
4. Then loosen the adjusting nut until the rear wheels are fully released. There should be no drag.
5. Lower vehicle and check operation.

1977–78 Rear Disc Brakes
1. Fully release parking brake, then place transmission in neutral and support vehicle at rear axle.
2. Tighten adjuster nut until levers on calipers just begin to move, then loosen adjuster nut until levers just return to stop position.
3. Apply and release parking brake. Check levers on caliper to determine if they are fully returned by attempting to pull lever rearward. If lever moves, the adjustment is too tight and must be readjusted.

VACUUM RELEASE PARKING BRAKE

The vacuum power unit will release the parking brakes automatically when the shift lever is moved into any drive position with the engine running. The brakes will not release automatically, however, when the shift lever is in neutral or park position with the engine running, or in any position with the engine off.

The power unit piston rod is attached to the release lever. Since the release lever pivots against the pawl, a slight movement of the release lever will disengage the pawl from the ratchet, allowing the brakes to release. The release lever pivots on a rivet pin in the pedal mount.

As shown in Fig. 12, hoses connect the power unit and the engine manifold to a vacuum release valve in the transmission neutral safety switch. Moving the transmission selector lever into any drive position with the engine running will open the release valve to connect engine manifold vacuum to one side of the actuating piston in the power unit. The pressure differential thus created will cause the piston and link to pull the release lever.

MASTER CYLINDER, REPLACE

1. Disconnect brake lines from master cylinder.
2. Remove nuts retaining master cylinder to brake booster.
3. Remove master cylinder.
4. Reverse procedure to install.

HYDRO-BOOST BRAKE BOOSTER, REPLACE

1. Working from inside of car under instrument panel, disconnect booster push rod link from brake pedal. To do this, proceed as follows:
2. Disconnect stop light switch wires at connector. Remove hairpin retainer. Slide switch off brake pedal pin just far enough for switch outer hole to clear pin. Then lift switch straight upward from pin. Slide master cylinder push rod and nylon washers and bushing off brake pedal pin.
3. Open hood and disconnect brake line at master cylinder outlet fitting.
4. Disconnect the pressure, steering gear and return lines, then plug lines and ports.
5. Remove Hydro-Boost to dash panel nuts and remove assembly from panel, sliding push rod link from engine side of dash panel.
6. Reverse procedure to install. To purge system, disconnect coil wire so that engine will not start. Fill power steering pump reservoir, then while engaging starter, pump brake pedal. Do not cycle steering wheel until all residual air has been purged from the hydro boost unit. Check fluid level, then connect coil wire and start engine. Apply brakes with a pumping action and cycle steering wheel, then check system for leaks.

VACUUM BRAKE BOOSTER, REPLACE

1. Disconnect battery ground cable.
2. Disconnect master cylinder from booster and position aside.

NOTE: It is not necessary to disconnect brake lines, but care should be taken to avoid twisting or kinking lines.

3. Disconnect manifold vacuum hose from booster check valve.
4. Working inside vehicle, disconnect stop lamp switch electrical connector under instrument panel.
5. Remove stop lamp switch retaining pin. Slide switch off brake pedal pin enough so outer plate of switch clears the pin, then remove switch from pin.
6. Remove booster-to-dash panel attaching screws.
7. Slide booster pushrod, nylon washers and bushing off brake pedal pin.
8. Slide pushrod out from engine side of dash panel and remove booster from vehicle.
9. Reverse procedure to install.

Rear Suspension

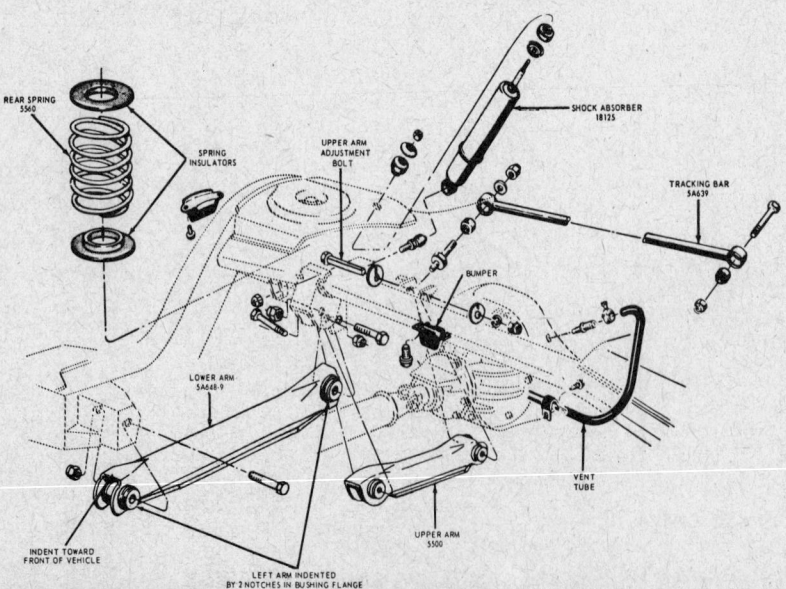

Fig. 1 Rear suspension (typical). 1977–78

SHOCK ABSORBER, REPLACE

1. With the rear axle supported properly disconnect shock absorber at upper mounting and compress it to clear hole in spring seat.
2. Disconnect shock absorber from stud on axle bracket.
3. Reverse procedure to install.

COIL SPRING, REPLACE

1. Raise rear of vehicle and support at frame. Support rear axle with a suitable jack.
2. Disconnect shock absorbers at lower mountings.
3. Disconnect brake line from rear brake hose and remove hose to bracket clip.
4. Lower axle to remove springs.

NOTE: On some models, it may be necessary to disconnect the right hand parking brake cable from right hand upper arm retainer before lowering axle.

5. Reverse procedure to install. Install an insulator between upper and lower seats and the spring on 1977–78 models and between upper seat and spring on 1979–84 models.

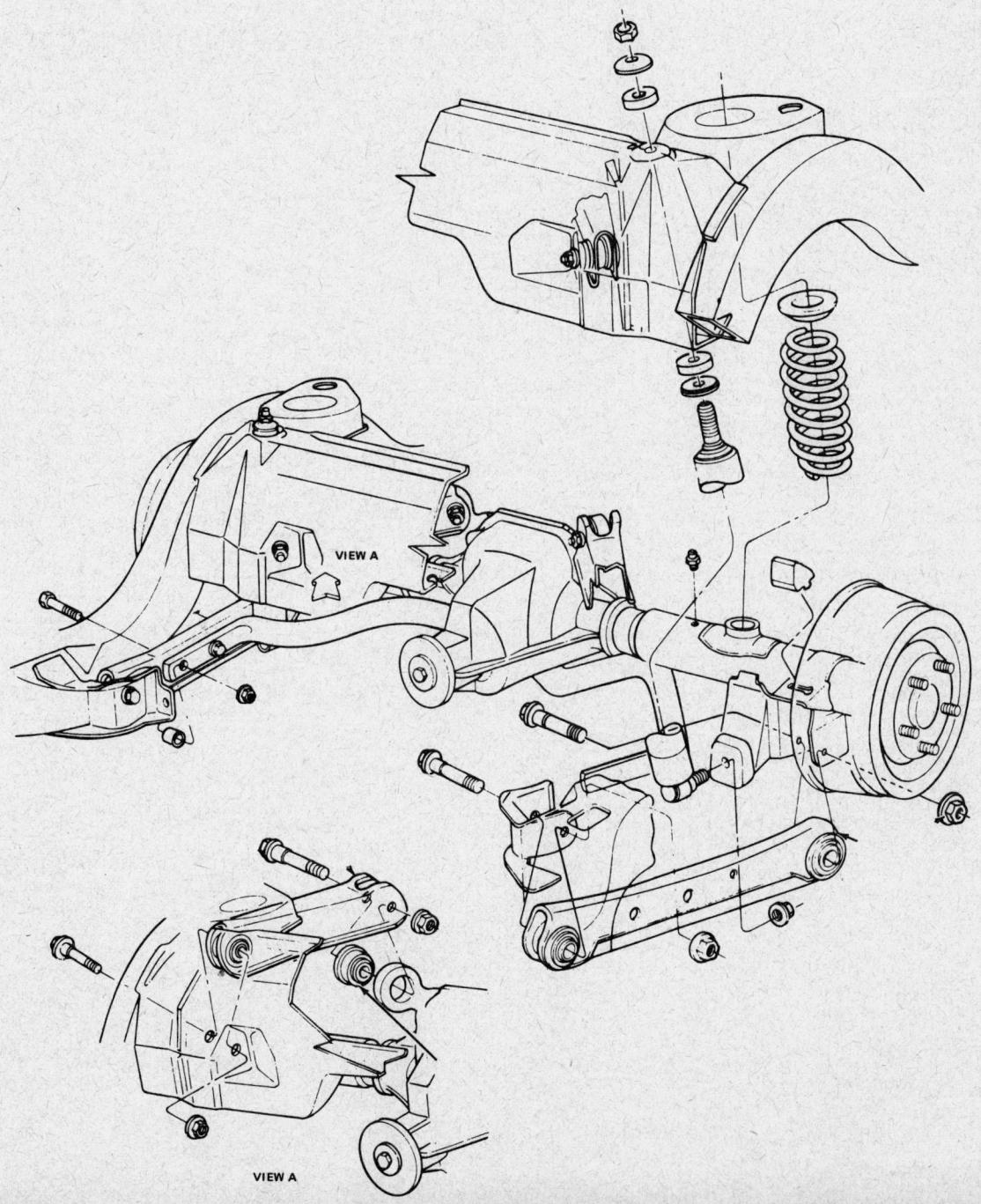

Fig. 2 Rear suspension. 1979–84

CONTROL ARMS, REPLACE

NOTE: Control arms must be replaced in pairs.

1. Raise rear of vehicle and support at frame. Support axle with a suitable jack.
2. On 1977–78 models, disconnect track bar from frame mounting bracket.
3. On 1979–84 models, remove stabilizer bar.
4. Lower axle and install a second jack under differential pinion nose.
5. On 1979–84 models, disconnect parking brake cable from upper arm retainer.
6. Disconnect control arm from axle bracket. On upper arms, disconnect arm from crossmember and on lower arms, disconnect arm from frame attachment bracket.
7. Reverse procedure to install.

TRACK BAR, REPLACE

1977–78
1. Remove cover from track bar axle attachment and disconnect track bar from mounting stud, Fig. 1.
2. Disconnect track bar from frame side rail.
3. Reverse procedure to install.

STABILIZER BAR, REPLACE

1979–84
1. Raise and support vehicle at frame side rails.
2. Support rear axle with a suitable jack and position axle so the shock absorbers are fully extended.
3. Remove bolts, nuts and spacers attaching stabilizer bar to lower arms, Fig. 2.
4. Remove stabilizer bar from vehicle.
5. Reverse procedure to install.

Front Suspension & Steering Section

FRONT SUSPENSION

1979–84

Referring to Fig. 1, note that the lower control arms pivot on two bolts and bushings attached to the crossmember. Previous models used only one bolt and bushing to attach the lower control arm to the suspension crossmember.

1977–78

Referring to Fig. 2, note that the lower control arm pivots on a bolt in the front crossmember. The struts, which are connected between the lower control arms and frame crossmember, prevent the control arms from moving forward and backward.

WHEEL ALIGNMENT

SERVICE BULLETIN

WHEEL BALANCING DIFFERS: On cars with disc brakes, dynamic balancing of the wheel-and-tire assembly on the car should not be attempted without first pulling back the shoe and lining assemblies from the rotor. If this is not done, brake drag may burn out the motor on the wheel spinner.

The drag can be eliminated by removing the wheel, taking out the two bolts holding the caliper splash shield, and detaching the shield. Then push the pistons into their cylinder bores by applying steady pressure on the shoes on each side of the rotor for at least a minute. If necessary, use waterpump pliers to apply the pressure.

After the pistons have been retracted, reinstall the splash shield and wheel. The wheel-and-tire assembly can then be dynamically balanced in the usual way. After the balancing job has been completed, be sure to pump the brake pedal several times until the shoes are seated and a firm brake pedal is obtained.

Caster and camber can be adjusted by loosening the bolts that attach the upper suspension arm to the shaft at the frame side rail, and moving the arm assembly in or out in the elongated bolt holes, Figs. 3 and 3A. Since any movement of the arm affects both caster and camber, both factors should be balanced against one another when making the adjustment.

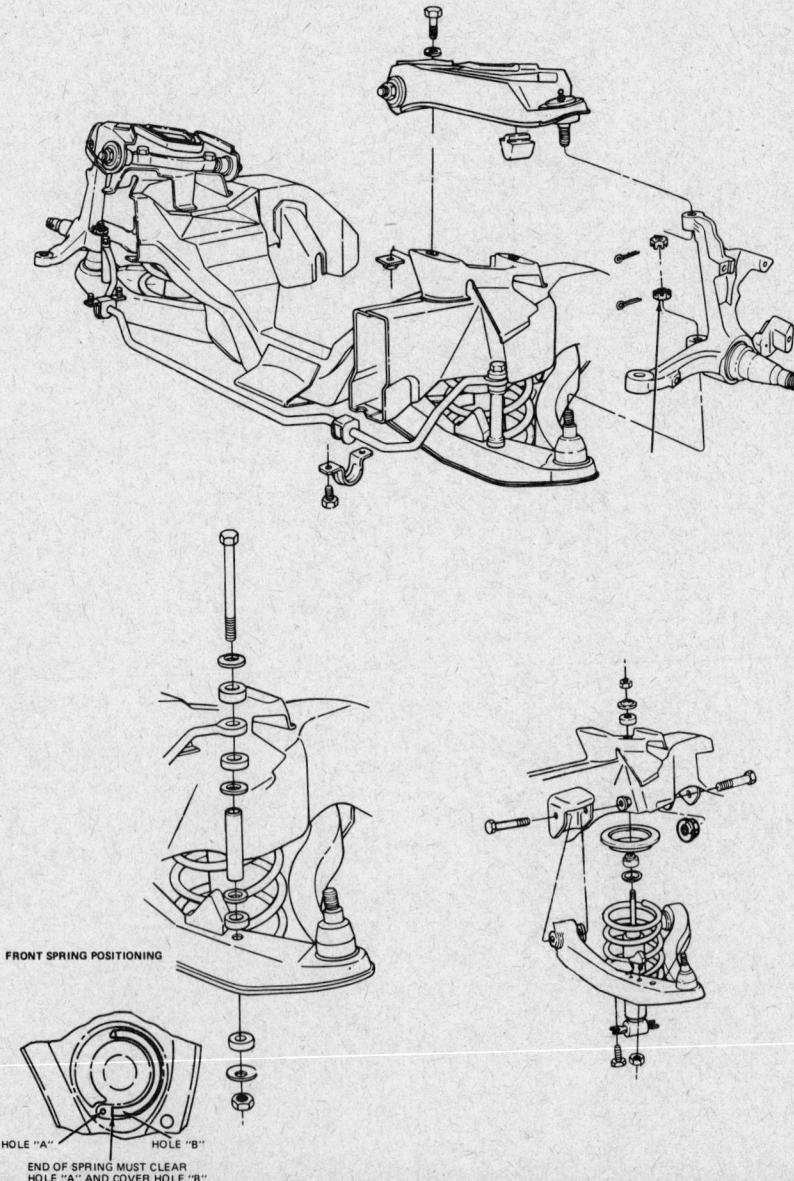

FRONT SPRING POSITIONING

HOLE "A"   HOLE "B"
END OF SPRING MUST CLEAR
HOLE "A" AND COVER HOLE "B"

Fig. 1 Front suspension. 1979–84

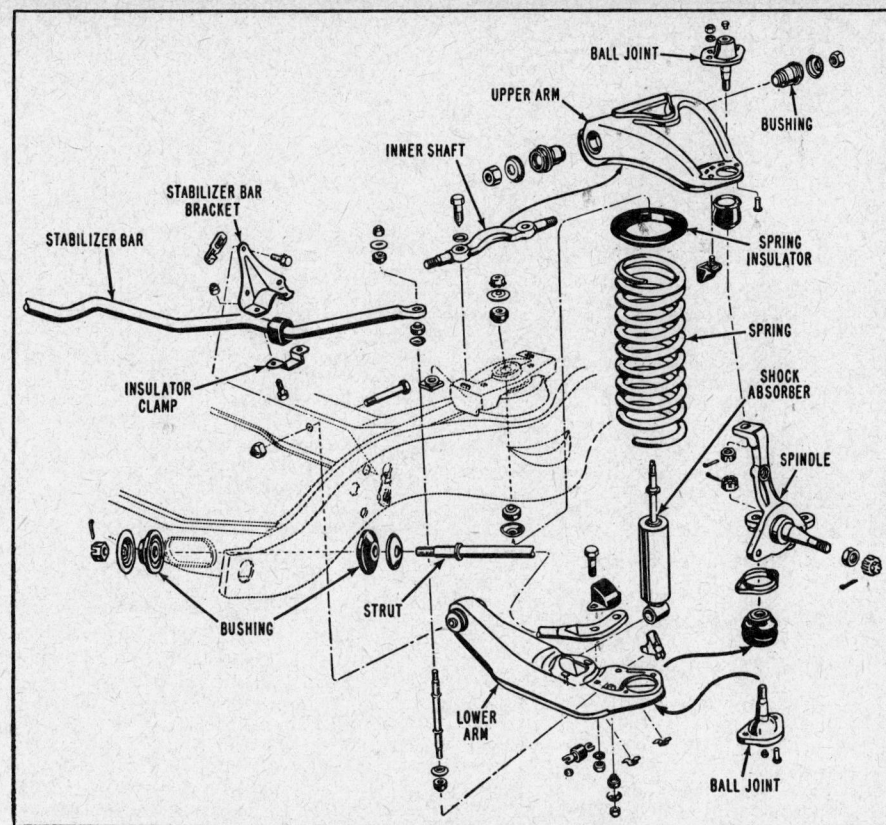

Fig. 2 Front suspension. 1977–78

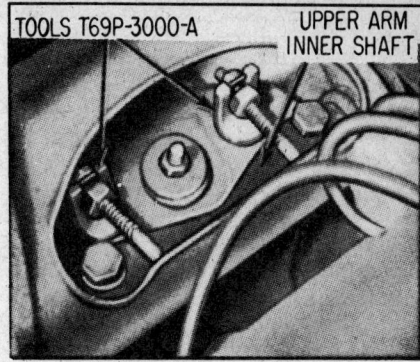

Fig. 3 Adjusting caster & camber. 1977–78

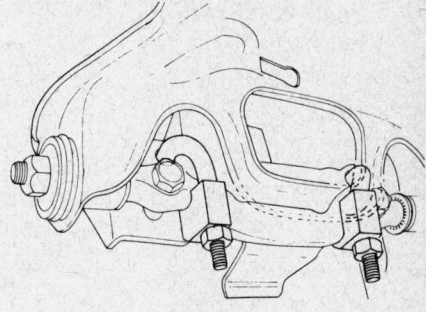

Fig. 3A Adjusting caster & camber. 1979–84

NOTE: On 1977–78 models, use alignment tool T69P-3000A, Fig. 3. On 1979–84 models, use alignment tool T79P-3000A, Fig. 3A. Install the tool with the pins in the frame holes and the hooks over the upper arm inner shaft. Tighten the hook nuts snug before loosening the upper arm inner shaft attaching bolts.

Caster, Adjust
1. Tighten the tool front hook nut or loosen the rear hook nut as required to increase caster to the desired angle.
2. To decrease caster, tighten the rear hook nut or loosen the front hook nut as required.

NOTE: The caster angle can be checked without tightening the inner shaft retaining bolts.

3. Check the camber angle to be sure it did not change during the caster adjustment and adjust if necessary.
4. Torque the upper arm inner shaft retaining bolts to 120–140 ft. lbs. and remove tool.

Camber, Adjust
1. Loosen both inner shaft retaining bolts.
2. Tighten or loosen the hook nuts as necessary to increase or decrease camber.
3. Recheck caster and readjust if necessary.
4. Torque upper arm inner shaft retaining bolts to 120–140 ft. lbs.

TOE-IN, ADJUST

Position the front wheels in their straight-ahead position. Then turn both tie rod adjusting sleeves an equal amount until the desired toe-in setting is obtained. Torque tie rod sleeve clamp bolt to 20–22 ft. lbs.

WHEEL BEARINGS, ADJUST

1. Raise and support vehicle so front wheels are free to turn.
2. Remove wheel cover, then the grease cap from hub.
3. Clean excess grease from end of spindle, then remove cotter pin and nut lock.
4. Back off adjusting nut three turns, then rock wheel assembly in and out several times to push shoe and linings away from rotor.
5. Torque adjusting nut to 17–25 ft. lbs. while rotating the wheel assembly.
6. Back off adjusting nut ½ turn, then retighten nut to 10–15 inch lbs.
7. Install nut lock on nut so castellations on lock are aligned with cotter pin hole in spindle, then install cotter pin.
8. Check wheel rotation. If wheel rotates roughly or makes noise, lubricate or replace bearings as necessary.

WHEEL BEARINGS, REPLACE

1. Raise and support front of vehicle, then remove tire and wheel assemblies.
2. Remove caliper mounting bolts.

NOTE: It is not necessary to disconnect the brake lines for this operation.

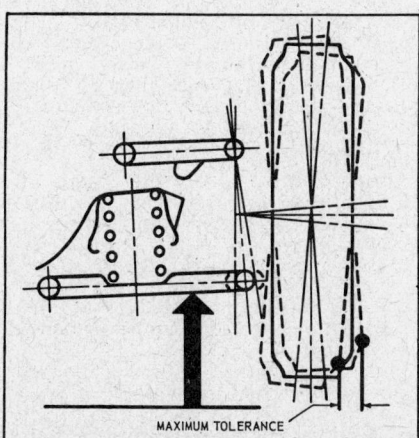

Fig. 4 Measuring lower ball joint radial play, which should not exceed ¼"

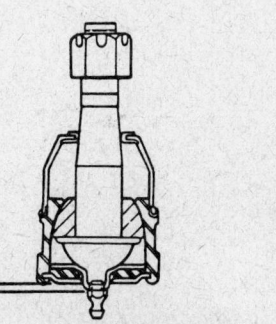

Fig. 5 Lower ball joint wear indicators. 1979–84

3. Slide caliper off of disc, inserting a spacer between the shoes to hold them in their bores after the caliper is removed. Position caliper assembly out of the way.

NOTE: Do not allow caliper to hang by brake hose.

4. Remove hub and disc assembly. Grease retainer and inner bearing can now be removed.
5. Reverse procedure to install.

CHECKING BALL JOINTS FOR WEAR

Upper Ball Joint

1. Raise car on floor jacks placed beneath lower control arms.
2. Grasp lower edge of tire and move wheel in and out.
3. As wheel is being moved in and out, observe upper end of spindle and upper arm.
4. Any movement between upper end of spindle and upper arm indicates ball joint wear and loss of preload. If any such movement is observed, replace upper ball joint.

NOTE: During the foregoing check, the lower ball joint will be unloaded and may move. Disregard all such movement of the lower ball joint. Also, do not mistake loose wheel bearings for a worn ball joint.

Lower Ball Joint

1977–78
1. Raise car on jacks placed under lower control arms as shown in Fig. 4. This will unload ball joints.
2. Adjust wheel bearings.
3. Attach a dial indicator to lower control arm and position so that its plunger rests against the inner side of the wheel rim adjacent to the lower ball joint.
4. Grasp tire at top and bottom and slowly move it in and out as shown in Fig. 4.
5. If reading on dial indicator exceeds 1/4", replace lower ball joint.

1979–84
These models are equipped with lower ball joint wear indicators, Fig. 5. To check ball joint for wear, support vehicle in normal driving position with both ball joints loaded. Observe the checking surface of the ball joint. If the checking surface is inside the cover, Fig. 5, replace the ball joint.

SHOCK ABSORBER, REPLACE

1. Remove nut, washer and bushing from shock absorber upper end.
2. Raise vehicle and install safety stands.
3. Remove two thread-cutting screws from lower end of shock absorber, then remove shock absorber.
4. Reverse procedure to install.

NOTE: If threads in lower arm become damaged, re-use original thread-cutting screws along with 5/16-18 locknuts.

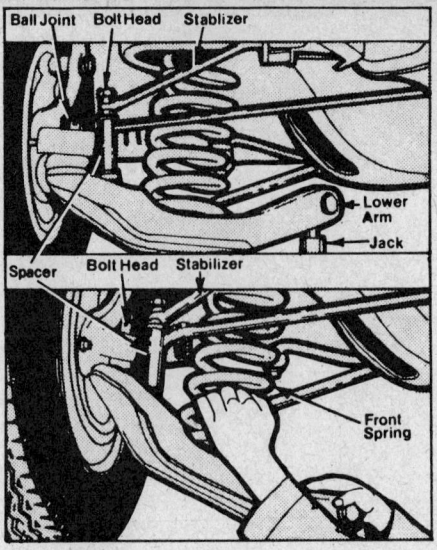

Fig. 6   Replacing coil spring. 1977–78

COIL SPRING, REPLACE

1979–84

1. Raise and support vehicle.
2. Remove wheel.
3. Disconnect stabilizer bar link from lower control arm.
4. Remove shock absorber.
5. Remove steering center link from pitman arm.
6. Compress coil spring with a suitable spring compressor, tool D-78P-5310-A or equivalent.
7. Remove two lower control arm pivot bolts and disengage arm from crossmember.
8. Remove spring from vehicle.
9. Reverse procedure to install. Torque stabilizer bar to lower control arm nuts to 9–12 ft. lbs. Torque lower control arm to crossmember bolts to 120–140 ft. lbs.

1977–78

1. Raise vehicle and support front end of frame with jack stands.
2. Disconnect shock absorber from lower arm, collapse shock absorber into the spring and place a jack under the lower arm for support, Fig. 6.
3. Remove strut and rebound bumper bolts and disconnect lower end of sway bar stud from lower arm.
4. Remove the nut and bolt retaining the inner end of the lower arm to the crossmember.
5. Carefully lower jack to relieve spring pressure on lower arm, then remove the spring.
6. Reverse procedure to install.

BALL JOINTS, REPLACE

NOTE: Ford Motor Company recommends that new ball joints should not be installed on used control arms and that the control arm be replaced if ball joint replacement is required. However, aftermarket ball joint repair kits which do not require control arm replacement, are available and can be installed using the following procedure.

The ball joints are riveted to the upper and lower control arms. The ball joints can be replaced on the car by removing the rivets and

retaining the new ball joint to the control arm with the attaching bolts, nuts and washers furnished with the ball joint kit.

When removing a ball joint, use a suitable pressing tool to force the ball joint out of the spindle.

POWER STEERING GEAR, REPLACE

1. Remove stone shield, if equipped.
2. Disconnect pressure and return lines from steering gear. Plug lines and ports in gear to prevent entry of dirt.
3. Remove two bolts that secure flex coupling to steering gear and to column.
4. Raise car and remove sector shaft nut.
5. Use a puller to remove pitman arm.
6. Support steering gear, then remove attaching bolts.
7. Work steering gear free of flex coupling and remove it from car.
8. Reverse procedure to install.

POWER STEERING PUMP, REPLACE

1978–84 Models

1. Disconnect power steering pump return line and allow power steering pump fluid to drain into a suitable container.
2. Disconnect power steering pump pressure hose from pump fitting.
3. On 1978–79 models, remove power steering pump mounting bracket attaching bolts, then disconnect drive belt from pulley and remove pump, pulley and mounting bracket as an assembly.
4. On 1980–84 models, disconnect drive belt from power steering pump pulley, remove pulley, then remove pump.
5. Reverse procedure to install. Torque pump to mounting bracket bolts to 30–45 ft. lbs.

NOTE: On Ford model CII power steering pump, torque pressure hose to pump fitting to 10–15 ft. lbs. End play on this fitting is normal and does not indicate a loose fitting.

1977 Models

Ford/TRW Pump
1. Disconnect power steering pump return line and allow power steering fluid to drain into a suitable container.
2. Disconnect pressure line from power steering pump.
3. Remove bolts from front of pump and nut at rear of pump attaching pump to mounting bracket, then disconnect drive belt from pulley and remove pump.
4. Reverse procedure to install. Torque pump to mounting bracket nut to 20–30 ft. lbs. and mounting bracket to pump bolts to 30–45 ft. lbs.

Saginaw Pump
1. Disconnect pressure and return lines from power steering pump, then cap lines and fittings.
2. Loosen power steering pump adjusting bracket nut, then remove bolts attaching power steering pump mounting bracket to A/C compressor mounting bracket, if equipped.
3. Disconnect drive belt from pulley, then remove power steering pump and bracket as an assembly.
4. Reverse procedure to install. Torque pump to mounting bracket nuts to 30–45 ft. lbs.

FORD & MERCURY
Compact & Intermediate Models

> **NOTE:** The 1977–84 Ford Mustang, Pinto, Mercury Bobcat and 1979–84 Capri are located elsewhere in this manual. Refer to the front of this manual for vehicle manufacturer's special service tool suppliers.

INDEX OF SERVICE OPERATIONS

ENGINE & SERIAL NUMBER LOCATION:

Engine code is fifth digit of serial number on 1977–80 models, or eighth digit of serial number on 1981–84 models. The serial number is stamped on a metal tag located on top left side dash and visible through windshield.

GRILLE IDENTIFICATION

1977 Comet

1977 Granada

1977 Maverick

1977 Monarch

1977 LTD II

1977 Thunderbird

1977–79 Cougar

1977–79 Cougar XR-7

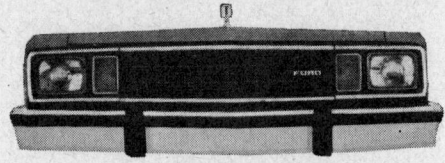

1978 Fairmont European Sport Option (ESO)

1978 Thunderbird

1978–79 LTD II

1978–80 Granada

1978–80 Monarch

1978–81 Fairmont

1978–81 Fairmont Futura

1978–83 Zephyr

1979 Thunderbird

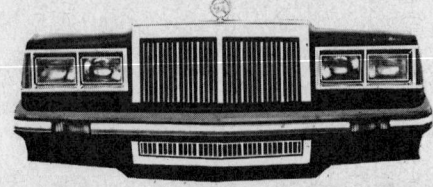

1980 Cougar

GRILLE IDENTIFICATION—Continued

1980 Thunderbird

1981 Cougar & 1982 Cougar Sta. Wag.

1981 Granada

1981—82 Thunderbird

1982 Cougar Exc. Sta. Wag.

1982 Granada

1982—83 Fairmont

1983—84 Cougar

1983—84 Ford LTD

1983—84 Mercury Marquis

1983—84 Thunderbird

GENERAL ENGINE SPECIFICATIONS

Year	Engine CID①/Liter	V.I.N. Code②	Carburetor	Bore and Stroke	Compression Ratio	Net H.P. @ R.P.M.③	Maximum Torque Ft. Lbs. @ R.P.M.	Normal Oil Pressure Pounds
1977	6-200, 3.3L④⑦	T	YFA, 1 Bbl.⑥	3.68 × 3.13	8.5	96 @ 4400	151 @ 2000	30—50
	6-200, 3.3L④⑤	T	YFA, 1 Bbl.⑥	3.68 × 3.13	8.5	97 @ 4400	153 @ 2000	30—50
	6-250, 4.1L⑤⑧	L	YFA, 1 Bbl.⑥	3.68 × 3.91	8.1	86 @ 3000	185 @ 1800	40—60
	6-250, 4.1L④⑤	L	YFA, 1 Bbl.⑥	3.68 × 3.91	8.1	98 @ 3600	190 @ 1400	40—60
	6-250, 4.1L④⑦	L	YFA, 1 Bbl.⑥	3.68 × 3.91	8.1	98 @ 3400	182 @ 1800	40—60
	V8-302, 5.0L⑤⑧	F	2700VV, 2 Bbl.⑪	4.00 × 3.00	8.1	122 @ 3400	222 @ 1400	40—65
	V8-302, 5.0L④⑦⑨	F	2150, 2 Bbl.⑪	4.00 × 3.00	8.4	122 @ 3200	237 @ 1600	40—65
	V8-302, 5.0L⑯⑰⑮	F	2150, 2 Bbl.⑪	4.00 × 3.00	8.4	130 @ 3400	243 @ 1800	40—65
	V8-302, 5.0L④⑤⑨	F	2150, 2 Bbl.⑪	4.00 × 3.00	8.4	134 @ 3600	245 @ 1600	40—65
	V8-302, 5.0L④⑤⑩	F	2150, 2 Bbl.⑪	4.00 × 3.00	8.4	137 @ 3600	245 @ 1600	40—65
	V8-351W, 5.8L④⑤⑨⑬	H	2150, 2 Bbl.⑪	4.00 × 3.50	8.3	135 @ 3200	275 @ 1600	40—65
	V8-351W, 5.8L④⑤⑬⑰⑮	H	2150, 2 Bbl.⑪	4.00 × 3.50	8.3	149 @ 3200	291 @ 1600	40—65
	V8-351M, 5.8L④⑤⑭⑰⑮	H	2150, 2 Bbl.⑪	4.00 × 3.50	8.0	161 @ 3600	285 @ 1800	50—75
	V8-351M, 5.8L⑤⑧⑭⑰⑮	H	2150, 2 Bbl.⑪	4.00 × 3.50	8.0	161 @ 3600	286 @ 1800	50—75
	V8-400, 6.6L④⑤⑰⑮	S	2150, 2 Bbl.⑪	4.00 × 4.00	8.0	173 @ 3800	326 @ 1600	50—75
	V8-400, 6.6L⑤⑧⑰⑮	S	2150, 2 Bbl.⑪	4.00 × 4.00	8.0	168 @ 3800	323 @ 1600	50—75

Continued

GENERAL ENGINE SPECIFICATIONS—Continued

Year	Engine CID①/Liter	V.I.N. Code②	Carburetor	Bore and Stroke	Compression Ratio	Net H.P. @ R.P.M.③	Maximum Torque Lbs. Ft. @ R.P.M.	Normal Oil Pressure Pounds
1978	4-140, 2.3L	Y	5200, 2 Bbl.⑪	3.781 × 3.126	9.0	88 @ 4800	118 @ 2800	50
	6-200, 3.3L	T	YFA, 1 Bbl.⑥⑱	3.68 × 3.13	8.5	85 @ 3600	250 @ 1600	30–50
	6-250, 4.1L	L	YFA, 1 Bbl.⑥	3.68 × 3.91	8.5	97 @ 3200	210 @ 1400	40–60
	V8-302, 5.0L⑧⑨⑲	F	2700VV, 2 Bbl.⑪	4.00 × 3.00	8.1	133 @ 3600	243 @ 1600	40–60
	V8-302, 5.0L④⑰	F	2150, 2 Bbl.⑪	4.00 × 3.00	8.4	134 @ 3400	248 @ 1600	40–60
	V8-302, 5.0L④⑨⑲⑮	F	2150, 2 Bbl.⑪	4.00 × 3.00	8.4	139 @ 3600	250 @ 1600	40–60
	V8-351, 5.8L⑬	H	2150, 2 Bbl.⑪	4.00 × 3.50	8.3	144 @ 3200	277 @ 1600	40–60
	V8-351, 5.8L⑭	H	2150, 2 Bbl.⑪	4.00 × 3.50	8.0	152 @ 3600	278 @ 1800	50–75
	V8-400, 6.6L	S	2150, 2 Bbl.⑪	4.00 × 4.00	8.0	166 @ 3800	319 @ 1800	50–75
1979	4-140, 2.3L	Y	5200, 2 Bbl.⑪	3.781 × 3.126	9.0	88 @ 4800	118 @ 2800	40–60
	6-200, 3.3L	T	YFA, 1 Bbl.⑥⑱	3.68 × 3.13	8.5	85 @ 3600	154 @ 1600	30–50
	6-250, 4.1L	L	YFA, 1 Bbl.⑥	3.68 × 3.91	8.6	97 @ 3200	210 @ 1400	40–60
	V8-302, 5.0L④⑰⑮	F	2150, 2 Bbl.⑪	4.00 × 3.00	8.4	133 @ 3400	245 @ 1600	40–65
	V8-302, 5.0L④⑨	F	2150, 2 Bbl.⑪	4.00 × 3.00	8.4	137 @ 3600	243 @ 2000	40–65
	V8-302, 5.0L⑧⑨	F	2700VV, 2 Bbl.⑪	4.00 × 3.00	8.4	138 @ 3800	239 @ 2200	40–65
	V8-302, 5.0L④⑲	F	2150, 2 Bbl.⑪	4.00 × 3.00	8.4	140 @ 3600	250 @ 1800	40–65
	V8-302, 5.0L⑧⑲	F	2700VV, 2 Bbl.⑪	4.00 × 3.00	8.4	143 @ 3600	243 @ 2200	40–65
	V8-351W, 5.8L④⑬⑯	H	2150, 2 Bbl.⑪	4.00 × 3.50	8.3	135 @ 3200	286 @ 1400	40–65
	V8-351W, 5.8L⑧⑬⑰	H	2150, 2 Bbl.⑪	4.00 × 3.50	8.0	149 @ 3800	258 @ 2200	50–75
	V8-351M, 5.8L④⑭⑰	H	2150, 2 Bbl.⑪	4.00 × 3.50	8.0	151 @ 3600	270 @ 2200	50–75
1980	4-140, 2.3L④⑳	A	5200, 2 Bbl.⑪	3.781 × 3.126	9.0	88 @ 4600	119 @ 2600	40–60
	4-140, 2.3L⑧⑳	A	6500, 2 Bbl.⑫	3.781 × 3.126	9.0	89 @ 4800	122 @ 2600	40–60
	4-140, 2.3L④㉑	A	5200, 2 Bbl.⑫	3.781 × 3.126	9.0	—	—	40–60
	4-140, 2.3L⑧㉑	A	6500, 2 Bbl.⑫	3.781 × 3.126	9.0	—	—	40–60
	6-200, 3.3L④	B	1946, 1 Bbl.⑫	3.68 × 3.13	8.6	91 @ 3800	160 @ 1600	30–50
	6-200, 3.3L⑧	B	1946C, 1 Bbl.⑫	3.68 × 3.13	8.6	—	—	30–50
	6-250, 4.1L④⑨	C	YFA, 1 Bbl.⑥	3.68 × 3.91	8.6	90 @ 3200	194 @ 1660	40–60
	V8-255, 4.2L⑲	D	2150, 2 Bbl.⑪	3.68 × 3.00	8.8	119 @ 3800	194 @ 2200	40–60
	V8-255, 4.2L⑯⑮	D	2150, 2 Bbl.⑪	3.68 × 3.00	8.8	115 @ 3800	191 @ 2000	40–60
	V8-255, 4.2L⑧⑨	D	2150, 2 Bbl.⑪	3.68 × 3.00	8.8	117 @ 3800	193 @ 2000	40–60
	V8-302, 5.0L⑨	F	2150, 2 Bbl.⑪	4.00 × 3.00	8.4	134 @ 3600	232 @ 1600	40–60
	V8-302, 5.0L④⑯⑮	F	2150, 2 Bbl.⑪	4.00 × 3.00	8.4	131 @ 3600	231 @ 1600	40–60
	V8-302, 5.0L⑧⑯⑮	F	2150, 2 Bbl.⑪	4.00 × 3.00	8.4	132 @ 3600	232 @ 1400	40–60
1981	4-140, 2.3L	A	6500, 2 Bbl.⑫	3.781 × 3.126	9.0	88 @ 4600	118 @ 2600	40–60
	6-200, 3.3L	B	1946, 1 Bbl.⑫	3.68 × 3.13	8.6	88 @ 3800	154 @ 1400	30–50
	V8-255, 4.2L④	D	2150, 2 Bbl.⑪	3.68 × 3.00	8.2	115 @ 3400	195 @ 2200	40–60
	V8-255, 4.2L⑧	D	7200VV, 2 Bbl.⑪	3.68 × 3.00	8.2	120 @ 3400	205 @ 2600	40–60
	V8-302, 5.0L④	F	2150, 2 Bbl.⑪	4.00 × 3.00	8.4	130 @ 3400	235 @ 1600	40–60
	V8-302, 5.0L⑧	F	7200VV, 2 Bbl.⑪	4.00 × 3.00	8.4	130 @ 3400	235 @ 1800	40–60
1982	4-140, 2.3L	A	6500, 2 Bbl.⑫	3.781 × 3.126	9.0	86 @ 4600	117 @ 2600	40–60
	6-200, 3.3L	B	1946, 1 Bbl.⑫	3.68 × 3.13	8.6	87 @ 3800	154 @ 1400	30–50
	V6-232, 3.8L④	3	2150, 2 Bbl.⑪	3.81 × 3.39	8.8	112 @ 4000	175 @ 2600	54–59
	V6-232, 3.8L⑧	3	7200VV, 2 Bbl.⑪	3.81 × 3.39	8.8	118 @ 4000	186 @ 2600	54–59
	V8-255, 4.2L④	D	2150, 2 Bbl.⑪	3.68 × 3.00	8.2	122 @ 3400	209 @ 2400	40–60
	V8-255, 4.2L⑧	D	7200VV, 2 Bbl.⑪	3.68 × 3.00	—	—	—	40–60
1983	4-140, 2.3L⑳	A	YFA, 1 Bbl.⑥	3.78 × 3.12	9.0	86 @ 4600	117 @ 2600	50
	4-140, 2.3L㉑	W	E.F.I.㉒	3.78 × 3.12	8.0	—	—	55
	6-200, 3.3L	X	1946, 1 Bbl.⑫	3.68 × 3.12	8.6	87 @ 3800	154 @ 1400	50
	V6-232, 3.8L	3	2150, 2 Bbl.⑪	3.8 × 3.4	8.7	112 @ 4000	175 @ 2600	40–60
	V8-302, 5.0L	F	E.F.I.㉒	4.00 × 3.00	—	—	—	40–60

Continued

GENERAL ENGINE SPECIFICATIONS—Continued

Year	Engine CID①/Liter	V.I.N. Code②	Carburetor	Bore and Stroke	Compression Ratio	Net H.P. @ R.P.M.③	Maximum Torque Lbs. Ft. @ R.P.M.	Normal Oil Pressure Pounds
1984	4-140, 2.3L⑳	A	YFA, 1Bbl.⑥	3.78 × 3.12	—	—	—	50
	4-140, 2.3L㉑	W	E.F.I.㉒	3.78 × 3.12	—	—	—	55
	V6-232, 3.8L	3	E.F.I.㉒	3.80 × 3.40	—	—	—	40–60
	V8-302, 5.0L	F	E.F.I.㉒	4.00 × 3.00	—	—	—	40–60

①—CID—cubic inch displacement.
②—On 1977–80 models, the fifth digit of the V.I.N. denotes engine code. On 1981–84 models, the eighth digit of the V.I.N. denotes engine code.
③—Ratings are NET—as installed on vehicle.
④—Except California.
⑤—With auto. trans.
⑥—Carter.
⑦—With manual trans.
⑧—California.
⑨—Granada & Monarch.
⑩—Comet & Maverick.
⑪—Motorcraft.
⑫—Holley.
⑬—Windsor engine.
⑭—Modified engine.
⑮—Thunderbird.
⑯—Cougar XR-7.
⑰—LTD II & Cougar.
⑱—Fairmont & Zephyr with auto. trans., Holley 1946.
⑲—Fairmont & Zephyr.
⑳—Non-Turbocharged.
㉑—Turbocharged.
㉒—Electronic fuel injection.

TUNE UP SPECIFICATIONS

The following specifications are published from the latest information available. This data should be used only in the absence of a decal affixed in the engine compartment.

★ When using a timing light, disconnect vacuum hose or tube at distributor and plug opening in hose or tube so idle speed will not be affected.

● When checking compression, lowest cylinder must be within 75% of the highest.

▲ Before removing wires from distributor cap, determine location of the No. 1 wire in cap, as distributor position may have been altered from that shown at the end of this chart.

☞ Spark plug types shown in this chart are recommendations of the original vehicle manufacturer and not MOTOR.

Check local sources for other spark plug manufacturers listings.

Year & Engine/V.I.N.	Spark Plug Type	Gap	Firing Order Fig. ▲	Ignition Timing BTDC① ★ Man. Trans.	Auto. Trans.	Mark Fig.	Curb Idle Speed② Man. Trans.	Auto. Trans.	Fast Idle Speed Man. Trans.	Auto. Trans.	Fuel Pump Pressure
1977											
6-200/T	BRF-82	.050	F	6°	6°	C	800	650D	1700③	1700③	5–7
6-250/L Exc. Calif.⑫⑬	BRF-82	.050	F	4°	6°	A	⑭	⑮	1700③	1700③	5–7
6-250/L Exc. Calif.⑧⑫⑯	BRF-82	.050	F	TDC	—	A	800	—	1700③	—	5–7
6-250/L Calif.	BRF-82	.050	F	—	8°	A	—	500/600D	—	2100③	5–7
V8-302/F Exc. Calif. & High Alt.⑦	ARF-52	.050	G	—	6°	B	—	700D	—	2100④	6–8
V8-302/F Exc. Calif. & High Alt.⑧	ARF-52	.050	G	6°	2°	B	800	650D	2100④	2100④	6–8
V8-302/F Exc. Calif. & High Alt.⑰	ARF-52	.050	G	—	2°	B	—	500/600D	—	2100④	6–8
V8-302/F Calif.⑦	ARF-52-6	.060	G	—	12°	B	—	500/600D	—	1900④	6–8
V8-302/F High Alt.⑫⑱	ARF-52-6	.060	G	—	12°	B	—	500/600D	—	1900④	6–8
V8-302/F High Alt.⑫⑲	ARF-52	.050	G	—	12°	B	—	500/650D	—	④⑳	6–8
V8-351W/H⑤⑧	ARF-52	.050	H	—	4°	B	—	625D	—	2100④	6–8
V8-351W/H⑤⑫⑰㉑	ARF-52	.050	H	—	14°	B	—	550/625D	—	2100④	6–8
V8-351W/H⑤⑫⑰㉒	ARF-52	.050	H	—	4°	B	—	625D	—	2100④	6–8
V8-351M/H Exc. Calif.⑥⑫⑰㉓	ARF-52	.050	H	—	10°	B	—	650D	—	1350③	6–8
V8-351M/H Exc. Calif.⑥⑫⑰㉔	ARF-52	.050	H	—	9°	B	—	650D	—	1350③	6–8
V8-351M/H Exc. Calif.⑥⑫⑰㉕	ASF-52	.050	H	—	8°	B	—	500/650D	—	1350③	6–8
V8-351M/H Calif.⑥⑫⑰㉖	ARF-52-6	.060	H	—	8°	B	—	500/600D	—	1350③	6–8

Continued

TUNE UP SPECIFICATIONS—Continued

The following specifications are published from the latest information available. This data should be used only in the absence of a decal affixed in the engine compartment.

★ When using a timing light, disconnect vacuum hose or tube at distributor and plug opening in hose or tube so idle speed will not be affected.

● When checking compression, lowest cylinder must be within 75% of the highest.

▲ Before removing wires from distributor cap, determine location of the No. 1 wire in cap, as distributor position may have been altered from that shown at the end of this chart.

☞ Spark plug types shown in this chart are recommendations of the original vehicle manufacturer and not MOTOR.

Check local sources for other spark plug manufacturers listings.

Year & Engine/V.I.N.	Spark Plug		Ignition Timing BTDC① ★				Curb Idle Speed②		Fast Idle Speed		Fuel Pump Pressure
	Type ☞	Gap	Firing Order Fig. ▲	Man. Trans.	Auto. Trans.	Mark Fig.	Man. Trans.	Auto. Trans.	Man. Trans.	Auto. Trans.	
1977—Continued											
V8-351M/H Calif.⑥⑫⑰㉗	ARF-52-6	.060	H	—	6°	B	—	500/600D	—	1350③	6–8
V8-400/S Exc. Calif.⑫⑰㉘	ARF-52	.050	H	—	8°	B	—	600D	—	1350③	6–8
V8-400/S Exc. Calif.⑫⑰㉙	ARF-52	.050	H	—	12°	B	—	600D	—	1350③	6–8
V8-400/S Exc. Calif.⑫⑰㉚	ARF-52	.050	H	—	10°	B	—	600D	—	1350③	6–8
V8-400/S Exc. Calif.⑫⑰㉛	ARF-52	.050	H	—	6°	B	—	600D	—	1350③	6–8
V8-400/S Exc. Calif.⑫⑰㉜	ARF-52	.050	H	—	8°	B	—	500/650D	—	1350③	6–8
V8-400/S Calif.⑰	ARF-52-6	.060	H	—	6°	B	—	500/600D	—	1350③	6–8
1978											
4-140/Y	AWSF-42	.034	D	6°	20°	E	850	800D	1600③	2000④	5–7㉝
6-200/T Exc. Calif. & High Alt.	BSF-82	.050	F	10°	10°	C	800	650D	1700③	1700③	5–7
6-200/T Calif.	BSF-82	.050	F	—	6°	C	—	650D	—	1700③	5–7
6-200/T High Alt.⑫㉞	BSF-82	.050	F	—	12°	C	—	650D	—	1700③	5–7
6-200/T High Alt.⑫㉟	BSF-82	.050	F	—	10°	C	—	650D	—	1700③	5–7
6-250/L Exc. Calif.	BSF-82	.050	F	4°	14°	A	800	600/700D㊱	1700③	1700③	5–7
6-250/L Calif.	BSF-82	.050	F	—	6°	A	—	600/700D㊱	—	2000③	5–7
V8-302/F Exc. Calif. & High Alt.㊲	ARF-52	.050	G	—	6°	B	—	600/675D㊱	—	④⑫㊳	6–8
V8-302/F Exc. Calif. & High Alt.⑧	ARF-52	.050	G	—	2°	B	—	600/675D㊱	—	2100④	6–8
V8-302/F Exc. Calif. & High Alt.⑰	ARF-52	.050	G	—	14°	B	—	600D	—	2100④	6–8
V8-302/F Calif.	ARF-52-6	.060	G	—	12°	B	—	600D	—	1800④	6–8
V8-302/F High Alt.	ARF-52	.050	G	—	14°	B	—	650/725D㊱	—	2000④	6–8
V8-351W/H⑤	ARF-52	.050	H	—	14°	B	—	600/675D㊱	—	2100④	6–8
V8-351M/H Exc. Calif. & High Alt.⑥⑫㊴	ASF-52	.050	H	—	8°	B	—	650D	—	1350③	6–8
V8-351M/H Exc. Calif. & High Alt.⑥⑫㊵	ASF-52	.050	H	—	14°	B	—	㊱㊶	—	1350③	6–8
V8-351M/H Exc. Calif. & High Alt.⑥⑫㊷	ASF-52	.050	H	—	12°	B	—	600/675D㊱	—	1350③	6–8
V8-351M/H Exc. Calif. & High Alt.⑥⑫㊸	ASF-52	.050	H	—	9°	B	—	600/675D㊱	—	1350③	6–8
V8-351M/H Calif.	ASF-52	.050	H	—	16°	B	—	600/650D㊱	—	2300④	6–8
V8-351M/H High Alt.	ASF-52	.050	H	—	12°	B	—	650D	—	2200④	6–8

Continued

TUNE UP SPECIFICATIONS—Continued

The following specifications are published from the latest information available. This data should be used only in the absence of a decal affixed in the engine compartment.

★ When using a timing light, disconnect vacuum hose or tube at distributor and plug opening in hose or tube so idle speed will not be affected.

● When checking compression, lowest cylinder must be within 75% of the highest.

▲ Before removing wires from distributor cap, determine location of the No. 1 wire in cap, as distributor position may have been altered from that shown at the end of this chart.

Spark plug types shown in this chart are recommendations of the original vehicle manufacturer and not MOTOR. Check local sources for other spark plug manufacturers listings.

Year & Engine/V.I.N.	Spark Plug Type	Gap	Ignition Timing BTDC[1]★ Firing Order Fig.▲	Man. Trans.	Auto. Trans.	Mark Fig.	Curb Idle Speed[2] Man. Trans.	Auto. Trans.	Fast Idle Speed Man. Trans.	Auto. Trans.	Fuel Pump Pressure
1978—Continued											
V8-400/S Exc. Calif. & High Alt.[12][44]	ASF-52	.050	H	—	13°	B	—	575/650D[36]	—	1350[3]	6-8
V8-400/S Exc. Calif. & High Alt.[12][45]	ASF-52	.050	H	—	14°	B	—	600/675D[36]	—	1350[3]	6-8
V8-400/S Calif.	ASF-52	.050	H	—	14°	B	—	600/675D	—	2300[4]	6-8
V8-400/S High Alt.	ASF-52	.050	H	—	8°	B	—	650D	—	2100[4]	6-8
1979											
4-140/Y Exc. Calif.	AWSF-42	.034	D	6°	20°	E	850/1300[36]	600/800D	[3][12][51]	2000[3]	5-7[33]
4-140/Y Calif.	AWSF-42	.034	D	6°	17°	E	850	600/750D	1800[3]	1800[3]	5-7[33]
6-200/T Exc. Calif.	[52]	.050	F	8°	10°	C	700/850[36]	650D	1600[3]	1700[3]	5-7
6-200/T Calif.	[52]	.050	F	—	6°	C	—	600/650D	—	2150[3]	5-7
6-250/L Exc. Calif.	[52]	.050	F	—	10°	A	—	600/700D	—	1700[3]	5-7
6-250/L Calif.	[52]	.050	F	—	6°	A	—	600/700D	—	2300[3]	5-7
V8-302/F Exc. Calif.	[46]	.050	G	12°	8°	B	800/850[36]	600/675D	2300[3]	2100[4]	6-8
V8-302/F Calif.	[53]	.060	G	—	12°	B	—	600/675D	—	1800[4]	6-8
V8-351W/H Exc. Calif.[5][12][49]	[46]	.050	H	—	15°	B	—	600/675D	—	2100[4]	6-8
V8-351W/H Exc. Calif.[5][12][50]	[46]	.050	H	—	10°	B	—	600/650D	—	2200[4]	6-8
V8-351M/H Exc. Calif.[6]	[46]	.050	H	—	12°	B	—	600/650D	—	2200[4]	6-8
V8-351M/H Calif.[6]	[46]	.050	H	—	14°	B	—	600/650D	—	2300[4]	6-8
1980											
4-140/A Exc. Calif.[12][47][55][56]	AWSF-42	.034	D	—	20°	E	—	800D	—	2000[3]	5-7[33]
4-140/A Exc. Calif.[12][47][55][57]	AWSF-42	.034	D	—	17°	E	—	800D	—	2000[3]	5-7[33]
4-140/A Exc. Calif.[47][58]	AWSF-42	.034	D	6°	6°	E	850	750D	1800[3]	2000[3]	5-7[33]
4-140/A Calif.[47]	AWSF-42	.034	D	6°	12°	E	850	750D	2000[3]	2000[3]	5-7[33]
4-140/A[48]	AWSF-32	.034	D	—	10°	E	—	800D	—	[3][12][59]	5-7[33]
6-200/B Exc. Calif.[12][37][55][60]	BSF-82	.050	F	—	7°	C	—	550/700D	—	2000[3]	5-7
6-200/B Exc. Calif.[12][37][55][61]	BSF-82	.050	F	—	10°	C	—	550/700D	—	2000[3]	5-7
6-200/B Exc. Calif.[37][58]	BSF-82	.050	F	[12][62]	10°	C	700	550/700D	1600[3]	2000[3]	5-7
6-200/B Exc. Calif.[58][63]	BSF-82	.050	F	—	10°	C	—	625/700D	—	2000[3]	5-7
6-250/C[55]	BSF-82	.050	F	8°	—	A	600	—	1700[3]	—	5-7
6-250/C[58]	BSF-82	.050	F	4°	10°	A	700/800	550/650D	1700[3]	1700[3]	5-7
V8-255/D Exc. Calif. & High Alt.[64]	ASF-42	.050	G	—	6°	B	—	[12][65]	—	[4][12][66]	6-8
V8-255/D Calif.[8]	ASF-42	.050	G	—	6°	B	—	500/650D	—	1800[4]	6-8
V8-255/D Calif.[64]	ASF-42	.050	G	—	6°	B	—	[12][67]	—	2000[4]	6-8

Continued

TUNE UP SPECIFICATIONS—Continued

The following specifications are published from the latest information available. This data should be used only in the absence of a decal affixed in the engine compartment.

★ When using a timing light, disconnect vacuum hose or tube at distributor and plug opening in hose or tube so idle speed will not be affected.

● When checking compression, lowest cylinder must be within 75% of the highest.

▲ Before removing wires from distributor cap, determine location of the No. 1 wire in cap, as distributor position may have been altered from that shown at the end of this chart.

Spark plug types shown in this chart are recommendations of the original vehicle manufacturer and not MOTOR.

Check local sources for other spark plug manufacturers listings.

Year & Engine/V.I.N.	Spark Plug Type	Gap	Firing Order Fig. ▲	Ignition Timing BTDC① ★ Man. Trans.	Auto. Trans.	Mark Fig.	Curb Idle Speed② Man. Trans.	Auto. Trans.	Fast Idle Speed Man. Trans.	Auto. Trans.	Fuel Pump Pressure
1980—Continued											
V8-255/D High Alt.㊲	ASF-42	.050	G	—	6°	B	—	500/650D	—	2000④	6–8
V8-302/F Exc. Calif. & High Alt.⑧	ASF-52	.050	G	—	8°	B	—	⑫㊻	—	2100④	6–8
V8-302/F Exc. Calif. & High Alt.⑫㊳㊽	ASF-52	.050	G	—	8°	B	—	⑫⑦⓪	—	2000④	6–8
V8-302/F Exc. Calif. & High Alt.⑫㊳㊛	ASF-52	.050	G	—	10°	B	—	500/650D	—	2000④	6–8
V8-302/F Calif.⑧	ASF-52	.050	G	—	6°	B	—	500/650D	—	2100④	6–8
V8-302/F Calif. ⑫㊳㊎	ASF-52	.050	G	—	10°	B	—	500/650D	—	2000④	6–8
V8-302/F Calif. ⑫㊴㊍	ASF-52	.050	G	—	6°	B	—	⑫⑦④	—	2100④	6–8
V8-302/F High Alt.⑧	ASF-52	.050	G	—	8°	B	—	500/650D	—	2000④	6–8
V8-302/F High Alt.㊳	ASF-52	.050	G	—	8°	B	—	⑫⑦⑤	—	2000④	6–8
1981											
4-140/A	AWSF-42	.034	D	6°	12°	E	850⑨	750D㊆	2000③	2300③	5–7㉝
6-200/B⑩⑫	BSF-92	.050	F	—	10°	C	—	600D	—	2000③	5–7㉝
6-200/B⑪⑫	BSF-92	.050	F	—	12°	C	—	600D	—	2000③	5–7㉝
V8-255/D Exc. Calif. ㊔	ASF-52	.050	G	—	10°	B	—	500D	—	1600③	6–8
V8-255/D Exc. Calif.㊲	ASF-52	.050	G	—	10°	B	—	500D	—	1700③	6–8
V8-255/D Calif.㊔	ASF-52	.050	G	—	8°	B	—	500/650D	—	1500③	6–8
V8-255/D Calif.㊲	ASF-52	.050	G	—	12°	B	—	500/650D	—	1500③	6–8
V8-302/F Exc. Calif.	ASF-52	.050	G	—	10°	B	—	500D	—	1600③	6–8
V8-302/F Calif.	ASF-52	.050	G	—	8°	B	—	500/675D	—	1600③	6–8
1982											
4-140/A Exc. Calif.	AWSF-42	.034	D	6°	12°	E	850	800D	1800③	2000③	5–7㉝
4-140/A Calif.	AWSF-42	.034	D	4°	12°	E	850	800D	1600③	1800③	5–7㉝
6-200/B Exc. High Alt.	BSF-92	.050	F	—	10°	C	—	450/600D	—	2000③	5–7㉝
6-200/B High Alt.	BSF-92	.050	F	—	12°	C	—	450/600D	—	2000③	5–7㉝
V6-232/3 Exc. Calif. & High Alt.	AGSP-52	.044	I	—	⑦⑧	J	—	550/650D	—	2200④	6–8
V6-232/3 Calif.	AGSP-52	.044	I	—	12°	J	—	550/650D	—	1200③	6–8
V6-232/3 High Alt.	AGSP-52	.044	I	—	12°	J	—	550/650D	—	2100③	6–8
V8-255/D Exc. High Alt.	ASF-52	.050	G	—	8°	B	—	500/650D	—	1500③	6–8
V8-255/D High Alt.	ASF-52	.050	G	—	14°	B	—	500/650D	—	1700③	6–8
1983											
4-140/A㊼	AWSF-44	.044	D	9°	9°	E	850	800	1800③	2000③	5–7㉝
4-140/W㊽	AWSF-32	.034	D	—	—	E	—	—	—	—	—
6-200/X Exc. High Alt.㊲	BSF-92	.050	F	—	10°	C	—	450/600	—	2000③	6–8
6-200/X High Alt.㊲	BSF-92	.050	F	—	12°	C	—	450/600	—	2000③	6–8
6-200/X Exc. Calif.㊵	BSF-92	.050	F	—	10°	C	—	450/550	—	2200③	6–8
6-200/X Calif.㊵	BSF-92	.050	F	—	10°	C	—	450/550	—	2100③	6–8

Continued

TUNE UP SPECIFICATIONS—Continued

The following specifications are published from the latest information available. This data should be used only in the absence of a decal affixed in the engine compartment.

★ When using a timing light, disconnect vacuum hose or tube at distributor and plug opening in hose or tube so idle speed will not be affected.

● When checking compression, lowest cylinder must be within 75% of the highest.

▲ Before removing wires from distributor cap, determine location of the No. 1 wire in cap, as distributor position may have been altered from that shown at the end of this chart.

☞ Spark plug types shown in this chart are recommendations of the original vehicle manufacturer and not MOTOR.

Check local sources for other spark plug manufacturers listings.

Year & Engine/V.I.N.	Spark Plug		Ignition Timing BTDC①★				Curb Idle Speed②		Fast Idle Speed		Fuel Pump Pressure
	Type ☞	Gap	Firing Order Fig. ▲	Man. Trans.	Auto. Trans.	Mark Fig.	Man. Trans.	Auto. Trans.	Man. Trans.	Auto. Trans.	
1983—Continued											
V6-232/3 Exc. Calif. & High Alt.	AWSF-52	.044	I	—	12°	J	—	550/650	—	2200④	6–8(33)
V6-232/3 Calif.	AWSF-52	.044	I	—	10°	J	—	550/700	—	2200④	6–8(33)
V6-232/3 High Alt.	AWSF-52	.044	I	—	12°	J	—	550/700	—	2100④	6–8(33)
V8-302/F	ASF-52	.050	G	—	—	B	—	550	—	—	(82)
1984											
4-140/A㊼	AWSF-44	.044	D	—	—	E	850	750	—	—	5–7
4-140/W㊽	AWSF-32	.034	D	—	—	E	—	—	—	—	—
V6-232/3	AWSF-52	.044	I	—	—	J	—	—	—	—	(81)
V8-302/F	ASF-52	.050	G	—	—	B	—	550	—	—	(82)

①—B.T.D.C.—Before top dead center.
②—Idle speed on manual trans. vehicles is adjusted in Neutral & on auto. trans. equipped vehicles is adjusted in Drive unless otherwise specified. Where two idle speeds are listed, the higher speed is with the A/C or throttle solenoid energized. On models equipped with vacuum release brake, whenever adjusting ignition timing or idle speed, vacuum line to brake release mechanism must be disconnected & plugged to prevent parking brake from releasing when selector lever is moved to Drive.
③—On kickdown step of cam.
④—On high step of fast idle cam.
⑤—Windsor engine.
⑥—Modified engine.
⑦—Comet & Maverick.
⑧—Granada & Monarch.
⑨—If mileage on vehicle is less than 100 mi., set idle at 100 RPM less than specified.
⑩—Calibration code 1-12B-R0.
⑪—Calibration code 1-12B-R10.
⑫—Refer to engine calibration code on engine identification label, located at rear of left valve cover on V6 & V8 engines, on front of valve cover on in line 4 & 6 cyl. engines. The calibration code is located on the label after the engine code number is preceded by the letter C and the revision code is located below the calibration code and is preceded by the letter R.
⑬—Calibration codes, man. trans. 7-8A-R2, 7-8A-R3 & 7-8A-R10; auto. trans. 7-29A-R1, 7-29A-R3 & 7-29A-R15.
⑭—Calibration code 7-8A-R2, 850 RPM; 6-8A-R3 & 7-8A-410, 800 RPM.
⑮—Calibration codes 7-29A-R1 & 7-29A-R3, 600D RPM; 7-29A-R15, less A/C 600D RPM, with A/C 700D RPM.
⑯—Calibration code 7-8A-R12.
⑰—LTD II, Cougar & Thunderbird.
⑱—Calibration codes, Comet & Maverick 7-11Z-R0; Granada & Monarch, 7-11Y-R2.
⑲—Calibration codes, 7-11Z-R4 & 7-11Z-R6; Granada & Monarch, 7-11Y-R4 & 7-11Y-R6.
⑳—Except calibration code 7-11Z-R4, 2000 RPM; calibration code 7-11Z-R4, 2100 RPM.
㉑—Calibration code 7-32B-R1.
㉒—Calibration codes 7-32B-R10 & 7-32B-R12.
㉓—Calibration codes 7-14A-R1 & 7-14B-R1.
㉔—Calibration codes 7-14A-R10, 7-14B-R10 & 7-14C-R11.
㉕—Calibration codes 7-34A-R0 & 7-34B-R0.
㉖—Calibration codes 7-14N-R0 & 7-14N-R12.
㉗—Calibration codes 7-14N-R13 & 7-14N-R17.
㉘—Calibration code 7-17B-R1.
㉙—Calibration code 7-17B-R15.
㉚—Calibration code 7-17B-R16.
㉛—Calibration code 7-17C-R1.
㉜—Calibration codes 7-37A-R0 & 7-37A-R1.
㉝—With pump to fuel tank return line pinched off & a new fuel filter installed.
㉞—Calibration code 8-7Z-R0.
㉟—Calibration code 8-7Z-R2.
㊱—With throttle solenoid energized. Higher idle speed is with A/C on & compressor clutch de-energized, if equipped.
㊲—Fairmont & Zephyr.
㊳—Calibration code 8-31B-R0, 1900 RPM; 8-11M-R0 & 8-11M-R16, 2100 RPM.
㊴—Calibration code 8-14H-R0.
㊵—Calibration codes 8-14A-R12 & 8-34A-R0.
㊶—Calibration code 8-14A-R12, 600/675D RPM; 8-34A-R0, 600/650D RPM.
㊷—Calibration code 8-14A-R22.
㊸—Calibration code 8-14A-R0.
㊹—Calibration codes 8-17A-R0 & 8-17C-R0.
㊺—Calibration code 8-37A-R0.
㊻—ASF-52 or ARF-52.
㊼—Except turbocharged engine.
㊽—Turbocharged engine.
㊾—Calibration code, 9-12E-R0.
㊿—Calibration code, 9-12G-R0.
(51)—Calibration codes 9-2A-RO & 9-2B-RO 1800 RPM; calibration codes 9-2C-RO & 9-2D-RO, 1600 RPM.
(52)—BSF-82 or BRF-82.
(53)—ASF-52-6 or ARF-52-6.
(54)—Models less Automatic Overdrive Transmission
(55)—Models less Thermactor pump.
(56)—Calibration code 9-21B-R10.
(57)—Calibration codes 0-21A-R0 & 0-21B-R0.
(58)—Models w/Thermactor pump.
(59)—Calibration codes 0-1H-R10, R11, R15 & 0-1S-R0, R10 & R11, 2000 RPM; calibration codes 0-1H-R19, R20 & 0-1S-R15, 2150 RPM.
(60)—Calibration code 0-27A-R3.
(61)—Calibration code 0-27A-R10.
(62)—Calibration code 0-6A-R0, 10° BTDC; calibration code, 0-6B-R1, 12° BTDC.
(63)—Cougar XR-7 & Thunderbird.
(64)—Cougar, Fairmont, Thunderbird & Zephyr.
(65)—Calibration codes 0-16C-R0 & R15, 500/650D; calibration code 0-16C-R13, 550/700D; calibration code 0-16C-R18, 550/625D; calibration code 0-16C-R19, 500/625D.
(66)—Except calibration code 0-16C-R0, 1800 RPM; calibration code 0-16C-R0, 2000 RPM.
(67)—Calibration code 0-16S-R14, 500/650D RPM; calibration code 0-16S-R17, 500/625D RPM.
(68)—Calibration code 9-11C-R1, 600/675D RPM; calibration code 0-11D-R0, 500/650D RPM.
(69)—Calibration codes 0-11A-R0 & R10.
(70)—Calibration code 0-11A-R0, 500/650D RPM; calibration code 0-11A-R10, 500/625D RPM.
(71)—Calibration code 0-11B-R0.
(72)—Calibration codes 0-11P-R12 & R13.
(73)—Calibration codes 0-11N-R0, R10, R11 & R13.
(74)—Calibration codes 0-11N-R0 & R10, 500/650D RPM; calibration codes 0-11N-R11 & R13, 500/625D RPM.
(75)—Calibration code 0-11W-R0, 500/700D RPM; calibration code 0-11W-R10, 550/625D RPM.
(76)—If mileage on vehicle is less than 100 mi., set idle at 50 RPM less than specified.

Continued

TUNE UP NOTES—Continued

(77)—Models with Automatic Overdrive Transmission.

(78)—Cougar & Granada, 10°BTDC; Cougar XR-7 & Thunderbird, 12°BTDC.

(79)—Exc. Calif., 700D; Calif., 650D; A/C blower on, A/C compressor off.

(80)—LTD & Marquis.

(81)—Frame rail mounted pump, 40–45; intake manifold mounted pump, 30.5.

(82)—Fuel tank mounted pump, 6; frame mounted pump, 39.

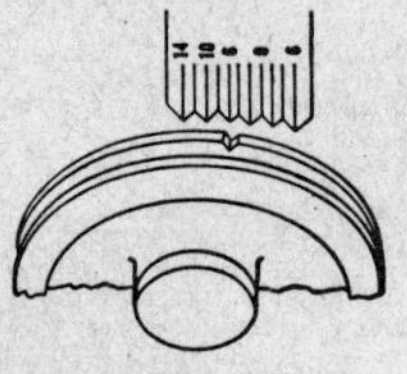

Fig. A

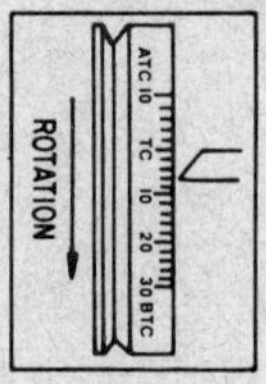
ROTATION
ATC10 TC 10 20 30BTC

Fig. B

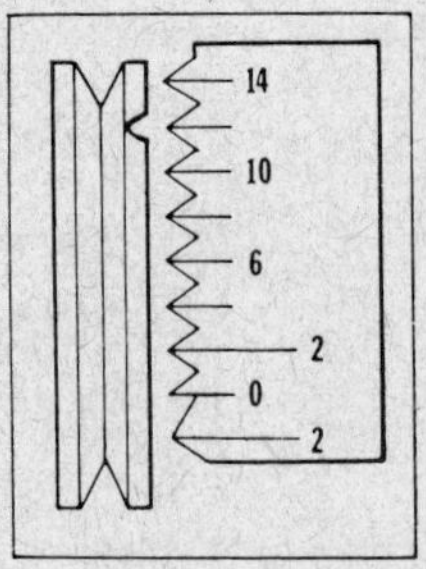
14
10
6
2
0
2

Fig. C

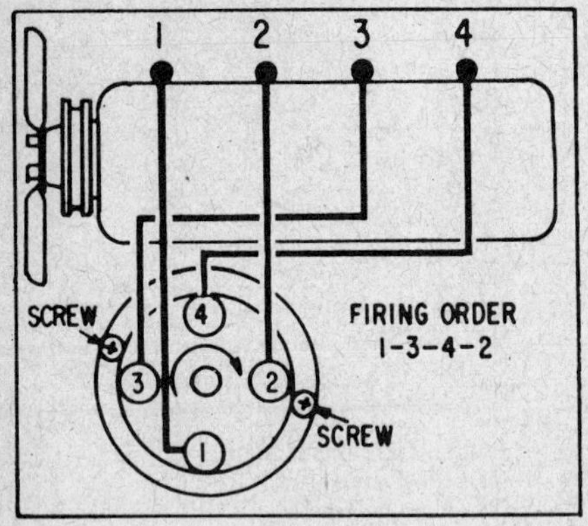
SCREW
FIRING ORDER
1-3-4-2
SCREW

Fig. D

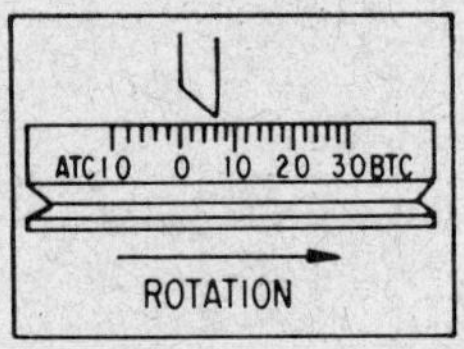
ATC10 0 10 20 30BTC
ROTATION

Fig. E

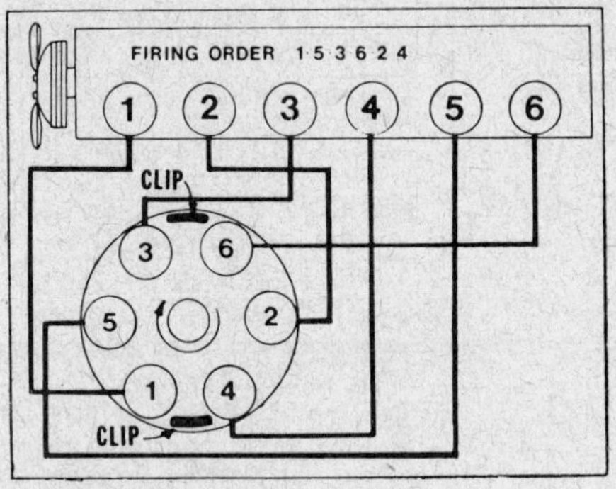
FIRING ORDER 1 5 3 6 2 4
CLIP
CLIP

Fig. F

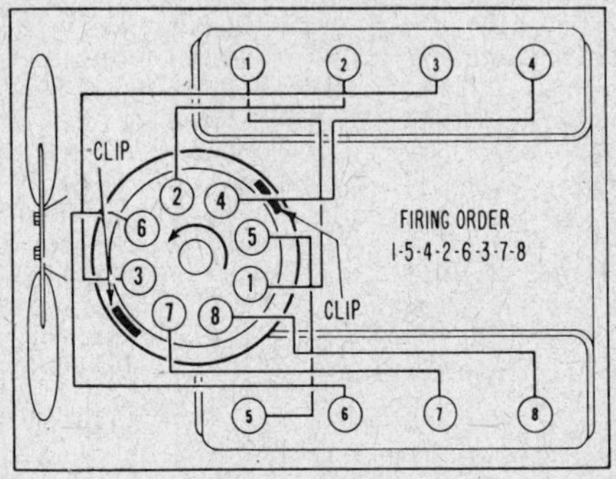
CLIP
FIRING ORDER
1-5-4-2-6-3-7-8
CLIP

Fig. G

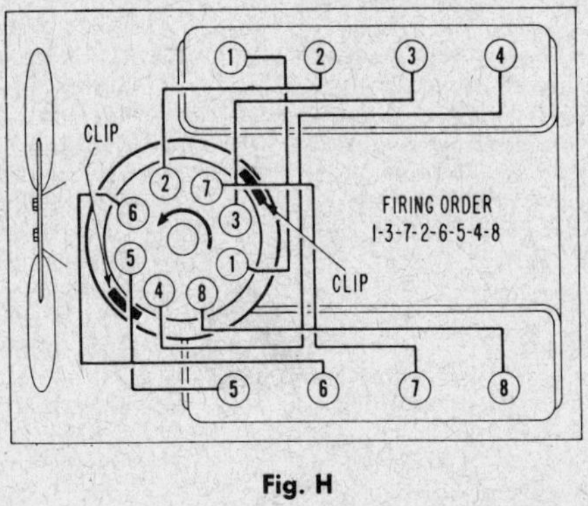
CLIP
FIRING ORDER
1-3-7-2-6-5-4-8
CLIP

Fig. H

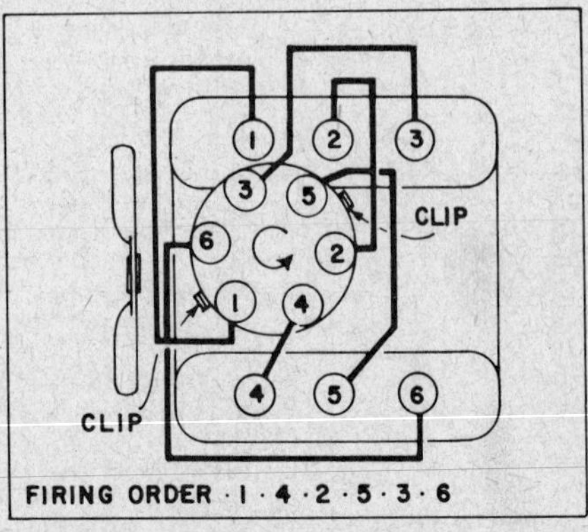
CLIP
CLIP
FIRING ORDER · 1 · 4 · 2 · 5 · 3 · 6

Fig. I

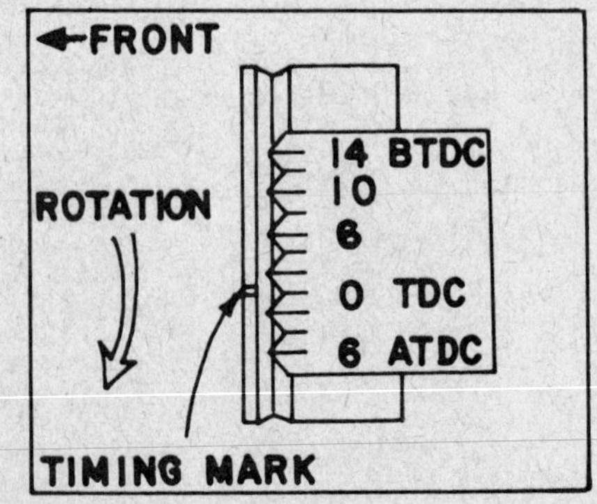
FRONT
14 BTDC
10
6
0 TDC
6 ATDC
ROTATION
TIMING MARK

Fig. J

DISTRIBUTOR SPECIFICATIONS

★Note: If unit is checked on vehicle, double the RPM and degrees to get crankshaft figures.

Distributor Ident. No.①	Centrifugal Advance Degrees @ RPM of Distributor				Vacuum Advance		Distributor Retard
	Advance Starts	Intermediate Advance		Full Advance	Inches of Vacuum to Start Plunger	Max. Adv. Dist. Deg. @ Vacuum	Max. Retard Dist. Deg. @ Vacuum
1977							
D5DE-AFA	−¾ to +1¼ @ 500	3–5¼ @ 700	—	6½ @ 1000	5	13¼ @ 15	—
D6DE-JA	1–4 @ 500	5–7¼ @ 700	—	9½ @ 1000	5	13¼ @ 15	—
D6AE-AA	0–2 @ 500	4–6 @ 700	7¾–9½ @ 1500	14 @ 2500	3	13¾ @ 11½	—
D7AE-BA	0–1 @ 425	2¾–4¾ @ 625	—	13½ @ 2250	3.5	15¼ @ 12	—
D7AE-CA	0–1 @ 700	3½–6 @ 1600	—	10¾ @ 2500	3	15½ @ 11	—
D7AE-DA	0–1 @ 450	3¾–5¾ @ 675	—	14 @ 2500	3.2	15½ @ 14½	—
D7BE-CA	—	—	—	—	—	—	—
D7BE-DA	0–1 @ 500	1¾–3¾ @ 600	—	8½ @ 2500	3	11¼ @ 11	—
D7BE-EA	0–1 @ 550	4¾–6¾ @ 625	—	13¾ @ 2450	3	11¼ @ 13½	—
D7BE-FA	0–1 @ 500	1–3 @ 575	—	8¼ @ 2500	3.1	7¼ @ 6½	—
D7DE-CA	0–1 @ 450	4¾–6¾ @ 700	—	15½ @ 2500	3	15¼ @ 11	—
D7DE-DA	—	—	—	—	—	—	—
D7DE-FA	0–1 @ 425	2½–4½ @ 575	—	13¾ @ 2500	3	15¼ @ 13½	—
D7DE-GA	0–1 @ 525	2¼–4¼ @ 700	—	7¼ @ 2500	3	13¼ @ 13	—
D7OE-CA	0–1 @ 450	2¾–4¾ @ 575	—	16 @ 2500	3.5	15¼ @ 14½	—
D7ZE-BA	0–1 @ 425	6–8 @ 650	—	16 @ 2500	3.5	13¼ @ 15.2	—
1978							
D7AE-UA	0–1 @ 650	0–2 @ 700	—	10½ @ 2500	4	13½ @ 15	—
D7BE-GA	0–1 @ 500	2–2¾ @ 600	—	8¾ @ 2500	3	7¼ @ 7	—
D7DE-AA	0–1 @ 500	1¾–4 @ 750	—	12½ @ 2500	3	13¼ @ 14	—
D7DE-CA	0–1 @ 450	5–8 @ 700	—	15¼ @ 2500	3	15¼ @ 11½	—
D7EE-CA	0–1 @ 800	1–3½ @ 1500	—	7½ @ 2500	2.3	13¾ @ 15¾	—
D7EE-DA	0–1 @ 510	3¾–5¾ @ 725	—	14 @ 2500	1.75	13¼ @ 12.4	—
D7EE-EA	0–1 @ 525	3.6–5.6 @ 725	—	14 @ 2500	2	13¼ @ 15¾	—
D8AE-BA	0–1 @ 450	4–6 @ 700	—	14 @ 2500	4.5	17¼ @ 14½	—
D8AE-CA	0–1 @ 1100	3½–6 @ 1600	—	9½ @ 2500	3	12½ @ 14	—
D8AE-GA	0–1 @ 450	3½–5½ @ 700	—	8¼ @ 2500	5.5	15¼ @ 16½	—
D8AE-HA	0–1 @ 450	4–6 @ 700	—	14 @ 2500	3.25	17¼ @ 13½	—
D8AE-JA	0–1 @ 700	2¾–6½ @ 1500	—	10½ @ 2400	3.25	15½ @ 13	—
D8AE-LA	0–1 @ 775	3½–5½ @ 1350	—	9¼ @ 2500	3.75	17¼ @ 14½	—
D8BE-CA	0–1 @ 1000	—	—	4¾ @ 2500	3	11¼ @ 11½	—
D8BE-EA	0–1 @ 550	2¾–4¾ @ 1100	—	9½ @ 2500	4.5	11¼ @ 12½	—
D8BE-FA	0–1 @ 500	1½–3½ @ 600	—	9½ @ 2500	3.5	11¼ @ 13½	—
D8BE-JA	0–1 @ 550	5½–7½ @ 1050	—	10½ @ 2500	3.5	9¼ @ 13	—
D8DE-CA	0–1 @ 1000	1–3 @ 600	—	4¾ @ 2500	3	11¼ @ 11½	—
D8DE-EA	0–1 @ 450	3–5 @ 600	—	12¼ @ 2500	2	13¼ @ 10.8	—
D8ZE-CA	0–1 @ 575	6–7¾ @ 1200	—	11½ @ 2500	2.5	12¼ @ 15.7	—
1979							
D7AE-UA	0–2 @ 730	—	—	10¼ @ 2500	2.3	13¼ @ 25	—
D7DE-AA	0–1 @ 525	1¾–4 @ 750	—	12½ @ 2500	3	15¼ @ 11	—
D7EE-CA	0–1 @ 800	1–3½ @ 1500	—	7½ @ 2500	2.3	13¼ @ 15¾	—
D7EE-DA	0–1 @ 510	3¾–5¾ @ 725	—	14 @ 2500	1.75	13¼ @ 12.4	—
D7EE-EA	0–1 @ 525	3.6–5.6 @ 725	—	14 @ 2500	2	13¼ @ 15¾	—
D7EE-HA	0–2½ @ 1200	—	—	7½ @ 2500	2.3	13¼ @ 15¾	—
D8BE-EA	0–1 @ 550	2¾–4¾ @ 1100	—	9½ @ 2500	4.5	11¼ @ 12½	—
D8BE-JA	0–1 @ 550	5½–7½ @ 1050	—	10½ @ 2500	3.5	9¼ @ 13	—
D8DE-CA	0–1 @ 475	1–3 @ 600	—	9 @ 2500	2	13¼ @ 10.8	—
D8DE-EA	0–1 @ 450	3–5 @ 600	—	12¼ @ 2500	3	13¼ @ 14	—
D8OE-AA	0–2¾ @ 500	6–7 @ 725	—	16.3 @ 2500	2	15¼ @ 25	—
D9AE-PA	0–3¾ @ 550	1¾–4⅛ @ 610	—	7⅛ @ 2500	2	17¼ @ 25	—

Continued

DISTRIBUTOR SPECIFICATIONS—Continued

★Note: If unit is checked on vehicle, double the RPM and degrees to get crankshaft figures.

Distributor Ident. No.①	Centrifugal Advance Degrees @ RPM of Distributor					Vacuum Advance		Distributor Retard
	Advance Starts	Intermediate Advance			Full Advance	Inches of Vacuum to Start Plunger	Max. Adv. Dist. Deg. @ Vacuum	Max. Retard Dist. Deg. @ Vacuum
1979—Continued								
D9BE-CA	0–1 @ 700	4 @ 1100	—	—	7½ @ 2500	4	12 @ 14	—
D9DE-CA	0–1 @ 1000	1–3 @ 600	—	—	6½ @ 2500	3	11¼ @ 11½	—
D9SE-AA	0–2 @ 500	2–4 @ 600	—	—	6¼ @ 2500	2.8	17¼ @ 25	—
D9TE-BA	0–1 @ 550	2¾–4¾ @ 1100	—	—	9½ @ 2500	4.5	11¼ @ 15¾	—
D9ZE-CA	0–3 @ 500	2¾–4⅞ @ 590	—	—	12¾ @ 2500	2.8	17¾ @ 15½	—
D97E-CA	0–1 @ 450	3–5 @ 600	—	—	13 @ 2500	4	8½ @ 13	—
1980								
D8BE-EA	1 @ 550	5 @ 1100	—	—	8 @ 2500	4.5	9½ @ 12.5	—
D8BE-JA	1 @ 550	7½ @ 1050	—	—	10½ @ 2500	3.5	9¼ @ 13	—
D9BE-DA	1 @ 675	4½ @ 925	—	—	9½ @ 2500	4.5	11¼ @ 13.5	—
D9DE-CA	1 @ 1000	3 @ 600	—	—	6½ @ 2500	4	11¼ @ 11.5	—
D9ZE-CA	3 @ 500	5 @ 590	—	—	13¾ @ 2500	4.8	17¼ @ 13.2	—
D94E-AA	—	—	—	—	—	—	—	—
E0EE-BA	2½ @ 610	3 @ 650	—	—	13 @ 2500	4	9¼ @ 25	—
E0EE-CA	2½ @ 580	5¾ @ 740	—	—	14 @ 2500	4½	13¼ @ 25	—
E0EE-DA	3½ @ 600	5¾ @ 730	—	—	14 @ 2500	5	13¼ @ 25	—
E0EE-FA	2½ @ 1140	—	—	—	8 @ 2500	5	9¼ @ 25	—
E0SE-CA	2 @ 635	5 @ 840	—	—	13 @ 2500	5	13¼ @ 25	—
E0ZE-AA	2 @ 635	5 @ 840	—	—	12 @ 2500	5	8½ @ 25	—
E0ZE-BA	1¾ @ 540	5 @ 760	—	—	11¼ @ 2500	4	11¼ @ 25	—
E0ZE-EA	2½ @ 540	5 @ 675	—	—	8 @ 2500	5	13 @ 25	—
1981								
D8BE-EA	—	3–5½ @ 1250	—	—	—	—	—	—
E0BE-BA	—	—	—	—	—	—	—	—
E0EE-BA	—	2½–6½ @ 1250	—	—	—	—	—	—
E0EE-DA	—	6–8½ @ 1250	—	—	—	—	—	—
E1BE-BA	—	—	—	—	—	—	—	—
E1BE-DA	—	—	—	—	—	—	—	—
E1SE-CA	—	—	—	—	—	—	—	—
E1SE-DA	—	—	—	—	—	—	—	—
E1SE-FA	—	—	—	—	—	—	—	—
1982								
E0EE-CA③	—	8.5–11 @ 1250	—	—	—	—	—	—
E0EE-CA④	—	7.5–10 @ 1250	—	—	—	—	—	—
E0EE-DA	—	8–11.5 @ 1250	—	—	—	—	—	—
E0EE-BA	—	9.5–12.5 @ 1250	—	—	—	—	—	—
E2BE-CA	—	8–11.5 @ 1250	—	—	—	—	—	—
E1BE-EA	—	9.5–11.5 @ 1250	—	—	—	—	—	—
E2DE-AA	—	5–7.5 @ 1250	—	—	—	—	—	—
E2SE-DA	—	8.5–11 @ 1250	—	—	—	—	—	—
E2SE-BA	—	9.5–11.5 @ 1250	—	—	—	—	—	—
E2SE-CA	—	11–13.5 @ 1250	—	—	—	—	—	—
E2SE-AA⑤	—	7–9.5 @ 1250	—	—	—	—	—	—
E1BE-DA	—	10–12.5 @ 1250	—	—	—	—	—	—
E2SE-AA②	—	10–12.5 @ 1250	—	—	—	—	—	—
1983								
E1BE-EA	—	9.5–11.5 @ 1250	—	—	—	—	—	—
E2BE-CA	—	8–10.5 @ 1250	—	—	—	—	—	—
E2SE-DA	—	8.5–10.5 @ 1250	—	—	—	—	—	—
E3AE-CA	—	8.5–10.5 @ 1250	—	—	—	—	—	—

Continued

DISTRIBUTOR SPECIFICATIONS—Continued

★Note: If unit is checked on vehicle, double the RPM and degrees to get crankshaft figures.

Distributor Ident. No.①	Centrifugal Advance Degrees @ RPM of Distributor				Vacuum Advance		Distributor Retard
	Advance Starts	Intermediate Advance		Full Advance	Inches of Vacuum to Start Plunger	Max. Adv. Dist. Deg. @ Vacuum	Max. Retard Dist. Deg. @ Vacuum
1983—Continued							
E3AE-DA	—	8.5–11 @ 1250	—	—	—	—	—
E3AE-EA	—	6.5–9 @ 1250	—	—	—	—	—
E3SE-DA	—	7.5–9.5 @ 1250	—	—	—	—	—
E3ZE-DA	—	3.5–5.5 @ 1250	—	—	—	—	—
E3ZE-FA	—	7.5–10.5 @ 1250	—	—	—	—	—
1984							
E4TE-BA	—	—	—	—	—	—	—
E4ZE-BA	—	—	—	—	—	—	—
EBZE-AA	—	—	—	—	—	—	—

①—Basic Ident. No. 12127.
②—California.
③—Models w/5-speed transmission.
④—Models w/4-speed transmission.
⑤—Exc. Calif.

STARTING MOTOR APPLICATIONS

Year	Engine/ V.I.N.	Ident. No.	Year	Engine/ V.I.N.	Ident. No.
1977	6-200/T①	D8BF-BA		V8-255/D, V8-302/F⑨	D8OF-AA
	6-200/T②	D8BF-AA		V8-255/D, V8-302/F⑩	E1AF-BA
	6-250/L, V8-302/F, V8-351/H⑤⑥	D6OF-AA	1981	4-140/A⑪	E1ZF-AA
				4-140/A⑫	E1ZF-BA
	6-250/L, V8-302/F, V8-351/H⑤⑦	D8OF-AA		4-140/A⑬	E2BF-AA
				6-200/B⑭	E1BF-BA
	V8-351/H⑧, V8-400/S⑥	D5AF-EA		6-200/B⑪⑮	E1BF-BA
	V8-351/H⑧, V8-400/S⑦	D8AF-AA		6-200/B⑮⑯	E1AF-BA
				V8-255/D, V8-302/F	E1AF-BA
1978	4-140/Y	EDD6EF-BA	1982	4-140/A	E2BF-AA
	6-200/T①	D8BF-CA		6-200/B⑰	E1AF-BA
	6-200/T②	D8BF-AA		6-200/B⑱	E1BF-BA
	6-250/L, V8-302/F, V8-351/H⑤	D8OF-AA		V6-232/3⑲	E2SF-AA
				V6-232/3⑳	E25F-AA
	V8-351/H⑧, V8-400/S	D8AE-AA		V8-255/D㉑	E1AF-BA
1979	4-140/Y	D8EF-AA		V8-255/D㉒	E3AF-AA
	6-200/T①	D8BF-CA	1983	4-140/A,W	E2BF-AA
	6-200/T②	D8BF-AA		6-200/X③	E3AF-AA
	6-250/L, V8-302/F, V8-351/H⑤	D8OF-AA		6-200/X④	E1BF-BA
				V6-232/3	E25F-AA
	V8-351/H⑧	D8AF-AA		V8-302/F	—
1980	4-140/A	D8EF-AA	1984	4-140/A,W	—
	6-200/B①	D8BF-CA		V6-232/3	—
	6-200/B②	D8BF-AA		V8-302/W	—
	6-250/C	D8OF-AA			

①—Automatic trans.
②—Manual trans.
③—Except Fairmont & Zephyr high alt.
④—Fairmont & Zephyr high alt.
⑤—Windsor engine.
⑥—Vehicles manufactured before 12-13-76.
⑦—Vehicles manufactured after 12-12-76.
⑧—Modified engine.
⑨—Vehicles manufactured before 3-24-80.

STARTING MOTOR APPLICATION NOTES—Continued

⑩—Vehicles manufactured after 3-23-80.
⑪—Vehicles manufactured before 3-21-81.
⑫—Vehicles manufactured between 3-21-81 and 5-1-81.
⑬—Vehicles manufactured after 5-1-81.
⑭—Thunderbird & XR-7.

⑮—Except Thunderbird & XR-7.
⑯—Vehicles manufactured after 3-20-81.
⑰—Except Thunderbird & XR-7 with C5 automatic trans., serial no. PEB-Z2.
⑱—Thunderbird & XR-7 with C5 automatic

trans., serial no. PEB-Z2.
⑲—Vehicles manufactured before 1-18-82.
⑳—Vehicles manufactured after 1-17-82.
㉑—Vehicles manufactured before 5-17-82.
㉒—Vehicles manufactured after 5-16-82.

ALTERNATOR & REGULATOR SPECIFICATIONS

Year	Color Code Stamp	Current Rating①		Field Current @ 75°F.		Voltage Regulator				Field Relay	
		Amperes	Volts	Amperes	Volts	Model No. (10316)	Voltage @ 75°F.	Contact Gap	Armature Air Gap	Armature Air Gap	Closing Voltage @ 75°F.
1977	Orange③⑦	40	15	2.9	12	D4AF-AA	13.5–15.3	④	④	④	2.5–4.0
	Green③⑦	60	15	2.9	12	D4AF-AA	13.5–15.3	④	④	④	2.5–4.0
	All⑧	70	15	2.9	12	D4TF-AA	13.5–15.3	④	④	④	2.5–4.0
	All⑧	90	15	2.9	12	D4TF-AA	13.5–15.3	④	④	④	2.5–4.0
1978	Orange③⑦	40	15	2.9	12	D4AF-AA	13.5–14.3	④	④	④	—
	Green③⑦	60	15	2.9	12	D4AF-AA	13.5–14.3	④	④	④	—
	Green③⑤⑦	60	15	4.0	12	D8BF-AA⑥	13.8–14.6	④	④	④	—
	Black③⑧	70	15	2.9	12	D4TF-AA	13.5–14.3	④	④	④	—
	Red③⑧	90	15	2.9	12	D4TF-AA	13.5–14.3	④	④	④	—
	Red③⑤⑧	90	15	4.0	12	D8BF-AA⑥	13.8–14.6	④	④	④	—
1979	Orange③⑤⑦	40	15	4.0	12	D8BF-AA⑥	13.8–14.6	④	④	④	—
	Green③⑤⑦	60	15	4.0	12	D8BF-AA⑥	13.8–14.6	④	④	④	—
	Black③⑤⑦	65	15	4.0	12	D8BF-AA⑥	13.8–14.6	④	④	④	—
	Black③⑤⑧	70	15	4.0	12	D8BF-AA⑥	13.8–14.6	④	④	④	—
	Red③⑤⑧	100	15	4.0	12	D8BF-AA⑥	13.8–14.6	④	④	④	—
1980–81	Orange③⑤⑦	40	15	4.0	12	D9BF-AB⑥	13.8–14.6	④	④	④	—
	Green③⑤⑦	60	15	4.0	12	D9BF-AB⑥	13.8–14.6	④	④	④	—
	Black③⑤⑦	65	15	4.0	12	D9BF-AB⑥	13.8–14.6	④	④	④	—
	Black③⑤⑧	70	15	4.0	12	D9BF-AB⑥	13.8–14.6	④	④	④	—
	Red③⑤⑧	100	15	4.0	12	D9BF-AB⑥	13.8–14.6	④	④	④	—
1982	Orange③⑤⑦	40	15	4.0	12	E1AF-AA⑥	13.8–14.6	④	④	④	—
	Green③⑤⑦	60	15	4.0	12	E1AF-AA⑥	13.8–14.6	④	④	④	—
	Black③⑤⑦	65	15	4.0	12	E1AF-AA⑥	13.8–14.6	④	④	④	—
	Black③⑤⑧	70	15	4.0	12	E1AF-AA⑥	13.8–14.6	④	④	④	—
	Red③⑤⑧	100	15	4.0	12	E1AF-AA⑥	13.8–14.6	④	④	④	—
1983	Orange③⑤⑦	40	15	4.25	12	—	—	—	—	—	—
	Black③⑤⑦	65	15	4.25	12	—	—	—	—	—	—
	Green③⑤⑦	60	15	4.25	12	—	—	—	—	—	—
	Black③⑤⑧	70	15	4.25	12	—	—	—	—	—	—
	Red③⑤⑧	100	15	4.25	12	—	—	—	—	—	—
1984	Orange	40	15	4.25	12	—	—	—	—	—	—
	Green	60	15	4.25	12	—	—	—	—	—	—
	Black	70	15	4.25	12	—	—	—	—	—	—
	Red	100	15	4.25	12	—	—	—	—	—	—

①—Current rating stamped on housing.
②—Voltage regulation stamped on cover.
③—Stamp color.
④—Not adjustable.
⑤—Solid state alternator.
⑥—Electronic voltage regulator. These units are color coded black for systems w/warning indicator lamp & blue for systems w/ammeter.
⑦—Rear terminal alternator.
⑧—Side terminal alternator.

VALVE SPECIFICATIONS

Year	Engine/V.I.N.	Valve Lash		Valve Angles		Valve Spring Installed Height	Valve Spring Pressure Lbs. @ In.	Stem Clearance		Stem Diameter, Standard	
		Int.	Exh.	Seat	Face			Intake	Exhaust	Intake	Exhaust
1977	6-200/T	.110–.160(4)		45	44	1 37/64	(18)	.0008–.0025	.0010–.0027	.3100–.3107	.3098–.3105
	6-250/L	.096–.184(4)		45	44	1 37/64	(19)	.0008–.0025	.0010–.0027	.3100–.3107	.3098–.3105
	V8-302/F	.096–.168(4)		45	44	(9)	(15)	.0010–.0027	.0015–.0032	.3416–.3423	.3411–.3418
	V8-351/H(8)	.096–.168(4)		45	44	(7)	(12)	.0010–.0027	.0015–.0032	.3416–.3423	.3411–.3418
	V8-351/H(5), 400/S	.125–.175(4)		45	44	1 53/64	226 @ 1.39	.0010–.0027	.0015–.0032	.3416–.3423	.3411–.3418
1978	4-140/Y	.040–.050(6)		45	44	1 9/16	189 @ 1.16	.0010–.0027	.0015–.0032	.3416–.3423	.3411–.3418
	6-200/T	.110–.160(4)		45	44	1 37/64	150 @ 1.22	.0008–.0025	.0010–.0027	.3100–.3107	.3098–.3105
	6-250/L	.096–.184(4)		45	44	1 37/64	150 @ 1.22	.0008–.0025	.0010–.0027	.3100–.3107	.3098–.3105
	V8-302/F(1)	.096–.168(4)		45	44	(14)	(15)	.0010–.0027	.0015–.0032	.3416–.3423	.3411–.3418
	V8-302/F(2)	(3)(4)		45	44	(14)	(15)	.0010–.0027	.0015–.0032	.3416–.3423	.3411–.3418
	V8-351/H(1)(8)	.096–.168(4)		45	44	(7)	(12)	.0010–.0027	.0015–.0032	.3416–.3423	.3411–.3418
	V8-351/H(2)(8)	.142(4)		45	44	(7)	(12)	.0010–.0027	.0015–.0032	.3416–.3423	.3411–.3418
	V8-351/H	.125–.175(4)		45	44	1 53/64	226 @ 1.39	.0010–.0027	.0015–.0032	.3416–.3423	.3411–.3418
	V8-400/S	.125–.175(4)		45	44	1 53/64	226 @ 1.39	.0010–.0027	.0015–.0032	.3416–.3423	.3411–.3418
1979	4-140/Y	.040–.050(6)		45	44	1 9/16	187 @ 1.16	.0010–.0027	.0015–.0032	.3416–.3423	.3411–.3416
	6-200/T	.110–.160(4)		45	44	1 37/64	150 @ 1.22	.0008–.0025	.0010–.0027	.3100–.3107	.3098–.3105
	6-250/L	.096–.184(4)		45	44	1 37/64	150 @ 1.22	.0008–.0025	.0010–.0027	.3100–.3107	.3098–.3105
	V8-302/F	.096–.165(4)		45	44	(9)	(10)	.0010–.0027	.0015–.0032	.3416–.3423	.3411–.3418
	V8-351/H(8)	.123–.173(4)		45	44	(11)	(17)	.0010–.0027	.0015–.0032	.3416–.3423	.3411–.3418
	V8-351/H(5)	.125–.175(4)		45	44	1 53/64	226 @ 1.39	.0010–.0027	.0015–.0032	.3416–.3423	.3411–.3418
1980	4-140/A	.040–.050(6)		45	44	1 9/16	167 @ 1.16	.0010–.0027	.0015–.0032	.3416–.3423	.3411–.3418
	6-200/B	.110–.184(4)		45	44	1 37/64	150 @ 1.22	.0008–.0025	.0010–.0027	.3100–.3107	.3098–.3105
	6-250/C	.096–.160(4)		45	44	1 37/64	150 @ 1.22	.0008–.0025	.0010–.0027	.3100–.3107	.3098–.3105
	V8-255/D	.071–.193(4)		45	44	(9)	(10)	.0010–.0027	.0015–.0032	.3416–.3423	.3411–.3418
	V8-302/F	.071–.193(4)		45	44	(9)	(13)	.0010–.0027	.0015–.0032	.3416–.3423	.3411–.3418
1981	4-140/A	.040–.050(6)		45	44	1 9/16	167 @ 1.16	.0010–.0027	.0015–.0032	.3416–.3423	.3411–.3418
	6-200/B	.110–.160(4)		45	44	1 37/64	150 @ 1.22	.0008–.0025	.0010–.0027	.3100–.3107	.3098–.3105
	V8-255/D	.096–.146(4)		45	44	(9)	(14)	.0010–.0027	.0015–.0032	.3416–.3423	.3411–.3418
	V8-302/F	.096–.146(4)		45	44	(9)	(14)	.0010–.0027	.0015–.0032	.3416–.3423	.3411–.3418
1982	4-140/A	.040–.050(6)		45	44	1 9/16	167 @ 1.16	.0010–.0027	.0015–.0032	.3416–.3423	.3411–.3418
	6-200/B	.110–.184(4)		45	44	1 19/32	150 @ 1.22	.0008–.0025	.0010–.0027	.3100–.3107	.3098–.3105
	V6-232/3	.088–.189(4)		45	44	1 47/64	215 @ 1.40	.0010–.0027	.0015–.0032	.3416–.3423	.3411–.3418
	V8-255/D	.096–.146(4)		45	44	(9)	(16)	.0010–.0027	.0015–.0032	.3416–.3423	.3411–.3418
1983	4-140/A,W	.040–.050(6)		45	44	1 9/16	149 @ 1.12	.0010–.0027	.0015–.0032	.3416–.3423	.3411–.3418
	6-200/X	.110–.184(4)		45	44	1 19/32	150 @ 1.22	.0008–.0025	.0010–.0027	.3100–.3107	.3098–.3105
	V6-232/3	.088–.189(4)		45	44	1 47/64	215 @ 1.40	.0010–.0027	.0015–.0032	.3416–.3423	.3411–.3418
	V8-302/F	.096–.146(4)		45	44	(9)	(20)	.0010–.0027	.0015–.0032	.3416–.3423	.3411–.3418
1984	4-140/A,W	.040–.050(6)		45	44	1 9/16	154 @ 1.12	.0010–.0027	.0015–.0032	.3416–.3423	.3411–.3418
	V6-232/3	.088–.189(4)		45	44	1 47/64	215 @ 1.40	.0010–.0027	.0015–.0032	.3416–.3423	.3411–.3418
	V8-302/F	.096–.146(4)		45	44	(9)	(20)	.0010–.0027	.0015–.0032	.3416–.3423	.3411–.3418

(1)—Early 1978 engines.
(2)—Late 1978 engines.
(3)—Exc. Calif., .121; Calif., .142.
(4)—Clearance is obtained at valve stem tip with hydraulic lifter collapsed. If clearance is less than the minimum install an undersize push rod; if clearance is greater than the maximum install on oversize push rod.

(5)—Modified engine.
(6)—Measured at cam with hydraulic lifter completely collapsed.
(7)—Intake, 1 51/64; Exhaust, 1 39/64.
(8)—Windsor engine.
(9)—Intake, 1 11/16 in.; exhaust, 1 19/32 in.
(10)—Intake, 201 @ 1.36; exhaust, 200 @ 1.20.
(11)—Intake, 1 25/32 in.; exhaust, 1 19/32 in.

(12)—Intake, 200 @ 1.34; exhaust, 200 @ 1.20.
(13)—Intake, 204 @ 1.36; exhaust, 200 @ 1.20.
(14)—Intake, 205 @ 1.36; exhaust, 200 @ 1.20.
(15)—Intake, 200 @ 1.31, exhaust 200 @ 1.20.
(16)—Intake, 205 @ 1.36; exhaust, 205 @ 1.15.
(17)—Intake, 226 @ 1.39; exhaust, 200 @ 1.20.
(18)—Intake, 156 @ 1.20; exhaust, 148 @ 1.23.
(19)—Intake, 156 @ 1.20; exhaust, 154 @ 1.20.
(20)—Intake, 205 @ 1.36; exhaust, 205 @ 1.05.

PISTONS, PINS, RINGS, CRANKSHAFT & BEARINGS

Year	Engine/V.I.N.	Piston Clearance	Ring End Gap[1] Comp.	Oil	Wristpin Diameter	Rod Bearings Shaft Diameter	Bearing Clearance	Main Bearings Shaft Diameter	Bearing Clearance	Thrust on Bear. No.	Shaft End Play
1977	6-200/T	.0013–.0021	.008	.015	.9121	2.1232–2.1240	.0008–.0015	2.2482–2.2490	.0008–.0015	5	.004–.008
	6-250/L	.0013–.0021	.008	.015	.9121	2.1232–2.1240	.0008–.0015	2.3982–2.3990	.0008–.0015	5	.004–.008
	V8-302/F	.0018–.0026	.010	.015	.9121	2.1228–2.1236	.0008–.0015	2.2482–2.2490	(5)	3	.004–.008
	V8-351/H[2]	.0018–.0026	.010	.015	.9121	2.3103–2.3111	.0008–.0015	2.9994–3.0002	.0008–.0015	3	.004–.008
	V8-351/H[6]	.0014–.0022	.010	.015	.9752	2.3103–2.3111	.0008–.0015	2.9994–3.0002	.0008–.0015	3	.004–.008
	V8-400/S	.0014–.0022	.010	.015	.9752	2.3103–2.3111	.0008–.0015	2.9994–3.0002	.0008–.0015	3	.004–.008
1978	4-140/Y	.0014–.0022	.010	.015	.9120	2.0464–2.0472	.0008–.0015	2.3986	.0008–.0015	3	.004–.008
	6-200/T	.0013–.0021	.008	.015	.9121	2.1232–2.1240	.0008–.0015	2.2486	.0008–.0015	5	.004–.008
	6-250/L	.0013–.0021	.008	.015	.9121	2.1232–2.1240	.0008–.0015	2.3986	.0008–.0015	5	.004–.008
	V8-302/F	.0018–.0026	.010	.015	.9121	2.1228–2.1236	.0008–.0015	2.2486	(5)	3	.004–.008
	V8-351M/H[2]	.0014–.0022	.010	.015	.9752	2.3103–2.3111	.0008–.0015	2.9998	.0008–.0015	3	.004–.008
	V8-351W/H[6]	.0018–.0026	.010	.015	.9122	2.3103–2.3111	.0008–.0015	2.9998	.0008–.0015	3	.004–.008
	V8-400/S	.0014–.0022	.010	.015	.9752	2.3103–2.3111	.0008–.0015	2.9998	.0008–.0015	3	.004–.008
1979	4-140/Y	.0014–.0022	.010	.015	.9121	2.0464–2.0472	.0008–.0015	2.3982–2.3990	.0008–.0015	3	.004–.008
	6-200/T	.0013–.0021	.008	.015	.9121	2.1232–2.1240	.0008–.0015	2.2482–2.2490	.0008–.0015	5	.004–.008
	6-250/L	.0013–.0021	.008	.015	.9121	2.1232–2.1240	.0008–.0015	2.3982–2.3990	.0008–.0015	5	.004–.008
	V8-302/F	.0018–.0026	.010	.015	.9121	2.1228–2.1236	.0008–.0015	2.2482–2.2490	(8)	3	.004–.008
	V8-351W/H[2]	.0018–.0026	.010	.015	.9121	2.3103–2.3111	.0008–.0015	2.9994–3.0002	.0008–.0015	3	.004–.008
	V8-351M/H[6]	.0003–.0005	.010	.015	.9752	2.3103–2.3111	.0008–.0015	2.9994–3.0002	.0008–.0015	3	.004–.008
1980	4-140/A[4]	.0014–.0022	.010	.015	.9121	2.0462–2.0472	.0008–.0015	2.3982–2.3990	.0008–.0015	3	.004–.008
	4-140/A[7]	.0034–.0042	.010	.015	.9121	2.0462–2.0472	.0008–.0015	2.3982–2.3990	.0008–.0015	3	.004–.008
	6-200/B	.0013–.0021	.008	.015	.9121	2.1232–2.1240	.0008–.0015	2.2482–2.2490	.0008–.0015	5	.004–.008
	6-250/C	.0013–.0021	.008	.015	.9121	2.1232–2.1240	.0008–.0015	2.3982–2.3990	.0008–.0015	5	.004–.008
	V8-255/D	.0018–.0026	.010	.015	.9121	2.1228–2.1236	.0008–.0015	2.2482–2.2490	(8)	3	.004–.008
	V8-302/F	.0018–.0026	.010	.015	.9121	2.1228–2.1236	.0008–.0015	2.2482–2.2490	(8)	3	.004–.008
1981	4-140/A	.0014–.0022	.010	.015	.9121	2.0462–2.0472	.0008–.0015	2.3982–2.3990	.0008–.0015	3	.004–.008
	6-200/B	.0013–.0021	.008	.015	.9121	2.1232–2.1240	.0008–.0015	2.2482–2.2490	.0008–.0015	5	.004–.008
	V8-255/D	.004–.0024	.010	.015	.9121	2.1228–2.1236	.0008–.0015	2.2482–2.2490	(8)	3	.004–.008
	V8-302/F	.0018–.0026	.010	.015	.9121	2.1228–2.1236	.0008–.0015	2.2482–2.2490	(8)	3	.004–.008
1982	4-140/A	.0014–.0022	.010	.015	.9121	2.0465–2.0472	.0008–.0015	2.3982–2.3990	.0008–.0015	3	.004–.008
	6-200/B	.0013–.0021	.008	.015	.9121	2.1232–2.1240	.0008–.0015	2.2482–2.2490	.0008–.0015	5	.004–.008
	V6-232/3	.0014–.0022	.010	.015	.9121	2.3103–2.3111	.0010–.0014	2.5190–2.5198	.0010–.0014	3	.004–.008
	V8-255/D	.0014–.0024	.010	.015	.9121	2.1228–2.1236	.0008–.0015	2.2482–2.2490	(3)	3	.004–.008
1983	4-140/A,W	.0014–.0022	.010	.015	.9121	2.0462–2.0472	.0008–.0015	2.2482–2.2490	.0008–.0015	5	.004–.008
	6-200/X	.0013–.0021	.008	.015	.9121	2.1232–2.1240	.0008–.0015	2.3982–2.3990	.0008–.0015	5	.004–.008
	V6-232/3	.0014–.0022	.010	.015	.9121	2.3103–2.3111	.0010–.0014	2.5190–2.5198	.0010–.0014	3	.004–.008
	V8-302/F	.0018–.0026	.010	.015	.9121	2.1228–2.1236	.0008–.0015	2.2482–2.2490	(9)	3	.004–.008
1984	4-140/A,W	.0030–.0038	.010	.015	.9121	2.0462–2.0472	.0008–.0015	2.3982–2.3990	.0008–.0015	5	.004–.008
	V6-232/3	.0014–.0032	.010	.015	.9121	2.3103–2.3111	.0010–.0014	2.5190–2.5198	.0010–.0014	3	.004–.008
	V8-302/F	.0018–.0026	.010	.015	.9121	2.1228–2.1236	.0008–.0015	2.2482–2.2490	(9)	3	.004–.008

①—Fit rings in tapered bores for clearance listed in tightest portion of ring travel.
②—Windsor engine.
③—No. 1, .0004–.0025; No. 2, 3, 4, 5, .004–.0015.
④—Non-Turbocharged.
⑤—No. 1: .0005–.0015; No. 2, 3, 4, 5: .0005–.0015.
⑥—Modified engine.
⑦—Turbocharged.
⑧—No. 1: .0001–.0015; No. 2, 3, 4, 5: .0004–.0015.
⑨—No. 1, .0004–.0025; No. 2, 3, 4, 5, .0004–.0015.

ENGINE TIGHTENING SPECIFICATIONS★

★ Torque specifications are for clean and lightly lubricated threads only. Dry or dirty
threads produce increased friction which prevents accurate measurement of tightness.

Year	Engine/V.I.N.	Spark Plugs Ft. Lbs.	Cylinder Head Bolts Ft. Lbs.	Intake Manifold Ft. Lbs.	Exhaust Manifold Ft. Lbs.	Rocker Arm Shaft Bracket Ft. Lbs.	Rocker Arm Cover Ft. Lbs.	Connecting Rod Cap Bolts Ft. Lbs.	Main Bearing Cap Bolts Ft. Lbs.	Flywheel to Crank-shaft Ft. Lbs.	Vibration Damper or Pulley Ft. Lbs.
1977–78	4-140/Y	5–10	80–90	14–21	16–23	—	4–7	30–36	80–90	54–65	100–120
	6-200/T, 250/L	10–15	70–75	—	18–24	30–35	3–5	21–26	60–70	75–85	85–100
	V8-302/F	10–15	65–72	23–25	18–24	⑤	3–5	19–24	60–70	75–85	70–90
	V8-351W/H③	10–15	105–112	23–25	18–24	⑤	3–5	40–45	95–105	75–85	70–90
	V8-351M/H①	10–15	95–105	④	18–24	18–25⑥	3–5	40–45	95–105	75–85	70–90
	V8-400/S	10–15	95–105	④	18–24	18–25⑥	3–5	40–45	95–105	75–85	70–90
1979	4-140/Y	5–10	80–90	14–21	16–23	—	5–8	30–36	80–90	56–64	100–120
	6-200/T	10–15	70–75	—	18–24	30–35	3–5	21–26	60–70	75–85	85–100
	6-250/L	10–15	70–75	—	18–24	30–35	3–5	21–26	60–70	75–85	85–100
	V8-302/F	10–15	65–72	23–25	18–24	18–25⑥	3–5	19–24	60–70	75–85	70–90
	V8-351W/H③	10–15	105–112	23–25	18–24	18–25⑥	3–5	40–45	95–105	75–85	70–90
	V8-351M/H①	10–15	95–105	④	18–24	18–25⑥	3–5	40–45	95–105	75–85	70–90
1980	4-140/A	5–10	80–90	⑦	16–23	—	6–8	30–36	80–90	56–64	100–120
	6-200/B	10–15	70–75	—	18–24	30–35	3–5	21–26	60–70	75–85	85–100
	6-250/C	10–15	70–75	—	18–24	30–35	3–5	21–26	60–70	75–85	85–100
	V8-255/D	10–15	65–72	23–25	18–24	18–25⑥	3–5	19–24	60–70	75–85	70–90
	V8-302/F	10–15	65–72	23–25	18–24	18–25⑥	3–5	19–24	60–70	75–85	70–90
1981	4-140/A	5–10	80–90	14–21	16–23	—	6–8	30–36	80–90	56–64	100–120
	6-200/B	10–15	70–75	—	18–24	30–35	3–5	21–26	60–70	75–85	85–100
	V8-255/D	10–15	65–72	18–20	18–24	18–25⑥	3–5	19–24	60–70	75–85	70–90
	V8-302/F	10–15	65–72	23–25	18–24	18–25⑥	3–5	19–24	60–70	75–85	70–90
1982	4-140/A	5–10	80–90	14–21	16–23	—	5–8	30–36	80–90	56–64	100–120
	6-200/B	10–15	70–75	—	18–24	30–35	3–5	21–26	60–70	75–85	85–100
	V6-232/3	15–22	②	18.4	15–22	18.4–25.8	3–5	31–36	65–81	54–64	93–121
	V8-255/D	10–15	65–72	18–20	18–24	18–25⑥	3–5	19–24	60–70	75–85	70–90
1983	4-140/A,W	5–10	80–90	14–21	16–23	—	5–8	30–36	80–90	56–64	100–120
	6-200/X	10–15	70–75	—	18–24	30–35	3–5	21–26	60–70	75–85	85–100
	V6-232/3	5–11	②	18.4	15–22	18.4–25.8	3–5	31–36	65–81	54–64	93–121
	V8-302/F	10–15	65–72	23–25	18–24	18–25⑥	3–5	19–24	60–70	75–85	70–90
1984	4-140/A,W	5–10	80–90	14–21	16–23	—	5–8	30–36	80–90	56–64	100–120
	V6-232/3	5–11	⑧	24	15–22	18.4–25.8	6.6–8.8	31–36	65–81	56–64	93–121
	V8-302/F	10–15	65–72	23–25	18–24	18–25⑥	3–5	19–24	60–70	75–85	70–90

①—Modified engine.
②—Tighten in 4 steps: 1, 47 ft. lbs.; 2, 55 ft. lbs.;
   3, 63 ft. lbs.; 4, 74 ft. lbs. Back off all bolts
   2–3 turns, retorque in 4 steps.
③—Windsor engine.
④—⁵/₁₆″ bolts, 19–25 ft. lbs.; ³/₈″ bolts, 22–32 ft.
   lbs.
⑤—1977 & early 1978 rocker arm stud nut,
   17–23 ft. lbs.; late 1978 fulcrum bolt to
   cylinder head, 18–25 ft. lbs.
⑥—Fulcrum bolt to cylinder head.
⑦—Except turbocharged engine, 14–21 ft. lbs;
   turborcharged engine, 13–18 ft. lbs.
⑧—Tighten in 4 steps: 1, 37 ft. lbs.; 2, 45 ft. lbs.;
   3, 52 ft. lbs.; 4, 59 ft. lbs. Back off all bolts
   2–3 turns, retorque in 4 steps.

WHEEL ALIGNMENT SPECIFICATIONS

Year	Model	Caster Angle, Degrees		Camber Angle, Degrees				Toe-In. Inch	Toe-Out on Turns, Deg	
		Limits	Desired	Limits		Desired			Outer Wheel	Inner Wheel
				Left	Right	Left	Right			
1977	Comet	−1 1/4 to +1/4	−1/2	−1/2 to +1	−1/2 to +1	+1/4	+1/4	1/8	18.36①	20
	Cougar	+3 1/4 to +4 3/4	+4	−1/4 to +1 1/4	−1/2 to +1	+1/2	+1/4	1/8	18.06	20
	Granada	−1 1/4 to +1/4	−1/2	−1/2 to +1	−1/2 to +1	+1/4	+1/4	1/8	18.43②	20
	Maverick	−1 1/4 to +1/4	−1/2	−1/2 to +1	−1/2 to +1	+1/4	+1/4	1/8	18.36①	20
	Monarch	−1 1/4 to +1/4	−1/2	−1/2 to +1	−1/2 to +1	+1/4	+1/4	1/8	18.43②	20
	LTD II	+3 1/4 to +4 3/4	+4	−1/4 to +1 1/4	−1/2 to +1	+1/2	+1/4	1/8	18.06	20
	Thunderbird	+3 1/4 to +4 3/4	+4	−1/4 to +1 1/4	−1/2 to +1	+1/2	+1/4	1/8	18.06	20
1978–79	Cougar	+3 1/4 to +4 3/4	+4	−1/4 to +1 1/4	−1/2 to +1	+1/2	+1/4	1/8	18.06	20
	Fairmont	+1/8 to +1 5/8	+7/8	−3/8 to +1 1/8	−3/8 to +1 1/8	+3/8	+3/8	5/16	19.74	20
	Granada	−1 1/4 to +1/4	−1/2	−1/2 to +1	−1/2 to +1	+1/4	+1/4	1/8	18.43②	20
	LTD II	+3 1/4 to +4 3/4	+4	−1/4 to +1 1/4	−1/2 to +1	+1/2	+1/4	1/8	18.06	20
	Monarch	−1 1/4 to +1/4	−1/2	−1/2 to +1	−1/2 to +1	+1/4	+1/4	1/8	18.43②	20
	Thunderbird	+3 1/4 to +4 3/4	+4	−1/4 to +1 1/4	−1/2 to +1	+1/2	+1/4	1/8	18.06	20
	Zephyr	+1/8 to +1 5/8	+7/8	−3/8 to +1 1/8	−3/8 to +1 1/8	+3/8	+3/8	5/16	19.74	20
1980	Cougar XR-7	+1/8 to +1 7/8	+1	−1/2 to +1 1/4	−1/2 to +1 1/4	+3/8	+3/8	3/16	19.84	20
	Fairmont, Sedan	+1/8 to +1 7/8	+1	−5/16 to +1 3/16	−5/16 to +1 3/16	+7/16	+7/16	3/16	19.74	20
	Fairmont, Sta. Wag.	−1/8 to +1 5/8	+3/4	−1/4 to +1 1/4	−1/4 to +1 1/4	+1/2	+1/2	3/16	19.74	20
	Granada	−1 1/4 to +1/4	−1/2	−1/2 to +1	−1/2 to +1	+1/4	+1/4	1/8	18.43②	20
	Monarch	−1 1/4 to +1/4	−1/2	−1/2 to +1	−1/2 to +1	+1/4	+1/4	1/8	18.43②	20
	Thunderbird	+1/8 to +1 7/8	+1	−1/2 to +1 1/4	−1/2 to +1 1/4	+3/8	+3/8	3/16	19.84	20
	Zephyr, Sedan	+1/8 to +1 7/8	+1	−5/16 to +1 3/16	−5/16 to +1 3/16	+7/16	+7/16	3/16	19.74	20
	Zephyr, Sta. Wag.	−1/8 to +1 5/8	+3/4	−1/4 to +1 1/4	−1/4 to +1 1/4	+1/2	+1/2	3/16	19.74	20
1981	Cougar	+1/8 to +1 7/8	+1	−5/16 to +1 3/16	−5/16 to +1 3/16	+7/16	+7/16	3/16	19.84	20
	Cougar XR-7	+1/8 to +1 7/8	+1	−1/2 to +1 1/4	−1/2 to +1 1/4	+3/8	+3/8	3/16	19.77	20
	Fairmont, Sedan	+1/8 to +1 7/8	+1	−5/16 to +1 3/16	−5/16 to +1 3/16	+7/16	+7/16	3/16	19.84	20
	Fairmont, Sta. Wag.	−1/8 to +1 5/8	+3/4	−1/4 to +1 1/4	−1/4 to +1 1/4	+1/2	+1/2	3/16	19.84	20
	Granada	+1/8 to +1 7/8	+1	−5/16 to +1 3/16	−5/16 to +1 3/16	+7/16	+7/16	3/16	19.84	20
	Thunderbird	+1/8 to +1 7/8	+1	−1/2 to +1 1/4	−1/2 to +1 1/4	+3/8	+3/8	3/16	19.77	20
	Zephyr, Sedan	+1/8 to +1 7/8	+1	−5/16 to +1 3/16	−5/16 to +1 3/16	+7/16	+7/16	3/16	19.84	20
	Zephyr, Sta. Wag.	−1/8 to +1 5/8	+3/4	−1/4 to +1 1/4	−1/4 to +1 1/4	+1/2	+1/2	3/16	19.84	20
1982	Cougar Sedan	+1/8 to +1 7/8	+1	−5/16 to +1 3/16	−5/16 to +1 3/16	+7/16	+7/16	3/16	19.84	20
	Cougar Sta. Wag.	+1/8 to +1 5/8	+3/4	−1/4 to +1 1/4	−1/4 to +1 1/4	+1/2	+1/2	3/16	19.84	20
	Cougar XR-7	+1/8 to +1 7/8	+1	−1/2 to +1 1/4	−1/2 to +1 1/4	+3/8	+3/8	3/16	19.73	20
	Fairmont	+1/8 to +1 7/8	+1	−5/16 to +1 3/16	−5/16 to +1 3/16	+7/16	+7/16	3/16	19.84	20
	Granada Sedan	+1/8 to +1 7/8	+1	−5/16 to +1 3/16	−5/16 to +1 3/16	+7/16	+7/16	3/16	19.84	20
	Granada Sta. Wag.	+1/8 to +1 5/8	+3/4	−1/4 to +1 1/4	−1/4 to +1 1/4	+1/2	+1/2	3/16	19.84	20
	Thunderbird	+1/8 to +1 7/8	+1	−1/2 to +1 1/4	−1/2 to +1 1/4	+3/8	+3/8	3/16	19.73	20
	Zephyr	+1/8 to +1 7/8	+1	−5/16 to +1 3/16	−5/16 to +1 3/16	+7/16	+7/16	3/16	19.84	20
1983	Cougar	+1/2 to +2	+1 1/4	−1/2 to +1	−1/2 to +1	+1/4	+1/4	3/16	19.73	20
	Fairmont	+1/8 to +2 1/8	+1 1/8	−5/16 to +1 3/16	−5/16 to +1 3/16	+7/16	+7/16	3/16	19.84	20
	LTD Sedan	+1/8 to +2 1/8	+1 1/8	−5/16 to +1 3/16	−5/16 to +1 3/16	+7/16	+7/16	3/16	19.84	20
	LTD Sta. Wagon	−1/8 to +1 7/8	+7/8	−1/4 to +1 1/4	−1/4 to +1 1/4	+1/2	+1/2	3/16	19.84	20
	Marquis Sedan	+1/8 to +2 1/8	+1 1/8	−5/16 to +1 3/16	−5/16 to +1 3/16	+7/16	+7/16	3/16	19.84	20
	Marquis Sta. Wagon	−1/8 to +1 7/8	+7/8	−1/4 to +1 1/4	−1/4 to +1 1/4	+1/2	+1/2	3/16	19.84	20
	Thunderbird	+1/2 to +2	+1 1/4	−1/2 to +1	−1/2 to +1	+1/4	+1/4	3/16	19.73	20
	Zephyr	+1/8 to +2 1/8	+1 1/8	−5/16 to +1 3/16	−5/16 to +1 3/16	+7/16	+7/16	3/16	19.84	20

Continued

WHEEL ALIGNMENT SPECIFICATIONS—Continued

Year	Model	Caster Angle, Degrees		Camber Angle, Degrees				Toe-In. Inch	Toe-Out on Turns, Deg	
		Limits	Desired	Limits		Desired			Outer Wheel	Inner Wheel
				Left	Right	Left	Right			
1984	Cougar	+1/4 to +1 3/4	+1	−1/2 to +1	−1/2 to +1	+1/4	+1/4	3/16	19.73	20
	LTD Sedan	+1/4 to +2 1/4	+1	−1/4 to +1 1/4	−1/4 to +1 1/4	+1/2	+1/2	3/16	19.84	20
	LTD Sta. Wagon	+1/4 to +2 1/4	+1	−1/4 to +1 1/4	−1/4 to +1 1/4	+1/2	+1/2	3/16	19.84	20
	Marquis Sedan	+1/4 to +2 1/4	+1	−1/4 to +1 1/4	−1/4 to +1 1/4	+1/2	+1/2	3/16	19.84	20
	Marquis Sta. Wagon	+1/4 to +2 1/4	+1	−1/4 to +1 1/4	−1/4 to +1 1/4	+1/2	+1/2	3/16	19.84	20
	Thunderbird	+1/4 to +1 3/4	+1	−1/2 to +1	−1/2 to +1	+1/4	+1/4	3/16	19.73	20

①—Power steering 18.13°. ②—Power steering 18.20°.

COOLING SYSTEM & CAPACITY DATA

Year	Model or Engine/V.I.N.	Cooling Capacity Qts.		Radiator Cap Relief Pressure, Lbs.	Thermo. Opening Temp.	Fuel Tank Gals.	Engine Oil Refill Qts. ①	Transmission Oil			Rear Axle Oil Pints
		Less A/C	With A/C					3 Speed Pints	4 Speed Pints	Auto. Trans. Qts. ②	
1977	6-200/T③	8.7	8.7	13	191	19.2	4	3 1/2	—	7 1/4	4 1/2
	6-200/T④	9.9	9.9	16	191	19.2	4	3 1/2	5	8 1/4	⑬
	6-250/L③	9.6	9.6	13	191	19.2	4	3 1/2	—	8 1/4	4 1/2
	6-250/L④	10.5	10.7	16	191	19.2	4	—	5	8 1/4	⑬
	V8-302/F③	13.5	14.1	13	191	19.2	4	3 1/2	—	10 1/4	4 1/2
	V8-302/F④	14.4	14.6	16	191	19.2	4	—	—	8 1/4	⑬
	V8-302/F⑭	14.8	15.1	16	191	⑦	4	—	—	10 1/4	5
	V8-351W/H④⑤	15.7	16.7	16	191	19.2	4	—	—	10 1/4	⑬
	V8-351W/H⑤⑭	15.9	16.2	16	191	⑦	4	—	—	⑧	5
	V8-351M/H⑨⑭	17.1	17.1	16	191	⑦	4	—	—	⑧	5
	V8-400/S⑭	17.1	17.1	16	191	⑦	4	—	—	⑩	5
1978	4-140/Y⑮	8.7	9.1	⑯	191	16	4	—	2.8	8	3.5
	6-200/T⑮	8.7	8.9	⑯	191	16	4	3 1/2	—	⑰	3.5
	6-250/L④	10.5	10.6	16	191	18	4	—	5	8 1/4	⑱
	V8-302/F⑮	13.5	14.1	⑯	191	16	4㉜	—	—	10	3 1/2
	V8-302/F④	14.2	14.3	16	191	18	4	—	5	8 1/4	⑱
	V8-302/F⑭	14.3	14.6	16	191	21	4	—	—	10 1/4	5
	V8-351W/H⑤⑭	15.4	15.7	16	191	21	4	—	—	⑧	5
	V8-351M/H⑨⑭	16.5	16.5	16	191	21	4	—	—	⑧	5
	V8-400/S⑭	16.5	16.5	16	191	21	4	—	—	⑧	5
1979	4-140/Y⑮	8.6	10.3	⑯	191	16	4	—	2.8	8	3 1/2
	6-200/T⑮	9	9	16	191	16	4	—	4 1/2	⑲	3 1/2
	6-250/L④	⑳	㉑	16	191	18	4	—	4 1/2	㉒	4 1/2
	V8-302/F⑮	13.9	14	16	195	16	4	—	4 1/2	10	3 1/2
	V8-302/F④	14.2	14.3	16	195	18	4	—	4 1/2	10	4 1/2
	V8-302/F⑭	14.3	14.6	16	195	21㉓	4	—	—	10	5
	V8-351W/H⑤⑭	15.4	15.7	16	195	21㉓	4	—	—	㉔	5
	V8-351M/H⑨⑭	16.5	16.5	16	195	21㉓	4	—	—	㉔	5

Continued

COOLING SYSTEM & CAPACITY DATA—Continued

Year	Model or Engine/V.I.N.	Cooling Capacity Qts. Less A/C	Cooling Capacity Qts. With A/C	Radiator Cap Relief Pressure, Lbs.	Thermo. Opening Temp.	Fuel Tank Gals.	Engine Oil Refill Qts. (1)	Transmission Oil 3 Speed Pints	Transmission Oil 4 Speed Pints	Transmission Oil Auto. Trans. Qts. (2)	Rear Axle Oil Pints
1980	4-140/A(25)	8.6	9	(16)	191	14	4	—	2.8	6.7	(27)
	4-140/A(26)	9.2	9.2	(16)	191	12.7	4½	—	3.5	—	(27)
	6-200/B	8.1	8.1	16	196	14	4	—	4½	(30)	(27)
	6-250/C	10.6	10.8	16	196	18	4	—	4½	(34)	(35)
	V8-255/D(15)	13.4	13.5	16	196	14	4(32)	—	—	10	(27)
	V8-255/D(4)	14.6	14.7	16	196	18	4	—	—	9.6	(35)
	V8-255/D(29)	13.2	13.3	16	196	17½	4(32)	—	—	10.1	5
	V8-302/F(4)	14.2	14.3	16	196	18	4	—	—	9.6	(35)
	V8-302/F(39)	12.7	12.8	16	196	17½	4(32)	—	—	(31)	5
1981	4-140/A(15)	8.6	9.2	(16)	191	14	4	—	2.8	(36)	(27)
	4-140/A(33)	8.6	9.2	(16)	191	14	4	—	4.5	6.8	3½
	6-200/B(15)	8.4	8.5	16	196	16	4	—	—	(37)	(27)
	6-200/B(33)	8.4	8.5	16	196	16	4	—	—	(37)	3½
	6-200/B(29)	8.4	8.5	16	196	17½	4	—	—	7.7	3½
	V8-255/D(15)	14.8	15.2	16	191	16	4(32)	—	—	9.6	(27)
	V8-255/D(33)	14.8	15.2	16	196	16	4(32)	—	—	9.6	3½
	V8-255/D(29)	14.9	15	16	191	18	4(32)	—	—	(31)	3½
	V8-302/F(29)	13.2	13.4	16	196	18	4(32)	—	—	12	3½
1982	4-140/A(15)(33)	8.6	9.4	(16)	191	16(6)	4	—	2.8	8	3½
	6-200/B(15)	8.4	8.5	16	196	16(6)	4	—	—	(11)	3½
	6-200/B(33)	10.7	10.8	16	196	16(6)	4	—	—	(11)	3½
	6-200/B(29)	8.4	8.5	16	196	21	4	—	—	(11)	3½
	V6-232/3(33)	8.4	8.5	16	196	16(6)	4	—	—	12	3½
	V6-232/3(29)	10.7	10.8	16	196	21	4	—	—	12	3½
	V8-255/D(29)	14.9	15	16	191	21	4	—	—	12	3½
1983	4-140/A(25)	8.6	9.4	(16)	191	16	4	—	2.8	8	(36)
	4-140/W(26)	8.4	8.7	(16)	191	18	4½	—	4.75(43)	—	(41)
	6-200/X	8.4	8.5	16	191	16	4	—	—	(39)	(36)
	V6-232/3	10.7	10.8	16	197	(37)	4	—	—	(40)	(36)
	V8-302/F	13.3	13.4	16	197	20.6	4	—	—	12	(36)
1984	4-140/A(25)	8.6	9.2	(16)	191	16	4	—	—	8	(41)
	4-140/W(26)	8.4	8.7	(16)	191	18	4½	—	5.6(43)	8	(41)
	V6-232/3	10.7	10.8	16	197	(42)	4	—	—	11	(41)
	V8-302/F	13.3	13.4	16	191	20.6	4	—	—	12	(41)

(1)—Add 1 qt. (½ qt. on turbocharged engines) with filter change.
(2)—Approximate. Make final check with dipstick.
(3)—Comet & Maverick.
(4)—Granada & Monarch.
(5)—Windsor engine.
(6)—With option extended range fuel tank, 20 gals.
(7)—Except sta. wag., 26½ gals.; sta. wag., 21¼ gals.
(8)—C4, 10¼ qts.; FMX, 11 qts.; C6, 12¼ qts.
(9)—Modified engine
(10)—FMX, 11 qts.; C6, 12¼ qts.
(11)—C3, 8 qts.; C5, 11 qts.
(12)—C3, 8 qts.; C4, w/10¼ in. torque converter, 7.2 qts.; C4 w/12 in. torque converter, 9.6 qts.
(13)—Models w/8 in. ring gear, 4½ pts.; models w/8.7" ring gear, 4 pts.; models w/4 wheel disc. brakes, 5 pts.
(14)—Cougar, LTD II & Thunderbird.
(15)—Fairmont & Zephyr.
(16)—Less A/C, 13 psi.; with A/C 16 psi.
(17)—C3, 8 qts.; C4, 6.7 qts.
(18)—Models w/2.47 rear axle ratio, 4 pts.; models w/3.00 rear axle ratio, 4½ pts.; models w/4 wheel disc brakes, 5 pts.
(19)—C3, 8 qts.; C4, 7½ qts.
(20)—Except Calif. 10.5 qts.; California, 10.7 qts.
(21)—Man. trans. 10.6 qts.; auto. trans. 10.8 qts.
(22)—C4, 8¼ qts.; Jatco, 8½ qts.
(23)—W/optional fuel tank, 27.5 gals.
(24)—C4, 10 qts.; FMX, 11 qts.
(25)—Non-turbocharged engine.
(26)—Turbocharged engine.
(27)—With 7.5 inch ring gear, 3.5 pts.; with 6.75 ring gear, 2.5 pts.
(28)—C3, 8 qts.; C4, 6.8 qts.
(29)—Cougar XR-7 & Thunderbird.
(30)—C3, 8 qts; C4, 7.1 qts.
(31)—C4, 10.1 qts; F10D auto. overdrive trans., 12 qts.
(32)—Dual sump oil pan. Remove both drain plugs to fully drain oil. One drain plug located at front of oil pan. Second drain plug located at left side of oil pan.
(33)—Cougar & Granada.
(34)—Jatco, 8.6 qts.; C4, 9.6 qts.
(35)—8 inch ring gear, 4.5 pts.; 9 inch ring gear, 5 pts.
(36)—Models with 7.5 inch ring gear, 3.5 pts.; models with 8.5 inch ring gears, 3.8 pts.
(37)—LTD & Marquis, 16 gal.; Thunderbird & Cougar, 21 gal.
(38)—Automatic 3 speed, 11 qts.; automatic 4 speed, 12 qts.
(39)—Fairmont & Zephyr except high alt., 11 qts.; Fairmont & Zephyr high alt. & LTD & Marquis sedan, Calif. & station wagon, 7.5 qts.; LTD & Marquis sedan except Calif., 10.3 qts.
(40)—C5, 11 qts.; auto overdrive, 11.4 qts.
(41)—Standard, 3¼ pts.; Traction-Lok, 3½ pts.
(42)—LTD & Marquis, 15.4 gals.; Cougar & Thunderbird, 20.6 gals.
(43)—Five Speed transmission.

REAR AXLE SPECIFICATIONS

Year	Ring Gear Diameter	Carrier Type	Ring Gear & Pinion Backlash Inch	Nominal Pinion Locating Shim, Inch	Pinion Bearing Preload				Differential Bearing Preload	Pinion Nut Torque Ft.-Lbs.①
					New Bearings With Seal Inch-Lbs.	Used Bearings With Seal Inch-Lbs.	New Bearings Less Seal Inch-Lbs.	Used Bearings Less Seal Inch-Lbs.		
1977–78	8.7″ WER③	Integral	.008–.012	.030	17–27	8–14	—	—	.008–.012②	140
1977–79	8″	Removal	.008–.012	.022	17–27	8–14	—	—	.008–.012⑥	170
	9″	Removal	.008–.012	.015	17–27④	8–14	—	—	.008–.012⑥	⑤
1978–79	7½″ WGX③	Integral	.008–.012	.030	17–27	8–14	—	—	.016⑦	140
1979	6¾″	Integral	.008–.012	.030	17–27	6–12	—	—	.016⑦	140
1980	6¾″	Integral	.008–.012	.030	17–27	6–12	—	—	.016⑦	140
	7½″ WGX③	Integral	.008–.012	.030	16–29	8–14	—	—	.016⑦	170
	9″	Removal	.008–.015	.030	17–27	8–14	—	—	.008–.012⑦	170
1981	6¾″ WGG③	Integral	.008–.015	.030	16–29	8–14	—	—	.016⑦	140
1981–84	7½″ WGX, WGZ③	Integral	.008–.015	.030	16–29	8–14	—	—	.016⑦	170

①—If torque cannot be obtained, install new spacer.
②—Case spread with new bearings. With used bearings .006–.010″.
③—Indentification tag prefix.
④—Solid spacer 13–33 inch-lbs.
⑤—With collapsible spacer 170 ft. lbs., with solid spacer 200 ft. lbs.
⑥—Case spread with new bearings. With used bearings .005–.008″.
⑦—Case spread across differential.

Electrical Section

STARTER, REPLACE

1978–83 Fairmont, Zephyr, 1981–82 Cougar, Granada & 1983–84 LTD, Marquis, Cougar & Thunderbird 4-140

1. Disconnect battery ground cable.
2. Raise vehicle on hoist.
3. Remove starter shield.
4. Disconnect starter cable from motor.
5. Remove starter attaching bolts and remove starter.

1980–82 Cougar XR-7, 1980–84 Thunderbird & 1983–84 Cougar V6-232, V8-255 & 302

1. Disconnect battery ground cable.
2. Raise vehicle and remove cross brace.
3. Remove starter motor attaching bolts, then lower starter motor and disconnect starter cable.
4. Reverse procedure to install.

1978–83 Fairmont, Zephyr, 1981–82 Cougar & Granada 6-200

1. Disconnect battery ground cable, then remove upper starter attaching bolt.
2. Remove exhaust heat shield, then disconnect starter cable from starter motor.
3. Raise vehicle and remove wishbone brace.
4. Remove lower starter mounting bolts, then remove starter motor.
5. Reverse procedure to install.

1978–83 Fairmont, Zephyr, 1981–82 Cougar & Granada & 1983–84 LTD & Marquis V6-232, V8-255 & 302

1. Disconnect battery ground cable.
2. Raise vehicle and remove wishbone brace.
3. Remove starter motor attaching bolts and remove starter assembly.
4. Disconnect starter cable from starter motor.
5. Reverse procedure to install.

1977–80 Granada & Monarch V8-302

1. Disconnect battery ground cable.
2. Disconnect starter cable from starter.
3. Remove engine mount through bolt and nut.
4. Remove two bolts retaining insulator to block and remove insulator.
5. Position a suitable jack under engine and raise engine.
6. Remove starter attaching bolts and starter.

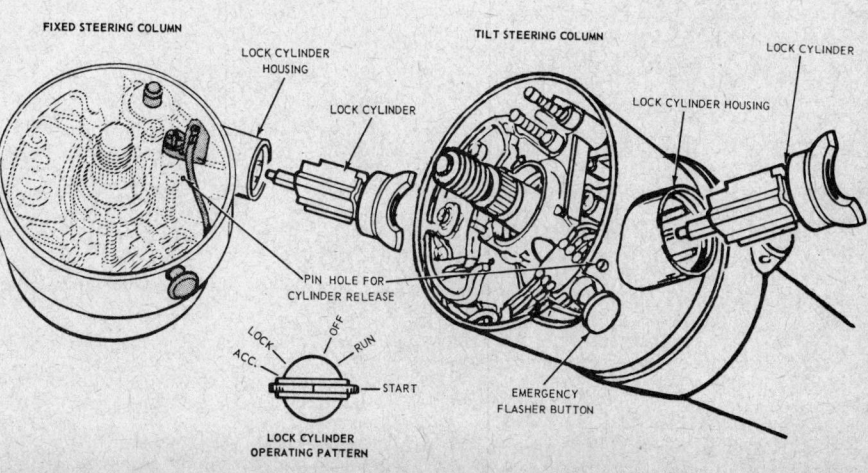

FIXED STEERING COLUMN

TILT STEERING COLUMN

LOCK CYLINDER HOUSING

LOCK CYLINDER

LOCK CYLINDER

LOCK CYLINDER HOUSING

PIN HOLE FOR CYLINDER RELEASE

LOCK
ACC.
OFF
RUN
START

LOCK CYLINDER OPERATING PATTERN

EMERGENCY FLASHER BUTTON

Fig. 1   Ignition lock

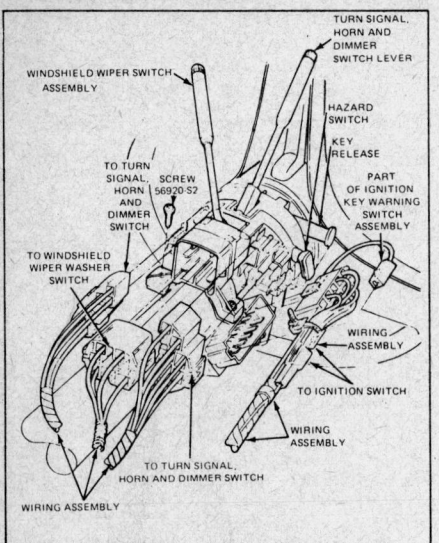

Fig. 2 Ignition switch. 1978—83 Fairmont, Zephyr, 1980—82 Cougar XR-7, 1980—84 Thunderbird, 1981—82 Cougar, Granada & 1981—84 Cougar, 1983—84 LTD & Marquis

1977—79 Cougar, LTD II & Thunderbird, 1977 Comet & Maverick

1. Disconnect battery ground cable.
2. Raise vehicle and disconnect starter cable at starter.
3. Remove starter attaching bolts and starter.
4. Reverse procedure to install.

NOTE: On engines equipped with a solenoid actuated starter, turn wheel to full right and remove the idler arm to frame bolts. On some models, it may be necessary to turn wheels aside to aid starter removal.

NOISY STARTER OR STARTER LOCKUP: If either of these situations occur, loosen the three mounting bolts enough to hand fit the starter properly into pilot plate. Then tighten starter mounting bolts, starting with top bolt. Starter should not be replaced until it has been proven noisy after proper alignment has been established by the above method.

IGNITION LOCK, REPLACE

1977—79

1. Disconnect the battery ground cable.
2. *Units With Fixed Steering Columns:* Remove steering wheel and trim pad. Insert a wire pin into the hole inside the column halfway down the lock cylinder housing, Fig. 1. *Units with Tilt Steering Columns:* Insert wire pin in the hole located on the outside of the flange casting next to the emergency flasher button, Fig. 1.
3. Place the gear shift lever in "Park" (with automatic trans) or "Reverse" (with manual trans) position, and turn the lock cylinder with the ignition key to "Run" position.

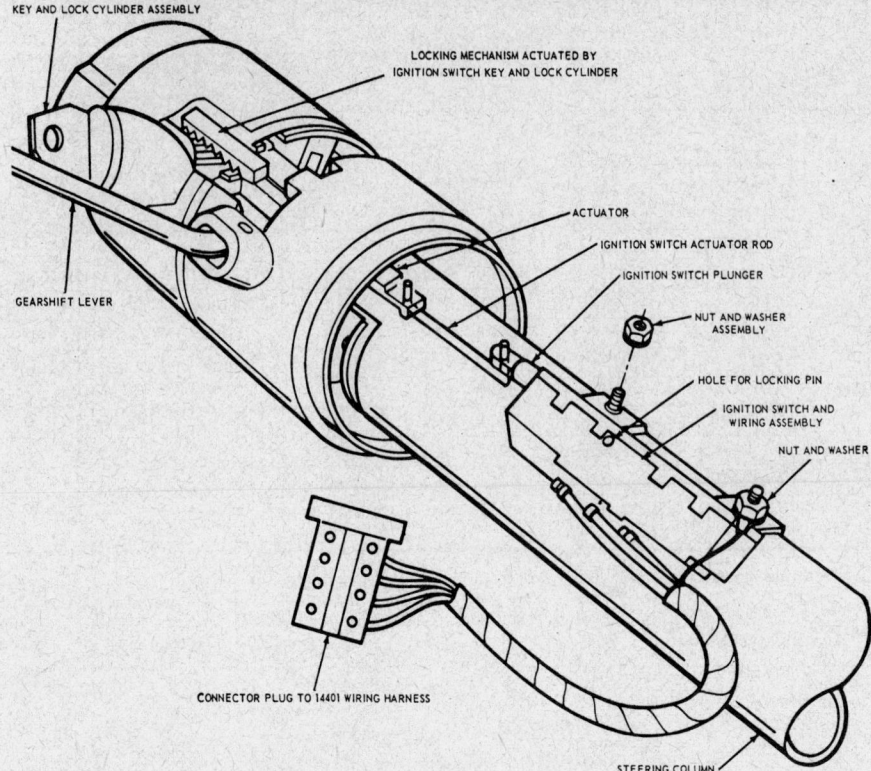

Fig. 3 Ignition switch installation 1977 Comet & Maverick

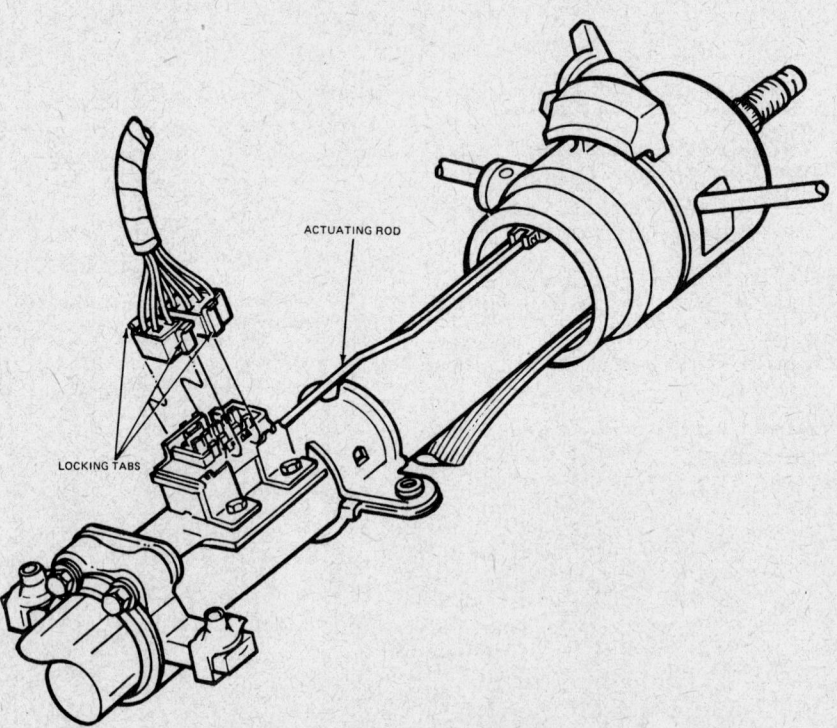

Fig. 4 Ignition switch installation. 1977—79 Cougar, LTD II & Thunderbird & 1977—80 Granada & Monarch

4. Depress the wire pin while pulling up on the lock cylinder to remove. Remove the wire pin.
5. To install insert the lock cylinder into housing in the flange casting, and turn the key to "Off" position. Be certain that the cylinder is fully inserted before turning to the "Off" position. This action will expend the cylinder retaining pin into the cylinder housing.
6. Turn the key to check for correct operation in all positions.

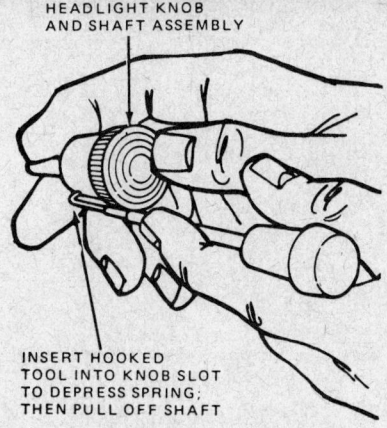

Fig. 5 Light switch knob removal. 1977–80 Granada, LTD II & Monarch

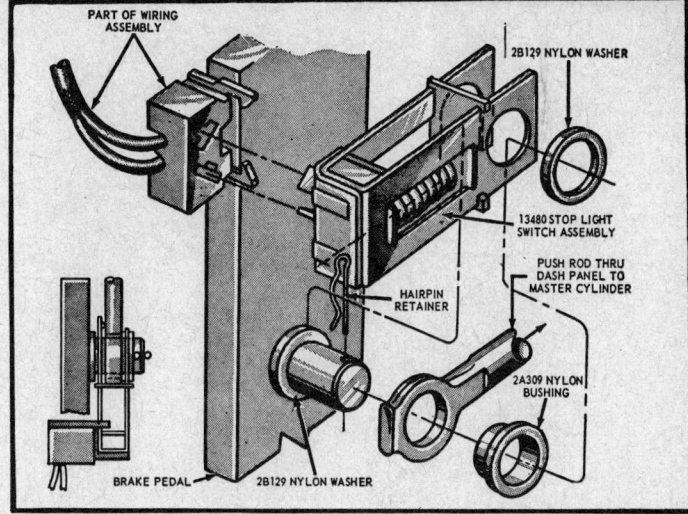

Fig. 7 Mechanical stop light switch.

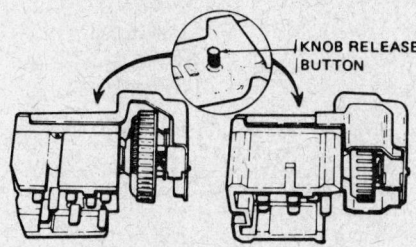

Fig. 6 Light switches. (Typical)

7. Install the steering wheel and trim pad on fixed column units.
8. Connect the battery ground cable.

1980–84

1. Disconnect battery ground cable.
2. On 1980 models, remove trim shroud.
3. On 1981–84 models equipped with tilt column, remove upper extension shroud by detaching from retaining clip at 9 o'clock position.
4. On 1981–84 models, remove both trim shroud halves.
5. On all models, disconnect key warning switch electrical connector.
6. Turn ignition key to "Run." Place gear shift lever in "Park" if equipped with column shift.
7. Insert a 1/8 inch diameter wire pin into hole in casting around lock cylinder. Remove lock cylinder while depressing retaining pin with wire.
8. Reverse procedure to install. Lock cylinder must be in "Run" and retaining pin depressed during installation. Following installation, turn the key to check for correct operation in all positions.

IGNITION SWITCH, REPLACE

1978–83 Fairmont & Zephyr; 1980–82 Cougar XR-7, 1980–84 Thunderbird; 1981–82 Granada; 1981–84 Cougar; 1983–84 LTD & Marquis

1. Disconnect battery ground cable.
2. On 1977–80 models, remove trim

shroud.
3. On 1981–84 models equipped with tilt column, remove upper extension shroud by detaching from retaining clip at 9 o'clock position.
4. On 1981–84 models, remove both trim shroud halves.
5. Disconnect ignition switch wire connector.
6. Drill out bolts that attach switch to lock cylinder housing using a 1/8 in. drill. Remove the two bolts using an easy-out or equivalent.
7. Disengage ignition switch from actuator pin, Fig. 2.
8. On 1978–81 models, adjust switch by sliding carrier to "Lock" position and inserting a drill bit through switch housing and into carrier. On 1978–79 models, insert a 7/16 inch drill bit. On 1980–81 models, insert a .050 inch drill bit.
9. On 1982–84 models, adjust switch by sliding carrier to "Run" position and inserting a 1/8 inch drill bit through housing and into carrier.
10. On 1978–81 models, rotate ignition key to "Lock" position, then install switch on actuator pin.
11. On 1982–84 models, rotate ignition key to the run position, which is approximately 90° from Lock position, then install ignition switch on actuator pin.
12. Install new switch to lock cylinder housing break away bolts and torque bolt until heads break away.
13. Remove drill bit from switch housing, then connect switch wire connector.
14. Connect battery ground cable and check switch for proper operation, then install steering column trim shroud.

Except 1978–83 Fairmont & Zephyr; 1980–82 Cougar XR-7, 1980–84 Thunderbird; 1981–82 Granada; 1981–84 Cougar; 1983–84 LTD & Marquis

1. On 1977–79 Cougar, LTD II and Thunderbird models, remove instrument cluster as described under Instrument Cluster, Replace.
2. On all models, remove steering column shroud and lower steering column from

brake support bracket.
3. Disconnect battery cable.
4. Disconnect switch wiring and remove two switch retaining nuts. Disconnect switch from actuator and remove switch, Figs. 3 and 4.
5. Move shift lever to "Park" position on automatic transmissions and Reverse on standard transmission units. Place ignition key in "Lock" position and remove the key.

NOTE: New replacement switches are pinned in the "Lock" position by a plastic shipping pin inserted in a locking hole in the switch. For an existing switch, pull plunger out as far as it will go then back one detent to "Lock" position and insert a 3/32" drill in locking hole to retain switch in Lock position.

6. With locking pin in place, install switch on steering column, determine mid position of actuator lash and tighten retaining bolts.
7. Remove locking pin.

LIGHT SWITCH, REPLACE

1. Disconnect battery ground cable.
2. On 1977–80 Granada, LTD II and Monarch models, to remove light switch knob, bend a discarded bowden cable into shape shown in Fig. 5. Insert hooked end of cable into knob slot to depress spring, then pull knob from shaft.
3. On all other models, remove control knob and shaft assembly, by placing knob in full "On" position, then pressing knob release button on switch and pulling out knob and shaft, Fig. 6. To gain access to the release button on Comet, Fairmont, Maverick and Zephyr models with air conditioning it may be necessary to first disconnect the left A/C duct.
4. On all models, remove bezel nut. Disconnect multiple plug connector, vacuum hoses if vehicle is equipped with headlight doors and remove switch.
5. Reverse procedure to install. On 1977–80 Granada, LTD II and Monarch models, align triangular holes in knob and shaft, then press knob onto shaft until knob

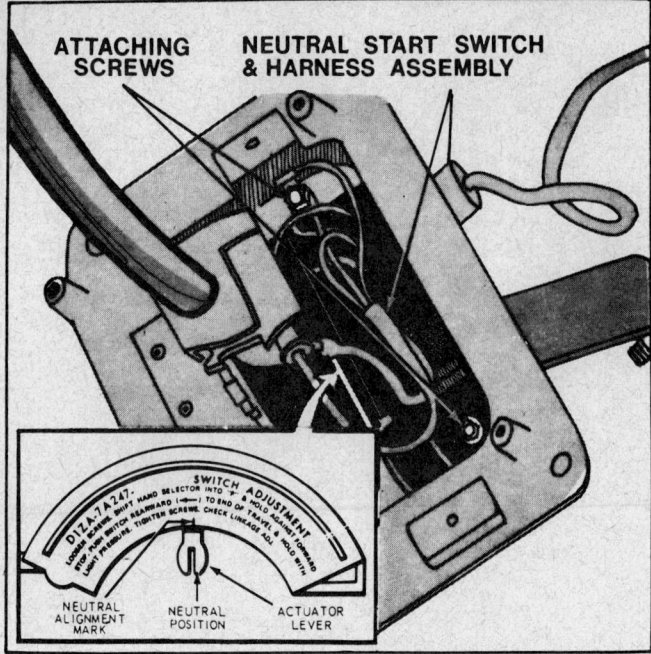

Fig. 8 Neutral safety switch. 1977–79 Cougar & LTD II with console

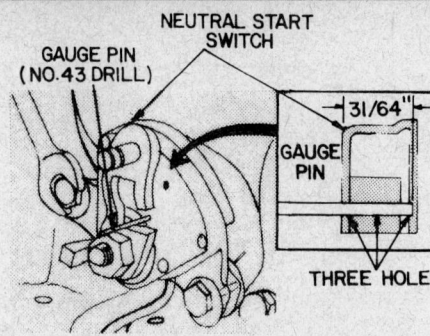

Fig. 9 Neutral safety switch. Transmission mounted

1977 Comet & Maverick; 1977–80 Monarch; 1977–82 Granada; 1978–83 Fairmont & Zephyr; 1980–82 Cougar XR-7; 1980–84 Thunderbird; 1981–84 Cougar; 1983–84 LTD & Marquis

Transmission Mounted Switch, Except Automatic Overdrive Transmission, Fig. 9

1. Remove downshift linkage rod from transmission downshift lever.
2. Apply penetrating oil to downshift lever shaft and nut; then remove downshift outer lever.
3. Remove switch attaching bolts.
4. Disconnect multiple wire connector and remove switch from transmission.
5. Install new switch.
6. With transmission manual lever in neutral, rotate switch and install gauge pin (#43 drill) into gauge pin holes.

NOTE: The shank end of the drill must be inserted 31/64 in. (15/32 in., 1983–84 models) into each of the gauge pin holes.

7. Tighten switch attaching bolts and remove gauge pin.
8. Complete the installation in reverse order of removal.

Transmission Mounted Switch, Automatic Overdrive Transmission

1. Disconnect battery ground cable.
2. Place transmission gear selector in manual low position.
3. Raise and support vehicle.
4. Disconnect electrical connector from neutral start switch. Lift connector straight up off switch using a long screwdriver under the rubber plug of connector.
5. Remove switch and "O" ring using socket No. T74P-77247-A or equivalent, and a 9½ inch extension.

NOTE: Use of any tools other than those specified may result in damage to the vehicle.

6. Reverse procedure to install. Torque switch to 7–10 ft. lbs.

TURN SIGNAL SWITCH, REPLACE

1978–83 Fairmont & Zephyr; 1980–82 Cougar XR-7; 1980–84 Thunderbird; 1981–82 Granada; 1981–84 Cougar; 1983–84 LTD & Marquis

1. Disconnect battery ground cable.

---

bottoms. On all other models, install knob and shaft by inserting shaft into the switch until a distinct click is heard. In some instances it may be necessary to rotate the shaft slightly until it engages the switch carrier.

STOP LIGHT SWITCH, REPLACE

1. Disconnect battery ground cable and disconnect wires at switch connector.

NOTE: On 1977–80 Granada and Monarch models with vacuum power brake units, loosen brake booster nut ¼ turn, thereby eliminating binding during removal.

2. Remove hairpin retainer and slide stop light switch, push rod, nylon washers and bushings away from brake pedal, and remove switch, Fig. 7.
3. Reverse procedure to install and on 1977–80 Granada and Monarch models, torque brake booster retaining nuts to 13-25 ft. lbs.

NEUTRAL SAFETY SWITCH, REPLACE

1977–79 Cougar, LTD II & Thunderbird Console

Removal & Adjustment, Fig. 8.
1. Place selector lever in neutral.
2. Raise vehicle and remove nut that secures shift rod to transmission manual lever.
3. Lower vehicle and remove selector level handle and dial housing.
4. Disconnect dial light and neutral start

switch wires at dash panel.

NOTE: On models with FMX transmission, disconnect seat belt warning circuit connector.

5. Remove selector lever and housing assembly.
6. Remove pointer back up shield attaching screws and remove shield.
7. Remove neutral start switch to selector lever housing attaching screws.
8. Push neutral start switch harness plug inward and remove switch and harness assembly.
9. Position switch and harness assembly on selector lever housing, then install but do not tighten attaching screws.

NOTE: Before installing switch and harness assembly, ensure selector lever is against neutral detent stop and actuator lever is properly aligned in neutral position.

10. Place selector lever in "Park" position and hold against forward stop.
11. Move neutral start switch rearward to end of its travel, then while holding switch in rearward position tighten attaching screws.
12. Install pointer back up shield, then position selector lever and housing assembly on console and install attaching bolts.
13. Connect dial indicator, neutral start switch and seat belt warning circuit (if equipped) wire connectors.
14. Install dial housing and shift lever handle, then place selector lever in "Drive" position.
15. Raise vehicle and install shift rod on transmission manual lever.
16. Check shift linkage adjustment, then lower vehicle and check operation of neutral start switch.

2. On 1981–84 models with tilt column, remove upper extension shroud. Unsnap shroud from retaining clip located at the 9 o'clock position.
3. On all models, remove trim shroud or shroud halves.
4. Remove turn signal switch lever from switch. Grasp lever and use a pulling and twisting motion while pulling lever straight out from switch.
5. Peel back foam shield from turn signal switch, then disconnect two electrical connectors from switch.
6. Remove turn signal switch attaching screws and the switch from vehicle.
7. Reverse procedure to install.

Except 1978–83 Fairmont & Zephyr; 1980–82 Cougar XR-7; 1980–84 Thunderbird; 1981–82 Granada; 1980–84 Cougar; 1983–84 LTD & Marquis

1. Remove retaining screw from underside of steering wheel spokes and lift off pad horn switch/trim cover and medallion as an assembly.
2. Disconnect horn switch wires from terminals.
3. Remove steering wheel retaining nut and remove steering wheel with suitable puller.
4. Remove turn signal switch lever by unscrewing it from steering column.
5. Remove shroud from under steering column.
6. Disconnect steering column wiring connector plugs and remove screws that secure switch to column.
7. On tilt column, remove wires and terminals from column plug. *NOTE: Record color code and position of wires before removing. A hole provided in the flange casting on fixed columns makes it unnecessary to separate wires from plug as the plug with wires can be guided through hole.*
8. Remove plastic cover sleeve from wiring harness and remove switch from top of column.

HORN SOUNDER, REPLACE

NOTE: On 1978–83 Fairmont, Zephyr, 1980–82 Cougar XR-7, 1980–84 Thunderbird, 1981–82 Granada, 1981–84 Cougar and 1983–84 LTD & Marquis, the horn sounder is located on the turn signal, headlight dimmer and horn lever. Refer to Turn Signal Switch Replace, when replacing lever.

The horn button used on some models may be removed by twisting the button counterclockwise. The horn switch on some models is part of the trim cover assembly and if defective, the trim cover must be replaced. The horn sounder on rim-blow steering wheels equipped with speed control cannot be replaced and if defective, the steering wheel assembly must be replaced. On rim-blow steering wheels without speed control, the horn sounder (plastic strip and copper insert) may be replaced using the following procedure:
1. Remove trim pad and disconnect lead wires.
2. Remove plastic cover and lift out horn insert on inner diameter of steering wheel.
3. Reverse procedure to install.

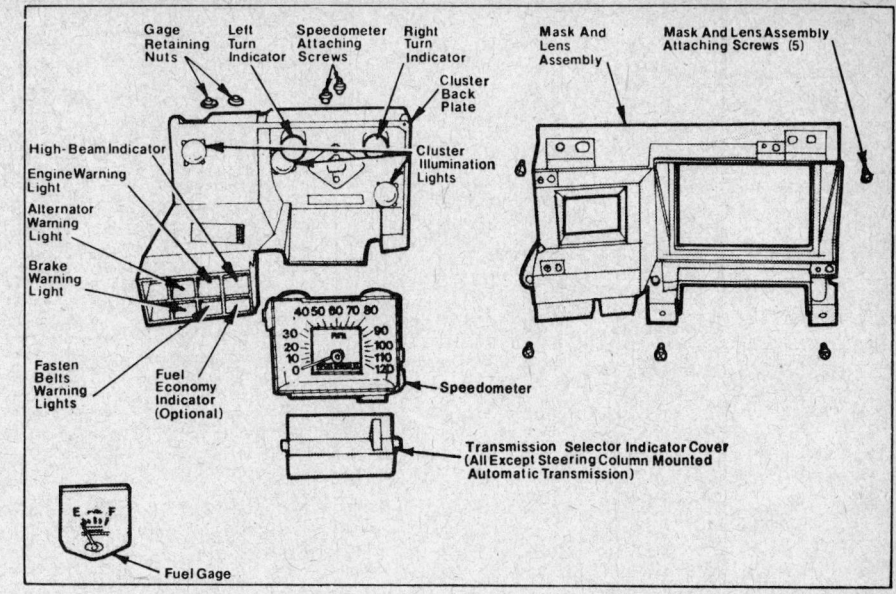

Fig. 10   Instrument cluster 1977–80 Granada & Monarch (Typical)

STEERING WHEEL, REPLACE

1. Disconnect battery ground cable.
2. Remove steering wheel trim pad, horn button or ring.

NOTE: On 1981–83 models with 4-spoke steering wheel, alternately push out on the cover retaining posts using a 9/32 inch rod through two access holes in back of steering wheel.

3. Disconnect horn and speed control wiring, if equipped.
4. Remove steering wheel nut.
5. Mark relationship between steering shaft and steering wheel hub for proper reinstallation.
6. Remove steering wheel with a suitable puller.
7. Reverse procedure to install.

INSTRUMENT CLUSTER, REPLACE

1980–82 Cougar XR-7, 1980–84 Thunderbird & 1983–84 Cougar, LTD & Marquis

STANDARD CLUSTER

1983–84 Cougar & Thunderbird
1. Disconnect battery ground cable.
2. Remove steering column shroud and instrument cluster trim cover.
3. Remove 6 instrument cluster-to-instrument panel attaching screws.
4. Pull cluster away from instrument panel and disconnect speedometer cable and cluster feed plugs.
5. Remove instrument cluster from vehicle.
6. Reverse procedure to install.

1981–84 Exc. 1983–84 Cougar & Thunderbird
1. Disconnect battery ground cable.
2. Disconnect speedometer cable, then remove instrument panel trim cover and steering column shroud.

3. Remove screw attaching transmission shift lever indicator cable bracket to steering column, then detach cable loop from pin on shift cane lever and remove plastic clamp from around steering column.
4. Remove four instrument cluster retaining screws, then disconnect cluster feed plug and remove instrument cluster.
5. Reverse procedure to install.

1980 Models
1. Disconnect battery ground cable.
2. Disconnect speedometer cable.
3. Remove steering column shroud and instrument cluster trim cover.
4. Remove six instrument cluster lens and mask attaching screws, then remove lens and mask.
5. Remove four instrument cluster attaching screws.
6. Disconnect cluster feed plug from printed circuit connector, then remove cluster assembly.
7. Reverse procedure to install.

ELECTRONIC CLUSTER
1. Disconnect battery ground cable.
2. Remove four instrument panel lower trim cover attaching screws, then remove trim cover.
3. Remove steering column shroud.
4. Remove six instrument cluster trim panel attaching screws, then remove trim panel.
5. Remove four instrument cluster to instrument panel attaching screws.
6. Remove screw attaching transmission selector lever indicator cable bracket to steering column, then detach cable loop from pin on steering column.
7. Carefully pull cluster assembly away from instrument panel.
8. Disconnect speedometer cable and cluster feed plug and ground wire from cluster back plate, then remove cluster assembly.
9. Reverse procedure to install.

1978–83 Fairmont, Zephyr & 1981–82 Cougar & Granada
1. Disconnect battery ground cable.

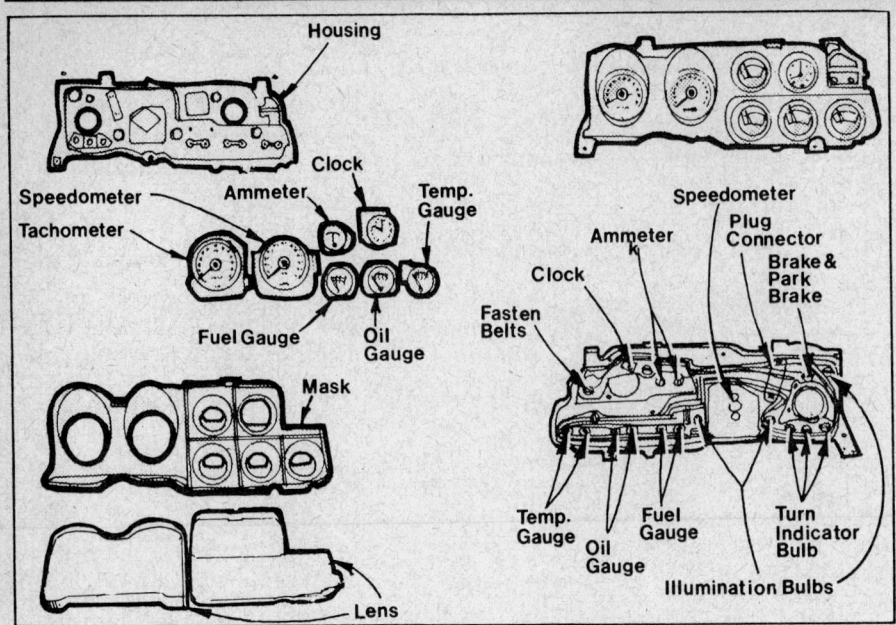

Fig. 11 Instrument cluster. 1977–79 Cougar, LTD II & Thunderbird with performance cluster

2. Remove steering column shroud.
3. Remove instrument cluster trim cover.
4. Remove screw retaining PRND21 control cable clamp to steering column. Then, disconnect the cable from pin on steering column. Remove plastic clamp from steering column.
5. Remove two upper and two lower screws retaining instrument cluster to instrument panel.
6. Pull cluster from instrument panel and disconnect speedometer cable.
7. Disconnect electrical connectors from instrument cluster.
8. Remove instrument cluster from vehicle.
9. Reverse procedure to install.

1977–80 Granada & Monarch

1. Disconnect battery ground cable.
2. Remove lower cluster cover from below steering column.
3. Remove steering column shroud.
4. On all models, remove headlamp switch knob and shaft assembly and bezel.
5. Remove four cluster finish panel attaching screws.
6. Using a right angle screwdriver, pry along edges of finish panel, thereby removing studs from retainers and remove finish panel.
7. Disconnect automatic transmission indicator cable and speedometer cable.

8. Remove four screws retaining cluster to instrument panel, then pull cluster out and disconnect feed plug from printed circuit, Fig. 10.
9. Disconnect wires from fuel gauge if equipped with low fuel warning light and remove cluster.
10. Reverse procedure to install

1977–79 Cougar XR7, LTD II & Thunderbird

1. Disconnect battery ground cable.
2. Remove upper and lower retaining screws from cluster trim cover and remove the cover, Figs. 11 and 12.
3. On 1977–79 models with standard cluster, remove clock or cover to cluster attaching screw and clock or cover to instrument panel retaining screw.
4. On all models, remove two upper and two lower screws retaining cluster to the panel.
5. Pull cluster away from panel and disconnect speedo cable.
6. Disconnect cluster feed plug from receptacle in printed circuit.
7. If equipped, remove Park, Belts and Fuel Economy lights from receptacles.
8. On Cougar, LTD II and Thunderbird models, disconnect overlay harness connector.
9. Remove cluster.
10. Reverse procedure to install.

1977 Comet & Maverick

1. Disconnect battery ground cable.
2. From under instrument panel, disconnect speedometer cable.
3. Remove two retaining screws at the top of the cluster and swing it down from the panel, Fig. 13.
4. Disconnect electrical connections and remove cluster.
5. Reverse procedure to install.

W/S WIPER MOTOR, REPLACE

1980–82 Cougar XR-7; 1980–84 Thunderbird; 1981–82 Granada; 1981–84 Cougar, Fairmont & Zephyr; 1983–84 LTD & Marquis

1. On 1983–84 Cougar and Thunderbird models, operate wipers and turn ignition key off when blades are straight up on the windshield.
2. On all models, disconnect battery ground cable.
3. On 1980–82 Cougar XR-7 and Thunderbird, and 1983–84 LTD and Marquis models, remove right hand wiper and blade assembly. On Fairmont, Granada, Zephyr, 1981–84 Cougar and 1983–84 Thunderbird models, remove both wiper arm and blade assemblies.
4. Remove cowl grille attaching screws, then remove cowl grille.
5. Remove clip, then disconnect linkage drive arm from motor crankpin.
6. Disconnect wire connector from wiper motor, then remove wiper motor attaching bolts and lift motor from cowl opening.

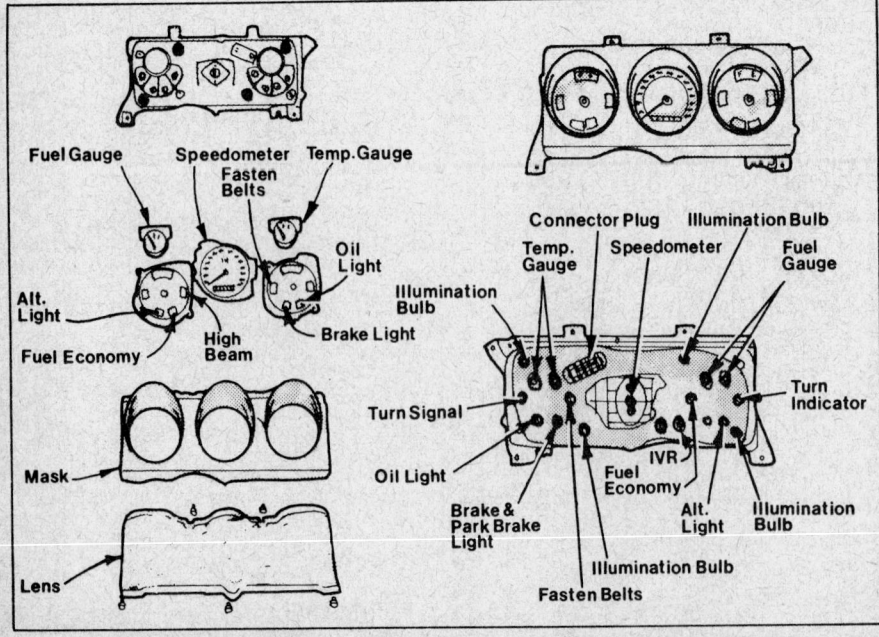

Fig. 12 Instrument cluster. 1977–79 Cougar, LTD II & Thunderbird with standard cluster

1978—80 Fairmont & Zephyr

1. Disconnect battery ground cable.
2. Remove left hand wiper arm from pivot shaft and place on cowl grille.
3. Remove cowl grille attaching screws, then raise left hand corner of cowl grille to gain access to linkage drive arm.
4. Disconnect linkage arm from motor output arm pin by removing retaining clip.
5. Disconnect wiper motor wire connector.
6. Remove wiper motor to cowl attaching bolts, then remove wiper motor.

1978—81 Fairmont, Zephyr, 1982 Cougar, Granada & 1983—84 LTD & Marquis Sta. Wag. Liftgate Wiper Motor

1. Disconnect battery ground cable.
2. Remove wiper arm and blade assembly.
3. Remove pivot shaft attaching nut and spacers.
4. On 1982—84 models, remove liftage inner trim panel.
5. On all models, remove license plate housing attaching screws, then disconnect lamp electrical connector and remove housing.
6. Disconnect wiper motor wire connector.
7. Remove linkage arm lock clip, then pry off arm and remove linkage.
8. Remove wiper motor and bracket attaching bolts, then remove motor and bracket.

1978—80 Granada & Monarch

1. Disconnect battery ground cable.
2. Remove instrument panel pad.
3. Remove speaker mounting bracket, then disconnect wire connector and remove speaker.
4. Remove defroster nozzle and air distribution duct.
5. Remove wiper motor to cowl attaching bolts, then remove wiper motor.

1977 Comet, Maverick, Granada & Monarch

1. Disconnect battery ground cable.
2. On all models, remove evaporator case center distribution duct assembly.
3. Working over top of brake support assembly, remove wiper motor pivot clip and disconnect linkage from motor arm.
4. Remove wiper motor attaching bolts and wiper motor.

NOTE: Some Granada and Monarch models may have an additional instrument panel brace which must be detached from the floor pan and swung to one side to provide access to wiper motor attaching bolts.

1977—79 Cougar, Thunderbird & LTD II

1. Disconnect battery ground cable.
2. Remove wiper arm and blade assembly.
3. Remove left cowl screen, then remove retaining clip and disconnect drive arm from motor crankpin.
4. Disconnect wire connectors from motor, then remove attaching bolts and motor.

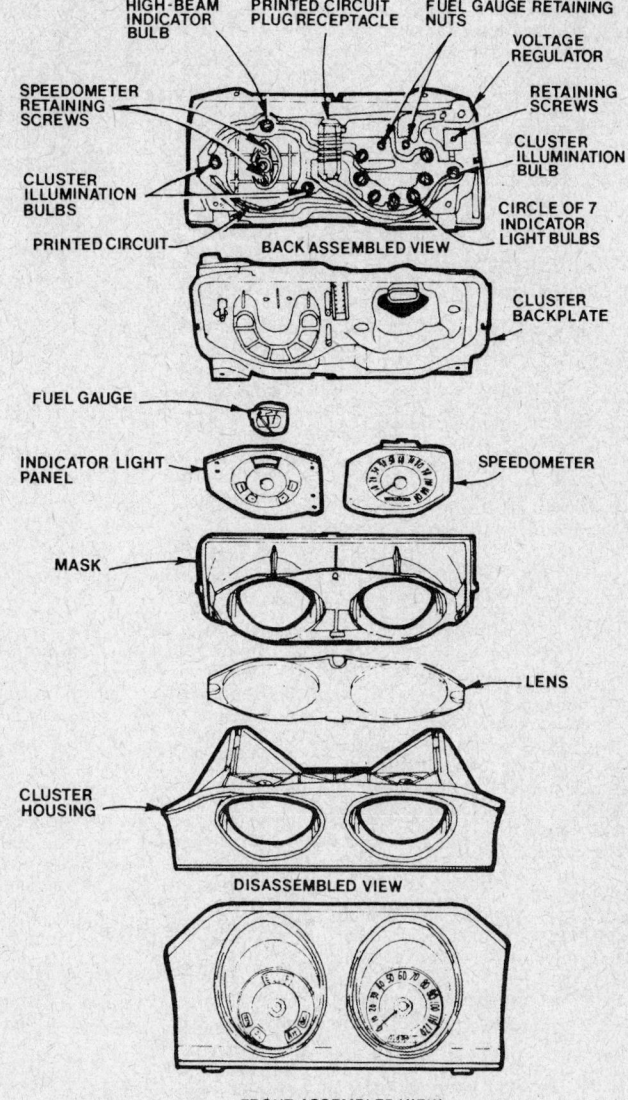

Fig. 13 Instrument cluster. 1977 Comet & Maverick

NOTE: If output arm catches on dash during removal, handturn arm clockwise so it will clear. Before installing ensure output arm is in "park" position.

W/S WIPER, TRANSMISSION REPLACE

1979—83 Fairmont & Zephyr; 1980—82 Cougar XR-7; 1980—84 Thunderbird; 1981—82 Granada; 1981—84 Cougar; 1983—84 LTD & Marquis

1. On 1983—84 Cougar and Thunderbird models, operate wipers and turn ignition key off when blades are straight up on windshield.
2. On all models, disconnect battery ground cable.
3. On all models except 1983—84 Cougar and Thunderbird, remove both wiper arm and blade assemblies.
4. On 1983—84 Cougar and Thunderbird models, remove right wiper arm and blade assembly.
5. On all models, remove cowl grille attaching screws and the cowl grille.
6. Remove retaining clip, then disconnect linkage drive arm from wiper motor crankpin.
7. On Fairmont, Granada, Zephyr and 1981—82 Cougar models, remove 4 bolts attaching left and right pivot shafts to cowl, then remove linkage assembly.
8. On Cougar XR-7, Thunderbird and 1983—84 LTD and Marquis models, remove 2 bolts attaching right pivot shaft to cowl, then remove nut, washer and spacer from left pivot shaft and remove linkage assembly.
9. On 1983—84 Cougar and Thunderbird models, remove pivot shaft attaching screws, then remove linkage assembly out through cowl chamber.
10. Reverse procedure to install.

1978 Fairmont & Zephyr

1. Disconnect battery ground cable.
2. Remove wiper arms and blade assemblies

from pivot shafts, then remove cowl grille attaching screws.

3. If left pivot shaft assembly is to be removed, disconnect linkage drive arm from right drive arm by removing retaining clip.
4. If right pivot shaft assembly is to be removed, disconnect linkage drive arm from motor and left drive arm by removing retaining clips.
5. Remove pivot shaft retaining screws, then remove linkage and pivot shaft assemblies.

1977–79 Cougar, LTD II & Thunderbird

1. Disconnect battery ground cable.
2. Remove wiper arm and blade assemblies.
3. Remove cowl screen. Screen snaps into cowl and the arm stop is integral with the screen.
4. Disconnect linkage drive arm from motor by removing retaining clip.
5. Remove pivot shaft retaining bolts and remove linkage and pivot shaft assemblies.

1977 Comet, Maverick & 1977–80 Granada & Monarch

Left Side:
1. Remove instrument cluster.
2. Remove wiper arm and blade.
3. Working through cluster opening, disconnect both pivot shaft links from motor drive arm by removing retaining clip.
4. Remove three pivot shaft assembly retaining bolts and remove assembly through cluster opening.
5. Reverse procedure to install.

Right Side:
1. Disconnect battery ground cable and remove wiper blade and arm.
2. On air conditioned units, remove right duct assembly.
3. From under the instrument panel, disconnect first left then right pivot shaft link from motor drive arm.
4. Reaching between utility shelf and instrument panel, remove pivot shaft retaining bolts and lower assembly out from under panel.
5. Reverse procedure to install.

W/S WIPER SWITCH, REPLACE

1977–79 Except Comet, Fairmont, Granada, Maverick, Monarch & Zephyr

1. Disconnect battery ground cable.
2. Remove wiper switch knob, bezel nut and bezel. The wiper switch knob is removed in the same manner as the headlight switch knob, Fig. 5.
3. Pull out switch from under panel and disconnect plug connector from switch.
4. Reverse procedure to install.

1979–83 Fairmont & Zephyr; 1980–82 Cougar XR-7; 1980–84 Thunderbird; 1981–82 Granada; 1981–84 Cougar; 1983–84 LTD & Marquis

1. Disconnect battery ground cable.

2. Remove four steering column shroud attaching screws, then grasp top and bottom of shroud and separate.
3. Using a screwdriver, disconnect wire connector from wiper switch.
4. Remove two wiper switch attaching screws, then remove switch.
5. Reverse procedure to install.

1978–81 Fairmont, Zephyr, 1982 Cougar, Granada & 1983–84 LTD & Marquis Sta. Wag. Liftgate Wiper Motor

1. Disconnect battery ground cable.
2. Remove wiper switch knob, then remove two bezel retaining screws.
3. Pull switch retainer away from instrument panel.
4. Remove wiper switch retaining nut, then separate switch from retainer.
5. Disconnect wire connector from wiper switch, then remove switch.
6. Reverse procedure to install.

1977–80 Granada, Monarch Column Mounted Switch

1. Disconnect battery ground cable.
2. Disconnect turn signal and wiper/washer switch wire connector.
3. Remove lower instrument panel shield.
4. Remove two screws and separate steering column cover halves.
5. Pull wire cover from bottom on column and remove cover.
6. With a screwdriver, disengage wiring shield tang and pry shield to remove.
7. Remove screw securing turn signal and windshield wiper/washer switch assembly to column, then remove the assembly.
8. Reverse procedure to install.

1977 Comet, & Maverick

1. Disconnect battery ground cable and remove switch knob.
2. On units without air conditioning, remove bezel nut and pull switch through panel. On air conditioned units, remove instrument cluster.
3. Disconnect wiring and remove switch.
4. Reverse procedure to install.

RADIO, REPLACE

NOTE: When installing radio, be sure to adjust antenna trimmer for peak performance.

1980–82 Cougar XR-7, 1980–84 Thunderbird & 1983–84 Cougar, LTD & Marquis

1. Disconnect battery ground cable.
2. Remove radio knobs, then remove instrument panel center trim panel.
3. Remove radio mounting plate attaching screws.
4. Pull radio to disengage from lower rear support bracket, then disconnect power antenna, speaker leads and floor switch lead, if equipped and remove radio.
5. Reverse procedure to install.

1978–83 Fairmont, Zephyr & 1981–82 Cougar & Granada

1. Disconnect battery ground cable.
2. Disconnect power lead, speaker leads and antenna lead from radio.
3. Remove control knobs, discs, control knob shaft nuts and washers.
4. Remove ash tray and bracket.
5. Remove radio rear support attaching nut.
6. Remove instrument panel lower reinforcement.
7. Remove heater or A/C floor ducts.
8. Remove radio from bezel and rear support, then lower radio from instrument panel.
9. Reverse procedure to install.

1977–80 Granada & Monarch

1. Disconnect battery ground cable.
2. Remove headlamp switch.
3. Remove knobs from heater and A/C control, windshield wiper switch and radio.
4. Remove instrument panel applique.
5. Disconnect antenna lead.
6. Remove radio bezel to instrument panel screws, then pull radio and bezel out to disconnect remaining electrical leads and remove radio from panel.
7. Remove rear support bracket and bezel from radio.
8. Reverse procedure to install.

1977–79 Thunderbird

1. Disconnect battery ground cable.
2. Pull radio knobs off shafts.
3. Remove nut from radio control shafts.
4. Remove radio rear support attaching screw at instrument panel.
5. Disconnect power and speaker wires at connectors.
6. Disconnect antenna lead and remove radio.
7. Reverse procedure to install.

1977 Comet, Maverick

1. Disconnect battery ground cable.
2. Disconnect power lead, speaker lead and antenna lead from radio.
3. Remove radio knobs, discs, control shaft nuts and washers.
4. Remove radio rear support attaching nut.
5. Remove radio from bezel and from rear support.
6. Reverse procedure to install.

1977–79 Cougar & LTD II

1. Disconnect battery ground cable.
2. Pull off radio control knobs.
3. Remove radio support to instrument panel attaching screw.
4. Remove bezel nuts from radio control shafts, then lower radio and disconnect speaker, power and antenna wire from radio.
5. Reverse procedure to install.

HEATER CORE, REPLACE

1983–84 Cougar & Thunderbird

Less Air Conditioning
1. Disconnect battery ground cable.
2. Remove steering column cover, then the instrument panel reinforcement under steering column opening.

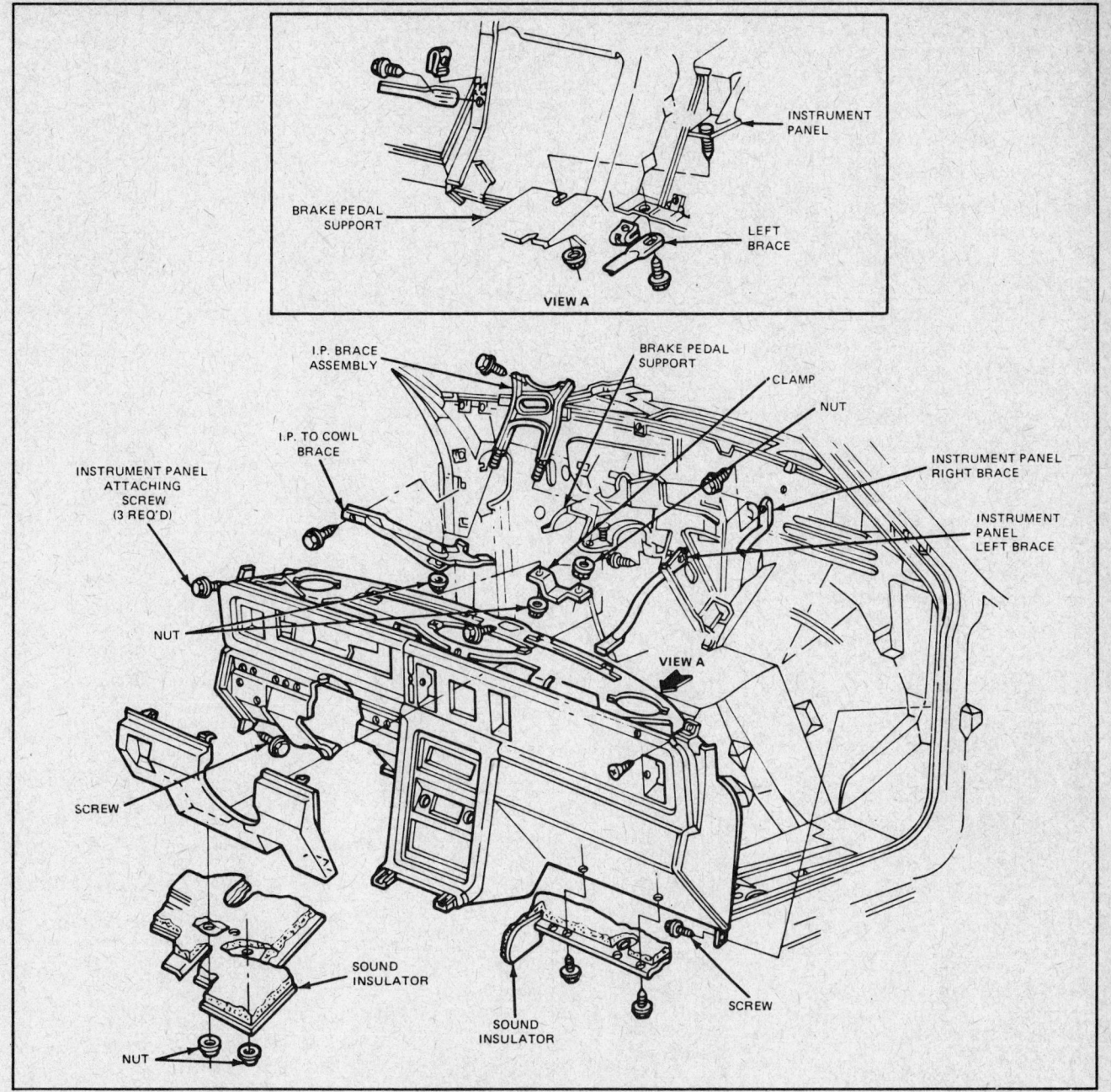

Fig. 14 Instrument panel. 1983—84 Cougar & Thunderbird

3. Remove 2 nuts securing hood latch release handle mounting bracket to brake pedal support under steering column.
4. Remove sound insulator from lower left side of instrument panel, Fig. 14.
5. Remove 2 steering column clamp attaching nuts and lower steering column to rest on front seat.
6. Remove instrument panel pad attaching screws and the pad.
7. Disconnect speedometer cable from speedometer.
8. Remove console cover or tray.
9. Remove 4 console switch panel cover attaching screws, then disconnect electrical connectors and remove switch panel.
10. Remove console attaching screws, then disengage console from instrument panel and position aside.
11. Remove 2 pins attaching glove compart-ment door straps to glove compartment and allow door to hang down on hinge.
12. Remove instrument panel brace attaching bolt from glove compartment opening.
13. Remove brake pedal support attaching nut from lower edge of instrument panel.
14. Remove instrument panel brace attaching bolt from lower edge of instrument panel on left side of console extension.
15. Remove instrument panel-to-cowl side panel attaching bolt from both sides of instrument panel.
16. Support instrument panel and remove 3 instrument panel-to-cowl top panel attaching screws.
17. Move instrument panel rearward, disconnect necessary electrical connectors and vacuum hoses, and rest panel on front seat.
18. Drain cooling system, then disconnect hoses from heater core. Cover hoses and heater core tubes to prevent leakage.
19. Remove 2 nuts securing heater case to dash panel from engine compartment.
20. Working in passenger compartment, remove screws attaching heater case support bracket and air inlet duct support bracket to cowl top panel.
21. Remove nut retaining bracket at left end of heater case to dash panel and nut securing bracket below case to dash panel.
22. Pull heater case away from dash panel to gain access to heater core access cover attaching screws.
23. Remove 5 heater core access cover attaching screws and the cover.
24. Remove heater core and seals from heater

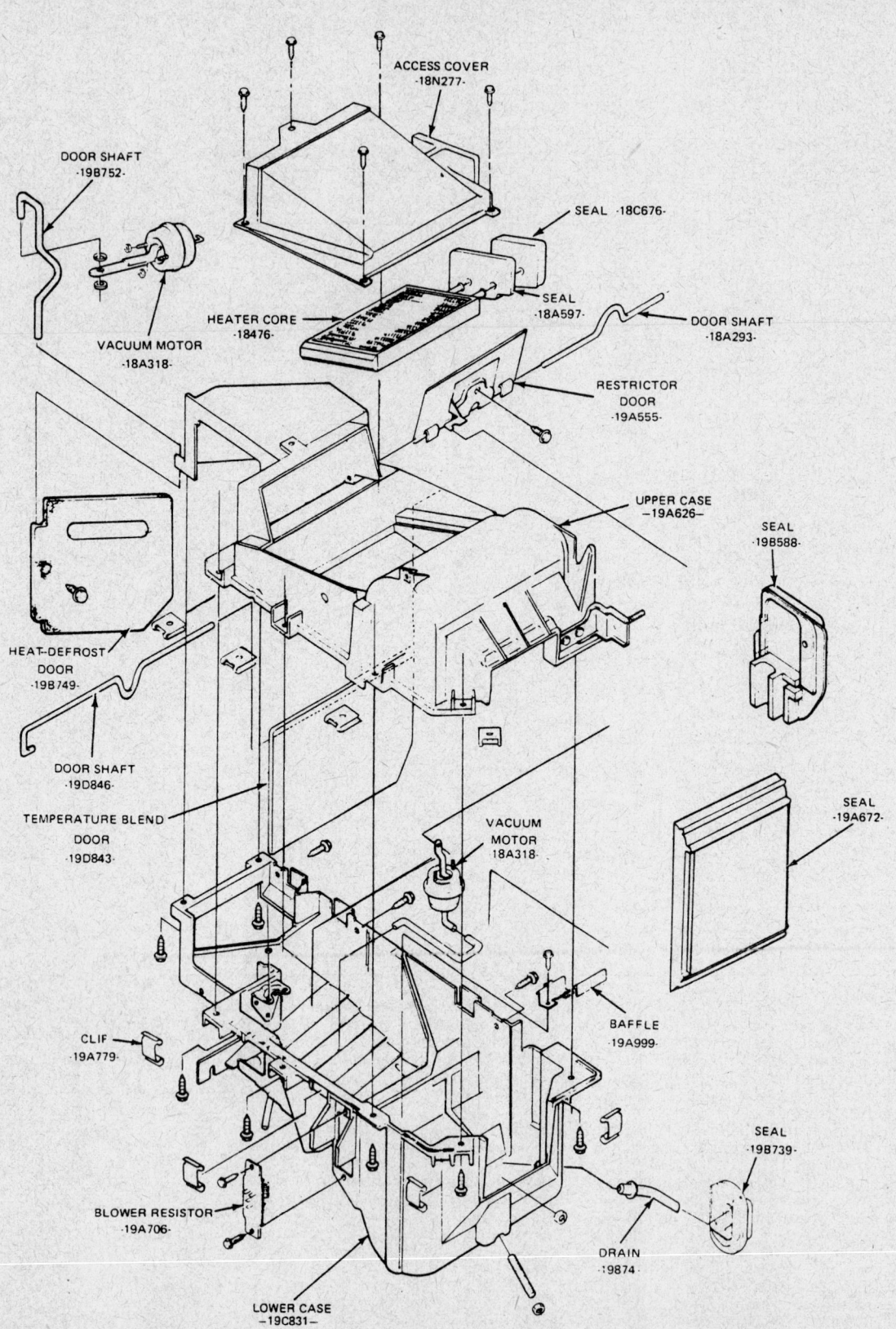

ACCESS COVER
-18N277-

DOOR SHAFT
-19B752-

SEAL -18C676-

SEAL
-18A597-

DOOR SHAFT
-18A293-

VACUUM MOTOR
-18A318-

HEATER CORE
-18476-

RESTRICTOR
DOOR
-19A555-

UPPER CASE
-19A626-

SEAL
-19B588-

HEAT-DEFROST
DOOR
-19B749-

DOOR SHAFT
-19D846-

TEMPERATURE BLEND
DOOR
-19D843-

VACUUM
MOTOR
-18A318-

SEAL
-19A672-

BAFFLE
-19A999-

CLIF
-19A779-

SEAL
-19B739-

BLOWER RESISTOR
-19A706-

DRAIN
-19874-

LOWER CASE
-19C831-

Fig. 15 Heater core less air conditioning. 1980–82 Cougar XR-7, 1980–84 Thunderbird & 1983–84 Cougar, LTD & Marquis

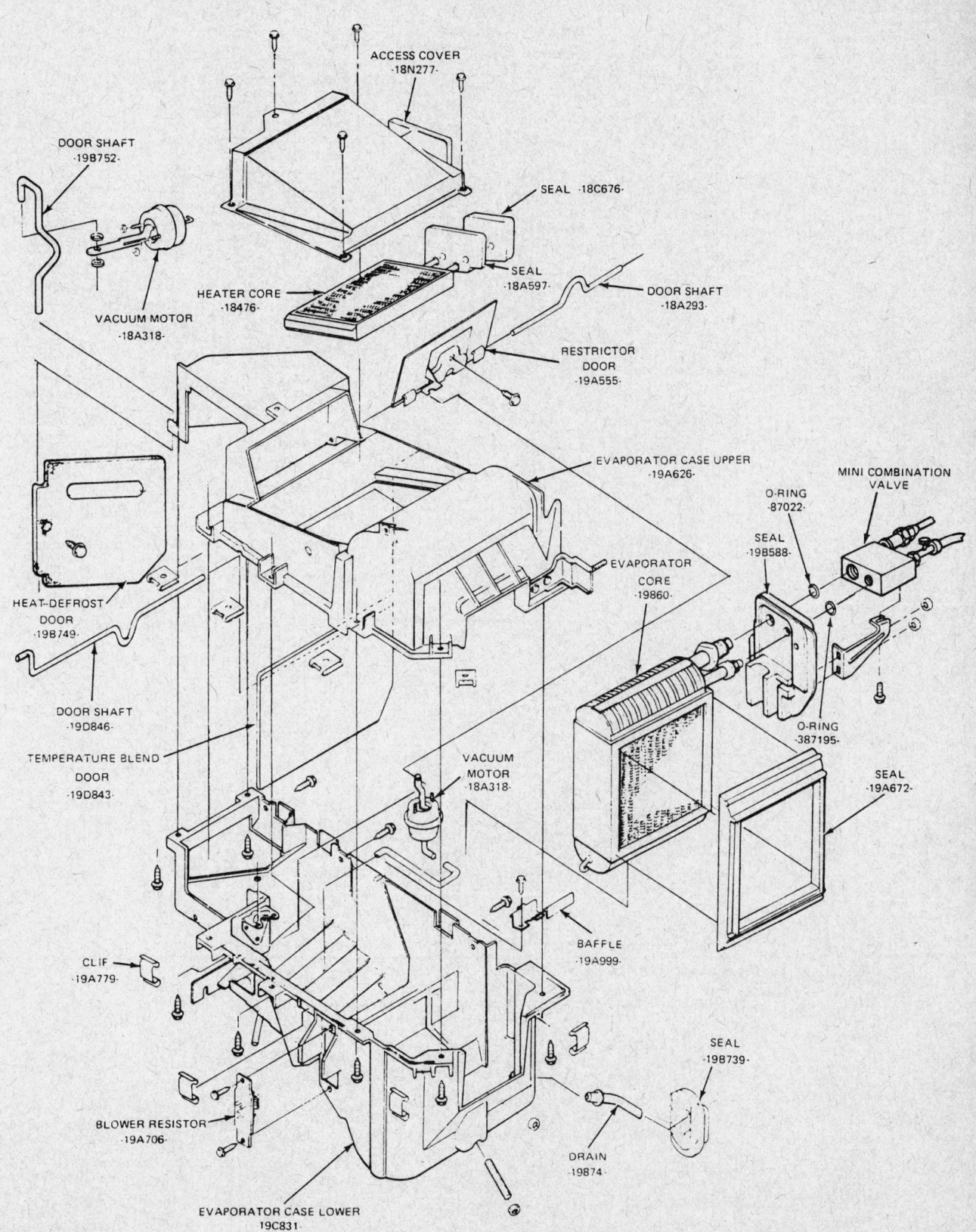

DOOR SHAFT
-19B752-

ACCESS COVER
-18N277-

SEAL -18C676-

VACUUM MOTOR
-18A318-

HEATER CORE
-18476-

SEAL
-18A597-

DOOR SHAFT
-18A293-

RESTRICTOR
DOOR
-19A555-

EVAPORATOR CASE UPPER
-19A626-

MINI COMBINATION
VALVE

O-RING
-87022-

SEAL
-19B588-

EVAPORATOR
CORE
-19860-

HEAT-DEFROST
DOOR
-19B749-

DOOR SHAFT
-19D846-

TEMPERATURE BLEND
DOOR
-19D843-

VACUUM
MOTOR
-18A318-

O-RING
-387195-

SEAL
-19A672-

CLIP
-19A779-

BAFFLE
-19A999-

SEAL
-19B739-

BLOWER RESISTOR
-19A706-

DRAIN
-19874-

EVAPORATOR CASE LOWER
19C831-

Fig. 16 Heater core with air conditioning. 1978–83 Fairmont, Zephyr, 1980–82 Cougar XR-7, 1980–84 Thunderbird, 1981–82 Granada, 1981–84 Cougar & 1983–84 LTD & Marquis

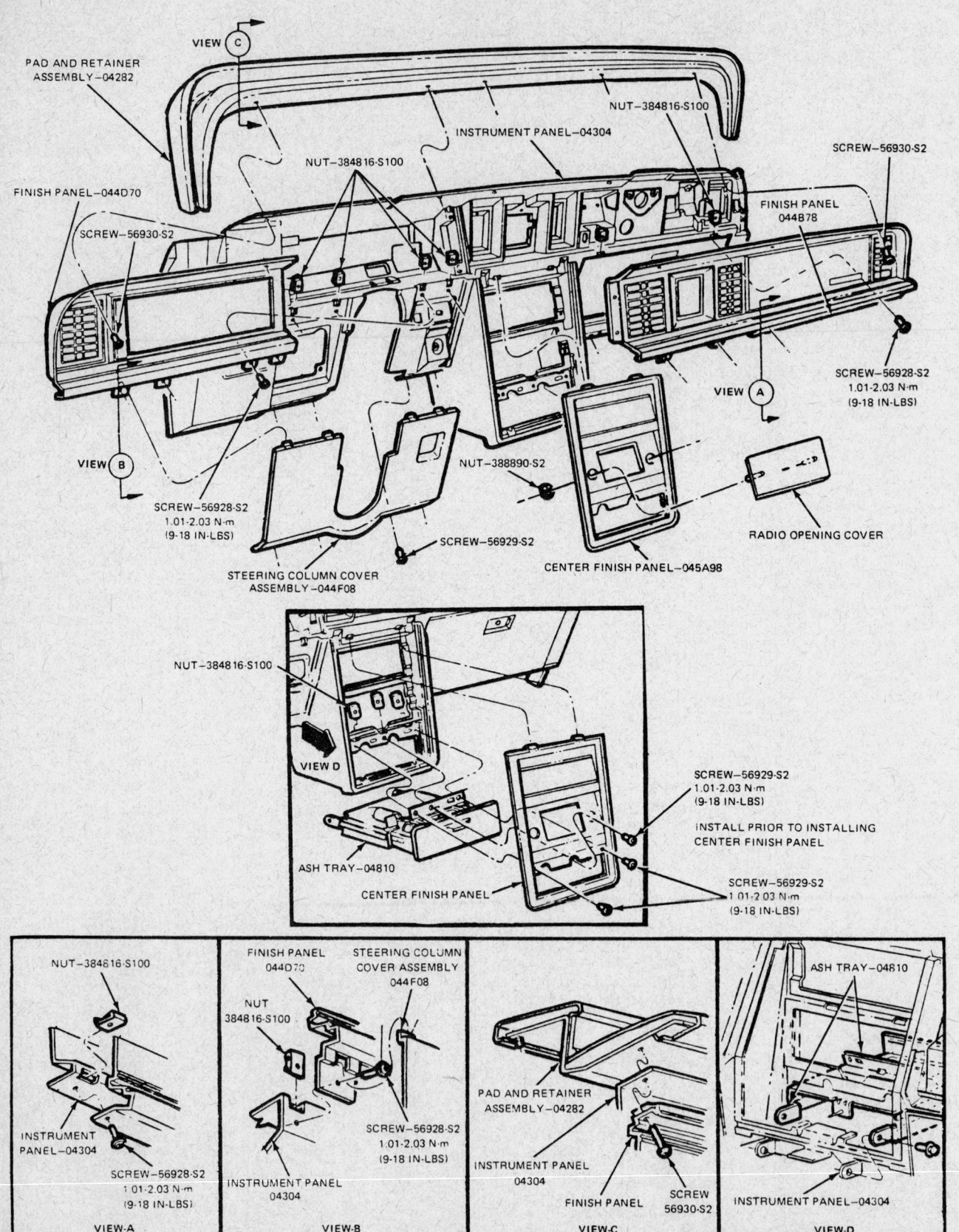

Fig. 17 Instrument panel trim panel (Typical). 1980-82 Cougar XR-7, Thunderbird & 1983-84 LTD & Marquis

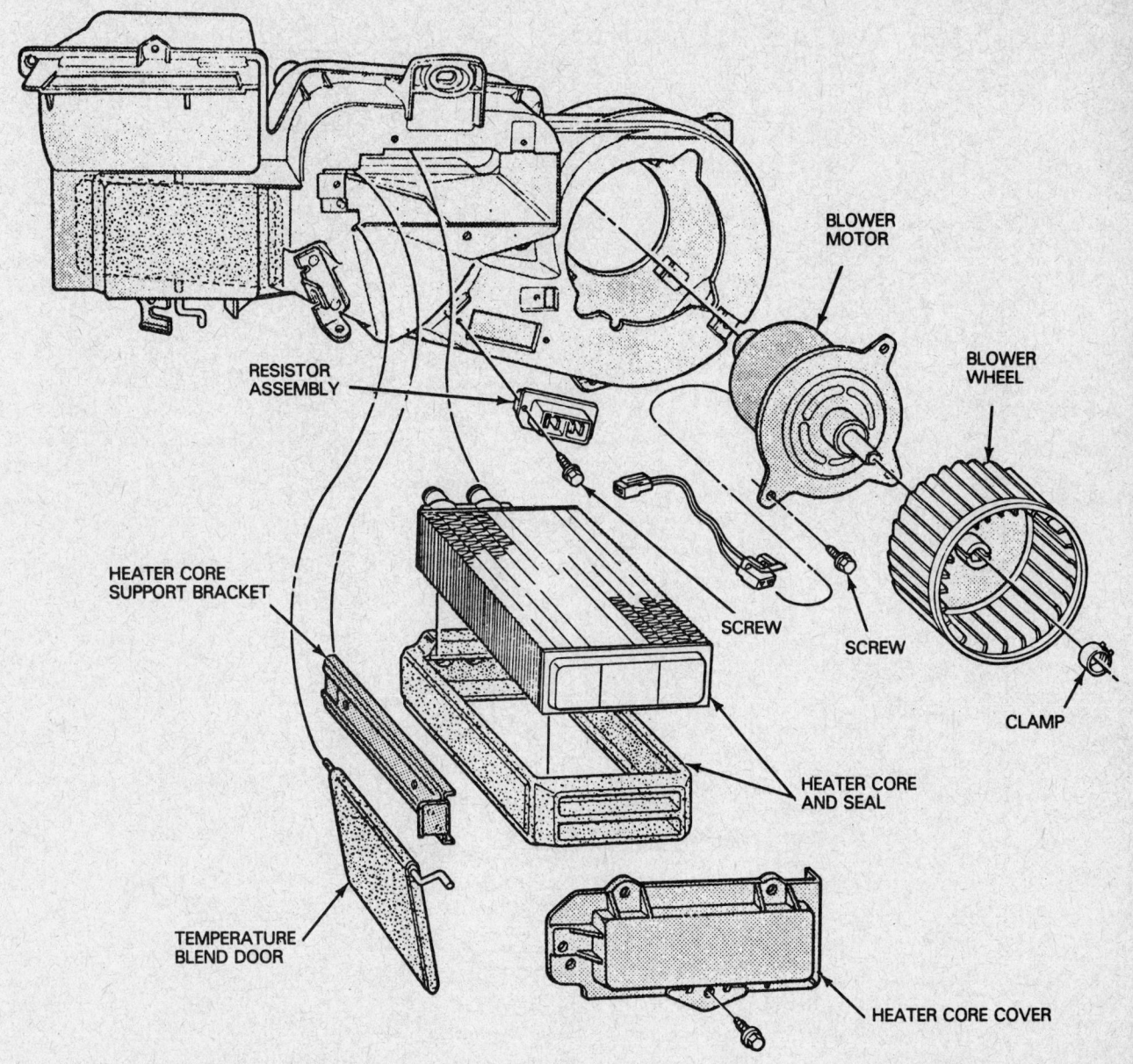

Fig. 18   Heater core assembly built after 11-1-81. 1982—83 Fairmont & Zephyr & 1982 Cougar & Granada

case, Fig. 15.
25. Remove the 2 seals from heater core tubes.
26. Reverse procedure to install.

With Air Conditioning

1. Perform steps 1 through 17 as described under "Heater Core, Replace," "1983—84 Cougar & Thunderbird, Less Air Conditioning."
2. Discharge refrigerant from A/C system at the service valve on suction line. When system is fully discharged, disconnect and cap high and low pressure lines.
3. Drain cooling system, then disconnect hoses from heater core. Cover hoses and heater core tubes to prevent leakage.
4. Remove screw securing air inlet duct and blower housing assembly support brace to cowl top panel.
5. Disconnect black vacuum supply hose

from in-line check valve in engine compartment.
6. Disconnect blower motor electrical connectors from harness.
7. Remove 2 evaporator case-to-dash panel attaching nuts from engine compartment.
8. Working in passenger compartment, remove evaporator case support bracket-to-cowl top panel attaching screw.
9. Remove nut securing bracket below evaporator case to dash panel.
10. Carefully remove evaporator case assembly from vehicle.
11. Remove 5 heater core access cover attaching screws and the cover.
12. Remove heater core and seals from evaporator case, Fig. 16.
13. Remove the 2 seals from heater core tubes.
14. Reverse procedure to install.

1980—82 Cougar XR-7, Thunderbird, 1983—84 LTD & Marquis

1. Disconnect battery ground cable.
2. Remove steering column cover assembly, then remove left and right finish panels, Fig. 17.
3. Remove two screws from sides of instrument panel pad and retainer assembly.
4. Remove pad and retainer assembly and upper finish panel.
5. Remove steering column attaching bolts, then carefully lower steering column just enough to allow access to transmission gear selector lever cable assembly. Reach between steering column and instrument panel, then carefully lift selector lever cable from lever and remove cable clamp from steering column tube.

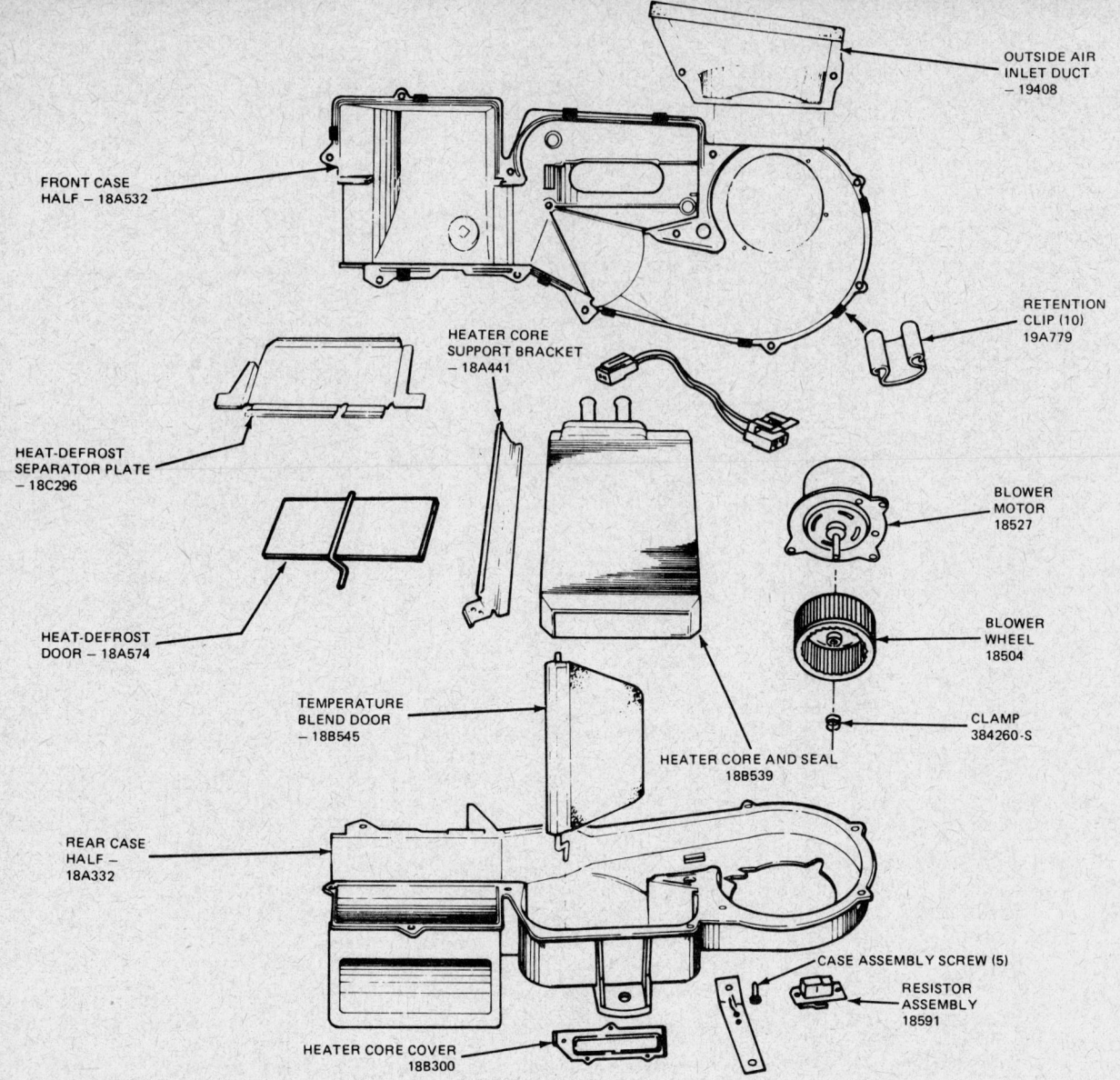

Fig. 19 Heater case assembly built prior to 11-1-81. 1978–82 Fairmont, Zephyr, 1981–82 Cougar & Granada

6. Lower steering column and allow to rest on front seat.
7. Remove screw attaching instrument panel to brake pedal support through steering column opening.
8. Disconnect temperature door cable from door and heater/evaporator cable bracket.
9. Disconnect vacuum hose connectors at evaporator housing.
10. Disconnect blower motor resistor wire from resistor on heater/evaporator case and blower motor feed wire at inline connector.
11. Support instrument panel, then remove three screws attaching top of instrument panel to cowl.
12. Remove one screw attaching each end of instrument panel to cowl side panels, then remove two screws attaching instrument panel to floor.
13. Move instrument panel rearward and disconnect speedometer cable and any wires

that will prevent instrument panel from being placed on front seat.

NOTE: Use care when removing instrument panel to prevent damage to panel or steering column surfaces.

14. On all 1980–81 models and 1982–84 models less A/C, perform steps 18 through 26 under "Heater Core, Replace," 1983–84 Cougar & Thunderbird, Less Air Conditioning."
15. On 1983–84 models with A/C, perform steps 2 through 14 under "Heater Core, Replace," "1983–84 Cougar & Thunderbird, With Air Conditioning."

1978–83 Fairmont, Zephyr & 1981–82 Cougar & Granada

SERVICE NOTE: Models with heater cases

built after 1-11-81 use a one piece case, Fig. 18. This type case cannot be separated and all interior case components must be removed and installed through openings in the case.

Less Air Conditioning
1. Disconnect battery ground cable and drain cooling system.
2. Disconnect heater hoses from heater core and seal the core tubes.
3. Remove glove box liner.
4. Remove instrument panel to cowl brace retaining screws and brace.
5. Place temperature control lever in the warm position.
6. Remove heater core cover retaining screws and the cover, Figs. 18 and 19.
7. From engine compartment, remove heater case assembly mounting stud nuts.
8. Push heater core tubes and seal toward passenger compartment to loosen heater core from case assembly.

9. Remove heater core through glove box opening.
10. Reverse procedure to install.

With Air Conditioning
1. Disconnect battery ground cable.
2. Remove screws attaching instrument cluster trim panel to instrument panel pad.
3. Remove instrument panel pad to instrument panel screws at each defroster opening.
4. Remove instrument panel pad edge to instrument panel screws, and pad.
5. Remove steering column lower cover to instrument panel screws then the cover.
6. On 1978 models, remove two nuts and bracket securing steering column to instrument panel and brake pedal support. Support steering column on front seat.
7. On 1979–84 models, proceed as follows:
   a. Remove steering column trim shroud attaching screws and the trim shrouds.
   b. Remove steering column attaching nuts, then carefully lower steering column just enough to allow access to transmission gear selector lever cable assembly. Reach between steering column and instrument panel and carefully lift selector lever cable from lever and remove cable clamp from steering column tube.
   c. Lower steering column and allow to rest on front seat.
8. On all models, remove instrument panel to brake pedal support screw at steering column opening.
9. Remove screw attaching lower brace to lower edge of instrument panel below radio.
10. Remove screw attaching the brace to lower edge of instrument panel.
11. Disconnect temperature control cable from blend door and evaporator case bracket.
12. Disconnect vacuum hose connectors from evaporator case.
13. Disconnect blower resistor wire connector from resistor on evaporator housing, then the blower motor feed wire at in-line connector.
14. Support instrument panel and, with an angle Phillips screwdriver, remove three screws attaching top of instrument panel to the cowl.
15. Remove screws attaching instrument panel to cowl side panels.
16. Move instrument panel rearward and disconnect speedometer cable and any wiring that will not permit the instrument panel to be positioned on the front seat.
17. On 1978–81 models, proceed as follows:
   a. Drain cooling system, then disconnect hoses from heater core and seal core tubes.
   b. From engine compartment, remove nuts retaining evaporator case to dash panel.
   c. From passenger compartment, remove screws attaching evaporator case support bracket and air inlet duct support bracket to cowl top panel.
   d. Remove one nut retaining bracket at left end of evaporator case to dash panel and one nut retaining bracket beneath the case to dash panel.
   e. Pull evaporator case assembly from dash panel.
18. On 1982–84 models, proceed as follows:
   a. Discharge refrigerant from A/C system at the service valve on suction line. When system is fully discharged, disconnect and cap high and lower

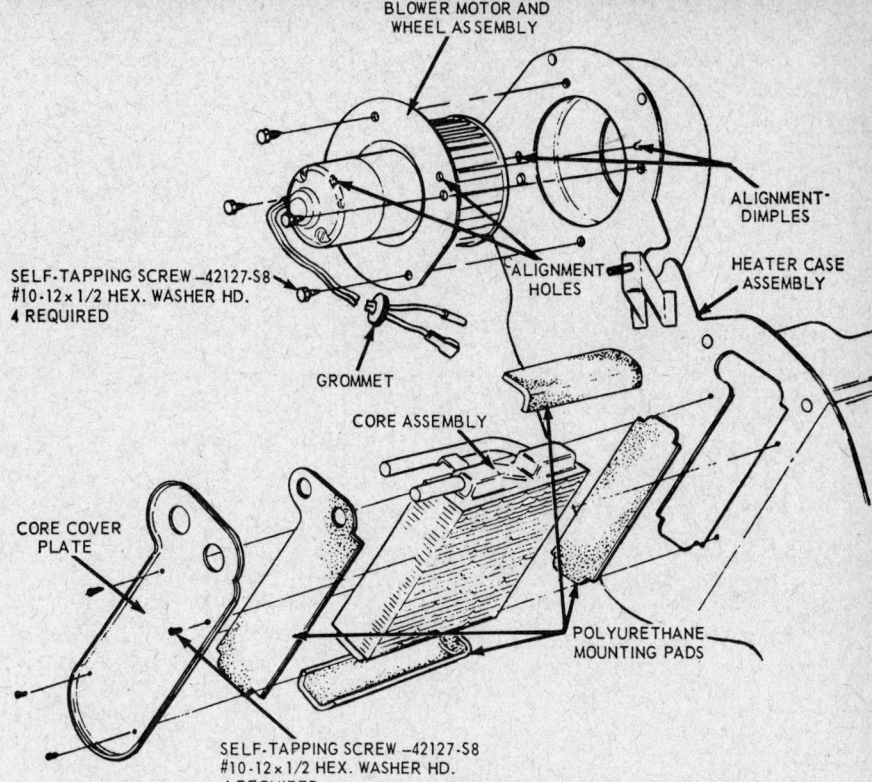

Fig. 20   Heater core & blower motor less air conditioning. 1977–80 Granada & Monarch; 1977–79 Cougar, LTD II & Thunderbird

pressure lines.
   b. Drain cooling system, then disconnect hoses from heater core. Cover hoses and heater core tubes to prevent leakage.
   c. Remove screw securing air inlet duct and blower housing assembly support brace to cowl top panel.
   d. Disconnect black vacuum supply hose from in-line check valve in engine compartment.
   e. Disconnect blower motor electrical connectors from harness.
   f. Disconnect electrical connector from blower motor resistor.
   g. Remove two evaporator case-to-dash panel attaching nuts from engine compartment.
   h. Working in passenger compartment, remove evaporator case support bracket-to-cowl top panel attaching screws.
   i. Remove screw retaining bracket below evaporator case to dash panel.
   j. Carefully remove evaporator case assembly from vehicle.
19. On all models, remove five heater core access cover attaching screws and the access cover, Fig. 16.
20. Remove heater core and seals from evaporator case.
21. Remove the two seals from heater core tubes.
22. Reverse procedure to install.

1977–80 Granada & Monarch
Less Air Conditioning
1. Drain cooling system and disconnect heater hoses from heater core.
2. Remove glove box and the right and floor air distribution ducts.
3. Disconnect heater control cables and wiring harness from resistor assembly. Remove right vent cable bracket from in-

strument panel.
4. Remove vent duct to upper cowl mounting bolt.
5. Remove heater case to dash panel nuts, then the heater case and vent duct assembly.
6. Remove core cover and seal, then slide core from case, Fig. 20.

With Air Conditioning
1. Disconnect battery ground cable and drain coolant system, then disconnect heater hoses from core at engine side of dash panel.

NOTE: Easier access may be obtained by first disconnecting suction hose and moving it out of the way.

---

2. Remove heat distribution duct from instrument panel, seat belt interlock module and glove box liner, then loosen right door sill scuff plate and remove right cowl side from trim panel.
3. Loosen instrument panel to right cowl side bolt and remove instrument panel brace bolt at lower rail under glove box.
4. Remove tunnel to cowl brace, located to left of evaporator plenum assembly, if equipped.
5. Remove defroster nozzle by removing instrument panel crash pad, removing radio speaker or panel cowl brace, removing four nozzle to cowl bracket screws and lifting defroster nozzle upward through crash panel, Fig. 21.
6. Disconnect vacuum hoses from A/C-Defrost and A/C-Heat door motors and remove vacuum harness to plenum clip screw, then remove the two A/C-Heat mounting nuts and swing door rearward on crankarm.

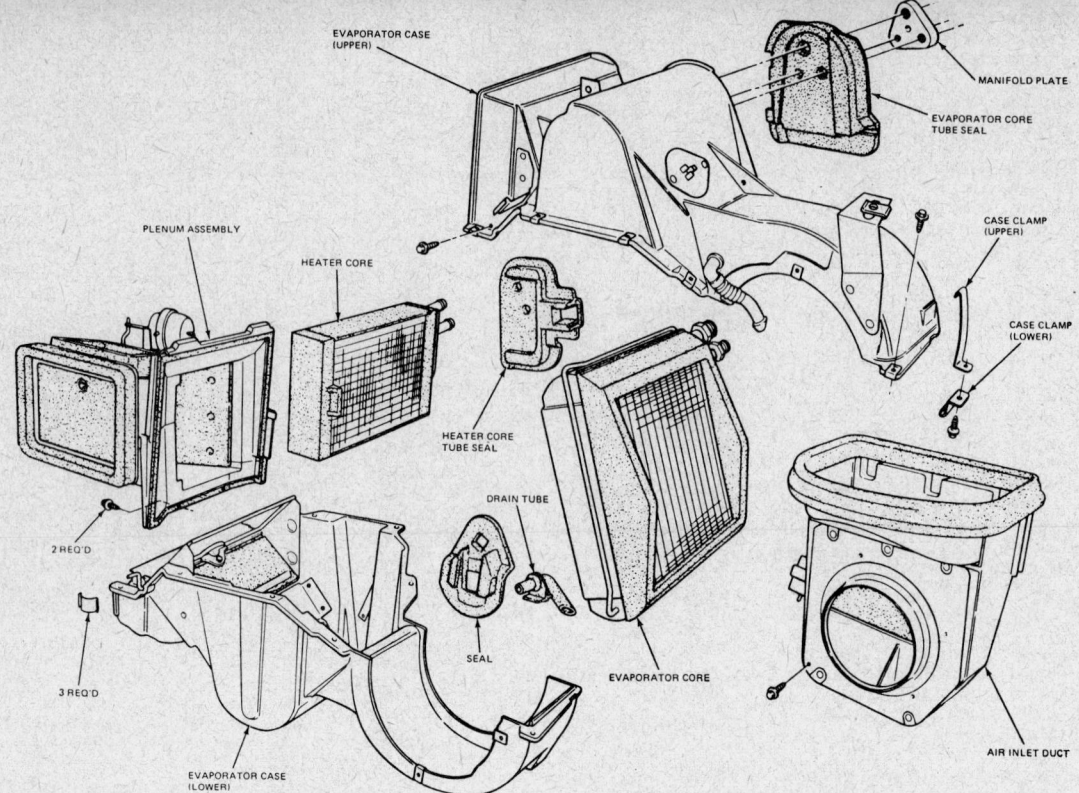

Fig. 21 Heater core. 1977—80 Granada & Monarch with air conditioning

7. Remove two plenum to left mounting bracket screws and remove the two screws and three clips securing plenum to evaporator case.
8. Swing bottom of plenum away from evaporator case and disengage S-clip on forward flange of plenum, then raise plenum to clear tabs on top of evaporator case.
9. Move plenum to left as far as possible (about 4 inches), pulling rearward on instrument panel to gain clearance.

NOTE: Use extreme care when pulling back on instrument panel to avoid cracking plastic panel. Also, there is very little clearance between plenum and wiper motor assembly.

10. Using tab molded into rear heater core seal, pull heater core to left, then as rear surface of heater core clears evaporator case, pull core rearward and downward to clear instrument panel.
11. Reverse procedure to install, making certain that heater core tube to dash panel seal is in place between evaporator case and dash panel.

1977—79 Cougar, LTD II & Thunderbird

Less Air Conditioning
1. Disconnect battery ground cable and drain cooling system.
2. Disconnect heater hoses from heater core and plug core openings.

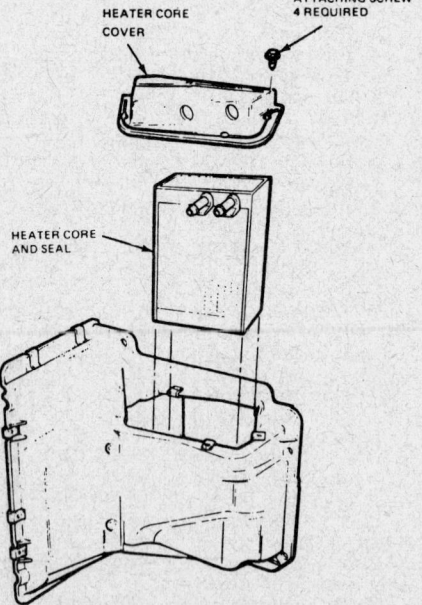

Fig. 22   Heater core with air conditioning 1977—79 Cougar, LTD II & Thunderbird

3. Remove heater assembly to dash retaining nuts.
4. Disconnect electrical wiring from door crank arms.
5. Disconnect electrical wiring from resistor and blower motor.

6. Remove glove box.
7. Remove right air duct control to instrument panel retaining nuts and bolts and the screws securing the right air duct, then remove the duct.
8. Remove heater assembly from vehicle.
9. Remove heater core cover pad and slide heater core from case, Fig. 20.

With Air Conditioning: 1977—79 Cougar, LTD II & Thunderbird
1. Disconnect battery ground cable and drain cooling system.
2. Disconnect heater hoses from heater core and plug core openings.
3. Remove heater core cover plate retaining screws and the plate.
4. Press downward on heater core and tip toward front of vehicle to release the heater core seal from housing Fig. 22.
5. Lift heater core from case and remove from vehicle.

1977 Comet & Maverick

Less Air Conditioning
1. Disconnect battery ground cable and drain engine cooling system.
2. Disconnect blower motor ground wire from fender apron at engine side of dash.
3. Disconnect heater hoses at engine block.
4. Remove heater assembly to dash panel mounting nuts.
5. Remove glove compartment and on all models remove right cowl trim panel.
6. Remove cable retaining clips and the

push nuts at door crank arms. Disconnect control cables from crank arms.

7. Remove defroster air duct from left side of heater assembly.
8. Disconnect motor lead from resistor assembly on bottom of heater.
9. Remove heater case to instrument panel support bracket mounting screw.
10. Pull heater hoses through dash panel and disconnect hoses from heater core.
11. Separate halves of heater and remove core, Fig. 23.

With Air Conditioning: 1977 Comet & Maverick

1. Disconnect battery ground cable and remove air cleaner.
2. Drain cooling system, then discharge refrigerant from A/C system.
3. Disconnect evaporator core tubes from expansion valve and heater hose from heater core.

NOTE: Place tape over evaporator core tubes and expansion valve fittings. Install plugs in heater hoses and core outlets to prevent coolant spillage.

---

4. Remove three A/C assembly to dash panel attaching nuts.
5. Remove lower instrument extension.
6. Remove radio.
7. On all models, disconnect right and left A/C register air duct assemblies from plenum chamber.
8. Remove floor distribution duct from blower housing.
9. On all models, disconnect vacuum lines from actuators and water valve
10. Remove any tape or clips retaining vacuum switch and control cable from door crank arm. Remove any vacuum lines to unit, then disconnect wires from A/C thermostat and resistor.
11. On 1977 models, disconnect blower motor wire connector and vacuum source line at connector and remove blower motor.
12. On all models, remove evaporator housing to cowl upper support attaching screw, then move assembly rearward to clear mounting studs.
13. Pull drain tube from floor pan, then lower evaporator assembly and remove from vehicle.
14. Remove clips and separate housing halves.
15. Remove water valve vacuum switch and blend air door shaft, door and door frame from lower half of housing.
16. Lift heater core out of lower housing.

BLOWER MOTOR, REPLACE

1978–83 Fairmont & Zephyr & 1981–82 Cougar & Granada Less Air Conditioning

1. Disconnect battery ground cable.
2. Remove screw securing right register duct mounting bracket to lower edge of instrument panel.
3. Remove screws securing ventilator control cable lever assembly to lower edge of instrument panel.
4. Remove glove box liner.
5. Remove plastic rivets securing grille to ventilator floor outlet, then the grille from the bottom of the ventilator assembly.
6. Remove right register duct and register assembly.

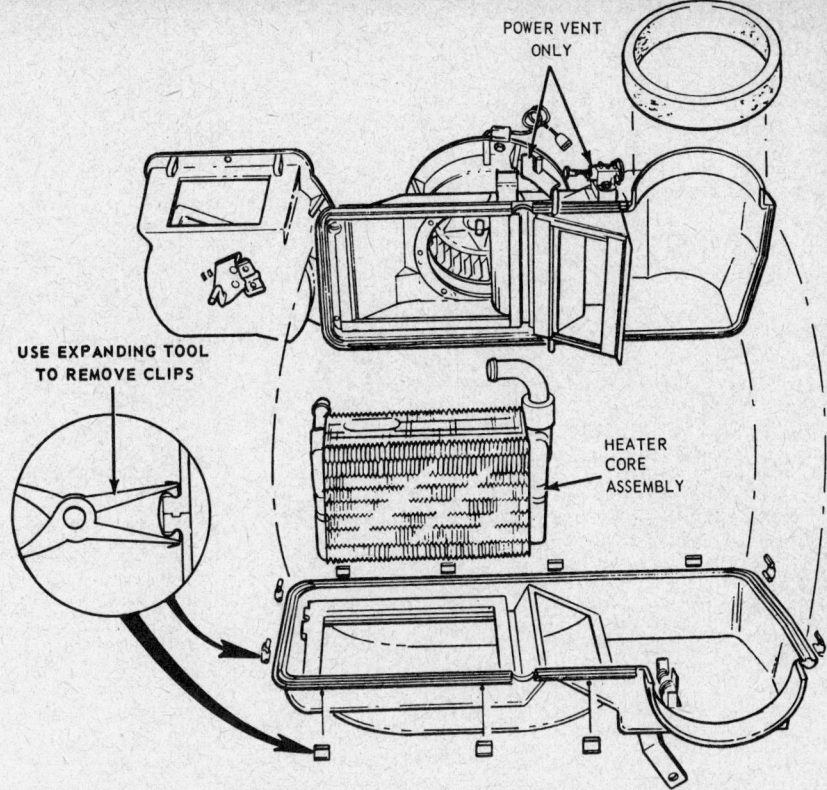

POWER VENT ONLY

USE EXPANDING TOOL TO REMOVE CLIPS

HEATER CORE ASSEMBLY

Fig. 23   Heater core less air conditioning. 1977 Comet & Maverick

7. Remove screws securing ventilator assembly to blower housing portion of the heater case assembly.
8. Slide ventilator assembly toward the right, then downward to remove from under instrument panel.
9. Remove push nut from door crank arm.
10. Remove control cable housing retaining screw, then control cable assembly from ventilator assembly.
11. On 1978–81 models, disconnect blower lead wire from case and push through hole in case. Remove right side cowl trim panel and the ground terminal lug retaining screw.
12. On 1982–84 models, remove hub clamp spring from blower wheel hub, then slide wheel off shaft.
13. On all models, remove blower motor attaching screws and the blower motor. On 1982–84 models, disconnect motor electrical connector before removing from vehicle.
14. Reverse procedure to install.

1978–83 Fairmont, Zephyr With Air Conditioning, 1980–82 Cougar XR-7, 1980–84 Thunderbird, 1983–84 Cougar, LTD & Marquis

1. Disconnect battery ground cable.
2. Remove glove box and disconnect vacuum hose from outside—recirc air door motor.
3. Remove instrument panel lower right to side attaching bolt.
4. Remove screw attaching support brace to top of air inlet duct.
5. Disconnect blower motor lead wire.
6. Remove nut securing blower motor housing lower bracket to evaporator case.
7. Remove side cowl trim panel and the blower ground wire screw.

8. Remove screw securing top of air inlet duct to evaporator case.
9. Move air inlet duct and blower housing assembly downward from evaporator case, Fig. 24.
10. Remove blower motor mounting plate screws and the blower motor.

NOTE: Do not remove mounting plate from motor.

---

11. Reverse procedure to install.

1977–80 Granada & Monarch

Less Air Conditioning

Remove heater case as outlined in the "1977–80 Granada & Monarch" procedure under "Heater Core, Removal," then remove screws securing blower motor to case, Fig. 20.

With Air Conditioning

1. Disconnect battery ground cable.
2. Loosen right door sill scuff plate and remove right cowl side trim panel, then remove right lower instrument panel to cowl side bolt.
3. Remove cowl to loosen instrument panel brace bolt, then disconnect wiring harness connectors from blower motor and remove cooling tube from motor.
4. Remove the four blower motor attaching screws and remove blower motor from scroll by pulling on lower edge of instrument panel to gain clearance.

NOTE: Use extreme care when pulling back on instrument panel to avoid cracking plastic panel.

---

5. Reverse procedure to install.

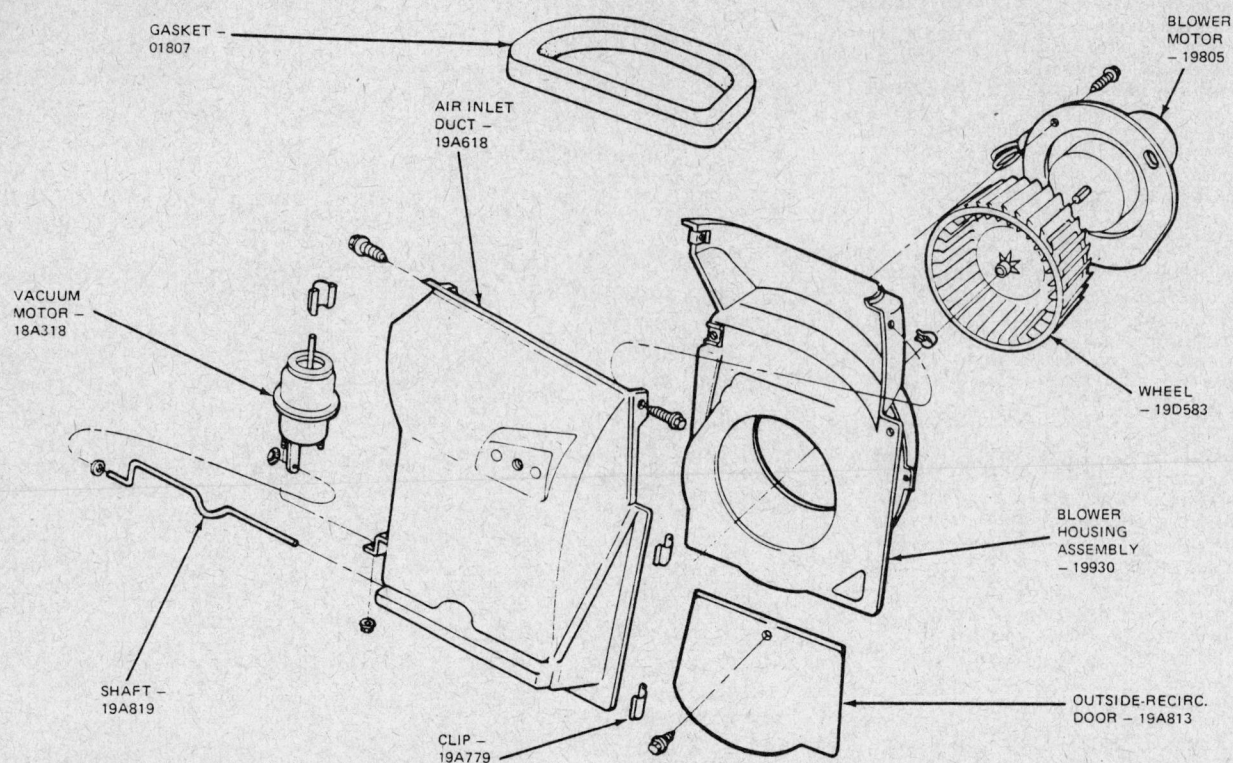

Fig. 24 Blower motor. 1978—83 Fairmont, Zephyr w/Air conditioning. 1980—82 Cougar XR-7, 1980—84 Thunderbird, 1983—84 Cougar & 1983—84 LTD & Marquis

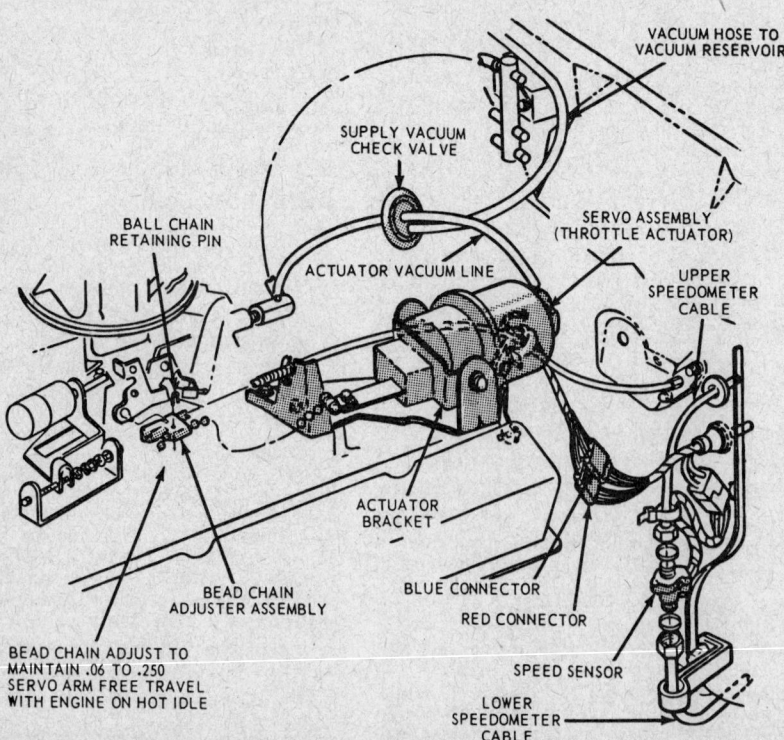

Fig. 25 Servo assembly & throttle linkage (typical)

1977—79 Cougar, Thunderbird & LTD II

Less Air Conditioning
1. Follow the procedure to remove the heater core as described previously.
2. Remove the heater assembly from the vehicle, and place it on a bench.
3. Remove the four mounting screws and remove the blower motor and wheel assembly from the blower, Fig. 20.
4. Reverse procedure to install.

With Air Conditioning: 1977—79 Cougar, LTD II & Thunderbird
1. Remove instrument panel pad, glove box and side cowl trim panel.
2. Remove instrument panel attachment on right side.
3. Remove one nut attaching blower motor housing to engine side of dash panel.
4. Remove one nut attaching blower motor to passenger compartment side of dash panel.
5. Remove one blower housing mounting bracket and cowl top inner screw.
6. Disconnect vacuum line from outside-recirculating air door vacuum motor.
7. Disconnect blower motor lead wire from connector and blower motor ground wire.
8. Remove blower housing assembly.
9. Remove blower motor and wheel as an assembly from blower housing.

1977 Comet & Maverick

Less Air Conditioning

1. Remove the heater core as described previously.
2. Disconnect the blower motor lead wire (orange) from the resistor.
3. Remove the four blower motor mounting plate nuts and remove the motor and wheel assembly from the heater assembly.

With Air Conditioning

NOTE: The blower housing must be removed to provide access to the blower motor.

1. Remove lower instrument panel extension.
2. Remove radio as described under "Radio, Replace."
3. Remove floor air distribution duct from bottom of blower housing. Remove blower housing mounting stud and lock plate.
4. Rotate the blower housing to unlock the slotted tabs on the blower housing from their lock pins on the evaporator housing. There are two tabs and two pins. Disconnect the red and yellow hoses at the vacuum motor on the blower housing. Disconnect the resistor and ground wires, and remove the blower housing.
5. Remove seven clips and separate blower motor housing halves.
6. Remove three blower motor mounting plate retaining nuts, and remove the motor and wheel assembly from the housing.
7. When installing be sure that the A/C Heat-Door is positioned properly before clipping the right and left housings together.

SPEED CONTROLS

Except 1979–83 Fairmont, Zephyr, 1980–82 Cougar XR-7, 1980–84 Thunderbird, 1981–82 Granada & 1981–84 Cougar & 1983–84 LTD & Marquis

Adjust bead chain to obtain .06–.25" actuator arm free travel when engine is at hot idle. The adjustment should be made to take as much slack as possible out of the chain without restricting the carburetor lever from returning to idle, Fig. 25.

On vehicles with a solenoid anti-diesel valve, perfom adjustment with ignition switch in the "ON" position.

1979–83 Fairmont, Zephyr, 1980–82 Cougar XR-7, 1980–84 Thunderbird, 1981–82 Granada, 1981–84 Cougar & 1983–84 LTD & Marquis

Bead Chain Adjustment

This adjustment should be made to remove as much slack as possible from the chain without restricting the carburetor lever from returning to the idle speed position. On vehicles equipped with a solenoid throttle positioner, the adjustment should be performed with the throttle positioner disengaged.

Vacuum Dump Valve

The vacuum dump valve is mounted on a moveable mounting bracket. The valve should be adjusted so that it is closed when the brake pedal is not depressed and opens when the brake pedal is depressed.

Actuator Cable Adjustment

1. Remove cable retaining clip.
2. On all carbureted models, deactivate the throttle positioner and set carburetor at hot idle.
3. On all models, pull the actuator cable to remove slack.
4. Insert cable retaining clip while maintaining light tension on the actuator cable.

Engine Section

NOTE: Refer to "FORD MUSTANG & PINTO ● MERCURY BOBCAT & CAPRI" Section for service procedures on the 2300 cc (4-140) engine & Turbocharged engine not covered in this section.

ENGINE MOUNTS

Caution: Whenever self-locking mounting bolts and nuts are removed, they must be replaced with new self-locking bolts and nuts.

SERVICE NOTE: On some 1982 Granada, 1982–83 Cougar and Thunderbird and 1983 LTD and Marquis models, a Silver colored flange nut which retains the engine mounts to No. 2 crossmember has replaced the black nut previously used. Reduce torque on this type nut to 50–65 ft. lbs.

1983–84 Cougar, LTD, Marquis & Thunderbird 4-140

1. Support engine using a suitable jack and wooden block placed under oil pan.
2. Remove fuel pump shield attaching screw, if equipped, from left hand engine support bracket.
3. On LTD and Marquis models, remove bolt securing lower end of engine damper to No. 2 crossmember bracket, Fig. 1.
4. On Cougar and Thunderbird models, remove through bolts from bottom of mounts, Fig. 1A.
5. Remove nuts and washers attaching both insulators to No. 2 crossmember.
6. Raise engine just enough to clear insulator studs from crossmember.
7. Remove insulator and bracket attaching bolts, then the insulator and bracket

assembly from vehicle.
8. Reverse procedure to install.

1978–83 Fairmont, Zephyr, 1980–82 Thunderbird, Cougar XR-7, 1981–82 Cougar, Granada & 1983 LTD & Marquis 6-200

1. Remove fan shroud screws.

2. Support engine with suitable jack and wooden block.
3. On LTD and Marquis models, remove engine damper lower bolt and No. 2 crossmember bracket, Fig. 1C.
4. On all models, remove nut and washer assemblies from insulators at No. 2 crossmember.
5. Raise engine with jack until insulator

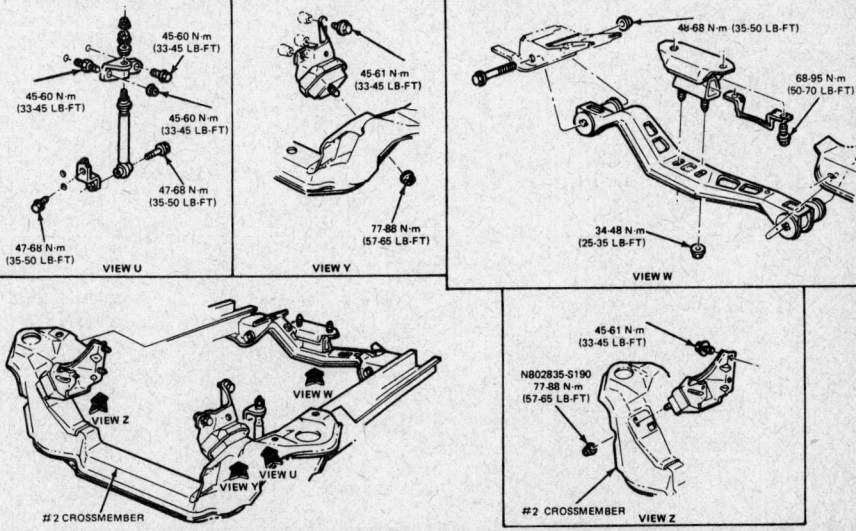

Fig. 1   Engine mounts. 1983–84 LTD & Marquis 4-140

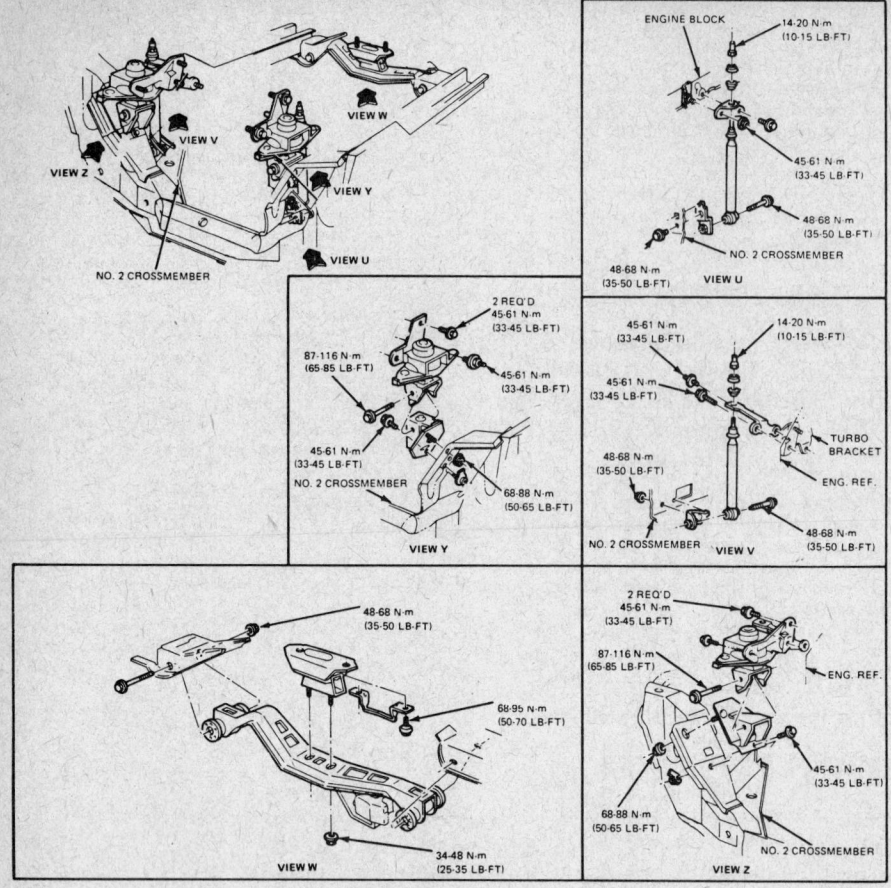

Fig. 1A Engine mounts. 1983–84 Cougar & Thunderbird 4-140

retaining nuts, Fig. 1D.

2. Using a wood block placed under the oil pan, raise the engine enough to clear the insulator.
3. Remove the retaining screws and nuts from the insulator(s). Remove the insulator(s).
4. Reverse procedure to install.

1983–84 V6-232

1. Remove fan shroud attaching screws.
2. Support engine using a suitable jack and wooden block placed under oil pan.
3. Remove nuts and washers attaching insulators to No. 2 crossmember, Fig. 2A.
4. On LTD and Marquis models, remove bolt securing lower end of engine damper to No. 2 crossmember bracket.
5. On all models, raise engine sufficiently to clear insulator studs from crossmember.
6. Remove fuel pump shield, if equipped, from right hand side of engine.
7. Disconnect oil cooler line attaching clips and starter ground cable from right hand engine support bracket.
8. Remove insulator and bracket attaching bolts, then the insulator and bracket assembly from vehicle.
9. Reverse procedure to install.

1982 V6-232

1. Support engine using a suitable jack and wooden block placed under oil pan.
2. Remove nut and washer attaching mount to chassis, then raise engine slightly, Fig. 2.
3. Remove bolts attaching engine mount and bracket to engine, then remove mount.
4. Reverse procedure to install.

1981 Cougar & Granada V8-255

1. Remove fan shroud attaching screws, then position shroud over fan.
2. Using a suitable jack with a wooden block placed under oil pan, support engine.

studs clear crossmember.

6. Disconnect bracket from engine and remove engine mount.
7. Reverse procedure to install. Torque fasteners according to Figs. 1B and 1C.

1977–80 Granada, Monarch & 1977 Comet & Maverick 6-200 & 250

1. Remove the insulator to support bracket

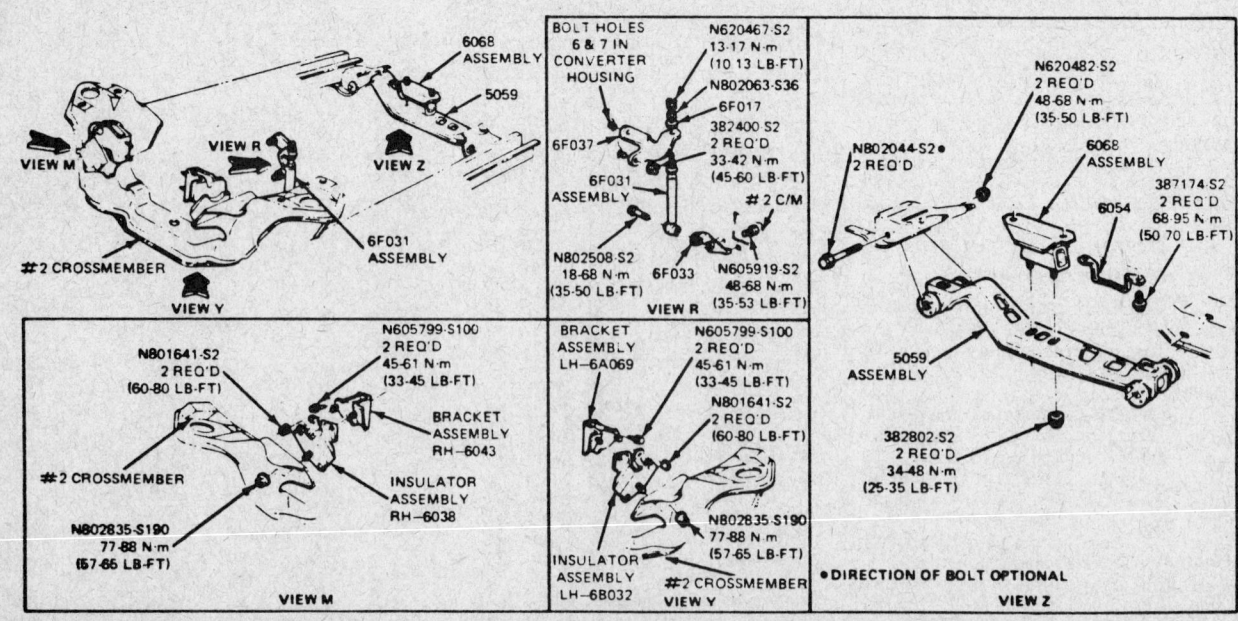

Fig. 1B Engine mounts. 1983 LTD & Marquis 6-200

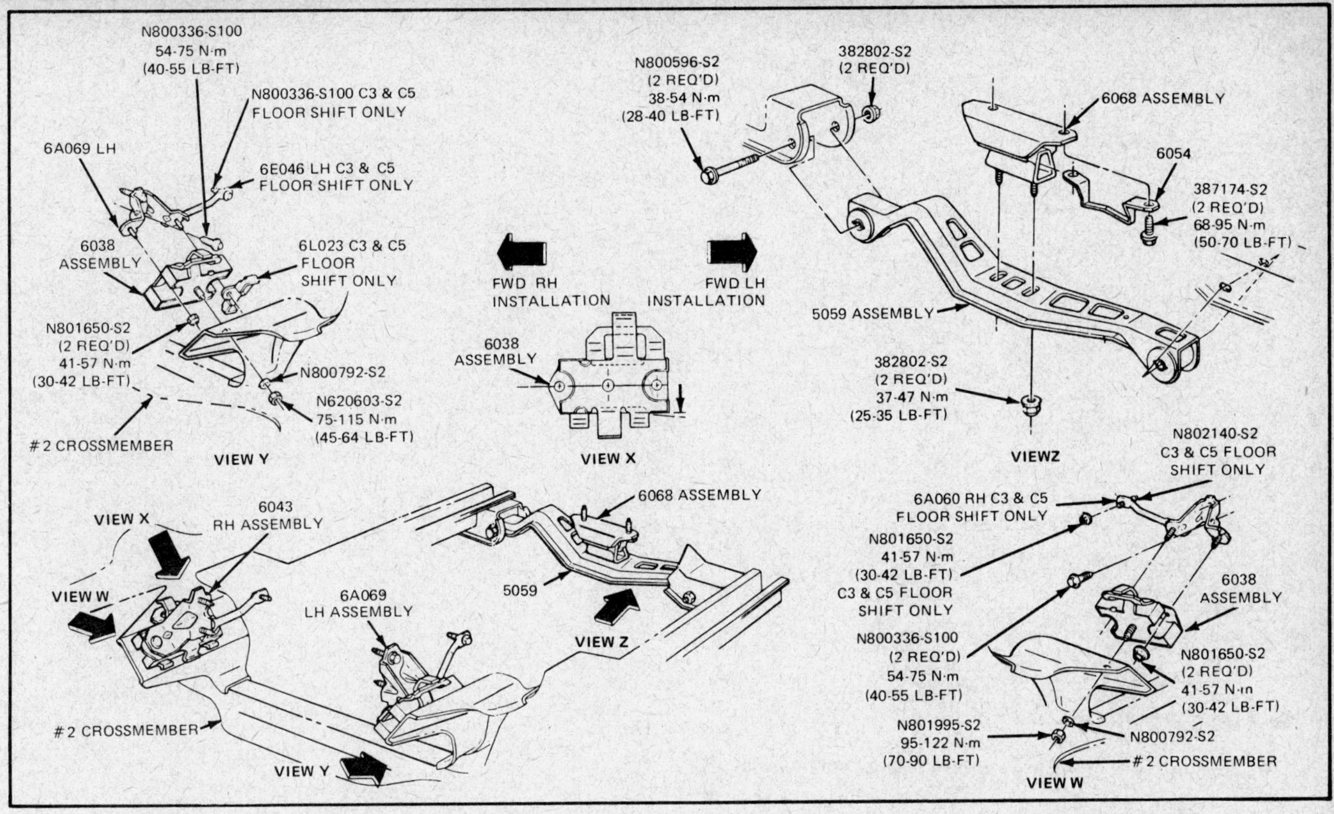

Fig. 1C Engine mounts. 1978—83 Fairmont, Zephyr, 1980—82 Cougar, XR-7, Thunderbird & 1981—82 Granada 6-200

3. Remove nut and through bolt attaching insulator to support bracket, Fig. 3.
4. Raise engine slightly, then remove insulator and bracket assembly to cylinder block attaching bolts.
5. Remove insulator assembly and heat shield, if equipped.
6. Reverse procedure to install.

1980—82 Cougar XR-7, 1983—84 Cougar & 1980—84 Thunderbird V8-255 & 302

1. Remove fan shroud attaching screws.
2. Using a suitable jack with a wooden block placed under oil pan, support engine.
3. Remove nut and through bolt attaching insulator to frame crossmember.
4. On 1983—84 models, disconnect shift linkage.
5. Raise engine slightly, then remove insulator and heat shield, if equipped, Fig. 3.
6. Reverse procedure to install.

1978—81 Fairmont & Zephyr V8-255 & 302

1. Remove fan shroud attaching screws.
2. Remove nuts attaching insulators to lower bracket, Fig. 3.
3. Raise engine slightly using a block of wood placed under the oil pan and a suitable jack.
4. Remove bolts attaching insulator to engine block.
5. Remove insulator assembly.
6. Reverse procedure to install.

1977 Comet, Maverick, 1977—80 Granada & Monarch V8-255, 302, 351W

1. Using a block of wood and jack placed under oil pan, support engine.
2. Remove through bolt attaching motor mount to crossmember, Figs. 4 and 5.
3. Remove engine mount to engine attaching bolts.
4. Raise engine slightly and remove engine mount and heat shield (if used).
5. Reverse procedure to install.

1977—79 V8-302 & 351W Except Comet, Fairmont, Granada, Maverick, Monarch & Zephyr

1. Remove fan shroud attaching screws.

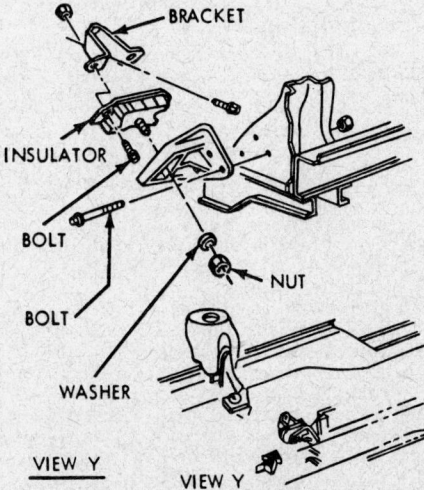

Fig. 1D Engine mounts. 1977 Comet & Maverick, 1977—80 Granada & Monarch 6-200, 250

2. Support engine using a block of wood placed under the oil pan and a suitable jack.
3. Remove nut and through bolt attaching insulator to frame crossmember, Fig. 6.
4. Raise engine slightly and remove insulator and heat shield, if equipped.
5. Reverse procedure to install.

1977—79 V8-351M & 400

1. Remove fan shroud attaching bolts.
2. Remove through bolt and nut attaching insulator to insulator support bracket, Fig. 7.
3. Raise engine slightly using a block of wood placed under the oil pan and a suitable jack.
4. Remove insulator assembly to engine block attaching bolts and lock washers.
5. Remove insulator and heat shield, if equipped.
6. Reverse procedure to install.

ENGINE, REPLACE
6-200 & 250

1. Remove battery ground cable.
2. Remove hood assembly.
3. Drain cooling system and oil pan.
4. Disconnect crankcase ventilation hose and remove air cleaner.
5. Disconnect canister purge hose from P.C.V. valve.
6. Disconnect radiator and heater hoses and remove all drive belts.
7. If equipped with automatic transmission, disconnect transmission oil cooler lines from radiator.

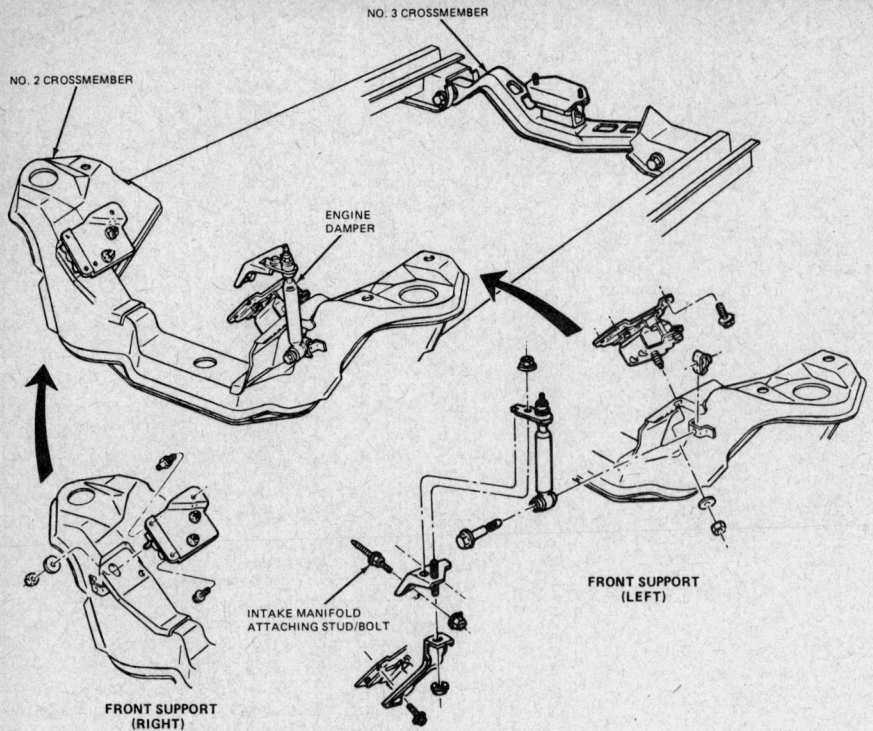

Fig. 2   Engine mount. 1982 V6-232

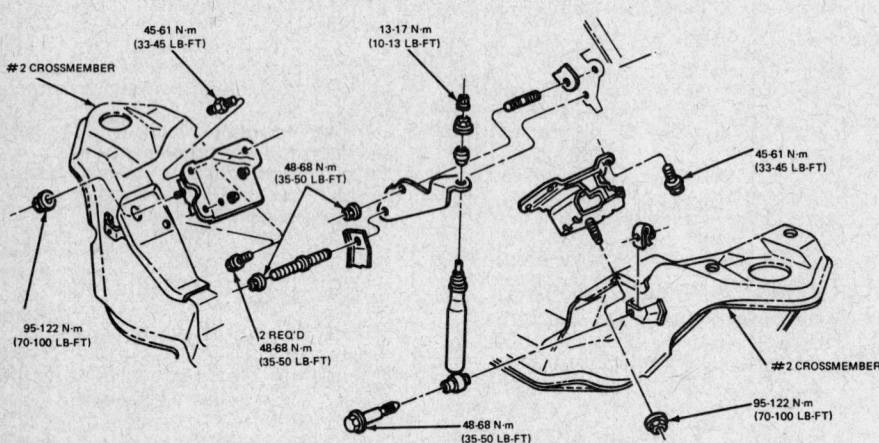

Fig. 2A   Engine mounts 1983—84 LTD & Marquis V6-232 (Typical of 1983—84 Cougar & Thunderbird)

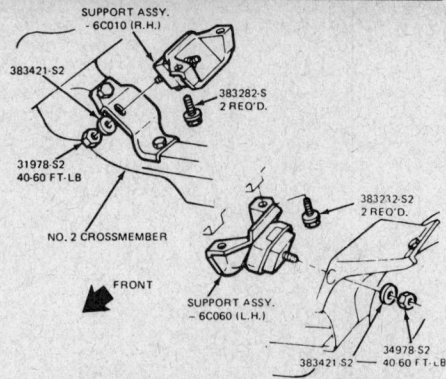

Fig. 3   Engine mounts (typical). 1978—81 Fairmont, Zephyr, 1980—82 Cougar XR-7, 1983—84 Cougar, 1980—84 Thunderbird & 1981 Cougar & Granada V8-255, 302

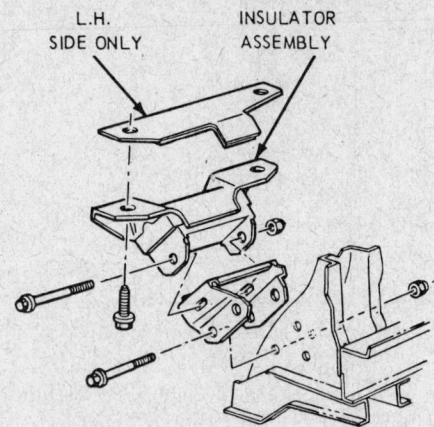

Fig. 4   Engine mounts. 1977 Comet & Maverick V8

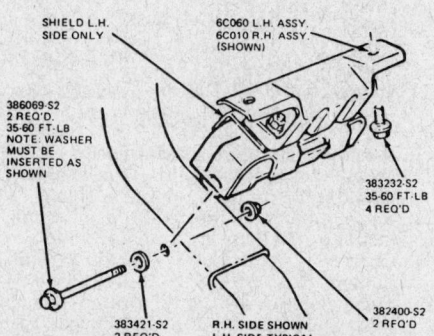

Fig. 5   Engine mounts. 1977—80 Granada & Monarch V8-255, 302, 351W

8. On all models, remove radiator, then the fan, spacer and pulley.
9. Disconnect alternator and starter wiring, then the accelerator cable from carburetor.
10. If equipped with Thermactor system, remove or disconnect components that may interfere with engine replacement.
11. If equipped with A/C, remove compressor from mounting bracket and position aside with refrigerant line attached.
12. On all models, disconnect and plug fuel pump inlet line.
13. Disconnect ignition coil wires, then the oil pressure and water temperature wiring from sending units.
14. Remove starter motor.
15. If equipped with manual transmission, disconnect clutch retracting spring, then the clutch equalizer shaft and arm bracket from underbody rail. Remove arm bracket and equalizer shaft.
16. On all models, raise vehicle and remove flywheel or converter housing upper attaching bolts.
17. Disconnect exhaust pipe from manifold. Loosen exhaust pipe clamp and slide off support bracket on engine.
18. Disconnect front engine mounts from underbody bracket.
19. Remove flywheel or converter housing cover.
20. If equipped with manual transmission, remove flywheel housing lower attaching bolts.
21. If equipped with automatic transmission, remove converter to flywheel bolts, then the converter housing lower attaching bolts.
22. On all models, lower vehicle and support transmission and flywheel or converter housing with a suitable jack.
23. Attach suitable lifting equipment to engine and remove engine from vehicle.
24. Reverse procedure to install.

V6-232

1. Disconnect battery ground cable, then drain cooling system and crankcase.
2. On models equipped with underhood light, disconnect electrical connector from the light.
3. Mark position of hood hinges, then remove hood.

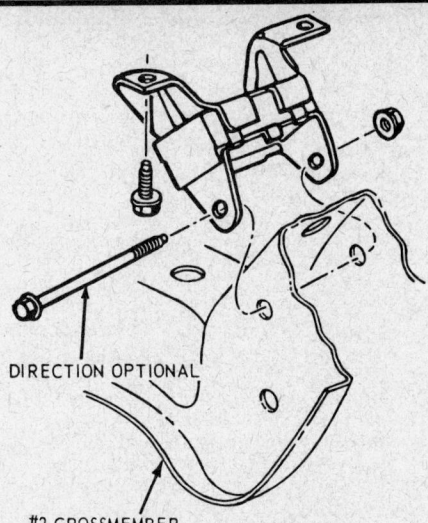

Fig. 6   Engine mounts, 1977–79 V8-302 351W exc. Comet, Fairmont, Granada, Maverick, Monarch & Zephyr

4. Remove air cleaner, air inlet duct and heat tube.
5. Remove fan shroud and fan assembly, then loosen accessory drive belt idler and remove drive belt and water pump pulley.
6. Disconnect upper and lower radiator hoses at radiator.
7. Disconnect Thermactor hose at air tube check valve, then remove air tube valve bracket attaching bolt at rear of right hand cylinder head.
8. Remove secondary wire from ignition coil.
9. Remove bolts attaching power steering pump mounting bracket, then remove pump and bracket assembly and position aside with hoses attached, if equipped.
10. On models with A/C, remove compressor mounting bracket attaching bolts, then remove compressor and mounting bracket assembly and secure to right hand shock absorber tower with refrigerant lines attached.
11. Remove alternator and position aside.
12. Disconnect heater hoses from water pump and heater tube.
13. On models equipped with speed control, disconnect servo chain at carburetor, then remove servo bracket attaching bolts and servo.
14. Disconnect all necessary vacuum hoses and wiring connectors.
15. Remove engine ground strap to dash panel attaching screw.
16. Disconnect transmission downshift linkage, throttle cable from carburetor, then remove throttle cable bracket attaching bolts.
17. Disconnect fuel line and PCV valve hose from carburetor, or flexible fuel lines from steel lines over the rocker arm cover, on models equipped with fuel injection.
18. Remove carburetor assembly from intake manifold. On models equipped with 7200 VV two barrel carburetor, remove spark knock intensity sensor and adapter assembly which is located between carburetor and thermostat housing.
19. With EGR spacer and phenolic gasket in position, install engine lifting plate T75T-6000-A or equivalent over carbure-

tor mounting studs, then install nuts.
20. Raise vehicle and disconnect fuel inlet hose from fuel pump. Cap fuel hose to prevent entry of dirt.
21. Remove inspection cover from torque converter housing, then remove nuts attaching flex plate to torque converter.
22. Remove starter motor.
23. Remove transmission cooler line retaining clips, then disconnect exhaust pipe from exhaust manifold.
24. Remove four lower engine to transmission attaching bolts, then lower vehicle.
25. Remove engine mount to crossmember attaching nuts.
26. Lower vehicle and position a suitable transmission jack under transmission. Raise jack just enough to support weight of transmission.
27. Remove two upper engine to transmission attaching bolts, then place a ¼ inch piece of plywood or other suitable material between engine and radiator to prevent damage to radiator.
28. Carefully raise engine slightly, then pull away transmission and lift from vehicle.

V8-255, 302 & 351W

1. Remove battery ground cable.
2. Remove hood.
3. Drain cooling system and oil pan.
4. Remove air cleaner and intake duct assembly.
5. Disconnect radiator and heater hoses, then remove all drive belts.
6. If equipped with automatic transmission, disconnect transmission oil cooler lines from radiator.
7. On all models, remove fan shroud attaching bolts, then the radiator, fan, spacer, pulley and shroud.
8. Remove alternator mounting bolts and position alternator aside with wiring attached.
9. Disconnect oil pressure and water temperature wiring from sending units, then the accelerator cable from carburetor.
10. Disconnect and plug fuel pump inlet line.
11. If equipped with automatic transmission, disconnect throttle valve vacuum line from intake manifold. Disconnect manual shift rod and the retracting spring at shift rod stud. Disconnect transmission filler tube bracket from engine block.
12. If equipped with Thermactor system, remove or disconnect engine components that may interfere with engine replacement.
13. If equipped with A/C, isolate and remove compressor.
14. If equipped with power steering, disconnect pump bracket from cylinder head and position assembly aside.
15. If equipped with power brakes, disconnect brake vacuum line from intake manifold.
16. On all models, remove flywheel or converter housing upper attaching bolts.
17. Disconnect ignition coil wiring.
18. On models equipped with EEC IV system, disconnect air charge temperature sensor, engine coolant temperature sensor and exhaust gas oxygen sensor electrical connectors.
19. On all models, disconnect wiring harness from left side rocker arm cover and position aside. Disconnect ground strap from engine block.
20. Raise front of vehicle. Disconnect starter wiring, then remove starter motor.
21. Disconnect exhaust pipes from manifolds.
22. Disconnect engine mounts from brackets

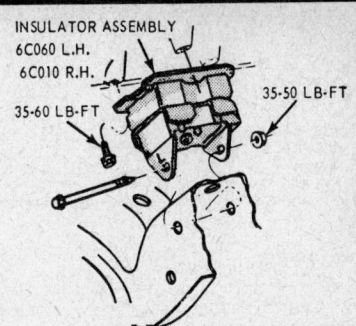

Fig. 7   Engine mounts. 1977–79 V8-400 & V8-351M

on frame.
23. If equipped with manual transmission, remove bolts attaching clutch equalizer bar to frame rail, then the equalizer from engine block. Remove remaining flywheel housing to engine bolts.
24. If equipped with automatic transmission, disconnect transmission oil cooler lines from retainer and remove converter housing inspection cover. Remove converter to flywheel bolts and secure converter in housing. Remove remaining converter housing to engine bolts.
25. On all models, lower vehicle and support transmission with a suitable jack.
26. Attach suitable engine lifting equipment to engine.
27. Lift engine slightly and pull forward to disengage from transmission, then remove engine from vehicle.
28. Reverse procedure to install.

V8-351M & 400

1. Remove battery ground cable.
2. Drain cooling system and oil pan.
3. Remove hood.
4. Remove air cleaner and air intake duct.
5. Disconnect radiator and heater hoses, then remove all drive belts.
6. If equipped with automatic transmission, disconnect transmission oil cooler lines from radiator.
7. On all models, remove fan shroud attaching bolts, then the radiator, fan, spacer, pulley and shroud.
8. Remove power steering pump brackets and position pump aside with lines attached.
9. If equipped with Thermactor system, remove or disconnect components that may interfere with engine replacement.
10. If equipped with A/C, isolate and remove compressor.
11. On all models, remove alternator bracket mounting bolts and position alternator aside with wiring attached. Disconnect alternator ground wire from engine block.
12. Remove wires from engine block and right hand cylinder head.
13. Disconnect and plug fuel pump inlet line.
14. Disconnect vacuum lines at rear of intake manifold. Disconnect vacuum control valve hoses and wiring, if equipped.
15. Disconnect accelerator cable or linkage from carburetor, then the transmission downshift linkage, if equipped.
16. Disconnect engine wiring harness from ignition coil, water temperature sending unit and oil pressure sending unit. Remove wiring harness from hold down clips.
17. Raise and support vehicle.

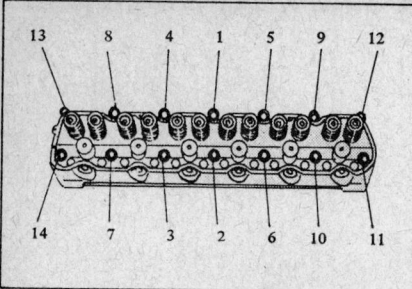

Fig. 8 Cylinder head tightening sequence. 1977 6-200 & 250

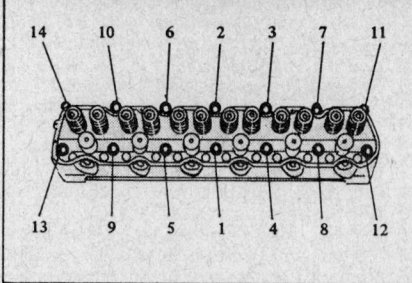

Fig. 8A Cylinder head tightening sequence. 1978–83 6-200 & 250

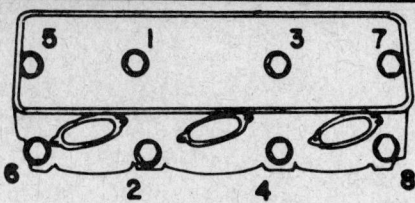

Fig. 9 Cylinder head tightening sequence. 1982–84 V6-232

18. Disconnect exhaust pipes from exhaust manifolds and remove the heat control valve, if equipped, or the manifold to pipe spacer.
19. Disconnect starter motor wiring and remove starter motor.
20. Remove engine front support through bolts and the starter motor cable clamp from right front engine support.
21. If equipped with automatic transmission, remove converter inspection cover, then the converter to flywheel bolts. Remove downshift rod, then the four lower converter housing to engine bolts and the adapter plate to converter housing bolt.
22. If equipped with manual transmission, disconnect clutch linkage from engine block and remove the four lower flywheel housing bolts.
23. On all models, lower the vehicle and remove the two upper converter housing or flywheel housing bolts.
24. Attach suitable engine lifting equipment to engine and support transmission with a suitable jack.
25. Raise engine slightly and pull forward to disengage from transmission, then remove engine from vehicle.
26. Reverse procedure to install.

CYLINDER HEAD, REPLACE

Tighten cylinder head bolts a little at a time in three steps in the sequence shown in the illustrations. Final tightening should be to the torque specifications listed in the *Engine Tightening* table. After tightening the bolts to specifications, *they should not be disturbed.*

6-200 & 250

1. Drain cooling system and remove air cleaner.
2. Disconnect exhaust pipe from manifold and pull it down.
3. Disconnect accelerator cable and trans-

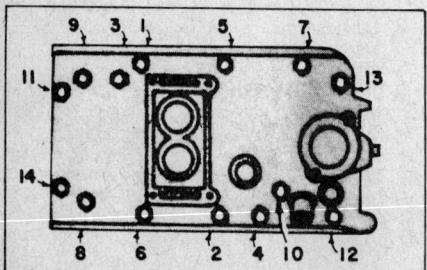

Fig. 10 Intake manifold tightening sequence. 1982–84 V6-232

mission downshift rod from carburetor.
4. Disconnect fuel inlet line at fuel filter hose, and distributor vacuum line at carburetor.
5. Disconnect coolant lines at carburetor spacer, if equipped. Remove radiator upper hose at outlet housing.
6. Disconnect distributor vacuum line at distributor. Disconnect carburetor fuel inlet line at fuel pump. Remove lines as an assembly.
7. Disconnect spark plug wires at plugs and temperature sending unit wire at sending unit.
8. Remove crankcase ventilation system. Remove hoses from Thermactor system as necessary for accessability.
9. Remove valve rocker arm cover.
10. Remove rocker arm shaft assembly.
11. Remove valve push rods.
12. Remove remaining cylinder head bolts and lift off head.
13. Reverse procedure to install. Torque cylinder head according to sequence shown in Figs. 8 and 8A in three steps: step 1, 50–55 ft. lbs.; step 2, 60–65 ft. lbs.; step 3, 70–75 ft. lbs.

V6-232

1. Disconnect battery ground cable, then drain cooling system.
2. Remove air cleaner, air intake duct and heat tube.
3. Loosen accessory drive belt idler and remove drive belt.
4. If left cylinder head is to be removed, proceed as follows:
   a. Remove oil filler cap.
   b. If equipped with power steering, remove pump bracket attaching bolts, then remove pump and bracket assembly and position pump aside with hoses attached.
   c. If equipped with A/C, remove compressor bracket attaching bolts, then position compressor and bracket assembly aside with refrigerant lines attached.
5. If right cylinder head is to be removed, proceed as follows:
   a. Remove Thermactor diverter valve and hose assembly.
   b. Remove accessory drive belt idler, then remove alternator.
   c. Remove Thermactor pump pulley, then remove Thermactor pump.
   d. Remove alternator mounting bracket.

NOTE: On models equipped with Tripminder, the fuel supply line from the fuel pump to the fuel sensor will have to be disconnected to gain access to the upper alternator bracket bolt.

e. Remove PCV valve.
6. Remove intake manifold and exhaust manifolds.
7. Remove rocker arm cover attaching screws, then loosen cover by using a putty knife under cover flange and remove cover. Do not use excess force when loosening rocker arm cover as cover may become damaged.
8. Loosen rocker arm fulcrum bolt enough to allow rocker arms to be rotated to one side, then remove push rods.

NOTE: Tag push rods so they can be installed in the same position.

9. Remove cylinder head attaching bolts, then remove cylinder head and gasket.
10. Reverse procedure to install. Apply a thin coating of pipe sealant D8AZ-19558-A or equivalent to the shorter cylinder head bolts which are installed on the exhaust manifold side of the cylinder head. Do not apply pipe sealant to long bolts which are installed on the intake manifold side of the cylinder head. Tighten cylinder head bolts in four steps to torque listed under Engine Tightening Specifications using sequence shown in Fig. 9. On 1982–83 models: step 1, 47 ft. lbs.; step 2, 55 ft. lbs.; step 3, 63 ft. lbs.; step 4, 74 ft. lbs. On 1984 models: step 1, 37 ft. lbs.; step 2, 45 ft. lbs.; step 3, 52 ft. lbs.; step 4, 59 ft. lbs. Loosen cylinder bolts approximately 2 to 3 turns, then retighten bolts in four steps to specified torque in sequence, Fig. 9. When installing intake manifold, tighten mounting bolts to torque specified under Engine Tightening Specifications in sequence shown in Fig. 10 in three steps:

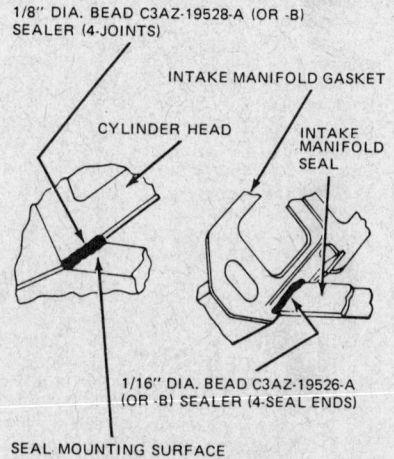

Fig. 11 Applying RTV sealer for intake manifold installation. 1980–84 V8-255, 302 & 1982–84 V6-232

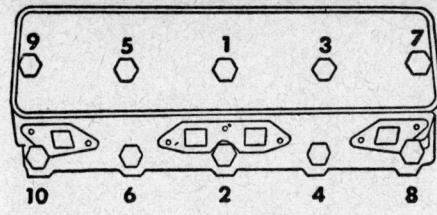

Fig. 12 Cylinder head tightening. V8 engines

step 1, 5 ft. lbs.; step 2, 10 ft. lbs.; step 3, 18 ft. lbs.

NOTE: Before installing intake manifold, apply a 1/8 inch bead of silicone rubber sealer D6AZ-19562-B or equivalent at mating surfaces of intake manifold, cylinder heads and cylinder block, Fig. 11. Also apply a 1/8 inch bead of sealer to the outer end of each intake manifold seal for the full width of the seal.

V8-255, 302, 351, 400

1. Remove intake manifold and carburetor as an assembly.
2. Disconnect battery ground cable at cylinder head.
3. If left head is being removed, remove A/C compressor (if equipped). Also remove and wire power steering pump out of the way. If equipped with Thermactor System, disconnect hose from air manifold on left cylinder head.
4. If right head is to be removed, remove alternator mounting bracket bolt and spacer, ground wire and air cleaner inlet duct.
5. If right head is to be removed on an engine with Thermactor System, remove air pump from bracket. Disconnect hose from air manifold.
6. Disconnect exhaust manifolds at exhaust pipes.
7. Remove rocker arm covers. If equipped with Thermactor System, remove check valve from air manifold.
8. On 1977 and early 1978 V8-302 and 351W engines, loosen rocker arm stud nut so that rocker arms can be rotated to one side. On V8-351M, 400 and late 1978 and 1979–84 V8-255, 302 and 351W, remove fulcrum bolts, oil deflector (if used), fulcrum and rocker arms. On all engines, remove push rods. Keep push rods and rocker arm components in order so they may be installed in original position.
9. Remove head bolts and lift head off block.
10. Reverse procedure to install. Torque cyl-

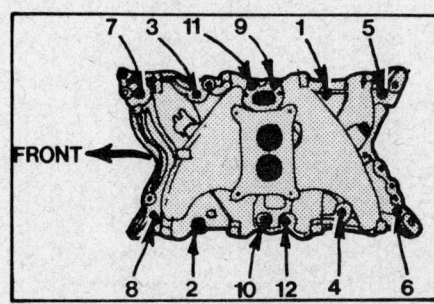

Fig. 14 Intake manifold tightening sequence V8-351M, 400

inder head bolts in sequence shown in Fig. 12, and torque intake manifold bolts in sequence shown in Figs. 13 and 14.

NOTE: On 1980–84 V8-255, 302 engines, before installing intake manifold, apply a 1/8 in. bead of silicone rubber sealer D6AZ-19563-A or B or equivalent at mating surfaces of intake manifold, cylinder heads and cylinder block, Fig. 11. Also apply a 1/16 in. bead of sealer to the outer end of each intake manifold seal for the full width of the seal.

SERVICE NOTE: On V8-302 engines equipped with cork intake manifold seals, both the front and rear seals should be replaced with RTV sealer. Apply a 1/4 inch bead of sealer to the front and rear sealing surfaces of engine block.

VALVE ARRANGEMENT
Front to Rear

Engine	Arrangement
4-140	E-I-E-I-E-I-E-I
6-200, 250	E-I-I-E-I-E-I-E-I-E-I-I-E
V6-232 Right	I-E-I-E-I-E
V6-232 Left	E-I-E-I-E-I
V8-255, 302 Right	I-E-I-E-I-E-I-E
V8-255, 302 Left	E-I-E-I-E-I-E-I
V8-351, 400 Right	I-E-I-E-I-E-I-E
V8-351, 400 Left	E-I-E-I-E-I-E-I

VALVE LIFT SPECS

Engine	Year	Intake	Exhaust
4-140	1978–84	.3997	.3997
6-200	1977–83	.372	.372
6-250	1977–80	.372	.372
V6-232	1982–84	.415	.417
V8-255	1980–82	.3753	.3753
V8-302	1976–77	.3823	.3884
	1978–79	.3823	.3980
	1980–81	.3753	.3909
	1983–84	.3753	.3909
V8-351W①	1977–79	.4186	.4186
V8-351M②	1977–79	.4065	.4065
V8-400	1977–78	.428	.4325

①—Windsor engine.
②—Modified engine.

VALVE TIMING
Intake Opens Before TDC

Engine	Year	Degrees
4-140	1978–84	22
6-200	1977–82	20
6-250	1977–80	18
V6-232	1982–84	13
V8-255	1980–82	16
V8-302	1977–81 & 1983–84	16
V8-351②	1977–79	23
V8-351①	1977–79	19.5
V8-400	1977–78	17

①—Modified.
②—Windsor engine.

VALVES, ADJUST
6-200 & 250

A .060 inch longer or a .060 inch shorter push rod is available to compensate for dimensional changes in the valve train. If clearance is less than the minimum, the .060 inch short-

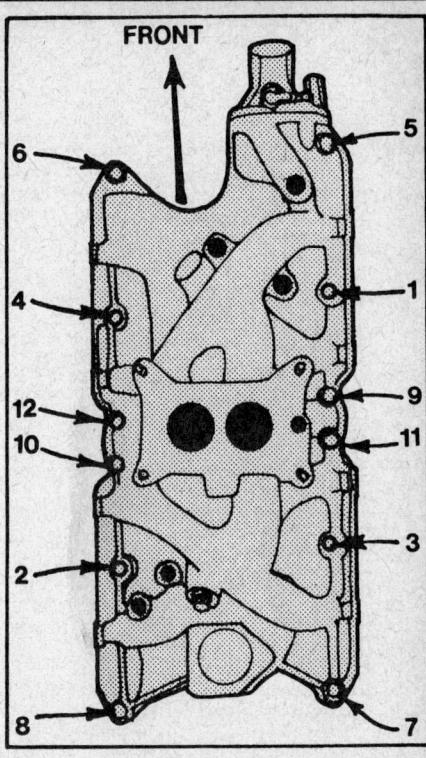

Fig. 13 Intake manifold tightening sequence V8-255, 302 & V8-351W

er push rod should be used. If clearance is more than the maximum, the .060 inch longer push rod should be used.

The procedure used to check the valve clearance is to rotate the crankshaft with an auxiliary starter switch until the No. 1 piston is near TDC at the end of the compression stroke, and then compress the valve lifter using tool 6513-K or equivalent, Fig. 15. At this point the following valves can be checked:

No. 1 Intake	No. 3 Exhaust
No. 1 Exhaust	No. 4 Intake
No. 2 Intake	No. 5 Exhaust

After the clearance of these valves have been checked, rotate the crankshaft until the No. 6 piston is on TDC at the end of its com-

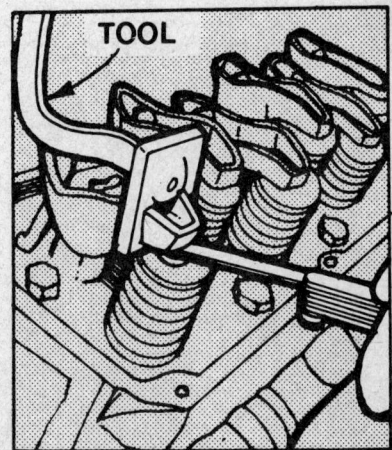

Fig. 15 Compressing lifter to check valve clearance. V8 engines (typical of 6 cylinder engines)

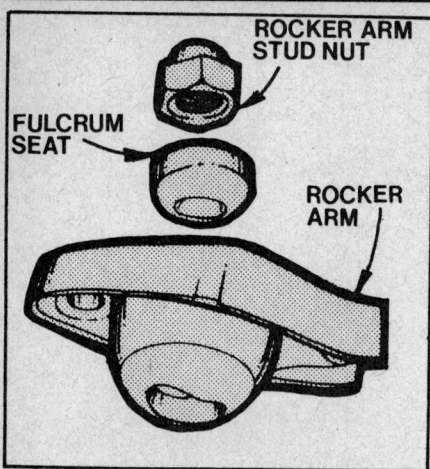

Fig. 16 Rocker arm assembly. 1977 & early 1978 V8-302, 351W

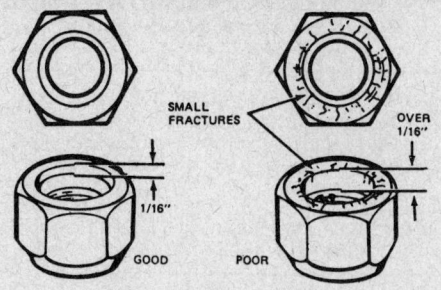

Fig. 17 Rocker arm stud nut. 1977 & early 1978 V8-302, 351W

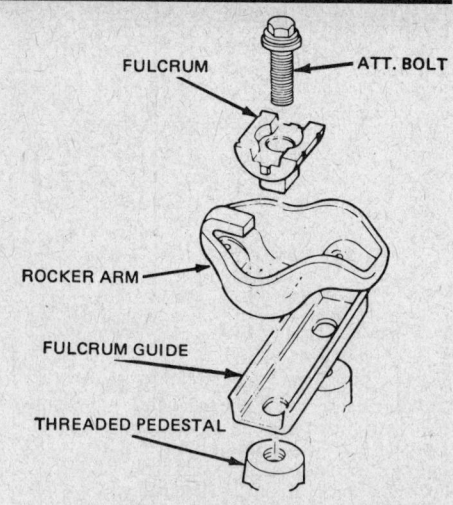

Fig. 18 Rocker arm assembly. V6-232 & Late 1978 & 1979–84 V8-255, 302, 351W

pression stroke (1 revolution of the crankshaft), and then compress the valve lifter using tool 6513-K or equivalent, Fig. 15, and check the following valves:

No. 2 Exhaust	No. 5 Intake
No. 3 Intake	No. 6 Intake
No. 4 Exhaust	No. 6 Exhaust

V6-232

A .060 inch longer or a .060 inch shorter push rod is available to compensate for dimensional changes in the valve train. If clearance is less than specified, the .060 inch shorter push rod should be used. If clearance is more than the maximum specified, the .060 inch longer push rod should be used.

Using an auxiliary starter switch crankshaft until No. 1 cylinder is at TDC compression stroke, then compress valve lifter using tool T82C-6500-A or equivalent, Fig. 15. At this point, the following valves can be checked:

No. 1 Intake	No. 3 Intake
No. 1 Exhaust	No. 4 Exhaust
No. 2 Exhaust	No. 6 Intake

After clearance on these valves has been checked, rotate crankshaft until No. 5 cylinder is at TDC compression stroke (1 revolu-

tion of crankshaft), and then compress valve lifter using tool No. T82C-6500-A or equivalent, Fig. 15, and check the following valves:

No. 2 Intake	No. 5 Intake
No. 3 Exhaust	No. 5 Exhaust
No. 4 Intake	No. 6 Exhaust

V8 Engines

For these engines, a .060″ longer or a .060″ shorter push rod is available to provide a means of compensating for dimensional changes in the valve train and rocker arm. If the clearance is less than the minimum, the .060″ shorter push rod should be used. If clearance is more than the maximum the .060″ longer push rod should be used.

1977 and early 1978 V8-302 and 351W engines use a positive stop rocker arm stud and nut, Fig. 16. Before checking valve lash, check condition of stud nut, Fig. 17. Torque stud nut to 18–22 ft. lbs.

Late 1978 and 1979–84 V8-255, 302 and 351W engines use a bolt and fulcrum attachment, Fig. 18.

To check valve clearance, proceed as follows:

1. Mark crankshaft pulley at three locations with number 1 location at TDC timing mark (end of compression stroke), number 2 location one half turn (180°) clockwise from TDC and number 3 location three quarter turn clockwise (270°) from TDC.
2. Turn the crankshaft to the number 1 location, then compress valve lifter using tool T71P-6513-A or equivalent, Fig. 15, and check the clearance on the following valves:

   V8-255, 302

No. 1 Intake	No. 1 Exhaust
No. 7 Intake	No. 5 Exhaust
No. 8 Intake	No. 4 Exhaust

   V8-351, 400

No. 1 Intake	No. 1 Exhaust
No. 4 Intake	No. 3 Exhaust
No. 8 Intake	No. 7 Exhaust

3. Turn the crankshaft to the number 2 location, then compress valve lifter using tool T71P-6513-A or equivalent, Fig. 15, and check the clearance on the following valves:

   V8-255, 302

No. 4 Intake	No. 2 Exhaust
No. 5 Intake	No. 6 Exhaust

   V8-351, 400

No. 3 Intake	No. 2 Exhaust
No. 7 Intake	No. 6 Exhaust

4. Turn the crankshaft to the number 3 location, then compress valve lifter using tool T71P-6513-A or equivalent, Fig. 15, and check the clearance on the following valves:

   V8-255, 302

No. 2 Intake	No. 3 Exhaust
No. 3 Intake	No. 7 Exhaust

No. 6 Intake	No. 8 Exhaust

V8-351, 400

No. 2 Intake	No. 4 Exhaust
No. 5 Intake	No. 5 Exhaust
No. 6 Intake	No. 8 Exhaust

adjust valve lash.

ROCKER ARM STUD, REPLACE

1977 & Early 1978 V8-302 & 351W

If it is necessary to replace a rocker arm stud, a rocker arm stud kit is available and contains a stud remover, Fig. 19, a stud installer, Fig. 20, and two reamers, one .006 in. and the other .015 in. If a .010 in. oversize stud is to be installed, use reamer T66P-6A527-B.

Rocker arm studs that have been broken or have damaged threads, may be replaced with standard size studs. Loose studs in the cylinder head may be replaced with .006, .010 or .015 in. oversize studs. Standard and oversize studs can be identified by measuring the stud

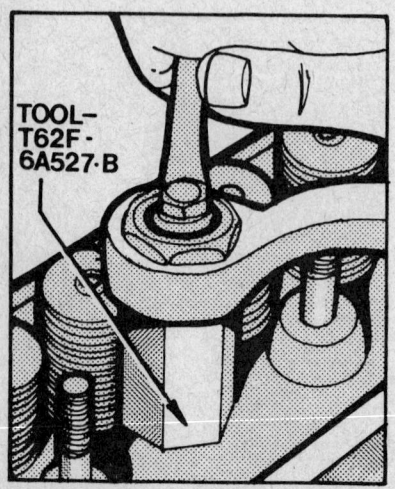

Fig. 19 Rocker arm stud removal 1977 & early 1978 V8-302 & 351W

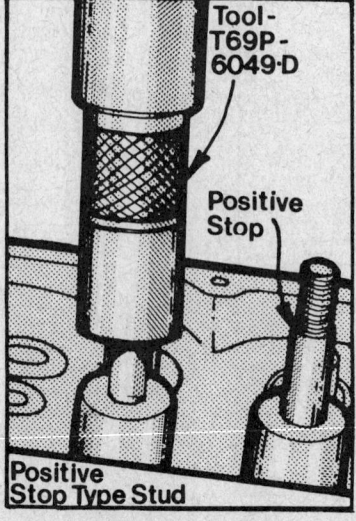

Fig. 20 Positive stop type rocker arm stud installation. 1977 & early 1978 V8-302 & 351W

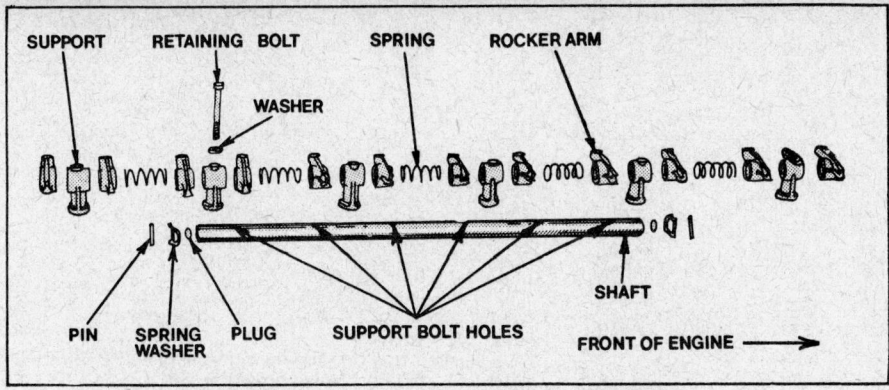

Fig. 21   Rocker arm shaft assembly. 6-200 & 250

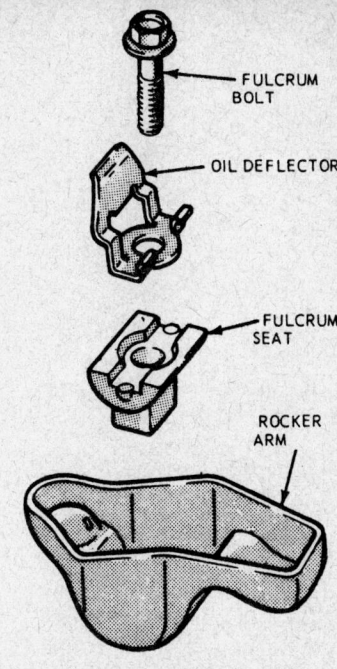

Fig. 22   Rocker arm assembly. V8-351M & 400

diameter within 1⅛ in. from pilot end of stud. The diameter of the rocker arm studs is as follows: standard .3714 to .3721 in.; .006 in. oversize, .3774 to .3781 in., 010 in. oversize, .3814 to .3821 in.; .015 in. oversize stud, .3864 to .3871 in.

When replacing a standard size stud with a .010 or .015 in. oversize stud, always use a .006 in. reamer before finishing with a .010 or .015 in. oversize reamer.

If a stud is broken off flush with the stud boss, use an easy-out to remove the broken stud, following the instructions of the tool manufacturer.

Installation
1. Position the piston of the cylinder being worked on at TDC compression stroke.
2. Locate stud properly with tool T69P-6049D, Fig. 20. Make sure tool bottoms on the head.
3. Lubricate rocker arm components and place rocker arm and fulcrum on the stud.
4. Thread nut onto the stud until it contacts the shoulder, then tighten nut to 18–22 ft lbs.

VALVE GUIDES

Valve guides consist of holes bored in the cylinder head. For service the guide holes can be reamed oversize to accommodate valves with oversize stems of .003, .015 and .030 inch from 1977–79 engine, .015 and .030 inch for 1980–84 engines.

ROCKER ARM SERVICE
6-200 & 250

Disassemble
1. To disassemble, remove pin and spring

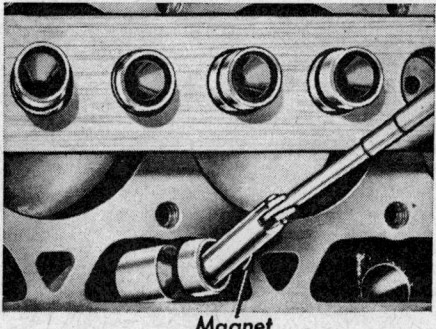

Magnet

Fig. 23   Removing valve lifter with magnetic rod

washer from each end of rocker shaft, Fig. 21.
2. Slide rocker arms, springs and supports off the shaft, being sure to identify location of parts for reassembly.
3. If it is necessary to remove the plugs from the shaft ends, drill or pierce the plug on one end. Then use a steel rod to knock out the plug on the opposite end. Working from the open end, knock out the remaining plug.

Assemble
1. Lubricate all parts with engine oil. Apply Lubriplate to the rocker arm pads.
2. If plugs were removed from shaft ends, use a blunt tool or large diameter pin punch and install a plug (cup side out) in each end of shaft.
3. Install spring washer and pin on one end of shaft.
4. Install rocker arms, supports and springs in order shown in Fig. 21. *Be sure oil holes in shaft are facing downward.*
5. Complete the assembly by installing remaining spring washer and pin.

V6-232

These engines use stamped steel rocker arms retained by a fulcrum seat which bolts directly to the cylinder head and guides the rocker arm. Torque fulcrum bolts in two steps as follows: For each valve rotate crankshaft until tappet rests on heel (base circle) of camshaft lobe and torque fulcrum bolt to 5–11 ft. lbs. After initial torquing all fulcrum bolts, final torque to 19–25 ft. lbs. Final torque may be done with camshaft in any position.

V8-255, 351M, 400 & Late 1978, 1979–81 V8-302, 351W & 1983–84 V8-302

These engines use stamped steel rocker arms retained by a fulcrum seat, Figs. 18 and 22. The fulcrum seat bolts directly to the cylinder head and guides the rocker arm.

SERVICE NOTE: Some 1981 V8-255 and V8-302 engines equipped with low profile rocker arm fulcrums (part No. E1TZ-6A528-A) may experience excessive oil displacement when engine is operated for extended periods during high ambient temperatures. This problem may be corrected by replacing original rocker fulcrums with part No. D7AZ-6A528-A.

VALVE LIFTERS, REPLACE
6-200 & 250

When necessary to replace valve lifters,

remove cylinder head and related parts as outlined previously. Then, using a magnet rod, Fig. 23, remove and install one lifter at a time to be sure they are placed in their original bores.

When installing, apply Lubriplate to each lifter foot and coat the remainder of lifter with oil before installation.

V6-232, V8-255, 302, 351 & 400

1. On V6-232 engine, disconnect secondary ignition wires from spark plugs using wire remover T74P-6666-A or equivalent. Remove ignition wire routing clips from rocker arm cover attaching bolt studs and position wires aside.
2. On all models, remove intake manifold.
3. Remove rocker arm covers. On engines with stud mounted rocker arms, loosen stud nuts and rotate rocker arms to one side. On other engines, remove fulcrum bolt, fulcrum, rocker arm and fulcrum guide (if used).
4. Remove push rods in sequence so they can be installed in their original bores.
5. Using a magnet rod, Fig. 23, remove the lifters and place them in a numbered rack so they can be installed in their original bores. *If the lifters are stuck in their bores by excessive varnish, etc., it may be necessary to use a plier-type tool to remove them. Rotate the lifter back and forth to loosen it from the gum or varnish.*
6. The internal parts of each lifter are matched sets. Do not intermix parts. Keep the assemblies intact until they are to be cleaned, Fig. 24.

TIMING CASE COVER, REPLACE

NOTE: To replace the seal in the timing gear

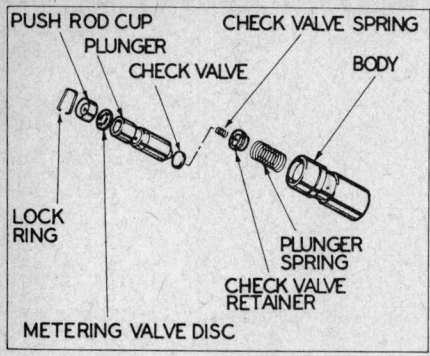

Fig. 24 Hydraulic valve lifter

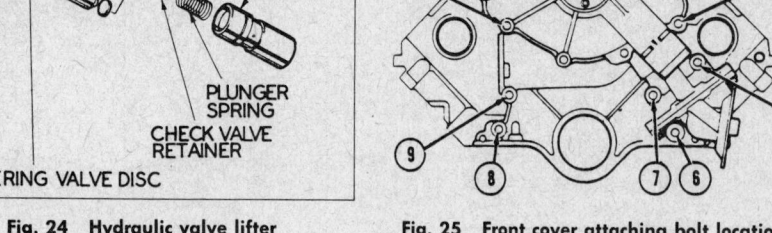

Fig. 25 Front cover attaching bolt locations. 1982–84 V6-232

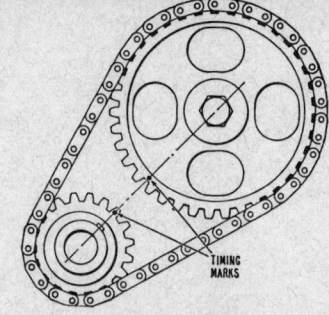

Fig. 26 Timing marks aligned for correct valve timing. 6-200 & 250

cover, it is necessary to remove the cover as outlined below.

6-200 & 250

Removal
1. Disconnect battery ground cable.
2. Drain cooling system and oil pan.
3. Disconnect radiator hoses from engine, then the transmission oil cooler lines from radiator, if equipped.
4. Remove radiator, then the drive belt, fan and pulley.
5. If equipped with A/C, remove condenser attaching bolts and position condenser forward with refrigerant lines attached. Remove compressor drive belt.
6. On all models, remove accessory drive pulley and the crankshaft damper with a suitable puller.
7. On 6-200 engines, remove front cover attaching screws from cover and oil pan. Pry cover from cylinder block slightly and cut oil pan gasket flush with front face of cylinder block.
8. On 6-250 engines, remove oil pan, then the front cover.
9. On all models, clean mating surfaces of cylinder block and front cover.

Installation
1. Apply oil resistant sealer to new front cover gasket and position gasket on front cover. Apply sealer to exposed area of gasket.
2. On 6-200 engines, apply sealer to gasket surface of oil pan. Cut and position the required portions of a new gasket on oil pan. Apply sealer to exposed areas of gasket, including the corners where contact is made with the front cover gasket.
3. On all models, install front cover.
4. Lubricate hub of crankshaft damper with Lubriplate or equivalent, then install damper. Torque attaching bolt to specifications.
5. On 6-250 engines, install oil pan.
6. On all models, install accessory drive pulley.
7. Reverse "Removal" steps 1 through 5 to complete installation.

V6-232

1. Disconnect battery ground cable, then drain cooling system.
2. Remove air cleaner and air intake duct.
3. Remove fan shroud attaching screws and fan and fan clutch attaching bolts, then remove fan and clutch assembly and shroud.
4. Loosen accessory drive belt idler, then

remove drive belt and water pump pulley.
5. On models equipped with power steering, remove pump bracket attaching bolts, then position pump aside with hoses attached.
6. On models equipped with A/C, remove compressor front support bracket.
7. Disconnect coolant bypass hose and heater hose at water pump and upper radiator hose at thermostat housing.
8. Disconnect ignition coil secondary wire from distributor cap, then remove distributor cap with ignition wires attached.
9. With No. 1 cylinder at TDC compression stroke, mark position of rotor to distributor housing and position of distributor housing to front cover.
10. Remove distributor hold down clamp, then lift distributor from front cover.
11. On models equipped with Tripminder, remove fuel flow meter support bracket. Do not remove flow meter or disconnect fuel lines.
12. On 1982–83 models, raise and support front of vehicle, then remove crankshaft pulley using a suitable puller.
13. On 1982–83 models, remove fuel pump shield, then disconnect fuel pump to carburetor fuel line at fuel pump.
14. On all models, remove fuel pump attaching bolts and position aside with fuel hose attached.
15. Remove oil filter, then disconnect lower radiator hose from water pump.
16. Remove oil pan as described under "Oil Pan, Replace."
17. Lower vehicle and remove from cover attaching bolts, Fig. 25.

NOTE: One of the front cover attaching bolts is located behind the oil filter adapter. Also tag bolts as they are removed so that they can be installed at the same location.

18. Remove ignition timing indicator, then remove front cover and water pump as an assembly.
19. Remove camshaft thrust button and spring from camshaft.
20. Reverse procedure to install. Before installing front cover attaching bolts at location 10, Fig. 25, coat threads of bolt with pipe sealant D8AZ-19558-A or equivalent. Also lubricate camshaft thrust button with polyethylene grease before installing. Torque front cover attaching bolts to 15 to 22 ft. lbs.

NOTE: If a replacement front cover is to be installed, the water pump, oil pump, oil filter

adapter and intermediate shaft must be removed from the front cover to be replaced and reinstalled on the replacement front cover. Also it may be necessary to rotate crankshaft 180° from the No. 1 cylinder TDC location to position fuel pump eccentric for fuel pump installation. When installing distributor, No. 1 cylinder must be at TDC position and marks made during removal must be aligned.

V8 Engines

1. To remove cover, drain cooling system and crankcase. Remove air cleaner and disconnect battery ground cable.
2. Remove water hose as necessary.
3. Remove generator support bolt at water pump, and loosen generator mounting bolts.
4. Remove fan, spacer and pulley.
5. Remove power steering drive belt (if equipped). If air conditioned, remove compressor drive belt.
6. Remove crankshaft pulley and adapter.
7. Remove fuel pump and lay it to one side with flexible fuel line attached.
8. Remove oil level dipstick tube bracket and oil filler tube bracket.
9. Remove oil pan-to-front cover bolts.
10. Remove cover and water pump as an assembly.
11. Drive out cover seal with a pin punch. Clean out recess in cover.
12. Coat a new seal with grease and drive seal in until it is fully seated in recess. Check seal after installation to be sure spring is properly positioned in seal.
13. Reverse removal procedure to install cover.

TIMING CHAIN

After removing the cover as outlined above, remove the crankshaft front oil slinger. Crank the engine until the timing marks are aligned as shown in Figs. 26, 27 and 28. Remove camshaft sprocket retaining bolt(s) and washer. Slide both sprockets and chain forward and remove them as an assembly.

Reverse the order of the foregoing procedure to install the chain and sprockets, being sure the timing marks are aligned.

CAMSHAFT, REPLACE
6-200 & 250

1. Remove air cleaner, then drain cooling system and crankcase.

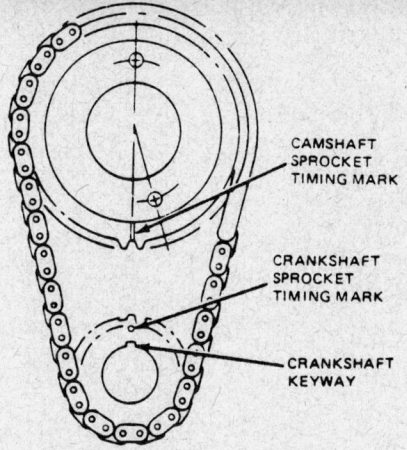

Fig. 27 Timing marks aligned for correct valve timing. 1982–84 V6-232

2. Remove radiator and grille.
3. On models equipped with A/C, remove condensor attaching bolts and position condensor aside.

NOTE: Do not disconnect refrigerant lines from condensor.

4. On 1977 models, disconnect accelerator retracting spring, then the accelerator control cable from carburetor.
5. On 1978–84 models, disconnect accelerator control cable from carburetor and bracket, then the bracket from carburetor.
6. On all models, disconnect fuel inlet line from fuel filter.
7. Disconnect connectors and vacuum hoses connected to cylinder head from carburetor.
8. Disconnect exhaust pipe from manifold. Pull pipe down and remove gasket.
9. On 1977 models, disconnect distributor vacuum line from distributor.
10. On all models, disconnect carburetor fuel inlet line from fuel pump.
11. Disconnect ignition wires from spark plugs and the high tension lead from ignition coil.
12. On 1977 models, remove distributor cap and ignition wires as an assembly. Disconnect primary wires from coil.
13. On all models, disconnect engine temperature sending unit electrical connector from sending unit.
14. On 1977–80 models, disconnect and plug flexible fuel line from fuel pump.
15. On all models, remove distributor, fuel pump and oil filter.

16. Remove crankcase vent hose, regulator valve, rocker arm cover, cylinder head and lifters.
17. Remove drive belt, fan and pulley, then the damper using a suitable puller.
18. On 1977–80 models, remove oil level dipstick.
19. On models with 6-250 engine, remove oil pan.
20. On 1977–80 models, remove oil pump and inlet tube assembly.
21. On all models, remove front cover, gasket, timing chain and sprockets.
22. Remove camshaft thrust plate, then the camshaft by pulling toward front of engine, Fig. 29.

CAUTION: Use care to avoid damaging crankshaft bearings.

23. Reverse procedure to install.

V6 & V8 Engines

1. Drain cooling system and remove radiator and grille.
2. If equipped with air conditioning:
   a. On 255, 302 and 351W engines, remove condensor retaining bolts and position condensor aside without disconnecting refrigerant lines.
   b. On V6-232, 351M and 400 engines, purge refrigerant from system and remove condensor.
3. Remove front cover, timing chain and sprockets.
4. Remove intake manifold.
5. Remove push rods and lifters.

NOTE: On 400 engines, make sure that number one cylinder is at top dead center position.

6. On V6-232 engine, remove oil pan.
7. Remove thrust plate, then carefully remove camshaft by pulling toward front of engine, Fig. 30.

CAUTION: Use care to avoid damaging camshaft bearings.

8. Reverse procedure to install.

PISTON & ROD ASSEMBLY

When installed, piston and rod assembly

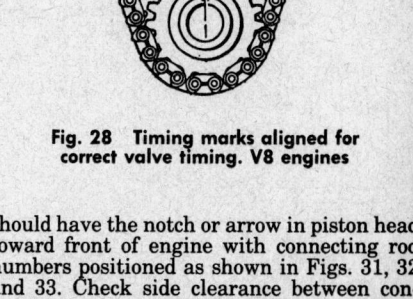

Fig. 28 Timing marks aligned for correct valve timing. V8 engines

should have the notch or arrow in piston head toward front of engine with connecting rod numbers positioned as shown in Figs. 31, 32 and 33. Check side clearance between connecting rods at each crankshaft journal. Clearance should be .0035–.0105 for 4-140, 6-200 and 6-250 engines, .0047–.0114 for V6-232 engine, and .010–.020 for V8-302, V8-351M, V8-351W and V8-400 engines.

PISTONS, PINS & RINGS

Pistons are available in standard sizes and oversizes of .003, .020, .030 and .040 in. Piston rings are available in standard sizes and oversizes of .020, .030 and .040 in. Piston pins are available in standard size and oversizes of .001 and .002 in.

MAIN & ROD BEARINGS

Main and rod bearings are available in standard sizes and undersizes of .001, .002, .010, .020 and .030 in.

CRANKSHAFT REAR OIL SEAL, REPLACE

1977–83

1. On all except V6-232 engines, remove oil pan and oil pump as described under "Oil Pan, Replace" and "Oil Pump, Replace."
2. Loosen all main bearing cap bolts, allowing crankshaft to drop slightly. Do not let crankshaft drop more than 1/32 inch.

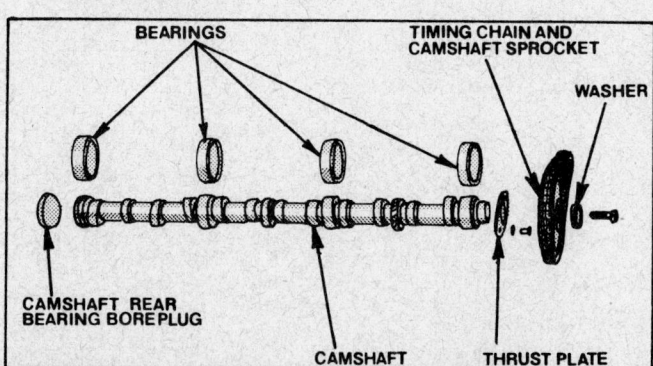

Fig. 29 Camshaft and related parts. 6-200 & 250

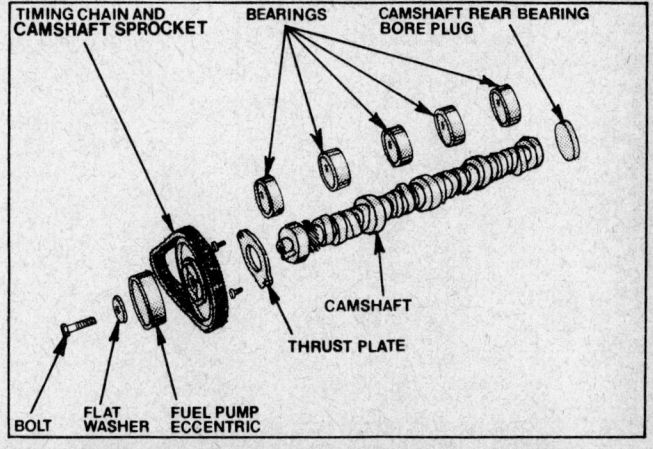

Fig. 30 Camshaft and related parts. V8 engines

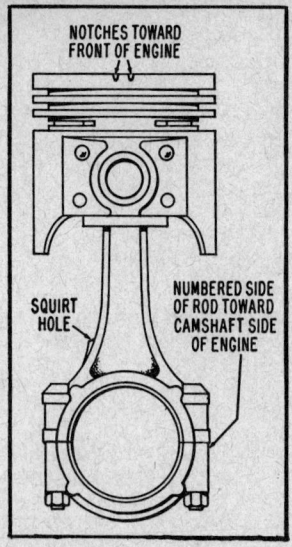

Fig. 31 Piston & rod assembly. 6-200 & 250 engines

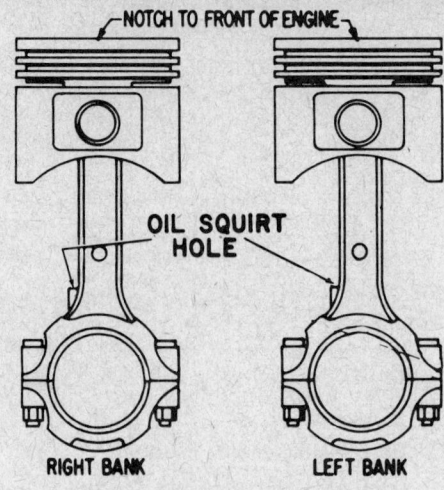

Fig. 32 Piston & rod assembly. 1982—84 V6-232

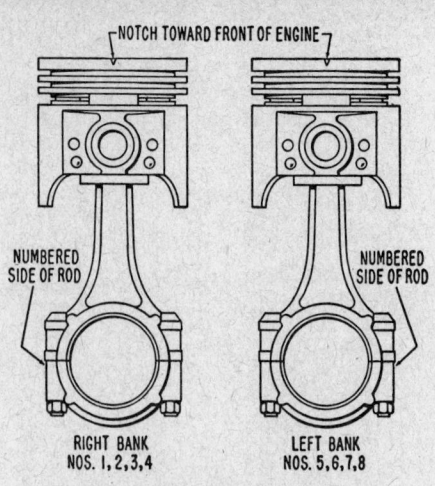

Fig. 33 Piston & rod assembly. V8s

3. Remove rear main bearing cap.
4. Remove old seals from both cylinder block and rear main bearing cap. To remove block half of seal, use a seal removal tool or install a small screw in one end of seal and pull on screw to remove seal.

NOTE: Use care to prevent damaging the crankshaft seal surfaces.

5. Carefully clean seal groove in block with a brush and solvent. Also clean seal groove in bearing cap. Remove the oil seal retaining pin from the bearing cap if so equipped. *The pin is not used with the split-lip seal.*
6. Dip seal halves in clean engine oil.

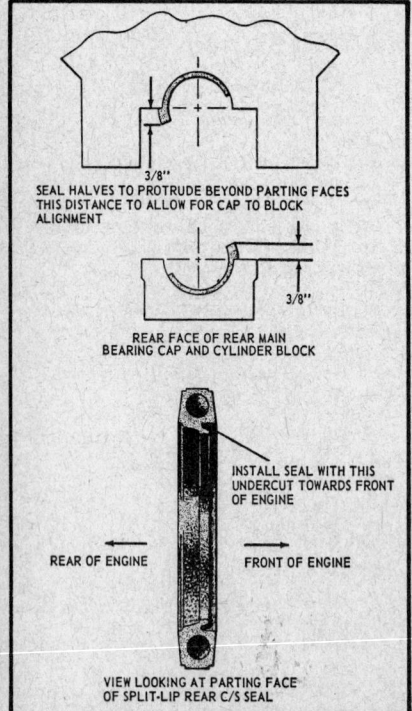

Fig. 34 Crankshaft rear seal installation. 1977–83 exc. 1982-83 V6-232

7. Carefully install upper seal half in its groove with undercut side of seal toward front of engine, Fig. 34, by rotating it on shaft journal of crankshaft until approximately 3/8″ protrudes below the parting surface. *Be sure no rubber has been shaved from outside diameter of seal by bottom edge of groove.*

NOTE: On V6-232 engines, seal ends should be flush with the block and cap.

8. Retighten main bearing caps and torque to specifications.
9. Install lower seal in main bearing cap with undercut side of seal toward front of engine, and allow seal to protrude about 3/8″ above parting surface to mate with upper seal upon cap installation.

NOTE: On V6-232 engines, install seals with locating tab facing rear of engine, then remove the tab, Fig. 34A.

10. Apply suitable sealer to parting faces of cap and block. Install cap and torque to

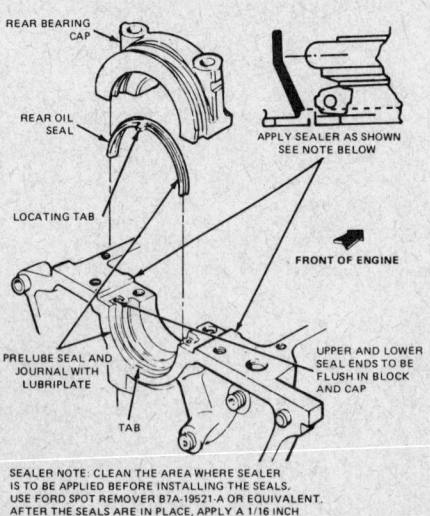

Fig. 34A Crankshaft rear seal installation. 1982-83 V6-232

specifications.

NOTE: If difficulty is encountered in installing the upper half of the seal in position, lightly lap (sandpaper) the side of the seal opposite the lip side using a medium grit paper. After sanding, the seal must be washed in solvent, then dipped in clean engine oil prior to installation.

SERVICE BULLETIN

A new crankshaft rear oil seal has been released for service. This new seal may be received when ordering an oil pan gasket kit and is installed in the same manner as described above, Fig. 35.

1984

1. Using a sharp tool, punch one hole into seal metal surface between seal lip and engine block.

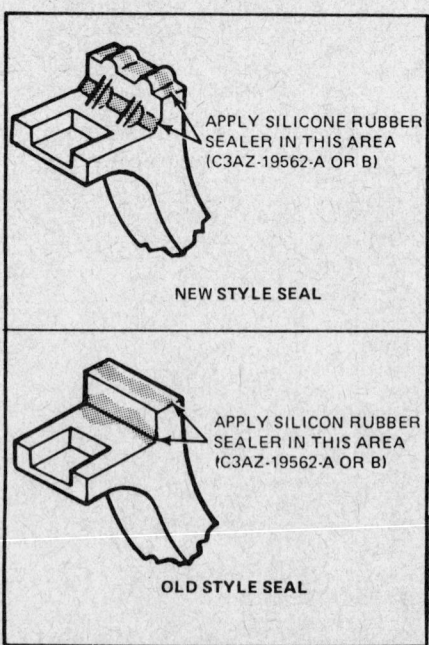

Fig. 35 Crankshaft oil seals

2. Remove seal using slide hammer No. T82L-9533-B or equivalent. Use care to prevent damaging the sealing surface.
3. Lubricate new seal with clean engine oil and install using tool No. T82L-6701-A or equivalent. Tighten bolts alternately to seat seal properly, Fig. 35A.

OIL PAN, REPLACE

1978–83 Fairmont & Zephyr, 1981–82 Granada & Cougar & 1983–84 Cougar, LTD, Marquis & Thunderbird 4-140

1. Disconnect battery ground cable.
2. Raise and support vehicle.
3. Drain cooling system and crankcase.
4. Remove right and left engine support nuts and washers or bolts.
5. Raise engine as far as possible using a suitable jack. Place wooden blocks between the mounts and chassis bracket or No. 2 crossmember pedestals, then remove jack.
6. Remove steering gear attaching nuts and bolts and the steering gear-to-flex coupling attaching bolt. Position steering gear forward and down.
7. Remove shake brace, then the starter motor.
8. Remove engine rear support-to-crossmember attaching nuts.
9. Raise and support transmission with a suitable jack.
10. Remove oil pan attaching bolts and the oil pan.
11. Reverse procedure to install.

1977 Comet & Maverick 6-200

1. Drain crankcase, then remove oil level dipstick and flywheel housing cover.
2. Remove oil pan and gasket.
3. Reverse procedure to install.

1978–83 Fairmont, Zephyr, 1980–82 Cougar XR-7, Thunderbird & 1981–82 Cougar & Granada 6-200 & 250

1. If equipped with automatic transmission, disconnect transmission oil cooler lines at radiator.
2. On all models, remove radiator top support, then the oil level dipstick.
3. Raise and support vehicle, and drain oil pan.
4. Remove nuts and bolts attaching sway bar to chassis and allow sway bar to hang downward.
5. Remove "K" brace.
6. Lower rack and pinion steering gear.
7. Remove starter motor.
8. Remove nuts attaching engine mounts to support brackets.
9. Loosen rear insulator to crossmember attaching bolts.
10. Slightly raise engine and place a 1/4 inch spacer between engine support insulator and chassis bracket.

NOTE: Loosen fan shroud attaching screws to prevent damage to fan when raising engine.

11. Support and raise transmission slightly with a suitable jack.
12. Remove oil pan attaching bolts and lower

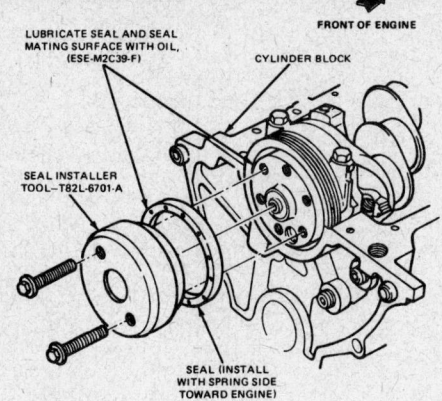

LUBRICATE SEAL AND SEAL MATING SURFACE WITH OIL, (ESE-M2C39-F)

FRONT OF ENGINE

CYLINDER BLOCK

SEAL INSTALLER TOOL–T82L-6701-A

SEAL (INSTALL WITH SPRING SIDE TOWARD ENGINE)

NOTE: REAR FACE OF SEAL MUST BE WITHIN 0.127mm (0.005-INCH) OF THE REAR FACE OF THE BLOCK

Fig. 35A Crankshaft rear seal installation. 1984

oil pan to crossmember.
13. Remove oil pump intermediate driveshaft, pick-up tube and screen assembly and allow components to drop into oil pan.
14. Position transmission oil cooler lines aside, if equipped, and remove oil pan from vehicle. It may be necessary to rotate crankshaft.
15. Reverse procedure to install.

1977–80 Granada & Monarch 6-250

1. On automatic transmission vehicles, disconnect transmission oil cooler lines at radiator.
2. Remove both radiator top support bolts, then raise vehicle and drain crankcase.
3. Remove the four bolts and nuts retaining sway bar to chassis and allow bar to hang down.
4. Remove starter motor, then remove both engine mount retaining nuts to support brackets.
5. Loosen but do not remove both rear mount insulator to crossmember bolts.
6. Raise front of engine and place 1 1/4 inch wooden blocks between engine mount and chassis bracket.
7. Lower engine and raise transmission slightly, then remove oil pan bolts and lower oil pan to crossmember.
8. Position crankshaft rear throw in the up position, then position transmission oil cooler lines aside and remove oil pan.
9. Reverse procedure to install.

1982 Cougar XR-7 & Granada, 1982–84 Cougar & Thunderbird & 1983–84 LTD & Marquis V6-232

1. Disconnect battery ground cable, then remove air cleaner and air intake duct.
2. Remove fan shroud attaching screws and position shroud over fan, then remove engine oil dipstick.
3. Remove vacuum solenoid(s) from dash panel and position on engine with vacuum hoses attached.
4. Raise and support front of vehicle, then remove exhaust pipe to exhaust manifold attaching nuts.
5. Drain crankcase, then remove oil filter.

6. Remove shift linkage bracket to converter housing attaching bolts.
7. Disconnect transmission oil cooler lines at radiator. Remove four converter cover attaching bolts, then remove converter cover.
8. Remove bolts attaching engine damper to No. 2 crossmember.
9. Disconnect steering gear at flex coupling, then remove steering gear to main crossmember attaching bolts and allow steering gear to rest on frame.
10. Remove nuts and bolts attaching from engine mounts to chassis, then raise engine approximately 2 to 3 inches and insert wooden block between engine mounts and frame.

NOTE: On some models, it may be necessary to raise engine as much as 5 inches to provide clearance for oil pan removal. On these models, transmission fluid dipstick tube may contact Thermactor air tube. If contact occurs, lower engine and remove dipstick and air tube.

11. Remove oil pan attaching bolts, then lower oil pan to crossmember.
12. Remove oil pump pickup tube attaching bolts and pickup tube bracket attaching nut, then lower pickup tube into oil pan.
13. Remove oil pan through front of vehicle, then remove oil pan gaskets and seals.
14. Reverse procedure to install. Using a small screwdriver, work tabs of oil pan seal into gap between rear main bearing cap and cylinder block, then with tabs positioned, work seal into groove on rear main bearing cap. Apply a 1/8 inch bead of silicone sealer D6AZ-19562-B or equivalent where front cover and cylinder block join and where rear main bearing cap and cylinder block join. Apply a 1/8 inch bead along oil pan rail surface of cylinder block and a 1/4 inch bead along front cover to oil pan surface.

1983–84 Cougar & Thunderbird V8-302

1. Disconnect battery ground cable.
2. Remove oil level indicator from left side of rear oil sump.
3. Remove air cleaner assembly.
4. Remove fan shroud attaching bolts and position shroud over fan.
5. Raise and support vehicle.
6. Drain engine oil and transmission fluid.
7. Disconnect driveshaft, then remove speedometer cable from transmission.
8. Remove transmission shift linkage lever from transmission.
9. Remove flywheel housing cover attaching bolts and the cover.
10. Remove flywheel-to-converter attaching bolts, then the transmission kickdown control shaft.
11. Remove gear selector valve rod, then the starter motor.
12. Remove catalytic converter and muffler inlet pipes.
13. Support transmission with a suitable jack and remove converter housing-to-cylinder block attaching bolts.
14. Remove No. 3 crossmember and rear insulator support assemblies.
15. Disconnect neutral start switch electrical connector from transmission.
16. Disconnect transmission oil cooler lines, then lower transmission and converter assembly from vehicle.

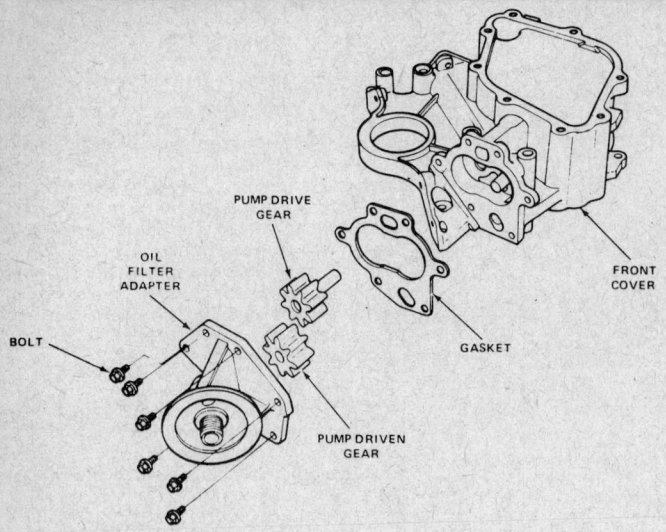

Fig. 36 Oil pump assembly. V6-232

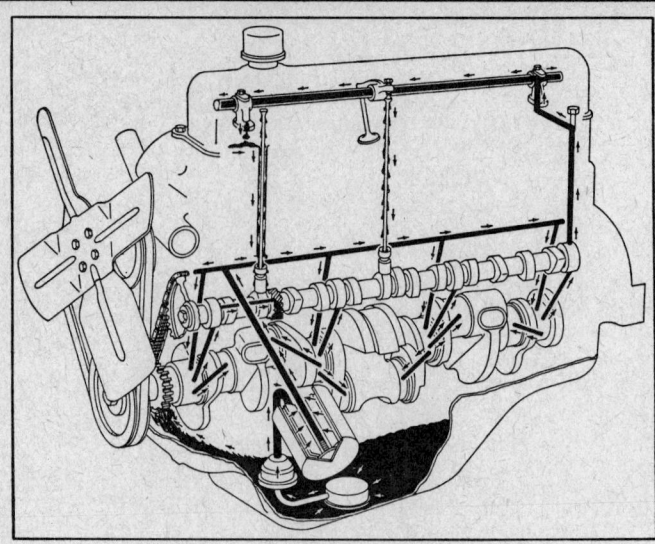

Engine oiling system. 6-200 & 250

17. Remove flywheel attaching bolts, then the engine rear cover plate.
18. Remove steering gear attaching bolts and position gear aside.
19. Raise engine sufficiently to provide clearance for oil pan removal.
20. Remove oil pan attaching bolts and the oil pan.
21. Reverse procedure to install.

1980–82 Cougar XR-7 & Thunderbird V8-255 & 302

1. Disconnect battery ground cable.
2. Remove fan shroud attaching screws and position shroud over fan, then remove dipstick and tube assembly.
3. Raise vehicle and drain crankcase.
4. Disconnect steering flex coupling, then remove two bolts attaching steering gear to main crossmember and let steering gear rest on frame away from oil pan.
5. Unclip and position splash pan away from ends of stabilizer.
6. Remove brackets attaching stabilizer bar to frame, then pull bar downward.
7. Remove transmission shift linkage bracket from frame rail.
8. Remove engine mount attaching bolts, then disconnect and plug transmission oil cooler lines.
9. Disconnect exhaust pipe at exhaust manifolds.
10. Loosen transmission mount nuts, then position a suitable jack under engine and raise engine until engine mount bolts clear frame mounts and pry engine as far forward as it will slide on the transmission mounts.
11. Position two wooden blocks between engine mounts and frame.
12. Remove oil pan attaching bolts, then lower oil pan to frame.
13. Remove oil pump attaching bolts and inlet tube attaching nut, then lower oil pump assembly into oil pan.
14. Remove oil pan. When removing, pull pan forward of stabilizer bar and steering gear flex coupling.

NOTE: It may be necessary to rotate the crankshaft so that oil pan will clear crankshaft counterweights.

15. Reverse procedure to install.

1978–81 Fairmont, Zephyr & 1981 Cougar & Granada V8-255 & 302

1. Remove fan shroud attaching bolts and position shroud over fan.
2. Raise and support vehicle, then drain oil pan.
3. Remove two bolts attaching steering gear to main crossmember and let steering gear rest on frame away from oil pan.
4. Remove engine mount attaching bolts.
5. Raise engine with a suitable jack and place wood blocks between engine mounts and frame.
6. Remove rear "K" braces.
7. Remove oil pan attaching bolts and lower oil pan to frame.
8. Remove oil pump attaching bolts and the inlet tube attaching nut, then lower pump into oil pan.
9. Remove oil pan, rotating crankshaft as necessary to provide clearance for oil pan.
10. Reverse procedure to install.

1977 Comet & Maverick & 1977–80 Granada & Monarch V8-302

1. Raise and support vehicle, then drain oil pan.
2. Remove stabilizer bar from chassis.
3. Remove engine front support through bolts, then the supports. If equipped, remove bolt and nut securing power steering lines to rear side of lower arm.
4. Remove idler arm bracket retaining bolts and pull linkage downward and aside.
5. Remove oil pan attaching bolts and the oil pan.
6. Reverse procedure to install.

1977–79 Cougar, LTD II & Thunderbird V8-302, 351 & 400

1. Remove oil level dipstick, then remove fan shroud retaining screws and position shroud over fan.
2. Raise vehicle and drain crankcase.
3. On 351M and 400 engines, remove starter.
4. Remove stabilizer retaining bolts and lower sway bar.
5. Remove engine mount through bolts, then raise engine and insert wooden blocks between engine mounts and brackets.
6. If equipped with automatic transmission, position oil cooler lines aside.
7. Remove oil pan retaining bolts and oil pan.
8. Reverse procedure to install.

OIL PUMP, REPLACE

6-200 & 250

1. Remove oil pan and related parts as directed above.
2. Unfasten and remove pump, gasket and intermediate drive shaft.
3. Prime pump by filling either the inlet or outlet port with engine oil. Rotate pump shaft to distribute oil within pump body.
4. Position intermediate drive shaft into distributor socket.
5. Position new gasket on pump housing. Insert intermediate drive shaft into oil pump.
6. Install pump and shaft as an assembly.
7. Install oil pan.

V6-232

On these engines, the oil pump is contained within the front cover, Fig. 36.

V8-255, 302, 351, 400

1. Remove oil pan as outlined above.
2. Remove pump inlet tube and screen.
3. Remove pump retaining bolts and remove pump, gasket and intermediate shaft.
4. To install, position intermediate drive shaft into distributor socket. With shaft seated in socket, stop on shaft should touch roof of crankcase. Remove shaft and position stop as necessary.
5. With new gasket on pump housing and stop properly positioned, insert intermediate shaft into oil pump. Install pump and shaft as a unit. *Do not force pump into*

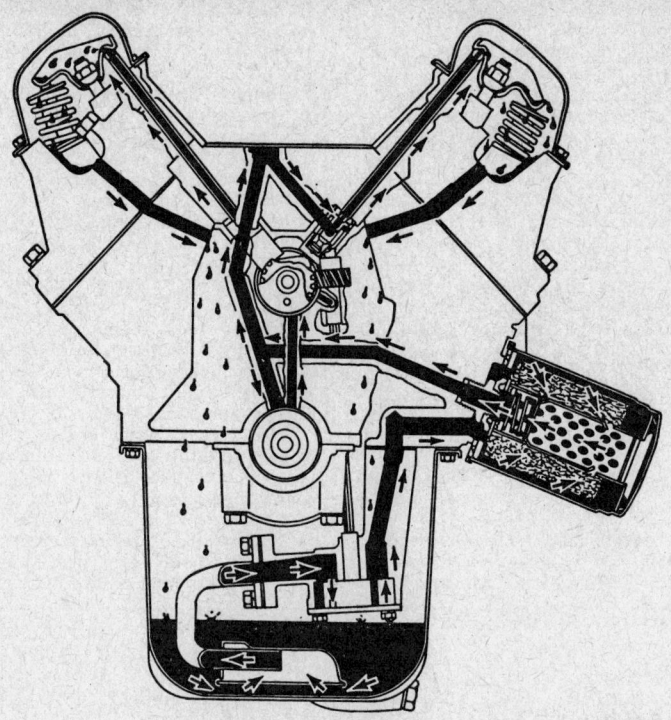

Engine oiling system. V8-255, 302, 351, 400

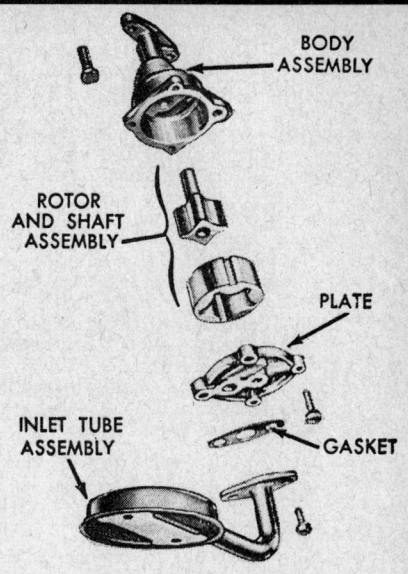

Fig. 37 Oil pump assembly.
6-200 & 250

① — 4 groves.
② — 5 grooves fixed.
③ — W/ absorber.
④ — W/ tensioner.

OIL PUMP, REPAIRS

V8-255, 302, 351, 400 & All Sixes

Referring to Figs. 36 thru 39, disassemble pump. To remove the oil pressure relief valve, insert a self-threading sheet metal screw of the proper diameter into the oil pressure relief valve chamber cap and pull cap out of chamber. Remove spring and plunger.

The inner rotor and shaft and the outer race are serviced as an assembly. One part should not be replaced without replacing the other.

position if it will not seat readily. The drive shaft hex may be misaligned with distributor shaft. To align, rotate shaft into new position.

4. Prime pump by filling either inlet or outlet port with engine oil. Rotate pump shaft to distribute oil within pump body.
5. Position new gasket on pump housing.
6. Insert intermediate drive shaft into oil pump.
7. Install pump and shaft as a unit.
8. Complete installation in reverse order of removal.

WATER PUMP, REPLACE

6-200 & 250

1. Drain cooling system, then remove Thermactor pump, power steering and A/C drive belts, if equipped.
2. Disconnect lower radiator hose, then remove fan belt, fan and drive clutch and water pump pulley.
3. Disconnect heater hose at water pump.
4. Remove water pump attaching bolts, then remove water pump.
5. Reverse procedure to install.

V6-232

1. Drain cooling system, then remove air cleaner and air intake duct.
2. Remove fan shroud attaching screws then

BELT TENSION DATA

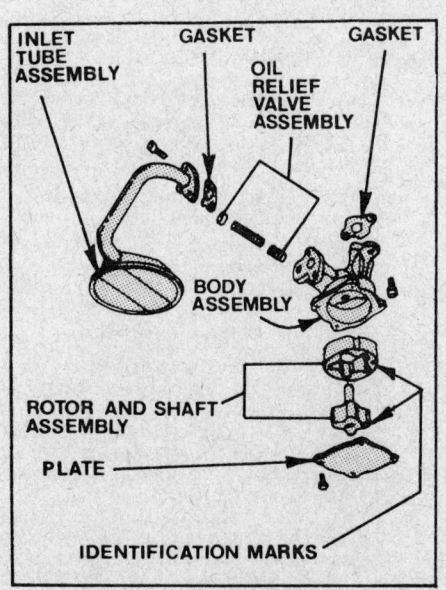

Fig. 38 Oil pump assembly.
V8-255, 302, 351W

	New	Used
1977–81		
Exc. 1/4" Belts.	140	105
1/4" Belts.	65	50
1981		
V Ribbed Belts		
4K①	105	100
5K②	125	120
5K③	108	108
6K②	155	150
6K④	113	113
1982–84		
Except 1/4"	140	105
1/4"		
Except Air Pump	65	50
Air Pump	110	105
Ribbed Belt		
4 Rib		
Except Air Pump	130	115
Air Pump	110	105
5 Rib	150	135
6 Rib		
V6	175	145
V8	113	110

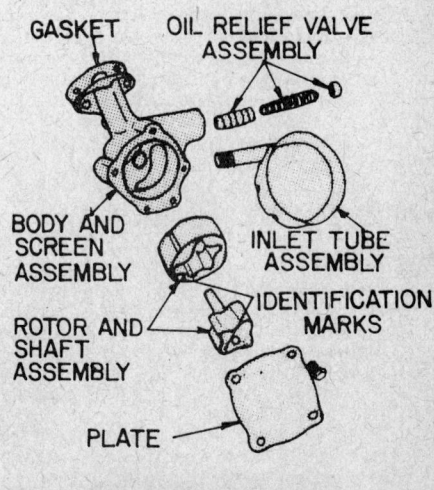

Fig. 39 Oil pump assembly.
V8-351M & 400

the fan and fan clutch attaching bolts. Remove fan and fan clutch and shroud.

3. Loosen accessory drive belt idler, then remove drive belt and water pump pulley.
4. On models equipped with power steering, remove pump mounting bracket attaching bolts, position pump aside with hoses attached.
5. On models equipped with A/C, remove compressor front support bracket.
6. Disconnect lower radiator hose, coolant bypass hose and heat hose from water pump.
7. On models equipped with Tripminder, remove fuel flow sensor support bracket. Do not disconnect fuel lines.
8. Remove water pump attaching bolts, then remove water pump.
9. Reverse procedure to install.

V8-255, 302 & 351W

1. Drain cooling system.
2. On 1978–84 models, remove carburetor air inlet tube.
3. On models equipped with a fan shroud,

remove shroud attaching bolts and position shroud over fan.
4. On all models remove fan, spacer and fan shroud.
5. Remove A/C compressor drive belt and idler pulley bracket, if equipped.
6. Remove alternator drive belt, then remove power steering drive belt and pump, if equipped.
7. Remove all accessory brackets attached to water pump, then remove water pump pulley.
8. Disconnect lower radiator hose, heater hose and bypass hose from water pump.
9. Remove water pump to front cover attaching bolts, then remove water pump.
10. Reverse procedure to install.

V8-351M & 400

1. Disconnect battery ground cable, then drain cooling system.
2. Remove air inlet tube and fan shroud attaching bolts, then position shroud rearward.
3. Remove fan and spacer from water pump shaft.
4. Remove A/C compressor drive belt lower

idler pulley and compressor mount to water pump bracket, if equipped.
5. Remove alternator and power steering drive belts, if equipped.
6. Remove water pump pulley.
7. Remove alternator bracket from water pump and position out of way.
8. Disconnect lower radiator hose, heater hose and bypass hose from water pump.
9. Remove water pump attaching bolts, then remove water pump.
10. Reverse procedure to install.

FUEL PUMP, REPLACE

1. Loosen fuel line connections, then retighten hand tight. Do not disconnect lines at this time.
2. Loosen fuel pump attaching bolts one or two turns. Apply hand force to break pump free from gasket.
3. Rotate engine slightly until pump cam lobe is near lowest position.
4. Disconnect inlet and outlet lines and the vapor return line from pump, if equipped.
5. Remove fuel pump attaching bolts and pump. Remove and discard gasket.
6. Reverse procedure to install.

Turbocharger Section

Refer to the "FORD MUSTANG & PINTO • MERCURY BOBCAT & CAPRI" Chapter for turbocharger service procedures.

Clutch & Transmission Section

CLUTCH PEDAL, ADJUST

1981–83 Fairmont, Zephyr, 1981–82 Cougar, Granada & 1983–84 LTD, Marquis & Thunderbird & 1984 Cougar

These models incorporate a self adjusting clutch mechanism. The adjust mechanism consists of a spring loaded rachet quadrant attached to the clutch cable. To accomplish this adjustment, grasp clutch pedal and pull upward, then slowly depress clutch pedal. If a click is heard during the procedure, an adjustment was necessary and has been accomplished. This procedure should be performed at least every 5000 miles.

1978–80 Fairmont & Zephyr

1978 4-140
1. From under vehicle, remove release lever return spring and dust shield.
2. Loosen clutch cable lock nut and adjusting nut at release lever.
3. Move release lever forward until free play is eliminated and hold lever in this position for adjustment.
4. Insert a .30 in. spacer against release lever cable spacer, then tighten adjusting nut against spacer finger tight.
5. Tighten lock nut against adjusting nut, using care not to disturb adjustment.

Torque lock nut to 5 to 8 ft. lbs. Cycle clutch pedal several times, then recheck free play. Free play at clutch pedal should be approximately 1½ in.
6. Install dust shield and return spring.

1978 6-200
1. Pull clutch toward front of vehicle until adjusting nut can be rotated. Rotate adjusting away from rubber insulator approximately .30 in. Do not rotate nylon nut until it is free of rubber insulator. If necessary, to free adjusting nut from dash insulator it may be necessary to remove clutch pedal bumper stop from clutch pedal. The clutch pedal bumper stop must be reinstalled before adjusting clutch pedal free play.
2. Release cable, then pull cable until free play at release lever is eliminated.
3. Rotate adjusting nut until it contacts rubber insulator, then index tabs into next notch. Free play at clutch pedal should be approximately 1½ in. Cycle clutch pedal several times and recheck free play.

1979–80 4-140 & V8-302
1. Remove dust shield, then loosen clutch cable locknut.
2. Turn adjusting nut as necessary to obtain a total clutch stroke of 5.3 inches on models with 4-140 engines, and 6.5 inches on models with V8-302 engines.

NOTE: Turning adjusting nut clockwise

will raise pedal and counterclockwise will lower pedal.

3. Tighten locknut against adjusting nut using care not to disturb the adjustment. Apply and release the clutch pedal several times and recheck pedal height.
4. On 1979 models, when clutch pedal is properly adjusted, the clutch pedal can be raised 2.7 inches on models with 4-140 engines, and 1.5 inches on models with V8-302 engines.

NOTE: This negative free play is normal and is required to provide for clutch facing wear.

5. Install dust shield.

1979–80 6-200
1. Pull cable toward front of vehicle until adjusting nut can be rotated. Do not rotate nylon adjusting nut until it is free of rubber insulator. To release nut from rubber insulator, it may be necessary to block the clutch release forward so the clutch is partially disengaged.
2. Rotate nut clockwise until 5.3 inches of clutch pedal stroke can be obtained when the nut has been reinstalled in the rubber insulator. Cycle the clutch pedal several times and recheck the adjustment. On 1979 models, when properly adjusted clutch pedal can be raised 2.7 inches.

NOTE: This negative free play is normal and is required to provide for clutch facing wear.

Except 1978–83 Fairmont, Zephyr, 1981–82 Cougar, Granada, 1983–84 LTD, Marquis & Thunderbird & 1984 Cougar

1. Disconnect clutch return spring from release lever.
2. On 1977–80 models remove locking pin, then on all models loosen adjusting nut.
3. Move release lever rearward until release bearing lightly contacts clutch pressure plate release fingers.
4. Slide rod until it seats in release lever pocket.
5. Insert proper feeler gauge (see below) between adjusting nut and swivel sleeve, then tighten adjusting nut finger tight against feeler gauge.
   1977 Comet & Maverick .136"
   1977–80 Granada & Monarch .136"
6. On 1977–80 models, rotate rod slightly to align flat with pin hole in adjusting nut, then install locking pin and remove feeler gauge.
7. On all models, connect return spring to release lever.
8. Depress clutch pedal a minimum of five times, then recheck free play setting with the feeler gauge. Check free travel of pedal which should be 7/8 to 1 1/8 inch.

CLUTCH, REPLACE

1978–83 Fairmont, Zephyr, 1981–82 Cougar, Granada, 1983–84 LTD, Marquis & Thunderbird & 1984 Cougar

NOTE: On 1981–84 models lift clutch pedal upward to disengage clutch cable self adjuster pawl and quadrant. Push quadrant forward, then detach cable from quadrant and allow quadrant to swing rearward slowly.

4-140
1. Raise vehicle and remove release lever spring and dust shield.
2. Loosen clutch cable lock nut and adjusting nut, then disconnect clutch cable from release lever.
3. Remove retaining clip, then remove clutch cable from clutch housing.
4. Remove starter motor.
5. Remove bolts attaching engine rear plate to lower front portion of fly-wheel housing.
6. Remove transmission and flywheel housing as described under "Transmission, Replace."
7. Remove clutch release lever from housing by pulling lever through opening in housing until retainer spring is disengaged from pivot.
8. On 1982–84 models, remove release bearing from release lever.
9. Remove pressure plate cover attaching bolts.

NOTE: Loosen bolts evenly to relieve spring tension without distorting cover. Mark cover and flywheel so that pressure plate can be installed in the same position.

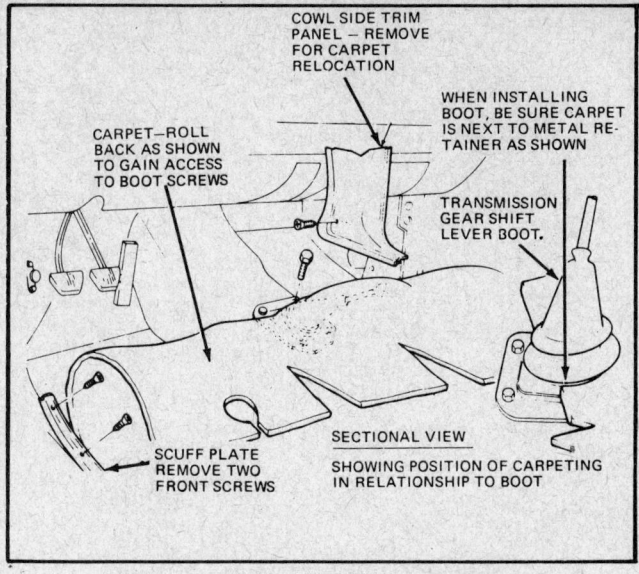

Fig. 1 Shift lever boot removal. 1978–83 Fairmont, Zephyr, 1981–82 Cougar, Granada & 1983–84 LTD & Marquis

10. Remove pressure plate and clutch disc from flywheel.
11. Reverse procedure to install. Adjust clutch pedal as described under "Clutch Pedal, Adjust."

6-200 & V8-302
1. Raise vehicle, then remove transmission as described under "Transmission, Replace."
2. Remove dust shield and loosen clutch cable adjusting nut, then disengage clutch cable from release lever.
3. Disengage clutch cable from flywheel housing.
4. Remove starter.
5. Remove bolts attaching engine rear plate to front lower portion of flywheel housing.
6. Remove bolts attaching housing to cylinder block.
7. Move housing back just far enough to clear pressure plate and remove housing.
8. Remove clutch release lever from housing by pulling lever through housing opening until retainer spring is disengaged from pivot.
9. Remove pressure plate cover attaching bolts.

NOTE: Loosen bolts evenly to relieve spring tension without distorting cover. Mark cover and flywheel so that pressure plate can be installed in the same position.

10. Remove pressure plate and clutch disc from flywheel.
11. Reverse procedure to install. Adjust clutch pedal as described under "Clutch Pedal, Adjust."

Except 1978–83 Fairmont, Zephyr, 1981–82 Cougar, Granada, 1983–84 LTD, Marquis & Thunderbird & 1984 Cougar

1. Remove transmission as described under Transmission, Replace.

2. Disconnect clutch release lever retaining spring.
3. Loosen clutch adjusting rod nuts and remove adjusting rod.
4. Remove starter motor.
5. Remove engine rear plate to lower flywheel housing attaching bolts.
6. Remove flywheel housing to engine attaching bolts and clutch equalizer bar pivot bracket, if equipped.
7. Move flywheel housing back just far enough to clear pressure plate and remove housing.

NOTE: Use care not to disturb clutch linkage.

8. Pull clutch release lever through opening in housing until retainer spring is disengaged from pivot.
9. Remove pressure plate cover attaching bolts.

NOTE: Loosen bolts evenly to relieve spring tension without distorting cover. Mark cover and flywheel so that pressure plate can be installed in the same position.

10. Remove pressure plate and clutch disc from flywheel.
11. Reverse removal procedure to install the clutch and adjust the pedal as outlned in Clutch Pedal, Adjust.

THREE SPEED TRANS. REPLACE

1977–78

1. Raise and support vehicle on a hoist or safety stands.
2. Disconnect electrical connectors from transmission.
3. Mark drive shaft so that it may be installed in the same position, then discon-

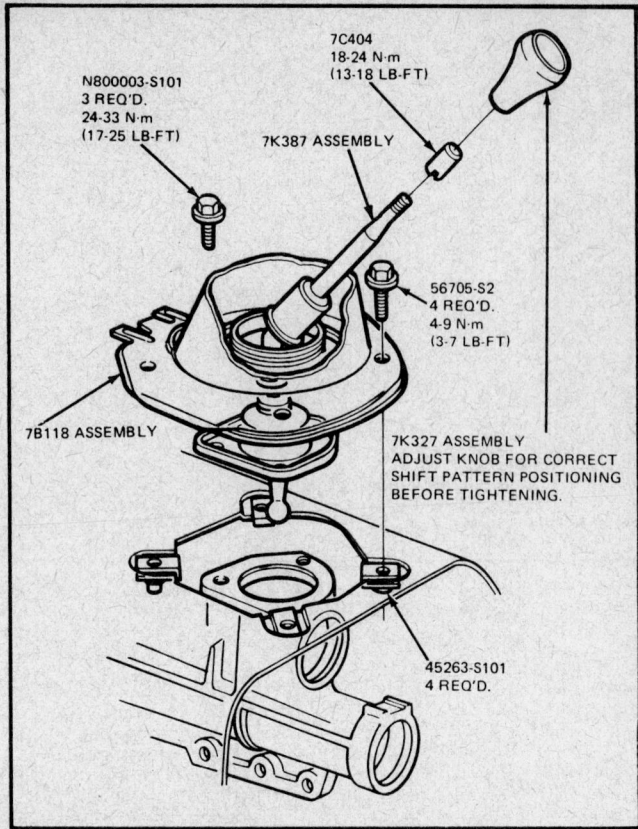

N800003-S101
3 REQ'D.
24-33 N·m
(17-25 LB-FT)

7C404
18-24 N·m
(13-18 LB-FT)

7K387 ASSEMBLY

56705-S2
4 REQ'D.
4-9 N·m
(3-7 LB-FT)

7B118 ASSEMBLY

7K327 ASSEMBLY
ADJUST KNOB FOR CORRECT
SHIFT PATTERN POSITIONING
BEFORE TIGHTENING.

45263-S101
4 REQ'D.

Fig. 2   Shift lever installation. 1978—83 Fairmont, Zephyr, 1981—82 Cougar, Granada & 1983—84 LTD & Marquis

nect it from rear U joint and remove it from output shaft.

NOTE: Plug extension housing to prevent loss of lubricant.

4. Disconnect speedometer cable and shift linkages from transmission.
5. Support transmission with suitable jack and remove engine rear support nuts. Remove the crossmember and rear support insulator.
6. Support engine and remove transmission.

NOTE: Do not depress clutch pedal with transmission removed.

FOUR SPEED OVERDRIVE TRANSMISSION, REPLACE

1979—80 Fairmont, Granada, Monarch & Zephyr

1. Raise vehicle and mark drive shaft so it can be installed in the same position, then disconnect driveshaft at rear U-joint flange. Slide driveshaft from transmission output shaft, then install an extension housing seal installation tool into extension housing opening to prevent lubricant spillage.
2. Disconnect speedometer cable from extension housing.
3. Remove shifter tower to turret assembly attaching screws, then remove shift tow-

er.
4. Support engine using a suitable jack, then remove extension housing to engine rear support attaching bolts.
5. Raise rear of engine slightly to relieve weight from crossmember, then remove crossmember to frame side support attaching bolts and remove crossmember.
6. Support transmission using a suitable jack, then remove bolts attaching transmission to flywheel housing.
7. Move transmission rearward until input shaft clears flywheel, then lower transmission from vehicle. It may be necessary to lower engine slightly to obtain clearance for transmission removal.
8. Reverse procedure to install.

1977—78 Granada & Monarch

1. Disconnect battery ground cable.
2. Remove shift lever boot bezel and the four shift lever boot to floor attaching screws. Lift boot upward.
3. Remove two bolts attaching shift lever to shift control, then the shift lever and boot.
4. From beneath vehicle, disconnect shift rods from shift control levers.
5. Disconnect back-up lamp switch electrical connector and remove switch from retainer by pulling and twisting the switch in both directions.

NOTE: Do not use pliers or other tools since damage to the switch may result.

6. Remove shift control assembly to extension housing attaching bolts, then the shift control assembly.

7. Raise vehicle and remove propeller shaft.
8. Disconnect speedometer cable from extension housing.
9. Support engine with a suitable jack and remove extension housing to engine rear support attaching bolts.
10. Support transmission with a suitable jack and release weight from crossmember. Remove bolts attaching crossmember to frame side supports and the crossmember.
11. Remove transmission to flywheel housing bolts.
12. Move transmission rearward and lower from vehicle.
13. Reverse procedure to install. Adjust shift linkage as outlined under "Gearshift Linkage".

FOUR SPEED TRANS., REPLACE

1978—83 Fairmont, Zephyr, 1981—82 Cougar, Granada & 1983—84 LTD & Marquis

1. Remove coin tray, then remove four screws attaching boot to floor pan and pull boot up on shift lever. Remove three lever attaching screws, then remove shift lever and boot assembly, Figs. 1 and 2.
2. From under hood, remove flywheel housing to engine block upper attaching bolts or nuts.
3. Raise and support vehicle.
4. Mark driveshaft so that it can be installed in the same position, then remove driveshaft and install a plug in transmission extension housing to prevent lubricant leakage.
5. Remove clutch release lever dust cover, then disconnect clutch cable from release lever.
6. Remove starter motor.
7. Remove speedometer cable attaching screw, then lift cable from extension housing.
8. Support rear of engine using a suitable jack, then remove bolts attaching crossmember to body.
9. Remove bolts attaching crossmember to extension housing and remove crossmember.
10. Lower engine as required to permit removal of bolts attaching flywheel housing to engine. Slide transmission rearward from engine and lower from vehicle.

NOTE: It may be necessary to slide mounting bracket forward from catalytic converter heat shield to provide clearance to move transmission rearward for removal.

11. Remove cover attaching bolts and drain lubricant.
12. Remove flywheel housing to transmission attaching bolts, then remove flywheel housing.
13. Reverse procedure to install.

FIVE SPEED TRANS., REPLACE

1983—84 Thunderbird & 1984 Cougar

1. Raise and support vehicle.

2. Mark driveshaft for assembly reference, then disconnect driveshaft from rear U-joint flange. Slide driveshaft from transmission output shaft, then install an extension housing seal installation tool into extension housing opening to prevent lubricant spillage.
3. Remove 4 catalytic converter attaching bolts and the converter with inlet pipe.
4. Remove rear transmission support attaching bolts.
5. Support engine and transmission using a suitable jack, then remove crossmember attaching bolts. Raise engine slightly and remove crossmember.
6. Lower transmission to gain access to 2 shift handle attaching bolts, then remove the bolts and shift handle.
7. Disconnect backup light electrical connector.
8. Remove speedometer cable retainer bolt, then the speedometer driven gear from transmission.
9. Remove transmission-to-flywheel attaching bolts.
10. Move transmission rearward until input shaft clears flywheel housing, then lower transmission from vehicle. It may be necessary to lower engine slightly to provide clearance for transmission removal

NOTE: Do not depress clutch pedal while transmission is removed from vehicle.

11. Reverse procedure to install.

GEARSHIFT LINKAGE, ADJUST

NOTE: *If the transmission shifts hard or will not engage, the gearshift levers may need adjusting at the cross-over. Move the shift lever through all positions to see that the cross-over operation is smooth. If not, adjust as follows:*

1977 3 Speed Column Shift

1. Place selector lever in Neutral position.
2. Loosen two gear shift rod adjusting nuts at transmission.

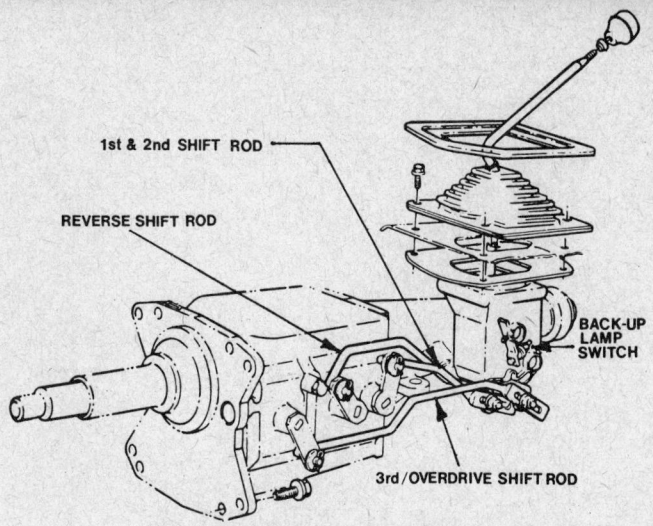

Fig. 3 Four speed overdrive gear shift linkage. 1977—78 Granada & Monarch

3. Check to ensure that transmission gear shift levers are in the Neutral position.
4. Fabricate an alignment pin from a piece of 3/16 in. drill rod bent into an L shape.
5. Insert alignment pin through 1st/reverse and 2nd/3rd gear shift levers and both holes in lower casting, then tighten two gear shift rod adjusting nuts.
6. Remove alignment pin, then start engine and check linkage for proper operation.

1977—78 3 Speed Floor Shift

NOTE: Floor shift linkages incorporate a transmission lock rod. This rod must be adjusted AFTER the shift linkage has been adjusted. With shift lever in Neutral and lock rod adjustment nut loose, align hole in steering column socket casting with alignment mark and insert a .180″ dia. rod. The casting must not rotate with the rod in this position.

1. Connect shift rods to transmission levers.

2. Ensure transmission is in neutral.
3. Insert alignment pin through hole in boot and into shift control assembly alignment hole.
4. Install slotted ends of shift rods over flats of studs in shift control assembly, then install and torque lock nuts.
5. Remove alignment pin.

1977—78 4 Speed Overdrive

1. Attach shift rods to transmission levers, Fig. 3.
2. Shift reverse lever (middle) clockwise to place transmission in reverse.
3. Insert alignment pin through hole in boot and into shift control assembly alignment hole.
4. Attach slotted ends of 1-2 and 3-overdrive shift rods over flats of studs on shift control assembly. Install lock nuts and torque to 10 to 20 ft. lbs.
5. Shift transmission to neutral and attach reverse lever. Torque lock nut to 10 to 20 ft. lbs.
6. Remove alignment pin.

Rear Axle, Propeller Shaft & Brakes

REAR AXLES

Ford WER Integral Carrier, Fig. 1

The gear set consists of a ring gear and an overhung drive pinion which is supported by two opposed tapered roller bearings. The differential case is a one-piece design with openings allowing assembly of the internal parts and lubricant flow. The differential pinion shaft is retained with a threaded bolt (lock) assembled to the case.

The roller type wheel bearings have no inner race, and the rollers directly contact the bearing journals of the axle shafts. The axle shafts do not use an inner and outer bearing

retainer. Rather, they are held in the axle by means of C-locks, Fig. 4. These C-locks also fit into a machined recess in the differential side gears within the differential case. There is no retainer bolt access hole in the axle shaft flange.

Ford WGF & WGG (6¾″ Ring Gear) Integral Carrier, Fig. 1A

This rear axle is an integral design hypoid with the centerline of the pinion set below the centerline of the ring gear. The semi-floating axle shafts are retained in the housing by ball bearings and bearing retainers at axle ends. The differential is mounted on two opposed

tapered roller bearings which are retained in the housing by removable caps. Differential bearing preload and drive gear backlash is adjusted by nuts located behind each differential bearing cup.

The drive pinion assembly is mounted on two opposed tapered roller bearings. Pinion bearing preload is adjusted by a collapsible spacer on the pinion shaft. Pinion and ring gear tooth contact is adjusted by shims between the rear bearing cone and pinion gear.

Ford WGX & WGZ Integral Carrier, Fig. 2

The gear set consist of a ring gear and an

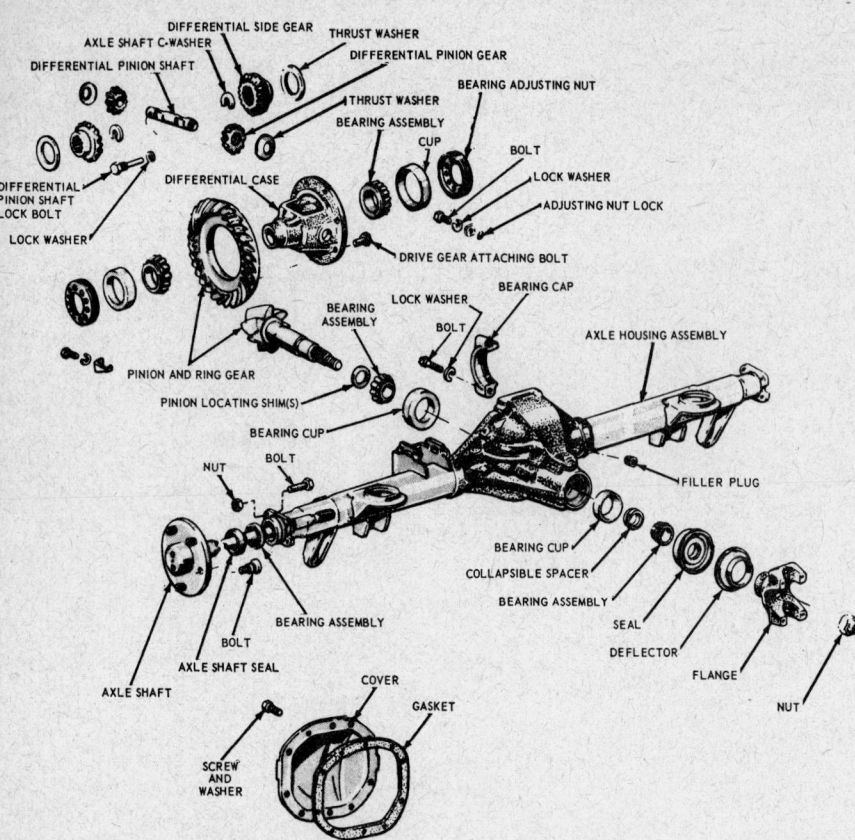

Fig. 1 Disassembled view of Ford WER integral carrier type rear axle assembly

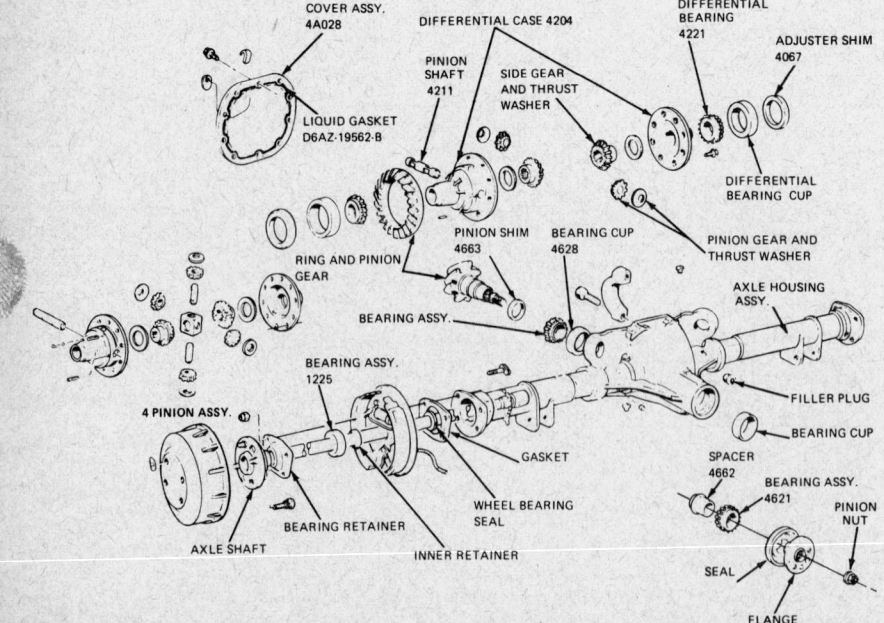

Fig. 1A Disassembled view of Ford WGF & WGG (6¾" Ring Gear) integral carrier type rear axle assembly

overhung drive pinion which is supported by two opposed tapered roller bearings. Pinion bearing preload is maintained by a collapsible spacer on the pinion shaft and adjusted by the pinion nut. The differential case is a one piece design with two openings to allow assembly of internal components and lubricant flow. The pinion shaft is retained with a threaded bolt assembled to the case. The differential case is mounted in the carrier between two opposed tapered roller bearings. The bearings are retained in the carrier by removable bearing caps. Differential bearing preload and ring gear backlash are adjusted by the use of shims located between the differential bearing cups and the carrier housing. Axle shafts are held in the housing by C-locks positioned in a slot on the axle shaft splined end, Fig. 4.

Removable Carrier Type

In these axles, Fig. 3, the drive pinion is straddle-mounted by two opposed tapered roller bearings which support the pinion shaft in front of the drive pinion gear, and a straight roller bearing that supports the pinion shaft at the rear of the pinion gear. The drive pinion is assembled in a pinion retainer that is bolted to the differential carrier. The tapered roller bearings are preloaded by a collapsible spacer between the bearings. The pinion is positioned by a shim or shims located between the drive pinion retainer and the differential carrier.

The differential is supported in the carrier by two tapered roller side bearings. These bearings are preloaded by two threaded ring nuts or sleeves between the bearings and the pedestals. The differential assembly is positioned for proper ring gear and pinion backlash by varying the adjustment of these ring nuts. The differential case houses two side gears in mesh with two pinions mounted on a pinion shaft which are held in place by a pin. The side gears and pinions are backed by thrust washers.

The axle shafts are of unequal length, the left shaft being shorter than the right. The axle shafts are mounted in sealed ball bearings which are pressed on the shafts.

Rear Axle, Replace

Leaf Spring Suspension
1. Raise vehicle and support at rear frame members.
2. Drain lubricant from axle.
3. Mark drive shaft and pinion flanges for reassembly, then disconnect drive shaft at rear axle U-joint and remove drive shaft from transmission extension housing. Install seal replacer tool in extension housing to prevent leakage.
4. Disconnect shock absorbers at lower mountings.
5. Remove rear wheels and brake drums, then disconnect brake lines at wheel cylinders.
6. Disconnect vent hose from vent tube, then remove vent tube from brake junction and axle housing.
7. Remove clips retaining brake lines to axle housing.
8. Support rear axle housing using a suitable jack, remove U-bolts and plates.
9. Lower rear axle and remove vehicle.
10. Reverse procedure to install.

Coil Spring Suspension
1. Raise rear of vehicle support at frame members and rear axle, then remove wheel and tire assembly.

2. Remove brake drums and disconnect brake lines at wheel cylinders.
3. Make marks on drive shaft yoke and pinion flange for reassembly, then disconnect drive shaft at rear U-joint and remove drive shaft from transmission extension housing. Install seal replacer tool in extension housing to prevent leakage.
4. Position a drain pan under differential carrier, then remove carrier attaching bolts and allow differential to drain.
5. Disconnect stabilizer bar, if equipped.
6. Disconnect shock absorbers from lower mountings.
7. Remove brake lines from retaining clips on rear axle housing, then remove brake line junction block retaining screw.
8. Position a suitable jack under axle housing to prevent housing from tilting when removing control arms.
9. Disconnect lower control arms from axle housing and position control arms downward.
10. Disconnect upper control arms from axle housing and position control arms upward.
11. Disconnect air vent line.
12. Lower axle slightly and remove coil springs and insulators.
13. Lower axle housing and remove from vehicle.

Axle Shaft, Replace

Removable Carrier Type
1. Remove wheel assembly.
2. Remove brake drum or rotor and caliper assembly.
3. Working through hole provided in axle shaft flange, Fig. 5, remove nuts that secure wheel bearing retainer.
4. Pull axle shaft out of housing. If bearing is a tight fit in axle housing use a slide hammer-type puller, Fig. 6. Remove brake backing plate and secure to frame rail with wire.
5. If the axle shaft bearing is to be replaced, loosen the inner retainer by nicking it deeply with a chisel in several places, Fig. 7. The bearing will then slide off easily.
6. Press bearing from axle shaft.
7. Inspect machined surface of axle shaft and housing for rough spots that would affect sealing action of the oil seal. Carefully remove any burrs or rough spots.
8. Press new bearing on shaft until it seats firmly against shoulder on shaft.
9. Press inner bearing retainer on shaft until it seats firmly against bearing.
10. If oil seal is to be replaced, use a hook-type tool to pull it out of housing, Fig. 8. Wipe a small amount of oil resistant sealer on outer edge of seal before it is installed, Fig. 9.

SERVICE NOTE: On 1977–78 Cougar, LTD II, Montego and Thunderbird models, if replacing an axle shaft of the sealed ball bearing design, the replacement assembly will have a tapered roller bearing. This tapered roller bearing is interchangeable with the ball bearing as an assembly only, however the inner oil seal must be removed before the tapered bearing shaft can be installed into the housing bore. The housing wheel bearing bore should be sanded with emery cloth before installing the bearing to provide a good sealing surface for the seal.

When removing a tapered roller bearing axle shaft, the outer bearing race may separate from the retaining ring and remain in the housing bore. If this occurs, the bearing must be removed and reinstalled on the shaft to

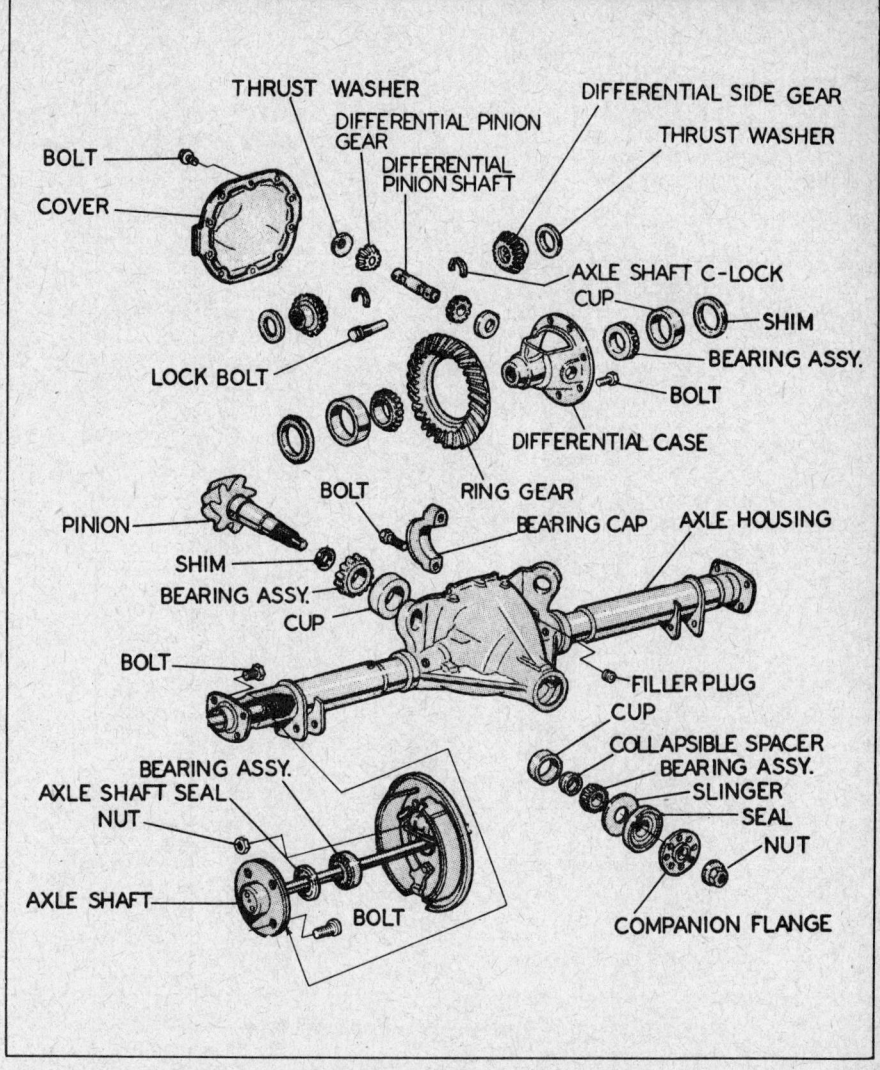

Fig. 2 Disassemble view of Ford WGX & WGZ integral carrier type rear axle assembly

prevent damage to the seal.

Installation
1. Place a new gasket on each side of brake carrier plate and slide axle shaft into housing.
2. Start the splines into the differential side gear and push the shaft in until bearing bottoms in housing.
3. Install retainer. On 1977 Comet, Granada, Maverick, Monarch and all 1978–80 models, torque retaining nuts to 20 to 40 ft. lbs. On 1977 models except Comet, Granada, Maverick and Monarch, torque retaining nuts to 35 to 55 ft. lbs.
4. Install brake drum or caliper and rotor and wheel assembly.

Ford WER Integral Carrier Type
1. Raise car on hoist and remove wheels.
2. Drain differential lubricant.
3. Remove brake drums.
4. Remove differential housing cover.
5. Position safety stands under rear frame member and lower hoist to allow axle to lower as far as possible.
6. Working through differential case opening, remove pinion shaft lock bolt and pinion shaft.

7. Push axle shaft(s) inward toward center of axle housing and remove C-lock(s) from housing, Fig. 4.
8. Remove axle shaft, using extreme care to avoid contact of shaft seal lip with any portion of axle shaft except seal journal.
9. Use a hook-type puller to remove seal and bearing, Fig. 8.

NOTE: Two types of bearings are used, Fig. 8A. One requires a light press fit in the housing flange, while on the other, a loose fit is acceptable. Therefore, if a loose fitting bearing is encountered, it does not indicate excessive wear or damage

10. Reverse procedure to install, using suitable driving tools, Fig. 9, to install seal and bearing. New seals are prepacked with lubricant and do not require oil soaking before installation.

Ford WGF & WGG Integral Carrier Type
1. Remove wheel and tire assembly, then remove nuts attaching brake drum to axle shaft flange and remove brake drum.
2. Working through opening in axle shaft flange, remove nuts securing axle shaft bearing retainer, Fig. 5.

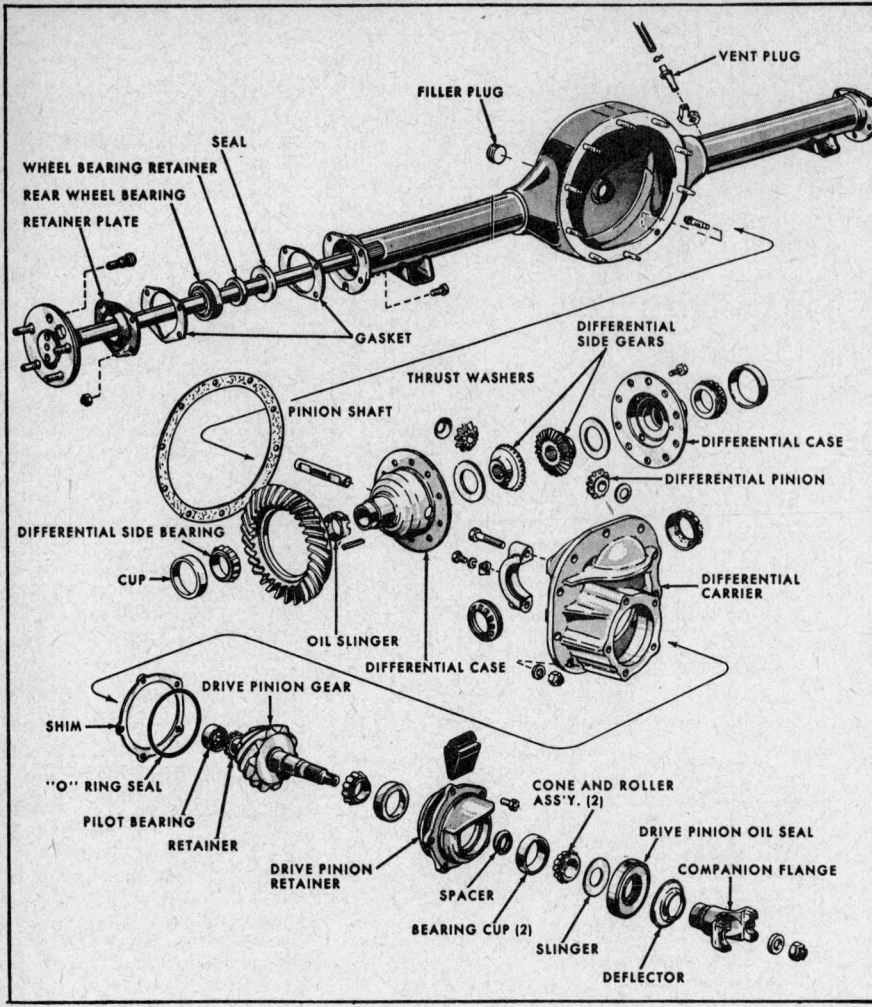

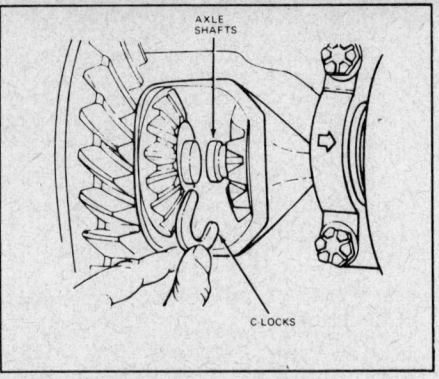

Fig. 4 Axle shaft C-lock. WER, WGX & WGZ integral type rear axle

Fig. 5 Removing nuts from wheel bearing retainer

Fig. 3 Rear axle assembly with removable carrier

3. Using a suitable puller, pull axle shaft from housing, Fig. 6.
4. Remove brake backing plate and attach to frame side rail with a piece of wire.
5. If rear wheel bearing is to be replaced, loosen inner retainer ring by nicking it deeply in several places with a chisel, Fig. 7, then slide retainer from axle shaft.
6. Press bearing from axle shaft using tool No. T71P-4621-B.
7. Using a hook type puller, remove oil seal from axle housing, Fig. 8.
8. Position bearing retainer and bearing on axle shaft, then using tool No. T62F-4621-A, press bearing onto shaft until firmly seated against shoulder.
9. Using bearing installation tool, press inner retainer onto shaft until retainer is firmly seated against bearing.
10. Wipe all lubricant from oil seal area of axle housing, then install oil seal using tool No. T79P-1177-A, Fig. 9.
11. Install gasket on housing flange, then install brake backing plate.
12. Carefully slide axle shaft into housing using care not to damage oil seal, then install bearing retainer attaching nuts and torque to 20 to 40 ft. lbs.
13. Install brake drum and retaining nuts, then install wheel and tire assembly.

Ford WGX & WGZ Integral Carrier Type
1. Raise and support rear of vehicle.
2. Remove wheel and tire assembly and brake drum.
3. Remove rear axle housing cover and drain lubricant.
4. Remove differential pinion lock screw and differential pinion shaft.

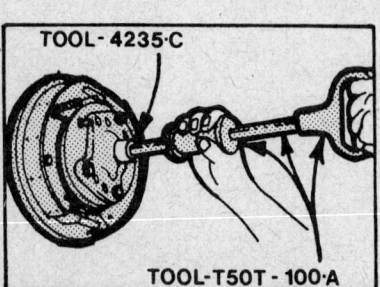

Fig. 6 Removing axle shaft with slide hammer-type puller

Fig. 7 Splitting bearing inner retainer for bearing removal

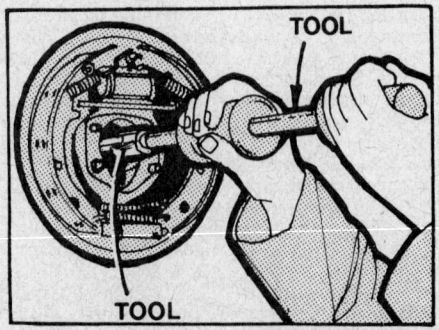

Fig. 8 Using hook-type tool to remove oil seal

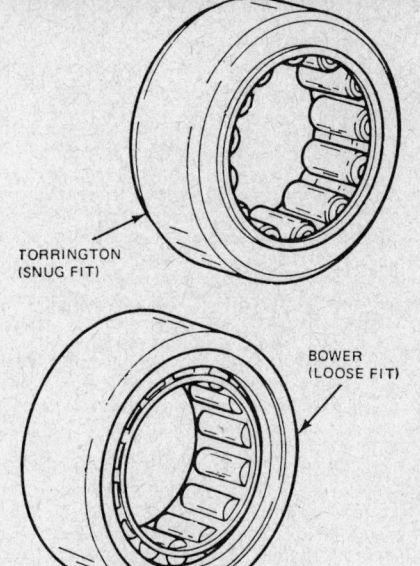

TORRINGTON
(SNUG FIT)

BOWER
(LOOSE FIT)

Fig. 8A   Axle shaft bearing identification. WER, WGX & WGZ integral type rear axle

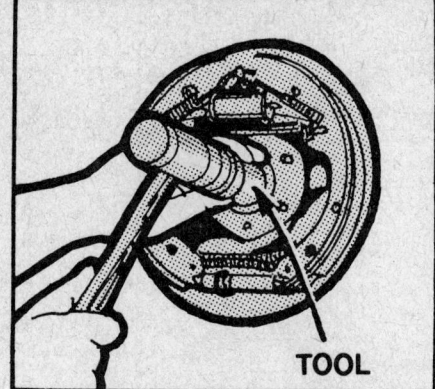

TOOL

Fig. 9   Using special driver to install oil seal

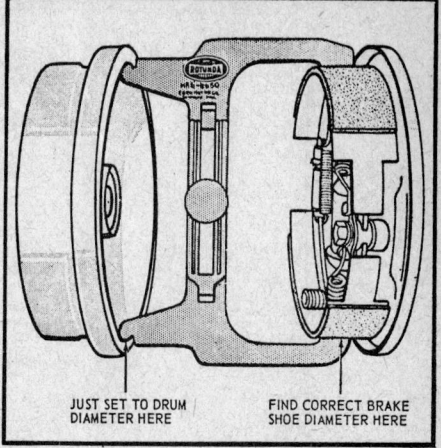

JUST SET TO DRUM DIAMETER HERE

FIND CORRECT BRAKE SHOE DIAMETER HERE

Fig. 10   Revised brake adjustment

5. Push axle shafts inward and remove C-locks, Fig. 4.
6. Remove axle shaft from housing using care not to damage oil seal.
7. Remove bearing and seal as an assembly using a suitable slide hammer, Fig. 8, if necessary.

NOTE: Two types of bearing are used, Fig. 8A. One requires a light press fit in the housing flange, while on the other a loose fit is acceptable. Therefore, if a loose fitting bearing is encountered, it does not indicate excessive wear or damage.

8. Lubricate bearing with rear axle lubricant and install bearing into housing bore using tool No. T78P-1225-A.
9. Install axle shaft seal into housing using tool No. T78P-1177-A, Fig. 9.
10. Reverse procedure to install axle shaft.

PROPELLER SHAFT, REPLACE

1. Mark relationship of driveshaft to pinion flange, then disconnect rear U-joint or companion flange from drive pinion flange.
2. Pull drive shaft toward rear of car until front U-joint yoke clears transmission extension housing and output shaft.
3. Install a suitable tool, such as a seal driver, in seal to prevent lube from leaking from transmission.
4. Before installing, check U-joints for freedom of movement. If a bind has resulted from misalignment after overhauling the U-joints, tap the ears of the drive shaft sharply to relieve the bind.
5. If rubber seal installed on end of transmission extension housing is damaged, install a new seal.
6. On a manual shift transmission, lubricate yoke spline with conventional transmission grease. On an automatic trans-

mission, lubricate yoke spline with special spline grease. *This spline is sealed so that transmission fluid does not "wash" away spline lubricant.*

7. Install yoke on transmission output shaft.
8. Install U-bolts and nuts which attach U-joint to pinion flange. Tighten U-bolts evenly to prevent binding U-joint bearings.

BRAKE ADJUSTMENTS

SERVICE BULLETIN

REVISED BRAKE ADJUSTMENT PROCEDURE: Some models use a new front and rear brake backing plate which omits the adjusting slot for manual brake adjustment. The backing plates have a partially stamped knock-out slot for use ONLY when the brake drums cannot be removed in a normal manner. The open slot is then covered with a rubber plug as used in the past to prevent contamination of the brakes.

When servicing a vehicle requiring a brake adjustment, the metal knock-out plugs should NOT be removed. Rather the drums should be removed and brakes inspected for a malfunction.

Although the brakes are self-adjusting, an initial adjustment will be necessary after a brake repair, such as relining or replacement. The initial adjustment can be obtained by the new procedure which follows:

1. Use the brake shoe adjustment gauge shown in Fig. 10 to obtain the drum inside diameter as shown. Tighten the adjusting knob on the gauge to hold this setting.
2. Place the opposite side of the gauge over the brake shoes and adjust the shoes by turning the adjuster screw until the gauge just slides over the linings. Rotate the gauge around the lining surface to assure proper lining diameter adjustment and clearance.
3. Install brake drum and wheel. Final adjustment is accomplished by making several firm reverse stops, using the brake pedal.

Self-Adjusting Brakes

These brakes, Fig. 11 have self-adjusting shoe mechanisms that assure correct lining-to-drum clearances at all times. The automatic adjusters operate only when the brakes are

applied as the car is moving rearward.

Although the brakes are self-adjusting, an initial adjustment is necessary after the brake shoes have been relined or replaced, or when the length of the star wheel adjuster has been changed during some other service operation.

Frequent usage of an automatic transmission forward range to halt reverse vehicle motion may prevent the automatic adjusters from functioning, thereby inducing low pedal heights. Should low pedal heights be encountered, it is recommended that numerous forward and reverse stops be made until satisfactory pedal height is obtained.

NOTE: If a low pedal condition cannot be corrected by making numerous reverse stops (provided the hydraulic system is free of air) it indicates that the self-adjusting mechanism is not functioning. Therefore, it will be necessary to remove the brake drum, clean, free up and lubricate the adjusting mechanism. Then adjust the brake, being sure the parking brake is fully released.

PARKING BRAKE, ADJUST

Rear Drum Brakes

1. Make sure parking brake is released.
2. Place transmission in neutral and raise the vehicle.
3. Tighten the adjusting nut against the cable equalizer to cause rear brakes to drag.
4. Then loosen the adjusting nut until the rear wheels are fully released. There should be no drag.
5. Lower vehicle and check operation.

Rear Disc Brakes

1. Fully release parking brake, then place transmission in neutral and support vehicle at rear axle.
2. Tighten adjuster nut until levers on calipers just start to move, then loosen the nut just enough to obtain full travel to the off position.

NOTE: If brake cables are replaced in any system having a foot-actuated control assembly, stroke parking brake control with about 100 pounds pedal effort, then repeat adjustment.

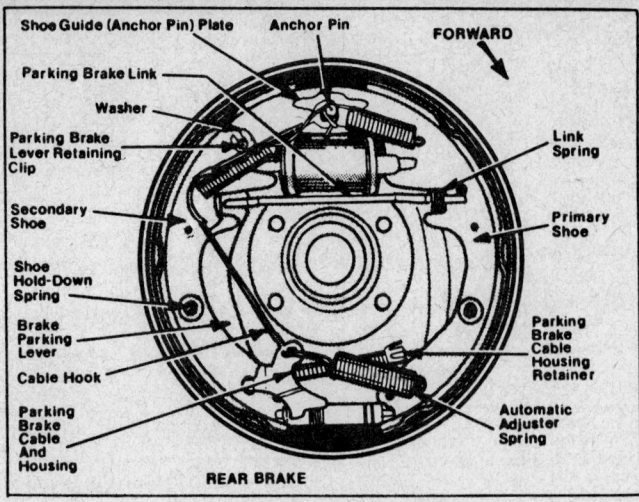

Fig. 11   Rear drum brake mechanism

3. The lever is in the off position when a 1/4 inch diameter pin can be freely inserted past the side of the lever into the 1/4 inch diameter holes in the cast iron housing.
4. Apply and release the parking brake, then apply and release the service brake pedal with moderate force. Check parking brake levers on calipers to determine if they are fully returned to the off position.

NOTE: If the 1/4 inch pin cannot be freely inserted, the adjustment is too tight. Repeat adjustment procedure. Also, if levers do not return to off position, parking and service brake function will be affected as the vehicle is driven.

Vacuum Release Unit

The vacuum power unit will release the parking brake automatically when the transmission selector lever is moved into any driving position with the engine running. The brakes will not release automatically, however, when the selector lever is in neutral or park position with the engine running, or in any other position with the engine off.

The lower end of the release handle extends out for alternate manual release in the event of vacuum power failure or for optional manual release at any time.

MASTER CYLINDER, REPLACE

1977–82 Less Power Brakes

1. Disconnect battery ground cable.
2. Disconnect stop light switch wires, remove hairpin retainer and slide stop light switch off brake pedal pin just far enough to clear end of pin. Then lift switch straight upward from pin.
3. Slide master cylinder push rod with nylon washers and bushings from brake pedal pin.
4. Remove brake tubes from outlet ports of master cylinder.
5. Remove lock nuts that secure master cylinder to dash panel and lift cylinder forward and upward from vehicle.
6. Reverse procedure to install.

1977–84 With Power Brakes

1. Disconnect brake lines from master cylinder.
2. On late 1983 and all 1984 models, disconnect brake warning lamp electrical connector.
3. On all models, remove master cylinder to power brake unit attaching nuts, then lift master cylinder from mounting studs.
4. Reverse procedure to install.

POWER BRAKE UNIT, REPLACE

1977–84 Except Hydro-Boost

1. Working under instrument panel, disconnect stop light switch wires at connector.
2. Remove hairpin type retainer. Slide stop light switch off brake pedal pin just far enough for the switch outer hole to clear the pin, then lower switch away from pin.
3. On 1977–79 Cougar and LTD II equipped with speed control, remove left cowl screen, then the 3 speed control servo mounting bracket attaching nuts, and position servo aside.
4. On all 1980–84 models equipped with speed control, remove control amplifier mounted to lower outboard booster stud and position aside.
5. On all models, slide booster push rod link and nylon washers off brake pedal pin.
6. On 1978–83 Fairmont, Zephyr, 1980–82 Cougar XR-7, 1980–84 Thunderbird, 1981–84 Cougar, Granada and 1983–84 LTD and Marquis, remove air cleaner. On models with 4-140 engine, disconnect accelerator cable from carburetor, then remove screw that secures accelerator cable to shaft bracket and remove cable from bracket. Remove two screws that secure accelerator shaft bracket to manifold and rotate bracket toward engine.
7. On 1977 Comet and Maverick with 6-250 engine, remove air cleaner and disconnect accelerator cable from carburetor.
8. On all 1977 Comet and Maverick models, remove fender to cowl brace.
9. On 1977–79 Cougar, LTD II, and Thunderbird models, equipped with speed control, remove left cowl screen, then remove servo mounting bracket attaching nuts and position servo cable.
10. On all models, disconnect brake line from master cylinder.
11. Disconnect vacuum hose from booster at check valve.
12. Unfasten and remove booster and bracket assembly from dash panel, sliding push rod link out from engine side of dash panel.

1977–80 Hydro-Boost

1. Disconnect stoplight switch wires at connector and remove hairpin retainer, then slide stoplight switch off brake pedal pin far enough for switch outer hole to clear pin and remove pin from switch.
2. Slide hydro-boost push rod and nylon washers and bushing off brake pedal pin.
3. Remove master cylinder and position to one side without disturbing hydraulic lines.

NOTE: It is not necessary to disconnect brake lines, but care should be taken not to deform lines.

4. Disconnect pressure, steering gear and return lines from booster, then plug lines and ports in hydro-boost to prevent entry of dirt.
5. Remove hydro-boost retaining nuts, and remove assembly sliding push rod link from engine side of dash panel.
6. Reverse procedure to install. To purge system, disconnect coil wire so that engine will not start. Fill power steering pump reservoir, then while engaging starter, pump brake pedal. Do not cycle steering wheel until all residual air has been purged from the hydro boost unit. Check fluid level, then connect coil wire and start engine. Apply brakes with a pumping action and cycle steering wheel, then check system for leaks.

Rear Suspension

SHOCK ABSORBER, REPLACE

1978–83 Fairmont & Zephyr; 1980–82 Cougar XR-7; 1980–84 Thunderbird; 1981–82 Granada; 1981–84 Cougar; 1983–84 LTD & Marquis

1. On sedans, open trunk to gain access to upper shock absorber attachment. On station wagons, remove side panel trim covers.
2. Remove rubber cap from shock absorber stud.
3. On all models, remove shock absorber attaching nut, washer and insulator.
4. Raise vehicle and support rear axle.
5. Compress shock absorber to clear hole in upper shock absorber tower.
6. On 1978–83 Fairmont and Zephyr, 1981–82 Cougar and Granada and 1983–84 LTD and Marquis models, remove nut or bolt and washer from shock absorber lower mounting stud, then the shock absorber. On 1980–82 Cougar XR-7, 1980–84 Thunderbird and 1983–84 Cougar models, remove shock absorber protective cover, then the shock absorber attaching bolt and shock absorber.
7. Reverse procedure to install. Torque upper shock mount to 14–26 ft. lbs. on 1978–81 models, or 24–26 ft. lbs. on 1982–84 models. Torque lower attaching bolt to 40–55 ft. lbs. on 1978–80 models, 65–70 ft. lbs. on 1981 models, 60–65 ft. lbs. on 1982 models, or 55–70 ft. lbs. on 1983–84 models.

Except 1978–83 Fairmont & Zephyr; 1980–82 Cougar XR-7; 1980–84 Thunderbird; 1981–82 Granada; 1981–84 Cougar; 1983–84 LTD & Marquis

1. Raise and properly support vehicle.

2. Disconnect shock absorber from its lower and upper mounting, then remove shock absorber.
3. Reverse procedure to install.

LEAF SPRINGS & BUSHINGS, REPLACE

1977 Comet & Maverick & 1977–80 Granada & Monarch

1. Raise rear of vehicle and support at frame. Support axle with a suitable jack.
2. Disconnect shock absorbers from lower mountings.
3. Lower jack and remove spring plate "U" bolts and spring plate, Fig. 1.
4. Raise axle to remove weight from spring and disassemble rear shackle.
5. Remove spring front mount bolt.
6. Replace spring front eye bushings as necessary, Figs. 2 and 3.
7. Reverse procedure to install.

STABILIZER BAR, REPLACE

1978–83 Fairmont & Zephyr; 1980–82 Cougar XR-7; 1980–84 Thunderbird; 1981–82 Granada; 1981–84 Cougar; 1983–84 LTD & Marquis

1. Raise and support rear of vehicle.
2. Remove four bolts attaching stabilizer bar to lower control arms.
3. Remove stabilizer bar from vehicle.

1977–79 Cougar, LTD II & Thunderbird

1. Remove bolts securing stabilizer bar to rear link assemblies on both sides, Fig. 4.
2. Remove nuts securing mounting bracket to lower mounting clamp and remove bar.
3. Reverse procedure to install.

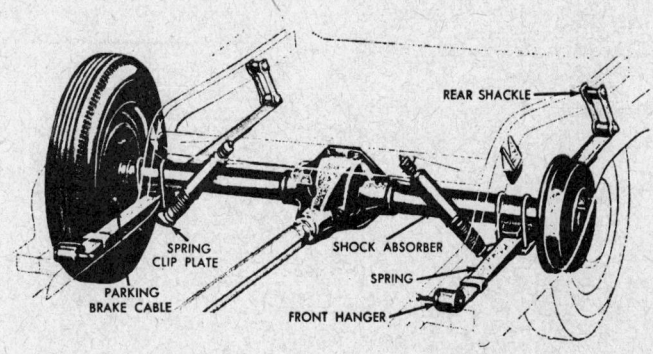

Fig. 1 Leaf spring suspension (typical)

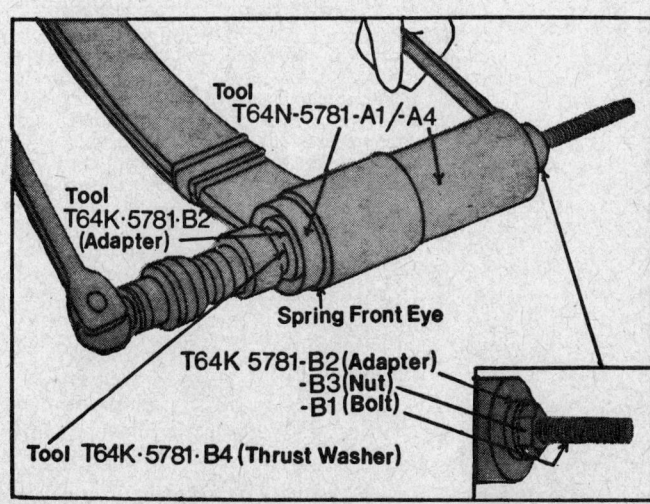

Fig. 2 Spring front bushing removal

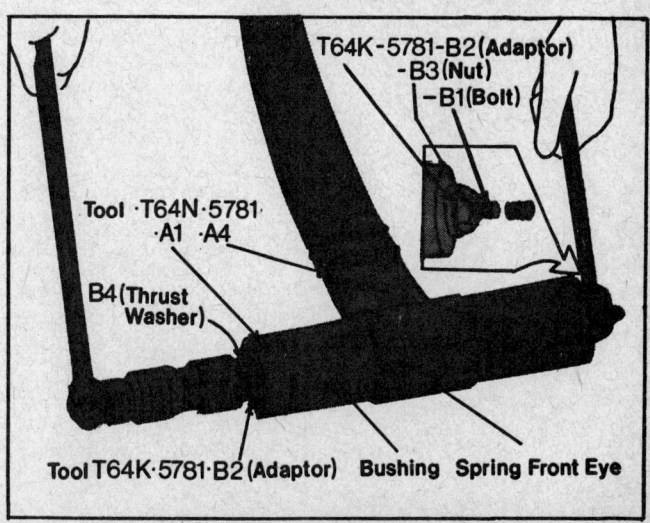

Fig. 3 Spring front bushing installation

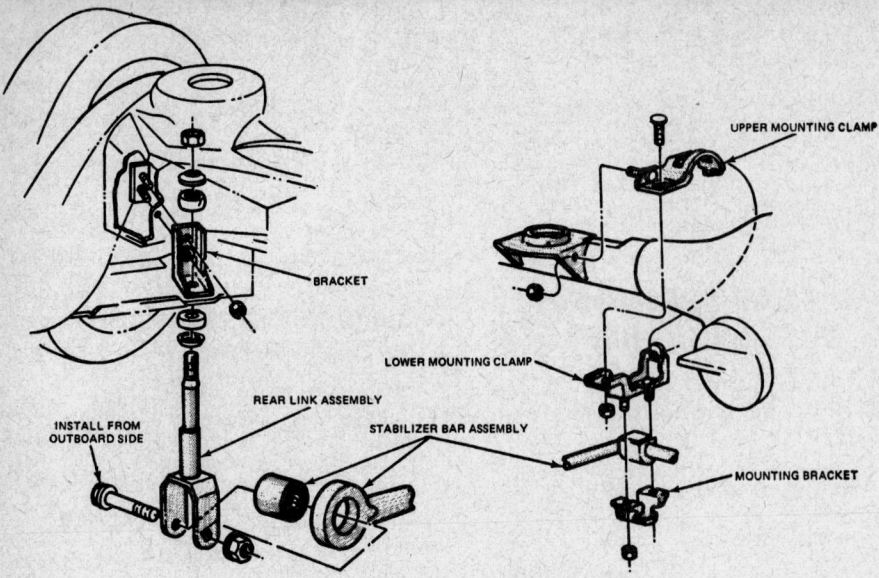

Fig. 4   Stabilizer bar installation 1977—79 Cougar, LTD II & Thunderbird

COIL SPRING, REPLACE

1978—83 Fairmont & Zephyr; 1980—82 Cougar XR-7; 1980—84 Thunderbird; 1981—82 Granada; 1981—84 Cougar; 1983—84 LTD & Marquis

1. Remove stabilizer bar as described under "Stabilizer Bar, Replace," if equipped.
2. Position a suitable jack under rear axle, then raise vehicle and support body at rear body crossmember.
3. Lower axle until shock absorbers are fully entended.

NOTE: Support axle with jack stands or a suitable jack.

4. Position a suitable jack under lower control arm pivot bolt and remove nut and bolt. Carefully and slowly lower the control arm until all spring tension is relieved.
5. Remove coil spring and insulators from vehicle, Fig. 5.

1977—79 Cougar, LTD II & Thunderbird

1. Raise rear of vehicle and support at frame. Support axle with a suitable jack.
2. Disconnect shock absorbers from lower mountings.
3. Lower axle to remove springs.
4. Reverse procedure to install. Install an insulator between upper and lower seats and spring.

CONTROL ARMS, REPLACE

NOTE: Upper and lower control arms must be replaced in pairs.

1978—83 Fairmont & Zephyr; 1980—82 Cougar XR-7; 1980—84 Thunderbird; 1981—82 Granada; 1981—84 Cougar; 1983—84 LTD & Marquis

Upper Arm
1. Raise vehicle and support body at rear body crossmember.
2. Remove upper arm pivot bolt and nut, Fig. 5.
3. Remove front pivot bolt and nut, then remove upper arm from vehicle.

Lower Arm
1. Remove stabilizer bar as described under "Stabilizer Bar, Replace," if equipped.
2. Position a suitable jack under rear axle, then raise vehicle and support body at rear body crossmember.
3. Lower axle until shock absorbers are fully extended.

NOTE: Support axle with jack stands or a suitable jack.

4. Position a suitable jack under lower control arm rear pivot bolt and remove nut bolt, Fig. 5. Carefully and slowly lower the control arm until all spring tension is relieved, then remove coil spring and insulators.
5. Remove lower control arm front pivot bolt and nut, then remove lower control arm assembly.

1977—79 Cougar, LTD II & Thunderbird

Upper Arm
1. Raise vehicle and support at frame side rails.
2. Lower axle and support axle under differential nose as well as under axle.
3. Remove nut and bolt attaching upper arm to axle housing, then disconnect arm from housing, Fig. 6.
4. Remove nut and bolt attaching upper arm to crossmember, then remove control arm from vehicle.

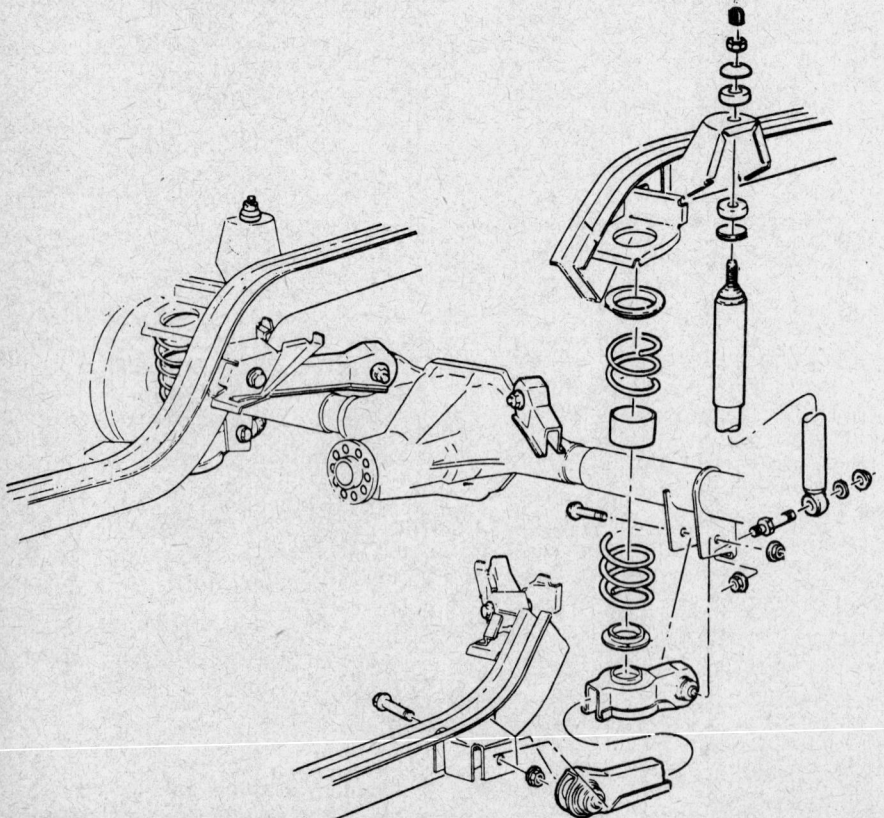

Fig. 5   Rear suspension (typical). 1978—83 Fairmont, Zephyr; 1980—82 Cougar XR-7, 1980—84 Thunderbird, 1981—82 Granada, 1981—84 Cougar & 1983—84 LTD & Marquis

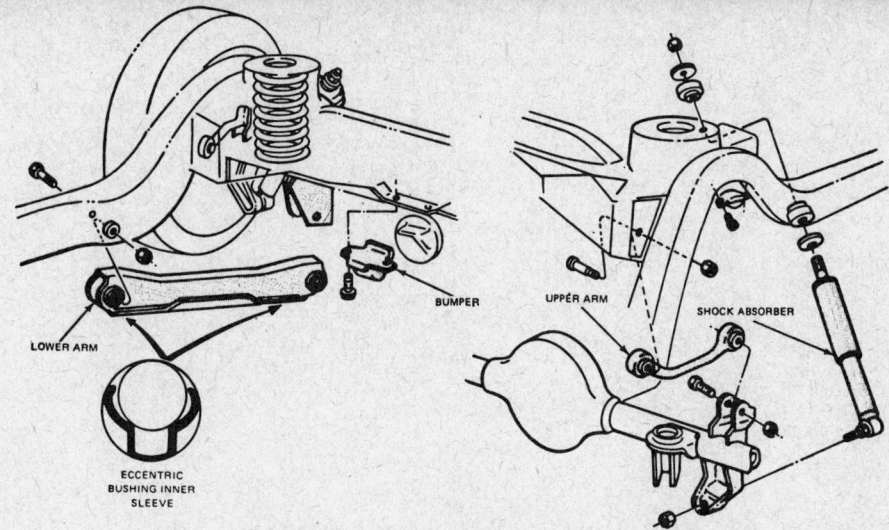

LOWER ARM

BUMPER

UPPER ARM

SHOCK ABSORBER

ECCENTRIC BUSHING INNER SLEEVE

Fig. 6   Rear suspension, 1977—79 Cougar, LTD II & Thunderbird

Lower Arm

1. Raise vehicle and support at frame side rails.
2. Lower axle until all spring tension is relieved.
3. Support axle under differential pinion nose as well as under axle.
4. Remove lower control arm pivot bolt and nut from axle bracket, then disconnect
arm from bracket, Fig. 6.
5. Remove pivot bolt and nut from frame bracket, then remove lower control arm from vehicle.

Front Suspension & Steering Section

FRONT SUSPENSION

1978—83 Fairmont & Zephyr; 1980—82 Cougar XR-7; 1980—84 Thunderbird; 1981—82 Granada; 1981—84 Cougar; 1983—84 LTD & Marquis

This suspension, Fig. 1, is a modified McPherson strut design, which uses shock struts and coil springs. The springs are mounted between the lower control arm and a spring pocket in the crossmember.

1977—79 Cougar, LTD II & Thunderbird

The front suspension, Fig 2, has the coil spring mounted on the lower arm.

1977 Comet & Maverick & 1977—80 Granada & Monarch

Referring to Fig. 3, each front wheel rotates on a spindle. The upper and lower ends of the spindle are attached to ball joints that are mounted to an upper and lower control arm. The upper arm pivots on a bushing and shaft assembly that is bolted to the underbody. The lower arm pivots on a bolt that is located in an underbody bracket.

A coil spring seats between the upper arm and the top of the spring housing. A double-acting shock absorber is bolted to the arm and the top of the spring housing.

Struts, which are connected between the lower control arms and the underbody, prevent the arms from moving fore and aft.

WHEEL ALIGNMENT

1983 Fairmont & Zephyr & 1983—84 Cougar, LTD, Marquis & Thunderbird

Caster

The caster angle of this suspension is factory pre-set and cannot be adjusted.

Camber

1. Remove pop rivet from camber plate.
2. Loosen 3 camber plate-to-body apron nuts.
3. Move top of shock strut as needed to bring camber angle within specifications, then tighten nuts.

NOTE: It is not necessary to replace the pop rivet.

1978—84 Fairmont & Zephyr; 1980—82 Cougar XR-7; 1980—82 Thunderbird; 1981—82 Granada; 1981—82 Cougar

Caster & Camber

The caster and camber angles of this suspension are factory pre-set and cannot be adjusted in the field.

1977 Comet & Maverick & 1977—80 Granada & Monarch

As shown in Fig. 4, caster is controlled by the front suspension strut. To obtain positive caster, loosen the strut rear nut and tighten the strut front nut against the bushing. To obtain negative caster, loosen the strut front nut and tighten the strut rear nut against the bushing. Torque strut to underbody nut to 70–80 ft. lbs.

Camber is controlled by the eccentric cam located at the lower arm attachment to the side rail. To adjust camber, loosen the camber adjustment bolt nut at the rear of the body bracket. Spread the body bracket at the camber adjustment bolt area just enough to permit lateral travel of the arm when the adjustment bolt is turned. Rotate the bolt and eccentric clockwise from the high position to increase camber or counterclockwise to decrease it. Torque lower arm to underbody bolt to 85–100 ft. lbs.

1977—79 Cougar, LTD II & Thunderbird

Caster and camber can be adjusted by loosening the bolts that attach the upper suspension arm to the shaft at the frame side rail, and moving the arm assembly in or out in the elongated bolt holes, Fig. 5. Since any movement of the arm affects both caster and camber, both factors should be balanced against one another when making the adjustment.

Install the tool with the pins in the frame holes and the hooks over the upper arm inner shaft. Tighten the hook nuts snug before loosening the upper arm inner shaft attaching bolts, Fig. 5.

Caster, Adjust

1. Tighten the tool front hook nut or loosen the rear hook nut as required to increase caster to the desired angle.
2. To decrease caster, tighten the rear hook nut or loosen the front hook nut as required.

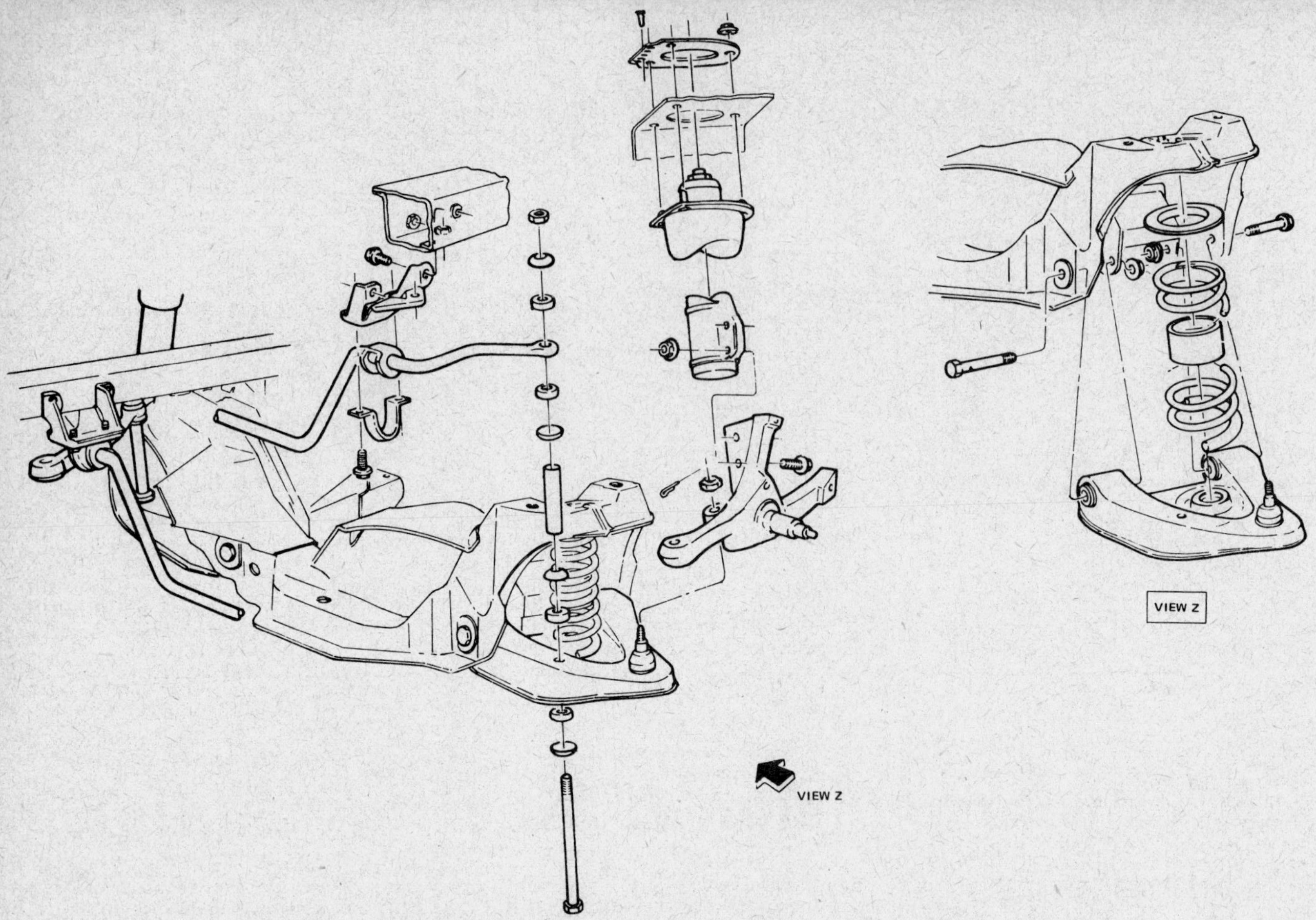

Fig. 1 Front suspension (typical). 1978–83 Fairmont & Zephyr, 1980–82 Cougar XR-7, 1980–84 Thunderbird, 1981–82 Granada, 1981–84 Cougar & 1983–84 LTD & Marquis

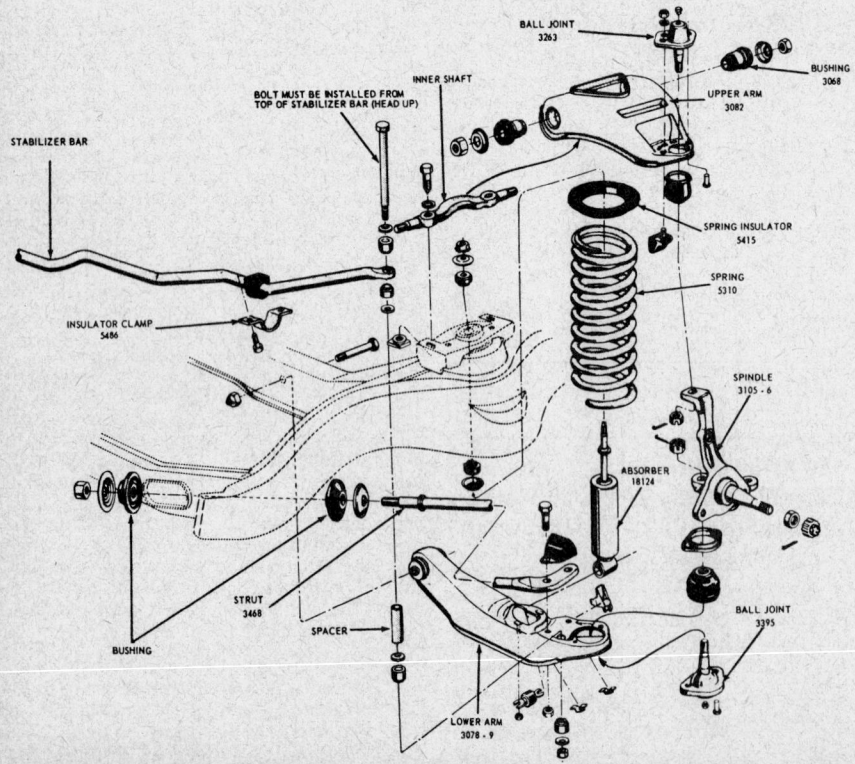

Fig. 2 Front suspension (typical). 1977–79 Cougar, LTD II & Thunderbird

NOTE: The caster angle can be checked without tightening the inner shaft retaining bolts.

3. Check the camber angle to be sure it did not change during the caster adjustment and adjust if necessary.
4. Torque the upper arm inner shaft retaining bolts to 120–140 ft. lbs. and remove tool.

Camber, Adjust

1. Install tool as previously outlined.
2. Loosen both inner shaft retaining bolts.
3. Tighten or loosen the hook nuts as necessary to increase or decrease camber.
4. Recheck caster angle. Torque upper arm inner shaft retaining bolts to 120–140 ft. lbs.

TOE-IN, ADJUST

1978–83 Fairmont & Zephyr; 1980–82 Cougar XR-7; 1980–84 Thunderbird; 1981–82 Granada; 1981–84 Cougar; 1983–84 LTD & Marquis

1. Check to see that steering shaft and steering wheel marks are in alignment and in the top position.
2. Loosen clamp screw on the tie rod bellows and free the seal on the rod to prevent

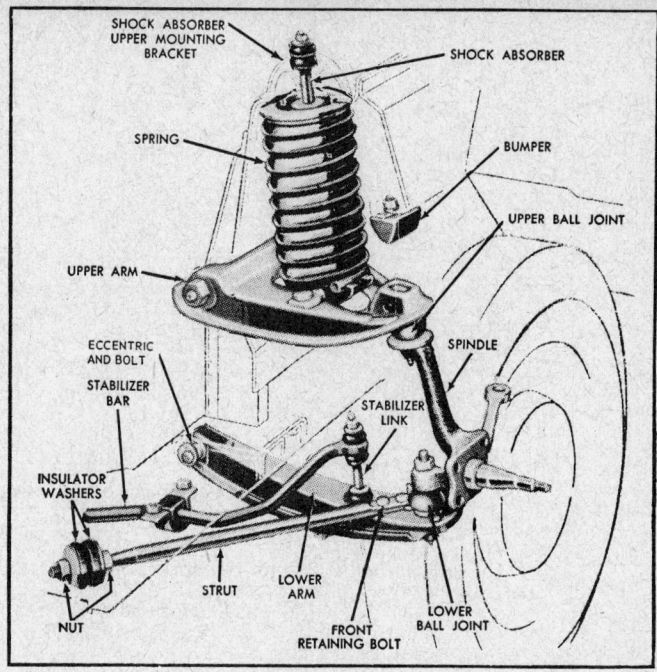

Fig. 3   Front suspension (typical). 1977 Comet & Maverick & 1977–80 Granada & Monarch

Fig. 4   Caster and camber adjustments. 1977 Comet & Maverick & 1977–80 Granada & Monarch

twisting of the bellows, Fig. 6

3. Place opened end wrench on flats of tie rod socket to prevent socket from turning, then loosen tie rod jam nuts.
4. Use suitable pliers to turn the tie rod inner end to correct the adjustment to specifications. Do not use pliers on tie rod threads. Turning to reduce number of threads showing will increase toe-in. Turning in the opposite direction will reduce toe-in.
5. Torque tie rod jam nuts to 33–50 ft. lbs. on 1977–81 models, or 43–50 ft. lbs. on 1982–84 models.

Exc. 1978–83 Fairmont & Zephyr; 1980–82 Cougar XR-7; 1980–84 Thunderbird; 1981–82 Granada; 1981–84 Cougar; 1983–84 LTD & Marquis

Check the steering wheel spoke position when the front wheels are in the straight-ahead position. If the spokes are not in the normal position, they can be adjusted while toe-in is being adjusted

1. Loosen clamp bolts on each tie rod end sleeve.
2. Adjust toe-in. If steering wheel spokes are in their normal position, lengthen or shorten both rods equally to obtain correct toe-in. If spokes are not in normal position, make necessary rod adjustments to obtain correct toe-in and steering wheel spoke alignment.

WHEEL BEARINGS, ADJUST

1. With wheel rotating, tighten adjusting nut to 17–25 ft. lbs.
2. Back off adjusting nut ½ turn, then retighten nut to 10–15 inch lbs. on 1977–83 models, or 10–12 inch lbs. on 1984 models.
3. Place nut lock on nut so that castellations

on lock are aligned with cotter pin hole in spindle and install cotter pin, Fig 7.
4. Check front wheel rotation, if it rotates noisily or rough, clean, inspect or replace wheel bearings as necessary.

WHEEL BEARINGS, REPLACE

(Disc Brakes)

1. Raise car and remove front wheels.
2. Remove caliper mounting bolts.

NOTE: It is not necessary to disconnect the brake lines for this operation.

---

3. Slide caliper off of disc, inserting a clean spacer between the shoes to hold them in their bores after the caliper is removed. Position caliper out of the way.

NOTE: Do not allow caliper to hang by

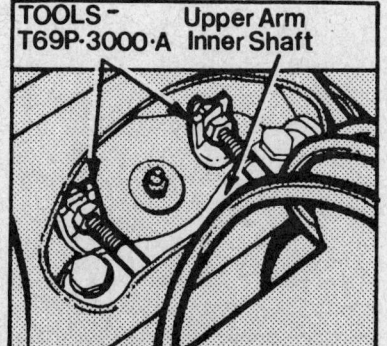

Fig. 5   Caster and Camber adjustment. 1977–79 Cougar, LTD II & Thunderbird

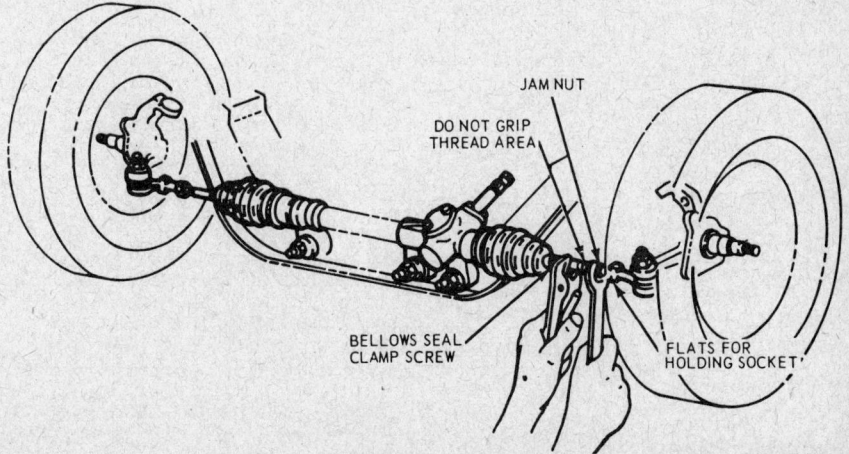

Fig. 6   Toe-in adjustment. 1978–84 Fairmont, Zephyr, 1980–82 Cougar XR-7, 1980–84 Thunderbird, 1981–82 Granada, 1981–84 Cougar & 1983–84 LTD & Marquis

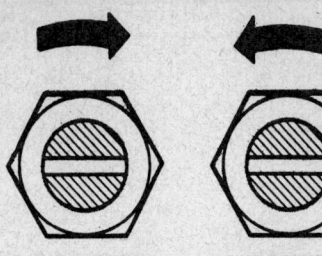

WITH WHEEL ROTATING, TORQUE ADJUSTING NUT, TO 17-25 FT. LBS.

BACK ADJUSTING NUT OFF 1/2 TURN

TIGHTEN ADJUSTING NUT TO 10-15 IN.-LBS.

INSTALL THE LOCK AND A NEW COTTER PIN

Fig. 7 Front wheel bearing adjustment

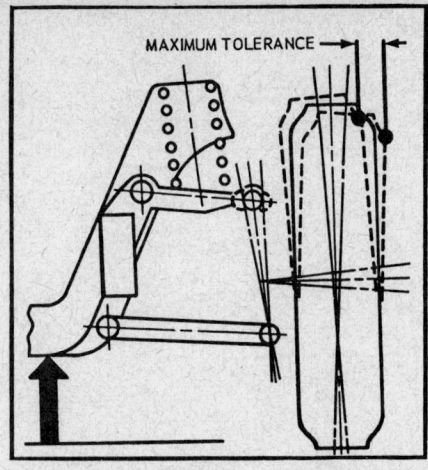

MAXIMUM TOLERANCE

Fig. 8 Measuring upper ball joint for radial play. 1977 Comet & Maverick

brake hose.

4. Remove hub and disc assembly. Grease retainer and inner bearing can now be removed.

CHECKING BALL JOINTS FOR WEAR

Upper Ball Joint

1977–80 Granada & Monarch

1. Raise car on frame contact hoist or by floor jacks placed beneath underbody until wheel falls to full down position.
2. Grasp the lower edge of tire and move the wheel in and out.
3. While the wheel is being moved observe any movement between the upper end of the spindle and upper arm. If any movement is observed replace the ball joint.

1977–79 Cougar, LTD II & Thunderbird

1. Raise vehicle and place floor jacks beneath lower control arms.
2. Grasp the lower edge of tire and move the wheel in and out.
3. While the wheel is being moved observe any movement between the upper end of the spindle and upper arm. If any movement is observed replace the ball joint.

1977 Comet & Maverick

1. Raise car on frame contact hoist or by floor jacks placed beneath underbody until wheel falls to full down position as shown in Fig. 8. This will unload upper ball joint.
2. With front wheel bearings properly adjusted, attach a dial indicator to the upper control arm and position the indicator so that its plunger rests against the inner side of the wheel rim adjacent to the upper arm ball joint.

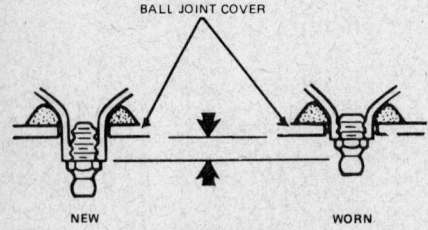

BALL JOINT COVER

NEW   WORN

CHECKING SURFACE

Fig. 9 Checking lower ball joint. 1978–83 Fairmont, Zephyr, 1980–82 Cougar XR-7, 1980–84 Thunderbird, 1981–82 Granada, 1981–84 Cougar & 1983–84 LTD & Marquis

3. Grasp tire at top and bottom and slowly move it in and out, Fig. 6. Reading on dial will indicate the amount of radial play. If reading exceeds ¼", replace the upper ball joint.

Lower Ball Joint

1978–83 Fairmont & Zephyr; 1980–82 Cougar XR-7; 1980–84 Thunderbird; 1981–82 Granada; 1981–84 Cougar; 1983–84 LTD & Marquis

1. Support vehicle in normal driving position with both ball joints loaded.
2. Clean area around grease fitting and checking surface.

NOTE: The checking surface is the round boss into which the grease fitting is installed.

3. The checking surface should project outside the cover, Fig. 9. If surface is inside cover replace lower arm assembly.

1977–79 Cougar, LTD II & Thunderbird

1. Raise vehicle and place floor jacks under the lower control arms, Fig. 10.
2. Adjust wheel bearings and place a dial indicator to the lower arm and position the indicator so that the plunger rests against the inner side of the wheel rim adjacent to the lower ball joint.
3. Grasp tire at top and bottom and move it slowly in and out. Reading on dial will indicate the amount of radial play. If reading exceeds ¼ inch replace the ball joint.

1977 Comet & Maverick, 1977–80 Granada & Monarch

1. With car jacked up as directed above, grasp the lower edge of the tire and move it in and out.
2. As wheel is being moved in and out, observe lower end of spindle and lower arm.
3. Any movement between lower end of spindle and lower arm indicates ball joint wear and loss of preload. If such movement is observed, replace lower arm and/or ball joint.

NOTE: During the foregoing check, the ball joints will be unloaded and may move. Therefore disregard any movement of the upper ball joint when checking the lower ball joint and any movement of the lower ball joint when checking the upper ball joint. Also, do not mistake loose wheel bearings for a worn ball joint.

BALL JOINTS, REPLACE

NOTE: Ford Motor Company recommends that new ball joints should not be installed on used control arms and that the control arm be replaced if ball joint replacement is required. However, aftermarket ball joint repair kits which do not require control arm replacement, are available and can be installed using the following procedure.

1978–83 Fairmont & Zephyr; 1980–82 Cougar XR-7; 1980–84 Thunderbird; 1981–82 Granada; 1981–84 Cougar; 1983–84 LTD & Marquis

These ball joints are not serviceable. If they require replacement, the control arm and ball joint must be replaced as an assembly.

Except 1978–83 Fairmont & Zephyr; 1980–82 Cougar XR-7; 1980–84 Thunderbird; 1981–82 Granada; 1981–84 Cougar; 1983–84 LTD & Marquis

The ball joints are riveted to the upper and lower control arms. The upper ball joint can be replaced by removing the rivets and retaining the new ball joint to the upper control arm with bolts, nuts and washers furnished with the ball joint repair kit. When removing an upper ball joint, use a suitable pressing tool to loosen the ball joint from the spindle.

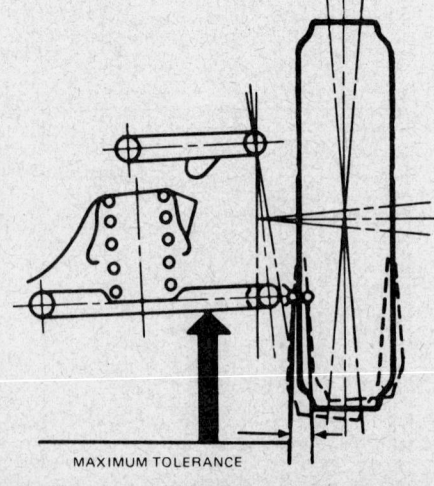

MAXIMUM TOLERANCE

Fig. 10 Measuring lower ball joint for radial play. 1977–79 Cougar, LTD II & Thunderbird

SHOCK STRUT, REPLACE

1978–83 Fairmont & Zephyr; 1980–82 Cougar XR-7; 1980–84 Thunderbird; 1981–82 Granada; 1981–84 Cougar; 1983–84 LTD & Marquis

1. Place ignition switch in the Unlocked position so that front wheels are free to move.
2. From engine compartment, remove one strut to upper mounting nut. Use a screwdriver in rod slot to hold rod stationary when removing nut.
3. Raise front of vehicle by lower control arms, then place safety stands under frame jack pads located rearward of wheels.
4. Remove wheel and tire assembly, then remove brake caliper, rotor assembly and dust shield.
5. Remove two nuts and bolts attaching lower strut to spindle.

NOTE: Gas pressurized struts (1983–84 Cougar, LTD, Marquis, and Thunderbird) must be held firmly during removal of the last spindle-to-strut bolt since gas pressure will cause strut to extend fully when bolt is removed.

6. Lift strut upward from spindle to compress rod, then pull downward and remove strut.
7. On 1983–84 models, remove jounce bumper.
8. Reverse procedure to install. Torque upper mount attaching nut to 60–75 ft. lbs. on 1978–82 models, or 55–92 ft. lbs. on 1983–84 models. Remove suspension load from lower control arm by lowering front of vehicle, then torque lower mounting nuts to 150–180 ft. lbs. on 1978–82 models, or 120–179 ft. lbs. on 1983–84 models.

SHOCK ABSORBER, REPLACE

1977 Comet & Maverick & 1977–80 Granada & Monarch

1. Raise hood and remove upper mounting bracket-to-spring tower retaining nuts.
2. Raise front of car and place safety stands under lower control arms.
3. Remove shock absorber lower retaining nuts and washers.
4. Lift shock absorber from spring tower.
5. Reverse procedure to install. Torque shock absorber upper attachment bolts to 10–16 ft. lbs., shock absorber upper bracket to body nuts to 32–48 ft. lbs. and shock absorber to spring seat to 8–12 ft. lbs.

1977–79 Cougar, LTD II & Thunderbird

1. Remove upper mounting nut, washer and bushing from shock absorber.
2. Raise vehicle and install safety stands.
3. Remove the shock absorber lower retaining screws and remove shock absorber. Torque shock absorber upper attachment bolts to 22–30 ft. lbs. and shock absorber to lower arm to 12–18 ft. lbs.

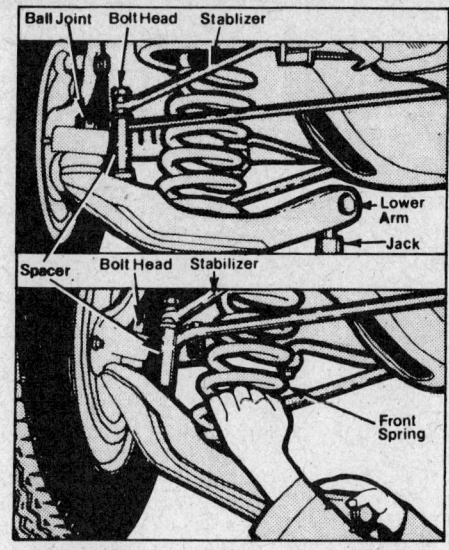

Fig. 11 Removing or installing front spring. 1977–79 Cougar, LTD II & Thunderbird

COIL SPRING, REPLACE

1978–83 Fairmont & Zephyr; 1980–82 Cougar XR-7; 1980–84 Thunderbird; 1981–82 Granada; 1981–84 Cougar; 1983–84 LTD & Marquis

1. Raise front of vehicle and position safety stands under jack pads located rearward of wheels, then remove wheel and tire assembly.
2. On 1982–84 models, disconnect caliper and wire it out of the way without disconnecting brake lines.
3. On all models, disconnect stabilizer bar link from lower control arm.
4. Remove steering gear attaching bolts, and position gear aside.
5. Disconnect tie rod from spindle using tool 3290-C, or equivalent.
6. Using spring compressor D78P-5310-A on 1978–81 models, or T82P-5310-A on 1982–84 models, compress spring until it is free from lower seat.
7. Remove two lower control arm pivot bolts and disengage control arm from frame, then remove spring from seat. If a replacement spring is to be installed, measure compressed length of spring being removed to assist in compressing and installing the replacement spring.
8. Reverse procedure to install. When installing spring, locate lower end of coil between two holes in lower control arm spring pocket. On 1978–81 models, torque control arm pivot bolt nuts to 200–220 ft. lbs., stabilizer bar link nut to 9 to 12 ft. lbs. and steering gear to crossmember attaching bolts to 90 to 100 ft. lbs. On 1982 models, torque lower control arm pivot nuts to 215 to 260 ft. lbs., stabilizer bar to lower control arm nut 6 to 12 ft. lbs. and steering gear to crossmember bolts to 90 to 100 ft. lbs. On 1983 models, torque control arm pivot nuts to 150–180 ft. lbs., stabilizer bar link nut to 6–12 ft. lbs., steering gear to crossmember nuts to 90–100 ft. lbs., and tie rod end to 35 ft. lbs.

1977 Comet & Maverick & 1977–80 Granada & Monarch

1. Remove shock absorber and upper mounting bracket as an assembly.
2. Raise car on hoist and install safety stands.
3. Remove wheel, hub and drum or caliper and rotor.
4. Install a suitable spring compressor and compress spring.
5. Remove two upper-arm-to-spring tower retaining nuts and swing upper arm outward from spring.
6. Release spring compressor. Then remove spring.
7. Reverse procedure to install. Torque upper arm and inner shaft to body nuts to 85–100 ft. lbs.

1977–79 Cougar, LTD II & Thunderbird

1. Raise vehicle and support front end of frame with jack stands.
2. Disconnect shock absorber from lower arm and place a jack under the lower arm for support, Fig. 11.
3. Remove strut and rebound bumper bolts and disconnect lower end of sway bar stud from lower arm.
4. Remove the nut and bolt that retains the inner end of the lower arm to the crossmember.
5. Carefully lower jack relieving spring pressure on the lower arm, then remove the spring.
6. Reverse procedure to install. Spring should be positioned on lower arm so that end is no more than 1/2 inch from depression in lower arm. Torque strut to lower arm bolts to 80–115 ft. lbs., stabilizer bar to lower arm to 9–12 ft. lbs. and lower arm inner pivot nut to 95–110 ft. lbs.

STABILIZER BAR &/OR INSULATOR

1978–83 Fairmont & Zephyr; 1980–82 Cougar XR-7; 1980–84 Thunderbird; 1981–82 Granada; 1981–84 Cougar; 1983–84 LTD & Marquis

1. Raise vehicle and place jack stands under lower control arms.
2. Disconnect stabilizer bar from links, then remove stabilizer insulator retaining clamps and remove stabilizer.
3. To remove insulator, cut insulators and plastic sleeves from stabilizer bar. Before installing new insulators, coat the necessary parts of the stabilizer with grease, then install the insulators and sleeves.
4. Reverse procedure to install stabilizer bar. Install new stabilizer link bolts with heads facing down and torque to 9–12 ft. lbs. on 1978–81 models, 6 to 12 ft. lbs. on 1982–84 models. Using new bolts, install stabilizer insulator retaining clamps and torque to 20 to 26 ft. lbs. on 1978 models, 14 to 16 ft. lbs. on 1979–80 models, 25 to 30 ft. lbs. on 1981 models, 20 to 25 ft. lbs. on 1982–84 models.

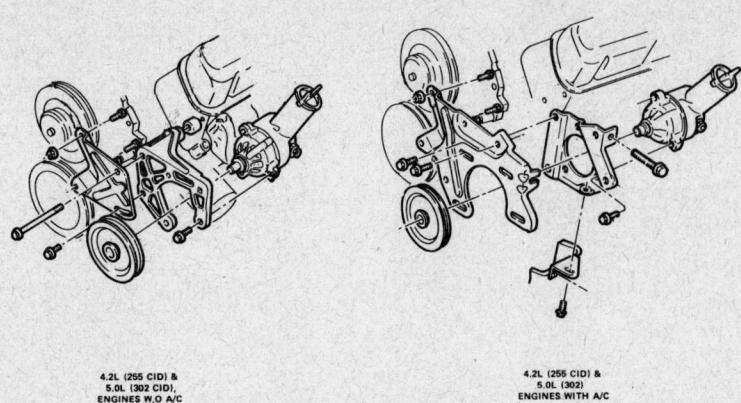

4.2L (255 CID) &
5.0L (302 CID),
ENGINES W.O A/C

4.2L (255 CID) &
5.0L (302)
ENGINES WITH A/C

Fig. 12 Power steering pump installation. Typical

POWER STEERING GEAR, REPLACE

Integral Power Rack & Pinion

1. Disconnect battery ground cable.
2. Remove bolt retaining flexible coupling to input shaft.
3. Turn ignition key "ON" and raise vehicle.
4. Remove the two tie rod end retaining nuts, then separate studs from spindle arms, using a suitable tool.
5. Support gear and remove attaching bolts, then lower gear enough to gain access to pressure and return lines, and remove bolt attaching the hose bracket to the gear.
6. Disconnect pressure and return lines and remove steering gear. Plug lines and ports to prevent entry of dirt.
7. Reverse procedure to install. Torque pressure and return line fittings to 10–15 ft. lbs., gear housing to crossmember mounting bolt to 80–100 ft. lbs., steering flex coupling bolt to 20–30 ft. lbs. and tie rod end to spindle arm nut to 35–47 ft. lbs.

NOTE: On some models, hoses can swivel when torqued properly. Do not over tighten.

Integral Power Steering Gear

1. Disconnect pressure and return lines from gear and plug openings to prevent entry of dirt.
2. Remove two bolts that secure flex coupling to gear and column.
3. Raise vehicle and remove pitman arm with suitable puller.
4. If vehicle is equipped with synchromesh transmission, remove clutch release retracting spring to provide clearance to remove gear.
5. Support gear and remove three gear attaching bolts.

MANUAL STEERING GEAR, REPLACE

Rack & Pinion

1. Disconnect battery ground cable, turn ignition "On" and raise vehicle.
2. Remove tie rod end retaining nuts and using ball joint separator, separate tie rod ends from spindle arms.
3. Remove pinion shaft to flexible coupling bolt and the bolts securing steering gear to crossmember.
4. Turn front wheels, then remove steering gear from left side of vehicle.
5. Reverse procedure to install. Torque connecting rod end to spindle arm nut to 35–47 ft. lbs. on 1977–80 models and 41–47 ft. lbs. on 1981–84 models. Torque flex coupling to 20–37 ft. lbs. and torque steering gear to crossmember bolts to 80–100 ft. lbs. on 1977–80 models and 90–100 ft. lbs. on 1981–84 models.

Except Rack and Pinion

1. Remove flex coupling bolts.
2. Remove pitman arm nut and remove arm from shaft using a puller.
3. With manual transmission it may be necessary to disconnect the clutch linkage and on V8 models it may be necessary to lower the exhaust system.
4. Unfasten and remove steering gear.
5. Reverse procedure to install. Torque steering gear to side rail bolts to 50–60 ft. lbs. and pitman arm to sector shaft nut to 200–225 ft. lbs.

POWER STEERING PUMP, REPLACE

1977–84 Models Exc. 1977 Models with TRW Pump

1. Disconnect return hose from power steer-ing pump and allow fluid to drain into a suitable container.
2. Remove pressure hose from power steering pump fitting.
3. On models less fixed pump, remove mounting bracket attaching bolts, then disconnect drive belt from pulley and remove pump.
4. On models with fixed pump, remove drive belt from pulley, then remove pulley and lift pump from engine compartment.
5. Reverse procedure to install, Fig. 12.

1977 Models with TRW Pump

1. Disconnect return hose from power steering pump and allow fluid to drain into a suitable container.
2. Disconnect pressure hose from pump, then remove front mounting bracket to pump attaching bolts. On models with V8 engine also remove nut attaching pump to rear of mounting bracket.
3. Disconnect drive belt from pulley, then remove pump from engine compartment.
4. Reverse procedure to install. Torque pump bracket front bolt to 30–45 ft. lbs., pump to bracket rear nut to 20–30 ft. lbs., pressure hose to pump nut to 28–37 ft. lbs. except on 302 cu. inch engines which are torqued to 25–34 ft. lbs. and return hose to pump to 12–24 inch lbs.

CONTROL VALVE, REPLACE

Non-Integral Power Steering

1. Disconnect fluid fittings at control valve and drain fluid from lines by turning wheels to left and right.
2. Loosen clamp at right-hand end of sleeve. Remove roll pin from steering arm-to-idler arm rod through slot in sleeve.
3. Using tool 3290-C, remove ball stud from sector shaft arm.

NOTE: The use of any other tool may result in damage to the control valve assembly.

4. Turn wheels fully to left and unthread control valve from idler arm rod.
5. Reverse procedure to install. Measure distance between center of left spindle connect-rod hole in idler arm to edge of control valve. Distance must be 2.55–2.65 inches. Torque valve sleeve clamp nut to 13–17 ft. lbs., ball stud nut to 35–47 ft. lbs., worm screw hose clamp to 30–60 in. lbs., return line to control valve to 16–25 ft. lbs., pressure line to control valve to 15–19 ft. lbs. and pressure and return lines to power cylinder to 15–19 ft. lbs. Connect short control valve to power cylinder hose to valve port "C" and other hose to valve port "A".

FORD MUSTANG & PINTO
MERCURY BOBCAT & CAPRI

INDEX OF SERVICE OPERATIONS

NOTE: Refer to the front of this manual for vehicle manufacturer's special service tool suppliers.

FORD MUSTANG & PINTO · MERCURY BOBCAT & CAPRI

ENGINE & SERIAL NUMBER LOCATION:

Engine code is fifth digit of serial number on 1977–80 models, or eighth digit of serial number on 1981–84 models. The serial number is stamped on a metal tag located on top left side dash and visible through windshield.

GRILLE IDENTIFICATION

1977–78 Mercury Bobcat

1977 Mustang II Cobra

1977 Pinto

1977 Pinto Wagon With Cruising Option

1977–78 Mustang

1978 Mustang II Cobra

1978 Pinto

1979–80 Bobcat

1979–81 Capri

1979–82 Mustang

1979–80 Pinto

1981 Mustang Cobra

1982 Capri

1982 Mustang GT

1983–84 Capri

1983 Mustang 1984 Mustang Exc. S.V.O.

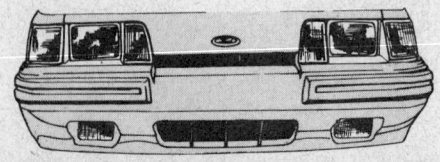

1984 Mustang S.V.O.

GENERAL ENGINE SPECIFICATIONS

Year	Engine CID/Liter①	V.I.N. Code②	Carburetor	Bore and Stroke	Compression Ratio	Net H.P. @ R.P.M.③	Maximum Torque Ft. Lbs. @ R.P.M.	Normal Oil Pressure Pounds
1977	4-140, 2.3L⑭	Y	5200, 2 Bbl.⑥	3.781 × 3.126	9.0	89 @ 4800	120 @ 3000	40–60
	4-140, 2.3L⑮	Y	5200, 2 Bbl.⑥	3.781 × 3.126	9.0	⑯	119 @ 3000	40–60
	V6-171, 2.8L⑰	Z	2150, 2 Bbl.⑥	3.66 × 2.70	8.7	90 @ 4200	139 @ 2600	40–55
	V6-171, 2.8L⑱	Z	2150, 2 Bbl.⑥	3.66 × 2.70	8.7	90 @ 4000	139 @ 2600	40–55
	V6-171, 2.8L⑲	Z	2150, 2 Bbl.⑥	3.66 × 2.70	8.7	88 @ 4000	138 @ 2600	40–55
	V6-171, 2.8L⑳	Z	2150, 2 Bbl.⑥	3.66 × 2.70	8.7	93 @ 4200	140 @ 2600	40–55
	V8-302, 5.0L㉑	F	2150, 2 Bbl.⑥	4.00 × 3.00	8.4	129 @ 3400	242 @ 2000	40–60
	V8-302, 5.0L㉒	F	2150, 2 Bbl.⑥	4.00 × 3.00	8.1	132 @ 3600	228 @ 1600	40–60
	V8-302, 5.0L⑤⑧	F	2150, 2 Bbl.⑥	4.00 × 3.00	8.4	139 @ 3600	247 @ 1800	40–60
1978	4-140, 2.3L	Y	5200, 2 Bbl.⑥	3.781 × 3.126	9.0	88 @ 4800	118 @ 2800	50
	V6-171, 2.8L	Z	2150, 2 Bbl.⑥	3.66 × 2.70	8.7	90 @ 4200	143 @ 2200	40–55
	V8-302, 5.0L⑧	F	2150, 2 Bbl.⑥	4.00 × 3.00	8.4	⑦	⑨	40–60
1979	4-140, 2.3L⑪	Y	5200, 2 Bbl.⑥	3.781 × 3.126	9.0	88 @ 4800	118 @ 2800	40–60
	4-140, 2.3L⑫	W	6500, 2 Bbl.④	3.781 × 3.126	9.0	—	—	40–60
	V6-171, 2.8L	Z	2700VV, 2 Bbl.⑥	3.66 × 2.70	8.7	102 @ 4400	138 @ 3200	40–60
	6-200, 3.3L⑤⑧	T	1946, 1 Bbl.④	3.68 × 3.13	8.5	85 @ 3600	154 @ 1600	30–50
	V8-302, 5.0L	F	⑩	4.00 × 3.00	8.4	140 @ 3600	250 @ 1800	40–65
1980	4-140, 2.3L⑪	A	5200, 2 Bbl.⑥	3.781 × 3.126	9.0	㉓	㉔	50
	4-140, 2.3L⑫	T	6500, 2 Bbl.④	3.781 × 3.126	9.0	—	—	55
	6-200, 3.3L⑧	B	1946, 1 Bbl.④	3.68 × 3.126	8.5	—	—	30–50
	V8-255, 4.2L⑧	D	2150, 2 Bbl.⑥	3.68 × 3.00	8.8	131 @ 2600	—	40–60
1981	4-140, 2.3L	A	5200, 2 Bbl.⑥⑬	3.781 × 3.126	9.0	88 @ 4600	118 @ 2600	40–60
	6-200, 3.3L⑧	B	1946, 1 Bbl.④	3.68 × 3.13	8.6	94 @ 4000	158 @ 1400	30–50
	V8-255, 4.2L⑧⑮	D	2150, 2 Bbl.⑥	3.68 × 3.00	8.2	120 @ 3400	205 @ 2600	40–60
	V8-255, 4.2L⑧⑭	D	7200VV, 2 Bbl.⑥	3.68 × 3.00	8.2	115 @ 3400	195 @ 2200	40–60
1982	4-140, 2.3L	A	5200, 2 Bbl.⑥⑬	3.781 × 3.126	9.0	㉕	㉖	40–60
	6-200, 3.3L	B	1946, 1 Bbl.④	3.68 × 3.13	8.6	87 @ 3800	154 @ 1400	40–60
	V8-255, 4.2L⑭	D	2150, 2 Bbl.⑥	3.68 × 3.00	8.2	83 @ 111	194 @ 1600	30–50
	V8-255, 4.2L⑮	D	7200VV, 2 Bbl.⑥	3.68 × 3.00	8.2	83 @ 111	194 @ 1600	40–60
	V8-302, 5.0L H.O.	F	2150A, 2 Bbl.⑥	4.00 × 3.00	8.4	160 @ 4200	247 @ 2400	40–60
1983	4-140, 2.3L⑪	A	YFA, 1 Bbl.㉚	3.781 × 3.126	9.0	90 @ 4600	122 @ 2600	40–60
	4-140, 2.3L⑫	W	E.F.I.㉙	3.781 × 3.126	8.0	—	—	40–60
	V6-232, 3.8L	3	2150, 2 Bbl.⑥	3.8 × 3.4	8.7	112 @ 4000	175 @ 2600	54–59
	V8-302 H.O., 5.0L	F	4180, 4 Bbl.④	4.0 × 3.0	8.3	174 @ 4200	244 @ 2400	40–60
1984	4-140, 2.3L⑪	A	YFA, 1 Bbl.㉚	3.781 × 3.126	—	—	—	40–60
	4-140, 2.3L⑫	W	E.F.I.㉙	3.781 × 3.126	—	—	—	40–60
	V6-232, 3.8L	3	E.F.I.㉙	3.8 × 3.4	—	—	—	54–59
	V8-302 H.O., 5.0L㉗	M	4180-C④	4.0 × 3.0	—	—	—	40–60
	V8-302 H.O., 5.0L㉘	M	E.F.I.㉙	4.0 × 3.0	—	—	—	40–60

①—CID—cubic inch displacement.
②—On 1977–80 vehicles the fifth digit in the VIN denotes engine code. On 1981–84 vehicles the eighth digit denotes engine code.
③—Net rating—as installed on vehicle.
④—Holley.
⑤—Auto. trans. exc. Calif.
⑥—Motorcraft.
⑦—Exc. Calif. 139 @ 3600; Calif. 133 @ 3600.
⑧—Refer to the Ford & Mercury—Compact & Intermediate Chapter for Service procedures on this engine.
⑨—Exc. Calif. 250 @ 1600; Calif. 243 @ 1600.
⑩—Calif. Motorcraft 2700VV; exc. Calif. Ford 2150.
⑪—Non-Turbocharged.
⑫—Turbocharged.
⑬—Some vehicles equipped with model 6500 Feedback Carburetor.
⑭—Exc. Calif.
⑮—Calif. only.
⑯—Sedan 88 @ 4800. Station Wagon 85 @ 4800.
⑰—Station Wagons, exc. Calif.
⑱—Sedans, Calif. only.
⑲—Station Wagons, Calif. only.
⑳—Sedans, exc. Calif.
㉑—Man. trans. exc. Calif.
㉒—Auto. trans. Calif. only.
㉓—Exc. Calif., 88 @ 4600; Calif. 89 @ 4800.
㉔—Exc. Calif., 119 @ 2600; Calif. 122 @ 2600.
㉕—Vehicles less A/C, 86 @ 4600; vehicles with A/C, 92 @ 4600.
㉖—Vehicles less A/C, 117 @ 2600; vehicles with A/C, 119 @ 2600.
㉗—Vehicles equipped with 5 speed manual trans.
㉘—Vehicles equipped with automatic overdrive trans.
㉙—Electronic fuel injection.
㉚—Carter.

TUNE UP SPECIFICATIONS

The following specifications are published from the latest information available. This data should be used only in the absence of a decal affixed in the engine compartment.

★ When using a timing light, disconnect vacuum hose or tube at distributor and plug opening in hose or tube so idle speed will not be affected.

● When checking compression, lowest cylinder must be within 75 percent of highest.

▲ Before removing wires from distributor cap, determine location of the No. 1 wire in cap, as distributor position may have been altered from that shown at the end of this chart.

Spark plug types shown in this chart are recommendations of the original vehicle manufacturer and not MOTOR. Check local sources for other spark plug manufacturers listings.

Year & Engine/V.I.N.	Spark Plug		Ignition Timing BTDC (1) ★				Curb Idle Speed (2)		Fast Idle Speed		Fuel Pump Pressure
	Type	Gap	Firing Order Fig. ▲	Man. Trans.	Auto. Trans.	Mark Fig.	Man. Trans.	Auto. Trans.	Man. Trans.	Auto. Trans.	
1977											
4-140, 2300 cc/Y Exc. Calif. High Alt.	AWRF-42	.034	G	6°	20°	E	850	600/800D	(3)(7)(8)	2000(3)	5–7(4)
4-140, 2300 cc/Y Calif.	AWRF-42	.034	G	6°	20°	E	(7)(9)	600/750D	1800(3)	1800(3)	5–7(4)
4-140, 2300 cc/Y High Alt.	AWRF-42	.034	G	6°	20°	E	550/850	(7)(10)	1800(3)	(3)(7)(11)	5–7(4)
V6-171, 2800 cc/Z Exc. Calif. (7)(12)	AWRF-42	.034	H	10°	—	F	850	—	1700(3)	—	3.5–6
V6-171, 2800 cc/Z Exc. Calif. (7)(13)	AWSF-42	.034	H	12°	12°	F	850	700/750D	1700(3)	1600(3)	3.5–6
V6-171, 2800 cc/Z Calif.	AWRF-42	.034	H	—	6°	F	—	600/750D	—	1800(5)	3.5–6
V8-302/F Exc. Calif. & High Alt.	ARF-52	.050	D	8°	4°	C	850	700D	2000(5)	2100(5)	6–8
V8-302/F Calif.	ARF-52-6	.060	D	—	12°	C	—	500/700D	—	1900(5)	6–8
V8-302/F High Alt. (7)(14)	ARF-52-6	.060	D	—	12°	C	—	500/700D	—	1900(5)	6–8
V8-302/F High Alt. (7)(15)	ARF-52	.050	D	—	12°	C	—	500/650D	—	2000(5)	6–8
1978											
4-140, 2300 cc/Y Exc. Calif. & High Alt. (7)(16)	AWSF-42	.034	G	6°	20°	E	(17)	800D	1600(3)	2000(3)	5–7(4)
4-140, 2300 cc/Y Exc. Calif. & High Alt. (7)(18)	AWSF-42	.034	G	6°	20°	E	850	600/800D	1800(3)	2000(3)	5–7(4)
4-140, 2300 cc/Y Calif. (7)(19)	AWSF-42	.034	G	6°	20°	E	(20)	750D	1800(3)	1800(3)	5–7(4)
4-140, 2300 cc/Y Calif. (7)(21)	AWSF-42	.034	G	6°	17°	E	850	750D	1850(3)	1850(3)	5–7(4)
4-140, 2300 cc/Y High Alt.	AWSF-42	.034	G	6°	20°	E	550/850	550/800D	1800(3)	2000(3)	5–7(4)
V6-171, 2800 cc/Z Exc. Calif.	AWSF-42	.034	H	10°	12°	F	700/850	650/750D(22)	1700(3)	1600(3)	3–6
V6-171, 2800 cc/Z Calif.	AWSF-42	.034	H	10°	6°	F	600/800	750D	1600(5)	1750(5)	3–6
V8-302/F Exc. Calif. & High Alt.	ARF-52	.050	D	10°	4°	C	(7)(22)(23)	(7)(22)(24)	2000(5)	2100(5)	6–8
V8-302/F Calif.	ARF-52-6	.060	D	—	10°	C	—	700D	—	1900(5)	6–8
V8-302/F High Alt.	ARF-52	.050	D	—	14°	C	—	650/725D(22)	—	2000(5)	6–8
1979											
4-140, 2300 cc/Y Exc. Calif. (25)	AWSF-42	.034	G	6°	20°	E	850/1300(22)	600/800D	(3)(7)(29)	2000(3)	5–7(4)
4-140, 2300 cc/Y Calif. (25)	AWSF-42	.034	G	6°	17°	E	850	600/750D	(3)(30)	(3)(30)	5–7(4)
4-140, 2300 cc/W (26)	AWSF-32	.034	G	2°	—	E	900/1300(22)	—	(3)(31)	—	5–7(4)

Continued

TUNE UP SPECIFICATIONS—Continued

The following specifications are published from the latest information available. This data should be used only in the absence of a decal affixed in the engine compartment.

★ When using a timing light, disconnect vacuum hose or tube at distributor and plug opening in hose or tube so idle speed will not be affected.

● When checking compression, lowest cylinder must be within 75 percent of highest.

▲ Before removing wires from distributor cap, determine location of the No. 1 wire in cap, as distributor position may have been altered from that shown at the end of this chart.

Spark plug types shown in this chart are recommendations of the original vehicle manufacturer and not MOTOR. Check local sources for other spark plug manufacturers listings.

Year & Engine/V.I.N.	Spark Plug Type	Gap	Firing Order Fig. ▲	Ignition Timing BTDC① ★ Man. Trans.	Auto. Trans.	Mark Fig.	Curb Idle Speed② Man. Trans.	Auto. Trans.	Fast Idle Speed Man. Trans.	Auto. Trans.	Fuel Pump Pressure
1979—Continued											
V6-171, 2800 cc/Z Exc. Calif.	AWSF-42	.034	H	10°	⑦㉞	F	850	650/750D	1300③	1600③	3–6
V6-171, 2800 cc/Z Calif.	AWSF-42	.034	H	—	6°	F	—	700D	—	1750⑤	3–6
6-200/T Exc. Calif.	BSF-82	.050	A	8°	10°	B	700/850㉒	650D	1600③	1700③	5–7
6-200/T Calif.	BSF-82	.050	A	—	6°	B	—	600/650D	—	2150③	5–7
V8-302/F Exc. Calif.	㉗	.050	D	12°	8°	C	800/875㉒	600/675D	2300⑤	2100⑤	6–8
V8-302/F Calif.	㉘	.060	D	—	12°	C	—	600/675D	—	1800⑤	6–8
1980											
4-140, 2300 cc/A Exc. Calif. ⑦㉓㉟㊲	AWSF-42	.034	G	—	20°	E	—	600/800D	—	2000③	5–7④
4-140, 2300 cc/A Exc. Calif. ⑦㉓㉟㊳	AWSF-42	.034	G	—	17°	E	—	650/800D	—	2000③	5–7④
4-140, 2300 cc/A Exc. Calif.㉕㊱	AWSF-42	.034	G	6°	6°	E	850	750D	2000③	1800③	5–7④
4-140, 2300 cc/A Calif.㉕	AWSF-42	.034	G	6°	12°	E	850	750D	2000③	2000③	5–7④
4-140, 2300 cc/T Exc. Calif.㉖	AWSF-42	.034	G	6°	10°	E	850	650/800D	1800③	③⑦㊴	④㊵
4-140, 2300 cc/T Calif.㉖	AWSF-42	.034	G	2°	10°	E	900	650/800D	1800③	③⑦㊶	④㊵
6-200/B Exc. Calif.㉟	BSF-82	.050	A	—	⑦㊷	B	—	550/700D	—	2000③	5–7
6-200/B Exc. Calif.㊱	BSF-82	.050	A	⑦㊸	10°	B	700/900	550/700D	1600③	2000③	5–7
6-200/B Calif.	BSF-82	.050	A	—	⑦㊹	B	—	600/700D	—	2300③	5–7
V8-255/D Exc. Calif.⑦㊺㊻	ASF-42	.050	D	—	6°	C	—	500D	—	2000⑤	6–8
V8-255/D Exc. Calif.⑦㊺㉜	ASF-42	.050	D	—	6°	C	—	550D	—	1800⑤	6–8
V8-255/D Calif.	ASF-42	.050	D	—	6°	C	—	550D	—	1800⑤	6–8
V8-255/D High Alt.	ASF-42	.050	D	—	6°	C	—	500D	—	2000⑤	6–8
1981											
4-140/A	AWSF-42	.034	G	6°	12°	E	850㉝	750D	2000③	2300③	5–7④
6-200/B	BSF-92	.050	A	8°	⑦㊼	B	700	600D	1800③	2000③	5–7
V8-255/D Exc. Calif.	ASF-52	.050	D	—	10°	C	—	500/650D	—	1600③	6–8
V8-255/D Calif.	ASF-52	.050	D	—	8°	C	—	500/650D	—	1500③	6–8
1982											
4-140/A Exc. Calif. & High Alt.	AWSF-42	.034	G	㊼	12°	E	850	800D	③㊾	2000③	5–7④
4-140/A Calif.⑦㊿	AWSF-32	.034	G	4°	—	E	850	—	1600③	—	5–7④

TUNE UP SPECIFICATIONS—Continued

The following specifications are published from the latest information available. This data should be used only in the absence of a decal affixed in the engine compartment.

★ When using a timing light, disconnect vacuum hose or tube at distributor and plug opening in hose or tube so idle speed will not be affected.

● When checking compression, lowest cylinder must be within 75 percent of highest.

▲ Before removing wires from distributor cap, determine location of the No. 1 wire in cap, as distributor position may have been altered from that shown at the end of this chart.

Spark plug types shown in this chart are recommendations of the original vehicle manufacturer and not MOTOR. Check local sources for other spark plug manufacturers listings.

Year & Engine/V.I.N.	Spark Plug Type	Gap	Firing Order Fig. ▲	Ignition Timing BTDC①★ Man. Trans.	Auto. Trans.	Mark Fig.	Curb Idle Speed② Man. Trans.	Auto. Trans.	Fast Idle Speed Man. Trans.	Auto. Trans.	Fuel Pump Pressure
1982—Continued											
4-140/A Calif.⑦㉛	AWSF-42	.034	G	4°	12°	E	850	800D	1600③	1800③	5–7④
4-140/A High Alt.	㉜	.034	G	6°	12°	E	850	800D	1800③	2000③	5–7④
6-200/B	BSF-92	.050	A	—	㉞	B	—	450/600D	—	2000③	5–7
V8-255/D Exc. High Alt.	ASF-52	.050	D	—	8°	C	—	500/700D	—	1500③	6–8
V8-255/D High Alt.	ASF-52	.050	D	—	14°	C	—	500/700D	—	1600③	6–8
V8-302/F	ASF-42	.044	I	12°	—	C	700/900	—	1500③	—	6–8
1983											
4-140/A㉕	AWSF-44	.044	G	9°	9°	E	850	800D	1800③	2000③	5–7
4-140/W㉖	AWSF-32	.034	G	10°	—	E	825–975㉠	—	㉠	—	—
V6-232/3 Exc. Calif. & High Alt.	AWSF-52	.044	J	—	10°	K	—	㊺	—	2200⑤	6–8㊼
V6-232/3 Calif.	AWSF-52	.044	J	—	8°	K	—	㊺	—	2200⑤	6–8㊼
V6-232/3 High Alt.	AWSF-52	.044	J	—	18°	K	—	㊺	—	2100⑤	6–8㊼
V8-302/F	ASF-42	.044	I	10°	—	C	700	—	2400⑤	—	6–8
1984											
4-140/A㉕	AWSF-44	.044	G	—	—	E	850	750D	—	—	5.5–6.5
4-140/W㉖	AWSF-32	.034	G	—	—	E	—	—	—	—	—
V6-232/3	AWSF-54	.044	J	—	—	K	—	—	—	—	㊾
V8-302/M㊽	ASF-42	.044	I	—	—	C	700	—	—	—	6.5–8.0
V8-302/M㊿	ASF-42	.044	I	—	—	C	—	—	—	—	⑨

①—B.T.D.C.—Before top dead center.

②—Idle speed on manual trans. vehicles is adjusted in Neutral & on auto. trans. equipped vehicles is adjusted in Drive unless otherwise specified. Where two idle speeds are listed, the higher speed is with the A/C or throttle solenoid energized.

③—On kickdown step of fast idle cam.

④—With pump to fuel tank line pinched off & a new fuel filter installed.

⑤—On high step of fast idle cam.

⑥—Except calibration code 1-12B-R10, 10° BTDC; calibration code, 1-12B-R10, 12° BTDC.

⑦—Refer to engine calibration code on engine identification label located at rear of left valve cover on V6 & V8 engines, on front of valve cover on inline 4 & 6 cyl. engines. The calibration code is located on the label after the engine codes number & is preceded by the letter C & the revision code is located below the calibration code is preceded by the letter R.

⑧—Except calibration code 7-2B-R16, 1600 RPM; calibration code 7-2B-R16, 1800 RPM.

⑨—Except calibration code 7-2N-R1, 800/850 RPM; calibration code 7-2N-R1, 650/850 RPM.

⑩—Calibration code 7-1X-RO, 550/750D RPM; 7-1X-R10, 550/800D RPM.

⑪—Calibration code 7-1X-RO, 1800 RPM; 7-1X-R10, 2000 RPM.

⑫—Calibration code 7-3A-R2.

⑬—Calibration codes, man. trans. 7-3A-R10; auto. trans., 7-4A-R2.

⑭—Calibration code 7-11X-R2.

⑮—Calibration codes 7-11X-R4 & 7-11X-R6.

⑯—Calibration codes, man. trans. 8-2A-RO & 8-2A-R10; auto. trans. 8-1A-RO & 8-1B-R10.

⑰—Calibration code 8-2A-RO, 850 RPM; 8-2A-R10, 900 RPM.

⑱—Calibration codes, man. trans., 8-2B-RO auto. trans. 8-21B-RO & 8-21B-R11.

⑲—Calibration codes, man. trans., 8-2N-RO & 8-2N-R11; auto. trans., 8-1N-RO.

⑳—Calibration code 8-2N-RO, 650/900 RPM, 8-2N-R11, 600/850 RPM.

㉑—Calibration codes, man. trans. 8-2P-RO & 8-2T-RO; auto. trans., 8-1R-R1.

㉒—With throttle solenoid energized. Higher idle speed is with A/C on & compressor clutch de-energized, if equipped.

㉓—Calibration code 8-10A-RO, 900/975 RPM; 8-10A-R10, 800/875 RPM.

㉔—Calibration code 8-31A-RO, 700/775D RPM; 8-31A-R10, 700/825 RPM.

㉕—Except turbocharged engine.

㉖—Turbocharged engine.

㉗—ASF-52 or ARF-52.

㉘—ASF-52-6 or ARF-52-6.

㉙—Calibration codes 9-2A-MRO & 9-2B-RO, 1800 RPM; calibration codes 9-2C-RO & 9-2D-RO, 1600 RPM.

㉚—Except Bobcat & Pinto, 1800 RPM; Bobcat & Pinto, 1850 RPM.

㉛—Except Calif., 1800 RPM; California, 1850 RPM.

㉜—Calibration code 0-16A-R12.

㉝—If mileage on vehicle is less than 100 mi., set idle speed 100 RPM less than specified.

㉞—Calibration code 9-4A-RO, 9° BTDC; calibration codes 9-4A-R10A & 9-4A-R10N, 6° BTDC.

㉟—Models less Thermactor air pump.

㊱—Models with Thermactor air pump.

㊲—Calibration code, 9-21B-R10.

㊳—Calibration codes, 0-21A-RO & 0-21B-RO & R10.

㊴—Except calibration code 0-1H-R20, 2000 RPM; calibration code 0-1H-R20, 2150 RPM.

㊵—Manual trans., 5–7 psi.; auto. trans. models use an electric fuel pump.

㊶—Except calibration code 0-1S-R15, 2000 RPM; calibration code 0-1S-R15, 2150 RPM.

㊷—Calibration code 0-27A-R3, 7° BTDC; calibration code 0-27A-R10, 10° BTDC.

㊸—Calibration code 0-6A-RO, 10° BTDC; calibration code 0-6A-R1, 12° BTDC.

㊹—Except calibration code 0-7P-R11, 10° BTDC;

Continued

TUNE UP NOTES—Continued

calibration code 0-7P-R11, 7° BTDC.
45—Except high altitude.
46—Calibration code 0-16A-R0.
47—Except calibration code 1-12B-R10, 10° BTDC; calibration code 1-12B-R10, 12° BTDC.
48—Vehicles equipped with 5 speed manual trans.
49—Vehicles equipped with automatic overdrive trans.

50—Calibration code 2-5N-R0.
51—Exc. calibration code 2-5N-R0.
52—Calibration code 2-5W-R0, AWSF-42; calibration code 2-6W-R0, AWSF-32.
53—Calibration codes 2-5A-R0 & 2-2B-R0, 6°; calibration codes 2-5C-R0 & 2-5C-R11, 4°.
54—Exc. high altitude, 10°; high altitude, 12°.
55—Calibration codes 2-5A-R0 & 2-5B-R0, 1800 RPM; calibration codes 2-5C-R0 & 2-5C-R11, 1600 RPM.

56—With A/C, 550/650D; less A/C, 450/550D.
57—If vehicle is equipped with Tripminder, return line should be pinched off when checking pressure.
58—Frame rail mounted pump, 40—45; intake manifold mounted pump, 30.5.
59—Fuel tank mounted pump, 6; frame mounted pump, 39.
60—Equipped w/ idle speed control.

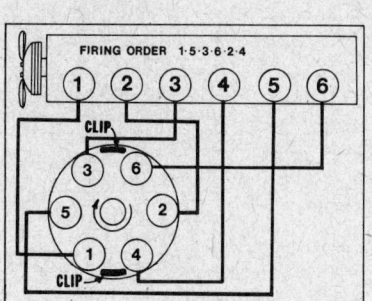

Fig. A

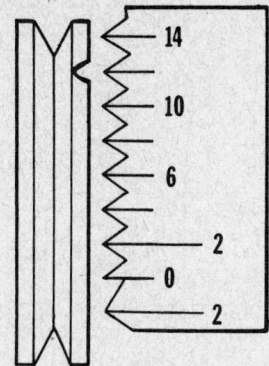

Fig. B

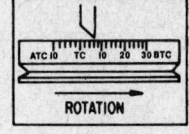

Fig. C

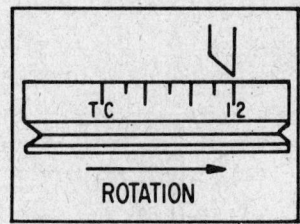

Fig. F

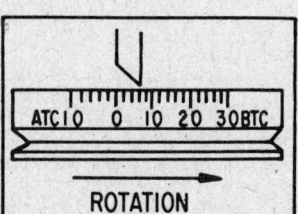

Fig. E

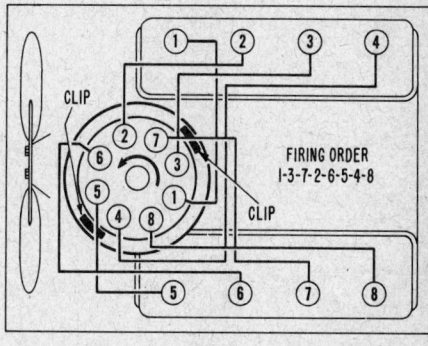

Fig. I

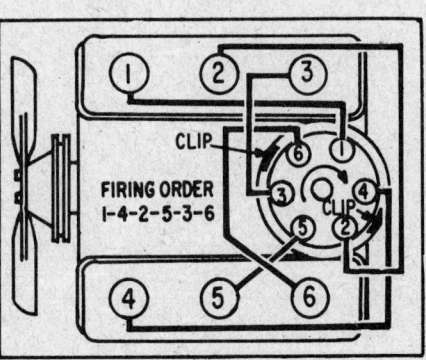

Fig. D

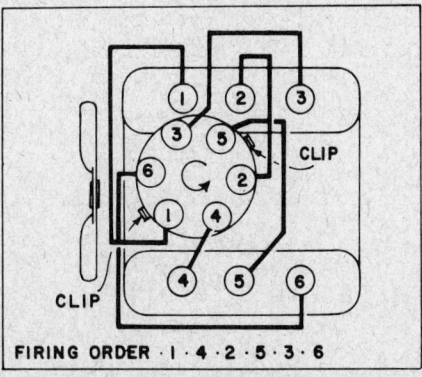

Fig. G

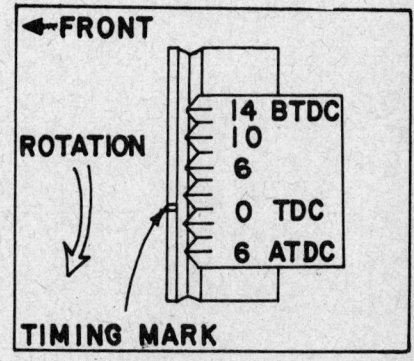

Fig. H

Fig. J

Fig. K

DISTRIBUTOR SPECIFICATIONS

★ If unit is checked on vehicle double the RPM and degrees to get crankshaft figures.

Distributor Part No.	Centrifugal Advance Degrees @ RPM of Distributor					Vacuum Advance		Distributor Retard
	Advance Starts	Intermediate Advance			Full Advance	Inches of Vacuum To Start Plunger	Max. Adv. Dist. Deg. @ Vacuum	Max. Ret. Dist. Deg. @ Vacuum
1977								
D7EE-CA	0–1 @ 800	1–3.5 @ 1500	—	—	7.5 @ 2500	2.3	13¼ @ 15.75	—
D7EE-DA	0–1 @ 510	3.75–5.75 @ 725	—	—	14 @ 2500	1.75	13¼ @ 12.4	—
D7EE-EA	0–1 @ 525	3.6–5.6 @ 725	—	—	14 @ 2500	2	13¼ @ 15.75	—
D7EE-GA	0–1 @ 525	3.75–5.75 @ 740	—	—	14 @ 2500	2.25	13¼ @ 15.75	—
D7EE-HA	0–1 @ 775	1.75–3.7 @ 1500	—	—	7.5 @ 2500	2	13¼ @ 15.75	—
D7OE-GA	0–1 @ 425	6–8 @ 650	—	—	16 @ 2500	3	13¼ @ 16	—
D7ZE-BA	0–1 @ 425	6–8 @ 650	—	—	16 @ 2500	3.5	13¼ @ 15.2	—
D7ZE-CA	0–1 @ 575	6.25–8.25 @ 1250	—	—	12 @ 2500	2.2	15¼ @ 16	—
77TF-AA	0–1 @ 625	5–7.5 @ 1000	—	—	10.5 @ 2100	4	10 @ 12	—
77TF-CA	0–1 @ 600	5–7.5 @ 1000	—	—	10.5 @ 2100	3.5	7 @ 8.5	—
77TF-DA	0–1 @ 600	5–7.5 @ 900	—	—	10.5 @ 2100	4.5	7 @ 10	—
1978								
D7DE-AA	0–1 @ 550	—	—	1¾–4 @ 750	12½ @ 2500	3	15¼ @ 11	—
D7DE-JA	0–1 @ 550	—	—	3½–5½ @ 650	10¾ @ 2500	3	13¼ @ 16	—
D7EE-CA	0–1 @ 800	—	—	1–3½ @ 1500	7½ @ 2500	2.3	13¼ @ 15.75	—
D7EE-DA	0–1 @ 510	—	—	3¾–5¾ @ 725	14 @ 2500	1.75	13¼ @ 12.4	—
D7EE-EA	0–1 @ 525	—	—	3⅝–5⅝ @ 725	14 @ 2500	2	13¼ @ 15.75	—
77TF-AA	0–1 @ 625	—	—	5–7½ @ 1000	10½ @ 2100	4	10 @ 12	—
77TF-CA	0–1 @ 600	—	—	5–7½ @ 900	10½ @ 2100	4.5	7 @ 10	—
77TF-HA	0–1 @ 600	—	—	5–7 @ 900	12 @ 2100	4.5	7 @ 10	—
D8ZE-BA	0–1 @ 425	—	—	6–8 @ 650	16 @ 2500	3.5	13¼ @ 14	—
D8ZE-CA	0–1 @ 575	—	—	6–7¾ @ 1200	11½ @ 2500	2.5	12¼ @ 15.7	—
1979								
77TF-CA	0–1 @ 600	5–7.5 @ 900	—	—	8–10.5 @ 2100	4.5	5–7 @ 10	—
79TF-FA	0–1 @ 600	4–7 @ 1000	—	—	10–12 @ 2100	4.5	2–4 @ 10	—
D7EE-CA	0–2.12 @ 1237	—	—	—	5–7.5 @ 2500	2.3	10.75–13.25 @ 15.75	—
D7EE-DA	0–2.25 @ 530	3.75–5.75 @ 725	—	—	11.5–14 @ 2500	1.75	10.75–13.26 @ 12.4	—
D7EE-EA	0–3 @ 500	3.25–5.5 @ 700	—	—	11.25–14 @ 2500	2	10.75–13.25 @ 15.75	—
D8DE-EA	0–1 @ 450	3–5 @ 600	—	—	9.25–12.25 @ 2500	2.5	10.75–13.25 @ 14.3	—
D9BE-CA	0–1 @ 575	2.75–4.75 @ 1050	—	—	6–8.75 @ 2500	2	10.75–13.25 @ 15.3	—
D9BE-DA	0–1 @ 550	2.75–4.75 @ 1100	—	—	7–9.5 @ 2500	4.5	8.75–11.25 @ 12.5	—
D9ZE-EA	0–2.5 @ 487	4.5–6.5 @ 662	—	—	10.5–13 @ 2500	1.8	10.75–13.25 @ 16.2	—
D9ZE-FA	0–2.5 @ 487	4.5–6.5 @ 662	—	—	10.5–13 @ 2500	1.8	8.75–11.25 @ 14.8	—
D9ZE-CA	0–1 @ 450	3–5 @ 600	—	—	9.5–12.25 @ 2500	2.8	14.75–17.25 @ 15.3	—
1980								
D8BE-EA	2 @ 760	2.7–4.75 @ 1100	—	—	6.7–9.5 @ 2500	2.4	8.75–11.25 @ 25	—
D94E-AA	—	—	—	—	—	—	—	—
D9BE-CA	—	—	—	—	—	—	—	—
D9BE-DA	2 @ 630	2.5–4.5 @ 925	—	—	5.9–9.75 @ 2500	1.8	8.75–11.25 @ 25	—
D9ZE-CA	—	—	—	—	—	—	—	—

Continued

DISTRIBUTOR SPECIFICATIONS—Continued

★ If unit is checked on vehicle double the RPM and degrees to get crankshaft figures.

Distributor Part No.	Centrifugal Advance Degrees @ RPM of Distributor					Vacuum Advance		Distributor Retard
	Advance Starts	Intermediate Advance			Full Advance	Inches of Vacuum To Start Plunger	Max. Adv. Dist. Deg. @ Vacuum	Max. Ret. Dist. Deg. @ Vacuum
1980—Continued								
EOEE-BA	2.4 @ 610	1.1–3.1 @ 650	—	—	10.2–13.1 @ 2500	2	6.75–9.25 @ 25	—
EOEE-CA	2.5 @ 580	3.75–5.75 @ 740	—	—	11.3–14 @ 2500	1.7	10.75–13.25 @ 25	—
EOEE-DA	3.2 @ 600	3.75–5.7 @ 730	—	—	11.6–14 @ 2500	2.1	10.75–13.25 @ 25	—
EOEE-EA	3.1 @ 500	4.3–6.75 @ 660	—	—	11.1–13.75 @ 2500	2	6.75–9.25 @ 25	—
EOEE-FA	2.6 @ 1140	—	—	—	5.1–7.9 @ 2500	2	6.75–9.25 @ 25	—
EOSE-CA	2 @ 635	2.8–4.6 @ 840	—	—	9.1–11.75 @ 2500	2.1	10.75–13.25 @ 25	—
EOZE-AA	3.3 @ 500	3–5.1 @ 620	—	—	9.9–12.7 @ 2500	2.3	10.75–13.25 @ 25	—
EOZE-BA	1.75 @ 540	2.95 @ 760	—	—	8.6–11.3 @ 2500	1.7	8.75–11.25 @ 25	—
EOZE-DA	—	—	—	—	—	—	—	—
EOZE-GA	3 @ 500	4.6–7:6 @ 650	—	—	10.6–13.4 @ 2500	2.2	10.75–13.25 @ 25	—
EOZE-HA	2.75 @ 500	.75–2.75 @ 535	—	—	6.6–9.3 @ 2500	2.2	6.75–9.25 @ 25	—
1981								
D8BE-EA	—	3–5.5 @ 1250	—	—	—	—	—	—
D9BE-DA	—	3–5.5 @ 1250	—	—	—	—	—	—
EOEE-BA	—	3.5–6.5 @ 1250	—	—	—	—	—	—
EOEE-DA	—	6–8.5 @ 1250	—	—	—	—	—	—
E1BE-BA	—	—	—	—	—	—	—	—
E1SE-CA	—	—	—	—	—	—	—	—
E1SE-EA	—	—	—	—	—	—	—	—
1982								
EOEE-CA	—	8.5–11 @ 1250	—	—	—	—	—	—
EOEE-CA①	—	7.5–10 @ 1250	—	—	—	—	—	—
EOEE-DA	—	8–11 @ 1250	—	—	—	—	—	—
EOEE-BA	—	9.5–12.5 @ 1250	—	—	—	—	—	—
E2BE-CA	—	8–10.5 @ 1250	—	—	—	—	—	—
E1BE-EA	—	9.5–11.5 @ 1250	—	—	—	—	—	—
E2BE-BA	—	7–9.5 @ 1250	—	—	—	—	—	—
E2SE-AA	—	10–12.5 @ 1250	—	—	—	—	—	—
E2ZE-DA	—	11–13 @ 1250	—	—	—	—	—	—
1983								
E3SE-BA	—	7.5–9.5 @ 1250	—	—	—	—	—	—
E3ZE-CA	—	11.5–13 @ 1250	—	—	—	—	—	—
E3ZE-DA	—	3.5–5.5 @ 1250	—	—	—	—	—	—
E3ZE-FA	—	8.5–11.5 @ 1250	—	—	—	—	—	—
E3ZE-HA	—	8.5–11 @ 1250	—	—	—	—	—	—
E3ZE-JA	—	8.5–11 @ 1250	—	—	—	—	—	—
1984								
E4ZE-AA	—	—	—	—	—	—	—	—

①—Manual transmission.

STARTING MOTOR APPLICATIONS

Year	Engine Model/V.I.N.	Ident. No.	Year	Engine Model/V.I.N.	Ident. No.	Year	Engine Model/V.I.N.	Ident. No.
1977	4-140/Y	D6EF-BA	1980	4-140/A	D8EF-AA		6-200/B	E1AF-BA
	V6-171/Z	D6EF-AA		6-200/B⑤	D8BF-CA		V8-255/D⑫	E1AF-BA
	V8-302/F①	D6OF-AA		6-200/B⑥	D8BF-AA		V8-255/D⑬	E3AF-AA
	V8-302/F②	D8OF-AA		V8-255/D	D8OF-AA		V8-302/F⑫	E1AF-BA
1978	4-140/Y	EDD6EF-BA	1981	4-140/A⑦	E1ZF-AA		V8-302/F⑬	E3AF-AA
	V6-171/Z③	D6EF-AA		4-140/A⑧	E1ZF-AB	1983	4-140/A	E2BF-AA
	V6-171/Z④	D8ZF-AA		4-140/A⑨	E2BF-AA		V6-232/A	E25F-AA
	V8-302/F	D8OF-AA		6-200/B⑤⑩	E1BF-BA		V8-302/F	E3AF-AA
1979	4-140/Y	D8EF-AA		6-200/B⑤⑪	E1AF-BA	1984	4-140/	—
	V6-171/Z	D8ZF-AA		6-200/B⑥	E1BF-AA		V6-232/	—
	6-200/T	D8BF-CA		V8-255/D	E1AF-BA		V8-302/	—
	V8-302/F	D8OF-AA	1982	4-140/A	E2BF-AA			

①—Vehicles manufactured before 2-1-77.
②—Vehicles manufactured after 1-31-77.
③—Vehicles manufactured before 3-15-78.
④—Vehicles manufactured after 3-14-78.
⑤—Automatic trans.
⑥—Manual trans.
⑦—Vehicles manufactured before 3-2-81.
⑧—Vehicles manufactured between 3-2-81 and 5-1-81.
⑨—Vehicles manufactured after 5-1-81.
⑩—Vehicles manufactured before 3-2-81.
⑪—Vehicles manufactured after 3-1-81.
⑫—Vehicles manufactured before 5-17-82.
⑬—Vehicles manufactured after 5-16-82.

REAR AXLE SPECIFICATIONS

Year	Ring Gear Diameter	Carrier Type	Ring Gear & Pinion Backlash Inch	Nominal Pinion Locating Shim, Inch	Pinion Bearing Preload				Differential Bearing Preload	Pinion Nut Torque Ft. Lbs.
					New Bearings With Seal Inch-Lbs.	Used Bearings With Seal Inch-Lbs.	New Bearings Less Seal Inch-Lbs.	Used Bearings Less Seal Inch-Lbs.		
1977–78	6¾" WGF②	Integral	.008–.012	.022	17–27	6–12	—	—	.004–.008①	140
1977–79	8"	Removable	.008–.012	.022	17–27	8–14	—	—	.004–.008①	170
1979	6¾" WGF, WGG②	Integral	.008–.012	.030	17–27	6–12	—	—	.016③	140
1979–80	7½" WGX, WGZ②	Integral	.008–.012	.030	17–27	8–14	—	—	.016③	140
1980	8, 9"	Removable	.008–.012	④	17–27	8–14	—	—	.005–.008①	170
1980	6¾" WGF, WGG②	Integral	.008–.015	.030	17–27	6–12	—	—	.016③	140
1981–82	7½" WGX②	Integral	.008–.015	.030	16–29	8–14	—	—	.016③	170
	6¾" WGG②	Integral	.008–.015	.030	16–29	8–14	—	—	.016③	140
1983–84	7½" WGX②	Integral	.008–.015	.030	16–29	8–14	—	—	.016③	170

①—Case spread with new bearings; with used bearings, .003–.005".
②—Identification tag code.
③—Case spread.
④—8 inch ring gear, .022"; 9 inch ring gear, .015".

ALTERNATOR & REGULATOR SPECIFICATIONS

Year	Make or Model	Current Rating		Field Current @ 75°F.		Voltage Regulator		Field Relay
		Amperes	Volts	Amperes	Volts	Make or Model	Voltage @ 75°F.	Closing Voltage @ 75°F.
1977	Orange①④	40	15	2.9	12	D4AF-AA	13.5–15.3	2.5–4.0
	Green①④	60	15	2.9	12	D4AF-AA	13.5–15.3	2.5–4.0
	All⑤	70	15	2.9	12	D4TF-AA	13.5–15.3	2.5–4.0
	All⑤	90	15	2.9	12	D4TF-AA	13.5–15.3	2.5–4.0
1978	Orange①④	40	15	2.9	12	D4AF-AA	13.5–15.3	—
	Green①④	60	15	2.9	12	D4AF-AA	13.5–15.3	—
	Green①④⑥	60	15	4.0	12	D8VF-AA⑦	13.8–14.6	—
	Black①⑤	70	15	2.9	12	D4AF-AA	13.5–15.3	—

Continued

ALTERNATOR & REGULATOR SPECIFICATIONS—Continued

Year	Make or Model	Current Rating		Field Current @ 75°F.		Voltage Regulator		Field Relay
		Amperes	Volts	Amperes	Volts	Make or Model	Voltage @ 75°F.	Closing Voltage @ 75°F.
	Red①⑤	90	15	2.9	12	D4AF-AA	13.5–15.3	—
	Red①⑤⑥	90	15	4.0	12	D8VF-AA⑦	13.8–14.6	—
1979	Orange①④⑥	40	15	4.0	12	D8VF-AA②⑦	13.8–14.6	—
	Green①④⑥	60	15	4.0	12	D8VF-AA②⑦	13.8–14.6	—
	Black①④⑥	65	15	4.0	12	D8VF-AA②⑦	13.8–14.6	—
	Black①⑤⑥	70	15	4.0	12	D8VF-AA②⑦	13.8–14.6	—
	Red①⑤⑥	100	15	4.0	12	D8VF-AA⑦	13.8–14.6	—
1980	Orange①④⑥	40	15	4.0	12	D9VF-AB③⑦	13.8–14.6	—
	Green①④⑥	60	15	4.0	12	D9VF-AB③⑦	13.8–14.6	—
	Black①④⑥	65	15	4.0	12	D9VF-AB③⑦	13.8–14.6	—
	Black①⑤⑥	70	15	4.0	12	D9VF-AB③⑦	13.8–14.6	—
1981	Orange①④⑥	40	15	4.0	12	—	13.8–14.6	—
	Green①④⑥	60	15	4.0	12	—	13.8–14.6	—
	Black①④⑥	65	15	4.0	12	—	13.8–14.6	—
	Black①⑤⑥	70	15	4.0	12	—	13.8–14.6	—
	Red①⑤⑥	100	15	4.0	12	—	13.8–14.6	—
1982	Orange①④⑥	40	15	4.0	12	E1TF-AA	13.8–14.6	—
	Green①④⑥	60	15	4.0	12	E1TF-AA	13.8–14.6	—
	Black①④⑥	65	15	4.0	12	E1TF-AA	13.8–14.6	—
	Black①⑤⑥	70	15	4.0	12	E1TF-AA	13.8–14.6	—
	Red①⑤⑥	90	15	4.0	12	E1TF-AA	13.8–14.6	—
1983	Orange①④⑥	40	15	4.25	12	E2TF-AA	—	—
	Green①④⑥	60	15	4.25	12	E2TF-AA	—	—
	Black①④⑥	65	15	4.25	12	E2TF-AA	—	—
	Black①⑤⑥	70	15	4.25	12	E2TF-AA	—	—
	Red①⑤⑥	100	15	4.25	12	E2TF-AA	—	—
1984	Orange①④⑥	40	15	4.25	12	E4TF-AA	—	—
	Green①④⑥	60	15	4.25	12	E4TF-AA	—	—
	Black①⑤⑥	70	15	4.25	12	E4TF-AA	—	—
	Red①⑤⑥	100	15	4.25	12	E4TF-AA	—	—

①—Color of identification tag.
②—Pinto & Bobcat use D8BF-AA.
③—Pinto & Bobcat use D9BF-AB.
④—Rear terminal alternator.
⑤—Side terminal alternator.
⑥—Solid state alternator.
⑦—Electronic voltage regulator. These units are color coded black for systems w/warning indicator lamp & blue for system w/ammeter.

WHEEL ALIGNMENT SPECIFICATIONS

Year	Model	Caster Angle, Degrees		Camber Angle, Degrees				Toe-In. Inch	Toe-Out on Turns, Deg.	
				Limits		Desired				
		Limits	Desired	Left	Right	Left	Right		Outer Wheel	Inner Wheel
1977–78	Mustang	+1/8 to +15/8	+7/8	−1/4 to +11/4	−1/4 to +11/4	+1/2	+1/2	1/8	18.84	20
1977–79	Bobcat & Pinto①	+1/4 to +13/4	+1	−1/4 to +11/4	−1/4 to +11/4	+1/2	+1/2	1/8	18.84	20
	Bobcat & Pinto②	−1/2 to +1	+1/4	−1/4 to +11/4	−1/4 to +11/4	+1/2	+1/2	1/8	18.84	20
1979	Capri & Mustang	+1/4 to +13/4	+1	−1/2 to +1	−1/2 to +1	+1/4	+1/4	5/16	19.74	20
1980	Bobcat & Pinto①	+1/4 to +13/4	+1	−1/4 to +11/4	−1/4 to +11/4	+1/2	+1/2	1/8	18.84	20
	Bobcat & Pinto②	−3/4 to +11/4	+1/4	−1/4 to +11/4	−1/4 to +11/4	+1/2	+1/2	1/8	18.84	20
1980–81	Capri & Mustang	+1/4 to +13/4	+1	−1/2 to +1	−1/2 to +1	+1/4	+1/4	3/16	19.84	20
1982	Capri & Mustang	+3/8 to +17/8	+11/8	−1/2 to +1	−1/2 to +1	+1/4	+1/4	3/16	19.84	20
1983	Capri & Mustang	+1/2 to +2	+11/4	−3/4 to +3/4	−3/4 to +3/4	Zero	Zero	3/16	19.84	20
1984	Capri & Mustang	+1/2 to +2	+11/4	−3/4 to +3/4	−3/4 to +3/4	Zero	Zero	3/16	19.84	20

①—Exc. sta. wag.   ②—Sta. wag.

FORD MUSTANG & PINTO • MERCURY BOBCAT & CAPRI

PISTONS, PINS, RINGS, CRANKSHAFT & BEARINGS

Year	Engine/V.I.N.	Piston Clearance	Ring End Gap[1]		Wristpin Diameter	Rod Bearings		Main Bearings			
			Comp.	Oil		Shaft Diameter	Bearing Clearance	Shaft Diameter	Bearing Clearance	Thrust on Bear. No.	Shaft End Play
1977–78	4-140/Y	.0014–.0022	.010	.015	.9121	2.0464–2.0472	.0008–.0015	2.3982–2.3990	.0008–.0015	3	.004–.008
	V6-171/Z	.0011–.0019	.015	.015	.9448	2.1252–2.1260	.0006–.0015	2.2433–2.2441	.0008–.0015	3	.004–.008
	V8-302/F	.0018–.0026	.010	.015	.9121	2.1228–2.1236	.0008–.0015	2.2482–2.2490	[5]	3	.004–.008
1979	4-140/W,Y	.0014–.0022	.010	.015	.9121	2.0464–2.0472	.0008–.0015	2.3982–2.3990	.0008–.0015	3	.004–.008
	V6-171/Z	.0011–.0019	.015	.015	.9448	2.1252–2.1260	.0006–.0016	2.2433–2.2441	.0008–.0015	3	.004–.008
	6-200/T[3]	.0013–.0021	.008	.015	.9121	2.1232–2.1240	.0008–.0015	2.2482–2.2490	.0008–.0015	3	.004–.008
	V8-302/F	.0018–.0026	.010	.015	.9121	2.1228–2.1236	.0008–.0015	2.2482–2.2490	[2]	3	.004–.008
1980	4-140/A[6]	.0014–.0022	.010	.015	.9121	2.0462–2.0472	.0008–.0015	2.3982–2.3990	.0008–.0015	3	.004–.008
	4-140/T[4]	.0034–.0042	.010	.015	.9121	2.0462–2.0472	.0008–.0015	2.3982–2.3990	.0008–.0015	3	.004–.008
	6-200/B[3]	.0013–.0021	.008	.015	.9121	2.1232–2.1240	.0008–.0015	2.2482–2.2490	.0008–.0015	3	.004–.008
	V8-255/D[3]	.0018–.0026	.010	.015	.9121	2.1328–2.1236	.0008–.0015	2.2482–2.2490	[2]	3	.004–.008
1981	4-140/A	.0014–.0022	.010	.015	.9121	2.0462–2.0472	.0008–.0015	2.3982–2.3990	.0008–.0015	3	.004–.008
	6-200/B[3]	.0013–.0021	.008	.015	.9121	2.1232–2.1240	.0008–.0015	2.2482–2.2490	.0008–.0015	3	.004–.008
	V8-255/D[3]	.0014–.0024	.010	.015	.9121	2.1328–2.1236	.0008–.0015	2.2482–2.2490	[2]	3	.004–.008
1982	4-140/A	.0014–.0022	.010	.015	.9121	2.0465–2.0472	.0008–.0015	2.3982–2.3990	.0008–.0015	3	.004–.008
	6-200/B[3]	.0013–.0021	.008	.015	.9121	2.1232–2.1240	.0008–.0015	2.2482–2.2490	.0008–.0015	3	.004–.008
	V8-255/D[3]	.0014–.0024	.010	.015	.9121	2.1228–2.1236	.0008–.0015	2.2482–2.2490	[7]	3	.004–.008
	V8-302 H.O./F[3]	.0018–.0026	.010	.015	.9121	2.1228–2.1236	.0008–.0015	2.2482–2.2490	[7]	3	.004–.008
1983	4-140/A[6]	.0014–.0022	.010	.015	.9121	2.0465–2.0472	.0008–.0015	2.3982–2.3990	.0008–.0015	3	.004–.008
	4-140/W[4]	.0030–.0038	.010	.015	.9121	2.0465–2.0472	.0008–.0015	2.3982–2.3990	.0008–.0015	3	.004–.008
	V6-232/3	.0014–.0022	.010	.015	.9121	2.3103–2.3111	.0010–.0014	2.5190–2.5198	.0010–.0014	3	.004–.008
	V8-302 H.O./F	.0018–.0026	.010	.015	.9121	2.1228–2.1236	.0008–.0015	2.2482–2.2490	[7]	3	.004–.008
1984	4-140/A[6]	.0030–.0038	.010	.015	.9121	2.0465–2.0472	.0008–.0015	2.3982–2.3990	.0008–.0015	3	.004–.008
	4-140/W[4]	.0030–.0038	.010	.015	.9121	2.0465–2.0472	.0008–.0015	2.3982–2.3990	.0008–.0015	3	.004–.008
	V6-232/3	.0014–.0032	.010	.015	.9122	2.3103–2.3111	.0010–.0014	2.5190–2.5198	.0010–.0014	3	.004–.008
	V8-302 H.O./M	.0018–.0026	.010	.015	.9122	2.1228–2.1236	.0008–.0015	2.2482–2.2490	[7]	3	.004–.008

[1]—Fit rings in tapered bores for clearance listed in tightest portion of ring travel.
[2]—No. 1, .0001–.0015; others, .0004–.0015.
[3]—Refer to the Ford & Mercury—Compact & Intermediate chapter for service procedures on this engine.
[4]—Turbocharged engine.
[5]—No. 1, .0001–.0015"; others, .0005–.0015.
[6]—Except turbocharged engine.
[7]—No. 1, .0004–.0025; others, .0004–.0015.

ENGINE TIGHTENING SPECIFICATIONS

★ Torque specifications are for clean and lightly lubricated threads only. Dry or dirty threads produce increased friction which prevents accurate measurement of tightness.

Year	Engine/V.I.N.	Spark Plugs Ft. Lbs.	Cylinder Head Bolts Ft. Lbs.	Intake Manifold Ft. Lbs.	Exhaust Manifold Ft. Lbs.	Rocker Arm Shaft Bracket Ft. Lbs.	Rocker Arm Cover Ft. Lbs.	Connecting Rod Cap Bolts Ft. Lbs.	Main Bearing Cap Bolts Ft. Lbs.	Flywheel to Crankshaft Ft. Lbs.	Vibration Damper or Pulley Ft. Lbs.
1977–78	4-140/Y	5–10	80–90	14–21	16–23	—	4–7	30–36	80–90	54–64	100–120
	V6-171/Z	10–15	65–80	[2]	20–30	43–49	3–5	21–25	65–75	47–51	92–103
	V8-302/F[1]	10–15	65–72	23–25	18–24	[3]	3–5	19–24	60–70	75–85	70–90
1979	4-140/W,Y	5–10	80–90	14–21	16–23	—	6–8	30–36	80–90	54–64	100–120
	V6-171/Z	10–15	65–80	[2]	20–30	43–49	3–5	21–25	65–75	47–51	92–103
	6-200/T[1]	10–15	70–75	—	18–24	30–35	3–5	21–26	60–70	75–85	85–100
	V8-302/F[1]	10–15	65–72	23–25	18–24	18–25[4]	3–5	19–24	60–70	75–85	70–90
1980–81	4-140/A[7]	5–10	80–90	14–21	16–23	—	6–8	30–36	80–90	56–64	100–120
	4-140/T[8]	5–10	80–90	13–18	16–23	—	6–8	30–36	80–90	56–64	100–120
	6-200/B[1]	10–15	70–75	—	18–24	30–35	3–5	21–26	60–70	75–85	85–100
	V8-255/D[1]	10–15	65–72	[5]	18–24	18–25[4]	3–5	19–24	60–70	75–85	70–90

Continued

ENGINE TIGHTENING SPECIFICATIONS—Continued

★ Torque specifications are for clean and lightly lubricated threads only. Dry or dirty threads produce increased friction which prevents accurate measurement of tightness.

Year	Engine/V.I.N.	Spark Plugs Ft. Lbs.	Cylinder Head Bolts Ft. Lbs.	Intake Manifold Ft. Lbs.	Exhaust Manifold Ft. Lbs.	Rocker Arm Shaft Bracket Ft. Lbs.	Rocker Arm Cover Ft. Lbs.	Connecting Rod Cap Bolts Ft. Lbs.	Main Bearing Cap Bolts Ft. Lbs.	Flywheel to Crankshaft Ft. Lbs.	Vibration Damper or Pulley Ft. Lbs.
1982	4-140/A	5–10	80–90	14–21	16–23	—	5–8	30–36	80–90	56–64	100–120
	6-200/B	10–15	70–75	—	18–24	30–35	3–5	21–26	60–70	75–85	85–100
	V8-255/D①	10–15	65–72	18–20	18–24	18–25④	3–5	19–24	60–70	75–85	70–90
	V8-302 H.O./F①	10–15	65–72	23–25	18–24	18–25④	3–5	19–24	60–70	75–85	70–90
1983	4-140/A⑦	5–10	80–90	14–21	16–23	—	5–8	30–36	80–90	56–64	100–120
	4-140/W⑧	5–10	80–90	14–21	16–23	—	5–8	30–36	80–90	54–64	100–120
	V6-232/3	5–11	⑥	18.4	15–22	18.4–25.8 ④	3–5	31–36	65–81	56–64	93–121
	V8-302 H.O./F	10–15	65–72	23–25	18–24	18–25④	3–5	19–24	60–70	75–85	70–90
1984	4-140/A⑦	5–10	80–90	14–21	16–23	—	5–8	30–36	80–90	56–64	100–120
	4-140/W⑧	5–10	80–90	14–21	16–23	—	5–8	30–36	80–90	56–64	100–120
	V6-232/3	5–11	⑨	24	15–22	18.4–25.8 ④	80–106⑩	31–36	65–81	54–64	93–121
	V8-302 H.O./M	10–15	65–72	23–25	18–24	18–25④	3–5	19–24	60–70	75–85	70–90

①—Refer to the Ford & Mercury—Compact & Intermediate Chapter for service procedures.
②—Bolt & nut, 15–18 ft. lbs.; stud, 10–12 ft. lbs.
③—1977 & early 1978 rocker arm stud nut, 17–23 ft. lbs.; late 1978 fulcrum bolt to cylinder head, 18–25 ft. lbs.
④—Rocker fulcrum bolt to cylinder head.
⑤—1980, 23–25 ft. lbs.; 1981, 18–20 ft. lbs.
⑥—Tighten in (4) steps: (1) 47 ft. lbs., (2) 55 ft. lbs., (3) 63 ft. lbs., (4) 74 ft. lbs., then back off all bolts 2–3 revolutions and repeat steps 1 through 4.
⑦—Except turbocharged engine.
⑧—Turbocharged engin.
⑨—Tighten in (4) steps; (1) 37 ft. lbs., (2) 45 ft. lbs., (3) 52 ft. lbs., (4) 59 ft. lbs., then back off all bolts 2–3 revolutions & repeat steps 1 through 4.
⑩—Inch lbs.

VALVE SPECIFICATIONS

Year	Engine/V.I.N.	Valve Lash Int.	Valve Lash Exh.	Valve Angles Seat	Valve Angles Face	Valve Spring Installed Height	Valve Spring Pressure Lbs. @ In.	Stem Clearance Intake	Stem Clearance Exhaust	Stem Diameter, Standard Intake	Stem Diameter, Standard Exhaust
1977	4-140/Y	.040–.050②		45	44	1.560	189 @ 1.16	.0010–.0027	.0015–.0032	.3416–.3423	.3411–.3418
	V6-171/Z	.014C	.016C	45	44	1.593	144 @ 1.222	.0008–.0025	.0018–.0035	.3159–.3167	.3149–.3156
	V8-302/F⑤	.096–.168⑥		45	44	③	④	.0010–.0027	.0015–.0032	.3416–.3423	.3411–.3418
1978	4-140/Y	.040–.050②		45	44	1.560	189 @ 1.16	.0010–.0027	.0015–.0032	.3416–.3423	.3411–.3418
	V6-171/Z	.014C	.016C	45	44	1.593	144 @ 1.222	.0008–.0025	.0018–.0035	.3159–.3167	.3149–.3156
	V8-302/F⑤⑦	.096–.168⑥		45	44	③	④	.0010–.0027	.0015–.0032	.3416–.3423	.3411–.3418
	V8-302/F⑤⑧	⑥⑨		45	44	③	④	.0010–.0027	.0015–.0032	.3416–.3423	.3411–.3418
1979	4-140/W, Y	.040–.050②		45	44	1.56	187 @ 1.16	.0010–.0027	.0015–.0032	.3416–.3423	.3411–.3418
	V6-171/Z	.014C	.016C	45	44	1.593	144 @ 1.222	.0008–.0025	.0018–.0035	.3159–.3167	.3149–.3156
	6-200/T⑤	.110–.160⑥		45	44	1 17/32	150 @ 1.22	.0008–.0025	.0010–.0027	.310–.3107	.3098–.3105
	V8-302/F⑤	.096–.165⑥		45	44	③	①	.0010–.0027	.0015–.0032	.3416–.3423	.3411–.3418
1980	4-140/A,T	.040–.050②		45	44	1.56	167 @ 1.16	.0010–.0027	.0015–.0032	.3416–.3423	.3411–.3418
	6-200/B⑤	.110–.184⑥		45	44	1.578	150 @ 1.22	.0008–.0025	.0010–.0027	.3100–.3107	.3098–.3105
	V8-255/D⑤	.123–.173⑥		45	44	③	①	.0010–.0027	.0015–.0032	.3416–.3423	.3411–.3418
1981	4-140/A	.040–.050②		45	44	1.56	167 @ 1.16	.0010–.0027	.0015–.0032	.3416–.3423	.3411–.3418
	6-200/B⑤	.110–.184⑥		45	44	1.58	150 @ 1.22	.0008–.0025	.0010–.0027	.3100–.3107	.3098–.3105
	V8-255/D⑤	.096–.146⑥		45	44	③	⑩	.0010–.0027	.0015–.0032	.3416–.3423	.3411–.3418
1982	4-140/A	.040–.050②		45	44	1.56	167 @ 1.16	.0010–.0027	.0015–.0032	.3416–.3423	.3411–.3418
	6-200/B⑤	.110–.184⑥		45	44	1.58	150 @ 1.22	.0008–.0025	.0010–.0027	.3100–.3107	.3098–.3105
	V8-255/D⑤	.096–.146⑥		45	44	③	⑪	.0010–.0027	.0015–.0032	.3416–.3423	.3411–.3418
	V8-302 H.O./F⑤	.096–.146⑥		45	44	③	⑪	.0010–.0027	.0015–.0032	.3416–.3423	.3411–.3418
1983	4-140/A,W	.040–.050②		45	44	1.56	167 @ 1.16	.0010–.0027	.0015–.0032	.3416–.3423	.3411–.3418
	V6-232/3⑤	.088–.189⑥		45	44	1.74	215 @ 1.40	.0010–.0027	.0015–.0032	.3416–.3423	.3411–.3418
	V8-302 H.O./F⑤	.123–.146⑥		45	44	⑫	⑬	.0010–.0027	.0015–.0032	.3416–.3423	.3411–.3418

FORD MUSTANG & PINTO • MERCURY BOBCAT & CAPRI

VALVE SPECIFICATIONS—Continued

Year	Engine/V.I.N.	Valve Lash Int.	Valve Lash Exh.	Valve Angles Seat	Valve Angles Face	Valve Spring Installed Height	Valve Spring Pressure Lbs. @ In.	Stem Clearance Intake	Stem Clearance Exhaust	Stem Diameter, Standard Intake	Stem Diameter, Standard Exhaust
1984	4-140/A,W	.040–.050②		45	44	1.56	167 @ 1.16	.0010–.0027	.0015–.0032	.3416–.3423	.3411–.3418
	V6-232/3⑤	.088–.189		45	44	1.74	215 @ 1.40	.0010–.0027	.0015–.0032	.3416–.3423	.3411–.3418
	V8-302 H.O./M	.123–.146⑥		45	44	⑫	⑬	.0010–.0027	.0015–.0032	.3416–.3423	.3411–.3418

①—Intake, 201 @ 1.36; exhaust, 200 @ 1.20.
②—Measured at cam with hydraulic valve lash adjuster completely collapsed.
③—Intake, 1¹¹/₁₆; exhaust, 1¹⁹/₃₂.
④—Intake 200 @ 1.31; exhaust 200 @ 1.20.
⑤—Refer to the Ford & Mercury—Compact & Intermediate Chapter for service procedures on this engine.

⑥—Clearance is obtained at valve stem tip with hydraulic lifter collapsed. If clearance is less than the minimum install an undersize push rod; if clearance is greater than the maximum install an oversize push rod.
⑦—Early 1978 engines. On these engines a stud & nut are used to retain rocker arm to cylinder head.

⑧—Late 1978 engines. On these engines a fulcrum bolt is used to retain rocker arm to cylinder head.
⑨—Except Calif., .121; California, .142.
⑩—Intake, 205 @ 1.36; exhaust 200 @ 1.20.
⑪—Intake, 205 @ 1.36; exhaust 205 @ 1.15.
⑫—Intake, 1²⁵/₃₂; exhaust, 1³⁹/₆₄.
⑬—Intake, 204 @ 1.33; exhaust, 205 @ 1.05.

COOLING SYSTEM & CAPACITY DATA

Year	Model or Engine/V.I.N.	Cooling Capacity, Qts. Less A/C	Cooling Capacity, Qts. With A/C	Radiator Cap Relief Pressure, Lbs.	Thermo. Opening Temp.	Fuel Tank Gals.	Engine Oil Refill Qts. ①	4 Speed Pints	5 Speed Pints	Auto. Trans. Qts. ②	Rear Axle Oil Pints
1977	4-140/Y	⑨	9.1	13	191	⑫	4	⑤	—	⑥	⑦
	V6-171/Z	⑩	9.2	13	191	④	4½⑧	⑤	—	⑥	⑦
	V8-302/F	16.3	16.3	13	191	16.5	4	⑤	—	⑥	4
1978	4-140/Y⑬	8.6	9.0	13	191	⑯	4	2.8	—	⑰	⑱
	4-140/Y⑭	8.8	9.1	13	191	13	4	3.5	—	⑰	⑱
	V6-171/Z⑬	8.5	9.2	13	191	⑯	4½⑧	2.8	—	⑰	⑱
	V6-171/Z⑭	⑮	9.0	13	191	13	4½⑧	3.5	—	⑰	⑱
	V8-302/F	14.6	14.6	13	191	16.5	4	3.5	—	7	⑱
1979	4-140/Y⑬	8.6	9.0	13	191	㉒	4	2.8	—	⑰	2.5
	4-140/Y⑲⑳	8.8	9.1	13	191	11.5	4⑧	2.8	—	⑰	2.5
	4-140/W⑲㉑	8.8	10.2	13	191	12.2	4⑧	4.5	—	⑰	3.5
	V6-171/Z⑬	8.5	9.1	13	195	㉒	4½⑧	2.8	—	⑰	4.5
	V6-171/Z⑲	8.6	9.1	16	195	12.2	4½⑧	4.5	—	⑰	3.5
	6-200/T	9.0	9.0	16	191	16	4	—	—	⑭	3.5
	V8-302/F	14	14.6	16	195	12.2	4㉖	4.5	—	③	3.5
1980	4-140/A⑬	8.6	8.9	13	191	㉒	4	2.8	—	㉔	㉓
	4-140/A⑲⑳	8.6	9	㉗	191	11.5	4	2.8	3.7	6.7	㉓
	4-140/T⑲㉑	9.2	9.2	16	191	12.5㉕	4½	3.5	3.7	6.7	㉓
	6-200/B⑲	8.1	8.1	16	191	12.5	4	4.5	—	⑰	㉓
	V8-255/D⑲	13.4	13.5	16	196	12.5	4㉖	—	—	10	㉓
1981	4-140/A⑲	8.6	9	㉗	191	12.5	4	2.8	3.7	㉔	—
	6-200/B⑲	8.4	8.4	16	196	12.5	4	4.5	—	㉙	㉘
	V8-255/D⑲	14.7	15	16	191	12.5	4㉖	—	—	9.6	㉘
1982	4-140/A⑲	8.6	9.4	㉗	191	15.4	4	2.8	3.7	8	㉘
	6-200/B⑲	8.4	8.4	16	196	15.4	4	—	—	⑪	㉘
	V8-255/D⑲	14.7	15	16	191	15.4	4	—	—	11	㉘
	V8-302 H.O./F⑲	13.1	13.4	16	196	15.4	4	4.5	—	—	㉘
1983	4-140/A⑳	8.6	9.4	㉗	191	15.4	4	2.8	—	8	㉚
	4-140/W㉑	10.5	10.5	㉗	191	15.4	4	—	5.6	—	㉚
	V6-232/3	—	—	16	196	15.4	4	—	—	11	㉚
	V8-302/F	13.1	13.4	16	196	15.4	4	4.5	—	—	3.5
1984	4-140/A⑳	8.6	9.4	㉗	191	15.4	4	2.8	—	8	㉜
	4-140/W㉑	10.5	10.5	㉗	191	15.4	4	—	5.6	8	㉜
	V6-232/3	10.7	10.8	16	196	15.4	4	—	—	11	㉜
	V8-302/M	13.1	13.4	16	196	15.4	4	—	—	11	3.5

Continued

COOLING SYSTEM & CAPACITY DATA—NOTES

①—Add 1 qt. with filter change unless otherwise noted.

②—Approximate. Make final check with dipstick.

③—C3 trans., 8 qts; C4 trans., 10 qts.

④—Exc. Sta. Wag., 13 gals.; Sta. Wag. 14 gals. Add 3½ gals. with auxiliary fuel tank.

⑤—Bobcat & Pinto, 2.8 pts.; Mustang, 3½ pts.

⑥—C3 trans., 8 qts.; C4 trans., 7¼ qts.

⑦—With 6¾″ ring gear Bobcat & Pinto, 2.2 pts.; Mustang, 3 pts.; units with 8 inch ring gear, 4 pts.

⑧—Add ½ qt. with filter change.

⑨—Bobcat & Pinto, 8.7 qts.; Mustang, 8.5 qts.

⑩—Bobcat & Pinto, 8.5 qts.; Mustang w/man. trans., 8.3 qts.; Mustang w/auto. trans., 8.8 qts.

⑪—C3, 8 qts.; C5, 11 qts.

⑫—Bobcat Calif. 11.7 gals.; Exc. Sta. Wag., 13 gals.; Sta. Wag., 14 gals. Add 3½ gals. with auxiliary fuel tank.

⑬—Bobcat & Pinto.

⑭—Mustang.

⑮—Man. trans., 8.3 qts.; Auto. trans., 8.8 qts.

⑯—Exc. Sta. Wag., 13 gals.; Sta. Wag., 14 gals.

⑰—C3 trans., 8 qts.; C4 trans., 7 qts.

⑱—6¾″ axle—Pinto & Bobcat 2.2 pts., Mustang, 3 pts., 8″ axle 4 pts.

⑲—Capri & Mustang.

⑳—Non-turbocharged.

㉑—Turbocharged.

㉒—Exc. Sta. Wag. & Calif. auto. trans. sedan, 13 gals.; Calif. auto. trans. sedan, 11.7 gals.; Sta. Wag., 14 gals.

㉓—6¾ inch axle, 2.5; 7½ inch axle, 3.5; 8 inch axle, 4.5.

㉔—C3, 8 qts.; C4, 6.7 qts.

㉕—Automatic transmission, 11.9 gal.

㉖—Dual sump oil. When draining oil, it is necessary to remove both drain plugs. One drain plug is located at front of oil pan. The second plug is located on left side of oil pan.

㉗—Less A/C, 13 psi.; with A/C, 16 psi.

㉘—6¾″ ring gear axle, 2.5 pts.; 7½″ ring gear axle, 3.5 pts.

㉙—C3, 8 qts.; C4 w/10¼ in. torque converter, 7.2 qts.; C4 w/12 in. torque converter, 9.6 qts.

㉚—Standard rear axle, 3.25 pts.; traction-lok rear axle, 3.55 pts.

Electrical Section

STARTER, REPLACE

1979–84 Capri & Mustang

1. Disconnect battery ground cable.
2. Raise and support front of vehicle.
3. On 1979–81 models with V8-255 engine, remove wishbone brace.
4. On 1981 models with 4-140 or 6-200 engine, remove starter heat shield.

NOTE: On models with 6-200 engine, remove heat shield by loosening lower starter attaching bolt and removing nut from stud.

5. On all models, disconnect starter cable from starter.
6. Remove starter motor attaching bolts and the starter.
7. Reverse procedure to install.

1977–78 Mustang & 1977–80 Bobcat & Pinto

1. Disconnect battery ground cable.
2. Raise vehicle and remove four bolts from crossmember under bell housing.

3. Remove flex coupling clamping screw from steering gear, then the three bolts attaching steering gear to crossmember.
4. Disconnect steering gear from flex coupling and pull gear down to gain access to starter.
5. Disconnect starter cable and remove three attaching bolts and starter.
6. Reverse procedure to install.

IGNITION LOCK, REPLACE

1980–84

1. Disconnect battery ground cable.
2. On 1981–84 models with tilt steering column, remove upper extension shroud. Unsnap shroud from retaining clip located at the 9 o'clock position.
3. On all models, remove trim shroud or shroud halves, then disconnect key warning switch electrical connector.
4. Place gear shift lever in PARK on models with automatic trans. or in any gear on models with manual trans.
5. Insert a ⅛ inch diameter pin in the hole in casting surrounding lock cylinder. Pull lock cylinder out of housing while depressing retaining pin.
6. To install, turn lock cylinder to RUN position and depress retaining pin.
7. Install lock cylinder into housing. Turn key to OFF position after checking that cylinder is fully seated and aligned in the interlocking washer.
8. Turn the key to check for proper operation in all positions.
9. Install trim shroud and extension shroud if applicable.
10. Reconnect battery ground cable.

1977–79

1. Disconnect battery ground cable.
2. Remove the steering wheel trim pad and the steering wheel. Insert a wire pin in the hole located inside the column halfway down the lock cylinder housing, Fig. 1.
3. Place the gear shift lever in PARK with auto. trans or in any gear (with manual trans. Turn the lock cylinder with the

ignition key to ON position.
4. Depress the wire while pulling up on the lock cylinder to remove. Remove the wire pin.
5. To install insert the lock cylinder into the housing in the flange casting, and turn the key to OFF position. This action will extend the cylinder retaining pin into the cylinder housing.
6. Turn the key to check for correct operation in all positions.
7. Install the steering wheel and trim pad. Reconnect the battery ground cable.

IGNITION SWITCH, REPLACE

1982–84 Capri & Mustang

Removal
1. Disconnect battery ground cable.
2. Remove steering column trim shroud.

NOTE: For tilt column only, remove upper extension shroud.

3. Disconnect electrical connector from switch, Fig. 2.
4. Rotate ignition key to On (Run) posi-

LOCK CYLINDER HOUSING

LOCK CYLINDER

PIN HOLE FOR CYLINDER RELEASE

LOCK
ACC.
OFF
RUN
START

LOCK CYLINDER OPERATING PATTERN

Fig. 1   Ignition lock

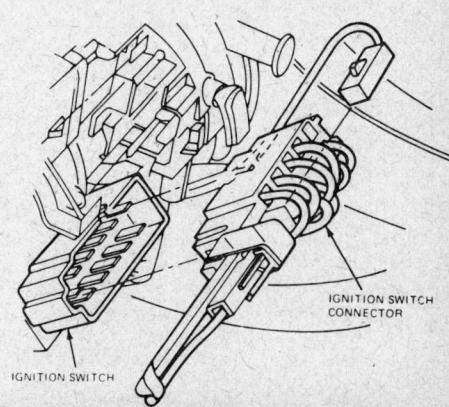

IGNITION SWITCH CONNECTOR

IGNITION SWITCH

Fig. 2   Ignition switch. 1979–84 Capri & Mustang

tion.

5. Drill out bolt heads securing switch to lock cylinder using a 1/8" twist drill. Remove bolts using an "Easy Out" or equivalent.
6. Disengage switch from the actuator pin.

Installation

1. Adjust switch by sliding the carrier to the switch On (Run) position.
2. Check to ensure that the ignition key lock cylinder is in the On (Run) position by rotating the key lock cylinder approximately 90 degrees from the Lock position.
3. Install switch onto the actuator pin.
4. Secure the switch with new break-off head bolts. Tighten bolts until heads shear.
5. Connect electrical connector to switch.
6. Install steering column trim shroud.

NOTE: For tilt column only, install upper extension shroud.

7. Connect battery ground cable.
8. Check for proper operation.

1979–81 Capri & Mustang

Removal
1. Disconnect battery ground cable.
2. Rotate ignition key to "Lock" position.
3. Remove steering column trim shroud.
4. Using a 1/8 inch twist drill, drill out the bolt heads securing the switch to the lock cylinder. Then, remove the bolts using an "Easy Out" or equivalent, Fig. 2.
5. Disengage the actuator rod from switch.
6. Disconnect electrical connector from switch.
7. Remove switch from vehicle.

Installation
1. With ignition key in "Lock" position, place switch on actuator rod.
2. Secure the switch with two new "Break-Off Head" bolts. Tighten the bolts until the heads shear.
3. Remove the locking pin from new switch, if installed.
4. Connect switch electrical connector.
5. Connect battery ground cable.
6. Check for proper operation.

Exc. 1979–84 Capri & Mustang

1. Remove shrouding from steering column and detach and lower steering column from brake support bracket.
2. Disconnect battery ground cable.
3. Disconnect switch wiring at plug, Fig. 3.
4. Remove two nuts that retain switch to column.
5. Lift switch vertically upward to disengage actuator rod from switch.
6. To install switch, both the locking mechanism at top of column and the switch must be in LOCK position for correct adjustment.
7. Move shift lever into PARK (with automatic transmission) or REVERSE (with manual transmission), turn the key to LOCK position and remove the key.

NOTE: *New switches, when received, are already pinned in LOCK position by a plastic shipping pin inserted in a locking hole on top of switch.*

8. Position the hole in the end of switch plunger to the hole in the actuator and install the connecting pin.
9. Position switch on column and install retaining nuts, but do not tighten them.
10. Move switch up and down along column to locate the mid-position of rod lash and then tighten nuts.
11. Remove the plastic or substitute locking pin, connect battery and check switch for proper start in PARK or NEUTRAL.

STOP LIGHT SWITCH, REPLACE

1. Disconnect wires at connector.
2. Remove hairpin retainer, slide switch, push rod and nylon washers and bushing away from the pedal and remove the switch, Fig. 4.
3. Reverse procedure to install.

NEUTRAL SAFETY, SWITCH, REPLACE

Removal
1. Remove downshift linkage rod from transmission downshift lever.
2. Remove downshift outer lever retaining nut and lever.
3. Remove two switch attaching bolts.
4. Disconnect wire connector and remove switch.

Installation
1. Install switch on transmission and replace attaching bolts.
2. With transmission manual lever in neutral, rotate switch and install gauge pin (No. 43 drill) into gauge pin hole, Fig. 5.
3. Tighten switch attaching bolts and remove gauge pin.
4. Install outer downshift lever and attaching nut.
5. Install downshift linkage rod to downshift lever.
6. Install switch wire connector and check operation of switch. The engine should start only with lever in NEUTRAL or PARK.

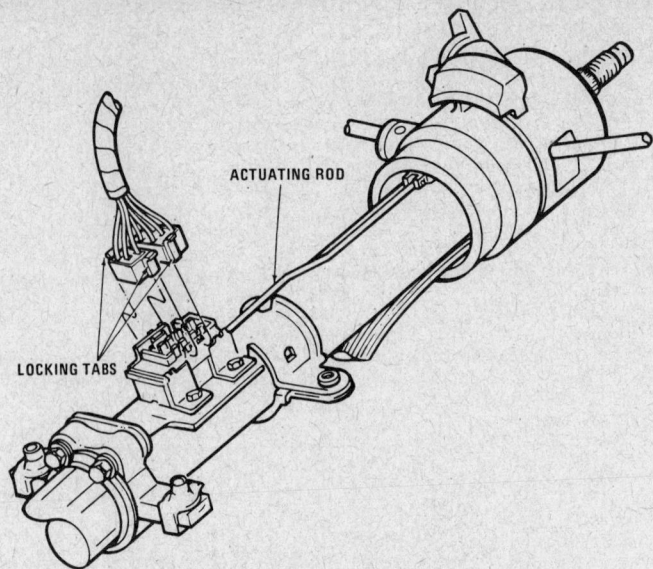

Fig. 3   Ignition switch installation. 1977–80 Bobcat & Pinto & 1977–78 Mustang

LIGHT SWITCH, REPLACE

1977–84 Mustang, 1980 Bobcat & Pinto, 1979–84 Capri

1. Disconnect battery ground cable.
2. Depress shaft release button by inserting a screwdriver through hole in underside of instrument panel, then remove knob and shaft.
3. Remove bezel nut, lower switch, disconnect electrical connector and remove switch.

1977–79 Bobcat & Pinto

1. Disconnect battery ground cable.
2. Remove instrument cluster as described further on.
3. Remove headlight switch knob and shaft assembly and retaining nut.
4. Disconnect connector plug from switch and remove switch from cluster opening.
5. Reverse procedure to install.

TURN SIGNAL SWITCH, REPLACE

1979–84 Capri & Mustang

1. Disconnect battery ground cable.
2. On models with tilt column, remove upper extension shroud by unsnapping shroud retaining clips at the 9 o'clock position.
3. Remove five attaching screws, then separate and remove two trim shroud halves.
4. Grasp turn signal switch lever by grasping and using a twisting pulling motion while pulling lever outward.
5. Peel back foam shield from turn signal switch, then disconnect two turn signal switch electrical connectors.
6. Remove two screws attaching turn signal switch to lock housing, then disengage switch from housing and remove.
7. Reverse procedure to install.

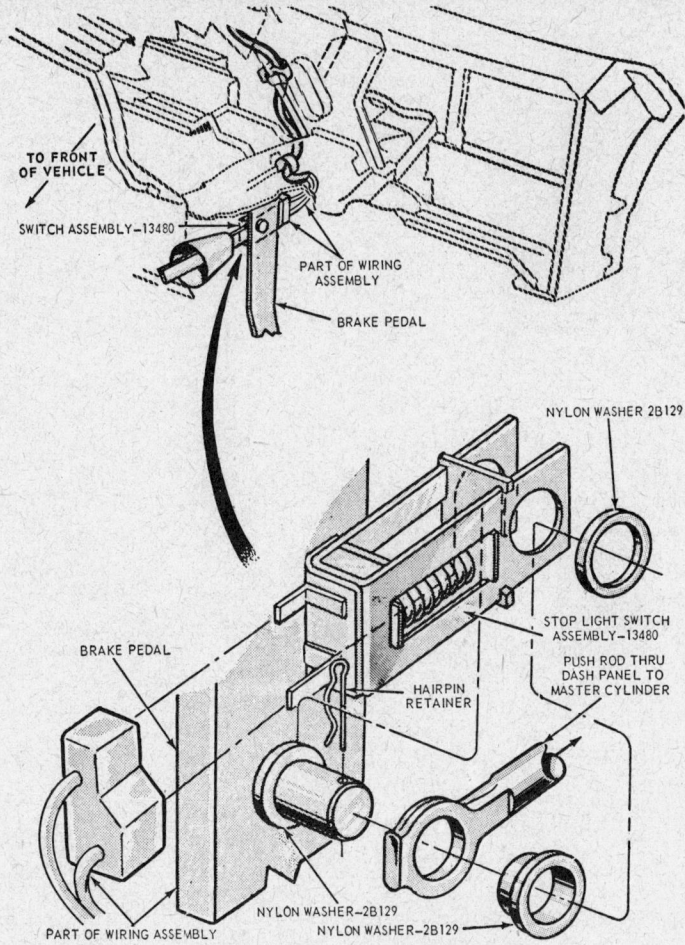

Fig. 4 Stoplight switch installation.

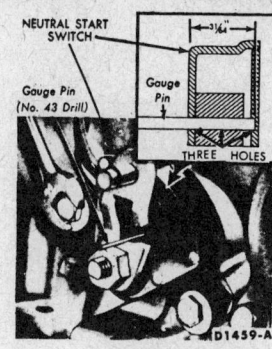

Fig. 5 Neutral safety switch adjustment. C4 units

2. Loosen forward steering column attaching nuts one or two turns.
3. Loosen rearward steering column attaching nuts 3/8 to 1/2 inch.
4. Disconnect wire connectors at printed circuit board and tachometer.
5. Disconnect speedometer cable.
6. Remove four cluster attaching screws and pull cluster out along angle of steering column, Fig. 7.

Auxiliary Cluster

1. Remove main cluster as described above.
2. Remove two screws attaching auxiliary cluster to instrument panel.
3. Remove auxiliary cluster mask from front of instrument panel.
4. Disconnect wire connector from printed circuit board, then remove auxiliary cluster through access provided by removal of main instrument cluster.

1977–78 Mustang

1. Disconnect battery ground cable.
2. On all models, remove instrument cluster trim cover.
3. Disconnect speedometer cable by pressing on flat section of quick disconnect.
4. Remove cluster retaining screws, pull cluster from instrument panel, disconnect electrical connectors, then remove cluster, Fig. 8.

WINDSHIELD WIPER MOTOR, REPLACE

1981–84

1. Disconnect battery ground cable, then remove right hand wiper arm and blade assembly.
2. Remove cowl grille, then remove clip and disconnect linkage drive arm from motor crank pin.
3. Disconnect wiper motor wire connector, then remove three motor attaching screws and pull motor through opening.
4. Reverse procedure to install.

1977–80

1. Loosen two nuts and disconnect wiper pivot shaft and link from the motor drive arm ball, on Bobcat and Pinto models. A link retaining clip is used on Capri & Mustang models.
2. Remove three motor attaching screws and lower motor away from under the left side of the instrument panel.

1977–78 Mustang & 1977–80 Bobcat & Pinto

1. Disconnect battery ground cable.
2. Remove steering wheel.
3. Unscrew turn signal switch lever from column.
4. Remove shroud from under steering column.
5. Disconnect steering column wiring connector plugs from bracket.
6. Remove turn signal switch attaching screws.
7. Remove plastic cover sleeve from wiring harness.
8. Pull switch and wiring up from steering columns.
9. Reverse procedure to install.

HORN SOUNDER, REPLACE

1979–84 Capri & Mustang

1. Disconnect battery ground cable, then remove steering column cover attaching screws and steering column cover.
2. With wire connectors exposed, carefully lift connector retaining tabs and disconnect connectors.
3. Remove switch attaching screws and the switch.
4. Reverse procedure to install.

1977–78 Mustang & 1977–80 Bobcat & Pinto

The horn sounder can be removed by depressing it and turning counter-clockwise or by removing retaining screws from under steering wheel spokes.

INSTRUMENT CLUSTER, REPLACE

1979–84 Capri & Mustang

1. Disconnect battery ground cable.
2. Remove three upper retaining screws from instrument cluster trim cover, then the trim cover.
3. Remove upper and lower screws retaining instrument cluster to instrument panel.
4. Pull cluster from panel slightly and disconnect speedometer cable and the printed circuit electrical connectors.
5. Remove instrument clusters from instrument panel, Fig. 6.
6. Reverse procedure to install.

1977–80 Bobcat & Pinto

Main Cluster

1. Remove two screws attaching upper half to lower half of steering column shroud, then remove lower half shroud.

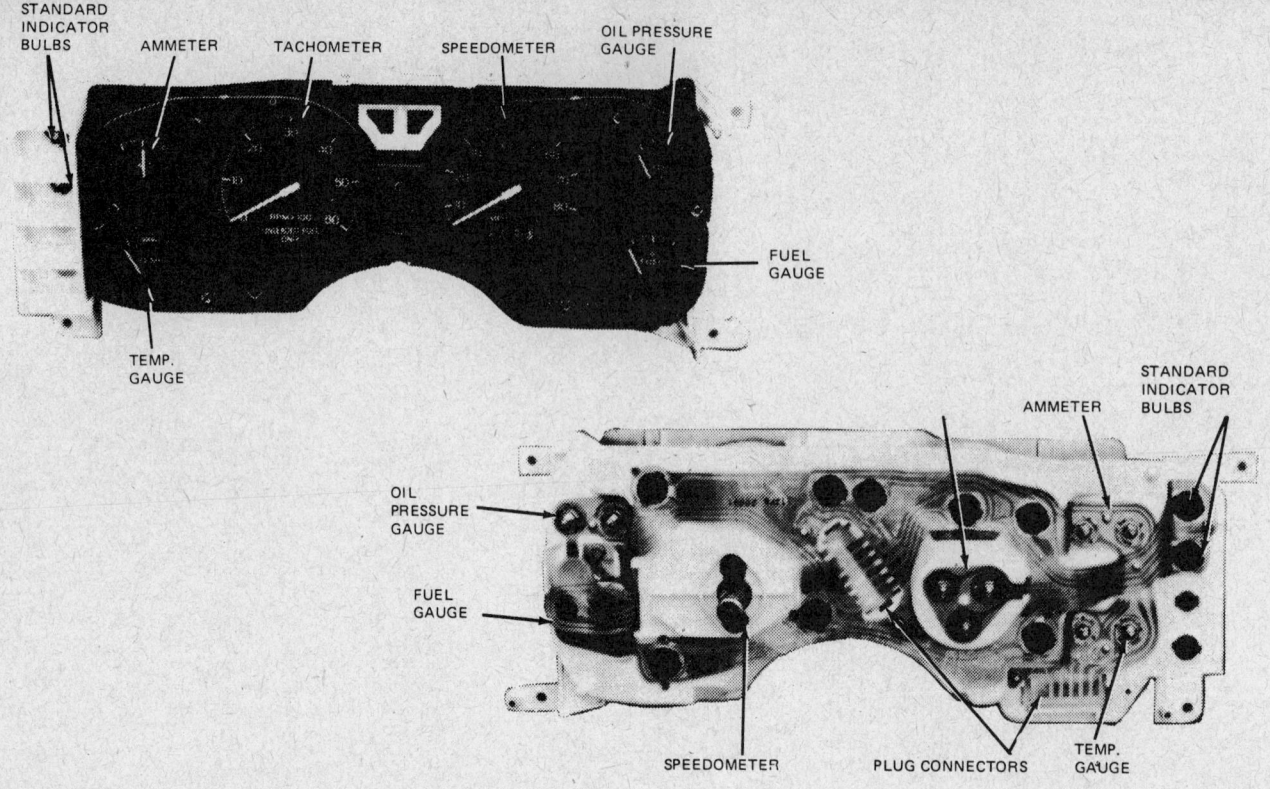

Fig. 6   Instrument cluster (Typical) 1979—84 Capri & Mustang

3. Disconnect wiper motor wires and remove motor.

WINDSHIELD WIPER TRANSMISSION, REPLACE

1981—84 Capri & Mustang

1. Disconnect battery ground cable, then remove right wiper arm and blade assembly from pivot shaft.
2. Remove cowl grille, then remove clip and disconnect linkage drive arm from wiper motor crank pin.
3. Remove two screws retaining right hand pivot shaft to cowl and large nut and spacer from left pivot shaft, then remove linkage assembly.
4. Reverse procedure to install.

1979—80 Capri & Mustang

1. Remove wiper motor and linkage cover for access to linkage.
2. Disconnect linkage drive arm from motor crank pin by removing the clip.
3. Remove bolts retaining right pivot shaft and the nut retaining left pivot shaft.
4. Remove assembly from vehicle.
5. Reverse procedure to install.

1979—80 Bobcat & Pinto

1. Disconnect battery ground cable, then remove wiper arms and blades from pivot shafts.

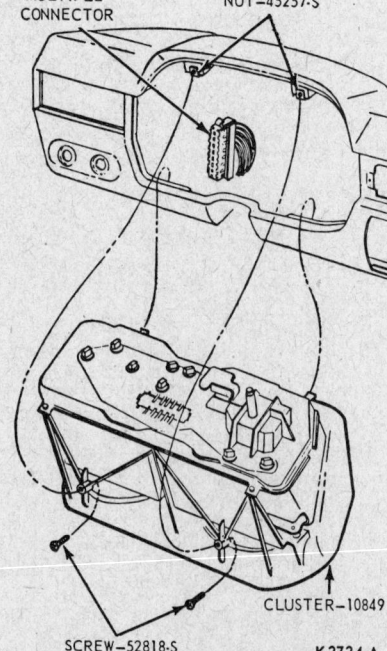

Fig. 7   Instrument-cluster removal (Typical). 1977—80 Bobcat & Pinto

2. Remove heater control cover from instrument panel to floor brace, then remove brace.
3. Remove glove box and door, trim panel located below glove box, floor heat distribution duct and center register.
4. Remove two wiring loom retainer attaching screws and pull wiring loom down and out of way.
5. Remove A/C defroster air distribution duct.
6. Loosen two nuts retaining wiper pivot shaft and link assembly to motor drive arm ball, then remove screws attaching both pivots.
7. Remove pivot shaft and link assembly from under left side of instrument panel.
8. Reverse procedure to install. Apply a 3/16 in. bead of sealer around each screw and main pivot stem before installing gasket.

1977—78 Bobcat, Mustang & Pinto

NOTE: On Bobcat & Pinto models equipped with air conditioning, remove blower motor to gain access to wiper transmission as described further on in this chapter.

1. Remove wiper arms and blades from pivot shafts.
2. Loosen two nuts retaining wiper pivot shaft and link assembly to the motor drive arm ball.
3. Remove three screws attaching each pivot shaft and remove assembly from under left side of instrument panel.

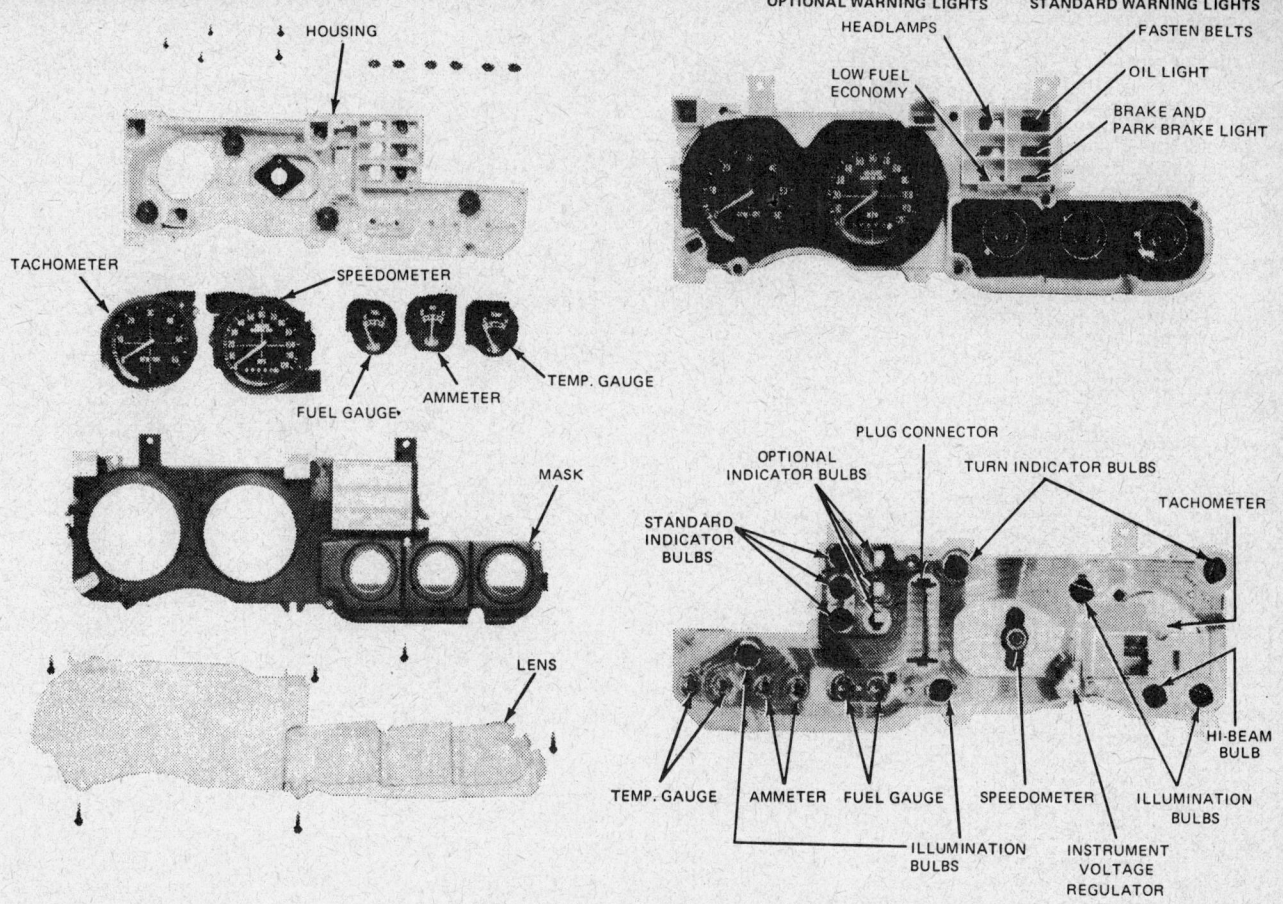

Fig. 8 Instrument cluster (Typical). 1977–78 Mustang

WINDSHIELD WIPER SWITCH, REPLACE

1979–84 Capri & Mustang

1. Disconnect battery ground cable.
2. Remove steering column shroud attaching screws and the shroud.
3. Disconnect electrical connector from wiper switch.
4. Remove wiper switch attaching screws and the switch.
5. Reverse procedure to install.

1977–78 Mustang

Dash Mounted Switch
1. Disconnect battery ground cable.
2. Remove switch knob and bezel nut, pull switch from panel, disconnect electrical connector and remove switch.

Column Mounted Switch
1. Disconnect battery ground cable.
2. Disconnect turn signal and wiper/washer switch wiring connector.
3. Remove lower instrument panel shield.
4. Pull wiring cover from bottom on column and remove cover.
5. With a screwdriver, disengage wiring shield tang and pry shield to remove.
6. Remove screw securing turn signal and wiper/washer switch assembly to column, then remove the assembly.

1977–80 Bobcat & Pinto

1. Remove instrument cluster as outlined previously.
2. Insert a thin bladed screwdriver into the slot in the switch knob and depress the spring. Then pull the knob from the switch shaft.
3. Remove wiper switch bezel nut. Then unplug wires and remove switch.

REAR WIPER MOTOR & LINKAGE, REPLACE

1979–82 Mustang & Capri

1. Disconnect battery ground cable.
2. Remove wiper arm and blade assembly.
3. Remove pivot shaft attaching nut and spacers.
4. Remove liftgate inner trim panel.
5. Disconnect electrical connector from wiper motor.
6. Remove 3 motor bracket attaching screws
7. Remove motor, bracket and linkage assembly from vehicle.
8. Reverse procedure to install.

REAR WIPER SWITCH, REPLACE

1979–82 Mustang & Capri

1. Disconnect battery ground cable.

2. Remove wiper switch knob.
3. Remove 2 bezel attaching screws, then pull switch retainer away from instrument panel.
4. Remove switch retaining nut and separate switch from retainer.
5. Disconnect electrical connector from switch and remove switch from vehicle.
6. Reverse procedure to install.

RADIO, REPLACE

NOTE: When installing radio, be sure to adjust antenna trimmer for peak performance.

1979–84 Capri & Mustang

1. Disconnect battery ground cable.
2. On 1982–84 models with console, remove console as follows:
   a. Remove gear shift lever opening plate. Lift plate up at front end and disengage from clip.
   b. Remove console panel moulding from center of console.
   c. Remove front ash tray.
   d. Remove 2 console-to-floor pan attaching screws located under the ash tray.

e. Open console storage compartment door and remove 4 console-to-floor pan attaching screws.
f. Disconnect all electrical connectors from console, then remove console from vehicle.
3. On all models, disconnect all electrical connectors from radio.
4. Remove control knobs, discs, control shaft nuts and washers.
5. Remove ash tray and bracket.
6. Remove radio rear support attaching nut.
7. Remove instrument panel lower reinforcement.
8. Remove A/C or heater floor ducts.
9. Remove radio from bezel and rear support, then lower from instrument panel.
10. Reverse procedure to install.

1977–78 Mustang

1. Disconnect battery ground cable.
2. Remove radio knobs, discs, shaft nuts and washers. Remove ash tray.
3. Remove radio rear support to instrument panel nut.
4. Lower radio, disconnect wiring and remove radio.

1977–80 Bobcat & Pinto

1. Disconnect battery ground cable.
2. Remove instrument panel trim brace cover.
3. Remove rear support to radio attaching bolt.
4. Remove four screws attaching the bezel to the instrument panel opening.
5. Pull radio out from instrument panel and disconnect speaker, power and antenna wires and remove radio.

HEATER CORE, REPLACE

Less Air Conditioning

1979–84 Capri & Mustang
1. Drain cooling system and disconnect battery ground cable.
2. Disconnect heater hoses from heater core and plug core openings.
3. Remove glove box liner.
4. Remove instrument panel to cowl brace retaining screws and the brace.
5. Move temperature control lever to warm position.
6. Remove the four heater core cover retaining screws, then the cover through the glove box opening.
7. Remove heater core assembly mounting stud nuts from engine compartment.
8. Push core tubes and seal toward passenger compartment to loosen core from case assembly.
9. Remove heater core from case through the glove box opening, Fig. 9.
10. Reverse procedure to install.

Exc. 1979–84 Capri & Mustang
1. Drain coolant and disconnect battery.
2. Disconnect blower motor ground wire at engine side of dash.
3. Disconnect heater hoses at engine block.
4. Remove four heater assembly-to-dash mounting nuts from the engine side of the dash.
5. Remove the glove box.
6. Disconnect control cables from heater.

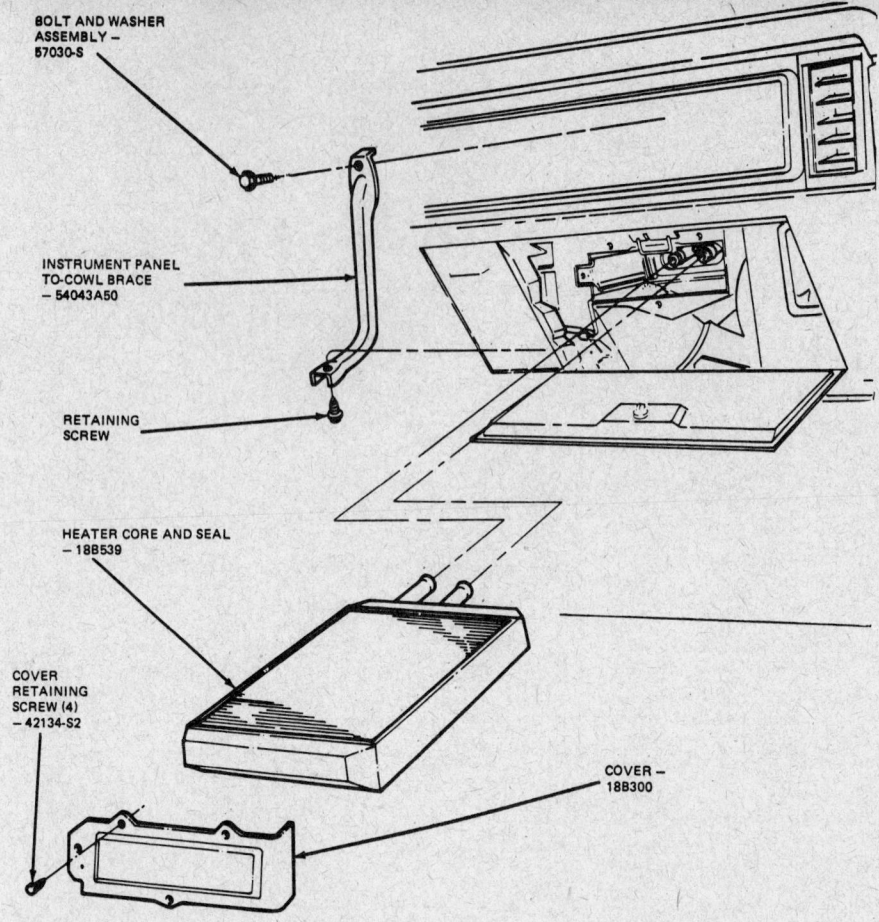

BOLT AND WASHER ASSEMBLY – 57030-S

INSTRUMENT PANEL TO-COWL BRACE – 54043A50

RETAINING SCREW

HEATER CORE AND SEAL – 18B539

COVER RETAINING SCREW (4) – 42134-S2

COVER – 18B300

Fig. 9 Heater core replacement. 1979–84 Capri & Mustang less A/C

Remove mounting bracket clips and disconnect cables from door crank arms.
7. Remove radio as outlined previously.
8. Working inside car, remove snap rivet that attaches the forward side of the defroster air duct to the plenum chamber. Move the air duct back into the defroster nozzle to disengage it from the tabs on the plenum chamber. Now, tilt the forward edge of the duct up and forward to disengage it from the nozzle and remove it from the left side of the heater assembly.
9. Remove heater case-to-instrument panel support bracket mounting screw and remove the heater case. At the same time, pull the two heater hoses in through the dash panel. Then disconnect the hoses from the heater core in the case.
10. Remove compression gasket from cowl air inlet.
11. Remove eleven clips from around the front and rear case flanges and separate the front and rear halves of the case, Fig. 10.
12. Lift heater core from front half of case.

With Air Conditioning

1979–84 Capri & Mustang
1. Disconnect battery ground cable.
2. Remove screws securing the left side of instrument panel pad retaining tabs to the instrument panel, in the upper right and left corners of the instrument panel cluster area.
3. Remove screws securing the right side of instrument panel pad retaining tabs to instrument panel, located in the two

openings at the top edge of the right instrument panel trim applique, above the glove box.
4. Remove screws securing leading edge of instrument panel pad to defroster openings. Use a magnetic or locking tang type phillips screwdriver. Do not let screws drop into defroster openings since plenum door damage may result.
5. Raise the overhanging edge of the instrument panel pad to clear retaining tabs and pull pad rearward to remove from top of instrument panel.
6. Remove screws attaching steering column opening lower cover to instrument panel, then the cover.
7. Remove steering column trim shrouds.
8. Remove nuts securing steering column to brake pedal support and lower steering column for access to gearshift selector lever and cable assembly.
9. Reach between steering column and instrument panel and lift selector lever cable off selector lever. Then, remove cable clamp from steering column tube.
10. Rest steering column on front seat.
11. Remove screw attaching instrument panel to brake pedal support at steering column opening.
12. Remove screw attaching lower brace to lower edge of instrument panel, below the radio.
13. Remove screw attaching brace to lower edge of instrument panel.
14. Disconnect temperature control cable from temperature blend door and evaporator case bracket.
15. Disconnect seven-port vacuum hose con-

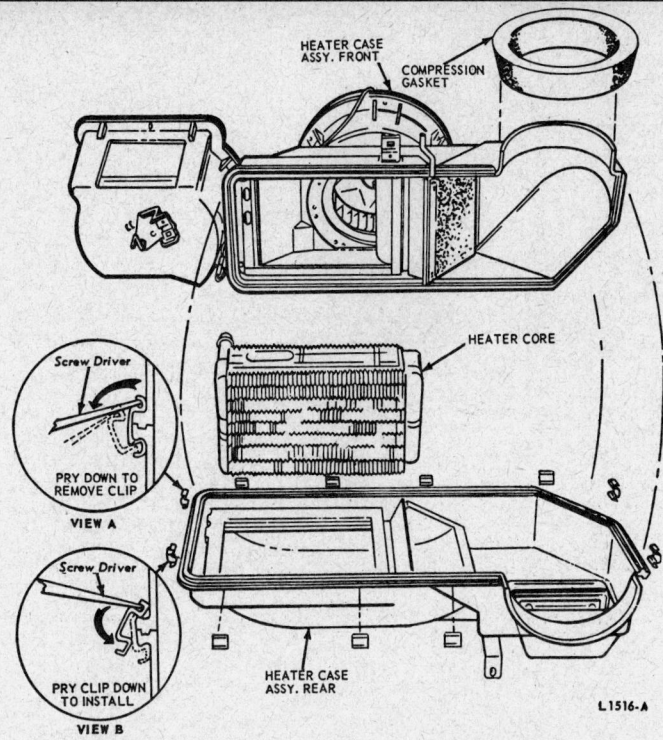

Fig. 10   Heater core removal 1977–78 Mustang & 1977–80 Bobcat & Pinto less A/C

nectors at evaporator case.

16. Disconnect blower resistor wire connector from resistor and the blower motor feed wire at in-line connector near the blower resistor wire connector.
17. Support instrument panel and remove three screws securing top of instrument panel to the cowl.
18. Remove screw at each side of instrument panel securing instrument panel to cowl side panels.
19. Move instrument panel rearward and disconnect speedometer cable and any wiring that will not permit the panel to lay on the front seat.
21. Drain cooling system.
22. On 1979–81 models, proceed as follows:
    a. Disconnect hoses from heater core.

Cover hoses and heater core tubes to prevent leakage.
    b. Remove 2 nuts securing evaporator case to dash panel from engine compartment.
    c. Working in passenger compartment, remove screws attaching evaporator case support bracket and air inlet duct support bracket to cowl top panel.
    d. Remove nut retaining bracket at left end of evaporator case to dash panel and nut securing bracket below case to dash panel.
    e. Pull evaporator case assembly from dash panel to gain access to heater core access cover-to-evaporator case attaching screws.
23. On 1982–84 models, proceed as follows:

a. Discharge refrigerant from A/C system at the service valve on suction line. When system is fully discharged, disconnect and cap high and low pressure lines.
b. Disconnect hoses from heater core. Cover hoses and heater core tubes to prevent leakage.
c. Remove screw securing air inlet duct and blower housing assembly support brace to cowl top panel.
d. Disconnect black vacuum supply hose from in-line check valve in engine compartment.
e. Disconnect blower motor electrical connectors from harness.
f. Disconnect electrical connector from blower motor resistor.
g. Remove 2 evaporator case-to-dash panel attaching nuts from engine compartment.
h. Working in passenger compartment, remove 2 evaporator case support bracket-to-cowl top panel attaching screws.
i. Remove screw securing bracket below evaporator case to dash panel.
j. Carefully remove evaporator case assembly from vehicle.
24. On all models, remove 5 heater core access cover attaching screws and the access cover.
25. Remove heater core and seals from evaporator case.
26. Remove the 2 seals from heater core tubes.
27. Reverse procedure to install.

1977–78 Mustang

1. Disconnect battery ground cable and remove the battery.
2. Drain cooling system and discharge A/C refrigerant system.
3. Remove instrument panel pad.
4. Remove radio speaker assembly.
5. Remove both "A" pillar mouldings.
6. Remove both side kick panel pad assemblies.
7. Remove the lower steering column cover.
8. Remove the steering column to cowl panel shake brace.
9. Remove accelerator pedal assembly and disconnect the two cables.
10. Remove the bottom bolt retaining center shake brace to instrument panel assembly.
11. Disconnect antenna lead from radio.
12. Disconnect the five connectors at the left cowl panel.
13. Disconnect electrical connector from wiper switch.
14. Disconnect the five connectors from the right cowl panel.
15. Disconnect electrical connector from dimmer switch assembly.
16. Disconnect the heater blower motor resistor.
17. Disconnect temperature control cable.
18. Remove the two evaporator to upper cowl bracket screws.
19. Disconnect the main wiring harness in the engine compartment and push the connectors into the passenger compartment.
20. Disconnect the three remaining connectors and push the connectors into the passenger compartment.
21. Disconnect the turn signal switch assembly.
22. Lower the steering column.
23. Disconnect electrical connectors from ignition switch.
24. Disconnect electrical connector from stop light switch assembly.

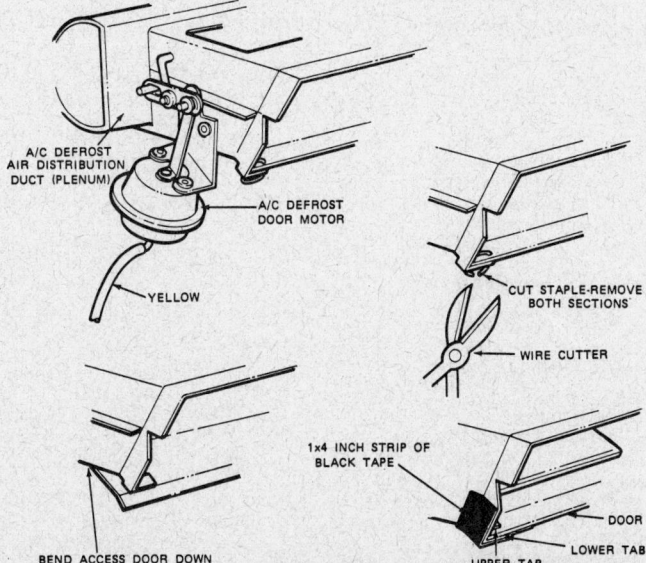

Fig. 11   A/C defrost air distribution duct fold down door. 1977–80 Bobcat & Pinto

25. Remove instrument panel to steering column center support bracket.
26. Remove instrument panel retaining bolts and the instrument panel.
27. Disconnect heater hoses from heater core.
28. Remove the two screws attaching evaporator manifold plate to expansion valve body.
29. Separate expansion valve body and STV housing manifold from evaporator manifold plate.
30. Remove four nuts retaining evaporator to dash panel and the evaporator assembly.
31. Remove the eight upper to lower case attaching screws.
32. Remove rubber seal from heater core tubes.
33. Remove upper half from evaporator case.
34. Remove air deflector mounting screw on lower case to left of heater core, then the air deflector and heater core.
35. Reverse procedure to install.

1977–80 Bobcat & Pinto
1. Disconnect battery ground cable, drain radiator and discharge refrigerant from A/C system.
2. Remove refrigerant lines and the front half of refrigerant manifold.

NOTE: Remove manifold mounting stud to ensure clearance for removal of evaporator case.

3. Disconnect heater hoses from core tubes and remove condensation drain hose in engine compartment.
4. Remove glove box.
5. Disconnect vacuum hoses from evaporator case and temperature control cable from blend door crank arm.
6. Remove heat distribution duct.
7. Remove staples retaining fold down door on plenum, Fig. 11. Bend fold down door from locating tabs on plenum and remove adapter duct.

NOTE: During installation, position fold down door between locating tabs and tape in place with two pieces of black tape, Fig. 11.

8. Remove blower motor and wheel from blower scroll.
9. Install a 1/4-20 hex washer head screw in mounting tab of inlet duct to upper cowl bracket, holding inlet duct in place.

NOTE: Leave screw in position during installation of case assembly.

10. Remove inlet duct to evaporator case screws.

NOTE: One upper case to inlet duct screw is located under outside-recirc. motor mounting bracket.

11. Remove evaporator to cowl bracket screws and the evaporator to dash panel nuts in engine compartment. Rotate evaporator down and away from instrument panel and remove from under panel.
12. Remove upper to lower case screws and rubber seal from heater core tubes.
13. Remove upper half of evaporator case and

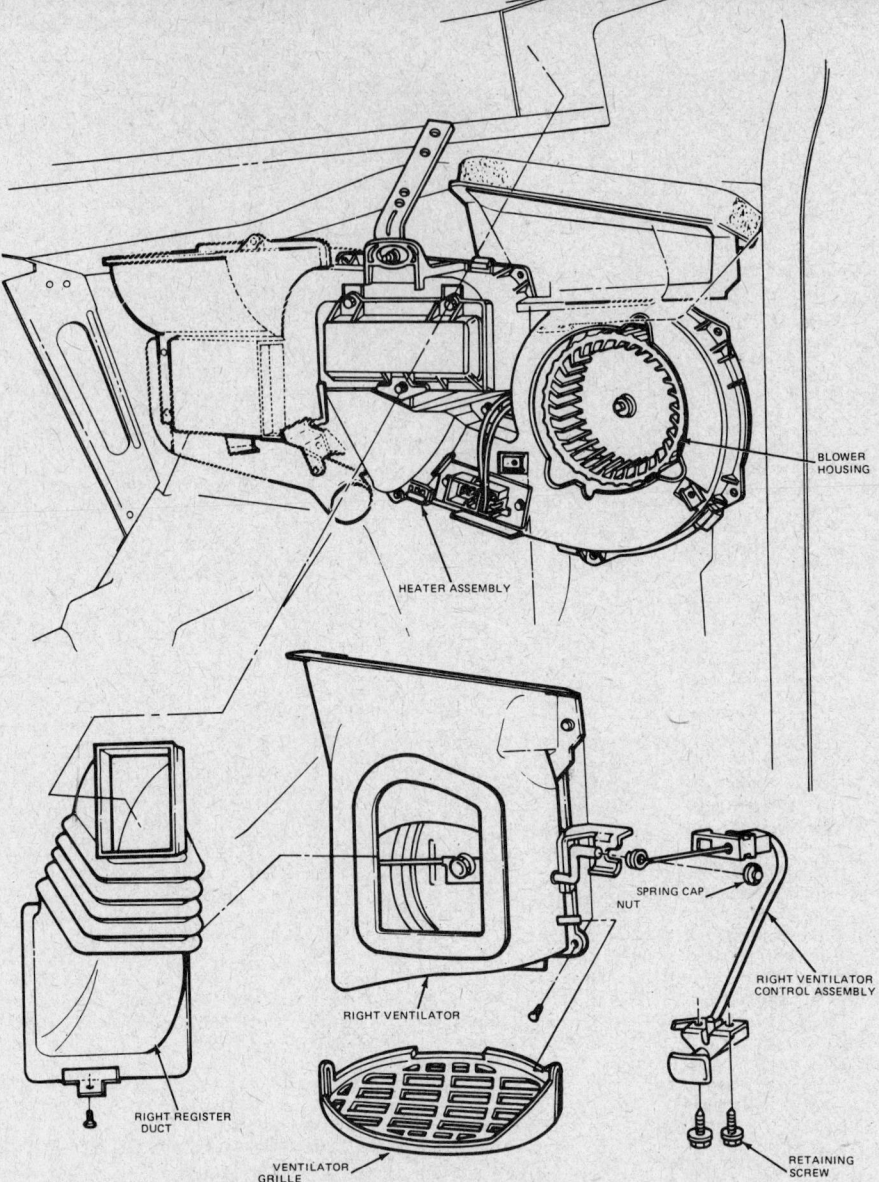

move rubber seal on evaporator core forward and pull evaporator core from lower case.
14. Remove heater core upper straps, air deflector mounting screw, then remove air deflector and heater core.

BLOWER MOTOR, REPLACE

Less Air Conditioning

1979–84 Capri & Mustang
1. Disconnect battery ground cable.
2. Remove right ventilator assembly as follows:
   a. Remove screw securing right register duct to lower edge of instrument panel, Fig. 12.
   b. Remove 2 screws securing ventilator control cable lever assembly to lower edge of instrument panel.
   c. Remove glove compartment liner to gain access to upper left ventilator attaching screw.
   d. Remove 2 plastic rivets securing grille to ventilator floor outlet opening. Remove grille from bottom of ventilator assembly to gain access to lower right ventilator assembly attaching screw.
   e. Remove right register duct and register assembly to gain access to upper right ventilator attaching screw.
   f. Remove 4 screws securing ventilator assembly to blower housing section of heater case.
   g. Move ventilator assembly to the right and down and remove from under instrument panel.
   h. Remove push nut from door crank arm.
   i. Remove control cable snap lock tab and the control cable assembly from ventilator assembly.
3. On 1979–81 models, remove blower motor as follows:

Fig. 12 Right ventilator assembly removal. 1979–84 Capri & Mustang less A/C

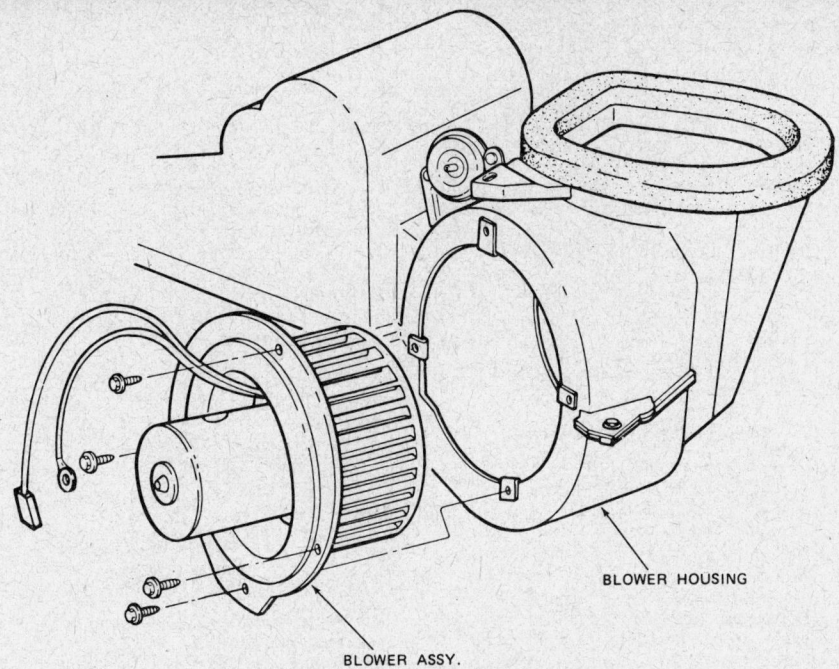

BLOWER HOUSING

BLOWER ASSY.

Fig. 13 Blower motor. (Typical)

a. Disconnect blower motor electrical connector from spade terminal of resistor assembly and push back through hole in case.
b. Remove right side trim panel to gain access to blower ground lug, then remove ground terminal lug attaching screw.
c. Remove blower motor flange attaching screws from inside blower housing.
d. Remove blower motor from housing.
4. On 1982–84 models, remove blower motor as follows:
   a. Remove hub clamp spring from blower wheel hub.
   b. Remove blower wheel from shaft.
   c. Remove blower motor flange attaching screws from inside blower housing.
   d. Slide blower motor out of housing and disconnect electrical connectors from motor.
   e. Remove blower motor from vehicle.
5. Reverse procedure to install.

Exc. 1979–84 Capri & Mustang
1. Follow procedure to remove the heater core as described previously.
2. Disconnect the blower motor lead wire (orange) from the resistor.
3. Remove the four blower mounting plate nuts and remove the motor and wheel assembly, Fig. 13.
4. Reverse procedure to install.

With Air Conditioning

1979–84 Capri & Mustang
1. Disconnect battery ground cable.
2. Remove glove box and disconnect hose from outside-recirculation door vacuum motor.
3. Remove instrument panel lower right to side cowl attaching bolt.
4. Remove screw attaching support brace to top of air inlet duct.
5. Disconnect blower motor feed wire at connector.
6. Remove nut retaining blower housing lower support bracket to evaporator case.
7. Remove side cowl trim panel.
8. Remove blower motor ground wire

screw.
9. Remove screw attaching top of air inlet duct to evaporator case.
10. Pull air inlet duct and blower housing assembly downward and away from evaporator case.
11. Remove four blower motor mounting plate screws, then the blower motor assembly from blower housing.

NOTE: Do not remove mounting plate from motor.

12. Reverse procedure to install.

Exc. 1979–84 Capri & Mustang
1. Remove glove box.
2. Remove four screws retaining blower motor and wheel to blower scroll.
3. Remove blower motor and wheel assembly.

NOTE: On 1977–80 models, it may be necessary to remove bolt securing instrument panel to right side cowl and pull instrument panel rearward to provide clearance for blower motor removal.

SPEED CONTROL

Bead Chain Adjustment

Adjust bead chain to obtain a taut chain with the engine at hot idle. The adjustment should be made as to remove as much slack as possible from the bead chain without restricting the carburetor lever from returning to idle. On vehicles equipped with a solenoid throttle positioner, perform adjustment with throttle positioner deactivated.

Actuator Cable Adjustment

1. Deactivate the throttle positioner.
2. Set carburetor at hot idle.
3. Pull the actuator cable to remove slack.
4. While maintaining light tension on the actuator cable, insert the cable retaining clip.

Vacuum Dump Valve

The vacuum dump valve is mounted on a moveable mounting bracket. The valve should be adjusted so that it is closed when the brake pedal is not depressed and opens when the brake pedal is depressed.

2300 cc Engine Section

NOTE: This U.S. built engine is designed to metric specifications and therefore metric tooling will be required.

ENGINE MOUNTS, REPLACE

1979—84 Capri & Mustang

1. Support engine using a wood block and jack placed under the engine.
2. Remove fan shroud, if necessary.
3. Remove screw attaching fuel pump shield to left hand support bracket, if so equipped.
4. Remove nut and washer assemblies attaching both insulators to the crossmember, Figs. 1 and 1A.
5. Disconnect transmission shift linkage.
6. Raise engine sufficiently to clear the insulator studs from the crossmember.
7. Remove bolts attaching insulator and bracket assembly from engine and remove insulator and bracket assembly.
8. Reverse procedure to install. Torque insulator and bracket assembly to 33–45 ft. lbs. Torque crossmember nut assemblies onto insulator studs to 70–100 ft. lbs.

1977—80 Bobcat & Pinto
1977—78 Mustang

1. Remove fan shroud screws and support engine with a suitable jack and place a piece of wood under oil pan.
2. Remove insulator to support bracket through bolt, Figs. 2 and 2A.
3. Remove support bracket mounting bolts, raise engine slightly, then remove support bracket.
4. Remove insulator to engine block bolts and insulator.
5. Reverse procedure to install.

ENGINE, REPLACE

1. Raise hood and secure in vertical position.
2. Drain coolant from radiator and oil from crankcase.
3. Remove air cleaner and exhaust manifold shroud.
4. Disconnect battery ground cable.
5. Remove radiator hoses and remove radiator and fan.
6. Disconnect heater hoses from water pump and carburetor choke fitting.
7. Disconnect wires from alternator and starter and disconnect accelerator cable from carburetor. On A/C vehicles, remove compressor from bracket and position it out of way with lines attached.
8. Disconnect flex fuel line from tank line and plug tank line.
9. Disconnect primary wire at coil and disconnect oil pressure and temperature sending unit wires at sending units.
10. Remove starter and raise vehicle to remove the flywheel or converter housing upper attaching bolts.
11. Disconnect inlet pipe at exhaust manifold. Disconnect engine mounts at underbody bracket and remove flywheel or converter housing cover.
12. On vehicle with manual shift, remove flywheel housing lower attaching bolts.
13. On vehicle with automatic transmission, disconnect converter from flywheel and remove converter housing lower attaching bolts. Disconnect transmission oil cooler lines if attached to engine at pan rail.
14. Lower vehicle and support transmission and flywheel or converter housing with a jack.
15. Attach engine lifting hooks to brackets and carefully lift engine out of engine compartment.

CYLINDER HEAD, REPLACE

1. Drain cooling system, then remove air cleaner assembly.
2. Remove heater hose-to-rocker arm cover retaining screw.
3. Remove distributor cap and ignition wires.
4. Remove spark plugs.
5. Disconnect all vacuum hoses necessary for cylinder head removal
6. Remove engine oil dipstick.
7. Remove rocker arm cover attaching bolts and the cover.
8. Remove intake manifold attaching bolts, then the intake manifold and carburetor as an assembly.

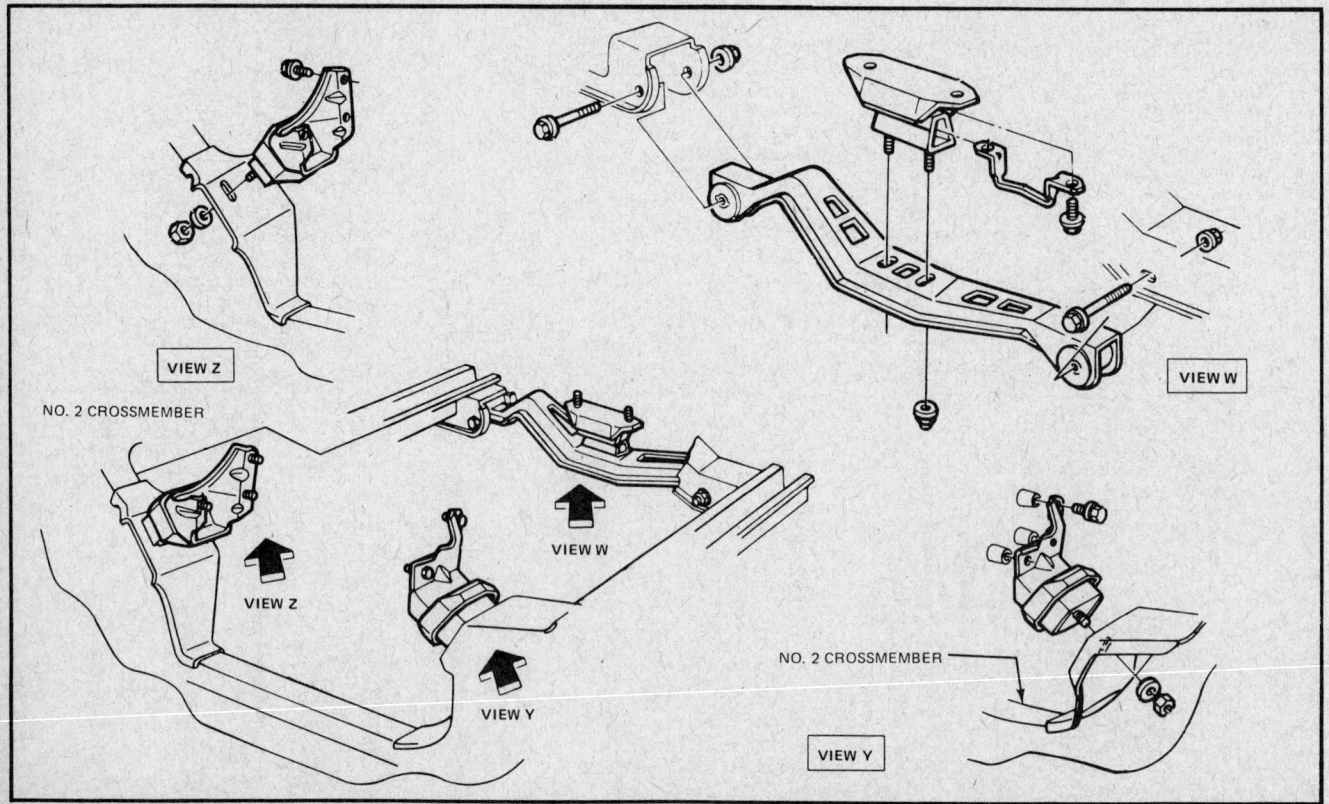

VIEW Z

NO. 2 CROSSMEMBER

VIEW W

VIEW W

VIEW Z

VIEW Y

NO. 2 CROSSMEMBER

VIEW Y

Fig. 1 Engine mounts. 1979–84 Capri & Mustang

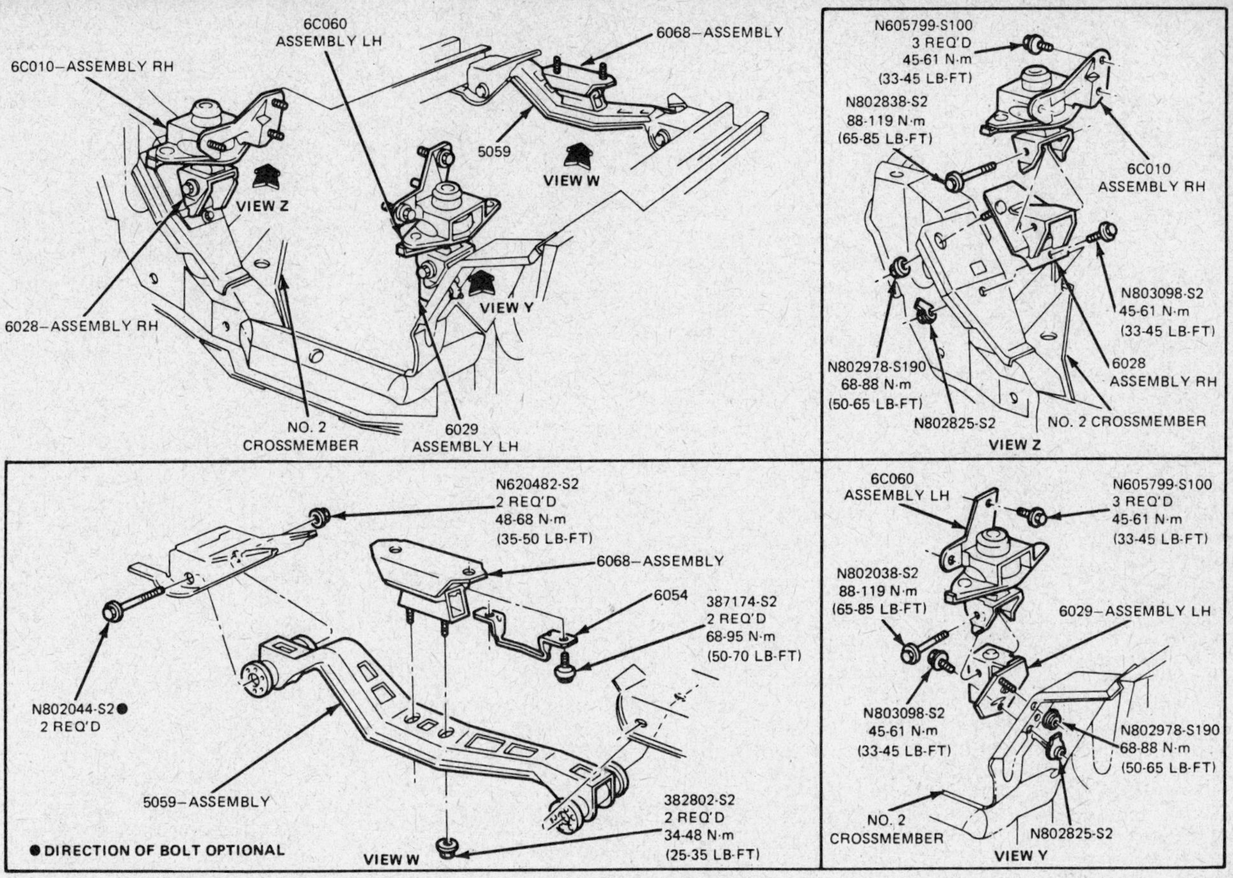

Fig. 1A Engine mount installation. 1983—84 4-140 turbocharged engine

9. Remove alternator drive belt, then the alternator mounting bracket attaching bolts.
10. Removing timing belt cover attaching bolts and the cover.
11. Loosen cam idler attaching bolts. Move idler to the unloaded position and retighten attaching bolts.
12. Remove timing belt from camshaft and auxiliary sprockets.
13. Remove heat stove from exhaust manifold.
14. Remove exhaust manifold, then the timing belt idler and two bracket bolts.
15. Remove timing belt idler spring stop from cylinder head, then disconnect oil sending unit electrical connector.
16. Remove cylinder head attaching bolts and the cylinder head.
17. Reverse procedure to install. Torque cylinder head bolts to specifications in sequence shown in Fig. 3 and intake manifold attaching bolts in sequence shown in

Fig. 4.

NOTE: When installing cylinder head, position camshaft in the 5 o'clock position, Fig. 3, allowing minimum protrusion of valves from cylinder head.

VALVE ARRANGEMENT

Front to Rear

2300 cc Engine . . . . E-I-E-I-E-I-E-I

VALVE LIFT SPECS.

Engine	Year	Intake	Exhaust
2300 cc	1977—83	.3997	.3997
2300 cc	1984	.3900	.3900

VALVE TIMING

Intake Opens Before TDC

Engine	Year	Degrees
2300 cc	1977—84	22

VALVES, ADJUST

The valve lash on this engine cannot be adjusted due to the use of hydraulic valve lash adjusters, Fig. 5. However, the valve train can be checked for wear as follows:
1. Crank engine to position camshaft with flat section of lobe facing rocker arm of valve being checked.
2. Remove rocker arm retaining spring.

NOTE: Late models do not incorporate the retaining spring.

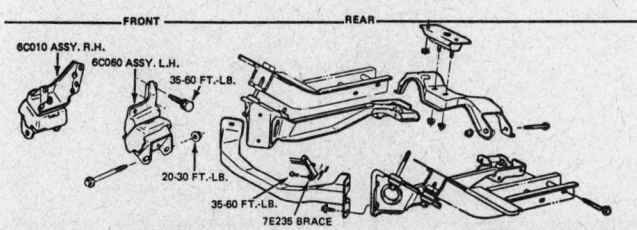

Fig. 2 Engine mount installation. 1977—78 Mustang

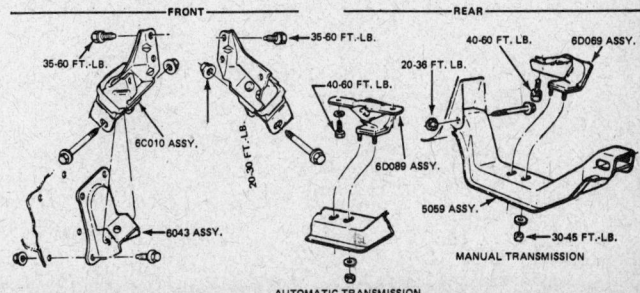

Fig. 2A Engine mount installation (typical). 1977—80 Bobcat & Pinto

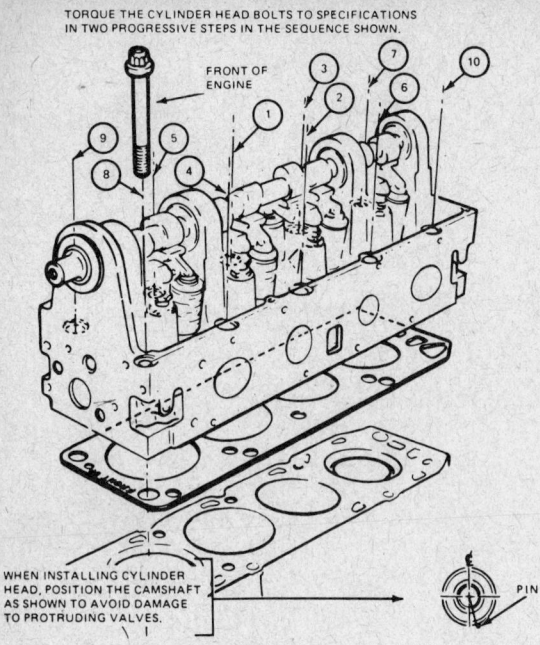

TORQUE THE CYLINDER HEAD BOLTS TO SPECIFICATIONS IN TWO PROGRESSIVE STEPS IN THE SEQUENCE SHOWN.

FRONT OF ENGINE

WHEN INSTALLING CYLINDER HEAD, POSITION THE CAMSHAFT AS SHOWN TO AVOID DAMAGE TO PROTRUDING VALVES.

PIN

Fig. 3   Cylinder head installation. 2300 cc engine

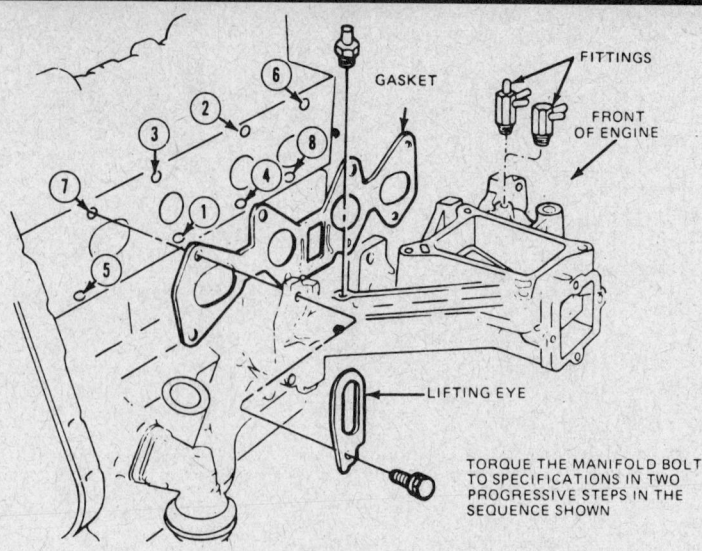

GASKET

FITTINGS

FRONT OF ENGINE

LIFTING EYE

TORQUE THE MANIFOLD BOLTS TO SPECIFICATIONS IN TWO PROGRESSIVE STEPS IN THE SEQUENCE SHOWN

Fig. 4   Intake manifold tightening sequence. 2300 cc engine

3. Collapse lash adjuster with tool T74P-6565B and insert correct size feeler gauge between rocker arm and camshaft lobe, Fig. 6. If clearance is not as listed in the "Valve Specifications" chart in front of this chapter, remove rocker arm and check for wear and replace as necessary. If rocker arm is found satisfactory, check valve spring assembled height and adjust as needed. If valve spring assembled height is within specifications listed in the front of this chapter, remove lash adjuster and clean or replace as necessary.

VALVE GUIDES

Valve guides consist of holes bored in the cylinder head. For service the guides can be reamed oversize to accommodate valves with oversize stems of .003, .015 and .030 inch.

ROCKER ARM SERVICE

1. Remove rocker arm cover.
2. Rotate camshaft until flat section of lobe faces rocker arm being removed.
3. With tool T74P-6565B, collapse lash adjuster and, if necessary, valve spring and slide rocker arm over lash adjuster.
4. Reverse procedure to install.

NOTE: Before rotating camshaft, ensure that lash adjuster is collapsed to prevent valve train damage.

LASH ADJUSTER, REPLACE

The hydraulic valve lash adjusters can be removed after rocker arm removal. There are two types of lash adjusters available, Type 1, being the standard lash adjuster, Fig. 7, and Type II, having a .020 inch oversize outside diameter, Fig. 8.

FRONT ENGINE SEALS, REPLACE

To gain access to the front engine seals, remove the timing belt cover and proceed as follows:

Crankshaft Oil Seal
1. Without removing cylinder front cover, remove crankshaft sprocket with tool

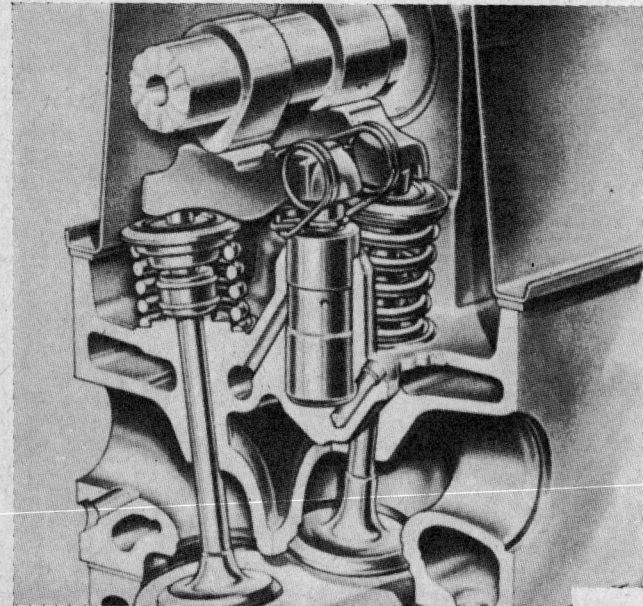

Fig. 5   Valve train installation. 2300 cc engine

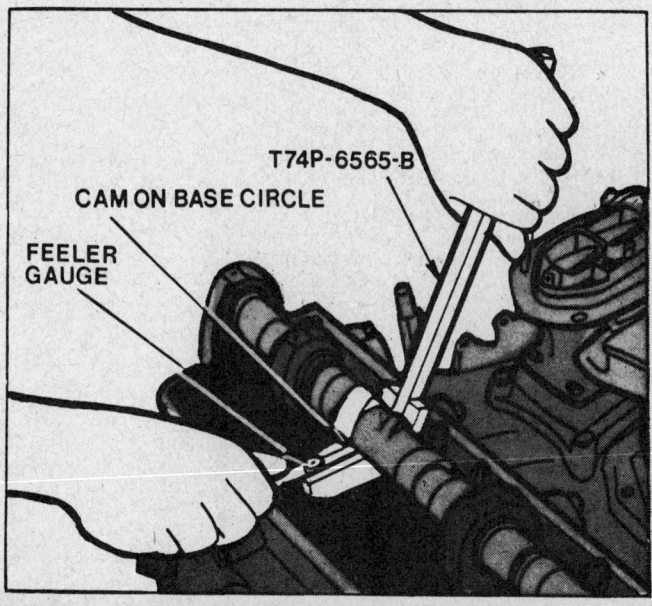

T74P-6565-B

CAM ON BASE CIRCLE

FEELER GAUGE

Fig. 6   Checking valve clearance. 2300 cc engine

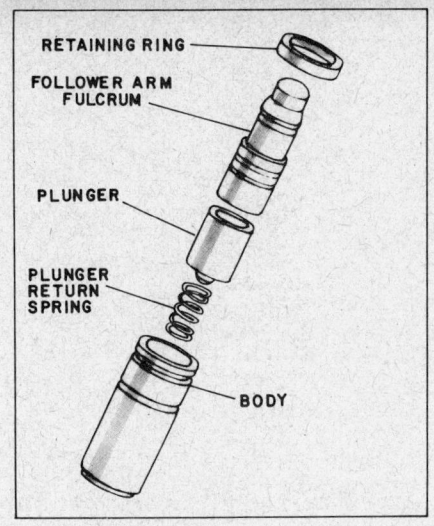

Fig. 7 Valve lash adjuster, Type I. 2300 cc engine

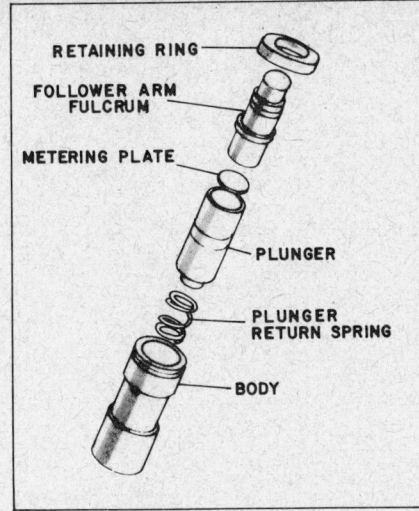

Fig. 8 Valve lash adjuster, Type II. 2300 cc engine

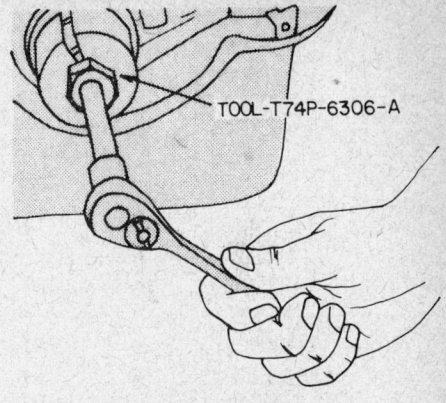

Fig. 9 Crankshaft sprocket removal. 2300 cc engine

T74P-6306A, Fig. 9.

2. Remove crankshaft oil seal with tool T74P-6700B, Fig. 10.
3. Install a new crankshaft oil seal with tool T74P-6150A, Fig. 11.
4. Install crankshaft sprocket with recess facing engine block, Fig. 12.

Camshaft & Auxiliary Shaft Oil Seals

1. Remove camshaft or auxiliary shaft sprocket with tool T74P-6256A, Fig. 13.
2. Remove oil seal with tool T74P-6700B, Fig. 14.
3. Install a new oil seal with tool T74P-6150A, Fig. 11.
4. Install camshaft or auxiliary shaft sprocket with tool T74P-6256A with center arbor removed.

TIMING BELT

1. Position crankshaft at TDC, No. 1 cylin-der compression stroke.
2. Remove timing belt cover, loosen belt tensioner, and remove belt from sprockets, Fig. 15. Tighten tensioner bolt, holding tensioner in position.

NOTE: Do not rotate crankshaft or camshaft after belt is removed. Rotating either component will result in improper valve timing.

---

3. To install belt, ensure timing marks are aligned, Fig. 16, and place belt over sprockets.
4. Loosen tensioner bolt, allowing tensioner to move against belt.
5. Rotate crankshaft two complete turns, removing slack from belt. Torque tensioner adjustment and pivot bolts and check alignment of timing marks, Fig. 16.
6. Install timing belt cover.

CAMSHAFT, REPLACE

1. Drain cooling system, then remove air cleaner assembly.
2. Disconnect ignition wires from spark plugs and rocker arm cover and position aside.
3. Disconnect all vacuum hoses necessary for camshaft removal.
4. Remove rocker arm cover attaching bolts and the cover.
5. Remove alternator drive belt.
6. Remove alternator mounting bracket attaching bolts and position bracket aside.
7. Remove upper radiator hose and disconnect lower hose.
8. Remove fan shroud. On models equipped with electric fan, remove fan and shroud as an assembly.
9. Remove timing belt cover attaching bolts and the cover.
10. Loosen cam idler attaching bolts. Move idler to the unloaded position and retighten attaching bolts.
11. Remove timing belt from camshaft and auxiliary sprockets.
12. Raise and support vehicle.
13. Remove right and left engine mount nuts and washers.

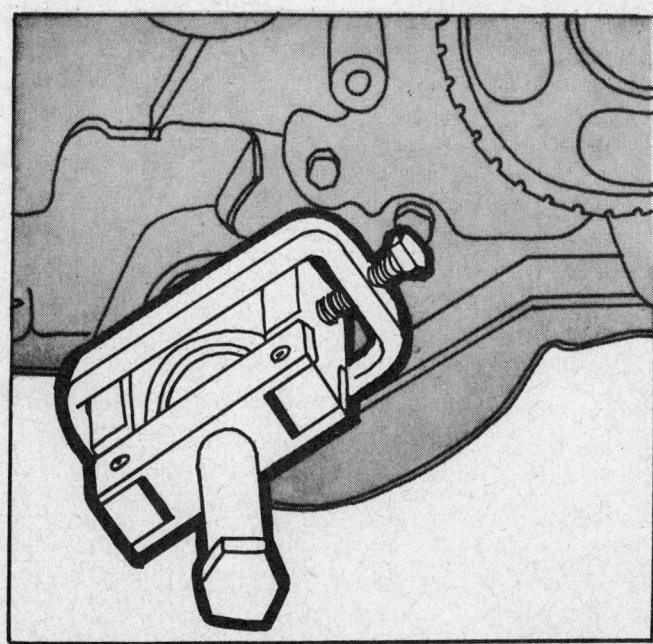

Fig. 10 Crankshaft front oil seal removal. 2300 cc engine

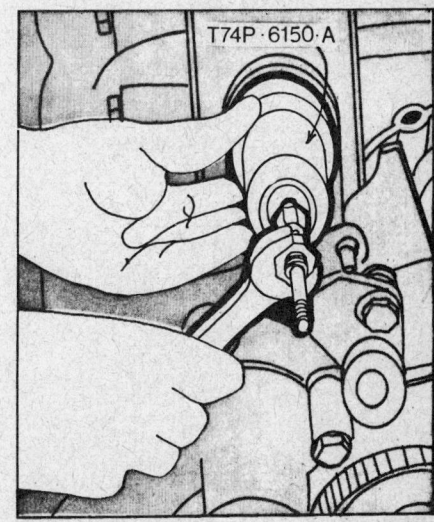

Fig. 11 Engine front seals installation. 2300 cc engine

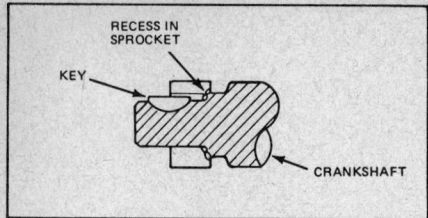

Fig. 12 Crankshaft sprocket installation. 2300 cc engine

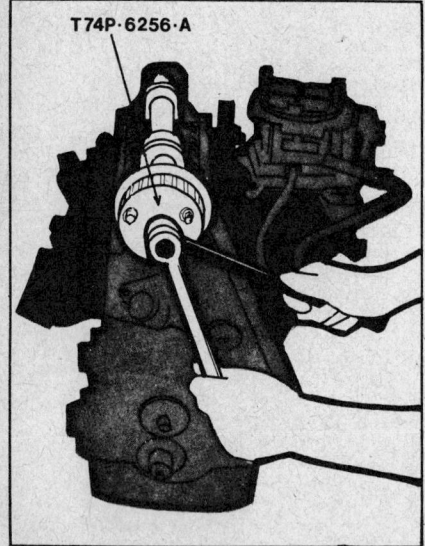

T74P·6256·A

Fig. 13 Camshaft & auxiliary shaft sprockets removal. 2300 cc engine

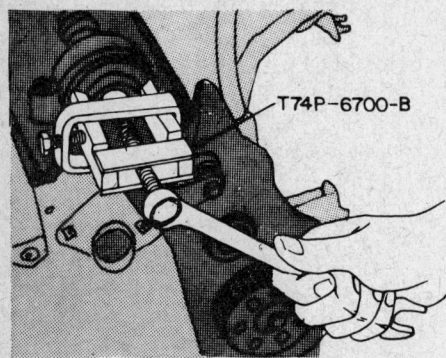

T74P-6700-B

Fig. 14 Camshaft & auxiliary shaft seals removal. 2300 cc engine

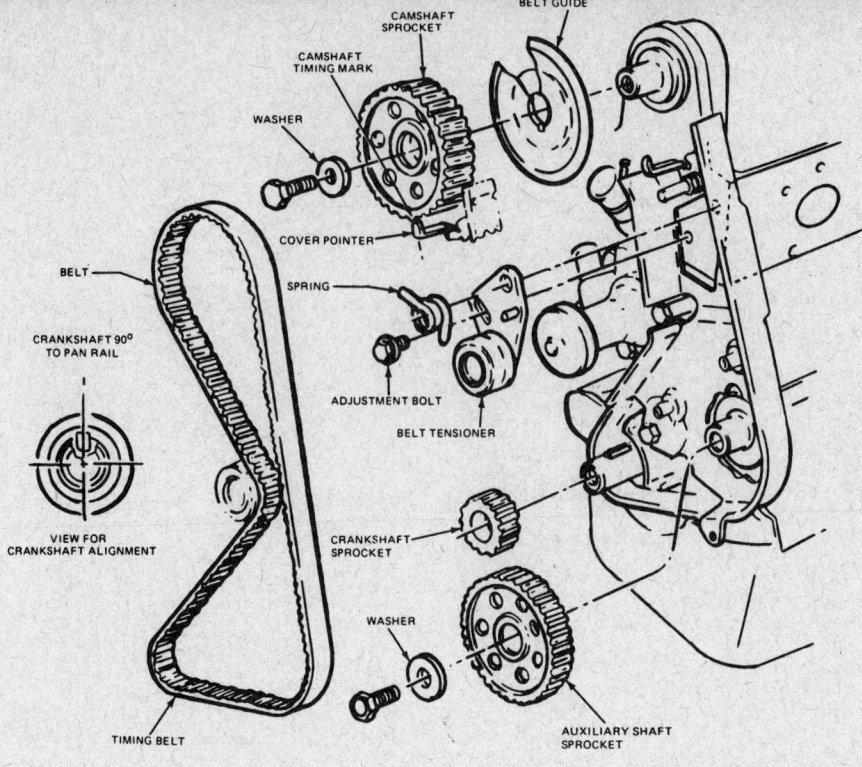

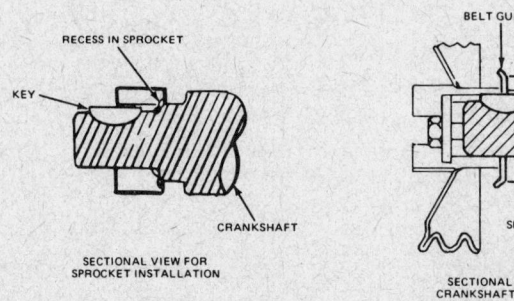

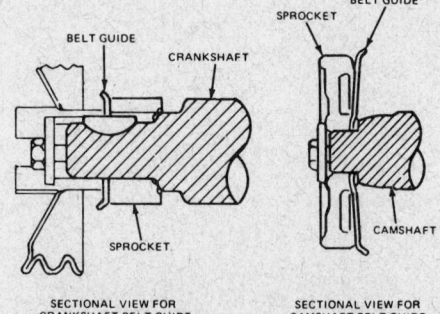

Fig. 15 Drive belt & sprockets installation. 2300 cc engine

14. Raise engine as far as possible using a suitable transmission jack with a block of wood positioned between jack and engine. Install wood blocks between No. 2 crossmember pedestals and engine mounts, then remove jack and lower vehicle.
15. Depress valve springs using tool No. T74P-6565-A or equivalent and remove camshaft followers.
16. Remove camshaft sprocket attaching bolt, then the sprocket using tool No. T-74P-6565-A, or equivalent.
17. Remove seal using tool No. T74P-6700-A, or equivalent.
18. Remove camshaft retainer attaching screws and the retainer.
19. Remove camshaft from cylinder head, Fig. 16A.
20. Reverse procedure to install.

NOTE: The camshaft sprocket attaching bolt should be replaced. If a new bolt is not available, coat threads of original bolt with D8AZ-19554-A sealer or equivalent, or wrap teflon tape around threads prior to installation.

PISTON & ROD, ASSEMBLE

Assemble the rod to the piston with the arrow or notch on top of piston facing front of engine, Fig. 17 and 17A.

Check side clearance between connecting rods at each connecting rod crankshaft journal. Clearance should be .0035–.0105 in.

PISTONS, PINS & RINGS

Oversize pistons are available in oversizes of .003″, .020″, .030″ and .040″. Oversize rings are available in .020″, .030″ and .040″ oversizes. Oversize pins are not available.

MAIN & ROD BEARINGS

Undersize main bearings are available in .002″, .020″, .030″ and .040″ undersizes. Undersize rod bearings are available in undersizes of .002″, .010″, .020″, .030″ and .040″.

The crankshaft and main bearings are installed with arrows on main bearing caps facing front of engine, Fig. 18. Install PCV baffle between bearing journals No. 3 and 4.

CRANKSHAFT OIL SEAL
1982–84

1. Remove oil pump, if necessary, as described under "Oil Pump, Replace".
2. Punch one hole into metal surface between seal and block using a sharp awl.
3. Screw the threaded end of slide hammer, tool No. T77L-9533-B or equivalent, into seal and remove seal. Use care to avoid damaging oil seal mating surface.
4. Apply suitable sealer to seal and block mating surfaces.

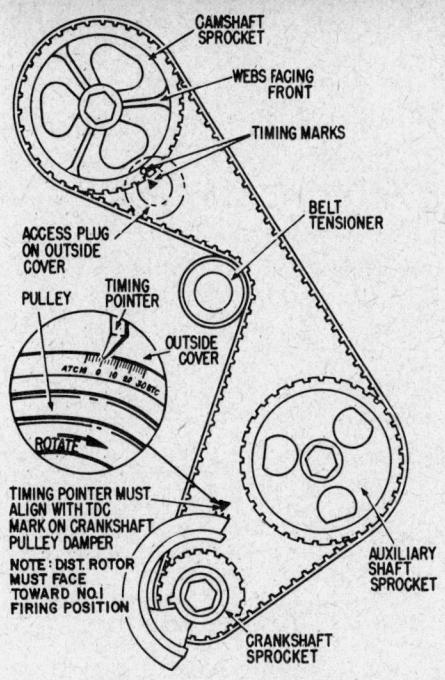

Fig. 16 Valve timing marks. 2300 cc engine

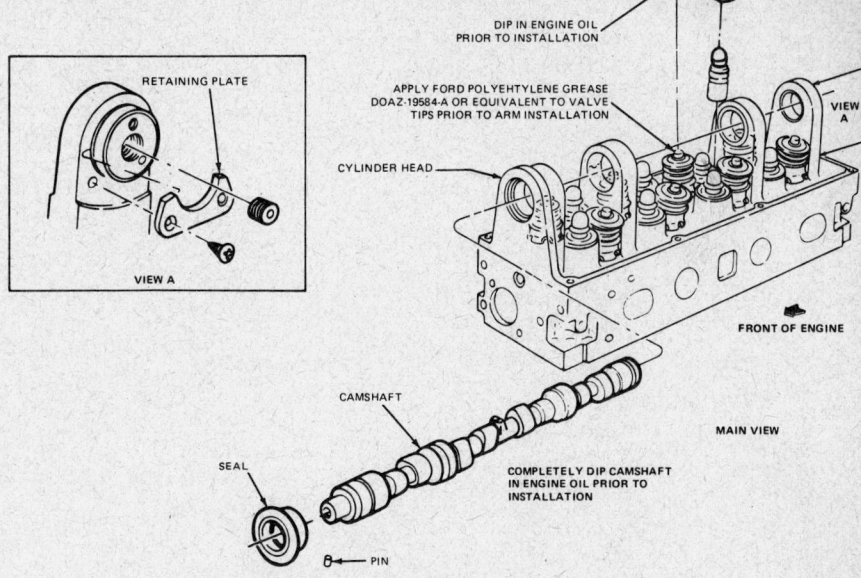

Fig. 16A Camshaft replacement. 2300 cc engine

5. Position seal on tool No. T82L-6701-A or equivalent, Fig. 19, and install seal. Tighten bolts alternately to ensure proper seating of the seal.
6. Install oil pump if previously removed.

1977–81

1. Remove oil pan.
2. Remove rear main bearing cap.
3. Loosen remaining bearing caps, allowing crankshaft to drop down about 1/32".
4. Install a sheet metal screw into seal and pull screw to remove seal.
5. Carefully clean seal groove in block with a brush and solvent. Also clean seal groove in bearing cap.
6. Dip seal halves in clean engine oil.
7. Carefully install upper seal half in its groove with locating tab toward rear of engine, Fig. 19A, by rotating it on shaft journal of crankshaft until approximately 3/8" protrudes below the parting surface. *Be sure no rubber has been shaved from outside diameter of seal by bottom edge of groove.*
8. Retighten main bearing caps and torque to specifications.

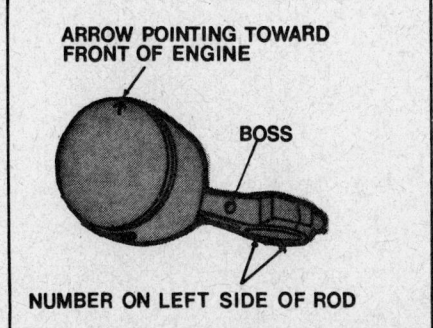

Fig. 17 Piston & rod. 1977-79 2300 cc engine

9. Install lower seal in main bearing cap with undercut side of seal toward front of engine, and allow seal to protrude about 3/8" above parting surface to mate with upper seal upon cap installation.
10. Apply suitable sealer to parting faces of cap and block. Install cap and torque to specifications.

NOTE: If difficulty is encountered in installing the upper half of the seal in position, lightly lap (sandpaper) the side of the seal opposite the lip side using a medium grit paper. After sanding, the seal must be washed in solvent, then dipped in clean engine oil prior to installation.

OIL PAN, REPLACE

1980–84

1. Disconnect battery ground cable.
2. Remove fan shroud. If equipped with electric fan, remove fan and shroud as an assembly.
3. On 1983–84 models, drain cooling system, then disconnect upper and lower hoses from radiator.
4. On all models, raise and support vehicle.
5. Drain engine oil, then remove right and left engine mount nuts and bolts or washers.
6. Raise engine as far as possible using a suitable jack with a block of wood positioned between jack and engine. Install wood blocks between mounts and chassis brackets or No. 2 crossmember pedestals, then remove jack.
7. Remove shake brace, then the sway bar attaching bolts and lower the sway bar.
8. Remove starter motor.
9. Remove steering gear attaching bolts and lower the gear.
10. Remove oil pan attaching bolts and the oil pan.

NOTE: The number four piston must be in the up position to allow clearance between crankshaft and rear of oil pan

for oil pan removal.

11. Reverse procedure to install.

1977–79

1. Drain crankcase and remove oil dipstick and flywheel inspection cover.
2. Disconnect steering cable from rack and pinion, then rack and pinion from crossmember and move forward to provide clearance.
3. Unfasten and remove oil pan. To install oil pan, refer to Fig. 20.

OIL PUMP, REPLACE

The oil pump, Fig. 21, can be removed after oil pan removal, Fig. 22.

OIL PUMP REPAIRS

1. Remove end plate and withdraw O ring from groove in body.
2. Check clearance between inner rotor tip and outer rotor lobe, Fig. 23. This should not exceed .012". Rotors are supplied only in a matched pair.
3. Check clearance between outer rotor and the housing, Fig. 24. This should not exceed .013".
4. Place a straightedge across face of pump

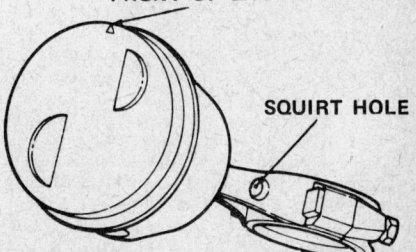

Fig. 17A Piston & rod. 1980-84 2300 cc engine

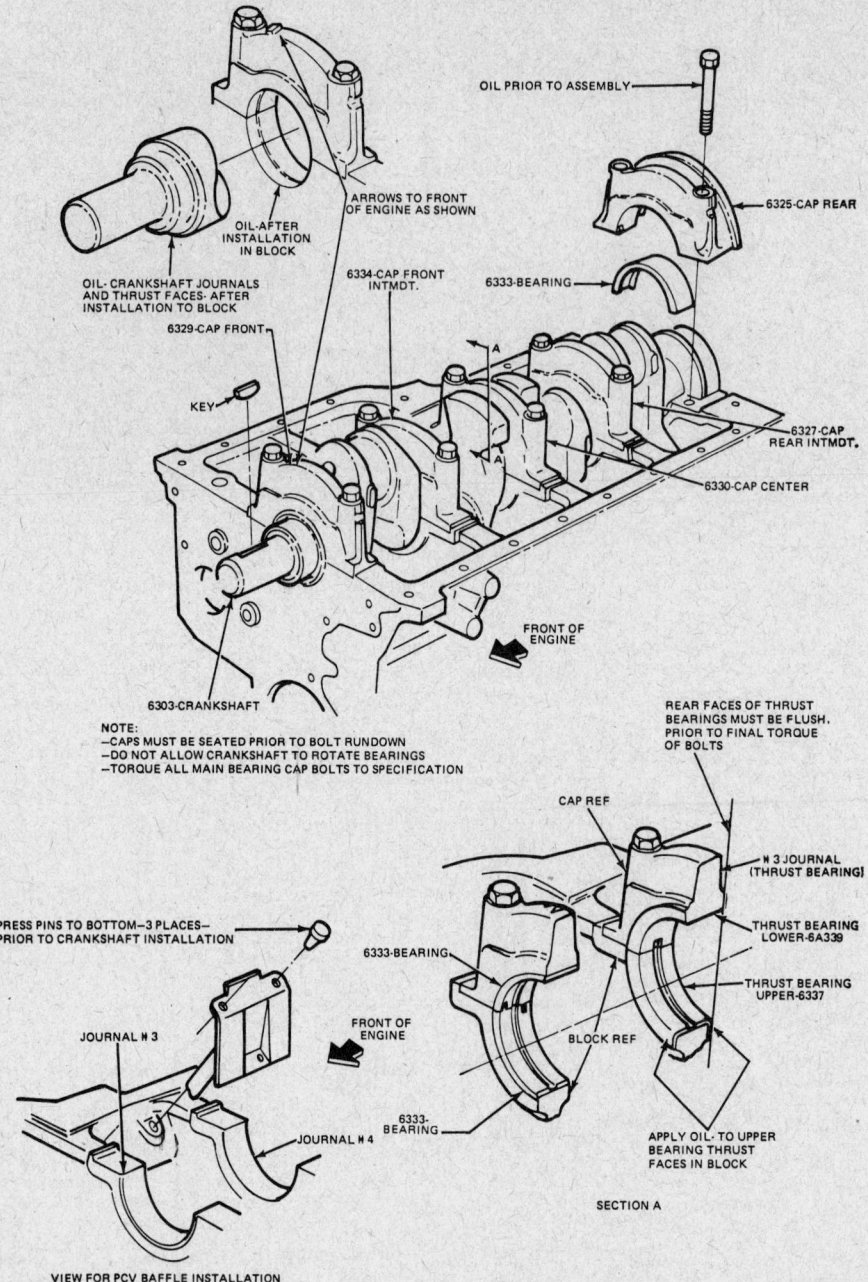

OIL PRIOR TO ASSEMBLY

6325-CAP REAR

ARROWS TO FRONT OF ENGINE AS SHOWN

OIL-AFTER INSTALLATION IN BLOCK

6334-CAP FRONT INTMDT.

6333-BEARING

OIL- CRANKSHAFT JOURNALS AND THRUST FACES- AFTER INSTALLATION TO BLOCK

6329-CAP FRONT

KEY

6327-CAP REAR INTMDT.

6330-CAP CENTER

FRONT OF ENGINE

6303-CRANKSHAFT

NOTE:
—CAPS MUST BE SEATED PRIOR TO BOLT RUNDOWN
—DO NOT ALLOW CRANKSHAFT TO ROTATE BEARINGS
—TORQUE ALL MAIN BEARING CAP BOLTS TO SPECIFICATION

REAR FACES OF THRUST BEARINGS MUST BE FLUSH, PRIOR TO FINAL TORQUE OF BOLTS

CAP REF

 # 3 JOURNAL (THRUST BEARING)

THRUST BEARING LOWER-6A339

THRUST BEARING UPPER-6337

PRESS PINS TO BOTTOM-3 PLACES— PRIOR TO CRANKSHAFT INSTALLATION

6333-BEARING

FRONT OF ENGINE

JOURNAL # 3

BLOCK REF

JOURNAL # 4

6333-BEARING

APPLY OIL- TO UPPER BEARING THRUST FACES IN BLOCK

SECTION A

VIEW FOR PCV BAFFLE INSTALLATION

Fig. 18 Crankshaft & main bearing installation. 2300 cc engine

body, Fig. 25. Clearance between face of rotors and straightedge should not exceed .004".
5. If necessary to replace rotor or drive shaft, remove outer rotor and then drive out retaining pin securing the skew gear to drive shaft and pull off the gear.
6. Withdraw inner rotor and drive shaft.

WATER PUMP, REPLACE

1. Drain cooling system and disconnect hos-

es from pump.
2. Loosen alternator and remove drive belt.
3. Remove fan, spacer and pulley.
4. Remove water pump attaching bolts and water pump after removing drive belt cover.

FUEL PUMP, REPLACE

1. Loosen fuel line connectors, then retight-

en hand tight. Do not disconnect lines at this time.
2. Loosen fuel pump attaching bolts one or two turns. Apply hand force to break pump free from gasket.
3. Rotate engine slightly until pump cam lobe is near it's lowest position.
4. Disconnect inlet and outlet lines and the vapor return line, if equipped, from pump.
5. Remove fuel pump attaching bolts and the pump. Remove and discard gasket.
6. Reverse procedure to install.

BELT TENSION DATA

	New Lbs.	Used Lbs.
1977–80 Exc. ¼ inch	140	110
¼ inch	65	50
1980		
Ribbed Belt w/o Tensioner	155	150
Ribbed Belt w/ Tensioner	130	130
1981		
Except ¼"	140	110
¼"	65	40
V Ribbed Belt		
4K	105	100
5K ①	125	120
5K ②	108	108
6K ①	155	150
6K ②	113	113
1982–84		
Except ¼"	140	105
¼"	65	50
V Ribbed Belt		
4 Rib		
Except Air Pump	130	115
Air Pump	110	105
5 Rib	150	135
6 Rib ①	113	110
6 Rib ③	160	145

①—W/ tensioner.
②—W/ absorber.
③—Fixed

LUBRICATE SEAL AND SEAL MATING SURFACE WITH OIL, (ESE-M2C39-F) OR EQUIVALENT

FRONT OF ENGINE

CYLINDER BLOCK

SEAL INSTALLER TOOL-T82L-6701-A

SEAL (INSTALL WITH SPRING SIDE TOWARD ENGINE)

NOTE: REAR FACE OF SEAL MUST BE WITHIN 0.127mm (0.005-INCH) OF THE REAR FACE OF THE BLOCK

Fig. 19 Crankshaft rear oil seal installation. 1983–84 2300 cc engine

REAR BEARING CAP

DIP SEALS IN ENGINE OIL BEFORE INSTALLING

REAR OIL SEAL

TAB

APPLY SEALER AS SHOWN SEE NOTE BELOW

FRONT OF ENGINE

UPPER AND LOWER SEAL ENDS TO BE FLUSH IN BLOCK AND CAP

TAB

SEALER NOTE: CLEAN THE AREA WHERE SEALER IS TO BE APPLIED BEFORE INSTALLING THE SEALS. USE FORD SPOT REMOVER B7A-19521-A OR EQUIVALENT. AFTER THE SEALS ARE IN PLACE, APPLY A 1/16 INCH BEAD OF C3AZ-19562-A OR B SEALER AS SHOWN. SEALER MUST NOT CONTACT SEALS.

Fig. 19A Crankshaft rear oil seal installation. 1977–82 2300 cc engine

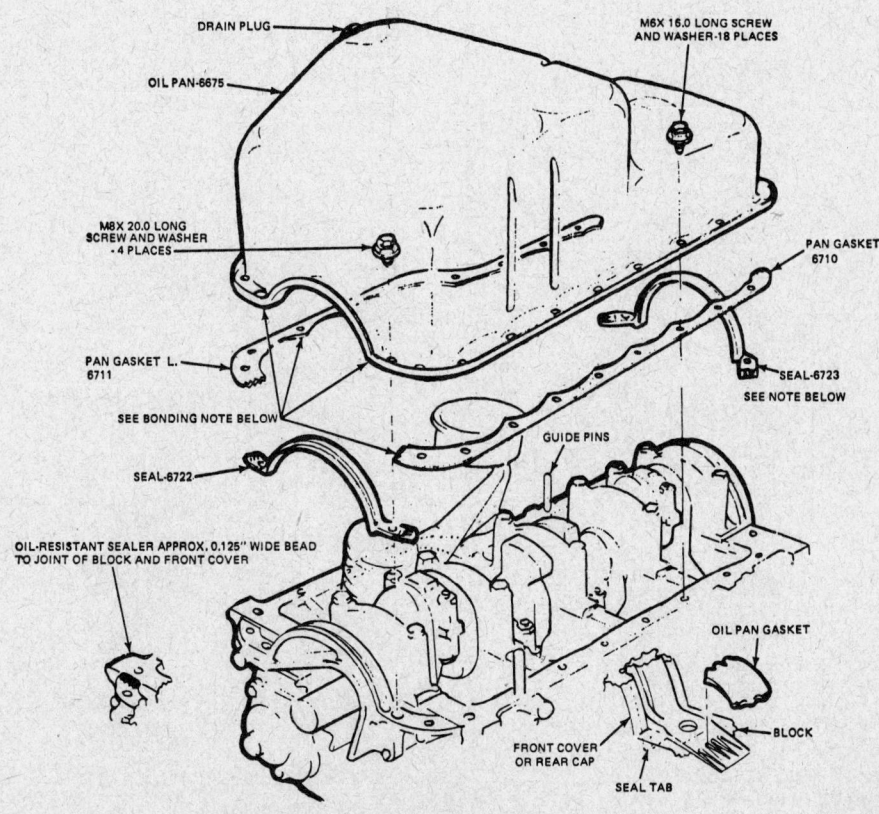

DRAIN PLUG

M6X 16.0 LONG SCREW AND WASHER-18 PLACES

OIL PAN-6675

M8X 20.0 LONG SCREW AND WASHER - 4 PLACES

PAN GASKET, R. 6710

PAN GASKET L. 6711

SEAL-6723 SEE NOTE BELOW

SEE BONDING NOTE BELOW

SEAL-6722

GUIDE PINS

OIL-RESISTANT SEALER APPROX. 0.125" WIDE BEAD TO JOINT OF BLOCK AND FRONT COVER

OIL PAN GASKET

FRONT COVER OR REAR CAP

BLOCK

SEAL TAB

1. APPLY GASKET ADHESIVE EVENLY TO OIL PAN FLANGE AND TO PAN SIDE GASKETS. ALLOW ADHESIVE TO DRY PAST WET STAGE, THEN INSTALL GASKETS TO OIL PAN.
2. APPLY SEALER TO JOINT OF BLOCK AND FRONT COVER. INSTALL SEALS TO FRONT COVER AND REAR BEARING CAP AND PRESS SEAL TABS FIRMLY INTO BLOCK. BE SURE TO INSTALL THE REAR SEAL BEFORE THE REAR MAIN BEARING CAP SEALER HAS CURED.
3. POSITION 2 GUIDE PINS AND INSTALL THE OIL PAN. SECURE THE PAN WITH THE FOUR M8 BOLTS SHOWN ABOVE.
4. REMOVE THE GUIDE PINS AND INSTALL AND TORQUE THE EIGHTEEN M6 BOLTS, BEGINNING AT HOLE A AND WORKING CLOCKWISE AROUND THE PAN.

Fig. 20 Oil pan installation. 2300 cc engine

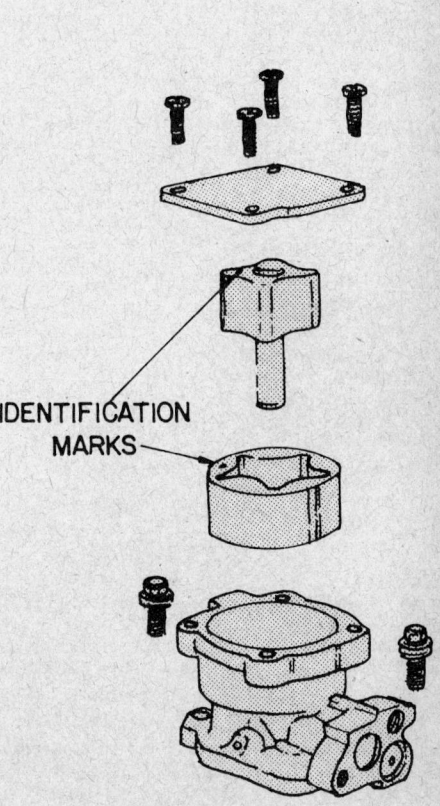

IDENTIFICATION MARKS

Fig. 21 Oil pump. 2300 cc engine

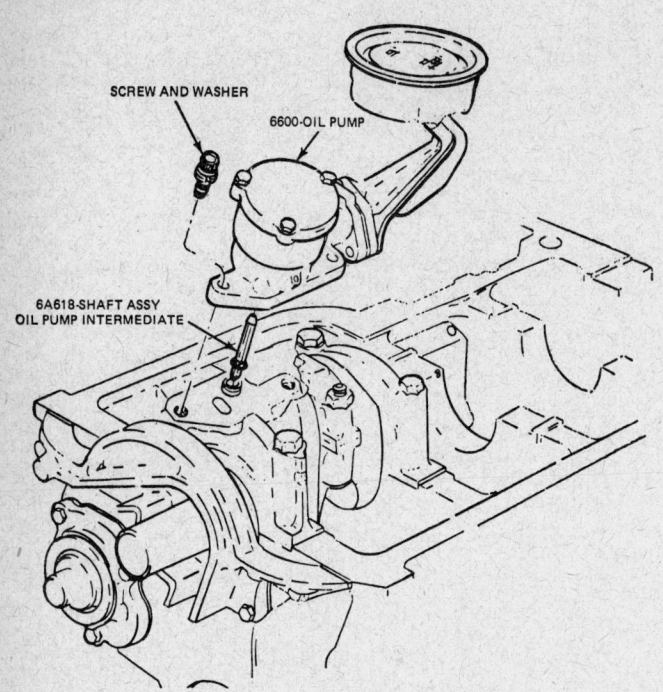

Fig. 22   Oil pump installation. 2300 cc engine

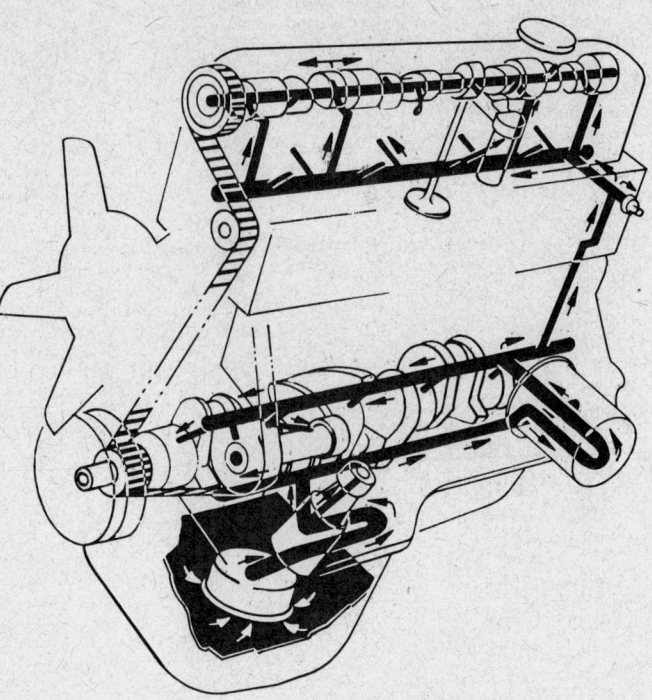

Engine oiling system. 2300 cc engine

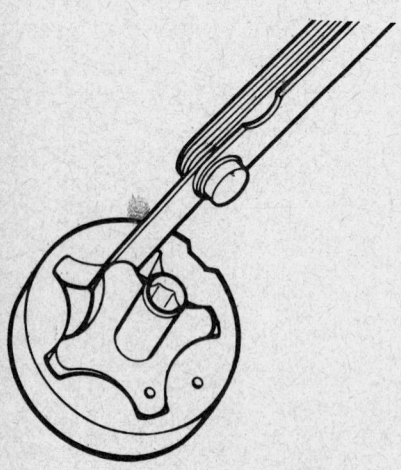

Fig. 23   Checking inner rotor tip clearance

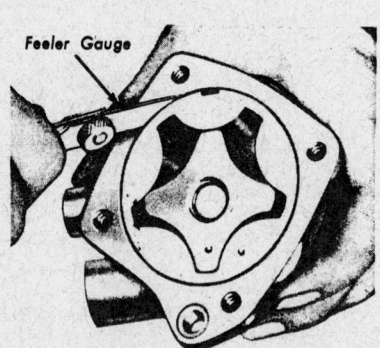

Fig. 24   Checking outer rotor to housing clearance. 2300 cc engine

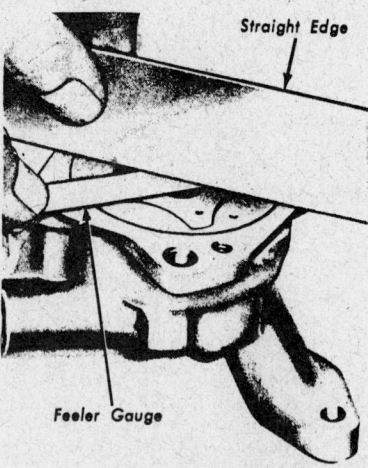

Fig. 25   Checking rotor end play. 2300 cc engine

2800 cc V6 Engine Section

ENGINE MOUNTS, REPLACE

1. Remove fan shroud screws and support engine with a suitable jack and a block of wood under the oil pan.
2. On all models except 1979 Capri and Mustang remove insulator to insulator support bracket through bolt, support bracket to frame bolts, raise engine slightly, then remove support bracket, Figs. 1 & 2.
3. On 1979 Capri and Mustang, remove nuts and washer attaching the insulator to the No. 2 crossmember pedestals. Lift engine slightly to disengage insulator stud from cross member, Fig. 1.
4. Remove bolt attaching fuel pump shield to left hand engine bracket, if equipped.
5. Remove insulator assembly to engine block bolts, then remove insulator and heat shield.

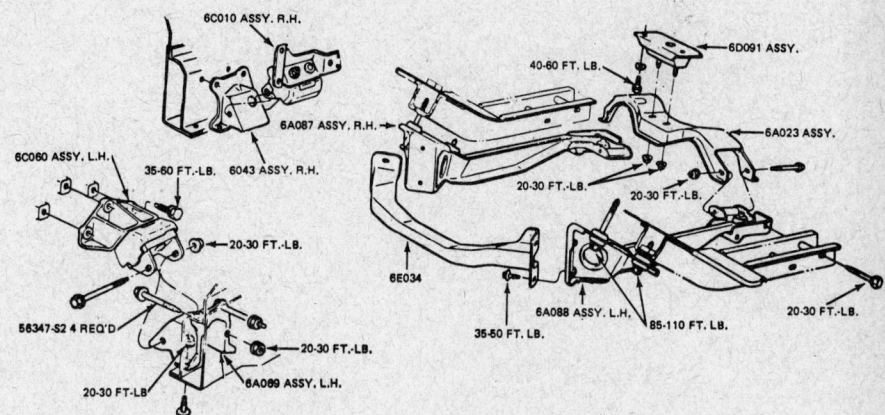

Fig. 1 Engine mounts (typical). 1977–78 Mustang

ENGINE, REPLACE

1. Disconnect battery cables and remove hood.
2. Remove air cleaner and intake duct.
3. Drain cooling system, disconnect radiator hoses from radiator, then remove radiator. Disconnect heater hoses from engine block and water pump.

NOTE: Remove fan shroud and position shroud over fan before removing radiator.

4. Remove alternator and bracket.
5. Disconnect ground wires from engine block.
6. Disconnect fuel tank line from fuel pump and plug line.
7. Disconnect all linkage from engine and wires from ignition coil.

NOTE: If equipped with Thermactor system, remove or disconnect system components interfering with engine removal.

8. Raise vehicle and place on jack stands.
9. Disconnect exhaust pipes from exhaust manifold and remove starter.
10. Remove engine front support through bolts or attaching nuts.
11. On vehicles equipped with automatic transmission, disconnect converter from flywheel, remove downshift rod, then remove converter housing to engine bolts and adapter plate to converter housing bolt.
12. On vehicles equipped with manual transmission, remove clutch linkage and bell housing to engine bolts.
13. On all models, lower vehicle and attach a suitable lifting sling to brackets on exhaust manifold.
14. Support transmission with a suitable jack, raise engine slightly and pull from transmission, then lift engine from engine compartment.

CYLINDER HEAD, REPLACE

1. Disconnect battery ground cable, disconnect linkage and drain coolant.
2. Remove distributor, coolant hoses, rocker arm covers, fuel line and filter, carburetor and intake manifold.
3. Remove rocker arm shaft, oil baffles and push rods.
4. Remove exhaust manifold.
5. Remove cylinder head bolts and cylinder head.
6. Reverse procedure to install. Torque cylinder head bolts in sequence shown in Fig. 3, and intake manifold bolts in sequence shown in Fig. 4.

VALVE ARRANGEMENT

Front to Rear

2800 cc engine—	
Right	I-E-I-E-E-I
Left	I-E-E-I-E-I

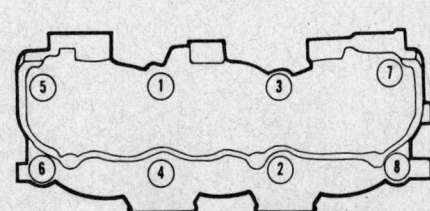

Fig. 3 Cylinder head tightening sequence. 2800 cc engine

VALVE LIFT SPECS.

Engine	Year	Intake	Exhaust
2800 cc	1977–79	.3730	.3730

VALVE TIMING

Intake Opens Before TDC

Engine	Year	Degrees
2800 cc	1977–79	20

VALVES, ADJUST

Cold Setting

1977–79

1. Remove all necessary components to allow removal of valve covers, then remove valve covers.
2. Slowly crank engine until intake valve for number 5 cylinder just starts to open. The camshaft is now correctly positioned to adjust valves on number 1 cylinder.
3. Refer to "Valves Specifications" chart, then using a feeler gauge of the specified clearance, adjust number 1 cylinder intake valve so that feeler gauge has a light to moderate drag, and a feeler gauge .001 inch greater is very tight, Fig. 5.

NOTE: Do not use a step-type "go/no-go" gauge. Also, when checking valve lash, insert gauge between rocker arm and front or rear of valve tip and move

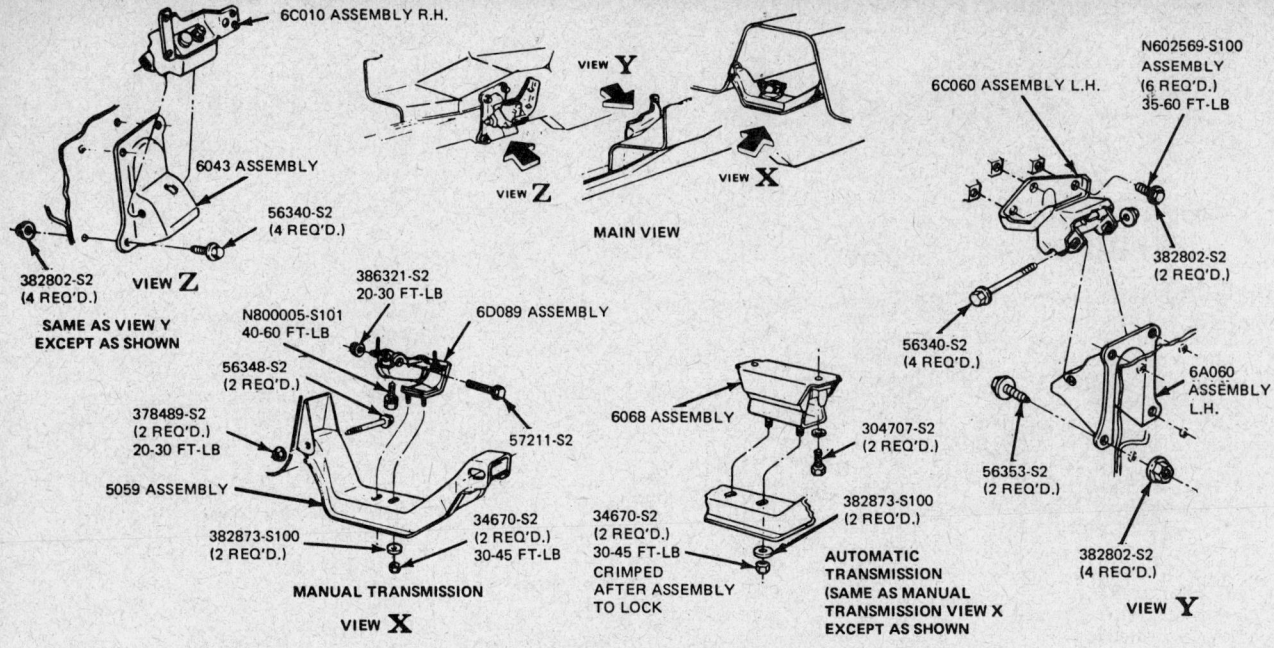

Fig. 2 Engine mounts (typical). 1977–79 Bobcat & Pinto

gauge toward opposite edge with a rearward or forward motion parallel to the crankshaft centerline. Inserting gauge at outboard edge, and moving inward toward carburetor, will produce an erroneous "feel" and result in excessively tight valves.

4. Using the same procedure as in step 3, adjust the number 1 cylinder intake valve using a feeler gauge of the specified clearance.
5. Adjust the remaining valves in sequence of firing order (1-4-2-5-3-6), by positioning the camshaft according to the following chart:

	With Intake Valve Just Opening for Cyl. No.					
	5	3	6	1	4	2
Adjust Both Valves For Cyl. No.	1	4	2	5	3	6

VALVE GUIDES

Valve guides consist of holes bored in the cylinder head. For service the guides can be reamed oversize to accomodate valves with oversize stems of .003, .015 and .030.".

ROCKER ARM SERVICE

1. Disconnect throttle rod from carburetor and remove rocker arm cover.
2. Remove rocker arm shaft stand bolts, rocker arm shaft assembly and oil baffle, Fig. 6.
3. Remove cotter pin and spring washer from ends of rocker shaft and slide rocker arms, springs and shaft supports off shaft, marking components for proper reassembly, Fig. 7.

4. Remove plugs from shaft ends by drilling a hole in one plug, insert a long rod through drilled plug and knock the opposite plug from shaft. Remove the drilled plug in same manner.
5. With a blunt tool, install plugs in end of rocker shafts with cup side out.
6. Install spring washer and cotter pin on one end of shaft and install components in proper sequence as marked during disassembly.

NOTE: Oil holes in rocker shaft must face downward during installation.

VALVE LIFTERS, REPLACE

Remove cylinder head as outlined previously and using a magnet, remove lifters from their bores.

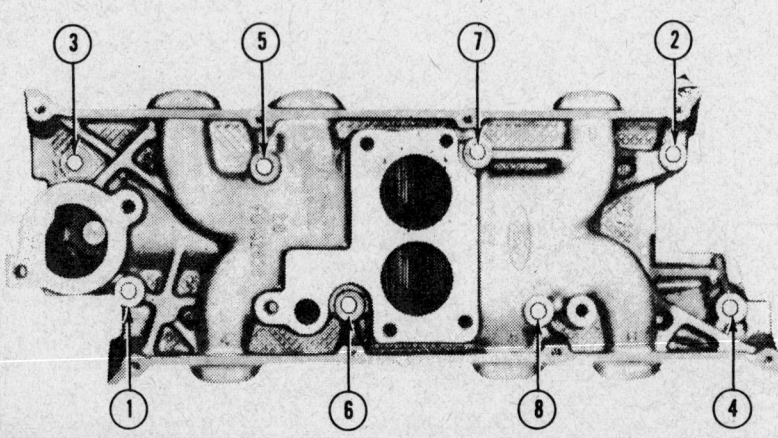

Fig. 4 Intake manifold tightening sequence. 2800 cc engine

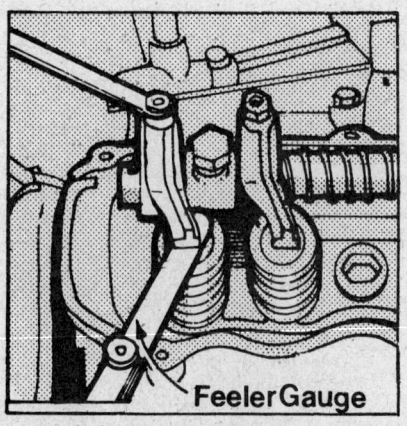

Fig. 5 Adjusting valve lash. 2800 cc engine

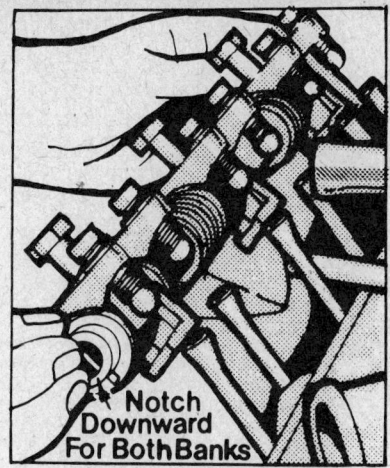

Notch Downward For Both Banks

Fig. 6 Rocker arm replacement. 2800 cc engine

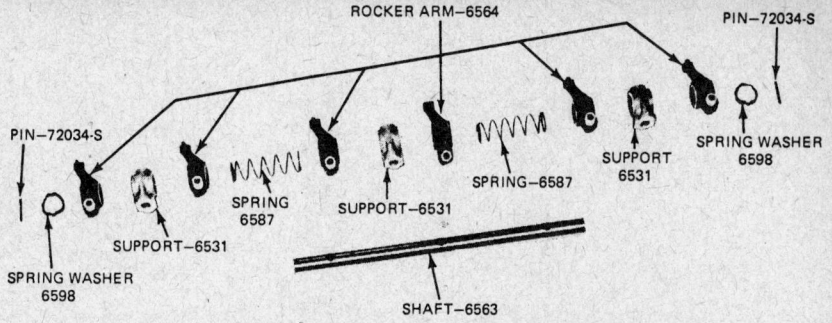

Fig. 7 Rocker arm shaft assembly. 2800 cc engine

TIMING CASE COVER

1. Remove oil pan as described further on.
2. Drain coolant and remove radiator, then remove any other components as necessary to obtain clearance.
3. If equipped, disconnect A/C compressor and bracket and place aside.
4. Remove alternator, Thermactor pump, drive belts, fan, water pump, hoses and harmonic balancer or pulley.
5. Remove cover retaining bolts and remove cover.

CRANKSHAFT FRONT OIL SEAL

The crankshaft front oil seal may be serviced without removing the cylinder front cover as follows:
1. Drain coolant and remove radiator, crankshaft pulley and water pump drive belt.
2. Pull oil seal from front cover, Fig. 8.
3. Install new oil seal with tool T72C-6150, Fig. 9.
4. Install crankshaft pulley, water pump drive belt, radiator, then refill cooling system.

TIMING GEARS

1. Drain, then remove radiator and oil pan.

2. Remove cylinder front cover and water pump.
3. Align timing marks, Fig. 10.
4. Using a suitable gear puller, remove crankshaft gear and key.
5. Remove camshaft gear with a suitable gear puller.

NOTE: Do not rotate crankshaft or camshaft with gears removed as rotation of either component can result in improper valve timing.

---

6. Install key in camshaft, then press camshaft gear onto camshaft.
7. Install key in crankshaft, then press crankshaft gear onto crankshaft with tool T72C-6150, Fig. 11, and make sure timing marks are aligned, Fig. 10.
8. Install cylinder front cover, water pump, radiator and oil pan.
9. Refill cooling system and oil pan. Start engine and adjust ignition timing, if necessary.

CAMSHAFT, REPLACE

1. Drain coolant, then remove radiator, fan, water pump pulley and belt.
2. Remove distributor, alternator, Thermactor pump, fuel line, filter, carburetor and intake manifold.
3. Remove rocker arm covers, rocker arm assemblies, pushrods and lifters. Identify pushrods and lifters so they can be reinstalled in their original location.
4. Remove oil pan as described further on.
5. Remove timing case cover as described previously.
6. Remove camshaft gear retaining bolt and

slide gear off shaft and remove camshaft thrust plate.
7. Carefully remove camshaft from engine using care to avoid damage to camshaft bearings Fig. 12.

PISTON & ROD ASSEMBLY

Assemble the piston to the rod with the notches facing front of engine and the numbered side of the rod toward left side of engine, Fig. 13.

PISTONS, PINS & RINGS

Oversize pistons and rings are available in .020″ and .040″ oversizes. Oversize pins are not available.

CRANKSHAFT REAR OIL SEAL

1. Remove transmission assembly.
2. On automatic transmission vehicles, remove flywheel.
3. On manual transmission vehicles, remove clutch assembly, flywheel, clutch housing and rear plate.
4. Punch two holes on opposite sides of seal just above bearing cap to cylinder block split line and install a sheet metal screw

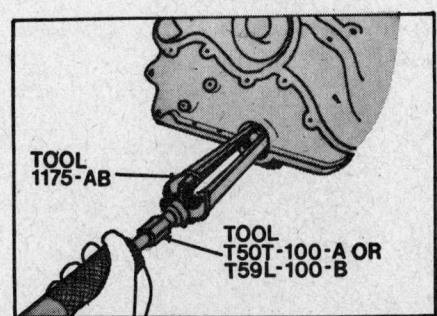

Fig. 8 Removing crankshaft front oil seal. 2800 cc engine

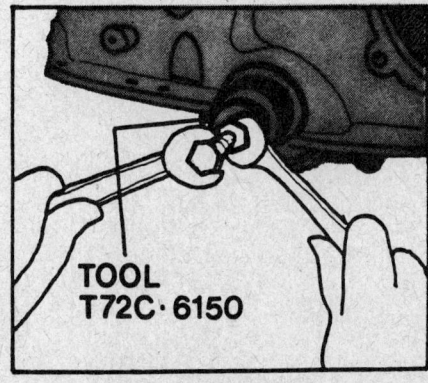

Fig. 9 Installing crankshaft front oil seal. 2800 cc engine

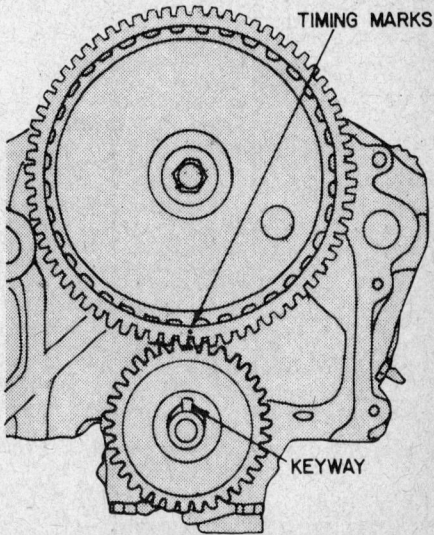

Fig. 10 Valve timing marks. 2800 cc engine

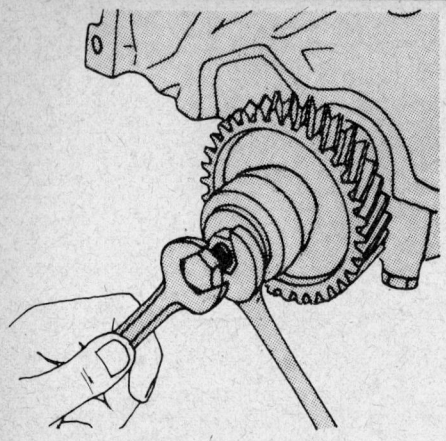

Fig. 11 Crankshaft gear installation. 2800 cc engine

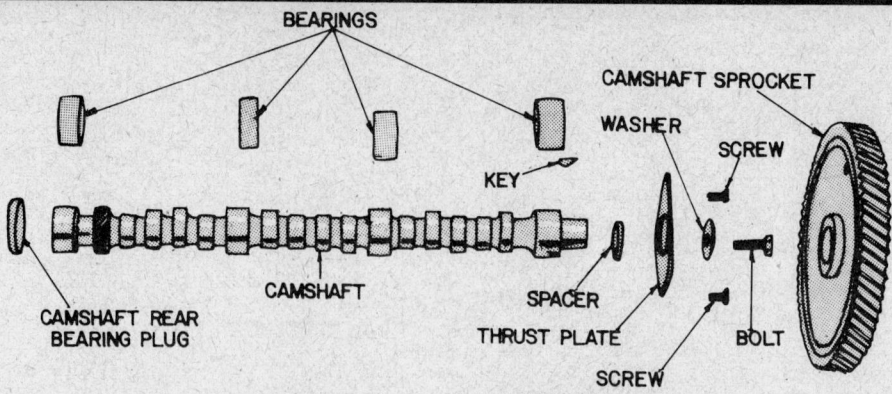

Fig. 12 Camshaft components. 2800 cc engine

in each hole. Using two large screwdrivers, pry evenly on both screws to remove seal, Fig. 14.

NOTE: Use care to avoid damaging the crankshaft oil seal surface.

5. Install new seal with tool T72C-6165, Fig. 15.

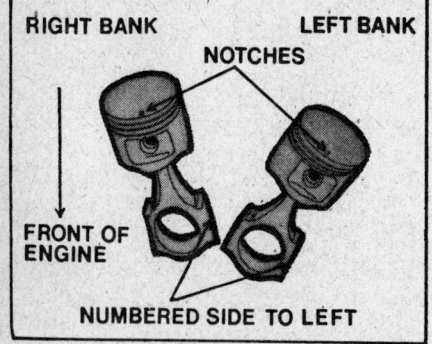

Fig. 13 Piston & rod. 2800 cc engine

OIL PAN, REPLACE

1979 Capri & Mustang

1. Disconnect battery ground cable.
2. Remove fan shroud attaching screws and position shroud over fan.
3. Raise and support vehicle, then drain oil pan.
4. Remove two bolts attaching steering gear to main crossmember and rest steering gear on frame away from oil pan.
5. Remove engine mount attaching nuts.
6. Raise engine with a suitable jack and place wood blocks between the engine mounts and the frame.
7. Remove rear "K" braces.
8. Remove oil pan attaching bolts and lower oil pan to frame.
9. Remove oil pump attaching bolts and lower oil pump into oil pan.
10. Remove oil pan. It may be necessary to rotate crankshaft to provide adequate clearance.
11. Reverse procedure to install.

Exc. 1979 Capri & Mustang

1. Disconnect battery ground cable.
2. Remove oil level dipstick.
3. Drain cooling system and disconnect upper and lower radiator hoses.
4. Remove fan shroud attaching bolts and place shroud over fan.
5. Raise vehicle and drain crankcase, then remove splash shield and starter.
6. If equipped with automatic transmission, disconnect cooler lines at radiator.

7. Disconnect steering gear and power steering hoses (if equipped) and position gear aside, then disconnect sway bar and rotate to allow clearance.
8. Remove engine front support nuts, then raise engine and place wood blocks between engine front supports and chassis.
9. Remove converter or clutch housing cover.
10. Remove oil pan bolts and oil pan.

OIL PUMP, REPLACE

The oil pump, Fig. 16, can be removed after oil pan removal.

OIL PUMP REPAIRS

1. Remove end plate and withdraw O ring from groove in body.
2. Check clearance between lobes of inner and outer rotors. This should not exceed .006". Rotors are supplied only in a matched pair.
3. Check clearance between outer rotor and the housing, Fig. 17. This should not exceed .010 inch.
4. Place a straightedge across face of pump body, Fig. 18. Clearance between face of rotors and straightedge should not exceed .005 inch.
5. If necessary to replace rotor or drive shaft, remove outer rotor and then drive out retaining pin securing the skew gear to drive shaft and pull off the gear.
6. Withdraw inner rotor and drive shaft.

Fig. 14 Removing crankshaft rear oil seal. 2800 cc engine

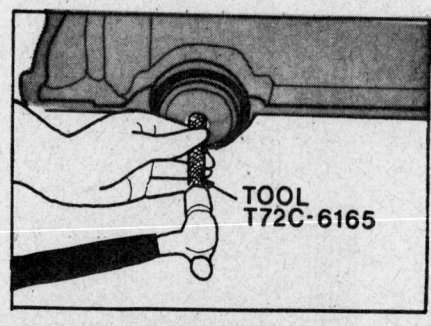

Fig. 15 Installing crankshaft rear oil seal. 2800 cc engine

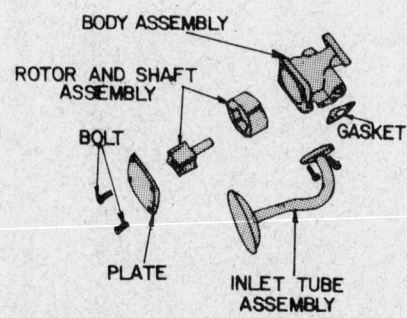

Fig. 16 Oil pump. 2800 cc engine

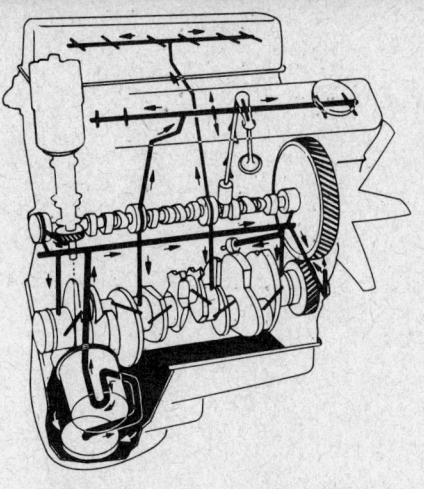

Engine oiling system. 2800 cc engine

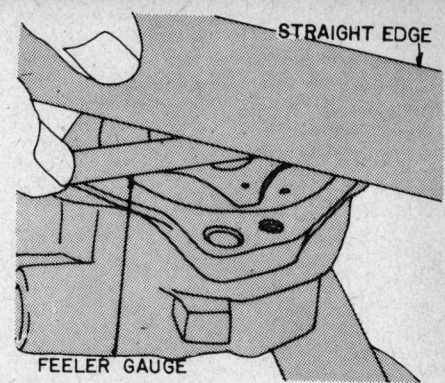

Fig. 17 Checking outer rotor to housing clearance. 2800 cc engine

Fig. 18 Checking rotor end play. 2800 cc engine

BELT TENSION DATA

	New Ft. Lbs.	Used Ft. Lbs.
1977–79 Exc. 1/4 inch	140	110
1/4 inch	65	50

WATER PUMP, REPLACE

1. Drain coolant and disconnect heater hose and lower radiator hose from pump.
2. Loosen alternator and remove drive belt.
3. Remove fan and pulley.
4. Remove water pump mounting bolts, water pump, water inlet housing and thermostat.

FUEL PUMP, REPLACE

1. Disconnect fuel lines from pump.
2. Remove fuel pump attaching bolts and fuel pump.

6-200 Engine Section

Refer to the Ford & Mercury—Compact & Intermediate chapter for service procedures on this engine not included in this section.

Oil Pan, Replace

1. If equipped with automatic transmission, disconnect transmission oil cooler lines from radiator, then remove the radiator top support.
2. Remove dipstick, then raise and support vehicle and drain crankcase.
3. Remove the four bolts and nuts retaining sway bar to chassis and allow sway bar to hang down.
4. Remove K-brace, then lower the rack and pinion steering gear.
5. Remove starter motor, then remove the two engine mounts to support bracket nuts and loosen the two rear insulator to crossmember retaining bolts.
6. Raise engine and place a 1 1/4 inch wooden block between each engine support insulator and chassis bracket, then lower engine onto wood blocks.
7. Using floor jack, raise transmission slightly, then remove the oil pan retaining bolts and lower oil pan onto crossmember.
8. Position transmission oil cooler lines aside and remove oil pan. If necessary, rotate engine so crankshaft throws clear oil pan rail.
9. Reverse procedure to install.

V6-232 Engine Section

Refer to Ford & Mercury—Compact & Intermediate Chapter for service procedures on this engine.

V8 Engine Section

NOTE: Refer to the Ford & Mercury—Compact & Intermediate chapter for service procedures on this engine not included in this section.

ENGINE MOUNTS, REPLACE

1979–84 Capri & Mustang

1. Remove fan shroud attaching screws, if necessary.
2. Remove nuts attaching insulators to lower bracket, Fig. 1.
3. Raise engine with a suitable jack and a block of wood placed under oil pan.
4. Remove insulator to engine block attaching bolts.
5. Remove insulator from vehicle.
6. Reverse procedure to install.

1977–78 Mustang

1. Remove fan shroud screws and support engine with a suitable jack and a block of wood under the oil pan.
2. Remove insulator to frame through bolt, Fig. 2.

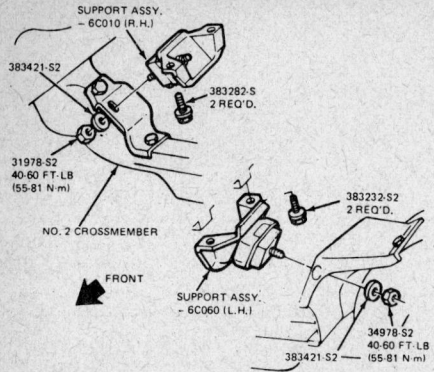

Fig. 1 Engine mount. 1979–84 Capri & Mustang

3. Remove insulator to engine block attaching bolts.
4. Raise engine slightly, then remove insulator and heat shield, if equipped.
5. Reverse procedure to install.

VALVES, ADJUST

The firing order of the 1982–84 V8-302 H.O. engine is 1-3-7-2-6-5-4-8, while the firing order for the 1977–79 V8-302 and 1980–82 V8-255 engines is 1-5-4-2-6-3-7-8. Therefore when adjusting valves on the 1982–84 V8-302 H.O. engine, refer to the procedure for the V8-351 engine in the "Ford & Mercury—Compact & Intermediate" chapter.

OIL PAN, REPLACE

1979–84

1. Disconnect battery cables.
2. Remove fan shroud retaining bolts and position fan shroud over fan.
3. On 1981–84 models, remove dipstick and tube assembly.

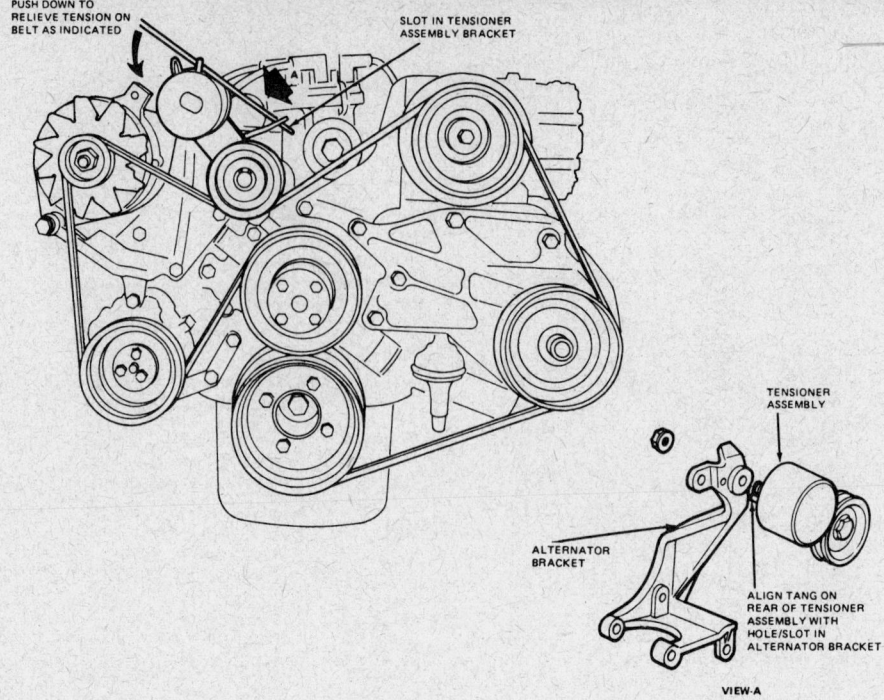

Fig. 3 Serpentine drive belt

4. On all models, raise and support vehicle, then drain crankcase.

NOTE: Some oil pans have dual oil sumps. Make sure to remove both drain plugs to thoroughly drain oil.

5. Remove the two bolts retaining steering gear to main crossmember and allow steering gear to rest on frame away from oil pan.
6. Remove engine mount retaining bolts, then raise engine and place a 2 x 4 inch wooden block between each engine mount and vehicle frame.
7. Remove rear K-braces
8. Remove oil pan retaining bolts and lower oil pan onto frame.
9. Remove oil pump retaining bolts and the inlet tube retaining nut from No. 3 main bearing cap stud. Lower the oil pump assembly into the oil pan.
10. Remove oil pan. If necessary, rotate engine so that crankshaft throws clear oil pan rail.
11. Reverse procedure to install.

1977–78

1. Disconnect battery cables.
2. Remove fan shroud retaining bolts and position fan shroud over fan.
3. Raise and support vehicle, then drain crankcase.
4. Remove the four crossmember retaining bolts and remove crossmember.
5. Remove retaining bolt from flex joint to release steering pinion shaft. Remove the 3 nuts and bolts retaining steering gear to crossmember. Remove the 4 bolts retaining sway bar to chassis and move sway bar down.
6. Remove starter motor.
7. Remove oil pan retaining bolts and oil pan.
8. Reverse procedure to install.

SERPENTINE DRIVE BELT

Some engines are equipped with a serpentine drive belt, Fig. 3, to drive the accessories in place of the usual arrangement. This "V" ribbed belt drives the fan/water pump, alternator, secondary air pump, optional A/C com-

Fig. 2 Engine mounts. 1977–78 Mustang

pressor and optional power steering pump.

The tensioner arm should be checked to ensure that the top edge of the arm is located between the two index marks scribed on the circumference next to the slot of the tensioner housing, Fig. 4. If the tensioner arm is not properly aligned, the drive belt and pulleys should be inspected for wear and binding. If the drive belt and pulleys are satisfactory, the tensioner must be replaced as outlined in the following procedure.

Drive belt & Tensioner, Replace

1. Insert a 16 inch pry bar or equivalent in the slot of the tensioner bracket, and using the tensioner housing as a fulcrum, push the pry bar downward to force the tensioner pulley upward, relieving tension on belt, Fig. 3.
2. Remove drive belt.

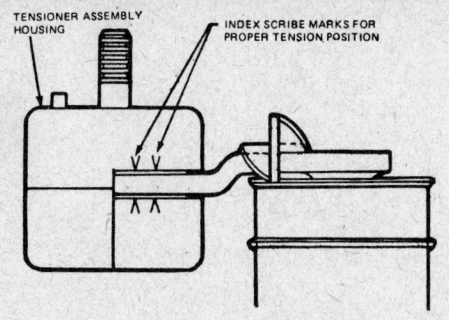

Fig. 4 Serpentine drive belt tensioner alignment marks

3. Remove bolt securing tensioner assembly to alternator bracket.
4. Remove tensioner assembly.
5. Position tensioner assembly so the tang, located on the rear of the assembly, is placed to fit in the hole or slot in alternator bracket.
6. Install the tensioner assembly bolt through the hole in the alternator bracket and torque bolt to 55-80 ft. lbs.
7. Install drive belt by inserting the pry bar as outlined in Step 1. Refer to decal located on top of the windshield washer/coolant expansion reservoir for proper belt routing.
8. Remove pry bar.
9. The drive belt is automatically tensioned when the tensioner arm is located between the two index marks, Fig. 4.

Turbocharger Section

DESCRIPTION

The turbocharger, Figs. 1 through 4, is an exhaust driven device which compresses the air-fuel mixture that is used to increase engine power on a demand basis, allowing a smaller, more economical engine to be used. An optional turbocharger is available on 1979–80 and 1984 Capri and Mustang models equipped with the 4-140 (2300cc) engine.

A turbine in the exhaust gas flow is connected through a shaft to the impeller (compressor). During normal, steady operation, the turbine does not rotate with sufficient speed to boost pressure to compress the air-fuel mixture. As the speed increases, the mixture is compressed, allowing the denser mixture to enter the combustion chambers and develop more engine power during the combustion cycle.

The intake manifold pressure (boost) is controlled by a wastegate valve which is used to bypass a portion of the exhaust gasses around the turbine at a predetermined point in the cycle, limiting the boost pressure.

A green light on the instrument panel indicates that the turbocharger is in a safe boost condition. A red light and buzzer are used to indicate a malfunction or if boost pressure exceeds a predetermined level.

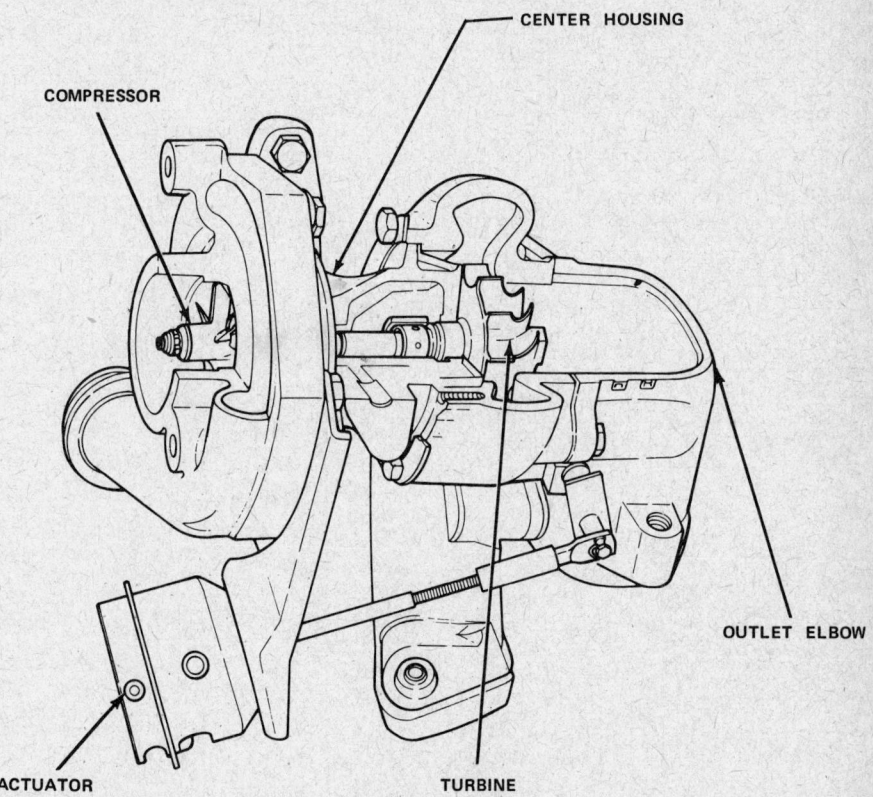

Fig. 1 Turbocharger

LUBRICATION

Turbochargers are lubricated from the engine oil system. These turbochargers operate at speeds up to 120,000 RPM which makes the lubrication of the bearings which support the shaft important for cooling as well as friction.

The oil enters the turbocharger through an inlet fitting in the center housing. This inlet fitting directs oil to the center housing bearings, the oil then drains from the turbocharger through a return hole in the center housing. When changing oil and filter on a turbocharged engine disconnect the ignition switch connector from the distributor then crank engine several times until the oil light goes out. Reconnect the ignition wire to the distributor. This procedure will aid in the filling of the oil system before starting engine.

NOTE: Engine oil on 1979–80 turbocharged engines must be changed every 3000 miles since turbocharger bearing damage may occur from oil contamination.

DIAGNOSIS, TESTING & TROUBLE SHOOTING

Prior to performing any diagnostic or testing procedure check all vacuum hoses and wiring for proper routing and connections, carburetor linkage for damage or any problems which may occur in a non-turbocharged engine.

CAUTION: A turbocharged engine has exhaust pipes located high in the engine compartment. Care must be taken to avoid accidental contact with hot exhaust pipes, since personal injury may occur.

Detonation With Turbo Light On

1. Improper grade of fuel being used.
2. Engine overheating.
3. Turbocharger wastegate actuator lines

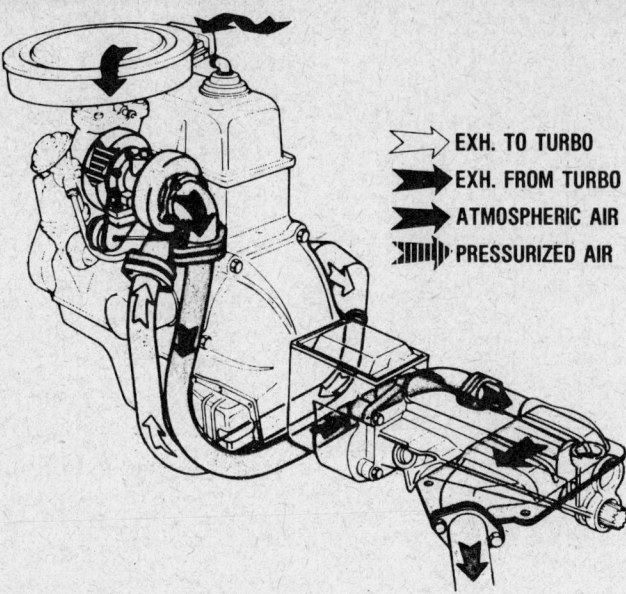

⇨ EXH. TO TURBO
➡ EXH. FROM TURBO
⬛➡ ATMOSPHERIC AIR
▥ PRESSURIZED AIR

Fig. 2   Turbocharger air flow. 1979–80

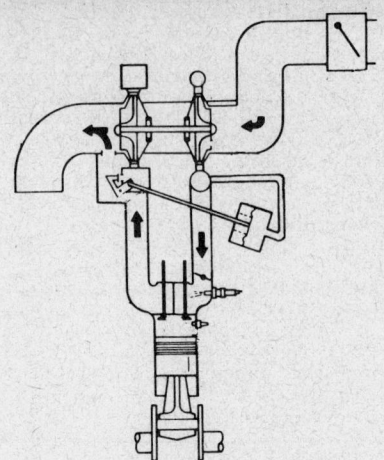

Fig. 3   Turbocharger air flow. 1984

loose or damaged.
4. Improper operation of turbocharger boost pressure control system.
5. Leaking turbocharger compressor oil seal.
6. Clogged PCV valve system.
7. Defective fuel pump or restriction in fuel system.
8. Low compression in one or more cylinders.
9. Contaminated fuel supply.
10. Defective thermostat or restriction in cooling system.
11. On 1979–80 models:
   a. Improper operation of pressure activated spark retard system.
   b. Improper operation of spark control system or spark delay valve.
   c. Defective or improperly adjusted carburetor.
   d. Defective or improperly adjusted distributor.

Engine Lacks Power Or Emits Black Exhaust Smoke

1. Partial or completely clogged air cleaner.
2. Loose compressor to intake manifold connections.
3. Vacuum leak at intake manifold.
4. Exhaust leak at engine exhaust manifold.
5. Leakage at turbocharger mounting flange.
6. Turbocharger rotating assembly binding or dragging.
7. Restrictions in compressor-to-intake manifold duct.
8. Restrictions in engine exhaust system.
9. Restriction in engine intake manifold.
10. On 1979–80 models, defective or improperly adjusted carburetor.
11. On all models, defective fuel pump or clogged fuel lines.
12. Transmission not shifting properly.
13. On 1979–80 models, defective spark control.
14. On all models, turbocharger wastegate not operating properly.

Excessive Oil Consumption Or Emits Blue Exhaust Smoke

1. Leaking or clogged turbocharger oil supply and drain lines or fittings.
2. Clogged air cleaner, fuel system, or evaporative control system.
3. Clogged PCV valve system.
4. On 1979–80 models, defective or improperly adjusted carburetor.
5. On all models, defective fuel pump.
6. Leaking vacuum lines or intake manifold.
7. EGR system not working properly.
8. Defective thermofactor system.
9. Cylinder compression low in one or more cylinders.
10. Leaking turbocharger compressor or turbine oil seals.
11. Check valve train for proper operation.

Wastegate Boost Pressure (In-Vehicle Test)

1979–80

1. Check that the wastegate actuator rod is attached to wastegate arm with retaining clip, Fig. 6.

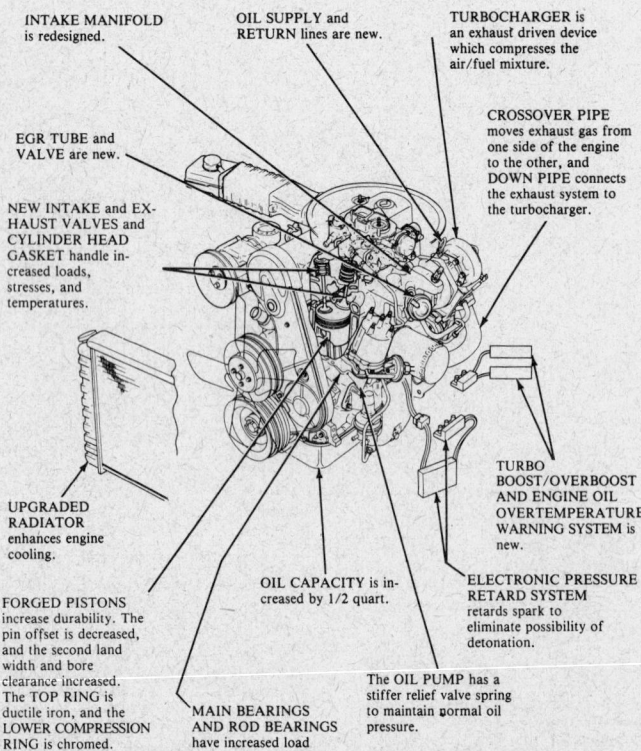

INTAKE MANIFOLD is redesigned.

OIL SUPPLY and RETURN lines are new.

TURBOCHARGER is an exhaust driven device which compresses the air/fuel mixture.

CROSSOVER PIPE moves exhaust gas from one side of the engine to the other, and DOWN PIPE connects the exhaust system to the turbocharger.

EGR TUBE and VALVE are new.

NEW INTAKE and EXHAUST VALVES and CYLINDER HEAD GASKET handle increased loads, stresses, and temperatures.

UPGRADED RADIATOR enhances engine cooling.

TURBO BOOST/OVERBOOST AND ENGINE OIL OVERTEMPERATURE WARNING SYSTEM is new.

ELECTRONIC PRESSURE RETARD SYSTEM retards spark to eliminate possibility of detonation.

FORGED PISTONS increase durability. The pin offset is decreased, and the second land width and bore clearance increased. The TOP RING is ductile iron, and the LOWER COMPRESSION RING is chromed.

OIL CAPACITY is increased by 1/2 quart.

MAIN BEARINGS AND ROD BEARINGS have increased load capacity.

The OIL PUMP has a stiffer relief valve spring to maintain normal oil pressure.

Fig. 4   Turbocharger system. 1979–80

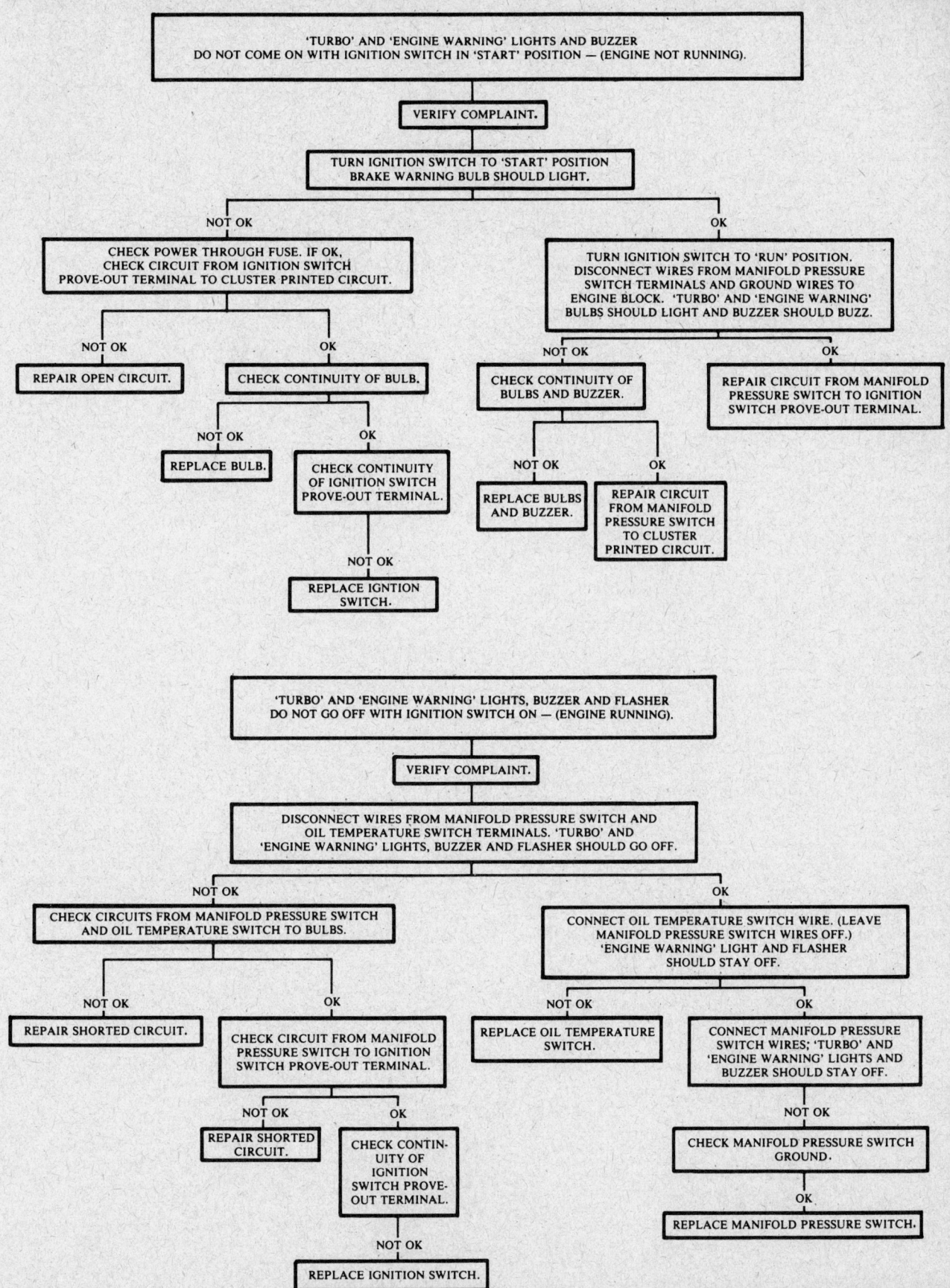

Fig. 5 Turbocharger boost/overboost warning system diagnosis. 1979–80

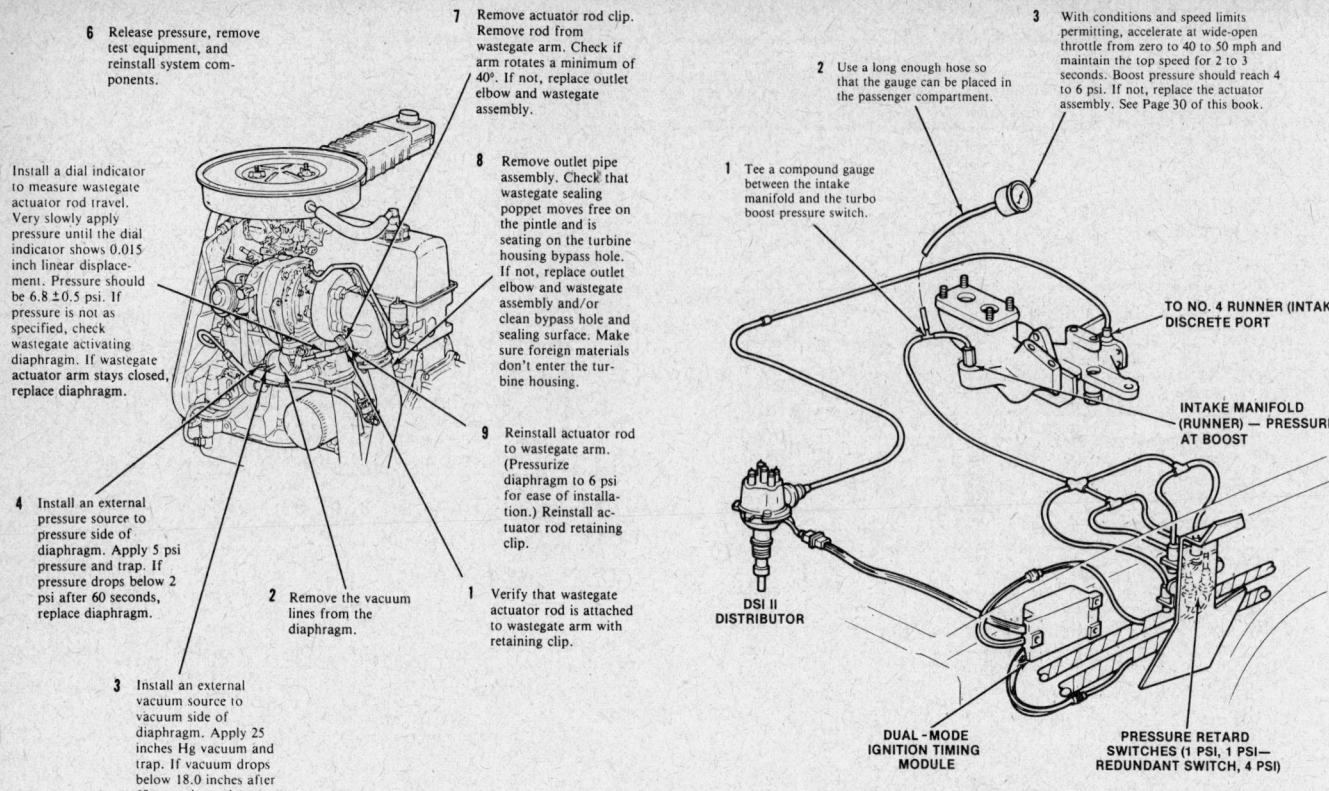

6 Release pressure, remove test equipment, and reinstall system components.

5 Install a dial indicator to measure wastegate actuator rod travel. Very slowly apply pressure until the dial indicator shows 0.015 inch linear displacement. Pressure should be 6.8 ±0.5 psi. If pressure is not as specified, check wastegate activating diaphragm. If wastegate actuator arm stays closed, replace diaphragm.

4 Install an external pressure source to pressure side of diaphragm. Apply 5 psi pressure and trap. If pressure drops below 2 psi after 60 seconds, replace diaphragm.

3 Install an external vacuum source to vacuum side of diaphragm. Apply 25 inches Hg vacuum and trap. If vacuum drops below 18.0 inches after 60 seconds, replace diaphragm.

7 Remove actuator rod clip. Remove rod from wastegate arm. Check if arm rotates a minimum of 40°. If not, replace outlet elbow and wastegate assembly.

8 Remove outlet pipe assembly. Check that wastegate sealing poppet moves free on the pintle and is seating on the turbine housing bypass hole. If not, replace outlet elbow and wastegate assembly and/or clean bypass hole and sealing surface. Make sure foreign materials don't enter the turbine housing.

9 Reinstall actuator rod to wastegate arm. (Pressurize diaphragm to 6 psi for ease of installation.) Reinstall actuator rod retaining clip.

2 Remove the vacuum lines from the diaphragm.

1 Verify that wastegate actuator rod is attached to wastegate arm with retaining clip.

Fig. 6 Testing wastegate boost pressure. 1979–80

3 With conditions and speed limits permitting, accelerate at wide-open throttle from zero to 40 to 50 mph and maintain the top speed for 2 to 3 seconds. Boost pressure should reach 4 to 6 psi. If not, replace the actuator assembly. See Page 30 of this book.

2 Use a long enough hose so that the gauge can be placed in the passenger compartment.

1 Tee a compound gauge between the intake manifold and the turbo boost pressure switch.

TO NO. 4 RUNNER (INTAKE) DISCRETE PORT

INTAKE MANIFOLD (RUNNER) — PRESSURE AT BOOST

DSI II DISTRIBUTOR

DUAL-MODE IGNITION TIMING MODULE

PRESSURE RETARD SWITCHES (1 PSI, 1 PSI— REDUNDANT SWITCH, 4 PSI)

Fig. 7 Compound gauge hook-up for boost pressure road test. 1979–80

2. Remove vacuum lines from the the diaphragm.
3. Install an external vacuum source to vacuum side of diaphragm, Fig. 6. Apply 25 inches vacuum and hold. If vacuum drops below 18.0 after 60 sec. replace diaphragm.
4. Install an external pressure source to the pressure side of diaphragm, Fig. 6. Apply 5 psi pressure and hold. If pressure drops below 2 psi after 60 seconds, replace diaphragm.
5. Using a dial indicator to measure wastegate actuator rod travel, Fig. 6, apply pressure until the dial indicator shows 0.015 inch linear displacement. Pressure should be about 6.8 psi. If pressure is not as specified, check wastegate activating diaphragm. If wastegate activating arm stays closed, replace diaphragm.
6. Release pressure, remove test equipment and reconnect vacuum lines to diaphragm.
7. Remove actuator rod clip. Remove rod from wastegate arm. Check to see if arm rotates a minimum of 40°. If it does not replace outlet elbow and wastegate assembly.
8. Remove outlet pipe assembly, then check that wastegate sealing poppet moves free and is seated on the turbine housing bypass hole. If not, replace outlet elbow and wastegate assembly and clean bypass hole and sealing surface.

CAUTION: Make sure foreign materials do not enter the turbine housing.

9. Reinstall actuator rod to wastegate arm. Reinstall actuator rod retaining clip.

Boost pressure (Road Test)

1979–80

1. Tee a compound gauge between the intake manifold and the turbo boost pressure switch, Fig. 7.
2. Use a long enough hose so that the gauge can be placed in the passenger compartment.
3. With conditions and speed limits permitting, accelerate at wide-open throttle from zero to 40 to 50 mph and maintain the top speed for 2 to 3 seconds. Boost pressure should reach 4 to 6 psi. If not replace the actuator assembly.

Electronic Pressure Retard System

1979–80

1. Check basic engine timing as described elsewhere in this manual.
2. Remove pressure activated retard switch assembly supply line, cap the open line and install an external pressure source to the pressure switch assembly.
3. Remove distributor vacuum line and plug it.
4. Connect a suitable tachometer to the engine.
5. Start engine and using a suitable tool increase engine idle speed to 1400 rpm.
6. Slowly apply pressure to the retard switch supply line, using a tachometer check that engine rpm does not change until 0.5 psi pressure is applied. Increase pressure to 1.0 psi. A 100 rpm drop should occur between 3.75 and 4.25 psi, but not before 3.75 psi.
7. If no rpm drop is noted in step 6, the pressure switch or ignition module may be defective.

TURBOCHARGER INTERNAL INSPECTION

1. Remove the turbocharger assembly following procedure found elsewhere in this section.
2. Remove wastegate actuator rod retaining clip and remove rod from the wastegate arm.
3. Scribe a line across the compressor housing and compressor backing plate to aid in reassembly.
4. Remove six compressor housing bolts, then remove wastegate actuator diaphragm.
5. Remove compressor housing from backing plate, then check for excessive oil on compressor wheel, backing plate and inner surface of housing. If excessive oil is detected, replace the center rotating housing assembly, Figs. 8 and 9.
6. If center housing rotating assembly is being replaced, pre-lubricate with engine oil.
7. Spin the compressor wheel. If rotating assembly binds or drags, replace the center housing rotating assembly.
8. Check turbine wheel for binding, blade cracking or bending, and excessive sludge build up. If any of these conditions exist, replace the turbocharger center rotating housing.
9. To check the turbocharger bearing clearances, remove turbine housing from center housing rotating assembly, and measure clearances.
10. Turbocharger bearing radial clearance
(a) Remove two bolts connecting the turbine oil outlet fitting to the center housing and remove the fitting Figs. 8 and 9.

Attach a dial indicator (Tool 4201-C) to the center housing so that the indicator plunger (Tool T79L-4201-A) extends through the oil outlet port and contacts the shaft Fig. 10.

(b) Manually apply pressure equally and simultaneously to both the compressor and the turbine wheels to move the shaft away from the dial indicator plunger as far as possible.

(c) Set the dial indicator to zero while holding the shaft away from the plunger tip.

(d) Manually apply pressure equally and simultaneously to both the compressor and turbine wheels to move the shaft towards the dial indicator plunger as far as possible. Note the maximum reading on dial indicator.

(e) Manually apply pressure equally and simultaneously to both the compressor and turbine wheels as required to move the turbine wheel assembly shaft away from the dial indicator as far as possible. The dial indicator should return to zero.

(f) Repeat steps 2, 3, 4, and 5 to make sure an accurate measurement has been made. If the bearing radial clearance is less then 0.003 inch or greater then 0.006 inch, replace the turbocharger center rotating housing assembly.

NOTE: Continued operation of a turbocharger having excessive bearing radial clearance will result in severe damage to the compressor and turbine wheels and the housings.

11. Turbocharger bearing axial clearance
(a) If not already done, remove five bolts connecting the turbine outlet elbow assembly and remove the elbow.

(b) Attach a dial indicator (Tool 4201-C) to the center housing so that the indicator plunger extends through the oil outlet port and contacts the shaft, Fig. 11.

(c) Manually push the turbine wheel assembly as far away from the dial indicator tip as possible.

(d) Set the dial indicator to zero while holding the turbine wheel away from the tip of the plunger.

(e) Manually push the turbine wheel assembly toward the dial indicator tip as far as possible.

(f) Repeat step 3 and check that the dial indicator returns to zero.

(g) Repeat steps 3, 4, 5, and 6 to make sure an accurate measurement has been made. If the bearing axial clearance is less than 0.001 inch or greater than 0.003 inch, replace the turbocharger center rotating housing assembly.

NOTE: Continued operation of a turbocharger having excessive bearing axial clearance will result in severe damage to the compressor and turbine wheels and housings.

TURBOCHARGER SERVICE

Before performing turbocharger service, note the following general precautions:
1. Clean area around turbocharger assembly with non-caustic solution before removal of assembly. Cover openings of engine assembly connections to prevent entry of foreign material while turbocharger is off engine.

2. When removing turbocharger assembly, do not bend, nick or in any way damage the compressor or turbine wheel blades. Any damage may result in rotating assembly imbalance, and failure of center housing, compressor, and/or turbine housings.

3. Before disconnecting the center housing from either the compressor or the turbine housing, scribe location of components for assembly in original position.

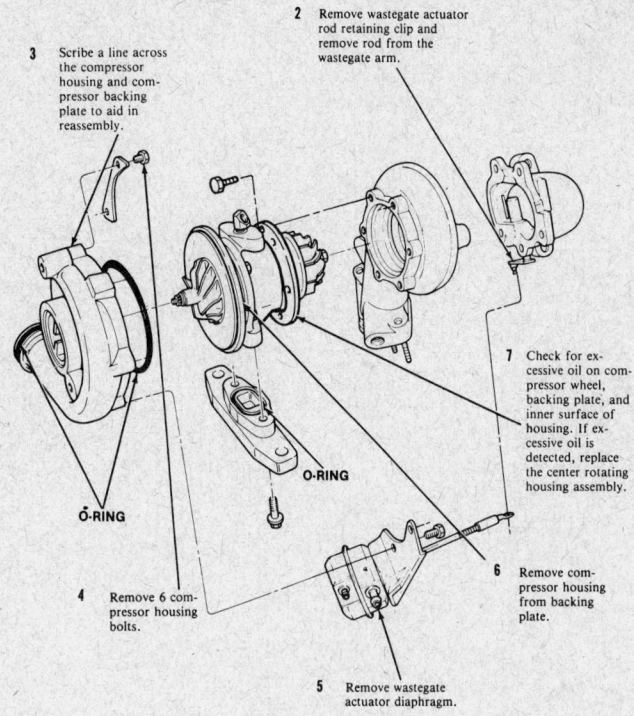

1 Remove the turbocharger from the engine

2 Remove wastegate actuator rod retaining clip and remove rod from the wastegate arm.

3 Scribe a line across the compressor housing and compressor backing plate to aid in reassembly.

7 Check for excessive oil on compressor wheel, backing plate, and inner surface of housing. If excessive oil is detected, replace the center rotating housing assembly.

O-RING

O-RING

4 Remove 6 compressor housing bolts.

6 Remove compressor housing from backing plate.

5 Remove wastegate actuator diaphragm.

Fig. 8 Exploded view of turbocharger. 1979–80

Wastegate Actuator Assembly, Replace

1. Disconnect two vacuum hoses from actuator.
2. Remove clip attaching actuator rod to wastegate arm.
3. Remove two bolts attaching actuator diaphragm assembly to compressor housing.
4. Reverse procedure to install.

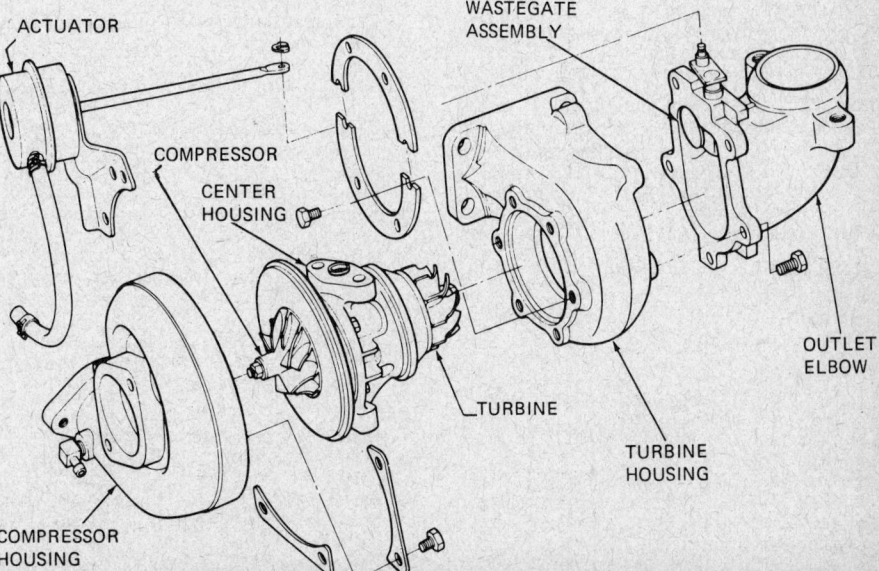

ACTUATOR

WASTEGATE ASSEMBLY

COMPRESSOR

CENTER HOUSING

TURBINE

OUTLET ELBOW

TURBINE HOUSING

COMPRESSOR HOUSING

Fig. 9 Exploded view of turbocharger. 1984

1 Remove turbocharger assembly from engine

2 Remove wastegate actuator rod retaining clip and remove rod from wastegate arm.

3 Remove 2 bolts connecting the turbine oil outlet fitting to the center housing and remove the fitting.

4 Attach a dial indicator (Tool 4201-C) to the center housing so that the indicator plunger (Tool T79L-4201-A) extends through the oil outlet port and contacts the shaft.

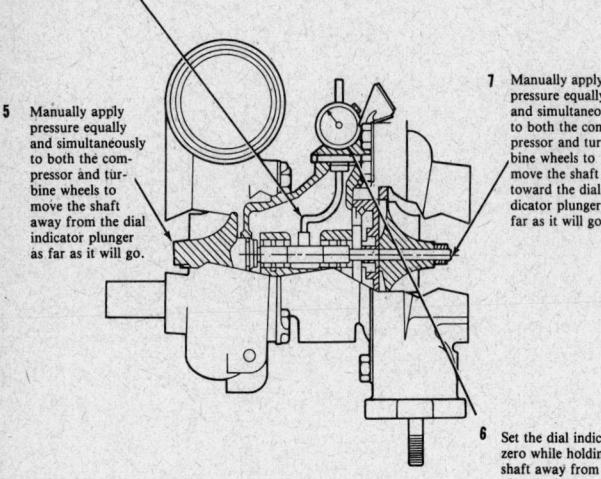

5 Manually apply pressure equally and simultaneously to both the compressor and turbine wheels to move the shaft away from the dial indicator plunger as far as it will go.

7 Manually apply pressure equally and simultaneously to both the compressor and turbine wheels to move the shaft toward the dial indicator plunger as far as it will go.

6 Set the dial indicator to zero while holding the shaft away from the plunger tip.

8 Repeat step 5 and note that the dial indicator returns to zero.

9 Repeat steps 5, 6, 7, and 8 to make sure an accurate measurement has been made. If the bearing radial clearance is less than 0.003 inch or greater than 0.006 inch, replace the turbocharger center rotating housing assembly.

Fig. 10 Checking turbocharger bearing radial clearance

1 Remove turbocharger assembly from engine

Remove wastegate actuator rod retaining clip and remove rod from the wastegate arm.

3 Remove 5 bolts connecting the turbine outlet elbow assembly and remove the elbow.

NOTE: One bolt is located inside the elbow housing.

4 Attach a dial indicator (Tool 4201-C) to the center housing so that the indicator plunger extends through the oil outlet port and contacts the shaft, as illustrated.

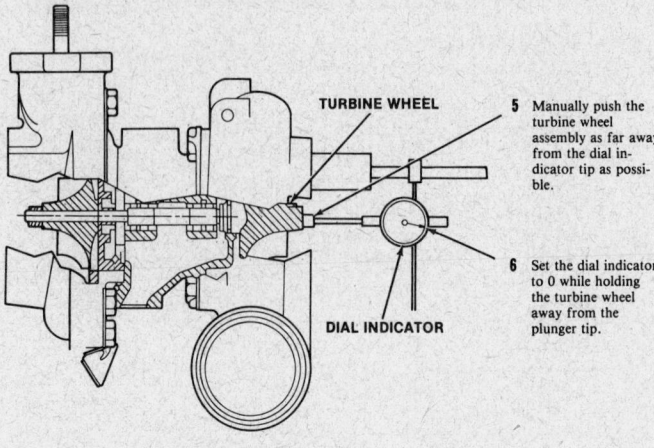

TURBINE WHEEL

DIAL INDICATOR

5 Manually push the turbine wheel assembly as far away from the dial indicator tip as possible.

6 Set the dial indicator to 0 while holding the turbine wheel away from the plunger tip.

7 Manually push the turbine wheel assembly toward the dial indicator tip as far as possible.

8 Repeat step 5 and note that the dial indicator returns to zero.

9 Repeat steps 5, 6, 7, and 8 to make sure an accurate measurement has been made. If the bearing axial clearance is less than 0.001 inch or greater than 0.003 inch, replace the turbocharger center rotating housing assembly.

Fig. 11 Checking turbocharger bearing axial clearance

Outlet Elbow & Wastegate Assembly, Replace

1979–80
1. Raise vehicle.
2. Loosen turbocharger exhaust pipe at catalytic converter.
3. Lower vehicle.
4. Disconnect turbocharger down pipe at outlet elbow and wastegate assembly.
5. Remove clip attaching actuator rod to wastegate linkage.
6. Remove five bolts attaching outlet and wastegate elbow assembly.
7. Reverse procedure to install.

1984
1. Disconnect turbocharger down pipe from outlet elbow and wastegate assembly.
2. Remove clip attaching actuator rod to wastegate linkage.
3. Remove 5 outlet and wastegate elbow assembly attaching bolts and the assembly.
4. Reverse procedure to install.

Turbine Outlet Elbow Assembly, Replace

1979–80
1. Disconnect turbocharger exhaust outlet pipe from elbow assembly.
2. Remove turbocharger heat shield.
3. Raise vehicle.
4. Disconnect turbocharger exhaust crossover pipe from the catalytic converter.
5. Lower car.
6. Remove clip attaching wastegate linkage to actuator rod.
7. Remove five bolts attaching outlet elbow to turbine housing.

NOTE: One bolt is located inside the outlet elbow.

8. Reverse procedure to install.

Turbocharger Assembly, Replace

1979–80
1. Remove air cleaner.
2. Remove turbocharger heat shield.
3. Raise vehicle.
4. Remove exhaust outlet pipe and exhaust down pipe.
5. Lower vehicle.
6. Remove boost control tube and oil supply line.
7. Remove throttle bracket.
8. Remove rear wastegate actuator vacuum line.
9. Remove EGR tube and dipstick tube.
10. Remove necessary vacuum hoses.
11. Remove four bolts attaching turbocharger to intake manifold.
12. Remove four bolts from turbocharger rear brace and remove turbocharger from engine.
13. Reverse procedure to install, replacing the three O-rings and greasing the compressor outlet O-ring.

1984
1. Disconnect battery ground cable.
2. Scribe hood hinge locations and remove hood.
3. Remove 2 throttle body discharge tube-to-turbocharger attaching bolts, then loosen upper hose clamp.
4. Disconnect vacuum hose and tubes from turbocharger.
5. Disconnect PCV tube from turbocharger air inlet elbow, then remove throttle body discharge tube and hose as an assembly.
6. Disconnect ground wire from air inlet elbow, then remove turbocharger oil supply line.
7. Disconnect oxygen sensor electrical connector from turbocharger.
8. Raise and support vehicle.
9. Disconnect exhaust pipe from turbocharger.
10. Remove lower oil return line from bottom of turbocharger.
11. Remove turbocharger bracket rear lower attaching bolt, then lower vehicle and remove front lower attaching bolt.
12. Remove 3 turbocharger stud nuts and lift assembly from engine.
13. Reverse procedure to install.

Compressor Housing, Replace

1979–80
To replace compressor housing, refer to Fig. 8 and follow the numerical sequence. Reverse sequence to install.

Turbine Housing, Replace

1979–80
1. Remove turbocharger assembly from engine as outlined previously in this section.
2. Remove wastegate actuator rod retaining clip and remove rod from wastegate arm.
3. Scribe a line across the turbine housing and center housing to aid in reassembly.
4. Remove six turbine housing bolts, then remove turbine housing from the center housing.
5. Reverse procedure to install.

Clutch & Transmission Section

CLUTCH PEDAL, ADJUST

1981—84 Capri & Mustang

These models incorporate a self adjusting clutch mechanism. The adjust mechanism consists of a spring loaded rachet quadrant attached to the clutch cable. To accomplish this adjustment, grasp clutch pedal and pull upward, then slowly depress clutch pedal. If a click is heard during the procedure, an adjustment was necessary and has been accomplished. This procedure should be performed at least every 5000 miles.

1979—80 Capri & Mustang

NOTE: These models do not require a free play adjustment. A clutch pedal height adjustment will be required instead.

1. From under vehicle remove dust shield.
2. Loosen clutch cable lock nut. Turn adjusting nut clockwise to raise clutch pedal and counter clockwise to lower clutch pedal. The total clutch pedal stroke should be 5.3 in. for 4-140 engine and 6.5 in. for V8-302 engine.
3. Torque lock nut to 5 to 8 ft. lbs., using care not to disturb adjustment.
4. Cycle clutch pedal several times, then recheck pedal height.
5. When clutch system is properly adjusted the clutch pedal can be raised approximately 2.7 in. on 4-140 engines and 1.5 in. for V8-302 engines, before contacting the clutch pedal stop.

1977—78 Mustang

1. Remove cable retaining clip at dash panel and remove cable retaining screw from fender apron.
2. Pull cable toward front of vehicle until nut can be rotated. Rotate nut from adjustment sleeve about 1/4 inch.
3. Release cable to neutralize the linkage and pull cable until free movement of release lever is eliminated.
4. Rotate adjusting nut toward adjustment sleeve until contact is made, then index into the next notch.

5. Install cable retaining clip, cable retaining bracket and retaining screw.

1977—80 Bobcat & Pinto

1. Loosen clutch cable lock nut at flywheel housing.
2. Pull cable toward front of vehicle so the nylon adjuster nut tabs are clear of the housing boss, then rotate nut toward vehicle front approximately 1/4 inch.
3. Release the cable, neutralizing the system, and pull cable forward again so release lever free movement is eliminated.
4. Rotate the adjusting nut until contact is made between index tab face and the housing, then index the tabs to engage the nearest housing groove.
5. Torque lock nut to 15 ft. lbs.

CLUTCH, REPLACE

1977—80 Bobcat & Pinto

1. Remove shift lever by removing knob and boot, then compress rubber spring and remove retaining snap ring. Bend shift lever lock tabs up and remove plastic dome nut from extension housing.
2. Raise vehicle on a hoist.
3. Disconnect drive shaft from U joint flange and slide drive shaft off transmission output shaft. Insert tool over output shaft to prevent loss of lubricant.
4. Disconnect speedometer cable and back-up light switch wire connector from extension housing.
5. Disconnect lower end of clutch cable at release lever.
6. Remove starter motor.
7. Remove bolts securing engine rear plate to front lower part of flywheel housing.
8. Support rear of engine using a suitable jack, then remove bolt attaching engine rear support. Also remove crossmember attaching bolts and remove the crossmember.
9. Remove bolts attaching flywheel housing to engine block.
10. Move transmission and flywheel housing assembly rearward until housing clears

the clutch pressure plate. Lower transmission and remove.
11. Unfasten and remove the pressure plate, marking same to assure correct assembly.

1977—78 Mustang & 1979—84 Capri & Mustang

NOTE: On 1981—84 Capri and Mustang, lift clutch pedal upward to disengage clutch cable self adjuster pawl and quadrant. Push quadrant forward, then detach cable from quadrant and allow quadrant to slowly swing rearward.

1. Loosen clutch cable adjusting nut to allow slack in cable. On 1979—84 models, disconnect cable from release lever.
2. Position gear shift lever in neutral, then remove lever attaching screws and the lever.
3. Raise and support vehicle.
4. On 1979—84 models, remove dust shield.
5. On all models, remove driveshaft. Cover extension housing to prevent leakage.
6. Disconnect electrical leads and speedometer cable from transmission.
7. Support rear of engine and remove crossmember, then lower engine as necessary and remove transmission attaching bolts and transmission.
8. Disconnect clutch release cable from lever and flywheel housing.
9. Disconnect starter cable and remove starter motor.
10. On models with V6 engine, remove number 2A crossmember. This crossmember is located behind the number 2 crossmember which supports the engine.
11. On all models, remove flywheel housing.
12. Evenly loosen and remove pressure plate attaching screws to prevent distortion of pressure plate. If pressure plate is to be reused, mark pressure plate and flywheel to assure correct assembly.

4 & 5 SPEED TRANS., REPLACE

The transmission is removed as described under "Clutch Replace".

Rear Axle, Propeller Shaft & Brakes

REAR AXLE

Integral Type

This rear axle, Figs. 1 and 2 is an integral design hypoid with the centerline of the pinion set below the centerline of the ring gear. The semi-floating axle shafts are retained in the housing by ball bearings and bearing retainers at axle ends.

The differential is mounted on two opposed tapered roller bearings which are retained in the housing by removable caps. Differential bearing preload and drive gear backlash is adjusted by nuts located behind each differential bearing cup.

The drive pinion assembly is mounted on two opposed tapered roller bearings. Pinion

bearing preload is adjusted by a collapsible spacer on the pinion shaft. Pinion and ring gear tooth contact is adjusted by shims between the rear bearing cone and pinion gear.

Removable Carrier Type

In these axles, Fig. 3, the drive pinion is straddle-mounted by two opposed tapered roller bearings which support the pinion shaft in front of the drive pinion gear, and a straight roller bearing that supports the pinion shaft at the rear of the pinion gear. The drive pinion is assembled in a pinion retainer that is bolted to the differential carrier. The tapered roller bearings are preloaded by a collapsible spacer between the bearings. The pinion is positioned by a shim or shims located

between the drive pinion retainer and the differential carrier.

The differential is supported in the carrier by two tapered roller side bearings. These bearings are preloaded by two threaded ring nuts or sleeves between the bearings and the pedestals. The differential assembly is positioned for proper ring gear and pinion backlash by varying the adjustment of these ring nuts. The differential case houses two side gears in mesh with two pinions mounted on a pinion shaft which is held in place by a pin. The side gears and pinions are backed by thrust washers.

The axle shafts are of unequal length, the left shaft being shorter than the right. The axle shafts are mounted in sealed ball bearings which are pressed on the shafts.

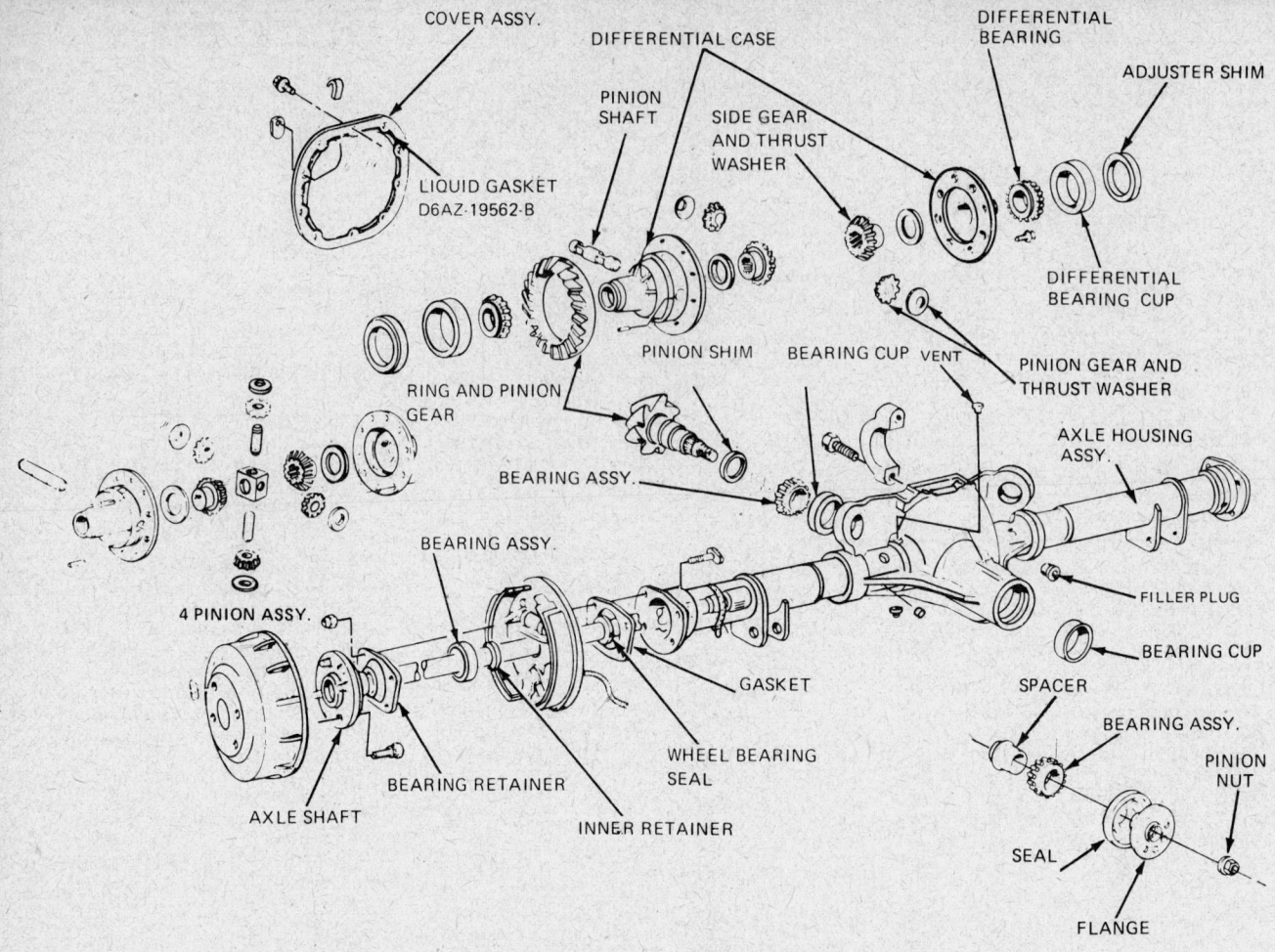

Fig. 1 Disassembled integral rear axle. 6¾ inch ring gear. 1979—83 (Typical of 1977—78)

REAR AXLE, REPLACE

1. Raise vehicle and support at rear frame members.
2. Drain lubricant from axle.
3. Mark drive shaft and pinion flanges for reassembly, then disconnect drive shaft at rear axle U-joint and remove drive shaft from transmission extension housing. Install seal replacer tool in extension housing to prevent leakage.
4. Disconnect shock absorbers at lower mountings.
5. Remove rear wheels and brake drums, then disconnect brake lines at wheel cylinders.
6. Disconnect vent hose from vent tube, then remove vent tube from brake junction and axle housing.
7. Remove clips retaining brake lines to axle housing.
8. Support rear axle housing using a suitable jack.
9. On models with coil springs, disconnect upper control arms from mountings on axle housing, then carefully lower axle assembly until spring tension is relieved and remove coil springs. Disconnect lower control arms from axle housing.
10. On models with leaf springs, remove U-bolts and plates.
11. Lower rear axle and remove from vehicle.
12. Reverse procedure to install.

AXLE SHAFT, BEARING & OIL SEAL, REPLACE

Integral Type

6¾ Inch Ring Gear
1. Remove wheel and tire from brake drum.
2. Remove Tinnerman nuts that secure brake drum to axle flange and remove brake drum.
3. Working through hole in each axle flange, remove nuts that secure wheel bearing retainer plate. Then pull the axle shaft assembly out of the housing being careful not to cut or rough up the seal.

NOTE: *The brake backing plate must not be dislodged. Replace one nut to hold the plate in place after shaft is removed.*

---

4. If wheel bearing is to be replaced, loosen inner retainer ring by nicking it deeply with a chisel in several places. It will then slide off.
5. Remove bearing from shaft.

7½ Inch Ring Gear
1. Raise and support vehicle.
2. Remove wheel and tire assembly, then the brake drum.
3. Clean all dirt from carrier cover area.
4. Remove housing cover to drain lubricant from rear axle.
5. Remove differential pinion shaft lock bolt and the shaft.
6. Move flanged end of axle shafts toward center of vehicle and remove "C" clip from button end of shaft.
7. Remove axle shaft from housing. Use care to avoid damaging the oil seal.
8. Remove bearing and seal as an assembly using a suitable slide hammer.
9. Reverse procedure to install. Lubricate new bearing with rear axle lubricant prior to installation. Apply suitable grease between lips of oil seal.

NOTE: The bearing should be installed using tool No. T78P-1225-A or equivalent, and the seal using tool No. T78P-1177-A or equivalent. If proper tools are not used, early bearing or seal failure may result. If seal becomes cocked in the bore during installation, it must be removed and replaced with a new one.

Removable Carrier Type

1. Remove wheel assembly.
2. Remove brake drum from flange.
3. Working through hole provided in axle shaft flange, remove nuts that secure wheel bearing retainer.
4. Pull axle shaft out of housing. If bearing is a tight fit in axle housing use a slide hammer-type puller.

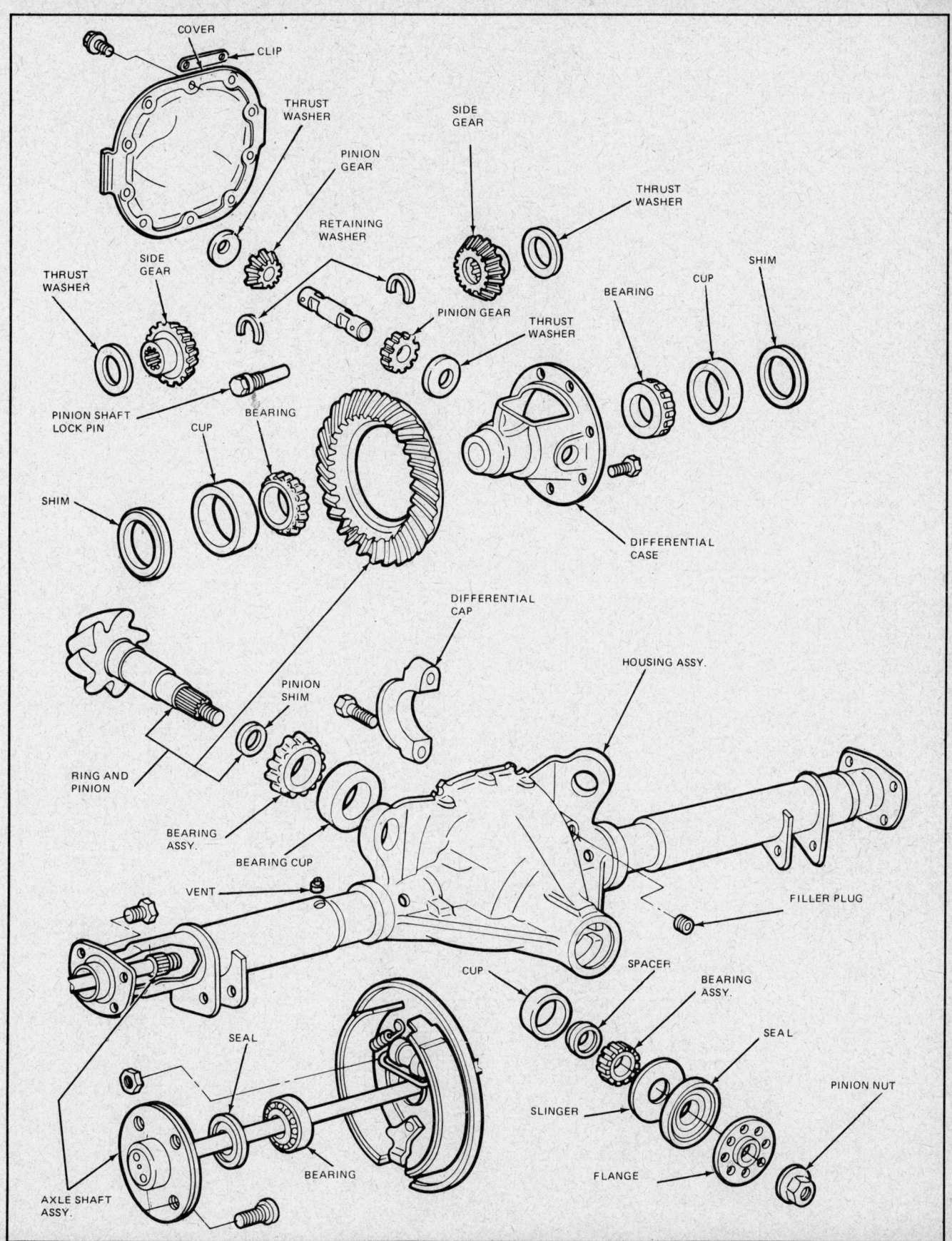

Fig. 2 Disassembled integral rear axle. 7½ inch ring gear

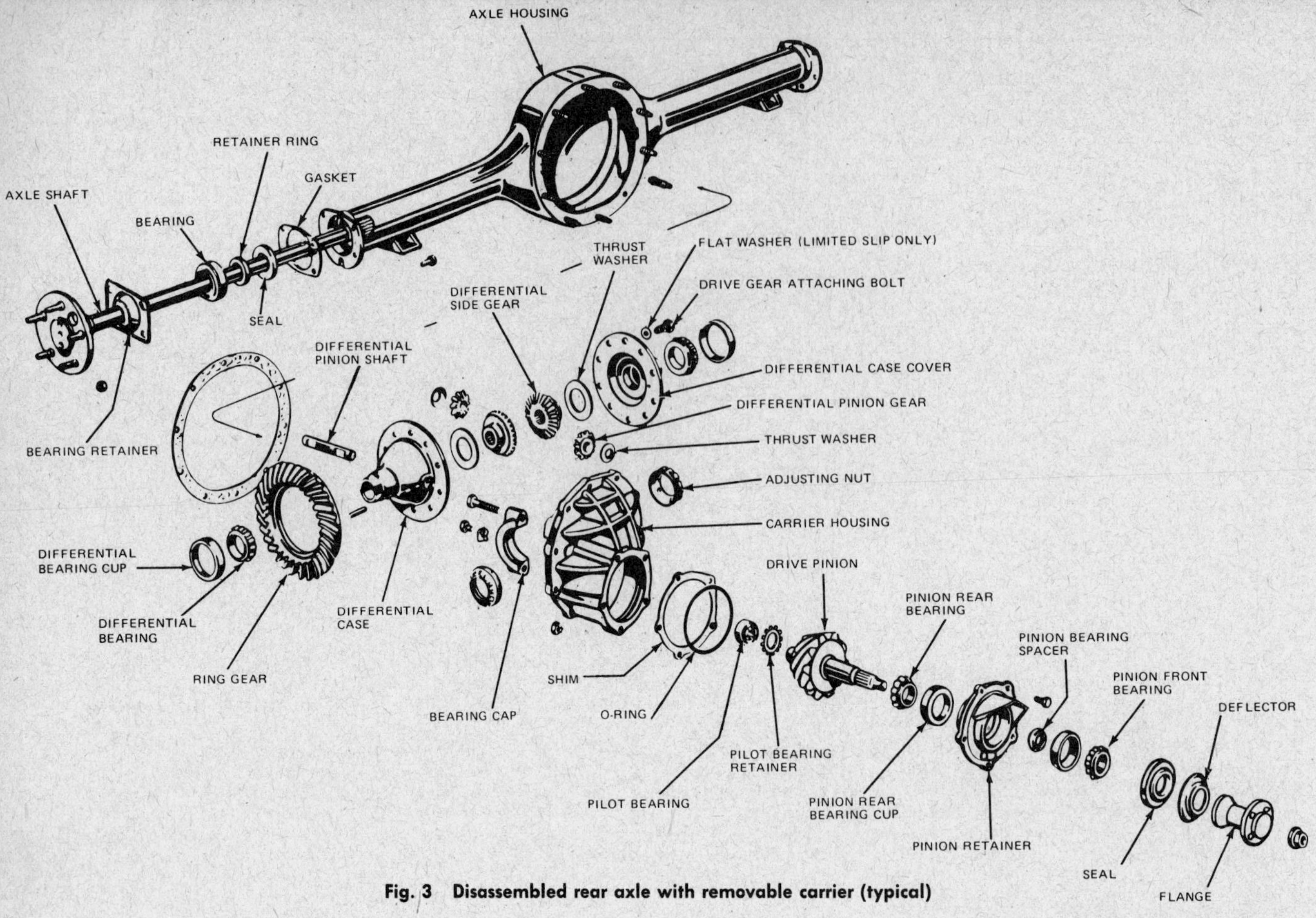

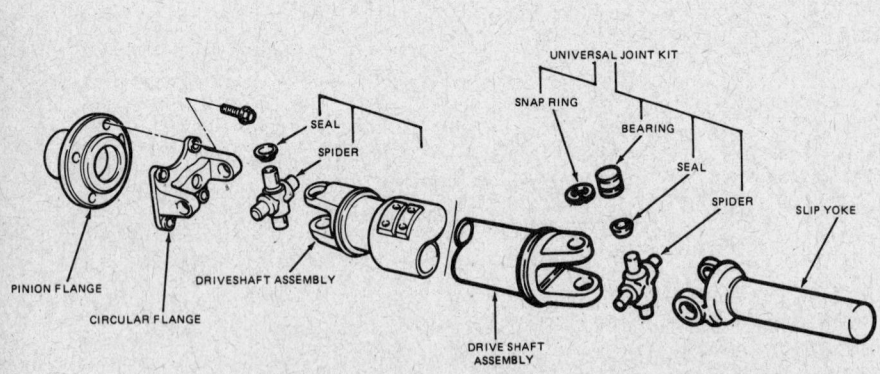

AXLE HOUSING

RETAINER RING

GASKET

AXLE SHAFT

BEARING

THRUST WASHER

FLAT WASHER (LIMITED SLIP ONLY)

DRIVE GEAR ATTACHING BOLT

SEAL

DIFFERENTIAL SIDE GEAR

DIFFERENTIAL CASE COVER

DIFFERENTIAL PINION SHAFT

DIFFERENTIAL PINION GEAR

BEARING RETAINER

THRUST WASHER

ADJUSTING NUT

CARRIER HOUSING

DIFFERENTIAL BEARING CUP

DRIVE PINION

PINION REAR BEARING

DIFFERENTIAL BEARING

PINION BEARING SPACER

DIFFERENTIAL CASE

PINION FRONT BEARING

RING GEAR

SHIM

DEFLECTOR

BEARING CAP

O-RING

PILOT BEARING RETAINER

PILOT BEARING

PINION REAR BEARING CUP

PINION RETAINER

SEAL

FLANGE

Fig. 3   Disassembled rear axle with removable carrier (typical)

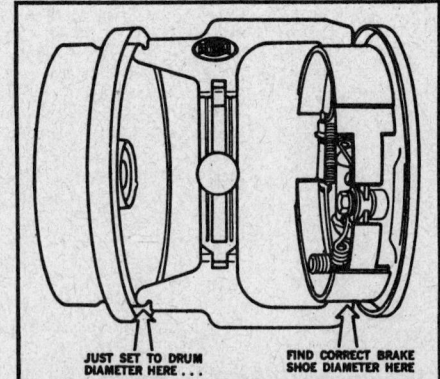

UNIVERSAL JOINT KIT

SNAP RING

SEAL

SPIDER

BEARING

SEAL

SPIDER

SLIP YOKE

PINION FLANGE

CIRCULAR FLANGE

DRIVESHAFT ASSEMBLY

DRIVE SHAFT ASSEMBLY

JUST SET TO DRUM DIAMETER HERE . . .

FIND CORRECT BRAKE SHOE DIAMETER HERE

Fig. 4   Drive shaft and universal joints disassembled (typical)   **Fig. 5   Brake adjustment**

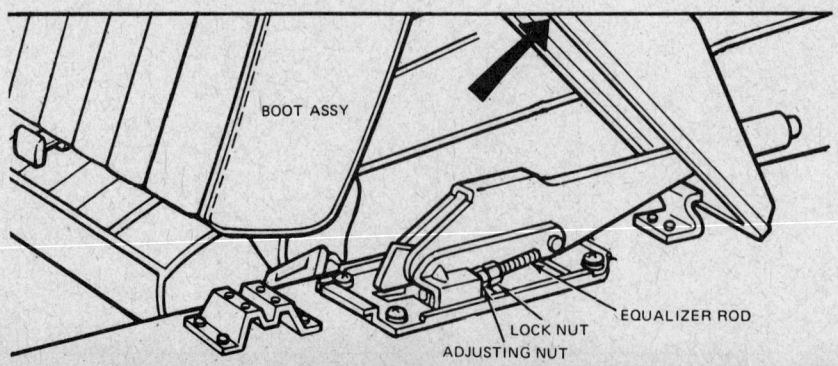

BOOT ASSY

EQUALIZER ROD

LOCK NUT

ADJUSTING NUT

Fig. 6   Parking brake adjustment

5. Remove brake backing plate.
6. If the axle shaft bearing is to be replaced, loosen the inner retainer by nicking it deeply with a chisel in several places. The bearing will then slide off easily.
7. Press bearing from axle shaft.
8. Inspect machined surface of axle shaft and housing for rough spots that would affect sealing action of the oil seal. Carefully remove any burrs or rough spots.
9. Press new inner bearing retainer on shaft until it seats firmly against shoulder on shaft.
10. Press inner bearing retainer on shaft until it seats firmly against bearing.
11. If oil seal is to be replaced, use a hook-type tool to pull it out of housing. Wipe a small amount of oil resistant sealer on outer edge of seal before it is installed.

Installation
1. Place a new gasket on each side of brake carrier plate and slide axle shaft into housing. Start the splines into the differential side gear and push the shaft in until bearing bottoms in housing.
2. Install retainer and tighten nuts to 20–40 ft. lbs.
3. Install brake drum and wheel.

PROPELLER SHAFT, REPLACE

1. To maintain balance, mark relationship of rear drive shaft yoke and the drive pinion flange of the axle if alignment marks are not visible.
2. Disconnect rear U-joint from companion flange, Fig. 4. Wrap tape around loose bearing caps to prevent them from falling off spider. Pull drive shaft toward rear of car until slip yoke clears transmission extension housing and the seal. Install tool in extension housing to prevent lubricant leakage.

BRAKE ADJUSTMENTS

The hydraulic drum brakes, Fig. 5, are self-adjusting and require a manual adjustment only after brake shoes have been replaced. The adjustment is made as follows:
1. Using tool No. 11-0001 on 1977–82 models, or tool No. D81L-1103-A on 1983–84 models, determine inside diameter of brake drum, Fig. 5.
2. Reverse tool and adjust brake shoes to fit the gauge. Hold automatic adjusting lever out of engagement while rotating adjusting screw, to prevent burring slots in screw.

PARKING BRAKE, ADJUST

1. Release parking brake.
2. Place transmission in Neutral and raise vehicle until rear wheels clear floor.
3. Tighten adjusting nut on equalizer rod at the control, Fig. 6, to cause the rear wheel brakes to drag.
4. Loosen adjusting nut until rear brakes are just free.

MASTER CYLINDER, REPLACE

Exc. Power Brakes

1. Disconnect battery ground cable.
2. Disconnect stoplight switch wires at connector. Remove spring retainer and slide stop light switch off brake pedal pin just far enough to clear end of pin, then lift switch straight upward from the pin.
3. Slide master cylinder push rod and nylon washers and bushings off brake pedal pin.
4. Remove brake tubes from master cylinder ports.
5. Unfasten and remove master cylinder by lifting forward and upward from vehicle.

Power Brakes

Disconnect brake tubes from master cylinder, then remove attaching nuts and slide master cylinder forward and upward from vehicle.

POWER BRAKE UNIT, REPLACE

1. Remove stoplight switch and slide booster push rod, bushing and inner nylon washer from brake pedal pin.
2. Remove air cleaner.
3. On all except Capri and Mustang with with V8 engine, disconnect accelerator cable from carburetor. Remove screws securing accelerator cable bracket to engine and rotate bracket toward engine. On models with 4-140 engine, disconnect inlet hose of choke water cover and position aside.
4. On Bobcat and Pinto, disconnect vacuum hoses from solenoid on fender apron, then remove the solenoid.
5. On 1977–78 Mustang with 4-140 or V6-171 engines, disconnect vacuum hose from EGR vacuum reservoir.
6. On all models, disconnect vacuum hose from power brake unit.
7. Disconnect hydraulic lines from master cylinder and cap open lines and ports.
8. Remove master cylinder.
9. From inside vehicle, remove power brake unit to dash panel attaching nuts.
10. On models with speed control, remove control amplifier which is mounted on the lower outboard booster stud and set aside.
11. On all models, work from engine compartment and move booster forward until booster studs clear the dash panel, then raise front of unit and remove from vehicle.

Rear Suspension

SHOCK ABSORBER, REPLACE

1979–84 Capri & Mustang

NOTE: On hatchback models, the upper shock absorber upper mounting is accessible from the luggage compartment. On hatchback and fastback models, remove side panel trim covers to gain access to the upper shock absorber mounting.

1. Disconnect shock absorber from upper mounting.
2. Raise vehicle and support rear axle.
3. Compress shock absorber to clear hole in upper shock absorber tower.
4. Disconnect shock absorber from lower mounting and remove shock absorber from vehicle.
5. Reverse procedure to install.

1977–78 Mustang & 1977–80 Bobcat & Pinto

1. With rear axle supported properly disconnect shock absorber from lower mounting.
2. Remove bolts securing upper mounting bracket to underbody.
3. Remove bracket from shock absorber.
4. Reverse procedure to install.

LEAF SPRINGS & BUSHINGS, REPLACE

1977–78 Mustang & 1977–80 Bobcat & Pinto

1. Raise rear of vehicle and support at frame. Support axle with a suitable jack.
2. Disconnect shock absorbers from lower mountings.
3. Lower jack and remove spring plate "U" bolts and spring plate, Fig. 1.
4. Raise axle to remove weight from spring and disassemble rear shackle.
5. Remove spring front mount bolt.
6. Replace spring front eye bushing as necessary, Figs. 2 and 3.
7. Reverse procedure to install.

COIL SPRING, REPLACE

1979–84 Capri & Mustang

1. Raise rear of vehicle and support at rear body crossmember.
2. Remove stabilizer bar, if equipped.
3. Lower axle housing until shock absorbers are fully extended.

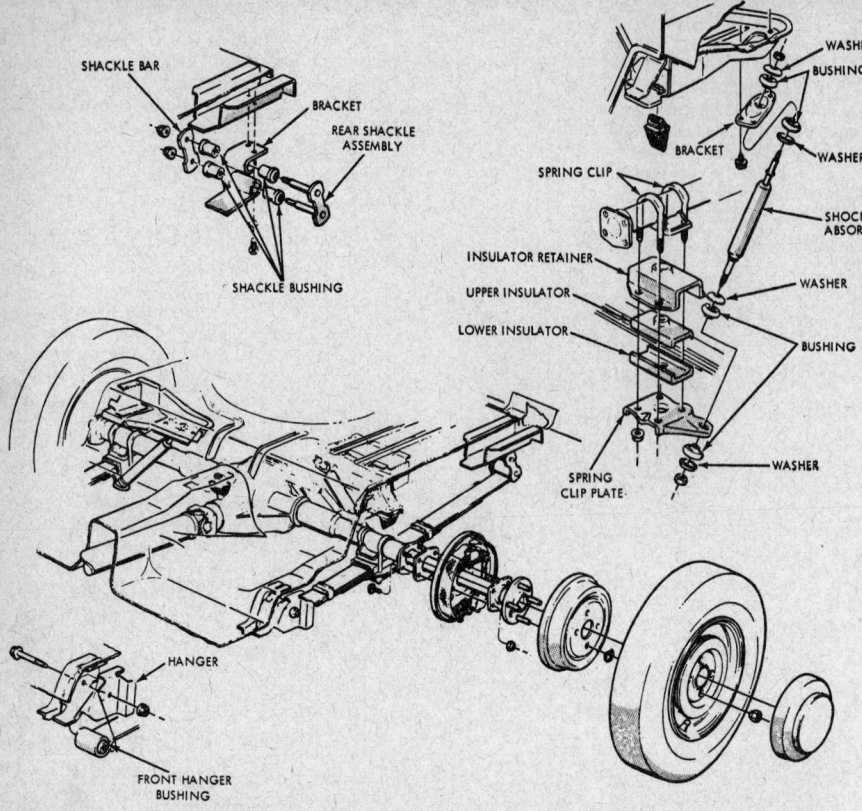

Fig. 1 Leaf spring rear suspension. 1977–78 Mustang & 1977–80 Bobcat & Pinto

NOTE: The axle housing must be supported with a suitable jack.

4. Position a suitable jack under lower control arm rear pivot bolt to support control arm, then remove pivot bolt.
5. Carefully lower the lower control arm until spring tension is relieved, then remove coil spring and insulator.
6. Reverse procedure to install. Torque lower control arm pivot bolt to 70 to 100 ft. 1979–80 and 1983–84 models, or 90–100 ft. lbs. on 1981–82 models, with suspension at curb height.

CONTROL ARMS & BUSHINGS, REPLACE
1979–84 Capri & Mustang

Upper Control Arm

1. Raise rear of vehicle and support at rear body crossmember.
2. Remove upper control arm rear and front pivot bolts, then remove control arm.
3. If control arm axle bracket bushings are to be replaced, refer to Figs. 5 and 6.
4. Position upper control arm into side rail bracket, then install front pivot bolt. Do not tighten bolt at this time.
5. Raise rear axle until upper control arm

rear pivot bolt hole is aligned with hole in axle housing, then install rear pivot bolt. Do not tighten bolt at this time.
6. Position suspension at curb height. Torque front pivot bolt to 70–100 ft. lbs. on 1979 and 1983–84 models, 85–120 ft. lbs. on 1980 models, or 100 ft. lbs. on 1981–82 models. Torque rear pivot bolt to 70–100 ft. lbs. on 1979–80 models, 100 ft. lbs. on 1981–82 models, or 80–104 ft. lbs. on 1983–84 models.

Lower Control Arms

1. Remove coil spring as described under "Coil Spring, Replace."
2. Remove lower control arm front pivot bolt and nut, then remove control arm.
3. Reverse procedure to install. Torque front pivot bolt to 70–100 ft. lbs. on 1979 models, 85–120 ft. lbs. on 1980 models, 100 ft. lbs. on 1981–82 models, or 80–104 ft. lbs. on 1983–84 models. Torque rear pivot bolt to 70–100 ft. lbs. on 1979–80 and 1983–84 models, or 100 ft. lbs. on 1981–82 models.

STABILIZER BAR, REPLACE
1979–84 Capri & Mustang

1. Raise and support rear of vehicle.
2. Remove four bolts attaching stabilizer bar to brackets on lower control arms.
3. Remove stabilizer bar from vehicle.
4. Reverse procedure to install. Torque horizontal bolts to 30–40 ft. lbs. and vertical bolts to 18–23 ft. lbs. on 1979 models. Torque all bolts to 15–20 ft. lbs. on 1980 models, 20 ft. lbs. on 1981 models, or 45–50 ft. lbs. on 1982–84 models.

AXLE DAMPERS, REPLACE
1984 Mustang & Capri with V8-302 Engine

1. Raise vehicle and support rear axle.
2. Remove rear wheel, then the axle damper rear attaching nut and pivot bolt, Fig. 7.
3. Remove axle damper forward attaching nut, the axle damper and spacer.
4. Reverse procedure to install. Torque attaching bolts to 50–60 ft. lbs.

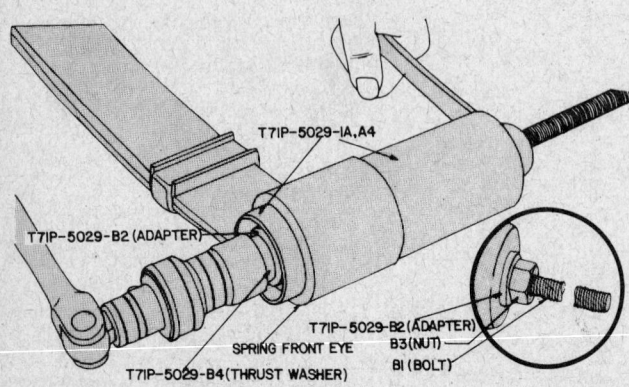

Fig. 2 Spring, front bushing removal. 1977–78 Mustang & 1977–80 Bobcat & Pinto

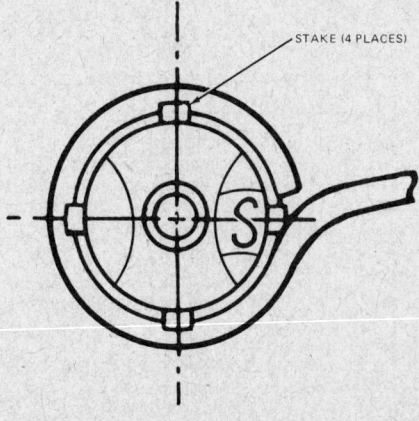

Fig. 3 Spring, front bushing installation. 1977–78 Mustang & 1977–80 Bobcat & Pinto

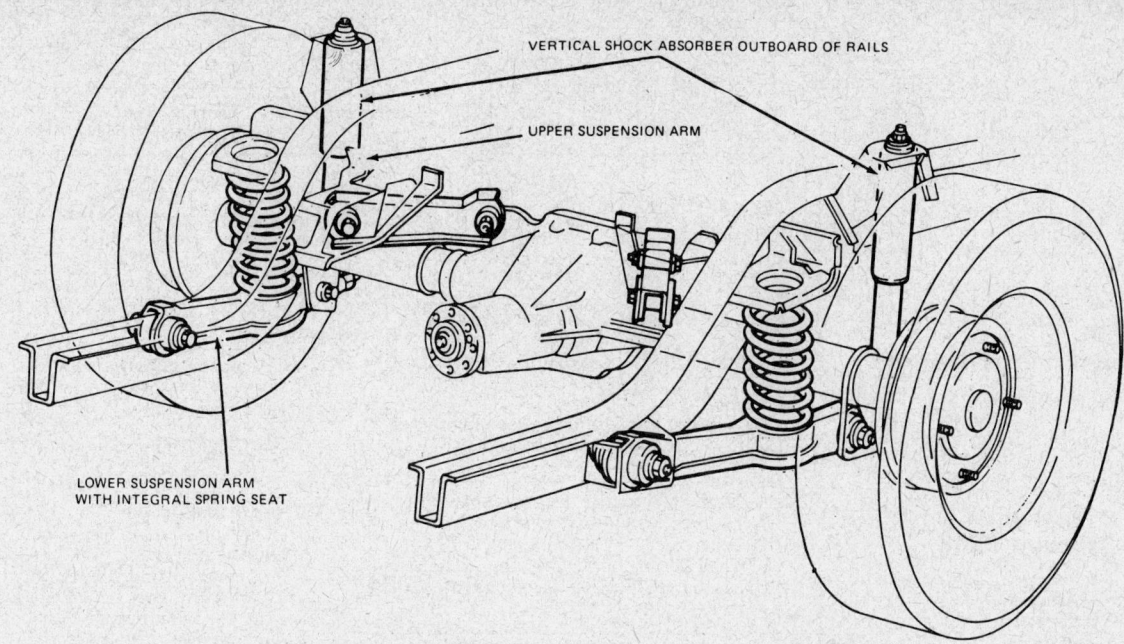

VERTICAL SHOCK ABSORBER OUTBOARD OF RAILS

UPPER SUSPENSION ARM

LOWER SUSPENSION ARM
WITH INTEGRAL SPRING SEAT

Fig. 4   Coil spring rear suspension. 1979—84 Capri & Mustang

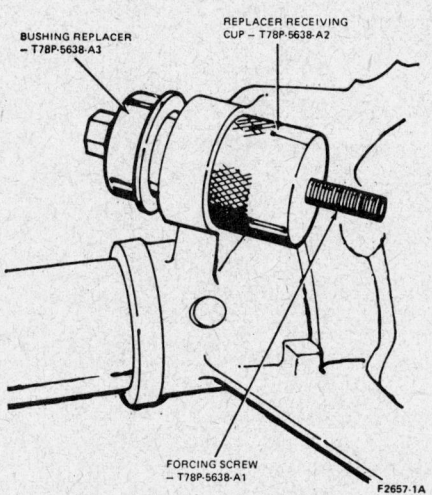

BUSHING REPLACER
– T78P-5638-A3

REPLACER RECEIVING
CUP – T78P-5638-A2

FORCING SCREW
– T78P-5638-A1

F2657-1A

Fig. 5   Upper control arm axle bracket bushing installation. 1979—84 Capri & Mustang

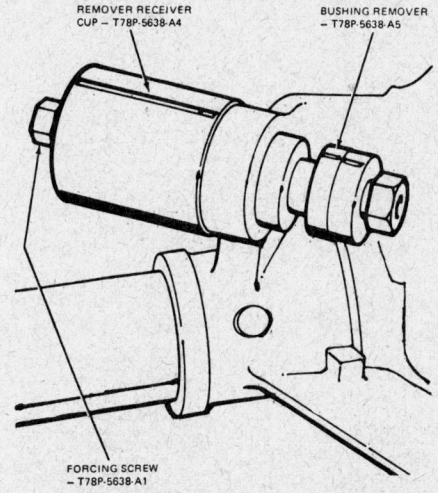

REMOVER RECEIVER
CUP – T78P-5638-A4

BUSHING REMOVER
– T78P-5638-A5

FORCING SCREW
– T78P-5638-A1

Fig. 6   Upper control arm axle bracket bushing removal. 1979—84 Capri & Mustang

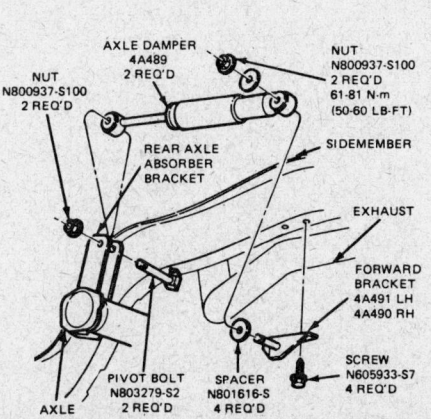

NUT
N800937-S100
2 REQ'D

AXLE DAMPER
4A489
2 REQ'D

NUT
N800937-S100
2 REQ'D

REAR AXLE
ABSORBER
BRACKET

SIDEMEMBER

EXHAUST

FORWARD
BRACKET
4A491 LH
4A490 RH

SCREW
N605933-S7
4 REQ'D

PIVOT BOLT
N803279-S2
2 REQ'D

SPACER
N801616-S
4 REQ'D

AXLE

Fig. 7   Axle damper assembly. 1984 Mustang & Capri with V8-305 engines

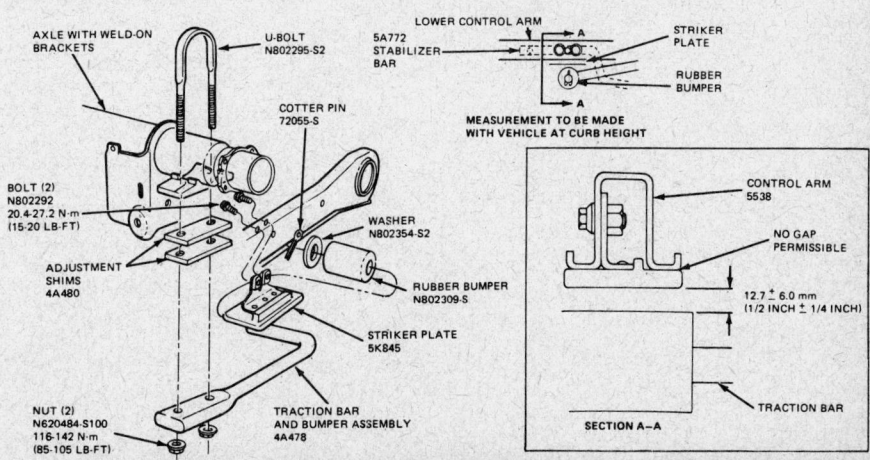

AXLE WITH WELD-ON
BRACKETS

U-BOLT
N802295-S2

COTTER PIN
72055-S

BOLT (2)
N802292
20.4-27.2 N·m
(15-20 LB-FT)

ADJUSTMENT
SHIMS
4A480

WASHER
N802354-S2

RUBBER BUMPER
N802309-S

STRIKER PLATE
5K845

NUT (2)
N620484-S100
116-142 N·m
(85-105 LB-FT)

TRACTION BAR
AND BUMPER ASSEMBLY
4A478

LOWER CONTROL ARM

5A772
STABILIZER
BAR

STRIKER
PLATE

RUBBER
BUMPER

MEASUREMENT TO BE MADE
WITH VEHICLE AT CURB HEIGHT

CONTROL ARM
5538

NO GAP
PERMISSIBLE

12.7 ± 6.0 mm
(1/2 INCH ± 1/4 INCH)

TRACTION BAR

SECTION A–A

Fig. 8   Traction bar assembly. 1984 Mustang & Capri with 2300cc turbocharged or V8-305 engines

TRACTION BAR, REPLACE

1984 Mustang & Capri with 2300cc Turbocharged or V8-302 Engines

1. Raise vehicle and support rear axle.

2. Remove traction bar to rear axle attaching bolts, then the traction bar, adjusting shims and "U" bolt, Fig. 8.
3. Remove cotter pin and washer, then the rubber bumper if necessary.
4. Reverse procedure to install, noting the following:

a. If rubber bumper is replaced, use tire mounting solution ESAM-1B6B or equivalent to ease installation.
b. Torque traction bar attaching nuts to 85–105 ft. lbs.
c. Adjust traction bar, as needed, by adding or subtracting shims, Fig. 8.

Front Suspension & Steering Section

FRONT SUSPENSION

1979–84 Capri & Mustang

The front suspension, Fig. 1, is of the modified McPherson strut design, which uses shock struts and coil springs. The springs are mounted between the lower control and a spring pocket in the crossmember.

1977–78 Mustang & 1977–80 Bobcat & Pinto

The upper and lower ends of the spindle are attached to upper and lower ball joints which are mounted in upper and lower arms. The upper arm pivots on a bushing and shaft assembly which is bolted to the frame. The lower arm pivots on a bolt in the front crossmember, Fig. 2.

WHEEL ALIGNMENT

1983–84 Capri & Mustang

Caster
The caster angle of this suspension is factory pre-set and cannot be adjusted.

Camber
1. Remove pop rivet from camber plate.
2. Loosen 3 camber plate-to-body apron nuts.
3. Move top of shock strut as needed to bring camber angle within specifications, then tighten nuts.

NOTE: It is not necessary to replace the pop rivet.

1979–82 Capri & Mustang

Caster & Camber
The caster and camber angles of this suspension are factory pre-set and can not be adjusted.

1977–78 Mustang & 1977–80 Bobcat & Pinto

Caster and Camber
1. Working inside front wheel housing, install special tool, one at each end of the upper arm inner shaft. Turn the special tool bolts inward until the bolt ends contact the body metal, Fig. 3.
2. Loosen the two upper arm inner shaft-to-body bolts. The upper shaft will move inboard until stopped by the tool bolt ends solidly contacting the body metal.

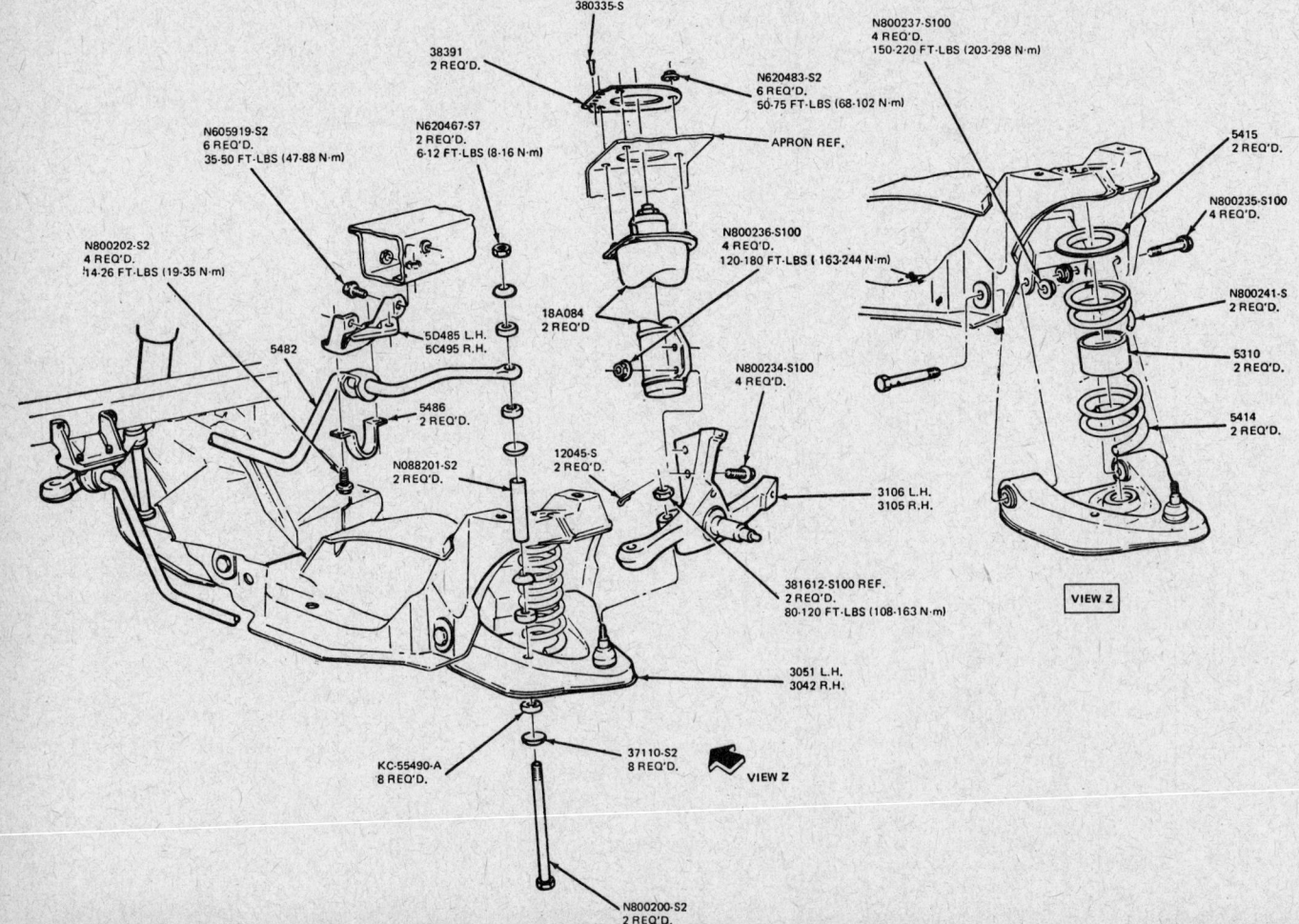

Fig. 1 Front suspension assembly. 1979–80 Capri & Mustang (Typical of 1981–84)

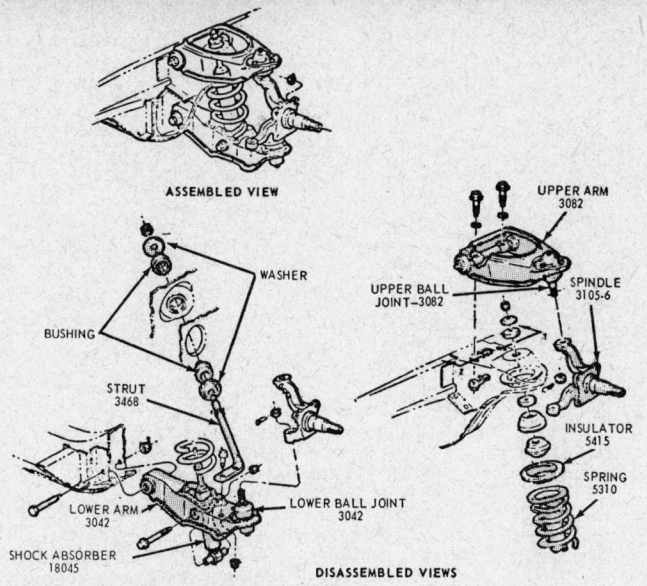

Fig. 2   Front suspension assembly (typical). 1977–78 Mustang & 1977–80 Bobcat & Pinto

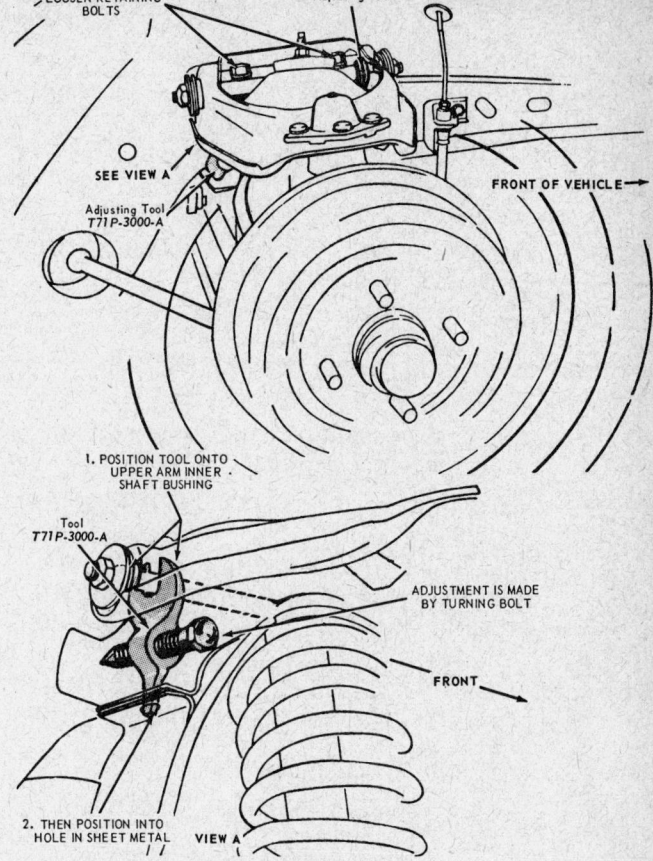

Fig. 3   Caster and camber adjustment. 1977–78 Mustang & 1977–80 Bobcat & Pinto

3. Turn the special tool bolts inward or outward until caster and camber are within specifications. Tightening these bolts on the special tool forces the arm outward; while loosening the bolts on the tools permits the arm and inner shaft to move inboard due to weight force.
4. When properly adjusted, torque shaft-to-body bolts to 95–120 ft. lbs., then remove the special tools.

TOE-IN, ADJUST

1. Check to see that steering shaft and steering wheel marks are in alignment and in the top position.
2. Loosen clamp screw on the tie rod bellows and free the seal on the rod to prevent twisting of the bellows, Fig. 4.
3. Loosen tie rod jam nut.
4. Use suitable pliers to turn the tie rod inner end to correct the adjustment to specifications. Do not use pliers on tie rod threads. Turning to reduce number of threads showing will increase toe-in. Turning in the opposite direction will reduce toe-in. On 1977–81 models, torque tie rod jam nuts to 35–50 ft. lbs. On 1982–84 models, torque to 43–50 ft. lbs.

WHEEL BEARINGS, ADJUST

1. Raise vehicle until wheel and tire clear floor.
2. Remove wheel cover and dust cap from hub.
3. Remove cotter pin and lock nut.
4. Loosen adjusting nut 3 turns, then rock wheel, hub and rotor assembly in and out several times to move shoe and linings away from rotor.
5. While rotating wheel assembly, torque the adjusting nut to 17–25 ft. lbs. to seat the bearings.
6. Back off the adjusting nut one half turn. Retighten the nut to 10–15 in. lbs. with a torque wrench or finger tight.
7. Locate the nut lock on the adjusting nut so the castellations on the lock are

aligned with the cotter pin hole in the spindle.
8. Install new cotter pin and replace dust cap and wheel cover.

WHEEL BEARINGS, REPLACE

(Disc Brakes)
1979–84 Capri & Mustang

1. Raise vehicle and remove front wheels.
2. Remove caliper mounting bolts.

NOTE: It is not necessary to disconnect the brake lines for this operation.

---

3. Slide caliper off of disc, inserting a clean spacer between the shoes to hold them in their bores after the caliper is removed. Position caliper out of the way.

NOTE: Do not allow caliper to hang by brake hose.

---

4. Remove hub and disc assembly. Grease retainer and inner bearing can now be removed.
5. Reverse procedure to install.

1977–78 Mustang & 1977–80 Bobcat & Pinto

1. Raise car and remove front wheels.
2. Use a 3/4″ wrench to loosen the large bolt at top of caliper assembly and washer at

the front of the caliper. Loosen it until it can be turned with the fingers.
3. Remove the smaller bolt at bottom of caliper with a 5/8″ wrench.
4. Insert a strong piece of wire carefully through the upper opening in the caliper and fasten it. Position the free end of the wire over the suspension upper arm.
5. When removing caliper from disc the brake pads must be held apart. Do this by inserting a piece of wood or cardboard. While holding the caliper, remove the large bolt in front. Now carefully slide the caliper back and slightly upward to remove it. While doing this, insert the wood or cardboard between the brake pads.
6. Carefully move caliper back to suspension upper arm and fasten loose end of wire so caliper will not drop.
7. Dust cap can now be removed from hub. Remove nut lock, etc. and rock disc to ease out washer and outer bearing. Disc can now be removed to service grease seal or inner bearing.

CHECKING BALL JOINTS FOR WEAR

Upper Ball Joint

1977–78 Mustang & 1977–80 Bobcat & Pinto
1. Raise car and place floor jacks beneath lower arms.
2. Grasp lower edge of tire and move wheel in and out.
3. As the wheel is being moved, notice any

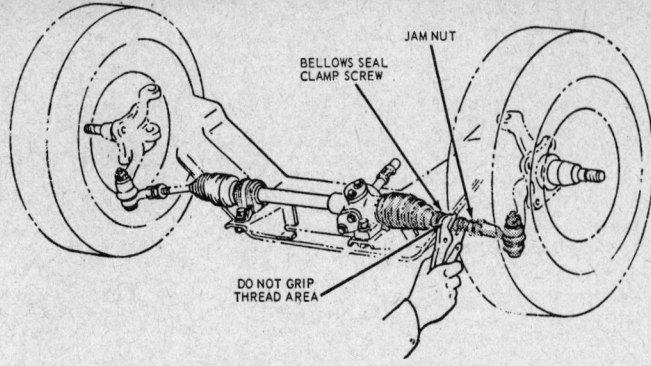
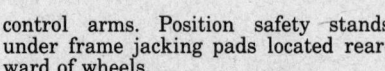

Fig. 4 Toe-in adjustment (typical)

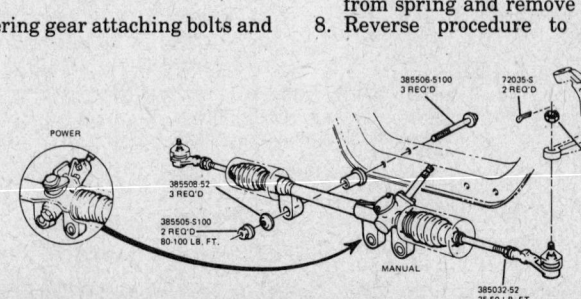

Fig. 5 Checking lower ball joint for wear. 1979–84 Capri & Mustang

movement between the upper end of the spindle and the upper arm. If movement is present, replace the ball joint.

Lower Ball Joint

1979–84 Capri & Mustang

Support vehicle in normal driving position with both ball joints loaded. Clean area around grease fitting and checking surface. The checking surface is the round boss into which the grease fitting is installed. The checking surface should project outside the ball joint cover, Fig. 5. If checking surface is inside the cover replace the lower control arm assembly.

1977–78 Mustang & 1977–80 Bobcat & Pinto

1. Raise vehicle and place jacks under lower arms as shown in Fig. 6.
2. Be sure wheel bearings are properly adjusted.
3. Attach a dial indicator to lower arm and position indicator so that plunger rests against inner side of wheel rim near lower ball joint.
4. Grasp tire at top and bottom and slowly move tire in and out. If the reading exceeds .250″, replace the joint.

SHOCK STRUT, REPLACE

1979–84 Capri & Mustang

1. Place ignition switch in the unlocked position.
2. From engine compartment, remove upper shock absorber mounting nut.
3. Raise front of vehicle and support lower

control arms. Position safety stands under frame jacking pads located rearward of wheels.
4. Remove wheel and tire assembly.
5. Remove caliper, rotor and dust shield.
6. Remove two bolts attaching shock absorber to spindle.
7. Lift strut upward from spindle to compress rod, then pull downward and remove shock absorber.
8. On 1983–84 models, remove jounce bumper.
9. Reverse procedure to install. Torque upper mounting nut to 60–75 ft. lbs. on 1979–82 models, or 55–92 ft. lbs. on 1983–84 models. Torque lower mounting nuts to 150–180 ft. lbs. on 1979–82 models, or 120–179 ft. lbs. on 1983–84 models.

SHOCK ABSORBER, REPLACE

1977–78 Mustang & 1977–80 Bobcat & Pinto

1. Disconnect upper end of the shock.
2. Raise vehicle and install safety stands.
3. Disconnect lower end of shock. It may be necessary to use a pry bar to free "T" shaped end of the shock from the lower end.
4. Reverse procedure to install. Torque shock absorber to lower arm nut to 70 ft. lbs. and shock absorber upper attachment to 26 ft. lbs.

COIL SPRING, REPLACE

1979–84 Capri & Mustang

1. Raise front of vehicle and place safety stands under jack pads located rearward of wheels, then remove wheel and tire assembly.
2. Disconnect stabilizer bar link from lower control arm.
3. Remove steering gear attaching bolts and

position gear out of way.
4. Using tool 3290-C, disconnect tie rod from spindle.
5. Install spring compressor D78P-5310-A on 1979–81 models, or T82P-5310A on 1982–84 models and compress coil spring until it is free of the spring seat.

NOTE: Ensure spring compressor is properly installed before compressing spring. Also ensure spring is sufficiently compressed to permit removal of lower control arm pivot bolts.

6. Remove two lower control arm pivot bolts, then disengage lower control arm and remove spring assembly, Fig. 1.

NOTE: Measure compressed length of spring and amount of curvature to aid in compressing and installing spring.

7. Reverse procedure to install. Ensure lower spring end is positioned between two holes in lower control arm spring pocket. Torque stabilizer bar to lower arm to 9 ft. lbs., steering gear to No. 2 crossmember to 95 ft. lbs. and tie rod to spindle to 40 ft. lbs. on 1979–81 models, or 35 ft. lbs. on 1982–84 models.

1977–78 Mustang & 1977–80 Bobcat & Pinto

1. Raise vehicle and support front end with safety stands.
2. Place a jack under lower arm to support it.
3. Disconnect lower end of shock.
4. Remove bolts that attach strut to lower arm.
5. Remove nut that retains shock to crossmember and remove the shock.
6. Remove nut and bolt that secures inner end of lower arm to crossmember.
7. Carefully lower jack to relieve pressure from spring and remove spring.
8. Reverse procedure to install. Torque

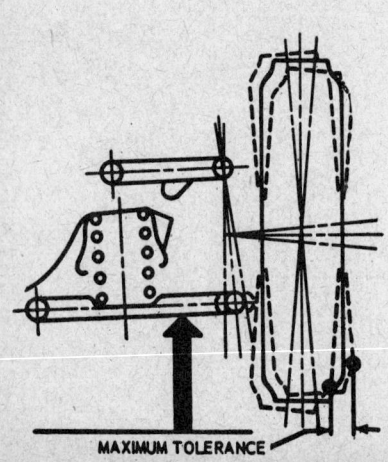

Fig. 6 Measuring lower ball joint play

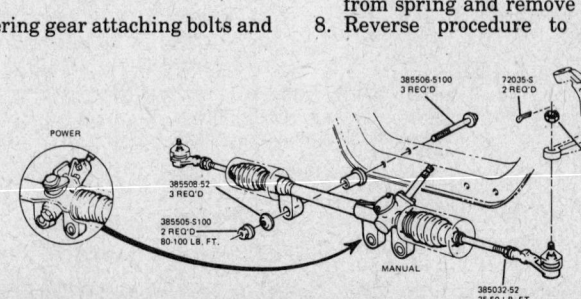

Fig. 7 Steering gear installation (typical)

shock to lower arm nut to 70 ft. lbs., strut to lower arm bolts to 40–60 ft. lbs., shock to crossmember nut to 22–30 ft. lbs. and lower arm to crossmember to 40–60 ft. lbs.

BALL JOINTS, REPLACE

1979–84 Capri & Mustang

On these models, the lower ball joint and lower control arm must be replaced as an assembly.

1977–78 Mustang & 1977–80 Bobcat & Pinto

NOTE: Ford Motor Company recommends that new ball joints should not be installed on used control arms and that the control arm be replaced if ball joint replacement is required. However, aftermarket ball joint repair kits which do not require control arm replacement, are available and can be installed using the following procedure.

The ball joints are riveted to the control arms. The ball joints can be replaced on the car by removing the rivets and replacing them with new attaching bolts, nuts and washers furnished with the kit.

When removing a ball joint, use a suitable pressing tool to force the ball joint out of the spindle.

STEERING GEAR, REPLACE

1979–84 Capri & Mustang

1. Disconnect battery ground cable.
2. Remove bolt attaching flexible coupling to input shaft.
3. Place ignition switch in the On position, then raise and support front of vehicle.
4. Remove cotter pins and nuts from tie rod ends, then using a suitable tool separate tie rods from spindle arms, Fig. 7.

5. Support steering gear, then remove two nuts, bolts and washers attaching steering gear to crossmember. On power steering gears, lower gear slightly and disconnect pressure and return lines. Cap lines and fittings to prevent entry of dirt.
6. Remove steering gear from vehicle.
7. Reverse procedure to install. Torque flexible coupling to input shaft bolt to 20–30 ft. lbs., tie rod to spindle arm nuts to 35–47 ft. lbs. and steering gear to crossmember bolts to 80–100 ft. lbs. Torque pressure line fitting at gear housing to 10–15 ft. lbs.

1977–78 Mustang, 1977–80 Bobcat & Pinto

Manual Steering Gear
1. Disconnect battery ground cable, turn ignition "On" and raise vehicle.
2. Remove tie rod end retaining nuts and using ball joint separator (tool 329OC), separate tie rod ends from spindle arms, Fig. 7.
3. Remove pinion shaft to flexible coupling bolt and the bolts securing steering gear to crossmember.

NOTE: On 1977–78 Mustang, the number 2A crossmember, located behind the front crossmember, must be removed to permit steering gear removal.

4. Turn front wheels, then remove steering gear from left side of vehicle.

Power Steering Gear
1. Disconnect battery ground cable.
2. Remove bolt retaining flexible coupling to input shaft.
3. Turn ignition key "On" and raise vehicle.
4. Remove the two tie rod end retaining nuts, then separate studs from spindle arms, using a suitable tool.
5. On Mustang models, remove the number 2A crossmember located behind the front crossmember to allow removal of steering gear retaining bolts.
6. Support gear and remove attaching bolts, then lower gear enough to gain access to pressure and return lines, and remove

bolt attaching the hose bracket to the gear.
7. Disconnect pressure and return lines and remove steering gear. Plug lines and ports to prevent entry of dirt.

POWER STEERING PUMP, REPLACE

1978–84

1. Disconnect return hose from power steering pump reservoir and allow fluid to drain into a suitable container.
2. Disconnect pressure hose from power steering pump fitting, then remove pump mounting bracket and disconnect drive belt from pulley.
3. On 2.3L, 3.8L and 5.0L which incorporate a fixed pump system, remove the belt from the pulley, and remove the pulley.
4. On all models, remove power steering pump.
5. Reverse procedure to install. Torque pump to mounting bracket bolts to 30–45 ft. lbs. and pressure hose to pump tube nut to 10–15 ft. lbs.

NOTE: End play of pressure hose to pump fitting is normal and does not indicate a loose fitting. Do not overtorque.

1977

1. Disconnect return line from power steering pump reservoir, and allow fluid to drain into a suitable container.
2. Disconnect pressure line from power steering pump.
3. Remove bolts attaching pump to front of mounting bracket. On 8 cylinder models, also remove nut attaching pump to rear of bracket.
4. Disconnect drive belt from pulley, then remove power steering pump.
5. Reverse procedure to install. Torque pressure hose to pump nut to 32 ft. lbs., pump to bracket front bolts to 30–45 ft. lbs., pump to bracket rear nut to 20–30 ft. lbs. and return hose to pump clamp to 12–24 in. lbs.

FORD ESCORT, EXP & TEMPO
MERCURY LN7, LYNX & TOPAZ

INDEX OF SERVICE OPERATIONS

NOTE: Refer to the front of this manual for vehicle manufacturer's special service tool suppliers.

ENGINE IDENTIFICATION

Engine code is eighth digit in serial number
(VIN) located on left side dash.

GRILLE IDENTIFICATION

1981 Escort

1981 Lynx

**1982 Escort; 1983 Escort GL, GLX, L & Sta. Wag;
1984 Escort GL & L**

1982–84 EXP

1982–83 LN7

1982 Lynx

**1983 Escort GT
1984 Escort GT & LX**

**1983 Lynx RS
1984 Lynx RS & LTS**

**1983 Lynx GS, L, LS & Sta. Wag.
1984 Lynx GS, L & Sta. Wag.**

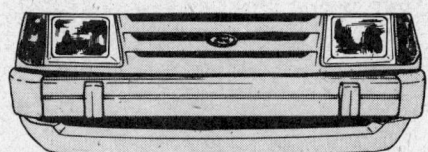

1984 Ford Tempo

1984 Mercury Topaz

GENERAL ENGINE SPECIFICATIONS

Year	Engine CID①/Liter	Engine VIN Code②	Carburetor	Bore and Stroke	Compression Ratio	Net H.P. @ R.P.M.③	Maximum Torque Ft. Lbs. @ R.P.M.	Normal Oil Pressure Pounds
1981	97.6, 1.6 L	2	740, 2 Bbl.④	3.15 × 3.13	8.8	65 @ 5200	85 @ 3000	40
1982	97.6, 1.6 L	2	740, 2 Bbl.④	3.15 × 3.13	8.8	70 @ 4600	89 @ 3000	30–50
1983	97.6, 1.6 L	2	740, 2 Bbl.④	3.15 × 3.13	8.8	—	—	—
	97.6, 1.6 L	2	EFI	3.15 × 3.13	9.5	88 @ 5400		
	97.6, 1.6 L H.O.	2	740, 2 Bbl.④	3.15 × 3.13	—		—	
1984	97.6, 1.6 L	2	740, 2 Bbl.④	3.15 × 3.13	8.8	—	—	30–50
	97.6, 1.6 L	5	EFI	3.15 × 3.13	9.5	—	—	30–50
	97.6, 1.6 L H.O.	4	740, 2 Bbl.④	3.15 × 3.13	9.0	—	—	30–50
	120, 2.0 L⑥	H	Fuel Injection	3.39 × 3.39	22.5	—	—	—
	140, 2.3 L⑦	R	6149, 1 Bbl.⑤	3.68 × 3.30	9.0	84 @ 4600	118 @ 2600	—

①—CID—Cubic inch displacement.
②—The eighth digit in the VIN denotes engine code.
③—Ratings are net—as installed in vehicle.
④—Motorcraft.
⑤—Holley.
⑥—Diesel.
⑦—Tempo & Topaz.

TUNE UP SPECIFICATIONS

The following specifications are published from the latest information available. This data should be used only in the absence of a decal affixed in the engine compartment.

★ When using a timing light, disconnect vacuum hose or tube at distributor and plug opening in hose or tube so idle speed will not be affected.

● When checking compression, lowest cylinder must be within 75 percent of highest.

▲ Before removing wires from distributor cap, determine location of the No. 1 wire in cap, as distributor position may have been altered from that shown at the end of this chart.

🖑 Spark plug types shown in this chart are recommendations of the original vehicle manufacturer and not MOTOR.

Check local sources for other spark plug manufacturers listings.

Year & Engine/V.I.N.	Spark Plug Type 🖑	Gap	Firing Order Fig. ▲	Ignition Timing BTDC① ★ Man. Trans.	Auto. Trans.	Mark Fig.	Curb Idle Speed Man. Trans.	Auto. Trans.②	Fast Idle Speed Man. Trans.	Auto. Trans.	Fuel Pump Pressure
1981											
4-97.6, 1.6L/2 Exc. Calif.	AGSP-32	.044	A	10°⑦	10°⑦	B	900③⑧	750D④	2400⑤⑨	2400⑤	4–6⑥
4-97.6, 1.6L/2 Calif.	AGSP-32	.044	A	10°⑦	6°⑦	B	900③⑧	750D④	2400⑤⑨	2400⑤	4–6⑥
1982											
4-97.6/2 Exc. Calif.⑩⑪⑫	AWSF-32	.044	A	—	12°⑦	B	—	800D③	—	2400⑤	4½–6½⑥
4-96.6/2 Exc. Calif. & High Alt.⑪⑬⑭	AWSF-32	.044	A	—	10°⑦	B	—	750D⑮	—	2400⑤	4½–6½⑥
4-97.6/2 Exc. High Alt.⑩⑪⑯	⑰	.044	A	6°⑦	—	B	800⑮	—	2400⑤	—	4½–6½⑥
4-97.6/2 Exc. High Alt.⑪⑬⑱	AWSF-32	.044	A	14°⑦	—	B	800⑮	—	2400⑤	—	4½–6½⑥
4-97.6/2 Exc. High Alt.⑪⑬⑲⑳	AWSF-32	.044	A	14°⑦	—	B	650/1300	—	2200⑤	—	4½–6½⑥
4-97.6/2 Exc. High Alt.⑪⑬㉑	AWSF-32	.044	A	12°⑦	—	B	800⑮	—	2400⑤	—	4½–6½⑥
4-97.6/2 Exc. High Alt.⑪⑬㉒	AWSF-32	.044	A	10°⑦	—	B	800⑮	—	2400⑤	—	4½–6½⑥
4-97.6/2 Calif.⑩⑪㉓	AWSF-32	.044	A	—	12°⑦	B	—	800D③	—	2400⑤	4½–6½⑥
4-97.6/2 Calif.⑩⑪㉔	AWSF-32	.044	A	—	8°⑦	B	—	800D③	—	2400⑤	4½–6½⑥
4-97.6/2 Calif.⑪⑬㉕	AWSF-32	.044	A	—	8°⑦	B	—	750D⑮	—	2400⑤	4½–6½⑥
4-97.6/2 Calif.⑪⑬㉖	AWSF-32	.044	A	—	10°⑦	B	—	750D⑮	—	2400⑤	4½–6½⑥
4-97.6/2 High Alt.⑩⑪㉗	AWSF-32	.044	A	8°⑦	—	B	800⑯	—	2400⑤	—	4½–6½⑥
4-97.6/2 High Alt.⑪⑬㉘	AWSF-32	.044	A	10°⑦	10°⑦	B	800⑯	750D⑮	2400⑤	2400⑤	4½–6½⑥
4-97.6 H.O./2㉙	AWSF-32	.044	A	10°⑦	10°⑦	B	—	750D⑮	—	2200⑤	4½–6½⑥
1983											
4-97.6/2 Exc. High Alt.⑪㉚	AWSF-34	.044	A	8°⑦	—	B	650	—	2100⑤	—	4½–6½⑥
4-97.6/2 Exc. High Alt.⑪㉙㉛	AWSF-32	.044	A	10°⑦	—	B	800㉜/1200㉝	—	2400⑤⑨	—	4½–6½⑥
4-97.6/2 Exc. High Alt.⑪㉞	AWSF-34	.044	A	—	10°⑦	B	—	750D	—	2400⑤	4½–6½⑥
4-97.6/2 Calif.⑪㊱	AWSF-34	.044	A	8°⑦	10°⑦	B	800㉜/1200㉝	750D	2200㉟	2400⑤	4½–6½⑥
4-97.6/2 Calif.⑪㉙㊲	AWSF-34	.044	A	—	14°⑦	B	—	750D	—	2400⑤	4½–6½⑥
4-97.6/2 High Alt.⑪㉙㊳	AWSF-32	.044	A	10°⑦	—	B	900㊴/1500㊵	—	2400⑤⑨	—	4½–6½⑥
4-97.6/2 High Alt.⑪㉙㊶	AWSF-34	.044	A	—	16°⑦	B	—	850D	—	2400⑤	4½–6½⑥
4-97.6 EFI/2⑪㊷	AWSF-24	.044	A	13°	—	B	㊺	—	—	—	39
4-97.6 EFI/2⑪㊸	AWSF-24	.044	A	15°	—	B	㊺	—	—	—	39
4-97.6 EFI/2 Exc. High Alt.⑪㊹	AWSF-24	.044	A	—	15°	B	㊺	—	—	—	39
1984											
4-97.6/2⑪	AWSF-34	.044	A	—	—	B	—	—	—	—	4–6⑥
4-97.6 H.O./4⑪㉙	AWSF-34	.044	A	—	—	B	—	—	—	—	4–6⑥
4-97.6 EFI/5⑪㊻	AWSF-24	.044	A	—	—	B	—	—	—	—	39
4-97.6 EFI/5⑪㊼	AWSF-22	.044	A	—	—	B	—	—	—	—	39
4-120 Diesel/H	—	—	—	—	—	—	—	—	—	—	113
4-140/R㊽	AWSF-62	.044	C	—	—	D㊾	—	—	—	—	4½–6½⑥
4-140/R㊽	AWSF-62	.044	C	—	—	E㊿	—	—	—	—	4½–6½⑥

Continued

TUNE UP NOTES—Continued

①—BTDC—Before top dead center.
②—D: Drive.
③—With A/C on, 1700 RPM, if equipped.
④—With A/C on, 1850 RPM, if equipped.
⑤—On kick down step of cam.
⑥—With pump to tank return pinched off.
⑦—At 800 RPM.
⑧—If mileage on vehicle is less than 100 mi., set at 750 RPM.
⑨—If mileage on vehicle is less than 100 mi., set at 2200 RPM.
⑩—Early production EXP & LN7.
⑪—Refer to engine calibration code on engine identification label, located at front of engine timing belt cover. The calibration code is located on the label below the engine sequence number (ESN) & is preceded by the letter C. The revision code is located next to the calibration code & is preceded by the letter R.
⑫—Calibration code 1-4E-R0.
⑬—Escort, Lynx & late production EXP & LN7.
⑭—Calibration code 2-4C-R0.
⑮—With A/C on, 1500N RPM, if equipped.

⑯—Calibration codes 1-3S-R0 & 1-3S-R11.
⑰—Calibration code 1-3S-R0, use AGSP-32; code 1-3S-R11, use AWSF-32.
⑱—Calibration codes 2-3A-R10 & 2-3C-R0.
⑲—Calibration codes 2-3D-R0, R1, R14 & R15.
⑳—Models less A/C & power steering.
㉑—Calibration code 2-3E-R0.
㉒—Calibration code 2-3G-R0.
㉓—Calibration code 1-4S-R0.
㉔—Calibration code 1-4S-R10.
㉕—Calibration code 2-4Q-R0.
㉖—Calibration code 2-4Q-R10.
㉗—Calibration code 1-3Y-R10.
㉘—Calibration code, man. trans. 2-3X-R0; auto. trans., 2-4X-R0.
㉙—High output engine.
㉚—Calibration code 3-3D-R01.
㉛—Calibration code 2-3B-R11.
㉜—With VOTM "off". If mileage on vehicle is less than 100 miles, set at 700 RPM.
㉝—With VOTM "on". If mileage on vehicle is less than 100 miles, set at 1100 RPM.
㉞—Calibration code 3-4C-R00.
㉟—If mileage on vehicle is less than 100 miles,

set at 2000 RPM.
㊱—Calibration code, man. trans., 3-3C-R00; auto. trans., 3-4Q-R01.
㊲—Calibration code 3-4T-R00.
㊳—Calibration code 2-3Y-R11.
㊴—With VOTM "off". If mileage on vehicle is less than 100 miles, set at 800 RPM.
㊵—With VOTM "on". If mileage on vehicle is less than 100 miles, set at 1400 RPM.
㊶—Calibration code 3-4Y-R00.
㊷—Calibration code 3-03A-R12.
㊸—Calibration code 3-03A-R13.
㊹—Calibration cdoe 3-04A-R10.
㊺—Idle speed not adjustable. Idle speed maintained by computer.
㊻—Except turbocharged engine.
㊼—Turbocharged engine.
㊽—Tempo & Topaz.
㊾—On manual transaxle models, a cover plate retained by two screws must be removed to view timing marks.
㊿—On automatic transaxle models, symbols are indented on outer face of flywheel.

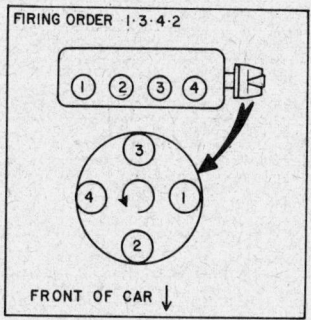

Fig. A

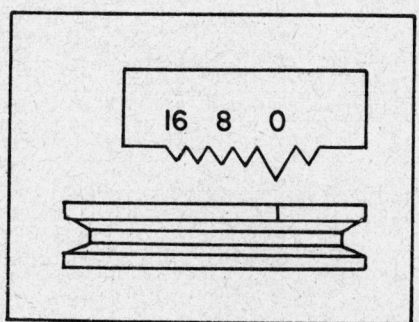

Fig. B

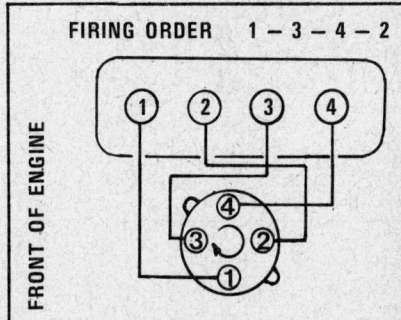

Fig. C

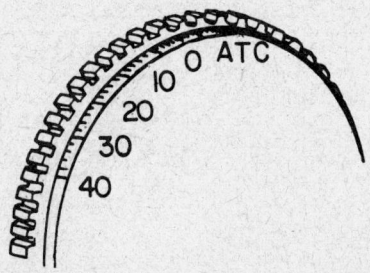

Fig. D

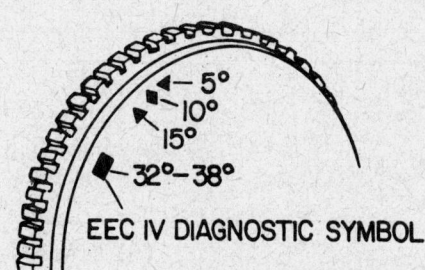

Fig. E

DISTRIBUTOR SPECIFICATIONS

★If unit is checked on vehicle, double the RPM and degrees to get crankshaft figures.

Distributor Part No.	Centrifugal Advance Degrees @ RPM of Distributor				Vacuum Advance		Distributor Retard
	Advance Starts	Intermediate Advance		Full Advance	Inches of Vacuum to start Plunger	Max. Adv. Dist. Deg. @ Vacuum	Max. Ret. Dist. Deg. @ Vacuum
1981							
E1EE-AB, AC, AE①②	—	—	9½–12 @ 1250	—	—	—	—	—
E1EE-AB, AC, AE①③	—	—	7½–10 @ 1250	—	—	—	—	—
E1EE-JA, JB②④	—	—	9½–12 @ 1250	—	—	—	—	—
E1EE-JA, JB③④	—	—	7½–10 @ 1250	—	—	—	—	—
1982							
E1EE-AB, AC, AE, AF①⑤	—	—	7½–10 @ 1250	—	—	—	—	—
E1EE-AB, AC, AE, AF①③	—	—	7½–10 @ 1250	—	—	—	—	—
E1EE-AB, AC, AE, AF①⑥	—	—	8½–11 @ 1250	—	—	—	—	—
E1EE-KA, KB②④⑤	—	—	7½–10 @ 1250	—	—	—	—	—
E1EE-KA, KB③④	—	—	5½–8 @ 1250	—	—	—	—	—
E2EE-EA, GA②④⑤	—	—	10–12 @ 1250	—	—	—	—	—
E2EE-EA, GA③④	—	—	⑦	—	—	—	—	—
E2EE-EA, GA④⑥	—	—	10–12 @ 1250	—	—	—	—	—
E2EE-FA①③	—	—	⑧	—	—	—	—	—
E2EE-FA①②⑤	—	—	⑨	—	—	—	—	—
E2EE-FA①⑥	—	—	11–13 @ 1250	—	—	—	—	—
E2EE-LA②④⑤	—	—	8½–11 @ 1250	—	—	—	—	—
E2EE-LA③④	—	—	8½–11 @ 1250	—	—	—	—	—
E2EE-LA④⑥	—	—	8½–11 @ 1250	—	—	—	—	—
E2EE-PA, RA②④⑤	—	—	7½–11 @ 1250	—	—	—	—	—
E2EE-PA, RA③④	—	—	7½–11 @ 1250	—	—	—	—	—
E2EE-PA, RA④⑥	—	—	7½–11 @ 1250	—	—	—	—	—
1983							
E3EE-DA①②⑤	—	—	8½–11 @ 1250	—	—	—	—	—
E3EE-DA①③	—	—	8½–11 @ 1250	—	—	—	—	—
E3EE-HA③④	—	—	7–9½ @ 1250	—	—	—	—	—
E3EE-PA①②⑤	—	—	7–9½ @ 1250	—	—	—	—	—
E3EE-RA③④	—	—	9½–11½ @ 1250	—	—	—	—	—
E3EE-RA④⑥	—	—	10½–12½ @ 1250	—	—	—	—	—
E3EE-TA①②⑤	—	—	8½–11½ @ 1250	—	—	—	—	—
E3EE-YA④⑥	—	—	9–11 @ 1250	—	—	—	—	—
E3EE-ZA①⑥	—	—	8–10½ @ 1250	—	—	—	—	—
1984							
E43E-AA	—	—	—	—	—	—	—	—

①—Man. Trans.
②—Except Calif.
③—Calif.
④—Auto Trans.
⑤—Except high altitude.
⑥—High altitude.

⑦—Calibration code 2-4Q-R0, 9–11 @ 1250; Calibration code 2-4Q-R10, 10–12 @ 1250.
⑧—Calibration code 2-3B-R10 & 2-3C-R11, 8½–11 @ 1250; Calibration code 2-3C-R0,

11–13 @ 1250; Calibration code 2-3E-R0, 9½–12 @ 1250.
⑨—Calibration code 2-3D-R0 & 2-3D-R1, 11–13 @ 1250; Calibration code 2-3D-R16, 9½–12 @ 1250.

STARTING MOTOR APPLICATIONS

Year	Engine Model/V.I.N.	Ident. No.①	Year	Engine Model/V.I.N.	Ident. No.①
1981	4-97.6, 1.6L/2	E1EF-AB	1984	4-97.6, 1.6L/2	—
1982	4-97.6, 1.6L/2	E1EF-AD		4-120, 2.0L/	—
1983	4-97.6, 1.6L/2	—		4-140, 2.3L/R	—

①—Basic ident. No., 11001.

ALTERNATOR & REGULATOR SPECIFICATIONS

Year	Ident. Stamp Color	Current Rating		Field Current @ 75°F.		Voltage Regulator				Field Relay	
		Amperes	Volts	Amperes	Volts	Ident. No. ①	Voltage @ 75°F	Contact Gap	Armature Air Gap	Armature Air Gap	Closing Voltage @ 75°F.
1981	Orange	40	15	4	12	D9BF-AB	13.8–14.6	—	—	—	—
	Green	60	15	4	12	D9BF-AB	13.8–14.6	—	—	—	—
	Black	65	15	4	12	D9BF-AB	13.8–14.6	—	—	—	—
1982–83	Orange	40	15	4	12	②	13.8–14.6				
	Green	60	15	4	12	②	13.8–14.6				
	Black	65	15	4	12	②	13.8–14.6				
1984	Orange	40	15	4.25	12	—					
	Green	60	15	4.25	12	—					
	Black	65	15	4.25	12	—					

①—Basic ident. No., 10316.
②—1982 Escort & Lynx, E1AF-AA; 1982 EXP & LN7, E1TF-AA; 1983 Escort & Lynx, E2AF-AA; 1983 EXP & LN7, E2TF-AA.

VALVE SPECIFICATIONS

Year	Engine	Valve Lash		Valve Angles		Valve Spring Installed Height	Valve Spring Pressure Lbs. @ In.	Stem Clearance		Stem Diameter	
		Int.	Exh.	Seat	Face			Intake	Exhaust	Intake	Exhaust
1981	4-97.6, 1.6L/2	.059–.194①		45	44	1.46	180 @ 1.09	.0008–.0027	.0015–.0032	.316	.315
1982	4-97.6, 1.6L/2	.059–.194①		45	44	1.46	180 @ 1.09	.0008–.0027	.0018–.0037	.316	.315
1983	4-97.6, 1.6L/2	.059–.194①		45	45.6	1.46	200 @ 1.09	.0008–.0027	.0018–.0037	.316	.315
	4-97.6, 1.6L/2 E.F.I. & H.O.	.059–.194①		45	45.6	1.46	206 @ 1.09	.0008–.0027	.0018–.0037	.316	.315
1984	4-97.6, 1.6/2	.059–.194①		45	45.6	1.46	200 @ 1.09	.0008–.0027	.0018–.0037	.316	.315
	4-97.6 (1.6)/4 H.O.	.059–.194①		45	45.6	1.46	200 @ 1.09	.0008–.0027	.0018–.0037	.316	.315
	4-97.6 (1.6)/5 E.F.I.	.059–.194①		45	45.6	1.46	200 @ 1.09	.0008–.0027	.0018–.0037	.316	.315
	4-120 (2.0)/H Diesel	—		45	45	—	—	.0016–.0029	.0018–.0031	.3141	.3140
	4-140 (2.3)/R②	.070–.170①		45	45.75	1.49	182 @ 1.10	.0018	.0023	.3415–.3422	.3411–.3418

①—With hydraulic valve lash adjuster completely collapsed.　　②—Tempo & Topaz

PISTONS, PINS, RINGS, CRANKSHAFT & BEARINGS

Year	Engine/VIN	Piston Clearance	Ring End Gap①		Wrist pin Diameter	Rod Bearings		Main Bearings		Thrust on Bear. No.	Shaft End Play
			Comp.	Oil		Shaft Diameter	Bearing Clearance	Shaft Diameter	Bearing Clearance		
1981–83	4-97.6, 1.6L/2	.0008–.0016	.012	.016	.8119–.8124	1.885–1.886	.0008–.0015	2.2826–2.2834	.0008–.0015	3	.004–.008
1984	4-97.6, 1.6L/2	.0018–.0026	.012	.016	.8119–.8124	1.885–1.886	.0008–.0015	2.2826–2.2834	.0008–.0015	3	.004–.008
	4-97.6, 1.6L/4 H.O.	.0018–.0026	.012	.016	.8119–.8124	1.885–1.886	.0008–.0015	2.2826–2.2834	.0008–.0015	3	.004–.008
	4-97.6, 1.6L/5 E.F.I.	.0018–.0026	.012	.016	.8119–.8124	1.885–1.886	.0008–.0015	2.2826–2.2834	.0008–.0015	3	.004–.008
	4-120, 2.0L/H Diesel	.0013–.0020	.0079	.0079	.9843–1.0234	2.005–2.006	.0012–.0020	2.359–2.360	.0012–.0020	3	.0016–.0111
	4-140, 2.3L/R②	.0013–.0021	.008	.015	.9119–.9124	2.123–1.124	.0008–.0015	2.248–2.249	.0008–.0015	3	.004–.008

①—Fit rings in tapered bores for clearance listed in tightest portion of ring travel.　　②—Tempo & Topaz.

ENGINE TIGHTENING SPECIFICATIONS

Year	Engine/VIN	Spark Plugs Ft. Lbs.	Cylinder Head Bolts Ft. Lbs.	Intake Manifold Ft. Lbs.	Exhaust Manifold Ft. Lbs.	Rocker Arm Shaft Bracket Ft. Lbs.	Rocker Arm Cover Ft. Lbs.	Connecting Rod Cap Bolts Ft. Lbs.	Main Bearing Cap Bolts Ft. Lbs.	Flywheel to Crankshaft Ft. Lbs.	Vibration Damper or Pulley Ft. Lbs.
1981–82	4-97.6, 1.6L/2	17–23	44①	12–15	15–20	7–11②	6–8	19–25	67–80	59–69	74–90
1983	4-97.6, 1.6L/2	8–15	44①	12–15	15–20	7–11②	6–8	19–25	67–80	54–64	74–90
1984	4-97.6, 1.6L/2, 4 & 5	8–15	③	12–15	15–20	7–11②	6–8	19–25	67–80	54–64	74–90
	4-120, 2.0L/H Diesel	④	—	11–16	15–19	—	⑤	50–54	60–65	130–137	115–123
	4-140, 2.3L/R⑥	5–10	⑦	15–23	⑧	⑨⑩	3–5	21–26⑪	60–74	54–64	82–103

①—Then tighten bolts an additional 1/2 turn in 1/4 turn increments after specified torque has been obtained.
②—Rocker arm stud to cylinder head.
③—Torque bolts to 30–45 ft. lbs., then turn bolts an additional 180 degrees in 90 degree increments.
④—Glow plug torque, 10–14 ft. lbs.
⑤—Cylinder head cover torque, 5–7 ft. lbs.
⑥—Tempo & Topaz.
⑦—Tighten bolts in 2 steps. Final torque of bolts must be 81 ft. lbs.
⑧—Tighten bolts in 2 steps. First to 5–7 ft. lbs., then 20–30 ft. lbs.
⑨—Tighten bolts in 2 steps. First to 4–7 ft. lbs., then 19–26 ft. lbs.
⑩—Rocker arm fulcrum bolt to cylinder head.
⑪—Connecting rod cap nut.

WHEEL ALIGNMENT SPECIFICATIONS

Year	Model	Caster Angle, Degrees		Camber Angle, Degrees					Toe-In Inch	Toe-Out on Turns, Deg.	
		Limits	Desired	Limits		Desired				Outer Wheel	Inner Wheel
				Left	Right	Left	Right				
1981	Front	+.55 to +2.05	+1.3	+1.4 to +2.9	+.95 to +2.45	+2.15	+1.7	①	②	20	
	Rear	—	—	−1.45 to +.25	−1.45 to +.25	−.6	−.6	0−.36	—	—	
1982–83	Front	+.55 to +2.05	+1.3	+1.4 to +2.9	+.95 to +2.45	+2.15	+1.7	①	③	20	
	Rear	—	—	−1.45 to +.25	−1.45 to +.25	−.6	−.6	.09	—	—	
1984	Front④	+.65 to +2.15	+1.4	+1.4 to +2.9	+.95 to +2.45	+2.15	+1.7	①	—	—	
	Rear④	—	—	−.40 to +2.1	−.40 to +2.1	−1.25	−1.25	0−.36	—	—	
	Front⑤	+.65 to +2.15	+1.4	+1.25 to +2.75	+.85 to +2.35	+2	+1.6	.12	—	—	
	Rear⑤	—	—	−.50 to +1	−.50 to +1	−.25	−.25	—	—	—	

①—Toe out, .10 inch.
②—Left wheel, 19.97°; right wheel, 17.04°.
③—Left wheel, 20°; right wheel, 17°.
④—All models, Except Tempo & Topaz.
⑤—Tempo & Topaz.

COOLING SYSTEM & CAPACITY DATA

Year	Model or Engine/VIN	Cooling Capacity, Qts.		Radiator Cap Relief Pressure, Lbs.	Thermo. Opening Temp.	Fuel Tank Gals.	Engine Refill Qts. ①	Transaxle Oil	
		Less A/C	With A/C					4 & 5 Speed Pints	Auto Trans. Qts. ①
1981	4-97.6, 1.6L/2	6.3	6.4	16	191	②	4③	5	9.8
1982	4-97.6, 1.6L/2	8	8	16	191	11.3	4③	5	9.8
1983	4-97.6, 1.6L/2	6.7	8	16	191	11.3	4③	④	8.3
1984	4-97.6, 1.6L/2	6.7	8.1	16	192	13	3.5	④	7.8
	4-120, 2.0/H	8.1	8.1	16	190	13	5	6.1	7.8
	4-140, 2.3/R	8.1	8.1	16	192	14	4	④	8.3

①—Approximate. Make final check with dipstick.
②—Models w/man. trans., 9 gals.; models w/ auto. trans., 10 gals.; models w/extended range option, 11.3 gals.
③—Includes filter.
④—4 speed trans., 5 pints; 5 speed trans., 6.1 pints.

Electrical Section

STARTER, REPLACE

1. Disconnect battery ground cable and raise and support vehicle. Disconnect starter cable from starter motor terminal.
2. On vehicles equipped with manual transmission, remove three nuts attaching roll restrictor brace to transmission-side starter studs and remove brace.
3. Remove two bolts attaching starter rear support bracket. Remove retaining nut from rear of starter stud bolt, then remove bracket.
4. Remove three starter mounting nuts or bolts and the starter.
5. Reverse procedure to install.

IGNITION SWITCH, REPLACE

1982-84

1. Disconnect battery ground cable, then remove five steering column shroud attaching screws.
2. Remove two bolts and two nuts attaching steering column to column bracket, then lower steering column assembly to seat and remove column shrouds.

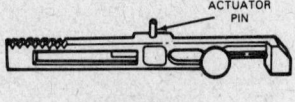

SWITCH ACTUATOR

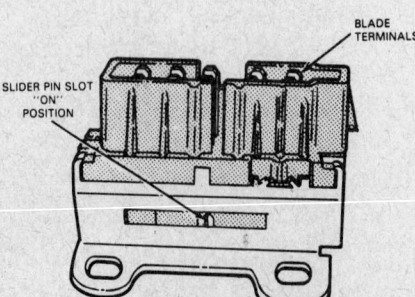

Fig. 1 Ignition switch. 1982-84

3. Disconnect ignition switch wire connector, then rotate ignition switch lock cylinder to the Run position.
4. Using a 1/8 inch drill bit, drill out shear bolts retaining ignition switch to lock cylinder housing.
5. Remove the two shear bolts using an easy out.
6. Detach ignition switch from actuator pin, then remove switch.
7. Check to ensure that ignition switch actuator pin slot and ignition switch lock cylinder are in the Run position.

NOTE: Replacement ignition switches are set in the Run position. The Run position on the ignition switch lock cylinder is located approximately 90° from the lock position.

8. Position ignition switch on actuator pin. It may be necessary to move switch slightly to align switch to column mounting bolt holes, Fig. 1.
9. Install and tighten shear bolts until heads break-off.
10. Connect wire connector to ignition switch, then connect battery ground cable and check ignition switch for proper operation.

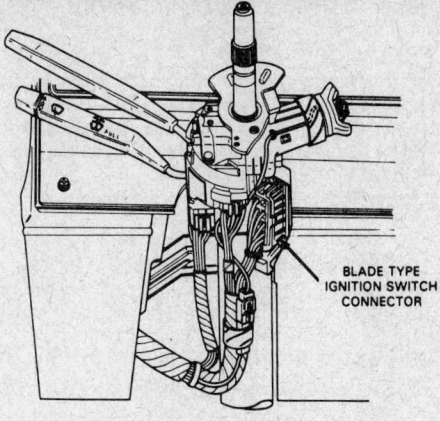

Fig. 1A   Ignition switch removal. 1981

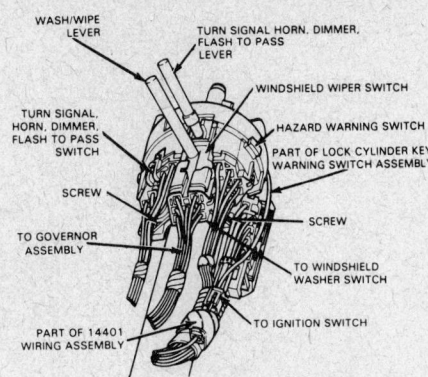

Fig. 2   Turn signal switch removal

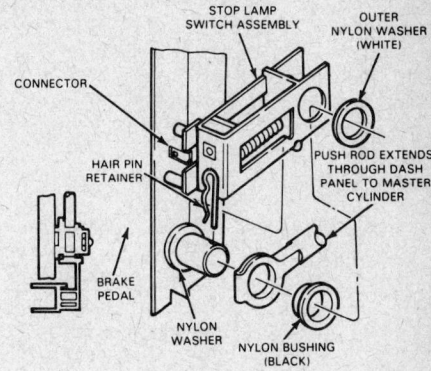

Fig. 3   Stop light switch

11. Position upper shroud on column, then raise steering column and install column mounting bracket to instrument panel attaching bolts. Torque bolts to 15 to 25 ft. lbs.
12. Position lower shroud on column and install attaching bolts.

1981

1. Disconnect battery ground cable.
2. Remove steering column upper and lower trim shroud. It may be necessary to loosen four steering column attaching nuts to facilitate shroud removal.
3. Disconnect ignition switch electrical connector, Fig. 1A.
4. Using a 1/8 in. drill, drill out the break-off head bolts attaching the switch to the lock cylinder.
5. Remove two switch retaining bolts using an easy out, then disengage the ignition switch from the actuator pin.
6. Adjust ignition switch by sliding carrier to the switch lock position, then insert a 1/16 in. drill bit through switch housing and into carrier.

NOTE: A replacement switch assembly includes an adjusting pin already installed.

7. Rotate lock cylinder to lock position and install switch onto actuator pin. Then install new break-off head bolts. Hand tighten the bolts.
8. Locate ignition switch upward on steering column until all travel in screw slots is used.
9. Hold switch in this position and tighten break off head bolts until heads break off. Remove adjustment drill bit, connect electrical connector, then install upper and lower trim shroud.

TURN SIGNAL SWITCH, REPLACE

1981–84

1. Disconnect battery ground cable, then remove the upper and lower trim shroud.

2. Grasp switch lever. Using a pulling and twisting motion, pull lever straight out from switch, Fig. 2.
3. Pull back switch cover from switch, then disconnect two switch electrical connectors.
4. Remove screws securing switch to lock cylinder housing, then the switch.
5. Reverse procedure to install.

STOPLIGHT LIGHT SWITCH, REPLACE

1981–84

1. Disconnect battery ground cable.
2. Disconnect electrical connector from switch.

NOTE: On vehicles equipped with standard brakes, the locking tab must be lifted before electrical connector can be removed.

3. On vehicles equipped with standard brakes, remove retainer, then slide the switch, push rod, white nylon washer and bushing away from pedal. Remove switch from vehicle, Fig. 3.
4. On vehicles equipped with power brakes, remove retainer and outer white nylon washer from pedal pin. Slide switch off brake pedal pin far enough so that outer side of plate of switch clears pin. Remove switch, Fig. 3.

STEERING WHEEL, REPLACE

1. Disconnect battery ground cable.
2. Remove steering hub cover assembly, then the steering wheel attaching nut. Discard nut.
3. Remove steering wheel from steering shaft using tool T67L3600A. Do not use a knock-off type steering wheel puller or strike end of steering column with a hammer since damage to steering column bearings will result.
4. Reverse procedure to install. Use a new wheel nut lnd torque to 13–20 ft. lbs.

INSTRUMENT CLUSTER, REPLACE

1981–84

1. Disconnect battery ground cable.
2. Remove steering column lower cover, then the four cluster opening finish panel retaining screws and the finish panel.
3. Remove two upper and two lower screws retaining instrument panel.
4. From under instrument panel, disconnect speedometer cable, then pull cluster away from instrument panel, Figs. 4 and 5. Disconnect cluster electrical connector.
5. Reverse procedure to install.

Auxiliary Cluster, Replace

EXP, LN7 & Tempo
1. Disconnect battery ground cable.
2. Pull trim cover at bottom edge and slide out of tabs at top edge.
3. Remove three cluster to console attaching screws. On Tempo models, remove four cluster to console attaching screws, then pull cluster outward and disconnect electrical connector.
4. Remove cluster from console.
5. Reverse procedure to install.

Temperature Gauge, Replace

Topaz
1. Disconnect battery ground cable.
2. Remove instrument cluster as described under "Instrument Cluster, Replace".
3. Remove retaining screws, mask and lens from cluster backplate.
4. Remove two gauge retaining nuts and gauge.
5. Reverse procedure to install.

Graphic Warning Display, Replace

Escort, Lynx, Tempo & Topaz
1. Disconnect battery ground cable, then remove console finish panel by prying at bottom edge to disengage retainers.
2. Remove module to console attaching screws, then pull module outward and disconnect electrical connector.
3. Remove module from console.
4. Reverse procedure to install.

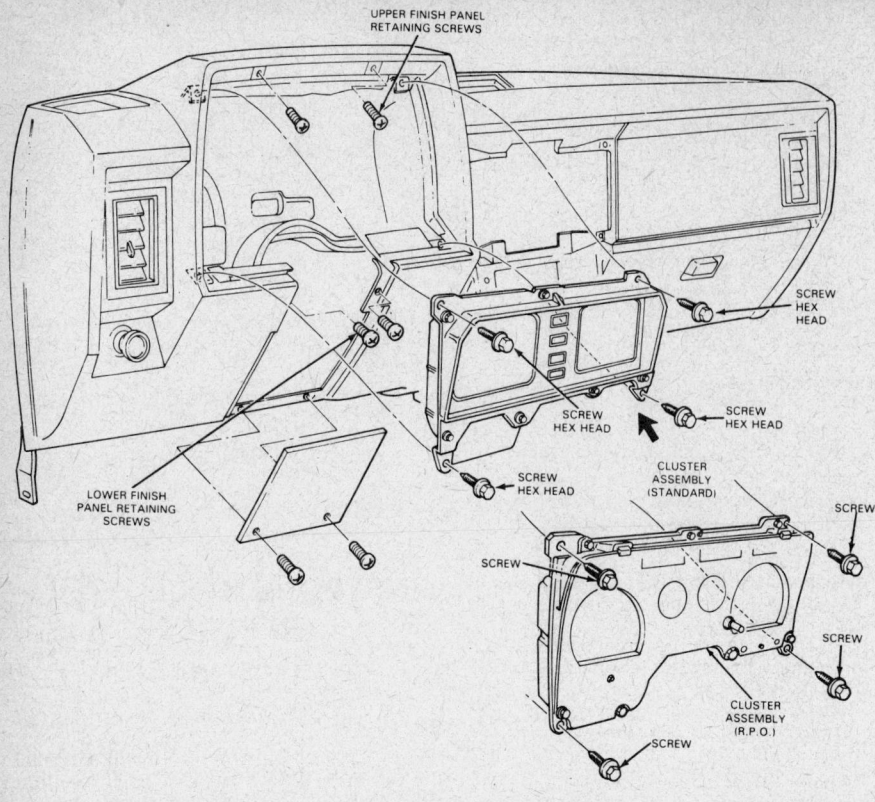

Fig. 4 Instrument cluster removal. 1981—83

HORN SOUNDER, REPLACE

NOTE: On these models, the horn sounder is located on the turn signal, headlight dimmer and horn lever. Refer to Turn Signal Switch, Replace when replacing lever.

HEADLAMP SWITCH, REPLACE

1981—83

1. Disconnect battery ground cable, then on vehicles without A/C, the left hand air vent control cable from the instrument panel.
2. Remove screws securing fuse panel bracket and position fuse panel to the side.
3. Place headlamp switch in the "On" position and depress the headlamp knob and shaft retainer button on headlamp switch. Remove knob and shaft assembly.
4. Remove headlamp switch bezel and disconnect electrical connector, then remove switch.
5. Reverse procedure to install.

1984

1. Disconnect battery ground cable.
2. Insert a thin flat blade under flange at side of headlamp switch to depress spring retaining clip. Twist blade to remove switch from one side.
3. Repeat step 2 for other side of headlamp switch.
4. Pull headlamp switch and electrical connector outward from instrument panel.
5. Disconnect headlamp switch electrical connector.
6. Reverse procedure to install.

RADIO, REPLACE

1981—83

1. Disconnect battery ground cable.
2. Remove A/C floor duct, if equipped.
3. Disconnect power, speaker and antenna leads from radio.
4. Remove knobs, discs, control shaft, nuts and washers from radio.

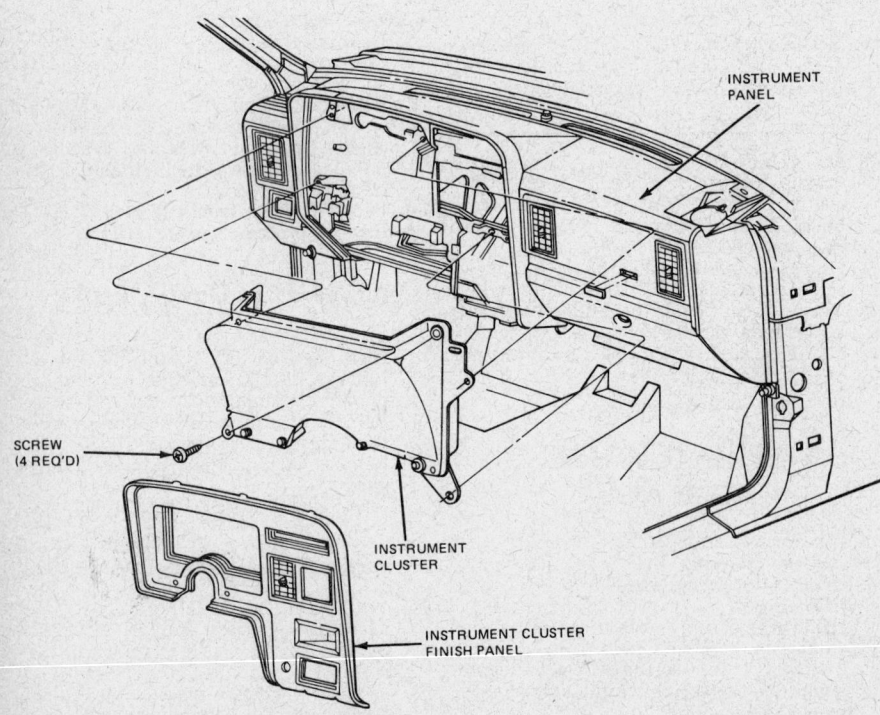

Fig. 5 Instrument cluster removal. 1984

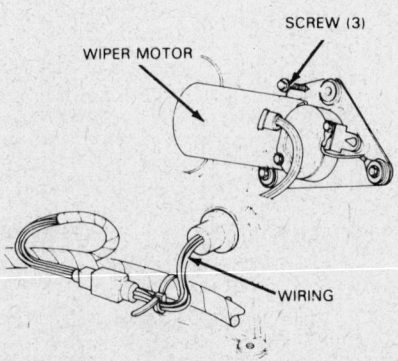

Fig. 6 Windshield wiper motor

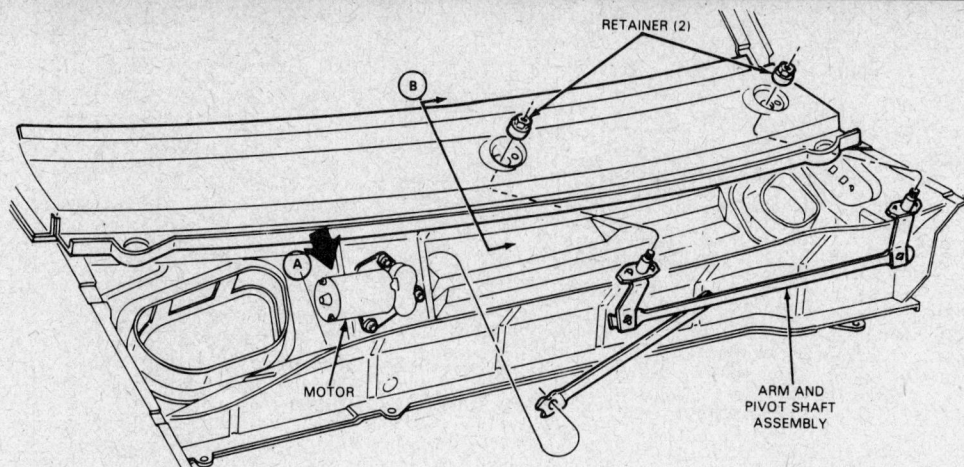

5. Remove ash tray and bracket, then the radio.
6. Remove radio rear support attaching nut.
7. Reverse procedure to install.

1984

1. Disconnect battery ground cable.
2. Remove radio knobs and instrument panel center trim panel.
3. Remove radio mounting plate screws, then pull radio outward to disengage lower rear support bracket.
4. Disconnect antenna and speaker leads from radio, then remove radio.
5. Remove nuts and washers from radio control shafts. Remove mounting plate.
6. Remove rear support retaining nut and support.
7. Reverse procedure to install.

W/S WIPER SWITCH

1981—84

NOTE: The switch handle is an integral part of the switch and cannot be removed separately.

1. Disconnect battery ground cable.
2. Remove upper steering column trim shroud, then disconnect electrical connector.
3. Pull back shield, then remove two screws securing switch. Remove switch.
4. Reverse procedure to install.

W/S WIPER MOTOR, REPLACE

1981—84

1. Disconnect battery ground cable.
2. Lift passenger side water shield cover

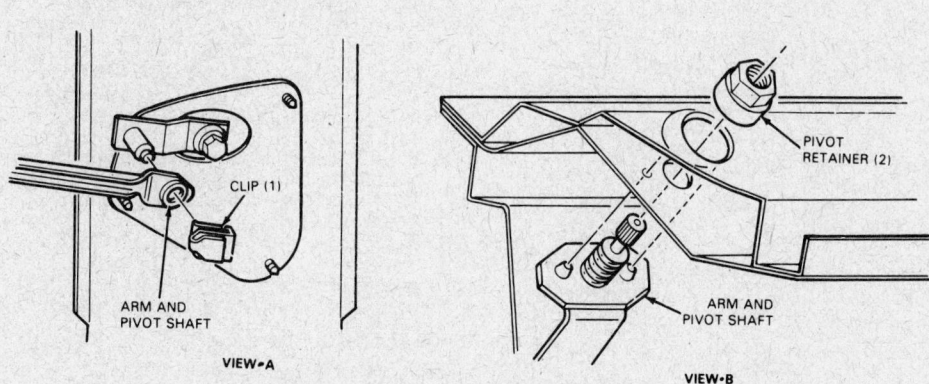

Fig. 7 Windshield wiper linkage, removal

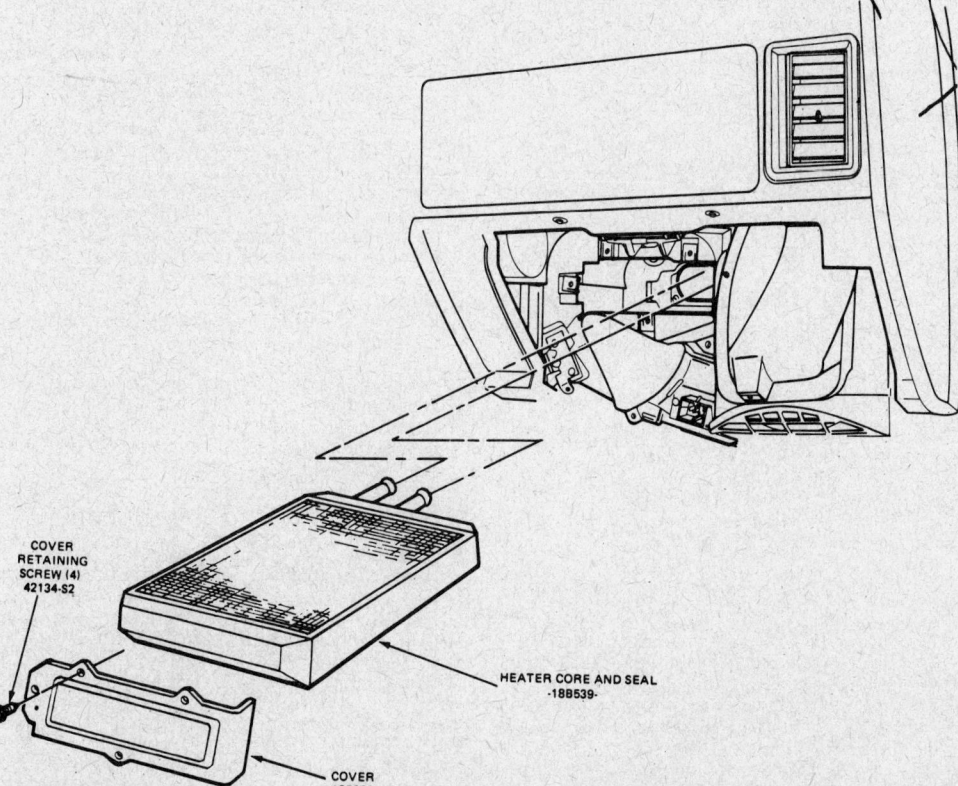

Fig. 8 Heater core removal, less air conditioning

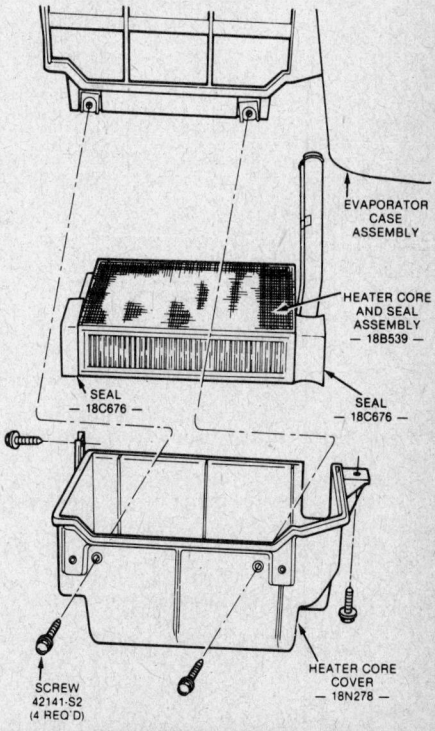

Fig. 9 Heater core removal, with air conditioning

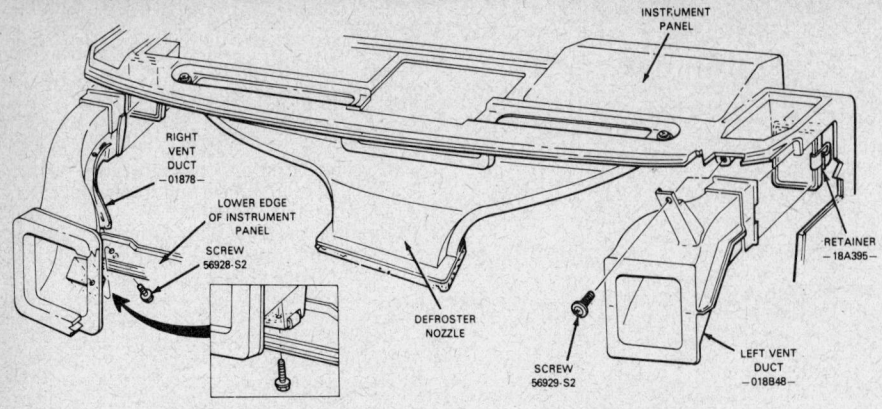

Fig. 9A Vent assembly removal. 1981–83

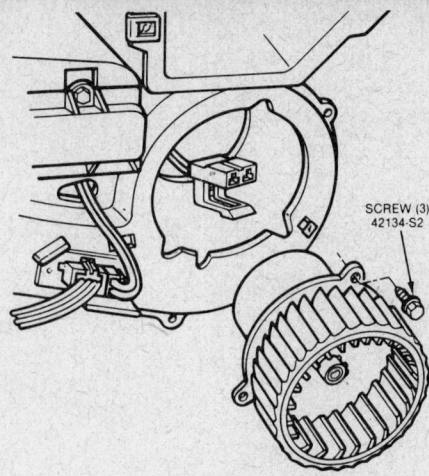

Fig. 11 Blower motor removal.
Less air conditioning

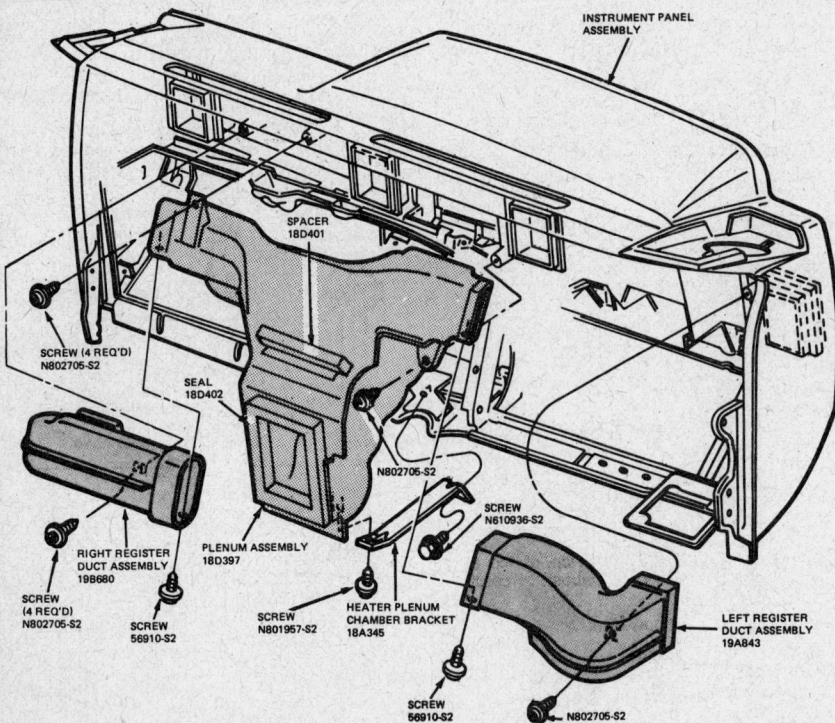

Fig. 10 Vent assembly removal. 1984

from cowl, then disconnect motor electrical connector.
3. Remove linkage retaining clip from motor arm, then the three bolts attaching motor to mounting bracket, Fig. 6.
4. Disconnect operating arm from motor, then separate motor from mounting bracket and remove from vehicle.
5. Reverse procedure to install.

W/S WIPER TRANSMISSION, REPLACE

1981–84

1. Remove wiper arm and blade assemblies from pivot shaft.
2. Disconnect battery ground cable.

3. Disconnect linkage drive arm from motor crank pin, then remove nut from each pivot shaft.
4. Remove linkage and pivots from cowl chamber, Fig. 7.
5. Reverse procedure to install.

HEATER CORE, REPLACE

Less Air Conditioning

1. Disconnect battery ground cable and drain cooling system.
2. Disconnect heater hoses from heater core and plug all open lines and fittings to prevent spillage.
3. Remove glove box and liner and move temperature lever to warm position.
4. Remove heater core cover, then working from engine compartment, loosen two

nuts attaching heater case assembly to dash panel.
5. Push heater core toward passenger compartment, then pull heater core through glove box opening and remove from vehicle, Fig. 8.
6. Reverse procedure to install.

With Air Conditioning

1. Disconnect battery ground cable and drain cooling system.
2. Disconnect heater hoses from heater core and plug all lines and fittings.
3. Remove floor duct from plenum.
4. Remove screws attaching heater core cover to plenum, then the cover and heater core, Fig. 9.
5. Reverse procedure to install.

BLOWER MOTOR, REPLACE

Less Air Conditioning

1. Disconnect battery ground cable.
2. Remove screws securing right ventilator control cable to instrument panel.
3. Remove screw securing right register duct to lower right edge of instrument panel.
4. Remove glove box and hinge bar from instrument panel.
5. Pull right register duct from installed position between air inlet duct and right register opening, Figs. 9A and 10.
6. Remove ventilator grille from bottom of ventilator assembly, then screws securing right ventilator assembly to blower housing.
7. Remove hub clamp spring from blower wheel hub, Fig. 11.
8. Pull blower wheel from blower shaft, then remove three blower motor flange attaching screws.
9. Pull blower motor from housing, disconnect electrical connector, then remove motor from vehicle.
10. Reverse procedure to install.

With Air Conditioning

1. Disconnect battery ground cable.
2. Remove glove box door and instrument panel lower reinforcement from instrument panel.
3. Disconnect blower motor electrical con-

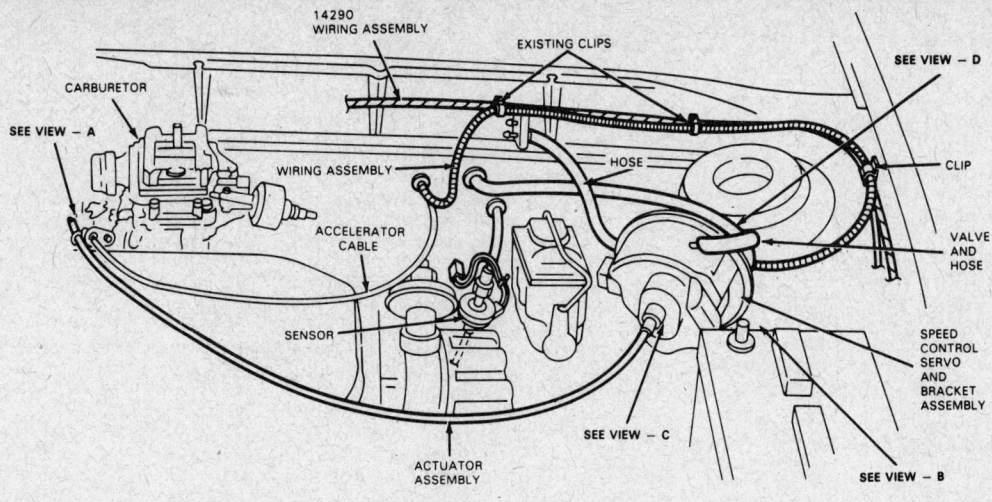

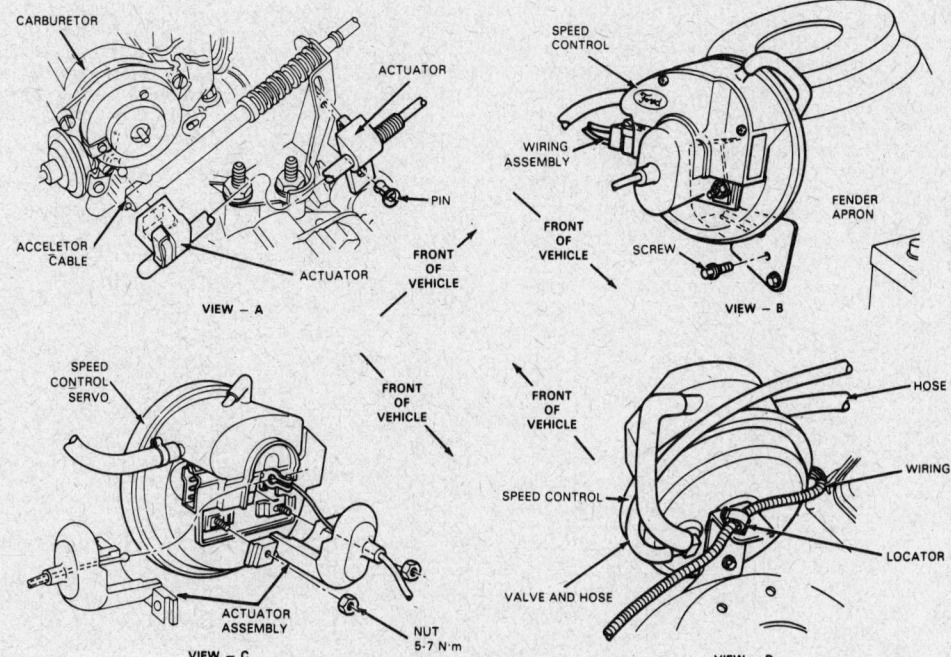

Fig. 12 Speed control actuator cable assembly

nector, then remove blower motor and mounting plate from evaporator housing.

4. Rotate motor until mounting plate flats clear edge of glove box opening, then remove motor.
5. Remove hub clamp wheel spring from blower wheel hub and remove blower wheel from motor shaft.
6. Reverse procedure to install.

SPEED CONTROLS

1981—84

Actuator Cable Adjustment
1. Remove cable retaining clip, then disengage throttle positioner.
2. Place carburetor throttle lever at the curb idle speed position.
3. Pull on actuator cable end tube to remove slack from cable, Fig. 12.
4. While maintaining light tension on actuator cable, insert cable retaining clip.

Vacuum Dump Valve Adjustment
1. Firmly depress brake pedal and hold in position.
2. Pull inward on dump valve until collar contacts retaining clip.
3. Position a .050 to .100 inch shim between pedal and dump valve button.
4. Pull brake pedal rearward to its normal position and allow dump valve to rachet into retaining clip.

Clutch Switch Adjustment

NOTE: This adjustment should be performed on models with manual transmission, when speed control will not engage.

1. Position and support clutch pedal in the full upward position against pedal stop.
2. Loosen switch attaching screw and slide switch forward toward clutch pedal, until clearance between switch plunger cap and switch housing is .030 inch, then tighten attaching screw.
3. Remove support holding clutch pedal in the full upward position and check speed control for proper operation. Ensure that speed control disengages when clutch pedal is depressed.

4-97.6 Gasoline Engine Section

ENGINE MOUNTS

Refer to Figs. 1 through 1E when replacing the engine mounts.

ENGINE, REPLACE

1. Disconnect battery ground cable, then mark location of hinges and remove hood.
2. Remove air cleaner, fresh air intake tube and hot air tube.
3. Drain cooling system, then disconnect secondary coil wire from distributor.
4. Remove alternator and thermactor pump.
5. Disconnect A/C compressor clutch wire from compressor.
6. On models with automatic transaxle, disconnect upper and lower oil cooler lines at radiator, then remove transmission oil cooler line clips.
7. Disconnect upper and lower radiator hoses.
8. Disconnect heater hoses from engine.
9. Disconnect wire connector from electric cooling fan and remove fan motor and shroud assembly, then remove radiator.
10. Remove power steering pump filler tube and cap pump opening to prevent fluid spillage, if equipped.
11. Disconnect all necessary vacuum hose and electrical connections.
12. Disconnect fuel supply and return hoses at metal connector to engine.
13. On models with automatic transaxle, disconnect throttle kickdown linkage.
14. Disconnect vacuum hose at power brake booster, if equipped.
15. Disconnect hose to thermactor valve, then disconnect accelerator cable at carburetor and bracket.
16. Disconnect fuel evaporation hose at metal tube located on left hand fender.
17. Loosen upper power steering pump pivot bolt, then remove upper pump to adjusting bracket attaching bolts, if equipped.
18. Remove upper rear thermactor pump bracket bolt, then install lifting eye.
19. Remove upper A/C compressor to mounting bracket attaching bolts, then remove clip retaining A/C compressor inlet line to exhaust manifold.
20. Raise and support vehicle, then loosen power steering pump lower adjusting bolt and remove drive belt. Remove power steering pump to lower bracket attaching bolts, then remove pump from bracket by passing pulley through adjusting bracket opening. Secure power steering pump against dash panel.
21. Remove heater supply and return tube clamps.
22. Remove starter motor ground cable and engine ground strap, then remove knee brace located at front of starter motor.
23. On models with manual transaxle, remove roll restrictor.
24. Remove starter motor and knee brace rear section, then disconnect exhaust pipe at inlet connector.
25. On models with automatic transaxle, remove converter cover and bracket. On models with manual transaxle, remove lower flywheel cover and brackets.
26. Using tool No. T81P-6312-A, remove crankshaft pulley.
27. On models with automatic transaxle, remove converter to flywheel attaching nuts, then remove lower converter housing to engine attaching bolts.
28. On models with manual transaxle, remove lower clutch housing to engine attaching bolts.
29. Remove coolant by pass hose from intake manifold, then remove lower No. 3-A engine mount bolt and nut from under insulator, Fig. 1.
30. Remove A/C compressor lower bracket bolt, if equipped.

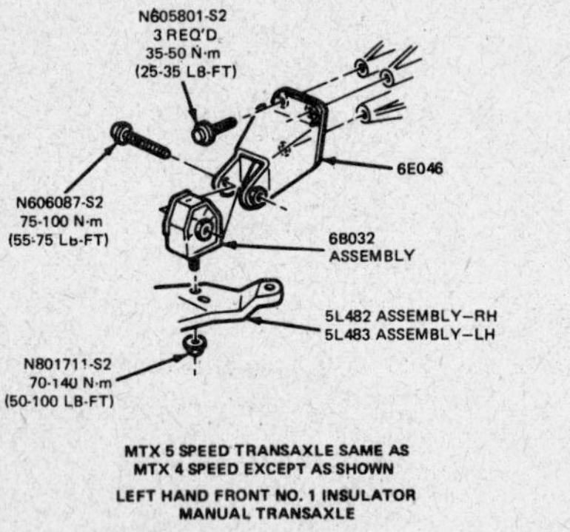

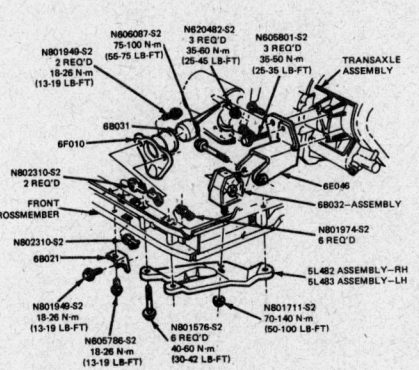

Fig. 1A Left hand front No. 1 insulator. 4 speed manual transaxle

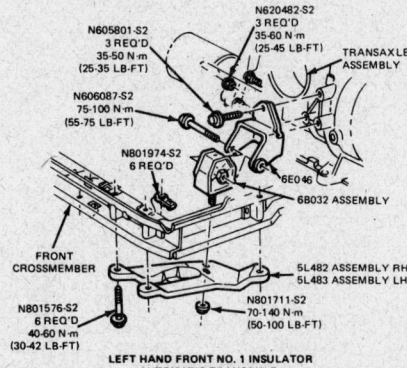

Fig. 1B Left hand front No. 1 insulator. Automatic transaxle

Fig. 1 Left hand front No. 1 insulator. 5 speed manual transaxle

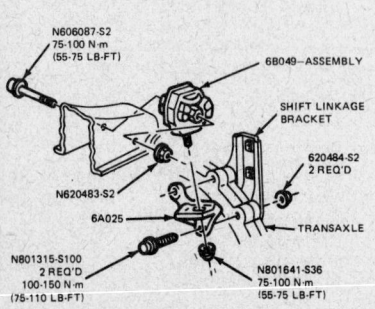

Fig. 1C Left hand rear No. 4 insulator. Automatic transaxle

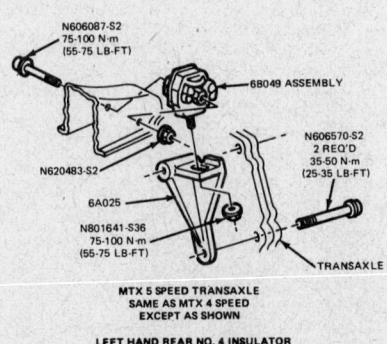

Fig. 1D Left hand rear No. 4 insulator. Manual transaxle

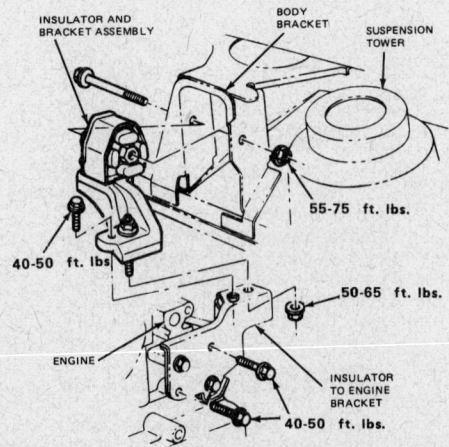

Fig. 1E Right hand No. 3A insulator. All

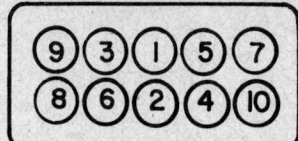

FRONT OF VEHICLE ↓

Fig. 2 Cylinder head bolt tightening sequence

31. Lower vehicle and attach a suitable lifting device to engine. Attach lifting device to engine using a 10mm bolt to exhaust side of cylinder head at the transaxle end and at lifting eye of thermacter pump bracket. A stabilizer chain may also be attached to alternator bracket bolt.
32. Remove engine mount No. 3-A through bolt, then remove engine mount, Fig. 1.
33. Remove A/C compressor bracket, if equipped.
34. On models with manual transaxle, remove timing belt cover.
35. Position a suitable transmission jack under transaxle.
36. On models with automatic transaxle, remove upper converter housing to engine attaching bolts. On models with manual transaxle, remove upper clutch housing to engine attaching bolts.
37. Remove engine from vehicle.

NOTE: On models with automatic transaxle, check to ensure that torque converter studs are free from flywheel before removing engine.

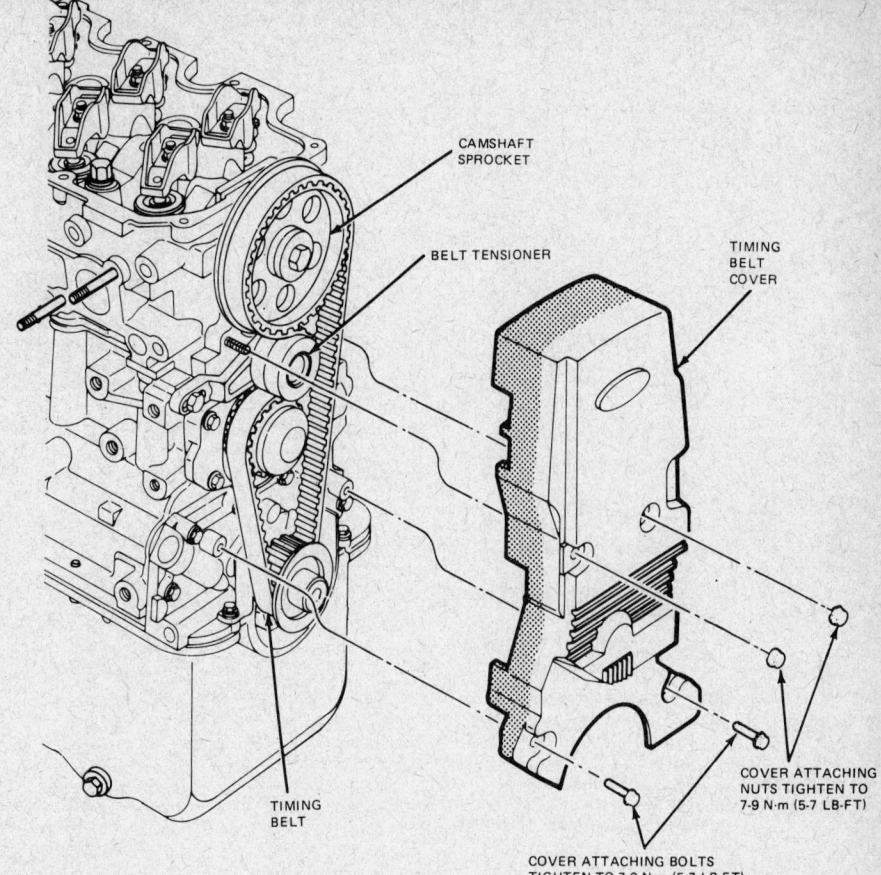

Fig. 3 Timing belt cover removal

CYLINDER HEAD, REPLACE

NOTE: Some engines may have an oversize camshaft. Engines having an oversize camshaft will be identified by a stamping marked ".38/OC" on the outside of the cylinder head above the No. 4 exhaust port. The camshaft will also be stamped ".38/OC" at the distributor drive end. If a cylinder head necessitating replacement incorporates an oversize camshaft, a standard size camshaft must be used with the replacement cylinder head.

1. Disconnect battery ground cable and drain coolant system.
2. Disconnect heater hose from intake manifold and radiator upper hose from cylinder head.
3. Disconnect cooling fan switch electrical connector.
4. Remove air cleaner assembly and PCV hose.
5. Disconnect all necessary vacuum hoses, then remove rocker arm cover.
6. Remove all accessory drive belts, then the crankshaft pulley.
7. Remove timing belt cover and bring No. 1 cylinder to TDC on compression stroke.
8. Remove distributor cap and spark plug wires as an assembly.
9. Loosen both belt tensioner attaching bolts using tool T81P-6254A or equivalent.

10. Position belt tensioner as far left as possible, then remove timing belt. Refer to "Timing Belt, Replace" for procedure. Discard used belt.
11. Disconnect EGR tube from EGR valve, then the PVS hose connectors using tool T81P-8564A or equivalent.
12. Disconnect choke cap electrical connector, fuel supply and return lines, accelerator cable and, if equipped, speed control cable.
13. Disconnect altitude compensator, if equipped, from dash panel and position on heater/A/C air intake.
14. Disconnect alternator air intake tube and alternator electrical connectors. Remove alternator and bracket.
15. On vehicles equipped with power steering, remove thermactor pump drive belt, thermactor pump and mounting bracket.
16. Raise and support vehicle, then disconnect exhaust pipe from exhaust manifold.
17. Lower vehicle, then remove cylinder head bolts and washers. Discard the bolts.
18. Remove cylinder head with intake and exhaust manifolds attached.

NOTE: Do not place cylinder head on flat surface as damage to the spark plugs or gasket surfaces may result.

19. Reverse procedure to install. Torque cylinder head bolts in sequence shown in Fig. 2. After torquing all bolts to specifications, refer to "Timing Belt, Replace" for belt tensioning data.

NOTE: Before installing cylinder head, the crankshaft must be rotated to position No. 1 piston at 90 degrees before top dead center. To position the piston, rotate crankshaft until pulley keyway is at the nine o'clock position. To time the valve train to this piston position, rotate camshaft until keyway is at the six o'clock position. The camshaft and crankshaft must not be rotated from this position until after the timing belt and gears have been installed.

VALVE ARRANGEMENT

Front to Rear

1.6 L . . . . I-E-I-E-I-E

CAM LOBE LIFT SPECS

Engine	Year	Intake	Exhaust
1.6L	1981–84	.229	.229
1.6L, E.F.I. & H.O.	1983–84	.240	.240

ARROW OR LUG TOWARD FRONT OF ENGINE

OIL SQUIRT HOLE

Fig. 4 Piston & rod assembly

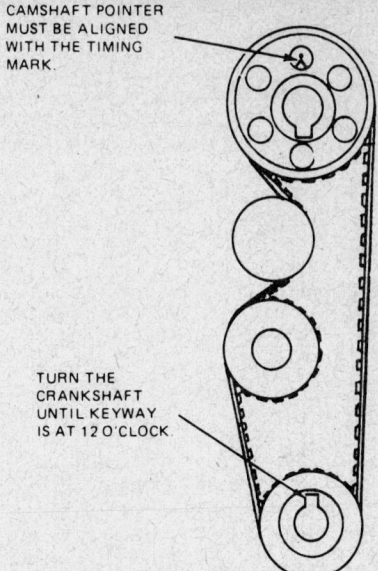

CAMSHAFT POINTER MUST BE ALIGNED WITH THE TIMING MARK.

TURN THE CRANKSHAFT UNTIL KEYWAY IS AT 12 O'CLOCK.

Fig. 5 Aligning camshaft to cylinder head timing marks

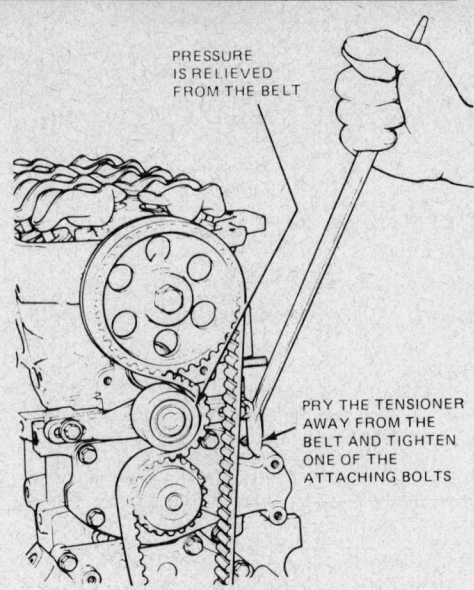

PRESSURE IS RELIEVED FROM THE BELT

PRY THE TENSIONER AWAY FROM THE BELT AND TIGHTEN ONE OF THE ATTACHING BOLTS

Fig. 6 Relieving timing belt tension

VALVE LIFT SPECS

Engine	Year	Intake	Exhaust
1.6 L	1981–84	.377	.377
1.6 L, E.F.I. & H.O.	1983–84	.396	.396

VALVE TIMING

Intake Opens Before TDC

Engine	Year	Degrees
1.6 L	1981	16
1.6 L	1982	20

VALVES, ADJUST

The 1.6L engines are equipped with overhead camshafts and hydraulic lash adjusters. Valve stem to rocker arm clearance is measured with the tappet completely collapsed. Perform the following procedure when measuring valve tappet clearance:

1. Rotate engine until No. 1 piston is on TDC of compression stroke.
2. Position suitable hydraulic lifter compressor tool onto rocker arm and slowly apply pressure to bleed tappet. Continue applying pressure until lifter plunger bottoms. Hold tappet in this position and check clearance between rocker arm and valve stem tip with feeler gauge. Collapsed tappet gap should be .059–.194 in. If clearance is less than specified, check for worn or damaged fulcrums, tappets or camshaft lobes.
3. With No. 1 piston on TDC of compression stroke, check the following valves for 1981 models:
   No. 1 intake & No. 1 exhaust.
   No. 2 intake & No. 3 exhaust.
   Rotate crankshaft 180° clockwise from above position and check the following valves:
   No. 2 exhaust & No. 3 intake.
   No. 4 intake & No. 4 exhaust.
4. With No. 1 piston on TDC of compression stroke, check the following valves for

1982–84 models:
No. 1 intake & No. 1 exhaust.
No. 2 intake.
Rotate crankshaft 180° from above position and check the following valves:
No. 3 intake & No. 3 exhaust
Rotate crankshaft another 180° from above position and check the following valves:
No. 4 intake & No. 4 exhaust.
No. 2 exhaust.

VALVE GUIDES

Valve guide reamers are available in oversizes of .003, .015 and .030 in. When reaming a valve guide to an oversize, use the reamer in sequence from the smallest oversize first, to the next largest, etc. Always reface the valve seat after the valve guide has been reamed and use a suitable tool to remove the corner that forms on the inner diameter of the top of the valve guide.

CAMSHAFT, REPLACE

1. Disconnect battery ground cable and remove air cleaner assembly.
2. Disconnect PCV hose and remove accessory drive belts.
3. Remove crankshaft pulley, then the timing belt cover, Fig. 3.
4. Remove valve cover, then rotate engine until No. 1 piston is on TDC of compression stroke.
5. Remove rocker arm hex flange nuts, fulcrums and rocker arms.
6. Remove fulcrum washers, then the tappets.
7. Remove crankshaft sprocket, then the timing belt. Refer to "Timing Belt, Replace" for procedure.
8. Remove camshaft sprocket, key and distributor assembly.
9. Loosen both timing belt tensioner attaching bolts using tool T81P-6254A or equivalent.
10. Remove camshaft thrust plate, then the fuel pump.
11. Remove ignition coil and bracket.
12. Remove camshaft from back of head

towards transaxle.
13. Reverse procedure to install. Lubricate camshaft with suitable oil before installing. Check camshaft seal for damage and wear.

PISTON & ROD ASSEMBLE

Assemble the piston to the rod with arrow or lug facing front of engine and numbered side of rod facing exhaust manifold side of engine, Fig. 4. Check side clearance between connecting rods at each connecting rod crankshaft journal. Clearance should be .004–.011 in.

PISTONS, RINGS & PINS

Standard size pistons and rings are color coded red or blue and oversize pistons and rings have .004 OS stamped on their dome. Piston to bore clearance should be .0008–.0016 in. on 1981 models, .0012–.0020 in. on 1982 models and .0018–.0026 in. on 1983–84 models. Measure cylinder bore and select a piston to ensure proper clearance. When the piston to bore clearance is in the lower 1/3 of the specified range, a red piston should be used; in the middle 1/3 range a blue piston should be used and in the upper 1/3 range a .004 OS piston should be used. Piston pins are not available in oversize.

MAIN & ROD BEARINGS

Main and rod bearings are available in standard size and undersizes of .001 and .002 in.

TIMING BELT, REPLACE

NOTE: Replacement of the timing belt when the belt tension is released is not necessary. Replace a damaged timing belt as required.

1. Disconnect battery ground cable and re-

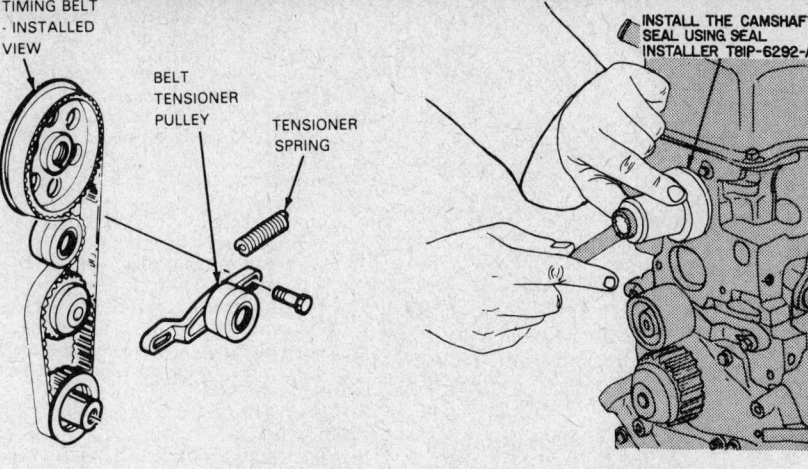

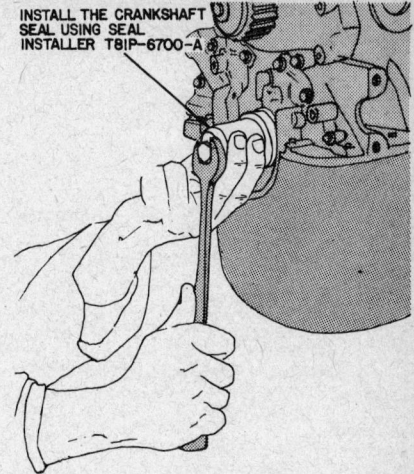

Fig. 8 Camshaft front oil seal installation

Fig. 9 Crankshaft front oil seal installation

NOTE: WHEN THE CRANKSHAFT KEYWAY IS AT THE 12 O'CLOCK POSITION, NUMBER ONE PISTON IS AT TDC. WHEN THE KEYWAY IS AT THE 9 O'CLOCK POSITION, NUMBER ONE PISTON IS 90° BEFORE TDC.

Fig. 7 Timing belt installed

move accessory drive belts.
2. Remove timing belt cover, Fig. 3.

NOTE: Align timing mark on camshaft sprocket with timing mark on cylinder head, Fig. 5.

3. Install timing belt cover and insure that timing mark on crankshaft pulley aligns with TDC mark on front cover. Remove timing belt cover.
4. Loosen both timing belt tensioner attaching bolts using tool T81P-6254A or equivalent.
5. Position belt tensioner away from belt as far as possible, then tighten one of the tensioner attaching bolts, Fig. 6.
6. Remove crankshaft pulley, then the timing belt. Discard timing belt, if damaged.
7. Install timing belt over gears in counterclockwise direction starting at crankshaft. Ensure belt span between crankshaft and camshaft is kept tight as belt is installed over remaining gears, Fig. 7.
8. Loosen belt tensioner attaching bolts and allow tensioner to locate against belt.
9. Tighten one tensioner attaching bolt using tool T81P-6254A or equivalent.
10. Install crankshaft pulley, drive plate and pulley attaching bolt.
11. Hold crankshaft pulley stationary using tool YA-826 or equivalent and torque pulley attaching bolt to 74–90 ft. lbs. (100–121 Nm).
12. To seat timing belt on sprocket teeth, proceed as follows:
    a. Connect battery ground cable.
    b. Crank engine for approximately 30 seconds.
    c. Disconnect battery ground cable.
    d. Turn crankshaft to align timing pointer on camshaft sprocket with timing

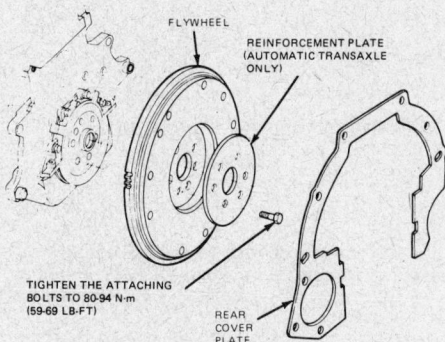

FLYWHEEL

REINFORCEMENT PLATE (AUTOMATIC TRANSAXLE ONLY)

TIGHTEN THE ATTACHING BOLTS TO 80-94 N·m (59-69 LB-FT)

REAR COVER PLATE

Fig. 10 Rear cover plate, removal

mark on cylinder head.
    e. Position timing belt cover on engine and confirm timing mark on crankshaft aligns with TDC pointer on the cover.

NOTE: If timing marks do not align, remove timing belt, align timing marks and repeat steps 7 thru 12.

13. Loosen belt tensioner attaching bolt tightened in step 9.
14. Secure crankshaft so it cannot rotate, then using tool No. D81P-6256 or equivalent and a torque wrench, turn camshaft sprocket counterclockwise. Tighten timing belt tensioner attaching bolt when torque wrench reads 27–32 ft. lbs., for a new timing belt and 10 ft. lbs., for a used timing belt.

NOTE: The engine must be cold when torque is applied to the camshaft sprocket. Do not set torque on a hot engine.

15. Remove crankshaft pulley and install timing belt cover.
16. Install accessory drive belts, crankshaft pulley and connect battery ground cable.

FRONT ENGINE OIL SEAL SERVICE

1. Remove timing belt as described under "Timing Belt, Replace".
2. Remove camshaft sprocket or crankshaft pulley as necessary.
3. Remove appropriate seal, Figs. 8 and 9.
4. Reverse procedure to install.

REAR CRANKSHAFT OIL SEAL SERVICE

1. Remove engine as described under "Engine, Replace".
2. Remove rear cover plate, Fig. 10, then the flywheel.
3. Using suitable tool, pierce seal metal casing.
4. Insert sheet metal screw into hole until screw forces seal out of retainer.
5. Reverse procedure to install using suitable seal installation tool to install seal.

INTAKE MANIFOLD, REPLACE

1. Disconnect battery ground cable and drain coolant system.
2. Disconnect heater hose from intake manifold and remove air cleaner assembly.
3. Disconnect vacuum hoses as necessary, then the electrical connectors from idle fuel solenoid, bowl vent and choke.
4. Remove EGR supply tube.
5. Raise and support vehicle, then disconnect PVS hose using tool T81P-8564A or equivalent.
6. Remove intake manifold nuts Nos. 2, 3, and 6, Fig. 11, then lower vehicle.
7. Disconnect fuel line at fuel filter and return line at carburetor.
8. Disconnect accelerator cable and, if equipped, speed control cable.
9. On vehicles equipped with automatic transmission, disconnect throttle valve linkage at carburetor, then remove cable bracket attaching bolts.
10. On vehicles equipped with power steering, remove thermactor pump drive belt,

OIL PUMP, REPLACE

1. Perform steps 1 thru 4 as described under "Timing Belt, Replace".
2. Remove timing belt from camshaft and crankshaft pulleys and water pump gear.
3. Raise and support vehicle, then drain engine oil.
4. Remove crankshaft pulley, then the timing belt. Discard timing belt.
5. Remove crankshaft drive plate assembly, then the crankshaft pulley and gear.
6. Disconnect starter electrical connectors, then remove knee brace from engine.
7. Remove starter, then the rear section of knee brace. Remove transmission inspection plate.
8. Remove oil pan retaining bolts, then the oil pan.
9. Remove oil pick up tube brace to cylinder block bolt.
10. Remove oil pump attaching bolts, oil pump and gaskets, Fig. 13.
11. Reverse procedure to install using suitable sealant on all pan gaskets.

OIL PUMP SERVICE

Refer to Fig. 14 and measure the following clearances:
a. Outer race to housing: .0027–.0055 in. (.069–.140 mm).
b. Outer race and rotor to cover: .001–.0025 in. (.040–.66 mm.).
c. Relief valve to bore: .007–.0031 in. (.02–.08 mm).

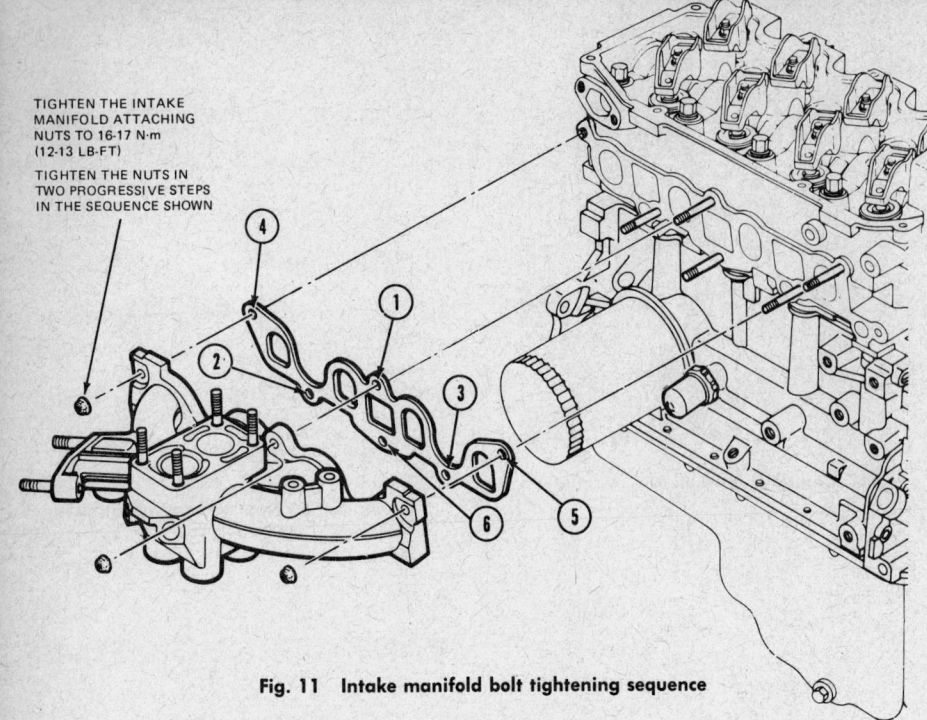

TIGHTEN THE INTAKE MANIFOLD ATTACHING NUTS TO 16-17 N·m (12-13 LB-FT)

TIGHTEN THE NUTS IN TWO PROGRESSIVE STEPS IN THE SEQUENCE SHOWN

Fig. 11 Intake manifold bolt tightening sequence

thermactor pump, mounting bracket and by-pass hose.
11. Remove fuel pump, then three remaining manifold attaching nuts. Remove intake manifold.

NOTE: Do not place manifold on flat surface as damage to gasket surfaces may result.

12. Reverse procedure to install. Tighten intake manifold stud nuts in sequence shown in Fig. 11 to torque listed in Engine Tightening Specifications.

OIL PAN, REPLACE

1. Disconnect battery ground cable, then raise and support vehicle.
2. Drain engine oil, then disconnect starter electrical connectors.
3. Remove knee brace, then the starter.
4. Remove transaxle knee braces, then the oil pan retaining bolts. Remove the oil pan and discard gaskets.

5. Reverse procedure to install using suitable sealant on all pan gaskets. Refer to Fig. 12 for oil pan bolt tightening sequence.

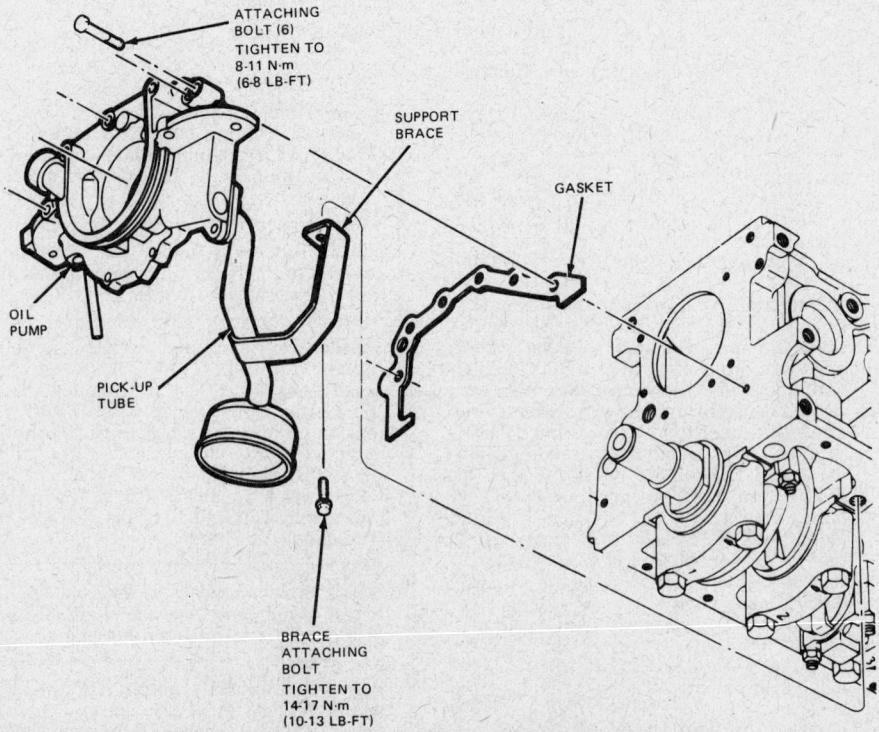

ATTACHING BOLT (6) TIGHTEN TO 8-11 N·m (6-8 LB-FT)

SUPPORT BRACE

GASKET

OIL PUMP

PICK-UP TUBE

BRACE ATTACHING BOLT TIGHTEN TO 14-17 N·m (10-13 LB-FT)

Fig. 13 Oil pump removal

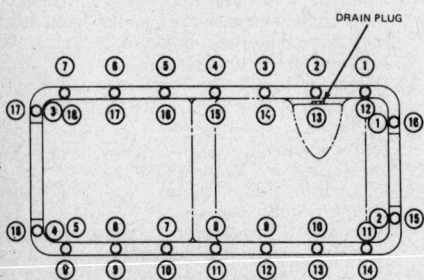

DRAIN PLUG

TIGHTEN THE ATTACHING BOLTS USING THE SEQUENCE INSIDE THE DIAGRAM RETIGHTEN THE ATTACHING BOLTS USING THE SEQUENCE OUTSIDE THE DIAGRAM

Fig. 12 Oil pan bolt tightening sequence

NOTE: An engine oil leak at the oil pump hex socket plug on some 1981–82 vehicles may be serviced by applying sealer to the oil pump hex plug threads above the pressure relief valve plug. Remove hex plug and clean plug threads with a suitable solvent. Apply sealer No. E0AZ-19554A or equivalent to the plug threads. Engines built prior to September of 1981 will have a 3/8 hex plug. Torque plug to 6–9 ft. lbs. Engines built after September of 1981 will have a shouldered hex plug with a white plastic sealing ring. Torque plug to 21–24 ft. lbs. These plugs are not interchangeable and must not be overtorqued.

NOTE: On some engines built after March 31, 1983, a new gerotor gear design oil pump is being used, Fig. 15. The oil pump, oil pan and crankshaft used on models equipped with gerotor gear type oil pumps are not interchangeable with those used with the crescent type oil pump.

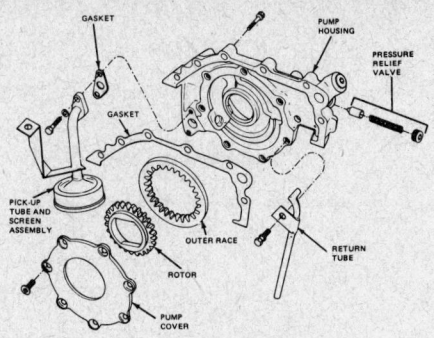

Fig. 14 Oil pump

FUEL PUMP, REPLACE

1. Loosen fuel supply attaching nut at fuel pump outlet and the fuel pump mounting bolts.
2. Manually rotate engine until pump push rod is positioned on low side of cam.
3. Disconnect fuel lines from fuel pump.
4. Remove pump mounting bolts, then the pump and gasket.
5. Reverse procedure to install.

WATER PUMP, REPLACE

1. Disconnect battery ground cable and drain coolant system.
2. Remove accessory drive belts, then the engine front timing cover.
3. Position No. 1 cylinder at TDC, then loosen both belt tensioner attaching bolts.
4. Secure tensioner as far left as possible, then remove timing belt. Discard timing belt.
5. Remove camshaft sprocket, then the rearward front timing cover stud.
6. Disconnect heater return tube hose connection at water pump inlet tube.
7. Remove water pump inlet tube fasteners, then the tube and gasket.
8. Remove water pump to cylinder block bolts, then the water pump.
9. Reverse procedure to install. Refer to "Timing Belt, Replace" for proper belt tensioning procedures.

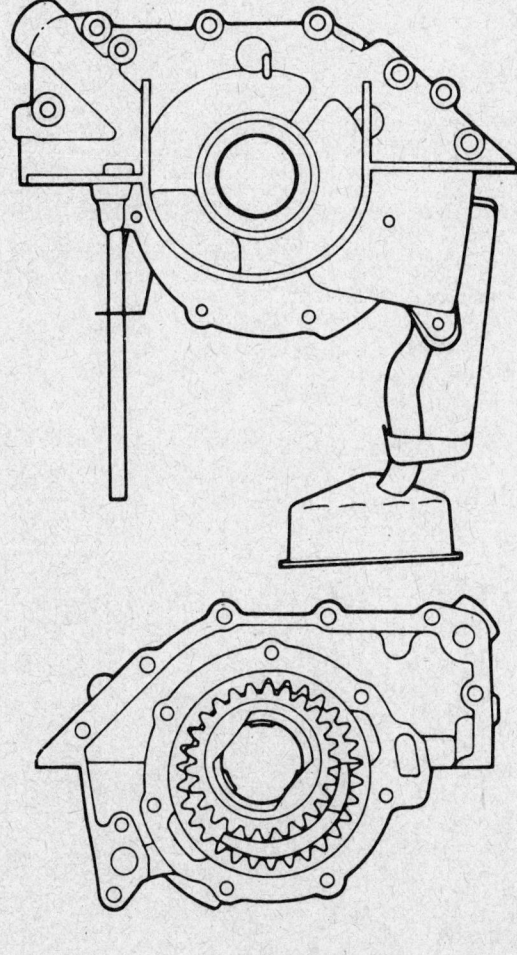

CRESCENT PUMP

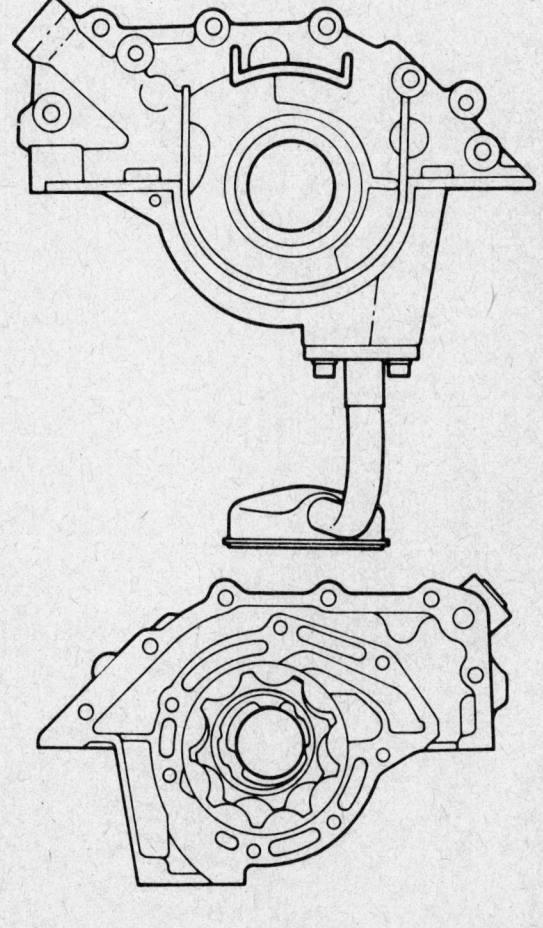

GEROTOR

Fig. 15 Crescent & gerotor type oil pumps

BELT TENSION DATA

		New	Used				
1981	¼ inch	50–80	40–60				
	4 ribbed	90–120	90–110				
	5 ribbed	110–140	110–130				

1982–83	¼ inch Air Pump	50–80	40–60
	4 ribbed All Others	90–130	90–120
	4 ribbed	110–150	100–130
	5 ribbed	130–170	120–150
1984	Air Pump (Low Mount)	90–130	80–100

Less Power Steering Air Pump (High Mount) & Power Steering		
Pump	50–90	40–60
Alternator	150–140	140–160

4-140 Gasoline Engine Section

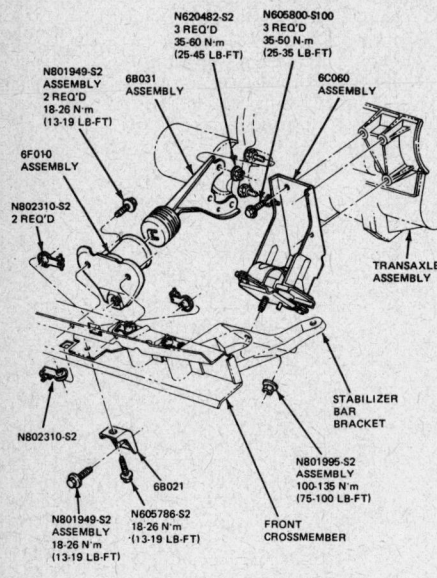

LEFT HAND FRONT NO. 1 INSULATOR
MTX 4 AND 5-SPEED APPLICATIONS

Fig. 1 Left hand front No. 1 insulator. 4 & 5 speed manual transaxle

ENGINE MOUNTS, REPLACE

Refer to Figs. 1 through 5 when replacing engine mounts.

ENGINE, REPLACE

NOTE: Engine and transaxle are removed as an assembly.

1. Mark position of hood hinges, then remove hood.
2. Disconnect battery ground cable, then remove air cleaner assembly.
3. Remove lower radiator hose and drain coolant from engine. Remove upper radiator hose from engine.
4. On models equipped with automatic transaxle, disconnect transaxle cooler lines from rubber hoses below radiator.
5. Remove coil assembly from cylinder head. Disconnect coolant fan electrical connector.

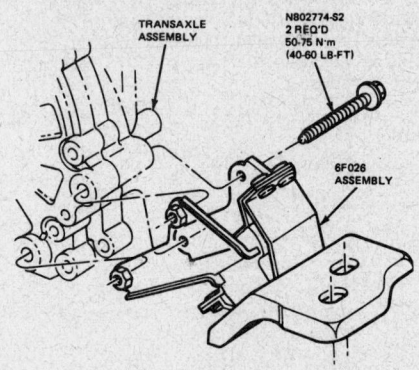

LEFT HAND REAR NO. 4 INSULATOR
MTX 5-SPEED AND ATX APPLIATIONS
(SAME AS MTX 4-SPEED EXCEPT AS SHOWN)

Fig. 4 Left hand rear No. 4 insulator. 5 speed manual & automatic transaxle

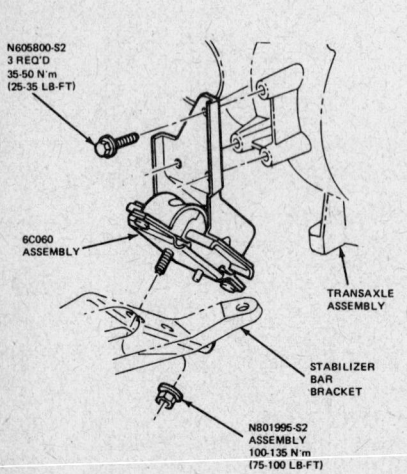

LEFT HAND FRONT NO. 1 INSULATOR
ATX APPLICATIONS

Fig. 2 Left hand front No. 1 insulator. Automatic transaxle

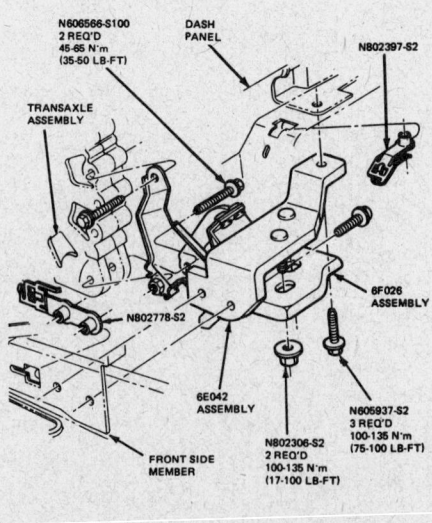

LEFT HAND REAR NO. 4 INSULATOR
MTX 4-SPEED APPLICATIONS

Fig. 3 Left hand rear No. 4 insulator. 4 speed manual transaxle

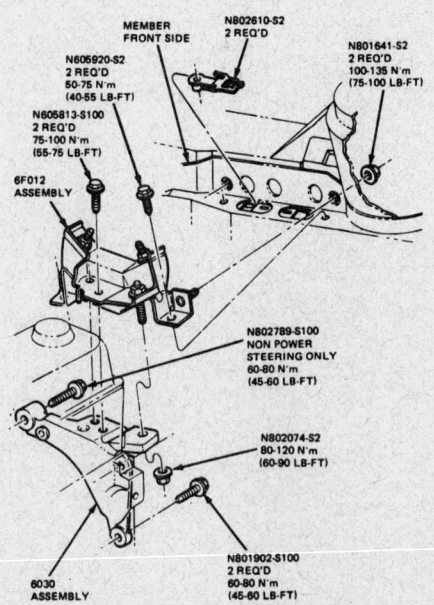

ALL APPLICATIONS

Fig. 5 Right hand No. 3A insulator. All

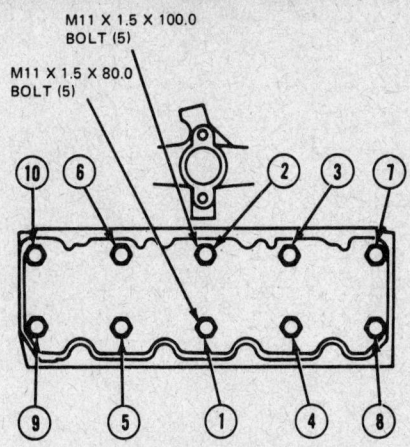

Fig. 6 Cylinder head bolt tightening sequence

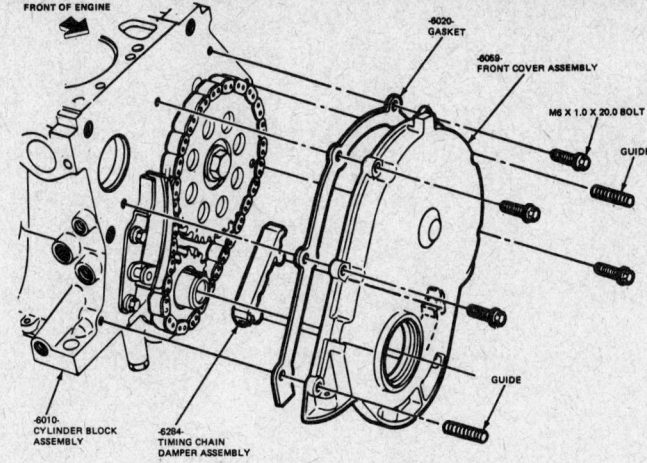

Fig. 7 Front cover removal

6. Remove radiator shroud, cooling fan and radiator.
7. Carefully discharge refrigerant from air conditioning system, if equipped. Remove inlet and outlet lines from compressor.
8. Mark and disconnect all electrical and vacuum lines from engine.
9. On models equipped with automatic transaxle, disconnect TV linkage from transaxle. On models equipped with manual transaxle, disconnect clutch cable from transaxle shift lever.
10. Disconnect accelerator linkage, fuel supply and return lines from engine.
11. Disconnect thermactor pump discharge hose from pump.
12. Disconnect power steering pressure and return lines from pump, if equipped. Remove power steering line bracket from cylinder head.
13. Install engine support tool No. T79P-6000-A or equivalent, to engine lifting eye.
14. Raise and support vehicle.
15. Remove starter cable from starter.
16. Remove air hose from catalytic converter.
17. Remove bolt securing exhaust pipe bracket to oil pan. Remove two exhaust pipes to exhaust manifold nuts, then pull exhaust pipe out of rubber insulating grommets and position aside.
18. Disconnect speedometer cable from transaxle.
19. Remove water pump inlet hose from engine.
20. Remove bolts securing control arms to body. Remove stabilizer bar bracket bolts and brackets.
21. Remove halfshaft assembly from transaxle.
22. On models equipped with manual transaxle, remove roll restrictor nuts from transaxle. Remove shift stabilizer bar to transaxle bolts. Remove shift mechanism to shift shaft nut and bolt from transaxle.
23. On models equipped with automatic transaxle, disconnect manual shift cable clip from transaxle shift lever. Remove manual shift linkage bracket bolts and bracket from transaxle.
24. Remove nuts and left hand rear No. 4 insulator mount bracket from body bracket.

25. Lower vehicle and install suitable lifting hoist to engine.

NOTE: Do not allow front wheels to touch floor.

26. Remove engine support tool No. T79L-6000-A or equivalent from engine.
27. Remove right hand No. 3 insulator intermediate bracket to engine bracket bolts and intermediate bracket to insulator nuts. Remove nut on the bottom of double ended stud which secures intermediate bracket to engine bracket. Remove bracket.
28. Carefully lower engine and transaxle assembly from vehicle.

CYLINDER HEAD, REPLACE

1. Disconnect battery ground cable.
2. Remove lower radiator hose and drain coolant from engine.
3. Disconnect heater hose from fitting located under intake manifold.
4. Disconnect upper radiator hose from cylinder head.
5. Disconnect electric cooling fan switch

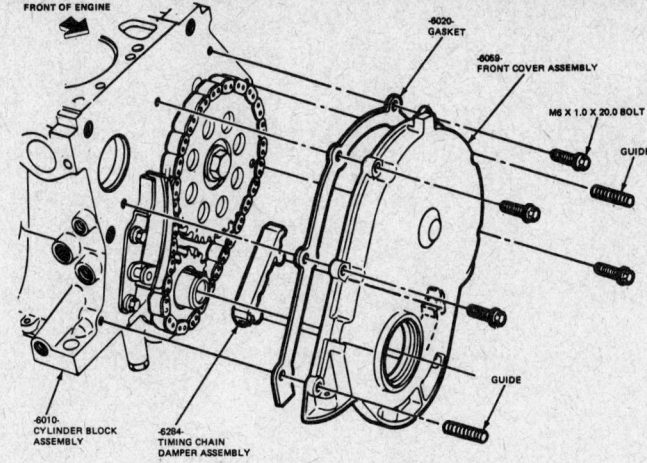

Fig. 8 Valve timing marks

from electrical connector.
6. Remove air cleaner assembly from engine.
7. Mark and disconnect all vacuum hoses from cylinder head.
8. Remove rocker arm cover.
9. Remove all accessory drive belts from engine.
10. Remove distributor cap and spark plug wires as an assembly.
11. Disconnect EGR tube from EGR valve. Disconnect choke cap wire.
12. Disconnect fuel supply and return lines from rubber connector.
13. Disconnect accelerator cable and speed control cable, if equipped.
14. Loosen thermactor pump belt pulley.
15. Raise and support vehicle.
16. Disconnect exhaust system from exhaust pipe. Lower vehicle.
17. Remove cylinder head bolts, cylinder head and gasket with thermactor pump, exhaust and intake manifolds attached.

NOTE: Do not lay cylinder head flat. Damage to spark plugs or gasket surfaces may result.

18. Reverse procedure to install. Torque cylinder head bolts in sequence shown in Fig. 6, to 53–59 ft. lbs.

ROCKER ARM COVER, REPLACE

1. Disconnect battery ground cable.
2. Remove oil filler cap.
3. Disconnect PCV hose from PCV valve.
4. Disconnect throttle linkage cable from rocker arm cover.
5. Disconnect speed control cable from rocker arm cover, if equipped.
6. Remove rocker arm cover bolts and cover.
7. Reverse procedure to install.

FRONT COVER OIL SEAL
Removal

NOTE: The following removal and installation

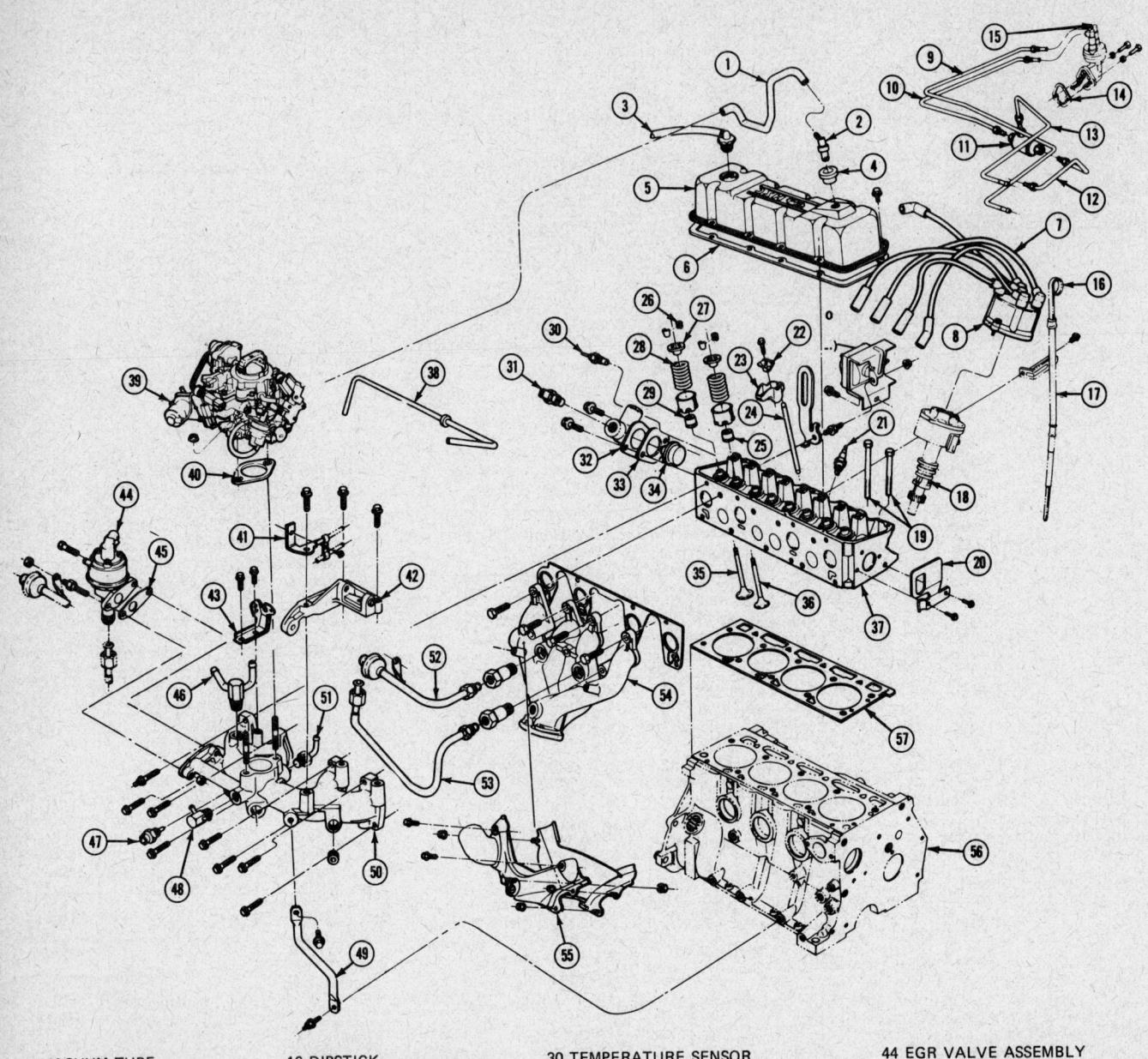

1 VACUUM TUBE
2 VENT VALVE ASSEMBLY
3 TUBE ASSEMBLY
4 GROMMET
5 ROCKER ARM COVER
6 ROCKER ARM COVER GASKET
7 SPARK PLUG WIRES
8 DISTRIBUTOR CAP
9 FUEL LINES
10 FUEL LINES
11 FUEL FILTER
12 FUEL FILTER LINES
13 FUEL FILTER LINES
14 FUEL PUMP GASKET
15 FUEL PUMP ASSEMBLY

16 DIPSTICK
17 DIPSTICK TUBE ASSEMBLY
18 DISTRIBUTOR
19 CYLINDER HEAD BOLTS
20 ENGINE LIFTING EYE
21 SPARK PLUG
22 ROCKER ARM FULCRUM
23 ROCKER ARM
24 PUSHROD
25 EXHAUST VALVE STEM SEAL
26 KEY
27 SPRING RETAINER
28 SPRING
29 INTAKE VALVE STEM SEAL

30 TEMPERATURE SENSOR
31 FAN SWITCH
32 WATER OUTLET CONNECTION
33 WATER OUTLET CONNECTION GASKET
34 THERMOSTAT ASSEMBLY
35 INTAKE VALVE
36 EXHAUST VALVE
37 CYLINDER HEAD
38 CARBURETOR FUEL LINE
39 CARBURETOR ASSEMBLY
40 CARBURETOR GASKET
41 BRACKET
42 BRACKET
43 ACCELERATOR SHAFT BRACKET

44 EGR VALVE ASSEMBLY
45 EGR VALVE GASKET
46 VACUUM FITTING
47 SENSOR
48 VACUUM FITTING
49 BRACE
50 INTAKE MANIFOLD ASSEMBLY
51 VACUUM FITTING
52 TUBE ASSEMBLY
53 TUBE ASSEMBLY
54 EXHAUST MANIFOLD
55 HEAT SHIELD
56 CYLINDER BLOCK
57 CYLINDER HEAD GASKET

Cylinder head assembly & components

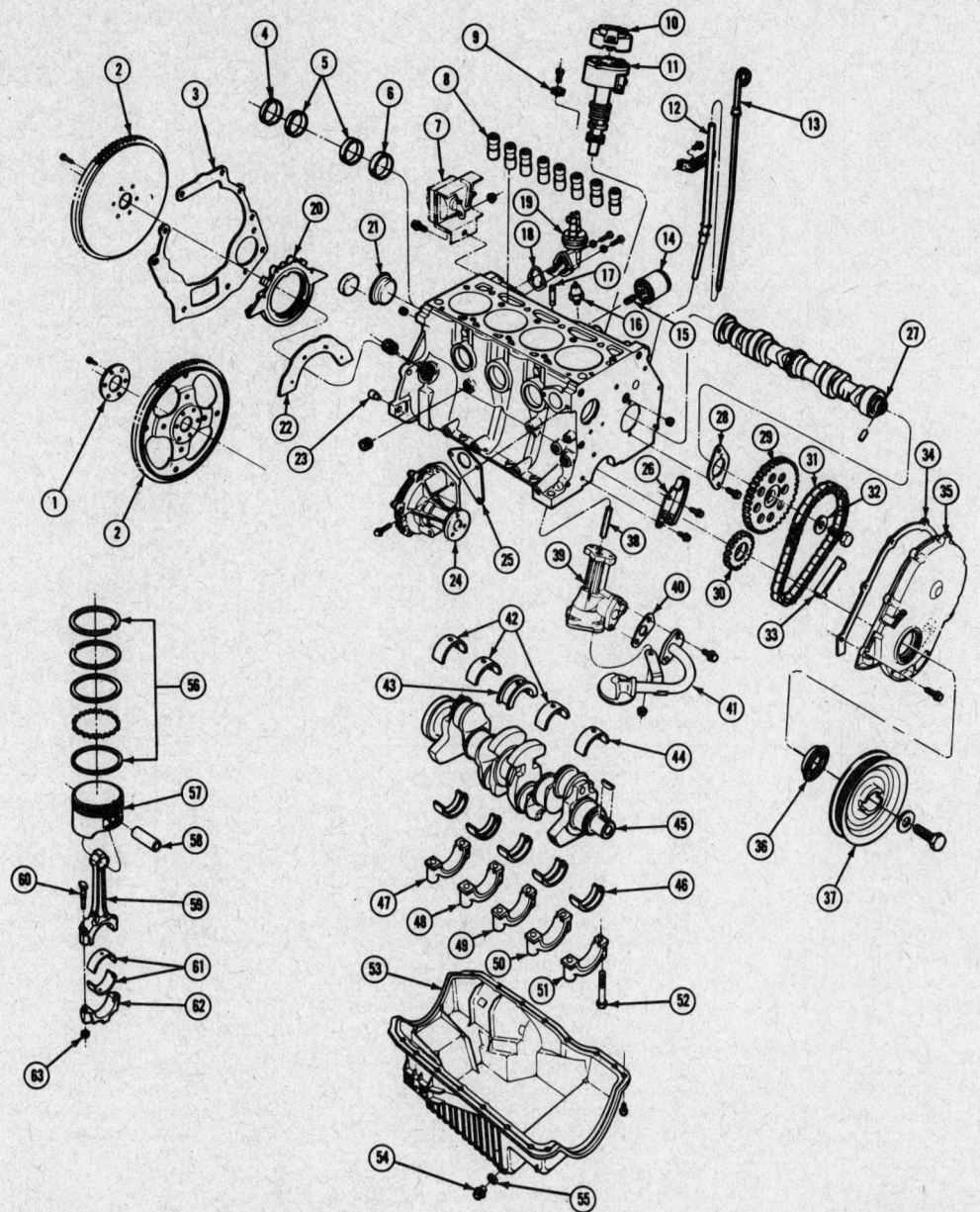

Cylinder block assembly & components

1 REINFORCEMENT PLATE	17 FUEL PUMP PUSHROD	33 TIMING CHAIN DAMPER	49 MAIN BEARING CAP
2 FLYWHEEL	18 FUEL PUMP GASKET	34 FRONT COVER GASKET	50 MAIN BEARING CAP
3 REAR COVER PLATE	19 FUEL PUMP	35 FRONT COVER	51 MAIN BEARING CAP FRONT
4 CAMSHAFT BEARING	20 RETAINER ASSEMBLY	36 SEAL	52 BOLT
5 CAMSHAFT BEARING	21 COVER	37 CRANKSHAFT PULLEY ASSEMBLY	53 OIL PAN ASSEMBLY
6 CAMSHAFT BEARING	22 GASKET	38 INTERMEDIATE DRIVESHAFT	54 DRAIN PLUG
7 COIL	23 DOWEL	39 OIL PUMP ASSEMBLY	55 WASHER
8 TAPPET ASSEMBLY	24 WATER PUMP ASSEMBLY	40 PICK-UP TUBE GASKET	56 PISTON RINGS
9 CLAMP	25 WATER PUMP GASKET	41 PICK-UP TUBE ASSEMBLY	57 PISTON
10 ROTOR	26 TENSIONER ASSEMBLY	42 UPPER MAIN BEARING	58 PISTON PIN
11 DISTRIBUTOR ASSEMBLY	27 CAMSHAFT	43 UPPER THRUST BEARING	59 CONNECTING ROD
12 TUBE	28 THRUST PLATE	44 UPPER MAIN BEARING FRONT	60 STUD
13 OIL DIPSTICK	29 CAMSHAFT SPROCKET	45 CRANKSHAFT	61 ROD BEARINGS
14 OIL FILTER	30 CRANKSHAFT SPROCKET	46 LOWER MAIN BEARING	62 ROD CAP
15 INSERT	31 TIMING CHAIN ASSEMBLY	47 REAR MAIN BEARING CAP	63 NUT
16 OIL PRESSURE SWITCH	32 WASHER	48 MAIN BEARING CAP	

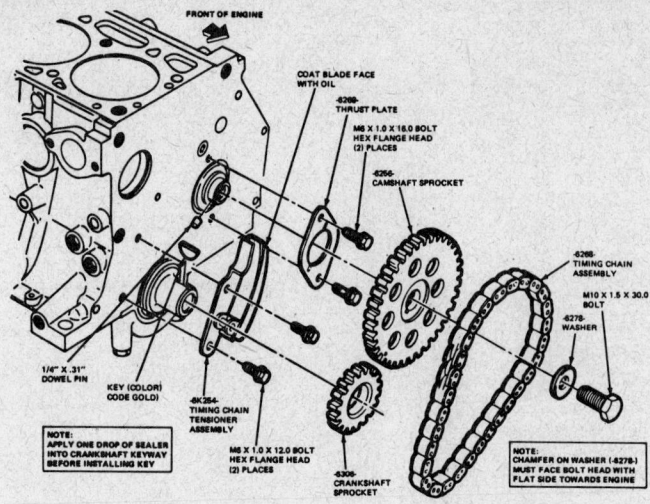

Fig. 9 Timing chain & sprockets removal

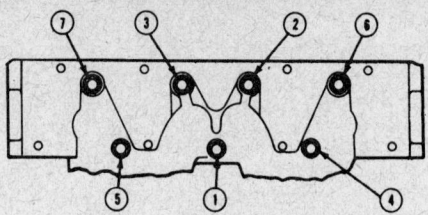

Fig. 10 Exhaust manifold bolt tightening sequence

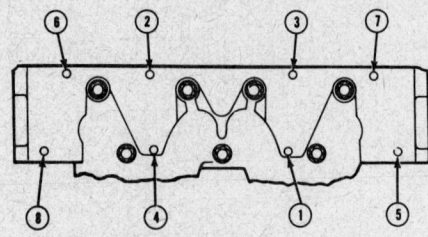

Fig. 11 Intake manifold bolt tightening sequence

procedure can only be performed with the engine removed from the vehicle. Remove engine as described under "Engine, Replace".

1. Remove bolt and washer from crankshaft pulley.
2. Using tool No. T77F-4220-B1 or equivalent, remove crankshaft pulley.
3. Using tool No. T74P-6700-A or equivalent, remove front cover oil seal.

Installation

1. Coat new front cover oil seal with a suitable lubricant.
2. Using tool No. T83T-4676-A or equivalent, install oil seal into front cover. Drive oil seal in until it is fully seated into front cover recess. Check oil seal after installation to ensure spring is properly positioned in oil seal.
3. Install crankshaft pulley, washer and bolt. Torque crankshaft pulley bolt to specification.

FRONT COVER, TIMING CHAIN & SPROCKETS, REPLACE

NOTE: The following procedure can only be performed with the engine removed from the vehicle. Remove engine as described under "Engine, Replace".

1. Remove dipstick, crankshaft pulley bolt, washer and pulley.
2. Remove front cover bolts and front cover, Fig. 7.
3. Align camshaft and crankshaft sprocket timing marks as shown in Fig. 8.
4. Remove camshaft sprocket bolt and washer.
5. Remove sprockets and timing chain from engine as an assembly, Fig. 9. Check timing chain vibration damper for wear. Replace if necessary.
6. Remove oil pan.
7. Reverse procedure to install. Ensure to align timing marks as shown in Fig. 7.

CAMSHAFT, REPLACE

NOTE: The following procedure can only be performed with the engine removed from the vehicle. Remove engine as described under "Engine, Replace".

1. Remove dipstick. Drain coolant and oil from engine.
2. Remove accessory drive belts and pulleys.
3. Position No. 1 piston at TDC with distributor rotor at No. 1 firing position, then remove distributor.
4. Remove cylinder head as described under "Cylinder Head, Replace".
5. Using a suitable magnet, remove hydraulic tappets and position in order so that they can be installed in their original locations. If tappets are stuck in their bores, use tool No. T70L-6500A or equivalent to remove tappets.
6. Loosen then remove fan drive belt, fan and crankshaft pulley.
7. Remove front cover as described under "Front Cover, Timing Chain & Sprockets, Replace".
8. Remove fuel pump, gasket and fuel pump push rod.
9. Remove timing chain, sprockets and timing chain tensioner as described under "Front Cover, Timing Chain & Sprockets, Replace".
10. Remove camshaft thrust plate. Carefully remove camshaft from engine to avoid damaging camshaft bearings, journals and lobes.
11. Reverse procedure to install. Lubricate camshaft with suitable oil before installing. Ensure No. 1 piston is at TDC with distributor rotor at No. 1 firing position.

MAIN BEARINGS

Main bearings are available in standard sizes and undersizes of .010, .020, .030 and .040 inch.

CRANKSHAFT REAR OIL SEAL, REPLACE

1. Remove engine and transaxle from vehi-

cle as described under "Engine, Replace".
2. Remove transaxle from engine.
3. Remove rear cover plate.
4. Using a suitable tool, punch a hole into the seal metal surface between the lip and block. Using Tool No. T77L-9533-B or equivalent, remove seal.
5. Reverse procedure to install.

INTAKE & EXHAUST MANIFOLD, REPLACE

1. Disconnect battery ground cable and drain coolant from engine.
2. Disconnect accelerator cable.
3. Remove air cleaner assembly and heat stove duct from heat shield.
4. Disconnect all vacuum lines from intake manifold.
5. Remove thermactor belt from pulley, thermactor hose and thermactor pump from engine.
6. Remove exhaust pipe to exhaust manifold nuts and disconnect exhaust pipe from exhaust manifold.
7. Remove exhaust manifold heat shield.
8. Disconnect EGO sensor electrical connector.
9. Disconnect thermactor check valve hose from tube assembly. Remove EGR valve bracket nuts and EGR valve bracket.
10. Disconnect water inlet hose from intake manifold.
11. Disconnect EGR hose from EGR valve.
12. Remove bolts, intake manifold and gasket from engine.
13. Remove bolts and exhaust manifold from engine.
14. Reverse procedure to install. Torque exhaust manifold bolts in two steps. Torque bolts in sequence shown in Fig. 10 to 7–10 ft. lbs., then 20–30 ft. lbs. Torque intake manifold bolts in sequence shown in Fig. 11 to 15–23 ft. lbs.

OIL PAN, REPLACE

1. Disconnect battery ground cable.
2. Raise and support vehicle.
3. Drain coolant and oil from engine.
4. On models equipped with manual trans-

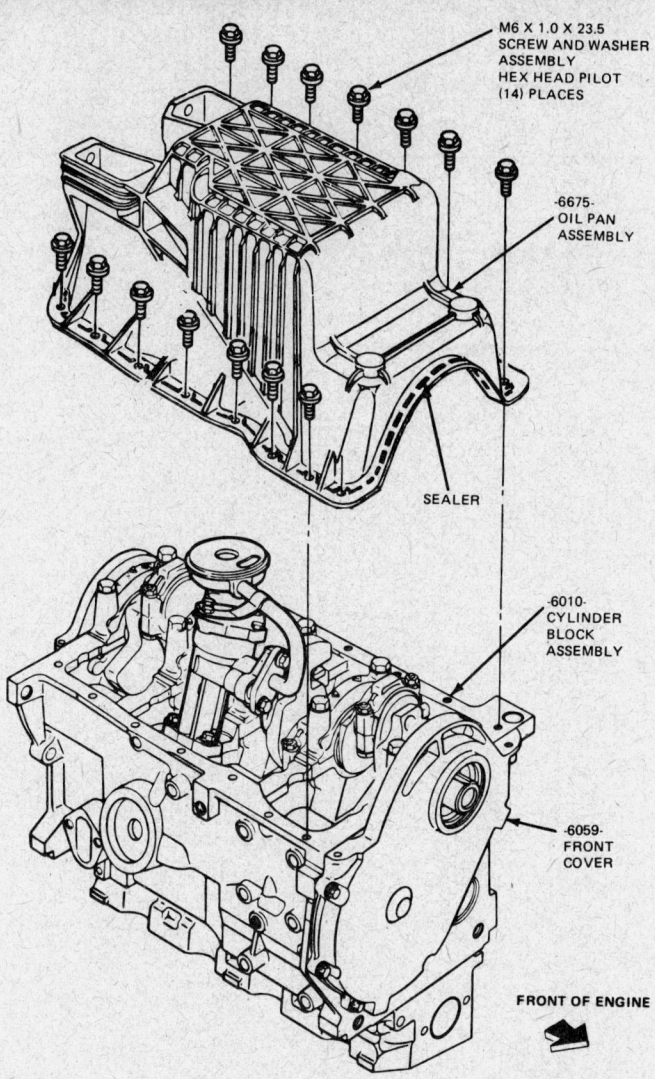

M6 X 1.0 X 23.5
SCREW AND WASHER
ASSEMBLY
HEX HEAD PILOT
(14) PLACES

-6675-
OIL PAN
ASSEMBLY

SEALER

-6010-
CYLINDER
BLOCK
ASSEMBLY

-6059-
FRONT
COVER

FRONT OF ENGINE

Fig. 12   Oil pan removal

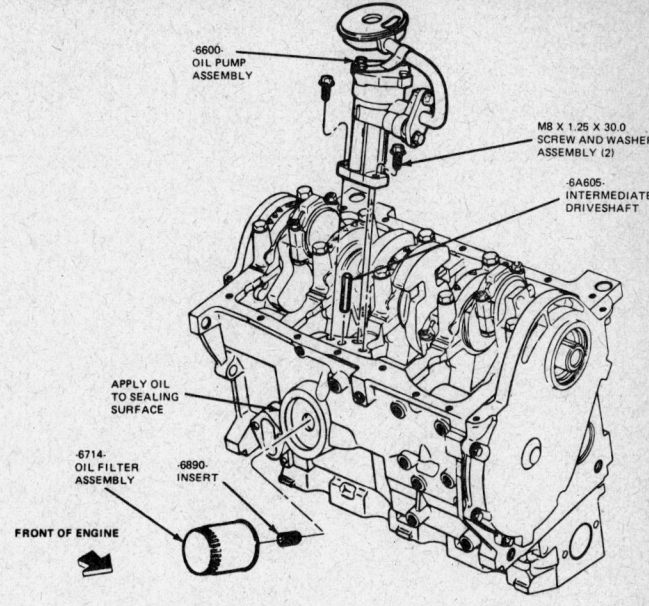

-6600-
OIL PUMP
ASSEMBLY

M8 X 1.25 X 30.0
SCREW AND WASHER
ASSEMBLY (2)

-6A605-
INTERMEDIATE
DRIVESHAFT

APPLY OIL
TO SEALING
SURFACE

-6714-
OIL FILTER
ASSEMBLY

-6890-
INSERT

FRONT OF ENGINE

Fig. 13   Oil pump removal

axle, remove roll restrictor.
5. Remove starter from engine.
6. Disconnect exhaust pipe from oil pan.
7. Remove engine coolant tube located at the lower radiator hose, at the water pump and from tabs on oil pan.
8. Remove oil pan bolts and oil pan, Fig. 12, from engine.
9. Reverse procedure to install.

OIL PUMP, REPLACE

1. Disconnect battery ground cable.
2. Remove oil pan as described under "Oil Pan, Replace".
3. Remove oil pump bolts and oil pump, Fig. 13, from engine. Remove intermediate driveshaft from oil pump.
4. Reverse procedure to install.

WATER PUMP, REPLACE

1. Disconnect battery ground cable and drain coolant from engine.
2. Loosen thermactor pump adjusting bolt and remove belt.
3. Remove thermactor air pump hose clamp, thermactor pump bracket bolts, pump

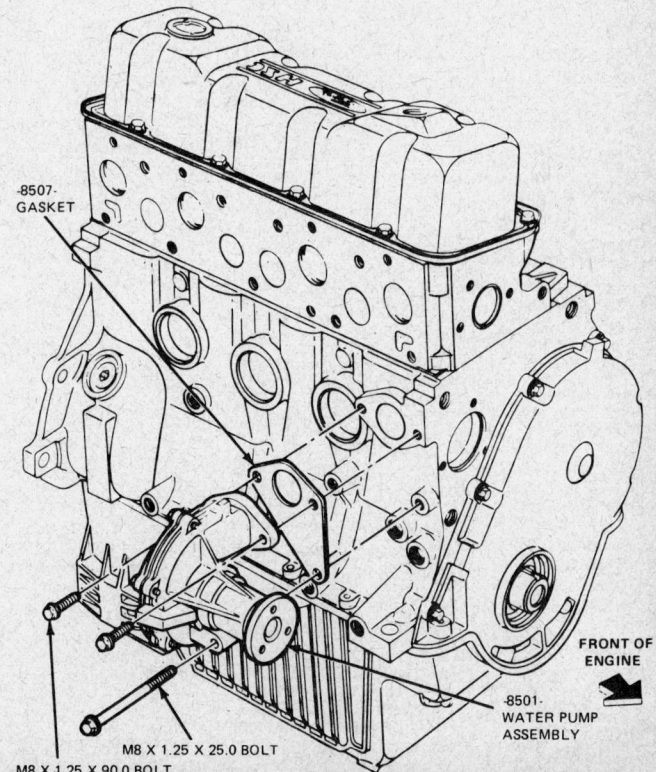

-8507-
GASKET

FRONT OF
ENGINE

-8501-
WATER PUMP
ASSEMBLY

M8 X 1.25 X 25.0 BOLT

M8 X 1.25 X 90.0 BOLT

Fig. 14   Water pump removal

and bracket assembly from engine.
4. Loosen water pump idler pulley bolt and remove belt from water pump pulley.
5. Remove water pump inlet tube.
6. Remove water pump bolts and water pump, Fig. 14.
7. Reverse procedure to install.

FUEL PUMP, REPLACE

1. Disconnect battery ground cable.
2. Disconnect fuel lines from fuel pump.
3. Remove fuel pump bolts, fuel pump and gasket.
4. Reverse procedure to install.

BELT TENSION DATA

	New Lbs.	Used Lbs.
Alternator, Power Steering & Air Conditioning	150–190	140–160
Water Pump & Air Pump	50–90	40–60

4-120 Diesel Engine Section

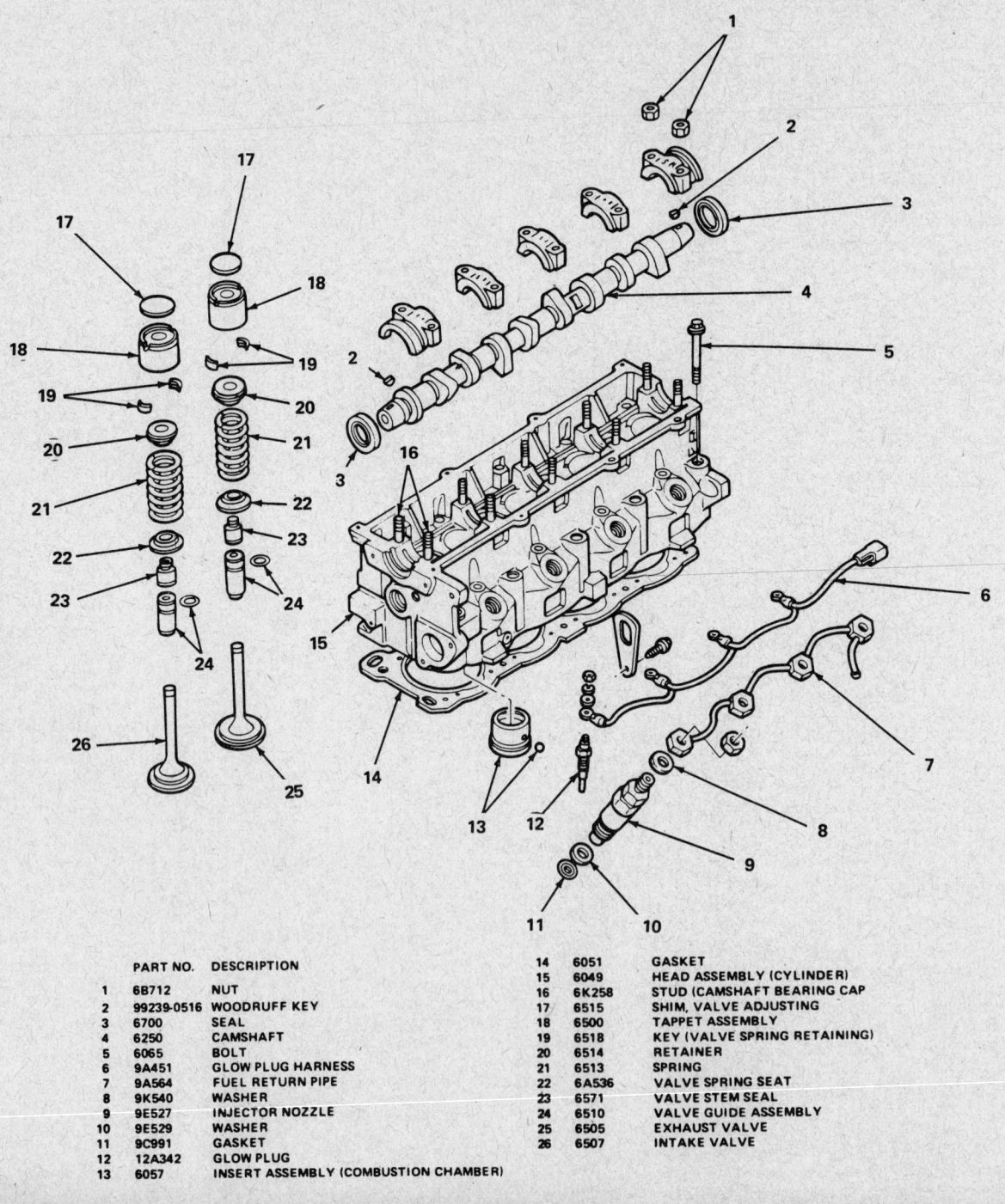

	PART NO.	DESCRIPTION			
1	6B712	NUT	14	6051	GASKET
2	99239-0516	WOODRUFF KEY	15	6049	HEAD ASSEMBLY (CYLINDER)
3	6700	SEAL	16	6K258	STUD (CAMSHAFT BEARING CAP
4	6250	CAMSHAFT	17	6515	SHIM, VALVE ADJUSTING
5	6065	BOLT	18	6500	TAPPET ASSEMBLY
6	9A451	GLOW PLUG HARNESS	19	6518	KEY (VALVE SPRING RETAINING)
7	9A564	FUEL RETURN PIPE	20	6514	RETAINER
8	9K540	WASHER	21	6513	SPRING
9	9E527	INJECTOR NOZZLE	22	6A536	VALVE SPRING SEAT
10	9E529	WASHER	23	6571	VALVE STEM SEAL
11	9C991	GASKET	24	6510	VALVE GUIDE ASSEMBLY
12	12A342	GLOW PLUG	25	6505	EXHAUST VALVE
13	6057	INSERT ASSEMBLY (COMBUSTION CHAMBER)	26	6507	INTAKE VALVE

Fig. 1 Cylinder head components

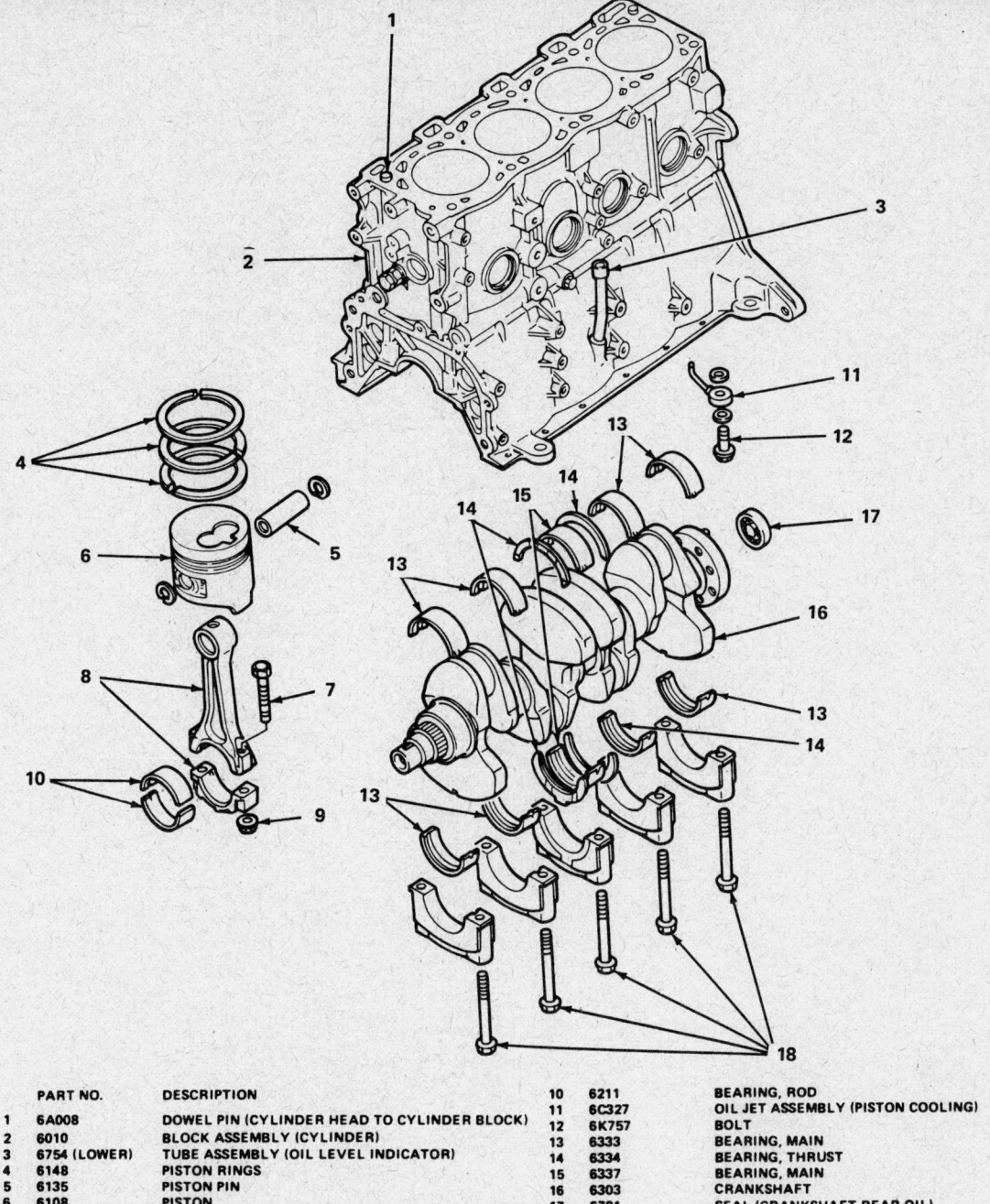

	PART NO.	DESCRIPTION			
			10	6211	BEARING, ROD
			11	6C327	OIL JET ASSEMBLY (PISTON COOLING)
1	6A008	DOWEL PIN (CYLINDER HEAD TO CYLINDER BLOCK)	12	6K757	BOLT
2	6010	BLOCK ASSEMBLY (CYLINDER)	13	6333	BEARING, MAIN
3	6754 (LOWER)	TUBE ASSEMBLY (OIL LEVEL INDICATOR)	14	6334	BEARING, THRUST
4	6148	PISTON RINGS	15	6337	BEARING, MAIN
5	6135	PISTON PIN	16	6303	CRANKSHAFT
6	6108	PISTON	17	6701	SEAL (CRANKSHAFT REAR OIL)
7	6214	BOLT	18	6345	BOLT
8	6200	ROD ASSEMBLY			
9	6212	NUT			

Fig. 1A   Cylinder block components

ENGINE, REPLACE

NOTE: Engine and transaxle are removed from vehicle as an assembly.

1. Disconnect battery ground cable located in luggage compartment.
2. Remove air cleaner assembly.
3. Remove lower radiator hose, then drain coolant from engine.
4. Disconnect cooling fan electrical connector.
5. Remove radiator shroud, cooling fan and radiator from vehicle.
6. Remove starter cable from starter.
7. Carefully discharge refrigerant from air conditioning system, if equipped. Disconnect pressure and return lines from compressor.
8. Mark then disconnect all electrical and vacuum lines from engine.
9. Disconnect clutch cable from transaxle shift lever.
10. Disconnect injection pump throttle linkage. Disconnect fuel supply and return lines from engine.
11. Disconnect power steering pressure and return lines from power steering pump, if equipped. Remove power steering line bracket from cylinder head.
12. Install engine support tool D79P-8000A or equivalent to engine lifting eye.
13. Raise and support vehicle.
14. Remove bolt securing exhaust pipe bracket to oil pan. Remove exhaust pipe to exhaust manifold nuts, then disconnect exhaust pipe from exhaust manifold.
15. Disconnect speedometer cable from transaxle.
16. Disconnect heater hoses from heater and oil cooler.
17. Remove bolts securing control arms to body. Remove stabilizer bar bracket bolts

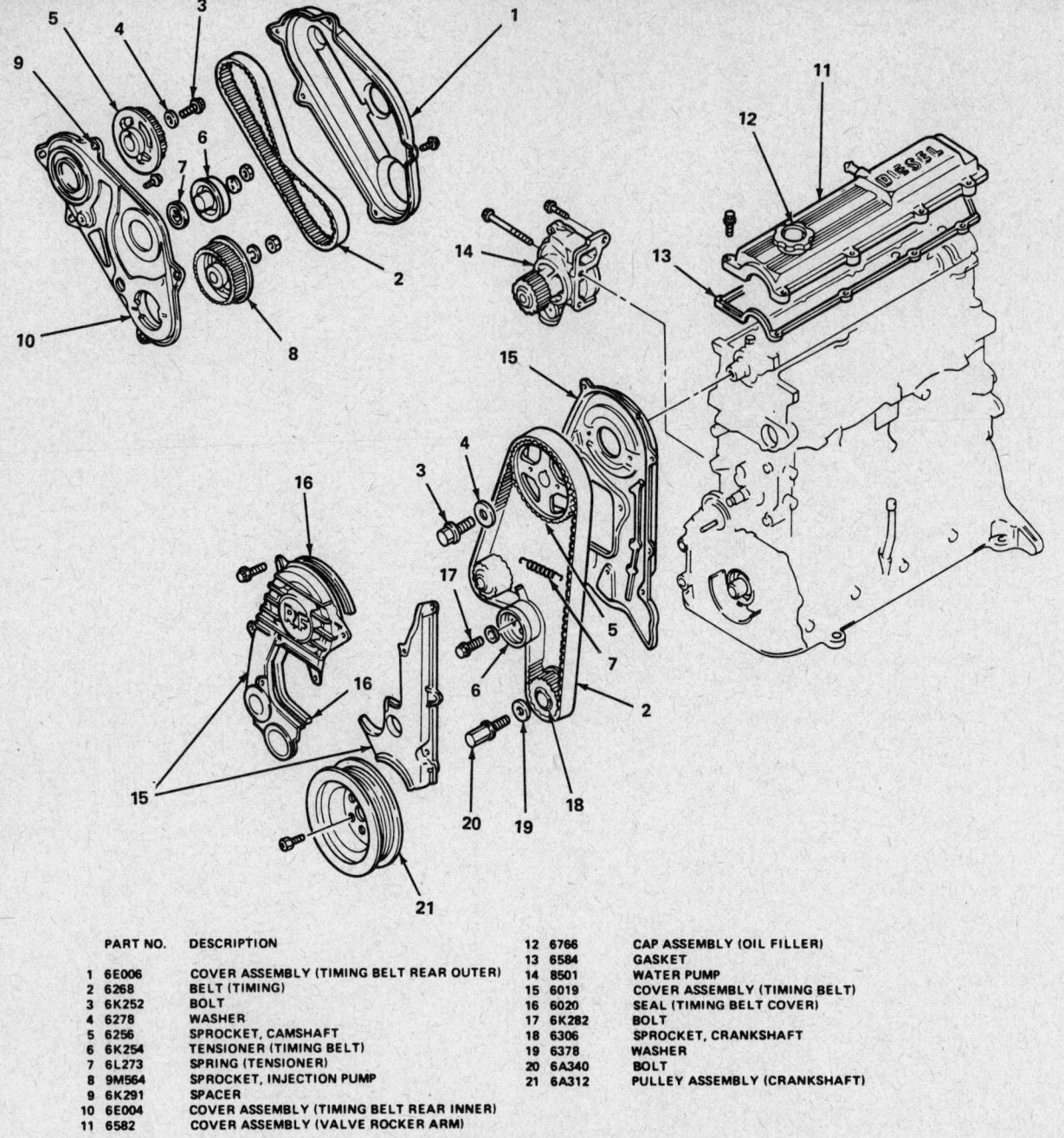

PART NO.	DESCRIPTION			
		12	6766	CAP ASSEMBLY (OIL FILLER)
		13	6584	GASKET
1	6E006	COVER ASSEMBLY (TIMING BELT REAR OUTER)	14	8501	WATER PUMP
2	6268	BELT (TIMING)	15	6019	COVER ASSEMBLY (TIMING BELT)
3	6K252	BOLT	16	6020	SEAL (TIMING BELT COVER)
4	6278	WASHER	17	6K282	BOLT
5	6256	SPROCKET, CAMSHAFT	18	6306	SPROCKET, CRANKSHAFT
6	6K254	TENSIONER (TIMING BELT)	19	6378	WASHER
7	6L273	SPRING (TENSIONER)	20	6A340	BOLT
8	9M564	SPROCKET, INJECTION PUMP	21	6A312	PULLEY ASSEMBLY (CRANKSHAFT)
9	6K291	SPACER			
10	6E004	COVER ASSEMBLY (TIMING BELT REAR INNER)			
11	6582	COVER ASSEMBLY (VALVE ROCKER ARM)			

Fig. 1B Timing belt, sprockets & related components

and bracket.

18. Remove halfshaft assembly from transaxle.

19. On models equipped with manual transaxle, remove shift stabilizer bar to transaxle bolts. Remove shift shaft nut and bolt from transaxle.

20. Remove lefthand rear No. 4 insulator mount bracket nuts and bracket from body bracket.

21. Remove lefthand front No. 1 insulator to transaxle mounting bolts.

22. Lower vehicle. Do not allow front wheels to touch floor.

23. Remove engine support tool D79P-8000A from engine lifting eye.

24. Remove righthand No. 3A insulator intermediate bracket to engine bracket

bolts, intermediate bracket to insulator nuts and bottom nut of double ended stud securing intermediate bracket to engine bracket. Remove bracket.

25. Lower engine and transaxle from vehicle.

26. Reverse procedure to install.

CYLINDER HEAD & PRE-CHAMBER, REPLACE

1. Disconnect battery ground cable and drain cooling system.

2. Remove camshaft cover, front and rear timing belt covers and belts.

3. Raise and support vehicle.

4. Disconnect exhaust pipe from exhaust manifold.

5. Lower vehicle.

6. Remove air inlet duct from air cleaner and intake manifold. Install cap, Fig. 2, onto intake manifold.

7. Remove all electrical connectors and vacuum hoses from temperature sensors.

8. Remove upper and lower coolant hoses and upper radiator hose from thermostat housing.

9. Remove injection lines from injection pump and nozzles. Cap all lines and fittings with cap set No. T84P-9395 or equivalent, Fig. 3.

10. Disconnect glow plug harness from engine harness.

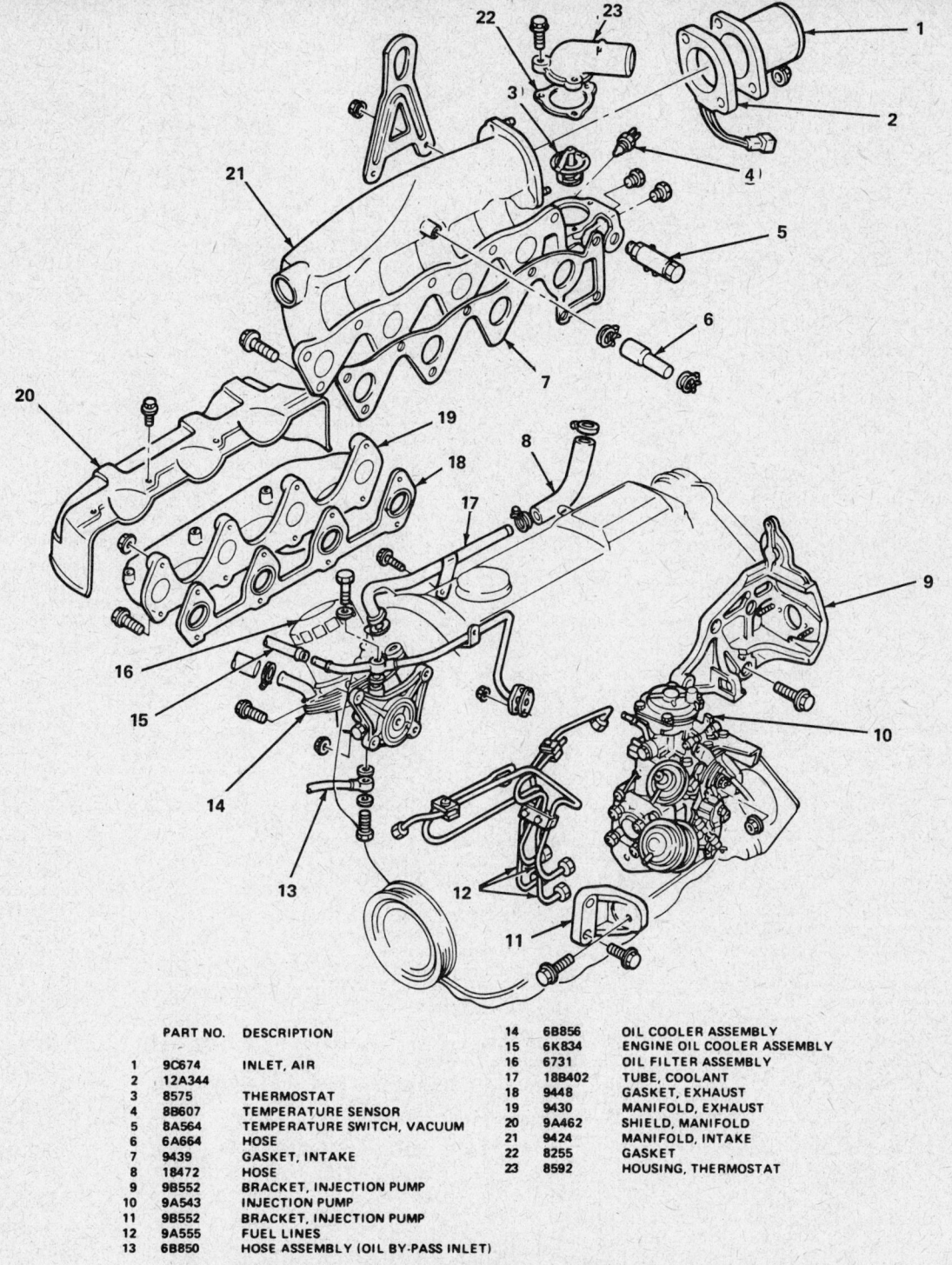

PART NO.	DESCRIPTION
1	9C674	INLET, AIR
2	12A344	
3	8575	THERMOSTAT
4	8B607	TEMPERATURE SENSOR
5	8A564	TEMPERATURE SWITCH, VACUUM
6	6A664	HOSE
7	9439	GASKET, INTAKE
8	18472	HOSE
9	9B552	BRACKET, INJECTION PUMP
10	9A543	INJECTION PUMP
11	9B552	BRACKET, INJECTION PUMP
12	9A555	FUEL LINES
13	6B850	HOSE ASSEMBLY (OIL BY-PASS INLET)

14	6B856	OIL COOLER ASSEMBLY
15	6K834	ENGINE OIL COOLER ASSEMBLY
16	6731	OIL FILTER ASSEMBLY
17	18B402	TUBE, COOLANT
18	9448	GASKET, EXHAUST
19	9430	MANIFOLD, EXHAUST
20	9A462	SHIELD, MANIFOLD
21	9424	MANIFOLD, INTAKE
22	8255	GASKET
23	8592	HOUSING, THERMOSTAT

Fig. 1C Intake manifold, exhaust manifold & injection pump components

11. Loosen cylinder head bolts in sequence shown in Fig. 4, then remove cylinder head.
12. Remove glow plugs.
13. Using a brass drift and hammer, remove pre-chambers from cylinder head, Fig. 5.
14. Clean pre-chamber cups, pre-chambers, cylinder head and crankcase gasket surfaces.
15. Install pre-chambers into cylinder head. Ensure pins are aligned with slots, Fig. 5.

16. Install glow plugs and torque to specification. Note the following:
    a. Using compressed air, blow out cylinder head bolt threads in crankcase.
    b. Install new cylinder head gasket. Ensure cylinder head oil feed hole is not restricted, Fig. 6.
    c. Measure dimension A, Fig. 7, of each cylinder head bolt. If dimension A is more than 4.5 in., replace cylinder head bolt.
    d. Rotate camshaft until both intake and exhaust valves for No. 1 cylinder are

closed. Rotate crankshaft clockwise until No. 1 piston is halfway up in the cylinder bore toward TDC.
    e. Install cylinder head.
    f. Before installing cylinder head bolts, paint a white reference mark on each bolt, Fig. 8, then apply a light coat of clean engine oil to bolt threads.
    g. Torque cylinder head bolts in sequence shown in Fig. 9 to 22 ft. lbs. Using the painted reference marks, tighten each cylinder head bolt in sequence an additional 90°, Fig. 8. Tighten cylinder

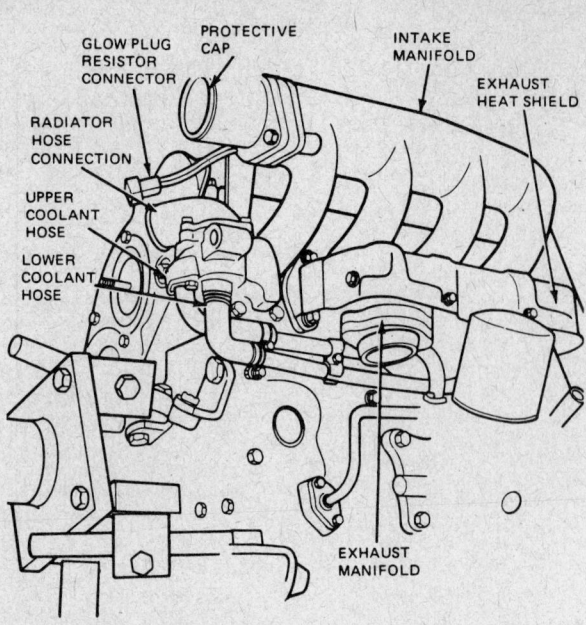

Fig. 2 Intake manifold removal

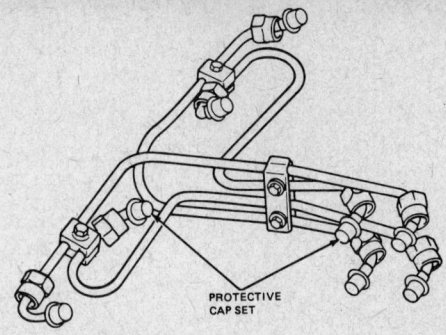

Fig. 3   Injection nozzle protective cap set

head bolts another 90° to complete cylinder head bolt installation.

17. Reverse procedure to install.

INTAKE MANIFOLD, REPLACE

1. Disconnect battery ground cable and drain cooling system.
2. Remove air inlet duct from air cleaner and intake manifold. Install cap, Fig. 2, onto intake manifold.
3. Disconnect resistor electrical connectors from glow plugs.
4. Remove breather hose from engine and upper radiator hose from thermostat housing.
5. Disconnect upper and lower coolant hoses from thermostat housing.
6. Disconnect electrical connectors from temperature sensors.
7. Remove intake manifold to cylinder head bolts, then the intake manifold.
8. Reverse procedure to install.

EXHAUST MANIFOLD, REPLACE

1. Disconnect battery ground cable.

2. Disconnect exhaust pipe from exhaust manifold.
3. Remove bolts securing heat shield to exhaust manifold.
4. Remove exhaust manifold to cylinder head nuts, then the exhaust manifold.
5. Reverse procedure to install.

VALVES, ADJUST

1. Disconnect breather hose from intake manifold and remove camshaft cover.
2. Rotate crankshaft until No. 1 piston is at TDC.
3. Using a suitable feeler gauge, check valve shim to cam lobe clearance for Nos. 1 and 2 intake valves and Nos. 1 and 3 exhaust valves, Fig. 10. Intake valve clearance should be .008–.011 in., exhaust valves clearance should be .011–.015 in.
4. Rotate crankshaft one complete revolution. Measure valve clearance for Nos. 3 and 4 intake valves and Nos. 2 and 4 exhaust valves. If measured clearance is not to specification, proceed as follows:

a. Rotate crankshaft until lobe of valve to be adjusted is facing downward.
b. Install cam follower retainer tool No. T84P-6513B or equivalent as shown in Fig. 11.
c. Rotate crankshaft until cam lobe is on base circle as shown in Fig. 12. Using tool No. T71P-19703C or equivalent, pry valve adjusting shim out of the cam follower, Fig. 12.

NOTE: Valve shims are available in thicknesses ranging from .134–.181 in. (3.40–4.60mm)

If the valve was tight, select a shim with a smaller thickness. If the valve was loose, select a shim with a larger thickness.

NOTE: Shim thickness is stamped on valve shim, Fig. 13. Install shim with numbers facing downward.

5. Rotate crankshaft until cam lobe is facing downward and remove cam follower retainer.
6. Recheck valve clearance. Repeat steps 2 thru 4 for each valve to be adjusted.

CAMSHAFT, REPLACE

1. Disconnect battery ground cable.

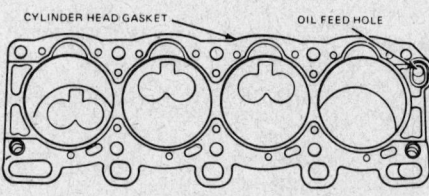

Fig. 6   Cylinder head gasket installation

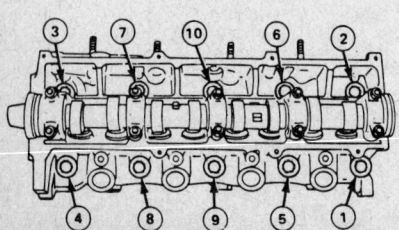

Fig. 4 Cylinder head bolt loosening sequence

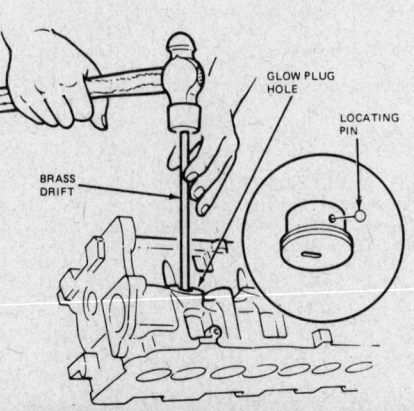

Fig. 5 Pre-chamber removal

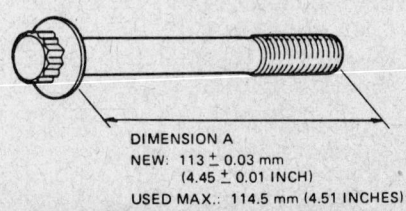

DIMENSION A
NEW: 113 ± 0.03 mm
(4.45 ± 0.01 INCH)
USED MAX.: 114.5 mm (4.51 INCHES)

Fig. 7 Cylinder head bolt dimension A

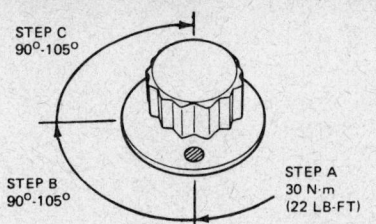

Fig. 8 Cylinder head bolt tightening steps

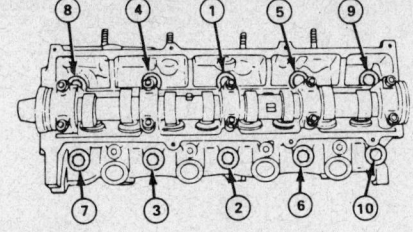

Fig. 9 Cylinder head bolt tightening sequence

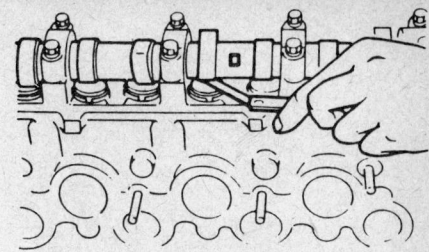

Fig. 10 Checking valve clearance

2. Disconnect breather hose from camshaft cover.
3. Remove camshaft cover bolts, then the camshaft cover.
4. Remove flywheel timing mark cover from clutch housing.
5. Rotate crankshaft until No. 1 cylinder is at TDC.
6. Remove front and rear timing belt covers.
7. Loosen front timing belt tensioner, then remove timing belt from camshaft sprocket.
8. Install an adjustable wrench onto camshaft boss, then loosen front camshaft sprocket bolt.
9. Hold camshaft with wrench then remove rear camshaft sprocket bolt.
10. Using tool Nos. T77F-4220B1 and D80L-625-4 or equivalents, remove camshaft sprockets. Retain camshaft sprocket woodruff keys.
11. Remove No. 1, 3 and 5 camshaft bearing caps.
12. Remove No. 2 and 4 camshaft bearing caps as follows:
    a. Loosen one of the camshaft bearing nuts two or three turns.
    b. Loosen the remaining camshaft bearing nuts one at a time, two or three turns.
    c. Repeat steps 12a and 12b, turning each nut two or three turns at a time, until all camshaft bearing cap nuts are loose.
13. Remove camshaft and discard camshaft seals.
14. Remove cam followers and note their location for installation in their original positions.
15. Reverse procedure to install. For installa-

tion of camshaft bearings, proceed as follows:

NOTE: Install camshaft bearings with arrows pointing toward front of engine. No. 2, 3 and 4 camshaft bearing caps have their numbers stamped on the top surface of the bearing cap. No. 1 and 5 bearing caps are not marked. No. 1 bearing cap has a slot to fit over camshaft thrust flange.

a. Install No. 2 and 4 bearing caps, tightening one of the nuts two or three turns.
b. Tighten the remaining nuts one at a time, two or three turns.
c. Repeat steps 15a and 15b, turning each nut two or three turns at a time until No. 2 and 4 bearing caps are seated.
d. Install No. 1, 3 and 5 bearing caps, and torque nuts to 15–19 ft. lbs.

FRONT TIMING BELT

Removal

1. With engine removed from vehicle, remove front timing belt upper cover bolts, then the upper cover.
2. Install flywheel holding tool T84P-6375 or equivalent onto flywheel.
3. Remove crankshaft pulley to crankshaft sprocket bolts.
4. Using tool Nos. T58P-6316 and T74P-6700B or equivalents, remove crankshaft pulley.
5. Remove front timing belt lower cover bolts, then the lower cover. Loosen tensioner pulley, then remove timing belt.

Installation

1. Align camshaft sprocket with timing

marks as shown in Fig. 14.

NOTE: Ensure crankshaft sprocket timing marks are aligned, Fig. 15.

2. Remove tensioner spring from front timing belt upper cover, then install spring into tensioner lever slot and over crankcase stud, Fig. 16.
3. Push tensioner lever toward water pump and tighten lock bolt.
4. Install timing belt as shown in Fig. 14. Adjust timing belt as described in "FRONT TIMING BELT, ADJUST".
5. Install front timing belt lower cover. Torque lower cover bolts to 5–7 ft. lbs.
6. Install crankshaft pulley. Torque pulley bolts to 17–24 ft. lbs.
7. Install front timing belt upper cover. Torque upper cover bolts to 5–7 ft. lbs.

REAR TIMING BELT, REPLACE

1. With engine removed from vehicle, remove rear timing belt cover bolts, then the rear cover.
2. Remove flywheel timing mark cover from clutch housing.
3. Rotate crankshaft until flywheel timing mark is at TDC on No. 1 cylinder, Fig. 17.

NOTE: Ensure injection pump and camshaft sprocket timing marks are aligned with their marks, Fig. 18.

4. Loosen tensioner locknut. Using a suitable tool, insert tool into tensioner slot, Fig. 19. Rotate tensioner clockwise, then tighten lock nut.
5. Remove rear timing belt.
6. Install rear timing belt as shown in Fig. 20.
7. Loosen tensioner lock nut and adjust timing belt as described under "REAR TIMING BELT, ADJUST".
8. Install rear timing belt cover. Torque the 6mm rear cover bolts to 5–9 ft. lbs., torque the 8mm rear cover bolts to 12–16 ft. lbs.

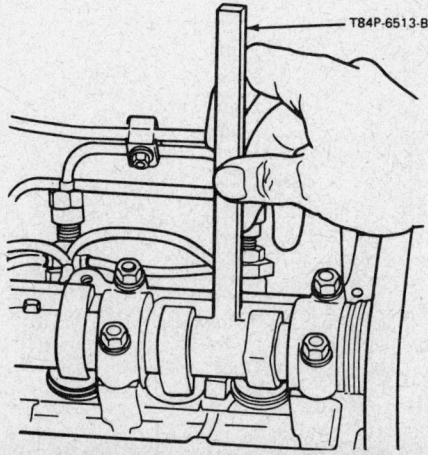

Fig. 11 Installing cam follower retainer

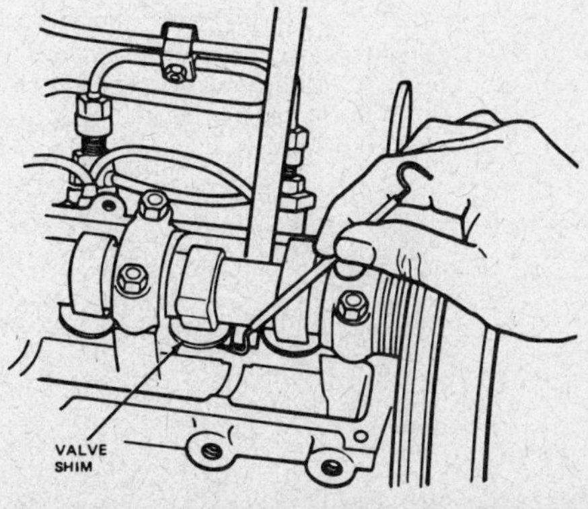

Fig. 12 Positioning cam lobe on base circle for valve shim removal

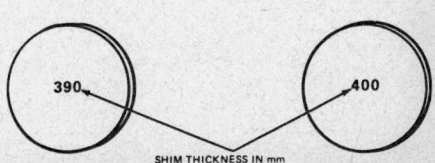

Fig. 13 Valve shim sizes

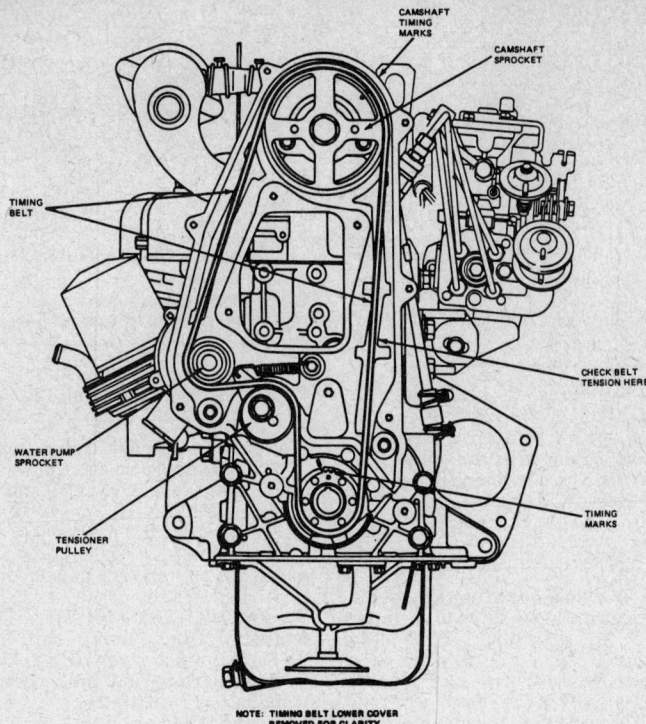

Fig. 14 Front timing belt installation

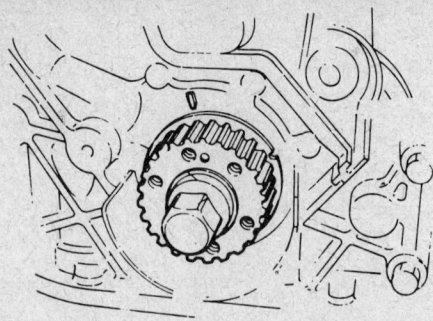

Fig. 15 Crankshaft pulley timing marks

with their marks, Fig. 18.

4. Torque tensioner lock nut to 15–20 ft. lbs.
5. Using a suitable belt tension gauge, check belt tension, Fig. 20. Belt tension should be 22–33 lbs.
6. Install rear timing belt cover. Torque the 6mm rear cover bolts to 5–9 ft. lbs., torque the 8mm rear cover bolts to 12–16 ft. lbs.
7. Install flywheel timing mark cover.

FRONT TIMING BELT, ADJUST

1. Remove flywheel timing mark cover.
2. Remove front timing belt upper cover.
3. Remove timing belt tension spring from front cover.
4. Install tensioner spring into belt tensioner lever and over crankcase stud, Fig. 16.
5. Loosen tensioner pulley lock bolt.
6. Rotate crankshaft pulley two revolutions clockwise until flywheel TDC timing mark aligns with pointer on rear cover plate, Fig. 17.

NOTE: Ensure front camshaft sprocket is aligned with its timing mark, Fig. 21.

7. Torque tensioner lock bolt to 23–34 ft. lbs. Using a suitable belt tension gauge, check belt tension, Fig. 14. Belt tension should be 33–44 lbs.
8. Remove tensioner spring and install spring into front cover.
9. Install front cover. Torque front cover bolts to 5–7 ft. lbs.
10. Install flywheel timing mark cover.

REAR TIMING BELT, ADJUST

1. Remove flywheel timing mark cover.
2. Remove rear timing belt cover.
3. Rotate crankshaft pulley two revolutions clockwise until flywheel TDC timing mark aligns with pointer on rear cover plate, Fig. 17.

NOTE: Ensure injection pump and camshaft sprocket timing marks are aligned

INJECTION PUMP, REPLACE

1. Disconnect battery ground cable located in luggage compartment.
2. Disconnect air inlet duct from air cleaner and intake manifold. Install cap, Fig. 2, onto intake manifold.
3. Remove rear timing belt cover and flywheel timing mark cover.
4. Remove rear timing belt as described under "REAR TIMING BELT, REPLACE".
5. Disconnect throttle and speed control cable, if equipped.
6. Disconnect vacuum lines from altitude compensator and cold start diaphragm.
7. Disconnect fuel supply and return lines from injection pump.
8. Disconnect electrical connector from fuel cut-off solenoid.

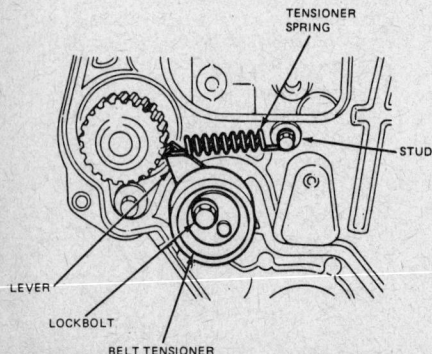

Fig. 16 Front timing belt tensioner spring installation

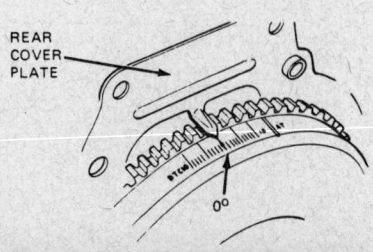

Fig. 17 Flywheel timing marks

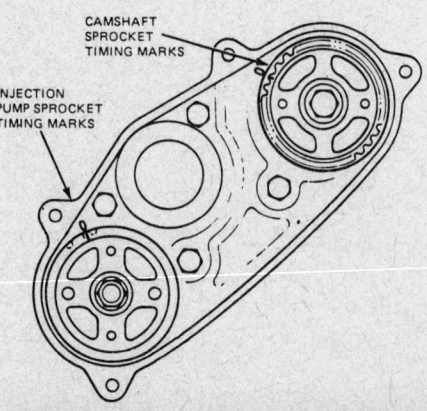

Fig. 18 Camshaft and injection pump timing marks

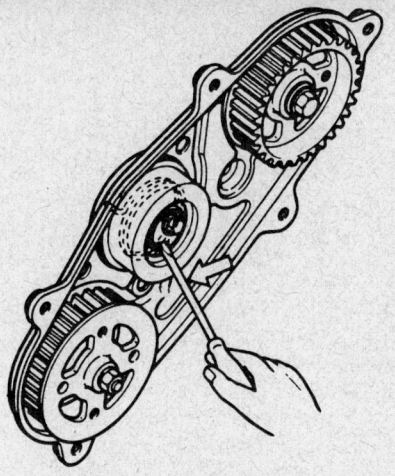

Fig. 19   Loosening tensioner pulley

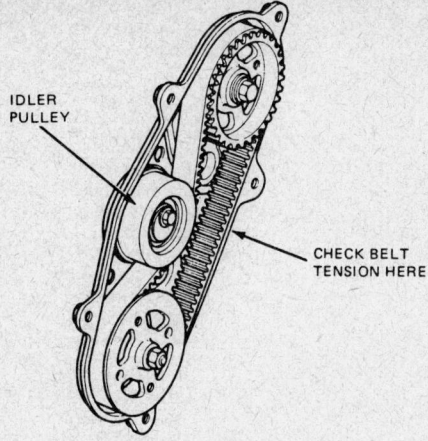

Fig. 20   Rear timing belt tensioner

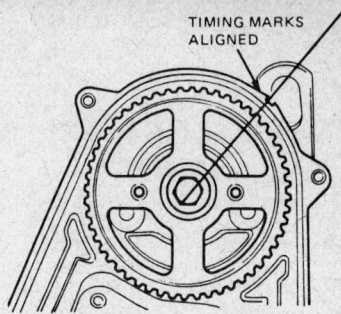

Fig. 21   Camshaft timing mark

9. Remove injection lines from injection pump and nozzles. Cap all lines and fittings with cap set No. T84P-9395 or equivalent, Fig. 3.
10. Rotate injection pump sprocket until injection pump and camshaft sprocket timing marks align with their marks, Fig. 18.
11. Install two M8 × 1.25 bolts into injection pump sprocket holes, Fig. 22, to secure injection pump sprocket. Remove injection pump sprocket bolt.
12. Using tool Nos. T77F-4220B1 and D80L-625-4 or equivalents, remove injection pump sprocket.
13. Remove bolt securing injection pump to pump front bracket.
14. Remove injection pump nuts, then the injection pump.
15. Reverse procedure to install.

PISTON & ROD ASSEMBLE

Pistons are available in standard size and oversize of .020 in. Install piston with an "F" mark, Fig. 23, on piston toward front of engine. Connecting rods have alignment marks stamped on one side of main bearing bore boss, Fig. 24. After piston and connecting rod assemblies have been installed, check side clearance between connecting rods on each crankshaft journal. Clearance should be .0043–.0103 inch.

MAIN & ROD BEARINGS

Main bearings are available in standard size and undersizes of .010, .020 and .030 inch. Connecting rod bearings are available in standard sizes and undersizes of .003, .010, .020, and .030 inch.

CRANKSHAFT REAR OIL SEAL, REPLACE

1. Disconnect battery ground cable.
2. Remove transaxle and clutch assemblies from engine.
3. Install flywheel holding tool No. T84P-6375A or equivalent, and remove flywheel bolts and flywheel.
4. Remove oil seal from crankshaft.
5. Reverse procedure to install.

OIL PAN, REPLACE

1. Disconnect battery ground cable.
2. Raise and support vehicle.
3. Remove oil pan bolts, then the oil pan.
4. Reverse procedure to install.

OIL PUMP, REPLACE

1. Disconnect battery ground cable.
2. With engine removed from vehicle, remove accessory drive belts.
3. Drain engine oil and remove oil pan.
4. Remove crankshaft pulley, front timing belt, front timing belt tensioner and crankshaft sprocket.
5. Remove bolts securing oil pump to crankcase, then the oil pump.
6. Reverse procedure to install.

BELT TENSION DATA

	New Lbs.	Used Lbs.
Alternator Exc. V ribbed Power Steering &	120–160	110–130
Air Conditioning	150–190	140–160

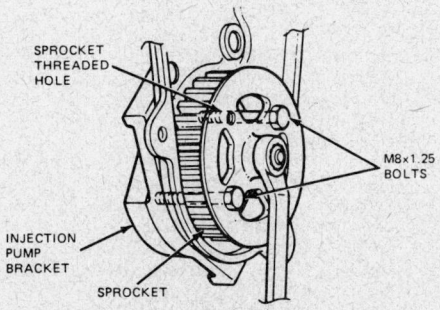

Fig. 22   Injection pump sprocket removal

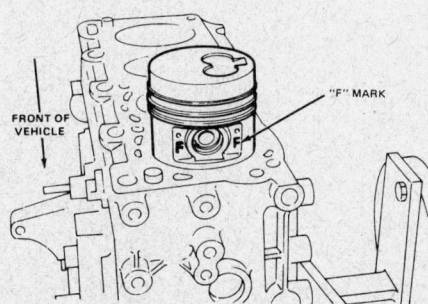

Fig. 23   Piston alignment

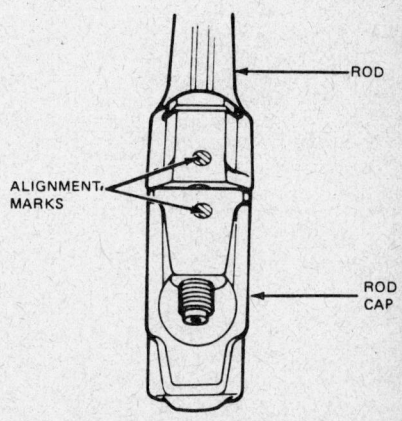

Fig. 24   Connecting rod cap alignment marks

Turbocharger Section

1984 ESCORT, EXP & LYNX

The turbocharger is used to increase engine power on a demand basis. As engine load increases and the throttle opens, more air-fuel mixture flows into the combustion chambers. As the increased flow is burned a larger volume of high energy exhaust gasses enters the engine exhaust system and is directed through the turbocharger turbine housing. Some of the exhaust gas energy is used to increase the speed of the turbine wheel which is connected to the compressor wheel. The increased speed of the compressor wheel compresses the air-fuel mixture and delivers the compressed air-fuel mixture to the intake manifold. The high pressure in the intake manifold allows a denser charge to enter the combustion chambers, in turn developing more engine power during the combustion cycle. Turbocharger output is governed by an integral wastegate which controls the passage of exhaust gas past the turbine. The electronic fuel injection system provides precise air-fuel mixture control. The fuel injectors at each cylinder intake port deliver more fuel when needed for high turbocharger boost power output.

The EEC-1V electronic engine control system provides precise control of fuel injection response to throttle position, air temperature, engine temperature, altitude and engine emission levels. The EEC-1V system also controls spark timing, exhaust gas recirculation and automatically shuts-off the air conditioner compressor at wide-open throttle to eliminate engine power drag when full engine output is needed.

Clutch & Transaxle Section

CLUTCH, ADJUST

The cable operated clutch control system, Fig. 1, is self adjusting and periodic adjustments are not required. If the clutch cable is replaced for any reason, an initial adjustment is performed by pulling the clutch pedal to its full upward position.

CLUTCH, REPLACE

1. Remove transmission as described under "Manual Transaxle, Replace" procedure.
2. Loosen pressure plate cover attaching bolts evenly to avoid distorting cover. If same pressure plate and cover are to be installed, mark cover and flywheel so pressure plate can be installed in original position.
3. Remove pressure plate and clutch disc from flywheel, Fig. 2.
4. Position clutch disc and pressure plate onto flywheel with flatter side of clutch disc facing toward flywheel.
5. Ensure three dowel pins on flywheel are aligned with dowel pins on pressure plate.
6. Snug tighten cover attaching bolts, then align clutch disc using tool T81P-7550A or equivalent. Torque bolts to 12–24 ft. lbs. (17–32 N.m.).
7. Remove alignment tool, then install transaxle and perform initial clutch adjustment.

GEARSHIFT LINKAGE, ADJUST, FIG. 3

Adjustment of the external gearshift linkage is not necessary and no provision is made for adjustment.

MANUAL TRANSAXLE, REPLACE

4 Speed

1. Disconnect battery ground cable and drain transaxle fluid.
2. Disconnect clutch cable from transaxle case.
3. Raise and support vehicle, then remove bolt securing brake hose routing clip to suspension strut bracket at both front wheels.
4. Remove lower control arm ball joint to steering knuckle bolt, then separate lower control arm from knuckle.

NOTE: Do not reuse nut and bolt. Plastic shield located behind rotor contains a molded pocket which accepts the lower

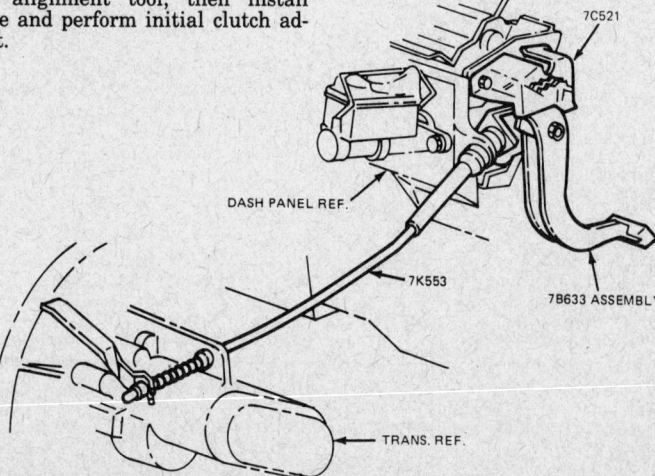

DASH PANEL REF.

7C521

7K553

7B633 ASSEMBLY

TRANS. REF.

Fig. 1 Clutch linkage

control arm ball joint. When separating control arm from knuckle, clearance for ball joint may be obtained by bending shield backward towards rotor. Failure to provide clearance for the ball joint may result in damage to the shield.

5. Remove right side inner constant velocity joint from transaxle, then wire halfshaft to underbody in level position to prevent damage to the assembly.
6. Repeat step 5 for removal of left side inner constant velocity joint. If joint cannot be pried from transaxle, insert tool T81P-4026A or equivalent through right hand side of case and tap out joint.
7. Disconnect front stabilizer bar at both lower control arms and discard nuts, then remove two front stabilizer bar brackets and the stabilizer bar.
8. Disconnect speedometer cable and back-up lamp switch electrical connector.
9. Remove three nuts from starter mounting studs which secure roll restrictor bracket. Remove engine roll restrictor and starter stud bolts.
10. Remove stiffener brace attaching bolts from lower portion of clutch housing, and the shift mechanism crossover spring.
11. Remove shift mechanism stabilizer bar to transaxle attaching bolt, and the shift mechanism to shift shaft attaching bolt. Remove shift mechanism from shift shaft.
12. Position suitable jack under transaxle, then loosen nut on rear mounting stud.
13. Remove three attaching bolts from rear mount, then three attaching bolts from front mount.
14. Lower jack until transaxle assembly clears rear mount. Support engine with suitable jack positioned under oil pan while transaxle is lowered.
15. Remove four engine to transaxle attaching bolts, then the transaxle from vehicle.
16. Reverse procedure to install.

5 Speed

1. Disconnect battery ground cable and drain transaxle fluid.
2. Wedge a seven inch wood block under clutch pedal.
3. Disconnect clutch cable from clutch re-

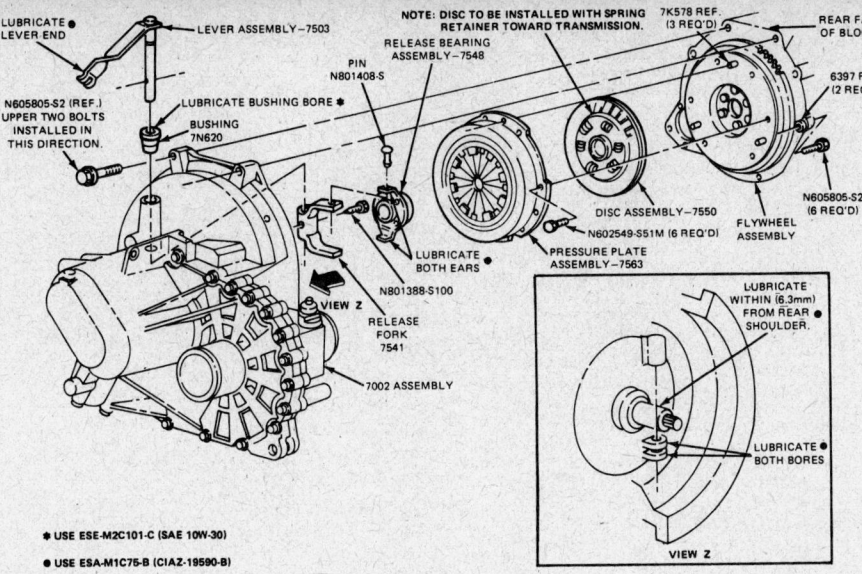

Fig. 2 Clutch assembly

DISASSEMBLED VIEW

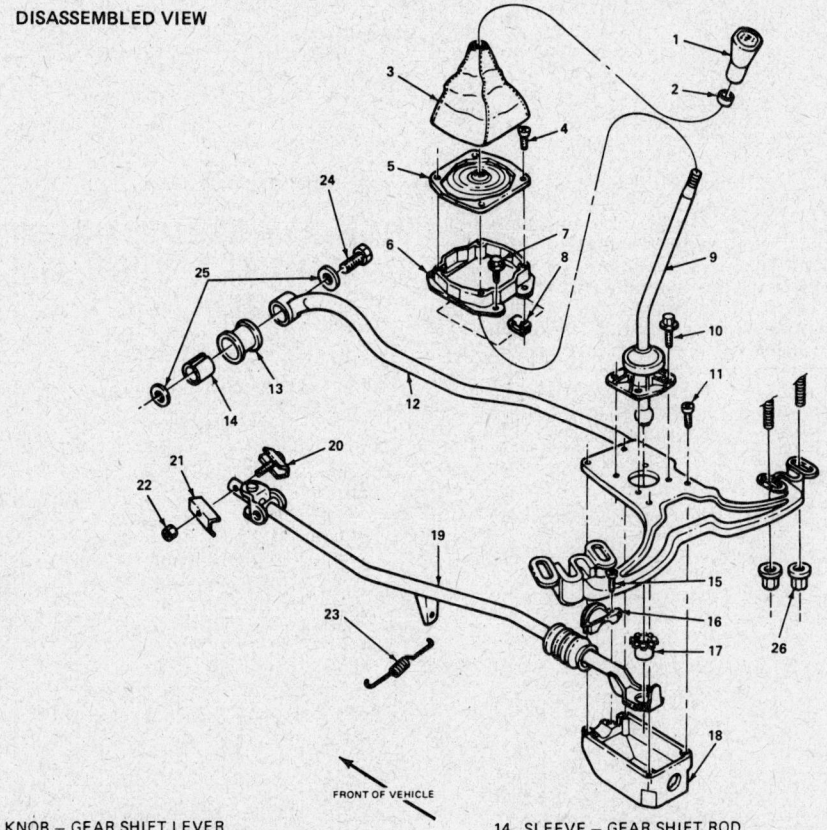

1. KNOB – GEAR SHIFT LEVER
2. NUT – SHIFT KNOB LOCKING
3. UPPER BOOT ASSEMBLY – GEAR SHIFT LEVER
4. SCREW – TAPPING (4 REQUIRED)
5. LOWER BOOT ASSEMBLY – GEAR SHIFT LEVER
6. BOOT RETAINER ASSEMBLY – GEAR SHIFT LEVER
7. BOLT – BOOT RETAINER (4 REQUIRED)
8. NUT – SPRING (4 REQUIRED)
9. LEVER ASSEMBLY – GEARSHIFT
10. BOLT – TAPPING (4 REQUIRED)
11. SCREW – TAPPING (4 REQUIRED)
12. SUPPORT ASSEMBLY (SHIFT STABILIZER BAR)
13. BUSHING – GEAR SHIFT STABILIZER BAR

14. SLEEVE – GEAR SHIFT ROD
15. SCREW – TAPPING (2 REQUIRED)
16. COVER – CONTROL SELECTOR
17. BUSHING – ANTI TIZZ
18. HOUSING – CONTROL SELECTOR
19. ASSEMBLY – SHIFT ROD AND CLEVIS
20. ASSEMBLY – CLAMP
21. CLAMP – GEAR SHIFT LEVER (2 REQUIRED)
22. NUT – CLAMP ASSEMBLY
23. RETAINING SPRING – GEAR SHIFT TUBE
24. BOLT -- STABILIZER BAR ATTACHING
25. WASHER – FLAT (2 REQUIRED)
26. ASSEMBLY – NUT/WASHER (4 REQUIRED)

Fig. 3 Gearshift linkage

lease shaft assembly, then remove the clutch cable casing from rib on top surface of transaxle case.

4. Remove two top transaxle to engine mounting bolts.
5. Remove top bolt that secures air management valve bracket to transaxle.
6. Raise vehicle, then remove lower control arm ball joint to steering knuckle attaching nut and bolt. Discard nut and bolt and repeat procedure on opposite side.
7. Pry lower control arm from knuckle on both sides of vehicle using suitable pry bar. Use care not to damage or cut ball joint.
8. Pry left inboard CV joint assembly from transaxle using suitable pry bar.

NOTE: Lubricant will drain from the seal at this time. Install two plugs.

9. Remove inboard CV joint from transaxle. Repeat procedure on other side.

NOTE: If the CV joint assembly cannot be pried from the transaxle, insert tool T81P-4026-A or other suitable tool through the left side and tap the joint out. Tool can be used from either side of the transaxle.

10. Wire left and right half shaft assemblies in level position.
11. Remove backup lamp switch connector from transaxle backlamp switch.
12. Remove engine roll restrictor bracket.
13. Remove three heater pipe bracket attaching screws, then remove engine roll restrictor.
14. Remove starter.
15. Disconnect shift mechanism from shaft.
16. Disconnect and remove control selector indicator switch arm from shift shaft.
17. Remove shift mechanism stabilizer bar to transaxle attaching bolt, then remove control selector indicator switch and bracket.
18. Remove speedometer cable from transaxle.
19. Remove two stiffener brace attaching bolts from lower position of clutch housing.
20. Position a jack under transaxle.
21. Remove two rear mount and air management valve to transaxle securing bolts, then remove three bolts attaching front mount to transaxle.
22. Lower transaxle support jack until transaxle clears rear mount and support engine with suitable jack. Use a suitable piece of wood between the jack and engine.
23. Remove remaining four engine-to-transaxle attaching bolts.
24. Remove transaxle from rear face of the engine and lower it from vehicle.

NOTE: The transaxle case casting may have sharp edges. Wear protective gloves when handling the transaxle assembly.

25. Reverse procedure to install. Torque the following as specified, engine-to-transaxle bolts 26–31 ft. lbs., front transaxle mount bolts 25–35 ft. lbs., rear transaxle mount bolts 40–51 ft. lbs., starter stud bolts 30–40 ft. lbs., starter nuts 25–30 ft. lbs.

Rear Suspension & Brakes Section

DESCRIPTION

Except Tempo & Topaz

These vehicles use a modified MacPherson strut independent rear suspension, Fig. 1. Each side consists of a shock strut, lower control arm, tie rod, spindle and a coil spring mounted between the lower control arm and body crossmember side rail.

Tempo & Topaz

These vehicles use a new MacPherson strut independent rear suspension, Fig. 2. Each side consists of a shock absorber strut assembly, two parallel control arms per side, tie rod, spindle and a jounce bumper and bracket.

The shock absorber strut assembly includes a rubber isolated top mount, upper spring seat, coil spring insulator, coil spring and a lower spring seat. the strut assembly is attached at the top by two studs, which retain the top mount of the strut to the inner body side panel. The lower end of the assembly is bolted to the spindle. The two control arms are attached to the underbody and spindle with nuts and bolts. The tie rod is attached to the underbody and the spindle. The jounce bumper bracket is bolted to the strut.

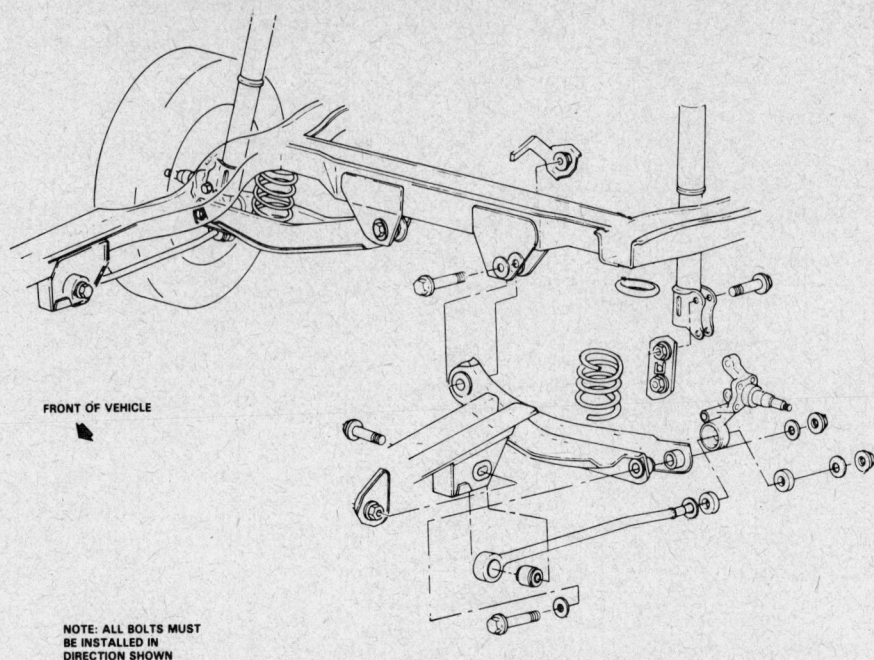

FRONT OF VEHICLE

NOTE: ALL BOLTS MUST BE INSTALLED IN DIRECTION SHOWN

Fig. 1 Rear suspension, exploded view. Except Tempo & Topaz

SHOCK STRUT, REPLACE

Except Tempo & Topaz

1. Raise and support vehicle.
2. Remove rear compartment access panels. On four-door models, remove quarter trim panel.

3. Loosen top shock strut attaching nut, then remove wheel assembly.
4. Remove clip retaining brake hose to rear shock and position hose aside.
5. Loosen but do not remove two nuts and bolts securing shock strut to spindle.
6. Remove top mounting nut, washer and rubber insulator, Fig. 3.
7. Remove two bottom mounting bolts, then the shock strut from the vehicle.
8. Reverse procedure to install.

SHOCK STRUT, UPPER MOUNT & SPRING, REPLACE

Tempo & Topaz

1. Raise and support vehicle. Loosen upper strut mount to body nuts located in luggage compartment.
2. Remove wheel assembly.
3. Place a suitable jack under control arms.
4. Remove brake hose bracket to strut bolt and position brake hose bracket aside.
5. Remove jounce bumper bracket.
6. Remove two upper mount to body nuts, then the strut.
7. Place strut, spring and upper mount assembly into a suitable spring compressor tool.

NOTE: Do not remove the spring from the strut without first compressing the spring.

8. With spring compressed, remove strut shaft to mount nuts. Remove spring, strut and mount, Fig. 4, from spring compressor tool.
9. Reverse procedure to install. Torque shaft nut to 35–50 ft. lbs., torque jounce bumper bracket to strut mount bolts to 70–90 ft. lbs., torque top mount to body nuts to 25–30 ft. lbs.

LOWER CONTROL ARM, REPLACE

Except Tempo & Topaz

1. Raise and support vehicle, then remove wheel assembly.

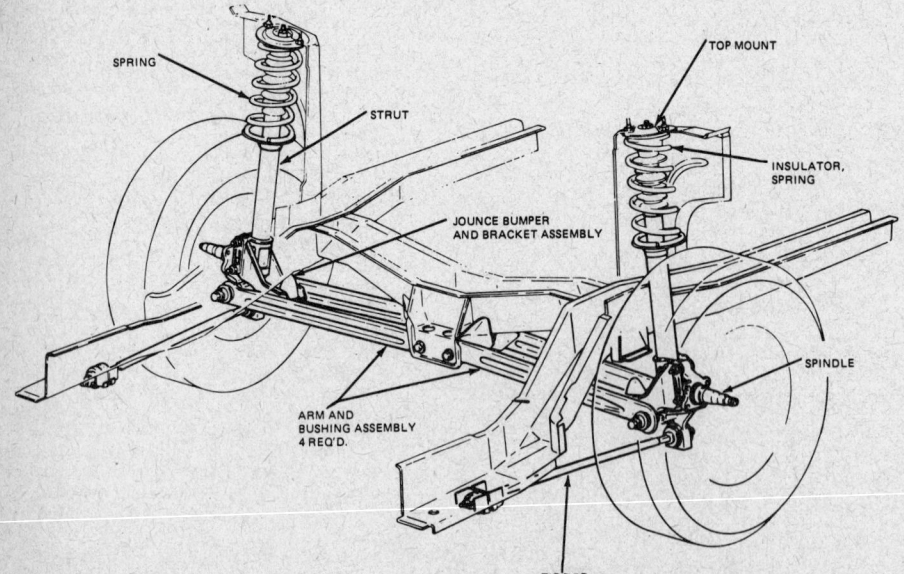

SPRING

STRUT

TOP MOUNT

INSULATOR, SPRING

JOUNCE BUMPER AND BRACKET ASSEMBLY

ARM AND BUSHING ASSEMBLY 4 REQ'D.

SPINDLE

TIE ROD

Fig. 2 Rear suspension components. Tempo & Topaz

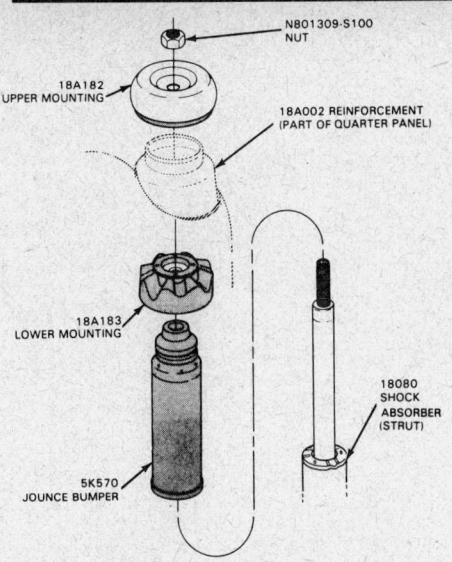

Fig. 3 Shock absorber strut upper mounting components. Except Tempo & Topaz

2. Place a suitable jack under lower control arm between spring and spindle mounting.

NOTE: Rear suspension should be at full rebound and the shock strut fully extended.

---

3. Remove control arm to body mounting nuts, then the control arm to spindle mounting nuts. Do not remove bolts.
4. Remove spindle end mounting bolt, then slowly lower jack until spring and spring insulator can be removed.
5. Remove bolts from body mountings, then the control arm from vehicle.
6. Reverse procedure to install.

Tempo & Topaz

1. Raise and support vehicle.
2. Remove wheel assembly.
3. Remove control arm to spindle nut and bolt.
4. Remove center mounting nut and bolt.
5. Remove control arm from vehicle.
6. Reverse procedure to install. Torque control arm to body bolt to 40–55 ft. lbs., torque control arm to spindle nut to 60–86 ft. lbs.

NOTE: When installing new control arms the bushing with the 10mm hole is installed toward the center of the vehicle and the bushing with the 12mm hole toward the spindle. The offset on the control arm must face up on the right side of the vehicle and down on the left side of the vehicle, Fig. 5. The flanged edge of the control arm stamping must face the rear of the vehicle.

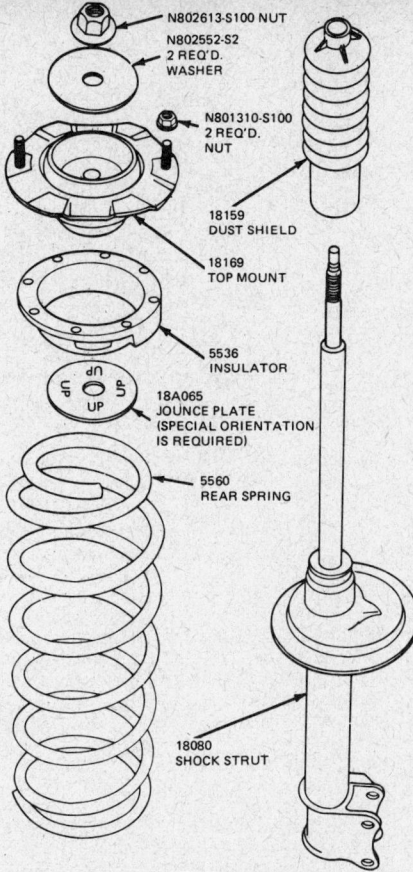

Fig. 4 Strut, spring & upper mount components. Tempo & Topaz

TIE ROD, REPLACE

Except Tempo & Topaz

1. Raise and support vehicle.
2. Scribe a reference mark on tie rod front bracket at bolt head centerline for use during reassembly.
3. Remove nut, washer and insulators attaching tie rod to spindle.
4. Remove nut and bolt attaching tie rod to body bracket, then the tie rod.

NOTE: It may be necessary to pry front

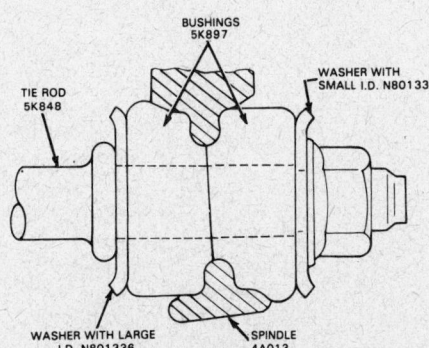

Fig. 6 Tie rod installation

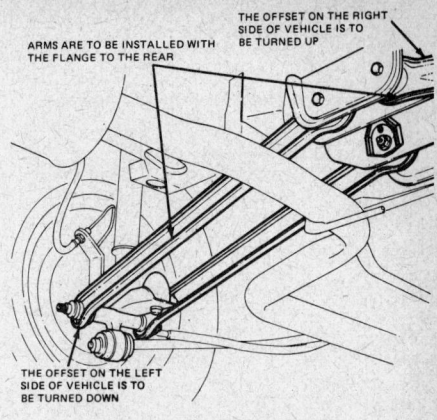

Fig. 5 Installing control arm. Tempo & Topaz

bracket sheet metal apart slightly to remove tie rod from body.

5. Place a new dished washer over tie rod end with flange toward middle of rod, Fig. 6.
6. Install tie rod through spindle bushings and place eye of rod into body bracket. Secure rod to bracket using a new nut and bolt. Do not tighten.
7. Place another dished washer over end of rod with flange toward end of rod, then install a new nut and torque to 65–75 ft. lbs.
8. Using suitable jack, raise lower control arm to curb height.
9. Align center of bolt head with reference mark on body bracket, then torque tie rod front bolt to 90–100 ft. lbs. This bolt must be installed with head inboard on vehicle.
10. Lower vehicle to ground.

Tempo & Topaz

1. Raise and support vehicle.
2. From inside of luggage compartment, loosen two strut top mount to body nuts.
3. Raise vehicle. Position a suitable jack under lower control arm with a piece of wood between jack and control arm.
4. Remove wheel assembly.
5. Remove two top mount studs, then tie rod to spindle retaining nut.
6. Remove tie rod to body retaining nut.
7. Lower jack until upper strut mount studs clear body mount holes.
8. Move spindle rearward until tie rod can be removed.
9. Place new washers and bushings on both ends of tie rod, Fig. 6.

NOTE: Front and rear bushings are not interchangeable. The rear bushings have indentations incorporated in them.

---

10. Insert tie rod into body bracket, then install new bushing, washer and nut. Do not tighten nut.
11. Pull back on spindle until tie rod can be installed into the spindle. Install new bushing, washer and nut. Do not tighten nut.
12. Raise jack enough to secure the two strut mounting studs in place.
13. Install two strut to body mount nuts. Torque nuts to 20–30 ft. lbs.

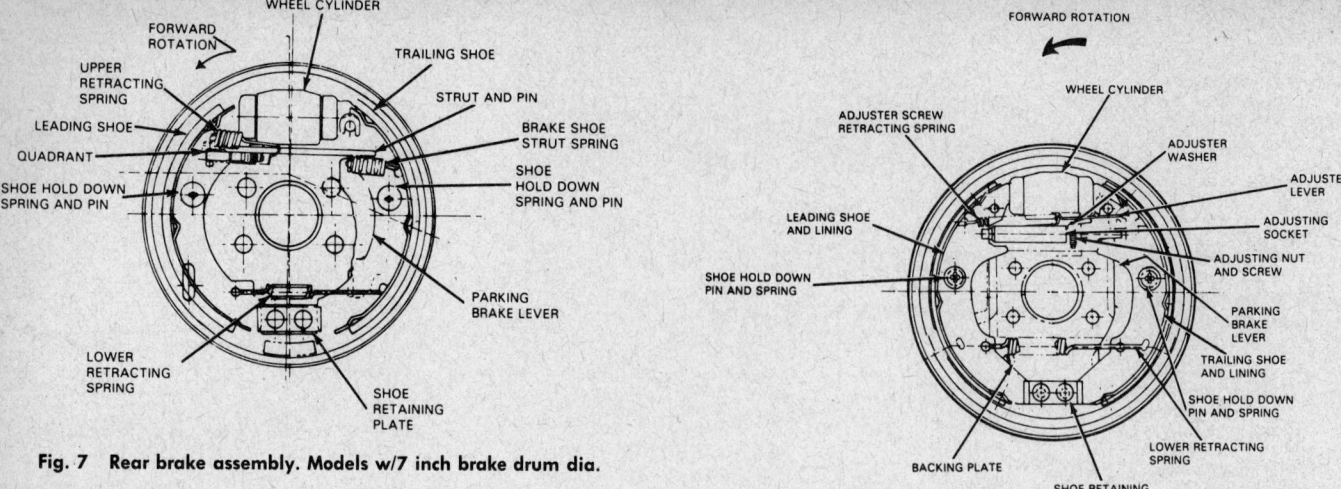

Fig. 7   Rear brake assembly. Models w/7 inch brake drum dia.

Fig. 8   Rear brake assembly. Models w/8 inch brake drum dia.

14. Using a suitable jack, raise lower control arm to curb height. Install tie rod nuts and torque to 52–74 ft. lbs.
15. Remove jack and install wheel assembly. Lower vehicle.

SPINDLE, REPLACE

Except Tempo & Topaz

1. Raise and support vehicle.
2. Remove wheel assembly, then the brake drum and wheel bearings.
3. Remove brake backing plate assembly, then the tie rod retaining nut and dished washer.
4. Remove two nuts and bolts securing strut to spindle.
5. Remove nut and bolt securing lower control arm to spindle, then the spindle.
6. Reverse procedure to install.

Tempo & Topaz

1. Raise and support vehicle.
2. Remove wheel assembly.
3. Remove brake drum. Remove brake flex hose bracket to strut bolt.

4. Remove brake backing plate to spindle bolts, then the brake backing plate.
5. Remove lower control arm to spindle bolt, washer and nut.
6. Remove tie rod nut, bushing and washer.
7. Remove spindle to strut bolts, then the spindle.
8. Reverse procedure to install. Torque spindle to strut bolts to 70–96 ft. lbs. Torque tie rod nut to 52–74 ft. lbs. Torque lower control arm to spindle nut to 60–86 ft. lbs.

COIL SPRING, REPLACE

Except Tempo & Topaz

1. Raise and support vehicle. Support lower control arm with suitable jack.
2. Remove tire and wheel assembly.
3. Remove nut, bolt and washer securing lower control arm to spindle.
4. Lower control arm until spring can be removed.
5. Reverse procedure to install. A new spring insulator must be used when replacing the spring.

BRAKE ADJUSTMENTS

Although the brakes are self-adjusting, Figs. 7 and 8, an initial adjustment will be necessary after a brake repair. The initial adjustment can be obtained as follows:

1. On 7 in. brakes, pivot adjuster quadrant until it meshes with knurled pin and is in third or fourth notch of the outboard end of the quadrant, Fig. 9.
2. On 8 in. brakes, determine inside diameter of drum brake surface using brake shoe gauge tool D81L-1103-A or equivalent. Adjust brake shoe diameter to fit guage. Hold automatic adjusting lever out of engagement while rotating adjusting screw and ensure that screw rotates freely.
3. Install drum and wheel assembly, then adjust wheel bearings as described in Fig. 10.
4. Complete adjustment by applying brakes several times, then check brake operation by making several stops from varying speeds.

NOTE: If brake drum cannot be removed for brake servicing, remove rubber plug from backing plate inspection hole. On 7 in. brakes,

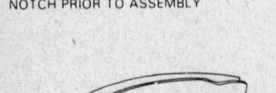

SET QUADRANT ON THIRD OR FOURTH NOTCH PRIOR TO ASSEMBLY

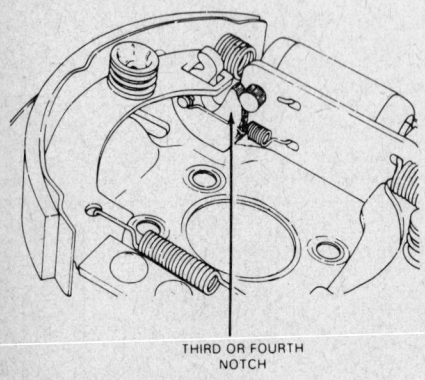

180 mm (7-INCH) REAR BRAKE

Fig. 9   Initial brake adjustment

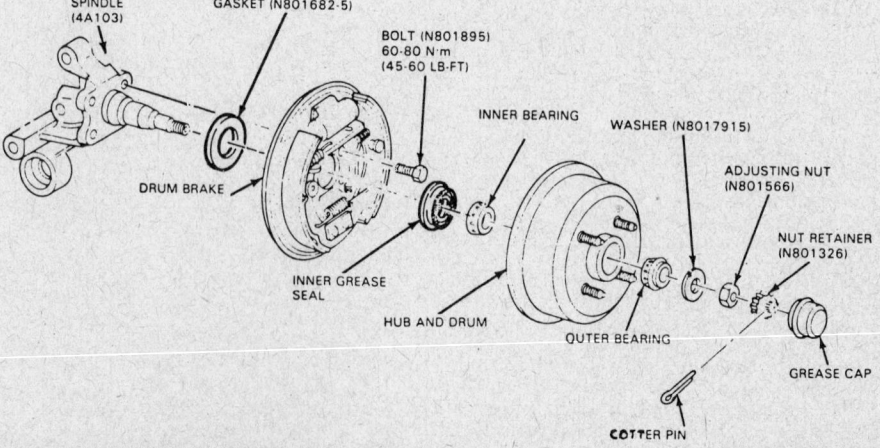

Fig. 10   Rear wheel bearing, assembly

insert a suitable tool into the hole until it contacts adjuster assembly pivot. Apply pressure sideways on the pivot point allowing adjuster quadrant to ratchet and release the brake adjustment. On 8 in. brakes remove the brake line to axle retention bracket. This will allow sufficient room for insertion of a suitable tool to disengage adjusting lever and back off the adjusting screw.

PARKING BRAKE, ADJUST

1. Pump brake pedal three times before making adjustment.
2. Place transmission in neutral, then raise and support vehicle.
3. Position parking brake control assembly in 12th notch position (two notches from full application). Tighten adjusting nut until rear wheel brakes drag slightly with control assembly fully released. Repeat procedure as necessary to ensure proper adjustment.
4. Reposition control assembly in 12th notch, then loosen adjusting nut enough to eliminate rear brake drag with the control assembly fully released.
5. Lower vehicle and check operation of parking brake.

MASTER CYLINDER, REPLACE

Less Power Brakes

1. Disconnect battery ground cable.

2. Disconnect stoplamp switch electrical connector and remove switch retainer.
3. Slide stoplamp switch off pedal pin far enough to clear end of pin, then remove switch from pin.
4. From inside engine compartment loosen two master cylinder attaching nuts, then slide master cylinder push rod, nylon washers and bushings from brake pedal pin.
5. Disconnect brake lines from master cylinder, then remove nuts securing master cylinder to dash panel. List cylinder forward and upward and remove from vehicle.
6. Reverse procedure to install.

With Power Brakes

1. Disconnect brake lines from master cylinder. Cap all lines and fittings.
2. On late 1983 models and all 1984 models, disconnect brake warning lamp switch wire connector.
3. Remove master cylinder to power brake unit attaching nuts, then remove master cylinder.
4. Reverse procedure to install.

POWER BRAKE UNIT, REPLACE

1. Remove master cylinder as described under Master Cylinder, Replace, Power Brakes.

2. From inside passenger compartment, disconnect stoplamp switch electrical connector.
3. Remove pushrod retainer and outer nylon washer from pedal pin, then slide switch along brake pedal far enough for outer hole to clear pin. Slide switch upward and remove.
4. Remove booster to dash panel attaching nuts, then slide booster pushrod and pushrod bushing from brake pedal pin.
5. From inside engine compartment, disconnect manifold vacuum hose from booster check valve.
6. Move booster forward until booster studs clear dash panel, then remove booster.
7. Reverse procedure to install.

REAR WHEEL BEARING, ADJUST

1. Raise and support vehicle. Remove dust cover from hub. Remove wheel assembly, if necessary.
2. Remove cotter pin and nut retainer.
3. Back off adjusting nut 1 full turn.
4. Torque adjusting nut, Fig. 10, to 17–25 ft. lbs., while rotating drum assembly.
5. Back off adjusting nut ½ turn, then retighten adjusting nut to 10–15 inch lbs. Position adjusting nut retainer over nut so slots are aligned with cotter pin hole, then install cotter pin.
6. Install dust cover, wheel assembly, if necessary and lower vehicle to ground.

Front Suspension & Steering Section

DESCRIPTION

These vehicles use a MacPherson type front suspension with the vertical shock absorber struts attached to the upper fender reinforcements and the steering knuckle, Fig. 1. The lower control arms are attached inboard to a crossmember and outboard to the steering knuckle through a ball joint to provide lower steering knuckle position.

WHEEL ALIGNMENT

Caster & Camber

Caster and camber angles are preset at the factory and cannot be adjusted.

Toe-In

To adjust toe-in, lock steering wheel in the straight ahead position using suitable steering wheel holder. Remove small outer clamp from steering boot to prevent boot from twisting during adjustment procedure. Loosen tie rod adjusting nuts, then adjust left and right tie rods until each wheel has ½ the desired total toe specification. Tighten tie rod adjusting nuts, replace steering gear rubber boots and tighten clamp. Remove steering wheel holding tool.

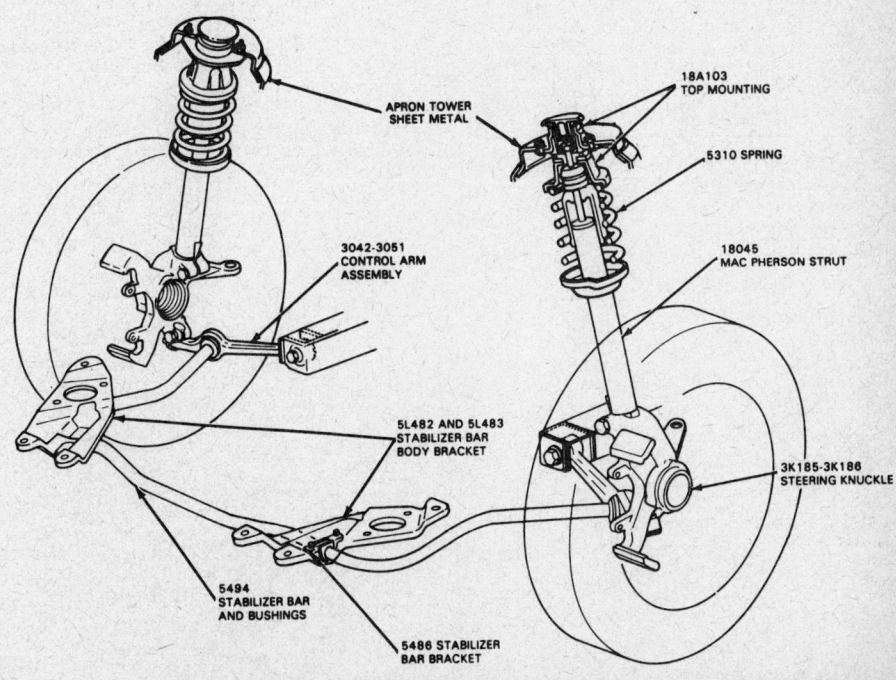

18A103 TOP MOUNTING

5310 SPRING

APRON TOWER SHEET METAL

3042-3051 CONTROL ARM ASSEMBLY

18045 MAC PHERSON STRUT

5L482 AND 5L483 STABILIZER BAR BODY BRACKET

3K185-3K186 STEERING KNUCKLE

5494 STABILIZER BAR AND BUSHINGS

5486 STABILIZER BAR BRACKET

Fig. 1 Front suspension

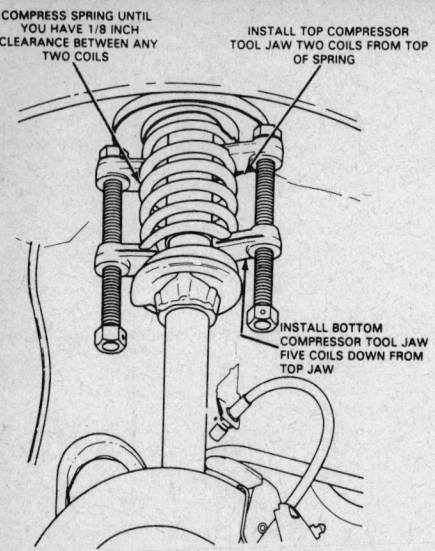

Fig. 2 **Installing coil spring compressor. Except Tempo & Topaz**

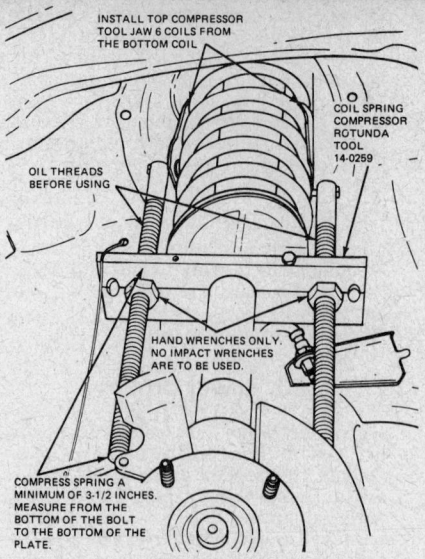

Fig. 3 **Installing coil spring compressor. Tempo & Topaz**

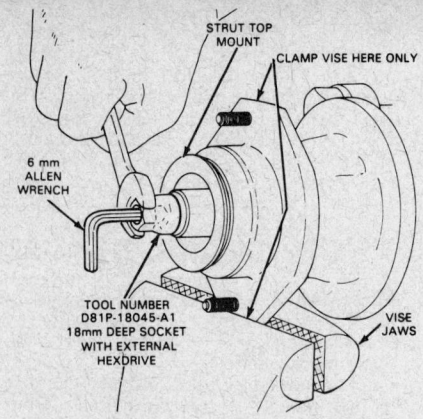

Fig. 4 **Removing shock absorber strut top mounting nut. 1981–82**

STRUT ASSEMBLY, REPLACE

1. Raise and support vehicle, then remove tire and wheel assembly.
2. Remove brake hose retaining bracket from strut.
3. On Tempo and Topaz models, remove brake calliper, brake rotor, and tie-rod end.
4. Place suitable jack under lower control arm and raise strut as far as possible without raising vehicle.
5. On models except Tempo and Topaz, install spring compressor tool No. T81P-5310A or equivalent by placing top jaw on second coil from top and bottom jaw so as to grip a total of 5 coils, then compress spring until there is about 1/8 inch between any 2 coils, Fig. 2.
6. On Tempo and Topaz models, install spring compressor tool No. 14-0259 or 86-0016 by placing top jaw on 5th or 6th coil from bottom, then compress spring a minimum of 3 1/2 inches, Fig. 3.

NOTE: Spring must be compressed before strut is removed to insure that no excessive force is applied to constant velocity universal joints.

7. Remove steering knuckle-to-strut pinch

bolt, then loosen two top mount to apron nuts and top strut shaft nut.

NOTE: When loosening or tightening strut-to-mount nut, hold 6mm Allen wrench, Fig. 4, or hold 8mm hex with a deep socket 1/4-inch drive wrench, Figs. 5 and 6, and turn only the nut.

8. Lower jack from control arm, then using a large screwdriver, spread knuckle-to-strut pinch joint.
9. Place block of wood 2 × 4 × 7 1/2 inches against knuckle shoulder. Using suitable pry bar between wood block and lower spring seat, separate strut from knuckle, Fig. 7.
10. Remove two top mounting nuts, then the strut, spring, and top mount assembly from vehicle.
11. On 1981–82 vehicles, install 18mm deep socket onto strut shaft nut. Insert 6mm Allen wrench into shaft end, then clamp mount into vise, Fig. 4.
12. On 1983–84 except Tempo and Topaz, place 18mm deep socket tool No. D81P-78045-A1 or equivalent on strut shaft nut. Place an 8mm deep socket, 1/4 inch

drive onto shaft end and clamp mount into vise, Fig. 5.
13. On Tempo and Topaz, place 18mm deep socket tool No. D81P-18045-A1 or equivalent on strut shaft nut. Insert an 8mm hex deep socket with 1/4-inch drive wrench and clamp strut into vise, Fig. 6.
14. On all vehicles, remove top shaft mounting nut from shaft while holding Allen wrench or 1/4-inch drive socket.

NOTE: Do not clamp directly on strut with vise as damage to strut may result.

15. Remove strut top mount components and, except on Tempo and Topaz, spring.

NOTE: On Tempo and Topaz models, check spring insulator for damage to splash shield.

16. On Tempo and Topaz models, remove spring compressor from strut and remove spring.
17. Reverse procedure to install. Refer to Figs. 8 and 9 for proper installation sequence of top mount components. On except Tempo and Topaz models, torque strut shaft nut to 48–62 ft. lbs., on Tempo

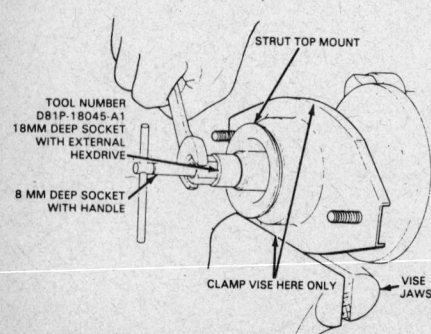

Fig. 5 **Removing shock absorber strut top mounting nut. 1983–84 exc. Tempo & Topaz**

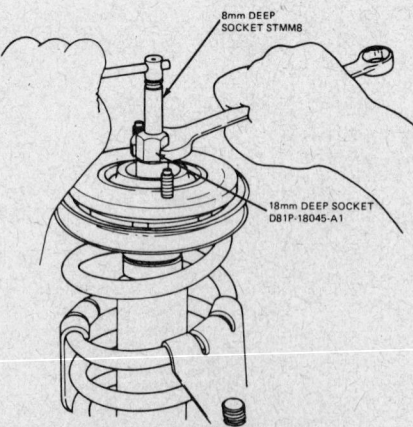

Fig. 6 **Removing shock absorber strut top mounting nut. Tempo & Topaz**

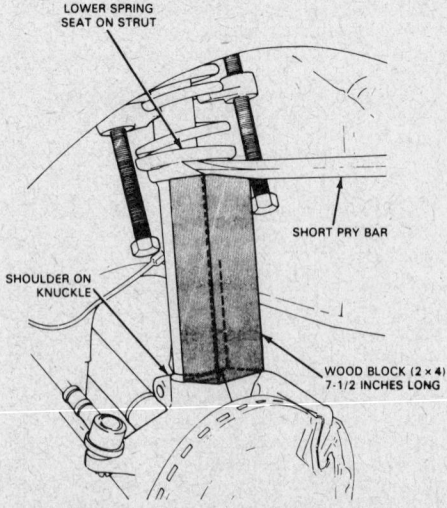

Fig. 7 **Separating shock absorber strut from knuckle**

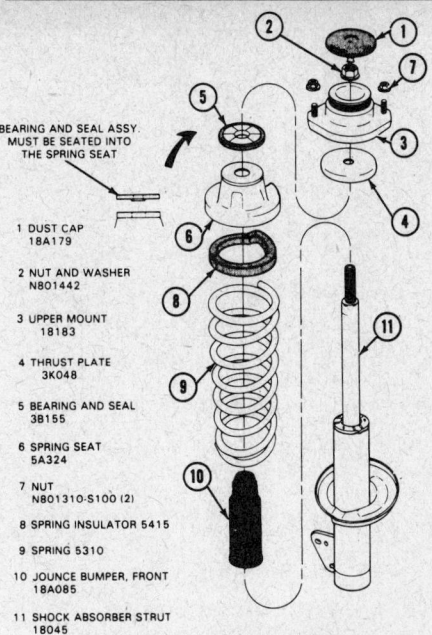

BEARING AND SEAL ASSY. MUST BE SEATED INTO THE SPRING SEAT

1 DUST CAP 18A179
2 NUT AND WASHER N801442
3 UPPER MOUNT 18183
4 THRUST PLATE 3K048
5 BEARING AND SEAL 3B155
6 SPRING SEAT 5A324
7 NUT N801310-S100 (2)
8 SPRING INSULATOR 5415
9 SPRING 5310
10 JOUNCE BUMPER, FRONT 18A085
11 SHOCK ABSORBER STRUT 18045

Fig. 8   Installation of shock absorber strut top mounting components. Except Tempo & Topaz

and Topaz models, torque strut shaft nut to 35–50 ft. lbs. Install new steering knuckle pinch nut and torque to 66–81 ft. lbs. On except Tempo and Topaz models, torque two top mount attaching nuts to 22–29 ft. lbs. On Tempo and Topaz models, torque two top mount attaching nuts to 25–30 ft. lbs.

CHECKING BALL JOINTS

1. Raise and support vehicle.
2. With suspension in full rebound position, grasp lower edge of tire and move wheel in and out, Fig. 10.
3. Observe lower end of knuckle and lower control arm as wheel is being moved in and out. Any movement between lower end of knuckle and lower arm indicates excessive ball joint wear.
4. If any movement is observed, install a new lower control arm assembly. The lower ball joint and control arm are serviced as an assembly only. Refer to Lower Control Arm, Replace in this section.

LOWER CONTROL ARM, REPLACE

1. Raise and support vehicle.

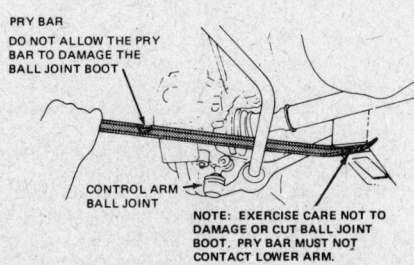

PRY BAR
DO NOT ALLOW THE PRY BAR TO DAMAGE THE BALL JOINT BOOT

CONTROL ARM BALL JOINT

NOTE: EXERCISE CARE NOT TO DAMAGE OR CUT BALL JOINT BOOT. PRY BAR MUST NOT CONTACT LOWER ARM.

Fig. 11   Separating ball joint from steering knuckle

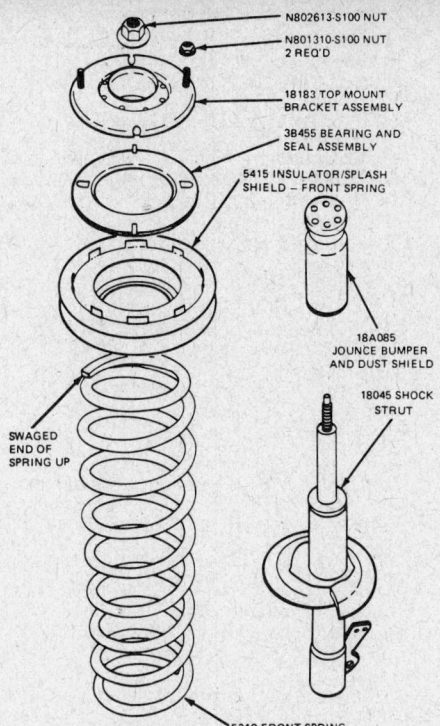

N802613-S100 NUT
N801310-S100 NUT 2 REQ'D
18183 TOP MOUNT BRACKET ASSEMBLY
3B455 BEARING AND SEAL ASSEMBLY
5415 INSULATOR/SPLASH SHIELD – FRONT SPRING
18A085 JOUNCE BUMPER AND DUST SHIELD
18045 SHOCK STRUT

SWAGED END OF SPRING UP

5310 FRONT SPRING

Fig. 9   Installation of shock absorber strut top mounting components. Tempo & Topaz

2. Remove nut from stabilizer bar, then the large dished washer.
3. Remove lower control arm inner pivot bolt and nut.
4. Remove lower control arm ball joint pinch bolt, then using a screwdriver, separate the control arm from the steering knuckle and remove from vehicle.

NOTE: Ensure steering column is in unlocked position. Do not use a hammer to separate ball joint from knuckle.

5. Reverse procedure to install. Torque pinch bolt and nut to 37–44 ft. lbs. On 1981–83 vehicles, torque lower control arm inner pivot nut to 44–55 ft. lbs. On 1984 vehicles, torque lower control arm inner pivot nut to 50–60 ft. lbs. Torque stabilizer bar nut to 98–115 ft. lbs.

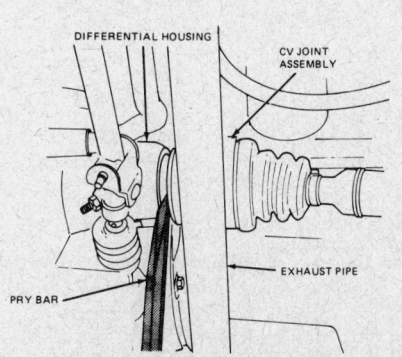

DIFFERENTIAL HOUSING
CV JOINT ASSEMBLY
EXHAUST PIPE
PRY BAR

Fig. 12   Removing halfshaft from differential housing

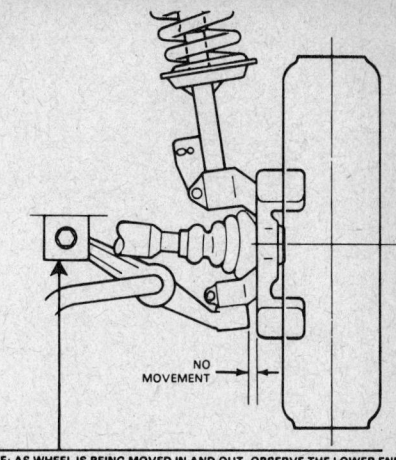

NO MOVEMENT

NOTE: AS WHEEL IS BEING MOVED IN AND OUT, OBSERVE THE LOWER END OF THE KNUCKLE AND THE LOWER CONTROL ARM. ANY MOVEMENT BETWEEN LOWER END OF THE KNUCKLE AND THE LOWER ARM INDICATES ABNORMAL BALL JOINT WEAR

Fig. 10   Checking lower ball joint

STEERING KNUCKLE, REPLACE

1. Raise and support vehicle, then remove wheel assembly.
2. Remove cotter pin from tie rod end stud, then the slotted nut.
3. Using tool 3290C and adapter T81P3504W, remove tie rod end from knuckle.
4. Remove brake caliper, then the hub from the driveshaft.
5. On 1984 vehicles, loosen two top mount nuts. Do not remove nuts.
6. Remove pinch bolt and nut securing lower arm to steering knuckle, then using a screwdriver, separate lower arm from knuckle.

NOTE: Ensure steering column is in unlocked position. Do not use a hammer to separate ball joint from knuckle.

7. Remove shock absorber strut to steering knuckle pinch bolt, then using a screwdriver, slightly open knuckle to strut pinch joint.
8. Remove steering knuckle from shock absorber strut, Fig. 7, then from the vehicle.
9. Reverse procedure to install. Torque

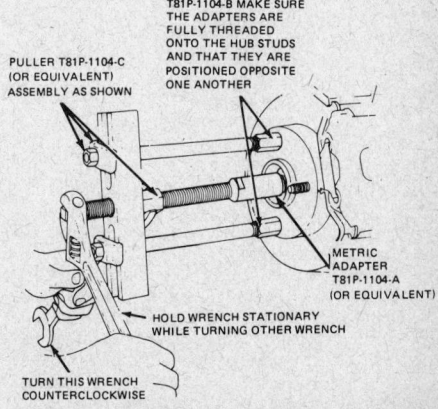

METRIC ADAPTERS T81P-1104-B MAKE SURE THE ADAPTERS ARE FULLY THREADED ONTO THE HUB STUDS AND THAT THEY ARE POSITIONED OPPOSITE ONE ANOTHER

PULLER T81P-1104-C (OR EQUIVALENT) ASSEMBLY AS SHOWN

METRIC ADAPTER T81P-1104-A (OR EQUIVALENT)

HOLD WRENCH STATIONARY WHILE TURNING OTHER WRENCH

TURN THIS WRENCH COUNTERCLOCKWISE

Fig. 13   Separating outer constant velocity joint from hub

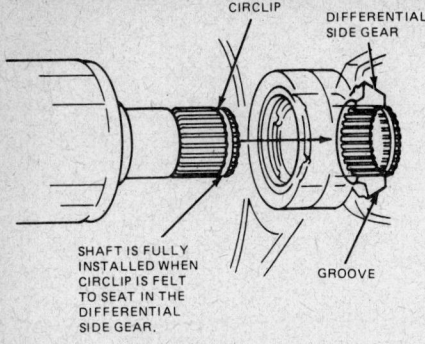

Fig. 14 Installing inner constant velocity joint into differential side gear

steering knuckle to shock strut assembly pinch bolt to 66–81 ft. lbs., torque lower control arm to steering knuckle pinch bolt to 37–44 ft. lbs. On 1984 vehicles, torque two top mount nuts to 25–30 ft. lbs. Install new slotted nut then torque to 23–35 ft. lbs.

STABILIZER BAR, REPLACE

1. Raise and support vehicle.
2. Remove stabilizer insulator mounting bracket bolts.
3. Remove stabilizer bar to control arm attaching bolts, then the stabilizer bar assembly.
4. Remove worn insulators from stabilizer bar.
5. Reverse procedure to install. Torque stabilizer bar to control arm attaching bolt to 98–115 ft. lbs. Torque stabilizer insulator mounting bracket bolts to 60–70 ft. lbs.

STEERING GEAR, REPLACE

Manual Steering

1. Disconnect battery ground cable, then turn ignition switch to "On" position.
2. Remove access panel from dash below steering column.
3. Remove intermediate shaft bolts at gear input shaft and at steering column shaft.
4. Using a wide blade screwdriver, spread slots enough to loosen intermediate shaft at both ends.
5. Turn steering wheel fully left to allow clearance for tie rod removal.
6. Remove tie rod ends from steering knuckles using tool 3290C and adapter T81P3504W. Turn right wheel to full left position.
7. Remove left tie rod end from tie rod, then on vehicles equipped with automatic transmission disconnect speedometer cable at transmission.
8. Disconnect secondary air tube at check valve, then exhaust pipes from exhaust manifold.
9. Remove exhaust hanger bracket from below steering gear. Wire exhaust system aside.
10. Remove gear mounting brackets and insulators, then separate gear from intermediate shaft while simultaneously pulling upward on shaft from inside vehicle.

NOTE: Right and left hand brackets and insulators are not interchangeable.

11. Rotate gear forward and downward to clear input shaft.
12. Ensure input shaft is in full left turn position, then remove gear through right side apron opening until left tie rod clears shift linkage.
13. Lower left side of gear and remove gear from vehicle.
14. Reverse procedure to install. Ensure input shaft is at full left turn stop and right wheel assembly is in full left turn position. Use caution not to damage steering gear bellows.

Power Steering

1. Disconnect battery ground cable, then turn ignition switch to "On" position.
2. Remove access panel from dash below steering column.
3. Remove four screws from dash panel steering column boot, then slide boot along intermediate shaft.
4. Remove intermediate shaft bolts at gear input shaft and from steering column shaft.
5. Using wide blade screwdriver, spread slot wide enough to loosen intermediate shaft at both ends.
6. Turn steering wheel to full left stop to facilitate gear removal.
7. On all 1981–82 vehicles except 1.6 L. engine and manual transmission without air conditioning, remove pressure switch electrical connector, then the switch.
8. On 1984 vehicles, remove air cleaner.
9. On vehicles equipped with air conditioning, except Tempo and Topaz models, secure liquid line above dash opening.
10. Disconnect secondary air tube at check valve, then the exhaust pipes from exhaust manifold. Secure exhaust system to the side.
11. Remove exhaust hanger brackets from below steering gear and from side apron.
12. Disconnect pressure and return lines from intermediate connector and drain fluid.
13. Remove tie rod ends from steering knuckles using tool 3290C and adapter T81P3504W. Turn right wheel to full left turn position.
14. On vehicles equipped with manual transmission, remove left tie rod end from tie rod.
15. On vehicles equipped with automatic transmission, disconnect speedometer cable from transmission.
16. On vehicles equipped with automatic transmission, disconnect shift cable assembly from transmission.
17. Except on Tempo and Topaz models, remove screws securing heater water tube to brace below oil pan.
18. Except on Tempo and Topaz models, remove nut from lower bolt securing engine mounting bracket to transmission housing. Tap bolt out as far as possible.
19. Remove gear mounting brackets and insulators.
20. Remove gear from intermediate shaft by pushing upward on shaft with bar while pulling gear downward.
21. Rotate gear downward and forward to clear input shaft.
22. Ensure input shaft is in full left turn position, then move gear through right side apron opening until left tie rod clears

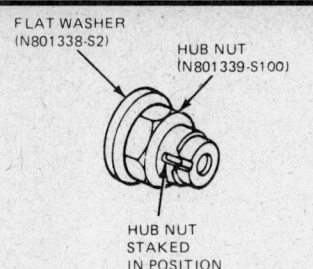

Fig. 15 Hub nut staking tool fabrication

opening. Use caution to avoid damaging bellows.
23. Lower left side of gear and remove gear from vehicle.
24. Reverse procedure to install.

POWER STEERING PUMP, REPLACE

With Diesel Engine

1. Remove drive belts.
2. On vehicles with air conditioning, remove alternator.
3. On vehicles with air conditioning, remove both braces from support bracket.
4. Disconnect power steering lines and drain fluid from pump.
5. Remove four bracket mounting bolts.
6. Install pulley removal tool No. T69L-10300-B or equivalent on pulley hub. Hold small hex head of tool and turn tool nut counterclockwise to remove pulley.
7. Remove pump from bracket.
8. Reverse procedure to install.

With Gasoline Engine

Escort, EXP, LN7 & Lynx
1. Remove air cleaner, thermactor pump drive belt and thermactor pump.
2. Remove power steering reservoir filler extension. Cover opening to prevent entry of dirt.
3. From underneath vehicle, loosen one power steering pump adjusting bolt and remove one pump to mounting bracket bolt, then disconnect return hose.
4. Form engine compartment, loosen one power steering pump adjusting bolt, then loosen pivot and remove drive belts.
5. Remove the remaining two power steering pump to bracket retaining bolts, then remove pump from bracket by passing pulley through adjusting bracket opening.
6. Disconnect pressure hose from power steering pump, then remove pump.
7. Reverse procedure to install.

Tempo & Topaz
1. Remove alternator drive belt.
2. Place alternator in upper most position.
3. Remove radiator overflow bottle.
4. Remove power steering pump drive belt.
5. Disconnect return line from pump.
6. Completely back off power steering pump pressure line nut. The pressure line will separate when the pump bracket is removed.
7. Remove power steering pump mounting bolts and pump.
8. Reverse procedure to install.

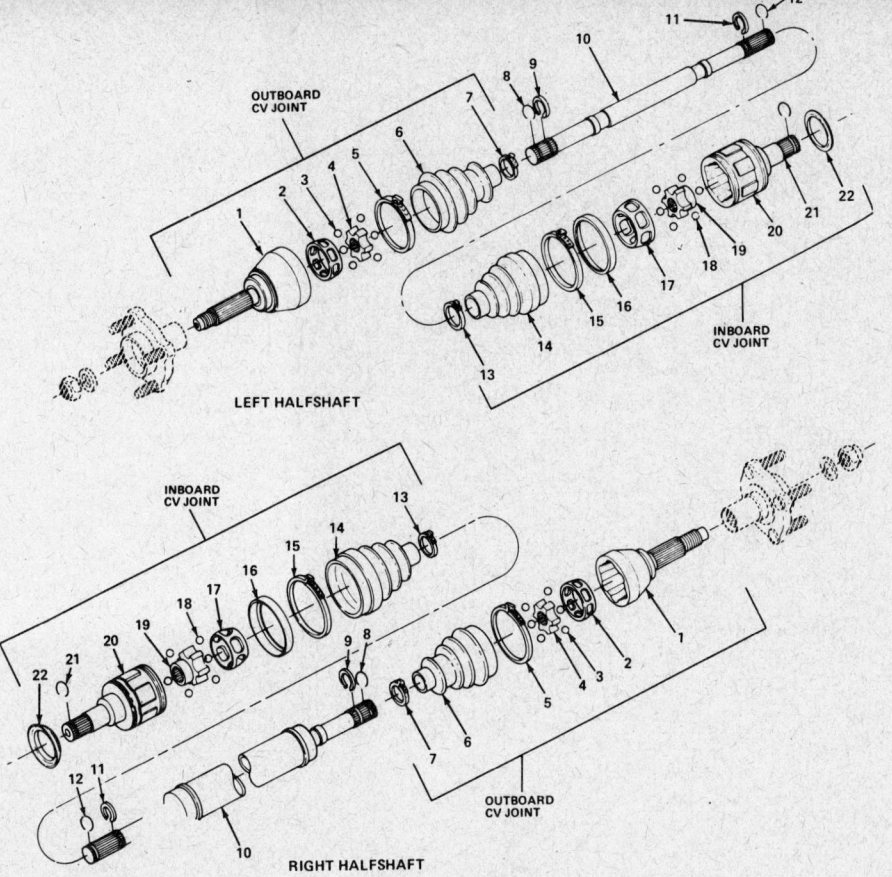

LEFT HALFSHAFT

RIGHT HALFSHAFT

LEGEND:

1. OUTER BEARING RACE AND STUB SHAFT ASSEMBLY
2. BEARING CAGE
3. BALL BEARINGS (6)
4. INNER BEARING RACE
5. BOOT CLAMP (LARGE)
6. BOOT
7. BOOT CLAMP (SMALL)
8. CIRCLIP
9. STOP RING
10. INTERCONNECTING SHAFT
11. STOP RING
12. CIRCLIP
13. BOOT CLAMP (SMALL)
14. BOOT
15. BOOT CLAMP (LARGE)
16. BEARING RETAINER
17. BEARING CAGE
18. BALL BEARINGS (6)
19. INNER BEARING RACE
20. OUTER BEARING RACE AND STUB SHAFT ASSEMBLY
21. CIRCLIP
22. DUST DEFLECTOR

Fig. 16 Halfshaft assemblies. 1981–82 & 1983 Early Models

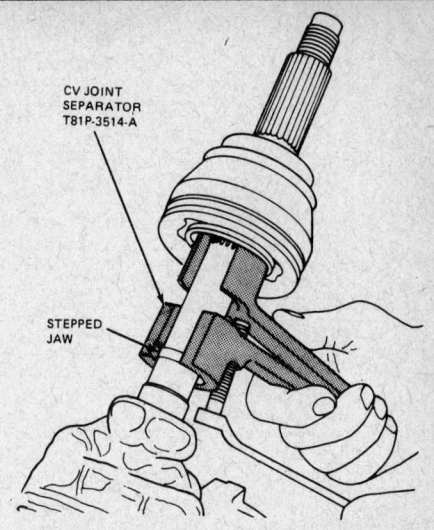

Fig. 17 Separating constant velocity joint from shaft. 1981–82 & 1983 Early Models

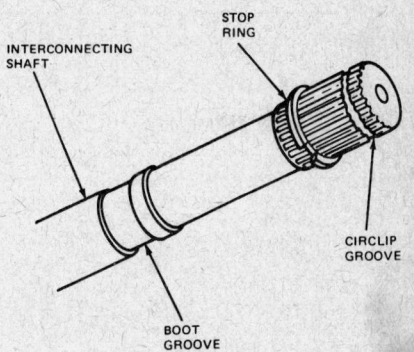

Fig. 18 Stub shaft stop ring

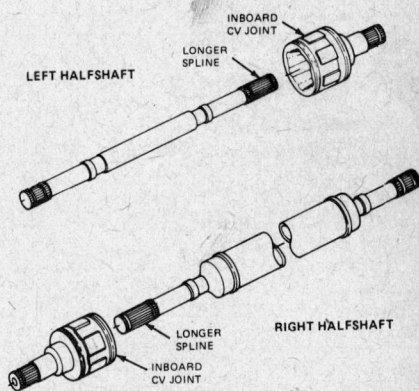

Fig. 19 Assembling constant velocity joints onto halfshafts

DRIVESHAFTS, REPLACE

NOTE: If removing both right and left side halfshafts, plugs T81P-1177B or equivalent must be installed. Failure to do so may result in dislocation of differential side gears, necessitating transaxle disassembly to re-align the gears. Also, halfshaft removal and installation procedures are the same for manual and automatic transaxles except for the following: due to automatic transaxle case configuration the right side halfshaft assembly must be removed first. Tool T81P-4026A or equivalent is then inserted into transaxle to remove left side inner constant velocity joint assembly from transaxle. If only the left side halfshaft is to be removed from the vehicle, remove right side halfshaft assembly from the transaxle case only and secure to underside of vehicle, then remove left side halfshaft assembly. The hub nut and lower control arm to steering knuckle attaching bolt and nut must be discarded after removal and new nuts and bolts installed.

1. Loosen hub nut without unstaking. Use of a chisel or similar tool to unstake nut may damage spindle threads.
2. Raise and support vehicle and remove wheel assemblies.
3. Remove bolt attaching brake hose routing clip to suspension strut.
4. Remove nut from ball joint to steering knuckle attaching bolt, then drive bolt from knuckle using suitable punch and hammer.
5. Separate ball joint from steering knuckle using pry bar, Fig. 11.

NOTE: Lower ball joints fit into a pocket formed in the plastic disc brake shield. The shield must be positioned away from the ball joint while removing ball joint from steering knuckle.

6. Remove halfshaft from differential housing using suitable pry bar. Use caution not to damage dust deflector located between shaft and case, Fig. 12. If an auto-

matic transaxle halfshaft assembly cannot be removed from differential by using a pry bar, insert a large bladed screwdriver between differential pinion shaft and inboard constant velocity joint stub shaft. Sharply tap on screwdriver handle, to free halfshaft from differential.

NOTE: Use caution not to damage differential oil seal, constant velocity joint boot or constant velocity joint dust deflector.

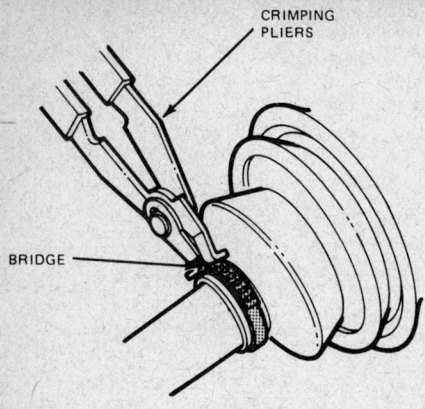

Fig. 20 Installing constant velocity joint clamp

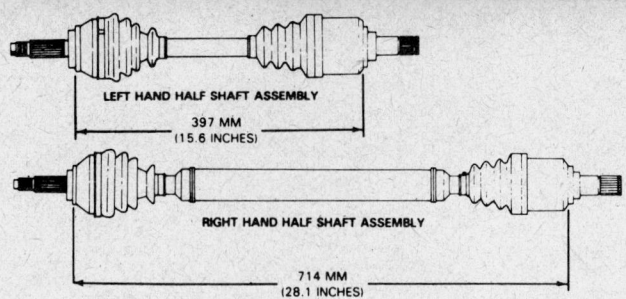

Fig. 21 Halfshaft assembled length. 1981–82 & 1983 Early Models

7. Separate outer constant velocity joint from hub using puller T81P-1104C or equivalent, Fig. 13, and adapters T81P-1104B and T81P-1104A or equivalent.

NOTE: Do not use a hammer to separate outboard constant velocity joint stub shaft from hub as damage to internal components may result.

8. Reverse procedure to install. Install new circlip on inboard constant velocity joint stub shaft. Align splines of inboard constant velocity joint stub shaft with splines in differential. Push joint into differential until circlip seats in side gear, Fig. 14. Torque new control arm to steering knuckle nut to 37–44 ft. lbs. Torque new hub nut to 180–200 ft. lbs., and stake nut, Fig. 15.

NOTE: If the hub nut cracks or splits during staking, remove and replace hub nut.

CONSTANT VELOCITY JOINT SERVICE

Replacement

1981–82 & Early 1983 Models, Fig. 16

Removal

NOTE: Service is the same for both inner and outer constant velocity joints.

1. Place halfshaft in suitable vice. Use caution not to damage boot or clamp.
2. Cut large boot clamp and remove from boot, then position boot upward on shaft. If boot only is being replaced due to damage, check joint grease for contamination. If joints were operating satisfactorily and grease is not contaminated, add grease and install new boot. If grease is contaminated, joint must be completely disassembled.
3. Separate constant velocity joint from shaft using tool T81P-3514A or equivalent, Fig. 17. If necessary, boot may be removed from shaft by cutting remaining clamp and removing boot.

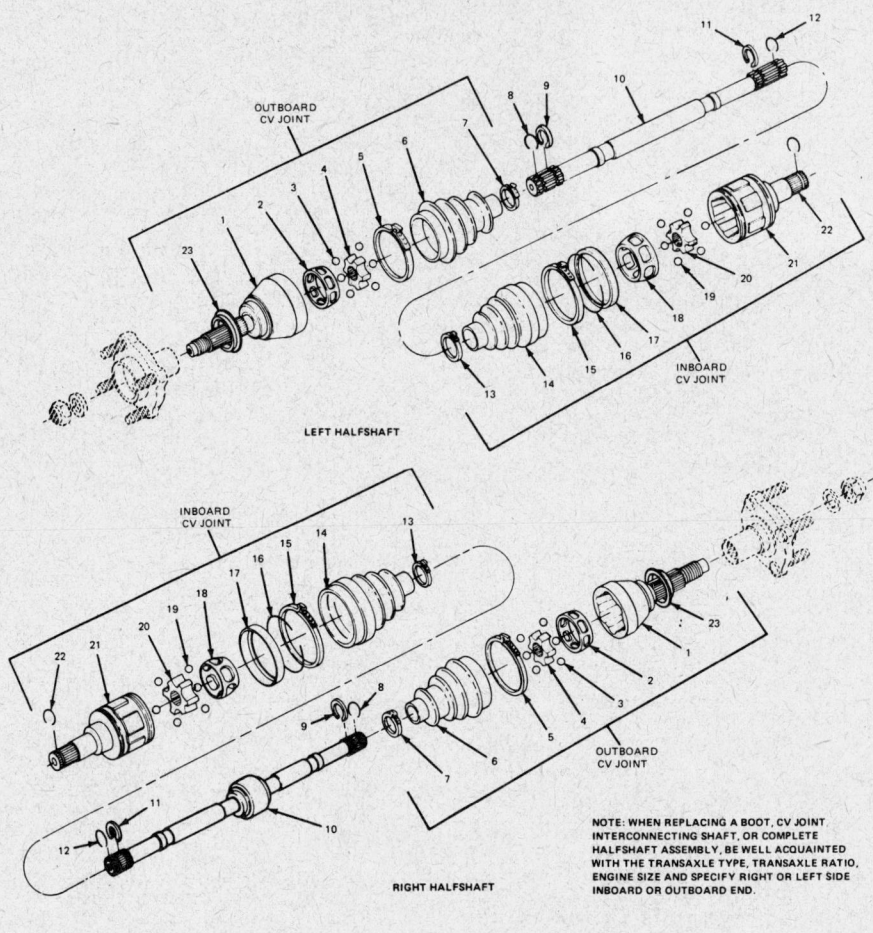

Fig. 22 Halfshaft assemblies. Late 1983 & 1984 models

LEGEND:
1. OUTER BEARING RACE AND STUB SHAFT ASSEMBLY
2. BEARING CAGE
3. BALL BEARINGS (6)
4. INNER BEARING RACE
5. BOOT CLAMP (LARGE)
6. BOOT
7. BOOT CLAMP (SMALL)
8. CIRCLIP
9. STOP RING
10. INTERCONNECTING SHAFT
11. STOP RING
12. CIRCLIP
13. BOOT CLAMP (SMALL)
14. BOOT
15. BOOT CLAMP (LARGE)
16. BEARING RETAINER (MTX 5-SPEED ONLY)
17. BEARING RETAINER (MTX 4-SPEED AND ATX)
18. BEARING CAGE
19. BALL BEARINGS (6)
20. INNER BEARING RACE
21. OUTER BEARING RACE AND STUB SHAFT ASSEMBLY
22. CIRCLIP
23. DUST SEAL

4. Remove circlip from end of shaft and discard. Inspect stop ring for damage and replace as necessary, Fig. 18.

Installation
1. Inspect splines at each end of shaft for damage and wear. Inner constant velocity joint must be installed onto longer splines, Fig. 19.
2. Ensure stop ring is in proper position, then install new circlip into groove nearest end of shaft.
3. Install joint boot until it seats in its groove, then install clamp. Tighten clamp securely but do not damage boot or cut clamp bridge, Fig. 20.

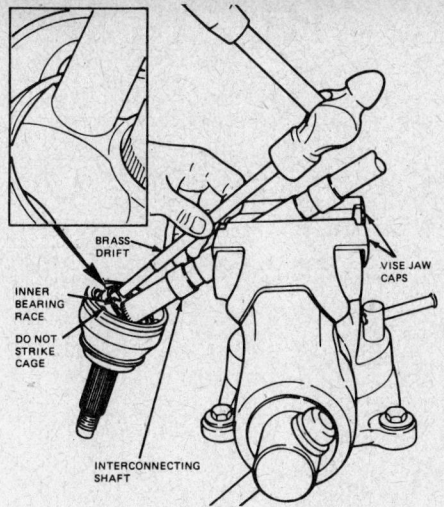

Fig. 23 Separating constant velocity joint from shaft. Late 1983 & 1984 models

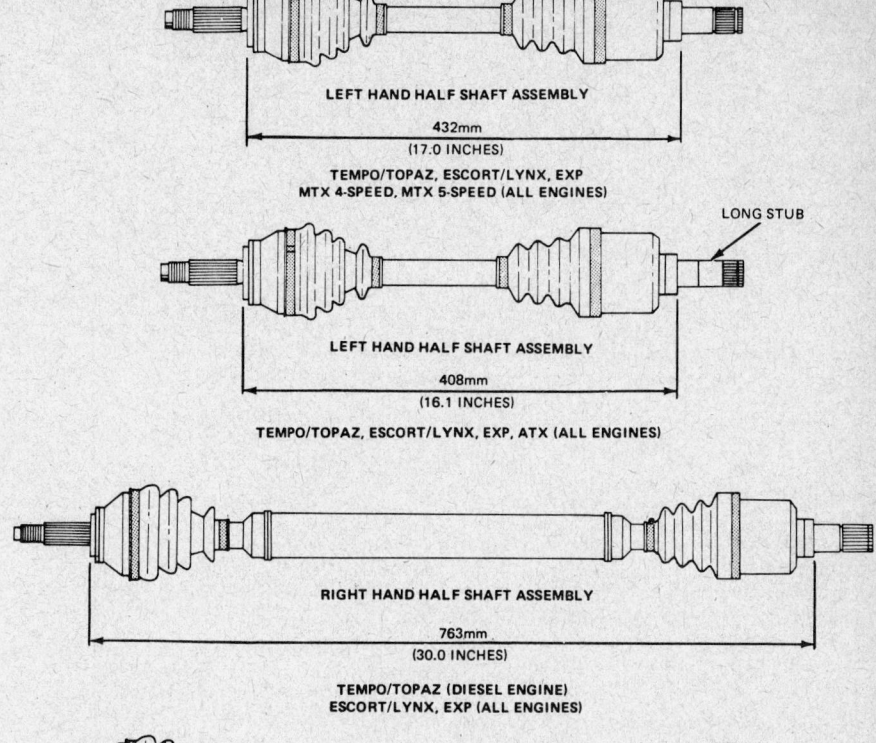

Fig. 24 Halfshaft assembled lengths. Late 1983 & 1984 models

4. Position boot upward towards end of shaft, then position constant velocity joint onto shaft and tap into position using plastic mallet. Joint is fully seated when circlip locks in groove cut into joint bearing inner race. Check for proper seating by trying to pull joint from shaft.
5. Lubricate joints with lubricant packs supplied with service kit. On outer joint, fill boot with 2/3 packet and pack joint with 1 1/3 packet of lubricant. On inner joint, fill boot with one packet and pack joint with one packet of lubricant. Use lubricant D8RZ-19590A or equivalent only.
6. Position boot over joint, then pry end of boot upward to release any trapped air.
7. Position joint inward or outward as necessary to adjust halfshaft to length shown in Fig. 21.
8. Ensure boot is seated in groove, then refer to step 3 for clamp installation.

Late 1983 & 1984 Models, Fig. 22

REMOVAL

Except Inboard Constant Velocity Joint & Boot, 5-Speed Manual Transaxle
1. Place halfshaft in suitable vise. Use caution not to damage boot or clamp.
2. Cut large boot clamp and remove from boot, then position boot upward on shaft. If boot only is being replaced due to damage, check joint grease for contamination. If joints were operating satisfactorily and grease is not contaminated, add grease and install new boot. If grease is contaminated, joint must be completely disassembled.
3. Place interconnecting shaft in a suitable vise and angle constant velocity joint so that inner bearing race is exposed, Fig. 23.
4. Using suitable drift and hammer, tap inner bearing race to dislodge internal circlip and separate constant velocity joint from interconnecting shaft, being careful not to drop joint.
5. Remove boot from shaft, cutting remaining clamp as necessary.
6. Remove circlip from end of shaft and dis-

card. Inspect stop ring for damage and replace as necessary, Fig. 18.

Inboard Constant Velocity Joint & Boot, 5-Speed Manual Transaxle
1. Remove large boot clamp, roll boot back, and wipe away excess grease.
2. Remove wire ring bearing retainer from outer race, then remove outer race.
3. Pull inner race and bearing assembly out until it rests on circlip, then, using suitable pliers, spread stop ring and move it back on shaft.

4. Slide inner race and bearing assembly down shaft to expose circlip, then remove circlip.
5. Remove inner race and bearing assembly and, if necessary, remove boot.

INSTALLATION

Except Inboard Constant Velocity Joint & Boot, 5-Speed Manual Transmission
1. Install new stop ring, if removed. Ensure that stop ring is properly seated in groove.

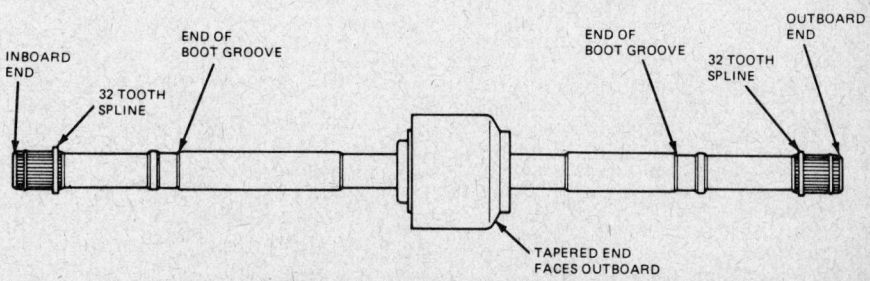

Fig. 25 Right hand interconnecting shaft. Late 1983 & 1984 models

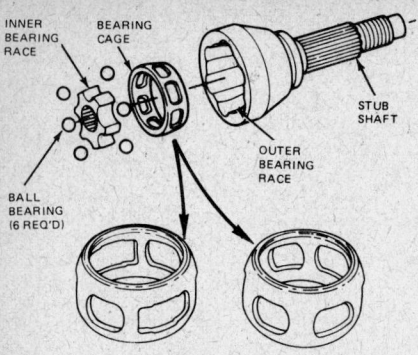

Fig. 26 Outer constant velocity joint bearing cage configuration

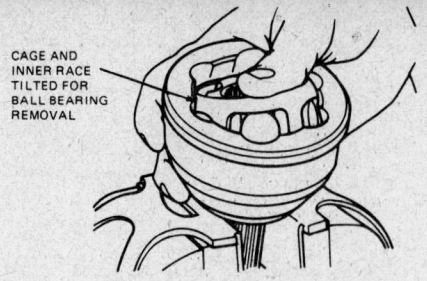

Fig. 27 Removing outer constant velocity joint bearings

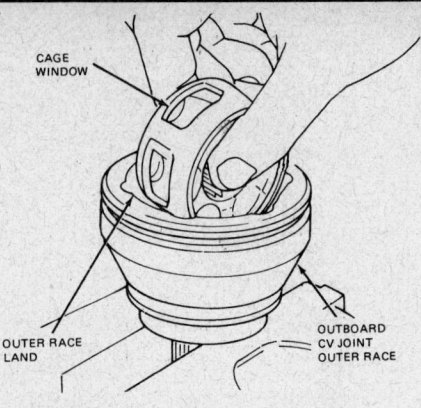

Fig. 28 Removing bearing cage and inner race assembly from outer constant velocity joint

2. Install new circlip in groove nearest end of shaft. To avoid over-expansion or twisting of circlip, start one end in groove and work circlip over stub shaft end and into groove.

NOTE: Interconnecting shafts are different depending on application. These shafts are non-symmetrical. Outboard end is approximately ¼ inch longer, from end of shaft to end of boot groove, than inboard end. Be careful to install inboard and outboard constant velocity joints to proper ends of shaft.

3. Install constant velocity joint boot, if removed, ensuring that boot is seated in groove. Tighten clamp securely, but not too tight.
4. Before positioning boot over constant velocity joint, pack joint and boot as follows:
   a. On inboard constant velocity joint, fill boot with 45 grams of grease and pack joint with 90 grams of grease.
   b. On outboard constant velocity joint, fill boot with 45 grams of grease and pack joint with 45 grams of grease.

CAUTION: Use only lubricant E2FZ-19590-A or equivalent.

5. Position boot upward toward end of shaft, then position constant velocity joint onto shaft and tap into position using plastic mallet. Joint is fully seated when circlip locks in groove cut into joint bearing inner race. Check for proper seating by trying to pull joint from shaft.

6. Remove all excess grease from external surfaces of constant velocity joint, then position boot over constant velocity joint and move joint in or out to adjust to proper length, Fig. 24.
7. Before installing boot clamp, insert dulled screwdriver blade between boot and outer bearing race to allow trapped air to escape.
8. Ensure that boot is seated in groove, then install clamp securely but not too tight.

Inboard Constant Velocity Joint & Boot, 5-Speed Manual Transmission

1. Move circlip and stop ring back into their respective grooves on shaft.

NOTE: Left hand interconnecting shaft is symmetrical and inboard and outboard constant velocity joints may be installed on either end. Right hand interconnecting shaft is non-symmetrical and care must be taken so that inboard and outboard constant velocity joints are correctly installed, Fig. 25.

2. Install constant velocity joint boot, if removed. Ensure that boot is seated in groove, then install clamp securely but not too tight.
3. Install new circlip in groove nearest end of shaft. To avoid over-expansion or twisting of circlip, start one end in groove and work circlip over stub shaft end and into groove.
4. Fill boot with 45 grams of grease and fill outer race with 90 grams of grease. Use only lubricant E2FZ-19590-A or equiva-

lent.
5. Push inner race and bearing assembly into outer race by hand.
6. Install ball retainer into groove inside outer race.
7. With boot positioned upward toward end of shaft, install constant velocity joint using suitable hammer. Ensure that splines are aligned before hammering constant velocity joint onto shaft.
8. Remove all excess grease from external surfaces of constant velocity joint, then position boot over constant velocity joint and move joint in or out to adjust to proper length, Fig. 24.
9. Before installing boot clamp, insert dulled screwdriver blade between boot and outer bearing race to allow trapped air to escape.
10. Ensure that boot is seated in groove, then install clamp securely but not too tight.

Disassembly & Assembly

Outer Joint

NOTE: Two different bearing cages are used on the outer joints. One type contains four equal sized windows and two elongated windows while the other type contains six windows of equal size, Fig. 26.

1. Position stub shaft in suitable vise with bearing facing upward.
2. Press downward on inner race until bearing can be removed, Fig. 27. Remove all six bearings in this manner.

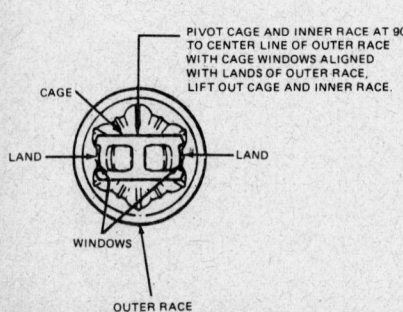

Fig. 29 Aligning inner cage and bearing race

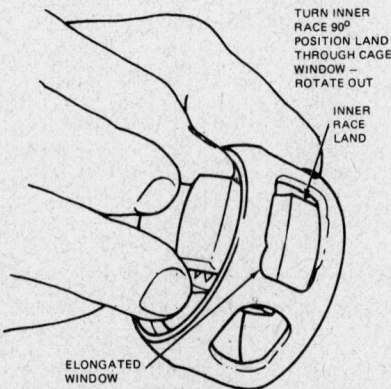

Fig. 30 Removing inner race from bearing cage

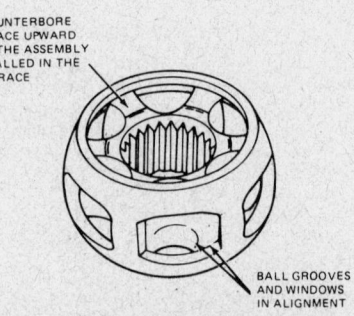

Fig. 31 Counterbore positioning and ball groove & window alignment

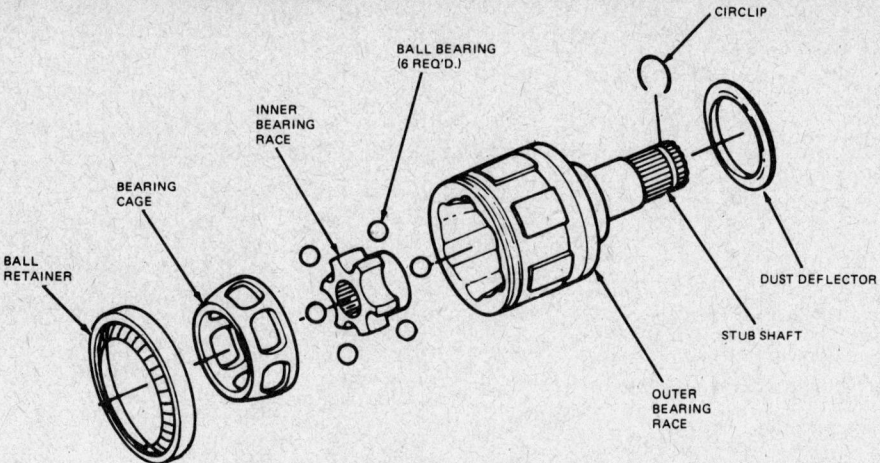

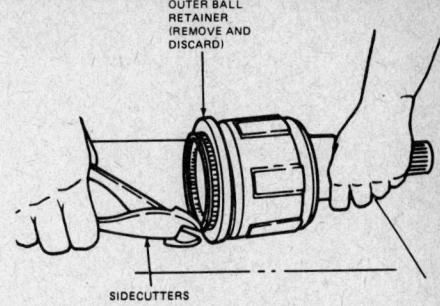

Fig. 33 Removing inner constant velocity joint outer ball retainer

Fig. 32 Inner constant velocity joint assembly

Fig. 34 Removing inner constant velocity joint inner race and bearing assembly

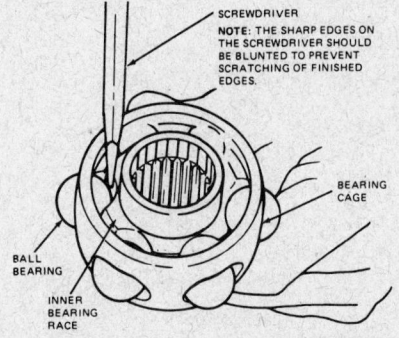

Fig. 35 Removing bearings from cage

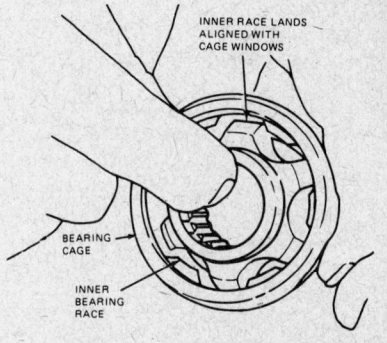

Fig. 36 Removing inner race from bearing cage

3. Pivot bearing cage and inner race assembly into position shown in Fig. 28. Align cage windows with outer race lands while pivoting cage, Fig. 29, then remove from outer race.

4. To separate inner race from cage, determine cage design and proceed as follows: on cages with six equal windows rotate inner race upward and remove from cage. On cages with two elongated windows, pivot inner race until it is in position shown in Fig. 28, then align one inner race band with one elongated window and position race through the window. Rotate inner race upward and remove from cage, Fig. 30.

5. Reverse procedure to assemble. Refer to Fig. 31 for ball groove and window alignment and proper counterbore positioning.

Inner Joint, Fig. 32

NOTE: On late 1983 and 1984 models with 5-speed manual transmission, disassembly of inboard constant velocity joint is performed during removal and assembly of inboard constant velocity joint is performed during installation as previously described.

1. Remove circlip from end of joint stub shaft, then using suitable cutters, cut and remove ball retainer, Fig. 33. Discard retainer since a new retainer is not required for assembly.

2. Gently tap joint on work surface until assembly can be removed by hand, Fig. 34.

3. Remove bearings from cage by prying with a dulled screwdriver. Use caution not to damage or scratch any components, Fig. 35.

4. Rotate inner race to align lands with cage windows, then remove race from bearing cage through wider end of cage, Fig. 36.

5. Reverse procedure to assemble.

LINCOLN

INDEX OF SERVICE OPERATIONS

NOTE: Refer to the front of this manual for vehicle manufacturer's special service tool suppliers.

SERIAL & ENGINE NUMBER LOCATION

Engine code is fifth digit of serial number on 1977—80 models, or eighth digit of serial number on 1981—84 models. The serial number is stamped on a metal tag located on top left side dash and visible through windshield.

GRILLE IDENTIFICATION

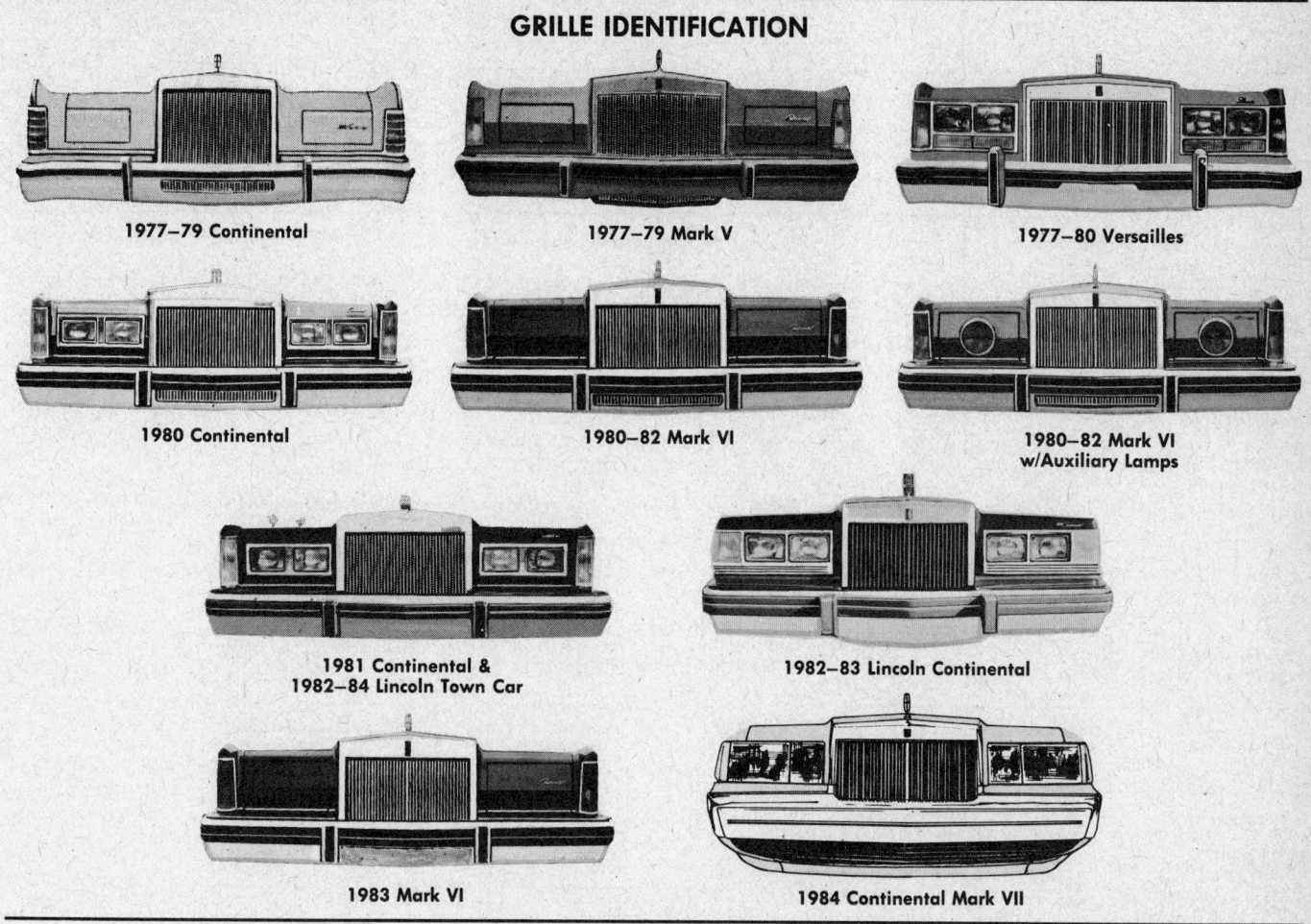

1977—79 Continental

1977—79 Mark V

1977—80 Versailles

1980 Continental

1980—82 Mark VI

1980—82 Mark VI w/Auxiliary Lamps

1981 Continental & 1982—84 Lincoln Town Car

1982—83 Lincoln Continental

1983 Mark VI

1984 Continental Mark VII

GENERAL ENGINE SPECIFICATIONS

Year	Engine C.I.D./Liter①	V.I.N. CODE②	Carburetor	Bore and Stroke	Compression Ratio	Net H.P. @ R.P.M.③	Maximum Torque Ft. Lbs. @ R.P.M.	Normal Oil Pressure Pounds
1977	V8-302, 5.0L	F	2150, 2 Bbl.④	4.00 × 3.00	8.1	122 @ 3400	222 @ 1400	40—60
	V8-351W, 5.8L	H	2150, 2 Bbl.④	4.00 × 3.50	8.1	135 @ 3200	275 @ 1600	45—65
	V8-400, 6.6L⑤	S	2150, 2 Bbl.④	4.00 × 4.00	8.0	179 @ 4000	329 @ 1600	45—75
	V8-400, 6.6L⑥	S	2150, 2 Bbl.④	4.00 × 4.00	8.0	181 @ 4000	331 @ 1600	45—75
	V8-460, 7.5L	A	4350, 4 Bbl.④	4.362 × 3.850	8.0	208 @ 4000	356 @ 2000	35—65
1978	V8-302, 5.0L	F	2150, 2 Bbl.④	4.00 × 3.00	8.1	133 @ 3600	243 @ 1600	40—60
	V8-400, 6.6L	S	2150, 2 Bbl.④	4.00 × 4.00	8.0	166 @ 3800	319 @ 1800	50—75
	V8-460, 7.5L	A	4350, 4 Bbl.④	4.362 × 3.850	8.0	210 @ 4200	357 @ 2200	35—65
1979	V8-302, 5.0L⑤	F	2150, 2 Bbl.④	4.00 × 3.00	8.4	130 @ 3600	237 @ 1600	40—65
	V8-302, 5.0L⑥	F	2150, 2 Bbl.④	4.00 × 3.00	8.4	133 @ 3600	236 @ 1400	40—65
	V8-400, 6.6L	S	2150, 2 Bbl.④	4.00 × 4.00	8.0	159 @ 3400	315 @ 1800	50—75
1980	V8-302, 5.0L	F	2150, 2 Bbl.④	4.00 × 3.00	8.4	132 @ 3600	232 @ 1400	40—60
	V8-302, 5.0L	F	⑦	4.00 × 3.00	8.4	129 @ 3600	231 @ 2000	40—60
	V8-351W, 5.8L	G	7200VV, 2 Bbl.④	4.00 × 3.50	8.3	140 @ 3400	265 @ 2000	40—60
1981	V8-302, 5.0L	F	⑦	4.00 × 3.00	8.4	130 @ 3400	230 @ 2000	40—60
1982	V6-232, 3.8L⑤	3	2150, 2 Bbl.④	3.81 × 3.39	8.8	112 @ 4000	175 @ 2600	54—59
	V6-232, 3.8L⑥	3	7200VV, 2 Bbl.④	3.81 × 3.39	8.8	118 @ 4000	186 @ 2600	54—59

Continued

GENERAL ENGINE SPECIFICATIONS—Continued

Year	Engine C.I.D./Liter①	V.I.N. CODE②	Carburetor	Bore and Stroke	Compression Ratio	Net H.P. @ R.P.M.③	Maximum Torque Ft. Lbs. @ R.P.M.	Normal Oil Pressure Pounds
	V8-302, 5.0L⑤	F	2150, 2 Bbl.④	4.00 × 3.00	8.4	—	—	40—60
	V8-302, 5.0L⑥	F	7200VV, 2 Bbl.④	4.00 × 3.00	8.4	131 @ 3400	229 @ 1200	40—60
	V8-302, 5.0L	F	⑦	4.00 × 3.00	8.4	134 @ 3400	232 @ 3200	40—60
1983	V8-302, 5.0L⑤	F	⑦	4.00 × 3.00	8.4	⑧	⑨	40—60
	V8-302, 5.0L⑥	F	⑦	4.00 × 3.00	8.4	130 @ 3200	240 @ 2000	40—60
1984	V8-302, 5.0L	F	⑦	4.00 × 3.00	8.4	—	—	40—60

①—C.I.D.—cubic inch displacement.
②—On 1977-80 vehicles the fifth digit in the VIN denotes engine code. On 1981-84 vehicles the eighth digit denotes engine code.
③—Ratings are net—as installed in vehicle.
④—Motorcraft.
⑤—Exc. Calif.
⑥—Calif.
⑦—Electronic Fuel Injection.
⑧—Single exhaust, 103 @ 3200; Dual exhaust 145 @ 3600.
⑨—Single exhaust, 240 @ 2000; Dual exhaust 245 @ 2200.

TUNE UP SPECIFICATIONS

The following specifications are published from the latest information available. This data should be used only in the absence of a decal affixed in the engine compartment.

★ When using a timing light, disconnect vacuum hose or tube at distributor and plug opening in hose or tube so idle speed will not be affected.

● When checking compression, lowest cylinder must be within 75 percent of highest.

▲ Before removing wires from distributor cap, determine location of No. 1 wire in cap, as distributor position may have been altered from that shown at the end of this chart.

Spark plug types shown in this chart are recommendations of the original vehicle manufacturer and not MOTOR.

Check local sources for other spark plug manufacturers listings.

Year & Engine/V.I.N.	Spark Plug Type	Gap	Ignition Timing BTDC①★ Firing Order Fig. ▲	Man. Trans.	Auto. Trans.	Mark Fig.	Curb Idle Speed② Man. Trans.	Auto. Trans.	Fast Idle Speed Man. Trans.	Auto. Trans.	Fuel Pump Pressure
1977											
V8-302/F Calif.	ARF-52	.050	D	—	12°	B	—	700D	—	—	6—8
V8-302/F High Alt.	ARF-52	.050	D	—	12°	B	—	500/650D	—	2000④	6—8
V8-351W/H⑤	ARF-52	.050	E	—	4°	B	—	625D	—	2100④	6—8
V8-400/S Calif.	ARF-52-6	.060	E	—	6°	B	—	500/600D	—	1350③	6—8
V8-460/A Exc. Calif. & High Alt.⑥⑦	ARF-52	.050	D	—	16°	B	—	525/650D	—	1350③	5.7—7.7
V8-460/A Exc. Calif. & High Alt.⑥⑧	ARF-52	.050	D	—	10°	B	—	⑨	—	1350③	5.7—7.7
V8-460/A High Alt.	ARF-52	.050	D	—	18°	B	—	500/600D	—	1350③	5.7—7.7
1978											
V8-302/F⑩	ARF-52	.050	⑪	—	30°⑫	B	—	625D	—	1900④	6—8
V8-400/S Exc. Calif. & High Alt.	ASF-52	.050	E	—	13°	B	—	575/650D⑬	—	1350③	6—8
V8-400/S Calif.	ASF-52	.050	E	—	16°	B	—	600/650D⑬	—	2300④	6—8
V8-400/S High Alt.	ASF-52	.050	E	—	8°	B	—	650D	—	2100④	6—8
V8-460/A Exc. Calif. & High Alt.⑥⑭	ARF-52	.050	D	—	16°	B	—	580/650D⑬	—	1350③	5.7—7.7
V8-460/A Exc. Calif. & High Alt.⑥⑮	ARF-52	.050	D	—	10°	B	—	580/650D⑬	—	1350③	5.7—7.7
1979											
V8-302/F Exc. Calif.⑩	⑯	.050	⑪	—	30°⑫	B	—	625D	—	1900④	6—8
V8-302/F Calif.⑩	⑯	.050	⑪	—	15°⑫	B	—	625D	—	2100④	6—8
V8-400/S Exc. Calif.	⑯	.050	E	—	14°	B	—	600/675D	—	2200④	6—8
V8-400/S Calif.⑥⑱	⑲	.060	E	—	14°	B	—	600/650D	—	2200④	6—8
V8-400/S Calif.⑥⑳	⑯	.050	E	—	16°	B	—	600/650D	—	2300④	6—8

Continued

TUNE UP SPECIFICATIONS—Continued

The following specifications are published from the latest information available. This
data should be used only in the absence of a decal affixed in the engine compartment.

★ When using a timing light, disconnect vacuum hose or tube at distributor and plug opening in hose or tube so idle speed will not be affected.

● When checking compression, lowest cylinder must be within 75 percent of highest.

▲ Before removing wires from distributor cap, determine location of No. 1 wire in cap, as distributor position may have been altered from that shown at the end of this chart.

Spark plug types shown in this chart are recommendations of the original vehicle manufacturer and not MOTOR.

Check local sources for other spark plug manufacturers listings.

Year & Engine/V.I.N.	Spark Plug Type	Gap	Firing Order Fig. ▲	Ignition Timing BTDC① ★ Man. Trans.	Auto. Trans.	Mark Fig.	Curb Idle Speed② Man. Trans.	Auto. Trans.	Fast Idle Speed Man. Trans.	Auto. Trans.	Fuel Pump Pressure
1980											
V8-302/F Versailles Exc. High Alt.	ASF-52	.050	⑪	—	6°	B	—	550D	—	④⑦㉒	6–8
V8-302/F Versailles Hign Alt.	ASF-52	.050	⑪	—	8°	B	—	550D	—	2100④	6–8
V8-302/F E.F.I. Exc. Versailles	ASF-52	.050	⑪	—	⑰	B	—	550D	—	2100㉓	—
V8-351W/G⑤⑩	ASF-52	.050	⑪	—	—	B	—	550/640D	—	1650㉑	6–8
1981											
V8-302/F E.F.I. Exc. Calif.	ASF-52	.050	⑪	—	⑰	B	—	550D	—	2200㉑	—
V8-302/F E.F.I. Calif.	ASF-52	.050	⑪	—	⑰	B	—	550D	—	2150㉑	—
1982											
V6-232/3 Exc. Calif.	AGSP-52	.044	A	—	12°	F	—	550/650D	—	2200④	6–8
V6-232/3 Calif.	AGSP-52	.044	A	—	12°	F	—	550/650D	—	2200③	6–8
V8-302/F Exc. Calif.	ASF-52	.050	D	—	12°	B	—	550D	—	1700③	6–8
V8-302/F High Alt.	ASF-52	.050	D	—	12°	B	—	550D	—	1700③	6–8
V8-302/F Calif.	ASF-52	.050	⑪	—	—	B	—	550D	—	—	6–8
V8-302/F E.F.I. Exc. Calif.	ASF-52	.050	⑪	—	⑰	B	—	550D	—	2200㉓	—
V8-302/F E.F.I. Calif.	ASF-52	.050	⑪	—	⑰	B	—	550D	—	2150㉓	—
1983											
V8-302/F E.F.I. Exc. Calif.	ASF-52	.050	⑪	—	⑰	B	—	550D	—	2200④	—
V8-302/F E.F.I. Calif.	ASF-52	.050	⑪	—	⑰	B	—	550D	—	2200④	—
1984											
V8-302/F E.F.I.	ASF-52	.050	⑪	—	⑰	B	—	—	—	—	—

①—B.T.D.C.—Before top dead center.
②—Idle speed on manual trans. vehicles is adjusted in Neutral & on auto. trans. equipped vehicles is adjusted in Drive unless otherwise specified. Where two idle speeds are listed, the higher speed is with the A/C or throttle solenoid energized. On models equipped with vacuum release brake, whenever adjusting ignition timing or idle speed, vacuum line to brake release mechanism must be disconnected & plugged to prevent parking brake from releasing when selector is moved to Drive.
③—On kickdown step of cam.
④—On high step of fast idle cam.
⑤—Windsor engine.
⑥—Refer to engine calibration code on engine

identification label, located at rear of left valve cover. The calibration code is located on the label after the engine code number and is preceded by the letter C and the revision code is located below the calibration code and is preceded by the letter R.
⑦—Calibration codes 7-19A-R1 & 7-19A-R17.
⑧—Calibration codes 7-19A-R2 & 7-19A-R3.
⑨—Calibration code 7-19A-R2, 525/650D RPM 7-19A-R3, 550/650D RPM.
⑩—Models equipped with Electronic Engine Control (EEC) System.
⑪—Firing order for V8-302, 1-5-4-2-6-3-7-8. Firing order for V8-351W, 1-3-7-2-6-5-4-8. Cylinder numbering (front to rear): Right bank 1-2-3-4, left bank 5-6-7-8. Refer to Fig. C for spark plug wire connections at distributor.

⑫—At 625 RPM. Ignition timing is not adjustable.
⑬—With throttle solenoid energized. Higher idle speed is with A/C on, compressor clutch de-energized, if equipped.
⑭—Calibration code 8-19A-R1.
⑮—Calibration codes 8-19B-R11 & 8-19B-R14.
⑯—ASF-52 or ARF-52.
⑰—Ignition timing is not adjustable.
⑱—Calibration code 9-17P-R0A.
⑲—ASF-52 or ARF-52-6.
⑳—Calibration code 9-17Q-R0.
㉑—On 2nd highest step of fast idle cam.
㉒—Calibration code 0-11E-R0, 2100 RPM; calibration code 0-11E-R13, 2200 RPM.
㉓—On 1st step of idle cam.

TUNE UP NOTES—Continued

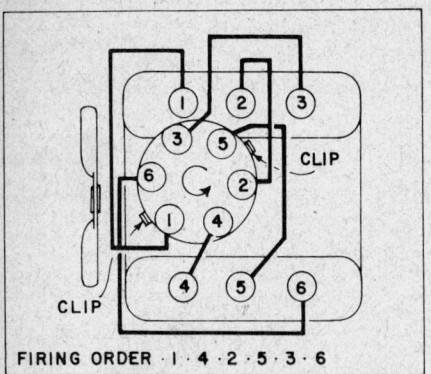

FIRING ORDER · 1·4·2·5·3·6

Fig. A

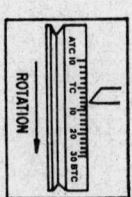

Fig. B

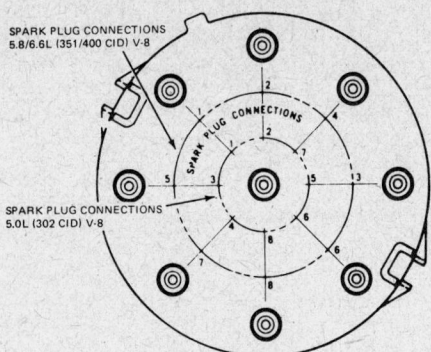

SPARK PLUG CONNECTIONS 5.8/6.6L (351/400 CID) V-8

SPARK PLUG CONNECTIONS 5.0L (302 CID) V-8

Fig. C

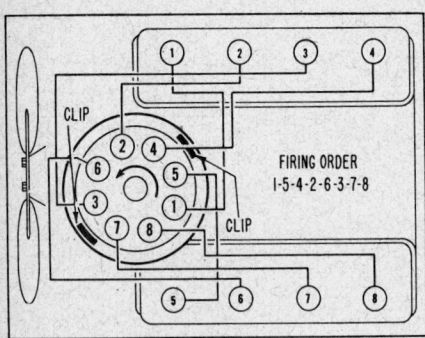

FIRING ORDER 1-5-4-2-6-3-7-8

Fig. D

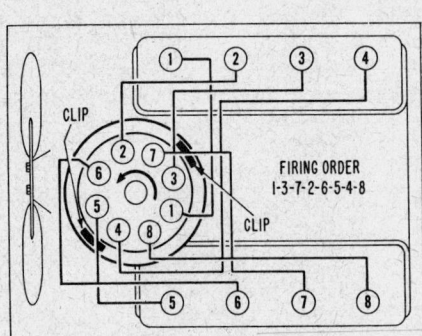

FIRING ORDER 1-3-7-2-6-5-4-8

Fig. E

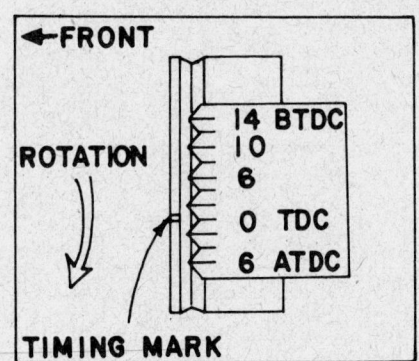

Fig. F

VALVE SPECIFICATIONS

Year	Engine Model/V.I.N.	Valve Lash ①		Valve Angles		Valve Spring Installed Height	Valve Spring Pressure Lbs. @ In.	Stem Clearance		Stem Diameter	
		Int.	Exh.	Seat	Face			Intake	Exhaust	Intake	Exhaust
1977	V8-302/F	.096–.168①		45	44	③	⑤	.0010–.0027	.0015–.0032	.3416–.3423	.3411–.3418
	V8-351W/H	.096–.168①		45	44	④	⑤	.0010–.0027	.0015–.0032	.3416–.3423	.3411–.3418
	V8-400/S	.100–.200①		45	44	1¹³⁄₁₆	226 @ 1.39	.0010–.0027	.0015–.0032	.3416–.3423	.3411–.3418
	V8-460/A	.075–.175①		45	44	1¹³⁄₁₆	②	.0010–.0027	.0010–.0027	.3416–.3423	.3416–.3423
1978–79	V8-302/F	.096–.168①		45	44	③	⑤	.0010–.0027	.0015–.0032	.3416–.3423	.3411–.3418
	V8-400/S	.125–.175①		45	44	1⁵³⁄₆₄	226 @ 1.39	.0010–.0027	.0015–.0032	.3416–.3423	.3411–.3418
	V8-460/A	.100–.150①		45	44	1¹³⁄₁₆	229 @ 1.33	.0010–.0027	.0010–.0027	.3416–.3423	.3416–.3423
1980	V8-302/F	.096–.163①		45	44	③	⑥	.001–.0027	.0015–.0032	.3416–.3423	.3411–.3418
	V8-351W/G	.096–.163①		45	44	④	⑥	.001–.0027	.0015–.0032	.3416–.3423	.3411–.3418
1981	V8-302/F	.096–.146①		45	44	③	⑥	.001–.0027	.0015–.0032	.3416–.3423	.3411–.3418
1982	V6-232/3	.088–.189①		45	44	1³⁄₄	215 @ 1.40	.001–.0027	.0015–.0032	.3416–.3423	.3411–.3418
	V8-302/F	.096–.146①		45	44	③	⑦	.001–.0027	.0015–.0032	.3416–.3423	.3411–.3418
1983	V8-302/F	.096–.146①		45	44	⑧	⑨	.001–.0027	.0015–.0032	.3416–.3423	.3411–.3418
1984	V8-302/F	.096–.146①		45	44	⑧	⑨	.001–.0027	.0015–.0032	.3416–.3423	.3411–.3418

① —Clearance is obtained at valve stem tip with hydraulic lifter collapsed. If clearance is less than minimum, install an undersize push rod; if clearance is greater than maximum, install an oversize push rod.

② —Intake, 229 @ 1.33; exhaust, 253 @ 1.33.
③ —Intake, 1¹¹⁄₁₆; exhaust, 1¹⁹⁄₃₂.
④ —Intake, 1⁵¹⁄₆₄; exhaust, 1³⁹⁄₆₄.
⑤ —Intake, 190–210 @ 1.31; exhaust, 190–210 @ 1.20.

⑥ —Intake, 204 @ 1.36; exhaust, 200 @ 1.20.
⑦ —Intake, 186–214 @ 1.36; exhaust, 195–215 @ 1.15.
⑧ —Intake, 1⁴³⁄₆₄–1⁴⁵⁄₆₄; exhaust, 1³⁷⁄₆₄–1³⁹⁄₆₄.
⑨ —Intake, 196–214 @ 1.36; exhaust, 195–215 @ 1.05.

DISTRIBUTOR SPECIFICATIONS

★ Note: If unit is checked on vehicle, double the RPM and degrees to get crankshaft figures.

Distributor Ident. No.①	Centrifugal Advance Degrees @ RPM of Distributor				Vacuum Advance		Distributor Retard
	Advance Starts	Intermediate Advance		Full Advance	Inches of Vacuum to Start Plunger	Max. Adv. Dist. Deg. @ Vacuum	Max. Retard Dist. Deg. @ Vacuum
1977							
D6AE-AA	0–2 @ 500	4–6 @ 700	7¼–9½ @ 1500	—	14 @ 2500	3	15¼ @ 11½	—
D6VE-CA	0–1 @ 450	7½–9½ @ 725	—	—	14 @ 2500	3.5	13¼ @ 15	—
D7AE-DA	0–1 @ 450	3¾–5¾ @ 675	—	—	14 @ 2500	3.2	15¼ @ 14½	—
D7DE-FA	−1 to +1½ @ 450	1¾–4½ @ 550	—	—	13¾ @ 2500	4.5	15¼ @ 12½	—
D7DE-GA	0–1 @ 525	2¼–4¼ @ 700	—	—	7¼ @ 2500	3	13½ @ 16	—
D7DE-HA	−1 to +½ @ 550	2–4 @ 750	—	—	6½ @ 2500	5	12½ @ 15	—
1978							
D7DE-AA	−1 to +½ @ 500	2¾–5 @ 1000	—	—	12½ @ 2500	3	15½ @ 16	—
D8DE-EA	0–3 @ 500	4–6½ @ 1000	—	—	12¼ @ 2500	3	13¼ @ 16	—
1979							
D9AE-YA	0–2 @ 630	2.25–4.25 @ 775	—	—	9.75–12.6 @ 2500	2	14.75–17.25 @ 25	—
D9AE-ACA	0–2 @ 725	—	—	—	7.5–10.25 @ 2500	2.4	6.9–9.25 @ 25	—
D8OE-AA	0–2.75 @ 500	6–7 @ 725	—	—	13.65–16.3 @ 2500	2	12.75–15.25 @ 25	—
D8DE-AA②	—	—	—	—	—	—	—	—
1980							
D94E-AA②	—	—	—	—	—	—	—	—
D94E-DA②	—	—	—	—	—	—	—	—
E0SE-CA	0–2 @ 635	2.8–4.6 @ 840	—	—	9.6–12.2 @ 2500	—	11.25–18.32 @ 25	—
E02E-EA	0–2.6 @ 540	3.5–5.5 @ 675	—	—	4.8–7.5 @ 2500	2.4	11.25–18.32 @ 25	—
1981							
D9AE-AA②	—	—	—	—	—	—	—	—
1982							
E2SE-BA③	—	9.5–11.5 @ 1250	—	—	—	—	—	—
E2SE-DA③	—	8.5–11 @ 1250	—	—	—	—	—	—
1983							
E3VE-AA②	—	—	—	—	—	—	—	—

①—Basic part No. 12127. ②—EEC system distributor. ③—V6-232, 3.8L engine.

REAR AXLE SPECIFICATIONS

Year	Model	Carrier Type	Ring Gear & Pinion Backlash Inch	Nominal Pinion Locating Shim, Inch	Pinion Bearing Preload				Differential Bearing Preload	Pinion Nut Torque Ft.-Lbs.
					New Bearings With Seal Inch-Lbs.	Used Bearings With Seal Inch-Lbs.	New Bearings Less Seal Inch-Lbs.	Used Bearings Less Seal Inch-Lbs.		
1977–80	All	Removable	.008–.012	④	17–27①	8–14①	—	—	②⑥	③
1980–84	All	Integral	.008–.015	.030	16–29	8–14	—	—	.016⑥	⑤

①—Bearing set with collapsible spacer; with solid spacer 13–33 inch-lbs.
②—With new bearings, 1977–80, .008–.012 inch; with used bearings, .005–.008 inch.
③—With collapsible spacer 170 ft. lbs., with solid spacer 200 ft. lbs.
④—With 8 inch ring gear, .022 inch; with 9 inch ring gear, .015 inch.
⑤—With 7.5 inch ring gear, 170 ft. lbs., with 8.5 inch ring gear 140 ft. lbs.
⑥—Case spread.

STARTING MOTOR APPLICATIONS

Year	Engine/V.I.N.	Ident. No.	Year	Engine/V.I.N.	Ident. No.
1977	V8-302/F, 351W/H	D8OF-AA	1980	V8-302/F	D8OF-AA
	V8-400/S	D5AF-EA		V8-351W/G	D8OF-AA
	V8-460/A	D6AF-AA	1981	V8-302/F	E1AF-BA
1978-79	V8-302	D8OF-AA	1982	V6-232/3	E25F-AA
	V8-400/S	D8AF-AA		V8-302/F	E1AF-BA
	V8-460/A	D8AF-AA	1983	V8-302/F	E3AF-AA
			1984	V8-302/F	—

ALTERNATOR & REGULATOR SPECIFICATIONS

Year	Ident. No.①	Current Rating②		Field Current @ 75°F.		Voltage Regulator	
		Amperes	Volts	Amperes	Volts	Ident. No. ③⑥	Voltage @ 75°F.
1977	Orange④⑨	40	15	2.9	12	D4AF-AA	13.5-15.3
	Green④⑨	60	15	2.9	12	D4AF-AA	13.5-15.3
	70 All⑤	70	15	2.9	12	D4AF-AA	13.5-15.3
	90 All⑤	90	15	2.9	12	D4TF-AA	13.5-15.3
1978	Orange④⑨	40	15	2.9	12	D4AF-AA	13.5-15.3
	Green④⑨	60	15	2.9	12	D4AF-AA	13.5-15.3
	Green④⑦⑨	60	15	4.0	12	D8BF-AA⑧	14.0-14.4
	Black④⑤	70	15	2.9	12	D4AF-AA	13.5-15.3
	Red④⑤	90	15	2.9	12	D4TF-AA	13.5-15.3
	Red④⑤⑦	90	15	4.0	12	D8BF-AA⑧	14.0-14.4
1979	Orange④⑨	40	15	4.0	12	D8BF-AA⑧	13.8-14.6
	Black④⑨	65	15	4.0	12	D8BF-AA⑧	14.0-14.4
	Green④⑨	60	15	4.0	12	D8BF-AA⑧	13.8-14.6
	Black④⑤	70	15	4.0	12	D8BF-AA⑧	14.0-14.4
	Red④⑤	100	15	4.0	12	D8BF-AA⑧	14.0-14.4
1980-81	Orange⑦⑨	40	15	4.0	12	D9BF-AB⑧	13.8-14.6
	Black⑦⑨	65	15	4.0	12	D9BF-AB⑧	13.8-14.6
	Green⑦⑨	60	15	4.0	12	D9BF-AB⑧	13.8-14.6
	Black⑤⑦	70	15	4.0	12	D9BF-AB⑧	13.8-14.6
	Red⑤⑦	100	15	4.0	12	D9BF-AB⑧	13.8-14.6
1982	Orange⑦⑨	40	15	4.0	12	E1AF-AA⑧	13.8-14.6
	Black⑦⑨	65	15	4.0	12	E1AF-AA⑧	13.8-14.6
	Green⑦⑨	60	15	4.0	12	E1AF-AA⑧	13.8-14.6
	Black⑤⑦	70	15	4.0	12	E1AF-AA⑧	13.8-14.6
	Red⑤⑦	100	15	4.0	12	E1AF-AA⑧	13.8-14.6
1983	Orange⑦⑨	40	15	4.25	12	E1ZF-FA⑧	—
	Black⑦⑨	65	15	4.25	12	E1ZF-FA⑧	—
	Green⑦⑨	60	15	4.25	12	E1ZF-FA⑧	—
	Black⑤⑦	70	15	4.25	12	E1ZF-FA⑧	—
	Red⑤⑦	100	15	4.25	12	E1ZF-ZA⑧	—
1984	Green⑦⑨	60	—	4.25	12	E4AF-AA⑧	—
	Black⑤⑦	70	—	4.25	12	E4AF-AA⑧	—
	Red⑤⑦	100	—	4.25	12	E4AF-AA⑧	—

①—Basic No. 10300.
②—Stamped on housing.
③—Stamped on cover.
④—Stamp color code.
⑤—Side terminal alternator.
⑥—Basic No. 10316.
⑦—Solid state alternator.
⑧—Electronic voltage regulator. These units are color coded black for system w/warning indicator lamp & blue for systems w/ammeter.
⑨—Rear terminal alternator.

PISTONS, PINS, RINGS, CRANKSHAFT & BEARINGS

Year	Engine/VIN	Piston Clearance	Ring End Gap①		Wristpin Diameter	Rod Bearings		Main Bearings			
			Comp.	Oil		Shaft Diameter	Bearing Clearance	Shaft Diameter	Bearing Clearance	Thrust on Bear. No.	Shaft End Play
1977–80	V8-351W④	.0018–.0026	.010	.015	.9121	2.3103–2.3111	.0008–.0015	2.9994–3.0002	.0008–.0015	3	.004–.008
1977–78	V8-460/A	.0014–.0022	.010	.015	1.040	2.4992–2.500	.0008–.0015	2.9994–3.0002	.0008–.0015	3	.004–.008
1977–81	V8-302/F	.0018–.0026	.010	.015	.9121	2.1228–2.1236	.0008–.0015	2.2482–2.2490	③	3	.004–.008
1977–79	V8-400/S	.0014–.0022	.010	.015	.9751	2.3103–2.3111	.0008–.0015	2.9994–3.0002	.0008–.0015	3	.004–.008
1982	V6-232/3	.0014–.0022	.010	.015	.9121	2.3103–2.3111	.001–.0014	2.5198–2.5190	.001–.0014	3	.004–.008
1982–83	V8-302/F	.0018–.0026	.010	.015	.9121	2.1228–2.1236	.0008–.0015	2.2482–2.2490	②	3	.004–.008
1984	V8-302/F	.0018–.0026	.010	.015	.9121	2.1228–2.1236	.0008–.0015	2.2482–2.2490	②	3	⑤

①—Fit rings in tapered bores for clearance listed in tightest portion of ring travel.
②—#1 .0004–.0025; others, .0004–.0015.
③—#1 .0001–.0015; others, .0005–.0015.
④—1977–79, H; 1980, G.
⑤—.012 Maximum.

ENGINE TIGHTENING SPECIFICATIONS★

★ Torque specifications are for clean and lightly lubricated threads only. Dry or dirty threads produce increased friction which prevents accurate measurement of tightness.

Year	Engine/V.I.N.	Spark Plugs Ft. Lbs.	Cylinder Head Bolts Ft. Lbs.	Intake Manifold Ft. Lbs.	Exhaust Manifold Ft. Lbs.	Rocker Arm Shaft Bracket Ft. Lbs.	Rocker Arm Cover Ft. Lbs.	Connecting Rod Cap Bolts Ft. Lbs.	Main Bearing Cap Bolts Ft. Lbs.	Flywheel to Crankshaft Ft. Lbs.	Vibration Damper or Pulley Ft. Lbs.
1977–78	V8-460/A	10–15	130–140	22–32	28–33	18–25①	5–6	40–45	95–105	75–85	70–90
1977–80	V8-351W⑧	10–15	105–112	23–25	18–24	③	3–5	40–45	95–105	75–85	70–90
	V8-400/S	10–15	95–105	②	18–24	18–25①	3–5	40–45	95–105	75–85	70–90
1977–84	V8-302/F	10–15	⑨	23–25	18–24	③	3–5	19–24	60–70	75–85	70–90
1982	V6-232/3	17–23	④	⑤	15–22	⑥	⑦	31–36	65–81	54–64	93–121

①—Rocker arm fulcrum bolt to cyl. head; or rocker arm stud nut.
②—5/16″ bolts, 19–25 ft. lbs.; 3/8″ bolts, 22–32 ft. lbs.
③—1977 & Early 1978 rocker arm stud nut, 17–23 ft. lbs.; Late 1978 & 1979–84, rocker arm fulcrum bolt to cylinder head, 18–25 ft. lbs.
④—Tighten bolts in 4 steps; #1, 47 ft. lbs.; #2, 55 ft. lbs.; #3, 63 ft. lbs.; #4, 74 ft. lbs.; then back off all bolts 2–3 turns and repeat sequence.
⑤—Tighten bolts in three steps; #1, 5.1 ft. lbs.; #2, 10.3 ft. lbs.; #3, 18.4 ft. lbs.
⑥—Rocker arm fulcrum bolt to cylinder head, tighten bolts in two steps; #1, 5.1–11.0 ft. lbs.; #2, 18.4–25.8 ft. lbs.
⑦—36–61 in. lbs.
⑧—1977–79, H; 1980, G.
⑨—Tighten bolts in two steps; #1, 55–65 ft. lbs.; #2, 65–72 ft. lbs.

COOLING SYSTEM & CAPACITY DATA

Year	Model or Engine	Cooling Capacity, Qts.		Radiator Cap Relief Pressure, Lbs.	Thermo. Opening Temp.	Fuel Tank Gals.	Engine Oil Refill Qts.①	Transmission Oil			Rear Axle Oil Pints
		Less A/C	With A/C					3 Speed Pints	4 Speed Pints	Auto. Trans. Qts.②	
1977	Lincoln	⑥	⑥	16	191	24.2⑦	4	—	—	⑤	5
	Mark V	⑨	⑨	16	191	24.2⑦	4	—	—	⑤	5
	Versailles	⑧	⑧	16	191	19.2	4	—	—	10	5
1978	Lincoln	⑩	⑩	16	191	24.2	4	—	—	12½	5
	Mark V	③	③	16	191	25	4	—	—	12½	5
	Versailles	14.3	14.3	16	191	19.2	4	—	—	10¼	5
1979	Lincoln	—	16.9	16	196	24.2	4	—	—	11.8	5
	Mark V	—	16.9	16	196	25	4	—	—	11.8	5
	Versailles	—	14.3	16	196	19.2	4	—	—	10	5
1980	Lincoln	—	13.4	16	196	18⑫	4⑪	—	—	12	⑬
	Mark VI	—	13.4	16	196	18⑫	4⑪	—	—	12	⑬
	Versailles	—	13.4	16	196	19.2	4	—	—	9.6	5
1981	Lincoln & Mark VI	—	13.4	16	195	18	4	—	—	12	4

Continued

COOLING SYSTEM & CAPACITY DATA—Continued

Year	Model or Engine	Cooling Capacity, Qts.		Radiator Cap Relief Pressure, Lbs.	Thermo. Opening Temp.	Fuel Tank Gals.	Engine Oil Refill Qts. ①	Transmission Oil			Rear Axle Oil Pints
		Less A/C	With A/C					3 Speed Pints	4 Speed Pints	Auto. Trans. Qts. ②	
1982–83	Town Car	—	13.4	16	195	18	4⑪	—	—	12.0	3¾
	Mark VI	—	13.4	16	195	18	4⑪	—	—	12.0	3¾
	Continental	—	④	16	195	⑭	4⑮	—	—	12.0	3.25
1984	Town Car	—	13.4	16	195	18	4⑪	—	—	12	4
	Mark VII	—	13.4	16	195	22.3	4⑪	—	—	12	3.5
	Continental	—	13.4	16	195	22.3	4⑪	—	—	12	3.5

①—Add one quart with filter change.
②—Approximate. Make final check with dipstick.
③—V8-400, 16.9 qts.; V8-460, 18.9 qts.
④—V8-302, 13.4 qts.; V6-232, 11.1 qts.
⑤—FMX, 11 qts.; C6, 12.2 qts.
⑥—V8-400, 17.1 qts.; V8-460, 18.5 qts.
⑦—Calif. V8-400, 20.0 gal.
⑧—V8-302, 14.6 qts.; V8-351, 15.7 qts.
⑨—V8-400, 17.5 qts.; V8-460, 19.4 qts.
⑩—V8-400, 16.9 qts.; V8-460, 18.7 qts.
⑪—Dual sump oil pan. When draining oil, it is necessary to remove both drain plugs. One drain plug is located at front of oil pan. The second drain plug is located on left side of oil pan.
⑫—V8-351W, 20 gal.
⑬—7.5 inch axle, 3.5 pts; 8.5 inch axle, 4 pts.
⑭—V8-302, 22.6 gals.; V6-232, 20 gals.
⑮—For V8-302 engines, refer to note ⑪.

WHEEL ALIGNMENT SPECIFICATIONS

Year	Model	Caster Angle, Degrees		Camber Angle, Degrees				Toe In. Inch	Toe Out on Turns, Deg. ①	
		Limits	Desired	Limits		Desired			Outer Wheel	Inner Wheel
				Left	Right	Left	Right			
1977	Versailles	−1¼ to +¼	−½	−½ to +1	−½ to +1	+¼	+¼	⅛	②	20
	Lincoln	+1¼ to +2¾	+2	−¼ to +1¼	−½ to +1	+½	+¼	⅛	18.16	20
	Mark V	+1¼ to +2¾	+2	−¼ to +1¼	−½ to +1	+½	+¼	3/16	18.09	20
1978–79	Lincoln	+1¼ to +2¾	+2	−¼ to +1¼	−½ to +1	+½	+¼	⅛	18.16	20
	Mark V	+3¼ to +4¾	+4	−¼ to +1¼	−½ to +1	+½	+¼	3/16	18.09	20
	Versailles	−1¼ to +¼	−½	−½ to +1	−½ to +1	+¼	+¼	⅛	②	20
1980	Versailles	−1¼ to +¼	−½	−½ to +1	−½ to +1	+¼	+¼	⅛	②	20
1980–81	Lincoln	+2¼ to +3¾	+3	−¼ to +1¼	−¼ to +1¼	+½	+½	1/16	18.51	20
	Mark VI	+2¼ to +3¾	+3	−¼ to +1¼	−¼ to +1¼	+½	+½	1/16	18.51	20
1982	Town Car	+2¼ to +3¾	+3	−¼ to +1¼	−¼ to +1¼	+½	+½	1/16	18.51	20
	Mark VI	+2¼ to +3¾	+3	−¼ to +1¼	−¼ to +1¼	+½	+½	1/16	18.51	20
	Continental	+⅛ to +1⅞	+1	−½ to +1¼	−½ to +1¼	+⅜	+⅜	3/16	19.13	20
1983	Town Car	+2¼ to +4	+3	−¼ to +1¼	−¼ to +1¼	+½	+½	1/16	18.51	20
	Mark VI	+2¼ to +4	+3	−¼ to +1¼	−¼ to +1¼	+½	+½	1/16	18.51	20
	Continental	+⅜ to +2⅛	+1¼	−½ to +1¼	−½ to +1¼	+⅜	+⅜	⅛	19.13	20
1984	Town Car	+2½ to +4	+3	−¼ to +1¼	−¼ to +1¼	+½	+½	1/16	—	—
	Mark VII③	+7/10 to +2½	+1¾	−¾ to +¾	−¾ to +¾	0	0	⅛	—	—
	Continental③	+7/10 to +2½	+1¾	−¾ to +¾	−¾ to +¾	0	0	⅛	—	—

①—Incorrect toe-out, when other adjustments are correct, indicates bent steering arms.
②—With power steering; 18.20 & Without 18.43.
③—Set ride height before performing alignment check.

Electrical Section

STARTER, REPLACE

1977–80 Versailles

1. Disconnect battery ground cable, then raise vehicle on a hoist.
2. Disconnect starter cable at starter terminal.
3. Remove through bolt and nut attaching motor mount insulator to mounting bracket.
4. Using a suitable jack raise engine.
5. Remove starter mounting bolts, then remove starter.
6. Reverse procedure to install.

1979–84 Except Versailles

1. Disconnect battery ground cable, then raise and support vehicle.
2. Disconnect starter cable at starter terminal, then remove starter mounting bolts.
3. Remove starter. On some models, it may be necessary to turn wheels to the left or right to gain clearance for removal.
4. Reverse procedure to install. Torque starter cable to starter motor bolt to 70–110 inch lbs.

1977–78 Except Versailles

1. Disconnect battery ground cable and support vehicle on hoist.
2. Disconnect cable and wires from solenoid.
3. On Mark V models, loosen the two front brace retaining bolts, then remove all other brace retaining bolts and allow brace to hang.
4. Turn wheels fully to the right and remove the two bolts attaching the steering idler arm to the frame.
5. Remove starter attaching bolts and remove starter.
6. Reverse procedure to install.

IGNITION LOCK, REPLACE

1980–84 Except Versailles

1. Disconnect battery ground cable.
2. On models with tilt wheel, remove upper column extension shroud by unsnapping from retaining clip at 9 o'clock position.
3. Remove steering column trim shroud.
4. Disconnect key warning switch electrical connector.
5. Turn ignition lock to "On" position.
6. Using a 1/8" pin or punch located in the 4 o'clock hole and 1¼ inch from outer edge of lock cylinder housing, depress retaining pin while pulling the lock cylinder from housing.
7. Turn lock cylinder to "On" position and insert cylinder into housing. Ensure that the lock cylinder is fully seated and aligned into the interlocking washer before turning key to "Off" position. This will permit the retaining pin to extend into the lock cylinder housing hole.
8. Rotate key to check for proper mechanical operation.
9. Connect key warning switch electrical connector.
10. Connect battery ground cable.
11. Check for proper operation.

1977–79 All & 1980 Versailles

1. Disconnect the battery ground cable.
2. **Units With Fixed Steering Columns:** Remove the steering wheel trim pad and steering wheel. Insert a wire pin in the hole located inside the column halfway down the lock cylinder housing, Fig. 1.
Units With Tilt Steering Columns: Insert wire pin in the hole located on the outside of the flange casting next to the emergency flasher button, Fig. 1.
3. Place the gear shift lever in *Park* position, and turn the lock cylinder with the ignition key to the *Run* position.
4. Depress the wire pin while pulling up on the lock cylinder to remove. Remove the wire pin.
5. To install insert the lock cylinder into the housing in the flange casting, and turn the key to the *Off* position. Be certain that the cylinder is fully inserted before turning to the *Off* position. This action will extend the cylinder retaining pin into the cylinder housing.
6. Turn the key to check for correct operation in all positions.
7. Install the steering wheel and trim pad on fixed column units.
8. Connect the battery ground cable.

IGNITION SWITCH, REPLACE

1982–84

1. Disconnect battery ground cable.
2. For tilt wheel only, remove upper column extension shroud by unsnapping from retaining clip at 9 o'clock position.
3. Remove steering column trim shrouds.
4. Disconnect ignition switch electrical connector. Turn the lock cylinder to the "On" position.
5. With a 1/8 inch drill, drill out the switch retaining bolt heads. Then, remove the bolts with an "Easy Out" or equivalent.
6. Disengage ignition switch from actuator and remove from vehicle, Fig. 2.
7. Adjust ignition switch by sliding the carrier to the switch "On" position.

NOTE: A replacement ignition switch will be pre-set in the "On" position.

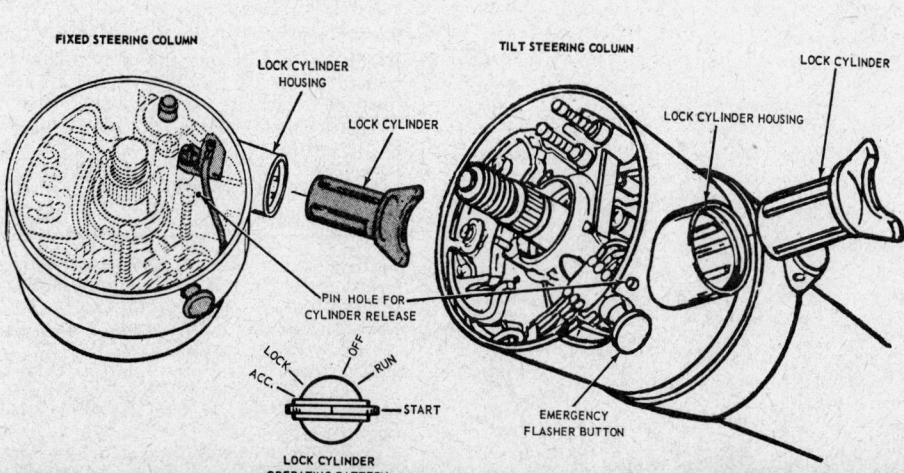

Fig. 1 Ignition lock cylinder. All 1977–79 models & 1980 Versailles

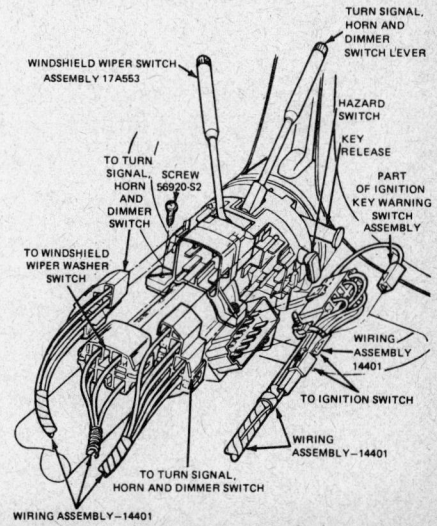

Fig. 2 Ignition switch installation. 1980–81 Continental & Mark VI & All 1982–84 models

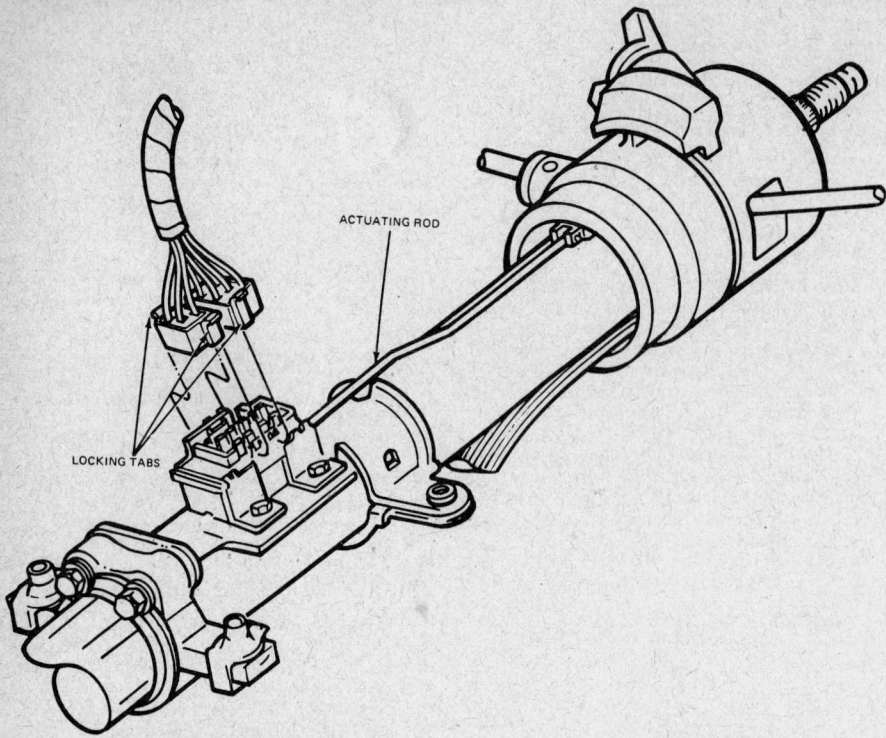

ACTUATING ROD

LOCKING TABS

Fig. 3   Ignition switch installation. 1977–79 Mark V & 1977–80 Versailles

8. Ensure the lock cylinder is in approximately the "On" position and install the ignition switch onto the actuator pin.
9. Install switch break-off head mounting bolts and tighten until heads shear.

10. Reconnect switch electrical connector and battery ground cable. Check the ignition switch for proper operation in all switch positions. Be sure the column is locked in the lock position.

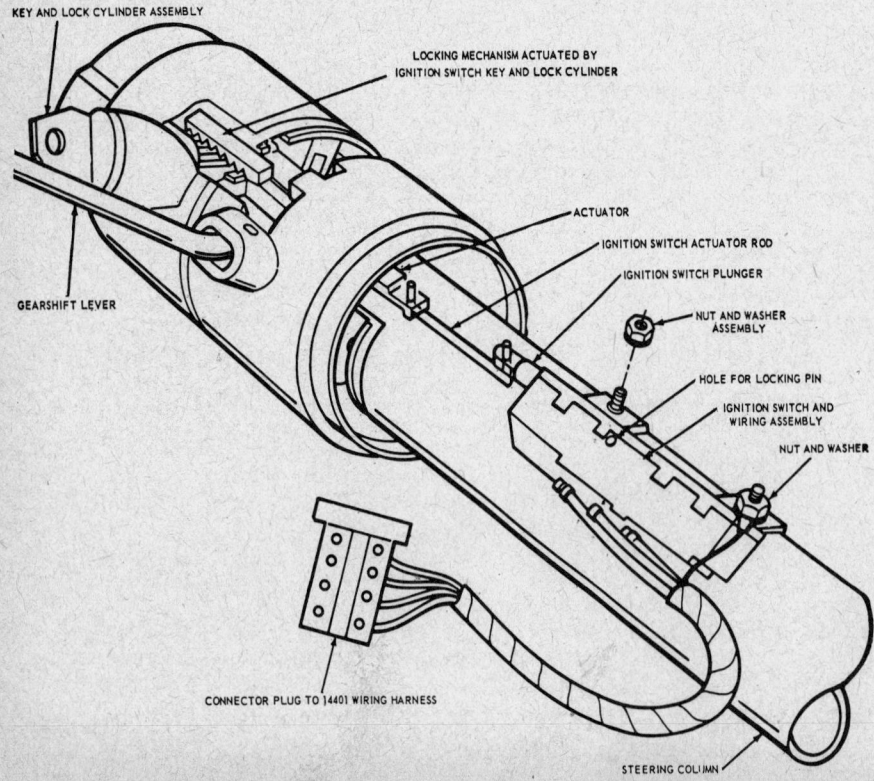

KEY AND LOCK CYLINDER ASSEMBLY

LOCKING MECHANISM ACTUATED BY IGNITION SWITCH KEY AND LOCK CYLINDER

ACTUATOR

IGNITION SWITCH ACTUATOR ROD

IGNITION SWITCH PLUNGER

NUT AND WASHER ASSEMBLY

HOLE FOR LOCKING PIN

IGNITION SWITCH AND WIRING ASSEMBLY

NUT AND WASHER

GEARSHIFT LEVER

CONNECTOR PLUG TO 14401 WIRING HARNESS

STEERING COLUMN

Fig. 4   Ignition switch installation. 1977–79 Continental

11. Reinstall shrouds.

1980–81 Continental & Mark VI

1. Disconnect battery ground cable.
2. Remove upper column shroud.
3. Disconnect ignition switch electrical connector.
4. With a ⅛ inch diameter twist drill, drill out the switch retaining bolt heads. Then, remove the bolts with a "Easy Out" or equivalent.
5. Disengage ignition switch from actuator and remove from vehicle, Fig. 2.
6. Adjust ignition switch by sliding the carrier to the switch "Lock" position. Insert a .050 inch drill or equivalent through the switch housing and into the carrier to prevent movement.

NOTE: A replacement ignition switch includes an installed adjusting pin.

7. Rotate ignition key to "Lock" positon.
8. Install ignition switch on actuator pin.
9. Install switch break-off head mounting bolts and tighten until the bolt heads shear.
10. Remove adjusting pin or drill.
11. Connect ignition switch electrical connector.
12. Connect battery ground cable and check for proper operation.
13. Install column shroud.

1977–79 Mark V & 1977–80 Versailles

1. Disconnect battery ground cable.
2. On 1977–79 Mark V, remove instrument cluster as described under "Instrument Cluster, Replace".
3. Remove steering column shroud, then detach and lower steering column from brake support bracket.
4. Disconnect switch wiring, then remove two nuts retaining switch to steering column, Fig. 3.
5. Lift switch vertically upward to disengage actuator rod, then remove switch.
6. When installing ignition switch, both locking mechanism at top of column and ignition switch must be in Lock position for correct adjustment. To hold mechanical parts in column in Lock position, move shift lever to Park, then turn key to Lock position and remove key.

NOTE: New replacement switches are pinned in Lock position by a metal pin inserted in locking hole located on side of switch. For existing switch, move switch carrier using a .010 in. diameter rod to lock detent. Insert a ⁵⁄₆₄ in. drill bit into lock hole on side of switch to hold switch in Lock position.

7. Connect switch plunger to actuator rod.
8. Position switch on column and install retaining nuts, but do not tighten.
9. Move switch up and down along column to locate mid-position of rod lash, then tighten switch retaining nuts.
10. Remove locking pin, then connect battery ground cable and check switch for proper operation.
11. Attaching steering column to brake support and install steering column shroud.
12. On 1977–79 Mark V models, install instrument cluster.

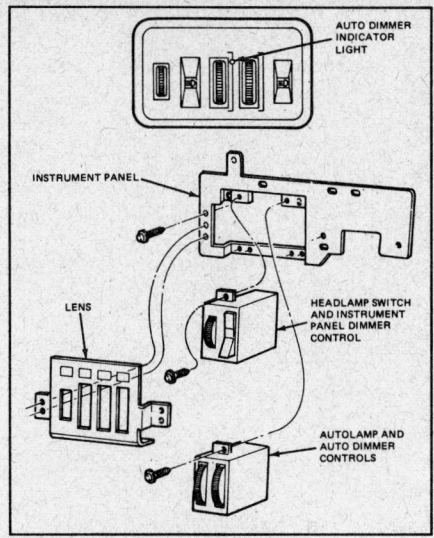

Fig. 4A   Light switch replacement. 1984 Continental & Mark VII

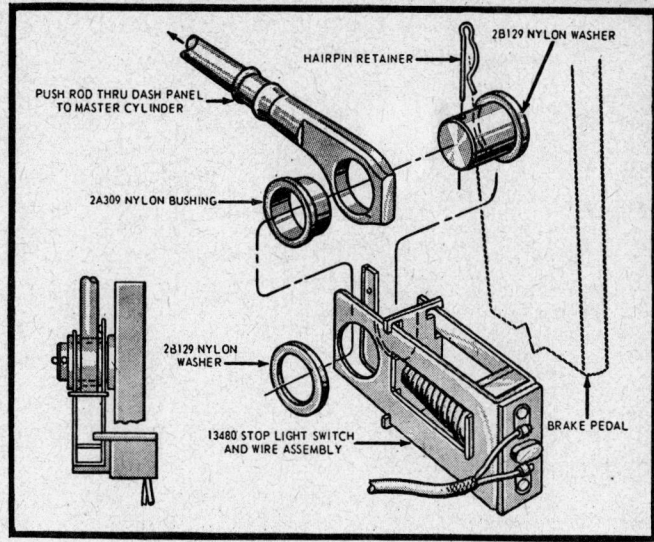

Fig. 6   Stop light switch 1977–84

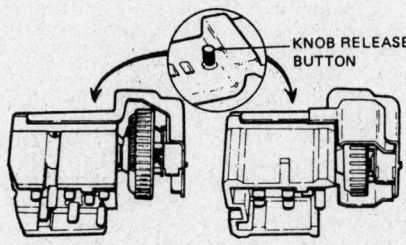

Fig. 5   Light switch. 1977–84 (typical). Exc. 1984 Continental & Mark VII

1977–79 Continental

1. Disconnect battery ground cable.
2. On 1978–79 models, remove instrument cluster as described under Instrument Cluster, Replace.
3. On all models remove shrouding from steering column and detach and lower steering column from brake support bracket.
4. Disconnect switch wiring at multiple plug, Fig. 4.
5. Remove two nuts that retain switch to column.
6. Detach switch plunger from actuator rod and remove the switch.
7. Move shift lever to Park position. Place ignition key in Lock position and remove the key.

NOTE: New replacement switches are pinned in the Lock position by a plastic shipping pin inserted in a locking hole in the switch. For an existing switch, pull plunger out as far as it will go then back one detent to Lock position and insert a 3/32" drill in locking hole to retain switch in Lock position.

8. With locking pin in place, install switch on steering column, determine mid position of actuator lash and tighten retaining bolts.
9. Remove locking pin.
10. Attach steering column to brake support and install shrouding.
11. On 1978–79 models, install instrument cluster.

LIGHT SWITCH, REPLACE

1984 Continental & Mark VII

1. Remove lens assembly attaching screws and the lens assembly.
2. Remove switch assembly attaching screws, then pull switch out from instrument panel, Fig. 4A.
3. Disconnect switch electrical connector and remove switch.
4. Reverse procedure to install.

1982–83 Continental

1. Disconnect battery ground cable.
2. Remove steering column trim shrouds.
3. Unsnap the instrument panel cluster lower moulding to expose five screws along bottom of cluster lens and remove.
4. Remove the left hand lower pad retaining screws and carefully tilt the pad out from under the cluster lens.
5. Disconnect the headlamp switch wiring connectors.
6. Insert a hooked tool into headlight switch knob slot and remove spring tension on knob, then pull off.
7. Remove switch retaining nut and lens.
8. Remove second nut and screw retaining the switch to lower pad and remove.
9. Reverse procedure to install.

1982–83 Mark VI & 1982–84 Town Car

1. Disconnect battery ground cable.
2. Insert a hooked tool into headlight switch knob slot and remove spring tension on knob, then pull off.
3. Remove steering column lower shroud and lower left hand instrument panel trim bezel.
4. Remove five headlight switch mounting bracket retaining screws.
5. Carefully pull switch and bracket from instrument panel and disconnect switch wiring.
6. On Mark VI models, mark and remove vacuum hoses from switch distributor valve.
7. Remove locknut and screw retaining switch to switch bracket.
8. Reverse procedure to install.

1980–81 Continental & Mark VI

1. Disconnect battery ground cable.
2. From instrument panel, depress light switch knob and shaft retainer button on side of switch and, while holding button in, pull knob and shaft assembly from switch, Fig. 5.
3. Unscrew trim bezel and remove lock nut.
4. From under instrument panel, pull switch from panel while tilting downward, disconnect electrical connector and remove switch.
5. Reverse procedure to install.

1977 Mark IV & 1977–79 Mark V

1. Disconnect battery ground cable.
2. Remove instrument cluster trim panel.
3. Remove the headlight switch mounting plate.
4. Remove bezel nut and disconnect multiple connector.
5. Remove vacuum lines, if so equipped.
6. Remove the switch.
7. Reverse procedure to install.

1977–79 Continental & 1977–80 Versailles

1. Disconnect battery ground cable.
2. Remove control knob and shaft by pressing knob release button and pulling it out of switch housing, Fig. 5.
3. Remove bezel nut and lower switch assembly.
4. Disconnect multiple plug and vacuum hoses at switch body and remove switch.
5. Reverse procedure to install.

STOP LIGHT SWITCH, REPLACE

1977–84

1. Disconnect wires at switch connector.
2. Remove hairpin retainer, slide switch, push rod and nylon washers and bushing away from brake pedal, and remove switch, Fig. 6.

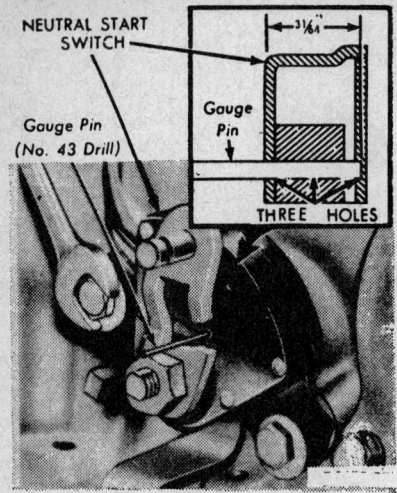

Fig. 7   Neutral safety switch. 1977—80
Versailles

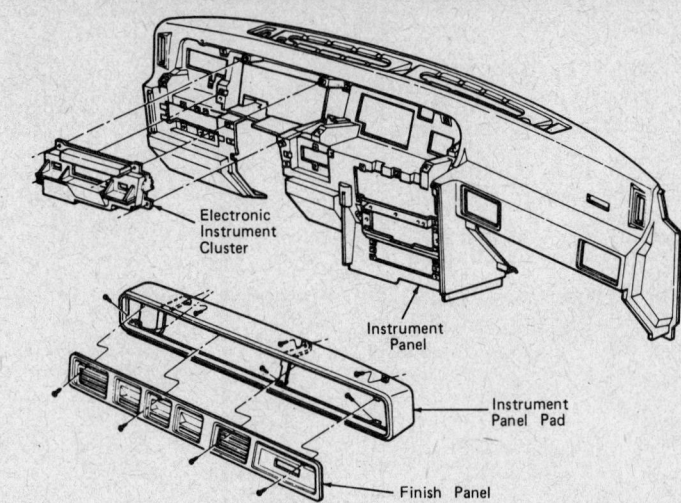

Fig. 7A   Electronic instrument cluster. 1984 Mark VII

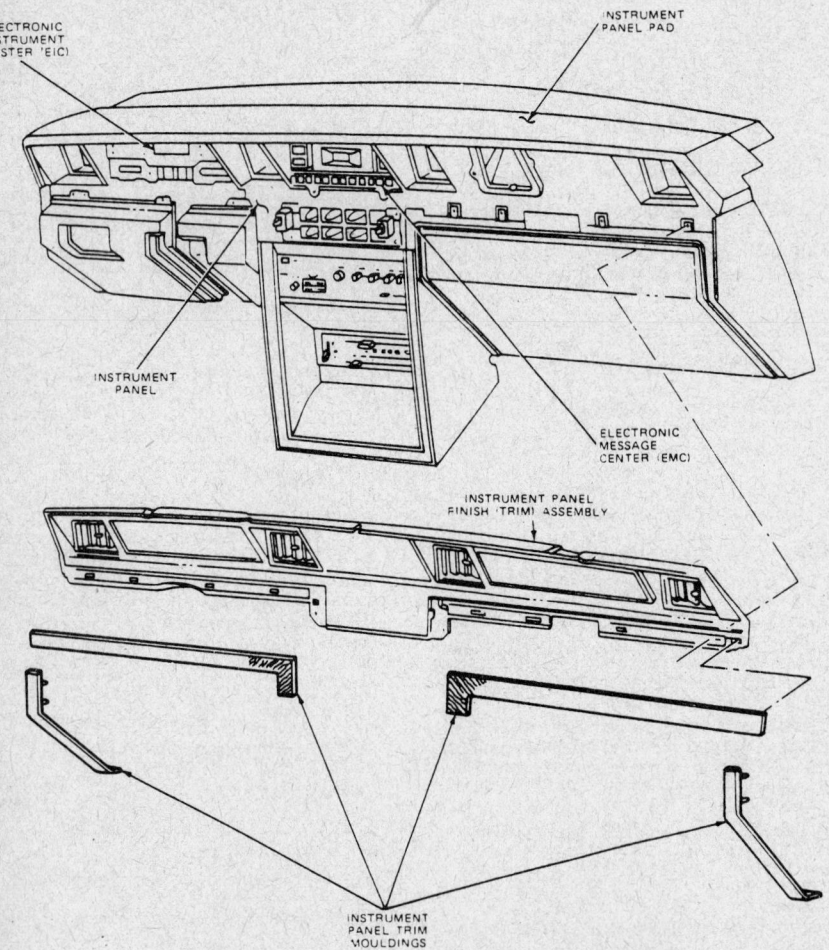

Fig. 7B   Electronic instrument panel. 1982—84 Continental

NOTE: On 1977—80 Versailles models, loosen brake booster nuts at pedal support approximately ¼ inch so booster is free to move to eliminate binding during switch removal.

3. Reverse above procedure to install.

NEUTRAL SAFETY SWITCH, REPLACE

1980—84 Continental & 1984 Mark VII With AOD Transmission

1. Disconnect battery ground cable.

2. Position transmission selector lever in "Lo" position.
3. Raise and support vehicle, then working from underneath vehicle, disconnect electrical harness from switch by lifting harness straight up off switch.
4. Using tool T74P-77247-A or equivalent, remove neutral start switch and O-ring seal by positioning tool over the extension housing area to gain access to switch.
5. Reverse procedure to install. Torque switch to 7—10 ft. lbs. using tool mentioned above.

1980—84 Town Car & 1980—83 Mark VI With AOD Transmission

1. Disconnect battery ground cable, then remove air cleaner assembly.
2. Position transmission selector lever in "Lo."
3. Disconnect electrical harness from switch by lifting harness straight up off switch.
4. Using tool T74P-77247-A or equivalent, remove neutral start switch and O-ring seal through access path at left side of dash panel.
5. Reverse procedure to install. Torque switch to 7—10 ft. lbs. using tool mentioned above.

1977—80 Versailles W/Floor Shift

Transmission Mounted Switch, Fig. 7
1. Remove downshift linkage rod from transmission downshift lever.
2. Apply penetrating oil to downshift lever shaft and nut; then remove downshift outer lever.
3. Remove switch attaching bolts.
4. Disconnect multiple wire connector and remove switch from transmission.
5. Install new switch.
6. With transmission manual lever in neutral, rotate switch and install gauge pin (#43 drill) into gauge pin holes.
7. Tighten switch attaching bolts and remove gauge pin.
8. Complete the installation in reverse order of removal.

1977—79 Except Versailles W/Floor Shift

The neutral safety switch has been elimi-

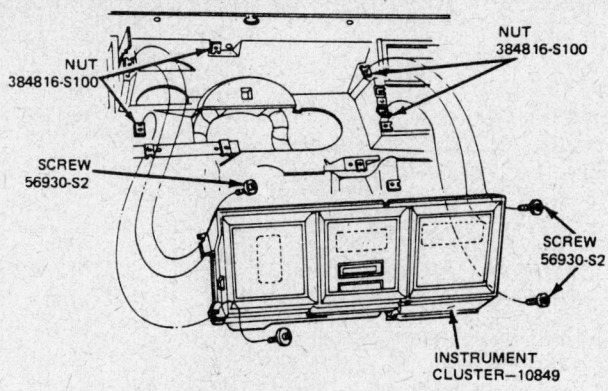

Fig. 7C Electronic instrument cluster. 1980–81 Continental & Mark VI, 1982–83 Mark VI & 1982–84 Town Car

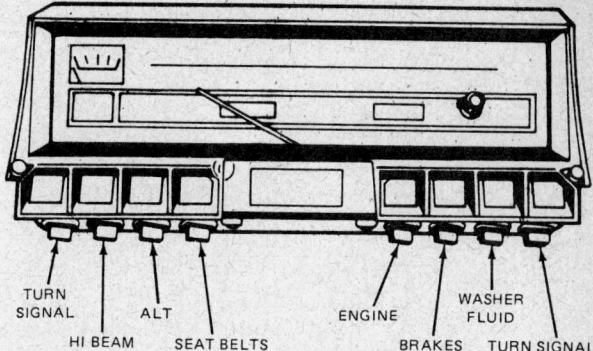

Fig. 8 Instrument cluster. 1978–79 Continental

nated and is replaced by a series of steps designed into the steering column selector lever hub casting.

TURN SIGNAL SWITCH, REPLACE

1980–84 All

1. Disconnect battery ground cable.
2. On models with tilt wheels, remove upper column extension shroud by unsnapping from retaining clip at 9 o'clock position.
3. Remove steering column cover attaching screws and the cover.
4. Carefully lift wiring connector plug retainer tabs and disconnect the plugs from switch.
5. Remove switch retaining screws and lift up switch assembly.
6. Reverse procedure to install.

1977–79

1. Remove retaining screw from underside of steering wheel spoke and lift off the pad horn switch/trim cover and medallion as an assembly.
2. Disconnect horn switch wires from terminals.
3. Remove steering wheel retaining nut and remove steering wheel using suitable puller.
4. Remove turn signal switch lever by unscrewing it from steering column.
5. Remove shroud from under steering column.
6. Disconnect steering column wiring connector plugs and remove the screws that secure switch assembly to the column.
7. On vehicles with tilt column, remove wires and terminals from steering column wiring connector plug.

NOTE: *Record the color code and location of each wire before removing it from connector. A hole provided in the flange on fixed columns makes it unnecessary to separate the wires from the connector plug. The plug with wires installed can be guided through the hole.*

8. Remove the plastic cover sleeve from the wiring harness and remove the switch and wires from the top of the column.

NOTE: *On models with speed control, transfer the ground brush located in the*

turn signal switch cancelling cam to the new switch assembly.

9. Reverse procedure to install.

HORN SOUNDER & STEERING WHEEL, REPLACE

1980–84 Except Versailles

Refer to "TURN SIGNAL SWITCH, REPLACE" for horn switch replacement.

1. Working from behind steering wheel, remove steering wheel hub cover by pushing retaining posts outward with a suitable drift.
2. Remove steering wheel to shaft retaining nut. Discard nut.
3. If no marks are present, scribe alignment marks on steering wheel and shaft to aid in installation.
4. Using a suitable puller, remove steering wheel from shaft.
5. Reverse procedure to install. Torque new retaining nut to 30–40 ft. lbs.

NOTE: On vehicles equipped with speed control, check slip ring for damage and slip ring grease for contamination before installing steering wheel.

1977–79 All & 1980 Versailles

1. Disconnect battery ground cable.
2. Remove screws from behind wheel spoke holding crash pad to wheel. Lift pad and disconnect horn wires. Disconnect speed control wires if used and remove pad.
3. Remove steering wheel nut. Install a suitable puller and remove steering wheel.
4. Reverse procedure to install.

INSTRUMENT CLUSTER, REPLACE

1984 Mark VII

1. Remove the four finish panel retaining screws, then rotate top of panel towards steering wheel and remove from vehicle, Fig. 7A.
2. Remove the six instrument panel pad retaining screws, then rotate pad toward steering wheel and remove from vehicle.
3. Remove the four instrument cluster to instrument panel retaining screws, then

pull cluster away from instrument panel.

4. Disconnect cluster electrical connector and remove cluster.
5. Reverse procedure to install.

1982–84 Continental

1. Disconnect battery ground cable.
2. Remove steering column shroud.
3. Snap off instrument panel mouldings.
4. Remove seventeen instrument panel assembly to instrument panel and instrument panel pad retaining screws, then remove trim assembly, Fig. 7B.
5. Disconnect PRND3L cable from steering column.
6. Remove four cluster retaining screws from instrument panel and move cluster away from instrument panel.
7. Disconnect wiring harness connector and remove cluster.
8. Reverse procedure to install.

1980–81 Continental & Mark VI; 1982–83 Mark VI & 1982–84 Town Car

Less Electronic Cluster
1. Disconnect battery ground cable.
2. Disconnect speedometer cable, then remove trim cover screws and remove trim cover.
3. Remove lower steering column cover screws and remove cover.
4. Remove PRND21 bracket retaining screw, then disconnect cable loop and bracket pin from steering column. Also remove the column bracket from column.
5. Remove cluster retaining screws, then disconnect electrical feed plug from connector and remove cluster.

With Electronic Cluster
1. Disconnect battery ground cable.
2. Remove steering column cover, lower instrument panel trim cover, keyboard trim panel and panel on left of column.
3. Remove the ten instrument cluster trim cover retaining screws, then remove trim cover.
4. Remove the four screws retaining instrument cluster to instrument panel and pull cluster forward. Disconnect both electrical plugs and ground wire from their receptacles, then disconnect speedometer cable by pressing on flat surface of plastic connector.
5. Remove PRND31 cable bracket retaining screw, then disconnect cable loop and bracket pin from steering column.
6. Remove plastic clamp from around steering column, then remove cluster, Fig. 7C.

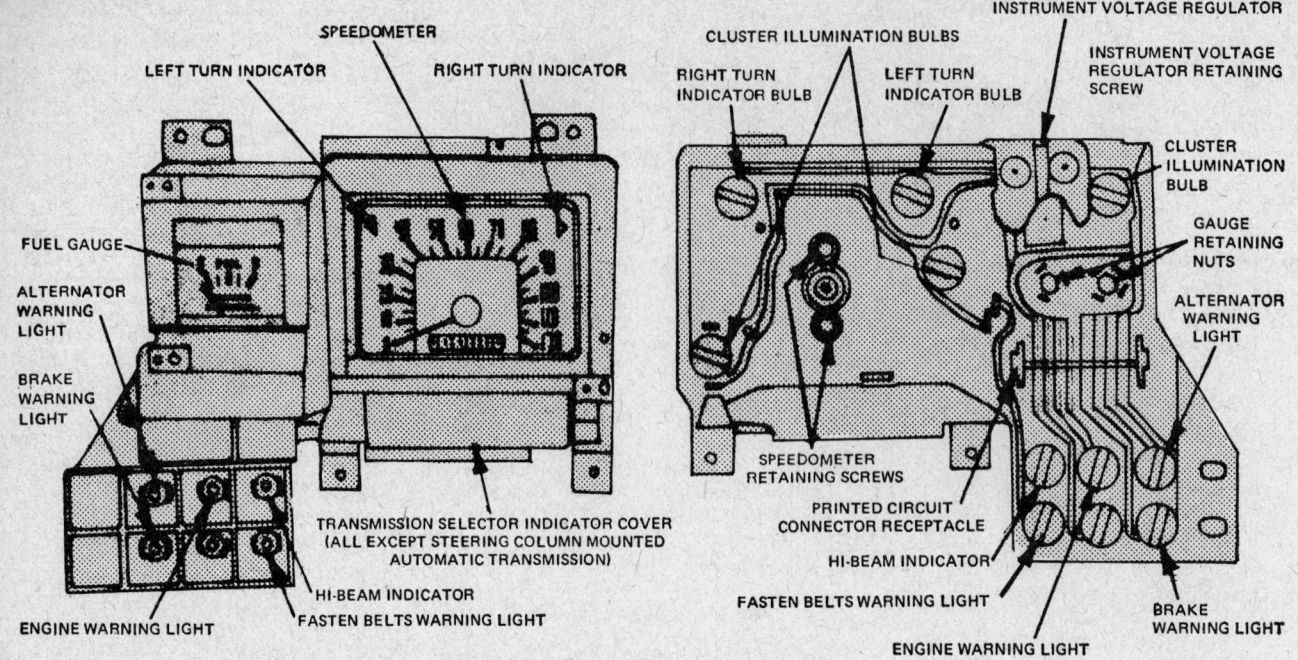

Fig. 9 Instrument cluster. 1977–80 Versailles

7. Reverse procedure to install.

1978–79 Continental

1. Disconnect battery ground cable.
2. Remove two steering column lower cover screws and remove lower cover.
3. Remove two instrument cluster trim cover attaching screws and remove trim cover.
4. Disconnect the cluster feed plug from behind the cluster.
5. Disconnect the speedometer cable. Unsnap and remove the steering column shroud cover. Unhook the shift indicator cable from the tab in the shroud retainer.
6. Remove screw attaching shift indicator cable bracket to the steering column. Disconnect cable loop from the pin on the steering column.
7. Remove the four cluster attaching screws and remove cluster assembly, Fig. 8.
8. Reverse procedure to install.

1977–80 Versailles

1. Disconnect battery ground cable.
2. Remove screws securing lower cluster applique beneath steering column.
3. Remove steering column shroud.
4. Remove headlamp switch knob and shaft

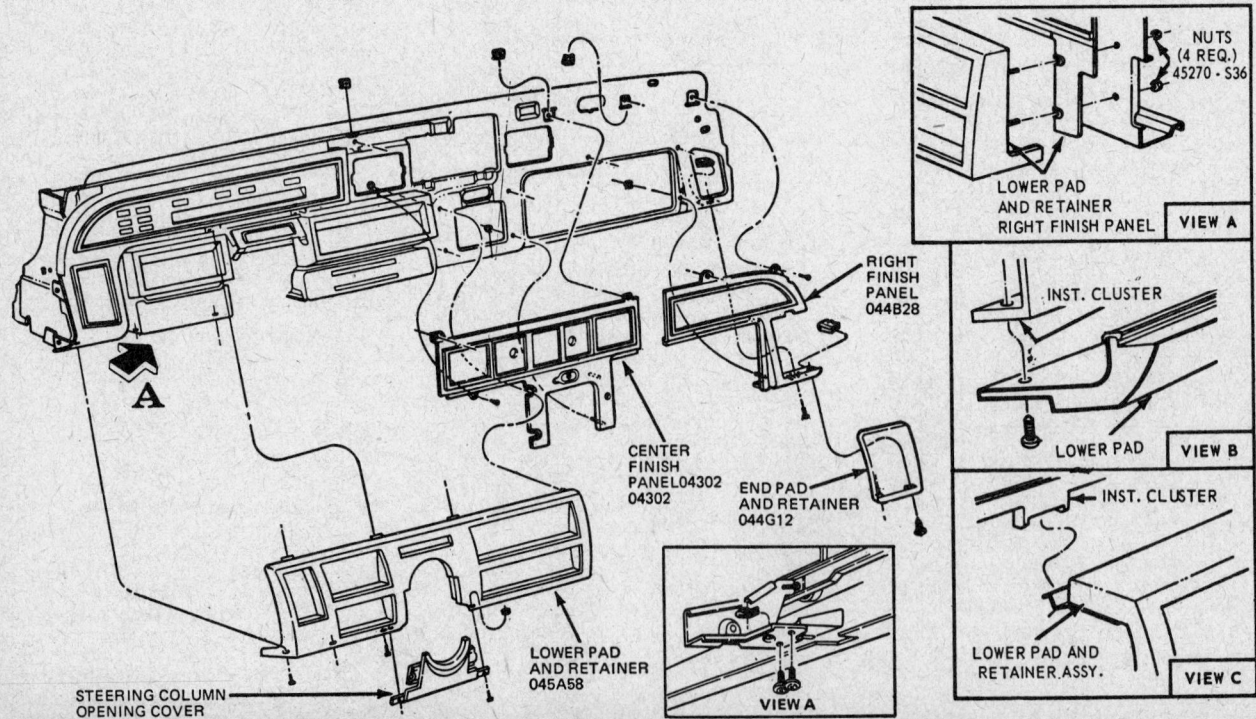

Fig. 10 Instrument panel lower pad removal (typical). 1977 Continental

5. Remove four screws from cluster front cover.
6. Using a right angle screwdriver, pry along edges of finish panel, thereby removing studs from retainers and remove finish panel.
7. Pull front cover slightly outward at top, then rearward at bottom to disengage cover to panel retainers.
8. Remove cluster front cover.
9. Remove screw attaching transmission indicator cable bracket to steering column and detach cable loop from pin on column.
10. Disconnect speedometer cable connector.
11. Remove four screws securing cluster to instrument panel.
12. Pull cluster from instrument panel and disconnect electrical connectors, Fig. 9.
13. Remove cluster from vehicle.
14. Reverse procedure to install.

1977 Continental

1. Disconnect battery ground cable.
2. Remove steering column trim shroud, then remove instrument panel lower pad as follows Fig. 10.
   a. From behind panel, remove the two nuts retaining right end of panel to instrument panel.
   b. From bottom edge, remove the five pad to instrument cluster screws.
   c. Remove the three left hand end finish panel retaining screws, then swing pad assembly outward to disengage tabs at top of cluster and remove pad assembly.
3. Disconnect lower instrument cluster electrical connector from printed circuit.
4. Remove PRND21 control cable to steering column screw.
5. Remove instrument cluster retaining screws, pull cluster from panel and disconnect electrical connector.
6. Remove instrument cluster, Fig. 11.
7. Reverse procedure to install.

1977–79 Mark V

1. Disconnect battery ground cable.
2. Remove three screws attaching upper access cover to instrument panel pad.
3. Remove one screw retaining lower cluster applique cover below steering column.
4. Squeeze lower half of steering column shroud together and separate lower half from upper.
5. Remove upper half of shroud from column.
6. Remove one screw attaching PRNDL control cable to steering column.
7. Remove heated backlite control knob.
8. Reach under panel and depress the button on side of headlight switch while withdrawing switch control knob and shaft. Remove headlight switch bezel.
9. Reach under panel and disconnect speedometer cable.
10. Remove wiper/washer control knob.
11. Remove threaded wiper/washer bezel.
12. Remove cigar lighter from its receptacle.
13. Remove four screws retaining cluster front cover. Remove one screw attaching shift indicator cable bracket to steering column and disconnect cable with transmission selector in PARK position.
14. Insert a right angle standard tip screwdriver along edges of finish panel withdrawing studs in sequence gradually around periphery of panel.
15. Remove two screws from cluster light baffle at cluster top.

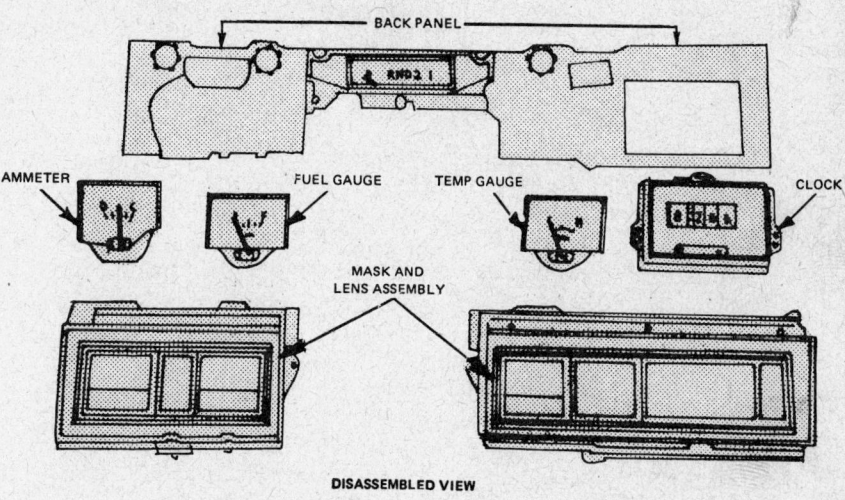

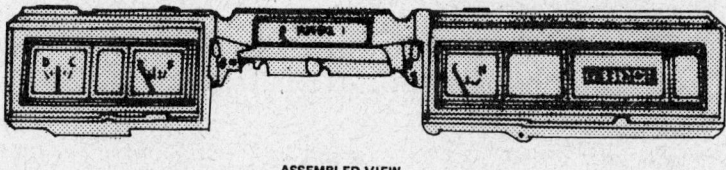

Fig. 11 Instrument cluster (typical). 1977 Continental

16. Remove five screws retaining cluster to instrument panel.
17. Pull cluster away from panel and disconnect printed circuit feed plug.
18. Tilt cluster out, bottom first, and move cluster toward center of vehicle, Fig. 12.
19. Reverse procedure to install.

W/S WIPER MOTOR, REPLACE

1984 Mark VII

1. Turn wipers on, then with wiper blades straight up on windshield, turn ignition key to "off" position.
2. Disconnect battery ground cable and remove arm and blade assemblies.
3. Remove left side trash screen.
4. Remove drive arm to motor crankpin retaining clip, then disconnect drive arm from crankpin.
5. Disconnect wiper motor electrical connector, then remove wiper motor retaining screws and the wiper motor from opening.
6. Reverse procedure to install.

1982–84 Continental

1. Disconnect battery ground cable.
2. Remove right hand side wiper and blade assembly.
3. Remove cowl top grille retaining screws and remove grille.
4. Disconnect linkage drive arm from the motor output arm crankpin by removing retainer clip.
5. Disconnect electrical connector and remove three motor attaching screws.
6. Pull the motor from the opening.
7. Reverse procedure to install.

1980–81 Continental & Mark VI; 1982–83 Mark VI & 1982–84 Town Car

1. Disconnect battery ground cable.
2. Disconnect right side washer nozzle hose clip and remove right side wiper arm and blade assembly from pivot shaft.

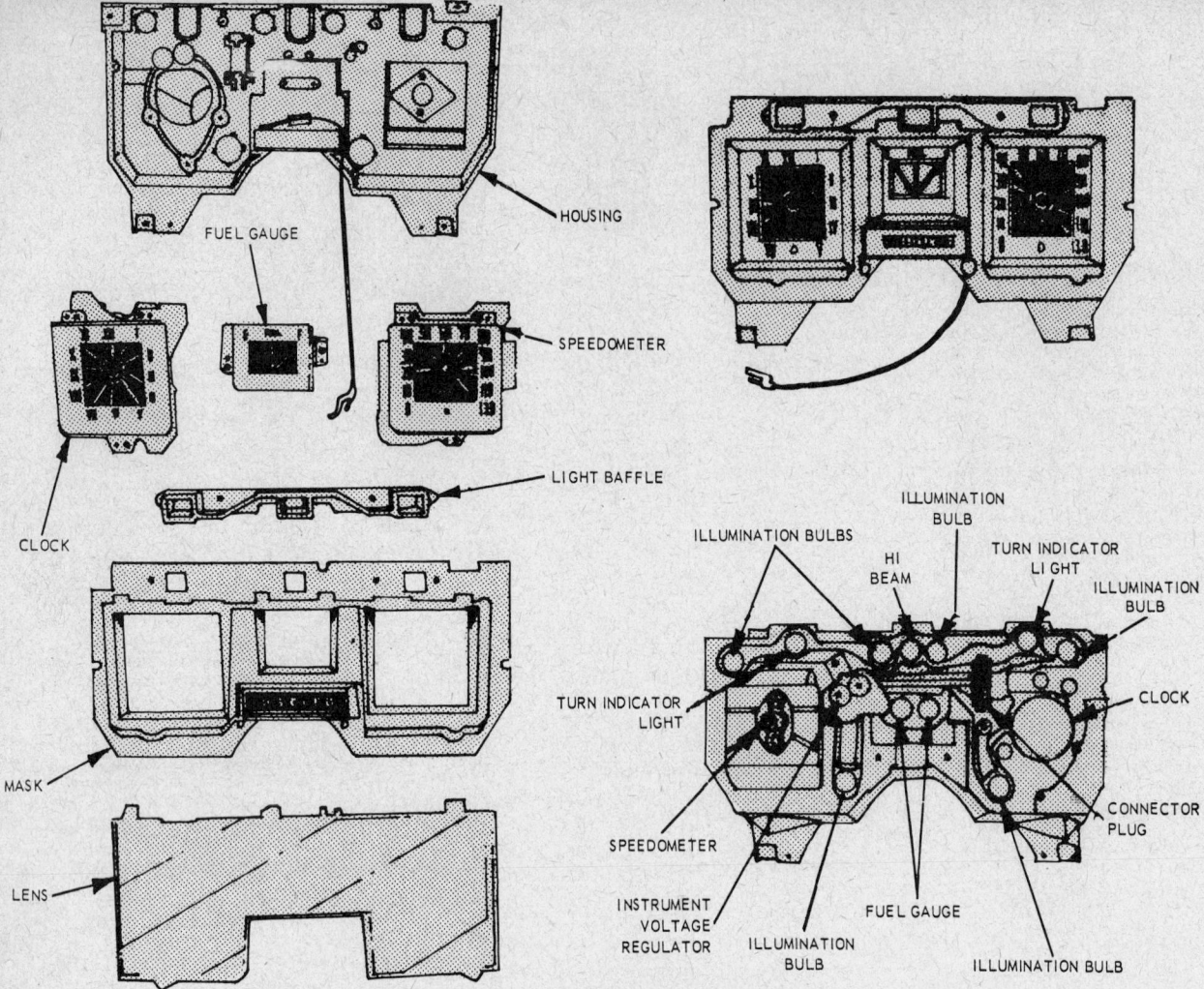

Fig. 12 Instrument cluster (Typical). 1977–79 Mark IV & V

3. Remove wiper motor linkage cover.
4. Disconnect linkage drive arm from the motor output arm crankpin by removing retainer clip.
5. Disconnect the wiring connectors from the motor.
6. Remove three bolts retaining the motor to the dash panel extension and the motor.
7. Reverse procedure to install.

1978–80 Versailles

1. Disconnect battery ground cable.
2. Remove eight instrument panel pad attaching screws, then remove pad.
3. Remove speaker mounting bracket, then disconnect wire connector and remove speaker.
4. Remove defroster nozzle and air distribution duct. Remove interlock module from bracket and disconnect multiple connector.
5. Remove wiper bracket to cowl attaching bolts and drive arm clip, then remove wiper motor.
6. Reverse procedure to install.

1977 Versailles

1. Disconnect battery ground cable.
2. Remove accelerator pedal and instrument panel to floor brace.

3. Remove drive arm clips and disconnect rod from drive arm.
4. Disconnect electrical connector and manual linkage.
5. Remove wiper motor retaining screws, then remove motor and bracket assembly.
6. Reverse procedure to install.

1977–79 Exc. Versailles

1. Disconnect battery ground cable.
2. Remove wiper arm and blade assemblies.
3. Remove left cowl screen for access through cowl opening.
4. Disconnect linkage drive arm from motor output arm crankpin by removing the retaining clip.
5. From engine side of dash, disconnect wire connectors from motor.
6. Remove bolts that retain motor to dash and remove the motor. If the output arm catches on dash during removal, hand-turn the arm clockwise so it will clear the opening in dash.

NOTE: *Before installing motor be sure the output arm is in the Park position.*

7. Reverse procedure to install.

W/S WIPER TRANSMISSION, REPLACE
1984 Mark VII

NOTE: The wiper transmission is mounted below the cowl top panel and can be reached by raising the hood. Because the pivot shaft and transmission assemblies are connected with unremovable plastic ball joints, the right and left pivot shafts and transmission are serviced as a unit.

1. Perform steps 1 and 2 as outlined under "W/S Wiper Motor, Replace" procedure.
2. Raise hood, then remove left and right cowl top grilles.
3. Remove drive arm to wiper motor crankpin retaining clip, then disconnect drive arm from crankpin.
4. Remove pivot shaft attaching screws, then guide transmission and pivots from cowl chamber.
5. Reverse procedure to install, ensuring wiper motor is in "Park" position.

1982–84 Continental

1. Disconnect battery ground cable.

2. Remove right hand side wiper arm and blade assembly.
3. Remove cowl top grille retaining screws and remove grille.
4. Disconnect linkage drive arm from the motor output arm crankpin by removing retainer clip.
5. Remove the right side pivot shaft retaining screws then, remove the large nut and spacer from the left side pivot shaft.
6. Remove linkage.
7. Reverse procedure to install.

1980–81 Continental & Mark VI; 1982–83 Mark VI & 1982–84 Town Car

1. Disconnect battery ground cable.
2. Remove wiper arm and blade assemblies from the pivot shafts.
3. Remove wiper motor and linkage cover for access to linkage.
4. Disconnect the linkage drive arm from the motor crank pin by removing the retaining clip.
5. Remove the six bolts retaining the left and right pivot shafts to the cowl, and remove the complete linkage assembly.
6. Reverse procedure to install.

1977–80 Versailles

Left Side:
1. Remove instrument cluster.
2. Remove wiper arm and blade.
3. Working through cluster opening, disconnect both pivot shaft links from motor drive arm by removing retaining clip.
4. Remove three pivot shaft assembly retaining bolts and remove assembly through cluster opening.
5. Reverse procedure to install.

Right Side:
1. Disconnect battery ground cable and remove wiper blade and wiper arm.
2. If air conditioned, remove right duct assembly by unclipping duct from right connector and sliding left end out of plenum chamber. Lower duct assembly out from under instrument panel.
3. From under the instrument panel, disconnect first left then right pivot shaft link from motor drive arm.
4. Reaching between utility shelf and instrument panel, remove pivot shaft retaining bolts and lower assembly out from under panel.
5. Reverse procedure to install.

1977–79 Mark V

1. Disconnect battery ground cable and remove wiper arm and blades.
2. Remove cowl top (left and center) retaining screws.
3. Disconnect linkage drive arm from the motor by removing retaining clip.
4. Remove pivot shaft retaining bolts and remove linkage and pivot shaft.

NOTE: When installing pivot shaft assemblies, be sure to force the linkage connecting clip into the locked position.

5. Reverse procedure to install.

1977–79 Continental

1. Disconnect battery ground cable.
2. Remove wiper arm and blade assemblies.
3. Remove left and center cowl screens for access to linkage.
4. Disconnect left linkage arm from the drive arm by removing the clip.

5. Remove three bolts retaining left pivot shaft assembly to the cowl and remove the left arm and pivot shaft assembly through cowl opening.
6. Disconnect linkage drive arm from motor crankpin by removing the clip.
7. Remove three bolts that connect the drive arm pivot assembly to the cowl and remove the pivot shaft drive arm and right arm as an assembly.
8. Reverse procedure to install.

W/S WIPER SWITCH, REPLACE

1980–84 All

1. Disconnect battery ground cable.
2. Remove the steering column cover screws and separate the two halves.
3. Remove wiper switch retaining screws, disconnect wiring connector and remove switch.
4. Reverse procedure to install.

1977–80 Versailles

NOTE: The wiper/washer switch is an integral part of the turn signal arm and cannot be replaced separately.

1. Disconnect battery ground cable.
2. Disconnect wiper/washer and turn signal electrical connector from under instrument panel.
3. Remove lower instrument panel shield retaining screws and shield.
4. Remove steering column cover screws and separate cover halves.
5. Remove wiring cover by pulling it, then remove wiring shield by prying out.
6. Using an internal bit screwdriver, remove wiper/washer and turn signal arm assembly.
7. Reverse procedure to install.

1977–79 Mark V

1. Disconnect battery ground cable.
2. Remove instrument cluster finish panel.
3. Remove switch mounting plate and disconnect cigar lighter and wiper switch wires.
4. Remove switch bezel nut and remove switch.
5. Reverse procedure to install.

1977–79 Continental

1. Disconnect battery ground cable.
2. Pull the knob and remove retaining nut and gasket from switch shaft.
3. Lower switch from behind instrument panel and disconnect the multiple connector.
4. Reverse procedure to install.

RADIO, REPLACE

NOTE: When installing radio, be sure to adjust antenna trimmer for peak performance.

1982–84 Continental & 1984 Mark VII

1. Disconnect battery ground cable.
2. Remove center instrument panel trim panel.

3. Remove four radio and mounting bracket to instrument panel retaining screws.
4. Push radio towards the front of vehicle and raise back end slightly so rear support bracket clears clip in instrument panel and carefully pull out radio.
5. Disconnect radio wiring and remove radio.
6. Remove rear support bracket.
7. Reverse procedure to install.

1980–81 Continental & Mark VI, 1982–83 Mark VI & 1982–84 Town Car

1. Disconnect battery ground able.
2. Remove radio plate to instrument panel retaining screws.
3. Pull radio rearward until the rear support bracket is clear of instrument panel.
4. Disconnect radio wiring and antenna lead. Remove radio.
5. Remove screws securing front bracket to radio and remove, remove rear support bracket.
6. Reverse procedure to install.

1978–79 Continental

1. Disconnect battery ground cable.
2. Remove the radio knobs and the screws attaching bezel to instrument panel.
3. Remove radio mounting plate attaching screws and pull radio to disengage it from lower rear support bracket.
4. Disconnect electrical leads and remove the radio.
5. Remove mounting plate and rear support from radio.
6. Reverse procedure to install.

1977–80 Versailles

1. Disconnect battery ground cable.
2. Remove headlamp switch.
3. Remove knobs from heater and A/C control, windshield wiper switch and radio.
4. Remove instrument panel applique.
5. Remove radio bezel to instrument panel screws, then pull radio and bezel out to disconnect antenna lead and electrical leads, then remove radio from panel.
6. Remove rear support bracket and bezel from radio.
7. Reverse procedure to install.

1977–79 Mark V

1. Disconnect battery ground cable.
2. Pull radio knobs and discs from shafts.
3. Remove twilight sentinel amplifier.
4. Remove air conditioning duct located under radio.
5. Remove radio rear support to panel screw, disconnect radio electrical leads and remove radio.
6. Reverse procedure to install.

1977 Continental

1. Disconnect battery ground cable.
2. Remove radio knobs and discs, then map light assembly.
3. Remove steering column shroud, ash tray door pad and instrument cluster panel pad.
4. Remove center register applique, then disconnect cigar lighter and glove box light switch electrical connectors.
5. Remove radio bracket to instrument panel tab nut and radio mounting bracket to instrument panel screws.
6. Pull radio out, disconnect wiring and remove radio.
7. Reverse procedure to install.

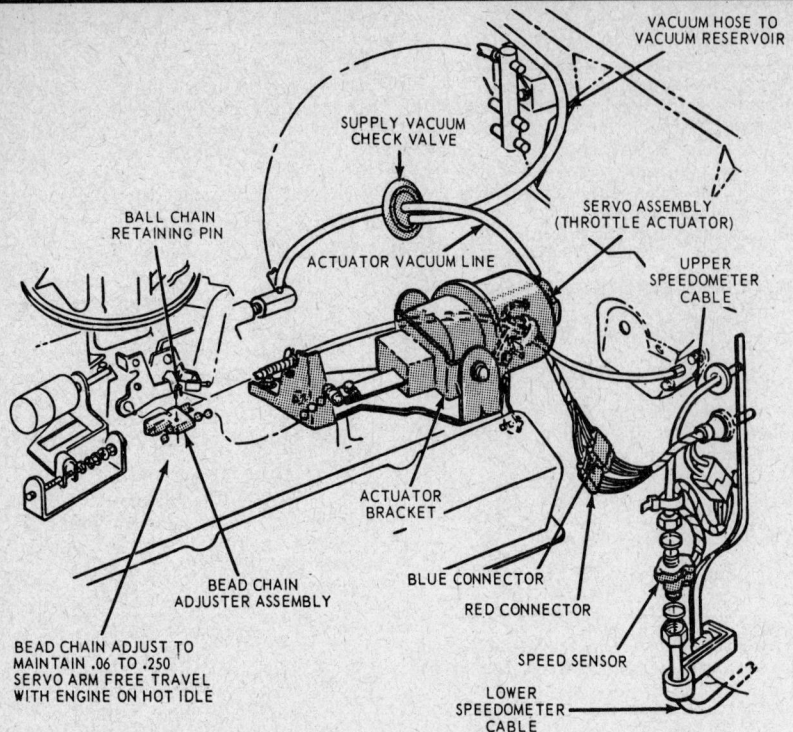

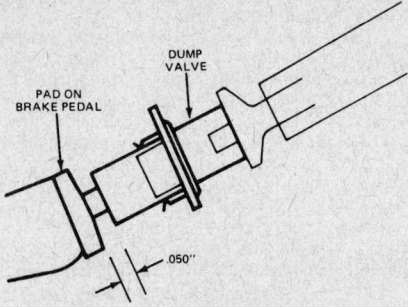

Fig. 13A Vacuum dump valve adjustment (typical)

Fig. 13 Servo assembly & throttle linkage installation. 1977–84 (typical)

SPEED CONTROLS, ADJUST

1977–84

Bead Chain

Adjust bead chain cable to obtain desired free travel with engine warm and carburetor at idle position. Desired free travel is 1/8–1/4 inch, Fig. 13. The adjustment should be made to take as much slack as possible out of the bead chain without restricting the carburetor lever from returning to idle. On vehicles with solenoid anti-diesel valve, perform the adjustment with the ignition switch in the ON position.

Actuator Cable

1. Remove actuator cable retaining clip from speed control connection adjuster.
2. Disengage throttle positioner.
3. With carburetor in hot idle position, pull the actuator cable end tube until all slack is removed from cable.
4. While maintaining light tension on cable, install cable retaining clip.

Vacuum Dump Valve

The vacuum dump valve is fully adjustable in its mounting bracket. When correctly adjusted, the valve should be closed when the brake pedal is in the released position, enabling the black housing of the valve to clear the adapter or pad on the brake pedal. If adjustment is necessary, hold the brake pedal down and push the dump valve forward through its adjustment collar. Position a .050 inch shim on the adapter or pad, Fig. 13A, then pull brake pedal fully rearward. Release brake pedal and remove shim. The white plunger on the valve should be in contact with the adapter or pad, while the threaded black housing should have sufficient clearance away from it.

HEATER CORE, REPLACE

1984 Mark VII

1. Remove instrument panel.
2. Discharge refrigerant from A/C system, then disconnect high and low pressure hoses. Cap hose ends to prevent entry of dirt and moisture.
3. Drain coolant and disconnect hoses from heater core. Plug hoses and core to prevent spillage.
4. Remove air inlet duct/blower housing assembly support brace to cowl top panel retaining screw.
5. Disconnect A/C wiring, if necessary, then working from engine compartment, remove the two evaporator case to dash panel retaining nuts.
6. Working from passenger compartment, remove evaporator case support bracket to cowl panel attaching screw.
7. Carefully pull evaporator case away from dash panel and remove from vehicle.
8. Remove heater core access cover to evaporator case attaching screws.
9. Remove heater core and seals from case, then remove seals from heater core tubes.
10. Reverse procedure to install.

1982–84 Continental

1. Disconnect battery ground cable.
2. Remove steering column cover assembly, then remove left and right finish panels, Fig. 7B.
3. Remove two screws from sides of instrument panel pad and retainer assembly.
4. Remove pad and retainer assembly and upper finish panel.
5. Remove steering column attaching bolts, then carefully lower steering column just enough to allow access to transmission gear selector lever cable assembly. Reach between steering column and instrument panel, then carefully lift selector lever cable from lever and remove cable clamp from steering column tube.
6. Lower steering column and allow to rest on front seat.
7. Remove screw attaching instrument panel to brake pedal support through steering column opening.
8. Disconnect temperature door cable from door and heater/evaporator cable bracket.
9. Disconnect vacuum hose connectors at evaporator housing.
10. Disconnect blower motor resistor wire from resistor on heater/evaporator case and blower motor feed wire at inline connector.
11. Support instrument panel, then remove three screws attaching top of instrument panel to cowl.
12. Remove one screw attaching each end of instrument panel to cowl side panels, then remove two screws attaching instrument panel to floor.
13. Move instrument panel rearward and disconnect speedometer cable and any wires that will prevent instrument panel from being placed on front seat.

NOTE: Use care when removing instrument panel to prevent damage to panel or steering column surfaces.

14. Drain cooling system, then disconnect heater hoses from heater core. Plug heater core tubes to prevent coolant spillage.
15. Discharge A/C system, then remove high and low side pressure hoses. Cap the hose openings to prevent entry of dirt or moisture.
16. From engine compartment, remove two nuts attaching heater/evaporator case to dash panel.
17. From passenger compartment, remove bolts attaching heater/evaporator case and air inlet duct support brackets to cowl top panel.
18. Remove one nut attaching bracket at left side of heater/evaporator case to dash panel, then remove one nut retaining bracket below case to dash panel.
19. Carefully pull case away from dash panel to gain access to heater core cover attaching bolts.
20. Remove five heater core cover attaching bolts, then remove cover
21. Remove heater core and seals from case, then remove seals from heater core tubes.
22. Reverse procedure to install.

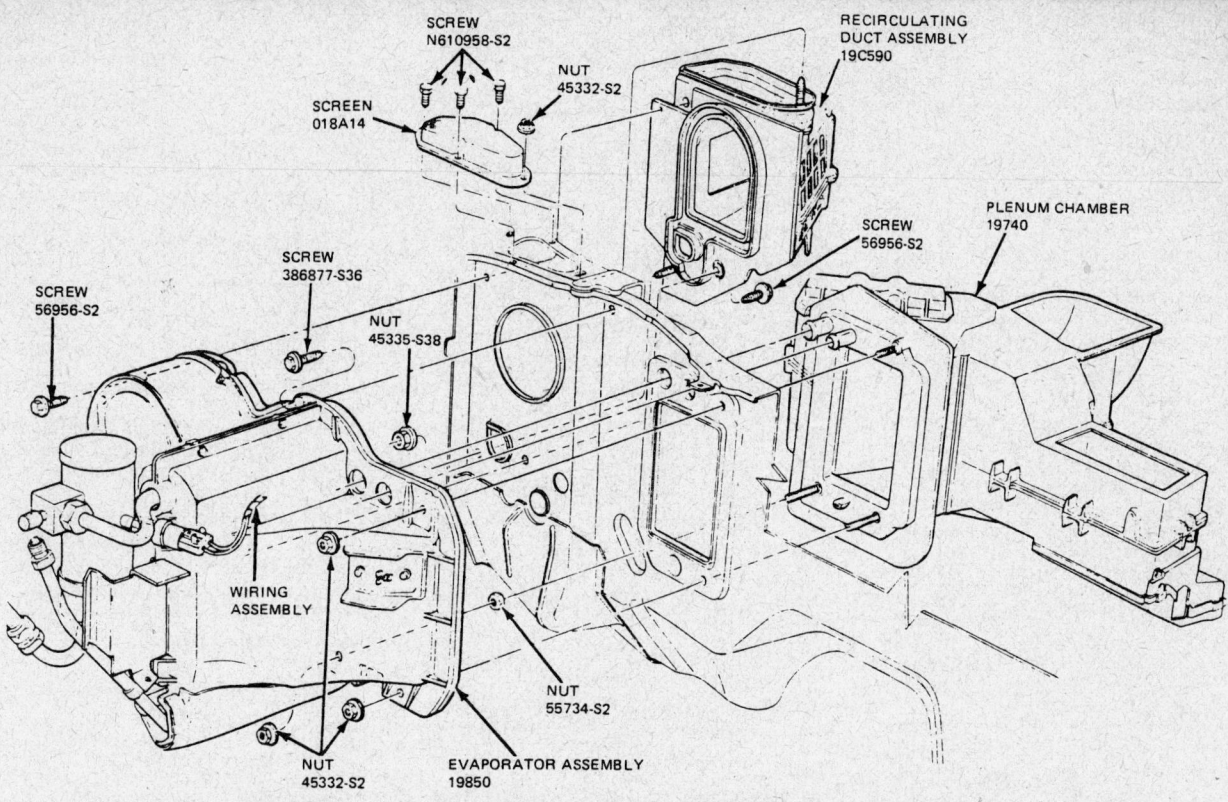

SCREW
N610958-S2

NUT
45332-S2

SCREEN
018A14

RECIRCULATING
DUCT ASSEMBLY
19C590

SCREW
386877-S36

NUT
45335-S38

SCREW
56956-S2

SCREW
56956-S2

PLENUM CHAMBER
19740

SCREW
56956-S2

WIRING
ASSEMBLY

NUT
55734-S2

NUT
45332-S2

EVAPORATOR ASSEMBLY
19850

Fig. 14 Plenum & air inlet duct assembly. 1980–81 Continental & Mark VI, 1982–83 Mark VI & 1982–84 Town Car

1980–81 Continental & Mark VI; 1982–83 Mark VI & 1982–84 Town Car Figs. 14 & 15

1. Disconnect battery ground cable.
2. Disconnect heater hoses from core. Plug hoses and heater core tubes to prevent coolant loss during core removal.
3. Remove one bolt located below the windshield wiper motor retaining left end of plenum to dash panel.
4. Remove one nut retaining the upper left corner of evaporator case to dash panel.
5. Disconnect vacuum supply hose from vacuum source, then push grommet and hose into passenger compartment.
6. Remove glove compartment, then loosen door sill plates and remove side cowl trim panels.

NOTE: On some models, it may be necessary to lower the steering column to remove the instrument panel. On these models, disconnect harnesses from multiple connectors and transmission shift indicator from column, then remove steering column to instrument panel brace attaching nuts and lower steering column to seat.

7. Disconnect speedometer cable from speedometer and antenna lead from radio.
8. Remove bolt retaining lower right end of insturment panel to side cowl, then remove instrument panel pad as follows:
   a. Remove screws retaining instrument panel pad to instrument panel at each defroster opening.
   b. Remove the one screw retaining each outboard end of pad to instrument panel.
   c. Remove the five screws retaining low-

er edge of instrument panel pad, then pull instrument panel pad rearward and remove it.
9. Disconnect temperature control cable housing from bracket at top of plenum, then disconnect cable from temperature

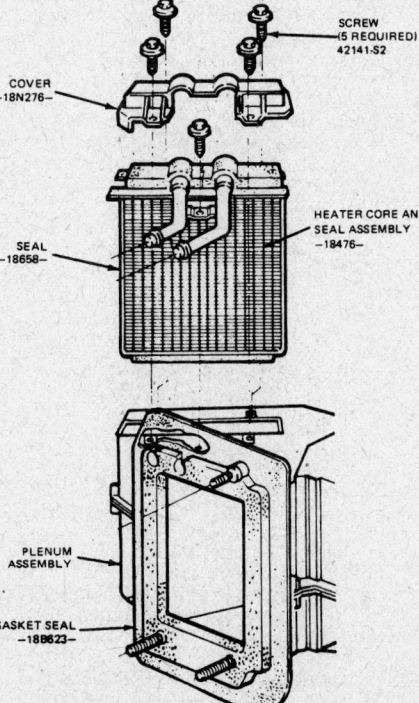

COVER
–18N276–

SCREW
(5 REQUIRED)
42141-S2

SEAL
–18658–

HEATER CORE AND
SEAL ASSEMBLY
–18476–

PLENUM
ASSEMBLY

GASKET SEAL
–18B623–

Fig. 15 Heater core removal. 1980–81 Continental & Mark VI, 1982–83 Mark VI & 1982–84 Town Car

blend door crank arm.
10. Remove push clip retaining the center register duct bracket to the plenum and rotate bracket to the right.
11. Disconnect vacuum jumper harness at multiple vacuum connector near the floor air distribution duct, then disconnect white vacuum hose from the outside-recirculating door vacuum motor.
12. Remove screws retaining the passenger side of floor air distribution duct to the plenum. It may be necessary to remove the two screws retaining the partial (lower) panel door vacuum motor to mounting bracket to gain access to right screw.
13. Remove the plastic push fastener retaining floor air distribution duct to left end of plenum and remove floor air distribution duct.
14. Remove nuts from the two studs along lower edge of plenum.
15. Carefully move plenum rearward to allow heater core tubes and stud at top of plenum to clear holes in dash panel. Remove plenum by rotating top of plenum forward, down and out from under instrument panel. Carefully pull lower edge of instrument panel rearward as necessary while rolling the plenum from behind the instrument panel.
16. Remove the four retaining screws from heater core cover and remove cover from plenum.
17. Remove heater core retaining screw then pull core and seal assembly from plenum assembly.
18. Reverse procedure to install.

1977–80 Versailles

1. Disconnect battery ground cable and drain cooling system.
2. Disconnect hoses from heater core. Plug heater core tubes to prevent coolant leakage.

3. Remove washer nut from plenum assembly mounting stud on engine side of dash panel.

4. Remove floor duct, seat belt interlock module and bracket, glove box liner and shields.

5. Loosen right door sill scuff plate, right A-pillar trim cover and right cowl side trim panel.

6. Loosen instrument panel to right cowl side bolt and remove instrument panel brace at lower rail below glove box opening.

7. If used, remove tunnel to cowl brace located on left side of plenum assembly.

8. Disconnect vacuum hoses from A/C-Defrost and Heat/Defrost door motors. Remove screw from clip retaining vacuum harness to plenum.

9. Remove the two Heat/Defrost door motor mounting nuts and swing motor rearward on door crankarm.

10. Remove the two screws retaining plenum to left mounting bracket, then remove the two screws and three clips retaining plenum to evaporator case.

11. Swing bottom of plenum away from evaporator case to disengage S-clip on forward flange of plenum, then raise plenum to clear tabs on top of evaporator case.

12. Move plenum to left while pulling instrument rearward to gain clearance. Use care to avoid cracking plastic.

NOTE: There is very little clearance between plenum and wiper motor assembly.

13. Pull heater core to the left, then as rear surface of heater core clears evaporator case, pull core rearward and downward to clear instrument panel.

14. Reverse procedure to install. Before installing core, make sure that heater core tube to dash panel seal is in place.

1977–79 Continental

1. Drain radiator and disconnect heater hoses from core.

2. On 1978–79 models, remove engine vacuum distribution connector, located on dash panel above heater core cover plate to provide clearance. Also remove electrical harness ground terminal located on dash panel above heater core plate.

3. On all models, remove heater core cover and gasket, then lift heater core and lower mounting gasket from evaporator housing, Fig. 16.

4. Reverse procedure to install.

1977–78 Mark V

1. Drain radiator and disconnect heater hoses from core.

2. Remove glove box, then heater air outlet register from plenum assembly by disengaging the snap clips.

3. Disconnect temperature control cable from blend door crank arm.

4. Remove vacuum hoses from high-low door motor, panel-defrost door motor and the in-line tee connector to temperature by-pass door motor.

5. Disconnect resistor wiring and remove plenum case flange screws, then remove

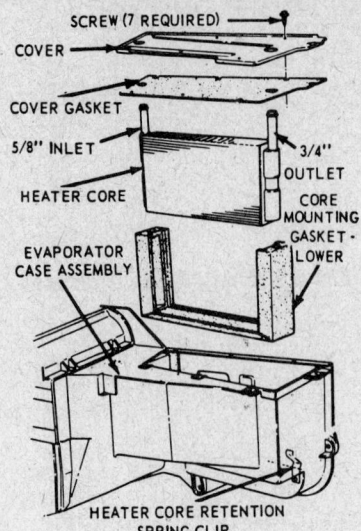

Fig. 16   Heater core removal. 1977–79 Continental

plenum case rear half.

6. Reverse procedure to install.

BLOWER MOTOR, REPLACE

1982–84 Continental & 1984 Mark VII

1. Disconnect battery ground cable.

2. Remove glove box and shield, then disconnect vacuum hose from outside-recirculating air door vacuum motor.

3. Remove instrument panel lower right to side cowl attaching bolt then, remove screw attaching support brace to top of air inlet duct.

4. Disconnect blower motor power lead at wire connector.

5. Remove blower motor housing lower support bracket to heater/evaporator attaching nut.

6. Remove side cowl trim panel.

7. Remove ashtray receptacle, then remove two screws securing instrument panel to transmission tunnel inside ashtray opening.

8. Remove screw attaching top of air inlet duct to heater/evaporator case.

9. Remove air inlet duct and blower housing assembly down and away from the evaporator case.

10. Remove assembly from vehicle, then remove four blower motor mounting plate screws and remove blower motor from housing.

11. Reverse procedure to install.

1980–81 Continental & Mark VI; 1982–83 Mark VI & 1982–84 Town Car

1. Disconnect battery ground cable.

2. Disconnect blower motor lead from wiring harness, then remove blower motor cooling tube from blower motor.

3. Remove the four blower motor retaining screws.

4. Rotate motor and wheel assembly slight-

ly to the right so that bottom edge of mounting plate follows contour of wheel well splash panel, then lift the motor and wheel assembly up and out of housing.

5. Reverse procedure to install.

1977–80 Versailles

1. Disconnect battery ground cable.

2. Remove glove box.

3. Loosen right door sill scuff plate, right A-pillar trim cover and remove right cowl side trim panel.

4. Remove right lower instrument panel to cowl side bolt.

5. Remove cowl to lower instrument panel brace bolt.

6. Disconnect electrical connector from motor.

7. Remove blower motor assembly retaining screws and then blower motor. Pull rearward on lower edge of instrument panel to gain clearance.

NOTE: Do not remove mounting plate from blower motor, as the plate location is critical and should not be changed.

8. Reverse procedure to install.

1977–78 Mark V

1. Remove glove box, recirculating air register and duct assembly.

2. Remove blower lower housing to dash screws.

3. Disconnect vacuum hose from outside-recirculating air door motor and remove motor from blower lower housing, leaving motor actuator connected to door crank arm.

4. Disconnect blower motor wiring and remove blower motor housing flange screws.

5. Separate upper and lower blower housing and remove lower housing and motor from under instrument panel.

6. Remove blower motor from lower housing.

7. Reverse procedure to install.

1977–79 Continental

1. Remove the hood.

2. Remove the right hood hinge and right fender inner support brace as an assembly.

3. Disconnect the blower motor air cooling tube from the motor.

4. Disconnect the motor lead wire from the harness and the ground wire from the dash panel.

5. Disconnect the rear section of the right front fender apron from the fender around the wheel opening (7 screws) and remove the two lower fender-to-cowl mounting screws.

6. Separate the fender apron from the fender wheel opening so that the apron can be pushed downward away from the blower motor.

7. Remove the four blower motor mounting plate screws. Move the motor and wheel forward out of the blower scroll and remove the assembly through the opening while applying pressure to the fender apron to enlarge the opening.

8. Reverse procedure to install.

Engine Section

ENGINE MOUNTS, REPLACE

CAUTION: Whenever self-locking mounting bolts and nuts are removed, they must be replaced with new self-locking bolts and nuts.

1980–83 Mark VI, 1980–84 Continental, 1982–84 Town Car & 1984 Mark VII

1. Remove fan shroud attaching screws, if necessary.
2. Remove the nut and through bolt attaching the insulator to the support bracket, Figs. 1, 1A and 1B.
3. Raise the engine slightly with a jack and a wood block placed under the oil pan.
4. Remove the engine insulator assembly to cylinder block attaching bolts. Remove the engine insulator assembly and the heat shield, if so equipped.
5. Reverse procedure to install.

1977–80 Versailles

1. On 1979–80 models, disconnect fan shroud from radiator and set shroud back on the fan. On all models, support engine using a jack and block of wood placed under oil pan.

2. Remove through bolt attaching insulator to insulator support bracket, Fig. 2.
3. Raise engine slightly and remove insulator and support bracket to engine attaching bolts.
4. Remove insulator and support bracket assembly.
5. Reverse procedure to install.

1977–79 Continental V8-400 & 1978 Continental V8-460

1. On Continental V8-400 models, discon-

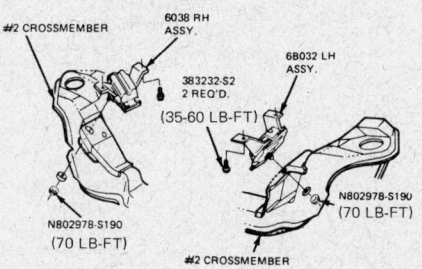

Fig. 1A   Engine mounts. 1982–84 Continental & 1984 Mark VII V8-302

nect transmission oil cooler lines from retaining bracket on block. On all models, remove fan shroud attaching bolts.
2. Remove through bolt attaching insulator to support bracket or crossmember, Figs. 3 and 3A.
3. Raise engine slightly using a jack and block of wood placed under oil pan.
4. Remove insulator to engine attaching bolts.
5. Remove insulator and heat shield, if equipped.
6. Reverse procedure to install.

1977 Continental V8-460

1. Block the rear wheels and set the parking brake. Raise front of vehicle and install safety stands.
2. Remove the bolts that attach the support bracket to the cylinder block, Fig. 3.
3. Place a block of wood between a jack and the front edge of the oil pan. Raise the engine high enough to provide clearance to remove the support and not damage the radiator.
4. Remove the through bolts from the support insulator. Lift the insulator from the number 2 crossmember.
5. Remove the bracket-to-insulator attach-

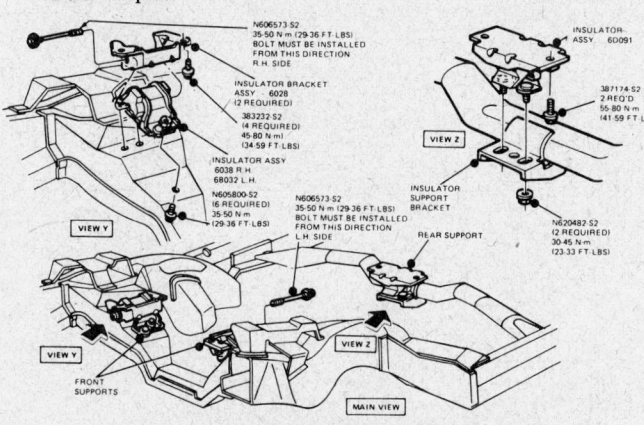

Fig. 1B   Engine mounts. 1980–81 Continental, 1980–83 Mark VI & 1982–84 Town Car V8-302, 351W

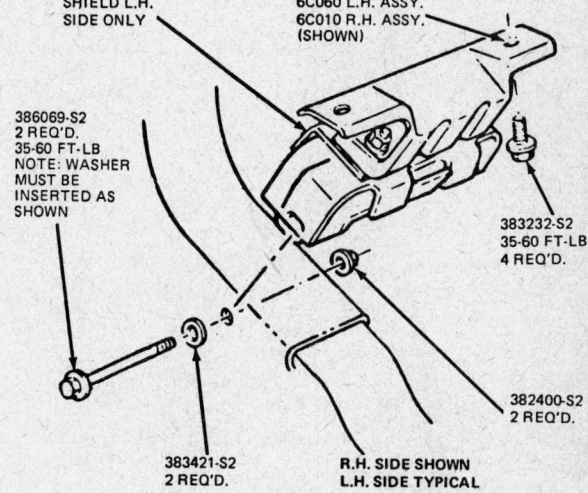

Fig. 2   Engine mounts. 1977–80 Versailles

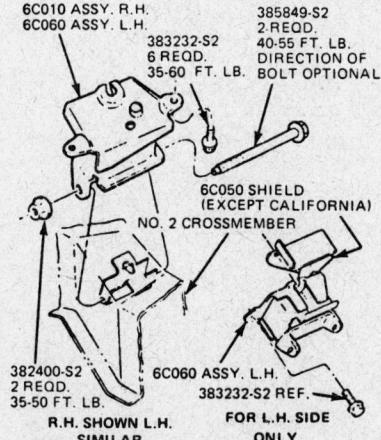

Fig. 3   Engine mounts. 1977–79 Continental V8-400

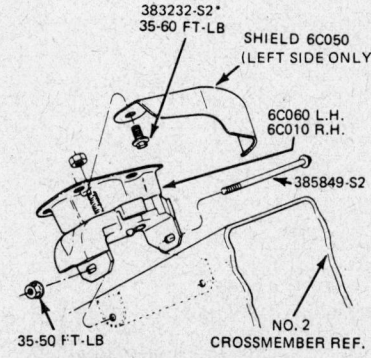

Fig. 3A   Engine mounts. 1977–78 Continental V8-460

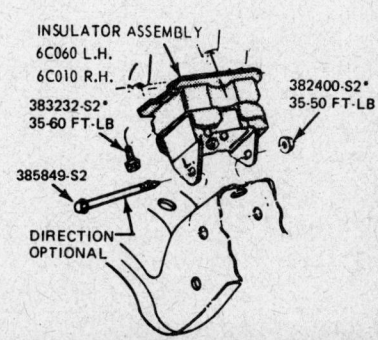

Fig. 4   Engine mounts. 1977–79 Mark V V8-460

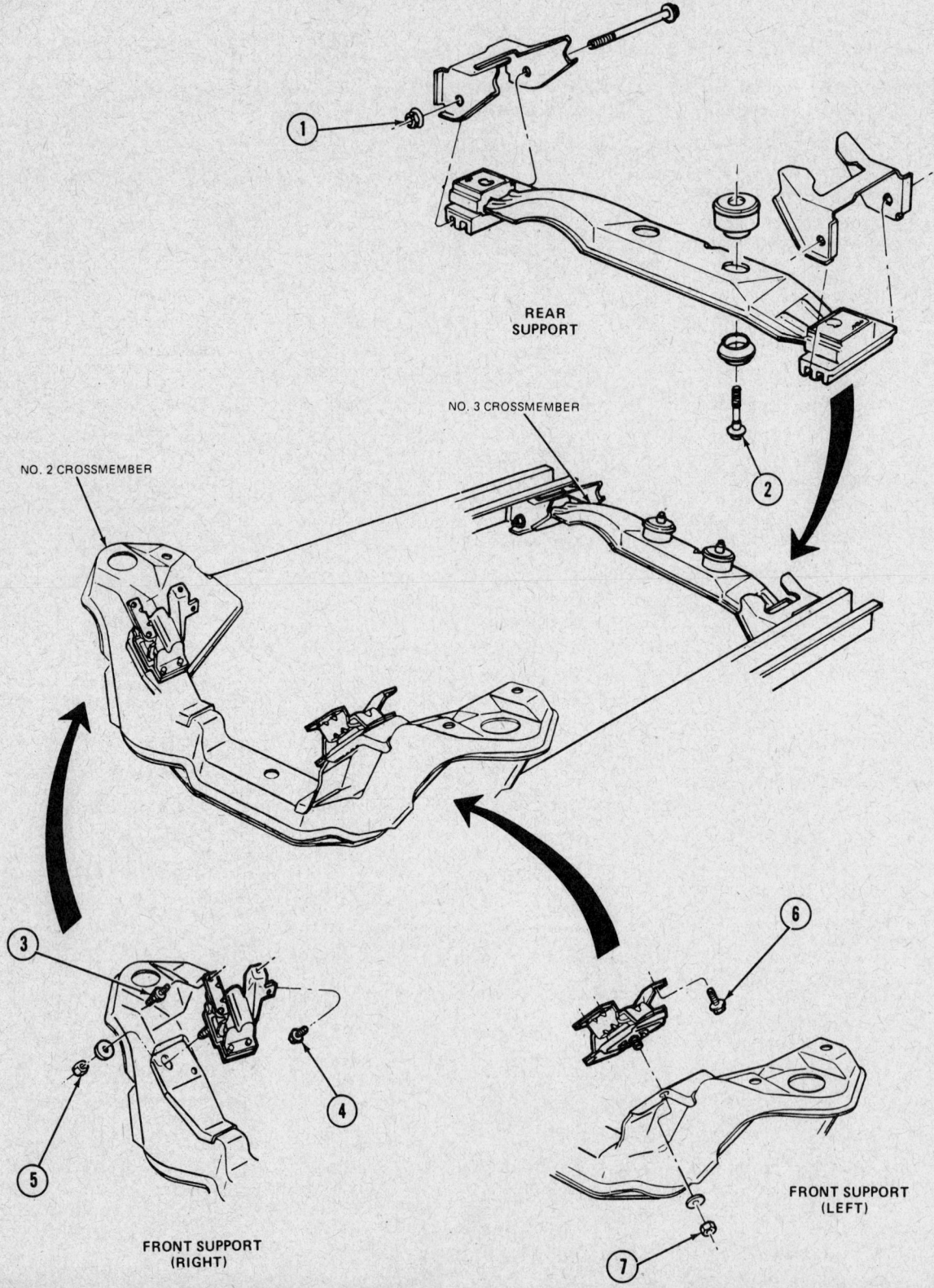

REAR
SUPPORT

NO. 3 CROSSMEMBER

NO. 2 CROSSMEMBER

FRONT SUPPORT
(RIGHT)

FRONT SUPPORT
(LEFT)

Fig. 1 Engine mounts. 1982 Continental V6-232

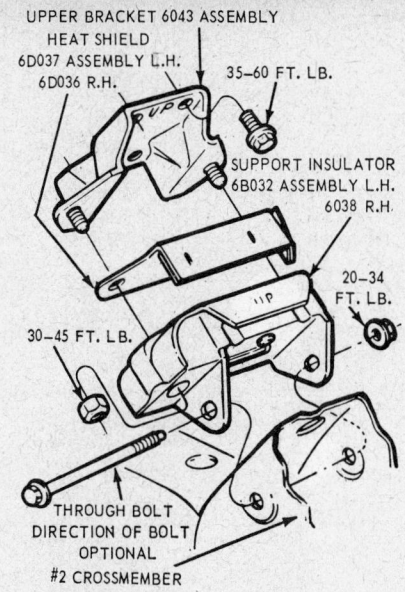

Fig. 5   Engine Mount. 1977–78 Mark V V8-460

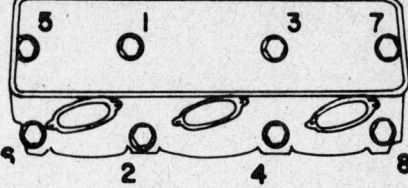

Fig. 6   Cylinder head tightening sequence. V6-232

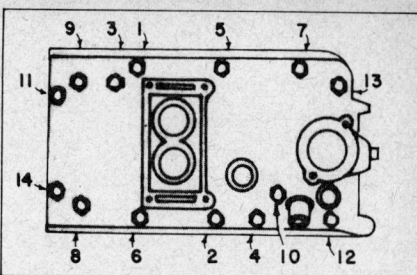

Fig. 6A   Intake manifold tightening sequence. V6-232

ing bolt and separate the units.

6. Reverse procedure to install.

1977–79 Mark V

1. Remove the fan shroud attaching screws and support the engine using a jack and a block of wood under the oil pan.
2. Remove the through bolt and nut attaching the insulator to the frame crossmember, Figs. 4 and 5.
3. Remove the insulator to upper bracket attaching nuts.
4. Raise the engine enough to remove the insulator and heat shield if so equipped.
5. If required, the upper bracket can now be removed by removal of the three screws holding the bracket to the cylinder block.
6. Reverse procedure to install.

ENGINE, REPLACE

1982 Continental V6-232

1. Disconnect battery ground cable, then drain cooling system and crankcase.
2. Mark position of hood hinges, then remove hood.
3. Remove air cleaner, air inlet duct and heat tube.
4. Remove fan shroud and fan assembly, then loosen accessory drive belt idler and remove drive belt and water pump pulley.
5. Disconnect upper and lower radiator hoses at radiator.
6. Disconnect Thermactor hose at air tube check valve, then remove air tube valve bracket attaching bolt at rear of right hand cylinder head.
7. Remove secondary wire from ignition coil.
8. Remove bolts attaching power steering pump mounting bracket, then remove pump and bracket assembly and position aside with hoses attached if equipped.
9. On models with A/C, remove compressor mounting bracket attaching bolts, then remove compressor and mounting bracket assembly and secure to right hand shock absorber tower with refrigerant lines attached.
10. Remove alternator and position aside.
11. Disconnect heater hoses from water pump

and heater tube.

12. On models equipped with speed control, disconnect servo chain at carburetor, then remove servo bracket attaching bolts and servo.
13. Disconnect all necessary vacuum hoses and wiring connectors.
14. Remove engine ground strap to dash panel attaching screw.
15. Disconnect transmission downshift linkage, throttle cable from carburetor, then remove throttle cable bracket attaching bolts.
16. Disconnect fuel line and PCV valve hose from carburetor.
17. Remove carburetor assembly from intake manifold. On models equipped with 7200 VV two barel carburetor, remove spark knock intensity sensor and adapter assembly which is located between carburetor and thermostat housing.
18. With EGR spacer and phenolic gasket in position, install engine lifting plate T75T-6000-A or equivalent over carburetor mounting studs, then install nuts.
19. Raise vehicle and disconnect fuel inlet hose from fuel pump. Cap fuel hose to prevent entry of dirt.
20. Remove inspection cover from torque converter housing, then remove nuts attaching flex plate to torque converter.
21. Remove starter motor.
22. Remove transmission cooler line retaining clips, then disconnect exhaust pipe from exhaust manifold.
23. Remove four lower engine to transmission attaching bolts, then lower vehicle.
24. Remove engine mount to crossmember attaching nuts.
25. Lower vehicle and position a suitable transmission jack under transmission. Raise jack just enough to support weight of transmission,
26. Remove two upper engine to transmission attaching bolts, then place a ¼ inch piece of plywood or other suitable material between engine and radiator to prevent damage to radiator.
27. Carefully raise engine slightly, then pull away from transmission and lift from vehicle.
28. Reverse procedure to install. Torque fasteners according to numbers in Fig. 1: 1, 35–50 ft. lbs.; 2, 50–70 ft. lbs.; 3, 35–60 ft. lbs.; 4, 35–60 ft. lbs.; 5, 70–90 ft. lbs.; 6, 35–50 ft. lbs.; 7, 70–90 ft. lbs.

1977–80 Versailles, 1980–83 Mark VI, 1980–84 Continental, 1982–84 Town Car & 1984 Mark VII

NOTE: On models equipped with Thermactor system, remove or disconnect components that will interfere with engine removal or installation.

1. Drain cooling system and crankcase.
2. Remove hood, then disconnect battery

and alternator ground cables from cylinder block.

3. Remove air cleaner and duct assembly.
4. Disconnect upper and lower radiator hoses from engine block and transmission oil cooler lines from radiator.
5. Remove bolts attaching fan shroud to radiator.
6. Remove radiator, fan, spacer, pulley and fan shroud.
7. Remove alternator mounting bolts and position alternator aside.
8. Disconnect oil pressure sending unit wire connector and fuel line at fuel pump. Plug fuel tank line.

NOTE: On models equipped with electronic fuel injection, relieve pressure at the schrader type valve on the fuel charging valve before disconnecting fuel lines.

9. Disconnect accelerator cable from carburetor and throttle valve vacuum line at intake manifold.
10. Disconnect transmission manual shift rod, then disconnect retracting spring at shift rod stud.
11. Disconnect transmission oil filler tube bracket from engine block.
12. On models equipped with A/C, isolate and remove compressor.
13. Remove power steering pump bracket from cylinder head and position pump aside. Position pump so that fluid will not drain from reservoir.
14. Disconnect heater hoses from water pump and intake manifold and temperature sending unit wire connector.
15. Remove converter housing to engine upper attaching bolts.
16. Disconnect primary wire connector from ignition coil, then remove wiring harness from left rocker arm cover and position out of way. Disconnect ground strap from block. On EEC-IV equipped vehicles, disconnect wiring at sensors.
17. Raise front of vehicle and remove starter.
18. Disconnect exhaust pipes from exhaust manifold, then remove engine support insulators from brackets on frame.
19. Disconnect transmission oil cooler lines from retainer and remove converter housing inspection cover.
20. Disconnect flywheel from converter, secure converter to converter housing.
21. Remove remaining converter housing to engine attaching bolts, then lower vehicle and support transmission using a suitable jack.
22. Attach engine lifting device to lifting brackets on intake manifold, then raise engine slightly and disconnect from transmission.
23. Carefully lift engine from engine compartment.
24. Reverse procedure to install.

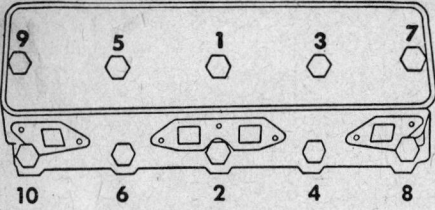

Fig. 7 Cylinder head tightening, V8 Engines

1977–79 Except Versailles

NOTE: Because of engine compartment tolerances, the engine should not be removed and installed with the transmission attached.

1. Disconnect battery ground cable, drain cooling system and crankcase and remove hood and air cleaner assembly.
2. Disconnect or remove all Thermactor components that may interfere with engine removal.
3. Disconnect hoses and oil cooler lines from radiator, then remove radiator, fan shroud and fan.
4. Remove all drive belts.
5. Disconnect power steering pump and alternator and position units out of the way.
6. If equipped with air conditioning, isolate and remove compressor.
7. Disconnect all hoses, lines and wiring from engine. Make certain to remove ground wires from block and right cylinder head.
8. Disconnect fuel line from pump and plug line.
9. Disconnect speed control at carburetor, if equipped.
10. Disconnect engine wiring harness.
11. Disconnect accelerator cable or linkage, then disconnect downshift linkage (if used).
12. Raise and properly support vehicle, then disconnect exhaust system from engine and remove starter.
13. Remove engine front support through bolts.
14. Remove converter cover, converter to flywheel bolts, and downshift rod.
15. Remove the four lower engine to clutch housing or converter housing bolts, then lower vehicle and remove the two upper engine to clutch housing or converter housing bolts.
16. Position jack under transmission, then using a suitable hoist, carefully remove engine from vehicle.
17. Reverse procedure to install.

CYLINDER HEAD, REPLACE

NOTES Before installing cylinder head, wipe off engine block gasket surface and be certain no foreign material has fallen into cylinder bores, bolt holes or in the valve lifter area. It is good practice to clean out bolt holes with compressed air.

Some cylinder head gaskets are coated with a special lacquer to provide a good seal once the parts have warmed up. Do not use any additional sealer on such gaskets. If the gasket does not have this lacquer coating, apply suitable sealer to both sides.

Tighten cylinder head bolts a little at a time in three steps in the sequence shown in the illustrations. Final tightening should be to

the torque specifications listed in the *Engine Tightening* table. After the bolts have been torqued to specifications, *they should not be disturbed.*

V6-232

1. Disconnect battery ground cable, then drain cooling system.
2. Remove air cleaner, air intake duct and heat tube.
3. Loosen accessory drive belt idler and remove drive belt.
4. If left cylinder head is to be removed, proceed as follows:
   a. Remove oil filler cap.
   b. If equipped with power steering, remove pump bracket attaching bolts, then remove pump and bracket assembly and position pump aside with hoses attached.
   c. If equipped with A/C, remove compressor bracket attaching bolts, then position compressor and bracket assembly aside with refrigerant lines attached.
5. If right cylinder head is to be removed, proceed as follows:
   a. Remove Thermactor diverter valve and hose assembly.
   b. Remove accessory drive belt idler, then remove alternator.
   c. Remove Thermactor pump pulley, then remove Thermactor pump.
   d. Remove alternator mounting bracket.

NOTE: On models equipped with Tripminder, then fuel supply line from the fuel pump to the fuel sensor will have to be disconnected to gain access to the upper alternator bracket bolt.

   e. Remove PCV valve.
6. Remove intake manifold, and exhaust manifolds.
7. Remove rocker arm cover and attaching screws, then loosen cover by using a putty knife under cover flange and remove cover. Do not use excess force when loosening rocker arm cover as cover may become damaged.
8. Loosen rocker fulcrum bolt enough to allow rocker arms to be rotated to one side, then remove push rods.

NOTE: Tag push rods so they can be installed in the same position.

9. Remove cylinder head attaching bolts, then remove cylinder head and gasket.
10. Reverse procedure to install. Apply a thin coating of pipe sealant D8AZ-19558-A or equivalent to the shorter cylinder head bolts which are installed on the exhaust manifold side of the cylinder head. Do not apply pipe sealant to long bolts which are installed on the intake manifold side of the cylinder head. Tighten cylinder head bolts in four steps to torque listed under Engine Tightening Specifications using sequence shown in Fig. 6. Loosen cylinder bolts approximately 2 to 3 turns, then retighten bolts in four steps to specified torque in sequence, Fig. 6. When installing intake manifold, tighten mounting bolts to torque specified under Engine Tightening Specifications in sequence shown in Fig. 6A.

NOTE: Before installing intake manifold, apply a 1/8 inch bead of silicone rubber sealer D6AZ-19562-B or equivalent at mating sur-

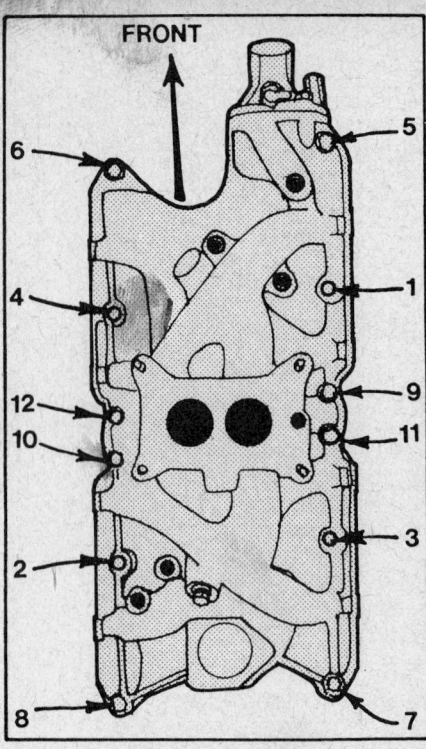

Fig. 7A Intake manifold tightening sequence. V8-302 & 351W

faces of intake manifold, cylinder heads and cylinder block. Also apply a 1/8 inch bead of sealer to the outer end of each intake manifold seal for the full width of the seal.

V8-302, 351W & 400

1. Remove intake manifold and carburetor as an assembly.
2. Disconnect battery ground cable at cylinder head.
3. If left head is being removed, remove A/C compressor (if equipped). Also remove and wire power steering pump out of the way. If equipped with Thermactor System, disconnect hose from air manifold on left cylinder head.
4. If right head is to be removed, remove alternator mounting bracket bolt and spacer, ground wire and air cleaner inlet duct, and A/C compressor bracket.
5. If right head is to be removed on an engine with Thermactor System, remove air pump from bracket. Disconnect hose from air manifold.
6. Disconnect exhaust manifolds at exhaust pipes.
7. Remove rocker arm covers. If equipped with Thermactor System, remove check valve from air manifold.
8. On 1977 V8-302, 351W and early 1978 V8-302 engines, loosen rocker arm stud nuts so that rocker arms can be rotated to one side. On V8-400 and late 1978 and 1979-84 V8-302 and 351W engines, remove fulcrum bolts, oil deflectors (if used), fulcrums and rocker arms. On all engines, remove push rods. Keep rocker arms and push rods in order so they can be installed in the same position.
9. Remove head bolts and lift head off block.
10. Reverse procedure to install. Torque cylinder head bolts in sequence shown in Fig. 7, and torque intake manifold bolts

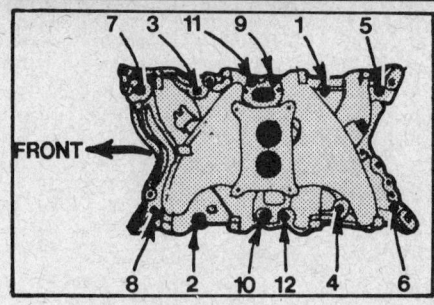

Fig. 8 Intake manifold tightening sequence. V8-400

in sequence shown in Figs. 7A and 8.

SERVICE NOTE

Some V8-302 engines may exhibit engine oil leakage at the front or rear intake manifold end seals. To correct this condition, RTV sealer should be used instead of the conventional cork seals provided in the gasket set.

Remove intake manifold and gaskets, then clean cylinder block and intake manifold sealing surfaces with suitable solvent. Install side runner gaskets onto cylinder block, then apply a 1/4 inch bead of RTV sealer across the front and rear sealing surfaces of the cylinder block. When applying the sealer, ensure sealer does not get inside engine, as damage may result. Install manifold and torque bolts to specifications.

SERVICE NOTE

Some 1981–82 V8-302 engines may exhibit excessive oil consumption caused by low profile rocker arm fulcrums, Part No. E1TZ-6A528-A, allowing excessive oil displacement when the engine is operated for an extended period during high ambient temperatures. To service the above problem, replace the fulcrums indicated above with new fulcrums, Part No. D7AZ-6A528-A.

V8-460

1. Remove intake manifold and carburetor

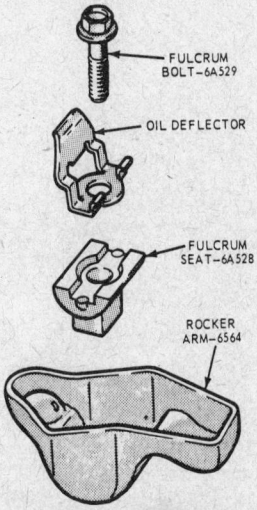

Fig. 11 Rocker arm & related parts. V8-400, 460

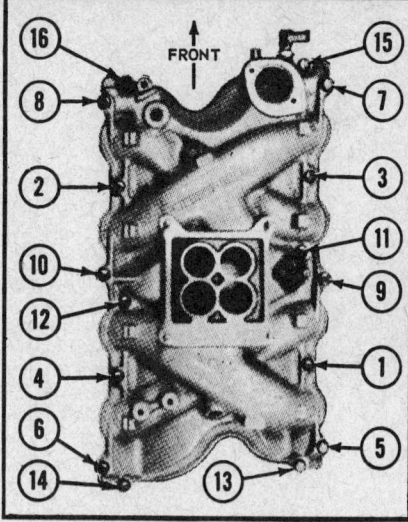

Fig. 9 Intake manifold tightening sequence. V8-460

as an assembly.
2. Disconnect muffler inlet pipe at exhaust manifold.
3. Loosen air conditioner compressor belt if so equipped.
4. Loosen alternator retaining bolts and remove bolt retaining alternator bracket to right head.
5. If air conditioned, purge system of refrigerent, then remove nuts retaining compressor bracket to water pump. Remove bolts retaining compressor to upper mounting bracket and lay compressor out of way. Remove compressor upper bracket from head.
6. If not air conditioned, remove bolts retaining power steering reservoir bracket to left head and position reservoir out of way.
7. Remove rocker arm covers and rocker arms. Remove push rods in sequence so they can be installed in their positions.
8. Remove head retaining bolts and lift head with exhaust manifold.

NOTE: If necessary to break gasket seal, pry at forward corners of cylinder heads against casting bosses provided on cylinder block. Avoid damaging machined surfaces on head and block.

9. Reverse procedure to install. Torque cylinder head bolts in sequence shown in Fig. 6, and torque intake manifold bolts in sequence shown in Fig. 9.

NOTE: *The cylinder head gaskets are marked "Top" or "Front" stamped near the front end of the gasket. The gasket is properly installed when the word is at the forward end of the engine and water passage holes line up. This results in the sealing beads on the right head gasket being inverted with respect to the left head gasket.*

VALVES, ADJUST
V6-232

A .060 inch longer or a .060 inch shorter push rod is available to compensate for dimensional changes in the valve train. If clearance is less than specified, the .060 inch shorter push rod should be used. If clearance is more

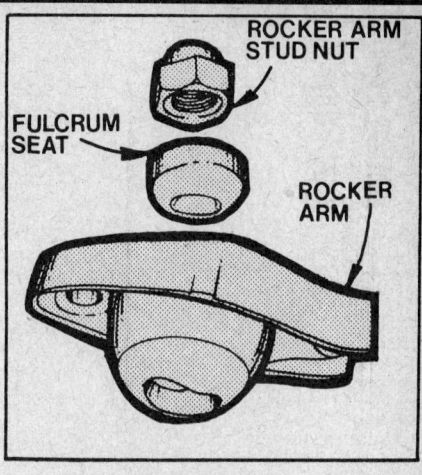

Fig. 10 Rocker arm assembly. 1977 & early 1978 V8-302 & 351W

than the maximum specified, the .060 inch longer push rod should be used.

Using an auxiliary starter switch crankshaft until No. 1 cylinder is at TDC compression stroke, then compress valve lifter using tool T82C-6500-A or equivalent, Fig. 14. At this point, the following valves can be checked:

No. 1 Intake	No. 3 Intake
No. 1 Exhaust	No. 4 Exhaust
No. 2 Exhaust	No. 6 Intake

After clearance on these valves has been checked, rotate crankshaft until No. 5 cylinder is at TDC compression stroke (1 revolution of crankshaft), and then compress valve lifter using tool No. T82C-6500-A or equivalent, Fig. 14, and check the following valves:

No. 2 Intake	No. 5 Intake
No. 3 Exhaust	No. 5 Exhaust
No. 4 Intake	No. 6 Exhaust

V8-302, 351, 400 & 460

To eliminate the need of adjusting valve lash, a positive stop rocker arm stud and nut is used on 1977 and early 1978 V8-302 and 351W engines, Fig. 10, and a positive stop fulcrum bolt and seat is used on V8-400 and 460 and late 1978 and 1979–84 V8-302 and 351W engines, Figs. 11 and 12.

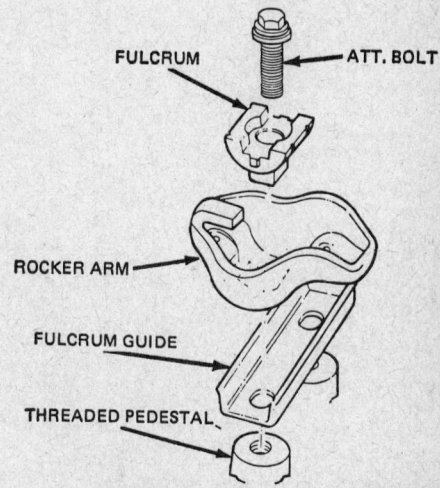

Fig. 12 Rocker arm & related parts. V6-232 & Late 1978 & 1979–84 V8-302 & 351W

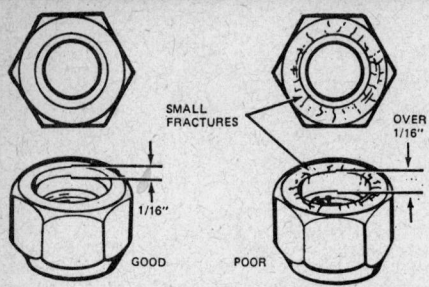

Fig. 13 Inspection or rocker arm stud nut. 1977 & early 1978 V8-302, 351W

It is very important that the correct push rod be used and all components be installed and torqued as follows:

1. Position the piston of the cylinder being worked on at TDC of its compression stroke.
2. On 1977 and early 1978 V8-302 and 351 engines, lubricate and install rocker arm and fulcrum seat on the stud. Thread nut onto the stud until it contracts the shoulder and torque to 17–23 ft. lbs.

NOTE: Each rocker arm stud nut should be inspected when adjusting valve clearance, Fig. 13.

3. On V8-400, 460 and late 1978 and 1979–84 V8-302 and 351W engines, install rocker arm, fulcrum seat and oil deflector. Install fulcrum bolt and torque to 18–25 ft. lbs.

A .060″ shorter push rod or a .060″ longer rod is available for service to provide a means of compensating for dimensional changes in the valve mechanism. Valve stem-to-rocker arm clearance should be as listed in the *Valve Specifications* table, with the hydraulic lifter completely collapsed, Fig. 14. Repeated valve grind jobs will decrease this clearance to the point that if not compensated for the lifters will cease to function.

When checking valve clearance, if the clearance is less than the minimum, the .060″ shorter push rod should be used. If clearance is more than the maximum, the .060″ longer push rod should be used. (See *Valve Specifications* table.) To check valve clearance, proceed as follows:

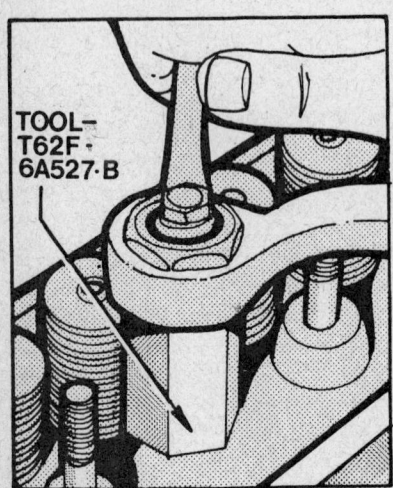

Fig. 15 Rocker arm stud removal. 1977 & early 1978 V8-302 & 351W

V8-302 & 351, 400 & 460

1. Mark crankshaft pulley at three locations, with number 1 location at TDC timing mark (end of compression stroke), number 2 location one half turn (180°) clockwise from TDC and number 3 location three quarter turn clockwise (270°) from number 2 location.
2. Turn the crankshaft to the number 1 location and check the clearance on the following valves:

V8-302 & 460

No. 1 Intake	No. 1 Exhaust
No. 7 Intake	No. 5 Exhaust
No. 8 Intake	No. 4 Exhaust

V8-351 & 400

No. 1 Intake	No. 1 Exhaust
No. 4 Intake	No. 3 Exhaust
No. 8 Intake	No. 7 Exhaust

3. Turn the crankshaft to the number 2 location and check the clearance on the following valves:

V8-302 & 460

| No. 5 Intake | No. 2 Exhaust |
| No. 4 Intake | No. 6 Exhaust |

V8-351 & 400

| No. 3 Intake | No. 2 Exhaust |
| No. 7 Intake | No. 6 Exhaust |

4. Turn the crankshaft to the number 3 location and check the clearance on the following valves:

V8-302 & 460

No. 2 Intake	No. 7 Exhaust
No. 3 Intake	No. 3 Exhaust
No. 6 Intake	No. 8 Exhaust

V8-351 & 400

No. 2 Intake	No. 4 Exhaust
No. 5 Intake	No. 5 Exhaust
No. 6 Intake	No. 8 Exhaust

VALVE ARRANGEMENT

Front to Rear

V6 Engine Right Bank	I-E-I-E-I-E
V6 Engine Left Bank	E-I-E-I-E-I
V8 Engine Right Bank	I-E-I-E-I-E-I-E
V8 Engine Left Bank	E-I-E-I-E-I-E-I

VALVE LIFT SPECS.

Engine	Year	Intake	Exhaust
V6-232	1982	.415	.417
V8-302	1977	.416	.434
	1978–79	.382	.398
	1980–84	.375	.390
V8-351W	1977	.416	.416
	1980	.411	.411
V8-400	1977–79	.428	.432
V8-460	1977–78	.437	.481

VALVE TIMING

Intake Opens Before TDC

Engine	Year	Degrees
V6-232	1982	13
V8-302①	1977–82	16
V8-302②	1980–81	17
V8-302②	1982	16
V8-351W	1977 & 80	23
V8-400	1977–79	17
V8-460	1977–78	8

①—Less EFI.
②—With EFI.

ROCKER ARM STUDS, REPLACE

1977 & Early 1978 V8-302, 351W

If necessary to replace a rocker arm stud, a rocker arm stud kit is available and contains

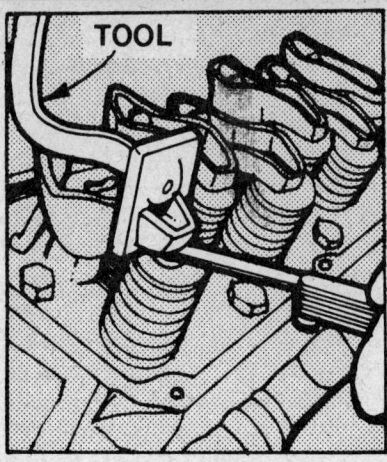

Fig. 14 Compressing lifter to check valve clearance

a stud remover, Fig. 15, a stud installer, Fig. 16, and two reamers, one .006″ and the other .015″. For .010″ oversize studs, use reamer T66P-6A527-B.

Rocker arm studs that are broken or have damaged threads may be replaced with standard studs. Loose studs in the head may be replaced with .006″, .010″ or .015″ oversize studs which are available for service.

When going from a standard size stud to a .015″ oversize stud, always use a .006″ reamer before finishing reaming with a .015″ reamer.

If a stud is broken off flush with the stud boss, use an easy-out to remove the broken stud, following the instructions of the tool manufacturer.

Installation

1. Position the piston of the cylinder to be worked on at TDC compression stroke.
2. Locate stud properly with tool T69P-6049D. Make sure tool bottoms on the head.
3. Lubricate rocker arm components and place rocker arm and fulcrum on the stud.
4. Thread nut onto the stud until it contacts the shoulder then tighten nut to 17–23 ft-lbs.

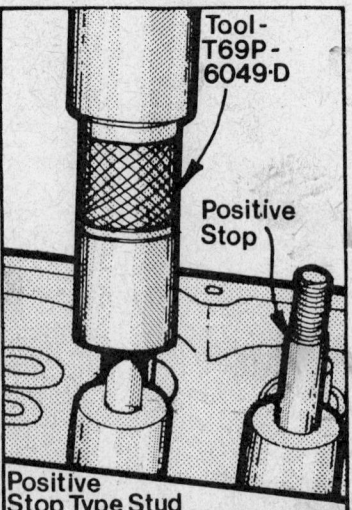

Fig. 16 Positive stop type rocker arm stud installation. 1977 & early 1978 V8-302 & 351W

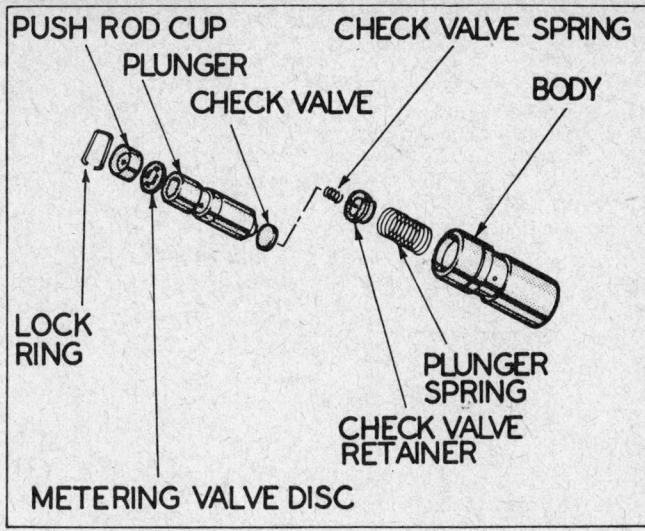

Fig. 17 Hydraulic valve lifter disassembled (typical)

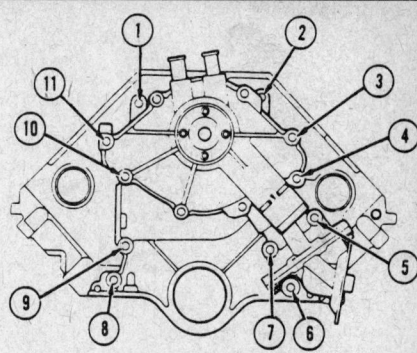

Fig. 17A Front cover attaching bolt location. V6-232

V6-232, V8-400, 460 & Late 1978 & 1979–83 V8-302 & 351W

The rocker arm is supported by a fulcrum bolt which fits through the fulcrum seat and threads into the cylinder head. To disassemble, remove the bolt, oil deflector, fulcrum seat and rocker arm, Figs. 11 and 12.

VALVE GUIDES

Valve guides in these engines are an integral part of the head and, therefore, cannot be removed. For service, guides can be reamed oversize to accommodate one of three service valves with oversize stems (.003″, .015″ and .030″).

Check the valve stem clearance of each valve (after cleaning) in its respective valve guide. If the clearance exceeds the service limits of .0055″, ream the valve guides to accommodate the next oversize diameter valve.

HYDRAULIC VALVE LIFTERS, REPLACE

NOTE: The internal parts of each hydraulic valve lifter assembly are a matched set. If these are mixed, improper valve operation may result. Therefore, disassemble, inspect and test each assembly separately to prevent mixing the parts.

Fig. 17, illustrates the type of hydraulic lifter used. See the *Trouble Shooting Chapter* under the heading *Engine Noises* for causes of hydraulic valve lifter noise. To replace valve lifters, proceed as follows:

1. Remove intake manifold and related parts.
2. Remove rocker arm covers.
3. Loosen rocker arm stud nuts or bolts and rotate rocker arms to the side.
4. Lift out push rods, keeping them in sequence in a rack so they may be installed in their original location.
5. Using a magnet rod, remove valve lifters and place them in sequence in a rack so they may be installed in their original location.
6. Reverse procedure to install.

TIMING CASE COVER, REPLACE

NOTE: If necessary to replace the cover oil seal the cover must first be removed.

V6-232

1. Disconnect battery ground cable and drain cooling.
2. Remove air cleaner and air duct assembly.
3. Remove fan shoud attaching, then remove fan and clutch assembly and fan shroud.
4. Loosen accessory drive belt idler, then remove drive belt and water pump pulley.
5. On models equipped with power steering, remove pump bracket attaching bolts, then position pump and bracket assembly aside with hoses attached.
6. If equipped with A/C, remove compressor front support bracket.
7. Disconnect by-pass hose, heater hoses and upper radiator hose from engine.
8. Position No. 1 cylinder at TDC compression stroke, then disconnect coil wire from distributor cap. Remove distributor cap and mark position of rotor to distributor body and distributor body to front cover. Remove distributor hold down clamp, then remove distributor.
9. On models equipped with Tripminder, remove fuel flow meter support bracket.
10. Raise vehicle and support, then remove crankshaft damper using a suitable puller.
11. Remove fuel pump shield, then remove fuel pump attaching bolts and position pump aside with fuel hose attached.
12. Remove oil filter, then disconnect lower radiator hose at water pump.
13. Remove oil pan as described under Oil Pan, Replace.
14. Lower vehicle, then remove front cover attaching bolts, Fig. 17A.

NOTE: One of the front cover attaching bolts is located behind the oil filter adapter.

15. Remove ignition timing indicator, then remove front cover and water pump as an assembly.
16. Reverse procedure to install. Coat threads of bolt located at position 10, Fig. 17A, with a suitable sealer before installing. Torque front cover attaching bolts to 15 to 22 ft. lbs.

NOTE: Lubricate camshaft thrust button with Polyethylene grease before installing front cover. Also ensure that thrust button and spring are properly seated.

V8-302, 351W

1. Drain cooling system and crankcase.
2. Remove fan shroud attaching bolts and position shroud over engine fan.
3. Remove engine fan, spacer and shroud.
4. Remove drive belts and A/C idler pulley bracket.
5. Remove power steering pump and position aside.
6. Remove all accessory brackets attached to water pump, then remove water pump pulley.
7. Disconnect lower radiator hose, heater hose and by-pass hose from water pump.
8. Remove crankshaft pulley from vibration damper.
9. Remove damper attaching screw and washer, then using a suitable puller, remove damper.
10. Disconnect fuel pump outlet line, then remove fuel pump attaching bolts and position pump aside.
11. Remove oil level dip stick.
12. Remove oil pan to front cover attaching bolts.
13. Remove front cover to engine block attaching bolts, then remove front cover and water pump as an assembly.

NOTE: Use a thin blade knife to cut oil pan gasket flush with cylinder block face prior to separating front cover from cylinder block.

14. Reverse procedure to install.

V8-400

1. Drain cooling system and disconnect battery ground cable.
2. Remove fan shroud attaching bolts then position shroud rearward.
3. Remove drive belts and A/C lower idler pulley.
4. Remove compressor mount to water pump bracket, if equipped.
5. Remove water pump pulley.

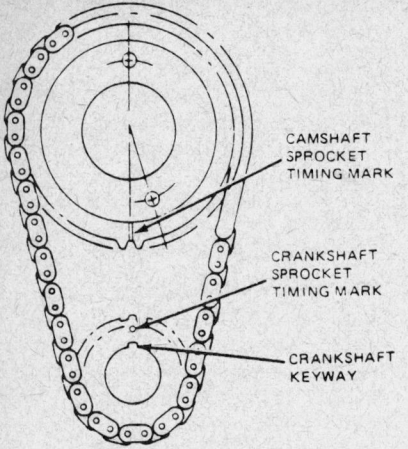

Fig. 18 Valve timing marks. V6-232

6. Remove alternator and power steering pump brackets from water pump and position aside.
7. Disconnect lower radiator hose and heater hose from water pump.
8. Remove crankshaft pulley and vibration damper attaching screw, then using a suitable puller, remove damper.
9. Remove timing pointer.
10. Remove front cover and water pump to engine block attaching bolts, then remove front cover and water pump as an assembly.
11. Reverse procedure to install.

V8-460

1. Drain cooling system and crankcase.
2. Remove engine fan and radiator shroud.
3. Disconnect upper and lower radiator hoses and transmission oil cooler lines from radiator.
4. Remove radiator upper support and radiator.
5. Remove drive belts and water pump pulley.
6. Remove A/C compressor support, if equipped.
7. Remove crankshaft pulley and vibration damper attaching screw, then remove damper using a suitable puller.
8. Remove woodruff key from crankshaft.
9. Loosen by-pass hose at water pump, then disconnect heater return hose from water pump.
10. Remove fuel pump.

11. Remove front cover to cylinder block attaching bolts, then remove front cover and water pump assembly.

NOTE: Using a thin blade knife, cut oil pan seal flush with cylinder block face prior to separating front cover from cylinder block.

12. Reverse procedure to install.

TIMING CHAIN, REPLACE

1. To remove the chain, first take off the timing chain cover as outlined previously.
2. Crank the engine until the timing mark on the camshaft sprocket is adjacent to the timing mark on the crankshaft sprocket, Figs. 18 & 18A.
3. Remove cap screws, lock plate and fuel pump eccentric from front of camshaft.
4. Place a screwdriver behind the camshaft sprocket and carefully pry the sprocket and chain off the camshaft.
5. Reverse the foregoing procedure to install the chain, being sure to align the timing marks as shown in Figs. 18 and 18A.

CAMSHAFT, REPLACE

If it is necessary to replace the camshaft only it may be accomplished without removing the engine from the chassis. But if the camshaft bearings are to be replaced the engine will have to be removed. To remove the camshaft, proceed as follows:

1980—84 V8-302, 351W & 1982 V6-232 Except Versailles

NOTE: It may be necessary to remove or reposition radiator, A/C compressor and grille components to provide adequate clearance.

1. To remove camshaft, remove front cover and timing chain.
2. Remove distributor cap and spark plug wires, then remove distributor.
3. Disconnect automatic transmission oil cooler lines from radiator and remove radiator.
4. Remove intake manifold and carburetor as an assembly.
5. Remove rocker arm covers.

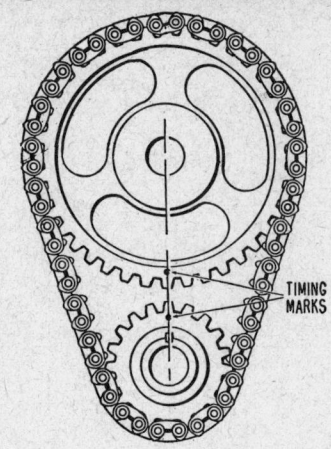

Fig. 18A Valve timing marks. V8 Engines

6. Loosen rocker arm fulcrum or bolts and rotate rocker arms to one side.
7. Remove push rods, keeping them in sequence in a rack so they may be installed in their original location.
8. Using a magnet, remove valve lifters and place them in a rack in sequence so they may be installed in their original location.
9. Remove camshaft thrust plate, and carefully pull camshaft from engine, using care to avoid damaging camshaft bearings.
10. Reverse procedure to install.

NOTE: Prior to installation of the camshaft, lubricate push rods and camshaft lobes with lubricant part No. D9AZ-19579-C or equivalent on V6-232 engines and D0AZ-19584-A or equivalent for V8-302 & 351W engines. Using engine oil SF, lubricate valve tappets & bores.

V8-302, 351W Versailles

1. Remove hood latch assembly, then disconnect A/C ambient temperature sensor wire connector and remove hood latch support brackets.
2. Remove condenser to radiator support attaching bolts, then remove fender to radiator support braces at each side of engine compartment.
3. Remove air dam and gasket located between radiator support and grille opening panel.
4. Carefully lift condenser upward until clearance is obtained to remove camshaft.
5. Remove cylinder front cover and timing chain as outlined previously.
6. Remove intake manifold and carburetor as an assembly.
7. Remove rocker covers. Loosen rocker arm stud nuts or fulcrum bolts and rotate rocker arms to the side.
8. Remove push rods and valve lifters in sequence so they can be installed in the same position.
9. Remove camshaft thrust plate, then carefully remove camshaft from engine, Fig. 19.

NOTE: When removing camshaft, use care not to damage camshaft bearings.

10. Reverse procedure to install.

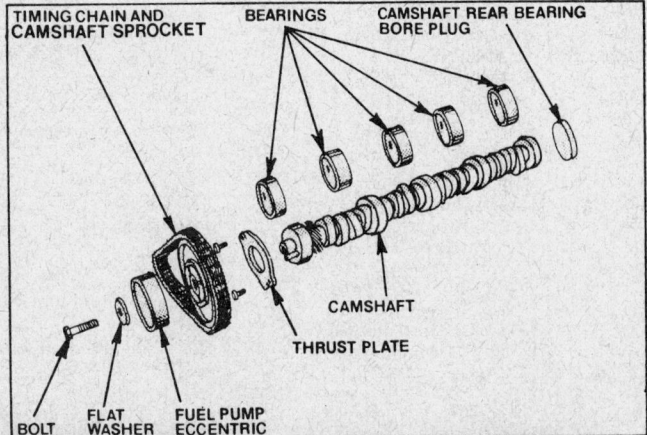

Fig. 19 Camshaft & related parts (typical). V8 engines

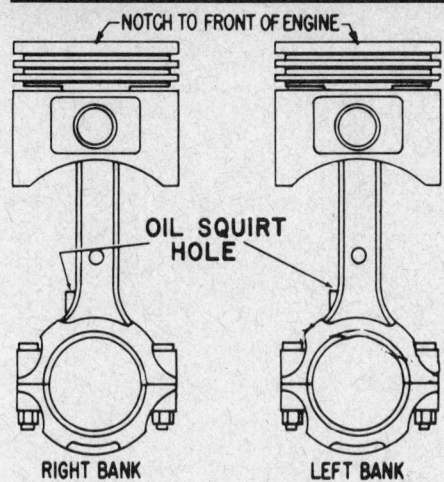

Fig. 20 Piston & rod assembly. V6-232

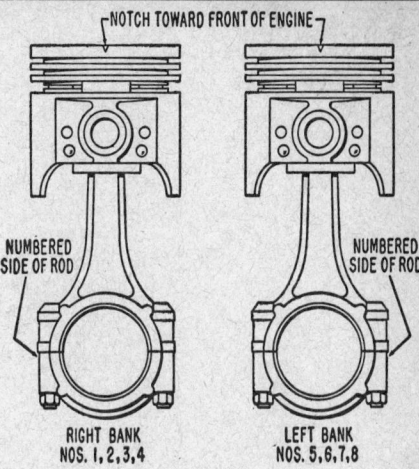

Fig. 20A Piston & rod assembly. V8 Engines

PISTONS, RINGS & PINS

Pistons are available in oversizes of .003, .020, .030 and .040".

Piston pins are available in oversizes of .001 and .002".

Rings are available in oversizes of .020, .030 and .040".

MAIN & ROD BEARINGS

Main and rod bearings are available in standard size and undersizes of .001, .002, .010, 020, .030 and .040".

CRANKSHAFT OIL SEAL, REPLACE

1977—83

1. Remove oil pan and oil pump, if necessary.
2. Remove rear bearing cap, Fig. 21.
3. Loosen remaining bearing caps, allowing crankshaft to drop down about 1/32".
4. Remove old seals from both cylinder block and rear main bearing cap. Use a brass rod to drift upper half of seal from cylinder block groove. Rotate crankshaft while drifting to facilitate removal.
5. Carefully clean seal groove in block with a brush and solvent. Also clean seal groove in bearing cap. Remove the oil seal retaining pin from the bearing cap if so equipped. *The pin is not used with the split-lip seal.*
6. Dip seal halves in clean engine oil.
7. Carefully install upper seal half in its groove with undercut side of seal toward front of engine, Fig. 22, by rotating it on shaft journal of crankshaft until approximately 3/8" protrudes below the parting surface. *Be sure no rubber has been shaved from outside diameter or seal by bottom edge of groove.*
8. Retighten main bearing caps and torque to specifications.
9. Install lower seal in main bearing cap with undercut side of seal toward front of engine, and allow seal to protrude about 3/8" above parting surface to mate with upper seal upon cap installation.
10. Apply suitable sealer to parting faces of cap and block. Install cap and torque to specifications.

NOTE: If difficulty is encountered in installing the upper half of the seal in position, lightly lap (sandpaper) the side of the seal opposite the lip side using a medium grit paper. After sanding, the seal must be washed in solvent, then dipped in clean engine oil prior to installation.

V8-400

1. Drain cooling system, then disconnect upper and lower radiator hose and transmission oil cooler lines from radiator.
2. If equipped with A/C, remove condenser.
3. Remove front cover and timing chain as outlined previously.
4. Remove fuel pump.
5. Remove intake manifold and carburetor as an assembly.
6. Remove rocker covers, then loosen fulcrum bolts and rotate rocker arms to the side.
7. Remove push rods and valve lifters in sequence so they can be installed in the same position.
8. Position No. 1 piston at TDC, then remove thrust plate and withdraw camshaft from engine, Fig. 19.

NOTE: When removing camshaft, use care not to damage camshaft bearings.

9. Reverse procedure to install.

V8-460

1. Drain crankcase and cooling system.
2. Remove timing cover, chain and sprockets as outlined previously.
3. Remove intake manifold and carburetor as an assembly.
4. Remove rocker arm covers. Back off rocker arm bolts, turn rocker arms sideways and remove push rods in sequence.
5. Remove valve lifters.
6. If air conditioned, unbolt and lay condenser on left fender. Secure in this position.
7. Remove grille.
8. Remove camshaft thrust plate bolts and carefully remove camshaft from front of engine, Fig. 19.
9. Reverse procedure to install.

PISTON & ROD, ASSEMBLE

If the old pistons are serviceable, make certain that they are installed on the rods from which they were removed. The assembly must be assembled as shown in Figs. 20 and 20A.

Check side clearance between connecting rods and crankshaft journal. Clearance should be .010–.020 inch for all engines except V6-232. V6-232 clearance should be .0047–.0114 inch.

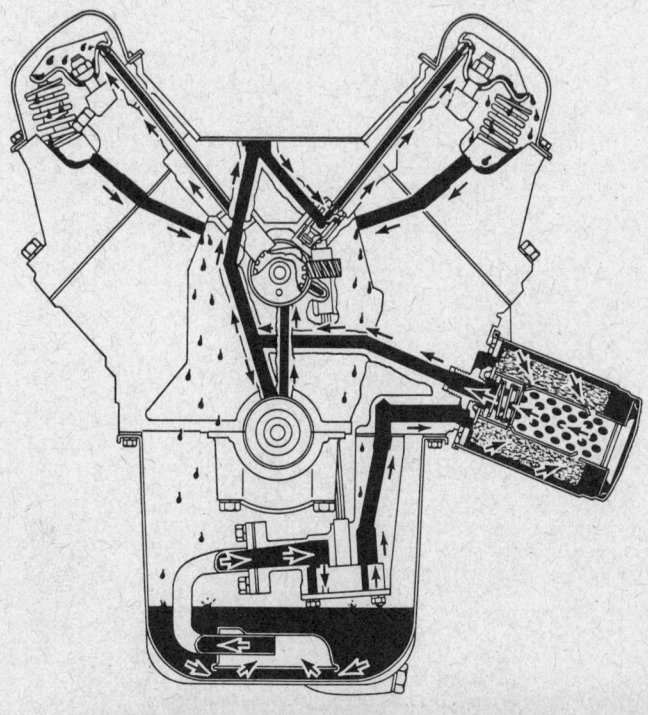

Engine lubrication (typical). V8 engine

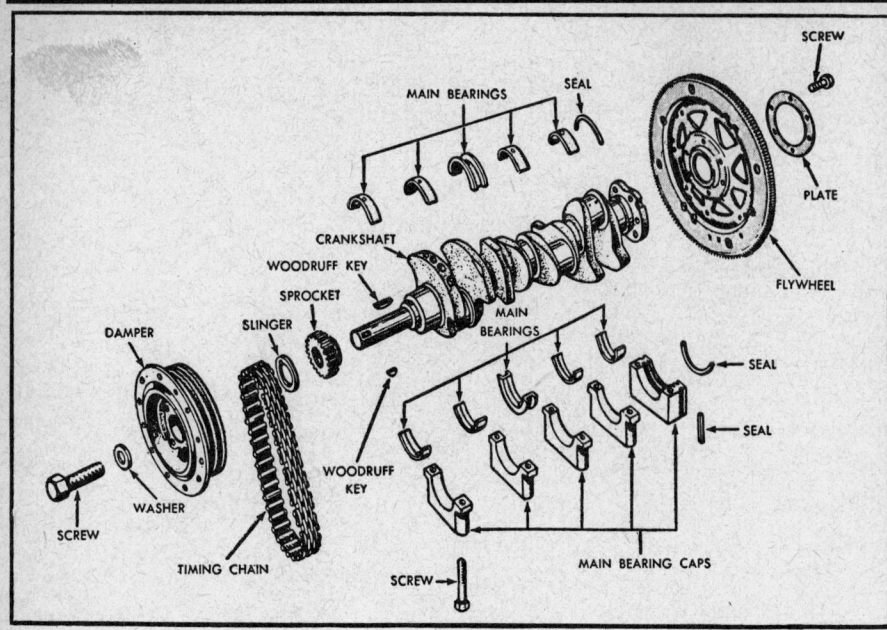

Fig. 21 Crankshaft and related parts. V8 Engines

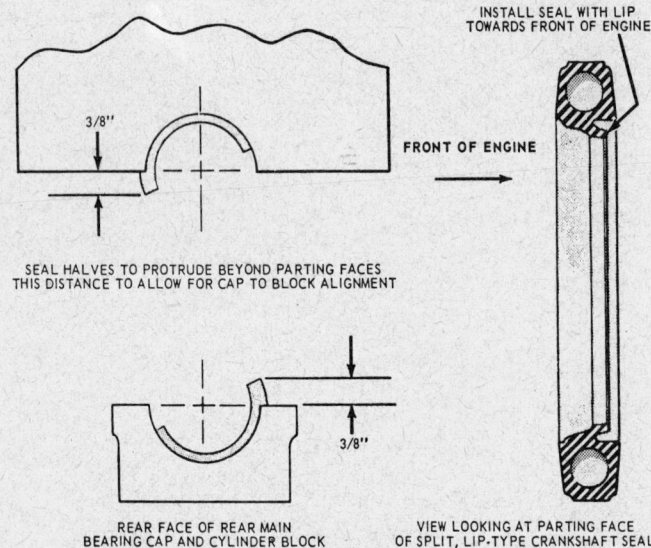

Fig. 22 Rear crankshaft seal installation. 1977–83

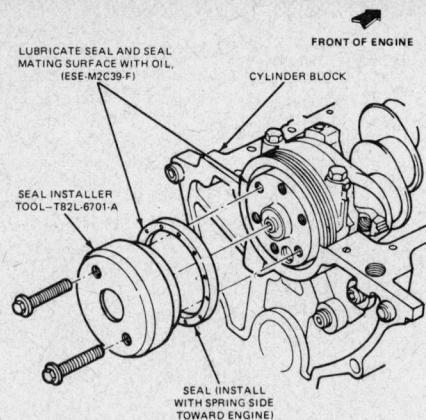

Fig. 22A Rear oil seal installation. 1984

1984

A new one-piece rear oil seal is used on 1984 engines. To replace the new type seal, proceed as follows:

1. Using a sharp awl, punch one hole into seal metal surface between seal lip and engine block.
2. Using slide hammer tool T82L-9533-B or equivalent, screw tool into hole in seal and remove seal by gently pulling rearward. Use caution to avoid damaging sealing surface.
3. Lubricate new seal with engine oil, then position seal on installer tool T82L-6701-A, or equivalent, Fig. 22A.
4. With spring end of seal facing towards engine, install tool, then alternately tighten bolts until rear face of seal is within .005 inch of the engine block.

OIL PAN, REPLACE

1982 Continental V6-232

1. Disconnect battery ground cable, then remove air cleaner and air intake duct.
2. Remove fan shroud attaching screws and position shroud over fan, then remove engine oil dipstick.
3. Remove vacuum solenoid from dash panel and position on engine with vacuum hoses attached.
4. Raise and support front of vehicle, then remove exhaust pipe to exhaust manifold attaching nuts.
5. Drain crankcase, then remove oil filter.
6. Remove shift linkage bracket to converter housing attaching bolts.
7. Disconnect transmission oil cooler lines at radiator. Remove four converter cover attaching bolts, then remove converter cover.
8. Remove bolts attaching engine damper to No. 2 crossmember.
9. Disconnect steering gear at flex coupling, then remove steering gear to main crossmember attaching bolts and allow steering gear to rest on frame.
10. Remove nuts and bolts attaching from engine mounts to chassis, then raise engine approximately 2 to 3 inches and insert wooden block between engine mounts and frame.

NOTE: On some models, it may be necessary to raise engine as much as 5 inches to provide clearance for oil pan removal. On these models, transmission fluid dipstick tube may contact Thermactor air tube. If contact occurs, lower engine and remove dipstick and air tube.

11. Remove oil pan attaching bolts, then lower oil pan to crossmember.
12. Remove oil pump pickup tube attaching bolts and pickup tube bracket attaching nut, then lower pickup tube into oil pan.
13. Remove oil pan through front of vehicle, then remove oil pan gaskets and seals.
14. Reverse procedure to install. Using a small screwdriver, work tabs of oil pan seal into gap between rear main bearing cap and cylinder block, then with tabs positioned, work seal into groove on rear main bearing cap. Apply a 1/8 inch bead of silicone sealer D6AZ-19562-B or equivalent where front cover and cylinder block join and where rear main bearing cap and cylinder block join. Apply a 1/8 inch bead along oil pan rail surface of cylinder block and a 1/4 inch bead along front cover to oil pan surface.

NOTE: When using silicone sealant, assembly must occur within 15 minutes after sealant application. After this time, the sealer may start to set, and its sealing effectiveness may be reduced.

1980–83 Mark VI, 1980–84 Continental, 1982–84 Town Car & 1984 Mark VII

1. Disconnect battery ground cable and remove air cleaner assembly.
2. Disconnect accelerator cable and kickdown rod from carburetor.

3. Remove accelerator mounting bracket bolts and bracket, then the EGR valve and cooler, if applicable.
4. Remove fan shroud attaching screws and position shroud over fan.
5. Disconnect wiper motor electrical connector and remove wiper motor.
6. Disconnect windshield washer hose.
7. Remove wiper motor mounting cover.
8. Remove oil level dipstick, then the dipstick tube retaining bolt from exhaust manifold.
9. If equipped with EGR cooler, remove Thermactor air dump tube retaining clamp, then the Thermactor crossover tube at rear of engine.
10. Raise and support vehicle, then drain engine oil.
11. On models equipped with EEC, remove transmission filler tube from oil pan and drain transmission fluid, then remove starter.
12. Disconnect fuel tank fuel line at fuel pump and plug line.

NOTE: Vehicles equipped with electronic fuel injection have high pressure at the electric fuel pump. Pressure must be relieved at the schrader type valve on the fuel charging assembly before disconnecting fuel supply and return lines.

13. Disconnect exhaust pipes from manifolds. Remove oxygen sensor, if applicable.
14. If equipped with EGR cooler, remove exhaust gas sensor from exhaust manifold, then the Thermactor secondary air tube to converter housing clamps.
15. On all models, remove dipstick tube from oil pan.
16. Loosen rear engine mount attaching nuts.
17. Remove engine mount through bolts.
18. Remove shift crossover bolts at transmission.
19. If equipped with EGR cooler, disconnect exhaust pipes from catalytic converter outlet, then the catalytic converter secondary air tube and inlet pipes to exhaust manifold.
20. On all models, disconnect transmission kickdown rod.
21. Remove torque converter housing cover.
22. Remove brake line retainer from front crossmember.
23. With a suitable jack, raise engine as far as possible.
24. Place a block of wood between each engine mount and chassis bracket. When engine is secured in this position, remove jack, then the low oil level sensor, if equipped.
25. Remove oil pan attaching bolts and lower the oil pan.
26. Remove oil pick-up tube bolts and lower tube in oil pan.
27. Remove oil pan from vehicle.
28. Reverse procedure to install.

1977–80 Versailles

1. Disconnect battery ground cable.
2. Remove two fan shroud attaching screws and loosen shroud to prevent damage when raising engine.
3. Raise vehicle and drain crankcase.
4. Remove stabilizer bar from chassis.
5. Remove right and left engine mount through bolts.
6. Loosen transmission oil cooler lines and move aside.
7. Raise engine and position 2 × 4 in. wooden blocks under engine mounts.
8. Remove oil pan attaching bolts and oil pan.

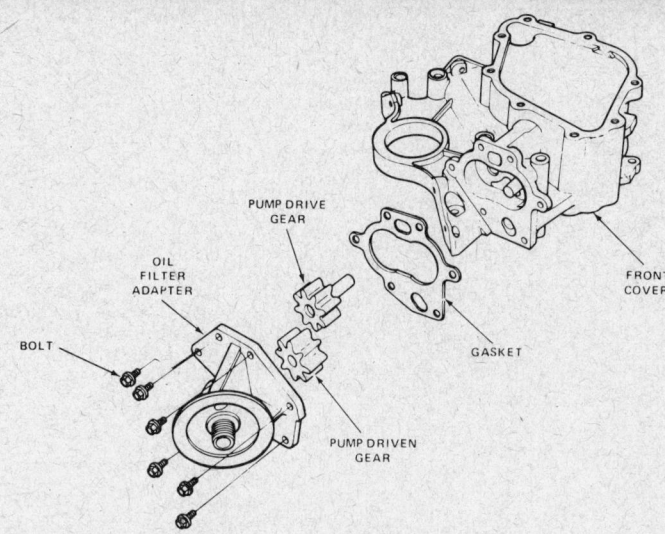

Fig. 23 Oil pump assembly. V6-232

NOTE: It will be necessary to rotate the crankshaft during removal so that rear crankshaft throw is in horizontal position to clear rear oil pan flange.

9. Reverse procedure to install.

1978–79—Continental & Mark V

1. Disconnect battery ground cable. Also disconnect transmission oil cooler lines from radiator and position aside.
2. Remove fresh air intake duct and radiator shroud attaching bolts, then position radiator shroud over fan.
3. Raise vehicle and drain crankcase.
4. On Mark V models, remove "X" brace located below oil pan.
5. On all models, remove end attachments of front stabilizer bar and rotate ends of bar downward to raise center of bar.
6. Support engine using a suitable jack, then remove engine support through bolts.
7. Raise engine and position wooden blocks 3 in. high between each engine support bracket and frame, then lower engine.
8. Remove oil pan attaching bolts, then lower pan to crossmember.
9. On models equipped with V8-400 engines, loosen oil pump and inlet tube and allow assembly to drop into the oil pan.
10. On all models, position rear crankshaft throw horizontally, then remove oil pan.

1977 Continental

1. Disconnect battery ground cable.
2. Disconnect radiator shroud from radiator.
3. Support vehicle on hoist and drain crankcase.
4. Remove starter retaining bolts.
5. Using a floor jack and wooden block under oil pan, raise engine enough to remove weight of engine from supports and remove through bolts from each support.
6. Remove the two forward support bolts from the right support insulator, then loosen the rear support bolt and pivot the insulator upward to gain access to the

converter support bolts. Remove converter support bolts and remove bracket from each side of oil pan.
7. Position a 1 inch wooden block under each engine support bracket and remove jack.
8. Remove front stabilizer bar end attachments and rotate ends of bar down to raise center of bar.
9. Remove oil filter.
10. Remove oil pan attaching bolts and remove oil pan.
11. Reverse removal procedure for installation.

1977 Mark IV & V

1. Disconnect battery ground cable.
2. Disconnect transmission oil cooler lines from radiator, then remove radiator shroud attaching bolts and position shroud over fan.
3. Support vehicle on hoist, then drain crankcase and remove oil filter.
4. Remove end attachments of front stabilizer bar and rotate ends of bar down to raise center of bar.
5. Support engine with floor jack and remove engine support through bolts.
6. Remove transmission oil cooler line attaching bolt from engine block and remove starter attaching bolts.
7. Raise engine enough to allow removal of right insulator heat shield, then position a wooden block 3 inches high between each engine support bracket and exhaust manifold. Lower engine allowing blocks to support engine.
8. Remove converter housing to cylinder block support attaching bolts and remove brackets.
9. Remove oil pan attaching bolts and lower pan to crossmember, then move transmission oil cooler lines upward and remove oil pan.
10. Reverse removal procedure for installation.

OIL PUMP, REPLACE

V6-232

On these engines, the oil pump is contained within the front cover, Fig. 23.

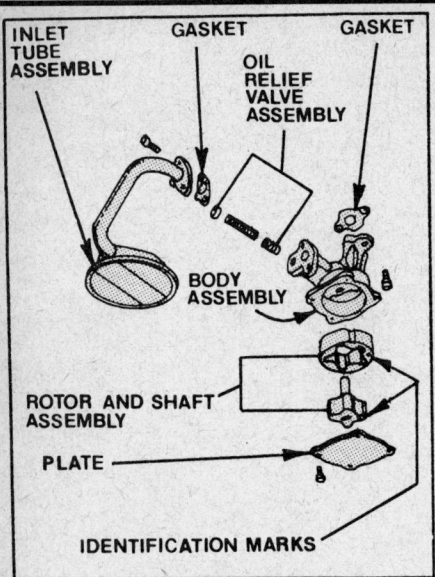

Fig. 23A Oil pump assembly. V8-302, 351W & 460

V8 Engines

1. Remove oil pan as previously described under "Oil Pan, Replace".
2. Remove the two attaching bolts and remove the oil pump assembly with gasket and drive shaft.
3. Reverse procedure to install.

OIL PUMP, SERVICE

V6-232 Engine

To disassemble, remove oil filter, if necessary, oil pump, cover bolts and cover. Lift oil pump gears from front cover pocket and remove cover gasket. Remove cotter pin from relief valve plug in pump housing. Drill a small hole and insert a self-tapping screw into the plug, then using pliers remove plug from pump housing. Remove retainer spring and relief valve from pump housing. Using a suitable solvent, thoroughly clean oil pump components. Inspect oil pump as follows:

1. Check oil pump cover gasket surface. Remove any remaining gasket material, burrs and nicks.
2. Position a straightedge across oil pump gears and gasket surface.
3. Using a feeler gauge, measure clearance between straightedge and gasket surface. Clearance should be .002–.005 inch. If clearance is less than .002 inch, proceed to step 4.
4. Using a micrometer, measure oil pump gear thickness. Gear thickness should be .872–.873 inch. If gear is less than .872 inch, replace gear and check reading.
5. Measure front cover gear pocket depth. Depth should be .868–.870 inch. If depth exceeds .870 inch, replace oil pump front cover.
6. Using a feeler gauge, measure side clearance between gear tooth and gear pocket side wall. Clearance should be .002–.005 inch. If clearance exceeds .005 inch, proceed to step 7.
7. Using a micrometer, measure gear diameter. Gear diameter should be 1.664–1.666 inch. If gear diameter is less than 1.664 inch, replace gear and check

reading.
8. Measure front cover gear pocket width. Width should be 1.671–1.674 inch. If width is less than 1.671, replace front cover.

V8 Engines

To disassemble, remove the pump cover plate, Figs. 23A and 24, and lift out the rotor and shaft. Remove cotter pin that secures relief valve plug in pump housing. Drill a small hole and insert a self-tapping screw into plug, then using pliers remove plug from pump housing. Then remove the retainer spring and relief valve from the pump housing. Inspect the pump as follows:

1. With all parts clean and dry, check the inside of the pump housing and the outer race and rotor for damage or excessive wear.
2. Check the mating surface of the pump cover for wear. If this surface is worn, scored or grooved, replace the cover.
3. Measure the clearance between the outer race and housing. This clearance should be .001–.013.
4. With the rotor assembly installed in the housing, place a straight edge over the rotor assembly and housing. Measure the clearance between the straight edge and the rotor and outer race. Recommended limits are .0016–.004".
5. Check the drive shaft-to-housing bearing clearance by measuring the O.D. of the shaft and the I.D. of the housing bearing. The recommended clearance limits are .0015–.0030".
6. Inspect the relief valve spring for a collapsed or worn condition.
7. Check the relief valve piston for scores and free operation in the bore. The specified clearance is .0015–.0030 inch.

BELT TENSION DATA

	New	Used
1977–80 1/4 inch	65	50
Exc. 1/4 inch	140	110
1981		
Except 1/4"	140	110
1/4"	65	40
V Ribbed Belt		
4 Rib	105	100
5 Rib①	125	120
5 Rib②	108	108
6 Rib①	155	150
6 Rib②	113	113
1982–84		
Except 1/4"	140	105
1/4"	65	50
V Ribbed Belt		
4 Rib		
Except Air Pump	130	115
Air Pump	110	105
5 Rib	150	135
6 Rib①	160	145
6 Rib②	113	110

①—W/ tensioner
②—W/ absorber

WATER PUMP, REPLACE

V6-232

1. Drain cooling system, then remove air cleaner and air intake duct.
2. Remove fan shroud attaching screws and fan and fan clutch attaching bolts, then remove fan and fan clutch assembly.
3. Loosen accessory drive belt idler, then remove drive belt and water pump pulley.

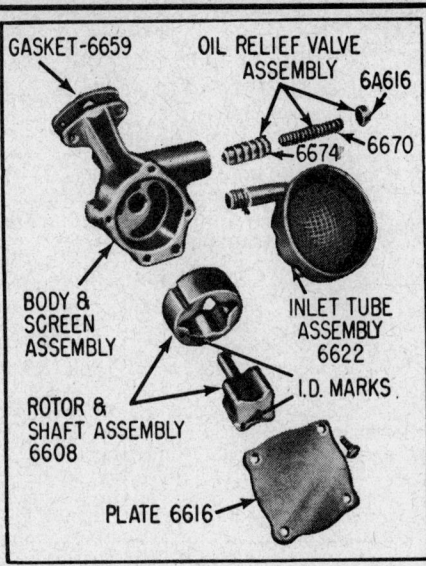

Fig. 24 Oil pump assembly. V8-400

4. On models equipped with power steering, remove pump mounting bracket attaching bolts, position pump aside with hoses attached.
5. On models equipped with A/C, remove compressor front support bracket.
6. Disconnect lower radiator hose, coolant bypass hose and heat hose from water pump.
7. On models equipped with Tripminder, remove fuel flow sensor support bracket. Do not disconnect fuel lines.
8. Remove water pump attaching bolts, then remove water pump.
9. Reverse procedure to install.

V8-302, 351W

1. Drain cooling system, then remove fan shroud attaching bolts and position shroud over fan.
2. Remove fan, spacer and shroud.
3. Remove drive belts, then remove A/C idler pulley bracket.
4. Remove power steering pump and position aside.
5. Remove all accessory brackets which attach to water pump, then remove water pump pulley.
6. Remove lower radiator hose, heater hose and by-pass hose from water pump.
7. Remove water pump to front cover attaching bolts, then remove water pump.
8. Reverse procedure to install.

V8-400

1. Drain cooling system, then disconnect battery ground cable.
2. Remove fan shroud attaching bolts and position shroud rearward.
3. Remove fan and spacer from water pump shaft.
4. Remove drive belts, then remove A/C lower idler pulley.
5. Remove A/C compressor mount from water pump bracket.
6. Remove water pump pulley.
7. Remove alternator and power steering bracket from water pump and position aside.
8. Disconnect lower radiator and heater hose from water pump.
9. Remove water pump attaching bolts and

water pump.
10. Reverse procedure to install.

V8-460

1. Drain cooling system and remove fan, fan shroud and drive belts.
2. Disconnect alternator bracket and position out of way.
3. Remove air pump pulley and pivot bolt, then disconnect adjusting bracket at pump. Remove upper bracket bolt and swing bracket out of way.
4. Remove power steering pump attaching bolts and position pump aside.
5. Remove A/C compressor and power steering pump and position aside.

NOTE: Secure compressor to left fender brace.

6. Remove A/C compressor bracket, then disconnect, radiator, heater and bypass hoses from water pump.
7. Remove water pump attaching bolts and water pump.
8. Reverse procedure to install.

FUEL PUMP, REPLACE

Mechanical Type

1. Disconnect fuel lines from fuel pump.
2. Remove fuel pump attaching bolts and the fuel pump and gasket.
3. Remove all gasket material from the pump and block gasket surfaces. Apply sealer to both sides of new gasket.
4. Position gasket on pump flange and hold pump in position against its mounting surface. Make sure rocker arm is riding on camshaft eccentric.
5. Press pump tight against its mounting.

Install retaining screws and tighten them alternately.
6. Connect fuel lines. Then operate engine and check for leaks.

NOTE: Before installing the pump, it is good practice to crank the engine so that the nose of the camshaft eccentric is out of the way of the fuel pump rocker arm when the pump is installed. In this way there will be the least amount of tension on the rocker arm, thereby easing the installation of the pump.

Electric Type

NOTE: When the electric fuel pump is removed from the fuel tank, all the rubber hoses, clamps and mounting gaskets should be replaced, as exposure to the air causes the hoses to become brittle and will lead to premature failure.

Removal

1. Remove air cleaner.
2. Attach tool T80L-9974-A or equivalent, to fuel diagnostic valve on the fuel charging assembly, then slowly depressurize fuel system.
3. Siphon fuel from fuel tank, then raise and support vehicle.
4. Disconnect fuel supply, return and vent lines at the left and right side rear axle frame kickdowns.
5. Disconnect electrical connector in front of fuel tank.
6. Disconnect and remove fuel filler tube.
7. Remove fuel tank support straps, then the fuel tank.
8. Clean all dirt accumulated around fuel pump attaching flange, then disconnect supply and return line fittings and the electrical connector.

9. Turn fuel pump lockring counterclockwise and remove lockring.
10. Remove fuel pump and bracket assembly from fuel tank. Discard seal ring.

Installation

1. Clean fuel tank mounting surface and seal ring groove.
2. Lightly coat new seal ring with heavy grease to hold it in place, then install into fuel ring groove.
3. Carefully install fuel pump and bracket assembly into tank, ensuring filter is not damaged during installation. Ensure locating keys are positioned in keyways and seal ring remains in groove.
4. Holding pump assembly in place, install lockring fingertight, ensuring all locking tabs are positioned under fuel tank ring tabs. Continue to turn lockring clockwise until ring contacts stop.
5. Connect fuel pump electrical connector, then lubricate fittings and reconnect fuel lines.
6. Install fuel tank and tighten support straps.
7. Reconnect fuel sender and fuel pump wiring harness, then lower vehicle.
8. Install fuel filler tube and reconnect vent line.
9. Lubricate fittings at right and left hand side of rear axle frame, reconnect finger tight, then tighten an additional 1/4 turn.
10. Fill fuel tank with at least 10 gallons of fuel and check for leaks.
11. Connect tool Y80L-9974-A or equivalent, onto fuel charging assembly diagnostic valve. Turn ignition key "ON" for approximately 3 seconds. Turn key "OFF," then back "ON" for another 3 seconds. Continue to perform this operation until gauge reads at least 35 psi. Check for leaks at all fittings. Correct as necessary.
12. Remove tool, start engine and recheck for leaks.

Rear Axle, Propeller Shaft & Brakes

REAR AXLES

Figs. 1 & 2 illustrate the rear axle assemblies used on these vehicles. When necessary to overhaul either one of these units, refer to the rear axle specifications table at the beginning of this chapter.

1980–84 Integral Carrier Type

The gear set consists of a ring gear and an overhung drive pinion which is supported by two opposed tapered roller bearings, Fig. 1. The differential case is a one-piece design with openings allowing assembly of the internal parts and lubricant flow. The differential pinion shaft is retained with a threaded bolt (lock) assembled to the case.

The roller type wheel bearings have no inner race, and the rollers directly contact the bearing journals of the axle shafts. The axle shafts do not use an inner and outer bearing retainer. Rather, they are held in the axle by means of C-locks. These C-locks also fit into a machined recess in the differential side gears within the differential case. There is no retainer bolt access hole in the axle shaft flange.

1977–80 Removable Carrier Type

In these axles, Fig. 2, the drive pinion is straddle-mounted by two opposed tapered roller bearings which support the pinion shaft in front of the drive pinion gear, and straight roller bearing that supports the pinion shaft at the rear of the pinion gear. The drive pinion is assembled in a pinion retainer that is bolted to the differential carrier. The tapered roller bearings are preloaded by a collapsible spacer between the bearings. The pinion is positioned by a shim or shims located between the drive pinion retainer and the differential carrier.

The differential is supported in the carrier by two tapered roller side bearings. These bearings are preloaded by two threaded ring nuts or sleeves between the bearings and pedestals. The differential assembly is positioned for proper ring gear and pinion backlash by varying the adjustment of these ring nuts. The differential case houses two side gears in mesh with two pinions mounted on a pinion shaft which is held in place by a pin. The side gears and pinions are backed by thrust washers.

The axle shafts are of unequal length, the left shaft being shorter than the right. The

axle shafts are mounted in tapered roller or ball bearings that are pressed on the shafts.

SERVICE BULLETIN

All Ford Built Rear Axles: Recent manufacturing changes have eliminated the need for marking rear axle drive pinions for individual variations from nominal shim thicknesses. In the past, these pinion markings, with the aid of a shim selection table, were used as a guide to select correct shim thicknesses when a gear set or carrier assembly replacement was performed.

With the elimination of pinion markings, use of the shim selection table is no longer possible and the methods outlined below must be used.

1. Measure the thickness of the original pinion depth shim removed from the axle. Use the same thickness upon installation of the replacement carrier or drive pinion. If any further shim change is necessary, it will be indicated in the tooth pattern check.
2. If the original shim is lost, substitute a nominal shim for the original and use the tooth pattern check to determine if further shim changes are necessary.

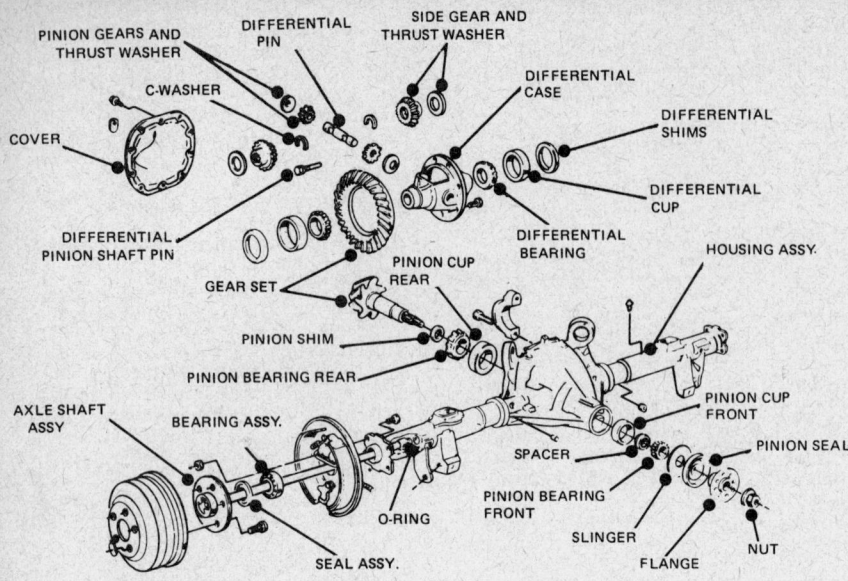

Fig. 1 Integral carrier type rear axle assembly (typical). 1980-84

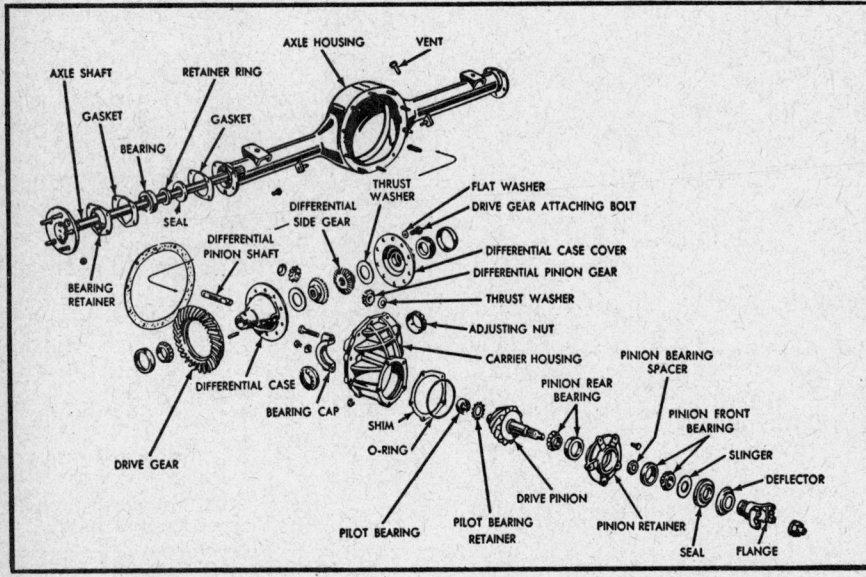

Fig. 2 Removable carrier type rear axle assembly (typical). 1977-80

REAR AXLE, REPLACE

1980-83 Mark VI, 1980-84 Continental, 1982-84 Town Car & 1984 Mark VII

1. Raise vehicle and position safety stands under the rear frame crossmember.
2. Disconnect drive shaft at companion flange and secure it to vehicle using wire.
3. Remove wheels and brake drums. If equipped with rear disc brakes, remove callipers from anchor plates and rotors from shafts.
4. Support axles housing with floor jack.
5. Disconnect brake line from clips that retain line to axle housing, then disconnect vent from rear axle housing.

NOTE: Some axle vents may be secured to the housing assembly through the brake junction block. When reinstalling, apply thread locking compound E0AZ-19554-B or equivalent to ensure proper retention.

6. Disconnect shock absorbers from axle housing.
7. Disconnect upper control arms from mountings on axle housing.
8. Lower axle housing assembly until coils springs are released, then remove springs.
9. Disconnect lower control arms from mountings on axle housing, then lower the axle housing and remove it from behicle.

10. Reverse procedure to install.

1977-80 Versailles

1. Raise vehicle and position safety stands under rear frame members.
2. Mark drive shaft yoke and pinion flange for reassembly, then disconnect drive shaft at rear axle U-joint and remove drive shaft from transmission extension housing. Install seal replacer tool in extension housing to prevent leakage.
3. Disconnect shock absorbers from lower mountings.
4. Remove wheel and tire assembly.
5. Remove calipers from anchor plates, then remove two retaining nuts and slide rotors off axle shafts.

NOTE: Secure calipers to frame with wire.

6. Remove vent tube from axle housing.
7. Remove brake lines from axle housing clips.
8. Support axle housing using a suitable jack, then remove spring clip nuts and plates.
9. Lower rear axle assembly and remove from vehicle.
10. Reverse procedure to install.

1977-79 Continental

1. Raise rear of vehicle and remove wheel and tire assembly.
2. On models equipped with rear drum brakes, remove brake drums, disconnect brake lines at wheel cylinders.
3. On models equipped with rear disc brakes, remove calipers from anchor plates, then remove two retaining nuts and slide rotors off axle shafts.

NOTE: Secure calipers to frame with wire.

4. Make marks on drive shaft yoke and pinion flange for reassembly, then disconnect drive shaft at rear axle U-joint and remove drive shaft from transmission extension housing. Install seal replacer tool in extension housing to prevent leakage.
5. Position a drain pan under differential carrier, then loosen carrier attaching bolts and allow axle to drain.
6. Disconnect anti-skid sensor wire connector from differential carrier, if equipped.
7. Position safety stands under frame rear members, then support axle housing using a suitable jack.
8. Disconnect brake lines from axle housing retaining clips.
9. Disconnect vent tube from rear housing.
10. Disconnect shock absorbers from lower mounting brackets.
11. Disconnect track bar from mounting stud on rear axle housing bracket.

NOTE: The axle housing mounting bracket has two holes; the track bar should be attached to the upper hole.

12. Lower rear axle housing until coil springs are released, then remove springs and insulators.
13. Disconnect suspension lower arms from axle housing, then disconnect suspension upper arms from housing.

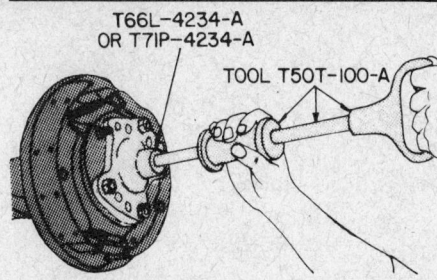

T66L-4234-A
OR T7IP-4234-A

TOOL T50T-100-A

Fig. 3   Removing axle shaft with slide hammer-type puller

14. Lower axle housing and remove from vehicle.
15. Reverse procedure to install.

1977–79 Mark V

1. Raise rear of vehicle and remove wheel and tire assembly.
2. On models equipped with rear drum brakes, remove brake drums and disconnect brake lines at wheel cylinders.
3. On models equipped with rear disc brakes, remove calipers from anchor plates, then remove two retaining nuts and slide rotors off axle shafts.

NOTE: Secure calipers to frame with wire.

4. Make marks on drive shaft yoke and pinion flange for reassembly, then disconnect drive shaft at rear axle U-joint and remove drive shaft from transmission extension housing. Install seal replacer tool in extension housing to prevent leakage.
5. Position a drain pan under differential carrier, then remove carrier attaching bolts and allow axle to drain.
6. Disconnect anti-skid sensor wire connector from differential carrier, then remove mounting bracket and sensor wiring from axle, if equipped.
7. Disconnect stabilizer, if equipped.
8. Disconnect shock absorber from lower mounting.
9. Remove brake line from retaining clips on rear axle housing, then remove brake line junction block retaining screw.
10. Position a suitable jack under axle housing to prevent housing from tilting when removing control arms.
11. Disconnect lower control arms from axle housing and position them downward.
12. Disconnect upper control arms from axle housing and position them upward.
13. Disconnect air vent line.

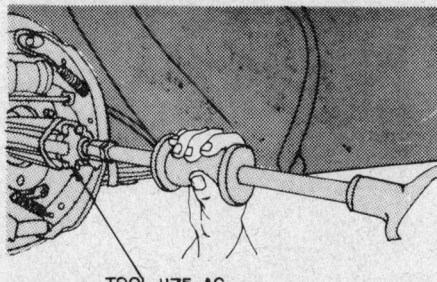

TOOL 1175-AC

Fig. 5   Using hook-type tool to remove oil seal

14. Lower axle housing slightly and remove coil springs and insulators.
15. Lower axle housing and remove from vehicle.
16. Reverse procedure to install.

AXLE SHAFTS & BEARINGS, REPLACE
Removable Carrier

SERVICE NOTE

If an axle shaft and bearing assembly is removed from a 1977–78 vehicle, and it is of the sealed bearing design, the replacement axle shaft assembly will be of the tapered roller bearing type. This type axle shaft assembly is completely interchangeable with the sealed bearing type as an assembly only. The inner oil seal must be removed before the tapered bearing shaft can be installed into the housing bore. In addition, the housing wheel bearing bore must be sanded with fine grit emery cloth before installation of the tapered type bearing to ensure a good sealing surface for the new wheel seal location.

If only a bearing replacement is required, however, the service bearing must be of the same design as the bearing removed.

1. Remove rear wheel assembly, then the brake drum or caliper and rotor assembly.
2. Remove axle shaft retainer nuts and bolts.
3. Pull axle shaft assembly from housing. It may be necessary to use a suitable slide hammer type puller, Fig. 3.
4. To replace wheel bearing on models equipped with tapered roller bearings:
   a. Drill a 1/4 inch hole in inner bearing retainer approximately 3/4 of the thickness of the bearing retainer deep.

NOTE: Do not drill completely through the bearing retainer since damage to the axle shaft may result.

   b. Place a cold chisel across the drilled hole and strike with a hammer to break retainer, then discard retainer, Fig. 4.
   c. Using suitable press and plates, press bearing from axle shaft. Do not apply heat since the heat will weaken the axle shaft bearing journal area.
   d. Install lubricated seal and bearing on axle shaft, ensuring the cup rib ring faces toward the axle flange.

NOTE: The lubricated seal of the bearing assembly used with drum brake installations is of a different length than the seal used on disc brake installations and are not interchangeable. For identification, the seal used on drum brake installations has a grey color outer rim and on disc brake installations, the seal has a black oxide appearance.

   e. Press new bearing into place, then the bearing retainer firmly against the bearing.
   f. Remove old bearing cup from axle housing with a suitable puller. Place new bearing cup on bearing and apply

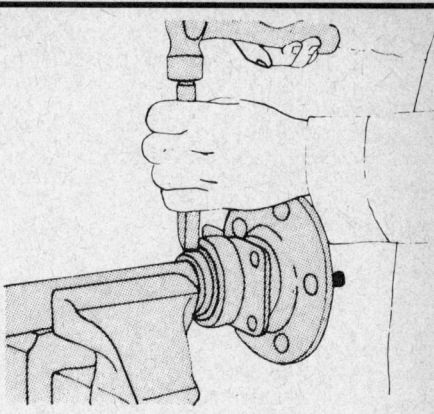

Fig. 4   Splitting bearing inner retainer for bearing removal

lubricant to outside diameter of seal and bearing cup and install in axle housing.

5. To replace wheel bearing on models equipped with ball bearings:
   a. Remove oil seal from axle housing, Fig. 5.
   b. Loosen bearing inner retaner by striking retainer ring in several places with a cold chisel and slide off shaft, Fig. 4.

NOTE: On some models, it may be necessary to drill a 1/4 inch hole in inner bearing retainer approximately 3/4 of the thickness of the bearing retainer deep before using the cold chisel.

   c. Using suitable press and plates, press bearing from shaft. Do not heat axle shaft since the heat will damage the shaft.
   d. Install outer retainer on shaft and press bearing into place. Press inner retainer onto shaft until firmly seated against bearing.
   e. Install oil seal into axle housing, Fig. 6.
6. On all units, slide axle shaft assembly into housing, engaging axle shaft splines in the side gear.
7. Install and torque axle shaft retainer nuts and bolts to 50–75 ft. lbs. on 1977 Continental, Mark IV and Mark V, 50–70 ft. lbs. on 1978–79 Continental and Mark V. On 1977 Versailles, torque disc brake anchor plate bolts to 90–120 ft. lbs. On

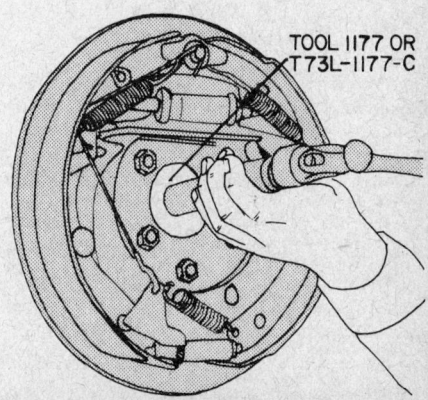

TOOL 1177 OR
T73L-1177-C

Fig. 6   Using special driver to install oil seal

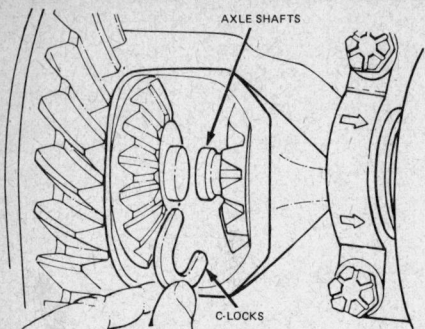

Fig. 7 Axle shaft "C" locks

1979 Versailles, torque axle shaft bearing retainer to 50–70 ft. lbs. On 1980 models, torque axle shaft bearing retainer to 20–40 ft. lbs.

Integral Carrier

1. Raise car on hoist and remove wheels.
2. Drain differential lubricant.
3. Remove brake drums.
4. Remove differential housing cover.
5. Position safety stands under rear frame member and lower hoist to allow axle to lower as far as possible.
6. Working through differential case opening, remove pinion shaft lock bolt and pinion shaft.
7. Push axle shaft(s) inward toward center of axle housing and remove C-lock(s) from housing, Fig. 7.
8. Remove axle shaft, using extreme care to avoid contact of shaft seal lip with any portion of axle shaft except seal journal.
9. Use a hook-type puller to remove seal and bearing, Fig. 8.
10. Reverse procedure to install, using suitable driving tools to install seal and bearing. Lubricate new bearing with rear axle lubricant and apply grease between the lips of the seal. Apply silicone sealant to

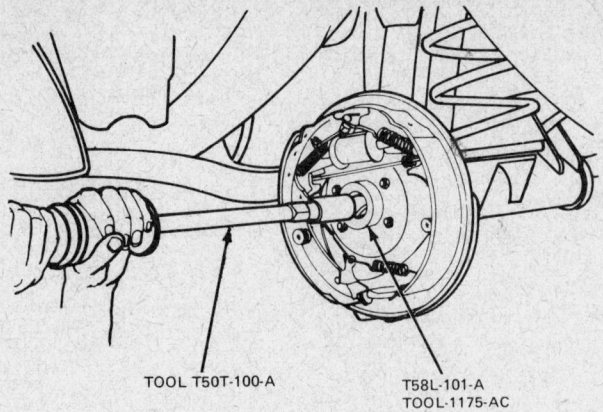

TOOL T50T-100-A
T58L-101-A
TOOL-1175-AC

Fig. 8 Removing axle shaft seal and bearing

carrier casting face as shown, Fig. 9, then install housing cover. Torque cover bolts to 30 ft. lbs.

PROPELLER SHAFT, REPLACE

To maintain proper drive line balance, mark the drive shaft, universal joints, slip yoke and companion flange before removing the shaft assembly so it can be reinstalled in its original position.
1. On Continental, Town Car, Versailles and Mark VI and VII vehicles, remove companion flange to drive pinion flange attaching bolts.
2. On Mark V models, disconnect rear U joint from companion flange. Tape loose bearing caps to spider.
3. On all models, pull drive shaft rearward until slip yoke clears transmission extension housing.
4. Reverse procedure to install.

BRAKE ADJUSTMENTS

These brakes, Fig. 10, have self-adjusting shoe mechanisms that assure correct lining-to-drum clearances at all times. The automatic adjusters operate only when the brakes are applied when the car is moving rearward.

Although the brakes are self-adjusting, an initial adjustment is necessary when the brake shoes have been relined or replaced, or when the length of the star wheel adjuster has been changed during some other service operation.

Frequent usage of an automatic transmission forward range to halt reverse vehicle motion may prevent the automatic adjusters from functioning, thereby inducing low pedal heights. Should low pedal heights be encountered, it is recommended that numerous forward and reverse stops be made until satisfactory pedal height is obtained.

NOTE: If a low pedal height condition cannot be corrected by making numerous reverse stops (provided the hydraulic system is free of air) it indicates that the automatic adjusting mechanism is not functioning. Therefore, it will be necessary to remove the brake drum, clean, free up and lubricate the adjusting mechanism. Then adjust the brakes, being sure the parking brake is fully released.

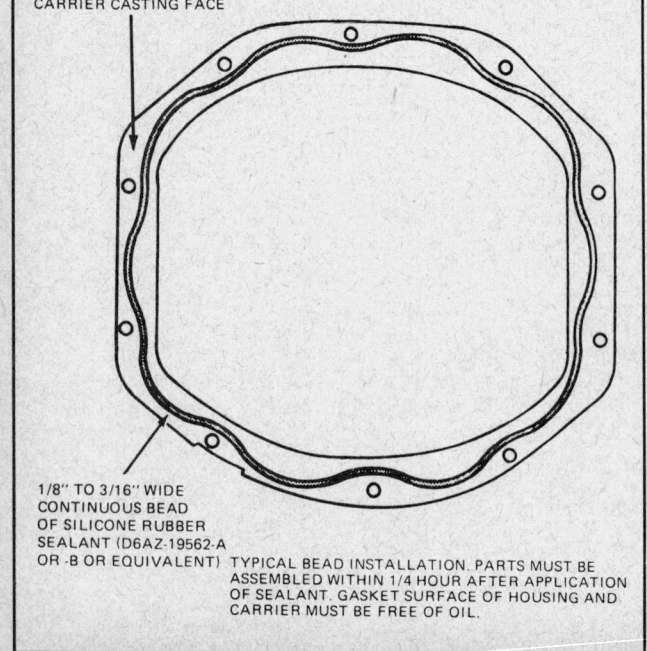

CARRIER CASTING FACE

1/8" TO 3/16" WIDE CONTINUOUS BEAD OF SILICONE RUBBER SEALANT (D6AZ-19562-A OR -B OR EQUIVALENT) TYPICAL BEAD INSTALLATION. PARTS MUST BE ASSEMBLED WITHIN 1/4 HOUR AFTER APPLICATION OF SEALANT. GASKET SURFACE OF HOUSING AND CARRIER MUST BE FREE OF OIL.

Fig. 9 Applying sealant to carrier casting face

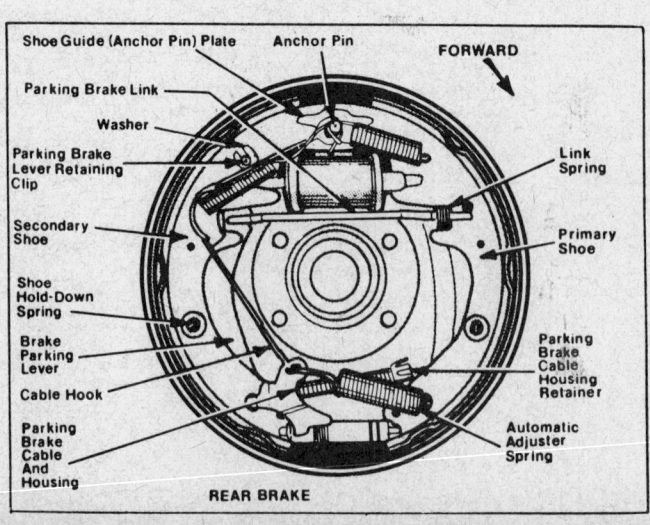

Shoe Guide (Anchor Pin) Plate
Anchor Pin
FORWARD
Parking Brake Link
Washer
Parking Brake Lever Retaining Clip
Secondary Shoe
Shoe Hold-Down Spring
Brake Parking Lever
Cable Hook
Parking Brake Cable And Housing
Link Spring
Primary Shoe
Parking Brake Cable Housing Retainer
Automatic Adjuster Spring
REAR BRAKE

Fig. 10 Rear brake assembly. 1977–84

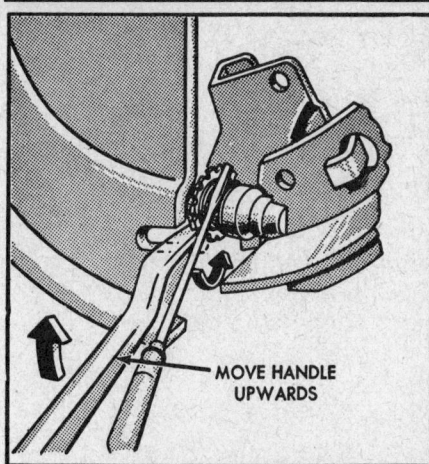

**Fig. 11 Backing off brake adjustment
by disengaging adjuster lever
with screwdriver**

Adjustment

SERVICE BULLETIN

When servicing a vehicle requiring a brake adjustment, the metal knock-out plugs should NOT be removed. Rather the drums should be removed and brakes inspected for a malfunction.

Although the brakes are self-adjusting, an initial adjustment will be necessary after a brake repair, such as relining or replacement. The initial adjustment can be obtained by the new procedure which follows:

NOTE: If after removing brake drum retaining nuts, the brake drum cannot be removed, pry rubber plug from backing plate. Insert a narrow screwdriver through hole in backing plate and disengage lever from adjusting screw. While holding lever away from adjusting screw, back off adjusting screw using a suitable tool to retract brake shoes, Fig. 11.

1. Use the brake shoe adjustment gauge shown in Fig. 12 to obtain the drum inside diameter as shown. Tighten the adjusting knob on the gauge to hold this setting.
2. Place the opposite side of the gauge over the brake shoes and adjust the shoes by turning the adjuster screw until the gauge just slides over the linings. Rotate the gauge around the lining surface to assure proper lining diameter adjustment and clearance.
3. Install brake drum and wheel. Final adjustment is accomplished by making several firm reverse stops, using the brake pedal.

PARKING BRAKES, ADJUST

Rear Disc Brakes

1. Fully release parking brake, then place transmission in neutral and support vehicle at rear axle.
2. Tighten adjuster nut until levers on calipers just begin to move, then loosen adjuster nut until levers just return to stop position.
3. Apply and release parking brake. Check levers on caliper to determine if they are fully returned by attempting to pull lever

rearward. If lever moves, the adjustment is too tight and must be readjusted.

Rear Drum Brakes

1. Make sure the parking brake is fully released.
2. Place transmission in neutral and raise the vehicle.
3. Tighten the adjusting nut against the cable equalizer to cause rear wheel brake drag. Then loosen the adjusting nut until the rear brakes are fully released. There should be no brake drag.
4. Lower the vehicle and check operation.

VACUUM RELEASE UNIT

The vacuum power unit will release the parking brake automatically when the transmission selector lever is moved into any driving position with the engine running. The brakes will not release automatically, however, when the selector lever is in neutral or park position with the engine running, or in any other position with the engine off.

The lower end of the release handle extends out for alternate manual release in the event of vacuum power failure or for optional manual release at any time.

To detect leaks in the vacuum release parking brake lines or to find disconnected or an improperly connected line, listen for a hissing sound along the line routings.

NOTE: Do not apply compressed air to the vacuum system when conducting a leak test. The actuator diaphram in the parking brake vacuum motor may be damaged.

Perform the following to detect leaks in the vacuum release system:

1. Start and operate engine at idle. Position transmission gear shift lever into Neutral and apply parking brake.
2. Position transmission gear shift lever into Drive and check parking brake sector to insure sector returns to its stop (zero travel position), when the parking brake releases.

NOTE: The parking brake vacuum release does not operate with the transmission in Reverse.

3. If parking brake does not release, disconnect vacuum line from parking brake release vacuum motor and connect a suitable vacuum gauge to the line. A minimum of 10 inches Hg is required to actuate the parking brake vacuum motor. If a minimum reading is obtained, replace parking brake release vacuum line. If a minimum reading is not obtained, replace parking brake vacuum release motor.

MASTER CYLINDER, REPLACE

1. Disconnect brake lines from master cylinder.
2. Remove two nuts attaching master cylinder to power brake unit.
3. Slide master cylinder off mounting studs and remove from vehicle.
4. Reverse procedure to install.

POWER BRAKE UNIT, REPLACE

Except Hydro Boost

1. Disconnect battery ground cable, then

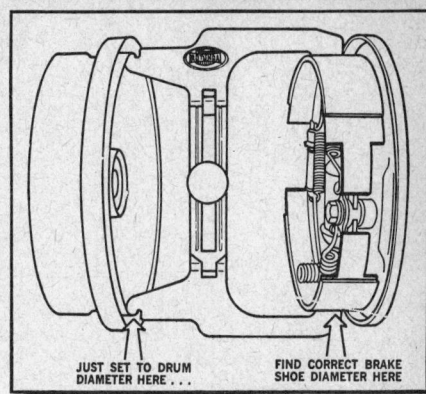

JUST SET TO DRUM DIAMETER HERE . . . **FIND CORRECT BRAKE SHOE DIAMETER HERE**

**Fig. 12 Brake adjustment
with gauge**

remove air cleaner.
2. Disconnect vacuum hose from power brake unit check valve.
3. Disconnect brake lines from master cylinder, then remove two nuts attaching master cylinder to power brake unit and remove master cylinder.
4. Working from under instrument panel, disconnect stop lamp switch wire connector, then remove clip and washer from brake pedal pin. Slide brake lamp switch off brake pedal pin just far enough for outer arm to clear pin, then remove switch. Slide power brake push rod and washer from brake pedal pin.
5. On models equipped with speed control, remove amplifier unit from lower power brake unit mounting stud.
6. Move power brake unit forward until studs clear dash panel, then remove unit.
7. Reverse procedure to install.

Hydro Boost

1. Disconnect stoplight switch wires at connector and remove hairpin retainer, then slide stoplight switch off brake pedal pin far enough for switch outer hole to clear pin and remove pin from switch.
2. Slide hydro-boost push rod and nylon washers and bushing off brake pedal pin.
3. Remove master cylinder and position to one side without disturbing hydraulic lines.

NOTE: It is not necessary to disconnect brake lines, but care should be taken not to deform lines.

4. Disconnect pressure, steering gear and return lines from booster, then plug lines and ports in hydro-boost to prevent entry of dirt.
5. Remove hydro-boost retaining nuts, and remove assembly sliding push rod link from engine side of dash panel.
6. Reverse procedure to install. To purge system, disconnect coil wire so that engine will not start. Fill power steering pump reservoir, then while engaging starter, pump brake pedal. Do not cycle steering wheel until all residual air has been purged from the hydro boost unit. Check fluid level, then connect coil wire and start engine. Apply brakes with a pumping action and cycle steering wheel, then check system for leaks.

Rear Suspension

Note: For air suspension service procedures on 1984 Continental & Mark VII, refer to Air Suspension Section.

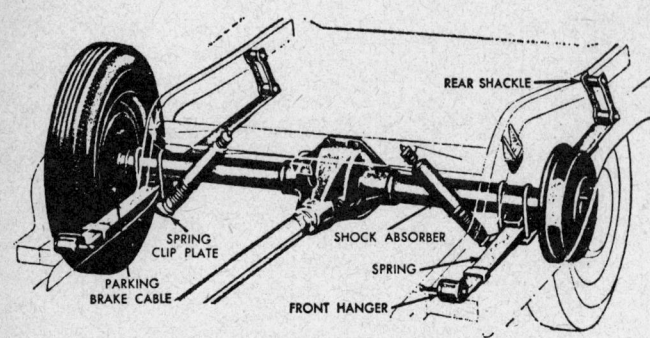

Fig. 1 Rear suspension (typical). 1977–80 Versailles

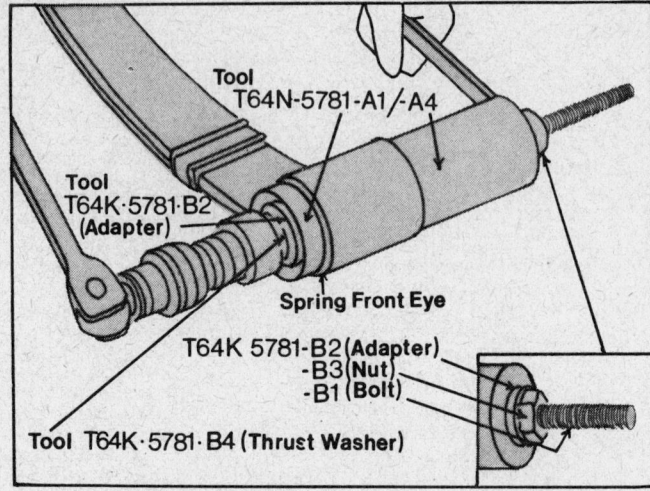

Fig. 2 Spring front bushing removal. 1977–80 Versailles

SHOCK ABSORBER, REPLACE

1982—84 Continental & 1984 Mark VII

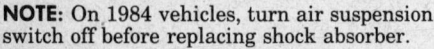

NOTE: On 1984 vehicles, turn air suspension switch off before replacing shock absorber.

1. Open trunk to gain access to upper shock absorber attachment.
2. Remove rubber cap if equipped, from shock absorber stud, then remove nut, washer and insulator.
3. Raise vehicle and support rear axle.
4. Remove lower shock absorber protective cover, then remove cross bolt and nut from lower shock absorber mounting bracket.
5. From underneath vehicle, compress shock absorber to clear hole in upper shock tower, then remove shock absorber.

NOTE: 1982–84 Continental & 1984 Mark VII are equipped with gas pressurized shock absorbers which extend unassisted during removal. Do not apply heat or flame to the shock absorber tube during removal.

6. Reverse procedure to install. While holding shock absorber in position, torque lower cross bolt to 59 ft. lbs. Lower vehicle and install upper mounting nut, washer and insulator and torque nut to 24 to 26 ft. lbs.

Except 1982—84 Continental & 1984 Mark VII

1. With the rear axle supported properly disconnect shock absorber at upper mounting and compress it to clear hole.
2. Disconnect shock absorber from lower attachment.
3. Reverse procedure to install.

NOTE: The 1984 Town Car is equipped with

gas pressurized shock absorbers which extend unassisted during removal. Do not apply heat or flame to the shock absorber tube during removal.

LEAF SPRINGS & BUSHINGS, REPLACE

1977—80 Versailles

1. Raise rear of vehicle and support at frame. Support axle with a suitable jack.
2. Disconnect shock absorbers from lower mountings.
3. Lower jack and remove spring plate "U" bolts and spring plate, Fig. 1.
4. Raise axle to remove weight from spring and disassemble rear shackle.
5. Remove spring front mount bolt.

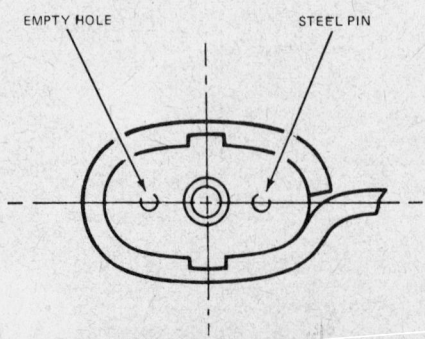

Fig. 3 Spring front bushing installation. 1977–80 Versailles

6. Replace spring front eye bushings as necessary, Figs. 2 and 3.
7. Reverse procedure to install.

COIL SPRINGS, REPLACE

1982—83 Continental

1. Remove stabilizer bar as described under Stabilizer Bar, Replace, if equipped.
2. Position a suitable jack under rear axle, then raise vehicle and support body at rear body crossmember.
3. Lower axle until shock absorbers are fully extended.

NOTE: Support axle with jack stands or a suitable jack.

4. Position a suitable jack under lower control arm pivot bolt and remove nut and bolt. Carefully and slowly lower the control arm until all spring tension is relieved.
5. Remove coil spring and insulators from vehicle, Fig. 4.

1980—81 Continental, 1980—83 Mark VI & 1982—84 Town Car

1. Raise rear of vehicle and support at frame side sills. Support rear axle with a suitable jack.
2. Disconnect shock absorbers and stabilizer bar from axle housing, Fig. 5.
3. Disconnect right hand parking brake cable from right hand upper arm retainer.
4. Lower the axle housing until coil springs are released.
5. Remove springs and insulators, Fig. 5.
6. Reverse procedure to install.

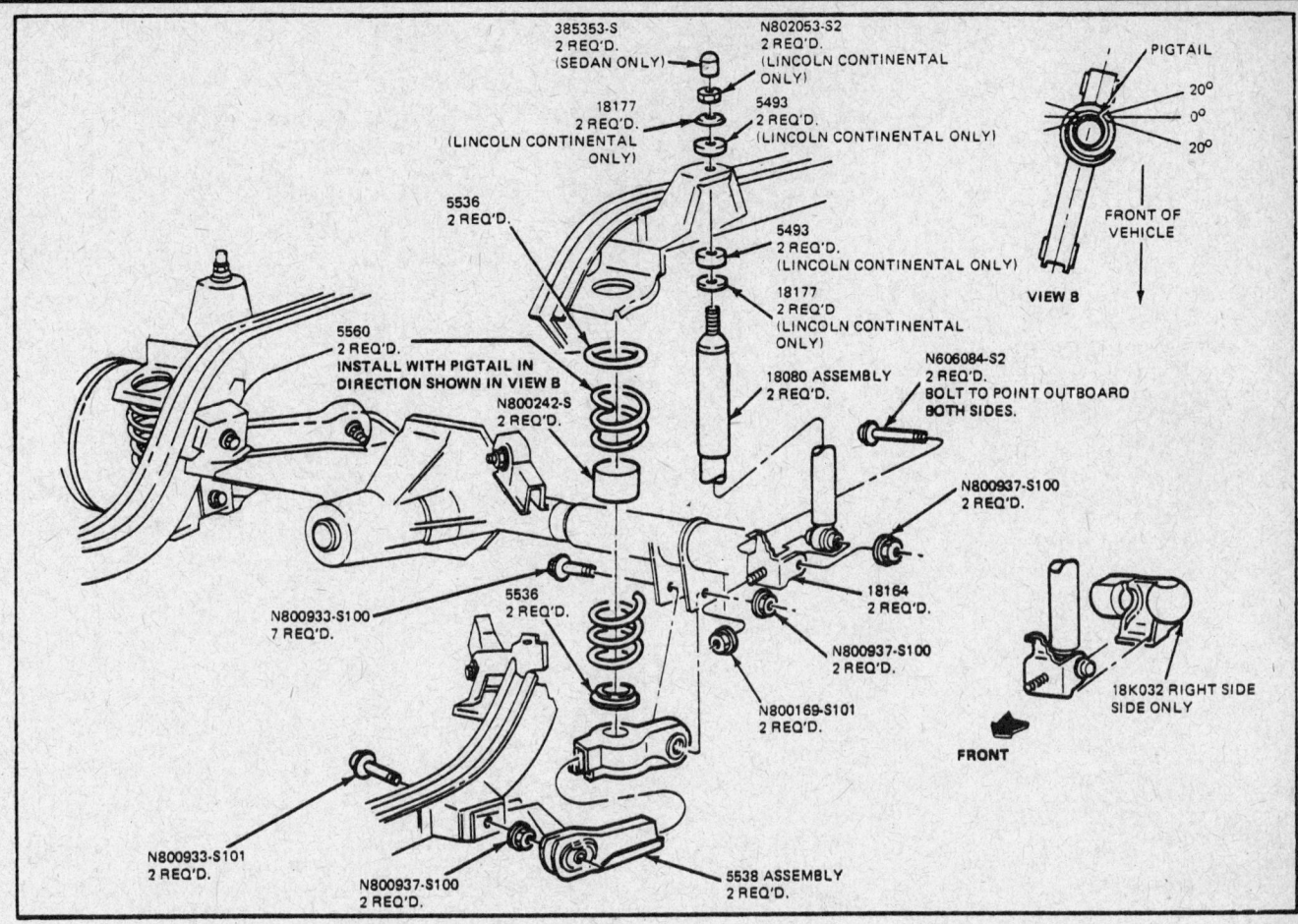

Fig. 4 Rear suspension. 1982–83 Continental

1977–79 Except Versailles

1. Raise rear of vehicle and support at frame. Support rear axle with a suitable jack.
2. Disconnect shock absorbers at lower mountings.
3. On 1977–79 Lincoln Continental models, disconnect brake hose at rear crossmember and remove hose to bracket clip.
4. Lower axle to remove springs.
5. Reverse procedure to install. On all models except 1977–79 Mark V, install an insulator between each seat and the spring, Fig. 6. On 1977–79 Mark V, an insulator is installed only between upper seat and the spring, Fig. 7.

CONTROL ARMS, REPLACE

1984 Continental & Mark VII

Upper Arm

NOTE: Always replace control arm in pairs. If one arm requires replacement, replace the same arm on the opposite side of the vehicle. Refer to "Air Suspension System" section for any procedures relating to this system.

1. Turn air suspension switch off.
2. Raise and support vehicle, then disconnect rear height sensor from side arm.

Note position of sensor adjustment bracket to aid in reassembly.
3. Remove upper arm to axle and upper arm to frame bracket pivot bolts and nuts.
4. Remove upper control arm.
5. Reverse procedure to install. Torque pivot bolts to 100 ft. lbs.

Lower Arm

1. Turn air suspension switch to off position, then raise and support vehicle and remove wheel assembly.
2. Vent air springs to atmosphere by removing air spring solenoid.
3. Remove the two air spring to lower control arm retaining bolts, and remove air spring from lower arm.
4. Remove control arm to frame and control arm to axle bracket pivot bolts and nuts.
5. Remove lower control arm.
6. Reverse procedure to install. Torque pivot bolts to 100 ft. lbs.

1982–83 Continental

Upper Arm

NOTE: Always replace control arms in pairs. Therefore, if one arm requires replacement, replace the same arm on the opposite side of the vehicle.

1. Raise vehicle and support body at rear body crossmember.
2. Remove upper arm pivot bolt and nut,

Fig. 5.
3. Remove front pivot bolt and nut, then remove upper arm from vehicle.
4. Reverse procedure to install. Torque upper arm pivot and front pivot bolts to 100 ft. lbs.

Lower Arm

NOTE: Always replace control arms in pairs. Therefore, if one arm requires replacement, replace the same arm on the opposite side of the vehicle.

1. Remove stabilizer bar as described under Stabilizer Bar, Replace, if equipped.
2. Position a suitable jack under rear axle, then raise vehicle and support body at rear body crossmember.
3. Lower axle until shock absorbers are fully extended.

NOTE: Support axle with jack stands or a suitable jack.

4. Position a suitable jack under lower control arm rear pivot bolt and remove nut bolt, Fig. 5. Carefully and slowly lower the control arm until all spring tension is relieved, then remove coil spring and insulators.
5. Remove lower control arm front pivot bolt and nut, then remove lower control arm assembly.

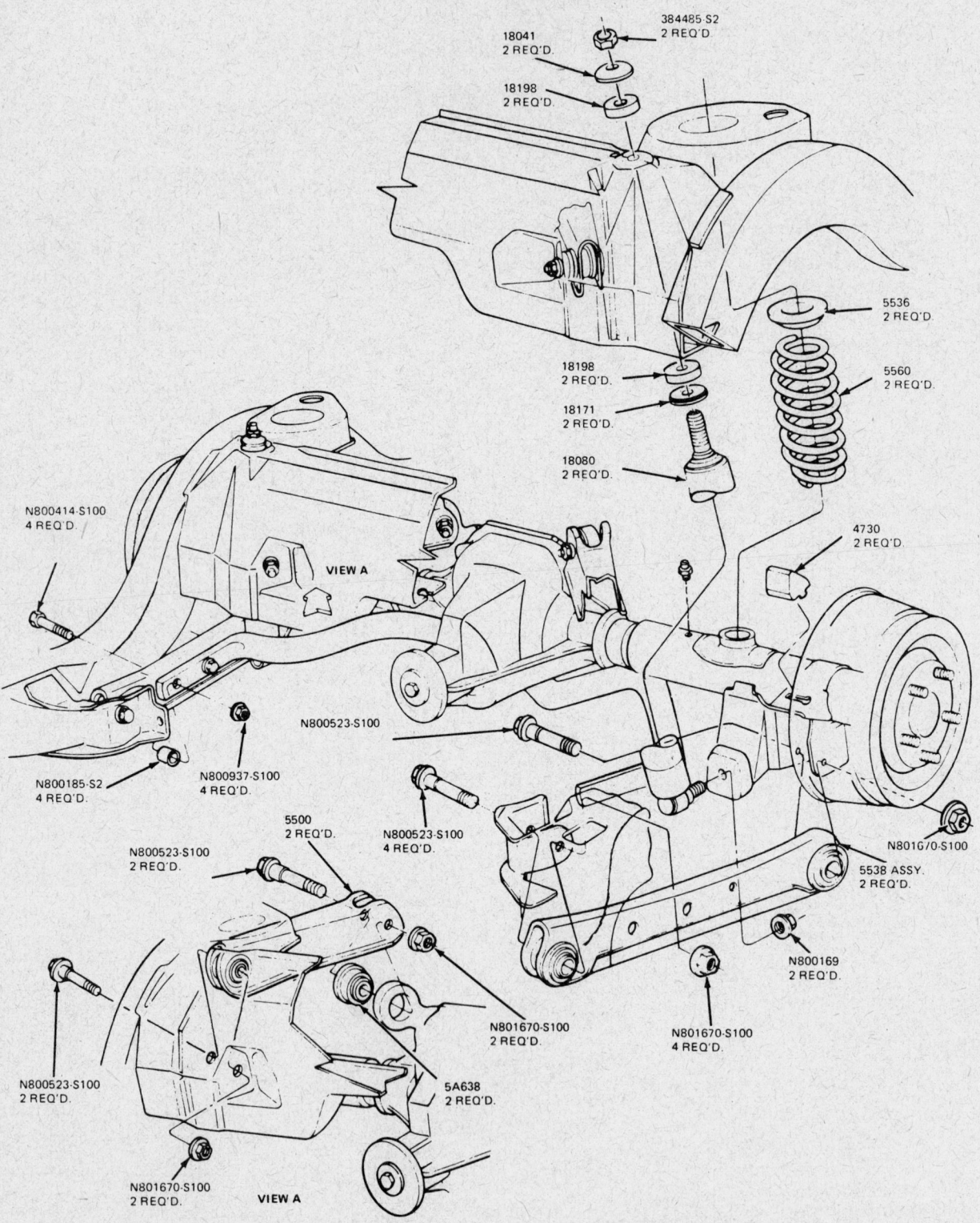

Fig. 5 Rear suspension. 1980–81 Continental, 1980–83 Mark VI & 1982–84 Town Car

18041
2 REQ'D.

384485-S2
2 REQ'D

18198
2 REQ'D.

5536
2 REQ'D.

18198
2 REQ'D.

5560
2 REQ'D.

18171
2 REQ'D.

18080
2 REQ'D.

N800414-S100
4 REQ'D.

VIEW A

4730
2 REQ'D.

N800523-S100

N800185-S2
4 REQ'D.

N800937-S100
4 REQ'D.

N801G70-S100

5538 ASSY.
2 REQ'D.

5500
2 REQ'D.

N800523-S100
4 REQ'D.

N800523-S100
2 REQ'D.

N800169
2 REQ'D.

N801670-S100
2 REQ'D.

N801670-S100
4 REQ'D.

N800523-S100
2 REQ'D.

5A638
2 REQ'D.

N801670-S100
2 REQ'D.

VIEW A

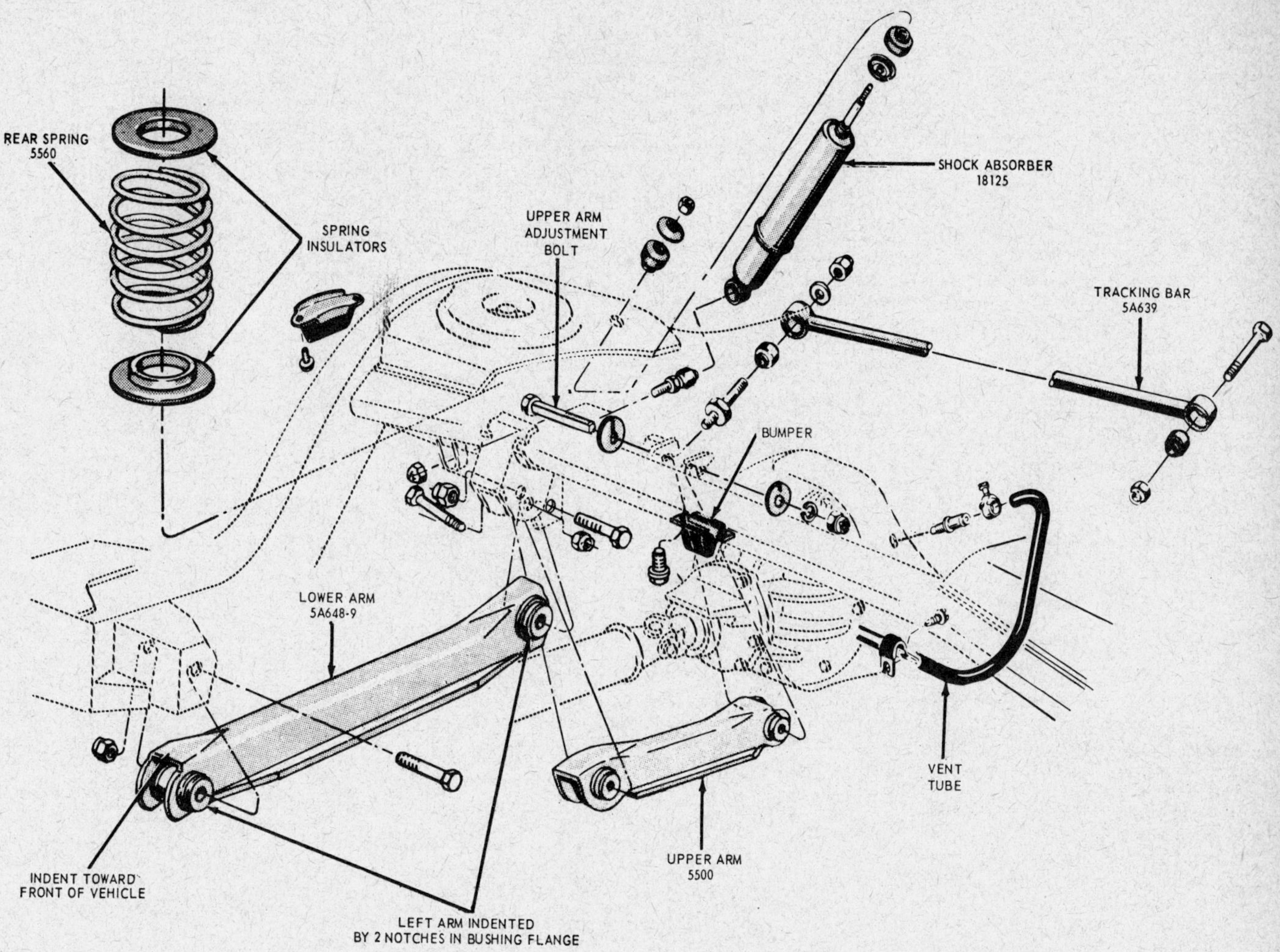

REAR SPRING
5560

SPRING
INSULATORS

UPPER ARM
ADJUSTMENT
BOLT

SHOCK ABSORBER
18125

TRACKING BAR
5A639

BUMPER

LOWER ARM
5A648-9

VENT
TUBE

INDENT TOWARD
FRONT OF VEHICLE

LEFT ARM INDENTED
BY 2 NOTCHES IN BUSHING FLANGE

UPPER ARM
5500

Fig. 6   Rear suspension (typical). 1977—79 Continental

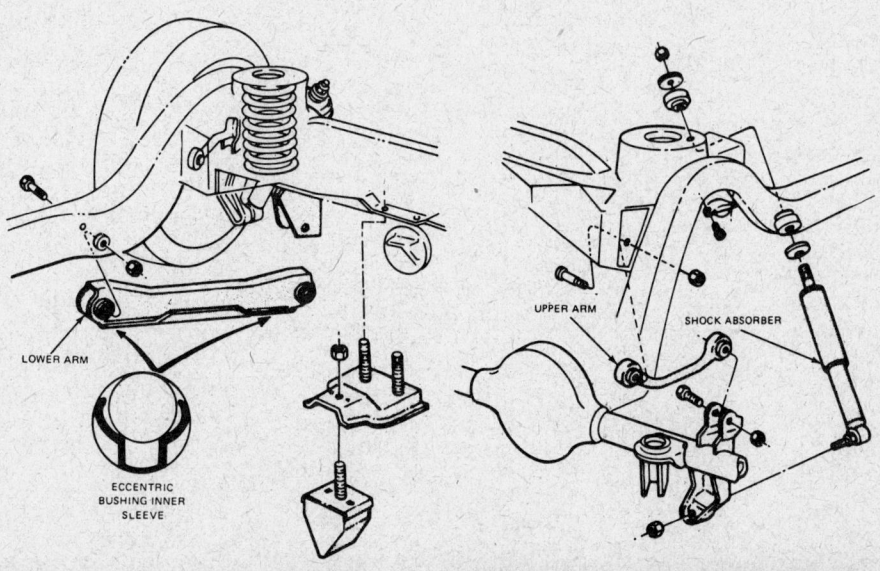

LOWER ARM

ECCENTRIC
BUSHING INNER
SLEEVE

UPPER ARM

SHOCK ABSORBER

Fig. 7   Rear suspension (typical). 1977—79 Mark V

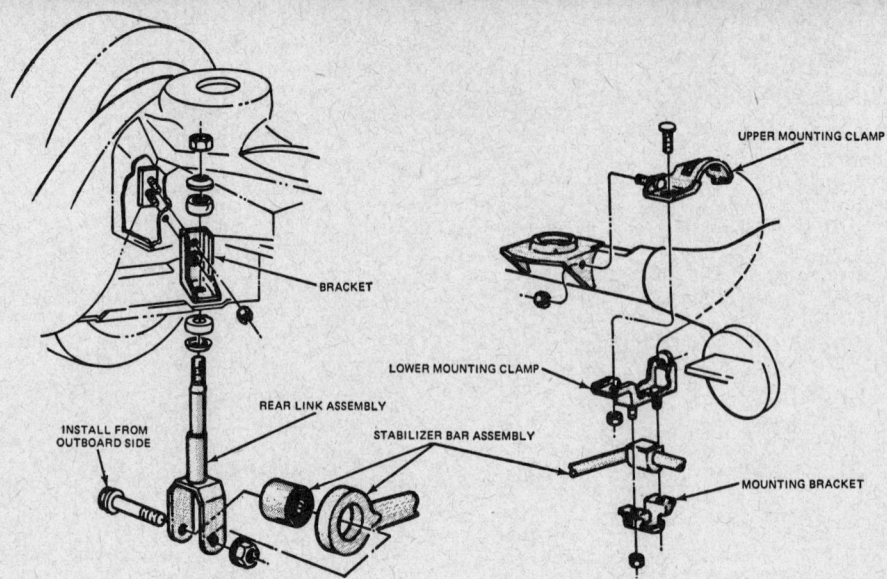

Fig. 8 Stabilizer bar installation. 1977–79 Mark V

1980–81 Continental, 1980–83 Mark VI & 1982–84 Town Car

NOTE: Always replace control arms in pairs. Therefore, if one arm requires replacement, replace the same arm on the opposite side of vehicle. Also, if both upper and lower control arms are to be removed at the same time, first remove both coil springs.

1. Raise vehicle and support at frame side rails with jack stands.
2. If removing lower control arm, disconnect stabilizer bar from arm.
3. With shock absorbers fully extended, support axle under differential pinion nose and under axle. If removing upper arm, disconnect parking brake cable from retainer.
4. Remove pivot bolts and nuts from axle and frame brackets, Fig. 5.
5. Remove control arm from vehicle.
6. Reverse procedure to install. Torque lower arm to axle bracket pivot bolt to 118 ft. lbs. and lower arm to frame pivot bolt to 135 ft. lbs.

1977–79 Except Versailles

NOTE: Upper and lower control arms are replaced in pairs.

1. Raise rear of vehicle and support at frame. Support axle with a suitable jack.

2. On all models except Mark V, disconnect track bar from frame mounting bracket.
3. Lower axle and install a second jack under differential pinion nose.
4. Disconnect control arm from axle bracket. On upper arms, disconnect arm from crossmember and on lower arms, disconnect arm from frame attachment bracket.
5. Reverse procedure to install.

STABILIZER BAR, REPLACE

1984 Continental & Mark VII

1. Turn air suspension switch off, then raise and support vehicle.
2. Remove stabilizer bar to link attaching nuts.
3. Remove stabilizer bar to bushing "U" clamp attaching nuts, then the stabilizer bar.
4. Reverse procedure to install.

1982–83 Continental

1. Raise and support rear of vehicle.
2. Remove four stabilizer bar to lower control arm attaching bolts.
3. Remove stabilizer bar from vehicle.
4. Reverse procedure to install. Torque stabilizer bar to lower control arm attaching bolts to 45 to 50 ft. lbs.

1980–81 Continental, 1980–83 Mark VI & 1982–84 Town Car

1. Raise rear of vehicle and support at frame side sills.
2. Lower axle housing until shock absorbers are fully extended.
3. Remove the four bolts, nuts and spacers retaining stabilizer bar lower control arms, then remove stabilizer bar, Fig. 5.
4. Reverse procedure to install. Torque bolts to 70–92 ft. lbs.

1977–79 Mark V

1. Remove bolts securing stabilizer bar to rear link assemblies on both sides, Fig. 8.
2. Remove nuts securing mounting bracket to lower mounting clamp and remove bar.
3. Reverse procedure to install.

TRACK BAR & BUSHINGS, REPLACE

1977–79 Continental

1. Remove cover from track bar axle attachment, then disconnect track bar from mounting stud.
2. Disconnect track bar from frame side rail.
3. Reverse procedure to install.

Front Suspension & Steering Section

NOTE: For air suspension service procedures on 1984 Continental & Mark VII, refer to Air Suspension Section.

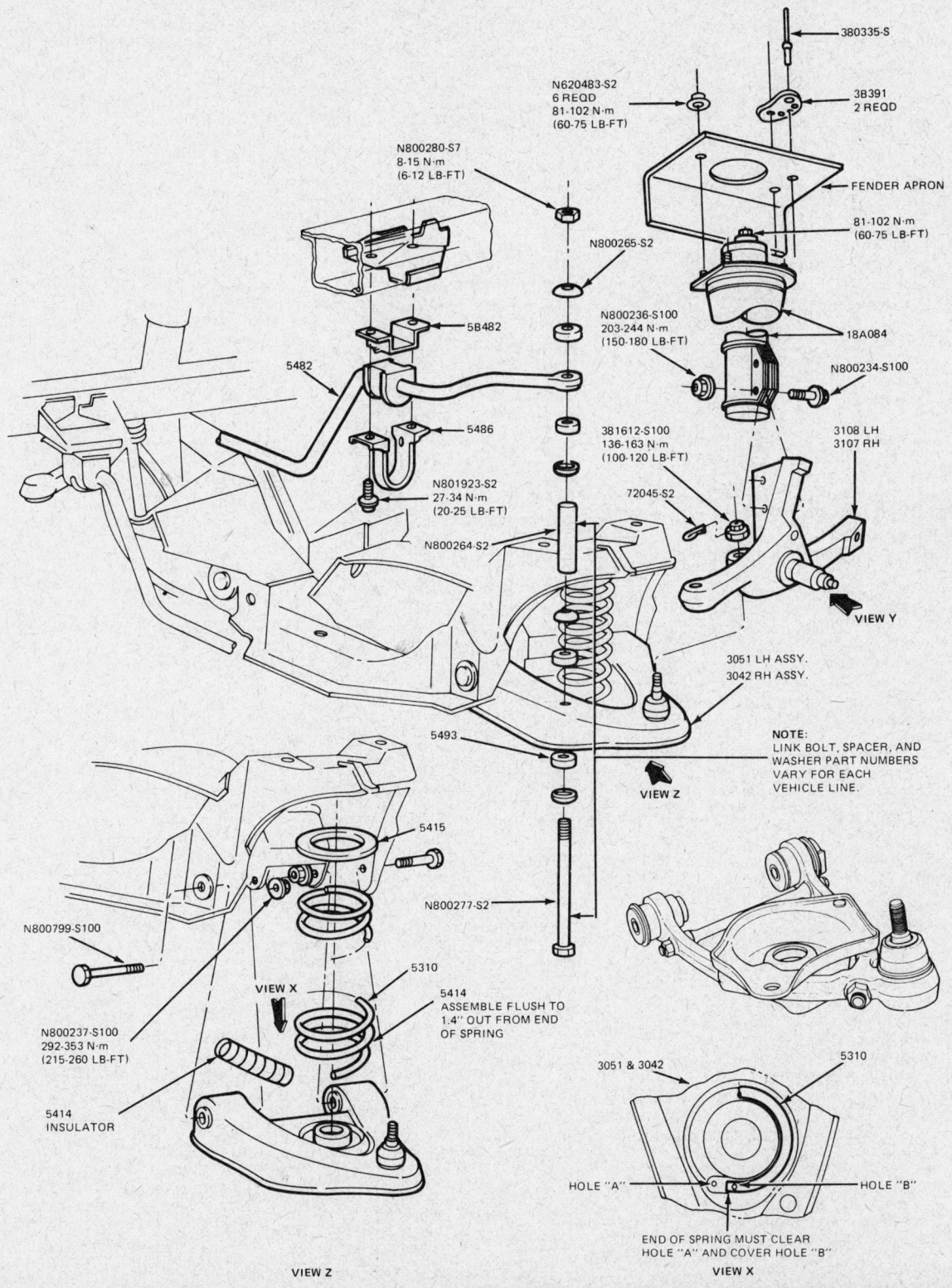

380335-S

N620483-S2
6 REQD
81-102 N·m
(60-75 LB-FT)

3B391
2 REQD

N800280-S7
8-15 N·m
(6-12 LB-FT)

FENDER APRON

N800265-S2

81-102 N·m
(60-75 LB-FT)

5B482

N800236-S100
203-244 N·m
(150-180 LB-FT)

18A084

5482

5486

N800234-S100

N801923-S2
27-34 N·m
(20-25 LB-FT)

381612-S100
136-163 N·m
(100-120 LB-FT)

72045-S2

3108 LH
3107 RH

N800264-S2

VIEW Y

3051 LH ASSY.
3042 RH ASSY.

5493

NOTE:
LINK BOLT, SPACER, AND
WASHER PART NUMBERS
VARY FOR EACH
VEHICLE LINE.

VIEW Z

5415

N800277-S2

N800799-S100

5310

VIEW X

5414
ASSEMBLE FLUSH TO
1.4" OUT FROM END
OF SPRING

N800237-S100
292-353 N·m
(215-260 LB-FT)

5414
INSULATOR

3051 & 3042

5310

HOLE "A"

HOLE "B"

END OF SPRING MUST CLEAR
HOLE "A" AND COVER HOLE "B"

VIEW Z

VIEW X

Fig. 1   Front suspension. 1982-83 Continental

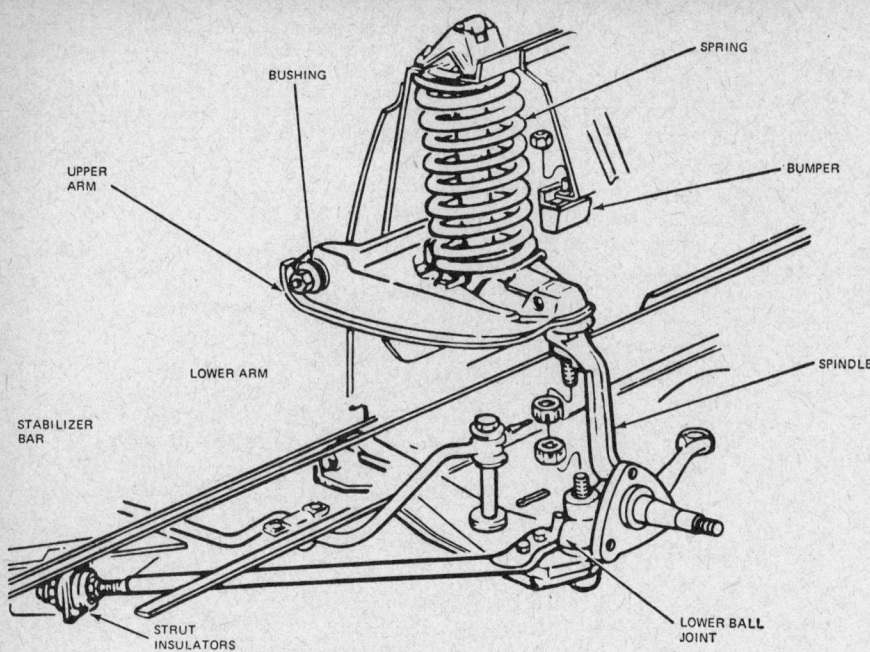

Fig. 2 Front suspension (typical). 1977–80 Versailles

ber adjustment bolt area just enough to permit lateral travel of the arm when the adjustment bolt is turned. Rotate the bolt and eccentric clockwise from the high position to increase camber or counterclockwise to decrease it.

Except Versailles, 1982–84 Continental & 1984 Mark VII

Caster and camber can be adjusted by loosening the bolts that attach the upper suspension arm to the shaft at the frame side rail, and moving the arm assembly in or out in the elongated bolt holes, Figs. 4 and 4A. Since any movement of the arm affects both caster and camber, both factors should be balanced against one another when making the adjustment.

Caster, Adjust
1. To adjust caster, install the adjusting tool as shown in Figs. 6 and 7.
2. Loosen both upper arm inner shaft retaining bolts and move either front or rear of the shaft in or out as necessary to increase or decrease caster angle. Then tighten bolt to retain adjustment.

Camber, Adjust
1. Loosen both upper arm inner retaining bolts and move both front and rear ends of shaft inward or outward as necessary to increase or decrease camber angle.
2. Tighten bolts and recheck caster and readjust if necessary.

FRONT SUSPENSION

1982–83 Continental

This suspension, Fig. 1, is a modified McPherson strut design, which uses shock struts and coil springs. The springs are mounted between the lower control arm and a spring pocket in the crossmember.

1977–80 Versailles

Referring to Fig. 2, each front wheel rotates on a spindle. The upper and lower ends of the spindle are attached to ball joints that are mounted to an upper and lower control arm. The upper arm pivots on a bushing and shaft assembly that is bolted to the underbody. The lower arm pivots on a bolt that is located in an underbody bracket.

A coil spring seats between the upper arm and the top of the spring housing. A double-acting shock absorber is bolted to the arm and the top of the spring housing.

Struts, which are connected between the lower control arms and the underbody, prevent the arms from moving fore and aft.

Except Versailles & 1982–83 Continental

Referring to Figs. 3 and 4, each wheel rotates on a spindle. The upper and lower ends of the spindle are attached to upper and lower ball joints that are mounted to an upper and lower control arm. The upper control arm pivots on a shaft assembly that is bolted to the frame. The lower control arm pivots on a bolt in the front crossmember. On 1977–79 models, the struts, which are connected between the lower control arms and frame crossmember, prevent the control arms from moving forward or backward.

WHEEL ALIGNMENT

1984 Continental & Mark VII

NOTE: Before performing wheel alignment check on these vehicles, set vehicle ride height as outlined in the "Air Suspension Section."

Caster & Camber

Caster is pre-set at the factory and is not adjustable.

To adjust camber, drill out pop rivet located on top of camber plate. Loosen the camber plate to body apron retaining nuts, then move the top of the shcok strut to the desired location. Retighten the retaining nuts. It is not necessary to replace the pop rivet after the camber adjustment is completed.

1982–83 Continental

Caster & Camber

The caster and camber angles of this suspension are factory pre-set and cannot be adjusted in the field.

1977–80 Versailles

Caster & Camber

As shown in Fig. 5, caster is controlled by the front suspension strut. To obtain positive caster, loosen the strut rear nut and tighten the strut front nut against the bushing. To obtain negative caster, loosen the strut front nut and tighten the strut rear nut against the bushing.

Camber is controlled by the eccentric cam located at the lower arm attachment to the side rail. To adjust camber, loosen the camber adjustment bolt nut at the rear of the body bracket. Spread the body bracket at the cam-

TOE-IN, ADJUST

1982–84 Continental & 1984 Mark VII

1. Check to see that steering shaft and steering wheel marks are in alignment and in the top position.
2. Loosen clamp screw on the tie rod bellows and free the seal on the rod to prevent twisting of the bellows, Fig. 8.
3. Place opened end wrench on flats of tie rod socket to prevent socket from turning, then loosen tie rod jam nuts.
4. Use suitable pliers to turn the tie rod inner end to correct the adjustment to specifications. Do not use pliers on tie rod threads. Turning to reduce number of threads showing will increase toe-in. Turning in the opposite direction will reduce toe-in.

Exc. 1982–84 Continental & 1984 Mark VII

Position the front wheels in their straight-ahead position. Then turn both tie rod adjusting sleeves an equal amount until the desired toe-in setting is obtained.

WHEEL BEARINGS, ADJUST

1. With wheel rotating, tighten adjusting nut to 17–25 ft. lbs.
2. Back off adjusting nut 1½ turn and retighten nut to 10–15 inch lbs.
3. Place nut lock on nut so that castellations on lock are aligned with cotter pin hole in spindle and install cotter pin.
4. Check front wheel rotation, if it rotates noisily or rough, clean, inspect or replace wheel bearings as necessary.

WHEEL BEARINGS, REPLACE

(Disc Brakes)

1. Raise car and remove front wheels.
2. Remove caliper mounting bolts.

NOTE: It is not necessary to disconnect the brake line for this operation.

3. Slide caliper off of the disc, inserting a spacer between the shoes to hold them in their bores after the caliper is removed. Position caliper assembly out of the way.

NOTE: Do not allow caliper to hang by brake hose.

4. Remove hub and disc. Grease retainer and inner bearing can now be removed.
5. Reverse procedure to install.

CHECKING BALL JOINTS FOR WEAR

Upper Ball Joint

1977–80 Versailles
1. Raise car on frame contact hoist or by floor jacks placed beneath underbody until wheel falls to full down position.
2. Grasp the lower edge of tire and move the wheel in and out.
3. While the wheel is being moved observe any movement between the upper end of the spindle and upper arm. If any movement is observed replace the ball joint.

1977–81 Continental, 1977–83 Mark V & VI & 1982–84 Town Car
1. Raise car on floor jacks placed beneath lower control arms.
2. Grasp lower edge of tire and move wheel in and out.
3. As wheel is being moved in and out, observe upper end of spindle and upper arm.
4. Any movement between upper end of spindle and upper arm indicates ball joint wear and loss of preload. If such movement is observed, replace upper ball joint.

NOTE: During the foregoing check, the lower ball joint will be unloaded and may move. Disregard all such movement of the lower joint. Also, do not mistake loose wheel bearings for a worn ball joint.

Lower Ball Joint

1982–84 Continental & 1984 Mark VII
1. Support vehicle in normal driving position with both ball joints loaded.
2. Clean area around grease fitting and checking surface.

NOTE: The checking surface is the round boss into which the grease fitting is installed.

3. The checking surface should project outside the cover, Fig. 9. If surface is inside

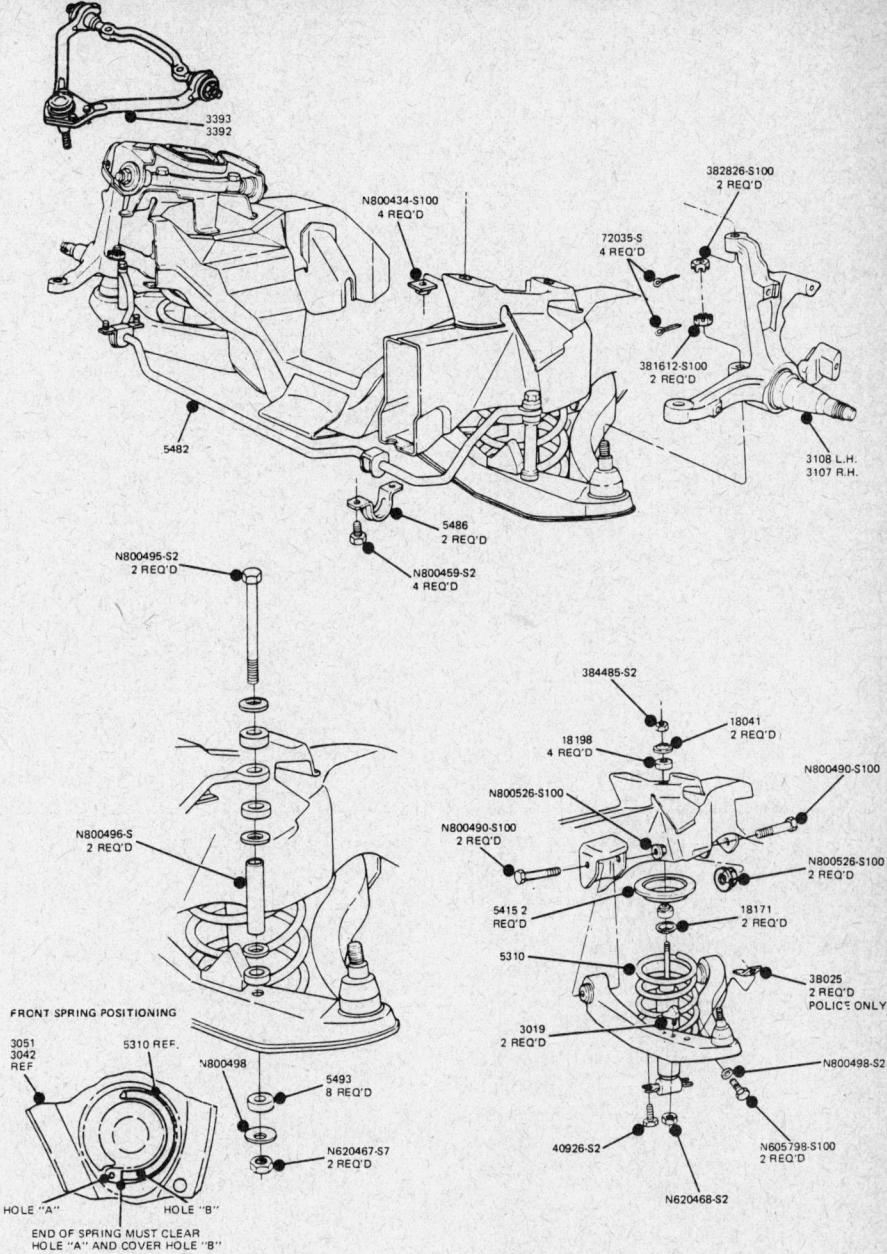

Fig. 3   Front suspension. 1980–81 Continental, 1980–83 Mark VI & 1982–84 Town Car

cover replace lower arm assembly.

1980–81 Continental, 1980–83 Mark VI & 1982–84 Town Car
These models are equipped with lower ball joint wear indicators, Fig. 9A. To check ball joint for wear, support vehicle in normal driving position with both ball joints loaded. Observe the checking surface of the ball joint. If the checking surface is inside the cover, replace the ball joint.

1977–80 Versailles
1. With car jacked up as directed above, grasp the lower edge of the tire and move it in and out.
2. As wheel is being moved in and out, observe lower end of spindle and lower

arm.
3. Any movement between lower end of spindle and lower arm indicates ball joint wear and loss of preload. If such movement is observed, replace lower arm and/or ball joint.

NOTE: During the foregoing check, the ball joints will be unloaded and may move. Therefore disregard any movement of the upper ball joint when checking the lower ball joint and any movement of the lower ball joint when checking the upper ball joint. Also, do not mistake loose wheel bearings for a worn ball joint.

1977–79 Except Versailles
1. Raise car on jacks placed under lower

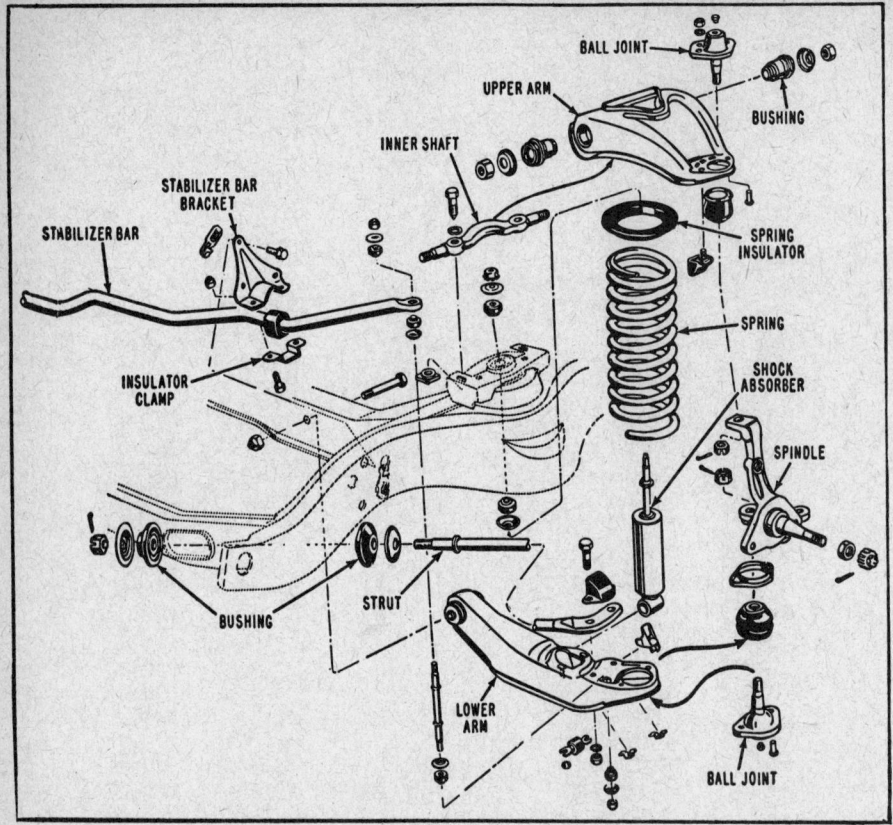

Fig. 4 Front suspension. 1977—79 Except Versailles

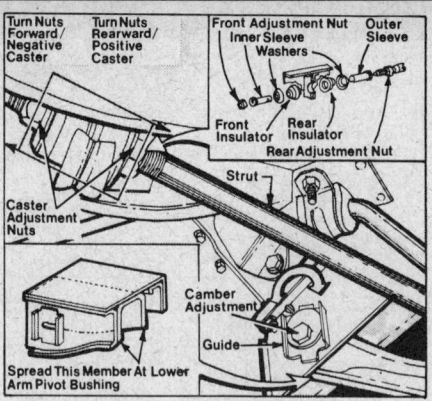

Fig. 5 Caster & camber adjustment. 1977—80 Versailles

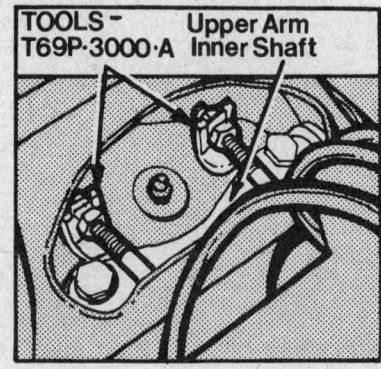

Fig. 6 Caster and camber adjusting tool. 1977—79 except Versailles

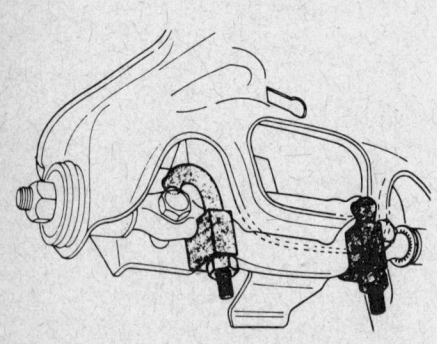

Fig. 7 Caster & camber adjusting tools. 1980—81 Continental, 1980—83 Mark VI & 1982—84 Town Car

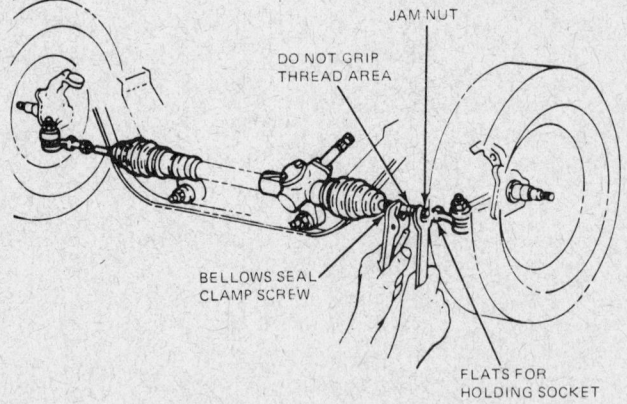

Fig. 8 Toe-in adjustment. 1982—84 Continental & 1984 Mark VII

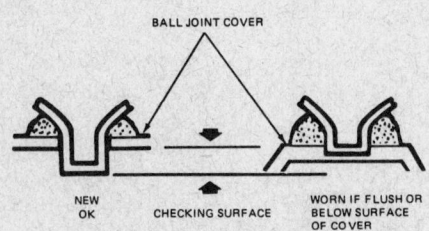

Fig. 9 Lower ball joint wear indicator. 1982—84 Continental & 1984 Mark VII

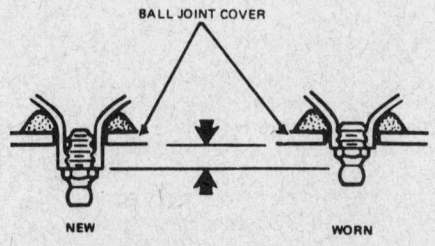

Fig. 9A Lower ball joint wear indicator. 1980—81 Continental, 1980—83 Mark VI & 1982—84 Town Car

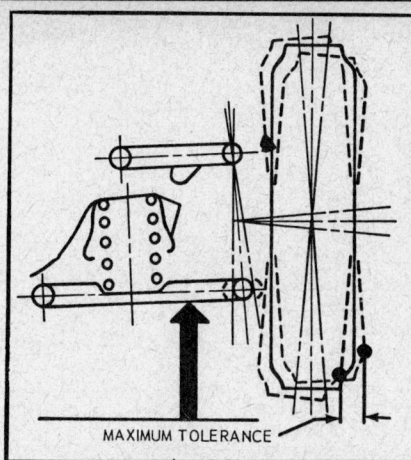

Fig. 10 Checking lower ball joint for wear. 1977–79 Exc. Versailles

control arms as shown in Fig. 10.
2. With a dial indicator attached to the lower arm, position indicator so that the plunger rests against inner side of wheel rim adjacent to lower ball joint.
3. Grasp tire at top and bottom and slowly move tire in and out. Note reading on dial, which is the radial play. If the reading exceeds 1/4", replace lower ball joint.

BALL JOINTS, REPLACE

1982–84 Continental & 1984 Mark VII

These ball joints are not serviceable. If they require replacement, the control arm and ball joint must be replaced as an assembly. Torque ball joint stud nut to 100–120 ft. lbs.

Except 1982–84 Continental & 1984 Mark VII

NOTE: Ford Motor Company recommends that new ball joints should not be installed on used control arms and that the control arm be replaced if ball joint replacement is required. However, aftermarket ball joint repair kits which do not require control arm replacement, are available and can be installed using the following procedure.

When replacing a riveted joint, remove the rivets and retain the new joint in its control arm with the bolts, nuts and washers furnished with the ball joint kit.
Use a suitable pressing tool to force the ball joint from the spindle.

SHOCK STRUT, REPLACE

1982–84 Continental & 1984 Mark VII

NOTE: On 1984 vehicles, turn air suspension switch off before removing shock strut. Refer to "Air Suspension System" section for proper procedure.

1. Place ignition switch in the Unlocked position so that front wheels are free to move.

2. From engine compartment, remove one strut to upper mounting nut. Use a screwdriver in rod slot to hold rod stationary when removing nut.
3. Raise front of vehicle by lower control arms, then place safety stands under frame jack pads located rearward of wheels.
4. Remove wheel and tire assembly, then remove brake caliper, rotor assembly and dust shield.
5. Remove two nuts and bolts attaching lower strut to spindle.

NOTE: When removing the second lower strut to spindle nut, hold strut firmly as gas pressure will cause strut to fully extend.

6. Lift strut upward from spindle to compress rod, then pull downward and remove strut.
7. Reverse procedure to install. Torque upper mount attaching nut to 60 to 75 ft. lbs. Remove suspension load from lower control arm by lowering front of vehicle, then torque lower mounting nuts to 150 to 180 ft. lbs.

SHOCK ABSORBER, REPLACE

1977–80 Versailles

1. Raise hood and remove upper mounting bracket-to-spring tower retaining nuts.
2. Raise front of car and place safety stands under lower control arms.
3. Remove shock absorber lower retaining nuts and washers.
4. Lift shock absorber from spring tower.
5. Reverse procedure to install.

1977–81 Continental, 1977–83 Mark V & VI & 1982–84 Town Car

1. Remove nut, washer and bushing from upper end of shock absorber.
2. Raise vehicle and support on stands.
3. Remove screws retaining shock absorber to lower control arm and remove shock absorber.
4. Reverse procedure to install.

COIL SPRING, REPLACE

1982–83 Continental

1. Raise front of vehicle and position safety stands under jack pads located rearward of wheels, then remove wheel and tire assembly.
2. Disconnect stabilizer bar link from lower control arm.
3. Remove steering gear attaching bolts, then position gear out of way.
4. Using tool 3290-C or equivalent, disconnect tie rod from spindle.
5. Using spring compressor D78P-5310-A or equivalent, compress spring until it is free from lower seat.
6. Remove two lower control arm pivot bolts and disengage control arm from frame, then remove spring from seat. If a re-

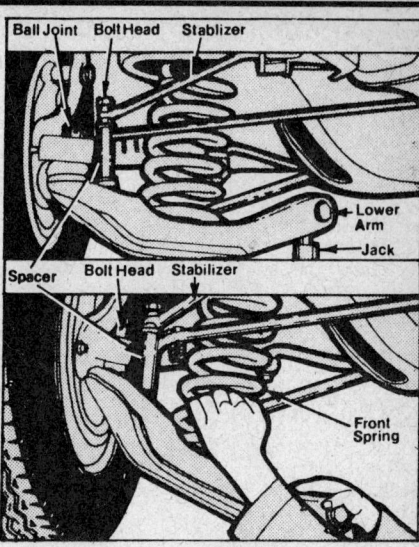

Fig. 11 Front spring replacement. Exc. Versailles

placement spring is to be installed, measure compressed length of spring being removed to assist in compressing and installing the replacement spring.
7. Reverse procedure to install. When installing spring, locate lower end of coil between two holes in lower control arm spring pocket. Torque control arm pivot bolt nuts to 215 to 260 ft.lbs., stabilizer bar link nut to 6 to 12 ft. lbs. and steering gear to crossmember attaching bolts to 90 to 100 ft. lbs.

1980–81 Continental, 1980–83 Mark VI & 1982–84 Town Car

1. Raise and support vehicle.
2. Remove wheel.
3. Disconnect stabilizer bar link from lower control arm.
4. Remove shock absorber.
5. Remove steering center link from pitman arm.
6. Compress coil spring with a suitable spring compressor, tool D-78P-5310-A or equivalent.
7. Remove two lower control arm pivot bolts and disengage arm from crossmember.
8. Remove spring from vehicle.
9. Reverse procedure to install. Torque pivot bolts to 120–140 ft. lbs.

NOTE: Tail end of spring must be positioned as shown in Fig. 3.

1977–80 Versailles

1. Remove shock absorber and upper mounting bracket as an assembly.
2. Raise car on hoist and install safety stands.
3. Remove wheel, tire, rotor and caliper assembly from spindle.
4. Install a suitable spring compressor and compress spring.
5. Remove two upper-arm-to-spring tower retaining nuts and swing upper arm outward from spring.
6. Release spring compressor, then remove spring.
7. Reverse procedure to install.

LINCOLN

1977–79 Except Versailles

1. Raise vehicle and support front end of frame with jack stands.
2. Disconnect shock absorber from lower arm and place a jack under the lower arm to support it, Fig. 11.
3. Remove strut and rebound bumper bolts and disconnect lower end of sway bar stud from lower arm.
4. Remove the nut and bolt retaining inner end of the lower arm to crossmember.
5. Carefully lower jack relieving spring pressure on the lower arm, then remove spring.
6. Reverse procedure to install.

POWER STEERING UNIT, REPLACE

Integral Power Rack & Pinion

1982–84 Continental & 1984 Mark VII
1. Disconnect battery ground cable.
2. Remove bolt retaining flexible coupling to input shaft.
3. Turn ignition key "On" and raise vehicle.
4. Remove the tie rod end retaining nuts, then separate studs from spindle arms.
5. Support gear and remove attaching bolts, then lower gear enough to gain access to pressure and return lines, and remove bolt attaching the hose bracket to the gear, and bolts from the crossmember.
6. Disconnect and cap pressure and return lines, then remove steering gear.
7. Reverse procedure to install. Torque pressure and return line fittings to 15–20 ft. lbs. Torque steering gear to crossmember bolts to 80–100 ft. lbs. Torque tie rod ends to spindle arm nuts to 35–47 ft. lbs.

1977–84 Integral Power Steering Gear

Exc. Versailles, 1982–84 Continental & 1984 Mark VII
1. Disconnect lines from steering gear and plug lines and ports.
2. Remove the two bolts securing flex coupling to steering gear and to column.
3. Raise vehicle and remove sector shaft nut and pitman arm.

NOTE: Do not damage the seals.

---

4. Support steering gear and remove three attaching bolts. Remove flex coupling clamp bolt and work steering gear free of coupling, then remove steering gear.
5. Reverse procedure to install.

Control Valve, Replace

Versailles
1. Disconnect fluid fittings at control valve and drain fluid from lines.
2. Loosen clamp at right-hand end of sleeve. Remove roll pin from steering arm-to-idler arm rod through slot in sleeve.
3. Using tool 3290-C, remove ball stud from sector shaft arm.

NOTE: The use of any other tool may result in damage to the control valve assembly.

---

4. Turn wheels fully to left and unthread control valve from idler arm rod.
5. Reverse procedure to install.

POWER STEERING PUMP, REPLACE

1980–84 Ford C11

Removal
1. Disconnect fluid return hose at reservoir and drain power steering fluid into a container.
2. Remove pressure hose from pump fitting. Do not remove fitting from pump.
3. Disconnect belt from pulley. If necessary, remove pulley from pump installing pulley remover tool T75L-3733-A or equivalent so small diameter threads engage in pump shaft. While holding small hex head, rotate tool nut to remove pulley. Do not apply in and out pressure on pump shaft as this will damage the internal thrust areas.
4. Remove pump.

Installation
1. Place pump in bracket and torque bolts to 30–45 ft. lbs.
2. If pulley was removed, install tool and while holding small hex head, turn tool nut clockwise to install pulley. Pulley must be flush within .010 inch of the end of the pump shaft. Do not apply in and out pressure on shaft. Remove tool.
3. Install pressure hose to pump fitting. Using tube nut wrench torque tube nut to 10–15 ft. lbs. Swivel and/or end play is normal.
4. Connect return hose to pump and tighten clamp. On vehicles with hydro-boost, connect lower return line.
5. On all vehicles, fill reservoir and check system for leaks.

1978–79 Ford C11

1. Disconnect fluid return line at the reservoir and allow fluid to drain into a suitable container.
2. Remove high pressure line from pump fitting.

NOTE: Do not remove the fitting from the pump.

---

3. Remove the pump mounting bracket and belt. Remove pump and bracket from vehicle.
4. Reverse procedure to install.

1977 Ford-TRW

1. Disconnect fluid return line at the reservoir and allow fluid to drain into a suitable container.
2. Disconnect high pressure line from the pump.
3. Remove bolts from the front of the pump and nut at the rear (8 cyl. only) attaching the pump to the pump bracket. Remove the belt and pump.
4. Reverse procedure to install.

1977–79 Saginaw

1. Disconnect the pressure and return lines from the pump and plug them to prevent entry of dirt or the loss of fluid.
2. Loosen the belt tension adjusting bolt.
3. Remove the pump mounting bracket attaching bolts.
4. Remove the pump, mounting bracket and pulley as an assembly.
5. Reverse procedure to install.

Air Suspension System

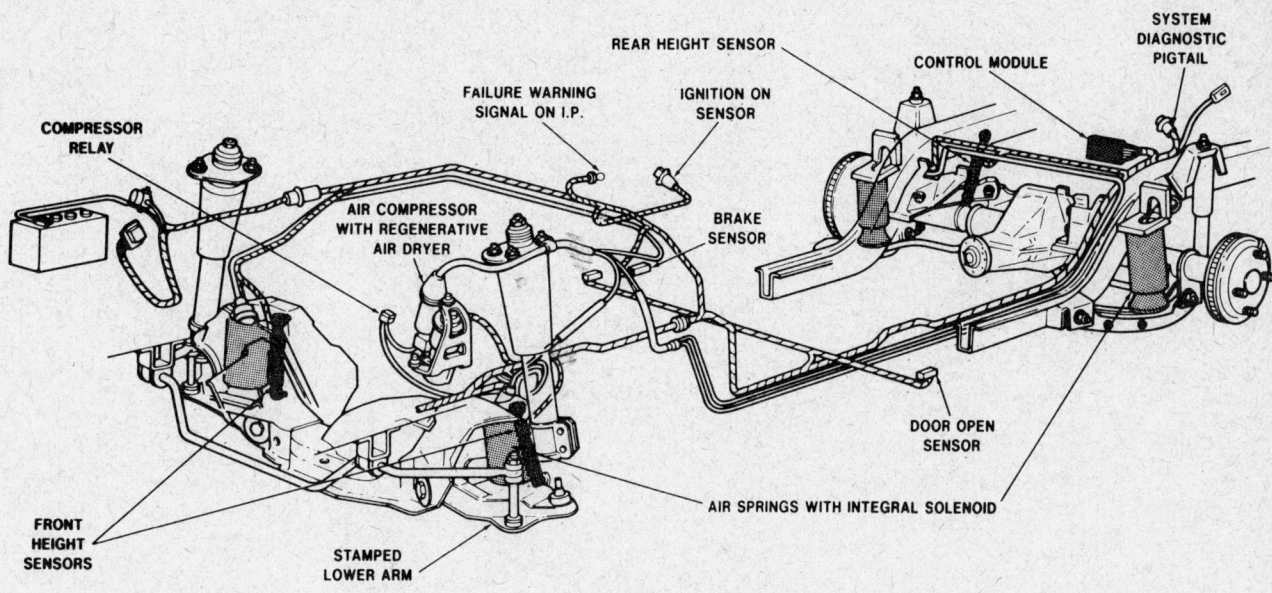

COMPRESSOR RELAY

FAILURE WARNING SIGNAL ON I.P.

REAR HEIGHT SENSOR

IGNITION ON SENSOR

CONTROL MODULE

SYSTEM DIAGNOSTIC PIGTAIL

AIR COMPRESSOR WITH REGENERATIVE AIR DRYER

BRAKE SENSOR

DOOR OPEN SENSOR

AIR SPRINGS WITH INTEGRAL SOLENOID

FRONT HEIGHT SENSORS

STAMPED LOWER ARM

Fig. 1   Air suspension system. 1984 Continental & Mark VII

DESCRIPTION

Used on 1984 Continental and Mark VII, the Air Suspension System, Fig. 1, is an air operated, microcompressor controlled suspension which replaces conventional coil springs with air springs and provides automatic front and rear load leveling.

The front air springs, Fig. 2, are mounted to the upper spring pocket in the crossmember and on the lower suspension arms as in conventional suspension systems. The rear springs, Fig. 3, are mounted ahead of the rear axle, outboard of the body side members and on the lower suspension arm.

A piston type electrically operated air compressor, attached to the left fender apron, supplies the air pressure necessary for system operation. All air passing through the system is filtered through a regenerative type dryer, located on the compressor manifold. A vent solenoid, also located on the manifold, controls exhaust air.

Air flow through the entire system is controlled by the interaction of the air compressor, solenoids, height sensors and the control module.

OPERATION

System operation is maintained by the addition or removal of air to or from the air springs, resulting in a predetermined front and rear suspension height. This predetermined height is known as the vehicle trim height. The trim height is controlled by three height sensors, two of which are located at the front wheels and a third at the rear suspension, Fig. 1. The height sensors are attached to the body and suspension arms and will lengthen or shorten, depending on the amount of suspension travel. As weight is added to the vehicle, the body settles, shortening the height sensors. The height sensors signal the control module, which then activates the air compressor through a relay, and signals the air spring solenoids to open. As the body rises, the height sensors lengthen. When the predetermined trim height is reached, the air compressor and solenoid valves are de-activated by the control module. As weight is removed, the body rises, lengthening the height sensors, and the height sensors signal the control module. The control module then opens the air compressor vent solenoid and the air spring solenoid valves. As the body lowers, the height sensors shorten. When the predetermined trim height is reached, the air compressor vent valve and air spring solenoid valves are closed by the control module.

The air required for leveling the vehicle is distributed from the air compressor to each spring by four nylon air lines which start at the dryer and end at the individual springs. Each air line is color coded to identify the spring to which they belong. The dryer is used to dry the air before it is delivered to each spring. The air required for compression and the vent air enter and exit through a common port on the compressor head. Vented air is controlled by a solenoid valve in the compressor head.

Electrical power to operate the system is distributed by the main body harness. The control module controls the air compressor relay, vent solenoid and the four air spring solenoids to provide the air requirements of the springs. The module also provides the power and ground circuits to the height sensors, while monitoring the input from the sensors and the Ignition Run/Brake and On/Door Open circuits. These inputs are used by the module in determining vehicle leveling requirements, which are then carried out by the air system components controlled by the module. The control module also provides for system self diagnosis, a routine for filling the air springs and operation of the system warning lamp.

Control Logic

Ignition Off

When the ignition switch is turned off, the system will continue to operate for approximately one hour. During this time, the system will service requests to lower the vehicle as required, provided no sensor was reading high at the time the ignition switch was turned off. Vent time is limited to 10 seconds for the rear springs and 3 seconds for the front. Approximately 1 hour after the ignition switch is turned off, the system will correct for a low vehicle height by activating the air compressor. Compressor run time is limited to 15 seconds for the rear springs and 30 seconds for the front.

Ignition In Run

When the ignition switch is first turned to the "RUN" position, the system will raise the vehicle as necessary. No down requests will be serviced for approximately 45 seconds. After the 45 second period, up and down requests will be serviced provided no door is open. If any door is open, no down requests will be serviced until the door is closed. However, if the brakes are applied with the doors closed, neither up nor down requests will be serviced

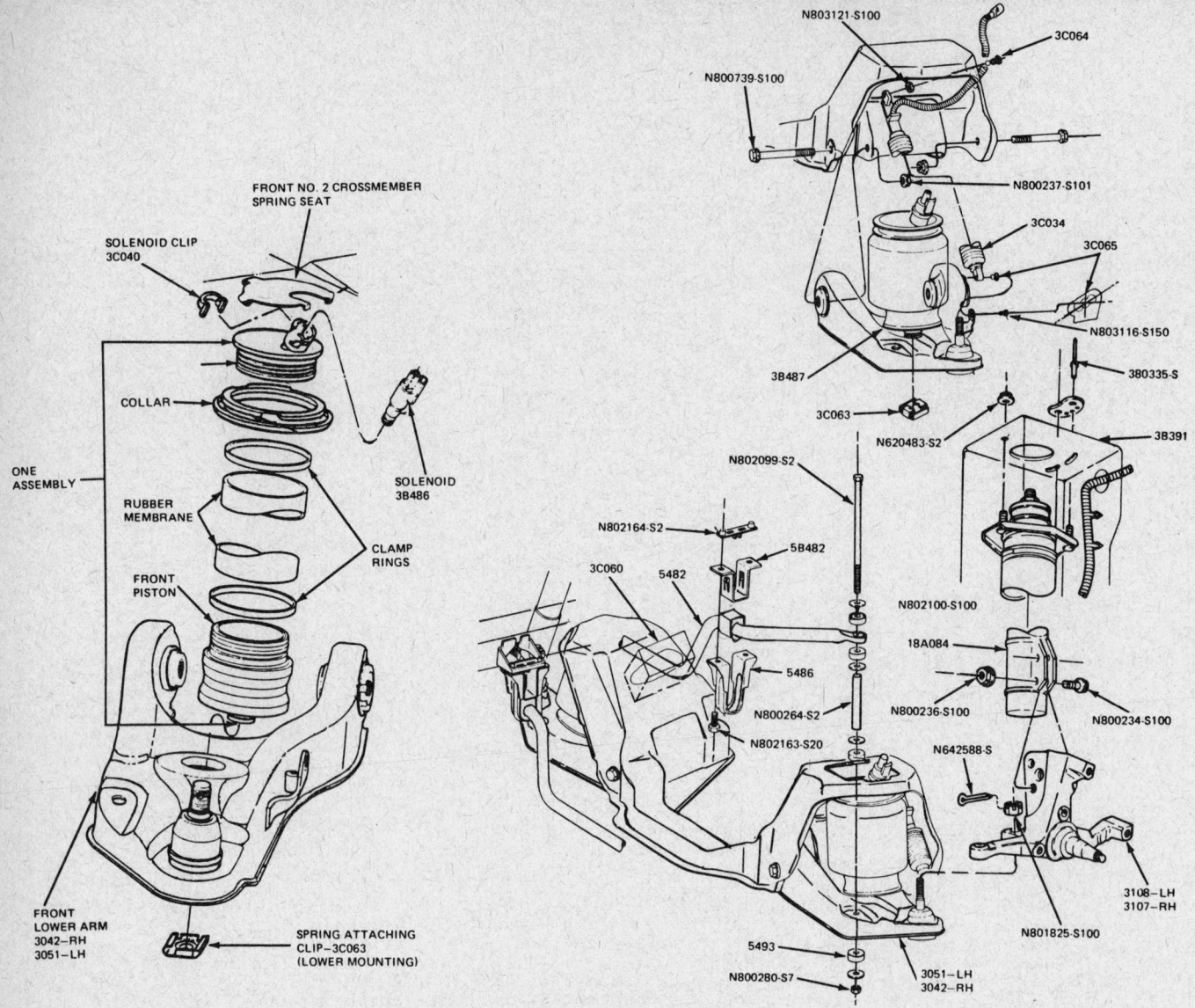

Fig. 2 Front suspension exploded view

except for a rear up request already in progress.

General Operating Conditions

1. Requests are serviced in the following Order: Rear Up, Front Up, Rear Down, Front Down.
2. With ignition in "Run," failure to service any request within 3 minutes will result in the activation of the warning lamp. The lamp will stay on during that complete ignition cycle. However, only the request that was being serviced will be affected. The control module will continue to service all other requests as usual.
3. The rear spring solenoids will always be operated in tandem, while the front solenoids may operate independently.
4. Front and rear requests are never serviced at the same time.
5. Turning the ignition from "Run" to "Off" will clear all memory in the control module, and the warning lamp may not indicate failure when the ignition is returned to the "On" position.

NOTE: When charging the battery, ensure ignition switch is off, as damage to the compressor or compressor relay may result.

SYSTEM WARNING LIGHT DIAGNOSIS

The "Check Suspension" warning light, located in the overhead console, serve the following diagnostic functions:
1. During normal operation with the ignition switch in the Run position and the "Check Suspension" light glowing, a possible air suspension problem is indicated.
2. During self diagnosis testing, the "Check Suspension" light blinks 1.8 times per second to indicate the diagnostic routine has been entered, then blinks the test number being run during the test sequence.
3. During "Air Spring Refill" procedure, the "Check Suspension" light blinks once every 2 seconds to indicate the air spring fill routine has been entered.

Observing the "Check Suspension" light during normal operation with the ignition switch On can aid in detecting the following Air Suspension System problems:
1. During normal operation, the "Check Suspension" light will glow for approximately one second and go out when ignition switch is turned from Off to Run position. The lamp does not operate with the ignition in the Off or Start position.
2. If "Check Suspension" light fails to go out after turning ignition switch from Off to Run position, no battery 12 volt power to the module is indicated.
3. If after turning ignition switch from Off to Run position, "Check Suspension" light glows for approximately one-half second, goes out and then glows continuously after five to eight seconds, a height sensor or harness problem is indicated.
4. If after turning ignition switch from Off to Run position, "Check Suspension" light comes on and glows continuously any

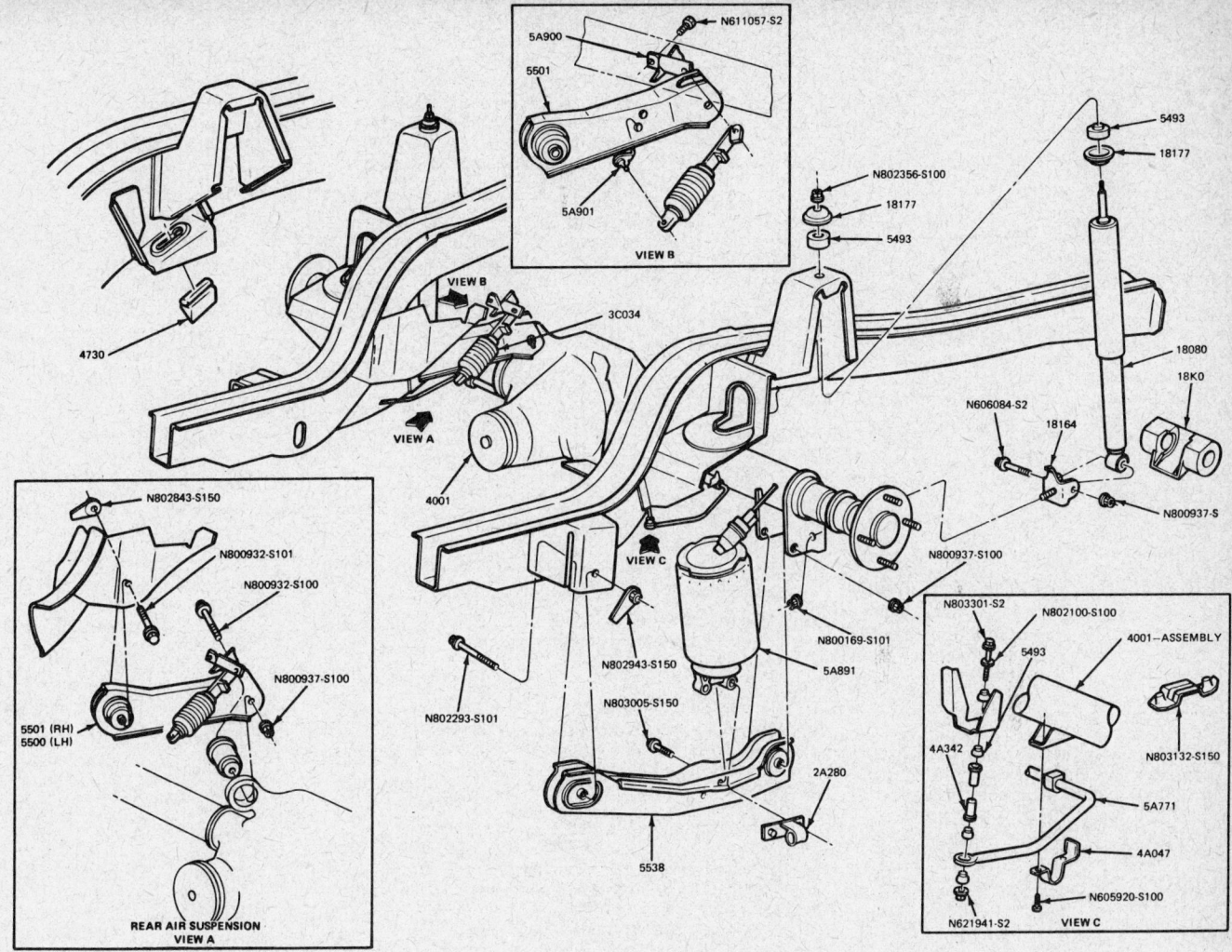

Fig. 3 Rear suspension exploded view

time after 8 seconds, an Air Suspension System problem is indicated.

5. Once the "Check Suspension" light comes On during an ignition On cycle, it will continue to glow for the duration of the ignition On cycle.

SYSTEM SELF DIAGNOSIS PROCEDURES

During these procedures, the following test equipment will be required:
1. A test light using a No. 194 bulb with pointed test probes.
2. A volt-ohmmeter.
3. A 150 PSI pressure gauge.

NOTE: Prior to attempting system self diagnosis, ensure all air lines and connections are tight and leak free. A suitable soap and water solution can be used to check for leaks.

System Self Diagnosis Description

During Self Diagnosis the following tests will be run:

Test 1

Test 1 is used in checking the rear suspension.

Test 2

Test 2 is used in checking the right front suspension.

Test 3

Test 3 is used in checking the left front suspension.

During tests 1 through 3, the following steps occur:
1. The rear, right front and left front of the vehicle will raise for 15 seconds, then continue raising an additional 15 seconds (30 seconds total maximum) or until a "Vehicle High" signal or illegal sensor reading is received from the rear/right front/left front height sensor.
2. The rear, right front and left front of the vehicle will lower for 30 seconds or until a "Vehicle Low" signal or illegal sensor reading is received from the rear, right front and left front height sensor.
3. The rear, right front and left front of the vehicle will raise for 30 seconds or until a "Vehicle Trim" signal or improper sensor reading is received from the rear, right front and left front height sensor.

NOTE: If the expected signal is not received within 30 seconds (total maximum), the test will stop and the warning light will glow con-

tinuously. If an improper sensor reading is obtained, the test will stop and the warning light will flash rapidly. The failed test may then be repeated by closing or opening the car door, or the next test may be started by opening and closing the car door twice within 15 seconds.

Test 4

During test 4, the compressor is cycled On and Off at .25 Hz. The compressor is limited to a maximum of 50 cycles.

Test 5

The compressor vent solenoid is cycled (open and closed) at 1 Hz.

Test 6

Left front solenoid is cycled (open and closed) at 1 Hz. and the compressor vent solenoid is opened. As the test progresses, the left front of the vehicle will drop slowly.

Test 7

Right front solenoid is cycled (open and closed) at 1 Hz. and the compressor vent solenoid is opened. As the test progresses, the right front of the vehicle will drop slowly.

Test 8

Right rear solenoid is cycled (open and closed) at 1 Hz. and the compressor vent solenoid is opened. As the test progresses, the right rear of the vehicle will drop slowly.

Test 9

Left rear solenoid is cycled (open and closed) at 1 Hz. and the compressor vent solenoid is opened. As the test progresses, the left rear of the vehicle will drop slowly.

Test 10

Disconnecting the diagnostic lead, depressing the brake pedal or turning ignition Off will return the module from diagnostics to the normal operating mode.

System Self Diagnosis

1. Check passenger compartment and luggage compartment for overloading, and unload as necessary. Allow vehicle to sit with the ignition switch in the Run position for five minutes, then proceed to step 2.
2. Cycle ignition switch to the Off, then Run position and observe the air suspension warning lamp. If lamp flashes or turns on, proceed to step 3. If lamp does not blink or turn on, refer to Step 1 of "System Will Not Enter Or Exit Self Diagnosis."
3. Connect battery charger to vehicle to reduce battery drain during diagnosis procedure. Turn ignition switch to the Off position, then ground diagnostic pigtail, Fig. 4. If pigtail is already grounded, unground and reground. Turn ignition switch to the Run position, and observe warning lamp. If warning lamp flashes continuously, proceed to step 4. If warning lamp flashes once, refer to step 10 of "System Will Not Enter Or Exit Self Diagnosis." If warning lamp stays on, refer to step 13 of "System Will Not Enter Or Exit Self Diagnosis."

NOTE: Do not start the engine, open the door, or depress the brake pedal until specifically instructed to do so.

---

4. To start test 1, open and close vehicle door. After test has been entered, a properly operating vehicle will raise the rear evenly for 15–30 seconds. If the rear of the vehicle is too high or too low, a maximum of 30 seconds is required to properly trim the vehicle. While test 1 is being performed, the warning lamp will flash the test number at a constant rate. Maximum test time is 90 seconds. After 90 seconds, observe warning lamp. If lamp flashes rapidly or stays on, then rear has failed test; proceed to step 5. If lamp flashes test number, then rear has passed test. Proceed to step 5. If warning lamp does not flash rapidly, stay on, or flash the test number, refer to step 22 of "System Will Not Enter Or Exit Self Diagnosis."
5. To start test 2, open and close vehicle door. If test 1 has failed, open and close the door twice. After test has been entered, a properly operating vehicle will raise the right front for 15–30 seconds. If the right front of the vehicle is too high or too low, a maximum of 30 seconds is required to properly trim the vehicle. While test 2 is being performed, the warning lamp will flash the test number at a constant rate. Maximum test time is 90 seconds. After 90 seconds, observe warning lamp. If lamp flashes rapidly or stays on, right front has failed test; proceed to step 6. If warning lamp flashes the test number, right front has passed test; proceed to step 6.

6. To start test 3, open and close vehicle door. If test 2 has failed, open and close the door twice. After test has been entered, a properly operated vehicle will raise the left front for 15–30 seconds. If the left front of the vehicle is too high or too low, a maximum of 30 seconds is required to properly trim the vehicle. While test 3 is being performed, the warning lamp will flash the test number at a constant rate. Maximum test time is 90 seconds. After 90 seconds, observe warning lamp. If lamp flashes rapidly or stays on, left front has failed test; proceed to step 7. If warning lamp flashes the test number, left front has passed test; proceed to step 7.
7. To start test 4, open and close vehicle door. If test 3 has failed, open and close the door twice. During this test the compressor should cycle on and off and the warning lamp should continuously flash the test number. If the compressor does not cycle on and off, compressor has failed test; proceed to step 8. If compressor cycles on and off, compressor has passed test; proceed to step 8.

NOTE: Rear of vehicle may raise during this test.

---

8. To start test 5, open and close vehicle door to cycle the vent solenoid. During this test, the vent solenoid should cycle on and off and the warning lamp should continuously flash the test number. If the vent solenoid does not cycle on and off, vent solenoid has failed test; proceed to step 9. If vent solenoid cycles on and off, vent solenoid has passed test. Proceed to step 9.
9. To start test 6, open and close vehicle door to cycle the left front air spring solenoid. Listen for air escaping from the vent solenoid, then ensure solenoid cycles at the left front wheel well opening. If left front air spring solenoid does not cycle or air is not escaping from the vent solenoid, left front air spring system has failed test; proceed to step 10. If left front air spring solenoid cycles and air is escaping from the vent solenoid, left front air spring system has passed test; proceed to step 10.

NOTE: The left front corner of the vehicle may drop during this test.

---

10. To start test 7, open and close vehicle door to cycle the right front air spring solenoid. Listen for air escaping from the vent solenoid, then ensure solenoid cycles at the right front wheel well opening. If the right front air spring solenoid does not cycle or air is not escaping from the vent solenoid, right front air spring system has failed test, proceed to step 11. If right front air spring solenoid cycles and air is escaping from the vent solenoid, right front air spring system has passed test; proceed to step 11.

NOTE: The right front corner of the vehicle may drop during this test.

---

11. To start test 8, open and close vehicle door to cycle the right rear air spring solenoid. Listen for air escaping from the vent solenoid, then ensure solenoid cycles at the

right rear wheel well opening. If the right rear air spring solenoid does not cycle or air is not escaping from the vent solenoid, right rear air spring system has failed test; proceed to step 12. If right rear air spring solenoid cycles and air is escaping from the vent solenoid, right rear air spring system has passed test; proceed to step 12.

NOTE: The right rear corner of the vehicle may drop during this test.

---

12. To start test 9, open and close vehicle door to cycle the left rear air spring solenoid. Listen for air escaping from the vent solenoid, then ensure the solenoid cycles at the left rear wheel well opening. If the left rear air spring solenoid does not cycle or air is not escaping from the vent solenoid, left rear air spring system has failed test; proceed to step 13. if the left rear air spring solenoid cycles and air is escaping from the vent solenoid, left rear air spring system has passed test; proceed to step 13.

NOTE: The left rear corner of the vehicle may drop during this test.

---

13. To start test 10, open vehicle door, then depress the brake pedal and observe the warning lamp. If warning lamp stops flashing, brake circuit has passed test and diagnostic procedure is completed. Unground the diagnostic pigtail and proceed to step 14. If warning lamp continues to flash, brake circuit has failed test. Refer to step 30 of "System Will Not Enter Or Exit Self Diagnosis."
14. If any failures have occurred during diagnosis, proceed to step 15. If no failures have occurred, air spring suspension system is satisfactory and no further diagnosis is required.
15. If the warning lamp flashed rapidly during steps 4 through 6, the module has read the sensor incorrectly; refer to step 1 of "Sensor Diagnosis." if the warning lamp did not flash rapidly, sensor is satisfactory; proceed to step 16.
16. If the warning lamp stayed on after the completion of step 4, check rear of vehicle, and refer to step 1 of "Rear Air Suspension Diagnosis." If warning lamp went out, proceed to step 17.
17. If the warning lamp stayed on after the completion of step 5, check right front of vehicle, and refer to step 1 of "Right Front Air Suspension Diagnosis." If warning lamp went out, right front of vehicle is satisfactory; proceed to step 18.
18. If warning lamp stayed on after the completion of step 6, check left front of vehicle, and refer to step 1 of "Left Front Air Suspension Diagnosis." If warning lamp went out, left front of vehicle is satisfactory; proceed to step 19.
19. If the right rear solenoid cycled and air escaped from the vent solenoid during step 11, right rear shock is satisfactory; proceed to step 20. If the solenoid did not cycle and air did not escape from the vent, refer to step 1 of "Rear Air Suspension Diagnosis."
20. If the left rear solenoid cycled and air escaped from the vent solenoid during step 12, left rear shock is satisfactory; refer to step 1 of "System Self Diagnosis." If solenoid did not cycle and air did not escape from the vent, refer to step 1 of "Rear Air Suspension Diagnosis."

System Will Not Enter Or Exit Self Diagnosis

1. If air suspension warning lamp bulb is burned out, replace bulb and perform "System Self Diagnosis" procedure. If bulb is not burned out, proceed to step 2.
2. Make a test lamp by attaching 2 test leads, with pointed probes, to a No. 194 lamp. Any other test lamp may cause damage to the air suspension system. Proceed to step 3.
3. Turn air suspension switch to the Off position, Fig. 4, and the ignition switch to the Off position. If the warning lamp is on, a short in circuit 687, Fig. 5, or ignition switch is indicated. Service circuit, then turn air suspension switch to the On position and perform "System Self Diagnosis" procedure. If the warning lamp is off, proceed to step 4.
4. Attach one lead of test lamp to circuit 640 at warning lamp, and the other lead to ground, Fig. 5. Turn ignition switch to Run position and observe the test lamp. If lamp is on, proceed to step 6. If lamp is off, proceed to step 5.
5. Check fuse in circuit 640, Fig. 5. If fuse is satisfactory, check for open in circuit 640, then perform "System Self Diagnosis" procedure. If fuse is not satisfactory, replace fuse, then check for short in circuit 640. If second fuse fails, perform "System Self Diagnosis" procedure.
6. Attach one lead of the test lamp to circuit 687 (pin 7) of the module connector and the other lead to ground, Fig. 5. Turn ignition switch to Run and observe test lamp. If test lamp is on, ignition circuit is satisfactory; proceed to step 7. If test lamp is off, check for open or short in circuit 687. Turn air suspension switch to the "On" position, then perform "System Self Diagnosis" procedure.
7. Attach one lead of the test lamp to circuit 687 (pin 7) of the module connector, Fig. 5, then turn ignition switch to Run and observe the test lamp. Attach the other lead of the test lamp to circuit 430 (pin 1) of the module connector, then move lead to pin 24, Fig. 5. If test lamp is on, ground circuit is satisfactory; proceed to step 8. If test lamp is off, check for open in circuit 430, then perform "System Self Diagnosis" procedure.
8. Using volt-ohmmeter, attach negative lead to ground and the positive lead to circuit 419 (pin 21) of the module connector, Fig. 5. Turn ignition switch to Run and observe voltage reading. If voltage is greater than 5 volts, warning circuit is satisfactory; proceed to step 9. If voltage is less than or equal to 5 volts, check for open in circuit 419 from the module connector to the warning lamp connector. Turn air suspension switch to "On" position, then perform "System Self Diagnosis" procedure.
9. Using volt-ohmmeter, attach negative lead to circuit 430 (pin 24) of the module connector and positive lead to circuit 418 (pin 20) of the module connector, Fig. 5. Observe voltage reading. If voltage is less than 11 volts, check for low battery or faulty connection, then perform "System Self Diagnosis" procedure. If voltage is greater than 11 volts, replace air suspension module, then perform "System Self Diagnosis" procedure.
10. Repeat steps 2 and 3 of "System Self Diagnosis" procedure and insure diagnostic pigtail is grounded. If warning lamp flashes once, proceed to step 11. If warning lamp flashes continuously, perform "System Self Diagnosis" procedure.
11. Use test lamp, described in step 2, for the following procedure.
12. Attach one lead of the test lamp to circuit 606 (pin 2) at the module connector and the other lead to circuit 687 (pin 7) at the module connector, Fig. 5. Turn ignition switch to the Run position, then ground and unground diagnostic pigtail. Observe the test lamp. If test lamp is on, then turns off, pigtail is satisfactory; refer to step 9. If lamp is on or off, check for open or short in circuit 606, then perform "System Self Diagnosis" procedure.
13. Open and close vehicle door and observe compressor. If compressor starts running, proceed to step 20. If compressor is already running or does not start to run, proceed to step 14.
14. Use test lamp, described in step 2, for the following procedure.
15. Attach one lead of the test lamp to circuit 418 (pin 20) at the module connector and the other lead to ground, Fig. 5. If test lamp is on, proceed to step 21. If test lamp is off, proceed to step 16.
16. Check fusible link in battery circuit 175. If fusible link is satisfactory, proceed to step 17. If fuse link is not satisfactory, replace fuse link and perform "System Self Diagnosis" procedure.
17. If air suspension switch is in On position, proceed to step 18. If switch is in Off position, place switch in On position and perform "System Self Diagnosis" procedure.
18. Attach one lead of test lamp to circuit 175 at the air suspension switch (pin 2), Fig. 5, on the battery side and the other lead to ground. If test lamp is on, proceed to step 19. If test lamp is off, check for open or short in circuit 175 from the air suspension switch (pin 2) to the battery, then perform "System Self Diagnosis" procedure.
19. Attach one lead of test lamp to circuit 418 at the air suspension switch (pin 1), Fig. 5, on the module side and the other lead to ground. If test lamp is on, check for open or short in circuit 418 from the air suspension switch (pin 1) to the battery, then perform "System Self Diagnosis" procedure. If test lamp is off, replace air suspension switch, then perform "System Self Diagnosis" procedure.
20. Disconnect module connector and observe warning lamp. If warning lamp is on, check for short to ground in circuit 419 from the module connector to the warning lamp, Fig. 5, then reconnect the module connector and perform "System Self Diagnosis" procedure. If warning lamp is off, warning lamp circuit is satisfactory; proceed to step 21.
21. Using volt-ohmmeter, attach negative lead to circuit 430 (pin 24) of the module connector and the positive lead to circuit 418 pin 20 at the module connector, Fig. 5. Observe voltage reading. If voltage is less than 11 volts, check for low battery or faulty connection, then perform "System Self Diagnosis" procedure. If voltage is greater than 11 volts, replace air suspension module, then perform "System Self Diagnosis" procedure.
22. Use test lamp, described in step 2, for the following procedure.
23. Attach one lead of test lamp to circuit 24 (pin 19) at the module connector and the other lead to ground, Fig. 5. Close vehicle door and observe test lamp. If test lamp is on, check for short to battery or ignition in circuit 24 or faulty door switch, then perform "System Self Diagnosis" procedure. If test lamp is off, proceed to step 24.
24. Open vehicle door and observe the test lamp. If test lamp is on, door circuit is satisfactory; proceed to step 25. If test lamp is off, check for open or short in circuit 24 or defective door switch, then perform "System Self Diagnosis" procedure.
25. Depress and release the brake pedal and observe the rear brake lights. If brake lights operate satisfactory, brake circuit is satisfactory; proceed to step 26. If brake lights do not operate satisfactorily, service as necessary and perform "System Self Diagnosis" procedure.
26. Disconnect compressor relay electrical connector, then perform steps 2 through 4 of "System Self Diagnosis" procedure. Observe warning lamp. If lamp flashes rapidly, stays on or flashes the test number, proceed to step 27. If lamp does not flash rapidly, stay on, or flash the test number, compressor circuit is satisfactory; refer to step 21.
27. With compressor relay connector disconnected, attach positive lead of volt-ohmmeter to circuit 417 (pin 2) on the harness side of the compressor connector and the negative lead to ground, Fig. 5. Observe ohmmeter reading. If ohmmeter reads

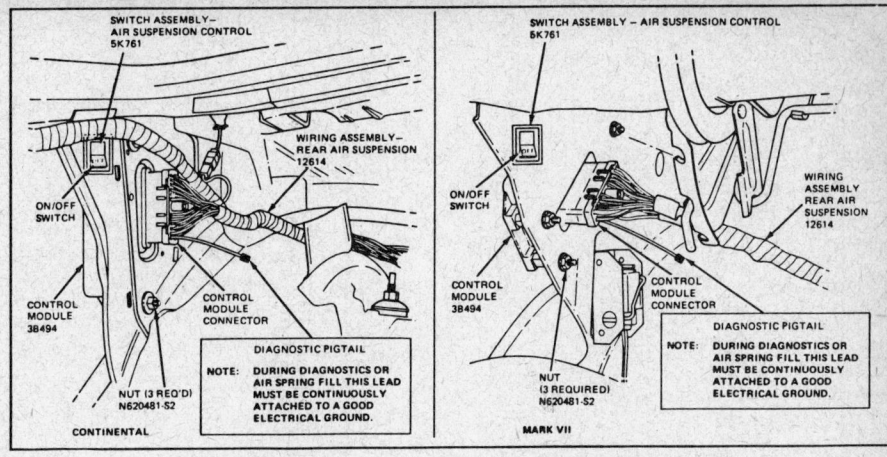

Fig. 4   Air suspension switch & diagnostic pigtail location

Wiring	Harness Side Connector	Pin Number	Function	Wire Harness			Circuit End Point
				Circuit	Color	Gauge	
Compressor (1)		1	Solenoid Feed	175	BK/Y D	16	Starter Relay
		2	Motor Feed	417	P/O	12	Compressor Relay
		3	Motor Ground	430	GY	14	Battery Ground Cable
		4	Solenoid Control	421	PK	18	Module Pin No. 23
Spring Solenoid (4)		1	Control	LR 429	P/LG H	18	Module Pin No. 9
			Control	RR 416	LB/BK	18	Module Pin No. 10
			Control	LF 415	LG/O	18	Module Pin No. 11
			Control	RF 414	O/R	18	Module Pin No. 12
		2	Feed	175	BK/Y D	16	Starter Relay
Front Height Sensor (2)		1	Ground	432	BK/PK D	20	Module Pin No. 14
		2	Feed — LF (RF)	431B (A)	PK/W H	20	Module Pin No. 4
		3	Logic Line B	RF 425	BR/PK H	20	Module Pin No. 16
			Logic Line B	LF 423	P/LG	20	Module Pin No. 17
		4	Logic Line A	RF 424	T	20	Module Pin No. 5
			Logic Line A	LF 422	PK/BK	20	Module Pin No. 6
Rear Height Sensor (1)	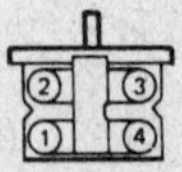	1	Ground	432	BK/PK D	20	Module Pin No. 14
		2	Feed	426	R/BK H	20	Module Pin No. 3
		3	Logic Line B	428	O/BK H	20	Module Pin No. 18
		4	Logic Line A	427	PK/BK H	20	Module Pin No. 13
Compressor Relay (1)	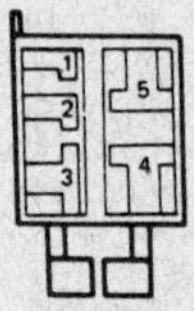	1	Control	420	DB/Y	18	Module Pin No. 22
		2	Feed (Coil)	175	BK/Y D	14	Starter Relay
		3	Feed (Contacts)	175	BK/Y D	14	Starter Relay
		4	Compressor Motor Feed	417	P/O	14	Compressor
		5	Compressor Motor Ground	430	GY	12	Battery Ground Cable
On/Off Switch (1)	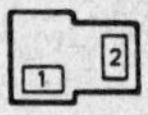	1	Feed to Module	418	DG/Y	14	Module Pin No. 20
		2	Feed to Switch	175	BK/Y D	14	Starter Relay
Warning Lamp (1)	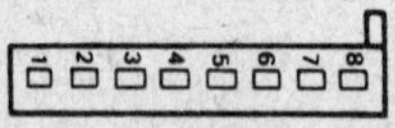	8	Control	419	DG/LG	20	Module Pin No. 21
		6	Feed	640	R/Y H	20	Fuse Panel
●	Ignition Switch (—14401—)		Ignition Sense	687	GY/Y	18	Module Pin No. 7
●	Stop Lamp Switch (—14A005—)		Brake Sense	511	LG	18	Module Pin No. 15
●	Courtesy Lamp Door Switch (—14488—)		Door Sense	24	DB/O H	20	Module Pin No. 19
Module (1)	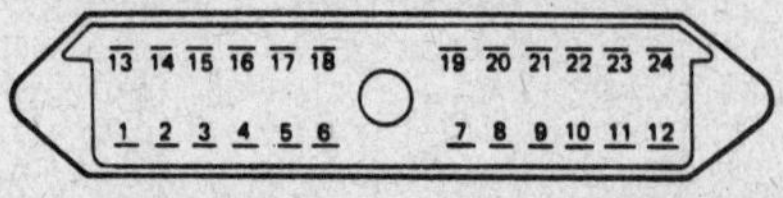						

Fig. 5   Air suspension system circuit identification

greater than 1000 ohms, proceed to step 28. If ohmmeter reads less than 1000 ohms, check for short to ground on circuit 417, then perform "System Self Diagnosis" procedure.

28. Disconnect compressor connector, then connect a jumper wire between pin 3 of the compressor connector and ground, Fig. 5. Using a suitable ammeter of 50 amp. capacity, attach negative lead to pin 3 of the compressor connector and positive lead to battery positive terminal. Measure current after compressor has run for 10 seconds. Do not allow the compressor to run for more than 60 seconds. If ammeter reads greater than 35 amps, replace compressor assembly, then perform "System Self Diagnosis" procedure. If amp meter reads less than 35 amps, proceed to step 29.

29. Perform step 28, but measure the battery voltage while the compressor is running. If voltage is greater than 11 volts, replace the air suspension module, then perform "System Self Diagnosis" procedure. If voltage is less than 11 volts, charge or replace battery, then perform "System Self Diagnosis" procedure.

30. Use test lamp, as described in step 2, for the following procedure.

31. Depress brake pedal and observe rear brake lights. If brake lights operate satisfactory, proceed to step 32. If brake lights do not operate satisfactory, service as necessary, then perform "System Self Diagnosis" procedure.

32. Attach one lead of test lamp to circuit 511 at the module connector and the other lead to ground, Fig. 5. Depress brake pedal and observe test lamp. If test lamp is on, replace air suspension module, then perform "System Self Diagnosis" procedure. If test lamp is off, check for open or short in circuit 511, then perform "System Self Diagnosis" procedure.

Sensor Diagnosis

1. If the warning lamp flashed during steps 4 through 6 of "System Self Diagnosis," proceed to step 2. If the warning lamp did not flash, proceed to step 11.

2. Attach one lead of test lamp to circuit 432 (pin 1) at the left front sensor connector, and the other lead to the battery positive terminal, Fig. 5. Observe test lamp. If test lamp is on, sensor ground circuit is satisfactory, proceed to step 5. If test lamp is off, proceed to step 3.

3. Without disconnecting module connector, attach one lead of test lamp to circuit 432 (pin 14) at the module connector and the other lead to battery (pin 20) at the module connector, Fig. 5. Observe test lamp. If test lamp is on, check for open in circuit 432, then perform "System Self Diagnosis" procedure. If test lamp is off, proceed to step 4.

4. Disconnect module connector and inspect sensor ground pin 14 and module ground pins 1 and 24 for corrosion and damage, Fig. 5. If corrosion or damage is found, service as necessary, then perform "System Self Diagnosis" procedure. If no corrosion or damage is found, replace the air suspension module, then perform "System Self Diagnosis" procedure.

5. Using volt-ohmmeter, attach negative lead to circuit 432 (pin 14) of the module connector and the positive lead to circuit 431 (pin 4) of the module connector, Fig. 5. Turn ignition switch to Run and observe voltage reading. If voltage is less than 1.0 volt and steady, proceed to step

6. If voltage reading is erratic or greater than 1.0 volt but less than 5 volts, check for open in circuit 426 or 431 between the module and sensors, then perform "System Self Diagnosis" procedure. If voltage is greater than 5 volts and steady, replace air suspension module, then perform "System Self Diagnosis" procedure.

6. Disconnect left front sensor wire connector while observing voltmeter. If voltage is less than 1.0 volt and steady, left front sensor is satisfactory; proceed to step 7. If voltage is erratic or greater than 1.0 volt, replace the left front sensor, then perform "System Self Diagnosis" procedure.

7. With left front sensor disconnected, disconnect the right front sensor wire connector and observe the volt-ohmmeter. If voltage is less than 1.0 volt and steady, right front sensor is satisfactory, proceed to step 8. If voltage is erratic or greater than 1.0 volt, replace right front sensor, then connect the left front sensor and perform "System Self Diagnosis" procedure.

8. With right front sensor disconnected, disconnect the rear sensor wire connector and observe the volt-ohmmeter. If the voltage is less than 1.0 volt and steady, rear sensor is satisfactory, proceed to step 9. If the voltage is erratic or greater than 1.0 volt, replace rear sensor, then connect the left and right front sensors and perform "System Self Diagnosis" procedure.

9. With rear sensor disconnected, disconnect the air suspension module. Using a volt-ohmmeter, attach negative test and lead to circuit 430 (pin 1) of the module connector and the positive lead to circuit 426 (pin 3) at the module connector, Fig. 5. Observe ohmmeter reading. If ohmmeter reads greater than 1000 ohms, proceed to step 10. If ohmmeter reads less than 1000 ohms, check for short to ground in circuit 426, then connect right and left front sensors, rear sensor and control module. Perform "System Self Diagnosis" procedure.

10. Move positive test lead of volt-ohmmeter to circuit 431 (pin 4) at module connector, Fig. 5, and observe ohmmeter reading. If ohmmeter reads greater than 1000 ohms, replace air suspension control module, then perform "System Self Diagnosis" procedure. If ohmmeter reads less than 1000 ohms, check for short to ground in circuit 431, then connect right and front sensors, rear sensor and control module. Perform "System Self Diagnosis" procedure.

11. If warning light flashed rapidly during step 4 of "System Self Diagnosis," proceed to step 12. If lamp did not flash rapidly, proceed to step 23.

12. Turn air suspension switch to the Off position, Fig. 4. Attach positive lead of volt-ohmmeter to circuit 432 (pin 1), Fig. 5, at the rear sensor, and the negative lead to ground and measure resistance. If resistance is greater than 5 ohms, check for open in circuit 432 between the module connector and the rear sensor, then perform "System Self Diagnosis" procedure. If resistance is less than 5 ohms, proceed to step 13.

13. Place the air suspension switch in On position, Fig. 4. Attach negative lead of volt-ohmmeter to circuit 432 (pin 1) of the rear sensor connector and the positive lead to circuit 426 (pin 2) of the sensor, Fig. 5. Turn ignition switch to Run position and measure voltage. If voltage is less than 1 volt and steady, check for open in circuit sensor power circuit 426 between module connector and rear sensor. Service circuit, then perform "System Self Diagnosis" procedure. If voltage is

greater than 1 volt or erratic, proceed to step 14.

14. Move positive lead to circuit 427 (pin 4) at rear sensor connector and measure voltage, Fig. 5. If voltage is greater than 1.5 volts or is erratic, proceed to step 18. If voltage is less than 1.5 volts, proceed to step 15.

15. Disconnect rear sensor connector and measure voltage. If voltage is greater than 1.5 volts, replace rear sensor, then perform "System Self Diagnosis" procedure. If voltage is less than 1.5 volts, proceed to step 16.

16. With rear sensor wiring disconnected, attach negative lead of volt-ohmmeter to circuit 432 (pin 14) of the module connector, Fig. 5. Attach positive lead of volt-ohmmeter to circuit 427 (pin 13) of the module connector, Fig. 5, and measure voltage. If voltage is greater than 1.5 volts, check for opens in circuit 427 between module and sensor. Service circuit, then perform "System Self Diagnosis" procedure. If voltage is less than 1.5 volts, proceed to step 17.

17. Disconnect module connector, then attach negative lead of volt-ohmmeter to module connector circuit 430 (pin 1), Fig. 5, and positive lead to circuit 427 (pin 13) at module connector. Measure circuit resistance. If resistance is greater than 1000 ohms, replace air suspension module and repeat "System Self Diagnosis" procedure. If resistance is less than 1000 ohms, check for short to ground in circuit 427 between module and rear sensor. Service circuit, then perform "System Self Diagnosis" procedure.

18. Move positive lead of volt-ohmmeter to rear sensor connector circuit 428 (pin 1), and measure voltage, Fig. 5. If voltage is greater than 1.5 volts or erratic, proceed to step 19. If voltage is less than 1.5 volts, proceed to step 20.

19. Repeat "System Self Diagnosis" steps 1 through 4 and observe warning lamp. If warning lamp is flashing rapidly, replace air suspension control module. If warning light is not flashing rapidly, perform complete "System Self Diagnosis" procedure.

20. Disconnect rear sensor connector and measure voltage. If voltage is greater than 1.5 volts, install new rear sensor, then perform "System Self Diagnosis" procedure. If voltage is less than 1.5 volts, proceed to step 21.

21. With rear sensor connected, attach negative lead of volt-ohmmeter to module connector circuit 432 (pin 14), Fig. 5. Attach positive lead to module connector circuit 428 (pin 18), Fig. 5, and measure voltage. If voltage is greater than 1.5 volts, check for open in sensor circuit 428 between module and rear sensor and repair as necessary. Repeat "System Self Diagnosis" procedure. If voltage is less than 1.5 volts, proceed to step 22.

22. Disconnect module connector and attach negative lead of a volt-ohmmeter to module connector circuit 430 (pin 1), then attach the positive lead to rear sensor circuit 428 (pin 18) at module connector, and measure circuit resistance. If resistance is greater than 1000 ohms, replace air suspension module, connect rear sensor and perform "System Self Diagnosis" procedure. If resistance is less than 1000 ohms, a short is indicated on rear sensor circuit 428 between module and rear sensor.

23. If the warning lamp flashed rapidly for step 4 of "System Self Diagnosis," proceed to step 24. If warning lamp did not flash

rapidly, proceed to step 35.

24. Attach one lead of test lamp to right front sensor ground circuit 432 (pin 1) and the second test lead to the positive battery terminal, Fig. 5, then observe test lamp. If the test lamp is on, sensor ground is satisfactory; proceed to step 25. If test lamp is off, an open is indicated in sensor ground circuit 432 between module connector and right front sensor. Service circuit, then perform "System Self Diagnosis" procedure.

25. Attach negative lead of suitable volt-ohmmeter to right front sensor connector ground circuit 432 (pin 1), then attach the positive test lead to sensor power circuit 431 (pin 2) at right front sensor connector, Fig. 5. Turn ignition to Run position and measure DC voltage. If voltage is less than 1.0 volts and steady, an open is indicated in sensor power circuit 431 from right front sensor to module. Service circuit, then perform "System Self Diagnosis" procedure. If voltage is erratic or greater than 1.0 volts, sensor is satisfactory; proceed to step 26.

26. Move positive test lead to right front sensor circuit 424 (pin 4) at connector and measure DC voltage, Fig. 5. If voltage is greater than 1.5 volts or is erratic, right front sensor is satisfactory; proceed to step 30. If voltage is less than 1.5 volts, proceed to step 27.

27. Disconnect connector at right front sensor and measure DC voltage. If voltage is greater than 1.5 volts, replace right front sensor and perform "System Self Diagnosis" procedure. If voltage is less than 1.5 volts, right front sensor is satisfactory; proceed to step 28.

28. With right front sensor disconnected, attach negative test lead of volt-ohmmeter to sensor connector circuit 432 (pin 1), and attach the positive lead to right front sensor connector circuit 424 (pin 4) at module connector, Fig. 5, then measure voltage. If voltage is greater than 1.5 volts, an open is indicated in right front sensor A circuit 424 between module and sensor. Service circuit, then perform "System Self Diagnosis" procedure. If voltage is less than 1.5 volts, proceed to step 29.

29. Disconnect module connector and attach negative lead of a volt-ohmmeter to module connector circuit 430 (pin 1), then attach positive lead to right front sensor circuit 424 (pin 5) at module connector and measure resistance, Fig. 5. If resistance is greater than 1000 ohms, replace air suspension module, connect right front sensor, then perform "System Self Diagnosis" procedure. If resistance is less than 1000 ohms, a short is indicated on right front sensor circuit 424 between module and right front sensor. Service circuit, then perform "System Self Diagnosis" procedure.

30. Move positive test lead to right front sensor connector circuit 425 (pin 3) at right front sensor and measure DC voltage, Fig. 5. If voltage is greater than 1.5 volts or is erratic, replace right front sensor, then proceed to step 31. If voltage is less than 1.5 volts, proceed to step 32.

31. Perform steps 2 through 5 of "System Self Diagnosis," if warning light flashes rapidly during step 5, replace air suspension control module, then perform "System Self Diagnosis" procedure. If warning light did not flash, perform "System Self Diagnosis" procedure.

32. Disconnect right front sensor connector and measure DC voltage. If voltage is greater than 1.5 volts, install new right

front sensor and perform "System Self Diagnosis" procedure. If DC voltage is less than 1.5 volts, proceed to step 33.

33. With right front sensor disconnected, attach negative lead of a suitable volt-ohmmeter to sensor circuit 432 (pin 14) at module connector, then attach positive lead to right front sensor circuit 425 (pin 16) at module connector and measure DC voltage. If voltage is greater than 1.5 volts, an open is indicated in right front sensor circuit 425 between module and sensor. Service and perform "System Self Diagnosis" procedure. If voltage is less than 1.5 volts, proceed to step 34.

34. Disconnect module connector and attach negative lead of a volt-ohmmeter to module connector circuit 430 (pin 1), then attach positive lead to right front sensor circuit 425 (pin 16) at module connector, Fig. 5, and measure resistance. If resistance is greater than 1000 ohms, replace air suspension module, connect right front sensor and perform "System Self Diagnosis" procedure. If resistance is less than 1000 ohms, a short is indicated on right front sensor circuit 425 between module and right front sensor. Service circuit, then perform "System Self Diagnosis" procedure.

35. Attach one lead of test lamp to sensor ground circuit 432 (pin 1) at left front sensor circuits, then attach the second test lead to positive battery terminal and observe test lamp. If test lamp is on, sensor ground is satisfactory; proceed to step 36. If test lamp is off, an open is indicated in sensor ground circuit 432 between module connector and left front sensor. Service circuit, then perform "System Self Diagnosis" procedure.

36. Attach negative lead of a volt-ohmmeter to sensor ground circuit 432 (pin 1) at left front sensor connector and attach the positive lead to sensor power circuit 431 (pin 2) at left front sensor connector, Fig. 5. Turn ignition to Run position and measure DC voltage. If voltage is greater than 1.0 volts or is erratic, sensor power circuit is satisfactory; proceed to step 37. If voltage is less than 1.0 volts and steady, an open is indicated in sensor power circuit 431 from left front sensor to module. Service circuit, then perform "System Self Diagnosis" procedure.

37. Move positive lead to left front sensor circuit 422 (pin 4) at left front sensor connector and measure DC voltage. If voltage is greater than 1.5 volts or is erratic, left front sensor circuit is satisfactory; proceed to step 41. If voltage is less than 1.5 volts proceed to step 38.

38. Disconnect left front sensor connector and measure DC voltage. If voltage is greater than 1.5 volts, replace left front sensor and perform "System Self Diagnosis" procedure. If voltage is less than 1.5 volts, left front sensor is satisfactory; proceed to step 39.

39. With left front sensor disconnected, attach negative lead of a volt-ohmmeter to sensor circuit 432 (pin 14) at module connector, then attach positive lead to right front sensor circuit 422 (pin 6) at module connector, Fig. 5, and measure DC voltage. If voltage is greater than 1.5 volts, an open is indicated in left sensor circuit 422 between module and sensor. Service circuit, then perform "System Self Diagnosis" procedure. If voltage is less than 1.5 volts, proceed to step 40.

40. Disconnect module connector and attach negative lead of a volt-ohmmeter to module connector circuit 430 (pin 1), then attach positive lead to left front sensor

circuit 422 (pin 6) at module connector, Fig. 5, and measure resistance. If resistance is greater than 1000 ohms, replace air suspension module, connect sensor and perform "System Self Diagnosis" procedure. If resistance is less than 1000 ohms, a short is indicated on left front sensor circuit 422 between module and left front sensor. Service circuit, then perform "System Self Diagnosis" procedure.

41. Move positive lead to left front sensor circuit 423 (pin 3) at connector and measure DC voltage. If voltage is greater than 1.5 volts or is erratic, replace left front sensor, then proceed to step 42. If voltage is less than 1.5 volts, proceed to step 43.

42. Perform steps 2 through 6 of "System Self Diagnosis." If warning lamp flashes rapidly during step 6, replace air suspension control module and perform "System Self Diagnosis" procedure. If warning lamp does not flash rapidly, perform "System Self Diagnosis" procedure.

43. Disconnect left front sensor connector and measure DC voltage. If DC voltage is greater than 1.5 volts or is erratic, install new left front sensor and perform "System Self Diagnosis" procedure. If voltage is less than 1.5 volts, left front sensor is satisfactory; proceed to step 44.

44. With left front sensor disconnected, attach negative lead of suitable volt-ohmmeter to module connector circuit 432 (pin 14), Fig. 5, then attach positive lead to left front sensor circuit 423 (pin 17) at module connector and measure DC voltage. If voltage is greater than 1.5 volts, an open is indicated in left front sensor circuit 423 between module and sensor. Service circuit, then perform "System Self Diagnosis" procedure. If voltage is less than 1.5 volts, proceed to step 45.

45. Disconnect module connector and attach negative lead of a volt-ohmmeter to module connector circuit 430 (pin 1), then attach positive lead to left front sensor circuit 423 (pin 17) at module connector, Fig. 5, and measure resistance. If resistance is greater than 1000 ohms, replace air suspension module, connect sensor and perform "System Self Diagnosis" procedure. If resistance is less than 1000 ohms, a short is indicated on left front sensor circuit 423 between module and left front sensor. Service circuit, then perform "System Self Diagnosis" procedures.

Rear Air Suspension Diagnosis

1. If compressor cycled during step 7 of "System Self Diagnosis," proceed to step 2. If the compressor did not cycle, proceed to step 1 of "Compressor Electrical Diagnosis."

2. If the right rear solenoid cycled during step 11 of "System Self Diagnosis," proceed to step 3. If the right rear solenoid did not cycle, proceed to step 12.

3. If the left front rear solenoid cycled during step 12 of "System Self Diagnosis," proceed to step 4. If the left front rear solenoid did not cycle, proceed to step 21.

4. If the vent solenoid cycled during step 8 of "System Self Diagnosis," proceed to step 5. If the vent solenoid did not cycle, proceed to step 1 of "Compressor Vent Solenoid Electrical Diagnosis."

5. Perform steps 2 and 3 of "System Self Diagnosis," then disconnect all air lines at compressor. Plug 3 of the 4 air line fittings and install a pressure gauge with a minimum of 150 psi to remaining fit-

ting, then open and close vehicle door and note pressure reading. If the pressure is greater than 120 psi, proceed to step 6. If the pressure is less than 120 psi, install new compressor and repeat "System Self Diagnosis" procedure.

6. Inspect rear sensor, ball studs and bracket for secure attachment. If attachment is secure, proceed to step 7. If connection is not secure, tighten as necessary and repeat "System Self Diagnosis" procedure.

7. Disconnect air lines at compressor leading to right and left rear air springs, then perform steps 2 and 3 of "System Self Diagnosis." Open and close vehicle door and verify escaping air from lines. If air is escaping from both lines, proceed to step 8. If air is escaping from only one line, proceed to step 10. If both lines fail to release air due to an absence of air in either spring, proceed to step 8.

8. If the vehicle failed steps 2 and 3 of "System Self Diagnosis," locate and service leak in faulty solenoid assembly. If vehicle passed steps 2 and 3, proceed to step 9.

9. Press down and release rear of vehicle. If rebound is high, replace compressor and repeat "System Self Diagnosis" procedure. If rebound is low, check for and repair leaking air line or fitting, then repeat "System Self Diagnosis" procedure.

NOTE: During the following test, rear of vehicle may fall. Use caution during procedure.

---

10. Reconnect rear air spring air lines to compressor, then perform steps 2 and 3 of "System Self Diagnosis." Disconnect affected rear air spring air line at solenoid, then open and close vehicle door and verify escaping air from affected air spring. If air is escaping from rear solenoid, repair leak or obstruction as necessary and repeat "System Self Diagnosis" procedure. If no air leak is present, proceed to step 11.

11. Inspect affected air spring and solenoid for leaks. If no leaks are present replace solenoid at affected air spring. If leaks are present service or replace spring or solenoid assembly. Perform "System Self Diagnosis" procedures.

12. Perform steps 2 and 3 of "System Self Diagnosis," then open and close vehicle door until warning lamp flashes test 8. Proceed to step 13.

13. Attach one lead of test lamp to circuit 416 at rear right solenoid connectors and attach the second lead to battery circuit 175 of right rear solenoid connector, Fig. 5, then observe test lamp. If test lamp is blinking, replace right rear solenoid and repeat "System Self Diagnosis" procedures. If test lamp is off, proceed to step 14. If test lamp is on, proceed to step 19.

14. Move test lead connected to circuit 416 to a suitable ground and observe test lamp. If test lamp is on, battery circuit is satisfactory; proceed to step 15. If test lamp is off, an open in circuit 175 is indicated between right rear solenoid and fuse link. Service wiring, then perform "System Self Diagnosis" procedures.

15. Without disconnecting module connector, attach one lead of test lamp to right rear solenoid circuit 416 (pin 10) at modular connector, Fig. 5. Attach the second lead to battery circuit 418 (pin 20) at module connector and observe test lamp. If lamp is blinking, open in circuit 416 is indi-

cated between module and right rear solenoid. Service circuit, then perform "System Self Diagnosis" procedures. If test lamp is off, proceed to step 16.

16. If warning lamp is blinking test 8, proceed to step 17. If warning lamp is not blinking, repeat step 12.

17. Disconnect module connector and inspect pins. If pins are satisfactory, proceed to step 18. If pins are not satisfactory, repair or replace as necessary and perform perform "System Self Diagnosis" procedures.

18. Attach negative lead of volt-ohmmeter to pin 1 of right rear solenoid and positive lead to pin 2 of right rear solenoid, Fig. 5, and measure circuit resistance. If resistance is greater than 13 ohms, replace air suspension control module and perform "System Self Diagnosis" procedure. If resistance is less than 13 ohms, replace right rear solenoid and air suspension module, then perform "System Self Diagnosis" procedures.

19. If warning lamp is blinking test 8, proceed to step 20. If warning lamp is not blinking, repeat step 12.

20. Disconnect module connector and observe test lamp. If test lamp is on, a short to ground is indicated on right rear solenoid circuit 416 between module and right rear solenoid. If test lamp is off, replace air suspension module.

21. Perform steps 2 and 3 of "System Self Diagnosis," then open and close vehicle door until warning lamp blinks test 9. Proceed to step 22.

22. Attach one lead of test lamp to left rear solenoid connector circuit 429 and attach the second lead to battery circuit 175 of same connector, Fig. 5, then observe test lamp. If test lamp is blinking, replace left rear solenoid and perform "System Self Diagnosis" procedures. If test lamp is off, proceed to step 23. If test lamp is on, proceed to step 28.

23. Move test lead connected to circuit 429 to a suitable ground, and observe test lamp. If test lamp is on, battery circuit is satisfactory; proceed to step 24. If test lamp is off, open or short to ground is indicated in circuit 418 between air suspension system on/off switch and right rear solenoid. Service circuit, then perform "System Self Diagnosis" procedures.

24. Without disconnecting module connector, attach one lead of test lamp to left rear solenoid circuit 429 (pin 9) at module connector and attach the second lead to battery circuit 418 (pin 20) at module connector, Fig. 5, and observe test lamp. If test lamp is blinking, an open is indicated in circuit between module and left rear solenoid. Service circuit, then perform "System Self Diagnosis" procedures. If test lamp is off, proceed to step 25.

25. If warning lamp is blinking test 9, proceed to step 26. If warning lamp is not blinking test 9, repeat step 21.

26. Disconnect module connector and inspect pins. If pins are satisfactory, proceed to step 27. If pins are not satisfactory, repair or replace as necessary and perform "System Self Diagnosis" procedures.

27. Attach negative lead of volt-ohmmeter to pin 1 of left rear solenoid and positive lead to pin 2 of left rear solenoid, Fig. 5, and measure circuit resistance. If resistance is greater than 13 ohms, replace air suspension control module. If resistance is less than 13 ohms, replace left rear solenoid and air suspension module, then perform "System Self Diagnosis" procedures.

28. If warning lamp is blinking test 9, pro-

ceed to step 29. If test lamp is not blinking test 9, repeat step 21.

29. Disconnect module connector and note test lamp indication. If test lamp is on, a short to ground is indicated in circuit 429 between module connector and left rear solenoid. Service circuit, then perform "System Self Diagnosis" procedures. If test lamp is off, replace air suspension module and perform "System Self Diagnosis" procedures.

Right Front Air Suspension Diagnosis

1. If vehicle passed step 4 of "System Self Diagnosis," proceed to step 2. If vehicle did not pass step 4, refer to step 1 of "Rear Air Suspension Diagnosis."

2. If the right front solenoid passed step 10 of "System Self Diagnosis," proceed to step 3. If the right front solenoid did not displace air, proceed to step 4. If right front solenoid displaces air but does not click, proceed to step 14.

3. Inspect right front sensor and ball stud for secure attachment. If sensor and stud are securely attached, proceed to step 6. If connection is not secure, tighten as necessary and perform "System Self Diagnosis" procedure.

4. Perform steps 2 and 3 of "System Self Diagnosis" procedure, then open and close vehicle door until warning lamp blinks test 7. Attach one end of test lamp to right front solenoid circuit 414 at right front solenoid connector and the second lead to battery circuit 175, Fig. 5, at the same connector and observe test lamp. If test lamp is blinking, electrical system is satisfactory; proceed to step 12.

5. Perform steps 2 and 3 of "System Self Diagnosis" procedures, then disconnect air lines at right front air spring solenoid. Open and close vehicle door twice and verify air escaping from spring solenoid line. If air is escaping, an obstruction or kink is indicated. Service right front air line, reconnect lines, then perform "System Self Diagnosis" procedure. If air is not escaping, proceed to step 6.

6. Reconnect air lines, then perform steps 2 and 3 of "System Self Diagnosis" procedures. Open and close vehicle door twice to verify air is not escaping from right front air spring or solenoid. If air is not leaking, service or replace right front air spring solenoid, then perform "System Self Diagnosis" procedure. If air is leaking, service or replace faulty right front air spring or solenoid, then perform "System Self Diagnosis" procedure.

7. Ground test lead connected to right front solenoid circuit 414 and observe test lamp. If test lamp is on, battery circuit is satisfactory; proceed to step 8. If test lamp is off, an open or short to ground is indicated in battery circuit between battery and right front solenoid.

8. Without disconnecting module connector, attach one lead of test lamp to right front solenoid circuit 414 (pin 12) at module connector and the second lead to battery circuit 418 (pin 20), Fig. 5, and observe test lamp. If test lamp is blinking, an open in the right front solenoid circuit 414 is indicated between module and right front solenoid. Service circuitry, then perform "System Self Diagnosis" procedure. If test lamp is off, proceed to step 9.

9. If the warning lamp is blinking test 7, proceed to step 10. If the warning lamp is not blinking test 7, repeat step 4.

10. Disconnect module connector and inspect pins. If pins are satisfactory, proceed to step 11. If pins are not satisfactory, repair or replace as necessary and perform "System Self Diagnosis" procedure.

11. Disconnect right front solenoid connector and attach negative lead of volt-ohmmeter to pin 1 of the right front solenoid connector, then attach the positive lead to pin 2 of the right front solenoid connector, Fig. 5, and measure circuit resistance. If resistance is greater than 13 ohms, replace air suspension control module. If resistance is less than 13 ohms, replace right front solenoid and air suspension module. Perform "System Self Diagnosis" procedure after each repair.

12. If warning lamp is blinking test 7, proceed to step 13. If warning lamp is not blinking, repeat step 4.

13. Disconnect module connector, leaving test lamp connected across circuits 414 and 175, and observe test lamp. If test lamp is on, a short to ground is indicated on right front solenoid circuit 414 between module connector and right front solenoid. Service and perform "System Self Diagnosis" procedure. if test lamp is off, replace air suspension module and perform "System Self Diagnosis" procedure.

14. Disconnect right front solenoid connector, then attach one lead of test lamp to right front solenoid circuit 414 on harness side of connector and the second lead to battery circuit 175, Fig. 5, on harness side of connector, and observe test lamp. If test lamp is on, a short to ground is indicated in solenoid circuit 414. Service circuit, then perform "System Self Diagnosis" procedure. If test lamp is off, replace solenoid and perform "System Self Diagnosis" procedure.

Left Front Air Suspension Diagnosis

1. If the vehicle passed step 4 of "System Self Diagnosis," proceed to step 2. If the vehicle did not pass step 4, refer to step 1 of "Rear Air Suspension Diagnosis."

2. If the left front solenoid passed step 9 of "System Self Diagnosis," proceed to step 3. If the solenoid did not displace air, proceed to step 4. If the solenoid displaced air but did not click, proceed to step 14.

3. Inspect left front sensor and ball stud for secure attachment. If sensor and stud are securely attached, proceed to step 6. If connection is not secure, tighten as necessary and perform "System Self Diagnosis" procedure.

4. Perform steps 2 and 3 of "System Self Diagnosis," then open and close vehicle door until warning lamp blinks test 6. Attach one lead of test lamp to left front solenoid circuit 415 at the left front solenoid connector and the second lead to battery circuit 175 of the same connector, Fig. 5, then observe test lamp. If test lamp is blinking, electrical system is satisfactory; proceed to step 5. If test lamp is off, proceed to step 7. If test lamp is on, proceed to step 12.

5. Perform steps 2 and 3 of "System Self Diagnosis," then disconnect left front air spring solenoid air lines. Open and close vehicle door three times to verify escaping air from spring solenoid. If air is escaping from solenoid, an obstruction or kink is indicated. Repair as necessary, reconnect air lines, then perform "System Self Diagnosis" procedure. If air is not escaping, proceed to step 6.

NOTE: Left front of vehicle will drop during this test.

6. Reconnect air lines, then perform steps 2 and 3 of "System Self Diagnosis" procedure. Open and close vehicle door three times to verify air is not escaping from left front air spring or solenoid. If air is not leaking, service or replace left front air spring solenoid, then perform "System Self Diagnosis" procedure. If air is leaking, service or replace faulty left front air spring or solenoid.

7. Ground test lead connected to circuit 415 and observe test lamp. If test lamp is on, battery circuit is satisfactory, proceed to step 8. If test lamp is off, an open or short is indicated in circuit 175 between battery and left front solenoid. Service circuit, then perform "System Self Diagnosis" procedure.

8. Without disconnecting module connector, attach one lead of test lamp to left front solenoid circuit 415 (pin 11) at module connector and the second lead to battery circuit 418 (pin 20), and observe test lamp, Fig. 5. If test lamp is blinking, an open is indicated in left front solenoid circuit between module and left front solenoid. Service circuit, then perform "System Self Diagnosis" procedure. If test lamp is off, proceed to step 9.

9. If warning lamp is blinking test 6, proceed to step 10. If warning lamp is not blinking, repeat step 4.

10. Disconnect module connector and inspect pins. If pins are satisfactory, proceed to step 11. If pins are not satisfactory, repair or replace as necessary and perform "System Self Diagnosis" procedure.

11. Disconnect left front solenoid connector and attach negative lead of volt-ohmmeter to pin 1 of left front solenoid connector, then attach the positive lead to pin 2 of left front solenoid connector, Fig. 5, and measure circuit resistance. If resistance is greater than 13 ohms, replace air suspension control module and perform "System Self Diagnosis" procedure. If resistance is less than 13 ohms, replace air suspension module and left front solenoid and perform "System Self Diagnosis" procedure.

12. If warning lamp is blinking test 6, proceed to step 13. If warning lamp is not blinking repeat step 4.

13. Disconnect module connector, leaving test lamp connected across circuits 415 and 175 and observe test lamp. If test lamp is on, a short to ground is indicated on left front solenoid circuit 415 between module connector and left front solenoid. Service and perform "System Self Diagnosis" procedure. If test lamp is off, replace solenoid and perform "System Self Diagnosis" procedure.

14. Disconnect left front solenoid connector, then attach one lead of test lamp to left front solenoid circuit 415 on harness side of connector and the second lead to battery circuit 175, Fig. 5, and observe test lamp. If test lamp is on, a short to ground is indicated in circuit 415; service circuit, then perform "System Self Diagnosis" procedure. If test lamp is off, replace solenoid and perform "System Self Diagnosis" procedure.

Compressor Electrical Diagnosis

1. Perform steps 2 and 3 of "System Self Diagnosis" procedure, then open and close vehicle door until warning lamp blinks test 4. During test 4 compressor

circuit will cycle 50 times (approximately 3 minutes), then turn off and will not cycle until test 4 is reentered. If the compressor relay is cycling, proceed to step 2. If the relay is not cycling, proceed to step 5.

2. Disconnect compressor connector and attach one lead of test lamp to compressor circuit 417 at harness side of connector, then ground the second test lamp lead and observe test lamp, Fig. 5. If test lamp is blinking, compressor circuit is satisfactory, proceed to step 3. If test lamp is on, replace compressor relay, reconnect connector and perform "System Self Diagnosis" procedure. If test lamp is off, proceed to step 4.

3. Move grounded test lamp lead to compressor ground circuit 430, Fig. 5, and observe test lamp. If test lamp is blinking, install a new compressor and perform "System Self Diagnosis" procedure. If test lamp is off, an open is indicated in ground circuit 430 between compressor and battery. Service circuit, then perform "System Self Diagnosis" procedure.

4. Connect compressor connector and perform step 1. Attach one lead of test lamp to compressor circuit 417 at compressor relay, Fig. 5, then ground the second test lead and observe test lamp. If test lamp is blinking, a short or open is indicated on circuit 417 between compressor and compressor relay. Service circuit, then perform "System Self Diagnosis" procedure. If test lamp is off, replace compressor relay, install connector and perform "System Self Diagnosis" procedure.

5. Attach one lead of test lamp to circuit 420 at compressor relay, Fig. 5, and the second lead to the positive battery terminal and observe test lamp. If test lamp blinks, module relay circuit is satisfactory; proceed to step 6. If test lamp is on, proceed to step 8. If test lamp is off, proceed to step 9.

6. Attach one lead of test lamp to circuit 175 at compressor relay (pin 2), Fig. 5, then ground the second lead and observe test lamp. If test lamp is on, replace compressor relay, install connector and perform "System Self Diagnosis" procedure. If test lamp is off, proceed to step 7.

7. Attach one lead of test lamp to battery circuit 175 at compressor relay (pin 3), Fig. 5, and ground the second lead, then observe test lamp. If test lamp is on, an open or short is indicated in jumper circuit 175. Service circuit, then perform "System Self Diagnosis" procedure. If test lamp is off, an open or short is indicated on battery circuit 175 between compressor relay and battery. Service circuit, then perform "System Self Diagnosis" procedure.

8. Disconnect module connector and observe test lamp. If test lamp is on, a short is indicated in relay circuit 420, Fig. 5. Service circuit, then perform "System Self Diagnosis" procedure. If test lamp is off, replace air suspension control module and perform "System Self Diagnosis" procedure.

9. Disconnect compressor relay connector and attach negative lead of volt-ohmmeter to pin 2 at compressor relay connector, then positive lead to pin 1, Fig. 5, and measure circuit resistance. If resistance is greater than 54 ohms, compressor relay is satisfactory; proceed to step 10. If resistance is less than 54 ohms, replace compressor relay and perform "System Self Diagnosis" procedure.

NOTE: Compressor relay failure may

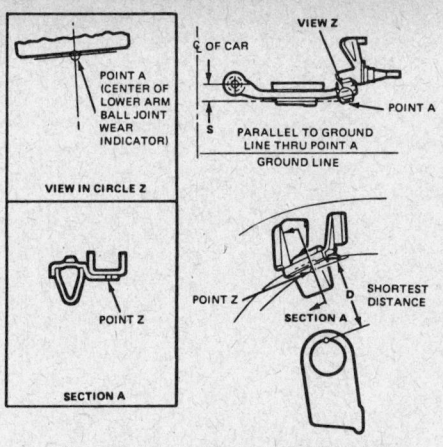

Fig. 6   Ride height "S" and "D" dimensions

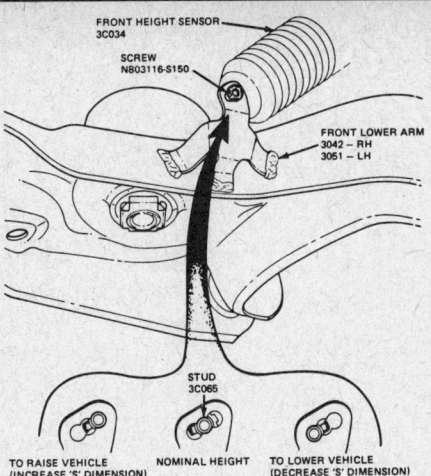

Fig. 7   Front suspension ride height adjustment

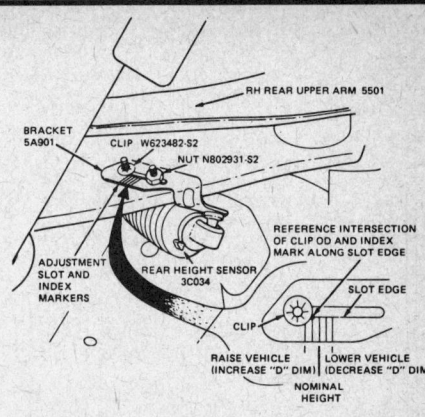

Fig. 8   Rear suspension ride height adjustment

have caused damage to air suspension control module.

10. Perform step 1. Without disconnecting module connector, attach one lead of test lamp to compressor relay circuit 420 (pin 22) and the second lead to battery circuit 418 (pin 20) at module connector, Fig. 5, and observe test lamp. If test lamp is blinking, an open in compressor relay circuit 420 is indicated between compressor relay and module. If test lamp is off, replace air suspension control module. After each repair, perform "System Self Diagnosis" procedure.

Compressor Vent Solenoid Electrical Diagnosis

1. Perform steps 2 and 3 of "System Self Diagnosis," then open and close vehicle door until warning lamp blinks test 5. Disconnect air compressor and attach one lead of test lamp to vent solenoid circuit 421 (pin 4) on harness side and the second lead to battery circuit 175 (pin 1), Fig. 5, then observe test lamp. If test lamp blinks, replace compressor assembly and perform "System Self Diagnosis" procedure. If test lamp is on, proceed to step 2. If test lamp is off, proceed to step 3.

2. Disconnect air suspension module connector and observe test lamp. If test lamp is on, a short is indicated in vent solenoid circuit 421 between compressor assembly and module. Service circuit, then perform "System Self Diagnosis" procedure. If test lamp is off, replace air suspension control module and perform "System Self Diagnosis" procedure.

3. Ground test lead connected to vent solenoid circuit 421 and observe test lamp. If test lamp is on, battery circuit is satisfactory; proceed to step 4. If test lamp is off, an open or short is indicated in battery circuit 175 between vent solenoid and battery. Service circuit, then perform "System Self Diagnosis" procedure.

4. Without disconnecting module connector, attach one lead of test lamp to vent solenoid circuit 421 (pin 23) at module connector and the second lead to battery circuit 418 (pin 20) at module connector, Fig. 5, and observe test lamp. If test lamp is blinking, an open is indicated in vent solenoid circuit 421 between module and compressor relay. Service circuit, then

perform "System Self Diagnosis" procedure. If test lamp is off, proceed to step 5.

5. If warning lamp is blinking test 5, proceed to step 6. If warning lamp is not blinking, repeat step 1.

6. Disconnect compressor connector. Attach negative lead of volt-ohmmeter to pin 4 at compressor connector, then the positive lead to pin 1 of compressor connector and measure circuit resistance. If resistance is greater than 27 ohms, replace air suspension control module and perform "System Self Diagnosis" procedure. If resistance is less than 27 ohms, replace compressor assembly and air suspension control module, then perform "System Self Diagnosis" procedure.

ADJUSTMENTS

Pre-Adjustment

This procedure must be performed before checking ride height and/or wheel alignment.

NOTE: If vehicle is significantly warmer or colder than test area, allow it to warm or cool to surrounding air temperature before performing the following procedure.

1. Turn ignition off, then exit vehicle.
2. Re-enter vehicle and turn ignition to "Run" position. Do not start engine.
3. Allow vehicle to level for approximately one minute, then push trunk release to open trunk area.
4. Turn ignition "Off" and exit vehicle.
5. Allow vehicle to vent to trim height (approximately 20 seconds), then close all doors and turn off air suspension switch in trunk, Fig. 4.

Ride Height, Adjust

Front Suspension

The front suspension ride height of "S" dimension, Fig. 6, is adjusted by moving the front left and/or right lower sensor attaching stud to one of the three adjustment positions as shown, Fig. 7. Loosen the attaching screw and adjust up or down as required. Changing

the sensor attachment point one position will result in a .50 inch change in the "S" dimension. The "S" dimension on 1984 vehicles should be .240 inch.

Rear Suspension

The rear suspension ride height of "D" dimension, Fig. 6, is adjusted by moving the rear sensor attaching bracket up or down in relation to the right rear upper control arm, Fig. 8. Loosen the attaching nut and position up or down as required. A change to the sensor attaching point by one index mark will result in a .250 inch change to the "D" dimension. The "D" dimension on 1984 vehicles should be 5.060 inches.

Wheel Alignment

Refer to "Front Suspension & Steering Section" for procedures.

COMPONENT REPLACE

Air Spring Solenoid, Replace

1. Turn air suspension switch off, then raise and support vehicle at body.
2. Remove wheel assembly.
3. Disconnect electrical connector and air line from air spring solenoid, then remove solenoid retaining clip.
4. Rotate solenoid counterclockwise to first stop, then pull outward to second stop and allow air to bleed from system as shown, Fig. 9.
5. Rotate solenoid counterclockwise to third stop and remove from air spring assembly.
6. Reverse procedure to install.

Air Spring, Replace

Removal

1. Remove air spring solenoid as outlined previously.
2. If replacing front spring, remove spring to lower control arm retaining clip. If replacing rear spring, remove retaining clip and/or bolts.
3. Push down on air spring collar spring clip, then rotate collar counterclockwise until spring releases from body spring seat.
4. Remove spring from vehicle.

Installation

1. Install air spring solenoid. If left side

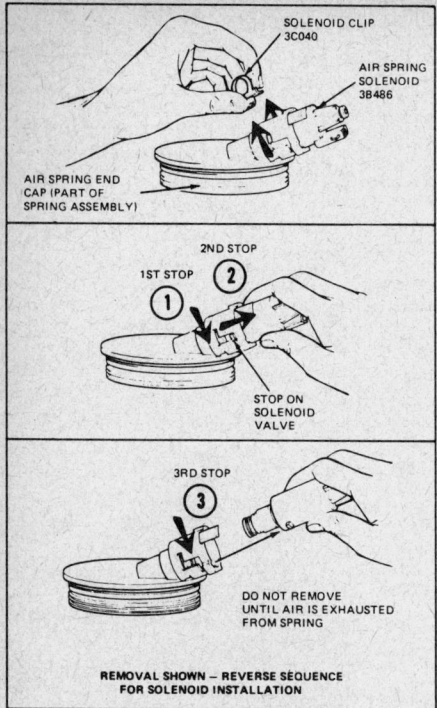

Fig. 9 Air spring solenoid removal

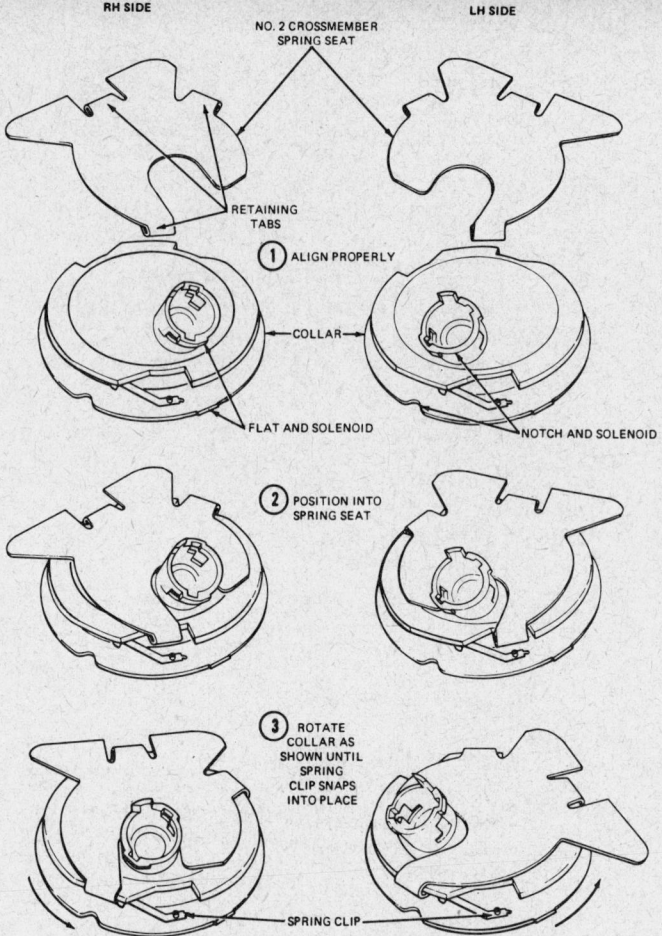

Fig. 10 Positioning solenoid onto spring collar

spring is being replaced, position solenoid so notch on spring collar is in line with centerline of solenoid. If right side spring is being replaced, position solenoid so flat on collar is in line with centerline of solenoid. Refer to Fig. 10 for correct positioning.

CAUTION: Do not attempt to install or inflate any air spring which has become unfolded. If any spring has been unfolded, refold spring as shown in Fig. 11, before installing into vehicle.

2. Install air spring into body spring seat, then rotate spring collar until spring clip snaps into position, Fig. 10.
3. Connect air line and electrical connector to solenoid.
4. Align and secure spring to lower control arm.

NOTE: The suspension must be at its full travel when replacing the springs, as damage to spring may result.

5. Replace wheel assembly.
6. Refill air springs as outlined in "Air Springs, Refill" procedure.

Control Module, Replace

1. Turn air suspension switch to "Off" position.
2. Remove left side luggage compartment trim panel, then disconnect wiring harness from module.
3. Remove the 3 control module retaining nuts, then the control module.
4. Reverse procedure to install.

Air Compressor/Dryer Assembly, Replace

1. Turn air suspension switch to "Off" position.
2. Disconnect compressor electrical connector.
3. Remove air line protector cap from dryer by releasing the 2 pins located at bottom of cap.
4. Disconnect air lines from dryer.
5. Remove air compressor/dryer assembly to mounting bracket retaining screws, then the assembly.
6. Reverse procedure to install.

Height Sensor, Replace

Front
1. Turn air suspension switch to "Off" position.
2. Working from engine compartment, disconnect sensor electrical connector.
3. Push connector through access hole at rear of shock tower, then raise and support vehicle.
4. Disconnect bottom and top ends of sensor from attaching studs as shown, Fig. 12.
5. Disconnect wiring harness from plastic clips on shock tower and remove sensor.
6. Reverse procedure to install.

Rear
1. Turn air suspension switch to "Off" position.
2. Working from luggage compartment, disconnect sensor electrical connector. Pull luggage compartment carpet back to gain access to sensor sealing grommet.
3. Raise and support vehicle, then disconnect bottom and top ends of sensor from the attaching studs, Fig. 12.
4. Pushing upwards, unseat sensor from grommet, then push sensor through floor pan into luggage compartment.
5. Reverse procedure to install.

AIR SPRING, REFILL

1. With suspension unloaded, turn air suspension switch to "On" position.
2. With driver's door open, turn ignition to Run for approximately 5 seconds, then return ignition to "Off" position.
3. Ground the diagnostic pigtail, Fig. 4, then with driver's door open and brakes applied, turn ignition to Run position. The warning lamp will blink continuously, indicating the spring refill sequence has been entered.
4. To fill the rear spring(s), close, then open the driver's door once. After a 6 second delay, the spring(s) will be filled for approximately 1 minute.

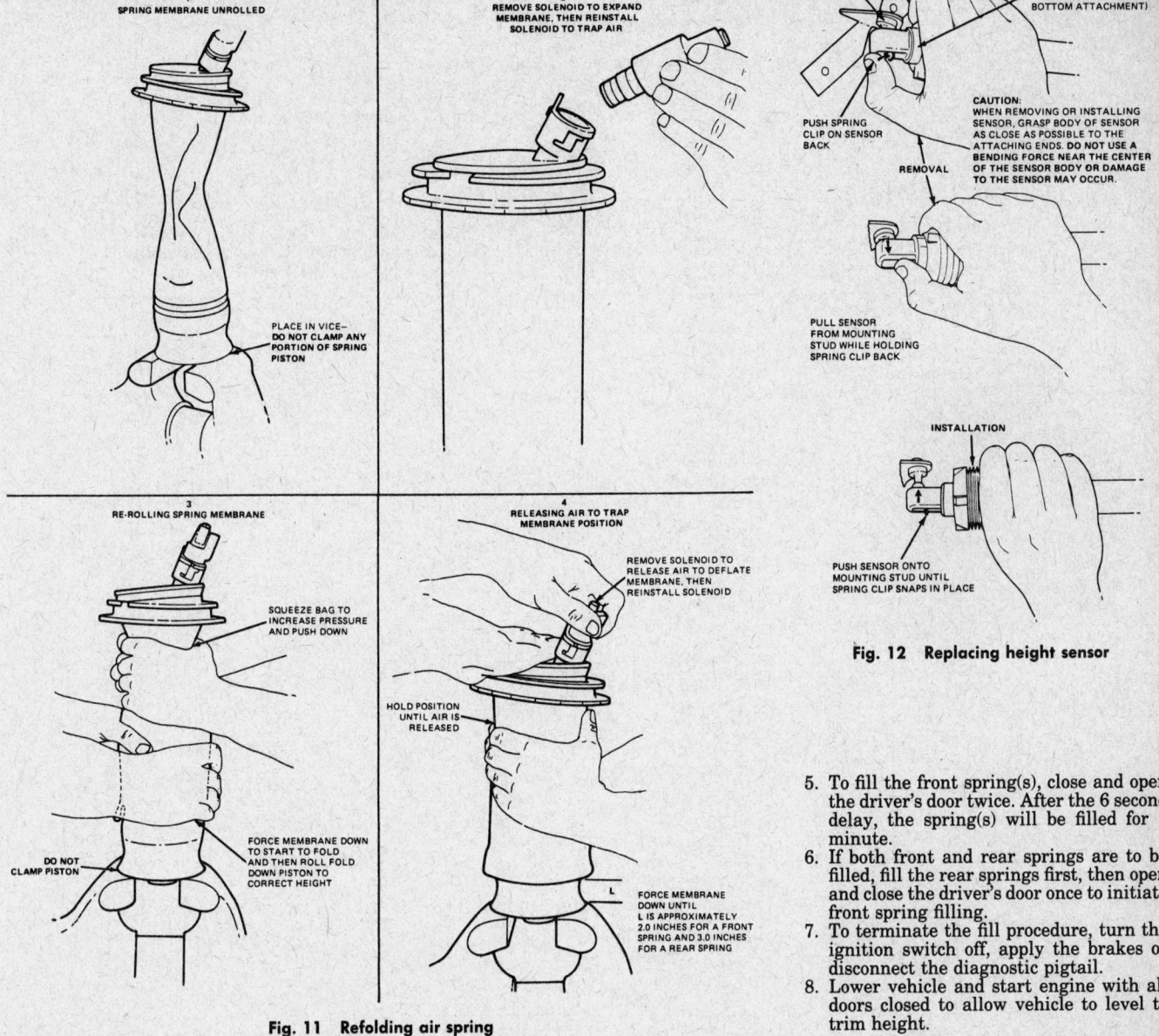

Fig. 11 Refolding air spring

1 — SPRING MEMBRANE UNROLLED
PLACE IN VICE— DO NOT CLAMP ANY PORTION OF SPRING PISTON

2 — REMOVE SOLENOID TO EXPAND MEMBRANE, THEN REINSTALL SOLENOID TO TRAP AIR

3 — RE-ROLLING SPRING MEMBRANE
SQUEEZE BAG TO INCREASE PRESSURE AND PUSH DOWN
DO NOT CLAMP PISTON
FORCE MEMBRANE DOWN TO START TO FOLD AND THEN ROLL FOLD DOWN PISTON TO CORRECT HEIGHT

4 — RELEASING AIR TO TRAP MEMBRANE POSITION
REMOVE SOLENOID TO RELEASE AIR TO DEFLATE MEMBRANE, THEN REINSTALL SOLENOID
HOLD POSITION UNTIL AIR IS RELEASED
FORCE MEMBRANE DOWN UNTIL L IS APPROXIMATELY 2.0 INCHES FOR A FRONT SPRING AND 3.0 INCHES FOR A REAR SPRING

SENSOR MOUNTING STUD (TYPICAL)
HEIGHT SENSOR (FRONT OR REAR, TOP OR BOTTOM ATTACHMENT)
PUSH SPRING CLIP ON SENSOR BACK
REMOVAL
CAUTION: WHEN REMOVING OR INSTALLING SENSOR, GRASP BODY OF SENSOR AS CLOSE AS POSSIBLE TO THE ATTACHING ENDS. DO NOT USE A BENDING FORCE NEAR THE CENTER OF THE SENSOR BODY OR DAMAGE TO THE SENSOR MAY OCCUR.
PULL SENSOR FROM MOUNTING STUD WHILE HOLDING SPRING CLIP BACK
INSTALLATION
PUSH SENSOR ONTO MOUNTING STUD UNTIL SPRING CLIP SNAPS IN PLACE

Fig. 12 Replacing height sensor

5. To fill the front spring(s), close and open the driver's door twice. After the 6 second delay, the spring(s) will be filled for 1 minute.
6. If both front and rear springs are to be filled, fill the rear springs first, then open and close the driver's door once to initiate front spring filling.
7. To terminate the fill procedure, turn the ignition switch off, apply the brakes or disconnect the diagnostic pigtail.
8. Lower vehicle and start engine with all doors closed to allow vehicle to level to trim height.

OLDSMOBILE 88, 98, TORONADO, 1977—79 OMEGA, CUTLASS EXC. CIERA & 1984 CRUISER

INDEX OF SERVICE OPERATIONS

NOTE: Refer to main index, "GM Front Wheel Drive," for front drive axle & drive link belt service procedures on 1977–84 Toronado. Also refer to the front of this manual for vehicle manufacturer's special service tool suppliers.

VEHICLE IDENTIFICATION PLATE:

1977—84 on left upper dash.

ENGINE NUMBER LOCATION

Buick built engines have the distributor located at the front of the engine. On 1979—84 models, the engine production code is located on front of right hand valve cover and top of left hand valve cover. On 1977—78 models, the engine production code is located on the right front of block.

Chevrolet built V8 engines have the distributor located at the rear of the engine with clockwise rotor rotation. On 1979—80 V8 engines, the engine production code is located front of right hand valve cover. On 1977—78 V8 engines, the code is stamped on the right hand side of engine.

Oldsmobile built engines have the distributor located at the rear of the engine with counter-clockwise rotor rotation and right side mounted fuel pump. The engine production code is located on the oil filler tube on 1977 thru early 1978 engines or on the left side valve cover on late 1978 & 1979—84 engines.

Pontiac built V8 engines have the distributor located at the rear of the engine with counter-clockwise rotor rotation and left side mounted fuel pump. On 1979 V8 engines, the engine production code is located on front of both left and right hand valve covers.

ENGINE IDENTIFICATION CODES

1977

Engine	Engine Code	V.I.N. Code
V6-231 Tr.[11][22]	RC, RD	A
V6-231 Man. Tr.[4][11]	SG	C
V6-231 Man. Tr.[2][11]	SU	C
V6-231 Auto. Tr.[4][11]	SI	C
V6-231 Auto. Tr.[2][11]	SK, SL	C
V6-231 Auto. Tr.[3][11]	SM, SN	C
V8-260 Man. Tr.[4]	OS, OT	F
V8-260 Auto. Tr.[4]	QC, QD, QE, QJ	F
V8-260 Auto. Tr.[3]	QU, QV	F
V8-305 Man. Tr.[4][6]	CPA	U
V8-305 Auto. Tr.[4][6]	CPY	U
V8-350 Auto. Tr.[4][6]	CHY, CUB	L
V8-350 Auto. Tr.[2][6]	CKR	L
V8-350 Auto. Tr.[3][6]	CKM	L
V8-350 Auto. Tr.[4]	QK, QL, QN, QO	R
V8-350 Auto. Tr.[4]	QP, QQ	R
V8-350 Auto. Tr.[3]	Q2, Q3	R
V8-350 Auto. Tr.[3]	Q6, Q7, Q8, Q9	R
V8-350 Auto. Tr.[2]	TB, TC, TU, TV	R
V8-350 Auto. Tr.[2]	TN, TO, TX, TY	R
V8-403 Auto. Tr.[4][15]	UJ, UK, UL, UN	K
V8-403 Auto. Tr.[3][15]	U2, U3	K
V8-403 Auto. Tr.[2][15]	VA, VB, VJ, VK	K
V8-403 Auto. Tr.[4][16]	UE	K
V8-403 Auto. Tr.[3][16]	U6	K
V8-403 Auto. Tr.[2][16]	VE	K

1978

Engine	Engine Code	V.I.N. Code
V6-231 Man. Tr.[4][11]	EA, ET	A
V6-231 Auto. Tr.[4][11]	EB, EC, EH, OH	A
V6-231 Auto. Tr.[4][11]	EI, EJ, EM, EN	A
V6-231 Auto. Tr.[3][11]	EG	A
V6-231 Auto. Tr.[2][11]	EE, EK, EL, OK	A
V8-260 Auto. Tr.[4]	QJ, QK, QX, QY	F
V8-260 Auto. Tr.[4]	QL, QB, QT, QU	F
V8-260 Auto. Tr.[4]	QD, QE	F
V8-260 Auto. Tr.[3]	Q4, Q5	F
V8-260 Auto. Tr.[2]	TJ, TK, TX, TY	F
V8-305 Man. Tr.[4][6][12]	CTH, CRW	U
V8-305 Auto. Tr.[4][6][12]	CTJ	U
V8-305 Auto. Tr.[3][6][12]	CPZ	U
V8-305 Auto. Tr.[2][6][12]	CRY, CRZ	U
V8-305 Auto. Tr.[4][6][13]	DAC, AG, AJ, AK	H
V8-305 Auto. Tr.[4][6][13]	CAJ, AM, AR	H
V8-305 Auto. Tr.[4][6][13]	CPE, AH	H
V8-350 Auto. Tr.[3][6]	CHL, CMC	L
V8-350 Auto. Tr.[2][6]	CHJ	L
V8-350 Auto. Tr.[4]	QO, QP, QQ, QS	R
V8-350 Auto. Tr.[3]	Q2, Q3	R
V8-350 Auto. Tr.[2]	TO, TP, TT, TU	R
V8-350 Auto. Tr.[2]	TQ, TS, TV, TW	R
V8-350 Auto. Tr.[5][18]	QB, QC, QV, QW	N
V8-350 Auto. Tr.[3][18]	Q6, Q7	N
V8-403 Auto. Tr.[4][15]	UA, UB, UD, UE	K
V8-403 Auto. Tr.[3][15]	U2, U3	K
V8-403 Auto. Tr.[2][15]	VA, VB, VJ, VK	K
V8-403 Auto. Tr.[4][16]	UC	K
V8-403 Auto. Tr.[3][16]	U4	K
V8-403 Auto. Tr.[2][16]	VC	K

1979

Engine	Engine Code	V.I.N. Code
V6-231 Man. Tr.[4][11]	NG, RA	A
V6-231 Auto. Tr.[4][11]	NJ, SJ, RB, SO	A
V6-231 Auto. Tr.[4][11]	NL, RX, SL, SR	A
V6-231 Auto. Tr.[4][11]	NK, RC, SK, SP	A
V6-231 Auto. Tr.[3][11]	RJ	A
V6-231 Auto. Tr.[2][11]	RG, RW	A
V8-260 Man. Tr.[4]	UC, UD	F
V8-260 Auto. Tr.[4]	UE, UJ, UK, UL	F
V8-260 Auto. Tr.[4]	UN, UO	F
V8-260 Auto. Tr.[3]	U5	F
V8-260 Auto. Tr.[2]	VC	F
V8-260 Man. Tr.[5][18]	UW, UX, V8, V9	P
V8-260 Auto. Tr.[5][18]	UP, UQ, V2, V7	P
V8-301 Auto. Tr.[4][14]	PXP, PYF	Y
V8-305 Auto. Tr.[4][6][12]	DTM	G
V8-305 Auto. Tr.[4][6][12]	DNJ	G
V8-305 Man. Tr.[4][6][13]	DNS	H
V8-305 Auto. Tr.[4][6][13]	DNT, DNW, DTX	H
V8-305 Auto. Tr.[3][6][13]	DTA	H
V8-305 Auto. Tr.[2][6][13]	DNX, DNY	H
V8-350 Auto. Tr.[3][6]	DRX, DRY	L
V8-350 Auto. Tr.[2][6]	DRJ	L
V8-350 Auto. Tr.[4][15]	QO, QN, UT, US	R
V8-350 Auto. Tr.[4][15]	UU, UV	R
V8-350 Auto. Tr.[3][15]	U9, TY	R
V8-350 Auto. Tr.[2][15]	VE, VK	R
V8-350 Auto. Tr.[4][16]	TW	R
V8-350 Auto. Tr.[3][16]	TY	R
V8-350 Auto. Tr.[2][16]	TX	R
V8-350 Auto. Cutlass Tr.[5][15][18]	VO, VN, T2, T3	N
V8-350 Auto. Tr.[5][15][18]	QQ, QP, QS, QT	N
V8-350 Auto. Tr.[5][15][18]	VO, VN, VQ	N
V8-350 Auto. Tr.[3][15][18]	V4, V6	N
V8-350 Auto. Tr.[5][16][18]	QU, T6	N
V8-350 Auto. Tr.[3][16][18]	QY, U3	N
V8-403 Auto. Tr.[4]	QB	K
V8-403 Auto. Tr.[3]	Q3	K
V8-403 Auto. Tr.[2]	TB	K

1980

Engine	Engine Code	V.I.N. Code
V6-231 Man. Tr.[1][11]	EA	A
V6-231 Auto. Tr.[1][11]	EB, EC, EO, EP	A
V6-231 Auto. Tr.[2][11]	OV, OW	A
V6-231 Auto. Tr.[1][11]	OX, OY	A
V8-260 Auto. Tr.[1]	QAC, QAD, QAF, QAH	F
V8-260 Auto. Tr.[1]	QBB, QBC, QBD	F
V8-260 Auto. Tr.[1]	QBF, QBH, QBJ	F
V8-305 Auto. Tr.[1][6]	CEA, CMC, CMD, CMF	H
V8-305 Auto. Tr.[2][6]	CEC, CMM	H
V8-307 Auto. Tr.[1][19]	TAA, TAB, TAR, TAS	Y
V8-307 Auto. Tr.[1][19]	TAT, TAU, TAX, TAW	Y
V8-307 Auto. Tr.[1][19]	TAJ, TAK, TAY, TAZ	Y
V8-307 Auto. Tr.[1][20]	TBA, TAM	Y
V8-307 Auto. Tr.[1][16]	TBB, TAN	Y
V8-350 Auto. Tr.[1][10]	UAN, UAR	R
V8-350 Auto. Tr.[1][19]	UAA, UAB, UAX, UAY	R
V8-350 Auto. Tr.[1][16][20]	UAC, UAN, UAZ, UBA	R
V8-350 Auto. Tr.[2][19][20]	UAD, UAF	R
V8-350 Auto. Tr.[2][16]	UAH	R
V8-350 Auto. Tr.[1][10][18]	VBP, VBR	N
V8-350 Auto. Tr.[1][18][19][20]	VBM, VBN, VCL, VCM	N
V8-350 Auto. Tr.[1][18][19]	VBS, VBT	N
V8-350 Auto. Tr.[1][16][18]	VBU	N
V8-350 Auto. Tr.[2][18]	VCF	N
V8-350 Auto. Tr.[2][18][19][20]	VCD	N
V8-350 Auto. Tr.[2][16][18]	VCH	N

1981

Engine	Engine Code	V.I.N. Code
V6-231 Man. Tr.[1][10][11]	NA	A
V6-231 Auto. Tr.[1][10][11]	NB	A
V6-231 Auto. Tr.[1][19][11]	NL	A
V6-231 Auto. Tr.[2][10][11]	NF, NT	A
V6-231 Auto. Tr.[2][19][11]	NC	A
V6-252 Auto. Tr.[16][11]		4
V8-260 Auto. Tr.[1][10]	QKA, QKB, QKH, QKJ	F
V8-260 Auto. Tr.[1][19]	OKJ, OKH, QKM	F
V8-260 Auto. Tr.[2][10]	QKC, QKK	F
V8-260 Auto. Tr.[2][19]	QKN	F
V8-307 Auto. Tr.[1][10]	TKA, TKB, TKJ, TKU	Y
V8-307 Auto. Tr.[1][10][19][20]	TKL, TLR	Y
V8-307 Auto. Tr.[1][16]	TKP, TLK	Y
V8-307 Auto. Tr.[2][10]	TKB	Y
V8-307 Auto. Tr.[2][19]	TKU	Y
V8-307 Auto. Tr.[1][19]		Y
V8-350 Auto. Tr.[1][10][18]	VKB, VKC, VNJ, VNK	N
V8-350 Auto. Tr.[1][10][18]	VLM, VLN, VLP, VNN	N
V8-350 Auto. Tr.[1][18][19]	VKH, VKJ, VLL, VLM, VLN, VNN, VNP, VNR, VNT	N
V8-350 Auto. Tr.[1][18][21]	VNH, VNK, VNW, VNX	N
V8-350 Auto. Tr.[1][18][20]	VKN, VLS, VNX, VNY	N
V8-350 Auto. Tr.[1][16][18]	VKU, VNX	N
V8-350 Auto. Tr.[2][10][18]	VLY, VNL	N
V8-350 Auto. Tr.[1][18][19][20][21]	VMJ, VNU	N
V8-350 Auto. Tr.[2][16][18]	VMT, VPA	N

1982

Engine	Engine Code	V.I.N. Code
V6-231 Auto. Tr.[1][10][23]	MA	A
V6-231 Auto. Tr.[1][19]	MK	A
V6-231 Auto. Tr.[2][10][23]	ML	A
V6-231 Auto. Tr.[2][19]	MM	A
V6-252 Auto. Tr.[1][20]	FT	4
V6-252 Auto. Tr.[1][16]	FV	4
V6-252 Auto. Tr.[2][20]	FT	4
V6-252 Auto. Tr.[2][16]	FW	4
V8-260 Auto. Tr.[1][19]	QAD, QAF	8

Continued

ENGINE IDENTIFICATION CODES—Continued

Engine	Engine Code	V.I.N. Code
1982—Continued		
V8-260 Auto.		
Tr.①⑲㉓	QAA, QAH	8
V8-260 Auto. Tr.②⑩	QAH	8
V8-260 Auto. Tr.②⑲㉓	QAC	8
V8-307 Auto. Tr.①㉓	TAD, TAF	Y
V8-307 Auto.		
Tr.①⑲⑳㉑	TAA, TAB, TAF, TAK, TAM	Y
V8-307 Auto. Tr.①⑯	TBB	Y
V8-307 Auto. Tr.②㉓	TAF	Y
V8-307 Auto.		
Tr.②⑲⑳㉑	TAB, TAF, TAK, TAM, TMR	Y
V8-307 Auto. Tr.②⑯	TBB	Y
V6-262 Auto. Tr.④⑱	UAA, UAD	V
V6-262 Auto. Tr.②⑱	UAA, UAD	V
V6-262 Auto. Tr.③⑱	UAJ	V
V8-350 Auto.		
Tr.④⑩⑱㉓	VAY, VAZ, VBA, VBB	N
V8-350 Auto.		
Tr.④⑱⑲	VAB, VAC, VAD	N
V8-350 Auto.		
Tr.④⑱㉑	VAK, VAL, VAM	N
V8-350 Auto. Tr.④⑱⑳	VAN, VAP	N
V8-350 Auto. Tr.④⑯⑱	VAW, VBP	N
V8-350 Auto.		
Tr.②⑩⑱㉓	VAY, VAZ, VBA, VBB	N
V8-350 Auto. Tr.②⑱⑲	VAB, VAC, VAD	N
V8-350 Auto. Tr.②⑱㉑	VAK, VAM	N
V8-350 Auto. Tr.②⑱⑳	VAN, VAP	N

Engine	Engine Code	V.I.N. Code
V8-350 Auto. Tr.②⑯⑱	VAW, VBP	N
V8-350 Auto. Tr.③⑩⑱㉓	VBC	N
V8-350 Auto. Tr.③⑲⑳	VAZ	N
V8-350 Auto. Tr.③⑱㉑	VAU	N
V8-350 Auto. Tr.③⑯⑱	VAX	N
1983		
V6-231 Auto. Tr.①⑩⑪	NR	A
V6-231 Auto. Tr.②⑩⑪㉓	NP, NH	A
V6-231 Auto. Tr.①⑪⑲㉑	NO	A
V6-231 Auto. Tr.②⑪⑲㉑	NS	A
V6-252 Auto. Tr.⑳	SO	4
V6-252 Auto. Tr.①⑯	SN	4
V6-252 Auto. Tr.②⑯	SR	4
V6-262 Auto.		
Tr.④⑩⑱㉓	UKA, UKB, UNH, UNJ	V
V6-262 Auto.		
Tr.②⑩⑱㉓	UKA, UKB, UNH, UNJ	V
V6-262 Auto. Tr.③⑩⑱㉓	UKC, UNK	V
V8-307 Auto. Tr.①⑮	TKN, TKP, TKY	Y
V8-307 Auto. Tr.②⑮	TKN, TKP, TKY	Y
V8-307 Auto. Tr.①⑯	TKH	Y
V8-307 Auto. Tr.②⑯	TKH	Y
V8-307 Auto. Tr.㉔	TLA	9
V8-350 Auto.		
Tr.④⑩⑱㉓	VKZ, VLA, VNA, VNB, VNC	N
V8-350 Auto.		
Tr.②⑩⑱㉓	VKZ, VLA, VNA, VNB, VNC	N

Engine	Engine Code	V.I.N. Code
V8-350 Auto. Tr.③⑩⑱㉓	VLB, VNC	N
V8-350 Auto.		
Tr.④⑱⑲⑳	VKB, VKC, VKK, VKL, VMR, VMT	N
V8-350 Auto.		
Tr.②⑱⑲⑳	VKB, VKC, VKK, VKL, VMR, VMT	N
V8-350 Auto.		
Tr.③⑱⑲⑳	VKD, VKK, VMW	N
V8-350 Auto.		
Tr.⑱㉑	VMA, VMB, VMS, VMU, VMW	N
V8-350 Auto.		
Tr.⑤⑯	VKR, VKS, VMX, VMY	N
V8-350 Auto. Tr.③⑯	VKT, VMZ	N

①—Except California.
②—California.
③—High altitude.
④—Exc. Calif. & High altitude.
⑤—Exc. high altitude.
⑥—Chevrolet built engine.
⑦—Omega.
⑧—Early production.
⑨—Late production.
⑩—Cutlass.
⑪—Buick built.
⑫—2 barrel carb.
⑬—4 barrel carb.
⑭—Pontiac Built engine.
⑮—Except Toronado.
⑯—Toronado.
⑰—Exc. even fire engine.
⑱—Diesel engine.
⑲—88.
⑳—98.
㉑—Custom Cruiser.
㉒—Even fire engine.
㉓—Cutlass Cruiser.
㉔—Hurst option.

GRILLE IDENTIFICATION

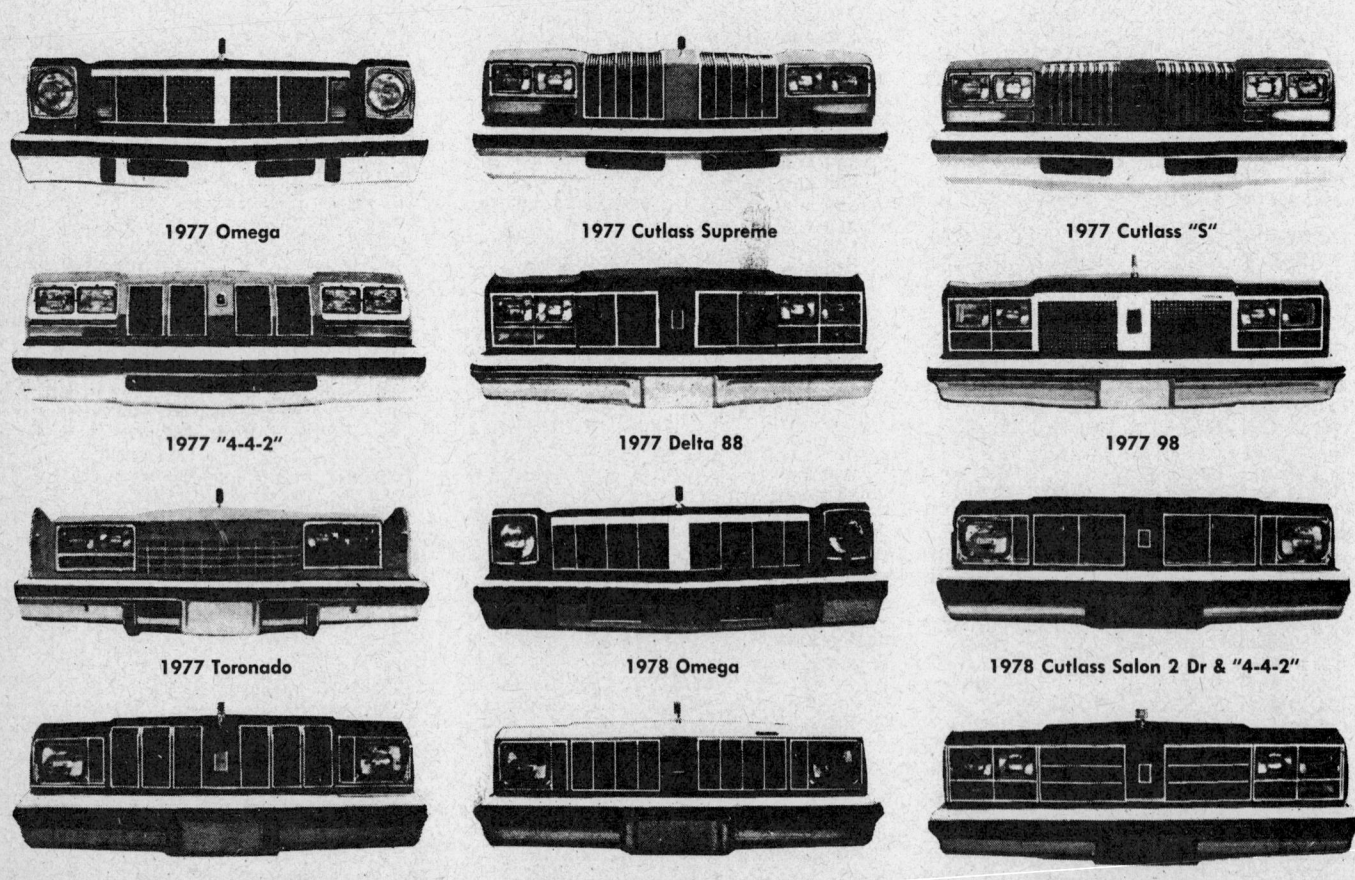

1977 Omega   1977 Cutlass Supreme   1977 Cutlass "S"

1977 "4-4-2"   1977 Delta 88   1977 98

1977 Toronado   1978 Omega   1978 Cutlass Salon 2 Dr & "4-4-2"

1978 Cutlass Brougham   1978 Cutlass Salon 4 Dr & Cruiser   1978 Delta 88 & Cruiser

Continued

GRILLE IDENTIFICATION—Continued

1978 98

1978 Toronado

1979 Omega Brougham

1979 Cutlass Supreme Brougham

1979 Cutlass Calais & Hurst Olds

1979 Cutlass Salon & "442"

1979 Cutlass Cruiser

1979 Cutlass Salon & Cruiser Brougham

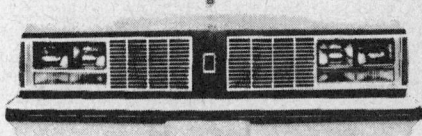

1979 Delta 88 Royale

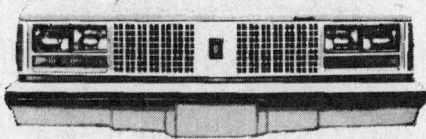

1979 98 Regency

1979 Custom Cruiser

1979 Toronado Brougham

1980 Cutlass Supreme

1980 Cutlass Supreme LS

1980 Cutlass Salon

1980 Cutlass "442"

1980 Delta 88 Royale

1980–81 Toronado

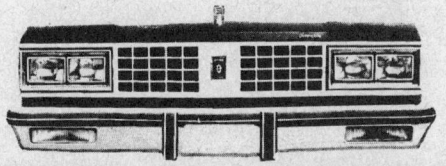

1980 98 Regency

Continued

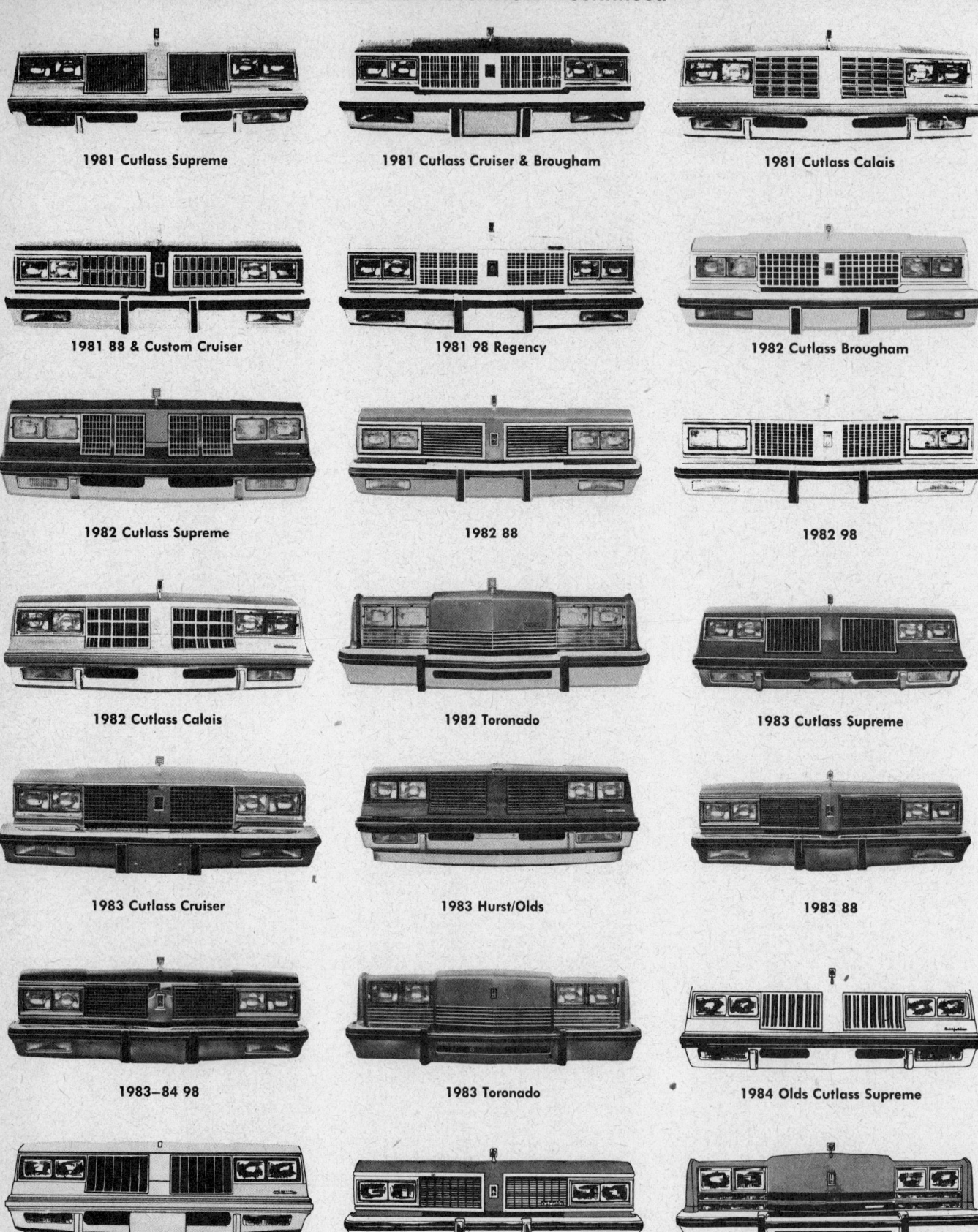

1981 Cutlass Supreme

1981 Cutlass Cruiser & Brougham

1981 Cutlass Calais

1981 88 & Custom Cruiser

1981 98 Regency

1982 Cutlass Brougham

1982 Cutlass Supreme

1982 88

1982 98

1982 Cutlass Calais

1982 Toronado

1983 Cutlass Supreme

1983 Cutlass Cruiser

1983 Hurst/Olds

1983 88

1983–84 98

1983 Toronado

1984 Olds Cutlass Supreme

1984 Hurst/Olds

1984 Olds Delta 88 & Custom Cruiser

1984 Olds Toronado

GENERAL ENGINE SPECIFICATIONS

Year	Engine CID①/Liter	V.I.N. Code②	Carburetor	Bore and Stroke	Compression Ratio	Net H.P. @ R.P.M.③	Maximum Torque Ft. Lbs. @ R.P.M.	Normal Oil Pressure Pounds
1977	V6-231, 3.8L⑨⑥	C	2GC, 2 Bbl.⑤	3.80 × 3.40	8.0	105 @ 3400	185 @ 2000	37
	V6-231⑨⑯	A	2GC. 2 Bbl.⑤	3.80 × 3.40	8.0	105 @ 3400	185 @ 2000	37
	V8-260, 4.3L	F	2MC, 2 Bbl.⑤	3.50 × 3.385	8.0	110 @ 3400	205 @ 1600	30—45
	V8-305, 5.0L④	U	2GC, 2 Bbl.⑤	3.736 × 3.48	8.5	145 @ 3800	245 @ 2400	32—40
	V8-350, 5.7L	R	M4MC, 4 Bbl.⑤	4.057 × 3.385	8.0	170 @ 3800	275 @ 2000	30—45
	V8-350, 5.7L⑩	R	M4MC, 4 Bbl.⑤	4.057 × 3.385	8.0	170 @ 3800	275 @ 2400	30—45
	V8-350, 5.7L④⑪	L	M4MC, 4 Bbl.⑤	4.00 × 3.48	8.5	170 @ 3800	270 @ 2400	32—40
	V8-403, 6.6L⑦	K	M4MC, 4 Bbl.⑤	4.351 × 3.385	8.0	185 @ 3600	320 @ 2000	30—45
	V8-403, 6.6L⑧	K	M4MC, 4 Bbl.⑤	4.351 × 3.385	8.0	200 @ 3600	330 @ 2400	30—45
1978	V6-231, 3.8L⑨	A	2GE, 2 Bbl.⑤	3.80 × 3.40	8.0	105 @ 3400	185 @ 2000	37
	V8-260, 4.3L	F	2GC, 2 Bbl.⑤	3.50 × 3.385	7.5	110 @ 2400	205 @ 1800	30—45
	V8-305, 5.0L④	U	2GC, 2 Bbl.⑤	3.736 × 3.48	8.5	145 @ 3800	245 @ 2400	32—40
	V8-305, 5.0L④	H	M4MC, 4 Bbl.⑤	3.736 × 3.48	8.5	160 @ 4000	235 @ 2400	32—40
	V8-350, 5.7L④	L	M4MC, 4 Bbl.⑤	4.00 × 3.48	8.5	160 @ 3800	260 @ 2400	32—40
	V8-350, 5.7L	R	M4MC, 4 Bbl.⑤	4.057 × 3.385	8.0	170 @ 3800	275 @ 2000	30—45
	V8-350, 5.7L⑫	N	Fuel Injection	4.057 × 3.385	22.5	120 @ 3600	220 @ 1600	30—45
	V8-403, 6.6L⑦	K	M4MC, 4 Bbl.⑤	4.351 × 3.385	8.0	185 @ 3600	320 @ 2200	30—45
	V8-403, 6.6L⑧	K	M4MC, 4 Bbl.⑤	4.351 × 3.385	8.0	190 @ 3600	325 @ 2000	30—45
1979	V6-231, 3.8L⑨	A	M2ME, 2 Bbl.⑤	3.80 × 3.40	8.0	115 @ 3800	190 @ 2000	37
	V8-260, 4.3L⑫	P	Fuel Injection	3.50 × 3.385	22.5	90 @ 3600	160 @ 1600	35
	V8-260, 4.3L	F	M2MC, 2 Bbl.⑤	3.50 × 3.385	7.5	105 @ 3600	205 @ 1800	30—45
	V8-301, 4.9L⑬	Y	M2MC, 2 Bbl.⑤	4.00 × 3.00	8.2	135 @ 3800	240 @ 1600	35—40
	V8-305, 5.0L④	G	M2MC, 2 Bbl.⑤	3.736 × 3.48	8.5	130 @ 3200	245 @ 2000	32—40
	V8-305, 5.0L④	H	M4MC, 4 Bbl.⑤	3.736 × 3.48	8.5	160 @ 4000	235 @ 2400	32—40
	V8-350, 5.7L④	L	M4MC, 4 Bbl.⑤	4.00 × 3.48	8.5	160 @ 3600	260 @ 2400	32—40
	V8-350, 5.7L⑦	R	M4MC, 4 Bbl.⑤	4.057 × 3.385	8.0	160 @ 3600	270 @ 2000	35
	V8-350, 5.7L⑧	R	M4MC, 4 Bbl.⑤	4.057 × 3.385	8.0	165 @ 3600	275 @ 2000	35
	V8-350, 5.7L⑫	N	Fuel Injection	4.057 × 3.385	22.5	125 @ 3600	225 @ 1600	30—45
	V8-403, 6.6L	K	M4MC, 4 Bbl.⑤	4.351 × 3.385	7.8	175 @ 3600	310 @ 2000	35
1980	V6-231, 3.8L⑨	A	M2ME, 2 Bbl.⑤	3.80 × 3.40	8.0	110 @ 3800	190 @ 1600	37
	V8-260, 4.3L	F	M2MC, 2 Bbl.⑤	3.50 × 3.385	7.5	105 @ 3400	195 @ 1600	30—45
	V8-305, 5.0L④⑭	H	M4MC, 4 Bbl.⑤	3.736 × 3.48	8.6	155 @ 4000	240 @ 1600	45
	V8-305, 5.0L④⑮	H	E4MC, 4 Bbl.⑤	3.736 × 3.48	8.6	155 @ 4000	230 @ 1600	45
	V8-307, 5.0L	Y	M4MC, 4 Bbl.⑤	3.80 × 3.385	7.9	150 @ 3600	245 @ 1600	30—45
	V8-350, 5.7L⑫	N	Fuel Injection	4.057 × 3.385	22.5	105 @ 3200	205 @ 1600	30—45
	V8-350, 5.7L	R	E4MC, 4 Bbl.⑤	4.057 × 3.385	8.0	160 @ 3600	270 @ 2000	30—45
1981	V6-231, 3.8L⑨	A	2ME, 2 Bbl.⑤	3.80 × 3.40	8.0	110 @ 3800	190 @ 1600	30—45
	V8-252, 4.1L⑨	4	M4MC, 4 Bbl.⑤	3.96 × 3.40	8.0	125 @ 4000	205 @ 2000	30—45
	V8-260, 4.3L	F	2MC, 2 Bbl.⑤	3.50 × 3.38	7.5	100 @ 3600	190 @ 1600	30—45
	V8-307, 5.0L	Y	2ME, 2 Bbl.⑤	3.80 × 3.38	8.0	140 @ 3600	240 @ 1600	30—45
	V8-307, 5.0L	Y	M4MC, 4 Bbl.⑤	3.80 × 3.38	8.0	140 @ 3600	240 @ 1600	30—45
	V8-350⑫	N	Fuel Injection	4.05 × 3.38	22.5	105 @ 3200	200 @ 1600	30—45
1982	V6-231, 3.8L⑨	A	E2ME, 2 Bbl.⑤	3.80 × 3.40	8.0	110 @ 3800	190 @ 1600	37
	V6-252, 4.1L⑨	4	E4ME, 4 Bbl.⑤	3.96 × 3.40	8.0	125 @ 4000	205 @ 1600	37
	V6-262, 4.3L⑫	V	Fuel Injection	4.05 × 3.38	21.6	85 @ 3600	165 @ 1600	30—45
	V8-260, 4.3L	8	E2ME, 2 Bbl.⑤	3.50 × 3.38	7.5	100 @ 3600	190 @ 1600	35
	V8-307, 5.0L	Y	E4ME, 4 Bbl.⑤	3.80 × 3.38	8.0	140 @ 3600	240 @ 1600	35
	V8-350, 5.7L⑫	N	Fuel Injection	4.05 × 3.38	22.5	105 @ 3200	200 @ 1600	30—45
1983	V6-231, 3.8L⑨	A	2 Bbl.⑤	3.80 × 3.40	8.0	110 @ 3800	190 @ 1600	37
	V6-252, 4.1L⑨	4	4 Bbl.⑤	3.96 × 3.40	8.0	125 @ 4000	205 @ 2000	37
	V6-262, 4.3L⑫	V	Fuel Injection	4.05 × 3.38	22.5	85 @ 3600	165 @ 1600	30—45
	V8-307, 5.0L⑰	Y	4 Bbl.⑤	3.80 × 3.38	8.0	140 @ 3600	240 @ 1600	30—45
	V8-307, 5.0L⑱	9	E4MC, 4 Bbl.⑤	3.80 × 3.38	—	180	245	30—45
	V8-350, 5.7L⑫	N	Fuel Injection	4.05 × 3.38	22.5	105 @ 3200	200 @ 1600	30—45

Continued

GENERAL ENGINE SPECIFICATIONS—Continued

Year	Engine CID①/Liter	Engine V.I.N. Code②	Carburetor	Bore and Stroke	Compression Ratio	Net H.P. @ R.P.M.③	Maximum Torque Ft. Lbs. @ R.P.M.	Normal Oil Pressure Pounds
1984	V6-231, 3.8L⑨	A	E2ME, 2 Bbl.⑤	3.80 × 3.40	8.0	110 @ 4000	190 @ 1600	37
	V6-252, 4.1L⑨	4	E4ME, 4 Bbl.⑤	3.96 × 3.40	8.0	125 @ 4000	205 @ 2000	37
	V6-262, 4.3L⑫	V	Fuel Injection	4.05 × 3.38	22.8	85 @ 3600	165 @ 1600	30—45
	V8-307, 5.0L⑰	Y	E4MC, 4 Bbl.⑤	3.80 × 3.38	8.0	140 @ 3600	240 @ 1600	30—45
	V8-307, 5.0L⑱	9	4 Bbl.	3.80 × 3.38	—	180 @ 4000	245 @ 3200	30—45
	V8-350, 5.7L⑫	N	Fuel Injection	4.05 × 3.38	22.7	105 @ 3200	200 @ 1600	30—45

①—CID—cubic inch displacement.
②—On 1977-80 vehicles, the fifth digit in the VIN denotes engine code. On 1981-83 vehicles, the eighth digit in the VIN denotes engine code.
③—All ratings are net—as installed in vehicle.
④—Chevrolet built engine. Distributor located at rear of engine, clockwise rotation.
⑤—Rochester.
⑥—Exc. even fire engine.
⑦—Exc. Toronado.
⑧—Toronado.
⑨—Buick built engine. Distributor located at front of engine.
⑩—Cutlass.
⑪—Omega.
⑫—Diesel.
⑬—Pontiac built engine. Distributor located at rear of engine, clockwise rotation.
⑭—Exc. Calif.
⑮—California.
⑯—Even fire engine.
⑰—Exc. Hurst option.
⑱—Hurst option.

TUNE UP SPECIFICATIONS

The following specifications are published from the latest information available. This data should be used only in the absence of a decal affixed in the engine compartment.

★ When using a timing light, disconnect vacuum hose or tube at distributor and plug opening in hose or tube so idle speed will not be affected.

● When checking compression, lowest cylinder must be within 70 percent of highest.

▲ Before removing wires from distributor cap, determine location of the No. 1 wire in cap, as distributor position may have been altered from that shown at the end of this chart.

Spark plug types in this chart are recommendations of the original vehicle manufacturer and not MOTOR.

Check local sources for other spark plug manufacturers listings.

Year & Engine/VIN	Spark Plug Type	Spark Plug Gap	Firing Order Fig. ▲	Ignition Timing BTDC①★ Man. Trans.	Ignition Timing BTDC①★ Auto. Trans.	Mark Fig.	Curb Idle Speed② Man. Trans.	Curb Idle Speed② Auto. Trans.	Fast Idle Speed Man. Trans.	Fast Idle Speed Auto. Trans.	Fuel Pump Pressure
1977											
V6-231/C⑩⑱	⑲	⑲	I	12°	12°	B⑳	600/800	600/670D㉑	—	—	3 Min.
V6-231/A⑩㊱	R46TSX	.060	A	—	15°	F⑳	—	600/670D㉑	—	—	3 Min.
V8-260/F	R46SZ	.060	J	16°⑤	㉒	G	750	550/650D⑥	900⑦	900⑦	5½-6½
V8-305/F⑭	R45TS	.045	H	8°	8°	C	600	500/650D	—	—	7½-9
V8-350/U, Exc. Calif.⑭㉓	R45TS	.045	H	—	8°	C	—	㉔	—	1600④	7½-9
V8-350/L, Exc. Calif. & High Alt.㉕	R46SZ	.060	J	—	20°⑤	G	—	550/650D⑥	—	900⑦	5½-6½
V8-350/R, Calif.㉕	R46SZ	.060	J	—	㉖	G	—	550/650D⑥	—	1000⑦	5½-6½
V8-350/R, High Alt.㉕	R46SZ	.060	J	—	20°⑤	G	—	600/700D⑥	—	1000⑦	5½-6½
V8-403/K, Exc. Calif. & High Alt.⑬	R46SZ	.060	J	—	㉗	G	—	550/650D⑥	—	900⑦	5½-6½
V8-403/K, Calif. & High Alt.⑬	R46SZ	.060	J	—	20°⑤	G	—	⑥㉘	—	1000⑦	5½-6½
V8-403/K, Toronado	R46SZ	.060	J	—	㉙	G	—	⑥㉚	—	⑦㉛	5½-6½
1978											
V6-231/A⑩	R46TSX	.060	A	15°	15°	F⑳	800	㉜	1850④	1850④	3 Min.
V8-260/F, Exc. Calif. & High Alt.	R46SZ	.060	J	18°⑤	20°⑤	G	650/800⑥	500/650D⑥	750⑦	800⑦	5½-6½
V8-260/F, Calif.	R46SZ	.060	J	—	18°⑤	G	—	500/650D⑥	—	800⑦	5½-6½
V8-260/F, High Alt.	R46SZ	.060	J	—	20°⑤	G	—	550/650D⑥	—	900⑦	5½-6½
V8-305/U, 2 Barrel Exc. Calif.⑭㉝	R45TS	.045	H	4°	4°	E	600/700	500/600D	1600④	1600④	7½-9

Continued

TUNE UP SPECIFICATIONS—Continued

The following specifications are published from the latest information available. This
data should be used only in the absence of a decal affixed in the engine compartment.

★ When using a timing light, disconnect vacuum hose or tube at distributor and plug opening in hose or tube so idle speed will not be affected.

● When checking compression, lowest cylinder must be within 70 percent of highest.

▲ Before removing wires from distributor cap, determine location of the No. 1 wire in cap, as distributor position may have been altered from that shown at the end of this chart.

Spark plug types in this chart are recommendations of the original vehicle manufacturer and not MOTOR.

Check local sources for other spark plug manufacturers listings.

Year & Engine/VIN	Spark Plug		Ignition Timing BTDC① ★				Curb Idle Speed②		Fast Idle Speed		Fuel Pump Pressure
	Type	Gap	Firing Order Fig. ▲	Man. Trans.	Auto. Trans.	Mark Fig.	Man. Trans.	Auto. Trans.	Man. Trans.	Auto. Trans.	
1978—Continued											
V8-305/U, 2 Barrel Calif. & High Alt.⑭	R45TS	.045	H	—	8°	E	—	㉟	—	1600④	7½–9
V8-305/H, 4 Barrel⑭	R45TS	.045	H	—	4°	E	—	500/600D	—	1600④	7½–9
V8-350/R⑭㉓	R45TS	.045	H	—	8°	E	—	㉔	—	1600④	7½–9
V8-350/R, Exc. Calif. & High Alt.㉕	R46SZ	.060	J	—	20°⑤	G	—	550/650D⑥	—	900⑦	5½–6½
V8-350/R, Calif. & High Alt.㉕	R46SZ	.060	J	—	20°⑤	G	—	㉘	—	1000⑦	5½–6½
V8-350 Diesel/N, Exc. High Alt.	—	—	—	—	4½°㊶㊷㊿	—	—	575/650D⑥	—	—	—
V8-350 Diesel/N, High Alt.	—	—	—	—	5½°㊶㊷㊿	—	—	575/650D⑥	—	—	—
V8-403/K, Exc. Calif. & High Alt.⑬	R46SZ	.060	J	—	㊲	G	—	550/650D⑥	—	900⑦	5½–6½
V8-403/K, Calif. & High Alt.⑬	R46SZ	.060	J	—	20°⑤	G	—	㉘	—	1000⑦	5½–6½
V8-403/K, Toronado	R46SZ	.060	J	—	㉙	G	—	⑥㉚	—	⑦㉛	5½–6½
1979											
V6-231/A, Exc. Calif. & High Alt.⑩	R46TSX	.060	A	15°	15°	F⑳	600/800⑥	550/670D⑥	2200	2200	3 Min.
V6-231/A, Calif. & High Alt.⑩	R46TSX	.060	A	—	15°	F⑳	—	600D	—	2200	3 Min.
V8-260/F, Exc. Calif. & High Alt.	R46SZ	.060	J	18°⑤	20°⑤	G	650/800⑥	500/625D⑥	750	800	5½–6½
V8-260/F, Calif.	R46SZ	.060	J	—	18°⑤	G	—	500/625D⑥	—	800	5½–6½
V8-260/F, High Alt.	R46SZ	.060	J	—	20°⑤	G	—	550/650D⑥	—	900	5½–6½
V8-260 Diesel/P, Exc. High Alt	—	—	—	3½°㊶㊷	4½°㊶㊷	—	575/695	590/650D	—	—	—
V8-260 Diesel/P, High Alt	—	—	—	4½°㊶㊷	5½°㊶㊷	—	575/695	590/650D	—	—	—
V8-301/Y⑮	R46TSX	.060	D	—	12°	L	—	500/650D⑥	—	2000	7–8½
V8-305/G, 2 Barrel⑭	R45TS	.045	H	4°	4°	E	600/700	500/600D⑥	1300	1600	7½–9
V8-305/H, 4 Barrel Exc. High Alt.⑭	R45TS	.045	H	4°	4°	E	700	500/600D⑥	1300	1600	7½–9
V8-305/H, 4 Barrel High Alt.⑭	R45TS	.045	H	—	8°	E	—	600/650D⑥	—	1750	7½–9
V8-350/L, Calif.⑭㉓	R45TS	.045	H	—	8°	E	—	500/600D⑥	—	1600	7½–9
V8-350/L, High Alt.⑭㉓	R45TS	.045	H	—	8°	E	—	600/650D⑥	—	1750	7½–9
V8-350/R Exc. Calif.㉕	R46SZ	.060	J	—	㊳	G	—	550/650D⑥	—	900	5½–6½
V8-350/R Calif.㉕	R46SZ	.060	J	—	20°⑤	G	—	500/600D⑥	—	1000	5½–6½
V8-350 Diesel/N, Exc. High Alt.	—	—	—	—	4½°㊶㊷㊿	—	—	575/650D⑥	—	—	—
V8-350 Diesel/N, High Alt.	—	—	—	—	5½°㊶㊷㊿	—	—	575/650D⑥	—	—	—
V8-403/K, Exc. Calif.	R46SZ	.060	J	—	20°⑤	G	—	550/650D⑥	—	900	5½–6½
V8-403/K, Calif.	R46SZ	.060	J	—	20°⑤	G	—	500/600D⑥	—	1000	5½–6½

TUNE UP SPECIFICATIONS—Continued

The following specifications are published from the latest information available. This
data should be used only in the absence of a decal affixed in the engine compartment.

★ When using a timing light, disconnect vacuum hose or tube at distributor and plug opening in hose or tube so idle speed will not be affected.

● When checking compression, lowest cylinder must be within 70 percent of highest.

▲ Before removing wires from distributor cap, determine location of the No. 1 wire in cap, as distributor position may have been altered from that shown at the end of this chart.

Spark plug types in this chart are recommendations of the original vehicle manufacturer and not MOTOR.

Check local sources for other spark plug manufacturers listings.

Year & Engine/VIN	Spark Plug Type	Gap	Firing Order Fig. ▲	Ignition Timing BTDC①★ Man. Trans.	Auto. Trans.	Mark Fig.	Curb Idle Speed② Man. Trans.	Auto. Trans.	Fast Idle Speed Man. Trans.	Auto. Trans.	Fuel Pump Pressure
1980											
V6-231/A⑧⑩	R45TS	.040	A	15°	15°	F⑳	600/800⑥	550/670D	2200	2000	3 Min.
V8-231/A⑩⑫	R45TSX	.060	A	—	15°	F⑳	—	550/620D	—	2200	3 Min.
V8-260/F	R46SX	.080	J	—	③	G	—	500/625D	—	700D	5½–6½
V8-305/H, Exc. Calif.⑭	R45TS	.045	H	—	4°	㉞	—	500/600D	—	1850	7½–9
V8-305/H, Calif.⑭	R45TS	.045	H	—	4°	㉞	—	550/650D	—	2200	7½–9
V8-307/Y	R46SX	.080	J	—	20°⑤	G	—	500/600D	—	700D	5½–6½
V8-350/R, Exc. Calif.	R46SX	.080	J	—	18°⑤	G	—	500/600D	—	700D	5½–6½
V8-350/R, Calif.	R46SX	.080	J	—	⑨	G	—	550/650D	—	700D	5½–6½
V8-350 Diesel/N, Exc. High Alt.	—	—	—	—	4½°㊶㊷㊿	—	—	600/750D	—	750D	—
V8-350 Diesel/N, High Alt.	—	—	—	—	5½°㊶㊷㊿	—	—	600/750D	—	750D	—
1981											
V6-231/A⑩	R45TS8	.080	A	15°	15°	F⑳	800	㊵	2200	1800	3 Min.
V6-252/4⑩	R45TS8	.080	A	—	15°	F⑳	—	550/690D	2200	2200	3 Min.
V8-260/F	R46SX	.080	J	—	㊳	G	—	㊵	—	700D	5½–6½
V8-307/Y, Exc. Calif.	R46SX	.080	J	—	⑯⑤	G	—	㊵	—	650D	5½–6½
V8-307/Y, Calif.	R46SX	.080	J	—	15°⑤	G	—	㊵	—	650D	5½–6½
V8-350 Diesel/N, Exc. High Alt.	—	—	—	—	4°㊶㊷㊿	—	—	600/750D	—	750D	—
V8-350 Diesel/N, High Alt.	—	—	—	—	5°㊶㊷㊿	—	—	600/750D	—	750D	—
1982											
V6-231/A	R45TS8	.080	A	—	15°	F⑳	—	㊵	—	2200	3 Min.
V6-252/4	R45TS8	.080	A	—	15°	F⑳	—	㊵	—	⑰	3 Min.
V6-262 Diesel/N, Exc. High Alt.	—	—	—	—	7°㊶㊸㊿	—	—	650D	—	725D	—
V6-262 Diesel/N, High Alt.	—	—	—	—	7°㊶㊹㊿	—	—	650D	—	725D	—
V8-260/8	R46SX	.080	J	—	20°⑤	G	—	㊵	—	700D	5½–6½
V8-307/Y	R46SX	.080	J	—	20°⑤	G	—	㊵	—	650D	5½–6½
V8-350 Diesel/N, Exc. High Alt.	—	—	—	—	4°㊶㊺㊿	—	—	600D	—	750D	—
V8-350 Diesel/N, High Alt.	—	—	—	—	4°㊶㊻㊿	—	—	600D	—	750D	—
1983											
V6-231/A	R45TS8	.080	A	—	15°	F⑳	—	㊵	—	2200	4¼–5¾
V6-252/4	R45TS8	.080	A	—	15°	F⑳	—	㊵	—	㊿	4¼–5¾
V6-262 Diesel/V	—	—	—	—	⑪㊿	—	—	660D	—	775D	—
V8-307/Y㊼	R46SX	.080	J	—	20°⑤	G	—	㊵	—	900D	6–7½
V8-307/9㊽	R46SX	.080	J	—	20°⑤	G	—	500D	—	900D	6–7½
V8-350 Diesel/N	—	—	—	—	㊾㊿	—	—	600D	—	750D	—

Continued

TUNE UP SPECIFICATIONS—Continued

The following specifications are published from the latest information available. This data should be used only in the absence of a decal affixed in the engine compartment.

★ When using a timing light, disconnect vacuum hose or tube at distributor and plug opening in hose or tube so idle speed will not be affected.

● When checking compression, lowest cylinder must be within 70 percent of highest.

▲ Before removing wires from distributor cap, determine location of the No. 1 wire in cap, as distributor position may have been altered from that shown at the end of this chart.

Spark plug types in this chart are recommendations of the original vehicle manufacturer and not MOTOR.

Check local sources for other spark plug manufacturers listings.

Year & Engine/VIN	Spark Plug Type	Gap	Firing Order Fig. ▲	Ignition Timing BTDC①★ Man. Trans.	Auto. Trans.	Mark Fig.	Curb Idle Speed② Man. Trans.	Auto. Trans.	Fast Idle Speed Man. Trans.	Auto. Trans.	Fuel Pump Pressure
1984											
V6-231/A	R45TS8	.080	A	—	15°	F⑳	—	④⓪	—	2200	4¼–5¾
V6-252/4	R45TS8	.080	A	—	15°	F⑳	—	④⓪	—	⑤⓪	4¼–5¾
V6-262 Diesel/V	—	—	—	—	⑪⑤⓵	—	675D	—	775D		—
V8-307/Y⑰	R46SX	.080	J	—	20°⑤	G	—	④⓪	—	700D	6–7½
V8-307/9⑱	R46SX	.080	J	—	20°⑤	G	—	500D	—	900D	6–7½
V8-350 Diesel/N	—	—	—	—	⑭⑨⑤⓵	—	600D	—	750D		—

①—BTDC—Before top dead center.
②—Idle speed on man. trans. vehicles is adjusted in Neutral & on auto. trans. equipped vehicles is adjusted in Drive unless otherwise specified. Where two idle speeds are listed, the higher the speed is with the A/C or idle solenoid energized.
③—88 & Cutlass except sta. wag., 20° at 1100 RPM; Cutlass sta. wag., 18° at 1100 RPM.
④—With cam follower or stop screw on high step of fast idle cam, EGR vacuum line disconnected & plugged & A/C off.
⑤—At 1100 RPM ALDL test lead grounded.
⑥—Idle speed with solenoid energized is adjusted with A/C on & compressor clutch wires disconnected.
⑦—With stop screw of low step of fast idle cam, EGR disconnected & plugged & A/C off.
⑧—Except Calif. & models w/Computer Controlled Catalytic Converter (C4) System.
⑨—Except Toronado, 18° at 1100 RPM; Toronado, 16° at 1100 RPM.
⑩—Buick built engine.
⑪—Injection timing, 7°ATDC at 1300 RPM.
⑫—California & models w/Computer Controlled Catalytic Converter (C4) system.
⑬—Except Toronado.
⑭—Chevrolet built engine.
⑮—Pontiac built engines.
⑯—Toronado, 15°BTDC. 88, Custom Cruiser & Cutlass Cruiser, except engine codes TMK, TML, TMN & TMS, 15°BTDC; engine codes TMK, TML, TMN & TMS, 18°BTDC.
⑰—Except Toronado Calif. models, 2200 RPM; Toronado California models, 2100 RPM.
⑱—Except even fire engine.
⑲—Early production, R46TS gapped at .040"; late production, R46TSX gapped at .060".
⑳—The harmonic balancer on these engines has two timing marks. The timing mark measuring 1/16 in. is used when setting timing with a hand held timing light. The mark measuring 1/8 in. is used when setting timing with magnetic timing equipment.
㉑—Idle speed with solenoid energized is adjusted with distributor vacuum advance hose disconnected & plugged, A/C on & compressor clutch wires disconnected.
㉒—Except Cutlass, 20°BTDC at 1100 RPM; Cutlass 18°BTDC at 1100 RPM.
㉓—Distributor located at rear of engine, rotor rotation clockwise.
㉔—Except high altitude, 500/650D RPM; high altitude, 600/650D RPM.
㉕—Distributor located at rear of engine, rotor rotation counter clockwise.
㉖—Omega & 88 except sta. wag., 18°BTDC at 1100 RPM; Cutlass, 88 sta. wag. & 98, 20°BTDC at 1100 RPM.
㉗—Cutlass except sta. wag., 88 & 98, 20°BTDC at 1100 RPM; Cutlass sta. wag., 22°BTDC at 1100 RPM.
㉘—Except high altitude, 550/650D RPM; high altitude, 600/700D RPM.
㉙—Equipped with Electronic Spark Timing (EST).
㉚—Except Calif.; high altitude, 550/650D RPM; California, 600/650D RPM; high altitude 600/700D RPM.
㉛—Except Calif. & high altitude, 900 RPM; California & high altitude, 1000 RPM.
㉜—Except 88 with A/C, 600D RPM; 88 with A/C, 600/670D RPM see note 21.
㉝—Except high altitude.
㉞—Early models, Fig. E; late models, Fig. K.
㉟—Except high altitude, 500/650D RPM; high altitude, 600/700D RPM.
㊱—Even fire engine.
㊲—88 except sta. wag. & 98, 18°BTDC at 1100 RPM; 88 sta. wag., 20°BTDC at 1100 RPM.
㊳—Except engine codes QN & QO, 20°BTDC at 1100 RPM; engine codes QN & QO, 18°BTDC at 1100 RPM.
㊴—Cutlass except sta. wag., 20°BTDC at 1100 RPM; Cutlass Cruiser & 88, 18°BTDC at 1100 RPM.
㊵—Idle speed is controlled by the idle speed control (ICS) motor or the idle load compensator (ILC).
㊶—ATDC—After top dead center.
㊷—At 1200 RPM.
㊸—At 1300 RPM. When operating at altitudes above 4000 ft., set at 8°ATDC.
㊹—At 1300 RPM. When operating at altitudes below 4000 ft., set at 6°ATDC.
㊺—At 1250 RPM. When operating at altitudes above 4000 ft., set at 5°ATDC.
㊻—At 1250 RPM. When operating at altitudes below 4000 ft., set at 3°ATDC.
㊼—Except Hurst option.
㊽—Hurst option.
㊾—Injection timing, 4°ATDC at 1250 RPM.
㊿—Except Toronado, 2200 RPM; Toronado, 2100 RPM.
⓵—Using diesel timing meter J-33075.

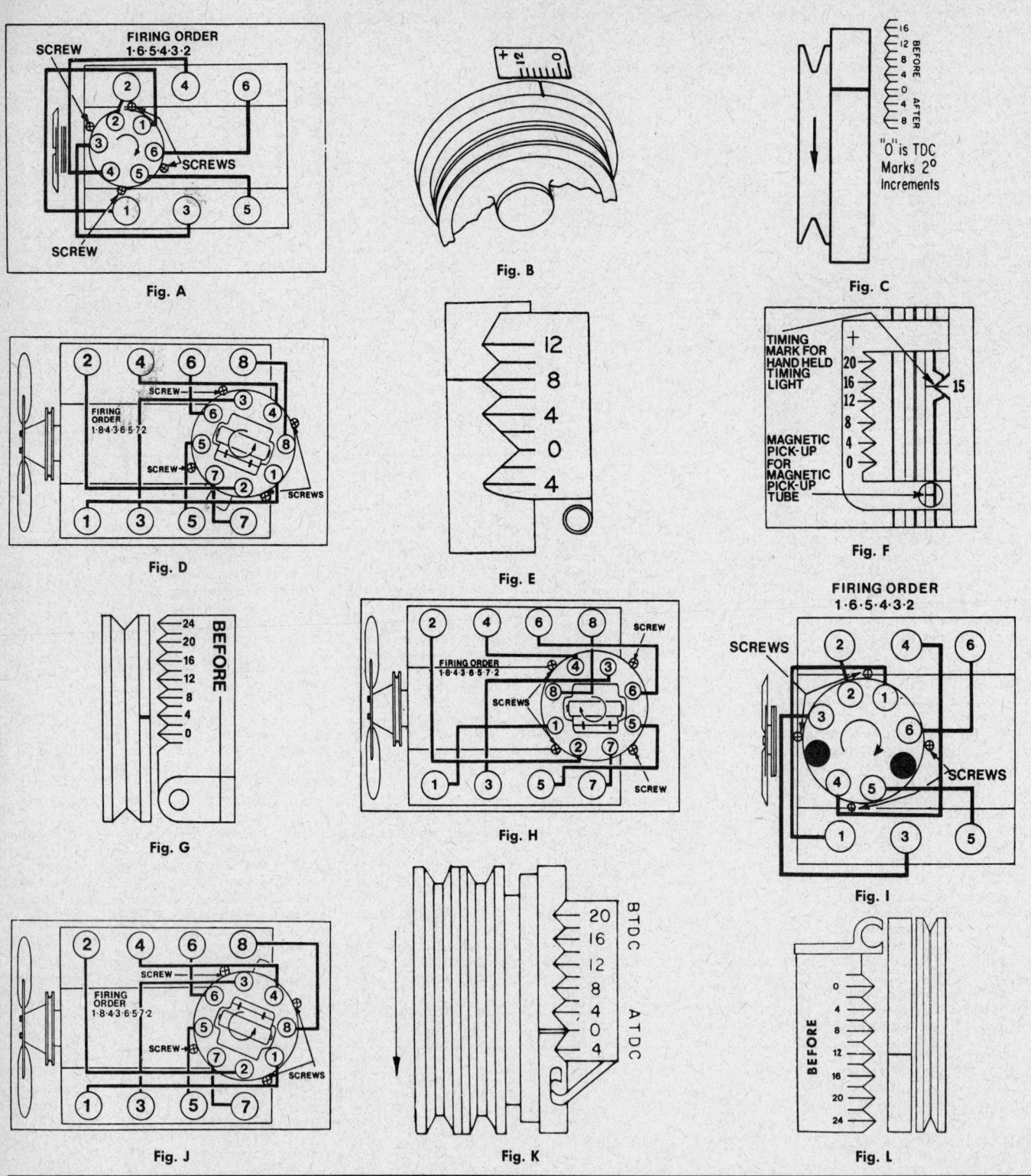

Fig. A

Fig. B

Fig. C

Fig. D

Fig. E

Fig. F

Fig. G

Fig. H

Fig. I

Fig. J

Fig. K

Fig. L

DISTRIBUTOR SPECIFICATIONS

★ Note: If unit is checked on vehicle, double the RPM and degrees to get crankshaft figures.

Distributor Part No.①	Centrifugal Advance Degrees @ RPM of Distributor					Vacuum Advance		Distributor Retard
	Advance Starts	Intermediate Advance			Full Advance	Inches of Vacuum to Start Plunger	Max. Adv. Dist. Deg. @ Vacuum	Max. Retard Dist. Deg. @ Vacuum
1977								
1103239	0 @ 600	7½ @ 1350	—	—	10 @ 2100	4	7½ @ 10	—
1103246	0 @ 600	5–7 @ 1000	—	—	12 @ 2100	3	9½ @ 13	—
1103248	0 @ 600	5–7 @ 1000	—	—	12 @ 2100	3	6 @ 9	—
1103259	0 @ 500	—	—	—	9½ @ 2000	6	12 @ 13	—
1103260	0 @ 500	—	—	—	9½ @ 2000	6	12 @ 13	—
1103262	0 @ 455	8½ @ 1188	—	—	13 @ 2233	4	15 @ 11	—
1103264	0 @ 500	—	—	—	6½ @ 1800	5	8 @ 11	—
1103266	0 @ 500	—	—	—	9½ @ 2000	5	8 @ 11	—
1110677	0–2.2 @ 765	8.9–11 @ 1800	—	—	11 @ 2500	6	12¾ @ 20	—
1110686	0–2.2 @ 890	3.2–5.5 @ 1300	—	—	11 @ 2500	6	4¾ @ 20	—
1112990②	—	—	—	—	—	—	—	—
1978								
1103313②	—	—	—	—	—	—	—	—
1103337	0 @ 550	6 @ 800	8 @ 1200	—	11 @ 2300	4	12 @ 10	—
1110731	0–2 @ 1000	—	—	—	9 @ 1800	4	8 @ 9	—
1978–79								
1103281	0 @ 500	5 @ 850	—	—	10 @ 1900	4	9 @ 12	—
1103282	0 @ 500	5 @ 850	—	—	10 @ 1900	4	10 @ 10	—
1103285	0 @ 600	6 @ 1000	—	—	11 @ 2100	4	12 @ 8	—
1103320	0 @ 455	8½ @ 1188	—	—	13 @ 2233	4	15 @ 11	—
1103322	0 @ 300	5½ @ 600	—	—	14½ @ 2000	6	12 @ 13	—
1103323	0 @ 500	—	—	—	9½ @ 2000	5	8 @ 11	—
1103324	0 @ 300	5½ @ 600	—	—	11½ @ 1800	6	12 @ 13	—
1103325	0 @ 500	—	—	—	6½ @ 1800	5	8 @ 11	—
1103342	0–2 @ 1000	—	—	—	9½ @ 2200	5–7	12 @ 13	—
1103346	0 @ 500	—	—	—	9½ @ 2000	6	12 @ 13	—
1103347	0 @ 500	—	—	—	6½ @ 1800	6	12 @ 13	—
1103353	0–1¾ @ 625	2½–3½ @ 850	—	3½–4½ @ 2000	6 @ 2250	3	10 @ 12	—
1103355	0 @ 455	8½ @ 1188	—	—	13 @ 2233	4	15 @ 9	—
1110695	0–3 @ 1000	—	—	—	9 @ 1800	7	12 @ 13	—
1979								
1103259	0 @ 500	—	—	—	10½ @ 2000	4	15 @ 11	—
1103260	0 @ 500	—	—	—	6¾ @ 1600	6	12 @ 13	—
1103262	0 @ 550	—	—	8½ @ 1175	14 @ 2500	4½	15½ @ 20	—
1103264	0 @ 500	—	—	—	8½ @ 1700	5	8 @ 11	—
1103266	0 @ 500	—	—	—	10½ @ 2000	5	8 @ 11	—
1103314	0 @ 413	5 @ 900	—	—	10½ @ 1700	4	12½ @ 12	—
1103368	0 @ 500	5 @ 850	—	—	10 @ 1900	4	5 @ 8	—
1103379	0 @ 500	5 @ 850	—	—	10 @ 1900	3	10 @ 7.5	—
1103396	0 @ 455	8½ @ 1188	—	—	13 @ 2233	5	15 @ 12	—
1110677	0 @ 640	—	—	—	10 @ 1800	5	12 @ 9.5	—
1110683	—	—	—	—	—	—	—	—
1110731	0 @ 950	—	—	7¼ @ 1800	8½ @ 2500	5	12¾ @ 20	—
1110766	0 @ 840	—	—	—	7½ @ 1800	4	12 @ 11	—
1110767	0 @ 840	—	—	—	7½ @ 1800	3	10 @ 12	—
1110768	0 @ 500	2½ @ 800	—	3 @ 1200	7½ @ 1800	3	10 @ 12	—
1110769	0 @ 500	2½ @ 800	—	3 @ 1200	7½ @ 1800	4	12 @ 11	—
1110770	0 @ 840	—	—	—	7½ @ 1800	3	10 @ 9	—
1110779	0 @ 840	—	—	—	7½ @ 1800	3	12 @ 9.5	—

Continued

DISTRIBUTOR SPECIFICATIONS—Continued

★ Note: If unit is checked on vehicle, double the RPM and degrees to get crankshaft figures.

Distributor Part No.①	Centrifugal Advance Degrees @ RPM of Distributor					Vacuum Advance		Distributor Retard
	Advance Starts	Intermediate Advance			Full Advance	Inches of Vacuum to Start Plunger	Max. Adv. Dist. Deg. @ Vacuum	Max. Retard Dist. Deg. @ Vacuum
1980								
1103384	0 @ 400	4 @ 600	8 @ 1000	—	10 @ 2000	4	7½ @ 12	—
1103386	0 @ 500	5 @ 850	—	—	10 @ 1900	4	8 @ 7.5	—
1103398	0 @ 300	5½ @ 600	—	—	11½ @ 1800	5	15 @ 13.7	—
1103412	0 @ 300	5½ @ 600	—	—	14½ @ 2000	4	15 @ 12.5	—
1103413	0 @ 500	—	—	—	6½ @ 1800	6	15 @ 13.7	—
1103414	0 @ 300	5½ @ 600	—	—	11½ @ 1800	6	12 @ 13	—
1103419	0 @ 300	5½ @ 600	—	—	11½ @ 1800	4	15 @ 11	—
1110552	0 @ 463	2 @ 650	3¼ @ 1250	—	7 @ 1700	3	12 @ 8	—
1110554	0 @ 840	—	—	—	7½ @ 1800	3	12 @ 12	—
1110555	0 @ 500	2½ @ 800	3 @ 1200	—	7½ @ 1800	4	12 @ 11	—
1110784②	—	—	—	—	—	—	—	—
1981								
1103451②	—	—	—	—	—	—	—	—
1103456②	—	—	—	—	—	—	—	—
1103466②	—	—	—	—	—	—	—	—
1110567②	—	—	—	—	—	—	—	—
1110573②	—	—	—	—	—	—	—	—
1110579②	—	—	—	—	—	—	—	—
1111386②	—	—	—	—	—	—	—	—
1982–83								
1103457②	—	—	—	—	—	—	—	—
1103470②	—	—	—	—	—	—	—	—

①—Stamped on distributor housing plate. ②—Equipped with Electronic Spark Timing (EST).

WHEEL ALIGNMENT SPECIFICATIONS

Year	Model	Caster Angle, Degrees		Camber Angle, Degrees					Toe-In. Inch	Toe-Out on Turns, Deg	
		Limits	Desired	Limits		Desired				Outer Wheel	Inner Wheel
				Left	Right	Left	Right				
1977	Omega③	−½ to −1½	−1	+¼ to +1¼	+¼ to +1¼	+¾	+¾	0 to ⅛	—	—
	Omega①	+½ to +1½	+1	+¼ to +1¼	+¼ to +1¼	+¾	+¾	0 to ⅛	—	—
	Cutlass②	+1½ to +2½	+2	+½ to +1½	0 to +1	+1	+½	0 to ⅛	—	—
	88, 98	+2½ to +3½	+3	+¼ to +1¼	+¼ to +1¼	+¾	+¾	1/16 to 3/16	—	—
	Toronado②	−½ to +½	0	−¼ to +¾	−¾ to +¼	+¼	−¼	−1/16 to +1/16	—	—
1978	Toronado	−½ to +½	0	−¼ to +¾	−¾ to +¼	+¼	−¼	−1/16 to +1/16	—	—
1978–79	Omega③	−½ to −1½	−1	+¼ to +1¼	+¼ to +1¼	+¾	+¾	+1/16 to +3/16	—	—
	Omega①	+½ to +1½	+1	+¼ to +1¼	+¼ to +1¼	+¾	+¾	+1/16 to +3/16	—	—
1978–83	Cutlass③	+½ to +1½	+1	0 to +1	0 to +1	+½	+½	+1/16 to +3/16	—	—
	Cutlass①	+2½ to +3½	+3	0 to +1	0 to +1	+½	+½	+1/16 to +3/16	—	—
	88, 98	+2½ to +3½	+3	+¼ to +1¼	+¼ to +1¼	+¾	+¾	+1/16 to +3/16	—	—
	Toronado	+2 to +3	+2½	−½ to +½	−½ to +½	0	0	−1/16 to +1/16	—	—
1984	Cutlass	+2½ to +3½	+3	0 to +1	0 to +1	+½	+½	+1/10 to +2/10	—	—
	88, 98	+2½ to +3½	+3	+3/10 to +13/10	+3/10 to +13/10	+4/5	+4/5	+1/10 to +2/10	—	—
	Custom Cruiser	+2½ to +3½	+3	+3/10 to +13/10	+3/10 to +13/10	+4/5	+4/5	+1/10 to +2/10	—	—
	Toronado	+2 to +3	+2½	−½ to +½	−½ to +½	0	0	−1/20 to +1/20	—	—

①—Power Steering.
②—Left and right side "camber" should be different at least ¼° and no more than ¾° with the left side having the greater (+) reading.
③—Manual Steering.

ENGINE TIGHTENING SPECIFICATIONS★

★ Torque specifications are for clean and lightly lubricated threads only. Dry or dirty threads produce increased friction which prevents accurate measurement of tightness.

Year	Engine Model/V.I.N.	Spark Plugs Ft. Lbs.	Cylinder Head Bolts Ft. Lbs.	Intake Manifold Ft. Lbs.	Exhaust Manifold Ft. Lbs.	Rocker Arm Shaft Bracket Ft. Lbs.	Rocker Arm Cover Ft. Lbs.	Connecting Rod Cap Bolts Ft. Lbs.	Main Bearing Cap Bolts Ft. Lbs.	Flywheel to Crankshaft Ft. Lbs.	Vibration Damper or Pulley Ft. Lbs.
1977	V6-231⑬⑮	20	80	45	25	30	4	40	100	60	175
	V8-260/F	25	85④	40	25	25①	7	42	80⑫	⑦	310
	V8-305/U②⑧	15	65	30	20	50⑤	45⑥	45	70	60	60
	V8-350/L②⑧	15	65	30	20⑩	50⑤	45⑥	45	70	60	60
	V8-350/R	25	130④	40④	25	25①	7	42	80⑫	⑦	310
	V8-403/K	25	130④	40④	25	25①	7	42	80⑫	⑦	310
1978	V6-231/A⑬	25	80	45	25	30	4	40	115	60	175
	V8-260/F	25	85④	40④	25	25①	7	42	80⑫	⑦	200–310
	V8-305②⑯	15	65	30	20	50⑤	45⑥	45	70	60	60
	V8-350/R②	15	65	30	20⑩	50⑤	45⑥	45	70	60	60
	V8-350/R	25	130④	40④	25	25①	7	42	80⑫	⑦	200–310
	V8-350/N⑨	—	130④	40④	25	25①	—	42	120	60	200–310
	V8-403/K	25	130④	40④	25	25①	15⑥	42	80⑫	⑦	200–310
1979	V6-231/A⑬	15	80	45	25	30	4	40	100	60	225
	V8-260/F	25	85④	40④	25	28①	7	42	80⑫	⑦	200–310
	V8-260/P⑨	—	85④	40④	25	28①	—	42	120	⑦	200–310
	V8-301/Y⑪	15	95	35	40	15⑤	6	30	70	95	160
	V8-305②⑯	22	65	30	20	50⑤	45⑥	45	70	60	60
	V8-350/L②	22	65	30	20⑩	50⑤	45⑥	45	70	60	60
	V8-350/R	25	130④	40④	25	28①	7	42	80⑫	⑦	200–310
	V8-350/N⑨	—	130④	40④	25	28①	—	42	120	60	200–310
	V8-403/K	25	130④	40④	25	28①	15⑥	42	80⑫	60	200–310
1980	V6-231/A⑬	15	80	45	25	30	4	40	100	60	225
	V8-260/F	25	85④	40④	25	28①	—	42	80⑫	60	200–310
	V8-305/H②	22	65	30	20	—	45⑥	45	70	60	60
	V8-307/Y	25	130④	40④	25	28①	—	42	70⑫	60	200–310
	V8-350/R	25	130④	40④	25	28①	—	42	80⑫	60	200–310
	V8-350/N⑨	—	130④	40④	25	28①	—	42	120	60	200–310
1981	V6-231/A⑬	15	80	45	25	30	4	40	100	60	225
	V6-252/4⑬	15	80	45	25	30	4	40	100	60	225
	V8-260/F	25	85④	40④	25	28①	—	42	80⑫	60	200–310
	V8-307/Y	25	130④	40④	25	28①	—	42	80⑫	60	200–310
	V8-350/N⑨	—	130④	40④	25	28①	—	42	120	60	200–310
1982–83	V6-231/A⑬	15	80	45	25	30	4	40	100	60	225
	V6-252/4⑬	15	80	45	25	30	4	40	100	60	225
	V6-262/V⑨	—	③	41	29	28①	—	42	⑰	48	160–350
	V8-260/8	25	85④	40④	25	28①	—	42	80⑰	60⑭	200–310
	V8-307/Y,9	25	125④	40④	25	28①	—	42	80⑰	60⑭	200–310
	V8-350/N⑨	—	130④	40④	25	28①	—	42	120	60	210–300
1984	V6-231/A⑬	15	80	45	25	30	4	40	100	60	225
	V6-252/4⑬	15	80	45	25	30	4	40	100	60	225
	V6-262/V⑨	—	③	41	31	28①	—	42	89	57	203–350
	V8-307/Y,9	25	125④	40④	25	28①	—	42	80⑫	60	200–310
	V8-350/N⑨	—	130④	40④	25	28①	—	42	120	60	200–310

①—Rocker arm pivot bolt to head.
②—Chevrolet built engine. Distributor located at rear of engine, clockwise rotation.
③—See text for procedure.
④—Clean and dip entire bolt in engine oil before tightening.
⑤—Rocker arm stud.
⑥—Inch lbs.
⑦—Auto. trans., 60 ft. lbs.; manual trans, 90 ft. lbs.
⑧—Omega.
⑨—Oldsmobile built diesel engine.
⑩—Inner bolts, 30 ft. lbs.
⑪—Pontiac built engine. Distributor located at rear of engine, clockwise rotation.
⑫—Rear 120 ft. lbs.
⑬—Buick built engine.
⑭—With automatic transmission.
⑮—V.I.N. code A, even fire engine; V.I.N. code C, exc. even fire engine.
⑯—V.I.N. code U on 1978 & G on 1979 denotes 2 barrel carb.; V.I.N. code H denotes 4 Bbl. carb.
⑰—1982, 107 ft. lbs; 1983, 89 ft. lbs.

DRIVE AXLE SPECIFICATIONS

Year	Model	Carrier Type	Ring Gear & Pinion Backlash		Pinion Bearing Preload			Differential Bearing Preload		
			Method	Adjustment	Method	New Bearings Inch-Lbs.	Used Bearings Inch-Lbs.	Method	New Bearings Inch-Lbs.	Used Bearings Inch-Lbs.
1977–78	Toronado	Integral	Shims	.005–.009	Shims	2–15	2–5	Shims	10–15①	5–7①
1977–84	Others	Integral	Shims	.005–.009	Spacer	24–32	8–12	Shims	②	②
1979–84	Toronado	Integral	Shims	.005–.007	Spacer	22	5	Shims	②	②

①—Over pinion bearing preload. ②—Slip fit plus .004 inch clearance on each side.

ALTERNATOR SPECIFICATIONS

Year	Model	Rated Hot Output Amps.	Field Current 12 Volts @ 80° F.	Year	Model	Rated Hot Output Amps.	Field Current 12 Volts @ 80° F.	Year	Model	Rated Hot Output Amps.	Field Current 12 Volts @ 80° F.
1977–78	1101016	80	—		1100122	63	—		1100239	55	—
	1101034	80	—		1100124	63	—		1100247	63	—
	1102394	37	4–4.5		1101038	70	—		1100260	78	—
	1102479	55	—		1101044	70	—		1100263	78	—
	1102840	55	—		1101065	70	—		1100297	42	—
	1102841	42	—		1101068	70	—		1100298	55	—
	1102842	63	—		1101071	70	—		1100300	63	—
	1102843	61	4–4.5		1101074	70	—		1101264	78	—
	1102844	63	—		1103103	63	—		1105022	78	—
	1102881	37	—		1103104	42	—		1105025	63	—
	1102913	61	—		1103112	63	—		1105027	63	—
	1103033	42	—		1103186	63	—		1105029	63	—
1979	1101016	80	—		1103186	63	—		1105032	78	—
	1101028	80	—	1980–82	1100110	42	—		1105041	78	—
	1101034	80	—		1100121	63	—		1105042	78	—
	1101043	80	—		1103151	63	—		1105194	78	—
	1101048	80	—	1981	1100110	42	—		1105198	85	—
	1102394	37	4–4.5		1100121	63	—		1105250	70	—
	1102479	55	4–4.5		1100156	55	—		1105343	85	—
	1102840	55	—		1101068	70	—	1984	1100200	78	—
	1102841	42	—	1981–82	1100164	55	—		1100239	55	—
	1102842	63	—		1101037	70	—		1100260	78	—
	1102843	61	—		1101045	85	—		1105025	66	—
	1102844	63	—		1101084	85	—		1105028	78	—
	1102860	63	—		1101088	70	—		1105041	78	—
	1102881	37	—	1982	1100164	55	—		1105197	70	—
	1103033	42	—		1100165	63	—		1105548	70	—
	1103042	63	—		1100190	85	—		1105564	66	—
	1103055	42	—		1100194	70	—		1105565	78	—
	1103056	63	—		1100195	85	—		1105566	66	—
	1103076	63	—		1100198	42	—		1105567	78	—
	1103098	63	—	1983	1100200	78	—		1105568	78	—
	1103099	63	—		1100230	42	—		1105569	78	—
1980	1100111	63	—								

①—At 85° F.

STARTING MOTOR APPLICATIONS

Year	Model/V.I.N.	Starter Number	Year	Model/V.I.N.	Starter Number
1977	V6-231⑧	1108797		V8-350 Diesel/N⑥	1109215
	V8-260/F	1108765		V8-350 Diesel/N⑥	1109216
	V8-305/U④	1109056		V8-350 Diesel/N⑦	1109214
	V8-305/U⑤	1108779		V8-350 Diesel/N⑦	1109218
	V8-350/L①	1109052	1981	V6-231/A	1109061
	V8-350/R②	1108765		V6-252/4⑥	1998227
	V8-403/K③	1108764		V6-252/4	1998205
	V8-403/K⑥	1108794		V8-260/F, V8-307/Y⑦	1109523
	V8-403/K⑦	1108795		V8-307/Y③⑥	1998205
1978	V6-231/A	1109061		V8-350 Diesel/N③⑥	1109216
	V8-260/F	1109523		V8-350 Diesel/N⑦	1109218
	V8-305①⑨	1109064	1982	V6-231/A	1998236
	V8-305③⑨	1109524		V6-252/4⑥	1998234
	V8-350/L①④	1109065		V6-252/4⑦	1998237
	V8-350/L①⑤	1109067		V6-262 Diesel/V	1998552
	V8-350/R②	1109072		V8-260/8	1109544
	V8-350 Diesel/N	1109213		V8-307/Y③⑥	1109544
	V8-403/K⑥	1109072		V8-307/Y⑦	1998237
	V8-403/K⑦	1109070		V8-350 Diesel/N③⑥	1998552
1979	V6-231/A	1109061		V8-350 Diesel/N⑦	1109495
	V8-260/F, V8-301/Y	1109523	1983	V6-231/A	1998236
	V8-260 Diesel/P	1109213		V6-252/4⑥	1998234
	V8-305④⑨	1109064		V6-252/4⑦	1998237
	V8-305⑤⑨	1109074		V6-262 Diesel/V	1998554
	V8-350/L①	1109065		V8-307/Y,9③⑥	1109544
	V8-350/R②⑥	1109072		V8-307/Y⑦	1998237
	V8-350/R②⑦	1108759		V8-350 Diesel/N③⑥	1998554
	V8-350 Diesel/N	1109213		V8-350 Diesel/N⑦	1109495
	V8-403/K	1109072	1984	V6-231/A	1998236
1980	V6-231/A	1109061		V6-252/4	1998237
	V8-260/F	1109523		V6-262 Diesel/V	1998556
	V8-265/S	1109523			22511854
	V8-305/H	1109524		V8-307/Y,9③⑥	1109544
	V8-307/Y⑥	1109523		V8-307/Y⑦	1998237
	V8-307/Y⑦	1998205		V8-350 Diesel/N③⑥	1998553
	V8-350/L⑥	1109072			22511854
	V8-350/L⑦	1998205		V8-350 Diesel/N⑦	1109495

①—Chevrolet built engine. Distributor located at rear of engine, clockwise rotation.
②—Oldsmobile built engine. Distributor located at rear of engine, counter-clockwise rotation.
③—Cutlass.
④—Auto. trans.
⑤—Manual trans.
⑥—88 & 98.
⑦—Toronado.
⑧—V.I.N. code A, even fire engine; V.I.N. code C, exc. even fire engine.
⑨—V.I.N. code U on 1978 models & G on 1979 models denotes 2 Bbl. carb.; V.I.N. code H denotes 4 Bbl. carb.

VALVE SPECIFICATIONS

Year	Model/V.I.N.	Valve Lash Int.	Valve Lash Exh.	Valve Angles Seat	Valve Angles Face	Valve Spring Installed Height	Valve Spring Pressure Lbs. @ In.	Stem Clearance Intake	Stem Clearance Exhaust	Stem Diameter Intake	Stem Diameter Exhaust
1977	V6-231(15)(11)	Hydraulic(6)		45	45	1.727	(9)	.0015-.0035	.0015-.0032	.3402-.3412	.3405-.3412
	V8-260/F	Hydraulic(6)		(2)	(13)	1.67	187 @ 1.27	.0010-.0027	.0015-.0032	.3425-.3432	.3420-.3427
	V8-305/U(8)	3/4 Turn(3)		46	45	(12)	200 @ 1.25	.0010-.0027	.0010-.0027	.3410-.3417	.3410-.3417
	V8-350/R	Hydraulic(6)		(2)	(13)	1.67	187 @ 1.27	.0010-.0027	.0015-.0032	.3425-.3432	.3420-.3427
	V8-350/L(8)	3/4 Turn(3)		46	45	(12)	200 @ 1.25	.0010-.0027	.0010-.0027	.3410-.3417	.3410-.3417
	V8-403/K	Hydraulic(6)		(2)	(13)	1.67	187 @ 1.27	.0010-.0027	.0015-.0032	.3425-.3432	.3420-.3427
1978	V6-231/A(11)	Hydraulic(6)		45	45	1.727	168 @ 1.33	.0015-.0035	.0015-.0032	.3401-.3412	.3405-.3412
	V8-260/F	Hydraulic(6)		(2)	(13)	1.670	187 @ 1.27	.0010-.0027	.0015-.0032	.3425-.3432	.3420-.3427
	V8-305(8)(16)	1 Turn(3)		46	45	1.718	200 @ 1.25	.0010-.0027	.0010-.0027	.3410-.3417	.3410-.3417
	V8-350/R	Hydraulic(6)		(2)	(13)	1.67	187 @ 1.27	.0010-.0027	.0015-.0032	.3425-.3432	.3420-.3427
	V8-350/L(8)	1 Turn(3)		46	45	1.718	200 @ 1.25	.0010-.0027	.0010-.0027	.3410-.3417	.3410-.3417
	V8-350/N(1)	Hydraulic(6)		(2)	(13)	1.670	151 @ 1.30	.0010-.0027	.0015-.0032	.3425-.3432	.3420-.3427
	V8-403/K	Hydraulic(6)		(2)	(13)	1.670	187 @ 1.27	.0010-.0027	.0015-.0032	.3425-.3432	.3420-.3427
1979	V6-231/A(11)	Hydraulic(6)		45	45	1.727	168 @ 1.34	.0015-.0035	.0015-.0032	.3402-.3412	.3405-.3412
	V8-260/F	Hydraulic(6)		(2)	(13)	1.670	187 @ 1.270	.0010-.0027	.0015-.0032	.3425-.3432	.3420-.3427
	V8-260/F(1)	Hydraulic(6)		(2)	(13)	1.670	151 @ 1.30	.0010-.0027	.0015-.0032	.3425-.3432	.3420-.3427
	V8-301/Y(7)	Hydraulic(6)		46	45	1.66	166 @ 1.296	.0010-.0027	.0010-.0027	.3418-.3425	.3418-.3425
	V8-305(16)(8)	1 Turn(3)		46	45	(5)	(10)	.0010-.0027	.0010-.0027	.3410-.3417	.3410-.3417
	V8-350/R	Hydraulic(6)		(2)	(13)	1.670	187 @ 1.270	.0010-.0027	.0015-.0032	.3425-.3432	.3427-.3420
	V8-350/L(8)	1 Turn(3)		46	45	(5)	(10)	.0010-.0037	.0010-.0037	.3410-.3417	.3410-.3417
	V8-350/N(1)	Hydraulic(6)		(2)	(13)	1.670	151 @ 1.30	.0010-.0027	.0015-.0032	.3425-.3432	.3420-.3427
	V8-403/K	Hydraulic(6)		(2)	(13)	1.670	187 @ 1.270	.0010-.0027	.0015-.0032	.3425-.3432	.3420-.3427
1980	V6-231/A(11)	Hydraulic(6)		45	45	1.727	168 @ 1.34	.0015-.0035	.0015-.0032	.3402-.3412	.3405-.3412
	V8-260/F	Hydraulic(6)		(2)	(13)	1.67	187 @ 1.27	.0010-.0027	.0015-.0032	.3425-.3432	.3420-.3427
	V8-305/H(8)	1 Turn(3)		46	45	1.70	(4)	.0010-.0027	.0010-.0027	.3410-.3417	.3410-.3417
	V8-307/Y	Hydraulic(6)		(2)	(13)	1.67	187 @ 1.27	.0010-.0027	.0015-.0032	.3425-.3432	.3420-.3427
	V8-350/R	Hydraulic(6)		(2)	(13)	1.67	187 @ 1.27	.0010-.0027	.0015-.0032	.3425-.3432	.3420-.3427
	V8-350/N(1)	Hydraulic(6)		(2)	(13)	1.67	151 @ 1.30	.0010-.0027	.0015-.0032	.3425-.3432	.3420-.3427
1981	V6-231/A(11)	Hydraulic(6)		45	45	1.727	(9)	.0015-.0035	.0015-.0032	.3401-.3412	.3405-.3412
	V6-252/4(11)	Hydraulic(6)		45	45	1.727	(9)	.0015-.0035	.0015-.0032	.3401-.3412	.3405-.3412
	V8-260/F	Hydraulic(6)		(2)	(13)	1.67	187 @ 1.27	.0010-.0027	.0015-.0032	.3425-.3432	.3420-.3427
	V8-307/Y	Hydraulic(6)		(2)	(13)	1.67	187 @ 1.27	.0010-.0027	.0015-.0032	.3425-.3432	.3420-.3427
	V8-350/N(1)	Hydraulic(6)		(2)	(13)	1.67	210 @ 1.22	.0010-.0027	.0015-.0032	.3425-.3432	.3420-.3427
1982-83	V6-231/A(11)	Hydraulic(6)		45	45	1.727	(14)	.0015-.0035	.0015-.0032	.3401-.3412	.3405-.3412
	V6-252/4(11)	Hydraulic(6)		45	45	1.727	(14)	.0015-.0035	.0015-.0032	.3401-.3412	.3405-.3412
	V6-262/V(1)	Hydraulic(6)		(2)	(13)	1.67	210 @ 1.22	.0010-.0027	.0015-.0032	.3425-.3432	.3420-.3427
	V8-260/8	Hydraulic(6)		(2)	(13)	1.67	187 @ 1.27	.0010-.0027	.0015-.0032	.3425-.3432	.3420-.3427
	V8-307/Y	Hydraulic(6)		(2)	(13)	1.67	187 @ 1.27	.0010-.0027	.0015-.0032	.3425-.3432	.3420-.3427
	V8-307/9	Hydraulic(6)		(2)	(13)	1.67	210 @ 1.22	.0010-.0027	.0015-.0032	.3425-.3432	.3420-.3427
	V8-350/N(1)	Hydraulic(6)		(2)	(13)	1.67	210 @ 1.22	.0010-.0027	.0015-.0032	.3425-.3432	.3420-.3427
1984	V6-231/A(11)	Hydraulic(6)		45	45	1.727	182 @ 1.34	.0015-.0035	.0015-.0032	.3401-.3412	.3405-.3412
	V6-252/4(11)	Hydraulic(6)		45	45	1.727	182 @ 1.34	.0015-.0035	.0015-.0032	.3401-.3412	.3405-.3412
	V6-262/V(1)	Hydraulic(6)		(2)	(13)	1.67	210 @ 1.22	.0010-.0027	.0015-.0032	.3425-.3432	.3420-.3428
	V8-307/Y	Hydraulic(6)		(2)	(13)	1.67	187 @ 1.27	.0010-.0027	.0015-.0032	.3425-.3432	.3420-.3427
	V8-307/9	Hydraulic(6)		(2)	(13)	1.67	210 @ 1.22	.0010-.0027	.0015-.0032	.3425-.3432	.3420-.3427
	V8-350/N(1)	Hydraulic(6)		(2)	(13)	1.67	210 @ 1.22	.0010-.0027	.0015-.0032	.3425-.3432	.3420-.3427

(1)—Oldsmobile built diesel engine.
(2)—Intake 45°, exhaust 31°.
(3)—Tighten rocker arm adjusting screw to eliminate all push rod end clearance. Then tighten screw the number of turns listed.
(4)—Intake, 180 @ 1.25; exhaust, 190 @ 1.16.
(5)—Intake, 1.70; Exhaust, 1.61.
(6)—No adjustment.
(7)—Pontiac built engine. Distributor located at rear of engine, clockwise rotation.
(8)—Chevrolet built engine. Distributor located at rear of engine, clockwise rotation.
(9)—Intake, 164 @ 1.34; exhaust, 182 @ 1.34.
(10)—Intake, 200 @ 1.25"; Exhaust 200 @ 1.16".
(11)—Buick built engine.
(12)—Intake, 1 21/32; exhaust, 1 19/32.
(13)—Intake 44°, exhaust 30°.
(14)—Intake, 220 @ 1.34; Exhaust 177 @ 1.450.
(15)—V.I.N. code A, even fire engine; V.I.N. code C, exc. even fire engine.
(16)—V.I.N. code U on 1978 models & G on 1979 models denotes 2 Bbl. carb.; V.I.N. code H denotes 4 Bbl. carb.

PISTONS, PINS, RINGS, CRANKSHAFT & BEARINGS

Year	Model/V.I.N.	Piston Clearance	Ring End Gap[1]		Wrist-pin Diameter	Rod Bearings		Main Bearings			
			Comp.	Oil		Shaft Diameter	Bearing Clearance	Shaft Diameter	Bearing Clearance	Thrust on Bear. No.	Shaft End Play
1977	V6-231[12][17]	.0008–.0020	.010	.015	.9392	2.000	.0005–.0026	2.4995	.0004–.0015	2	.004–.008
	V8-260/F	.0010–.0020	.010	.015	.9805	2.1238–2.1248	.0004–.0033	[3]	[11]	3	.0035–.0135
	V8-305/U[8]	.0025–.0035	.010	.015	.9272	2.199–2.200	.0013–.0035	[13]	[14]	5	.002–.006
	V8-350/L[8]	.0025–.0035	.010	.015	.9272	2.199–2.200	.0013–.0035	[13]	[14]	5	.002–.006
	V8-350/R	.0010–.0020	.010	.015	.9805	2.1238–2.1248	.0004–.0033	[3]	[11]	3	.0035–.0135
	V8-403/K	.0010–.0020	.010	.015	.9805	2.1238–2.1248	.0004–.0033	[3]	[11]	3	.0035–.0135
1978	V6-231/A[12]	.0008–.0020	.010	.015	.9392	2.000	.0005–.0026	2.4995	.0004–.0015	2	.004–.008
	V8-260/F	.0010–.0020	.010	.015	.9805	2.1238–2.1248	.0004–.0033	[3]	[11]	3	.0035–.0135
	V8-305[8][18]	.0007–.0017	.010	.015	.9272	2.0986–2.0998	.0013–.0035	[13]	[14]	5	.002–.006
	V8-350/L[8]	.0007–.0017	.010	.015	.9272	2.0986–2.0998	.0013–.0035	[13]	[14]	5	.002–.006
	V8-350/R	.0010–.0020	.010	.015	.9805	2.1238–2.1248	.0004–.0033	[3]	[11]	3	.0035–.0135
	V8-350/N[6]	.0050–.0060	.015	.0015	1.0951	2.1238–2.1248	.0005–.0026	2.9993–3.0003	[11]	3	.0035–.0135
	V8-403/K	.0010–.0020	.010	.015	.9805	2.1238–2.1248	.0004–.0033	[3]	[11]	3	.0035–.0135
1979	V6-231/A[12]	.0008–.0020	.010	.015	.9392	2.2487–2.2495	.0003–.0018	2.4995	.0005–.0026	2	.004–.008
	V8-260/F	.00075–.00175	[5]	.015	.9805	2.1238–2.1248	.0004–.0033	[3]	[11]	3	.0035–.0135
	V8-260/P[6]	.00050–.00060	[15]	.015	1.0951	2.1238–2.1248	.0005–.0026	2.9993–3.0003	[11]	3	.0035–.0135
	V8-301/Y[7]	.0025–.0033	.010	.015	.9400		.0005–.0025	3.000	.0002–.0020		.003–.009
	V8-305[8][18]	.0007–.0017	.010	.015	.9272	2.0986–2.0998	.0013–.0035	[13]	[14]	5	.002–.006
	V8-350/L[8]	.0007–.0017	.010	.015	.9272	2.0986–2.0998	.0013–.0035	[13]	[14]	5	.002–.006
	V8-350/R	.00075–.00175	[5]	.015	.9805	2.1238–2.1248	.0004–.0033	[3]	[11]	3	.0035–.0135
	V8-350/N[6]	.0050–.0060	.015	.015	1.0951	2.1238–2.1248	.0005–.0026	2.9993–3.0003	[11]	3	.0035–.0135
	V8-403/K	.0005–.0015	[5]	.015	.9805	2.1238–2.1248	.0004–.0033	[3]	[11]	3	.0035–.0135
1980	V6-231/A[12]	.0011–.0023	.013	.015	.9392	2.2487–2.2495	.0004–.0033	2.4995	.0003–.0018	2	.003–.009
	V8-260/F	.00075–.00175	.010	.015	.9805	2.1238–2.1248	.0004–.0033	[2]	[11]	3	.0035–.0135
	V8-305/H[8]	.0007–.0042	[10]	.010	.9272	2.099–2.100	.0013–.0035	[13]	[14]	5	.002–.007
	V8-307/Y	.0005–.0015	.010	.015	.9805	2.1238–2.1248	.0004–.0033	[2]	[11]	3	.0035–.0135
	V8-350/L	.00075–.00175	.010	.015	.9805	2.1238–2.1248	.0005–.0026	[2]	[11]	3	.0035–.0135
	V8-350/N[6]	.0050–.0060	.015	.015	1.0951	2.1238–2.1248	.0005–.0026	3.00	[11]	3	.0035–.0135
1981	V6-231/A, 252/4[12]	.0008–.0020	.013	.015	.9392	2.2487–2.2495	.0005–.0026	2.4995	.0003–.0018	2	.003–.009
	V8-260/F	.00075–.00175	.010	.015	.9805	2.1238–2.1248	.0004–.0033	[16]	[11]	3	.0035–.0135
	V8-307/Y	.00075–.00175	.010	.015	.9805	2.1238–2.1248	.0005–.0026	[16]	[11]	3	.0035–.0135
	V8-350/N[6]	.005–.006	.015	.015	1.0951	2.1238–2.1248	.0005–.0026	3.00	[11]	3	.0035–.0135
1982–83	V6-231/A, 252/4[12]	.0008–.0020	.013	.015	.9392	2.2487–2.2495	.0005–.0026	2.4995	.0003–.0018	2	.003–.009
	V6-262/V[6]	.0035–.0045	[19]	[20]	1.0951	2.2490–2.2510	.0003–.0025	2.9993–3.0003	[4]	3	.0035–.0135
	V8-260/8	.00075–.00175	.010	.015	.9805	2.1238–2.1248	.0004–.0033	[16]	[11]	3	.0035–.0135
	V8-307/Y,9	.00075–.00175	.010	.015	.9805	2.1238–2.1248	.0004–.0033	[2]	[11]	3	.0035–.0135
	V8-350/N[6]	.003–.004	[19]	.015	1.0951	2.1238–2.1248	.0005–.0026	2.9993–3.0003	[9]	3	.0035–.0135
1984	V6-231/A, 252/4[12]	.0008–.0020	.010	.015	.9392	2.2487–2.2495	.0005–.0026	2.4995	.0003–.0018	2	.0030–.0110
	V6-262/V[6]	.0035–.0045	[19]	.010	1.0951	2.2490–2.2510	.0005–.0025	2.9993–3.0003	[4]	3	.0035–.0135
	V8-307/Y,9	.00075–.00175	.010	.015	.9805	2.1238–2.1248	.0004–.0033	[2]	[11]	3	.0035–.0135
	V8-350/N[6]	.0035–.0045	[19]	.010	1.0951	2.1238–2.1248	.0005–.0026	2.9993–3.0003	[9]	3	.0035–.0135

[1]—Fit rings in tapered bores for clearance listed in tightest portion of ring travel.
[2]—No. 2-3-4-5, 2.4990–2.4995; No. 1, 2.4993–2.4998.
[3]—No. 1: 2.4988–2.4998; Nos. 2, 3, 4, 5: 2.4985–2.4995.
[4]—Nos. 1, 2 & 3, .0005–.0021; No 4, .0020–.0034.
[5]—Refer to text under "Piston Rings".
[6]—Diesel.
[7]—Pontiac built engine. Distributor located at rear of engine, clockwise rotation.

[8]—Chevrolet built engine. Distributor located at rear of engine, clockwise rotation.
[9]—Nos. 1, 2, 3 & 4, .0005–.0021; No. 5, .0020–.0034.
[10]—Top—.010"; No. 2—.013".
[11]—No. 1, 2, 3, 4: .0015–.0021; No. 5: .0015–.0031.
[12]—Buick built engine.
[13]—No. 1: 2.4484–2.4493; No. 2, 3, 4: 2.4481–2.4490; No. 5: 2.4479–2.4488.
[14]—No. 1: .0008–.0020; No. 2, 3, 4:

.0011–.0023; No. 5: .0017–.0032.
[15]—Top—.012"; No. 2—.010".
[16]—No. 2-3-4-5, 2.4990–2.4995; No. 1, 2.4993–2.4998.
[17]—V.I.N. code A, even fire engine; V.I.N. code C, exc. even fire engine.
[18]—V.I.N. code U on 1978 models & G on 1979 models denotes 2 Bbl. carb.; V.I.N. code H denotes 4 Bbl. carb.
[19]—Top—.019"–.027"; No. 2—.013"–.021".
[20]—.015"–.055"

COOLING SYSTEM & CAPACITY DATA

Year	Model or Engine/V.I.N.	Cooling Capacity, Qts. Less A/C	Cooling Capacity, Qts. With A/C	Radiator Cap Relief Pressure, Lbs.	Thermo. Opening Temp.	Fuel Tank Gals.	Engine Oil Refill Qts. [1]	Transmission Oil 3 Speed Pints	Transmission Oil 4 Speed Pints	Transmission Oil 5 Speed Pints	Auto. Trans. Qts. [2]	Rear Axle Oil Pints
1977	6-231 Omega[8][43]	12.7	13.7	15	195	21	4	3	—	—	[14]	3½
	6-231 Cutlass[8][43]	16.9	17.0	15	195	22	4	3	—	—	[10]	4¼
	6-231[8][13][43]	11.5	11.4	15	195	[13][16]	4	—	—	—	[14]	3½
	8-260/F Omega	16.8	17.8	15	195	21	4	—	—	3½	[14]	3½
	8-260/F Cutlass	16.9	17.0	15	195	22	4	—	—	3½	[14]	4¼
	8-260/F[13]	15.5	15.3	15	195	[13][16]	4	—	—	—	[14]	3½
	8-305/U Omega	—	—	15	195	21	4	3	—	—	[14]	3½
	8-350 Omega[44]	15.6	16.6	15	195	21	4	—	—	—	[14]	3½
	8-350 Cutlass[44]	15.1	15.3	15	195	22	4	—	—	—	[14]	4¼
	8-350[13][44]	13.8	13.7	15	195	[13][16]	4	—	—	—	[14]	4¼
	8-403/K Cutlass	16.3	16.4	15	195	22	4	—	—	—	[14]	4¼
	8-403/K[13]	14.9	14.8	15	195	24½[16]	4	—	—	—	[14]	4¼
	8-403/K Toronado	17.2	17.4	15	195	26	5	—	—	—	[17]	4[3]
1978	V6-231/A Omega[8]	12.75	12.75	15	195	21	4	3.5	—	3.5	[10]	3½
	V6-231/A Cutlass[8]	12	12	15	195	17.5[24]	4	3.5	—	3.5	[14]	4¼
	V6-231/A 88[8]	12.25	12.25	15	195	25.3	4	—	—	—	[14]	[27]
	V8-260/F Cutlass	16.25[19]	16.25[19]	15	195	17.5[24]	4	—	—	3.5	[14]	4¼
	V8-260/F 88	16.25[20]	16.25[20]	15	195	25.3	4	—	—	—	[14]	[27]
	V8-305 Omega[45]	15.75[19]	16.0[19]	15	195	21	4	—	2.5	—	[10]	3½
	V8-305 Cutlass[45]	15.5[21]	15.5[21]	15	195	17.5[24]	4	—	2.5	—	[14]	4¼
	V8-350 Omega[44]	16	16.75	15	195	21	4	—	—	—	[10]	3½
	V8-350 Cutlass[44]	15.5	16.25	15	195	17.5[24]	4	—	—	—	[14]	4¼
	V8-350/N Diesel	18	18	15	195	27.25[16]	7[7][26]	—	—	—	[14]	[27]
	V8-350[13][44]	14	15.5	15	195	[5]	4	—	—	—	[14]	[27]
	V8-403/K[13]	15.75	16.5	15	195	25.3[16]	4	—	—	—	[14]	[27]
	V8-403/K Toronado	17.5[23]	17.5[23]	15	195	26	5	—	—	—	[17]	4[3]
1979	V6-231/A Omega[8]	12.75	12.75	15	195	21	4	3	—	—	[10]	3½
	V6-231/A Cutlass[8]	13.25	13.25	15	195	18.1[24]	4	3	3	—	[14]	4¼
	V6-231/A 88[8]	13.25	13.25	15	195	25	4	—	—	—	[14]	[27]
	V6-260/F Cutlass	16.25[19]	16.25[19]	15	195	18.1[24]	4	—	—	3½	[14]	4¼
	V8-260/F Cutlass[22]	20	20	15	195	19.8	7[7][25]	—	—	3½	[14]	4¼
	V8-260/F 88	16.25[20]	16.25[20]	15	195	25	4	—	—	—	[14]	[27]
	V8-301/Y 88	20[11]	20[11]	15	195	25	5[29]	—	—	—	[14]	[27]
	V8-305 Omega[45]	15.75[19]	16[19]	15	195	21	4	—	3	—	[10]	3½
	V8-305 Cutlass[45]	15.5[21]	15.5[21]	15	195	18.1[24]	4	—	3	—	[14]	4¼
	V8-350 Omega[44]	16[19]	16[19]	15	195	21	4	—	—	—	[10]	3½
	V8-350 Cutlass[9][44]	15.5[21]	15.5[21]	15	195	18.1[24]	4	—	—	—	[14]	4¼
	V8-350 Cutlass[31][44]	14.5[32]	15[32]	15	195	18.1[24]	4	—	—	—	[14]	4¼
	V8-350/N Cutlass[22]	17.5	17.5	15	195	19.8	7[7][26]	—	—	—	[14]	4¼
	V8-350[13][44]	14.5[33]	14.5[33]	15	195	[34]	4	—	—	—	[14]	[27]
	V8-350/N[13][22]	18	18	15	195	27	7[7][26]	—	—	—	[14]	[27]
	V8-350 Toronado[44]	15[35]	15[35]	15	195	20	4	—	—	—	[36]	3¼[3]
	V8-350/N Toronado[22]	18.5	18.5	15	195	22.8	7[7][26]	—	—	—	[36]	3¼[3]
	V8-403/K[13]	15.75[37]	16.5	15	195	25[16]	4	—	—	—	[14]	[27]
1980	V6-231/A Cutlass[8]	13	13	15	195	18[24]	4	3	—	—	[37]	4½
	V6-231/A 88[8]	13	13	15	195	25	4	—	—	—	[37]	[27]
	V8-260/F Cutlass	16[25]	16[25]	15	195	18[24]	4	—	—	—	[37]	4¼
	V8-305/H Cutlass	15¼[38]	15¼[38]	15	195	18[24]	4	—	—	—	[12]	4¼
	V8-307/Y 88 & 98	15½[39]	15½[39]	15	195	25[16]	4	—	—	—	[12]	[27]
	V8-307/Y Toronado	16¼	16¼	15	195	21	4	—	—	—	[36]	3¼[3]
	V8-350/R Cutlass	15	15	15	195	18[24]	4	—	—	—	[37]	4¼
	V8-350/R 88 & 98	14½[35]	14½[35]	15	195	25[16]	4	—	—	—	[12]	[27]
	V8-350/R Toronado	15½[32]	15½[32]	15	195	21	4	—	—	—	[36]	3¼[3]

Continued

COOLING SYSTEM & CAPACITY DATA—Continued

Year	Model or Engine/V.I.N.	Cooling Capacity, Qts. Less A/C	With A/C	Radiator Cap Relief Pressure, Lbs.	Thermo. Opening Temp.	Fuel Tank Gals.	Engine Oil Refill Qts. (1)	Transmission Oil 3 Speed Pints	4 Speed Pints	5 Speed Pints	Auto. Trans. Qts. (2)	Rear Axle Oil Pints
	V8-350/N Cutlass(22)	17¼	17¼	15	195	19¾(24)	7(7)(26)	—	—	—	(40)	4¼
	V8-350/N 88 & 98(22)	18¼	18	15	195	27(16)	7(7)(26)	—	—	—	(37)	(27)
	V8-350/N Toronado(22)	18	18	15	195	23	7(7)(26)	—	—	—	(36)	3¼(3)
1981	V6-231/A Cutlass(8)	13(41)	13(41)	15	195	18	4	3	—	—	(42)	4¼
	V6-231/A 88(8)	13	13	15	195	25	4	—	—	—	(42)	4¼
	V6-252/4 98	12.8	12.8	15	195	25	4	—	—	—	(18)	4¼
	V6-252/4 Toronado	13.1	13.1	15	195	21	4	—	—	—	(18)	3¼(3)
	V8-260/F Cutlass	15.9(25)	15.5(25)	15	195	18	4	—	—	—	(42)	4¼
	V8-260/F 88	16.5(20)	16.2(20)	15	195	25(16)	4	—	—	—	(42)	4¼
	V8-307/Y Cutlass	14.9(33)	15.6	15	195	18	4	—	—	—	(42)	4¼
	V8-307/Y 88 & Cust. Cruiser	15.6(21)	15.3(21)	15	195	25(16)	4	—	—	—	(30)	4¼
	V8-307/Y 98	16.2	16.2	15	195	25	4	—	—	—	(18)	4¼
	V8-307/Y Toronado	16.5	16.5	15	195	21	4	—	—	—	(28)	3¼(3)
	V8-350/N Cutlass(22)	17.4	17.3	15	195	19¾(4)	7(7)(26)	—	—	—	(30)	4¼
	V8-350/N 88 & 98(22)	18.3	18	15	195	27(16)	7(7)(26)	—	—	—	(42)	4¼
	V8-350/N Toronado(22)	18	18	15	195	23	7(7)(26)	—	—	—	(28)	3¾(3)
1982	V6-231/A Cutlass(8)	13(41)	13(41)	15	195	18	4	—	—	—	(6)	(4)
	V6-231/A 88(8)	13	13	15	195	25(16)	4	—	—	—	(6)	(4)
	V6-252/4 98	12.8	12.8	15	195	25	4	—	—	—	(6)	(4)
	V6-252/4 Toronado	13.1	13.1	15	195	21	4	—	—	—	(6)	3¼(3)
	V6-262/V(22)	14.5	15.3	15	195	19.75	7(7)(26)	—	—	—	(6)	(4)
	V8-260/8	16.5(20)	16.2(20)	15	195	25(16)	4	—	—	—	(6)	(4)
	V8-307/Y Cutlass	14.9(33)	15.6	15	195	25(16)	4	—	—	—	(6)	(4)
	V8-307/Y 88 & Custom Cruiser	15.6(21)	15.3(21)	15	195	25(16)	4	—	—	—	(6)	(4)
	V8-307/Y 98	16.2	16.2	15	195	25	4	—	—	—	(6)	(4)
	V8-307/Y Toronado	16.5	16.5	15	195	21	4	—	—	—	(6)	3¼(3)
	V8-350/N Cutlass(22)	17.4	17.3	15	195	19.75(24)	7(7)(26)	—	—	—	(6)	(4)
	V8-350/N 88 & 98(22)	18	18	15	195	26.5(16)	7(7)(26)	—	—	—	(6)	(4)
	V8-350/N Toronado(22)	18.1	18.1	15	195	22.75	7(7)(26)	—	—	—	(6)	3¼(3)
1983	V6-231/A Cutlass	13(46)	13(46)	15	195	18	4	—	—	—	(6)	(4)
	V6-231/A 88	13	13	15	195	25(16)	4	—	—	—	(6)	(4)
	V6-252/4 98	12.5	12.5	15	195	25	4	—	—	—	(6)	(4)
	V6-252/4 Toronado	13.25	13.25	15	195	21	4	—	—	—	(6)	3¼(3)
	V6-262/V(22)	13.75	14.25	15	195	19.8(48)	6(7)(26)	—	—	—	(6)	(4)
	V8-307/Y Cutlass	14.75	15.5	15	195	18	4	—	—	—	(6)	(4)
	V8-307/Y 88	15.5(47)	15.3(47)	15	195	25	4	—	—	—	(6)	(4)
	V8-307/Y 98	15.25(47)	15.25(47)	15	195	25	4	—	—	—	(6)	(4)
	V8-307/Y Toronado	16.25	16.25	15	195	21	4	—	—	—	(6)	3¼(3)
	V8-350/N Cutlass	17.5	17.5	15	195	19.8	7(7)(26)	—	—	—	(6)	(4)
	V8-350/N 88 & 98	18.25	18	15	195	26	7(7)(26)	—	—	—	(6)	(4)
	V8-350/N Toronado	18.25	18.25	15	195	22.8	7(7)(26)	—	—	—	(6)	3¼(3)
1984	V6-231/A Cutlass	13(46)	13(46)	15	195	18.2	4	—	—	—	(6)	(4)
	V6-231/A 88	13	13	15	195	25(16)	4	—	—	—	(6)	(4)
	V6-252/4 Toronado	—	12.5	15	195	21	4	—	—	—	(6)	3⅓(3)
	V6-262/V(22) Cutlass	13.6	14.4	15	195	19.8	6(7)(26)	—	—	—	(6)	(4)
	V8-307/Y Cutlass	14.9	15.6	15	195	18.2	4	—	—	—	(6)	(4)
	V8-307/Y 88 & 98	15.6(47)	15.3(47)	15	195	25	4	—	—	—	(6)	(4)
	V8-307/Y Toronado	—	16.4	15	195	21	4	—	—	—	(6)	3⅓(3)
	V8-350/N Cutlass	17.4	17.3	15	195	19.8	7(7)(26)	—	—	—	(6)	(4)
	V8-350/N 88 & 98	18.3	18	15	195	27(16)	7(7)(26)	—	—	—	(6)	(4)
	V8-350/N Toronado	—	18.2	15	195	22.8	7(7)(26)	—	—	—	(6)	3⅓(3)

Continued

2-793

COOLING SYSTEM & CAPACITY DATA NOTES—Continued

①—Add one quart with filter change.
②—Approximate; make final check with dipstick.
③—Final drive
④—7.5 inch ring gear, 3.5 pints; 8.5 inch ring gear, 4.25 pints.
⑤—Delta 88 sedan & Calif. coupe, 21 gals.; Custom Cruiser, 22 gals.; all others 25.3 gals.
⑥—THM 200C, oil pan 4⅛ qts.; total capacity, 10½ qts. THM 2004R, oil pan 5 qts.; total capacity, 11 qts. THM 250C & 350C, oil pan 3⅛ qts.; total capacity 10 qts. THM 325-4L, oil pan 5½ qts.; total capacity 13 qts.
⑦—Recommended diesel engine oil—1978, use oil designation SE/CD; 1979–80, use oil designation SE/CC; 1981, use oil designation SF/CC, SF/CD or SE/CC; 1982–84 use oil designation SF/CC or SF/CD.
⑧—Buick built engine.
⑨—Chevrolet built engine. Distributor located at rear of engine, clockwise rotation.
⑩—Oil pan only 3 qts. After overhaul 10 qts.
⑪—Trailer towing, 21 qts.
⑫—T.H.M. 200 & 200C, oil pan 3½ qts.; after overhaul 9½ qts.; T.H.M. 250C, oil pan 4 qts., after overhaul 10 qts.; T.H.M. 350 & 350C, oil pan 3¼ qts., after overhaul 12¼ qts.; T.H.M. 400, oil pan 3 qts., after overhaul 10 qts.

⑬—Full size cars.
⑭—Turbo Hydro-matic 200: Oil pan only, 3 qts.; after overhaul, 9 qts. T.H. 250, 350 & 400: pan only, 3 qts.; after overhaul 10 qts.
⑮—Delta 88 except Calif. V8-350: 21 gals.; Calif. V8-350 & Ninety-Eight models: 24½ gals.
⑯—Custom Cruiser 22 gallons.
⑰—Oil pan only 4 qts. after overhaul 12 qts.
⑱—Oil pan, 3½ qts.; after overhaul, 11¼ qts.
⑲—Heavy duty & trailer towing, 16.75 qts.
⑳—Trailer towing, 17.0 qts.; Heavy duty, 17.25 qts.
㉑—Heavy duty & trailer towing, 16.25 qts.
㉒—Diesel engine.
㉓—Trailer towing, 17.25 qts.
㉔—Cutlass Cruiser, 18.25 gals.
㉕—Heavy duty cooling system & trailer tow, 16½ qts.
㉖—Includes filter.
㉗—Exc. 7.5" ring gear, 4.25 pts.; 7.5" ring gear, 3.5 pts.
㉘—Oil pan, 5¼ qts.; after overhaul, 13½ qts.
㉙—With or without filter change.
㉚—T.H.M. 200-4R, oil pan 3½ qts., after overhaul 11¼ qts.; T.H.M. 250C, oil pan 3¼ qts., after overhaul 10 qts.
㉛—Oil pan, 4¼ qts., after overhaul, 10½ qts.
㉜—Trailer towing, 15.25 qts.

㉝—Heavy duty & trailer towing, 15.5 qts.
㉞—Delta 88 Calif. models & models with power seats, 20.7 gals.; Custom Cruiser, 22 gals.; all other models, 25 gals.
㉟—Heavy duty, 16 qts.; trailer towing 15.5 qts.
㊱—Oil pan, 5 qts.; after overhaul, 12 qts.
㊲—T.H.M. 200 & 200C, oil pan 3½ qts., after overhaul 9½ qts.; T.H.M. 350 & 350C, oil pan 3¼ qts., after overhaul 12¼ qts.
㊳—With heavy duty cooling system, 16 qts.
㊴—High capacity, 16¼ qts., heavy duty trailer tow, 16 qts.
㊵—Oil pan, 3½ qts.; after overhaul 9½ qts.
㊶—With heavy duty or trailer tow, 13.6 qts.
㊷—T.H.M. 200C, oil pan 4¼ qts., after overhaul 10½ qts.; T.H.M. 250C & 350C, oil pan 3¼ qts., after overhaul 10 qts.
㊸—V.I.N. code A, even fire engine; V.I.N. code C, exc. even fire engine.
㊹—V.I.N. code R, Oldsmobile built engine; V.I.N. code L, Chevrolet built engine.
㊺—V.I.N. code U on 1978 models & G on 1979 models denotes 2 Bbl. carb.; V.I.N. code H denotes 4 Bbl. carb.
㊻—With high capacity, 13.25 qts.
㊼—High capacity cooling, 16.25 qts.; heavy duty trailer tow, 16 qts.
㊽—Cutlass Cruiser, 18 qts.

Electrical Section

IGNITION LOCK, REPLACE

1979–84

1. Remove steering wheel as described under Horn Sounder and Steering Wheel, Replace.
2. Remove turn signal switch as described under Turn Signal Switch. Replace, then remove buzzer switch.
3. Place ignition switch in Run position, then remove lock cylinder retaining screw and lock cylinder.
4. To install, rotate lock cylinder to stop while holding housing, Fig. 1. Align cylinder key with keyway in housing, then push lock cylinder assembly into housing until fully seated.
5. Install lock cylinder retaining screw. Torque screw to 40 in. lbs. for standard columns. On adjustable columns, torque retaining screw to 22 in. lbs.
6. Install buzzer switch, turn signal switch and steering wheel.

1977–78

1. Follow the procedure to remove the turn signal switch as described further on.
2. Position the lock assembly in "Run" position. Insert a long thin screwdriver into the slot as shown in Fig. 2 and pull outward on lock assembly to remove.
3. To install lock, hold lock cylinder sleeve and rotate knob clockwise against stop, then insert cylinder with key on cylinder sleeve aligned with keyway in housing. Push in to abutment of cylinder and sector, then rotate knob counterclockwise, maintaining a light inward push on cylinder until drive section of cylinder mates with drive shaft. Push in until ring snaps into groove and lock cylinder is secured.

STARTER, REPLACE

NOTE: Upon removal of starter, note if any shims are used. If shims are used, they should be reinstalled in their original location during installation.

If starter is noisy during cranking, remove one .015 inch double shim or add one .015 inch single shim to the outer bolt. If starter makes a high pitched whine after firing, add .015 inch double shims until noise ceases.

1979 V8-260 Diesel W/Man. Trans.

1. Disconnect battery ground cable.

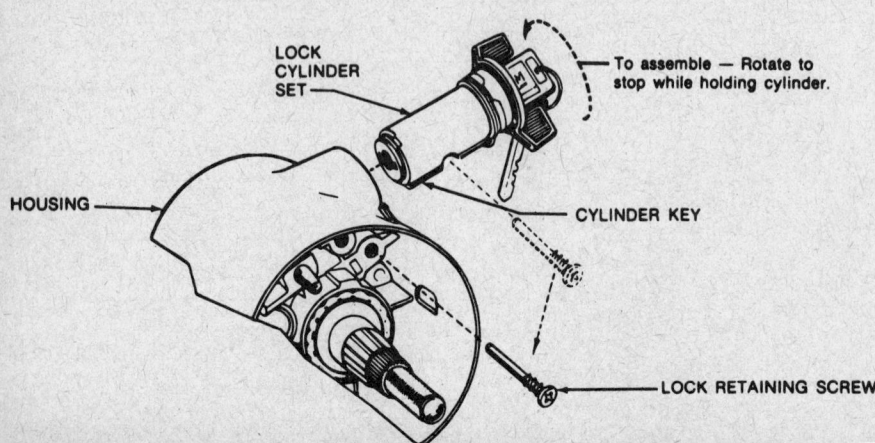

Fig. 1 Ignition lock removal. 1979–84

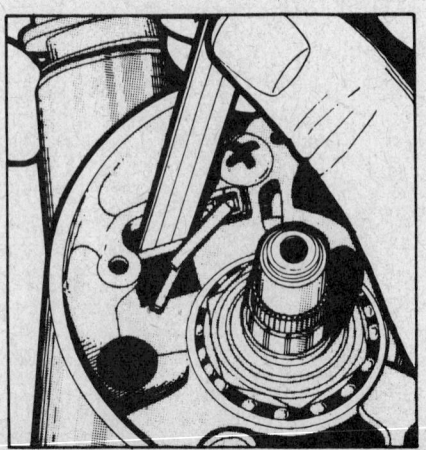

Fig. 2 Ignition lock removal. 1977–78

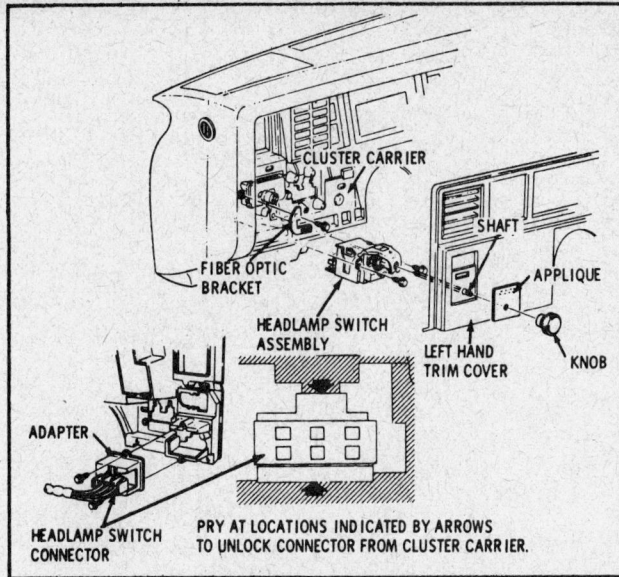

Fig. 3 Headlight switch. 1979—84 Toronado

Fig. 4 Headlight switch. 1978—84 Cutlass

2. Remove fan shroud attaching screws and leave shroud loose.
3. Remove clutch equalizer shaft, if equipped.
4. Support engine with a suitable jack, disconnect engine mounts and raise engine approximately 1½ inches.
5. Disconnect starter wiring.
6. Remove starter attaching bolts and the starter.
7. Reverse procedure to install. If shims were removed, they must be installed in their original location.

1977—84 V6-231 & 252

1. Disconnect battery ground cable, then raise and support vehicle.
2. On vehicles with automatic transmission, disconnect exhaust crossover pipe and disconnect oil cooler lines at transmission, then remove flywheel housing cover.
3. On vehicles with manual transmission, remove front crossmember to body bolts, right and left brace to crossmember bolts, then remove crossmember.
4. Remove starter bolts, then lower the starter, disconnect electrical leads and remove starter.
5. Reverse procedure to install.

1977—84 Exc. Toronado, V6-231 & 252 & V8-260 Diesel With Man. Trans.

1. Disconnect battery ground cable, then raise and support vehicle.
2. On all except V8-305 and 350 Chev. built engine:
   a. Remove upper support retaining bolts.
   b. On V8 engines, remove flywheel housing cover.
3. On V8-305 and 350 Chev. built engine, disconnect starter brace, then remove the wire guide retaining bolts.
4. Remove starter retaining bolts, then lower starter, disconnect electrical leads and remove starter.
5. Reverse procedure to install.

1977—84 Toronado

1. Disconnect battery ground cable, then raise and support vehicle.
2. Remove starter attaching bolts and position starter so that starter wiring can be disconnected.
3. Disconnect starter wiring, then lower starter from vehicle.
4. Reverse procedure to install. If shims were removed, they must be installed in their original location.

IGNITION SWITCH, REPLACE

1977—84

1. Disconnect battery ground cable.
2. On models with regular steering column, turn ignition lock to "Off-Unlock" position. On models with tilt and telescope steering column, turn ignition lock to "Accessory" position.
3. Remove cover attaching bolts, loosen toe pan clamp bolts and remove trim cap from lower part of panel.
4. Remove bracket retaining nuts and lower steering column to the seat.
5. Disconnect and remove switch.
6. On models equipped with column mounted dimmer switch, remove two switch attaching screws, then remove switch and disconnect wire connector.
7. Be sure that lock is in same position as when switch was removed then install switch onto actuator and column.
8. Connect wiring and reinstall column. On models with column mounted dimmer switch, install and adjust dimmer switch as described under "Column Mounted Dimmer Switch."

LIGHT SWITCH, REPLACE

1979—84 Toronado

1. Disconnect battery ground cable.
2. Remove headlamp switch knob, radio

knobs and steering column trim cover.
3. Remove four screws from underside of left hand trim cover, Fig. 3.
4. Remove left hand sound absorber, then carefully pull left hand trim cover from instrument panel.

NOTE: It may be necessary to disconnect shift indicator cable clip and lower steering column slightly to remove left hand trim cover.

5. Remove two screws attaching switch to instrument cluster carrier, then pull switch rearward to remove.
6. To disconnect wire connector, remove two connector attaching screws, then pry connector at locations shown in Fig. 3.
7. Reverse procedure to install.

1978—84 Cutlass

1. Disconnect battery ground cable.
2. Remove cluster pad assembly.
3. Remove two headlight switch mounting screws, then pull switch away from panel adapter.
4. To disconnect wire connector, pry connector at locations indicated by arrows as shown in Fig. 4. Pull connector out, then slide to left and push forward to remove.
5. Reverse procedure to install. Refer to Fig. 4, to install wire connector.

1977—81 88 & 98

1. Disconnect battery ground cable.
2. Rotate headlight switch so notch on switch faces downward. Bend a ⅛ inch hook on a piece of stiff wire. Use the wire hook in the notch to pull the knob retainer clip and pull knob off shaft.
3. Remove twilight sentinel knob.
4. Position steering column collar upward and remove column lower trim cover.
5. Remove two screws securing trim cover to cluster carrier.
6. Pull trim cover from clips.
7. Remove light switch mounting plate screws.
8. Pull switch through opening and disconnect electrical connector.
9. Remove nut and switch from mounting plate.
10. Reverse procedure to install.

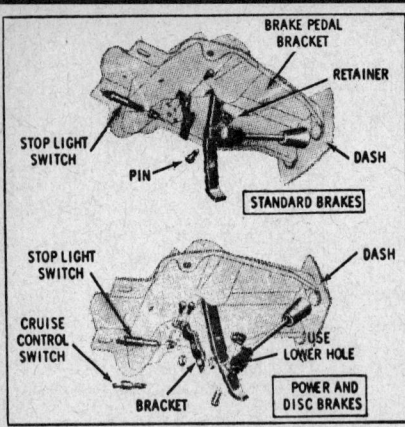

Fig. 5 Brake switch installation. 1977–84

1982–84 88 & 98

1. Disconnect battery ground cable.
2. Remove steering column trim cover, gage cluster and headlamp switch knob.
3. Remove two screws attaching left side trim cover to cluster carrier, then remove trim cover by pulling rearward.
4. Remove two screws attaching mounting plate to cluster carrier.
5. Pull switch and mounting plate rearward and disconnect electrical connector.
6. Remove nut and separate mounting plate from switch.
7. Reverse procedure to install.

1977–78 Toronado

1. Disconnect battery ground cable.
2. Without disconnecting vacuum hoses or electrical connectors, remove heater or air conditioning control.
3. Remove switch escutcheon and pull switch through heater or air conditioning control opening in cluster and disconnect electrical connector.
4. Reverse procedure to install.

1977 Cutlass

Less Air Conditioning
1. Disconnect battery ground cable.
2. Remove steering column trim cover.
3. Pull switch to "On," and push in button on switch rear, then pull switch knob and shaft from switch.
4. Remove switch escutcheon, pull switch from panel and disconnect electrical connector.
5. Reverse procedure to install.

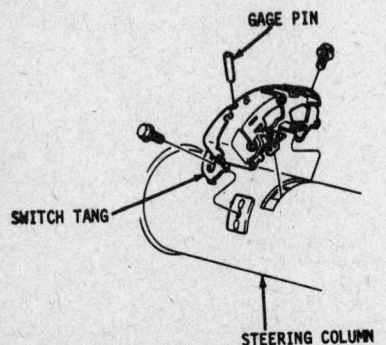

Fig. 7 Back-up light switch adjustment. 1977–79 88 & 98, 1978–79 Cutlass & 1979 Toronado

With Air Conditioning
1. Disconnect battery ground cable.
2. Remove steering column trim cover and disconnect A/C outlet hose.
3. Disconnect parking brake release cable.
4. Remove screws securing left hand control panel and pull control panel from instrument panel.
5. Disconnect switch electrical connector.
6. Pull switch to "On" and push in button on switch rear, then pull switch knob and shaft from switch.
7. Remove switch escutcheon and switch.
8. Reverse procedure to install.

1977–79 Omega

1. Disconnect battery ground cable.
2. Disconnect multiple connector from switch.
3. Pull knob out to headlight "On" position, then depress spring-loaded button on switch body and pull knob out of switch assembly.
4. Remove switch escutcheon.
5. Remove switch from rear of panel.
6. Reverse procedure to install.

STOP LIGHT SWITCH

1977–84

The stop light switch is attached to the brake pedal bracket and is actuated by the brake pedal arm, Fig. 5. When installing the switch, insert switch into tubular clip until switch body seats on tube clip. Pull brake pedal rearward until it contacts brake pedal stop. This moves the switch in the tubular clip providing proper adjustment.

CLUTCH START SWITCH

1977–81

All cars equipped with a manual transmission use a clutch start switch which is mounted on the pedal bracket. The switch closes when the clutch is depressed and completes solenoid connection. When installing switch, no adjustment is necessary.

NEUTRAL START & BACK-UP LIGHT SWITCH, REPLACE

1977 Cutlass, 1977–79 Omega & 1977–78 Toronado

1. Place gear selector in "Neutral" for column shift models, or "Park" for console shift models.
2. Remove screws attaching switch to steering column, then remove switch.
3. Disconnect wiring connectors. Connect wiring connectors to new switch.
4. Position new switch on steering column and loosely install screws.
5. Install .090 inch gauge pin in switch as shown in Fig. 6.
6. Rotate switch until gauge pin aligns with the alignment hole in inner plastic slide.
7. Torque switch attaching screws to 20 inch lbs. and remove gauge pin.

NOTE: Do not overtorque attaching screws.

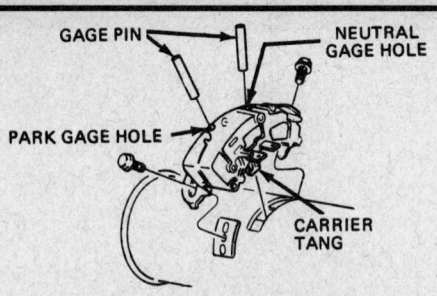

Fig. 6 Back-up light or neutral start/back-up light switch adjustment

8. Ensure vehicle will start in "Park" or "Neutral" only. If not, repeat procedure.

BACK-UP LIGHT SWITCH, REPLACE

1977–79 88 & 98, 1978–79 Cutlass & 1979 Toronado

1. Place gear selector in "Neutral".
2. Remove screws attaching switch to steering column, then remove switch.
3. Disconnect wiring connectors. Connect wiring connectors to new switch.
4. Position new switch on steering column, aligning the switch carrier tang in the switch tube slot.
5. Install attaching screws and tighten.

NOTE: No adjustment is required. The switch is pinned in the proper position with a plastic shear pin.

6. If adjustment is required:
   a. Place gear selector in "Neutral".
   b. Loosen switch attaching screws.
   c. While rotating switch on column, insert a .096 inch gauge pin in neutral gauge hole a depth of 3/8 inch, Fig. 7.
   d. Tighten attaching screws and remove gauge pin.

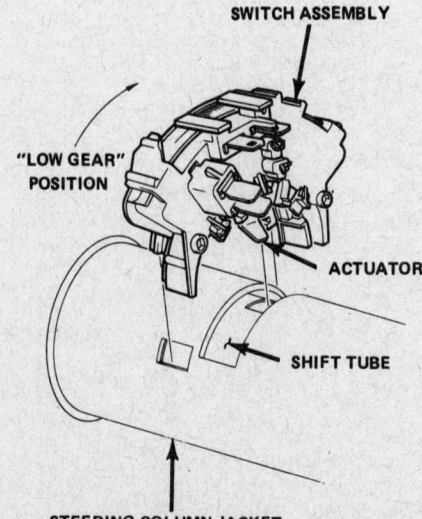

Fig. 7A Back-up light switch installation. 1981 V-8 Toronado & 1982–84 models

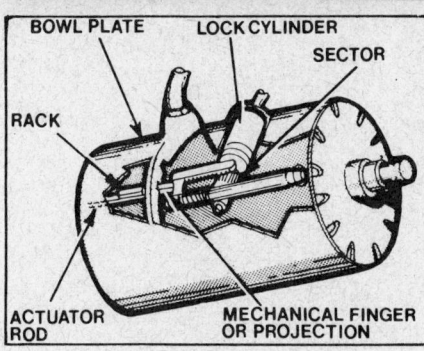

Fig. 8 Mechanical neutral start system with standard column. 1977—84 88, 98, 1978—84 Cutlass 1979—84 Toronado

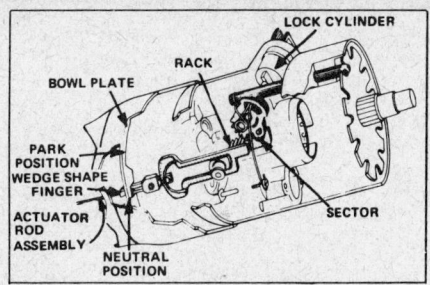

Fig. 9 Mechanical neutral start system with tilt column. 1977—84 88, 98, 1978—84 Cutlass 1979—84 Toronado

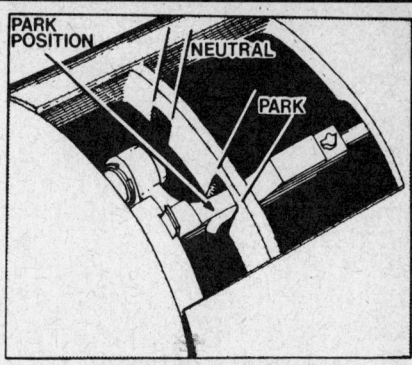

Fig. 10 Mechanical neutral start system in Park position. 1977—84 88, 98, 1978—84 Cutlass 1979—84 Toronado

1980—81 Models Exc. 1981 V8 Toronado

1. On 1980 models and 1981 models with column shift, place gear selector in "Neutral". On 1981 models with console shift, place gear selector in "Park".
2. Remove screws attaching switch to steering column, then remove switch.
3. Disconnect wiring connectors. Connect wiring connectors to new switch.
4. Position new switch on steering column and loosely install screws.
5. Install .096 inch gauge pin in switch as shown in Fig. 6.
6. Rotate switch until gauge pin aligns with the alignment hole in inner plastic slide.
7. On 1981 models with console shift, rotate shift bowl clockwise to remove free play, then lightly hold against stop.
8. Tighten attaching screws and remove gauge pin.
9. Ensure vehicle will start in "Park" and "Neutral" only. If not, repeat procedure.

1981 V8 Toronado & 1982—84 Models

1. Place gear selector in "Neutral".
2. Gently rock back-up light switch out of steering column.
3. Disconnect wiring connectors. Connect wiring connectors to new switch.
4. Align switch actuator with hole in shift tube, Fig. 7A.
5. Position connector side of switch into lower jacket cut out.

6. Push down front of switch, ensuring switch tangs snap into holes in steering column jacket.
7. Adjust switch by placing gear selector in "Park" position. The switch main housing and housing back should ratchet, providing proper adjustment.

NEUTRAL START SYSTEM

1977—84 88 & 98, 1978—84 Cutlass & 1979—84 Toronado

Actuation of the ignition switch is prevented by a mechanical lockout system, Figs. 8 and 9, which prevents the lock cylinder from rotating when the selector lever is out of Park or Neutral. When the selector lever is in Park or Neutral, the slots in the bowl plate and the finger on the actuator rod align allowing the finger to pass through the bowl plate in turn actuating the ignition switch, Fig. 10. If the selector lever is in any position other than Park or Neutral, the finger contacts the bowl plate when the lock cylinder is rotated, thereby preventing full travel of the lock cylinder.

TURN SIGNAL SWITCH, REPLACE

1977—84 Tilt & Telescope

1. Disconnect battery ground cable and remove steering wheel.
2. Remove instrument panel lower trim panel, then disconnect turn signal harness connector. Remove connector from packet mounting bracket and wrap tape around connector and wires to prevent wires from snagging when removing switch, Fig. 11.
3. Remove four bolts securing column bracket assembly to mast jacket.
4. Disconnect shift indicator.
5. Hold column in position and remove two nuts securing column bracket assembly. Then, remove bracket and turn signal wiring connector. Loosely re-install bracket to hold column in place.
6. Remove rubber bumper and plastic retainer.
7. Using a suitable compressor, Fig. 12, depress lock plate far enough to remove "C" ring from shaft.

NOTE: On Tilt & Telescope, compressor must be positioned on large lips of cancelling cam.

8. Remove lock plate and carrier assembly, then the upper bearing spring.
9. On models less column mounted dimmer switch, place turn signal lever in right turn position and unscrew lever. Lift tilt lever and position in center position.
10. On models with column mounted dimmer switch, remove actuator arm screw and actuator arm, then remove turn signal lever by pulling straight out to disengage.
11. Push in hazard warning knob, then remove screw and hazard warning knob.
12. Remove turn signal switch attaching screws, then pull switch and wiring from top of column.

1977—84 Exc. Tilt & Telescope

1. Disconnect battery ground cable.
2. Remove steering wheel.
3. Remove cover screws and cover.
4. Using suitable compressor, depress lock plate far enough to remove the "C" ring from shaft.
5. Remove lock plate, cancelling cam, spring and signal lever.
6. Depress hazard warning knob then unscrew knob and remove.
7. On models less column mounted dimmer switch, position lever in right turn position and remove three switch attaching screws.
8. On models with column mounted dimmer switch, remove actuator arm screw and actuator arm, then remove turn signal lever by pulling straight out to disengage.

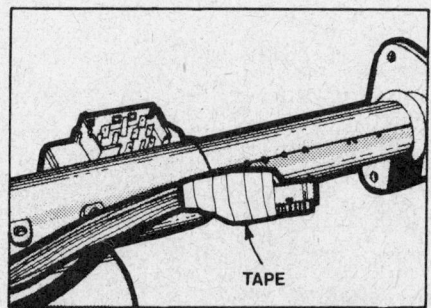

Fig. 11 Taping turn signal connector and wires

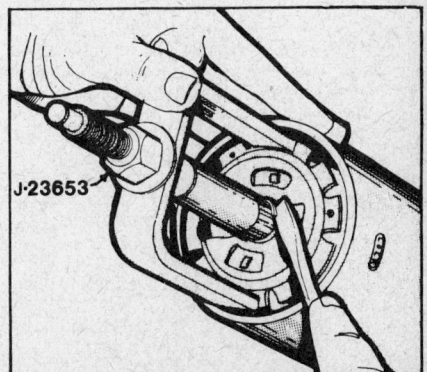

J-23653

Fig. 12 Compressing lock plate and removing retaining ring

9. Remove panel lower trim cap, disconnect switch harness and remove bolts attaching bracket to column jacket.
10. Disconnect shift indicator if equipped.
11. Remove two nuts holding column in position, remove bracket and wire protector while holding column in position then loosely install bracket to hold column in place.
12. Tape switch wires at connector keeping wires flat, then carefully remove wires and switch.

COLUMN-MOUNTED DIMMER SWITCH, REPLACE

1977–84 88, 98, 1978 Cutlass & 1979–84 Toronado

1. Disconnect battery ground cable.
2. Remove instrument panel lower trim and on models with A/C, remove A/C duct extension at column.
3. Disconnect shift indicator from column and remove toe-plate cover screws.
4. Remove two nuts from instrument panel support bracket studs and lower steering column, resting steering wheel on front seat.
5. Remove dimmer switch retaining screw and the switch. Tape actuator rod to column and separate switch from rod.

NOTE: On 1978–84 models, two screws are used to retain dimmer switch to steering column.

6. Reverse procedure to install. To adjust switch, depress dimmer switch slightly and install a 3/32 inch twist drill to lock the switch to the body. Force switch upward to remove lash between switch and pivot. Torque switch retaining screw to 35 inch lbs. and remove tape from actuator rod. Remove twist drill and check for proper operation.

HORN SOUNDER & STEERING WHEEL, REPLACE

1. Disconnect battery ground cable.
2. For tilt and telescope steering column proceed as follows:
   a. Remove pad assembly retaining screws, disconnect connector and remove pad assembly.
   b. Move locking lever counterclockwise until full release is obtained. Scribe a mark on the plate assembly where the two screws attach plate assembly to locking lever (for ease of installation) and remove the two screws.
   c. Unscrew and remove plate assembly.
3. For standard wheel, pull up on horn cap retainer assembly and disconnect horn contacts.
4. For Deluxe wheel, remove three screws from pad assembly and disconnect connectors.
5. On sport wheel, pull up on and remove emblem and horn contact assembly from wheel.
6. On Wood Grain wheel, carefully pry horn cap assembly from wheel.
7. On all models, remove steering wheel nut

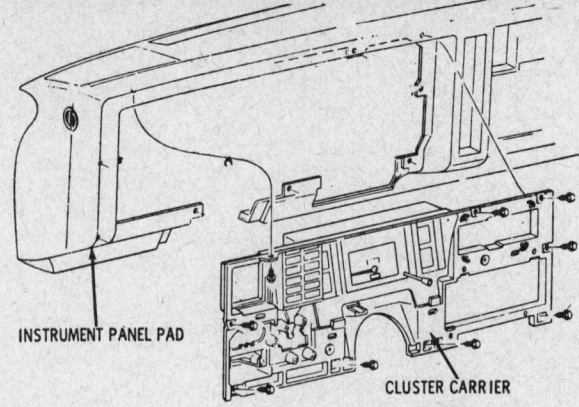

Fig. 13 Instrument cluster. 1979–84 Toronado

and using a suitable puller, remove steering wheel.

NOTE: Some vehicles have a snap ring on the end of the steering shaft which must be removed before removing steering wheel nut.

8. Reverse procedure to install.

INSTRUMENT CLUSTER, REPLACE

NOTE: On some 1980–84 models, a yellow flag with the word emissions will rotate into the odometer window at 30,000 mile intervals indicating either a catalyst or oxygen sensor change is required. After performing the required maintenance, reset the emissions flag as follows:
a. On Cutlass models, remove cluster pad assembly. On 88, 98 and Toronado, remove left hand trim cover.
b. On all models, remove trip odometer reset knob, if equipped.

c. Remove screws attaching cluster lens to cluster assembly and remove lens.
d. Using a pointed tool inserted at an angle to engage flag wheel detents, rotate flag wheel downward. When flag wheel is reset, the alignment mark will be in center of odometer window.

1979–84 Toronado

1. Disconnect battery ground cable.
2. Remove headlamp switch knob, radio knobs and steering column trim cover.
3. Remove four screws from underside of left hand trim cover.
4. Remove left hand sound absorber, then pull left hand trim cover from instrument panel.

NOTE: It may be necessary to disconnect shift indicator cable clip and lower steering column slightly to remove left hand trim cover.

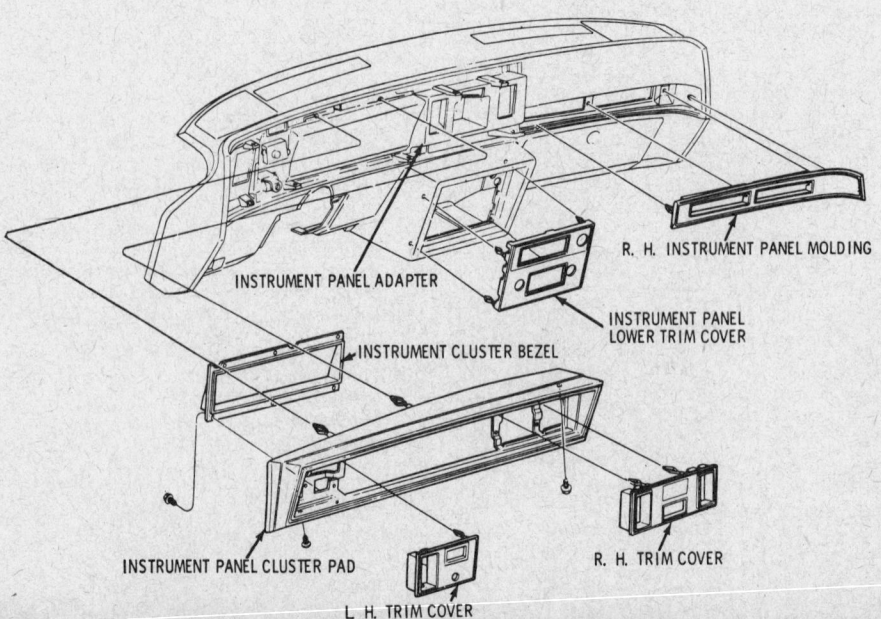

Fig. 14 Instrument panel cluster pad. 1978–84 Cutlass

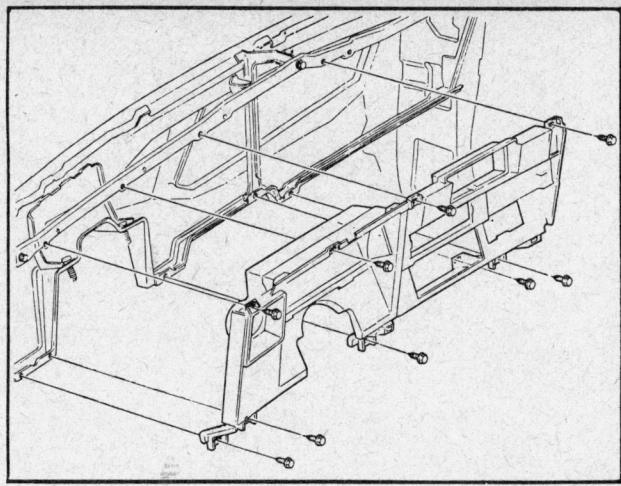

Fig. 15   Instrument cluster. 1977–84 88 & 98

5. Remove two screws attaching headlamp switch to cluster carrier, then pull switch from carrier.
6. Remove windshield wiper switch, then remove radio from instrument panel.
7. Remove four screws attaching heater-A/C control to cluster. Pull control out of cluster and disconnect wiring, vacuum lines and temperature control cable, then remove control assembly.
8. Unlock headlamp switch, windshield wiper, cruise control and defogger switch connectors from cluster carrier, then disconnect speedometer cable.
9. Remove nine cluster carrier attaching screws, then remove cluster carrier, Fig. 13.

1978–84 Cutlass

1. Disconnect battery ground cable.
2. Remove right hand and left hand trim panels, Fig. 14.
3. Remove the 7 screws retaining cluster pad to panel adapter.
4. Pull panel pad to disengage it from retaining clips and remove pad assembly, Fig. 14.
5. Remove steering column trim cover, then disconnect shift indicator clip from shift bowl.
6. Remove the 4 screws retaining cluster assembly, then disconnect speedometer cable and electrical connectors and remove cluster assembly.
7. Reverse procedure to install.

1977–84 88 & 98

1. Disconnect battery ground cable.
2. Rotate headlight switch so notch on switch faces downward. Bend a 1/8 inch hook on a piece of stiff wire. Use the wire

hook in the notch to pull the knob retainer clip and pull knob off shaft.
3. Remove twilight sentinel knob.
4. Position steering column collar upward and remove column lower trim cover.
5. Remove two screws securing trim cover to cluster carrier, Fig. 15.
6. Pull trim cover from clips.
7. Remove radio knobs and cigar lighter.
8. Remove two screws securing to panel, Fig. 15.
9. Pull trim cover from panel clips.
10. Remove radio as outlined under "Radio, Removal."
11. Remove A/C-heater control attaching screws, pull control outward and disconnect control cables and electrical connectors.
12. Remove switches, clock and disconnect ash tray lamp.
13. Remove right hand outside remote mirror control screws.
14. Disconnect shift indicator cable clip.
15. Remove steering column bolts at floor pan and the nuts from the steering column bracket. Then, lower the steering column and rest steering wheel on seat.
16. Disconnect speedometer cable.
17. Remove instrument panel cluster carrier bolts and the two instrument panel screws, Fig. 15.
18. Remove center air duct screws.
19. Pull cluster outward to disconnect electrical connectors.
20. Remove cluster carrier, Fig. 15.

1977–78 Toronado

CAUTION: On vehicles equipped with an Air Cushion Restraint system, turn ignition switch to "Lock," disconnect battery ground cable and tape end, thereby deactivating system.

1. Disconnect battery ground cable.
2. Disconnect electrical connections at flood lamp or map lamp and remove lamp.
3. Carefully pry speakers from clips, disconnect electrical connections and remove speakers.
4. Remove instrument panel pad screws through speaker openings.
5. Remove screws from lower left outside edge of instrument panel pad, instrument cluster above speedometer, lower right hand corner of glove box and glove box top edge.
6. Pull at center edge of instrument panel pad, releasing clips holding instrument panel pad to windshield edge and remove instrument panel pad.
7. Disconnect the right hand instrument panel cover from lower trim panel and remove glove box door.

NOTE: Cover is secured by one screw and five studs pushed through clips mounted in lower panel.

8. If equipped with air conditioning, disconnect upper right hand air hose from duct.
9. On all models, disconnect electrical connectors from clock, trunk release and glove box lamp.
10. Remove the upper trim panel.
11. Disconnect the left hand instrument panel cover, slide steering column cover up the column and pull the left hand

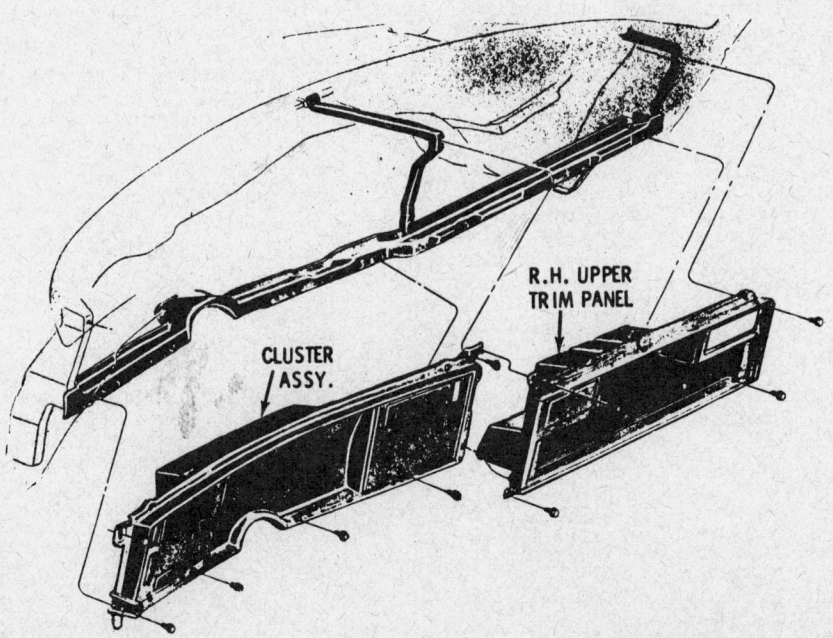

CLUSTER ASSY.

R.H. UPPER TRIM PANEL

Fig. 16   Instrument cluster. 1977–78 Toronado

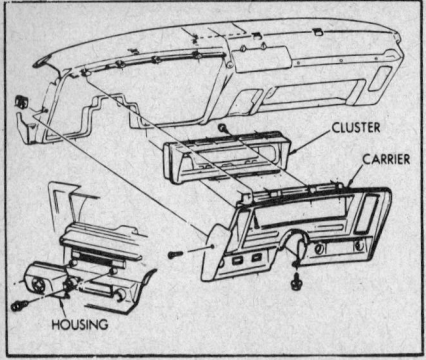

Fig. 17 Instrument cluster (Typical). 1977–79 Omega

instrument panel cover from lower trim panel.

NOTE: Cover is secured by six studs pushed through clips mounted in lower panel.

12. If equipped with air conditioning, disconnect upper left hand air hose from duct.
13. On all models, disconnect temperature and defroster cables from heater case and remove radio to radio support nut.
14. Remove instrument cluster attaching screws, Fig. 16, pull cluster outward and disconnect speedometer cable.
15. Disconnect electrical connectors from instrument cluster and the vacuum harness from air conditioning or heater control.
16. Disconnect radio electrical connectors, pull fiber optic element from washer fluid indicator lens and remove screw from windshield wiper switch ground.
17. Remove three screws securing wiring harness to lower corners of instrument cluster, then disconnect harness from three retaining clips.
18. Remove instrument cluster assembly.

1977–79 Omega

1. Disconnect battery ground cable.
2. Remove shift indicator needle from shift bowl and lower steering column.

NOTE: Apply protective material to mast jacket to prevent damage to painted surfaces.

3. Remove three screws from front of heater control securing it to cluster.

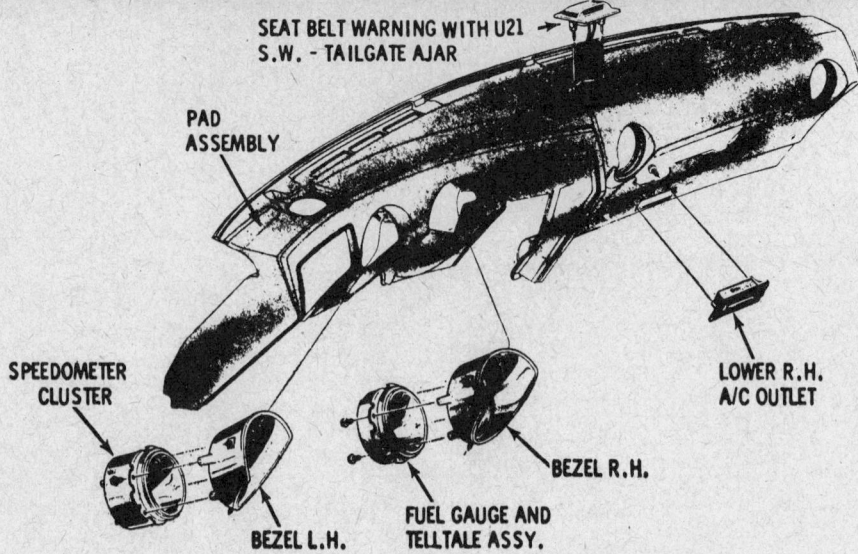

Fig. 18 Instrument cluster. 1977 Cutlass

4. Remove radio knobs, washers, bezel nuts and front support at lower edge of instrument cluster. This allows radio to remain in the panel.
5. Remove screws at top, bottom and side of cluster securing it to instrument panel, Fig. 17.
6. Tilt cluster forward and reach behind to disconnect speedo cable, speed-minder and electrical connectors and lift cluster out of carrier after removing screws.

1977 Cutlass

Speedometer Cluster

1. Disconnect battery ground cable.
2. With automatic transmission column shift, remove lower trim cover (below steering column) then disconnect shift indicator clip on shift bowl.
3. On all models, lower steering column.
4. Disconnect speedo cable from speedometer.
5. Remove three cluster attaching screws and pull cluster out carefully so shift indicator needle is not damaged. Disconnect wiring connector and remove cluster.

Fuel Gauge & Telltale Assembly

1. Perform steps 1 through 3 as outlined under "Speedometer Cluster" procedure.
2. Remove three assembly attaching screws and pull assembly out of pad, Fig. 18.
3. Disconnect wiring connectors and remove assembly.

W/S WIPER MOTOR, REPLACE
1977–84

1. Raise hood and remove cowl screen or grille.
2. Reach through cowl opening and loosen transmission drive link attaching nuts to motor crankarm.
3. Disconnect wiring and washer hoses.
4. Disconnect transmission drive link from motor arm.
5. Remove motor attaching screws.
6. Remove motor while guiding crankarm through opening.

W/S WIPER TRANSMISSION, REPLACE
1977–84

Rectangular Motor

1. Remove wiper arms and blades.
2. Raise hood and remove cowl vent screen or grille.
3. Disconnect wiring from motor.
4. Loosen, do not remove, transmission drive link to motor crankarm attaching nuts and disconnect drive link from crankarm.

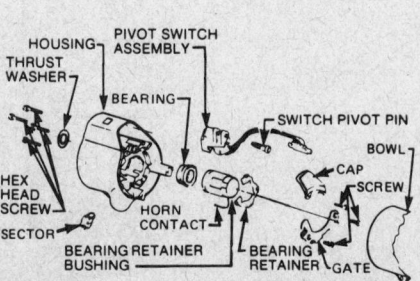

Fig. 19 W/S wiper switch removal & installation. 1982–84 models w/ standard steering column

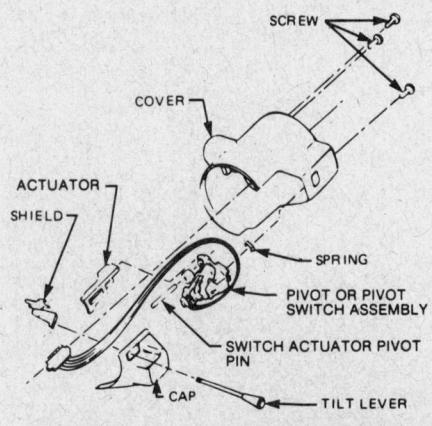

Fig. 19A W/S wiper switch removal & installation. 1982–84 models w/ tilt steering column

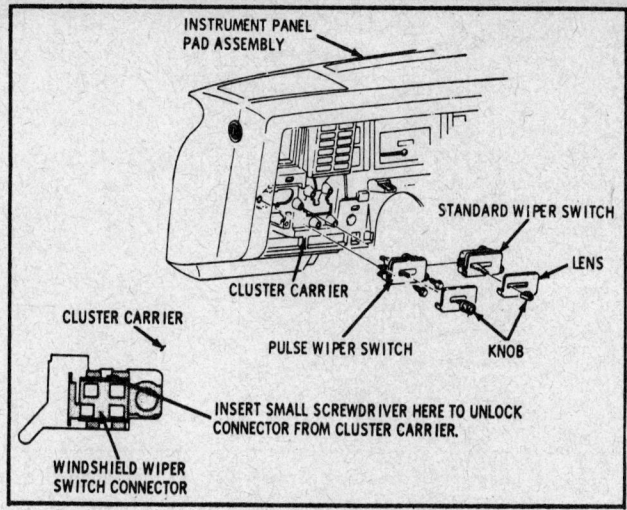

Fig. 20 Windshield wiper switch. 1979-81 Toronado

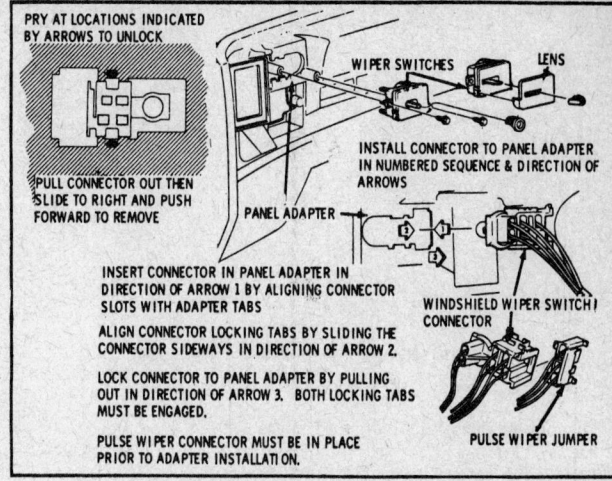

Fig. 21 Windshield wiper switch. 1978-81 Cutlass

5. Remove right and left transmission to body attaching screws and guide transmission and linkage out through cowl opening.

Round Motor

1. Raise hood and remove cowl vent screen.
2. On 1977-84 except Toronado, remove right and left wiper arm and blade assemblies. On 1977-84 Toronado, remove arm and blade only from transmission to be removed.
3. Loosen, do not remove, attaching nuts securing transmission drive link to motor crankarm.

NOTE: On 1977-84 Toronado, if only the left transmission is to be removed, it will not be necessary to loosen attaching nuts securing the right transmission drive link to the motor.

4. Disconnect drive link from motor crankarm.
5. On 1977-84 except Toronado, remove right and left transmission to body attaching screws. On 1977-84 Toronado, remove the attaching screws securing only the transmission to be removed.
6. Remove transmission and linkage by guiding it through opening.

W/S WIPER SWITCH, REPLACE

1982-84 All

1. Remove steering wheel as described under "Horn Sounder and Steering Wheel, Replace."
2. Remove turn signal switch as described under "Turn Signal Switch, Replace."
3. Remove ignition lock as described under "Ignition Lock, Replace."
4. Remove and install cover and wiper switch as shown in Figs. 19 and 19A.
5. Reverse steps 1 through 3 to install.

1979-81 Toronado

1. Disconnect battery ground cable.
2. Remove headlamp switch knob, radio knobs and steering column trim cover.

3. Remove four screws from under side of left hand trim cover.
4. Remove left hand sound absorber, then carefully pull left hand trim cover from instrument panel.

NOTE: It may be necessary to disconnect shift indicator cable clip and lower steering column slightly to remove left hand trim cover.

---

5. Remove two screws attaching switch to cluster, then pull switch rearward to remove, Fig. 20.

1978-81 Cutlass

1. Disconnect battery ground cable.
2. Remove cluster pad assembly.
3. Remove switch retaining screws, then pull switch out to remove, Fig. 21.
4. Reverse procedure to install.

1977-81 88 & 98

1. Disconnect battery ground cable.
2. Rotate headlight switch knob so that notch on back of switch knob is down. Bend a 1/8 in. hook on paper clip wire and use in notch to pull knob retainer clip while pulling knob off shaft.
3. Remove twilight sentinel knob, if equipped.
4. Move steering column collar up and snap out lower trim cover.
5. Remove two trim cover attaching screws, then pull trim cover out of clips.
6. Remove switch mounting plate screws, then pull switch through opening, disconnect wire connector and remove switch.

1977-78 Toronado

1. Disconnect battery ground cable.
2. Remove air conditioning or heater control without disconnecting vacuum harness or electrical connectors.
3. Remove headlamp switch escutcheon and pull headlamp switch through air conditioning or heater control opening without removing electrical connector.
4. Remove windshield wiper switch knob and two switch attaching nuts through air conditioning or heater control open-

ing, then pull switch through opening, disconnect electrical connector and remove switch.

1977 Cutlass

1. Disconnect battery ground cable.
2. Remove steering column trim cover screws and if equipped with air conditioning, disconnect outlet hose.
3. Disconnect parking brake cable.
4. Remove left hand control panel screws, pull control panel from instrument panel and disconnect wiring.
5. Remove electrical connector from wiper switch, wiper switch knob, switch retaining screws and switch.

1977-79 Omega

1. Disconnect battery ground cable.
2. Remove switch electrical connector, switch retaining screws and switch from behind instrument panel.

RADIO, REPLACE

NOTE: When installing radio, be sure to adjust antenna trimmer for peak performance.

1979-84 Toronado

1. Disconnect battery ground cable.
2. Remove headlamp switch knob, radio knobs and steering column trim cover.
3. Remove four screws from underside of left hand trim cover.
4. Remove left hand sound absorber, then pull left hand trim cover from instrument panel.

NOTE: It may be necessary to disconnect shift indicator cable clip and lower steering column slightly to remove left hand trim cover.

---

5. Remove right hand sound absorber.
6. Remove screw attaching instrument panel wiring harness to radio bracket and screw attaching radio to tie bar. Move tone generator aside, if equipped.
7. Remove four screws attaching radio mounting plate to cluster carrier.

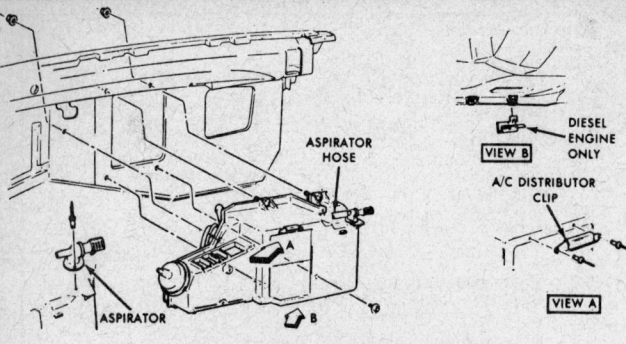

Fig. 22 Heater core. 1979–84 Toronado

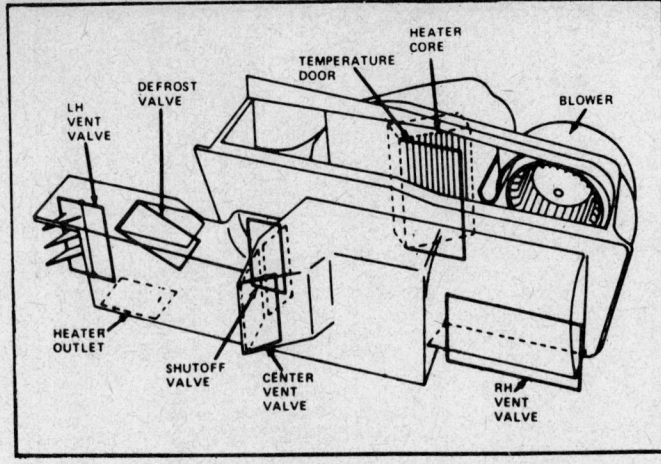

Fig. 23 Heater core and blower motor (less air conditioning). 1977–84 88 & 98

8. Disconnect antenna lead and radio wiring.
9. Pull radio and mounting plate rearward to remove.

1978–84 Cutlass

1. Disconnect battery ground cable.
2. Remove instrument panel lower trim cover.
3. Remove the 4 radio mounting plate screws, and the screw from radio support bracket on lower instrument panel tie bar.
4. Pull radio outward, then disconnect antenna and electrical connectors and remove radio.
5. Reverse procedure to install.

1977–84 88 & 98

1. Disconnect battery ground cable.
2. Remove radio knobs, cigar lighter and right hand trim panel cover.
3. Remove radio bracket to lower tie bar screw and the four mounting plate screws.
4. Pull radio out, then disconnect the electrical connectors and antenna lead, and remove radio.
5. Reverse procedure to install.

1977–78 Toronado

1. Disconnect battery ground cable.
2. Disconnect all wiring from radio.
3. Disconnect throttle cable, then remove throttle lever and reinforcement.
4. Remove radio support bracket to tie-bar screw.
5. Remove radio knobs and two nuts securing radio to instrument cluster.
6. Lower radio and remove from behind instrument panel.

1977–79 Omega

1. Disconnect battery cable.
2. Remove ash tray and housing as necessary.
3. Remove knobs, controls, washers, trim plate and nuts from radio.
4. Remove hoses from center A/C distribution duct as necessary.
5. Disconnect all leads to radio.
6. Remove screws or nuts from radio rear mounting bracket and remove radio.

1977 Cutlass

1. Disconnect battery ground cable.
2. Remove four screws from steering column

trim cover and remove cover.
3. Remove knobs from radio by pulling outward on knobs.
4. Remove nuts from front of radio.
5. Remove four screws holding R.H. Control Panel to dash and gently pull panel outward and up.
6. Remove screw from radio support bracket.
7. Remove four screws holding ash tray housing to tie bar and remove housing assembly.
8. Disconnect all leads and remove radio.

HEATER CORE, REPLACE

1979–84 Toronado

1. Disconnect battery ground cable, then drain cooling system.
2. Disconnect heater hoses at heater core, then install plugs in core outlets to prevent spillage.
3. Remove instrument panel sound absorbers, then lower steering column.
4. Remove instrument cluster as described under Instrument Cluster, Replace.
5. Remove radio front speakers.
6. Remove three screws attaching manifold to heater case.
7. Remove four upper and three lower instrument panel attaching screws.
8. Disconnect parking brake release cable.
9. Disconnect instrument wiring harness from dash wiring assembly.
10. Disconnect right hand remote control mirror cable from instrument panel pad.
11. Disconnect speedometer cable from clip and temperate control cable at heater case.
12. Disconnect radio and A/C wiring, vacuum lines and all wiring necessary to remove instrument panel assembly. If equipped with pulse wiper, remove wiper switch and unlock wire connector from cluster carrier, then separate pulse wiper jumper harness from wiper switch wire connector.
13. Remove instrument panel and wiring harness assembly.
14. Remove defroster ducts, then disconnect lines from actuators.
15. Remove blower motor resistor.
16. From engine side of dash panel, remove three heater and A/C case retaining nuts.
17. From passenger compartment, remove

screws and clip retaining heater and A/C case to dash panel.
18. Remove heater and A/C case, then remove heater core from case, Fig. 22.

1977–84 88 & 98

Less A/C
1. Disconnect battery ground cable.
2. Disconnect blower resistor and blower motor wiring.
3. Drain cooling system into a suitable container, then remove heater hoses from heater core.
4. Remove seven screws attaching heater and blower case to plenum case, then remove case.

NOTE: The heater temperature air valve can be removed at this time by disconnecting valve cable and tapping hinge pin down until it clears the upper pivot, then lift valve and hinge pin out of lower pivot, Fig. 23.

5. Remove four screws securing heater core shroud, then shroud and core, Fig. 23.
6. Remove core mounting screws and clamps, then separate core from shroud.
7. Reverse procedure to install. Replace sealer as necessary during installation to prevent air and water leaks.

With A/C
1. Disconnect battery ground cable.
2. Disconnect blower resistor and blower motor wiring.
3. Disconnect A/C wiring, then heater core ground strap.
4. Remove thermostatic switch and diagnostic connector (if equipped).
5. Remove right half of hood seal, then seven screws attaching air inlet screen. Remove screen.
6. Remove five bolts attaching case to dash, nine upper to lower case attaching screws around flange and two upper to lower case attaching screws located inside plenum.
7. Remove upper case by lifting straight up, then off, Fig. 24.
8. Remove accumulator bracket, then lift evaporator out of case.
9. Remove heater hoses, then lift heater core out of case.
10. Reverse procedure to install. Replace sealer as necessary during installation to prevent air and water leaks.

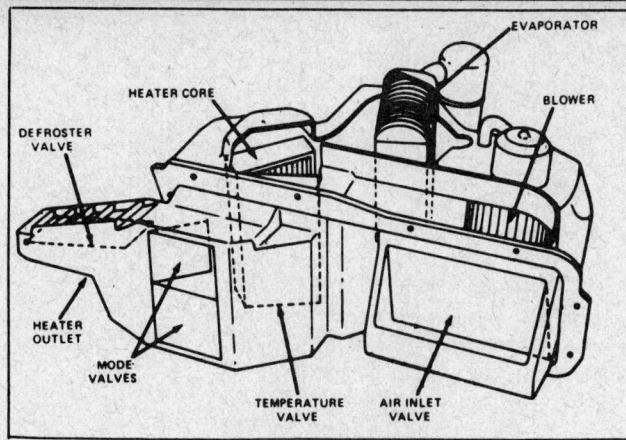

Fig. 24   Heater core and blower motor (with air conditioning). 1977—84 88 & 98

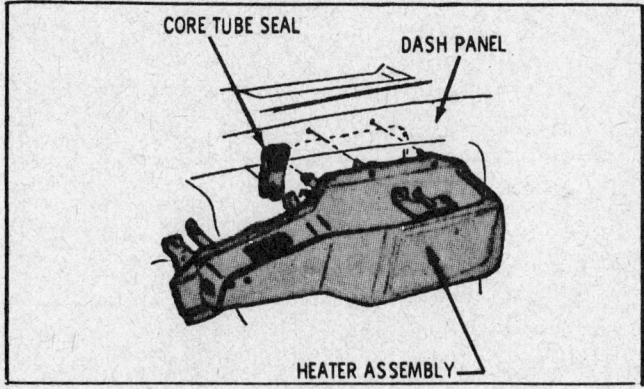

Fig. 26   Heater core. 1977—79 Omega (Typical)

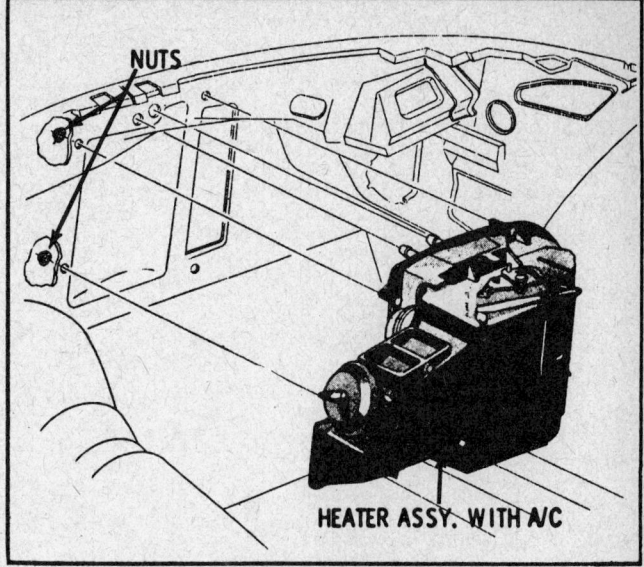

Fig. 25   Heater core. 1977—78 Toronado & 1977 Cutlass (Typical)

1977—78 Toronado

1. Disconnect battery ground cable and drain radiator.
2. Disconnect heater hoses and plug hoses and core openings to prevent coolant loss.
3. Remove heater case to dash panel attaching nuts, Fig. 25.
4. Remove instrument panel trim cover and the heater case to cowl bolts.
5. Remove lower air duct.
6. Remove instrument panel pad, then electrical connectors from glovebox light and clock.
7. Remove right hand upper trim panel and on models equipped with A/C, remove manifold from heater case.
8. On all models, remove defroster duct from heater case and disconnect lower dash trim panel.
9. Disconnect temperature and defroster cables, then the vacuum hose from heater case. Remove heater case from dash, then core from case.

Intermediate Models Less A/C

1978—84 Cutlass

1. Disconnect battery ground cable and drain cooling system.
2. Disconnect heater hoses.
3. Disconnect electrical connectors from heater module.
4. Remove module front cover screws.
5. Remove heater core from module.
6. Reverse procedure to install.

1977 Cutlass

1. Disconnect battery ground cable and drain radiator.
2. Disconnect heater hoses and plug hoses and core openings to prevent coolant loss.
3. Remove heater case attaching nuts and screws, disconnect control cables and remove case from dash, then core from case, Fig. 25.

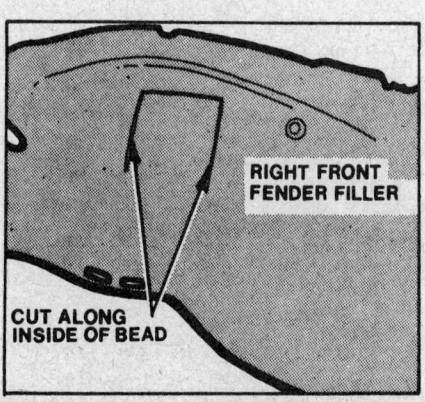

Fig. 27   Blower motor access hole location. 1977—78 Toronado

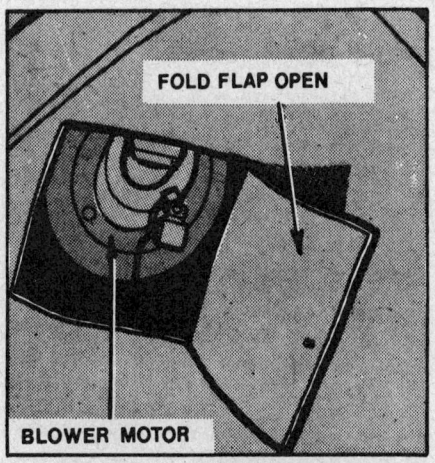

Fig. 28   Removing blower motor. 1977—78 Toronado

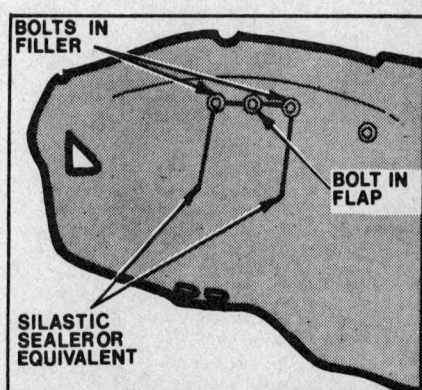

Fig. 29   Sealing blower motor access hole. 1977—78 Toronado

1977-79 Omega

1. Disconnect battery ground cable and drain radiator.
2. Disconnect heater hoses and plug hoses and core openings to prevent coolant loss.
3. Remove heater case retaining nuts from engine side of dash, Fig. 26.
4. Remove glove box and door, then pull heater case from dash.
5. Disconnect blower resistor electrical connector and control cables from case, then remove heater case from dash and core from case.

Intermediate Models With A/C

1978-84 Cutlass

1. Disconnect battery ground cable and drain cooling system.
2. Disconnect heater hoses from core.
3. Remove retention bracket and ground strap.
4. Remove module rubber seal and screen.
5. Remove right hand W/S wiper arm.
6. Remove attaching screws from the diagnostic connector, hi-blower relay and thermostatic switch.
7. Disconnect all electrical connectors from top of module.
8. Remove top cover from module.
9. Remove heater core from module.
10. Reverse procedure to install.

1977 Cutlass

1. Disconnect battery ground cable and drain radiator.
2. Remove glove box and the center A/C manifold.
3. Disconnect vacuum hoses and temperature cable from heater case.
4. Disconnect heater hoses and plug hoses and core openings to prevent coolant loss.
5. Remove heater case to dash panel attaching bolts, then heater case from dash and core from case, Fig. 25.

1977-79 Omega

1. Disconnect battery and drain coolant.
2. Disconnect upper heater hose from core.
3. Remove right front fender skirt bolts and lower skirt to gain access to lower heater hose clamp. Disconnect lower hose and remove lower right hand heater core and case attaching nut.
4. Remove glove box and door.
5. Remove recirculation vacuum diaphragm at right kick panel.
6. Remove heater outlet (at bottom of heater case).
7. Remove cold air distributor duct from heater case.
8. Remove heater case extension screws and separate extension from case.
9. Disconnect cables and wiring and remove case and core assembly, Fig. 26.
10. Separate core from case.

BLOWER MOTOR, REPLACE

1979-84 Toronado

1. Disconnect battery ground cable.
2. Disconnect hi blower relay electrical connectors, then remove relay.
3. Remove screws securing blower motor, then remove blower motor.
4. Reverse procedure to install. Apply continuous bead of suitable sealer to blower motor mounting.

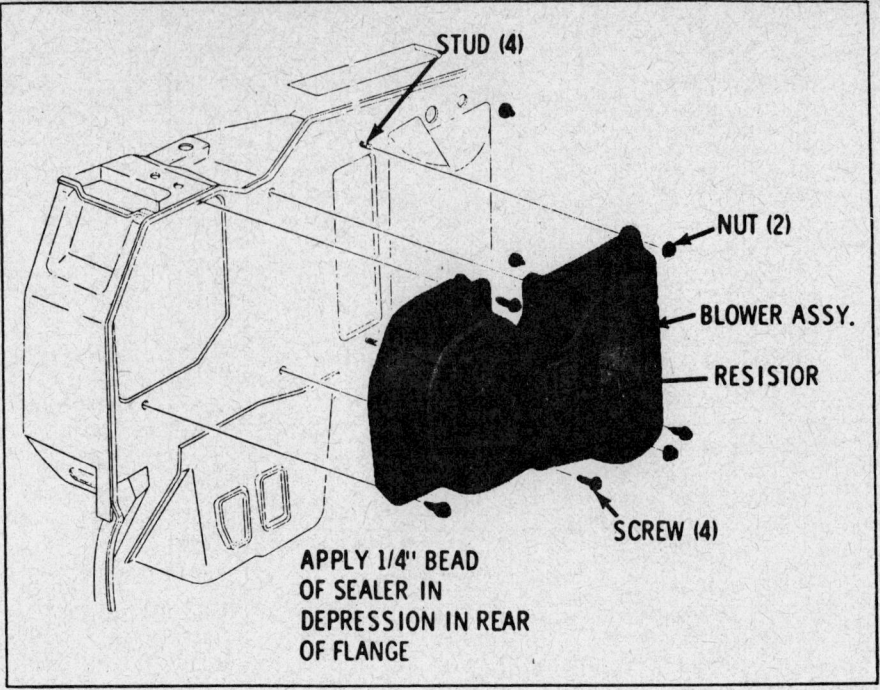

APPLY 1/4" BEAD OF SEALER IN DEPRESSION IN REAR OF FLANGE

STUD (4)
NUT (2)
BLOWER ASSY.
RESISTOR
SCREW (4)

Fig. 30   Blower motor. 1977 Cutlass

1977-84 88 & 98

1. Disconnect battery ground cable.
2. Disconnect blower motor ground and feed wires.
3. Remove six blower motor attaching screws and blower motor, Figs. 23 and 24.

1977-78 Toronado

1. Disconnect battery ground cable.
2. Raise vehicle and remove right front wheel.
3. Referring to Fig. 27, cut along inside of bead.
4. Fold flap over to expose blower motor, Fig. 28.

5. Remove blower motor attaching screws and the blower motor through opening.

NOTE: After blower motor installation, the access hole must be sealed as follows:

a. Drill a hole in flap and install a 5/16 inch self tapping bolt with a large flat washer, Fig. 29.
b. Close flap and drill two holes in inner filler panel and install two 5/16 inch self tapping bolts with large flat washers, Fig. 29.
c. With a suitable sealer, seal edge of flap. Do not use weatherstrip adhesive.

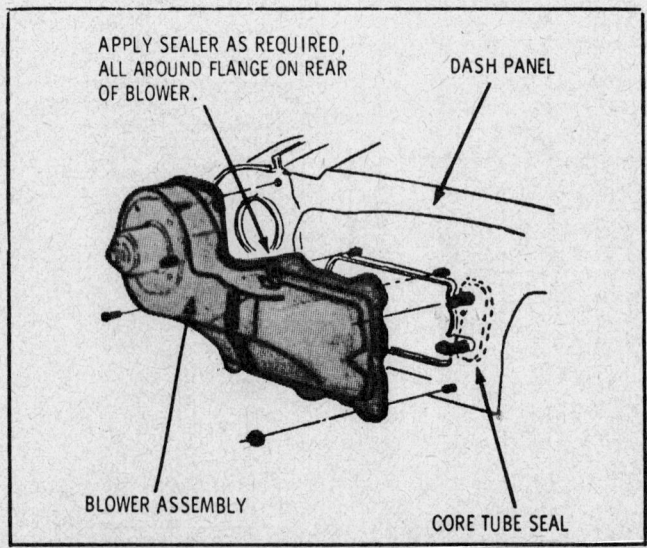

APPLY SEALER AS REQUIRED, ALL AROUND FLANGE ON REAR OF BLOWER.

DASH PANEL

BLOWER ASSEMBLY

CORE TUBE SEAL

Fig. 31   Blower motor. 1977-79 Omega (Typical)

1977-84 Intermediate Models

1978-84 Cutlass
1. Disconnect battery ground cable.
2. If equipped with air conditioning, disconnect cooling tube from blower motor.
3. On all models, disconnect electrical connector from blower motor.
4. Remove blower motor retaining screws and the blower motor.
5. Reverse procedure to install.

1977 Cutlass, Less A/C
1. Remove the right front fender filler panel.
2. Disconnect the blower motor wiring.
3. Remove the five nuts and two screws securing the inlet assembly to dash.
4. Disengage the inlet assembly from the studs and remove from the car. The blower motor can be removed from the inlet assembly by removing the attaching screws, Fig. 30. The fan is held to the motor shaft by a nut and lock-washer.

1977-79 Omega, Less A/C
1. Disconnect battery and detach hoses from clips on right fender skirt.
2. Raise vehicle on hoist.
3. Remove fender skirt attaching bolts except those retaining the skirt to radiator support.
4. Pull out then down on skirt and place block of wood between skirt and fender to allow clearance for blower motor removal.
5. Disconnect blower motor cooling tube and electrical connections at blower motor.
6. Remove blower motor attaching screws and remove blower motor, Fig. 31. Gently pry motor flange if sealer acts as an adhesive.

1977 Cutlass, with A/C
1. Disconnect battery ground cable and blower motor feed wire.
2. Remove screws securing blower motor to dash, then the blower motor, Fig. 30.
3. Reverse procedure to install.

1977-79 Omega, with A/C
1. Disconnect the battery cable.
2. Remove the fender filler plate attaching bolts and position it forward and inboard.
3. Disconnect the blower feed wire.
4. Remove the blower motor attaching screws and blower motor.

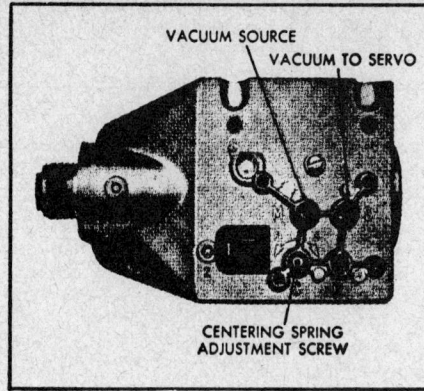

Fig. 32 Centering spring adjustment. 1977—78 Models with flyweight regulator

CRUISE CONTROL, ADJUST

System Release Switches, Adjust

Insert switches into tubular clip until the switch seats on clip. Then, pull brake pedal rearward against stop. The switches will be moved in the clip, thereby providing the proper adjustment.

Servo Linkage, Adjust

UNITS WITH SERVO ROD Except 1978-80 V8-305
With curb idle speed properly adjusted and the carburetor in curb idle position with the engine off, install servo rod retainer in hole that provides clearance between retainer and servo bushing. Some clearance is required, however, do not exceed the width of one hole.

1978-80 V8-305
Screw rod into link with ignition "Off" and fast idle cam off and throttle closed. Hook rod through tab on servo. Adjust length so link assembles over end of stud, then install retainer.

UNITS WITH BEAD CHAIN
Assemble chain to be taut with carburetor in hot idle position and the idle solenoid deenergized. Place chain into swivel cavities which permits chain to have slight slack. Place retainer over swivel and chain assembly. Retainer must be made to rest between balls. Cut off chain flush with side of swivel to remove excess length. Chain slack should not exceed one half diameter of ball stud, .150 inch, when measured at hot idle position.

UNITS WITH CABLE Except 1979 V8-301
With throttle closed, ignition and fast idle cam off, adjust cable jam nuts until free play is removed from cable sleeve at carburetor without holding throttle open. Torque jam nuts to 50 in. lbs. Ensure servo boot is over cable washer.

1979 V8-301
1. Set carburetor choke to hot idle position.
2. With cable connected to vacuum servo, pull steel tube of servo as far as it will go and check if one of the cross holes in the steel tube aligns with carburetor lever pin.
3. If one of the cross holes in the steel tube aligns with carburetor lever pin, install the tube, washer and cotter pin.
4. If none of the cross holes in the steel aligns with carburetor lever pin, move tube rearward to align the next closest hole and install cable, washer and cotter pin.

CAUTION: Do not stretch cable to make adjustment, as this will prevent carburetor from returning to normal idle.

Centering Spring, Adjust

1977-78 Models with Flyweight Regulator
1. If speed control system holds speed three or more mph higher than selected speed, turn centering spring adjusting screw (C) toward (S) 1/32″ or less, Fig. 32.
2. If speed control system holds speed three or more mph below selected speed, turn centering spring adjusting screw (C) toward (F) 1/32″ or less. *Do not move adjustment screw (R).*

Orifice Tube Adjustment

1977-84 Models with Transducer Regulator
If the cruising speed is lower than the engagement speed, loosen the orifice tube locknut and turn the tube outward; if higher turn the tube inward. Each 1/4 turn will alter the engagement-cruising speed difference one mph. Tighten locknut after adjustment and check the system operation.

Gasoline Engine Section

See Chevrolet Chapter for Service Procedures on V8-305 & 1977—79 V8-350 with distributor at rear of engine, clockwise distributor rotor rotation. See Buick Chapter for Service Procedures on V6-231, V6-252 Engine. See Pontiac Chapter for Service Procedures on 1979 V8-301.

ENGINE MOUNTS

1979—84 Toronado

1. Raise and support vehicle.
2. Remove front splash shield.
3. Remove two screws from engine mount bracket to engine mount on each side, Fig. 1.
4. Place a suitable lifting device under the harmonic balancer and raise engine only enough to remove each mount.
5. Reverse procedure to install.

1977—84 V8 Exc. Toronado

Removal or replacement of a motor mount can be accomplished by supporting the weight of the engine at the area of the mount to be replaced, Figs. 2 thru 4.

1977—78 Toronado

Refer to Fig. 5 to replace engine mounts.

ENGINE, REPLACE

1977—84 V8 Exc. Toronado

1. Mark hood hinge before removing to aid in proper alignment upon reassembly.
2. Drain radiator and disconnect battery.
3. Disconnect radiator hoses, heater hoses, vacuum hoses, power steering pump hoses (if necessary), starter cable at junction block, engine-to-body ground strap, fuel hose from fuel line, wiring and accelerator linkage.
4. Remove fan blade and pulley, coil and upper radiator support.
5. Raise car.
6. Disconnect exhaust pipes at manifolds.
7. Remove torque converter cover and the three bolts securing converter to flywheel.
8. Remove engine mount bolts, then three transmission to engine bolts on right side.
9. Remove starter with wiring attached and position aside.
10. Lower vehicle and support engine with suitable lifting equipment.
11. Support transmission with a suitable jack and remove three left hand transmission to engine bolts.
12. Remove engine from vehicle.

1979—84 Toronado

1. Disconnect battery ground cable and drain cooling system.
2. Remove radiator upper support.
3. Remove air cleaner assembly.

4. Scribe hood hinge locations and remove hood.
5. Disconnect engine ground strap.
6. Disconnect upper and lower radiator hoses from engine.
7. Disconnect transmission oil cooler lines from radiator.
8. Disconnect heater hoses from water pump and water control valve.
9. Remove radiator, fan and the shroud.
10. Disconnect power steering pump bracket from engine and position aside without disconnecting lines.
11. Disconnect A/C compressor bracket from engine and position aside without disconnecting lines.
12. Disconnect fuel lines.
13. Disconnect throttle cable, vacuum hoses and electrical connections.
14. Disconnect left hand exhaust pipe from manifold.
15. On left side of engine, remove through bolt and bracket securing final drive to engine.
16. Raise and support vehicle.
17. Remove flywheel shield.
18. Disconnect right hand exhaust pipe from manifold.
19. Disconnect starter motor wiring and remove starter motor.
20. Remove converter to flywheel bolts. Mark location of converter on flywheel for alignment during installation.
21. Remove splash shield.
22. Remove engine front mounting attaching nuts.
23. Remove two bolts securing right hand

output shaft support brackets. Using a sharp tool, scribe a mark around the washers as far as possible. Use these scribe marks to position bracket upon installation.
24. Remove lower right hand transmission to engine attaching bolts. One bolt retains the modulator line clip.
25. Use a suitable length of chain to retain final drive in vehicle.
26. Lower vehicle and attach suitable engine lifting equipment to engine.
27. Remove the remaining transmission to engine bolts. It may be necessary to raise or lower transmission with a suitable jack to facilitate bolt removal.
28. Raise engine and remove from vehicle.
29. Reverse procedure to install.

1977—78 Toronado

1. Drain radiator and remove hood, marking hinge as a guide for reassembly.
2. If equipped with venturi shroud, unhook strap, remove seal to venturi ring clips and move towards radiator.
3. Remove air cleaner and hot air pipe.
4. Disconnect engine ground strap, upper and lower radiator hoses, transmission oil cooler lines and heater hoses.
5. Remove upper radiator baffle, radiator, fan shroud and venturi components, if equipped.
6. Disconnect power steering pump bracket from engine without disconnecting oil lines. Position pump and bracket assembly aside.

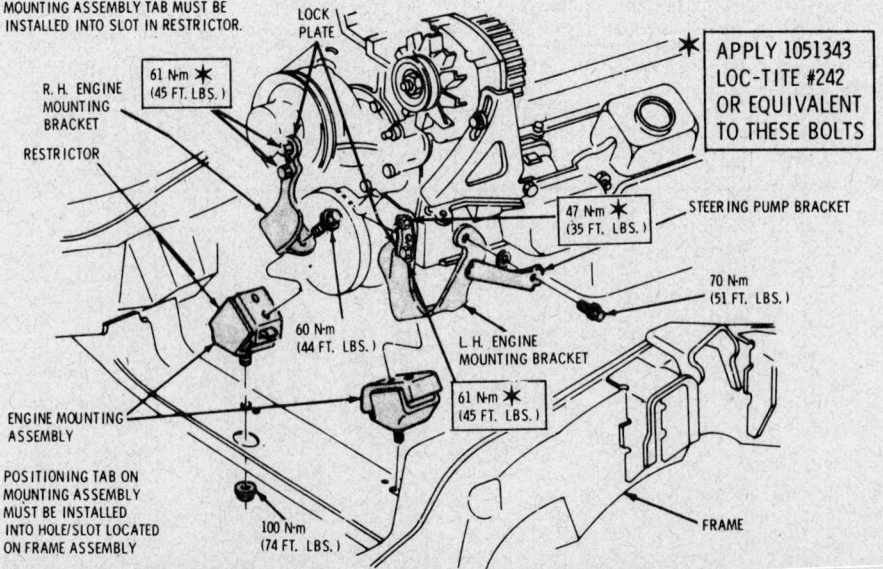

MOUNTING ASSEMBLY TAB MUST BE INSTALLED INTO SLOT IN RESTRICTOR.

LOCK PLATE

R. H. ENGINE MOUNTING BRACKET

RESTRICTOR

61 N·m (45 FT. LBS.)

★ APPLY 1051343 LOC-TITE #242 OR EQUIVALENT TO THESE BOLTS

47 N·m (35 FT. LBS.)

STEERING PUMP BRACKET

70 N·m (51 FT. LBS.)

60 N·m (44 FT. LBS.)

L. H. ENGINE MOUNTING BRACKET

61 N·m (45 FT. LBS.)

ENGINE MOUNTING ASSEMBLY

POSITIONING TAB ON MOUNTING ASSEMBLY MUST BE INSTALLED INTO HOLE/SLOT LOCATED ON FRAME ASSEMBLY

100 N·m (74 FT. LBS.)

FRAME

Fig. 1 Front engine mounts. 1979—84 Toronado

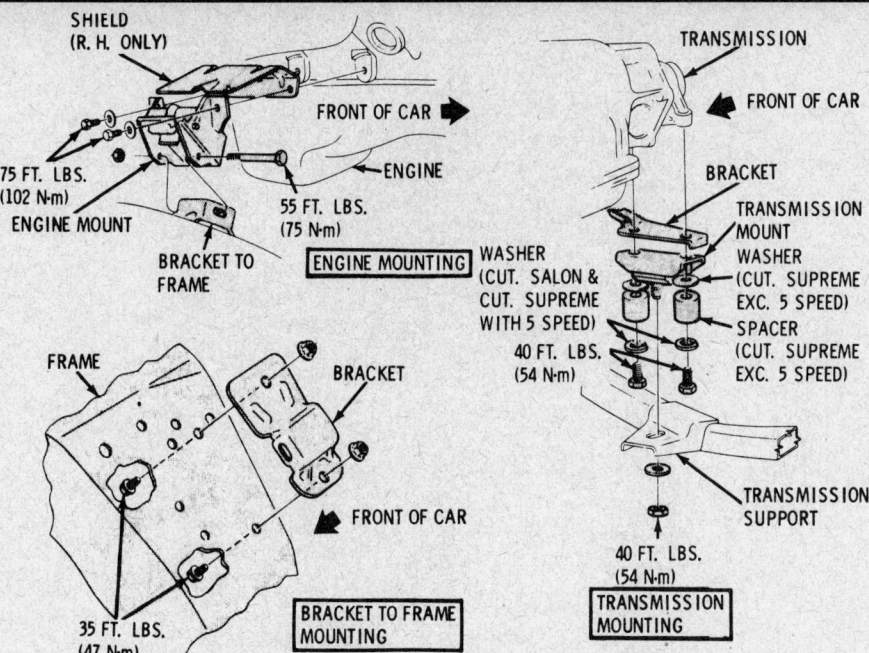

Fig. 2 Engine mounts. 1978–84 Cutlass

and lower vehicle.
19. Install suitable engine lifting equipment and remove remaining engine to transmission bolts.

NOTE: It may be necessary to raise or lower the transmission using a suitable jack with a wood block placed between the jack and transmission.

20. Remove engine from vehicle.
21. Reverse procedure to install.

CYLINDER HEAD, REPLACE

Head gaskets used on these engines are of a special composition material that is not to be used with a sealer.

Prior to installation, clean the head bolts and dip in engine oil. Tighten head bolts in steps and in the sequence shown in Fig. 7. Final torquing should be to the specifications listed in "Engine Tightening Specifications".

V8-260, 307, 350, 403

1. Disconnect battery ground cable.
2. Drain radiator and cylinder block.
3. Remove intake and exhaust manifolds.
4. Remove ground strap from left cylinder head.
5. Remove rocker arm bolts, pivots, rocker arms and push rods. Keep rocker arms, pivots and push rods in order so they can be installed in the same position.
6. Remove cylinder head attaching bolts and remove cylinder head.
7. Reverse procedure to install. Torque cylinder head bolts in sequence shown in Fig. 7 and torque intake manifold bolts in sequence shown in Fig. 8.

VALVE ARRANGEMENT

Front to Rear

V6-231①	E-I-I-E-I-E
V6-252①	E-I-I-E-I-E
V8-260, 307, 350③, 403	I-E-I-E-E-I-E-I
V8-301④	E-I-I-E-E-I-I-E
V8-305, 350②	E-I-I-E-E-I-I-E

①—Refer to Buick chapter for service procedures.
②—Refer to Chevrolet chapter for service procedures.
③—Oldsmobile engine.
④—Refer to Pontiac chapter for service procedures.

VALVE LIFT SPECS.

Engine	Year	Intake	Exhaust
V6-231②	1977–78	.383	.366
V6-231②	1979–84	.357	.366
V6-252②	1981–84	.357	.366
V8-260	1977–82	.395	.400
V8-301③	1979	.357	.376
V8-305①	1977–79	.3727	.4100
V8-305①	1980	.357	.390
V8-307④	1981–84	.400	.400
V8-307⑤	1983–84	.440	.440
V8-350	1977–80	.400	.400
V8-350①	1977–80	.390	.410
V8-403	1977–79	.400	.400

①—Refer to Chevrolet chapter for service procedures.
②—Refer to Buick chapter for service procedures.
③—Refer to Pontiac chapter for service procedures.
④—Exc. Hurst Olds.
⑤—Hurst Olds.

7. Disconnect A/C compressor bracket from engine without disconnecting refrigerant lines. Position compressor and bracket assembly aside.
8. Disconnect fuel lines at fuel pump, throttle cable, vacuum hoses and electrical connections.
9. Disconnect exhaust pipes from manifolds.
10. Raise vehicle.
11. Loosen upper left hand flywheel cover bolt.
12. Remove starter, then the remaining flywheel cover bolts and pivot cover from

upper left hand bolt slot.
13. Mark relationship between converter and flywheel, then remove converter to flywheel bolts.
14. Remove engine front mounting attaching nuts.
15. Remove right hand output shaft support bracket bolts. Mark position of bracket to assist assembly.
16. From vehicle left side, remove final drive to engine through bolt and bracket.
17. Remove lower right hand transmission to engine attaching bolts.
18. Attach final drive support chain, Fig. 6,

Fig. 3 Engine mounts. 1978–84 88 & 98

VALVE TIMING

Intake Opens Before TDC

Engine	Year	Degrees
V6-231②	1977-78	17
V6-231②	1979-84	16
V6-252②	1981-84	16
V8-260	1977-82	14
V8-301③	1979	16
V8-305①	1977-80	28
V8-307	1980-84	20
V8-350	1977-80	16
V8-350①	1977-79	28
V8-403	1977-79	16

①—Refer to Chevrolet chapter for service procedures.
②—Refer to Buick chapter for service procedures.
③—Refer to Pontiac chapter for service procedures.

ROCKER ARMS

NOTE: V8 engines use valve rotators, Fig. 9. The rotator operates on a sprag clutch principle utilizing the collapsing action of a coil spring to give rotation to the rotor body which turns the valve.

V8-260, 307, 350, 403

1. Remove valve cover.
2. Remove flanged bolts, rocker arm pivot and rocker arms, Fig. 9.
3. When installing rocker arm assemblies, lubricate wear surfaces with suitable lubricant. Torque flanged bolts to 25 ft. lbs.

VALVE ROTATORS

The rotator operates on a Sprag clutch principle utilizing the collapsing action of coil spring to give rotation to the rotor body which turns the valve, Fig. 9.

To check rotator action, draw a line across rotator body and down the collar. Operate engine at 1500 rpm, rotator body should move around collar. Rotator action can be in either direction. Replace rotator if no movement is noted.

When servicing valves, valve stem tips should be checked for improper wear pattern which could indicate a defective valve rotator, Fig. 10.

VALVES

Whenever a new valve is installed or after grinding valves, it will be necessary to measure valve stem height using the Special Tool shown in Figs. 11 and 12.

On V8-260, 307, 350 and 403 engines, there should be a minimum clearance of .015 inch between gauge surface and the valve stem, Fig. 11.

Check valve rotator height, Fig. 12. If valve stem tip extends less than .005 inch above rotator, replace the valve.

Lacking this tool the only alternative is to lay flat feeler gauges on the retainer and check the distance between the retainer and valve stem tip.

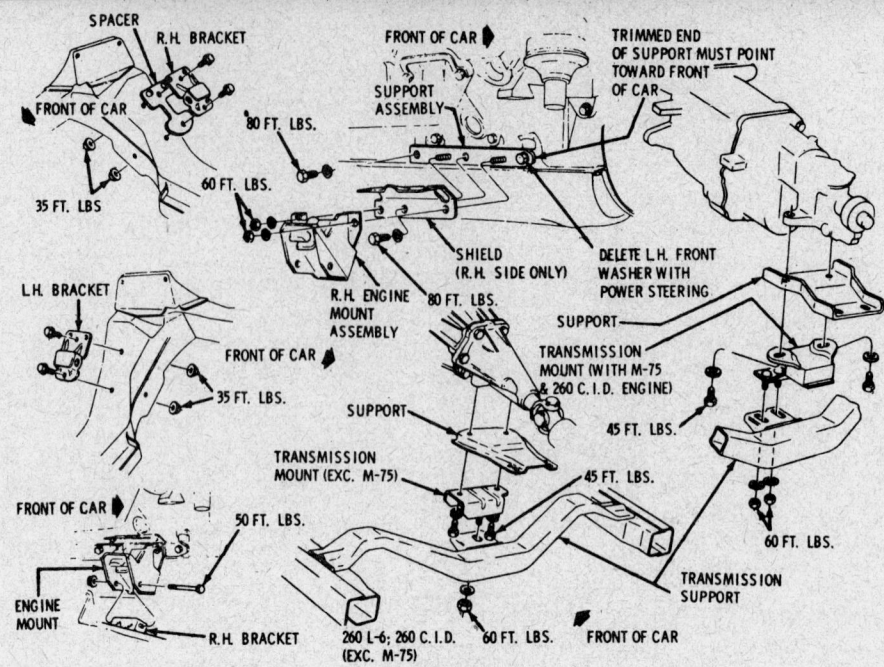

Fig. 4   Engine mounts. 1977 Omega (Typical)

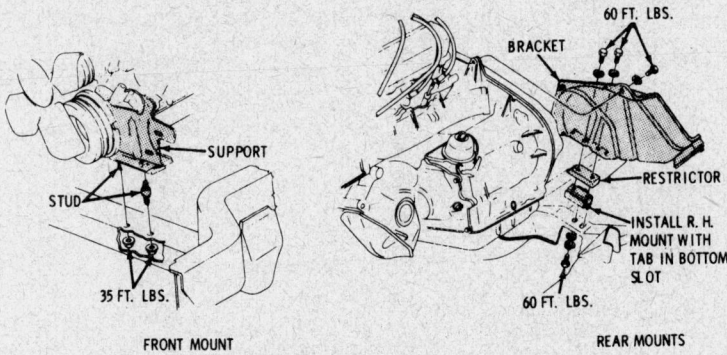

Fig. 5   Front engine mount. 1977-78 Toronado

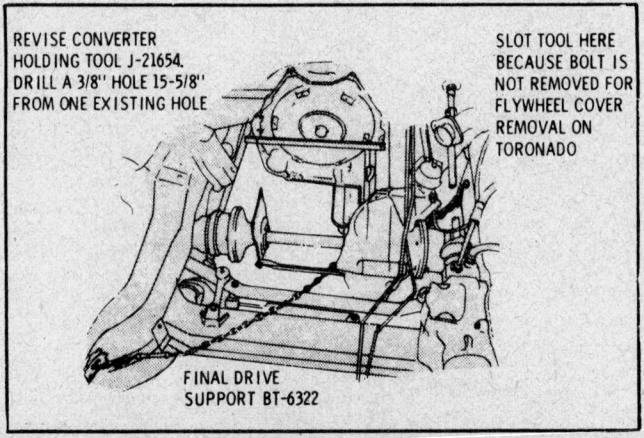

Fig. 6   Final drive supporting tool

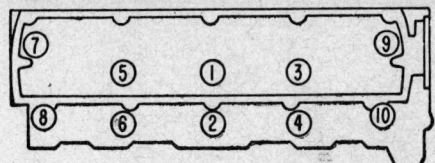

Fig. 7   Cylinder head tightening sequence. V8-260, 307, 350, 403

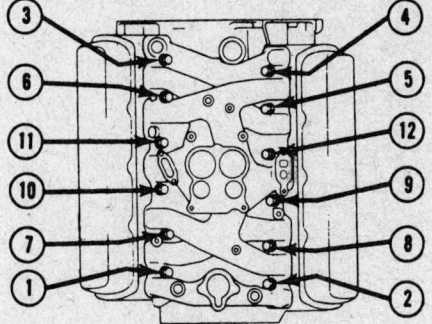

Fig. 8   Intake manifold tightening sequence. V8-260, 307, 350, 403

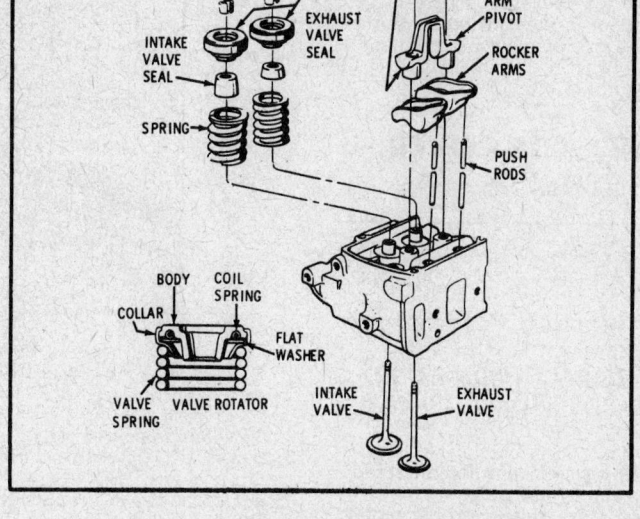

Fig. 9   Cylinder head exploded. 1977—84 V8

VALVE GUIDES

V8-260, 307, 350, 403

Valve stem guides are not replaceable, due to being cast in place. If valve guide bores are worn excessively, they can be reamed oversize.

If a standard valve guide bore is being reamed, use a .003″ or .005″ oversize reamer. For the .010″ oversize valve guide bore, use a .013″ oversize reamer. If too large a reamer is used and the spiraling is removed, it is possible that the valve will not receive the proper lubrication.

NOTE: Occasionally a valve guide will be oversize as manufactured. These are marked on the cylinder head as shown in Fig. 13. If no markings are present, the guide bores are standard. If oversize markings are present, any valve replacement will require an oversize valve. Service valves are available in standard diameters as well as .003″, .005″, .010″ and .013″ oversize.

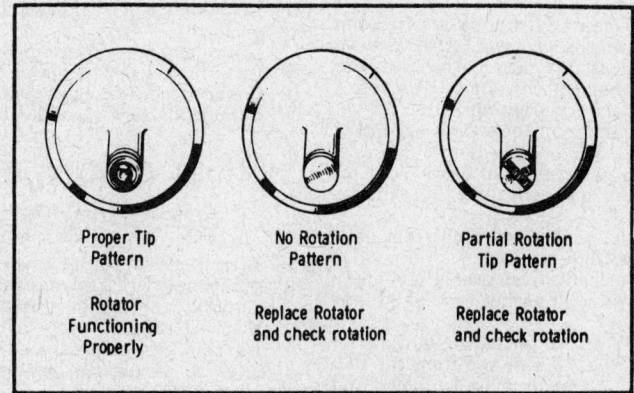

Fig. 10   Checking valve stems for rotator malfunction

VALVE LIFTERS

Valve lifters are available in standard size and an oversize of .010 inch. An "O" is etched on the side of the .010 inch oversize lifter for identification. Also, the cylinder block near the valve lifter bore is marked with an "O". Ensure valve lifters are re-installed in original bores.

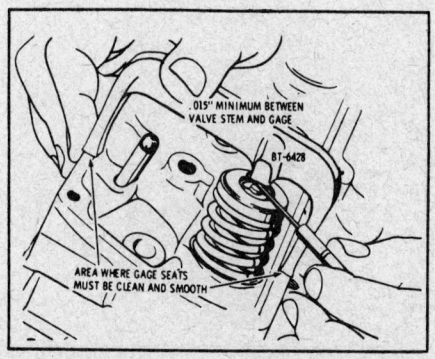

Fig. 11   Measuring valve stem height. V8-260, 307, 350, 403

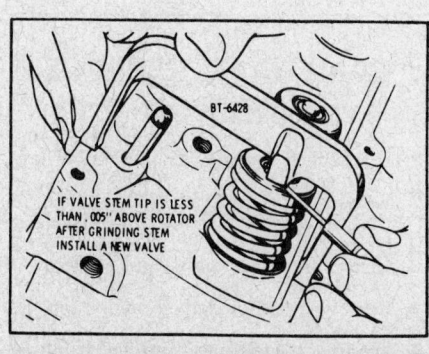

Fig. 12   Measuring valve retainer or valve rotator height. V8-260, 307, 350, 403

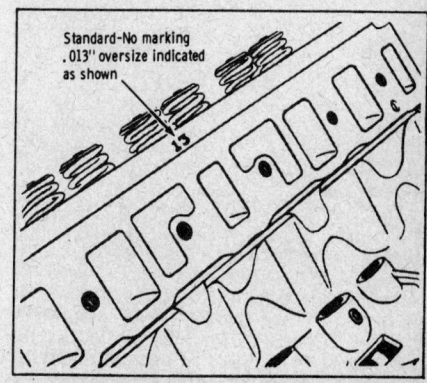

Fig. 13   Valve guide bore marking. V8-260, 307, 350, 403

Plungers are not interchangeable because they are selectively fitted to the bodies at the factory.

If plunger and body appear satisfactory blow off with air to remove all particles of dirt. Install the plunger in the body without other parts and check for free movement. A simple text is to be sure that the plunger will drop of its own weight in the body, Fig. 14.

TIMING CASE COVER, REPLACE

NOTE: When it becomes necessary to replace the cover oil seal, the cover need not be removed.

1977–82 V8-260, 1980–84 307, 1977–80 350 & 1977–79 403

1. Disconnect battery ground cable.
2. Drain cooling system and disconnect radiator hoses and bypass hose.
3. Remove all drive belts, fan and pulley, crankshaft pulley and harmonic balancer, and accessory brackets.
4. Remove timing indicator and water pump.
5. Remove remaining front cover attaching bolts and the front cover. Also, remove the dowel pins. It may be necessary to grind a flat on the dowel pin to provide a rough surface for gripping.
6. Grind a chamfer on one end of each dowel pin.
7. Cut excess material from front end of oil pan gasket on each side of cylinder block.
8. Trim approximately 1/8 inch from each end of new front pan seal.
9. Install new front cover gasket and apply suitable sealer to gasket around coolant holes.
10. Apply RTV sealer to mating surfaces of cylinder block, oil pan and front cover.
11. Place front cover on cylinder block and press downward to compress seal. Rotate cover right and left and guide oil pan seal into cavity with a small screwdriver.

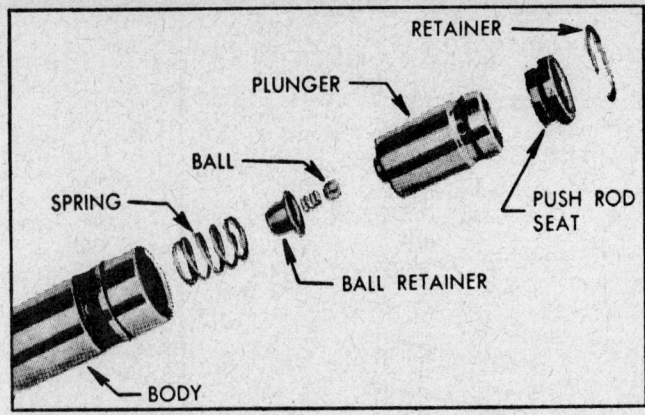

Fig. 14 Hydraulic valve lifter (typical)

12. Apply engine oil to bolts.
13. Install two bolts finger tight to retain cover.
14. Install the two dowel pins, chamfered end first.
15. Install timing indicator and water pump and torque bolts as shown in Figs. 15 and 16.
16. Install harmonic balancer and crankshaft pulley.
17. Install accessory brackets.
18. Install fan and pulley and drive belts.
19. Connect radiator hoses and bypass hose.
20. Connect battery ground cable.

TIMING CHAIN, REPLACE

V8-260, 307, 350, 403

1. After removing front cover, remove fuel pump eccentric, oil slinger, crankshaft sprocket, chain and camshaft sprocket.
2. Install camshaft sprocket, crankshaft sprocket and timing chain together, aligning timing marks as shown in Fig. 17.
3. Install fuel pump eccentric with flat side rearward, Fig. 18. Then install oil slinger and replace front cover.

NOTE: The valve timing marks, Figs. 17 and 18, do not indicate TDC compression stroke for No. 1 cylinder, which is used for distributor installation. If distributor was removed, install timing chain and sprockets, aligning timing marks, Figs. 17 and 18, then rotate engine until No. 1 cylinder is on compression stroke and camshaft timing mark is 180° from valve timing position shown in illustrations, then install distributor.

CAMSHAFT, REPLACE

V8-260, 307, 350, 403

1. Disconnect battery ground cable and drain radiator.
2. Remove upper radiator baffle and disconnect upper radiator hose from water outlet.
3. Disconnect transmission oil cooler lines at radiator.
4. Remove radiator fan shroud, then the radiator.
5. Disconnect fuel lines from fuel pump.
6. Remove air cleaner and disconnect throttle cable.

7. Remove all drive belts and position alternator, power steering pump and air conditioning compressor aside.
8. Disconnect by-pass hose from water pump and all electrical and vacuum connections from engine.
9. Remove distributor.
10. Raise vehicle and drain oil pan.
11. Remove exhaust cross-over pipe and the starter.
12. Disconnect exhaust pipe from manifold.
13. Install engine support bar.
14. Remove engine mount to bracket bolts, raise engine and remove engine mounts.
15. Remove flywheel cover and engine oil pan.
16. Place wood blocks between exhaust manifolds and cross-member to support engine, then remove engine support bar.
17. Remove crankshaft pulley and balancer, then the engine front cover.
18. Lower vehicle and remove valve covers, intake manifold, rocker arms, push rods and valve lifters.

NOTE: Note position of the valve train components to ensure installation in original location.

Front Cover Attaching Bolts (5/16")
Torque To 22 ft. lbs.

Self
Tapping
Water
Pump
Attaching
Screws.
Use Oil On Installation.
Torque To 13 ft. lbs.

Torque To 35 ft. lb.
-Toronado 50 ft. lb.

Fig. 15 Engine front cover bolts. 1977–78 V8-260, 350, 403

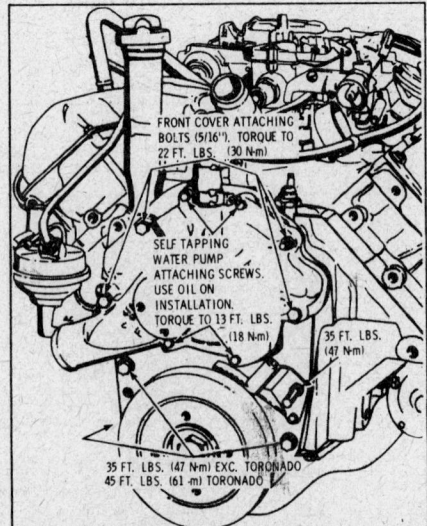

FRONT COVER ATTACHING BOLTS (5/16"), TORQUE TO 22 FT. LBS. (30 N·m)

SELF TAPPING WATER PUMP ATTACHING SCREWS. USE OIL ON INSTALLATION. TORQUE TO 13 FT. LBS. (18 N·m)

35 FT. LBS. (47 N·m)

35 FT. LBS. (47 N·m) EXC. TORONADO
45 FT. LBS. (61 ·m) TORONADO

Fig. 16 Engine front cover bolts. 1979–84 V8-260, 307, 350 & 403

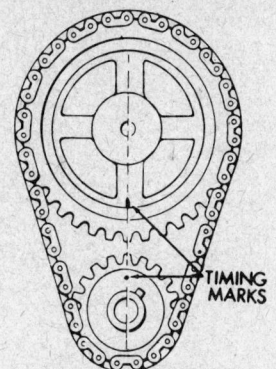

Fig. 17   Timing chain position.
V8-260, 307, 350, 403

19. If equipped with A/C, discharge refrigerant and remove condenser.
20. Remove fuel pump eccentric, camshaft sprocket, oil slinger and timing chain.
21. Slide camshaft from front of engine.
22. Reverse procedure to install.

NOTE: *To insure proper camshaft installation, and to provide initial lubrication, it is extremely important that the camshaft be coated with GM Concentrate (Part No. 1051396).*

PISTON & ROD, ASSEMBLE

Lubricate the piston pin hole and piston pin to facilitate installation of pin, then position the connecting rod with its respective piston as shown in Figs. 19, 19A and 20. Measure connecting rod side clearance using a suitable feeler gauge, clearance should be .006–.020 inch.

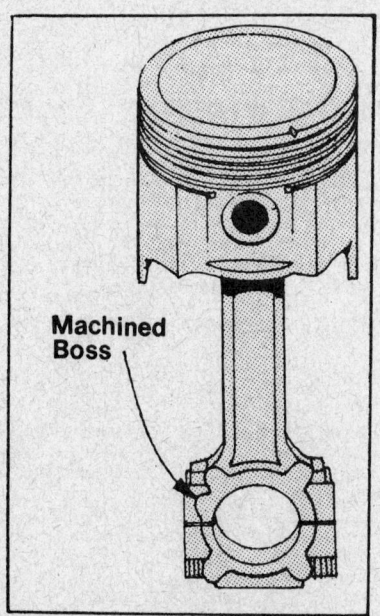

Fig. 20   Assembly of piston to rod.
1977–79 V8-403

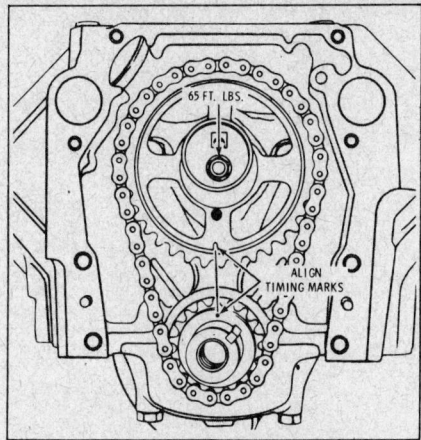

Fig. 18   Fuel pump eccentric.
V8-260, 307, 350, 403, 455

Fig. 19A   Assembly of piston to rod.
1980–84 V8-260, 307 & 350

PISTONS, RINGS & PINS

NOTE: On 1979–84 V8-260, 307, 350 and 403, different types of piston compression rings

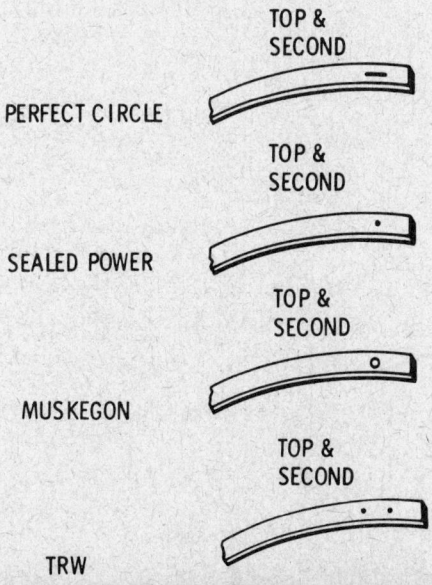

Fig. 21   Piston compression ring identification.
1979–84 V8-260, 307, 350 & 403

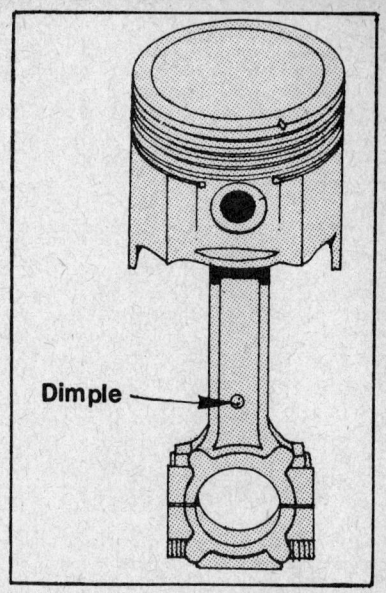

Fig. 19   Assembly of piston to rod.
1977–79 V8-260, 307 & 350

are used, refer to Fig. 21 for piston ring identification. On V8-260 engines, piston ring end gap should be .009–.019 in. for Sealed Power piston rings and .010–.020 in. for Perfect Circle and Muskegon piston rings. On V8-307 engines, piston ring end gap should be .009–.019 in. for Sealed Power piston rings and .010–.020 in. for TRW piston rings. On V8-350 engines, piston ring end gap should be .010–.020 in. for Sealed Power piston rings and .013–.023 in. for Perfect Circle and Muskegon piston rings. On V8-403 engine, piston ring end gap should be .009–.019 in. for Sealed Power piston rings and .010–.020 in. for Perfect Circle piston rings.

Pistons are available in standard sizes and oversizes of .010 and .030".

Rings are available in standard sizes and oversizes of .010 and .030".

MAIN & ROD BEARINGS

Main bearings are available in standard sizes and undersizes of .0005, .001, .0015, .002, .010 and .020".

Rod bearings are available in standard sizes and undersizes of .001, .002, .005, .010, .012 and .020 inch.

NOTE: Main bearing clearances not within

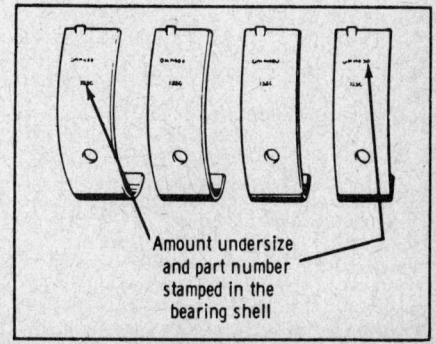

Fig. 22   Main bearing size location.
V8-260, 307, 350, 403

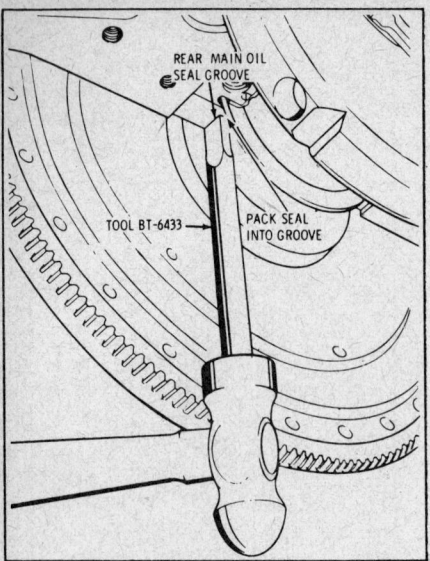

Fig. 23 Packing upper rear main bearing oil seal

specifications must be corrected by the use of selective upper and lower shells. Figs. 22 illustrate the undersize identification marking on the bearing tang.

REAR CRANKSHAFT SEAL SERVICE

Since the braided fabric seal used on these engines can be replaced only when the crankshaft is removed, the following repair procedure is recommended.

1. Remove oil pan and bearing cap.
2. Drive end of old seal gently into groove, using a suitable tool, until packed tight. This may vary between 1/4 and 3/4 inch depending on amount of pack required.
3. Repeat previous step for other end of seal.
4. Measure and note amount that seal was driven up on one side. Using the old seal removed from bearing cap, cut a length of seal the amount previously noted plus 1/16 inch.
5. Repeat previous step for other side of seal.
6. Pack cut lengths of seal into appropriate side of seal groove. A packing tool, BT-6433, Fig. 23, may be used since the tool has been machined to provide a built-in stop. Use tool BT-6436 to trim the seal flush with block, Fig. 24.
7. Install new seal in lower bearing cap.

OIL PAN, REPLACE

Exc. Toronado

1. Remove distributor cap and align rotor with No. 1 firing position.
2. Disconnect ground cable, remove dip stick and drain oil pan.
3. Remove upper radiator support and fan shroud attaching screws.
4. Remove flywheel cover and starter.
5. Disconnect exhaust pipes and crossover pipe on single exhaust models.
6. Disconnect engine mounts and raise engine.
7. Remove oil pan bolts and oil pan.
8. Reverse procedure to install. Torque oil pan bolts to 10 ft. lbs.

1980–84 Toronado

1. Disconnect battery ground cable.
2. Raise and support vehicle, then remove three final drive to transmission bolts.
3. Disconnect frame braces, then disconnect idler arm and pitman arm from relay rod.
4. Separate drive axles from output shafts.
5. Remove battery cable bracket from output shaft support.
6. Disconnect output shaft support from engine block.
7. Support transmission with suitable jack, then remove final drive assembly.
8. Remove splash shield and starter motor.
9. Drain engine oil and remove oil pan.
10. Reverse procedure to install.

1979 Toronado

1. Disconnect battery ground cable.
2. Disconnect shroud from upper radiator support.
3. Remove right hand axle cotter pin, retainer and nut.
4. Raise vehicle and remove right wheel.
5. Disconnect right hand tie rod end using tool J-6627 or BT 7101.
6. Disconnect right hand upper ball joint.
7. Remove bolts attaching drive axle to right hand output shaft, then the output shaft.
8. Disconnect starter wiring and remove starter.
9. Remove splash shield.
10. Disconnect pitman arm and idler arm from intermediate rod using tool J-24319-01 or a suitable puller.
11. Drain pan oil.
12. Remove front engine mount to frame nuts.
13. Disconnect shroud from lower radiator support.
14. Using suitable equipment, raise the front of the engine.
15. Remove the right engine mount.
16. Remove oil pan attaching bolts and oil pan.
17. Reverse procedure to install. Torque oil pan attaching bolts to 10 ft. lbs.

1977–78 Toronado

1. Remove engine as outlined previously.
2. Remove dipstick, drain oil and remove mount from front cover.
3. Unfasten and remove oil pan.
4. Apply sealer to both sides of pan gaskets (cork) and install on block.
5. Install front and rear rubber seals.
6. Wipe lube on seal area and install pan. Torque 5/16" bolts to 15 ft-lbs and 1/4" bolts to 10 ft-lbs.
7. Install mount on front cover and install engine.

OIL PUMP REPAIRS

V8-260, 307, 350, 403

1. Remove oil pan and pump baffle. Remove attaching screws and remove pump and drive shaft extension.
2. To service the pump, refer to Fig. 25.
3. To install, insert the drive shaft extension through the opening in the block until the shaft mates into the distributor drive gear. Position pump onto rear main bearing cap and torque the attaching bolts to 35 ft-lbs.
4. Install oil pump baffle and pan.

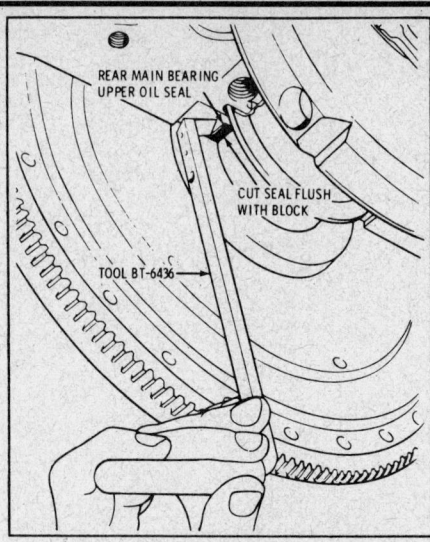

Fig. 24 Trimming upper rear main bearing oil seal

BELT TENSION DATA

	New Lbs.	Used Lbs.
1981–84		
V6 All		
Air Conditioning	145	80
A.I.R. Pump	80	45
Alternator	145	70
Power Steering	170	90
Vacuum Pump	80	45
V8 All		
Air Conditioning	170	90
A.I.R. Pump	80③	45③
Alternator	160④	80④
Power Steering	170	90
Vacuum Pump	125	55
1979–80		
5/16" Belts	80	50
3/8" Belts①	140	70
3/8" Belts②	140	60
15/32" Belts	165	90
1977–78		
V8 All	110–140	70

①—Except cogged belts.
②—Cogged belts.
③—3/8" belts; new, 145; used, 70.
④—Cogged belts; new, 145; used, 55.

WATER PUMP, REPLACE

V8-260, 307, 350, 403

1. Drain cooling system and remove heater and lower hoses from pump.
2. Loosen pulley belts and remove fan and pulley. On air conditioned cars, remove clutch fan assembly and pulley.
3. Remove pump from front cover.

FUEL PUMP, REPLACE

1. Disconnect fuel line fron fuel pump.
2. Remove fuel pump mounting bolts and the fuel pump.
3. Remove all gasket material from the pump and block gasket surfaces. Apply sealer to both sides of new gasket.
4. Position gasket on pump flange and hold pump in position against its mounting surface. Make sure rocker arm is riding on camshaft eccentric.
5. Press pump tight against its mounting. Install retaining screws and tighten them alternately.
6. Connect fuel lines. Then operate engine and check for leaks.

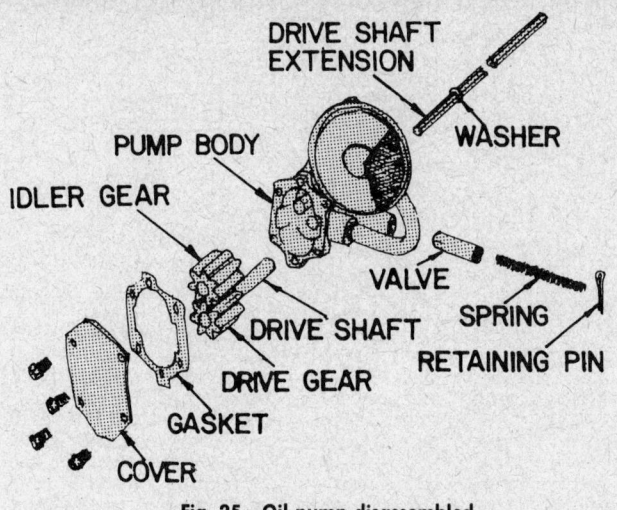

Fig. 25 Oil pump disassembled.
V8-260, 307, 350, 403 (Typical)

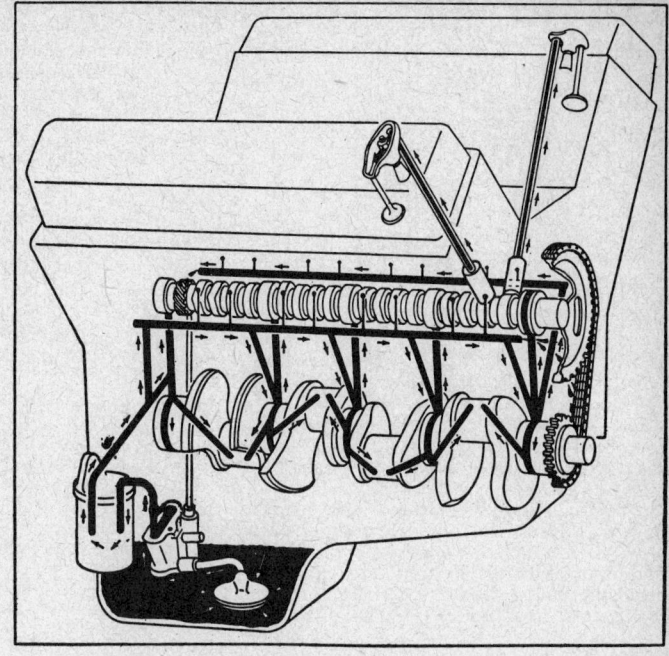

Engine lubrication. V8-260, 307, 350, 403 (Typical)

Diesel Engine Section

DIESEL ENGINE SECTION INDEX

DESCRIPTION

Engine Construction

The Oldsmobile four stroke cycle diesel engine is basically the same in construction as the Oldsmobile gasoline engine. The cylinders are numbered 1,3,5,7 on the left bank and 2,4,6,8 on the right bank on 8 cylinder engines or 1, 3 and 5 on the left bank and 2, 4 and 6 on the right bank on 6 cylinder engines. The firing order is 1-8-4-3-6-5-7-2 on 8 cylinder engines or 1-6-5-4-3-2 on 6 cylinder engines. The major differences between the diesel and gasoline versions is in the cylinder heads, combustion chamber, fuel distribution system,

air intake manifold and method of ignition. The cylinder block, crankshaft, main bearings, connecting rods, pistons and pins are of heavy construction due to the high compression ratio required to ignite the diesel fuel. The diesel fuel is ignited when the heat developed in the combustion chamber during the compression stroke reaches a certain temperature.

The valve train operates the same as in the gasoline engine, but are of special design and material for diesel operation. The stainless steel pre-chamber inserts in the cylinder head combustion chambers are serviced separately from the cylinder head. With the cylinder head removed, these pre-chamber inserts can be driven from the cylinder head after remov-

ing the glow plugs or injection nozzles. The glow plugs are threaded into the cylinder head and the injection nozzles are retained by a bolt and clamp. The injection nozzles are spring loaded and calibrated to open at a specified fuel pressure.

Fuel System

The fuel injection pump is mounted on top of the engine and is gear driven by the camshaft and rotates at camshaft speed. This high pressure rotary pump injects a metered amount of fuel to each cylinder at the proper time. Six or eight high pressure fuel delivery pipes from the injection pump to the injection nozzles, Figs. 1 and 1A, are the same length to

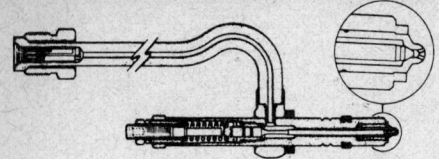

Fig. 1   Fuel injection nozzle. 1978–79

prevent any difference in timing from cylinder to cylinder. The fuel injection pump provides the required timing advance under all operating conditions. Engine speed is controlled by a rotary fuel metering valve, Figs. 2 and 2A. When the accelerator is depressed, the throttle cable opens the metering valve and allows more fuel to be delivered to the engine. The injection pump also incorporates a low pressure transfer pump to deliver fuel to the fuel line to the high pressure pump, Figs. 2 and 2A.

The fuel filter is located between the mechanical fuel pump and the injection pump on 8 cylinder engines, or between the electric fuel pump and the injection pump on 6 cylinder engines. The diaphragm type mechanical fuel pump used on 8 cylinder engines is mounted on the right hand side of the engine and is driven by a cam on the crankshaft. The electric fuel pump used on 6 cylinder engines is mounted on the engine. The fuel tank at the rear of the vehicle is connected by fuel pipes to the mechanical fuel pump. Excess fuel returns from the fuel injection pump and injection nozzles to the fuel tank through pipes and hoses.

NOTE: Injection nozzles on 1980–84 diesel engines do not use a fuel return line.

"Water in Fuel" System

This system is available on some 1980 and all 1981–84 models. These vehicles have a "Water in Fuel" light mounted in the instrument panel. The "Water in Fuel" light has a bulb check feature and should light for 2 to 2½ seconds when the ignition is turned on. If not, the bulb is burned out or there is an open in the wiring circuit. When there is water in the fuel, the light will come back on and remain on after a 15 to 20 second delay.

A water sensing probe, mounted on the fuel sender, actuates the instrument panel light when it is partially covered with water. About 1 to 2½ gallons of water must be present in the fuel tank to cause the sensor light to activate.

If the "Water in Fuel" lamp goes on while the vehicle is being driven, the fuel system should be checked for water. If the lamp goes on immediately after refueling and before the vehicle is moved, there is a large quantity of water in the tank and should be removed immediately.

The water may be removed from the tank with a pump or by siphoning. The pump or siphon hose should be connected to the quarter inch fuel return hose (the smaller of the two hoses), located under the hood near the fuel pump. Refer to "Purging Water From Fuel Tank" procedure.

Housing Pressure Cold Advance (HPCA)

This feature is used on all 1981–84 engines and advances the injection timing 3° during cold operation. This circuit is actuated by a temperature switch calibrated to open the cir-

cuit at 125° F. Below the switching point, housing pressure is decreased from 10 to 0 psi which advances the injection timing 3°. Above the switching point, the switch opens, de-energizing the solenoid and the housing pressure is returned to 10 psi. The fast idle solenoid is energized by the same switch and closes when the temperature falls below 95° F.

Housing Pressure Altitude Advance (HPAA)

Used on 1984 engines (exc. Calif.), the HPAA is used to meet emission standards at both low and high altitudes. Altitude compensation is achieved through timing changes and EGR modification and is controlled by an altitude sensitive switch.

Timing is controlled by two pressure regulators, the Housing Pressure Cold Advance, located in the injection pump, and the Housing Pressure Altitude Advance solenoid in the fuel return line.

The HPAA solenoid regulates housing pres-

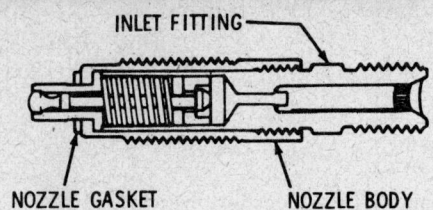

Fig 1A   Fuel injection nozzle. 1980–84

sure according to altitude. When the solenoid is activated, the glass check ball seats, regulating pressure at its calibrated value. When the solenoid is de-activated, the check ball moves off its seat, opening the fuel return line and preventing pressure regulation. It is possible for both the HPCA and the HPAA to regulate housing pressure at the same time. Likewise, it is also possible to have just the HPCA or the HPAA regulate pressure singularly. The HPCA must be energized and not regulating to allow the HPAA solenoid to regulate at its calibrated value.

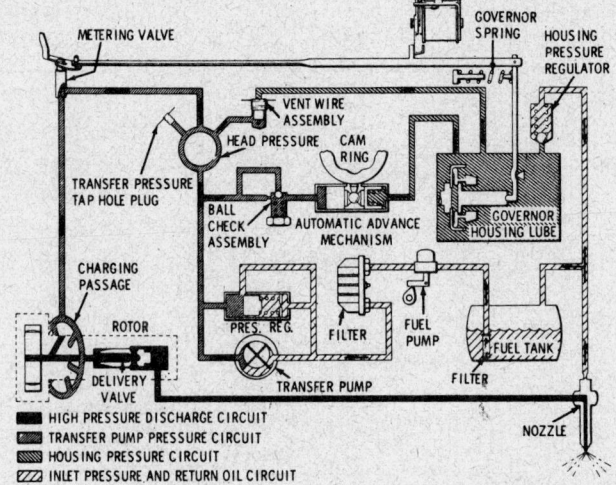

Fig. 2   Fuel injection pump circuit, V8 engine

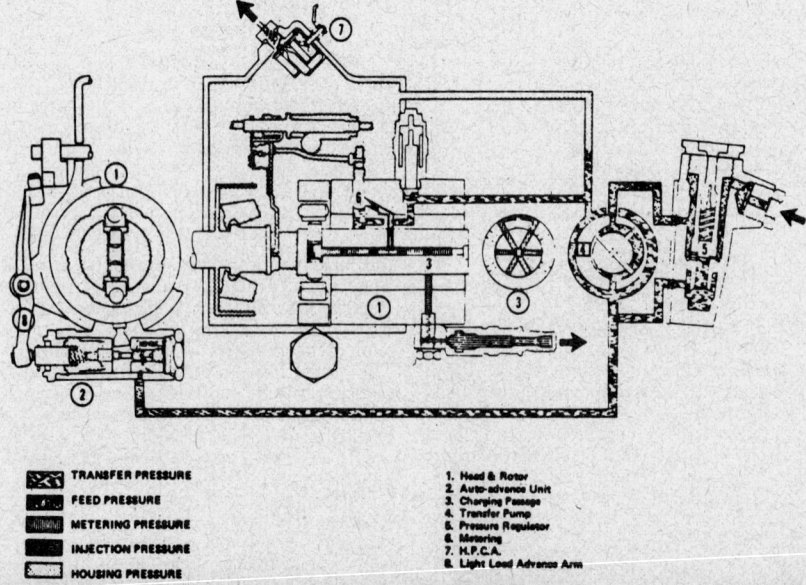

Fig. 2A   Fuel injection pump circuit. V6 engine

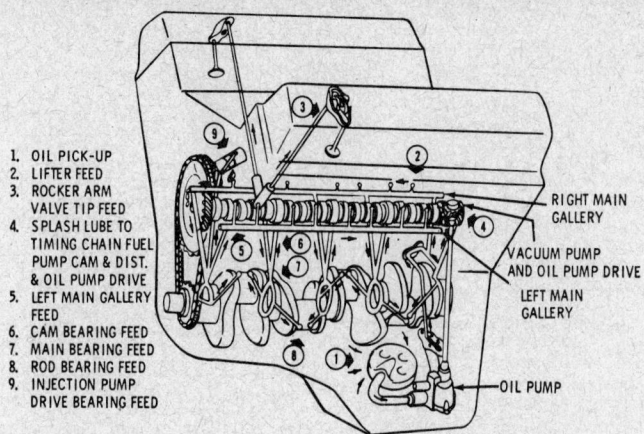

1. OIL PICK-UP
2. LIFTER FEED
3. ROCKER ARM VALVE TIP FEED
4. SPLASH LUBE TO TIMING CHAIN FUEL PUMP CAM & DIST. & OIL PUMP DRIVE
5. LEFT MAIN GALLERY FEED
6. CAM BEARING FEED
7. MAIN BEARING FEED
8. ROD BEARING FEED
9. INJECTION PUMP DRIVE BEARING FEED

Fig. 3 Engine lubricating system. Typical. (V6 engine similar)

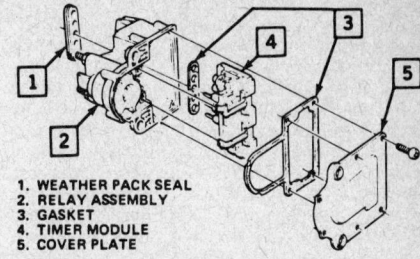

1. WEATHER PACK SEAL
2. RELAY ASSEMBLY
3. GASKET
4. TIMER MODULE
5. COVER PLATE

Fig. 3A Glow plug control module. 1984

Engine Lubrication System

NOTE: On 1978 engines, the recommended diesel engine oil designation is SE/CD. On 1979—80 engines, the recommended diesel engine oil designation is SE/CC. On 1981 engines, the recommended diesel engine oil is SF/CC, SF/CD or SE/CC. On 1982—84 engines the recommended diesel engine oil is SF/CC or SF/CD.

The diesel engine lubrication system is basically the same as the gasoline engine. The fuel injection pump driven gear is lubricated by oil directed through a passage from the top of the camshaft bearing, Fig. 3. An angled passage in the shaft portion of the driven gear directs the oil to the rear driven gear bearing. At the front of the right oil gallery, a small orifice sprays oil to lubricate the fuel pump eccentric cam on the crankshaft and timing chain.

Engine Cooling System

The diesel engine cooling system is the same as the gasoline engine except the radiator incorporates two oil coolers. One cooler is used to cool the transmission fluid and the other cooler is used to cool the engine oil.

Engine Electrical System

1984

A new glow plug system is used for 1984

diesel engines. A self-limiting feature regulates maximum temperature, while the glow plugs are programmed to shut off automatically should the vehicle not be started within the specified time period.

System Components

The glow plug control module, Fig. 3A, is an integral assembly that includes the timer functions, lamp switch and glow plug relay. The control module serves the following functions:

1. Controls wait lamp operation, which varies according to system voltage and/or ambient temperature.
2. Controls system shutdown timing depending on voltage and ambient temperature.
3. An overvoltage function that protects the glow plugs from failure, should higher than normal voltages be incurred.
4. A thermal cutout function that disengages the glow plug system when module temperatures are greater than 113°F.
5. A power relay function that switches the voltage applied to the glow plugs.
6. A quick reset function that permits the module to recycle quickly, after initial shutdown time.

This control module can only be used with glow plugs that regulate their own temperature. The new glow plugs used have positive temperature coefficient properties, which mean they have low resistance values at low temperatures and high resistance values at high temperatures. The new plugs offer a fast

temperature rise similar to past fixed resistance plugs, plus improved and simpler glow plug control.

System Operation

The glow plug control circuit, Fig. 3B, operates the glow plug system in three steps: pre-glow, after-glow and off. During pre-glow, the circuit activates the wait lamp and heats the glow plugs until they are sufficiently warm to start the engine. During after-glow, the circuit deactivates the wait lamp, but continues to apply power to the glow plugs. During the Off cycle, the circuit removes power from the glow plugs and keeps it off until the engine is restarted.

As stated previously, the glow plug control module controls all circuit functions. The thermal controls open the pre-glow and after-glow switches to end the respective cycles, and are responsive to engine temperature. When the system is energized with the engine cold, both switches are in the "Cold" position. As time passes, current flow heats the thermal controls, moving both switches toward their "HOT" position. The time needed for each switch to reach its "HOT" position is dependent upon how cold the engine and control module were when the system was first energized. As the pre-glow switch reaches the "HOT" position, the wait lamp deactivates and the engine may now be started. The control module continues to operate, whether the engine is started or not, since the after-glow switch has not yet reached its "HOT" position. Current flow continues to heat the thermal control. When the thermal control reaches full temperature, the after-glow switch moves to "HOT", opening the path to ground from the coil of the glow plug relay. This allows current flow to bypass the coil of the reset relay. With the path to ground now open, current must flow to bypass the coil of the reset relay. With the path to ground now open, current must flow to ground through the reset relay coil. The glow plug relay de-energizes, removing power to the glow plugs. The reset relay now energizes, opening the contact of the relay and locking off the thermal controls. When the ignition switch is turned off, the reset relay contact closes, and the glow plug module is ready to repeat the cycle. If the engine is above 140°F. when restarted, the thermal controls will be "HOT", energizing the reset relay and preventing glow plug operation.

The over-voltage protector protects the glow plugs should battery voltage rise above 14 volts. When the protector senses over 14 volts, it opens the circuit to the glow plug relay coil and prevents current from flowing to the glow plugs. After a short time, the protector closes the circuit. If battery voltage is still above 14 volts, it will reopen the circuit again. The protector continues to cycle in this way as long as the over-voltage condition exists and as long as glow plug operation is needed.

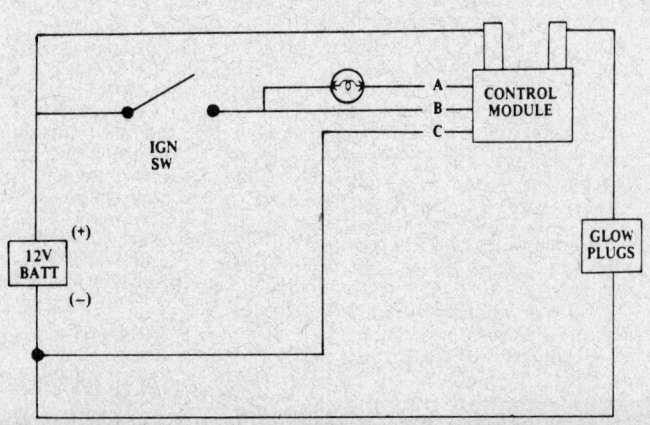

Fig. 3B Glow plug control circuit schematic. 1984

1978-83

Eight glow plugs are used to pre-heat the pre-chamber to aid in starting. The type 1 glow plugs are 12 volt heaters and are activated when the ignition switch is turned to the "Run" position. The type 1 system uses steady current applied to 12 volt glow plugs. The type 2 glow plug system uses 6 volt glow plugs with a controlled pulsating current applied to them for starting. The type 2 glow plug system uses an electromechanical controller to control glow plug temperature, preglow time, wait/start lights and after glow time. The 1980-83 Cutlass Electronic Glow Plug Control System uses an electronic module and a control sensor to control glow plug temperature, the glow plug relay and the wait light. On this system a coolant temperature switch controls the fast idle solenoid through a fast idle relay. The 6 volt and 12 volt glow plugs are not interchangeable and can be identified by the wire connector spade. The 6 volt glow plugs have a $5/16$ in. wire connector spade, while the 12 volt glow plugs have a $1/4$ in. wire connector spade. The glow plugs remain activated for a short time after starting then are automatically turned "Off". Two 12 volt batteries connected in parallel are required for the higher electical load due to the glow plugs and starter motor. The diesel starter motor is larger than the gasoline engine starter and is designed to crank the engine at least the 100 RPM required for starting. An alternator supplies charging current to both batteries at the same time and there are no switches or relays in the charging circuit.

DIESEL ENGINE ELECTRICAL DIAGNOSIS

1978-83

Refer to Figs. 4 through 27I for diesel engine electrical diagnosis.

ROUGH IDLE DIAGNOSIS

Check for mechanical malfunctions such as incorrect idle speed or injection pump timing, or leaking nozzles or high pressure lines. If rough idle is still evident, refer to "Glow Plug Resistance Check".

Glow Plug Resistance Check

1981-84

1. Using multi-meter J-29125 (1981-83) or J-29125A (1984), set left selector switch to "OHMS", right selector switch to 200 ohms and center slide switch to "D.C. LO".

   NOTE: If another ohmmeter is used, different values will result. Tools J-29125 and J-29125A were used in the development of this procedure. Their use is required if similar readings are to be obtained.

2. Start engine, allow it to reach normal operating temperature, then disconnect all feed wires from glow plugs. Turn heater to "On" position.
3. Disconnect alternator two wire connector.
4. Using tachometer J-26925, or equivalent, adjust idle speed screw to obtain worst engine idle roughness condition. Do not exceed 900 RPM.
5. Allow engine to run at worst idle speed for approximately one minute, then attach an alligator clip to black test lead of meter. Ground black test lead to fast idle solenoid (1983-84) or engine lift strap (1981-82).
6. Write down the engine firing order on a piece of paper, then with engine idling, probe each glow plug terminal and record the resistance values on each cylinder in the firing sequence.

   NOTE: If vehicle is equipped with an electric cooling fan, record resistance values with cooling fan inoperative. Do not disconnect cooling fan circuitry. The resistance values are dependent on the temperature in each cylinder, and therefore, can indicate cylinder output.

7. If a resistance reading on any cylinder is 1.3-1.4 ohms for 1984 vehicles, or 1.2-1.3 for 1981-83 vehicles, check engine for a mechanical problem. Make a compression check of the lowest reading cylinder and the cylinders which fire before and after. Correct cause of low compression before proceeding to fuel system.
8. On 1984 vehicles, install glow plug luminosity probe, from tool J-33075, into cylinder with lowest resistance value. Observe combustion light flashes of probe. The flashes will usually be erratic and in sequence with the misfire. If not, move to the next lowest reading cylinder, until the misfire is found.
9. On all vehicles, observe the results of all glow plug resistance readings, looking for differences between cylinders. Rough engines will normally have a difference of .4 ohms or more between cylinders in the firing sequence. To correct rough engine idle, it will be necessary to raise or lower the resistance values on one or more of the offending cylinders by replacing the injection nozzles.
10. Remove nozzle from the cylinder(s) affecting idle performance. Determine the pop off pressure of the nozzle and check the nozzle for leakage and spray pattern. Refer to tool manufacturer for proper testing procedures. Install nozzles with higher pop off pressures to lower resistance values, and nozzles with lower pop off pressures to raise values. A change of 30 psi nozzle pressure will result in a .1 ohm difference in resistance. Use new nozzles on new vehicles and broken in nozzles on vehicles with 1500 or more miles, if possible.

    NOTE: Whenever a nozzle is cleaned or replaced, crank the engine and watch for air bubbles at the nozzle inlet before connecting the injection pipe. If bubbles are evident, clean or replace the nozzle.

11. Connect injection pipe, restart engine and check idle quality. If idle quality is still not acceptable, repeat steps 6 through 10.
12. After making additional nozzle changes, check idle quality again.
13. If problem moves from cylinder to cylinder and resistance values do not change as nozzles are changed, the injection pump may be defective.

NOTE: Always recheck cylinders at same engine RPM. Sometimes cylinder readings may not indicate that an improvement has been made, even though the engine may idle better. A nozzle with a tip leak can allow more fuel than required into a cylinder, raising the glow plug resistance value. This will steal fuel from the next nozzle in the firing order and will result in that glow plug having a lower resistance value. If this is evident, remove and check the nozzle with the high reading. If it is leaking, it may be responsible for the rough idle. If low readings are evident on a glow plug and it does not change with a nozzle change, switch glow plugs between the good and bad cylinder. If the reading of each cylinder is not the same as before the switch, then the glow plug cannot be used for rough idle diagnosis.

WATER IN FUEL SYSTEM DIAGNOSIS

Water in Fuel Lamp Does Not Go On

If the likelihood of water in the fuel tank exists and the Water In Fuel lamp is off, siphon the fuel tank to check for water by connecting a pump to the fuel return line. If at least 3 gallons of water are siphoned from the tank, proceed as follows:

1. Disconnect Water In Fuel electrical lead at fuel tank and ground the lead. If lamp does not go on, proceed to step 4. If it does, check for at least 8 volts at the electrical lead. If no voltage is present, replace the Water In Tank light bulb.
2. Ground the Water In Tank electrical lead. If lamp does not go on, check for open circuit in wiring, Fig. 27J.
3. Remove fuel level sender and Water in Fuel detector unit from fuel tank.
4. Check connections to "Water In Fuel". If satisfactory, check detector unit as follows:
   a. Remove detector from fuel sender unit, Fig. 27K.
   b. Connect the detector to a bulb and power source as shown in Fig. 27L. The lamp should go on when the detector probe is lowered into the container of water $3/8$ inch or less. Make sure water is grounded to negative side of battery.

Water In Fuel Lamp Stays On

Under this condition, siphon the tank to check for water by connecting a pump to the fuel return line. If no water is present, proceed as follows:

1. Disconnect the Water In Fuel electrical lead near the fuel tank. If lamp does not go off, proceed to step 2. If lamp goes off, remove fuel level sender and check detector as described previously under "Water In Fuel Lamp Does Not Go On".
2. Check for short circuit in wire between the "Water In Fuel" connection at the fuel tank and the dash indicator lamp, Fig. 27G.

ENGINE MOUNTS

Refer to Figs. 28, 28A, 28B, 28C and 28D for engine mount installation.

DIESEL ENGINE DIAGNOSIS

Condition	Possible Cause	Correction
ENGINE WILL NOT CRANK	1. Loose or corroded battery cables 2. Discharged batteries 3. Starter Inoperative	1. Check connections at battery, engine block and starter solenoid. 2. Check charging system. 3. Check starting system.
ENGINE CRANKS SLOWLY— WILL NOT START (Minimum Engine Crank Speed— 100 RPM)	1. Battery cable connections loose or corroded 2. Batteries undercharged 3. Wrong engine oil	1. Check connections at battery, engine block and starter. 2. Check charging system. 3. Drain and refill with recommended oil.
ENGINE CRANKS NORMALLY— WILL NOT START	1. Incorrect starting procedure 2. Incorrect or contaminated fuel 3. No fuel to nozzles 4. No fuel to injection pump 5. Plugged fuel return system 6. Pump timing incorrect 7. Glow plug control system inoperative 8. Glow plugs inoperative 9. Internal engine problems 10. No voltage to fuel solenoid 11. Restricted fuel tank filter.	1. Use recommended starting procedure. 2. Flush fuel system and install correct fuel. 3. Loosen injection line at a nozzle. Do not disconnect. Use care to direct fuel away from sources of ignition. Wipe connection to be sure it is dry. Crank 5 seconds. Fuel should flow from injection line. Tighten connection. If fuel does not flow, check fuel solenoid operation as follows: Connect a 12 volt test lamp from wire at injection pump solenoid to ground. Turn ignition to "ON". Lamp should light. If lamp does not light, check wiring to solenoid. 4. Remove line at inlet to injection pump fuel filter. Connect hose from line to metal container. Crank engine. If no fuel is discharged, test the fuel supply pump. If the pump is OK, check the injection pump fuel filter and replace if plugged. If filter and inlet line to injection pump are OK, replace injection pump. 5. Disconnect fuel return line at injection pump and route hose to a metal container. Connect a hose to the injection pump connection and route it to the metal container. Crank the engine; if engine starts and runs, correct restriction in fuel return system. 6. Make certain that pump timing mark is aligned with mark on adapter. 7. Refer to Diesel Engine Electrical System Diagnosis. 8. Refer to Diesel Engine Electrical System Diagnosis. 9. Correct as necessary. 10. Connect a 12 volt test lamp from injection pump solenoid to ground. Turn ignition to "On", lamp should light. If lamp lights, remove test lamp and connect and disconnect solenoid connector and listen for solenoid operation. If solenoid does not operate, remove injection pump for repairs. If lamp does not light, refer to Diesel Engine Electrical System Diagnosis. 11. Remove fuel tank and check filter.
ENGINE STARTS BUT WILL NOT CONTINUE TO RUN AT IDLE	1. No fuel in tank 2. Incorrect or contaminated fuel 3. Limited fuel to injection pump 4. Fuel solenoid disengaged with ignition switch in the "ON" position 5. Restricted fuel return system	1. Install correct fuel in tank. 2. Flush fuel system and install correct fuel. 3. Test the fuel supply pump. Replace as necessary. 4. Connect a 12 volt test lamp from wire at injection pump solenoid to ground. Turn ignition to "ON". Lamp should light. Turn ignition to "START". Lamp should light. If lamp does not light in both positions, check wiring to solenoid. 5. Disconnect fuel return line at injection pump and route hose to a metal container. Connect a hose to injection pump connection and route to metal container. Crank engine; if engine starts and runs, correct restriction in fuel return system.

Condition	Possible Cause	Correction
ENGINE STARTS BUT WILL NOT CONTINUE TO RUN AT IDLE (Cont'd)	6. Fast idle solenoid inoperative	6. With engine cold, start car; solenoid should move to support injection pump lever in "fast idle position" for about 5 seconds. If solenoid does not move, refer to Electrical System Diagnosis.
	7. Low idle incorrectly adjusted	7. Adjust idle screw to specification.
	8. Pump timing incorrect	8. Make certain that timing mark, on injection pump, is aligned with mark on adapter.
	9. Glow plug control system malfunction	9. Refer to Diesel Engine Electrical System Diagnosis.
	10. Injection pump malfunction	10. Install replacement pump.
	11. Internal engine problems	11. Correct as necessary.
ENGINE STARTS, IDLES ROUGH, WITHOUT ABNORMAL NOISE OR SMOKE	1. Low idle incorrectly adjusted	1. Adjust idle screw to specification.
	2. Injection line leaks	2. Wipe off injection lines and connections. Run engine and check for leaks. Correct leaks.
	3. Restricted fuel return system	3. Disconnect fuel return line at injection pump and route hose to a metal container. Connect a hose to the injection pump connection and route it to the metal container. Crank the engine; if engine starts and runs, correct restriction in fuel return system.
	4. Incorrect or contaminated fuel	4. Flush fuel system and install correct fuel.
	5. Nozzle(s) inoperative	5. With engine running, loosen injection line fitting at each nozzle in turn. Use care to direct fuel away from sources of ignition. Each nozzle should contribute to rough running. If nozzle is found that does not change idle quality, it should be replaced.
	6. Internal fuel leak at nozzle(s)	6. Disconnect fuel return system from nozzles on one bank at a time. With the engine running, observe the normal fuel seepage at the nozzles. Replace any nozzle with excessive fuel leakage.
	7. Fuel supply pump malfunctions	7. Test the fuel supply pump. Replace if necessary.
	8. Uneven fuel distribution to cylinders	8. Install new or reconditioned nozzles, one at a time, until condition is corrected as indicated by normal idle.
ENGINE STARTS AND IDLES ROUGH WITH EXCESSIVE NOISE AND/OR SMOKE	1. Injection pump timing incorrect	1. Be sure timing mark on injection pump is aligned with mark on adapter.
	2. Nozzle(s) inoperative	2. With engine running, crack injection line at each nozzle, one at a time. Use care to direct fuel away from sources of ignition. Each nozzle should contribute to rough running. If a nozzle is found that does not affect idle quality or changes noise and/or smoke, it should be replaced.
	3. High pressure lines incorrectly installed	3. Check routing of each line. Correct as required.
ENGINE COLD, STARTS AND IDLES ROUGH WITH EXCESSIVE NOISE AND/OR SMOKE, BUT CLEARS UP AFTER WARM-UP	1. Incorrect starting procedure	1. Advise operator on correct procedure. (See owners manual.)
	2. Injection pump timing incorrect	2. Check timing with J-33075 timing meter and reset if needed.
	3. Insufficient engine break-in time	3. Break in engine 2000 miles or more.
	4. Air in system	4. Install a section of clear plastic tubing on the fuel return fitting from the engine. Evidence of bubbles in fuel when cranking or running indicates the presence of an air leak in the suction fuel line.
	5. Inoperative glow plug	5. Replace faulty glow plug.
	6. Nozzle(s) malfunction	6. Remove and clean or replace.
	7. Housing pressure cold advance inoperative	7. Check operation and repair.
ENGINE MISFIRES BUT IDLES CORRECTLY	1. Plugged fuel filter	1. Replace filter.
	2. Incorrect injection pump timing	2. Be sure that timing mark on injection pump and adapter are aligned.
	3. Incorrect or contaminated fuel	3. Flush fuel system and install correct fuel.

Condition	Possible Cause	Correction
ENGINE WILL NOT RETURN TO IDLE	1. External linkage misadjustment or failure	1. Reset linkage or replace as required.
	2. Internal injection pump malfunction	2. Install replacement injection pump.
FUEL LEAKS ON GROUND—NO ENGINE MALFUNCTION	1. Loose or broken fuel line or connection	1. Examine complete fuel system, including tank, supply, injection and return system. Determine source and cause of leak and repair.
	2. Internal injection pump failure	2. Install replacement injection pump.
SIGNIFICANT LOSS OF POWER	1. Incorrect or contaminated fuel	1. Flush fuel system and install correct fuel.
	2. Pinched or otherwise restricted return system	2. Examine system for restriction and correct as required.
	3. Plugged fuel tank vent	3. Remove fuel cap. If "hissing" noise is heard, vent is plugged and should be cleaned.
	4. Restricted supply	4. Examine fuel supply system to determine cause of restriction. Repair as required.
	5. Plugged fuel filter	5. Remove and replace filter.
	6. External compression leaks	6. Check for compression leaks at all nozzles and glow plugs, using "Leak-Tec" or equivalent. If leak is found, tighten nozzle clamp or glow plug. If leak persists at a nozzle, remove it and reinstall with a new carbon stop seal and compression seal.
	7. Plugged nozzle(s)	7. Remove nozzles, check for plugging and have repaired or replaced.
	8. Internal engine problem	8. Correct as necessary.
NOISE—"RAP" FROM ONE OR MORE CYLINDERS	1. Air in fuel system	1. Check for leaks and correct.
	2. Air in high pressure line(s)	2. Crack line at nozzle(s) and bleed air at each cylinder determined to be causing noise. Use care to direct fuel away from sources of ignition and be sure to carefully retighten lines.
	3. Nozzle(s) sticking open or with very low blowoff pressure	3. Replace the nozzle(s) causing the problem.
	4. Internal engine problem	4. Correct as necessary.
NOISE—SIGNIFICANT OVERALL COMBUSTION NOISE INCREASE WITH EXCESSIVE BLACK SMOKE	1. Timing not set to specification	1. Align timing marks on adapter and injection pump.
	2. Internal engine problem	2. Check for presence of oil in the air crossover. If present, determine cause and correct.
	3. Injection pump housing pressure out of specifications.	3. Check housing pressure. If incorrect, replace fuel return line connector assembly.
	4. Internal injection pump problem	4. Replace pump.
NOISE—INTERNAL OR EXTERNAL	1. Fuel supply pump, alternator, water pump, valve train, vacuum pump, bearings etc.	1. Inspect and correct as necessary.
ENGINE OVERHEATS	1. Coolant system leak or oil cooler system leak	1. Check for leaks and correct as required.
	2. Belt failure	2. Replace.
	3. Thermostat malfunction, head gasket failure or internal engine problem	3. Inspect and correct as necessary.
INSTRUMENT PANEL OIL WARNING LAMP "ON" AT IDLE	1. Oil cooler or oil cooler line restricted	1. Remove restriction in cooler or cooler line.
	2. Internal engine problem	2. Correct as necessary.
ODOR OR SMOKE— EXCESSIVE AND NOT PREVIOUSLY COVERED	1. Same as Gasoline Engines	1. Correct as necessary. Refer to Trouble-Shooting Chapter.
ENGINE WILL NOT SHUT OFF WITH KEY	1. Injection pump solenoid does not drop out	1. Refer to electrical diagnosis. If problem is determined to be internal with the injection pump, replace the injection pump.
	2. Injection pump solenoid return spring failed	2. Replace injection pump.

NOTE: With engine at idle, pinch the fuel return line at the injection pump to shut off engine.

1
IGN. SWITCH
-"OFF"-

WAIT LAMP - OFF
START LAMP - OFF
GLOW PLUGS - OFF

2
IGN. SWITCH
-"RUN"-

WAIT LAMP - ON
START LAMP - OFF
GLOW PLUGS - ON

3
IGN. SWITCH
-"RUN"-

WAIT LAMP - OFF
START LAMP - ON
GLOW PLUGS - ON

⬇ SEE ✳ 1

4
IGN. SWITCH
-"START"-

WAIT LAMP - OFF
START LAMP - OFF
GLOW PLUGS - ON

5
IGN. SWITCH
-"RUN"-

WAIT LAMP - OFF
START LAMP - OFF
GLOW PLUGS - ON

⬇ SEE ✳ 2 & 3

6
IGN. SWITCH
-"RUN"-

WAIT LAMP - OFF
START LAMP - OFF
GLOW PLUGS - OFF

✳ 1: If the ignition is left in the "RUN" position 2-5 minutes before turning it to "START" the Glow Plugs and Lamps turn off. This prevents discharging the battery. Turn ignition "OFF" then to "RUN" and wait for Start Lamp. (Voltage to the starter solenoid is also directed to the module and is the signal that the ignition switch was turned to the Start position).

✳ 3: Engine did not start. Ign. switch still in "RUN" position. "GEN" lamp on. Electronic control starts over after 2-4 second delay (step 2). Wait lamp on. Start lamp off, and Glow Plugs on.

CHECK DIESEL AND GAGES FUSES

✳ 2: Engine Running - Generator voltage to turn off the "GEN" lamp is also directed to the module. 9 volts or more indicates the engine is running. Glow plugs remain on the same length of time between No. 5 and 6 as they did between No. 2 and 3.

✳ 4: The extra light bulb is behind the I. P. and located so it cannot be seen. It's purpose is to provide more current to the generator field coil when starting and idling the engine.

✳ 5: Diode prevents generator feedback to fuel solenoid when ignition is turned off. The diode is located behind the instrument cluster and may be serviced separately.

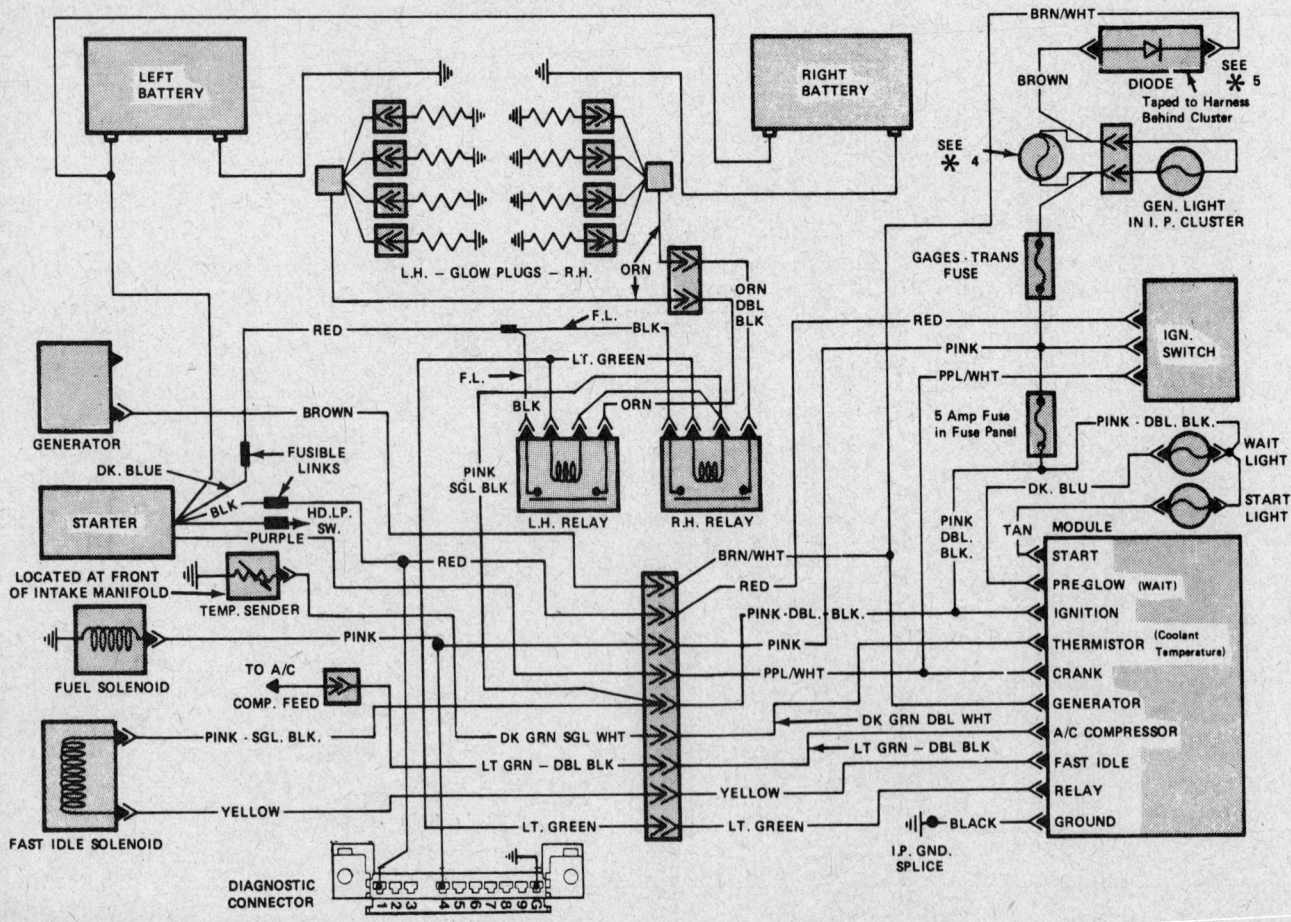

Fig. 4   Diesel engine electrical system. 1978–79 88 & 98 Type 1

1	2	3	4	5	6
IGN. SWITCH -"OFF"-	IGN. SWITCH -"RUN"-	IGN. SWITCH -"RUN"-	IGN. SWITCH -"START"-	IGN. SWITCH -"RUN"-	IGN. SWITCH -"RUN"-
WAIT LAMP - OFF	WAIT LAMP - ON	WAIT LAMP - OFF	WAIT LAMP - OFF	WAIT LAMP - OFF	WAIT LAMP - OFF
START LAMP - OFF	START LAMP - OFF	START LAMP - ON	START LAMP - OFF	START LAMP - OFF	START LAMP - OFF
GLOW PLUGS - OFF	GLOW PLUGS - ON	GLOW PLUGS - ON	GLOW PLUGS - ON	GLOW PLUGS - ON	GLOW PLUGS - OFF
		⬇ SEE ✱ 1		⬇ SEE ✱ 2 & 3	

✱ 1: If the ignition is left in the "RUN" position 2-5 minutes before turning it to "START", the Glow Plugs and Lamps turn off. This prevents discharging the battery. Turn ignition "OFF" then to "RUN" and wait for Start Lamp. (Voltage to the starter solenoid is also directed to the module and is the signal that the ignition switch was turned to the Start position).

✱ 2: Engine Running - Generator voltage to turn off the "GEN" lamp is also directed to the module. 9 volts or more indicates the engine is running. Glow plugs remain on the same length of time between No. 5 and 6 as they did between No. 2 and 3.

✱ 3: Engine did not start. Ign. switch still in "RUN" position. "GEN" lamp on. Electronic control starts over after 2-4 second delay (step 2). Wait lamp on. Start lamp off, and Glow Plugs on.

✱ 4: The extra light bulb is behind the I. P. and located so it cannot be seen. It's purpose is to provide more current to the generator field coil when starting and idling the engine.

✱ 5: Diode prevents generator feedback to fuel solenoid when ignition is turned off. The diode is located behind the instrument cluster and may be serviced separately.

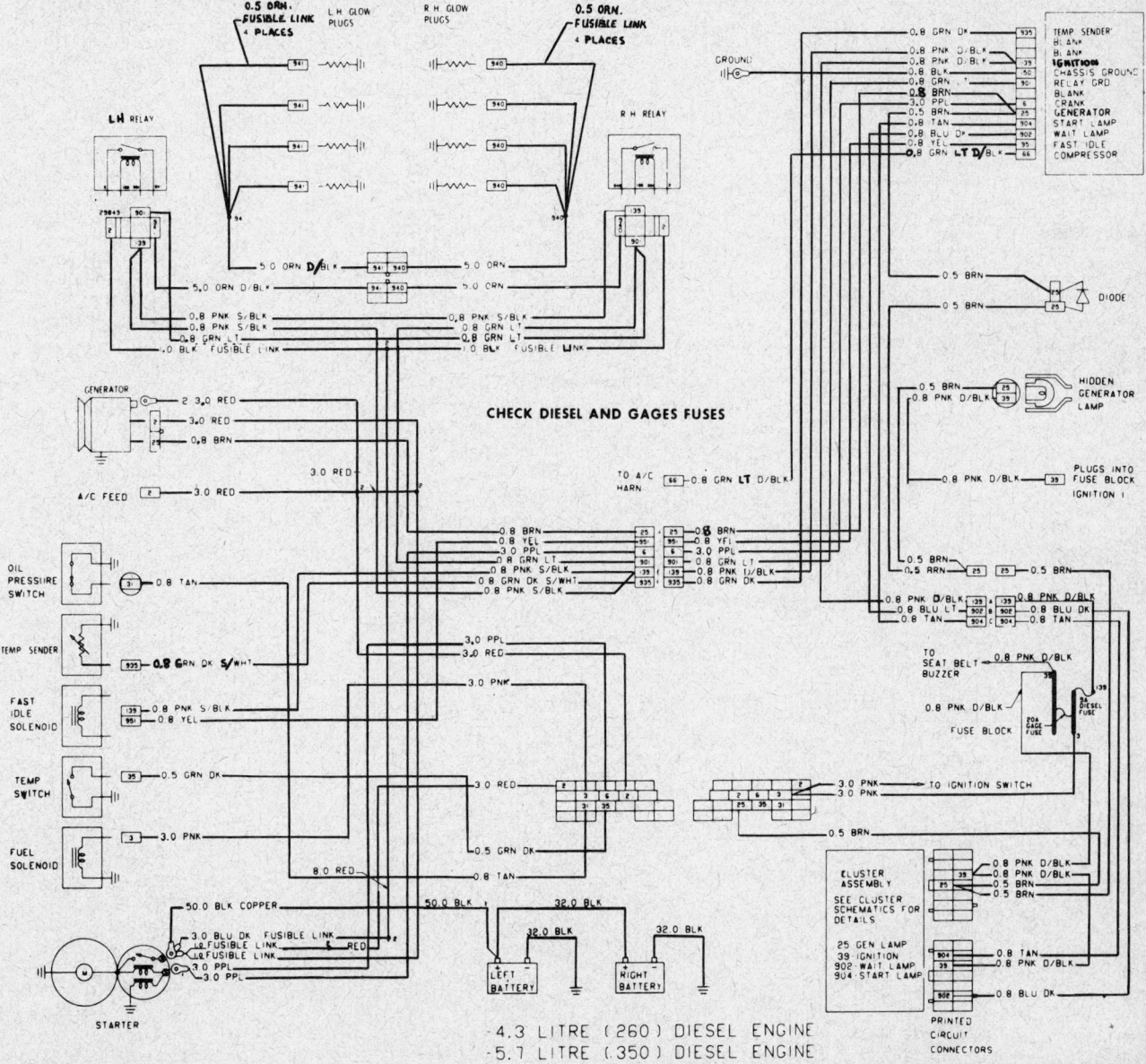

CHECK DIESEL AND GAGES FUSES

-4.3 LITRE (260) DIESEL ENGINE
-5.7 LITRE (350) DIESEL ENGINE

Fig. 5   Diesel engine electrical system. 1979 Cutlass Type 1

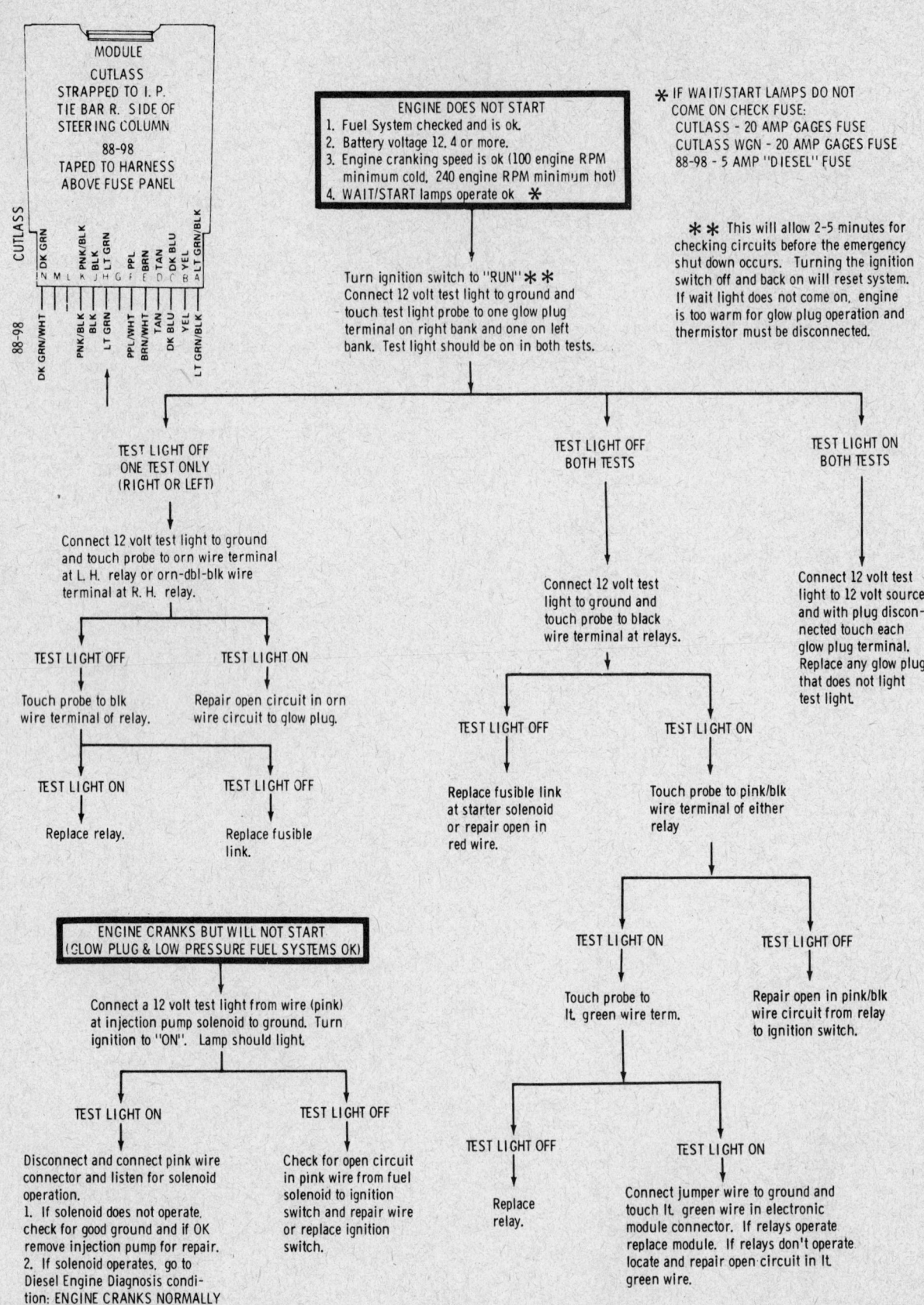

Fig. 6   Diesel engine electrical diagnosis, part 1 of 5. 1978–79 Type 1

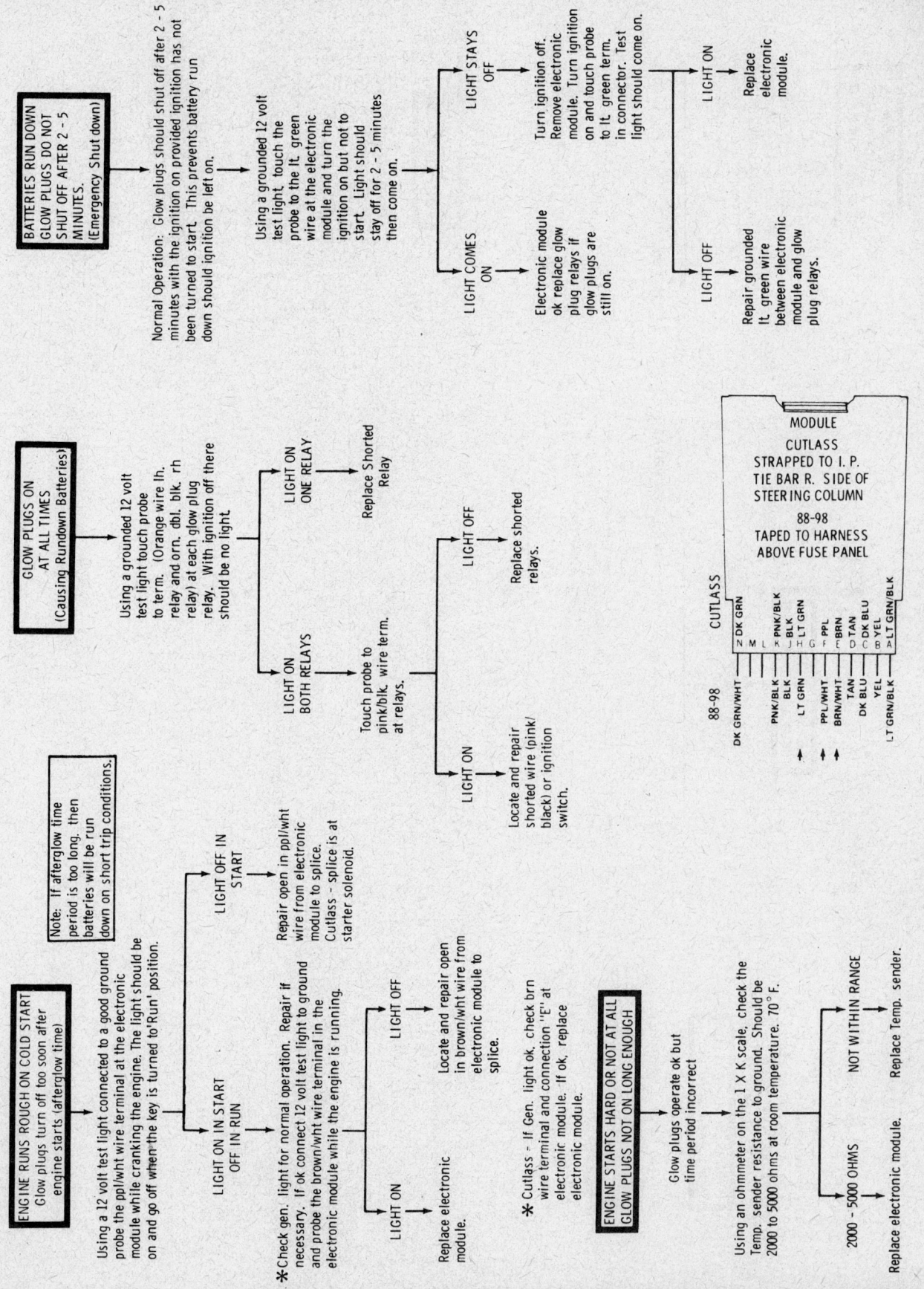

Fig. 7 Diesel engine electrical diagnosis, part 2 of 5. 1978–79 Type 1

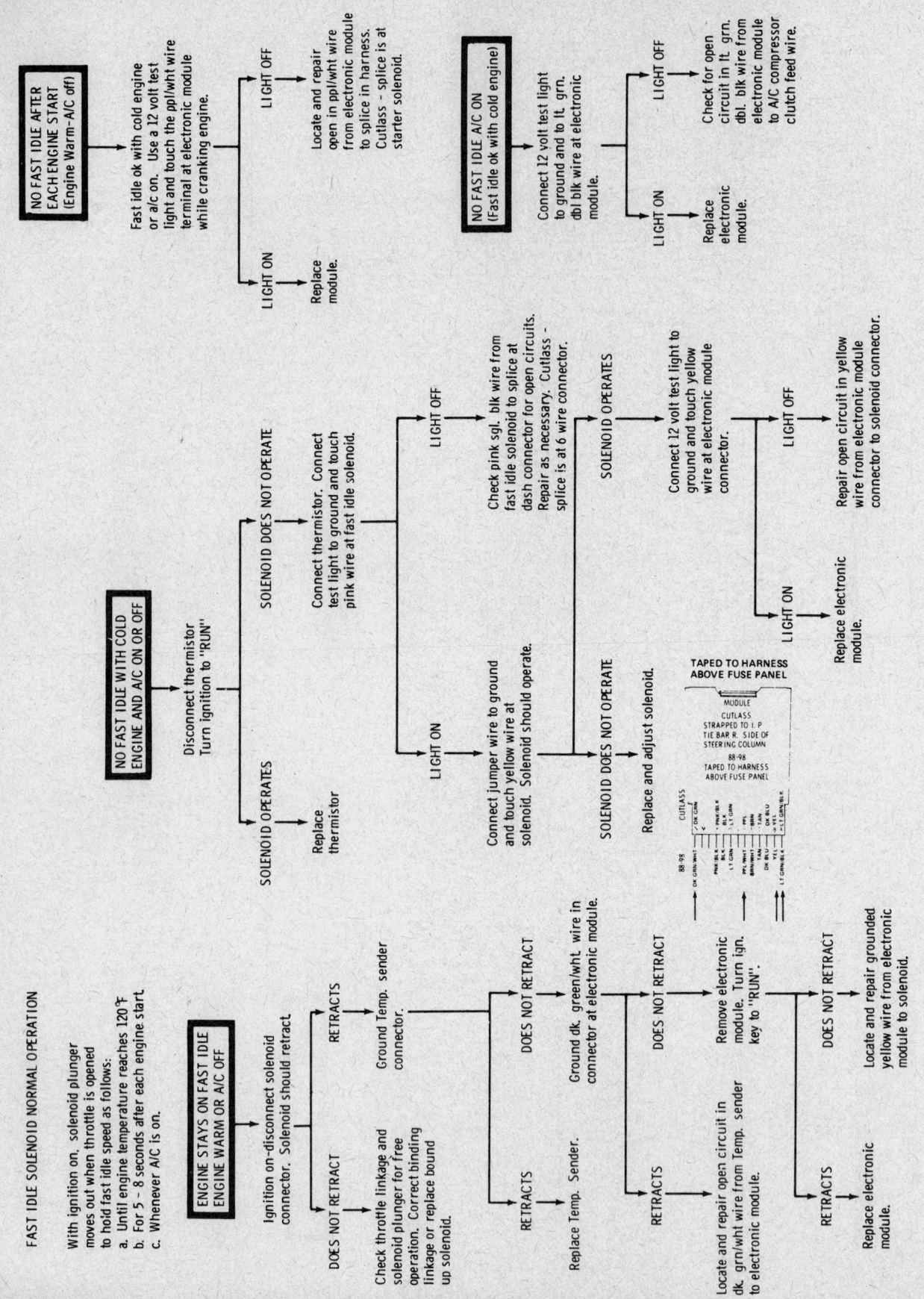

NO FAST IDLE AFTER EACH ENGINE START (Engine Warm-A/C off)

Fast idle ok with cold engine or a/c on. Use a 12 volt test light and touch the ppl/wht wire terminal at electronic module while cranking engine.

LIGHT OFF → Locate and repair open in ppl/wht wire from electronic module to splice in harness. Cutlass - splice is at starter solenoid.

LIGHT ON → Replace module.

NO FAST IDLE A/C ON (Fast idle ok with cold engine)

Connect 12 volt test light to ground and to lt. grn. dbl blk wire at electronic module.

LIGHT OFF → Check for open circuit in lt. grn. dbl. blk wire from electronic module to A/C compressor clutch feed wire.

LIGHT ON → Replace electronic module.

NO FAST IDLE WITH COLD ENGINE AND A/C ON OR OFF

Disconnect thermistor. Turn ignition to "RUN".

SOLENOID DOES NOT OPERATE → Connect thermistor. Connect test light to ground and touch pink wire at fast idle solenoid.

LIGHT OFF → Check pink sgl. blk wire from fast idle solenoid to splice at dash connector for open circuits. Repair as necessary. Cutlass - splice is at 6 wire connector.

SOLENOID OPERATES → Connect 12 volt test light to ground and touch yellow wire at electronic module connector.

LIGHT OFF → Repair open circuit in yellow wire from electronic module connector to solenoid connector.

LIGHT ON → Replace electronic module.

LIGHT ON → Connect jumper wire to ground and touch yellow wire at solenoid. Solenoid should operate.

SOLENOID DOES NOT OPERATE → Replace and adjust solenoid.

SOLENOID OPERATES → Replace thermistor

```
TAPED TO HARNESS
ABOVE FUSE PANEL

MODULE
CUTLASS
STRAPPED TO I. P.
TIE BAR R. SIDE OF
STEERING COLUMN

88-98
TAPED TO HARNESS
ABOVE FUSE PANEL

                    CUTLASS
            DK GRN
            PNK/BLK
            BLK
            LT GRN
            PPL
            BRN
            TAN
            DK BLU
            YEL
            LT GRN/BLK
88-98
DK GRN/WHT
PNK/BLK
BLK
LT GRN
PPL/WHT
BRN/WHT
TAN
DK BLU
YEL
LT GRN/BLK
```

FAST IDLE SOLENOID NORMAL OPERATION

With ignition on, solenoid plunger moves out when throttle is opened to hold fast idle speed as follows:
a. Until engine temperature reaches 120°F
b. For 5 - 8 seconds after each engine start.
c. Whenever A/C is on.

ENGINE STAYS ON FAST IDLE ENGINE WARM OR A/C OFF

Ignition on-disconnect solenoid connector. Solenoid should retract.

RETRACTS → Ground Temp. sender connector.

DOES NOT RETRACT → Check throttle linkage and solenoid plunger for free operation. Correct binding linkage or replace bound up solenoid.

RETRACTS → Replace Temp. Sender.

DOES NOT RETRACT → Ground dk. green/wht. wire in connector at electronic module.

RETRACTS → Locate and repair open circuit in dk. grn/wht wire from Temp. sender to electronic module.

DOES NOT RETRACT → Remove electronic module. Turn ign. key to "RUN".

RETRACTS → Replace electronic module.

DOES NOT RETRACT → Locate and repair grounded yellow wire from electronic module to solenoid.

Fig. 8   Diesel engine electrical diagnosis, part 3 of 5. 1978—79 Type 1

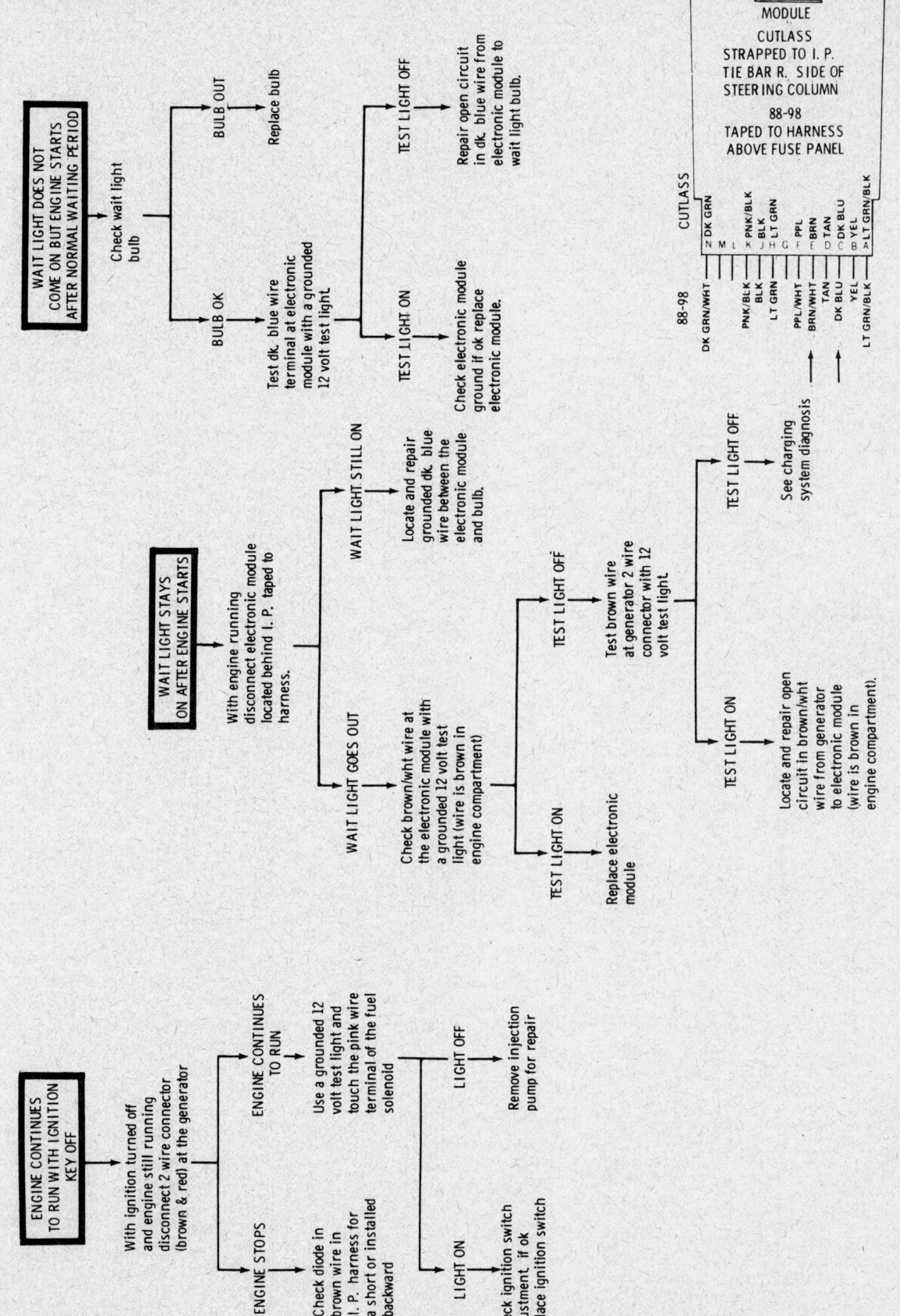

Fig. 9 Diesel engine electrical diagnosis, part 4 of 5. 1978–79 Type 1

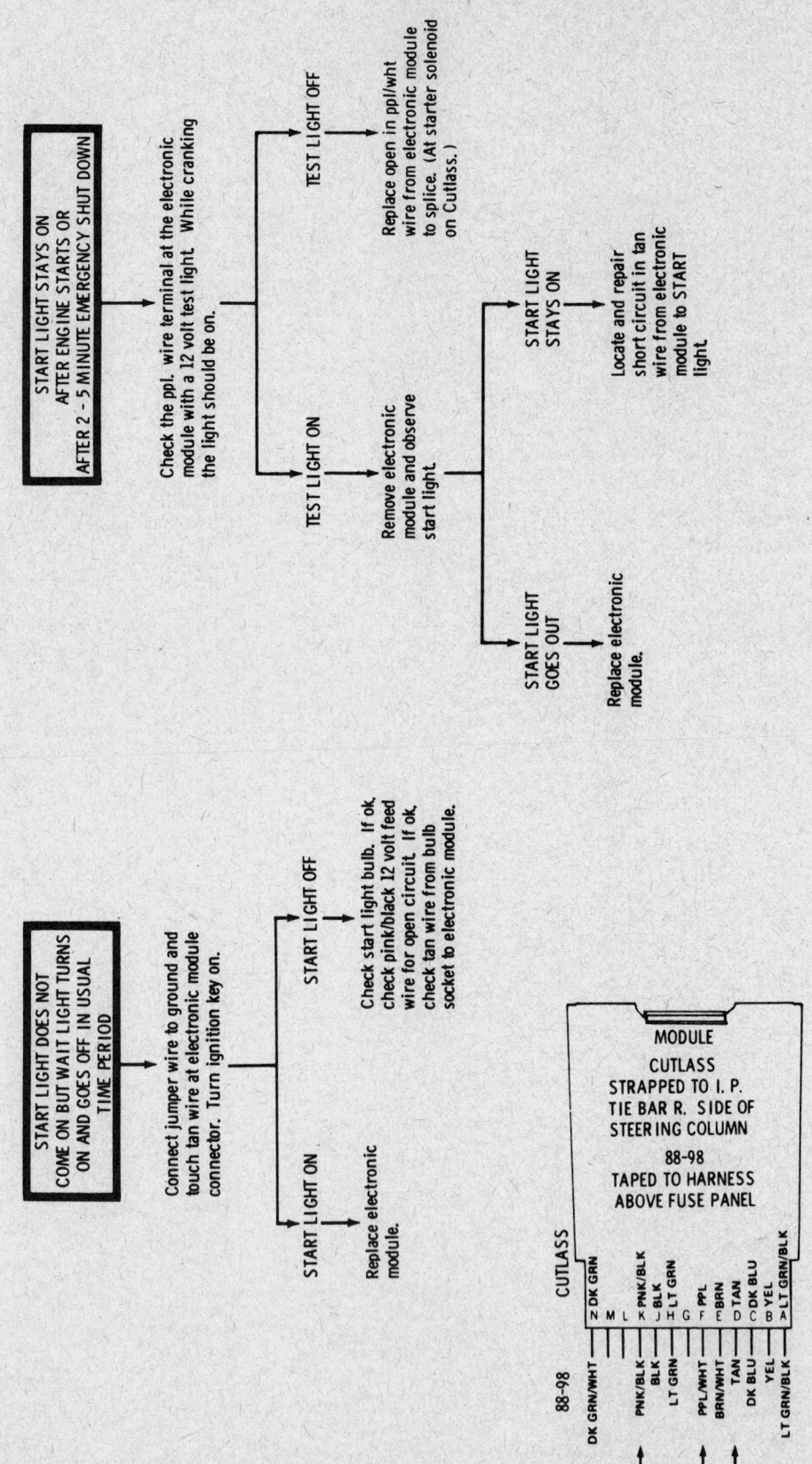

Fig. 10   Diesel engine electrical diagnosis, part 5 of 5. 1978–79 Type 1

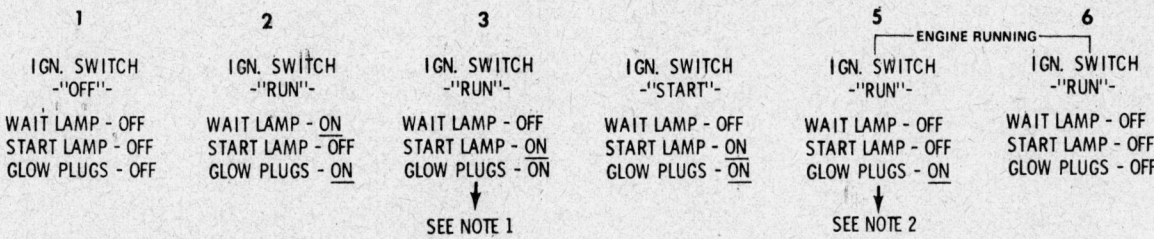

1	2	3	4	5	6
IGN. SWITCH -"OFF"-	IGN. SWITCH -"RUN"-	IGN. SWITCH -"RUN"-	IGN. SWITCH -"START"-	IGN. SWITCH -"RUN"-	IGN. SWITCH -"RUN"-
WAIT LAMP - OFF	WAIT LAMP - ON	WAIT LAMP - OFF	WAIT LAMP - OFF	WAIT LAMP - OFF	WAIT LAMP - OFF
START LAMP - OFF	START LAMP - OFF	START LAMP - ON	START LAMP - ON	START LAMP - OFF	START LAMP - OFF
GLOW PLUGS - OFF	GLOW PLUGS - ON	GLOW PLUGS - ON	GLOW PLUGS - ON	GLOW PLUGS - ON	GLOW PLUGS - OFF
		↓ SEE NOTE 1		↓ SEE NOTE 2	

ENGINE RUNNING (spanning 5–6)

NOTE 1: If the ignition is left in the "Run" position without starting the engine, the glow plugs will continue to pulse on/off until batteries run down. (About 4 hours when coolant switch is open.)

NOTE 3: Do not manually energize or by-pass the glow plug relay as glow plugs will be damaged instantly.

NOTE 2: Glow plugs will pulse on/off for about 30 seconds after engine starts. Then turn off and remain off as long as engine temperature is above about 120°F (49°C).

NOTE 4: Diodes prevent glow plug operation when the engine is warm (above 120°) the engine is not running and key is in RUN.

IMPORTANT: Do Not use more than a 2—3 candle power test light when making circuit checks.

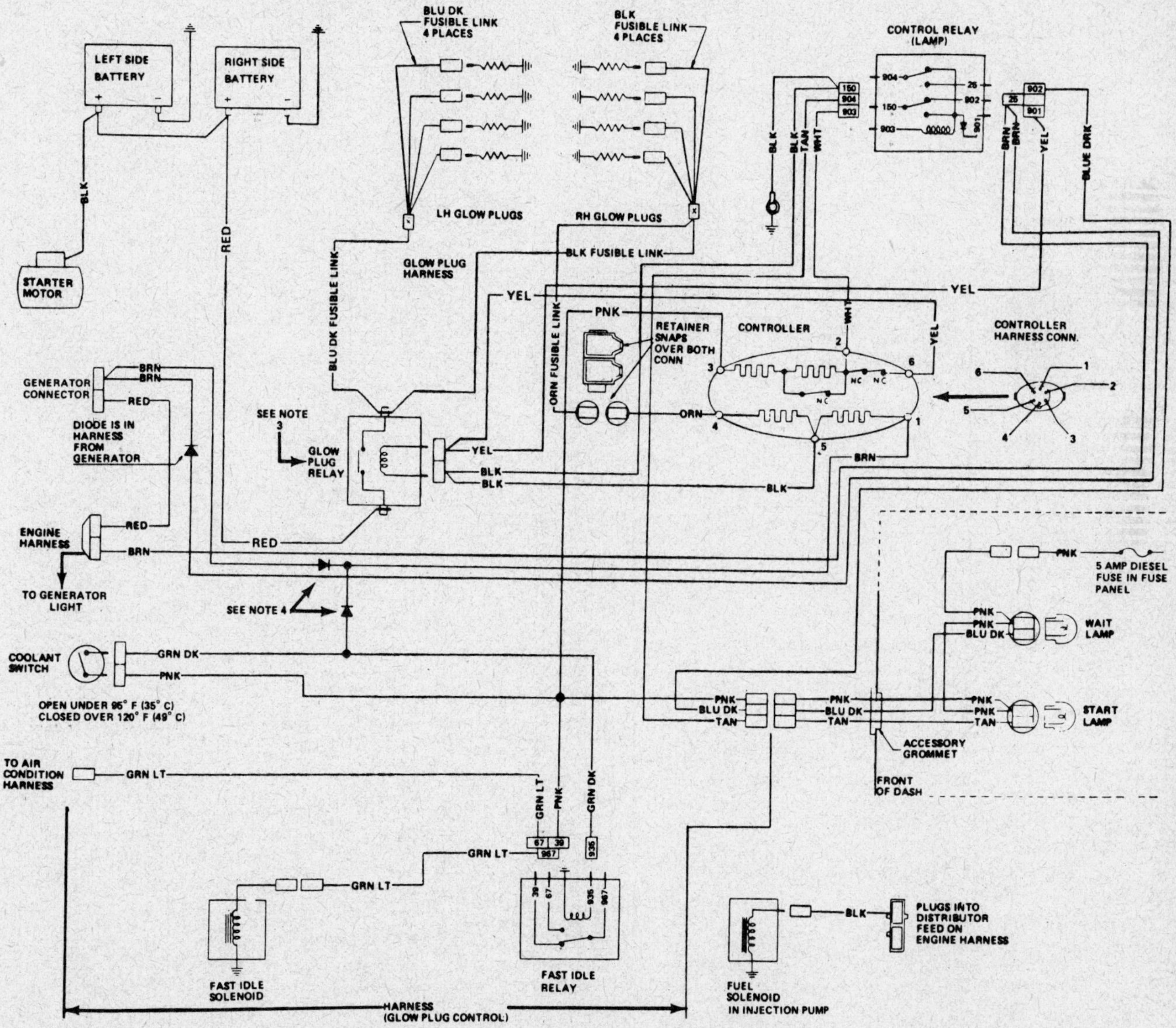

Fig. 11 Diesel engine electrical system. 1978 Type 2

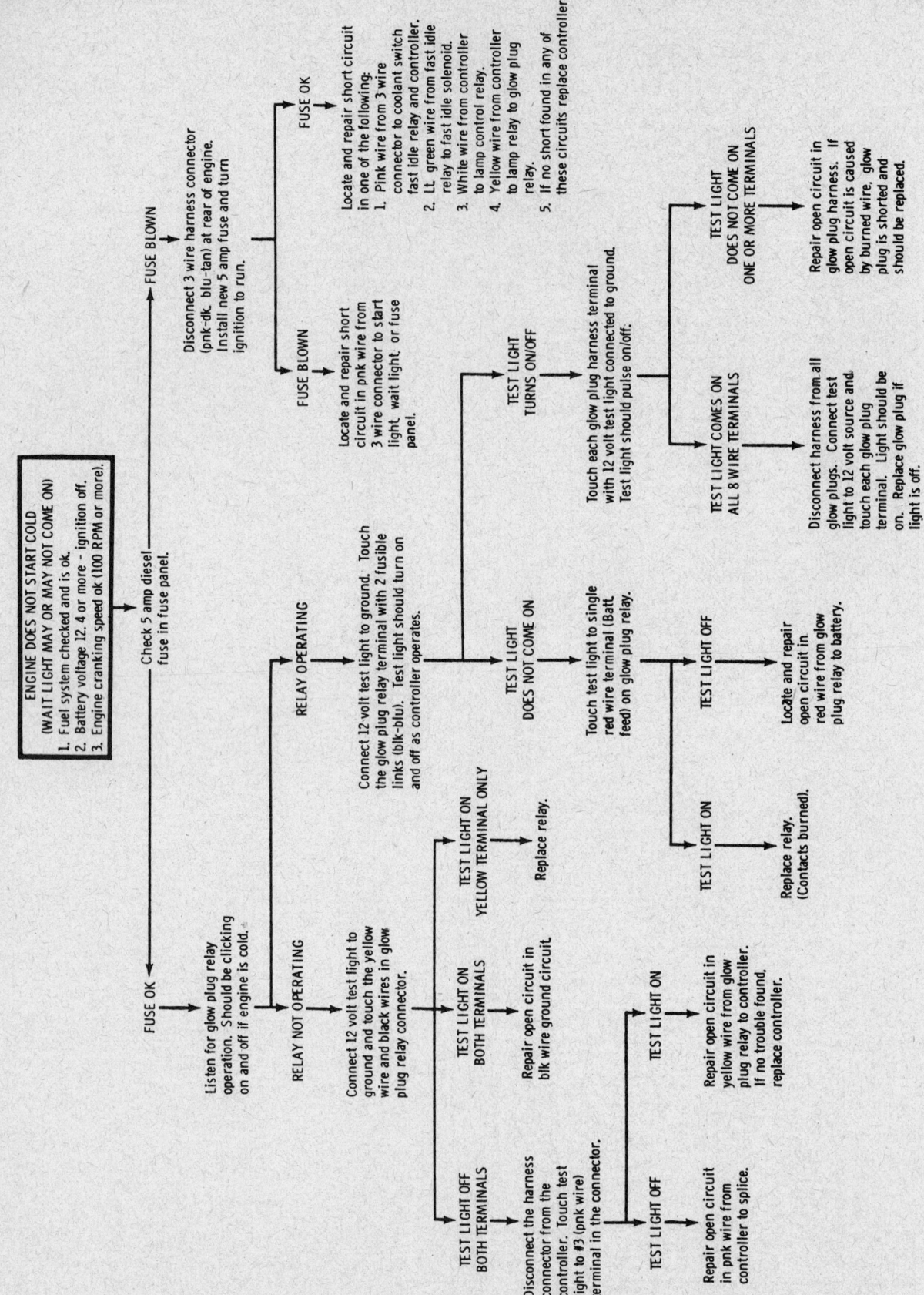

Fig. 12   Diesel engine electrical diagnosis, part 1 of 4, 1978 Type 2

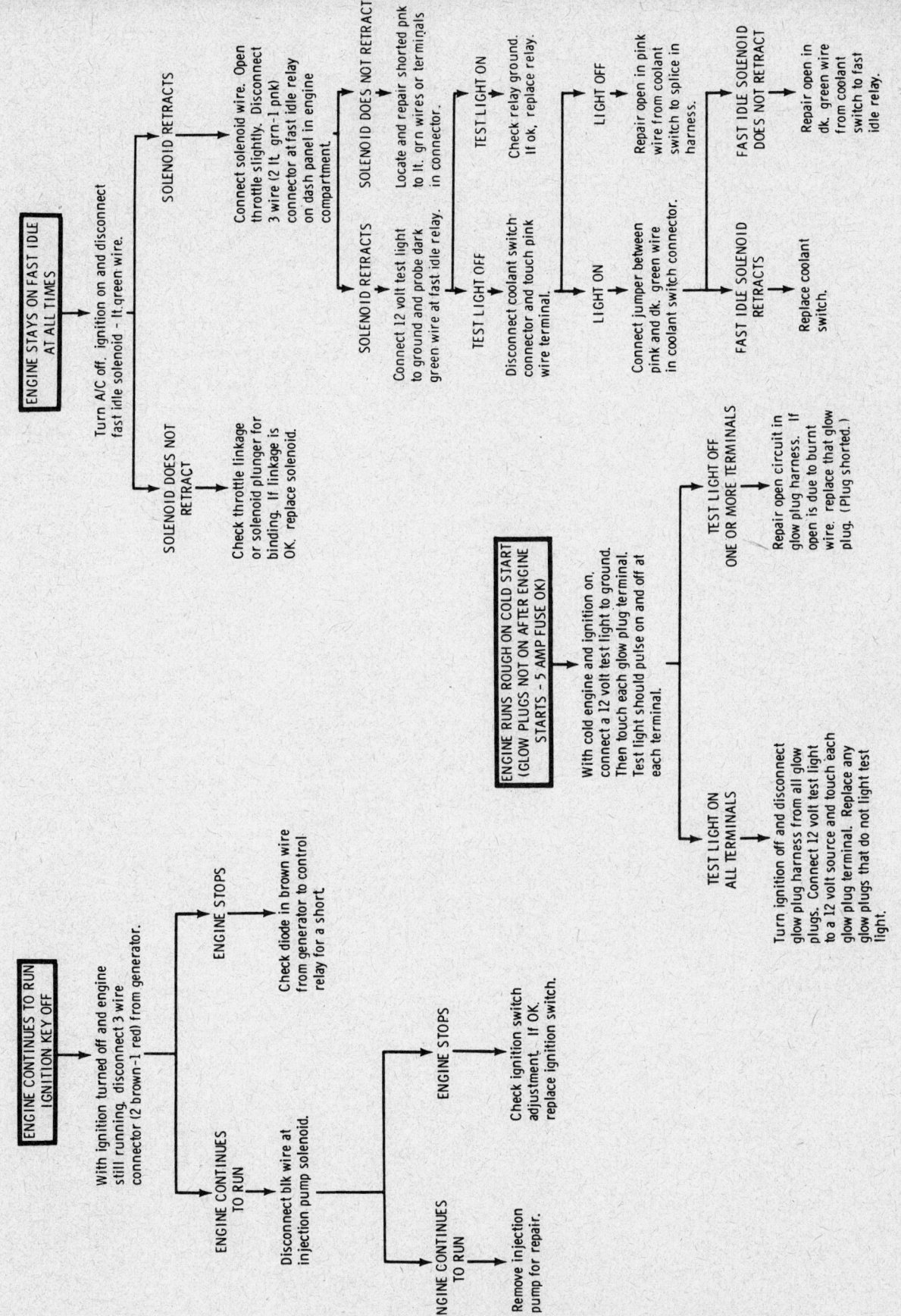

Fig. 13 Diesel engine electrical diagnosis, part 2 of 4. 1978 Type 2

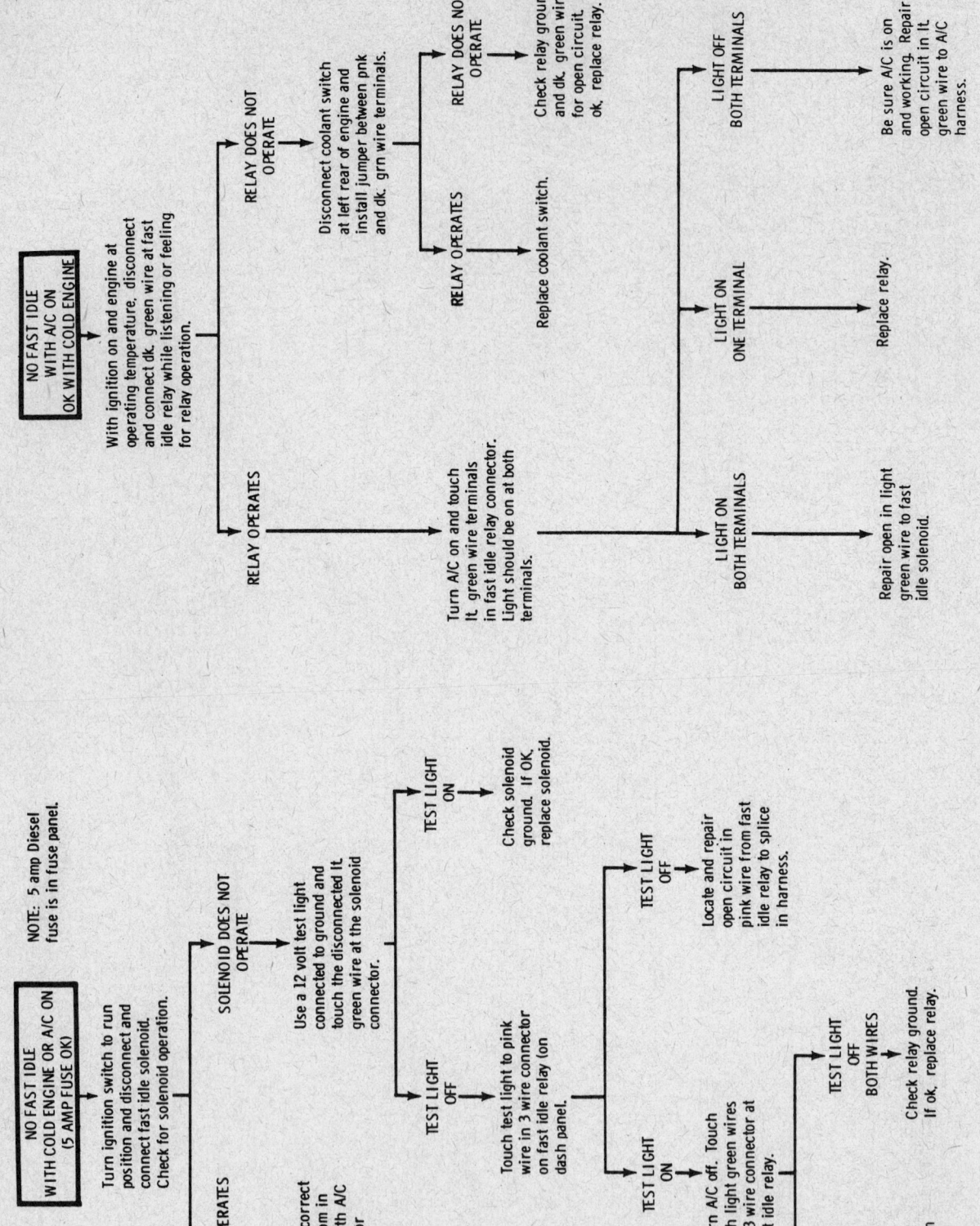

Fig. 14   Diesel engine electrical diagnosis, part 3 of 4. 1978 Type 2

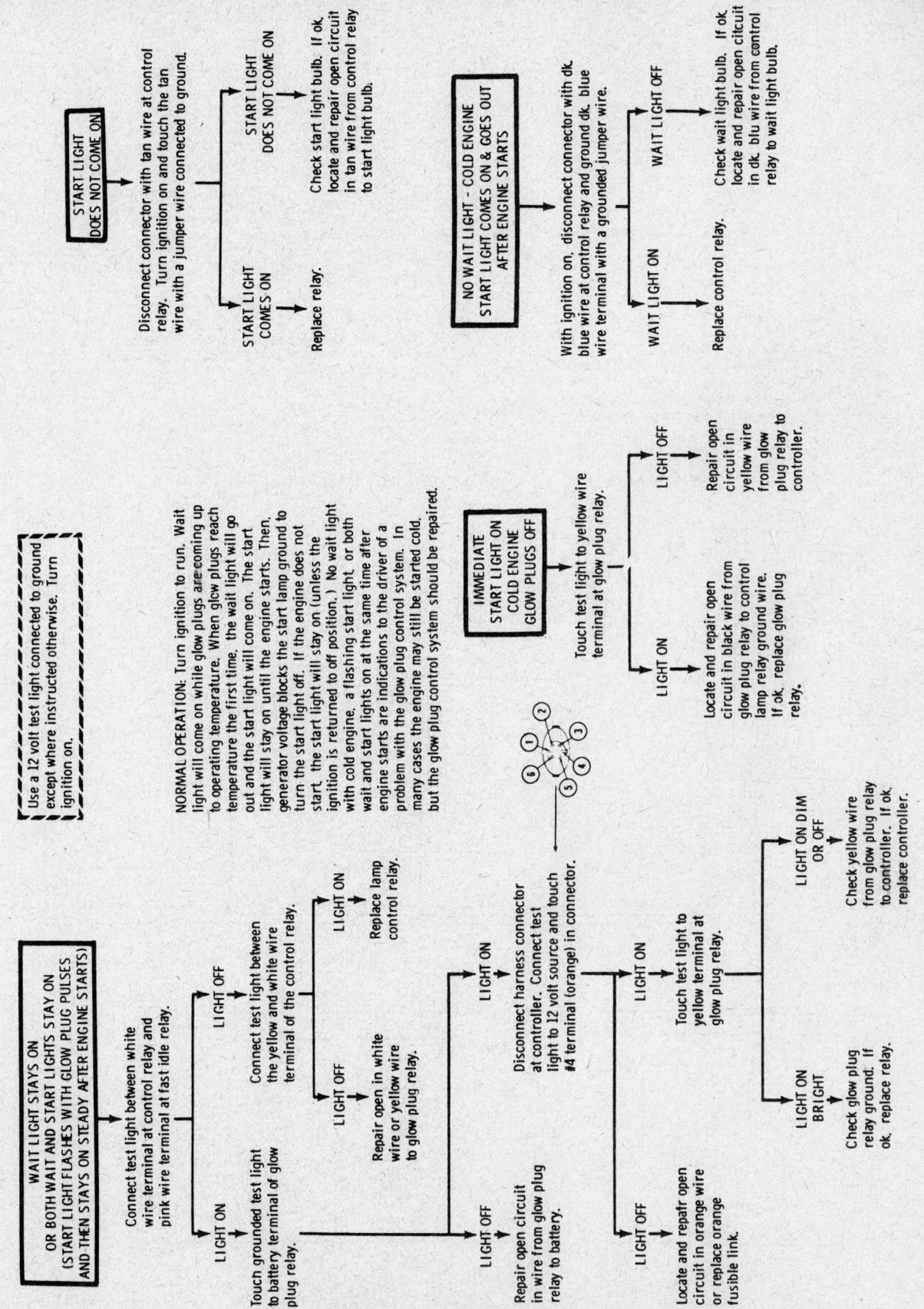

Fig. 15   Diesel engine electrical diagnosis, part 4 of 4. 1978 Type 2

1	2	3	4	5	6
				ENGINE RUNNING	
IGN. SWITCH -"OFF"-	IGN. SWITCH -"RUN"-	IGN. SWITCH -"RUN"-	IGN. SWITCH -"START"-	IGN. SWITCH -"RUN"-	IGN. SWITCH -"RUN"-
WAIT LAMP - OFF	WAIT LAMP - ON	WAIT LAMP - OFF	WAIT LAMP - OFF	WAIT LAMP - OFF	WAIT LAMP - OFF
START LAMP - OFF	START LAMP - OFF	START LAMP - ON	START LAMP - ON	START LAMP - OFF	START LAMP - OFF
GLOW PLUGS - OFF	GLOW PLUGS - ON	GLOW PLUGS - ON	GLOW PLUGS - ON	GLOW PLUGS - ON	GLOW PLUGS - OFF
		SEE NOTE 1		SEE NOTE 2	

NOTE 1: If the ignition is left in the "Run" position without starting the engine, the glow plugs will continue to pulse on/off until batteries run down. (About 4 hours when coolant switch is open.)

NOTE 3: Do not manually energize or by-pass the glow plug relay as glow plugs will be damaged instantly.

NOTE 2: Glow plugs will pulse on/off for about 30 seconds after engine starts. Then turn off and remain off as long as engine temperature is above about 120°F (49°C).

IMPORTANT: Do Not use more than a 2–3 candle power test light when making circuit checks.

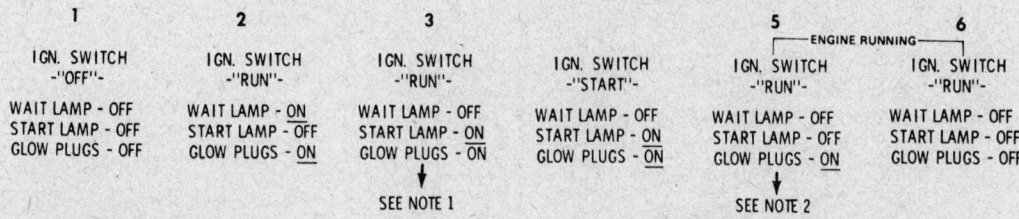

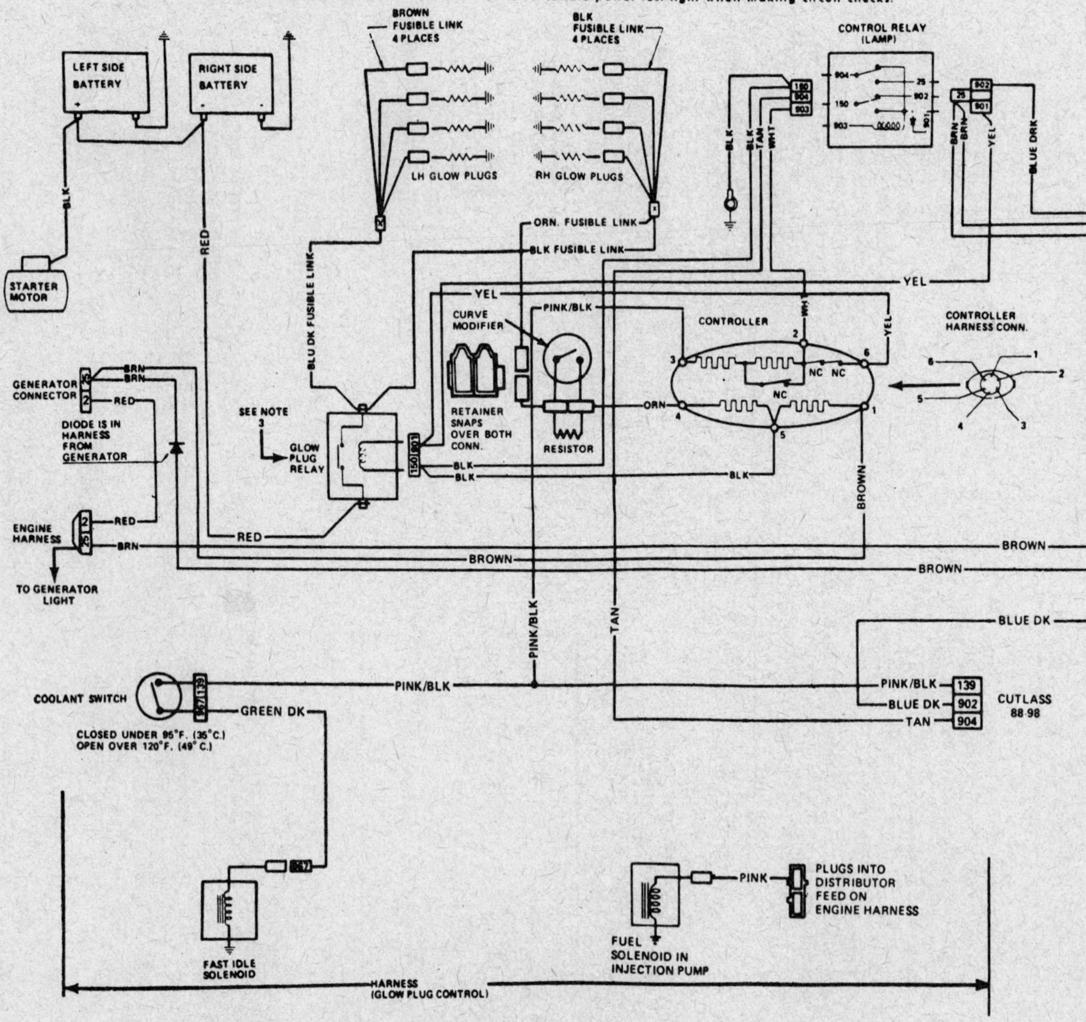

Fig. 16 Diesel engine electrical system. 1979 V8-260 Type 2

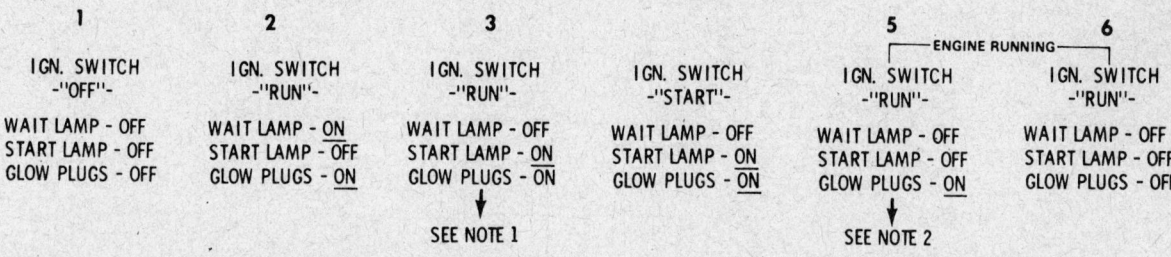

1	2	3	4	5	6
IGN. SWITCH -"OFF"-	IGN. SWITCH -"RUN"-	IGN. SWITCH -"RUN"-	IGN. SWITCH -"START"-	ENGINE RUNNING IGN. SWITCH -"RUN"-	IGN. SWITCH -"RUN"-
WAIT LAMP - OFF	WAIT LAMP - ON	WAIT LAMP - OFF	WAIT LAMP - OFF	WAIT LAMP - OFF	WAIT LAMP - OFF
START LAMP - OFF	START LAMP - OFF	START LAMP - ON	START LAMP - ON	START LAMP - OFF	START LAMP - OFF
GLOW PLUGS - OFF	GLOW PLUGS - ON	GLOW PLUGS - ON	GLOW PLUGS - ON	GLOW PLUGS - ON	GLOW PLUGS - OFF
		SEE NOTE 1		SEE NOTE 2	

NOTE 1: If the ignition is left in the "Run" position without starting the engine, the glow plugs will continue to pulse on/off until batteries run down. (About 4 hours when coolant switch is open.)

NOTE 3: Do not manually energize or by-pass the glow plug relay as glow plugs will be damaged instantly.

NOTE 2: Glow plugs will pulse on/off for about 30 seconds after engine starts. Then turn off and remain off as long as engine temperature is above about 120° F (49° C).

NOTE 4: Diodes prevent glow plug operation when the engine is warm (above 120°) the engine is not running and key is in RUN.

IMPORTANT: Do Not use more than a 2–3 candle power test light when making circuit checks.

Fig. 17   Diesel engine electrical system, part 1 of 2. 1979 V8-350 Type 2

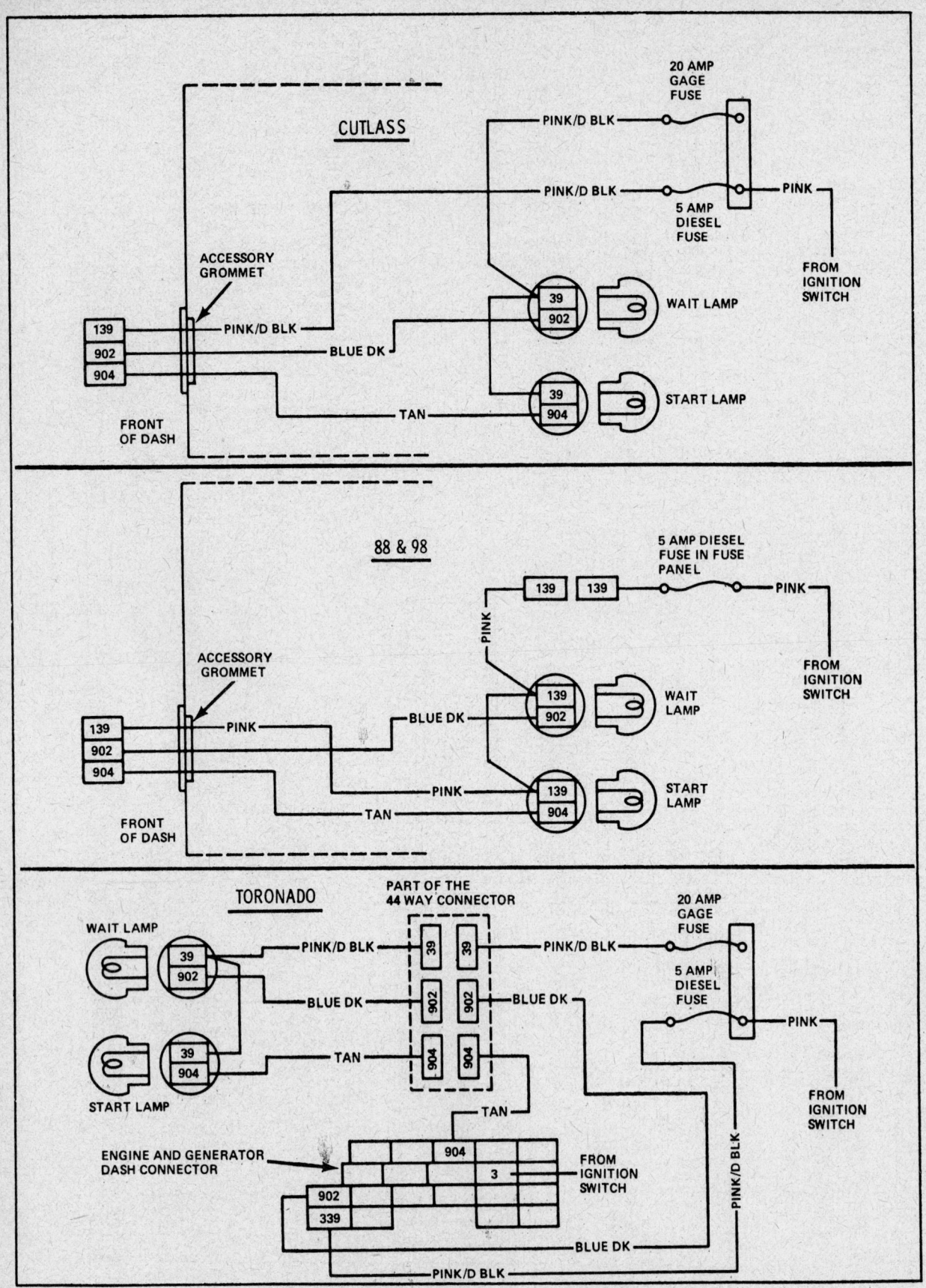

Fig. 18   Diesel engine electrical system, part 2 of 2. 1979 V8-350 Type 2

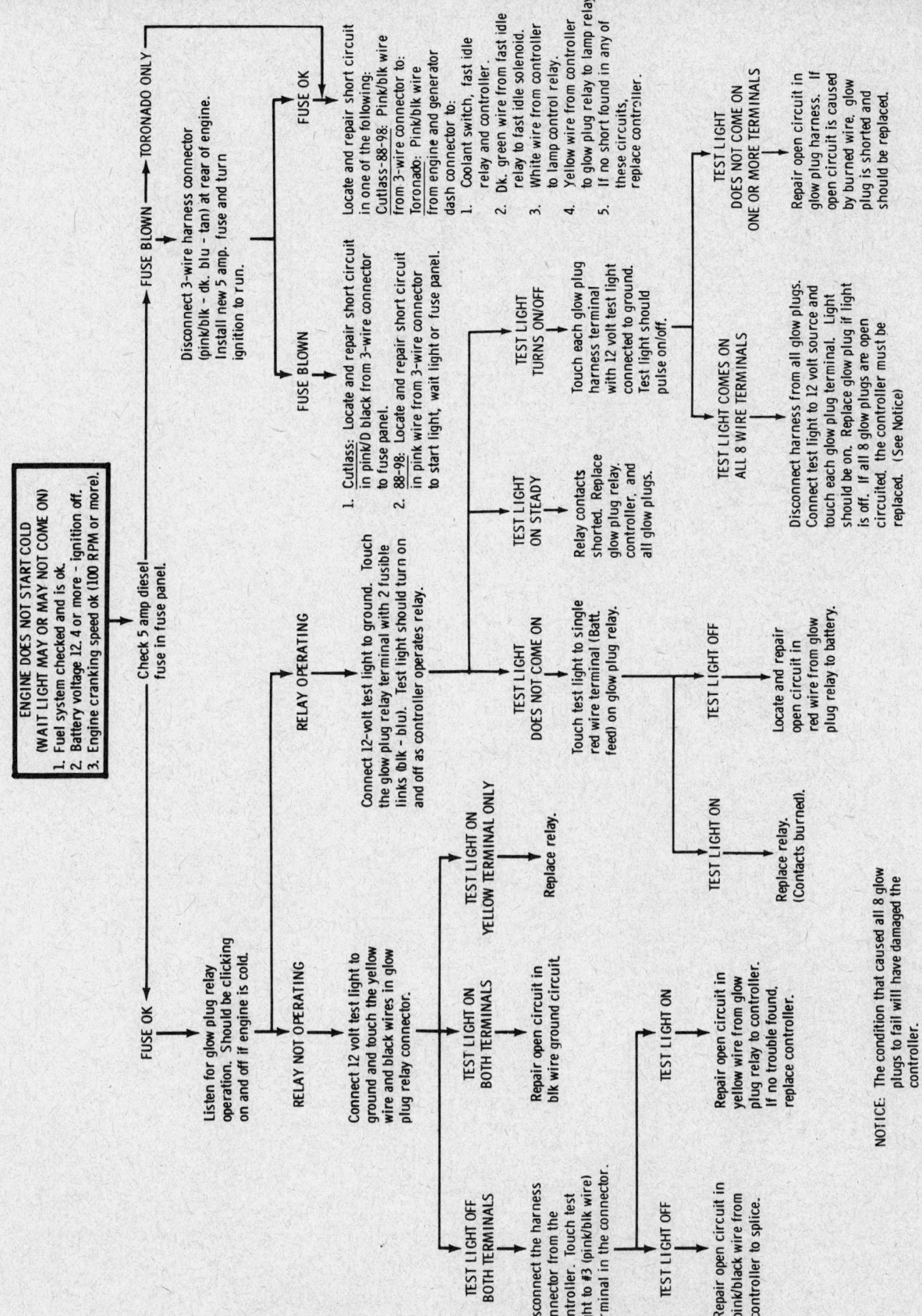

Fig. 19 Diesel engine electrical diagnosis, part 1 of 5. 1979 V8-260 (4.3 litre) & 350 (5.7 litre) Type 2

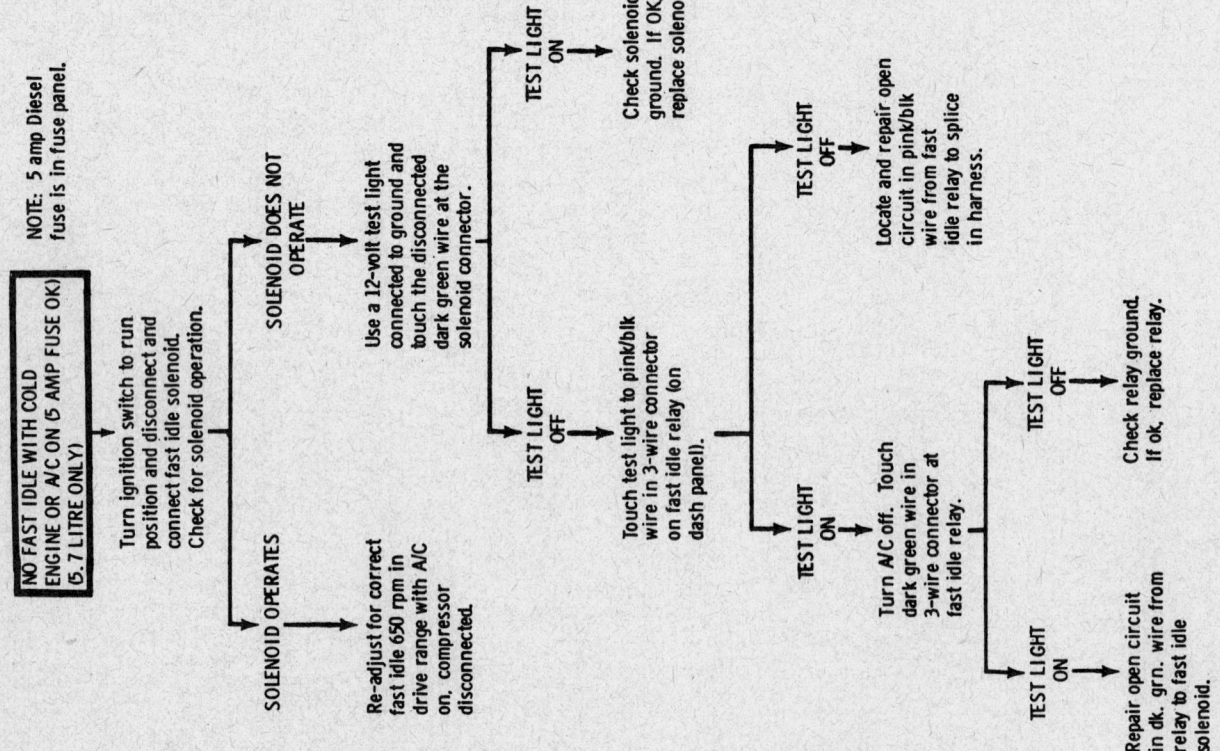

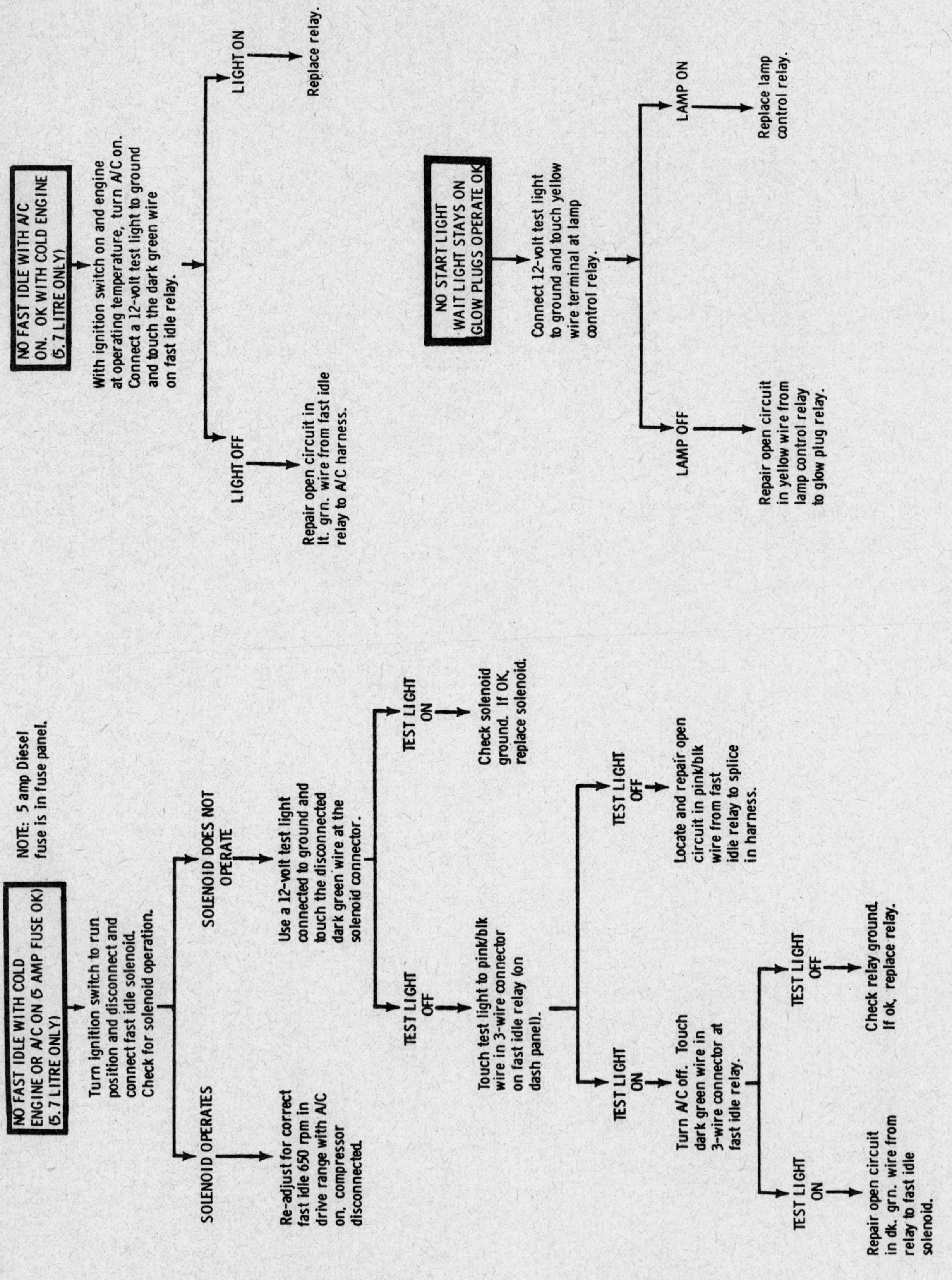

Fig. 20   Diesel engine electrical diagnosis, part 2 of 5. 1979 V8-260 (4.3 litre) & 350 (5.7 litre) Type 2

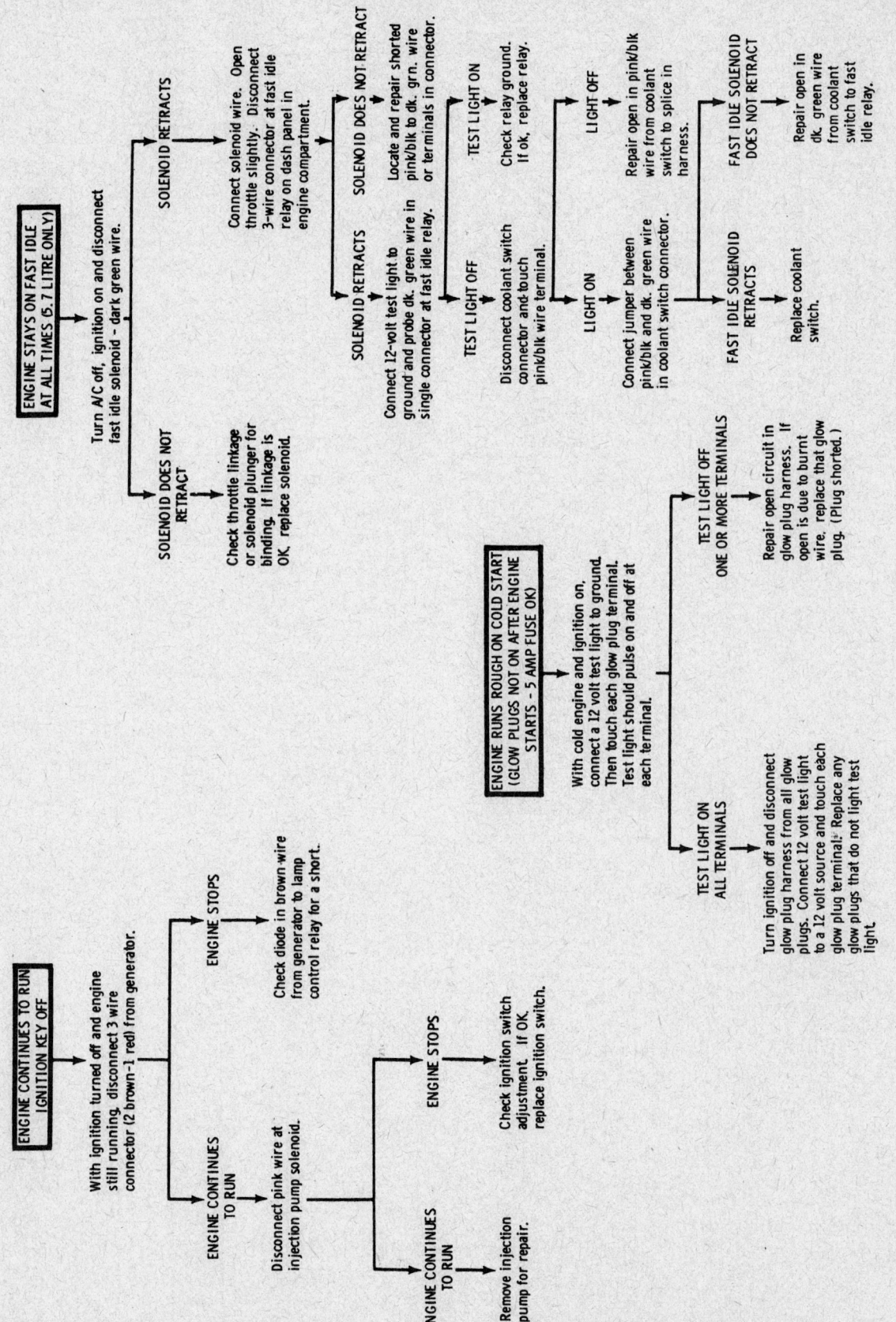

Fig. 21   Diesel engine electrical diagnosis, part 3 of 5. 1979 V8-260 (4.3 litre) & 350 (5.7 litre) Type 2

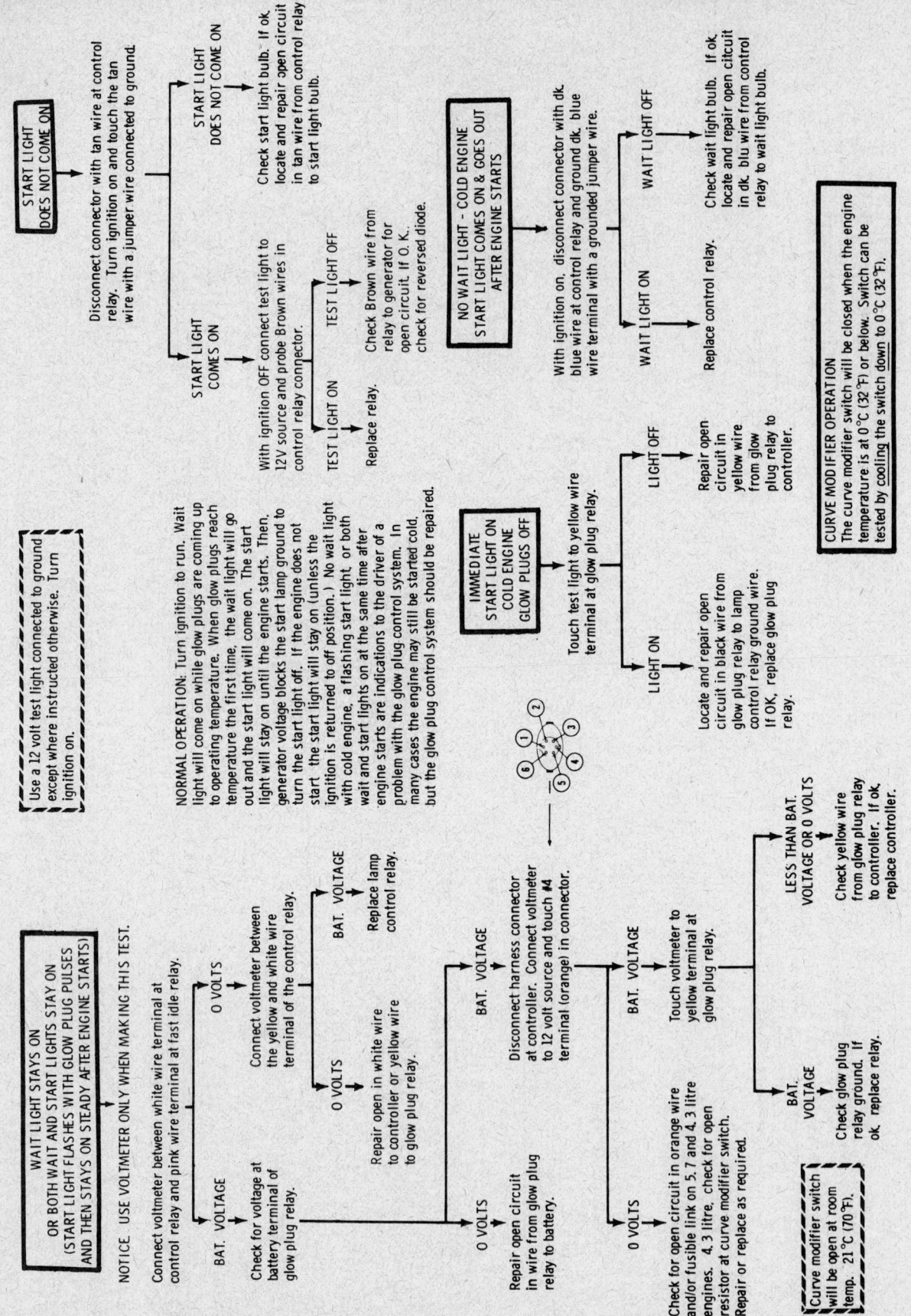

START LIGHT DOES NOT COME ON

Disconnect connector with tan wire at control relay. Turn ignition on and touch the tan wire with a jumper wire connected to ground.

START LIGHT DOES NOT COME ON

Check start light bulb. If ok, locate and repair open circuit in tan wire from control relay to start light bulb.

START LIGHT COMES ON

With ignition OFF connect test light to 12V source and probe Brown wires in control relay connector.

TEST LIGHT OFF

Check Brown wire from relay to generator for open circuit. If O. K. check for reversed diode.

TEST LIGHT ON

Replace relay.

NO WAIT LIGHT – COLD ENGINE START LIGHT COMES ON & GOES OUT AFTER ENGINE STARTS

With ignition on, disconnect connector with dk. blue wire at control relay and ground dk. blue wire terminal with a grounded jumper wire.

WAIT LIGHT OFF

Check wait light bulb. If ok, locate and repair open circuit in dk. blu wire from control relay to wait light bulb.

WAIT LIGHT ON

Replace control relay.

CURVE MODIFIER OPERATION
The curve modifier switch will be closed when the engine temperature is at 0°C (32°F) or below. Switch can be tested by cooling the switch down to 0°C (32°F).

Use a 12 volt test light connected to ground except where instructed otherwise. Turn ignition on.

NOTICE USE VOLTMETER ONLY WHEN MAKING THIS TEST.

NORMAL OPERATION: Turn ignition to run. Wait light will come on while glow plugs are coming up to operating temperature. When glow plugs reach temperature the first time, the wait light will go out and the start light will come on. The start light will stay on until the engine starts. Then, generator voltage blocks the start lamp ground to turn the start light off. If the engine does not start the start light will stay on (unless the ignition is returned to off position.) No wait light with cold engine, a flashing start light, or both wait and start lights on at the same time after engine starts are indications to the driver of a problem with the glow plug control system. In many cases the engine may still be started cold, but the glow plug control system should be repaired.

IMMEDIATE START LIGHT ON COLD ENGINE GLOW PLUGS OFF

Touch test light to yellow wire terminal at glow plug relay.

LIGHT OFF

Repair open circuit in yellow wire from glow plug relay to controller.

LIGHT ON

Locate and repair open circuit in black wire from glow plug relay to lamp control relay ground wire. If OK, replace glow plug relay.

WAIT LIGHT STAYS ON OR BOTH WAIT AND START LIGHTS STAY ON (START LIGHT FLASHES WITH GLOW PLUG PULSES AND THEN STAYS ON STEADY AFTER ENGINE STARTS)

Connect voltmeter between white wire terminal at control relay and pink wire terminal at fast idle relay.

BAT. VOLTAGE

Check for voltage at battery terminal of glow plug relay.

0 VOLTS

Connect voltmeter between the yellow and white wire terminal of the control relay.

BAT. VOLTAGE

Replace lamp control relay.

0 VOLTS

Repair open in white wire to controller or yellow wire to glow plug relay.

0 VOLTS

Repair open circuit in wire from glow plug relay to battery.

Disconnect harness connector at controller. Connect voltmeter to 12 volt source and touch #4 terminal (orange) in connector.

BAT. VOLTAGE

Touch voltmeter to yellow terminal at glow plug relay.

LESS THAN BAT. VOLTAGE OR 0 VOLTS

Check yellow wire from glow plug relay to controller. If ok, replace controller.

BAT. VOLTAGE

Check glow plug relay ground. If ok. replace relay.

0 VOLTS

Check for open circuit in orange wire and/or fusible link on 5.7 and 4.3 litre engines. 4.3 litre, check for open resistor at curve modifier switch. Repair or replace as required.

Curve modifier switch will be open at room temp. 21°C (70°F).

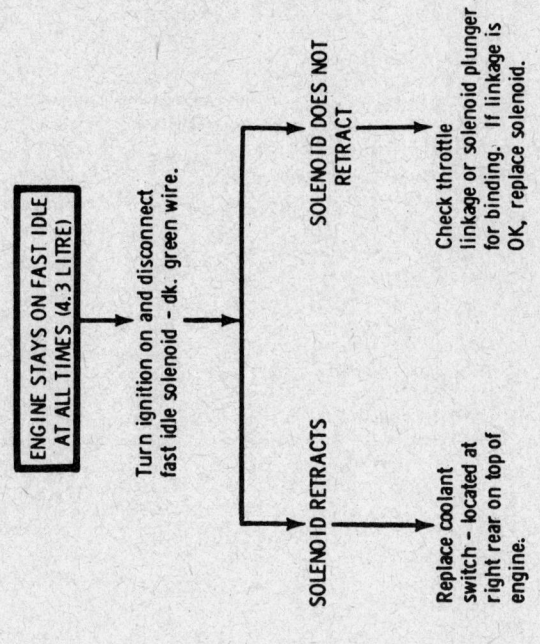

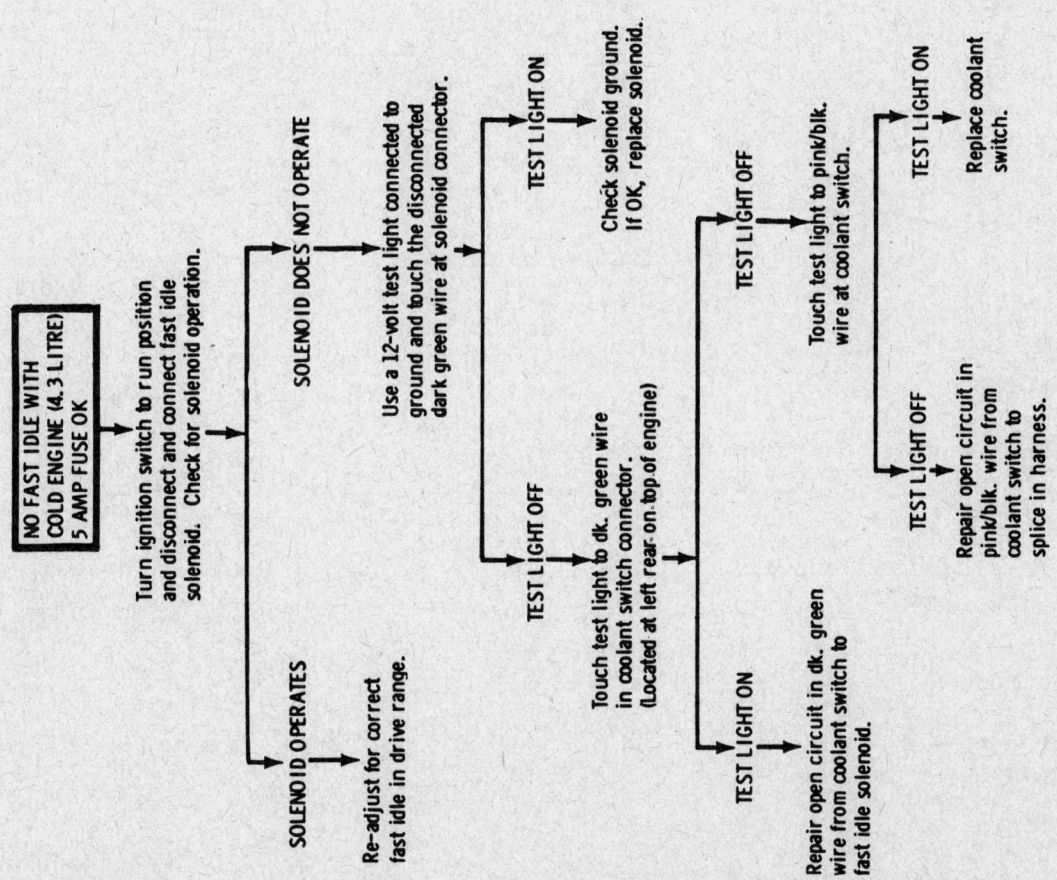

Fig. 23   Diesel engine electrical diagnosis, part 5 of 5. 1979 V8-260 (4.3 litre) Type 2

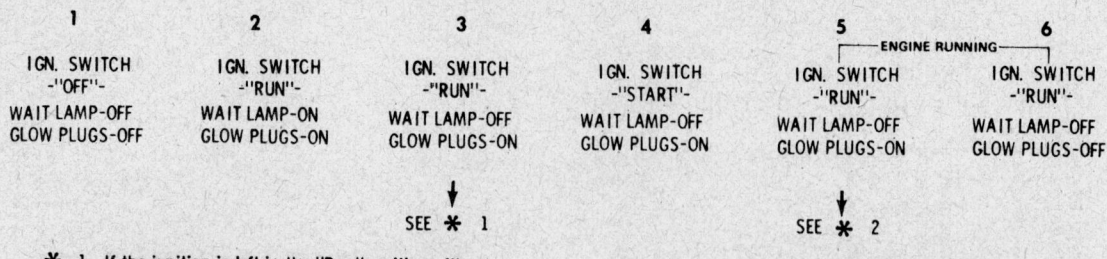

1	2	3	4	5	6
IGN. SWITCH -"OFF"-	IGN. SWITCH -"RUN"-	IGN. SWITCH -"RUN"-	IGN. SWITCH -"START"-	IGN. SWITCH -"RUN"-	IGN. SWITCH -"RUN"-
WAIT LAMP-OFF	WAIT LAMP-ON	WAIT LAMP-OFF	WAIT LAMP-OFF	WAIT LAMP-OFF	WAIT LAMP-OFF
GLOW PLUGS-OFF	GLOW PLUGS-ON	GLOW PLUGS-ON	GLOW PLUGS-ON	GLOW PLUGS-ON	GLOW PLUGS-OFF

ENGINE RUNNING (over 5 and 6)

SEE ✱ 1 (under 3)   SEE ✱ 2 (under 4)

✱ 1: If the ignition is left in the "Run" position without starting the engine, the glow plugs will continue to pulse on/off until batteries run down. (About 4 hours when coolant switch is open.)

✱ 3: Do not manually energize or by-pass the glow plug relay as glow plugs will be damaged instantly.

✱ 2: Glow plugs will pulse on/off for about 30 seconds after engine starts. Then turn off and remain off as long as engine temperature is above about 120°F (49°C).

✱ 4: Diodes prevent glow plug operation when the engine is warm (above 120°) the engine is not running and key is in RUN.

IMPORTANT: Do Not use more than a 2–3 candle power test light when making circuit checks.

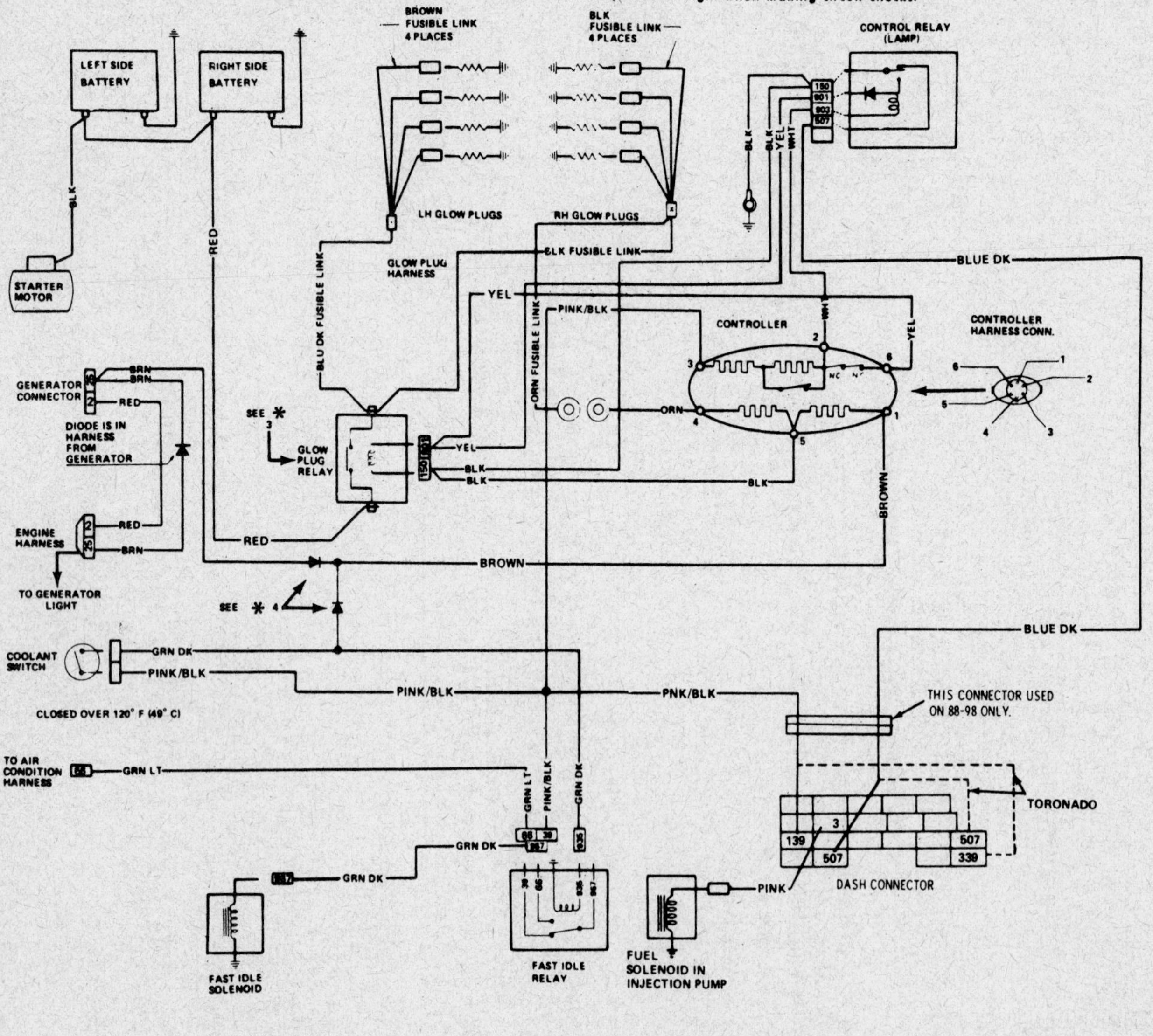

Fig. 24 Diesel engine electrical system, part 1 of 2. 1980–83 88, 98 & Toronado Type 2

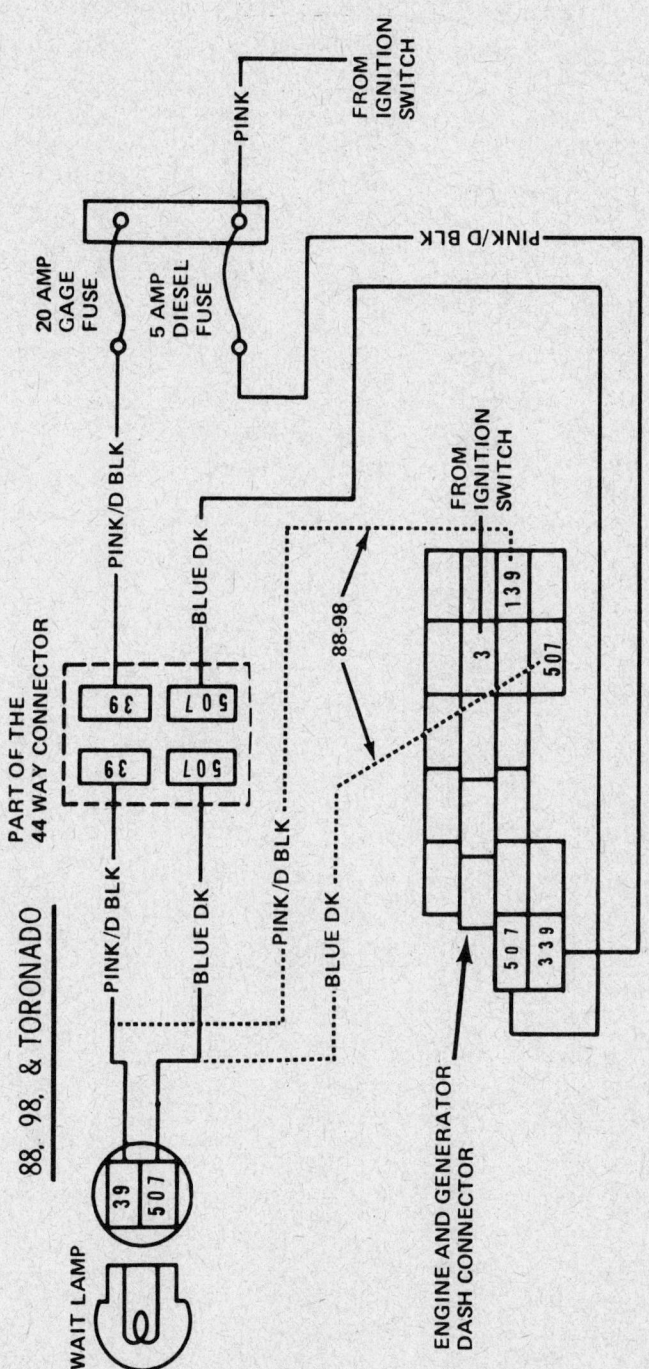

Fig. 24A Diesel engine electrical system, part 2 of 2. 1980–83 88, 98 & Toronado Type 2

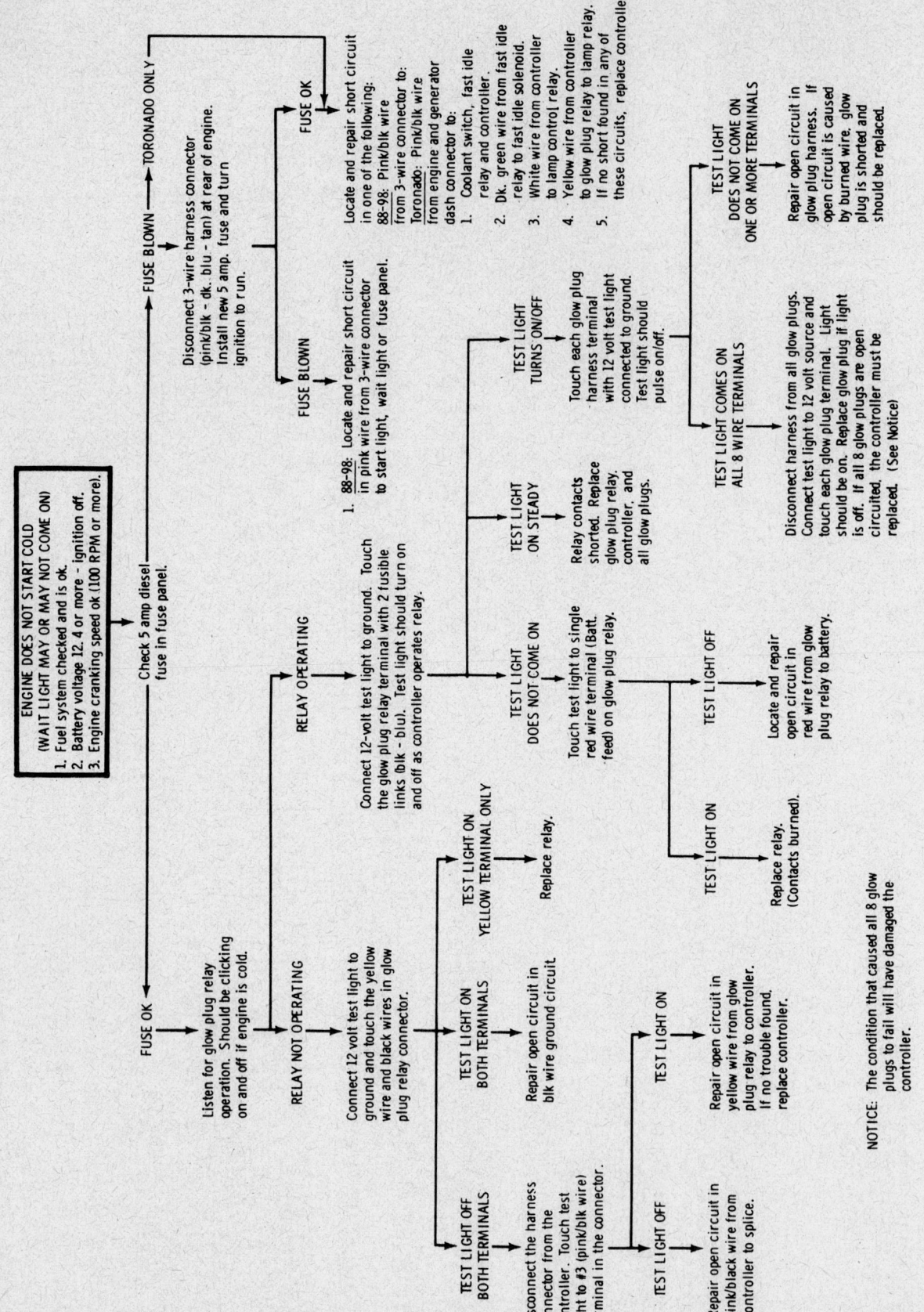

Fig. 25 Diesel engine electrical diagnosis, part 1 of 4. 1980–83 Type 2 exc. Cutlass

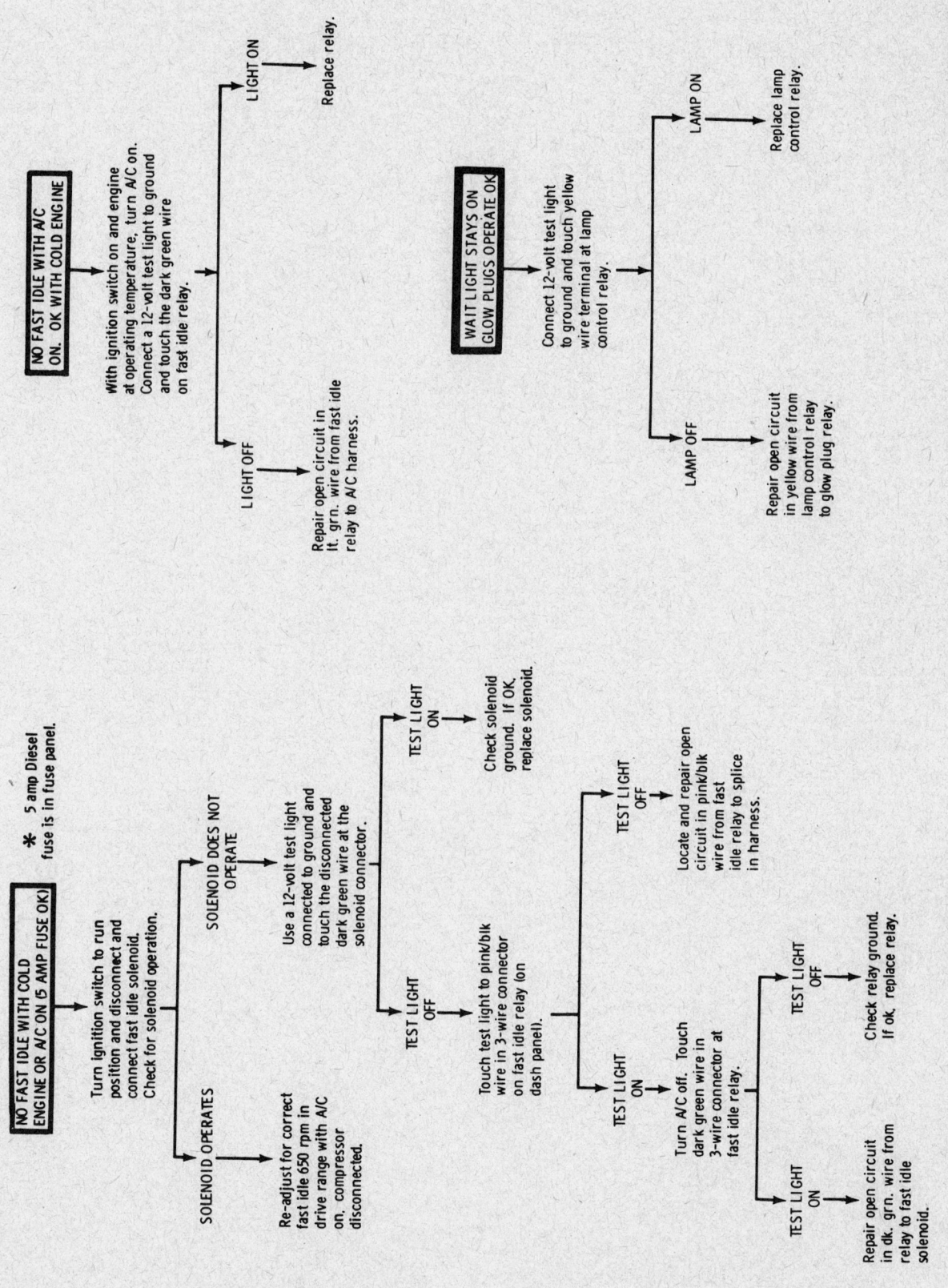

NO FAST IDLE WITH A/C ON. OK WITH COLD ENGINE

With ignition switch on and engine at operating temperature, turn A/C on. Connect a 12-volt test light to ground and touch the dark green wire on fast idle relay.

LIGHT ON → Replace relay.

LIGHT OFF → Repair open circuit in lt. grn. wire from fast idle relay to A/C harness.

WAIT LIGHT STAYS ON GLOW PLUGS OPERATE OK

Connect 12-volt test light to ground and touch yellow wire terminal at lamp control relay.

LAMP ON → Replace lamp control relay.

LAMP OFF → Repair open circuit in yellow wire from lamp control relay to glow plug relay.

* 5 amp Diesel fuse is in fuse panel.

NO FAST IDLE WITH COLD ENGINE OR A/C ON (5 AMP FUSE OK)

Turn ignition switch to run position and disconnect and connect fast idle solenoid. Check for solenoid operation.

SOLENOID DOES NOT OPERATE → Use a 12-volt test light connected to ground and touch the disconnected dark green wire at the solenoid connector.

SOLENOID OPERATES → Re-adjust for correct fast idle 650 rpm in drive range with A/C on, compressor disconnected.

TEST LIGHT ON → Check solenoid ground. If OK, replace solenoid.

TEST LIGHT OFF → Touch test light to pink/blk wire in 3-wire connector on fast idle relay (on dash panel).

TEST LIGHT OFF → Locate and repair open circuit in pink/blk wire from fast idle relay to splice in harness.

TEST LIGHT ON → Turn A/C off. Touch dark green wire in 3-wire connector at fast idle relay.

TEST LIGHT OFF → Check relay ground. If ok, replace relay.

TEST LIGHT ON → Repair open circuit in dk. grn. wire from relay to fast idle solenoid.

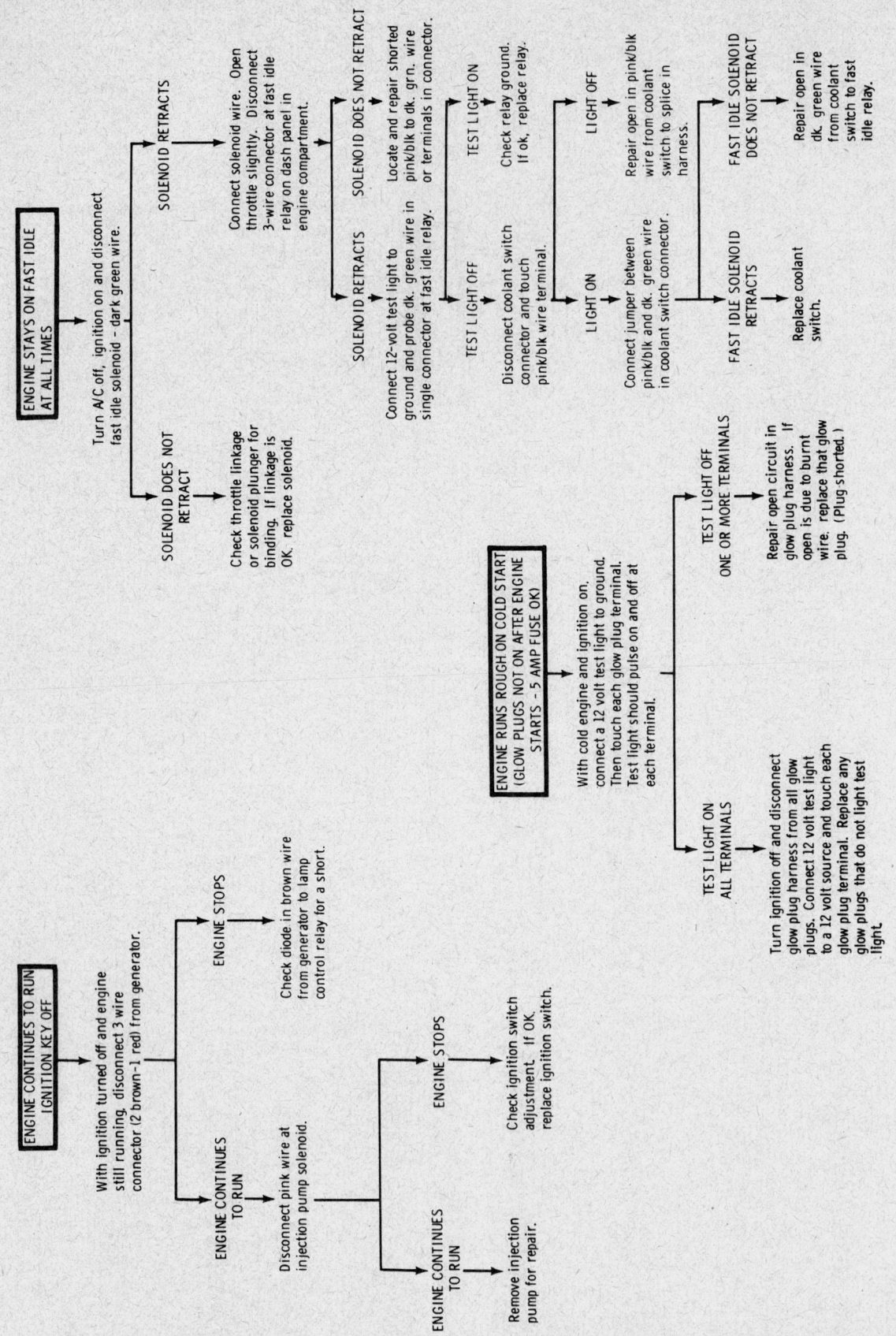

ENGINE STAYS ON FAST IDLE AT ALL TIMES

Turn A/C off, ignition on and disconnect fast idle solenoid - dark green wire.

SOLENOID RETRACTS

Connect solenoid wire. Open throttle slightly. Disconnect 3-wire connector at fast idle relay on dash panel in engine compartment.

SOLENOID DOES NOT RETRACT

Check throttle linkage or solenoid plunger for binding. If linkage is OK, replace solenoid.

SOLENOID RETRACTS

Connect 12-volt test light to ground and probe dk. green wire in single connector at fast idle relay.

SOLENOID DOES NOT RETRACT

Locate and repair shorted pink/blk to dk. grn. wire or terminals in connector.

TEST LIGHT OFF

Disconnect coolant switch connector and touch pink/blk wire terminal.

TEST LIGHT ON

Check relay ground. If ok, replace relay.

LIGHT ON

Connect jumper between pink/blk and dk. green wire in coolant switch connector.

LIGHT OFF

Repair open in pink/blk wire from coolant switch to splice in harness.

FAST IDLE SOLENOID RETRACTS

Replace coolant switch.

FAST IDLE SOLENOID DOES NOT RETRACT

Repair open in dk. green wire from coolant switch to fast idle relay.

ENGINE RUNS ROUGH ON COLD START (GLOW PLUGS NOT ON AFTER ENGINE STARTS - 5 AMP FUSE OK)

With cold engine and ignition on, connect a 12 volt test light to ground. Then touch each glow plug terminal. Test light should pulse on and off at each terminal.

TEST LIGHT OFF ONE OR MORE TERMINALS

Repair open circuit in glow plug harness. If open is due to burnt wire, replace that glow plug. (Plug shorted.)

TEST LIGHT ON ALL TERMINALS

Turn ignition off and disconnect glow plug harness from all glow plugs. Connect 12 volt source to a 12 volt source and touch each glow plug terminal. Replace any glow plugs that do not light test light.

ENGINE CONTINUES TO RUN IGNITION KEY OFF

With ignition turned off and engine still running, disconnect 3 wire connector (2 brown–1 red) from generator.

ENGINE STOPS

Check diode in brown wire from generator to lamp control relay for a short.

ENGINE CONTINUES TO RUN

Disconnect pink wire at injection pump solenoid.

ENGINE STOPS

Check ignition switch adjustment. If OK, replace ignition switch.

ENGINE CONTINUES TO RUN

Remove injection pump for repair.

NORMAL OPERATION: Turn ignition to run. Wait light will come-on while glow plugs are coming up to operating temperature. When glow plugs reach temperature the first time, the wait light will go out to indicate the engine is ready to start. No wait light with cold engine, or a continuous wait light after the engine starts are indications to the driver of a problem with the glow plug control systems. In many cases the engine may still be started cold, but the glow plug system should be repaired.

NO WAIT LIGHT - COLD ENGINE

With ignition on, disconnect connector with dk. blue wire at control relay and ground dk. blue wire terminal with a grounded jumper wire.

WAIT LIGHT OFF → Check wait light bulb. If ok locate and repair open circuit in dk. blu wire from control relay to wait light bulb.

WAIT LIGHT ON → Replace control relay.

Use a 12 volt test light connected to ground except where instructed otherwise. Turn ignition on.

WAIT LIGHT STAYS ON-AFTER ENGINE STARTS

NOTICE: USE VOLTMETER ONLY WHEN MAKING THIS TEST.

Connect voltmeter between white wire terminal at control relay and pink wire terminal at fast idle relay.

BAT. VOLTAGE → Check for voltage at battery terminal of glow plug relay.

0 VOLTS → Connect voltmeter between the yellow and white wire terminal of the control relay.

BAT. VOLTAGE → Replace lamp control relay.

0 VOLTS → Repair open in white wire to controller or yellow wire to glow plug relay.

BAT. VOLTAGE → Disconnect harness connector at controller. Connect voltmeter to 12 volt source and touch #4 terminal (orange) in connector.

0 VOLTS → Repair open circuit in wire from glow plug relay to battery.

BAT. VOLTAGE → Touch voltmeter to yellow terminal at glow plug relay.

0 VOLTS → Check for open circuit in orange wire and/or fusible link. Repair or replace as required.

LESS THAN BAT. VOLTAGE OR 0 VOLTS → Check yellow wire from glow plug relay to controller. If ok, replace controller.

BAT. VOLTAGE → Check glow plug relay ground. If ok. replace relay.

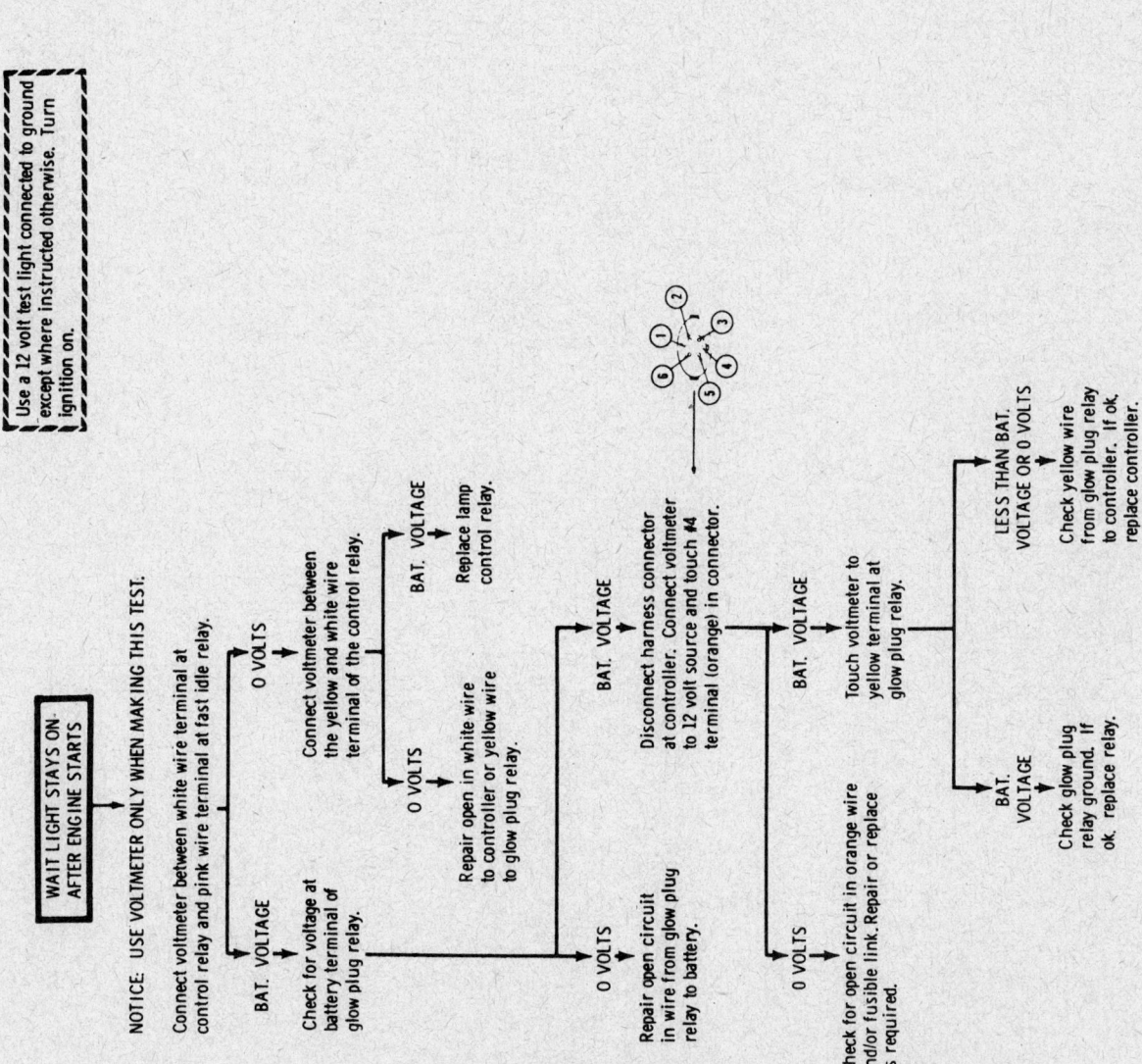

Fig. 25C Diesel engine electrical diagnosis, part 4 of 4. 1980–83 Type 2 exc. Cutlass

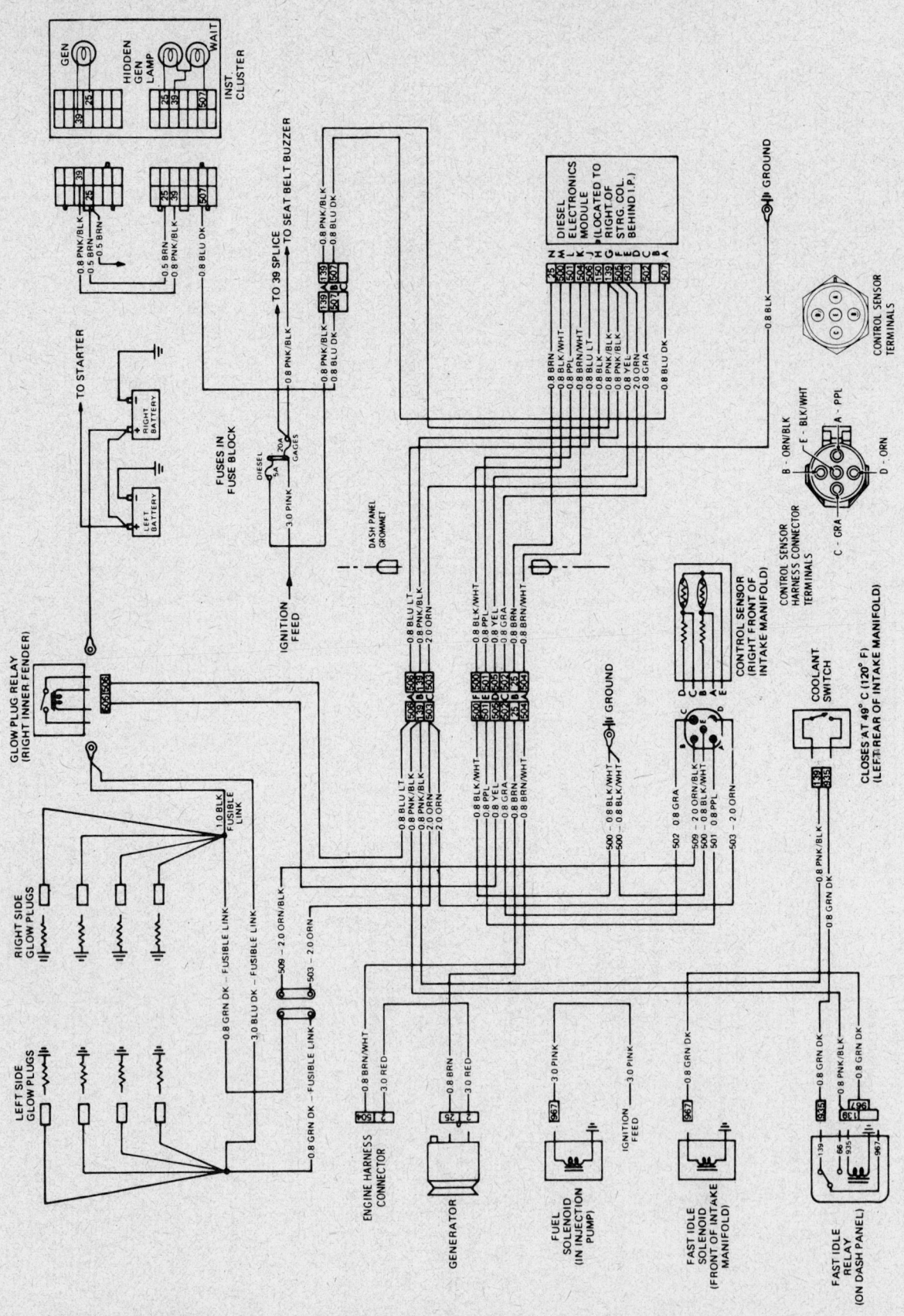

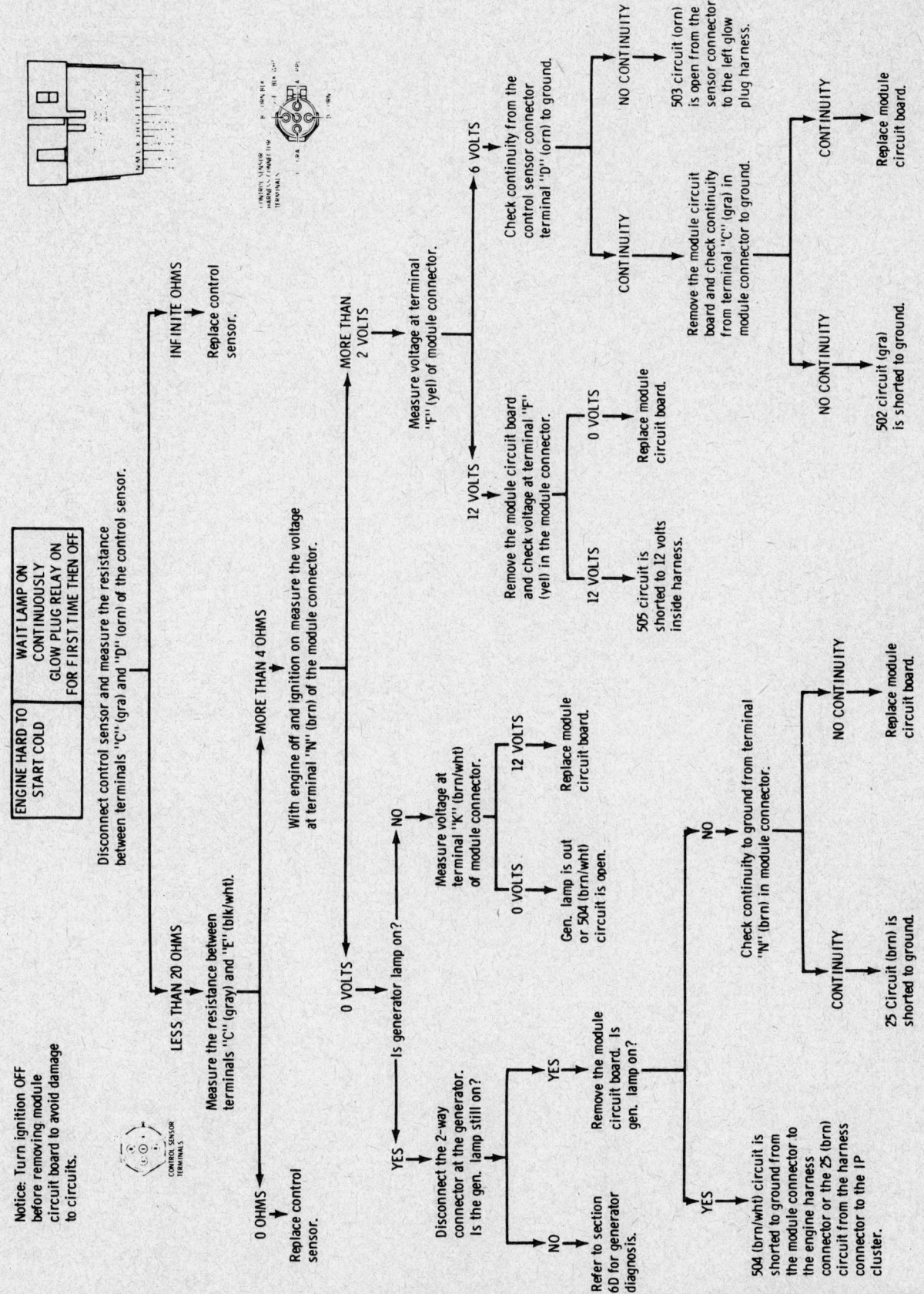

Fig. 27 Diesel engine electrical diagnosis, part 1 of 10. 1980-83 Cutlass with V8 engine

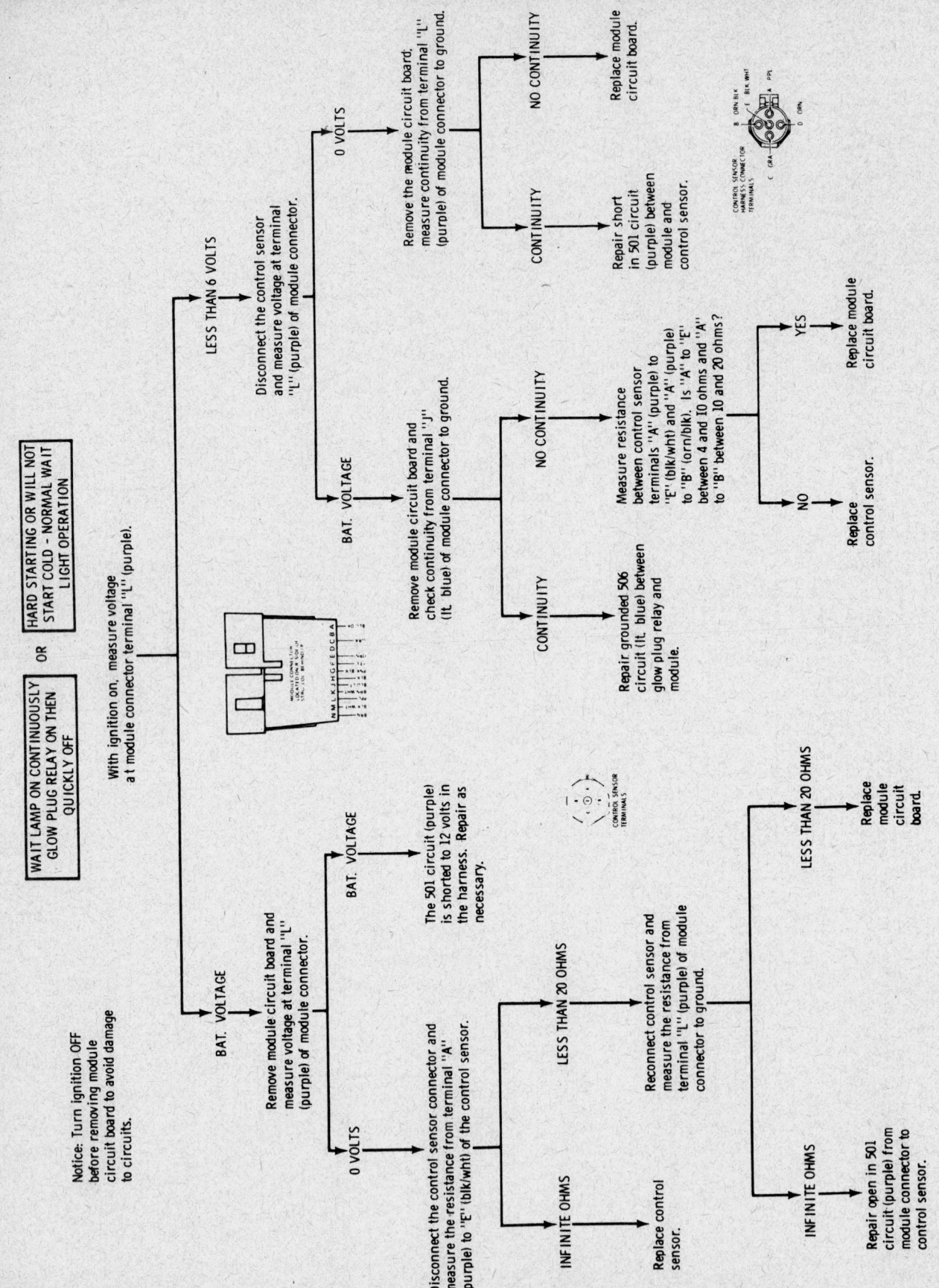

Fig. 27A   Diesel engine electrical diagnosis, part 2 of 10. 1980—83 Cutlass with V8 engine

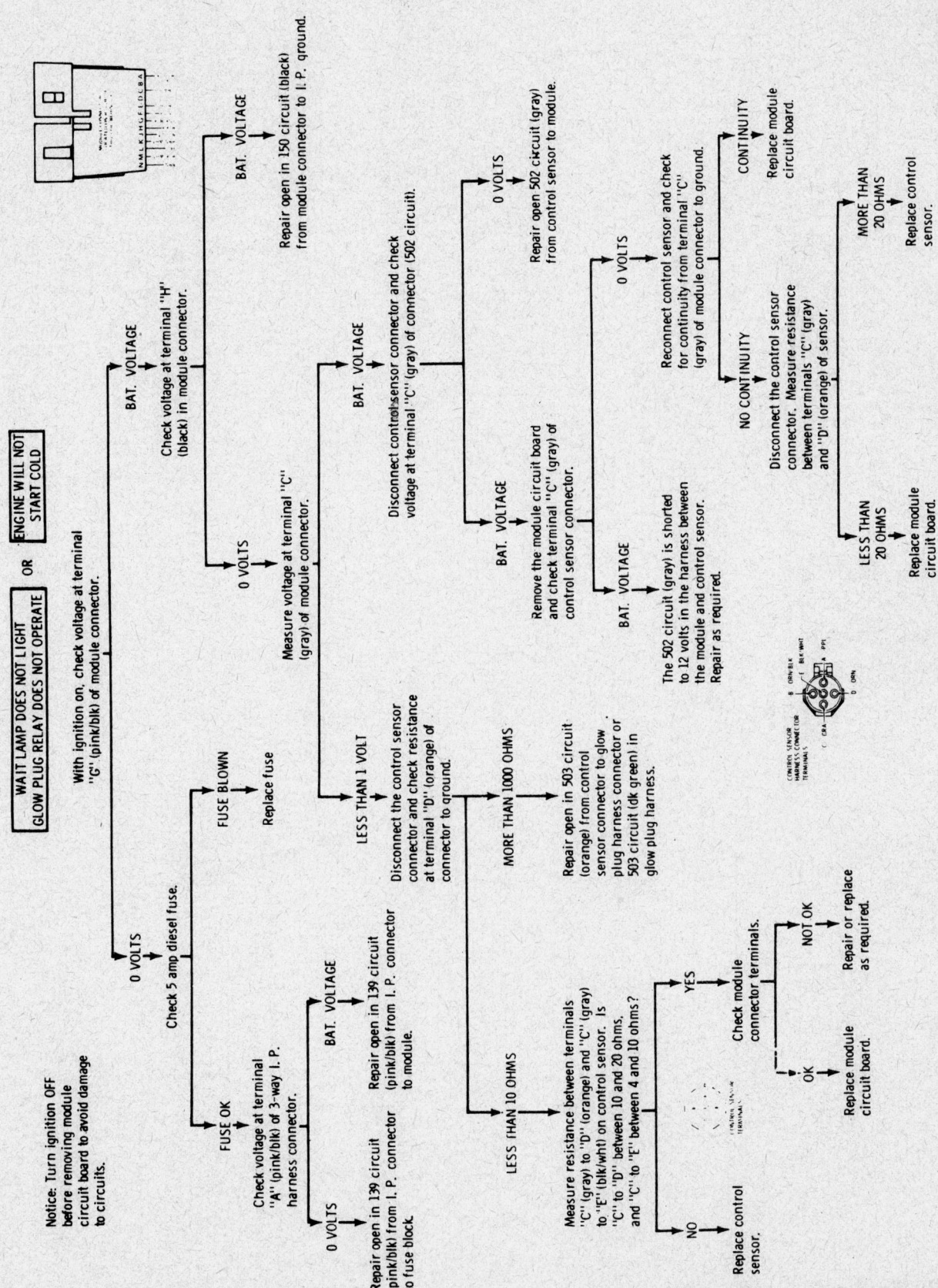

Fig. 27B   Diesel engine electrical diagnosis, part 3 of 10. 1980–83 Cutlass with V8 engine

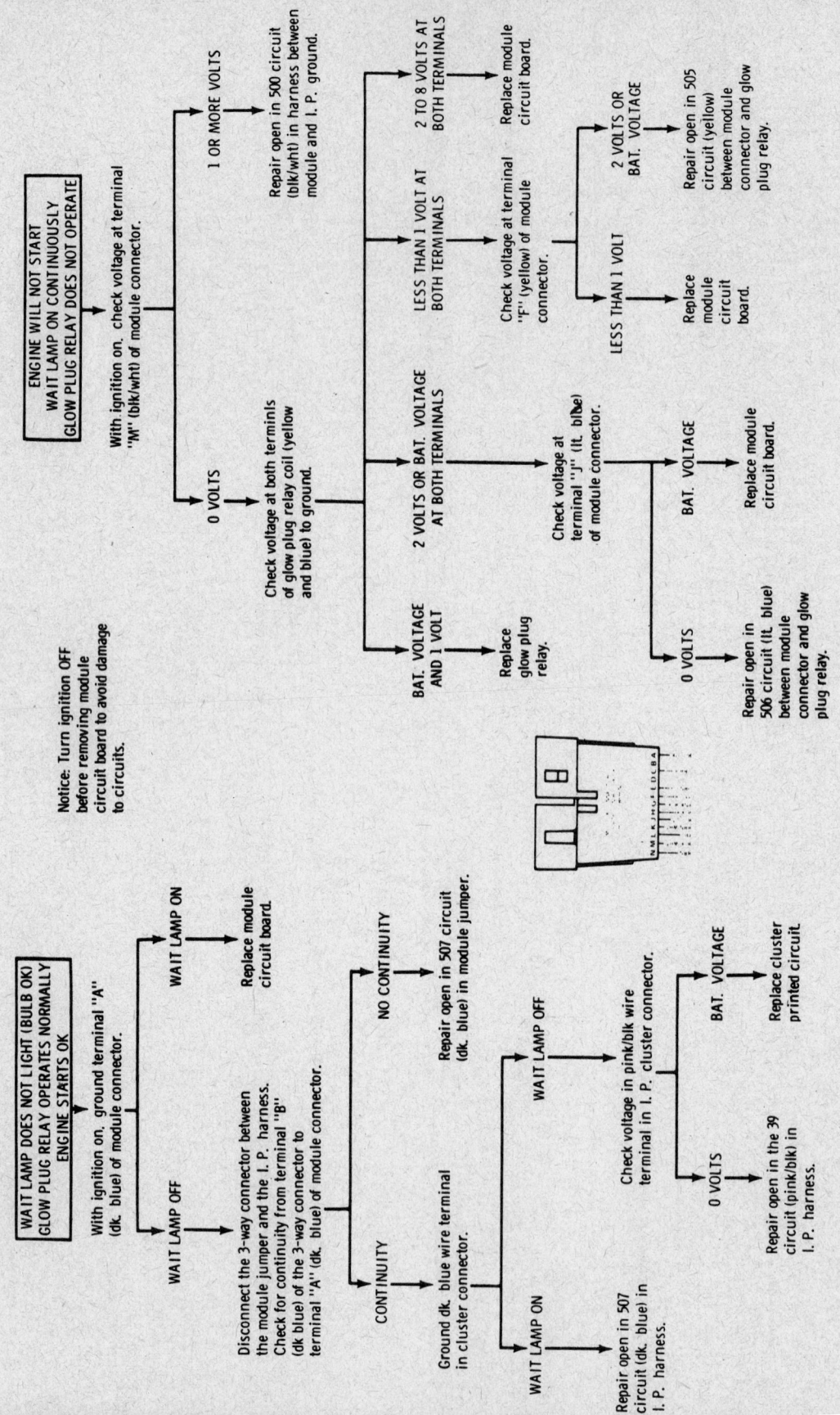

ENGINE WILL NOT START WAIT LAMP ON CONTINUOUSLY GLOW PLUG RELAY DOES NOT OPERATE

With ignition on, check voltage at terminal "M" (blk/wht) of module connector.

1 OR MORE VOLTS → Repair open in 500 circuit (blk/wht) in harness between module and I. P. ground.

2 TO 8 VOLTS AT BOTH TERMINALS → Replace module circuit board.

LESS THAN 1 VOLT AT BOTH TERMINALS → Check voltage at terminal "F" (yellow) of module connector.

2 VOLTS OR BAT. VOLTAGE → Repair open in 505 circuit (yellow) between module connector and glow plug relay.

LESS THAN 1 VOLT → Replace module circuit board.

0 VOLTS → Check voltage at both terminls of glow plug relay coil (yellow and blue) to ground.

2 VOLTS OR BAT. VOLTAGE AT BOTH TERMINALS → Check voltage at terminal "J" (lt. blue) of module connector.

BAT. VOLTAGE → Replace module circuit board.

0 VOLTS → Repair open in 506 circuit (lt. blue) between module connector and glow plug relay.

BAT. VOLTAGE AND 1 VOLT → Replace glow plug relay.

Notice: Turn ignition OFF before removing module circuit board to avoid damage to circuits.

WAIT LAMP DOES NOT LIGHT (BULB OK) GLOW PLUG RELAY OPERATES NORMALLY ENGINE STARTS OK

With ignition on, ground terminal "A" (dk. blue) of module connector.

WAIT LAMP ON → Replace module circuit board.

WAIT LAMP OFF → Disconnect the 3-way connector between the module jumper and the I. P. harness. Check for continuity from terminal "B" (dk blue) of the 3-way connector to terminal "A" (dk. blue) of module connector.

NO CONTINUITY → Repair open in 507 circuit (dk. blue) in module jumper.

CONTINUITY → Ground dk. blue wire terminal in cluster connector.

WAIT LAMP OFF → Check voltage in pink/blk wire terminal in I. P. cluster connector.

BAT. VOLTAGE → Replace cluster printed circuit

0 VOLTS → Repair open in the 39 circuit (pink/blk) in I. P. harness.

WAIT LAMP ON → Repair open in 507 circuit (dk. blue) in I. P. harness.

Fig. 27C   Diesel engine electrical diagnosis, part 4 of 10. 1980–83 Cutlass with V8 engine

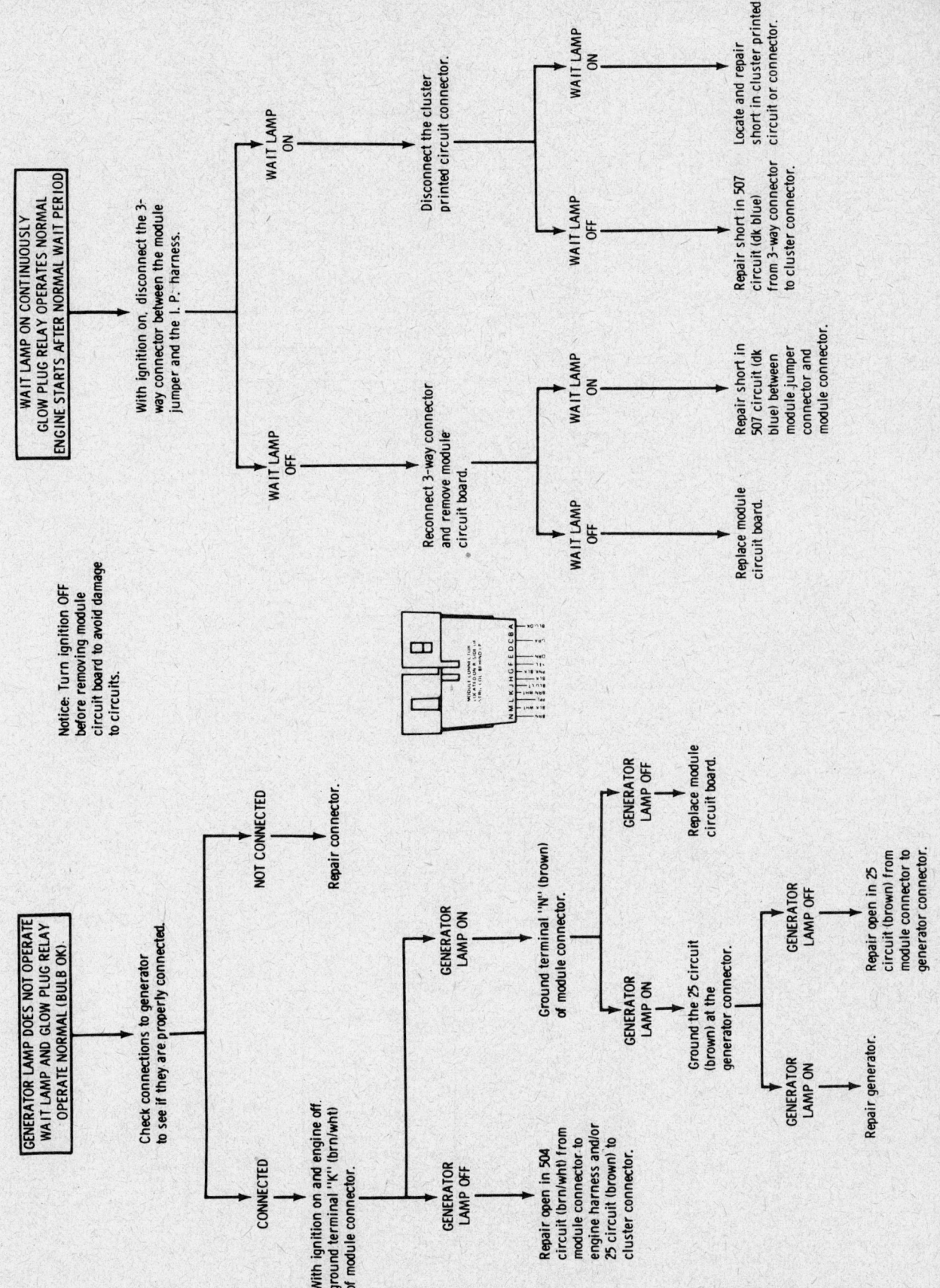

Fig. 27D   Diesel engine electrical diagnosis, part 5 of 10. 1980—83 Cutlass with V8 engine

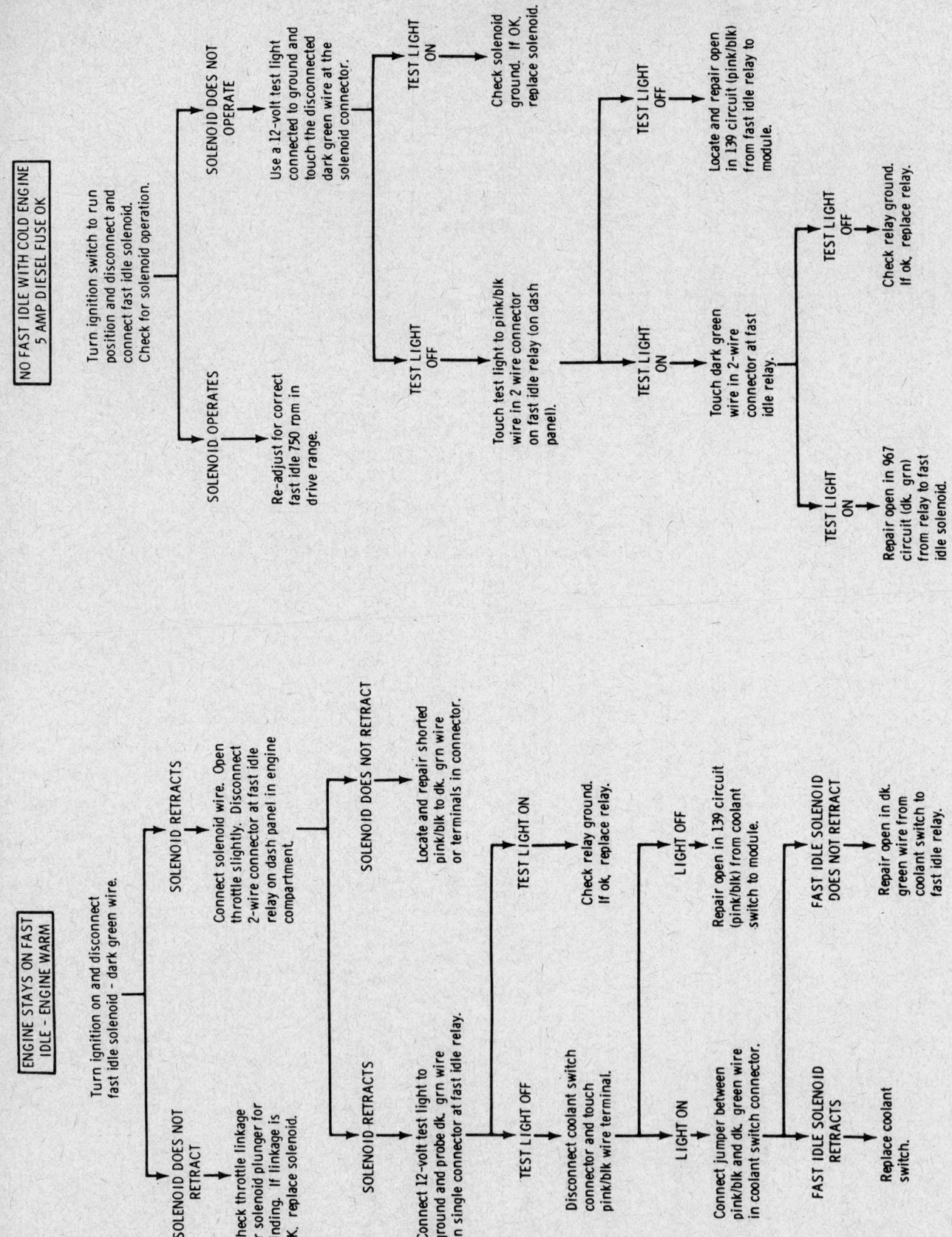

Fig. 27E   Diesel electrical diagnosis, part 6 of 10. 1980–83 Cutlass with V8 engine

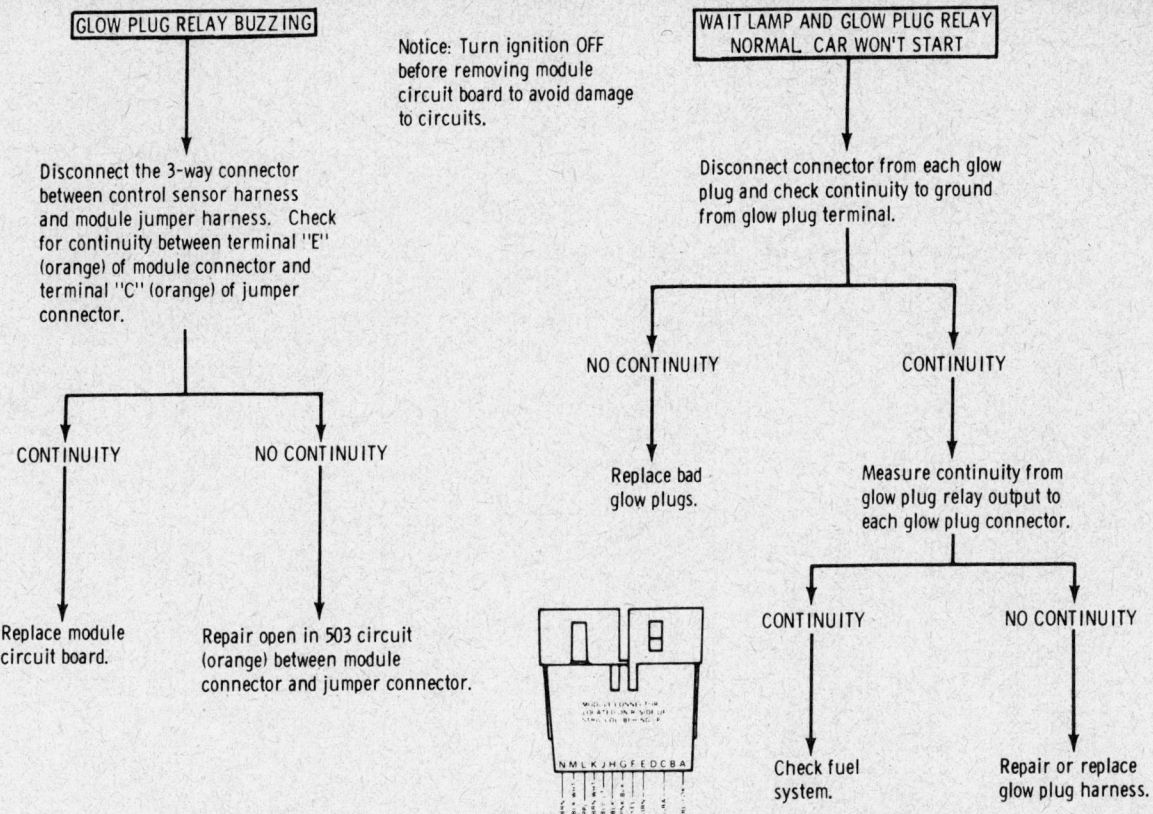

Fig. 27F   Diesel engine electrical diagnosis, part 7 of 10. 1980—83 Cutlass with V8 engine

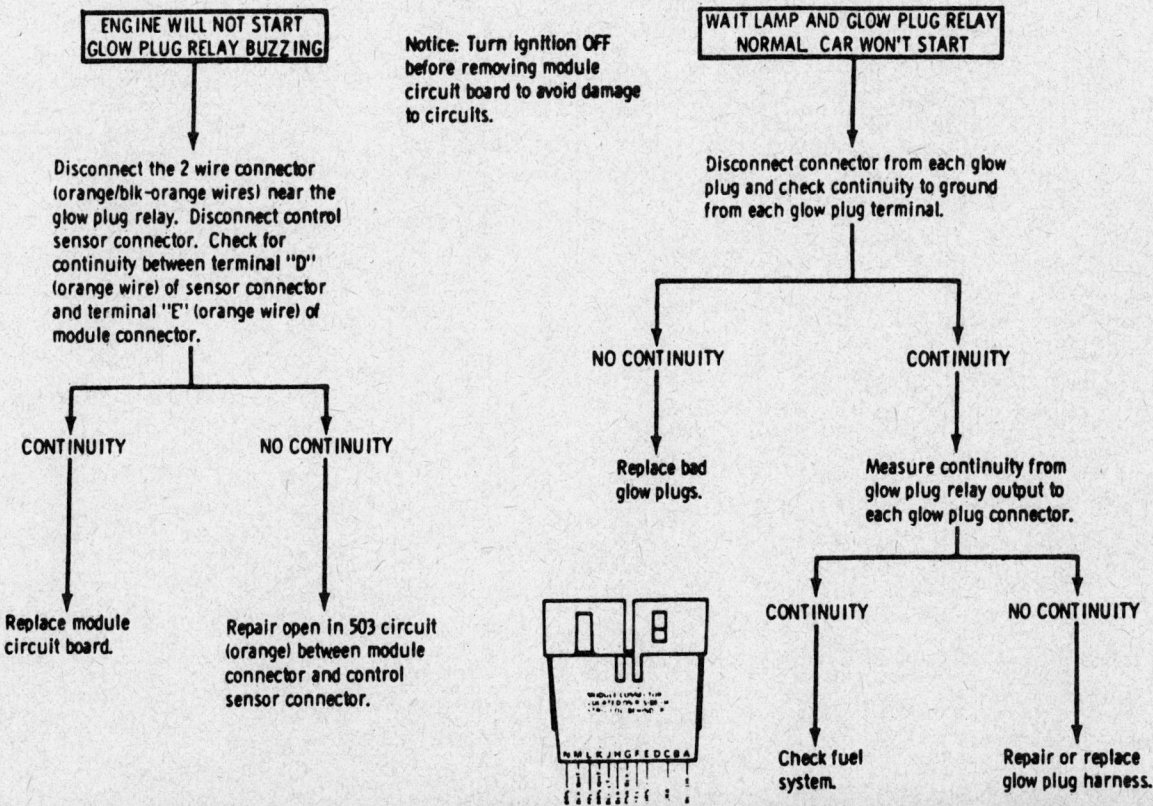

Fig. 27G   Diesel engine electical diagnosis, part 10 of 10. 1982—83 Cutlass V6 engine

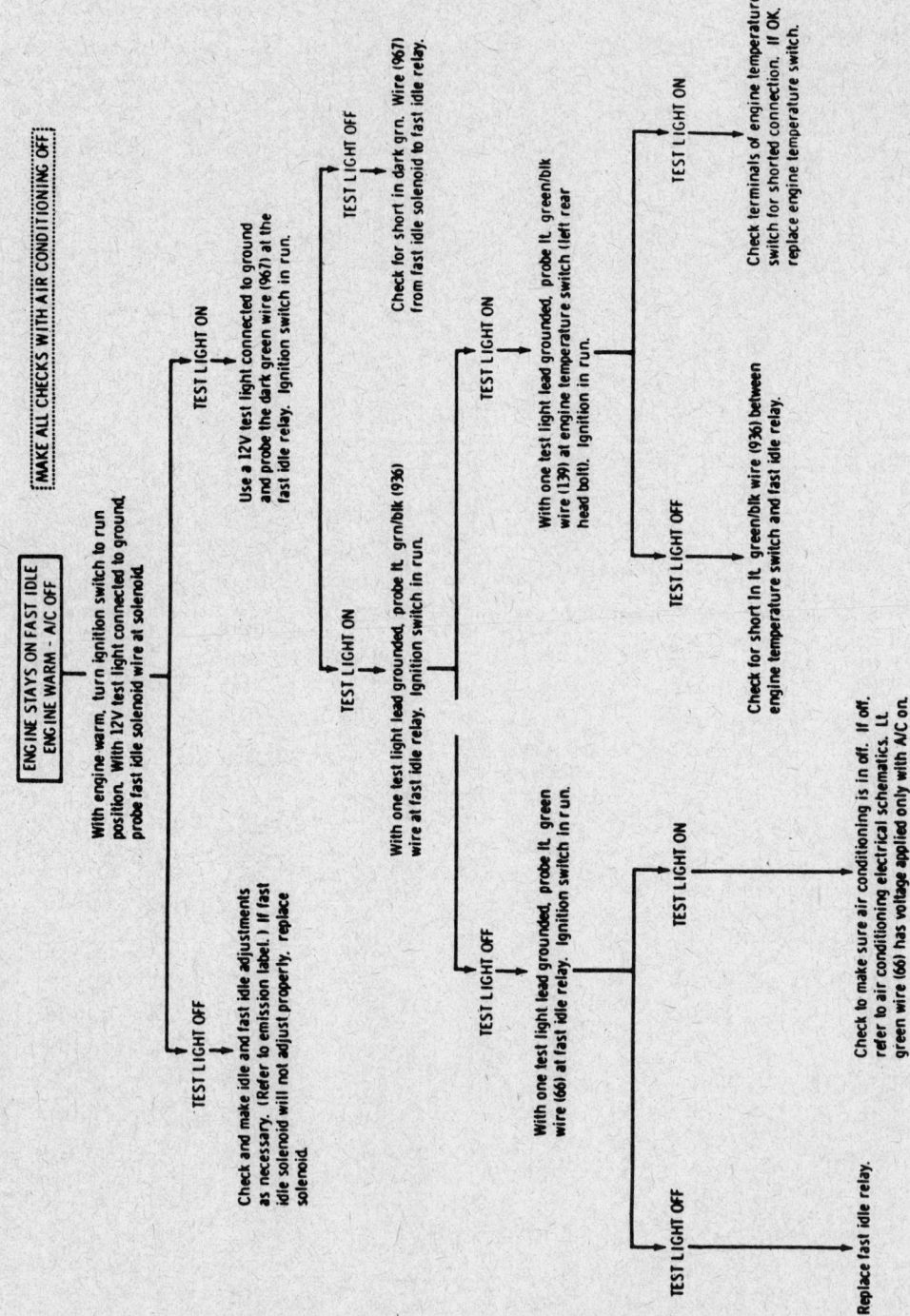

MAKE ALL CHECKS WITH AIR CONDITIONING OFF

ENGINE STAYS ON FAST IDLE ENGINE WARM - A/C OFF

With engine warm, turn ignition switch to run position. With 12V test light connected to ground, probe fast idle solenoid wire at solenoid.

TEST LIGHT OFF — Check and make idle and fast idle adjustments as necessary. (Refer to emission label.) If fast idle solenoid will not adjust properly, replace solenoid.

TEST LIGHT ON — Use a 12V test light connected to ground and probe the dark green wire (967) at the fast idle relay. Ignition switch in run.

TEST LIGHT OFF — Check for short in dark grn. Wire (967) from fast idle solenoid to fast idle relay.

TEST LIGHT ON — With one test light lead grounded, probe lt. grn/blk (936) wire at fast idle relay. Ignition switch in run.

TEST LIGHT OFF — With one test light lead grounded, probe lt. green wire (66) at fast idle relay. Ignition switch in run.

TEST LIGHT ON — Check to make sure air conditioning is in off. If off, refer to air conditioning electrical schematics. Lt. green wire (66) has voltage applied only with A/C on.

TEST LIGHT OFF — Replace fast idle relay.

TEST LIGHT ON — With one test light lead grounded, probe lt. green/blk wire (39) at engine temperature switch (left rear head bolt). Ignition in run.

TEST LIGHT OFF — Check for short in lt. green/blk wire (936) between engine temperature switch and fast idle relay.

TEST LIGHT ON — Check terminals of engine temperature switch for shorted connection. If OK, replace engine temperature switch.

Fig. 27H   Diesel engine electrical diagnosis, part 8 of 10. 1982–83 Cutlass V6 engine

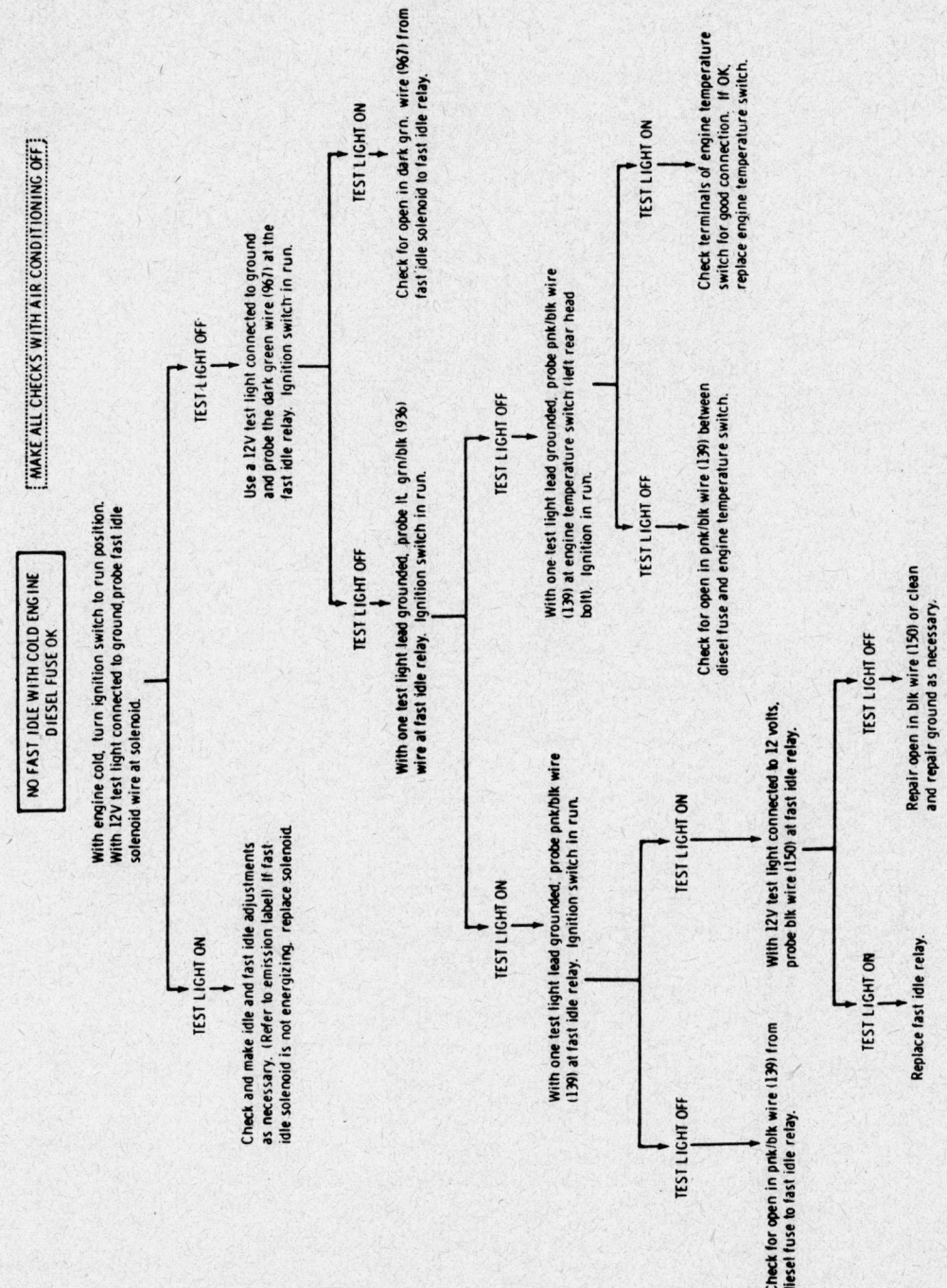

Fig. 271   Diesel engine electrical diagnosis, part 9 of 10. 1982–83 Cutlass V6 engine

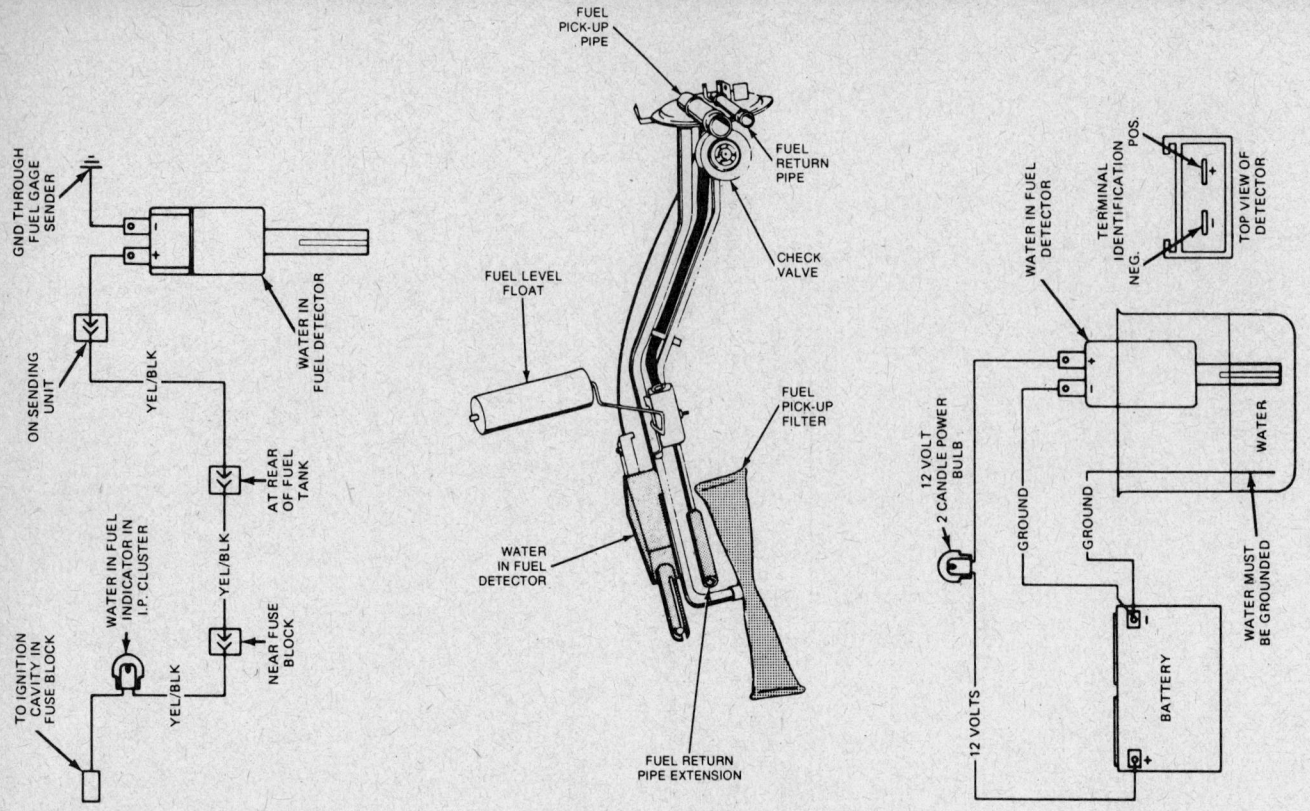

Fig. 27J Water In Fuel System wiring circuit

Fig. 27K Water in Fuel System fuel level sender and water detector

Fig. 27L Checking water detector operation

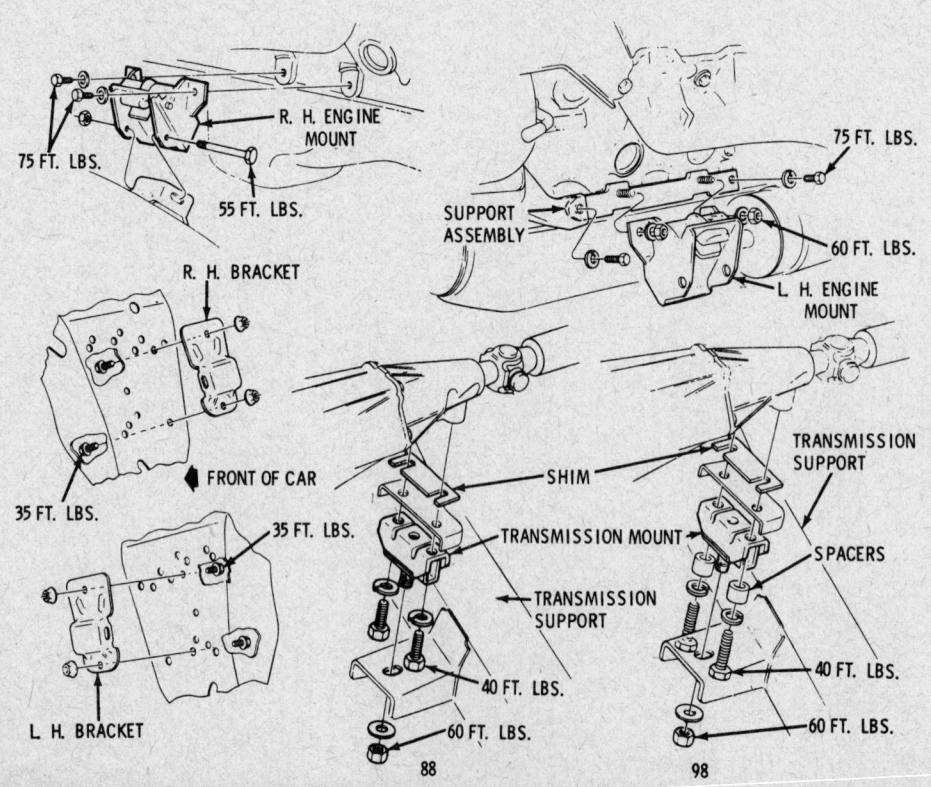

Fig. 28 Diesel engine mounts. 1978 88 & 98

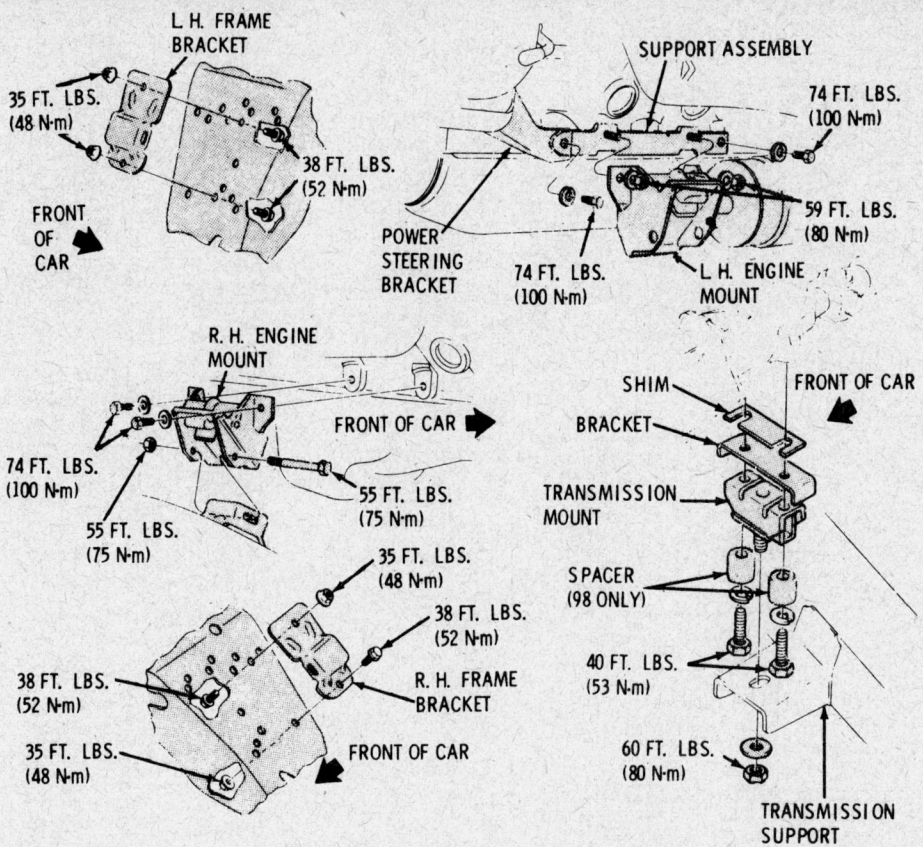

Fig. 28A Diesel engine mount. 1979—84 88 & 98

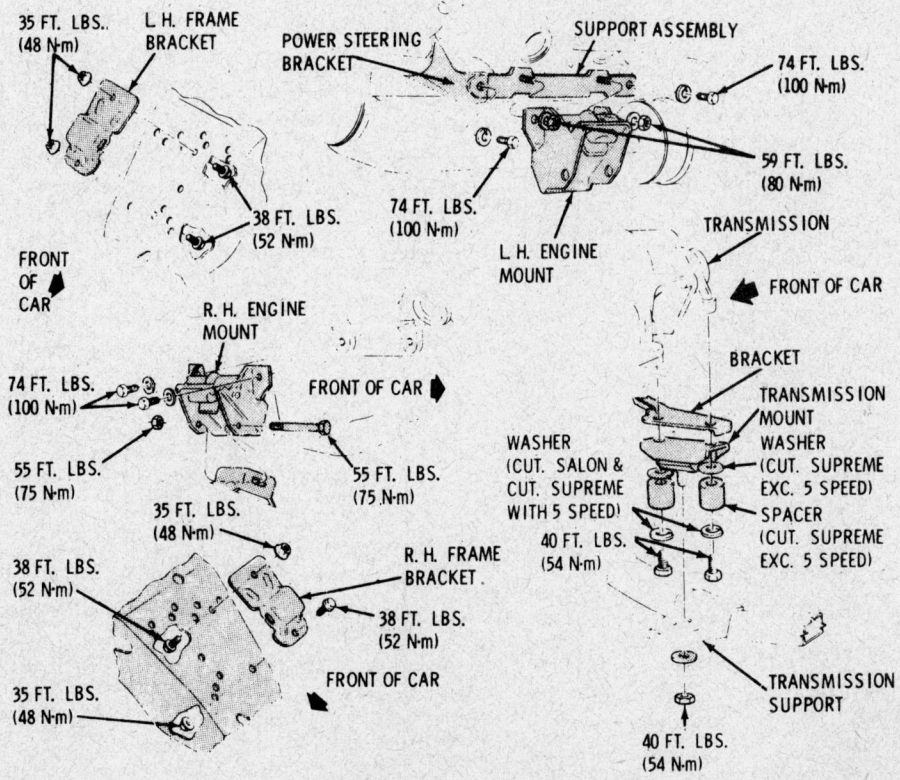

Fig. 28B Diesel engine mount. 1979—84 Cutlass V8 engine

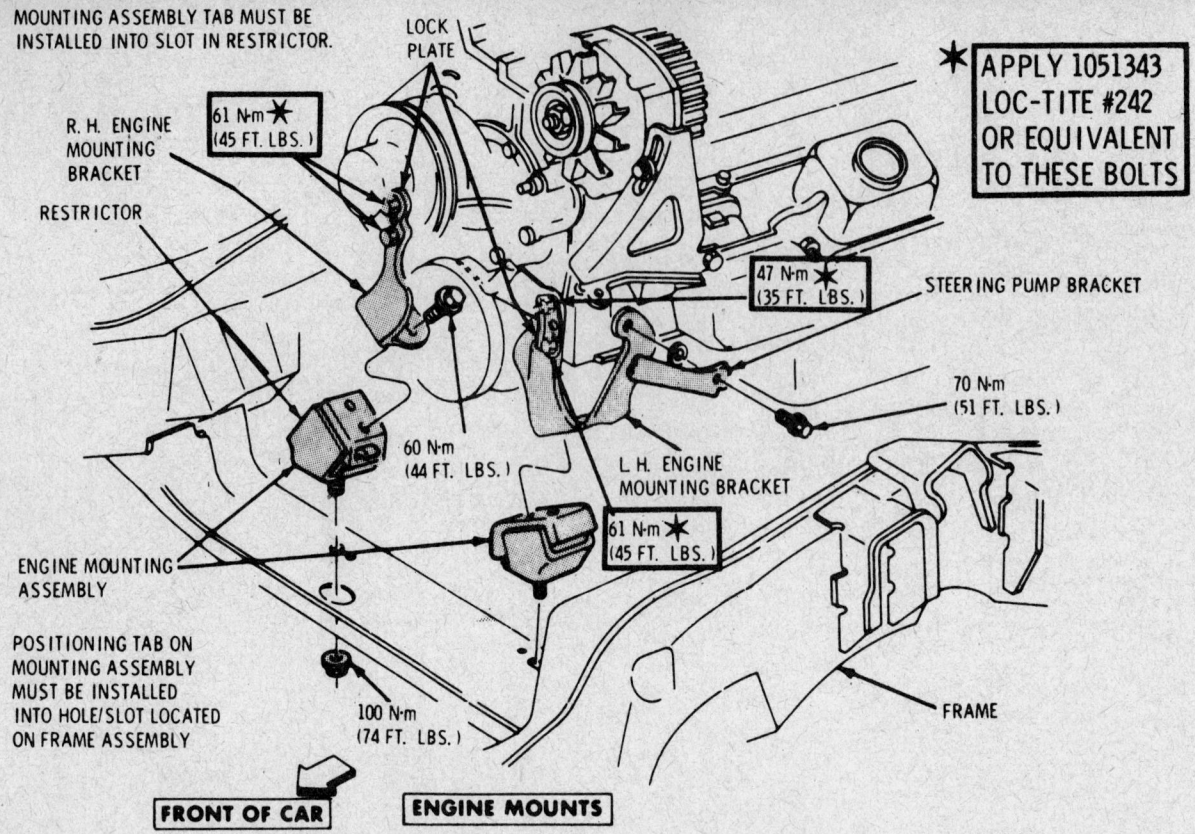

MOUNTING ASSEMBLY TAB MUST BE INSTALLED INTO SLOT IN RESTRICTOR.

LOCK PLATE

R. H. ENGINE MOUNTING BRACKET

61 N·m ⋆ (45 FT. LBS.)

RESTRICTOR

⋆ APPLY 1051343 LOC-TITE #242 OR EQUIVALENT TO THESE BOLTS

47 N·m ⋆ (35 FT. LBS.)

STEERING PUMP BRACKET

70 N·m (51 FT. LBS.)

60 N·m (44 FT. LBS.)

L. H. ENGINE MOUNTING BRACKET

61 N·m ⋆ (45 FT. LBS.)

ENGINE MOUNTING ASSEMBLY

POSITIONING TAB ON MOUNTING ASSEMBLY MUST BE INSTALLED INTO HOLE/SLOT LOCATED ON FRAME ASSEMBLY

100 N·m (74 FT. LBS.)

FRAME

FRONT OF CAR   ENGINE MOUNTS

Fig. 28C Diesel engine mount. 1978–84 Toronado

ENGINE, REPLACE

Exc. Toronado

1. Disconnect ground cable from batteries and drain cooling system.
2. Remove air cleaner.
3. Scribe hood hinge locations and remove hood.
4. Disconnect ground wires at inner fender and the engine ground strap at right cylinder head.
5. Disconnect radiator hoses, oil cooler lines, heater hoses, vacuum hoses, power steering hoses from gear, A/C compressor with brackets and hoses attached, fuel pump hose from fuel pump and the wiring.
6. Remove hairpin clip from bellcrank, on all except 6 cylinder engine.
7. Remove throttle and throttle valve cables from intake manifold brackets and position cables aside.
8. Remove upper radiator support and the radiator on all except 6 cylinder engine.
9. Raise and support vehicle.

10. Disconnect exhaust pipes from exhaust manifold.
11. Remove torque converter cover and the three bolts securing torque converter to flywheel.
12. Remove engine mount bolts or nuts.
13. Remove three engine to transmission bolts on the right side.
14. Disconnect starter wiring and remove starter.
15. Lower vehicle.
16. Attach suitable engine lifting equipment to engine. Support transmission with a suitable jack.
17. Remove the three engine to transmission bolts on the left side.

18. Remove engine from vehicle.
19. Reverse procedure to install.

1979–84 Toronado

1. Disconnect battery ground cable and drain cooling system.
2. Remove radiator upper support.
3. Remove air cleaner assembly.
4. Scribe hood hinge locations and remove hood.
5. Disconnect engine ground strap.
6. Disconnect upper and lower radiator hoses from engine.
7. Disconnect transmission oil cooler lines from radiator.

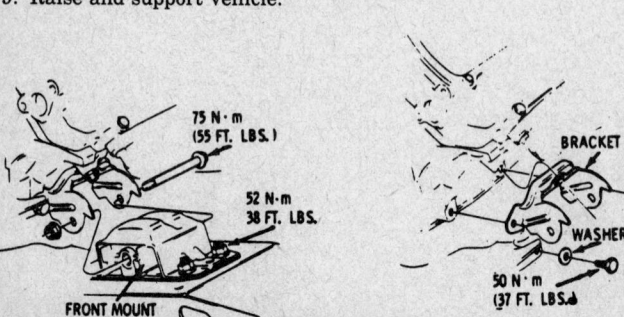

75 N·m (55 FT. LBS.)

52 N·m 38 FT. LBS.

BRACKET

WASHER

50 N·m (37 FT. LBS.)

FRONT MOUNT

Fig. 28D Motor mounts. 1982–84 Cutlass V6 engine

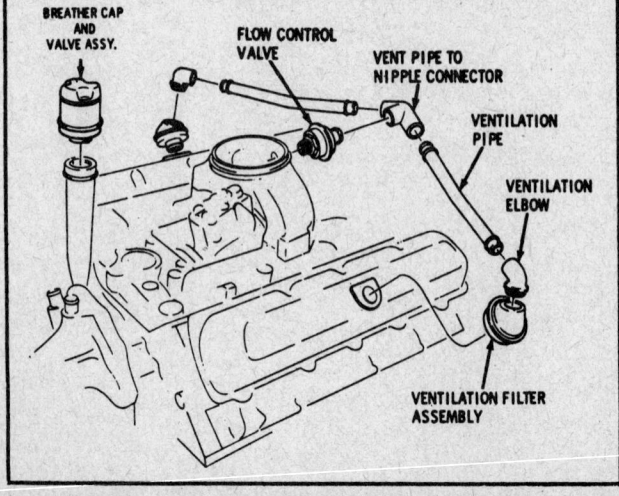

BREATHER CAP AND VALVE ASSY.

FLOW CONTROL VALVE

VENT PIPE TO NIPPLE CONNECTOR

VENTILATION PIPE

VENTILATION ELBOW

VENTILATION FILTER ASSEMBLY

Fig. 28E Crankcase ventilation system. V8 engine

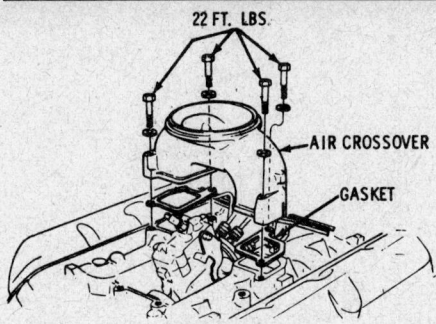

Fig. 29 Air crossover installation. Typical

8. Disconnect heater hoses from water pump and water control valve.
9. Remove radiator, fan and the shroud.
10. Disconnect power steering pump bracket from engine and position aside without disconnecting lines.
11. Disconnect A/C compressor bracket from engine and position aside without disconnecting lines.
12. Disconnect fuel lines.
13. Disconnect throttle cable, vacuum hoses and electrical connections.
14. Disconnect left hand exhaust pipe from manifold.
15. On left side of engine, remove through bolt and bracket securing final drive to engine.
16. Raise and support vehicle.
17. Remove flywheel shield.
18. Disconnect right hand exhaust pipe from manifold.
19. Disconnect starter motor wiring and remove starter motor.
20. Remove converter to flywheel bolts. Mark location of converter on flywheel for alignment during installation.
21. Remove splash shield.
22. Remove engine front mounting attaching nuts.
23. Remove two bolts securing right hand output shaft support brackets. Using a sharp tool, scribe a mark around the washers as far as possible. Use these scribe marks to position bracket upon installation.
24. Remove lower right hand transmission to engine attaching bolts. One bolt retains the modulator line clip.
25. Use a suitable length of chain to retain final drive in vehicle.
26. Lower vehicle and attaching suitable engine lifting equipment to engine.
27. Remove the remaining transmission to engine bolts. It may be necessary to raise or lower transmission with a suitable jack to facilitate bolt removal.
28. Raise engine and remove from vehicle.
29. Reverse procedure to install.

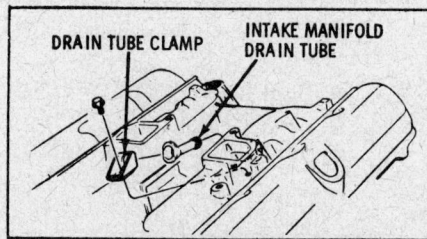

Fig. 31 Intake manifold drain tube installation

INTAKE MANIFOLD, REPLACE

V8 Engine

1. Disconnect ground cables from batteries.
2. Remove air cleaner assembly.
3. Drain cooling system, then disconnect upper radiator hose and thermostat bypass hose from water pump outlet. Disconnect heater hose and vacuum hose from water control valve.
4. Remove breather pipes from valve covers and air crossover, Fig. 28E.
5. Remove air crossover and cap intake manifold, Fig. 29.
6. Disconnect throttle rod and return spring. If equipped with Cruise Control, remove servo.
7. Remove hairpin clip from bellcrank and disconnect the cables. Remove throttle and throttle valve cables from intake manifold brackets and position cables aside.
8. Disconnect wiring as necessary.
9. Disconnect or remove alternator and A/C compressor brackets as necessary.
10. Disconnect fuel line from fuel pump and filter and remove fuel filter and bracket.
11. Disconnect lines from injector nozzles and remove injection pump, refer to "Injection Nozzle Replace, Injection Pump & Lines". Cap all open fuel line lines and fittings.
12. Disconnect fuel return line from injection pump.
13. Disconnect vacuum lines at vacuum pump. Remove vacuum pump, if equipped with A/C, or oil pump drive assembly, if less A/C, Fig. 30.
14. Remove intake manifold drain tube, Fig. 31.
15. Remove intake manifold bolts and the intake manifold.
16. Remove adapter seal and injection pump adapter.
17. Reverse procedure to install. Torque intake manifold bolts in sequence, Fig. 32, to specifications.

V6 Engine

1. Disconnect battery ground cable and remove air cleaner.
2. Drain cooling system, then disconnect upper radiator hose and thermostat bypass hose from water outlet.
3. Disconnect heater inlet hose and on models equipped with air conditioning, the water valve vacuum line.
4. Disconnect crankcase ventilation pipe from air crossover, Fig. 32A. Remove air crossover.
5. Remove fuel pump and plug all open lines and fittings.
6. Remove fuel injection pump as described under "Injection Pump, Replace".
7. Disconnect electrical connectors as necessary.
8. Remove cruise control servo, if equipped.
9. Disconnect fuel lines and position aside. Disconnect vacuum lines as necessary.
10. Remove drain tube, then remove intermediate pump adapter, Fig. 32B.
11. Remove intake manifold bolts and the intake manifold.
12. Reverse procedure to install. Lubricate intake manifold bolts with engine oil before installing, then torque bolts as specified in sequence shown in Fig. 32C. Apply chassis grease to seal area of intake manifold and pump adapter and to inside and outside diameter of seal and seal area of

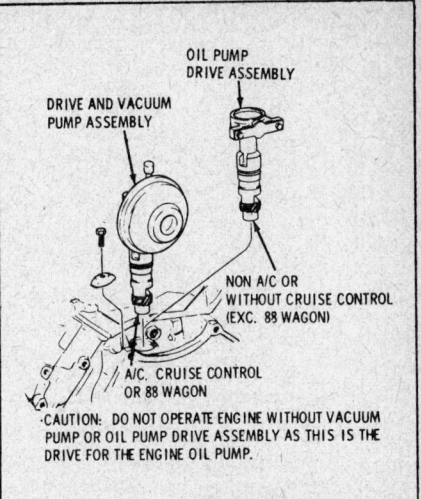

Fig. 30 Vacuum pump & oil pump drive assembly

tool J-28425 or equivalent. Install seal onto tool, then install seal.

CYLINDER HEAD, REPLACE

SERVICE NOTE

V8-350

New head bolts with increased torque capacity were introduced into production during March 1980 and are now available, Fig. 32D.

When replacing a cylinder head, it is recommended new head bolts be used if they have not already been installed in the engine. When installing later production model head bolts, be sure to clean and oil the threads. Before installation of the cylinder head, ensure bolt holes are tapped deep enough into the block. Blow out any chips or liquid in the bolt holes. Then position cylinder head on cylinder block without the cylinder head gasket. Install bolt and tighten by hand until bolt head contacts the cylinder head. This will indicate that the holes are tapped deep enough into the block, allowing for proper torque. For cylinder head bolt location, part number and size, refer to Fig. 32E.

New design head gaskets are available for service and will supersede previous gaskets

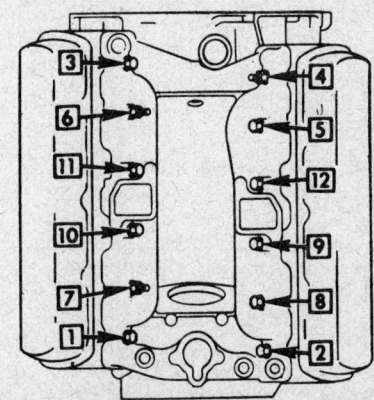

Fig. 32 Intake manifold tightening sequence. V8 engine

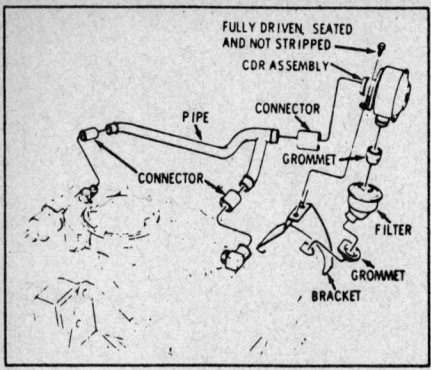

Fig. 32A Crankcase ventilation system. V6 engine

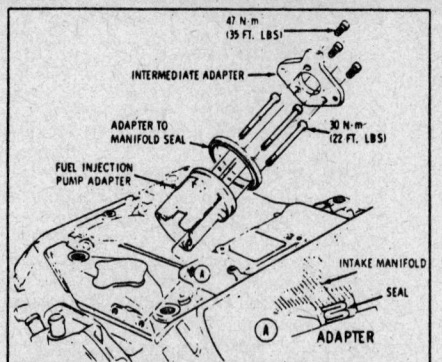

Fig. 32B Removing intermediate pump adapter. V6 engine

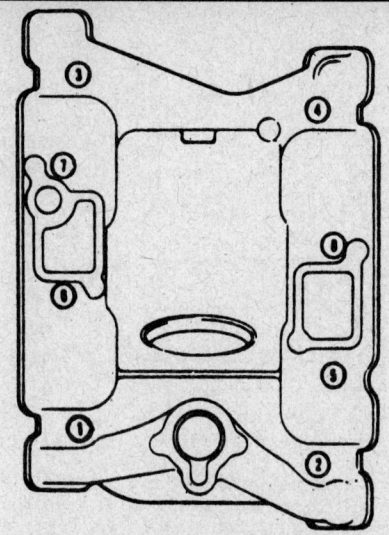

Fig. 32C Intake manifold bolt tightening sequence. V6 engine

used on V8-350 diesel engines. These gaskets are the same gaskets recommended for use on engines using .030 inch oversize pistons and will now be used for all applications. The use of these gaskets on standard engines should prevent loss of compression due to the gasket sealing ring falling into the combustion chamber. On 1978–80 and 1983 engines, use new gasket, Part No. 22519416. This gasket is evident by the grey seal located on the gasket face. On 1981–82 engines, use new gasket, Part No. 22510719, evident by the purple seal on the gasket face. No gasket sealer should be used on either gasket during installation.

When servicing cylinder head, ensure that prechambers are not recessed into cylinder head or protrude out of cylinder head more than .004 inch, since head gasket leakage may result. Measure the difference between flat or prechamber and the flat surface of cylinder head at two or more points around circumference of prechamber, using a straight edge and feeler gauge. If prechamber is recessed more than specified, replace prechamber or cylinder head, depending on which is at fault. If prechamber protrudes more than specified, grind top of prechamber for a flush fit, or replace as necessary.

1. Remove intake manifold as outlined previously.
2. Remove valve cover. It may be necessary to remove any interfering accessory brackets.
3. Disconnect glow plug wiring.
4. Remove ground strap from right cylinder

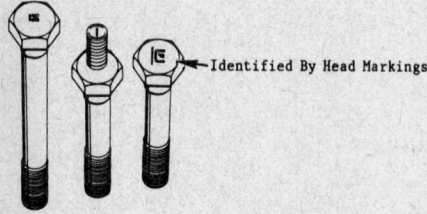

Fig. 32D Cylinder head bolt markings

head, if removing.
5. Remove rocker arm bolts, pivots, rocker arms and push rod. Note locations of valve train components so they can be installed in original locations.
6. Remove fuel return lines from injection nozzles if equipped.
7. Remove exhaust manifold.
8. Remove engine block drain plug on side of block that cylinder head is being removed.
9. Remove cylinder head bolts and cylinder head. On 1982 V8 diesel remove TCC temperature switch located on exposed right rear cylinder head bolt.
10. If necessary to remove pre-chamber, remove a glow plug or injection nozzle, then tap out pre-chamber with a suitable drift, Fig. 33.
11. Reverse procedure to install. Do not use any sealing compound on cylinder head gasket. On 8 cylinder engines, torque cylinder head bolts in sequence, Fig. 34, to 100 ft. lbs., then to 130 ft. lbs. On 6 cylinder engines, torque cylinder head bolts except bolts 5, 6, 11, 12, 13 and 14, Fig. 34A, to 142 ft. lbs. Torque bolts 5, 6, 11, 12, 13 and 14 to 59 ft. lbs.

ROCKER ARMS

NOTE: This engine uses valve rotators, Fig. 35. The rotator operates on a sprag clutch principle utilizing the collapsing action of a coil spring to give rotation to the rotor body which turns the valve.

SERVICE NOTE

Some 1978–83 V8-350 diesel engines may experience valve train ticking noise and/or exhaust backfire. This condition may be caused by premature wear of the rocker arm pivots. Two types of rocker arm pivots were used on these engines. Type 1 pivot assemblies, Fig. 35A, are the only ones showing premature wear. It is therefore recommended

that only Type 2 pivot assemblies, Fig. 35B, be used when servicing the engine for the above mentioned condition.

1. Remove valve cover.
2. Remove flanged bolts, rocker arm pivot and rocker arms, Fig. 35.
3. When installing rocker arm assemblies, lubricate wear surfaces with suitable lubricant. Torque flanged bolts to 25 ft. lbs. On 8 cylinder engines or 28 ft. lbs. on 6 cylinder engines.

VALVE ROTATORS

The rotator operates on a Sprag clutch principle utilizing the collapsing action of coil spring to give rotation to the rotor body which turns the valve, Fig. 35.

To check rotator action, draw a line across rotator body and down the collar. Operate engine at 1500 rpm, rotator body should move around collar. Rotator action can be in either direction. Replace rotator if no movement is noted.

When servicing valves, valve stem tips should be checked for improper wear pattern which could indicate a defective valve rotator, Fig. 36.

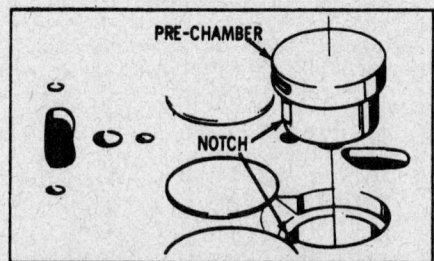

Fig. 33 Pre-chamber installation

LOCATION NUMBER	PART NUMBER	SIZE
1	22510580	1/2 - 13 x 3.10
2	22510582	1/2-13 x 3.10 stud end
3	22510579	1/2 - 13 x 4.30
4	22510585	1/2 - 13 x 4.30 stud end

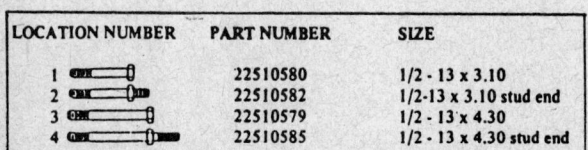

Fig. 32E Cylinder head bolt identification

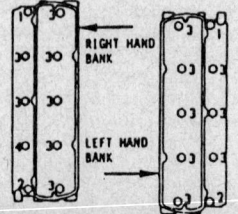

Fig. 34 Cylinder head tightening sequence. V8 engine

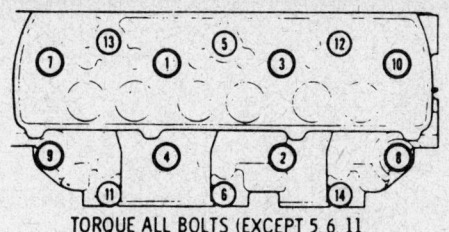

TORQUE ALL BOLTS (EXCEPT 5, 6, 11, 12, 13 & 14) TO 193 N·m (142 FT. LBS.). NUMBERS 5, 6, 11, 12, 13 & 14 TORQUE TO 80 N·m (59 FT. LBS.).

Fig. 34A Cylinder head bolt tightening sequence. V6 engine

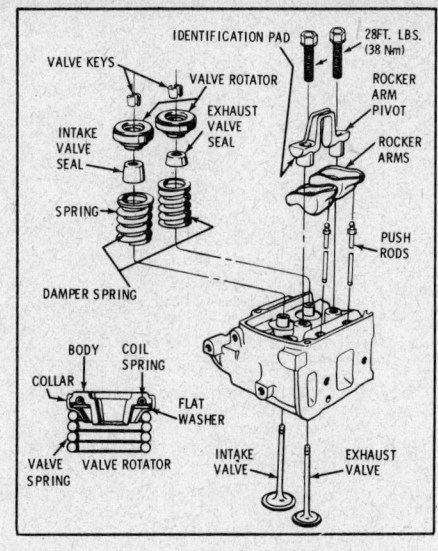

Fig. 35 Cylinder head exploded view

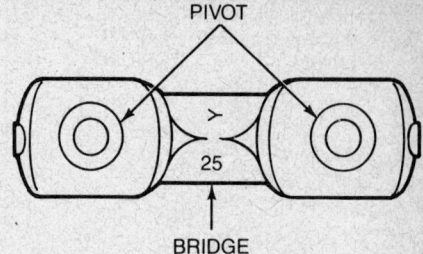

Fig. 35A Type 1 rocker arm pivot. 1978—83 V8-350 diesel

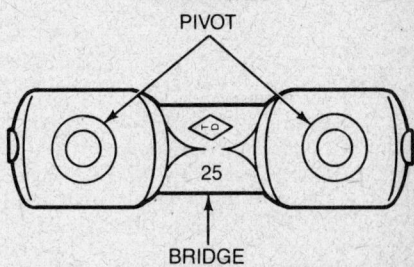

Fig. 35B Type 2 rocker arm pivot. 1978—83 V8-350 diesel

VALVE LIFT SPECS.

Engine	Year	Intake	Exhaust
V8-260, 350 Diesel	1978–84	.375	.376
V6-262 Diesel	1982–84	.375	.375

VALVE ARRANGEMENT

V8-260, 350 Diesel . . . . I-E-I-E-E-I-E-I
V6-262 Diesel . . . . I-E-E-I-E-I

VALVE TIMING
Intake Opens Before TDC

Engine	Year	Degrees
V8-260, 350 Diesel	1978–84	16
V6-262 Diesel	1982–84	16

VALVES

Whenever a new valve is installed or after grinding valves, it is necessary to measure the valve stem height with the special tool as shown in Fig. 37.

There should be at least .015 inch clearance between the gauge and end of valve stem. If clearance is less than .015 inch, remove valve and grind end of valve stem as required.

Check valve rotator height, Fig. 38. If valve stem end is less than .005 inch above rotator, the valve is too short and a new valve must be installed.

VALVE GUIDES

Valve stem guides are not replaceable, due to being cast in place. If valve guide bores are worn excessively, they can be reamed oversize.

If a standard valve guide bore is being reamed, use a .003″ or .005″ oversize reamer. For the .010″ oversize valve guide bore, use a

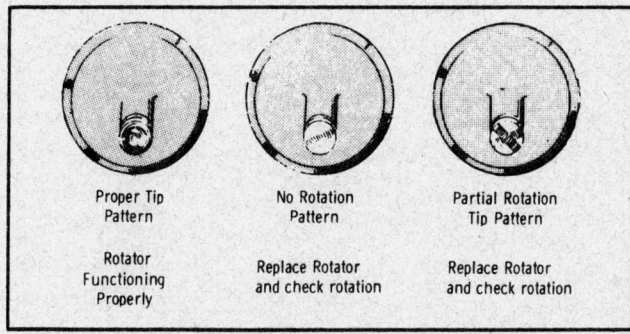

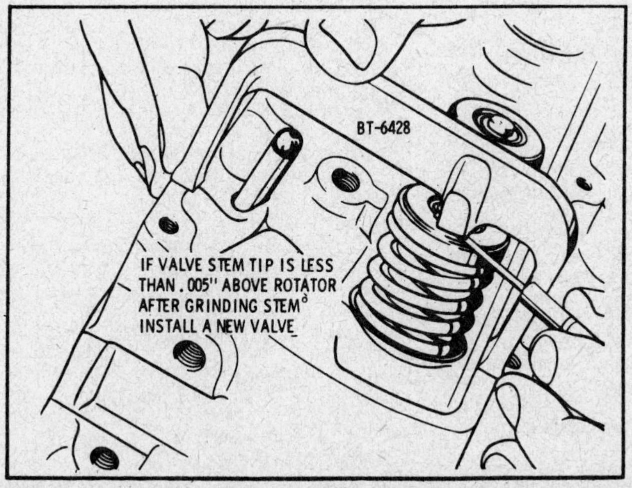

Fig. 36 Checking valve stem for rotator malfunction

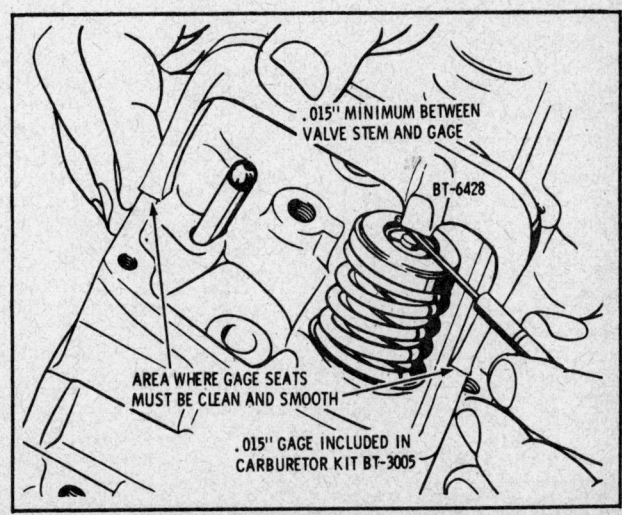

Fig. 37 Measuring valve stem height

Fig. 38 Measuring valve rotator height

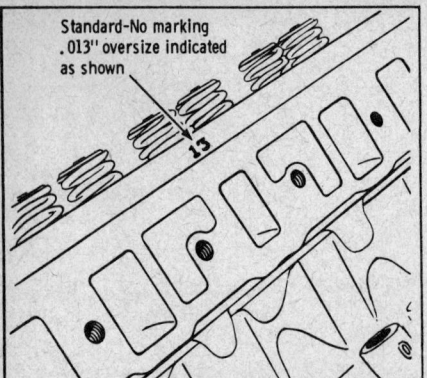

Fig. 39 Valve guide bore marking

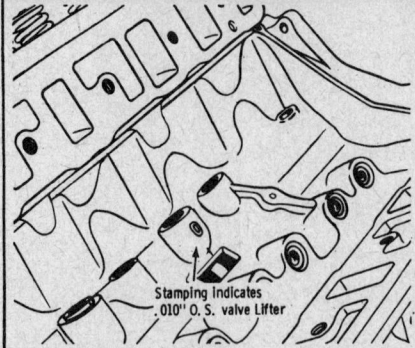

Fig. 40 Oversize valve lifter bore marking

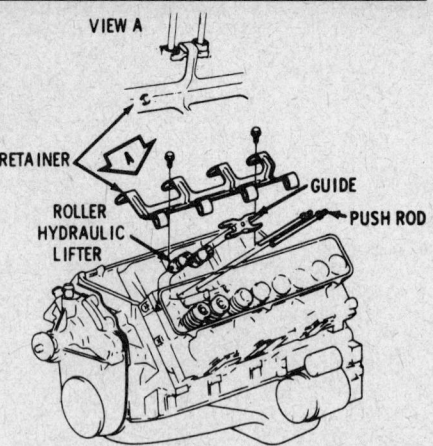

Fig. 40A Hydraulic roller lifter retainer and guide. 1981–84 (Typical)

.013″ oversize reamer. If too large a reamer is used and the spiraling is removed, it is possible that the valve will not receive the proper lubrication.

NOTE: Occasionally a valve guide will be oversize as manufactured. These are marked on the cylinder head as shown in Fig. 39. If no markings are present, the guide bores are standard. If oversize markings are present, any valve replacement will require an oversize valve. Service valves are available in standard diameters as well as .003″, .005″, .010″ and .013″ oversize.

VALVE LIFTERS, REPLACE

NOTE: Some engines have both standard and .010 inch oversize valve lifters. The .010 inch oversize valve lifters are etched with a "0" on the side of the lifter. Also, the cylinder block will be marked if an oversize lifter is used, Fig. 40.

1. Remove intake manifold as outlined previously.
2. Remove valve covers, rocker arm assemblies and push rods. Note location of valve train components so they can be installed in original position.
3. On 1981–84 models, remove the hydraulic lifter retainer bolts, Fig. 40A.
4. Remove valve lifters.
5. Reverse procedure to install.

NOTE: Plungers are not interchangeable because they are selectively fitted to the bodies at the factory.

VALVE LIFTERS, SERVICE

1. Remove valve lifters, refer to "Valve Lifters, Replace."
2. Using a small screwdriver, remove retainer ring, Figs. 41 and 41A.
3. Remove pushrod seat, oil metering valve, plunger, and plunger spring.
4. Remove check ball retainer from plunger, then remove ball and spring.
5. Clean parts in a suitable solvent.

NOTE: Do not interchange parts between lifters. If any parts are worn, replace lifter.

6. Inspect all parts for nicks, burrs or scoring. If any parts are defective, replace lifter.
7. On 1981–84 roller lifters, inspect roller. It should rotate freely, but without excessive play, also check for missing or broken needle bearing. If any parts are defective, replace lifter.
8. Apply a coating of light engine oil to all lifter surfaces.
9. Install ball check spring and retainer into plunger. Ensure retainer flange is pressed tight against bottom of recess in plunger.
10. Install plunger spring over check retainer.
11. Hold plunger with spring up and insert in lifter body. Hold plunger vertically to prevent cocking spring.
12. Submerge lifter assembly in clean diesel fuel or kerosene, then install oil metering valve and push rod seat into lifter and install retaining ring.

VALVE LIFTER BLEED DOWN

If the intake manifold has been removed and if any rocker arms have been removed or loosened, it will be necessary to remove those lifters, disassemble them, drain the oil from them and reassemble. Refer to "Valve Lifters, Service."

If the intake manifold has not been removed, but rocker arms have been loosened or removed, the valve lifters must be bled down to prevent possible valve to piston interference by using the following procedure:

1. Prior to installing rocker arms, rotate crankshaft pulley to a position 32° BTDC (before top dead center). This is approximately 2 inches counterclockwise from 0° pointer.
2. If the right side valve cover was removed only, remove cylinder No. 1 glow plug and determine if No. 1 piston is in the correct

position, this can be determined by compression pressure.

3. If the left side valve cover was removed only, rotate crankshaft until No. 5 cylinder intake valve push rod is .28 inch above the No. 5 cylinder exhaust valve push rod.
4. If removed, install cylinder No. 5 pivot and rocker arms. Alternately torque the bolts until the intake valve begins to open and stop tightening.

NOTE: When torquing rocker arms, use only hand wrenches to prevent engine damage.

5. Install remaining rocker arms except No. 3 exhaust valve. Torque bolt to 25 ft. lbs. on 1978–80 models and 28 ft. lbs. on 1981–84.
6. If removed, install No. 3 exhaust rocker arm and pivot, but do not torque beyond the point that the valve would be fully opened. This is indicated by a strong resistance while turning the pivot retaining bolt. Going beyond this point would bend the push rod.

NOTE: While performing step 6, torque bolt slowly allowing the lifter to bleed down.

7. Finish torquing No. 5 rocker arm pivot bolt slowly, allowing valve lifter to bleed down. Do not torque beyond the point that the valve would be fully opened. This is indicated by a strong resistance while turning the pivot retaining bolt. Going beyond this point would bend the push rod.
8. Do not turn the crankshaft for at least 45 minutes while lifters bleed down.

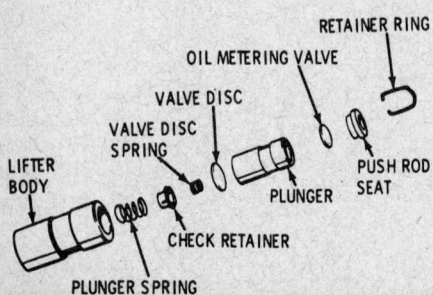

Fig. 41 Valve lifter exploded view. 1978–80

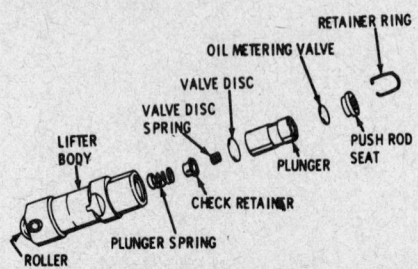

Fig. 41A Hydraulic roller lifter assembly exploded view. 1981–84

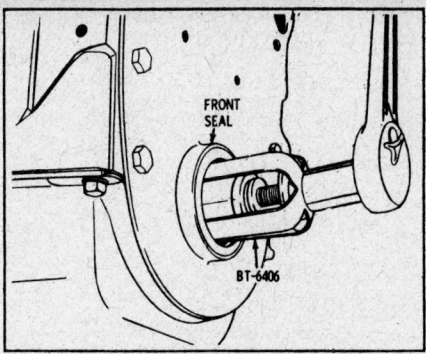

Fig. 42 Front oil seal removal

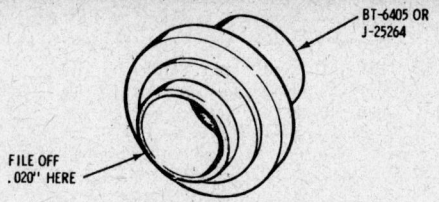

Fig. 43 Modifying tool for front oil seal installation

Fig. 45 Dowel pin chamfer

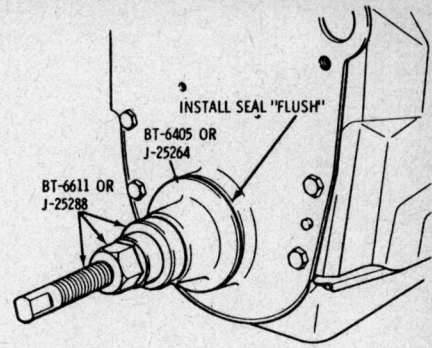

Fig. 44 Front oil seal installation

NOTE: Do not rotate the engine until the valve lifters have bled down, otherwise engine damage might occur.

FRONT OIL SEAL, REPLACE

1. Disconnect ground cables from batteries.
2. Remove accessory drive belts.
3. Remove crankshaft pulley and harmonic balancer.
4. Using tool BT-6406, remove front oil seal, Fig. 42.
5. Apply suitable sealer to outside diameter of new oil seal.
6. File .020 inch from flange of tool No. J-25264, Fig. 43, to prevent tool from contacting oil slinger before seal is properly seated in front cover.
7. Using tool BT-6611, install new oil seal, Fig. 44.
8. Install harmonic balancer and crankshaft pulley.
9. Install and tension accessory drive belts.

ENGINE FRONT COVER, REPLACE

1. Disconnect ground cables from batteries.
2. Drain cooling system and disconnect radiator hoses and bypass hose.
3. Remove all drive belts, fan and pulley, crankshaft pulley and harmonic balancer, and accessory brackets.

4. Remove timing indicator and water pump.
5. Remove remaining front cover attaching bolts and the front cover. Also, remove the dowel pins. It may be necessary to grind a flat on the dowel pin to provide a rough surface for gripping.
6. Grind a chamfer on one end of each dowel pin, Fig. 45.
7. Cut excess material from front end of oil pan gasket on each side of cylinder block.
8. Trim approximately 1/8 inch from each end of new front pan seal.
9. Install new front cover gasket and apply suitable sealer to gasket around coolant holes.
10. Apply RTV sealer to mating surfaces of cylinder block, oil pan and front cover.
11. Place front cover on cylinder block and press downward to compress seal. Rotate cover right and left and guide oil pan seal into cavity with a small screwdriver.
12. Apply engine oil to bolts.
13. Install two bolts finger tight to retain cover.
14. Install the two dowel pins, chamfered end first.
15. Install timing indicator and water pump and torque bolts as shown in Fig. 46.
16. Install harmonic balancer and crankshaft pulley.
17. Install accessory brackets.
18. Install fan and pulley and drive belts.

19. Connect radiator hoses and bypass hose.
20. Connect ground cables to batteries.

TIMING CHAIN & GEARS, REPLACE

1. Remove front cover as outlined previously. On 6 cylinder engines, loosen rocker arm pivot bolts evenly so that some lash is present between rocker arms and valves.
2. Remove oil slinger, cam gear, crank gear and timing chain.
3. Remove fuel pump eccentric from crankshaft.
4. Install key in crankshaft, if removed.
5. Install fuel pump eccentric, if removed.
6. Install cam gear, crank gear and timing chain with timing marks aligned, Fig. 47.

NOTE: With the timing marks aligned in Fig. 47, No. 6 cylinder is in the firing position. To place No. 1 cylinder in the firing position, rotate crankshaft one complete revolution. This will bring the camshaft gear mark to top and No. 1 cylinder will be in the firing position.

7. Install oil slinger.
8. Install front cover.

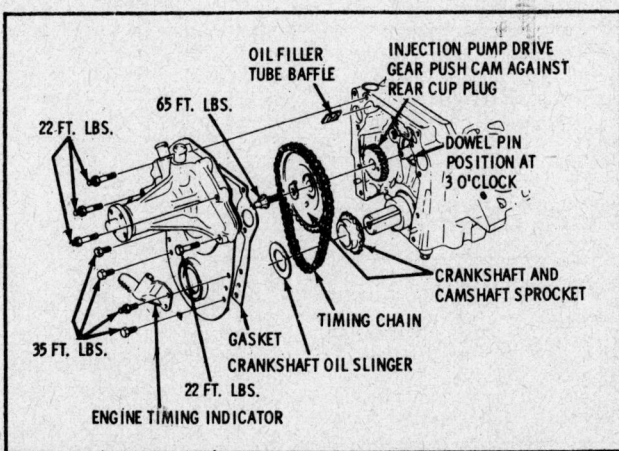

Fig. 46 Engine front cover installation. Typical

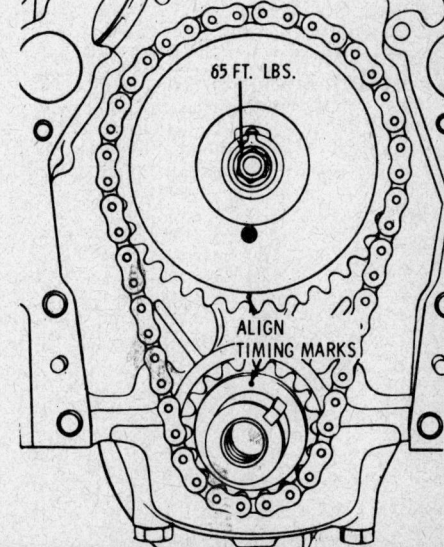

Fig. 47 Valve timing marks

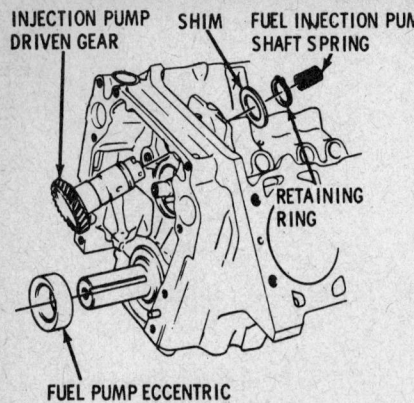

Fig. 48 Fuel injection pump driven gear installation

CAMSHAFT & INJECTION PUMP DRIVE & DRIVEN GEARS, REPLACE

1. Disconnect ground cables from batteries.
2. Drain cooling system.
3. Remove radiator upper baffle.
4. Disconnect upper radiator hose at water outlet and hose support clamp.
5. Disconnect cooler lines at radiator.
6. Remove fan shroud and radiator.
7. Remove intake manifold as outlined previously.
8. Remove engine front cover as outlined previously.
9. Remove valve covers.
10. Remove rocker arm bolts, pivots, rocker arms and push rod. Note valve train component locations to install components in original locations.
11. If equipped with A/C, discharge refrigerant system and remove condenser.
12. On all models, remove timing chain and gears as outlined previously.
13. Position camshaft dowel pin at 3 o'clock position.
14. While holding the camshaft rearward and rocking the injection pump driven gear slide, slide the injection pump drive gear from camshaft.
15. Remove injection pump adapter, snap ring, selective washer, injection pump driven gear and spring, Fig. 48.

NOTE: On some 1980 diesel vehicles, the fuel injection pump shaft spring, Fig. 48, may be missing. The absence of this spring could affect the idle characteristics of the engine. The spring is available as

Fig. 49A Piston & rod assembly. 1982–84 V6-262 & V8-350

part No. 22502241.

16. Slide camshaft from front of engine.
17. Reverse procedure to install. Check injection pump driven gear end play. If end play is not .002–.006 inch, replace selective washer, Fig. 48. Selective washers are available from .080 to .115 inch in increments of .003 inch.

PISTON & ROD ASSEMBLE

1978–81 V8

Assemble piston to rod and install in cylinder block. On 8 cylinder engines, the piston is installed with the valve depression facing toward the crankshaft. Also, there are two different pistons used in this engine. In cylinder numbers 1, 2, 3 and 4, the large valve depression faces the front of the engine, Fig. 49. In cylinder numbers 5, 6, 7 and 8 the large valve depression faces the rear of the engine, Fig. 49. The pistons are interchangeable between cylinder numbers 1, 3, 6 and 8 and 2, 4, 5 and 7. Check connecting rod side clearance. Clearance should be .006–.020 inch.

1982–84 V6 & V8

Install piston and rod assembly so that notch at top of piston is facing toward front of engine, Fig. 49A. Check connecting rod side clearance. Clearance should be .006–.020 inch on V8 engines or .008–.021 on V6 engines.

PISTONS, RINGS & PINS

SERVICE NOTE

Some V8-350 diesel engines may exhibit excessive oil consumption, low compression and/or excessive blowby. These conditions may be caused by stuck or frozen piston rings. To correct the above mentioned problem, proceed as follows:

1. With engine warm, remove all glow plugs from cylinders.
2. Using top engine cleaner Part No. 1050002, or equivalent, divide contents of can equally into each cylinder. Allow engine to soak for 24 hours.
3. Crank engine with glow plugs removed to expel excess cleaner.
4. Install glow plugs and start engine.

Pistons are available in standard sizes and oversizes of .010 and .030″ on 8 cylinder engines or in standard size and oversize of .010 inch on 6 cylinder engines.

Rings are available in standard sizes and oversizes of .010 and .030″.

MAIN & ROD BEARINGS

SERVICE NOTE

Beginning with 1981 production engines, a new ¼ inch longer main bearing cap bolt is used on V8-350 engines. To accommodate the longer bolts, all holes in the cylinder block have a ¼ inch deeper tap and counter bore.

Main bearings are available in standard sizes and undersizes of .0005, .0010 and .0015

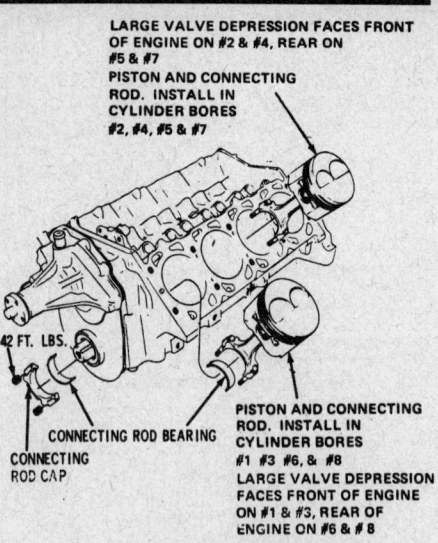

Fig. 49 Piston & rod installation. 1978–81 V8 engine

inch. The amount of undersize and part number is stamped on the bearing shell, Fig. 50.

Rod bearings are available in standard sizes and an undersize of .010 inch.

REAR CRANKSHAFT SEAL SERVICE

Since the braided fabric seal used on these engines can be replaced only when the crankshaft is removed, the following repair procedure is recommended.

1. Remove oil pan and bearing cap.
2. Drive end of old seal gently into groove, using a suitable tool, until packed tight. This may vary between ¼ and ¾ inch depending on amount of pack required.
3. Repeat previous step for other end of seal.
4. Measure and note amount that seal was driven up on one side. Using the old seal removed from bearing cap, cut a length of seal the amount previously noted plus 1/16 inch.
5. Repeat previous step for other side of seal.
6. Pack cut lengths of seal into appropriate side of seal groove. A packing tool, BT-6433, Fig. 51, may be used since the tool has been machined to provide a built-in stop. Use tool BT-6436 to trim the seal flush with block, Fig. 52.
7. Install new seal in lower bearing cap.

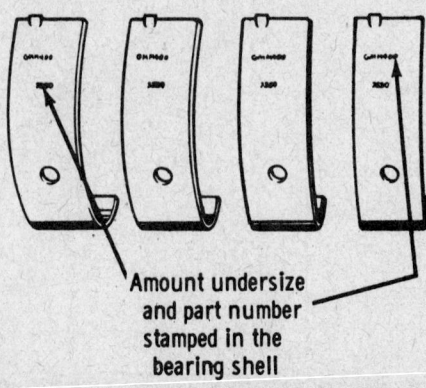

Fig. 50 Main bearing identification

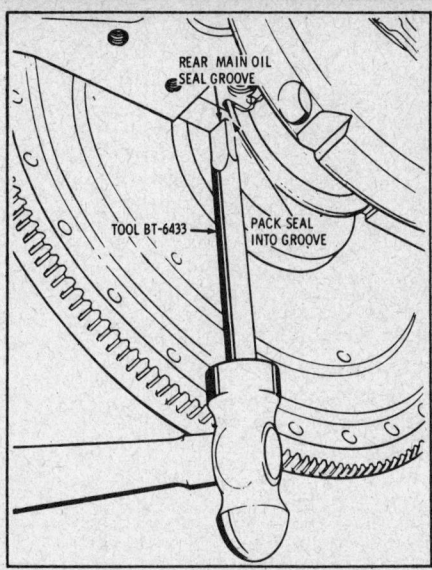

Fig. 51 Packing upper rear main bearing seal

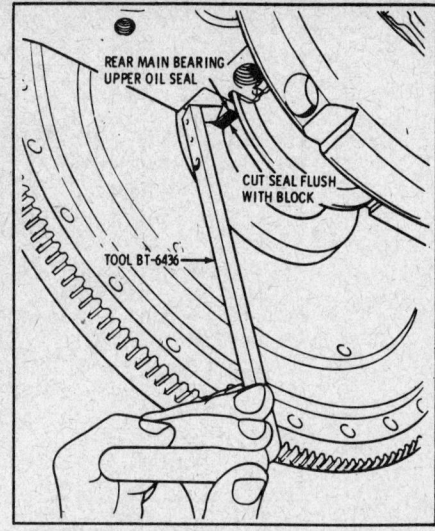

Fig. 52 Trimming upper rear main bearing seal

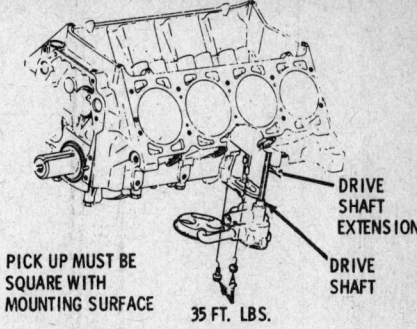

PICK UP MUST BE SQUARE WITH MOUNTING SURFACE

Fig. 53 Oil pump installation. Typical

OIL PAN, REPLACE

NOTE: On 1978 engines, the recommended diesel engine oil designation is SE/CD. On 1979—80 engines, the recommended diesel engine oil designation is SE/CC. On 1981 engines, the recommended diesel engine oil is SF/CC, SF/CD and SE/CC. On 1982—84 engines the recommended diesel engine oil is SF/CC or SF/CD.

1978—84 Cutlass, 88, 98

1. Disconnect ground cables from batteries.
2. Remove oil pump drive and vacuum pump, if equipped with A/C, or oil pump drive, if less A/C.
3. Remove oil dipstick.
4. Remove radiator upper support and fan shroud attaching screws.
5. Raise and support vehicle and drain oil pan.
6. Remove flywheel cover.
7. Disconnect exhaust and crossover pipes from exhaust manifold.
8. Remove oil cooler lines at filter base.

9. Disconnect starter wiring and remove starter.
10. Remove engine mounts from engine block, then raise front of engine with suitable equipment.
11. Remove oil pan attaching bolts and the oil pan.
12. Reverse procedure to install. Torque oil pan attaching bolts to 10 ft. lbs.

1979 Toronado

1. Disconnect battery ground cable.
2. Disconnect shroud from upper radiator support.
3. Remove right hand axle cotter pin, retainer and nut.
4. Raise vehicle and remove right wheel.
5. Disconnect right hand tie rod end using tool J-6627 or BT 7101.
6. Disconnect right hand upper ball joint.
7. Remove bolts attaching drive axle to right hand output shaft, then the output shaft.
8. Disconnect starter wiring and remove starter.
9. Remove splash shield.
10. Disconnect pitman arm and idler arm from intermediate rod using tool J-24319-01 or a suitable puller.

11. Drain pan oil.
12. Remove front engine mount to frame nuts.
13. Disconnect shroud from lower radiator support.
14. Using suitable equipment, raise the front of the engine.
15. Remove the right engine mount.
16. Remove oil pan attaching bolts and oil pan.
17. Reverse procedure to install. Torque oil pan attaching bolts to 10 ft. lbs.

1980—84 Toronado

1. Disconnect battery ground cables.
2. Remove three final drive to transmission bolts, then raise and support vehicle.
3. Disconnect frame brace retaining bolts. Disconnect idler arm and pitman arm from relay rod.
4. Disconnect drive axles from output shafts.
5. Disconnect battery cable bracket from output shaft support.
6. Disconnect output shaft support from engine block.
7. Position suitable jack under final drive, then remove final drive.
8. Remove splash shield and starter motor.
9. Drain oil, then remove oil pan.

NOTE: To remove oil pan on 1982—84 models, engine murt be raised 1—1½ inch using tool No. BT-6501, or equivlent.

10. Reverse procedure to install.

OIL PUMP, REPLACE & SERVICE

Replacement

1. Remove oil pan as outlined previously.
2. Remove oil pump to rear main bearing cap attaching bolts, Fig. 53.
3. Remove oil pump and drive shaft extension.
4. Reverse procedure to install. Torque attaching bolts to 35 ft. lbs.

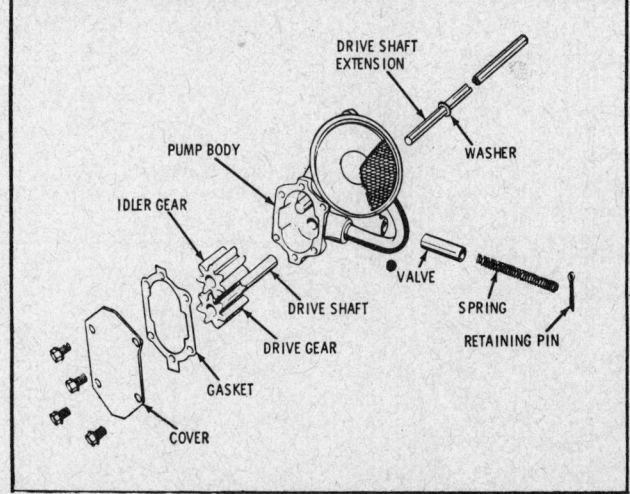

Fig. 54 Oil pump disassembled

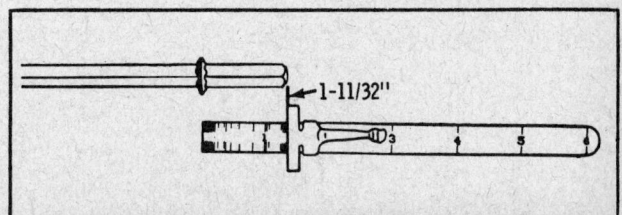

Fig. 55 Oil pump driveshaft extension. V8 engines

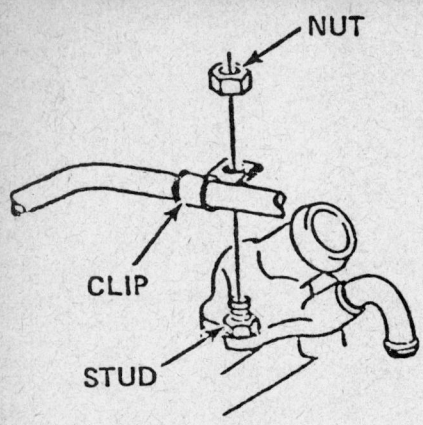

Fig. 55A Installing fuel line stud & clip assembly

Service

Disassembly

1. Remove oil pump drive shaft extension, Fig. 54. Do not attempt to remove washers from drive shaft extension. The drive shaft extension and washers is serviced as an assembly.
2. Remove cotter pin, spring and pressure regulator valve.

NOTE: Apply pressure on pressure regulator bore before removing cotter pin since the spring is under pressure.

3. Remove oil pump cover attaching screws and the oil pump cover and gasket.
4. Remove drive gear and idler gear from pump body.

Inspection

1. Check gears for scoring or other damage, replace if necessary.
2. Proper end clearance is .0005–.0075 inch.
3. Check pressure regulator valve, valve spring and bore for damage. Proper bore to valve clearance is .0025–.0050 inch.
4. Check extension shaft ends for wear, Fig. 55.

Assembly

1. Install gears and shaft in oil pump body.
2. Check gear end clearance by placing a straight edge over the gears and measure the clearance between the straight edge and gasket surface. If end clearance is excessive, check for scores in cover that would bring the clearance over specified limits.
3. Install cover and torque attaching screws to 8 ft. lbs.
4. Install pressure regulator valve, closed end first, into bore, then the valve spring and cotter pin.

WATER PUMP, REPLACE

V6-262

1. Disconnect battery ground cables and drain cooling system.
2. Remove fan clutch and fan, then disconnect radiator inlet hose at radiator.
3. Remove upper radiator support.
4. Remove drive belt and water pump pulley.

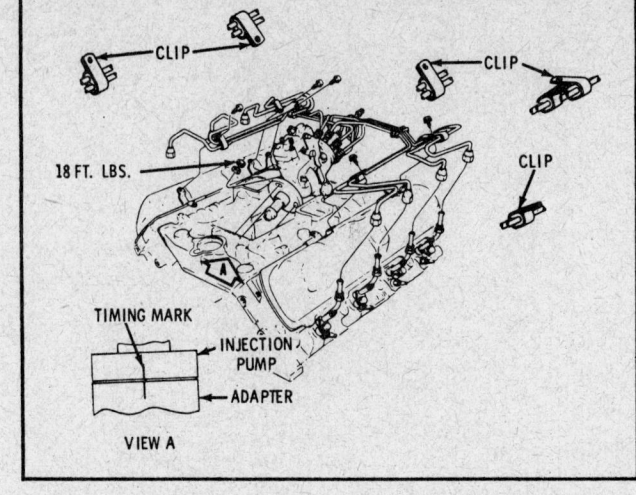

Fig. 56 Fuel injection pump timing marks. Typical

Fig. 57 Fuel injection pump connections. 1978–80

5. Remove vacuum pump and bracket assembly, then the cruise control servo mounting bracket, if equipped.
6. Remove power steering pump and brackets and position aside. Do not disconnect hoses from pump.
7. Disconnect heater and radiator outlet hoses at water pump, then loosen thermostat bypass hose clamp.
8. Remove water pump to front cover and water pump and front cover to block retaining bolts.
9. Remove water pump from front cover.
10. Reverse procedure to install. Coat gaskets with suitable sealer and water pump and front cover to block retaining bolts with primer and adhesive, Part No. 1052624, or equivalent.

NOTE: Failure to use the above mentioned primer and adhesive may cause coolant leaks and/or loss of bolt torque.

V8-350

1. Disconnect ground cables from batteries.
2. Drain cooling system.
3. Loosen drive belts and remove fan and pulley assembly.
4. Disconnect all hoses from water pump.
5. Remove water pump attaching screws and the water pump, Fig. 46.
6. Reverse procedure to install.

BELT TENSION DATA

	New Lbs.	Used Lbs.
1982–84③		
3/8"①	160	80
3/8"②	145	55
7/16"	170	90
1979–81		
5/16" Belts	80	50
3/8" Belts①	140	70
3/8" Belts②	140	60
15/32" Belts	165	90
1978		
3/8" Belts	150	70
15/32" Belts	165	90

①—Except cogged belts.
②—Cogged belts.
③—V8 engine only. V6 engine serpentine drive belt is self adjusting.

MECHANICAL FUEL PUMP, REPLACE

SERVICE NOTE

Some diesel engines may exhibit a condition of hard cold starts. If this condition exists, check the fuel pump housing for a crack in the area where the fuel line is connected to the fuel pump, which may allow air to enter the system. The cracked fuel pump housing could be caused by the fuel line vibrating.

To correct this condition, remove the right hand thermostat housing bolt and install stud, part No. 6270979. Disconnect fuel line at the fuel pump and install clip, part No. 343463 onto fuel line as shown in Fig. 55A. Install washer face nut, part No. 10008001. Replace the fuel pump and connect the fuel line.

1. Disconnect fuel lines from pump.
2. Remove fuel pump mounting bolts and the fuel pump.
3. Remove all gasket material from the pump and block gasket surfaces. Apply sealer to both sides of new gasket.
4. Position gasket on pump flange and hold pump in position against its mounting surface. Make sure rocker arm is riding on crankshaft eccentric.
5. Press pump tight against its mounting. Install retaining screws and tighten them alternately.

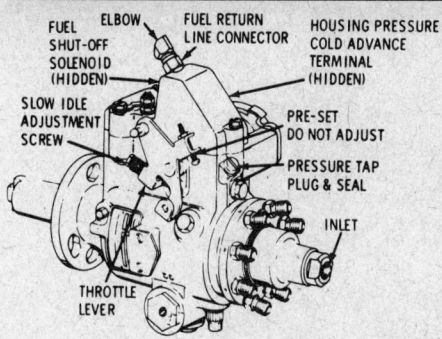

Fig. 57A   Fuel injection pump connections. 1981-84 V8 engine

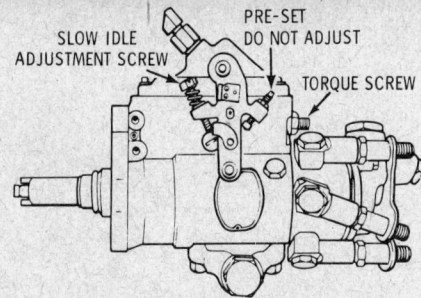

Fig. 57B   Fuel injection pump housing torque screw. 1982-84 V6 engine

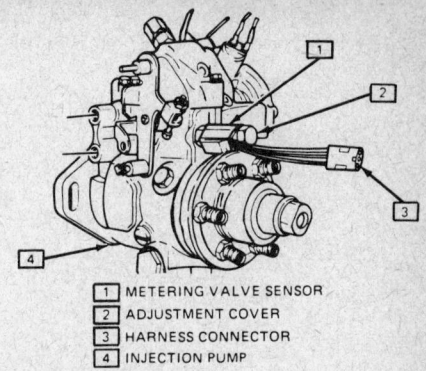

1. METERING VALVE SENSOR
2. ADJUSTMENT COVER
3. HARNESS CONNECTOR
4. INJECTION PUMP

Fig. 57C   Metering valve sensor. 1984 V6-262 (Calif.)

6. Connect fuel lines. Then operate engine and check for leaks.

NOTE: Before installing the pump, it is good practice to crank the engine so that the nose of the crankshaft eccentric is out of the way of the fuel pump rocker arm when the pump is installed. In this way there will be the least amount of tension on the rocker arm, thereby easing the installation of the pump.

INJECTION PUMP TIMING

Less Timing Meter

1. The mark on the injection pump adapter must be aligned with the mark on the injection pump flange, Fig. 56.
2. To adjust:
   a. Loosen the injection pump retaining nuts with tool J-26987.
   b. Align the mark on the injection pump flange with the mark on the injection pump adapter, Fig. 56.
   c. Torque injection pump retaining nuts to 35 ft. lbs. (V6) or 18 ft. lbs. (V8).

With Timing Meter J-33075

NOTE: Certain engine malfunctions can cause inaccurate timing readings. Engine malfunctions should be corrected before adjusting pump timing. The marks on the pump and pump adapter will normally be aligned within .030 (V8) or .050 (V6) inch.

1. Place transmission in Park, apply parking brake and block drive wheels.
2. Start engine and allow to reach normal operating temperature.
3. Shut engine off.
4. Remove air cleaner assembly, install cover J-26996-1 then disconnect EGR valve hose.
5. Clean dirt from engine probe holder and crankshaft balancer rim.
6. Clean lens on both ends of glow plug probe. Look through probe to ensure that it is clean.
7. Remove glow plug from No. 1 (V6) or No. 3 (V8) cylinder. Insert glow plug probe into glow plug opening and torque probe to 8 ft. lbs.
8. Set timing meter selector to A (V6) or B (V8), then connect meter battery leads.
9. Disconnect generator two lead connector,

then start engine and adjust idle speed to specifications.
10. Observe timing meter, wait approximately two minutes, then observe timing meter again. When meter stabilizes, compare timing reading to specifications. If timing is as specified, proceed to step 16. If timing is not as specified, proceed to next step.
11. Turn engine off and note relative position of marks on pump flange and adapter.
12. Loosen nuts or bolts holding pump to adapter, then rotate pump to the left (advance) or right (retard) as necessary. Torque retaining nuts or bolts to 18 (V8) or 35 (V6) ft. lbs.

NOTE: Move pump gradually when adjusting timing. On V8 engines, the width of the adapter timing mark is equal to approximately 1 degree. On V6 engines, the width of the mark is equal to approximately 2/3 of a degree.

13. Start engine and recheck timing. Reset timing, if necessary.
14. On V8 engines, adjust pump rod.
15. On all engines, reset curb and fast idle speeds.
16. Disconnect timing meter and install removed glow plug. Torque glow plug to 12 (V8) or 15 (V6) ft. lbs.
17. Connect generator two lead connector, install air cleaner assembly and reconnect EGR valve hose.

SERVICE NOTE

The timing marks on the injection pump and adapter should be close to being lined up after timing the engine. If they are not, and the engine still exhibits poor performance, the timing may still be incorrect. A misfiring cylinder can result in incorrect timing. When this occurs, it is necessary that timing be checked in an alternate cylinder. Timing can be checked in cylinders 2 or 3 on V8 engines, or 1 or 4 on V6 engines. If a difference exists between cylinders, try both positions to determine which timing performs best.

If the engine continues to run poorly and excessive exhaust smoke is evident, check the housing pressure cold advance (1981-84) for proper operation. If the advance is operating properly, a stuck or frozen injection pump advance piston may be at fault. This piston is used on 1980-84 vehicles and can be checked by pushing in on the bottom of the face cam lever on the right side of the injection pump. If the piston is free, the timing will retard and cause the engine to run roughly. If no change is evident, the piston is sticking and must be repaired.

FUEL INJECTION PUMP HOUSING FUEL PRESSURE CHECK

1. Remove air crossover and install screened covers J-29657 (V6 engines) or J-26996-10 (V8 engines) or equivalent.
2. Remove fuel return pressure tap plug or torque screw, Figs. 57, 57A and 57B. If equipped with torque screw, add second nut to lock nut and back out screw with nuts attached to avoid disturbing the adjustment.
3. Install the seal from the pressure tap plug on the pressure tap adapter, tool J-28526, then install the adapter into pump housing.
4. Connect a low pressure gauge to the adapter.
5. Connect pick-up tachometer, tool J-26925, to the engine.
6. Check pressure with engine operating at 1000 RPM in Park. The pressure should be 8-12 PSI with no more than a 2 PSI fluctuation.
7. If pressure reading is zero on 1981-84 models, check operation of housing pressure cold advance as follows:
   a. Disconnect housing cold pressure advance electrical connector.
   b. If pressure reading is still zero, remove injection pump cover and check operation of advance solenoid. Repair or replace as necessary.
   c. If pressure is as specified with housing cold pressure advance electrical connector disconnected, check operation of temperature switch located on cylinder head bolt.
8. If pressure is still low, replace fuel return line connector assembly. If pressure is too high, fuel return system or HPAA may be restricted. Remove return line at injection pump. Install fitting and short piece of hose to allow return flow to empty into a small container.
9. If pressure is lower than before, correct restriction in fuel line.
10. If pressure is still too high, replace fuel return line connector assembly. If assembly is replaced check injection pump timing and adjust if necessary.
11. If pressure remains too high, remove injection pump for repair.
12. Remove tachometer, pressure gauge and adapter.
13. Install a new pressure tap plug seal on the pressure tap plug and install plug into housing.
14. Remove screened covers and install air crossover.

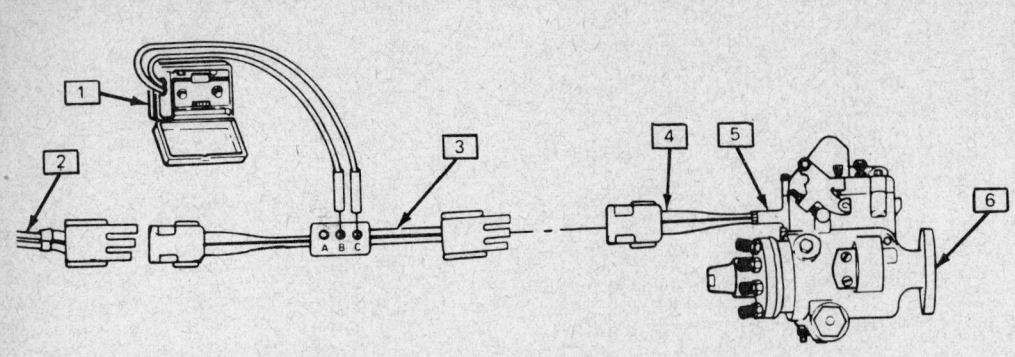

1	DIGITAL VOLT METER
2	ENGINE HARNESS
3	MVS TEST HARNESS (BT-8342 OR J-34678)
4	MVS HARNESS
5	METERING VALVE SENSOR
6	INJECTION PUMP

Fig. 57D Metering valve sensor test connections

V-REF	4.5	4.6	4.7	4.8	4.9	5.0	5.1	5.2	5.3	5.4	5.5
MVS VOLTAGE (In "D" 650 RPM)	.53-.55	.54-.56	.55-.57	.57-.59	.58-.60	.59-.61	.60-.62	.61-.63	.63-.65	.64-.66	.65-.67

MVS VOLTAGE TABLE

Fig. 57E Metering valve sensor voltage chart

METERING VALVE SENSOR

Used on 1984 California V6-262 engines with Diesel Electronic Control System, the metering valve sensor, Fig. 57C, is a variable type resistor that electrically signals the diesel ECM as to metering valve position.

Testing

1. Block drive wheels, apply parking brake and place transmission in Park.
2. Start engine, allow it to reach normal operating temperature, then shut engine off.
3. Remove air cleaner.
4. Remove air crossover, then install cover J-29657, or equivalent.
5. Disconnect metering valve sensor harness and attach test harness J-34678 or BT-8342 as shown, Fig. 57D.
6. Install tachometer J-26925, or equivalent, then torque metering valve sensor to pump attaching bolts to 30 inch lbs.
7. Start engine, accelerate to 1500 RPM for 10–20 seconds to stabilize fuel flow, then return engine to idle.
8. Place transmission in Drive and set idle speed to 650 RPM.
9. Using voltmeter J-29124, or equivalent, set meter at 20V scale and measure voltage between terminals A and C of test harness, Fig. 57D. Observe and record voltage (V-REF) reading.
10. Measure voltage between terminals B and C of test harness. Observe and record MVS voltage reading.
11. Shift transmission into Park, then compare voltages recorded in steps 9 and 10 with specifications in chart, Fig. 57E.

Voltages should be within ranges shown.
12. With gear selector in Park, measure voltage between terminals B and C as throttle is quickly opened to wide open throttle position. Voltage should range from less than 1 volt at idle to over 4 volts as throttle approaches wide open position.
13. If MVS voltage is as specified in steps 11 and 12, the sensor is operating properly. If voltage is not as specified, proceed to "Adjustment" procedure.
14. Connect sensor harness, start engine and adjust idle speed to specifications.
15. Install air crossover, then the air cleaner.

Adjustment

1. With engine off, hold metering valve sensor assembly and carefully remove hole plug. Use caution to prevent sensor assembly from moving.
2. Using tool J-24182-2, or equivalent, turn adjustment screw clockwise to increase voltage reading, or counterclockwise to decrease reading. Turn adjustment screw in 1/8 turn increments.

NOTE: It may be necessary to file tool J-24182-2, to enable it to enter sensor assembly.

3. Install hole plug finger tight, then perform steps 7 through 11 of testing procedure. If voltages are not within chart specifications, readjust sensor as necessary.
4. Install hole plug using a new "O" ring seal, then hold sensor assembly and torque hole plug to 30 inch lbs.
5. Connect sensor harness, start engine and check for fuel leaks.
6. Adjust idle speed to specifications, then install air crossover and air cleaner.

INJECTION PUMP, REPLACE

Injection Pump & Lines

Removal
1. Disconnect ground cables from batteries.
2. Remove air cleaner.
3. Remove filters and pipes from valve cov-

ers and air crossover, Fig. 28E and 32A.
4. Remove air crossover and plug intake manifold, Fig. 29.
5. Disconnect throttle rod and return spring on V8 engines or throttle cable and TV detent cable from pump throttle lever.
6. Remove bellcrank.
7. Remove throttle and throttle valve cables from intake manifold brackets and position cables aside.
8. Remove fuel lines to fuel filter, then the fuel filter, Fig. 58 and 58A.
9. Disconnect fuel line at fuel pump and remove fuel line. If equipped with A/C, remove rear compressor brace.
10. Disconnect fuel return line from injection pump, Fig. 59, 59A and 58A.
11. Slide clamp from fuel return lines at injector nozzles and remove fuel return lines from each bank.
12. Disconnect injection pump lines at injector nozzles, Figs. 60 and 60A. It is necessary to use two wrenches.
13. Remove nuts retaining injection pump with tool No. J-26987.
14. Remove injection pump and cap all lines and fittings.

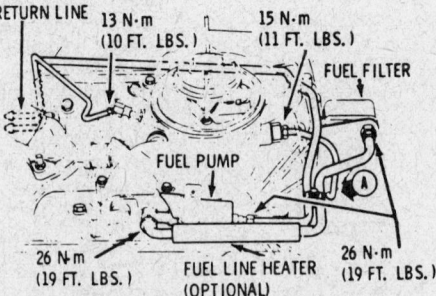

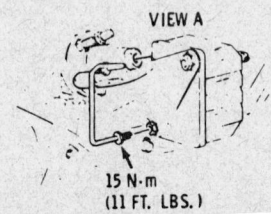

VIEW A

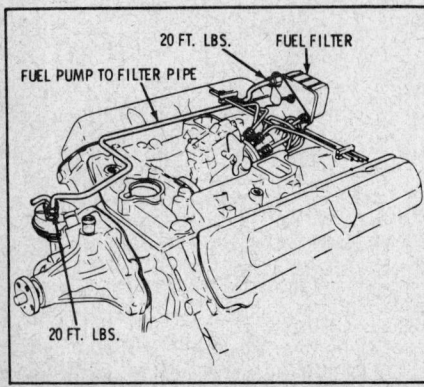

Fig. 58 Fuel filter & lines. V8 engine

Fig. 58A Fuel filter & lines. V6 engine

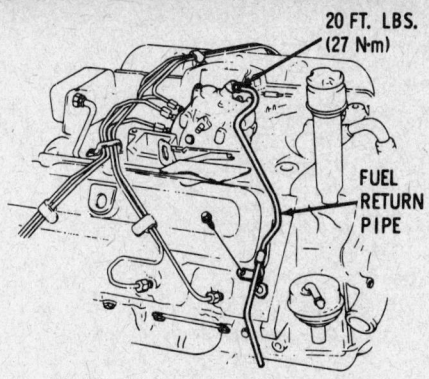

Fig. 59A Fuel return line. 1980—84 V8 engine

Installation

1. Align offset tang on pump drive shaft with pump driven gear, Fig. 61, and install injector pump.
2. Loosely install the injector pump retaining nuts and lock washers. Connect fuel lines to injector pump and torque line fittings to 25 ft. lbs., Figs. 60 and 60A.
3. Connect fuel return lines to injector nozzles and injector pump.
4. Align mark on injection pump with line on adapter and torque retaining nuts to 18 ft. lbs. on V8 engines or 35 ft. lbs. on V6 engines.
5. Adjust throttle rod.
6. Install fuel line from fuel pump to fuel filter, Fig. 58 and 58A. If equipped with A/C, install rear compressor brace.
7. Install bellcrank and hairpin clip.
8. Install throttle and throttle valve cables, to intake manifold brackets and attach to bellcrank. Adjust throttle valve cable.
9. Connect throttle rod and return spring on V8 engines or throttle cable and TV cable on V6 engines.
10. Crank engine and check for fuel leaks.
11. Remove plugs from intake manifold and install air crossover, Fig. 29.
12. Install tubes in flow control valve in air crossover and ventilation filters in valve covers, Fig. 28E and 32A.
13. Install air cleaner.

Injection Pump

Removal

1. Disconnect battery ground cable and remove air cleaner assembly.
2. Remove crankcase ventilation filters and pipes from the valve covers and air crossover.
3. Remove the air crossover, Fig. 29, and install intake manifold screened covers J-

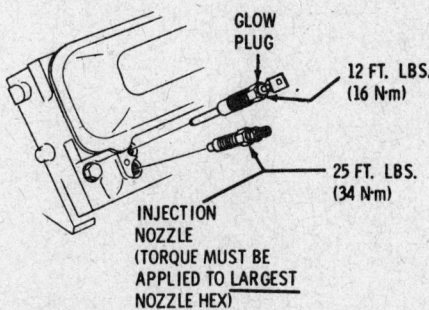

Fig. 60A Injection nozzle installation. 1980—84

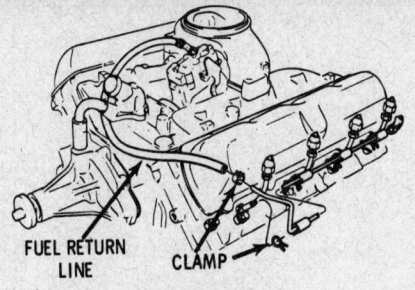

L. H. SIDE OF ENGINE

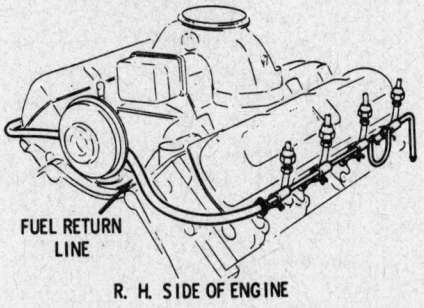

Fig. 59 Fuel return lines. 1978—79

26996-10.
4. Disconnect the throttle rod and throttle return spring.
5. Remove bellcrank.
6. Remove throttle and TV detent cables from intake manifold brackets and position cables aside.
7. Remove fuel lines to fuel filter, then the fuel filter, Figs. 58 & 58A.
8. Disconnect fuel line at fuel pump and remove fuel line. If equipped with A/C remove rear compressor brace.
9. Disconnect fuel return line from injection pump, Figs. 59, 59A and 58A.
10. Disconnect the injection line clamps closest to pump.
11. Disconnect the injection lines from pump and cap all openings.
12. Remove three nuts retaining injection pump, using tool No. J-26987.
13. Remove pump and discard the pump to adapter O-ring.

Installation

1. Align offset tang on pump drive shaft with pump driven gear, Fig. 61.
2. Install new pump to adapter O-ring, then install the pump fully seating pump by hand.
3. Align mark on injection pump with line on adapter and torque retaining nuts to 18 ft. lbs.
4. Remove caps from the openings and con-

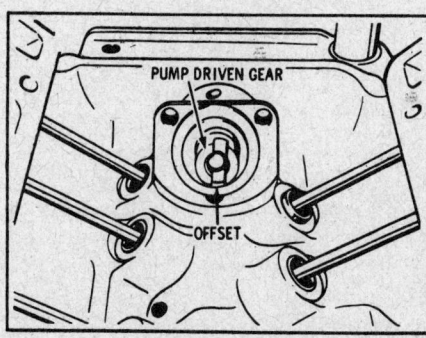

Fig. 61 Offset on fuel injection pump driven gear

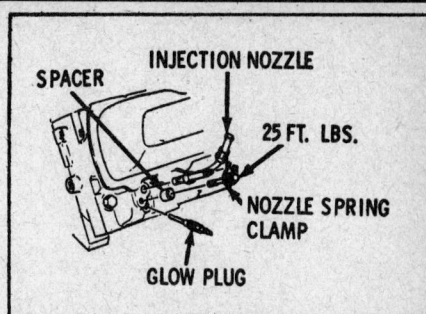

Fig. 60 Injection nozzle installation. 1978—79

nect the injection lines to the pump.
5. Install injection line clamps.
6. Connect the fuel return line.
7. Reconnect the fuel line at the fuel pump. If equipped with A/C, install the rear compressor brace.
8. Install the fuel filter and fuel filter to injection pump line.
9. Install throttle and TV detent cables on intake manifold.
10. Install bellcrank.
11. Install throttle rod and throttle return spring.
12. Remove screened covers from intake manifold, then install air crossover.
13. Install pipes and hoses in the air crossover and ventilation filters in valve covers.
14. Install air cleaner assembly and connect battery ground cable.

INJECTION PUMP ADAPTER, ADAPTER SEAL & NEW TIMING MARK

1. Remove injection pump as outlined previously.
2. Remove injection pump adapter, Fig. 62.
3. Remove seal from injection pump adapter.
4. File mark off injection pump adapter. Do not file mark from injection pump.
5. Position engine to No. 1 cylinder firing position. Align marks on balancer with zero mark on indicator. The injection pump driven gear should be offset to the right when No. 1 cylinder is at top dead center.
6. Loosely install injection pump adapter.
7. Install seal in injection pump adapter with tool J-28425, Fig. 63.
8. Torque injection pump adapter bolts to 25 ft. lbs.
9. Install timing tool J-26896 into injection

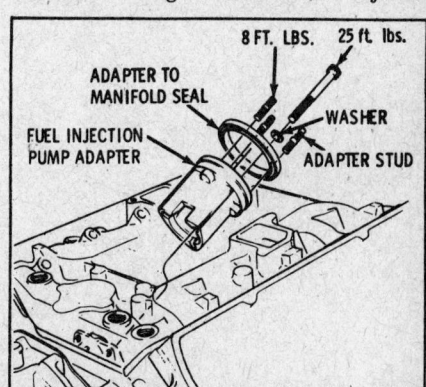

Fig. 62 Fuel injection pump adapter installation

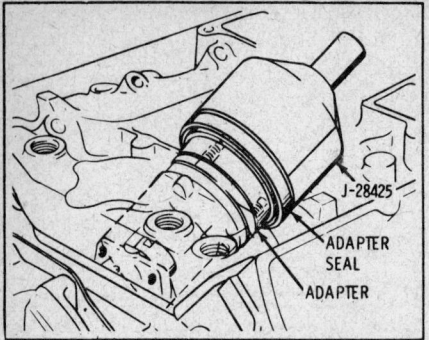

Fig. 63 Fuel injection pump adapter seal installation

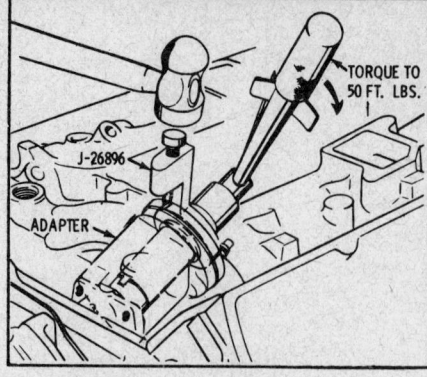

Fig. 64 Marking fuel injection pump adapter with new timing mark

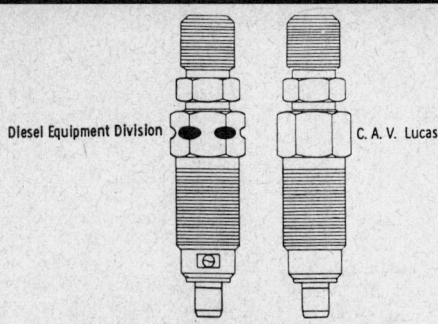

Fig. 64A Injection nozzle identification

pump adapter. Rotate torque wrench counterclockwise to obtain a 50 ft. lbs. reading, then mark injection pump adapter, Fig. 64.

10. Install injection pump as outlined previously.

INJECTION NOZZLE, REPLACE

1981–84

SERVICE NOTE

Injection nozzle body leaks may be corrected by loosening the inlet fitting and retorquing to 45 ft. lbs. on DED type injection nozzles, and 19 ft. lbs. on CAV type injection nozzles, Fig. 64A. In the event this does not correct the leak, remove the inlet fitting. Using a piece of crocus cloth, press and rotate the end of the inlet fitting against the crocus cloth back and forth about six times. After polishing has been performed, flush inlet fitting using diesel fuel and install fitting onto pump.

1. Remove fuel lines, using a backup wrench on upper injection nozzle hex.
2. Remove nozzle by applying torque to largest nozzle hex, Fig. 60A.
3. Cap nozzle and lines to prevent entry of dirt. Also remove copper gasket from cylinder head if gasket did not remain with nozzle.
4. Reverse procedure to install. Torque nozzle to 25 ft. lbs. When tightening nozzle,

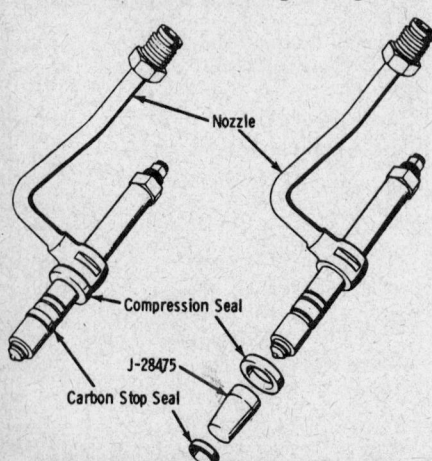

Fig. 65 Injection nozzle seal installation

torque must be applied to largest nozzle hex. Torque fuel line to 25 ft. lbs. using a backup wrench on upper injection nozzle hex.

1978–79

1. Remove fuel line from injector nozzle.
2. Remove fuel line clamps from all nozzles on bank where nozzle is being removed. Remove fuel return line from nozzle being replaced.
3. Remove nozzle hold down clamp and spacer, Fig. 60, then the nozzle with tool J-26952.
4. Cap nozzle inlet line and tip of nozzle.
5. Reverse procedure to install. Install new seals on injection nozzles, Fig. 65. Torque nozzle hold down clamp bolt to 25 ft. lbs.

NOTE: 1979 diesel engines use two different types of connections to attach the high pressure fuel lines to the injection nozzles. Before replacing an injection nozzle or high pressure fuel line, it is necessary to determine which type of connection is used, either the "Flare Type" or "Ferrule Type", Fig. 66. Also, check the replacement part to ensure that the proper connection is used.

TRANSMISSION VACUUM VALVE, REPLACE

1. Note location of the valve vacuum hoses, then disconnect the vacuum hoses.
2. Remove the two valve attaching bolts and the valve.
3. Reverse procedure to install.

THROTTLE SHAFT SEAL, REPLACE

1981–84

V8 Engine
1. Disconnect both battery ground cables.
2. Remove air cleaner and air crossover and install air screens J-26996-2 or J-26996-10.
3. Disconnect injection pump fuel solenoid, housing pressure cold advance wires and fuel return pipe, Fig. 66A.
4. Remove throttle rod, vacuum regulator valve, return spring and throttle cable bracket.
5. Place tool J-29601 over throttle shaft and pin, then position spring clip of tool over throttle shaft advance cam and tighten

wing nut. Without loosening wing nut, pull tool off shaft. This will provide proper alignment during reassembly, Fig. 66B.

6. Drive pin from throttle shaft and remove shaft advance cam and fiber washer. Remove any burrs from shaft which may have resulted from pin removal.
7. Clean injection pump cover, upper portion of pump, throttle shaft and guide stud area. Position several shop cloths in engine valley area to absorb fuel.
8. Remove injection pump cover and screws.

CAUTION: Use care to avoid any foreign matter from entering pump when cover is removed. If any object or foreign matter enter pump, it must be removed before engine is started as injection pump damage or engine damage may occur.

9. Note position of metering valve spring before removal as its position must be duplicated exactly during reassembly, Fig. 66C.
10. Remove guide stud and washer, noting parts before removal.
11. Rotate min-max governor assembly up for clearance then remove it, Fig. 66C. If idle governor spring becomes disengaged from throttle block, it must be reinstalled with tightly wound coils toward throttle block.
12. Remove throttle shaft assembly and inspect shaft for unusual wear or damage, replace if necessary. It may be necessary to loosen nuts at injection pump mounting flange and injection pump slightly to allow throttle shaft to clear intake manifold.
13. Inspect throttle shaft bushings in pump housing for damage or unusual wear. If replacement of bushings is necessary, it must be performed by a qualified repair facility.
14. Remove throttle shaft seals. Do not cut seals to remove, as any nicks in the seal

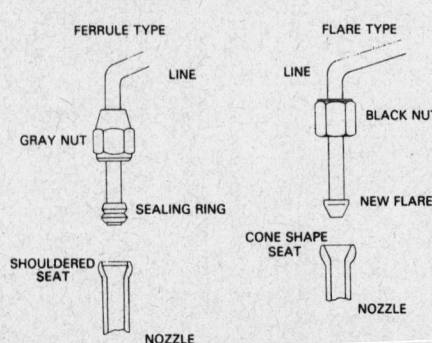

Fig. 66 Injection nozzle connections. 1979

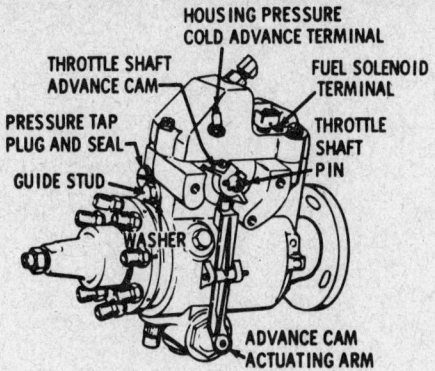

Fig. 66A Injection pump right side view. 1981–84. V8 engine

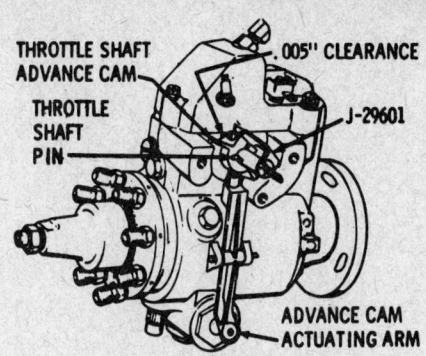

Fig. 66B Installing tool J-29601 on injection pump. 1981–84. V8 engine

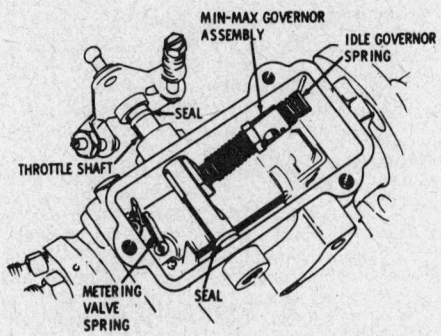

Fig. 66C Injection pump with cover removed. 1981–84. V8 engine

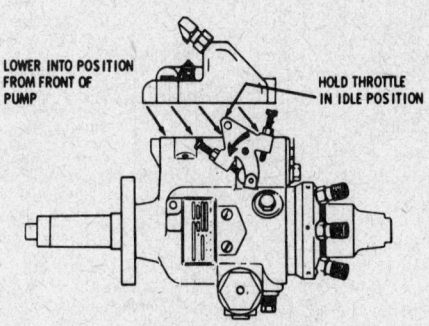

Fig. 66D Installing injection pump cover. 1981–84. V8 engine

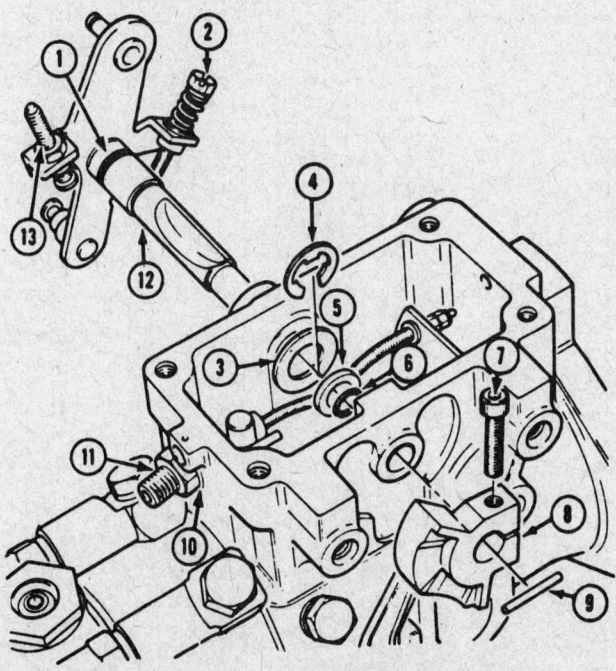

1. Rubber "O" ring
2. Idling adjuster screw
3. Thrust washer
4. "E" type circlip
5. Thrust washer
6. Rubber "O" ring
7. Clamp screw
8. Light load advance cam
9. Pin
10. Locknut and rubber "O" ring
11. Torque screw
12. Throttle shaft
13. Maximum speed adjustment screw (Do not adjust)

Fig. 66E Throttle shaft & seals. V6 engine

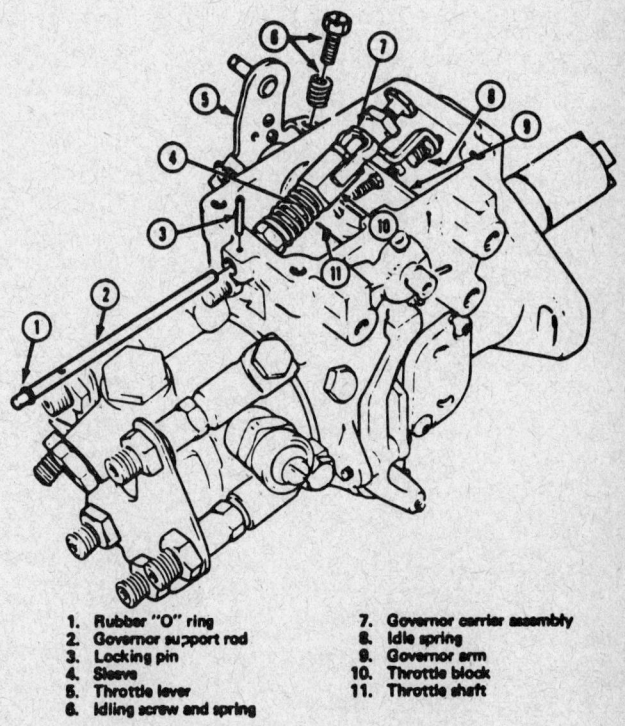

1. Rubber "O" ring
2. Governor support rod
3. Locking pin
4. Sleeve
5. Throttle lever
6. Idling screw and spring
7. Governor carrier assembly
8. Idle spring
9. Governor arm
10. Throttle block
11. Throttle shaft

Fig. 66F Governor assembly. V6 engine

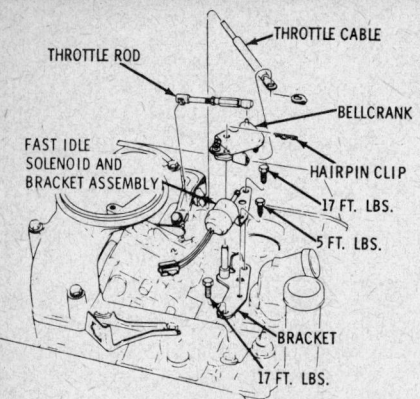

Fig. 67   Throttle linkage. V8 engine

seat will cause leakage.

15. Install new shaft seals, lubricated with chassis grease. Use care to avoid cutting seals on sharp edges of shaft.
16. Carefully slide throttle shaft into pump to point where min-max governor assembly will slide back onto throttle shaft, Fig. 66C.
17. Rotate min-max governor assembly downward, then hold in position and slide throttle shaft and governor into position.
18. Install new fiber washer, throttle shaft advance cam (do not tighten screw at this time) and a new throttle shaft drive pin, Fig. 66A.
19. Align throttle shaft advance cam so tool J-20601 can be installed over throttle shaft, pins in slots and spring clip over advance cam.
20. Insert a .005 inch feeler gauge between cam and fiber washer, then tighten cam screw and remove tool J-29601.
21. Install guide stud with new washer, assuring that upper extension of metering valve spring slides on top of guide stud. Torque guide studs to 85 inch lbs.

CAUTION: Over torquing may strip the aluminum threads in the housing.

22. Hold throttle in idle position and install new pump cover seal. Making sure that screws are not in cover, position cover

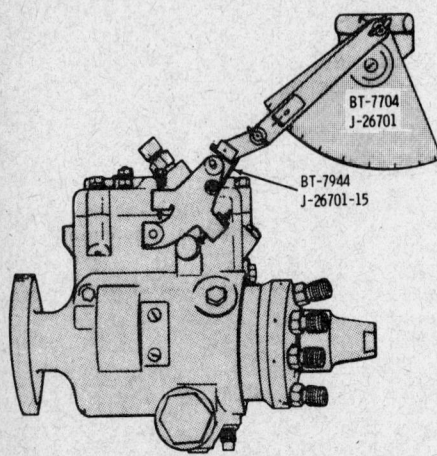

Fig. 69   Transmission vacuum valve adjustment. 1979-84 (Typical)

about ¼ inch forward toward shaft end and above ⅛ inch above pump, Fig. 66D. Move cover rearward and downward into position, using care to avoid cutting seal, then reinstall cover screws. Each screw must have a flat washer and internal lock washer, with flat washer against pump cover. Torque screws to 37 inch lbs. and install vacuum regulator.

23. Reconnect both battery ground cables, then turn ignition switch to run position and touch pink solenoid wire to solenoid. A clicking noise should be heard as the wire is connected and disconnected. If not, the linkage may be jammed in the wide open position and the engine must not be started. Proceed to step 24. If clicking is heard, connect pump solenoid and housing pressure cold advance wires and proceed to step 25.
24. Remove cover, then ground solenoid lead (opposite hot lead) and connect pink wire. With ignition switch in run position, the solenoid in the cover should move the linkage. If not, the solenoid must be replaced. Minimum voltage across solenoid terminals must be 12 volts. Reinstall cover and repeat step 23.
25. Install throttle cable bracket, throttle rod, throttle cable and return springs. Make sure timing marks on pump and adapter are aligned and make sure nuts retaining pump are tight. Install fuel return pipe.
26. Start engine and check for fuel leaks.

NOTE: Rough idle may be due to air in the pump. Allow sufficient time for air to purge by allowing engine to idle. It may be necessary to turn engine off to allow air bubbles to rise to top of pump where they will be purged.

27. Adjust Transmission Vacuum Valve as described further on, then remove intake manifold screens and install air crossover and air cleaner.

V6 Engine

1. Remove air crossover and install cover J-29657 or equivalent.
2. Disconnect fuel return pipe, Fig. 58A, then remove governor control cover screws and the cover.
3. Remove fast idle solenoid and vacuum regulator valve.
4. Disconnect throttle cable and TC detent cable.
5. Disconnect throttle return spring.
6. Install tool J-29601 or equivalent over throttle shaft with slots of tool engaging vacuum regulator valve lock pin. Place spring clip of tool over throttle shaft advance cam and tighten wing nut. Without loosening wing nut, pull tool off of shaft.
7. Remove lock pin from throttle shaft, Fig. 66E.
8. Remove rollpin from pump housing and remove governor support rod.
9. Tilt governor carrier assembly by lifting end nearest drive end of pump and remove carrier from pump housing.
10. Remove clamping screw from light load cam, then remove cam.
11. Remove E clip from throttle shaft, then remove throttle shaft from pump.
12. Remove and discard 0 rings.
13. Check throttle shaft assembly and governor housing bores for damage and wear and replace as necessary.
14. Lubricate shaft and 0 rings with oil and assemble larger 0 rings onto shaft.

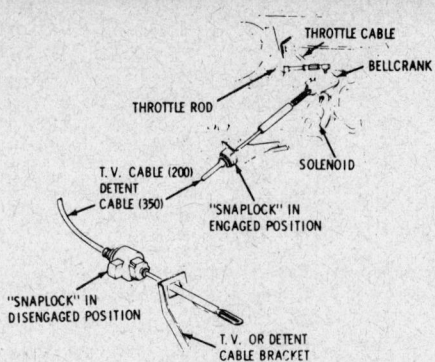

Fig. 68   Throttle valve or detent cable adjustment

15. Install throttle shaft into housing until thrust washers can be installed onto shaft in original positions. Install smaller 0 ring onto shaft.
16. Assemble light load advance cam onto shaft and install but do not tighten clamping screw.
17. Install E clip into throttle shaft recess. If new throttle shaft is installed, shaft end play must be checked and adjusted by selective fitting of thrust washers. Throttle shaft end play should be .006-.012 inch.
18. Install new pin onto head of shaft. Align throttle shaft advance cam until tool J-29601 or equivalent can be installed over throttle shaft. Tighten cam screw, then remove tool J-29601.
19. Rotate throttle lever forwards to the drive end of pump. Install governor carrier assembly onto pump housing and engage lug on underside of throttle block with cut away notch in throttle shaft.
20. Lubricate governor support rod and new 0 ring, then install 0 ring onto support rod using tool J-33096 or equivalent.
21. Insert plain end of rod through rear of governor housing and into carrier assembly sleeve.
22. Install support rod into housing and install new locking pin, Fig. 66F.
23. Install governor cover and fuel return pipe.
24. Install throttle return springs and connect throttle cable.
25. Connect TV detent cable.
26. Install vacuum regulator valve and fast idle solenoid.
27. Start engine and check for leaks. Install air crossover and air cleaner.

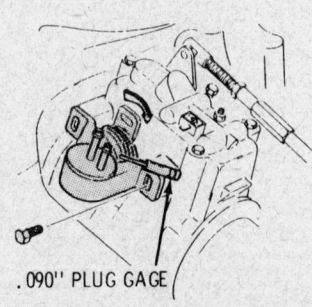

Fig. 70   Transmission vacuum valve adjustment. 1978

PUMP COVER SEAL AND/OR GUIDE STUD, REPLACE

1981—84

1. Disconnect both battery ground cables.
2. Remove air cleaner and air crossover and install air screens J-26996-2 or J-26996-10.
3. Disconnect injection pump fuel solenoid, housing pressure cold advance wires and fuel return pipe.
4. Clean injection pump cover, upper portion of pump and guide stud area. Position shop cloths to absorb fuel.
5. Remove injection pump cover, then remove screws from cover.

CAUTION: Use care to avoid any foreign matter from entering pump when cover is removed. If any object or foreign matter enter pump, it must be removed before starting engine as injection pump damage or engine damage may occur.

---

6. Note position of metering valve spring before removal as its position must be duplicated exactly during reassembly, Fig. 66C.
7. Remove guide stud and washer, noting location of parts before removal.
8. Refer to steps 21 thru 27 under "Throttle Shaft Seal, Replace" procedure for reassembly of "Pump Cover Seal And/Or Guide Stud".

THROTTLE ROD, ADJUST

1. If equipped with Cruise Control, remove clip from Cruise Control rod, then the rod from bellcrank.
2. Remove throttle valve cable from bellcrank, Fig. 67.
3. Loosen the throttle rod locknut and shorten the rod several turns.
4. Rotate the bellcrank to the full throttle stop, then lengthen the throttle rod until the injection pump lever contacts the injection pump full throttle stop. Release the bellcrank.
5. Tighten the throttle rod locknut.
6. Connect the throttle valve cable and Cruise Control rod, if equipped, to bellcrank.

THROTTLE VALVE OR DETENT CABLE, ADJUST

1. Remove throttle rod from bellcrank, Fig. 68.
2. Push snap lock to disengaged position.
3. Rotate bellcrank to full throttle stop position and push in snap lock until flush with cable end fitting. Release bellcrank.
4. Connect the throttle rod.

TRANSMISSION VACUUM VALVE, ADJUST

1979—84

1. Remove air crossover, then install screened covers J26996-2.
2. Remove throttle rod from throttle lever on V8 models or disconnect throttle cable and TV detent cable on V6 models, then loosen transmission vacuum valve injection pump bolts.
3. Install carburetor angle gauge J26701-15 and adapter on injection pump throttle lever, Fig. 69.
4. Rotate throttle lever to the wide open position and set angle gauge to zero degrees.
5. Center bubble in level, then set angle gauge to 49 degrees on 1979 units, 50 degrees on 1980 units, 58 degrees on 1981—84 V8 engines or 49° on V6 engines.
6. Rotate throttle lever so level bubble is centered.
7. Attach a suitable vacuum pump to center port of vacuum valve and install a vacuum gauge to outside port of vacuum valve, then apply 12 inches of vacuum on 1979 units, 18—22 inches of vacuum on 1980—84 units.
8. Rotate vacuum valve clockwise to obtain 8½ to 9 inches of vacuum on 1979 units, 7 to 8 inches of vacuum on 1980 units, 8.6 to 9.2 inches of vacuum on 1981 units and 10.6 inches of vacuum on 1982—84 units, then tighten vacuum valve bolts. Remove vacuum gauge and vacuum pump.
9. Install throttle rod to bellcrank, on V8 models or connect throttle cable and TV detent cable on V6 models, then remove screened covers and install air crossover.

1978

1. Remove throttle rod from bellcrank.
2. Loosen transmission vacuum valve attaching bolts to disengage valve from injection pump shaft.
3. Hold the injection pump lever against injection pump full throttle stop, rotate vacuum valve to full throttle position and insert a .090 inch diameter pin to hold the valve in the full throttle position, Fig. 70.
4. Rotate assembly clockwise until the injection pump shaft lever is contacted, then tighten the valve attaching bolts.
5. Remove pin and release lever.
6. Connect throttle rod.

PURGING WATER FROM FUEL TANK

1980—84 Models With Water In Fuel Detector

On these vehicles, any water in the fuel tank may be purged by siphoning or using a pump. The pump or siphon hose should be connected to the ¼ inch fuel return hose (smaller of the two hoses) under the hood near the fuel pump. Purging should continue until all water is removed from the fuel tank. Also, remove fuel filler cap while purging, and replace cap when completed.

CAUTION: Use all safety precautions while handling the fuel/water mixture.

Clutch & Transmission Section

CLUTCH PEDAL, ADJUST

1977—81

Exc. 1978—81 Cutlass

1. Loosen lower push rod swivel lock nut, Figs. 1 and 2.
2. Disconnect pedal return spring.
3. Rotate clutch lever and shaft assembly until clutch pedal firmly contacts rubber bumper on dash brace.
4. Push outer end of clutch fork rearward until throwout bearing lightly contacts clutch plate.
5. Remove lower push rod swivel retaining clip and install swivel in the gauge (Upper) hole. Reinstall retaining clip.
6. Increase length of push rod until lash is removed.

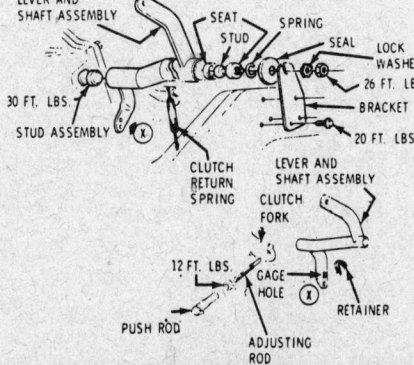

Fig. 1 Clutch linkage. 1977—79 Omega

7. Install swivel in lower hole of lever and shaft assembly, then install retaining clip.
8. Tighten lock nut against swivel. Do not change rod length.
9. Connect pedal return spring.
10. Free pedal play should be ⅞ to 1½ inch on 1977—79 Omega or ¾ to 1¼ inch on 1977 Cutlass.

1978—81 Cutlass

1. Disconnect clutch return spring.
2. Rotate clutch lever and shaft assembly until clutch pedal firmly contacts rubber bumper on bracket.
3. Push outer end of clutch fork rearward until release bearing lightly contacts clutch plate.
4. Install lower push rod "A", Fig. 3, in

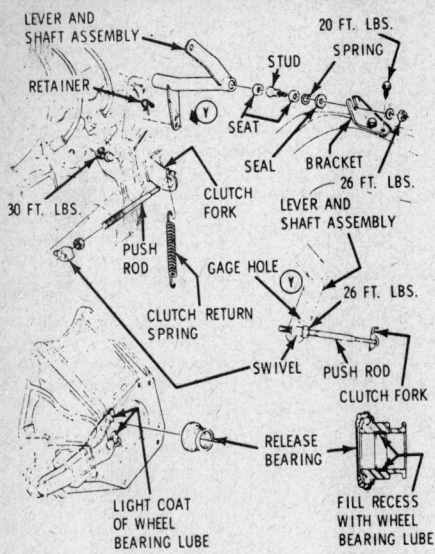

Fig. 2 Clutch linkage. 1977 Cutlass

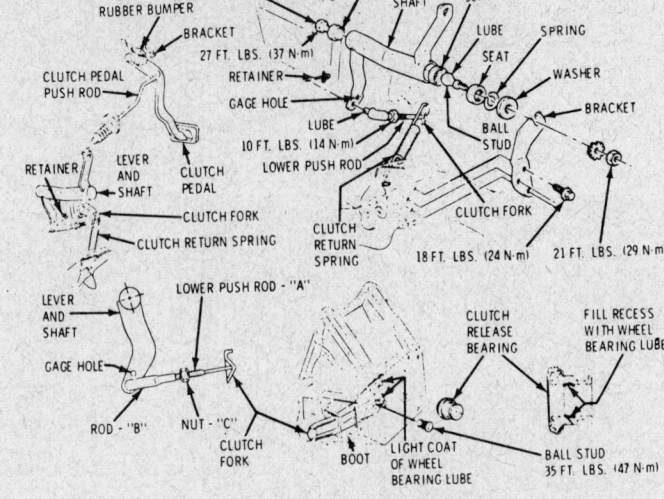

Fig. 3 Clutch linkage. 1978–81 Cutlass

clutch fork and rod "B", Fig. 3, in gauge (Upper) hole.
5. Increase length of push rod "A" until all lash is removed.
6. Install rod "B" in lower hole of lever and shaft, then the retaining clip.
7. Tighten lock nut "C" against rod "B", Fig. 3. Do not change rod length.
8. Connect return spring.
9. Free pedal play should be 11/16 to 5/8 inch.

CLUTCH, REPLACE

1977–81

1. Remove transmission.
2. Disconnect clutch release spring and clutch rod.
3. Remove clutch release bearing.
4. Remove flywheel housing, leaving starter attached to engine. Release yoke and ball stud will remain in housing.
5. Scribe mark on clutch cover to flywheel for correct assembly.
6. Unfasten and remove clutch cover and disc.

NOTE: Loosen pressure plate bolts alternately, one turn at a time.

7. Reverse removal procedure to install clutch and adjust clutch pedal free play.

THREE SPEED MANUAL TRANS., REPLACE

1977–81

1. On models with floor shift, remove shift lever from shifter assembly.
2. Raise car and remove drive shaft.
3. Disconnect shift rods from shift levers and the TCS switch wiring, if equipped.
4. Support rear of engine.
5. Remove cross support bar-to-rear transmission mount attaching bolts.
6. Remove catalytic converter support bracket.
7. Disconnect parking brake cables from cross support and remove cross support bar.
8. If equipped with dual exhaust it may be necessary to disconnect left-hand exhaust pipe at exhaust manifold to provide clearance.
9. Disconnect speedometer cable.
10. Remove transmission upper attaching bolts and install aligning studs in the bolt holes.
11. Remove lower bolts and remove transmission.
12. Reverse procedure to install.

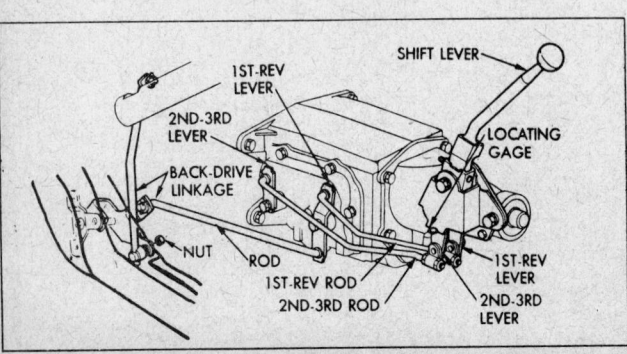

Fig. 4 Three speed shift linkage (typical)

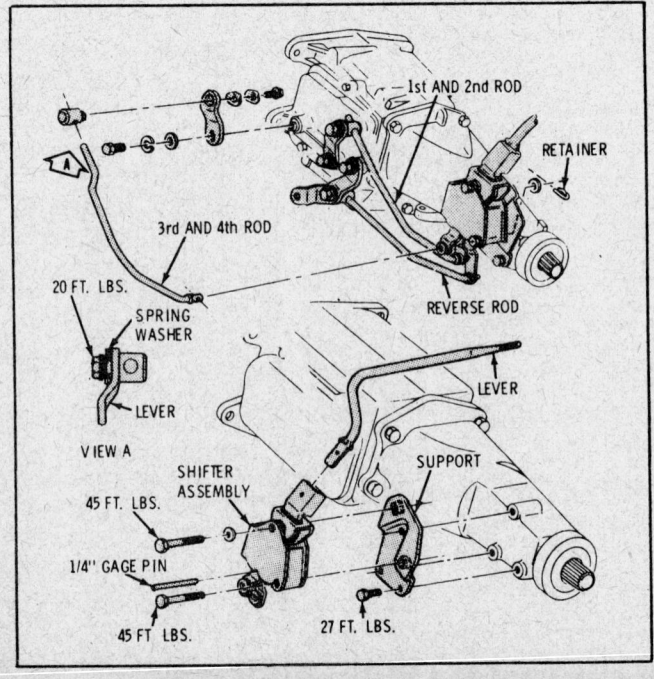

Fig. 5 Four speed shift linkage. 1978–80

3 SPEED SHIFT LINKAGE, ADJUST

1977—80 Column Shift

1. Place transmission in reverse and raise vehicle.
2. Loosen swivel bolts on shift rods at transmission, ensuring rods are free to move in swivels.
3. Hold 1st-reverse column relay lever in position, push up on shift rod until detent in column is felt, then torque swivel bolt to 20 ft. lbs. on 1978—79 Omega, 26 ft. lbs. on 1977 Omega, 23 ft. lbs. on 1977 Cutlass and 20 ft. lbs. on 1980 Cutlass.
4. Place transmission in Neutral, insert 3/16 inch rod through column relay lever into alignment hole and torque swivel nut to 20 ft. lbs. on 1978—79 Omega, 26 ft. lbs. on 1977 Omega, 23 ft. lbs. on 1977 Cutlass and 20 ft. lbs. on 1980 Cutlass.
5. Lower vehicle and check shift operation.
6. Place transmission in reverse, turn ignition switch to lock position and ensure that the key can be removed, steering wheel will not turn and transmission will not shift out of reverse.
7. Place ignition switch in run position, shift transmission to second gear, ensure that steering wheel will turn and key can not be removed from ignition switch.

1978—81 Floor Shift

1978—81 Cutlass
1. Place ignition switch in "Off" position, then raise vehicle.
2. Remove retainers from shift rods, then place transmission shift levers in neutral.
3. Place control lever in neutral position. Align levers and insert gauge pin into levers and bracket.

4. Loosen nuts on 1st-reverse shift rod and adjust trunion and pin assembly, then tighten nuts.
5. Loosen nuts on 2nd-3rd shift rod and adjust trunion and pin assembly, then tighten nuts.
6. Remove gauge pin, then check linkage for proper operation.

4 SPEED TRANS., REPLACE

1977—80

1. Raise vehicle and drain transmission.
2. Remove propeller shaft.
3. Disconnect speedometer cable and back-up light switch from transmission.
4. Disconnect transmission control rod and lever assemblies from shifter shafts. Position rods aside.
5. Remove crossmember to transmission mount bolts.
6. Remove catalytic converter support bracket.
7. Support engine with a suitable jack and remove crossmember to frame bolts, then the crossmember.
8. Remove transmission to clutch housing upper retaining bolts and install guide pins in holes.
9. Remove the transmission to clutch housing lower retaining bolts, slide transmission rearward and remove from vehicle.
10. Reverse procedure to install.

4 SPEED SHIFT LINKAGE, ADJUST

1977—80

1. Turn ignition switch to "Off" position and raise vehicle.
2. Loosen lock nuts on shift rod swivels, Fig. 5. The rods should pass freely through the swivels.
3. Place transmission shift levers in neutral.
4. Place shift control lever in neutral. Align control levers and install a suitable pin into levers and bracket.
5. Tighten 1st.-2nd. shift rod nut against swivel.
6. Tighten 3rd.-4th. shift rod nut against swivel.
7. Tighten reverse shift control rod nut.
8. Remove pin from control lever assembly and check for proper operation.

5 SPEED TRANS., REPLACE

1977—79

1. Remove Shifter assembly.
2. Raise vehicle and remove propeller-shaft.
3. Disconnect speedometer cable from transmission.
4. Remove crossmember to transmission bolts.
5. Remove catalytic converter support bracket.
6. Support engine and remove crossmember.
7. Remove transmission to clutch housing upper retaining bolts and install guide pins.
8. Remove transmission to clutch housing lower bolts and slide transmission rearward, then remove from vehicle.
9. Remove back-up lamp switch and fill plug. Tilt transmission and drain fluid.
10. Reverse procedure to install.

Toronado Drive Link Belt

For service procedures on Toronado drive link belt or sprockets, refer to the Main Index.

Rear Axle, Propeller Shaft & Brakes

REAR AXLE
1979—84 Toronado

On these models the hub and wheel bearing is incorporated into one assembly which eliminates the need for wheel bearing adjustment and does not require periodic maintenance.

Wheel Bearing & Spindle, Replace

REAR DISC BRAKES
Removal
1. Raise and support rear of vehicle.
2. Remove tire and wheel assembly.

3. Mark a wheel stud and a corresponding place on the rotor to assist in installation if bearing is not replaced.
4. Disconnect brake line at bracket on control arm.
5. Remove caliper and rotor assembly.
6. Remove four nut and bolts securing the spindle to the control arm and remove bearing assembly Fig. 1.

Installation

NOTE: Before installing bearing, remove all rust and corrosion from bearing mounting surfaces. Lack of a flat surface may result in early bearing failure. A slip fit must exist between the bearing and the control arm assembly.

1. Install rear spindle, shield and plate to lower control arm with four nut and bolt assemblies. Tighten to 32 ft. lbs. Fig. 1.
2. If bearing was not replaced install rotor using reference marks made at time of removal.
3. Install brake caliper assembly.
4. Connect brake line at bracket on control arm, tighten and bleed brake system.

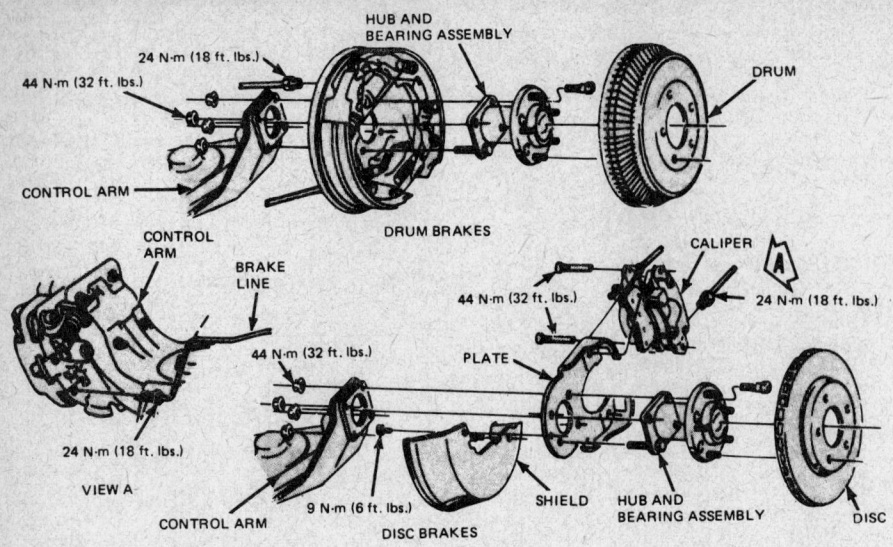

Fig. 1 Wheel bearing and hub assembly removal 1979—84 Toronado

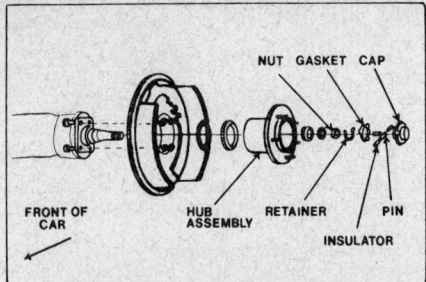

Fig. 3 Rear wheel hub & spindle with True-Track brake. 1977—78

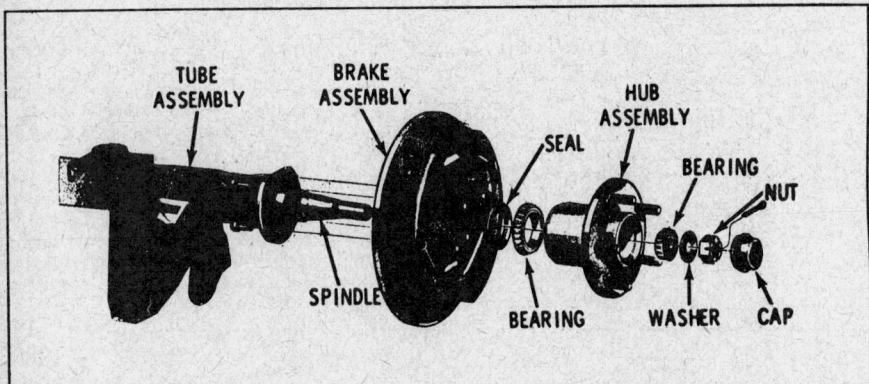

Fig. 2 Rear wheel hub & spindle less True-Track brake. 1977—78

5. Install wheel and tire assembly. Tighten to 100 ft. lbs.
6. Remove support and lower car.

REAR DRUM BRAKES
Removal
1. Raise and support rear of vehicle.
2. Remove tire and wheel assembly.
3. Remove brake drum.
4. Remove four nuts attaching rear wheel bearing assembly to control arm.
5. Remove wheel bearing and four attaching bolts, Fig. 1.

Installation

NOTE: Before installing bearing, remove all rust and corrosion from bearing mounting surfaces. Lack of a flat surface for any reason may result in early bearing failure. A slip fit must exist between the bearing and the control arm assembly.

1. Install four nuts and bolts attaching wheel bearing to rear control arm assembly, Fig. 1.
2. Install brake drum.
3. Install wheel and tire assembly, tighten to 100 ft. lbs.
4. Remove supports and lower car.

1977—78 Toronado

The rear wheel spindles are a press fit and bolted to the rear axle assembly, Figs. 2 and 3. As shown, tapered roller bearings are used in the rear wheels.

Wheel Bearing Adjustment

Adjustment of the rear wheel bearings should be made while revolving the wheel at least three times the speed of the nut rotation when taking torque readings.
1. Check to make sure that hub is completely seated on wheel spindle.
2. While rotating wheel, tighten spindle nut to 25 to 30 ft-lbs. Make certain all parts are properly seated and that threads are free.
3. Back nut off 1/2 turn, then retighten nut to finger-tight and install cotter pin.
4. If cotter pin cannot be installed in either of the two holes in the spindle, back nut off until cotter pin can be installed.
5. The rear hub must be rotated at least three revolutions during tightening of spindle nut. The final adjustment to be finger-tight to provide .001—.005" bearing end play.
6. Peen end of cotter pin snug against side of nut. If it can be moved with a finger,

vibration may cause it to wear and break.

Wheel Spindle, Replace

Removal
1. Raise and support rear of car and remove hub.
2. Disconnect brake line at wheel cylinder.
3. Unfasten and remove brake backing plate and position out of the way.
4. Remove bolts securing spindle to axle.
5. Use a suitable puller to remove spindle from axle to tube.

Installation
1. Start spindle into axle tube assembly with keyway facing up and install backing plate to spindle attaching bolts. Using a suitable slide hammer, drive spindle into tube while tightening bolts until spindle is fully seated.
2. Remove slide hammer and bolts.
3. Install new gasket on wheel spindle.
4. Install brake backing plate and tighten nuts to 40 ft-lbs.
5. Connect brake line to wheel cylinder, tightening fitting to 14 ft-lbs.
6. Install rear hub.

Rear Axle, Replace

1977—78
1. Raise and support rear of car with jack stands at rear frame pads ahead of rear wheel opening.
2. Remove rear wheels and hubs.
3. Disconnect brake lines at wheel cylinders.
4. Disconnect parking brake cable at equalizer.
5. Disconnect rubber brake hose at underbody connector.
6. Support axle with a suitable jack.
7. If equipped with True Track brakes, disconnect wiring connector from underbody connector.
8. Disconnect shock absorbers from lower mountings.
9. Lower axle and remove coil spring.
10. Remove brake backing plate attaching bolts and position plates aside.
11. Disconnect upper and lower control arms from axle.
12. Lower axle from vehicle.
13. Reverse procedure to install.

Exc. Toronado

Figs. 4 and 5 illustrate the rear axle assemblies used on conventional models. When necessary to overhaul any of these units, refer to the *Rear Axle Specifications* table in this chapter.

Integral Carrier
Type "B" & "O" (Except 7½")

As shown in Fig. 4, the drive pinion is mounted on two tapered roller bearings that are preloaded by two selected spacers. The drive pinion is positioned by shims located between a shoulder on the pinion and the rear bearing. The front bearing is held in place by a large nut.

The differential is supported in the carrier by two tapered roller side bearings. These are preloaded by inserting shims between the bearings and the pedestals. The differential assembly is positioned for ring gear and pinion backlash by varying these shims.

Type C, G, K, M, O (7½") & P

In these rear axles, Fig. 5, the rear axle housing and differential carrier are cast into an integral assembly. The drive pinion assembly is mounted in two opposed tapered roller bearings. The pinion bearings are preloaded by a spacer behind the front bearing. The pinion is positioned by a washer between the head of the pinion and the rear bearing.

The differential is supported in the carrier by two tapered roller side bearings. These bearings are preloaded by spacers located between the bearings and carrier housing. The differential assembly is positioned for proper ring gear and pinion backlash by varying these spacers. The differential case houses two side gears in mesh with two pinions mounted on a pinion shaft which is held in place by a lock pin. The side gears and pinions are backed by thrust washers.

Rear Axle, Replace

Construction of the axle assembly is such that service operations may be performed with the housing installed in the vehicle or with the housing removed and installed in a holding fixture. The following procedure is necessary only when the housing requires replacement.

1977–79 Omega
1. Raise vehicle and support axle using a suitable jack.
2. Disconnect shock absorbers from axle housing.
3. Disconnect properller and support out of way.
4. Remove rear wheel, brake drums and axle shafts.
5. Disconnect brake lines from clips on axle tubes.
6. Remove backing plates and support from frame using wire.
7. Remove lower spring pad brackets, then shift axle to clear springs.
8. Reverse procedure to install.

1977–84 Except Omega
1. Raise car and remove rear wheels, drums and axle shafts.
2. Disconnect brake line from wheel cylinders.
3. Unfasten and support backing plates with wire hooks to frame kickup.
4. Disconnect shock absorbers at housing.
5. Position jack stands under frame rear torque boxes, then disconnect upper control arms and slowly lower axle housing to stands.
6. Remove springs.

7. Remove propeller shaft and support front of axle housing at companion flange to prevent assembly from rotating when the lower control arms are disconnected.
8. Remove lower control arm bolts at axle housing.
9. Remove support at companion flange and lower axle housing.
10. Remove assembly to bench and transfer parts to new axle housing.
11. Reverse procedure to install.

Axle Shaft, Replace

Type C, G, K, M, O (7½") & P
1. Raise vehicle and remove wheel and brake drum.
2. Clean all dirt from area of carrier cover.
3. Drain lubricant from carrier by removing cover.
4. Remove differential pinion shaft lock screw and shaft.

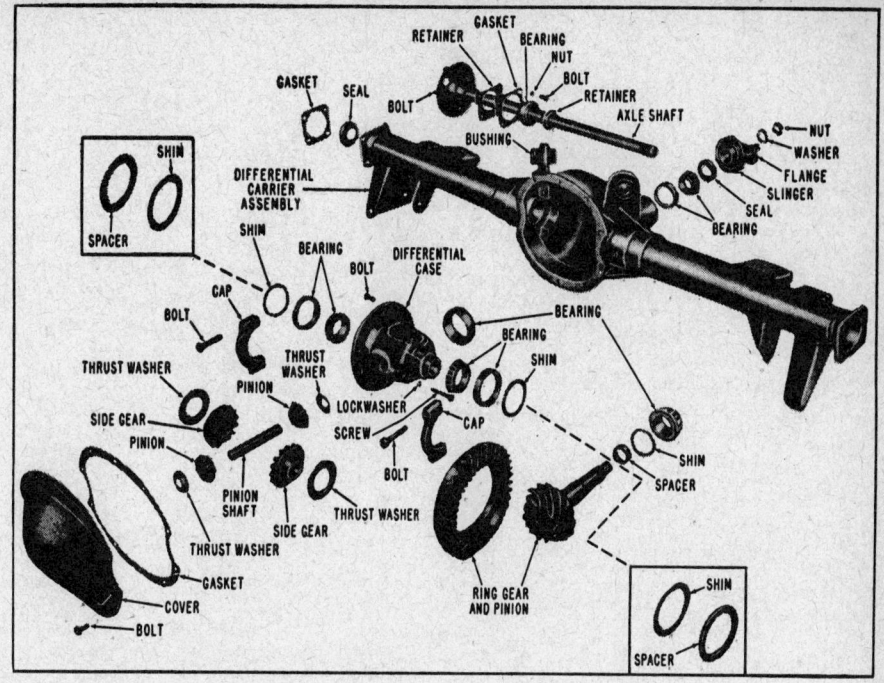

Fig. 4   Integral carrier type rear axle. 1977–84 Type B & O (Except 7½") axle

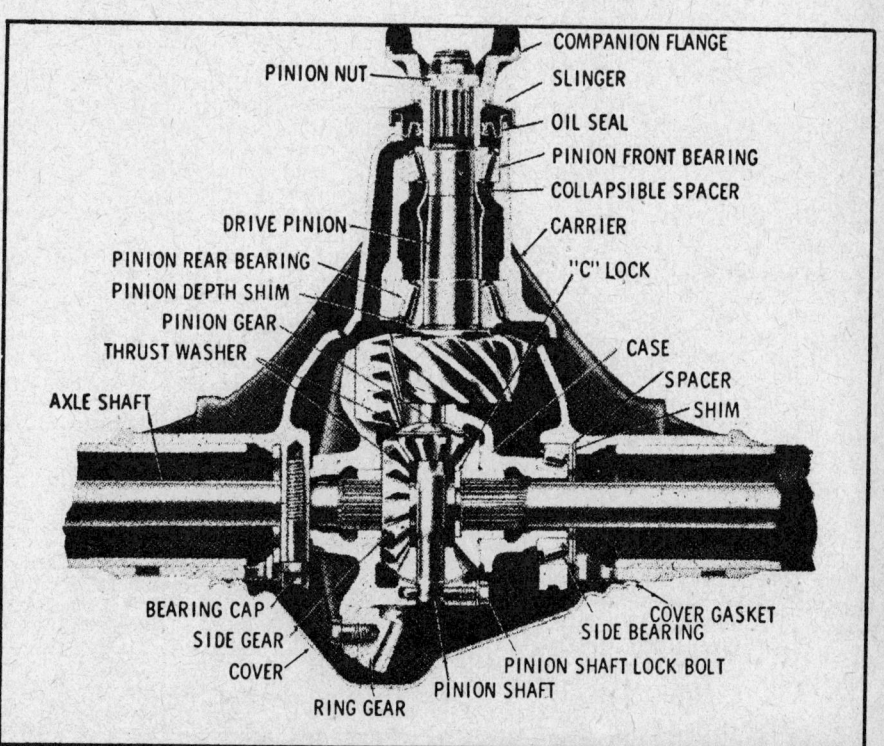

Fig. 5   Integral carrier type differential. 1977–84 Types C, G, K, M, O (7½") & P axle

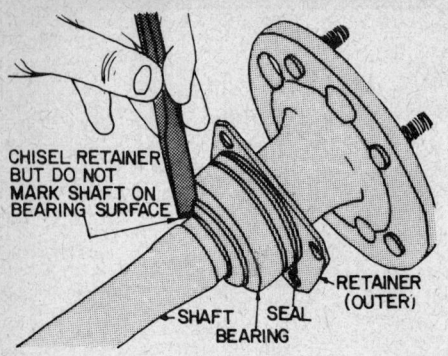

Fig. 6 Removing axle shaft bearing retainer

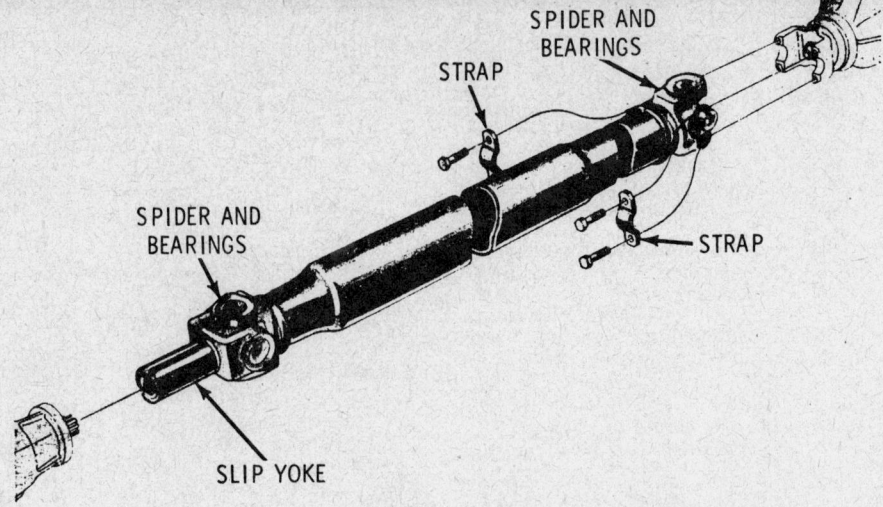

Fig. 7 Propeller shaft installation 1977–84 all (Typical)

5. Push flanged end of axle shaft toward center of vehicle and remove "C" lock from button end of shaft.
6. Remove axle shaft from housing, being careful not to damage oil seal.
7. Reverse procedure to install.

Type B & O (Except 7½")
1. Remove wheel and brake drum.
2. Remove axle bearing retainer (4 nuts).

NOTE: On 1977–81 8½ inch axles, new retainers are used and can be identified by a raised area around the axle shaft opening. This raised area provides proper seating of the seal and bearing.

3. Pull axle shaft from housing. If bearing is a tight fit in housing, use a slide hammer-type puller. Do not drag shaft over seal as this may damage axle seal.
4. Attach one axle bearing retainer nut to hold brake backing plate in position.
5. Before installing axle shaft, examine oil seal. The seals have feathered edges which form a tight seal around the shaft. If these edges are damaged in any way, seal must be replaced. Examine seal surface on shaft; if it is not smooth, dress it down with very fine emery cloth.
6. Reverse removal procedure to install axle shaft, being sure to grease outside of axle bearing, seal surface on axle shaft and bore of axle housing with differential lubricant. Place new gasket and bearing retainer over studs, install nuts and tighten to 40 ft. lbs. on all 1977 models and 35 ft. lbs. on all 1978–84 models.
7. Bearings should be replaced if found to be rough or have greater than .020" end play. Remove bearing only when new bearing is to be installed; once removed it must not be reused.
8. With axle shaft removed from housing, split bearing retainer with a chisel, Fig. 6.
9. Press bearing off shaft.
10. Press new bearing on shaft up against shoulder on shaft.
11. Press retainer on shaft up against bearing.
12. Reverse removal procedure to install axle shaft.

PROPELLER SHAFT

1977–84

The propeller shaft is of one or two piece construction with a single or double U-joint securing the shaft to the companion flange,

Fig. 7.
1. Mark propeller shaft and companion flange so they can be installed in the same position.
2. On 1977–84 models, remove strap bolts, Fig. 7. Use a piece of tape or wire to hold universal joint bearing caps in place.
3. Lower rear of shaft and slide rearward.
4. Reverse procedure to install. If drive shaft yokes do not have vent holes, lubricate internal splines with engine oil. If drive shaft yokes have vent holes apply lubricant No. 1050169 or equivalent to internal splines prior to installation. Torque strap bolts to 14–16 ft. lbs.

BRAKE ADJUSTMENTS

These brakes have self adjusting shoe mechanisms that assure correct lining-to-drum clearances at all times. The automatic adjusters operate only when the brakes are applied as the car is moving rearward.

Although the brakes are self-adjusting, an initial adjustment is necessary after the brake shoes have been relined or replaced, or when the length of the star wheel adjuster has been changed during some other service operation.

Frequent usage of an automatic transmission forward range to halt reverse vehicle motion may prevent the automatic adjusters from functioning, thereby inducing low pedal heights. Should low pedal heights be encountered, it is recommended that numerous forward and reverse stops be made until satisfactory pedal height is obtained.

NOTE: If a low pedal height condition cannot be corrected by making numerous reverse stops (provided the hydraulic system is free of air) it indicates that the self-adjusting mechanism is not functioning. Therefore, it will be necessary to remove the brake drum, clean, free up and lubricate the adjusting mechanism. Then adjust the brakes as follows, being sure the parking brake is fully released.

Adjustment

NOTE: Inasmuch as there is no way to adjust these brakes with the drums installed, the fol-

lowing procedure is mandatory after new linings are installed or if it becomes necessary to change the length of the brake shoe adjusting screw.

1. With brake drums removed, position the caliper shown in Fig. 9 to the inside diameter of the drum and tighten the clamp screw.
2. Next position brake shoe end of the caliper tool over the brake shoes as shown in Fig. 10.
3. Rotate the gauge slightly around the shoes to insure that the gauge contacts the linings at the largest diameter.
4. Adjust brake shoes until the gauge is a snug fit on the linings at the point of largest lining diameter.

NOTE: If it is necessary to back off the brake shoe adjustment, it will be necessary to hold the adjuster lever away from the adjuster screw, Fig. 11.

PARKING BRAKE, ADJUST

Depress parking brake pedal 3 clicks on all models except 1977–79 Omega and 1977 88 and 98 and all 1978–84 models. Depress parking brake pedal 2 clicks on 1977 Omega and 6 clicks on 1977 88 and 98 and 2 clicks on all 1978–84 models. Tighten adjusting nut until left rear wheel can just be rotated rearward using both hands and cannot be rotated forward. Release parking brake, rear wheels should turn freely in either direction with no brake drag.

POWER BRAKE UNIT, REPLACE

Hydro-Boost

1978–84

NOTE: Pump brake pedal several times with engine off to deplete accumulator of fluid.

1. Remove two nuts attaching master cylin-

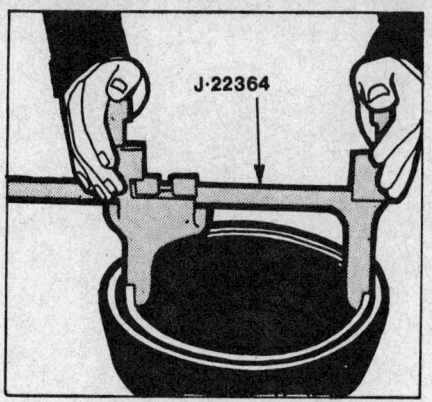

Fig. 9 Brake shoe gauge measuring inside diameter of brake drum. 1977–84

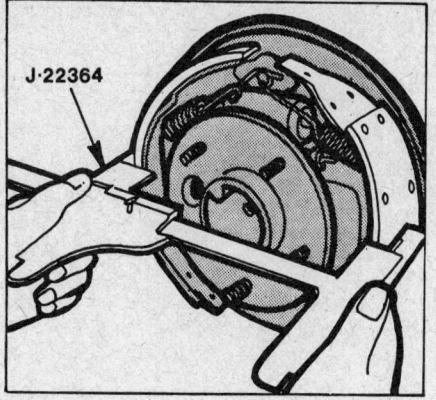

Fig. 10 Brake shoe gauge measuring outside diameter of brake shoes. 1977–84

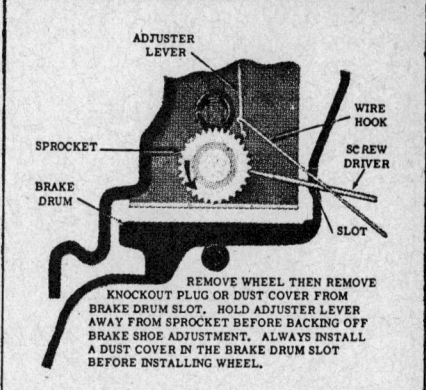

Fig. 11 Backing off brake shoe adjustment

der to booster, then move master cylinder away from booster with brake lines attached.
2. Remove three hydraulic lines from booster. Plug and cap all lines and outlets.
3. Remove retainer and washer securing booster push rod to brake pedal arm.
4. Remove four nuts attaching booster unit to dash panel.
5. From engine compartment, loosen booster from dash panel and move booster push rod inboard until it disconnects from brake pedal arm. Remove spring washer from brake pedal arm.
6. Remove booster unit from vehicle.
7. Reverse procedure to install. To purge system, disconnect feed wire from injection pump. Fill power steering pump reservoir, then crank engine for several seconds and recheck power steering pump fluid level. Connect injection pump feed wire and start engine, then cycle steering wheel from stop to stop twice and stop engine. Discharge accumulator by depressing brake pedal several times, then check fluid level. Start engine, then turn steering wheel from stop to stop and turn engine off. Check fluid level and add fluid as necessary. If foaming occurs, stop engine and wait for approximately one hour for foam to dissipate, then recheck fluid level.

Vacuum Booster

1. Disconnect vacuum hose from vacuum cylinder and cover openings to prevent entrance of dirt.
2. Disconnect pipes from master cylinder outlets and cover openings in master cylinder and end of pipes to prevent entrance of dirt.
3. Disconnect push rod from brake pedal.

4. Unfasten and remove power brake unit.
5. Reverse procedure to install.

BRAKE MASTER CYLINDER, REPLACE

1. Be sure area around master cylinder is clean, then disconnect the hydraulic lines at master cylinder. Plug or tape end of line to prevent entrance of dirt or loss of brake fluid.
2. On Omega models with manual brakes, remove push rod to brake pedal clevis pin.
3. On Cutlass models with manual brakes, remove push rod to brake pedal pin.
4. Remove master cylinder retaining nuts and the master cylinder.
5. Reverse procedure to install.

Rear Suspension

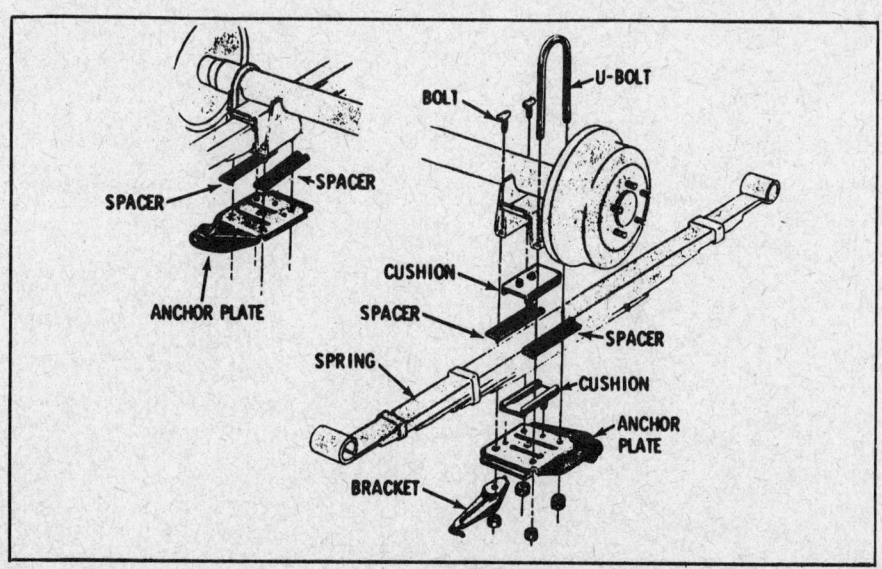

Fig. 1 Rear suspension (typical). 1977–79 Omega

SHOCK ABSORBER, REPLACE

1. With rear axle properly supported, disconnect shock absorber from upper mounting.
2. Disconnect shock absorber from lower mounting.
3. Reverse procedure to install.

LEAF SPRINGS & BUSHINGS, REPLACE
1977–79 Omega

1. Support vehicle at frame and support rear axle, relieving tension from spring.
2. Disconnect shock absorbers from lower mountings and loosen spring front mounting bolt.
3. Remove spring retainer bracket to underbody screws, lower rear axle and remove retainer bracket.

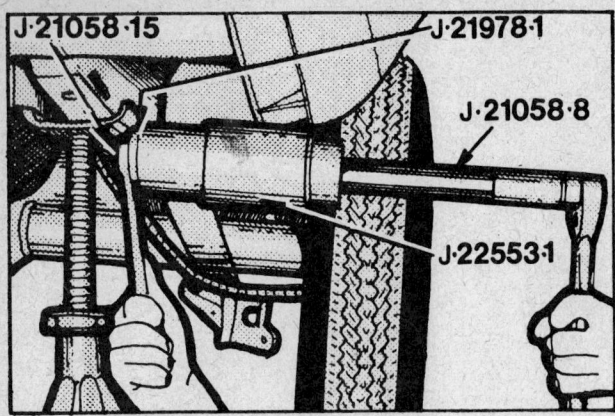

Fig. 2   Leaf spring bushings removal. 1977-79 Omega

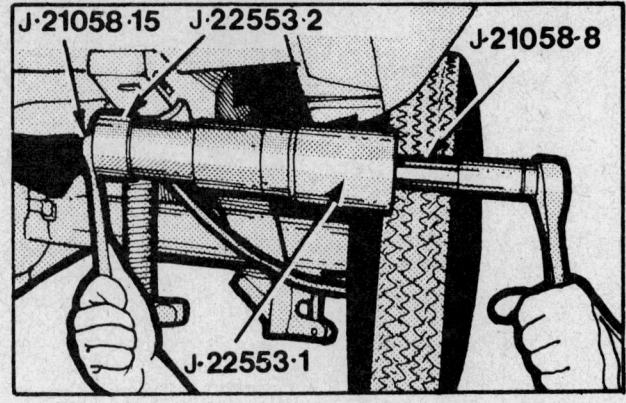

Fig. 3   Leaf spring bushings installation. 1977-79 Omega

4. Disconnect parking brake cable from spring plate bracket.
5. Remove "U" bolts and spring plate, Fig. 1.
6. Support spring, remove spring front mounting bolt and rear shackle bolts.
7. Replace spring eye bushings and rear shackle frame bushings as necessary, Figs. 2 and 3.
8. Reverse procedure to install.

COIL SPRING, REPLACE

1977-84 Except Omega & Toronado

1. Position a suitable jack under rear axle housing and raise rear of vehicle, then support frame side rails with support stands. Do not lower jack.
2. Disconnect brake line at axle housing.
3. Disconnect upper control arms at axle housing.
4. Disconnect shock absorber at lower mounting, then carefully lower rear axle assembly.

NOTE: Use care not to stretch or kink brake hoses.

5. Remove coil spring from vehicle.

1979-84 Toronado

1. Raise and support rear of vehicle, then remove wheel and tire assembly.
2. Remove stabilizer bar as described under Stabilizer Bar, Replace.
3. Using a suitable jack support lower control arm.
4. Disconnect automatic level air line at shock absorber. If removing left hand spring from vehicle, disconnect automatic level control link from ball pivot at control arm.
5. Disconnect shock absorber from upper and lower mountings and remove shock absorber.
6. Carefully lower control arm until spring tension is relieved, then remove spring and insulator, Fig. 4.
7. Reverse procedure to install. Locate bottom end of spring between dimples on lower control arm assembly.

1977-78 Toronado

1. Support vehicle at frame.
2. With rear axle properly supported, dis-

connect shock absorbers from lower mountings, Fig. 5.
3. Carefully lower rear axle and remove springs.

NOTE: It may be necessary to compress springs, using a suitable spring compressor, to facilitate removal.

4. Reverse procedure to install. On 1977-78 models, springs must be properly indexed, Fig. 6.

CONTROL ARMS & BUSHINGS, REPLACE

NOTE: Replace control arms one at a time to prevent axle assembly misalignment, making installation difficult.

Upper Control Arms

Exc. Toronado
1. Support vehicle at frame and rear axle.
2. Remove control arm front and rear mount bolts.

3. Replace axle housing bushing as necessary, Figs. 7 thru 10.
4. On 1978-84 models, replace control arm bushings as necessary, Figs. 11 and 12.
5. Reverse procedure to install. Tighten control arm bolts with vehicle at curb height.

1977-78 Toronado
1. Support vehicle at frame and rear axle.
2. Remove control arm front and rear mounting bolts.
3. Replace control arm bushings as necessary.

NOTE: When installing upper control arm rear bushing, reverse tool # J-21474-13.

4. Reverse procedure to install. Tighten control arm bolts with vehicle at curb height.

Lower Control Arms All Exc. Toronado

Follow "Upper Control Arms" procedure for replacement of lower control arms. On 1977 models, control arm bushings are not serviceable. On 1978-84 models, replace control arm bushings as shown in Figs. 11 and 12.

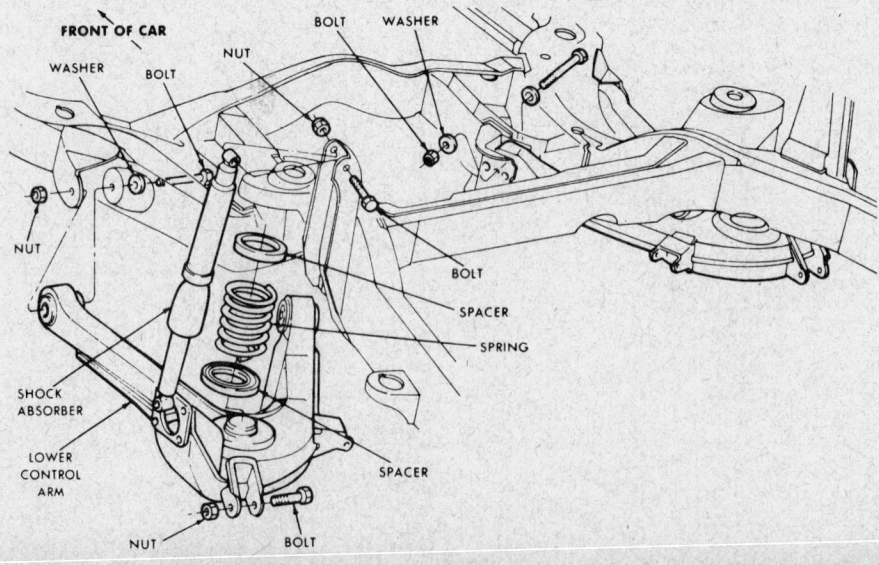

Fig. 4   Rear suspension. 1979-84 Toronado

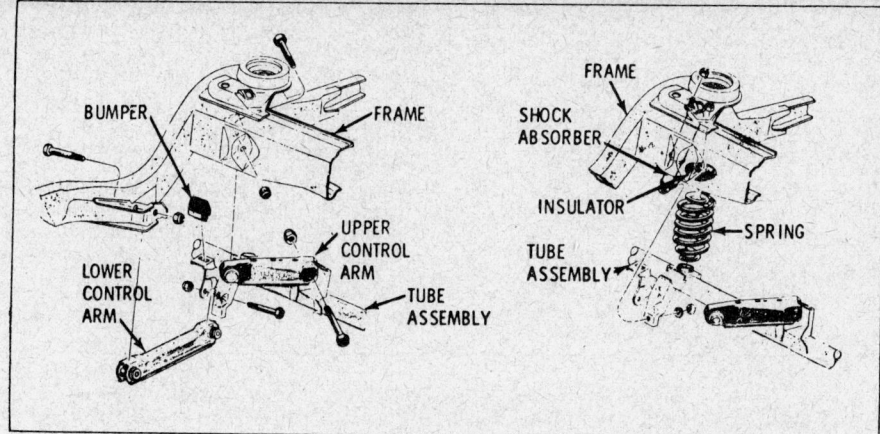

Fig. 5   Rear suspension. 1977–78 Toronado

PIGTAIL ON FRAME END OF SPRING MUST POINT TO RIGHT SIDE OF CAR WITHIN LIMITS SHOWN

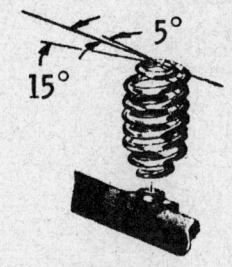

Fig. 6   Rear coil spring installation. 1977–78 Toronado

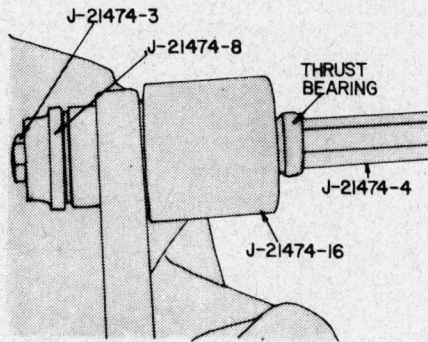

Fig. 7   Upper control arm axle bracket bushing removal. 1977 models

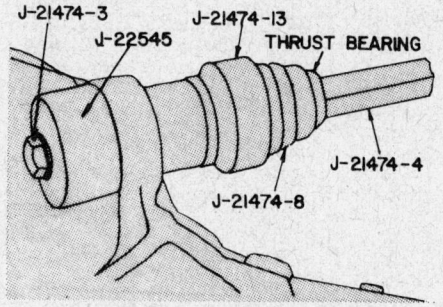

Fig. 8   Upper control arm axle bracket bushing installation. 1977 models

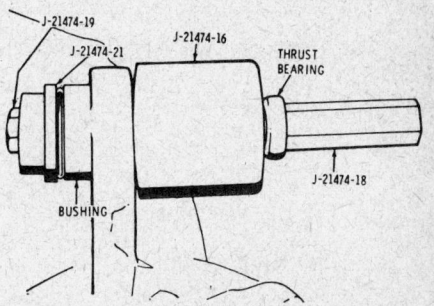

Fig. 9   Upper control arm axle bracket bushing removal. 1978–84 models

1979–84 Toronado

1. Raise and support rear of vehicle, then remove wheel and tire assembly.
2. Remove stabilizer bar as described under Stabilizer Bar, Replace.
3. Disconnect brake line bracket from control arm, then remove caliper assembly.
4. Mark a wheel stud and a corresponding point of the rotor for alignment, then remove rotor.
5. If left hand control arm is to be removed, disconnect automatic level control link from ball pivot on control arm.
6. Using a suitable jack support control arm.
7. Disconnect air line from shock absorber, then disconnect shock absorber from up-

per and lower mountings and remove shock absorber.
8. Carefully lower the control arm until spring tension is relieved, then remove spring and insulator.
9. Remove two bolts mounting control arm to frame and remove control arm, Fig. 8.
10. Reverse procedure to install.

1977–78 Toronado

Follow "Upper Control Arms" procedure for replacement of lower control arms.

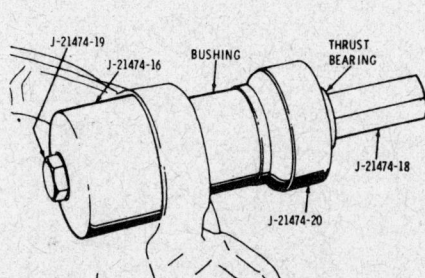

Fig. 10   Upper control arm axle bracket bushing installation. 1978–84 models

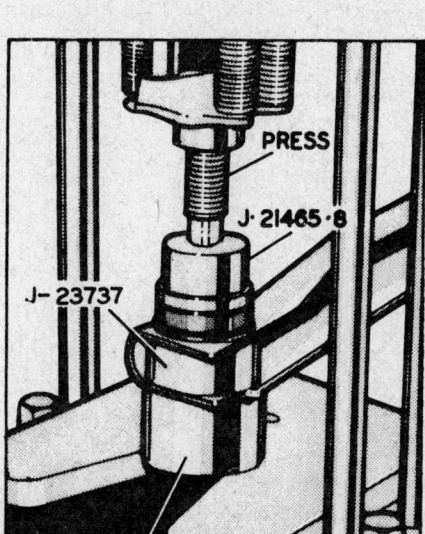

Fig. 11   All front & lower control arm rear bushing removal. 1978–84 models

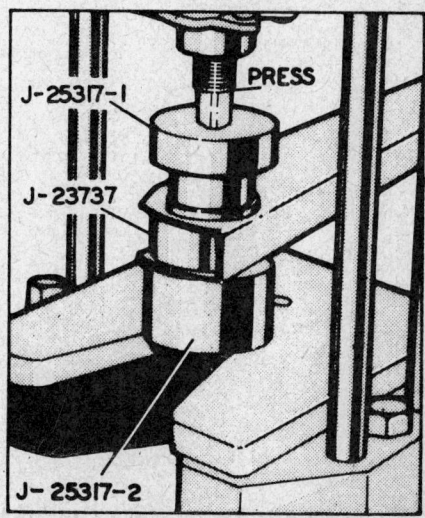

Fig. 12   All front & lower control arm rear bushing installation. 1978–84 models

STABILIZER BAR, REPLACE

Exc. 1979–84 Toronado

1. Support vehicle at rear axle.
2. Remove bolts attaching stabilizer bar to the lower control arms, Fig. 13.
3. Reverse procedure to install.

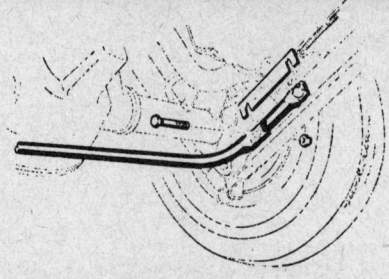

Fig. 13   Stabilizer bar installation (typical)

1979–84 Toronado

1. Raise and support rear of vehicle.
2. Remove nuts and bolts securing front of stabilizer bar to control arms.
3. Remove inside nut and bolt from each side of stabilizer bar link, then loosen outside nut and bolt on the stabilizer link.
4. Rotate bottom parts of link to one side and slip stabilizer out of bushings.

Front Suspension & Steering Section

> Refer to Main Index for Front Drive Axle Service. For Front Suspension and Steering service procedures on 1977–84 Toronado, refer to Cadillac chapter, "Front Suspension and Steering, Eldorado & 1980–84 Seville" section.

FRONT SUSPENSION

As shown in Figs. 1 and 2, the front suspension is of the conventional "A" frame design with ball joints. Double acting shock absorbers are mounted within the coil springs. Caster and camber are controlled by shims.

WHEEL ALIGNMENT

1977–84

Camber and caster are adjusted by shims placed between the upper pivot shafts and the frame. In order to remove or install shims, *do not remove weight from front wheels.* Loosen pivot shaft-to-frame bolts. To gain access to these bolts, loosen top and rear fasteners on fender filler plate aprons.

To decrease positive caster, add shim at the front bolt. To increase positive caster, remove shim at the front bolt.

To increase camber, remove shims at both front and rear bolt. To decrease camber, add shims at both bolts.

By adding or subtracting an equal amount of shims from both front and rear bolts, camber will change without affecting caster adjustment.

TOE-IN, ADJUST

1977–84

To adjust the toe-in, loosen the clamps at both ends of the adjustable tubes at each tie rod. Then turn the tubes an equal amount until the toe-in is correct. When the tie rods are mounted ahead of the steering knuckle, they must be decreased in length to increase toe-in. When the tie rods are mounted behind the steering knuckle, they must be increased in length to increase toe-in.

NOTE: *The steering knuckle and steering arm "rock" or tilt as front wheel rises and falls. Therefore, it is vitally important to position the bottom face of the tie rod end parallel with the machined surface at the outer end of the steering arm when tie rod length is adjusted. Severe damage and possible failure can result unless this precaution is taken. The tie rod sleeve clamps must be straight down to provide clearance.*

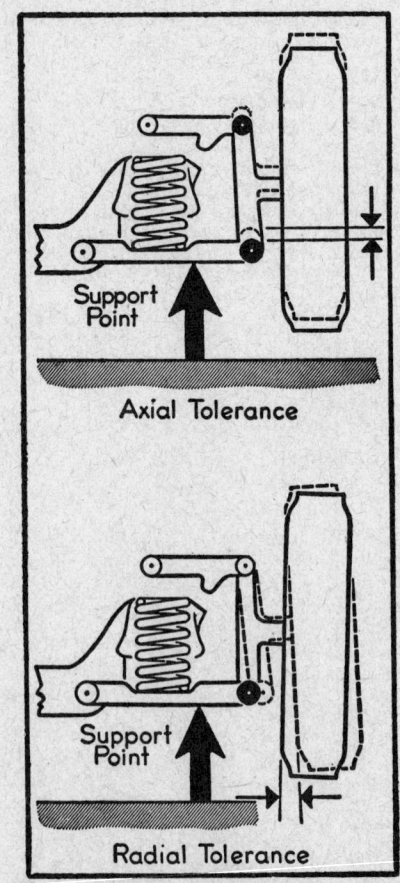

Fig. 3   Checking ball joints for wear

Fig. 1   Front suspension. 1977–84 Full Size (Typical)

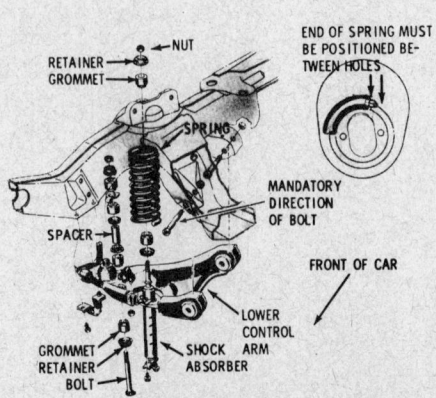

Fig. 2   Front suspension. 1977–84 Exc. Full Size

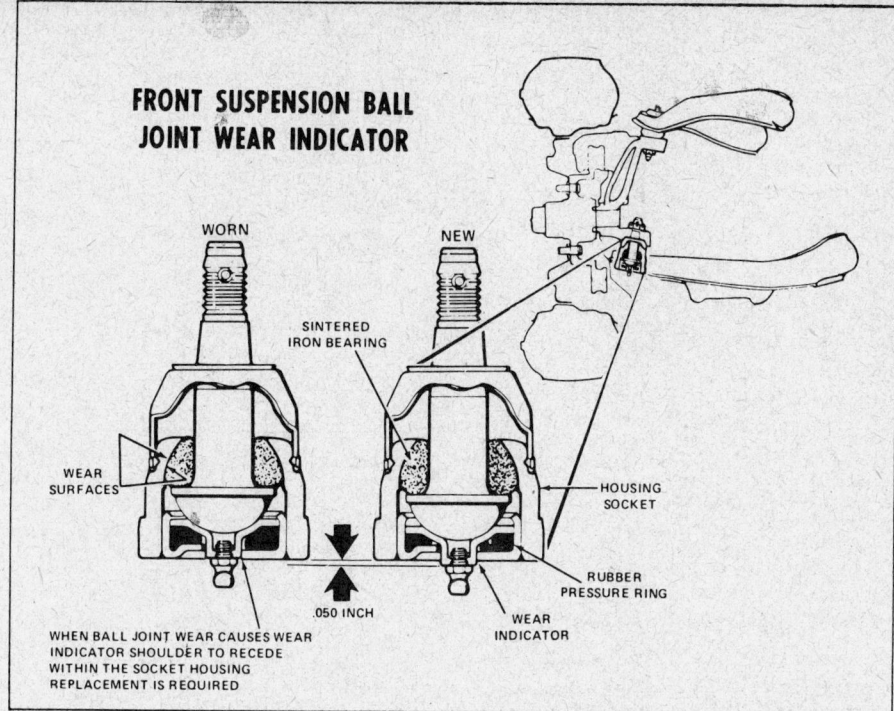

Fig. 4 Ball joint wear indicator. 1977–84

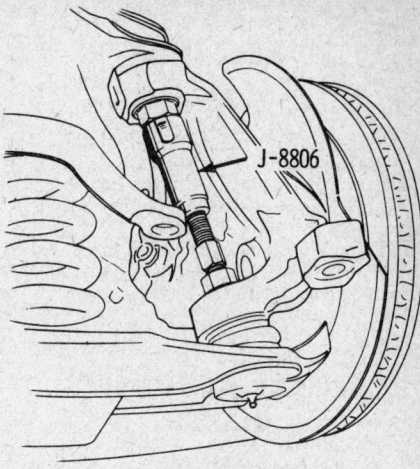

Fig. 5 Removing lower ball joint stud from knuckle

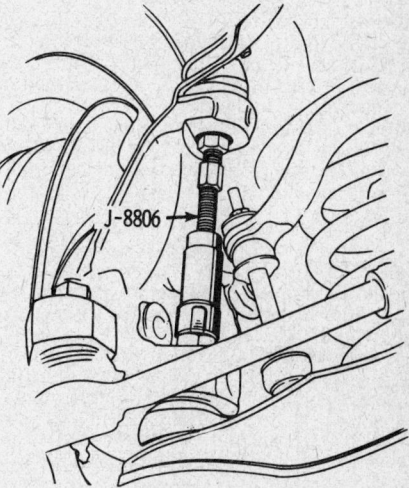

Fig. 6 Removing upper ball joint stud from knuckle

CHECKING BALL JOINTS FOR WEAR

1977–84

If loose ball joints are suspected, first be sure the front wheel bearings are properly adjusted and that the control arms are tight. Then check ball joints for wear as follows:

Referring to Fig. 3, raise wheel with a jack placed under the lower control arm as shown. Then test by moving the wheel up and down to check axial play, and rocking it at the top and bottom to measure radial play.

1977–79 Omega

1. Upper ball joint should be replaced if looseness exceeds .125″.

1977–84 Cutlass

1. Upper ball joint should be replaced if looseness exceeds .125″.

NOTE: A wear indicator is built into the lower ball joint, Fig. 4.

1977–84 Full Size Cars

1. Upper ball joint should be replaced if looseness exceeds .125″.

NOTE: A wear indicator is built into the lower ball joint. Refer to Fig. 4.

BALL JOINTS, REPLACE

On some models the ball joints are riveted to the control arms. All service ball joints, however, are provided with bolt, nut and washer assemblies for replacement purposes.

Some ball joints are pressed into the control arms, in which case they may be pressed out and new ones installed.

LOWER BALL JOINT

1. Raise vehicle and support at frame. Remove wheel.
2. Support lower control arm with a suitable jack.
3. Remove cotter pin and loosen stud nut 2–3 turns. Using tool No. J-8806 or equivalent, break ball joint loose from the knuckle, Fig. 5.
4. Remove stud nut and lower the control arm. Position knuckle assembly aside.
5. Pry ball joint seal retainer from joint and remove seal.
6. Press ball joint from lower control arm with suitable tools.
7. Reverse procedure to install. Torque ball joint stud nut to the following specifications:

Year	Model	Ft. Lbs.
1982–84	All	70
1981	All	90
1980	All	90①
1978–79	All	83 Min.
1977	Cutlass	95
	88 & 98	105

①—Before installing stud nut, tool No. J-29194 must be used to seat the stud on the steering knuckle. Torque tool to 40 ft. lbs., then remove tool and install and torque stud nut.

UPPER BALL JOINT

1. Raise vehicle and support at frame. Remove wheel.
2. Support lower control arm with suitable jack or jack stand.
3. Remove cotter pin and loosen stud nut 2–3 turns. Using tool No. J-8806 or equivalent, break ball joint loose from the knuckle, Fig. 6.
4. Remove stud nut and support knuckle assembly to prevent damage to brake hose.
5. Using a 1/8 inch twist drill, drill the 4 ball joint rivets approximately 1/4 inch. Then drill off rivets heads using a 1/2 inch twist drill.
6. Punch out rivets and remove lower ball joint.
7. Install new ball joint in lower control arm and torque attaching bolts to 8 ft. lbs.
8. Reverse procedure to assemble. Torque ball joint stud nut to the following specifications:

Year	Model	Ft. Lbs.
1982–84	All	50
1981	All	65
1980	All	65①
1978–79	All	60 Min.
1977	All	70

①—Before installing stud nut, tool No. J-29193 must be used to seat the stud on the steering knuckle. Torque tool to 40 ft. lbs., then remove tool and install and torque stud nut.

WHEEL BEARINGS, REPLACE

1977–84

1. Raise car and remove front wheels.
2. Remove brake pads and caliper assembly but do not disconnect brake line. Suspend caliper from a wire loop or hook to avoid strain on the brake hose.
3. Remove grease cap, cotter pin and nut. Pull off hub and disc assembly. Grease retainer and inner bearing can now be removed.

WHEEL BEARINGS, ADJUST

1978–84

1. While rotating hub assembly, tighten spindle nut to 12 ft. lbs. to insure bearings are properly seated.
2. Back off nut to the just loose position.
3. Hand tighten spindle nut, then loosen nut until either hole in spindle aligns with slot in nut. Do not back off more than ½ flat.
4. Install cotter pin, then measure hub assembly end play. There will be .001 to .005 in. end play when bearings are properly adjusted.

1977

1. While rotating hub assembly, tighten nut o 30 ft-lbs to insure all parts are properly seated.
2. Back off nut ½ turn.
3. Retighten nut finger tight and install retaining ring or cotter key if possible. If unable to install retaining ring or cotter key, back off nut (not to exceed 1/12 of a turn) until tabs on clip align with serrations in nut.

SHOCK ABSORBER, REPLACE

1977–84

1. Remove upper attaching nut, retainer and grommet from shock absorber.
2. Remove two bolts and washers attaching shock absorber to lower control arm and remove shock absorber.
3. To install, position grommet and retainer over shock and slide shock up through spring and frame. Install and tighten attaching nut and lower cap-screws.

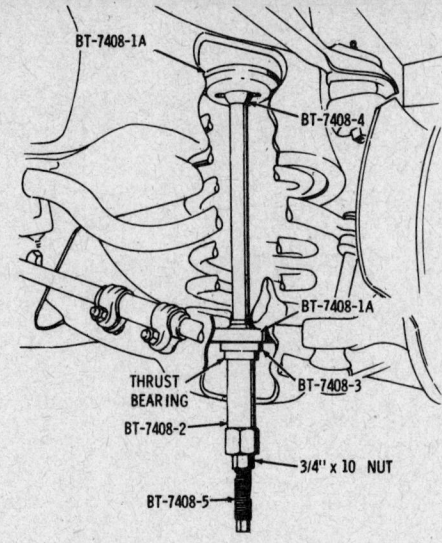

Fig. 7   Replacing coil spring. 1977–84

COIL SPRING, REPLACE

IMPORTANT: Left and right coil springs should not be interchanged. Spring part number is stamped on outer side of end coil.

1977–84

1. Place transmission in Neutral.
2. Disconnect shock absorber from upper mounting.
3. Raise vehicle and support at frame. Remove wheel.
4. Disconnect stabilizer bar from lower control arm.
5. Remove shock absorber.
6. Install lower plate BT-7408-1A or 1B, Fig. 7, with pivot ball seat facing downward into spring coils. Rotate plate to fully seat it in lower control arm spring seat.
7. Install upper plate BT-7408-1A or 1B, Fig. 7, with pivot ball seat facing upward into spring coils. Insert ball nut BT-7408-4 through spring coils and onto upper plate.
8. Install rod BT-7408-5 through shock absorber opening in lower control arm and through the upper and lower plates. Depress lock pin on shaft and thread into upper ball nut BT-7408-4. Ensure lock pin is fully extended above ball nut upper surface.
9. With ball nut tang engaged in slot in upper plate, rotate upper plate until it con-

tacts upper spring seat.
10. Install lower pivot ball, thrust bearing and nut on rod and rotate nut until coil spring is compressed enough to be free in the seat.
11. Remove lower control arm pivot bolts. Move control arm rearward and remove coil spring.
12. Reverse procedure to install.

MANUAL STEERING GEAR, REPLACE

1. Remove two flex coupling flange nuts.

NOTE: On 1977–84 models, remove coupling shield.

2. Hoist and support car with stands under outer ends of lower control arms.
3. Remove nut and use a puller to remove pitman arm.
4. Remove gear-to frame bolts.
5. Position steering linkage out of the way and withdraw gear assembly from under car.
6. Reverse procedure to install unit.

POWER STEERING GEAR, REPLACE

1. Remove coupling flange hub bolt.

NOTE: On 1977–84 models, remove coupling shield.

2. Disconnect hoses from gear and cap gear and hose fittings.
3. Remove pitman arm nut and, using a suitable puller, remove pitman arm.
4. Remove gear-to-frame bolts. Permit lower shaft to slide free of coupling flange, then remove gear with hoses attached.

POWER STEERING PUMP, REPLACE

To replace the power steering pump, loosen pump adjusting bolts and position pump so that drive belt can be removed from pump pulley. Disconnect hydraulic lines from pump and plug all lines and openings to prevent entry of dirt. Remove bolts securing pump or pump and bracket to engine and remove pump from vehicle. It may be necessary, depending on engine and vehicle model, to remove other accessories and components from front of engine to facilitate steering pump removal.

PONTIAC
(Exc. Astre, Fiero, Sunbird, 1000 & Front Wheel Drive)

INDEX OF SERVICE OPERATIONS

NOTE: Refer to the front of this manual for vehicle manufacturer's special service tool suppliers.

SERIAL NUMBER LOCATION

1977–84: On plate fastened to upper left instrument panel area, visible through windshield.

On 1977–80, the 5th digit represents engine identification code. On 1981–84 the 8th digit represents engine identification code.

ENGINE IDENTIFICATION

Buick built engines have the distributor located at the front of the engine. On 1977 V6-231 engines, the engine identification code is located on a machined pad on the right side of block near the head to block parting line. On 1978–82 V6-231 engines, the engine identification code is located on the front of the left rocker arm cover. On 1983–84 V6-231 engines, the engine identification code is located on the left side engine to transmission mounting flange below the cylinder head. On 1982 V6-252 engines, the engine identification code is located on the left rear engine block. On V8-350 engines, the engine identification code is located on the front of the left rocker arm cover.

Chevrolet built engines have the distributor located at the rear of the engine, with clockwise rotor rotation. On V6-173 and 229, V8-305 and V8-350 engines, the engine identification code is located on a machined surface on the front of the block below the right cylinder head.

Oldsmobile built engines have the distributor located at the rear of the engine with counter clockwise rotor rotation and right side mounted fuel pump. On 1981 V8-307 engine, the engine identification code is located on the right side valve cover. On 1977 V8-350 and V8-403 engines, the engine identification code is located on the oil filler tube. On 1978–80 V8-350 and 1978–79 V8-403 engines, the engine identification code is located on the front of the left rocker arm cover. On 1980–82 V8-350 diesel engines, the engine identification code is located on the right side valve cover. On 1983–84 V8-350 diesel engines, the engine identification code is located on the left front of the engine below the cylinder head.

Pontiac built V8 engines have the distributor located at the rear of the engine with counter clockwise rotor rotation and left side mounted fuel pump. On 1977–78 4-151 engines, the engine identification code is located on the distributor mounting pad. On 1982–84 4-151 engines, the engine identification code is located on the left side engine to transmission mounting flange above the starter. On 1980–81 V8-265 engines, the engine identification code is located on the front of the left and right hand valve covers. On V8-301, V8-350 and V8-400 engines, the engine identification code is located on a machined surface on the front of the engine block below the right cylinder head.

ENGINE CODES

1977

CODE	TRANS.	V.I.N. Code (9)	ENGINE
WF	(7)	V	4-151(1)
WH	(7)	V	4-151(1)
YR	(6)	V	4-151(1)
YS	(6)(11)	V	4-151(1)
SG	(4)(11)	C	V6-231(1)(13)
SI	(6)(11)	C	V6-231(1)(13)
SJ	(6)(11)	C	V6-231(1)(13)
SK	(6)(11)	C	V6-231(1)(13)
SL	(6)(11)	C	V6-231(1)(13)
SM	(6)(11)	C	V6-231(1)(13)
SN	(6)(11)	C	V6-231(1)(13)
SU	(4)(11)	C	V6-231(1)(13)
RC,RD	(17)	A	V6-231
HK	(6)	Y	V8-301(1)
WB	(5)	Y	V8-301(1)
YH	(6)	Y	V8-301(1)
YW	(6)	Y	V8-301(1)
YX	(6)	Y	V8-301(1)
CPR	(6)	U	V8-305(1)
CRA	(6)	U	V8-305(1)(14)
CKR	(6)	L	V8-350(2)(14)
CKM	(6)	L	V8-350(2)(14)
Q2	(6)	R	V8-350(2)(12)
Q3	(6)	R	V8-350(2)(12)
Q6	(6)	K	V8-350(2)(12)
Q7	(6)	K	V8-350(2)(12)
Q8	(6)	K	V8-350(2)(12)
Q9	(6)	R	V8-350(2)(12)
QP	(6)	R	V8-350(2)(12)
QQ	(6)	K	V8-350(2)(12)
TK	(6)	R	V8-350(2)(12)
TL	(6)	R	V8-350(2)(12)
TN	(6)	R	V8-350(2)(12)
TO	(6)	R	V8-350(2)(12)
TX	(6)	R	V8-350(2)(12)
TY	(6)	R	V8-350(2)
Y9	(6)	P	V8-350(2)
YA	(6)	P	V8-350(2)
YB	(6)	P	V8-350(2)
WA	(6)	Z	V8-400(2)
XA	(6)	Z	V8-400(2)
Y4	(6)	Z	V8-400(2)
Y6	(6)	Z	V8-400(2)
Y7	(6)	Z	V8-400(2)
YC	(6)	Z	V8-400(2)
YD	(6)	Z	V8-400(2)
YU	(6)	Z	V8-400(2)
U2	(6)	K	V8-403(2)(12)
U3	(6)	K	V8-403(2)(12)
UA	(6)	K	V8-403(2)(12)
UB	(6)	K	V8-403(2)(12)

1977—Cont'd

CODE	TRANS.	V.I.N. Code (9)	ENGINE
VA	(6)	K	V8-403(2)(12)
VB	(6)	K	V8-403(2)(12)
VJ	(6)	K	V8-403(2)(12)
VK	(6)	K	V8-403(2)(12)

1978

CODE	TRANS.	V.I.N. Code (9)	ENGINE
YB,YC	(6)	V	4-151(1)
EA	(6)	A	V6-231(1)(13)
EC,EE,EI	(6)	A	V6-231(1)(13)
EJ,EK,EL	(6)	A	V6-231(1)(13)
OE,OH,OK,OR	(6)	A	V6-231(1)(13)
XA,XB,XC	(6)	Y	V8-301(1)
XD,XF	(6)	Y	V8-301(1)
XH,XU,XW	(6)	W	V8-301(2)
CPF	(6)	H	V8-305(2)(14)
CPH,CPZ,CRU	(6)	U	V8-305(1)(14)
CRY,CRZ,CJJ	(6)	U	V8-305(1)(14)
CTH	(4)	U	V8-305(1)(14)
CTK,CTM,CTS	(6)	U	V8-305(1)(14)
CTT,CTU,CTW	(6)	U	V8-305(1)(14)
CTX,CTY,CTZ	(6)	U	V8-305(1)(14)
MA,MB	(6)	X	V8-350(2)(13)
TO,TP,TQ	(6)	R	V8-350(2)(12)
TS,Q2,Q3	(6)	R	V8-350(2)(12)
CHJ,CHL,CMC	(6)	L	V8-350(2)(14)
CHR	(4)	L	V8-350(2)(14)
WC	(4)	Z	V8-400(2)
XJ,XK	(6)	Z	V8-400(2)
X7,X9	(6)	Z	V8-400(2)
Y,YA,YH	(6)	Z	V8-400(2)
YJ,YK	(6)	Z	V8-400(2)
U2,U3	(6)	K	V8-403(2)(12)
U5,U6	(6)	K	V8-403(2)(12)
VA,VB	(6)	K	V8-403(2)(12)
VD,VE	(6)	K	V8-403(2)(12)

1979

CODE	TRANS.	V.I.N. Code (9)	ENGINE
NA,NG	(4)	A	V6-231(1)(10)(13)
NB,NJ,NK	(6)	A	V6-231(1)(10)(13)
NC	(4)	A	V6-231(1)(8)(13)
NE	(6)	A	V6-231(1)(3)(13)
NH	(6)	A	V6-231(1)(8)(13)
NL,NM	(6)	A	V6-231(1)(10)(13)
RA	(6)	A	V6-231(1)(10)(13)
RB,RC,RX	(6)	A	V6-231(1)(10)(13)
RG,RW,RY	(6)	A	V6-231(1)(8)(13)
PWA,PWB	(4)	W	V8-301(1)(10)
PXF,PXH	(6)	Y	V8-301(1)(10)
PXL,PXN,PXS	(6)	Y	V8-301(1)(10)
PXP,PXR	(6)	Y	V8-301(1)(10)

1979—Cont'd

CODE	TRANS.	V.I.N. Code (9)	ENGINE
PXT,PXU,PXW	(6)	W	V8-301(2)(10)
PX4,PX6	(6)	W	V8-301(2)(10)
PX7,PX9	(6)	Y	V8-301(1)(10)
DND,DNK	(6)	G	V8-305(1)(8)(10)
DNJ,DTL	(6)	G	V8-305(1)(10)(14)
DNX,DNY	(6)	H	V8-305(2)(8)(14)
DTA	(6)	H	V8-305(2)(14)
DTK,DTM	(4)	G	V8-305(1)(10)(14)
SA,SC,SD	(6)	X	V8-350(2)(10)(13)
DNX,DRY	(6)	L	V8-350(2)(3)(14)
DRJ	(6)	L	V8-350(2)(3)(14)
U9	(6)	R	V8-350(2)(3)(12)
VK	(6)	R	V8-350(2)(8)(14)
PWH	(4)	Z	V8-400(2)(10)
Q3	(6)	K	V8-403(2)(10)(12)
TB,TD,TE	(6)	K	V8-403(2)(8)(12)
QB	(6)	K	V8-403(2)(3)(12)
QE,QL,QJ	(6)	K	V8-403(2)(10)(12)

1980

CODE	TRANS.	V.I.N. Code (9)	ENGINE
CLA	(4)	K	V6-229(10)(14)
CLB,CLC	(6)	K	V6-229(10)(14)
EA,EX,OJ	(4)	A	V6-231(10)(13)
EB,EC,EO,EP	(6)	A	V6-231(10)(13)
EZ,OA,OK,OL	(6)	A	V6-231(10)(13)
EF,EG,ES,ET	(6)	A	V6-231(8)(13)
OB,OC,OM,ON	(6)	A	V6-231(10)(13)
XH,XR,X6	(6)	S	V8-265(10)
XT,XW,X3,X9	(6)	W	V8-301(10)
XN,YN,YR	(6)	W	V8-301(10)
YL	(6)	T	V8-301(10)
CEC,CEL,CEM	(6)	H	V8-305(8)(14)
ML,MV	(6)	X	V8-350(10)(13)
UAD,UAF	(6)	R	V8-350(8)(12)
VBN,VBT,VCD, VCP	(6)	N	V8-350(1)(16)

1981

CODE	TRANS.	V.I.N. Code (9)	ENGINE
NA,NZ	(4)	A	V6-231(10)(13)
NB,NL,RA	(6)	A	V6-231(10)(13)
NC,ND,RB	(6)	A	V6-231(8)(13)
RK,RL,RC,RD	(6)	A	V6-231(13)
AU,AW,AZ	(6)	S	V8-265
BA,DB,DC	(6)	S	V8-265
DH,DJ	(6)	S	V8-265
WAV	(6)	S	V8-265
WDB	(6)	S	V8-265(10)
WDH	(6)	S	V8-265(10)
WBD,WBJ	(6)	W	V8-301
WBO	(6)	T	V8-301(15)
DHA,DHB,DHC	(5)(6)	H	V8-305(14)

Continued

ENGINE CODES—Continued

1981—Cont'd

CODE	TRANS.	V.I.N. Code ⑨	ENGINE
DHD,DHF,DHH	⑤⑥	H	V8-305⑭
DHJ,DHK,DHU	⑤⑥	H	V8-305⑭
DHZ	④	H	V8-305⑩⑭
DHZ	⑥	H	V8-305⑧⑭
DKB,D6A,D6B	⑤⑥	H	V8-305⑭
D6C,D6D	⑤⑥	H	V8-305⑭
TKA,TKB,TKC	⑥	Y	V8-307⑫
TKJ,TKM	⑥	Y	V8-307⑩⑫
TKL,TKR	⑥	Y	V8-307⑫
TKP,TKT,TKU	⑥	Y	V8-307⑫
TKX,TKY,TKZ	⑥	Y	V8-307⑫
TLA,TLB,TLD	⑥	Y	V8-307⑫
TLF,TLH,TLJ	⑥	Y	V8-307⑫
TLK,TLL,TLM,TLN	⑥	Y	V8-307⑫
VKB,VKC,VKH	⑥	N	V8-350⑫⑯
VKJ,VKN,VKR	⑥	N	V8-350⑫⑯
VKU,VKY,VLA	⑥	N	V8-350⑫⑯
VLC,VLD,VLK	⑥	N	V8-350⑫⑯
VLL,VLN,VLP	⑥	N	V8-350⑫⑯
VL8,VLY,VMJ	⑥	N	V8-350⑫⑯
VMT,VMX,VMY	⑥	N	V8-350⑫⑯
VNA,VNB,VNC	⑥	N	V8-350⑫⑯
VND,VNE	⑥	N	V8-350⑫⑯

1982

CODE	TRANS.	V.I.N. Code ⑨	ENGINE
X3A,X3C,X3F	④	2	4-151
X3H,X5A,X5F,X5H	⑥	2	4-151
CBT,CBU,CBW	⑤⑥	1	V6-173⑭
CBX,CB2,CJB	⑥	1	V6-173⑭
C7A,C7B,C7C,C7D	⑥	1	V6-173⑭
MA,MG,MC	⑥	A	V6-231⑬
MK,ML,MM	⑥	A	V6-231⑬
FA,FB,FC	⑥	4	V6-252⑬
FD,FE,FF	⑥	4	V6-252⑬
FG,FH,FJ,FK	⑥	4	V6-252⑬
CFA,CFB,CFC,CFD	⑥	H	V8-305⑭
CFF,CFH,CFR,C2R	⑥	H	V8-305⑭
C2S,C2T,C2U,C2W	⑥	H	V8-305⑭
CFT,CFW,CFY,			
CF2,CRA	⑥	H	V8-305⑭
CEJ,CFK,CFM,CFN	⑥	7	V8-305⑭
VAB,VAC,VAD,VAK	⑥	N	V8-350⑫⑯
VAL,VAM,VAN,VAP	⑥	N	V8-350⑫⑯
VAS,VAU,VAW,			
VAX	⑥	N	V8-350⑫⑯
VAY,VAZ,VBA,VBB	⑥	N	V8-350⑫⑯
VBC,VBP,VBU,VBW	⑥	N	V8-350⑫⑯

1983

CODE	TRANS.	V.I.N. Code ⑨	ENGINE
YMM,YMT		2	4-151
DAA,DAB,DAC,DAD		2	4-151
DAF,DAJ,DAK,D6A		2	4-151
D6B,D6C,D6D		1	V6-173⑭
—		L	V6-173 H.O.⑭
DBA,DBB,DBC,DBD		9	V6-229⑭
DBF,DBH		9	V6-229⑭
ND,NG,NH,NJ,NL		A	V6-231⑬
DDB,DDC,DDD,DDF		H	V8-305⑭
DDH,DDJ,DDK,DDM		H	V8-305⑭
DDN,DDS,DDW,DDY		H	V8-305⑭
DDZ,DGN,DRA,DSC		H	V8-305⑭
DUK,DVA,D5B,D5C		H	V8-305⑭
D5D,D5F,D5H,D5N		H	V8-305⑭
D5R		H	V8-305⑭
DDA,DUA		S	V8-305 TBI⑭
VKB,VKC,VKD,VKK		N	V8-350⑫⑯
VKL,VKR,VKS,VKT		N	V8-350⑫⑯
VKZ,VLA,VLB,VLP		N	V8-350⑫⑯
VLS,VLT,VLW,VMR		N	V8-350⑫⑯
VMS,VMT,VMU,VMW		N	V8-350⑫⑯
VMX,VMY,VMZ,VNA		N	V8-350⑫⑯
VNB,VNC,VND,VNF		N	V8-350⑫⑯
VNH,VNJ		N	V8-350⑫⑯

①—Two barrel carburetor.
②—Four barrel carburetor.
③—Hi Altitude.
④—Manual trans.
⑤—Four speed manual trans.
⑥—Automatic trans.
⑦—Five speed manual trans.
⑧—California.
⑨—On 1977–80 vehicles, the fifth digit in the V.I.N. denotes engine code. On 1981–84 vehicles, the eighth digit in the V.I.N. denotes engine code.
⑩—Exc. California.
⑪—Except even fire engine.
⑫—See Oldsmobile chapter for service procedures.
⑬—See Buick chapter for service procedures.
⑭—See Chevrolet chapter for service procedures.
⑮—Turbocharged engine.
⑯—Diesel.
⑰—Even fire engine.

GRILLE IDENTIFICATION

1977 Ventura

1977 LeMans, Sports Cpe, & GT

1977 Grand LeMans

1977 Grand Prix

1977–78 Firebird Trans Am

1977–78 Formula Firebird

1977–79 Phoenix

1978 Bonneville & Grand Safari

1978 Catalina

1977–78 Firebird, Esprit

1977 Catalina

1977 Bonneville & Grand Safari
Continued

GRILLE IDENTIFICATION—Continued

1978–79 Grand Am

1978 Grand LeMans, LeMans Safari

1978 Grand Prix

1979 Grand LeMans, Grand LeMans Safari & Grand Am 4 Dr.

1979 Bonneville Brougham & Safari

1979 Catalina

1979 Grand Prix

1978–81 Firebird Formula

1979–81 Firebird Trans Am

1980 Grand Am

1980 Grand LeMans

1980 Grand Prix

1980 Bonneville & Catalina

1981 Bonneville

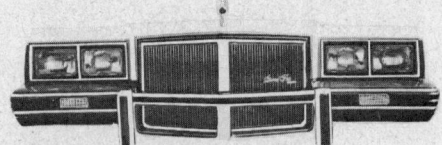

1981 LeMans

1981 Grand Prix

1982 Bonneville

1982 Grand Prix

1982–83 Firebird; 1984 Firebird Exc. Trans. Am

1983–84 Bonneville

1983–84 Grand Prix

1983–84 Pontiac Parisienne

GENERAL ENGINE SPECIFICATIONS

Year	Engine CID①/Liter	Engine V.I.N. Code②	Carburetor	Bore and Stroke	Compression Ratio	Net H.P. @ R.P.M.③	Maximum Torque Ft. Lbs. @ R.P.M.	Normal Oil Pressure Pounds
1977	4-151, 2.5L	V	5210C, 2 Bbl.⑨	4.00 × 3.00	8.3	88 @ 4400	128 @ 2400	30—45
	V6-231, 3.8L⑦	C	2GC, 2 Bbl.⑤	3.80 × 3.40	8.0	105 @ 3200	185 @ 2000	37
	V6-231, 3.8L⑦	A	2GE, 2 Bbl.⑤	3.80 × 3.40	8.0	105 @ 3200	185 @ 2000	37
	V8-301, 4.9L	Y	M2MC, 2 Bbl.⑤	4.00 × 3.00	8.2	135 @ 4000	⑩	38—42
	V8-305, 5.0L④	U	2GC, 2 Bbl.⑤	3.736 × 3.48	8.5	145 @ 3800	245 @ 2400	32—40
	V8-350, 5.7L④	L	M4MC, 4 Bbl.⑤	4.00 × 3.48	8.5	170 @ 3800	270 @ 2400	32—40
	V8-350, 5.7L	P	M4MC, 4 Bbl.⑤	3.88 × 3.75	7.6	170 @ 4000	280 @ 1800	55—60
	V8-350, 5.7L⑥	R	M4MC, 4 Bbl.⑤	4.057 × 3.385	8	170 @ 3800	275 @ 2000	37
	V8-400, 6.6L	Z	M4MC, 4 Bbl.⑤	4.12 × 3.75	7.6	180 @ 3600	325 @ 1600	55—60
	V8-400, 6.6L⑪	Z	M4MC, 4 Bbl.⑤	4.12 × 3.75	8.0	200 @ 3600	⑫	55—60
	V8-403, 6.6L⑥	K	M4MC, 4 Bbl.⑤	4.351 × 3.385	8.0	185 @ 3600	320 @ 2200	30—45
1978	4-151, 2.5L	V	5210C, 2 Bbl.⑨	4.00 × 3.00	8.3	85 @ 4400	123 @ 2800	36—41
	V6-231, 3.8L⑦	A	2GC, 2 Bbl.⑤	3.80 × 3.40	8.0	105 @ 3400	185 @ 2000	37
	V8-301, 5.0L	Y	M2MC, 2 Bbl.⑤	4.00 × 3.00	8.2	140 @ 3600	235 @ 2000	35—40
	V8-301, 5.0L	W	M4MC, 4 Bbl.⑤	4.00 × 3.00	8.2	150 @ 4000	240 @ 2000	35—40
	V8-305, 5.0L④⑬	U	2GC, 2 Bbl.⑤	3.736 × 3.48	8.4	135 @ 3800	240 @ 2000	32—40
	V8-305, 5.0L④⑭	H	M4MC, 4 Bbl.⑤	3.736 × 3.48	8.4	145 @ 3800	245 @ 2400	32—40
	V8-350, 5.7L⑦	X	M4MC, 4 Bbl.⑤	3.80 × 3.85	8.0	155 @ 3400	280 @ 1800	—
	V8-350, 5.7L④	L	M4MC, 4 Bbl.⑤	4.00 × 3.48	8.2	160 @ 3800	260 @ 2400	32—40
	V8-350, 5.7L⑥	R	M4MC, 4 Bbl.⑤	4.057 × 3.385	7.9	170 @ 3800	275 @ 2000	30—45
	V8-350, 5.7L④	L	M4MC, 4 Bbl.⑤	4.00 × 3.48	8.2	170 @ 3800	270 @ 2400	32—40
	V8-400, 6.6L	Z	M4MC, 4 Bbl.⑤	4.12 × 3.75	7.7	180 @ 3600	325 @ 1600	35—40
	V8-400, 6.6L⑪	Z	M4MC, 4 Bbl.⑤	4.12 × 3.75	8.1	220 @ 4000	320 @ 2800	55—60
	V8-403, 6.6L⑥	K	M4MC, 4 Bbl.⑤	4.351 × 3.385	7.9	185 @ 3600	320 @ 2000	30—45
1979	V6-231, 3.8L⑦	A	M2ME, 2 Bbl.⑤	3.80 × 3.40	8.0	115 @ 3800	185 @ 2000	37
	V6-231, 3.8L⑦	A	M2ME, 2 Bbl.⑤	3.80 × 3.40	8.0	115 @ 3800	190 @ 2000	37
	V6-231, 3.8L⑦	A	M2ME, 2 Bbl.⑤	3.80 × 3.40	8.0	135 @ 3800	190 @ 2000	37
	V8-301, 4.9L	Y	M2MC, 2 Bbl.⑤	4.00 × 3.00	8.1	130 @ 3200	245 @ 2000	35—40
	V8-301, 4.9L	Y	M2MC, 2 Bbl.⑤	4.00 × 3.00	8.1	135 @ 3800	240 @ 1600	35—40
	V8-301, 4.9L	W	M4MC, 4 Bbl.⑤	4.00 × 3.00	8.1	150 @ 4000	⑮	35—40
	V8-305, 5.0L④	G	M2MC, 2 Bbl.⑤	3.736 × 3.48	8.4	125 @ 3200	245 @ 2000	32—40
	V8-305, 5.0L④	H	M4MC, 4 Bbl.⑤	3.736 × 3.48	8.4	130 @ 3200	245 @ 2000	32—40
	V8-305, 5.0L④	H	M4MC, 4 Bbl.⑤	3.736 × 3.48	8.4	155 @ 4000	225 @ 2400	32—40
	V8-350, 5.7L⑦	X	M4MC, 4 Bbl.⑤	3.80 × 3.85	8.0	155 @ 3400	280 @ 1800	34
	V8-350, 5.7L⑥	R	M4MC, 4 Bbl.⑤	4.057 × 3.385	7.9	160 @ 3600	270 @ 2000	30—45
	V8-350, 5.7L④	L	M4MC, 4 Bbl.⑤	4.00 × 3.48	8.2	165 @ 3800	260 @ 2400	32—40
	V8-400, 6.6L	Z	M4MC, 4 Bbl.⑤	4.12 × 3.75	8.1	220 @ 4000	320 @ 2800	35—40
	V8-403, 6.6L⑥	K	M4MC, 4 Bbl.⑤	4.351 × 3.385	7.9	175 @ 3600	310 @ 2000	30—45
	V8-403, 6.6L⑥	K	M4MC, 4 Bbl.⑤	4.351 × 3.385	7.9	185 @ 3600	315 @ 2000	30—45
1980	V6-229, 3.8L④	K	M2ME, 2 Bbl.⑤	3.376 × 3.48	8.6	115 @ 4000	175 @ 2000	45
	V6-231, 3.8L⑦	A	M2ME, 2 Bbl.⑤	3.80 × 3.40	8.0	115 @ 3800	188 @ 2000	37
	V8-265, 4.3L	S	M2ME, 2 Bbl.⑤	3.75 × 3.00	8.3	120 @ 3600	210 @ 1600	35—40
	V8-301, 4.9L	W	M4ME, 4 Bbl.⑤	4.00 × 3.00	8.2	150 @ 4000	240 @ 2000	35—40
	V8-301, 4.9L⑯	W	M4ME, 4 Bbl.⑤	4.00 × 3.00	8.2	170 @ 4400	240 @ 2200	55—60
	V8-301, 4.9L⑭	T	M4ME, 4 Bbl.⑤	4.00 × 3.00	7.5	205 @ 4000	310 @ 2800	55—60
	V8-305, 5.0L④	H	E4ME, 4 Bbl.⑤	3.736 × 3.48	8.4	150 @ 3800	230 @ 2400	45
	V8-350, 5.7L⑦	X	M4MC, 4 Bbl.⑤	3.80 × 3.85	—	—	—	37
	V8-350, 5.7L⑥	R	E4MC, 4 Bbl.⑤	4.057 × 3.385	—	160 @ 3600	270 @ 2000	30—45
	V8-350, 5.7L⑥⑧	N	Fuel Injection	4.057 × 3.385	22.5	105 @ 3200	205 @ 1600	30—45
1981	V6-231, 3.8L⑥	A	E2ME, 2 Bbl.⑤	4.00 × 3.00	8.0	110 @ 3800	190 @ 1600	35—40
	V8-265, 4.3L	S	E2ME, 2 Bbl.⑤	3.75 × 3.00	8.3	120 @ 4000	205 @ 2000	35—40
	V8-301, 4.9L⑯	W	E4ME, 4 Bbl.⑤	4.00 × 3.00	8.1	135 @ 3600	235 @ 3600	35—40
	V8-301, 4.9L⑭	T	E4ME, 4 Bbl.⑤	4.00 × 3.00	7.5	200 @ 4000	340 @ 2000	55—60

Continued

GENERAL ENGINE SPECIFICATIONS—Continued

Year	Engine CID①/Liter	V.I.N. Code②	Carburetor	Bore and Stroke	Compression Ratio	Net H.P. @ R.P.M.③	Maximum Torque Ft. Lbs. @ R.P.M.	Normal Oil Pressure Pounds
1981	V8-305, 5.0L④	H	E4ME, 4 Bbl.⑤	3.736 × 3.48	8.6	145 @ 3800	240 @ 2400	30—45
	V8-307, 5.0L⑥	Y	E4ME, 4 Bbl.⑤	3.80 × 3.385	8.5	145 @ 3800	240 @ 2000	30—45
	V8-350, 5.7L⑥⑧	N	Fuel Injection	4.057 × 3.385	22.5	105 @ 3200	205 @ 1600	37
1982	4-151, 2.5L	2	T.B.I.	4.00 × 3.00	8.2	90 @ 4000	132 @ 2800	36—41
	V6-173, 2.8L④	1	E2SE, 2 Bbl.⑤	3.50 × 3.00	8.5	102 @ 4800	142 @ 2400	50—65
	V6-231, 3.8L⑦	A	E2ME, 2 Bbl.⑤	3.80 × 3.40	8.0	110 @ 3800	190 @ 1600	37
	V6-252, 4.1L⑦	4	E4ME, 4 Bbl.⑤	3.965 × 3.40	8.0	125 @ 3800	210 @ 2000	37
	V8-305, 5.0L④	H	E4ME, 4 Bbl.⑤	3.736 × 3.48	8.6	145 @ 4000	240 @ 2000	50—65
	V8-305, 5.0L④	7	T.B.I.	3.736 × 3.48	9.5	165 @ 4200	240 @ 2400	50—65
	V8-350, 5.7L⑥⑧	N	Fuel Injection	4.057 × 3.385	22.5	105 @ 3200	200 @ 1600	35
1983	4-151, 2.5L	2	T.B.I.	4.00 × 3.00	8.2	92 @ 4000	134 @ 2800	36—41
	V6-173, 2.8L④	1	E2SE, 2 Bbl.⑤	3.50 × 3.00	8.5	107 @ 4800	145 @ 2100	50—65
	V6-173 H.O., 2.8L④	L	E2SE, 2 Bbl.⑤	3.50 × 3.00	8.9	135 @ 5400	145 @ 2400	50—65
	V6-229, 3.8L④	9	E2ME, 2 Bbl.⑤	3.736 × 3.48	8:6	110 @ 4200	170 @ 2000	50—65
	V6-231, 3.8L⑦	A	E2ME, 2 Bbl.⑤	3.80 × 3.40	8.0	110 @ 3800	190 @ 1600	37
	V8-305, 5.0L④	H	E4ME, 4 Bbl.⑤	3.736 × 3.48	8.6	150 @ 4000	240 @ 2400	50—65
	V8-305, 5.0L④	S	T.B.I.	3.736 × 3.48	9.5	175 @ 4200	250 @ 2800	50—65
	V8-305 H.O., 5.0L④	G	E4ME, 4 Bbl.⑤	3.736 × 3.48	9.5	190 @ 4800	240 @ 3200	50—65
	V8-350, 5.7L⑥⑧	N	Fuel Injection	4.057 × 3.385	22.5	105 @ 3200	200 @ 1600	30—45
1984	4-151, 2.5L	2	T.B.I.	4.00 × 3.00	9.0	92 @ 4400	132 @ 2800	36—41
	V6-173, 2.8L④	1	E2SE, 2 Bbl.⑤	3.50 × 3.00	8.5	107 @ 4800	145 @ 2100	50—65
	V6-173 H.O., 2.8L④	L	E2SE, 2 Bbl.⑤	3.50 × 3.00	8.9	125 @ 5400	145 @ 2400	50—65
	V6-231, 3.8L⑦	A	E2ME, 2 Bbl.⑤	3.80 × 3.40	8.0	110 @ 3800	190 @ 1600	37
	V8-305, 5.0L④	H	E4ME, 4 Bbl.⑤	3.736 × 3.48	8.6	150 @ 4000	240 @ 2400	50—65
	V8-305, H.O., 5.0L④	G	E4ME, 4 Bbl.⑤	3.736 × 3.48	9.5	190 @ 4800	240 @ 3200	50—65
	V8-350, 5.7L⑥⑧	N	Fuel Injection	4.057 × 3.385	22.5	105 @ 3200	200 @ 1600	30—45

①—CID—Cubic Inch displacement.
②—VIN Code—On 1977-80 vehicles the fifth digit in the VIN denotes engine code. On 1981-84 vehicles the eighth digit in the VIN denotes engine code.
③—Ratings are net—as installed in vehicle.
④—See Chevrolet chapter for service procedures on this engine.
⑤—Rochester.
⑥—See Oldsmobile chapter for service procedures on this engine.
⑦—See Buick chapter for service procedures on this engine.
⑧—Diesel engine.
⑨—Holley.
⑩—Manual trans., 235 @ 2400. Auto. trans., 245 @ 2200.
⑪—High performance Trans Am engine.
⑫—Manual trans., 325 @ 2400; Auto. trans., 325 @ 2200.
⑬—High altitude.
⑭—Turbocharged engine.
⑮—Manual trans., 240 @ 2400; Auto. trans., 240 @ 2200.
⑯—E/C (electronic engine control).

TUNE UP SPECIFICATIONS

The following specifications are published from the latest information available. This data should be used only in the absence of a decal affixed in the engine compartment.

★ When using a timing light, disconnect vacuum hose or tube at distributor and plug opening in tube or hose so idle speed will not be affected.

● When checking compression, lowest cylinder must be within 70% of the highest.

▲ Before removing wires from distributor cap, determine location of the No. 1 wire in cap, as distributor position may have been altered from that shown at the end of this chart.

Spark plug types shown in this chart are recommendations of the original vehicle manufacturer and not MOTOR.

Check local sources for other spark plug manufacturers listings.

Year & Engine/V.I.N.	Spark Plug Type	Gap	Ignition Timing BTDC①★ Firing Order Fig.▲	Man. Trans.	Auto. Trans.	Mark Fig.	Curb Idle Speed② Man. Trans.	Auto. Trans.	Fast Idle Speed Man. Trans.	Auto. Trans.	Fuel Pump Pressure
1977											
4-151/V	R44TSX	.060	F		14°	B	⑱	⑲	2200⑤	2400⑤	4—5½
V6-231/C⑳	㉑	㉑	G	12°	12°	C㉒	600/800	600D㉓	—		4¼—5¾

Continued

TUNE UP SPECIFICATIONS—Continued

The following specifications are published from the latest information available. This data should be used only in the absence of a decal affixed in the engine compartment.

★ When using a timing light, disconnect vacuum hose or tube at distributor and plug opening in tube or hose so idle speed will not be affected.

● When checking compression, lowest cylinder must be within 70% of the highest.

▲ Before removing wires from distributor cap, determine location of the No. 1 wire in cap, as distributor position may have been altered from that shown at the end of this chart.

☞ Spark plug types shown in this chart are recommendations of the original vehicle manufacturer and not MOTOR.

Check local sources for other spark plug manufacturers listings.

Year & Engine/V.I.N.	Spark Plug Type ☞	Gap	Firing Order Fig. ▲	Ignition Timing BTDC① ★ Man. Trans.	Auto. Trans.	Mark Fig.	Curb Idle Speed② Man. Trans.	Auto. Trans.	Fast Idle Speed Man. Trans.	Auto. Trans.	Fuel Pump Pressure
1977—Continued											
V6-231/A㉔	R46TSX	.060	D	—	15°	E㉒	—	600/670D㉕	—	—	4¼–5¾
V8-301/Y	R46TSX	.060	O	16°	12°	A	750/850	550/650D	1750	1750	7–8½
V8-305/U	R45TS	.045	P	—	8°	R	—	500/650D	—	—	7½–9
V8-350/P㉖	R45TSX	.060	P	—	16°	H	—	575/650D	—	1800	7½–9
V8-350/L㉗	R45TS	.045	P	—	8°	H	—	㉘	—	1600	7½–9
V8-350/R㉙	R46SZ	.060	M	—	㉚	J	—	㉛	—	1000	5½–6½
V8-400/Z	R45TSX	.060	O	18°	㉜	I	775	㉝	1800	1800	7–8½
V8-403/K Exc. Calif. & High Alt.	R46SZ	.060	M	—	22°⑦	J	—	550/650D	—	900	5½–6½
V8-403/K Calif. & High Alt.	R46SZ	.060	M	—	20°⑦	J	—	㉞	—	1000	5½–6½
1978											
4-151/V	R43TSX	.060	F	—	14°⑰	B	—	㊱	—	⑤ ㊲	4½–5
V6-231/A	R46TSX	.060	D	15°	15°	E㉒	800	㊳	—	—	4½–5.9
V8-301/Y 2 Barrel	R46TSX	.060	O	—	12°	A	—	550/650D	—	2200	7–8½
V8-301/W 4 Barrel	R45TSX	.060	O	—	12°	A	—	550/650D	—	2300	7–8½
V8-305/U Exc. Calif. & High Alt.	R45TS	.045	P	4°	4°	R	600/700	500/600D	1600	1600	7½–9
V8-305/U Calif.	R45TS	.045	P	—	6°	R	—	500/600D	—	1600	7½–9
V8-305/U High Alt.	R45TS	.045	P	—	8°	R	—	600/700D	—	1600	7½–9
V8-350/L㉗	R45TS	.045	P	6°	8°	H	700	⑩	1300	1600	7½–9
V8-350/R㉙	R46SZ	.060	M	—	20°⑦	J	—	550/650D	—	⑪	5½–6½
V8-350/X⑬	R46TSX	.060	N	—	15°	E㉒	—	550D	—	1500	⑭
V8-400/Z	R45TSX	.060	O	16°	㉜	I	775	㉝	1800	1800	7–8½
V8-403/K	R46SZ	.060	M	—	20°⑦	J	—	㉛	—	1000	5½–6½
1979											
V6-231/A	R46TSX	.060	D	15°	15°	E㉒	600/800	㉟	2200	2200	4½–5.9
V8-301/Y 2 Barrel	R46TSX	.060	O	—	12°	A	—	500/650D	—	2000	7–8½
V8-301/W 4 Barrel	R45TSX	.060	O	14°	12°	A	700/800	500/650D	2000	2200	7–8½
V8-305/G 2 Barrel Exc. Calif.	R45TS	.045	P	4°	4°	R	600/700	500/600D	1300	1600	7½–9
V8-305/G 2 Barrel Calif.	R45TS	.045	P	—	4°	R	—	600/650D	—	1950	7½–9
V8-305/H 4 Barrel	R45TS	.045	P	—	4°	R	—	500/600D	—	1600	7½–9
V8-350/L㉗	R45TS	.045	P	—	8°	R	—	⑩	—	1600	7½–9
V8-350/R㉙	R46SZ	.060	M	—	20°⑦	J	—	500/600D	—	1000	5½–6½
V8-350/X⑬	R46TSX	.060	N	—	15°	E㉒	—	550D	—	1550	⑭
V8-400/Z	R45TSX	.060	O	18°	—	I	775	—	1800	—	7–8½
V8-403/K	R46SZ	.060	M	—	20°⑦	J	—	500/600D	—	1000	5½–6½
1980											
V6-229/K	R45TS	.045	Q	10°	10°	R	700/750	600/675D	1750	1750	4½–6
V6-231/A Exc. Calif.	R45TS	.040	D	15°	15°	E㉒	600/800	500/670D	2200	2000	3 Min.

TUNE UP SPECIFICATIONS—Continued

The following specifications are published from the latest information available. This
data should be used only in the absence of a decal affixed in the engine compartment.

★ When using a timing light, disconnect vacuum hose or tube at distributor and plug opening in tube or hose so idle speed will not be affected.

● When checking compression, lowest cylinder must be within 70% of the highest.

▲ Before removing wires from distributor cap, determine location of the No. 1 wire in cap, as distributor position may have been altered from that shown at the end of this chart.

Spark plug types shown in this chart are recommendations of the original vehicle manufacturer and not MOTOR.

Check local sources for other spark plug manufacturers listings.

Year & Engine/V.I.N.	Spark Plug		Ignition Timing BTDC (1) ★				Curb Idle Speed (2)		Fast Idle Speed		Fuel Pump Pressure
	Type	Gap	Firing Order Fig. ▲	Man. Trans.	Auto. Trans.	Mark Fig.	Man. Trans.	Auto. Trans.	Man. Trans.	Auto. Trans.	
1980—Continued											
V6-231/A Calif.	R45TSX	.060	D	—	15°	E(22)	—	550/620D	—	2200	3 Min.
V8-265/S	R45TSX	.060	O	—	10°	A	—	550/650D	—	2200	7–8½
V8-301/W(12)	R45TSX	.060	O	—	12°	A	—	550/650D	—	2500	7–8½
V8-301/W(6)	R45TSX	.060	O	—	12°	A	—	550D	—	2500	7–8½
V8-301/T(9)	R45TSX	.060	O	—	8°	A	—	600/650D	—	2400	7–8½
V8-305/H	R45TS	.045	P	—	4°	(4)	—	550/650D	—	2200	7½–9
V8-350/X Exc. Calif.(13)	R45TSX	.060	N	—	15°	E(22)	—	550/670D	—	1850	3 Min.
V8-350/R Calif.(29)	R46SX	.080	M	—	18°(7)	J	—	550/650D	—	700	5½–6½
V8-350 Diesel/N	—	—	—	—	(3)(40)	—	—	575/750D	—	—	—
1981											
V6-231/A	R45TS8	.080	D	15°	15°(47)	E(22)	800N	(16)	2200	1800	3 Min.
V8-265/S	R45TSX	.060	O	—	12°(51)	A	—	450D	—	2000	7–8½
V8-301/W Exc. Turbo	R45TSX	.060	O	—	12°(51)	A	—	450D	—	2000	7–8½
V8-301 Turbo/T	R45TSX	.060	O	—	6°(51)	A	—	450D	—	2400	7–8½
V8-305/H	R45TS	.045	P	6°(47)	—	L	800N	—	2200	—	7½–9
V8-307/Y	R46SX	.080	M	—	15°(7)(47)	J	—	(16)	—	650D	5½–6½
V8-350 Diesel/N	—	—	—	—	(3)(41)	—	—	600D	—	750D	—
1982											
4-151 T.B.I./2	R44TSX	.060	K	8°(48)	8°(48)	S	(16)(42)	650D(16)	(16)	(16)	—
V6-173/1	R43CTS	.045	T	10°(47)	10°(47)	U	850/1100N	600/700D	2600	2500	6–7½
V6-231/A	R45TS8	.080	D	—	15°(47)	E(22)	—	500D	—	2000	4¼–5¾
V6-252/4	R45TS8	.080	D	—	15°(47)	E(22)	—	500D	—	—	4¼–5¾
V8-305/H	R45TS	.045	P	6°(47)	6°(47)	L	700/800N	500/600D	1800(49)	2200(49)	7½–9
V8-305 T.B.I./7	R45TS	.045	P	—	6°(50)	L	—	500D(39)	—	1000(39)	—
V8-350 Diesel/N(43)	—	—	—	—	(3)(44)	—	—	600D	—	750D	—
V8-350 Diesel/N(45)	—	—	—	—	(3)(46)	—	—	600D	—	750D	—
1983											
4-151 T.B.I./2	R44TSX	.060	K	—	8°(48)	S	—	(16)	—	(16)	—
V6-173/1	R43CTS	.045	T	10°(47)	10°(47)	U	775/1100N	600/750D	2500	2500	6–7½
V6-173 H.O./L	R42CTS	.045	T	10°(47)	10°(47)	U	800/1100N	725/850D	2600	2700	6–7½
V6-229/9	R45TS	.045	Q	—	TDC	R	—	(16)	—	(16)	4½–6
V6-231/A	R45TS8	.080	D	—	15°	E(22)	—	(16)	—	2200	4¼–5¾
V8-305/H	R45TS	.045	P	6°(47)	6°(47)	L	700/800N	500/600D	1800(49)	2200(49)	7½–9
V8-305 T.B.I./S	R45TS	.045	P	—	6°(50)	L	—	(39)	—	(39)	—
V8-305 H.O./G	R45TS	.045	P	—	—	L	700	500D	—	—	7½–9
V8-350 Diesel/N	—	—	—	—	(3)(8)	—	—	600D	—	750D	—
1984											
4-151/2	R44TSX	.060	K	—	—	S	(16)	(16)	(16)	(16)	—
V6-173/1	R43CTS	.045	T	—	—	U	800	600D	—	—	—
V6-173/L	R42CTS	.045	T	—	—	U	—	—	—	—	—

Continued

TUNE UP SPECIFICATIONS—Continued

The following specifications are published from the latest information available. This
data should be used only in the absence of a decal affixed in the engine compartment.

★ When using a timing light, disconnect vacuum hose or tube at distributor and plug opening in tube or hose so idle speed will not be affected.

● When checking compression, lowest cylinder must be within 70% of the highest.

▲ Before removing wires from distributor cap, determine location of the No. 1 wire in cap, as distributor position may have been altered from that shown at the end of this chart.

☞ Spark plug types shown in this chart are recommendations of the original vehicle manufacturer and not MOTOR.

Check local sources for other spark plug manufacturers listings.

Year & Engine/V.I.N.	Spark Plug		Firing Order Fig. ▲	Ignition Timing BTDC①★			Curb Idle Speed②		Fast Idle Speed		Fuel Pump Pressure
	Type ☞	Gap		Man. Trans.	Auto. Trans.	Mark Fig.	Man. Trans.	Auto. Trans.	Man. Trans.	Auto. Trans.	
1984—Continued											
V6-231/A	R45TS8	.080	D	—	—	E㉒	—	—	—	—	—
V8-305/H	R45TS	.045	P	—	—	L	700	500D	—	—	—
V8-305 H.O./G	R45TS	.045	P	—	—	L	700	500D	—	—	—
V8-350 Diesel/N	—	—	—	③⑧		—	—	600/750D	—	750D	—

①—BTDC—Before top dead center.
②—Idle speed on man. trans. vehicles is adjusted in Neutral & on auto. trans. equipped vehicles is adjusted in Drive unless otherwise specified. Where two idle speeds are listed, the higher speed is with the A/C or idle solenoid energized.
③—Using Diesel Timing Meter J-33075.
④—Early models, Fig. R; late models, Fig. L.
⑤—On high step of fast idle cam with A/C off.
⑥—E/C (electronic control) engine.
⑦—At 1100 RPM.
⑧—Set at 4° ATDC at 1250 RPM.
⑨—Turbocharged engine.
⑩—Except high altitude, 500/600D RPM; high altitude, 600/650D RPM.
⑪—Except Calif., 900 RPM; California, 1000 RPM.
⑫—Except E/C (electronic control) & turbocharged engines.
⑬—Distributor located at front of engine.
⑭—Less A/C, 5–6½ psi.; with A/C, 5.9–7.4 psi.
⑮—On Grand LeMans & LeMans models, set to 575D RPM.
⑯—Idle speed is controlled by the idle speed control (ICS) motor or the idle load compensator (ILC).
⑰—At 1000 RPM.
⑱—Less A/C, 500/1000 RPM; with A/C, 500/1200 RPM.
⑲—Less A/C, 500/650D RPM; with A/C, 650/850D RPM.
⑳—Except Even-Fire engine.
㉑—R46TS gapped at .040" or R46TSX gapped at .060".
㉒—The harmonic balancer on these engines has two timing marks. The mark measuring 1/16 in. is used when setting timing with a hand

held timing light. The mark measuring 1/8 in. is used when setting timing with magnetic timing equipment.
㉓—On Ventura, Phoenix & full size models with A/C, set to 600/670D RPM.
㉔—Even-Fire engine.
㉕—On full size models, idle speed with solenoid energized is set with A/C on.
㉖—Distributor located rear of engine, rotor rotation counter clockwise. Fuel pump located left side of engine.
㉗—Distributor located rear of engine, rotor rotation clockwise.
㉘—Except high altitude 500/650D RPM; high altitude, 600/650D RPM.
㉙—Distributor located rear of engine, rotor rotation counter clockwise. Fuel located right side of engine.
㉚—Except Firebird, Phoenix & Ventura Calif. models, 20° BTDC at 1100 RPM; Firebird, Phoenix & Ventura California models, 18° BTDC at 1100 RPM.
㉛—Except high altitude, 550/650D RPM; high altitude, 600/700D RPM.
㉜—Except Firebird high performance engine (engine code Y6), 16° BTDC; Firebird high performance engine (engine code Y6), 18° BTDC.
㉝—Except Firebird high performance engine (engine code Y6), 575/650D RPM; Firebird high performance engine (engine code Y6), 600/700D RPM.
㉞—Except high altitude, 550/650D RPM; high altitude, 600/650D RPM.
㉟—Less idle solenoid, 600D RPM; with idle solenoid, 550/670D RPM.
㊱—Less A/C, 500/650D RPM; with A/C, 650/850D RPM.
㊲—Engine code YB, 2200 RPM; engine code YC, 2400 RPM.

㊳—Less idle solenoid, 600D RPM; with idle solenoid, 600/670D RPM.
㊴—Idle speed controlled by Idle Air Control (IAC) assembly.
㊵—Except high altitude, 4½° ATDC at 1200 RPM; high altitude, 5½° ATDC at 1200 RPM.
㊶—Except high altitude, 4° ATDC at 1200 RPM; high altitude, 5° ATDC at 1200 RPM.
㊷—Less A/C, 850 RPM; with A/C, 900 RPM.
㊸—Models less High Altitude Emissions Package.
㊹—At altitudes below 4000 ft., set 4° ATDC at 1250 RPM; at altitudes above 4000 ft., set at 5° ATDC at 1250 RPM.
㊺—Models w/ High Altitude Emissions Package.
㊻—At altitudes below 4000 ft., set at 3° ATDC at 1250 RPM; at altitudes above 4000 ft., set at 4° ATDC at 1250 RPM.
㊼—With distributor 4-wire connector disconnected.
㊽—Ground diagnostic connector located under dash. The check engine light should flash on & off when in diagnostic mode. Check average ignition timing of cylinder Nos. 1 & 4, and reset as necessary. After completing timing check, remove ground from diagnostic connector & ensure check engine light is off.
㊾—With EGR vacuum hose disconnected and plugged. Check adjustments within 15 seconds after placing throttle on high step of fast idle cam.
㊿—When checking ignition timing, disconnect Electric Spark Timing bypass connector (tan wire w/black stripe) to place EST in bypass mode.
51—With distributor by-pass pigtail (blue connector) grounded.

TUNE UP NOTES—Continued

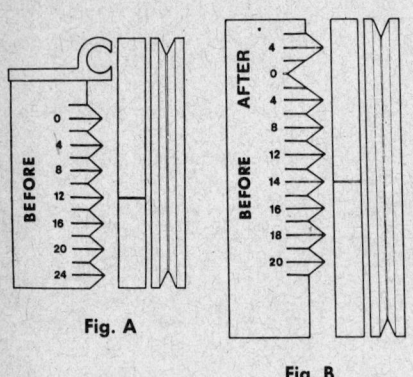

Fig. A

Fig. B

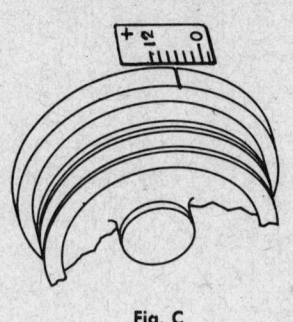

Fig. C

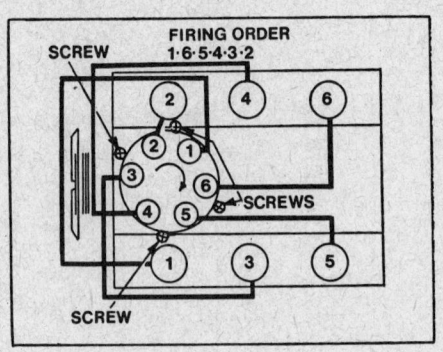

Fig. D

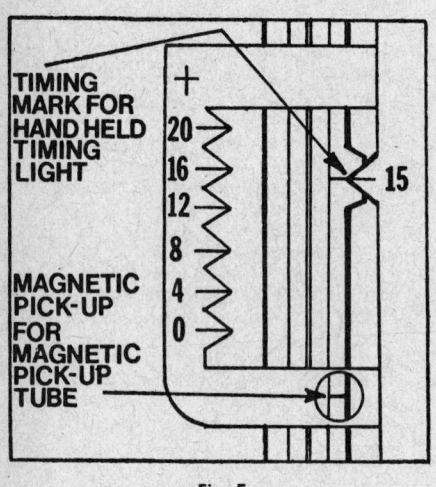

Fig. E

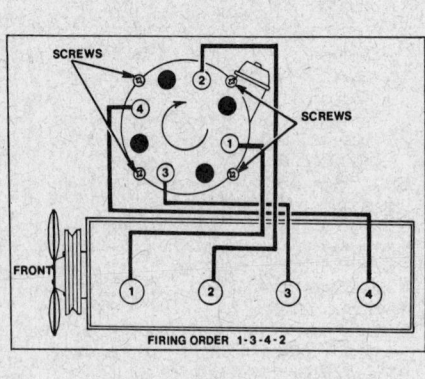

Fig. F

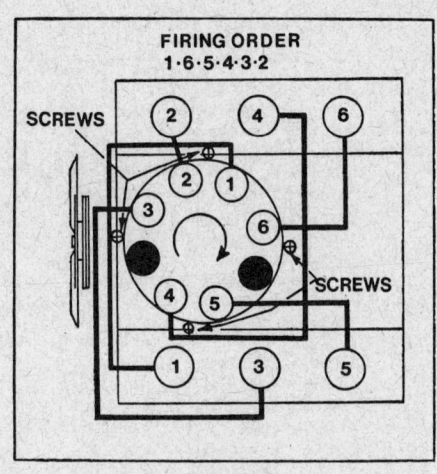

Fig. G

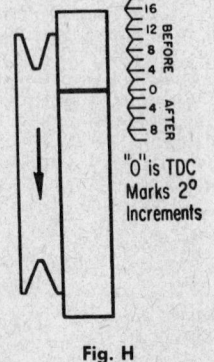

Fig. H

Fig. I

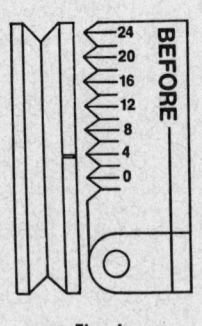

Fig. J

Continued

TUNE UP NOTES—Continued

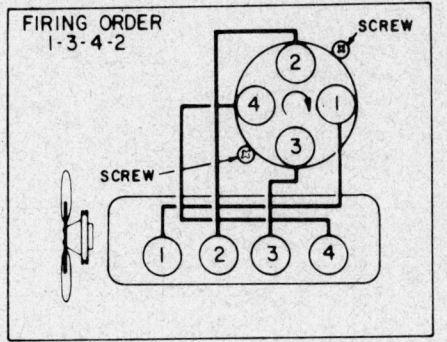

Fig. K

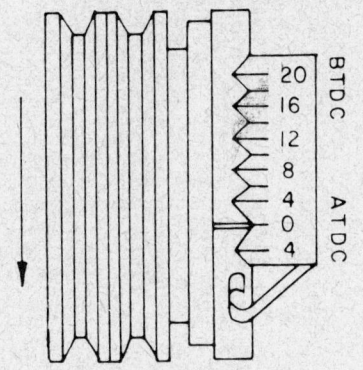

Fig. L

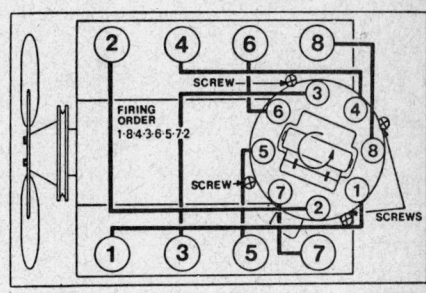

Fig. M

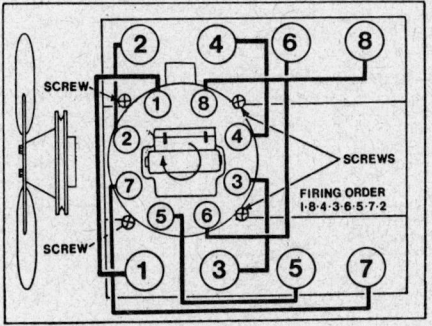

Fig. N

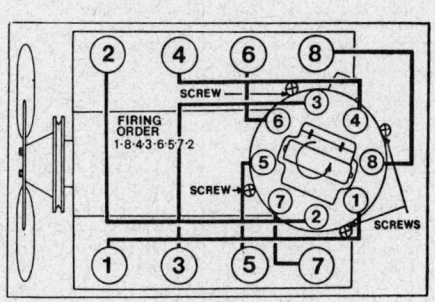

Fig. O

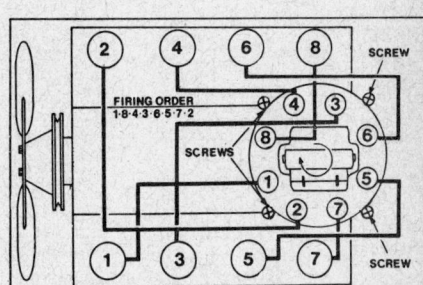

Fig. P

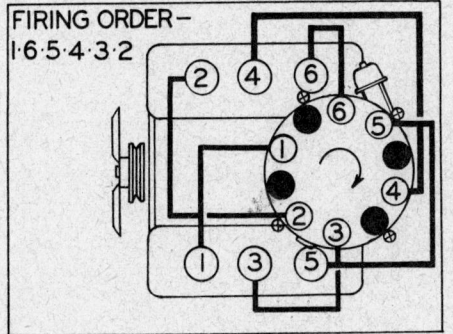

Fig. Q

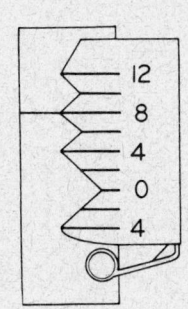

Fig. R

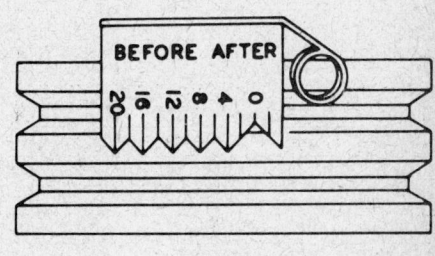

Fig. S

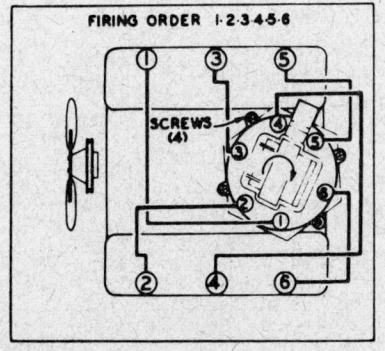

Fig. T

Fig. U

DISTRIBUTOR SPECIFICATIONS

★ Note: If unit is checked on vehicle, double the RPM and degrees to get crankshaft figures.

| Distributor Part No.① | Centrifugal Advance Degrees @ RPM of Distributor | | | | | Vacuum Advance | |
	Advance Starts	Intermediate Advance			Full Advance	Inches of Vacuum to Start Plunger	Max. Adv. Dist. Deg. @ Vacuum
1977							
1103231	0 @ 600	—	—	—	10 @ 2200	3.5	10 @ 12
1103257	0 @ 600	2 @ 700	—	—	8.5 @ 1800	5	10 @ 10
1103259	0 @ 500	—	—	—	9.5 @ 2000	6	12 @ 13
1103260	0 @ 500	—	—	—	6.5 @ 1800	6	12 @ 13
1103263	0 @ 600	—	—	—	10 @ 2200	3.5	10 @ 9
1103264	0 @ 500	—	—	—	6.5 @ 1800	5	8 @ 11
1103266	0 @ 500	—	—	—	9.5 @ 2000	5	8 @ 11
1103269	0 @ 500	4.5 @ 1000	—	—	8.5 @ 2300	5	10 @ 10
1103271	0 @ 500	4 @ 700	—	—	10 @ 2200	5	12.5 @ 11
1103272	0 @ 413	5 @ 900	—	—	10¾ @ 1715	4	12.5 @ 12
1103273	0 @ 500	8.5 @ 1300	—	—	9.5 @ 1800	4	12.5 @ 12
1103276	0 @ 400	2 @ 500	—	—	—	5	10 @ 10
1103278	0 @ 600	2 @ 700	—	—	8 @ 2200	5	10 @ 10
1110677	—	—	—	—	—	—	—
1110686	—	—	—	—	—	—	—
1978							
1103281	0 @ 500	5 @ 850	—	—	10 @ 1900	4	9 @ 12
1103282	0 @ 500	5 @ 850	—	—	10 @ 1900	4	10 @ 10
1103285	0 @ 600	6 @ 1000	—	—	11 @ 2100	4	5 @ 8
1103310	0 @ 500	5.5 @ 1000	—	—	7 @ 2200	4	12.5 @ 12
1103314	0 @ 413	5 @ 900	—	—	10.7 @ 1700	4	12.5 @ 12
1103315	0 @ 500	4 @ 700	—	—	10 @ 2200	5	12.5 @ 11
1103316	0 @ 500	4.5 @ 1000	—	—	8.5 @ 2300	4	12.5 @ 12
1103323	0 @ 500	—	—	—	9.5 @ 2000	5	8 @ 11
1103325	0 @ 500	—	—	—	6.5 @ 1800	5	8 @ 11
1103329	0 @ 600	—	—	—	10 @ 2200	3.5	10 @ 9
1103337	0 @ 550	6 @ 800	—	—	8 @ 1200	4	12 @ 10
1103342	—	2 @ 1000	—	—	9.5 @ 2200	7	12 @ 13
1103343	0 @ 400	2.25 @ 508	—	—	8.25 @ 1820	4	12.5 @ 11
1103346	0 @ 500	—	—	—	9.5 @ 2000	6	12 @ 13
1103347	0 @ 500	—	—	—	6.5 @ 1800	6	12 @ 13
1103359	0 @ 500	4.5 @ 1000	—	—	8.5 @ 2300	5	10 @ 10
1110695	0–3 @ 1000	—	—	—	9 @ 1800	6	12 @ 13
1110731	0–2 @ 1000	—	—	—	9 @ 1800	6	8 @ 9
1979							
1103281	1 @ 575	5 @ 850	—	—	10 @ 1900	4	10 @ 13
1103282	1 @ 600	5 @ 850	—	—	10 @ 1900	3.5	11 @ 11
1103285	1 @ 675	6 @ 1000	—	—	11 @ 2100	4	12 @ 7
1103314	1 @ 525	5 @ 900	—	—	10.5 @ 1725	4	12.5 @ 13
1103315	0 @ 500	3.5 @ 1000	—	—	8.5 @ 2300	6	12.5 @ 12
1103324	2 @ 400	5.5 @ 600	—	—	11.5 @ 1800	6	12.5 @ 12.5
1103325	1 @ 700	—	—	—	6.5 @ 1800	5	8.5 @ 11.5
1103342	1 @ 1100	—	—	—	8.5 @ 2200	6	13 @ 15
1103346	1 @ 650	—	—	—	9.5 @ 2000	6	12.5 @ 13.5
1103353	1.5 @ 600	6 @ 800	8 @ 1200	—	11 @ 2350	3.5	12 @ 11
1103379	1 @ 575	5 @ 850	—	—	10 @ 1900	2.5	11 @ 8.5
1103399	1 @ 575	4 @ 700	—	—	10 @ 2200	4	12.5 @ 13
1103400	1 @ 525	4.5 @ 1000	—	—	8.5 @ 2350	4	12.5 @ 12
1110766	1 @ 975	—	—	—	7.5 @ 1800	4	12.5 @ 11.5

Continued

DISTRIBUTOR SPECIFICATIONS—Continued

★ Note: If unit is checked on vehicle, double the RPM and degrees to get crankshaft figures.

Distributor Part No.①	Centrifugal Advance Degrees @ RPM of Distributor				Full Advance	Vacuum Advance	
	Advance Starts	Intermediate Advance				Inches of Vacuum to Start Plunger	Max. Adv. Dist. Deg. @ Vacuum
1979—Continued							
1110767	1 @ 975	—	—	—	7.5 @ 1800	3.5	10.5 @ 12.5
1110768	1 @ 625	—	—	—	7.5 @ 1800	3.5	10.5 @ 12.5
1110769	1 @ 625	—	—	—	7.5 @ 1800	4	12.5 @ 12.5
1110770	1 @ 975	—	—	—	7.5 @ 3600	3	10.5 @ 9.5
1980							
1103282	1.25 @ 600	5 @ 850	—	—	10 @ 1900	5	10 @ 11
1103407	1 @ 600	8 @ 1000	—	—	11.5 @ 2200	4.5	10 @ 10.5
1103413	0 @ 500	—	—	—	6.5 @ 1800	6	15 @ 13
1103425	1 @ 675	4.5 @ 1000	—	—	9 @ 2300	4.5	10 @ 10.5
1103444	.5 @ 600	8 @ 1000	—	—	12 @ 2200	7.5	9.5 @ 13.5
1103447	1 @ 1100	—	—	—	8.5 @ 2200	7.0	12 @ 14.6
1103450	1 @ 575	—	—	—	9.5 @ 1600	4.5	10 @ 10.5
1110552	1 @ 600	3 @ 1250	—	—	7 @ 1700	3.5	12 @ 8.5
1110554	0 @ 840	—	—	—	7.5 @ 1800	3	12 @ 12
1110555	1 @ 600	3 @ 1200	—	—	7.5 @ 1800	4.5	12 @ 9.5
1110558	1 @ 675	4.5 @ 1200	—	—	7 @ 2000	3.5	8 @ 12
1110559	.25 @ 600	4.5 @ 1200	—	—	7 @ 2000	3.5	8 @ 14
1110560	1 @ 725	3.5 @ 1000	—	—	7 @ 2200	5.0	10.5 @ 10.5
1110752	1 @ 775	4.5 @ 1200	—	—	7 @ 2050	4	8 @ 7.5
1110769	1 @ 600	3 @ 1200	—	—	7.5 @ 1800	4.5	12 @ 9.5
1981							
1103443②	—	—	—	—	—	—	—
1103451②	—	—	—	—	—	—	—
1103453②	—	—	—	—	—	—	—
1103466②	—	—	—	—	—	—	—
1110573②	—	—	—	—	—	—	—
1111386②	—	—	—	—	—	—	—
1982							
1103460②	—	—	—	—	—	—	—
1103470②	—	—	—	—	—	—	—
1110583②	—	—	—	—	—	—	—
1110597②	—	—	—	—	—	—	—
1103494②	—	—	—	—	—	—	—
1983							
1103460②	—	—	—	—	—	—	—
1103470②	—	—	—	—	—	—	—
1103539②	—	—	—	—	—	—	—
1103519②	—	—	—	—	—	—	—
1110584②	—	—	—	—	—	—	—

①—Stamped on distributor housing plate.　②—Equipped with Electronic Spark Timing (EST).

PONTIAC—Exc. Astre, Fiero, Sunbird, 1000 & Front Wheel Drive

STARTING MOTOR APPLICATIONS

Year	Model/V.I.N.	Starter Number	Year	Model/V.I.N.	Starter Number
1977	4-151/V	1109412		V8-265/S, 301/T,W	1109523
	V6-231/A, C	1108797		V8-305/H	1109524
	V8-301/Y	1108758		V8-350/X	1109061
	V8-305/V	1109056		V8-350/R⑥	1109072
	V8-350/L③	1108796		V8-350 Diesel/N	1109213
	V8-350/R⑥	1108765	1981	V6-231/A	1109061
	V8-350/P⑤, 400/Z	1108759		V8-265/S, 301/T,W	1109523
	V8-403/K	1108794		V8-305/H②	1109524
1978	4-151/V	1109521		V8-305/H⑦	1109074
	V6-231/A	1109061		V8-307/Y	1998205
	V8-301/W,Y	1109523		V8-350 Diesel/N	1109216
	V8-305/H⑫	1109524	1982	4-151/2	1109533
	V8-305/V①⑬	1109064		V6-173/1	1109535
	V8-305/V⑬④	1109074		V6-231/A	1998236
	V8-350/L①③	1109065		V6-252/4	1998234
	V8-350/L③④	1109067		V8-305/H,7	⑭
	V8-350/X⑧	1109061		V8-350 Diesel/N	1998552
	V8-350/R⑥, 403/K	1109072	1983	4-151/2	1109556
	V8-400/Z	1108759		V6-173/L,1	1109535
1979	V6-231/A	1109061		V6-229/9	1998236
	V8-301/W,Y	1109523		V6-231/A	1998236
	V8-305/G⑨	1109064⑪		V8-305/G,H,S	1109534⑮
	V8-305/H⑩	1109524		V8-350 Diesel/N	1998554
	V8-350/L③	1109065	1984	4-151/2	1998450
	V8-350/X⑧	1109061		V6-173/L,1	1998427
	V8-350/R⑥, 403/K	1109072		V6-231/A⑯	1998236
	V8-400/Z	1108759		V6-231/A⑰	1998452
1980	V6-229/K	1109524		V8-305/G,H	1998430⑮
	V6-231/A	1109061		V8-350 Diesel/N	1998554

①—Auto. trans.
②—Except Firebird.
③—Distributor located rear of engine, rotor rotation clockwise.
④—Manual trans.
⑤—Distributor located at rear of engine, rotor rotation counter clockwise. Fuel pump located left side of engine.
⑥—Distributor located rear of engine, rotor rotation counter clockwise. Fuel pump located right side of engine.
⑦—Firebird
⑧—Distributor located front of engine.
⑨—Two barrel Carb.
⑩—Four barrel Carb.
⑪—With high output option, 1102844.
⑫—LeMans & Grand Prix.
⑬—Firebird & Phoenix.
⑭—Models less 4 spd. man. trans., #1109534; models w/ 4 spd. man. trans., #1998240.
⑮—With high output option, 1998466.
⑯—Exc. Parisienne.
⑰—Parisienne.

ALTERNATOR SPECIFICATIONS

Year	Model	Rated Hot Output Amps	Field Current 12 Volts @ 80°F.	Year	Model	Rated Hot Output Amps	Field Current 12 Volts @ 80°F.	Year	Model	Rated Hot Output Amps	Field Current 12 Volts @ 80°F.
1977	1101016	80	4.0–4.9		1102840	55	4.0–4.5		1102908	63	—
	1102389	42	—		1102841	42	—		1102909	61	—
	1102394	37	4.0–4.5		1102842	63	—	1978–79	1101016	80	—
	1102478	55	—		1102843	61	—		1102389	42	—
	1102479	55	—		1102844	63	—		1102391	61	—
	1102485	42	—		1102854	63	—		1102392	63	—
	1102486	61	4.0–4.5		1102881	37	—		1102394	37	4.0–4.5
	1102491	37	4.0–4.5		1102906	61	—		1102478	55	4.0–4.5

2-898

Continued

ALTERNATOR SPECIFICATIONS—Continued

Year	Model	Rated Hot Output Amps	Field Current 12 Volts @ 80°F.	Year	Model	Rated Hot Output Amps	Field Current 12 Volts @ 80°F.	Year	Model	Rated Hot Output Amps	Field Current 12 Volts @ 80°F.
	1102479	55	4.0—4.5	1980	1101038	70	—	1983	1100200	78	4.0—4.5
	1102480	61	4.0—4.5		1103043	42	—		1100226	37	4.0—4.5
	1102485	42	—		1103103	63	—		1100230	42	—
1978–79	1102486	61	4.0—4.5		1103104	42	—		1100239	55	—
	1102495	37	—		1103112	63	—		1100246	63	4.0—4.5
	1102841	42	—	1981	1101037	70	—		1100247	55	4.0—4.5
	1102842	63	—		1101038	70	—		1100263	78	4.0—4.5
	1102843	61	—		1103088	55	—		1100270	78	4.0—4.5
	1102844	63	—		1103091	63	—		1100300	63	—
	1102854	63	—		1103103	63	—		1105022	78	4.0—4.5
	1102901	61	—	1982	1100110	42	—		1105798	63	—
	1102909	61	—		1100179	42	—		1105343	85	—
	1102910	63	—		1103187	42	—	1984	1100200	78	—
	1102913	61	—		1100121	63	—		1100239	56	—
	1103033	61	—		1103197	63	—		1100260	78	—
1979	1101024	80	—		1100199	63	—		1105197	70	—
	1102860	63	—		1101037	70	—		1105443	94	—
	1102908	63	—		1101088	70	—		1105444	94	—
	1103055	42	—		1100187	70	—		1105493	94	—
	1103056	63	—		1101449	70	—		1105548	85	—
	1103058	63	—		1101045	85	—		1105565	78	—
	1103076	63	—		1101443	85	—				

①—At 5500 RPM.

VALVE SPECIFICATIONS

Year	Model/V.I.N.	Valve Lash Int.	Valve Lash Exh.	Valve Angles Seat	Valve Angles Face	Valve Spring Installed Height	Valve Spring Pressure Lbs. @ In.	Stem Clearance Intake	Stem Clearance Exhaust	Stem Diameter Intake	Stem Diameter Exhaust
1977	4-151/V	Hydraulic⑦		46	45	1.66	176 @ 1.254	.0017—.0030	.0017—.0030	.3400	.3400
	V6-231/C⑥	Hydraulic⑭		45	45	1.727	168 @ 1.327	.0015—.0032	.0015—.0032	.3405—.3412	.3405—3412
	V6-231/A⑥	Hydraulic⑭		45	45	1.727	182 @ 1.340	.0015—.0035	.0015—.0032	.3402—.3412	.3405—3412
	V8-301/Y	Hydraulic⑦		46	45	1.69	170 @ 1.26	.0017—.0020	.0017—.0020	.3400	.3400
	V8-305V①	¾ Turn②		46	45	⑩	⑤	.0010—.0027	.0010—.0027	.3410—.3417	.3410—.3417
	V8-350/L①⑰	¾ Turn②		46	45	⑨	⑤	.0010—.0027	.0010—.0027	.3410—.3417	.3410—.3417
	V8-350/R⑫⑯	Hydraulic⑬		⑩	⑪	1.67	187 @ 1.27	.0010—.0027	.0015—.0032	.3425—.3432	.3420—.3427
	V8-350/P⑮	Hydraulic⑦		③	⑧	1.549	131 @ 1.185	.0016—.0033	.0021—.0038	.3412—.3419	.3407—.3414
	V8-400/Z	Hydraulic⑦		③	⑧	1.549	131 @ 1.185	.0016—.0033	.0021—.0038	.3412—.3419	.3407—.3414
	V8-403/K⑯	Hydraulic⑬		⑩	⑪	1.67	187 @ 1.27	.0010—.0027	.0015—.0032	.3425—.3432	.3420—.3427
1978	4-151/V	Hydraulic⑦		46	45	1.66	176 @ 1.254	.0010—.0027	.0010—.0027	.3425—.3418	.3425—.3418
	V6-231/A	Hydraulic⑬		45	45	1.727	168 @ 1.340	.0015—.0035	.0015—.0032	.3402—.3412	.3405—.3412
	V8-301/Y	Hydraulic⑦		46	45	1.66	166 @ 1.296	.0010—.0027	.0010—.0027	.3425—.3418	.3425—.3418
	V8-305/V①	1 Turn②		46	45	1.70	200 @ 1.25	.0010—.0027	.0010—.0027	.3410—.3417	.3410—.3417
	V8-350/L①⑰	1 Turn②		46	45	1.70	200 @ 1.25	.0010—.0027	.0010—.0027	.3410—.3417	.3410—.3417
	V8-350/R⑫⑯	Hydraulic⑬		⑩	⑪	1.67	187 @ 1.270	.0010—.0027	.0015—.0032	.3432—.3425	.3427—.3420
	V8-350/P⑥⑭	Hydraulic⑬		45	45	1.727	175 @ 1.34	.0015—.0035	.0015—.0032	.3720—.3730	.3730—.3723
	V8-400/Z	Hydraulic⑦		③	⑧	1.549	131 @ 1.185	.0016—.0033	.0021—.0038	.3425	.3425
	V8-403/K⑯	Hydraulic⑬		⑩	⑪	1.670	187 @ 1.270	.0010—.0027	.0015—.0032	.3432—.3425	.3427—.3420
1979	V6-231/A	Hydraulic⑬		45	45	1.727	④	.0015—.0035	.0015—.0032	.3402—.3412	.3405—.3412
	V8-301/W,Y	Hydraulic⑬		46	45	1.66	166 @ 1.296	.0010—.0027	.0010—.0027	.3418—.3425	.3418—.3425
	V8-305/G,H①	Hydraulic⑬		46	45	1.70	200 @ 1.25	.0010—.0027	.0010—.0027	.3410—.3417	.3410—.3417

Continued

VALVE SPECIFICATIONS—Continued

| Year | Model/V.I.N. | Valve Lash | | Valve Angles | | Valve Spring Installed Height | Valve Spring Pressure Lbs. @ In. | Stem Clearance | | Stem Diameter | |
		Int.	Exh.	Seat	Face			Intake	Exhaust	Intake	Exhaust
	V8-350/L①⑰	Hydraulic⑬		46	45	1.70	200 @ 1.25	.0010–.0027	.0010–.0027	.3410–.3417	.3410–.3417
	V8-350/R⑫⑯	Hydraulic⑬		45	46	1.67	187 @ 1.270	.0010–.0027	.0015–.0032	.3425–.3432	.3420–.3427
	V8-350/X⑥⑭	Hydraulic⑬		45	45	1.727	175 @ 1.34	.0015–.0035	.0015–.0032	.3720–.3730	.3730–.3723
	V8-400/Z	Hydraulic⑦		③	⑧	1.549	131 @ 1.185	.0016–.0033	.0021–.0038	.3412–.3419	.3407–.3414
	V8-403/K	Hydraulic⑬		⑩	⑪	1.670	187 @ 1.270	.0010–.0027	.0015–.0032	.3425–.3432	.3420–.3427
1980	V6-229/K①	1 Turn②		46	45	1.70	200 @ 1.25	.0010–.0027	.0010–.0027	.3410–.3417	.3410–.3417
	V6-231/A⑥	Hydraulic⑬		45	45	1.727	④	.0015–.0035	.0015–.0032	.3401–.3412	.3405–.3412
	V8-265/S	Hydraulic⑦		46	45	1.66	175 @ 1.29	.0010–.0027	.0010–.0027	.3418–.3425	.3418–.3425
	V8-301/T,W	Hydraulic⑦		46	45	1.66	175 @ 1.29	.0010–.0027	.0010–.0027	.3418–.3425	.3418–.3425
	V8-305/L①	1 Turn②		46	45	1.70	200 @ 1.25	.0010–.0027	.0010–.0027	.3410–.3417	.3410–.3417
	V8-350/X⑥⑭	Hydraulic⑬		45	45	1.727	182 @ 1.34	.0015–.0035	.0015–.0032	.3401–.3412	.3405–.3412
	V8-350/R⑫⑯	Hydraulic⑬		⑩	⑪	1.67	187 @ 1.27	.0010–.0027	.0015–.0032	.3425–.3432	.3420–.3427
	V8-350 Diesel/N⑯	Hydraulic⑬		⑩	⑪	1.67	151 @ 1.30	.0010–.0027	.0015–.0032	.3425–.3432	.3420–.3427
1981	V6-231/A⑥	Hydraulic⑬		45	45	1.727	④	.0015–.0035	.0015–.0032	.3401–.3412	.3405–.3412
	V8-265/S	Hydraulic⑦		46	45	1.66	175 @ 1.29	.0010–.0027	.0010–.0027	.3425	.3425
	V8-301/T,W	Hydraulic⑦		46	45	1.66	175 @ 1.29	.0010–.0027	.0010–.0027	.3425	.3425
	V8-305/L①	1 Turn②		46	45	1.70	200 @ 1.25	.0010–.0027	.0010–.0027	.3425–.3432	.3420–.3427
	V8-307/Y⑯	Hydraulic⑬		⑩	⑪	1.67	189 @ 1.27	.0010–.0027	.0015–.0032	.3425–.3432	.3420–.3427
	V8-350 Diesel/N⑯	Hydraulic⑬		⑩	⑪	1.67	210 @ 1.3	.0010–.0027	.0015–.0032	.3425–.3432	.3420–.3427
1982	4-151/2	Hydraulic⑬		46	45	1.69	160 @ 1.25	.0010–.0027	.0010–.0027	.3418–.3425	.3418–.3425
	V6-173/1①	1½ Turns②		46	45	1.57	195 @ 1.18	.0010–.0027	.0010–.0027	.3409–.3417	.3409–.3417
	V6-231/A⑥	Hydraulic⑬		45	45	1.727	182 @ 1.34	.0015–.0035	.0015–.0032	.3401–.3412	.3405–.3412
	V6-252/4⑥	Hydraulic⑬		45	44	1.727	182 @ 1.34	.0015–.0035	.0015–.0032	.3401–.3412	.3405–.3412
	V8-305/H,7①	1 Turn②		46	45	1.70	200 @ 1.25	.0010–.0027	.0010–.0027	.3425–.3432	.3420–.3427
	V8-350 Diesel/N⑯	Hydraulic⑬		⑩	⑪	1.67	210 @ 1.22	.0010–.0027	.0015–.0032	.3425–.3432	.3420–.3427
1983–84	4-151/2	Hydraulic⑬		46	45	1.69	160 @ 1.25	.0010–.0027	.0010–.0027	.3418–.3425	.3418–.3425
	V6-173/1,L①	1½ Turns②		46	45	1.57	195 @ 1.18	.0010–.0027	.0010–.0027	.3409–.3417	.3409–.3417
	V6-229/9	1 Turn②		46	45	1.17	200 @ 1.25	.0010–.0027	.0010–.0027	.3410–.3417	.3410–.3417
	V6-231/A⑥	Hydraulic⑬		45	45	1.72	182 @ 1.34	.0015–.0035	.0015–.0032	.3410–.3412	.3405–.3412
	V8-305/①	1 Turn②		46	45	1.70	200 @ 1.25	.0010–.0027	.0010–.0027	.3425–.3432	.3420–.3427
	V8-350 Diesel/N⑯	Hydraulic⑬		⑩	⑪	1.67	210 @ 1.22	.0010–.0027	.0015–.0032	.3425–.3432	.3420–.3427

①—For service on this engine, see Chevrolet Chapter.
②—Turn rocker arm stud nut until all lash is eliminated, then tighten nut the additional turns listed.
③—Intake 30°, exhaust 45°.
④—Intake 164 ± 5 @ 1.340; Exhaust 182 ± 8 @ 1.340.
⑤—Intake 174–186 @ 1.25; Exhaust 184–196 @ 1.16.
⑥—See Buick chapter for service procedures.
⑦—No adjustment. On V8's, rocker arms are correctly positioned when ball retainer nuts are tightened to 20 ft. lbs.
⑧—Intake 29°, exhaust 44°.
⑨—Intake, 135.1 @ 1.13; Exhaust, 140.8 @ 1.12.
⑩—Intake, 45°; exhaust, 31°.
⑪—Intake, 44°; exhaust, 30°.
⑫—Distributor located at rear of engine, counter
clockwise rotor rotation. Fuel pump located right side of engine.
⑬—No adjustment.
⑭—Distributor located at front of engine.
⑮—Distributor located at rear of engine, counter clockwise rotor rotation. Fuel pump located left side of engine.
⑯—See Oldsmobile Chapter for service procedures.
⑰—Distributor located at rear of engine, clockwise rotor rotation.

PISTONS, PINS, RINGS, CRANKSHAFT & BEARINGS

| Year | Model/V.I.N. | Piston Skirt Clearance | Ring End Gap① | | Wrist-pin Diameter | Rod Bearings | | Main Bearings | | Thrust on Bear. No. | Shaft End Play |
			Comp. ⑱	Oil ⑱		Shaft Diameter	Bearing Clearance	Shaft Diameter	Bearing Clearance		
1977	4-151/V	.0025–.0033	.010	.010	.940	2.000	.0005–.0026	2.2983–2.2993	.0002–.0022	5	.0015–.0085
	V6-231/C⑩	.0008–.0020	.010	.015	.93925	1.991–2.000	.0005	2.4995	.0004–.0015	2	.004–.008
	V6-231/A⑩	.0008–.0020	.013	.015	.93925	2.2491	.0005–.0026	2.4995	.0004–.0015	2	.003–.009
	V8-301/Y	.0025–.0033	.010	.035	.927	2.000	.0005–.0025	3.00	.0004–.0020	5	.003–.009
	V8-305/L⑧	.0007–.0017	.010	.015	.9270	2.099–2.100	.0013–.0035	②	④	5	.002–.006
	V8-350/L⑧⑪	.0007–.0017	⑨	.015	.9270	2.099–2.100	.0013–.0035	②	④	5	.002–.006
	V8-350/P⑯	.0025–.0023	.010	.035	.980	2.25	.0005–.0025	3.00	.0004–.0015	5	.003–.009
	V8-350/R⑬⑥	.0005–.0015	.010	.015	.9805	2.1238–2.1248	.0004–.0033	⑮	⑤	3	.0035–.0135
	V8-400/Z	.0025–.0033	.010	.035	.9802	2.25	.0005–.0025	3.00	.0004–.0015	5	.003–.009
	V8-403/K⑬	.0003–.0017	.010	.015	.9805	2.1238–2.1248	.0004–.0033	⑮	⑤	3	.0035–.0135

Continued

PISTONS, PINS, RINGS, CRANKSHAFT & BEARINGS—Continued

Year	Model/V.I.N.	Piston Skirt Clearance	Ring End Gap① Comp.⑱	Oil⑱	Wrist-pin Diameter	Rod Bearings Shaft Diameter	Bearing Clearance	Main Bearings Shaft Diameter	Bearing Clearance	Thrust on Bear. No.	Shaft End Play
1978	4-151/V	.0025–.0033	⑨	.015	.940	2.00	.0005–.0026	2.30	.0002–.0022	5	.0035–.0085
	V6-231/A⑩	.0008–.0020	.013	.015	.93925	2.2491	.0005–.0026	2.4995	.0004–.0015	2	.003–.009
	V8-301/W,Y	.0025–.0033	.010	.035	.940	2.25	.0005–.0025	3.00	.0002–.0020	4	.003–.009
	V8-305/H,V⑧	.0007–.0017	.010	.010	.92715	2.009–2.100	.0013–.0035	②	④	5	.002–.006
	V8-350/L⑧⑪	.0007–.0017	⑨	.015	.92715	2.009–2.100	.0013–.0035	②	④	5	.002–.006
	V8-350/X⑩⑦	.008–.0020	.010	.015	.93915	1.991–2.000	.0005–.0026	2.9995	.0004–.0015	3	.003–.009
	V8-350/R⑬⑥	.001–.002	.010	.015	.9805	2.1238–2.1248	.0005–.0026	⑮	⑤	3	.0035–.0135
	V8-400/Z	.0025–.0033	.010	.035	.9802	2.25	.0005–.0025	3.00	.0002–.0017	4	.003–.009
	V8-403/K⑬	.001–.002	.010	.015	.9805	2.1238–2.1248	.0005–.0026	⑮	⑤	3	.0035–.0135
1979	V6-231/A⑩	.0008–.0020	.013	.015	.9392	2.2487–2.2495	.0005–.0026	2.4995	.0003–.0018	2	.003–.009
	V8-301/W,Y	.0025–.0033	.010	.035	.940	2.25	.0005–.0025	3.000	.0002–.0020	4	.003–.009
	V8-305/ G,H⑧	.0007–.0017	.010	.015	.9271	2.0986–2.0998	.0013–.0035	②	④	5	.002–.006
	V8-350/L⑧⑪	.0007–.0017	.010	.015	.9271	2.0986–2.0998	.0013–.0035	②	④	5	.002–.006
	V8-350/ X⑩⑥	.0008–.0020	.013	.015	.9392	1.991–2.000	.0005–.0026	3.000	.0004–.0015	3	.003–.009
	V8-350/R⑬⑦	.00075–.00175	③	.015	.9805	2.1238–2.1248	.0004–.0033	2.4985–2.4995	⑤	3	.0035–.0135
	V8-400/Z	.0025–.0033	.010	.035	.940	2.25	.0005–.0025	3.000	.0002–.0020	4	.003–.009
	V8-403/K⑬	.0005–.0015	③	.015	.9805	2.1238–2.1248	.0004–.0033	2.4985–2.4995	⑤	3	.0035–.0135
1980	V6-229/K⑧	.0007–.0017	.010	.015	.9271	2.0986–2.0998	.0013–.0035	②	④	4	.002–.006
	V6-231/A⑩	.0008–.0020	.013	.015	.9392	2.2487–2.2495	.0005–.0026	2.4995	.0003–.0018	2	.003–.009
	V8-265/S	.0025–.0033	.010	.035	.927	2.00	.0005–.0026	3.000	.0002–.0018	4	.0035–.0085
	V8-301/W⑫	.0025–.0033	.010	.035	.927	2.25	.0005–.0026	3.000	.0004–.0020	4	.006–.022
	V8-301/T⑭	.0017–.0025	.010	.035	—	2.25	.0005–.0026	3.000	.0004–.0020	4	.006–.022
	V8-305/H⑧	.0007–.0017	.010	.015	.9271	2.0986–2.0998	.0013–.0035	②	④	5	.002–.006
	V8-350/X⑩⑥	.0008–.0020	.013	.015	.9392	1.991–2.000	.0005–.0026	3.000	.0004–.0015	3	.003–.009
	V8-350/R⑬⑦	.00075–.00175	.010	.015	.9805	2.1238–2.1248	.0005–.0026	2.4985–2.4995	⑤	3	.0035–.0135
	V8-350/N⑬	.005–.006	.015	.015	1.0951	2.1238–2.1248	.0005–.0026	2.9993–3.0003	⑰	3	.0035–.0135
1981	V6-231/A⑩	.008–.0020	.013	.015	.9392	2.2487–2.2495	.0005–.0026	2.4995	.0003–.0018	2	.003–.009
	V8-265/S	.0017–.0025	.010	.035	.940	2.00	.0005–.0026	3.00	.0002–.0018	4	.003–.009
	V8-301/T,W	.0017–.0025	.010	.035	.940	2.00	.0005–.0026	3.00	.0002–.0018	4	.003–.009
	V8-305/H⑧	.0007–.0017	.010	.015	.9271	2.090–2.100	.0013–.0035	②	④	5	.002–.007
	V8-307/Y⑬	.0005–.0015	.009	.015	.9805	2.1238–2.1248	.0004–.0033	⑮	⑤	3	.0035–.0135
	V8-350/N⑬	.0005–.0006	.015	.015	1.0951	2.1238–2.1248	.0005–.0026	3.00	⑰	3	.0035–.0135
1982	4-151/2	⑲	.010	.015	.940	2.000	.0005–.0026	2.300	.0005–.0022	5	.0035–.0085
	V6-173/1⑧	.0017–.003	.010	.020	.905	2.0303–2.031	.0014–.0037	⑳	.002–.003	3	.002–.007
	V6-231/A⑩	.0008–.0020	.013	.015	.9392	2.2487–2.2495	.0005–.0026	2.4995	.0003–.0018	2	.003–.009
	V6-252/4⑩	.0008–.0020	.013	.015	.9392	2.2487–2.2495	.0005–.0026	2.4995	.0003–.0018	2	.003–.009
	V8-305/H,7⑧	.0007–.0017	.010	.015	.9271	2.0986–2.0998	.0018–.0039	②	④	5	.002–.007
	V8-350/N⑬	.005–.006	.015	.015	1.0946	2.1238–2.1248	.0005–.0026	2.9993–3.0003	⑰	3	.0035–.0135
1983–84	4-151/2	⑲	.010	.015	.940	2.000	.0005–.0026	2.300	.0005–.0022	5	.0035–.0085
	V6-173/1,L⑧	.0017–.003	.010	.020	.905	2.0303–2.031	.0014–.0037	⑳	.002–.003	3	.002–.007
	V6-229/9⑧	.0007–.0017	.010	.015	.927	2.0986–2.0998	.0013–.0035	②	④	4	.004–.008
	V6-231/A⑩	.0008–.0020	.010	.015	.939	2.2487–2.2495	.0005–.0026	2.4995	.0003–.0018	2	.003–.009
	V8-305/⑧	.0007–.0017	.010	.015	.927	2.0986–2.0998	.0018–.0039	②	④	5	.002–.006
	V8-350/N⑬	.005–.006	.015	.015	1.094	2.1238–2.1248	.0005–.0026	2.993–3.0003	⑰	3	.0035–.0135

①—Fit rings in tapered bores for clearance listed in tightest portion of ring travel.
②—No. 1, 2.4484–2.4493; Nos. 2, 3, 4, 2.4481–2.4490; No. 5, 2.4479–2.4488.
③—Refer to text in Oldsmobile Chapter Engine Section under Piston, Rings & Pins.
④—No. 1, .0008–.0020; Nos. 2, 3, 4, .0011–.0023; No. 5, .0017–.0032.
⑤—No. 1, 2, 3, 4, .0005–.0021; No. 5, .0015–.0031.
⑥—Distributor located at rear of engine, counter clockwise rotor rotation. Fuel pump located right side of engine.
⑦—Distributor located at front of engine.
⑧—For service on this engine, see Chevrolet Chapter.
⑨—No. 1, .013"; No. 2, .010".
⑩—See Buick chapter for service procedures.
⑪—Distributor located at rear of engine, clockwise rotor rotation.
⑫—Except turbocharged engine.
⑬—See Oldsmobile Chapter for service procedures.
⑭—Turbocharged engine.
⑮—No. 1—2.4988–2.4998; No. 2, 3, 4, 5; 2.4985–2.4995.
⑯—Distributor located at rear of engine, counter clockwise rotor rotation. Fuel pump located left side of engine.
⑰—No. 1, 2, 3 & 4; .0005–.0021; No. 5, .0020–.0034.
⑱—Clearances specified are minimum gaps.
⑲—Top of bore, .0025–.0033; bottom of bore, .0017–.0041.
⑳—Nos. 1, 2 & 4, 2.5336–2.5345; No. 3, 2.5328–2.534.

PONTIAC—Exc. Astre, Fiero, Sunbird, 1000 & Front Wheel Drive

REAR AXLE SPECIFICATIONS

Year	Model	Carrier Type	Ring Gear & Pinion Backlash		Pinion Bearing Preload			Differential Bearing Preload		
			Method	Adjustment	Method	New Bearings Inch-Lbs.	Used Bearings Inch-Lbs.	Method	New Bearings Inch-Lbs.	Used Bearings Inch-Lbs.
1977–84	Exc. 1983–84 Parisienne	Integral	Shims	.006–.008	[1]	20–25	10–15	Shims	35–40	20–25
1983–84	Parisienne	Integral	Shims	.005–.008	Spacer	15–30[2]	10–15[2]	Shims	—	—

[1]—Tighten pinion shaft nut with inch-pound torque wrench.

[2]—Use inch-pound torque wrench on pinion shaft nut.

ENGINE TIGHTENING SPECIFICATIONS ★

★ Torque specifications are for clean and lightly lubricated threads only. Dry or dirty threads produce increased friction which prevents accurate measurement of thickness.

Year	Model/V.I.N.	Spark Plugs Ft. Lbs.	Cylinder Head Bolts Ft. Lbs.	Intake Manifold Ft. Lbs.	Exhaust Manifold Ft. Lbs.	Rocker Arm Ft. Lbs.	Rocker Arm Cover Ft. Lbs.	Connecting Rod Cap Bolts Ft. Lbs.	Main Bearing Cap Bolts Ft. Lbs.	Flywheel to Crankshaft Ft. Lbs.	Vibration Damper or Pulley Ft. Lbs.
1977	V6-231/C	20	75	45	25	30[11]	5	40	100	55	150
	V6-231/A	15	80	45	25	30[11]	4	40	100	60	225
	V8-301/Y	15	90	35	40	20	7	30	70[7]	95	160
	V8-305/V[4]	15	65	30	20[6]	—	45[5]	45	70	60	60
	V8-350/L[4][14]	15	65	30	20[6]	—	45[5]	45	70	60	60
	V8-350/P[15]	15	95	35	40	20	7	40	100[3]	95	160
	V8-350/R[8][16]	25	130	40	25	25	—	42	80[3]	60	260
	V8-400/Z	15	95	35	40	20	7	40	100[3]	95	160
	V8-403/K	25	130	40	25	25	—	42	80[3]	60	260
1977–78	4-151/V	15	95	[13]	[13]	20	85[5]	30	65	55	160
1978–79	V6-231/A[12]	15	80	45	25	30[11]	4	40	100	60	225
	V8-301/W,Y	15	95	35	40	20	6	30	70[2]	95	160
	V8-305/G,H[4]	[1]	65	30	20[6]	—	45[5]	45	70	60	60
	V8-350/L[4][14]	[1]	65	30	20[6]	—	45[5]	45	70	60	60
	V8-350/R[8][16]	25	130[9]	40[9]	25	25	—	42	80[3]	[10]	260
	V8-350/X[12][17]	15	80	45	25	30	4	40	100[3]	60	225
	V8-400/Z	15	95	35	40	20	6	40	100[3]	95	160
	V8-403/K	25	130[9]	40[9]	25	25	—	42	80[3]	[10]	260
1980–81	V6-229/K[4]	22	65	30	20	—	45[5]	45	70	60	60
	V6-231/A[12]	15	80	45	25	30[11]	4	40	100	60	225
	V8-265/S	15	95	35	40	20	6	30	70[2]	95	160
	V8-301/W[18]	15	95	35	40	20	6	30	70[2]	95	160
	V8-301/T[19]	20	93	37	40	20	7	28	100[2]	—	163
	V8-305/H[4]	22	65	30	20[6]	—	45[5]	45	70	60	60
	V8-350/X[12][17]	15	80	45	25	30[11]	4	40	100	60	225
	V8-350/R[8][16]	25	130[9]	40[9]	25	28	—	42	80[3]	60	200–310
	V8-350 Diesel/N[8]	—	130[9]	40[9]	25	28	—	42	120	60	200–310
1981	V8-307/Y[8]	25	130[9]	40[9]	25	28	—	42	80[3]	60	200–310
1982	4-151/2	15	85	29	44	20	6	32	70	44	160
	V6-173/1[4]	7–15	65–75	20–25	22–28	43–49[21]	6–9	34–40	63–74	45–55	75
	V6-231/A[12]	15	80	45	25	30[11]	4	40	100	60	225
	V6-252/4[12]	15	80	45	20	30[11]	4	40	100	60	225
	V8-305/H,7[4]	22	65	30	20[6]	—	4	45	70	60	60
	V8-350 Diesel/N[8]	—	130[9]	40[9]	25	28	—	42	120	60	200–310
1983	4-151/2	15	85	29	44	20	6	32	70	[20]	200
	V6-173/1,L[4]	7–15	70	23	25	46[21]	8	37	69	50	75
	V6-229/9[4]	22	65	30	20	—	45[5]	45	70	60	60
	V6-231/A[12]	15	80	45	25	30[11]	4	40	100	60	225
	V8-305/G,H,S[4]	22	65	30	20[6]	—	45[5]	45	70	60	60
	V8-350/N[8]	—	130[9]	40[9]	25	28	—	42	120	60	200–310
1984	4-151/2	15	92	29	44	20	6	32	70	44	200
	V6-173/1,L[4]	7–15	70	23	25	46[21]	8	37	69	50	66–84
	V6-231/A[12]	15	80	45	25	30[11]	4	40	100	60	225
	V8-305/G,H[4]	22	65	30	20[6]	—	45[5]	45	70	60	60
	V8-350/N[8]	—	130[9]	40[9]	25	28	—	42	120	60	200–310

Continued

ENGINE TIGHTENING SPECIFICATION NOTES

①—1978, 15; 1979 22.
②—Rear, 100.
③—Rear 120.
④—For service on this engine, see Chevrolet Chapter.
⑤—Inch pounds.
⑥—Inside bolts 30 ft. lbs.
⑦—Rear, 100 ft. lbs.
⑧—For service on this engine, see Oldsmobile Chapter.
⑨—Clean & dip entire bolt in engine oil before tightening.
⑩—Exc. manual trans. 60 ft. lbs.; manual trans. 90 ft. lbs.
⑪—Rocker arm shaft to cylinder head.
⑫—See Buick chapter for service procedures.
⑬—Intake to exhaust manifold bolts, 40 ft. lbs.; manifold to cylinder head nuts, 30 ft. lbs.; manifold to cylinder head bolts, 40 ft. lbs.
⑭—Distributor located at rear of engine, clockwise rotor rotation.
⑮—Distributor located at rear of engine, counter clockwise rotor rotation. Fuel pump located left side of engine.
⑯—Distributor located at rear of engine, counter clockwise rotor rotation. Fuel pump located right side of engine.
⑰—Distributor located front of engine.
⑱—Except turbocharged engine.
⑲—Turbocharged engine.
⑳—Automatic transmission, 63; Manual transmission, 77.
㉑.—Rocker arm stud.

COOLING SYSTEM & CAPACITY DATA

Year	Model or Engine/V.I.N.	Cooling Capacity, Qts.		Radiator Cap Relief Pressure, Lbs.	Thermo. Opening Temp.	Fuel Tank Gals.	Engine Oil Refill Qts. ①	Transmission Oil				Rear Axle Oil Pints
		Less A/C	With A/C					3 Speed Pints	4 Speed Pints	5 Speed Pints	Auto Trans. Qts. ②	
1977	4-151/V Ventura	12.4	12.4	14–17	195	21	4	3.5	2.4	3.5	3⑮	3½
	V6-231/C Ventura	13.8	13.8	14–17	195	21	4	3.5	2.4	3.5	3⑮	3½
	V6-231/C LeMans	14.5	14.5	14–17	195	22	4	3.5	—	—	4⑧	4.25
	V6-231/C Firebird	13.2	13.2	14–17	195	21	4	3.5	2.5	—	4⑧	4.25
	V6-231/C Pontiac	12.9	12.9	14–17	195	21	4	—	—	—	⑯	⑰
	V8-301/Y Ventura	19.8	20.2㉓	14–17	195	21	5½	3.5	2.4	3.5	3⑱	3½
	V8-301/Y LeMans	20.2	20.8㉓	14–17	195	22	5½	3.5	—	—	⑯	4.25
	V8-301/Y Firebird	19.5	19.5	14–17	195	21	5½	3.5	2.5	—	4⑧	4.25
	V8-301/Y Pontiac	18.6	19.8㉓	14–17	195	21	5½	—	—	—	⑯	⑰
	V8-301/Y Grand Prix	20.5	21.1㉓	14–17	195	25	5½	—	—	—	3¾⑧	4.25
	V8-305/U Ventura	17	18	14–17	195	21	4	3.5	2.4	3.5	3⑱	3½
	V8-350/L,R Ventura	16.6	16.6	14–17	195	21	4	3.5	2.4	3.5	3⑧	3½
	V8-350/P LeMans⑲	21.7	23.9㉓	14–17	195	22	5	3.5	—	—	⑯	4.25
	V8-350/R LeMans⑳	16.7	17.5㉓	14–17	195	22	4	3.5	—	—	⑯	4.25
	V8-350/P Firebird⑲	20.3	23㉓	14–17	195	21	5	3.5	2.5	—	4⑧	4.25
	V8-350/R Firebird⑳	16	18.2㉓	14–17	195	21	4	3.5	2.5	—	4⑧	4.25
	V8-350/P Pontiac⑲	15	16.2㉓	14–17	195	21	5	—	—	—	⑯	⑰
	V8-350/R Pontiac⑳	15	16.2㉓	14–17	195	21	4	—	—	—	⑯	⑰
	V8-350/P Grand Prix⑲	21.9	24.1㉓	14–17	195	25	5	—	—	—	3¾⑧	4.25
	V8-350/R Grand Prix⑳	17	17.8㉓	14–17	195	25	4	—	—	—	3¾⑧	4.25
	V8-400/Z LeMans	21.7	23.9㉓	14–17	195	22	5	3.5	—	—	⑯	4.25
	V8-400/Z Firebird㉑	21.1	22.9	14–17	195	21	5	3.5	2.5	—	4⑧	4.25
	V8-400/Z Firebird㉒	20.4	21.2	14–17	195	21	5	3.5	2.5	—	4⑧	4.25
	V8-400/Z Firebird	—	23㉓	14–17	195	21	5	3.5	2.5	—	4⑧	4.25
	V8-400/Z Pontiac	21.7	23.9㉓	14–17	195	21	5	—	—	—	⑯	⑰
	V8-400/Z Grand Prix	21.9	24.1㉓	14–17	195	25	5	—	—	—	3¾⑧	4.25
	V8-403/K LeMans	17.9	18.7㉓	14–17	195	22	4	3.5	—	—	⑯	4.25
	V8-403/K Firebird	17.1	19.4㉓	14–17	195	21	4	3.5	2.5	—	4⑧	4.25
	V8-403/K Pontiac	16.1	17.3㉓	14–17	195	21	4	—	—	—	⑯	⑰
	V8-403/K Grand Prix	18.2	19.0㉓	14–17	195	25	4	—	—	—	3¾⑧	4.25
1978	4-151/V Phoenix	11.8	11.8	14–17	195	21	3	3.5	2.5	3.5	3⑫	3½
	V6-231/A Phoenix	14.0	14.1	14–17	195	21	4	3.5	2.5	—	3⑫	3½
	V6-231/A LeMans	14.3	14.2	14–17	195	17⑤	4	3.5	2.4	—	3⑫	3½
	V6-231/A Firebird	14.0	14.0	14–17	195	21	4	3.5	2.5	—	3④	4¼
	V6-231/A Grand Prix	14.3	14.2	14–17	195	15	4	3.5	—	—	3⑫	3½
	V6-231/A Pontiac	14.2	14.1	14–17	195	21	4	—	—	—	3⑫	⑰
	V8-301/W,Y LeMans	20.3	20.2	14–17	195	15⑤	5	—	—	—	3⑫	3½
	V8-301/W,Y Grand Prix	20.3	20.2	14–17	195	15	5	—	—	—	3⑫	3½
	V8-301/W,Y Pontiac	20.2	20.1	14–17	195	21	5	—	—	—	3⑫	⑰
	V8-305/H,U Phoenix	16.8	17.0	14–17	195	21	4	—	2.5	—	3⑫	3½
	V8-305/H,U LeMans	17.7	17.4	14–17	195	15⑤	4	—	—	—	3⑫	3½
	V8-305/H,U Firebird	17.2	17.2	14–17	195	21	4	—	3.5	—	3④	4¼
	V8-305/H,U Grand Prix	17.7	17.4	14–17	195	15	4	—	—	—	3⑫	3½

COOLING SYSTEM & CAPACITY DATA—Continued

Year	Model or Engine/V.I.N.	Cooling Capacity, Qts.		Radiator Cap Relief Pressure, Lbs.	Thermo. Opening Temp.	Fuel Tank Gals.	Engine Oil Refill Qts. ①	Transmission Oil				Rear Axle Oil Pints
		Less A/C	With A/C					3 Speed Pints	4 Speed Pints	5 Speed Pints	Auto Trans. Qts. ②	
1978	V8-350/L,R Phoenix	17.1	17.8	14–17	195	21	4	—	—	—	3(12)	4¼
	V8-350/L,R LeMans	17.7	18.1	14–17	195	15(5)	4	—	—	—	3(12)	3½
	V8-350/L,R Firebird	17.2	17.2	14–17	195	21	4	—	3.5	—	3(4)	4¼
	V8-350/X Pontiac(6)	16.6	18.5	14–17	195	21	4	—	—	—	3(12)	4¼
	V8-350/L,R Pontiac	16.5	19.1	14–17	195	21(7)	4	—	—	—	3(12)	4¼
	V8-400/Z Firebird	19.7	22.0	14–17	195	21	5	—	2.4	—	3(4)	4¼
	V8-400/Z Pontiac	26.3	20.3	14–17	195	21	5	—	—	—	3(12)	4¼
	V8-403/K Firebird	17.4	18.0	14–17	195	21	4	—	—	—	3(4)	4¼
	V8-403/K Pontiac	17.7	23.0	14–17	195	21	4	—	—	—	3(12)	4¼
1979	V6-231/A Phoenix	14	14	14–17	195	21	4	3.5	3.5	—	3(34)	(17)
	V6-231/A LeMans	14.2	14	14–17	195	18	4	3.5	3.5	—	3(34)	3½
	V6-231/A Firebird	14	14	14–17	195	21	4	3.5	2.5	—	3(34)	4¼
	V6-231/A Grand Prix	14.2	14	14–17	195	18	4	3.5	3.5	—	3(34)	3½
	V6-231/A Pontiac	13.9	13.9	14–17	195	21	4	3.5	2.5	—	3(34)	(31)
	V8-301/W,Y Firebird	(26)	(26)	14–17	195	21	4(33)	3.5	2.5	—	3(34)	4¼
	V8-301/W,Y LeMans	20.3(32)	20.3(32)	14–17	195	18	4(33)	3.5	3.5	—	3(34)	3½
	V8-301/W,Y Grand Prix	20.3(29)	20.3(29)	14–17	195	18	4(33)	3.5	2.5	—	3(34)	4¼
	V8-301/W,Y Pontiac	20.2	20.2	14–17	195	21	4(33)	—	—	—	3(34)	(31)
	V8-305/G,H Phoenix	16.8(11)	17(11)	14–17	195	21	4	3.5	3.5	—	3(34)	(17)
	V8-305/G,H LeMans	17.7(30)	18.3	14–17	195	18	4	3.5	3.5	—	3(34)	3.5
	V8-305/G,H Firebird	17.2(11)	17.8	14–17	195	21	4	3.5	2.5	—	3(34)	4¼
	V8-305/G,H Grand Prix	17.7(30)	18.3	14–17	195	18	4	3.5	3.5	—	3(34)	3½
	V8-350/L,R,X Phoenix	17.1	17.8	14–17	195	21	4	3.5	3.5	—	3(34)	(17)
	V8-350/L,R,X LeMans	17.7(30)	18.3	14–17	195	18	4	3.5	3.5	—	3(34)	3.5
	V8-350/L,R,X Firebird	17.2	17.8	14–17	195	21	4	3.5	2.5	—	3(34)	4¼
	V8-350/L,R,X Pontiac	17	23	14–17	195	21	4	—	—	—	3(34)	(31)
	V8-400/Z Firebird	19.7(24)	20.3(24)	14–17	195	21	5	3.5	2.5	—	3(34)	4¼
	V8-403/K Firebird	17.4(25)	18	14–17	195	21	4	3.5	2.5	—	3(34)	4¼
	V8-403/K Pontiac	17(30)	23(30)	14–17	195	21	4	—	—	—	3(34)	(31)
1980	V6-229/K LeMans	18.5	18.5	15	195	18.1	4	3.5	—	—	(3)	3.5
	V6-231/A LeMans	13.3	13.3	15	195	18.1	4	3.5	—	—	(3)	3.4
	V6-231/A Firebird	14	14	15	195	20.8	4	3.5	—	—	(3)	4¼
	V6-231/A Grand Prix	13.3	13.3	15	195	18.1	4	—	—	—	(3)	3.5
	V6-231/A Pontiac	13.3	13.3	15	195	25(14)	4	—	—	—	(3)	(17)
	V8-265/S LeMans	20.3	20.3	15	195	18.1	4(33)	—	—	—	(3)	3.5
	V8-265/S Firebird	21.6	21.6	15	195	20.8	4(33)	—	—	—	(3)	4¼
	V8-265/S Grand Prix	20.3	20.3	15	195	18.1	4(33)	—	—	—	(3)	3.5
	V8-265/S Pontiac	21.1	21.1	15	195	25(14)	4(33)	—	—	—	(3)	(17)
	V8-301/T LeMans	20.3	20.3	15	195	18.1	4(33)	—	—	—	(3)	3.5
	V8-301/T Firebird	21.6	21.6	15	195	20.8	4(33)	—	—	—	(3)	4¼
	V8-301/T Grand Prix	20.3	20.3	15	195	18.1	4(33)	—	—	—	(3)	3.5
	V8-301/T Pontiac	21.1	21.1	15	195	25(14)	4(33)	—	—	—	(3)	(17)
	V8-305/H LeMans	18.5	18.5	15	195	18.1	4	—	—	—	(3)	3.5
	V8-305/H Firebird	17.3	17.3	15	195	20.8	4	—	—	—	(3)	4¼
	V8-305/H Grand Prix	18.2	18.2	15	195	18.1	4	—	—	—	(3)	3.4
	V8-305/H Pontiac	20.1	20.1	15	195	25(14)	4	—	—	—	(3)	(17)
	V8-350/X Pontiac(19)	14.8	14.8	15	195	25(14)	4	—	—	—	(3)	(17)
	V8-350/R Pontiac(20)	16.4	16.4	15	195	25(14)	5(33)	—	—	—	(3)	(17)
	V8-350 Diesel/N Pontiac	18.2	18.2	15	195	27(14)	7(35)	—	—	—	(3)	(17)
1981	V6-231/A LeMans	13.1	13.1	15	195	18.1	4	3½	—	—	(9)	3.5
	V6-231/A Firebird	13.1	13.1	15	195	20.8	4	3½	—	—	(9)	4.2
	V6-231/A Grand Prix	13.1	13.1	15	195	18.1	4	—	—	—	(10)	3.5
	V6-231/A Pontiac	13.1	13.3	15	195	25	4	—	—	—	(13)	(17)

Continued

COOLING SYSTEM & CAPACITY DATA—Continued

Year	Model or Engine/V.I.N.	Cooling Capacity, Qts. Less A/C	With A/C	Radiator Cap Relief Pressure, Lbs.	Thermo. Opening Temp.	Fuel Tank Gals.	Engine Oil Refill Qts. ①	Transmission Oil 3 Speed Pints	4 Speed Pints	5 Speed Pints	Auto Trans. Qts. ②	Rear Axle Oil Pints
1981	V8-265/S LeMans	20.3	20.3	15	195	18.1	4㉝	—	—	—	⑨	3.5
	V8-265/S Firebird	20.9㊱	20.9㊱	15	195	20.8	4㉝	—	—	—	⑨	4.2
	V8-265/S Grand Prix	20.3	20.3	15	195	18.1	4㉝	—	—	—	⑩	3.5
	V8-265/S Pontiac	19	19	15	195	25	4㉝	—	—	—	⑬	⑰
	V8-301/W LeMans	20.3㉗	21	15	195	18.1	4㉝	—	—	—	⑨	3.5
	V8-301/W Firebird	20.9㊱	20.9㊱	15	195	20.8	4㉝	—	—	—	⑨	4.2
	V8-301/T Firebird	23	23	15	195	20.8	5㉝	—	—	—	⑨	4.2
	V8-305/H Firebird	17.2	17.2	15	195	20.8	4	—	—	—	⑨	4.2
	V8-307/Y Pontiac	15.6㉘	15.3㉘	15	195	25⑭	4	—	—	—	⑬	⑰
	V8-350/N Grand Prix	17	17	15	195	19.8	7㉟	—	—	—	⑩	3.5
	V8-350/N Pontiac	17	17	15	195	27⑭	7㉟	—	—	—	⑬	⑰
1982	4-151/2 Firebird	12.8	13	15	195	16	3㉝	—	3.5	—	㊳	3.5
	V6-173/1 Firebird	12.5	12.5	15	195	16	4㉝	—	3.5	—	㊳	3.5
	V6-231/A Bonneville	13	13	15	195	18	4	—	—	—	㊴	3.5
	V6-231/A Grand Prix	13	13	15	195	18	4	—	—	—	㊴	3.5
	V6-252/4 Bonneville	13	13	15	195	18	4	—	—	—	㊴	3.5
	V6-252/4 Grand Prix	13	13	15	195	18	4	—	—	—	㊴	3.5
	V8-305/H Firebird	15	15	15	195	16	4	—	—	—	㊳	3.5
	V8-305 E.F.I./7 Firebird	15	15	15	195	16	4	—	—	—	㊳	3.5
	V8-350 Diesel/N Bonneville	17.3	17.3	15	195	19.8⑤	7㊲	—	—	—	㊴	3.5
	V8-350 Diesel/N Grand Prix	17.3	17.3	15	195	19.8	7㊲	—	—	—	㊴	3.5
1983	4-151/2 Firebird	12.8	13	15	195	16	3㉝	—	4.3	5.3	㊶	3.5
	V6-173/1 Firebird	12.5	12.5	15	195	16	4㉝	—	—	5.3	㊶	3.5
	V6-173/L H.O. Firebird	12.5	12.5	15	195	16	4㉝	—	—	5.3	㊶	3.5
	V6-229/9 Parisienne	14.3	14.3	15	195	25⑭	4㉝	—	—	—	㊹	㊸
	V6-231/A Bonneville	13	13	15	195	17.5⑤	4	—	—	—	㊵	3.5
	V6-231/A Grand Prix	13	13	15	195	17.5	4	—	—	—	㊵	3.5
	V8-305/H Bonneville	15.3	15.9	15	195	17.5	4	—	—	—	㊵	3.5
	V8-305/G,H Firebird	15	15	15	195	16	4	—	—	5.3	㊶	3.5
	V8-305/H Grand Prix	15.3	15.9	15	195	17.5	4	—	—	—	㊵	3.5
	V8-305 TBI/S Firebird	15	15	15	195	16	4	—	—	—	㊶	3.5
	V8-305/H Parisienne	15.5	15.5	15	195	25⑭	4	—	—	—	㊹	㊸
	V8-350 Diesel/N Bonneville	17.3	17.3	15	195	19.8	7㊲	—	—	—	㊵	3.5
	V8-350 Diesel/N Grand Prix	17.3	17.3	15	195	19.8	7㊲	—	—	—	㊵	3.5
	V8-350 Diesel/N Parisienne	18.3	18.3	15	195	27⑭	7㊲	—	—	—	㊹	㊸
1984	4-151/2 Firebird	12.8	13	15	195	15.9	3㉝	—	4.3	5.3	㊶	3.5
	V6-173/1,L Firebird	12.5	12.5	15	195	15.9	4㉝	—	—	5.3	㊶	3.5
	V6-231/A Bonneville	13	13	15	195	18.1	4	—	—	—	㊷	3.5
	V6-231/A Grand Prix	13	13	15	195	18.1	4	—	—	—	㊷	3.5
	V6-231/A Parisienne	11.75	11.75	15	195	25⑭	4	—	—	—	㊷	㊸
	V8-305/H Bonneville	15.25	15.25	15	195	18.1	4	—	—	—	㊷	3.5
	V8-305/H Firebird	17.2	17.2	15	195	15.9	4	—	—	5.3	㊶	㊸
	V8-305/H Grand Prix	15.3	16.1	15	195	18.1	4	—	—	—	㊷	3.5
	V8-305/H Parisienne	15.25	15.25	15	195	25⑭	4	—	—	—	㊷	㊸
	V8-305 H.O./G Firebird	17.2	17.2	15	195	15.9	7㊲	—	—	5.3	㊶	3.5
	V8-350 Diesel/N Bonneville	17.2	17.2	15	195	19.8	7㊲	—	—	—	㊷	3.5
	V8-350 Diesel/N Grand Prix	17.2	17.2	15	195	19.8	7㊲	—	—	—	㊷	3.5
	V8-350 Diesel/N Parisienne	18.3	18.3	15	195	27⑭	7㊲	—	—	—	㊷	㊸

COOLING SYSTEM & CAPACITY DATA NOTES

①—Add one quart with filter change.
②—Approximate. Make final check with dipstick.
③—THM 200—oil pan, 3.5 qts.; after overhaul, 9½ qts. THM 250 & 350—oil pan, 2¾ qts.; after overhaul, 10¼ qts.
④—Oil pan only. After overhaul 10 qts.
⑤—Station Wagons, 18 gals.
⑥—Distributor located at front of engine.
⑦—Station Wagons 24 gals.
⑧—Oil pan only. After overhaul 9½ qts.
⑨—T.H.M. 200/C, oil pan 4.15 qts., after overhaul 10.55 qts.; T.H.M. 250/C, oil pan 2¾ qts., after overhaul 10.25 qts.; T.H.M. 350/C, oil pan 3.15 qts., after overhaul 10 qts.; T.H.M. 350/O, oil pan 3.15 qts. after overhaul 11.45 qts.
⑩—T.H.M. 200/C, oil pan 4.25 qts., after overhaul 10.55 qts.; T.H.M. 250/C, oil pan 2.75 qts., after overhaul, 10.25 qts.; T.H.M. 350/C, oil pan 3.15 qts., after overhaul 10 qts.
⑪—With heavy duty cooling system, 17.8 qts.
⑫—Oil pan only. After overhaul; THM 200, 9 qts. THM 350, 10 qts.
⑬—T.H.M. 200/C, oil pan 4.25 qts., after overhaul 10.55 qts.; T.H.M. 250/C, oil pan 2.75 qts., after overhaul 10.25 qts.; T.H.M. 350/C, oil pan 3.15 qts., after overhaul 10 qts.; T.H.M. 200-4R, oil pan 5.05 qts., after overhaul 11 qts.
⑭—Station Wagons 22 gals.
⑮—Oil pan only. After overhaul 6¾ qts.
⑯—THM 200, oil pan only 3 qts.; after overhaul 8¾ qts. THM 350, oil pan only 4 qts.; after overhaul 9.6 qts. THM 400, oil pan only 3¾ qts.; after overhaul 9½ qts.
⑰—7½ inch axle 3½ pints. 8½ & 8¾ inch axle 4¼ pints.
⑱—Oil pan only. After overhaul 8¾ qts.
⑲—With fuel pump located on driver side of engine.
⑳—With fuel pump located on passenger side of engine.
㉑—Manual trans.
㉒—Auto. trans.
㉓—Vehicles equipped with A/C and/or heavy duty cooling system.
㉔—With heavy duty cooling system, 21.7 qts.
㉕—With heavy duty cooling system, 18.1 qts.
㉖—With 2 barrel carb., 19.9 qts. With 2 barrel carb., 20.5 qts. With 2 barrel carb. and heavy duty cooling system, 20.4 qts. With 4 barrel carb. and heavy duty cooling system, 21 qts.
㉗—With heavy duty cooling system, 21 qts.
㉘—With heavy duty cooling system, 16.2 qts.
㉙—With heavy duty cooling system, 20.8 qts.
㉚—With heavy duty cooling system, 18.5 qts.
㉛—Exc. Station Wagon, 3.5 pts.; Station Wagon, 4.25 pts.
㉜—With heavy duty cooling system, 20.8 qts.
㉝—With or without filter change.
㉞—Oil pan only. After overhaul 9 qts.
㉟—Includes filter. Recommended diesel engine oil—on 1980 units, use oil designated SE/CC; on 1981 units, use engine oil designated SF/CC, SF/CD or SE/CC.
㊱—With heavy duty cooling system, 21.6 qts.
㊲—Includes filter. Recommended diesel engine oil—on 1982–84 units, use oil designated SF/CD or SF/CC.
㊳—Oil pan only, 3.5 qts.; after overhaul, 5 qts.
㊴—T.H.M. 250C, oil pan only, 2.75 qts.; after overhaul, 10.25 qts. T.H.M. 350C, oil pan only, 3.15 qts.; after overhaul, 10.15 qts.
㊵—T.H.M. 250C, oil pan only, 2.75 qts.; after overhaul, 10.25 qts. T.H.M. 350C, oil pan only, 3.25 qts.; after overhaul, 10.15 qts.
㊶—T.H.M. 200C, oil pan only, 4¼ qts.; after overhaul, 10½ qts.; T.H.M. 700-4R, oil pan only, 4.7 qts.; total capacity, 11½ qts.
㊷—T.H.M. 200C, oil pan only, 4¼ qts.; after overhaul, 10½ qts. T.H.M. 200-4R, oil pan only, 3.48 qts.; after overhaul, 11.05 qts.; T.H.M. 250C, oil pan only, 3.15 qts.; after overhaul, 10.0 qts. T.H.M. 700-4R, oil pan only, 4.7 qts; after overhaul 11.5
㊸—7½ inch axle, 3.5 pints; 8½ inch axle, 4.3 pints; 8¾ inch axle, 5.4 pints.
㊹—T.H.M. 200C, oil pan, 3.5 qts.; after overhaul, 5 qts. T.H.M. 350C, oil pan, 3 qts.; after overhaul, 10 qts.

WHEEL ALIGNMENT SPECIFICATIONS

Year	Model	Caster Angle, Degrees		Camber Angle, Degrees					Toe-In, Inch	Toe-Out on Turns, Deg.	
		Limits	Desired	Limits		Desired				Outer Wheel	Inner Wheel
				Left	Right	Left	Right				
1977	Ventura②	−1½ to −½	−1	+.3 to +1.3	+.3 to +1.3	+.8	+.8	0 to 1/8	—	—
	Ventura③	+½ to +1½	+1	+.3 to +1.3	+.3 to +1.3	+.8	+.8	0 to 1/8	—	—
	Firebird	+½ to +1½	+1	+½ to +1½	+½ to +1½	+1	+1	0 to 1/8	—	—
	LeMans②	+½ to +1½	+1	+½ to +1½	0 to +1	+1	+½	0 to 1/8	—	—
	LeMans③	①	+2	+½ to +1½	0 to +1	+1	+½	0 to 1/8	—	—
	Grand Prix	+4.5 to +5.5	+5	+½ to +1½	0 to +1	+1	+½	0 to 1/8	—	—
	Pontiac	+2½ to +3½	+3	+.3 to 1.3	+.3 to 1.3	+.8	+.8	1/8 to 1/4	—	—
1978	Phoenix②	−1.5 to −.5	−1	+.3 to 1.3	+.3 to 1.3	+.8	+.8	1/16 to 3/16	—	—
	Phoenix③	+.5 to +1.5	+1	+.3 to 1.3	+.3 to 1.3	+.8	+.8	1/16 to 3/16	—	—
	Firebird	+.5 to +1.5	+1	+.5 to +1.5	+.5 to +1.5	+1	+1	1/16 to 3/16	—	—
	Intermediate②	+.5 to +1.5	+1	0 to +1	0 to +1	+.5	+.5	1/16 to 3/16	—	—
	Intermediate③	+2.5 to +3.5	+3	0 to +1	0 to +1	+.5	+.5	1/16 to 3/16	—	—
	Pontiac	+2.5 to +3.5	+3	+.3 to 1.3	+.3 to 1.3	+.8	+.8	1/16 to 3/16	—	—
1979	Phoenix②	−1.5 to −.5	−1	+.3 to 1.3	+.3 to 1.3	+.8	+.8	1/16 to 3/16	—	—
	Phoenix③	+.5 to +1.5	+1	+.3 to 1.3	+.3 to 1.3	+.8	+.8	1/16 to 3/16	—	—
	Firebird	+.5 to +1.5	+1	+.5 to +1.5	+.5 to +1.5	+1	+1	1/16 to 3/16	—	—
	LeMans②	+.5 to +1.5	+1	0 to +1	0 to +1	+.5	+.5	1/16 to 3/16	—	—
	LeMans③	+2.5 to +3.5	+3	0 to +1	0 to +1	+.5	+.5	1/16 to 3/16	—	—
	Grand Prix	+2.5 to +3.5	+3	0 to +1	0 to +1	+.5	+.5	1/16 to 3/16	—	—
	Pontiac	+2.5 to +3.5	+3	.3 to 1.3	.3 to 1.3	+.8	+.8	1/16 to 3/16	—	—
1980	Firebird	+.5 to +1.5	+1	+.5 to +1.5	+.5 to +1.5	+1	+1	1/16 to 3/16	—	—
	LeMans②	+.5 to +1.5	+1	0 to +1	0 to +1	+.5	+.5	1/16 to 3/16	—	—
	LeMans③	+2.5 to +3.5	+3	0 to +1	0 to +1	+.5	+.5	1/16 to 3/16	—	—
	Grand Prix	+2.5 to +3.5	+3	0 to +1	0 to +1	+.5	+.5	1/16 to 3/16	—	—
	Pontiac	+2.5 to +3.5	+3	+.3 to 1.3	+.3 to 1.3	+.8	+.8	1/16 to 3/16	—	—

Continued

WHEEL ALIGNMENT SPECIFICATIONS—Continued

Year	Model	Caster Angle, Degrees		Camber Angle, Degrees				Toe-In. Inch	Toe-Out on Turns, Deg.	
		Limits	Desired	Limits		Desired			Outer Wheel	Inner Wheel
				Left	Right	Left	Right			
1981	Firebird	+.5 to +1.5	+1	+.5 to +1.5	+.5 to +1.5	+1	+1	1/16 to 3/16	—	—
	LeMans	+2.5 to +3.5	+3	−.4 to +.6	−.4 to +.6	+.1	+.1	1/16 to 3/16	—	—
	Grand Prix	+2.5 to +3.5	+3	−.4 to +.6	−.4 to +.6	+.1	+.1	1/16 to 3/16	—	—
	Pontiac	+.5 to +1.5	+1	+.3 to +1.3	+.3 to +1.3	+.8	+.8	1/16 to 3/16	—	—
1982	Firebird	+2.5 to +3.5	+3	+1/2 to +1 1/2	+1/2 to +1 1/2	+1	+1	1/8 to 1/4	—	—
	Grand Prix	+2.5 to +3.5	+3	0 to +1	0 to +1	+.5	+.5	1/16 to 3/16	—	—
	Bonneville	+2.5 to +3.5	+3	0 to +1	0 to +1	+.5	+.5	1/16 to 3/16	—	—
1983–84	Firebird	+2.5 to +3.5	+3	+.5 to +1.5	+.5 to +1.5	+1	+1	④	—	—
	Grand Prix	+2.5 to +3.5	+3	0 to +1	0 to +1	+5	+5	1/16 to 3/16	—	—
	Bonneville	+2.5 to +3.5	+3	0 to +1	0 to +1	+5	+5	1/16 to 3/16	—	—
	Parisienne	+2.5 to +3.5	+3	+.3 to +1.3	+.3 to +1.3	+.8	+.8	1/16 to 3/16	—	—

①—Exc. radial tires, +1/2 to +1 1/2; Radial tires +1 1/2 to +2 1/2.
②—Manual Steering.
③—Power steering.
④—Toe-in degrees per wheel, −.3° to +.7°.

Electrical Section

STARTER, REPLACE

NOTE: Upon removal of starter, note if any shims are used. If shims are used, they should be reinstalled in their original location during installation.

If starter is noisy during cranking, remove one .015 inch double shim or add one .015 inch single shim to the outer bolt. If starter makes a high pitched whine after firing, add .015 inch double shims until noise ceases.

1. Disconnect battery ground cable.
2. Disconnect brace from starter and swing brace forward, then remove heat shields, if used.
3. On 4-151, disconnect wiring from starter, then remove retaining bolts and starter.
4. On all other engines, remove starter retaining bolts, then lower starter, disconnect wiring and remove starter.
5. Reverse procedure to install.

IGNITION LOCK, REPLACE

1979–84

1. Remove steering wheel as described under Horn Sounder and Steering Wheel.
2. Remove turn signal switch as described under Turn Signal Switch, Replace, then remove buzzer switch.
3. Place ignition switch in "Run" position, then, remove lock cylinder retaining screw and lock cylinder.
4. To install, rotate lock cylinder to stop while holding housing, Fig. 1. Align cylinder key with keyway in housing, then push lock cylinder assembly into housing until fully seated.
5. Install lock cylinder retaining screw. Torque screw to 40 in. lbs. for standard columns. On adjustable columns, torque retaining screw to 22 in. lbs.
6. Install buzzer switch, turn signal switch and steering wheel.

1977–78

1. Follow the procedure to remove the turn signal switch as described further on.
2. Remove the lock cylinder in "Run" position by inserting a thin tool (screwdriver or knife blade), Fig. 2, into the slot next to the switch mounting screw boss (right hand slot) and depress spring latch at bottom of slot, which releases lock. Remove lock by pulling out of housing.

NOTE: If this is the first time the lock cylinder is being removed, the slot will be covered by a thin casting "flash" which is easily broken when inserting thin tool.

3. To install, hold lock cylinder sleeve and rotate knob clockwise against stop, then insert cylinder into housing with key on lock cylinder sleeve aligned with keyway in housing. Push into abutment of cylinder and lock sector.
4. Push in until latch snaps into groove and lock cylinder is secured in housing.

IGNITION SWITCH, REPLACE

1. Disconnect battery ground cable.
2. Position ignition key in off-unlock position on standard columns, or ACC on tilt columns.
3. Remove lower portion of instrument panel, then toe-pan trim cover.
4. Remove shift indicator cable clip from shift bowl, if equipped with column shift.
5. Loosen toe-pan clamp bolts, then remove switch attaching screws.
6. Disconnect electrical wiring from switch, then remove switch from steering column.
7. Position new switch slider in same position as old switch slider, Fig. 3.
8. Install new switch.

LIGHT SWITCH, REPLACE

1977–81 & 1983–84 Full Size

1. Disconnect battery ground cable.

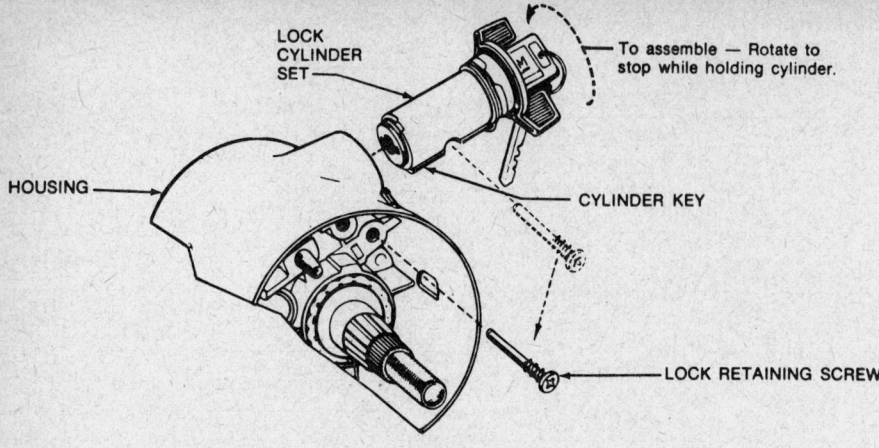

Fig. 1 Ignition lock replacement. 1979—84 models

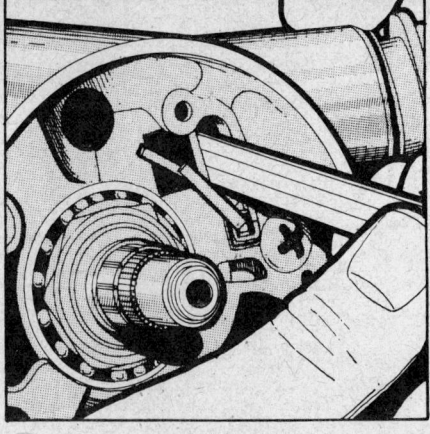

Fig. 2 Ignition lock replace. 1977—78

2. Pull headlight knob to "ON" position, then reach under instrument panel, depress switch shaft release button and pull knob and shaft assembly from switch.
3. Remove switch retaining nut, wire connector and switch.
4. Reverse procedure to install.

1977—84 Intermediate Size

1. Disconnect battery ground cable.
2. Remove left side lower trim panel.
3. Remove instrument panel bezel attaching screws, then bezel.
4. Pull headlight knob to "ON" position, then remove light switch mounting plate to cluster attaching screws and pull assembly rearward.
5. Depress switch shaft retainer and pull out knob and shaft assembly.
6. Remove wiring connector from switch, then switch.
7. Disassemble light switch from bracket.
8. Reverse procedure to install.

1977—81 Firebird

1. Disconnect battery ground cable.
2. Remove lower cover from steering column.
3. Reach up under left side of instrument cluster and depress light switch shaft retainer while pulling on shaft.
4. Remove switch to carrier retaining nut.
5. Remove instrument cluster retaining screws, and tilt right side of cluster out.
6. Disconnect electrical connectors from switch, then remove switch.
7. Reverse procedure to install.

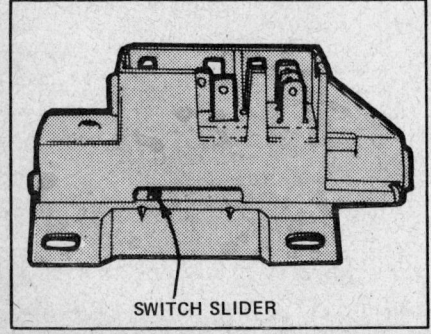

SWITCH SLIDER

Fig. 3 Ignition switch. 1977—84 (typical)

1982—84 Firebird

1. Remove right and left lower trim plates.
2. Remove instrument panel cluster trim plate.
3. Remove two retaining screws from switch assembly.
4. Depress side tangs and pull switch assembly from instrument panel.
5. Reverse procedure to install.

STOP LIGHT SWITCH, REPLACE

Except 1982—84 Firebird

The stop light switch has a slip fit in the mounting sleeve which permits positive adjustment by pulling the brake pedal up firmly against the stop. The pedal arm forces the switch body to slip in the mounting sleeve bushing to position the switch properly.
1. Disconnect wires from switch and remove switch from bracket.
2. Position new switch in bracket and push in to maximum distance. Brake pedal arm moves switch to correct distance on rebound. Check if pedal is in full return position by lifting slightly by hand.
3. Connect switch wires by inserting plug on switch.

1982—84 Firebird

1. Remove left hand side hush panel.
2. Located under instrument panel, disconnect wire connector from switch at brake pedal support.
3. Remove switch from mounting bracket.
4. Depress brake pedal and install new switch into clip, until shoulder on switch bottoms out against clip.
5. If adjustment of the switch is necessary, the switch may be rotated or pulled in the clip. Electrical contact should be made when brake pedal is depressed .053 inch from its fully released position.

NEUTRAL SAFETY SWITCH, REPLACE

NOTE: Some models use a combination neutral start and back-up light switch, while others use a separate back-up light switch.

Both switches are serviced in the following manner.

1982—84 Self-Adjusting Type

1. Place gear selector in "Neutral."
2. Gently rock switch out of steering column.
3. Disconnect wiring connectors. Connect wiring connectors to new switch.
4. Align switch actuator with hole in shift tube, Fig. 4.
5. Position connector side of switch into lower jacket cut out.
6. Push down front of switch, ensuring switch tangs snap into holes in steering column jacket.
7. Adjust switch by placing gear selector in "Park" position. Switch main housing and housing back should ratchet, providing proper adjustment.

1977—84 Manual Adjust Type, Exc. 1982—84 Firebird

1. Lock steering column in "Park" position

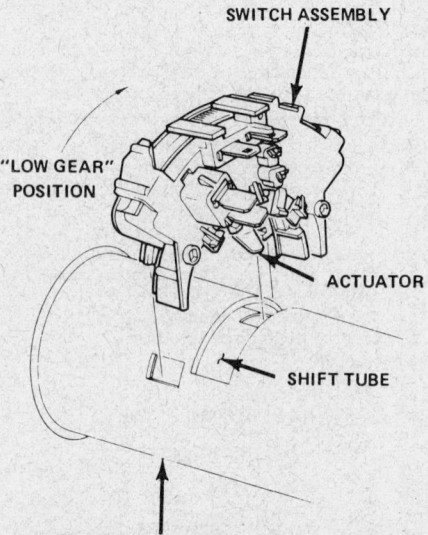

Fig. 4 Self-adjusting type neutral safety switch (typical)

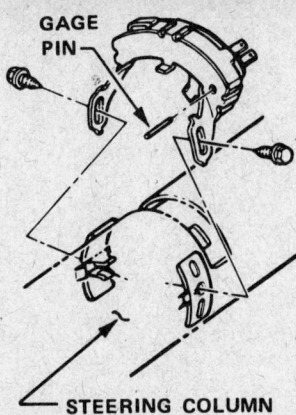

Fig. 5 Manual adjust type neutral safety switch. Manual transmission (typical)

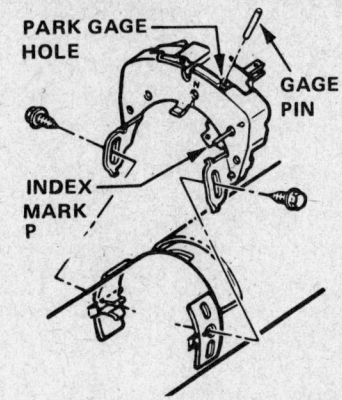

Fig. 6 Manual adjust type neutral safety switch. Automatic transmission (typical)

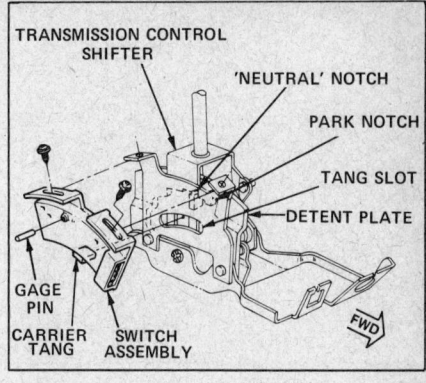

Fig. 7 Neutral safety switch. 1982–84 Firebird

for automatic transmissions and "Reverse" for manual transmissions, then remove screws attaching switch to steering column.
2. Remove switch electrical connectors, then switch.
3. Connect wiring connector to new switch.
4. Position new switch on steering column, aligning switch carrier tang in shift selector tube slot.
5. Install attaching screws and tighten.

NOTE: The switch is held in the proper position with a plastic sheer pin. No additional pinning is required.

6. Adjust switch by loosening attaching screws, then inserting a .096 inch gauge pin in gauge hole of switch, Figs. 5 and 6.
7. Rotate switch in clockwise direction until freeplay is eliminated and gauge pin slides in gauge hole to a depth of 3/8 inch.
8. Tighten attaching screws and remove gauge pin.

1982–84 Firebird

1. Remove floor console cover.
2. Disconnect wire connectors from backup lamp/neutral start switch.
3. Position gear shift lever into Neutral position.
4. Remove two screws securing neutral

starter switch, then remove switch.
5. Ensure gear shift lever is in Neutral position before installing switch.
6. Install new switch in position on gear shift lever. Ensure pin on gear shift lever is in slot of switch. Tighten switch and torque to 14–19 inch lbs., Fig. 7.
7. Move gear shift lever out of Neutral position to break plastic shear pin.
8. Connect electrical connectors to switch. Apply parking brake and start vehicle. Ensure vehicle starts only in Park or Neutral positions.
9. Turn ignition off and install floor console cover.

MECHANICAL NEUTRAL START SYSTEM

1977–81 Full Size, 1978–81 Grand Am, Grand Prix & LeMans & 1982–84 Bonneville & Grand Prix & 1983–84 Parisienne

Actuation of the ignition switch is prevented by a mechanical lockout system, Figs. 8 and 9, which prevents the lock cylinder from rotating when the selector lever is out of Park or Neutral. When the selector lever is in Park or Neutral, the slots in the bowl plate and the finger on the actuator rod align allowing the finger to pass through the bowl plate in turn actuating the ignition switch, Fig. 10. If the

selector lever is in any position other than Park or Neutral, the finger contacts the bowl plate when the lock cylinder is rotated, thereby preventing full travel of the lock cylinder.

CLUTCH START SWITCH

All cars equipped with a manual transmission use a clutch start switch which is mounted on the pedal bracket. The switch closes when the clutch is depressed and completes solenoid connection. When installing switch, no adjustment is necessary.

TURN SIGNAL SWITCH, REPLACE

1977–84

NOTE: *On tilt column, the column must first be lowered from panel.*

1. Disconnect battery ground cable, then remove steering wheel using puller.

CAUTION: *Do not hammer on end of shaft as hammering could collapse shaft or loosen plastic injections which maintain column rigidity.*

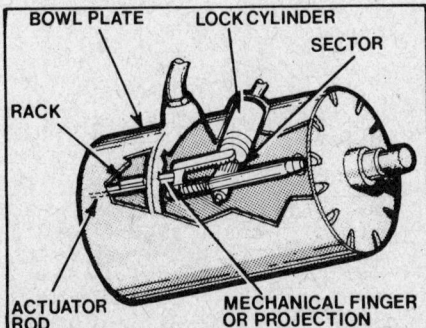

Fig. 8 Mechanical neutral start system with standard column. 1977–81 Full size models, 1978–81 Grand Am, Grand Prix and LeMans & 1982–84 Bonneville & Grand Prix & 1983–84 Parisienne

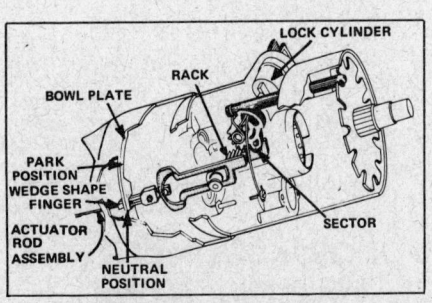

Fig. 9 Mechanical neutral start system with tilt column. 1977–81 Full size models, 1978–81 Grand Am, Grand Prix and LeMans & 1982–84 Bonneville & Grand Prix & 1983–84 Parisienne

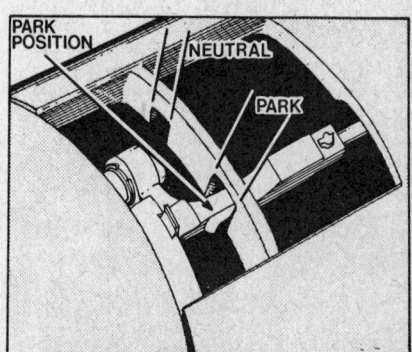

Fig. 10 Mechanical neutral start system in Park position. 1977–81 Full size models, 1978–81 Grand Am, Grand Prix and LeMans & 1982–84 Bonneville & Grand Prix & 1983–84 Parisienne

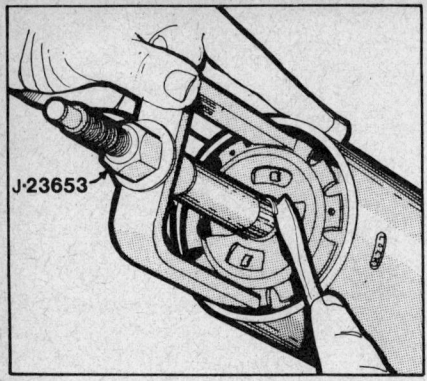

Fig. 11   Compressing lock plate and removing retaining ring

J·23653

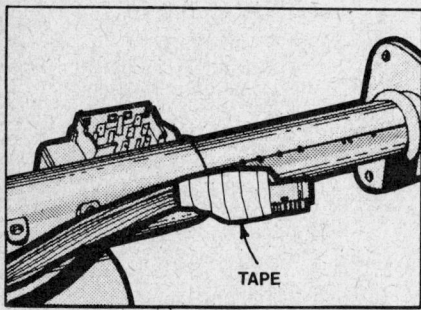

TAPE

Fig. 12   Taping turn signal connector & wires

2. Remove cover by prying out with a screwdriver at slots provided in cover for this purpose.
3. Depress lock plate and pry round wire lock ring out of shaft groove, Fig. 11. Remove lock plate.
4. Slide upper bearing preload spring and turn signal cancelling cam off shaft.
5. Remove turn signal lever.

NOTE: On models with column mounted dimmer switch, remove actuator arm screw and actuator arm before removing turn signal lever.

6. Push hazard warning switch in and unscrew knob.
7. Pull turn signal wiring connector out of bracket on jacket and disconnect.
8. Remove three turn signal switch screws.
9. Remove shift indicator cable, if equipped.
10. Lower steering column from instrument panel and remove wire protector, then pull switch straight up with wire protector and remove housing.

NOTE: Place tape around upper part of connector and wires to prevent snagging when switch is being removed, Fig. 12

COLUMN-MOUNTED DIMMER SWITCH, REPLACE

1977–81 Full Size, 1978–81 Grand Prix & LeMans & 1982–84 Bonneville, Grand Prix & Firebird & 1983–84 Parisienne

1. Disconnect battery ground cable.

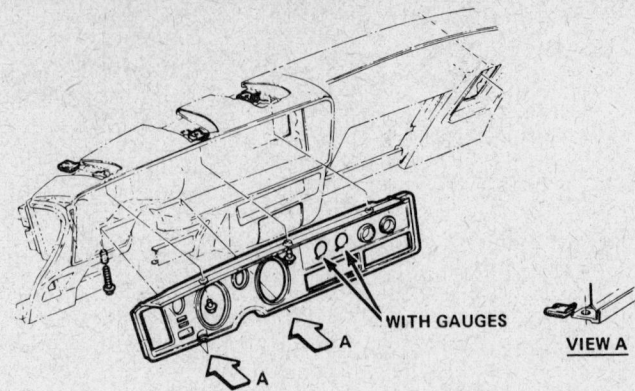

WITH GAUGES

VIEW A

Fig. 13   Instrument panel. 1977–81 Firebird

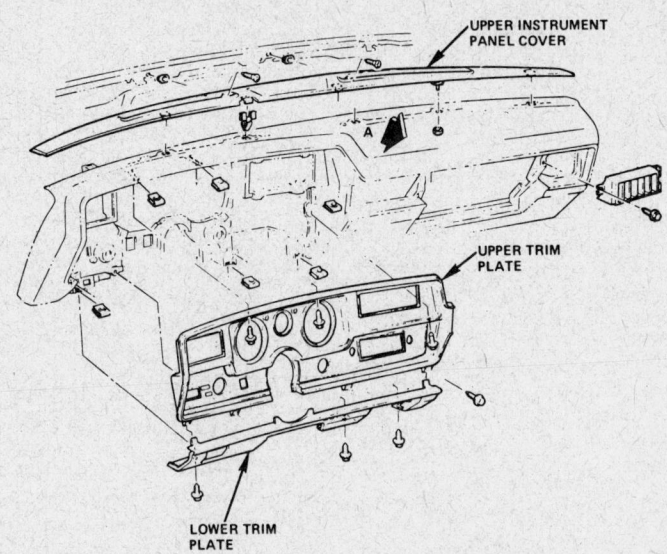

UPPER INSTRUMENT PANEL COVER

UPPER TRIM PLATE

LOWER TRIM PLATE

Fig. 14   Instrument panel. 1977 LeMans less optional instrument cluster

2. Remove instrument panel lower trim and on models with A/C, remove A/C duct extension at column.
3. Remove toe-plate cover screws.
4. Remove two nuts from instrument panel support bracket studs and lower steering column, resting steering wheel on front seat.
5. Remove dimmer switch retaining screw(s) and the switch. Tape actuator rod to column and separate switch from rod.
6. Reverse procedure to install. To adjust switch, depress dimmer switch slightly and install a 3/32 inch twist drill to lock the switch to the body. Force switch upward to remove lash. Torque retaining screws to 35 inch lbs. and remove tape from actuator rod. Remove twist drill and check for proper operation.

HORN SOUNDER & STEERING WHEEL, REPLACE

Except 1982–84 Firebird

1. Disconnect battery ground cable.

2. Remove screws attaching horn pad assembly to steering wheel.
3. Disconnect horn contact from steering wheel.
4. Remove steering wheel nut retainer and attaching nut.
5. Using suitable steering wheel puller, remove steering wheel. Note position of steering wheel to shaft.
6. Reverse procedure to install.

1982–84 Firebird

1. Disconnect battery ground cable.
2. Remove steering wheel shroud screws on underside of steering wheel.
3. Remove steering wheel shroud and horn contact lead assembly from the steering wheel.
4. Remove snap ring and steering wheel nut.
5. Using steering wheel puller tool No. J-2927 or equivalent, remove steering wheel. Note position of steering wheel to shaft.
6. Reverse procedure to install.

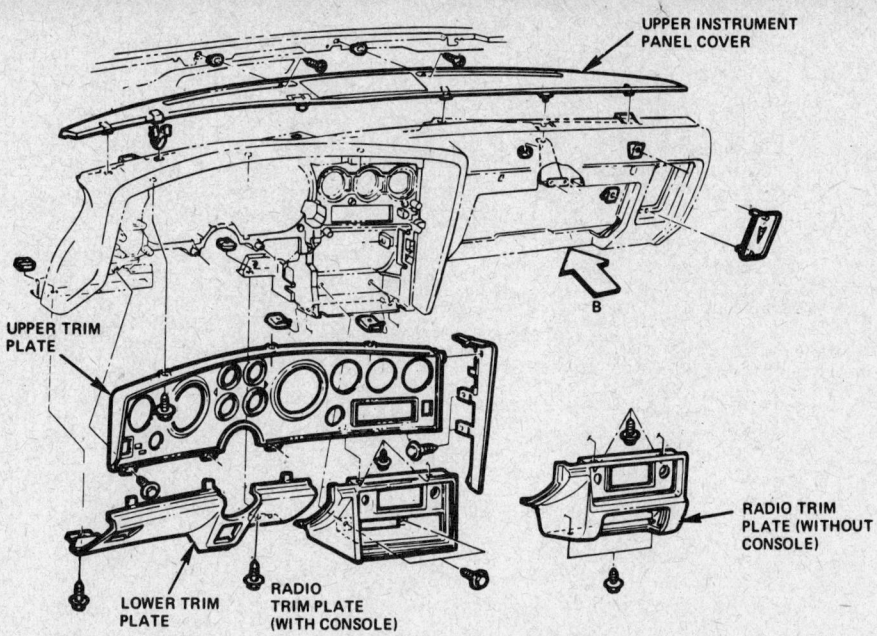

Fig. 15 Instrument panel. 1977 Grand Prix & LeMans with optional instrument cluster

INSTRUMENT CLUSTER, REPLACE

1977–84 Models Exc. 1977 Ventura, 1977–79 Phoenix, 1982–84 Firebird & 1983–84 Parisienne

1. Disconnect battery ground cable.
2. Remove upper and lower instrument panel trim plates, Figs. 13 through 17.
3. Remove instrument panel bezel attaching screws and bezel, if equipped.
4. On column mounted shift models, remove shift indicator cable.
5. On Firebird, loosen steering column nuts and lower column approximately ½ inch.
6. On all models, remove cluster retaining screws, pull cluster outward and disconnect speedometer cable and printed circuit connector, if equipped.
7. Remove lower bezel anti-rattle clips, if equipped, then instrument cluster, Figs. 17 through 21.
8. Reverse procedure to install.

1983–84 Parisienne

1. Disconnect battery ground cable.
2. Remove four steering column lower cover screws and cover.
3. If equipped with automatic transmission, disconnect shift indicator cable from steering column.
4. Remove two steering column to instrument panel screws and lower steering column.

CAUTION: Use extreme care when lowering steering to prevent damage to column assembly.

5. Remove six screws and three snap-in fasteners from perimeter of instrument cluster lens, Fig. 22.
6. Remove two screws from upper surface of grey sheet metal trim plate.
7. Remove two stud nuts from lower corner of cluster.
8. Disconnect speedometer cable and pull cluster from instrument panel.
9. Disconnect electrical connectors from cluster and remove from vehicle.
10. Reverse procedure to install.

1982–84 Firebird

1. Disconnect battery ground cable, then remove right and left lower trim plates, Fig. 23.
2. Remove instrument cluster trim plate.
3. Remove six cluster attachment screws, pull cluster back and disconnect speedometer cable.
4. Disconnect necessary electrical connections.
5. Remove trip odometer and cluster lens.
6. Reverse procedure to install.

1977 Ventura & 1977–79 Phoenix

1. Disconnect battery ground cable.
2. Remove steering column trim panel, Fig. 24.
3. On 1977–79 models, remove hush panel.
4. Remove three screws retaining heater or A/C control panel to instrument panel carrier.
5. Remove radio control knobs, bezels and nuts.
6. Remove screws at top, bottom and side of carrier securing it to instrument panel pad.
7. Disconnect shift quadrant indicator cable at shaft bowl (if automatic), remove two steering column to panel nuts.
8. Remove toe plate cover and five tow plate to cowl screws, lower column from panel and protect it with shop towels or tape.
9. Remove ground wire screw from under left side of panel pad above kick pad and disconnect speedo cable from under dash.
10. Tilt carrier and cluster rearward, disconnect printed circuit and cluster ground connectors and rest assembly on top of column.
11. Remove screws from cluster to carrier assembly and remove cluster.
12. Reverse procedure to install.

W/S WIPER MOTOR, REPLACE

1. Raise hood and remove cowl screen or grille.

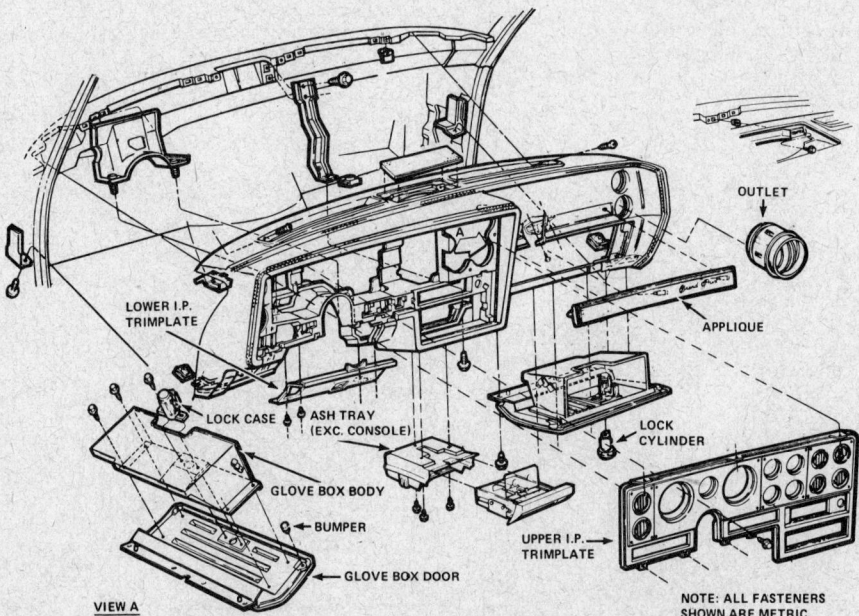

Fig. 16 Instrument panel. 1978–80 Grand Am, 1978–81 LeMans, 1978–84 Grand Prix & 1982–84 Bonneville

2. Disconnect wiring and washer hoses.
3. Reaching through opening, loosen transmission drive link to crankarm attaching nuts.
4. Remove drive link from motor crankarm.
5. Remove three motor attaching screws and remove motor while guiding crankarm through opening.
6. Reverse procedure to install.

W/S WIPER TRANSMISSION, REPLACE

With Rectangular Motor
1. Remove wiper arms and blades.
2. Raise hood and remove cowl vent screen or grille.
3. Disconnect wiring from motor.
4. Loosen, but do not remove, transmission drive link to motor crankarm attaching nuts and disconnect drive link from crankarm.
5. Remove right and left transmission to body attaching screws and guide transmission and linkage assembly out through opening.

NOTE: When installing, motor must be in Park position.

With Round Motor
1. Raise hood and remove cowl vent screen.
2. On Intermediates and 1977–84 full size models, remove right and left wiper arm and blade assemblies.
3. Loosen, but do not remove, attaching nuts securing transmission drive link to motor crankarm.
4. Disconnect transmission drive link from motor crankarm.
5. On Intermediate and 1977–84 full size models, remove right and left transmission to body attaching screws.
6. Remove transmission and linkage assembly by guiding it through opening.

NOTE: When installing, motor must be in Park position.

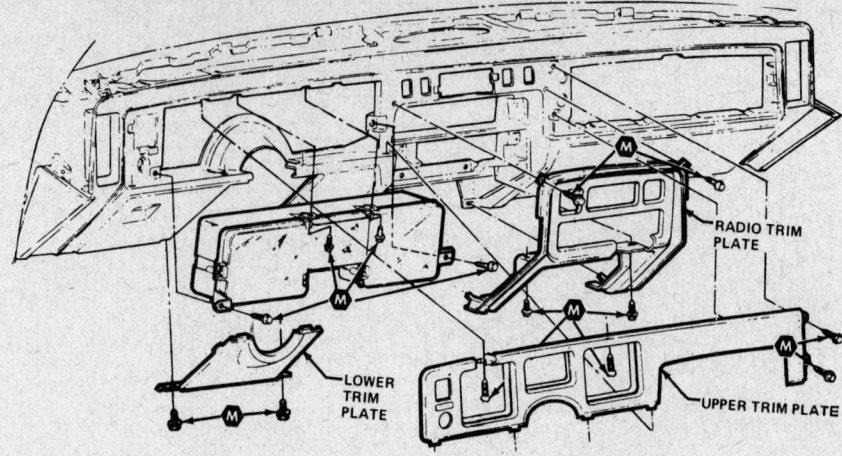

Fig. 17 Instrument panel and cluster. 1977–81 Full Size

W/S WIPER SWITCH, REPLACE

1982–84 Exc. 1983 Parisienne
1. Remove steering wheel as described under Horn Sounder and Steering Wheel, Replace.
2. Remove turn signal switch as described under Turn Signal Switch, Replace.
3. Remove ignition lock and buzzer as described under Ignition Lock, Replace.
4. Remove and install cover and wiper switch as shown in Fig. 25 & 25A.
5. Reverse remaining procedure to install.

1983 Parisienne
1. Disconnect battery ground cable.
2. Pull headlight switch knob to ON position.
3. Reach up under instrument panel and depress headlight switch shaft release button, then pull out switch shaft and knob assembly.

4. Remove four screws securing control shroud to instrument panel.

NOTE: When removing control shroud to instrument panel screws, one screw is hidden above cigar lighter knob while another is hidden above headlamp switch shaft location.

4. Remove control shroud, then two remaining screws.
5. Remove wiper switch electrical connector, then light bulb and socket from rear of switch.
6. Remove switch.
7. Reverse procedure to install.

1977–81 Exc. Phoenix & Ventura
1. Disconnect battery ground cable. Remove upper and lower instrument panel trimplates.
2. Remove switch mounting plate and disconnect connector.
3. Remove switch retaining screws and remove switch.

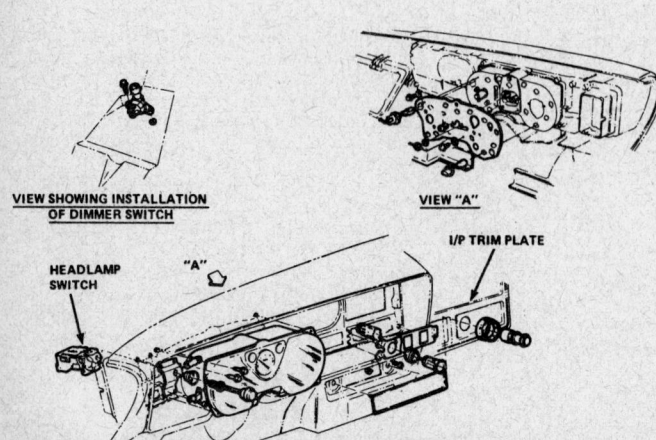

VIEW SHOWING INSTALLATION OF DIMMER SWITCH

VIEW "A"

I/P TRIM PLATE

HEADLAMP SWITCH

"A"

Fig. 18 Instrument cluster. 1977–81 Firebird

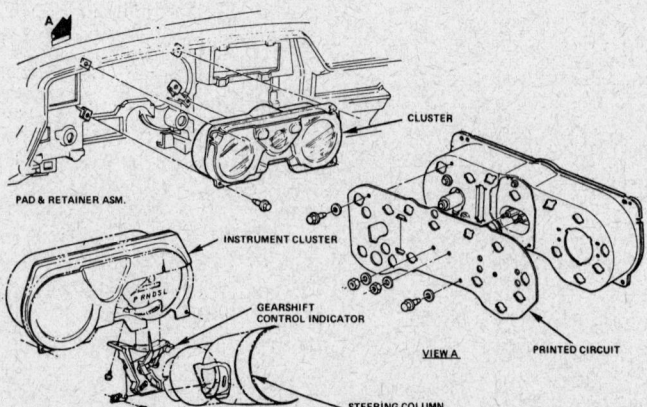

PAD & RETAINER ASM.

CLUSTER

INSTRUMENT CLUSTER

GEARSHIFT CONTROL INDICATOR

STEERING COLUMN

VIEW A

PRINTED CIRCUIT

Fig. 19 Instrument cluster. 1977 LeMans less optional instrument cluster

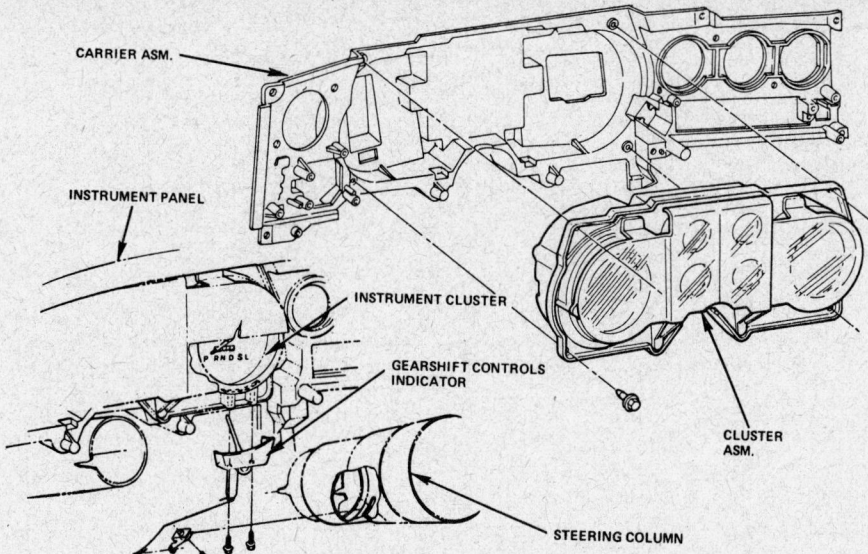

Fig. 20 Instrument cluster. 1977 Grand Prix & LeMans with optional instrument cluster

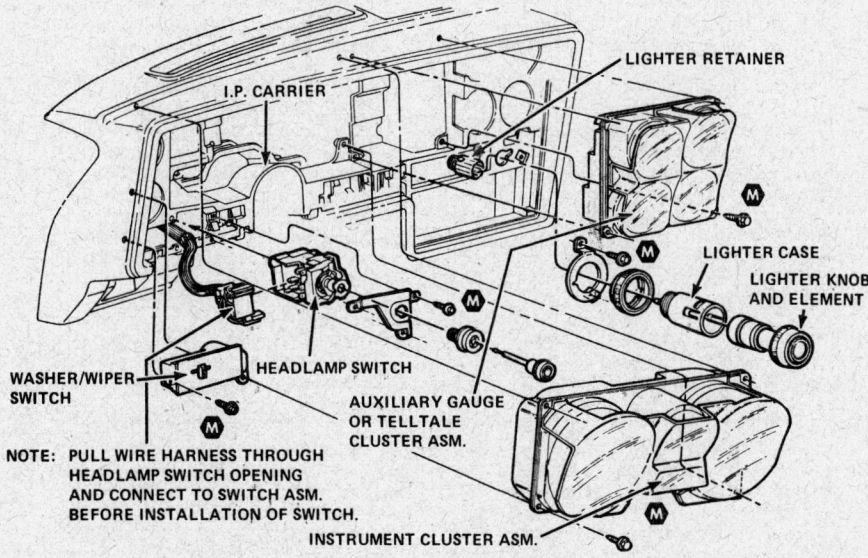

Fig. 21 Instrument cluster. 1978—80 Grand Am, 1978—81 LeMans, 1978—84 Grand Prix & 1982—84 Bonneville

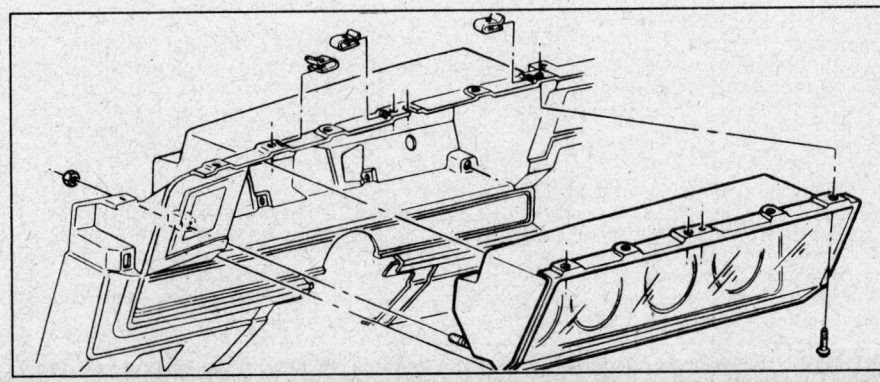

Fig. 22 Instrument cluster. 1983—84 Parisienne

1977—79 Phoenix & Ventura

1. Disconnect battery ground cable.
2. From under dash, disconnect wiring from switch.
3. Remove screws retaining switch to lower instrument panel and remove switch from panel.

RADIO, REPLACE

NOTE: When installing radio, be sure to adjust antenna trimmer for peak performance.

1983—84 Parisienne

1. Disconnect battery ground cable.
2. Remove control knobs from control shafts.
3. Remove three radio trim plate attaching screws.
4. Remove two screws and bottom nut attaching radio bracket to instrument panel.
5. Disconnect antenna lead and wire connector from radio.
6. Remove radio with mounting bracket attached from instrument panel.
7. Remove bracket from radio.
8. Reverse procedure to install.

1978—81 Grand Am, Grand LeMans, Grand Prix, LeMans & 1982—84 Bonneville & Grand Prix

1. Disconnect battery ground cable.
2. Remove upper and lower trim plates.
3. If equipped with console, move shift lever fully rearward.
4. On all models, remove four radio attaching screws from front of radio.
5. Open glove box door and lower by releasing spring clip.
6. Loosen radio rear attaching nut and pull radio outward slightly.
7. Disconnect electrical leads from radio and remove radio from vehicle.
8. Reverse procedure to install.

1977—81 Full Size

1. Disconnect battery ground cable.
2. Remove upper trim plate.
3. Remove radio trim plate by removing the two top screws and ash tray assembly, then disconnect cigar lighter electrical connector and remove the two small screws and large screw retaining ash tray bracket.
4. Remove two screws securing radio.
5. Pull radio from instrument panel opening and disconnect electrical leads from radio.
6. Remove radio from vehicle. Remove bezel nuts from front of radio to remove front trim plate if new radio is installed.
7. Reverse procedure to install.

1977 LeMans

1. Disconnect battery and remove radio knobs and bezels.
2. Remove upper and lower trimplates.

3. Remove radio retaining screws.
4. Remove radio from opening, disconnect connections and antenna lead-in while radio is being pulled out.
5. If new unit is being installed, remove bushing from old unit and install on replacement unit.

1977 Grand Prix & Grand LeMans

1. Disconnect battery ground cable.
2. Remove radio knobs and bezels, then the hex nut from right hand tuning shaft.
3. Remove radio trim plate.
4. Remove radio and radio bracket to instrument panel retaining screws.

NOTE: Radio and bracket must be removed as an assembly.

5. Remove radio and bracket from instrument panel, disconnect wiring harness and antenna lead, then separate bracket from radio.

1977–79 Phoenix & Ventura

1. Disconnect battery ground cable.
2. Remove "hush" panel, if equipped.
3. Remove radio knobs, bezels, nuts and side braces screw and disconnect wiring and antenna.
4. Remove radio from under dash.

1982–84 Firebird

1. Disconnect battery ground cable.
2. Remove radio and A/C heater console trim plate.
3. Remove four radio to console attaching screws, then pull radio outward and disconnect wire connectors and antenna lead.
4. Reverse procedure to install.

1977–81 Firebird

1. Disconnect battery ground cable.
2. Remove glove box and door and right lower A/C duct if equipped.
3. Remove radio knobs and hex nuts and trim plate.
4. Disconnect all leads to radio.
5. Remove radio bracket and radio from passenger side of instrument panel through glove box opening.

HEATER CORE, REPLACE

Without Air Cond.

Parisienne
1. Disconnect battery ground cable and drain cooling system.
2. Disconnect heater hoses from heater core. Plug core outlets to prevent coolant spillage.
3. Disconnect wire connectors from module cover, then remove front module cover attaching screws and cover.
4. Remove heater core from module.
5. Reverse procedure to install.

1982–84 Firebird
1. Disconnect battery ground cable.
2. Drain radiator and remover heater hoses

1	TRIM PLATE ASM.-CLUSTER
2	BOLT/SCREW
3	COVER, LOWER R.H.
4	COVER, LOWER L.H.
5	LOWER TRIM PLATE ASM. (LH)
6	LOWER TRIM PLATE ASM. (RH)
7	HEATER ONLY
8	I.P. LOWER REINF.
9	BRACKET
10	CONVENIENCE CENTER MOUNTING BRACKET

VIEW A
(HEATER ONLY)

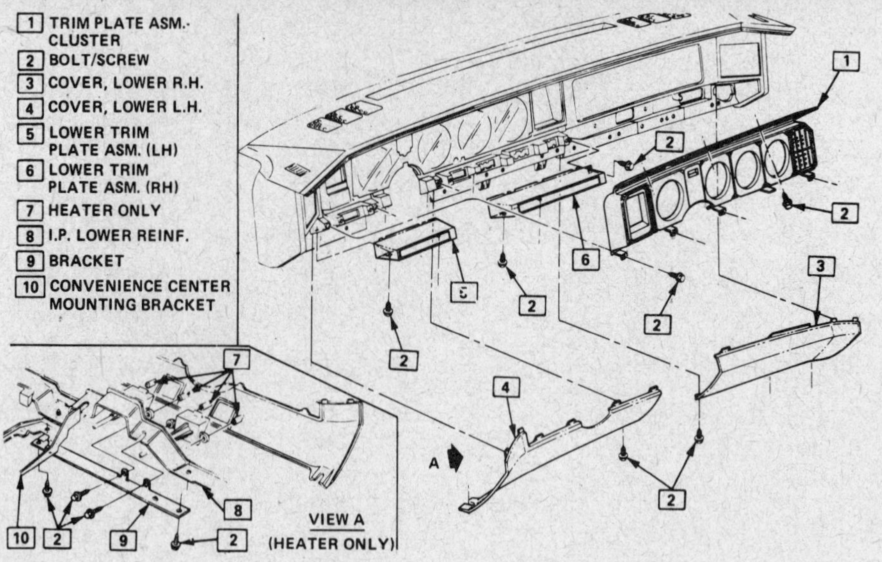

Fig. 23 Instrument cluster. 1982–84 Firebird

from heater core.
3. Remove right lower hush panel.
4. Remove right lower instrument trim panel.
5. Vehicles equipped with the V8-305 EFI engine, remove ESC module.
6. Remove lower right instrument panel carrier to cowl screw.
7. Remove four heater case cover screws.
8. Remove heater case cover.
9. Remove core support plate and baffle screws.
10. Remove heater core, support plate and baffle from case.
11. Reverse procedure to install.

1978–81 Grand Am, Grand LeMans, Grand Prix, LeMans & 1982–84 Bonneville & Grand Prix
1. Disconnect battery ground cable and drain cooling system.
2. Disconnect heater hoses.
3. Disconnect electrical connectors from heater module.
4. Remove module front cover screws.
5. Remove heater core from module.
6. Reverse procedure to install.

1977–81 Full Size
1. Disconnect battery ground cable.
2. Disconnect hoses from heater core and plug core tubes to prevent spilling coolant.
3. Remove retaining screws from around heater core cover.
4. Remove heater core cover, then heater core from module, Fig. 26.
5. Reverse procedure to install.

1977–81 Firebird
1. Drain radiator and disconnect heater hoses from core.
2. Remove retaining nuts from core case studs on engine side of dash.
3. Inside car, remove glove box and door on Firebird and heater outlet from case on Firebird.
4. Remove defroster duct retaining screw from heater case and pull entire heater assembly from firewall.
5. Disconnect control cables and wiring and

remove assembly.
6. Remove core tube seal and core retaining strips and remove core.

1977–79 Phoenix & Ventura
1. Drain radiator and disconnect heater hoses from core.
2. Disconnect battery ground cable.
3. Remove retaining nuts from core case studs on engine side of dash.
4. Remove glove box and door.
5. On all models, drill out lower right hand heater case stud with 1/4 inch drill from inside vehicle.
6. Pull entire heater core and case assembly from firewall.
7. Disconnect cables and wiring and remove assembly from car.
8. Remove core tube seal and core retaining strips and remove core.

With Air Cond.

1983–84 Parisienne
1. Disconnect battery ground cable and drain cooling system.
2. Disconnect heater hoses from heater core. Plug core outlets to prevent coolant spillage.
3. Remove heater core retainer bracket and ground strap.
4. Remove module rubber seal and module screen.
5. Remove right hand windshield wiper arm.
6. Remove high blower relay, then thermostatic switch mounting screws.
7. Disconnect wire connector at top of module, then remove module top cover.
8. Remove heater core from module.
9. Reverse procedure to install.

1982–84 Bonneville & Grand Prix
1. Disconnect negative battery cable.
2. Discharge air conditioning system and drain cooling system.
3. Remove both windshield wipers and wiper stops.
4. Remove cover windshield molding and leaf screens.
5. Remove lower windshield molding brackets, bolts from upper half of module case,

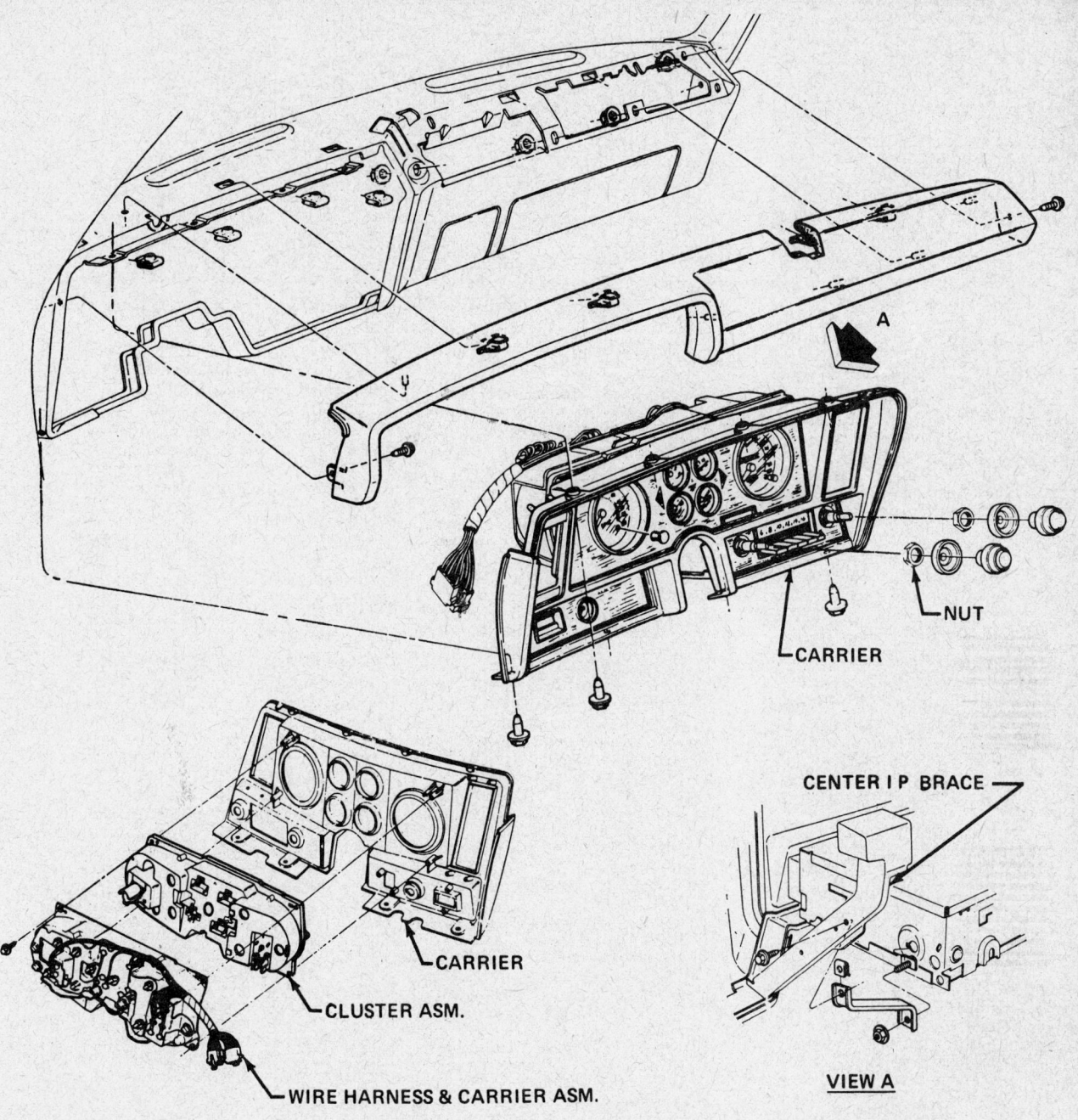

Fig. 24   Instrument panel and cluster. 1977 Ventura & 1977–79 Phoenix

all electrical connections and module cover.

6. Remove heater core clamp bolt and remove heater core.
7. Reverse procedure to install.

1982–84 Firebird

1. Disconnect battery ground cable.
2. Drain radiator and remove heater hoses from heater core.
3. Remove right lower hush panel.
4. Remove right lower instrument trim panel.
5. Vehicles equipped with the V8-305 TBI engine, remove ESC module.

6. Remove lower right instrument panel carrier to cowl screw.
7. Remove four heater case cover screws.
8. Remove heater case cover.
9. Remove core support plate and baffle screws.
10. Remove heater core, support plate and baffle from case.
11. Reverse procedure to install.

1978–81 Grand Am, Grand LeMans, Grand Prix & LeMans

1. Disconnect battery ground cable.
2. Remove right hand windshield wiper arm and blade assembly.
3. Drain cooling system, then disconnect

heater hoses at heater core and plug core openings.
4. Remove bracket and ground strap.
5. Remove module cover as follows:
   a. Remove seals and screens, then disconnect wire connector.
   b. Loosen and move up lower windshield reveal moulding, then remove reveal moulding cowl brackets.
   c. Tape a strip of wood below lower edge of windshield over module to prevent damage to windshield.
   d. Remove all cover attaching screws, then cut through sealing material along cowl.
   e. Carefully pry cover off from side, then

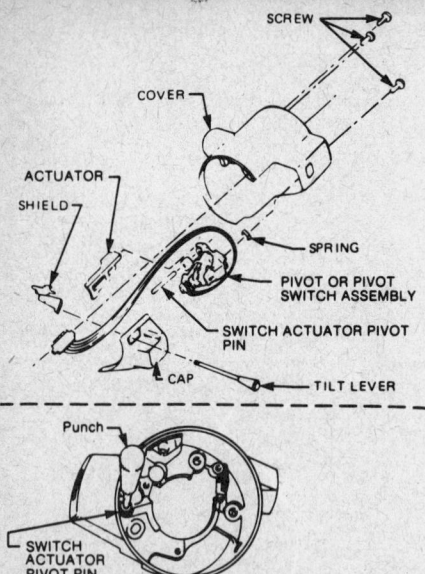

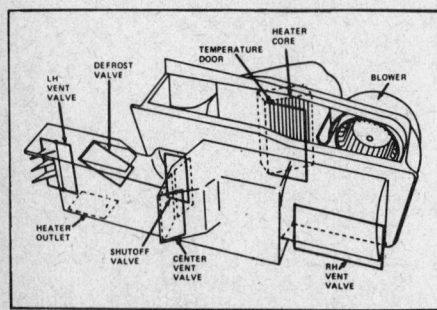

Fig. 25 Windshield wiper switch removal & installation. 1982–84 models less tilt wheel

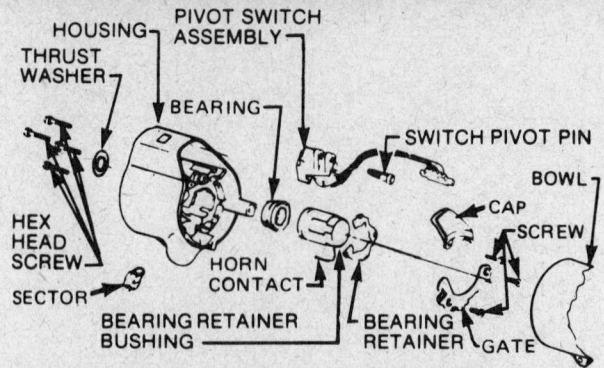

Fig. 25A Windshield wiper switch removal & installation. 1982–84 models less tilt wheel

lift cover away from flange of fender cowl brace.

f. Remove heater core and seal from module.

1977–81 Full Size
1. Disconnect battery ground cable.
2. Remove right half of hood seal from air inlet screen.
3. Remove air inlet screen.
4. Remove screws securing top of module, then disconnect electrical connectors from electrical components on top of module.
5. Remove thermostatic switch mounting screws from top of module.
6. Remove A/C diagnostic connector mounting screws and position aside.
7. Remove top of module.
8. Disconnect and remove heater core from module.
9. Reverse procedure to install.

1977 LeMans, Grand Am & Grand Prix
1. Drain radiator and disconnect heater hoses from core.
2. Remove glove box, cold air duct and heater outlet and defroster duct screw.
3. Disconnect heater core case from dash. Remove blower motor resistor to gain access to case upper retaining nut.
4. Move case assembly rearward, freeing case studs from cowl and remove assembly.

5. Disconnect temperature cable and vacuum hoses from case and remove screws securing core inside of case.

1977–81 Firebird
1. Drain radiator.
2. Remove glove box and door.
3. Remove cold air duct (lower right hand duct) and remove left and center lower A/C ducts.
4. Jack right front area of car and place on safety stand.
5. Remove rocker panel trim on right side and remove screws holding forward portion of rocker panel trim attaching bracket.
6. Remove three lower fender bolts at rear of fender.
7. Remove four fender to skirt bolts at rear of wheel opening.
8. Remove two fender skirt bolts near blower motor area.
9. Pry rear portion of fender out at bottom to gain access to hose clamp on lower core hose and disconnect hose.
10. Disconnect water pump to core hose at core.
11. Remove heater case retaining nuts under hood at dash.
12. Remove two heater case retaining bolts (inside car).
13. Remove console, if equipped. If equipped with tape player, remove console with tape player intact. If equipped with tape player and no console, remove tape player.
14. Disconnect temperature cable at heater case.
15. Remove heater outlet duct.
16. Remove lower defroster duct screw at heater case.
17. Remove right kick panel.
18. Remove heater core and case.
19. Disconnect vacuum hoses from heater case.
20. Remove core from case.

1977–79 Phoenix & Ventura
1. Disconnect battery and drain coolant.
2. Remove upper heater hose from core.
3. Remove right front fender skirt bolts and lower skirt to gain access to lower heater hose clamp. Disconnect lower hose and remove lower right hand heater core and case attaching nut.
4. Remove glove box and door.
5. Remove recirculation vacuum diaphragm at right kick panel.
6. Remove heater outlet (at bottom of heater case).
7. Remove cold air distributor duct from heater case.

8. Remove heater case extension screws and separate extension from case.
9. Disconnect cables and wiring and remove case and core assembly.
10. Separate core from case.

BLOWER MOTOR, REPLACE

1978–81 Grand Am, Grand LeMans, Grand Prix, LeMans & 1982–84 Bonneville and Grand Prix & 1983–84 Parisienne
1. Disconnect battery ground cable.
2. If equipped with air conditioning, disconnect cooling tube from blower motor.
3. On all models, disconnect electrical connector from blower motor.
4. Remove blower motor retaining screws and the blower motor.
5. Reverse procedure to install.

1977–81 Full Size Without Air Cond.
1. Disconnect battery ground cable.
2. Disconnect blower motor electrical lead.
3. Remove blower motor retaining screws and remove blower motor, Fig. 26.
4. Reverse procedure to install.

1977–81 Full Size With Air Cond.
1. Disconnect battery ground cable.
2. Remove right half of hood seal from air inlet screen.
3. Remove air inlet screen.
4. Remove screws securing top of module, then disconnect electrical connectors from electrical components on top of module.
5. Remove thermostatic switch mounting screws from top of module.
6. Remove A/C diagnostic connector mounting screws and position aside.
7. Remove top of module.

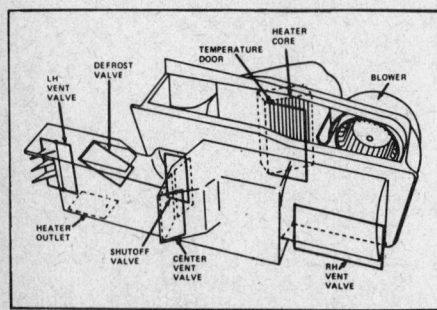

Fig. 26 Heater core & blower motor (less air conditioning). 1977–81 Full size

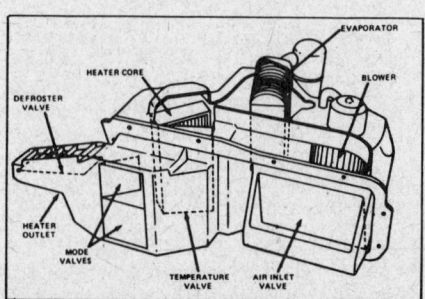

Fig. 27 Heater core & blower motor (with air conditioning). 1977–81 Full size

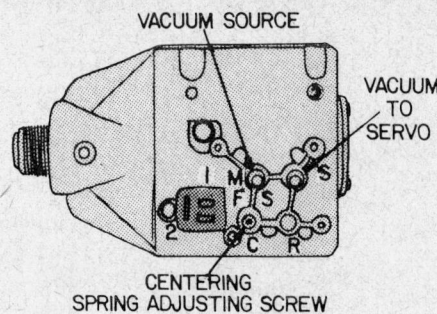

Fig. 28 Centering spring adjustment. Early model flyweight type regulator

8. Disconnect and remove blower motor from module, Fig. 27.
9. Reverse procedure to install.

1977–84 Firebird
1. Disconnect battery ground cable.
2. Disconnect wire connector. On models with A/C, disconnect cooling tube.
3. Remove motor attaching screws and nuts, then remove blower motor assembly from case.
4. Reverse procedure to install.

1977 Grand Prix & LeMans
1. Disconnect blower motor feed wire.
2. Remove blower motor retaining screws.
3. Remove blower motor.

1977–79 Phoenix & Ventura
1. Disconnect battery and detach hoses from clips on right fender skirt.
2. Raise vehicle on hoist.
3. Remove fender skirt attaching bolts except those retaining the skirt to radiator support.
4. Pull out then down on skirt and place block of wood between skirt and fender to allow clearance for blower motor removal.
5. Disconnect blower motor cooling tube and electrical connections at blower motor.
6. Remove blower motor attaching screws and remove blower motor. Gently pry motor flange if sealer acts as an adhesive.

SPEED CONTROLS

1977–84 Cruise Control

Brake Release Switches, Adjust
Apply brake pedal and push both switches forward as far as possible. Pull pedal forcibly rearward to adjust switches.

Centering Spring Adjustment Exc. Cruise Master Units
If speed control holds speed three or more mph higher than selected speed, turn centering screw (C) clockwise 1/8 turn or less, Fig. 28.

If speed control holds speed three or more mph below selected speed, turn centering adjustment screw (C) counterclockwise 1/8 turn or less. *Do not move adjustment screw (R)*.

Orifice Tube Adjustment, Cruise Master Units
To check engagement speed, engage the system at 55 mph. If vehicle cruises below the engagement speed, loosen the locknut and screw the orifice tube outward. If vehicle cruises above the engagement speed, loosen the locknut and screw the orifice tube inward, Fig. 29.

NOTE: Approximately 1/4 turn of the orifice tube will change the cruise speed about 1 mph. Also, do not remove orifice tube as it cannot be reinstalled once removed.

Bead Chain Adjustment, 1977–84 Buick Built Engines
Assemble chain to be taut with carburetor in hot idle position and the idle solenoid deenergized. Place chain into swivel cavities which permits chain to have slight slack. Place retainer over swivel and chain assembly. Retainer must be made to rest between balls. Cut off chain flush with side of swivel to remove excess length. Chain slack should not exceed one half diameter of ball stud, .150 inch, when measured at hot idle position.

Cable Adjustment, 1977–84 Pontiac Built Engines
1. Set carburetor choke to hot idle position.
2. With cable connected to vacuum servo, pull steel tube of servo as far as it will go and check if one of the cross holes in the steel tube aligns with carburetor lever pin.
3. If one of the cross holes in the steel tube aligns with carburetor lever pin, install the tube, washer and cotter pin.
4. If none of the cross holes in the steel aligns with carburetor lever pin, move tube rearward to align the next closest hole and install cable, washer and cotter pin.

CAUTION: Do not stretch cable to make adjustment, as this will prevent carburetor from returning to normal idle.

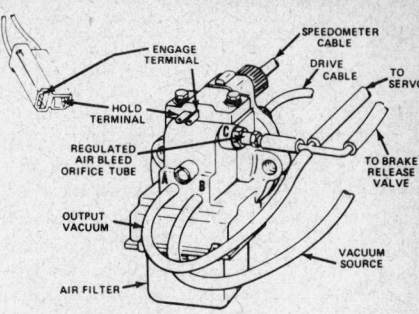

Fig. 29 Orifice tube adjustment. Late model transducer type regulator

Cable Adjustment, 1982–84 Chevrolet Built Engines Less Electronic Fuel Injection
1. Assemble cable to cable bracket and throttle lever.
2. Install cable assembly onto servo bracket.
3. Place throttle in fully closed position. Attach servo chain to cable assembly with first two beads of servo chain hanging loose outside cable assembly clip.
4. Adjust cable assembly jam nuts until there is a .03 inch clearance between throttle lever stud pin and end of slot on throttle cable assembly. Torque jam nuts to 35–48 inch lbs. Pull rubber boot over washer on cable.

Cable Adjustment, 1982–83 Chevrolet Built Engines With Electronic Fuel Injection
1. Assemble cable to cable bracket and TBI lever and servo bracket.
2. Place throttle in fully closed position. Attach servo chain to cable assembly with first two beads of servo chain hanging loosely outside cable assembly clip.
3. Adjust cable jam nuts until cable sleeve at TBI unit is tight but not holding throttle open. Torque jam nuts to 35–48 inch lbs. Pull rubber boot over washer on cable.

Rod Adjustment, 1977–84 Oldsmobile Built Engines
Adjust length of rod to minimum slack with carburetor in hot idle position and the engine static.

Rod Adjustment, 1977–84 Chevrolet Built Engines
Screw rod into link with ignition "Off" and fast idle cam off and throttle closed. Hook rod through tab on servo. Adjust length so link assemblies over end of stud, then install retainer.

Engine Section

For service on V6-231, 252 & 1978—80 V8-350 engines with distributor located at front of engine, see Buick Chapter.

For service on V6-173, V6-229, V8-305 & all 1977—80 V8-350 engines with distributor located at rear of engine and fuel pump located on right side of engine, see Chevrolet Chapter.

For service on all V8-307, 350, 350 Diesel & 403 engines with distributor located at rear of engine, fuel pump located on right side of engine and oil filler tube located on engine front cover, see Oldsmobile Chapter.

ENGINE MOUNTS, REPLACE

4-151

1977—78
1. Remove insulator to engine bracket through bolt(s), Fig. 1.
2. Raise engine to release weight off front mounts.
3. Remove insulator and separate from engine bracket.

1982—84
1. Disconnect battery ground cable.
2. Raise and support front of vehicle.
3. Remove mount through bolts on left and right hand side, Fig, 1A.
4. Raise front of engine and remove mount to engine attaching bolts, then remove mounts.
5. Reverse procedure to install.

1977—81 V8-265, 301, 350 & 400

1. Disconnect battery ground cable.
2. Raise engine to release weight off front mounts.
3. Remove bolts fastening engine insulators to engine, Fig. 2.
4. Raise engine just clear of insulator.
5. Remove insulator.

ENGINE, REPLACE

1977—81

1. Disconnect battery cables at battery and drain cooling system.
2. Scribe alignment marks on hood and remove hood from hinges.
3. Disconnect all wiring, ground straps, fuel lines and vacuum hoses from engine.

NOTE: On V8 engines, remove thermal feed switch, located on rear of left cylinder head on all models except Ventura. On Venture models, switch is located on the right cylinder head.

---

4. Remove air cleaner and upper radiator shield assembly.
5. Disconnect radiator hoses and heater hoses at engine.
6. Remove fan and disconnect accelerator linkage.
7. If equipped with power steering or air conditioning, remove pump and/or compressor from mountings and set aside. Do not disconnect hoses.
8. On V8, disconnect transmission vacuum modulator line and power brake vacuum line at carburetor and fold back out of way.
9. Raise vehicle on hoist and drain crankcase.
10. Disconnect exhaust pipe from manifold and remove starter.
11. If equipped with automatic transmission, remove converter cover and three converter retaining bolts and slide converter to rear.
12. With manual transmission, disconnect clutch linkage and remove clutch cross shaft.
13. Remove four lower bell housing bolts.
14. Disconnect transmission filler tube support and starter wire harness shield from cylinder head.

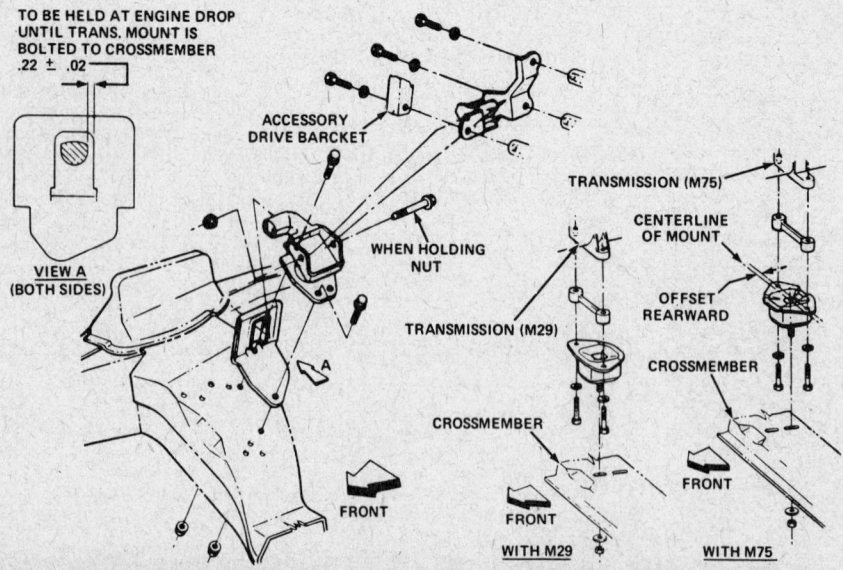

Fig. 1 Engine mounts. 1977—78 4-151

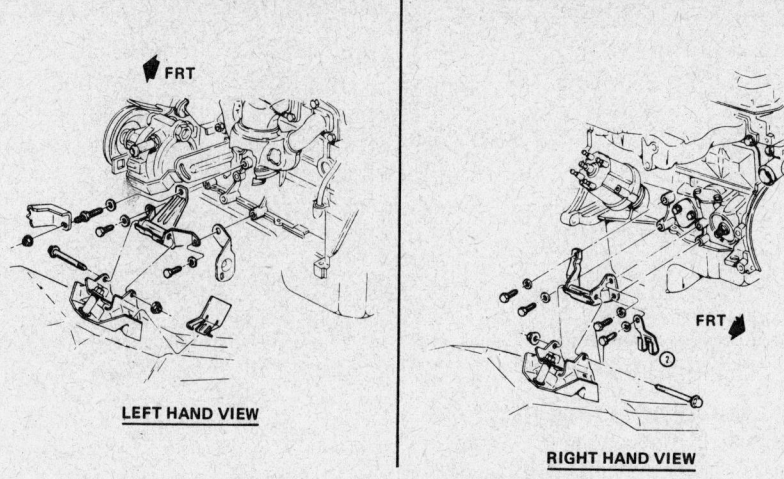

LEFT HAND VIEW

RIGHT HAND VIEW

Fig. 1A   Engine mounts. 1982–84 4-151

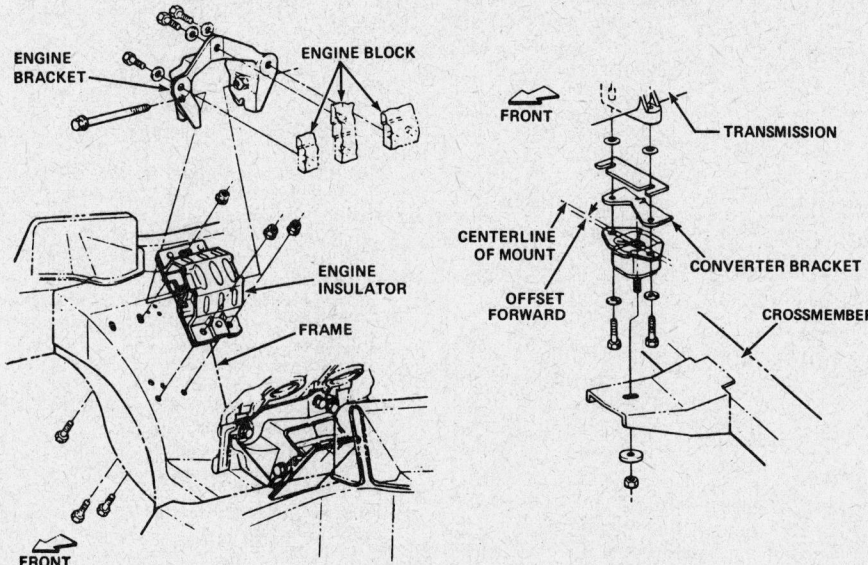

Fig. 2   Engine mounts (typical). V8-265, 301, 350 & 400

15. Remove two front motor mount to frame bracket bolts.
16. Lower vehicle and using a jack and block of wood, support transmission.
17. Support weight of engine with suitable lifting device.
18. Remove two remaining bell housing bolts.
19. Raise transmission slightly.
20. Position engine forward to free it from transmission and remove from car by tilting front of engine up.

1982–84 4-151

1. Disconnect battery ground cable.
2. Drain cooling system.
3. Scribe alignment marks on hood, then remove hood from hinges.
4. Remove A/C compressor, brackets and position aside.
5. Remove upper and lower radiator hoses from engine.

6. Remove fan assembly.
7. On models with auto. trans., remove radiator and shroud assembly. On models with manual transmission, remove upper half of radiator shroud.
8. Disconnect power steering hoses, then remove power steering pump from mounting brackets.
9. Disconnect engine wiring at bulkhead connection.
10. Disconnect inlet and return fuel lines at flex hoses.
11. Remove vacuum brake hose from filter.
12. Disconnect engine to body ground strap from rear of cylinder head.
13. From inside of vehicle, remove right hand hush panel, then disconnect E.C.M. harness from E.C.M. unit.
14. Remove splash shield from right fender and feed E.C.M. harness from inside of vehicle.
15. Disconnect heater hoses from heater core.
16. Disconnect throttle linkage and canister

hose from E.F.I. assembly.
17. Raise and support vehicle.
18. Disconnect electrical connectors from transmission.
19. Remove flywheel dust cover.
20. On models equipped with automatic transmission, remove torque converter to flywheel bolts.
21. Remove bell housing to engine bolts.
22. Disconnect exhaust pipe at manifold, then remove exhaust pipe support at bell housing.
23. Disconnect catalytic converter at tail pipe joint, then remove converter and exhaust pipe assembly.
24. Disconnect starter wiring, then remove starter assembly.
25. On models equipped with manual transmission, remove clutch fork return spring.
26. Remove motor mount through bolts.
27. Lower vehicle, then using a suitable jack and block of wood, support transmission.
28. Support weight of engine with suitable lifting device.
29. Remove engine from vehicle. On models equipped with manual transmission, swing engine slightly to the right to remove clutch swing arm from ball.

CYLINDER HEAD, REPLACE

4-151

1. Drain cooling system and remove air cleaner.
2. Disconnect accelerator and fuel and vacuum lines at carburetor.
3. Remove intake and exhaust manifolds.
4. Remove bolts attaching alternator bracket to cylinder head.
5. If equipped with power steering or A/C, remove right side front bracket.
6. Disconnect temperature sending unit wiring harness, battery ground cable and radiator and heater hoses.
7. Disconnect spark plug wires and remove spark plugs.
8. Remove rocker cover, then back off rocker arm nuts.
9. Pivot rocker arms to clear push rods and remove push rods.
10. Remove cylinder head attaching bolts and cylinder head.
11. Reverse procedure to install. Coat cylinder head bolts with sealer. Torque bolts in sequence as shown in Figs. 3 & 4. When installing intake and exhaust manifolds, refer to Figs. 5, 6 and 7 for bolt tightening sequence.

V8-301, 350 & 400

1. Drain cooling system and remove air cleaner.
2. Remove intake manifold, push rod cover and rocker arm cover.
3. Loosen all rocker arm nuts and move rocker arms off push rods.
4. Remove push rods, keeping them in order so they may be installed in their original locations.
5. Detach exhaust crossover pipe from manifolds.
6. Remove battery ground strap and engine ground strap on left head or engine ground strap.
7. Unfasten and remove head with exhaust manifold attached.

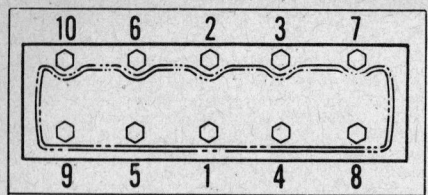

Fig. 3 Cylinder head tightening sequence. 1977–78 4-151

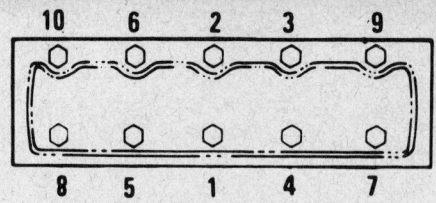

Fig. 4 Cylinder head tightening sequence. 1982–84 4-151

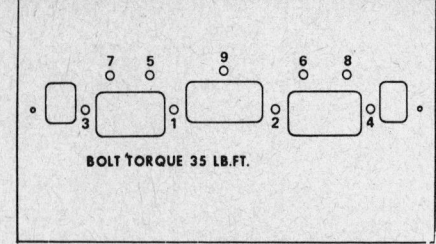

BOLT TORQUE 35 LB.FT.

Fig. 5 Manifold tightening sequence. 1977–78 4-151

CAUTION: *Use extreme care when handling heads as the rocker arm studs are hardened and may crack if struck.*

NOTE: *If left head is being removed, it will be necessary to raise head off dowel pins, move it forward and maneuver it in order to clear power steering and power brake equipment if so equipped.*

8. Reverse procedure to install. On V8-301, coat cylinder head bolts with sealer.
9. On 1977–82 engines, torque cylinder heads to specifications in sequence shown in Fig. 8.

ROCKER ARM STUDS, REPLACE

With Screw in Studs

1. On V8-301, drain cooling system.
2. Remove rocker arm cover.
3. Remove rocker arm and nut.
4. Using a deep socket, remove rocker stud.
5. Install new stud and tighten to 50 ft. lbs.

NOTE: On V8-301, coat lower rocker arm stud threads with sealer.

6. Install rocker arm and tighten nut to 20 ft. lbs.
7. Install rocker cover using new gasket.

VALVE ARRANGEMENT

Front to Rear

Four Cyl. E-I-I-E-E-I-I-E
V8s . . . . E-I-I-E-E-I-I-E

VALVE LIFT SPECS.

Year	Engine	Intake	Exhaust
1977	4-151	.406	.406
	V6-231②	.383	.366
	8-301⑤	.377	.377
	8-301⑥	.364	.364
	8-305⑧	.3727	.410
	8-350①③	.400	.400
	8-350④	.364	.364
	8-350⑧⑫	.390	.410
	8-400	.364	.364
	8-403	.400	.400
1978	4-151	.406	.406
1978–82	V6-231②	.383	.366
1978–79	V8-301	.364	.364
	V8-305	.3727	.410
	V8-350①③	.400	.400
	V8-350⑧⑫	.390	.410
	V8-350②⑨	.323	.339
	V8-400	.364	.364
	V8-403①	.400	.400
1979	V6-231②	.357	.366
1980	V6-229⑫	.373	.410
	V8-350①③	.400	.400
	V8-350②⑨	.357	.366
1980–82	V6-231②	.357	.366
	V8-265	.364	.364
	V8-301⑩	.350	.350
	V8-301⑪	.364	.364
	V8-305⑫	.357	.390
1981	V8-350①⑦	.376	.376
	V8-307①	.400	.400
1982–84	4-151	.398	.398
	V6-173⑫	.231	.262
	V6-252②	.358	.366

①—Refer to Oldsmobile Chapter for service procedures.
②—Refer to Buick Chapter for service procedures.
③—Distributor located at rear of engine, counter-clockwise distributor rotor rotation. Fuel pump located at right side of engine.
④—Distributor located at rear of engine, counter-clockwise distributor rotor rotation. Fuel pump located at left side of engine.
⑤—Std. trans.
⑥—Auto. trans.
⑦—Diesel.
⑧—Distributor located at rear of engine, clockwise distributor rotor rotation.
⑨—Distributor located at front of engine.
⑩—Except E/C (Electronic control) engine.
⑪—E/C (Electronic control) engine.
⑫—Refer to Chevrolet Chapter for service procedures.

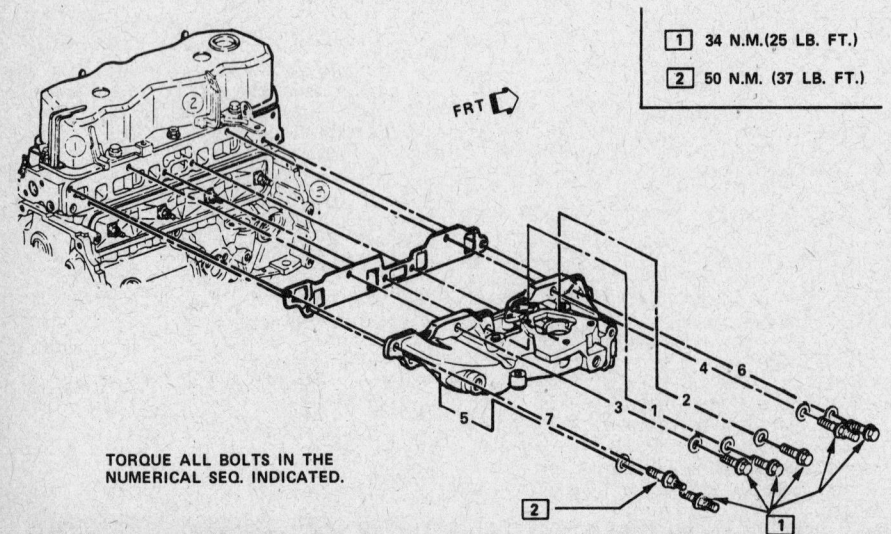

| 1 | 34 N.M. (25 LB. FT.) |
| 2 | 50 N.M. (37 LB. FT.) |

FRT

TORQUE ALL BOLTS IN THE NUMERICAL SEQ. INDICATED.

Fig. 6 Intake manifold tightening sequence. 1982–84 4-151

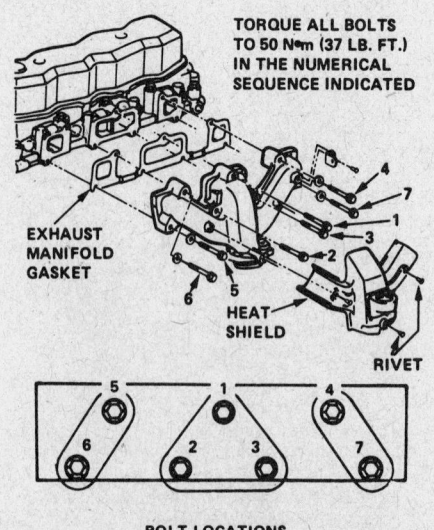

TORQUE ALL BOLTS TO 50 N·m (37 LB. FT.) IN THE NUMERICAL SEQUENCE INDICATED

EXHAUST MANIFOLD GASKET

HEAT SHIELD

RIVET

BOLT LOCATIONS

Fig. 7 Exhaust manifold tightening sequence. 1982–84 4-151

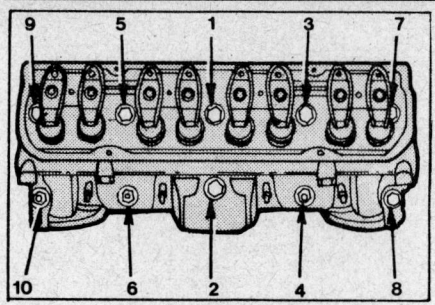

Fig. 8 Cylinder head tightening sequence. V8-301, 350 & 400

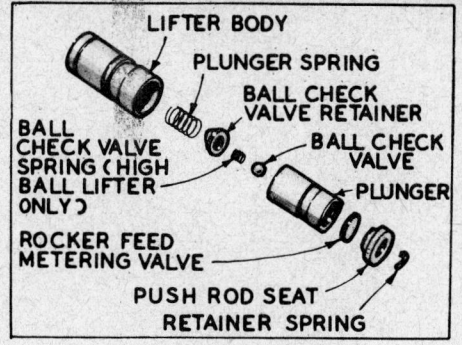

Fig. 9 Hydraulic valve lifter

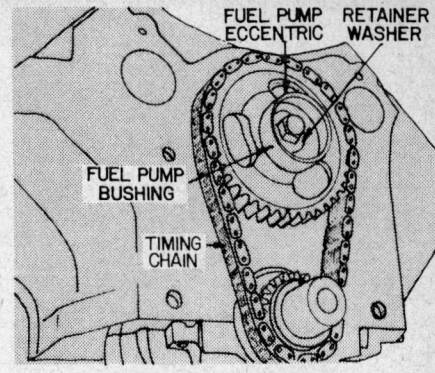

Fig. 10 Front of engine with timing case cover removed. V8 engines

VALVE TIMING

Intake Opens Before TDC

Engine	Year	Degrees
4-151	1977	23
	1978–82	33
V6-229⑮	1980	42
V6-231⑮	1977–82	16
8-265	1980	27
8-265	1981	16
8-301	1977⑤	31
	1977⑥	27
	1978①	27
	1978②	14
	1979①	16
	1979②⑤	27
	1979②⑥	16
	1981⑫	16
	1981⑬	17
8-305⑭	1977–80	28
8-305⑭	1981–82	44
8-307⑧	1981	20
8-350③	1977	29
8-350④⑧	1977–82	16
8-350⑦⑭	1977–79	28
8-350⑨⑮	1978–79	13.5
	1980	16
	1977–78⑤⑩	21
	1977–78⑥⑩	29
	1977–79⑪	16
8-403⑧	1977–79	16

①—2 bar. carb.
②—4 bar. carb.
③—Distributor located at rear of engine, counter clockwise distributor rotor rotation. Fuel pump located at left side of engine.
④—Distributor located at rear of engine, counter clockwise distributor rotor rotation. Fuel pump located at right side of engine.
⑤—Std. trans.
⑥—Auto. trans.
⑦—Distributor located at rear of engine, clockwise distributor rotor rotation.
⑧—Refer to Oldsmobile Chapter for service procedures.
⑨—Distributor located at front of engine.
⑩—Except T/A engine.
⑪—T/A engine.
⑫—Except E/C (Electronic Control) engine.
⑬—E/C (Electronic Control) engine.
⑭—Refer to Chevrolet Chapter for service procedures.
⑮—Refer to Buick Chapter for service procedures.

VALVE GUIDES

Valve guides are cast integral with the cylinder head. Valves with oversize stems are available in .001″, .003″ and .005″ larger than standard.

Oversize reamers are required to enlarge valve guide holes to fit the oversize stems. best results when installing .005″ oversize valve stem use a .003″ oversize reamer first and then ream to .005″ oversize. Always reface the valve and valve seat after reaming valve guide. Valves are marked .001, .003 or .005 with colored ink.

VALVE LIFTERS, REPLACE

1. Remove intake manifold.
2. Remove push rod cover and valve cover.
3. Loosen rocker arm, then rotate rocker arm off push rod and remove push rod.
4. Remove lifter, Fig. 9.

NOTE: If more than one lifter is to be removed, identify lifters and push rods, so they can be reinstalled in their original locations.

5. Reverse procedure to install. Torque rocker arm ball nut to 20 ft. lbs.

TIMING CASE COVER, REPLACE

NOTE: If necessary to replace the cover oil seal it can be accomplished without removing the timing chain cover.

V8s

1. Drain cooling system.
2. Loosen alternator adjusting bolts.
3. Remove fan and accessory drive belts.
4. Remove fan and pulley.
5. Remove water pump.
6. Disconnect radiator hoses.
7. Remove fuel pump.
8. Remove vibration damper.
9. Remove front four oil pan-to-timing chain cover screws.
10. Remove cover attaching screws.
11. Pull cover forward to clear studs and remove.

4-151

1. Disconnect battery ground cable.
2. Remove torsional damper and the two oil pan to front cover screws.
3. Remove front cover retaining screws.
4. Pull cover forward just enough to permit cutting of oil pan front seal, then cut oil

pan front seal flush with cylinder block at both sides and remove front cover.
5. Reverse procedure to install.

TIMING CHAIN, REPLACE

V8 Engines

1. Remove timing chain cover.
2. Remove fuel pump eccentric, bushing and timing chain cover oil seal, Fig. 10.
3. Align timing marks to simplify proper positioning of sprockets during assembly, Fig. 11.

NOTE: The valve timing marks, Fig. 11, does not indicate TDC, compression stroke for No. 1 cylinder for use during distributor installation. When installing the distributor, rotate engine until No. 1 cylinder is on compression stroke and the camshaft timing mark is 180° from the valve timing position shown in Fig. 11.

4. Slide off chain and sprockets.
5. Install new chain and sprockets, making sure timing marks are aligned exactly on a straight line passing through the shaft centers, Fig. 11. Camshaft should extend through sprocket so that hole in fuel pump eccentric will locate on shaft.

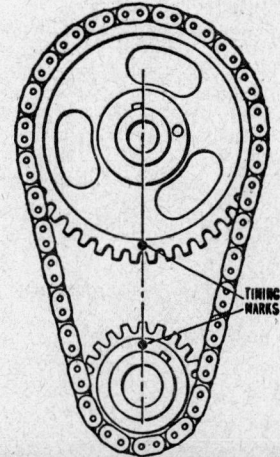

Fig. 11 Valve timing marks. V-8 engines

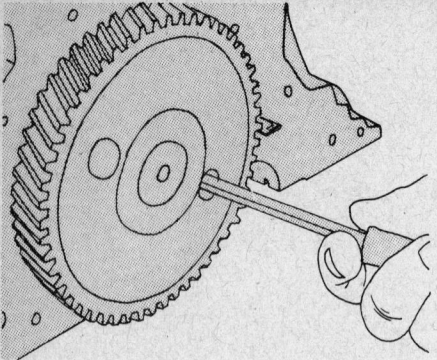

Fig. 12 Camshaft thrust plate screw removal. 4-151

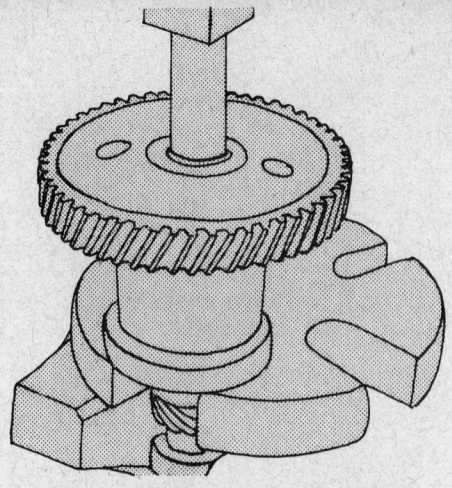

Fig. 13 Camshaft gear removal. 4-151

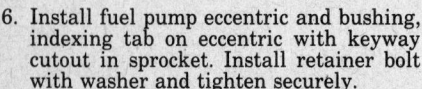

Fig. 14 Camshaft gear installation & thrust plate clearance check. 4-151

6. Install fuel pump eccentric and bushing, indexing tab on eccentric with keyway cutout in sprocket. Install retainer bolt with washer and tighten securely.
7. Making sure hollow dowels are in place in block, place timing chain cover gasket over studs and dowels.
8. Install cover, making sure O-ring seal is in place.

CAMSHAFT, REPLACE

4-151

1. Disconnect battery ground cable.
2. Drain oil pan and radiator.
3. Remove radiator, fan and water pump pulley.
4. Remove distributor, spark plugs and fuel pump.
5. Remove push rod cover and valve cover, then loosen rocker arms and rotate rocker arms off push rods.
6. Remove push rods and valve lifters.

NOTE: Identify push rods and lifters so they can be reinstalled in their original locations.

7. Remove harmonic balancer and timing gear cover.
8. Remove camshaft thrust plate retaining screws, Fig. 12, and carefully pull camshaft out of engine.

NOTE: Use care to avoid damaging camshaft bearings.

9. To remove gear, proceed as follows:
   a. Support gear on press using a suitable sleeve, Fig. 13, then press camshaft out of gear using a socket or other suitable tool.

NOTE: Thrust plate must be positioned so that woodruff key in shaft does not damage thrust plate when camshaft is pressed out.

   b. To install gear, firmly support camshaft at back of front journal in press using plate adapters.
   c. Place gear spacer ring and thrust plate cover end of shaft and install woodruff key.
   d. Press gear until it bottoms against the gear spacer ring. Check end clearance which should be .0015 to .0050 inch, Fig. 14. If clearance is less than specified, the spacer ring should be replaced. If clearance is greater than specified, the thrust plate should be replaced.
10. Carefully install camshaft making sure that marks are aligned as shown in Fig. 15. Torque thrust plate retaining screws to 75 inch lbs.

NOTE: The valve timing marks shown in Fig. 15 do not indicate TDC compression stroke for No. 1 cylinder for use during distributor installation. Before installing distributor, turn crankshaft one complete revolution to firing position of No. 1 cylinder (TDC compression stroke), then install distributor in its original position and align shaft so that rotor points toward No. 1 cylinder in distributor cap.

11. Reverse procedure to install remaining components.

All V8s

The camshaft and camshaft bearings can be replaced with the engine installed in the car or with engine removed and disassembled for overhaul. However, to replace the rear camshaft bearing without removing and completely disassembling the engine, the propeller shaft, transmission and clutch housing must first be removed. The procedure for removing the camshaft is as follows:

1. Drain cooling system and remove air cleaner.
2. Disconnect radiator and heater hoses, distributor vacuum hose and spark plug wires.

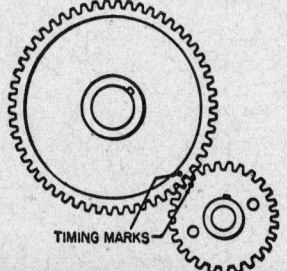

Fig. 15 Valve timing marks. 4-151

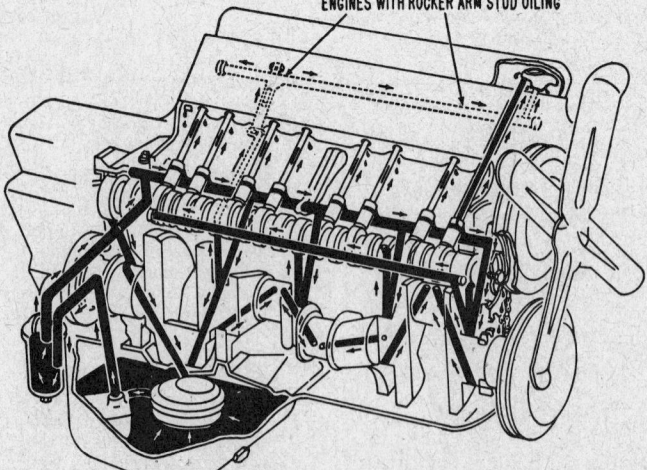

Engine oiling system. V8s

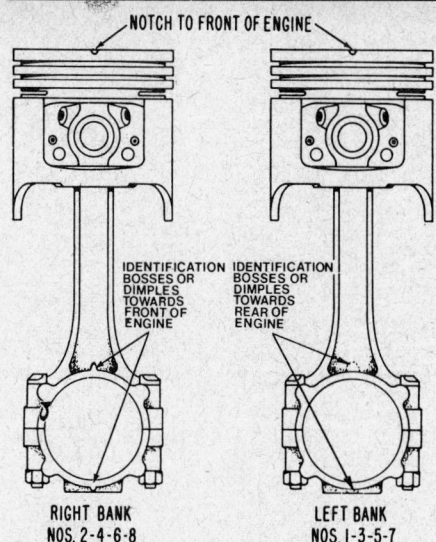

Fig. 16 Piston & rod assembly. 1977–79
V8-400 & 1977 V8-350. (Oil spurt hole toward
camshaft)

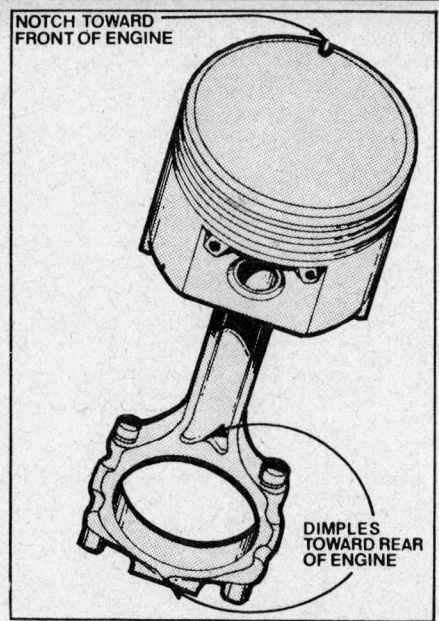

Fig. 17 Piston & rod assembly. 4-151, V8-265
& 301 less turbo

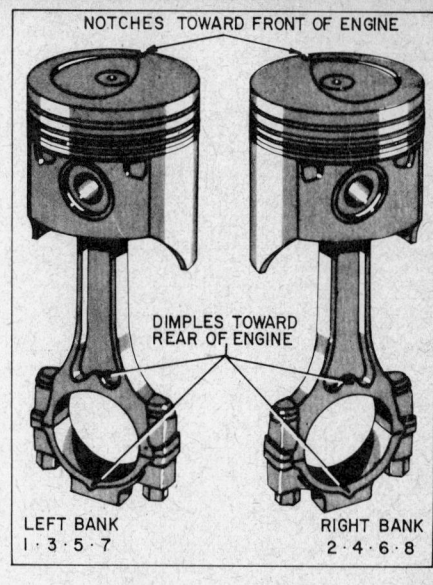

Fig. 18 Piston & rod assembly. V8-301 turbo

3. Disconnect carburetor linkage, fuel lines and wire connector from temperature sending unit.
4. Remove hood latch brace.
5. Remove radiator, fan and pulleys.
6. On air conditioned cars, remove alternator and its mounting bracket.
7. Remove crankcase ventilator hose or outlet pipe.
8. Remove distributor.
9. Remove rocker arm covers.
10. Remove intake manifold. *Make certain "O" ring seal between intake manifold and timing chain cover is retained and installed during assembly.*
11. Remove push rod cover.
12. Loosen rocker arm ball retaining nuts so that rocker arms can be disengaged from push rods and turned sideways.
13. Remove push rods and hydraulic lifters, keeping them in proper sequence so that they may be returned to their original locations.
14. Remove vibration damper.
15. Remove fuel pump.
16. Remove timing chain cover.
17. Remove fuel pump eccentric and fuel pump bushing.
18. Remove chain and sprockets.
19. Remove camshaft thrust plate and carefully pull camshaft from engine. *Clearance for camshaft removal is very limited and, in cases where engine mounts are worn excessively, it may be necessary to raise the front of the engine to permit removal.*

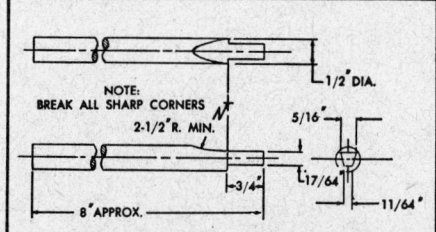

Fig. 19 Rear main bearing oil seal
tool V8-301, 350, 400

PISTON & ROD, ASSEMBLE

Assemble pistons and rods as indicated in Figs. 16, 17 and 18.

When installing connecting rod and piston assemblies into V8-301 engines, the raised notches at bearing end of each connecting rod must all face toward the rear of the engine. When installing connecting rod and piston assemblies in V8-350 and 400 engines, the raised notches at the bearing end of each connecting rod in the right bank cylinders (2, 4, 6 and 8) must face front of engine. Connecting rods installed in the left bank cylinders (1, 3, 5 and 7) must have all the raised notches facing toward the rear of the engine, Fig. 16.

On all engines, the notch cast in the piston heads must face the front of the engine when the piston and connecting rod assemblies are installed.

Correct piston and connecting rod assembly installation is extremely important as incorrect installation could cause an engine knock.

Upon installation, measure the connecting rod side clearance using a suitable feeler gauge. Measurement obtained should be .006–.022 inch for 4-151, V8-265, 301, 350 and .012–.017 inch for V8-400.

PISTONS, PINS & RINGS

Pistons and rings are available in standard sizes and oversizes of .005, .010, .020 and .030 inch.

Piston pins are available in oversizes of .001 and .003".

MAIN & ROD BEARINGS

Main bearings are available in standard sizes and undersizes of .001 and .002".

Rod bearings are available in standard sizes and undersizes of .001 and .002".

CRANKSHAFT REAR OIL SEAL, REPLACE

V8s

1. Remove oil pan, oil pump and pump drive shaft.
2. Remove oil baffle and cylinder block-to-oil baffle tube.
3. Remove rear main bearing cap.
4. Use tool shown in Fig. 19 made from brass bar stock to pack upper seal as follows:
   a. Insert tool against one end of oil seal in cylinder block and drive seal gently into groove until tool bottoms.
   b. Remove tool and repeat at other end of seal in cylinder block.
5. Clean block and bearing cap parting line thoroughly.
6. Form a new seal in cap.
7. Remove newly formed seal from cap and cut four pieces about 3/8" long from this seal.
8. Work two 3/8" pieces into each end of the gaps which have been made at the end of seal in cylinder block. Without cutting off the ends, work these seal pieces in until

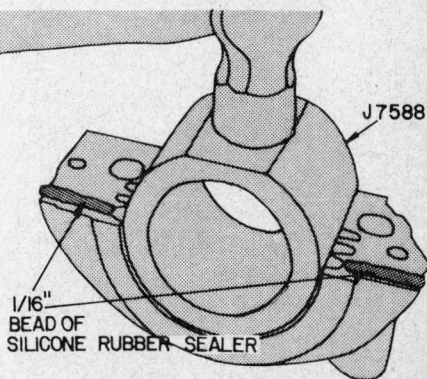

Fig. 20 Installing rear main bearing oil
seal. V8-265, 301, 350, 400 engines

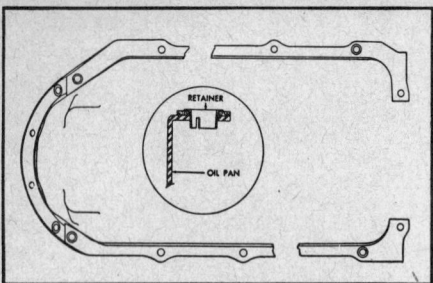

Fig. 21 Installing oil pan gasket retainers. V8-265, 301, 350 & 400 engines

flush with parting line, being sure that no fibers are protruding over the metal adjacent to the groove.

9. Form another new seal in the cap, Fig. 20.
10. Assemble the cap to the block and torque to specifications.
11. Remove cap and inspect parting line to insure that no seal material has been compressed between the block and cap.
12. Apply a 1/16″ bead of sealer from the center of the seal to the external cork groove.
13. Reassemble the cap and torque to specifications.

4-151

1977–78 Models W/ Two Piece Type Seal

NOTE: Crankshaft rear oil seal can be removed without removal of crankshaft.

1. Remove oil pan and rear main bearing cap.
2. Remove upper half of seal by tapping on one end with a blunt punch until other end of seal protrudes far enough to be removed with pliers. Remove lower half of seal by prying out with a small screwdriver.
3. Install upper half of seal by pushing into plate with lip toward front of engine. Install lower half of seal by pushing with a hammer handle until seal is rolled into place.
4. Torque bearing cap bolts to specifications and install oil pan.

1982–84 Models W/One Piece Type Seal

NOTE: Crankshaft rear oil seal can be re-

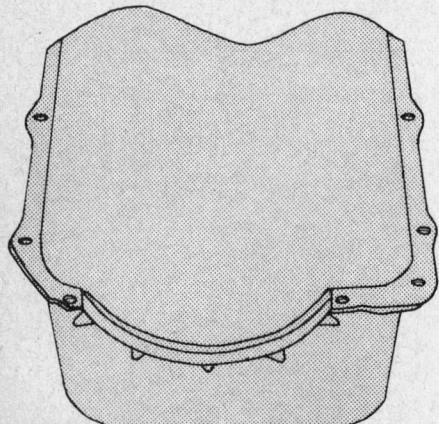

Fig. 23 Rear oil pan gasket positioned in oil pan. V8-265, 301, 350 & 400 engines

placed without removal of crankshaft or oil pan.

1. Disconnect battery ground cable.
2. Remove transmission.
3. Remove flywheel retaining bolts, then flywheel.
4. On all models, remove seal using suitable screwdriver.
5. Reverse procedure to install.

NOTE: To facilitate installation, apply a light coat of engine oil to outside sealing surface of new seal, then evenly press seal into place.

OIL PAN, REPLACE

4-151

1. Disconnect battery ground cable and remove engine fan.
2. Raise vehicle and drain oil pan.
3. Disconnect exhaust pipe at manifold and loosen hanger bracket.
4. Remove starter and place aside, then remove flywheel housing inspection cover.
5. Raise engine slightly to remove weight from engine mounts and remove both brackets to engine mount bolts.
6. Remove oil pan bolts, then raise engine to allow oil pan removal and remove oil pan.
7. Reverse procedure to install.

V8-301, 350 & 400 Pontiac Built Engines

1. Disconnect battery ground cable and remove fan.
2. Make sure that all hoses and wiring are properly routed to avoid binding or stretching when engine is raised.
3. On some air conditioned vehicles, it will be necessary to remove A/C compressor from mounting brackets and place aside for clearance.
4. Remove distributors cap, then raise vehicle and drain engine oil.
5. Disconnect exhaust pipes from manifolds, then remove starter and flywheel housing cover.
6. Rotate crankshaft until number on cylinder is at bottom dead center.
7. Remove engine mount through bolts.
8. Remove oil pan bolts, then raise engine just enough to allow oil pan removal and remove oil pan.
9. Reverse procedure to install. Install gasket as shown in Figs. 21, 22 and 23.

OIL PUMP, REPLACE

4-151

Remove oil pan. Remove the two flange mounting bolts and nut and remove pump.

Remove the four cover retaining screws, cover, gears and shaft and regulator parts, Fig. 24.

CAUTION: Do not attempt to remove or disturb oil pick-up tube.

Clean and inspect pump. If any of the following conditions are found, the oil pump should be replaced:
1. Inspect pump body for cracks or wear.
2. Inspect gears for excessive wear or damage.

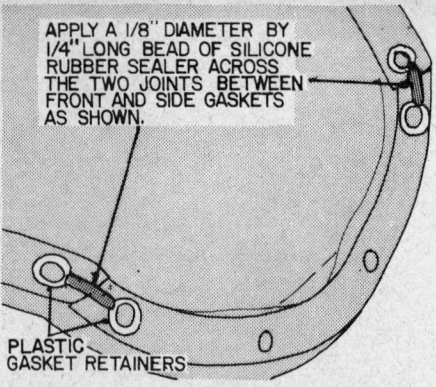

Fig. 22 Front oil pan gasket overlapping side gasket, V8-265, 301, 350 & 400 engines

3. Inspect shaft for looseness in housing.
4. Inspect inside of cover for wear which may permit oil to leak past the ends of the gears.
5. Inspect oil pick-up screen.

To assemble, install drive gear and shaft in housing, then install idler gear with smooth side facing cover. Install cover and screws and torque screws to 105 inch lbs. Make sure that shaft turns freely. Install regulatory valve spring, retainer and pin.

To install pump, align drive shaft with distributor tang, then position pump on engine and install retaining bolts and nut. Torque bolts and nut to 115 inch lbs. on 1977–78 models. On 1982–84 models torque bolts and nuts to 20 to 22 ft. lbs.

V8 Engines

Remove oil pan. While holding pump in place, remove attaching screws. Lower the pump away from the block with one hand while removing the oil pump drive shaft with the other.

Remove oil screen and pressure regulator parts. Detach cover from pump body and take out gears, Fig. 25.

Examine all parts for damage and assemble. Do not attempt to change oil pressure by varying length of pressure regulator spring.

Position drive shaft in distributor and oil pump drive gear. Place pump in position in

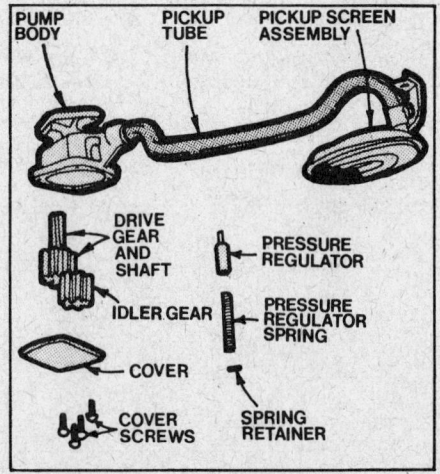

Fig. 24 Oil pump disassembled. 4-151

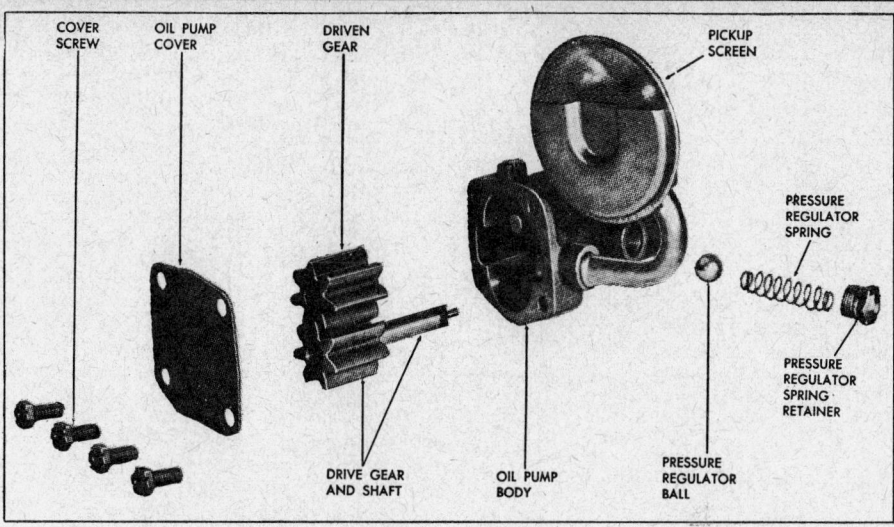

COVER SCREW · OIL PUMP COVER · DRIVEN GEAR · PICKUP SCREEN · PRESSURE REGULATOR SPRING · PRESSURE REGULATOR SPRING RETAINER · DRIVE GEAR AND SHAFT · OIL PUMP BODY · PRESSURE REGULATOR BALL

Fig. 25   Oil pump disassembled. V8 Pontiac engines

the block, indexing the drive shaft with pump drive gear shaft. Install attaching screws with lock washers and tighten securely.

Removal and installation of pump does not affect distributor timing since the oil pump and distributor drive gear are mounted on the distributor shaft.

BELT TENSION DATA

	New Lbs.	Used Lbs.
1977		
Air Conditioning		
Exc. 4-151 &		
V8-305, 350①	135–165	100–105
4-151	110–140	75–80
V8-305, 350①	135–165	80
Air Pump		
V6-231	60–80	50–55
V8-305, 350①	120–150	55
V8-350②, 403	110–140	75–80
Alternator		
Exc. V8-305,		
350①	110–140	75–80
V8-305, 350①	120–150	55
Power Steering		
V6-231, V8-301,		
350③, 400	135–165	100–105
4-151,		
V8-350②, 403	110–140	75–80
V8-305, 350①	120–150	55

BELT TENSION DATA—Cont'd

	New Lbs.	Used Lbs.
1978–81		
Air Conditioning		
Exc. 4-151	135–145	90–100
4-151	120–130	70–80
Air Pump		
Exc. V6-231	120–130	70–80
V6-231	65–75	45–55
Alternator		
All	120–130	70–80
Power Steering		
Exc. 4-151	135–145	90–100
4-151	120–130	70–80
1982		
5/16″ Wide	80	50
3/8″ Wide	140	70
15/32″ Wide	165	90
7/16″ Wide	165	90
1983–84		
Air Conditioning		
4-151	165	90
Generator		
4-151		
With A/C	165	90
Without A/C	145	70
Power Steering		
4-151	145	70

BELT TENSION DATA—Cont'd

①—Distributor located at rear of engine, clockwise distributor rotor rotation.
②—Distributor located at rear of engine, counter clockwise distributor rotor rotation. Fuel pump located at right side of engine.
③—Distributor located at rear of engine, counter clockwise distributor rotor rotation. Fuel pump located at left side of engine.

WATER PUMP, REPLACE

NOTE: Water pump is serviced as an assembly only.

1. Disconnect battery cable and drain cooling system.
2. Loosen alternator adjusting bolt and remove fan belt.
3. Remove fan and pulley.
4. On 1977–78 V8 engine, remove alternator front bracket.
5. Disconnect radiator and heater hose at pump, then remove water pump retaining bolts and pump.
6. Reverse procedure to install. Torque water pump retaining bolts to 15 ft. lbs. except on 1977–78 4-151 engines. On 1977–78 4-151 engines, torque water pump retaining bolts to 20 ft. lbs.

FUEL PUMP, REPLACE

1. Disconnect fuel lines from pump.
2. Remove pump retaining bolts and pump.
3. Remove all gasket material from the pump and block gasket surfaces. Apply sealer on both sides of new gasket.
4. Position gasket on pump flange and hold pump in position against its mounting surface. Make sure rocker arm is riding on camshaft eccentric.
5. Press pump tight against its mounting. Install retaining screws and tighten them alternately.
6. Connect fuel lines. Then operate engine and check for leaks.

SERVICE NOTE: Before installing the pump, it is good practice to crank the engine so that the nose of the camshaft eccentric is out of the way of the fuel pump rocker arm when the pump is installed. In this way there will be the least amount of tension on the rocker arm, thereby easing the installation of the pump.

Diesel Engine Section

Refer to the Oldsmobile chapter for service procedures on this engine.

Turbocharger Section

DESCRIPTION

The turbocharger, Figs. 1 and 2, is used to increase engine power on demand, while maintaining the capability of good fuel economy.

As engine load increases and the throttle opens, more air-fuel mixture flows into the combustion chambers. As the increased flow is burned, a larger volume of high energy exhaust gasses enters the engine exhaust system and is directed through the turbocharger turbine housing, Fig. 3. Some of the exhaust gas energy is used to increase the speed of the turbine wheel which is connected to the compressor wheel. The increased speed of the compressor wheel compresses the air-fuel mixture from the carburetor and delivers the compressed air-fuel mixture to the intake manifold, Fig. 3. The high pressure in the intake manifold allows a denser charge to enter the combustion chambers, in turn developing more engine power during the combustion cycle.

The intake manifold pressure (Boost) is controlled to a maximum value by an exhaust gas bypass valve (Wastegate), Fig. 3. The wastegate allows a portion of the exhaust gas to bypass the turbine wheel, thereby not increasing turbine speed. The wastegate is operated by a spring loaded diaphragm device sensing the pressure differential across the compressor. When intake manifold pressure reaches a set value above ambient pressure, the wastegate begins to bypass the exhaust gas.

An Electronic Spark Control System is used to retard ignition timing up to 18°–22° to minimize detonation. The power enrichment vacuum regulator (PEVR) is used to control vacuum flow to the carburetor power piston.

NOTE: Engine oil on turbocharged engines must be changed every 3000 miles since turbocharger bearing damage may occur from oil contamination. Before starting engine after changing oil and filter, disconnect ignition switch wire connector (pink wire) from distributor. Crank engine several times, not to exceed 30 seconds for each interval, until oil light goes out, then reconnect ignition switch wire connector to distributor.

DIAGNOSIS & TESTING

Prior to performing any diagnostic or testing procedure check all vacuum hoses and wiring for proper routing and connections, carburetor linkage for freedom of movement, wastegate linkage for damage or any problems which may occur in a non-turbocharged engine.

CAUTION: A turbocharged engine has exhaust pipes located high in the engine compartment. Care must be taken to avoid accidental contact with hot exhaust pipes since personal injury may occur.

Wastegate-Boost Pressure Test

1. Inspect actuator linkage for damage.
2. Check tubing from compressor housing to actuator assembly and the return tubing

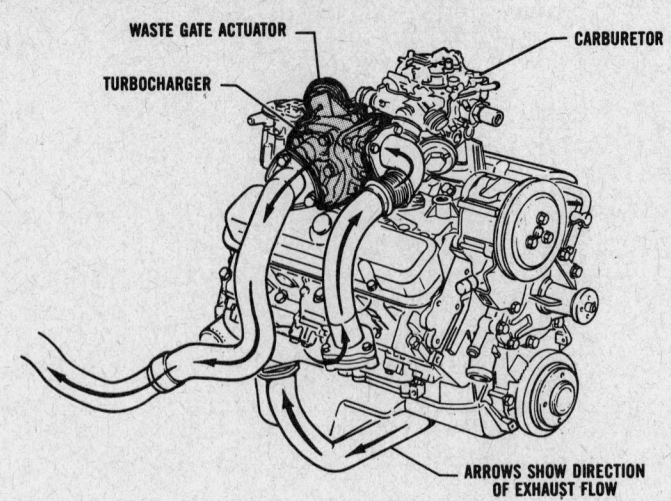

Fig. 1 Turbocharger assembly installation

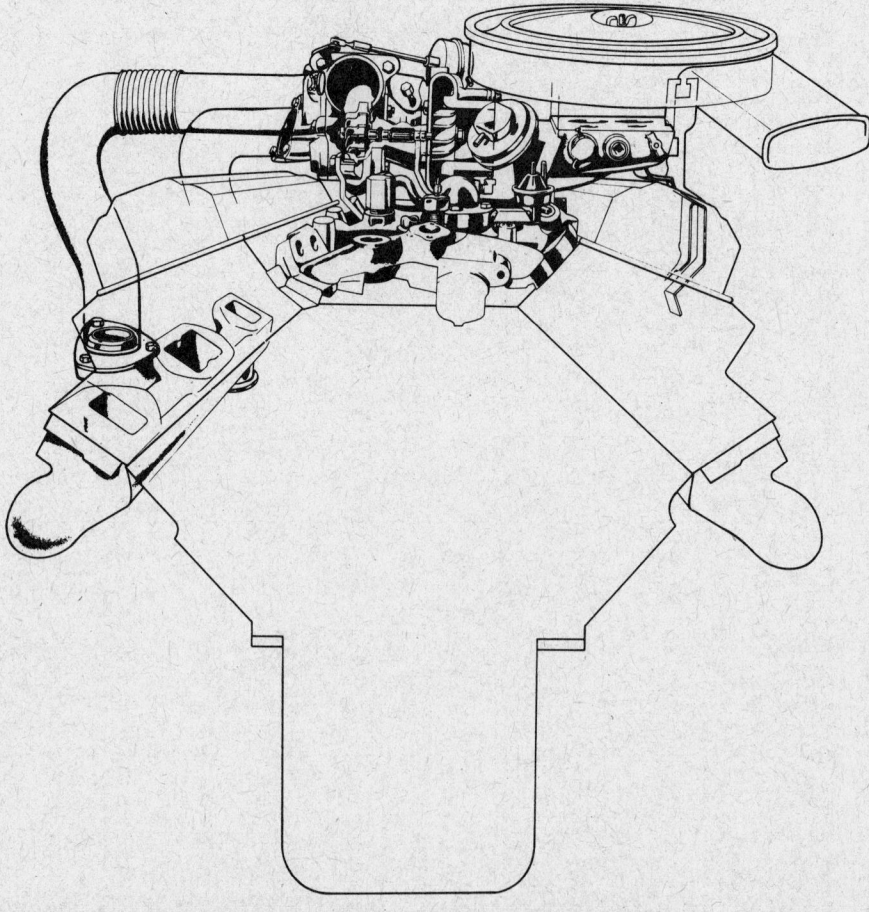

Fig. 2 Sectional view of turbocharger assembly

from the actuator to the PCV tee.

3. Tee the hand operated vacuum/pressure pump J-23738 into the tubing from the compressor housing to the actuator. At approximately 8.5–9.5 psi. the lever should begin to move and actuate the wastegate. If not, replace actuator assembly and calibrate assembly to open at 9 psi. Use J-23738 or perform "Road Test" as outlined below to measure boost pressure.

Road Test

1. Tee the compound gauge J-28474 into the tubing between compressor housing and actuator assembly with a sufficient length of hose to place the guage in the passenger compartment.
2. With conditions and speed limits permitting, perform a zero to 40–50 mph wide open throttle acceleration and maintain top speed for two to three seconds. Boost pressure should reach 8.5–9.5 psi. If not, replace actuator assembly and, using tool J-23738, calibrate to open at 9 psi.

Power Enrichment Vacuum Regulator (PEVR) Test

1. Inspect PEVR and attaching hoses for deterioration, cracking or other damage and replace as necessary.
2. Tee one hose of manometer J-23951 between yellow stripped input hose and input port. Connect other hose directly to PEVR output port.
3. Start engine and operate at idle speed. There should be no more than 14″ H_2O difference between manometer readings. If difference is greater than 14″ H_2O, replace PEVR.
4. Remove PEVR from intake manifold and install a plug in intake manifold PEVR bore. Connect input and output hoses to PEVR.
5. Tee gauge J-28474 into output hose of PEVR.
6. Start engine and operate at idle speed. The gauge reading from the output port should be 8–10″ Hg.
7. Apply 3 psi. to manifold signal port of PEVR. Vacuum reading from output port should be 1.4–2.6″ Hg. If difficulty is encountered in measuring level of vacuum, apply 5 psi. to manifold signal port of PEVR. There should be no vacuum output from PEVR.
8. If PEVR does not perform as described above, replace PEVR.

TURBOCHARGER INTERNAL INSPECTION

1. Remove the turbocharger assembly but do not separate the center housing rotating assembly from the turbine housing.
2. Manually operate the wastegate linkage and using a small mirror, observe wastegate movement in the elbow assembly. Replace the elbow assembly if the wastegate fails to open or close.
3. Check for loose backplate to center housing rotating assembly bolts and tighten, if necessary.
4. Spin the compressor wheel. If rotating assembly binds or drags, replace the center housing rotating assembly.
5. Inspect center rotating housing assembly for sludge in the oil drain area. Clean, if minor, or replace center housing rotating assembly if excessively sludged or coked.

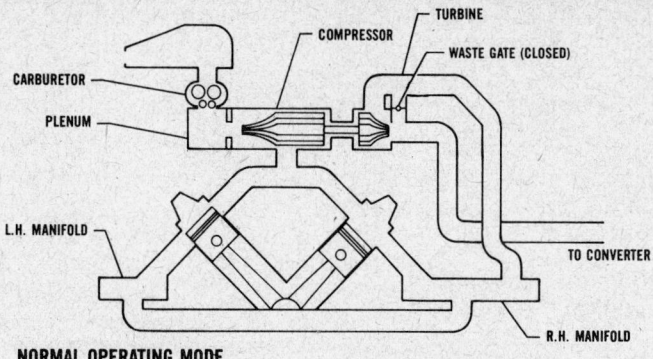

NORMAL OPERATING MODE

(labels: CARBURETOR, PLENUM, COMPRESSOR, TURBINE, WASTE GATE (CLOSED), L.H. MANIFOLD, TO CONVERTER, R.H. MANIFOLD)

Fig. 3 Turbocharger operating schematic

6. Inspect compressor oil seal for damage or leakage on the compressor wheel side of the backplate. Replace center housing rotating assembly if oil seal damage or leakage is present.
7. If compressor wheel is damaged or severely coked, replace center housing rotating assembly.
8. If center housing rotating assembly is being replaced, pre-lubricate with engine oil.
9. Inspect compressor housing and turbine housing. If either housing is gouged, nicked or distorted, replace if necessary.
10. Remove turbine housing from center housing rotating assembly and check the journal bearing radial clearance and thrust bearing axial clearance as follows:
    a. Journal bearing radial clearance.
    (1) Attach a rack and pinion type dial indicator (Starrett model 656-517 or equivalent with a two inch long, ¾ to 1 inch offset extension rod) to the center housing so the indicator plunger extends through the oil output port and contacts the turbine wheel assembly shaft. If required, a dial indicator mounting adapter can be utilized.
    (2) Manually apply pressure equally and at the same time to both the compressor wheel and turbine wheel as required to move the turbine wheel assembly shaft away from the dial indicator as far as possible.
    (3) Zero the dial indicator.
    (4) Manually apply pressure equally and at the same time to both the compressor and turbine wheels as required to move the turbine wheel assembly shaft toward the dial indicator plunger as far as possible. Note maximum reading on dial indicator.

NOTE: To ensure that the dial indicator reading is the maximum obtainable, roll the wheels slightly in both directions while applying pressure.

    (5) Manually apply pressure equally and at the same time to both the compressor and turbine wheels as required to move the turbine wheel assembly shaft away from the dial indicator as far as possible. The dial indicator should return to zero.

    (6) Repeat steps 2 through 5 as required to ensure the maximum clearance between the center housing bores and the shaft bearing diameters, as indicated by the maximum shaft travel, has been obtained.
    (7) If the maximum bearing radial clearance is less than .003 inch or greater than .006 inch, replace the center housing rotating assembly.

NOTE: Continued operation of a turbocharger having excessive bearing radial clearance will result in severe damage to the compressor and turbine wheels and the housings.

    b. Thrust bearing axial clearance.
    (1) Mount a dial indicator (Starrett model 25-141 or equivalent) at the turbine end of the turbocharger so the dial indicator plunger contacts the end of the turbine wheel assembly.
    (2) Manually move the compressor wheel and turbine wheel assembly in each direction shown on the indicator dial.
    (3) Repeat step 2 to ensure the maximum clearance between the thrust bearing components, as indicated by the maximum turbine wheel assembly travel, has been obtained.
    (4) If the maximum thrust bearing axial clearance is less than .001 inch or greater than .003 inch, replace the center housing rotating assembly.

NOTE: Continued operation of a turbocharger having excessive thrust bearing axial clearance will result in severe damage to the compressor and turbine wheels and the housings.

SERVICE

Before performing turbocharger service, note the following general cautions:

1. Clean area around turbocharger assembly with a non-caustic solution before service. Cover openings of engine assembly connections to prevent entry of foreign material.

2. When removing the assembly, do not bend, nick or in any way damage the compressor or turbine wheel blades. Any damage may result in rotating assembly imbalance, failure of the center housing rotating assembly, and failure of the compressor and/or turbine housing.
3. Before disconnecting center housing rotating assembly from either compressor housing or turbine housing, scribe location of components for assembly in original position.

Wastegate Actuator Assembly, Replace

1. Disconnect two vacuum hoses from actuator.
2. Remove clip from wastegate linkage to actuator rod.
3. Remove two bolts attaching actuator and the actuator.
4. Reverse procedure to install.

Elbow Assembly, Replace

1. Raise and support vehicle, then disconnect turbocharger exhaust outlet pipe and catalytic converter at intermediate pipe.
2. Lower vehicle and disconnect turbocharger exhaust outlet pipe from elbow assembly.
3. Disconnect turbocharger inlet pipe at elbow assembly and loosen at exhaust manifold, then position inlet pipe out of way.
4. Remove wastegate linkage to actuator rod retainer.
5. Disconnect elbow assembly support bracket bolts at elbow and loosen bracket bolts at intake manifold, then position bracket out of way.
6. Remove bolts attaching elbow assembly to turbine housing, then remove elbow assembly from vehicle.
7. Reverse procedure to install.

Center Housing Rotating Assembly, Replace

1. Remove elbow assembly as described under "Elbow Assembly, Replace".
2. Remove oil feed and return lines from housing.
3. Remove six bolts, three clamps and three lock plates attaching turbine housing to center housing rotating assembly.
4. Reverse procedure to install.

Compressor Housing, Replace

1. Remove elbow assembly and center housing rotating assembly as described previously.
2. Remove air cleaner and EGR valve and heat shield.
3. Remove six bolts attaching compressor housing to plenum.
4. Remove three bolts attaching compressor housing to intake manifold, then remove compressor.
5. Reverse procedure to install.

Turbocharger & Actuator Assembly, Replace

1. Disconnect exhaust inlet and outlet pipes from turbocharger.
2. Remove air cleaner, then disconnect accelerator, cruise control and detent linkages at carburetor and linkage bracket from plenum.
3. Disconnect fuel line at carburetor and necessary vacuum hoses.
4. Drain approximately three quarts of coolant from cooling system, then disconnect coolant hoses from front and rear of plenum.
5. Disconnect EGR pipe at intake manifold fitting.
6. Remove two bolts attaching turbine housing to bracket on intake manifold, then remove three bolts attaching compressor housing to intake manifold.
7. Remove turbocharger and actuator with carburetor and plenum assembly still attached, from engine. Disconnect vacuum hoses as necessary.
8. Remove six bolts attaching turbocharger and actuator assembly to plenum and carburetor assembly.
9. Remove oil drain from center housing rotating assembly.
10. Reverse procedure to install.

Plenum, Replace

1. Remove turbocharger and actuator assembly as described under "Turbocharger and Actuator Assembly, Replace".
2. Remove throttle bracket and two bolts attaching carburetor to plenum, then remove plenum.
3. Reverse procedure to install.

ECS Detonation Sensor, Replace

1. Squeeze side of metal connector to wire from controller and gently pull straight up to remove. Do not pull on wire.
2. Using a deep socket, remove ECS detonation sensor.
3. Reverse procedure to install.

Clutch & Transmission Section

CLUTCH PEDAL, ADJUST

1. Disconnect return spring from clutch fork.
2. Rotate clutch lever and shaft assembly until clutch pedal is firmly seated against rubber bumper on dash brace.
3. Push outer end of clutch fork rearward until release bearing lightly contacts diaphragm spring fingers.
4. Disconnect lower push rod from lever and shaft assembly and install it in gauge hole.
5. Rotate fork rod finger tight until all lash has been removed from linkage.
6. Remove swivel from gauge hole and install it in hole furthest from lever and shaft assembly. When adjusting a new clutch on 1978–79 Phoenix and Ventura models, if necessary shorten push rod 5/16 inch by turning rod an additional 2½ turns to eliminate clutch interference.
7. Install washers and retainer, then tighten lock nut being careful not to change length of rod.
8. Reconnect return spring and check pedal free travel. Free travel should be approximately 1.0 inch on all except 1978–79 Phoenix and Ventura models. On 1978–79 Phoenix and Ventura models, free travel should be 1¾ to 2⅜ inch for a new clutch and 7/8 to 15/16 inch for a used clutch, Fig. 1.

NOTE: On 1978–79 Phoenix, when adjusting

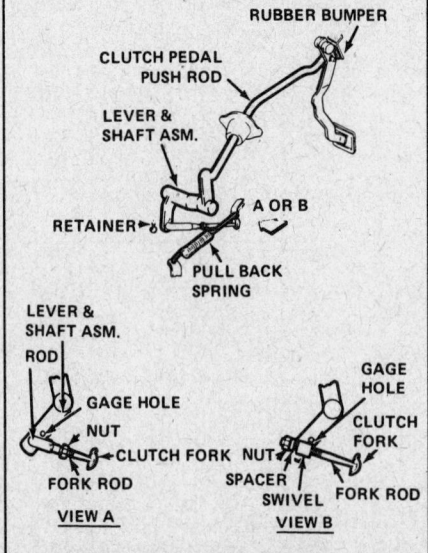

Fig. 1   Clutch pedal, adjust

a used clutch, check for diaphragm finger to clutch disc spring pocket interference when pressing pedal fully to the floor. If interference exists as indicated by a grinding or scraping noise, increase free travel sufficiently to eliminate contact.

CLUTCH, REPLACE

1. Remove transmission as described under "Transmission, Replace."
2. Disconnect clutch fork push rod and spring.
3. Remove flywheel housing from engine.
4. Slide clutch fork from ball stud and remove fork from dust boot.
5. Install a dummy shaft to support clutch assembly during removal.
6. Mark clutch plate and flywheel to ensure reassembly in the same position.
7. Loosen clutch cover to flywheel bolts one turn at a time until spring pressure is relieved, then remove mounting bolts and clutch cover and disc.

THREE-SPEED MANUAL TRANS., REPLACE

1. Disconnect battery ground cable.

2. Raise vehicle and drain lubricant from transmission.
3. Scribe mark on companion flange and drive shaft yoke, then remove drive shaft.
4. Disconnect speedometer cable and back-up light switch wire connector.
5. On models with column shift, disconnect transmission shift levers from transmission shifter shafts. On models with floor shift, it will also be necessary to remove shifter assembly to shifter support bolts and remove shifter assembly from transmission.
6. Remove crossmember to transmission mount bolts and catalytic converter to transmission bracket, if equipped, then remove crossmember to frame bolts.
7. Raise transmission and remove crossmember.
8. Remove transmission to clutch housing upper attaching bolts and install guide pins.
9. Remove transmission to clutch housing lower attaching bolts, then slide transmission straight back on guide pins until main drive splines are clear of clutch plate and remove transmission from vehicle.
10. Reverse procedure to install.

SHIFT LINKAGE
3 SPEED TRANS., ADJUST

Column Shift
1. Place shift lever in reverse position and ignition switch in Lock position.
2. Raise vehicle and loosen shift control rod swivel lock nuts.
3. Pull down slightly on 1st–reverse control rod attached to column lever to remove slack in column mechanism, then tighten lock nut at transmission.
4. Unlock ignition switch and position shift lever in neutral position. Position column lower levers in neutral, then align gauge holes in levers and insert 3/16 in. gauge pin.

NOTE: Alignment holes are located on lower side of levers.

5. Support rod and swivel to prevent movement of assembly and tighten 2nd–3rd control rod lock nut.
6. Remove alignment tool from column levers and check shifter operation. Place shift lever in reverse and check interlock control.

NOTE: With shift lever in reverse, ignition key must move freely to Lock position. It must not be possible to obtain Lock position in any other selector position than reverse.

Floor Shift
1. Place ignition switch in off position, then raise vehicle.
2. Loosen lock nuts at swivels on shift rods. Rods should pass freely through swivels.
3. Shift shift levers into neutral at transmission.
4. Place shift control lever in neutral detent, then align control assembly levers and insert a 3/16 in. gauge pin into lever alignment slot.
5. Tighten locknuts at shift rod swivels and remove gauge pin.
6. Place shift control lever in reverse position and ignition switch in Lock position. Loosen lock nut at back drive control rod swivel, then pull down on rod slightly to remove slack in column mechanism and tighten clevis jam nut.
7. Check interlock control, ignition key should move freely to and from Lock position.
8. Lower vehicle and check adjustment.

4 SP. TRANS., REPLACE

Follow procedure outlined for three-speed model.

NOTE: For 1982–84 Firebird, torque arm must be removed after step 2 of three speed transmission removal procedure. Refer to "Rear Axle, Propeller Shaft and Brake Section" of this chapter for torque arm removal procedure.

SHIFT LINKAGE
4 SPEED TRANS, ADJUST

1. Place selector lever in neutral.
2. Loosen trunnion nuts on transmission control rod.
3. Place transmission lever and bracket assembly in neutral and install a gauge pin through hole and slot provided in bracket.
4. Position lever on transmission in neutral.
5. Tighten trunnion nuts and remove gauge pin.
6. Position shift lever in Reverse, set steering column lever in Lock position and lock ignition. Push up on control rod to remove clearance and tighten nut of adjusting swivel.

5 SP. TRANS., REPLACE

1. Disconnect battery ground cable.
2. From inside vehicle, remove screws attaching bezel to tunnel, then remove bezel by slipping over boot and shift lever.
3. With shift lever in neutral, hold boot out of way and remove four bolts attaching shift lever to transmission, then remove shift lever assembly.
4. Raise vehicle and scribe a mark on companion flange and drive shaft yoke, then remove drive shaft.
5. Remove bolts attaching catalytic converter support bracket to transmission.
6. Remove two bolts attaching transmission mount to support.
7. Raise transmission and remove two long end bolts, then remove transmission support.
8. Disconnect speedometer cable and back-up light switch wire connector.
9. Remove transmission to clutch housing upper attaching bolts and install guide pins.
10. Remove transmission to clutch housing lower attaching bolts, then slide transmission back on guide pins until main drive gear splines clear clutch plate and remove transmission from vehicle.

Rear Axle, Propeller Shaft & Brake Section

REAR AXLES

Figs. 1 and 2 illustrate the rear axle assemblies used on 1977–84 conventional models. When necessary to overhaul either of these units, refer to the *Rear Axle Specifications* table in this chapter.

1977–84

In this rear axle, Fig. 1, the rear axle housing and differential carrier are cast into an integral assembly. The drive pinion assembly is mounted in two opposed tapered roller bearings. The pinion bearings are preloaded by a spacer behind the front bearings. The pinion is positioned by a shim between the head of the pinion and the rear bearing.

The differential is supported in the carrier by two tapered roller side bearings. These bearings are preloaded by shims located between the bearings and carrier housing. The differential assembly is positioned for proper ring gear and pinion backlash by varying these shims. The differential case houses two side gears in mesh with two pinions mounted on a pinion shaft which is held in place by a lock screw. The side gears and pinions are backed by thrust washers.

Rear Axle, Replace

Except 1982–84 Firebird
It is not necessary to remove rear axle assembly from vehicle to perform any normal service operation. However, if any part of housing is damaged, rear axle assembly may be removed and installed using the following procedure.
1. Raise car and place a floor jack under center of axle housing so it starts to raise rear axle assembly. Place jack stands solidly under frame members on both sides.
2. Disconnect rear U-joint from drive pinion flange and support propeller shaft out of the way.
3. Remove both axle shafts.
4. Support both brake backing plates out of the way.
5. Disconnect rear brake hose bracket by removing top cover bolt. Remove brake line from housing by bending back tabs.
6. Loosen remaining cover bolts, break loose cover about 1/8 inch and allow lube to drain.

7. Disconnect shock absorbers at axle housing.
8. On models with coil springs:
   a. Disconnect upper control arms at axle housing.
   b. Slowly lower jack until all spring tension is relieved and remove springs.
   c. Disconnect lower control arms and remove axle assembly.
9. On models with leaf springs.
   a. While supporting spring, remove rear shackle from spring.
   b. Lower spring and remove nut and bolt from spring front bushing, remove spring.
   c. Remove axle assembly.

1982–84 Firebird

1. Hoist car and support at frame and under rear axle housing.
2. Disconnect both shock absorbers and remove bolt from left side of track bar to axle.
3. Remove bolt from brake line junction block at axle housing and disconnect brake lines from junction block.
4. Lower rear axle assembly and remove springs.
5. Remove rear wheels and drums and remove rear axle cover and drain lube.
6. Disconnect brake lines from axle housing clips.
7. Remove axle shafts, brake backing plates, lower control arms and torque arm from axle housing.
8. Disconnect drive shaft from rear axle flange and place aside after marking for reinstallation.
9. Remove rear axle housing.
10. Reverse procedure to install.

Axle Shaft, Replace

NOTE: Design allows for axle shaft end play of .018 inches max. on 1977 "B" and "O" (8½ inch) axles; .022 inches max. on 1977 "C," "G," "K" and "O" (7½ inch) axles; .032 inches max. on 1977–81 "P" (8¾ inch) axles; and .002–.020 inches max. on 1978–81 "C," "G," "K," "O" and "P" (7½ and 8½ inch) axles. The axle type identification marks for 1977–84

except 1978–81 "B" axles will be stamped on right rear axle tube, on forward side. 1978–81 "B" axles will have a tag attached by a cover bolt at the seven o'clock position. This end play can be checked with wheel and brake drum removed by measuring difference between end of housing and axle shaft flange while moving the axle shaft in and out by hand.

TYPE "B & O" (EXCEPT 7½")

1. To remove, take off wheels and brake drums.
2. Remove nuts holding retainer plates and brake backing plates. Pull retainers clear of bolts and reinstall two lower nuts finger tight to hold backing plate in position.
3. Use a slide hammer-type puller to remove axle shaft, Fig. 3.

Axle Shaft Bearing

1. Press axle shaft bearing off shaft.
2. Press new bearing against shoulder on shaft.

CAUTION: Outer retainer plate which retains bearing in housing must be on axle shaft before bearing is installed. A new outer retainer gasket must be installed after bearing. Use care not to wedge outer retainer between bearing and shoulder of shaft. Do not press bearing and inner retainer on in one operation.

3. Press new inner retainer ring against bearing.

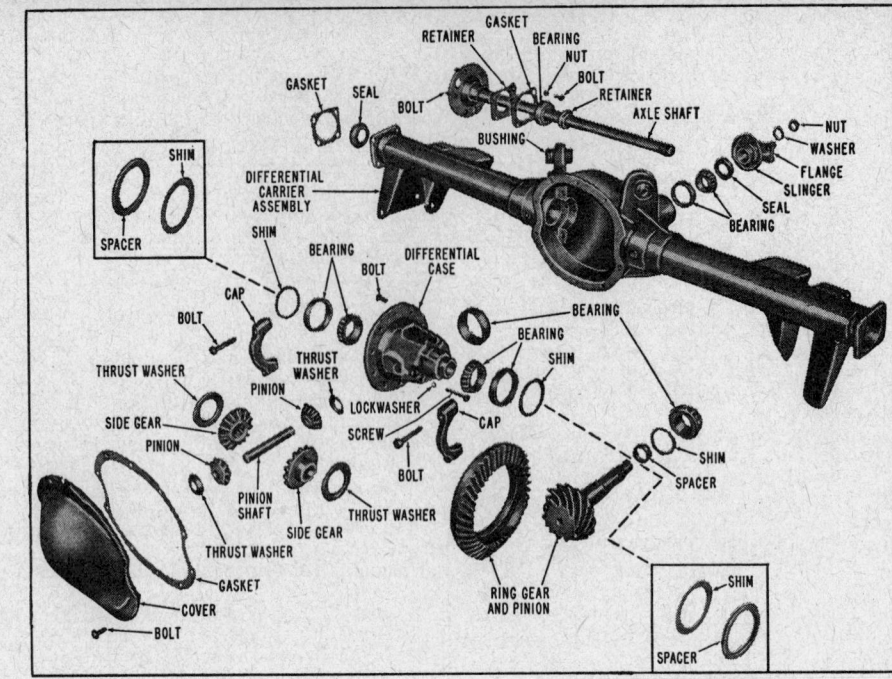

Fig. 1 Rear Axle assembly exploded. Except "C" lock axle retention

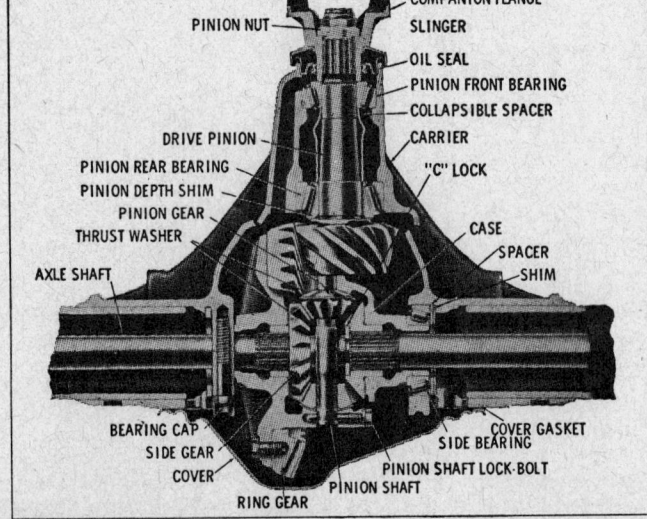

Fig. 2 Rear Axle assembly exploded. With "C" lock retention

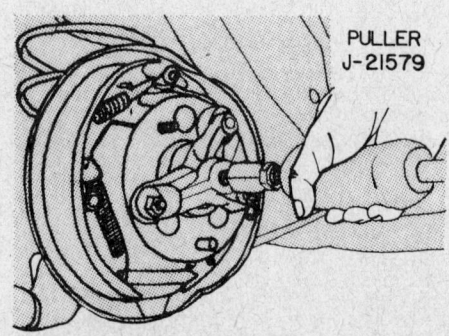

Fig. 3 Removing axle shaft with slide hammer-type puller

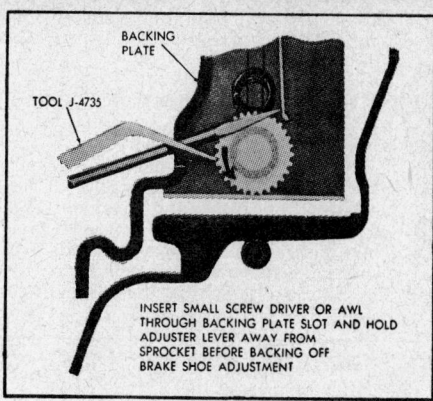

Fig. 4 Backing off adjusting screw

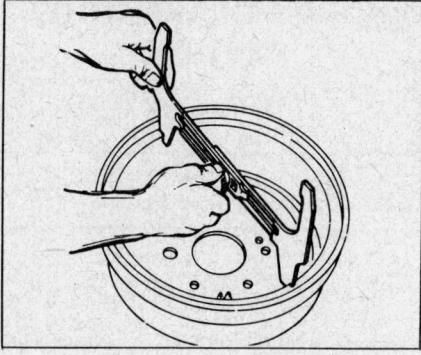

Fig. 5 Measuring brake drum inside diameter

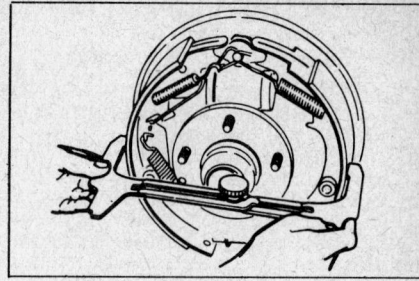

Fig. 6 Checking brake shoe lining clearance

Axle Shaft Seal

1. Insert suitable tongs behind seal and pull straight out to remove seal.
2. Apply sealer to outside diameter of new seal.
3. Position seal over a suitable installer and drive straight into axle housing until tool bottoms on bearing shoulder in housing.

Axle Shaft, Install

1. Apply a coat of wheel bearing grease in bearing recess of housing. Also lightly lubricate the axle shaft with rear axle lube from the sealing surface to about 6" inboard.
2. Install *new* axle housing-to-brake backing plate gasket.
3. Install brake assembly with backing plate in proper position.
4. With a *new* outer retainer gasket in proper position, insert axle shaft until splines engage differential. *Do not allow shaft to drag on seal.*
5. Drive axle shaft into position.
6. Place new outer retainer gasket and retainer over studs and install nuts.
7. Install brake drums and wheels.

TYPE "C", "G", "K", "O" (7½") & "P" AXLE

1. Raise and support car leaving the rear wheels and differential suspended.
2. Remove rear wheels and brake drums.
3. Remove differential cover and drain lubricant.
4. Remove pinion shaft lock bolt and pinion shaft.
5. Push axle shaft inward to permit removal of "C" locks then remove axle shaft.
6. Install axle shaft bearing and seal remover and remove the bearing and seal.

PROPELLER SHAFT, REPLACE

One type of propeller shaft is used on all vehicles. The type being used is a one-piece shaft with two single cardan type U-joints.

Two methods of retention are used at the rear of the propeller shaft. The first method uses a pair of straps retained by bolts, while the second method uses a set of bolted flanges.

1. Raise and properly support vehicle, then mark relationship of propeller shaft to companion flange in order to insure correct alignment during reassembly.
2. Disconnect rear U-joint by removing strap bolts of flange bolts.

NOTE: If U-joint bearing cups are loose, tape them together to avoid dropping and losing needle rollers.

3. Remove propeller shaft by pulling rearward.

CAUTION: Support propeller shaft during removal. Do not allow propeller shaft to drop or allow universal joints to bend to an extreme angle.

4. Reverse procedure to install, making sure that alignment marks are properly aligned. Torque strap retaining bolts to 15 ft. lbs. Torque flange bolts to 45 ft. lbs.

BRAKE ADJUSTMENTS

1977—84 Self-Adjusting Brakes

These brakes have self-adjusting shoe mechanisms that assure correct lining-to-drum clearances at all times. The automatic adjusters operate only when the brakes are applied as the car is moving rearward.

Although the brakes are self-adjusting, an initial adjustment is necessary after the brake shoes have been relined or replaced, or when the length of the star wheel adjuster has been changed during some other service operation.

Frequent usage of an automatic transmission forward range to half reverse vehicle motion may prevent the automatic adjusters from functioning, thereby inducing low pedal heights. Should low pedal heights be encountered, it is recommended that numerous forward and reverse stops be made until satisfactory pedal height is obtained.

If a low pedal height condition cannot be corrected by making numerous reverse stops (provided the hydraulic system is free of air) it indicates that the self-adjusting mechanism is not functioning. Therefore, it will be necessary to remove the drum, clean, free up and lubricate the adjusting mechanism. Then adjust the brakes as follows, being sure the parking brake is fully released.

Adjustment

1. Knock out lanced area from brake backing plate with a suitable punch.

NOTE: If this is done with drum installed on car, drum must be removed and brake area cleaned of all metal particles.

2. Turn brake adjusting screw with tool J6166 or equivalent until brake shoes are expanded to where wheel can just be turned by hand. Amount of effort to turn wheels should be same at all four wheels.
3. While holding adjusting lever out of engagement with a suitable screw driver, Fig. 4, back off adjusting screw several notches and check for drag. If brakes still drag, back off adjusting screw one or two more notches.

NOTE: Brakes should be free of drag when screw has been backed off approximately 12 notches. Heavy drag at this point indicates tight parking brake cables.

4. Install new adjusting hole cover in brake backing plate cover.
5. Check parking brake adjustment.

NOTE: The recommended method of adjusting the brakes is by using the Drum-to-Brake Shoe Clearance Gauge shown in Fig. 5 to check the diameter of the brake drum inner surface. Turn the tool to the opposite side and fit over the brake shoes by turning the star wheel until the gauge just slides over the linings, Fig. 6. Rotate the gauge around the brake shoe lining surface to assure proper clearance.

PARKING BRAKE, ADJUST

CAUTION: Adjustment of parking brake cable is necessary whenever rear brake cables are disconnected. The need for parking brake adjustment is indicated if parking brake pedal travel is less than 9 ratchet clicks or more than 17 ratchet clicks. It is also important that parking brake cables are not adjusted too tightly as brake drag will occur. Incorrect cable tension can damage brake system and cause premature wear to brake linings.

1977–84, Less Rear Disc Brakes

1. Raise and support rear of vehicle.
2. Apply parking brake pedal two to three ratchet clicks on all except 1977–81 full size models, and six ratchet clicks on 1977–81 full size models.
3. Tighten adjusting nut until left rear wheel can just be rotated rearward but is locked when forward rotation is attempted.
4. Release parking brake and check to ensure that rear wheels rotate freely in either direction with no brake drag.

1979–84 Firebird With Rear Disc Brakes

1. Lubricate parking brake cables at underbody rub points and at equalizer hooks. Check for free movement of all cables.
2. Ensure parking brake hand lever is in fully released position.
3. Raise and support rear of vehicle.
4. Hold brake cable stud from turning and tighten equalizer nut until cable slack is removed.
5. Ensure caliper levers are against stops on caliper housing after tightening equalizer nut.
6. If levers are off the stops, loosen cable until levers return to stops.
7. Operate parking brake lever several times to check adjustment. After cable adjustment is performed, parking brake lever should travel 14 clicks with approximately 150 ± 20 pounds force of handle effort using tool J-28662.
8. Lower vehicle and ensure levers are against caliper stops. If necessary back off parking brake adjuster to keep levers against stops.

POWER BRAKE UNIT, REPLACE

Hydro-Boost

NOTE: Pump brake pedal several times with engine off to deplete accumulator of fluid.

1. Remove two nuts attaching master cylinder to booster, then move master cylinder away from booster with brake lines attached.
2. Remove three hydraulic lines from booster. Plug and cap all lines and outlets.
3. Remove retainer and washer securing booster push rod to brake pedal arm.
4. Remove four nuts attaching booster unit to dash panel.
5. From engine compartment, loosen booster from dash panel and move booster push rod inboard until it disconnects from brake pedal arm. Remove spring washer from brake pedal arm.
6. Remove booster unit from vehicle.
7. Reverse procedure to install. To purge system, disconnect feed wire from injection pump. Fill power steering pump reservoir, then crank engine for several seconds and recheck power steering pump fluid level. Connect injection pump feed wire and start engine, then cycle steering wheel from stop to stop twice and stop engine. Discharge accumulator by depressing brake pedal several times, then check fluid level. Start engine, then turn steering wheel from stop to stop and turn engine off. Check fluid level and add fluid as necessary. If foaming occurs, stop

engine and wait for approximately one hour for foam to dissipate, then recheck fluid level.

Vacuum Booster

1. Remove vacuum check valve.
2. If brake booster and master cylinder are being removed as an assembly, disconnect hydraulic lines and cover openings in master cylinder and lines to avoid entry of dirt. If only brake booster is to be removed, remove master cylinder retaining nuts and position master cylinder aside.

CAUTION: Be careful not to bend or kink hydraulic lines.

3. Remove clevis pin retainer from brake pedal.
4. Remove brake booster retaining nuts and remove brake booster.
5. Reverse procedure to install.

BRAKE MASTER CYLINDER, REPLACE

1977–84

1. Disconnect brake lines from two outlets on master cylinder and tape end of lines to prevent entrance of dirt.
2. On models less power brakes, disconnect master cylinder push rod from brake pedal.
3. Remove two nuts attaching master cylinder to dash or power brake unit and remove master cylinder from vehicle.

Rear Suspension

SHOCK ABSORBER, REPLACE

NOTE: If vehicle is equipped with Superlift shock absorbers, bleed system air pressure through service valve before disconnecting lines at shock absorber fittings.

1. With rear axle supported properly, disconnect shock absorber from lower mounting nut. Use a wrench to prevent mounting stud rotation.
2. Disconnect shock absorber from upper mounting nut.
3. Reverse procedure to install.

LEAF SPRING & BUSHINGS, REPLACE

1977–81 Firebird & 1977–79 Phoenix & Ventura

1. Raise and support vehicle so that axle can be raised and lowered.
2. Lower axle assembly to relieve tension

rom spring.
3. Disconnect shock absorber from lower mounting, Fig. 1.
4. Loosen spring eye to bracket retaining bolt.
5. Remove bolts attaching spring retainer bracket to under body.

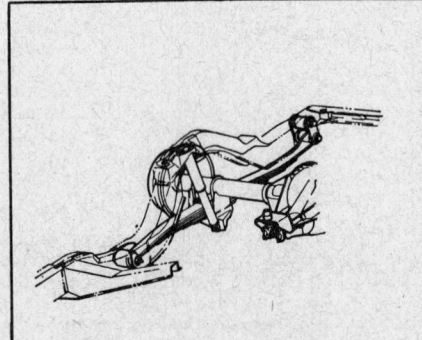

Fig. 1   Leaf spring suspension (typical) 1977 Ventura, 1977–79 Firebird, 1977–79 Phoenix

6. Lower axle assembly to permit access to spring retainer bracket, and remove bracket from spring.
7. Pry parking brake cable out of retainer bracket mounted on anchor plate.
8. Remove lower spring plate to axle bracket retaining nuts.
9. Remove upper and lower cushions and anchor plate.
10. Support spring, then remove lower bolt from spring rear shackle. Separate shackle and remove spring from vehicle.
11. To replace bushings, refer to Figs. 2 and 3.
12. Reverse procedure to install.

Leaf Spring Service

NOTE: The main leaf may be serviced separately, however, if any of the smaller leaves require replacement, the entire assembly must be replaced.

1. Clamp spring in a vise, remove spring clips and center bolt, then carefully open vise, allowing spring to expand.
2. Replace main leaf and use a drift to align center bolt holes, compress spring in a vise, remove drift and install new center

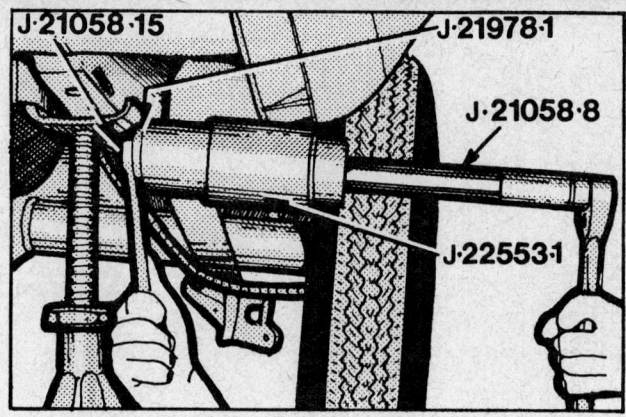

Fig. 2   Leaf spring front bushing removal

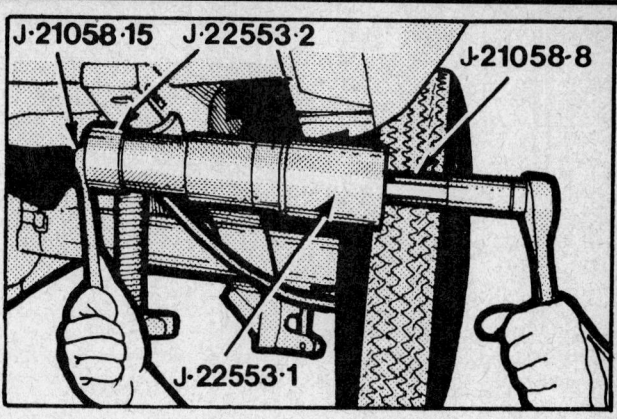

Fig. 3   Leaf spring front bushing installation

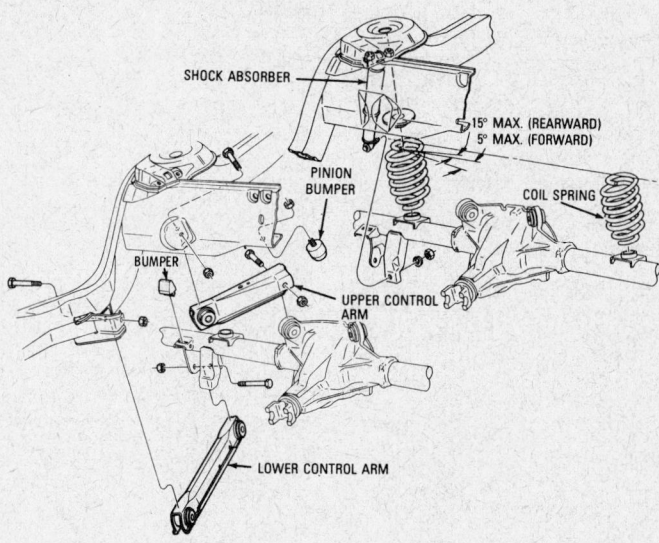

Fig. 4   Coil spring suspension (typical) Except 1982–84 Firebird

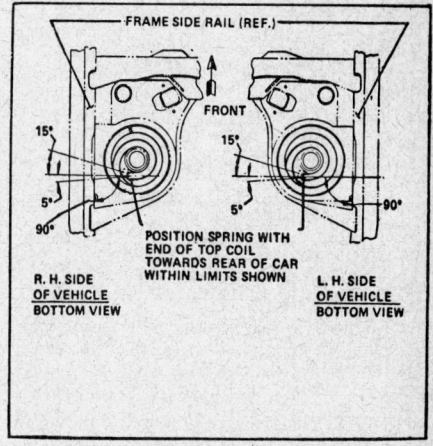

Fig. 4A   Indexing coil springs. 1977–81 & 1983–84 Full Size and 1977–84 Intermediates

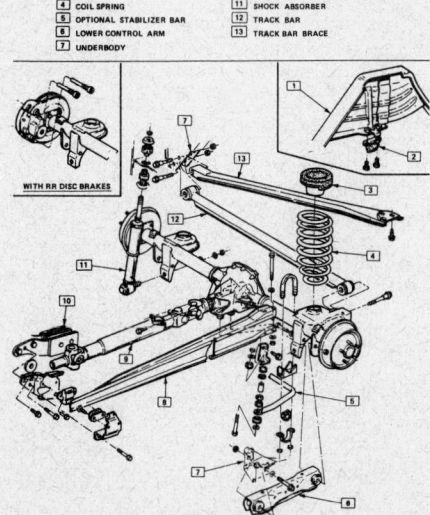

1 RAIL	8 TORQUE ARM
2 JOUNCE BUMPER	9 PROP SHAFT
3 SPRING INSULATOR ASM.	10 DAMPER ASM. WITH 4 CYL. ENGINE
4 COIL SPRING	11 SHOCK ABSORBER
5 OPTIONAL STABILIZER BAR	12 TRACK BAR
6 LOWER CONTROL ARM	13 TRACK BAR BRACE
7 UNDERBODY	

Fig. 5   Coil spring suspension. 1982–84 Firebird

bolt.

3. Align spring leaves and bend spring clips into position.

NOTE: Overtightening spring clips will bind spring action.

COIL SPRING, REPLACE

1977–84 All Exc. Firebird, Phoenix & Ventura

1. Support vehicle at frame rails and support rear axle with a suitable jack.
2. Remove brake line connector block bolt at axle housing.
3. Release brake line from clips on axle housing as necessary.
4. Disconnect upper control arms from axle housing, Fig. 4.
5. Disconnect shock absorbers from lower mountings.
6. Lower rear axle. Do not permit the rear brake hose to kink or stretch.
7. When the axle has been lowered sufficiently to provide clearance for coil spring removal, remove coil spring.
8. Reverse procedure to install. Ensure that coil springs are properly indexed, Fig. 4A.

1982–84 Firebird

1. Raise car on suitable hoist and support rear axle on adjustable type lifting device.
2. Loosen track bar bolt at body brace and remove track bar mounting bolt at axle assembly, Fig. 5.
3. Disconnect rear brake hose clip at underbody and remove both shock absorber lower attaching nuts.
4. Remove prop shaft from vehicles with four cylinder engines.
5. Lower rear axle and remove coil spring and insulators.
6. Reverse procedure to install.

CONTROL ARMS & BUSHINGS, REPLACE

NOTE: Replace control arms one at a time to prevent axle misalignment, making installation difficult.

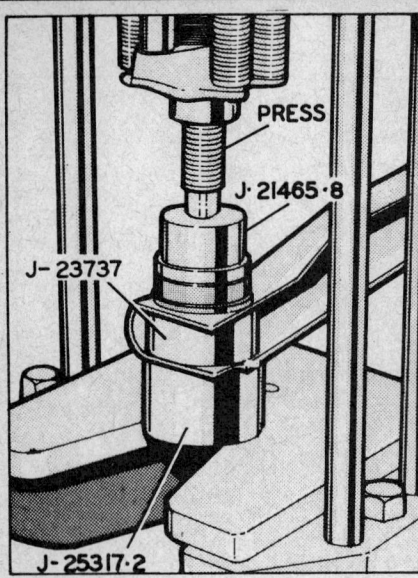

PRESS

J·21465·8

J-23737

J-25317·2

Fig. 6 All front & lower control arm rear bushing removal. 1978–1984 models

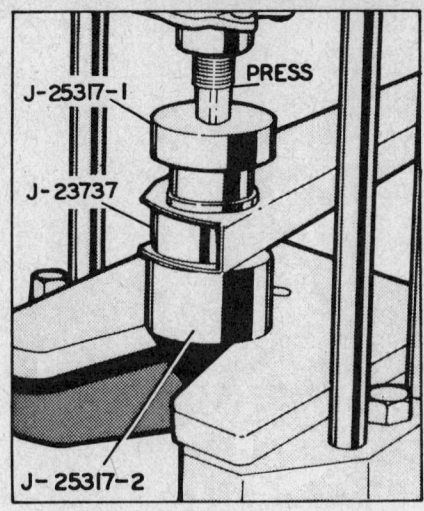

J-25317-1

PRESS

J-23737

J-25317-2

Fig. 7 All front & lower control arm rear bushing installation. 1978–84 models

GRIND TOOL OFF AS SHOWN

J-21474-3
J-21474-8   J-21474-4
J-21474-16

THRUST BEARING & WASHER

Fig. 8 Upper control arm rear bushing removal. 1977 models (Typical)

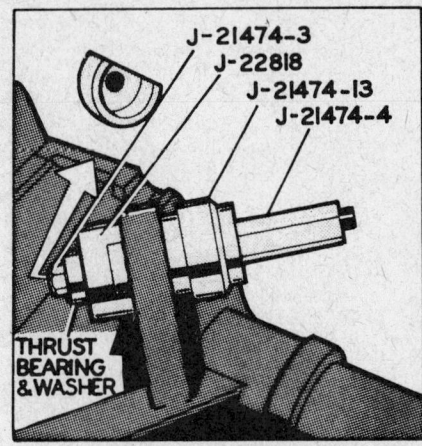

J-21474-3
J-22818
J-21474-13
J-21474-4

THRUST BEARING & WASHER

Fig. 9 Upper control arm rear bushing installation. 1977 models (Typical)

Upper Control Arms

NOTE: 1982–84 Firebird uses a single torque arm in place of upper control arms. Refer to "Torque Arm, Replace" & Fig. 5.

1. Support vehicle at frame and rear axle.
2. Remove control arm front and rear mounting bolts.

NOTE: On some vehicles, disconnect the shock absorber lower mounting stud to provide clearance. Also, use a suitable jack under the nose of differential housing to aid bolt removal.

3. Replace bushings as necessary, Figs. 6 thru 11.

NOTE: On 1977 models, bushings in control arms can only be serviced by replacing control arms.

4. Reverse procedure to install. Tighten control arm bolts with vehicle at curb height.

Lower Control Arms

Follow "Upper Control Arms" procedure for replacement of lower control arms. Lower control arm bushings are serviceable, Figs. 6 & 7.

NOTE: On models equipped with a stabilizer bar, remove stabilizer bar outlined under "Stabilizer Bar & Bushings, Replace" procedure before removing lower control arm mounting bolts.

TORQUE ARM, REPLACE

1. Raise vehicle on suitable hoist and support rear axle assembly with adjustable jack.
2. Loosen track bar bolt at body brace and remove track bar bolt at axle assembly.
3. Disconnect rear brake hose clip at underbody and remove both shock absorber lower attaching nuts.
4. Remove prop shaft from vehicles with four cylinder engine.
5. Lower rear axle and remove coil springs.

NOTE: Coil springs must be removed before removing torque arm to avoid rear axle forward twist which may cause vehicle damage.

6. Remove torque arm rear attaching bolts, front torque arm outer bracket and re-

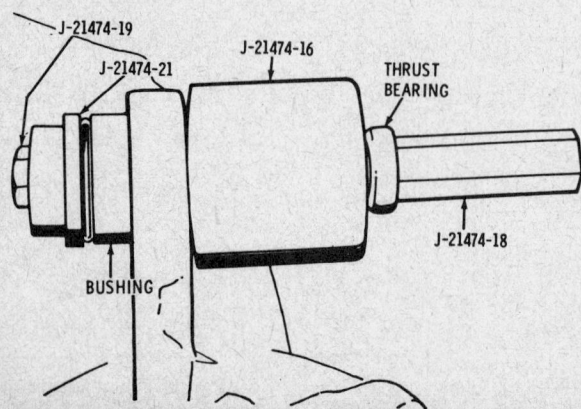

J-21474-19
J-21474-21
J-21474-16
THRUST BEARING
J-21474-18
BUSHING

Fig. 10 Upper control arm rear bushing removal. 1978–84 models

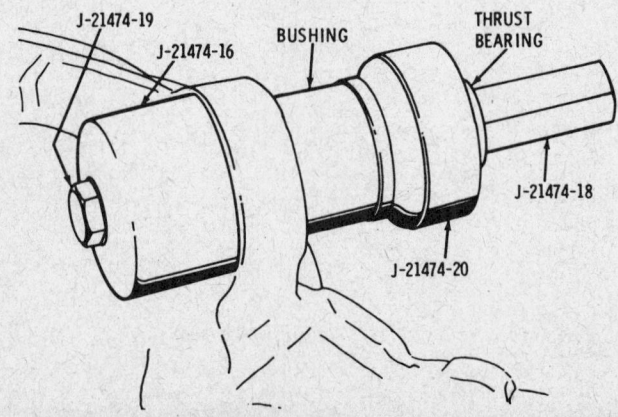

J-21474-19
J-21474-16
BUSHING
THRUST BEARING
J-21474-18
J-21474-20

Fig. 11 Upper control arm rear bushing installation. 1978–84 models

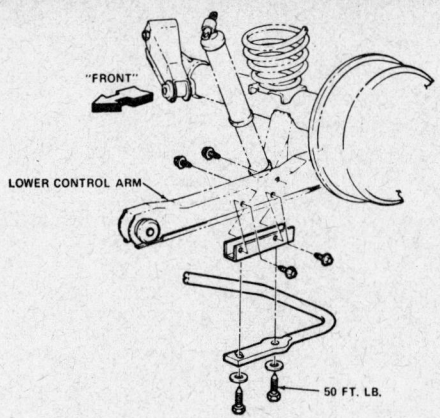

Fig. 12 Stabilizer bar installation. 1977–78 intermediates & all full size

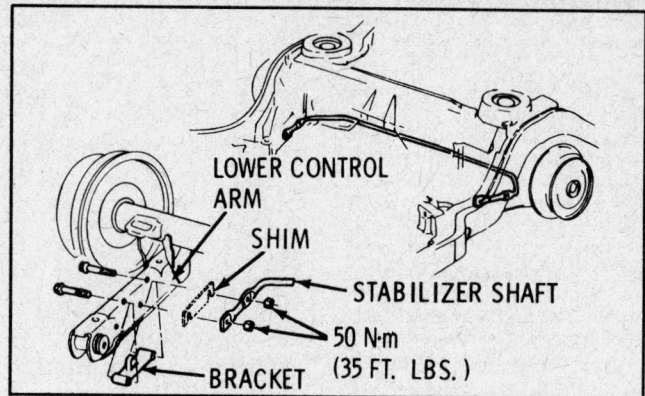

Fig. 13 Stabilizer bar installation. 1977–84 intermediates

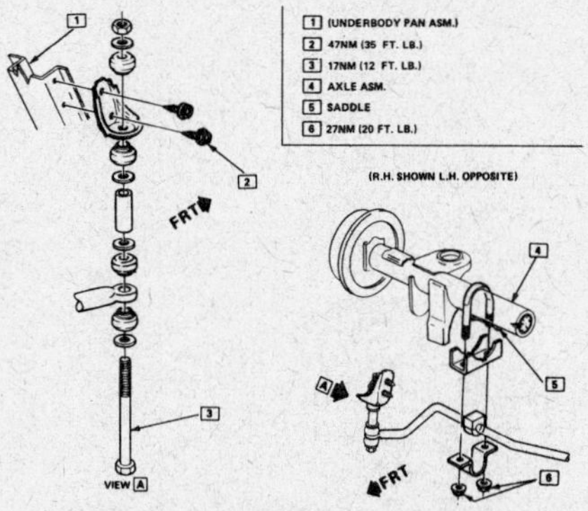

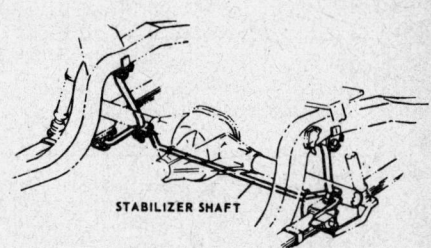

Fig. 15 Stabilizer bar installation. 1977 Ventura, 1977–81 Firebird & 1977–79 Phoenix

Fig. 14 Stabilizer bar installation. 1982–84 Firebird

STABILIZER BAR, REPLACE

Models With Coil Springs

Exc. 1982–84 Firebird
1. With vehicle supported at rear axle, remove bolts attaching stabilizer bar to lower control arms, Figs. 12 and 13.
2. If equipped with shims, note number and location.
3. Reverse procedure to install. Tighten attaching bolts with vehicle at curb height.

1982–84 Firebird
  Refer to Fig. 14 for removal and installation procedures.

Models With Leaf Springs

1. Raise and support rear of vehicle.
2. Remove clamping bolts to disconnect lower end of each support assembly from stabilizer shaft, Fig. 15.
3. Remove insulator and bracket from below each spring and shock absorber anchor plate.
4. Reverse procedure to install making sure that slit in insulators are positioned toward front of vehicle.

move torque arm.
7. Reverse procedure to install. Torque track bar mounting nut at axle to 93 ft. lbs. and torque track bar to body bracket nut to 58 ft. lbs.

Front Suspension & Steering Section

FRONT SUSPENSION

Exc. 1982–84 Firebird

The front suspension is of the conventional "A" frame design with coil springs and ball joints. The ball joints have a "fixed boot" grease seal for protection against the entry of dirt and water. The steering knuckles and spindles are of integral design.

On most models, an integral steering knuckle which is a combination steering knuckle, brake caliper support and steering arm is used. On other models, the steering knuckle is of the conventional type with a separate steering arm.

Rubber bushings at the inner ends of the upper control arms pivot on shafts attached to the car frame. Caster and camber adjustments are made with shims at this point, Fig. 1. Direct acting shock absorbers operate within the coil springs.

1982–84 Firebird

The front suspension is designed to allow each wheel to compensate for changes in the road surface level without appreciably affecting the opposite wheel. Each wheel is independently connected to the frame by a steering knuckle, strut assembly, ball joint, and lower control arm. The steering knuckles

move in a prescribed three dimensional arc. The front wheels are held in proper relationship to each other by two tie rods which are connected to the steering knuckles and to a relay rod assembly.

Coil springs are mounted between the spring housings on the front crossmember and the lower control arms. The upper portion of each strut assembly extends through the fender well and attaches to the upper mount assembly with a nut, Fig. 2.

The inner ends of the lower control arm have pressed in bushings. Bolts, passing through the bushings, attach the arm to the suspension crossmember. The lower ball joint assembly is a press fit in the arm and attaches to the steering knuckle with a torque prevailing nut.

WHEEL ALIGNMENT

Exc. 1982–84 Firebird

Caster and camber adjustments are made by placing shims between the upper pivot shafts and frame, Fig. 3. Both adjustments can be made at the same time. In order to remove or install shims, raise car to remove weight from front wheel, then loosen control arm shaft-to-frame bolts.

NOTE: Shim pack thickness should not exceed .40 inch maximum on 1977–84 models. Also, difference between front and rear shim packs should not exceed 3/8 inch maximum.

1. To increase negative caster, add shims to front bolt or remove shims from rear bolt.
2. To decrease negative caster (increase positive caster), remove shims from front bolt or add shims to rear bolt.
3. To increase positive camber, remove shims from both front and rear bolts.
4. To decrease positive camber (increase negative camber), add shims to both front and rear bolts.

NOTE: *By adding or subtracting an equal amount of shims from front and rear bolts, camber will be changed without affecting caster.*

5. After proper shim pack has been installed, torque pivot shaft mounting bolts to 70 to 75 ft. lbs. on all models except 1981–84 Intermediates, and 45 ft. lbs. on 1981–84 Intermediates.

1982–84 Firebird

Caster and camber can be adjusted by moving the position of the upper strut mount assembly.
1. Remove dust cap and fender bolt.
2. Attach J-29724, using original fender bolt and tighten the turnbuckle, Fig. 4.
3. Loosen three nuts attaching mount assembly.
4. Adjust camber by rotating the turnbuckle to allow the mount assembly to move inboard or outboard, Fig. 5.
5. Adjust the caster by lightly tapping the mount assembly forward or rearward, Fig. 6
6. When correct camber and caster readings have been obtained to specifications, tighten the three nuts attaching the mount assembly to 20 ft. lbs.
7. Remove tool J-29724, and install fender bolt and dust cap.

TOE-IN, ADJUST

1. Remove steering wheel trim cover or horn button and set gear on high point by turning steering wheel until mark on end of shaft is exactly at top. This mark locates high point or middle travel of steering gear.
2. Loosen tie rod clamp bolts and turn both adjuster sleeves an equal amount until toe-in is set to specifications. To increase toe-in, turn left tie rod adjuster sleeve in direction of forward rotation of wheels. Turn right tie rod adjuster sleeve in opposite direction.
3. Make sure front wheels are straight

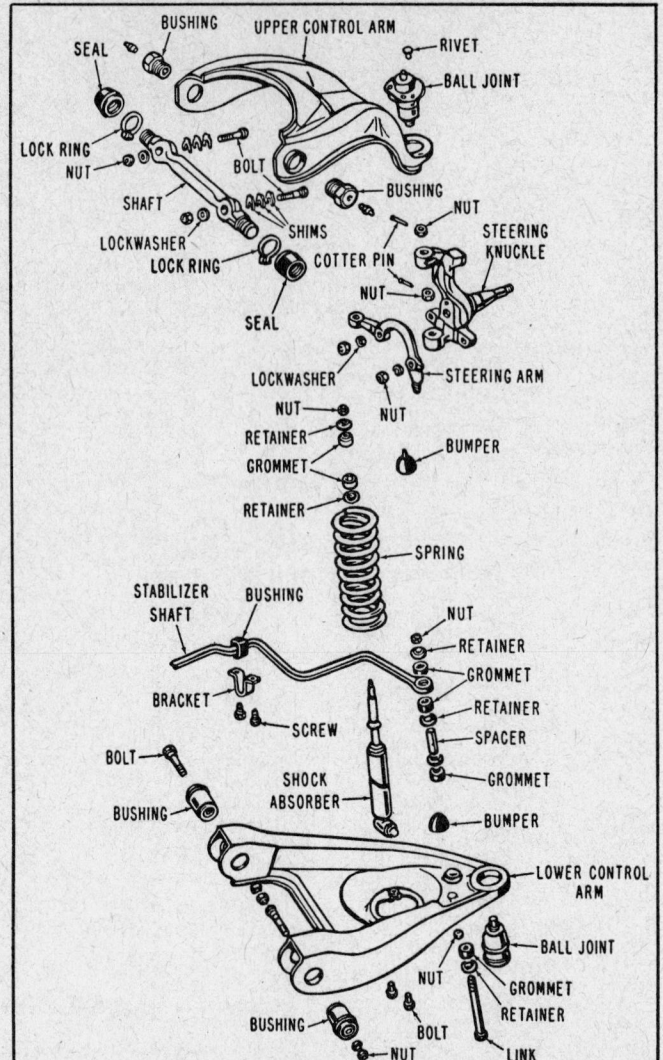

Fig. 1   Disassembled view of front suspension. 1977–84 (typical), Exc. 1982–84 Firebird

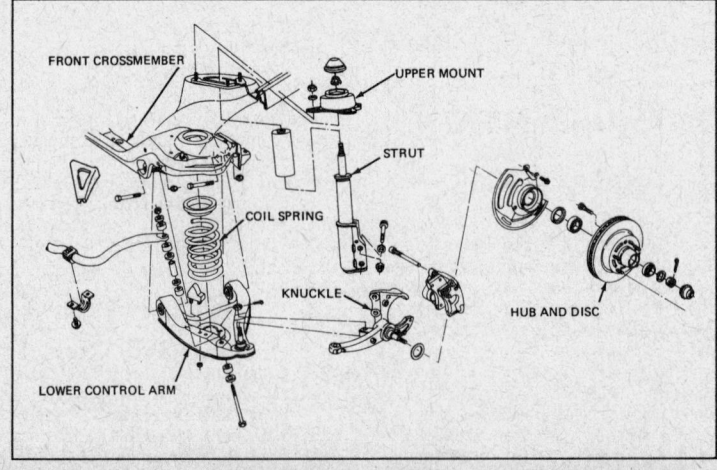

Fig. 2   Disassembled view of front suspension. 1982–84 Firebird

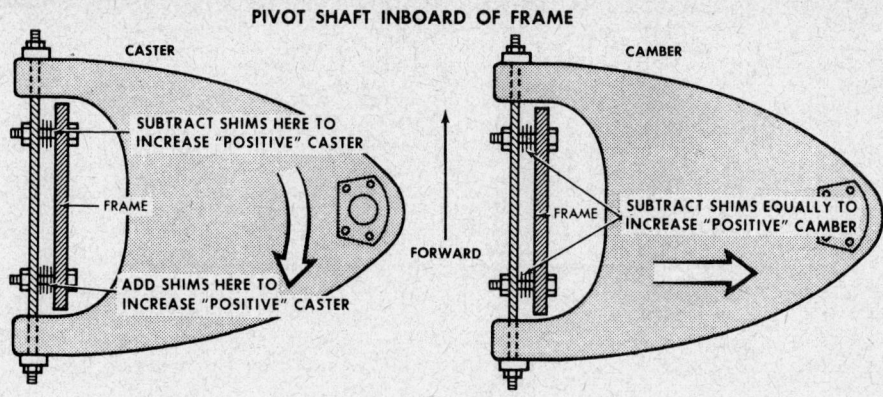

PIVOT SHAFT INBOARD OF FRAME

Fig. 3   Caster and camber shim location

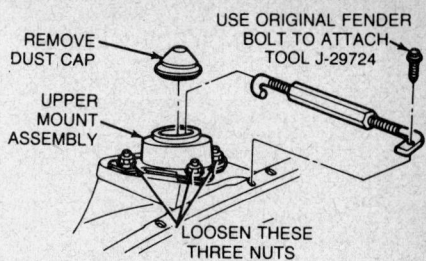

Fig. 4   Installing tool J-29724, for caster and camber adjustment. 1982–84 Firebird

ahead by measuring from a reference point at same place on each side of frame center to front of wheel rims. If measurements are unequal, turn both tie rod adjuster sleeves in same direction (so as not to change toe-in) until measurements become equal. Recheck toe-in and re-adjust as necessary.

4. Torque tie rod clamp bolts to 15 ft. lbs.

NOTE: Open end clamps should be located to a vertical down position. Refer to Figs. 7 and 8.

WHEEL BEARINGS, ADJUST

1. While rotating wheel, torque spindle nut to 12 ft. lbs.
2. Back off spindle nut until just loose, then retighten by hand.
3. Loosen spindle nut until cotter pin can be inserted, however, do not loosen spindle nut more than 1/2 flat.
4. With bearing properly adjusted, there should be .001–.005 inch end play.

WHEEL BEARINGS, REPLACE

(Disc Brakes)

1. Raise vehicle and remove front wheels.

2. Remove brake hose support to caliper mounting bracket screw.
3. Remove caliper to mounting bracket bolts.

NOTE: Do not place strain on brake hose.

4. Remove spindle nut, and disc and hub assembly. Grease retainer and inner bearing can now be removed.

CHECKING BALL JOINTS FOR WEAR

Except 1982–84 Firebird

Before checking ball joints for wear, make sure the front wheel bearings are properly adjusted and that the control arms are tight.

Referring to Fig. 9, raise wheel with a jack placed under the lower control at the point Shown. Then test by moving the wheel up and down to check axial play, and rocking it at the top and bottom to measure radial play.

1. Upper ball joint should be replaced if there is any noticeable looseness at this joint.

   If the ball joint is the type using a built in rubber pre-load cushion it will be necessary to remove the ball stud from the knuckle. Then replace the ball joint retaining nut on the ball stud. Using a socket and torque wrench, measure amount of torque required to turn the ball stud in its socket. If any torque is required, the ball joint is satisfactory. If no torque is required, the ball joint must be replaced.
2. A visual wear indicator is built into the lower ball joint on all models, Fig. 10.

CHECKING FRONT SUSPENSION FOR WEAR

1982–84 Firebird

1. Raise vehicle with floor jack placed under frame torque box, located behind front wheel.
2. Place steering wheel in locked position, then place suitable dial indicator on outside perimeter of wheel.
3. Test by moving wheel back and forth

without moving steering wheel. Gauge reading should not exceed .108 inch.

4. If gauge reading is not within specifications, A thorough front end inspection should be performed and parts replaced as necessary.

BALL JOINTS, REPLACE

Except 1982–84 Firebird

On all models the upper ball joint is riveted to the control arm. All service ball joints, however, are provided with bolt, nut and washer assemblies for replacement purposes.

The lower ball joint is pressed into the control arm. They may be pressed out and new joints pressed in.

Upper Ball Joint

1. Raise vehicle and support lower control arm.
2. Remove wheel assembly.
3. Remove upper ball joint stud from steering knuckle, Fig. 11.
4. Drill or chisel rivet heads from ball joint rivets. Then, drive rivets from control arm with a suitable punch.
5. Install new ball joint and torque retaining bolts to 9 ft. lbs. except on 1983–84 Parisienne, and 13 ft. lbs. for 1983–84 Parisienne.
6. Install ball joint stud into steering knuckle and torque to 60 ft. lbs. for 1977 models, 64 ft. lbs. for 1978–79 models, 88 ft. lbs. for 1980 models and 65 for 1981–84 models.
7. Install cotter pin.
8. Install wheel assembly and lower vehicle.

Lower Ball Joint

1. Raise vehicle and support lower control arm under spring seats.

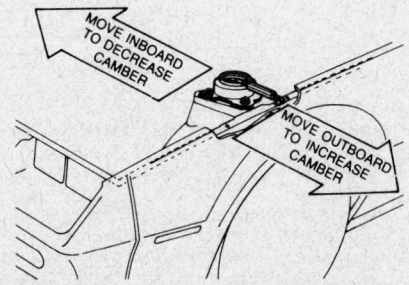

Fig. 5   Camber adjustment. 1982–84 Firebird

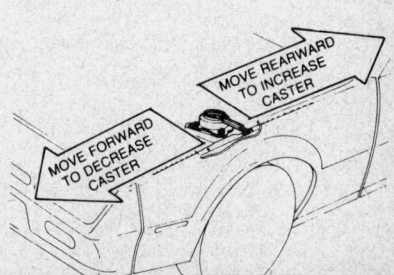

Fig. 6   Caster adjustment. 1982–84 Firebird

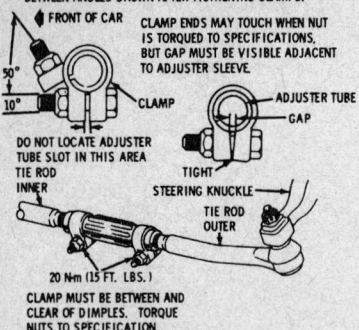

BOLTS MUST BE INSTALLED IN DIRECTION SHOWN. ROTATE BOTH INNER AND OUTER TIE ROD HOUSINGS REARWARD TO THE LIMIT OF BALL JOINT TRAVEL BEFORE TIGHTENING CLAMPS. WITH THIS SAME REARWARD ROTATION ALL BOLT CENTERLINES MUST BE BETWEEN ANGLES SHOWN AFTER TIGHTENING CLAMPS.

Fig. 7   Tie rod clamp and sleeve positioning. Except 1982–84 Firebird

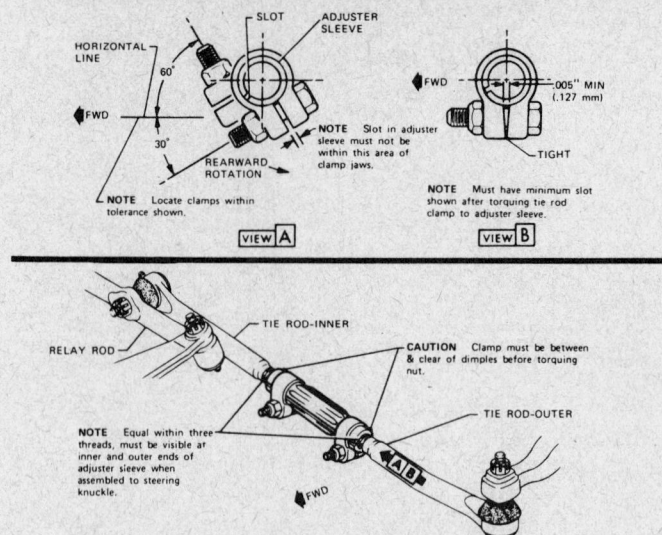

Fig. 8   Tie rod clamp and sleeve positioning. 1982–84 Firebird & 1983–84 Parisienne

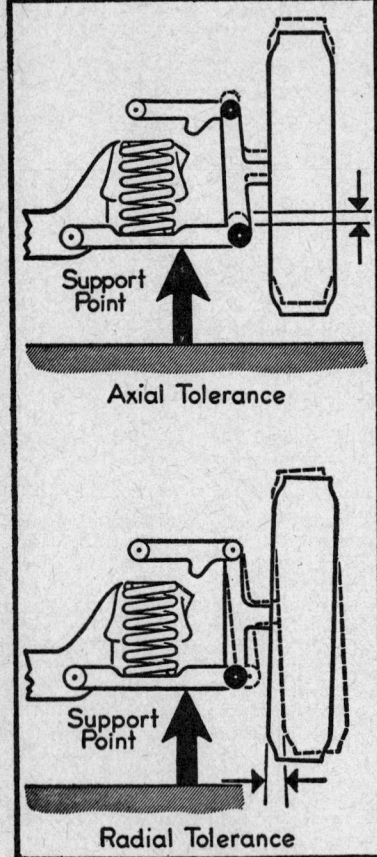

Fig. 9   Checking ball joints for wear

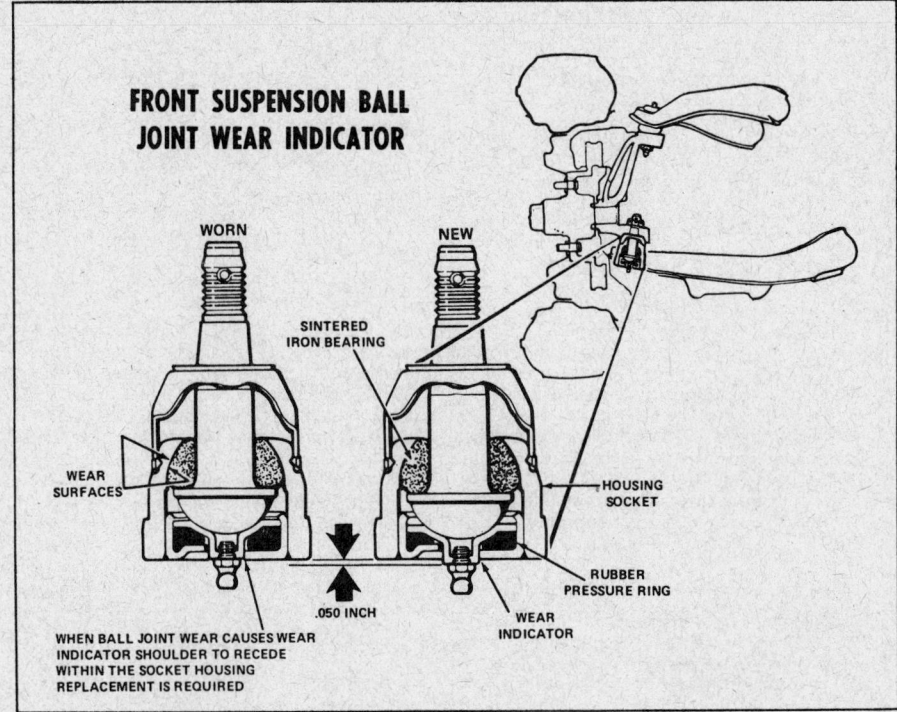

FRONT SUSPENSION BALL JOINT WEAR INDICATOR

Fig. 10   Lower ball joint wear indicator. 1977–84 Exc. 1982–84 Firebird

2. Remove brake drum and backing plate or caliper.
3. Remove lower ball joint stud from steering knuckle, Fig. 11.
4. With a screwdriver, pry ball joint seal and retainer from ball joint.
5. Press lower ball joint from control arm.
6. Press new ball joint into lower control arm.
7. Install ball joint stud into steering knuckle and torque nut to 70 ft. lbs. for 1977 models, 83 ft. lbs. for 1978–80 models, and 90 ft. lbs. for 1981–84 models.
8. Install cotter pin.

9. Install brake backing plate and drum or caliper, then the wheel assembly.

1982–84 Firebird

1. Raise and support vehicle.
2. Remove tire and wheel assembly.
3. Place a suitable floor jack under control arm spring seat.

CAUTION: Floor jack must remain under control arm spring seat during removal and installation to retain spring and control arm in position.

4. Remove cotter pin and loosen nut. Use tool J-24292A to break ball joint loose from steering knuckle.
5. Remove tool and separate joint from knuckle.
6. Guide lower control arm out of opening in splash shield with a suitable tool.
7. Remove grease fittings, and install special tools as shown in Fig. 12.
8. Reverse procedure to install. Torque ball stud nut to 90 ft. lbs.

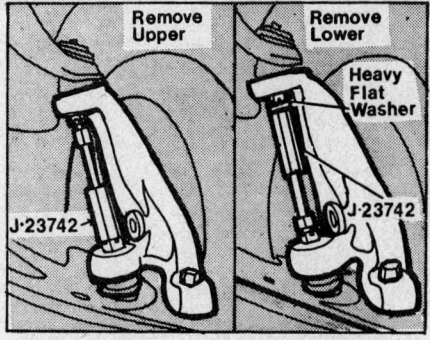

Fig. 11 Removing ball joint studs from steering knuckle.

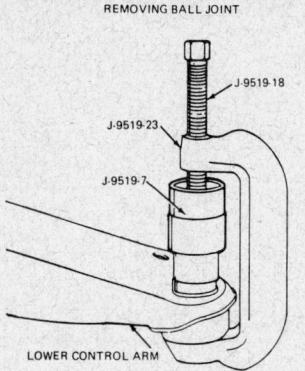
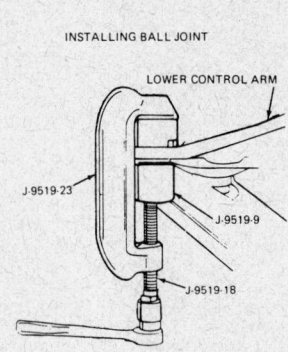

Fig. 12 Removing & installing ball joint. 1982–84 Firebird

SHOCK ABSORBER, REPLACE

Except 1982–84 Firebird

Hold the shock absorber upper stem from turning with a suitable wrench and remove the nut and grommet. Remove the lower shock absorber pivot from the lower control arm and pull the shock absorber and mounting out at the bottom of the spring housing.

To install, reverse the removal procedure. Torque upper retaining nut to 10 ft. lbs. Torque shock absorber lower retaining bolts to 20 ft. lbs.

STRUT, REPLACE

1982–84 Firebird

1. Raise and support vehicle.
2. Remove tire and wheel assembly.
3. Support lower control arm with jack-stand.
4. Remove brake hose bracket.
5. Remove two strut-to-knuckle bolts.
6. Remove cover from upper mount assembly.
7. Remove nut from upper end of strut assembly.
8. Remove strut and shield.
9. Reverse procedure to install. Torque nuts to 52 ft. lbs.

COIL SPRING, REPLACE

1977–84, Except 1982–84 Firebird

1. Support vehicle at frame and remove wheel.
2. Disconnect shock absorber from lower control arm and push shock absorber through hole in lower control arm up into spring.
3. Remove stabilizer link nut, link, spacer, grommets and retainer.
4. Support lower control arm with tool J-23028 bolted onto a suitable jack.

5. Install a safety chain through spring and lower control arm, remove the two lower control arm to frame crossmember pivot bolts. Lower jack, allowing spring to expand and remove spring.
6. Reverse procedure to install. Torque lower control arm to frame attaching nuts, with weight of vehicle on wheels, to specifications listed below:

Year	Nuts, Ft. Lbs.
1977	
Full Size, Grand Prix & LeMans	95
Firebird	90
Phoenix & Ventura	105
1978–79	
Phoenix	92
1978–80	
Grand Prix & LeMans	70
Full Size	124
Firebird	90
1981	
Grand Prix & LeMans	65
Full Size	95
Firebird	95
1982–84	
Intermediates	65
1983–84	
Parisienne	90

1982–84 Firebird

1. Raise and support vehicle.
2. Remove tire and wheel assembly.
3. Remove stabilizer link and bushings at lower control arm.
4. Remove pivot bolt nuts.

NOTE: Do not remove pivot bolts at this time.

5. Install adapter tool No. J-23028 or equivalent adapter to floor jack and place into position with supporting bushings.
6. Install jackstand under outside frame on opposite side of vehicle.
7. Raise tool No. J-23028 enough to remove both pivot bolts.
8. Lower tool No. J-23028 carefully and remove spring.

9. Remove ball joint from steering knuckle using tool No. J-24292A or equivalent as outlined under "Ball Joint, Replace".
10. Replace bushings in lower control arm.
11. Reverse procedure to install. Torque nut to 70 ft. lbs.

STEERING GEAR, REPLACE

1. Use puller to remove pitman arm from steering gear shaft.
2. Remove flex coupling shield, if equipped, then scribe a mark on worm shaft flange and steering shaft and disconnect lower flange from steering shaft.
3. Unfasten gear housing from frame (3 bolts) and remove from car.

POWER STEERING GEAR, REPLACE

1. Remove flex coupling shield if equipped, then scribe mark on worm shaft flange and steering shaft and disconnect lower flange from steering shaft.
2. Disconnect pressure and return hoses from gear housing.
3. Raise vehicle and disconnect pitman arm from shaft.
4. Remove gear housing to frame bolts and remove steering gear assembly.
5. Reverse procedure to install.

POWER STEERING PUMP, REPLACE

1. Disconnect battery ground cable.
2. Remove power steering pump belt drive, then remove pulley from pump.
3. Disconnect pressure and return line from power steering pump. Cap lines and fittings to prevent entry of dirt.
4. Remove pump and bracket from engine as an assembly, then remove bracket from pump.
5. Reverse procedure to install.

PONTIAC FIERO

INDEX OF SERVICE OPERATIONS

NOTE: Refer to the front of this manual for vehicle manufacturer's special service tool suppliers.

PONTIAC FIERO

VEHICLE IDENTIFICATION NUMBER LOCATION

The vehicle identification number is located on top of instrument panel, lower left.

ENGINE NUMBER LOCATION

The engine code stamping is located on vertical pad on front of block below cylinder head.

ENGINE V.I.N. CODE

The eigth digit of the seventeen digit V.I.N. code denotes engine code.

ENGINE IDENTIFICATION CODE

Year	Engine	V.I.N. Code	Engine Code
1984	4-151	R	—

GRILLE IDENTIFICATION

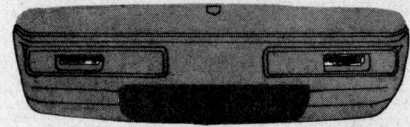

1984 Pontiac Fiero

GENERAL ENGINE SPECIFICATIONS

Year	Engine CID①/Liter	V.I.N. Code	Carburetor	Bore and Stroke	Compression Ratio	Net H.P. @ R.P.M.②	Maximum Torque Ft. Lbs. @ R.P.M.	Normal Oil Pressure Pounds
1984	4-151, 2.5L	R	E.F.I.③	4.0 × 3.0	9.0	92 @ 4000	134 @ 2800	36—41

①—CID—Cubic inch displacement. ②—Ratings are net as installed in vehicle. ③—Electronic fuel injection.

TUNE UP SPECIFICATIONS

The following specifications are published from the latest information available. This data should be used only in the absence of a decal affixed in the engine compartment.

★ When using a timing light, disconnect vacuum hose or tube at distributor and plug opening in hose or tube so idle speed will not be affected.

● When checking compression, lowest cylinder must be within 70 percent of highest.

▲ Before removing wires from distributor cap, determine location of the No. 1 wire in cap, as distributor position may have been altered from that shown at the end of this chart.

Spark plug types shown in this chart are recommendations of the original vehicle manufacturer and not MOTOR. Check local sources for other spark plug manufacturers listings.

Year & Engine/V.I.N.	Spark Plug Type	Gap	Ignition Timing BTDC①★ Firing Order Fig. ▲	Man. Trans.	Auto. Trans.	Mark Fig.	Curb Idle Speed② Man. Trans.	Auto. Trans.	Fast Idle Speed Man. Trans.	Auto. Trans.	Fuel Pump Pressure
1984											
4-151/R	R44TSX	.060	A	—	—	B	—	—	—	—	—

①—BTDC—Before top dead center.
②—Idle speed on man. trans. vehicles is adjusted in Neutral, & on auto. trans. equipped vehicles is adjusted in Drive unless otherwise specified. Where two idle speeds are listed, the highest speed is with the A/C or idle solenoid energized.

FIRING ORDER 1-3-4-2

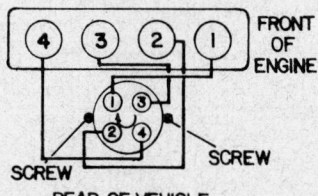

Fig. A

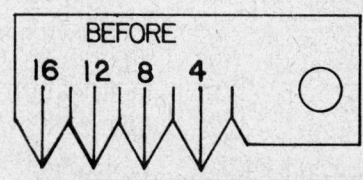

Fig. B

PONTIAC FIERO

VALVE SPECIFICATIONS

Year	Engine/V.I.N.	Valve Lash		Valve Angles		Valve Spring Installed Height	Valve Spring Pressure Lbs. @ In.	Stem Clearance		Stem Diameter	
		Int.	Exh.	Seat	Face			Intake	Exhaust	Intake	Exhaust
1984	4-151/R	Hydraulic①		46	45	1.69	151 @ 1.254	.0010–.0027	.0010–.0027	.3420–.3430	.3420–.3430

①—No adjustment.

WHEEL ALIGNMENT SPECIFICATIONS

Year	Model	Caster Angle, Degrees		Camber Angle, Degrees				Toe-In. mm	Toe-Out on Turns, Deg.①	
		Limits	Desired	Limits		Desired			Outer Wheel	Inner Wheel
				Left	Right	Left	Right			
1984	All①	+3°–+7°②	+5°	−.3°–+1.3°	−.3°–+1.3°	+.5°	+.5°	1.6	—	—
	All③	—	—	−1.5°–+.5°	−1.5°–.5°	−1°	−1°	1.6	—	—

①—Front wheel alignment.　　②—Left & right side should be equal within 2°.　　③—Rear wheel alignment.

PISTONS, PINS, RINGS, CRANKSHAFT & BEARINGS

Year	Engine V.I.N.	Piston Clearance Top of Skirt	Ring Gap①		Wristpin Diameter	Rod Bearings		Main Bearings			Shaft End Play
			Comp.	Oil		Shaft Diameter	Bearing Clearance	Shaft Diameter	Bearing Clearance	Thrust on Bear. No.	
1984	4-151/R	.0025–.0030	.010	.020	.940	2.000	.0005–.0026	2.300	.0005–.0022	5	.0035–.0085

①—Fit rings in tapered bores for clearance given in tightest portion of ring travel. Clearances specified are minimum gaps.

ALTERNATOR SPECIFICATIONS

Year	Model	Rated Hot Output Amps.
1984	—	66

STARTING MOTOR APPLICATIONS

Year	Model	Starter Number
1984	All	1109564
	All	1998429

ENGINE TIGHTENING SPECIFICATIONS★

★Torque specifications are for clean and lightly lubricated threads only. Dry or dirty threads produce increased friction which prevents accurate measurement of tightness.

Year	Engine Model/ V.I.N.	Spark Plugs Ft. Lbs.	Cylinder Head Bolts Ft. Lbs.	Intake Manifold Ft. Lbs.	Exhaust Manifold Ft. Lbs.	Rocker Arm Stud Ft. Lbs.	Rocker Arm Cover Ft. Lbs.	Connecting Rod Cap Bolts Ft. Lbs.	Main Bearing Cap Bolts Ft. Lbs.	Flywheel to Crankshaft Ft. Lbs.	Vibration Damper or Pulley Ft. Lbs.
1984	4-151/R	7–15	92①	29	44	20②	6	32	70	44	200

①—Requires thread sealer.　　②—Rocker arm bolt.

Continued

BRAKE SPECIFICATIONS

Year	Model	Wheel Cylinder Bore Diameter			Master Cylinder Bore Diameter		
		Disc Brake	Front Drum Brake	Rear Drum Brake	With Disc Brakes	With Drum Brakes	With Power Brakes
1984	All	2.52	—	—	1.00	—	1.00

COOLING SYSTEM & CAPACITY DATA

Year	Model or Engine/V.I.N.	Cooling Capacity, Qts.		Radiator Cap Relief Pressure, Lbs.	Thermo. Opening Temp.	Fuel Tank Gals.	Engine Oil Refill Qts.	Transaxle Oil	
		Less A/C	With A/C					Manual Transaxle Pts.	Auto. Transaxle Qts. ①
1984	All	13.0	13.4	15	195	10.5	3②	5.9	③

①—Approximate; make final check with dip-stick.   ②—With or without filter change.   ③—Oil pan capacity, 4 qts.; total capacity, 6 qts.

Electrical Section

STARTER, REPLACE

1. Disconnect battery ground cable.
2. Disconnect solenoid wires from starter motor.
3. Raise and support vehicle.
4. Remove rear starter bracket attaching bolt and the 2 starter motor-to-engine bolts.
5. Remove starter motor through front of converter toward front of engine.
6. Reverse procedure to install.

IGNITION LOCK, REPLACE

1. Remove turn signal switch as described under "Turn Signal Switch, Replace."
2. Remove key warning buzzer switch.

3. Turn lock cylinder to Run position, then remove retaining screw and the lock cylinder, Fig. 1.
4. Reverse procedure to install. Turn lock cylinder to Run position before installing key warning buzzer switch.

IGNITION & DIMMER SWITCHES, REPLACE

1. Remove turn signal switch as described under "Turn Signal Switch, Replace."
2. Refer to Figs. 2 and 3 to replace ignition and dimmer switches.

TURN SIGNAL SWITCH, REPLACE

1. Disconnect battery ground cable.
2. Remove steering wheel as described under "Steering Wheel, Replace."
3. Refer to Fig. 4 to replace turn signal switch.

STEERING WHEEL, REPLACE

1. Disconnect battery ground cable.

To assemble, rotate to stop while holding cylinder.

LOCK CYLINDER

LOCK RETAINING SCREW

CLIP

COVER

KEY WARNING BUZZER SWITCH

Fig. 1 Lock cylinder replacement

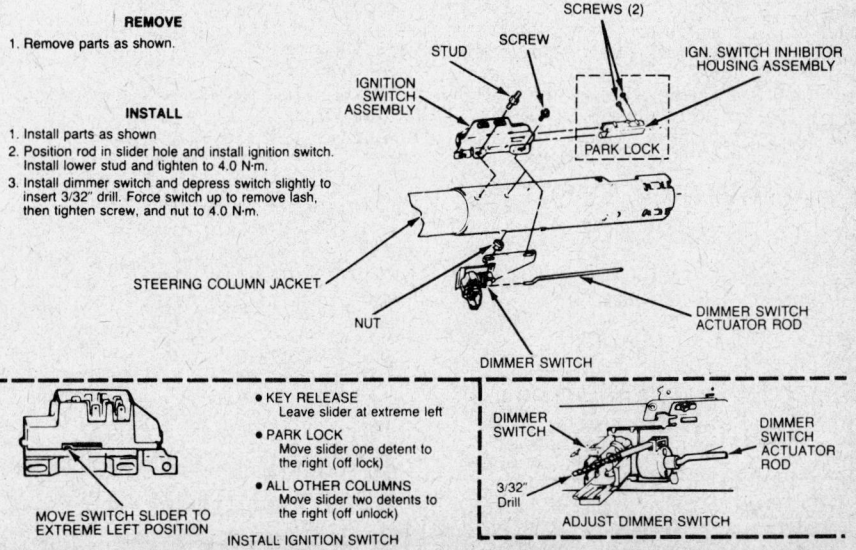

REMOVE
1. Remove parts as shown.

INSTALL
1. Install parts as shown
2. Position rod in slider hole and install ignition switch. Install lower stud and tighten to 4.0 N·m.
3. Install dimmer switch and depress switch slightly to insert 3/32" drill. Force switch up to remove lash, then tighten screw, and nut to 4.0 N·m.

SCREWS (2)

STUD   SCREW

IGN. SWITCH INHIBITOR HOUSING ASSEMBLY

IGNITION SWITCH ASSEMBLY

PARK LOCK

STEERING COLUMN JACKET

NUT

DIMMER SWITCH ACTUATOR ROD

DIMMER SWITCH

● KEY RELEASE
Leave slider at extreme left

● PARK LOCK
Move slider one detent to the right (off lock)

● ALL OTHER COLUMNS
Move slider two detents to the right (off unlock)

MOVE SWITCH SLIDER TO EXTREME LEFT POSITION

INSTALL IGNITION SWITCH

DIMMER SWITCH

3/32" Drill

DIMMER SWITCH ACTUATOR ROD

ADJUST DIMMER SWITCH

Fig. 2 Ignition & dimmer switch replacement. Except tilt column

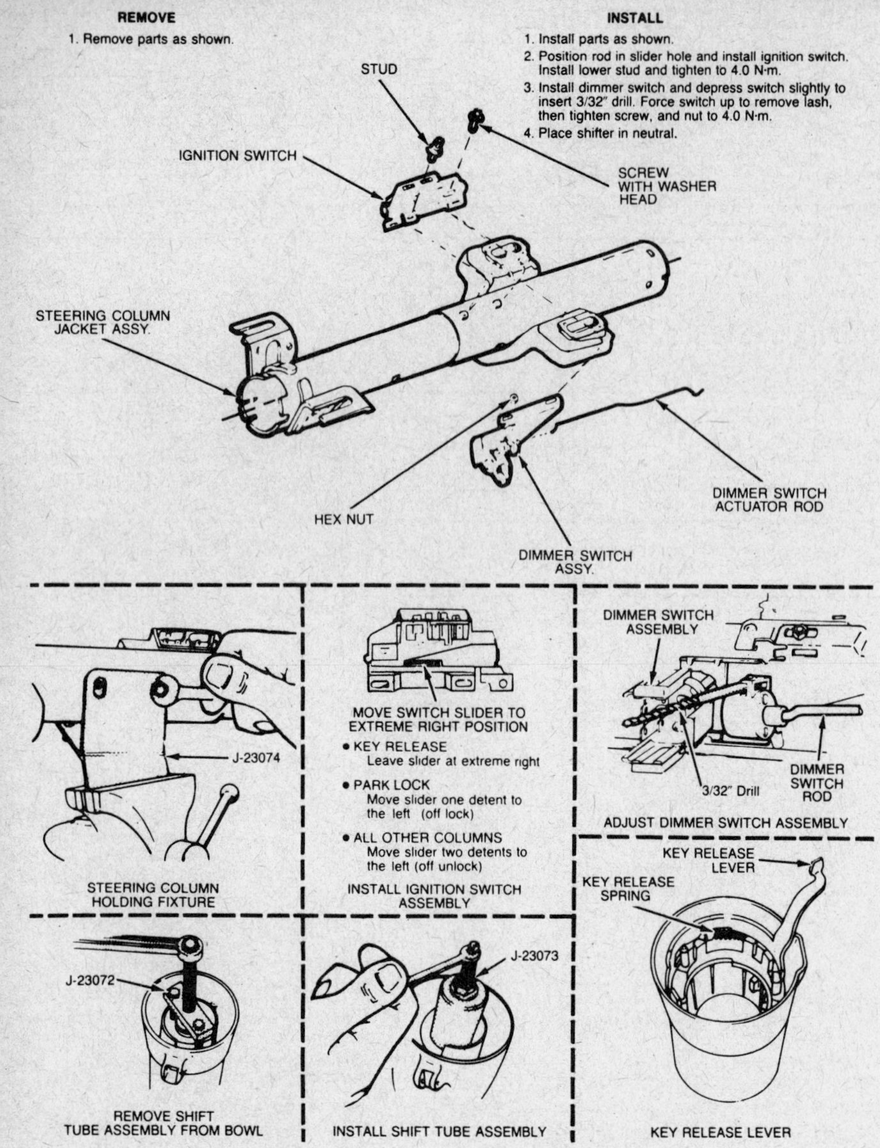

REMOVE
1. Remove parts as shown.

INSTALL
1. Install parts as shown.
2. Position rod in slider hole and install ignition switch. Install lower stud and tighten to 4.0 N·m.
3. Install dimmer switch and depress switch slightly to insert 3/32" drill. Force switch up to remove lash, then tighten screw, and nut to 4.0 N·m.
4. Place shifter in neutral.

STUD

IGNITION SWITCH

SCREW WITH WASHER HEAD

STEERING COLUMN JACKET ASSY.

HEX NUT

DIMMER SWITCH ASSY.

DIMMER SWITCH ACTUATOR ROD

J-23074

STEERING COLUMN HOLDING FIXTURE

MOVE SWITCH SLIDER TO EXTREME RIGHT POSITION
- KEY RELEASE
  Leave slider at extreme right
- PARK LOCK
  Move slider one detent to the left (off lock)
- ALL OTHER COLUMNS
  Move slider two detents to the left (off unlock)

INSTALL IGNITION SWITCH ASSEMBLY

DIMMER SWITCH ASSEMBLY

3/32" Drill

ADJUST DIMMER SWITCH ASSEMBLY

DIMMER SWITCH ROD

J-23072

REMOVE SHIFT TUBE ASSEMBLY FROM BOWL

J-23073

INSTALL SHIFT TUBE ASSEMBLY

KEY RELEASE LEVER

KEY RELEASE SPRING

KEY RELEASE LEVER

Fig. 3   Ignition & dimmer switch replacement. Tilt column

REMOVE
1. Remove parts as shown.

INSTALL
1. Install parts as shown.

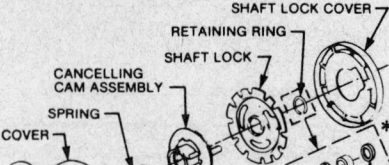

SHAFT LOCK COVER
RETAINING RING
SHAFT LOCK
CANCELLING CAM ASSEMBLY
SPRING
COVER
SHAFT LOCK RETAINER
CARRIER SNAP RING RETAINER
SPACERS
RETRACTED STRG SHAFT BUMPER

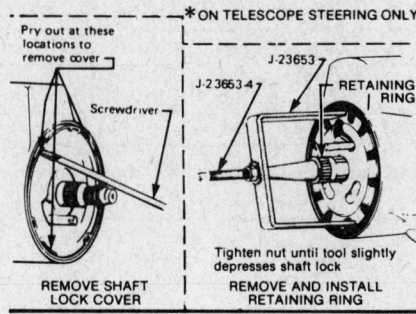

Pry out at these locations to remove cover

Screwdriver

REMOVE SHAFT LOCK COVER

*ON TELESCOPE STEERING ONLY

J-23653-4   J-23653

RETAINING RING

Tighten nut until tool slightly depresses shaft lock

REMOVE AND INSTALL RETAINING RING

REMOVE
1. Remove parts as shown.

INSTALL
1. Install parts as shown.

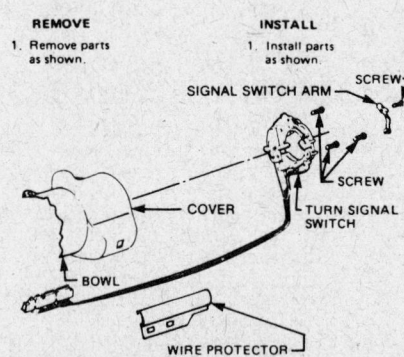

SIGNAL SWITCH ARM   SCREW

SCREW

TURN SIGNAL SWITCH

COVER

BOWL

WIRE PROTECTOR

Fig. 4   Turn signal switch replacement

2. Remove horn button.
3. Remove retainer and steering wheel retaining nut.
4. Remove steering wheel using puller J-1859-03 or equivalent.
5. Reverse procedure to install.

W/S WIPER SWITCH, REPLACE

1. Remove ignition lock as described under "Ignition Lock, Replace."
2. Refer to Figs. 5 and 6 to replace wiper switch.

W/S WIPER PULSE MODULE, REPLACE

NOTE: The pulse module is located under the instrument panel on the right hand steering column support bracket.

1. Disconnect battery ground cable.
2. Remove instrument panel steering column cover.
3. Disconnect electrical connectors from module.
4. Disconnect module ground wire.
5. Remove module attaching bolt and the module.
6. Reverse procedure to install.

STOP LAMP SWITCH, ADJUST

Insert switch into retainer until switch body seats on retainer. Pull brake pedal rearward until clicks are no longer audible.

BACKUP LIGHT/NEUTRAL START SWITCH, REPLACE

NOTE: On vehicles equipped with automatic

transmission, the neutral start and backup light switches are combined into one unit and must be replaced as an assembly.

Manual Transmission

1. Disconnect battery ground cable.
2. Remove shift trim plate cover.
3. Disconnect electrical connector from switch, Fig. 7.
4. Remove switch retainer and the switch.
5. Reverse procedure to install.

Automatic Transmission

1. Disconnect battery ground cable.
2. Open deck lid, then open retaining clip and disconnect electrical connector from switch.
3. Pry cable from pivot pin at bottom of shift lever, then remove lever-to-transmission shaft attaching nut.
4. Remove 2 switch-to-transaxle attaching bolts and the switch, Fig. 8.
5. Reverse procedure to install, noting the following:

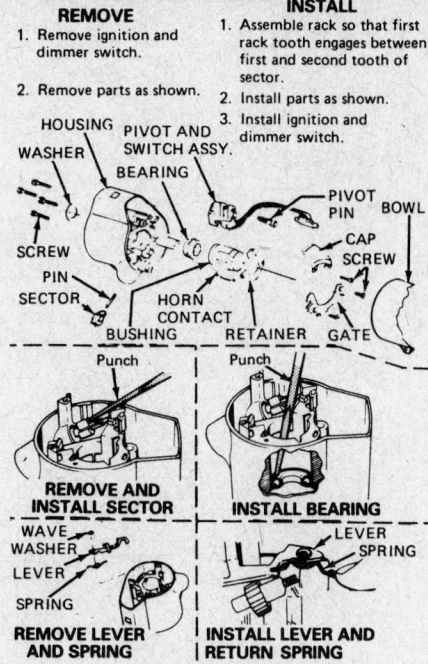

REMOVE
1. Remove ignition and dimmer switch.
2. Remove parts as shown.

INSTALL
1. Assemble rack so that first rack tooth engages between first and second tooth of sector.
2. Install parts as shown.
3. Install ignition and dimmer switch.

REMOVE AND INSTALL SECTOR

INSTALL BEARING

REMOVE LEVER AND SPRING

INSTALL LEVER AND RETURN SPRING

Fig. 5 Windshield wiper switch replacement. Except tilt column

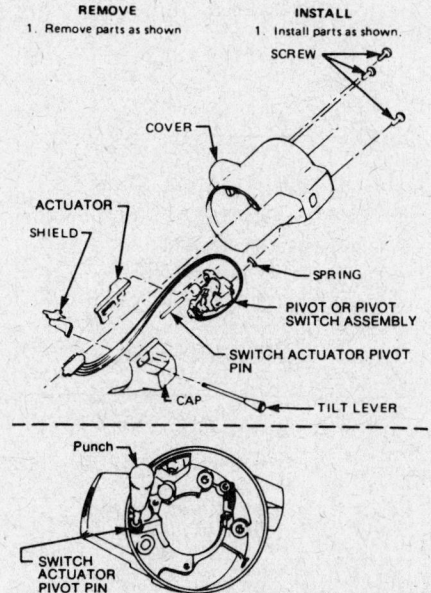

REMOVE
1. Remove parts as shown.

INSTALL
1. Install parts as shown.

REMOVE AND INSTALL PIVOT AND SWITCH ASSEMBLY

Fig. 6 Windshield wiper switch replacement. Tilt column

a. Transmission must be in Neutral when installing switch.
b. Torque switch attaching bolts to 20 ft. lbs.
c. Torque lever attaching nut to 20 ft. lbs. while holding lever out of Park.

BACKUP LIGHT/NEUTRAL START SWITCH, ADJUST

Automatic Transmission
1. Shift transmission into Neutral.

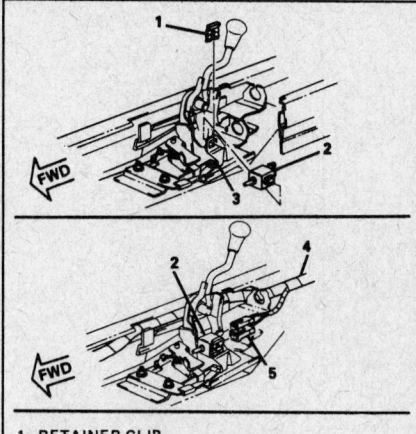

1—RETAINER CLIP
2—BACK-UP LAMP SWITCH ASSEMBLY
3—MANUAL TRANSMISSION CONTROL ASSEMBLY
4—MAIN HARNESS ASSEMBLY
5—BACK-UP LAMP SWITCH CONNECTOR

Fig. 7 Backup light switch replacement. Manual transmission

2. Align flats in switch insert with flats on transmission shaft, and slide switch over shaft.
3. Install attaching bolts hand tight.
4. Insert a 2.34 inch diameter gauge pin into adjustment hole, then rotate switch until pin drops to .354 inch.
5. Torque attaching bolts to 20 ft. lbs. and remove gauge pin.

CLUTCH START SWITCH, REPLACE
1. Disconnect battery ground cable.
2. Disconnect electrical connector from switch.
3. Remove switch attaching bolt. Rotate switch to disconnect shaft from clutch pedal hole, then remove switch from vehicle, Fig. 9.
4. Reverse procedure to install.

HEADLAMP SWITCH, REPLACE
1. Disconnect battery ground cable.
2. Remove 4 switch attaching screws.
3. Pull switch out of panel and disconnect electrical connectors, then remove switch from vehicle.
4. Reverse procedure to install.

NOTE: When replacing switch, install lower attaching screws first.

INSTRUMENT CLUSTER, REPLACE
1. Disconnect battery ground cable.
2. Remove rear cluster cover, front trim plate and steering column cover.
3. Remove instrument cluster attaching screws.
4. Pull cluster rearward and disconnect all

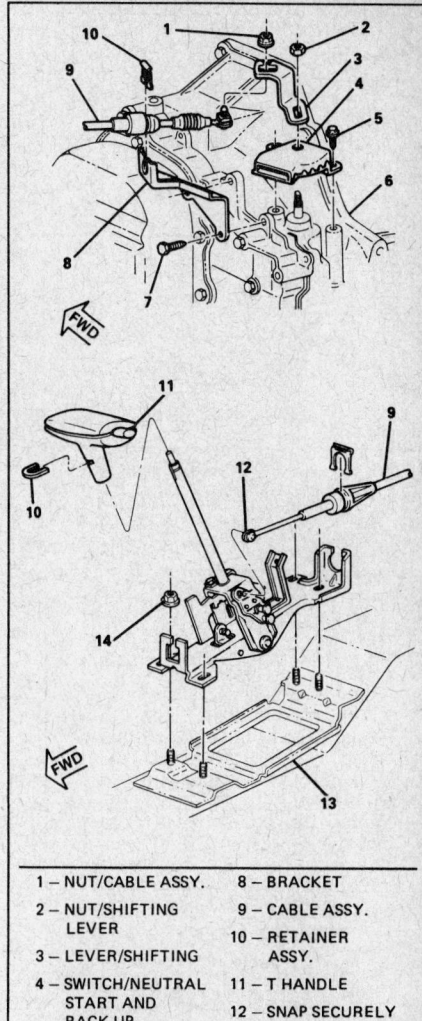

1 — NUT/CABLE ASSY.
2 — NUT/SHIFTING LEVER
3 — LEVER/SHIFTING
4 — SWITCH/NEUTRAL START AND BACK-UP
5 — BOLT/NEUTRAL START SWITCH (2)
6 — TRANSAXLE
7 — BOLT/BRACKET
8 — BRACKET
9 — CABLE ASSY.
10 — RETAINER ASSY.
11 — T HANDLE
12 — SNAP SECURELY ONTO PIN
13 — GEAR SHIFT SUPPORT
14 — NUT 23 N·M (17 FT. LB.)

Fig. 8 Backup light/neutral start switch replacement. Automatic transmission

electrical connectors, then remove cluster from vehicle, Fig. 10.
5. Reverse procedure to install.

RADIO, REPLACE
1. Disconnect battery ground cable.
2. Remove shift knob and both ash trays.
3. Remove 4 shift plate attaching bolts and the plate.
4. Remove front trim plate, then the front pad attaching screws and front pad.
5. Remove radio attaching screws.
6. Pull radio rearward and disconnect all electrical connectors, then remove radio from vehicle.
7. Reverse procedure to install.

W/S WIPER MOTOR, REPLACE
1. Disconnect battery ground cable.

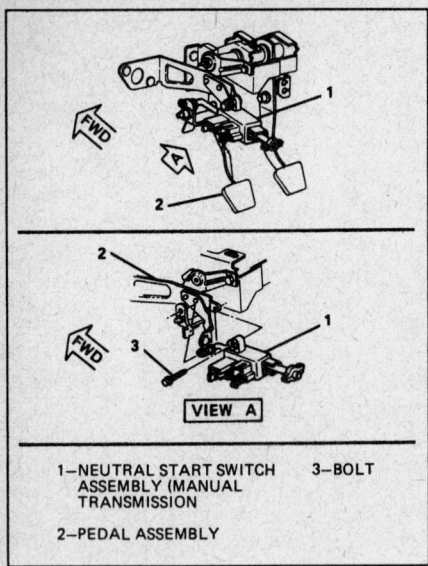

1—NEUTRAL START SWITCH ASSEMBLY (MANUAL TRANSMISSION
2—PEDAL ASSEMBLY
3—BOLT

Fig. 9   Clutch start switch replacement

2. Remove both wiper arms using tool No. J-8966 or equivalent.
3. Remove cowl top vent screen.
4. Remove drive link from crank arm.
5. Disconnect electrical connectors from wiper motor.
6. Remove wiper motor attaching screws and the motor.
7. Reverse procedure to install. Torque motor attaching screws to 40–58 inch lbs. and drive link attaching nuts to 49–80 inch lbs.

W/S WIPER TRANSMISSION, REPLACE

1. Remove both wiper arms using tool No. J-8966 or equivalent.
2. Remove cowl top vent screen.
3. Remove drive link from crank arm.
4. Remove 6 cowl panel attaching screws and the cowl panel.
5. Remove transmission assembly from vehicle.
6. Reverse procedure to install. Torque cowl attaching screws and drive link attaching nuts to 49–80 inch lbs.

BLOWER MOTOR, REPLACE

1. Disconnect battery ground cable.
2. Remove cooling tube from blower motor.
3. Disconnect blower motor electrical connections.
4. Remove 5 blower motor attaching screws and the blower motor assembly, Fig. 11.
5. Remove fan cage attaching screw and slide cage off motor shaft.
6. Reverse procedure to install.

HEATER CORE, REPLACE

Less Air Conditioning

1. Disconnect battery ground cable.

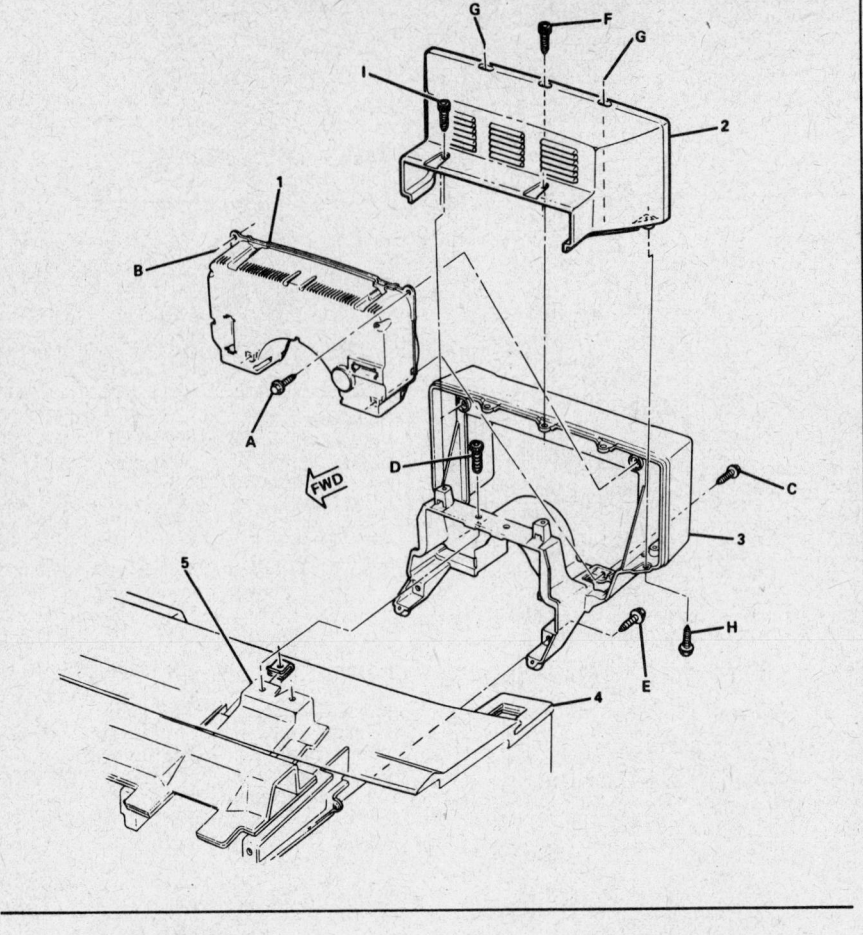

1 — CLUSTER ASM.
2 — REAR CLUSTER COVER
3 — CLUSTER HOUSING ASM.
4 — I/P
5 — STEERING COL. SUPT.

A — INSTALL THIS BOLT/SCREW FIRST
B — INSTALL THIS BOLT/SCREW SECOND
C — INSTALL THIS BOLT/SCREWS THIRD
D — INSTALL THIS BOLT/SCREWS FOURTH
E — INSTALL THIS BOLT/SCREW FIFTH
F — INSTALL THIS BOLT/SCREW SIXTH
G — INSTALL THIS BOLT/SCREWS SEVENTH
H — INSTALL THIS BOLT/SCREWS EIGHTH
I — INSTALL THESE BOLT/SCREWS LAST

Fig. 10   Instrument cluster

2. Disconnect all electrical connectors from rear of heater case.
3. Remove forward courtesy lamp bulb socket, if equipped.
4. Remove windshield washer fluid tank.
5. Disconnect heater hoses from heater core, then remove heater core grommets. Plug hoses to prevent spillage.
6. Remove heater case cover attaching screws and the cover, Fig. 11.
7. Remove heater core retainer and the heater core.
8. Reverse procedure to install.

With Air Conditioning

1. Disconnect battery ground cable.
2. Disconnect heater hoses from heater core. Plug hoses to prevent spillage.
3. Remove speaker grille and the speaker.
4. Remove heater core cover, then the heater core retainers and heater core.
5. Reverse procedure to install.

CRUISE CONTROL, ADJUST

Servo Cable, Adjust

1. Install cable assembly end onto throttle body unit lever stud, with cable installed in bracket, and secure with retainer.
2. Pull servo end of cable toward servo without moving injector lever.
3. Connect pin to tab with retainer.

NOTE: If a tab hole does not line up with pin, move cable away from servo until the next closest hole aligns, then connect pin to tab.

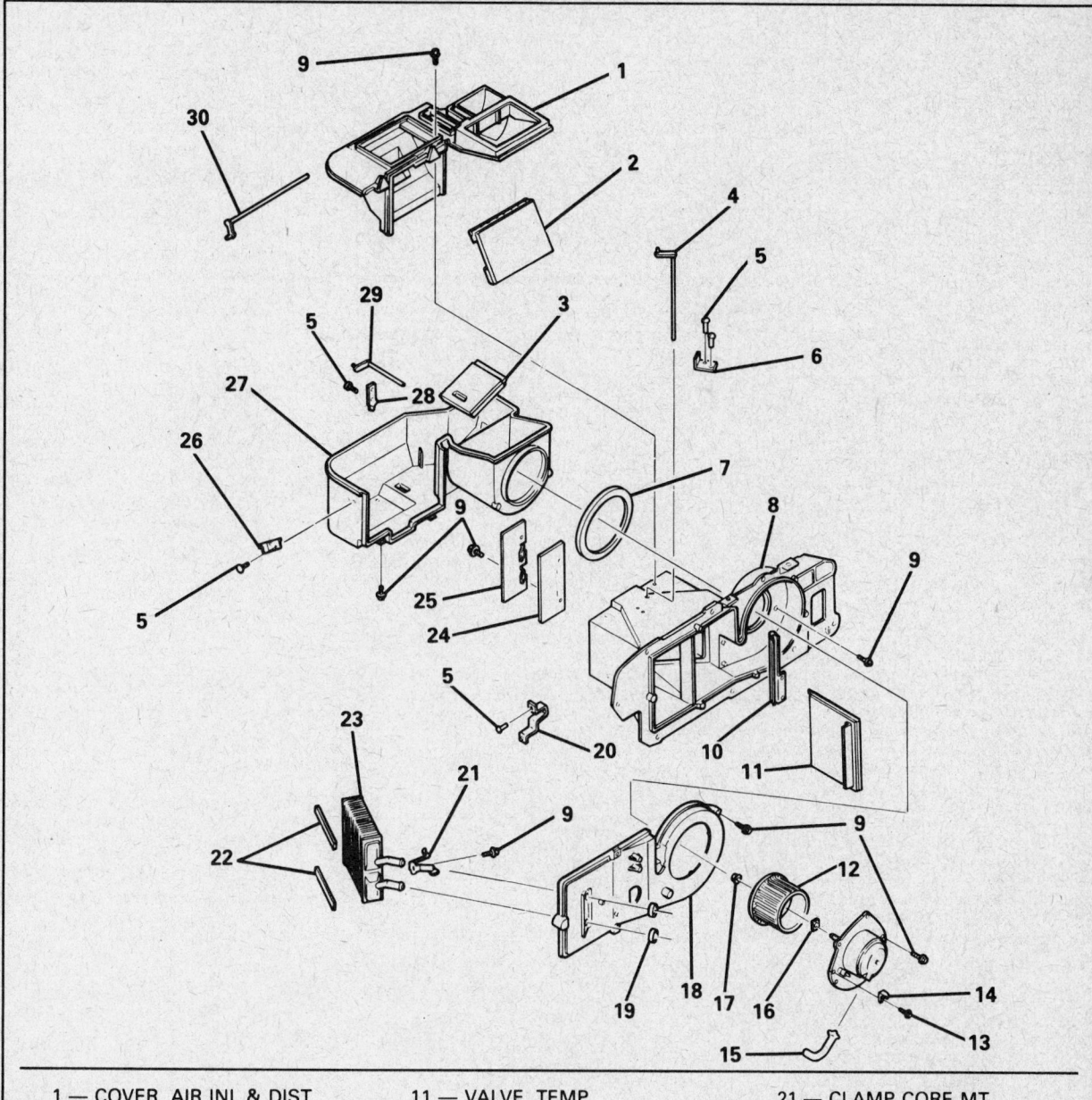

Fig. 11 Heater core & blower motor. Models less A/C

1 — COVER, AIR INL & DIST
2 — VALVE, VENT
3 — VALVE, DEFR
4 — SHAFT, W/LVR, TEMP VLV
5 — RIVET, TRUSS HD
(9/16" x 1/4")
6 — BRACKET, CBL MTG
7 — SEAL, HTR & BLO CASE
8 — CASE, HTR
9 — SCREW, HWH TAP
(M4.2 x 1.41 x 13)
10 — BAFFLE, AIR

11 — VALVE, TEMP
12 — FAN, BLO
13 — SCREW, HWH TAP
(M4.2 x 1.41 x 14)
14 — TERMINAL, BLO MTR GRD
15 — TUBE, MTR CLG
16 — WASHER, FAN SUPT
17 — NUT, BLO FAN
18 — COVER, BLO
19 — SEAL, HTR CORE TUBE
20 — BRACKET, MT

21 — CLAMP, CORE MT
22 — SEAL, HTR CORE
23 — CORE, HTR
24 — SEAL, HTR CORE CASE
25 — CLIP, HTR CORE MT
26 — BRACKET, CBL MT
27 — CASE, AIR INL & DISTR
28 — BRACKET, CBL MT
29 — SHAFT, W/LVR, DEFR VLV
30 — SHAFT, W/LVR, VENT VLV

4-151 Engine Section

ENGINE MOUNTS, REPLACE

1. Raise and support vehicle.
2. Remove engine mount-to-chassis attaching nuts, Fig. 1.
3. On models equipped with A/C, remove forward torque reaction rod attaching bolts.
4. On all models, raise engine slightly using a suitable engine lifting device. Raise engine only enough to provide clearance for mount removal.
5. Removal 2 upper mount-to-engine support bracket attaching nuts and the engine mount.
6. Reverse procedure to install.

ENGINE, REPLACE

1. Disconnect battery cables, then drain cooling system.
2. Remove rear compartment lid.

NOTE: Do not remove torsion rod retaining bolts.

3. Remove air cleaner, then disconnect throttle and transaxle cables.
4. Disconnect all necessary vacuum hoses from non-engine components.
5. Disconnect heater hose from intake manifold.
6. Disconnect fuel lines and remove fuel filter.
7. Disconnect fuel pump relay and oxygen sensor electrical connectors.
8. On models equipped with automatic transaxle, disconnect transaxle cooler lines.
9. On models equipped with manual transaxle, remove slave cylinder.
10. On all models, disconnect engine ground strap.
11. Disconnect radiator and heater hoses.
12. Disconnect engine harness connector from bulkhead.
13. On models equipped with A/C, discharge refrigerant from system, then disconnect and cap lines from A/C compressor.
14. Remove rear console.
15. Disconnect electronic control module (ECM) electrical connector through bulkhead panel.
16. Install engine support fixture, tool No. J-28467 or equivalent to engine.
17. Mark the engine strut bracket and attaching bolt for assembly reference, then remove bolt and bracket.
18. Raise and support vehicle.
19. Remove rear wheels.
20. On models equipped with automatic transaxle, remove torque converter attaching bolts.
21. Disconnect parking brake cable.
22. Remove brake calipers and suspend from frame with a piece of wire. Do not suspend calipers by brake hoses.
23. Mark struts for proper realignment as described under "Strut Assembly, Replace" in the "Rear Axle, Rear Suspension & Brakes" section, then remove strut attaching bolts.
24. Disconnect any remaining electrical connectors interfering with engine removal.
25. Remove engine cradle attaching bolts.
26. Release parking brake cables from cradle using tool No. J-34065 or equivalent.
27. Support engine, transaxle and cradle assembly with a suitably dolly, then lower vehicle and remove engine support fixture.

NOTE: When lowering vehicle, ensure outboard ends of lower control arms are properly supported.

28. Raise vehicle and slide engine, transaxle and cradle assembly out from under vehicle.
29. Separate engine from transaxle.
30. Reverse procedure to install.

CYLINDER HEAD, REPLACE

1. Drain cooling system.
2. Raise and support vehicle.
3. Disconnect exhaust pipe from exhaust manifold, then lower vehicle.
4. Remove oil dipstick tube and air cleaner.
5. Disconnect throttle body injection unit electrical connectors and vacuum hoses.
6. Remove EGR base plate, then disconnect heater hose from intake manifold.
7. Remove ignition coil lower attaching bolt, then disconnect wiring from coil.
8. Disconnect all electrical connectors from cylinder head and intake manifold.
9. Remove engine strut attaching bolt from upper engine support.
10. Remove alternator drive belt.
11. Disconnect throttle and throttle valve cables from intake manifold.
12. Disconnect upper radiator hose from cylinder head.
13. Remove rocker arm cover, then the rocker arms and push rods.
14. Remove cylinder head attaching bolts, then lift cylinder head and intake and exhaust manifolds as an assembly from cylinder block.
15. Reverse procedure to install. Coat threads of cylinder head bolts with a suitable sealing compound, then install bolts finger tight. Torque cylinder head bolts to specifications in sequence shown, Fig. 2.

ROCKER ARM STUDS

Rocker arm studs which are cracked or have

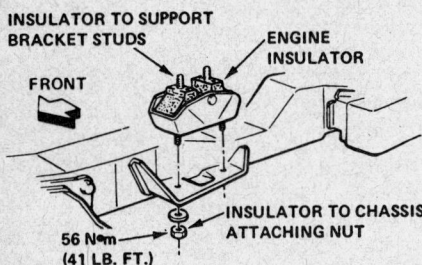

Fig. 1 Engine mounts

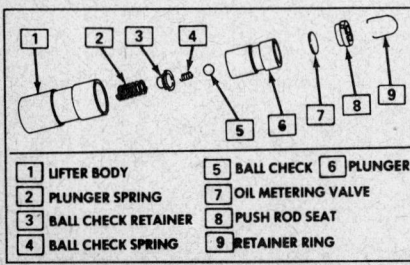

Fig. 3 Hydraulic valve lifter

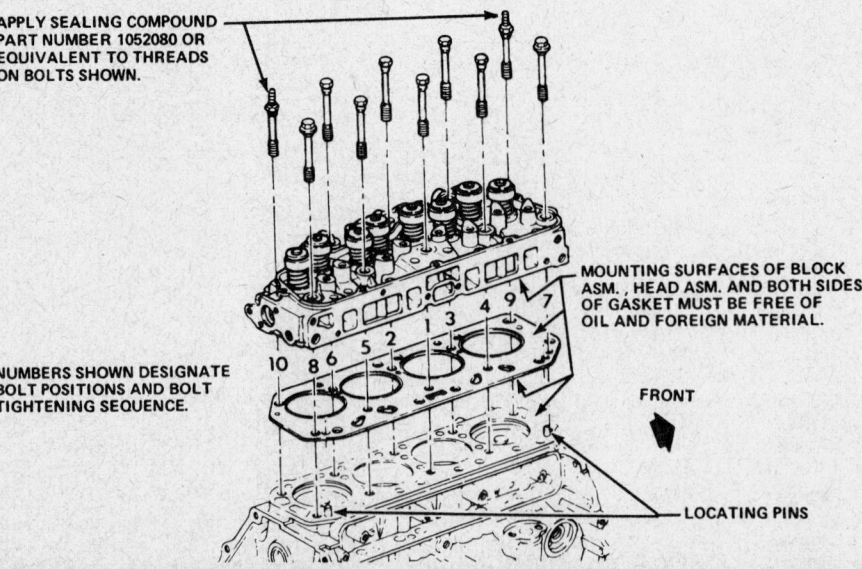

Fig. 2 Cylinder head bolt tightening sequence

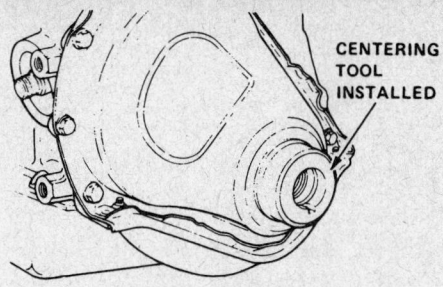

Fig. 4 Engine front cover installation

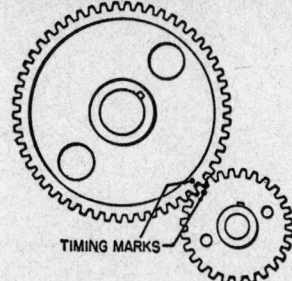

Fig. 5 Valve timing marks

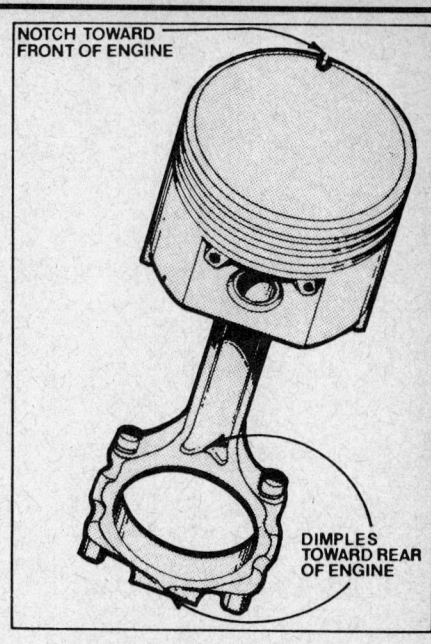

Fig. 6 Piston & rod assembly

damaged threads can be removed from the cylinder head using a deep well socket. Install and torque new rocker arm stud to 75 ft. lbs.

VALVE ARRANGEMENT

Front to rear

I-E-I-E-E-I-E-I

VALVE LIFT SPECS.

Year	Intake	Exhaust
1984	.398	.398

VALVE TIMING

Intake Opens Before TDC

Year	Degrees
1984	33

VALVE GUIDES

Valve guides are an integral part of the cylinder head and are not removable. If valve stem clearance becomes excessive, the valve guide should be reamed to the next oversize and the appropriate oversize valves installed. Valves are available in oversizes of .003 and .005 inch.

VALVE LIFTERS

Failure of a hydraulic valve lifter, Fig. 3, is generally caused by an inadequate oil supply or dirt. An air leak at the intake side of the oil pump or excessive oil in the engine will produce air bubbles in the oil supply to the lifters, causing them to collapse. This is a probable cause of trouble when several lifters fail to function, but air in oil is not likely to cause failure of a single unit.

Valve lifters can be removed after removing rocker arm cover, intake manifold and push rod cover. Loosen rocker arm stud nut and rotate rocker arm so push rod can be removed, then remove valve lifter. It may be necessary to use tool No. J-3049 to facilitate lifter removal.

ENGINE FRONT COVER, REPLACE

1. Remove drive belts, then the right rear inner splash shield.
2. Remove pulley attaching bolt, then the pulley and hub from shaft.
3. Remove oil pan-to-front cover attaching screws and the front cover.
4. Clean cylinder block and front cover sealing surfaces, then position oil pan front seal on front cover.
5. Apply a 3/8 inch wide by 3/16 inch thick bead of RTV sealer to joint formed at oil pan and front cover.
6. Apply a 1/4 inch wide by 1/8 inch thick bead of RTV sealer on front cover to block mating surface.
7. Install centering tool No. J-23042 in front cover seal, Fig. 4.
8. Install front cover. Install 2 attaching screws finger tight, then install remaining screws and torque all screws to 90 inch lbs.
9. Remove centering tool and install pulley, hub, splash shield and drive belts.

TIMING GEARS

When necessary to install a new camshaft gear, the camshaft will have to be removed as the gear is a pressed fit on the camshaft. The camshaft is held in place by a thrust plate retained to the engine by two capscrews which are accessible through the two holes in the gear web.

To remove gear, use an arbor press and a suitable sleeve to properly support gear on its steel hub.

Before installing gear, assemble thrust plate and gear spacer ring, then press gear onto shaft until it bottoms against spacer ring. The thrust plate end clearance should be .0015–.0050 inch. If clearance is less than .0015 inch, the spacer ring should be replaced. If clearance is greater than .0050 inch, the thrust plate should be replaced.

The crankshaft gear can be replaced using a puller and two bolts in the tapped holes of the gear.

When installing timing gears, ensure marks on gears are properly aligned, Fig. 5.

NOTE: The valve timing marks, Fig. 5, do not indicate TDC compression for No. 1 cylinder for use during distributor installation. When installing the distributor, rotate engine until No. 1 cylinder is on compression stroke and the camshaft timing mark is 180° from the valve timing position shown in Fig. 5.

CAMSHAFT, REPLACE

1. Remove engine as described under "Engine, Replace." Do not separate engine from transaxle.
2. Remove rocker arm cover, then loosen rocker arm stud nuts. Pivot rocker arms clear of push rods and remove the rods.
3. Remove distributor, then the alternator and mounting brackets.
4. Remove front engine mount and bracket assembly.
5. Remove oil pump drive shaft.
6. Remove front cover as described under "Engine Front Cover, Replace."
7. Remove camshaft thrust plate attaching screws.
8. Carefully remove camshaft and gear through front of block.
9. Reverse procedure to install. When installing camshaft, align crankshaft and camshaft timing marks on gear teeth, Fig. 5.

PISTONS & RODS, ASSEMBLE

Assemble piston to rod with notch on piston facing toward front of engine and the raised notch side of rod at bearing end facing toward rear of engine, Fig. 6.

Upon installation, measure connecting rod side clearance using a suitable feeler gauge. Clearance should be .006–.022 inch.

PISTONS, PINS & RINGS

Pistons and rings are available in standard size and oversizes of .010, .020 and .030 inch. Piston pins are available in oversizes of .001 and .003 inch.

MAIN & ROD BEARINGS

Main and rod bearings are available in standard size and oversizes of .001, .002 and .010 inch.

OIL PAN, REPLACE

1. Install engine support fixture, tool No. J-28467 or equivalent, and raise engine slightly to relieve tension from cradle mounts, Fig. 7.
2. Raise and support vehicle.

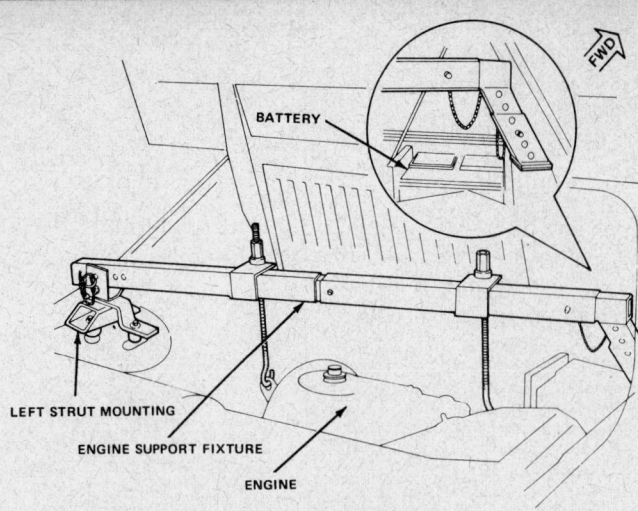

Fig. 7 Engine support fixture

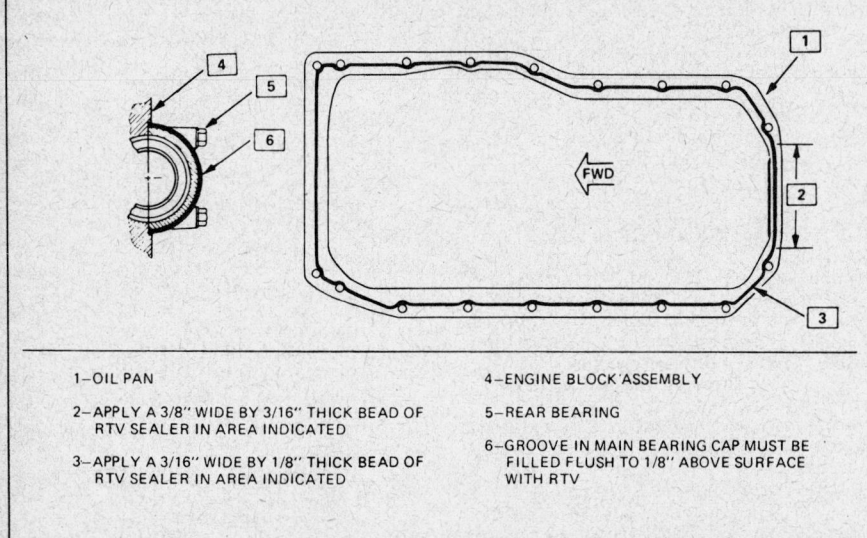

Fig. 8 Oil pan installation

1—OIL PAN

2—APPLY A 3/8″ WIDE BY 3/16″ THICK BEAD OF RTV SEALER IN AREA INDICATED

3—APPLY A 3/16″ WIDE BY 1/8″ THICK BEAD OF RTV SEALER IN AREA INDICATED

4—ENGINE BLOCK ASSEMBLY

5—REAR BEARING

6—GROOVE IN MAIN BEARING CAP MUST BE FILLED FLUSH TO 1/8″ ABOVE SURFACE WITH RTV

1	PUMP BODY	6	SPRING RETAINER
2	PICKUP TUBE	7	COVER SCREWS
3	PICKUP SCREW ASSEMBLY	8	COVER
4	PRESSURE REGULATOR VALVE	9	IDLER GEAR
5	PRESSURE REGULATOR SPRING	10	DRIVE GEAR AND SHAFT

Fig. 9 Exploded view of oil pump

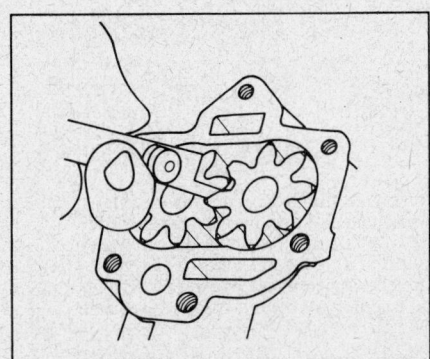

Fig. 10 Measuring oil pump gear backlash

3. Disconnect exhaust pipe from exhaust manifold, then remove rear wheels.
4. Disconnect both lower control arms and toe link rods from knuckle.
5. Disconnect parking brake cable from cradle.
6. Remove engine and transmission attaching bolts.
7. Remove cradle attaching bolts and the cradle.
8. Drain engine oil, then remove front engine mount-to-support bracket attaching nuts.
9. Disconnect exhaust pipe from rear transaxle mount.
10. Remove starter and flywheel cover, then the upper alternator bracket.
11. Remove lower alternator and engine support brackets.
12. Remove oil pan retaining bolts and the oil pan.
13. Reverse procedure to install, noting the following:
    a. Apply RTV sealer as shown in Fig. 8.
    b. Install 2 bolts in front cover after all other pan attaching bolts have been

torqued to 75 inch lbs. Torque front cover bolts to 90 inch lbs.
    c. When installing cradle, first install front cradle attaching bolts and nuts finger tight, then note the following torques: rear cradle bolts, 76 ft. lbs.; front cradle nut, 67 ft. lbs.; engine mount bolts, 42 ft. lbs.; rear mount bolts, 18 ft. lbs.; front mount bolts, 36 ft. lbs.; lower control arm-to-knuckle bolts, 33 ft. lbs.; lower control arm-to-cradle bolts, 69 ft. lbs.; tow rod-to-knuckle bolts, 35 ft. lbs.; exhaust pipe-to-manifold bolts, 25 ft. lbs.

OIL PUMP SERVICE

Removal

1. Remove oil pan as described under "Oil Pan, Replace."
2. Remove oil pump attaching bolts and nuts, then the oil pump and screen as an assembly.

Disassembly

1. Drain residual oil from pump.
2. Remove suction pipe and screen assembly from pump.
3. Remove pump cover attaching screws, then the pump cover and gears, Fig. 9.
4. Remove pump regulator valve. Remove plug, spring and ball from valve.

Inspection

1. Inspect pump housing and cover for wear or damage, and replace if necessary.
2. Inspect pressure regulator valve for scoring or sticking. Burrs may be removed with a fine oil stone, however more extensive damage requires replacement of valve.
3. Inspect idler gear shaft for wear or damage, and replace if necessary.
4. Inspect pressure regulator spring for lack of tension or distortion, and replace if necessary.
5. Inspect suction pipe and screen, and clean or replace as necessary.

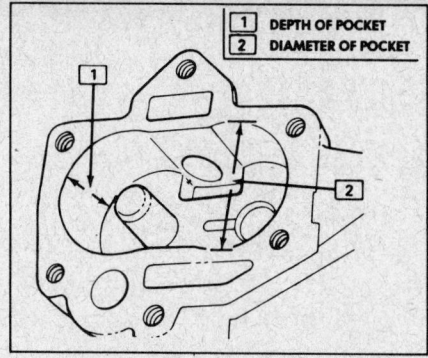

Fig. 11   Measuring oil pump gear pocket

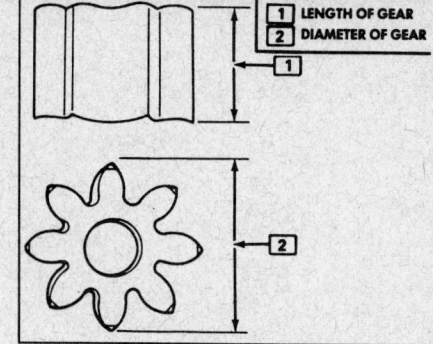

Fig. 12   Measuring oil pump gears

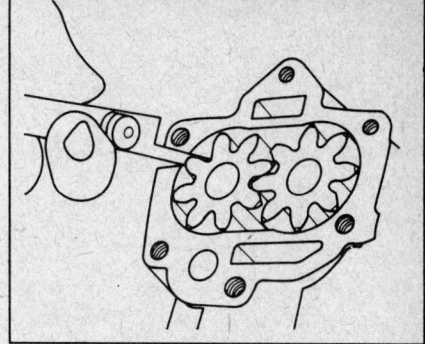

Fig. 13   Measuring oil pump gear side clearance

NOTE: If suction pipe is permanently pressed into the pump body, and if it is loose or has been removed, a new pipe must be installed.

6. Inspect gears and driveshaft for wear or damage and replace as necessary.
7. Install gears into housing and measure gear backlash, Fig. 10. Backlash should measure .009–.015 inch.
8. Measure pump housing gear pocket depth and diameter, Fig. 11. Depth should measure .995–.998 inch and diameter 1.503–1.506 inches.
9. Measure length and diameter of gears, Fig. 12. Length of both gears should be .999–1.002 inch and diameter should be 1.498–1.500 inches.
10. Measure gear side clearance, Fig. 13. Side clearance should measure no more than .004 inch.
11. Measure gear end clearance, Fig. 14. End clearance should be .002–.005 inch.
12. If any measurements taken in steps 7 through 11 are not within specifications, replace oil pump components as necessary.

Assembly

1. Lubricate all internal components with clean engine oil and pack all pump cavities with petroleum jelly.
2. Install pump gears into housing.
3. Install pump cover, pressure regulator valve and spring. Torque cover attaching bolts to 10 ft. lbs. and the pressure regulator valve plug to 15 ft. lbs.
4. Apply suitable sealer to new pipe, then tap pipe into position using a plastic hammer and tool No. J-8369.

Installation

1. Align oil pump shaft with tang on oil

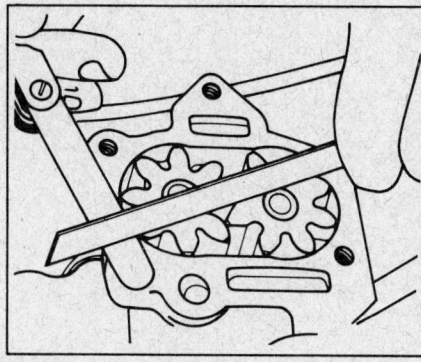

Fig. 14   Measuring oil pump gear end clearance

pump drive shaft, then install pump on block, positioning pump flange over oil pump drive shaft lower bushing.
2. Install pump attaching bolts and torque to 20 ft. lbs.
3. Install oil pan.

CRANKSHAFT REAR OIL SEAL, REPLACE

NOTE: The rear main oil seal is a one-piece seal which can be replaced without removing the oil pan or crankshaft.

1. Remove transaxle and flywheel.
2. On models equipped with manual transaxle, remove pressure plate and disc.
3. On all models, remove rear main bearing oil seal using a suitable screwdriver. Use care not to scratch crankshaft.
4. Reverse procedure to install. Lubricate outside of seal to ease assembly.

WATER PUMP, REPLACE

1. Disconnect battery ground cable and drain cooling system.
2. Remove accessory drive belts.
3. Disconnect lower radiator hose from water pump.
4. Remove water pump attaching bolts and the pump.
5. Reverse procedure to install. Apply a 1/8 inch bead of suitable sealer to pump sealing surface, and install pump before sealer dries.

FUEL PUMP, REPLACE

1. Release pressure from fuel system as follows:
   a. Remove fuel pump fuse from fuse block, then start and run engine until engine stalls from fuel starvation.
   b. Energize starter for approximately 3 seconds to release any residual pressure from system.
   c. Turn ignition off and replace fuel pump fuse.
2. Disconnect battery ground cable.
3. Raise and support vehicle.
4. Remove fuel tank from vehicle.
5. Remove fuel meter/pump assembly. Turn cam lock ring counterclockwise, then lift assembly from fuel tank and remove pump from meter.
6. Lift pump up into attaching hose while pulling away from bottom support. When pump is clear of lower support, remove assembly from rubber connector.

NOTE: Use care to avoid damage to rubber insulator and strainer during removal.

7. Reverse procedure to install.

Clutch & Transaxle Section

HYDRAULIC CLUTCH, BLEED

NOTE: Extreme cleanliness must be maintained while bleeding the clutch system. Do not use linty rags, and ensure no dirt enters the system, particularly at the supply tank. Never add previously used fluid to the supply tank as it may be contaminated or have an excessive moisture content.

1. Fill supply tank with suitable brake fluid.
2. Remove floormat or any other object which may impede full travel of clutch pedal.
3. Back out bleed screw on slave cylinder until fluid can be pumped out (approximately ½ turn).
4. Depress clutch pedal fully, then apply three short, rapid strokes.
5. Release pressure to allow clutch pedal to return quickly to its stop.
6. Repeat steps 2 and 3 until all air has been released from bleed screw.
7. Close bleed screw immediately following last downward stroke of pedal when air bubbles no longer appear.

CLUTCH, REPLACE

1. Remove transaxle as described under "Manual Transaxle, Replace."
2. Mark position of pressure plate to flywheel for assembly reference.
3. Gradually loosen pressure plate attaching bolts until spring pressure is relieved.
4. Support pressure plate and remove mounting bolts, pressure plate and driven disc, Fig. 1.

MANUAL TRANSAXLE SHIFT CABLE, ADJUST

1. Disconnect battery ground cable.
2. Shift transaxle into first gear.
3. Loosen shift cable attaching nuts "E" on transaxle levers "D" and "F," Fig. 2.
4. Remove console and trim plates to provide access to shifter.
5. With transaxle in first gear, insert a yoke clip to retain lever, Fig. 2, view "D."
6. Insert a No. 22 or 5/32 inch drill bit into alignment hole at side of shifter assembly, Fig. 2, view "C."
7. Remove backlash from transaxle by rotating lever "D" in direction of arrow while torquing nut "E" on lever "F" to 20 ft. lbs., Fig. 2.
8. Remove drill bit and yoke from shifter.
9. Install console and trim pads.
10. Connect battery ground cable, then road test vehicle and check shifter for proper operation. If "hang-up" is encountered when shifting in the 1–2 gear range, and the shift cables are properly adjusted, it may be necessary to change the shifter shaft selective washer. Perform the following procedure to determine correct

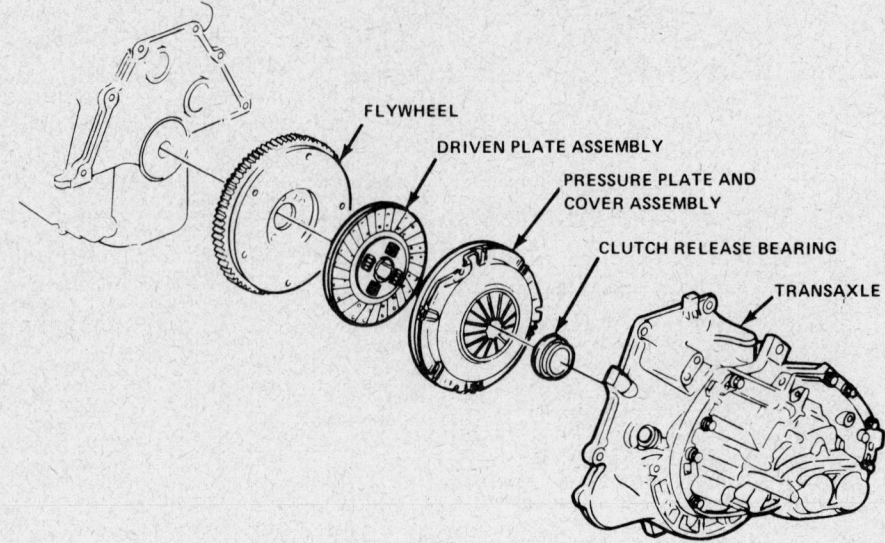

Fig. 1   Clutch assembly

washer thickness:
a. Remove reverse inhibitor fitting spring and washer from end of housing, then place shifter shaft in second gear.
b. Measure dimension "A," Fig. 3, which is the distance between end of housing and shoulder just behind end of shaft.
c. Apply a 9–13 lb. load on opposite end of shaft, then measure dimension "B," Fig. 3, which is distance between end of housing and end of shifter shaft major diameter.
d. Subtract dimension "B" from dimension "A" to obtain dimension "C."
e. Refer to chart, Fig. 4, to determine correct thickness shim.

MANUAL TRANSAXLE, REPLACE

1. Disconnect battery ground cable, then remove air cleaner.
2. Disconnect ground cable from transaxle.
3. Disconnect shift and select cables from transaxle.
4. Remove upper transaxle-to-engine attaching bolts.
5. Install engine support fixture, tool No. J-28467 or equivalent, Fig. 5.
6. Raise and support vehicle.
7. Remove rear wheels, then disconnect axle shafts from transaxle as described in the "Drive Axle, Rear Suspension & Brakes" section under "Drive Axle, Replace."
8. Remove heat shield from catalytic converter, then disconnect exhaust pipe from exhaust manifold.
9. Remove engine mount and transaxle mount-to-cradle attaching nuts.
10. Support cradle with a suitable jack, then remove front and rear cradle-to-body

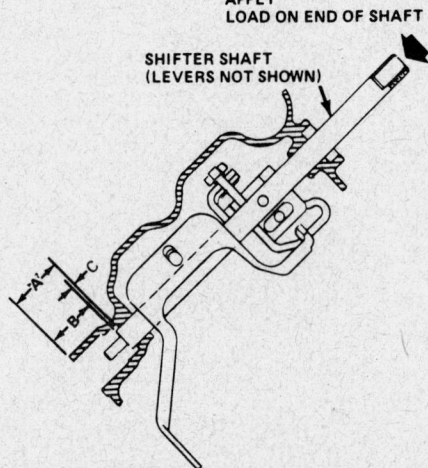

Fig. 3   Manual transaxle shifter shaft selective washer measurement

attaching bolts.
11. Lower cradle from vehicle and position aside.
12. Remove starter and inspection cover shields, then the starter motor.
13. Remove flywheel-to-converter attaching bolts.
14. Support transaxle with a suitable jack, then remove lower transaxle-to-engine attaching bolts and lower transaxle assembly from vehicle.
15. Reverse procedure to install.

NOTE: When installing cradle, work into position on rear mounts, then raise front into position.

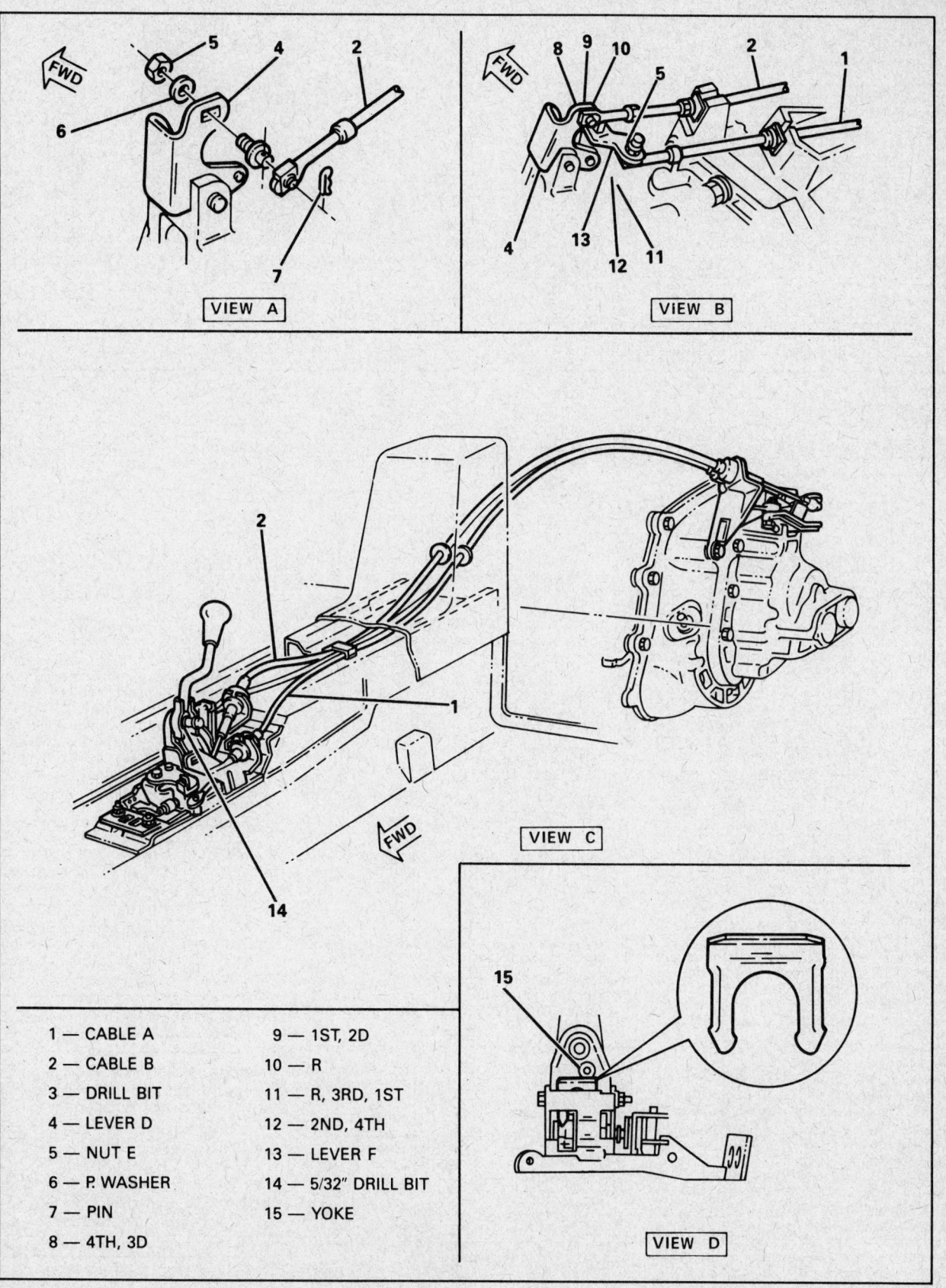

VIEW A

VIEW B

VIEW C

VIEW D

1 — CABLE A	9 — 1ST, 2D
2 — CABLE B	10 — R
3 — DRILL BIT	11 — R, 3RD, 1ST
4 — LEVER D	12 — 2ND, 4TH
5 — NUT E	13 — LEVER F
6 — P. WASHER	14 — 5/32" DRILL BIT
7 — PIN	15 — YOKE
8 — 4TH, 3D	

Fig. 2 Manual transaxle shift cable adjustment

Dimension "C" Fig. 3 Inch (mm)	Ident. Color & No. of Stripes	Shim Part No.
.0708 (1.8)	3 White	14008235
.0827 (2.1)	1 Orange	476709
.0945 (2.4)	2 Orange	476710
.1063 (2.7)	3 Orange	476711
.1181 (3.0)	1 Blue	476712
.1299 (3.3)	2 Blue	476713
.1417 (3.6)	3 Blue	476714
.1535 (3.9)	1 White	476715
.1654 (4.2)	2 White	476716

Fig. 4   Shifter shaft selective washer identification

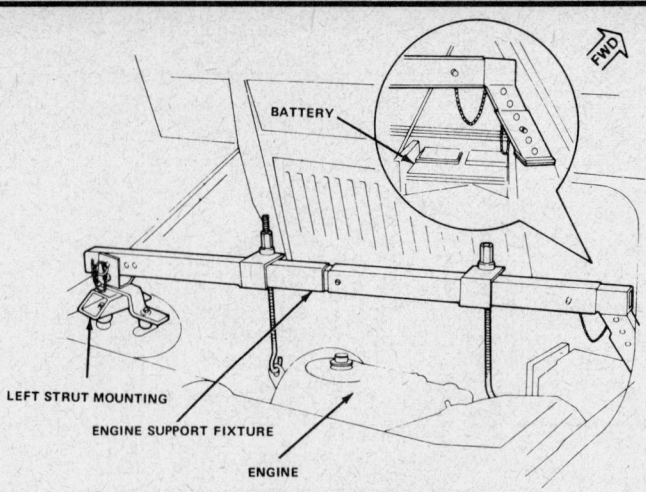

Fig. 5   Engine support fixture

Drive Axle, Rear Suspension & Brakes

DESCRIPTION

The drive axles are completely flexible assemblies which consist of an inner and outer constant velocity joint connected by an axle shaft. The inner constant velocity joint has the capability of moving in and out, whereas the outer joint does not.

The rear suspension, Fig. 1, is a MacPherson strut design. The lower control arms pivot from the engine cradle. The cradle uses isolation mounts to the body and conventional rubber bushings at the lower control arm pivots. A rubber mount isolates the upper end of the strut.

DRIVE AXLE, REPLACE

NOTE: It is important that the axle not be overextended. When one or both ends of the shaft are disconnected, over-extending the joint may cause separation of internal components, which could lead to failure of the joint.

1. Remove and discard hub nut.
2. Raise and support vehicle.
3. Remove wheel and tire assembly.
4. Install axle shaft boot seal protector J-27812 on outer seal and J-33162 on inner seal, Fig. 2.
5. Disconnect toe link rod from knuckle assembly.
6. Disconnect parking brake cables from engine cradle.
7. Remove brake line bracket from underbody in inner wheel house opening.
8. Remove axle shaft from hub and bearing assembly using tool No. J-28733 or equivalent.
9. Support axle shaft and remove clamp bolt from lower control arm ball stud.
10. Separate knuckle from lower control arm.

11. Move strut, knuckle and caliper assembly away from body, and secure in this position.
12. Disengage snap rings retaining drive axle using tools J-33008 and J-2619-01, then carefully pull drive axles from transaxle.
13. Reverse procedure to install. Torque hub nut to 70 ft. lbs., toe link rod nut to 15 ft. lbs., and lower control arm ball stud nut to 33 ft. lbs.

DRIVE AXLE SERVICE

Refer to Figs. 3, 4 and 5 for service procedures on drive axle assembly.

WHEEL ALIGNMENT

Camber

1. Loosen both strut-to-knuckle attaching bolts sufficiently to allow movement between strut and knuckle.
2. Move top of tire inboard or outboard until camber is within specifications, then torque both strut-to-knuckle bolts to 140 ft. lbs.

NOTE: If complete torque cannot be applied to bolts due to inaccessibility, tighten bolts just enough to hold camber position, then remove wheel and wire and apply final torque.

Toe-In

1. Loosen jam nuts on toe link rod, then rotate rods until toe-in is within specifications, Fig. 6.
2. Torque jam nuts to 47 ft. lbs.

NOTE: Use care not to twist or damage rubber boots.

WHEEL BEARING, REPLACE

Removal

1. On vehicles equipped with steel wheels, remove hub cap and loosen hub nut, then raise and support vehicle and remove wheel and tire assembly.
2. On vehicles equipped with 14 inch aluminum wheels, set parking brake, then raise and support vehicle and remove wheel and tire assembly.
3. On all models, install drive axle boot protector J-33162.
4. Remove and discard hub nut.
5. Remove brake caliper and rotor. Suspend caliper from frame with a piece of wire.
6. Remove hub and bearing attaching bolts.

NOTE: If the old bearing is being reinstalled, mark attaching bolts and corresponding holes for installation reference, Fig. 7.

7. Remove hub and bearing assembly using tool No. J-28671 or equivalent, Fig. 8.

NOTE: If assembly is heavily corroded, ensure hub and bearing are loose in knuckle before using puller tool.

8. Replace knuckle seal if installing new bearing.

CAUTION: Do not move drive axle until hub nut is installed and torqued to specifications.

Installation

1. Clean and inspect knuckle bore and bear-

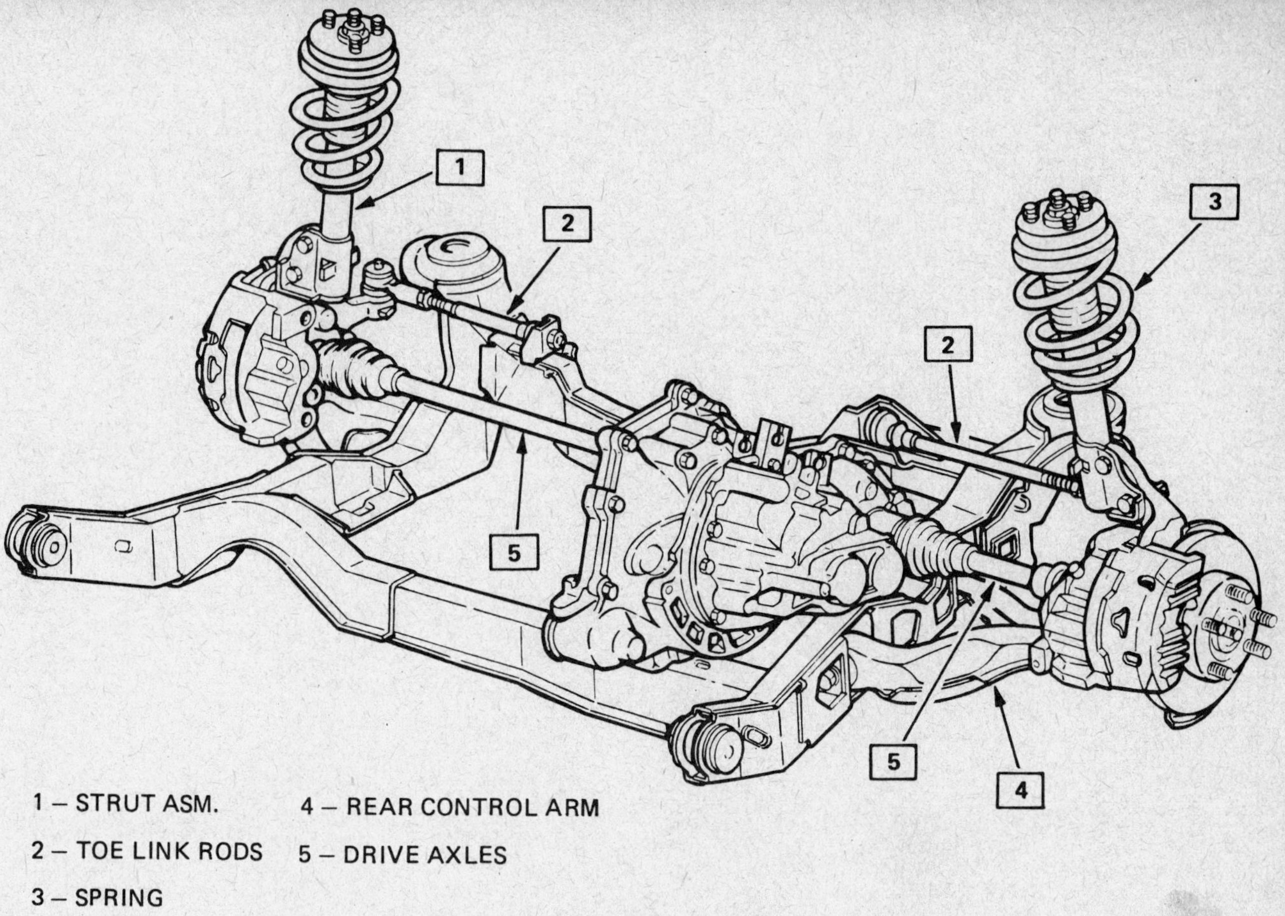

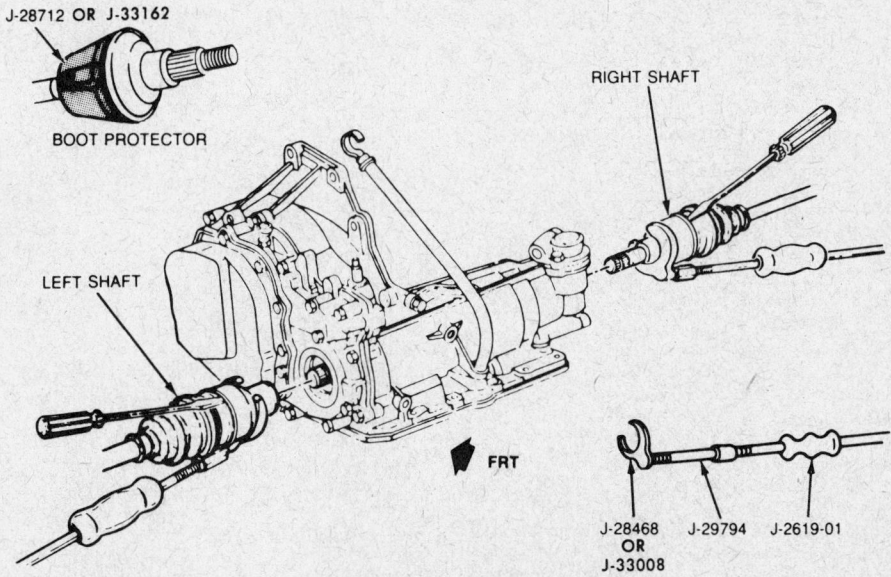

1 – STRUT ASM.   4 – REAR CONTROL ARM

2 – TOE LINK RODS 5 – DRIVE AXLES

3 – SPRING

Fig. 1   Rear suspension

J-28712 OR J-33162

BOOT PROTECTOR

RIGHT SHAFT

LEFT SHAFT

FRT

J-28468
OR
J-33008   J-29794   J-2619-01

Fig. 2   Drive axle removal

ing mating surfaces for dirt, nicks and burrs.
2. If installing new knuckle seal, apply suitable grease to seal and knuckle bore, then press seal into knuckle using tool No. J-28671 or equivalent.
3. Install hub and bearing assembly onto

axle shaft. Torque attaching bolts to 55–70 ft. lbs.
4. Install hub nut and torque to 74 ft. lbs.
5. Install brake rotor and caliper.
6. Install wheel and tire assembly, then lower vehicle and torque hub nut to 200 ft. lbs.

LOWER BALL JOINT, REPLACE

1. Raise and support vehicle.
2. Remove wheel and tire assembly, then the ball stud clamp bolt.
3. Disconnect ball joint from knuckle by tapping with a mallet.
4. Replace ball joint as shown in Fig. 9.

LOWER CONTROL ARM & BUSHINGS, REPLACE

1. Raise and support vehicle.
2. Remove wheel and tire assembly, then the ball joint clamp bolt.
3. Disconnect ball joint from knuckle by tapping with a mallet.
4. Remove lower control arm pivot bolts from frame.
5. Replace lower control arm and bushings as shown in Fig. 10.

REAR KNUCKLE, REPLACE

Refer to Fig. 11 for removal and installation procedures.

STRUT ASSEMBLY, REPLACE

1. Remove engine compartment cover.

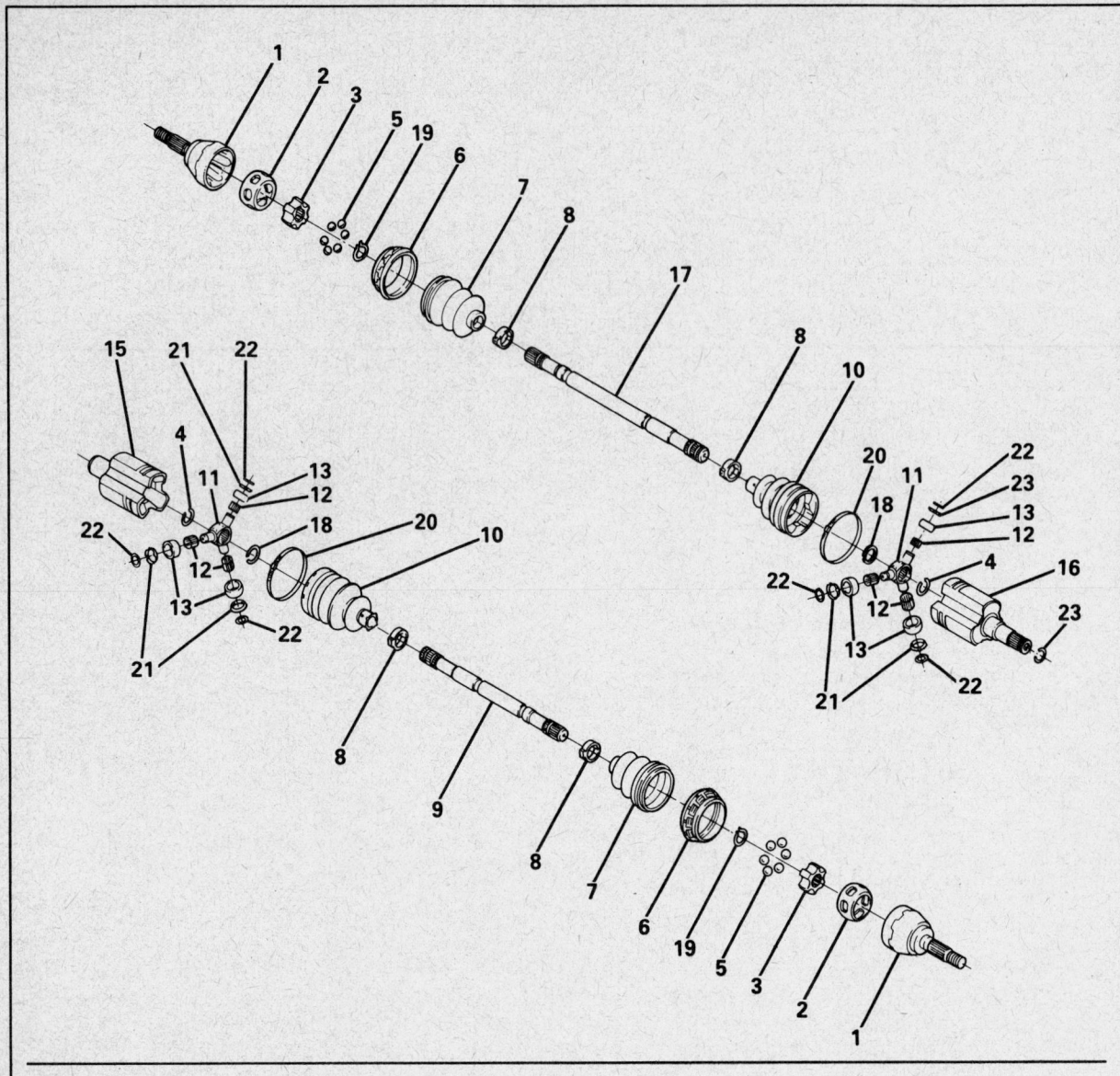

Fig. 3 Exploded view of drive axle

1 — RACE, C.V. JOINT OUTER
2 — CAGE, C.V. JOINT
3 — RACE, C.V. JOINT INNER
4 — RING, SHAFT RETAINING
5 — BALL (6)
6 — RETAINER, SEAL
7 — SEAL, C.V. JOINT
8 — CLAMP, SEAL RETAINING
9 — SHAFT, AXLE (LH)
10 — SEAL, TRI-POT JOINT
11 — SPIDER, TRI-POT JOINT
12 — ROLLER, NEEDLE

13 — BALL, TRI-POT JOINT (3)
14 — THIS NO. NOT USED
15 — HOUSING ASSY, TRI-POT (LH)
16 — HOUSING ASSY, TRI-POT (RH)
17 — SHAFT, AXLE (RH)
18 — RING, SPACER
19 — RING, RACE RETAINING
20 — CLAMP, SEAL RETAINING
21 — RETAINER, NEEDLE
22 — RING, NEEDLE RETAINER
23 — RING, JOINT RETAINING

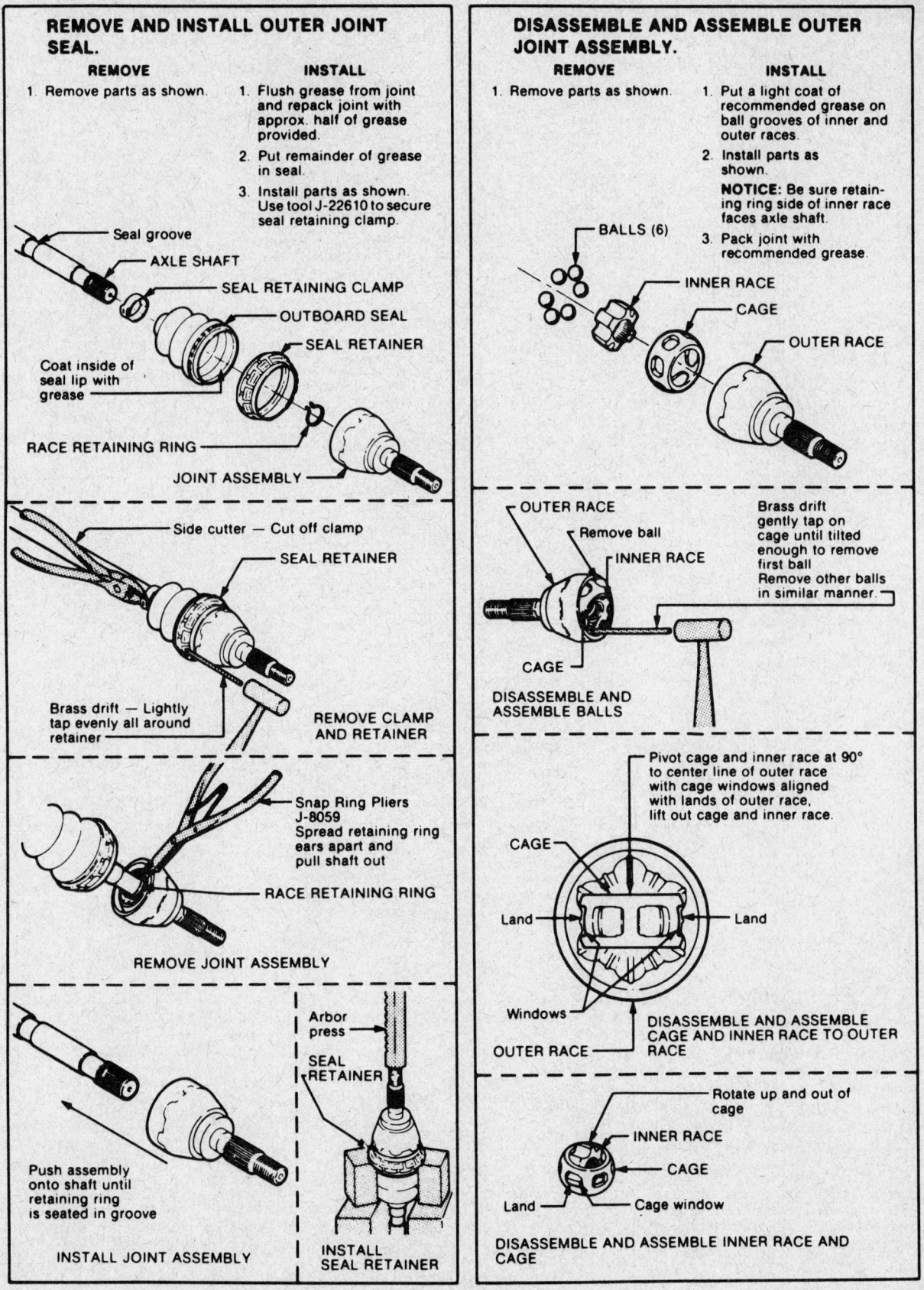

REMOVE AND INSTALL OUTER JOINT SEAL.

REMOVE

1. Remove parts as shown.

INSTALL

1. Flush grease from joint and repack joint with approx. half of grease provided.
2. Put remainder of grease in seal.
3. Install parts as shown. Use tool J-22610 to secure seal retaining clamp.

Seal groove
AXLE SHAFT
SEAL RETAINING CLAMP
OUTBOARD SEAL
SEAL RETAINER
Coat inside of seal lip with grease
RACE RETAINING RING
JOINT ASSEMBLY

Side cutter — Cut off clamp
SEAL RETAINER
Brass drift — Lightly tap evenly all around retainer
REMOVE CLAMP AND RETAINER

Snap Ring Pliers J-8059 Spread retaining ring ears apart and pull shaft out
RACE RETAINING RING
REMOVE JOINT ASSEMBLY

Push assembly onto shaft until retaining ring is seated in groove
INSTALL JOINT ASSEMBLY

Arbor press
SEAL RETAINER
INSTALL SEAL RETAINER

DISASSEMBLE AND ASSEMBLE OUTER JOINT ASSEMBLY.

REMOVE

1. Remove parts as shown.

INSTALL

1. Put a light coat of recommended grease on ball grooves of inner and outer races.
2. Install parts as shown.
   NOTICE: Be sure retaining ring side of inner race faces axle shaft.
3. Pack joint with recommended grease.

BALLS (6)
INNER RACE
CAGE
OUTER RACE

OUTER RACE
Remove ball
INNER RACE
CAGE
Brass drift gently tap on cage until tilted enough to remove first ball Remove other balls in similar manner.
DISASSEMBLE AND ASSEMBLE BALLS

Pivot cage and inner race at 90° to center line of outer race with cage windows aligned with lands of outer race, lift out cage and inner race.
CAGE
Land
Land
Windows
OUTER RACE
DISASSEMBLE AND ASSEMBLE CAGE AND INNER RACE TO OUTER RACE

Rotate up and out of cage
INNER RACE
CAGE
Land
Cage window
DISASSEMBLE AND ASSEMBLE INNER RACE AND CAGE

Fig. 4 Outer constant velocity joint & seal service

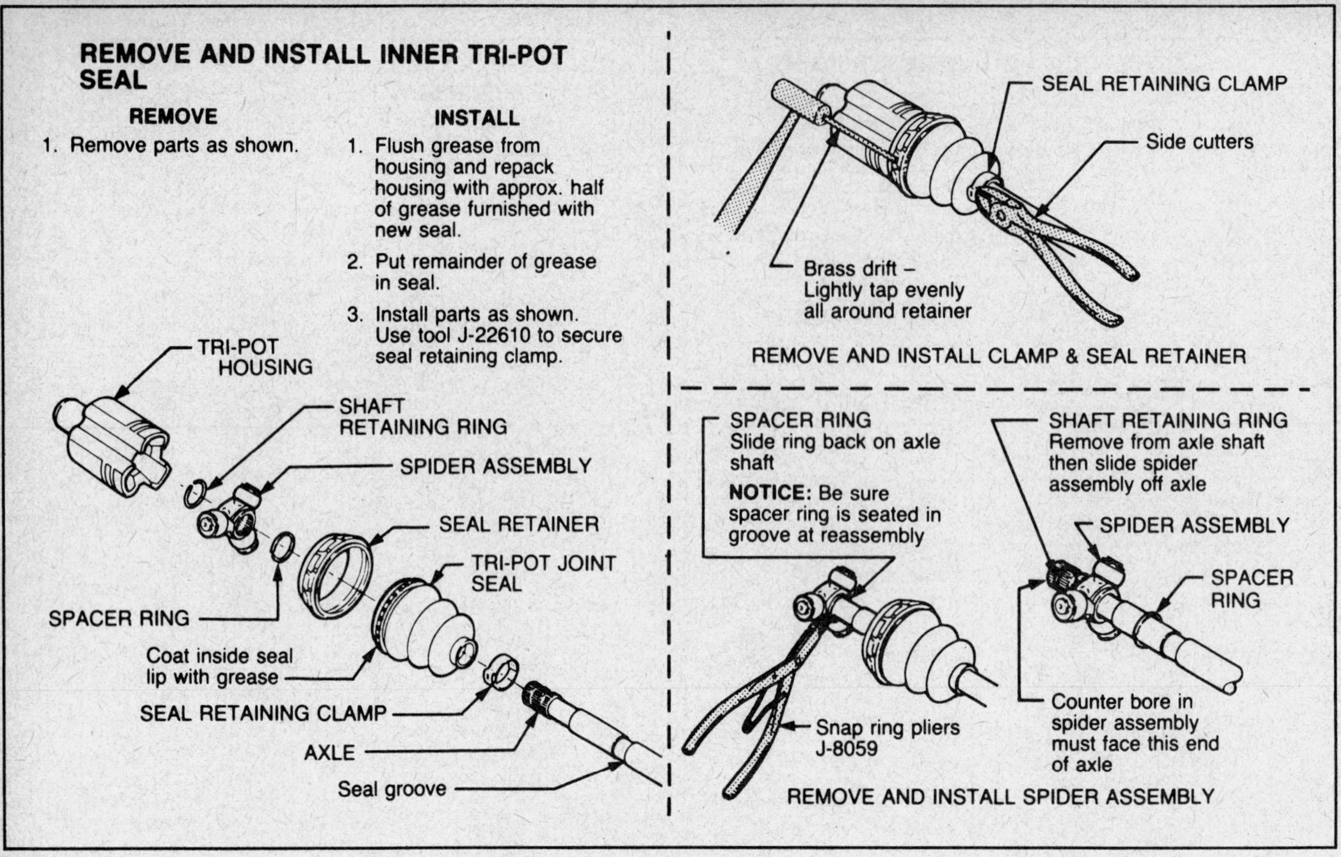

REMOVE AND INSTALL INNER TRI-POT SEAL

REMOVE
1. Remove parts as shown.

INSTALL
1. Flush grease from housing and repack housing with approx. half of grease furnished with new seal.
2. Put remainder of grease in seal.
3. Install parts as shown. Use tool J-22610 to secure seal retaining clamp.

TRI-POT HOUSING

SHAFT RETAINING RING

SPIDER ASSEMBLY

SEAL RETAINER

TRI-POT JOINT SEAL

SPACER RING

Coat inside seal lip with grease

SEAL RETAINING CLAMP

AXLE

Seal groove

SEAL RETAINING CLAMP

Side cutters

Brass drift — Lightly tap evenly all around retainer

REMOVE AND INSTALL CLAMP & SEAL RETAINER

SPACER RING
Slide ring back on axle shaft
NOTICE: Be sure spacer ring is seated in groove at reassembly

SHAFT RETAINING RING
Remove from axle shaft then slide spider assembly off axle

SPIDER ASSEMBLY

SPACER RING

Counter bore in spider assembly must face this end of axle

Snap ring pliers J-8059

REMOVE AND INSTALL SPIDER ASSEMBLY

Fig. 5   Inner tri-pot seal replacement

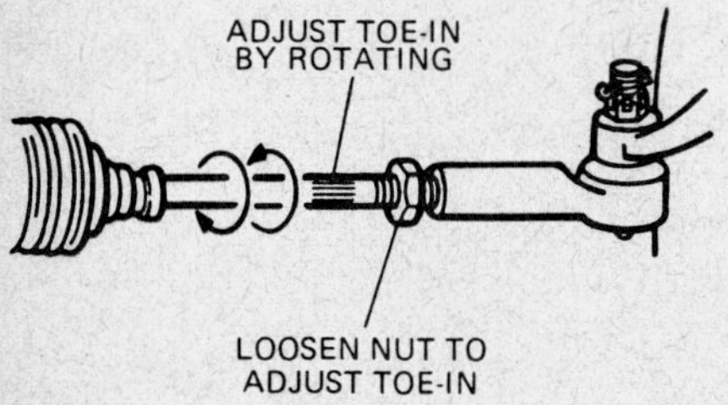

ADJUST TOE-IN BY ROTATING

LOOSEN NUT TO ADJUST TOE-IN

Fig. 6   Toe-in adjustment

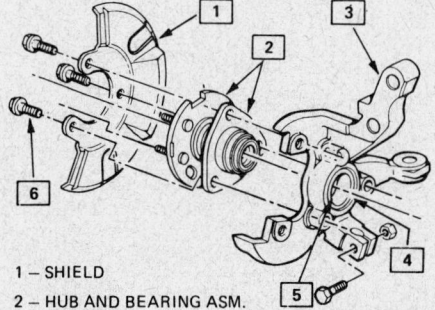

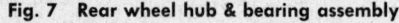

1 — SHIELD
2 — HUB AND BEARING ASM.
3 — KNUCKLE
4 — KNUCKLE SEAL ASM.
5 — FILL HUB BEARING CAVITY BETWEEN SEALING LIPS WITH .8 GRAMS OF CHASSIS LUBRICANT.
6 — BOLT 75-95 N·m (55-70 FT. LB.)

Fig. 7   Rear wheel hub & bearing assembly

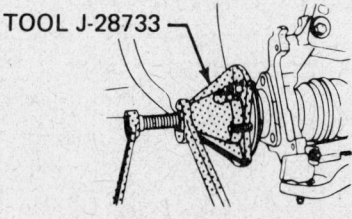

TOOL J-28733

Fig. 8   Hub & bearing assembly removal

2. Remove three upper strut nuts and washers, Fig. 12.
3. Loosen wheel lug nuts, then raise vehicle and support at rear control arm.
4. Remove wheel and tire assembly, then the brake line retaining clip.
5. Scribe strut and knuckle, Fig. 13, for assembly reference.

NOTE: When servicing the jounce bumper, strut mount, strut shield, spring seal or spring insulator, the strut and knuckle must be scribed as shown in Fig. 13 to maintain the original camber setting. However, it will be necessary to check toe-in setting and adjust as necessary.

When servicing the strut damper, knuckle or rear ride spring, the scribe marks should not be made. However, it will be necessary to check both toe-in and camber settings and correct as necessary.

6. Remove strut attaching nuts and bolts,

then the strut assembly and spacer plate.
7. Reverse procedure to install. Torque knuckle attaching nuts to 140 ft. lbs., and upper strut attaching nuts to 18 ft. lbs.

STRUT ASSEMBLY, SERVICE

Disassembly

1. Clamp strut compressor, tool No. J-

26854, in a suitable vise.
2. Install strut assembly into bottom adapter of compressor and install bottom adapter, Fig. 14. Ensure strut and locating pins are fully engaged.
3. Rotate strut assembly until top mounting assembly lip is aligned with compressor support notch.
4. Install upper adapter onto top spring seal, Fig. 14, so long stud is at high location to strut flange.
5. Rotate compressor forcing screw clockwise until top support flange contacts top adapter, and continue turning screw to compress strut spring.
6. Install second upper adapter over spring seat assembly, then rotate forcing screw counterclockwise until strut spring tension is relieved.
7. Remove top adapters, bottom adapter and strut.

ASSEMBLY

1. Perform steps 1 and 2 as outlined in the

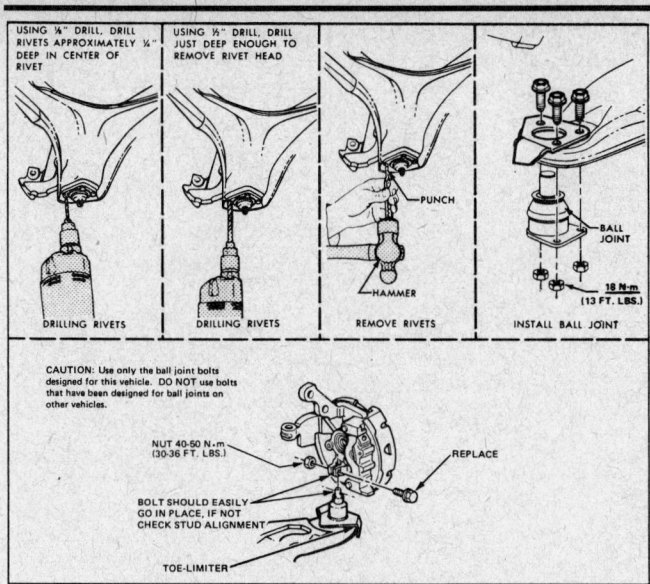

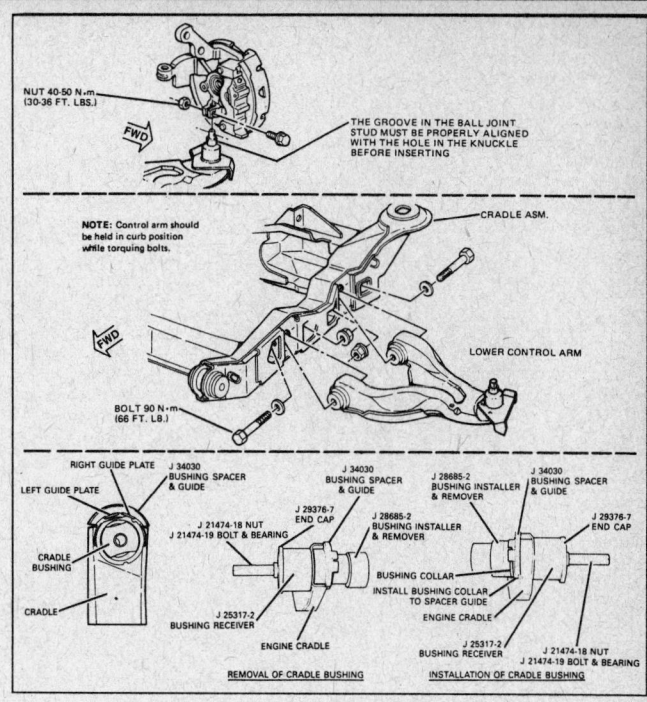

Fig. 9 Lower ball joint replacement

Fig. 10 Lower control arm & bushing replacement

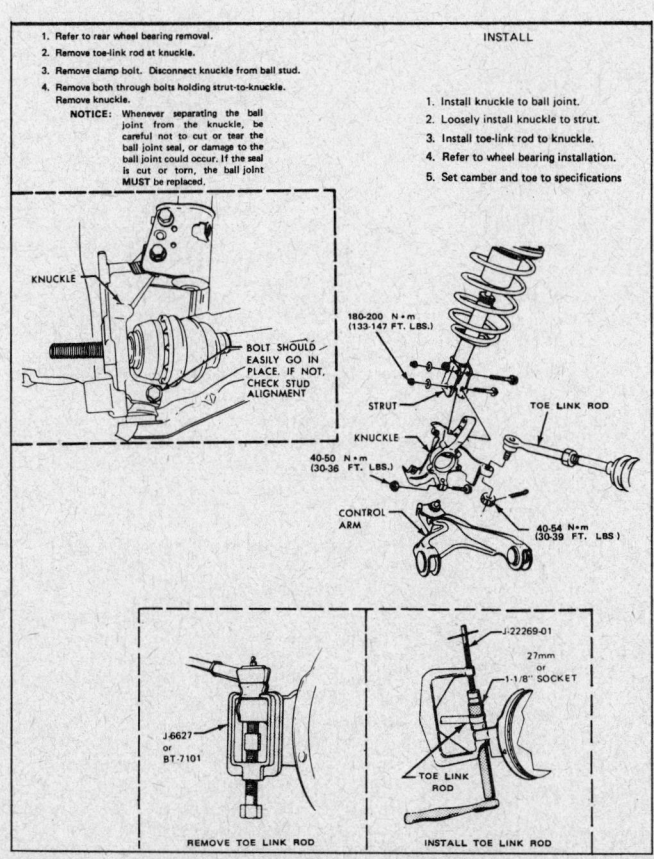

1. Refer to rear wheel bearing removal.
2. Remove toe-link rod at knuckle.
3. Remove clamp bolt. Disconnect knuckle from ball stud.
4. Remove both through bolts holding strut-to-knuckle. Remove knuckle.
   NOTICE: Whenever separating the ball joint from the knuckle, be careful not to cut or tear the ball joint seal, or damage to the ball joint could occur. If the seal is cut or torn, the ball joint MUST be replaced.

INSTALL

1. Install knuckle to ball joint.
2. Loosely install knuckle to strut.
3. Install toe-link rod to knuckle.
4. Refer to wheel bearing installation.
5. Set camber and toe to specifications

Fig. 11 Rear knuckle replacement

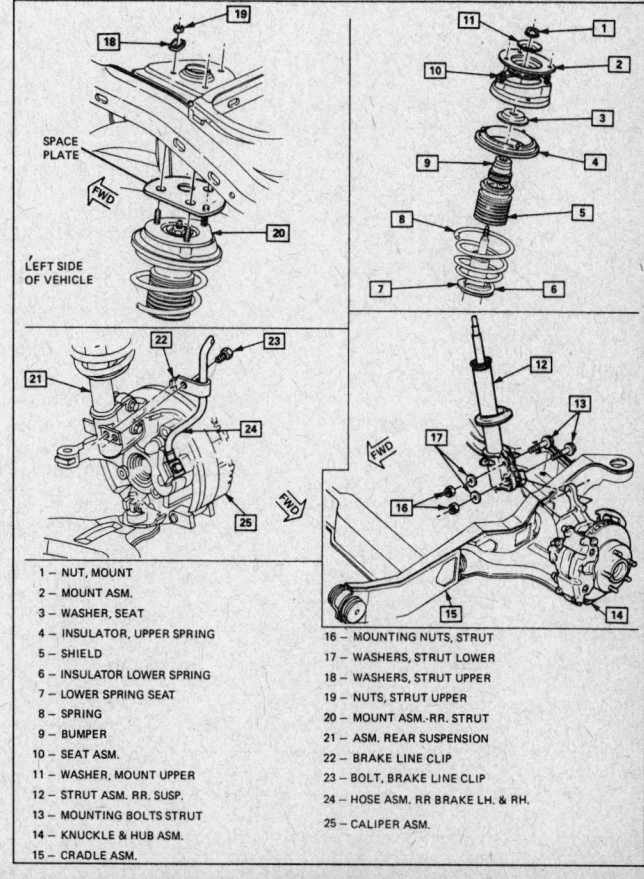

1 — NUT, MOUNT
2 — MOUNT ASM.
3 — WASHER, SEAT
4 — INSULATOR, UPPER SPRING
5 — SHIELD
6 — INSULATOR LOWER SPRING
7 — LOWER SPRING SEAT
8 — SPRING
9 — BUMPER
10 — SEAT ASM.
11 — WASHER, MOUNT UPPER
12 — STRUT ASM. RR. SUSP.
13 — MOUNTING BOLTS STRUT
14 — KNUCKLE & HUB ASM.
15 — CRADLE ASM.
16 — MOUNTING NUTS, STRUT
17 — WASHERS, STRUT LOWER
18 — WASHERS, STRUT UPPER
19 — NUTS, STRUT UPPER
20 — MOUNT ASM.-RR. STRUT
21 — ASM. REAR SUSPENSION
22 — BRAKE LINE CLIP
23 — BOLT, BRAKE LINE CLIP
24 — HOSE ASM. RR BRAKE LH. & RH.
25 — CALIPER ASM.

Fig. 12 Strut assembly replacement

PONTIAC FIERO

1. USING A SHARP TOOL, SCRIBE THE KNUCKLE ALONG THE LOWER OUTBOARD STRUT RADIUS, AS IN VIEW A.
2. SCRIBE THE STRUT FLANGE ON THE INBOARD SIDE, ALONG THE CURVE OF THE KNUCKLE, AS IN VIEW B.
3. MAKE A CHISEL MARK ACROSS THE STRUT/KNUCKLE INTERFACE, AS IN VIEW C.
4. ON REASSEMBLY, CAREFULLY MATCH THE MARKS TO THE COMPONENTS.

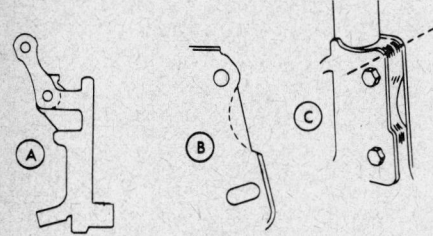

Fig. 13 Scribing strut & knuckle

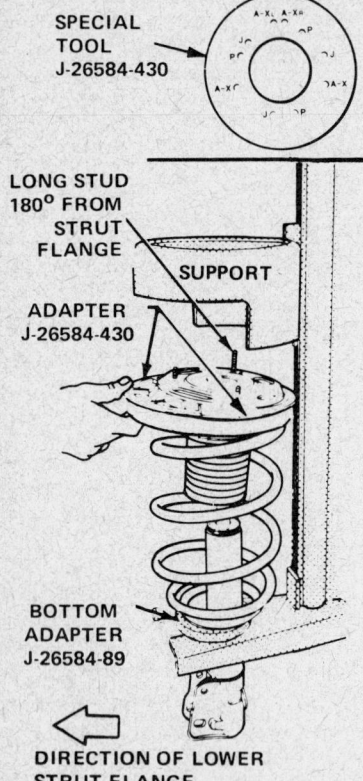

SPECIAL TOOL J-26584-430

LONG STUD 180° FROM STRUT FLANGE

SUPPORT

ADAPTER J-26584-430

BOTTOM ADAPTER J-26584-89

← DIRECTION OF LOWER STRUT FLANGE

Fig. 14 Removing damper & coil spring from strut

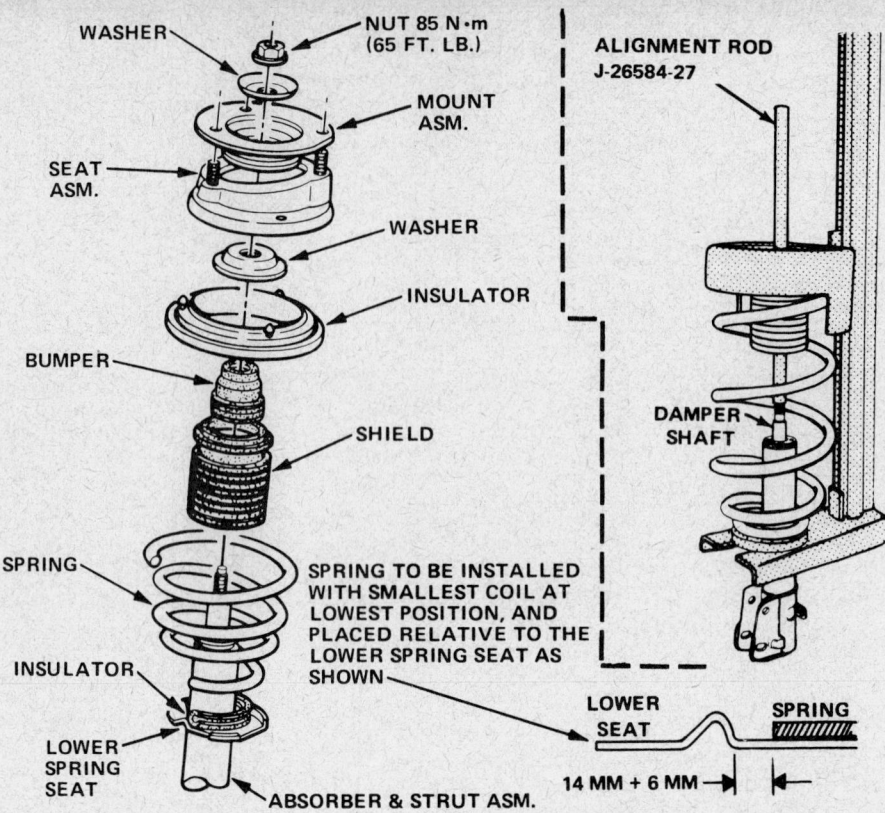

WASHER

NUT 85 N·m (65 FT. LB.)

MOUNT ASM.

SEAT ASM.

WASHER

INSULATOR

BUMPER

SHIELD

SPRING

SPRING TO BE INSTALLED WITH SMALLEST COIL AT LOWEST POSITION, AND PLACED RELATIVE TO THE LOWER SPRING SEAT AS SHOWN

INSULATOR

LOWER SPRING SEAT

ABSORBER & STRUT ASM.

ALIGNMENT ROD J-26584-27

DAMPER SHAFT

LOWER SEAT   SPRING

14 MM + 6 MM

Fig. 15 Strut assembly alignment & components

"Disassembly" procedure.
2. Rotate strut assembly until mounting flange is facing outward, opposite compressor forcing screw.
3. Install strut components, Fig. 15. Ensure spring is properly seated on bottom spring plate.
4. Install strut spring seat assembly on top of spring with long stud positioned 180° from strut mounting flange.
5. Install top adapter over spring seat assembly.
6. Rotate compressor forcing screw until compressor top support just contacts top adapter. Do not compress spring.
7. Install strut alignment rod through top spring seat and thread onto damper shaft hand tight, Fig. 15.
8. Rotate compressor forcing screw clockwise to compress spring until damper shaft is exposed enough so nut can be threaded securely, then install the nut. Ensure damper shaft comes through center of spring seat opening to prevent damage.

NOTE: Do not compress spring until bottomed.

9. Remove alignment rod, then install mount and torque nut to 65 ft. lbs.
10. Rotate compressor forcing screw counterclockwise and remove strut assembly from compressor.

PARKING BRAKE, ADJUST

1. Jack up both rear wheels with parking brake fully released.
2. Apply suitable lubricant to groove in equalizer nut.
3. Remove slack from cable by tightening equilizer nut while preventing brake cable stud from turning.

NOTE: After tightening nut, ensure caliper levers are against stops on caliper housing. If levers are not against stops, loosen cable until they return.

4. Activate parking brake several times to check adjustment. The parking brake lever should move 5–8 notches when a force is applied perpendicularly at a midway point on handle grip.
5. Lower rear wheels and ensure levers are on caliper stops. If necessary, back off parking brake adjuster to keep levers on stops.

MASTER CYLINDER, REPLACE

1. Disconnect both brake lines from master cylinder.
2. Remove 2 master cylinder attaching nuts and the master cylinder.
3. Reverse procedure to install. Torque master cylinder attaching nuts to 22–30 ft. lbs., and brake line nuts to 120–180 inch lbs.

POWER BRAKE UNIT, REPLACE

1. Remove 2 master cylinder-to-power brake unit attaching nuts, and position master cylinder aside with brake lines attached.
2. Disconnect power brake unit pushrod from brake pedal.
3. Remove power brake unit attaching nuts and the power brake unit.
4. Reverse procedure to install. Torque attaching nuts to 22–30 ft. lbs.

Front Suspension & Steering Section

DESCRIPTION

The front suspension, Fig. 1, is a conventional short and long arm design with coil springs. The control arms are attached with bolts and bushings at the inner pivot points, and are attached to the steering knuckle/front wheel spindle assembly at the outer pivot points.

WHEEL ALIGNMENT

Camber

1. Remove upper ball joint as described under "Upper Ball Joint, Replace."
2. Camber may be increased approximately 1° by rotating ½ turn and reinstalling with flat of upper flange on inboard side of control arm, Fig. 2.

Caster

1. Remove upper control arm as described under "Upper Control Arm, Replace."
2. Adjust caster by installing washers between legs of upper control arm, Fig. 3.

NOTE: When caster is adjusted, two washers totalling .472 inch (12mm) must be installed, with one at each end of locating tube.

Toe-In

1. Loosen jam nuts on toe link rod, then rotate rods until toe-in is within specifications, Fig. 4.
2. Torque jam nuts to 47 ft. lbs.

NOTE: Use care not to twist or damage rubber boots.

WHEEL BEARING, ADJUST

1. Raise and support vehicle.
2. Remove wheel and tire assembly.
3. Remove dust cap from hub, then the cotter pin from spindle and spindle nut.
4. Torque spindle nut to 12 ft. lbs. while rotating wheel forward by hand.
5. Back off spindle nut until just loose, then hand tighten nut and back off again until either hole in spindle lines up with hole in nut.

NOTE: Do not back off nut more than ½ flat.

6. Install new cotter pin, then measure hub end play. With bearing properly adjusted, end play should measure .001–.005 inch.

WHEEL BEARING, REPLACE

Removal

1. Raise and support vehicle.
2. Remove wheel and tire assembly, then disconnect brake caliper from steering knuckle and suspend from frame with a piece of wire. Do not let brake lines support weight of caliper.
3. Remove hub dust cap, cotter pin, spindle nut and washer.
4. Remove hub and bearing from spindle.
5. Remove outer bearing from hub, then pry out grease seal and remove inner bearing. Discard seal.

Installation

1. Clean all grease from hub, spindle and bearing.
2. Apply a thin film of suitable grease to spindle at outer bearing seat and the inner bearing seat, shoulder and seal seat.
3. Apply grease inboard of each bearing race in hub.
4. Completely fill bearing cone and roller assemblies with grease.
5. Install inner bearing into hub and apply additional grease outboard of bearing.
6. Install new grease seal flush with hub and lubricate seal lip with a thin coating of grease.
7. Install hub and rotor assembly onto spindle, then position outer bearing in race.
8. Install washer and nut, then adjust bearing as previously described.
9. Install brake caliper, then the wheel and tire assembly.

UPPER BALL JOINT, REPLACE

1. Raise and support vehicle.
2. Remove wheel and tire assembly, then support lower control arm with a suitable jack.
3. Remove upper ball joint stud nut, then reinstall nut finger tight.
4. Install tool No. J-26407 with cup end over lower ball joint stud nut. Rotate threaded end of tool until upper stud is free of steering knuckle, then remove tool and nut from stud, Fig. 5.
5. Remove 2 ball joint-to-upper control arm attaching bolts and nuts.
6. Note position of flat on ball joint for proper installation, then remove ball joint from vehicle.
7. Reverse procedure to install. Torque ball joint-to-upper control arm attaching bolts to 28 ft. lbs. Torque stud nut to 35 ft. lbs., then tighten nut up to an additional ⅙ turn to align cotter pin hole.

LOWER BALL JOINT, REPLACE

The lower ball joint is permanently attached to the lower control arm and cannot be serviced separately. If the lower ball joint requires replacement, the entire lower control arm must be replaced.

SHOCK ABSORBER, REPLACE

1. Raise and support vehicle.
2. Remove wheel and tire assembly, then the 2 shock absorber upper attaching bolts.
3. Remove shock absorber lower attaching bolts and nut, Fig. 1.
4. Remove shock absorber from vehicle.
5. Reverse procedure to install. Torque upper attaching bolts to 20 ft. lbs., and lower attaching bolt to 35 ft. lbs.

STABILIZER BAR, REPLACE

1. Raise and support vehicle.
2. Remove stabilizer bar attaching bolt and nut and associated components from lower control arms, Fig. 1.
3. Remove stabilizer bar clamp and the stabilizer bar from vehicle.
4. Reverse procedure to install. Torque clamp attaching bolts to 15 ft. lbs., and stabilizer bar attaching bolt to 16 ft. lbs.

LOWER CONTROL ARM & COIL SPRING, REPLACE

1. Raise vehicle and support at frame crossmember.
2. Remove wheel and tire assembly, then disconnect stabilizer bar from lower control arm.
3. Disconnect tie rod from steering knuckle, then the shock absorber from lower control arm.
4. Support lower control arm with a suitable jack, then remove lower ball joint stud nut and press ball joint out of steering knuckle, using tool No. J-26407, Fig. 6. Position steering knuckle and hub aside.
5. Loosen lower control arm pivot bolts.
6. Install a safety chain through coil spring, then slowly lower jack and remove spring, Fig. 1.
7. Remove lower control arm attaching bolts and the lower control arm.

NOTE: It may be necessary to loosen or remove steering gear attaching bolts to gain access to the control arm attaching bolt at the crossmember.

8. Reverse procedure to install, noting the following:
   a. Install control arm attaching bolts finger tight. Do not torque bolts until all other components have been assembled and torqued to specifications.
   b. Torque ball joint stud nut to 55 ft. lbs.
   c. Torque stabilizer bar attaching bolt to 16 ft. lbs.
   d. Torque tie rod attaching nut to 29 ft. lbs.

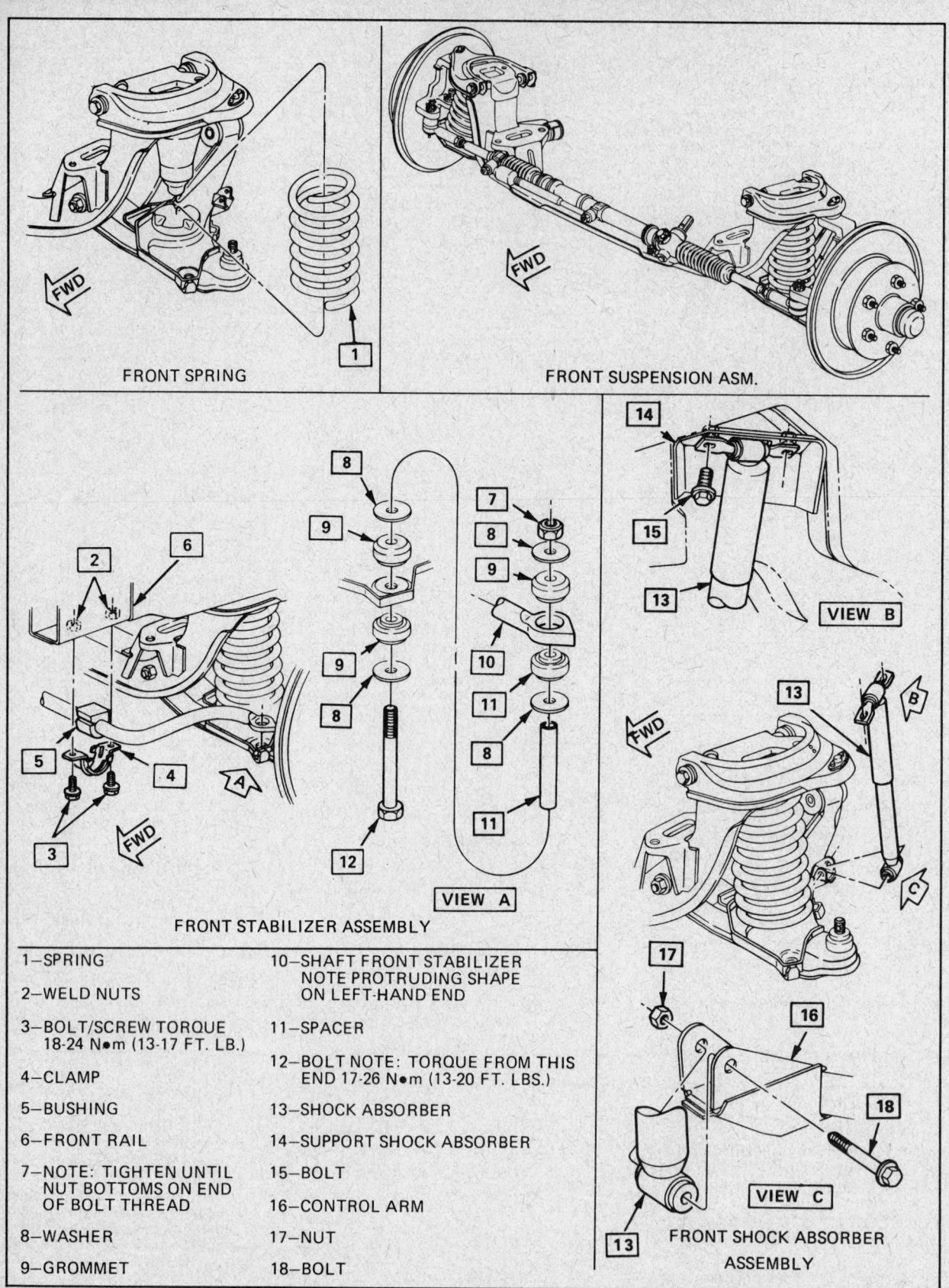

FRONT SPRING

FRONT SUSPENSION ASM.

FRONT STABILIZER ASSEMBLY

VIEW A

VIEW B

VIEW C

FRONT SHOCK ABSORBER ASSEMBLY

1—SPRING

2—WELD NUTS

3—BOLT/SCREW TORQUE 18-24 N•m (13-17 FT. LB.)

4—CLAMP

5—BUSHING

6—FRONT RAIL

7—NOTE: TIGHTEN UNTIL NUT BOTTOMS ON END OF BOLT THREAD

8—WASHER

9—GROMMET

10—SHAFT FRONT STABILIZER NOTE PROTRUDING SHAPE ON LEFT-HAND END

11—SPACER

12—BOLT NOTE: TORQUE FROM THIS END 17-26 N•m (13-20 FT. LBS.)

13—SHOCK ABSORBER

14—SUPPORT SHOCK ABSORBER

15—BOLT

16—CONTROL ARM

17—NUT

18—BOLT

Fig. 1 Front suspension

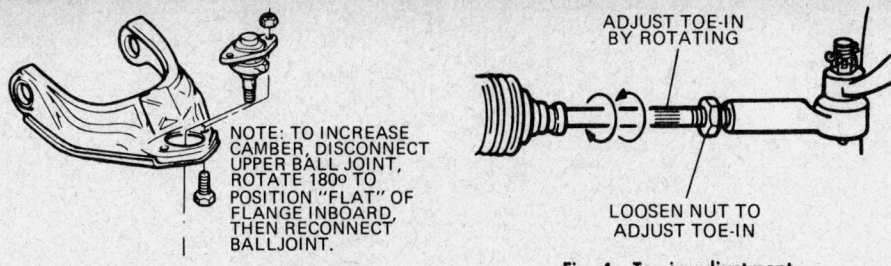

NOTE: TO INCREASE CAMBER, DISCONNECT UPPER BALL JOINT, ROTATE 180° TO POSITION "FLAT" OF FLANGE INBOARD, THEN RECONNECT BALLJOINT.

Fig. 2 Camber adjustment

ADJUST TOE-IN BY ROTATING

LOOSEN NUT TO ADJUST TOE-IN

Fig. 4 Toe-in adjustment

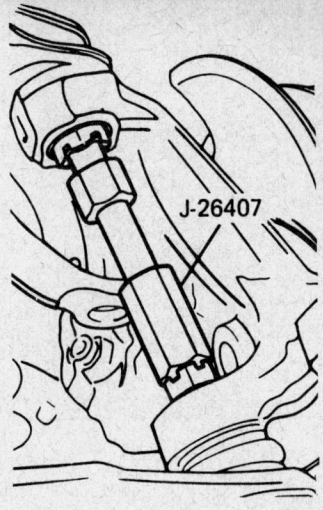

J-26407

Fig. 5 Upper ball joint removal

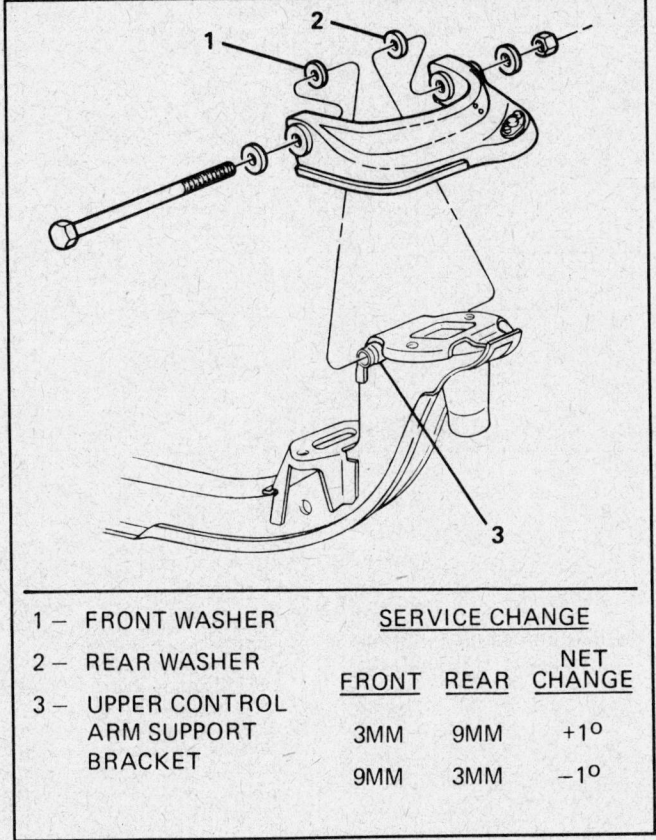

1 — FRONT WASHER	SERVICE CHANGE		
2 — REAR WASHER	FRONT	REAR	NET CHANGE
3 — UPPER CONTROL ARM SUPPORT BRACKET	3MM	9MM	+1°
	9MM	3MM	−1°

Fig. 3 Caster adjustment

HEAVY FLAT WASHER

J-26407

Fig. 6 Lower ball joint removal

e. Torque shock absorber lower attaching bolt to 35 ft. lbs.
f. If steering gear attaching bolts have been loosened or removed, install new bolts and torque to 21 ft. lbs.
g. Torque control arm-to-body attaching bolt to 62 ft. lbs. and control arm-to-crossmember nut to 52 ft. lbs.

UPPER CONTROL ARM, REPLACE

1. Raise and support vehicle.
2. Remove wheel and tire assembly, then the rivet securing brake line clip to upper control arm.
3. Support lower control arm with a suitable jack, then remove upper ball joint as

described under "Upper Ball Joint, Replace."
4. Remove control arm attaching bolt and the control arm from vehicle.
5. Reverse procedure to install. Torque control arm attaching bolt to 66 ft. lbs.

NOTE: Washers and shims, Fig. 3, must be installed in their original positions unless a change in caster angle is desired.

CROSSMEMBER BUMPER, REPLACE

1. Remove coil spring as described under "Lower Control Arm & Coil Spring,

Replace."
2. Remove crossmember bumper from vehicle.
3. Reverse procedure to install.

STEERING KNUCKLE, REPLACE

1. Raise and support vehicle. Support lower control arm with a suitable jack.
2. Remove wheel and tire assembly, then disconnect brake caliper from steering knuckle and suspend from frame with a piece of wire. Do not let brake lines support weight of caliper.

NOTE: Install a block of wood between

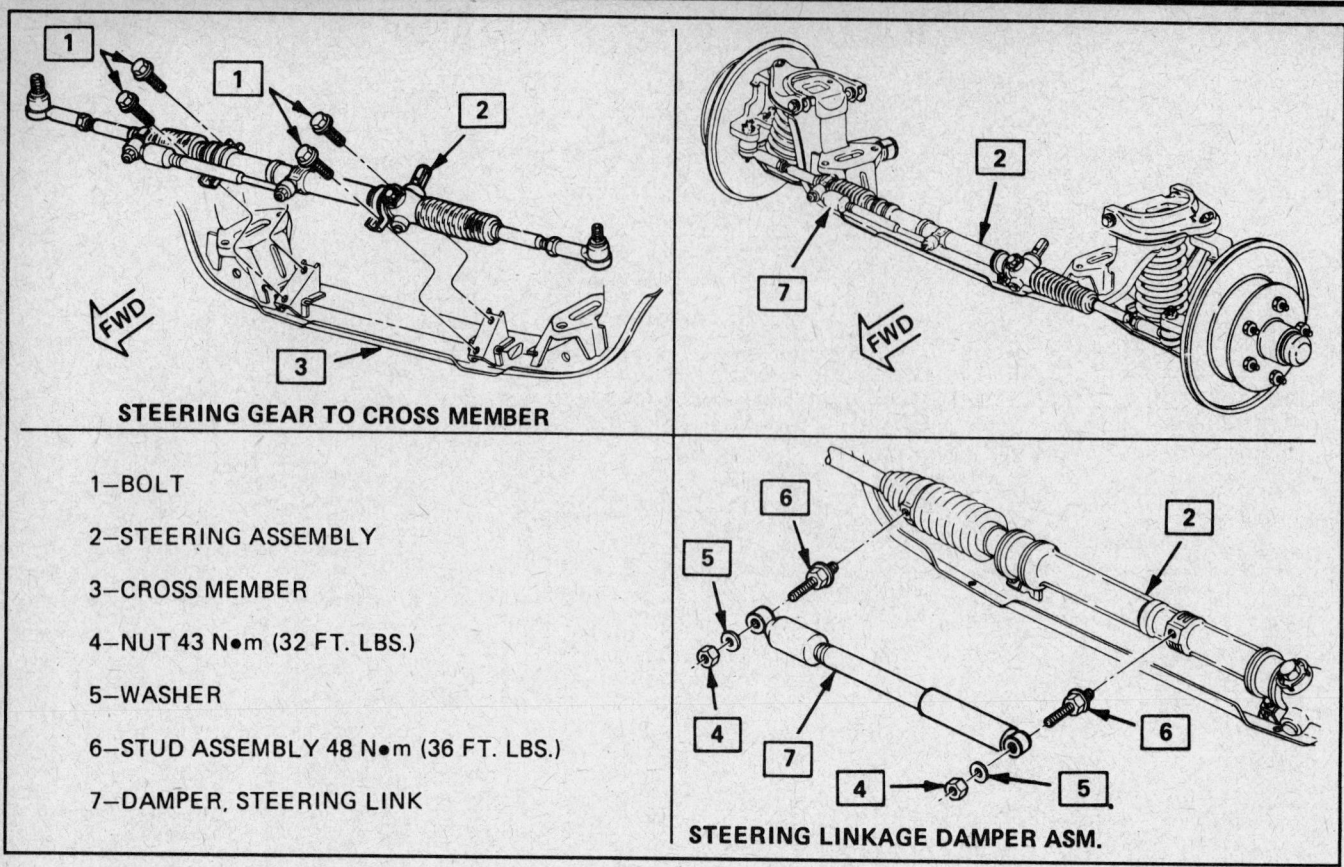

1—BOLT

2—STEERING ASSEMBLY

3—CROSS MEMBER

4—NUT 43 N•m (32 FT. LBS.)

5—WASHER

6—STUD ASSEMBLY 48 N•m (36 FT. LBS.)

7—DAMPER, STEERING LINK

STEERING GEAR TO CROSS MEMBER

STEERING LINKAGE DAMPER ASM.

Fig. 7   Steering gear replacement

---

brake shoes to hold piston in caliper bore.

3. Remove hub, disc and splash shield.
4. Remove both ball joint studs as previously described.
5. Disconnect tie rod end from steering knuckle.
6. Press both ball joint studs from steering knuckle using tool No. J-26407 or equivalent.
7. Remove ball joint stud nuts, then the steering knuckle.
8. Reverse procedure to install, noting the following torques: lower ball joint stud nut, 55 ft. lbs.; upper ball joint stud nut, 35 ft. lbs.; splash shield bolts, 7 ft. lbs.; tie rod nut, 29 ft. lbs.

MANUAL STEERING GEAR, REPLACE

1. Raise and support vehicle.
2. Remove both front crossmember braces.
3. Remove flex coupling pinch bolt from shaft.
4. Remove outer tie rod cotter pins and nuts on both sides, and disconnect tie rods from steering knuckles.
5. Remove 4 steering gear attaching bolts and the steering gear, Fig. 7.
6. Reverse procedure to install, noting the following torques: flex coupling bolt, 46 ft. lbs.; steering gear bolts, 21 ft. lbs.; tie rod nuts, 29 ft. lbs., plus up to an additional 1/6 turn to align cotter pin hole; front crossmember brace bolts, 20 ft. lbs.

GM FRONT WHEEL DRIVE

INDEX

1977–78 Drive Axles

GENERAL DESCRIPTION

Each drive axle, Fig. 1, consists of an axle shaft with a ball type constant velocity joint at the outboard end and a tri-pot type at the inboard end. The torsional damper on the right hand shaft is not serviceable and must be replaced as a unit.

The inboard joint is not only flexible to operate at various angles, but can also move in and out as required by suspension movement.

RIGHT DRIVE AXLE

1. Disconnect battery ground cable and remove wheel and wheel disc.

NOTE: If drive axle is to be removed, remove cotter pin and loosen but do not remove spindle nut.

2. Raise vehicle so front vehicle weight is supported at lower control arms.
3. Loosen right front shock absorber lower mounting nut, then, using a screwdriver, pry shock absorber at mount inner sleeve until it contacts nut.

NOTE: Do not remove shock absorber from lower mount since lower control arm may drop.

4. Place a short piece of rubber hose on both lower control arm torsion bar connectors.
5. Remove screws and lockwashers securing right drive axle to output shaft.
6. Position inboard end of axle rearward toward starter to provide access to output shaft.
7. Remove output shaft support strut to final drive housing screw, then the two screws securing right output shaft support to the engine.

8. Slide output shaft outboard to disengage splines, then move inboard end of the assembly forward and downward until clear of vehicle.
9. Using a block of wood and a hammer, strike end of drive axle to unseat axle at hub.

NOTE: Loosen spindle nut just enough to allow axle to unseat.

10. Rotate axle inboard and forward, guiding axle over front cross-member and from under vehicle.
11. Reverse procedure to install.

LEFT DRIVE AXLE

1. Raise and support vehicle with jack stands underneath frame side rails.
2. Remove wheel and tire and drive axle spindle nut.
3. Remove the six drive axle to output shaft screws and lock washers.

NOTE: Discard the six screws and lockwashers. Use new screws during reassembly.

4. Loosen shock absorber upper bolt, then remove the ball joint cotter pin and nut and remove brake hose clip from joint stud.
5. Using a hammer, strike knuckle in area of ball joint. Lift up on upper arm and remove joint stud from steering knuckle.

CAUTION: Use care to avoid damaging brake hose.

6. Remove brake hose bracket from frame, then carefully tip disc and knuckle assembly out at upper end to extent of brake hose.

CAUTION: To prevent damaging the brake hose, wire the assembly to upper control arm so brake hose does not support weight of knuckle assembly.

7. Rotate inner end of drive axle toward front of vehicle, then guide drive axle out of knuckle and remove drive axle.
8. Remove output shaft retaining bolt.

NOTE: To prevent output shaft from rotating, install two screws in output shaft flange.

9. Remove output shaft by pulling straight out.

CAUTION: Use care when removing output shaft to avoid damaging oil seal.

10. Reverse procedure to install.

OUTER CONSTANT VELOCITY JOINT

1. Remove inner and outer seal clamps by cutting with a chisel, then slide seal down axle shaft to gain access to joint.
2. Wipe excess grease from joint and spread snap ring and slide joint off spline, Fig. 2.
3. Remove inner race snap ring, Fig. 3.
4. Hold constant velocity joint in one hand, then tilt cage and inner race so that one ball can be removed, Fig. 4. Continue until all balls have been removed.

NOTE: It may be necessary to tap outer cage to rotate it.

5. Turn cage 90° with slot in cage aligned with short land on outer race and lift cage out of race, Fig. 5.

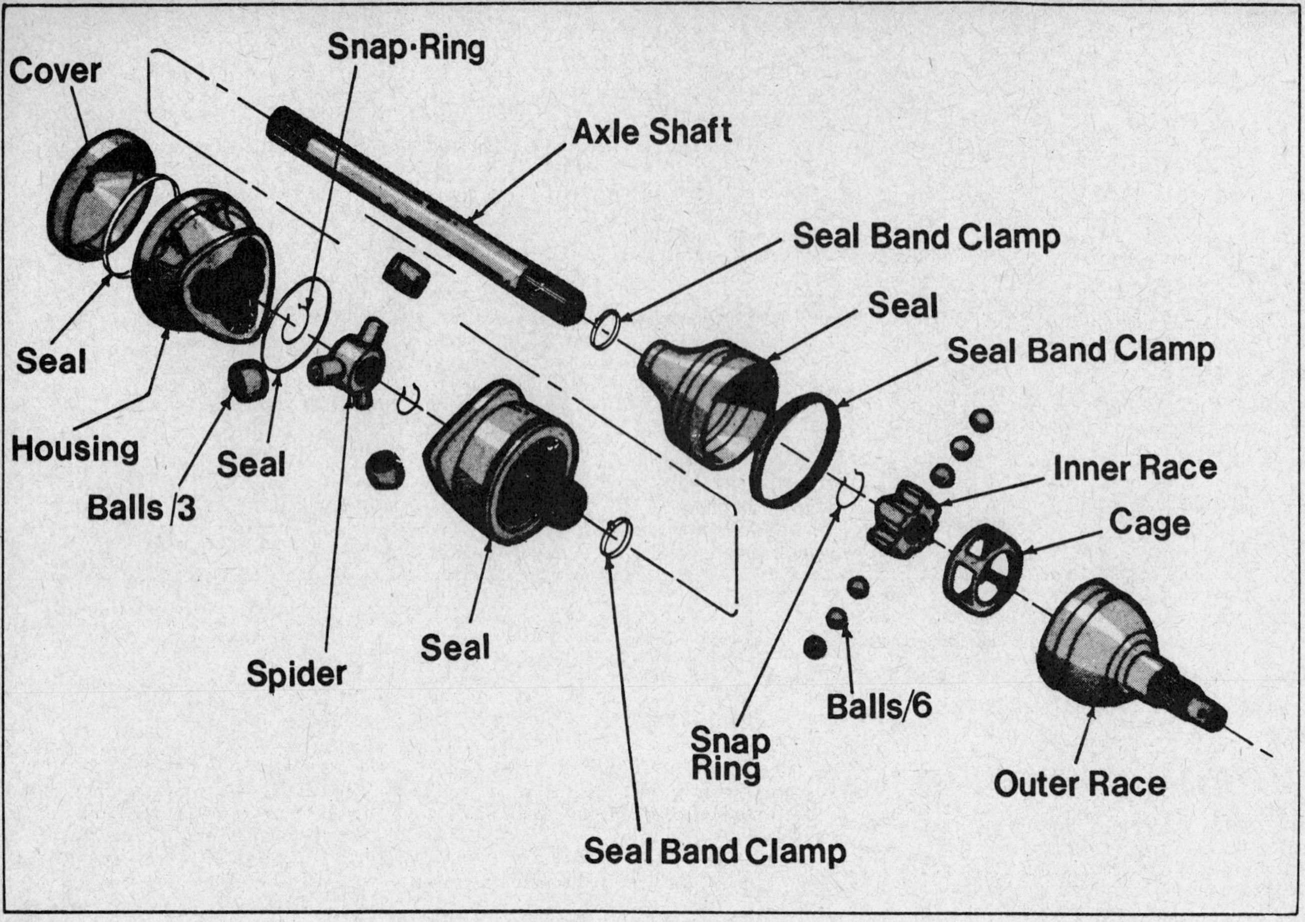

Fig. 1 Exploded view of front drive axle. 1977—78

6. Turn short land of inner race 90° in line with hole in cage. Lift land on inner race up through hole in cage, then turn up and out to separate, Fig. 6.
7. Reverse procedure to install, using new seal clamps, Fig. 7. Cut off excess strap.

INNER CONSTANT VELOCITY JOINT

1. Remove small seal clamp bank by cutting it with a chisel.
2. Remove large end of seal from joint housing by prying up crimped edges on seal adapter. Drive seal adapter and seal off joint housing with hammer and chisel, Fig. 8.

NOTE: Use care when removing seal adapter not to damage adapter or seal.

3. Slide seal and adapter down axle shaft until joint is exposed.

NOTE: Do not allow spider leg balls to fall off accidentally as adapter is moved.

4. Remove spider leg balls.
5. Remove spider outer snap ring, Fig. 9.
6. Tap spider assembly from shaft.
7. Reverse procedure to install, being sure to stake seal adapter to joint housing, Fig. 10.

RIGHT HAND OUTPUT SHAFT

1. Disconnect negative battery cable.

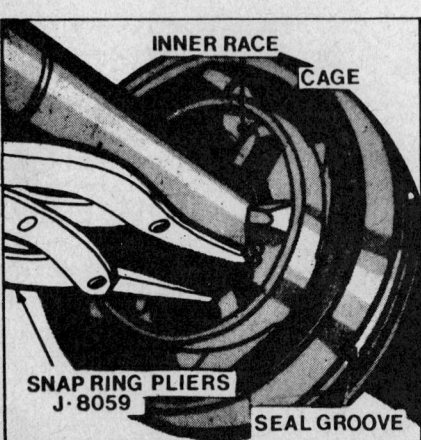

Fig. 2 Removing outer joint from axle

Fig. 3 Removing and installing inner snap ring

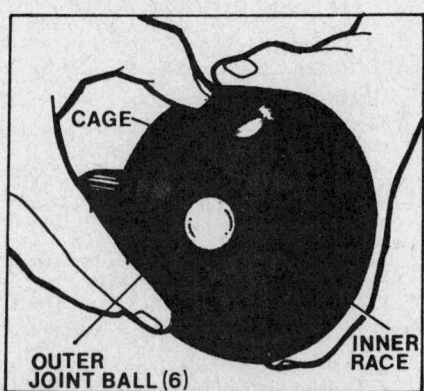

Fig. 4 Removing balls from outer joint

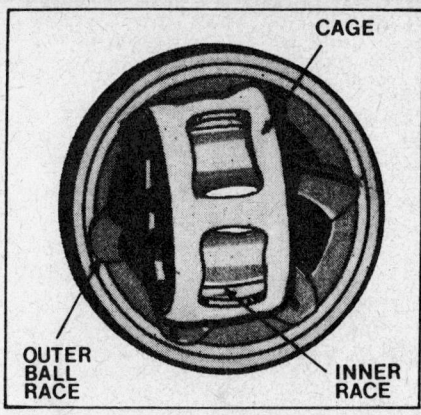

Fig. 5 Removing cage and inner race

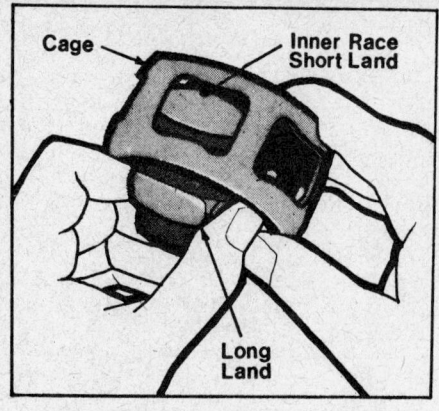

Fig. 6 Removing inner race from cage

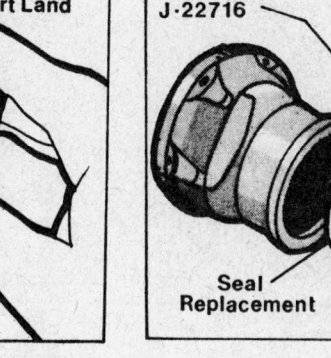

Fig. 7 Installing new seal clamp

2. Raise car and install a short length of rubber hose on lower control arm torsion bar connector, Fig. 11.
3. Remove six drive axle-to-output shaft bolts and lock washers.
4. Remove output shaft support mounting bolts.
5. Rotate inboard end of drive axle rearward.
6. Pull output shaft out until it clears final drive then lower splined end and remove from car.
7. Reverse procedure to install.

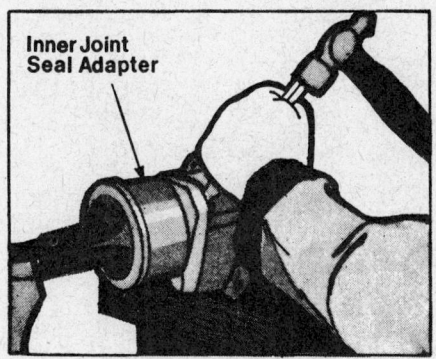

Fig. 8 Removing seal adapter

RIGHT HAND OUTPUT SHAFT BEARING, REPLACE

1. Remove output shaft as described above.
2. Remove three output shaft bearing retainer-to-support bolts.
3. Using two fabricated steel plates and four 3/8 × 24 bolts five inches long, Fig. 12, tighten bolts alternately to press out bearing.
4. Reverse procedure to install.

LEFT HAND OUTPUT SHAFT

1. Remove left drive axle.
2. Remove output shaft retaining bolt and pull shaft out of final drive.
3. Reverse procedure to install.

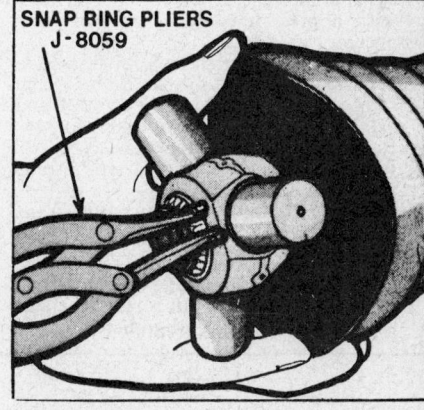

Fig. 9 Removing spider snap ring

FINAL DRIVE, REPLACE

The final drive unit it not serviced, but is replaced as a unit.
1. Disconnect negative battery cable.
2. Remove approximately one gallon of fluid from transmission, then remove transmission and filler tube and plug tube hole.
3. Remove bolts "A" and "B" and nut "H", Fig. 13.
4. Remove bolt securing transmission oil cooler lines to final drive.
5. Remove nut from large through bolt, joining final drive support bracket to final drive.
6. Disconnect left front engine mount support bracket from engine, and final drive support bracket from left front engine mount support.
7. Remove right output shaft as outlined above.

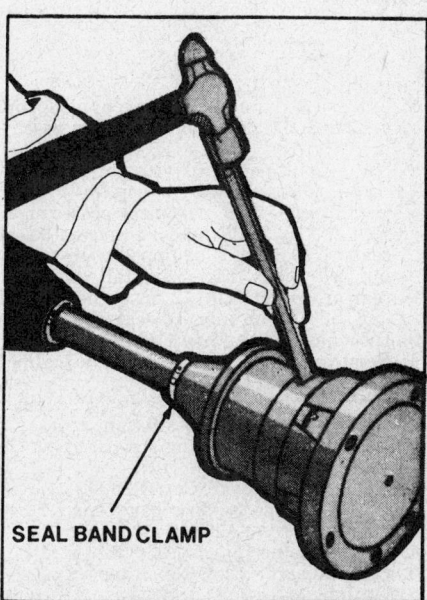

Fig. 10 Installing seal adapter on joint housing

Fig. 11 Rubber hose location

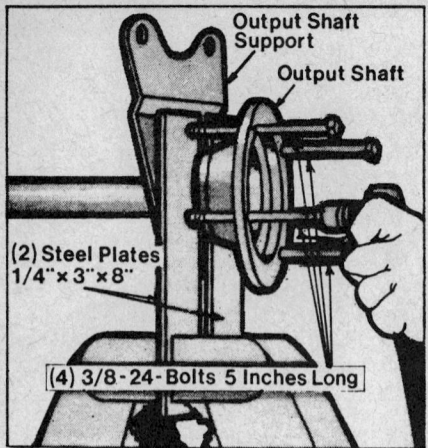

Fig. 12   Removing right hand output shaft support and bearing

8. Remove six left output shaft-to-drive axle bolts and lock washers.
9. Loosen final drive cover screws and drain fluid, then remove cover.
10. Compress left hand inner constant velocity joint and secure drive axle to frame with a piece of wire to provide clearance.
11. Disconnect left tie strut from crossmember and loosen strut to side rail bolt. Then rotate strut outboard until clear of final drive.
12. Remove final drive support bracket.
13. Remove remaining final drive-to-transmission bolts and nut "G."
14. Disengage final drive splines from transmission.

NOTE: To avoid damage to seals, final drive unit should be supported by a suitable jack and proper alignment must be

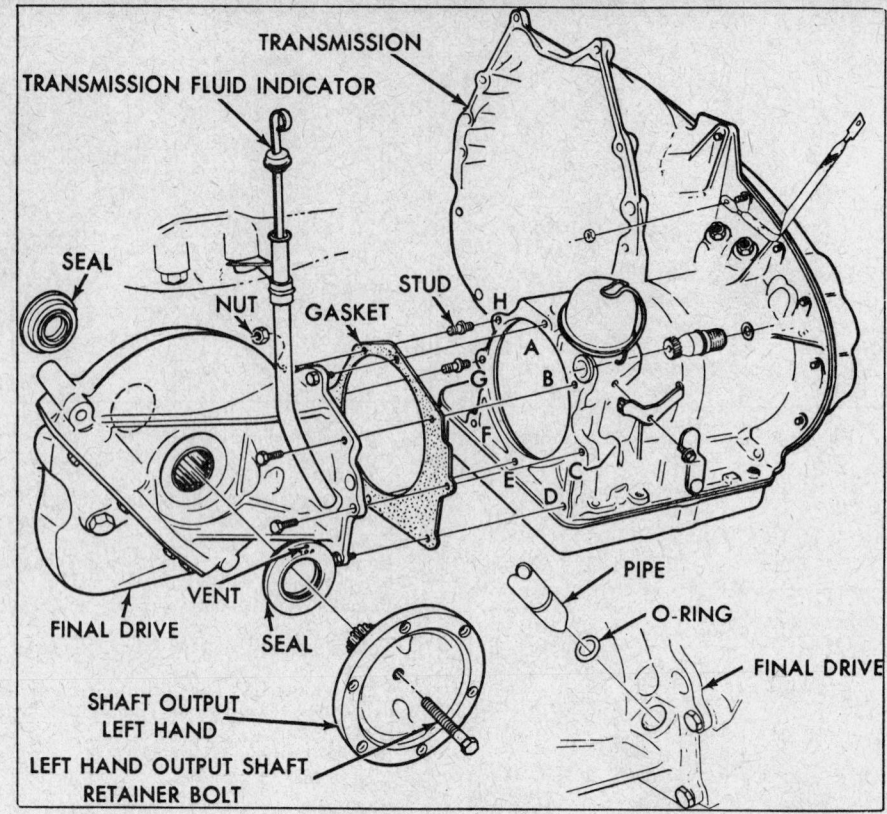

Fig. 13   Final drive attachment

maintained throughout removal.

15. Remove final drive unit from underside of car by sliding unit toward front of car, permitting ring gear to rotate up over

steering linkage, and work unit free from car.
16. Reverse procedure to install, being very careful to maintain proper final drive-to-transmission alignment to prevent seal damage.

1979–84 Drive Axles

DESCRIPTION

NOTE: On 1979 Eldorado, Riviera and Toronado models, two different types of driving axles are used. Early type driving axles can be identified by a groove on the drive axle, while the late type driving axle has no groove, Fig. 1.

The front wheel drive system, Figs. 2 and 3, consists of a final drive unit, left and right hand output shafts and drive axles. On 1979–84 Eldorado, Riviera and Toronado and 1980–84 Seville models, the output shafts are splined to the side gears and are retained by a retaining ring. Each drive axle, Figs. 4 and 5, consists of an axle shaft, with a ball type constant velocity joint at the outboard end and a tri-pot joint at the inboard end. On 1980–84 Citation, Omega, Phoenix, Skylark and 1982–84 Cavalier, Celebrity, Century, Cutlass Ciera, Cimarron, Firenza, 2000, Skyhawk and 6000 models, two different types of drive axle design is used. Both designs use the same ball type constant velocity joint at the outboard end. One design uses a ball type constant velocity joint at the inboard end, Fig.

6, the other design uses a tri-pot joint at the inboard end, Fig. 7. Both designs incorporate male splines which lock on the transaxle gears with snap rings, except for the left side inboard joint used with the automatic transaxles. The left side inboard joint used on automatic transaxles models utilizes a female spline which installs over a transaxle stub shaft.

DRIVE AXLE, REPLACE
1980–84 Citation, Omega, Phoenix, Skylark; 1982–84 Celebrity, Century, Cutlass Ciera, 6000; 1983–84 Cavalier, Cimarron, Firenza, 2000 & Skyhawk

NOTE: On models equipped with tri-pot joints on inboard axles, care must be taken not to over extend joints. When either or both ends are disconnected, over extending the tri-pot joint could result in internal joint separation.

Removal
1. Remove hub nut, then raise and support vehicle and remove wheel and tire assembly.
2. On vehicles equipped with ball type constant velocity inboard joints, Fig. 6, install axle shaft boot seal protector J-28712, Fig. 3, on inboard and outboard seals. On vehicles equipped with tri-pot inboard joints, Fig. 7, install axle boot seal protector J-28712 on outboard seal and J-33162 on inboard seal, Fig. 3.
3. Disconnect brake line clip at strut.
4. Remove disc brake caliper and caliper support.
5. Mark cam bolt to ensure proper camber alignment during installation.
6. Remove bolts attaching steering knuckle to strut.
7. Using tool J-28468 or J-33008 and J-2619-01, Fig. 3, disengage snap rings retaining drive axles.
8. Separate steering knuckle from strut.
9. Carefully pull drive axles from transaxle. On vehicles equipped with tri-pot inboard joints, Fig. 7, do not over extend joints.
10. Using tool J-28733, remove axle shaft from hub and bearing assssembly.

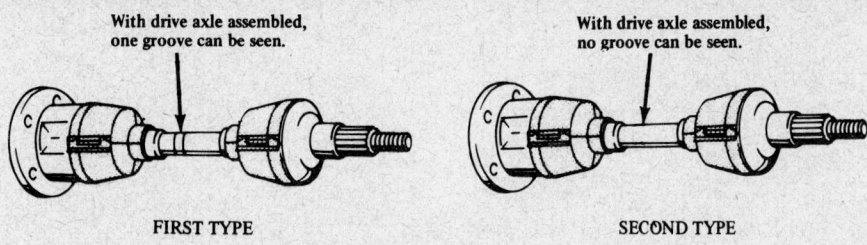

Fig. 1   Drive axle identification. 1979 Eldorado, Riviera & Toronado

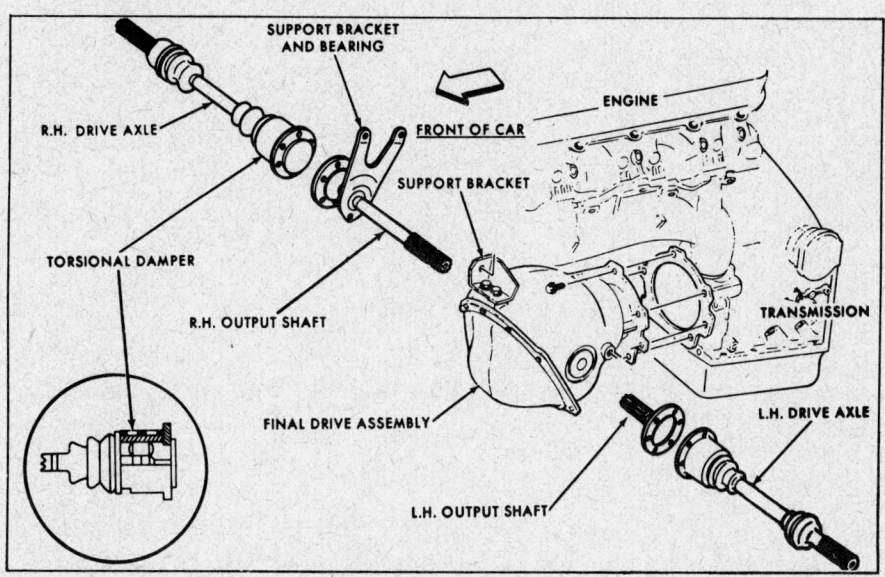

Fig. 2   Front wheel drive components. 1979—84 Eldorado, Riviera & Toronado; 1980—84 Seville

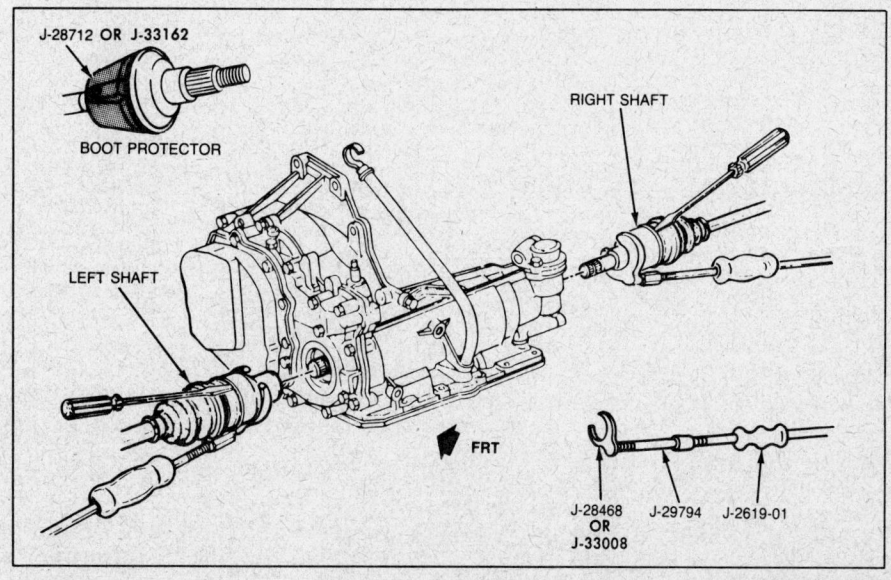

Fig. 3   Front wheel drive components. 1980—84 Citation, Omega, Phoenix & Skylark; 1982—84 Cavalier, Celebrity, Century, Cimarron, Cutlass Ciera, Firenza, 2000, Skyhawk & 6000

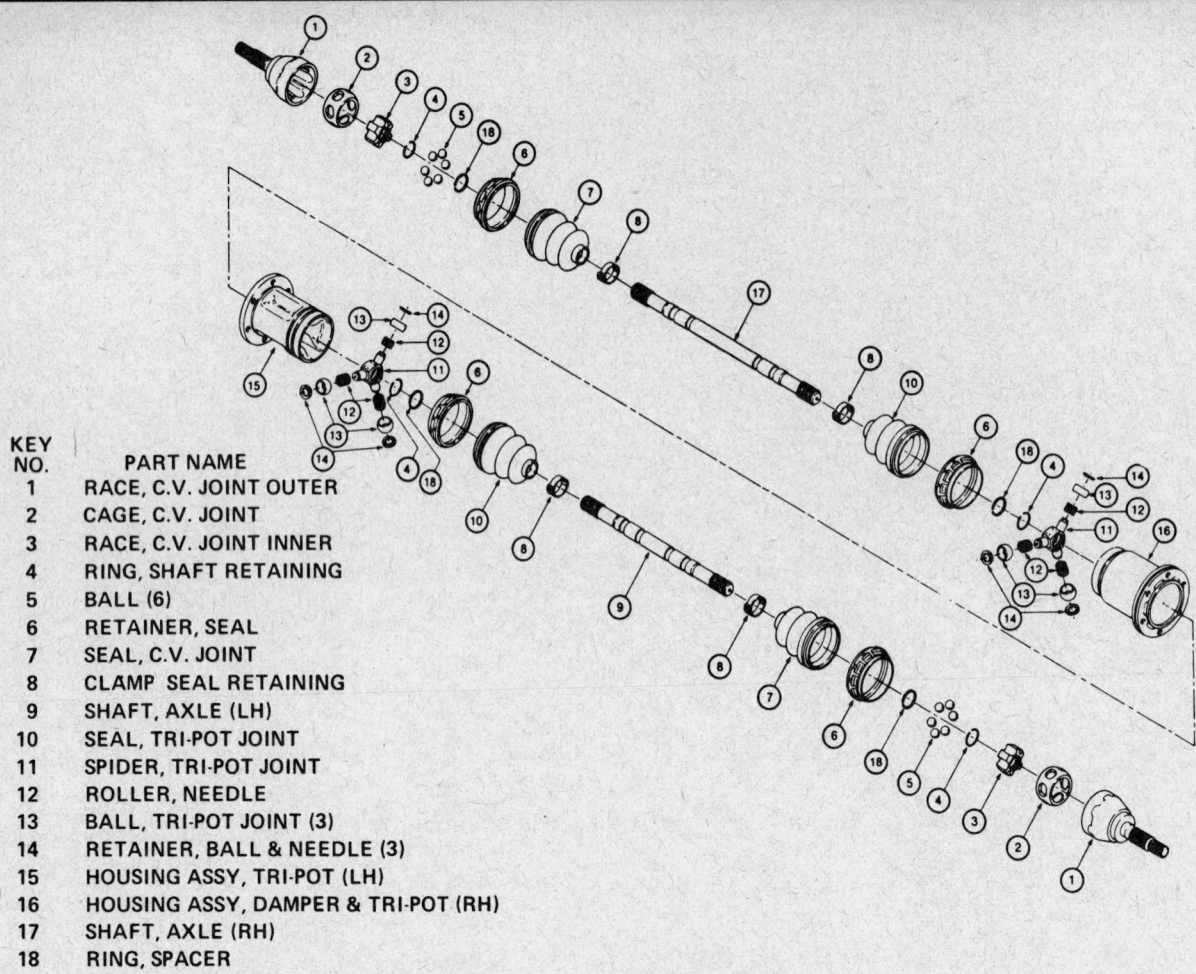

KEY NO.	PART NAME
1	RACE, C.V. JOINT OUTER
2	CAGE, C.V. JOINT
3	RACE, C.V. JOINT INNER
4	RING, SHAFT RETAINING
5	BALL (6)
6	RETAINER, SEAL
7	SEAL, C.V. JOINT
8	CLAMP SEAL RETAINING
9	SHAFT, AXLE (LH)
10	SEAL, TRI-POT JOINT
11	SPIDER, TRI-POT JOINT
12	ROLLER, NEEDLE
13	BALL, TRI-POT JOINT (3)
14	RETAINER, BALL & NEEDLE (3)
15	HOUSING ASSY, TRI-POT (LH)
16	HOUSING ASSY, DAMPER & TRI-POT (RH)
17	SHAFT, AXLE (RH)
18	RING, SPACER

Fig. 4 Exploded view of drive axle. 1979 Eldorado, Riviera & Toronado early type

Installation

1. Loosely install drive axle to steering knuckle and transaxle.
2. Loosely attach steering knuckle to strut bracket.
3. Install disc brake caliper, torque attaching bolts to 30 ft. lbs.
4. Install drive axle to steering knuckle. The drive axle is an interference fit. Install hub nut, when shaft begins to rotate, insert a brass drift in slot on rotor to prevent shaft from turning. It will take approximately 70 ft. lbs. of torque to seat axle shaft.
5. Apply load on hub by lowering vehicle on jack stand. Align cam bolt alignment marks, then torque nut to 140 ft. lbs.
6. Using a screwdriver in groove provided on inner retainer, install axle shaft on transaxle, Fig. 3. Tap on screwdriver until axle shaft is seated in transaxle.
7. Connect brake line clip to strut bracket, then install wheel and tire assembly and lower vehicle.
8. Torque hub nut to 225 ft. lbs. on 1980-82 models and to 185 ft. lbs. on 1983-84 models.

1982 Cavalier, Cimarron, Firenza, 2000 & Skyhawk

NOTE: On models equipped with tri-pot joints on inboard axles, care must be taken not to over extend joints. When either or both ends are disconnected, over extending the tri-pot joint could result in internal joint separation.

Removal

1. Remove hub nut, then raise and support vehicle and remove wheel and tire assembly.
2. On vehicles equipped with ball type constant velocity inboard joints, Fig. 6, install axle shaft boot seal protector J-28712, Fig. 3, on inboard and outboard seals. On vehicles equipped with tri-pot inboard joints, Fig. 7, install axle boot seal protector J-28712 on outboard seal and J-33162 on inboard seal, Fig. 3.
3. Remove disc brake caliper, rotor and caliper support.

NOTE: Prior to beginning next step, it is suggested to mark cam bolt to ensure proper camber alignment during installation.

4. Remove strut to steering knuckle attaching bolts, then seperate steering knuckle from strut bracket.
5. Using tool J-28468 or J-33008 with extension J-29794, remove axle shaft from transaxle, Fig. 3.
6. Using tool J-28733, remove axle shaft from hub and bearing assembly.

Installation

1. Loosely install drive axle to steering knuckle and transaxle.
2. Loosely attach steering knuckle to strut bracket.
3. Remove one hub to steering knuckle attaching bolt and install a longer bolt through hub cutout to prevent hub from turning. Install hub nut and washer and torque to 70 ft. lbs.
4. Remove long bolt and install original hub and bearing to steering knuckle attaching bolt. Torque bolts to 63 ft. lbs.
5. Install disc brake caliper and rotor. Torque caliper attaching bolts to 21-35 ft. lbs.
6. Using a screwdriver in groove provided on inner retainer, install axle shaft into transaxle, Fig. 3. Tap on screwdriver until axle shaft is seated in transaxle.
7. Torque steering knuckle to strut bracket attaching bolts to 140 ft. lbs.
8. Install wheel and tire and lower vehicle.
9. Torque hub nut to 185 ft. lbs.

RIGHT HAND DRIVE AXLE, OUTPUT SHAFT & SEAL, REPLACE

1979-84 Eldorado, Riviera & Toronado; 1980-84 Seville

Removal
1. Disconnect battery ground cable.

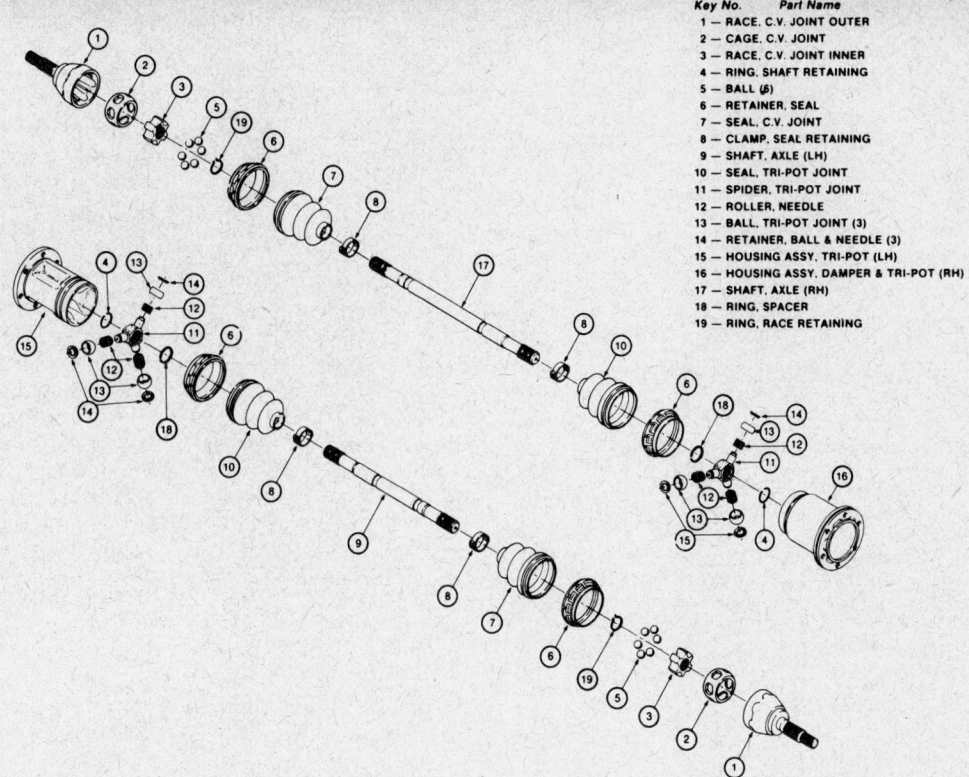

Key No.   Part Name
1 — RACE, C.V. JOINT OUTER
2 — CAGE, C.V. JOINT
3 — RACE, C.V. JOINT INNER
4 — RING, SHAFT RETAINING
5 — BALL (6)
6 — RETAINER, SEAL
7 — SEAL, C.V. JOINT
8 — CLAMP, SEAL RETAINING
9 — SHAFT, AXLE (LH)
10 — SEAL, TRI-POT JOINT
11 — SPIDER, TRI-POT JOINT
12 — ROLLER, NEEDLE
13 — BALL, TRI-POT JOINT (3)
14 — RETAINER, BALL & NEEDLE (3)
15 — HOUSING ASSY, TRI-POT (LH)
16 — HOUSING ASSY, DAMPER & TRI-POT (RH)
17 — SHAFT, AXLE (RH)
18 — RING, SPACER
19 — RING, RACE RETAINING

Fig. 5   Exploded view of drive axle. 1979—84, Eldorado, Riviera & Toronado late type. 1980—84 Seville

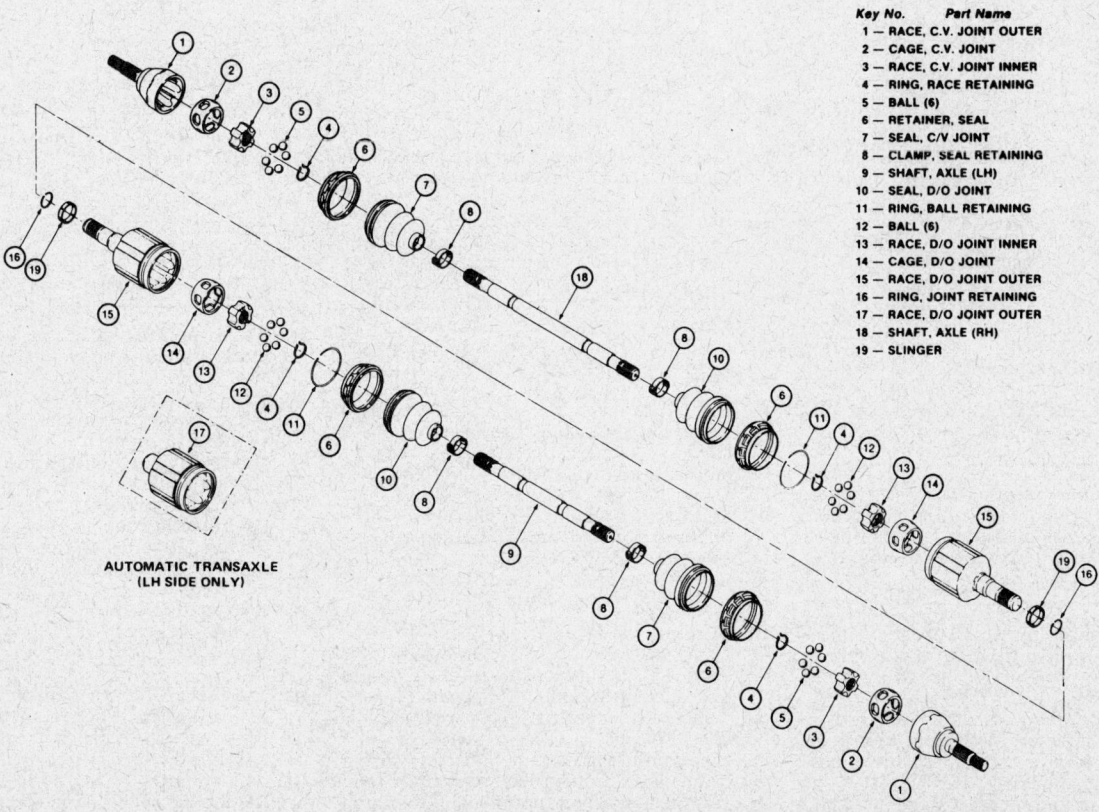

Key No.   Part Name
1 — RACE, C.V. JOINT OUTER
2 — CAGE, C.V. JOINT
3 — RACE, C.V. JOINT INNER
4 — RING, RACE RETAINING
5 — BALL (6)
6 — RETAINER, SEAL
7 — SEAL, C/V JOINT
8 — CLAMP, SEAL RETAINING
9 — SHAFT, AXLE (LH)
10 — SEAL, D/O JOINT
11 — RING, BALL RETAINING
12 — BALL (6)
13 — RACE, D/O JOINT INNER
14 — CAGE, D/O JOINT
15 — RACE, D/O JOINT OUTER
16 — RING, JOINT RETAINING
17 — RACE, D/O JOINT OUTER
18 — SHAFT, AXLE (RH)
19 — SLINGER

AUTOMATIC TRANSAXLE
(LH SIDE ONLY)

Fig. 6   Exploded view of drive axle with ball type constant velocity inboard joint. 1980—84 Citation, Omega, Phoenix & Skylark;
1982—84 Cavalier, Celebrity, Century, Cimarron, Cutlass Ciera, Firenza, 2000, Skyhawk & 6000

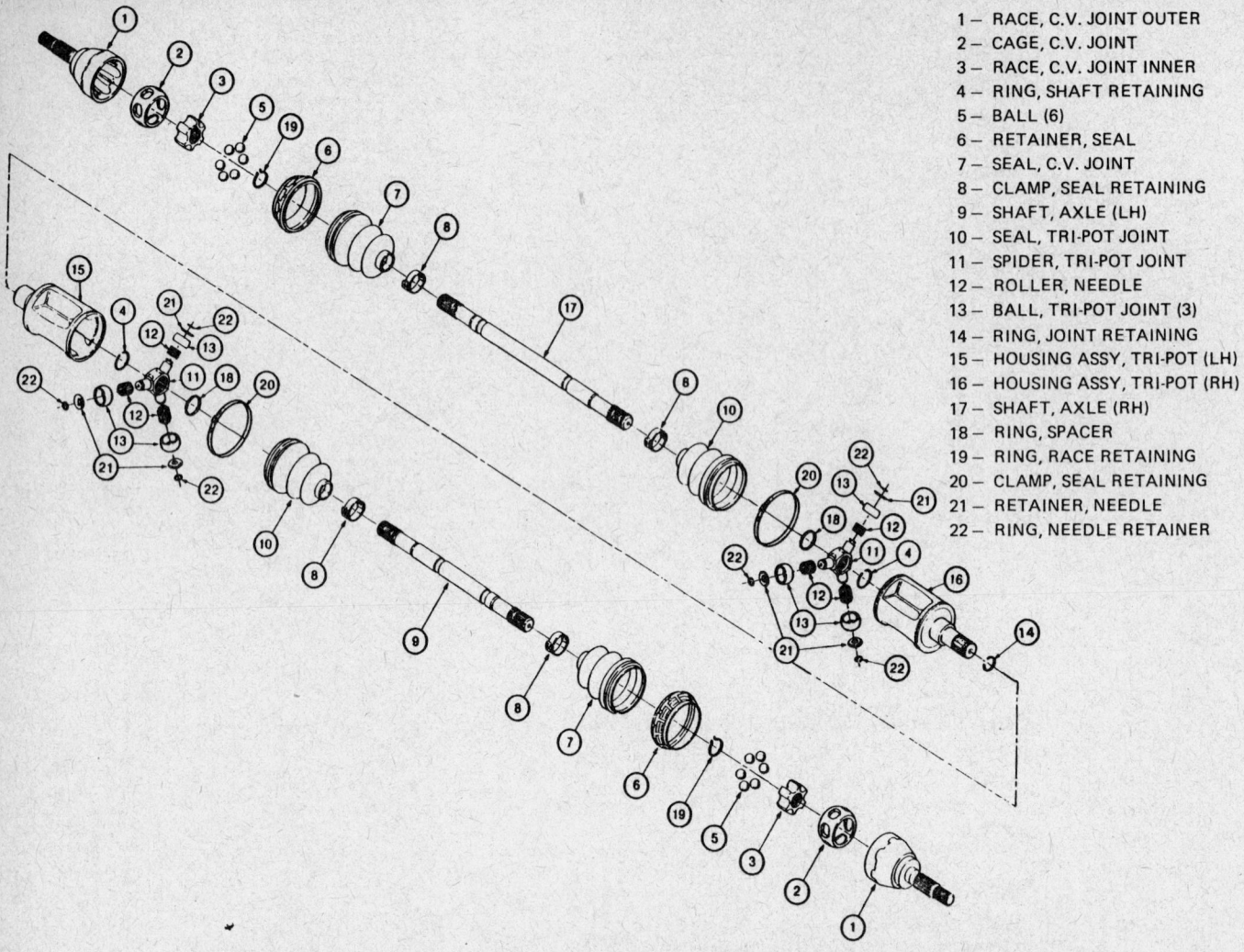

1 — RACE, C.V. JOINT OUTER
2 — CAGE, C.V. JOINT
3 — RACE, C.V. JOINT INNER
4 — RING, SHAFT RETAINING
5 — BALL (6)
6 — RETAINER, SEAL
7 — SEAL, C.V. JOINT
8 — CLAMP, SEAL RETAINING
9 — SHAFT, AXLE (LH)
10 — SEAL, TRI-POT JOINT
11 — SPIDER, TRI-POT JOINT
12 — ROLLER, NEEDLE
13 — BALL, TRI-POT JOINT (3)
14 — RING, JOINT RETAINING
15 — HOUSING ASSY, TRI-POT (LH)
16 — HOUSING ASSY, TRI-POT (RH)
17 — SHAFT, AXLE (RH)
18 — RING, SPACER
19 — RING, RACE RETAINING
20 — CLAMP, SEAL RETAINING
21 — RETAINER, NEEDLE
22 — RING, NEEDLE RETAINER

Fig. 7 Exploded view of drive axle with tri-pot inboard joint. 1980—84 Citation, Omega, Phoenix & Skylark; 1982—84 Cavalier, Celebrity, Century, Cimarron, Cutlass Ciera, Firenza, 2000, Skyhawk & 6000

2. Raise front of vehicle and place jack stands under front frame horns.
3. Remove wheel and tire assembly.
4. Remove cotter pin, nut and shield from tie rod pivot, then using puller J-24319, detach tie rod end from steering knuckle.
5. Install drive shaft seal protector J-28712, then remove cotter pin, nut and washer from drive axle, then remove six screws attaching drive axle to output shaft.

NOTE: To prevent axle shaft from rotating when removing nut or attaching screws, insert a drift through opening on top of caliper into corresponding rotor vane.

6. Remove cotter pin and nut from upper ball joint stud nut, then remove brake hose clip from stud and loosely reinstall nut.
7. Using a hammer and brass drift, rap on steering knuckle to free upper ball joint stud. Use care not to damage brake hose or steering knuckle.
8. Remove nut and separate upper ball joint from steering knuckle.
9. Guide drive axle out of steering knuckle and remove from vehicle.

10. Remove two screws attaching battery cable retainer to support and remove two screws attaching output support to engine, then rotate support downward.
11. Remove front nut and bolt from right hand frame brace, then pivot brace outward to provide clearance.
12. Using a plastic mallet, drive on flange end of output shaft until shaft releases from retaining ring, then remove output shaft and support. Use care not to damage output shaft seal surfaces or splines.
13. Using a suitable pry bar, pry output shaft seal out of housing. Pry at two or three different places to avoid cocking seal. Use care not to damage housing.

Installation

1. Using tool No. J-28518, install output shaft seal. Rotate tool to maintain proper alignment when installing seal.
2. Apply wheel bearing grease between lips of seal.
3. Index splines of output shaft with splines of side gear in final drive assembly, then install shaft by tapping on flange end with a soft faced mallet until retaining ring snaps into shaft groove. Ensure shaft is securely locked into position.

NOTE: When installing output shaft, use care not to damage seal.

4. Align output shaft support and engine block attaching screw holes, then install two support attaching screws. Torque screws to 50 ft. lbs.
5. Install two screws attaching battery cable retainer to support.
6. Guide drive axle into position and install splined end axle into steering knuckle.
7. Position upper ball joint stud into steering knuckle, then place brake hose clip on stud and install stud nut. Torque stud nut to 60 ft. lbs., then install cotter pin. The nut may be tightened an additional 1/6 turn to align cotter pin slots.
8. Install six screws attaching output shaft to drive axle. Torque screws to 60 ft. lbs.
9. Install drive axle washer, nut, retainer and cotter pin. Torque nut to 175 ft. lbs. Align cotter pin slot by rotating retainer and bend cotter pin so that retainer is held snugly.
10. Install tie rod pivot on steering knuckle. Torque nut to 44 ft. lbs. The nut may be tightened an additional 1/6 turn to align cotter pin slots.

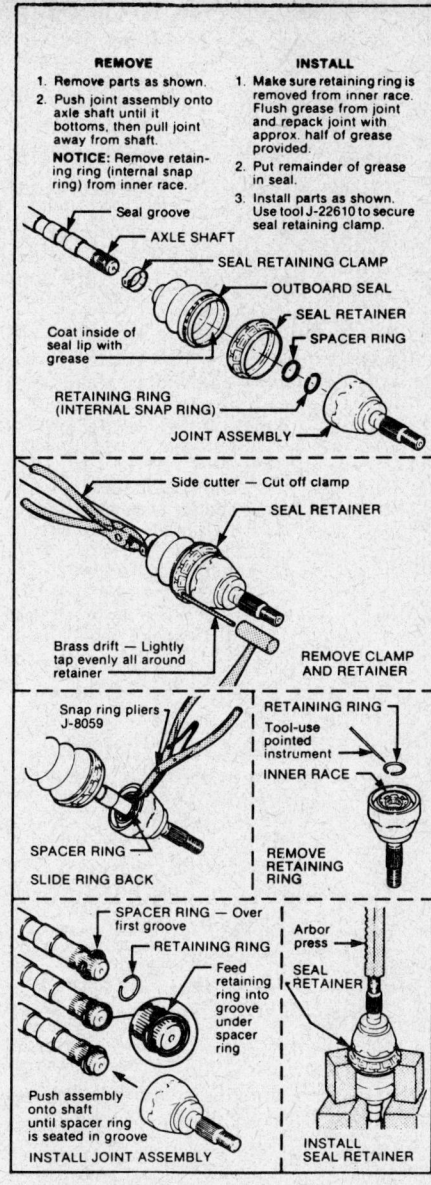

Fig. 8 Outer constant velocity joint seal removal & installation. 1979 Eldorado, Riviera & Toronado early type

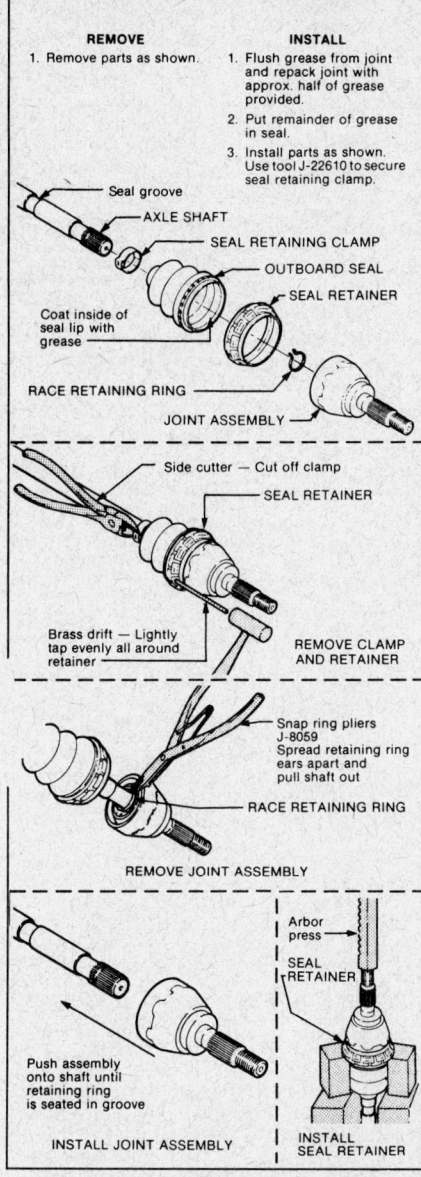

Fig. 9 Outer constant velocity joint seal removal & installation. 1979–84 Eldorado, Riviera, Toronado late type & 1980–84 All models

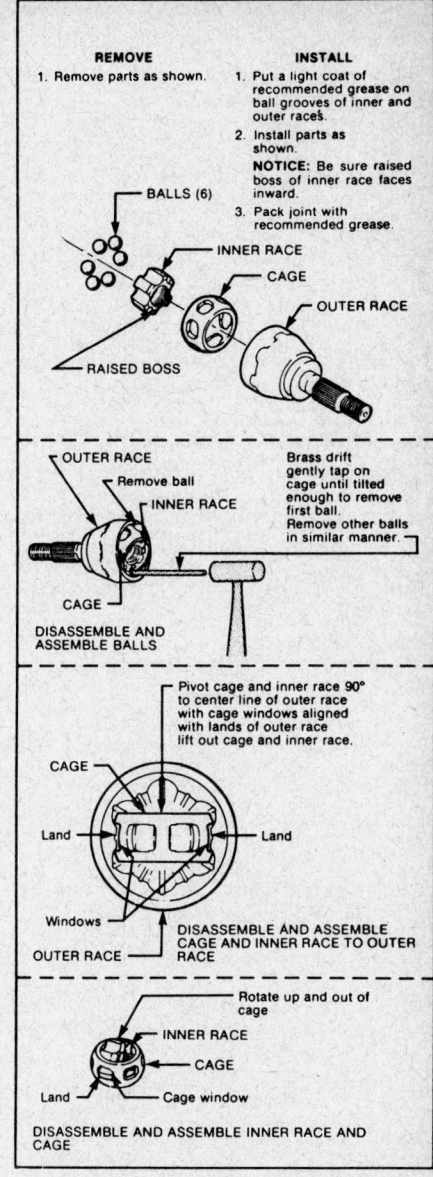

Fig. 10 Outer constant velocity joint disassembly & assembly. 1979–84 All models

11. Install right hand frame brace bolt and nut. Torque belt to 50 ft. lbs.
12. Install front wheel and tire assembly, then lower vehicle and connect battery ground cable.
13. Check output shaft seal for leakage.

LEFT HAND DRIVE AXLE, OUTPUT SHAFT & SEAL, REPLACE

1979–84 Eldorado, Riviera & Toronado; 1980–84 Seville

Removal
1. Raise front of vehicle and place jack stands under front frame horns.
2. Remove wheel and tire assembly.

3. Remove cotter pin, nut and shield from tie rod pivot, then using puller J-24319, detach tie rod end from steering knuckle.
4. Remove cotter pin, nut and washer from drive axle, then remove six screws attaching drive axle to output shaft.

NOTE: To prevent drive axle from rotating when removing nut or attaching screws, insert a drift through opening on top of caliper into corresponding rotor vane.

5. Remove cotter pin and nut from upper ball joint stud nut, then remove brake hose clip from stud and loosely reinstall nut.
6. Using a hammer and brass drift, rap on steering knuckle to free upper ball joint stud. Use care not to damage brake hose or steering knuckle.

7. Remove nut and separate upper ball joint from steering knuckle.
8. Guide drive axle out of steering knuckle and remove from vehicle.
9. Remove front nut and bolt from left hand frame brace, then pivot brace outward to provide clearance.
10. Using a hammer and brass drift, drive on flange end of output shaft until shaft releases from retaining ring, then remove output shaft.
11. Using a suitable pry bar, pry output shaft seal from housing. Pry at two or three locations to avoid cocking seal. Use care not to damage housing.

Installation
1. Using tool No. J-28518, install output shaft seal. Rotate tool to maintain proper alignment when installing seal.
2. Apply wheel bearing grease between lips of seal.

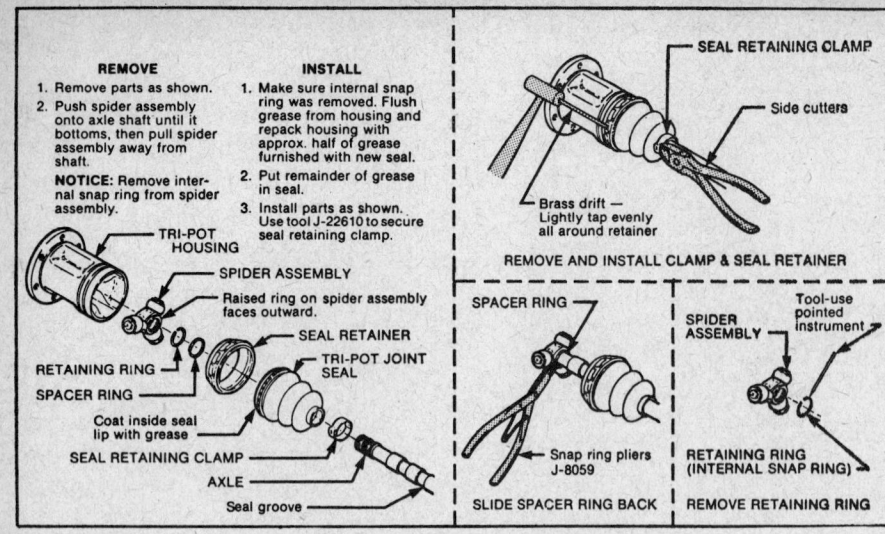

Fig. 11 Inner tri-pot seal removal & installation. 1979 Eldorado, Riviera & Toronado early type

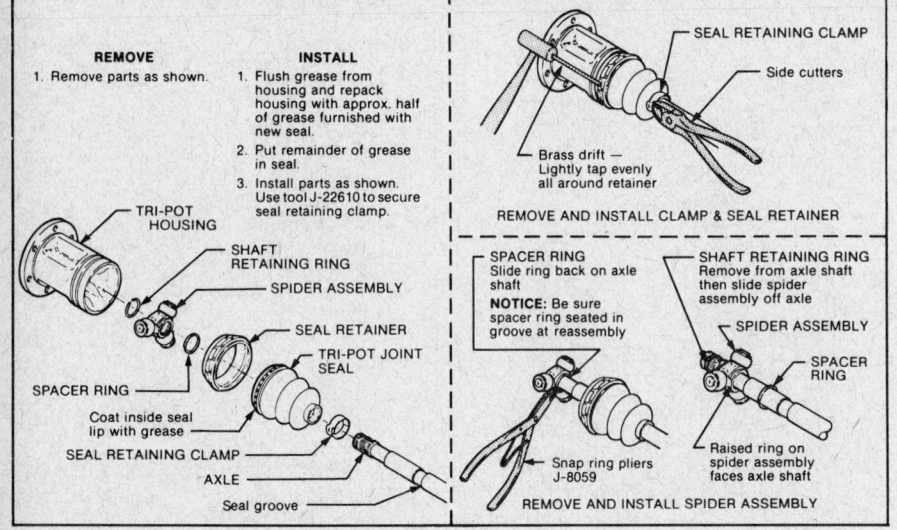

Fig. 12 Inner tri-pot seal removal & installation. 1979—84 Eldorado, Riviera & Toronado late type. 1980—84 Seville

3. Index splines of output shaft with splines of side gear in final drive assembly then install shaft by tapping center of flange end with a soft faced mallet until retaining ring snaps into shaft groove. Ensure shaft is securely locked into position.

NOTE: When installing output shaft, use care not to damage seal.

4. Guide drive axle into position and install splined end into steering knuckle.
5. Position upper ball joint stud into steering knuckle, then place brake hose clip on stud and install nut. Torque nut to 60 ft. lbs., then install cotter pin. The nut may be tightened an additional 1/6 turn to align cotter pin slots.
6. Install six screws attaching output shaft to drive axle. Torque screws to 60 ft. lbs.
7. Install drive axle water nut, retainer and cotter pin. Torque nut to 175 ft. lbs. and bend cotter pin so that retainer is held snugly.
8. Install tie rod pivot on steering knuckle. Torque nut to 44 ft. lbs. The nut may be tightened an additional 1/6 turn to align cotter pin slots.
9. Install left hand frame brace bolt and nut. Torque bolt to 50 ft. lbs.
10. Install wheel and tire assembly, then lower vehicle and check output shaft seal for leakage.

RIGHT HAND OUTPUT SHAFT SUPPORT BEARING, REPLACE

1979—84 Eldorado, Riviera & Toronado; 1980—84 Seville

1. Remove right hand output shaft as described under Right Hand Drive Axle, Output Shaft and Seal, Replace.
2. Remove three screws securing bearing retainer to support.
3. Install tool No. J-22912 between flange end of output shaft and flat area of shaft support, with flat surface of tool against flat area of shaft support. Position assembly on a suitable press and press shaft support, bearing, retainer and slinger from output shaft.
4. Remove bearing from output shaft support.
5. Lubricate output shaft support and bearing, then position bearing into support.
6. Pack bearing with wheel bearing grease, then install retainer and three attaching screws.
7. Place assembled components and slinger on output shaft, then position components and output shaft on a press. Using a standard 1¼ in. inside diameter pipe, press bearing and assembled components onto shaft.
8. Check to ensure bearing and support rotate smoothly, then install right hand output shaft.

OUTER CONSTANT VELOCITY JOINT & SEAL, REPLACE

1979—84 Eldorado, Riviera Toronado; 1980—84 Seville, Citation, Omega, Phoenix & Skylark; 1982—84 Cavalier, Celebrity, Century, Cimarron, Cutlass Ciera, Firenza, 2000, Skyhawk & 6000

For removal and installation procedures refer to Figs. 8, 9 and 10.

INNER TRI-POT SEAL, REPLACE

1979—84 Eldorado, Riviera & Toronado; 1980—84 Seville

For removal and installation procedures refer to Figs. 11 and 12.

1980—84 Citation, Omega, Phoenix & Skylark; 1982—84 Cavalier, Celebrity, Century, Cimarron, Cutlass Ciera, Firenza, 2000, Skyhawk & 6000

For removal and installation procedures, refer to Fig. 13.

INNER CONSTANT JOINT & SEAL, REPLACE

1980—84 Citation, Omega, Phoenix & Skylark; 1982—84 Cavalier, Celebrity, Century, Cimarron, Cutlass Ciera, Firenza, 2000, Skyhawk & 6000

For removal and installation procedures, refer to Figs. 14 and 15.

FINAL DRIVE, REPLACE

1980—84 Citation, Omega, Phoenix & Skylark; 1982—84 Cavalier, Celebrity, Century, Cimarron, Cutlass Ciera, Firenza, 2000, Skyhawk & 6000

On these models, the final drive unit is an integral component of the transaxle assembly.

1979—84 Eldorado, Riviera & Toronado; 1980—84 Seville

1. Disconnect battery ground cable.
2. Raise front of vehicle and position jack stands under front frame horns.
3. Remove right and left hand frame brace front attaching bolts, then position braces to provide clearance.
4. Position drain pan under final drive cover, then loosen cover and allow lubricant to drain.
5. Remove final drive cover attaching screws, cover and gasket.
6. Remove screws attaching right and left output shafts to drive axles. Separate output shaft flanges from drive axles to permit clearance of final drive assembly with shafts installed.
7. Remove two screws attaching battery cable retainer to right hand output shaft support, then remove two screws securing support to engine. Rotate support downward to provide clearance for removal.
8. Remove final drive to transmission attaching screws that secures rear of final drive shield, then loosen support bracket screw that secure front of shield and remove shield.
9. Remove five remaining final drive to transmission attaching screws.
10. Remove screws attaching final drive support bracket to engine block.
11. Using tool J-24319, disconnect steering linkage intermediate shaft from pitman and idler arms. Push linkage forward to ensure adequate clearance for final drive assembly removal.
12. Slide final drive assembly forward, off transmission splined shaft and remove unit with output shafts attached. Use care not to damage output shaft seal or splines.
13. Reverse procedure to install. Torque final drive to transaxle attaching bolts to 30 ft. lbs., support bracket bolts to 50 ft. lbs. and output shaft to drive shaft attaching bolts to 60 ft. lbs.

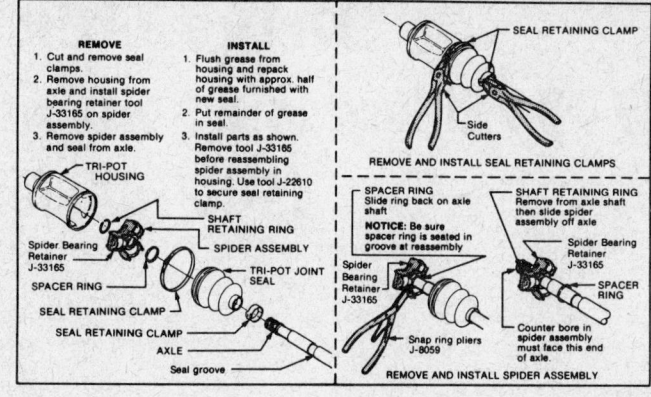

Fig. 13   Inner tri-pot seal removal & installation. 1980—84 Citation, Omega, Phoenix & Skylark; 1982—84 Cavalier, Celebrity, Century, Cimarron, Cutlass Ciera, Firenza, 2000, Skyhawk & 6000

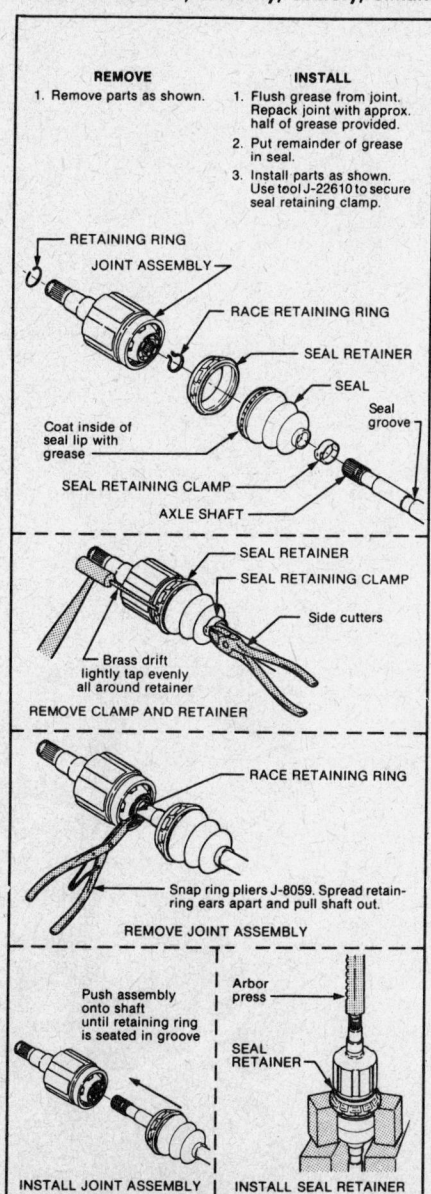

Fig. 14   Inner constant velocity joint seal removal & installation. 1980—84 Citation, Omega, Phoenix & Skylark; 1982—84 Cavalier, Celebrity, Century, Cimarron, Cutlass Ciera, Firenza, 2000, Skyhawk & 6000

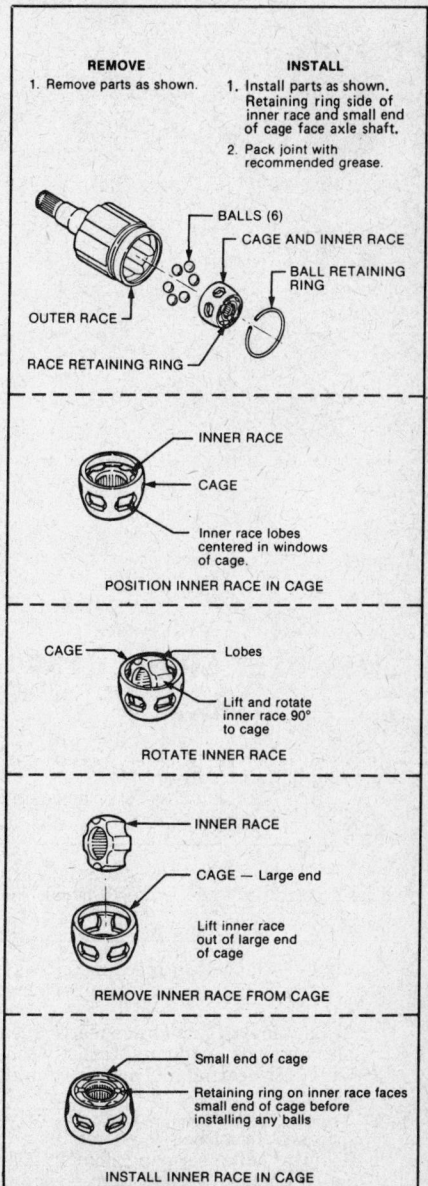

Fig. 15   Inner constant velocity joint removal & installation. 1980—84 Citation, Omega, Phoenix & Skylark; 1982—84 Cavalier, Celebrity, Century, Cimarron, Cutlass Ciera, Firenza, 2000, Skyhawk & 6000

Drive Link Belt
1977–84 Eldorado & Toronado; 1979–84 Riviera;
1980–84 Seville

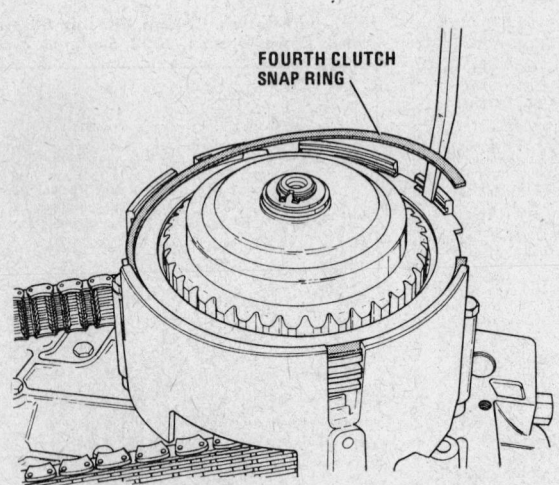

FOURTH CLUTCH SNAP RING

Fig. 1 Fourth gear clutch snap ring removal. 1982–84 models

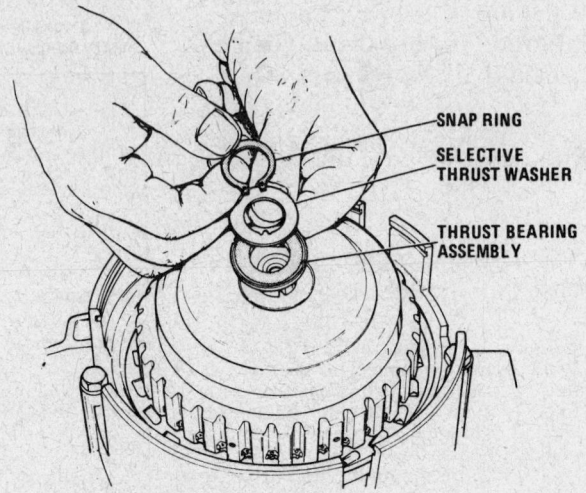

SNAP RING

SELECTIVE THRUST WASHER

THRUST BEARING ASSEMBLY

Fig. 2 Turbine shaft snap ring, selective thrust washer and thrust bearing assembly. 1982–84 models

LINK BELT SPROCKETS

Removal

After removal of transmission assembly, proceed as follows:

1. Remove sprocket housing cover attaching bolts, then cover.

NOTE: Do not hit the cover to remove it. Use a suitable putty knife to break the case to cover seal.

---

2. On 1982–84 models, proceed as follows:
   a. Remove fourth gear clutch snap ring, Fig. 1.
   b. Remove fourth gear clutch plates, then turbine shaft snap ring, thrust washer, thrust bearing and overdrive unit, Fig. 2.
   c. Remove overdrive carrier to drive sprocket thrust bearing assembly.
   d. Remove bolts securing fourth gear clutch housing to case, then housing.
   e. Remove clutch housing to case "O" ring.
3. On all models, remove sprocket bearing retaining snap rings from retaining grooves in support housings located under drive and driven sprockets, Fig. 3.

J-4646

Fig. 3 Removing or installing retaining snap rings. All models

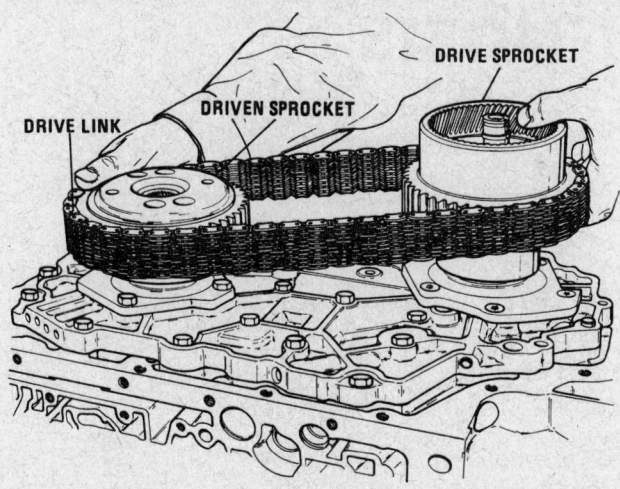

Fig. 4 Removing or installing sprockets and link assembly. All models

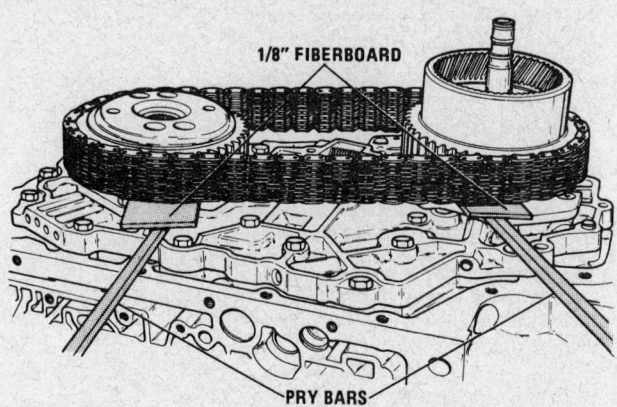

Fig. 5 Removing tight sprockets

THICKNESS	IDENTIFICATION NO. AND/OR COLOR
1.63mm - 1.73mm (0.063" - 0.067")	1 — Gray
1.81mm - 1.91mm (0.070" - 0.074")	2 — Dark Green
1.99mm - 2.09mm (0.077" - 0.081")	3 — Pink
2.17mm - 2.27mm (0.084" - 0.088")	4 — Brown
2.35mm - 2.45mm (0.091" - 0.095")	5 — Light Blue
2.53mm - 2.63mm (0.098" - 0.102")	6 — White
2.71mm - 2.81mm (0.105" - 0.109")	7 — Yellow
2.89mm - 2.99mm (0.112" - 0.116")	8 — Light Green
3.07mm - 3.17mm (0.119" - 0.123")	9 — Orange
3.25mm - 3.35mm (0.126" - 0.130")	10 — Violet
3.43mm - 3.53mm (0.133" - 0.137")	11 — Red
3.61mm - 3.71mm (0.140" - 0.144")	12 — Dark Blue

Fig. 6 Overdrive unit end play selective thrust washer thickness chart. 1982—84 models

NOTE: Do not attempt to remove snap rings from beneath sprockets. Leave snap rings in a loose position between sprockets and bearing assemblies.

4. Remove drive and driven sprockets, link belt, bearings and turbine shaft simultaneously by alternately pulling upwards on driven support housing, Fig. 4.

NOTE: If sprockets and link belt are difficult to remove, place a small piece of masonite or similiar material between the sprockets and pry bar. Alternately pry upward under each sprocket. Do not pry on chain links or aluminum case, Fig. 5.

5. Remove link belt from drive and driven sprockets.

Installation

1. Place link belt around drive and driven sprockets so links engage teeth of sprockets and colored guide link which has etched numerals is facing link cover.
2. Simultaneously position link belt, drive and driven sprockets into support housing, Fig. 4.
3. Install sprocket assembly to support housing snap rings.
4. On 1982—84 models, proceed as follows:
   a. Install new "O" ring in case.
   b. Position fourth gear clutch housing on case, then install retaining bolts and torque to 17 ft. lbs.
   c. Place overdrive carrier to drive support thrust bearing in position.
   d. Install overdive unit into fourth gear clutch housing, then thrust bearing, thrust washer and turbine shaft snap ring, Fig. 2.
   e. Lubricate clutch plates with transmission fluid, then install in the following order: 1 steel plate, 1 composition plate, 2 steel plates, 1 composition plate and 1 backing plate (micro-finish down).
   f. Install fourth gear clutch snap ring, Fig. 1.
   g. Position suitable dial indicator on turbine shaft end, then set indicator to zero. Move turbine shaft upward by pushing up from the convertor side. The overdrive unit end play should be .004 in. to .029 in. If overdrive unit is outside specifications, a corrective selective thrust washer should be chosen, Fig. 6, and installed as shown in Fig. 2.
5. On all models, install sprocket housing cover and gasket. Torque bolts to 8 ft. lbs. on 1978—81 models or 3 ft. lbs. on 1982—84 models.

GM ENGINE ELECTRICAL PLUG-IN DIAGNOSIS

1977–82 FULL SIZE MODELS EXCEPT CADILLAC

1977–82 full size models are equipped with two electrical diagnostic connectors, Figs. 1, 2 and 3. The A/C connector is located on top of the A/C module and the engine electrical connector is located on the left fender panel. The following diagnostic procedures require the use of a jumper wire and a voltmeter.

Engine Electrical Diagnosis

Some diagnostic connector wires are spliced into the individual unit feed wire, instead of being connected directly to the connector on the unit. The connector on the unit should be checked before starting a repair. The splice can be checked by connecting a voltmeter to the connector on the unit and the voltage should be the same as at the terminal at the diagnostic connector.

Cranking tests are performed with the engine at any temperature, however, if the engine is extremely hot or cold, the voltage readings obtained will be lower than specified. To determine which of the following problems apply, turn the ignition key to "Start".

   a. Poor cranking, or solenoid clicks or chatters.

   b. Solenoid makes no sound, no cranking.

   c. Starter runs (spins), engine does not crank.

For all cranking problems, check for a damaged battery, loose or corroded terminals and cables and repair as necessary. If satisfactory, check battery state of charge indicator or specific gravity. If state of charge indicator is "Green" or the specific gravity is 1.200 or more, select condition in the following charts and perform checks with a voltmeter. The parking brakes should be applied with automatic transmission in "Park" and manual transmission in "Neutral", clutch released and the ignition key in the "Start" position. If the state of charge indicator is "Dark" or the specific gravity is less than 1.200, charge battery and recheck condition. Check charging system condition and also for a battery drain.

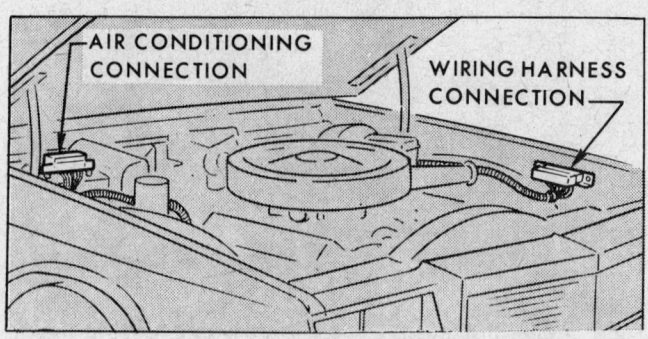

Fig. 1 Diagnostic connector location. 1977–82 models

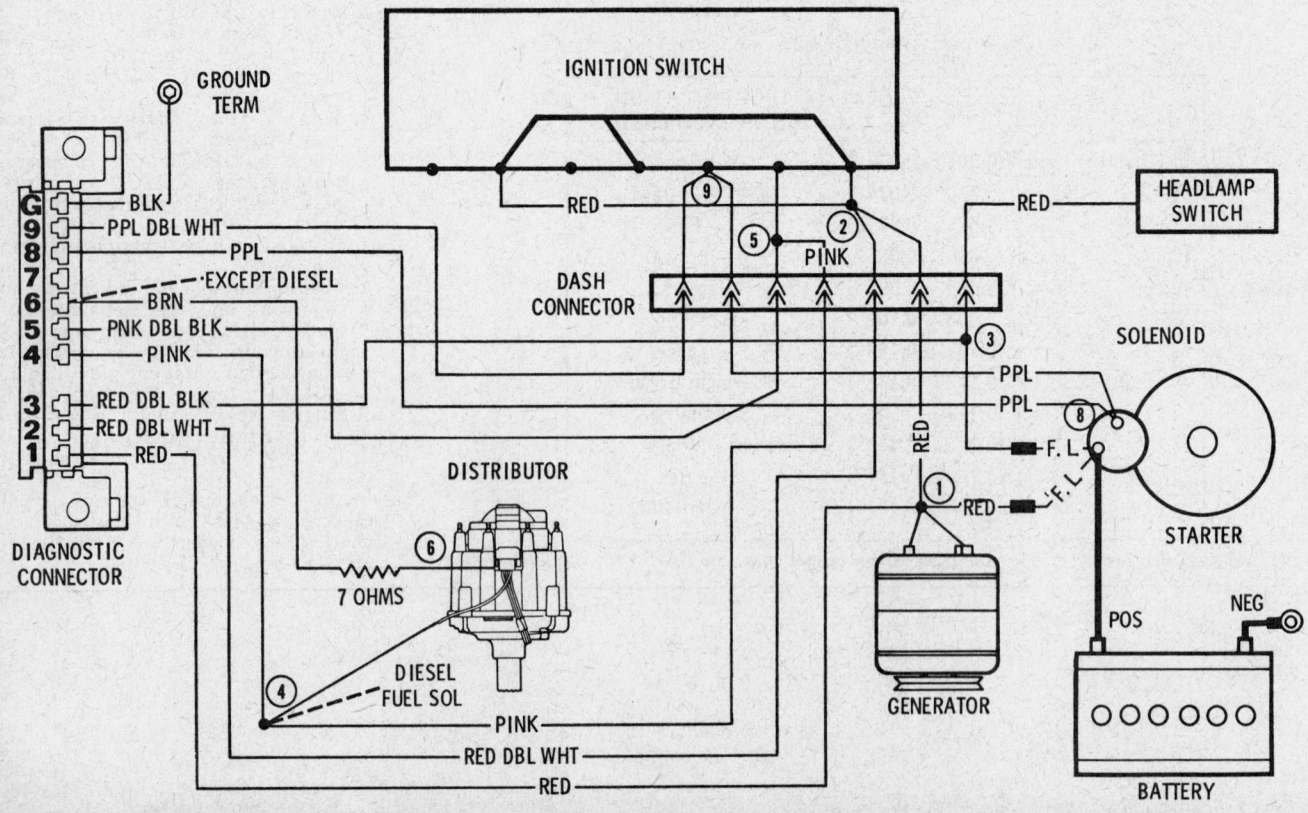

Fig. 2 Engine electrical wiring circuit. 1977–78 models

GM ENGINE ELECTRICAL PLUG-IN DIAGNOSIS

VOLTMETER CONNECTIONS	VOLTAGE READING	CORRECTION
POOR CRANKING, OR SOLENOID CLICKS OR CHATTERS		
1. 1 and G	9 volts or more	More voltmeter lead from G to engine block, key in "Start". 9 volts or more—Remove starter for repair. Under 9 volts—Check battery ground cable connections at engine block and at battery.
	Under 9 volts	Go to test 2.
2. Bat. Pos. and Bat. Neg. at battery	9.6 volts or more	Go to test 3.
	Under 9.6 volts	Perform battery load test. If OK, remove starter for repair.
3. Bat. Pos. at Battery and 1	.7 volts or more	Check positive cable terminals for clean, tight connections and condition of cable. Check fusible link (solenoid to generator harness).
	Under .7 volts	Check battery ground cable condition and connections.
SOLENOID MAKES NO SOUND—NO CRANKING		
1. 8 and G (Key in Start)	7 volts or more	Remove starter for repair.
	Under 7 volts	Go to test 2.
2. 1 and G	9 volts or more	Go to test 5.
	Under 9 volts	Go to test 3.
3. Bat. Pos. and Bat. Neg. at Battery	9.6 volts or more	Go to test 4.
	Under 9.6 volts	Perform battery load test. If OK, remove starter for repair.
4. Bat. Pos. at Battery and 1	.7 volts or more	Check positive cable terminals for clean, tight connections and condition of cable. Check fusible link (solenoid to generator harness).
	Under .7 volts	Check battery ground cable condition and connections.
5. 9 and G (Key in Start)	7 volts or more	Check purple wire from ignition switch through engine/generator to starter solenoid for open/loose connections.
	Under 7 volts	Go to test 6.
6. 2 and G	7 volts or more	Replace ignition switch.
	Under 7 volts	Check battery wire (red) from ignition switch through engine/generator dash connector to splice for open/loose connection.

GM ENGINE ELECTRICAL PLUG-IN DIAGNOSIS

VOLTMETER CONNECTIONS	VOLTAGE READING	CORRECTION

STARTER RUNS (SPINS), ENGINE DOES NOT CRANK

Check flywheel gear teeth. If OK, remove starter for repair.

IGNITION MISS OR WILL NOT START (CRANKS OK)

Make a secondary output check (except diesel) using a calibrated spark gap or out-put meter. HEI system should produce at least 25,000 volts (25KV) cranking or engine idling. If not, follow procedure below. If satisfactory, check spark plugs, spark plug cables, distributor cap and rotor.

If car will not start, make voltage checks cranking. If it will start, make checks running. Both cranking and running voltages are given.

VOLTMETER CONNECTIONS	VOLTS CRANKING	VOLTS IDLING
1. 6 and G (Except Diesel)	7 or more	9.6 or more—Check HEI distributor.
	Under 7	Under 9.6—Go to test 2.
2. 4 and G	7 or more	9.6 or more—7 volts or more at HEI battery terminal, check the HEI distributor (fuel solenoid on diesel).
	Under 7	Under 9.6—Go to test 3.
3. 5 and G	7 or more	9.6 or more—Check for open circuit or loose connection in wire from bat. terminal on distributor (fuel solenoid on diesel) through engine dash connector to ignition switch.
	Under 7	Under 9.6—Replace ignition switch.

ALTERNATOR WARNING LIGHT "ON" ENGINE RUNNING

1. Check alternator belt, adjust or replace as needed.
2. Check gauges/trans. fuse, if blown check for short circuit in pink dbl. wht. str. wire from fuse panel to instrument cluster and/or trunk release.
3. Remove 2 wire connector from alternator, if warning light turns off remove alternator for repair. If warning light stays on, check for short circuit in brown wire from alternator connector through engine dash connector to instrument cluster connector (alternator warning, light circuit).

LOW BATTERY, BUT ALTERNATOR LIGHT INDICATES NO PROBLEM

1. Adjust or replace alternator belt as needed.
2. Charge battery.
3. Run engine at 1500 to 2000 RPM for one minute with lights on high beam, heater on high, radio and defogger blower on.

1 and G	Under 12.5 volts	Remove alternator for repair.
	12.5 volts or more	Check for battery drain and driving habits. If no defect is found, make alternator output check.

OVERCHARGING

1. Connect voltmeter to terminal 1 and G. Run engine at 1500 to 2000 RPM until voltmeter reaches maximum, do NOT run engine more than one minute.

1 and G	15.5 or more	Remove alternator for repair.
	Under 15.5 volts	Check for extended driving conditions in hot weather.

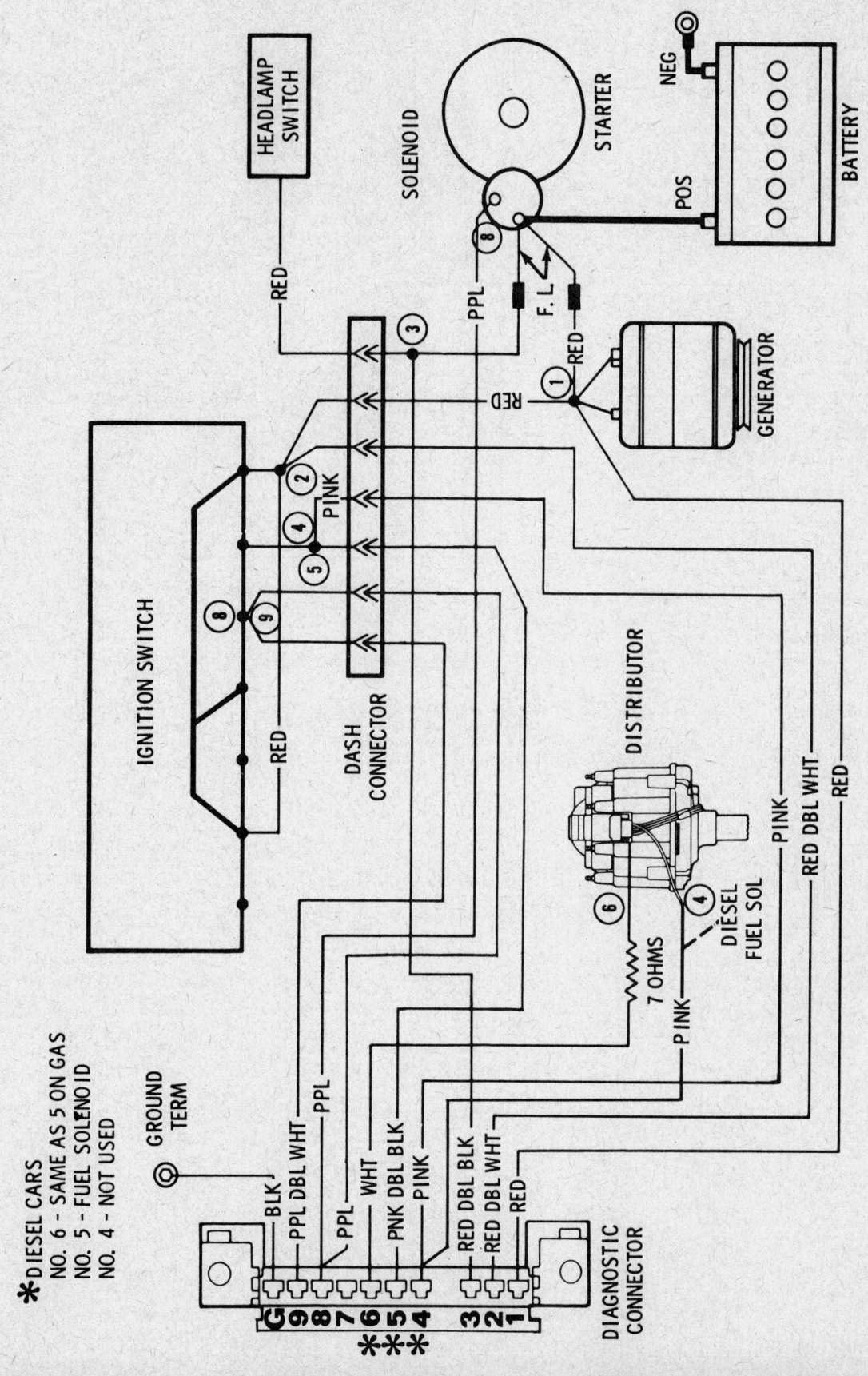

Fig. 3   Engine electrical wiring circuit. 1979–82 models

GM ENGINE ELECTRICAL PLUG-IN DIAGNOSIS

1977—82 CHEV. CHEVETTE & 1981—82 PONT. 1000

Electrical Diagnosis

This vehicle is equipped with either one or two "Master Electrical Connectors," Fig. 4. One connector is the "Engine Electrical Master Diagnostic Connector" and the other is the "Air Conditioning Electrical Master Diagnostic Connector." These connectors are used to diagnose electrical malfunctions in the air conditioning, charging, cranking and ignition systems.

CAUTION: When performing any of the following tests, ensure transmission is in Neutral on manual transmission models or Park on automatic transmission models. Also, fully apply the parking brake.

Engine Electrical Diagnostic Tests, Fig. 5

NOTE: The following tests are performed with a 14 gauge jumper wire and the ignition switch in the "Off" position.

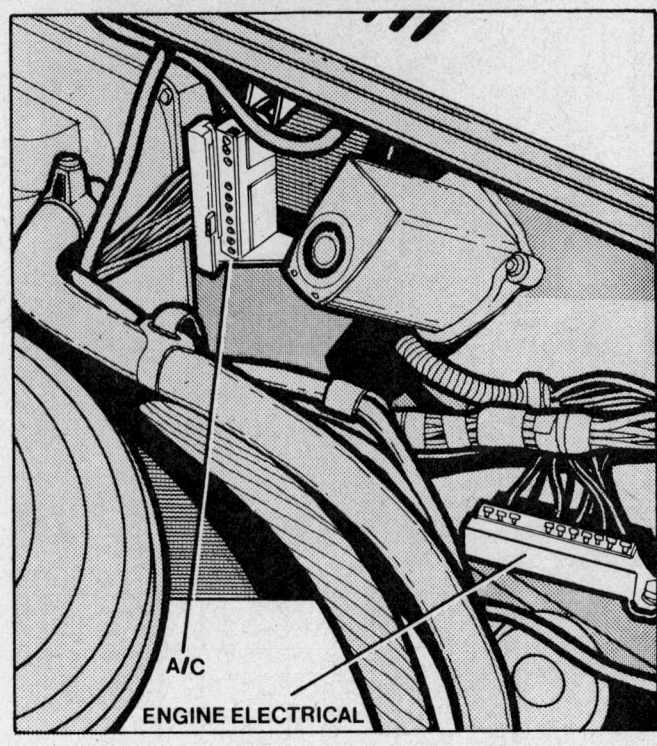

Fig. 4 Master electrical diagnostic connector locations

Starter Does Not Crank Or Cranks Slowly

Test T-1
1. Connect jumper wire between terminal Nos. 1 and 8.
2. If malfunction remains there may be an open wire between terminal No. 8 and the starter solenoid "S" terminal, a faulty connection at the starter solenoid "S" terminal or a poor connection at battery or starter. If the wiring and connections are satisfactory, the starter solenoid may be defective.
3. If starter cranks in step 1, proceed to Test T-2.

Test T-2
1. Connect jumper wire between terminals Nos. 1 and 9.
2. If malfunction remains, the neutral starter switch may be defective or faulty neutral starter switch wiring.
3. If starter cranks in step 1, the ignition switch may be defective or improperly connected.

Engine Cranks But Will Not Start

Test T-3
1. Check for ignition output by removing a spark plug wire, insert an extension into the boot and crank engine while holding the spark plug wire with insulated pliers approximately 1/4 inch (6 mm) from engine block.
2. If spark is noted in step 1, the malfunction is not in ignition system (excluding the spark plugs).
3. If no spark occurs in step 1, proceed to Test T-4.

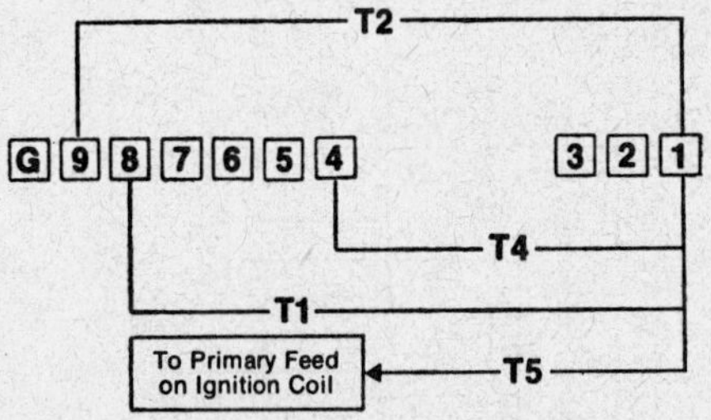

Test T-4
1. Connect jumper wire between terminals Nos. 1 and 4 and crank engine.
2. If engine starts, the ignition switch may be defective or not connected properly.
3. If engine does not start in step 1, proceed to Test T-5.

Test T-5
1. Connect jumper wire between terminal No. 1 and the ignition coil primary feed terminal and crank engine.
2. If engine starts, there is an open wire between test terminal No. 4 and the coil or a faulty coil connection.
3. If engine does not start, the H.E.I. system is malfunctioning.

Fig. 5 Engine electrical diagnostic test connections

Flasher Locations

Car	1977 TSF	1977 HWF	1978 TSF	1978 HWF	1979 TSF	1979 HWF	1980 TSF	1980 HWF	1981 TSF	1981 HWF	1982 TSF	1982 HWF	1983 TSF	1983 HWF	1984 TSF	1984 HWF
American Motors	3	(7)	3	(2)	3	3	12	3	12	3	12	3	12	3	12	3
Astre & Vega	5	3	—	—	—	—	—	—	—	—	—	—	—	—	—	—
Buick, Regal, Riviera & 1977–81 Century	4	3	3	3	3	3	3	3	3	3	3	3	3	3	3	3
Buick Skylark & 1982–84 Century	10	3	10	3	10	3	6	15	6	15	6	15	6	15	6	15
Cadillac Brougham & DeVille	3	3	3	3	3	3	6	4	6	4	6	4	6	4	6	4
Cadillac Seville & Eldorado	4(8)	3	4(8)	3	3	3	6	4	6	4	6	4	6	4	6	4
Camaro & Firebird	4	3	4	3	4	3	4	3	4	3	6	6	6	6	6	6
Capri & Mustang	7	7	7	7	4	4	14	4	14	4	14	4	14	4	14	4
Cavalier, Cimarron, 2000, 1982–84 Skyhawk, Firenza & 1984 Sunbird	—	—	—	—	—	—	—	—	—	—	5	3	5	3	5	3
Chevelle, Malibu & Monte Carlo	4	3	3	3	3	3	3	3	3	3	3	3	3	3	3	3
Chevette & 1000	13	3	13	3	13	3	13	3	13	3	13	3	13	3	13	3
Chevrolet Full Size	3	3	3	3	3	3	3	3	3	3	3	3	3	3	3	3
Chevrolet Citation & Celebrity	—	—	—	—	—	—	6	15	6	15	6	15	6	15	6	15
Chevrolet Nova	10	3	10	3	10	3	—	—	—	—	—	—	—	—	—	—
Chrysler, Imperial & 1977–81 LeBaron	5(12)	3	5(12)	3	7(12)	6(12)	7(12)	6(12)	7(12)	6(12)	3	3	3	3	3	3
Chrysler E Class, Excutive, 1982–84 LeBaron & 1983–84 New Yorker	—	—	—	—	—	—	—	—	—	—	4	5	4	5	4	5
Chrysler Laser	—	—	—	—	—	—	—	—	—	—	—	—	—	—	—	—
Comet & Maverick	4	3	—	—	—	—	—	—	—	—	—	—	—	—	—	—
Cordoba & Mirada	13	(4)	14	4	9	3	5	5	5	5	3	3	3	3	3	3
Corvette	16	3	16	3	3	3	3	3	3	3	3	3	—	—	7	7
Cougar, LTD II & Thunderbird	4	4	4	4	4	4	4	4	4	(14)	4	(14)	4	4	4	4
Dodge & Plymouth Full Size	5	3	5	3	7	6	7	6	7	6	—	—	—	—	—	—
Dodge & Plymouth Intermed.	(9)	3(10)	(9)	3	(1)	3	3	3	3	3	3	3	3	3	3	3
Dodge Aries, 400, 600 & Plymouth Reliant	—	—	—	—	—	—	—	—	3	3	4	5	4	5	4	5
Dodge Daytona	—	—	—	—	—	—	—	—	—	—	—	—	—	—	—	—
Horizon, Omni & 1983–84 Charger & Turismo	—	—	3	3	3	3	3	3	3	3	3	3	3	3	3	3
Escort, EXP, LN7 & Lynx	—	—	—	—	—	—	—	—	4	5	4	5	4	5	4	5
Ford & Mercury Full Size	3	4	3	3	3	3	5	5	5	5	5	5	5	5	5	5
Fairmont, Zephyr & 1983–84 LTD & Marquis	—	—	14	11	14	11	4	4	4	14	4	14	4	14	4	14
Ford Pinto & Mercury Bobcat	11	11	11	11	6	6	6	6	—	—	—	—	—	—	—	—
Ford Tempo & Mercury Topaz	—	—	—	—	—	—	—	—	—	—	—	—	—	—	5	5
Granada, Monarch & Versailles	10	4	10	4	10	4	10	4	4	14	4	14	—	—	—	—
Grand Am, Grand Prix, LeMans & 1982–84 Bonneville	3(6)	3	3	3	3	3	3	3	3	3	3	3	3	3	3	3
Lincoln	10(5)	3	10(5)	3	3(3)	3	5	5	5	5	5(15)	5(15)	5(15)	5(15)	5	5
Monza, Starfire, 1977–80 Skyhawk & Sunbird	12	12	12(11)	4	12(11)	4	12	4	—	—	—	—	—	—	—	—
Oldsmobile	3	3	3	3	3	3	3	3	3	3	3	3	3	3	3	3
Oldsmobile Cutlass (Exc. Ciera & 1984 Cruiser)	4	3	3	3	3	3	3	3	3	3	3	3	3	3	3	3
Olds. Omega, Cutlass Ciera & 1984 Cruiser	10	3	10	3	10	3	6	15	6	15	6	15	6	15	6	15
Oldsmobile Toronado	4	3	4	3	3	3	3	3	3	3	6	4	6	4	6	4
Pontiac Full Size, 1977–81, 1983–84	3	3	3	3	3	3	3	3	3	3	—	—	3	3	3	3
Pont. Phoenix, Ventura & 6000	10	3	10	3	10	3	6	15	6	15	6	15	6	15	6	15
Pontiac Fiero	—	—	—	—	—	—	—	—	—	—	—	—	—	—	5	16

TSF: Turn Signal Flasher.   HWF: Hazard Warning Flasher.

①—Location 9 on Magnum. Location 3 on Aspen, Diplomat & Volaré.
②—Location 3 on Concord & Gremlin. Location 4 on Matador. Location 5 on Pacer.
③—Location 10 on Mark V.
④—On right side of brake pedal support.
⑤—Location 3 on Mark V.
⑥—Location 4 on LeMans.
⑦—Location 6 on Gremlin & Hornet. Location 4 on Matador. Location 5 on Pacer.
⑧—On underside of steering column cover on Eldorado models.
⑨—Location 3 on Aspen, Diplomat & Volaré. Location 13 on Charger, Fury, Magnum & Monaco.
⑩—On right side of brake pedal support on Charger, Fury & Monaco.
⑪—Location 5 on Monza "S" Coupe, Sunbird Coupe & all Sta. Wag.
⑫—Location 3 on LeBaron. Location 5 on Imperial.
⑬—Location 3 on Eldorado.
⑭—Location 14 on Cougar. Location 4 on Cougar XR-7 & Thunderbird.
⑮—Location 4 on Lincoln Continental.

1984 CARBURETOR ADJUSTMENT SPECIFICATIONS

The following carburetor specifications are the latest additions to the "Carburetor Chapter". Refer to the "Carburetor Chapter," page 3—140 for the location of adjustments.

CARTER YF & YFA SERIES ADJUSTMENT SPECIFICATIONS

Year	Carb. Model No.	Float Level	Float Drop	Fast Idle Cam Setting	Dechoke or Unloader Setting	Pulldown Setting	Choke Setting
AMERICAN MOTORS							
1984	7452	.600	—	.175	.280	—	—
	7453	.600	—	.175	.280	—	—
	7454	.600	—	.175	.280	—	—
	7455	.600	—	.175	.280	—	—

HOLLEY MODEL 6510-C ADJUSTMENT SPECIFICATIONS

Year	Carb. Model No.	Float Level	Float Drop	Fast Idle Cam	Vacuum Break	Unloader	Choke Coil	Secondary Throttle Stop Screw
1984	14068690	.500	—	.080	.270	.350	—	①
	14068691	.500	—	.080	.270	.350	—	①
	14068692	.500	—	.080	.300	.350	—	①

①—Refer to text for procedure.

HOLLEY MODEL 6520 ADJUSTMENT SPECIFICATIONS

Year	Model No.	Float Level	Float Drop	Acc. Pump Hole No.	Choke Vacuum Kick	Choke Setting
1984	R40071A	.480	1.875	3	.080	—
	R40122A	.480	1.875	2	.080	—
	R400581A	.480	1.875	2	.070	—
	R400641A	.480	1.875	3	.080	—
	R400651A	.480	1.875	3	.080	—
	R400811A	.480	1.875	2	.080	—
	R400821A	.480	1.875	2	.080	—
	R401071A	.480	1.875	2	.055	—

MIKUNI CARBURETOR ADJUSTMENT SPECIFICATIONS

Year	Model No.	Float Level	Fast Idle Opening At 68°F	Choke Breaker Opening At 14°F	Unloader Opening At 32°F
1984	4243740①	.779	—	.067	.051
	4243743①	.779	—	.067	.051

①—Chrysler identification number.

Continued

1984 CARBURETOR ADJUSTMENT SPECIFICATIONS

ROCHESTER 2SE & E2SE ADJUSTMENT SPECIFICATIONS

Year	Carb. Production No.	Float Level	Accel. Pump	Choke Coil Lever	Choke Rod	Vacuum Break Primary	Vacuum Break Secondary	Air Valve Rod	Choke Setting	Unloader	Secondary Lockout
GENERAL MOTORS											
1984	17084356	9/32	—	.085	22°	25°	30°	1°	—	30°	.025
	17084357	9/32	—	.085	22°	25°	30°	1°	—	30°	.025
	17084358	9/32	—	.085	22°	25°	30°	1°	—	30°	.025
	17084359	9/32	—	.085	22°	25°	30°	1°	—	30°	.025
	17084368	1/8	—	.085	22°	25°	30°	1°	—	30°	.025
	17084370	1/8	—	.085	22°	25°	30°	1°	—	30°	.025
	17084430	11/32	—	.085	15°	26°	38°	1°	—	42°	.025
	17084431	11/32	—	.085	15°	26°	38°	1°	—	42°	.025
	17084434	11/32	—	.085	15°	26°	38°	1°	—	42°	.025
	17084435	11/32	—	.085	15°	26°	38°	1°	—	42°	.025
	17084452	5/32	—	.085	28°	25°	35°	1°	—	45°	.025
	17084453	5/32	—	.085	28°	25°	35°	1°	—	45°	.025
	17084455	5/32	—	.085	28°	25°	35°	1°	—	45°	.025
	17084456	5/32	—	.085	28°	25°	35°	1°	—	45°	.025
	17084458	5/32	—	.085	28°	25°	35°	1°	—	45°	.025
	17084532	5/32	—	.085	28°	25°	35°	1°	—	45°	.025
	17084632	9/32	—	.085	28°	25°	35°	1°	—	45°	.025
	17084633	9/32	—	.085	28°	25°	35°	1°	—	45°	.025
	17084635	9/32	—	.085	28°	25°	35°	1°	—	45°	.025
	17084636	9/32	—	.085	28°	25°	35°	1°	—	45°	.025

ROCHESTER DUAL-JET 2MC, M2MC, M2ME 200, 210 & M2ME ADJUSTMENT SPECIFICATIONS

Year	Carb. Production No.	Float Level	Pump Rod Hole	Pump Rod Adj.	Choke Coil Lever	Choke Rod	Vacuum Break Rich	Vacuum Break Lean	Vacuum Break Front	Vacuum Break Rear	Choke Unloader	Choke Setting
1984	17082130	3/8	—	—	.120	20°	—	—	27°	—	38°	—
	17082132	3/8	—	—	.120	20°	—	—	27°	—	38°	—
	17084191	5/16	—	—	.120	18°	—	—	28°	24°	32°	—
	17084193	5/16	—	—	.120	17°	—	—	27°	25°	35°	—
	17084194	5/16	—	—	.120	17°	—	—	27°	25°	35°	—
	17084195	5/16	—	—	.120	17°	—	—	27°	25°	35°	—

ROCHESTER QUADRAJET E4M & M4M SERIES ADJUSTMENT SPECIFICATIONS

Year	Carb. Production No.	Float Level	Pump Rod Hole	Pump Rod Adj.	Fast Idle (Bench) Turns	Choke Coil Lever	Choke Rod	Vacuum Break Front	Vacuum Break Rear	Air-Valve Dash-Pot	Choke Setting	Choke Unloader	Air Valve Spring Wind-Up
1984	17084201	11/32	—	—	—	.120	20°	27°	—	.025	—	38°	7/8
	17084205	11/32	—	—	—	.120	38°	27°	—	.025	—	38°	7/8
	17084208	11/32	—	—	—	.120	20°	27°	—	.025	—	38°	7/8
	17084209	11/32	—	—	—	.120	38°	27°	—	.025	—	38°	7/8
	17084210	11/32	—	—	—	.120	20°	27°	—	.025	—	38°	7/8
	17084240	5/16	—	—	—	.120	24.5°	24°	—	.025	—	32°	1
	17084244	5/16	—	—	—	.120	24.5°	24°	—	.025	—	32°	1
	17084246	5/16	—	—	—	.120	24.5°	22°	24°	.025	—	32°	1
	17084248	5/16	—	—	—	.120	24.5°	24°	—	.025	—	32°	1
	17084252	7/16	—	—	—	.120	14°	27°	41°	.025	—	35°	1/2
	17084254	7/16	—	—	—	.120	14°	27°	41°	.025	—	35°	1/2

GARRET-AIRESEARCH T-3 TURBOCHARGER SECTION
Chrysler Corp. 4-135 (2.2L) Turbo Engine

DESCRIPTION

The turbocharged engine is similar to the standard 4-135 engine. However, many components have been upgraded in order to withstand the more than fifty percent higher power output generated by the turbocharger. This upgrading includes more durable intake and exhaust valve materials, better sealing piston rings, a larger capacity oil pump, select-fit bearings, and a revised camshaft. Dished piston tops are incorporated to lower the compression ratio to 8.1.

The turbocharged engine integrates a Garrett-AiResearch T-3 center housing and wastegate assembly with a Chrysler built compressor and turbine housing, and exhaust outlet elbow, Fig. 1. The wastegate is calibrated to regulate maximum boost pressure at 7.5 psi. Turbo boost begins at 1200 RPM, rises to 7.2 psi at 2050 RPM, and peaks at 7.5 psi at 6000 RPM.

This turbocharger also incorporates a water cooled turbine end shaft bearing which lowers bearing temperatures, especially after a hot shut-off, to increase the durability of the turbocharger, Fig. 2.

TURBOCHARGER, REPLACE

1. Disconnect battery ground cable and drain cooling system.
2. Raise and support vehicle.
3. Disconnect exhaust pipe at articulated joint and the oxygen sensor at electrical connectors.
4. Remove turbocharger housing to block support bracket.
5. Loosen oil drain back tube connector hose clamps and move tube down on block nipple.
6. Disconnect turbocharger coolant tube nut at block outlet below steering pump bracket and disconnect coolant tube at tube support bracket.
7. Lower vehicle.
8. Remove air cleaner assembly, including throttle body adapter, hose, and air cleaner box with block support bracket.
9. Disconnect accelerator linkage, throttle body electrical connector, and vacuum hoses.
10. Loosen throttle body to turbocharger inlet hose clamps.
11. Remove 3 throttle body to intake manifold attaching screws, then the throttle body.
12. Loosen turbocharger discharge hose end clamps.
13. Relocate fuel rail by removing 4 bracket screws from intake manifold and the 2 bracket to heat shield retaining clips, then lift and secure fuel rail, with injectors, wiring harness, and fuel lines intact, up out of way.
14. Remove 3 heat shield to intake manifold attaching screws, then the heat shield.
15. Disconnect coolant return tube and hose assembly from turbocharger housing to water box, then remove tube support bracket from cylinder head and remove tube and hose assembly.
16. Disconnect oil feed line from oil sending unit hex tee and turbocharger bearing housing, then remove support bracket.
17. Remove 4 turbocharger to exhaust manifold attaching nuts.
18. Remove turbocharger assembly by lifting it off exhaust manifold studs while pushing downward toward passenger side of unit, and lift turbocharger up and out of engine compartment.
19. Reverse procedure to install, noting the following:
    a. Position turbocharger assembly on exhaust manifold studs, ensuring that turbocharger discharge tube is properly positioned between intake manifold and turbocharger.
    b. Apply suitable anti-seize compound to threads of exhaust manifold studs and torque 4 turbocharger attaching nuts to 30 ft. lbs.
    c. Torque oil feed line tube nuts to 125 inch lbs., then install and tighten support bracket screw.
    d. Torque 3 heat shield to intake manifold screws to 105 inch lbs.
    e. Torque coolant tube nuts to 30 ft. lbs. and install bracket screw.
    f. Torque 4 fuel rail bracket to intake manifold retaining screws to 250 inch lbs. and install shield to bracket clips.
    g. Torque discharge tube hose clamp to 35 inch lbs.
    h. Torque 3 throttle body to intake manifold screws to 250 inch lbs.
    i. Torque throttle body hose clamps to 35 inch lbs.
    j. Connect accelerator linkage, electrical connector, and vacuum hoses.
    k. Torque 2 hose adaptor to throttle body screws to 55 inch lbs. and the air cleaner box support bracket screws to 40 ft. lbs.
    l. Torque coolant tube nut to block connector to 30 ft. lbs.
    m. Position oil drain back hose and torque clamps to 30 inch lbs.
    n. Install turbocharger to block support bracket and install screws finger tight. Torque block screw to 40 ft. lbs., then torque screw to turbocharger housing to 20 ft. lbs.
    o. Torque articulated joint shoulder bolts to 250 inch lbs.
    p. Fill cooling system and connect negative battery terminal.

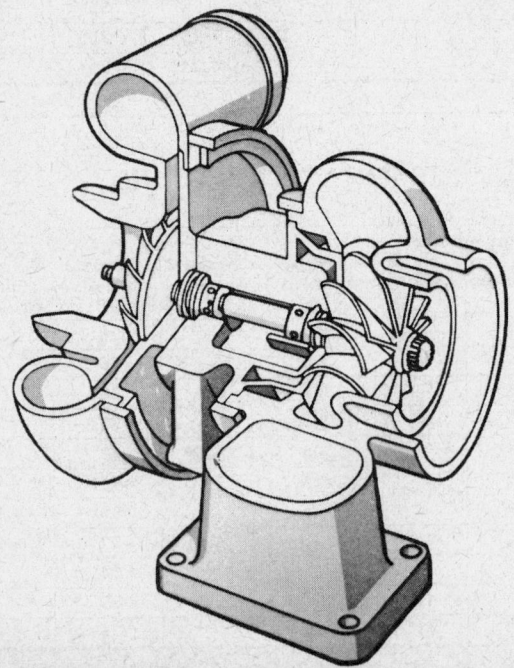

Fig. 1 Section view of Garret-AiResearch T3 type turbocharger

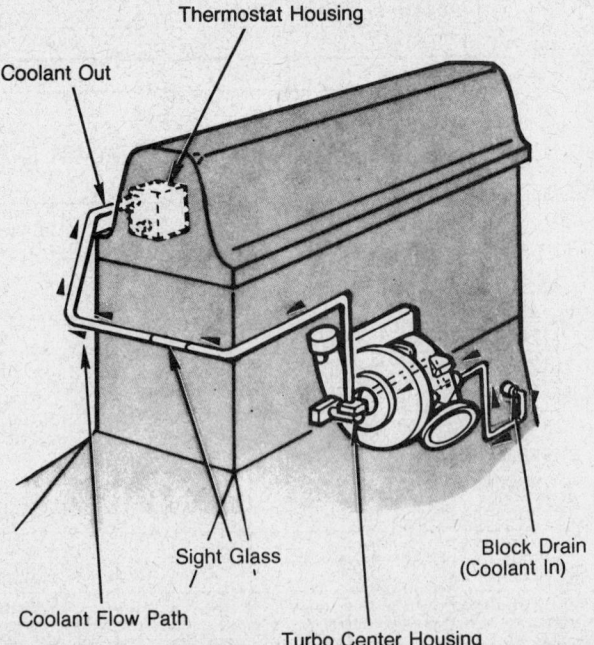

Thermostat Housing

Coolant Out

Sight Glass

Coolant Flow Path

Turbo Center Housing

Block Drain (Coolant In)

Fig. 2 Turbocharger water cooling system

EMISSION MAINTENANCE REMINDER INDICATORS

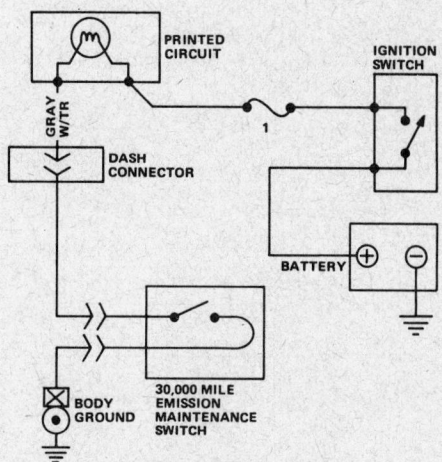

Fig. 1 Emission control maintenance lamp wiring circuit. 1980–81 AMC models

AMERICAN MOTORS

Emission Control Maintenance Lamp

1980–81 Models

The emission maintenance lamp will illuminate at 30,000 mile intervals to indicate that required service for oxygen sensor should be performed. After performing the required service, the emission maintenance switch must be reset. The switch is located between the upper and lower speedometer cables in the engine compartment on left hand side of dash panel. To reset, turn spring loaded reset screw counterclockwise approximately 1/4 turn to the reset detent position.

1982–83 Models W/ 4-151 Engine

The emission maintenance lamp will illuminate after 1000 hours of engine operation indicating that required service for oxygen sensor should be performed. After performing the required service, the emission maintenance E-cell timer must be replaced. The E-cell timer is located in the passenger compartment within the wiring harness leading to the feedback system micro processor. Remove E-cell timer (printed circuit board) from its enclosure and install a replacement E-cell timer.

CHRYSLER CORP.

Oxygen Sensor Maintenance Reminder System

1980 Models

When the vehicle has been operated for 30,000 miles, a warning lamp will illuminate on the instrument cluster to remind the operator that the oxygen sensor must be replaced as soon as possible. The reminder system can be either mechanical, Fig. 3, or electronic, Fig. 4.

After the prescribed maintenance has been performed, the switch must be reset for the next 30,000 mile period. To reset the switch and extinguish the warning lamp on a mechanical system, rotate the reset screw on the switch, Fig. 3. An electronic system may be reset by removing 9 volt battery from module and inserting a suitable rod into the hole in module case.

GENERAL MOTORS CORP.

Oxygen Sensor Maintenance Reminder Flag

1978–79 Monza, Starfire & Sunbird W/ 4-151 Calif. Engine

At every 15,000 mile interval, a "Sensor"

Fig. 2 Emission control maintenance lamp wiring circuit. 1982–83 AMC models w/ 4-151 engine

flag will appear in a window in the speedometer face or across part of the odometer to remind the operator that the oxygen sensor must be replaced as soon as possible.

After the prescribed maintenance has been performed, the flag must be reset for the next 15,000 mile service interval. This is accomplished by gaining access to the speedometer head, then on 1978 models, pulling down on the reset cable until a positive stop is felt, Fig. 5. On 1979 models, the speedometer lens assembly must be removed, then using a suitable pointed tool, rotate flag wheel downward using the left edge of flag wheel detents until flag wheel turns no further, Fig. 6. On all models, when the flag wheel is properly reset, alignment mark on flag wheel should be centered in window or odometer.

1979 Calif. V6-231 Turbocharged Models W/ 2 Bbl. Carb. & C4 (Computer Controlled Catalytic Converter) System

At every 15,000 mile interval, a "Sensor"

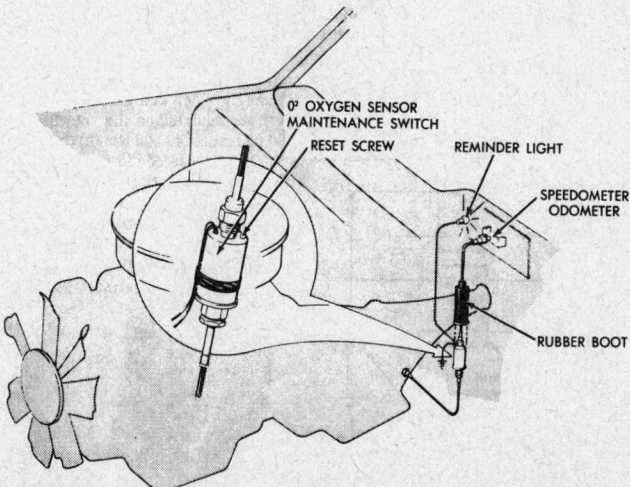

Fig. 3 Oxygen sensor maintenance reminder system. 1980 Chrysler Corp. mechanical type

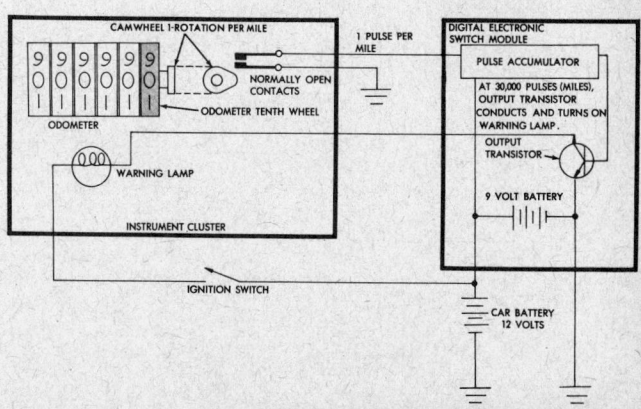

Fig. 4 Oxygen sensor maintenance reminder system. 1980 Chrysler Corp. electronic type

EMISSION MAINTENANCE REMINDER INDICATORS

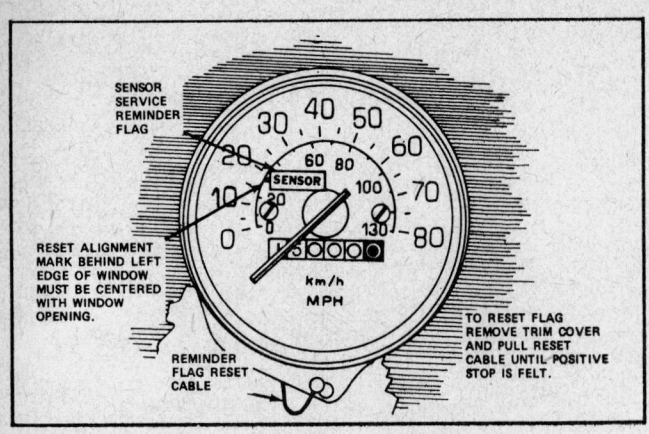

Fig. 5   Oxygen sensor reset. 1978 GM models (if equipped)

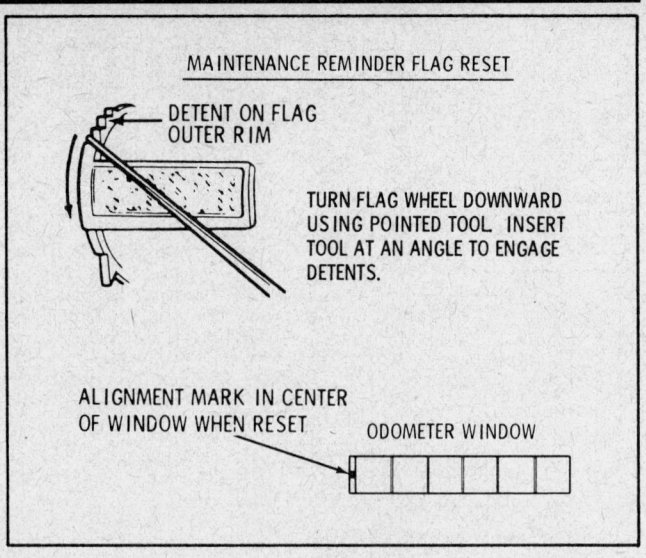

Fig. 6   Oxygen sensor reset. 1979–80 GM models (if equipped)

flag will appear across part of the odometer to remind the operator the oxygen sensor must be replaced.

After the prescribed maintenance has been performed, the flag must be reset for the next 15,000 mile interval. This is accomplished by gaining access to the speedometer head, then removing the speedometer lens. Using a suitable pointed tool, rotate flag wheel downward using the left edge of flag wheel detents until flag wheel turns no further, Fig. 6. When flag wheel is properly reset, alignment mark on flag wheel should be centered in odometer.

Emissions Maintenance Reminder Flag

1980 Models W/ C4 (Computer Controlled Catalytic Converter) System

At every 30,000 mile interval, an "Emission" flag will appear across part of the odometer to remind the operator the oxygen sensor must be replaced.

After the prescribed maintenance has been performed, the flag must be reset for the next 30,000 mile interval. This is accomplished by gaining access to the speedometer head, then removing the speedometer lens. Using a suitable pointed tool, rotate flag wheel downward using the left edge of flag wheel detents until flag wheel turns no further, Fig. 6. When flag wheel is properly reset, alignment mark on flag wheel should be centered in odometer.

FORD MOTOR CO. 2.0L DIESEL STARTER SERVICE
1984 Escort, Lynx, Tempo & Topaz

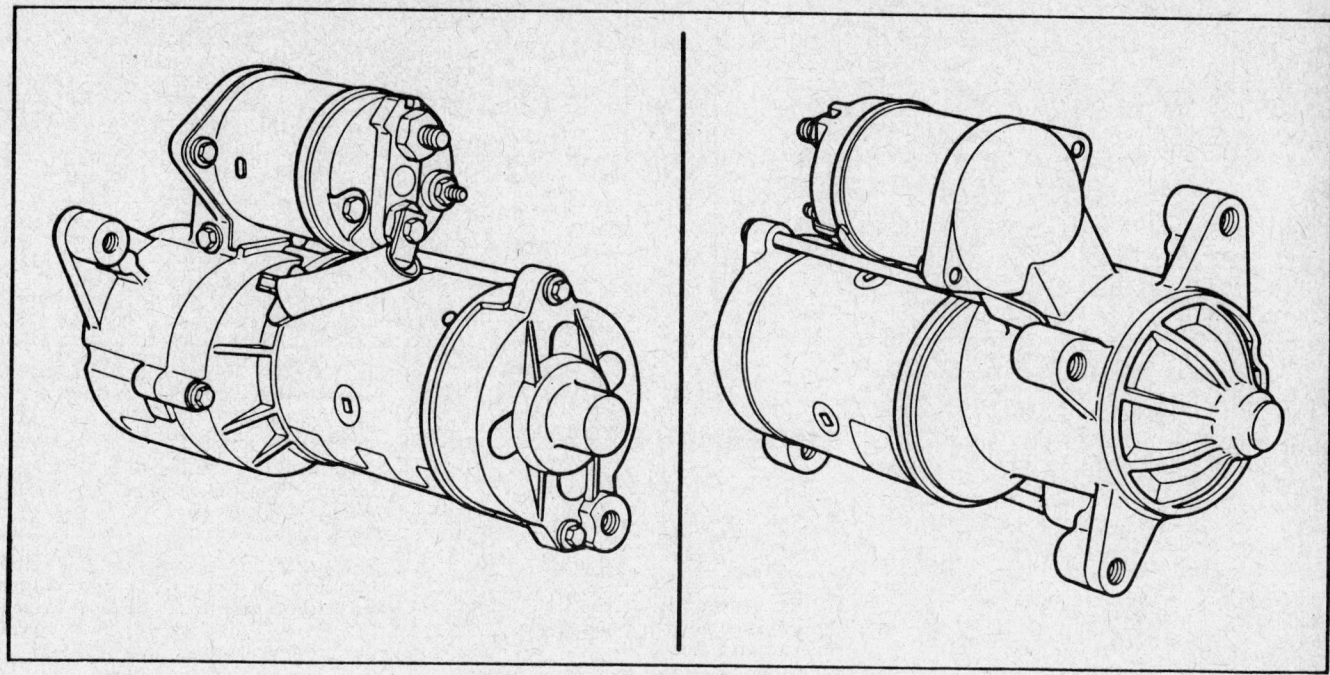

Fig. 1 Ford front wheel drive diesel engine starting motors

DESCRIPTION

This type starting motor, Fig. 1, has the solenoid mounted on the starter housing. When the starter relay contacts are closed, the solenoid is energized and the starter drive is engaged to start the engine. During engine starting, the starter is protected from excessive speed by an overrunning clutch in the drive. Current flows through the solenoid energizing coil until the solenoid plunger reaches the end of its travel, at which time the plunger closes a set of contacts that bypass the energizing coil. The holding coil keeps the starter drive engaged and passes current to the starting motor.

TROUBLESHOOTING
Starter Cranks Slowly

1. Attempt to jump start engine. If engine can be jump started, check condition of battery and recharge or replace as necessary.
2. If engine can not be jump started, clean and tighten connections at starter, relay and battery ground on engine and check starter circuit for a short to ground.
3. If engine still cannot be jump started, replace starting motor.

Starter Does Not Operate; Solenoid Clicks

1. Perform "Starter Cranks Slowly" diagno-

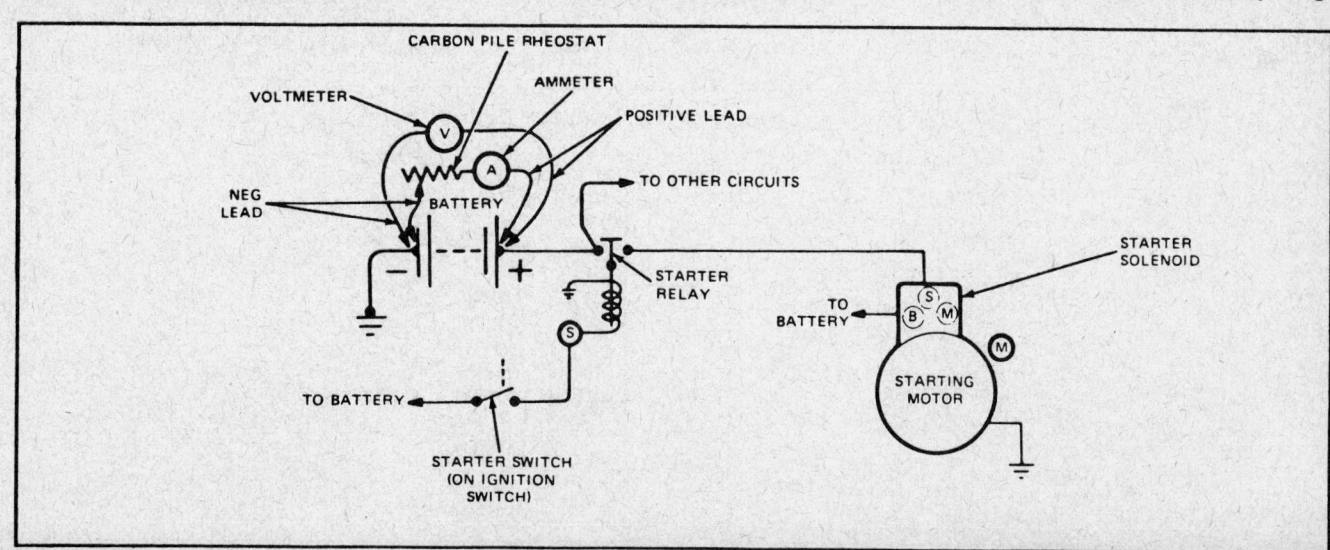

Fig. 2 Connections for starter load test

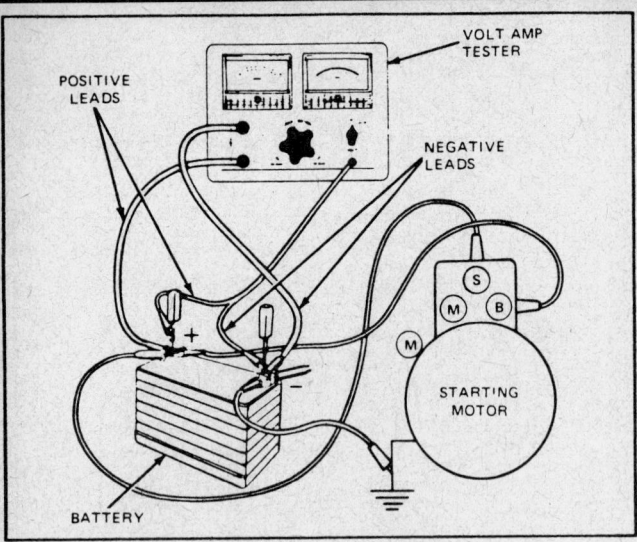

Fig. 3 Connections for starter no-load test

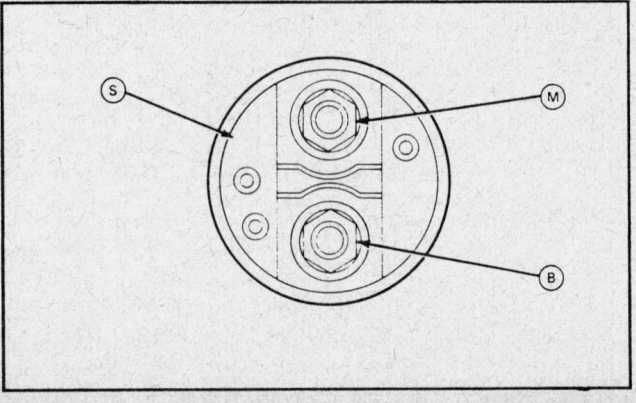

Fig. 4 Testing armature windings for continuity

sis as previously described.

2. Clean and tighten starter and relay electrical connections, ensuring there are no loose wire strands at eyelets.
3. Connect suitable jumper wire between starter solenoid terminals B and M. If engine still does not crank, replace starting motor.

Starter Does Not Crank; Relay Chatters or Does Not Click

1. Perform "Starter Cranks Slowly" diagnosis as previously described.
2. Disconnect push-on connector from relay terminal S and clean or repair as necessary.
3. If push-on connector is satisfactory, attempt to start engine with transmission in Neutral, push-on connector disconnected and relay terminal S jumpered to battery positive connection at relay.
4. If engine still does not crank, replace starter relay.

Starter Spins But Does Not Crank Engine

1. Remove driveshaft and check for corrosion. Clean or replace as necessary.
2. If driveshaft is not corroded, replace drive assembly.

IN-VEHICLE TESTS

Starter Load Test

1. Connect test equipment to starter circuit as shown in Fig. 2.

   NOTE: Ensure no current is flowing through ammeter and carbon pile rheostat portion of circuit.

2. Disconnect electrical connectors from starter relay and connect a suitable remote starter switch between battery positive terminal and starter relay terminal S.
3. Crank engine with ignition Off and note voltmeter reading.
4. Stop cranking engine, then reduce rheostat resistance until voltmeter reading is equal to that obtained while cranking engine. The ammeter will not indicate starter current draw under load.

BENCH TESTS

Starter No-Load Test

NOTE: This test can be used to determine if

windings are open or shorted, armature is rubbing, or armature shaft is bent.

1. Connect test equipment to starter as shown in Fig. 3 and note voltmeter reading with starter running.

   NOTE: Ensure no current is flowing through ammeter and carbon pile rheostat portion of circuit.

2. Disconnect starter from battery, then reduce rheostat resistance until voltmeter reading is equal to that obtained in step 1. The ammeter will now indicate starter no-load current draw.

Armature & Field Grounded Circuit Test

NOTE: This test can be used to determine if the winding insulation is damaged, permitting a conductor to contact armature core or frame.

1. Check armature windings using a suitable ohmmeter, Fig. 4. If ohmmeter does not indicate infinite resistance, the armature windings are grounded.
2. Measure resistance between yoke and field terminal, Fig. 5. Ohmmeter should indicate infinite resistance.
3. Confirm continuity between yoke lead wires using an ohmmeter.

Solenoid Test

1. Check for continuity between solenoid S

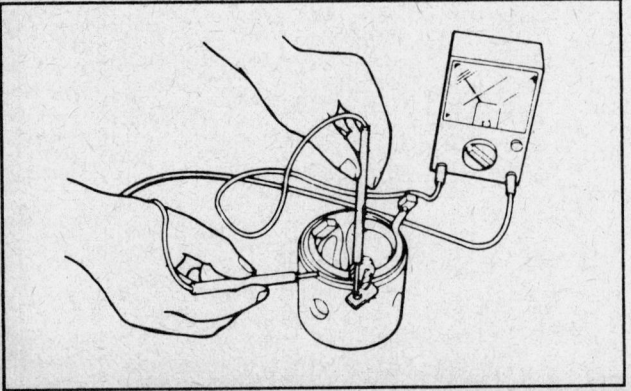

Fig. 5 Testing field coils for continuity

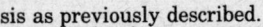
Fig. 6 Solenoid terminals

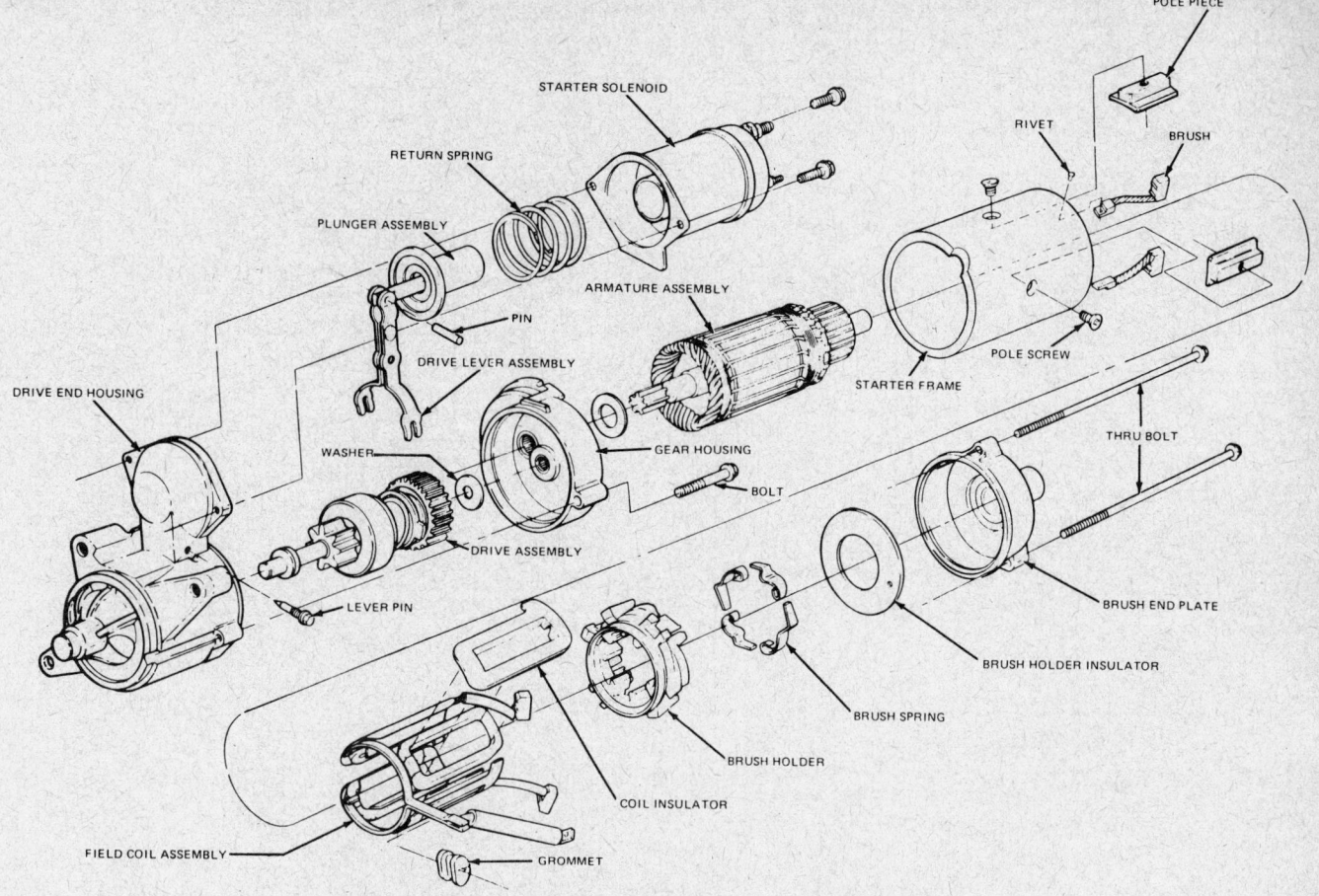

Fig. 7 Exploded view of Ford front wheel drive diesel engine starting motor

terminal and ground, and between S and M terminals, Fig. 6.
2. If there is no continuity, replace solenoid.

STARTING MOTOR SERVICE

Disassembly

1. Disconnect field coil connection from solenoid motor terminal.
2. Remove solenoid attaching screws, then rotate solenoid 90° and remove solenoid and plunger return spring, Fig. 7.
3. Remove field frame through bolts and the brush end plate.
4. Remove brush springs and brushes, then the brush holder. Note position of brush holder for assembly reference.
5. Remove frame and armature assemblies.
6. Remove gear housing attaching bolt and the gear housing.
7. Remove plunger and lever assembly attaching bolt and the assembly.
8. Remove gear, output shaft and drive assembly.
9. Remove thrust washer, retainer and drive stop ring, then slide drive assembly off output shaft.

Inspection

1. Clean drive assembly, field coils, arma-ture, gear and housing using compressed air or a brush.
2. Inspect armature windings for burned or broken insulation or open connections at commutator.
3. Measure commutator runnout. If commutator is more than .005 inch out of round, repair or replace as necessary.
4. Inspect brush holder for damage and replace as necessary.
5. Measure brush length and replace if worn to .25 inch or less.
6. Inspect field coils and insulators for damage or burns and replace as necessary.
7. Check continuity of coil and brush connections and repair or replace as necessary.
8. Inspect gears, output shaft spline and drive pinion for damage and replace as necessary.

Assembly

1. Apply a thin coat of Lubriplate 777 or equivalent on output shaft spline.
2. Slide drive assembly onto shaft, then install a new stop ring, retainer and thrust washer.
3. Install shaft and drive assembly into drive end housing.
4. Install plunger and lever assembly and torque attaching bolt to 7–11 ft. lbs. Ensure notches in lever engage flange ears of starter drive.
5. Install lubricated gear and washer on end of output shaft.
6. Install gear housing and torque attaching bolt to 5–7 ft. lbs.
7. Lubricate pinion, then install armature and washer on end of shaft.
8. Position grommet around field lead and press into notch in starter frame.
9. Install frame assembly to gear housing, ensuring grommet is properly positioned.
10. Install brush holder, then the brush springs and brushes.

NOTE: Ensure positive brush leads are installed in correct slots to prevent grounding.

11. Install brush end plate and through bolts. Torque through bolts to 5–7 ft. lbs.

NOTE: Threaded hole in brush plate must be properly positioned to accommodate vacuum pump support bracket installation.

12. Install return spring on solenoid plunger.
13. Install solenoid and torque attaching bolts to 5–7 ft. lbs. Apply suitable sealer to mating surface of solenoid case flange, gear and drive end housings.
14. Connect motor field terminal to solenoid M terminal and torque to 20–30 inch lbs.

DELCOTRON SI VOLTAGE REGULATOR TESTS

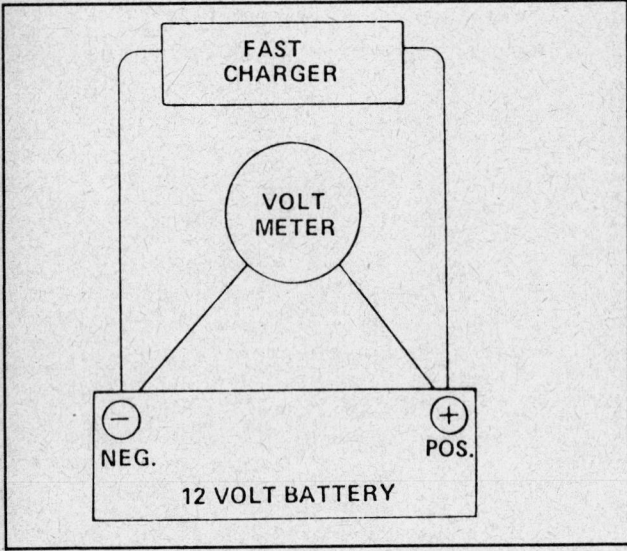

Fig. 1 On-car voltage regulator test

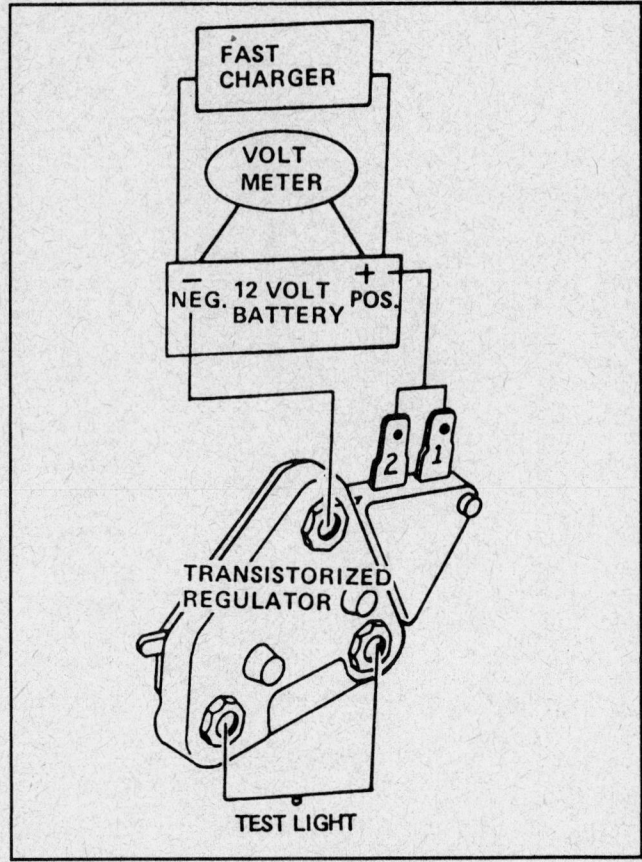

Fig. 2 Off-car voltage regulator test

ON-CAR TEST

1. Connect a suitable voltmeter and fast charger to battery, Fig. 1.
2. Turn ignition on and slowly increase charge rate, while observing voltmeter and generator warning light.
3. The generator warning light should dim when voltmeter reads 13.5–16.0 volts. If not, replace voltage regulator.

OFF-CAR TEST

1. Connect a suitable voltmeter, fast charger and test light to regulator, Fig. 2. Test light should be illuminated.
2. Turn charger on and slowly increase charge rate, while observing voltmeter and test light.
3. The test light should go out when voltmeter reads 13.5–16.0 volts. If not, replace voltage regulator.

AIR CONDITIONING

CONTENTS

A/C System Testing

PERFORMANCE TEST

The system should be operated for at least 15 minutes to allow sufficient time for all parts to become completely stabilized. Determine if the system is fully charged by the use of test gauges and sight glass if one is installed on system. Head pressure will read from 180 psi to 220 psi or higher, depending upon ambient temperature and the type unit being tested. The sight glass should be free of bubbles if a glass is used in the system. Low side pressures should read approximately 15 psi to 30 psi, again depending on the ambient temperature and the unit being tested. It is not feasible to give a definite reading for all types of systems used, as the type control and component installation used on a particular system will directly influence the pressure readings on the high and low sides, Fig. 1.

The high side pressure will definitely be affected by the ambient or outside air temperature. A system that is operating normally will indicate a high side gauge reading between 150–170 psi with an 80°F ambient temperature. The same system will register 210–230 psi with an ambient temperature of 100°F. No two systems will register exactly the same, which requires that allowance for variations in head pressures must be considered. Following are the most important normal readings likely to be encountered during the season.

Ambient Temp.	High Side Pressure
80	150–170
90	175–195
95	185–205
100	210–230
105	230–250
110	250–270

Evaporator Pressure Gauge Reading	Evaporator Temperature F°	High Pressure Gauge Reading	Ambient Temperature
0	-21°	45	20°
0.6	-20°	55	30°
2.4	-15°	72	40°
4.5	-10°	86	50°
6.8	- 5°	105	60°
9.2	0°	126	70°
11.8	5°	140	75°
14.7	10°	160	80°
17.1	15°	185	90°
21.1	20°	195	95°
22.5	22°	220	100°
23.9	24°	240	105°
25.4	26°	260	110°
26.9	28°	275	115°
28.5	30°	290	120°
37.0	40°	305	125°
46.7	50°	325	130°
57.7	60°		
70.1	70°		
84.1	80°		
99.6	90°		
116.9	100°		
136.0	110°		
157.1	120°		
179.0	130°		

Fig. 1 Pressure-temperature relationship (Typical). Conditions equivalent to 30 mph or 1750 engine rpm

Relative Temperature of High and Low Sides

The high side of the system should be uniformly hot to the touch throughout. A difference in temperature will indicate a partial blockage of liquid or gas at this point.

The low side of the system should be uniformly cool to the touch with no excessive sweating of the suction line or low side service valve. Excessive sweating or frosting of the low side service valve usually indicates an expansion valve is allowing an excessive amount of refrigerant into the evaporator.

Evaporator Output

At this point, provided all other inspection tests have been performed, and components have been found to operate as they should, a rapid cooling down of the interior of the vehicle should result. The use of a thermometer is not necessary to determine evaporator output. Bringing all units to the correct operating specifications will insure that the evaporator performs as intended.

DISCHARGING & EVACUATING SYSTEM

Service Note

On all American Motor models equipped with

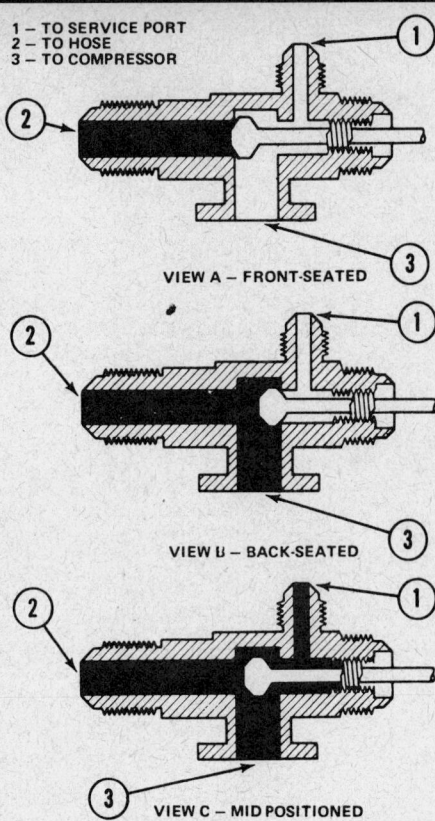

1 – TO SERVICE PORT
2 – TO HOSE
3 – TO COMPRESSOR

VIEW A – FRONT-SEATED

VIEW B – BACK-SEATED

VIEW C – MID POSITIONED

Fig. 2 Service valve positions (Typical). American Motors

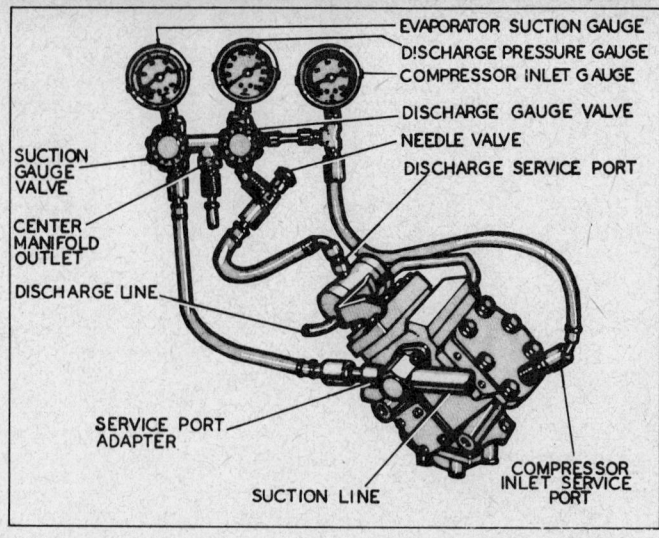

EVAPORATOR SUCTION GAUGE
DISCHARGE PRESSURE GAUGE
COMPRESSOR INLET GAUGE
DISCHARGE GAUGE VALVE
NEEDLE VALVE
DISCHARGE SERVICE PORT
SUCTION GAUGE VALVE
CENTER MANIFOLD OUTLET
DISCHARGE LINE
SERVICE PORT ADAPTER
SUCTION LINE
COMPRESSOR INLET SERVICE PORT

Fig. 3 Manifold gauge set connections. Chrysler Airtemp RV2 compressor

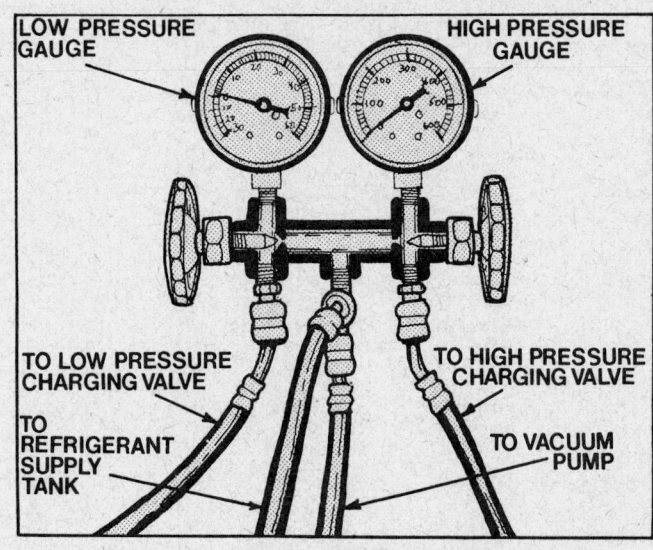

LOW PRESSURE GAUGE
HIGH PRESSURE GAUGE
TO LOW PRESSURE CHARGING VALVE
TO HIGH PRESSURE CHARGING VALVE
TO REFRIGERANT SUPPLY TANK
TO VACUUM PUMP

Fig. 4 Manifold gauge set hose connections (Typical). Except Chrysler Airtemp RV2 compressor

the York 2 cylinder compressor, 1981 California models equipped with 6-258 engine and Sankyo 5 cylinder rotary compressor and all 1982–83 models, it is not necessary to discharge refrigerant system for compressor removal. The compressor can be isolated from the system, eliminating need for recharging when performing compressor service or oil level check. Proceed as follows:

Isolating Compressor From System

1. Connect pressure gauge and manifold set, then close both gauge hand valves and crack (mid-position) both service valves, Fig. 2.
2. Start engine and operate air conditioning.
3. Slowly turn suction service valve clockwise toward the front seated position, Fig. 2. When pressure reading drops to zero or less stop engine and finish front-seating suction service valve, then front-seat discharge service valve, Fig. 2.
4. Slowly loosen oil sump filler plug to relieve any internal pressures in the compressor.

NOTE: A face shield should be worn when loosening the oil filler plug.

5. Compressor is now isolated from system, service valve can be removed from compressor. Plug all openings to prevent entry of dirt and moisture.

Purging Compressor of Air

The compressor must be purged of air whenever it has been isolated from the system for oil level check or compressor service.

1. Connect service valve and lines to compressor, then cap service gauge ports on both service valves.
2. Back-seat suction valve to allow refrigerant to enter compressor.
3. Place discharge service valve in mid-position, then loosen discharge service valve gauge port cap to allow refrigerant to force air from compressor.
4. Back-seat discharge service valve and tighten gauge port cap.
5. Remove manifold and gauge set.

Discharging System

1. Connect gauges into system, Figs. 3 and 4, and adjust controls for maximum cooling. *This is necessary when the system has not been operating to return excess oil to the compressor.*
2. Operate engine for 10 to 15 minutes to stabilize the system at 1500–1750 rpm.
3. Adjust engine speed to slow idle, then shut off engine and controls.
4. Open low side hand manifold valve slightly, using a container to catch oil and refrigerant. *Do not discharge the refrigerant near an open flame as a toxic gas (phosgene) can result.*
5. On AMC, Chrysler and Ford full size models, open high side manifold valve slightly. On Ford (except full size) and GM models, allow all refrigerant to discharge through the low side fitting only.

NOTE: Open hand valve(s) only enough to bleed refrigerant from system. Too rapid purging will draw excessive oil from compressor and system.

6. On AMC, Chrysler and Ford full size models, close gauge manifold hand valves when refrigerant ceases to bleed from discharge hose and manifold gauges read zero. On Ford (except full size) and GM models, when refrigerant ceases to bleed

from the discharge hose on the low side, crack open the high side hand valve to check for any remaining pressure. If pressure does exist, allow high side to discharge slowly. This condition indicates a high side restriction, and it must be diagnosed and corrected before evacuating and charging the system.

Evacuate System with Vacuum Pump

Vacuum pumps suitable for removing air and moisture from A/C systems are commercially available. A specification for system pump-down used here is 28 to 29½" vacuum. This reading can be attained at or near sea level only. For each 1000 feet of altitude this operation is being performed, the reading will be 1" vacuum lower. As an example, at 5000 feet elevation, only 23–24½" of vacuum can be obtained.

CAUTION: The system must be completely discharged before it can be evacuated. Damage to vacuum pump may result if pressurized refrigerant is allowed to enter.

AMC, Chrysler & Ford Full Size Models
1. With gauges connected into system, remove cap from vacuum hose connector. Install center hose from gauge manifold to vacuum pump connector. Mid-position high and low side compressor service valves (if used). Open high and low side gauge manifold hand valves.
2. Operate vacuum pump a minimum of 30 minutes for air and moisture removal. Watch compound gauge that system pumps down into a vacuum. System will reach 28–29½" vacuum in not over 5 minutes. If system does not pump down, check all connections and leak-test if necessary.
3. Close gauge manifold hand valves and shut off vacuum pump.
4. Check ability of system to hold vacuum. Watch compound gauge to see that gauge does not rise at a faster rate than 1" vacuum every 4 or 5 minutes. If compound gauge rises at too rapid a rate, install partial charge and leak-test. Then evacuate system as outlined above.
5. If system holds vacuum, charge system with refrigerant.

Ford (Except Full Size) & GM Models
1. With hand gauges connected into system, remove cap from vacuum hose connector. Install hand gauge manifold center hose to vacuum pump connector. Open low side gauge manifold hand valve only.
2. Ensure low side gauge is calibrated correctly. It should be reading zero. If not, adjust calibration.
3. Evacuate system with the vacuum pump until the low pressure gauge reads at least 28" of vacuum. Continue evacuating system for an additional 15 minutes for routine system servicing or 20 to 30 minutes, if any parts have been replaced.
4. When system evacuation is complete, close low side gauge manifold hand valve, then turn vacuum pump off.
5. Check ability of system to hold vacuum. Watch low side gauge to see that gauge does not rise at a faster rate than 1" vacuum every 4 or 5 minutes. if low side gauge rises at too rapid a rate, install partial charge and leak test. Evacuate system again.

6. If system holds vacuum, charge system with refrigerant.

Evacuate System Using Charging Station

A vacuum pump is built into the charging station and is constructed to withstand repeated and prolonged use without damage. Complete moisture removal from the system is possible only with a vacuum pump constructed for the purpose.

CAUTION: The system must be completely discharged before it can be evacuated. Damage to the vacuum pump may result if pressurized refrigerant is allowed to enter.

AMC, Chrysler & Ford Full Size Models
1. Connect hose to vacuum pump if system was discharged through charging station.
2. Open high and low side gauge valves of charging station.
3. Connect station into 110-volt current.
4. Engage "Off-On" switch to vacuum pump according to directions of specific station being used.
5. System should pump down into a 28–29½" vacuum in not more than 5 minutes. If system fails to meet this specification, repair as necessary.
6. Operate pump a minimum of 30 minutes to remove all air and moisture.
7. Close high and low side gauge valves. Open switch to turn off pump.
8. Check ability of system to hold vacuum by watching compound gauge to see that it does not rise at a rate higher than 1" of vacuum every 4 or 5 minutes: If rise rate is not within specifications, repair system as necessary. If rise rate is within specifications, charge system with refrigerant.

Ford (Except Full Size Models) & GM Models
1. Connect hose to vacuum pump, if system was discharged through charging station.
2. Open low side gauge hand valve of charging station.
3. Connect station into 110 volt current.
4. Engage "Off-On" switch to vacuum pump according to instructions for specific station being used.
5. Evacuate system with the vacuum pump until the low pressure gauge reads at least 28" of vacuum. Continue evacuating system for an additional 15 minutes for routine system servicing or 20 to 30 minutes, if any parts have been replaced.
6. Close low side gauge hand valve, then turn vacuum pump off.
7. Check ability of system to hold vacuum. Watch low side gauge to see that gauge does not rise at a faster rate than 1" vacuum every 4 to 5 minutes. If low side gauge rises at too rapid a rate, install partial charge and leak test. Then evacuate system again.
8. If system holds vacuum, charge system with refrigerant.

CHARGING THE SYSTEM
American Motors

Charging Procedure With Multi-Refrigerant Can Opener
1. Connect pressure gauge and manifold assembly J-23575 or equivalent. Keep both service valves in mid-position.

2. Close both gauge hand valves and disconnect service hose from vacuum pump.
3. Connect service hose to center of refrigerant can opener. Close valves on dispenser.
4. Attach refrigerant cans to opener. Refer to A/C Data Table for proper weight of refrigerant for vehicle being serviced.
5. Open one petcock valve and loosen center service hose at gauge to allow refrigerant to purge air from hose. Tighten hose and close petcock valve.
6. Open suction gauge hand valve and one petcock valve. Do not open high pressure gauge hand valve.
7. Start engine and set A/C system controls to maximum cooling position. Compressor will help pull refrigerant gas into suction side of system.

NOTE: Refrigerant cans can be placed in pan of water no hotter than 125°F to aid charging process.

8. When first can is empty, open next valve to continue charging until specified amount of refrigerant is in system. Frost line on can may be used as a guide when specifications call for using part of full can. If a scale is available, weigh cans before and during charging procedure to ensure accurate filling.
9. When system is fully charged, close suction gauge hand valve and all petcock valves.
10. Operate system for 5–10 minutes to allow it to stabilize and to determine if system cycles properly.
11. After checking operation of system, backseat suction and discharge service valves to normal operating position by turning valves fully counterclockwise.
12. Loosen pressure gauge and manifold assembly service hoses to release refrigerant trapped in hoses. Remove pressure gauge and manifold assembly and install dust caps on fittings.

Using Charging Station J-23500-01
1. After discharging and evacuating system, close low pressure valve on charging station. Fully open left hand refrigerant control valve at base of cylinder and high pressure valve on charging station and allow required charge of refrigerant to enter high side of system. When full charge has entered system, close refrigerant control valve and high pressure valve on charging station.

CAUTION: Do not permit level of liquid to drop below zero mark on cylinder sight glass.

2. After charging is completed, close manifold gauges and check high and low pressures and system operation.

CAUTION: Read gauges with high and low pressure valves closed on charging station. Low pressure gauge can be damaged if both high and low pressure valves are opened.

3. Close all valves on charging station and close refrigerant drum valve when all operations are finished.
4. After completing operational check, backseat suction and discharge service valves to their normal operating position by turning them fully counter-clockwise.

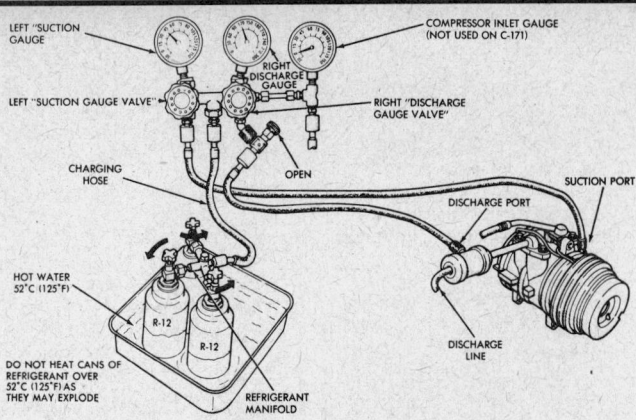

Fig. 5 Complete charging of system. Chrysler

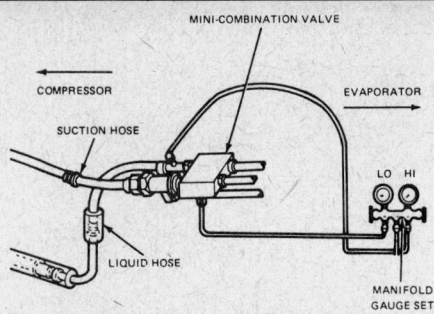

Fig. 6 Service connections for systems with mini-combination valve. 1981 Ford

5. Disconnect high and low pressure charging hoses from compressor.
6. Open valve on top of cylinder to remove remaining refrigerant as charging cylinder is not designed to store refrigerant.
7. Replace quick seal caps on compressor service valves.

Chrysler Corp.

Charging With 14 Ounce Cans

CAUTION: Never use cans to charge into high pressure side of system (compressor discharge port) or into system at high temperature, as high system pressure transferred into charging can may cause it to explode.

1. Attach center hose from manifold gauge set to refrigerant dispensing manifold. Turn refrigerant manifold valves completely counterclockwise to open fully, and remove protective caps from refrigerant manifold.
2. Screw refrigerant cans into manifold, ensuring gasket is in place and in good condition. Torque can and manifold nuts to 6–8 ft. lbs.
3. Turn refrigerant manifold valves clockwise to puncture cans, and close manifold valves, Fig. 5.
4. Loosen charging hose at gauge set manifold and turn a refrigerant valve counterclockwise to release refrigerant and purge air from charging hose. When refrigerant gas escapes from loose connection, retighten hose.
5. Fully open all refrigerant manifold valves being used and place refrigerant cans into pan of hot water at 125°F to aid transfer of refrigerant gas.

CAUTION: Do not heat refrigerant cans over 125°F as they may explode.

Place water pan and refrigerant cans on scale and note weight.
6. Connect a jumper wire across cycling clutch switch terminals located on suction line near H valve so clutch will remain engaged.
7. Start engine and set controls to A/C low blower position. Low pressure cut-out switch will prevent clutch from engaging until refrigerant is added to system. If clutch does engage, replace switch before continuing.
8. Charge through suction side of system by slowly opening suction manifold valve.

Adjust valve so charging pressure does not exceed 50 psig.
9. Adjust engine speed to fast idle of 1400 RPM.
10. After specified refrigerant charge has entered system, close gauge set manifold valves, refrigerant manifold valves, and reconnect wiring.

Charging With Bulk Refrigerant Supply

CAUTION: Only a charging bottle may be used to charge liquid refrigerant through the compressor discharge muffler. Never charge with liquid through compressor inlet or suction line ports, as damage to compressor is likely to occur. Do not run compressor while adding liquid refrigerant.

1. Warm charging bottle in pan of 125°F water. Do not heat R-12 with a torch, as it may explode.
2. Loosen charging hose at gauge set manifold and slowly open refrigerant supply valve until refrigerant has purged air from hose. Retighten the hose.
3. Place refrigerant container upside down on scale and note weight.
4. Open refrigerant supply valve and compressor discharge gauge valve to charge system. When scale indicates proper amount of charge has entered system, close valves.
    If required amount of refrigerant does not enter system, close compressor discharge valve on manifold gauge set. Turn charging bottle right side up so gas, not liquid, will enter system. Start engine and set A/C control in A/C position. Slowly open suction line valve on manifold gauge set. The compressor will draw refrigerant into system. Charging line valve should be set so suction pressure does not exceed 50 psig.

Ford Motor Co.

Charging From Small Containers

When charging from small cans, do not open manifold gauge set high pressure (discharge) gauge valve, as this can cause containers to explode.
1. Connect a suitable refrigerant dispensing valve and valve retainer such as Motorcraft tool YT-280 or equivalent to the refrigerant can.
2. Connect manifold gauge set to system, Figs. 6 and 7. Connect hose normally connected to R-12 tank to special valve on small can adaptor. Make sure valve is closed (full clockwise position).

3. When can is connected, charge system according to procedure under "Charging From Drum." When can is empty, close valve and remove can. Connect new can open valve and continue charging until correct weight of refrigerant has entered system. Note capacity of refrigerant cans. When specifications require use of a portion of a can, weigh it to ensure proper amount of refrigerant is installed.

Charging From Drum

1. With manifold gauge set valves closed to center hose, disconnect vacuum pump from manifold gauge set.
2. Connect center hose of manifold gauge set to refrigerant drum.
3. Purge air from center hose by loosening hose at manifold gauge set and open refrigerant drum valve. When refrigerant escapes from hose, tighten center hose connection at manifold gauge set.
4. On vehicles so equipped, disconnect wire harness connector at clutch cycling pressure switch. Install jumper wire across terminals of connector.
5. On all models, open manifold gauge set low side valve and allow refrigerant to enter system. Refrigerant can must be kept upright if vehicle low pressure service gauge port is not on suction accumulator/drier or suction accumulator fitting.
6. When system stops drawing refrigerant in, start engine and set control lever to A/C position and blower switch to "HI" position to draw remaining refrigerant into system.
7. When specified weight of refrigerant is in system, close gauge set low pressure valve and refrigerant supply valve.
8. On vehicles so equipped, remove jumper wire from clutch cycling pressure switch connector and connect connector to pressure switch.
9. On all models, operate system until pressures stabilize to check operation and system pressures. During high ambient temperatures, a high volume fan may be necessary to blow air through the radiator and condensor to cool engine and prevent excessive refrigerant system pressures.
10. When charging is complete and system operating pressures are normal, disconnect manifold gauge set from vehicle and install protective caps on service gauge port valves.

General Motors

J 23500-01 Charging Station Method

Use instructions provided with charging station with the following exceptions:
1. Do not connect high pressure line to A/C system.

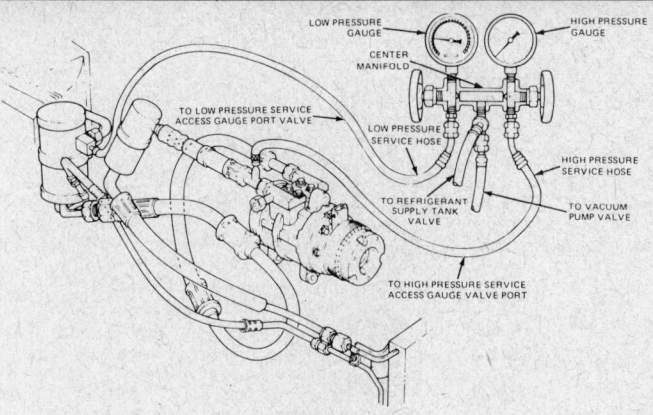

Fig. 7 Refrigerant system service connections. Ford fixed orifice systems

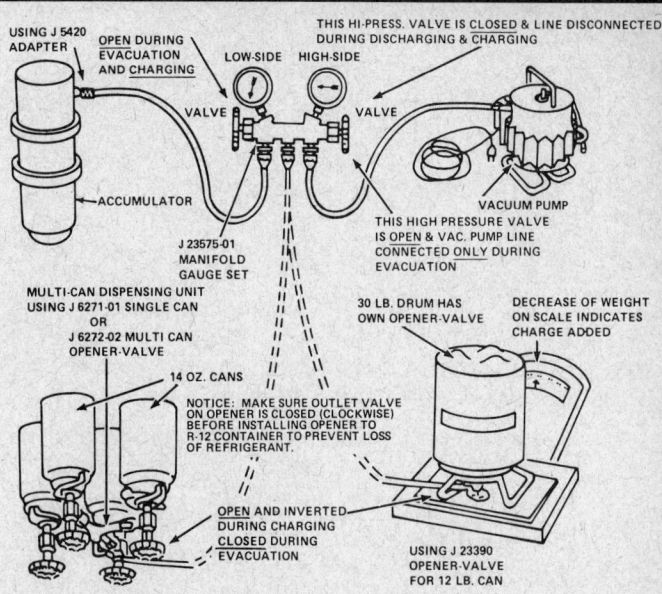

Fig. 8 Charging C.C.O.T. A/C system. General Motors

2. Always keep high pressure valve closed on charging station.
3. Perform all evacuation and charging through accumulator low-side pressure service fitting.

Use of these procedures will prevent charging station from being accidentally exposed to high-side vehicle system pressure.

Disposable Can Or Refrigerant Drum Method

If R-12 drum is used, place on scale and note total weight before charging. During charging, watch scale to determine amount of R-12 used.

If 14 ounce R-12 cans are used, close tapping valve, then attach cans following instructions included with manifold adaptor.

Charging Of System

1. Start engine and allow to warm up (choke off, normal idle). Set A/C control lever to OFF.
2. With R-12 drum or cans inverted, open R-12 supply valve and allow 1 lb. of liquid R-12 to flow into system through low-side service fitting on accumulator, Fig. 8.
3. When 1 lb. of refrigerant has entered system, engage compressor by setting A/C lever to NORM and blower switch to HI to draw in remainder of charge. Cooling condenser with a large fan will speed up charging procedure by maintaining condenser temperature below charging cylinder temperature.
4. Close refrigerant supply valve and run engine for 30 seconds to clear lines and gauges.
5. With engine running, remove charging low-side hose adapter from accumulator service fitting. Unscrew rapidly to avoid excessive refrigerant loss.

CAUTION: Do not remove a gauge line from its adaptor when line is connected to A/C system. To disconnect line, always remove line adaptor from service fitting. Do not remove charging hose at gauge set while attached to accumulator, as system will be discharged due to depressed Schrader valve.

6. Replace protective cap on accumulator fitting and turn engine off.
7. Check system for leaks.
8. Start engine and check for proper system pressures.

LEAK TEST SYSTEM

The propane torch Halide Leak Detector is the most widely used of the detection devices. Therefore, only the procedure for this device will be given. The procedure is the same for any electronic detector, except that the pick-up device registers the presence of refrigerant by a flashing light or high pitched squeal instead of changing the color of the flame. All other steps in preparing the system and leak testing are the same and can be followed as outlined below:

1. Stabilize system at 1500–1750 rpm. If system is empty of refrigerant, it will be necessary to install a partial charge before continuing. With gauges connected into system, adjust A/C controls for maximum cooling. Operate for 10 to 15 minutes, then shut off car engine.
2. Light leak detector. Open valve to a low flame that will not blow itself out. Warm up until copper element turns cherry red. Lower flame until flame tip is even with or slightly below center of element. *For electronic tester, follow preparation procedure as given in operating instructions.*
3. Move leak detector pick-up under hoses, joints, seals, and any possible place for a leak to occur.

NOTE: Freon 12 refrigerant is heavier than air and will move downward. If concentration of refrigerant is located, move pick-up upward to locate leak. Do not inhale fumes produced by burning refrigerant.

4. Watch for color change of flame: Pale blue, no refrigerant; yellow, small amount of refrigerant; purplish-blue, large amount of refrigerant. Repair system as necessary if leaks are located.
5. Check sensitivity of reaction plate. Pass pick-up hose over empty can or crack open refrigerant container; flame should show violent reaction. If no color change, replace reaction plate, following instructions accompanying leak detector. *Too high a flame will result in short life to reaction plate and poor reaction and will soon burn out element.*
6. Charge system if repairs were necessary.

A/C System Servicing

OIL CHARGE

Delco Air & Frigidaire Compressors Models With Cycling Clutch

Oil Charge-Component Replacement

If there are no signs of excessive leakage, add the following amount of oil depending on component to be replaced.

Evaporator .... 3 ounces
Condenser .... 1 ounce

If accumulator or compressor are to be replaced, drain oil from component to be replaced and measure, then add same amount of new oil to replacement component plus one additional ounce.

CAUTION: On 1981–83 units, if accumulator is replaced, two additional ounces of oil must be added to replace amount captured by desiccant in old accumulator.

NOTE: The radial 4 cylinder compressor does not have an oil sump.

Oil Charge-Leak Condition

On models with axial 6 cylinder compressor, both accumulator and compressor must be removed and oil drained and measured in cases of excessive oil leakage. If oil recovered is 4 ounces or more, add same amount of new refrigerant oil to system. If amount of oil recovered is less than 4 ounces, add 6 ounces of new refrigerant oil to system.

On models with radial 4 cylinder compressor, it will only be necessary to remove and drain and measure oil from accumulator assembly in cases of excessive oil leakage. The radial 4 cylinder compressor does not have an oil sump, therefore it is not necessary to remove compressor in cases of oil leakage. On 1977–80 units, if amount of oil recovered is 2 ounces or more, add same amount of new refrigerant oil to system. If amount of oil recovered is less than 2 ounces, add two ounces of new refrigerant oil to system. On 1981–83 units, if amount of oil recovered is 3 ounces or more, add the same amount of new refrigerant oil to system. If amount recovered is less than 3 ounces, add 3 ounces of new refrigerant oil to system.

NOTE: On 1977–80 units, if accumulator is replaced one additional ounce of oil must be added to replace amount captured by desiccant in old accumulator. On 1981–83 units, if accumulator is replaced two additional ounces of oil must be added to replace amount captured by desiccant in old accumulator.

Models Less Cycling Clutch

RADIAL 4 CYLINDER COMPRESSOR

Component Replacement

When replacing a system component, oil should be added to the system as follows. If compressor is operating, idle engine for 10 minutes with A/C controls set for maximum cooling and high blower prior to discharging system.

Add additional oil as specified if any of components are replaced.

Condenser .... 1 ounce
Evaporator .... 1 ounce
VIR .... 3 ounce
Accumulator .... 1 ounce

Compressor Replacement

1. Discharge system and remove compressor from vehicle.
2. Position compressor with shaft end up and allow oil to drain from suction and discharge ports into a container calibrated in ounces.
3. Drain oil from new compressor, then add same amount of new refrigerant oil to new compressor as was drained from original compressor.

NOTE: If system was flushed the total oil capacity must be added to the compressor as specified in the *A/C Data Table.*

4. Install new compressor and charge system.

Component Rupture, Fast Discharge

1. Repair leak and flush system.
2. Remove compressor and drain oil.
3. Add total capacity as specified in A/C *Data Table* of new refrigerant oil to suction port of compressor.
4. Install compressor, charge system and perform leak check.

Slow Leak

1. If refrigerant loss has occurred over an extended period of time, add 3 ounces of refrigerant oil to system.
2. Recharge system.

System Performance Evaluation

When system performance, efficiency and proper oil charge are in doubt, the system should be flushed and the total capacity, as specified in the *A/C Data Table,* of new refrigerant oil be added to the compressor prior to any further checks of the system.

AXIAL 6 CYLINDER COMPRESSOR

Oil Charge

1. Idle engine for 10 minutes at 1250 rpm with system controls set for maximum cooling and high blower speed.
2. Stop engine, discharge system and remove compressor.
3. With compressor in a horizontal position and drain plug down, remove plug and drain oil into a measured container.
4. If 4 ounces or more of oil was drained, add the same amount to the compressor. If less than 4 ounces of oil was drained, add 6 ounces of oil to compressor.

Compressor Replacement

1. Idle engine for 10 minutes at approximately 1250 rpm at maximum cooling and high blower speed to distribute oil in system.
2. Remove compressor from vehicle.

3. Remove plug and allow oil to drain from compressor into a container calibrated in ounces.
4. Drain oil from new compressor.
5. If amount drained from original compressor is more than four ounces, add the same amount of new refrigerant oil to the new compressor plus amount lost during discharge.
6. If amount of oil drained from original compressor is less than 4 ounces, add 6 ounces of new refrigerant oil to the new compressor plus amount lost during discharge.

Component Replacement

Whenever a component of the A/C system is replaced, if not pre-charged by factory, measured quantities of refrigeration oil should be added to the component to assure that the total oil charge in the system is correct before the unit is placed into operation.

The oil is poured directly into the replacement component. If an evaporator is installed, pour oil into the inlet pipe with the pipe held vertically so the oil will drain into the evaporator core. No additional oil is required if valves and hoses are replaced.

Add additional oil as specified if any of the following components are replaced.

Evaporator (front or rear) .... 3 ounces
Condenser .... 1 ounce
VIR .... 1 ounce
Accumulator .... 1 ounce
Receiver .... 1 ounce

NOTE: If the system is flushed with sufficient quantity of a flushing agent that would remove oil from the system, install the full amount specified in the *A/C Data Table.* On a newly installed system, install the full capacity of oil prior to operation. On systems containing metal particles in the oil, replace or overhaul the compressor, replace the receiver-dehydrator or VIR dessicant and install a high capacity, low pressure drop filter in the liquid line to the filter to protect the expansion valve and new compressor from damage due to foreign particles.

C-171

1. Discharge system and remove suction and discharge lines from compressor.
2. Remove compressor assembly from vehicle, then drain compressor oil from suction and discharge ports.
3. Add 5 fl. oz. of refrigerant oil to compressor through suction port.
4. Install compressor assembly and, using new gaskets, attach suction and discharge lines.
5. Evacuate and charge system.
   If any of the following components are to be replaced, oil must be added to the system:
   Evaporator .... 2 ounces
   Condenser .... 1 ounce
   Filter-Drier .... 1 ounce

1977–80 Motorcraft Axial 6 Cyl Compressor

Refer to Delco Air and Frigidaire for oil charge procedure.

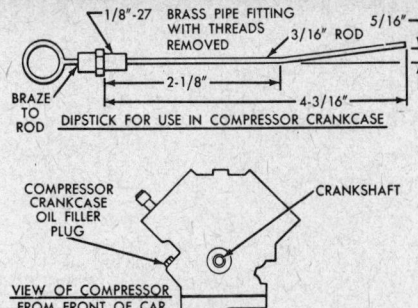

Fig. 1 Air Temp compressor oil level dipstick fabrication and filler plug location

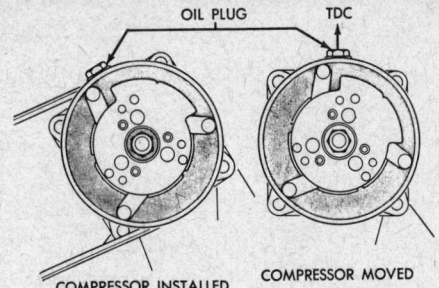

Fig. 2 Positioning compressor for oil level check. Sankyo compressor

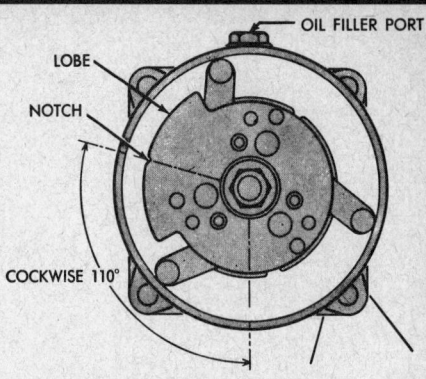

Fig. 3 Positioning front plate for oil level check. Sankyo compressor

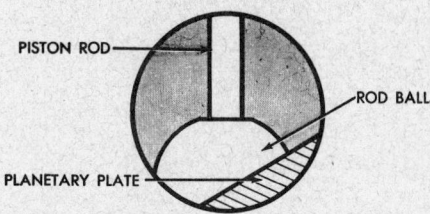

Fig. 4 Top piston rod as viewed through oil filler port. Sankyo compressor

When other air conditioning system components are replaced, measured amounts of 500 viscosity oil should be added to the component to ensure total oil charge is correct. Clean refrigerant oil should be added as follows:

Evaporator core . . . . 3 fluid ounces
Condenser . . . . 1 fluid ounce
Accumulator: Drain oil from accumulator through pressure switch fitting and measure. Add equal amount plus 1 ounce clean refrigerant oil to new accumulator.

Replacement of other components such as valves or hoses does not require the addition of any refrigerant oil.

OIL LEVEL CHECK

NOTE: The oil level of these compressors should be checked whenever refrigerant has been lost due to leakage or through normal system servicing.

Chrysler Air Temp Compressors

RV2 Compressor

1. Connect gauge and manifold assembly, Fig. 3, and slowly discharge refrigerant system. Near completion of discharge, flush dipstick with existing freon. This will ensure dipstick is clean and at approximately the same temperature as refrigerant oil in compressor sump.
2. Carefully remove compressor oil sump filler plug, then insert dipstick into hole until it bottoms in sump, Fig. 1.

NOTE: When removing compressor oil sump filler plug a face shield should be worn. Refrigerant dissolved in compressor oil could cause oil to purcolate out through filler plug opening.

3. Remove dipstick and measure oil level, refer to A/C Specification Tables. Add refrigerant oil as necessary to bring oil level within limits.

NOTE: Oil level should be checked only after refrigerant has boiled off and oil surface has stabilized.

4. If any of the following components are to be replaced, it will be necessary to add additional oil to system.
   Evaporator . . . . 2 ounces
   Condenser . . . . 1 ounce
   Filter Drier . . . . 1 ounce
5. On all models, install filler plug, then

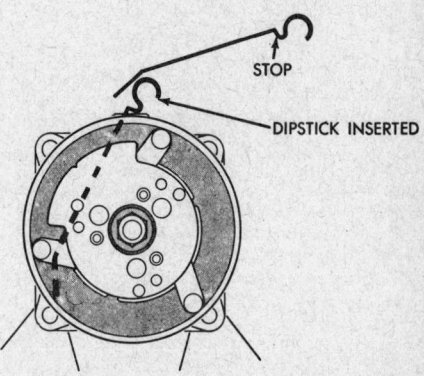

Fig. 5 Checking oil level. Sankyo compressor

evacuate and recharge system.

C–171 Compressor

1. Discharge refrigerant from system.
2. On 1979 models, drain and discard oil through drain plug at bottom of compressor. On 1980–83 models, remove compressor from vehicle, then invert compressor and allow oil to drain from suction and discharge ports.
3. On 1979 models, install drain plug and torque to 90–130 inch lbs., then remove suction line and add 5 fluid ounces of clean refrigerant oil through suction port. Then install suction line using a new gasket.
4. On 1980–83 models, add 5 fluid ounces of clean refrigerant oil through suction port, then install compressor and connect suction and discharge lines using new gaskets.
5. Evacuate and recharge system.

NOTE: The C–171 compressor contains 9 to 10 ounces of refrigerant oil. While the A/C system is in operation, the oil is carried through the entire system by the refrigerant. Some of the oil will be retained in the various components of the system. If a replacement evaporator coil is installed, add 2 ounces of refrigerant oil to system. If a replacement condenser coil or filter-drier is installed, add one additional ounce of refrigerant oil to system. This additional oil must be added to compensate for oil removed with the component. Replacement compressors are charged with 9 to 10 ounces of refrigerant oil, therefore before installing a replacement compressor, approximately 4 ounces of refrigerant oil should be drained from the compressor.

1980–83 Ford FS6 & Nippondenso 6 Cyl. Compressors

1. If compressor is not seized, operate engine at 1000 to 1500 RPM with A/C on maximum cooling and high blower for approximately 10 minutes.
2. Discharge refrigerant system, then remove compressor from vehicle.
3. Remove drain plug from compressor and pour refrigerant oil into a calibrated container.
4. If oil drained is less than 3 ounces, add 6 ounces of new refrigerant oil to compressor.
5. If oil drained is between 3 and 6 ounces, add the same amount of new refrigerant oil to the compressor.
6. If oil drained is more than 6 ounces, only add six ounces to compressor.

NOTE: Replacement compressors are charged with 10 ounces of refrigerant oil. Before installing a replacement compressor, the oil must be drained and only 6 ounces of oil reinstalled into the replacement compressor. When certain other refrigerant system components are replaced, the oil level must be adjusted to compensate for oil retained in these components. When installing a replacement evaporator core, add 3 ounces of oil to evaporator. When installing a replacement condenser or accumulator, add 1 ounce of oil to the component.

Ford HR-980 Radial 4 Cylinder Compressor

A new service replacement compressor contains 8 fluid ounces of refrigerant oil. Before installing replacement compressor, drain 4 fluid ounces of oil from compressor in order to maintain total system oil charge within specified limits.

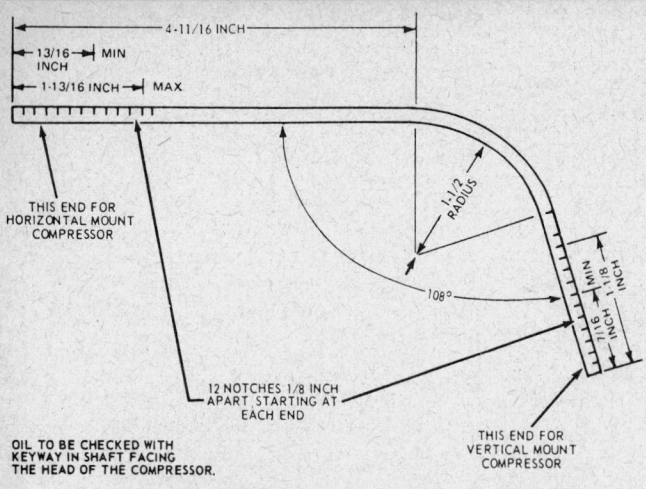

Fig. 6   York compressor oil level dipstick fabrication. Ford Motor Co. models

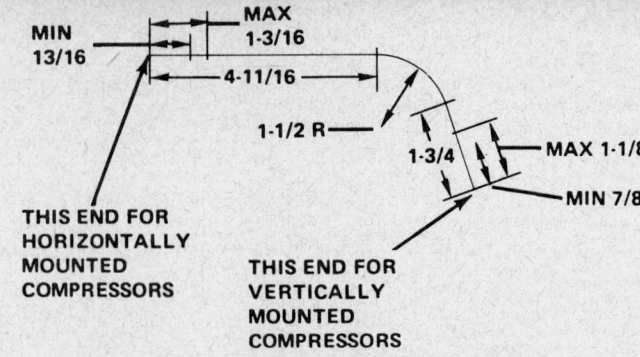

Fig. 7   York compressor oil level dipstick fabrication. American Motors

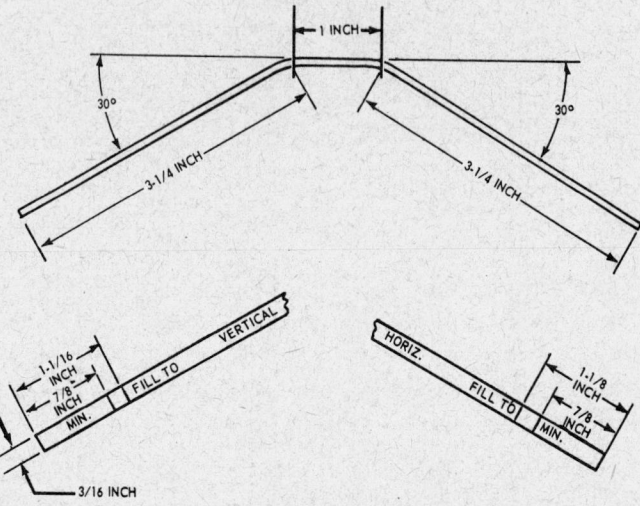

Fig. 8   Tecumseh compressor oil level dipstick fabrication. Ford Motor Co. models

Sankyo 5 Cyl. Rotary Compressor

1979 Chrysler Corp. Models
1. Disconnect and plug vacuum hose from water valve.
2. With engine at idle speed, operate A/C system for 10 minutes in Max A/C mode, high blower speed and temperature control set at maximum heat.
3. Shut off engine and reconnect water valve vacuum hose, then slowly discharge the A/C system.
4. Loosen compressor mounting bolts and remove belt, then rotate compressor so that oil filler tube is at top dead center position, Fig. 2.
5. Thoroughly clean area around oil filler plug and remove plug.

CAUTION: Use care when removing the filler plug to prevent the dissolved refrigerant in the crankcase oil from percolating out through the filler plug opening. This action will stop as soon as the refrigerant has boiled away. Also, the oil level should be measured only after the refrigerant has boiled away and the oil surface has stabilized.

6. Rotate front plate of clutch hub so that notch in center of lobe is indexed 110° from bottom, Fig. 3. In this position, the ball end of the piston rod aligns with oil filler port, Fig. 4.
7. Looking at front plate with lobe notch at upper left in the 110° position, insert dipstick (tool C-4504) diagonally from upper right to lower left until stop contacts the filler port surface, Fig. 5.

NOTE: Before inserting dipstick, clean and cool the dipstick with refrigerant.

8. Remove dipstick and note oil level. The dipstick is marked in eight increments and each increment represents one ounce of oil. Add oil if necessary to bring level within specifications.

1981 American Motors California Models W/ 6–258 Engine & All 1982–83
When installing a replacement compressor, proceed as follows:
1. Isolate compressor from system, then remove compressor.
2. Remove oil plug from compressor, then drain refrigerant oil into a calibrated container.
3. Drain refrigerant oil from compressor to be installed.
4. Add the same amount of refrigerant oil removed from compressor to be replaced plus 1 ounce to the compressor to be installed.
5. Install drain plug, then install and purge air from compressor.

Tecumseh & York

1. Connect manifold gauge set, Fig. 4, then operate system for approximately 10 minutes or until system pressures stabilize. This will allow oil in the system to return to compressor sump.
2. On American Motors models, isolate compressor as outlined earlier.
3. On Ford Motor Co. models, discharge entire refrigerant system.
4. On all models, slowly loosen compressor oil filler plug to relieve any internal pressures in compressor.

NOTE: A face shield should be worn when loosening or removing oil filler plug.

5. Insert clean dipstick into filler plug hole until it bottoms in sump, Figs. 6, 7 and 8.

NOTE: On York compressors ensure keyway in shaft faces head of compressor before checking oil level.

6. Remove dipstick and measure oil level. Refer to "A/C Data Table" and add refrigerant oil as necessary. Install filler plug and "O" ring.
7. On American Motors models, purge air from compressor.
8. On Ford Motor Co. models, evacuate and recharge system.

Nippondenso

1. Operate compressor for 10 to 15 minutes at maximum cooling to stabilize system.
2. Discharge system and remove compressor from vehicle. Remove drain plug and measure amount of oil drained from compressor.
3. If less than three ounces of oil were drained from compressor, add six ounces of refrigerant oil to drained service replacement compressor.
4. If between three and six ounces of oil were drained from compressor, oil is properly distributed throughout system. Add an equal amount of refrigerant oil to drained service replacement compressor.
5. Never add more than six ounces of refrigerant oil to a replacement compressor and never install a replacement compressor containing more than six ounces of refrigerant oil. Clean refrigerant oil should be added to the following replacement components:

Evaporator . . . . 3 ounces
Condenser . . . . 1 ounce
Accumulator . . . . 1 ounce

AIR CONDITIONING SPECIFICATIONS

Year	Model	Refrigerant Capacity, Lbs.	Refrigeration Oil			Compressor Clutch Air Gap Inch
			Viscosity	Total System Capacity, Ounces	Compressor Oil Level Check, Inches	
AMERICAN MOTORS						
1977	Matador	3	③	7	⑧	—
	Gremlin, Hornet	2	③	7	⑧	—
	Pacer	2 1/8	③	7	⑧	—
1978	AMX, Concord, Gremlin	2	③	7	⑧	—
	Matador	3	③	7	⑧	—
	Pacer	2 1/8	③	7	⑧	—
1979	AMX, Concord, Spirit	2	③	7	⑧	—
	Pacer	2 1/8	③	7	⑧	—
1980	York 2 Cyl. Comp.	⑱	③	7	⑧	—
	Delco Air 4 Cyl. Comp.	⑱	525	6	①	.020–.040
1981	York 2 Cyl. Comp.	2	③	7	⑧	—
	Delco Air 4 Cyl. Comp.	2	525	6	①	.020–.040
	Sankyo 5 Cyl. Comp.	2	500	7–8	①	.016–.031
1982–83	All	2	500	7–8	①	.016–.031
BUICK—EXC. SKYHAWK, 1980–83 SKYLARK & 1982–83 CENTURY						
1977–79	Skylark	3 1/2	525	④	①	⑲
	Century & Regal	3 3/4	525	④	①	⑲
	Electra, LeSabre, Riviera	3 3/4	525	④	①	⑲
1980	Century, Regal, Riviera	3 1/2	525	④	①	⑲
	Electra & LeSabre	3 3/4	525	④	①	⑲
1981	Century, Regal, Riviera	3 1/4	525	④	①	⑲
	Electra & LeSabre	3 1/2	525	④	①	⑲
1982–83	Regal & Riviera	3 1/4	525	6	①	.020–.040
	Electra & LeSabre	3 1/2	525	6	①	.020–.040
CADILLAC—EXC. CIMARRON						
1977–79	All Exc. Seville	⑥	525	⑩	①	⑲
1977–79	Seville	3 1/2	525	10	①	⑲
1980–81	All	3 3/4	525	6	①	⑲
1982	All	3 1/4	525	6	①	.020–.040
1983	All	3 1/2	525	6	①	.020–.040
CHEVROLET—CAMARO, CHEVROLET, MALIBU, MONTE CARLO & NOVA						
1977–79	Nova	3 1/2	525	④	①	⑲
1977–80	Exc. Camaro, Nova	3 3/4	525	④	①	⑲
1977–81	Camaro	3 1/4	525	④	①	⑲
1981–82	Caprice, Impala	3 1/2	525	④	①	⑲
	Malibu, Monte Carlo	3 1/4	525	④	①	⑲
1982–83	Camaro	3	525	6	①	.020–.040
1983	Caprice, Impala	3 1/2	525	6	①	.020–.040
	Malibu, Monte Carlo	3 1/4	525	6	①	.020–.040
1982–83 CHEV. CAVALIER, BUICK SKYHAWK, CAD. CIMARRON, OLDS. FIRENZA & PONT. 2000						
1982–83	All	2 3/4	525	6	①	.020–.040
1982–83 CHEV. CELEBRITY, BUICK CENTURY, OLDS. CUTLASS CIERA & PONT. 6000						
1982	All	2 3/4	525	6	①	.020–.040
1983	All	2 3/4	525	㉑	①	㉒
CHEVROLET CHEVETTE & PONTIAC 1000						
1977–81	All	2 1/4	525	④	①	⑲
1982–83	All	2 1/4	525	6	①	.020–.040

Continued

AIR CONDITIONING SPECIFICATIONS—Continued

Year	Model	Refrigerant Capacity, Lbs.	Refrigeration Oil			Compressor Clutch Air Gap Inch
			Viscosity	Total System Capacity, Ounces	Compressor Oil Level Check, Inches	
1980–83 CHEVROLET CITATION, BUICK SKYLARK, OLDS OMEGA & PONTIAC PHOENIX						
1980–83	All	2³/₄	525	5¹/₂–6¹/₂	①	.020–.040
1977–80 CHEVROLET MONZA, BUICK SKYHAWK, OLDS STARFIRE & PONTIAC SUNBIRD						
1977–80	Monza	2¹³/₁₆	525	④	①	⑲
1977	Skyhawk	3	525	6	①	.020–.040
	Sunbird	3¹/₄	525	6	①	.020–.040
1977–78	Starfire	2¹/₂	525	6	①	.020–.040
1978–80	Skyhawk	2¹/₂	525	6	①	.020–.040
	Sunbird	2¹/₂	525	6	①	.020–.040
1979–80	Starfire	⑨	525	6	①	.020–.040
CHEVROLET VEGA & PONTIAC ASTRE						
1977	Astre	2¹/₂	525	5¹/₂–6¹/₂	①	.020–.040
	Vega	2¹³/₁₆	525	5¹/₂–6¹/₂	①	.020–.040
CHEVROLET CORVETTE						
1977–81	All	3	525	④	①	⑲
1982	All	3	525	6	①	.020–.040
CHRYSLER CORP. REAR WHEEL DRIVE CHRYSLER						
1977	Newport & New Yorker	2³/₄	500	10–12	2³/₈②	—
	Cordoba & LeBaron	2⁵/₈	500	10–12	2³/₈②	—
1978–79	All	2⁵/₈	500	⑤	⑰	⑳
1980	Newport & New Yorker	2⁷/₈	500	⑤	⑰	.020–.035
	Cordoba & LeBaron	2⁵/₈	500	⑤	⑰	.020–.035
1981	All	2⁵/₈	500	⑤	⑰	.020–.035
1982–83	All	2⁵/₈	500	9–10	⑦	.020–.035
DODGE						
1977	Monaco	2³/₄	500	10–12	2³/₈②	—
	Exc. Monaco	2⁵/₈	500	10–12	2³/₈②	—
1978–79	All	2⁵/₈	500	⑤	⑰	⑳
1980	St. Regis	2⁷/₈	500	⑤	⑰	.020–.035
	Exc. St. Regis	2⁵/₈	500	⑤	⑰	.020–.035
1981	All	2⁵/₈	500	⑤	⑰	.020–.035
1982–83	All	2⁵/₈	500	9–10	⑦	.020–.035
PLYMOUTH						
1977	Gran Fury	2³/₄	500	10–12	2³/₈②	—
	Fury & Volaré	2⁵/₈	500	10–12	2³/₈②	—
1978–79	All	2⁵/₈	500	⑤	⑰	⑳
1980	Gran Fury	2⁷/₈	500	⑤	⑰	.020–.035
	Volaré	2⁵/₈	500	⑤	⑰	.020–.035
1981	All	2⁵/₈	500	⑤	⑰	.020–.035
1982–83	All	2⁵/₈	500	9–10	⑦	.020–.035
CHRYSLER CORP. FRONT WHEEL DRIVE						
1978–79	Horizon & Omni	2¹/₈	500	7–8	⑪	⑳
1980–81	Horizon & Omni	2¹/₈	500	⑤	⑦	.020–.035
1981	Aries & Reliant	2³/₈	500	⑤	⑦	.020–.035
1982–83	Horizon, Omni, Charger, Turismo, O24 & TC3	2¹/₈	500	9–10	⑦	.020–.035
	Exc. Horizon, Omni, Charger, Turismo, O24 & TC3	2³/₈	500	9–10	⑦	.020–.035

Continued

AIR CONDITIONING SPECIFICATIONS—Continued

Year	Model	Refrigerant Capacity, Lbs.	Refrigeration Oil			Compressor Clutch Air Gap Inch
			Viscosity	Total System Capacity, Ounces	Compressor Oil Level Check, Inches	
FORD—FULL SIZE						
1977–79	All	4¼	525	10½	①	.022-.057
1980	All	3¼	⑫	⑬	①	⑭
1981–82	All	3¼	500	13	①	.021-.036
1983	All	3¼	500	10	①	.021-.036
FORD—COMPACT & INTERMEDIATE (EXC. MUSTANG & PINTO)						
1977–78	Granada	4¼	525	10½	①	.022-.057
1977–79	York Comp.	⑮	③	10	②⑧	—
	Tecumseh Comp.	⑮	③	11	②⑧	—
1979–80	Granada	4	525	10½	①	.022-.057
1980–81	York Comp.	3½	③	10	②⑧	—
	Tecumseh	3½	③	11	②⑧	—
1982	Ford FS-6	2½	500	13	①	.021-.036
1982–83	York Comp.	2½	③	10	②⑧	—
	Tecumseh 2 Cyl. Comp.	2½	③	11	②⑧	—
1983	Ford FS-6	2½	500	10	①	.021-.036
	Tecumseh HR-980 Comp.	2½	500	8	①	.021-.036
FORD ESCORT, EXP & TEMPO; MERCURY LYNX, LN7 & TOPAZ						
1981	Escort & Lynx	2½	500	13	①	.021-.036
1982	All	2⁹⁄₁₆	500	10	①	.021-.036
1983	Escort & Lynx	2⁹⁄₁₆	500	10	①	.021-.036
	EXP & LN7	2⁵⁄₁₆	500	10	①	.021-.036
1984	Tempo & Topaz	2⁹⁄₁₆	500	10	①	.021-.036
FORD MUSTANG & MERCURY CAPRI						
1977–78	York Comp.	3¼	③	10	②⑧	—
	Tecumseh Comp.	3¼	③	11	②⑧	—
1979–81	York Comp.	3½	③	10	②⑧	—
	Tecumseh Comp.	3½	③	11	②⑧	—
1982–83	York Comp.	2½	③	10	②⑧	—
	Tecumseh 2 Cyl. Comp.	2½	③	11	②⑧	—
1983	Nippondenso 6P148 Comp.	2½	500	10	①	.021-.036
	Tecumseh HR-980 Comp.	2½	500	8	①	.021-.036
FORD PINTO & MERCURY BOBCAT						
1977–80	York Comp.	2¼	③	10	②⑧	—
	Tecumseh Comp.	2¼	③	11	②⑧	—
LINCOLN						
1977–78	Mark V	4½	525	10½	①	.022-.057
	Lincoln	4¼	525	10½	①	.022-.057
1977–78	Versailles	4¼	525	10½	①	.022-.057
1979–80	Exc. Versailles	4¼	⑫	⑬	①	⑭
	Versailles	4	⑫	⑬	①	.022-.057
1981–82	All exc. 1982 Continental	3	500	13	①	.021-.036
1982	Continental	2½	500	13	①	.021-.036
1983	Continental	2½	500	10	①	.021-.036
	Exc. Continental	3	500	10	①	.021-.036

AIR CONDITIONING SPECIFICATIONS—Continued

Year	Model	Refrigerant Capacity, Lbs.	Refrigeration Oil: Viscosity	Refrigeration Oil: Total Sytem Capacity, Ounces	Refrigeration Oil: Compressor Oil Level Check, Inches	Compressor Clutch Air Gap Inch
MERCURY—FULL SIZE						
1977–79	All	4¼	525	10½	①	.022–.057
1980	All	3¼	⑫	⑬	①	⑭
1981–82	All	3¼	500	13	①	.022–.036
1983	All	3¼	500	10	①	.021–.036
MERCURY—COMPACT & INTERMEDIATE (EXC. BOBCAT & CAPRI)						
1977–78	Monarch	4¼	525	10½	①	.022–.057
1977–79	York Comp.	⑯	③	10	②⑧	—
	Tecumseh Comp.	⑯	③	11	②⑧	—
1979–80	Monarch	4	525	10½	①	.022–.057
1980–81	York	3½	③	10	②⑧	—
	Tecumseh	3½	③	11	②⑧	—
1983	Ford FS-6	2½	500	13	①	.021–.036
1982–83	York Comp.	2½	③	10	②⑧	—
	Tecumseh 2 Cyl. Comp.	2½	③	11	②⑧	—
1983	Ford FS-6	2½	500	10	①	.021–.036
	Tecumseh HR-980 Comp.	2½	500	8	①	.021–.036
OLDSMOBILE—88, 98, TORONADO, 1977–79 OMEGA & CUTLASS EXC. CIERA						
1977–79	Omega	3½	525	④	①	⑲
1977–80	All exc. Omega	3¾	525	④	①	⑲
1981	Cutlass	3¼	525	④	①	⑲
1981	All exc. Cutlass	3½	525	④	①	⑲
1982–83	Cutlass	3¼	525	6	①	.020–.040
1982–83	All exc. Cutlass	3½	525	6	①	.020–.040
PONTIAC—EXC. ASTRE, SUNBIRD, 1000 & FRONT WHEEL DRIVE						
1977	Ventura	3½	525	④	①	⑲
1977–79	Phoenix	3½	525	④	①	⑲
1977–79	All exc. Ventura, Phoenix & Firebird	3¾	525	④	①	⑲
1977–81	Firebird	3¼	525	④	①	⑲
1980	Gran Prix & LeMans	3¾	525	④	①	⑲
1980–81	All exc. Gran Prix & LeMans	3½	525	④	①	⑲
1981	Gran Prix & LeMans	3¼	525	④	①	⑲
1982–83	All exc. Firebird & Parisienne	3¼	525	6	①	.020–.040
1982–83	Firebird	3	525	6	①	.020–.040
1983	Parisienne	3½	525	6	①	.020–.040

①—Note that "Oil level inches" cannot be checked. Refer to total capacity in ounces. See text for procedure.
②—Dipstick reading with compressor installed.
③—Suniso 5G or Capella E.
④—Axial comp., 10 oz.; radial comp., 6 oz.
⑤—With RV2 compressor, 10–12 ounces. With Sankyo Compressor, 7–8 ounces. With C-171 compressor, 9 ounces.
⑥—With one evaporator, 3¾. With two evaporators, 5.
⑦—Refer to text for C-171 compressor.
⑧—York Comp.—Vertical mount., 7/8–1 1/8; horizontal mount., 13/16–1 3/16. Tecumseh Comp.—Vertical mount., 7/8–1 3/8; horizontal mount., 7/8–1 5/8.
⑨—With axial compressor, 3 lbs.; with radial compressor, 2½ lbs.
⑩—With one evaporator, 10½. With two evaporators, 13½.
⑪—On Sankyo compressor oil level should be at the third to fourth increment on the dipstick which represents 3 to 4 ounces of oil. Refer to text for procedure. On C-171 compressor, refer to text for procedure.
⑫—Motorcraft compressor, 525 viscosity; Nippondenso compressor, 500 viscosity.
⑬—Motorcraft compressor, 10½ ounces; Nippondenso compressor, 13 ounces.
⑭—Motorcraft compressor, .022–.057"; Nippondenso compressor, .021–.036".
⑮—Maverick, 1 7/8; LTD II & Thunderbird, 4¼; Fairmont, 3½.
⑯—Comet, 1 7/8; Cougar, 4¼; Zephyr, 3½.
⑰—RV2 compressor, 2 3/8 inches. On Sankyo compressors, the oil level should be at the third to fourth increment on the dipstick which represents 3 to 4 ounces of oil. Refer to text for procedure. On C-171 compressor, refer to text.
⑱—AMX, Concord & Spirit, 2; Pacer, 2 1/8.
⑲—R-4 compressor, .020–.040", A-6 compressor, .022–.057".
⑳—RV-2 compressor, non-adjustable; Sankyo compressor, .016–.032"; C-171 compressor, .020–.035.
㉑—Axial comp., 8 oz.; radial comp., 6 oz.
㉒—Axial comp., .015–.025"; radial comp., .020–.040".

CHARGING VALVE LOCATIONS

Year & Model	High Press.	Low Press.
AMERICAN MOTORS		
1977–79	Compressor	Compressor
1980–83	①	①
BUICK (EXC. SKYHAWK, 1980–83 SKYLARK & 1982–83 CENTURY)		
1977–83	⑨	Accumulator
CADILLAC (EXC. CIMARRON)		
1977–79	⑤	Accumulator
1980–83	⑨	Accumulator
CHEVROLET, CAMARO, MALIBU, MONTE CARLO & NOVA		
1977–83	⑨	Accumulator
1982–83 CHEVROLET CAVALIER, BUICK SKYHAWK, CADILLAC CIMARRON, OLDSMOBILE FIRENZA & PONTIAC 2000		
1982–83	⑨	Accumulator
1982–83 CHEVROLET CELEBRITY, BUICK CENTURY, OLDSMOBILE CUTLASS CIERA & PONTIAC 6000		
1982–83	⑨	Accumulator
CHEVROLET CHEVETTE & PONTIAC 1000		
1977–79	Dis. Pres. Sw.	Accumulator
1980–81	Muffler	Accumulator
1982–83		Accumulator

Year & Model	High Press.	Low Press.
1980–83 CHEVROLET CITATION, BUICK SKYLARK, OLDSMOBILE OMEGA & PONTIAC PHOENIX		
1980–83	Muffler	Accumulator
CHEVROLET CORVETTE		
1977	VIR	VIR
1978–82	⑨	Accumulator
CHEVROLET VEGA & PONTIAC ASTRE		
1977	Dis. Pres. Sw.	Accumulator
CHRYSLER		
1977	Compressor	Compressor
1978–83	⑫	Compressor
DODGE (ALL)		
1977	Compressor	Compressor
1978–83	⑫	Compressor
FORD EXC. TEMPO		
1977–79⑩	Compressor	Compressor
1977–79⑪	⑤	STV
1980–81⑩	⑭	⑬
1980–81⑪	⑤	Accumulator
1982–83⑯	⑤	⑥
1982–83⑰	⑤	Accumulator
FORD TEMPO & MERCURY TOPAZ		
1984	⑤	⑥
LINCOLN		
1977–80④	⑤	⑬
1977–81⑮	⑤	Accumulator
1982–83⑱	⑤	Accumulator
1982–83⑲	⑤	⑥

Year & Model	High Press.	Low Press.
MERCURY EXC. TOPAZ		
1977–79⑩	Compressor	Compressor
1977–79⑪	⑤	STV
1980–81⑩	⑭	⑬
1980–81⑪	⑤	Accumulator
1982⑯	⑤	⑥
1982–83⑰	⑤	Accumulator
1977–80 MONZA, SKYHAWK, STARFIRE & SUNBIRD		
1977–79	⑦	⑧
1980	⑨	Accumulator
OLDSMOBILE—88, 98, TORONADO, 1977–79 OMEGA & CUTLASS (EXC. CIERA)		
1977③	Compressor	VIR
1977–81②	Compressor	Accumulator
1982–83	⑨	Accumulator
PLYMOUTH (ALL)		
1977	Compressor	Compressor
1978–83	⑫	Compressor
PONTIAC (EXC. ASTRE, SUNBIRD, 1000 & FRONT WHEEL DRIVE)		
1977–83	⑨	Accumulator
THUNDERBIRD		
1977–79	Compressor	⑥
1980–81	⑤	⑬
1982–83	⑤	⑥

①—On models with 6 cylinder engine, the high and low pressure service ports are located on the compressor; On models with 4 cylinder engine, the high and low pressure service ports are located on service valve adapter.
②—Except VIR system.
③—With VIR.
④—Versailles.
⑤—On high pressure line from compressor.

⑥—On low pressure line from compressor.
⑦—4 cyl. eng., on line from condenser; 6 cyl. & 8 cyl. eng., Dis. Press. Switch.
⑧—4 cyl. & 6 cyl. eng. on VIR; 8 cyl. eng., on accumulator.
⑨—High pressure vapor line or muffler.
⑩—2 cyl. compressor.
⑪—6 cyl. compressor.
⑫—With RV2 compressor, on compressor. With

Sankyo or C-171 compressor, on muffler.
⑬—On combination valve.
⑭—On liquid line at combination valve.
⑮—Except Versailles.
⑯—Except full size
⑰—Full size
⑱—Except Lincoln Continental
⑲—Lincoln Continental

VARIABLE SPEED FANS

Fig. 1 Typical variable-speed fan installed

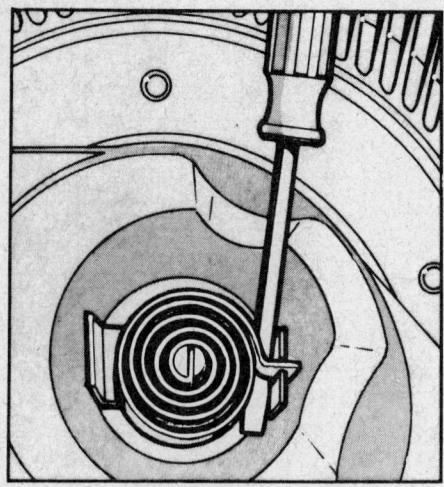

Fig. 4 Disconnecting bi-metal spring

The fan drive clutch, Fig. 1, is a fluid coupling containing silicone oil. Fan speed is regulated by the torque-carrying capacity of the silicone oil. The more silicone oil in the coupling the greater the fan speed, and the less silicone oil the slower the fan speed.

Two types of fan drive clutches are in use. On one, Fig. 2, a bi-metallic strip and control piston on the front of the fluid coupling regulates the amount of silicone oil entering the coupling. The bi-metallic strip bows outward with a decrease in surrounding temperature and allows a piston to move outward. The piston opens a valve regulating the flow of silicone oil into the coupling from a reserve chamber. The silicone oil is returned to the reserve chamber through a bleed hole when the valve is closed.

On the other type of fan drive clutch, Fig. 3, a heat-sensitive, bi-metal spring connected to an opening plate brings about a similar result. Both units cause the fan speed to increase with a rise in temperature and to decrease as the temperature goes down.

In some cases a Flex-Fan is used instead of a Fan Drive Clutch. Flexible blades vary the volume of air being drawn through the radiator, automatically increasing the pitch at low engine speeds.

Fan Drive Clutch Test

CAUTION: Do not operate the engine until the fan has been first checked for possible cracks and separations.

Run the engine at a fast idle speed (1000 rpm) until normal operating temperature is reached. This process can be speeded up by blocking off the front of the radiator with cardboard. Regardless of temperatures, the unit must be operated for at least five minutes immediately before being tested.

Stop the engine and, using a glove or a cloth to protect the hand, immediately check the effort required to turn the fan. If considerable effort is required, it can be assumed that the coupling is operating satisfactorily. If very little effort is required to turn the fan, it is an indication that the coupling is not operating properly and should be replaced.

If the clutch fan is the coiled bi-metal spring type, it may be tested while the vehicle is being driven. To check, disconnect the bi-metal spring, Fig. 4, and rotate 90° counter clockwise. This disables the temperature-controlled free-wheeling feature and the clutch performs like a conventional fan. If this cures the overheating condition, replace the clutch fan.

Service Procedure

CAUTION: To prevent silicone fluid from draining into fan drive bearing, do not store or place drive unit on bench with rear of shaft pointing downward.

The removal procedure for either type of fan clutch assembly is generally the same for all cars. Merely unfasten the unit from the water pump and remove the assembly from the car.

The type of unit shown in Fig. 2 may be partially disassembled for inspection and cleaning. Take off the capscrews that hold the assembly together and separate the fan from the drive clutch. Next remove the metal strip on the front by pushing one end of it toward the fan clutch body so it clears the retaining bracket. Then push the strip to the side so that its opposite end will spring out of place. Now remove the small control piston underneath it.

Check the piston for free movement of the coupling device. If the piston sticks, clean it with emery cloth. If the bi-metal strip is damaged, replace the entire unit. These strips are not interchangeable.

When reassembling, install the control piston so that the projection on the end of it will contact the metal strip. Then install the metal strip with any identification numerals or letters facing the clutch. After reassembly, clean the clutch drive with a cloth soaked in solvent. Avoid dipping the clutch assembly in any type of liquid. Install the assembly in the reverse order of removal.

The coil spring type of fan clutch cannot be disassembled, serviced or repaired. If it does not function properly it must be replaced with a new unit.

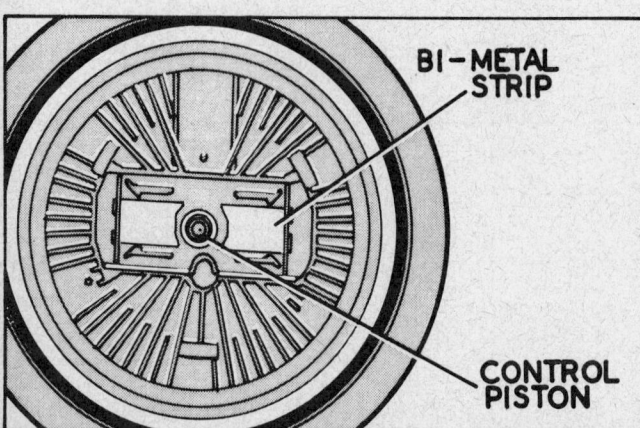

Fig. 2 Variable-speed fan with flat bi-metal thermostatic spring

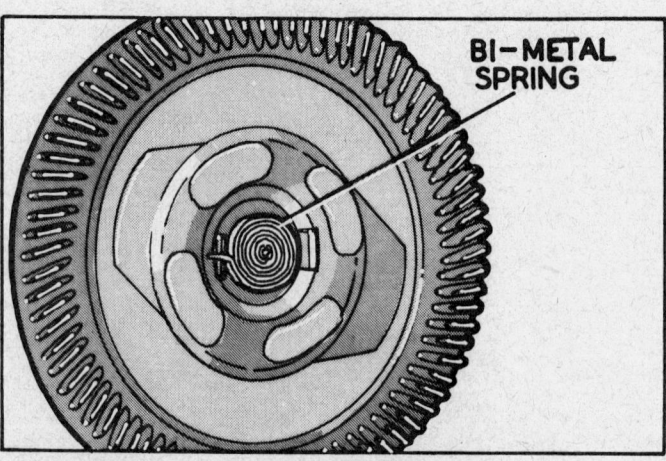

Fig. 3 Variable-speed fan with coiled bi-metal thermostatic spring

ELECTRIC ENGINE COOLING FANS

> **CAUTION:** On models equipped with electric engine cooling fans, the battery ground cable should be disconnected whenever underhood service is performed.

1977–79 MONZA, STARFIRE & 1978–79 SUNBIRD W/V8 ENGINE & A/C

These models are equipped with an auxiliary electric engine cooling fan located in front of the radiator. The fan is thermostatically controlled by a thermostatic switch located at the rear of the right hand cylinder head. When engine temperature reaches approximately 235 degrees F, the thermostatic switch will close and the fan will operate to provide supplemental air flow in addition to that which is supplied by the engine cooling fan.

To replace the fan and motor assembly, disconnect wire connector and ground strap, then remove attaching bolts and fan and motor assembly, Fig. 1.

1979–82 CORVETTE AUXILIARY FAN

Description

Current is supplied to the auxiliary fan motor through a 30 amp. circuit breaker located in the fuse panel. The fan motor is controlled by an engine temperature switch located at the rear of the right hand cylinder head. When engine temperature reaches approximately 238 degrees F, the engine temperature switch will close and the fan motor will operate to provide supplementary air flow in addition to that supplied by the engine cooling fan. When engine temperature decreases to approximately 201 degrees F, the engine temperature switch will open and current will no longer be supplied to the fan motor. The fan motor will only operate when the ignition switch is in the "Run" position.

Fan Motor, Replace

1. Disconnect battery ground cable, then remove fresh air scoop.
2. Remove engine cooling fan, then disconnect fan motor wire connector from vehicle wire connector. Remove retainer se-

curing fan motor wiring to chassis, if equipped.
3. Remove upper fan shroud mounting bolts, then remove fan shroud and auxiliary fan motor as an assembly.
4. Remove nuts attaching auxiliary fan motor to fan shroud, then disconnect wiring from fan motor and remove motor.
5. Reverse procedure to install.

1978–83 CHRYSLER FRONT WHEEL DRIVE MODELS

Description

The fan is controlled by a fan switch which is located on the radiator, Fig. 2. The switch will automatically turn on when coolant temperature reaches 193 to 207 degrees F. On models with A/C, when the A/C system is in operation, the fan motor will operate continually regardless of engine coolant temperature. When the ignition switch is turned off the fan motor will stop operating, except on 1981–82 models equipped with 2.6 L engine and air conditioning. On 1981–82 models equipped with 2.6 L engines and air conditioning, the fan will remain operating with ignition off for approximately 5 minutes if ambient temperature at radiator is above a predetermined level.

Radiator Fan Switch

The radiator fan switch is located on left hand radiator tank. The switch is normally open and incorporates a bimetal disc which pushes the plunger when coolant temperature reaches approximately 200 degrees F. If the

fan motor turns on and off at the appropriate temperature, the switch is operating properly.

To check switch continuity, drain coolant until level is below switch. The switch can be viewed by looking downward through the radiator filler neck. Disconnect electrical connector from switch and remove switch from radiator. Dip switch into an oil bath which has achieved a temperature of 208 degrees F or higher and check switch for continuity using a test lamp or ohmmeter. If continuity is not indicated, replace switch.

Ambient Temperature Switch

The ambient temperature switch is used on air conditioned 1981–82 2.6 L engines only. The switch is located on the radiator cooling fan mounting bracket and is used in conjunction with the time delay relay to activate the radiator cooling fan for approximately 5 minutes with engine off during periods of radiator ambient temperature of 105° F. or above.

The switch is tested using a suitable ohmmeter. When the switch is cold, continuity should not exist. When the switch is warmed to 105° F. or above, continuity should be present. Replace if defective.

Electric Fan Motor

Diagnosis
Disconnect wire connector from fan motor terminal, then connect a 14 gauge jumper wire from battery to fan motor terminal. If fan motor does not operate properly, replace fan motor.

Fan Motor, Replace
1. Disconnect wire connectors from fan mo-

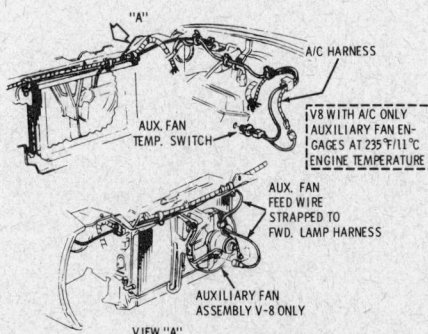

Fig. 1 Auxiliary electric engine cooling fan. 1977–79 Monza, Starfire & 1978–79 Sunbird W/V8 engine & A/C

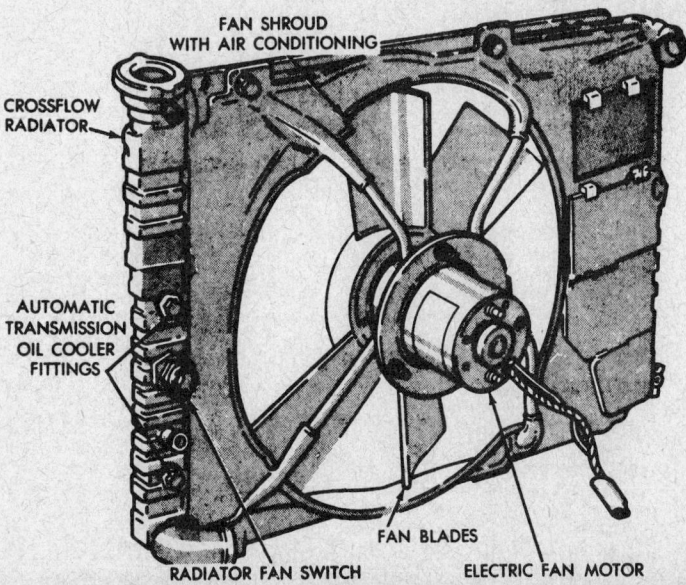

Fig. 2 Electric engine cooling fan. 1978–83 Chrysler front wheel drive models

tor and fan switch, then drain cooling system.
2. Disconnect upper and lower radiator hoses from radiator. On models equipped with automatic transmission, disconnect fluid cooling hoses from radiator, if necessary.
3. Remove upper fan shroud attaching screws, then lift shroud upward and out of bottom shroud retaining clips, separating shroud from radiator.

NOTE: When removing shroud from radiator, use care not to damage fan or radiator cooling fins.

4. Remove fan motor to shroud attaching screws, then while supporting fan motor and shaft, remove fan motor retaining clip and fan motor.
5. Reverse procedure to install.

Electric Fan Motor Relay

The fan motor relay is used on models equipped with A/C. The relay is located on the left hand shock absorber housing. If radiator fan switch and fan motor test results are satisfactory, but fan motor will not operate the fan motor relay is then suspected. After replacing relay, disconnect wire connector from radiator fan switch and connect a 14 gauge jumper wire between wire connector terminals. Place ignition switch in the Accessory position. Fan motor should operate.

On 1981–82 models equipped with 2.6 L engines, the electric engine cooling fan relay also contains the time delay, which operates the cooling fan when ignition is off and the radiator ambient temperature is 105° F. or above.

1980–83 CITATION, OMEGA, PHOENIX, SKYLARK & 1982–83 CAVALIER, CELEBRITY, CENTURY, CIMARRON, CUTLASS CIERA, FIRENZA, SKYHAWK, 2000 & 6000

Description

The single speed electric cooling fan is used on all models except those equipped with V6 gasoline engines with heavy duty cooling systems and all diesel engines, which use a two-speed electric motor. The fan motor is operated by the cooling fan relay on single speed models or cooling fan relay and cooling fan speed control on two speed models. On single speed models, when coolant temperature exceeds 230 degrees F., the cooling fan temperature switch closes. On two-speed models, when the coolant temperature reaches 226 (diesel 223) degrees F., the low speed cooling fan temperature switch closes, and at 239 (diesel 246) degrees F., the high speed cooling fan temperature switch closes. On all models, when the cooling fan temperature switch closes on single speed models, or the low speed cooling fan temperature switch closes on two

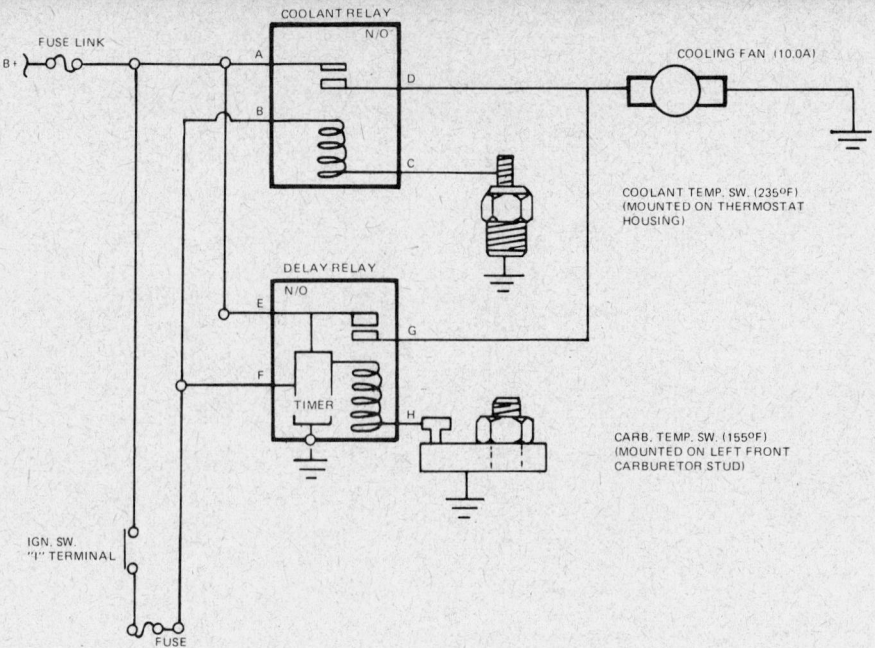

Fig. 3   Electric engine cooling fan wiring diagram. 1980 Fairmont, Zephyr & 1980–81 Capri & Mustang less A/C

speed models, it allows current to pass through the choke heater fuse or fuel pump fuse (depending on model) and cooling fan relay coil to ground, thus closing the relay contacts. On single speed models, when the relay contacts are closed, current flows through a fusible link to the fan motor. On two speed models when the relay contacts are closed, current flows through a fusible link, then cooling fan speed control low speed contacts, and into the fan motor. On two speed models, when the high speed cooling fan temperature switch closes, the solid state circuitry of the cooling fan speed control is grounded, causing cooling fan speed control high speed contacts to close and cooling fan motor to operate at high speed. On single speed models, when coolant temperature falls below a predetermined level, the cooling fan temperature switch opens and current is no longer supplied to the fan motor. On two speed models, when coolant temperature falls below the high speed cooling fan temperature switch predetermined level, the contacts open, opening the ground circuit to the cooling fan speed control and causing the fan motor to operate at low speed. When the coolant temperature falls below the low speed cooling fan temperature switch predetermined level, the contacts open, causing the cooling fan relay to open and shut off current to the cooling fan speed control and the cooling fan motor. On 1980 models and 1982–83 diesel engined models with A/C, a second switch (diesel engine models use two switches) which senses compressor head pressure to the condensor, is used to activate the fan motor when the A/C compressor is operating. On all models equipped with A/C, the cooling fan relay is grounded whenever the A/C selector switch is in the Max., Normal or Bi-Level position, causing the cooling fan to operate. On some automatic transmission models with gasoline V6 engines, the electric engine cooling fan operates when the torque converter clutch is engaged.

Troubleshooting

1. If fan motor does not operate, check the following:
   a. Check for blown fuse.
   b. Check fusible link.
   c. Disconnect wire connector from engine coolant temperature switch. With ignition "On", ground end of wire. Fan motor should operate.
2. If cooling fan operates whenever the ignition switch is in the Run position, check the following:
   a. Check cooling fan temperature switch, compressor pressure switch, if equipped and other related mechanical components.
   b. Check cooling fan relay.

Fan Motor, Replace

1. Disconnect battery ground cable, then disconnect wire connector from fan motor.
2. Detach front lamp wiring harness from fan motor, then remove harness from fan motor frame.
3. Remove fan motor frame to radiator support attaching bolts, then remove fan motor.
4. Reverse procedure to install. Torque fan to radiator support attaching bolts to 85 inch lbs.

1980 FAIRMONT & ZEPHYR & 1980–81 CAPRI & MUSTANG W/4-140 TURBO ENGINE

Description

Two thermal switches are used to activate the cooling fan motor. When engine tempera-

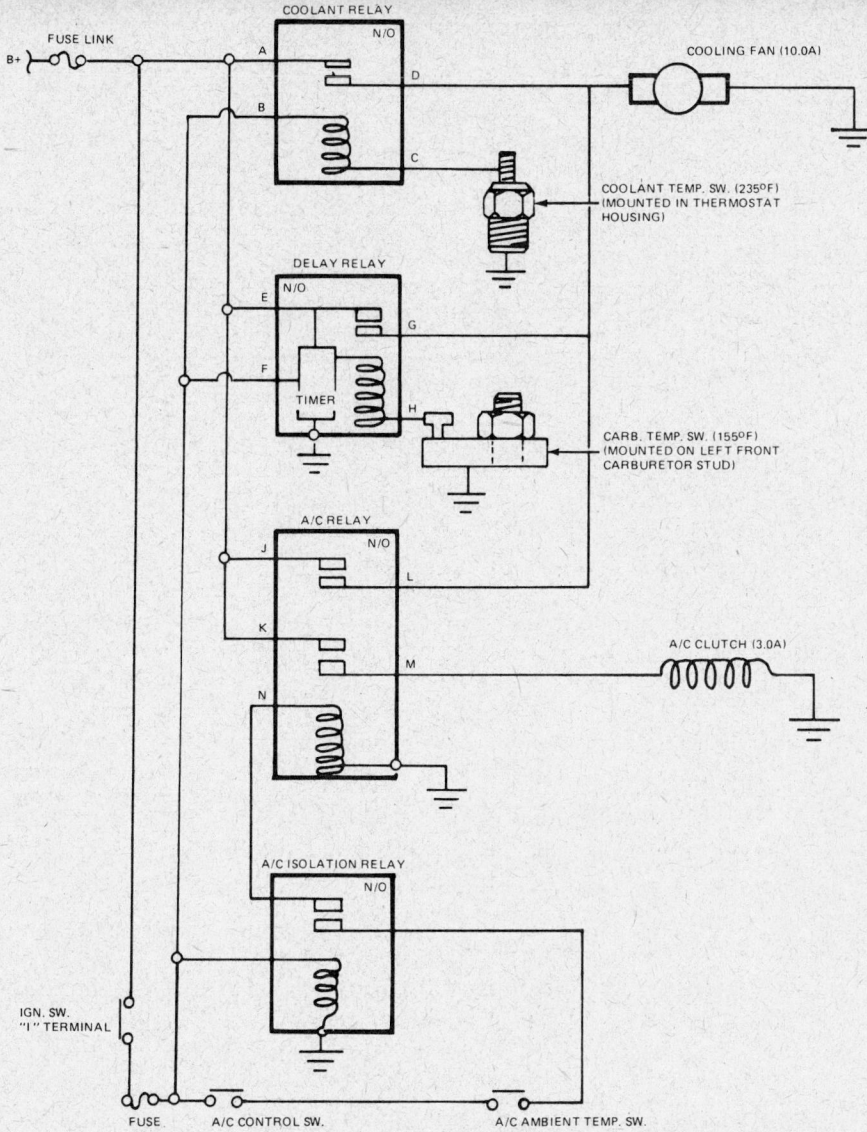

Fig. 4   Electric engine cooling fan wiring diagram. 1980 Fairmont, Zephyr & 1980–81 Capri & Mustang 4-140 Turbo with A/C

Delay Relay Check

Disconnect coolant relay wire connector, then place ignition switch in the On position and connect a jumper wire from carburetor temperature switch to ground. If fan motor operates, replace carburetor temperature switch. If fan motor fails to operate, disconnect delay relay wire connector and check for battery voltage at connector terminals E and F. If battery voltage is not indicated, trace circuits and repair as necessary. If battery voltage is indicated, check for continuity between delay relay connector terminals G and H. If continuity does not exist, trace circuit and repair as necessary. If continuity does exist, replace delay relay.

A/C Relay Check

Disconnect A/C compressor clutch lead and connect a jumper wire from battery to compressor clutch. If compressor clutch does not click, replace clutch. If compressor clutch clicks, disconnect coolant and delay relay wire connectors, then disconnect ambient temperature switch wire connector and connect a jumper wire between ambient temperature switch connector terminals. Place ignition switch in the On position and turn on A/C controls. The fan motor should be operating and the compressor clutch should click. If neither occurs, disconnect A/C relay wire connector and check for battery voltage at connector terminals N, J and K. If battery voltage is not indicated, check circuit and repair as necessary. If A/C fuse continues to blow, check for short in circuit, otherwise replace relay. If when jumper wire was connected between ambient switch wire connector terminals only the fan motor operated or only the A/C clutch clicked, or if neither occurred and battery voltage was indicated at A/C relay terminals N, J and K, check for continuity between A/C relay connector terminals L and M. If continuity does not exist, trace circuit and repair as necessary. If continuity does exist, replace A/C relay.

Fan Will Not Stop Operating

With ignition switch and A/C controls in the off position, disconnect A/C relay wire connector, then disconnect coolant relay. If fan stops operating, replace relay that was disconnected at time fan stopped operating. If fan continues to operate, connect a jumper wire from carburetor temperature switch to ground and cycle ignition switch on and off. If fan does not stop operating after approximately 20 minutes, replace delay relay.

Fan Motor, Replace

1. Detach wiring harness retainer from fan shroud, and disconnect fan motor wire connector.
2. Remove four fan shroud and fan motor assembly to radiator attaching screws, then remove shroud and motor assembly.
3. Remove retainer clip from end of fan motor shaft and remove fan blade.
4. Remove three nuts attaching fan motor to shroud, then remove fan motor.
5. Reverse procedure to install.

ture reaches 221 degrees F, the coolant temperature switch will close, thus activating the normally open coolant relay which supplies current to the fan motor. After engine has been turned off, extreme underhood temperatures may develop, causing fuel vaporization in the carburetor, which could cause a no start or hard starting condition. When carburetor temperature reaches 155 degrees F, the carburetor switch closes providing battery voltage to the fan motor relay which operates the fan motor. When the carburetor temperature switch closes, it also activates a timer which allows the fan motor to operate for a period of approximately 15 to 20 minutes. On models equipped with A/C, the engine cooling fan will operate whenever the compressor clutch is in operation.

Diagnosis, Figs. 3 & 4

Fan Motor Check

Disconnect fan motor wire connector, then connect jumper wires between battery and motor connector terminal with brown yellow wire and motor connector terminal with black wire to ground. If motor fails to operate, replace fan motor. If motor operates, proceed to next test.

Coolant Relay Check

Disconnect delay relay wire connector, then place ignition switch in the On position and connect a jumper wire from coolant temperature switch to ground. If fan motor operates, replace coolant temperature switch. If motor fails to operate, disconnect coolant relay wire connector and check for battery voltage at connector terminals A and B. If battery voltage is not indicated, trace circuit to ignition switch and battery and repair as necessary. If battery voltage is indicated, check for continuity between coolant relay wire connector terminals C and D, with coolant temperature switch connected to ground. If continuity does not exist, repair circuit. If continuity does exist, replace coolant relay.

FORD & MERCURY EXC. 1980 FAIRMONT & ZEPHYR & 1980–81 CAPRI & MUSTANG W/4-140 TURBO ENGINE

Description

The cooling fan is activated by the thermal

ELECTRIC ENGINE COOLING FANS

Year	Engine	Models	With Fuel Economy Package	With Auto. Trans.	With Power Brakes	With Air Conditioning	With High Output Engine	With Fuel Injection	System Type
1981	1.6L	Escort & Lynx	—	—	—	No	—	—	1
	1.6L	Escort & Lynx	—	—	—	Yes	—	—	7
1982	1.6L	Escort, EXP, LN7 & Lynx	—	—	—	No	—	—	1
	1.6L	Escort, EXP, LN7 & Lynx	—	—	No	Yes	—	—	3
	1.6L	Escort, EXP, LN7 & Lynx	—	—	Yes	Yes	—	—	4
	2.3L	Fairmont & Zephyr	Yes	—	—	No	—	—	1
	2.3L	Capri & Mustang	—	—	—	—	—	—	5
	2.3L	Cougar, Fairmont Granada & Zephyr	No	—	—	Yes	—	—	5
1983	1.6L	Escort, EXP, LN7 & Lynx	No	Yes	—	No	No	No	1
	1.6L	Escort, EXP, LN7 & Lynx	Yes	No	—	No	No	No	2
	1.6L	Escort, EXP, LN7 & Lynx	No	Yes	Yes	Yes	—	No	8
	1.6L	Escort, EXP, LN7 & Lynx	No	No	—	—	No	No	12
	1.6L	Escort, EXP, LN7 & Lynx	No	No	—	Yes	Yes	No	10
	1.6L	Escort, EXP, LN7 & Lynx	No	—	—	Yes	No	Yes	9
	2.3L	All	Yes	—	—	No	—	—	2
	2.3L	All	No	—	—	No	—	—	1
	2.3L, 3.3L	All	No	—	—	Yes	—	—	6
	3.8L	Exc. Capri & Mustang	No	—	—	Yes	—	—	6
	3.8L	Capri & Mustang	No	—	—	Yes	—	—	5
1984	2.3L	Tempo & Topaz	Yes	—	—	No	—	—	2
	2.3L	Tempo & Topaz	No	—	—	Yes	—	—	11

Fig. 5 Electric engine cooling fan system application chart

switch when engine coolant temperature reaches approximately 221 degrees F. The fan will continue to operate until coolant temperature drops to approximately 185 to 193 degrees F, at which time the thermal switch opens, releasing the relay contacts which supply current to the fan motor. On models equipped with A/C, the fan motor will continue to operate whenever the compressor clutch is operating regardless of coolant temperature. On some models, two fuses are used to protect the fan motor and thermal switch. A 16 amp fuse is located in the fan motor relay at the left hand dash panel near the steering column. There is also an 8 amp fuse located in the fuse panel. Cycling of the cooling fan will cause the temperature gauge to read between mid and upper range of the gauge range.

Trouble Shooting

For troubleshooting procedures on Ford and Mercury models except 1980 Fairmont and Zephyr and 1980–81 Capri and Mustang with 4-140 turbocharged engine, refer to Fig. 5 to determine which Electric Engine Cooling Fan system applies to a particular model.

TYPE 1 & 2, FIGS. 6 & 7
1. Check cooling fan fusible link. If fusible link is not blown, go to step 2. If blown, repair and retest.
2. Disconnect fan motor electrical connector, then connect a jumper wire from motor ground connection to a known good ground and a jumper wire from battery positive to motor B+ connection. If motor does not run, replace motor. If motor runs, reconnect electrical connector and proceed to step 3.
3. On type 2 systems, turn ignition "On." On both systems disconnect coolant temperature switch connector, then connect a jumper wire from connector to ground. If motor runs, check switch ground. If ground is satisfactory, replace coolant temperature switch. If motor does not run, proceed to step 4.
4. Using an ohmmeter, check continuity of wire 197 from temperature switch to fan relay. If no continuity exists, check circuit 197 for opens. If continuity exists, connect a jumper wire from coolant temperature switch connector to ground and proceed to step 5.

5. Disconnect fan relay wire connector then, connect a jumper wire from wire terminal 37 to 228. If motor runs, replace fan relay. If motor does not run, check circuit 37 for opens.

TYPE 3, FIG. 8
1. Check cooling fan fusible link. If fusible link is not blown, go to step 2. If blown, repair and retest.
2. Disconnect coolant temperature switch

COOLING FAN

COOLANT FAN RELAY 228

37
37 N.O.

BATTERY FUSIBLE LINK (IN 14401 HARNESS)

COOLANT TEMPERATURE SWITCH

197

COLOR CODES

CIRCUIT NUMBER	COLOR
37	Y
197	T/O HASH
228	BR/Y

Fig. 6 Electric engine cooling fan wiring diagram. Type 1

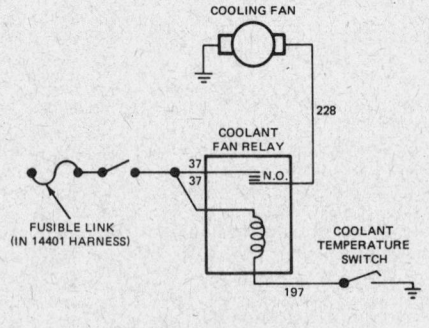

COOLING FAN

228

COOLANT FAN RELAY

37
37 N.O.

FUSIBLE LINK (IN 14401 HARNESS)

COOLANT TEMPERATURE SWITCH

197

COLOR CODES

CIRCUIT NUMBER	COLOR
37	Y
197	T/O HASH
228	BR/Y

Fig. 7 Electric engine cooling fan wiring diagram. Type 2

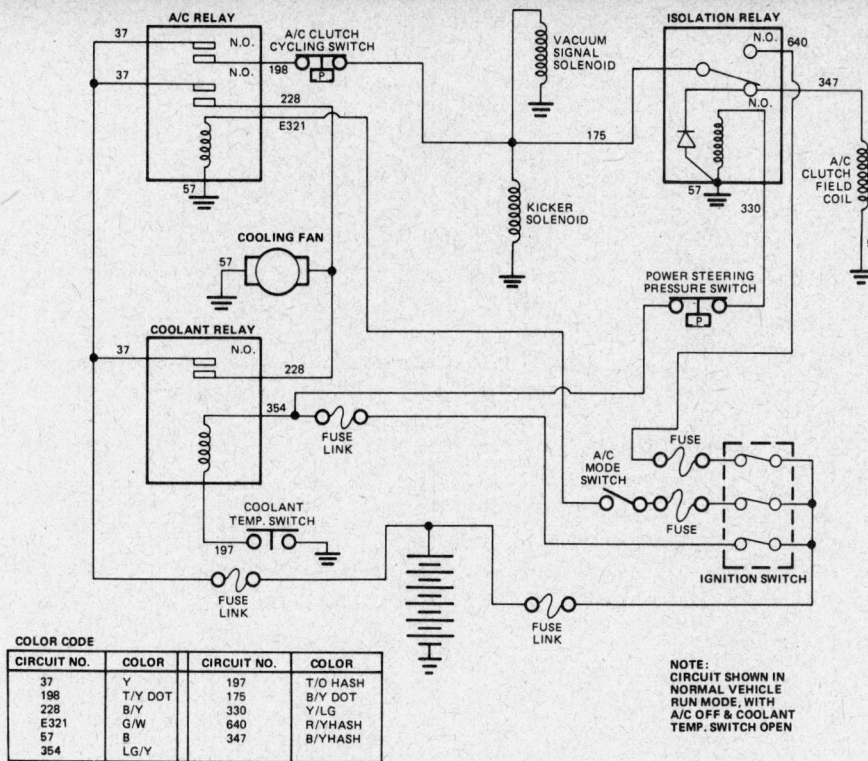

Fig. 8 Electric engine cooling fan wiring diagram. Type 3

COLOR CODE			
CIRCUIT NO.	COLOR	CIRCUIT NO.	COLOR
37	Y	197	T/O HASH
198	T/Y DOT	175	B/Y DOT
228	B/Y	330	Y/LG
E321	G/W	640	R/YHASH
57	B	347	B/YHASH
354	LG/Y		

NOTE:
CIRCUIT SHOWN IN
NORMAL VEHICLE
RUN MODE, WITH
A/C OFF & COOLANT
TEMP. SWITCH OPEN

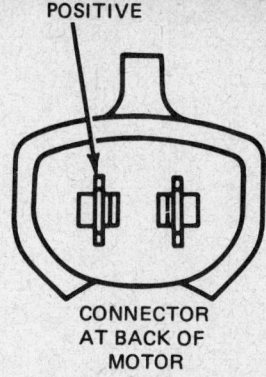

Fig. 9 Fan motor terminal identification.
Type 3, 4 & 7

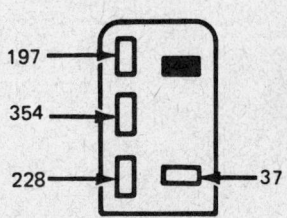

Fig. 10 Cooling fan relay wire connector
terminal identification. Type 3

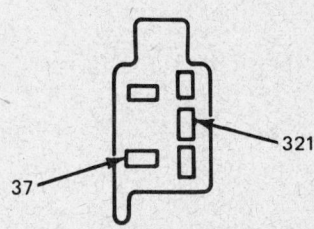

Fig. 11 A/C relay wire connector terminal
identification. Type 3, 4 & 7

connector, then connect a jumper wire from connector to ground and turn ignition "On." If fan motor does not run, proceed to step 3. If fan motor does run, primary system is operating satisfactory. If complaint is overheating, replace coolant temperature switch.

3. Reconnnect coolant temperature switch connector. Set A/C controls on maximum and turn ignition "On." If fan motor does not run, proceed to step 4. If fan motor runs, system is satisfactory.

4. Disconnect fan motor electrical connector, then connect a jumper wire from motor ground connection to a known good ground and a jumper wire from battery positive to motor B+ connection, Fig. 9. If motor does not run, replace motor. If motor runs, reconnect electrical connection and proceed to step 5.

5. Disconnect cooling fan relay connector and turn ignition "On." Using a test light, check for voltage at terminals 37 and 354, Fig. 10. If there is no voltage at one or both terminals, service relay feed circuits. If voltage at both terminals, proceed to step 6.

6. Connect jumper wire between terminals 354 and 228, Fig. 10. If fan motor does not run, repair wiring from relay connector to motor connector. If motor runs, disconnect jumper wire and proceed to step 7.

7. Using an ohmmeter, check continuity of wire 228 from relay connector to coolant temperature switch connector. If no continuity exists, repair wires and/or connectors. If continuity exists, replace cooling fan relay and recheck step 2.

8. Disconnect A/C relay connector. Using an ohmmeter, check continuity of wire 228 from relay to motor. If no continuity exists, repair wires and/or connectors. If continuity exists, proceed to step 9.

9. Reconnect fan motor connector, then disconnect A/C relay connector. Set A/C controls on maximum and turn ignition "On." Using a test light, check for voltage at terminals 37 and 321, Fig. 11. If there is no voltage at one or both terminals, service relay feed circuits or A/C control and recheck step 3. If there is voltage at both terminals, go to step 10.

10. Connect jumper wire to base of relay and connect to known good ground. If fan motor does not run, replace relay and recheck step 3. If fan motor runs, clean relay ground.

TYPE 4, FIG. 12

1. Check cooling fan fuse and fusible link. If fuse or fusible link is not blown, proceed to step 2. If fuse or fusible link is blown, repair or replace as necessary and retest.

2. Disconnect coolant temperature switch connector, then connect a jumper wire from connector to ground and turn ignition "On." If fan motor does not run, proceed to step 5. If fan motor runs, primary system is operating satisfactory. If complaint is overheating, replace coolant temperature switch.

3. Reconnect coolant temperature switch connector. Set A/C controls on maximum and turn ignition "On." If fan motor does not run, proceed to step 10. If fan motor does run, secondary system is operating satisfactorily, except possibly the coolant temperature switch. If complaint is overheating, proceed to step 4.

4. Using an ohmmeter, check coolant temperature switch body to thermostat housing for continuity. If no continuity exists, tighten switch until continuity exists.

Start engine and allow to warm up thoroughly. If fan motor runs, system is satisfactory. If fan motor does not run, replace coolant temperature switch.

5. Disconnect cooling fan motor connector, then connect a jumper wire from motor ground connection to a known good ground and a jumper wire from battery positive to motor B+ connection, Fig. 9. If fan motor does not run, replace motor. If fan motor runs, proceed to step 6.

6. Using an ohmmeter, check fan motor ground. If continuity exists, proceed to step 7. If continuity does not exist, repair ground.

7. Remove jumper wires, then reconnect fan motor connector. Disconnect cooling fan relay connector and switch ignition "On." Using a test light, check for voltage at terminals 37 and 354, Fig. 13. If there is no voltage at one or both terminals, repair relay feed circuits. If there is voltage at both terminals, proceed to step 8.

8. Jump terminals 37 to 228 of cooling fan relay connector, Fig. 13. If fan motor does not run, repair wiring from relay connector to fan motor connector. (Check capacitor, if equipped.) If fan motor runs, proceed to step 9.

9. Remove jumper wires. Using an ohmmeter, check continuity of wire 354 from relay connector to coolant temperature switch connector, Fig. 13. If continuity does not exist, repair wires and/or connec-

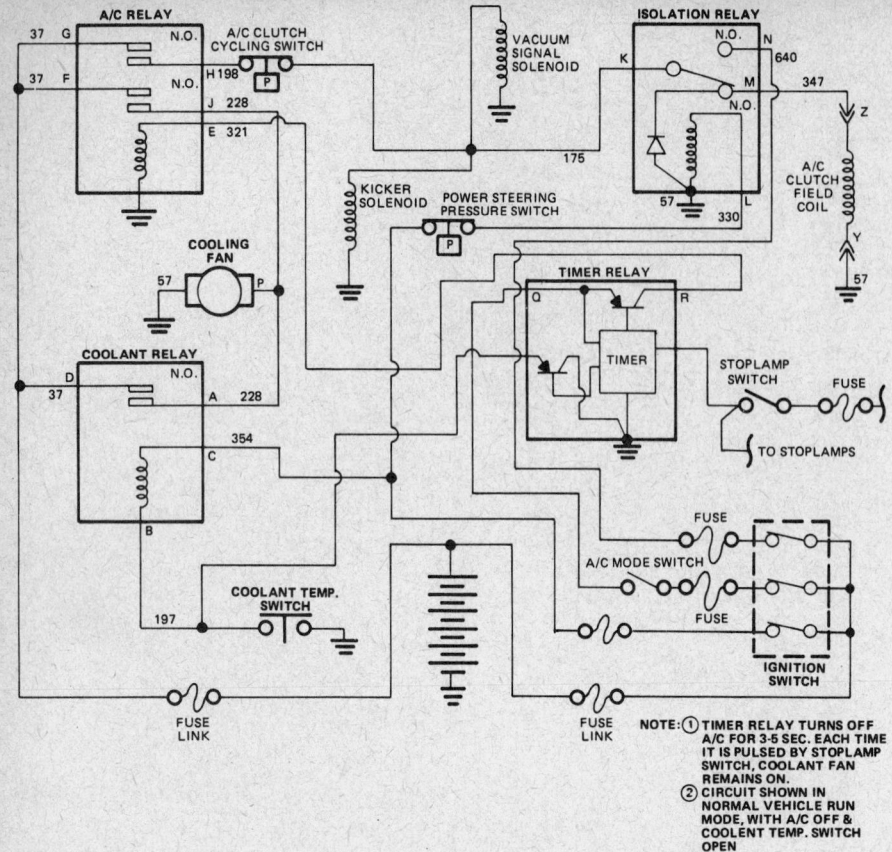

Fig. 12 Electric engine cooling fan wiring diagram. Type 4

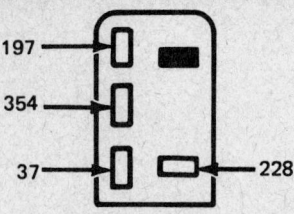

Fig. 13 Cooling fan relay connector terminal identification. Type 4 & 7

tors. If continuity does exist, replace cooling fan relay and retest.

10. Disconnect A/C relay connector. Using an ohmmeter, check continuity of wire 228 from relay to motor. If continuity does not exist, repair wires and/or connectors. If continuity does exist, proceed to step 11.

11. Reconnect fan motor connector, then disconnect A/C relay connector. Set A/C controls on maximum and turn ignition "On." Using a test light, check for voltage at terminals 37 and 321, Fig. 11. If there is no voltage at terminal 37, repair relay connector feed circuit. If there is no voltage at terminal 321, proceed to step 13. If there is voltage at both terminals, proceed to step 12.

12. Reconnect A/C relay connector. Connect jumper wire to base of relay to a known good ground. If fan motor does not run, replace relay and retest step 4. If fan motor runs, clean relay ground.

13. Using a test light, test for voltage at circuit 296 of A/C function control harness. If voltage exists, proceed to step 14. If no voltage exists, repair feed wire from fuse box.

14. Using an ohmmeter, check continuity of terminals 296 to 321 in A/C function control. Continuity should only exist in the following positions: A/C Max., A/C Norm. and Defrost. If continuity is not satisfactory, replace A/C function control. If continuity is satisfactory, proceed to step 15.

15. Using an ohmmeter, check continuity of circuit 321 from A/C function control to A/C relay. If continuity does not exist, repair wiring and/or connectors. If continuity does exist, repeat step 11.

TYPE 5 & 6, FIGS. 14 & 15

Fan Motor Inoperative

1. Check cooling fan fuses and fusible link. If fuses or fusible link are not blown, proceed to step 2. If fuses or fusible link are blown, repair or replace as necessary, and retest.

2. Disconnect fan motor electrical connector, then connect a jumper wire from motor ground connection to a known good ground and a jumper wire from battery positive to motor B+ connection. If motor does not run, replace motor. If motor runs, reconnect electrical connector and proceed to step 3.

3. Disconnect coolant temperature switch connector, then connect a jumper wire from connector to ground and turn ignition "On." If fan motor does not run, proceed to step 4. If motor does run, check switch ground, and if satisfactory, replace coolant temperature switch.

4. Turn ignition "Off," then remove jumper wire installed in step 3. Using an ohmmeter, check continuity of circuit 45 from cooling fan controller terminal #1 to coolant temperature switch. The controller, Fig. 16, is located under instrument panel near steering column. If continuity does not exist, check wire circuit 45 for opens. If continuity does exist, jump coolant temperature switch to ground and proceed to step 5.

5. Without disconnecting wiring connector from controller, Fig. 16, connect battery positive to circuit 68 at controller (terminal #8). If fan motor runs, check ignition feed circuits for opens. If fan motor does not run, remove jumper wire and proceed

to step 6.

6. Disconnect cooling fan wiring connector at controller, Fig. 16. Using a jumper wire, connect battery positive current to circuit 228 (terminal #5). If fan motor does not run, check circuit 228 for opens. If motor runs, remove jumper and proceed to step 7.

7. Using a jumper wire, connect circuit 175 to 228 (terminals #2 & 5) at the cooling fan motor controller connector. If motor does not run, check circuit 175 for opens. If motor does run, replace cooling fan controller, then remove jumper wire from temperature switch and reconnect connector.

Fan Motor Operates When Engine Overheats, Does Not Operate With A/C On

1. Set A/C controls selector lever in A/C position and turn ignition "On." If A/C clutch does not engage, proceed to step 2. If A/C clutch does engage, proceed to step 7.

2. Check fuse in fuse panel. If blown, replace. If fuse is not blown, proceed to step 3.

3. Disconnect A/C clutch cycle pressure switch. Use a jumper wire to jump across connector. If A/C clutch does not engage, proceed to step 5. If A/C clutch does engage, proceed to step 4.

4. Check A/C system for low refrigerant charge. If charge is insufficient, leak test, service and charge system. If charge is satisfactory, replace clutch cycling pressure switch.

5. Using a test light, check for voltage on 348 circuit at clutch cycling pressure switch. If there is no voltage, proceed to step 6. If there is voltage, repair open 347 circuit to A/C clutch.

6. Using a test light, test for voltage on 296 and 348 circuits at A/C function selector switch in instrument panel. If there is voltage on 296 but not on 348, replace A/C control assembly. If there is no voltage on 296 circuit, trace circuits 296 and 297 toward ignition switch.

7. Using a test light, check for voltage on 347 circuit (terminal #6) of cooling fan controller, Fig. 16. If there is no voltage, repair open 347 circuit. If voltage does exist, proceed to step 8.

8. Leaving connector attached to controller, ground 57 circuit (terminal #4) of controller. If fan motor runs, repair ground circuit. If fan does not run, replace controller.

TYPE 7, FIG. 17

1. Check cooling fan fuses located in the fuse

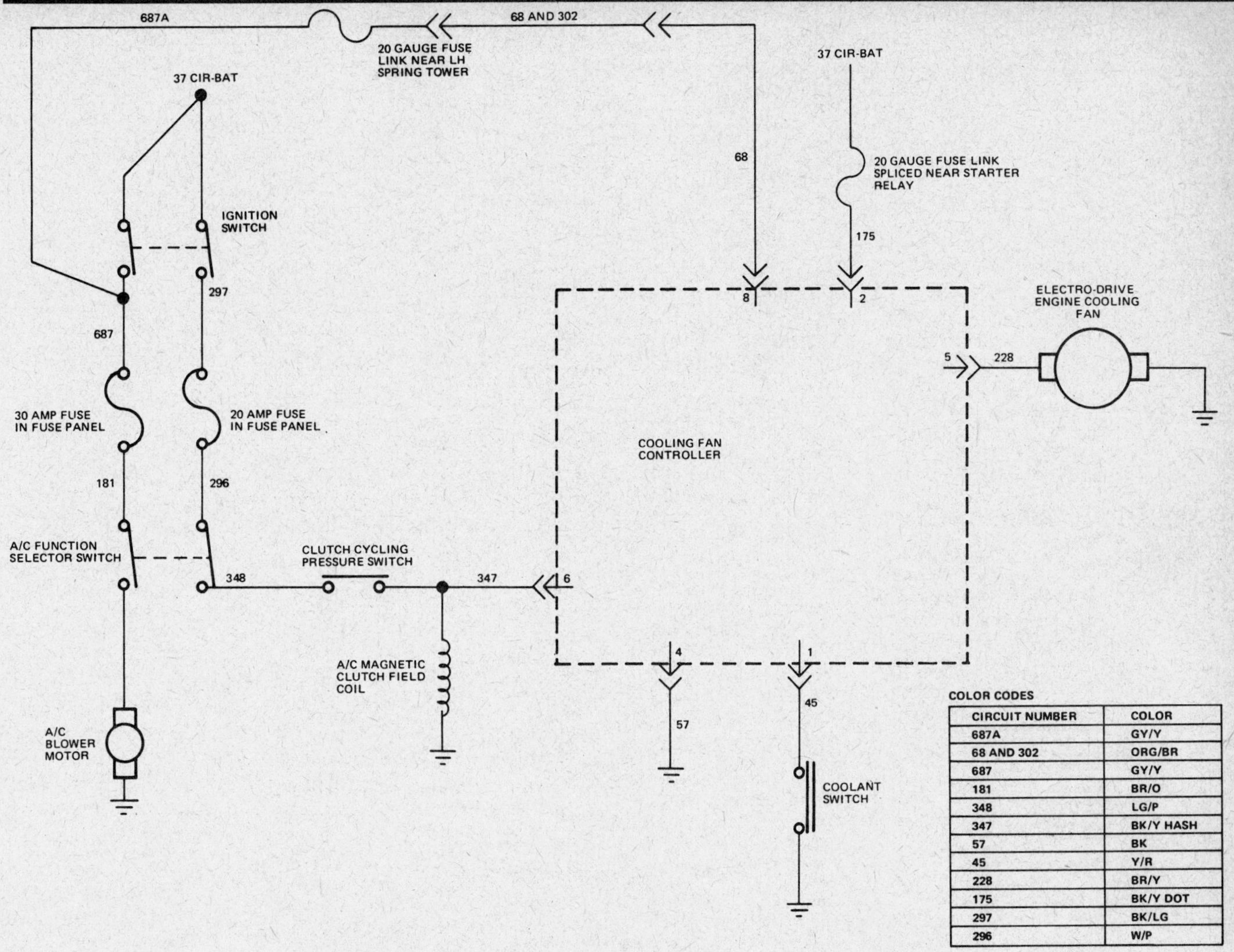

687A

68 AND 302

20 GAUGE FUSE LINK NEAR LH SPRING TOWER

37 CIR-BAT

37 CIR-BAT

IGNITION SWITCH

297

68

20 GAUGE FUSE LINK SPLICED NEAR STARTER RELAY

175

ELECTRO-DRIVE ENGINE COOLING FAN

687

8

2

5   228

30 AMP FUSE IN FUSE PANEL

20 AMP FUSE IN FUSE PANEL

COOLING FAN CONTROLLER

181

296

A/C FUNCTION SELECTOR SWITCH

CLUTCH CYCLING PRESSURE SWITCH

348

347

6

A/C MAGNETIC CLUTCH FIELD COIL

4

1

A/C BLOWER MOTOR

57

45

COOLANT SWITCH

COLOR CODES	
CIRCUIT NUMBER	COLOR
687A	GY/Y
68 AND 302	ORG/BR
687	GY/Y
181	BR/O
348	LG/P
347	BK/Y HASH
57	BK
45	Y/R
228	BR/Y
175	BK/Y DOT
297	BK/LG
296	W/P

Fig. 14   Electric engine cooling fan wiring diagram. Type 5

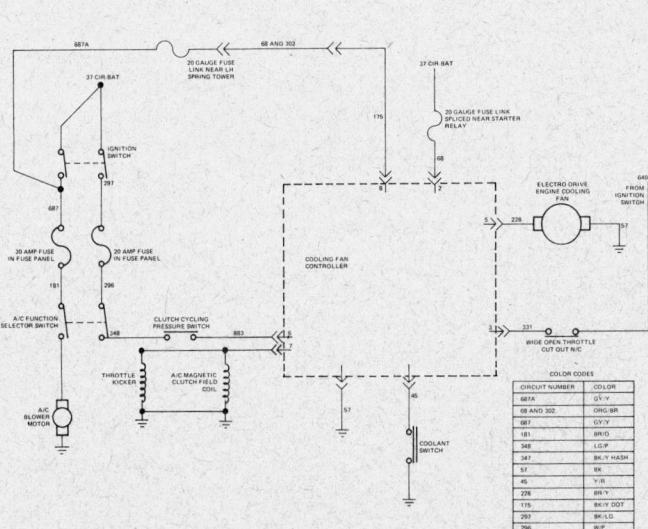

Fig. 15   Electric engine cooling fan wiring diagram. Type 6

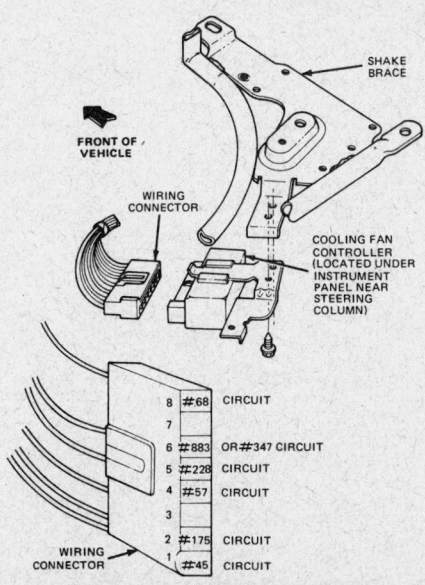

SHAKE BRACE

FRONT OF VEHICLE

WIRING CONNECTOR

COOLING FAN CONTROLLER (LOCATED UNDER INSTRUMENT PANEL NEAR STEERING COLUMN)

8   #68   CIRCUIT
7
6   #883   OR #347 CIRCUIT
5   #228   CIRCUIT
4   #57   CIRCUIT
3
2   #175   CIRCUIT
1   #45   CIRCUIT

WIRING CONNECTOR

Fig. 16   Cooling fan controller terminal identification. Type 5 & 6

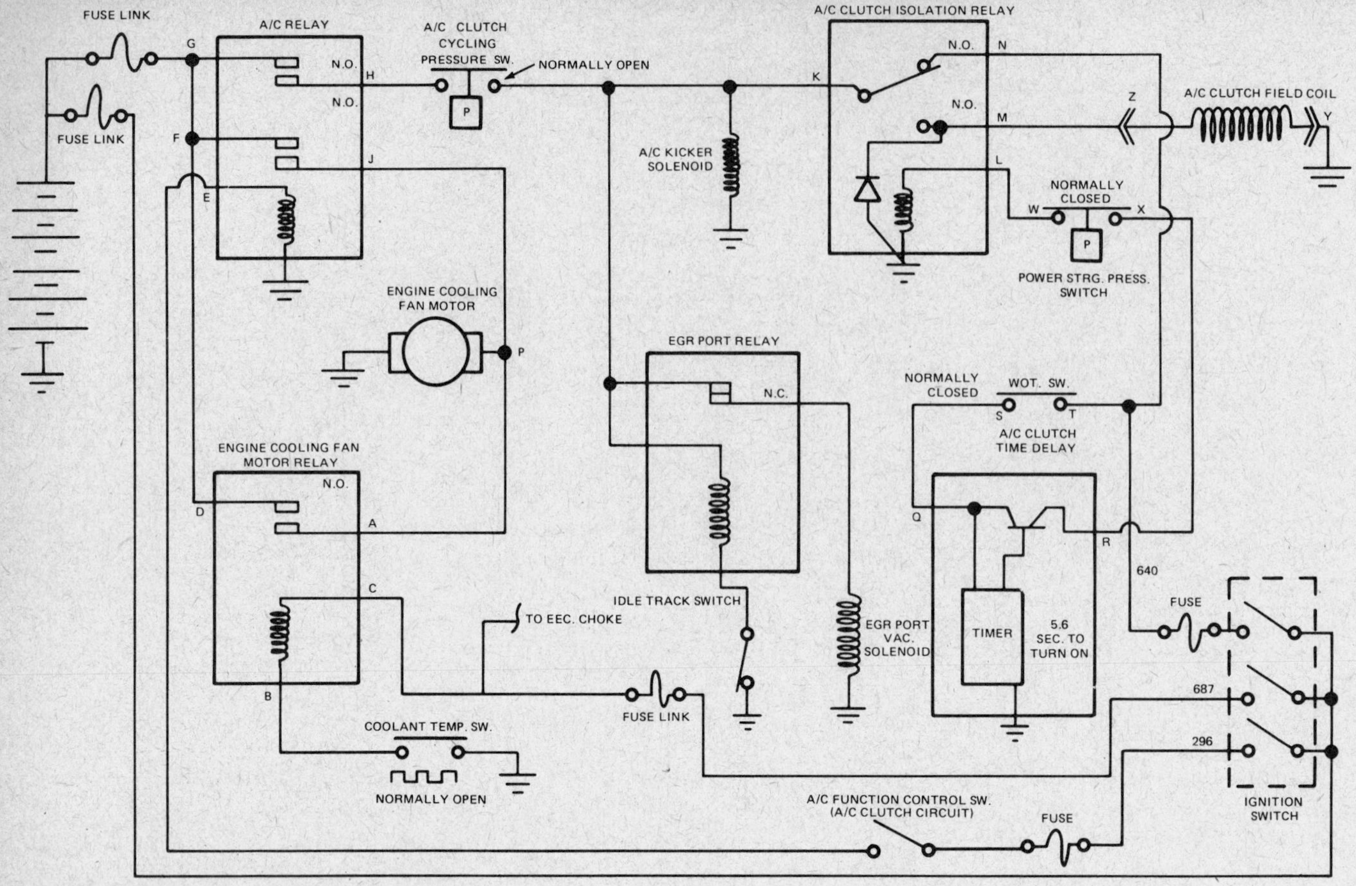

ELECTRIC ENGINE COOLING FANS

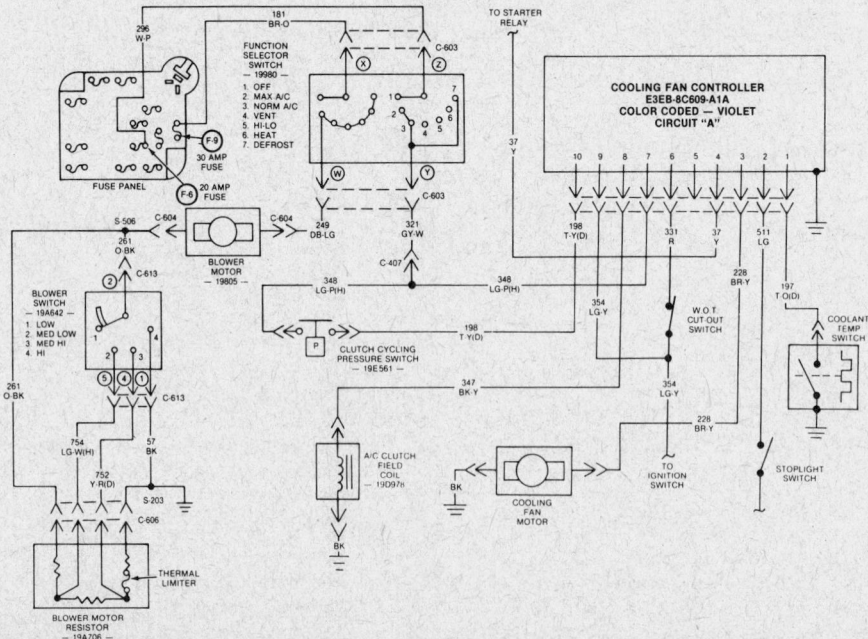

Fig. 17 Electric engine cooling fan wiring circuit. Type 7

panel and fan motor relay. If fuse is not blown, proceed to step 2. If fuse is blown, replace and retest.

2. Disconnect wire connector at coolant temperature switch, then connect a jumper wire between connector terminal and ground and place ignition switch in the Run position. If fan motor operates, proceed to step 3. If fan motor fails to operate, proceed to step 5.

3. If vehicle is equipped with A/C, proceed to step 4. On models less A/C, the system is operating properly and if overheating has occured, replace coolant temperature switch.

4. Connect wire connector to coolant temperature switch, then place A/C control at Max. A/C and ignition switch in Run position. If fan motor operates, system is satisfactory. If fan motor fails to operate, proceed to step 9.

5. Disconnect wire connector at fan motor, then connect a jumper wire between fan motor positive terminal and battery and fan motor negative terminal and ground, Fig. 9. If fan motor operates, proceed to step 6. If fan motor fails to operate, replace fan motor.

6. Disconnect jumper wires and reconnect fan motor wire connector. Disconnect wire connector at fan motor relay, then place ignition switch in the run position and check for voltage at connector terminals 37 and 197, Fig. 13. If no voltage is indicated at one or both terminals, trace circuit and repair as necessary. If voltage

Fig. 18 Electric engine cooling fan wiring circuit. Type 8

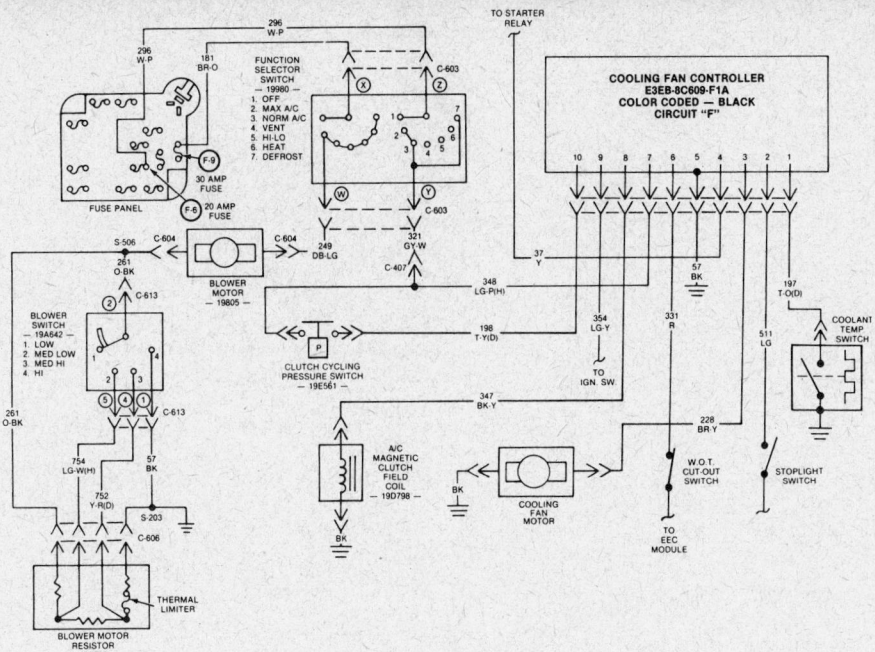

Fig. 19 Electric engine cooling fan wiring diagram. Type 9

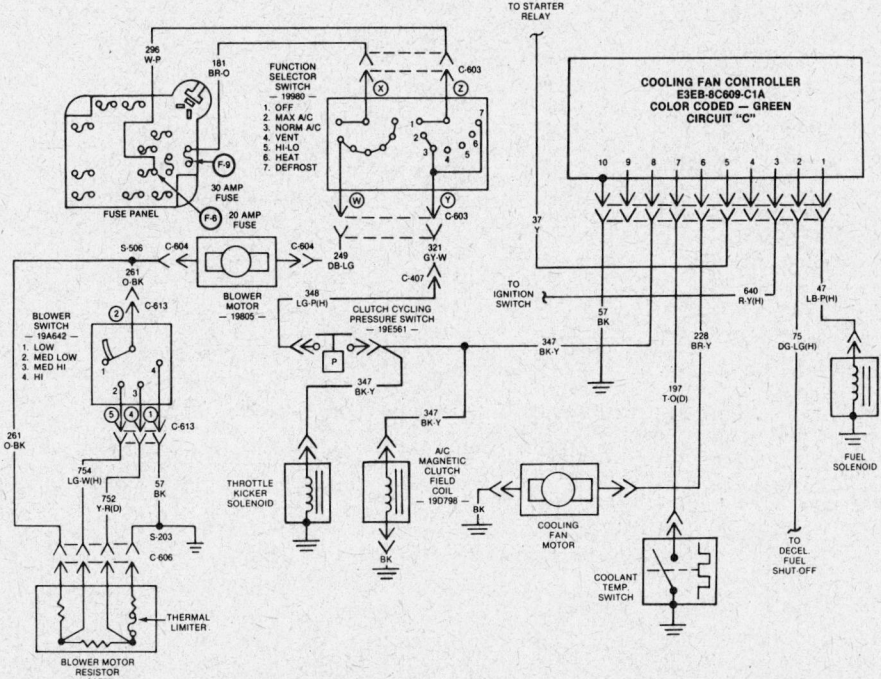

Fig. 20 Electric engine cooling fan wiring diagram. Type 10

10. Connect fan motor relay and disconnect wire connect at A/C relay, then place A/C control Max. A/C and ignition switch in Run position. Check for voltage at wire connector terminals 37 and 321, Fig. 11. If voltage is available at both terminals, proceed to step 11. If voltage is not available at one or both terminals, trace circuit and repair as necessary. If problem is not found in circuit, check A/C control and repair as necessary. Proceed to step 4.

11. Connect a jumper wire from A/C relay base to ground. If fan motor operates, clean relay ground surfaces. If fan motor fails to operate, replace relay and proceed to step 4.

TYPE 8, 9, 10 & 11, FIGS. 18, 19, 20 & 21

1. Check cooling fan fuse and fusible link. If satisfactory, proceed to step 2. If fuse or fusible link is blown, repair or replace as necessary and retest.

2. Bring engine to operating temperature and above while operating A/C to determine when cooling does or does not operate. If cooling fan operates during A/C operation only, proceed to step 3. If cooling fan does not operate at any time, proceed to step 13. If cooling fan operates only during high engine temperature, proceed to step 6.

3. Disconnect coolant temperature switch connector, then connect a jumper wire from connector to ground. If fan motor operates, proceed to step 4. If fan motor does not operate, proceed to step 5.

4. Using a suitable ohmmeter, check temperature switch body to thermostat housing continuity. If continuity does not exist (poor ground), tighten switch until continuity exists, then recheck operation. If continuity does exist between switch and thermostat housing, replace temperature switch.

5. Disconnect cooling fan controller connector, then using a suitable ohmmeter, check continuity of 197 circuit from controller to temperature switch. If continuity exists, replace controller. If no continuity exists, service 197 circuit.

6. With engine running, engage A/C clutch. If clutch engages, proceed to step 7. If clutch does not engage, check fuse. If satisfactory, proceed to step 9.

7. Inspect wide open throttle switch to determine position. If switch is open, replace or adjust as necessary. If switch is closed, proceed to step 8.

8. Disconnect cooling fan controller connector, then check for voltage at 354 circuit. If no voltage exists, service 354 circuit as necessary. If voltage exists, replace cooling fan controller.

9. Disconnect cooling fan controller connector, then turn ignition and A/C "On." Check for voltage at 198 circuit. If voltage exists, replace cooling fan controller. If voltage does not exist, proceed to step 10.

10. Disconnect A/C clutch cycling pressure switch, then using a suitable jumper wire, jump across connector. Check again for voltage at 198 circuit. If voltage exists, proceed to step 11. If voltage does not exist, proceed to step 12.

11. Check A/C system for sufficient charge. If charge is insufficient, replace clutch cycling pressure switch.

12. Disconnect A/C control assembly connector, then jump 296 circuit to 321 circuit and check for voltage at 198 and 348 circuits at cooling fan controller connector. If voltage exists at both circuits, replace function selector switch. If voltage exists at 198 circuit only, service 348 circuit.

is indicated at both circuits, proceed to step 7.

7. Connect a jumper wire between relay wire connector terminals 37 and 228, Fig. 13. If fan motor operates, proceed to step 8. If fan motor fails to operate, trace circuit from wire connector to motor connector and repair as necessary.

8. Disconnect jumper wire from relay wire connector, then check for continuity of circuit 354 from relay wire connector,

Fig. 13, to coolant temperature switch wire connector. If continuity exists, replace fan relay and perform step 2. If continuity does not exist, check circuit and repair as necessary.

9. Disconnect wire connector at A/C relay and check circuit 228 from relay wire connector, Fig. 13, to fan motor wire connector. If continuity exists, proceed to step 10. If continuity does not exist, trace circuit and repair as necessary.

ELECTRIC ENGINE COOLING FANS

13. Disconnect fan motor electrical connector, then connect a jumper wire from motor ground connection to a known good ground and a jumper wire from battery positive to motor B+ connection. If fan motor does not run, replace motor. If fan motor runs, proceed to step 14.

14. Remove jumper wire, then reconnect fan motor connector. Disconnect fan motor controller connector. With ignition "On," check for voltage at controller connector 37 and 354 circuits. If voltage exists at both circuits, proceed to step 15. If no voltage exists at one or both circuits, service circuit(s).

15. Using a jumper wire, jump circuit 37 to 228 circuit at cooling fan controller connector. If fan motor runs, replace cooling fan controller. If fan motor does not run, service motor ground.

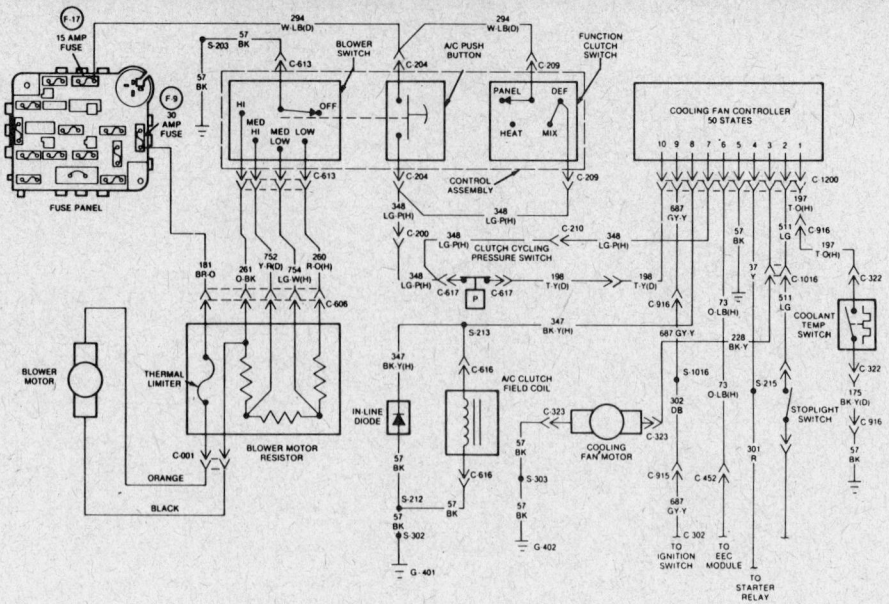

Fig. 21   Electric engine cooling fan wiring circuit. Type 11

TYPE 12, FIG. 22

1. Refer to steps 1 through 5 of Type 8, 9 & 10 electric engine cooling fan systems, then continue using the following procedures.

2. With engine running, engage A/C clutch. If clutch engages, proceed to step 3. If clutch does not engage, check fuse. If satisfactory, proceed to step 4.

3. Disconnect cooling fan controller connector, then check for voltage at 640 and 37 circuits. If voltage exists at both circuits, replace controller. If voltage does not exist at one or both circuits, service circuits as necessary.

4. Disconnect A/C clutch cycling pressure switch, then using a suitable jumper wire, jump across connector. Check to see if A/C clutch engages. If clutch engages, proceed to step 5. If clutch does not engage, proceed to step 6.

5. Check A/C system for sufficient charge. If charge is insufficient, leak test, repair and recharge system, then retest. If charge is sufficient, replace clutch cycling pressure switch.

6. Disconnect A/C control assembly connector, then jump 296 circuit to 321 circuit and check for voltage at black/yellow wire of clutch connector. If voltage exists, replace function selector switch. If voltage does not exist, service 321, 347 or 348 circuit.

7. Remove jumper wire from A/C clutch cycling pressure switch connector and connect to pressure switch.

Fan Motor, Replace

1981–83 ESCORT, LYNX; 1982–83 EXP, LN7; 1984 TEMPO & TOPAZ

1. Disconnect battery ground cable, then disconnect fan motor wire connector and detach wire loom clip from fan shroud.

2. Remove two nuts attaching fan motor and shroud, then remove fan motor and shroud assembly from vehicle.

3. Remove nut or clip retaining fan blade to fan motor shaft, then remove fan blade.

NOTE: The nut retaining the fan blade to the motor shaft has a left handed thread. The nut should be rotated clockwise to loosen and counter-clockwise to tighten.

4. Remove three nuts and washers attaching fan motor to shroud, then remove fan motor.

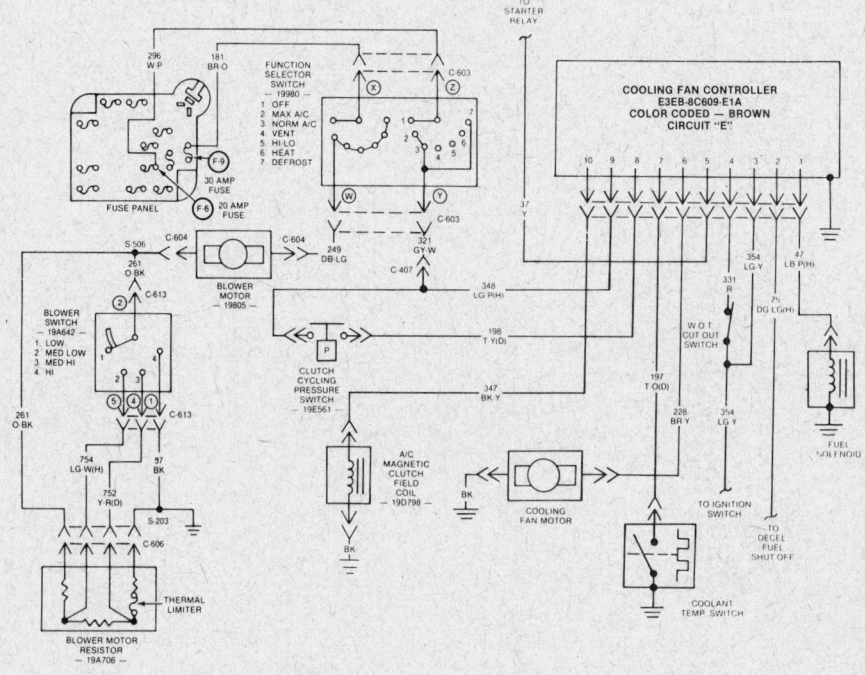

Fig. 22   Electric engine cooling fan wiring diagram. Type 12

5. Reverse procedure to install. Torque fan motor to fan shroud attaching nuts to 6.6 to 9.6 ft. lbs., fan blade to fan motor retaining nut to 30 to 40 inch lbs. and fan shroud to radiator attaching nuts to 80 to 100 inch lbs.

ALL EXC. 1981–83 ESCORT, LYNX; 1982–83 EXP, LN7; 1984 TEMPO & TOPAZ

1. Disconnect battery ground cable, then remove wiring from routing clip.

2. Disconnect fan motor wiring connector.

3. Remove four screws securing mounting bracket and remove fan assembly from vehicle.

4. Remove fan blade retaining clip, then remove fan.

5. Remove nuts securing fan motor to mounting bracket.

6. Reverse procedure to install. Torque fan motor attaching nuts to 70–95 in. lbs., fan shroud to radiator attaching bolts, 70–95 in. lbs.

DASH GAUGES

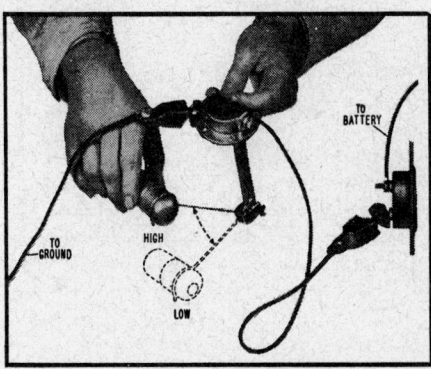

Fig. 1 Hook-up for testing dash gauge with a spare tank unit

terminals, indicator gauge terminals, or open circuit in wiring harness and printed circuit between components.
5. Connect test lamp or voltmeter ground lead to ground terminal in sending unit wiring harness connector. Light should pulse or meter reading should fluctuate as in step 2. If not, locate open in ground circuit.

NOTE: Do not apply battery voltage to system or ground output terminals of IVR, as damage to system components or wiring circuits may result.

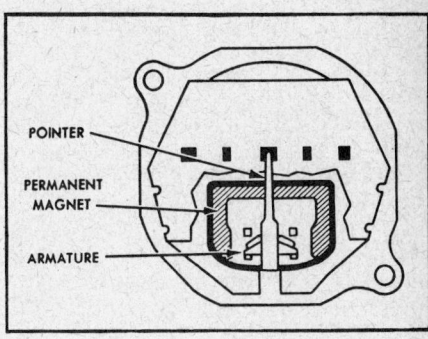

Fig. 2 Conventional type ammeter (typical)

TESTING

Gauge failures are often caused by defective wiring or grounds. The first step in locating trouble should be a thorough inspection of all wiring, terminals and printed circuits. If wiring is secured by clamps, check to see whether the insulation has been severed thereby grounding the wire. In the case of a fuel gauge installation, rust may cause failure by corrosion at the ground connection of the tank unit.

CONSTANT VOLTAGE REGULATOR TYPE (CVR)

The Constant Voltage Regulator (CVR) type indicator is a bimetal-resistance type system consisting of an Instrument Voltage Regulator (IVR), an indicator gauge, and a variable resistance sending unit. Current to the system is applied to the gauge terminals by the IVR, which maintains an average-pulsating value of 5 volts.

The indicator gauge consists of a pointer which is attached to a wire-wound bimetal strip. Current passing through the coil heats the bimetal strip, causing the pointer to move. As more current passes through the coil, heat increases, moving the pointer farther.

The circuit is completed through a sending unit which contains a variable resistor. When resistance is high, less current is allowed to pass through the gauge, and the pointer moves very little. As resistance decreases due to changing conditions in system being monitored, more current passes through gauge coil, causing pointer to move farther.

These procedures apply to Chrysler Corp., Ford, Mercury, and earlier AMC vehicles.

Operational Test

1. Disconnect wiring harness connector at sending unit. Connect a test lamp or voltmeter between terminal in wiring harness connector and ground.
2. With ignition switch in ON position, light should pulse or meter reading should fluctuate.
3. If lamp lights but does not pulse, or if meter reading remains steady, check ground to IVR. If ground is satisfactory, IVR is defective.
4. If lamp fails to light, or if meter reads 0 volts, check for open circuit across IVR

Dash Gauge Test

1. Disconnect battery ground cable and remove gauge from vehicle.
2. Connect ohmmeter between gauge terminals and read coil winding resistance.
3. An upward movement of ohmmeter needle from 10 ohms to 14 ohms is normal, as test current of ohmmeter causes a temperature rise in gauge coil windings.
4. If ohmmeter reads below 10 ohms or above 14 ohms, gauge is defective.

Sending Unit Tests

Fuel Tank Gauge
1. Disconnect wiring harness connector at sending unit and connect ohmmeter between ground terminal and resistor terminal on sending unit.
2. Meter should read 8–86 ohms. If reading shows no continuity (infinite reading), check ground connection to tank gauge.
3. If ground is satisfactory, but reading is not within specification, tank unit is defective.
4. If reading is within specification, remove fuel tank gauge from vehicle and connect ohmmeter between resistor terminal and ground terminal (metal housing on single terminal units).
5. Observe meter while slowly moving float rod between empty and full stops. Meter should read 60–86 ohms at empty stop and 8–12 ohms at full stop. Change in readings should be smooth, without hesitation or jumping.
6. If tank unit fails to operate as outlined, unit is defective.

NOTE: Before installing fuel tank gauge, connect wiring harness connector to gauge and move float rod from empty to full position with ignition key in ON position. If dash gauge reading is incorrect, check IVR and dash gauge. If system tests prove satisfactory, but system still does not operate correctly, check that tank gauge rod is not bent or binding and that float is not damaged, loose or filled with fuel.

Oil & Temperature Sending Units
1. Test dash gauge and IVR as outlined above.
2. If system is satisfactory, start engine and allow it to reach operating temperature.

3. If no reading is indicated on the gauge, check the sending unit-to-gauge wire by removing the wire from the sending unit and momentarily ground this wire to a clean, unpainted portion of the engine.
4. If the gauge still does not indicate, the wire is defective. Repair or replace the wire.
5. If grounding the new or repaired wire causes the dash gauge to indicate, the sending unit is faulty.

VARIABLE VOLTAGE TYPE

The variable voltage type dash gauge consists of two magnetic coils to which battery voltage is applied. The coils act on the gauge pointer and pull in opposite directions. One coil is grounded directly to the chassis, while the other coil is grounded through a variable resistor within the sending unit. Resistance through the sending unit determines current flow through its coil, and therefore pointer position.

When resistance is high in the sending unit, less current is allowed to flow through its coil, causing the gauge pointer to move toward the directly grounded coil. When resistance in the sending unit decreases, more current is allowed to pass through its coil, increasing the magnetic field. The gauge pointer is then attracted toward the coil which is grounded through the sending unit.

These procedures apply to GM and AMC (exc. CVR) vehicles.

System Test

Following is the method of quickly checking the gauge system to determine which component (sender or receiver) of a given system is defective.

System Testing

1. Use a spare gauge tank unit known to be correct.
2. To test whether the dash gauge in question (fuel, oil or temperature) is functioning, disconnect the wire at the gauge which leads to the sending unit.
3. Attach a wire lead from the dash gauge terminal to the terminal of the "test" tank gauge, Fig. 1.
4. Ground the test tank unit to an unpainted portion of the dash panel and move the float arm.

3–25

5. If the gauge operates correctly, the sending unit is defective and should be replaced.
6. If the gauge does not operate during this test, the dash gauge is defective and should be replaced.

AMMETERS

The ammeter is an instrument used to indicate current flow into and out of the battery. When electrical accessories in the vehicle draw more current than the alternator can supply, current flows from the battery and the ammeter indicates a discharge (−) condition. When electrical loads of the vehicle are less than alternator output, current is available to charge the battery, and the ammeter indicates a charge (+) condition. If battery is fully charged, the voltage regulator reduces alternator output to meet only immediate vehicle electrical loads. When this happens, ammeter reads zero.

Conventional Ammeter

A conventional ammeter must be connected between the battery and alternator in order to indicate current flow. This type ammeter, Fig. 2, consists of a frame to which a permanent magnet is attached. The frame also supports an armature and pointer assembly. Current in this system flows from the alternator through the ammeter, then to the battery or from the battery through the ammeter into the vehicle electrical system, depending on vehicle operating conditions.

When no current flows through the ammeter, the magnet holds the pointer armature so that the pointer stands at the center of the dial. When current passes in either direction through the ammeter, the resulting magnetic field attracts the armature away from the effect of the permanent magnet, thus giving a reading proportional to the strength of the current flowing.

Trouble Shooting

When the ammeter apparently fails to register correctly, there may be trouble in the wiring which connects the ammeter to the alternator and battery or in the alternator or battery itself.

To check the connections, first tighten the two terminal posts on the back of the ammeter. Then, following each wire from the ammeter, tighten all connections on the ignition switch, battery and alternator. Chafed, burned or broken insulation can be found by following each ammeter wire from end to end.

All wires with chafed, burned or broken insulation should be repaired or replaced. After this is done, and all connections are tightened, connect the battery cable and turn on the ignition switch. The needle should point slightly to the discharge (−) side.

Start the engine and speed it up a little above idling speed. The needle should then move to the charge side (+), and its movement should be smooth.

If the pointer does not behave correctly, the ammeter itself is out of order and a new one should be installed.

Shunt Type Ammeter

American Motors, Ford, 1981–82 Chrysler Corp.

The shunt type ammeter is actually a specially calibrated voltmeter. It is connected to read voltage drop across a resistance wire (shunt) between the battery and alternator.

The shunt is located either in the vehicle wiring or within the ammeter itself.

When voltage is higher at the alternator end of the shunt, the meter indicates a charge (+) condition. When voltage is higher at the battery end of the shunt, the meter indicates a discharge (−) condition. When voltage is equal at both ends of the shunt, the meter reads zero.

Trouble Shooting

Ammeter accuracy can be determined by comparing reading with an ammeter of known accuracy.
1. With engine stopped and ignition switch in RUN position, switch on headlamps and heater fan. Meter should indicate a discharge (−) condition.
2. If ammeter pointer does not move, check ammeter terminals for proper connection and check for open circuit in wiring harness. If connections and wiring harness are satisfactory, ammeter is defective.
3. If ammeter indicates a charge (+) condition, wiring harness connections are reversed at ammeter.

ALTERNATOR INDICATOR LIGHT

Delcotron SI Integral Charging System

This system features an integral solid state regulator mounted inside the alternator slip ring end frame. The alternator indicator lamp is installed in the field wire circuit connected between the ignition "Ign." terminal and alternator No. 1 terminal, Fig. 3. The resistance provided by the alternator warning light circuit is needed to protect the diode trio. The alternator indicator lamp should light when the ignition switch is turned on before engine is started. If lamp does not light, either lamp is burned out or indicator lamp wiring has an open circuit. After engine is started, the indicator lamp should be out at all times. If indicator lamp comes on, alternator belt may be loose, alternator or regulator may be defective, charging circuit may be defective or fuse may be blown.

Motorcraft Alternator

The indicator lamp glows when field relay fails to close. When ignition is in the On position, battery current flows through the charge indicator lamp and a parallel resistor, and through regulator to field, and the lamp comes on. Vehicles with electronic voltage regulator have a 500 ohm resistor. On all others the resistor is 15 ohms. When the alternator builds up enough voltage to close the field relay the charge indicator lamp will go out. Place ignition switch in the Run position with the engine stopped. The lamp should light. If not, the bulb is burned out or indicator lamp has an open circuit.

On vehicles with electro-mechanical or transistorized regulators, an open resistor wire in the alternator charging circuit will usually cause the indicator lamp to remain on until engine speed is increased to approximately 2000 rpm. In some cases the lamp will remain on above 2000 rpm. The charge indicator lamp may be tested using a test light containing a No. 67 or 1155 bulb. Disconnect regulator wire connector from regulator, then place ignition switch in the Run position. Place one test lamp lead on regulator wire connector "l" terminal and other lead on regulator base. Test lamp will light if circuit is in proper working order. If 15 ohm resistor or circuit is open, indicator lamp will operate at full brightness and test lamp will not light.

OIL PRESSURE INDICATOR LIGHT

Many cars utilize a warning light on the instrument panel in place of the conventional dash indicating gauge to warn the driver when the oil pressure is dangerously low. The warning light is wired in series with the ignition switch and the engine unit—which is an oil pressure switch.

The oil pressure switch contains a diaphragm and a set of contacts. When the ignition switch is turned on, the warning light circuit is energized and the circuit is completed through the closed contacts in the pressure switch. When the engine is started, build-up of oil pressure compresses the diaphragm, opening the contacts, thereby breaking the circuit and putting out the light.

Trouble Shooting

NOTE: On some 1978–83 General Motors

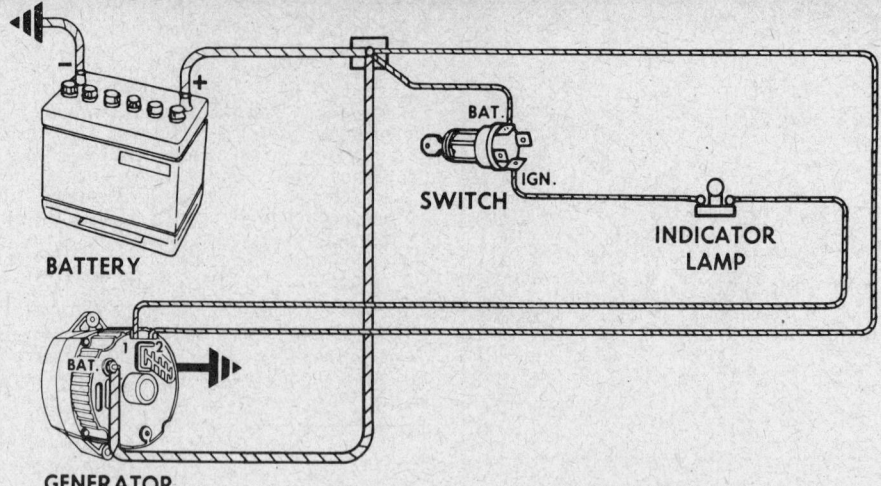

Fig. 3 Charge indicator lamp wiring. Delco SI type charging system

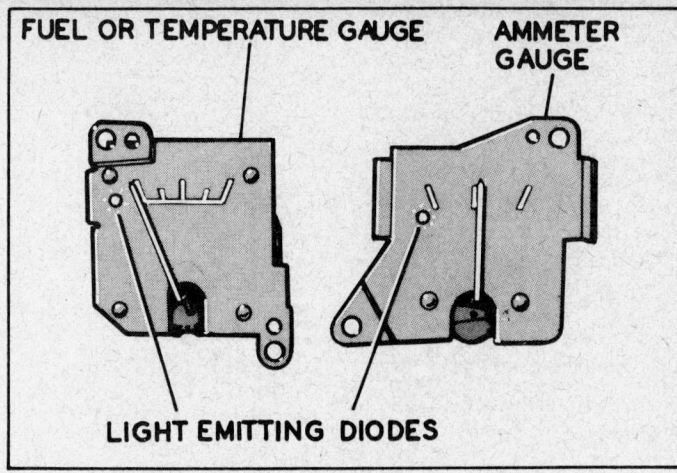

FUEL OR TEMPERATURE GAUGE   AMMETER GAUGE

LIGHT EMITTING DIODES

Fig. 4 Gauges Incorporating the L.E.D. system

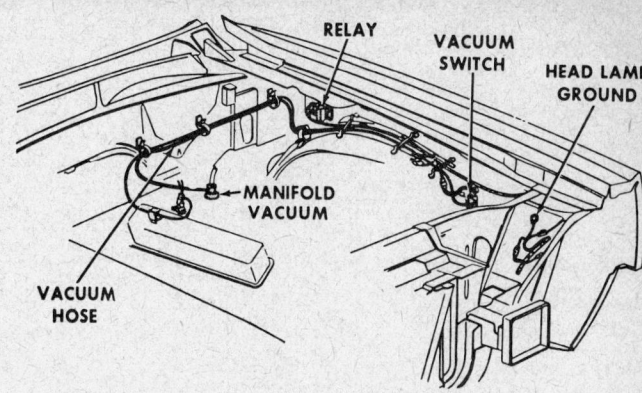

RELAY   VACUUM SWITCH   HEAD LAMP GROUND

MANIFOLD VACUUM

VACUUM HOSE

Fig. 5 Fuel pacer system. 1977 Charger, Cordoba, Coronet & Fury; 1977 Monaco (Typical)

models, the oil pressure indicator light also serves as the electric choke defect indicator. If Oil or Eng. indicator light does not light, check to ensure electric choke is not disconnected at carburetor. Also check for defect in electric choke heater, blown gauge fuse or defect in lamp or wiring circuit. If indicator light stays on with engine running possible causes are: oil pressure is low, switch to indicator light wiring has an open circuit, oil pressure switch wire connector has disconnected or on some models, gauge or radio fuse has blown.

The oil pressure warning light should go on when the ignition is turned on. If it does not light, disconnect the wire from the engine unit and ground the wire to the frame or cylinder block. Then if the warning light still does not go on with the ignition switch on, replace the bulb.

If the warning light goes on when the wire is grounded to the frame or cylinder block, the engine unit should be checked for being loose or poorly grounded. If the unit is found to be tight and properly grounded, it should be removed and a new one installed. (The presence of sealing compound on the threads of the engine unit will cause a poor ground).

If the warning light remains lit when it normally should be out, replace the engine unit before proceeding further to determine the cause for a low pressure indication.

The warning light sometimes will light up or will flicker when the engine is idling, even though the oil pressure is adequate. However, the light should go out when the engine is speeded up. There is no cause for alarm in such cases; it simply means that the pressure switch is not calibrated precisely correct.

TEMPERATURE INDICATOR LIGHT

Trouble Shooting

If the red light is not lit when the engine is being cranked, check for a burned out bulb, an open in the light circuit, or a defective ignition switch.

If the red light is lit when the engine is running, check the wiring between light and switch for a ground, temperature switch defective, or overheated cooling system.

NOTE: *As a test circuit to check whether the red bulb is functioning properly, a wire which is connected to the ground terminal of the ignition switch is tapped into its circuit. When the ignition is in the "Start" (engine cranking) position, the ground terminal is grounded inside the switch and the red bulb will be lit. When the engine is started and the ignition switch is in the "On" position, the test circuit is opened and the bulb is then controlled by the temperature switch.*

CHRYSLER GAUGE ALERT SYSTEM

L.E.D. (Light Emitting Diode)

The fuel, temperature and ammeter gauges are equipped with a L.E.D. (Light Emitting Diode) mounted in each of the gauge dials, Fig. 4. This diode will illuminate and alert the driver that the system the gauge is monitoring is malfunctioning. The electronic sensor circuit is mounted on the gauge housing. The printed circuit board is permanently attached and is not serviceable. If the L.E.D. is malfunctioning, the gauge and the printed circuit board must be replaced as an assembly.

Operation

Fuel Gauge
When gauge indicator shows approximately 1/8 of a tank of fuel remaining, the L.E.D. will light alerting the driver of a low fuel situation.

Temperature Gauge
When gauge indicator shows engine temperature approximately 240 to 260 degrees F. the L.E.D. will light alerting the driver of an overheat condition.

Ammeter Gauge
This L.E.D. operates independently of the gauge indicator and monitors system voltage. The L.E.D. will alert the driver of three charging system potential malfunctions.
1. A discharging condition, caused by excessive electrical demand on charging system, (engine at idle rpm).
2. A weak or defective battery with ignition

switch in the "ON" position, (before the ignition switch is moved to the "START" position).
3. A weak or defective battery with minimum demand on charging system, while vehicle is being used in stop and go driving (intermittent L.E.D. illumination occurring).

Testing

Fuel and Temperature L.E.D.
Use testor C-3826 for diagnosing systems.

Ammeter L.E.D.

NOTE: Only if battery and charging system are functioning properly can the following test be performed.

Turn ignition switch to the "ON" position and turn on headlights, windshield wipers and stoplights. This will cause excessive demand on charging system activating the L.E.D. immediately or within approximately one minute. If the L.E.D. does not light there is a malfunction in the system. If L.E.D. lights, run engine at approximately 2000 rpm, L.E.D. should stop emitting light, if the L.E.D. continues to emit light there is a malfunction in the system.

NOTE: In all cases of system malfunctions the complete gauge must be replaced.

CHRYSLER FUEL PACER SYSTEM

The Fuel Pacer system, Figs. 5 and 6, incorporates a vacuum switch, relay, vacuum hoses, diodes and the use of the left front fender mounted turn signal indicator lamp. When engine vacuum falls below 4½ inches Hg., electrical contacts in the vacuum switch close, causing the indicator lamp to light, therefore indicating excessive fuel consumption by the engine.

The Fuel Pacer system overrides the blinking action of the fender mounted left turn indicator lamp. However, an inline diode is incorporated in the circuit so the complete turn signal system is not affected. A second in-line diode is placed in the fender mounted indicator lamp feed wire, preventing feedback through the main harness and therefore avoiding some accessories from functioning when the hazard warning flashers are "On", with the ignition switch in the "Accessory" position.

1977 System Tests

Test 1

1. Disconnect vacuum hose from vacuum switch and connect an external vacuum source to the switch.
2. Turn ignition switch to "On" position and observe fender mounted turn indicator lamp. If indicator lamp is lit, the vacuum switch is satisfactory. If not, check the following: defective wiring or connections supplying current through vacuum switch to indicator lamp, burnt indicator bulb or a defective vacuum switch.

Test 2

1. With an external vacuum source connected to the vacuum switch and the ignition switch in the "On" position, apply increasing vacuum to the switch and observe fender mounted indicator lamp.
2. Indicator lamp should turn off at approximately 4½ inches of vacuum. If not, increase vacuum until switch does go out. If lamp goes out, the switch is out of adjustment, requiring readjustment. If lamp does not go out regardless of amount of vacuum applied, the switch is defective, requiring replacement.

Vacuum Switch Adjustment

1977

1. Install a vacuum gauge on the engine.
2. Operate vehicle, noting the vacuum reading at which the indicator lamp glows. This also may be accomplished by carefully loading the engine with the brakes applied.
3. Remove vacuum switch adjusting screw cap.
4. To decrease vacuum setting, turn adjusting screw counter-clockwise. To increase vacuum setting, turn adjusting screw clockwise.
5. Install adjusting screw cap.
6. Operate vehicle or load engine, noting the vacuum reading at which the indicator lamp glows. It may be necessary to readjust switch to obtain desired setting.

BOOST/OVERBOOST WARNING SYSTEM

1979–80 Capri & Mustang, W/Turbocharged 4-140 Engine

Two calibrated pressure switches provide the driver visual indication that turbo boost pressure is satisfactory and visual and audible indication when turbo boost pressure is unsatisfactory. One switch will illuminate the green Turbo lamp located on the instrument panel when turbo boost pressure levels are within satisfactory limits. The second pressure switch will turn off the green Turbo lamp and illuminate the red engine warning lamp and sound the audible buzzer when excessive turbo boost pressure or high engine oil temperatures are encountered. When the red

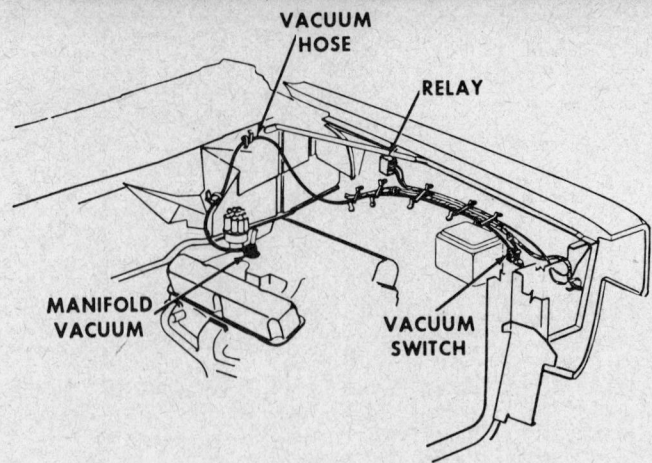

Fig. 6   Fuel pacer system. 1977 Chrysler, Gran Fury & Royal Monaco (Typical)

engine lamp is constant and buzzer sounds, the turbocharger is in an overboost condition, reduce engine speed immediately until buzzer ceases and warning lamp goes off. When the red engine warning light flashes on and off with no buzzer, this indicates excessive engine oil temperature, reduce engine speed to approximately 2500 RPM. The engine warning lamp should go out within 5 minutes. When the red engine warning lamp flashes on and off and buzzer sounds simultaneously, excessive turbo overboost and/or high engine oil temperatures are occuring, reduce engine speed immediately.

NOTE: Whenever the engine warning lamp has illuminated or the audible buzzer sounds, the vehicle should be inspected as soon as possible to determine the cause.

With ignition switch in start position and engine not operating, the warning lamps should glow and the buzzer should sound to indicate the electrical circuits are operating properly. If warning lamps do not glow or if buzzer does not sound, the boost/overboost electrical system should be checked as soon as possible.

SPEEDOMETERS

The following material covers only that service on speedometers which can be performed by the average service man. Repairs on the units themselves are not included as they require special tools and extreme care when making repairs and adjustments and only an experienced speedometer mechanic should attempt such servicing.

The speedometer has two main parts—the indicator head and the speedometer drive cable. When the speedometer fails to indicate speed or mileage, the cable or housing is probably broken.

Speedometer Cable

Most cables are broken due to lack of lubrication or a sharp bend or kink in the housing.

A cable might break because the speedometer head mechanism binds. If such is the case, the speedometer head should be repaired or replaced before a new cable or housing is installed.

A "jumpy" pointer condition, together with a sort of scraping noise, is due, in most instances, to a dry or kinked speedometer cable. The kinked cable rubs on the housing and winds up, slowing down the pointer. The cable then unwinds and the pointer "jumps".

To check for kinks, remove the cable, lay it on a flat surface and twist one end with the fingers. If it turns over smoothly the cable is not kinked. But if part of the cable flops over as it is twisted, the cable is kinked and should be replaced.

Lubrication

The speedometer cable should be lubricated with special cable lubricant every 10,000 miles.

Fill the ferrule on the upper end of the housing with the cable lubricant. Insert the cable in the housing, starting at the upper end. Turn the cable around carefully while feeding it into the housing. Repeat filling the ferrule except for the last six inches of cable. Too much lubricant at this point may cause the lubricant to work into the indicating hand.

Installing Cable

During installation, if the cable sticks when inserted in the housing and will not go through, the housing is damaged inside or kinked. Be sure to check the housing from one end to the other. Straighten any sharp bends by relocating clamps or elbows. Replace housing if it is badly kinked or broken. Position the cable and housing so that they lead into the head as straight as possible.

Check the new cable for kinks before installing it. Use wide, sweeping, gradual curves when the cable comes out of the transmission and connects to the head so the cable will not be damaged during its installation.

If inspection indicates that the cable and housing are in good condition, yet pointer action is erratic, check the speedometer head for possible binding.

The speedometer drive pinion should also be checked. If the pinion is dry or its teeth are stripped, the speedometer may not register properly.

The transmission mainshaft nut must be tight or the speedometer drive gear may slip on the mainshaft and cause slow speed readings.

ELECTRIC CLOCKS

Regulation of electric clocks used on automobiles is accomplished automatically by merely resetting the time. If the clock is running fast, the action of turning the hands back to correct the time will automatically cause the clock to run slightly slower. If the clock is running slow, the action of turning the hands forward to correct the time will automatically cause the clock to run slightly faster (10 to 15 seconds day).

A lock-out feature prevents the clock regulator mechanism from being reset more than once per wind cycle, regardless of the number of times the time is reset. After the clock rewinds, if the time is then reset, automatic regulation will take place. If a clock varies over 10 minutes per day, it will never adjust sufficiently, and must be repaired or replaced.

Winding Clock When Connecting Battery or Clock Wiring

The clock requires special attention when reconnecting a battery that has been disconnected for any reason, a clock that has been disconnected, or when replacing a blown clock fuse. *It is very important that the initial wind by fully made.* The procedure is as follows:

1. Make sure that all other instruments and lights are turned off.
2. Connect positive cable to battery.
3. Before connecting the negative cable, press the terminal to its post on the battery. Immediately afterward strike the terminal against the battery post to see if there is a spark. If there is a spark, allow the clock to run down until it stops ticking, and repeat as above until there is no spark. Then immediately make the permanent connection before the clock can again run down. The clock will run down in approximately two minutes.
4. Reset clock after all connections have been made. *The foregoing procedure should also be followed when reconnecting the clock after it has been disconnected, or if it has stopped because of a blown fuse. Be sure to disconnect battery before installing a new fuse.*

Trouble Shooting

If clock does not run, check for blown "clock" fuse. If fuse is blown check for short in wiring. If fuse is not blown check for open circuit.

With an electric clock, the most frequent cause of clock fuse blowing is voltage at the clock which will prevent a complete wind and allow clock contacts to remain closed. This may be caused by any of the following: discharged battery, corrosion on contact surface of battery terminals, loose connections at battery terminals, at junction block, at fuse clips, or at terminal connection of clock. Therefore, if in reconnecting battery or clock it is noted that the clock is not ticking, always check for blown fuse, or examine the circuits at the points indicated above to determine and correct the cause.

Fig. 7   Typical vacuum gauge

FIBER OPTIC MONITORING SYSTEM

Fiber optics are non-electric light conductors made up of coated strands which, when exposed to a light source at one end, will reflect the light through their entire length, thereby illuminating a monitoring lens on the instrument panel or fender without the use of a bulb when the exterior lights are turned on.

LOW FUEL WARNING SYSTEM

The switch type consists of an indicator light and a low fuel warning switch located on the instrument panel.

The warning switch contacts are closed by the difference in voltage potential between the fuel gauge terminals. This voltage differential will activate the warning switch when the fuel tank is less than 1/4 full and, in turn, cause the indicator to light.

Trouble Shooting

This system incorporates an indicator light. With ignition switch turned to "ON", the indicator should light. If not, check bulb and all electrical connections. On General Motors switch type, replace warning switch if bulb and connections prove satisfactory. On Ford switch type systems, perform additional tests outlined below.

Improper operation of the warning switch will be indicated when the light remains "ON" when tank is more than 1/4 full. To test system, disconnect connector on warning switch and turn ignition "ON". Starting with the terminal on the end opposite the blank position, connect a jumper wire between the battery positive terminal and connector terminal. The indicator on instrument panel should light. If not, replace warning switch. Skip the next connector terminal and connect a test lamp between the battery positive terminal and connector terminal. The test lamp should light. If not, trace wire from

ignition switch for an open circuit. Test the remaining connector terminals with the test lamp making connections between ground and terminal connectors. If lamp fails to light, trace particular wire for an incomplete circuit.

LOW WASHER FLUID INDICATOR

There are two types of low washer fluid indicating systems used on GM cars. They are the mechanical type and electrically controlled type. The mechanical type consists of a float and rod assembly, sending unit and a fiber optic. The electrically controlled type consists of a float, magnet, contact points and a resistor.

On the mechanical type, the upper end of the rod extends into the sending unit and has colored red and green portions. When the windshield wipers are activated, a lamp bulb in the sending unit lights either the red or green sections of the rod. The colored light is then picked up by the fiber optic and is transmitted through it to the tell tale lens. The lens will show red or green depending upon washer fluid level.

The electrically controlled indicator is activated when the windshield wipers are engaged. A slight amount of current flows from the wiper motor to the washer bottle float unit. This current will either pass through the contact points or the resistor which is in parallel with the points. When the washer fluid level is high, the magnet holds the contact points open. The current will now flow through the resistor where it is reduced so the indicator will not light. When the washer fluid level is low, the float drops and the magnet will separate from the cap assembly allowing the current to pass through the contact points and activate the indicator light.

Trouble Shooting

On the mechanical indicating system, if the tell tale lens fails to glow when the windshield wipers are activated, check lamp bulb in sending unit and see that fiber optic is not broken.

On the electrically controlled system, the first item to check is the indicator bulb. With the windshield wipers "ON", connect a jumper wire between the two terminals on the washer bottle cap. The indicator should then light. If not, replace bulb. If the bulb is found to be satisfactory, remove cap and float assembly from washer bottle. Float should be able to move to the bottom of the stem and the magnet should separate from the cap. If not, replace float and cap assembly.

VACUUM GAUGE

This gauge, Fig. 7, measures intake manifold vacuum. The intake manifold vacuum varies with engine operating conditions, carburetor adjustments, valve timing, ignition timing and general engine condition.

Since the optimum fuel economy is directly proportional to a properly functioning engine, a high vacuum reading on the gauge relates to fuel economy. For this reason some manufacturers call the vacuum gauge a "Fuel Economy Indicator." Most gauges have colored

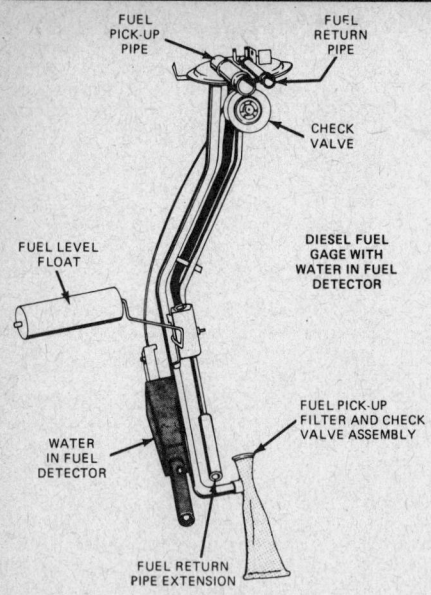

FUEL PICK-UP PIPE

FUEL RETURN PIPE

CHECK VALVE

FUEL LEVEL FLOAT

DIESEL FUEL GAGE WITH WATER IN FUEL DETECTOR

WATER IN FUEL DETECTOR

FUEL PICK-UP FILTER AND CHECK VALVE ASSEMBLY

FUEL RETURN PIPE EXTENSION

FUEL TANK PURGE PROCEDURE

Cars which have a "Water in Fuel" light may have the water removed from the fuel tank with a pump or by siphoning. The pump or siphon hose should be hooked up to the 1/4 inch fuel return hose (smaller of the two fuel hoses) above the rear axle or under the hood near the fuel pump. Siphoning should continue until all water is removed from the fuel tank. Use a clear plastic line or observe filter bowl on draining equipment to determine when clear fuel begins to flow. Be sure to remove the cap on fuel tank while using this purge procedure. Replace the cap when finished. The same precautions for handling gasoline should be observed when purging diesel fuel tanks.

Fig. 8 Water in fuel indicator & tank purge procedure. 1981—83 GM with diesel engine

CONDITION	POSSIBLE SOURCE	ACTION	LOCATION
• Taillamp L.E.D. Illuminated/False Indication	• Bad Bulb • Open Wire	• Replace Bulb • Check Cir. 14/102	• Rear Running Lamps • 14401 Connector to Module
• Headlamp L.E.D. Illuminated or False Indications	• Bad Headlamp Bulb • Non-Halogen Bulb • Open Wire	• Replace Headlamp • Replace with Halogen Bulb • Check Cir. 13 or 108	• Headlamp • 14401 Connector to Module
• Brake Lamp L.E.D. Illuminated or False Indication	• Bad Bulb • Open Wire	• Replace Bulb • Check Cir. 5 and 105, 9 and 104	• Tail lamp • Console
• Low Fuel L.E.D. Illuminated or False Indication	• Low Fuel • Warning Switch (Inoperative)	• Fill Gas Tank • Replace	• Gas Tank • Console
• Washer Fluid L.E.D. Illuminated or False Indication	• Low Washer Fluid • Warning Switch (Inoperative)	• Fill Washer Reservoir • Replace	• Under Hood • Windshield Washer Reservoir
• (Test) No L.E.D.'s Will Illuminate	• No Voltage • Open Wire	• Check Fuse • Check Cir. 296-57D	• Fuse Panel • 14401 Connector to Module
• (Test) One or More L.E.D.'s Will Not Illuminate	• Bad L.E.D.'s	• Replace Indicator	• Console

Fig. 9 Graphic display warning indicator diagnosis chart

sectors the green sector being the "Economy" range and red the "Power" range. Therefore, the vehicle should be operated with gauge registering in the green sector or a high numerical number, Fig. 7, for maximum economy.

LOW COOLANT LEVEL INDICATOR

Some General Motors vehicles use a buzzer or indicator lamp to indicate a low coolant level condition. The buzzer or lamp is activated by a sensor, located in the radiator, when the coolant level becomes one quart or more low.

FUEL USAGE GAUGE

1978—83 Buick & Cadillac

Operation

This system consists of green and amber indicator lights located on the fuel gauge or telltale lamp cluster, a switch mounted on the instrument panel behind the gauges and an interconnecting vacuum hose and tee. The system operates on engine vacuum through a dual contact vacuum sensing switch. When the accelerator is operated slowly and smoothly, engine vacuum remains high and the switch passes current to the green indicator light which indicates economical fuel consumption. When the accelerator pedal is depressed rapidly, vacuum decreases and the switch passes current to the amber indicator light, which indicates high fuel consumption. The amber indicator light will glow when the ignition switch is in the "On" position with the engine stopped.

Functional Test
1. With ignition switch in the "On" position, ground each terminal at the economy switch. Both green and amber indicator lights should glow. If not check for burned out bulbs.
2. With ignition switch in "On" position, amber indicator light should glow. If not, check for loose or disconnected wires at fuel economy switch or for poor ground. If amber indicator light still does not glow replace switch.
3. Start engine and allow to idle, the green indicator light should glow. If not, check for leaking, plugged or kinked vacuum hose between vacuum source and fuel economy switch. Check for loose or disconnected wires at economy switch or poor ground. If green indicator lamp still does not glow, replace switch.

TURBO-POWER INDICATOR

1978—83 Buick V6-231 Turbo-Charged Engine

Century, Regal and Riviera models utilize two lights located in the lower right hand gauge area. The yellow light indicates moderate acceleration and the orange light indicates power or heavy acceleration. When neither light is illuminated, the indication visible is a green paint band signifying economy. LeSabre models utilize three lights located at the bottom of the fuel gauge. On light acceleration or cruising, a green light indicates economy. Moderate acceleration activates a yellow indicator light. The orange light is activated during heavy acceleration.

WATER IN FUEL INDICATOR

1981—83 General Motors With Diesel Engine

The Water In Fuel warning system employs an electronic water detector, mounted inside the fuel tank, on the fuel gauge sending unit. The detector provides a warning when 1—2½ gallons of water are present in the fuel tank by lighting a warning lamp on the instrument panel. The sending unit assembly also contains a provision for siphoning-off water in the tank through the fuel return line, Fig. 8.

The water in fuel lamp will come on for 2—5 seconds each time ignition is switched to RUN position to insure that the lamp is operating. If there is water in the fuel, the warning lamp will come back on after a 15—20 second delay and remain on.

Trouble Shooting

If warning indicator fails to light during bulb check, disconnect wiring harness connector at fuel gauge sending unit, containing a yellow/black stripe wire. With ignition switch in RUN position, connect yellow/black stripe wire to ground, using a suitable jumper wire. If lamp lights, problem is in water detector. If lamp fails to light, check for open circuit between sender and warning lamp, a burned out bulb, or a blown fuse.

If warning lamp remains on at all times, disconnect wiring harness connector at fuel tank sending unit with ignition switch in RUN position. If warning lamp remains on, check for short circuit to ground between sender and warning lamp. If warning lamp goes out when harness is disconnected, first purge water in fuel tank, Fig. 8, then recheck circuit. If lamp remains on with harness connected to sending unit, water detector is defective.

DRIVER REMINDER PACKAGE

1983 Toronado

The driver reminder package incorporates several warning and reminder features into one system. The system uses three distinct sounds, and warning and reminder lights on

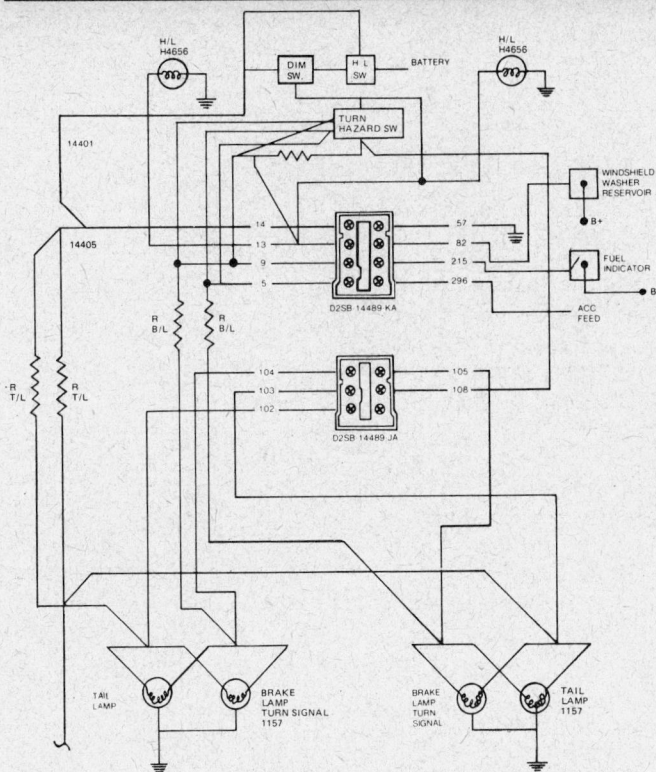

Fig. 10 Graphic display warning indicator wiring diagram. 1979–81 Ford & Mercury Exc. Escort & Lynx (Mustang/Capri & Fairmont/Zephyr sedan shown, typical of other models)

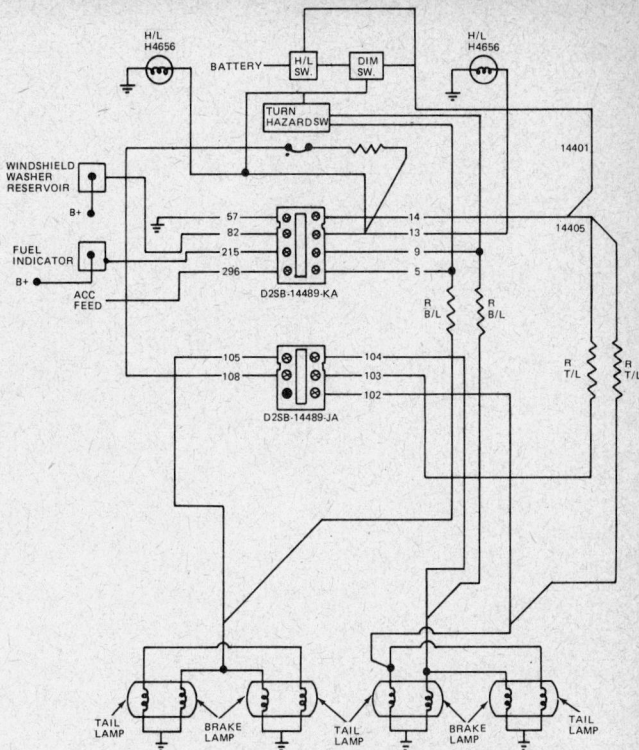

Fig. 11 Graphic display warning indicator wiring diagram. 1982–83 Ford & Mercury Exc. Escort & Lynx (Mustang/Capri & Fairmont/Zephyr sedan shown, typical of other models)

the center instrument cluster.

If engine coolant level is 3 quarts or more low, a red LOW COOLANT warning light will illuminate and a fast-pulsed tone will be heard. The light will remain lit and the tone will be heard until coolant is added to the cooling system. The light will also illuminate during engine starting as a bulb check.

When the headlight switch is in the ON position and the ignition is off, a red LIGHTS ON warning light will illuminate and a fast-pulsed tone will be heard. Turning the headlight switch to the right will dim the instrument panel lights and shut off the tone.

When there is less than approximately 3 gallons of fuel in the tank, an amber LOW FUEL warning light will illuminate and a steady 5 second tone will be heard, however the lamp may not light until fuel level is diminished to as low as 1/2 gallon. The light will remain lit until fuel is added to the tank. This warning light will also illuminate during engine starting as a bulb check.

The amber LOW WASH FLUID reminder light will illuminate while the windshield wipers are operated if the washer fluid reservoir is less than approximately 1/3 full. This light will remain lit during wiper operation until fluid is added.

Additional tones used to warn operator of potential problems are: engine overheating, fast-pulsed tone; malfunction in the charging system, fast-pulsed tone; seat belt reminder, slow-pulsed tone; key reminder, steady tone.

GRAPHIC DISPLAY WARNING INDICATOR SYSTEM

1979–83 Ford/Mercury

Operation

This system is equipped with five L.E.D. (light emitting diodes) located on console, which will indicate running lamp failure, headlamp failure, brake lamp or low w/s washer fluid or fuel level. If lamp is burned out, L.E.D. will illuminate, indicating bulb failure. Application of emergency flasher or rear turn signal when turn signal/stop lamp bulb is burned out will cause L.E.D. to flash. When w/s washer fluid or fuel is below a predetermined level, corresponding L.E.D. will illuminate.

Trouble Shooting, Fig. 9

1. Depress graphic indicator button with ignition switch in ACC or Run position. All of L.E.D. should illuminate. If not, check fuse.
2. Check to ensure that indicator module wire connector is properly installed.
3. Visually check vehicle for lamp outage, low w/s washer fluid level and low fuel indicator on instrument panel.
4. If any of the above components are not operating properly, repair inoperative

circuit and recheck operation, Figs. 10 through 13.

LAMP-OUT WARNING SYSTEM

1981–83 Thunderbird & XR-7; 1982 Lincoln Continental; 1983 LTD & Marquis

The lamp-out warning system monitors low-beam headlamps, tail lamps and brake lamps. The system consists of a warning module, a wiring harness and a set of three indicator lamps located on the upper tier of the instrument panel.

The wiring harness used with the system uses special resistance wire to ensure proper system operation. To prevent malfunctioning of the system, the lengths of these wires should never be altered.

The warning module contains a printed circuit board and logic circuitry. Normal operating voltage is 10–15 volts, however the unit will withstand up to 24 volts for a period of 15 minutes.

The lamp-out warning system operates when the ignition is in ACC or RUN position.

If one or more low beam lamps are burned out when headlamps are energized in low

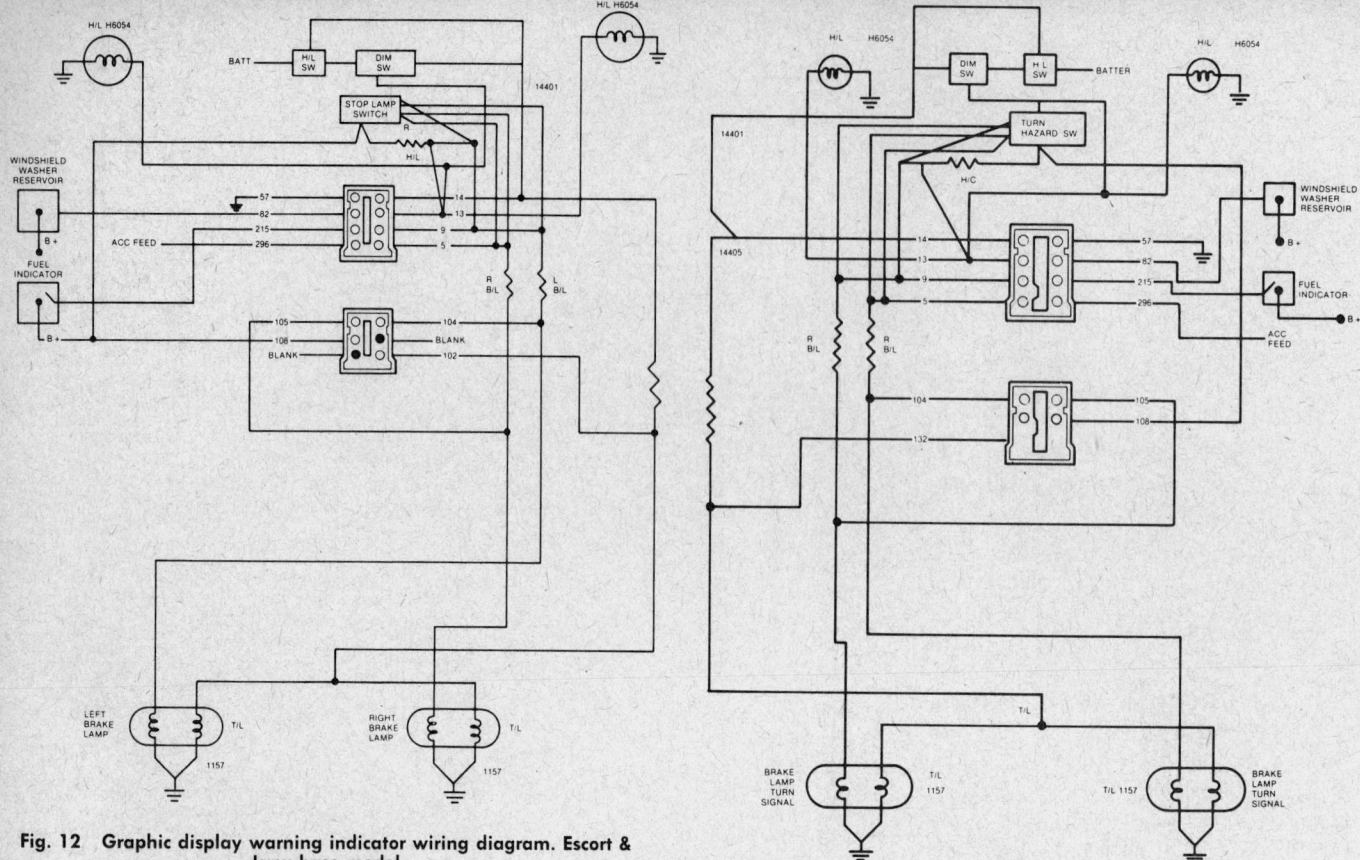

Fig. 12 Graphic display warning indicator wiring diagram. Escort & Lynx base model

Fig. 13 Graphic display warning indicator wiring diagram. Escort & Lynx Exc. base model

beam mode, the low beam Out indicator will illuminate. The tail lamp Out indicator will illuminate when running lamps are energized and one or more tail lamps are burned out. The brake lamp Out indicator will light when brake lights are energized and one or more brake lamps are burned out.

When ignition key is in START position, all three warning lights should illuminate.

1981–83 Lincoln Town Car & Mark VI

The lamp-out warning system monitors low beam headlamps, tail lamps and brake lamps. Each assembly is equipped with three outputs connected to the electronic message center module which displays the appropriate warning message.

Lamp outages are sensed by measuring change in voltage drop across a section of wiring harness by a transistor-diode bridge which provides logic level signals to external message center.

The lamp-out warning module contains a printed circuit board and logic circuitry. Normal operating voltage is 10–15 volts, however the unit will withstand up to 24 volts for a period of 15 minutes.

The lamp-out warning system operates when ignition is in ACC or RUN position.

If one or more low beam lamps are burned out when headlamps are energized in low beam mode, the headlamp outage message will flash. The tail lamp outage indicator will flash when headlamp switch is energized and one or more tail lamps are burned out. The brake lamp outage indicator will flash when brake or turn signal is applied and one or more brake lamps are burned out. The brake lamp indicator will also be illuminated if turn signal or emergency flasher is activated with message center on and one or more lamps burned out.

When the "check out" button on message center is depressed with ignition in ACC or RUN position, all lamp-out warning displays should illuminate.

1983 Lincoln Continental

The lamp-out warning system monitors rear lamps and headlamps by measuring change in voltage across a section of wiring harness with a transistor-bridge diode. Warning indicators are located on either side of the tripminder.

The lamp-out warning system operates when ignition is in ACC or RUN position.

The rear outage light will illuminate when headlamp switch is energized and one or more tail lamps are burned out, or when one or more brake lamps are burned out and brake or turn signal is applied. The rear lamp indicator will also light if turn signal or emergency flasher is applied with one or more brake lamps out.

When the headlamp switch is energized in low beam mode and one or more low beam lamps are burned out, headlamp outage light will illuminate.

When the ignition key is in START position, both warning lights should illuminate.

STARTING MOTORS & SWITCHES

CONTENTS

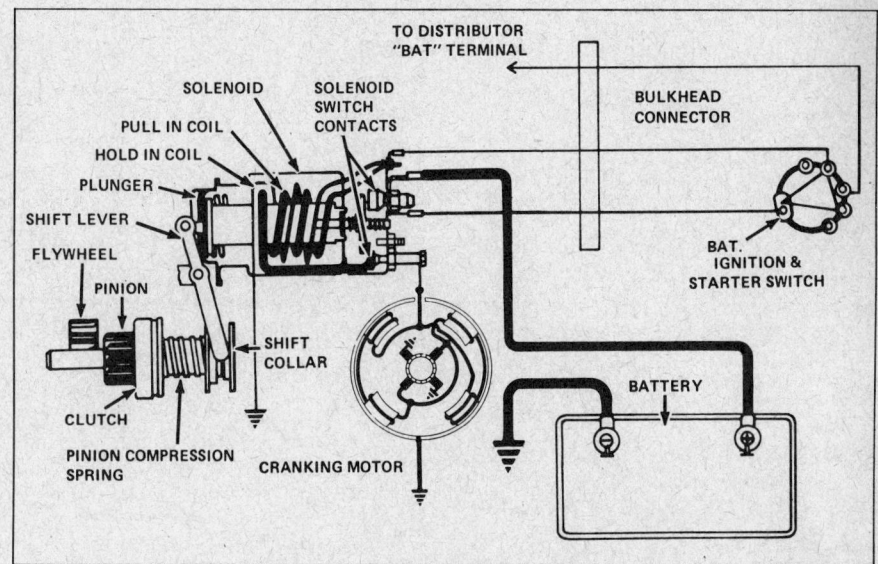

Fig. 1 Wiring diagram of a typical starting circuit

STARTER TROUBLE CHECK-OUT

When trouble develops in the starting motor circuit, and the starter cranks the engine slowly or not at all, several preliminary checks can be made to determine whether the trouble lies in the battery, in the starter, in the wiring between them, or elsewhere. Many conditions besides defects in the starter itself can result in poor cranking performance.

To make a quick check of the starter system, turn on the headlights. They should burn with normal brilliance. If they do not, the battery may be run down and it should be checked with a hydrometer.

If the battery is in a charged condition so that lights burn brightly, operate the starting motor. Any one of three things will happen to the lights: (1) They will go out, (2) dim considerably or (3) stay bright without any cranking action taking place.

If Lights Go Out

If the lights go out as the starter switch is closed, it indicates that there is a poor connection between the battery and starting motor. This poor connection will most often be found at the battery terminals. Correction is made by removing the cable clamps from the terminals, cleaning the terminals and clamps, replacing the clamps and tightening them securely. A coating of corrosion inhibitor (vaseline will do) may be applied to the clamps and terminals to retard the formation of corrosion.

If Lights Dim

If the lights dim considerably as the starter switch is closed and the starter operates slowly or not at all, the battery may be run down, or there may be some mechanical condi-

tion in the engine or starting motor that is throwing a heavy burden on the starting motor. This imposes a high discharge rate on the battery which causes noticeable dimming of the lights.

Check the battery with a hydrometer. If it is charged, the trouble probably lies in either the engine or starting motor itself. In the engine, tight bearings or pistons or heavy oil place an added burden on the starting motor. Low temperatures also hamper starting motor performance since it thickens engine oil and makes the engine considerably harder to crank and start. Also, a battery is less efficient at low temperatures.

In the starting motor, a bent armature, loose pole shoe screws or worn bearings, any of which may allow the armature to drag, will reduce cranking performance and increase current draw.

In addition, more serious internal damage is sometimes found. Thrown armature windings or commutator bars, which sometimes occur on over-running clutch drive starting motors, are usually caused by excessive over-running after starting. This is the result of such conditions as the driver keeping the starting switch closed too long after the en-

gine has started, the driver opening the throttle too wide in starting, or improper carburetor fast idle adjustment. Any of these subject the over-running clutch to extra strain so it tends to seize, spinning the armature at high speed with resulting armature damage.

Another cause may be engine backfire during cranking which may result, among other things, from ignition timing being too far advanced.

To avoid such failures, the driver should pause a few seconds after a false start to make sure the engine has come completely to rest before another start is attempted. In addition, the ignition timing should be reset if engine backfiring has caused the trouble.

Lights Stay Bright, No Cranking Action

This condition indicates an open circuit at some point, either in the starter itself, the starter switch or control circuit. The solenoid control circuit can be eliminated momentarily by placing a heavy jumper lead across the

Fig. 2 Checking voltage drop between vehicle frame and grounded battery terminal post

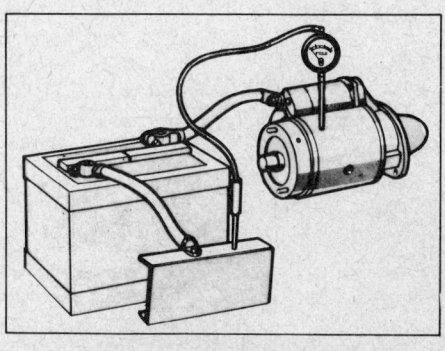

Fig. 3 Checking voltage drop between vehicle frame and starter field frame

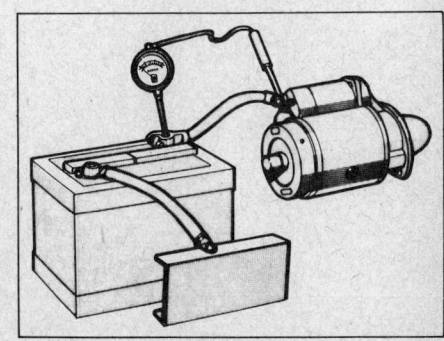

Fig. 4 Checking voltage drop between ungrounded battery terminal post and battery terminal on solenoid

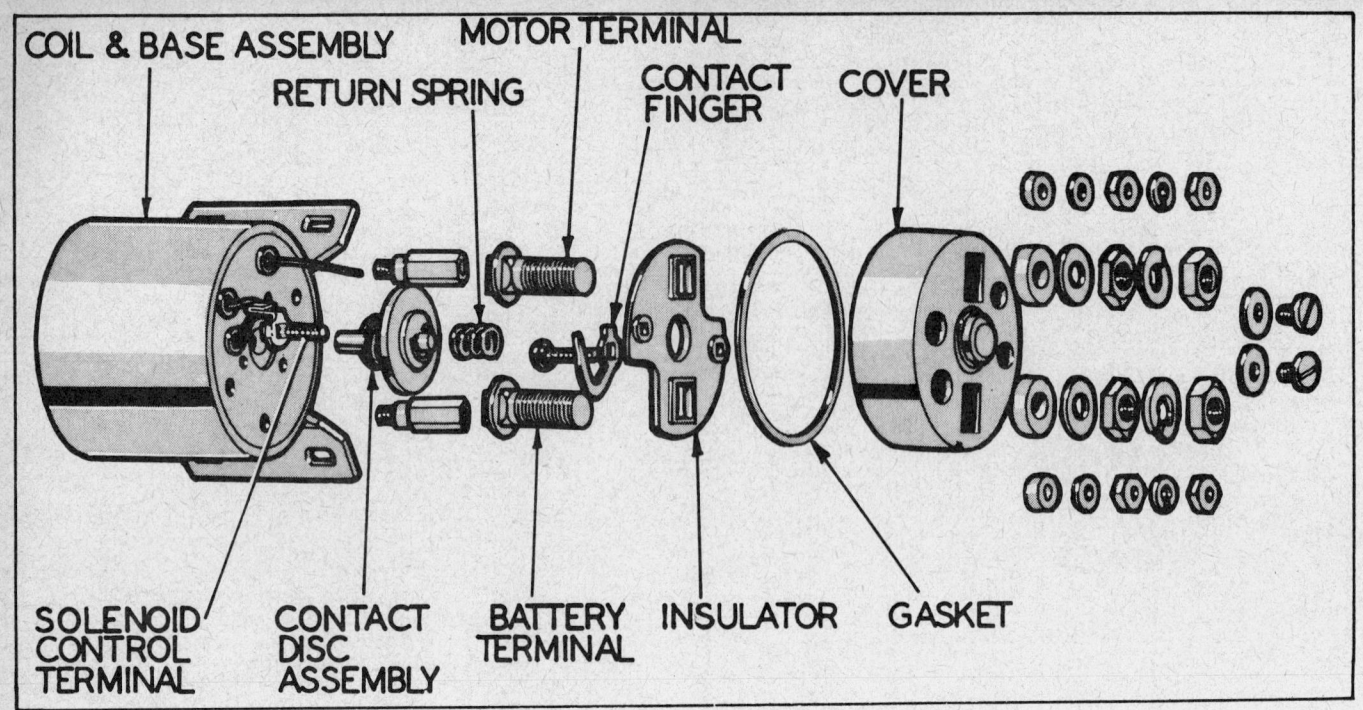

COIL & BASE ASSEMBLY MOTOR TERMINAL
RETURN SPRING CONTACT FINGER COVER

SOLENOID CONTROL TERMINAL CONTACT DISC ASSEMBLY BATTERY TERMINAL INSULATOR GASKET

Fig. 5 Solenoid switch, exploded view (Typical)

solenoid main terminals to see if the starter will operate. This connects the starter directly to the battery and, if it operates, it indicates that the control circuit is not functioning normally. The wiring and control units must be checked to locate the trouble, Fig. 1.

If the starter does not operate with the jumper attached, it will probably have to be removed from the engine so it can be examined in detail.

Checking Circuit With Voltmeter

Excessive resistance in the circuit between the battery and starter will reduce cranking performance. The resistance can be checked by using a voltmeter to measure voltage drop in the circuits while the starter is operated. There are three checks to be made:

1. Voltage drop between car frame and grounded battery terminal post (not cable clamp), Fig. 2.
2. Voltage drop between car frame and starting motor field frame, Fig. 3.
3. Voltage drop between insulated battery terminal post and starting motor terminal stud (or the battery terminal stud of the solenoid), Fig. 4.

Each of these should show no more than one-tenth (0.1) volt drop when the starting motor is cranking the engine. Do not use the starter for more than 30 seconds at a time to avoid overheating it.

If excessive voltage drop is found in any of these circuits, make correction by disconnecting the cables, cleaning the connections carefully, and then reconnecting the cables firmly in place. A coating of vaseline on the battery cables and terminal clamps will retard corrosion.

NOTE: On some cars, extra long battery cables may be required due to the location of the battery and starter. This may result in somewhat higher voltage drop than the above recommended 0.1 volt. The only means of

determining the normal voltage drop in such cases is to check several of these vehicles. Then when the voltage drop is well above the normal figure for all cars checked, abnormal resistance will be indicated and correction can be made as already explained.

SOLENOID SWITCHES

The solenoid switch on a cranking motor not only closes the circuit between the battery and the cranking motor but also shifts the drive pinion into mesh with the engine flywheel ring gear. This is done by means of a linkage between the solenoid switch plunger and the shift lever on the cranking motor.

Fig. 5 shows a solenoid switch used on vehicles with 12-volt systems. Like other solenoid switches, this type is energized by the battery through a separate starting switch. Note, however, that the switch includes an additional small terminal and contact finger. This

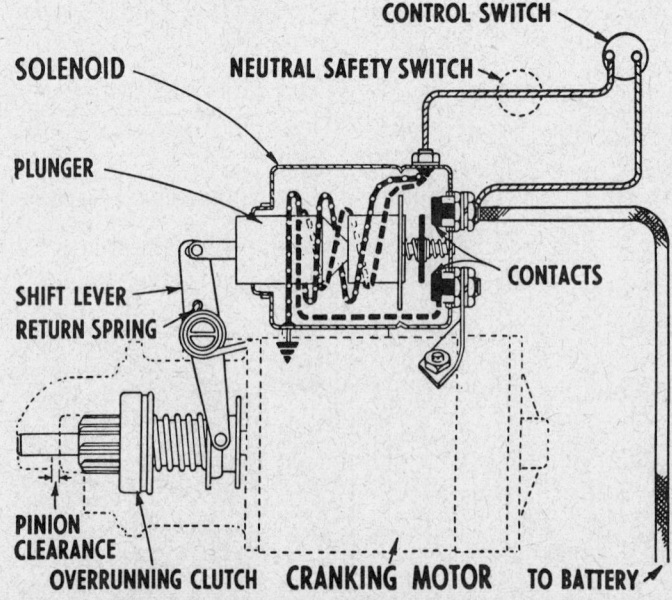

CONTROL SWITCH
SOLENOID NEUTRAL SAFETY SWITCH
PLUNGER
CONTACTS
SHIFT LEVER
RETURN SPRING
PINION CLEARANCE
OVERRUNNING CLUTCH CRANKING MOTOR TO BATTERY

Fig. 6 Solenoid switch wiring circuit (Typical)

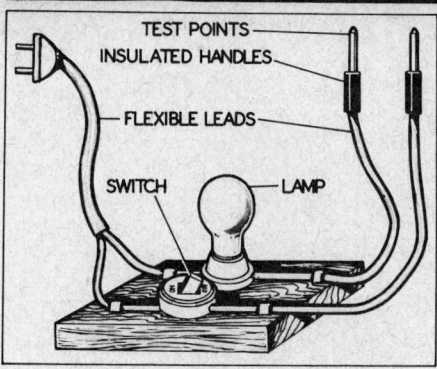

Fig. 7 A simple tester for use in making continuity and ground tests on armature and field windings

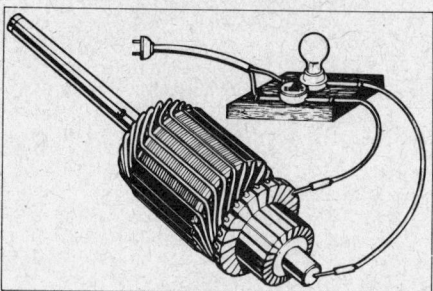

Fig. 8 Checking armature for grounds. If lamp lights armature is grounded and should be replaced

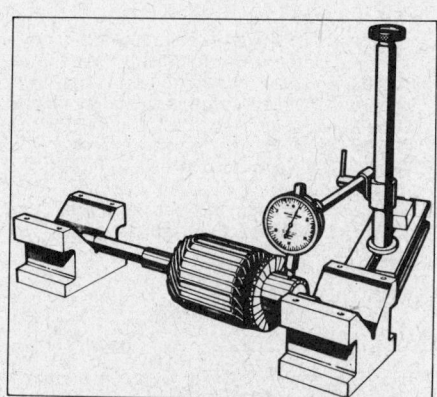

Fig. 9 Measuring commutator runout with dial indicator. Mount shaft in V blocks and rotate commutator. If runout exceeds .003", commutator should be turned in a lathe to make it concentric

terminal has no functional duty in relation to the switch, but is used to complete a special ignition circuit during the cranking cycle only. When the solenoid is in the cranking position, the finger touches the contact disk and provides a direct circuit between the battery and ignition coil.

When reassembling the switch the contact finger should be adjusted to touch the contact disk before the disk makes contact with the main switch terminals. There should be 1/16" to 3/32" clearance between the contact disk and the main terminals when the finger touches.

Fig. 6 is a wiring circuit of a typical solenoid switch. There are two windings in the sole-

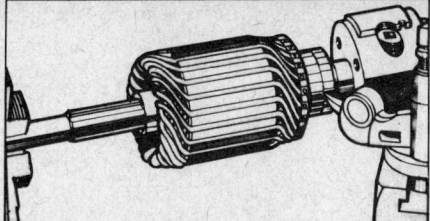

Fig. 10 Turning commutator in a lathe. Take light cuts until worn or bad spots are removed. Then remove burrs with No. 00 sandpaper

noid; a pull-in winding (shown as dashes) and a hold-in winding (shown dotted). Both windings are energized when the external control switch is closed. They produce a magnetic field which pulls the plunger in so that the drive pinion is shifted into mesh, and the main contacts in the solenoid switch are closed to connect the battery directly to the cranking motor. Closing the main switch contacts shorts out the pull-in winding since this winding is connected across the main contacts. The magnetism produced by the hold-in winding is sufficient to hold the plunger in, and shorting out the pull-in winding reduces drain on the battery. When the control switch is opened, it disconnects the hold-in winding from the battery. When the hold-in winding is disconnected from the battery, the shift lever spring withdraws the plunger from the solenoid, opening the solenoid switch contacts and at the same time withdrawing the drive pinion from mesh. Proper operation of the switch depends on maintaining a definite balance between the magnetic strength of the pull-in and hold-in windings.

This balance is established in the design by the size of the wire and the number of turns specified. *An open circuit in the hold-in winding or attempts to crank with a discharged battery will cause the switch to chatter.*

To disassemble the solenoid, remove nuts, washers and insulators from the switch terminal and battery terminal. Remove cover and take out the contact disk assembly.

STARTING MOTOR SERVICE

To obtain full performance data on a starting motor or to determine the cause of abnormal operation, the starting motor should be submitted to a no-load and torque test. These tests are best performed on a starter bench tester with the starter mounted on it.

From a practical standpoint, however, a simple torque test may be made quickly with the starter in the car. Make sure the battery is fully charged and that the starter circuit wires and terminals are in good condition. Then operate the starter to see if the engine turns over normally. If it does not, the torque developed is below standard and the starter should be removed for further checking.

Remove the starter from the engine as outlined in the vehicle chapters, disassemble it as outlined further on and make the tests as suggested in Figs. 8 through 13.

CHRYSLER REDUCTION GEAR STARTER

This reduction gear starting motor, Fig. 14,

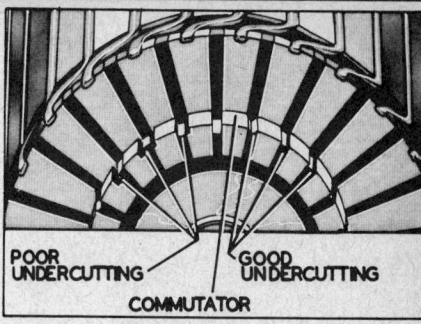

Fig. 11 Good undercutting should be .002" wider than mica insulation, 1/64" deep and exactly centered so that there are no burrs on the mica. Do not undercut molded commutators

Fig. 12 Checking armature for short circuit. As armature is rotated by hand, steel strip (hacksaw blade) will vibrate if short circuit exists

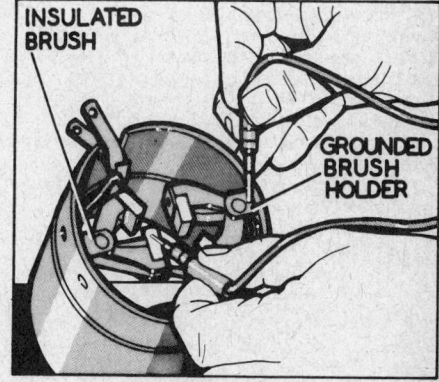

Fig. 13 Testing field coils for grounds. If a ground is present, lamp will light

has an armature-to-engine crankshaft ratio of 2 to 1 or a 3 1/2 to 1 reduction gear set is built into the motor assembly. The starter utilizes a solenoid shift. The housing of the solenoid is integral with the starter drive end housing.

Disassembly

1. Place gear housing of starter in a vise with soft jaws. *Use vise as a support*

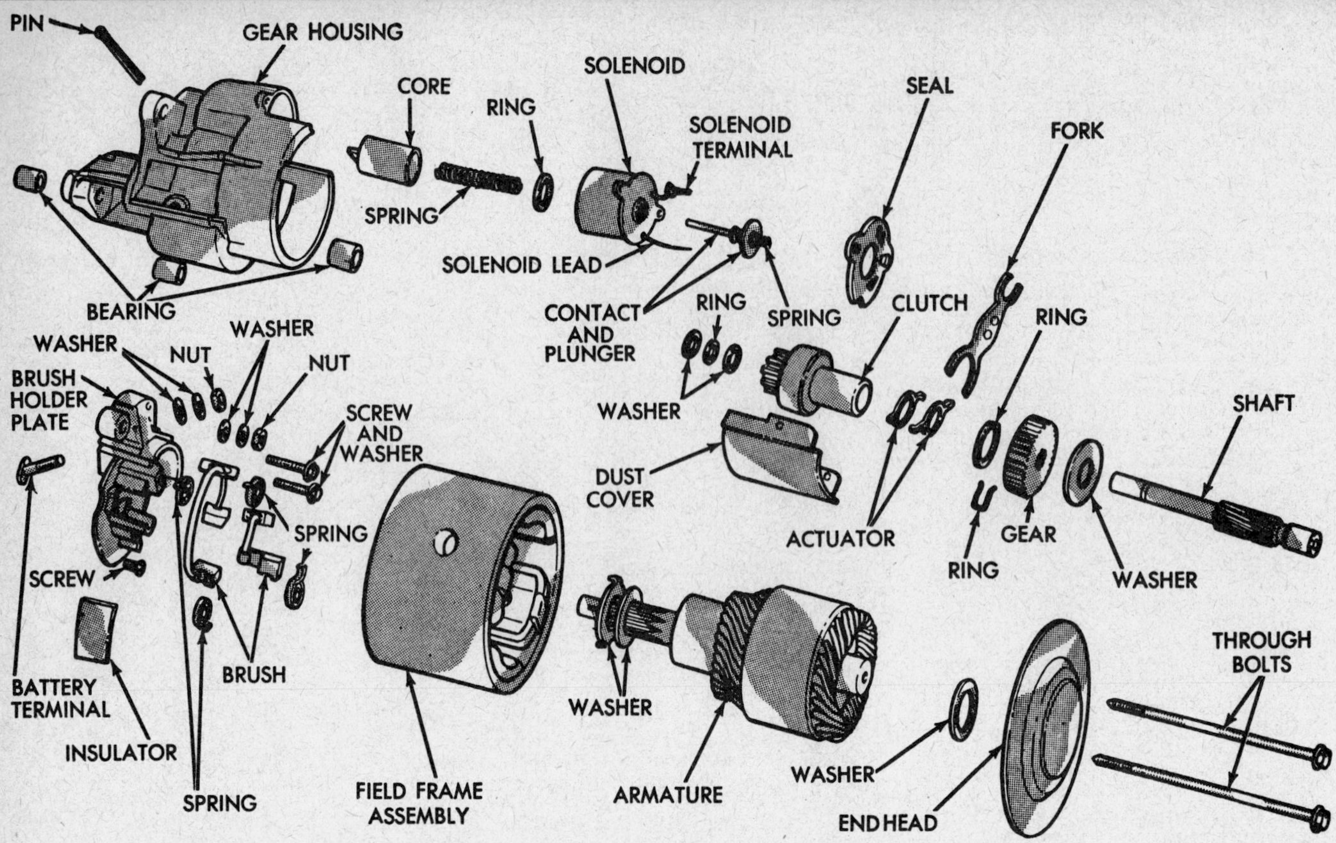

STARTING MOTORS & SWITCHES

Fig. 14 Chrysler built reduction gear starting motor

fixture only; do not clamp.

2. Remove through bolts and starter end head assembly.
3. Carefully remove armature from gear housing and field frame assembly.
4. Pull field frame assembly from gear housing to expose terminal screw.
5. Support terminal screw with a finger, then remove terminal screw, Fig. 15.
6. Remove field frame assembly.
7. Remove nuts attaching solenoid and brush holder plate assembly to gear housing, then remove the solenoid and brush plate assembly.
8. Remove nut, steel washer and insulating washer from solenoid terminal.
9. Unwind solenoid lead wire from brush terminal, Fig. 16, and remove screws securing solenoid to brush plate, then remove the solenoid from brush plate.

10. Remove nut from battery terminal on brush plate, then the battery terminal.
11. Remove solenoid contact and plunger assembly from solenoid, Fig. 17, then the return spring from the solenoid moving core.
12. Remove dust cover from gear housing, Fig. 18.
13. Release retainer clip positioning driven gear on pinion shaft, Fig. 19.

NOTE: The retainer clip is under tension. Therefore, it is recommended that a cloth be placed over the retainer clip when released, preventing it from springing away.

14. Remove pinion shaft "C" clip, Fig. 20.

15. Push pinion shaft toward rear of housing, Fig. 21, and remove retainer ring and thrust washers, clutch and pinion assembly, with the two shift fork nylon actuators as an assembly, Fig. 22.
16. Remove driven gear and thrust washer.
17. Pull shifting fork forward and remove solenoid moving core, Fig. 23.
18. Remove shifting fork retainer pin, Fig. 24, and remove clutch shifting fork assembly.

Reassembly

NOTE: *The shifter fork consists of two spring steel plates assembled with two rivets, Fig. 25. There should be about 1/16" side movement to insure proper pinion gear engagement. Lubri-*

Fig. 15 Terminal screw replacement

Fig. 16 Unwinding solenoid lead wire

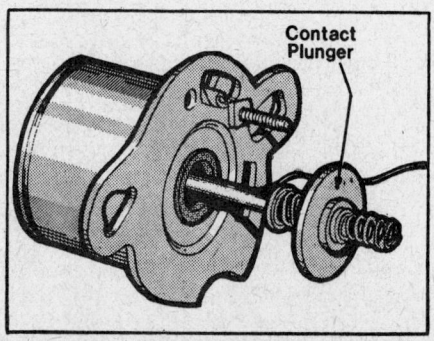

Fig. 17 Solenoid contact & plunger

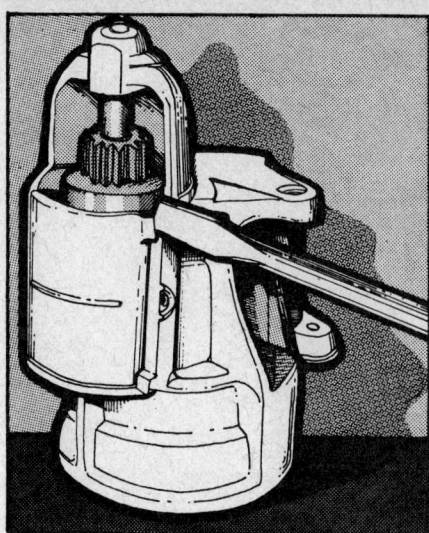

Fig. 18   Dust cover removal, all (Typical)

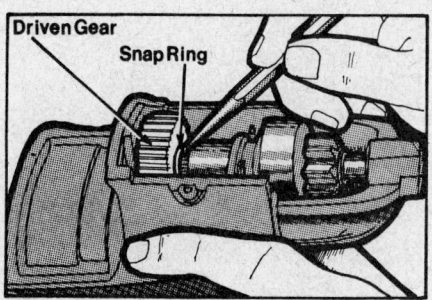

Fig. 19   Driven gear snap ring replacement, all (Typical)

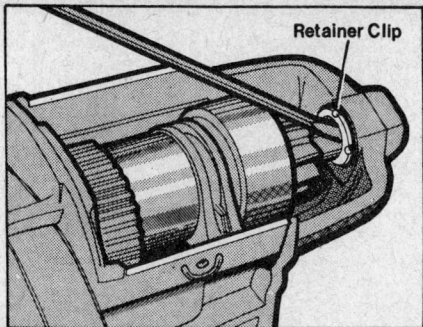

Fig. 20   Pinion shaft "C" clip replacement

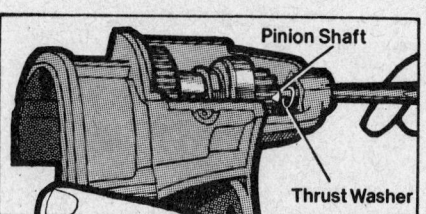

Fig. 21   Removing pinion shaft

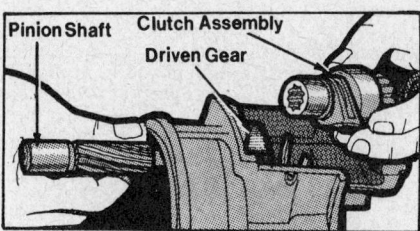

Fig. 22   Clutch assembly replacement (Typical)

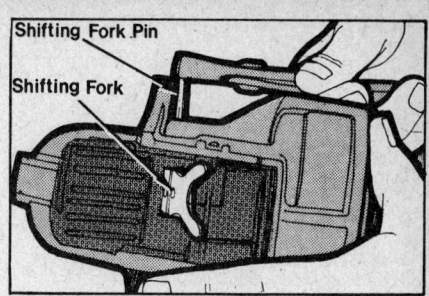

Fig. 24   Shifter fork pin replacement, all (Typical)

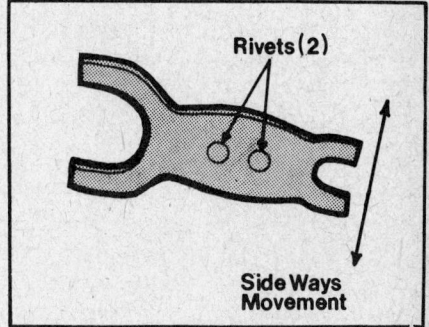

Fig. 25   Shifter fork assembly (Typical)

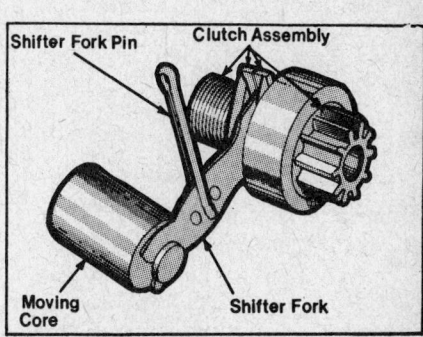

Fig. 26   Shifter fork & clutch assembly (Typical)

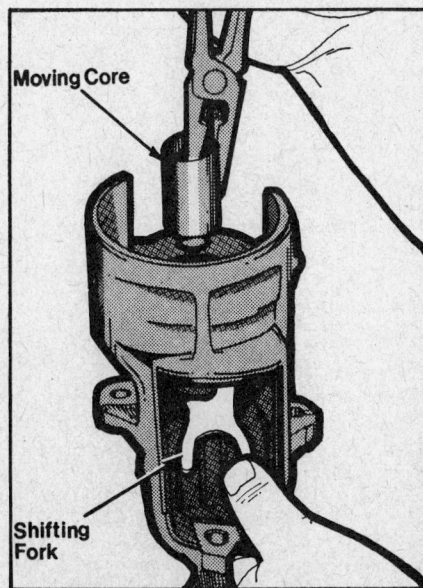

Fig. 23   Solenoid core replacement (Typical)

cate between plates sparingly with SAE 10 engine oil.

1. Position shift fork in drive housing and install fork retaining pin, Fig. 24. One tip of pin should be straight, *the other tip should be bent at a 15 degree angle away from housing. Fork and pin should operate freely after bending tip of pin.*
2. Install solenoid moving core and engage shifting fork, Fig. 23.
3. Enter pinion shaft in drive housing and install friction washer and driven gear.
4. Install clutch and pinion assembly, Fig. 22, thrust washer, retaining ring, and thrust washer.
5. Complete installation of pinion shaft, engaging fork with clutch actuators, Fig. 26. *Friction washer must be positioned on shoulder of splines of pinion shaft before driven gear is positioned.*
6. Install driven gear snap ring, Fig. 19, then the pinion shaft retaining ring or "C" clip, Fig. 20.
7. Install starter solenoid return spring into movable core bore.

NOTE: Inspect starter solenoid switch contacting washer. If top of washer is burned, disassemble contact switch plunger assembly and reverse the washer.

8. Install solenoid contact plunger assembly into solenoid, Fig. 17. Ensure contact spring is properly positioned on shaft of solenoid contact plunger assembly.
9. Install battery terminal stud in brush holder.

NOTE: Inspect contacts in brush holder. If contacts are badly burned, replace brush holder with brushes and contacts as an assembly.

10. Position seal on brush holder plate.
11. Install solenoid lead wire through hole in brush holder, Fig. 27, then the solenoid stud, insulating washer, flat washer and nut.
12. Wrap solenoid lead wire around brush terminal post, Fig. 16, and solder with a high temperature resin core solder and resin flux.
13. Install brush holder attaching screws.
14. Install solenoid coil and brush plate assembly into gear housing bore and posi-

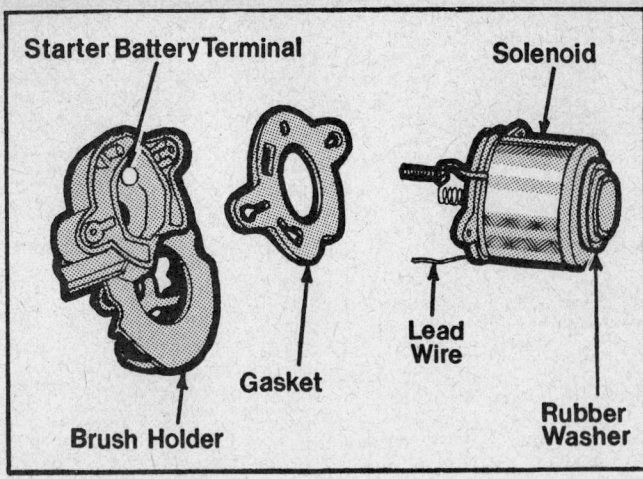

Fig. 27 Solenoid to brush holder plate assembly (Typical)

Fig. 28 Solenoid & brush holder installation (Typical)

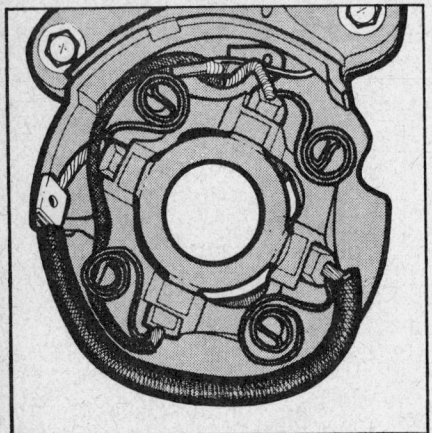

Fig. 29 Installing brushes & armature thrust washer (Typical)

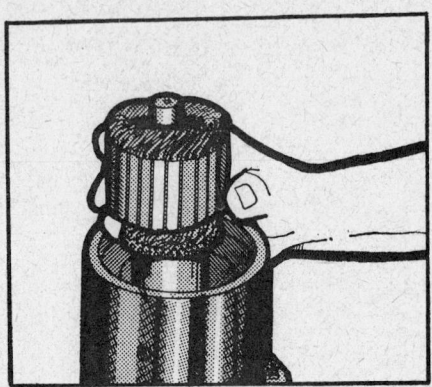

Fig. 30 Armature installation (Typical)

tion brush plate assembly into starter gear housing, Fig. 28. Then, install and tighten housing attaching nuts.

15. Install brushes with armature thrust washer, Fig. 29. This holds brushes out and facilitates proper armature installation.
16. Install brush terminal screw, Fig. 15.
17. Position field frame on gear housing and install armature into field frame and starter gear housing, Fig. 30, carefully engaging splines of shaft with reduction gear by rotating armature slightly to engage splines.
18. Install thrust washer on armature shaft.
19. Install starter end head assembly, then the through bolts.

DELCO-REMY STARTERS Except 1978—83 Olds Built Diesel

This type staring motor, Fig. 31, has the solenoid shift lever mechanism and the solenoid plunger enclosed in the drive housing, thus protecting them from exposure to road dirt, icing conditions and splash. They have an extruded field frame and an overrunning clutch type of drive. The overrunning clutch is operated by a solenoid switch mounted to a flange on the drive housing.

Solenoid

The solenoid is attached to the drive end housing by two screws. The angle of the nose of the plunger provides a greater bearing area between the plunger and core tube. A molded push rod, Fig. 32, is assembled in the contact assembly. A shoulder molded on the push rod and a cup that can easily be assembled to the rod and locked into position over two molded bosses holds the contact assembly in place.

To disassemble the cup from the push rod, push in on the metal cup and rotate 1/4 turn so the molded bosses on the rod are in line with openings in the cup; then slide the metal cup off the rod.

To assemble the metal cup on the rod, locate the parts on the rod as shown and align the large openings in the cup with the molded bosses on the rod; then push in on the cup and rotate it 1/4 turn so the small bosses on the rod fall into the keyways of the cup.

Maintenance

Most motors of this type have graphite and oil impregnated bronze bearings which ordinarily require no added lubrication except at times of overhaul when a few drops of light engine oil should be placed on each bearing before reassembly.

Since the motor and brushes cannot be inspected without disassembling the unit, there is no service that can be performed with the unit assembled on the vehicle.

Free Speed Test

With the circuit connected as shown in Fig. 33, use a tachometer to measure armature revolutions per minute. Failure of the motor to perform to specifications may be due to tight or dry bearings, or high resistance connections.

Pinion Clearance

There is no provision for adjusting pinion clearance on this type motor. When the shift lever mechanism is correctly assembled, the pinion clearance should fall within the limits of .010 to .140″. When the clearance is not within these limits, it may indicate excessive wear of the solenoid linkage or shift lever yoke buttons.

Pinion clearance should be checked after the motor has been disassembled and reassembled. To check, disconnect motor field coil connector from solenoid terminal and insulate end. Connect one battery lead to solenoid switch terminal and the other lead to the solenoid frame, Fig. 34. Using a jumper lead connected to the solenoid motor terminal, momentarily flash the lead to the solenoid frame. This will shift the pinion into the cranking position until the battery is disconnected.

After energizing the solenoid with the clutch shifted toward the pinion stop retainer, push the pinion back toward the commutator end as far as possible to take up any slack movement; then check the clearance with feeler gauge, Fig. 35.

Disassembling Motor

NOTE: The 5 MT series starting motor will be used on some 1978—83 models, Fig. 36. On this type starting motor, the field coils and pole shoes are permanently bonded to the motor frame. The frame and field coils must be replaced as an assembly.

Normally the motor should be disassembled only so far as necessary to repair or replace defective parts.

1. Disconnect field coil connectors from sole-

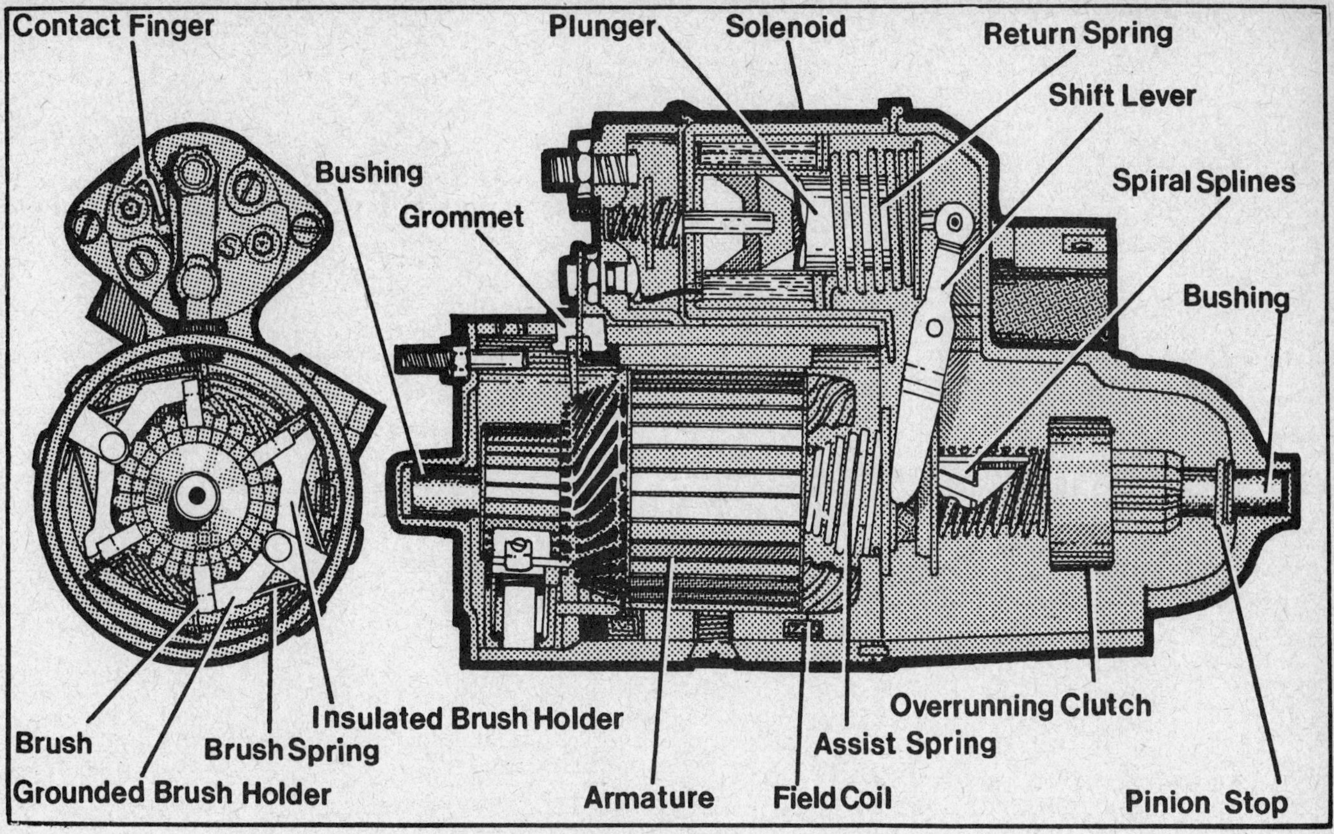

Contact Finger · Plunger · Solenoid · Return Spring · Shift Lever · Bushing · Grommet · Spiral Splines · Bushing · Brush · Insulated Brush Holder · Brush Spring · Grounded Brush Holder · Armature · Field Coil · Assist Spring · Overrunning Clutch · Pinion Stop

Fig. 31   Delco-Remy starter with enclosed shift lever

noid "motor" terminal.
2. Remove thru bolts.
3. Remove commutator end frame and field frame assembly.
4. Remove armature assembly from drive housing. On some models it may be necessary to remove solenoid and shift lever assembly from the drive housing before removing the armature assembly. *Important: When solenoid is installed, apply sealing compound between field frame and solenoid flange, Fig. 37.*
5. Remove overrunning clutch from armature shaft as follows:
   a) Slide thrust collar off end of armature shaft, Fig. 38.
   b) Slide a standard 1/2" pipe coupling, a 5/8" deep socket or other metal cylinder of suitable size onto shaft so end of coupling or cylinder butts against edge of retainer. Tap end of coupling with

hammer, driving retainer toward armature and off snap ring, Fig. 39.
   c) Remove snap ring from groove in shaft. If snap ring is too badly distorted during removal, use a new one when reassembling the clutch.
   d) Slide retainer, clutch and assist spring from armature shaft.

Reassembling Motor, Figs. 36 & 40

1. Lubricate drive end and splines of armature shaft with lubricant 1960954 or equivalent.
2. Place "assist" spring on drive end of shaft next to armature, with small end against lamination stack.
3. Slide clutch assembly onto armature shaft with pinion outward.
4. Slide retainer onto shaft with cupped surface facing end of shaft.
5. Stand armature on end on wood surface with commutator down. Position snap ring on upper end of shaft and hold in place with a block of wood. Hit wood block with a hammer forcing snap ring over end of shaft, Fig. 41. Slide snap ring into groove, squeezing it to ensure a good fit in groove.
6. Assemble thrust collar on shaft with shoulder next to snap ring.
7. Position retainer and thrust collar next to snap ring. With clutch pressed against assist spring, for clearance next to retainer, use two pairs of pliers at the same time (one pair on either side of shaft) to grip retainer and thrust collar. Then squeeze until snap ring is forced into retainer, Fig. 42.

8. Lubricate drive end housing bushing with lubricant 1960954 or equivalent. Make sure thrust collar is in place against snap ring and retainer; then slide armature and clutch assembly into place in drive housing.
9. Attach solenoid and shift lever assembly to drive housing. Be sure lever buttons are located between sides of clutch collar.
10. Position field frame over armature, *applying sealing compound between frame and solenoid flange* (Fig. 37). Position frame against drive housing, using care to prevent damage to brushes.
11. Lubricate commutator end frame bushing with lubricant 1960954 or equivalent. Make sure leather brake washer is on

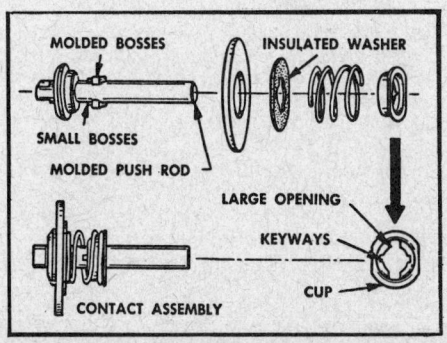

MOLDED BOSSES · INSULATED WASHER · SMALL BOSSES · MOLDED PUSH ROD · LARGE OPENING · KEYWAYS · CUP · CONTACT ASSEMBLY

Fig. 32   Solenoid contact assembly

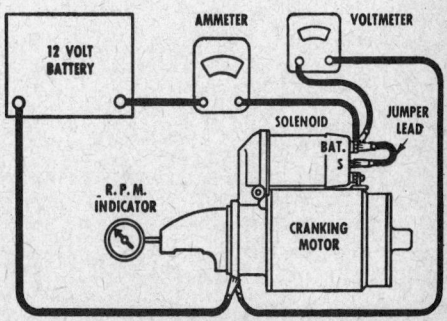

12 VOLT BATTERY · AMMETER · VOLTMETER · SOLENOID · JUMPER LEAD · BAT. · S · R.P.M. INDICATOR · CRANKING MOTOR

Fig. 33   Connections for checking free speed of motor

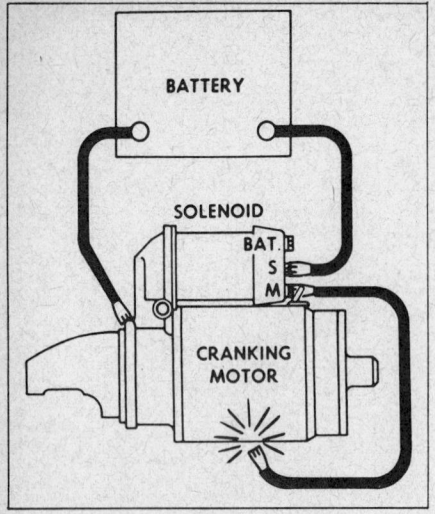

Fig. 34 Connections for checking pinion clearance

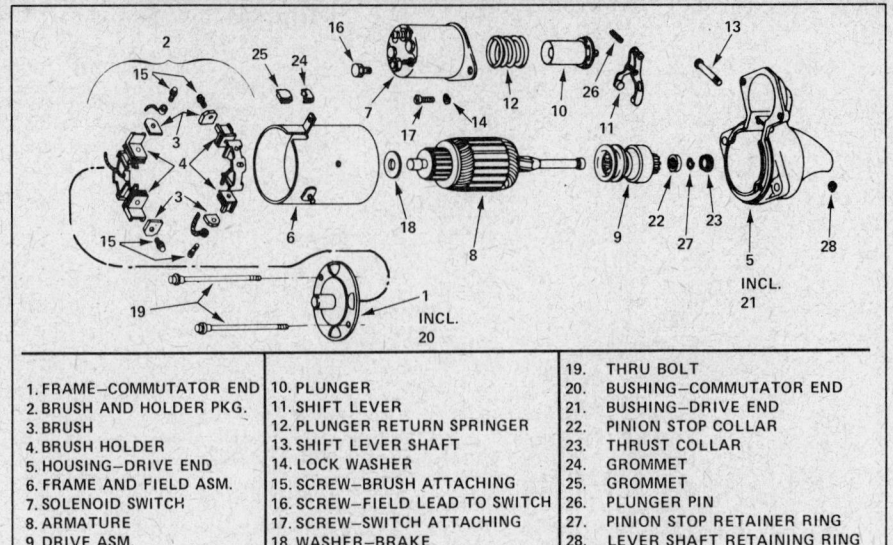

1. FRAME—COMMUTATOR END	10. PLUNGER	19. THRU BOLT
2. BRUSH AND HOLDER PKG.	11. SHIFT LEVER	20. BUSHING—COMMUTATOR END
3. BRUSH	12. PLUNGER RETURN SPRINGER	21. BUSHING—DRIVE END
4. BRUSH HOLDER	13. SHIFT LEVER SHAFT	22. PINION STOP COLLAR
5. HOUSING—DRIVE END	14. LOCK WASHER	23. THRUST COLLAR
6. FRAME AND FIELD ASM.	15. SCREW—BRUSH ATTACHING	24. GROMMET
7. SOLENOID SWITCH	16. SCREW—FIELD LEAD TO SWITCH	25. GROMMET
8. ARMATURE	17. SCREW—SWITCH ATTACHING	26. PLUNGER PIN
9. DRIVE ASM.	18. WASHER—BRAKE	27. PINION STOP RETAINER RING
		28. LEVER SHAFT RETAINING RING

Fig. 36 Disassembled view of Delco-Remy 5MT series starting motor

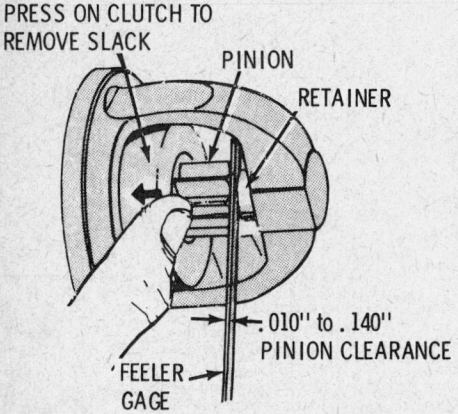

Fig. 35 Checking pinion clearance

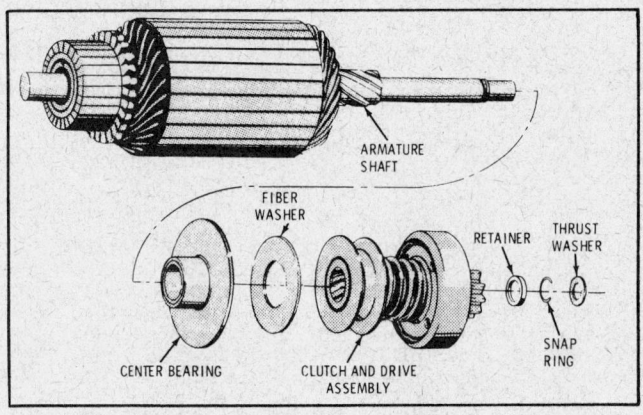

Fig. 38 View of armature and over-running clutch

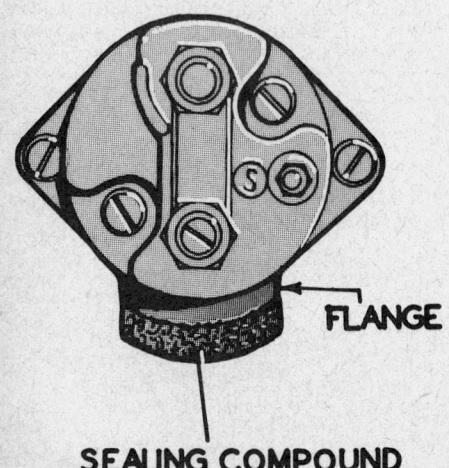

Fig. 37 Sealing solenoid housing to frame

armature shaft; then slide commutator end frame onto shaft.

12. Install thru bolts and tighten securely.
13. Reconnect field coil connectors to solenoid "motor" terminal.

Olds Built Diesel

25 & 27 MT Series

1978–81 ALL, 1982 CAPRICE & IMPALA & 1982-83 ELDORADO, RIVIERA, SEVILLE & TORONADO

Disassemble

1. Remove screw from field coil connector and solenoid mounting screws, then rotate solenoid 90° and remove solenoid with plunger return spring, Fig. 43.
2. Remove two through bolts, then commutator end frame with washer.
3. Remove end frame assembly from drive gear housing.
4. Remove shift lever pivot bolt.
5. Remove center bearing screws, then remove drive gear housing from armature shaft. Shift lever and plunger assembly, should fall from starter clutch.
6. Remove thrust washer or collar from armature shaft.
7. Position a 5/8 in. deep socket over shaft against retainer, then tap socket to move retainer off snap ring.
8. Remove snap ring from groove in shaft, then remove retainer, clutch assembly, fiber washer and center bearing from armature shaft.
9. Remove roll pin and separate shift lever and plunger.
10. Remove brush pivot pin and brush spring, then replace brushes as necessary.

Assemble

1. Lubricate drive end of armature with lubricant 1960954 or equivalent.
2. Install center bearing with bearing facing toward armature winding, then install fiber washer on armature shaft, Fig. 43.
3. Position clutch assembly on armature

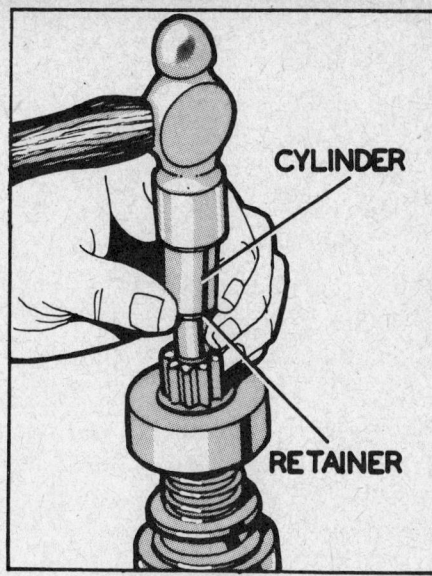

Fig. 39 Removing over-running clutch snap ring retainer

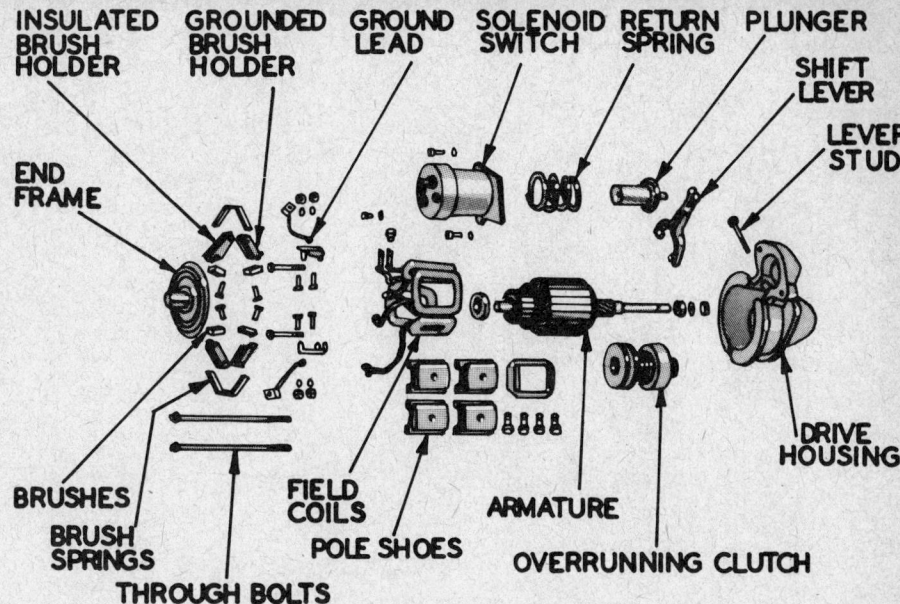

Fig. 40 Disassembled view of Delco-Remy 10MT series starting motor

shaft with pinion facing away from armature.

4. Position retainer on armature shaft with cupped side facing end of shaft.
5. Install snap ring into groove on armature shaft, then install thrust washer.
6. Using two pliers, grip retainer and thrust washer or collar and squeeze until snap ring is forced into retainer and is held securely in groove on armature shaft.
7. Lubricate drive end housing bushing with lubricant 1960954 or equivalent.
8. Engage shift lever yoke with clutch and slide complete assembly into drive gear housing.
9. Install center bearing attaching screws and shift lever pivot bolt.
10. Install solenoid on drive gear housing.
11. Apply sealer No. 1050026 or equivalent to solenoid flange where field frame contacts solenoid.

12. Position field frame against drive gear housing on alignment pin, using care to prevent damage to brushes.
13. Lubricate commutator end frame bushing with lubricant 1960954 or equivalent.
14. Install washer on armature shaft and slide end frame onto shaft, then install and tighten through bolts.
15. Connect field coil connector to solenoid terminal, then check pinion clearance.

15 MT/GR Series

1982–83 EXC. ELDORADO, RIVIERA, SEVILLE, TORONADO & 1982 CAPRICE & IMPALA

Disassemble
1. Remove screw from field coil connector and field frame thru bolts, Fig. 44.
2. Separate field frame and drive gear assemblies, then remove armature and commutator end frame from field frame.
3. Remove solenoid attaching screws and solenoid from drive housing.
4. Remove retaining ring, shift lever shaft and housing thru bolts, then separate drive assembly, drive housing and gear housing.
5. Remove overrunning clutch from drive shaft as follows:
   a. Remove thrust washer from drive shaft.
   b. Slide a ⅝ inch deep socket or a piece of pipe of suitable size over shaft and butt it against retainer. Lightly tap tool to move retainer off snap ring.
   c. Remove snap ring from groove in shaft. If snap ring is too badly distorted, a new one must be used when reassembling the clutch.
   d. Remove retainer and clutch assembly from drive shaft.

Assemble

NOTE: The roller bearings are pre-lubricated and must not be lubricated during assembly of starter motor.

1. Slide clutch assembly onto drive shaft and position retainer with cupped side toward end of shaft, snap ring and washer.

2. Using two pairs of pliers, force snap ring into retainer and groove, in shaft, Fig. 42.
3. Install plunger and shift lever into drive housing with lever shaft and retaining ring.
4. Place washer over drive shaft on side of gear opposite drive assembly, then lubricate gear teeth with lubricant 1960954, or equivalent.
5. Assemble gear housing with attaching screws and attach solenoid to drive housing.
6. Lubricate bushing in commutator end frame with lubricant 1960954, or equivalent, then slide washer on commutator end of armature shaft.
7. Assemble armature, field frame and commutator end frame to gear housing with thru bolts.
8. Attach field coil connector to solenoid terminal.

V6 Diesel Aluminum Starter (Mitsubishi)

1982–83 CELEBRITY, CENTURY, CUTLASS CIERA & 6000

Disassemble
1. Remove nut from field coil connector, solenoid switch mounting screws and solenoid switch, Fig. 45.

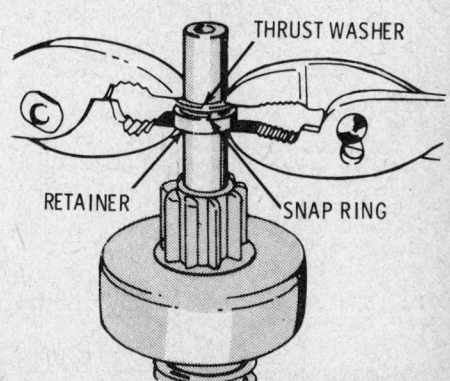

Fig. 42 Installing snap ring into retainer

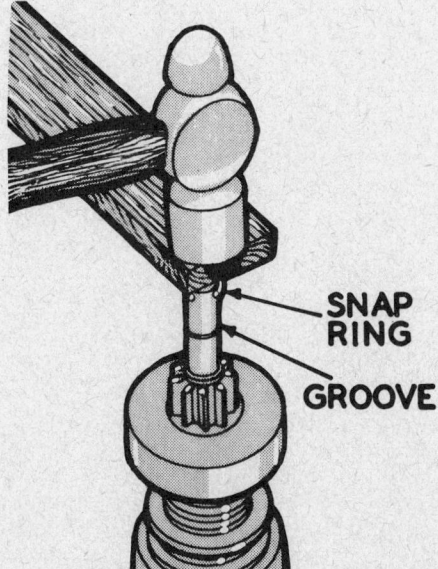

Fig. 41 Installing snap ring onto armature shaft

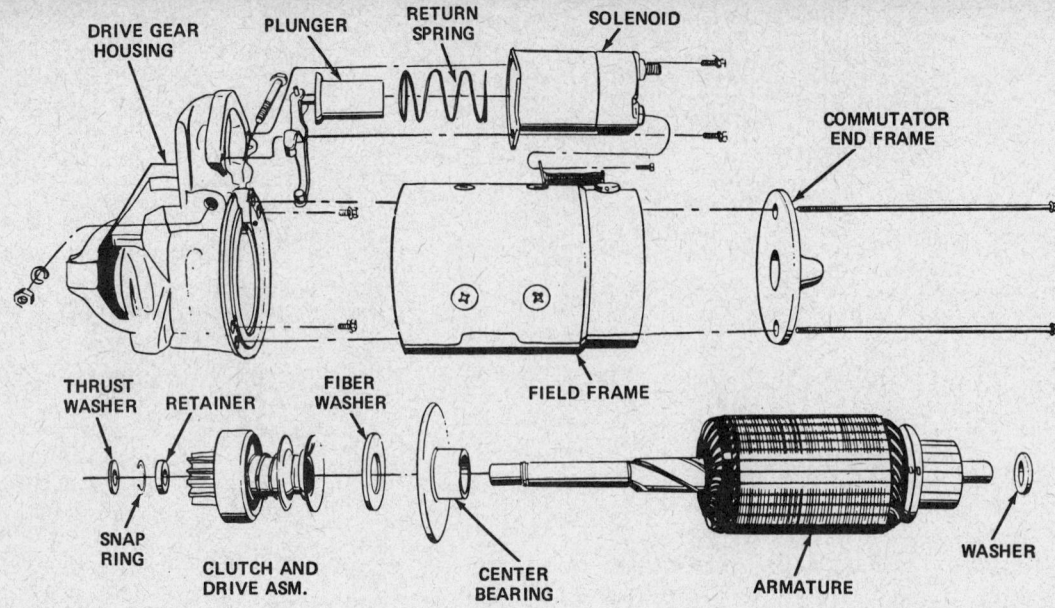

Fig. 43 Disassembled view of Delco-Remy 25 MT & 27 MT series starting motor. Olds built diesel. 1978—81 all, 1982 Caprice & Impala & 1982—83 Eldorado, Riviera, Seville & Toronado

NOTE: Some starters may have shims between solenoid switch and drive end housing, used to set drive pinion position.

2. Remove thru bolts and brush holder retaining screws.
3. Remove commutator end frame from armature and bearing assembly.
4. Remove field frame assembly and armature from center housing.
5. Bend back each brush spring so that each brush can be backed away from armature approximately 1/4 inch, then release spring to hold brushes in backed out position, Fig. 46.
6. Remove armature from field frame and brush holder.
7. Remove pinion shaft cover on center housing by removing two screws, C-washer and plate, Fig. 47.
8. Remove center housing retaining bolts, center housing and shim thrust washer(s).
9. Remove reduction gear, spring holder and lever springs.
10. Slide a 5/8 inch socket, or piece of pipe of suitable size, over shaft against stopper, then tap tool to move stopper off ring, Fig. 48.
11. Remove ring, stopper and drive pinion. If ring is distorted, a new one must be used on reassembly.
12. Remove pinion shaft and lever assembly, noting direction of levers and lever holders.

Assemble
1. Lubricate bearing surfaces and splines of pinion shaft assembly, nylon lever holders, and both ends of lever with lubricant 2960954, or equivalent.
2. Install lever assembly on overrunning clutch, Fig. 49.

NOTE: If lever is not positioned properly, pinion travel will be incorrect, causing a lock-up in the clutch mechanism.

3. Install pinion shaft and lever assembly into drive end housing.
4. Slide spring, drive pinion and stopper

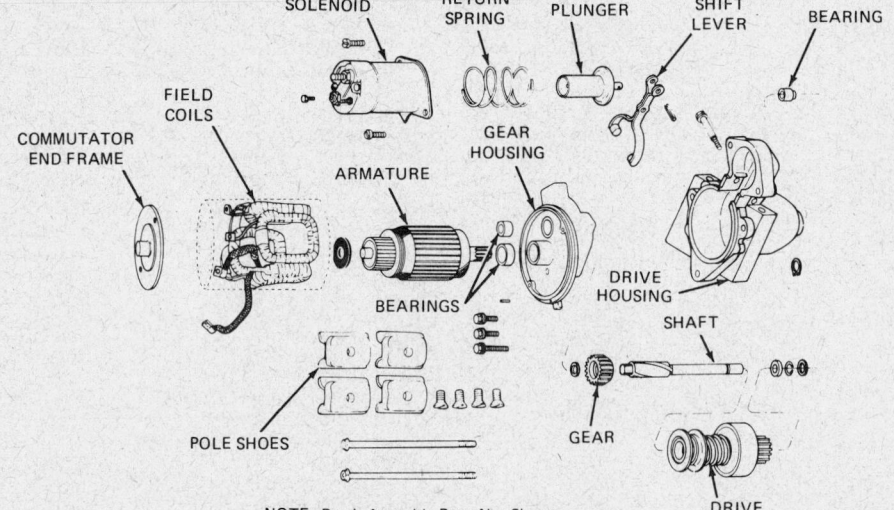

NOTE: Brush Assembly Parts Not Shown

Fig. 44 Disassembled view of 15MT/GR starting motor. Olds built diesel. 1982—83 Exc. Eldorado, Riviera, Seville, Toronado & 1982 Caprice & Impala

ring over pinion shaft with cupped surface of stopper facing end of shaft.
5. Install ring into groove on pinion shaft while forcing drive pinion and stopper down against drive end housing.
6. Force stopper over ring with tool J-22888, Fig. 50.
7. Install the two lever springs and spring holder into drive end housing.
8. Lubricate reduction gear teeth with lubricant 1960954, or equivalent.
9. Install gear and shim thrust washers onto pinion shaft assembly.
10. Assemble center housing to drive end housing, then install and tighten the two attaching bolts.
11. If the drive end housing, pinion shaft, reduction gear, shim washer(s), or center housing were replaced, pinion shaft end play must be checked as follows:
    a. Install plate and C-washer onto end of pinion shaft, then mount drive end housing in a suitable holding fixture.
    b. Insert feeler gauge between C-washer and cover plate, rotate pinion shaft

with a screwdriver and measure end play, Fig. 51. Proper end play is .004—.020 inch.
    c. If end play does not fall within limits, remove plate, C-washer and center bracket, add or remove shim thrust washers as needed, and recheck clearance.
    d. Fill cap one-half full with lubricant 1960954, or equivalent, and install the cap. Install and tighten the two attaching bolts.
12. Install armature, carefully engaging splines of shaft with reduction gear by slightly rotating armature to engage splines.
13. Install field frame and brush holder assembly on center housing.

NOTE: The rubber grommet for the field coil lead must be installed in the locating ribs, Fig. 52.

14. Install brushes by prying back on springs

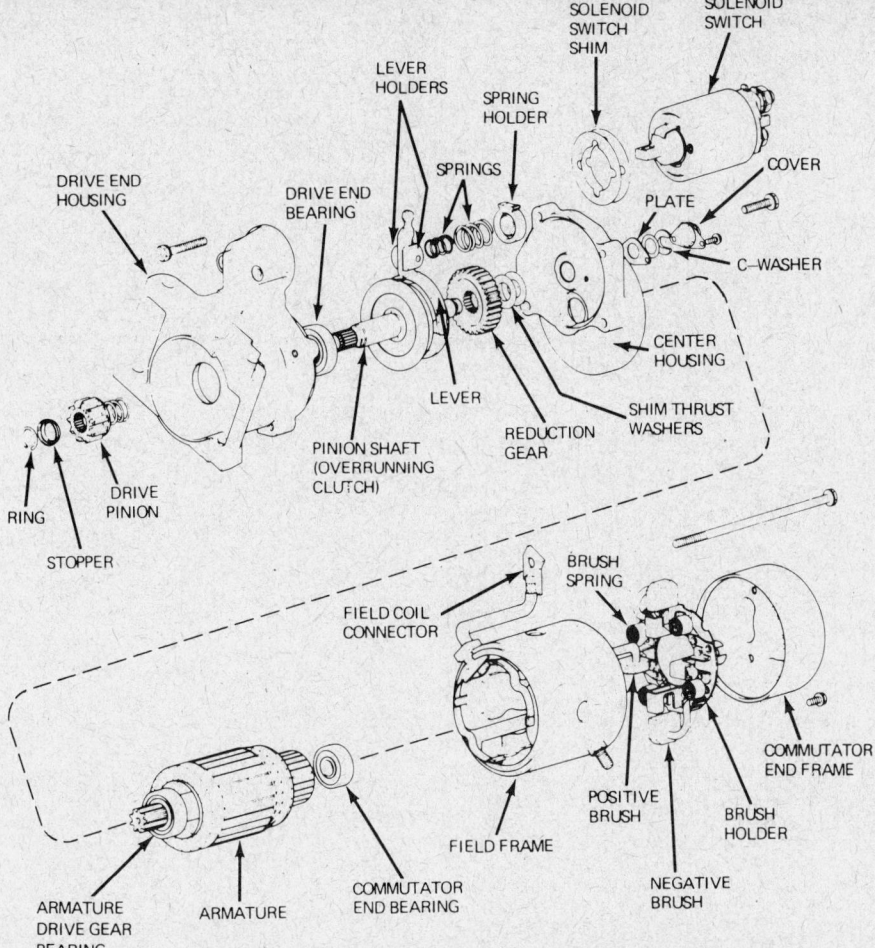

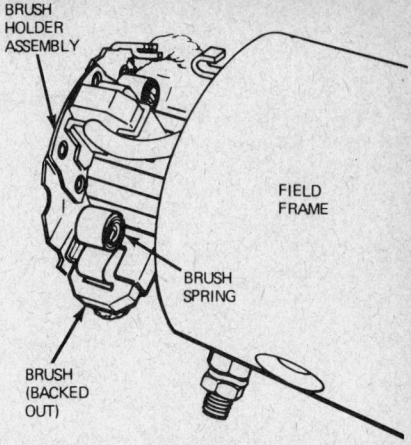

Fig. 46 Brush holder assembly

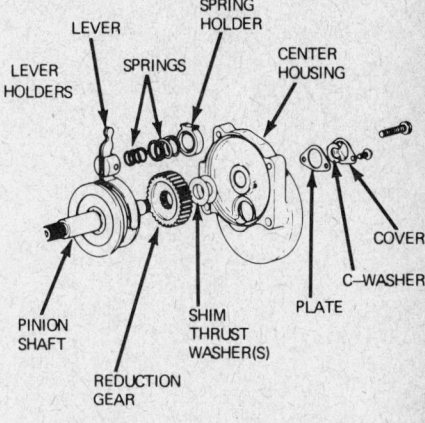

Fig. 47 Disassembled view of pinion shaft (overrunning clutch) assembly

Fig. 45 Disassembled view of V6 diesel aluminum starter. (Mitsubishi). 1982–83 Celebrity, Century, Cutlass Ciera & 6000

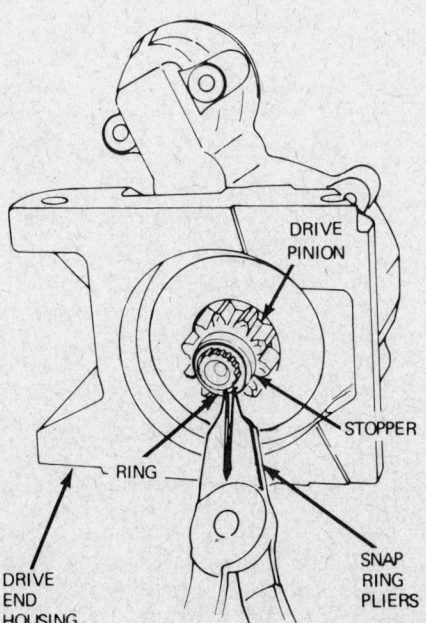

Fig. 48 Removing pinion shaft ring

to allow brushes to seat against commutator bars.

15. Install commutator end frame onto field frame with alignment marks lined up, Fig. 53.
16. Install and tighten brush holder screws and thru bolts.
17. Install solenoid switch and shims on drive end housing, ensuring that slot in plunger engages with top of lever, then install and tighten the two bolts.
18. Connect field coil connector to solenoid switch terminal.

Pinion Clearance Check
1. Disconnect field coil connector from solenoid terminal and insulate carefully.
2. Connect one 12 volt battery lead to solenoid switch terminal and other lead to starter motor frame.
3. Flash a jumper lead momentarily from solenoid motor terminal to starter motor frame. This will shift pinion into cranking position until battery is disconnected.
4. Push pinion back as far as possible to take up any movement, then check pinion clearance using a feeler gauge. Pinion clearance should be .010–.140 in. On V6 diesel aluminum starter, clearance should be .020–.080 inch. If clearance is not within limits, check for improper installation or worn parts and replace as necessary.

NOTE: On V6 diesel aluminum starter, clearance may be adjusted by adding or removing

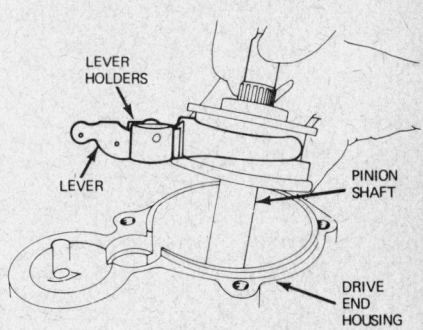

Fig. 49 Installing lever assembly on overrunning clutch

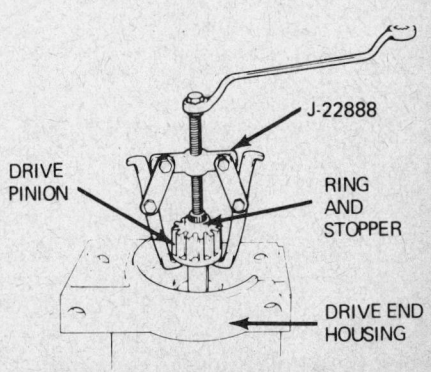

Fig. 50 Installing stopper on overrunning clutch

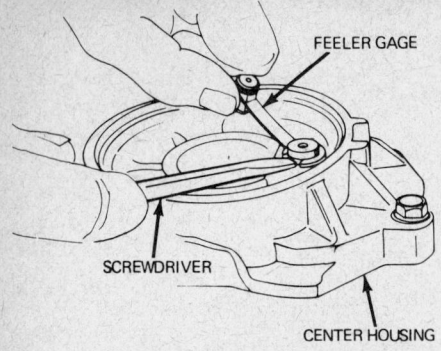

Fig. 51 Checking pinion shaft end play

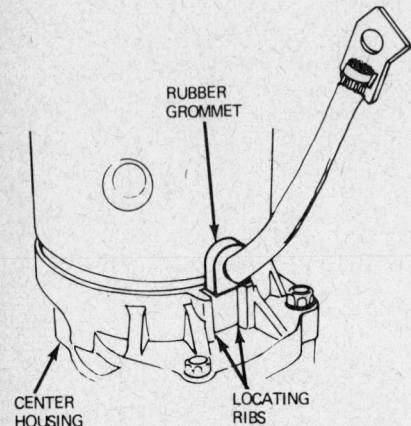

Fig. 52 Installing field frame and brush holder assembly

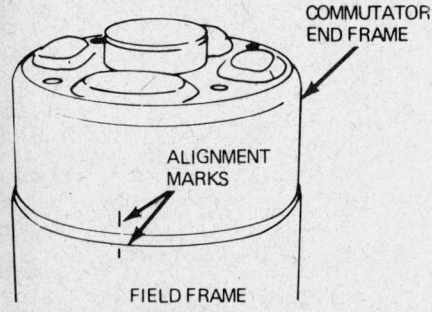

Fig. 53 Installing commutator end frame on field frame

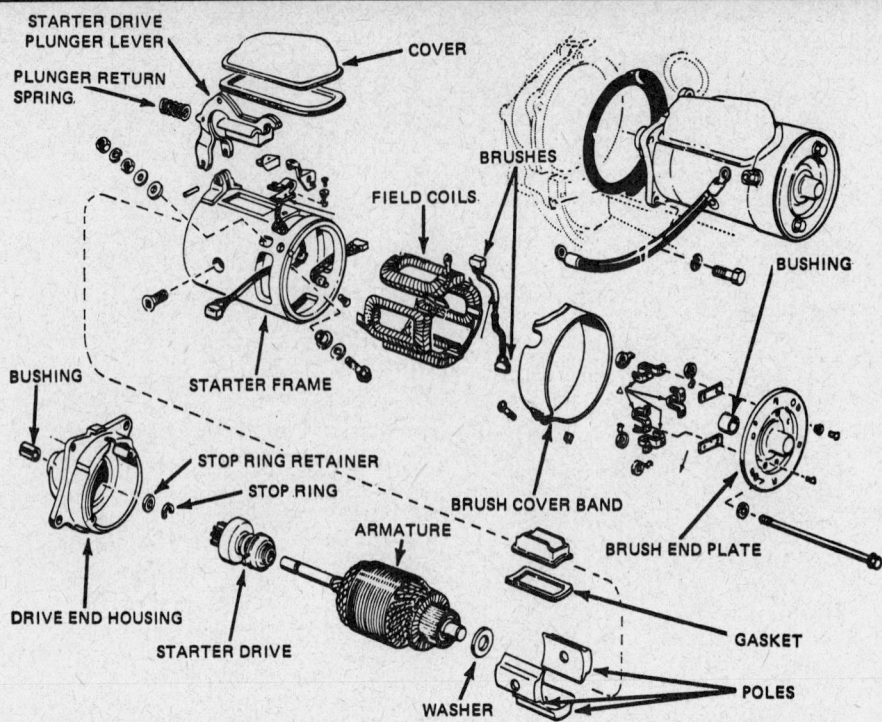

Fig. 54 Ford Motorcraft positive engagement starting motor. 1977 except V6-2800cc engine

by the field coil pulls the moveable pole, which is part of the lever, downward to its seat. When the pole is pulled down, the lever moves the drive assembly into the engine flywheel, Fig. 58.

When the moveable pole is seated, it functions as a normal field pole and opens the contact points. With the points open, current flows through the starter field coils, energizing the starter. At the same time, current also flows through a holding coil to hold the movable pole in its seated position.

When the ignition switch is released from the start position, the starter relay opens the circuit to the starting motor. This allows the return spring to force the lever back, disengaging the drive from the flywheel and returning the movable pole to its normal position.

1977 Units

Disassemble, Figs. 54 & 55

It may not be necessary to disassemble the starter completely to accomplish repair or replacement of certain parts. Thus, before

shims located between the switch and front bracket. Adding shims decreases amount of movement. Shims are available in thicknesses of .010 and .020 inch.

FORD MOTORCRAFT STARTER WITH INTEGRAL POSITIVE ENGAGEMENT DRIVE

This type starting motor, Figs. 54 through 57, is a four pole, series parallel unit with a positive engagement drive built into the starter. The drive mechanism is engaged with the flywheel by lever action before the motor is energized.

When the ignition switch is turned on to the start position, the starter relay is energized and supplies current to the motor. The current flows through one field coil and a set of contact points to ground. The magnetic field given off

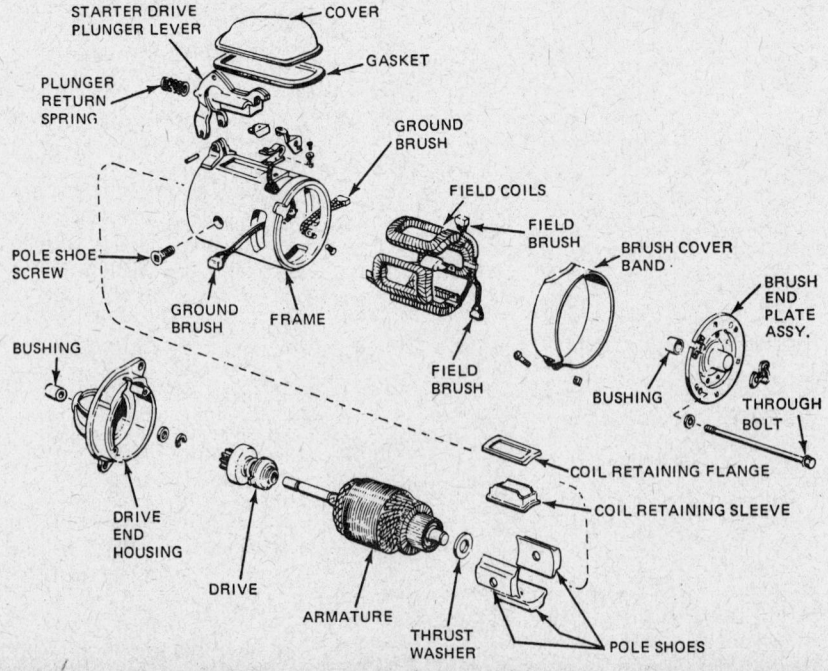

Fig. 55 Ford Motorcraft positive engagement starting motor. 1977 V6-2800cc engine

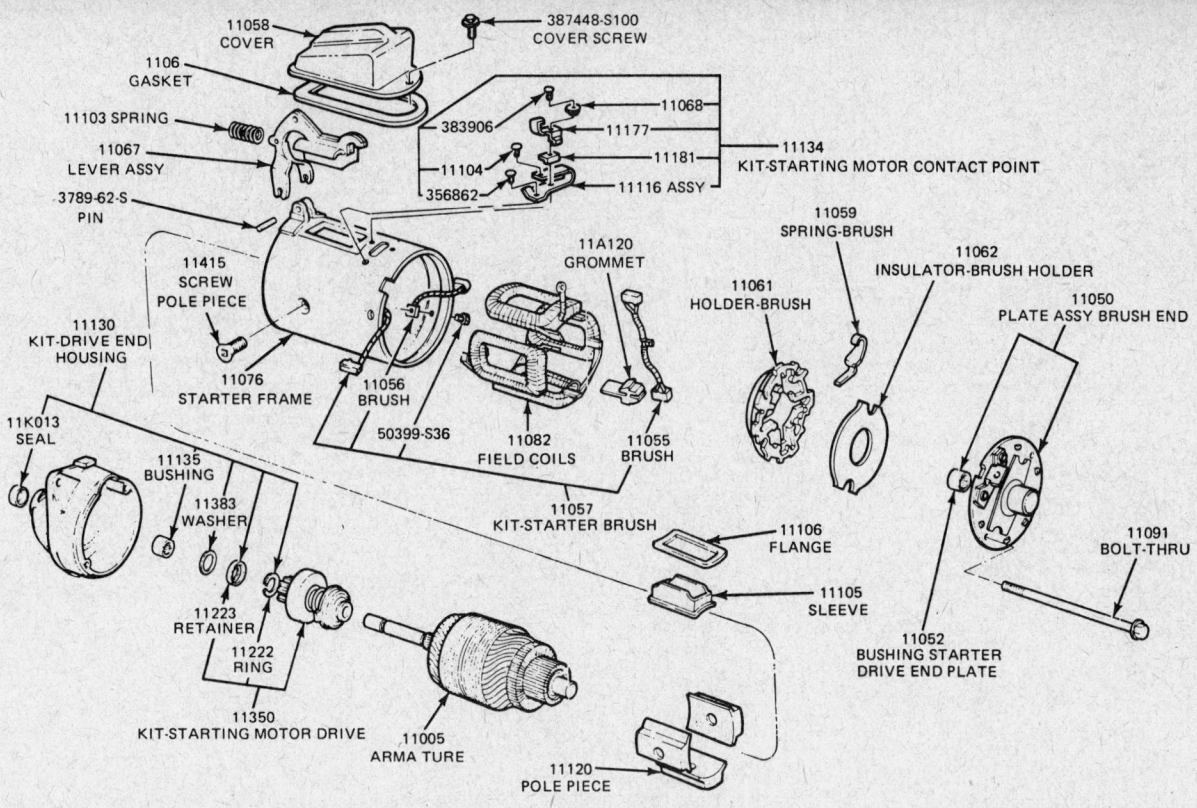

Fig. 56 Ford Motorcraft positive engagement starting motor. 1978–79 V6-2800cc, 1978–83 4-2300cc & 1982–83 1600cc engines (Typical)

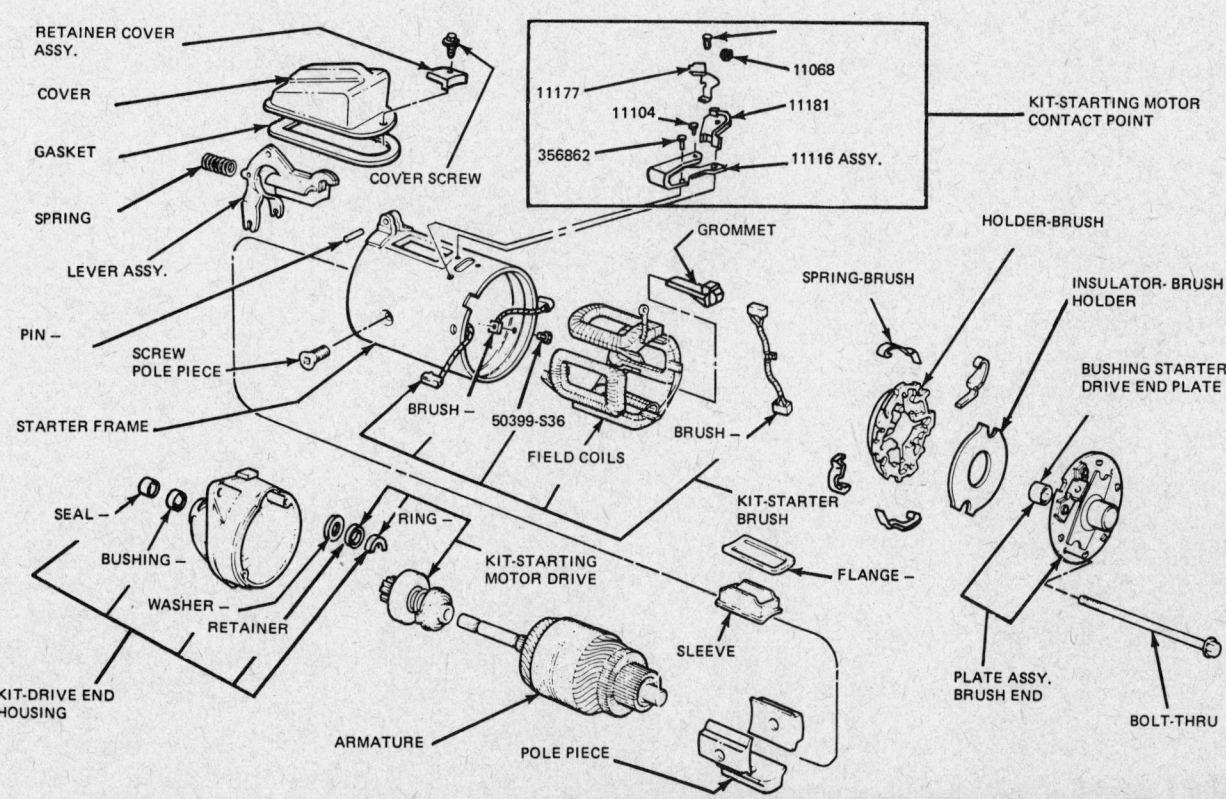

Fig. 57 Ford Motorcraft positive engagement starting motor. 1978–83 except 4-1600cc, 4-2300cc & V6-2800cc engines (Typical)

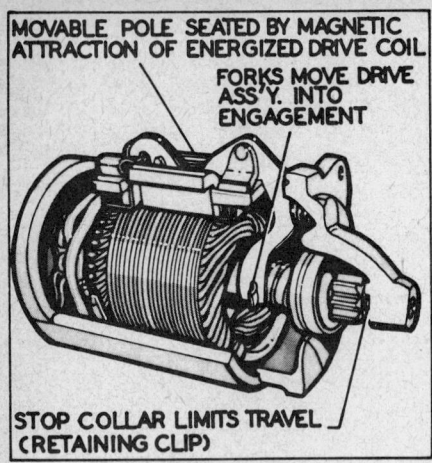

MOVABLE POLE SEATED BY MAGNETIC ATTRACTION OF ENERGIZED DRIVE COIL

FORKS MOVE DRIVE ASS'Y. INTO ENGAGEMENT

STOP COLLAR LIMITS TRAVEL (RETAINING CLIP)

Fig. 58   Starter drive engaged

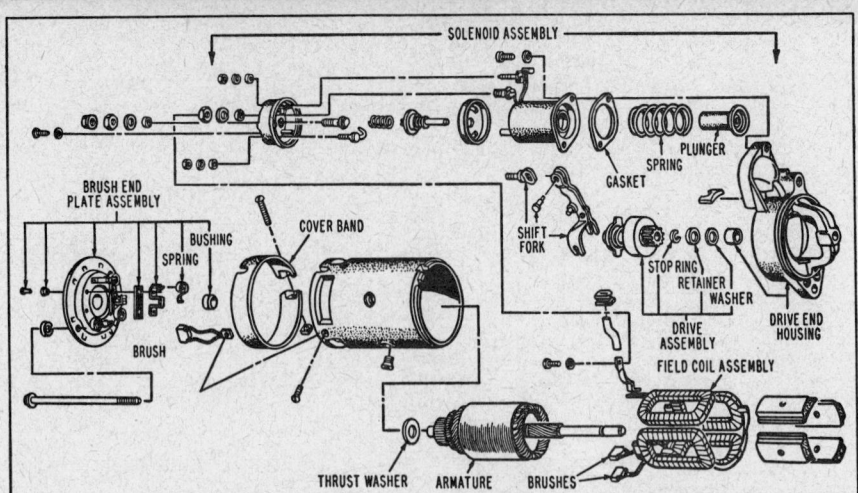

SOLENOID ASSEMBLY

BRUSH END PLATE ASSEMBLY

BUSHING
SPRING

COVER BAND

BRUSH

PLUNGER
SPRING
GASKET

SHIFT FORK

STOP RING
RETAINER
WASHER

DRIVE ASSEMBLY

DRIVE END HOUSING

FIELD COIL ASSEMBLY

THRUST WASHER   ARMATURE   BRUSHES

Fig. 61   Ford Motorcraft solenoid actuated starter, exploded view

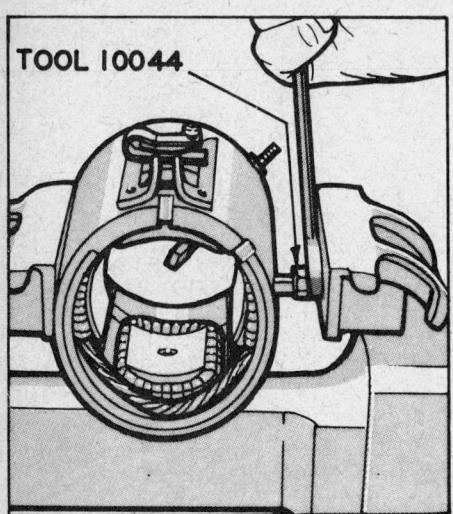

TOOL 10044

Fig. 59   Removing field coil pole shoe screws

disassembling the motor, remove the cover band and starter drive actuating lever cover. Examine brushes to make sure they are free in their holders. Replace brushes if defective or worn beyond their useful limit. Check the tension of each brush spring with a pull scale. Spring tension should not be less than 45 ounces. If disassembly is necessary, proceed as follows:

1. Remove cover band and starter drive actuating lever cover.
2. Remove through bolts, starter drive gear housing, drive gear retaining clip cup and starter drive actuating lever return spring.
3. Remove pivot pin retaining starter gear actuating lever and remove lever and armature.

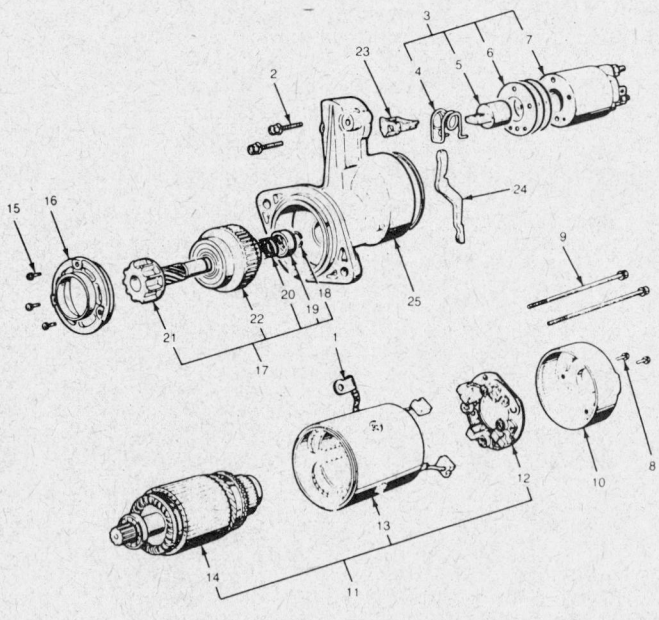

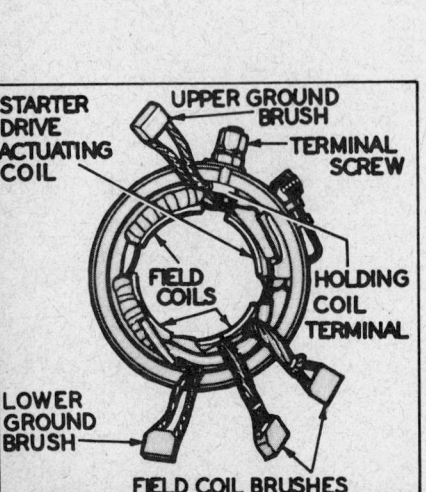

STARTER DRIVE ACTUATING COIL

UPPER GROUND BRUSH

TERMINAL SCREW

FIELD COILS

HOLDING COIL TERMINAL

LOWER GROUND BRUSH

FIELD COIL BRUSHES

Fig. 60   Field coil assembly

DISASSEMBLY ORDER

1 Lead wire	14 Armature
2 Bolt	15 Screw
3 Solenoid assembly	16 Bearing retainer
4 Torsion spring	17 Pinion assembly
5 Plunger	18 Pinion stop retainer
6 Adjusting plates	19 Pinion stop retainer clip
7 Solenoid	20 Return spring
8 Screw	21 Pinion shaft
9 Through bolt	22 Clutch
10 Rear cover	23 Dust cover
11 Motor assembly	24 Shift lever
12 Brush holder	25 Gear case
13 Yoke	

Fig. 62   Hitachi S13-62A starter

4. Remove and discard spring clip retaining starter drive gear to end of armature shaft, and remove starter drive gear.
5. Remove commutator brushes from brush holders and remove brush end plate.
6. Remove two screws retaining ground brushes to frame.
7. On the field coil that operates the drive gear actuating lever, bend tab up on field retainer and remove retainer.
8. Remove field coil retainer screws, Fig. 59. Unsolder field coil leads from terminal screw, and remove pole shoes and coils from frame.
9. Remove starter terminal nut and related parts. Remove any excess solder from terminal slot.

Assemble, Figs. 54 & 55
1. Install starter terminal, insulator, washers and retaining nut in frame, Fig. 60. Be sure to position slot in screw perpendicular to frame end surface.
2. Install field coils and pole pieces. As pole shoe screws are tightened, strike frame several sharp blows with a soft-faced hammer to seat and align pole shoes, then stake the screws.
3. Install solenoid coil retainer and bend tabs to retain tabs to frame.
4. Solder field coils and solenoid wire to starter terminal, using rosin core solder.
5. Check for continuity and grounds in the assembled coils.
6. Position solenoid coil ground terminal over ground screw hole nearest starter terminal.
7. Position ground brushes to starter frame and install retaining screws, Fig. 60.
8. Position starter brush end plate to frame with end plate boss in frame slot.
9. Install drive gear to armature shaft and install a new retaining spring clip.
10. Position fiber thrust washer on commutator end of armature shaft and install armature in frame.
11. Install starter drive actuating lever to frame and starter drive, and install pivot pin.
12. Position actuating lever return spring and drive gear housing to frame and install through bolts. Do not pinch brush leads between brush plate and frame.
13. Install brushes in holders, being sure to center brush springs on brushes.
14. Position drive gear actuating lever cover on starter and install brush cover band.

1978-83 Units

Disassemble, Figs. 56 & 57
1. Remove cover screw, cover, through bolts, starter drive end housing and starter drive plunger lever return spring.
2. Remove plunger lever retaining pin, then remove lever and armature.
3. Remove stop ring retainer from armature shaft, then remove stop ring and starter drive gear assembly.
4. Remove brush end plate and insulator assembly.
5. Remove brushes from brush holder, then remove brush holder. Note position of brush holder to end terminal.
6. Remove two screws retaining ground brushes to frame.
7. Bend up edges of sleeve inserted in frame, then remove sleeve and retainer.
8. Detach field coil ground wire from copper tab on frame.

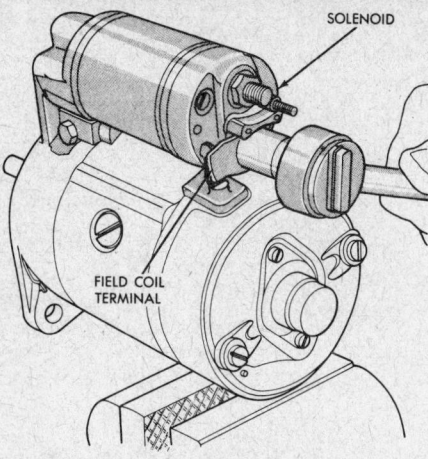

Fig. 63 Disconnecting coil wire from solenoid (typical). Bosch units

9. Using tool No. 10044-A, remove three coil retaining screws, Fig. 59. Cut field coil connection at switch post lead and pole shoes and coils from frame.
10. Cut positive brush leads from field coils, as close to field connection as possible.

Assemble, Figs. 56 & 57
1. Position pole pieces and coils in frame, then install retaining screws using tool No. 10044-A, Fig. 59. As pole shoes are tightened, strike frame several times with a soft faced mallet to seat and align pole shoes, then stake screws.
2. Install plunger coil sleeve and retainer, then bend tabs to retain coils to frame.
3. Position grommet on end terminal, then insert terminal and grommet into notch on frame.
4. Solder field coil to starter terminal post strap.

NOTE: Use 300 watt soldering iron and rosin core solder.

5. Check coils for continuity and grounds.
6. Position brushes to starter frame and install retaining screws.
7. Apply a thin coat of Lubriplate 777 or equivalent to armature shaft splines.
8. Install drive gear assembly on armature shaft, then install stop ring and stop ring retainer.
9. Install armature into starter frame.
10. Position starter drive gear plunger to frame and starter drive assembly, then install pivot assembly. Fill end housing bearing bore approximately 1/4 full with grease, then position drive end housing to frame.
11. Install brush holder, then insert brushes into holder and install brush springs.

NOTE: Ensure positive brush leads are properly positioned in slots on brush holder.

12. Install brush end plate. Ensure brush end plate insulator is properly positioned.
13. Install through bolts, then install starter drive plunger lever cover and tighten retaining screw.

FORD MOTORCRAFT SOLENOID ACTUATED STARTER

Description

The solenoid assembly, in this unit, is mounted to a flange on the starter drive housing which encloses the entire shift lever and solenoid plunger mechanism. The solenoid incorporates a pull-in winding and a hold-in winding.

Operation

As the solenoid is energized, it shifts the starting motor pinion into mesh with the engine flywheel ring gear.
At the same time, the solenoid contacts are closed and battery current flows to the motor, turning it and the engine.
After the engine starts, the starter drive is disengaged when the ignition switch is returned from the start position to the run position and the solenoid spring pushes the shift lever back, disengaging the starter drive from the flywheel ring gear.
The starting motor is protected by an over-running clutch built into the starter drive.

Disassembly, Fig. 61

1. Disconnect the copper strap from the starter terminal of the solenoid, remove the retaining screws and remove solenoid.
2. Loosen retaining screw and slide brush cover band back on frame.
3. Remove commutator brushes from holders. Hold each spring away from the brush with a hook while sliding brush from holder.
4. Remove through bolts and separate end plates and frame.
3. Remove commutator brushes from holders. Hold each spring away from the brush with a hook while sliding brush from holder.
4. Remove through bolts and separate end plates and frame.
5. Remove solenoid plunger and shift fork assembly.
6. Remove armature and drive assembly from frame. Remove drive stop ring and slide drive assembly from shaft. Remove fiber thrust washer from commutator end of shaft.
7. Remove drive stop ring retainer from shaft.

Reassembly, Fig. 61

1. Install drive assembly on shaft and install new stop ring.
2. Install solenoid plunger and shift fork.
3. Place new retainer in drive housing and install armature and drive in housing. Be sure shift lever tangs properly engage drive assembly.
4. Install fiber washer on commutator end of shaft and position frame to drive housing, being sure to index frame and drive housing correctly.
5. Install brush plate assembly being sure to index it properly, install through bolts and tighten to 55-75 inch lbs.
6. Install brushes by pulling each spring away from holder with a hook to allow entry of the brush. Center the brush springs on the brushes. Press insulated brush leads away from all other components to prevent possible shorts.
7. Install rubber gasket and solenoid.

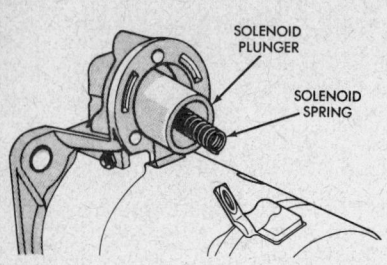

Fig. 64 Solenoid plunger removal. Bosch units for A-404 auto. transaxle or 1983 A-460 man. transaxle

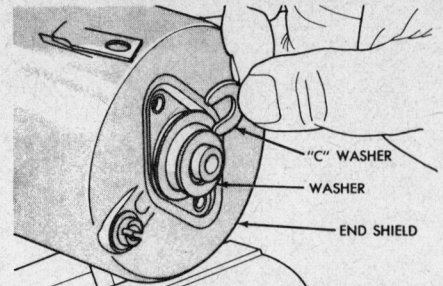

Fig. 65 "C" washer & bearing washer removal. Bosch units

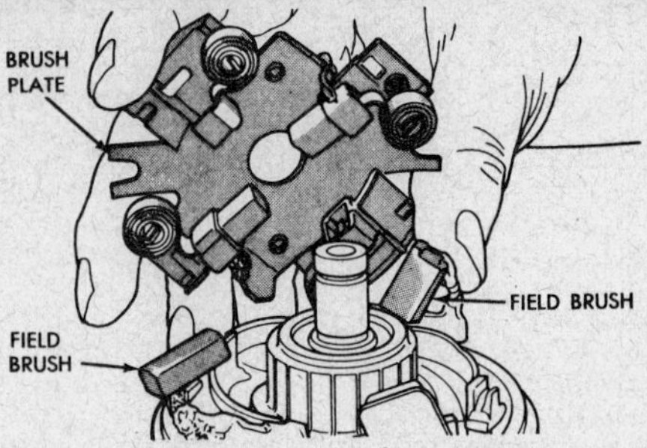

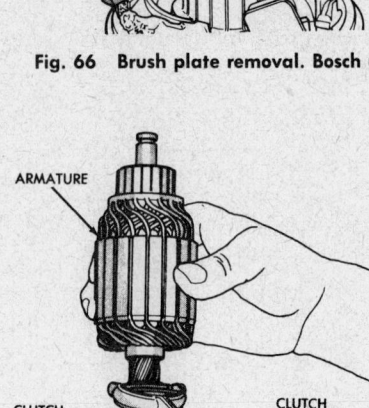

Fig. 66 Brush plate removal. Bosch units

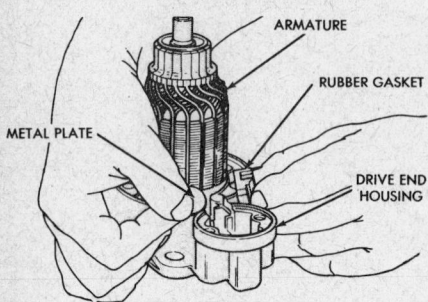

Fig. 67 Metal plate & rubber gasket removal. Bosch units

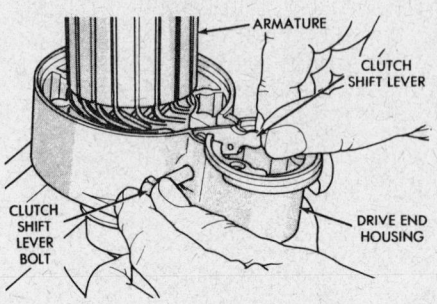

Fig. 68 Shift lever bolt removal. Bosch units

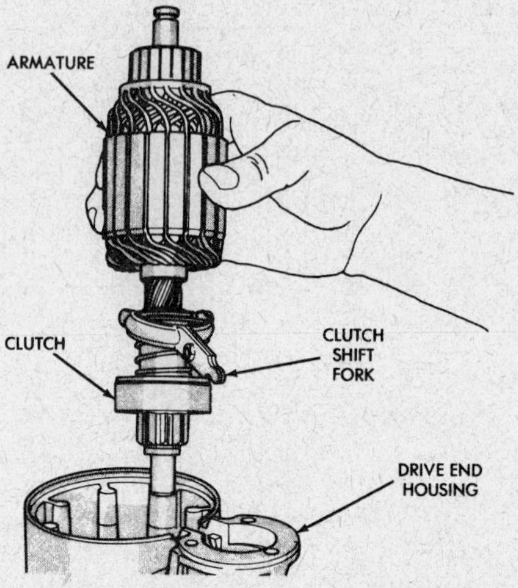

8. Connect copper strap to starter terminal of solenoid.
9. Position cover band and tighten retaining screw.
10. Connect starter to battery and check operation.

HITACHI S13-62A STARTER

Disassembly

1. Disconnect solenoid lead wire.
2. Remove solenoid to starter attaching bolts and remove the solenoid from the shift lever, Fig. 62.

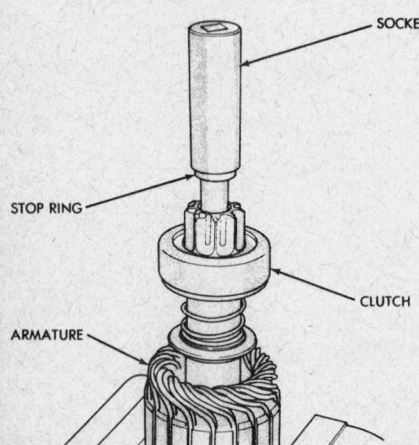

Fig. 70 Pressing stop collar from snap ring. Bosch units except models w/A-412 man. transaxle

3. Remove the solenoid torsion spring.
4. Remove starter through bolts and separate the rear cover.
5. Using long-nose pliers, remove brushes and brush holder from the armature.
6. Remove the frame and armature together as an assembly from the gear case.
7. Remove two screws from gear drive housing and separate drive housing and solenoid.
8. Remove two pinions from gear case, then remove the overrunning clutch and retainer.
9. Remove the solenoid return spring.
10. Remove the steel ball from the overrunning clutch.

Assemble

1. Reverse disassembly procedure to assemble, noting the following:
   a. Be sure to install the steel ball and solenoid return spring.
   b. Use caution not to get oil or other contaminants on brushes or armature.
   c. Always replace O-rings with new ones.
   d. Lubricate all necessary parts prior to assembly.

BOSCH & NIPPONDENSO STARTER MOTORS

Chrysler Corp. Front Wheel Drive Models

Description
Bosch units are painted black, while Nippondenso units have an aluminum covered drive side with a yellowish color elsewhere. The starter drive is of the overrunning clutch

type with a solenoid switch mounted on the starting motor.

Bosch Starter

1.7 L Engine W/A-404 Auto. Transaxle or A-412 or 1983 A-460 Man. Transaxle
1. Disconnect field coil wire from solenoid terminal, Fig. 63.
2. Remove solenoid mounting screws and the solenoid. On automatic transaxle, or 1983 A-460 manual transaxle units, remove solenoid plunger from shift fork, Fig. 64.
3. Remove end shield bearing cap, then the "C" washer and bearing washer, Fig. 65.
4. Remove through bolts and the end

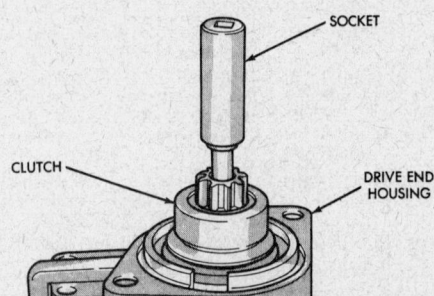

Fig. 69 Armature assembly & shift fork. Bosch units for A-404 auto. transaxle or 1983 A-460 man. transaxle

Fig. 71 Pressing stop collar from snap ring. Bosch units for A-412 man. transaxle

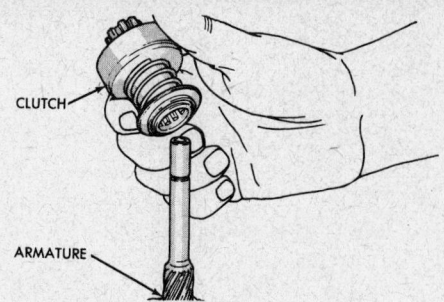

Fig. 72 Clutch removal (Typical). Bosch units

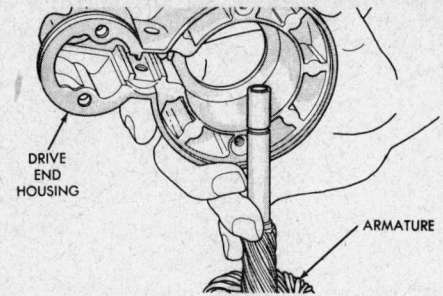

Fig. 73 Drive end housing removal. Bosch units for A-412 man. transaxle

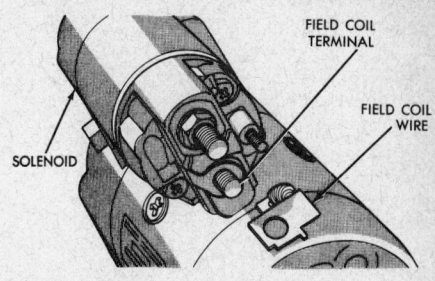

Fig. 74 Field coil terminal identification. Nippondenso units except 2.6 L engine

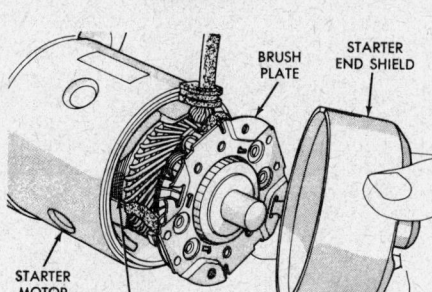

Fig. 75 Starter end plate removal. Nippondenso units for 1.6 L engine W/A-460 man. transaxle

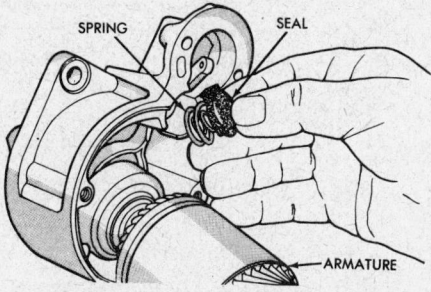

Fig. 76 Rubber seal & spring removal. Nippondenso units for 1.6 L engine W/A-460 man. transaxle

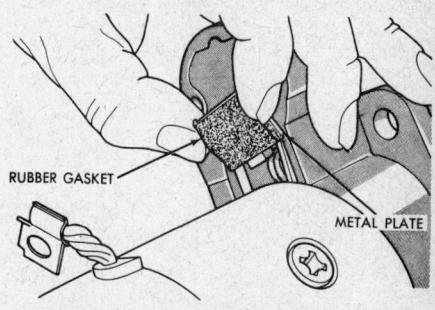

Fig. 77 Rubber gasket & metal plate removal. Nippondenso units for A-404 auto. transaxle & A-412 & 1983 A-460 man. transaxle

shield.
5. Remove both field brushes and the brush plate, Fig. 66.
6. Remove field frame from starter.
7. Remove rubber gasket and metal plate, Fig. 67.
8. Remove clutch lever pivot bolt, Fig. 68.
9. On automatic transaxle, or 1983 A-460 manual transaxle units, remove armature assembly and shift lever from drive end housing, Fig. 69.
10. On all models, press stop collar off snap ring, Figs. 70 and 71, and remove snap ring.
11. Remove stop collar and clutch, Fig. 72.
12. On A-412 manual transaxle units, remove drive end housing from armature, Fig. 73.
13. Reverse procedure to assemble.

1981–82 1.7 L Engine W/A-460 Man. Transaxle; 1981–83 2.2 L Engine W/A-413 Auto. Transaxle or A-460 or A-465 Man. Transaxle
1. Remove nut from solenoid field coil terminal, then remove field coil strap from ter-

minal, Fig. 63.
2. Remove three solenoid attaching screws, then work solenoid from shift fork and remove solenoid.
3. Remove two starter motor end shield bearing cap attaching screws and remove end shield cap, C-washer and bearing washer, Fig. 65.
4. Remove starter motor through bolts, then remove starter motor brush end shield.
5. Remove two starter motor brushes by prying the brush retaining springs back, then remove brush plate, Fig. 66.
6. Slide field frame from armature, then remove armature and clutch assembly from drive end housing.
7. Remove rubber seal and clutch lever bolt from drive end frame, then remove clutch lever.
8. Position armature in a suitable vise, then using a socket, press collar from pinion gear stop snap ring, Fig. 70. Remove snap ring from armature shaft using snap ring pliers.
9. Remove stop collar and clutch assembly from armature shaft, Fig. 72.
10. Reverse procedure to assemble.

Nippondenso Starter

1.6 L Engine W/A-460 Man. Transaxle
1. Remove nut from solenoid field coil terminal, then disconnect field coil wire from solenoid terminal, Fig. 74.
2. Remove solenoid attaching screws, then remove solenoid.
3. Remove starter motor through bolts, then remove front support bracket.
4. Remove brush plate attaching screws, then remove end plate, Fig. 75.
5. Pry brush plate springs back, then remove the two brushes from their holders.
6. Remove brush plate, then slide field frame off armature.
7. Remove rubber seal and spring from drive end housing, Fig. 76.
8. Remove armature and clutch assembly from drive end housing.
9. Remove shift lever assembly from drive end housing. Remove bushings from shift lever.
10. Using a suitable socket, press stop collar off snap ring, Fig. 82, then remove snap

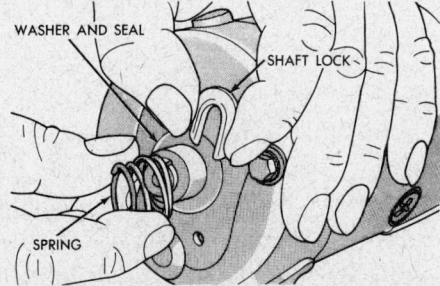

Fig. 78 Armature shaft lock, washer & spring removal. Nippondenso units for A-404 auto. transaxle & A-412 & 1983 A-460 man. transaxle

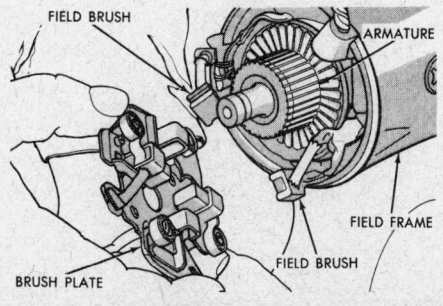

Fig. 79 Brush plate removal. Nippondenso units except 2.6 L engine

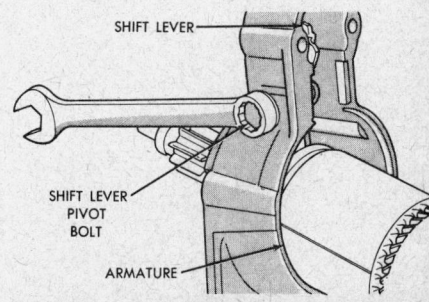

Fig. 80 Shift lever pivot removal. Nippondenso units for A-404 auto. transaxle & A-412 & 1983 A-460 man. transaxle

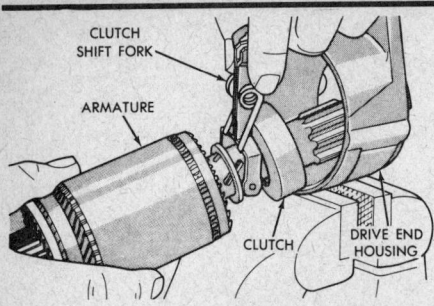

Fig. 81 Armature assembly removal. Nippondenso units for A-404 auto. transaxle & A-412 man. transaxle

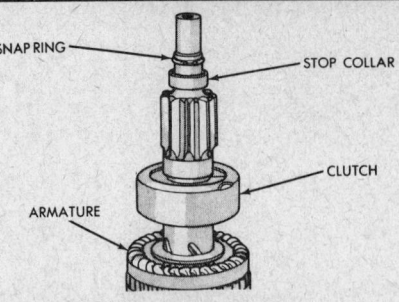

Fig. 82 Stop collar, snap ring & clutch assembly. Nippondenso units except 2.6 L engine

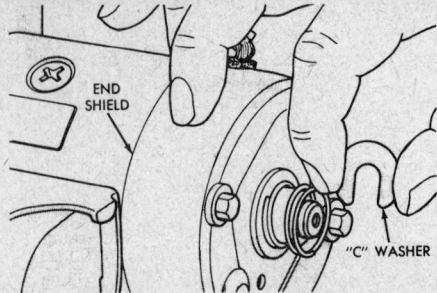

Fig. 83 C-washer removal. Nippondenso units for A-413 auto. transaxle & A-460 or A-465 man. transaxle. Exc. 1983 1.7 L W/A-460

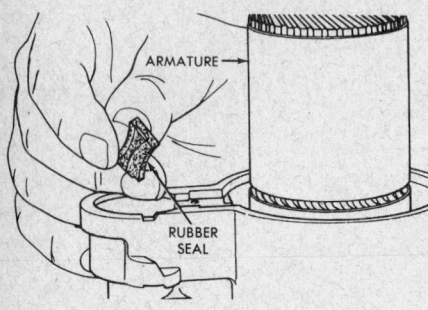

Fig. 84 Rubber seal removal. Nippondenso units for A-413 auto. transaxle & A-460 or A-465 man. transaxle. Exc. 1983 1.6 L & 1.7 L W/A-460

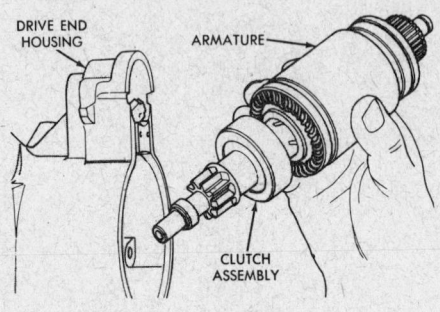

Fig. 85 Armature & clutch assembly removal. Nippondenso units for A-413 auto. transaxle & A-460 or A-465 man. transaxle. Exc. 1983 1.6 L & 1.7 L W/A-460

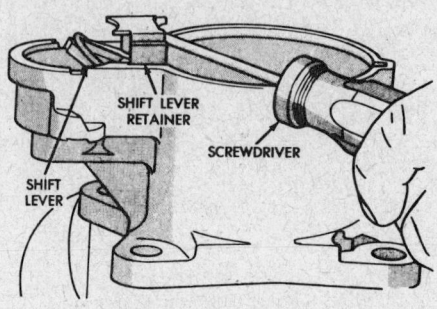

Fig. 86 Clutch shift lever retainer. Nippondenso units for A-413 auto. transaxle & A-460 or A-465 man. transaxle. Exc. 1983 1.6 L & 1.7 L W/A-460

ring and stop collar.
11. Remove clutch assembly from armature shaft.
12. Reverse procedure to assemble.

1.7 L Engine W/A-404 Auto. Transaxle or A-412 or 1983 A-460 Man. Transaxle
1. Disconnect field coil wire from solenoid terminal, Fig. 74.
2. Remove solenoid mounting screws and the solenoid.
3. Remove rubber gasket and metal plate, Fig. 77.
4. Remove bearing cover mounting screws and the bearing cover.
5. Remove armature shaft lock, washer, spring and seal, Fig. 78.
6. Remove through bolts and the commutator end frame cover.
7. Remove field brushes and the brush plate, Fig. 79.

8. Remove field frame from starter.
9. Remove shift lever pivot bolt, Fig. 80.
10. Remove armature assembly and shift lever from drive end housing, Fig. 81.
11. Press stop collar off snap ring, Fig. 82.
12. Remove snap ring, stop collar and clutch, Fig. 82.
13. Reverse procedure to assemble.

1981–82 1.7 L Engine W/A-460 Man. Transaxle; 1981–83 2.2 L Engine W/A-413 Auto. Transaxle or A-460 or A-465 Man. Transaxle
1. Remove nut from solenoid field coil terminal, then remove field coil strap, Fig. 74.
2. Remove two nuts attaching solenoid to starter housing, then work solenoid from shift fork and remove solenoid.
3. Remove two attaching screws end shield

bearing cap, then remove end shield cap, C-washer, bearing spring and bearing washer, Fig. 83.
4. Remove two starter motor through bolts, then remove starter motor brush end shield.
5. Pry back on brush spring and remove field brushes, then remove brush plate, Fig. 79.
6. Remove field frame from armature, then remove rubber seal from drive end housing, Fig. 84.
7. Remove armature and clutch assembly from drive end frame, Fig. 85.
8. Remove clutch lever retainer from drive end frame, then remove clutch lever, Fig. 86.
9. Press stop collar from snap ring, then remove snap ring, stop collar and clutch, Fig. 82.
10. Reverse procedure to assemble.

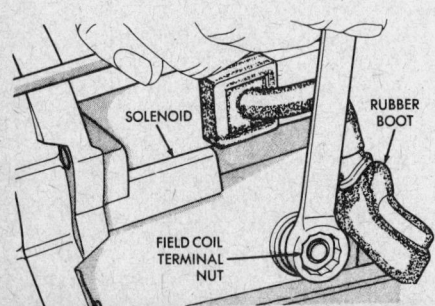

Fig. 87 Field coil terminal nut removal. Nippondenso units for 2.6 L engine

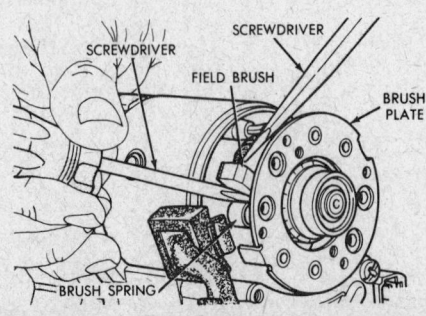

Fig. 88 Field brush removal. Nippondenso units for 2.6 L engine

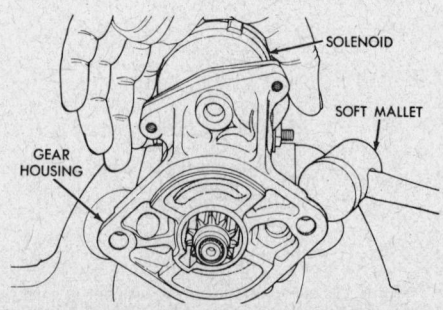

Fig. 89 Separating solenoid from gear and housing. Nippondenso units for 2.6 L engine

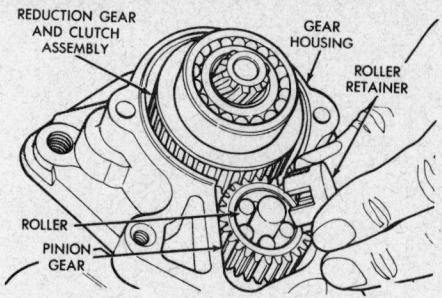

Fig. 90 Pinion roller retainer removal. Nippondenso units for 2.6 L engine

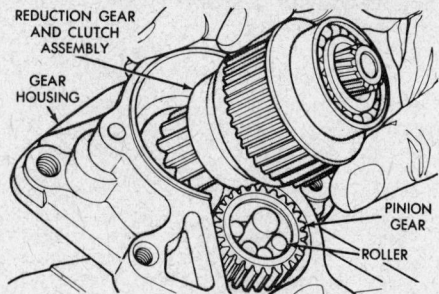

Fig. 91 Reduction gear & clutch assembly removal. Nippondenso units for 2.6 L engine

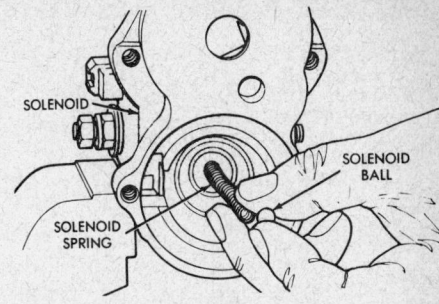

Fig. 92 Solenoid ball & spring removal. Nippondenso units for 2.6 L engine

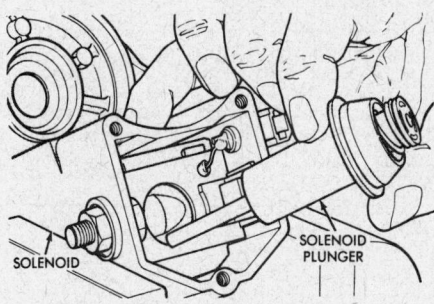

Fig. 93 Solenoid plunger removal. Nippondenso units for 2.6 L engine

2.6 L Engine

1. Pull rubber boot from field coil terminal, then remove nut from field coil terminal stud, Fig. 87.
2. Remove field coil lead from field coil terminal stud.
3. Remove two starter motor through bolts, then remove two screws from starter motor end shield.
4. Remove upper left solenoid attaching screw retaining field coil lead retainer, then remove field coil lead retainer.
5. Remove starter motor brush end shield.
6. Pry back on brush retaining springs and remove brushes, then remove brush plate, Fig. 88.
7. Slide armature from field frame, then remove field frame from gear end frame.
8. Remove two gear end frame to solenoid attaching screws, then using a soft faced mallet separate solenoid from end frame, Fig. 89.
9. Remove reduction gear pinion roller retainer from gear end frame, Fig. 90.
10. Remove reduction gear and clutch assembly from gear end frame, Fig. 91.
11. Remove pinion gear from gear end frame, then remove pinion gear rollers.
12. Remove solenoid ball and spring, Fig. 92, then remove two remaining solenoid cover screws from solenoid and remove solenoid cover.
13. Remove solenoid plunger from solenoid housing, Fig. 93.
14. Reverse procedure to assemble.

STARTER DRIVE TROUBLES

Starter drive troubles are easy to diagnose and they usually cannot be confused with ordinary starter difficulties. If the starter does not turn over at all or if it drags, look for trouble in the starter or electrical supply sys-

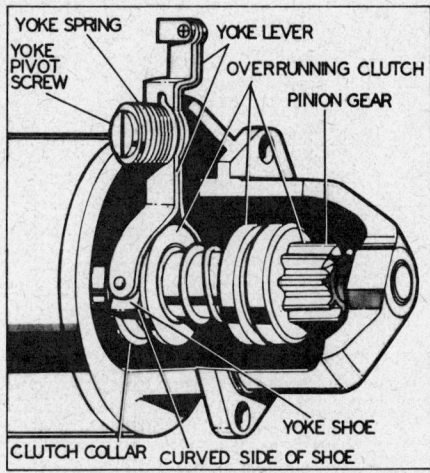

Fig. 94 Overrunning clutch drive. When assembling, make sure curved sides of yoke shoes are toward gear end of clutch. Reversed yoke shoes can cause improper meshing of pinion

tem. Concentrate on the starter drive or ring gear if the starter is noisy, if it turns but does not engage the engine, or if the starter won't disengage after the engine is started. After the starter is removed, the trouble can usually be located quickly.

Worn or chipped ring gear or starter pinion are the usual causes of noisy operation. Before replacing either or both of these parts try to find out what caused the damage. With the Bendix type drive, incomplete engagement of the pinion with the ring gear is a common cause of tooth damage. The wrong pinion clearance on starter drives of the over-running clutch type leads to poor meshing of the pinion and ring gear and too rapid tooth wear.

A less common cause of noise with either type of drive is a bent starter armature shaft. When this shaft is bent, the pinion gear alternately binds and partly meshes with the ring gear. Most manufacturers specify a maximum of .003″ radial run-out on the armature shaft.

When Clutch Drive Fails

The over-running clutch type drive seldom becomes so worn that it fails to engage since it is directly activated by a fork and lever, Fig. 94. The only thing that is likely to happen is that, once engaged, it will not turn the engine because the clutch itself is worn out. A much more frequent difficulty and one that rapidly wears ring gear and teeth is partial engage-

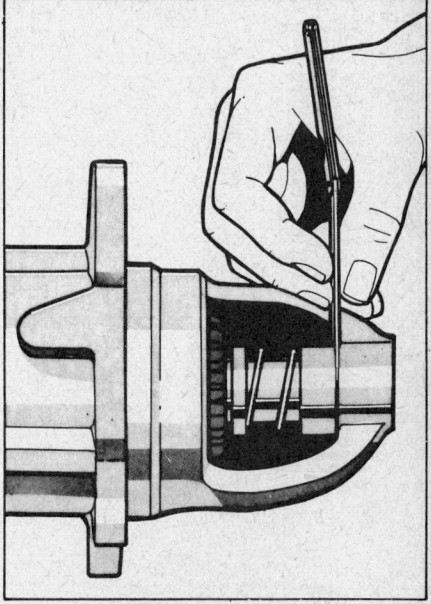

Fig. 95 Measuring overrunning clutch drive stop clearance. Do not compress anti-drift spring as this will give an incorrect clearance. If clearance is not present there is danger of the drive housing being broken as gear or collar slams back against it

ment. Proper meshing of the pinion is controlled by the end clearance between the pinion gear and the starter housing or pinion stop, if used.

The clearance is set with the starter off the car and with the drive in the engaged position. To check the clearance, supply current to the starter solenoid with the electrical connection between starter and solenoid removed. Supplying current to the solenoid but not the starter will prevent the starter from rotating during the test. Take out all slack by pushing lightly on the starter drive clutch housing while inserting a feeler gauge between pinion and housing or pinion stop, Fig. 95.

On late model cars, the solenoids are completely enclosed in the starter housing and the pinion clearance is not adjustable. If the clearance is not correct, the starter must be disassembled and checked for excessive wear of solenoid linkage, shift lever mechanism, or improper assembly of parts.

Failure of the over-running clutch drive to disengage is usually caused by binding between the armature shaft and the drive. If the drive, particularly the clutch, shows signs of overheating it indicates that it is not disen-

STARTING MOTORS & SWITCHES

gaging immediately after the engine starts. If the clutch is forced to over-run too long, it overheats and turns a bluish color. For the cause of the binding, look for rust or gum between the armature shaft and the drive, or for burred splines. Excess oil on the drive will lead to gumming, and inadequate air circulation in the flywheel housing will cause rust.

Over-running clutch drives cannot be overhauled in the field so they must be replaced. In cleaning, never soak them in a solvent because the solvent may enter the clutch and dissolve the sealed-in lubricant. Wipe them off lightly with kerosene and lubricate them

sparingly with SAE 10 or 10W oil.

When Bendix Drive Fails

When a Bendix type drive doesn't engage the cause usually is one of three things: either the drive spring is broken, one of the drive spring bolts has sheared off, or the screwshaft threads won't allow the pinion to travel toward the flywheel. In the first two cases, remove the drive by unscrewing the set screw under the last soil of the drive spring and replace the broken parts. Gummed or rusty

screwshaft threads are fairly common causes of Bendix drive failure and are easily cleaned with a little kerosene or steel wool, depending on the trouble. Here again, as in the case of over-running clutch drives, use light oil sparingly, and be sure the flywheel housing has adequate ventilation. There is usually a breather hole in the bottom of the flywheel housing which should be open.

The failure of a Bendix drive to disengage or to mesh properly is most often caused by gummed or rusty screwshaft threads. When this is not true, look for mechanical failure within the drive itself.

STARTING MOTOR SPECIFICATIONS

Starter Make	Starter Model Number	Brush Spring Tension, Ounces	Free Speed Test			Solenoid	
			Amps	Volts	RPM	Hold-In Windings	Pull-In Windings
Bosch	5206255	—	47	11	6600	—	—
	5206260	—	47	11	6600	—	—
	5213045	—	47	11	6600	—	—
	5213080	—	47	11	6600	—	—
	5213395	—	47	11	6600	—	—
Chrysler	3755250	32–36	90	11	5700	13–15	8–9
	3755900	32–36	90	11	3700	13–15	8–9
	4111855	32–36	90	11	5700	13–15	8–9
	4111860	32–36	91	11	5700	13–15	8–11
Delco-Remy	1100214	—	—	—	—	—	—
	1100215	—	—	—	—	—	—
	1100534	35①	45–70	10	7000–11900	—	—
	1100941	—	—	—	—	—	—
	1102844	35①	60–85②	9	6800–10300	—	—
	1103519	—	—	—	—	—	—
	1108415	35①	35–75②	9	6000–9000	—	—
	1108758	35①	55–80②	9	3500–6000	14.5–16.5	13–15.5
	1108759	35①	65–95②	9	7500–10500	—	—
	1108762	35①	55–80②	9	3500–6000	14.5–16.5	13–15.5
	1108764	35①	65–95②	9	7500–10000	—	—
	1108765	35①	55–80②	9	3500–6000	14.5–16.5	13–15.5
	1108771	35①	50–75②	9	6500–10000	—	—
	1108772	35①	50–75②	9	6500–10000	—	—
	1108774③	35①	50–80②	9	5500–10500	—	—
	1108774④	35①	60–88②	9	6500–10100	—	—
	1108779	35①	50–80②	9	5500–10000	—	—
	1108790	35①	55–80②	9	3500–6000	—	—
	1108794	35①	65–95②	9	7500–10000	14.5–16.5	13–15.5
	1108795	35①	65–95②	9	7500–10000	—	—
	1108796	35①	65–95②	9	7500–10000	—	—
	1108797	35①	55–80②	9	5500–10000	14.5–16.5	13–15.5
	1108799	35①	50–80②	9	5500–10500	14.5–16.5	13–15.5
	1109038	35①	65–95②	9	7000–10500	—	—
	1109039	35①	65–95②	9	7000–10500	—	—
	1109052	35①	65–95②	9	7500–10500	14.5–16.5	13–16.5
	1109056	35①	50–80②	9	5500–10500	14.5–16.5	13–15.5
	1109059	35①	65–95②	9	7500–10500	—	—
	1109061	35①	65–85②	9	6800–10300	17–19	24–27
	1109062	35①	65–95②	9	7500–10500	17–19	24–27
	1109063	—	—	—	—	—	—
	1109064	35①	60–85②	9	6800–10300	17–19	24–27
	1109065	35①	65–95②	9	7500–10500	17–19	24–27

Continued

STARTING MOTOR SPECIFICATIONS—Continued

Starter Make	Starter Model Number	Brush Spring Tension, Ounces	Free Speed Test			Solenoid	
			Amps	Volts	RPM	Hold-In Windings	Pull-In Windings
	1109067	35①	65–95②	9	7500–10500	—	—
	1109070	35①	65–95②	9	7500–10500	—	—
	1109072	35①	65–95②	9	7500–10500	17–19	24–27
	1109074	35①	60–85②	9	6800–10300	15–20	20–30
	1109213	35①	40–140②	9	8000–13000	—	—
	1109214	35①	40–140②	9	8000–13000	—	—
	1109215	35①	40–140②	9	8000–13000	—	—
	1109216	35①	120–210②	10.6	9000–13400	15–20	20–30
	1109218	35①	120–210②	10.6	9000–13400	—	—
	1109412	35①	50–75②	9	6500–10500	—	—
	1109414	35①	50–75②	9	6500	—	—
	1109495	35①	120–210	11	9000–13400	—	—
	1109521	35①	45–75②	9	6500–9700	—	—
	1109522	—	—	—	—	—	—
	1109523	35①	45–70②	9	7000–11900	17–23	16–18
	1109524	35①	45–70②	9	7000–11900	17–23	16–18
	1109526	35①	45–70②	9	7000–11900	15–20	20–30
	1109530	35①	85⑥	9	6800–10300	15–20	20–30
	1109531	—	—	—	—	—	—
	1109532	—	—	—	—	—	—
	1109533	35①	45–70②	9	7000–11900	13–19	23–30
	1109534	35①	45–70	9	7000–11900	—	—
	1109535	35①	45–70②	9	7000–11900	13–19	26–38
	1109537	35①	45–75②	9	6500–9700	13–19	46–60
	1109544	35①	45–70	9	7000–11900	—	—
	1109551	35①	55–85②	10	6000–12000	13–19	23–30
	1109556	35①	55–85	10	6000–12000	—	—
	1109560	35①	50–75	10	6000–11900	—	—
	1109562	35①	45–70②	9	7000–11900	13–19	23–30
	1109564	35①	50–74	10	6000–11900	—	—
	1998204	35①	60–85②	9	6800–10300	17–19	24–27
	1998205	35①	65–95②	9	7500–10500	17–19	24–27
	1998217	—	—	—	—	—	—
	1998227	35①	65–95②	9	7500–10500	—	—
	1998233	—	—	—	—	—	—
	1998234	35①	65–95②	9	7500–10500	—	—
	1998236	35①	60–85②	9	6800–10300	—	—
	1998237	35①	65–95②	9	7500–10500	—	—
	1998240	35①	60–85②	9	6800–10300	—	—
	1998241	35①	70–110	9	6500–10700	—	—
	1998552	35①	160–220	9	4000–5500	—	—
	1998553	35①	160–220	9	4000–5500	15–20	30–40
	1998554	35①	160–240	10	4400–6300⑤	—	—
	1998556	35①	55–85	9	6000–12000	13–19	23–30
	3236659	—	45–70	9	7000–11900	—	—
Hitachi	94238758	—	—	—	—	—	—
Mitsubishi	22515863	—	125–170	10	3200–4100⑤	—	—
Motorcraft	D5AF-EA	80	80	12	—	—	—
	D6AF-AA	40	70	12	—	—	—
	D6BF-AA	80	80	12	—	—	—
	D6BF-BA	80	80	12	—	—	—
	D6DF-AA	80	80	12	—	—	—
	D6EF-AA	40①	70	12	—	—	—

STARTING MOTORS & SWITCHES

STARTING MOTOR SPECIFICATIONS—Continued

Starter Make	Starter Model Number	Brush Spring Tension, Ounces	Free Speed Test			Solenoid	
			Amps	Volts	RPM	Hold-In Windings	Pull-In Windings
	D6EF-BA	40①	70	12	—	—	—
	D6OF-AA	80	80	12	—	—	—
	D8AF-AA	80	80	12	—	—	—
	D8AF-BA	80	80	12	—	—	—
	D8BF-AA	40	70	12	—	—	—
	D8BF-AA⑦	80	80	12	—	—	—
	D8BF-AA⑧	40–80	85	12	—	—	—
	D8BF-CA⑦	80	80	12	—	—	—
	D8BF-CA⑧	40–80	85	12	—	—	—
	D8DF-AA	80	80	12	—	—	—
	D8EF-AA⑦	40	70	12	—	—	—
	D8EF-AA⑨	40	80	12	—	—	—
	D8EF-AA⑩	80	80	12	—	—	—
	D8OF-AA⑦	80	80	12	—	—	—
	D8OF-AA⑪	40–80	85	12	—	—	—
	D8ZF-AA	40①	70	12	—	—	—
	E1AF-BA	40–80	85	12	—	—	—
	E1BF-AA	40–80	85	12	—	—	—
	E1BF-BA	40–80	85	12	—	—	—
	E1EF-AB	80	80	12	—	—	—
	E1EF-AD	80	80	12	—	—	—
	E1EF-11001-BA	—	67	12	7380–9356	—	—
	E1ZF-AA	80	80	12	—	—	—
	E1ZF-BA	80	80	12	—	—	—
	E2BF-AA	80	80	12	—	—	—
	E25F-AA	40–80	85	12	—	—	—
	⑫	80	80	12	—	—	—
	⑬	40–80	85	12	—	—	—
	3212235	40	65	12	9250	—	—
	3229844	40	65	12	9250	—	—
	3231371	—	77	12	8900–9600	—	—
	3231372	—	67	12	7380–9356	—	—
	3238665	—	67	12	7380–9356	—	—
	3250032	—	69	12	6709–10843	—	—
Nippondenso	5206265	—	47	11	6600	—	—
	5206270	—	47	11	6600	—	—
	5213085	—	47	11	6600	—	—
	5213190	—	85	11	3700	—	—
	5213235	—	47	11	6600	—	—
	5213295	—	47	11	6600	—	—
	5213301	—	47	11	6600	—	—
	5213645	—	47	11	6600	—	—

①—Minimum.
②—Includes solenoid.
③—1977–78.
④—1979.
⑤—Pinion speed.
⑥—Maximum.
⑦—1977–79.
⑧—1980.
⑨—1980 Mustang, Capri, Pinto and Bobcat.
⑩—1980 Exc. Mustang, Capri, Pinto and Bob-cat.
⑪—1980–81.
⑫—1983 four cylinder Ford models.
⑬—1983 six and eight cylinder Ford models.

ALTERNATOR SYSTEMS

CONTENTS

INTRODUCTION

Alternators are composed of the same functional parts as the conventional D.C. generator but they operate differently: The field is called a rotor and is the turning portion of the unit. A generating part, called a stator, is the stationary member, comparable to the armature in a D.C. generator. The regulator, similar to those used in a D.C. system, regulates the output of the alternator-rectifier system.

The power source of the system is the alternator. Current is transmitted from the field terminal of the regulator through a slip ring to the field coil and back to ground through another slip ring. The strength of the field regulates the output of the alternating current. This alternating current is then transmitted from the alternator to the rectifier where it is converted to direct current.

These alternators employ a three-phase stator winding in which the phase windings are electrically 120 degrees apart. The rotor consists of a field coil encased between interleaved sections producing a magnetic field with alternate north and south poles. By rotating the rotor inside the stator the alternating current is induced in the stator windings. This alternating current is rectified (changed to D.C.) by silicon diodes and brought out to the output terminal of the alternator.

Diode Rectifiers

Six silicon diode rectifiers are used and act as electrical one-way-valves. Three of the diodes have ground polarity and are pressed or screwed into a heat sink which is grounded. The other three diodes (ungrounded) are pressed or screwed into and insulated from the end head; these diodes are connected to the alternator output terminal.

Since the diodes have a high resistance to the flow of current in one direction and a low resistance in the opposite direction, they may be connected in a manner which allows current to flow from the alternator to the battery in the low resistance direction. The high resistance in the opposite direction prevents the flow of current from the battery to the alternator. Because of this feature no circuit breaker is required between the alternator and battery.

SERVICE PRECAUTIONS

1. Be certain that battery polarity is correct when servicing units. Reversed battery polarity will damage rectifiers and regulators.

2. If booster battery is used for starting, be sure to use correct polarity in hook up.

3. When a fast charger is used to charge a vehicle battery, the vehicle battery cables should be disconnected *unless the fast charger is equipped with a special Alternator Protector,* in which case the vehicle battery cables need not be disconnected. Also the fast charger should never be used to start a vehicle as damage to rectifiers will result.

4. Lead connections to the grounded rectifiers (negative) on Chrysler units should never be soldered as the excessive heat may damage the rectifiers.

5. Unless the system includes a load relay or field relay, grounding the alternator output terminal will damage the alternator and/or circuits. This is true even when the system is not in operation since no circuit breaker is used and the battery is applied to the alternator output terminal at all times. The field or load relay acts as a circuit breaker in that it is controlled by the ignition switch.

6. When adjusting the voltage regulator, do not short the adjusting tool to the regulator base as the regulator may be damaged. The tool should be insulated by taping or by installing a plastic sleeve.

7. Before making any "on vehicle" tests of the alternator or regulator, the battery should be checked and the circuit inspected for faulty wiring or insulation. loose or corroded connections and poor ground circuits.

8. Check alternator belt tension to be sure the belt is tight enough to prevent slipping under load.

9. The ignition switch should be off and the battery ground cable disconnected before making any test connections to prevent damage to the system.

10. The vehicle battery must be fully charged or a fully charged battery may be installed for test purposes.

Bosch Type K1 Alternator

DESCRIPTION

The main components of the Bosch type K1 alternator, Figs. 1 and 2, are the front and rear housings, stator windings, rotor and rectifying diodes. Current is supplied to the rotor through slip rings and two brushes which, on integral regulator units, are built into the voltage regulator positioned on the rear housing. The rotor is supported in the front and rear housings by ball bearings. The stator windings are assembled inside a laminated core which forms part of the alternator frame. A diode plate containing three positive and three negative diodes is soldered to the stator winding leads. Alternator field current is supplied through a diode trio which is also connected to the stator windings. A capacitor which is mounted to the rear housing, protects the diode plate assembly from high voltages and suppresses radio noises. On all units, the

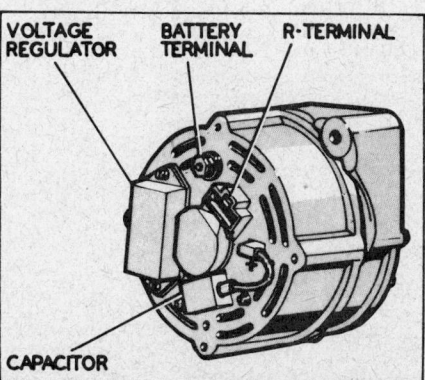

VOLTAGE REGULATOR   BATTERY TERMINAL   R-TERMINAL

CAPACITOR

Fig. 1   Bosch Type K1 alternator with integral regulator

voltage regulator is solid state, which is not serviceable or adjustable. On integral regulator units, the voltage regulator can be replaced without disassembling the alternator.

IN-VEHICLE TESTING

Integral Regulator Units

Indicator Lamp Diagnosis

NOTE: If indicator lamp lights with engine operating, indicating a no charge condition perform the following test.

1. Check alternator belt tension and adjust as necessary.
2. Start engine and measure battery voltage

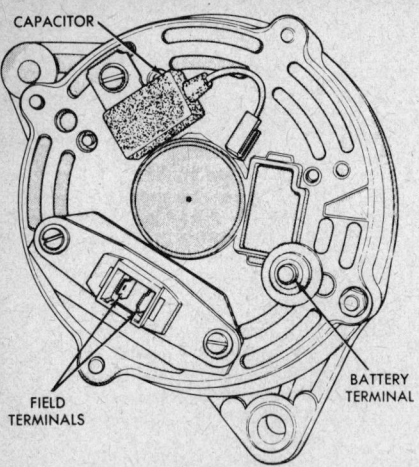

Fig. 2   Rear view of Bosch Type K1 alternator less integral regulator

using a suitable voltmeter.
3. Raise engine speed to fast idle.
4. Ground the metal sleeve on the voltage regulator to the alternator housing and check voltage reading, Fig. 3. If voltage reading is higher than reading obtained in step 2, the regulator is defective and should be replaced. If voltage reading is lower or remains the same, the alternator must be removed and repaired.

Undercharged Battery
Refer to diagnosis charts, Figs. 4 and 5 for test procedure.

Overcharged Battery
Refer to diagnosis chart, Fig. 6 for test procedure.

Exc. Integral Regulator Units
For procedures on these units, refer to Chrysler Alternators under "In Vehicle Testing."

ALTERNATOR DISASSEMBLY

Integral Regulator Units, Fig. 7

1. Scribe marks on alternator front and rear housings for use during reassembly.
2. Remove regulator and brush holder retaining screws and washers, then tilt regulator and brush holder assembly and remove from rear housing.
3. Disconnect condenser wire, then remove retaining screws, washer and condenser.
4. Remove through bolts, then separate front housing and rotor assembly from stator and rear housing assembly. Remove wave washer from rear housing.

NOTE: Place a piece of tape over rear housing bearing and slip ring end of rotor shaft to prevent entry of dirt. Do not use tape which will leave a gummy deposit on rotor shaft. If brushes are to be reused, clean with a soft dry cloth.

5. Remove battery terminal nuts and washers. Note positioning of components for reassembly.

6. Position rotor assembly in a vise, then remove shaft nut, lockwasher, pulley, key and fan from rotor shaft.

NOTE: When positioning rotor in vise, tighten vise only enough to permit loosening of shaft nut. Overtightening may cause damage to rotor.

7. Remove bearing retainer attaching screws from front housing, then remove rotor assembly.
8. Remove stator and diode assembly from rear housing.
9. Unsolder stator leads from diode plate assembly.
10. Separate drive housing from rotor shaft.
11. Press rear bearing from rotor shaft using a suitable press and support.

NOTE: The rear rotor shaft bearing must be replaced if it is found to be insufficiently lubricated. Do not attempt to lubricate or reuse a dry bearing.

12. Press front bearing from rotor shaft.

Exc. Integral Regulator Units, Fig. 8

1. Mount alternator in a suitable vise using mounting lug as a clamping point.
2. Remove pulley nut, lockwasher, pulley, spacer, fan and key.
3. Remove brush holder mounting screw, then brush holder.
4. Disconnect capacitor lead from terminal, then remove capacitor mounting screw and capacitor.
5. Remove ground stud nut and washer. Scribe alignment marks on alternator housings to aid in reassembly.
6. Remove alternator through bolts, then pry between stator and drive end shield with a suitable screwdriver. Carefully separate rotor and housing assembly from stator and rectifier housing assembly.
7. Using a suitable press, press rotor from drive end housing, then remove front bearing retaining screws and press out front bearing.
8. Remove battery terminal stud nut, lockwasher, flat washer and insulators from rear end housing.
9. Remove rectifier assembly mounting screws, then remove rectifier and stator assembly.
10. Using a suitable soldering gun and a pair of long nosed pliers as a heat sink, unsolder stator to rectifier leads.
11. Remove inner battery terminal stud insulator, then remove rear housing bearing dust and oil seal.
12. Using a suitable puller, remove rear bearing from rotor assembly.

BENCH TESTS

Rotor & Slip Ring Test

To test rotor for grounds, set ohmmeter to 1000 scale, then place one ohmmeter lead on rotor shaft and contact other ohmmeter lead to slip ring, Fig. 9. Repeat test with other slip ring. The ohmmeter should indicate an infinite reading. If ohmmeter indicates other than infinite reading, a short to ground exists. Inspect soldered connections at slip rings to ensure they are not grounded against the

Fig. 3   Voltage regulator grounding sleeve. Integral regulator unit

rotor coil. Inspect rotor coil and replace if damaged.

On American Motors models, to test rotor for an open circuit, set ohmmeter to 1 scale, then contact ohmmeter leads to slip rings, Fig. 10. Ohmmeter reading should be 3.0 to 3.7 ohms. If an infinite reading is obtained, rotor winding has an open circuit.

On Chrysler models, to test rotor for an open circuit, check for continuity across slip rings, Fig. 10. If continuity does not exist, field coil is defective and rotor should be replaced.

On American Motors models only, to check rotor for short circuit, connect a 12 volt battery and ammeter in series with slip rings, Fig. 11. Field current at 12 volts and 80 degrees F should be between 3.5 and 5 amps. If reading is above 5 amps, shorted windings are indicated. Winding resistance and ammeter readings will vary with temperatures. A reading below the specified value indicates excessive resistance. This test can also be performed by connecting an ohmmeter between the two slip rings. If resistance is below 3 ohms, at 80 degrees F, the winding is shorted. If reading is above 3.7 ohms at 80 degrees F, winding has excessive resistance.

Stator Winding Test

To test stator for short circuit, set ohmmeter to 1000 scale, then connect one ohmmeter lead to stator core and the other ohmmeter lead to one of the three stator leads, Fig. 12. The ohmmeter should indicate an infinite reading. If ohmmeter indicates other than infinite reading, the stator is grounded and should be replaced.

To test stator for continuity, set ohmmeter to 1 scale, then contact ohmmeter leads to two of the stator leads, Fig. 13. Test all three stator leads in this manner. Equal readings should be obtained for each pair. An infinite reading would indicate an open stator winding. Check junction splice for poor solder connection and resolder as necessary. Recheck stator continuity, if an open still exists replace stator. A reading of more than one ohm indicates a poor solder splice, check junction splice.

NOTE: Shorted stator windings are difficult to locate without special equipment. If other tests indicate normal, but alternator fails to supply rated output, shorted stator windings are indicated.

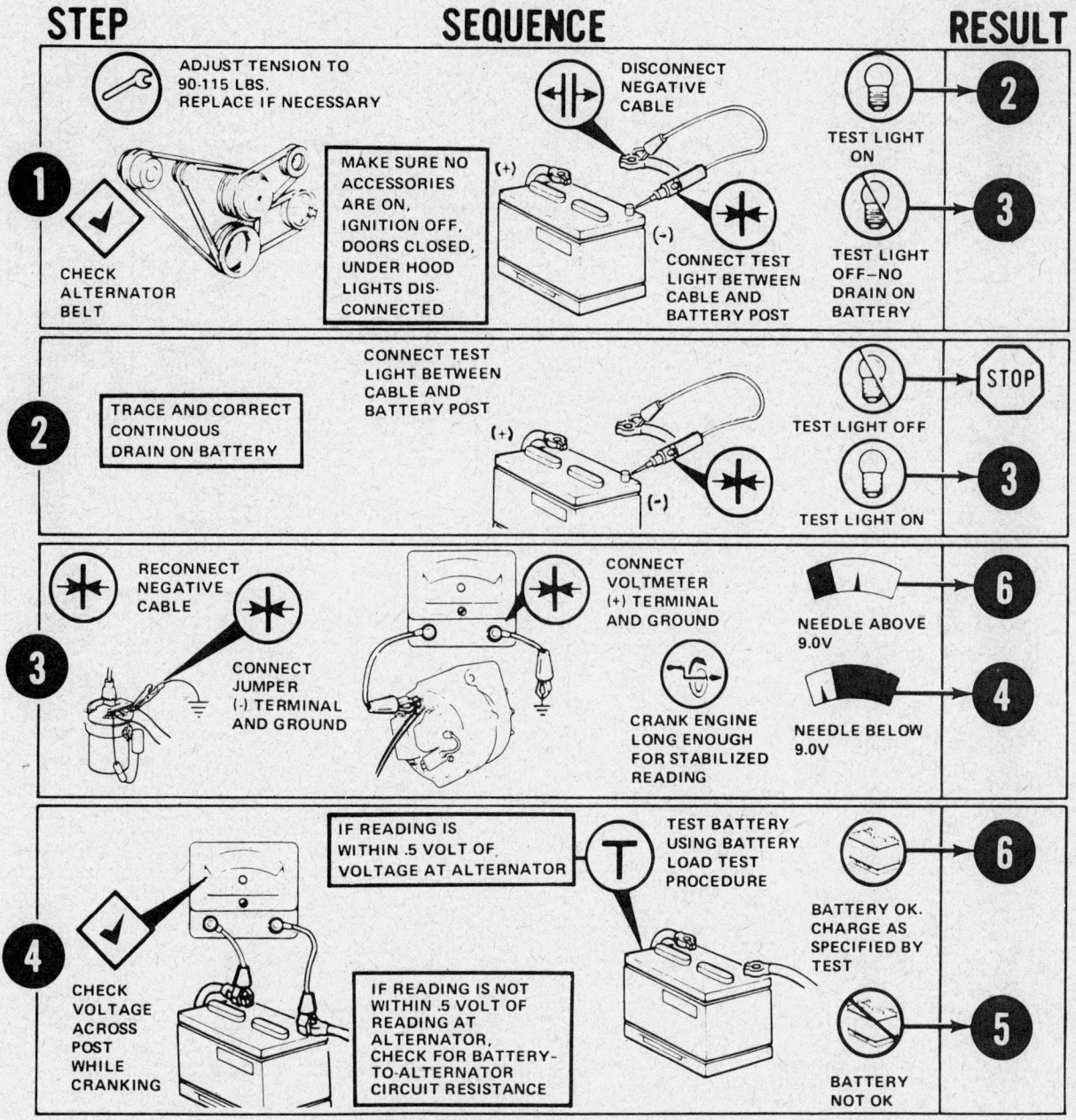

STEP   **SEQUENCE**   **RESULT**

1 CHECK ALTERNATOR BELT — ADJUST TENSION TO 90-115 LBS. REPLACE IF NECESSARY / MAKE SURE NO ACCESSORIES ARE ON, IGNITION OFF, DOORS CLOSED, UNDER HOOD LIGHTS DISCONNECTED / DISCONNECT NEGATIVE CABLE / CONNECT TEST LIGHT BETWEEN CABLE AND BATTERY POST → TEST LIGHT ON → **2** / TEST LIGHT OFF—NO DRAIN ON BATTERY → **3**

2 TRACE AND CORRECT CONTINUOUS DRAIN ON BATTERY — CONNECT TEST LIGHT BETWEEN CABLE AND BATTERY POST → TEST LIGHT OFF → **STOP** / TEST LIGHT ON → **3**

3 RECONNECT NEGATIVE CABLE / CONNECT JUMPER (-) TERMINAL AND GROUND / CONNECT VOLTMETER (+) TERMINAL AND GROUND / CRANK ENGINE LONG ENOUGH FOR STABILIZED READING → NEEDLE ABOVE 9.0V → **6** / NEEDLE BELOW 9.0V → **4**

4 CHECK VOLTAGE ACROSS POST WHILE CRANKING / IF READING IS WITHIN .5 VOLT OF VOLTAGE AT ALTERNATOR / IF READING IS NOT WITHIN .5 VOLT OF READING AT ALTERNATOR, CHECK FOR BATTERY-TO-ALTERNATOR CIRCUIT RESISTANCE / TEST BATTERY USING BATTERY LOAD TEST PROCEDURE → BATTERY OK. CHARGE AS SPECIFIED BY TEST → **6** / BATTERY NOT OK → **5**

Fig. 4   Bosch K1 alternator with integral regulator undercharged battery test chart. Part 1 of 2

Diode Test

Unsolder stator winding leads at junctions. Bend lead wires as little as possible to avoid damaging wires. Set ohmmeter to 1 scale, then contact one ohmmeter lead to diode plate and the other ohmmeter lead to the individual diode junctions, Fig. 14. Each combination of terminals tested should give one high reading and one low reading. High and low readings will vary slightly with temperature. If one high and one low reading is not observed for all diodes, replace diode plate assembly.

ALTERNATOR ASSEMBLY

Integral Regulator Units, Fig. 7

1. Fill cavity between retainer plate and bearing one quarter full with Bosch lubricant FT1v34 or equivalent. Do not overfill.
2. Install front bearing, retainer and collar into front housing. Press rear bearing onto rotor shaft. Install wave washer into rear housing.

NOTE: Use care not to misalign bearings.

3. Install rotor into front housing.
4. Solder stator leads to diode plate assembly, then install stator assembly on rear housing.
5. Remove tape from rear housing bearing and rotor shaft, then position front and rear housings together, aligning scribe marks made during disassembly.
6. Install and tighten through bolts.
7. Position key, fan, pulley and washer on

ALTERNATOR SYSTEMS

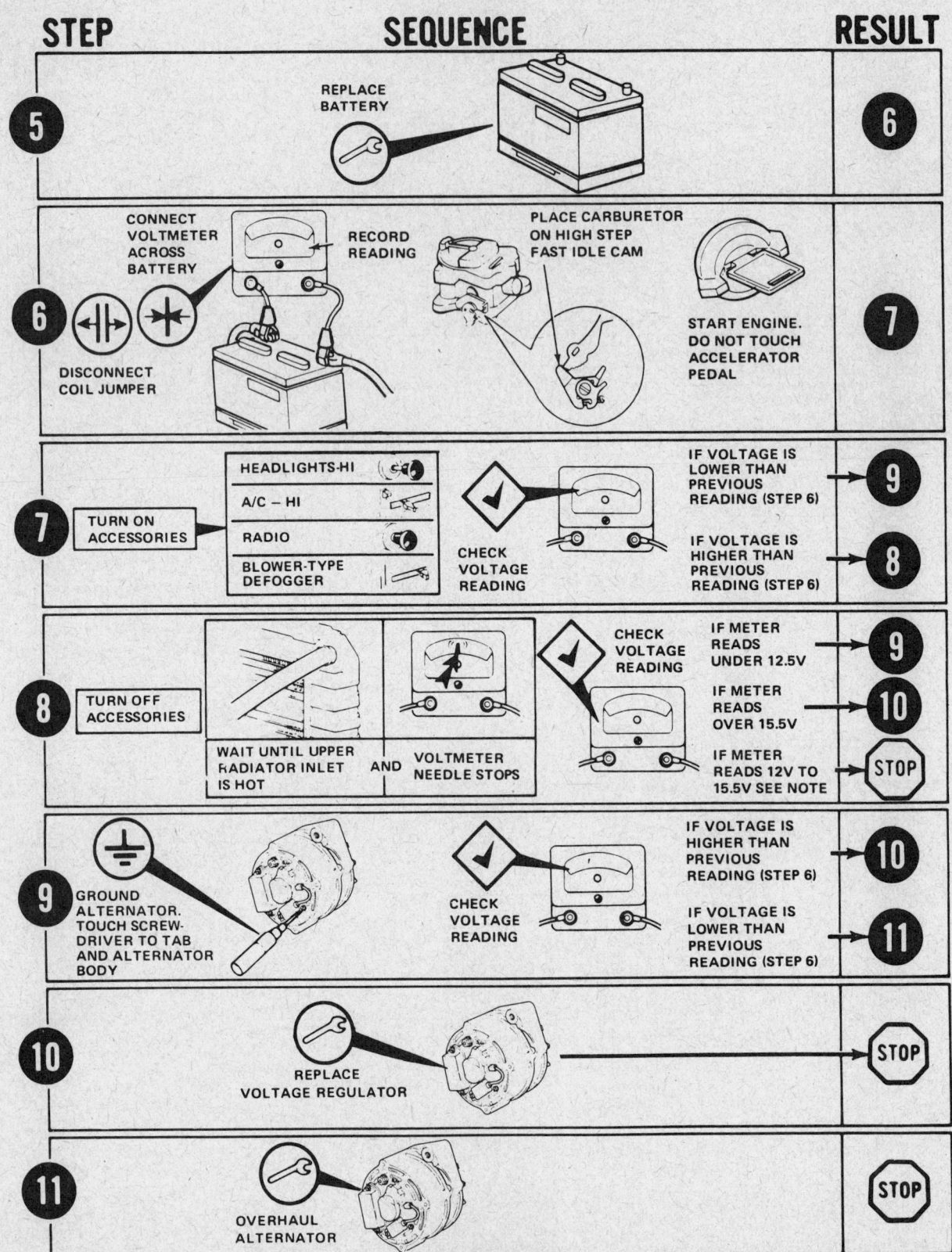

STEP — **SEQUENCE** — **RESULT**

5 REPLACE BATTERY → **6**

6 DISCONNECT COIL JUMPER / CONNECT VOLTMETER ACROSS BATTERY / RECORD READING / PLACE CARBURETOR ON HIGH STEP FAST IDLE CAM / START ENGINE. DO NOT TOUCH ACCELERATOR PEDAL → **7**

7 TURN ON ACCESSORIES — HEADLIGHTS-HI / A/C – HI / RADIO / BLOWER-TYPE DEFOGGER — CHECK VOLTAGE READING
- IF VOLTAGE IS LOWER THAN PREVIOUS READING (STEP 6) → **9**
- IF VOLTAGE IS HIGHER THAN PREVIOUS READING (STEP 6) → **8**

8 TURN OFF ACCESSORIES / WAIT UNTIL UPPER RADIATOR INLET IS HOT AND VOLTMETER NEEDLE STOPS / CHECK VOLTAGE READING
- IF METER READS UNDER 12.5V → **9**
- IF METER READS OVER 15.5V → **10**
- IF METER READS 12V TO 15.5V SEE NOTE → STOP

9 GROUND ALTERNATOR. TOUCH SCREW-DRIVER TO TAB AND ALTERNATOR BODY / CHECK VOLTAGE READING
- IF VOLTAGE IS HIGHER THAN PREVIOUS READING (STEP 6) → **10**
- IF VOLTAGE IS LOWER THAN PREVIOUS READING (STEP 6) → **11**

10 REPLACE VOLTAGE REGULATOR → STOP

11 OVERHAUL ALTERNATOR → STOP

Fig. 5   Bosch K1 alternator with integral regulator undercharged battery test chart. Part 2 of 2

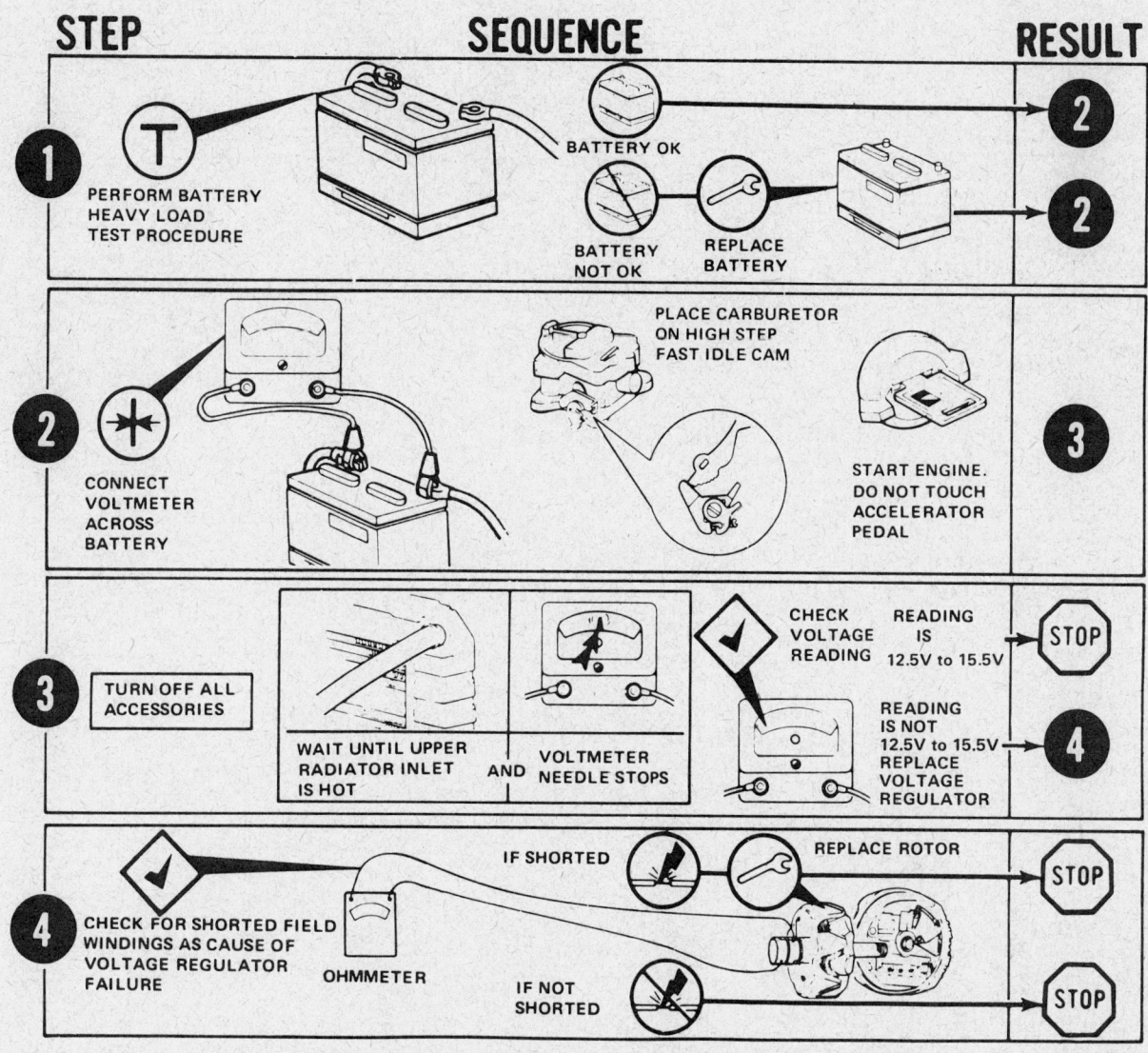

Fig. 6 Bosch K1 alternator with integral regulator overcharged battery test chart

rotor shaft, then install pulley nut.
8. Place rotor in a vise and tighten pulley nut. Tighten vise only enough to permit tightening of pulley nut.
9. Install nuts and washer on battery terminal.
10. Install condenser on rear housing and connect condenser lead.
11. Install voltage regulator and brush assembly on rear housing.

Exc. Integral Regulator Units, Fig. 8

1. Using a suitable press, install rear bearing on rotor assembly until bearing bottoms.
2. Install rear housing bearing dust and oil seal, then inner battery terminal stud insulator.
3. Using long nosed pliers as a heat sink, solder stator leads to rectifier assembly, then install stator and rectifier assembly in rear end housing. Tighten screws securely.
4. Install battery terminal stud insulators, flat washer, lock washer and stud nut.
5. Using a suitable press, install drive end housing bearing, then install bearing retainer and attaching screws.
6. Using a suitable press, install drive end housing onto rotor.
7. Align marks made previously, then install stator and rectifier housing assembly over rotor and housing assembly.
8. Install alternator through bolts and tighten securely.
9. Install ground stud washer and nut, then install capacitor to rear end housing.
10. Position brush holder in rear end housing, then install attaching screws and tighten securely.
11. Install rotor fan key, fan, spacer, pulley, lockwasher and nut. Tighten pulley nut securely.

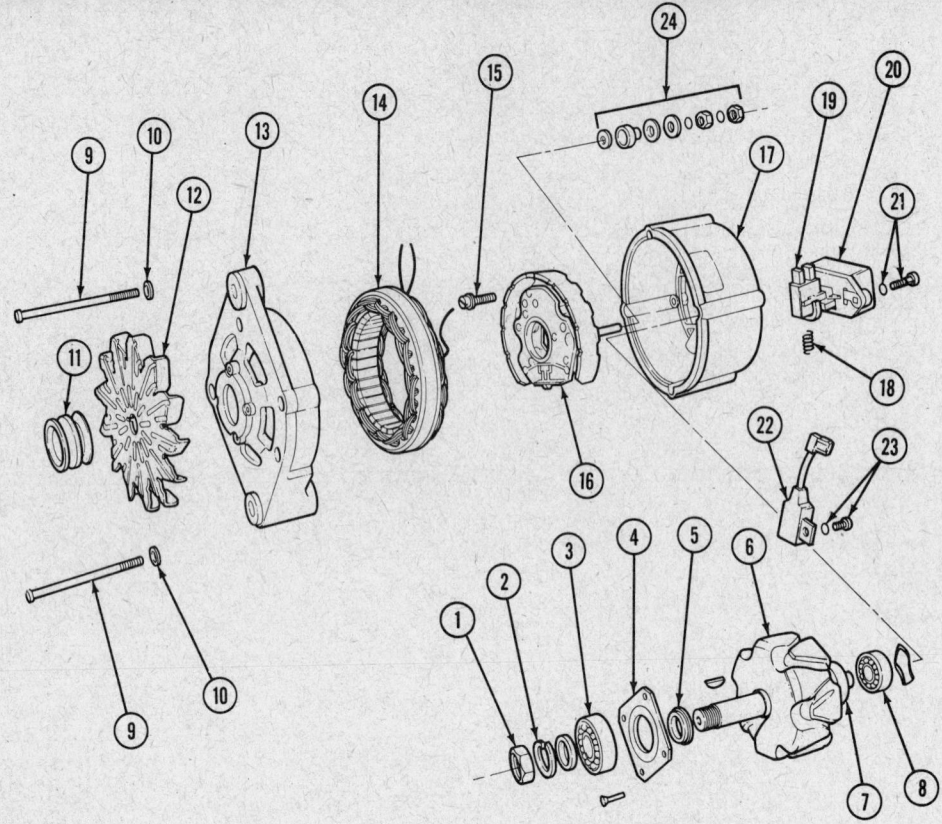

1. PULLEY NUT	9. THROUGH-SCREW	17. REAR HOUSING
2. LOCKWASHER	10. WASHER	18. COMPRESSION SPRING
3. BEARING	11. PULLEY	19. CARBON BRUSH SET
4. COVER PLATE	12. FAN	20. REGULATOR
5. COLLAR	13. FRONT HOUSING	21. SPRING WASHER AND SCREW
6. ROTOR	14. STATOR	22. SUPPRESSION CAPACITOR
7. COLLECTOR RING	15. WASHER AND SCREW ASSEMBLY	23. SPRING WASHER AND SCREW
8. BEARING	16. RECTIFIER	24. BATTERY TERMINAL NUTS AND WASHERS

Fig. 7 Exploded view of Bosch Type K1 alternator with integral regulator

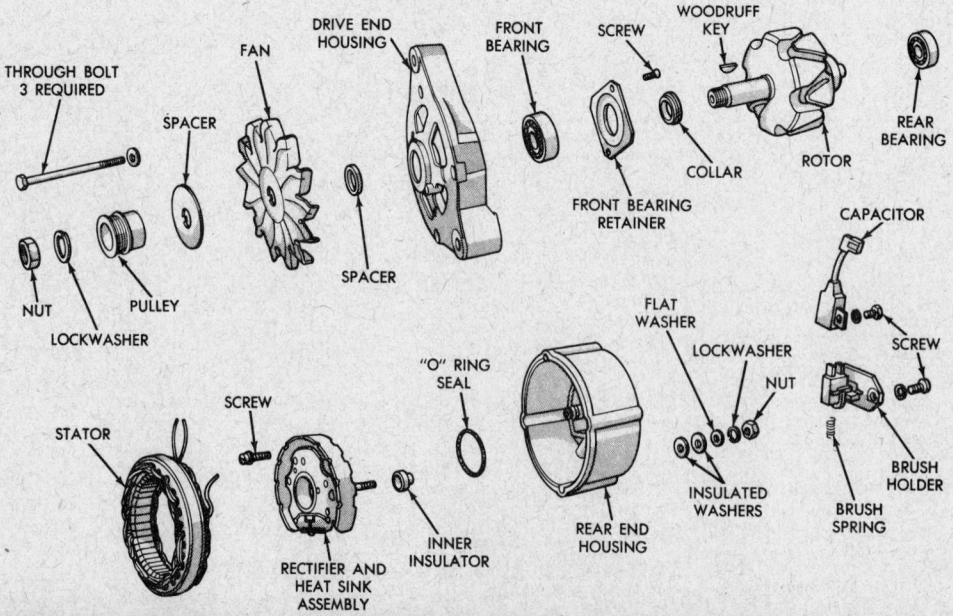

Fig. 8 Exploded view of Bosch Type K1 alternator less integral regulator

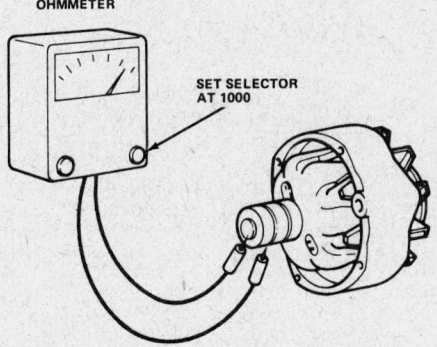

Fig. 9   Rotor short to ground test

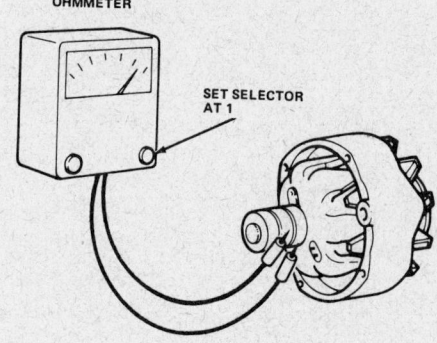

Fig. 10   Rotor open circuit test

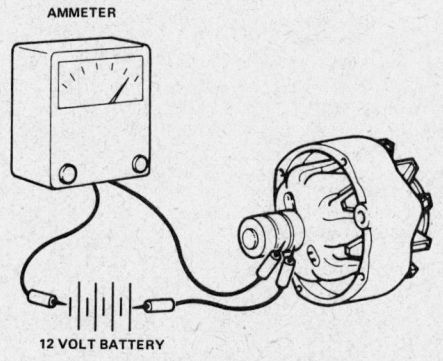

Fig. 11   Rotor internal short test. Integral regulator models

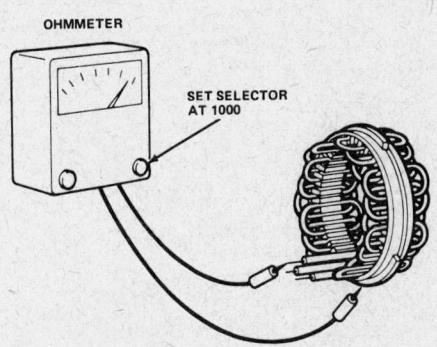

Fig. 12   Stator short to ground test

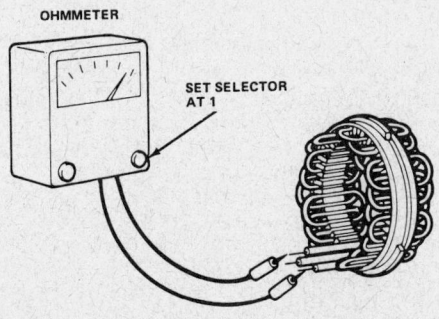

Fig. 13   Stator continuity test

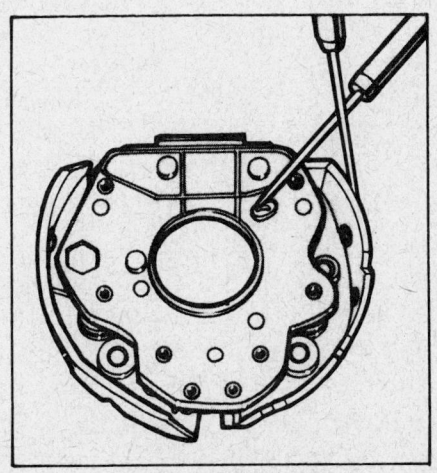

Fig. 14   Diode test

Chrysler Alternators

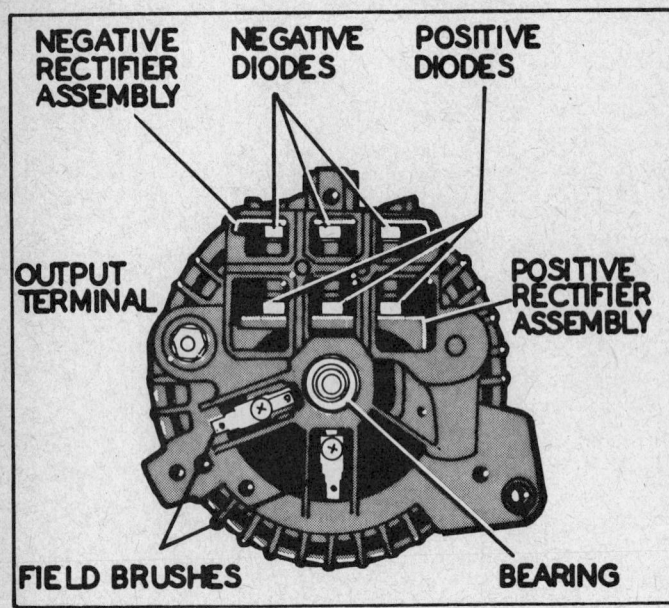

Fig. 1   Alternator assembly exc. 100 & 114 amp units. 1977—83

NEGATIVE RECTIFIER ASSEMBLY — NEGATIVE DIODES — POSITIVE DIODES — OUTPUT TERMINAL — POSITIVE RECTIFIER ASSEMBLY — FIELD BRUSHES — BEARING

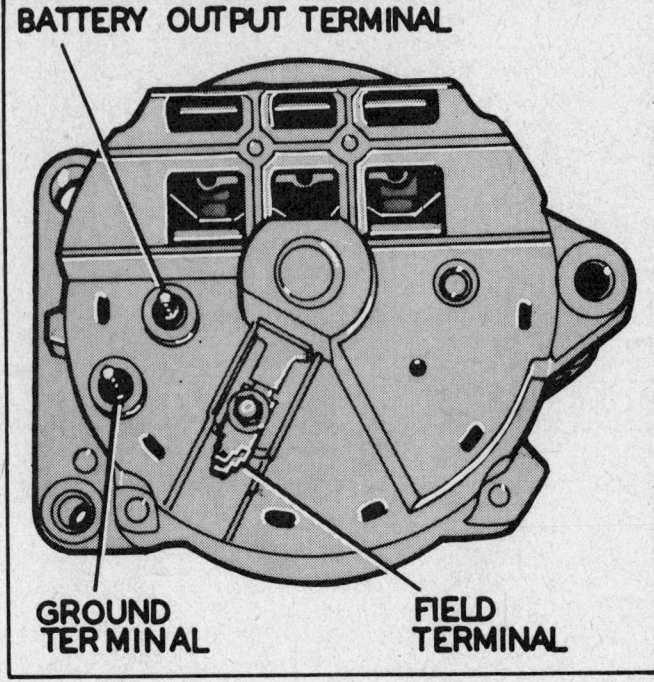

Fig. 3   100 & 114 amp alternator assembly. 1977—83

BATTERY OUTPUT TERMINAL — GROUND TERMINAL — FIELD TERMINAL

All Chrysler alternators except the 100 and 114 amp units are equipped with six silicon rectifiers, Figs. 1 and 2. The 100 and 114 amp alternators are equipped with twelve silicon rectifiers, Figs. 3 and 4.

IN-VEHICLE TESTING

NOTE: When testing alternators except 100 and 114 amp units, use a 0–100 amp ammeter. When testing 100 and 114 amp alternators, use a 0–150 amp ammeter.

Charging Circuit Resistance Test

1. Disconnect battery ground cable. Disconnect "Batt" lead at the alternator.

2. Complete test connections as per Fig. 5.
3. Connect battery ground cable, start engine and operate at idle.
4. Adjust engine speed and carbon pile to obtain 20 amps in the circuit and check voltmeter reading. Reading should not exceed .7 volts. If a voltage drop is indicated, inspect, clean and tighten all connections in the circuit. A voltage drop test at each connection can be performed to isolate the trouble.

Current Output Test

1. Disconnect battery ground cable, complete test connections as per Fig. 6 and

start engine and operate at idle. *Immediately after starting, reduce engine speed to idle.*

2. Adjust the carbon pile and engine speed in increments until a speed of 1250 RPM and 15 volts are obtained on all units except 100 and 114 amp alternators. On 100 and 114 amp alternators, obtain engine speed of 900 RPM and 13 volts.

CAUTION: While increasing speed, do not allow voltage to exceed 16 volts.

3. Check ammeter reading. Output current should be within specifications.

Voltage Regulator Test

NOTE: Battery must be fully charged for test to be accurate.

1. Connect test equipment, Fig. 7.
2. Start and run engine at 1250 RPM with all lights and accessories turned "Off." Voltage should be as specified in Fig. 8.
3. It is normal for the vehicle ammeter to indicate an immediate charge, then gradually return to the normal position.
4. If voltage is below limits or is fluctuating, proceed with the following:
   a. Check voltage regulator for proper ground. The ground is obtained through the regulator case to mounting screws, then to the vehicle sheet metal.
   b. With ignition switch "Off", disconnect voltage regulator connector. Turn ig-

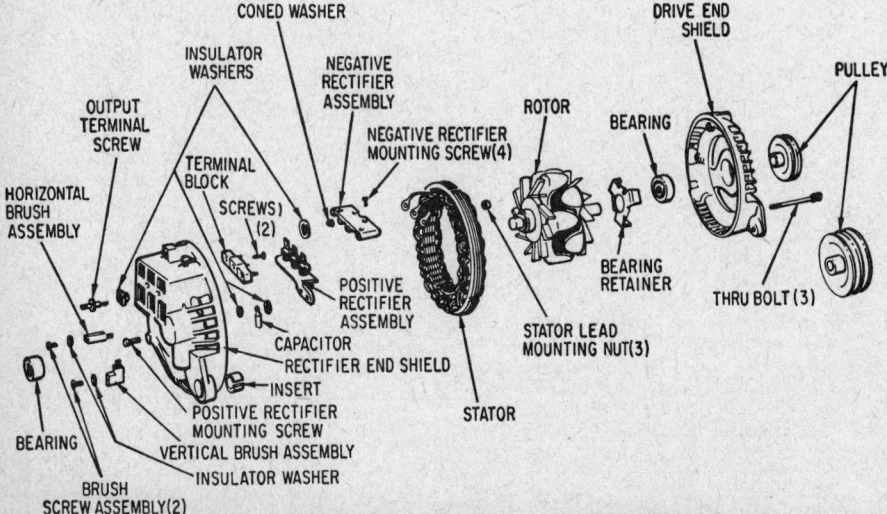

Fig. 2   Alternator disassembled exc. 100 & 114 amp units (typical) 1977—83

OUTPUT TERMINAL SCREW — CONED WASHER — INSULATOR WASHERS — NEGATIVE RECTIFIER ASSEMBLY — NEGATIVE RECTIFIER MOUNTING SCREW(4) — DRIVE END SHIELD — PULLEY — ROTOR — BEARING — HORIZONTAL BRUSH ASSEMBLY — TERMINAL BLOCK — SCREWS(2) — POSITIVE RECTIFIER ASSEMBLY — CAPACITOR — RECTIFIER END SHIELD — INSERT — POSITIVE RECTIFIER MOUNTING SCREW — VERTICAL BRUSH ASSEMBLY — INSULATOR WASHER — BEARING RETAINER — BEARING — STATOR LEAD MOUNTING NUT(3) — STATOR — THRU BOLT (3) — BRUSH SCREW ASSEMBLY(2)

nition "On" and check for battery voltage at the wiring harness terminal. Both green and blue leads should have battery voltage.

c. If voltage regulator was grounded properly and battery voltage was present at the green and blue leads, replace voltage regulator except on systems incorporating a field-loads relay. On systems with a field-loads relay, test the relay as outlined under "Field-Loads Relay Test." If relay tests satisfactory, replace voltage regulator. On all systems, repeat test.

5. If voltage is above limits, refer to Steps 4B and 4C.

BENCH TESTS

If the alternator performance does not meet current output specification limits, it will have to be disassembled for further tests and servicing.

To remove the alternator, disconnect the battery ground cable and the leads at the alternator. Then unfasten and remove the alternator from the vehicle.

Field Coil Draw

1. Place alternator on an insulated surface.
2. On all units, connect a jumper wire between one alternator field terminal and the negative terminal of a fully charged battery.
3. Connect test ammeter positive lead to the other alternator field terminal and the ammeter negative lead to the positive battery terminal.
4. On 1979–83 units except 100 and 114 amp, connect a jumper wire between alternator end shield and negative terminal of battery.
5. On all units, slowly rotate rotor by hand and note ammeter reading. On units except 100 and 114 amp, field current at 12 volts should be 4.5 to 6.5 amps. On 100 and 114 amp units, field current should be 4.75 to 6.0 amps.
6. A low rotor coil draw is an indication of high resistance in the field coil circuit, (brushes, slip rings or rotor coil). A high rotor coil draw indicates shorted rotor coil or grounded rotor. No reading indicates an open rotor or defective brushes.

ALTERNATOR REPAIRS EXCEPT 100 & 114 AMP UNITS

Disassembly

To prevent possible damage to the brush assemblies, they should be removed before disassembling the alternator. Both brushes are insulated and mounted in plastic holders.

1. Remove both brush screws, insulating nylon washers and remove brush assemblies, Fig. 2.

NOTE: The stator is laminated; do not burr it or the end shield.

2. Remove through bolts and pry between stator and drive end shield with a screwdriver. Carefully separate drive end shield, pulley and rotor from stator and diode rectifier shield, Fig. 9.
3. The pulley is an interference fit on the rotor shaft; therefore, a suitable puller must be used to remove it, Fig. 10.

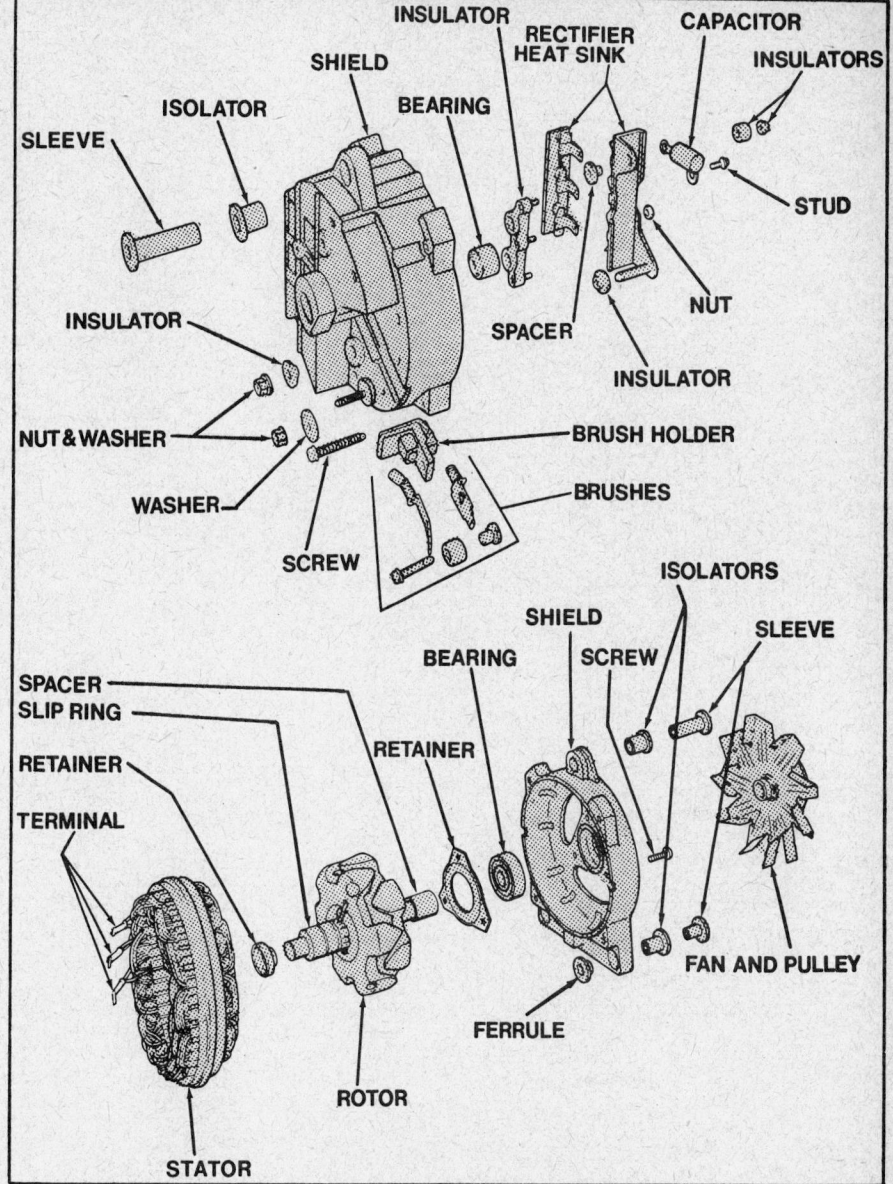

Fig. 4   100 & 114 amp alternator disassembled. 1977–83

4. Pry drive end bearing spring retainer from end shield with a screwdriver, Fig. 11.
5. Support end shield and tap rotor shaft with a plastic hammer to separate rotor from end shield.
6. The drive end ball bearing is an interference fit with the rotor shaft; therefore, a suitable pulley must be used to remove it, Fig. 12.
7. To remove rectifiers and heat sinks, loosen screws securing negative rectifier and heat sink assembly to end shield, remove the two outer screws and lift assembly from end shield. Remove nuts securing positive rectifier and heat sink assembly to insulated terminals in end shield. Then, remove capacitor ground screw and lift insulated washer, capacitor and positive rectifier and heat sink assembly from end shield.
8. The needle roller bearing in the rectifier end shield is a press fit. If it is necessary to remove the rectifier end frame needle bearing, protect the end shield by supporting the shield when pressing out the bearing as shown in Fig. 13.

Testing Diode Rectifiers

A special Rectifier Tester Tool C-3829 provides a quick, simple and accurate method to test the rectifiers without the necessity of disconnecting the soldered rectifier leads. This instrument is commercially available and full instructions for its use are provided. Lacking this tool, the rectifiers may be tested with a 12 volt battery and a test lamp having a No. 67 bulb. The procedure is as follows:

1. Remove nuts securing stator windings, positive and negative rectifier straps to terminal block. Remove stator winding terminals and pry stator from end shield.
2. Connect one side of test lamp to positive battery post and the other side of the test lamp to a test probe. Connect another test probe to the negative battery post, Fig. 14.

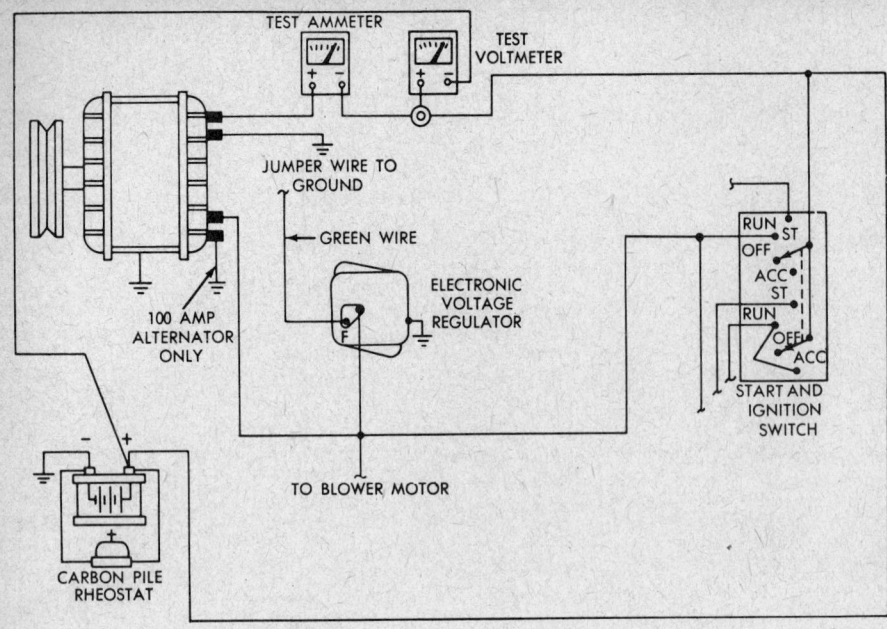

Fig. 5 Charging circuit resistance test. 1977—83 alternators

does not light, the stator has an open circuit.

4. Install new stator if one tested is defective.

Testing Rotor

The rotor may be tested electrically for grounded, open or shorted field coils as follows:

Grounded Field Coil Test: Connect an ohmmeter between each slip ring and the rotor shaft. The ohmmeter should indicate infinite resistance. If reading is zero or higher, rotor is grounded.

Open or Shorted Field Coil Test: Connect an ohmmeter between slip rings and note reading. Ohmmeter reading should be between 1.5 and 2 ohms at room temperature. A reading of 2.5 to 3 ohms, would indicate that the alternator was operated at high underhood temperature, however the rotor is still satisfactory. A reading above 3.5 ohms would indicate a high resistance in rotor coils and further testing or replacement of rotor is required. If resistance is below 1.5 ohms, the field coil is shorted.

Replacing Slip Rings

NOTE: Slip rings are not serviced as a separate item. Rotor replacement is required when the slip rings are defective.

3. Contact heat sink with one probe and strap on top of rectifier with the other probe.
4. Reverse position of probes. If test lamp lights in one direction only, the rectifier is satisfactory. If test lamp lights in both directions, the rectifier is shorted. If test lamp lights in neither direction, the rectifier is open.

NOTE: *Possible cause of an open or a blown rectifier is a faulty capacitor or a battery that has been installed on reverse polarity. If the battery is installed properly and the rectifiers are open, test the capacitor capacity, which should be .50 microfarad plus or minus 20%.*

Testing Stator

1. Separate stator from end shields.
2. Using a 12 volt test lamp, Fig. 15, test stator for grounds. Contact one test probe to any pin on stator frame and the other to each stator lead. If lamp lights, stator is grounded.

NOTE: Remove varnish from stator frame pin to ensure proper electrical connection.

3. Use a 12-volt test lamp to test stator for continuity. Contact one stator lead with one probe and the remaining two leads with the other probe, Fig. 16. If test lamp

Alternator Assemble

1. Press grease retainer onto rotor shaft using tool No. C-3921, Fig. 17. The grease retainer is properly positioned when the inner bore of the installed tool bottoms on the rotor shaft.
2. Install diode end shield bearing, Fig. 18.
3. Install drive end bearing in end shield with bearing retainer plate to hold bearing in position. Place assembly on rotor shaft and press into position, Fig. 19.
4. Press pulley onto rotor shaft until it contacts inner race of bearing, Fig. 20.

NOTE: Do not exceed 6800 lbs.

5. Install output terminal stud and insulator through end shield. Then place positive heat sink assembly over studs, guiding rectifier straps over studs.
6. Place capacitor terminal over capacitor end stud and install capacitor shoulder insulator. Ground the capacitor bracket to end shield with a metal screw. Install and tighten positive heat sink lockwashers and nuts.
7. Slide negative rectifier and heat sink assembly into place, position straps on terminal block studs, then install and tighten attaching screws.
8. Position stator on diode end shield.
9. Position rotor end shield on stator and diode end shield.
10. Align through bolt holes in stator, diode end shield and drive end shield.
11. Compress stator and both end shields by hand and install through bolts, washers and nuts.
12. Install field brush into vertical and horizontal holders. Place an insulating

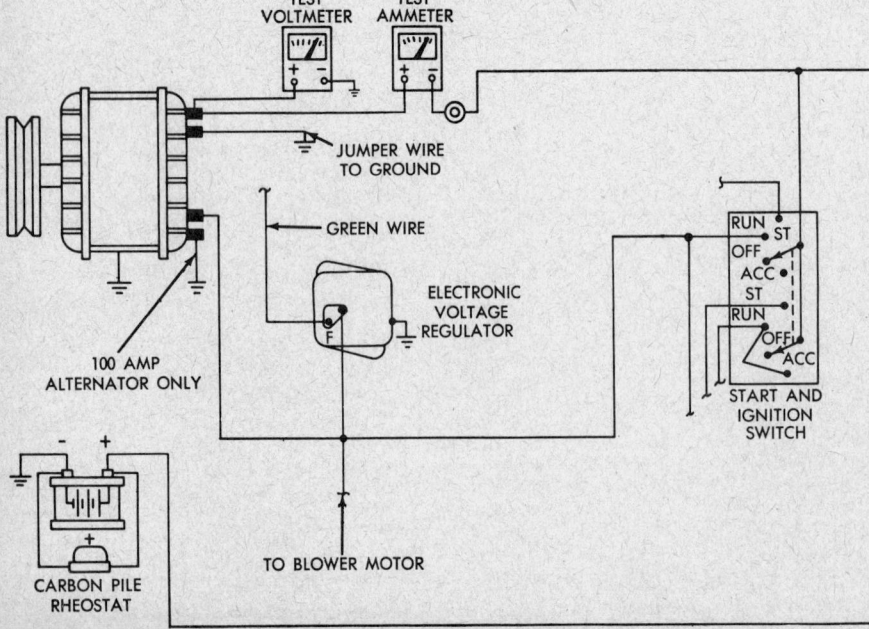

Fig. 6 Current output test. 1977—83 alternators

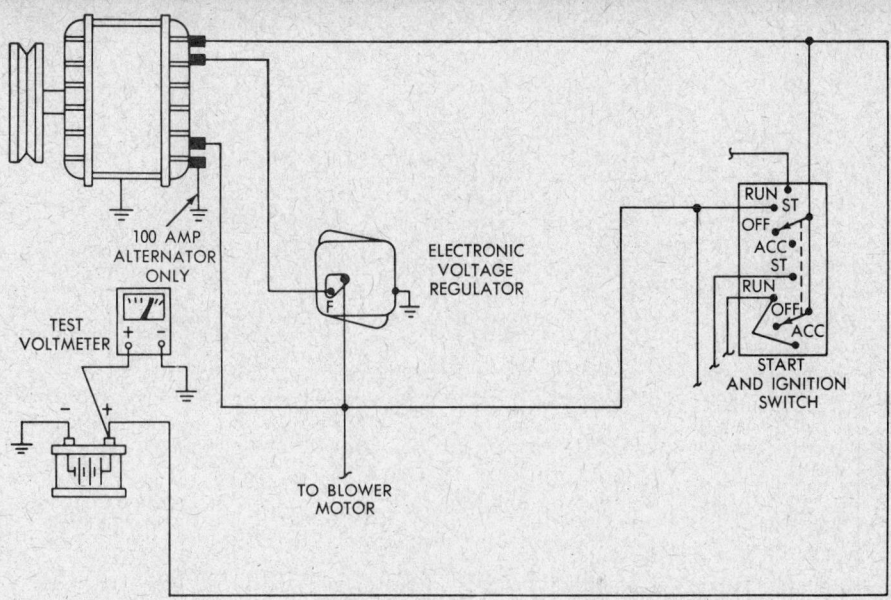

Fig. 7   Voltage regulators test. 1977–83 alternators

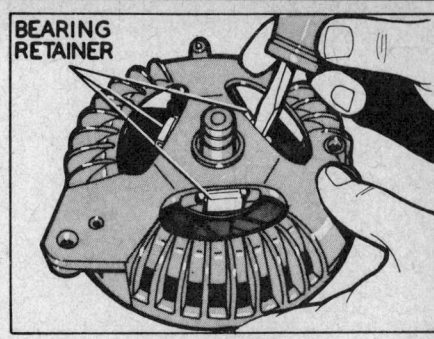

Fig. 11   Disengaging bearing retainer from end shield

Ambient Temperature Near Regulator	−20°F	80°F	140°F	Above 140°F
1977–83	14.9–15.9	13.9–14.6	13.3–13.9	Less than 13.6

Fig. 8   Voltage regulator test specifications

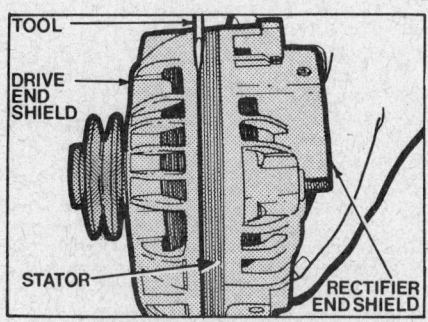

Fig. 9   Separating drive end shield from stator

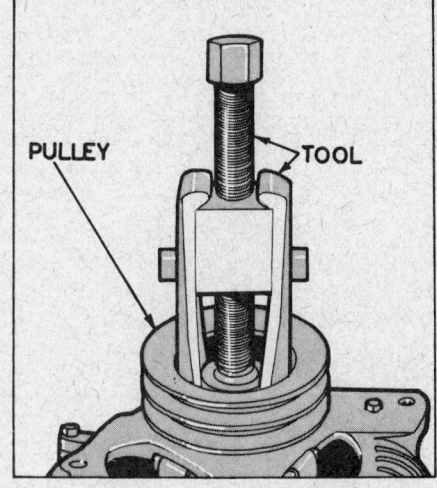

Fig. 10   Removing pulley

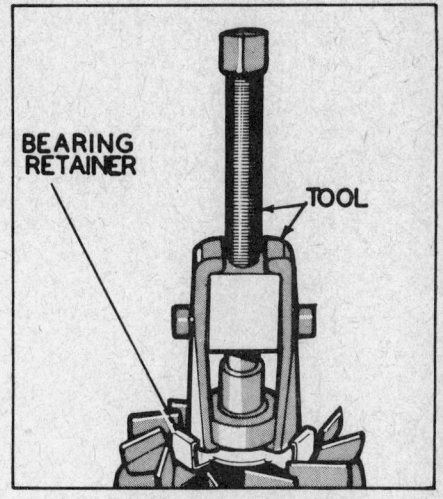

Fig. 12   Removing bearing from rotor shaft

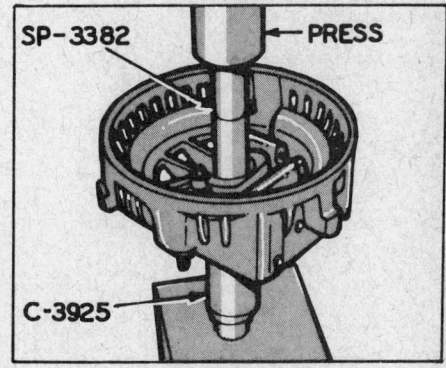

Fig. 13   Removing rectifier end shield bearing

washer on each field brush terminal and install lock-washers and attaching screws.

NOTE: Ensure brushes are not grounded.

13. Rotate pulley slowly by hand to be sure rotor fans do not touch diodes, capacitor lead and stator connections.
14. Install alternator and adjust drive belt.
15. Connect leads to alternator.
16. Connect battery ground cable.
17. Start and operate engine and observe alternator operation.
18. If necessary, test current output and regulator voltage setting.

100 & 114 AMP ALTERNATOR
Disassembly & Testing

Separating End Shields
1. Remove brush holder screw and insulating washer, then lift brush holder from end shield.
2. Remove the through bolts, then using a screwdriver, pry between the stator and end shield in the slot provided to separate end shields, Fig. 21.

Rectifier Testing
1. Remove stator winding leads to terminal block stud nuts, Fig. 22.
2. Lift stator winding leads and pry stator from end shield.
3. Using a 12 volt battery and a test lamp equipped with a #67 bulb, test rectifiers as follows:
   a. Connect one test probe to rectifier heat sink and the other test probe to the metal strap on top of rectifier, Fig. 23. Reverse the probes.
   b. If test lamp lights in one direction and does not light in the other, rectifier is satisfactory. If test lamp lights in both

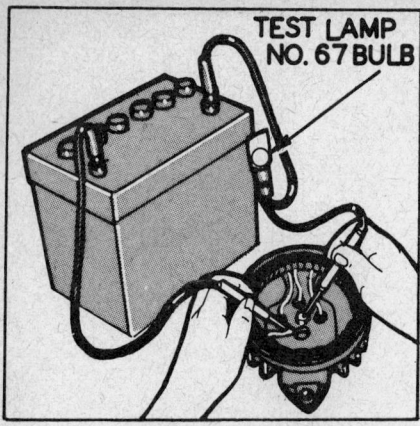

Fig. 14 Testing diodes with a test lamp

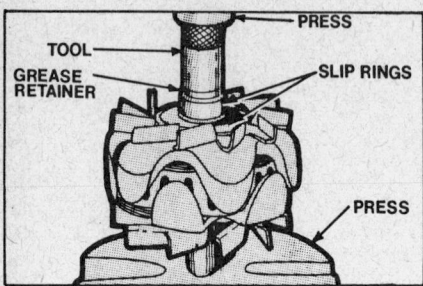

Fig. 17 Installing bearing grease retainer

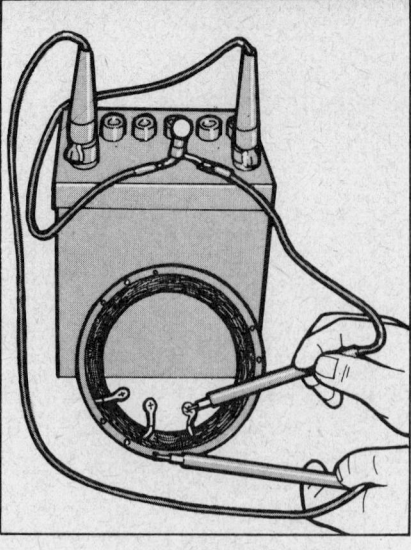

Fig. 15 Testing stator for grounds

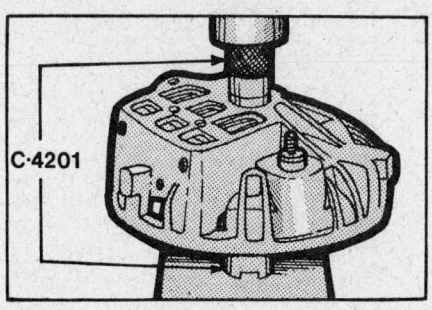

Fig. 18 Installing diode end shield bearing

Fig. 16 Testing stator windings for continuity (typical)

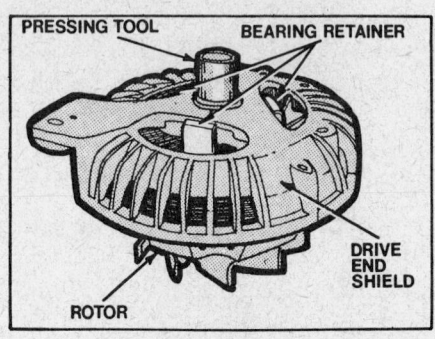

Fig. 19 Installing drive end shield and bearing

directions, rectifier is shorted. If test lamp does not light in either direction, rectifier is open.

Rectifier & Heat Sink Assembly Removal

1. Remove nut and insulator securing positive heat sink assembly to end shield stud.
2. Remove capacitor attaching screw.
3. Remove nut and insulator securing positive heat sink assembly stud to end shield, then remove positive heat sink assembly, Fig. 24, noting location of the insulators.
4. Remove screws securing negative heat sink assembly to end shield, then the negative heat sink assembly, Fig. 25.
5. Remove terminal block, then the capacitor and insulator.

Stator Testing

1. Contact one test lamp probe to outer diameter of stator frame and the other probe to each of the stator lead terminals, one at a time, Fig. 26.
2. If test lamp lights, the stator lead is grounded, requiring replacement.

NOTE: The stator windings are Delta Wound, therefore the windings cannot be tested for opens or shorts using a test lamp. If the stator is not grounded, and all other electrical circuits and alternator components test satisfactory, the stator may be open or shorted.

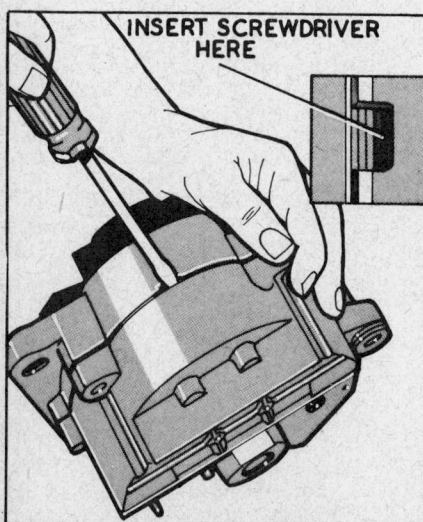

Fig. 21 Separating end shields. 100 & 114 amp units

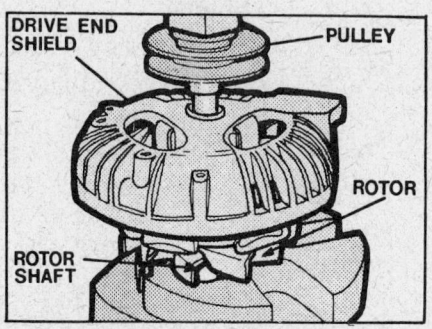

Fig. 20 Installing pulley

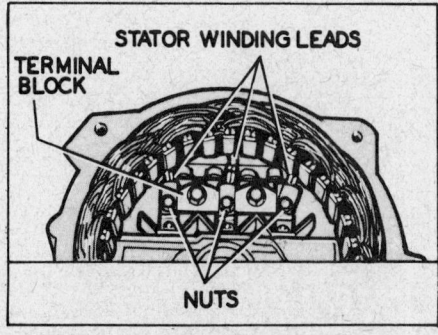

Fig. 22 Removing stator winding leads. 100 & 114 amp units

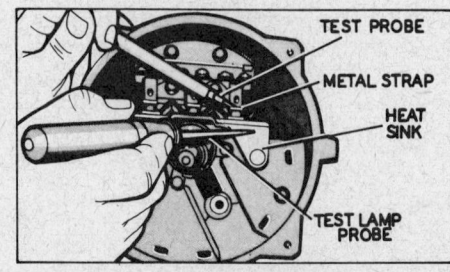

Fig. 23 Testing rectifiers with a test lamp. 100 & 114 amp units

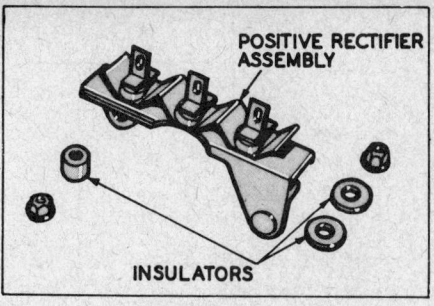

Fig. 24 Positive rectifier assembly.
100 & 114 amp units

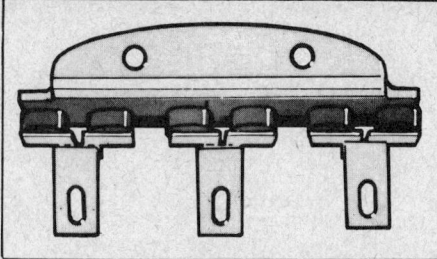

Fig. 25 Negative rectifier assembly.
100 & 114 amp units

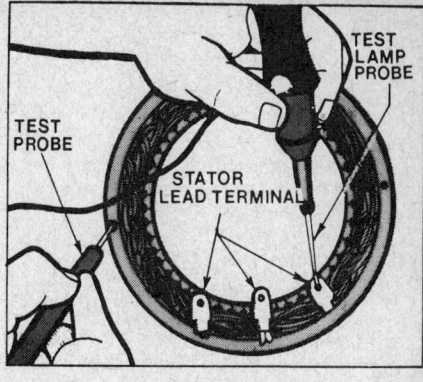

Fig. 26 Testing stator. 100 & 114 amp units

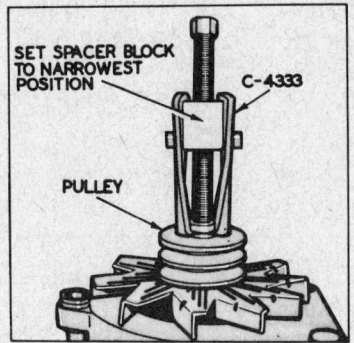

Fig. 27 Removing pulley. 100 & 114 amp
units

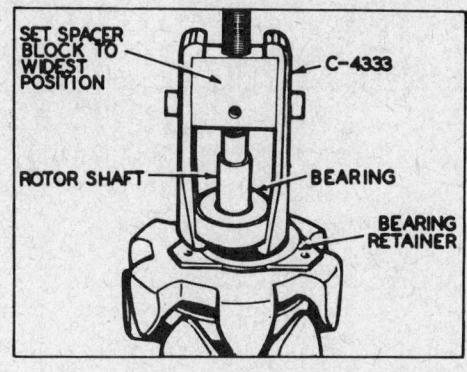

Fig. 28 Removing bearing from rotor shaft.
100 & 114 amp units

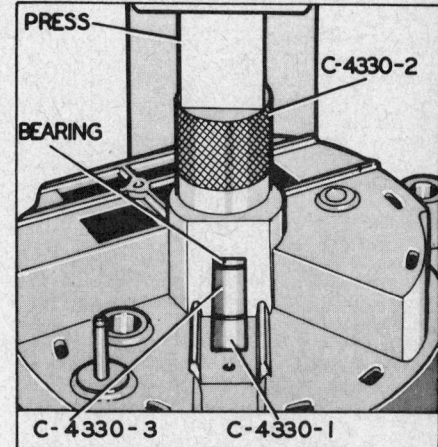

Fig. 29 Removing rectifier end shield
bearing. 100 & 114 amp units

Pulley & Bearing Removal

1. Remove pulley with a suitable puller, Fig. 27.
2. Remove bearing retainer to drive end shield attaching screws.
3. Support end shield and using a mallet, tap rotor from end shield.
4. Remove bearing with a suitable puller, Fig. 28.
5. If necessary to remove needle roller bearing in rectifier end shield, use tool C-4330, Fig. 29.

Rotor Testing

Grounded Field Coil Test: Connect a test lamp between each slip ring and the rotor shaft, Fig. 30. If test lamp lights, the rotor is grounded, requiring replacement.

Open Field Coil Test: Connect a test lamp between the slip rings, Fig. 31. If test lamp does not light, the rotor is open, requiring replacement.

Shorted Field Coil Test: Connect an ohmmeter between the slip rings, Fig. 31. If reading is below 1.7 ohms, the rotor is shorted.

High Resistance Test: with an ohmmeter connected across the slip rings, reading should be between 1.7 and 2.1 ohms at 80°F. If not, replace rotor.

Assembly

1. Press grease retainer onto rotor shaft, Fig. 29 (Omit tool C-4330-3).
2. Place rectifier end shield bearing on base of tool C-4330-1, Fig. 29 (Omit tool C-4330-3), then place rectifier end shield on top of bearing. Using tool C-4330-2, press end shield onto bearing until end shield contacts press base.
3. Install drive end bearing and retainer in drive end shield.
4. Position bearing and drive end shield on rotor and while supporting base of rotor shaft, press end shield onto shaft. Ensure rotor spacer is in place before pressing bearing and end shield on shaft.

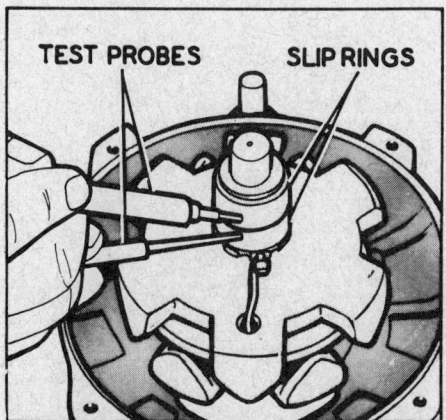

Fig. 30 Testing rotor for opens or shorts
100 & 114 amp units

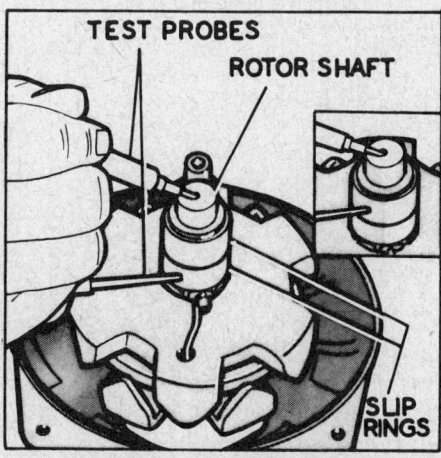

Fig. 31 Testing rotor for grounds
100 & 114 amp units

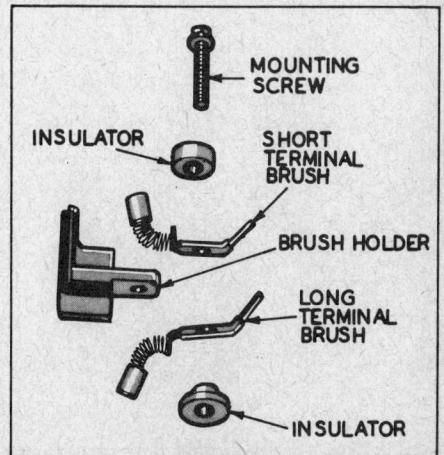

Fig. 32 Assembling field brushes.
100 & 114 amp units

5. Press pulley onto rotor shaft until it contacts inner race of bearing.

NOTE: Do not exceed 6800 lbs.

6. Place insulator and capacitor on positive heat sink mounting stud, then install capacitor mounting screw.
7. Place terminal block into position in rectifier end shield and install mounting screws.
8. Place negative heat sink into position, ensuring metal straps are properly located over studs on terminal block, then install negative heat sink mounting screws.

9. Place insulator over positive heat sink stud and install positive heat sink assembly into position in end shield, ensuring metal straps are properly located over terminal block studs. From inside end shield, place insulator on positive heat sink mounting stud, then install mounting nut. From outside end shield, place insulator on positive heat sink stud, then install mounting nut.
10. Place stator over rectifier end shield and install terminals on terminal block. Then, press stator pins into end shield and install terminal nuts.

NOTE: Route leads to avoid contact with

rotor or sharp edge of negative heat sink.

11. Place rotor and drive end shield assembly over stator and rectifier end shield assembly, aligning bolt holes. Compress stator and both end shields, then install and torque through bolts to 40–60 inch lbs.
12. Install field brushes into brush holder with long terminal on bottom and the short terminal on top, Fig. 32. Then, install insulators and mounting screw.
13. Place brush holder on end shield, ensure it is properly seated and tighten mounting screw.
14. Slowly rotate pulley to ensure rotor poles do not contact stator winding leads.

Delcotron Type SI Integral Charging System

DESCRIPTION

These units, Figs. 1 thru 6, feature a solid state regulator mounted inside the alternator slip ring end frame, along with the brush holder assembly. All regulator components are enclosed in a solid mold with no need or provision for adjustment of the regulator. A rectifier bridge, containing six diodes and connected to the stator windings, changes A.C. voltage to D.C. voltage which is available at the output terminal. Generator field current is supplied through a diode trio which is also connected to the stator windings. The diodes and rectifiers are protected by a capacitor which is also mounted in the end frame.

NOTE: General Motors units incorporate a resistor in the warning indicator circuit. Fig. 7.

Some alternators used on diesel engines are equipped with an R terminal for the tachometer. On these units, if the alternator pulley is to be replaced, a pulley of the same diameter as the one removed must be installed, otherwise tachometer may provide inaccurate readings.

No maintenance or adjustments of any kind are required on this unit.

TROUBLE SHOOTING

SERVICE NOTE

If a condition of a dimly lit "No Charge" indicator lamp occurs under heavy electrical load on 1982 and some 1983 Cadillac Brougham and Deville models with Digital Fuel Injection, it may be caused by insufficient filtering of the "No Charge" indicator bulb.

This condition is not caused by a low charging rate but, by the alternator charging at near maximum capacity, with alternator voltage output in excess of battery voltage. This causes a voltage potential difference across the indicator lamp terminals, resulting in a dim bulb glow.

This condition can be checked by thoroughly testing the charging system. If all systems are satisfactory, the indicator lamp should be removed and a filter (GM part No. 25076102) installed over the bulb. The bulb should then

be reinstalled.

Undercharged Battery

1. Disconnect battery ground cable.
2. Disconnect wire at "BAT" terminal of alternator, connect ammeter, positive lead to "BAT" terminal and negative lead to wire.
3. Connect battery ground cable.
4. Turn on all accessories, then connect a carbon pile regulator across battery.
5. Operate engine at moderate speed, adjust carbon pile regulator to obtain maximum current output.
6. If ammeter reading is within 10 amps of rated output, alternator is not at fault.

NOTE: Alternator rated output is stamped on alternator frame.

7. If ammeter reading is not within 10 amps

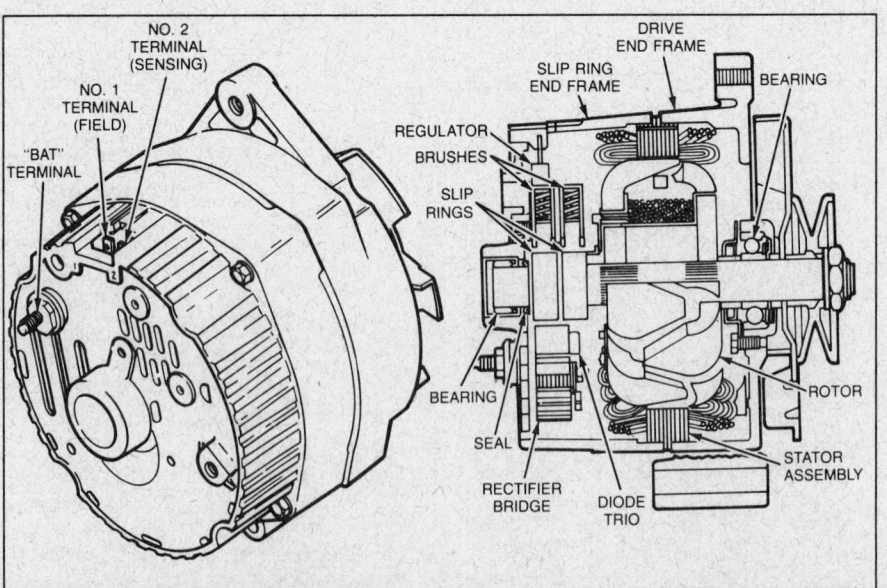

Fig. 1   Delcotron type 10 SI alternator (typical)

Fig. 2   Cross-sectional view of 10 SI alternator

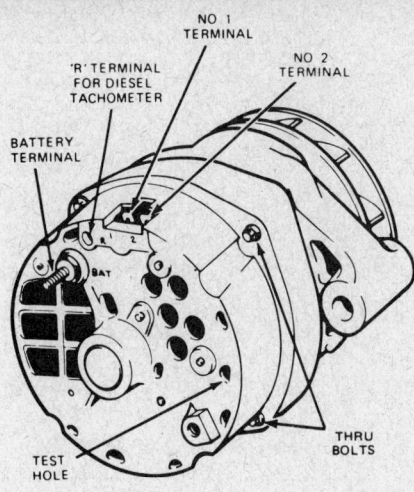

Fig. 3 Delcotron type 12 SI alternator

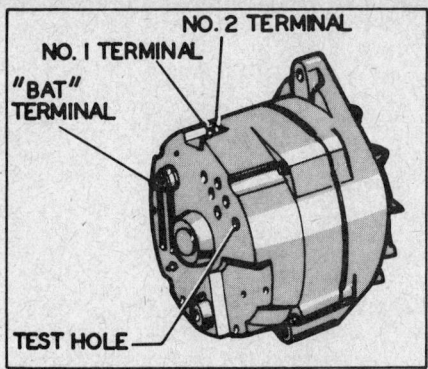

Fig. 4 Delcotron type 15 SI alternator

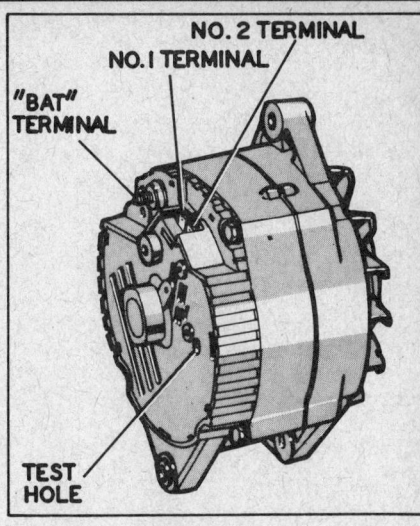

Fig. 5 Delcotron type 27 SI alternator

of rated output, ground field winding by inserting screw driver in end frame hole, contacting tab, Fig. 8.

NOTE: Do not insert screwdriver deeper than one inch since tab is usually located within 3/4 inch of casing surface.

8. If reading is within 10 amps of rated output, regulator must be replaced. If reading is not within limits, check field winding, diode trio, rectifier bridge and stator.
9. Turn off all accessories and disconnect ammeter and carbon pile regulator.

Overcharging Battery

1. Remove alternator from vehicle and separate end frames as outlined under "Alternator Disassembly."
2. Check field winding, if shorted replace rotor and regulator.
3. Connect ohmmeter from brush clip to end

frame, set meter on low scale and note reading. Fig. 9.
4. Reverse leads, if both readings are zero remove screw from brush clip and inspect sleeve and insulator.
5. If sleeve and insulator are in good condition, then regulator is at fault and must be replaced.

ALTERNATOR DISASSEMBLY

NOTE: When pressing bearings or seals from end frames, support frames from inside.

1. Scribe mark across end frames and stator ring so parts can be installed in same position.
2. Remove four through bolts, then using screw driver in stator slot pry end frames apart. Fig. 10.

NOTE: Brushes may fall from holders and become contaminated with bearing grease, if so they must be cleaned prior to assembly.

3. Place tape over slip ring end frame bearing and shaft at slip ring end.
4. Remove nut, washer, pulley, fan and collar from rotor shaft, then slide drive end frame from shaft.
5. Remove bearing, retainer and seal from drive and frame.
6. Remove stator lead attaching nuts, then pry stator from slip ring end frame.
7. Remove capacitor, diode trio, rectifier bridge and battery terminal stud.

NOTE: On diesel engine alternators equipped with R terminal for tachometer, the R terminal nut and jumper strap must be removed, before removing the rectifier bridge and battery terminal.

8. Remove resistor (if equipped), brush holder and regulator.
9. Remove bearing and seal from slip ring end frame.

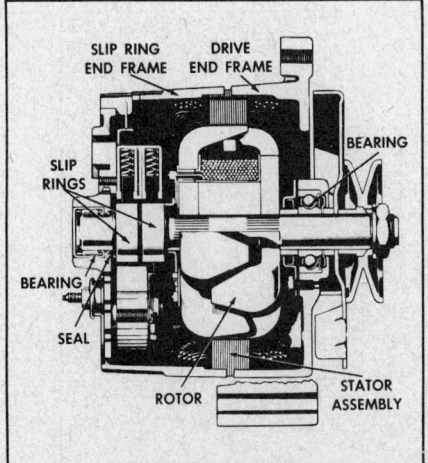

Fig. 6 Sectional view of Delcotron type SI alternator (typical)

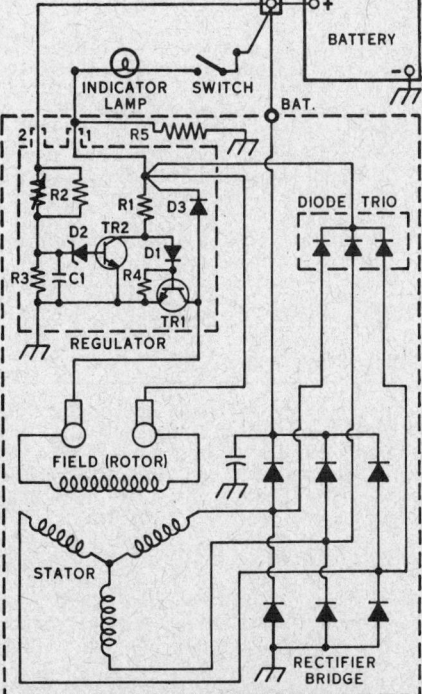

Fig. 7 Wiring diagram of charging circuit. 1977–83 G.M. vehicles

Fig. 8 Grounding field windings

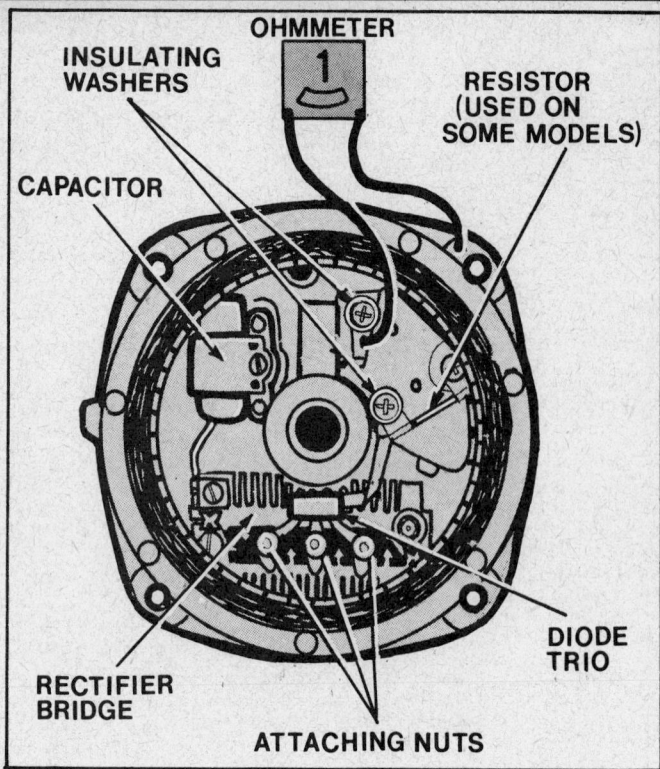

Fig. 9   Testing brush clip

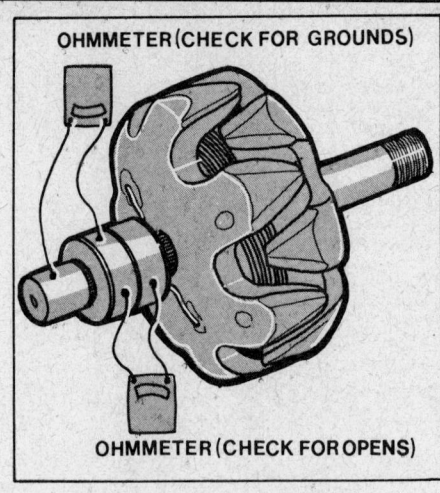

Fig. 11   Testing rotor & slip rings

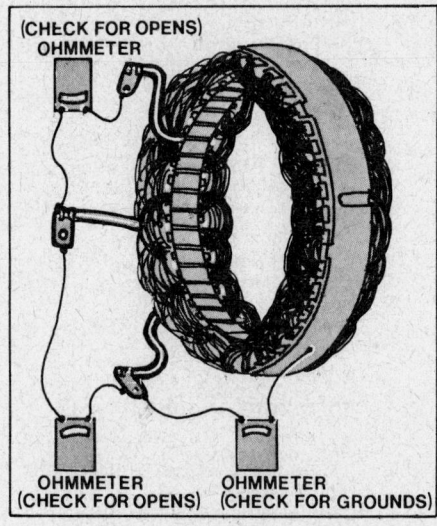

Fig. 12   Testing stator winding

BENCH TESTS

Rotor & Slip Ring Test

NOTE: Ohmmeter must be at low scale setting during this test.

1. Inspect rotor for wear or damage.
2. Touch ohmmeter leads to slip rings. Fig. 11.
3. If no reading is obtained an open circuit exists in windings.
4. If reading below 2.4 ohms on G.M., or 2.2 ohms on A.M.C. vehicles, is obtained, winding is shorted.
5. If a reading above 3 ohms, or 3.5 ohms on 1982–83 G.M. vehicles, is obtained, excessive resistance exists in windings.
6. Connect one ohmmeter lead to rotor shaft and touch slip rings with other lead, if any reading is obtained there is a ground in the circuit. Fig. 11.

NOTE: If any of the above problems are present the rotor assembly must be replaced.

Stator Winding Test

1. Inspect stator for discolored windings, loose connections and damage.
2. Connect an ohmmeter from stator lead to frame, if any reading is obtained windings are grounded. Fig. 12.
3. On 10 SI and 12 SI units, connect ohmmeter between stator leads, if reading is high when connected between each pair of leads, an open circuit exists in windings. The stator windings on 15 SI and 27 SI units cannot be checked for open circuits.

NOTE: Shorted windings are difficult to locate without special equipment. If other tests indicate normal, but rated alternator output cannot be obtained the windings are probably shorted.

Diode Trio

1. With diode unit removed, connect an ohmmeter to the single connector and to one of the three connectors. Fig. 13
2. Observe the reading. Reverse ohmmeter leads.
3. Reading should be high with one connection and low with the other. If both readings are the same, unit must be replaced.
4. Repeat between the single connector and each of the three connectors.

NOTE: There are two diode units differing in appearance. These are completely interchangeable.

The diode unit can be checked for a grounded brush lead while still installed in the end frame by connecting an ohmmeter from the brush lead clip to the end frame as in Steps 1 and 2 above. If both readings are zero, check for a grounded brush or brush lead.

Rectifier Bridge Test

1. Connect a suitable ohmmeter between grounded heat sink and one of the three flat metal clips surrounding the studs, Fig. 14.
2. Observe the reading then reverse leads.
3. Reading should be high with one connection and low with the other. If both readings are the same, unit must be re-

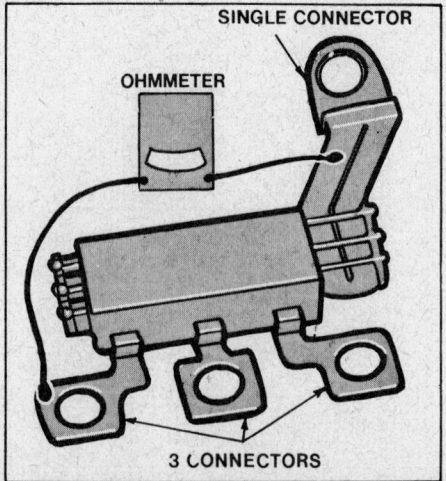

Fig. 13   Testing diode trio

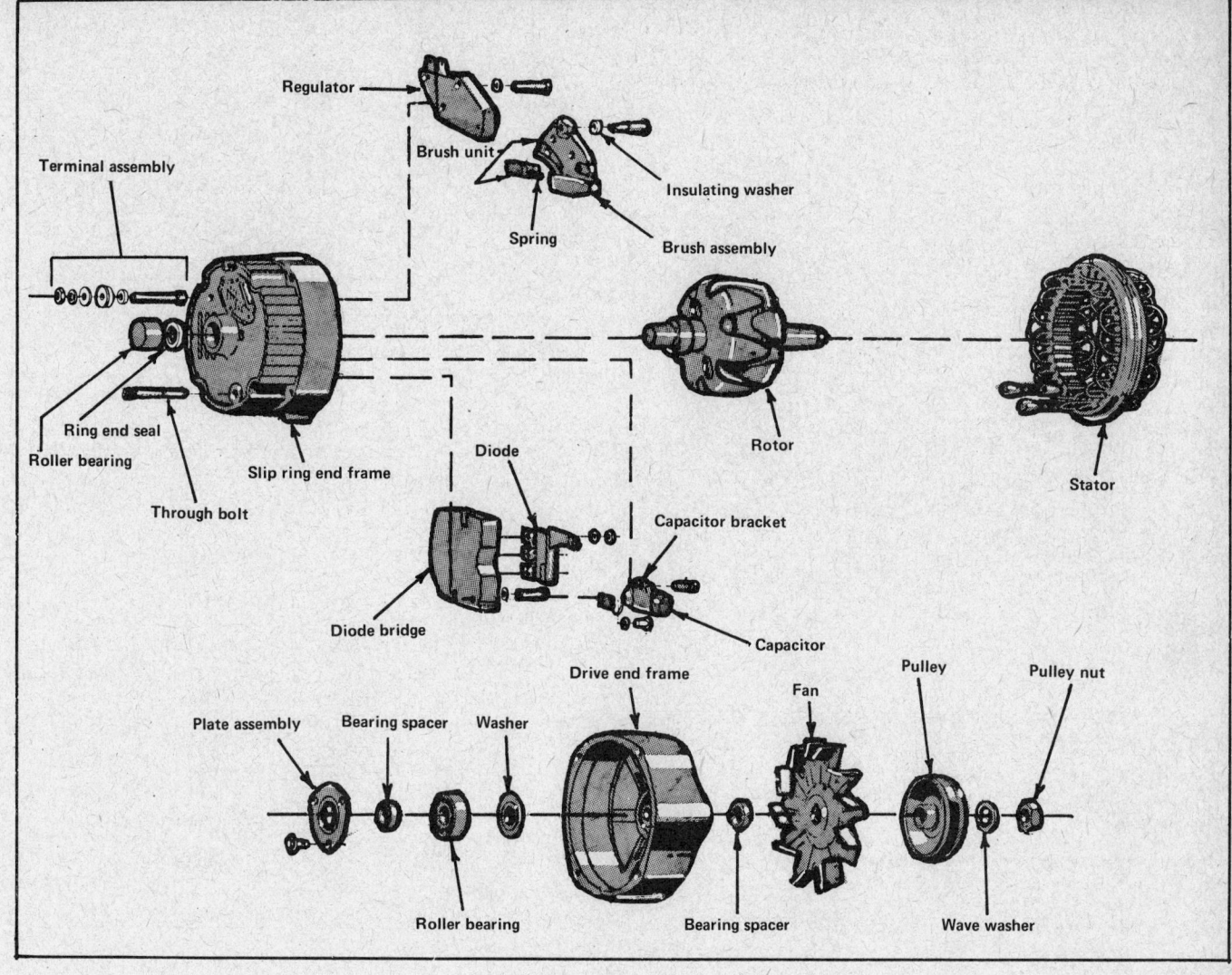

Fig. 10 Alternator disassembled

placed.
4. Repeat test for each of the other terminals.
5. Repeat entire test between insulated heat sink and three flat metal clips surrounding the studs.

Voltage Regulator/Brush Lead Test

Connect an ohmmeter from the brush lead clip to the end frame, note reading, then reverse connections. If both readings are zero, either the brush lead clip is grounded or the regulator is defective.

ALTERNATOR ASSEMBLY

NOTE: When pressing bearings or seals, end frames must be supported from inside.

1. Lightly lubricate seal and position on slip ring end frame with lip facing toward rotor. Fig. 10.
2. Press seal part way into housing.
3. On 10 S, 12 SI and 27 SI units, position

bearing and end plug on slip ring end frame, press bearing and plug in until flush with end frame. On 15 SI units, refer to Fig. 15, when installing slip ring end frame bearing.
4. Place regulator in end frame, install brushes and springs in brush holder, use pin to hold brushes in compressed position.

NOTE: Insulating washers are installed under two of the attaching screws, Fig. 16.

5. Install rectifier bridge and battery terminal stud.
6. On diesel engine alternators equipped with R terminal for tachometer, install plastic insulating washer on R terminal stud, then position terminal stud into end frame. Install fiber insulating washer, jumper strap and nut on R terminal stud. Position jumper strap on rectifier bridge, then tighten R terminal stud.
7. Install diode trio, ensure current only flows one way through single connector.
8. Install capacitor.

NOTE: On 15 SI units, the capacitor lead uses a push clip connector to attach to the rectifier bridge instead of a screw, Fig. 17.

9. Install stator, check the three leads for continuity, ensure stator is not grounded against case or holder.
10. On 1977–82 10 SI and 27 SI units, position slinger on drive end frame, then press ball bearing into end frame, Fig. 18. On 1977–82 and early production 1983 15 SI and 27 SI units, refer to Fig. 19, when installing drive end bearing. On late production 1983 15 SI and 27 SI units and 1983 10 SI and 12 SI units, refer to Fig. 20.
11. Fill seal cavity ¼ full with special alternator lubricant, then install retainer.
12. Install rotor in drive end frame, then install collar, fan, pulley, washer and nut.
13. Align scribe marks on end frames and stator plate, install through bolts and remove brush retaining pins.

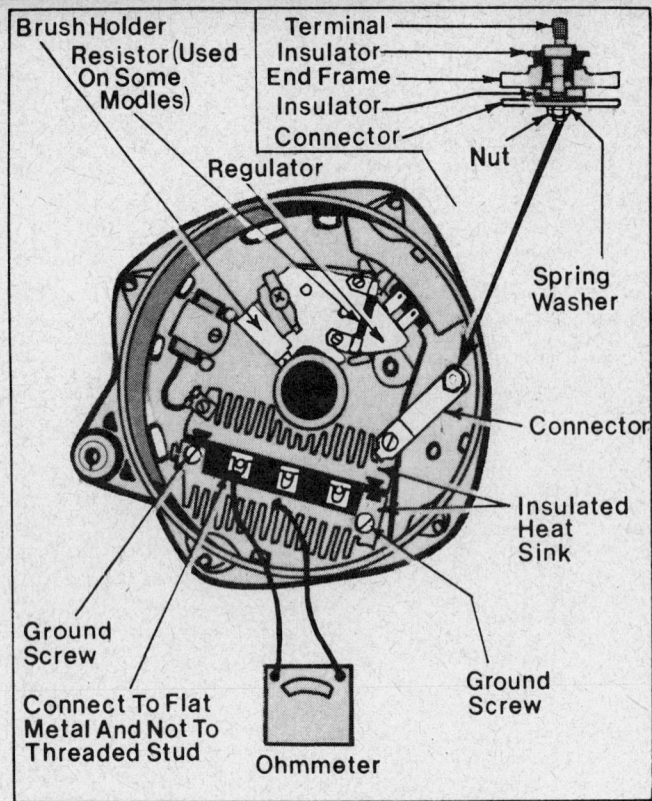

Fig. 14   Testing rectifier bridge diodes

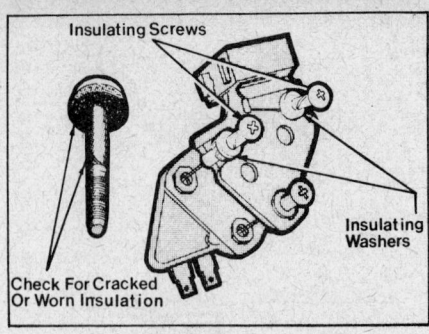

Fig. 16   Brush holder & regulator installation

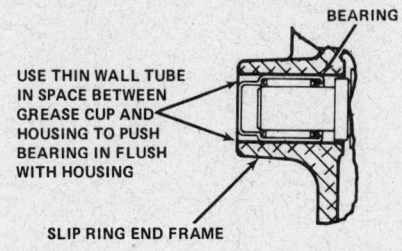

Fig. 15   Installing slip ring end frame bearing. 15 SI units

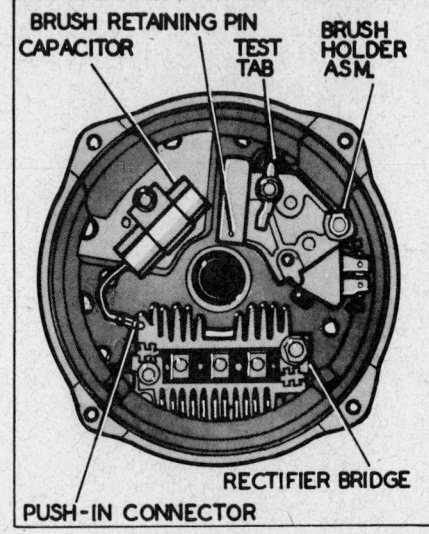

Fig. 17   Slip ring end frame. 15 SI units

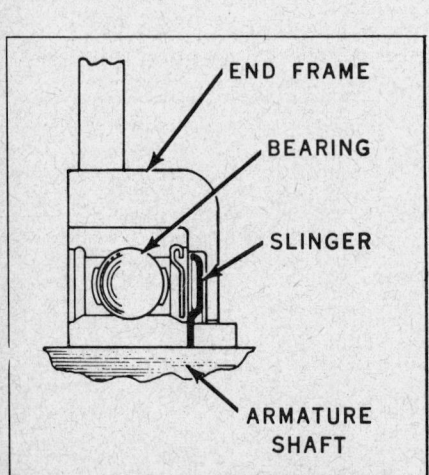

Fig. 18   Drive end frame bearing & slinger installed. 1977–82 10 SI & 27 SI units

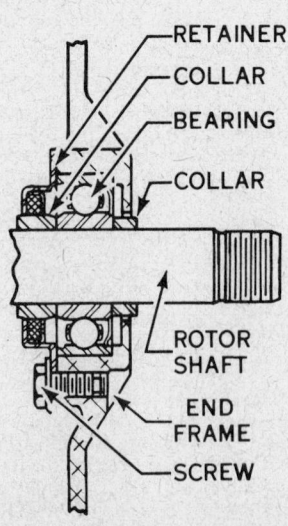

Fig. 19   Drive end frame bearing. 1977–82 15 SI & 1983 early production 15 SI & 27 SI units

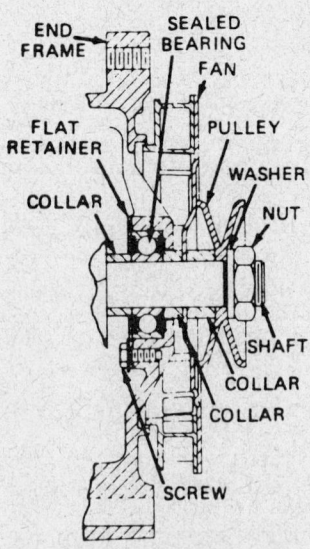

Fig. 20   Drive end frame bearing. 1983 10 SI & 12 SI & 1983 late production 15 SI & 27 SI

Ford Motorcraft Alternator

CONTENTS

GENERAL

A charge indicator lamp or ammeter can be used in charging system.

If a charge indicator lamp is used in the charging system, Figs. 1, 3 and 5, the system operation is as follows: when the ignition switch is turned ON, a small electrical current flows through the lamp filament (turning the lamp on) and through the alternator regulator to the alternator field. When the engine is started, the alternator field rotates and produces a voltage in the stator winding. When the voltage at the alternator stator terminal reaches about 3 volts, the regulator field relay closes. This puts the same voltage potential on both sides of the charge indicator lamp causing it to go out. When the field relay has closed, current passes through the regulator A terminal and is metered to the alternator field.

If an ammeter is used in the charging system, Figs. 2, 4 and 6, the regulator 1 terminal and the alternator stator terminal are not used. When the ignition switch is turned ON, the field relay closes and electrical current passes through the regulator A terminal and is metered to the alternator field. When the engine is started, the alternator field rotates causing the alternator to operate.

Some 1978 and all 1979-83 Ford vehicles are equipped with new electronic voltage regulators, Figs. 7 and 8. These solid state regulators are used in conjunction with other new components in the charging system such as an alternator with a higher field current requirement, a warning indicator lamp shunt resistor (500 ohms) and a new wiring harness with a new regulator connector. When replacing system components, note the following precautions:

1. Always use the proper alternator in the system. If the 1978-83 alternator is installed on previous model systems, it will destroy the electro-mechanical regulator. If the older model alternator is used on the new system, it will have a reduced output.
2. Do not use an electro-mechanical regulator in the new system since the wiring harness connector will not index properly with this type of regulator.
3. The new electronic regulators are color coded for proper installation. The black color coded unit is installed in systems equipped with a warning indicator lamp. The blue color coded regulator is installed in systems equipped with an ammeter.
4. The new systems use a 500 ohm resistor on the rear of the instrument cluster on vehicles equipped with a warning indicator lamp. Do not replace this resistor with the 15 ohm resistance wire used on previous systems.

On the new systems with an indicator lamp, closing the ignition switch energizes the warning lamp and turns on the regulator output stage. The alternator receives maximum field current and is ready to generate an output voltage. As the alternator rotor speed increases, the output and stator terminal voltages increase from zero to the system regulation level determined by the regulator setting. When the ignition switch is turned off, the solid state relay circuit turns the output stage off, interrupting current flow through the regulator so there is not a current drain on the battery.

On vehicles equipped with an ammeter, the operating principle is similar.

NOTE: The ammeter indicates current flow into (charge) or out of (discharge) the vehicle battery.

SYSTEM TESTING

NOTE: The operations and on vehicle test procedures for the side terminal alternator are same as for rear terminal alternator. However, the internal wiring, Figs. 3 through 6, and bench test procedures differ.

In-Vehicle Voltmeter Test

NOTE: *All lights and electrical systems in the off position, parking brake applied, transmission in neutral and a charged battery (at least 1.200 specific gravity).*

1. Connect the negative lead of the voltmeter to the negative battery cable clamp (not bolt or nut).

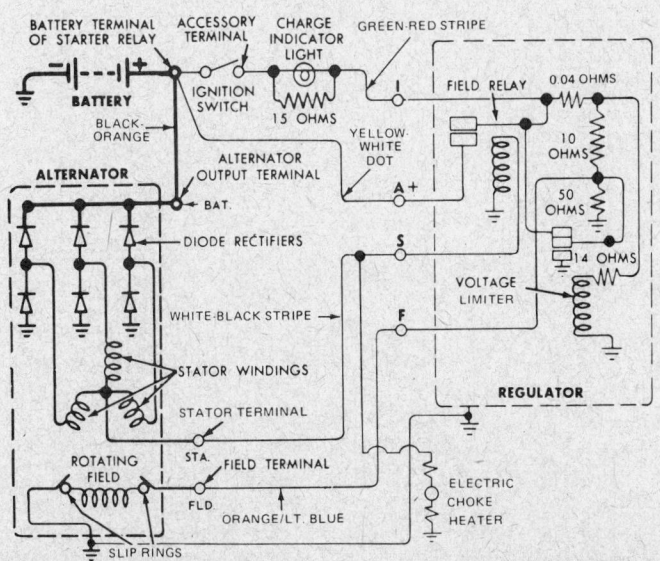

Fig. 1 Indicator light rear terminal alternator charging circuit

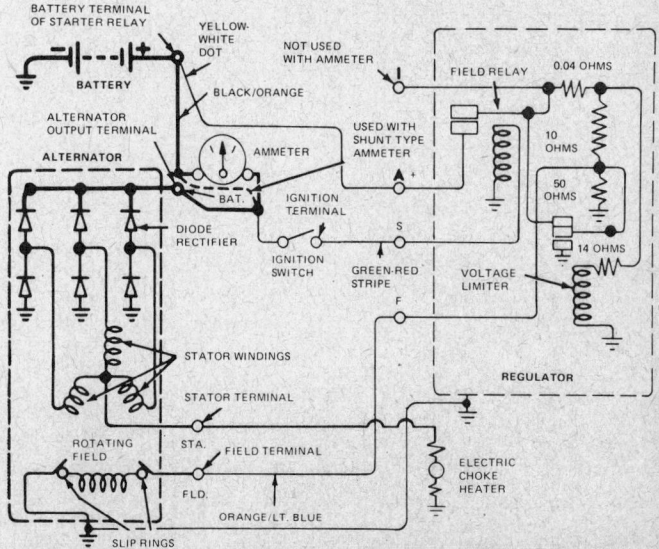

Fig. 2 Ammeter rear terminal alternator charging circuit

ALTERNATOR SYSTEMS

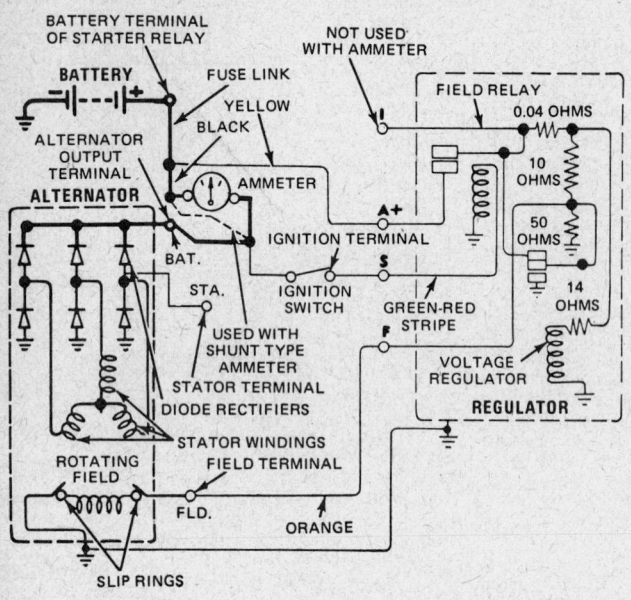

Fig. 3 Indicator light side terminal alternator charging system.
70 amp system

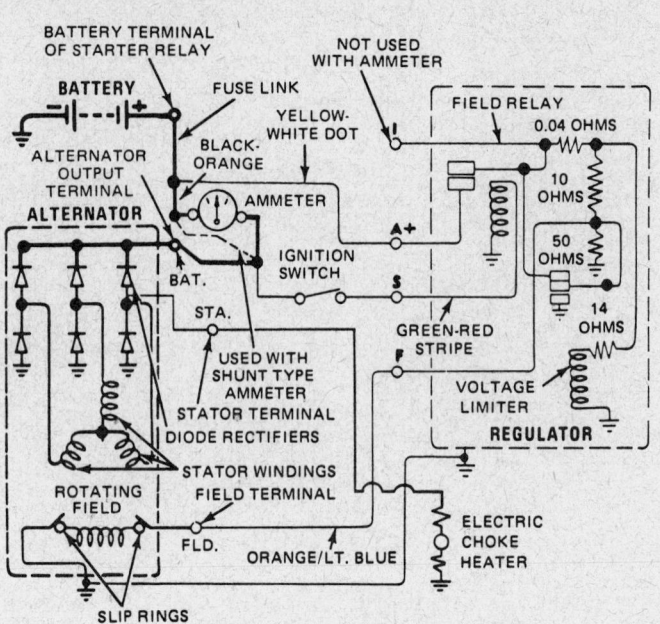

Fig. 4 Ammeter side terminal alternator charging system.
70 amp system

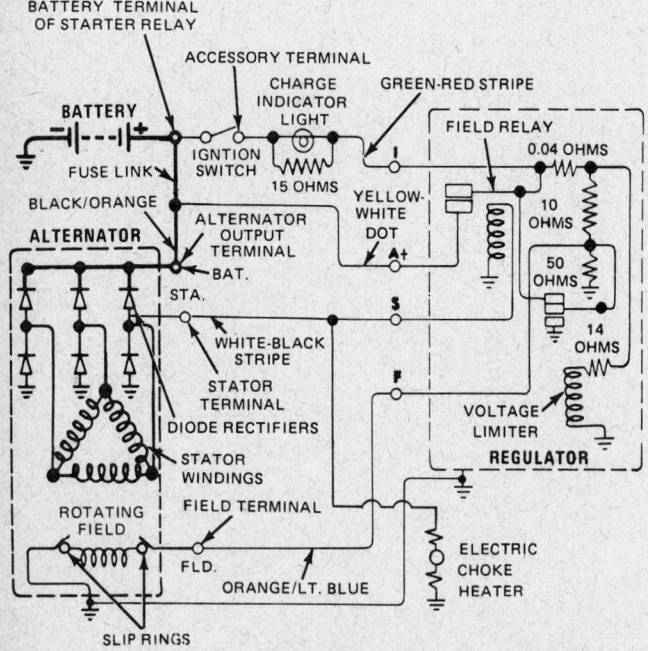

Fig. 5 Indicator light side terminal alternator charging system.
90 amp system

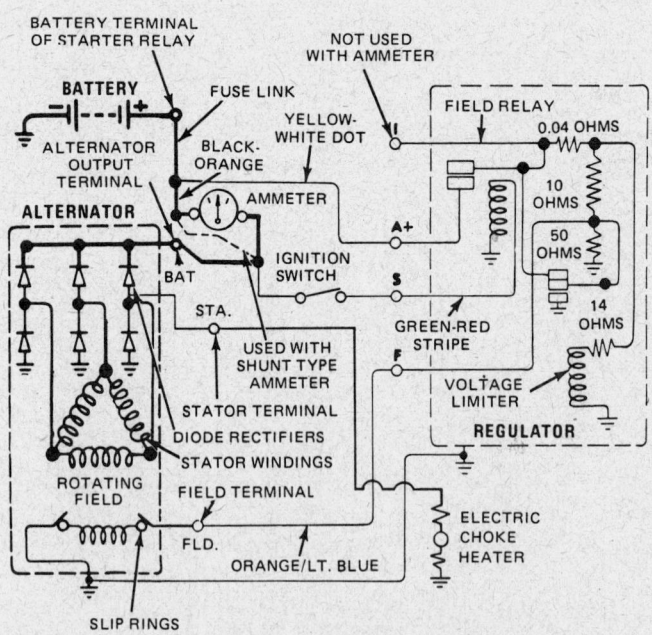

Fig. 6 Ammeter side terminal alternator charging system.
90 amp system

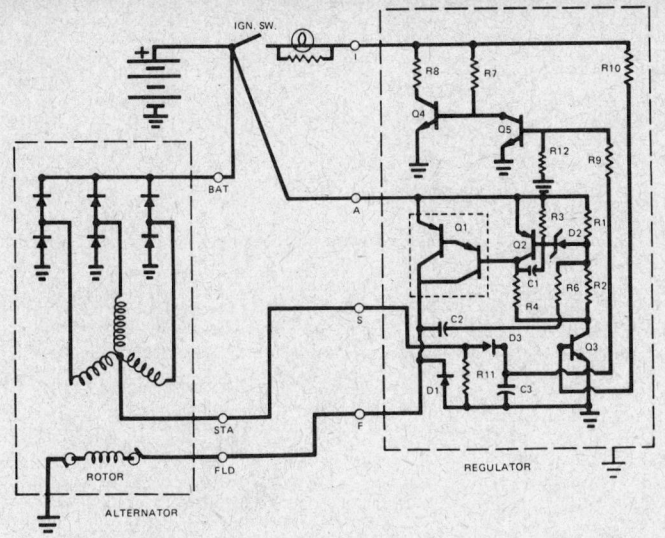

Fig. 7 Indicator light charging system with electronic voltage regulator

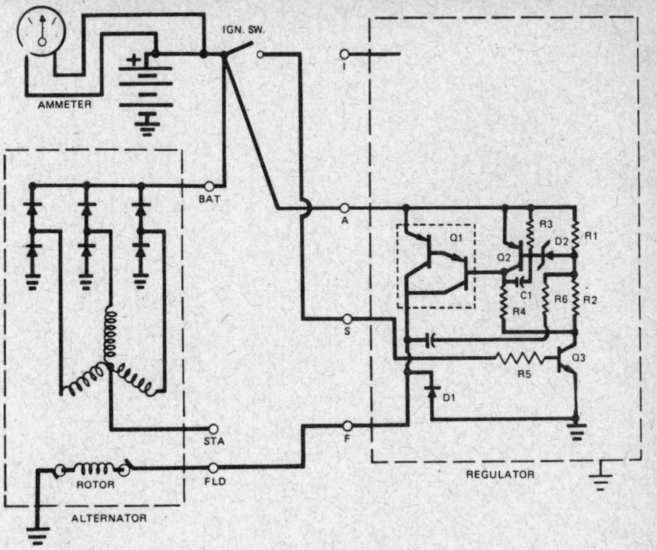

Fig. 8 Ammeter charging system with electronic voltage regulator

2. Connect the positive lead of the voltmeter to the positive battery cable clamp (not bolt or nut).
3. Record the battery voltage reading shown on the voltmeter scale.
4. Connect the red lead of a tachometer to the distributor terminal of the coil and the black tachometer lead to a good ground.
5. Then, start and operate the engine at approximately 1500 rpm. With no other electrical load (foot off brake pedal and car doors closed), the voltmeter reading should increase but not exceed (2 volts) above the first recorded battery voltage reading. The reading should be taken when the voltmeter needles stops moving.
6. With the engine running, turn on the heater and/or air conditioner blower motor to high speed and headlights to high beam.
7. Increase the engine speed to 2000 rpm. The voltmeter should indicate a minimum reading of 0.5 volts above the battery voltage, Fig. 9.

NOTE: *If the above tests indicate proper voltage*

readings, the charging system is operating normally. Proceed to "Test Results" if a problem still exists.

TEST RESULTS

1. If voltmeter reading indicates 2 volts over battery voltage (over voltage), proceed as follows:
   a. Stop the engine and check the ground connections between the regulator and alternator and/or regulator to engine. Clean and tighten connections securely and repeat the *Voltmeter Test Procedures.*
   b. If *over voltage* condition still exists, disconnect the regulator wiring plug from the regulator and repeat the *Voltmeter Test Procedures.*
   c. If *over voltage* still exists with the regulator wiring plug disconnected, repair the short in the wiring harness between the alternator and regulator. Then, replace the regulator and connect the regulator wiring plug to the regulator and repeat the *Voltmeter Test Procedures.*

2. On 1977 units, if voltmeter does not indicate more than 1/2 volt above battery voltage, proceed as follows:
   a. Check for presence of battery voltage at alternator BAT terminal and the regulator plug A terminal, Fig. 10. Repair the wiring if no voltage is present at these terminals, and repeat the *Voltmeter Test Procedures.*
   b. If voltmeter reading does not increase 1/2 volt above battery voltage, proceed to next step.
   c. Before performing other tests, the field circuit (regulator plug to alternator) must be checked for a grounding condition. If the field circuit is grounded and the jumper wire is used as a check at the regulator wiring plug from the A to F terminals, Fig. 10, excessive current will cause heat damage to the regulator wiring plug terminals and may burn the jumper wire, Fig. 10. Also, if the field circuit was grounded, the connector wire inside the regulator will be burned open and an under voltage condition will result.
   d. The field circuit should be checked with the regulator wiring plug disconnected and an ohmmeter connected

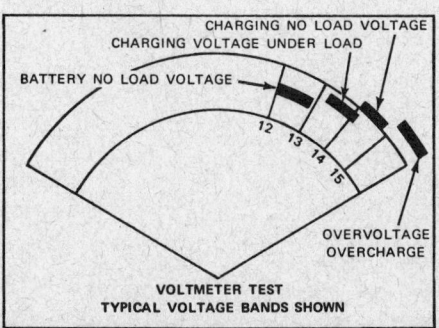

Fig. 9 Voltmeter test scale

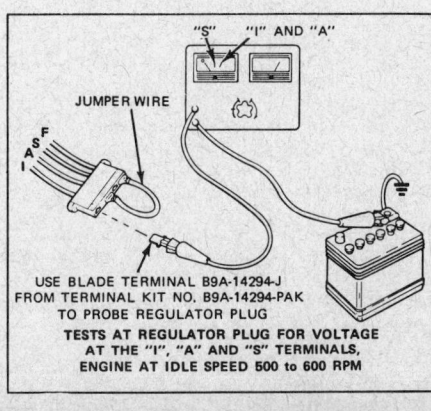

Fig. 10 Regulator plug voltage test

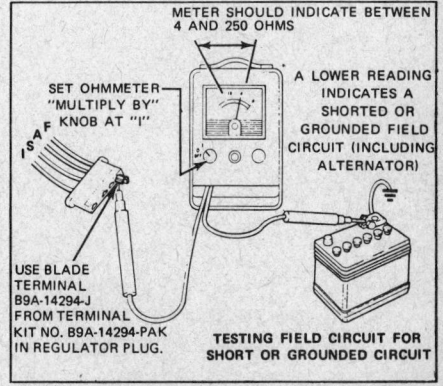

Fig. 11 Testing field circuit with ohmmeter

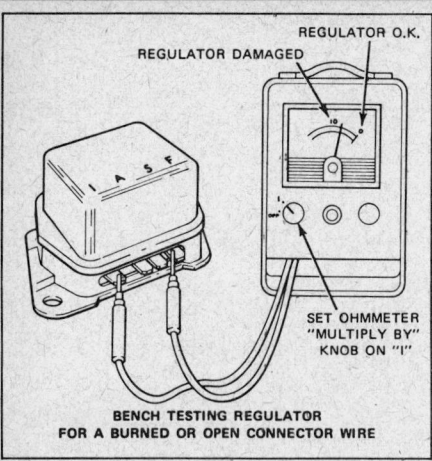

Fig. 12 Testing regulator for a burned or open connector wire

from the *F* terminal of the regulator wiring plug to the battery ground. The ohmmeter should indicate between 4 and 250 ohms, Fig. 11.

e. A check for the regulator burned-open wire is made by connecting an ohmmeter from the *I* to *F* terminals of the regulator, Fig. 12. The reading should indicate *O* (no resistance). If the reading indicates approximately *10 ohms*, the connector wire inside the regulator is burned open. *The field circuit grounded condition must be found and repaired before installing a new regulator.*

3. On 1978–83 units, if voltmeter does not indicate more than ½ volt above battery voltage, proceed as follows:

a. Disconnect voltage regulator wire connector and connect an ohmmeter between wire connector F terminal and ground. Ohmmeter reading should indicate more than 3 ohms. If reading is less than 3 ohms, repair grounded field circuit and repeat Voltmeter Test procedure.

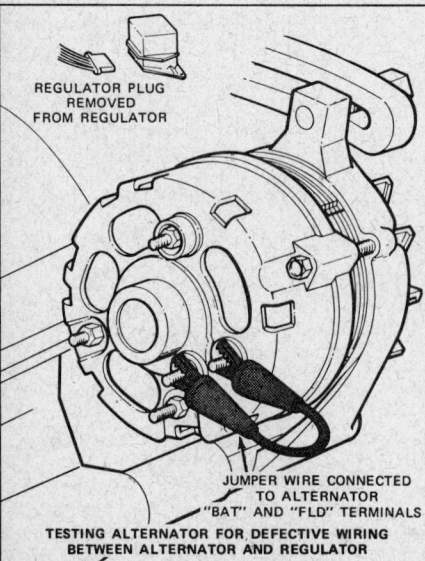

Fig. 14 Rear terminal alternator. Jumper wire connection

b. If ohmmeter reading is more than 3 ohms, connect a jumper wire between voltage regulator wire connector terminals A and F, Fig. 13, then repeat Voltmeter Test procedure. If voltmeter reading is now more than ½ volt above battery voltage, the voltage regulator or wiring is defective, refer to Regulator Test.

c. If voltmeter still indicates less than ½ volt, disconnect jumper wire from voltage regulator wire connector and leave connector disconnected from regulator. Connect a jumper wire between alternator FLD and BAT terminals, Figs. 14 and 15, then repeat Voltmeter Test procedures.

d. If voltmeter reading now indicates ½ volt or more above battery voltage, repair alternator to regulator wiring harness.

e. If voltmeter still indicates less than ½ volt above battery voltage, stop engine and move voltmeter positive lead to alternator BAT terminal.

f. If voltmeter now indicates battery voltage, the alternator should be removed, inspected and repaired. If zero volts is indicated, repair BAT terminal wiring.

Field Circuit and Alternator Tests

1. If the field circuit is satisfactory, disconnect the regulator wiring plug at the regulator and connect the jumper wire from the *A* to the *F* terminals on the regulator wiring plug, Fig. 13.
2. Repeat the *Voltmeter Test Procedures.*
3. If the *Voltmeter Test Procedures* still indicate a problem of under voltage, remove the jumper wire at the regulator plug and leave the plug disconnected from the regulator, Figs. 14 and 15. Connect a jumper wire to the *FLD* and *BAT* terminals on the alternator, Figs. 14 and 15.
4. Repeat the *Voltmeter Test Procedures.*
5. If the *Voltmeter Test* are now satisfactory, repair the wiring harness from the alternator to the regulator. Then, remove the jumper wire at the alternator and connect the regulator wiring plug to the regulator.
6. Repeat the *Voltmeter Test Procedures,* to be sure the charging system is operating normally.
7. If the *Voltmeter Test* results still indicate under voltage, repair or replace the alternator. With the jumper wire removed, connect the wiring to the alternator and regulator.
8. Repeat the *Voltmeter Test Procedures.*

Diode Test

Test Procedure
1. Disconnect electric choke, if equipped.
2. Disconnect voltage regulator wiring connector.
3. Connect a jumper wire between the "A" and "F" terminals of the voltage regulator wiring connector, Fig. 13.
4. Connect voltmeter to battery clamps. Then, start and idle engine.
5. Observe and note voltmeter reading.
6. Move the voltmeter positive lead to the alternator "S" terminal and note voltage reading.

Test Results
1. If voltmeter reading is within ½ of battery voltage, the diodes are satisfactory.
2. If voltmeter reading is approximately 1.5 volts, the alternator has a shorted nega-

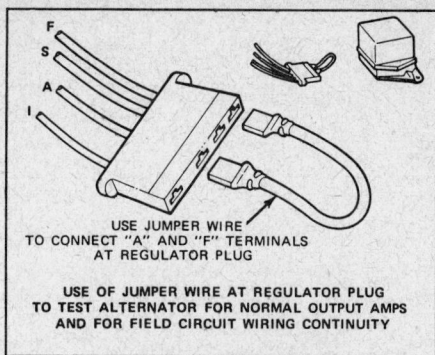

USE OF JUMPER WIRE AT REGULATOR PLUG TO TEST ALTERNATOR FOR NORMAL OUTPUT AMPS AND FOR FIELD CIRCUIT WIRING CONTINUITY

Fig. 13 Regulator plug. Jumper wire connection

tive diode or a grounded stator winding.
3. If voltmeter reading is approximately 1.5 volts less than battery voltage, the alternator has a shorted positive diode.
4. If voltage reading is approximately 1 to 1.5 volts less than ½ battery voltage, the alternator has an open positive diode.
5. If voltage reading is 1 to 1.5 volts above ½ battery voltage, the alternator has an open negative diode.
6. Reconnect electric choke into circuit after tests are completed, if equipped.

Regulator Tests

S Circuit Test—With Ammeter

1. Connect the positive lead of the voltmeter to the *S* terminal of the regulator wiring plug Fig. 10. Turn the ignition switch to the *ON* position. *Do not start the engine.*
2. The voltmeter reading should indicate battery voltage.
3. If there is *no* voltage reading, disconnect the positive voltmeter lead from the positive battery clamp and repair the *S* wire lead from the ignition switch to the regulator wiring plug.
4. Connect the positive voltmeter lead to the positive battery cable terminal and repeat the *Voltmeter Test Procedures.*

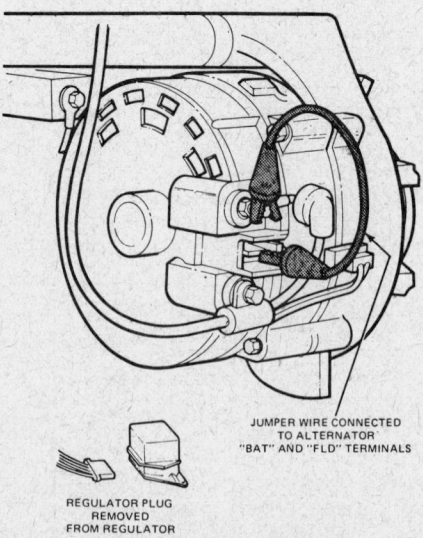

Fig. 15 Side terminal alternator. Jumper wire connector

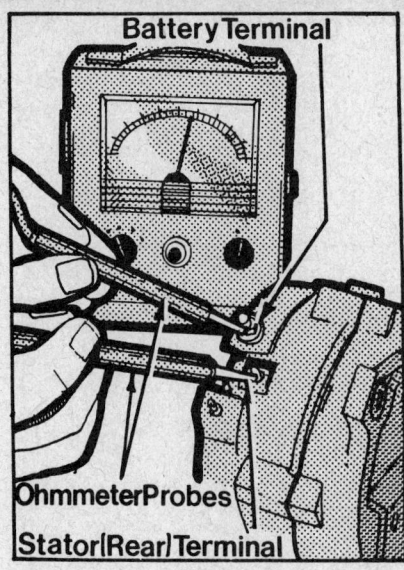

Fig. 16 Side terminal alternator rectifier short or grounded & stator grounded test

S and I Circuit Test—With Indicator Light

1. Disconnect regulator wiring plug, then install a suitable jumper wire between connector "A" and "F" terminals, Fig. 13.
2. With the engine idling, connect the positive lead of the voltmeter to the *S* terminal and then to the *I* terminal of the regulator wiring plug. Fig. 10. The voltage of the *S* circuit should read approximately 1/2 of the *I* circuit.
3. If no voltage is present, repair the alternator or the wiring circuit at fault. Reconnect the positive voltmeter lead to the positive battery cable terminal and repeat the *Voltmeter Test Procedures.*
4. If the above tests are satisfactory, install a new regulator.
5. Then, remove the jumper wire from the regulator wiring plug and connect the wiring plug to the regulator. Repeat the *Voltmeter Test Procedures.*

Bench Tests

Rectifier Short or Grounded and Stator Grounded Test

Using a suitable ohmmeter, connect one probe to the alternator BAT terminal, Fig. 16, the other probe to the STA terminal (rear blade terminal). Then, reverse the ohmmeter probes and repeat the test. A reading of about 60 ohms should be obtained in one direction and no needle movement with the probes reversed. A reading in both directions indicates a bad positive diode, a grounded positive diode plate or a grounded BAT terminal.

Perform the same test using the STA and GND (ground) terminals of the alternator. A reading in both directions indicates either a bad negative diode, a grounded stator winding, a grounded stator terminal, a grounded positive diode plate, or a grounded BAT terminal.

Infinite readings (no needle movement) in all four probe positions in the preceeding tests indicates an open STA terminal lead connection inside the alternator.

Field Open of Short Circuit Test

Using a suitable ohmmeter, connect the alternator field terminal with one probe and the ground terminal with the other probe, Fig. 17. Then, spin the alternator pulley. The ohmmeter reading should be between 3.5 and 250 ohms on 1977 units, 2.4 and 25 ohms on 1978–80 units 2.4 and 100 ohms on 1981–83 units, and should fluctuate while the pulley is turning. An infinite reading (no meter movement) indicates an open brush lead, worn or stuck brushes, or a bad rotor assembly. An ohmmeter reading less than 3.5 ohms on 1977 units or 2.4 ohms on 1978–83 units indicates a grounded brush assembly, a grounded field terminal or a bad rotor.

Diode Test

To test one set of diodes, contact one probe of a suitable ohmmeter to the terminal bolt, Figs. 18 and 19 and contact each of the three stator lead terminals with the other probe. Reverse the probes and repeat the test. All diodes should show a low reading of about 60 ohms in one direction, and an infinite reading (no needle movement) with the probes reversed. Repeat the preceding tests for the other set of diodes except that the other terminal screw is used.

If the meter readings are not as specified, replace the rectifier assembly.

Stator Coil Open or Grounded Test

Disassemble the stator from the alternator, using a suitable ohmmeter connected between each pair of stator leads (3 different ways). The ohmmeter must show equal readings for each pair or stator leads. Replace the stator if the readings are not the same.

Connect the ohmmeter probes to one of the

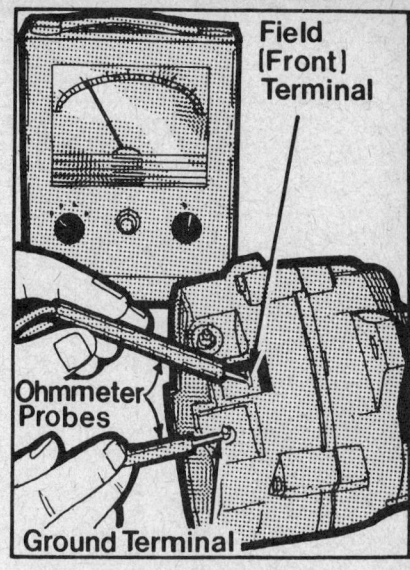

Fig. 17 Side terminal alternator field open or short circuit test

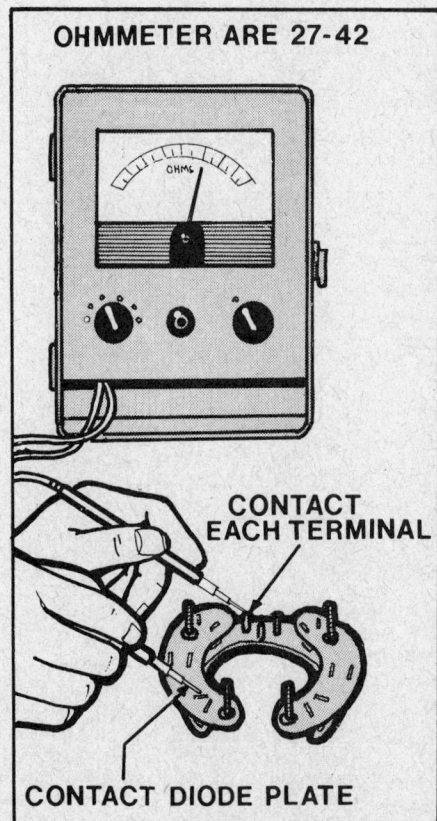

Fig. 18 Rear terminal diode test

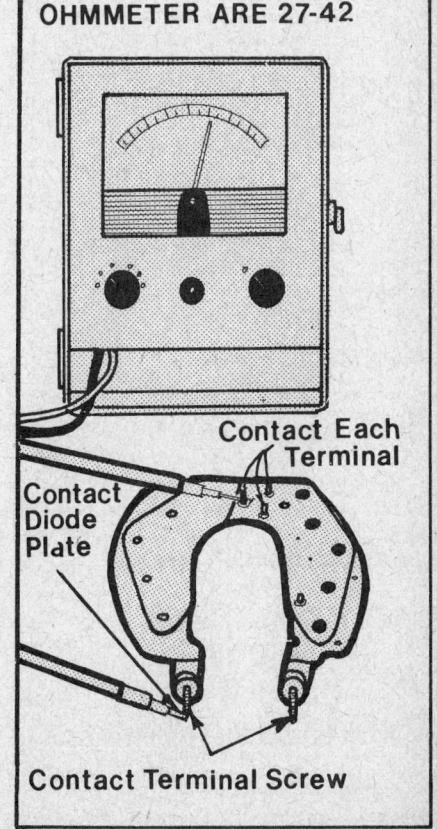

Fig. 19 Side terminal alternator diode test

ALTERNATOR SYSTEMS

stator leads and to the stator laminated core. Be sure that the probe makes a good electrical connection with the stator core. The meter should show an infinite reading (no meter movement). If the meter does not indicate an infinite reading (needle moves), the stator winding is shorted to the core and must be replaced. Repeat this test for each stator lead.

Rotor Open or Short Circuit Test

Disassemble the front housing and rotor from the rear housing and stator.

Contact each ohmmeter probe to a rotor slip ring. The meter reading should be 3.5 to 4.5 ohms on 1977 units, 2.4 to 4.9 ohms on 1978–80 units, and 2.0 to 3.5 ohms on 1981–83 units. A higher reading indicates a damaged slip ring solder connection or a broken wire. A lower reading indicates a shorted wire or slip ring.

Contact one ohmmeter probe to a slip ring and the other probe to the rotor shaft. The meter reading should be infinite (no deflection). A reading other than infinite indicates the rotor is shorted to the shaft. Inspect the slip ring soldered terminals to be sure they are not bent and touching the rotor shaft, or that excess solder is not grounding the rotor coil connections to the shaft. Replace the rotor if it is shorted and cannot be repaired.

REGULATOR ADJUSTMENTS

1977–78 Transistorized Regulator

The only adjustment of this regulator is the voltage limiter adjustment. This adjustment is made with regulator at normal operating temperature. Remove the regulator cover and using a fiber rod, turn voltage adjusting screw clockwise to raise voltage setting or counterclockwise to lower voltage setting, Fig. 20. Refer to the "Alternator & Regulator Specifications" as listed in the individual car chapters for proper voltage setting.

1977–78 Electro-Mechanical & 1978–83 Electronic Regulators

These regulators are factory calibrated and sealed and no adjustment is possible. If regulator calibration values are not within specifications, the regulator must be replaced.

ALTERNATOR REPAIRS
Rear Terminal Alternator

NOTE: Use a 100 watt soldering iron.

Disassembly

1. Mark both end housings and the stator with a scribe mark for assembly, Fig. 21.
2. Remove the three housing through bolts.
3. Separate the front housing and rotor from the stator and rear housing.
4. Remove all the nuts and insulators from the rear housing and remove the rear housing from the stator and rectifier assembly.

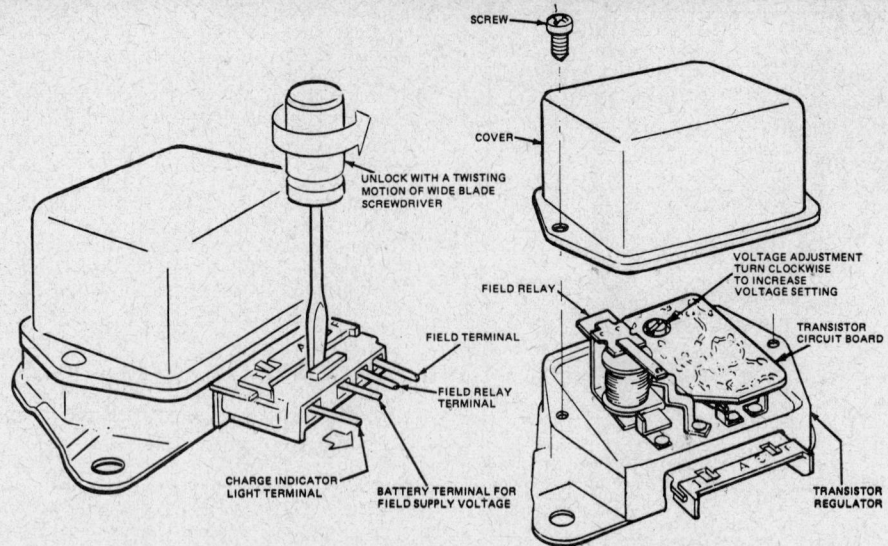

Fig. 20 Transistorized regulator adjustment, 1977–78

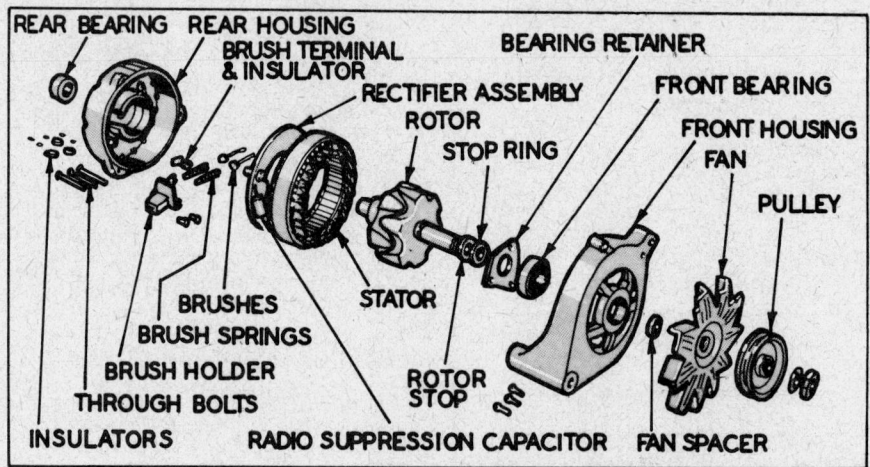

Fig. 21 Disassembled rear terminal alternator

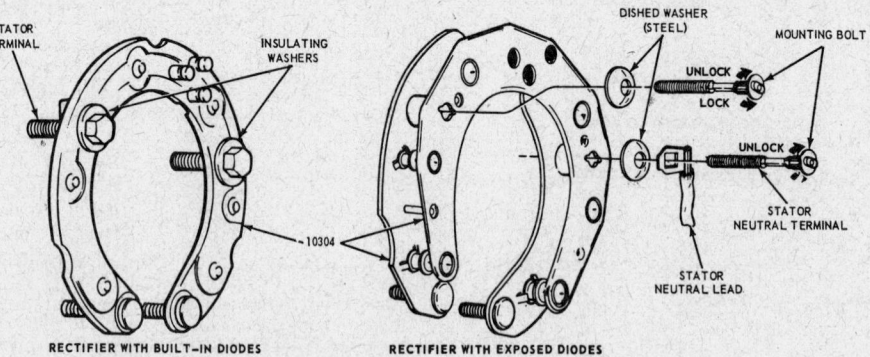

Fig. 22 Rectifier assembly

5. Remove the brush holder mounting screws and remove the holder, brushes, brush springs, insulator and terminal.
6. If replacement is necessary, press the bearing from the rear housing, supporting the housing on the inner boss.
7. If the rectifier assembly is being replaced, unsolder the stator leads from the printed-circuit board terminals, and separate the stator from the rectifier assembly.
8. Original production alternators will have one of two types of rectifier assembly circuit boards, Fig. 22; one has the circuit board spaced away from the diode plates with the diodes exposed. Another type is a single circuit board with built-in diodes.

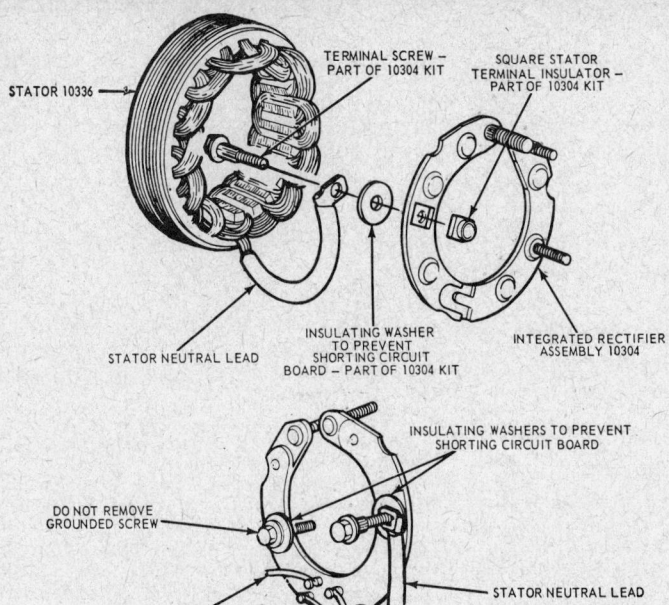

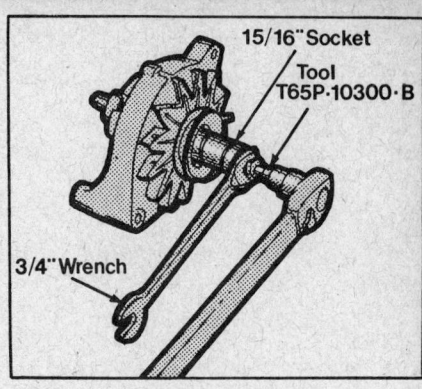

Fig. 24 Typical pulley removal

Fig. 23 Stator terminal installation.
Integral rectifier circuit board

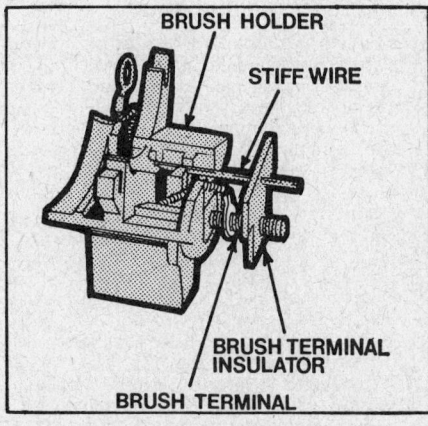

Fig. 25 Brush holder assembly

If the alternator rectifier has an exposed diode circuit board, remove the screws from the rectifier by rotating the bolt heads 1/4 turn clockwise to unlock them and then remove the screws, Fig. 22. Push the stator terminal screw straight out on a rectifier with the diodes built into the circuit board, Fig. 22. Avoid turning the screw while removing to make certain that the straight knurl will engage the insulators when installing. Do not remove the grounded screw, Fig. 23.

9. Remove the drive pulley nut, Fig. 24, then, pull the lockwasher, pulley, fan, fan spacer, front housing and rotor stop from the rotor shaft.

10. Remove the three screws that hold the front end bearing retainer, and remove the retainer. If the bearing is damaged or has lost its lubricant, support the housing close to the bearing boss and press out the old bearing from the housing.

11. Perform a diode test and a field open or short circuit test.

Assembly

NOTE: Refer to "Cleaning and Inspection" procedures before reassembly.

1. The rotor, stator and bearings must not be cleaned with solvent. Wipe these parts off with a clean cloth.

2. Press the front bearing in the front housing bearing boss (put pressure on the outer race only), and install the bearing retainer, Fig. 21.

3. If the stop-ring on the rotor drive shaft was damaged, install a new stop-ring. Push the new ring on the shaft and into the groove.

NOTE: *Do not open the ring with snap ring pliers as permanent damage will result.*

4. Position the rotor stop on the drive shaft with the recessed side against the stop-ring.

5. Position the front housing, fan spacer, fan, pulley and lock washer on the drive shaft and install the retaining nut. Torque the retaining nut, Fig. 24, to 60–100 ft lbs.

Fig. 26 Typical brush lead positions

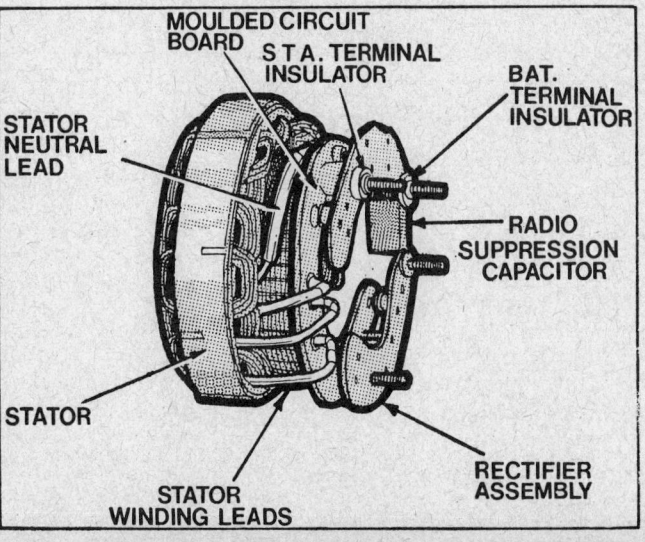

Fig. 27 Stator lead connections

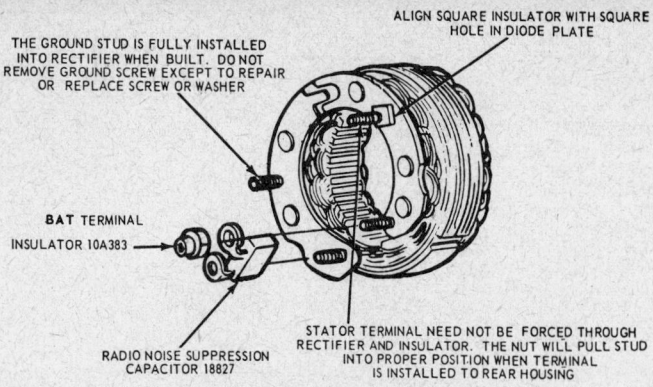

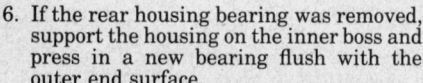

Fig. 28 Fiber-glass circuit board terminal insulators

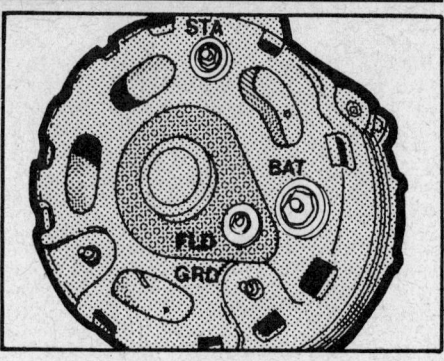

Fig. 29 Alternator terminal locations

6. If the rear housing bearing was removed, support the housing on the inner boss and press in a new bearing flush with the outer end surface.

7. Place the brush springs, brushes, brush terminal and terminal insulator in the brush holder and hold the brushes in position by inserting a piece of stiff wire in the brush holder, Fig. 25.

8. Position the brush holder assembly in the rear housing and install the mounting screws. Position the brush leads in the brush holder, Fig. 26.

9. Wrap the three stator winding leads around the circuit board terminals and solder them. Position the stator neutral lead eyelet on the stator terminal screw and install the screw in the rectifier assembly, Fig. 27.

10. For a rectifier with the diodes exposed insert the special screws through the wire lug, dished washers and circuit board, Fig. 22. Turn them 1/4 turn counterclockwise to lock them. For single circuit boards with built in diodes, insert the screws straight through the wire lug, insulating washer and rectifier into the insulator, Fig. 23.

NOTE: The dished washers are to be used only on the circuit board with exposed diodes, Fig. 22. If they are used on the single circuit board, a short circuit will occur. A flat insulating washer is to be used between the stator terminal and the board when a single circuit board is used,

Fig. 23.

11. Position the radio noise suppression capacitor on the rectifier terminals. On the circuit board with exposed diodes, install the STA and BAT terminal insulators, Fig. 27. On the single circuit board, position the square stator-terminal insulator in the square hole in the rectifier assembly, Fig. 23. Position the BAT terminal insulator, Fig. 28.

Position the stator and rectifier assembly in the rear housing. Make certain that all terminal insulators are seated properly in the recesses, Fig. 27. Position the STA (black), BAT (red) and FLD (orange) insulators on the terminal bolts, and install the retaining nuts, Fig. 29.

12. Wipe the rear end bearing surface of the rotor shaft with a clean lint-free rag.

13. Position the rear housing and stator assembly over the rotor and align the scribe marks made during disassembly. Seat the machined portion of the stator core into the step in both end housings. Install the housing through bolts. Remove the brush retracting wire, and put a daub of water-proof cement over the hole to seal it.

Side Terminal Alternator
Disassembly

NOTE: Use a 200 watt soldering iron.

1. Mark both end housings and the stator with a scribe mark for use during assembly, Fig. 30.

2. Remove the four housing through bolts, and separate the front housing and rotor from the rear housing and stator. Slots are provided in the front housing to aid in disassembly. *Do not separate the rear housing from the stator at this time.*

3. Remove the drive pulley nut, Fig. 24. Remove the lockwasher, pulley, fan and fan spacer from the rotor shaft.

4. Pull the rotor and shaft from the front housing, and remove the spacer from the rotor shaft, Fig. 30.

5. Remove three screws retaining the bearing to the front housing. If the bearing is damaged or has lost its lubricant, remove the bearing from the housing. To remove the bearing, support the housing close to the bearing boss and press the bearing from the housing.

6. Unsolder and disengage the three stator leads from the rectifier, Fig. 31.

7. Lift the stator from the rear housing.

8. Unsolder and disengage the brush holder lead from the rectifier.

9. Remove the screw attaching the capacitor lead to the rectifier.

10. Remove four screws attaching the rectifier to the rear housing, Fig. 31.

11. Remove the two terminal nuts and insulator from outside the housing, and remove the rectifier from the housing.

12. Remove two screws attaching the brush holder to the housing and remove the brushes and holder.

13. Remove sealing compound from rear housing and brush holder.

14. Remove one screw attaching the capaci-

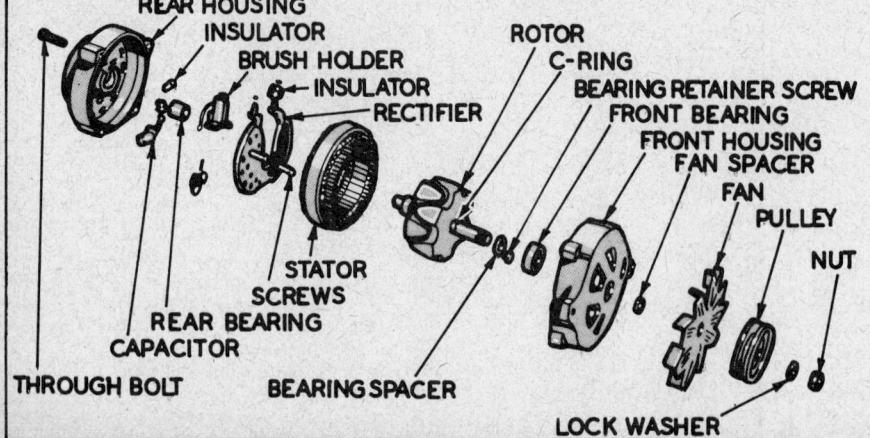

Fig. 30 Disassembled side terminal alternator

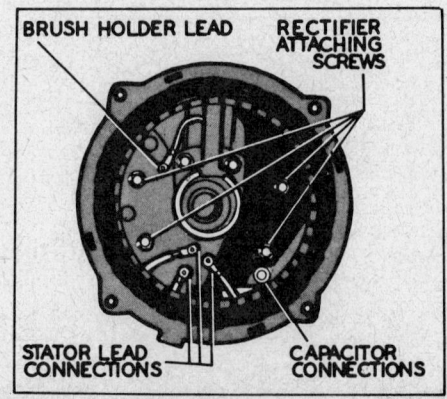

Fig. 31 Stator lead connections

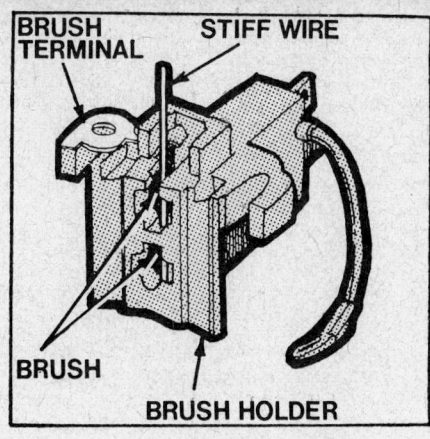

Fig. 32   Brush holder assembly

tor to the rear housing and remove the capacitor.

15. If bearing replacement is necessary, support the rear housing close to the bearing boss and press the bearing out of the housing from the inside.

Assembly

NOTE: Refer to "Cleaning and Inspection" procedures before reassembly.

1. If the front housing bearing is being replaced, press the new bearing in the housing.

    NOTE: *Put pressure on the bearing outer race only.* Then, install the bearing retaining screws.

2. Place the inner spacer on the rotor shaft and insert the rotor shaft into the front housing and bearing.
3. Install the fan spacer, fan, pulley, lockwasher and nut on the rotor shaft, Fig. 24.
4. If the rear bearing is being replaced, press a new bearing in from inside the housing until it is flush with the boss outer surface.
5. Position the brush terminal on the brush holder, Fig. 32. Install the springs and brushes in the brush holder, and insert a piece of stiff wire to hold the brushes in place, Fig. 32.
6. Position the brush holder in the rear housing and install the attaching screws. Push the brush holder toward the rotor shaft opening and tighten the brush holder attaching screws.
7. Position the capacitor to the rear housing and install the attaching screw.
8. Place the two cup shaped (rectifier) insulators on the bosses inside the housing, Fig. 33.
9. Place the insulator on the BAT (large) terminal of the rectifier, and position the rectifier in the rear housing. Place the outside insulator on the BAT terminal, and install the nuts on the BAT and GRD terminals *finger tight.*
10. Install but do not tighten the four rectifier attaching screws.
11. Tighten the BAT and GRD terminal nuts on the outside of the rear housing. Then, tighten the four rectifier attaching screws.
12. Position the capacitor lead to the rectifier

and install the attaching screw.
13. Press the brush holder lead on the rectifier pin and solder securely, Fig. 31.
14. Position the stator in the rear housing and align the scribe marks. Press the three stator leads on the rectifier pins and solder securely, Fig. 31.
15. Position the rotor and front housing into the stator and rear housing. Align the scribe marks and install the four through bolts. Tighten two opposing bolts and then the two remaining bolts.
16. Spin the fan and pulley to be sure nothing is binding within the alternator.
17. Remove the wire retracting the brushes, and place a daub of waterproof cement over the hole to seal it.

Brush Replacement

Removal

1. Mark both end housings and the stator with a scribe mark for use during assembly.
2. Remove the four housing through bolts, and separate the front housing and rotor from the rear housing and stator. Slots are provided in the front housing to aid in disassembly.

    NOTE: Do not separate the rear *housing and stator.*

3. Unsolder and disengage the brush holder lead from the rectifier.
4. Remove the two brush holder attaching screws and lift the brush holder from the rear housing.
5. Remove the brushes from the brush holder.

Installation

1. Insert the brushes into the brush holder and position the terminal on the brush holder.
2. Depress the brushes and insert a 1½ inch piece of stiff wire, Fig. 32, to hold the brushes in the retracted position.
3. Position the brush holder to the rear housing, inserting the wire used to retract the brushes through the hole in the rear housing.
4. Install the brush holder attaching screws. Push the brush holder toward the rotor shaft opening and tighten the attaching screws.
5. Press the brush holder lead on the rectifier pin and solder securely.
6. Position the rotor and front housing into the stator and rear housing. Align the scribe marks and install the four through bolts. Tighten two opposing bolts and then the two remaining bolts.
7. Spin the fan and pulley to be sure nothing is binding within the alternator.
8. Remove the wire retracting the brushes, and place a daub of waterproof cement over the hole to seal it.

Rectifier Replacement

Removal

1. Mark both end housings and the stator with a scribe mark for use during assembly, Fig. 30.
2. Remove the four housing through bolts, and separate the front housing and rotor from the rear housing and stator. Slots are provided in the front housing to aid in disassembly.

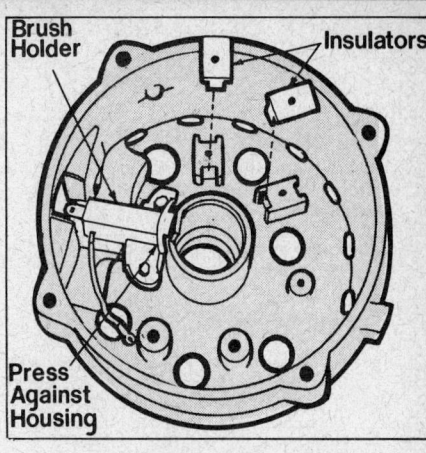

Fig. 33   Brush holder and rectifier insulators installed

NOTE: *Do not separate the rear housing and stator at this time.*

3. Unsolder and disengage the three stator leads from the rectifier, Fig. 31. Lift the stator from the rear housing.
4. Unsolder and disengage the brush holder lead from the rectifier.
5. Remove the screw attaching the capacitor lead to the rectifier.
6. Remove four screws attaching the rectifier to the rear housing, Fig. 31.
7. Remove two terminal nuts and insulator from outside the housing, and remove the rectifier from the housing.

Installation

1. Insert a piece of wire through the hole in the rear housing to hold the brushes in the retracted position.
2. Place the two cup shaped (rectifier) insulators on the bosses inside the housing, Fig. 33.
3. Place the insulator on the BAT (large) terminal of the rectifier, and position the rectifier in the rear housing. Place the outside insulator on the BAT terminal, and install the nuts on the BAT and GRD terminals finger tight.
4. Install but do not tighten the four rectifier attaching screws.
5. Tighten the BAT and GRD terminal nuts on the outside of the rear housing. Then, tighten the four rectifier attaching screws.
6. Position the capacitor lead to the rectifier and install the attaching screw.
7. Press the brush holder lead on the rectifier pin and solder securely, Fig. 31.
8. Position the stator in the rear housing and align the scribe marks. Press the three stator leads on the rectifier pins and solder securely, Fig. 31.
9. Position the rotor and front housing into the stator and rear housing. Align the scribe marks and install the four through bolts. Partially tighten all four through bolts. Then, tighten two opposing bolts and then the two remaining bolts.
10. Spin the fan and pulley to be sure nothing is binding within the alternator.
11. Remove the wire retracting the brushes in the brush holder, and place a daub of waterproof cement over the hole in the rear housing to seal it.

Cleaning and Inspection Procedures

NOTE: When rebuilding a high temperature alternator, use only high temperature rectifier assembly and bearings. If standard parts are used, alternator failure will occur.

1. The rotor, stator, and bearings must not be cleaned with solvent. Wipe these parts off with a clean cloth.
2. Rotate the front bearing on the drive end of the rotor drive shaft. Check for any scraping noise, looseness or roughness that will indicate that the bearing is excessively worn. Look for excessive lubricant leakage. If any of these conditions exist, replace the bearing.
3. Inspect the rotor shaft at the rear bearing surface for roughness or severe chatter marks. Replace the rotor assembly if the shaft is not smooth.
4. Place the rear end bearing on the slip-ring end of the shaft and rotate the bearing on the shaft. Make the same check for noise, looseness or roughness as was made for the front bearing. Inspect the rollers and cage for damage. Replace the bearing if these conditions exist, or if the lubricant is lost or contaminated.
5. Check the pulley and fan for excessive looseness on the rotor shaft. Replace any pulley or fan that is loose or bent out of shape. Check the rotor shaft for stripped or damaged threads. Inspect the hex hole in the end of the shaft for damage.
6. Check both the front and rear housing for cracks. Check the front housings for stripped threads in the mounting gear. Replace defective housings.
7. Check all wire leads on both the stator and rotor assemblies for loose soldered connections, and for burned insulation. Resolder poor connections. Replace parts that show burned insulation.
8. Check the slip rings for nicks and surface roughness. If the slip rings are badly damaged, the entire rotor will have to be replaced, as it is serviced as a complete assembly.
9. Replace any parts that are burned or cracked. Replace brushes and brush springs that are not to specification.

Mitsubishi Alternator

DESCRIPTION

On these units the regulator is incorporated into the alternator rear housing, Figs. 1 and 2. The electronic voltage regulator has the ability to vary regulated system voltage upward or downward as temperature changes. No voltage regulated adjustments are required on these units.

IN-VEHICLE TESTS

Voltage Regulator Test

1. With ignition switch in the Off position, disconnect battery positive cable and connect an ammeter between battery positive post and battery cable, Fig. 3.
2. Connect a voltmeter between alternator L terminal and ground, Fig. 3. Voltmeter should indicate zero voltage. If voltage is present, the alternator or charging system wiring is defective.
3. Place ignition switch in the On position and note voltmeter reading. Voltmeter reading should be 1 volt or less, if a higher reading is indicated, the alternator should be removed for bench tests.
4. Connect a tachometer to engine, then start and operate engine at approximately 2000 to 3000 RPM and note ammeter reading.

NOTE: When starting engine, ensure that no starting current is applied to ammeter.

5. If ammeter reading is 5 amps or less, check voltmeter reading with engine operating at 2000 to 3000 RPM. The charging voltage should be 14.4 volts at 68 degrees F.
6. If ammeter reading is above 5 amps, continue to charge battery until reading drops to less than 5 amps and check voltmeter reading at 2000 to 3000 RPM. If voltage is not within limits, remove alternator for bench tests.

Current Output Test

1. With ignition switch in the Off position, disconnect battery ground cable, then disconnect battery lead from alternator output terminal.
2. Connect an ohmmeter set at the 0 to 100 amp scale between alternator output terminal and the disconnected battery lead, Fig. 4.
3. Connect positive lead of voltmeter to alternator output terminal and negative lead to ground, Fig. 4.
4. Connect suitable tachometer to engine and reconnect battery ground cable.
5. Connect a variable carbon pile regulator between battery terminals. When installing carbon pile regulator, ensure that regulator is in the Open or Off position.
6. Adjust carbon pile regulator and accelerate engine to the specified RPM, noting ammeter and voltmeter readings, Fig. 5.
7. If ammeter reading is less than specified, the alternator should be removed for bench tests.

ALTERNATOR, DISASSEMBLE

1. Position alternator with mounting lug in a soft jawed vise, then remove three alternator through bolts, Fig. 1.
2. Using a screwdriver, pry between stator and drive end frame, then carefully separate drive end frame and rotor from stator and rectifier end frame.
3. Remove pulley nut, pulley, fan and pulley spacer from rotor shaft, then lift drive end housing from rotor.
4. Remove front and rear dust shields from drive end housing.
5. Remove drive end housing bearing retainer, then using a suitable socket, tap

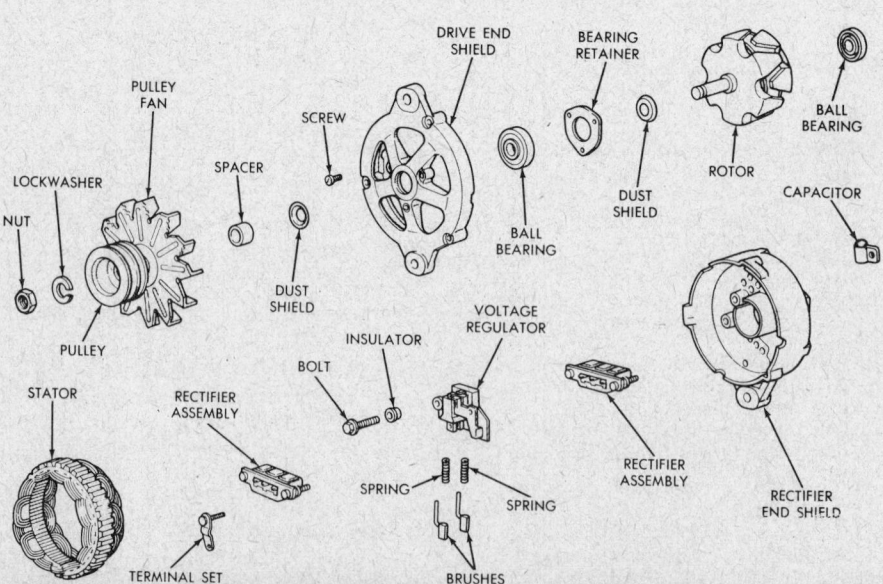

Fig. 1   Disassembled view of Mitsubishi alternator

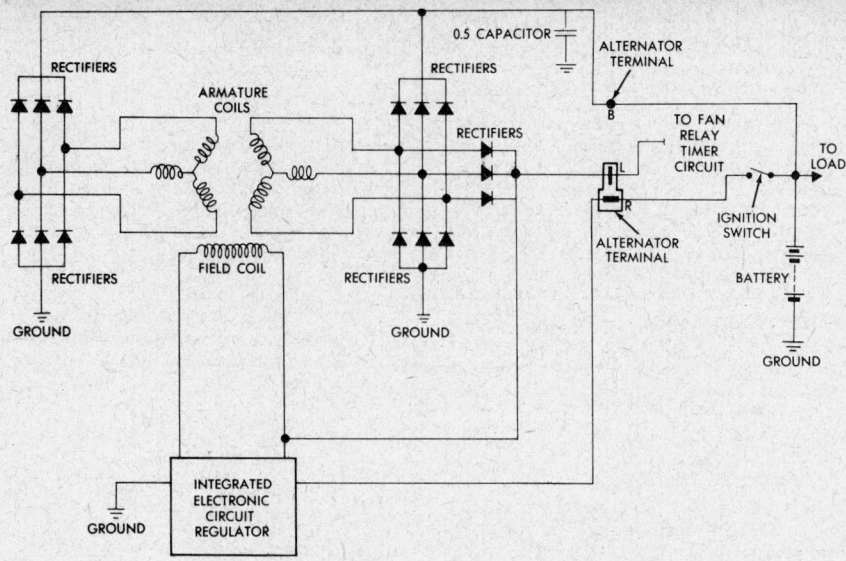

Fig. 2 Wiring diagram of Mitsubishi charging system

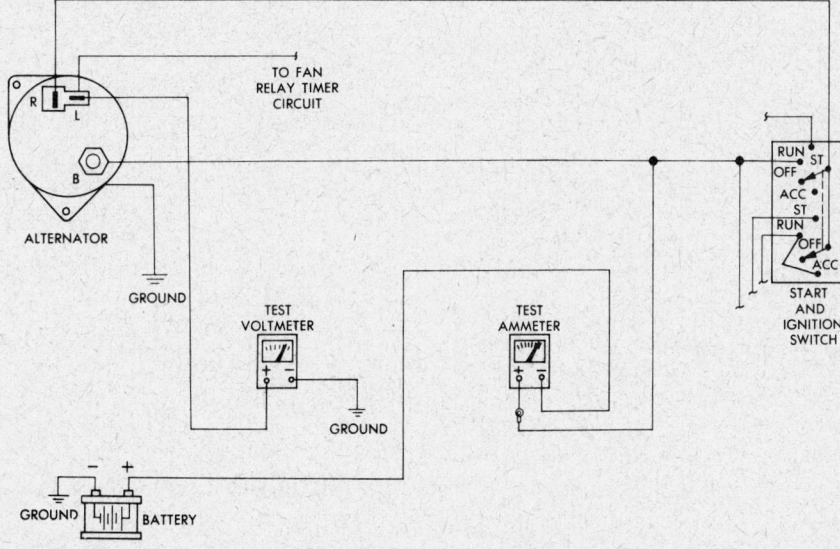

Fig. 3 Voltage regulator test connections

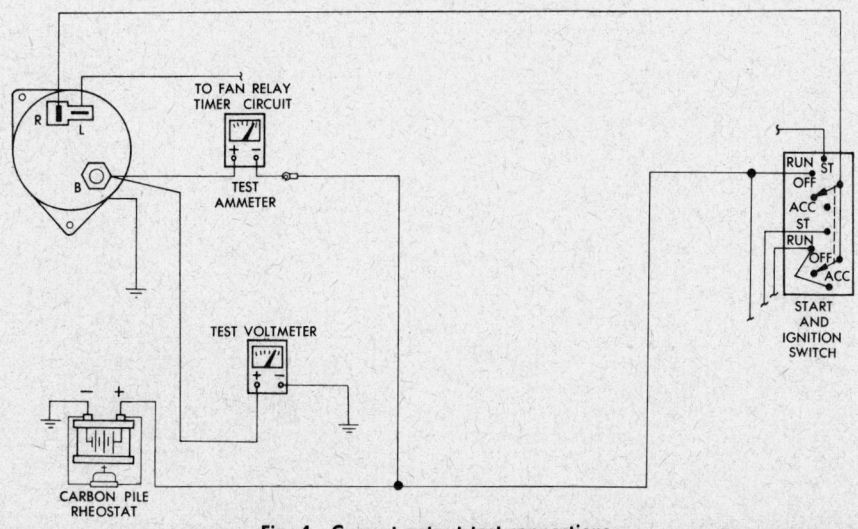

Fig. 4 Current output test connections

Engine RPM	Alternator Current Output Hot or Cold At 13.5 Volts
50	17—25 Amps
1000	63—70 Amps
2000	74 Amps

Fig. 5 Alternator output test specifications

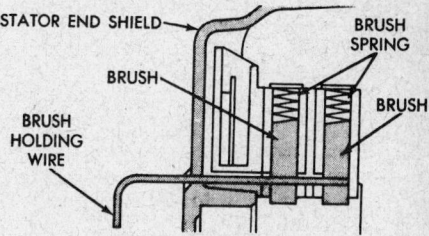

Fig. 6 Positioning brushes for rotor installation

bearing from drive end housing.

6. Unsolder six stator leads from rectifier terminals, then remove stator assembly from rectifier end housing.
7. Remove four screws attaching rectifiers to end housing, then remove brush holder and screw attaching regulator to end housing.
8. Remove nut from alternator B terminal and disconnect capacitor lead.
9. Remove rectifier and regulator assembly from end housing.
10. Unsolder joint attaching one of the rectifiers to the regulator, then remove the other rectifier by sliding the battery stud out of the regulator.

BENCH TESTS

Rotor Test

Check for continuity between field coil and slip rings. If continuity does not exist, the rotor assembly must be replaced. Check for continuity between slip rings and rotor shaft. If continuity exists, the rotor assembly should be replaced.

Stator Coil Test

Using an ohmmeter, check for continuity between stator leads. If continuity does not exist, replace stator.

Rectifier Test

Using an ohmmeter, check for continuity between stator coil lead terminal and heat sink, then reverse ohmmeter leads. Continuity should exist with only one connection. If continuity exists with both connections, the diode is short circuited and the rectifier assembly should be replaced.

Using an ohmmeter, check rectifier diodes for continuity, then reverse ohmmeter leads. If continuity or an open circuit is indicated with both connections, the diode is defective and rectifier assembly must be replaced.

Brush & Brush Spring Inspection

Check brush length, a brush worn to .315 inch or less should be replaced. Check brush spring tension, brush spring tension should be .7 to 1 lb.

ALTERNATOR, ASSEMBLE

Refer to Alternator, Disassemble and reverse procedure to assemble. When installing rotor, push brushes into holder and insert a suitable piece of wire, Fig. 6. After rotor has been installed, remove wire from brushes.

Hitachi LR155-12B Alternator

DESCRIPTION

This alternator is a solid state unit which incorporates an integral regulator. A vacuum pump is attached to the rear cover and is driven off the alternator shaft.

ALTERNATOR, DISASSEMBLE, FIG. 1

1. Scribe reference marks on front and rear covers for use during reassembly.
2. Remove bolts securing vacuum pump. Holding the center plate, remove pump in direction in line with rotor shaft, Fig. 1.
3. Remove brush cover, then remove the screws securing the brushes and remove.
4. Remove through bolts, and carefully separate the alternator body into front and rear sections. Ensure the stator coils remain with the rear section.

NOTE: When separating sections care must be taken not to damage the oil seal in the rear section. Taping the vacuum pump drive splines will provide some protection.

5. Clamp the rotor assembly in a suitable vise, then remove the pulley nut, pulley, front cover and rotor.
6. Remove front cover bearing retainer screws, then remove the bearing.
7. Remove nuts securing "B" terminal and diode holder, then remove the screw inside the stator.

NOTE: Use care to note the position of any insulating washers to ensure correct installation.

8. Using long-nose pliers as a heatsink, separate diodes from the stator by melting away solder on stator coils, diodes and "L" terminal leads.
9. Unsolder connections on IC regulator holder plate terminal, and remove regulator.
10. Inspect all parts for wear or abnormal damage and replace or repair as necessary.

BENCH TESTS

Rotor & Slip Ring Test

1. Visually inspect slip rings for contamination or roughness. If rings are roughened, dress with fine sandpaper. If rings are contaminated, they may be cleaned with an alcohol saturated cloth.
2. Measure outside diameter of rings. Minimum diameter is 1.181 inches.
3. Check resistance of rotor coil across slip rings, Fig. 2. Ohmmeter should read 4.2 ohms at 68 degrees F.
4. Check for continuity across slip ring and rotor core or shaft, Fig. 3. If continuity exists, replace parts as necessary.
5. Check front and rear ball bearings for binding or abnormal noise and replace as necessary.

Stator Winding Test

1. Check for continuity across stator coils, Fig. 4. If there is no continuity, replace coils.
2. Measure resistance across coil and terminal N. Ohmmeter should read .05 ohms at 68 degrees F.
3. Check for continuity across one of the stator coils and stator core, Fig. 5. If continuity exists, replace coil.

Brushes, Inspect

Measure length of brushes. Standard brush length is .787 inch and minimum length is .551 inch. Brushes are marked with a line to indicate wear limit.

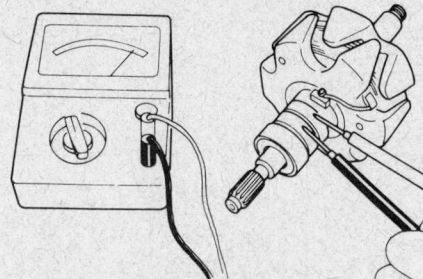

Fig. 2   Testing rotor & slip rings for open circuit

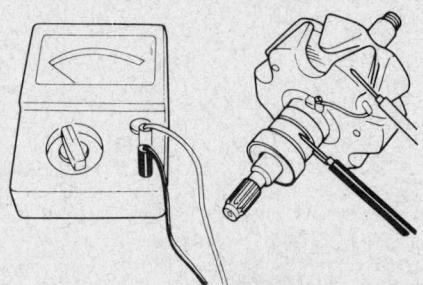

Fig. 3   Testing rotor & slip rings for grounds

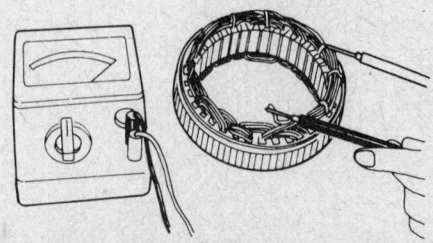

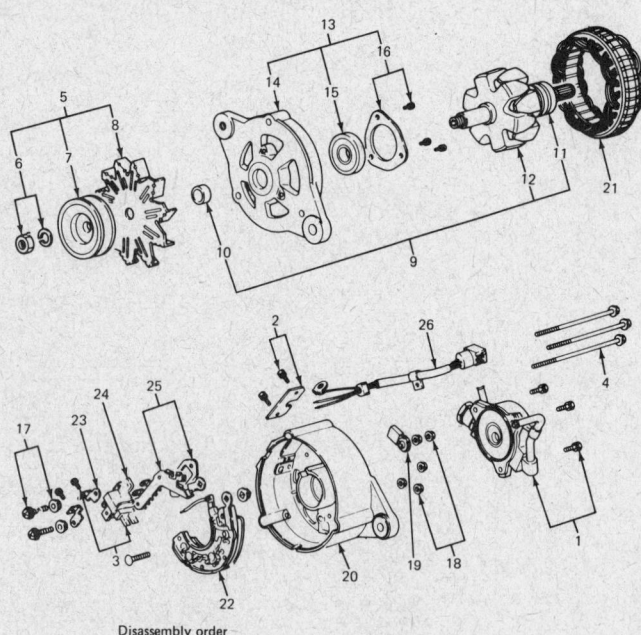

Disassembly order

1. Vacuum pump
2. Cover
3. Brush
4. Through bolt
5. Pulley assembly
6. Pulley nut
7. Pulley
8. Fan
9. Rotor assembly
10. Spacer
11. Ball bearing
12. Rotor
13. Front cover assembly
14. Front cover
15. Ball bearing
16. Bearing retainer
17. Screw
18. Terminal bolt and nut
19. Condenser
20. Rear cover
21. Stator
22. Diode
23. Holder plate
24. Brush holder
25. IC regulator assembly
26. Lead wire

▲ See disassembly procedures for details.

Fig. 1   Hitachi LR155-12B alternator

Fig. 4   Testing stator coils for open circuit

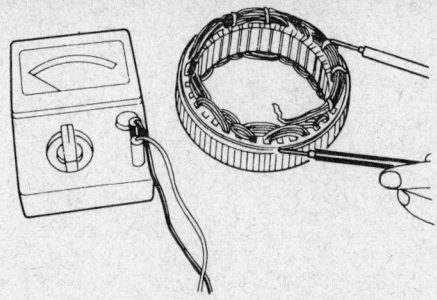

Fig. 5 Testing stator coils for grounds

Diode Test

1. Check for continuity across terminals, Fig. 6. If continuity exists, diode is satisfactory. If there is no continuity, replace diode.
2. Check for continuity with polarities reversed. If there is no continuity, diode is satisfactory. If there is continuity at any point, replace diode.

NOTE: Auxiliary diodes are not provided with terminal and a continuity test should be made across terminals of conventional diodes.

Regulator Test

NOTE: To perform regulator tests, the following measuring instruments will be needed: resistor (10 ohms, 3 watts). . . . R1, variable resistor (0–300 ohms, 3 watts). . . . Rv, battery (12 volts, 2 pieces). . . . BAT1, BAT2, DC voltmeter (0–30 volts).

1. Connect instruments as shown in Fig. 7.
2. Measure voltage at BAT1 (V1). Voltmeter reading should be 10–13 volts.
3. Measure voltage between terminals F and E (V2). Voltmeter reading should be approximately 2 volts.

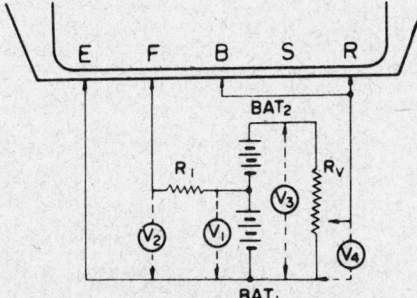

Fig. 8 Testing IC regulator

U.V.W. INDICATES STATOR COIL LEAD TERMINALS

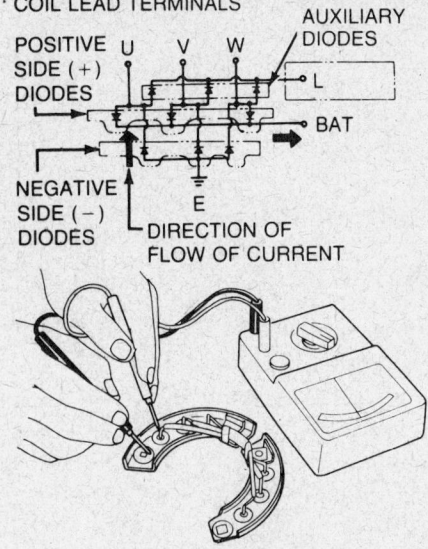

Fig. 6 Testing diodes

4. Measure voltage between BAT1 and BAT2 (V3) with terminal S disconnected. Voltmeter reading should be 20–26 volts.
5. Measure voltage between terminals E and F while varying resistance gradually with variable resistor. Voltage should increase from 2 volts to 10–13 volts without any interruption. If voltage increase is interrupted, replace regulator.
6. Measure voltage between intermediate tap on variable resistor and terminal E (V4) without actuating variable resistor. Voltmeter should read 14.0–14.6 volts, or regulator must be replaced.
7. Connect instruments as shown in Fig. 8.
8. Measure voltage between terminals B and E while gradually increasing voltage with variable resistor. Voltage should increase from approximately 2 volts to 10–13 volts. If voltage does not vary, replace regulator.
9. Check voltage between intermediate tap of variable resistor and terminal E without actuating variable resistor. Voltmeter should read 14.5–16.6 volts, or regulator must be replaced.

Vacuum Pump, Inspect

1. Measure length of vanes. Vanes should measure .511–.531 inch, or must be replaced.
2. Measure inside diameter of pump housing. Diameter should be 2.2440–2.2441 inches.
3. Apply light pressure to check valve with a screwdriver and ensure smooth operation of valve.
4. Inspect inner face of rear cover for signs of

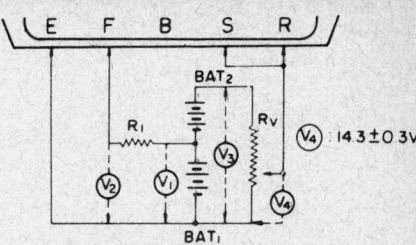

Fig. 7 Testing IC regulator

oil leakage and inspect oil seal for excessive wear or damage.
5. If rear seal requires replacement, remove old seal from rear cover side with a screwdriver and install new seal with seal installer, Fig. 9.

ALTERNATOR, ASSEMBLE FIG. 1

1. Solder the IC regulator wires to the IC regulator, Fig. 1.
2. Using long-nose pliers as a heatsink and working as quickly as possible, solder stator coil leads and diode leads.
3. Clamp the rotor in a suitable vise, install front cover, pulley and pulley nut.
4. Install rear cover over rotor, remove tape on splines. Insert and tighten through bolts.
5. Install brushes into brush holder, and install brush cover.
6. Install vacuum pump. Torque bolts to 4–5 ft. lbs. If necessary, pour approximately 5 cc of engine oil into the vacuum pump filler port.

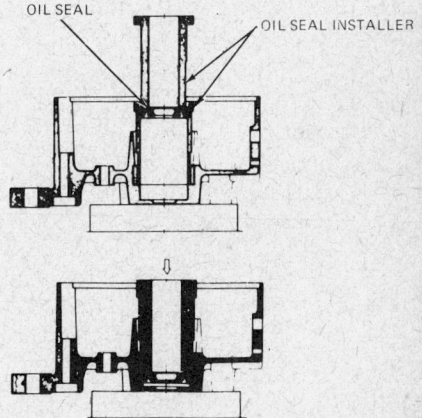

Fig. 9 Replacing vacuum pump oil seal

UNIVERSAL JOINTS

SERVICE NOTES

Before disassembling any universal joint, examine the assembly carefully and note the position of the grease fitting (if used). Also, be sure to mark the yokes with relation to the propeller shaft so they may be reassembled in the same relative position. Failure to observe these precautions may produce rough car operation which results in rapid wear and failure of parts, and place an unbalanced load on transmission, engine and rear axle.

When universal joints are disassembled for lubrication or inspection, and the old parts are to be reinstalled, special care must be exercised to avoid damage to universal joint spider or cross and bearing cups.

NOTE: Some late model cars use an injected nylon retainer on the universal joint bearings. When service is necessary, pressing the bearings out will sheer the nylon retainer. Replacement with the conventional steel snap ring type is then necessary.

CROSS & ROLLER TYPE

Figs. 1 and 2 illustrate typical examples of universal joints of this type. They all operate on the same principle and similar service and replacement procedures may be applied to all.

Disassembly

1. Remove snap rings (or retainer plates) that retain bearings in yoke and drive shaft.
2. Place U-joint in a vise.
3. Select a wrench socket with an outside diameter slightly smaller than the U-joint bearings. Select another wrench socket with an inside diameter slightly larger than the U-joint bearings.
4. Place the sockets at opposite bearings in

the yoke so that the smaller socket becomes a bearing pusher and the larger socket becomes a bearing receiver when the vise jaws come together, Fig. 3. Close vise jaws until both bearings are free of yoke and remove bearings from the cross or spider.

5. If bearings will not come all the way out, close vise until bearing in receiver socket protrudes from yoke as much as possible without using excessive force. Then remove from vise and place that portion of

bearing which protrudes from yoke between vise jaws. Tighten vise to hold bearing and drive yoke off with a soft hammer.

6. To remove opposite bearing from yoke, replace in vise with pusher socket on exposed cross journal with receiver socket over bearing cup. Then tighten vise jaws to press bearing back through yoke into receiving socket.

7. Remove yoke from drive shaft and again place protruding portion of bearing be-

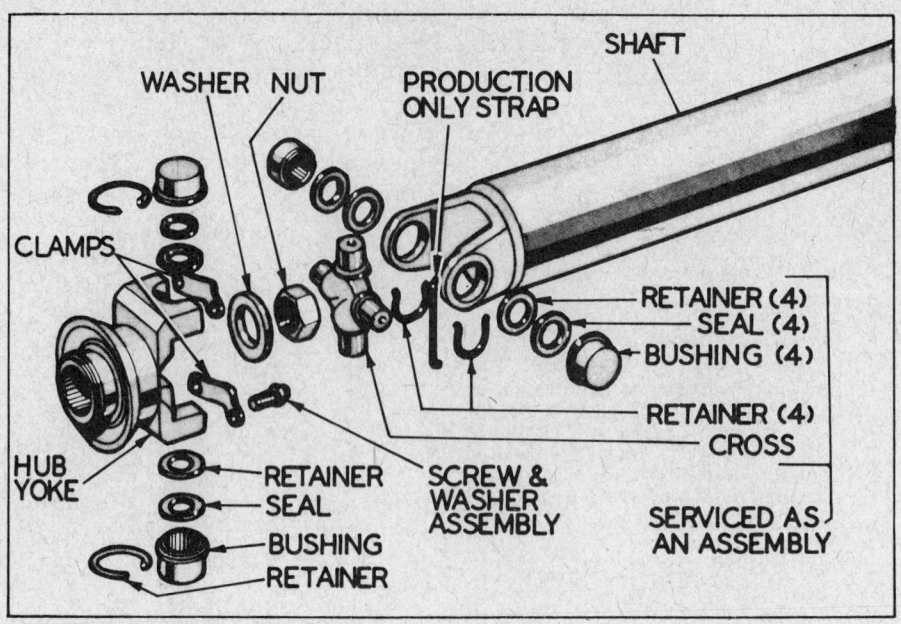

Fig. 1 Cross and roller type universal joint. Chrysler-built cars

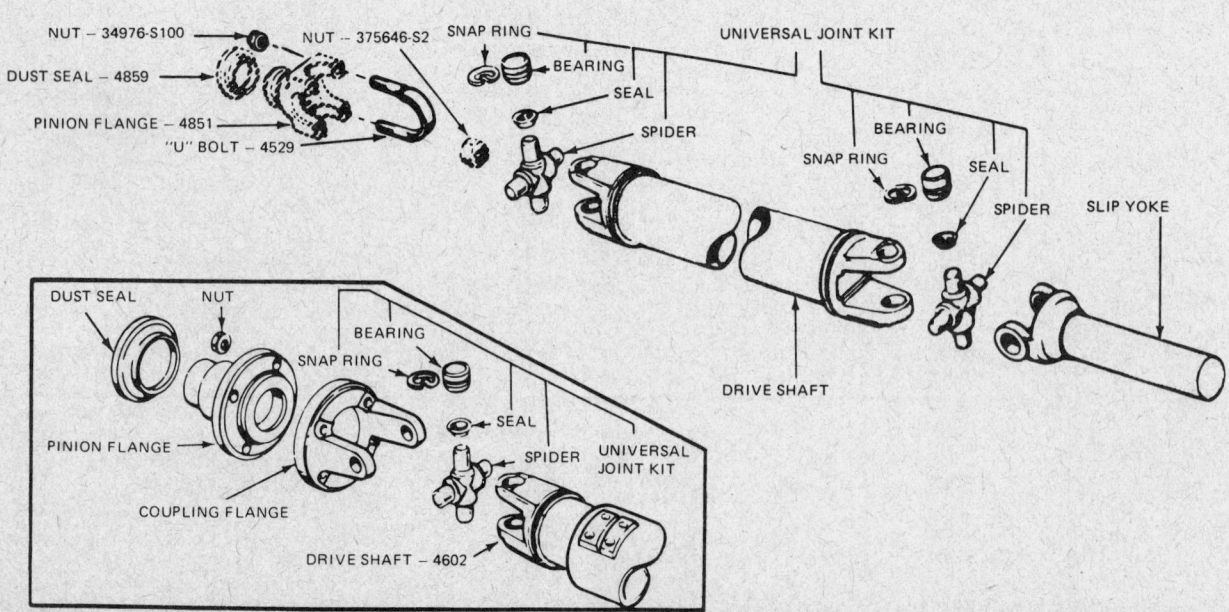

Fig. 2 Cross and roller universal joints & propeller shaft (Typical)

Fig. 3 Removing bearings from yoke using small and large wrench sockets as pusher and receiver tools, respectively

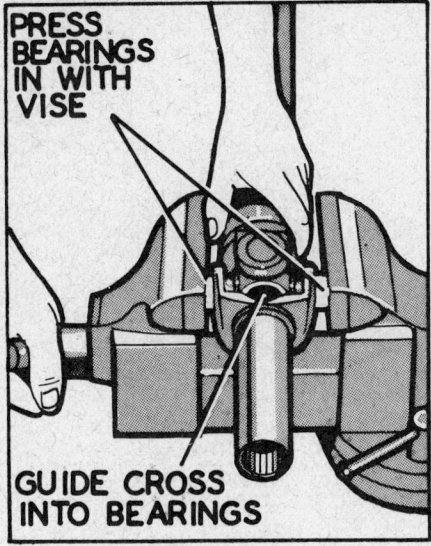

Fig. 4 Installing bearings into drive shaft yoke

Fig. 5 Some units have locating lugs which must face propeller shaft when installed

tween vise jaws. Then tighten vise to hold bearing while driving yoke off bearing with soft hammer.

8. Turn spider or cross 1/4 turn and use the same procedure to press bearings out of drive shaft.

Reassembly

1. If old parts are to be reassembled, pack bearing cups with universal joint grease. *Do not fill cups completely or use excessive amounts as over-lubrication may damage seals during reassembly.* Use new seals.

2. If new parts are being installed, check new bearings for adequate grease before assembling.

3. With the pusher (smaller) socket, press one bearing part way into drive shaft. Position spider into the partially installed bearing. Place second bearing into drive shaft. Fasten drive shaft in vise so that bearings are in contact with faces of vise jaws, Fig. 4. *Some spiders are provided with locating lugs which must face toward drive shaft when installed, Fig. 5.* Press bearings all the way into position and install snap rings or retainer plates.

5. Install bearings in yoke in same manner. When installation is completed, check U-joint for binding or roughness. If free movement is impeded, correct the condition before installation in vehicle.

CONSTANT VELOCITY TYPE

This type of U-joint, Fig. 6, is composed of two conventional cross and roller joints connected with a special link yoke. Because the two joint angles are the same, even though the usual U-joint fluctuation is present within the unit, the acceleration of the front joint (within the yoke) is always neutralized by the deceleration of the rear joint (within the yoke) and vice versa. The end result is the front and rear propeller shafts always turn at a constant velocity.

Disassemble Constant Velocity U-Joint

1. Mark yokes before disassembly to be sure reassembly is made in same relative position of components, Fig. 7.

2. Disassemble rear section of constant velocity U-joint first as follows:

3. Remove snap rings from bearings using a punch.

4. Place rear propeller shaft yoke in a vise. Shaft must be supported horizontally and link yoke must be free to move vertically, Fig. 8.

5. Using a pipe coupling or a wrench socket with the inside diameter slightly larger than outside diameter of bearing, Fig. 8, drive link yoke downward until about 1/4" of bearing projects from yoke. *Do not attempt to drive yoke down farther than ball socket will allow easily.*

6. Rotate shaft 180 degrees and repeat Steps 3, 4 and 5.

7. Clamp 1/4" projecting portion of either bearing in vise and remove bearing by driving link yoke upward. Remove other bearing in same manner, Fig. 9.

8. Separate spider, shaft yoke and shaft from link yoke.

9. To remove bearings from shaft yoke, clamp spider in vise with its jaws bearing against ends of spider journals. Yoke must be free to move vertically between jaws of vise.

10. Using the same bearing remover tool as in Step 5, apply force on shaft yoke around bearing. Drive yoke downward until bearing is free of yoke.

Centering Ball Replacement

1. With CV joint disassembled, position inner part of tool J-23677 on centering ball, Fig. 10.

2. Install outer cylinder of tool J-23677 over inner part, thread nut onto tool and pull centering ball off stud.

3. Place replacement ball on stud and using a suitable tool, drive ball onto stud until it seats firmly against shoulder at base of stud.

4. Assemble ball seats and related parts into ball cavity as shown in Fig. 11. All parts must be adequately lubricated with lubricant provided with kit.

5. Lubricate centering ball seal with approved lubricant and install with sealing lip tipping inward. Fill ball cavity with lubricant.

Reassemble Constant Velocity U-Joint

All yokes must be carefully assembled using the marks made before disassembly for reference. Assemble front section of constant velocity joint first.

1. Position spider inside splined yoke. Install bearings by pressing between vise jaws. Make sure that spider journals enter bearings squarely to avoid damage, Fig. 12.

2. Fully install bearings and install snap rings.

3. Position splined yoke and spider inside link yoke and install bearings into link yoke in same manner as for splined yoke.

4. Position spider inside rear propeller shaft yoke and install bearings.

5. Lubricate ball and socket with a high grade of extreme pressure grease.

6. Position spider of rear propeller shaft assembly in link yoke.

7. Engage socket with ball of splined yoke assembly. *Make sure that all reference marks are properly aligned.*

8. Install bearings into link yoke in same manner as above while holding spring loaded ball and socket assembly together to make sure that spider journals enter bearing squarely.

1977 Lincoln

These vehicles incorporate a double cardan type constant velocity joint at each end of the drive shaft, Fig. 13. Each double cardan has a center yoke (cage), a centering socket yoke and a stud yoke which is welded to each end of the tube assembly. The splines on the yoke and transmission output shaft permit the drive shaft to move in and out as the axle moves up and down. All drive shaft assemblies are balanced and should be kept free of undercoating.

Disassembly

1. Mark location of spiders, center yoke and centering socket yoke as related to stud yoke.

NOTE: The spiders must be assembled with bosses in their original position to provide proper clearance.

2. Remove snap rings that secure bearings in front of center yoke, then position tool, Fig. 14, and thread clockwise until bearing protrudes about 3/8 inch out of yoke.

3. Remove drive shaft from vise and tighten bearing in vise then tap the center yoke,

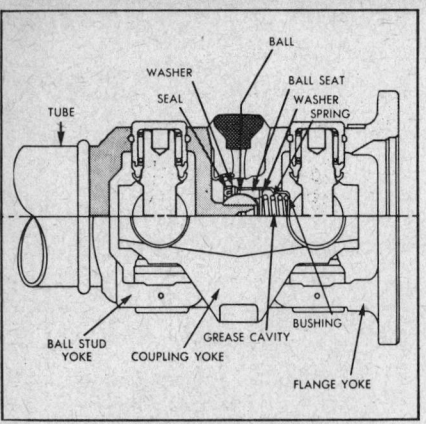

Fig. 6 Cross-section of typical GM constant velocity U-joint

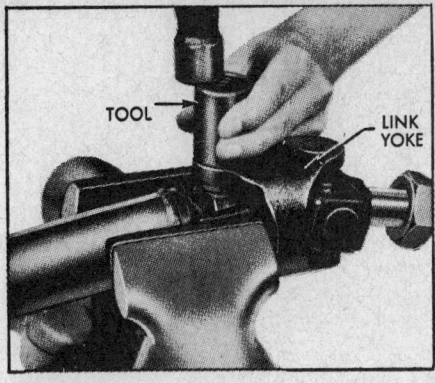

Fig. 8 Driving bearing from link yoke

Fig. 9 Removing bearing

Fig. 15, to free it from bearing.
4. Remove the two bearings from the spider, Fig. 16, then reposition the tool on the yoke and move the remaining bearing in the opposite direction so that it protrudes about 3/8 inch out the yoke.
5. Grip bearing in a vise, then drive the center yoke freeing it from bearing, Fig. 15, and remove spider from center yoke.
6. Pull centering socket yoke off center stud, Fig. 17, then remove rubber seal from centering ball stud.
7. Remove the snap rings from center and drive shaft yokes, then position tool on drive shaft yoke, Fig. 18, and press bearing outward until inside of center yoke almost contacts the slinger ring at the front of the drive shaft yoke.

NOTE: Pressing beyond this point can distort the slinger ring. Fig. 19 shows the interference point.

8. Clamp exposed end of bearing in a vise and drive the center yoke with a soft face hammer freeing it from bearing, then reposition tool and press on spider to remove opposite bearing.
9. Remove center yoke from spider and remove spider from drive shaft yoke in same manner.
10. Clean all serviceable parts in cleaning solvent. If using a repair kit, use all parts supplied in kit. If driveshaft is damaged, it should be replaced to insure a balanced assembly.

Assembly
1. Position spider in shaft yoke making sure

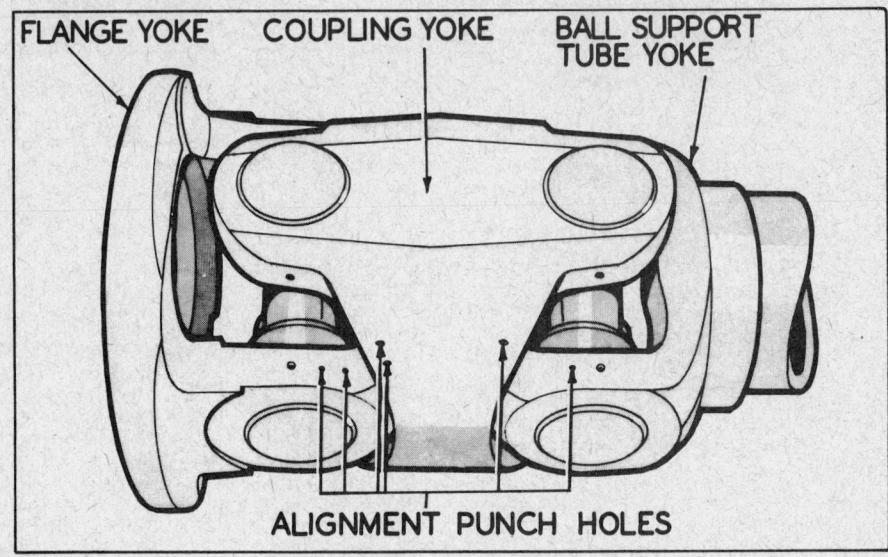

Fig. 7 Marking constant velocity joint

that spider bosses (or lubrication plugs) will be in original position. Press in bearing cups and install snap rings.
2. Position center yoke over spider ends then press in bearing cups and install snap rings.
3. Install new seal on centering stud and position centering socket yoke on stud.
4. Place front spider in center yoke making sure that spider bosses (or lubrication plugs) are properly positioned. Press in bearing cups and install snap rings.
5. Applying pressure on centering socket, install remaining bearing cup.
6. If using a repair kit, remove plug from each spider and lubricate universal joints. Reinstall plug.

1977-80 Versailles

These models use a one-piece driveshaft with a constant velocity universal joint between the driveshaft and companion flange, Fig. 20.

Disassembly
1. Mark relative positions of the spiders, center yoke and centering socket yoke to the companion flange.
2. Install tool CJ91B, Fig. 14. Thread tool

clockwise until bearing protrudes approximately 3/8 inch from yoke.
3. Remove driveshaft from vise.
4. Tighten the bearing in a vise and tap on yoke to free bearing from center yoke, Fig. 15. Do not tap on driveshaft tube.

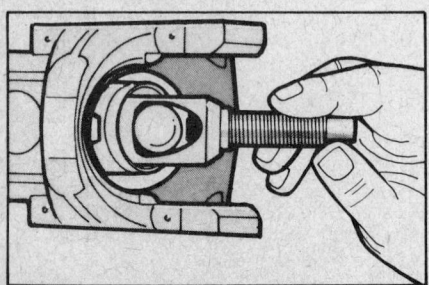

Fig. 10 Removing centering ball with tool J-23677

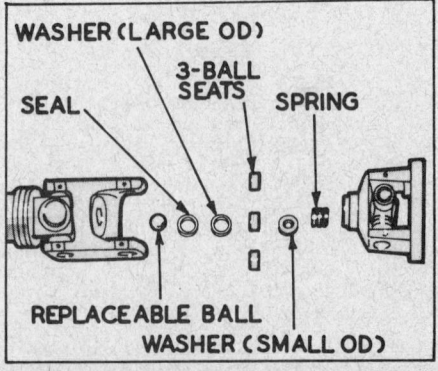

Fig. 11 Centering ball assembly

5. Repeat steps 2 through 4 on remaining bearings.
6. Remove spider from center yoke.
7. Remove bearings from driveshaft yoke as outlined in steps 2 through 4. Remove spider from yoke.
8. Insert a screwdriver into centering ball socket, located in companion flange, and pry out rubber seal. Remove retainer, three piece ball seat, washer and spring from ball socket.

Assembly

1. Inspect centering ball socket assembly for worn or damaged components and replace the assembly if necessary.
2. Insert spring, washer, three piece ball seat and retainer into ball socket.
3. With a suitable tool, install centering ball socket seal.
4. Place spider in driveshaft yoke. Ensure that spider bosses are in the original posi-

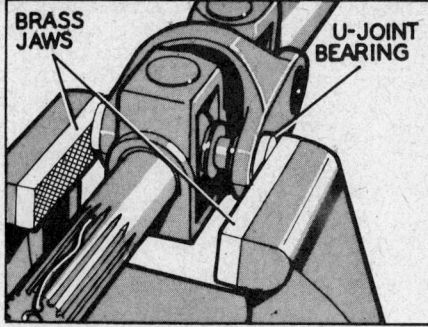

Fig. 12 Installing bearings

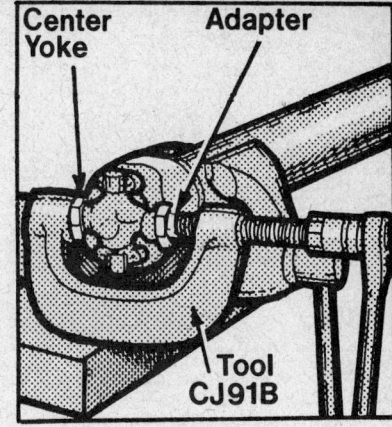

Fig. 14 Partially pressing bearing from center yoke

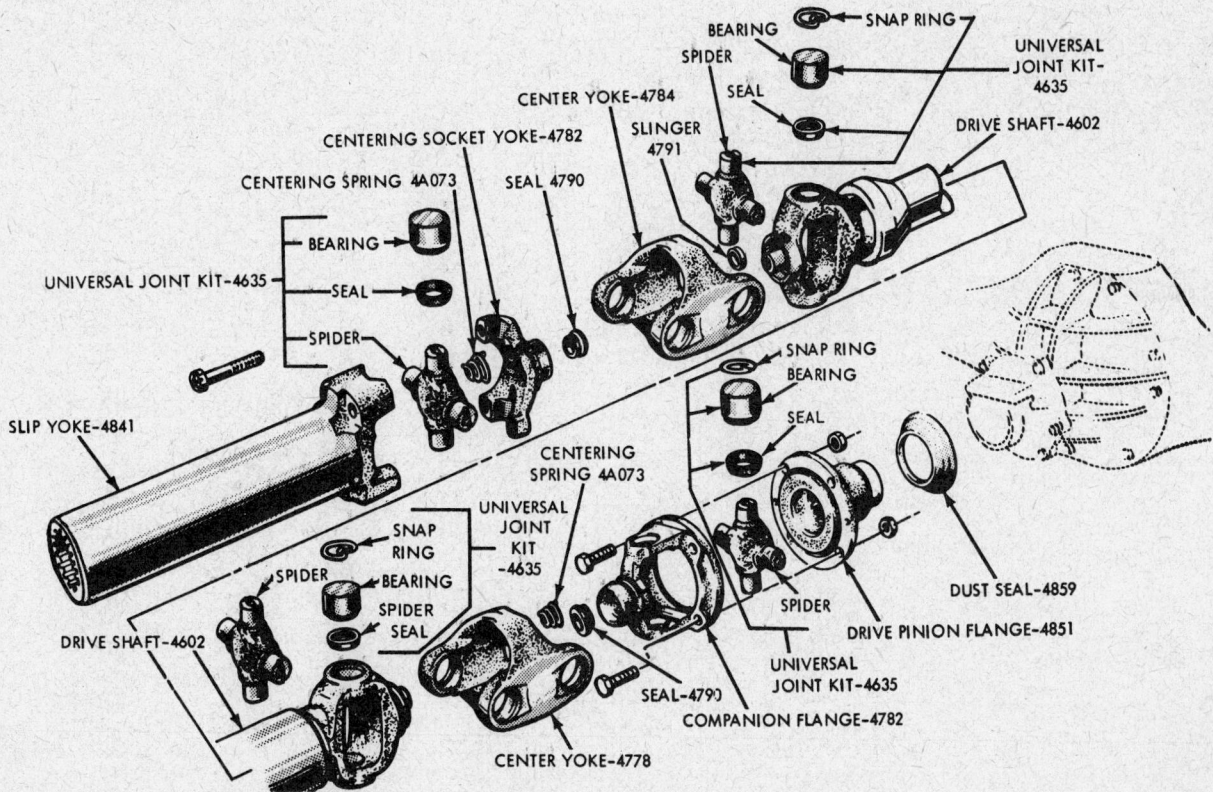

Fig. 13 Constant velocity type universal joint 1977 Lincoln

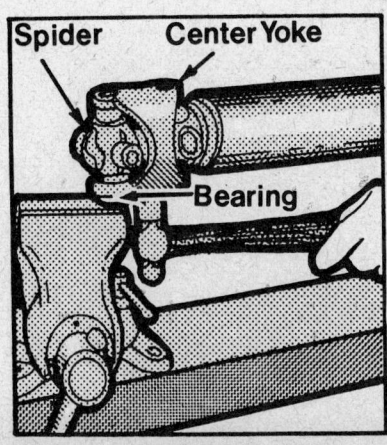

Fig. 15 Removing bearing from center yoke

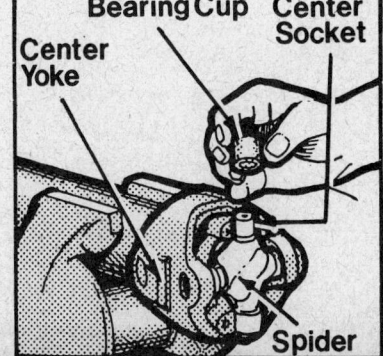

Fig. 16 Removing bearing cup from spider

UNIVERSAL JOINTS

Fig. 17 Removing center socket yoke

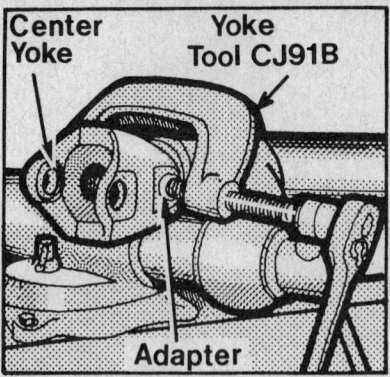

Fig. 18 Removing bearing from rear of center yoke

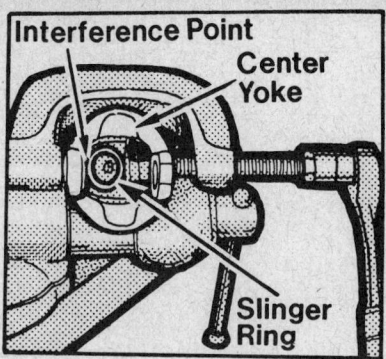

Fig. 19 Center yoke interference point

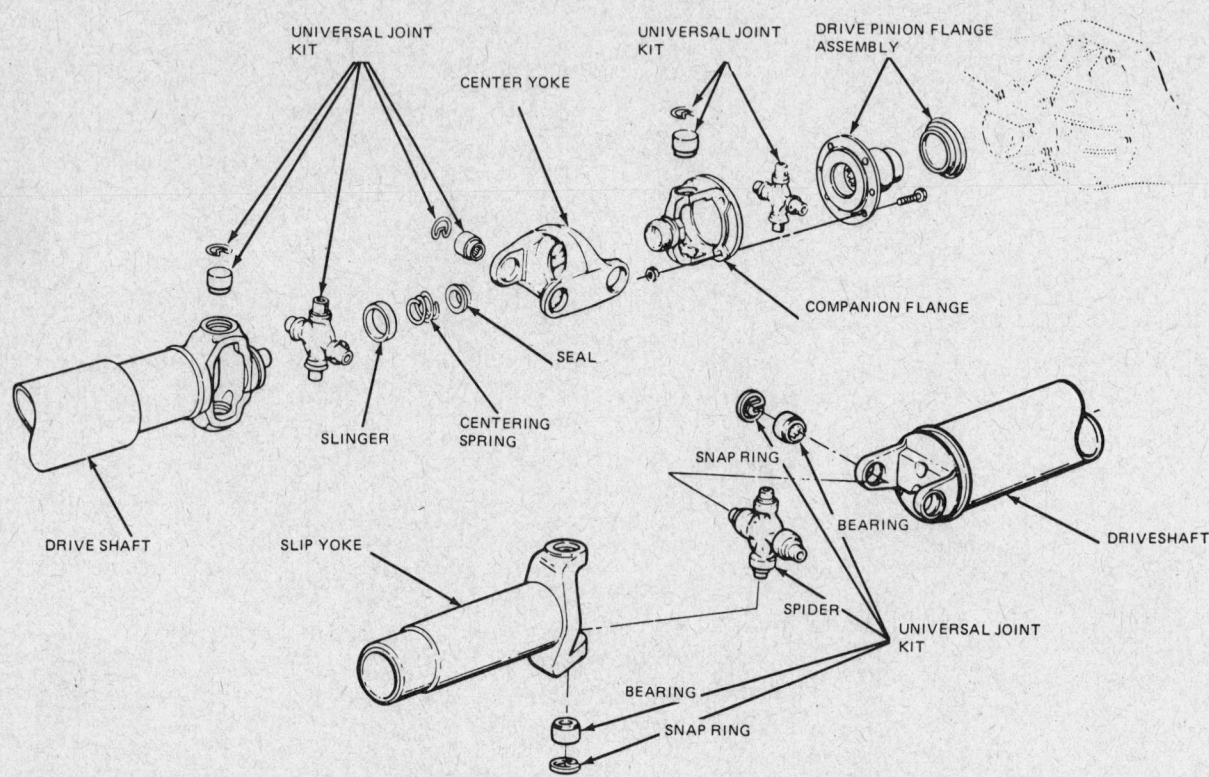

Fig. 20 Constant velocity universal joint, 1977–80 Versailles

tion. Press in bearing cups with tool CJ91B. Install snap rings.

5. Place center yoke over spider ends and press in bearing cups. Install snap rings.
6. Install spider in companion flange yoke. Ensure that spider bosses are in original positions. Press on bearing cups and install snap rings.
7. Place center yoke over spider ends and press in bearing cups. Install snap rings.

1978–79 Lincoln, Fig. 21

NOTE: Refer to the "General Motors, Centering Ball Replacement" procedure for centering ball service.

Disassembly

1. Mark position of all yokes so that original positions can be maintained during assembly.
2. Support driveshaft in a suitable vise.
3. Install tool CJ91B, Fig. 14. Tighten tool clockwise until the plastic retaining the bearing is sheared and the bearing protrudes approximately 3/8 inch from yoke.
4. Remove driveshaft from vise and tighten bearing in vise, then tap the center yoke, Fig. 15, to free yoke from bearing.
5. Repeat steps 2 through 4 on opposite bearing.
6. Remove remainder of the sheared plastic retaining rings from the grooves in the yokes. The sheared plastic may prevent the bearing cups from being properly pressed in place and seated.

Assembly

1. Ensure all alignment marks are properly positioned, then partially install one bearing cup into yoke.
2. Insert spider into yoke so the journal seats freely into bearing cup.
3. Partially install opposite bearing cup.
4. With tool CJ91B, press both bearing cups into yoke. Move the spider when pressing in the bearing cups. If any binding is felt, check the needle bearings.
5. When one of the retaining ring grooves clears the inside of the yoke, install the retaining ring.
6. Press in the remaining bearing cup until the retaining ring can be installed. If difficulty is encountered, tap the yoke with a hammer to aid in seating the retaining rings.

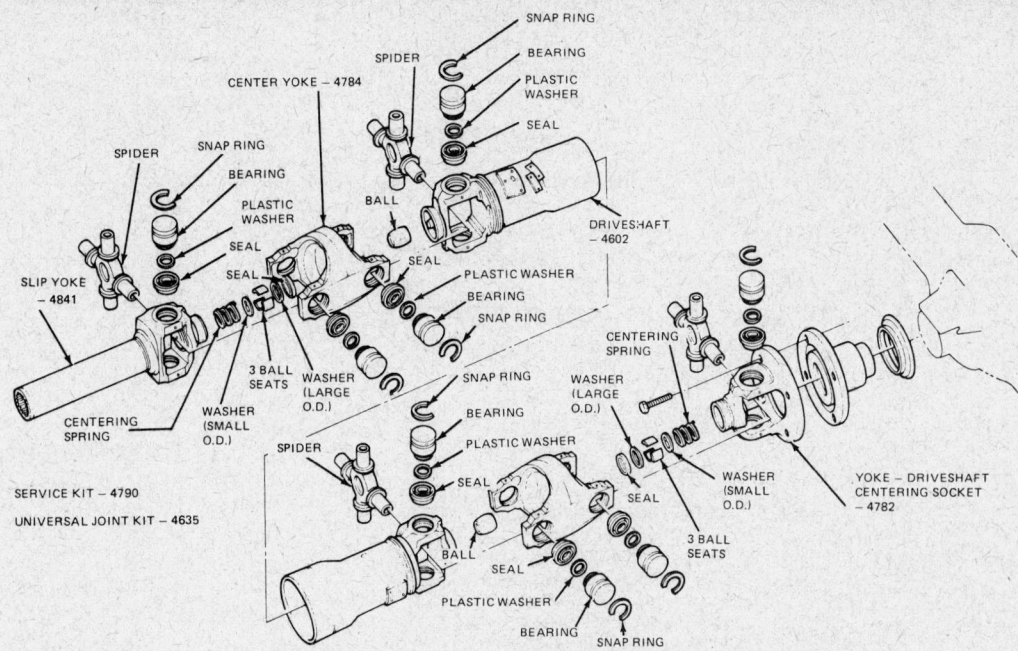

Fig. 21 Drive shaft and universal joints exploded view. 1978–79 Lincoln

1980–82 Cougar XR7 & Thunderbird & 1982–83 Continental, Fig. 22

NOTE: When rear U-joint disassembly is required, new U-joints should be installed.

Disassembly
1. Mark position of all yokes so that original position can be maintained during assembly.
2. Support driveshaft in suitable vise.
3. Remove two snap rings that secure rear spider bearing to center yoke.
4. Install tool T74P-4635-C, Fig. 23. Tighten tool until bearing cup extends approximately 3/8 inch from yoke.
5. Remove driveshaft from vise and grip bearing cup in vise. Tap on center yoke to free bearing from yoke.
6. Repeat steps 2 through 5 on opposite bearing.
7. Pull flanged center socket yoke off center stud.
8. Remove spider from flanged center socket yoke following steps 2 through 5.
9. Remove snap rings from center yoke and studs. Install tool T74P-4635-C on driveshaft stud yoke and press bearing cup outward until inside of center yoke almost contacts slinger ring attached to stud yoke. Grip protruding bearing cup in vise and tap on yoke center to remove. Repeat this step on opposite bearing.

Assembly
1. Install front spider in driveshaft stud yoke. Press in bearing cups using tool T74P-4635-C and install snap rings.
2. Install center yoke over spider ends and

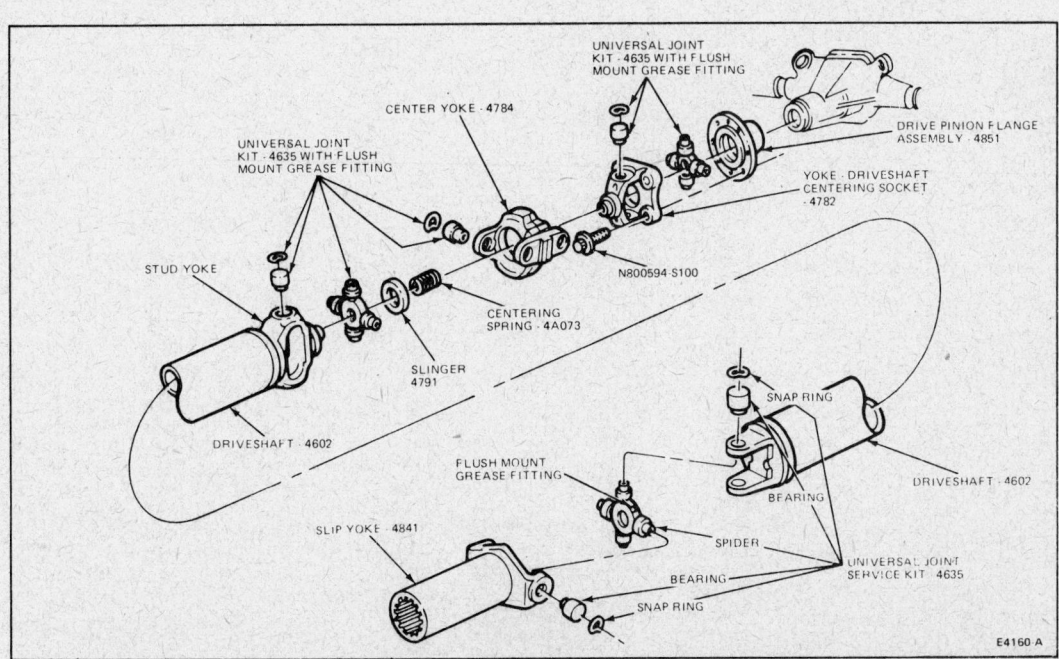

Fig. 22 Drive shaft and universal joint exploded view. 1980–82 Cougar XR7 & Thunderbird & 1982–83 Continental

UNIVERSAL JOINTS

press in bearing cup assemblies using tool T74P-4635-C. Install snap rings.
3. Install rear spider in flanged center socket yoke and press in bearing cup assemblies using tool T74P-4635-C. Install snap rings.
4. Pack inside of ball with ESW-MIC147-A and place centering spring inside ball

stud yoke.
5. Assemble flanged center socket yoke to ball stud and center yoke by guiding ball onto stud while flexing spider in flange. Press in center yoke bearing cup assemblies using tool T74P-4635-C. Install snap rings.
6. Rap center yoke to free joint.

7. Remove grease plug from each spider and lubricate all U-joints with ESW-M1C147-A. Install plugs.

NOTE: Flush type grease fittings are required to insure proper clearance during normal vehicle operation.

DISC BRAKES

CONTENTS

Fig. 1   Checking rotor for lateral runout

SERVICE PRECAUTIONS

Brake Shoes, Linings & Calipers

Remove wheels and inspect brake disc, caliper and linings. The wheel bearings should be inspected at this time and repacked if necessary. Do not get any grease on the linings.

On all models except Chevrolet Corvette, and Chrysler front wheel drive models, the brake shoe and lining assemblies should be replaced if the lining is worn to within 1/32 inch of rivet heads (riveted linings) or brake shoe (bonded linings). On Chevrolet Corvette, the brake shoe and lining assemblies should be replaced when the lining is the approximate thickness of the brake shoe. On Chrysler front wheel drive models, the brake shoe and lining assemblies should be replaced when the combined thickness of the shoe and lining is 5/16 inch or less. It is recommended that both front and/or rear wheel sets be replaced whenever a respective shoe and lining assembly is replaced.

If a visual inspection does not adequately determine the condition of the linings, the brake shoe and lining assemblies should be removed and inspected. If shoes do not require replacement, reinstall them in their original positions. Brake shoes and linings should also be replaced if cracked or damaged.

If the caliper is cracked or fluid leakage through the casting is evident, it must be replaced as a unit.

Brake Roughness

The most common cause of brake chatter on disc brakes is a variation in thickness of the disc. If roughness or vibration is encountered during highway operation or if pedal pumping

is experienced at low speeds, the disc may have excessive thickness variation. To check for this condition, measure the disc at 12 points with a micrometer at a radius approximately one inch from edge of disc. If thickness measurements vary by more than .0005", the disc should be replaced with a new one.

Excessive lateral runout of braking disc may cause a "knocking back" of the pistons, possibly creating increased pedal travel and vibration when brakes are applied.

Before checking the runout, wheel bearings should be adjusted. The readjustment is very important and will be required at the completion of the test to prevent bearing failure. Be sure to make the adjustment according to the recommendations given under *Front Wheel Bearings, Adjust* in the car chapters.

Brake Disc Service

Servicing of disc brakes is extremely critical due to the close tolerances required in machining the brake disc to insure proper brake operation.

The maintenance of these close controls of the shape of the rubbing surfaces is necessary to prevent brake roughness. In addition, the surface finish must be non-directional and maintained at a micro inch finish. This close control of the rubbing surface finish is necessary to avoid pulls and erratic performance and promote long lining life and equal lining wear of both left and right brakes.

In light of the foregoing remarks, refinishing of the rubbing surfaces should not be attempted unless precision equipment, capable of measuring in micro inches (millionths of an inch) is available.

To check lateral runout of a disc, mount a dial indicator on a convenient part (steering knuckle, tie rod, disc brake caliper housing) so that the plunger of the dial indicator contacts the disc at a point one inch from the outer edge, Fig. 1. If the total indicated runout exceeds specifications, install a new disc.

To check parallelism (thickness variation), mount dial indicators, Fig. 2, so the plunger contacts rotor approximately 1 inch from outer edge. If parellelism exceeds specifications, replace rotor.

General Precautions

1. Grease or any other foreign material must be kept off the caliper, surfaces of the disc and external surfaces of the hub,

Fig. 2.   Checking rotor parallelism (Thickness variation)

during service procedures. Handling the brake disc and caliper should be done in a way to avoid deformation of the disc and nicking or scratching brake linings.

2. If inspection reveals rubber piston seals are worn or damaged, they should be replaced immediately.

3. During removal and installation of a wheel assembly, exercise care so as not to interfere with or damage the caliper splash shield, or bleeder screw.

4. Front wheel bearings should be adjusted to specifications.

5. Be sure vehicle is centered on hoist before servicing any of the front end components to avoid bending or damaging the disc splash shield on full right or left wheel turns.

6. Before the vehicle is moved after any brake service work, be sure to obtain a firm brake pedal.

7. The assembly bolts of the two caliper housings should not be disturbed unless the caliper requires service.

Inspection of Caliper

Should it become necessary to remove the caliper for installation of new parts, clean all parts in alcohol, wipe dry using lint-free

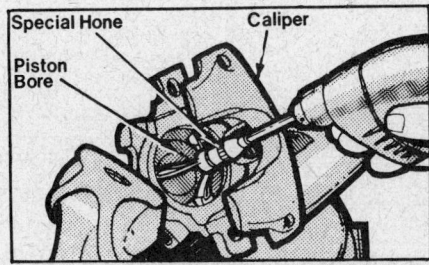

Fig. 3   Honing caliper piston bore

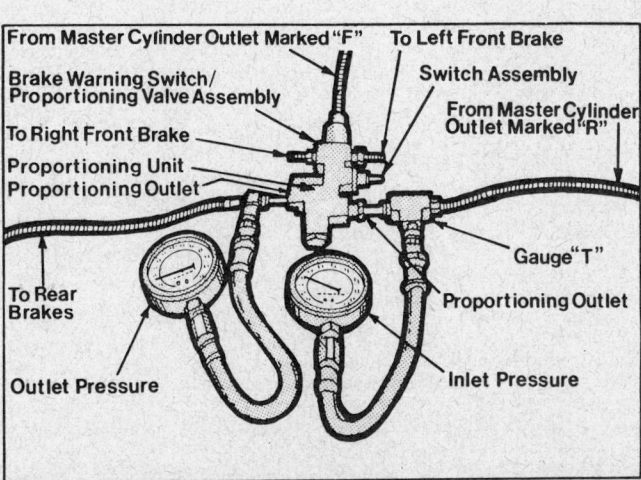

Fig. 4   Gauge hook-up for testing proportioning valve (typical)

DISC BRAKES

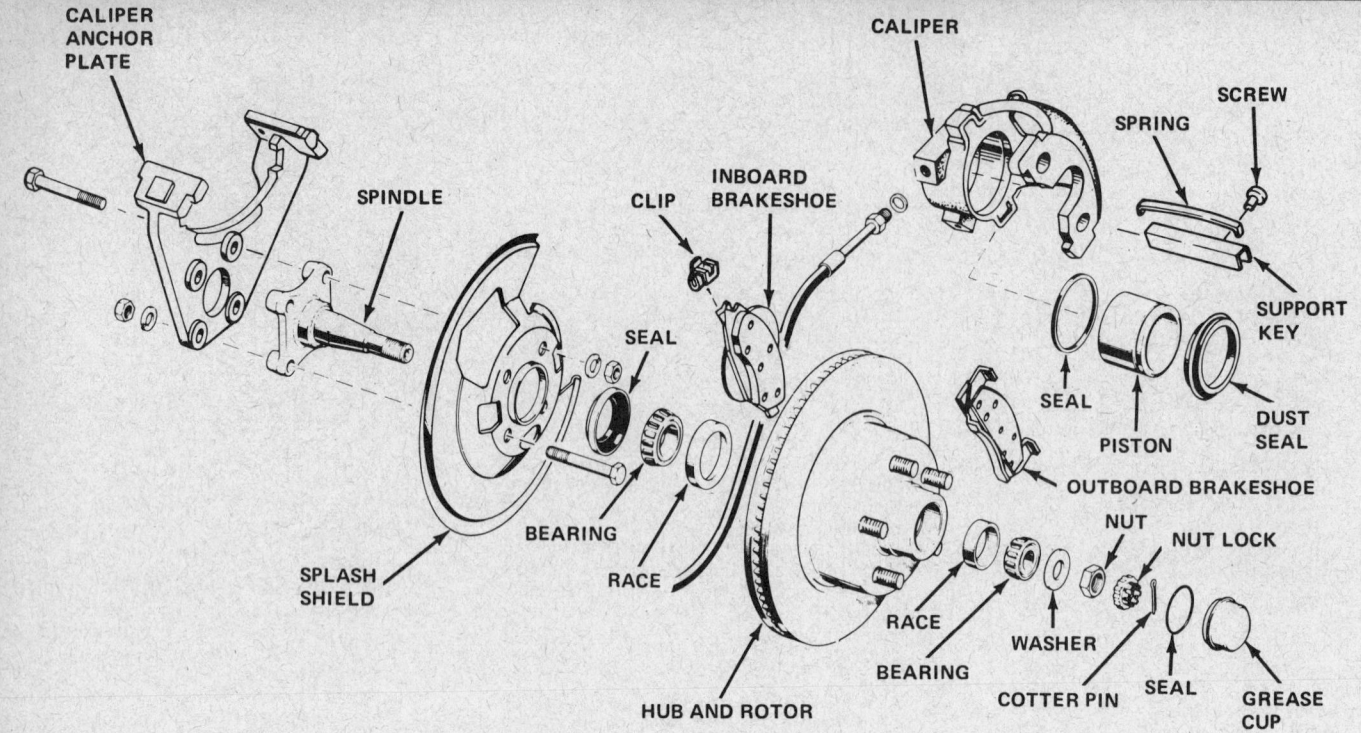

Fig. 5 Bendix sliding caliper disc brake (Typical)

cloths. Using an air hose, blow out drilled passages and bores. Check dust boots for punctures or tears. If punctures or tears are evident, new boots should be installed upon reassembly.

Inspect piston bores in both housings for scoring or pitting. Bores that show light scratches or corrosion can usually be cleaned with crocus cloth. However, bores that have deep scratches or scoring may be honed, provided the diameter of the bore is not increased more than .002". If the bore does not clean up within this specification, a new caliper housing should be installed (black stains on the bore walls are caused by piston seals and will do no harm).

When using a hone, Fig. 3, be sure to install the hone baffle before honing bore. The baffle is used to protect the hone stones from damage. Use extreme care in cleaning the caliper after honing. Remove all dust and grit by flushing the caliper with alcohol. Wipe dry with clean lint-less cloth and then clean a second time in the same manner.

Bleeding Disc Brakes

NOTE: Pressure bleeding is recommended for all hydraulic disc brake systems.

The disc brake hydraulic system can be bled manually or with pressure bleeding equipment. On vehicles with disc brakes the brake pedal will require more pumping and frequent checking of fluid level in master cylinder during bleeding operation.

Never use brake fluid that has been drained from hydraulic system when bleeding the brakes. Be sure the disc brake pistons are returned to their normal positions and that the shoe and lining assemblies are properly seated. Before driving the vehicle, check brake operation to be sure that a firm pedal has been obtained.

Proportioning Valve

The proportioning valve (when used), Fig. 4, provides balanced braking action between front and rear brakes under a wide range of braking conditions. The valve regulates the hydraulic pressure applied to the rear wheel cylinders, thus limiting rear braking action when high pressures are required at the front brakes. In this manner, premature rear wheel skid is prevented.

Testing Proportioning Valve

When a premature rear wheel slide is obtained on a brake application, it usually is an indication that the fluid pressure to the rear wheels is above the 50% reduction ratio for the rear line pressure and that malfunction has occured within the proportioning valve.

To test the valve, install gauge set shown in Fig. 4 in brake line between master cylinder and proportioning valve, and at output end of proportioning valve and brake line as shown. Be sure all joints are fluid tight.

Have a helper exert pressure on brake pedal (holding pressure). Obtain a reading on master cylinder output of approximately 700 psi. While pressure is being held as above, reading on valve outlet should be 550–610 psi. If the pressure readings do not meet these specifications, the valve should be removed and a new valve installed.

BENDIX SLIDING CALIPER

This sliding caliper disc brake assembly incorporates a hub and rotor assembly, caliper, brake shoes and linings, caliper anchor plate and a splash shield, Fig. 5.

Cooling fins are cast into the rotor between the two braking surfaces to ventilate and cool the rotor. The sliding caliper is positioned in, and slides on, the abutment surfaces on the

leading and trailing edges of the caliper anchor plate. A caliper support key, located between the forward edge of the caliper and abutment surface, is secured with a retaining screw. A support spring is installed between the support key and caliper to maintain tension on the support key.

The caliper is a one-piece casting containing the piston, piston seal and dust seal, Fig. 6. The hydraulic seal between the caliper piston and piston bore is achieved by a square cut piston seal, located in a machined groove in the piston bore. The dust seal seats in a recess machined on the edge of the piston bore and into a groove in the caliper piston.

Caliper Removal

1. Siphon two-thirds of brake fluid from master cylinder reservoir serving front disc brakes.
2. Raise vehicle, support on jackstands and remove front wheels.
3. Bottom the caliper piston in bore. Insert a screwdriver between inboard shoe and piston, then pry piston back into bore. The piston can also be bottomed in the bore with a large "C" clamp.
4. Using a 1/4 inch allen wrench, remove support key retaining screw, Fig. 7.
5. Drive caliper support key and spring from anchor plate with a suitable drift and hammer, Fig. 8.
6. Lift caliper from anchor plate and off rotor, Fig. 9. Hang caliper from coil spring with wire. Do not allow caliper to hang from brake hose.
7. Remove inboard brake shoe from anchor plate, then the anti-rattle spring from the brake shoe, Fig. 10. Remove teflon slipper plate from leading anchor abutment surface, if equipped.
8. Remove outboard brake shoe from caliper, Fig. 11. It may be necessary to loosen the brake shoe with a hammer to permit shoe removal.

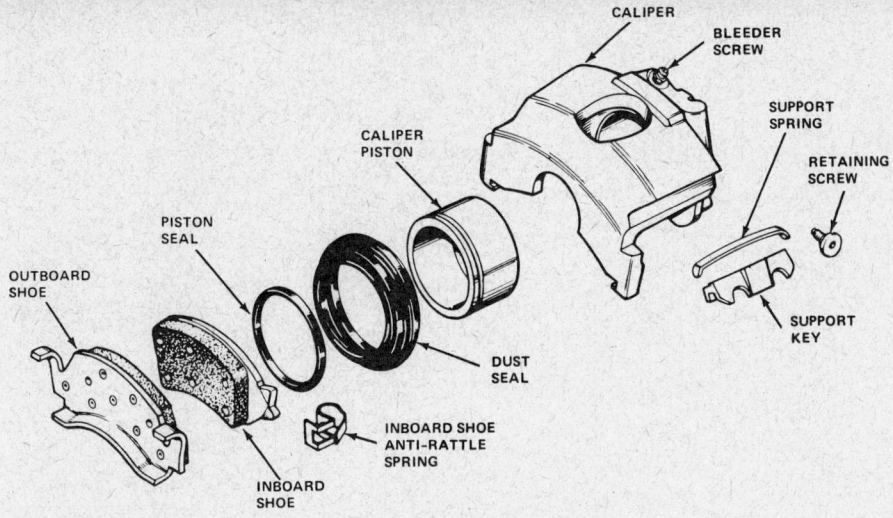

Fig. 6 Caliper assembly

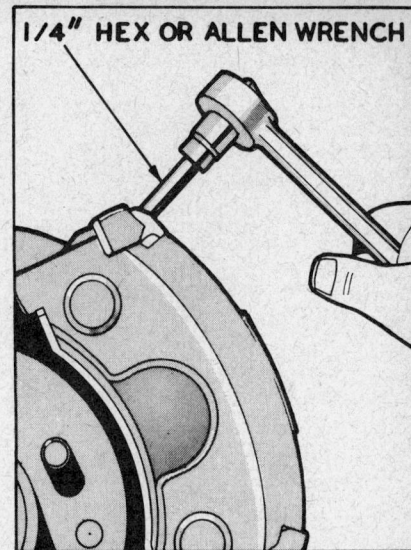

Fig. 7 Removing support key retaining screw

Caliper Disassembly

1. Drain brake fluid from caliper.
2. Position caliper with shop cloths, Fig. 12, and apply compressed air to fluid inlet port to ease piston from bore.

NOTE: Do not attempt to catch piston or to protect it when applying compressed air since personal injury is possible.

3. Remove dust seal from piston, then the piston seal from bore, Fig. 6. Use wooden or plastic tool to remove piston seal since metal tools may damage piston.
4. Remove bleeder screw.

Caliper Assembly

1. Coat square cut piston seal with clean brake fluid, then install seal into piston bore. Work seal into groove with clean fingers.
2. Install bleeder screw and plastic cap.

3. Lubricate dust seal and tool J-24387 with clean brake fluid, then place dust seal on tool, allowing 1/4 inch of tool to extend past small lip of dust seal, Fig. 13.
4. Place dust seal and tool over piston bore, then work large lip of dust seal into seal groove, Fig. 14. Ensure dust seal is fully seated.
5. Lubricate caliper piston and insert through tool. Center piston in bore and use a hammer handle to apply pressure to install piston halfway into bore, Fig. 14.

NOTE: On some models, disc brake caliper pistons may develop a light coating of rust under the dust seal and outboard of the piston seal. This rust may cause the piston to not fully retract. Before installing piston, apply a light coating of dielectric compound 8126688, or equivalent, to

caliper piston bore, Fig. 14A.

6. Remove tool J-24387 and seat small lip of dust seal in caliper piston groove, then bottom piston in bore.

Brake Shoe & Lining, Replace

The procedures to remove & install the brake shoe and lining assemblies are outlined under "Caliper Removal" and "Caliper Installation". It is not necessary to disconnect the brake hose, however, use caution not to twist or kink hose.

Caliper Installation

1. Clean and lubricate abutment surfaces of caliper and the anchor plate with a suitable molydisulfide grease, Fig. 15.
2. Install inboard brake shoe anti-rattle

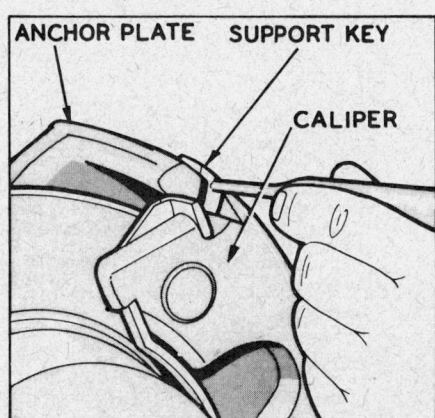

Fig. 8 Removing support key

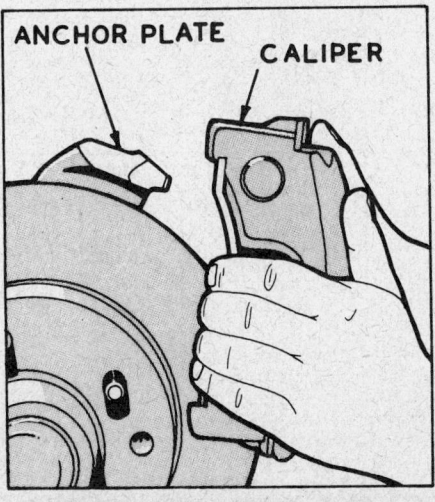

Fig. 9 Removing or installing caliper

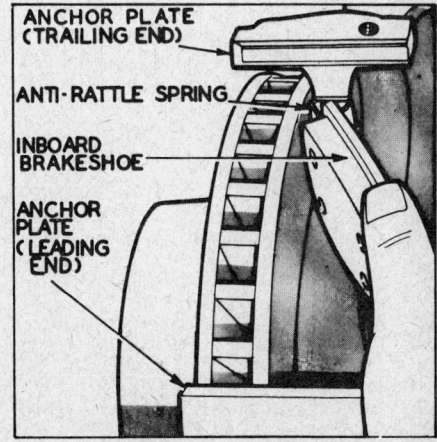

Fig. 10 Removing or installing inboard brake shoe

DISC BRAKES

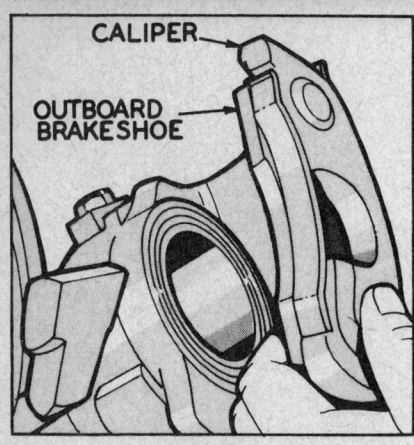

Fig. 11 Removing or installing outboard brake shoe

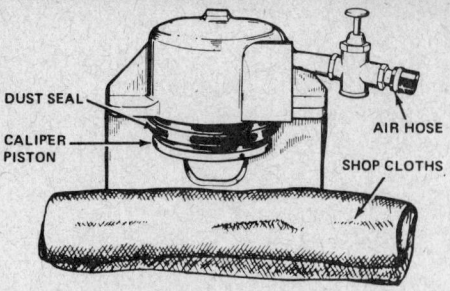

Fig. 12 Removing piston from caliper

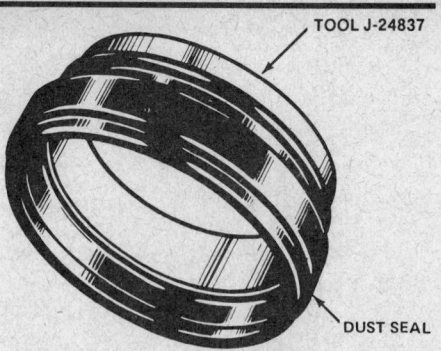

Fig. 13. Dust seal & installer tool assembly

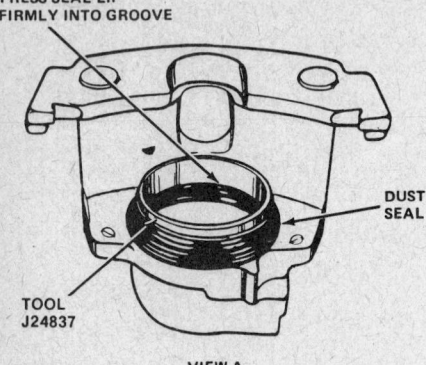

VIEW A

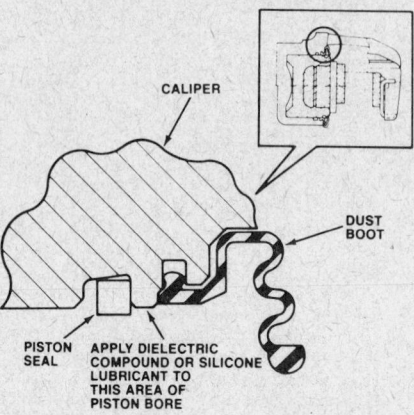

Fig. 14A Lubricating caliper piston bore

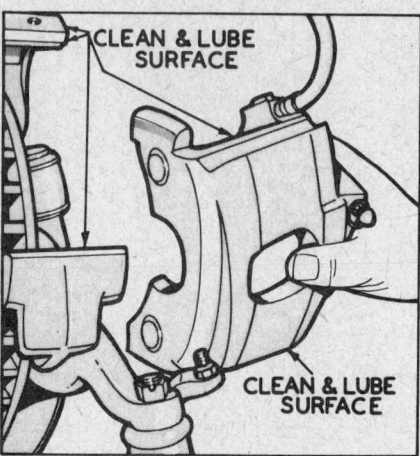

Fig. 15 Caliper & anchor plate abutment surfaces

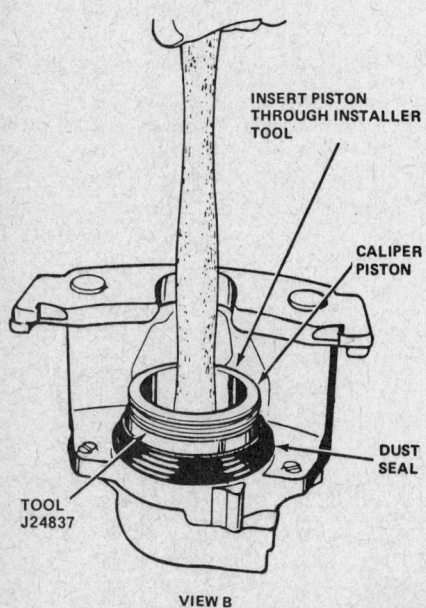

VIEW B

A42886

Fig. 14 Installing dust seal & caliper piston

Fig. 16 Installing inboard brake shoe anti-rattle spring

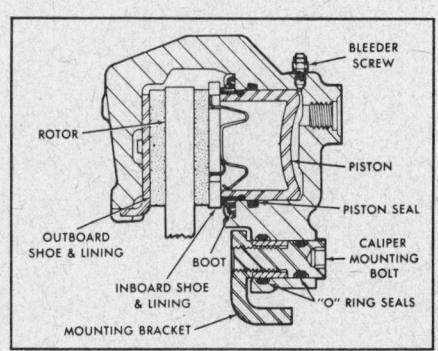

Fig. 17 Single piston disc brake assembly

spring on brake shoe rear flange, ensure looped section of clip is facing away from rotor, Fig. 16. Install teflon slipper plate on leading anchor abutment surface, if equipped.

3. Install inboard brake shoe on caliper anchor plate, Fig. 10.
4. Install outboard brake shoe in caliper, Fig. 11. Ensure the shoe flange is seated fully into outboard arms or caliper. It may be necessary to use a hammer to seat the shoe.
5. Place caliper assembly over rotor and position in caliper anchor plate. Ensure dust boot is not torn or mispositioned by inboard brake shoe during caliper installation.
6. Align caliper with anchor plate abutment surfaces, then insert support key and spring between abutment surfaces, then insert support key and spring between abutment surfaces at the trailing end of caliper and anchor plate. With a hammer and brass drift, drive caliper support key and spring into position, then install and torque support key retaining screw to 15 ft. lbs.
7. Refill master cylinder to within 1/4" of rim. Press brake pedal several times to seat shoes.
8. Install front wheels and lower vehicle.

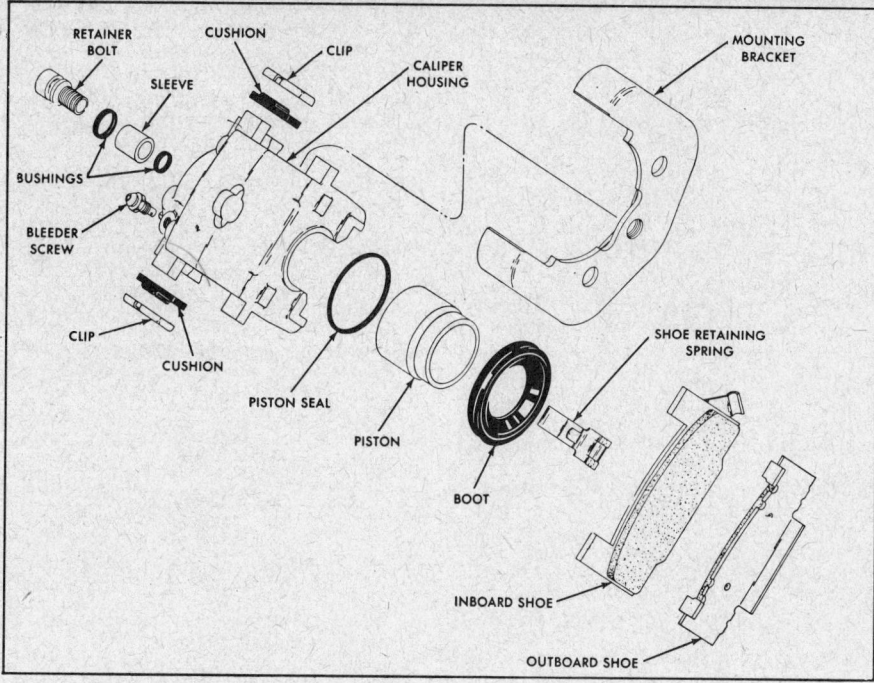

Fig. 18   Delco-Moraine single piston disc brake with single mounting bolt

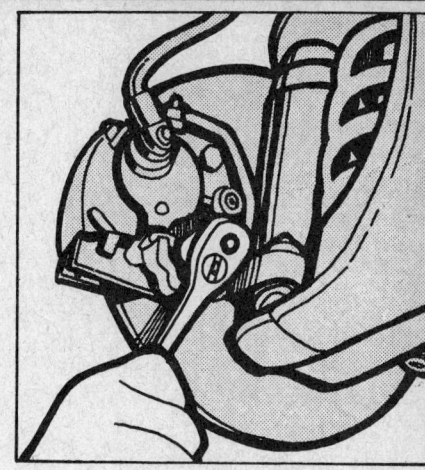

Fig. 19   Removing mounting bracket from steering knuckle

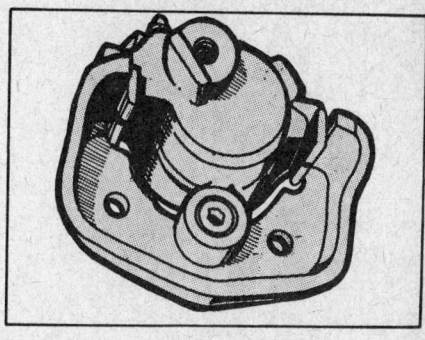

Fig. 20   Bracket assembly installed on caliper

DELCO-MORAINE SINGLE PISTON

W/Single Mounting Bolt

This single piston sliding caliper assembly, Figs. 17 and 18, incorporates a one piece housing with the inboard side of the housing bored for the piston. A seal within the housing bore provides a hydraulic seal between the piston and housing wall.

A spring steel scraper (wear sensor) is incorporated on each inboard shoe. When shoe lining has worn to within .030 inch of the shoe, the sensor scrapes the rotor and emits an audible high frequency sound indicating that the linings should be replaced.

The caliper assembly slides on a mounting sleeve which is secured by a mounting bolt. Upon brake application fluid pressure against the piston forces the inboard shoe against the inboard side of the rotor. This action causes the caliper to slide until the outboard shoe comes in contact with the rotor.

Caliper Removal

1. Siphon brake fluid from master cylinder to bring level to ⅓ full, discard brake fluid removed.
2. Raise vehicle and remove wheel and tire assembly.
3. Install a 7 inch C-clamp on caliper with solid end of clamp on caliper housing and screw end on metal portion of outboard brake shoe. Tighten clamp until piston bottoms in caliper bore, then remove clamp.
4. Disconnect brake hose from caliper and remove copper gaskets, cap end of brake hose.

NOTE: If only brake shoes are to be replaced do not disconnect brake hose.

5. Remove the two mounting brackets to steering knuckle bolts, Fig. 19.

NOTE: Do not remove socket head retaining bolt. Support caliper when removing second bolt to prevent caliper from falling.

6. Slide caliper from rotor.

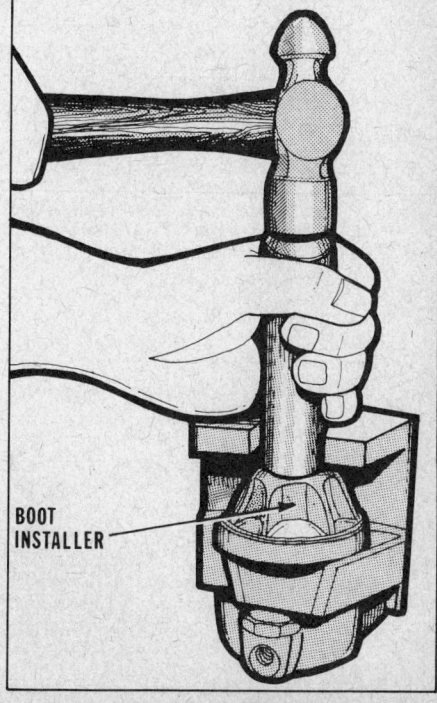

Fig. 23   Installing boot on caliper

Fig. 21   Removing and installing cushions

Fig. 22   Removing piston boot

DISC BRAKES

NOTE: If only brake shoes are to be replaced support caliper from suspension using wire. Do not stretch or kink brake hose.

Brake Shoe Removal

1. Remove caliper as described under "Caliper Removal".
2. Remove brake shoes, if retaining spring does not come off with inboard shoe remove it from piston.

Caliper Disassembly

1. Using clean brake fluid clean exterior of caliper.
2. Drain brake fluid from caliper.
3. Remove caliper mounting bracket bolt and slide bracket from caliper, Fig. 20, then remove sleeve and bushing from bolt and bushing from caliper mounting hole, Fig. 18.
4. Remove clips if still in place, then remove cushions, Fig. 21.
5. Pad interior of caliper with clean shop towels, then direct compressed air through caliper inlet hole to remove piston.

NOTE: Use only enough air pressure to ease piston out of bore.

CAUTION: Do not place fingers in front of piston for any reason when applying compressed air. This could result in serious personal injury.

6. Using a screwdriver carefully pry boot from caliper, Fig. 22.
7. Remove piston seal from caliper bore using a piece of wood or plastic.

NOTE: Do not use metal tool to remove piston seal as it may damage caliper bore.

8. Remove bleeder valve.

Caliper Assembly

1. Lubricate caliper bore and piston seal with clean brake fluid, then position seal in caliper bore groove.
2. Lubricate piston with clean brake fluid and install boot into piston groove with fold facing the open end of piston, Fig. 18.
3. Insert piston into caliper, then using care to avoid unseating seal, force piston into caliper.

NOTE: To force piston into caliper a force of 50–100 pounds will be required.

4. Position outside diameter of boot into caliper counterbore and seat with suitable boot installer. Fig. 23.

CAUTION: Ensure that retaining ring molded into boot is not bent and that boot is installed fully and evenly below and around the caliper, as dirt and moisture may enter caliper and cause damage and corrosion.

5. Install bleeder screw.

Fig. 24   Fitting brake pad to caliper

6. Position and stretch cushions over caliper lugs, fitting the heavy section in the lug recess and saw-tooth edges of cushions facing out, Fig. 21.
7. Using silicone lubricant, liberally lubricate sleeve and bushings and the unthreaded portion of the retainer bolt. Install the larger bushing in the caliper hole groove and install the sleeve. Install the smaller bushing in the retainer bolt groove.
8. With caliper clamped in a vise, position clips over cushions and squeeze mounting bracket over clips, aligning the bolt hole. Move bracket against retainer boss on caliper and install retainer bolt. Torque bolt to 28 ft. lbs., (38 N-m).

NOTE: Considerable force may be required to squeeze bracket over cushions and clips on caliper. Start open end of bracket over ends of clips near the boot and move the bracket toward the closed end of caliper.

Brake Shoe Installation

1. Position retaining spring on inboard shoe, place single leg in brake shoe hole, then snap two other legs over notch in shoe.

NOTE: Some inboard replacement brake pads incorporate wear sensors and have a specific left and right hand assembly. Properly installed, the wear sensor will face toward the rear of caliper.

2. Install shoe in caliper.
3. Position caliper over rotor, align mounting holes, install and torque bolts to 70 ft. lbs., (95 N-m).
4. Using suitable pliers clinch outboard shoe to caliper, place lower jaw of pliers on bottom edge of shoe, place upper jaw of pliers on shoe tab, squeeze pliers and bend tab, Fig. 24. Clinch other end of shoe in same manner. Outboard end play should be zero to .005 inch., (zero to 0.127 mm).
5. Install wheel and tire assembly and lower vehicle.
6. Add brake fluid to within ¼ inch from top of master cylinder.

NOTE: Pump brake pedal several times to ensure it is firm before moving vehicle.

Caliper Installation

1. Install caliper as described under "Brake Shoe Installation", then install brake hose with new copper gaskets, torque fitting to 21 ft. lbs., (29 N-m), if removed, bleed brake system.

NOTE: Brake hose fitting must be against machined surface on caliper to ensure proper hose positioning.

DELCO-MORAINE OPPOSED PISTONS

These brakes are used on all four wheels. The components of the disc brake system are shown in Fig. 25. The caliper assemblies replace the conventional wheel cylinder, brake shoes and linings, and the disc replaces the brake drum.

The caliper assembly contains four pistons, two acting on each shoe with one shoe on each side of the disc.

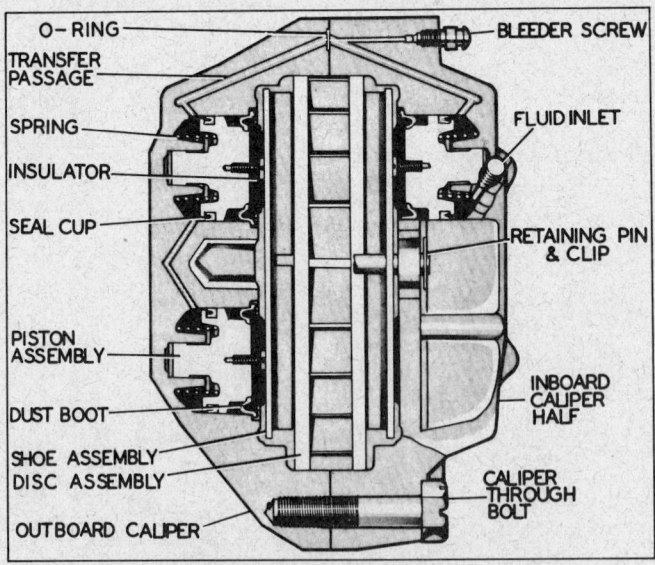

Fig. 25   Delco-Moraine opposed piston disc brake assembly

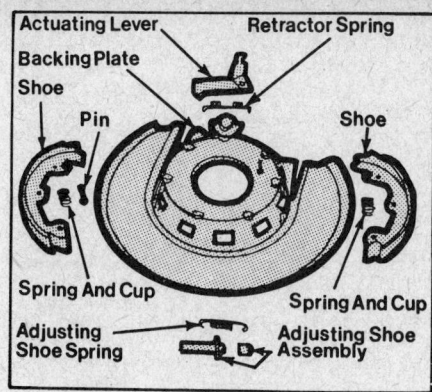

Fig. 26 Delco-Moraine parking brake components

The brake disc is riveted to the hub flange at the front wheel and to the spindle flange at the rear wheel. The disc rotates through the caliper assembly, which is bolted to a support that is attached to the steering knuckle at the front wheel and the spindle support bolts at the rear wheel. The disc has cooling fins between the two shoe reacting surfaces. When a disc must be replaced, the rivets can be drilled out and then the wheel studs will be used for disc retention purposes.

A miniature set of brake shoes, mounted on a flange plate and shield assembly attached to the rear wheel spindle support bolts, are used for vehicle parking, Fig. 26.

Removing Lining

1. To prevent overflow, remove two thirds of brake fluid from master cylinder.
2. Support vehicle on hoist and remove wheel.
3. Remove cotter pin from inboard end of retaining pin.
4. Remove inboard and outboard shoe by pulling up.

Installing Lining

1. Install inboard and outboard shoe one at a time. Use two screwdrivers to push pistons back as shoes are inserted, Fig. 27.
2. Install retaining pin through outboard caliper half, outboard shoe, inboard shoe and inboard caliper half. Insert a new $3/32 \times 5/8$ inch plated cotter pin through retaining pin.
3. Repeat above procedure at each wheel where shoes are to be replaced.
4. Refill master cylinder, then install wheel and lower vehicle.

CAUTION: Do not move vehicle until a firm brake pedal has been obtained.

Calipers

The caliper assembly, Fig. 28, incorporates two halves retained by bolts at the flange end. The two halves contain fluid crossover passages from one to the other, sealed with "O" rings.

The bleeder screw is threaded into a passage drilled to intersect the fluid crossover passage. The bleeder screws are located at the front of each caliper. There are two bleeder screws, one inboard, one outboard at the rear wheels, and one bleeder screw at the inboard side at the front wheel. It is necessary, therefore, to remove the rear wheel when bleeding the rear caliper.

Removing Caliper

1. Support vehicle on hoist and remove wheel.
2. On front caliper, disconnect brake hose from support bracket. On rear caliper, disconnect tubing from inboard caliper. Tape open tube or line end to prevent entry of dirt.
3. Remove caliper mounting bolts and remove caliper.

Disassembling Caliper

1. Remove brake hose from front caliper.
2. Remove cotter pin from retaining pin, then remove pin and shoe assembly from caliper.
3. Remove caliper retaining bolts and sepa-

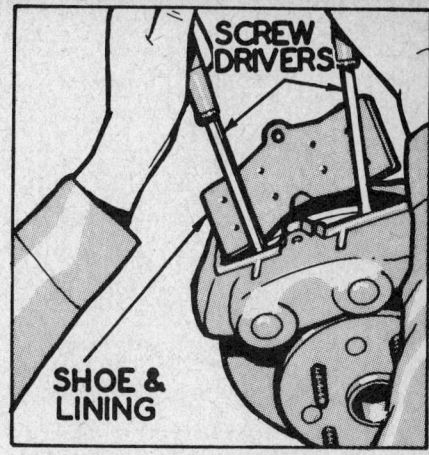

Fig. 27 Installing Delco Moraine disc brake shoes

rate caliper halves, then remove the two O-rings from fluid transfer cavities in ends of caliper halves.
4. Push piston into caliper as far as it will move, then insert a screwdriver under inner edge of steel ring in boot and using piston as a fulcrum, pry piston boot from its seat in caliper half.

CAUTION: Use care not to puncture seal when removing pistons from caliper.

5. Remove pistons and springs from caliper half, then remove boot and seal from piston.

Cleaning & Inspection

1. Clean all metal parts using clean brake fluid, removing all traces of dirt and grease.

CAUTION: Never use mineral base cleaning solvents as they can cause deterioration of rubber parts or make them soft and swollen.

2. Using air pressure, blow out all fluid passages in caliper halves, making sure that these passages are not obstructed.
3. Discard all rubber parts and replace with new service kit parts.
4. Inspect piston bores. They must be free of scores and pits. A damaged bore will cause leaks and unsatisfactory brake operation. If either caliper half is damaged to the extent that polishing with fine crocus cloth will not restore to satisfactory condition, replace the caliper half.
5. Check fit of piston in bore using a feeler gauge. Clearance should be as follows:
   $1\frac{7}{8}$ inch bore   .0045–.010
   $1\frac{3}{8}$ inch bore   .0035–.009
If bore is not damaged and clearance exceeds specifications, only a new piston will be required.

Assembling Caliper

1. Install seal in piston groove which is closest to flat end of piston. The seal lip must face toward large end of piston.

NOTE: Make certain seal lips are in

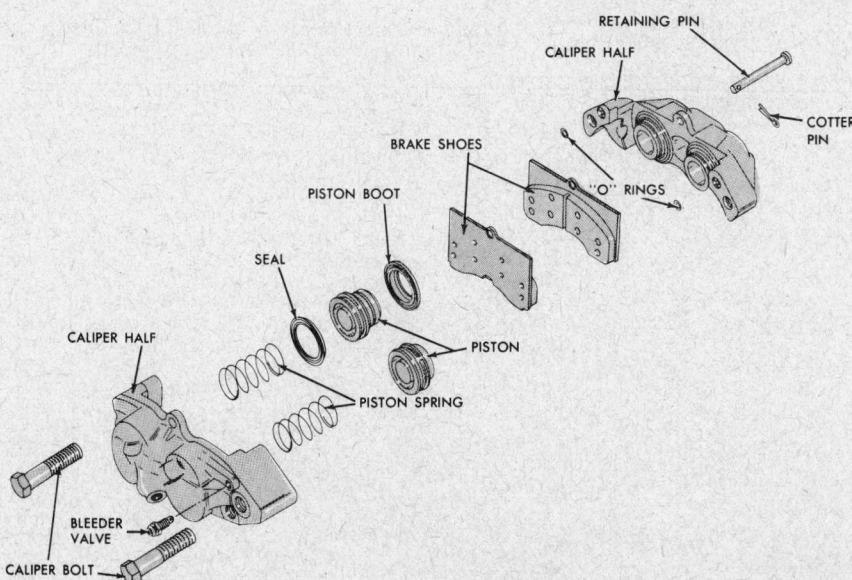

Fig. 28 Delco-Moraine disc brake caliper components

DISC BRAKES

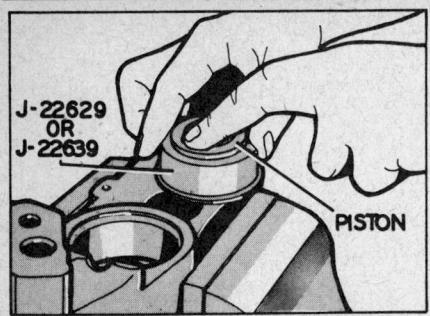

Fig. 29   Installing piston in caliper

piston groove and do not extend over step in end of groove.

2. Place spring in piston bore, then lubricate seal with brake fluid.
3. Install piston assembly in bore using tool J-22591, 22629 or 22639, Fig. 29. Use care not to damage seal lip as piston is pressed past edge of bore.
4. Install piston boot in groove closest to concave end of piston with fold in boot facing toward end of piston with seal attached.

NOTE: On 1979–83 models, apply a bead of suitable sealer (GM 1052366 or equivalent into piston boot groove, then install boot into groove.

5. Make certain that piston slides smoothly into bore until end of piston is flush with end of bore. If not, recheck piston assembly and position of piston spring and seal.
6. Using boot seal installer tool J-22592, J-22628 or J-22638, Fig. 30, over piston, seat steel boot retaining ring evenly into counterbore.

NOTE: Boot retaining ring must be flush or below machined face of caliper. Any distortion or uneven seating could allow corrosive elements to enter bore. On 1979–83 models, push pistons into bore fully and hold in place. Apply a bead of suitable sealer (GM 1052366 or equivalent) onto outer edge of boot retaining ring to form a seal between retaining ring and caliper housing.

7. Install O-rings in cavities around brake fluid transfer holes at both ends of outboard caliper halves. Lubricate caliper bolts with Delco Brake Lube #540032 (or equivalent) or clean brake fluid, then secure caliper halves together and torque front caliper housing bolts to 130 ft. lbs. and rear caliper housing bolts to 60 ft. lbs.

Installing Caliper

1. Mount caliper over disc, then using two screwdrivers, depress pistons so that caliper can be lowered into place.

NOTE: Use care not to damage boots on edge of disc as caliper is installed.

2. Install mounting bolts and torque to 70 ft. lbs.

CAUTION: If reusing old shoe assemblies, be sure to install shoes in same location

3—100

---

from which removed.

3. Install disc pads as outlined previously.
4. Place a new copper gasket on male end of front wheel brake hose and install brake hose in calipers. With wheels straight ahead, pass female end of hose through support bracket, then making certain that tube seat is clean, connect brake line tube nut to caliper and tighten securely.
5. Allowing hose to seek a normal position, without twist, insert hose fitting in support bracket and secure with "U" shaped retainer, then while turning steering geometry from stop to stop, check that hose does not contact other parts at anytime. If contact does occur, remove "U" shaped retainer and twist hose in a direction that will eliminate hose contact. Reinstall retainer and recheck for hose contact. If satisfactory, place steel tube connecter in hose fitting and tighten securely.
6. If rear caliper is being serviced, connect brake line to caliper.
7. Bleed brakes and install wheels.

CAUTION: Do not move vehicle until a firm pedal has been obtained.

Service Summary

1. There is no brake shoe adjustment on the disc brakes.
2. The groove in the brake shoe is an indicator of brake wear. When the groove is just about gone it is time for shoe replacement.
3. When replacing shoes it is necessary to siphon fluid from master cylinder reservoir to make room for fluid to return to the reservoir when pushing the caliper pistons back into their bores to make room for the thickness of the new shoes.
4. The shoes have a directional arrow on the back of the shoe plate. This arrow points to the forward rotation of the disc, and the purpose is for aligning the grain of the lining material in relation to the disc.
5. When bleeding the calipers, the rear wheel must be removed to reach the outboard bleeder screw.
6. A retaining clip of thin metal is used to hold the pistons into the bores while installing the new brake shoes.
7. The caliper assembly is removable, after disconnecting the brake line, by remov-

Fig. 31   Kelsey-Hayes floating caliper single piston disc brake (typical)

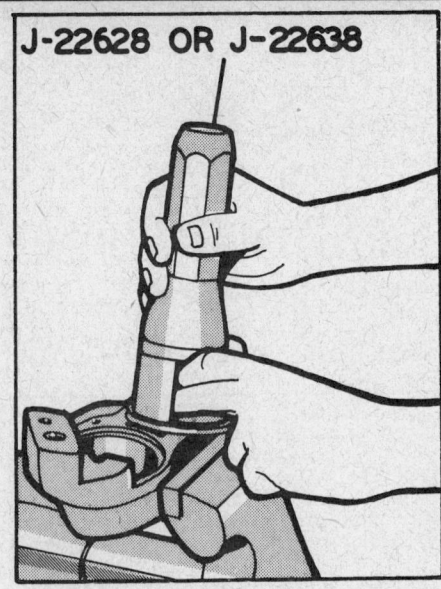

Fig. 30   Installing boot seal in caliper

ing the two mounting bolts and lifting the assembly off the disc.

8. The disc is riveted to the spindle flange in production. However, the rivets may be drilled out and the wheel studs and nuts are sufficient to hold the new disc in place when replacing the disc.
9. The rear wheel spindle must be removed to gain access to the parking brake shoes. It is necessary then to remove the caliper, the axle drive shaft, the spindle drive shaft yoke and remove the spindle and disc as an assembly from the wheel support. You now have access to the parking brake shoes the same as any other conventional bendix type brake shoe, Fig. 26.
10. If the car is equipped with the special optional knock-off hub assemblies, the adapters must be removed to gain access to the parking brake adjustment.

KELSEY-HAYES DUAL PIN FLOATING CALIPER

This type brake is a floating caliper, single piston, ventilated unit, actuated by the hydraulic system, Fig. 31. The caliper assembly, Fig. 32, is made up of a floating caliper assembly and an anchor plate. The anchor plate is bolted to the wheel spindle arm by two bolts. The caliper is attached to the anchor plate through two spring steel stabilizers. The caliper slides on two guide pins which also attach to the stabilizers. A single piston is used. The cylinder bore contains a piston with a molded rubber dust boot to seal the cylinder bore from contamination and also to return the piston to the released position when hydraulic pressure is released. Also a rubber piston seal is used to provide sealing between cylinder and piston.

Service Precautions

In addition to the precautions described at the beginning of this chapter, the following must be observed:

1. If the piston is removed for any reason the piston seal must be replaced.
2. During removal and installation of a wheel assembly, use care not to interfere with and damage the caliper splash shield or the bleeder screw fitting.
3. Be sure the vehicle is centered on the

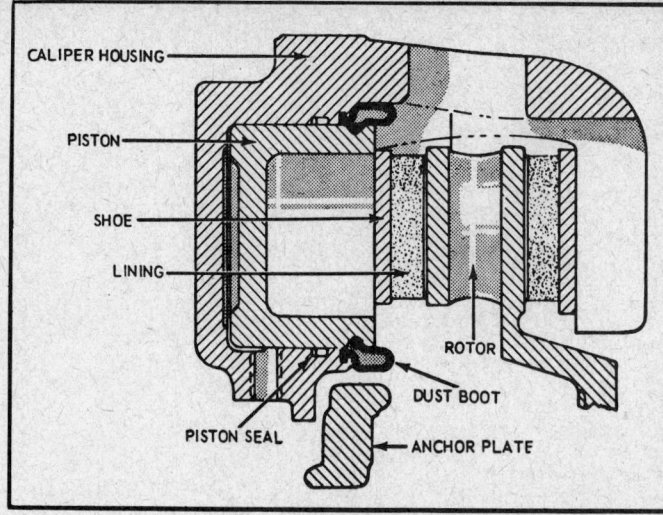

Fig. 32 Kelsey-Hayes floating caliper single piston disc brake (typical)

certain that metal portion of shoe is fully in recess of caliper and adaptor.

2. Holding inboard shoe assembly in place, carefully slide caliper down into position in adaptor and over rotor. Align guide pin holes of adaptor and inboard and outboard shoes.

3. Press in on end of guide pin and thread pin into adaptor using extreme care not to cross threads. Torque guide pins from 33 ft. lbs. making sure that tabs of positioners are over machined surfaces of caliper.

4. If caliper was removed, connect brake hose to caliper and tighten securely, then open bleeder screw and allow caliper to fill with fluid. Make certain that all air bubbles have escaped when bleeding caliper.

CAUTION: Do not move vehicle until a firm brake pedal has been obtained.

Caliper Disassembly

1. Open bleeder screw and drain brake fluid from caliper then place caliper assembly in a soft jawed vise.

CAUTION: Do not overtighten vise as excessive pressure will cause bore distortion and binding of piston.

2. To remove piston place a cloth over piston and apply compressed air to fluid port in caliper, Fig. 34. Use extreme care to avoid damage to piston or bore. Allow dust boot to remain in caliper groove as piston is withdrawn.

3. Using a small wooden or plastic stick, work piston seal out of its groove and discard seal.

NOTE: Do not use screwdriver to remove piston seal as it could scratch bore or burr edges of seal groove.

4. Remove bleeder screw.

Cleaning & Inspection

1. Clean all parts with brake fluid and wipe

hoist before servicing any front end components to avoid bending or damaging the rotor splash shield on full right or left wheel turns.

4. The proportioning valve should not be disassembled or adjustments attempted on it.

5. The wheel and tire must be removed separately from the brake rotor.

6. The caliper assembly must be removed from the spindle prior to removal of shoe and lining assembly.

7. Do not attempt to clean or restore oil or grease soaked brake linings. When contaminated linings are found, linings must be replaced in complete axle sets.

Removing Lining & Caliper

1. Support vehicle on hoist and remove wheel assembly.

2. Remove two thirds of brake fluid from

reservoir that serves disc brakes.

3. If caliper is to be removed, disconnect front brake hose from tube from mounting bracket and plug brake tube to prevent loss of fluid.

NOTE: If pistons are to be removed, leave flex brake line connected to tube at mounting bracket.

4. Remove caliper guide pins, Fig. 33.
5. Slide outboard and inboard shoe assembly out of caliper and adaptor.
6. Remove inner and outer bushings from caliper.

Installing Lining & Caliper

1. Install new inner and outer bushings Fig. 33, then slide shoe and lining assembly into place in caliper and adaptor making

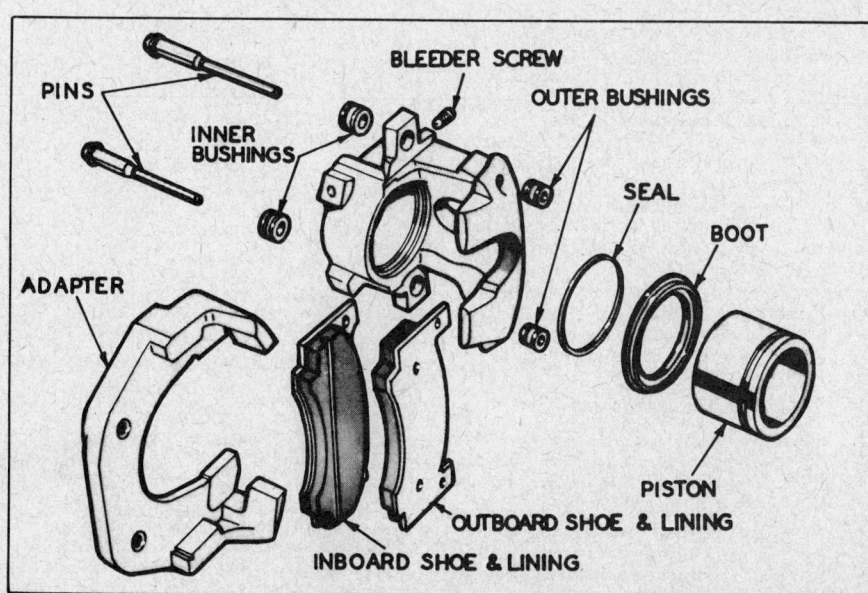

Fig. 33 Single piston disc brake caliper disassembled.

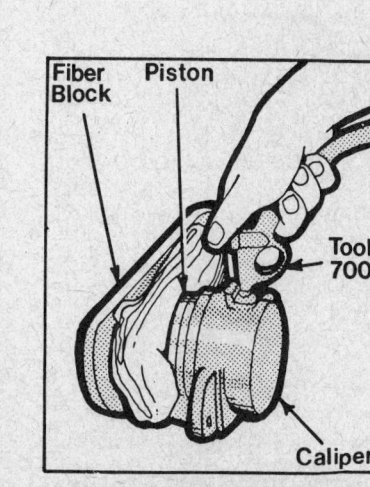

Fig. 34 Removing piston with air pressure

dry, then blow out all drilled passages using compressor.

2. Inspect bore for scoring, pitting or corrosion. A deeply scored or corroded caliper should be replaced, although light scores and stains may be removed.

NOTE: If piston is pitted, scored or worn, replace piston.

3. Using crocus cloth, polish any discolored or stained area. Using finger pressure rotate crocus cloth in cylinder bore. Do not slide cloth in and out of bore under pressure or use any other form of abrasive or abrasive cloth. Black stains on bore wall are caused by piston seals and will do no harm.

4. Bores that have deep scratches or scores, should be honed providing that the diameter of the bore is not increased more than .002 inch.

5. Using a feeler gauge, check clearance of piston in bore. Clearance should be .002-.006 inch. If clearance exceeds this specification, replace caliper assembly.

Caliper Assembly

1. Dip new piston seal in clean brake fluid and install in bore groove. Seal should be positioned and gently worked around groove until properly seated.

2. Dip new dust boot in clean brake fluid and install in caliper by working into outer groove. Boot will seem larger than diameter of groove but will snap into place when properly seated in groove. Slide forefinger around inside of boot to be sure it is seated.

3. Dip piston in clean brake fluid, then with fingers spreading boot, work piston into boot and carefully down the bore until bottomed.

CAUTION: To avoid cocking, force must be uniformly applied on piston.

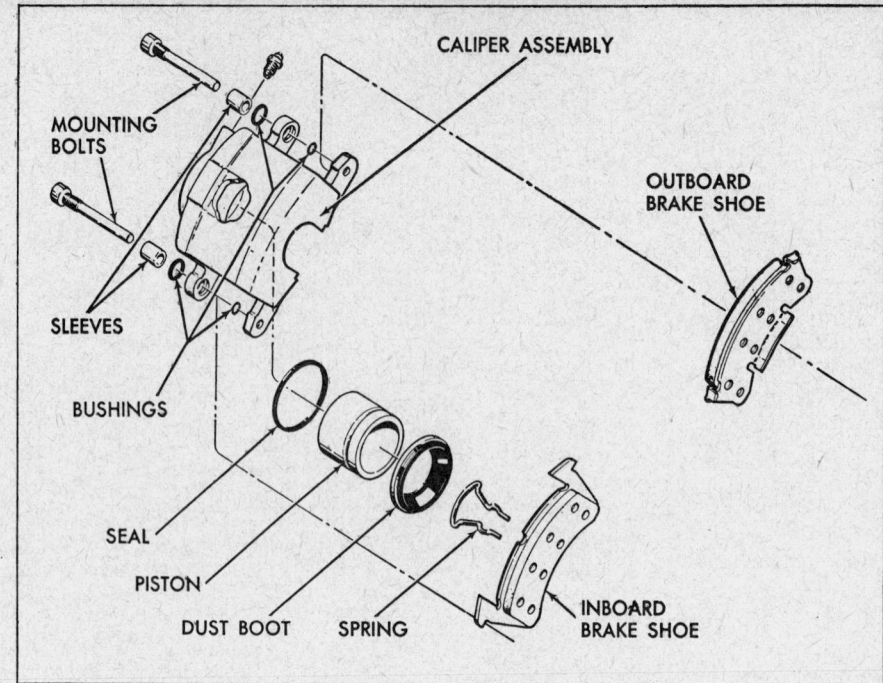

Fig. 35 Exploded view of caliper assembly (Typical). Delco Moraine single piston w/dual bolt mounting (Types 1 & 2)

DELCO-MORAINE SINGLE PISTON W/DUAL MOUNTING BOLTS (TYPE 1)

This single piston sliding caliper assembly, Fig. 35, incorporates a one piece housing with the inboard side of the housing bored for the piston. A seal within the housing bore provides a hydraulic seal between the piston and housing wall.

A spring steel scraper (wear sensor) is incorporated on each inboard shoe. When the shoe lining has worn to within .030 inch of the shoe, the sensor scrapes the rotor and emits an audible high frequency sound indicating that the linings should be replaced.

The caliper assembly slides on the mounting bolts. Upon brake application, fluid pressure against the piston forces the inboard shoe and lining assembly against the inboard side of the disc. This action causes the caliper assembly to slide until the outboard lining comes into contact with the disc. As pressure builds up, the linings are pressed against the disc with increased force.

Caliper Removal

1. Siphon enough brake fluid out of the master cylinder to bring fluid level to 1/3 full to avoid fluid overflow when the caliper piston is pushed back into its bore.

2. Raise vehicle and remove front wheels.

3. Using a "C" clamp, as illustrated in Fig. 36, push piston back into its bore.

4. Remove two mounting bolts, Fig. 37, and lift caliper away from disc.

Brake Shoe Removal

1. Remove caliper assembly as outlined above.

2. Remove inboard shoe. Dislodge outboard shoe and position caliper on the front suspension so the brake hose will not support the weight of the caliper.

3. Remove shoe support spring from piston.

4. Remove two sleeves from inboard ears of the caliper.

5. Remove four rubber bushings from the grooves in each of the caliper ears.

Brake Shoe Installation

1. Lubricate new sleeves, rubber bushings,

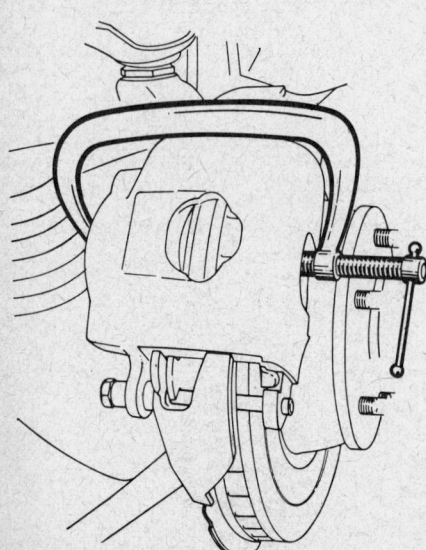

Fig. 36 Compressing piston and shoes with "C" clamp

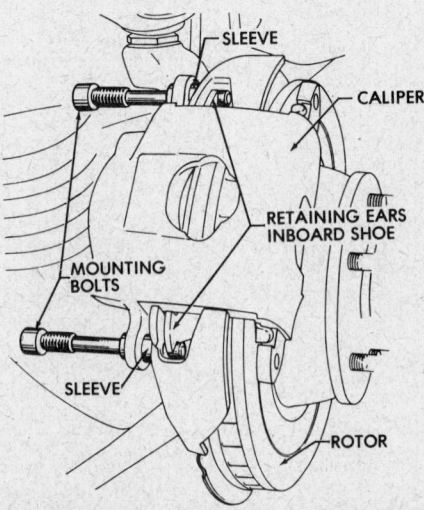

Fig. 37 Caliper & mounting bolts

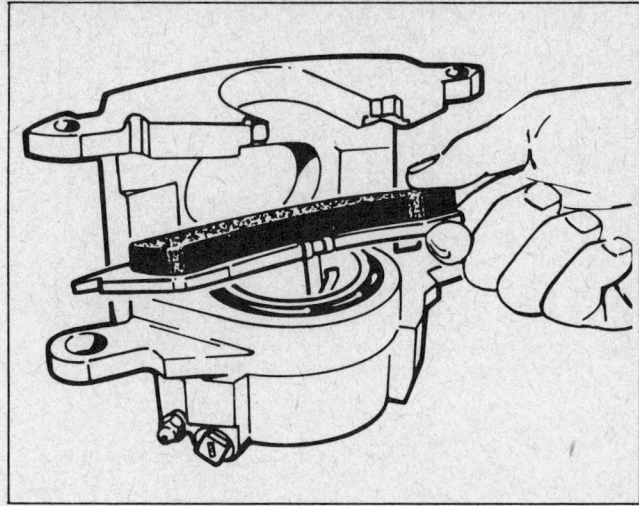

Fig. 38   Installing support spring

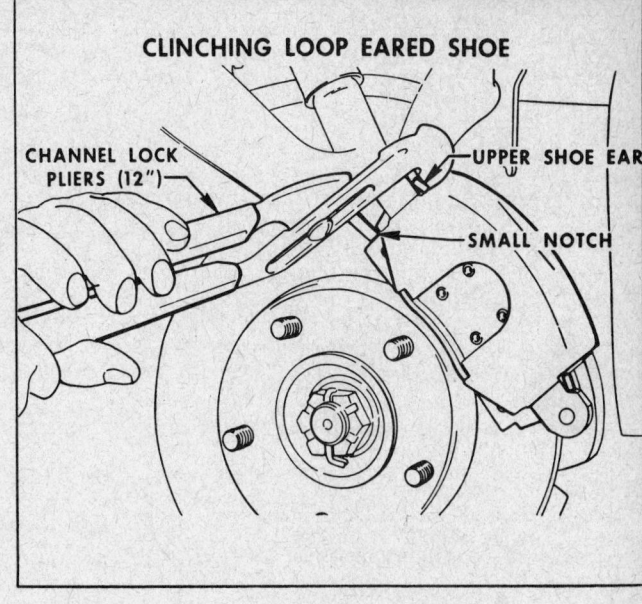

CLINCHING LOOP EARED SHOE

CHANNEL LOCK PLIERS (12")   UPPER SHOE EAR   SMALL NOTCH

Fig. 39   Clinching loop eared brake shoe

bushing grooves and mounting bolt ends with Delco Silicone Lube or its equivalent.
2. Install new bushings and sleeves in caliper ears.

NOTE: Position the sleeve so that the end toward the shoe is flush with the machined surface of the ear.

3. Install shoe support spring by positioning single tang end of spring into notch cut at top of inboard shoe. Press remaining end of spring over bottom edge of shoe until shoe is engaged securely, Fig. 38.
4. Position inboard shoe with spring attached into caliper with ear end facing downward and bottom end facing upward with spring resting on inside diameter of piston. Press downward on both ends of shoe until shoe contacts piston and support spring contacts piston inside diameter.

NOTE: Some inboard replacement brake pads incorporate wear sensors and have a specific left and right hand assembly. Properly installed, the wear sensor will face toward the rear of caliper.

5. Position outboard shoe in caliper with shoe ears over caliper ears and tab at bottom of shoe engaged in caliper cutout.

6. With shoes installed, lift caliper and rest bottom edge of outboard lining on outer edge of brake disc to be sure there is no clearance between outboard shoe tab and caliper abutment.
7. Install caliper and torque mounting bolts to 30–40 ft. lbs. on 1977–80 models. On 1981–83 vehicles, torque to 28 ft. lbs.
8. Clinch upper ears of outboard shoe by positioning pliers with one jaw on top of upper ear and one jaw in notch on bottom shoe opposite ear, Fig. 39. Ears are to be flat against caliper housing with no radial clearance. If clearance exists, repeat clinching procedure.

NOTE: Before moving vehicle, pump brake pedal several times to be sure it is firm. Do not move vehicle until a firm pedal is obtained. On 1981–83 models with low drag calipers, apply approximately 175 pounds of pressure to the brake pedal three times to properly seat the caliper and related components.

Disassembling Caliper

1. Remove caliper as outlined above.
2. Disconnect hose from steel line, remove U shaped retainer and withdraw hose from frame support bracket.
3. After cleaning outside of caliper, remove brake hose and discard copper gasket.
4. Drain brake fluid from caliper.
5. Pad caliper interior with clean shop towels and use compressed air to remove piston, Fig. 40.

NOTE: Use just enough air pressure to ease piston out of bore. Do not blow piston out of bore.

CAUTION: Do not place fingers in front of piston in an attempt to catch or protect it when applying compressed air. This could result in serious injury.

6. Carefully pry dust boot out of bore.

7. Using a small piece of wood or plastic, remove piston seal from bore.

NOTE: Do not use a metal tool of any kind to remove seal as it may damage bore.

8. Remove bleeder valve.

Assembling Caliper

1. Lubricate caliper piston bore and new piston seal with clean brake fluid. Position seal in bore groove.
2. Lubricate piston with clean brake fluid and assemble a new boot into the groove in the piston so the fold faces the open end of the piston, Fig. 41.
3. Using care not to unseat the seal, insert piston into bore and force the piston to the bottom of the bore.
4. Position dust boot in caliper counterbore and install, using suitable seal installer, Fig. 42.

NOTE: Check the boot installation to be sure the retaining ring moulded into the boot is not bent and that the boot is installed below the caliper face and evenly all around. If the boot is not fully installed, dirt and moisture may enter the bore and cause corrosion.

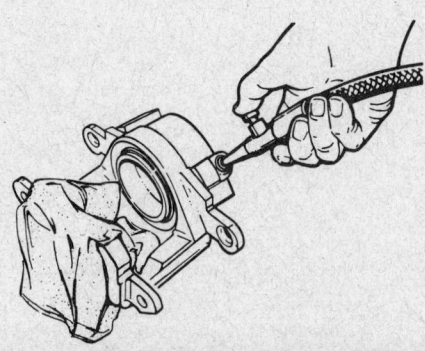

Fig. 40   Removing piston from caliper

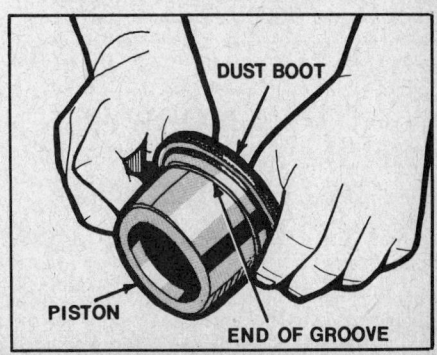

DUST BOOT

PISTON   END OF GROOVE

Fig. 41   Installing boot to piston

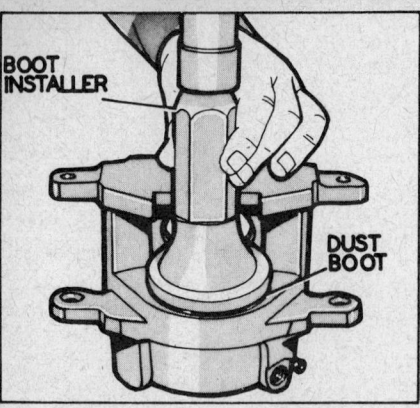

Fig. 42 Installing boot to caliper

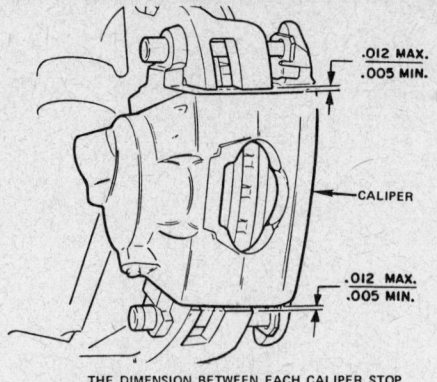

THE DIMENSION BETWEEN EACH CALIPER STOP AND THE CALIPER SHOULD BE .005"—.012"

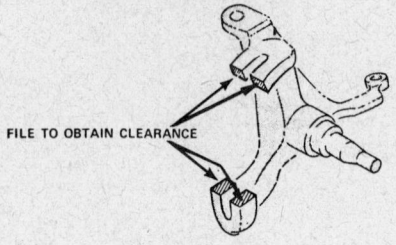

FILE TO OBTAIN CLEARANCE

Fig. 43 Checking clearance between caliper & stops

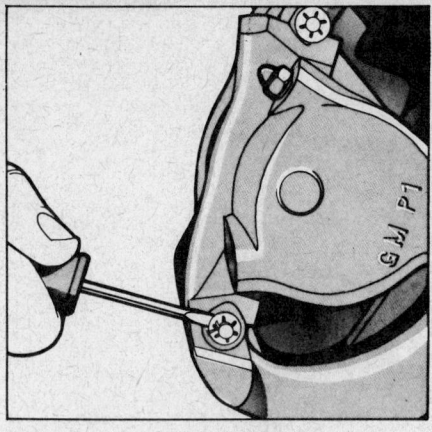

Fig. 44 Removing stamped nuts from mounting pins

5. Install the brake hose in the caliper using a new copper gasket.
6. Install shoes and re-install caliper assembly.

Caliper Installation

1. Position caliper over disc, lining up holes in caliper with holes in mounting bracket. If brake hose was not disconnected during removal, be sure not to kink it during installation.
2. Start mounting bolts through sleeves in inboard caliper ears and the mounting bracket, making sure ends of bolts pass under ears on inboard shoe.

NOTE: Right and left calipers must not be interchanged.

3. Push mounting bolts through to engage holes in the outboard ears. Then thread mounting bolts into bracket.
4. Torque mounting bolts to 30–40 ft. lbs. on 1977–80 models. On 1981–83 vehicles, torque to 28 ft. lbs.
5. Check the dimensions between each caliper stop and caliper, Fig. 43.
6. If brake hose was removed, reconnect it and bleed the calipers.
7. Replace front wheels, lower vehicle and add brake fluid to master cylinder to bring level to ¼" from top.

NOTE: Before moving vehicle, pump brake pedal several times to be sure it is firm. Do not move vehicle until a firm pedal is obtained. On 1981–83 models with low drag calipers, apply approximately 175 pounds of pressure to the brake pedal three times to properly seat the caliper and related components.

DELCO-MORAINE SINGLE PISTON W/DUAL BOLT MOUNTING (TYPE 2)

The single piston caliper assembly, Fig. 35, incorporates a one piece housing, with the inboard side of the housing bored for the piston. A seal within the housing bore provides a hydraulic seal between the piston and housing wall.

A spring steel scraper (wear sensor) is incorporated on each inboard shoe. When the shoe lining has worn to within .030 inch of the shoe, the sensor scrapes the rotor and emits an audible high frequency sound indicating that the linings should be replaced.

The caliper slides on the mounting sleeves which are secured by two mounting pins. Upon brake applications, fluid pressure against the piston forces the inboard shoe and lining assembly against the inboard side of the disc. This action causes the caliper assembly to slide until the outboard lining comes in contact with the disc. As pressure builds up, the linings are pressed against the disc with increased force.

Lining Removal

1. Remove one half the total brake fluid capacity to front master cylinder to prevent reservoir overflow when the caliper piston is pushed back in its bore.
2. Raise and properly support vehicle.
3. Position a 7 inch C-clamp on caliper so that solid end rests against the inside of the caliper and the screw end rests on the back side of the outer shoe. Tighten C-clamp until the caliper moves enough to push the piston to the bottom of the piston bore, then remove clamp.
4. Remove the two mounting pin snap rings or stamped nuts, Fig. 44, and slide out mounting pins, Fig. 45.
5. Lift caliper off disc and remove inner and outer by sliding out.

CAUTION: Do not permit brake hose to support weight of caliper. Support caliper by tying it to the suspension or control arm.

6. If caliper is to be removed, disconnect brake line.

Lining Installation

1. Install new sleeves with bushings on caliper grooves, Fig. 46.

NOTE: The "shouldered end" of sleeve must be installed toward outside.

2. Install inner shoe on caliper and slide shoe ears over sleeve, Fig. 47. Install the outer shoe in the same manner.

NOTE: Some inboard replacement brake pads incorporate wear sensors and have a specific left and right hand assembly. Properly installed, the wear sensor will face toward the rear of caliper.

CAUTION: If pads are being re-used, they must be installed in same location as when removed.

3. Mount caliper on steering knuckle. If brake line was disconnected, reconnect and torque bolt to 22 ft. lbs.

NOTE: To avoid overflow, it may be necessary to remove half of brake fluid capacity from master cylinder.

4. Install mounting pins from outside in and install snap rings or stamped nuts, Fig. 47. Nuts should be pressed on as far as possible using a suitable size socket that just seats on outer edge of nut.
5. Install wheel assembly and lower vehicle.
6. Add brake fluid to within ¼ inch from top of master cylinder and test brake operation to insure a firm brake pedal before moving vehicle.

Caliper Disassembly

1. Remove caliper as described under "Lining Removal".
2. Drain brake fluid from caliper and clean exterior of caliper using clean brake fluid.
3. Using clean towels, pad interior of caliper

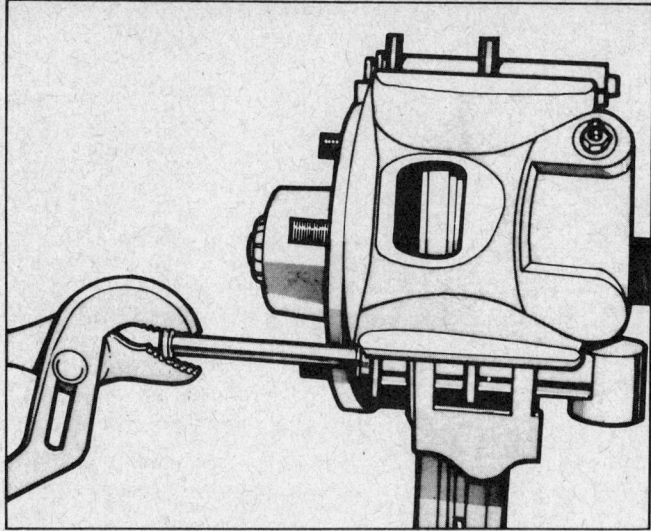

Fig. 45   Removing mounting pins

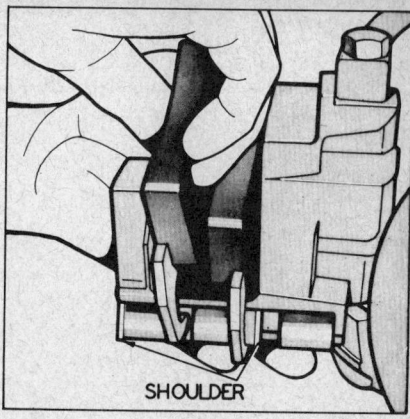

SHOULDER

Fig. 46   Mounting sleeves & brake shoe installation

and remove piston by applying just enough compressed air to fluid inlet port to ease piston out of bore.

CAUTION: Do not place fingers in front of piston in an attempt to catch or protect it when applying compressed air.

4. Carefully using a screwdriver so as not to scratch piston bore, pry dust boot out of piston bore, Fig. 48.
5. Using a piece of wood or plastic so as not to damage bore, remove piston seal from its groove in caliper bore.
6. Remove bleeder screw.

Cleaning & Inspection

1. Clean all metal parts in clean brake fluid, then using clean filtered air, dry parts and blow out all passages in caliper and bleeder valve.

NOTE: Always use clean brake fluid to clean caliper parts. Never use mineral base cleaning solvents as they can cause rubber parts to deteriorate and become soft and swollen, also the use of lubricated

compressed air will leave a film of oil on metal parts that may damage rubber parts when they come in after reassembly.

2. Inspect piston surface for scoring, nicks, corrosion and worn or damaged plating. If any surface defects are detected, replace piston.

CAUTION: The piston outside surface is the primary sealing surface in the caliper. It is manufactured and plated to close tolerances, therefore refinishing by any means or the use of any abrasive is not recommended.

3. Check caliper bore for same defects as piston. The piston bore is not plated and stains or minor corrosion may be polished with crocus cloth.

CAUTION: Do not use emery cloth or any other form of abrasive and thoroughly clean caliper after use of crocus cloth. If caliper cannot be cleaned up in this manner, replace caliper.

Caliper Assembly

NOTE: The dust boot and piston seal are to be replaced each time that the caliper is disassembled.

1. Lubricate piston bore and new piston seal with clean brake fluid, then position seal in caliper bore groove.
2. Lubricate piston with clean brake fluid and assemble a new boot into groove in piston, Fig. 49.
3. Install piston into bore using care not to unseat seal, then force piston to bottom of bore.

NOTE: Approximately 50–100 pounds of force are required to push piston to bottom of bore.

4. Position dust boot in caliper counterbore and seat boot using suitable boot installer, Fig. 42.

NOTE: Check boot installation to make sure that retaining ring moulded into boot is not bent and that boot is installed evenly all around. If boot is not fully installed, dirt and moisture may enter bore.

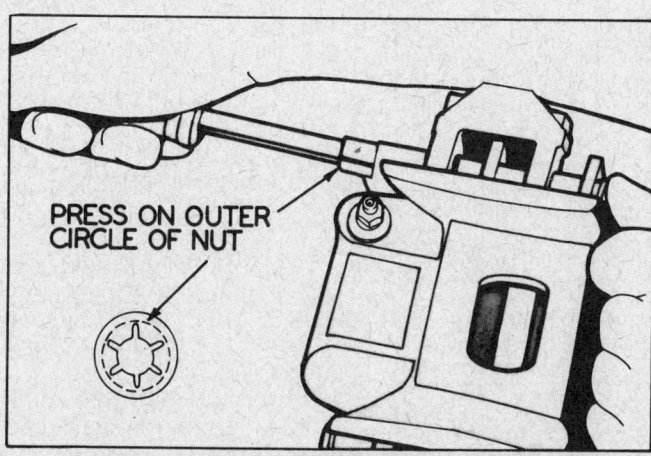

PRESS ON OUTER CIRCLE OF NUT

Fig. 47   Installing stamped nuts on mounting pins

SEAL

Fig. 48   Dust boot seal removal

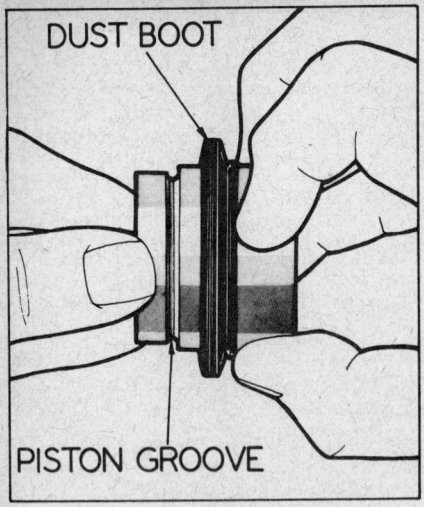

Fig. 49 Installing piston on boot

DELCO-MORAINE SINGLE PISTON W/DUAL BOLT MOUNTING (TYPE 3)

The caliper has a single piston and is mounted to the support bracket by two mounting bolts, Fig. 50. The caliper assembly slides on the two mounting bolts. Upon brake application, fluid pressure against the piston forces the inboard shoe and lining assembly against the inboard side of the disc. This action causes the caliper assembly to slide until the outboard lining comes into contact with the disc. As pressure builds up the linings are pressed against the disc with increased force.

Caliper Removal

1. Remove approximately 2/3 of brake fluid from master cylinder.
2. Raise and support front of vehicle, then remove wheel and tire assembly.
3. Position C-clamp as shown in Fig. 51, tighten C-clamp until piston bottoms in piston bore, then remove C-clamp.
4. If caliper assembly is being removed for service, remove brakeline fitting mounting bolt, Fig. 52. If only shoe and lining assemblies are to be replaced, do not disconnect brake line fitting from caliper.

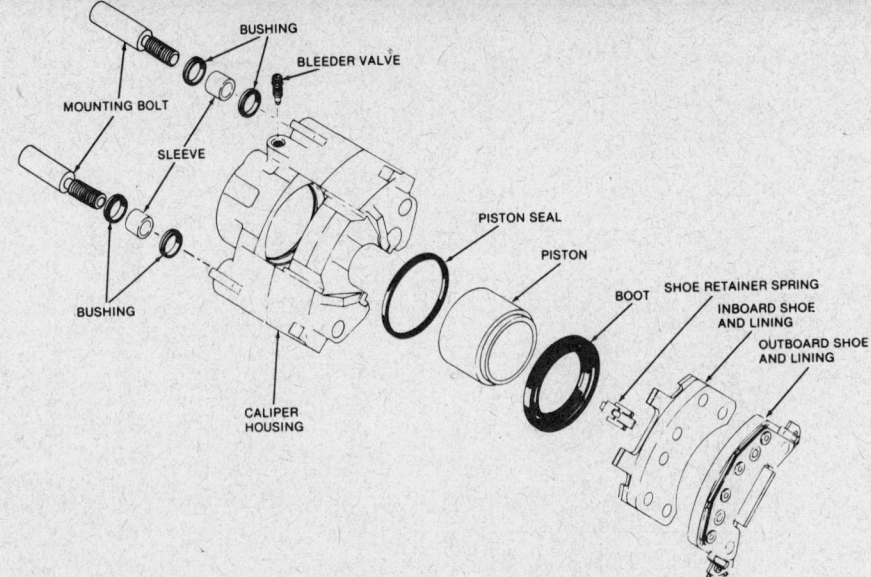

Fig. 50 Exploded view of caliper assembly. Delco Moraine single piston w/dual bolt mounting (Type 3)

5. Remove allen head caliper mounting bolts, Fig. 53. If bolts show signs of corrosion, use new bolts when installing caliper assembly.
6. Remove caliper assembly from disc. If only shoe and lining assemblies are to be replaced, using a length of wire suspend caliper from spring coil. Never allow caliper to hang from brake hose.

Shoe & Lining Removal

1. Remove caliper assembly as described under Caliper Removal.
2. Remove shoe and lining assemblies from caliper, Fig. 50.
3. Remove sleeves and bushings from grooves in caliper mounting bolt holes, Fig. 50.

Caliper Disassemble

1. Use clean shop towels to pad interior of caliper assembly, then remove piston by

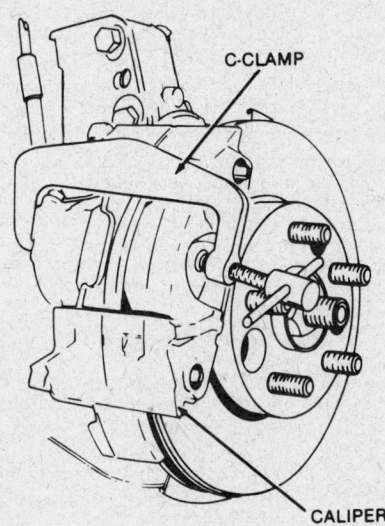

Fig. 51 Compressing piston & shoes with C-clamp

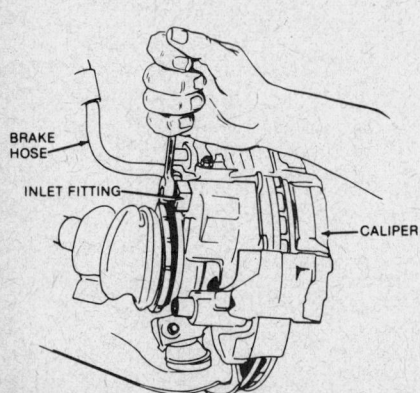

Fig. 52 Disconnecting brake line fitting from caliper

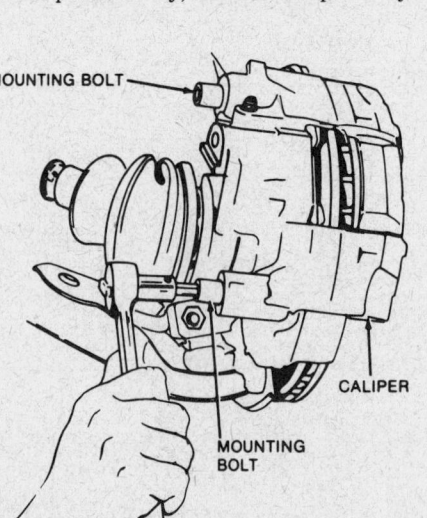

Fig. 53 Removing caliper mounting bolts

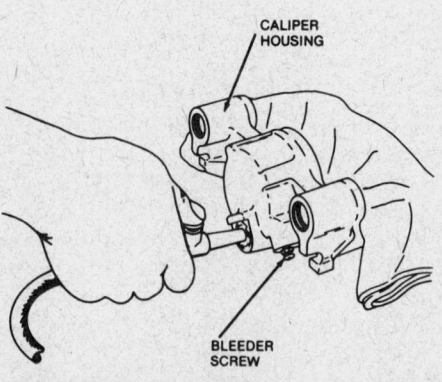

Fig. 54 Applying compressed air to caliper line port

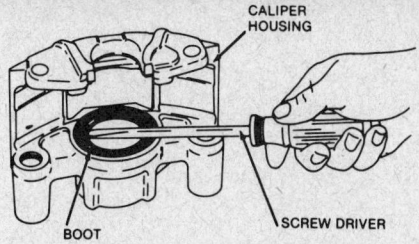

Fig. 55   Removing dust boot

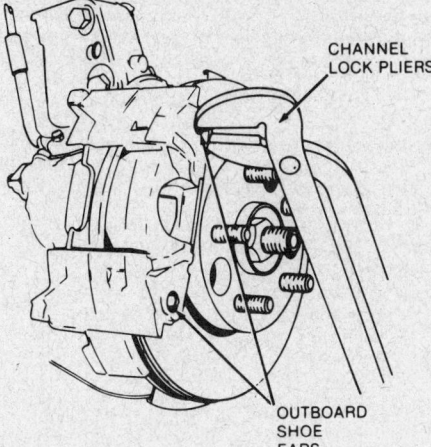

Fig. 58   Clinching outboard shoe to caliper

directing compressed air into caliper brake line inlet hole, Fig. 54.

NOTE: Use just enough air pressure to ease piston out of bore.

CAUTION: Do not place fingers in front of piston for any reason when applying compressed air. This could result in serious personal injury.

2. Remove bleeder screw from caliper body.

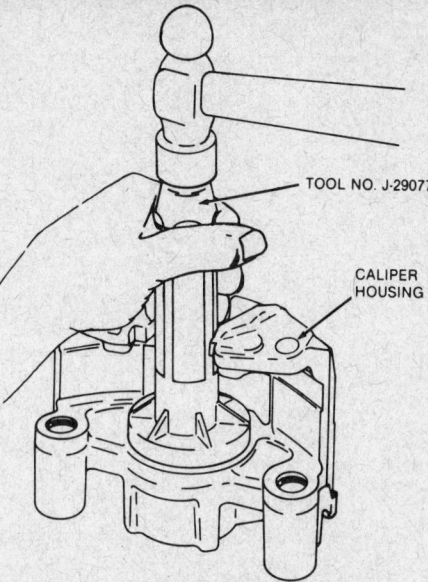

Fig. 56   Seating dust boot in caliper

3. Using a suitable screwdriver, remove dust boot from caliper bore, Fig. 55.
4. Using a piece of wood or plastic, remove piston seal from groove in caliper bore.

NOTE: Do not use any type of metal tool to remove piston seal, since damage to caliper bore may result.

5. Inspect piston for corrosion, scoring, nicks, wear and damage to chrome plating. If any of the above defects are found, replace piston.
6. Inspect caliper bore for corrosion, scoring, nicks, and wear. Light corrosion can be polished out using crocus cloth. If crocus cloth fails to remove corrosion, the caliper housing must be replaced.

Caliper Assemble

1. Lubricate piston seal with clean brake fluid, then install piston seal into caliper

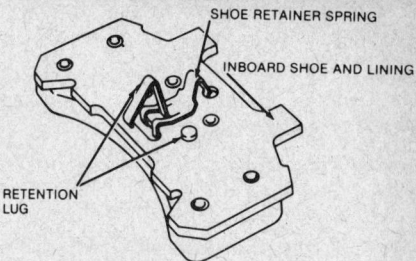

Fig. 57   Installing retainer spring on inboard shoe

bore groove. Check to ensure that piston seal is not twisted.
2. Lubricate caliper bore with clean brake fluid.
3. Insert piston into caliper bore of caliper, then force piston down until piston bottoms in bore.
4. Position outer diameter of dust boot in caliper housing counterbore, then seat boot as shown in Fig. 56.
5. Install bleeder screw on caliper housing.

Shoe & Lining Installation

1. Install outboard shoe and lining assembly into caliper housing.
2. Install retaining spring onto inboard shoe and lining assembly, Fig. 57, then install inboard shoe into caliper housing.
3. On 1980–81 models, using suitable pliers, clinch outboard shoe and lining assembly ears to caliper housing, Fig. 58.
4. On 1982–83 models, to clinch caliper to brake outboard shoe proceed as follows:
   a. To seat shoe flange to caliper, tightly position a large flat blade screwdriver between outboard shoe flange and hat section of rotor, Fig. 58A.
   b. Pressurize the hydraulic system by moderately applying brake pedal, then using suitable tool, clamp the outboard shoe tightly to the caliper.
   c. Position a ball peen hammer on outboard shoe tab, Fig. 58B, then using a larger brass hammer, lightly tap the ball peen hammer to bend the outboard shoe tab. Tabs must be bent around casting to approximately 45 degrees.
   d. After both tabs have been bent pressure should be released and outboard shoe should be locked into position. If shoe is loose, repeat steps a. through d.

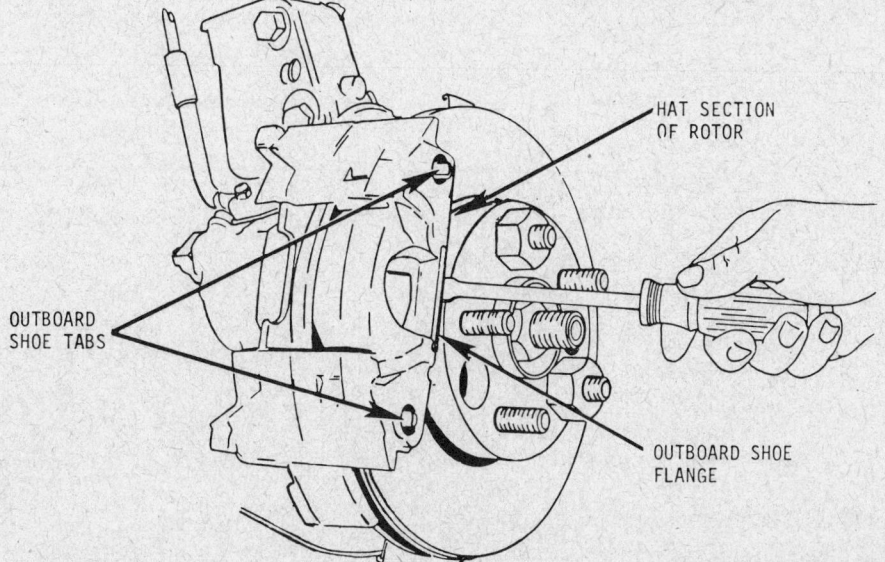

Fig. 58A   Screwdriver in position between outboard shoe flange & hat section of rotor

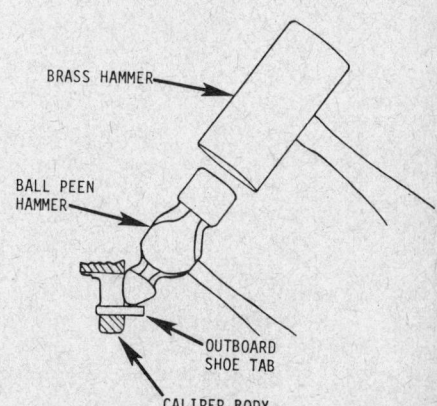

Fig. 58B   Ball peen hammer in position on outboard shoe tab

NOTE: If an outboard shoe is removed from the caliper, or the tabs unclinched for any reason, then it will be necessary to replace the disc shoe and lining assemblies. Do not reclinch outboard shoe locking tabs after having removed shoe from caliper.

Caliper Installation

1. Position caliper assembly over disc and align mounting bolt holes. If brake hoses were not disconnected during removal, use care not to kink hoses during installation.
2. Install mounting bolts and torque to 21 to 35 ft. lbs., Fig. 53.
3. If brake line fitting was disconnected during removal, install brake line fitting and torque retaining bolt to 18 to 30 ft. lbs., Fig. 52.
4. Fill master cylinder. Bleed brake system if brake line was disconnected and recheck master cylinder fluid level.
5. Install wheel and tire assembly on vehicle, then lower vehicle and check brake system operation.

FORD SLIDING CALIPER

The caliper assembly is made up of a sliding caliper housing assembly and an anchor plate, Fig. 59.

The anchor plate is bolted to the wheel spindle arm. Two angular machined surfaces on the upper end of the caliper housing contact mating machined surfaces of the anchor plate. A steel, plated key and a caliper support spring is fitted between the angular machined surfaces of the lower end of the caliper and the machined surface of the anchor plate. The key is held in position with a retaining screw. The caliper is held in position against the mating surfaces of the anchor plate by means of the caliper support spring. A brake shoe anti-rattle spring clip is provided on the anchor plate at the lower end of the inner brake shoe and lining assembly. The inner and outer

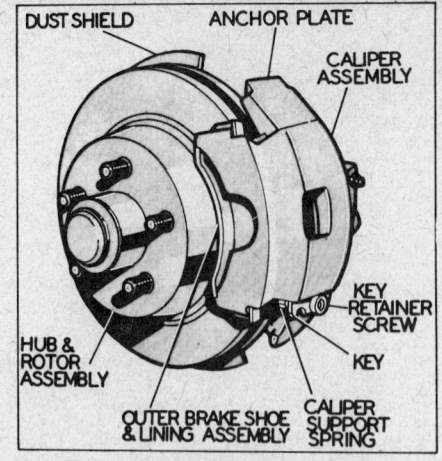

Fig. 59 Ford sliding caliper disc brake

brake shoe assemblies are not interchangeable.

The sliding caliper contains a single cylinder and a piston with a molded dust boot to seal the cylinder bore from contamination. A square section rubber piston seal is positioned in a groove in cylinder bore to provide sealing between cylinder and piston.

Caliper Removal

1. Raise car and suppor with safety stands. Block both rear wheels if a jack is used.
2. Remove wheel and tire assembly from hub.
3. Disconnect brake hose from caliper.
4. Remove retaining screw from caliper retaining key, Fig. 59.
5. Slide caliper retaining key and support spring either inward or outward from anchor plate. Use hammer and drift, if necessary, to remove the key and caliper support spring. Use care to avoid damaging the key.
6. Lift caliper assembly away from anchor

plate by pushing caliper down against anchor plate and rotate upper end upward out of anchor plate, Fig. 60.
7. Remove inner shoe and lining from anchor plate. The brake shoe anti-rattle clip (inner shoe only) may become displaced at this time and if so, reposition it on anchor plate, Fig. 61. Tap lightly on outer shoe and lining to free it from caliper.
8. Clean caliper, anchor plate and rotor assemblies and inspect them for signs of fluid leakage, wear or damage. If either lining is worn to within 1/32″ of any rivet head, both shoe and lining assemblies must be replaced. Also, if necessary to replace shoes and lining on one wheel, they must be replaced on both wheels to maintain equal brake action.

Caliper Disassembly

1. With caliper removed as described previously, disconnect brake hose. Cap hose and plug caliper inlet to prevent fluid loss.
2. With caliper on work bench, remove inlet plug and drain fluid from housing.
3. Place a wooden block or an old brake pad into the caliper, then place a shop cloth between wooden block and piston.
4. Apply air pressure slowly to caliper inlet port to remove piston, Fig. 62.

NOTE: If high pressure is applied quickly, piston may pop out and cause injury. A cocked or seized piston can be eased out by rapping sharply on piston end with a soft brass hammer.

5. Remove boot from piston and seal from caliper cylinder bore.

Caliper Assembly

1. Lubricate piston seal with clean brake fluid and piston seal in its cylinder bore groove.
2. Assemble dust boot on caliper housing by seating boot flange in the outer groove of cylinder bore, making sure it is fully seated.
3. Coat piston with clean brake fluid and install in cylinder bore.
4. Spread dust boot over piston as piston is installed and then bottom piston in the bore. Seat dust boot in its piston groove.

Caliper Installation

1. If new shoe and lining assemblies are to

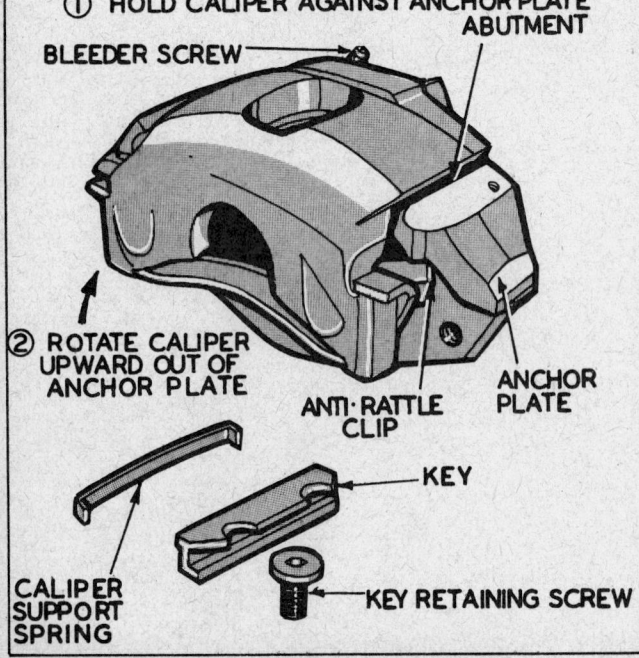

Fig. 60 Removing caliper assembly

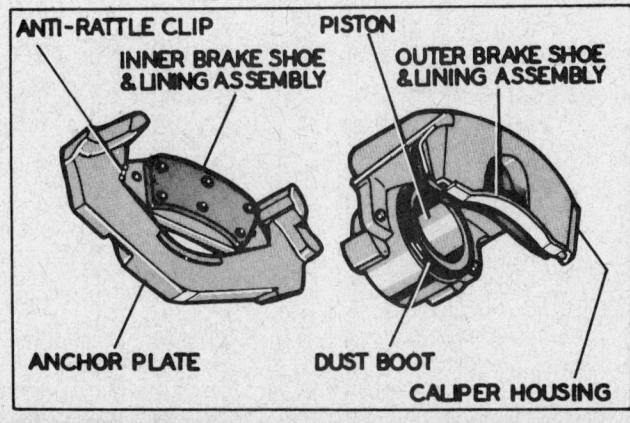

Fig. 61 Caliper and outer shoe removed from anchor plate

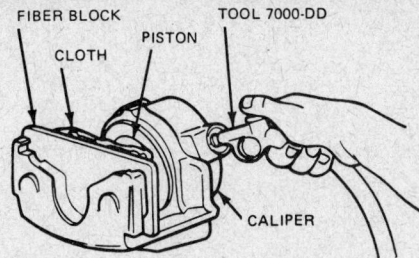

Fig. 62 Removing piston from caliper

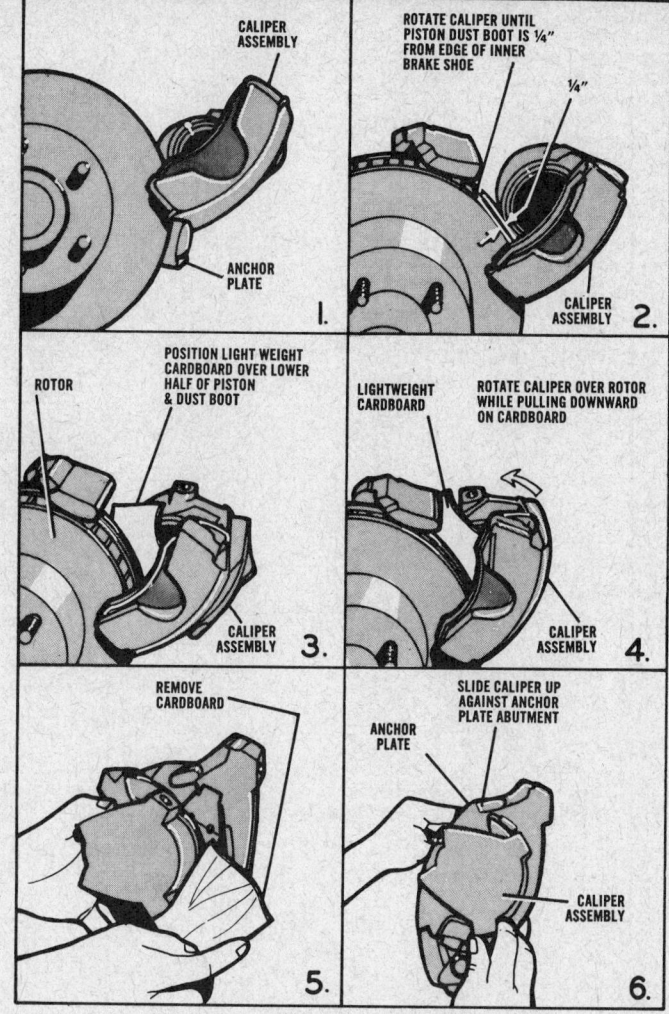

Fig. 63 Installing caliper assembly

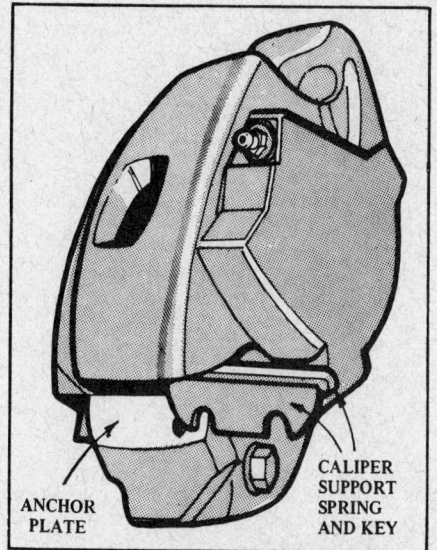

Fig. 64 Installing caliper support spring and retaining key

be installed, use a 4″ C-clamp and a block of wood 1¾″ × 1″ and about ¾″ thick to seat the caliper piston in its bore. This must be done to provide clearance for the caliper to fit over new shoes when installed.

2. Be sure brake shoe anti-rattle clip is in place on lower inner brake shoe support on anchor plate with pigtail of clip toward inside of anchor plate. Position inner shoe and lining on anchor plate with lining toward rotor, Fig. 61.

3. Install outer shoe and lining with lower flange ends against the caliper leg abutments and the brake shoe upper flanges over the shoulders on caliper legs. The shoe upper flanges fit tightly against the shoulder machined surfaces. If the same brake shoes and linings are to be used, be sure they are installed in their original positions.

4. Remove C-clamp if used, from the caliper (the piston will remain seated in its bore).

5. Position caliper housing lower V groove on anchor plate lower abutment surface, Fig. 63. Refer to Figs. 63 and 64 to complete assembly following steps shown.

Connect brake hose, bleed brakes and replace wheel.

6. Install key retaining screw and torque to 12–20 ft. lbs.

Brake Shoe & Lining, Replace

The procedure to replace the shoe and lining assemblies is the same as the caliper removal discussed previously with the exception that it is not necessary to disconnect the brake hose. Use care to avoid twisting or stretching the brake hose.

Hub & Rotor Removal

1. Remove caliper and shoes as previously described. If no repairs are necessary on the caliper it is not necessary to disconnect the brake hose. The caliper can be temporarily secured to the upper suspension arm. Do not remove the anchor plate and be careful not to stretch or twist the brake hose.

2. Remove grease cap from wheel spindle and remove cotter pin and nut lock from wheel bearing adjustment nut.

3. Remove wheel bearing adjusting nut and

grasp the hub and rotor and pull it out far enough to loosen the washer and outer wheel bearing. Then push it back in and remove the washer, outer wheel bearing and remove the hub and rotor.

KELSEY-HAYES SLIDING CALIPER

This sliding caliper single piston system uses a one piece hub and is actuated by the hydraulic system and disc assembly, Fig. 65. Alignment and positioning of the caliper is achieved by two machined guides or "ways" on the adaptor, while caliper retaining clips allow lateral movement of the caliper, Fig. 66. Outboard shoe flanges are used to position and locate the shoe on the caliper fingers, Fig. 67, while the inboard shoe is retained by the adaptor, Fig. 68. Braking force applied onto the outboard shoe is transferred to the caliper, while braking force applied onto the inboard shoe is transferred directly to the adaptor.

A square cut piston seal provides a hydraulic seal between the piston and the cylinder bore, Fig. 65. A dust boot with a wiping lip installed in a groove in the cylinder bore and

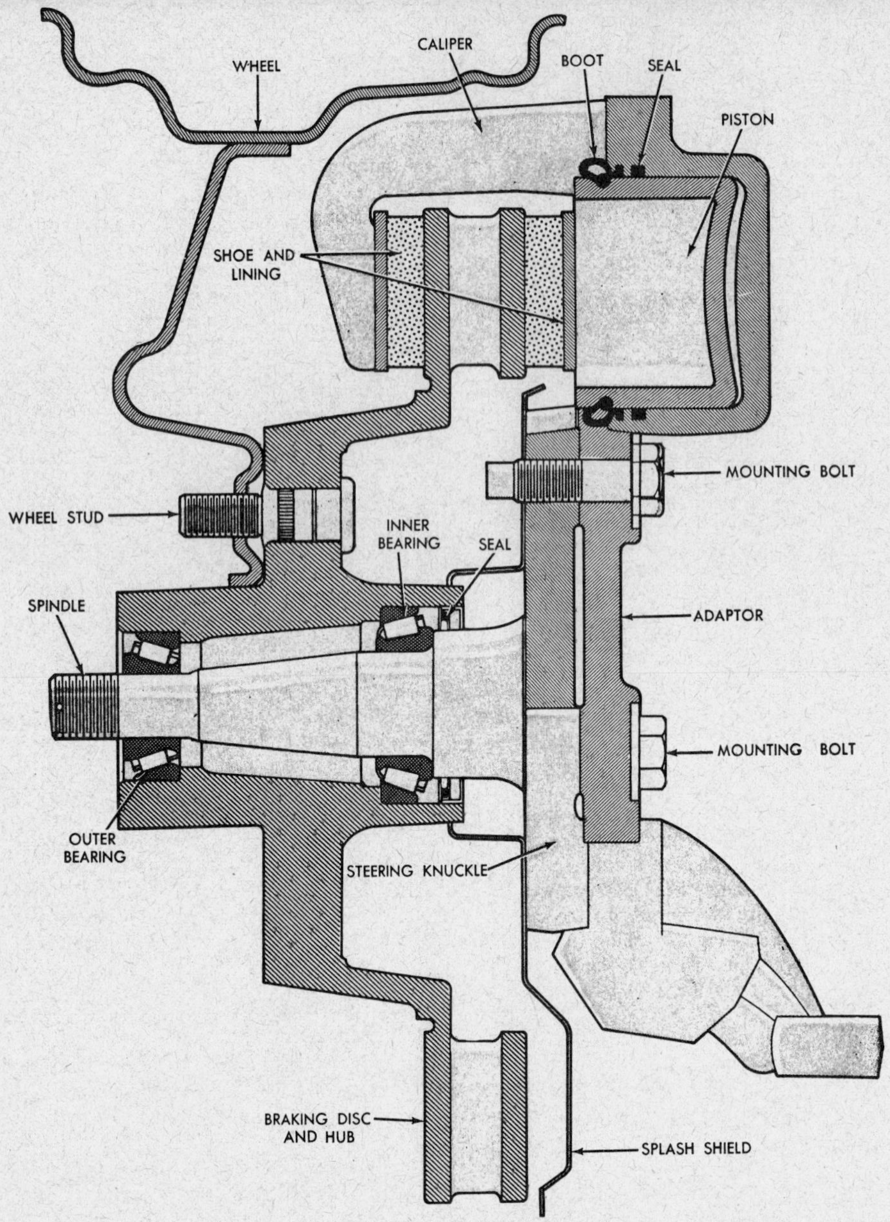

WHEEL CALIPER BOOT SEAL

PISTON

SHOE AND LINING

WHEEL STUD

SPINDLE

INNER BEARING SEAL

MOUNTING BOLT

ADAPTOR

MOUNTING BOLT

OUTER BEARING

STEERING KNUCKLE

BRAKING DISC AND HUB

SPLASH SHIELD

Fig. 65 Sectional view of Kelsey-Hayes sliding caliper front disc brake

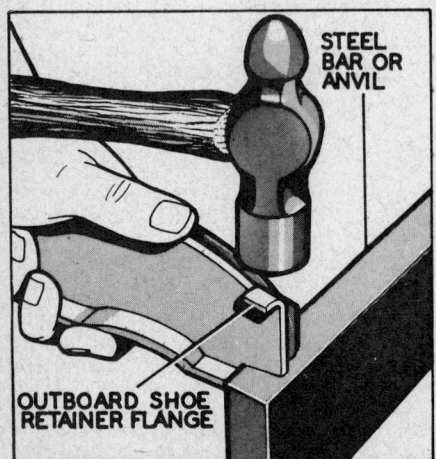

STEEL BAR OR ANVIL

OUTBOARD SHOE RETAINER FLANGE

Fig. 67 Fitting outboard shoe retaining flange

piston, prevents contamination in the piston and cylinder bore area. Adjustment between the disc and the shoe is obtained automatihcally by the outward relocation of the piston as the inboard lining wears and inward movement of the caliper as the outboard lining wears.

Caliper Removal

1. Raise the vehicle and remove front wheel.
2. Remove caliper retaining clips and anti-rattle springs, Fig. 66.
3. Remove caliper from disc by slowly sliding caliper assembly out and away from disc.

NOTE: Use some means to support caliper. Do not let caliper hang from hydraulic line.

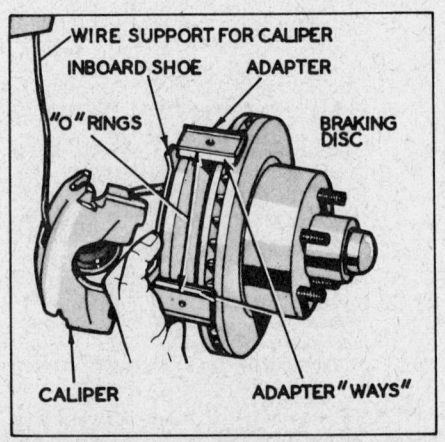

WIRE SUPPORT FOR CALIPER

INBOARD SHOE   ADAPTER

"O" RINGS

BRAKING DISC

CALIPER

ADAPTER "WAYS"

Fig. 68 Replacing inboard shoe

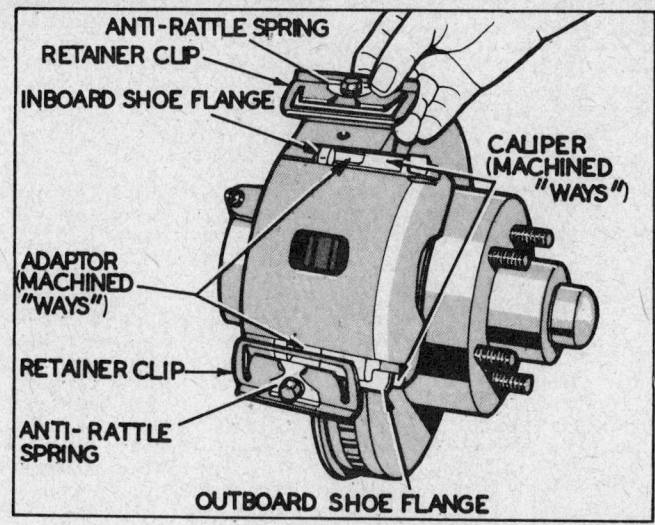

Fig. 66   Caliper machined "ways" and assembly retention

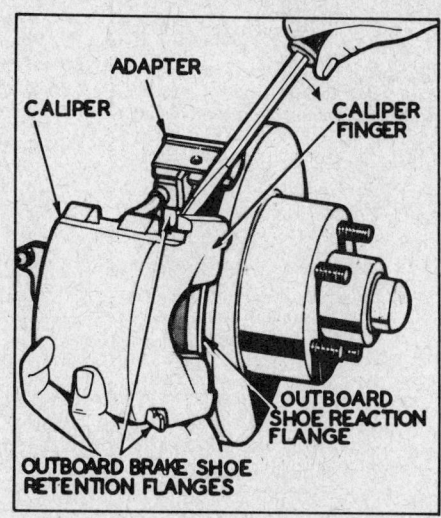

Fig. 69   Removing outboard shoe

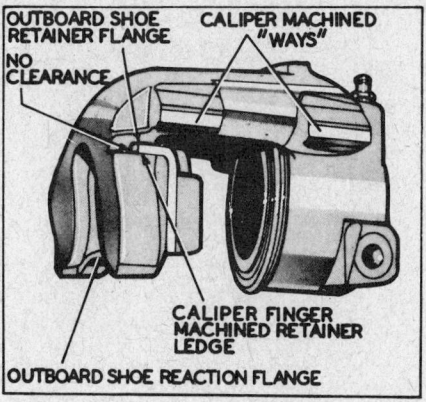

Fig. 70   Positioning outboard shoe onto caliper finger machined retainer ledge

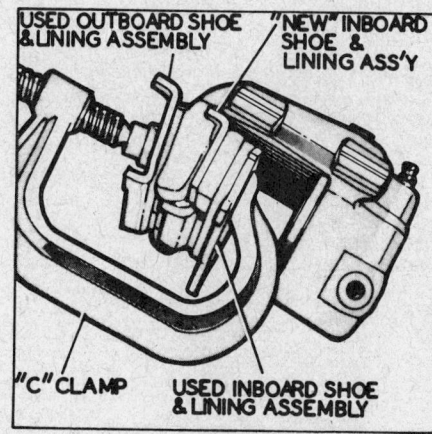

Fig. 71   Installing outboard shoe using "C" clamp

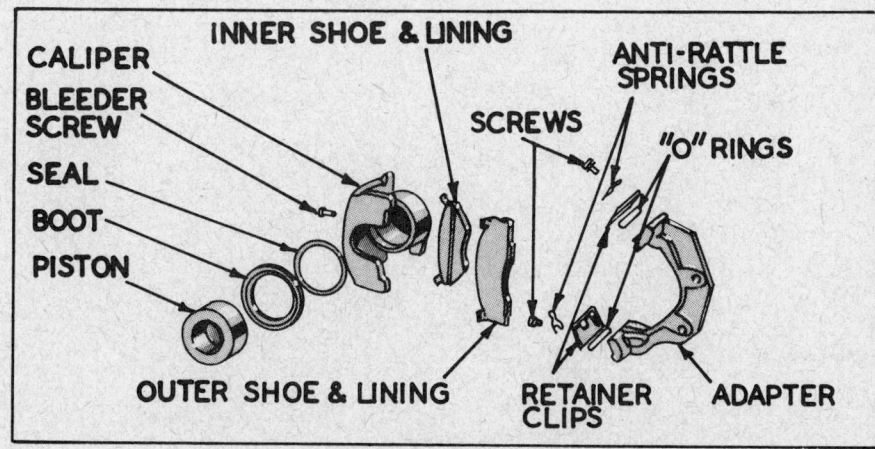

Fig. 72   Exploded view of a Kelsey-Hayes sliding caliper disc brake

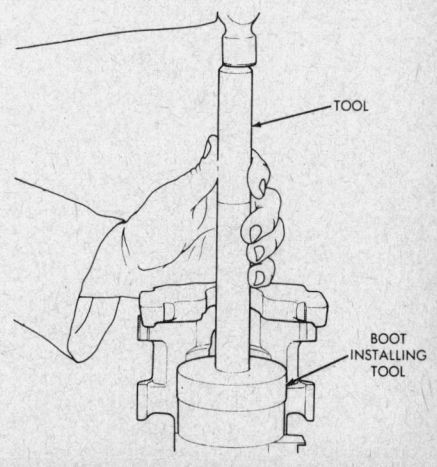

Fig. 72A   Installing piston dust boot. 1981-83 models

DISC BRAKES

Brake Shoe Removal

1. Remove caliper aassembly as outlined above.
2. Remove outboard shoe by prying between the shoe and the caliper fingers, Fig. 69, since flanges on outboard shoe retain caliper firmly.

NOTE: Caliper should be supported to avoid damage to the flexible brake hose.

3. Remove inboard brake shoe from the adaptor, Fig. 68.

Brake Shoe Installation

NOTE: Remove approximately 1/3 of the brake fluid out of the reservoir to prevent overflow when pistons are pushed back into the bore.

1. With care, push piston back into bore until bottomed.
2. Install new outboard shoe in recess of caliper.

NOTE: No free play should exist between brake shoe flanges and caliper fingers, Fig. 70.

If up and down movement of the shoe shows free play, shoe must be removed and flanges bent to provide a slight interference fit, Fig. 67. Reinstall shoe after modification, if shoe can not be finger snapped into place, use light "C" clamp pressure, Fig. 71.

3. Position inboard shoe with flanges inserted in adaptor "ways," Fig. 68.
4. Carefully slide caliper assembly into adaptor and over the disc while aligning caliper on machined "ways" of adaptor.

NOTE: Make sure dust boot is not pulled out from groove when piston and boot slide over the inboard shoe.

5. Install anti-rattle springs and retaining clips and torque retaining screws to 180 inch-pounds.

NOTE: The inboard shoe anti-rattle spring is to be installed on top of the retainer spring plate, Fig. 56.

Caliper Disassembly

1. With caliper and shoes removed as described previously, place caliper onto the upper control arm and slowly depress brake pedal, in turn hydraulically pushing piston out of bore.

NOTE: Pedal will fall when piston passes bore opening.

2. Support pedal below first inch of pedal travel to prevent excessive fluid loss.
3. To remove piston from the opposite caliper, disconnect flexible brake line at frame bracket, from vehicle side where piston has been removed previously and plug tube to prevent pressure loss. By depressing brake pedal this piston can also be hydraulically pushed out.
4. Mount caliper in a vise equipped with protector jaws.

NOTE: Excessive vise pressure will distort caliper bore.

5. Remove the dust boot, Fig. 72.
6. Insert a suitable tool such as a small, pointed wooden or plastic object between the cylinder bore and the seal and work seal out of the groove in the piston bore.

NOTE: A metal tool such as a screwdriver should not be used since it can cause damage to the piston bore or burr the edges of the seal groove.

Caliper Assembly

1. Dip new piston seals in clean brake fluid. Work seal gently into the groove (using clean fingers) until seal is properly seated, make sure that seal is not twisted or rolled.

NOTE: Old seals should never be reused.

2. On 1981–82 models, install piston into bore and push past seal until piston bottoms in bore.
3. Lubricate piston boot generously with clean brake fluid. On 1977–80 models, using finger pressure, install into caliper by pushing into outer groove of the caliper bore. When properly positioned in groove boot will snap into place. Double check to make sure boot is properly installed and seated by running finger around the inside of the boot. On 1981–82 models, install piston boot with tool C-4689 and handle C-4171, Fig. 72A.
4. On 1977–80 models, plug high pressure inlet to caliper and bleeder screw hole and coat piston with a generous amount of lubricant. Spread boot with finger and work piston into boot while pressing down on piston. As piston is depressed, entrapped air below piston will force boot around piston and into its groove.
5. On 1977–80 models, remove the plug and apply uniform force to the piston (avoid cocking piston) until piston bottoms in bore.
6. Install brake hose to caliper using new seal washers.
7. Install caliper and shoes as described under "Brake Shoe Installation."

CHRYSLER CORP. FRONT WHEEL DRIVE DUAL PIN FLOATING CALIPER DISC BRAKE

Operation

The single piston floating caliper disc brake assembly consists of the hub and disc brake rotor assembly, caliper, shoes and linings, splash shield and adapter, Fig. 73.

The caliper assembly floats on two rubber bushings riding on two steel guide pins threaded into the adapter. The bushings are inserted on the inboard portion of the caliper. Two machined abutments on the adapter position and align the caliper fore and aft. Guide pins and bushings control caliper and piston seal movement to assist in maintaining proper shoe clearance.

All braking force is taken directly by the adapter. The steel piston used on 1978–82 Horizon & Omni models is 1.89 inches in diameter. The plastic piston used on 1981–82 Aries & Reliant, 1982 LeBaron and 400 and the phenolic piston used on 1983 Omni, Horizon, Reliant, 400, 600, Aries, LeBaron, E-Class & New Yorker, are 2.13 inches in diameter.

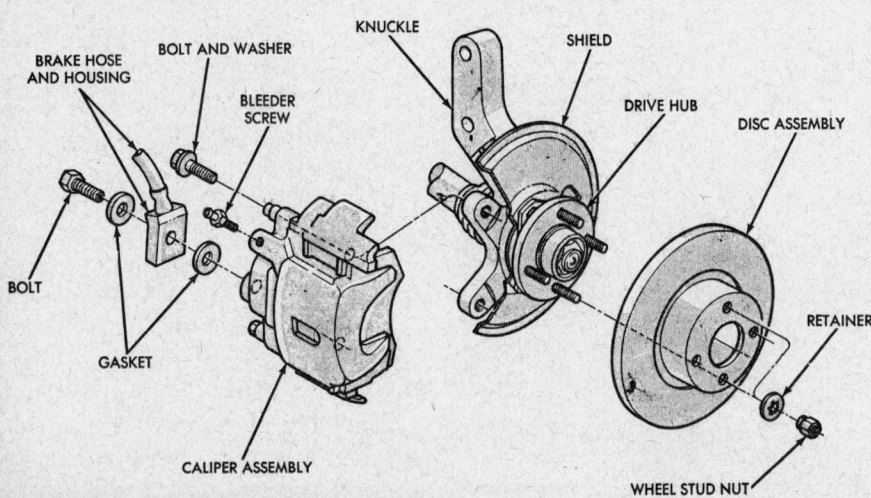

Fig. 73 Dual pin floating caliper disc brake. Chrysler front wheel drive models

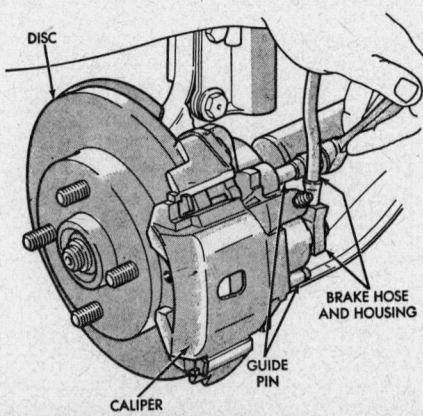

Fig. 74 Removing caliper guide pins

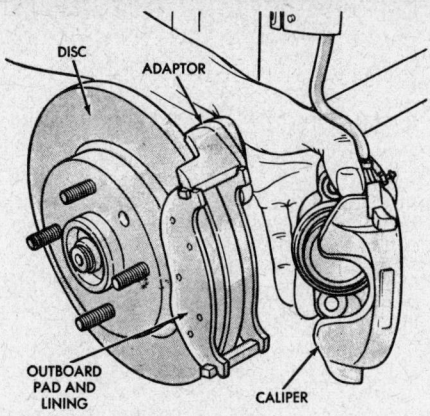

Fig. 75 Removing caliper

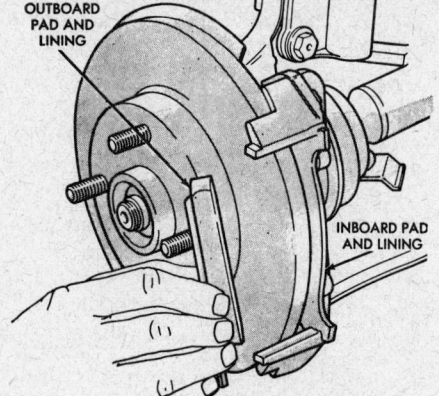

Fig. 76 Removing outboard pad & lining assembly

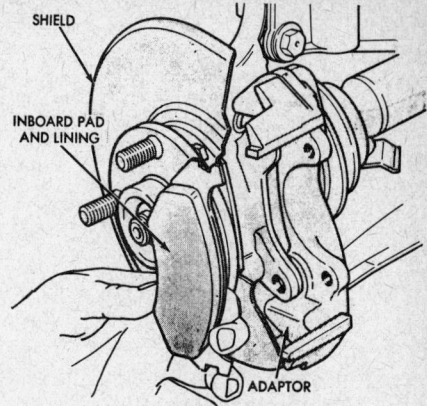

Fig. 78 Removing inboard pad & lining assembly

Brake Shoe & Lining, Replace

Omni, Horizon & 1983 Charger & Turismo

1. Raise and support front of vehicle, then remove wheel and tire assembly.
2. Remove caliper guide pins and anti-rattle spring, Fig. 74.
3. Carefully slide caliper assembly away from disc, Fig. 75. Support caliper assembly to prevent damage to brake hose.
4. Remove outboard shoe and lining assembly from adapter, Fig. 76.
5. Remove rotor from drive axle flange and studs, Fig. 77.
6. Remove inboard shoe and lining assembly from adapter, Fig. 78.
7. Carefully push piston into caliper bore.

NOTE: Remove some brake fluid from reservoir to prevent overflowing when pushing piston into caliper bore.

8. Position inboard shoe and lining on adapter. Ensure metal portion of shoe is properly positioned in recess of adapter.
9. Install rotor over studs and drive flange.
10. While holding outboard shoe in position on adapter, carefully position adapter over disc brake rotor.
11. Carefully lower caliper over disc brake rotor and adapter.
12. Install guide pins through bushings, caliper and adapter.
13. Press in on guide pins and thread pin into adapter. Torque pins to 25 to 40 ft. lbs.
14. Install wheel and tire assembly, then lower vehicle.

Aries, Reliant, 1982–83 LeBaron & 400, 1983 E-Class, New Yorker & 600

1. Raise and support vehicle, then remove wheel and tire assemblies.
2. Remove hold down spring from caliper assembly by pressing spring outward.
3. Loosen, but do not remove, caliper guide pins, then remove caliper from disc. Inboard shoe will remain inside caliper. Support caliper assembly to prevent damage to hydraulic brake hose.

NOTE: Remove caliper guide pins only if bushings or sleeves are to be replaced.

4. Remove inboard shoe from caliper and outboard shoe from adapter.
5. Push caliper piston into bore.

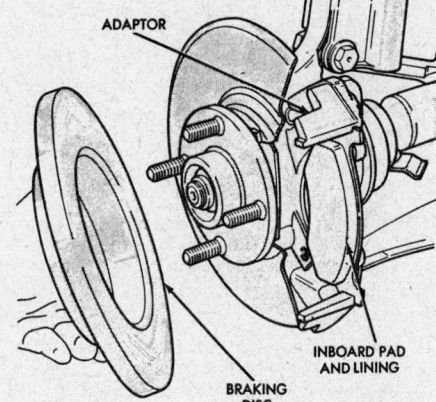

Fig. 77 Removing disc brake rotor from hub

NOTE: Remove some brake fluid from master cylinder reservoir to prevent overflowing when piston is pushed into bore.

6. Install new inboard shoe into caliper with retainer positioned in piston bore.
7. Install outboard shoe onto adapter.
8. Position caliper over brake disc and adapter, then torque guide pins to 18–22 ft. lbs.
9. Install hold down spring, then install tire and wheel assemblies and lower vehicle to ground.
10. Check master cylinder reservoir for proper level of brake fluid and add as necessary.

Caliper Overhaul

Disassemble, Fig. 79 & 79A

1. Remove caliper assembly as described under Brake Shoe & Lining, Replace.
2. With brake hose attached to caliper, carefully depress brake pedal to push piston out of caliper bore. Prop brake pedal to any position below first inch of brake pedal travel to prevent brake fluid loss.
3. If pistons are to be removed from both cal-

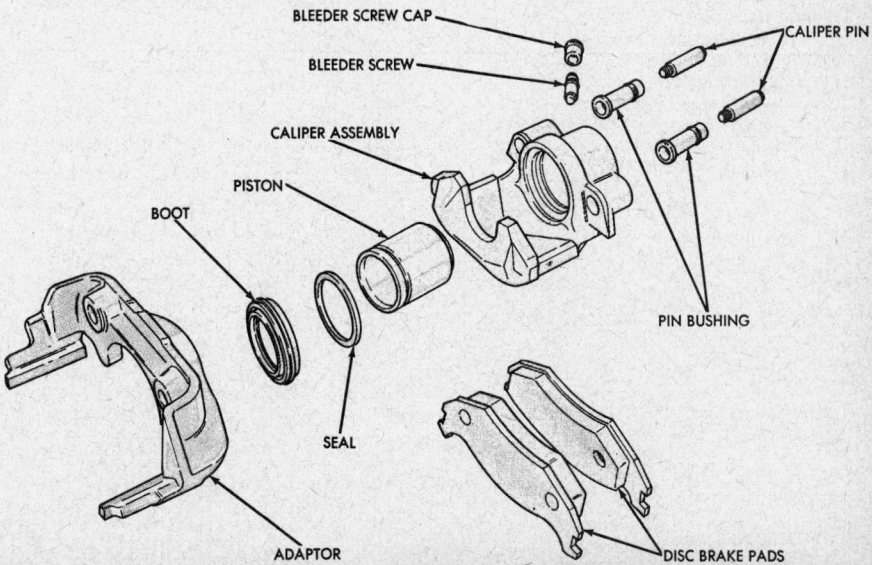

Fig. 79 Disassembled view of disc brake caliper. Omni, Horizon & 1983 Charger & Turismo

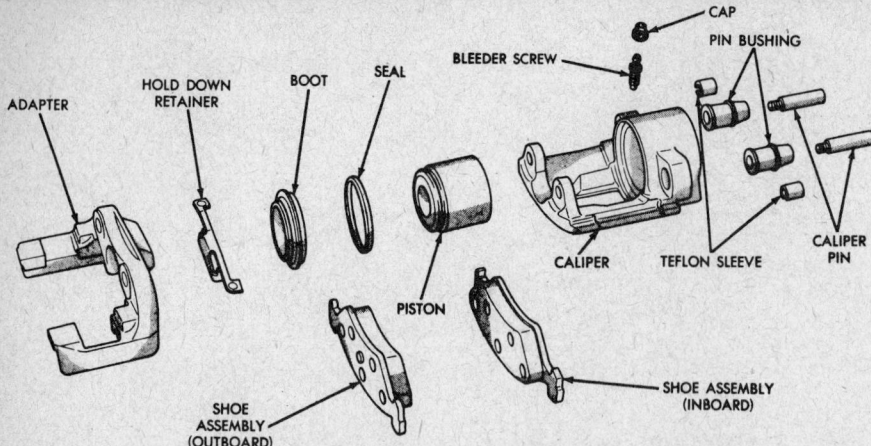

Fig. 79A Disassembled view of disc brake caliper. Aries, Reliant, 1982—83 LeBaron & 400, 1983 E-Class, New Yorker & 600

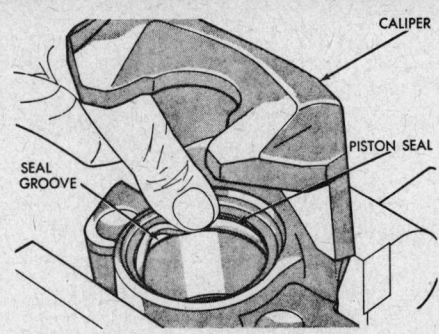

Fig. 80 Installing piston seal

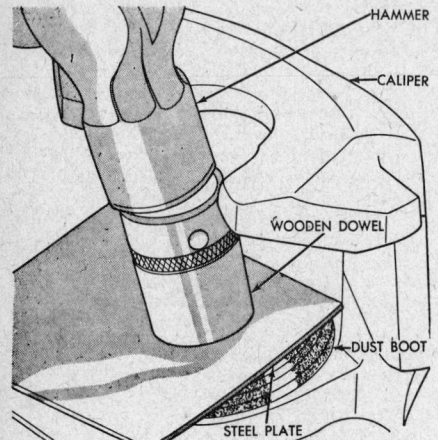

Fig. 81 Installing piston dust boot

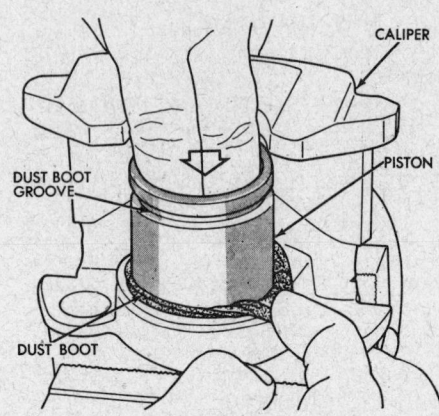

Fig. 82 Installing caliper piston

discard.

7. Using a small wooden or plastic stick, remove seal from groove in piston bore and discard.

8. Using a suitable tool, remove bushings from caliper.

Inspection

1. Clean all components using alcohol or other suitable cleaning solvent, then blow dry using compressed air. With compressed air blow out drilled passages and bores.

2. Inspect piston bore for pitting or scoring. Light scratches or corrosion can usually be cleared with crocus cloth. Bores that have deep scratches or scoring should be honed with tool No. C-4095, providing bore diameter is not increased by more than .001 in. If scratches or scoring cannot be cleared up, or if caliper bore is increased by more than .001 in., replace caliper housing.

NOTE: When using hone C-4095, coat hone and caliper bore with clean brake fluid. After honing carefully clean boot and seal grooves with a stiff non-metallic brush. Flush caliper with clean brake fluid and wipe dry with a clean lintless cloth, then flush and wipe caliper dry again.

---

3. Replace piston if found to be scored, pitted or if plating is severely worn or if caliper bore was honed. Black stains on steel pis-

ton are caused by piston seal and are not cause for replacing piston.

Assemble, Fig. 79 & 79A

1. Mount caliper in a soft jawed vise.

2. Lubricate piston seal with clean brake fluid and install seal in caliper bore groove, Fig. 80. Ensure seal is properly seated.

3. Lubricate piston boot with clean brake fluid and install boot in caliper bore groove, Fig. 81.

4. Using a hammer and small steel plate or a suitable C-clamp, drive into caliper until seated, Fig. 82. Ensure boot is properly seated in caliper bore.

5. Plug brake hose inlet boss and bleeder screw hole, then lubricate piston with

ipers, disconnect brake hose at frame bracket after removing piston, then cap brake line and repeat procedure to remove piston from other caliper.

4. Disconnect brake hose from caliper.

5. Mount caliper in a soft jawed vise.

6. Support caliper and remove dust boot and

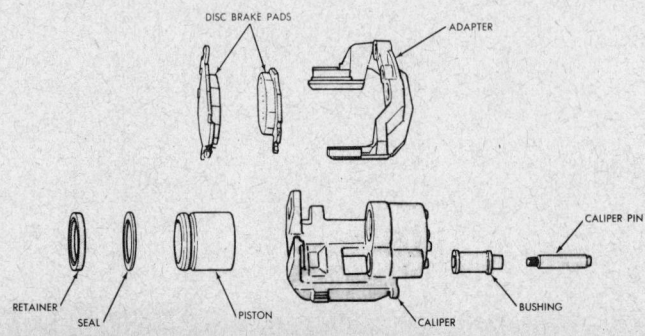

Fig. 83 Disassembled view of Kelsey-Hayes single pin floating caliper

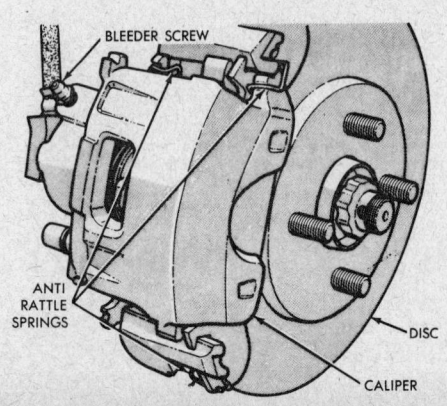

Fig. 84 Anti-rattle spring location

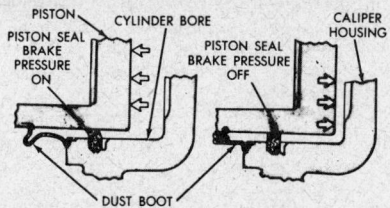

Fig. 85 Sectional view of piston seal & dust boot

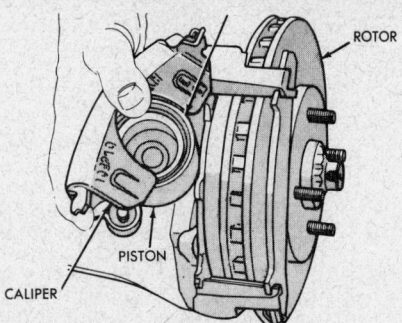

Fig. 86 Removing caliper

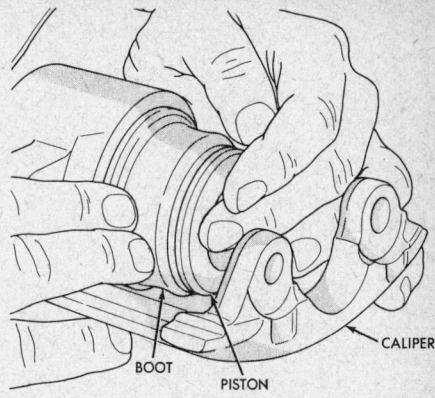

Fig. 87 Piston installation

clean brake fluid.

6. Spread boot with finger and work piston into boot, then press down on piston.
7. Remove plug and carefully push piston down in bore until bottomed.
8. Compress flanges of guide pin bushings and install bushings on caliper housing. Ensure that bushing flanges extend evenly over caliper housing on both sides.

NOTE: On Aries, Reliant, 1982–83 LeBaron, 400, 1983 E-Class, New Yorker & 600 models, remove teflon sleeves from guide pin bushings prior to installing bushings into caliper. After bushings are installed into caliper, reinstall teflon sleeves into bushings.

9. Connect brake hose to brake line at frame bracket.
10. Install caliper on vehicle as described under Brake Shoe & Lining, Replace.
11. Check brake fluid level of master cylinder reservoir, then open caliper bleed screw and bleed brake system. Continue bleeding procedure until firm pedal is obtained.

KELSEY-HAYES SINGLE PIN FLOATING CALIPER DISC BRAKE

Operation

The caliper assembly consists of a rotor,

caliper, shoes and linings, and adapter, Fig. 83. The single piston caliper assembly floats through a rubber bushing on a single pin, threaded into the adapter. The bushing is inserted into the inboard portion of the caliper. Two machined abutments on the adapter, position and align the caliper fore and aft. The guide pin and bushing controls the movement of the caliper and the piston seal, to assist in maintaining proper shoe clearance.

This assembly has three anti-rattle clips. One is on top of the inboard shoe, one clip is on the bottom of the outboard shoe, and one clip is on top of the caliper, Fig. 84.

All of the braking force is taken directly by the adapter. The caliper is a one piece casting with the inboard side containing a single piston cylinder bore. The phenolic piston is 2.13 inches in diameter.

A square cut rubber piston seal is located in a machined groove in the caliper bore and provides a seal between piston and caliper bore, Fig. 85.

A molded rubber dust boot installed in a groove in the cylinder bore and piston keeps contamination from the caliper bore and piston. The boot mounts in the caliper bore and in a groove in the piston, Fig. 85.

Brake Shoe & Lining, Replace

Removal

1. Remove brake fluid until reservoir is half

full.
2. Raise and support front of vehicle, then remove wheel and tire assembly.
3. Remove caliper guide pin and anti-rattle clips.
4. Remove caliper from disc by sliding caliper assembly out and away from braking disc, Fig. 86. Suspend caliper with wire so as not to damage flexible brake hose.
5. Remove outboard brake lining, then lift off rotor and remove inboard brake lining.

Installation

1. Push piston back into cylinder bore with uniform pressure until it is bottomed, Fig. 87.
2. Position inboard shoe and lining on adapter, then install rotor.
3. While holding outboard shoe in position on adapter, carefully position caliper over disc brake rotor.

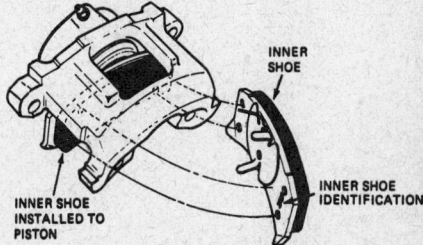

Fig. 89 Installing inner brake shoe on caliper

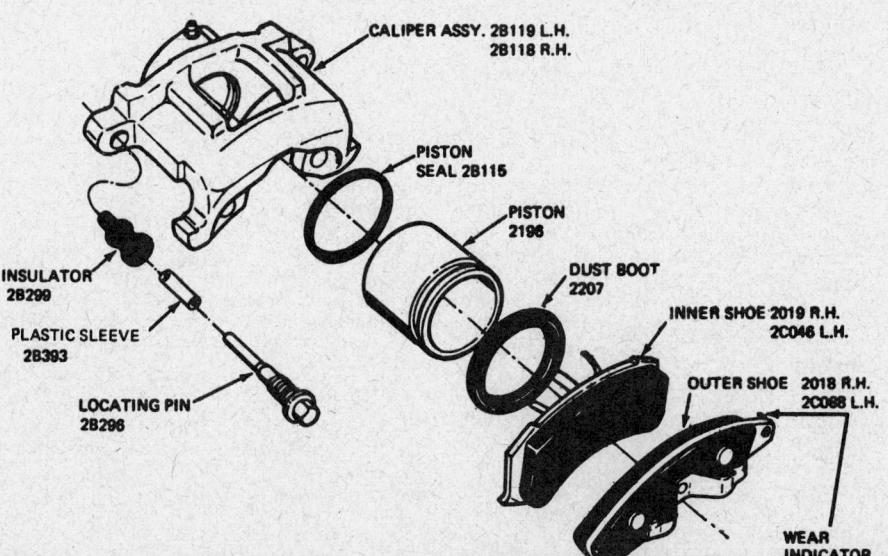

Fig. 88 Kelsey-Hayes pin slider disc brake caliper (Typical)

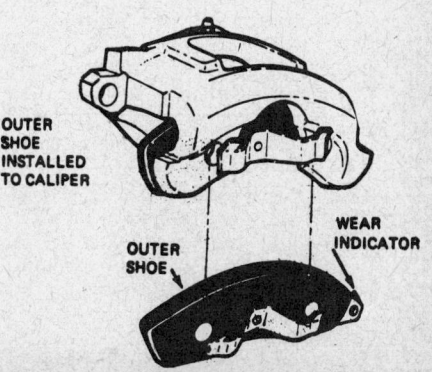

Fig. 90 Installing outer brake shoe on caliper

DISC BRAKES

4. Lower caliper over rotor and adapter.
5. Install guide pin through bushing, caliper and adapter.
6. Press in on guide pin and thread pin into adapter. Torque pin to 25 to 40 ft. lbs.
7. Install wheel and tire assembly, then lower vehicle.

Caliper Overhaul

Refer to Caliper Overhaul under "Chrysler Corp. Front Wheel Drive Dual Pin Floating Caliper Disc Brake" for procedure.

KELSEY-HAYES PIN SLIDER DISC BRAKE

Operation

The caliper assembly consists of a pin slider caliper housing, inner and outer shoe and lining assemblies and a single piston, Fig. 88. The caliper slides on two pins which also act as attaching bolts between caliper and the combination anchor plate and spindle. The outer brake shoe and lining assembly is longer than the inner brake shoe and lining assembly. Inner and outer shoe and lining assemblies are attached to the caliper by spring clips riveted to the shoe surfaces. The inner shoe is attached to the caliper by installing the spring clip to the inside of the caliper piston. The outer shoe clips directly to the caliper housing. A wear indicator is incorporated which emits a noise when the lining is worn to a point when replacement is necessary. Inner and outer shoes are of left and right hand and are not interchangeable.

NOTE: The inner shoe and lining on Capri, Fairmont, Mustang, and Zephyr with V8-302 engine has a replaceable single finger anti-rattle clip and an insulator held in position by the clip. The shoe is slotted to accept the snap on clip which loads the assembly against the caliper bridge. The inner shoe on the Capri and Mustang with 2300cc and 2800cc has a single finger anti-rattle clip similar to the Fairmont and Zephyr inner shoe, holding the shoe down against the spindle ledge. The clip does not lock into the piston. The insulator is also riveted to the shoe and is not replaceable.

Brake Shoe & Lining, Replace

Removal
1. Remove brake fluid until reservoir is half full.
2. Raise and support front of vehicle, then remove wheel and tire assembly.
3. Remove caliper locating pins.
4. Lift caliper assembly from spindle and adapter plate, then remove outer shoe from caliper assembly.

NOTE: On 1982–83 Lincoln Continental models, slip shoe down caliper leg until clip is disengaged.

5. Remove inner shoe and lining assembly.

NOTE: On 1982–83 Lincoln Continental models, pull shoe straight out of piston. This could require a force as high as 20–30 lbs.

6. Suspend caliper from inner fender housing with wire to avoid damaging brake hose.
7. Remove and discard locating pin insulators and plastic sleeves.

Installation
1. Using a 4 in. C-clamp and a block of wood 2¾ × 1 in. and approximately ¾ in. thick, seat caliper piston in bore, then remove C-clamp and wooden block.

NOTE: On 1982–83 Lincoln Continental, late 1983 Escort, EXP, LN7 and Lynx and 1984 Tempo and Topaz models, the piston is made of phenolic material. Do not seat piston in bore by applying C-clamp directly to piston. Extra care must be taken during this procedure to prevent damage to the piston. Metal or sharp objects cannot come into direct contact with the piston or damage may result.

2. Install locating pin insulators and plastic sleeves on caliper housing. Ensure insulators and sleeves are properly positioned.
3. Install inner shoe and lining assembly on caliper piston, Fig. 89.

NOTE: Inner brake shoes are marked LH (left hand) and RH (right hand) and must be installed on the proper caliper. Use care to not bend spring clips too far during installation in piston, otherwise distortion and rattles may result.

4. Install outer brake shoe and lining assembly, Fig. 90. Ensure that shoes are installed on proper caliper. Make sure that clip and buttons on shoe are properly seated.

NOTE: The outer shoe can be identified as left hand and right hand by the wear indicator which must be installed toward front of vehicle.

5. Install locating pins and torque to 30–40 ft. lbs.

NOTE: On 1982–83 Lincoln Continental and 1980–83 Ford and Mercury full size and Lincoln models, torque locating pins to 40–60 ft. lbs. On 1981–83 Escort, EXP, LN7 and Lynx and 1984 Tempo and Topaz, torque to 18–25 ft. lbs.

CAUTION: On 1982–83 models except Lincoln Continental, ensure that two round torque buttons are firmly seated in the two holes of outer caliper leg and that shoe is held tightly against housing by spring clip. A temporary loss of brakes may occur if buttons are not properly seated.

6. Refill master cylinder, then install wheel and tire assembly and lower vehicle.
7. Pump brake pedal several times to position brake linings before moving vehicle.

Caliper, Replace

Removal

NOTE: Before removing calipers, mark left and right hand calipers so they can be installed in the same position.

1. Raise and support front of vehicle, then remove wheel and tire assembly.
2. Loosen brake tube fitting which connects brake tube to fitting on frame and plug brake tube. Remove retaining clip from brake hose and bracket, then disconnect brake hose from caliper.
3. Remove caliper locating pins.
4. Lift caliper from rotor and spindle anchor plate assembly.

NOTE: On late 1983 Escort, EXP, LN7, and Lynx and 1984 Tempo and Topaz with phenolic caliper piston, do not pry directly against the piston or damage may result.

Installation
1. Install caliper assembly over rotor with outer shoe against rotor braking surface during installation on spindle and anchor plate to prevent pinching of piston boot between inner brake shoe and piston.

NOTE: Ensure calipers are installed in the correct position.

2. Install locating pins. Torque locating pins to 30 to 40 ft. lbs.

NOTE: On 1982–83 Lincoln Continental and 1980–83 Ford and Mercury full size and Lincoln models, torque locating pins to 40–60 ft. lbs. On 1981–83 Escort, EXP LN7 and Lynx and 1984 Tempo and Topaz, torque to 18–25 ft. lbs.

3. Connect brake hose to caliper and tighten hose fitting.
4. Position upper end of brake hose in bracket and install retaining clip. Remove plug from brake line, then connect brake hose fitting to brake line. Torque fitting to 10 to 18 ft. lbs.
5. Bleed brake system and centralize pressure differential valve.
6. Install wheel and tire assembly, then lower vehicle.
7. Pump brake pedal several times to position brake shoes before moving vehicle.

Caliper Overhaul

Disassemble, Fig. 88
1. Remove caliper assembly from vehicle as described under Caliper, Replace.
2. Position fiber block and shop towels between caliper piston and caliper housing, then apply compressed air to caliper brake line fitting bore to force piston from caliper.
3. Remove dust boot from caliper assembly.
4. Remove pistol seal from cylinder and discard.

Inspection
Clean all metal parts with isopropyl alcohol, then clean and dry passages and grooves with compressed air. Check caliper and piston for damage and wear and replace as necessary.

Assemble, Fig. 88
1. Lubricate piston seal with clean brake fluid, then install seal in caliper bore.

NOTE: Ensure seal is firmly seated in groove.

2. Install dust boot in outer groove of caliper bore.
3. Coat piston with clean brake fluid and install piston in caliper bore. Spread dust boot over piston as it is installed. Seat dust boot in piston groove.
4. Install caliper assembly as described under "Caliper, Replace."

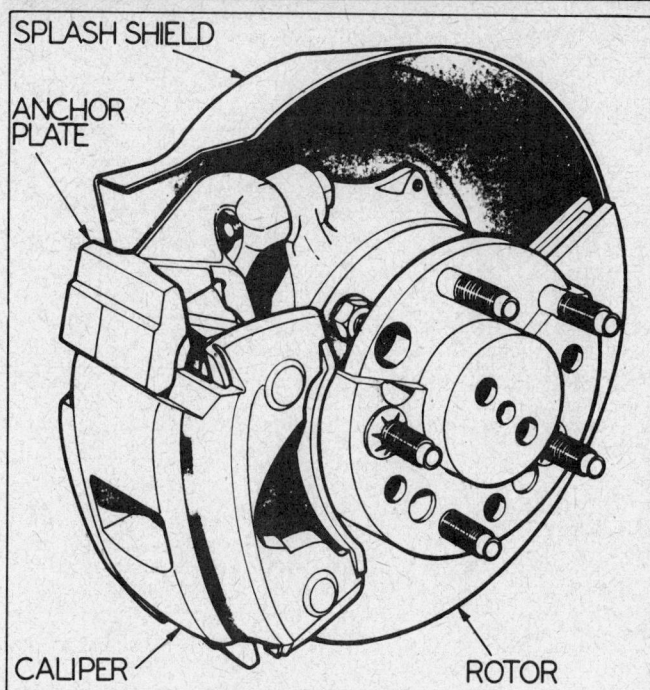

SPLASH SHIELD

ANCHOR PLATE

CALIPER

ROTOR

Fig. 91   Rear disc brake

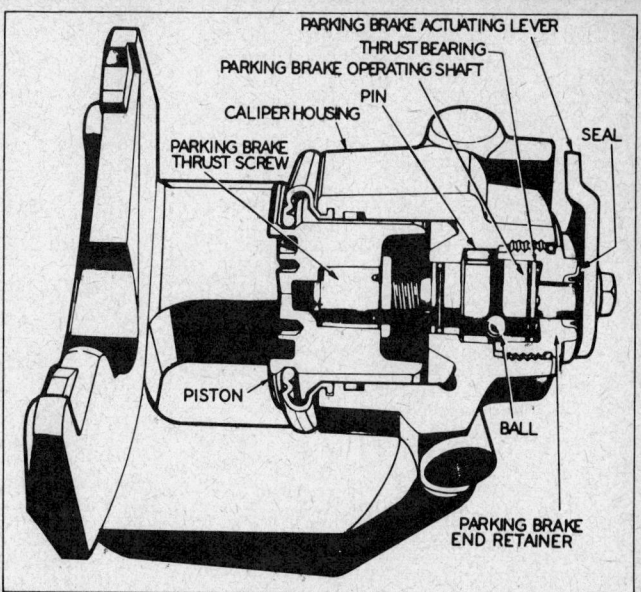

PARKING BRAKE ACTUATING LEVER
THRUST BEARING
PARKING BRAKE OPERATING SHAFT
CALIPER HOUSING
PIN
SEAL
PARKING BRAKE THRUST SCREW
PISTON
BALL
PARKING BRAKE END RETAINER

Fig. 92   Caliper housing cutaway to show parking brake mechanism

FORD REAR WHEEL DISC BRAKE & PARKING BRAKE

Sliding caliper rear disc brakes are used on some 1977–80 models and on the 1982–83 Lincoln Continental, Fig. 91. The caliper is basically the same as the larger front wheel caliper, however, a parking brake mechanism and a larger inner brake shoe anti-rattle spring have been added, Fig. 92. A hydraulically powered brake booster (Hydroboost) provides the power assist for this four wheel disc brake system.

The parking brake lever, located at the rear of the caliper, is actuated by a cable system similar to rear drum brake applications. When the parking brake is applied, the cable rotates the lever and operating shaft. Three steel balls, placed in pockets between the opposing heads of the operating shaft and thrust screw, roll between ramps formed in the pockets and force the thrust screw away from the operating shaft, in turn, driving the caliper piston and brake shoe assembly against the rotor. An automatic adjuster in the assembly compensates for lining wear and maintains proper clearance in the parking brake mechanism.

The cast iron rotors are ventilated by curved fins located between the braking surfaces and are designed to cause the rotor to act as an air pump when the vehicle is traveling forward. The rotors are not interchangeable and are identified by a Right or Left marking cast inside the hat section of the rotor. The rotor is secured to the axle flange in the same manner as a rear brake drum. A splash shield is bolted to a forged axle adapter to protect the inboard rotor surface.

Caliper Removal

NOTE: After performing any service work, obtain a firm brake pedal before moving vehicle.

1. Raise vehicle and support on safety stands, then remove tire and wheel assemblies.
2. Disconnect fitting on rear brake tube from hose end fitting at frame mounted bracket and plug end of brake tube to prevent loss of fluid and entry of dirt. Remove horseshoe retaining clip from hose fitting and disengage hose from bracket.

NOTE: On Granada, Monarch and Versailles models, disconnect hose bracket from axle spring seat. On Lincoln Continental, Ford and Mercury models, disconnect hose end fitting from caliper. On Granada, Mark IV, Mark V, Monarch, Thunderbird and Versailles models, remove hollow retaining bolt, connecting hose fitting to caliper.

3. Disconnect parking cable from lever, Fig. 93, using care to avoid kinking or cutting cable or return spring, then remove retaining screw from caliper retaining key, Fig. 94. On 1982–83 Lincoln Continental, remove caliper locating pins.
4. Slide caliper retaining key and support spring from anchor plate, Fig. 94. If necessary, use a hammer and brass drift, being careful to avoid damaging key on sliding ways or hitting parking brake lever.

NOTE: If caliper cannot be removed due to

rust build-up on outer edge of rotor, scrape off loose scale, being careful not to damage braking surfaces. If rotor wear or scoring prevents removal of caliper, it will be necessary to loosen caliper end retainer 1/2 turn maximum, to allow piston to be forced back into its bore. To loosen end retainer, remove parking brake lever and mark or scribe end retainer and caliper housing to be sure that end retainer is not loosened more than 1/2 turn, then force piston back in its bore, Fig. 92, and move caliper back and forth to center rotor and remove caliper. If retainer must be loosened more than 1/2 turn, use caution, as the seal between the thrust screw and housing may be broken and brake fluid will enter parking brake mechanism chamber. In this case, the end retainer must be removed and the internal parts cleaned and lubricated.

5. On all except 1982–83 Lincoln Continental, remove inner shoe and lining assembly from anchor plate, then tap lightly on outer shoe and lining assembly to free it from caliper. Mark each shoe for identification if they are to be reused.
6. On 1982–83 Lincoln Continental, proceed as follows:
   a. Remove outer shoe and lining assembly from anchor plate, then remove rotor retainer nuts and rotor from axle shaft.
   b. Remove inner brake shoe and lining assembly from anchor plate and mark each shoe for identification if they are to be reused.
   c. Remove anti-rattle clip from anchor plate, then remove flexible hose from caliper by removing hollow retaining bolt.

Cleaning & Inspection

Clean caliper, anchor plate and rotor assembly and inspect for signs of brake fluid leakage, excessive wear or damage. The caliper must be inspected for leakage both in piston boot area and operating shaft seal area. Lightly sand or wire brush any rust or corrosion from caliper and anchor plate sliding

DISC BRAKES

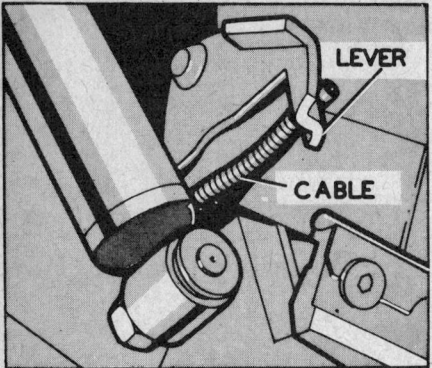

Fig. 93 Parking lever & cable installation

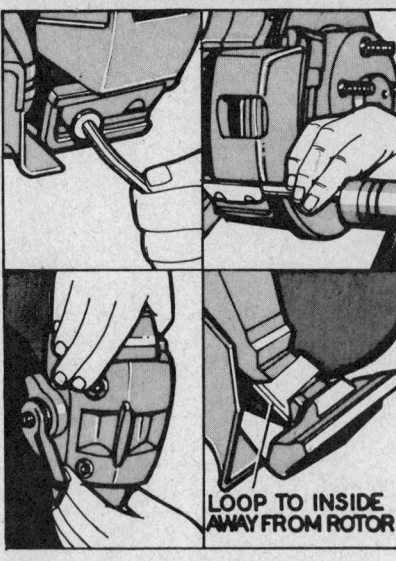

Fig. 94 Removing rear caliper assembly

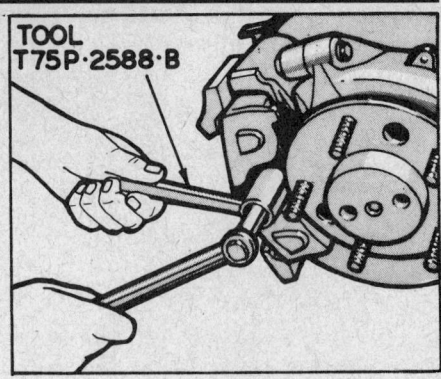

Fig. 95 Adjusting piston depth for lining installation

surfaces and inner brake shoe abutment surfaces in anchor plate. Inspect brake shoes for wear. If either lining is within 1/32 inch of any rivet head, replace both shoe and lining assemblies from both wheels in order to maintain equal brake action.

NOTE: On 1982–83 Lincoln Continental models, linings must not be worn to within less than 1/8 inch of shoe surface.

Caliper Installation

1. If end retainer has been loosened only 1/2 turn, reinstall caliper in anchor plate using key. Do not install shoe and lining assembly. Torque end retainer to 75–95 ft. lbs. and install parking brake actuating lever on its keyed spline. Lever arm must point down and rearward so that parking brake cable will pass freely under axle. Torque retainer screw to 16–22 ft. lbs.

NOTE: Parking brake lever must rotate freely after torquing retainer screw.

2. Remove caliper from anchor plate. If new shoe and lining assemblies are to be installed, the piston must be bottomed in caliper bore using tool T75P-2588-B to provide clearance. Remove rotor and install caliper without lining and shoe assemblies in anchor plate using key only. Install tool and while holding shaft, rotate tool handle counterclockwise until the tool seats firmly against piston, Fig. 95. Loosen handle about 1/4 turn, and while holding handle rotate tool shaft clockwise until piston is fully bottomed in bore (piston will continue to turn even after it is bottomed). Turn tool handle until there is no further inward movement of piston and there is a firm seating force, then remove caliper from mounting plate and reinstall rotor.

NOTE: For use on 1982–83 Lincoln Continental models, tool T75P-2588-B must be slightly modified, Fig. 95.

3. Making certain that brake shoe anti-rattle clip is in place in lower inner brake shoe support on anchor plate with loop of clip toward inside of anchor plate, Fig. 94, position inner brake shoe and lining assembly on anchor plate. On 1982 Lin-

coln Continental models, install rotor and two retaining nuts.

4. Install outer brake shoe with lower flange ends against caliper abutments and brake shoe upper flanges over shoulders on caliper legs. The shoe upper flanges fit tightly against machined shoulder surfaces.

NOTE: If old brake shoes and lining assemblies are re-used, be certain the shoes are installed in their original positions as marked for identification during removal.

5. Lubricate caliper and anchor sliding ways with M1C-167-A (LPS-ESA-100) grease, using care to prevent lubricant from getting on braking surfaces, then position caliper housing lower V-groove on anchor plate lower abutment surfaces. On 1982–83 Lincoln Continental models, use D7AE-019590, or equivalent grease.

6. Rotate caliper until it is completely over rotor, being careful not to damage piston dust boot, then pull caliper outboard until inner shoe and lining is firmly seated against rotor. Measure clearance between outer lining and rotor which should be 1/16 inch or less, Fig. 96. On 1982–83 Lincoln Continental models, clearance must be between 1/32 and 3/32 inch. If it is greater, remove caliper and move piston outward

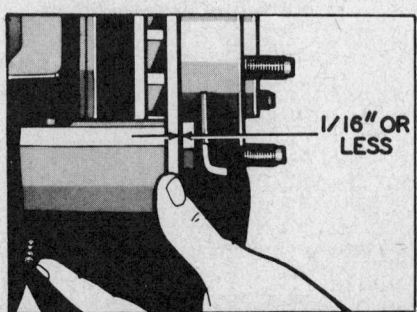

Fig. 96 Checking lining clearance

to narrow gap. Follow precedure in step 2 and note that 1/4 turn of the shaft counter-clockwise, moves piston about 1/16 inch.

CAUTION: A clearance greater than specified limit may allow adjuster to be pulled out of piston when service brake is applied, causing parking brake to fail to adjust. It will then be necessary to replace piston/adjuster assembly.

7. While holding caliper against anchor plate upper abutment surfaces, center caliper over lower anchor plate abutment, then position caliper support spring and key in slot and slide them into opening between lower end of caliper and lower anchor plate abutment until key semi-circular slot is centered over retaining screw threaded hole in anchor plate.

8. Install key retaining screw and torque to 12–16 ft. lbs., then reinstall brake hose on caliper. On Lincoln and Ford Mercury models, place a new gasket on fitting and torque to 20–30 ft. lbs. On 1982–83 Lincoln Continental and all Granada, Mark IV, Mark V, Monarch, Thunderbird and Versailles models, place a new gasket on each side of the fitting outlet, then install the attaching bolt through the washers and fitting and torque to 17–25 ft. lbs. (20–30 ft. lbs. on 1982–83 Lincoln Continental models).

NOTE: On Granada, Monarch and Versailles models, ensure the pin in the hose fitting engages the mating hole in the caliper before torquing the bolt.

9. On all except 1982–83 Lincoln Continental models, position upper end of flexible hose in bracket and install retaining clip, then connect brake tube to hose and torque fitting to 10–15 ft. lbs.

NOTE: Do not twist or coil brake hose, the stripe on the hose must be kept straight.

10. On 1982–83 Lincoln Continental models, lubricate pins and inside of insulator with D7AZ-19A331-A or equivalent silicone grease and add one drop of Loctite EOAC-19554-A, or equivalent, to locating pin threads. Install locating pins through caliper insulators and into anchor plate and torque to 29–37 ft. lbs.

11. Connect parking brake lever to lever on caliper.
12. Bleed brake system, then with engine running pump brake pedal lightly about 40 times allowing 1 second between pedal applications. An alternate with engine off is to pump brake pedal lightly about 10 times to discharge accumulator, then pump brake pedal firmly about 30 times. Check parking brake for excessive travel or very light effort, if so, repeat pumping brake pedal, and if necessary check parking brake cable tension.
13. Install wheel and torque nuts to 70–115 ft. lbs.

NOTE: Before moving vehicle, make certain that a firm brake pedal has been obtained.

Shoe & Lining Removal & Installation

To remove shoe and lining assemblies, follow "Caliper Removal" procedure and omit step 2 as it is not necessary to disconnect brake hose. After removing caliper, support it with a length of wire to avoid damaging brake hose. To install shoe and lining assemblies, follow "Caliper Installation" procedure, making certain that proper parking brake adjustment is obtained.

Caliper Overhaul

Disassemble
1. Remove caliper assembly as described previously.
2. Remove caliper end retainer, operating shaft, thrust bearing and balls, Fig. 97.
3. Remove thrust screw anti-rotation pin with a magnet or tweezers. If pin cannot be removed with a magnet or tweezers, proceed with the following procedure:
   a. With tool T75P-2588B, force piston approximately one inch from caliper bore.
   b. Push piston back into caliper housing with tool, then with tool in position, hold tool shaft in place and rotate handle counter-clockwise until thrust screw clears anti-rotation pin. Remove thrust screw and anti-rotation pin.
4. Remove thrust screw by rotating with ¼ inch allen wrench.
5. Install tool T75P-2588-A through back of caliper housing and remove piston assembly, Fig. 98.

CAUTION: Use care not to damage polished surface in thrust screw bore and do not attempt to remove or press adjuster can, as it is a press fit in piston.

6. Remove and discard piston seal, boot, thrust O-ring seal, end retainer, O-ring and end retainer lip seal.

Cleaning & Inspection
1. Clean all metal parts with alcohol, then using clean, dry compressed air, blow out and dry all grooves and passages making sure the caliper bore and component parts are free of any foreign material.
2. Inspect caliper bore for damage or excessive wear. The thrust screw must be smooth and free of pits. If piston is pitted, scored or chrome plating is worn, replace piston and adjuster assembly.
3. Adjuster can must be bottomed in piston to be properly seated and provide consis-

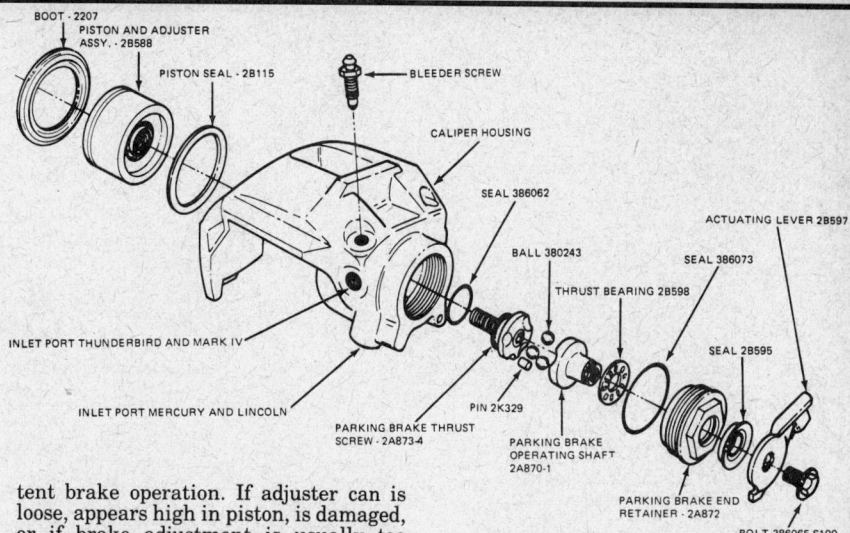

Fig. 97 Rear disc brake caliper assembly

tent brake operation. If adjuster can is loose, appears high in piston, is damaged, or if brake adjustment is usually too tight, too loose or not functioning, replace piston/adjuster assembly. Check adjuster operation by assembling thrust screw into piston/adjuster assembly, then pull the two parts apart about ¼ inch and release them, Fig. 99. When pulling on the two parts, the brass drive ring must remain stationary causing the nut to rotate. When releasing the two parts, the nut must remain stationary and drive ring must rotate. If action does not follow this pattern, replace piston/adjuster assembly.
4. Inspect ball pockets, threads, grooves, bearing surfaces of thrust screw, operating shaft, balls and anti rotation pin for wear, brinnelling or pitting. Replace operating shaft, balls, thrust screw and anti rotation pin if any of these parts are worn or damaged. A polished appearance on the ball paths is acceptable if there is no sign of wear into the surface.
5. Inspect thrust bearing for corrosion, pitting or wear and replace as necessary.
6. Inspect end plug bearing surface for wear

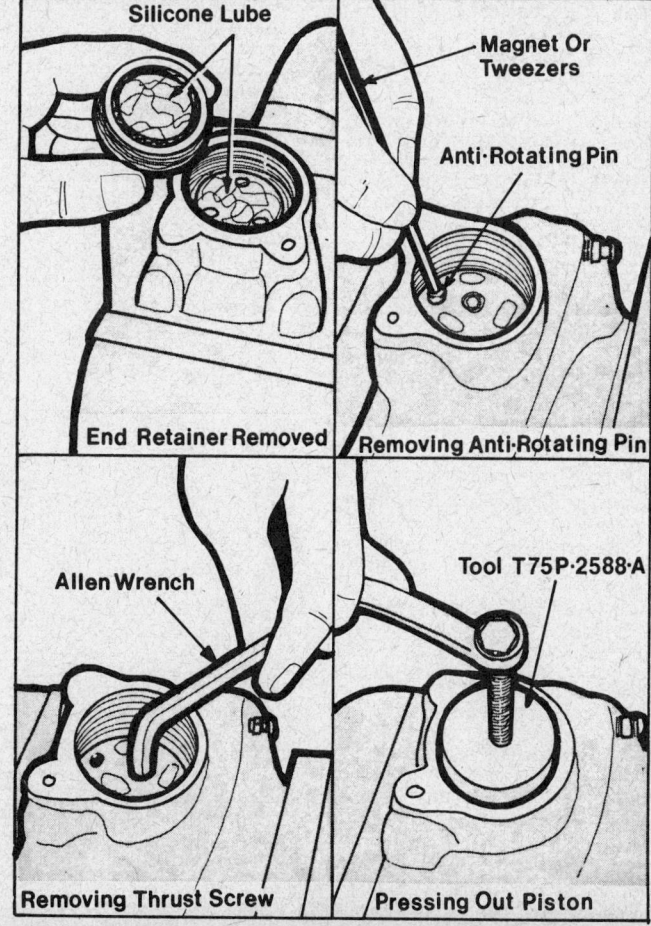

Fig. 98 Disassembling rear disc brake caliper

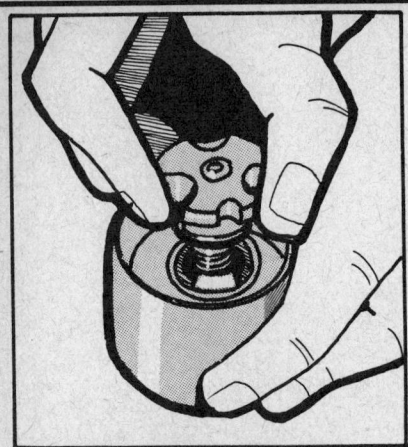

Fig. 99   Checking parking brake adjuster operation

or brinnelling and replace as necessary. A polished appearance on bearing surface is acceptable if there is no sign of wear into surface.

7. Inspect operating lever for damage and replace as necessary.

Assemble

1. Coat new caliper piston seal with clean brake fluid and install it in caliper making certain that seal is not twisted and is fully seated in groove.
2. Install new dust boot by seating flange squarely in outer groove of caliper bore, then coat piston/adjuster assembly with clean brake fluid and install it in caliper bore. Spread dust boot over piston as it is installed and seat dust boot in piston groove.
3. Install caliper in vise, Fig. 100, and fill piston/adjuster assembly with clean brake fluid.
4. Coat new thrust screw O-ring with clean brake fluid and install it in thrust screw groove, then install thrust screw into piston adjuster assembly until top surface of thrust screw is flush with bottom of threaded bore, being careful to avoid cutting O-ring seal. Index notches on thrust screw and caliper housing and install anti-rotation pin.

NOTE: The thrust screw and operating shafts are not interchangeable from side to side since the ramp direction in the ball pockets are different. The pocket surfaces of the operating shaft and thrust screws are stamped "R" (Right) and "L" (Left).

5. Place a ball in each of three pockets of thrust screw and apply a liberal amount of silicone grease M1C-169-A on parking brake components, then install operating shaft on balls.
6. Coat thrust bearing with silicone grease and install it on operating shaft, then install a new lip seal and O-ring on end retainer.
7. Lightly coat O-ring seal and lip seal with silicone grease and install end retainer in caliper. Firmly hold operating shaft against internal mechanism while installing end retainer to prevent mislocation of balls. If lip seal moves out of position, reseat seal. Torque end retainer to 75–95 ft. lbs.

NOTE: Parking brake lever must rotate freely after torquing.

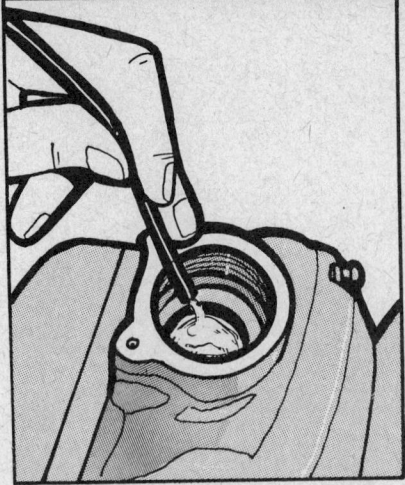

Fig. 100   Filling piston/adjuster assembly

8. Install parking brake lever on keyed spline facing down and rearward. Torque retaining screw to 16–22 ft. lbs.
9. Bottom piston using tool T75P-2588-B, Fig. 101, and install caliper as described previously.

DELCO-MORAINE REAR DISC BRAKE

Operation, Figs. 102, 103 & 104

Upon application of brake, the cone and piston move out as one part. The nut remains stationary on the high lead screw and a gap develops between the cone and nut. When lining wear occurs, the cone and piston do not return to their original position, thereby leaving a small gap equal to the lining wear between the nut and cone. The adjusting spring causes the nut to rotate on the high lead screw to close the gap and adjust the caliper.

Upon application of parking brake, the lever rotation causes the high lead screw to turn and the nut to move down the screw,

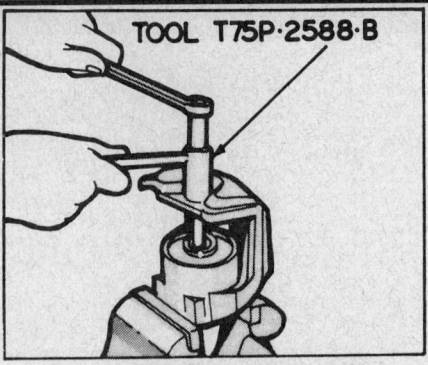

Fig. 101   Bottoming piston in caliper

thereby loading through the cone and the cone-clutch interface of the piston, resulting in a clamp load on the linings. When the parking brake is released, the cone rotates on the clutch interface to adjust the caliper. The clutch interface prevents the cone from turning when the parking brake is applied.

Caliper Removal

CAUTION: Do not mix power steering fluid with brake fluid. If brake seals contact steering fluid or steering seals contact brake fluid, damage will result.

1. Remove two thirds of the total brake fluid capacity from the master cylinder front reservoir, to prevent overflow of brake fluid.
2. Support vehicle on a hoist and remove tire and wheel assembly.
3. Install one nut with flat side facing rotor to prevent rotor from falling out when caliper is removed.
4. Loosen parking brake cable tension at equalizer, then remove cable from parking brake lever and remove return spring, lock nut, lever, lever seal and anti-friction washer.

NOTE: Lever must be held in place while removing nut.

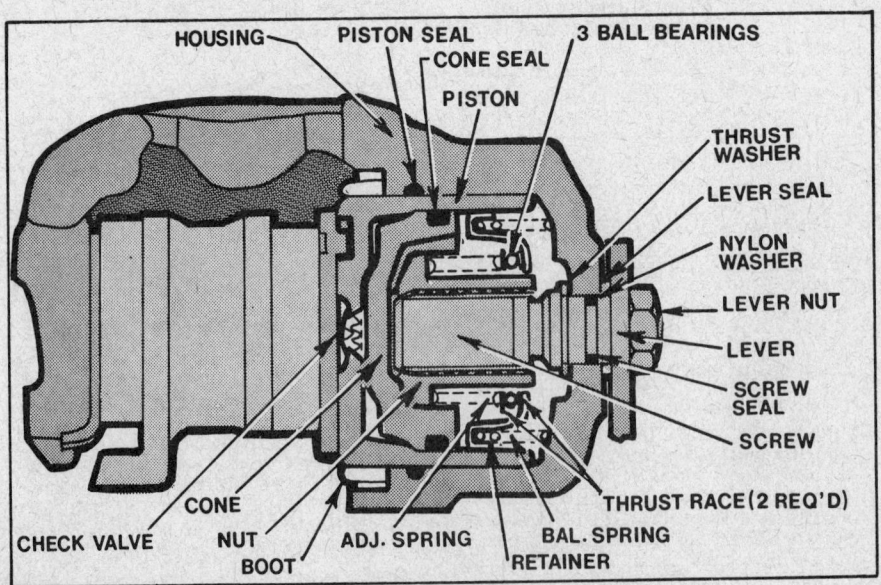

Fig. 102   Delco-Moraine rear disc brake

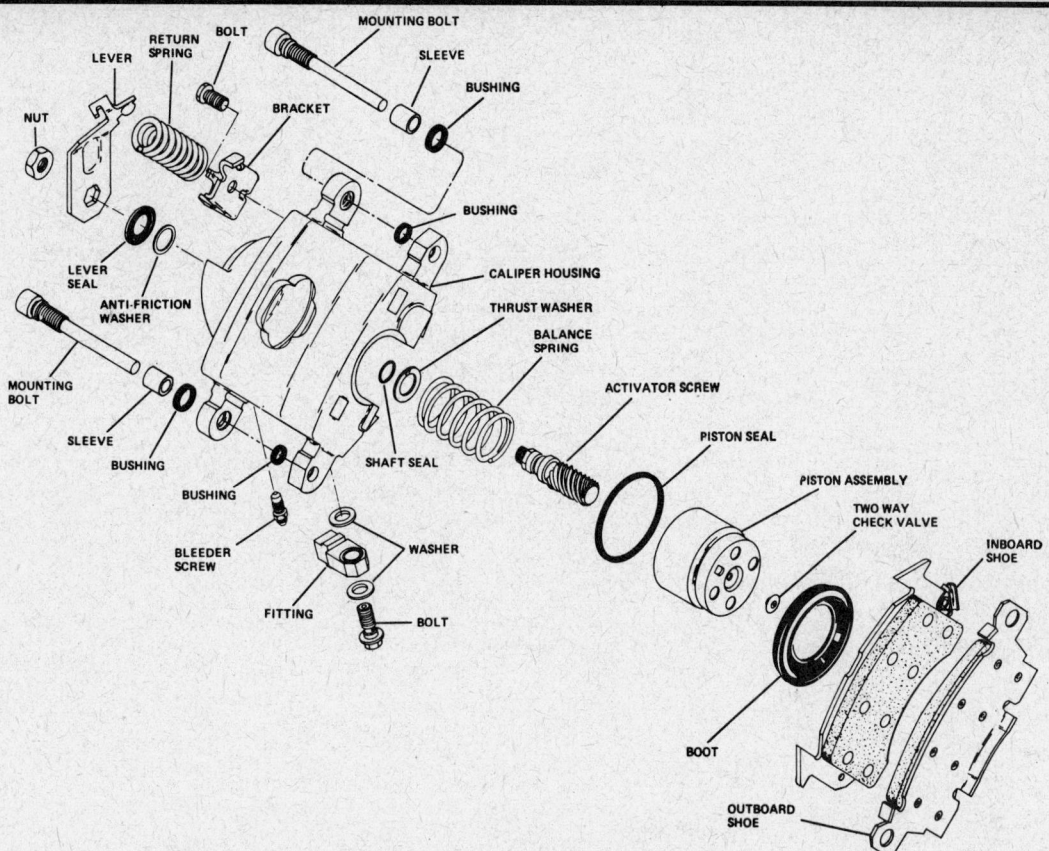

Fig. 103   Rear disc brake caliper disassembled. 1977–78 Eldorado, 1977–78 Riviera, 1977–79 Cadillac Seville & Brougham & 1978–80 Electra

5. Clean surface in area of lever seal, then using a 7 inch (or larger) C-clamp, with the solid end on lever stop and screw end on back of outboard lining, turn clamp until piston is bottomed in caliper.

NOTE: Do not position C-clamp on actuator screw.

6. Before removing clamp, lubricate housing surface under lever seal with silicone lubricant.
7. Install a new anti-friction washer, a new lever seal and lever.

NOTE: Install lever on hex with arm pointing downward.

8. Rotate lever toward front of vehicle and while holding in this position, install nut and torque to 25 ft. lbs. and rotate lever back to stop.
9. Install lever return spring and remove C-clamp.

NOTE: On Cadillac springs are color coded, red for the right hand caliper and black for the left hand caliper.

10. Disconnect brake line from caliper and plug openings to prevent loss of fluid and entry of dirt.
11. On all calipers except Eldorado and right hand Brougham remove the brass bolt from the block.

NOTE: If brake line nut is seized, brass bolt and block can be removed with brake

line attached by removing bolt. Plug openings to prevent loss of fluid and entry of dirt.

12. Remove caliper mounting bolts and remove caliper.
13. Reverse procedure to install and torque caliper mounting bolts to 30 ft. lbs.

NOTE: When installing brass bolt and block, use two new copper gaskets. Torque bolt or connector to 30 foot-pounds.

Inspection

1. Clean corrosion and dirt from face of piston. Inspect piston and check valve area for fluid leakage, indicated by excessive moisture around boot area.
2. Inspect dust boot for cuts, cracks or other damage which may affect its sealing ability. If leaks are present, replace dust boot.

NOTE: Do not use compressed air to clean caliper as it may unseat the dust boot.

3. Inspect piston boot seal. Replace boot seal if leakage is indicated.
4. Inspect for leaks at threaded end of actuator screw. Replace seal if leakage is indicated. If bore is nicked or scratched, replace caliper.

Caliper Overhaul

Disassembly

1. Clamp caliper in a vise and remove the two mounting sleeves and four bushings,

Fig. 103 and 104.
2. Remove brake shoes and lever return spring.
3. Rotate parking brake lever back and forth to remove piston from housing, Fig. 105. If piston will not move from housing, remove lock nut, lever and anti-friction washer. With a 9/16 inch wrench, rotate screw clockwise on right hand caliper or counter-clockwise on left hand caliper until the piston moves from housing.

NOTE: Pad caliper with shop cloths when removing piston.

4. Remove piston assembly and balance spring.
5. Remove lock nut, lever, lever seal and anti-friction washer if not removed previously.
6. Push screw from housing, then remove piston seal and boot.

Assembly

1. Install new piston seal.
2. Install new boot onto piston assembly with lip of boot located in piston groove.
3. Install new thrust washer and seal on actuator screw.
4. Install actuator screw into piston assembly. The piston assemblies are identified by a stamped letter on the adjuster nut end. "L" denote left hand and "R" denotes right hand. The caliper housing is also marked with a letter. The parking brake will not function if the caliper and actuator screw are located on the wrong side of vehicle.
5. Coat piston seal with clean brake fluid. Install balance spring into piston and

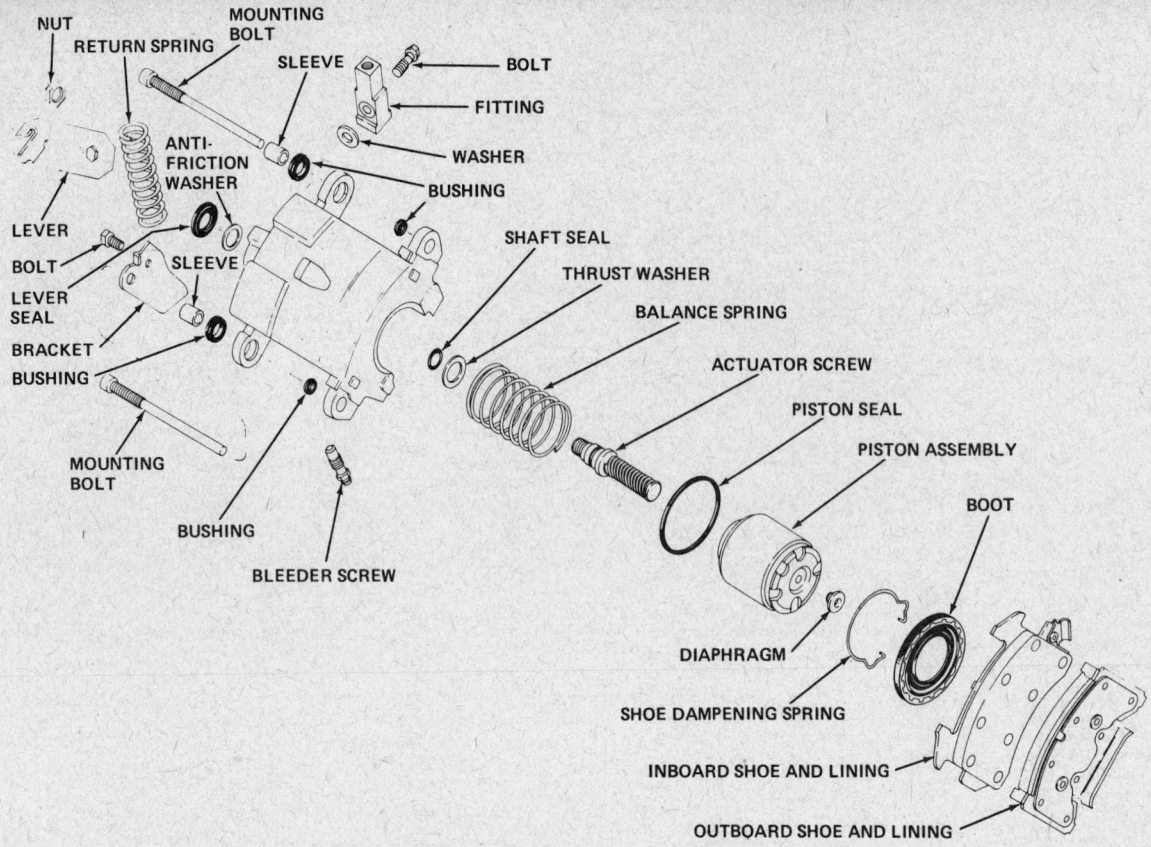

Fig. 104   Rear disc brake caliper disassembled. 1982–83 Camaro, 1979–83 Eldorado, Firebird, Riviera & Toronado & 1980–83 Seville

install assembly into caliper housing, Fig. 106.

6. With tool J-23072, push piston fully into caliper housing, Fig. 107.

NOTE: The piston must be pushed straight into caliper to prevent damage to the actuator screw seal as it passes through hole in rear of piston bore.

7. Before removing tool J-23072, install lubricated anti-friction washer, new lever seal, lever and lock nut. Position lever away from stop, rotate forward and hold lever in position, then torque nut to 25 ft. lbs.

8. Remove tool J-23072, rotate lever back to stop and install return spring.

NOTE: On Cadillac the return springs are color coded red for right hand and black for left hand.

9. With tool J-26296, drive boot until seal bottoms in caliper housing, Fig. 108.

Shoe & Lining Replacement

1. Remove caliper as described previously and remove shoe and lining.

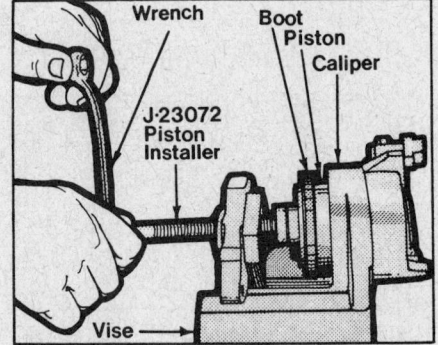

Fig. 107   Installing piston into caliper

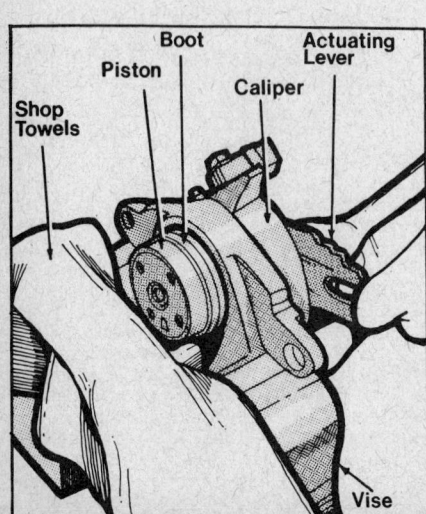

Fig. 105   Removing piston from bore

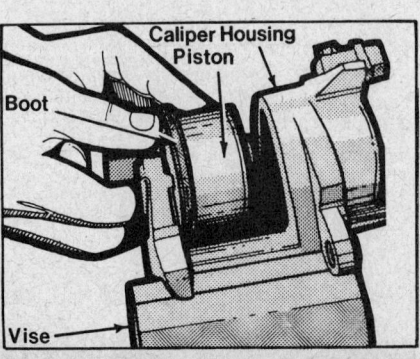

Fig. 106   Positioning piston in caliper

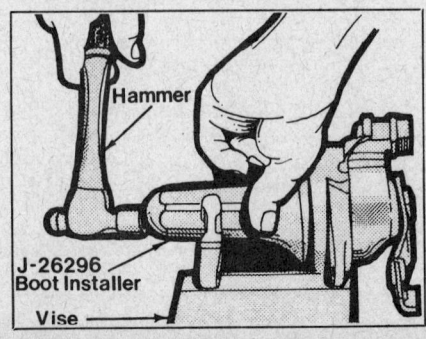

Fig. 108   Driving boot into caliper

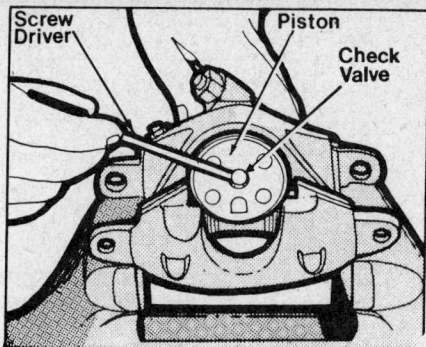

Fig. 109 Removing piston check valve

2. Remove and discard the two caliper mounting sleeves and the four bushings. Using silicone lubricant, install new bushings and seals.

NOTE: Sleeves are installed in inner bushings.

3. Remove and discard piston check valve and install a new one, Fig. 109.

CAUTION: Front brake shoes must not be installed on rear calipers.

4. Position new inboard shoe assembly on piston. The D-shaped tab must fit into indentation in piston. If piston requires rotation, use tool J-7642 to rotate it, Fig. 110.

NOTE: Install new spring retainers on all exc. Eldorado outboard shoe assembly.

5. Install new outboard shoe assembly onto caliper. Install caliper and torque mounting bolts to 30 ft. lbs.

AMERICAN MOTORS DUAL PIN SLIDING CALIPER

Operation

This dual pin sliding caliper assembly incorporates a hub and rotor assembly, a caliper, brake shoes and linings, caliper anchor plate, adapter bracket and splash shield on Spirit and Concord models, Fig. 111. On Eagle models, the caliper assembly incorporates a rotor which mounts to the hub assembly, a caliper, brake shoes and linings, caliper anchor plate and splash shield, Fig. 112.

The caliper used on all models has a 2.6 inch diameter piston. The caliper is positioned over the rotor and slides on two mounting pins which maintain caliper position relative to the rotor and caliper anchor plate. The caliper is a one-piece casting with a groove machined in the bore to hold the square cut piston seal to maintain a hydraulic seal between the piston and bore wall. The dust boot is seated in a machined recess in the top of the piston bore and a groove in the piston exterior surface.

The inner and outer brakeshoes are positioned by the caliper anchor plate. The brakeshoe anti-rattle clip is positioned between the brakeshoe and caliper anchor plate. The brake linings are riveted to the shoes and the inner and outer brake shoes are not interchangeable.

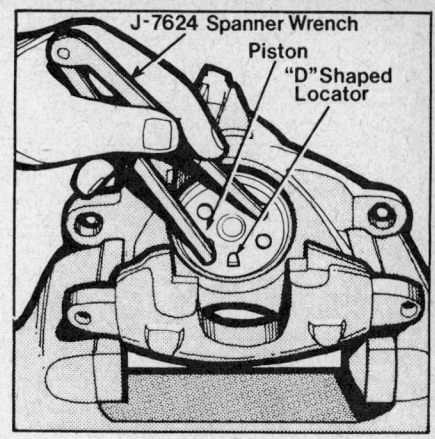

Fig. 110 Rotating piston in bore

Brake Shoe & Linings, Replace

Removal

1. Drain and discard approximately ⅔ of the brake fluid from the larger brake fluid reservoir.
2. Raise and support vehicle, then remove tire and wheel assembly.
3. Using a suitable screwdriver, pry piston fully into caliper bore.

NOTE: If piston cannot be bottomed in cylinder bore using a screwdriver, use a "C" clamp.

4. Using a 7 mm Allen wrench, remove caliper mounting pins.
5. Lift caliper from anchor plate and off rotor.

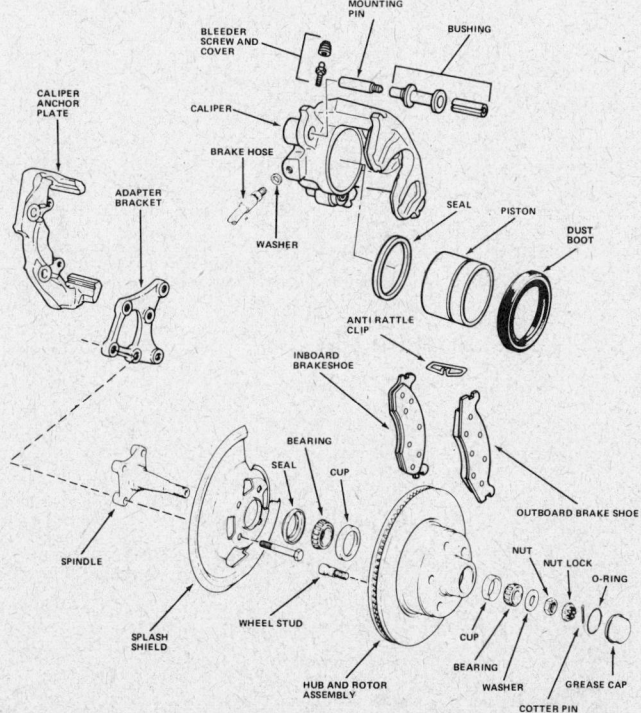

Fig. 111 American Motors dual pin slider disc brake assembly. 1982–83 Spirit & Concord

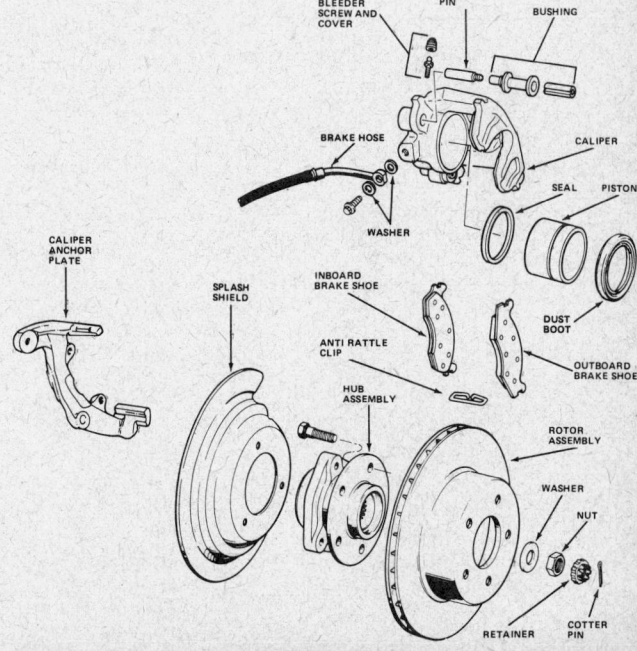

Fig. 112 American Motors dual pin slider disc brake assembly. 1982–83 Eagle

6. Suspend caliper from coil spring with suitable wire to prevent damaging brake hose.
7. Hold anti-rattle clip against caliper anchor plate and remove outer brake shoe.

NOTE: Note position of anti-rattle clip for assembly reference.

8. Remove inner brake shoe from caliper anchor plate, then anti-rattle clip.
9. Wipe inside of caliper with dry, clean cloth and inspect piston bore for leakage. If leakage is present, refer to "Caliper Overhaul".

NOTE: Do not clean caliper with compressed air as damage to the dust boot may result.

Installation

1. Inspect caliper and anchor plate abutment surfaces for rust and corrosion. If rust and corrosion are evident, clean surfaces with wire brush.
2. Lightly lubricate caliper and anchor plate abutment surfaces with Molydisulfide grease.
3. Install anti-rattle clip on trailing end of anchor plate. Ensure split end of clip faces away from rotor.
4. While holding anti-rattle clip in position, install inner and outer brake shoes.
5. Install caliper over rotor and into position on adapter.
6. Install caliper mounting pins. Torque to 26 ft. lbs.
7. Fill master cylinder with clean brake fluid, then pump brake pedal several times to position caliper piston and brake shoes.
8. Install tire and wheel assembly, then lower vehicle.
9. Check brake fluid and refill as necessary.

NOTE: Before moving vehicle, ensure a firm brake pedal is obtained.

Caliper Overhaul

Removal

1. Follow steps 1 through 3 of Removal procedure under "Brake Shoe and Linings, Replace."
2. Clean dirt from brake hose fittings.
3. Disconnect brake hose from caliper, then cap open lines to prevent entry of dirt.

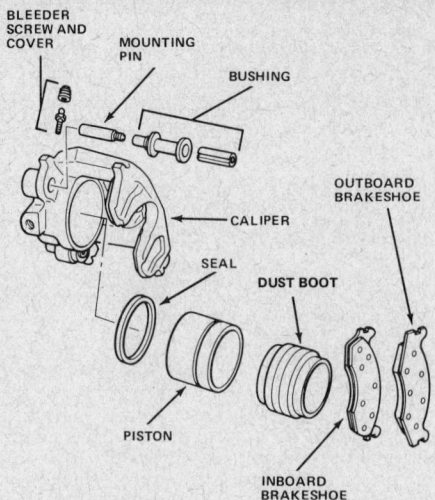

Fig. 113 Disassembled view of disc brake caliper. 1982–83 American Motors

4. Discard hose fitting washer.
5. Remove caliper following steps 4 through 8 of Removal procedure under "Brake Shoe and Linings, Replace."

Disassembly

1. Clean caliper exterior with suitable brake cleaning solvent.
2. Drain caliper, then place on clean work surface.
3. Pad caliper interior with clean shop cloths, then using compressed air, gently apply just enough air pressure into caliper fluid inlet hole to ease piston out of bore.

NOTE: Do not place fingers in front of piston in an attempt to catch or protect it when applying compressed air. This could result in serious injury.

4. Using a suitable screwdriver, pry dust boot from bore using care not to damage piston bore, Fig. 113.
5. Using a pencil or other suitable wooden object, remove piston seal.

Inspection

1. Clean all parts in brake cleaning solvent or brake fluid, then blow out caliper fluid passages with filtered compressed air.
2. Inspect caliper mounting pins for corrosion, replace as necessary.

NOTE: Do not attempt to clean or polish caliper mounting pins with abrasives as protective plating will be removed.

3. Inspect caliper piston. If nicked, scratched, corroded or protective plating is worn off, replace.

NOTE: Do not attempt to refinish piston in any way as protective plating will be removed, leading to corrosion and eventual failure.

4. Inspect caliper bore. If nicked, scratched, worn, cracked, or badly corroded, replace caliper.

NOTE: Minor corrosion and stains can be removed from caliper bore with crocus cloth. Do not attempt to clean caliper bore with any other abrasives.

Assembly

1. Lubricate piston bore and seal with brake fluid, then work seal into piston groove using fingers only.
2. Lubricate piston with brake fluid, then slide metal portion of dust seal over open end of piston and pull rearwards until seal boot seats in piston groove, then push metal portion of seal forward until retainer is flush with rim and seal fold snaps into position.
3. Insert piston and seal assembly into bore. Do not unseat piston seal.
4. Using a hammer handle, press piston in bore.
5. Using tool No. J-33028, install dust seal in caliper housing.
6. Install bleeder screw and tighten securely.
7. Install replacement plastic sleeves and rubber bushings in caliper ears.

Installation

1. Follow steps 1 through 6 of Installation procedures under "Brake Shoe and Linings, Replace."
2. Install replacement hose fitting washer on brake hose, then install hose in caliper and torque to 25 ft. lbs.
3. Fill master cylinder with clean brake fluid and bleed brakes.
4. Install tire and wheel assembly, then lower vehicle.
5. Check brake fluid and refill as necessary.

NOTE: Before moving vehicle, ensure a firm brake pedal is obtained.

Disc Brake Rotor Specifications

CAR	Year	Nominal Thickness	Minimum Refinish Thickness	Thickness Variation Parallelism	Lateral Runout (T.I.R.)	Finish (Micro-In.)
AMERICAN MOTORS						
Matador	1977–78	1.190	1.120	.0005	.003	15–80
Exc. Matador	1977–80	.880	.810	.0005	.003	15–80
Exc. Eagle	1981–83	—	.815	.0005	.003	15–80
Eagle	1981–83	—	.815	.0005	.004	15–80
BUICK (EXC. SKYHAWK, 1980–83 SKYLARK & 1982–83 CENTURY)						
Full Size	1977–78⑬	1.040	.980	.0005	.005	30–80
	1978–79⑭	.974	.921	.0005	.003③	—
	1979⑬	1.040	.980	.0005	.004③	30–80
	1980–83⑬	1.040	.980	.0005	.004③	⑤
	1980–83⑭	.974	.921	.0005	.004③	⑤
Intermediate	1977–78	1.040	.980	.0005	⑮	30–80
	1979–83	1.040	.980	.0005	.004	30–80
CADILLAC (EXC. CIMARRON)						
All⑬	1977	1.037	.980	.0005	.005	19.7–59
All⑭	1977	.974	.911	.0005	.003	15.7–78.7
All⑬	1978	1.038	.981	.0005	.005	19.7–59.1
All⑭	1978	.975	.911	.0005	.003	15.76–78.8
Exc. Eldorado⑬	1979	1.037	.980	.0005	.005	—
Exc. Eldorado⑭	1979	.974	.921	.0005	.003	—
Eldorado⑬	1979	1.036	—	.0005	.005	—
Eldorado⑭	1979	1.035	—	.0005	.005	—
Exc. Eldorado & Seville⑬	1980–81	1.037	—	.0005	.005	—
Eldorado & Seville⑬	1980–81	1.036	—	.0005	.005	—
Eldorado & Seville⑭	1980–81	1.036	—	.0005	.005	—
All	1982–83	1.000	—	.0005	.004	
CHEVROLET (CAMARO, CHEVROLET, CORVETTE, MALIBU, MONTE CARLO & NOVA)						
Corvette	1977–82	1.250	1.230	.0005	.005	20–60
All exc. Corvette	1977–83	1.030	.980	.0005	.004	20–60

CAR	Year	Nominal Thickness	Minimum Refinish Thickness	Thickness Variation Parallelism	Lateral Runout (T.I.R.)	Finish (Micro-In.)
1982–83 CHEV. CAVALIER • BUICK SKYHAWK • CAD. CIMARRON • OLDS FIRENZA • PONT. 2000						
All	1982–83	.885	.830	.0005	.002	—
CHEVROLET CHEVETTE • PONTIAC 1000						
All	1977	.50 (12.7 mm)	.456 (11.58 mm)	.003 (.08 mm)	.005 (.13 mm)	20–60 (.5–1.6 micro/m)
	1978–83	.4334 (11 mm)	.390 (9.9 mm)	.0005 (.013 mm)	.005 (.13 mm)	20–60 (.5–1.6 micro/m)
1980–83 CHEV. CITATION, BUICK SKYLARK, OLDS. OMEGA & PONT. PHOENIX • 1982–83 CHEV. CELEBRITY, BUICK CENTURY, OLDS CUTLASS CIERA & PONT. 6000						
All	1980	1.040	.980	.0005	.005	30–80
All	1981–83	.885	.830	.0005	.004	12–50
1977–80 CHEV. MONZA • BUICK SKYHAWK • OLDS. STARFIRE • PONT. SUNBIRD						
All	1977–80	.880	.830	.0005	.005	20–60
CHEVROLET VEGA • PONTIAC ASTRE						
All	1977	.500	.455	.0005	.005	20–60
CHRYSLER, DODGE & PLYMOUTH						
Full Size	1977–78	1.250	1.180	.0005	.004	15–80
	1979–83	1.010	.940	.0005	.004	15–80
Imperial	1981–83	1.010	.940	.0005	.004	15–80
Intermediate (Exc. Below)	1977–83	1.010	.940	.0005	.004	15–80
Aspen, Valiant & Volare	1977–80	1.010	.940	.0005	.004	15–80
Omni & Horizon	1978–80	.490	.431	.0005	⑪	15–80
	1981–83	.498	.431	.0005	.005	15–80
Charger & Turismo	1983	.498	.431	.0005	.005	15–80
Aries & Reliant	1981–83	.935	.882	.0005	.005	15–80
400 & LeBaron	1982–83	.935	.882	.0005	.005	15–80
600, E-Class & New Yorker	1983	.935	.882	.0005	.005	15–80

Continued

DISC BRAKES

DISC BRAKE ROTOR SPECIFICATIONS—Continued

CAR	Year	Nominal Thickness	Minimum Refinish Thickness	Thickness Variation Parallelism	Lateral Run-out (T.I.R.)	Finish (Micro-In.)
FORD MOTOR COMPANY						
Ford & Mercury Full Size	1977–78	1.180⑦	1.120⑧	.0005②	.003⑨	15–80
	1979	1.030⑦	.972⑧	.0005	.003⑨	15–80
	1980–83	1.030	.972	.0005	.003	10–80
Ford & Mercury Intermediate	1977–79①	1.180	1.120	.0005	.003	15–80
	1980④	.870	.810	.0005	.003	15–80
	1981–83④	.870	.810	.0005	.003	15–125
Comet & Maverick	1977	.870	.810	.0005	.003	15–80
Granada, Monarch & Versailles	1977–80	.870⑦	.810⑧	.0005	.003⑨	15–80
	1981–82	.870	.810	.0005	.003	15–125
Lincoln Continental, Mark V, VI & Town Car	1977–79	1.180⑦	1.120⑧	.0025⑩	.003⑨	15–80
	1980–83⑥	1.030	.972	.0005	.003	10–80
	1982–83⑯	1.030⑦	.972⑧	.0005	.003⑨	15–125 ⑰
Capri, Mustang, Pinto & Bobcat	1977–80	.870	.810	.0005	.003	15–80
	1981–83	.870	.810	.0005	.003	15–125
Fairmont & Zephyr	1978–80	.870	.810	.0005	.003	15–80
	1981–83	.870	.810	.0005	.003	15–125

CAR	Year	Nominal Thickness	Minimum Refinish Thickness	Thickness Variation Parallelism	Lateral Run-out (T.I.R.)	Finish (Micro-In.)
Escort, EXP, LN7 & Lynx	1981–83	.945 (24 mm)	.882 (22.4 mm)	—	.003 (.075 mm)	16–79
Tempo & Topaz	1984	.945 (24 mm)	.882 (22.4 mm)	.0005	.003	15–80
OLDSMOBILE (88, 98, TORONADO, 1977–79 OMEGA & CUTLASS EXC. CIERA)						
88, 98 & Custom Cruiser	1977–81	1.040	.965	.0005	⑫	30–50
	1982	1.020	.984	.0005	.004	—
Intermediate	1977–81	1.040	.980	.0005	.004	30–50
	1982–83	1.020	.984	.0005	.004	—
Toronado	1977–78	1.245	1.185	.0005	.002	30–50
	1979–80	1.040	1.020	.0005	.005	19–80
	1981	1.020	.960	.0005	.005	19–80
	1982–83	1.020	.984	.0005	.004	19–80
PONTIAC (EXC. ASTRE, SUNBIRD, 1000 & FRONT WHEEL DRIVE)						
Bonneville & Catalina	1977–80	1.040	.980	.0005	.005	20–60
	1981–83	1.030	.980	.0005	.005	30–80
Grand Am, Grand Prix & LeMans	1977–80	1.040	.980	.0005	.005	20–60
	1981–83	1.030	.980	.0005	.005	30–80
Firebird	1977–80	1.030	.980	.0005	.004	20–60
	1981–83	1.030	.980	.0005	.004	30–80
Parisienne	1983	1.030	.980	.0005	.004	20–60
Phoenix & Ventura	1977–79	1.040	.980	.0005	.004	20–60

①—1977–1979 Cougar, LTD II & Thunderbird.
②—1977–78 Mercury, Front disc. .0004, 1977–78 rear disc. 0005.
③—1979–83 Riviera, .005.
④—Cougar, Cougar XR-7, Thunderbird & 1983 LTD & Marquis.
⑤—Exc. Riviera, 30–80; Riviera, 19–80.
⑥—Mark VI & Town Car.
⑦—Rear disc. .945.
⑧—Rear disc. .895.
⑨—Rear disc. .004.
⑩—Rear disc. .0004.
⑪—1978, .003; 1979–80, .005.
⑫—Exc. Olds 88 w/V8-403 engine, .004; Olds 88w/V8-403 engine, .005.
⑬—Front.
⑭—Rear.
⑮—1977–78 Skylark, .005; 1977–78 except Skylark, .004.
⑯—Continental.
⑰—Rear disc brake, 15-80.

Disc Brake Caliper Specifications

Year	Model	Caliper Bore Dia. In.
AMERICAN MOTORS		
1977–78	Matador	3.1
1977–83	Exc. Matador	2.6
BUICK (EXC. SKYHAWK, 1980–83 SKYLARK & 1982–83 CENTURY)		
1977	All	2 15/16
1978	Century & Regal	2 7/16

Year	Model	Caliper Bore Dia. In.
1979–81	Exc. Century & Regal	2 15/16
	Century & Regal	2 7/16
	Riviera	2 1/2
1982–83	Exc. Century, Regal & Riviera	2 15/16
	Regal & Riviera	2 1/2
	Exc. Regal & Riviera	2 15/16

Year	Model	Caliper Bore Dia. In.
CADILLAC (EXC. CIMARRON)		
1977–78	All	2 15/16
1979	Eldorado	2 1/2
	Exc. Eldorado	2 15/16
1980–83	Eldorado & Seville	2 1/2
	Brougham & DeVille	2 15/16

Continued

DISC BRAKE CALIPER SPECIFICATIONS—Continued

Year	Model	Caliper Bore Dia. In.
CHEVROLET (CAMARO, CHEVROLET, CORVETTE, MALIBU, MONTE CARLO & NOVA)		
1977	Corvette	①
	Exc. Corvette	2¹⁵/₁₆
1978–81	Exc. Malibu, Monte Carlo & Corvette	2¹⁵/₁₆
	Malibu & Monte Carlo	2½
	Corvette	①
1982	Camaro	②
	Malibu & Monte Carlo	2½
	Chevrolet	2¹⁵/₁₆
	Corvette	①
1983	Camaro	②
	Malibu & Monte Carlo	2½
	Chevrolet	2¹⁵/₁₆
1984	Corvette	③

1982–83 CHEV. CAVALIER • BUICK SKYHAWK • CAD. CIMARRON • OLDS FIRENZA • PONTIAC 2000

Year	Model	Caliper Bore Dia. In.
1982–83	All	2.24

CHEVROLET CHEVETTE • PONTIAC 1000

Year	Model	Caliper Bore Dia. In.
1977–82	All	1⁷/₈
1983	All	2.05

1980–83 CHEV. CITATION • BUICK SKYLARK • OLDS OMEGA • PONT. PHOENIX

Year	Model	Caliper Bore Dia. In.
1980–83	All	2.24

1982–83 CHEV. CELEBRITY • BUICK CENTURY • OLDS. CUTLASS CIERA • PONT. 6000

Year	Model	Caliper Bore Dia. In.
1982–83	All	2.24

1977–80 CHEV. MONZA • BUICK SKYHAWK • OLDS. STARFIRE • PONT. SUNBIRD

Year	Model	Caliper Bore Dia. In.
1977–80	All	2½

Year	Model	Caliper Bore Dia. In.
CHEVROLET VEGA • PONTIAC ASTRE		
1977	All	1⁷/₈
CHRYSLER CORP. FRONT WHEEL DRIVE		
1978–80	All	1.89
1981–82	Omni & Horizon	1.894
	Exc. Omni & Horizon	2.130
1983	All	2.130
CHRYSLER CORP. REAR WHEEL DRIVE		
1977	Chrysler, Royal Monaco & Gran Fury	3.1
	LeBaron & Diplomat	2.755
	Volaré, Fury, Cordoba, Aspen, Charger & Monaco	2³/₄
1978	Chrysler	3.102
	Exc. Chrysler	2.755
1979–83	All	2.755
FORD & MERCURY—Full Size Models		
1977–78	All	3.10④
1979–83	All	2.88④
FORD & MERCURY—Compact & Intermediate Models		
1977	Maverick & Comet	2.60
	Granada & Monarch	2.60
	Cougar, LTD II & Thunderbird	3.10
1978–79	Cougar, LTD II & Thunderbird	3.10
	Fairmont & Zephyr	2.36
	Granada & Monarch	2.60
1980	Cougar, XR-7 & Thunderbird	2.36

Year	Model	Caliper Bore Dia. In.
	Fairmont & Zephyr	2.36
	Granada & Monarch	2.60
1981–83	All	2.36
FORD MUSTANG & PINTO • MERCURY BOBCAT & CAPRI		
1977–79	All	2.6
1980	Bobcat & Pinto	2.6
	Capri & Mustang	2.36
1981–83	Capri & Mustang	2.36
FORD ESCORT, EXP & TEMPO • MERCURY LN7, LYNX & TOPAZ		
1981–83	All	2.125
1984	Tempo & Topaz	2.36
LINCOLN		
1977–79	Exc. Versailles	3.1④
	Versailles	2.6⑤
1980	Exc. Versailles	2.88
	Versailles	2.6⑤
1981	Lincoln & Mark VI	2.88
1982–83	Exc. Continental	2.88
	Continental	2.38⑤
OLDSMOBILE (EXC. FIRENZA, STARFIRE, 1980–83 OMEGA & 1982–83 CUTLASS CIERA)		
1977–81	Exc. Cutlass	2¹⁵/₁₆
	Cutlass	2½
1982–83	Cutlass & Toronado	2½
	88, 98 & Custom Cruiser	2¹⁵/₁₆
PONTIAC (EXC. ASTRE, SUNBIRD, 1000 & FRONT WHEEL DRIVE)		
1977	All	2.9375
1978–81	Exc. Grand Prix & LeMans	2.9375
	Grand Prix & LeMans	2.5
1982–83	Exc. Firebird	2.9375
	Firebird	⑥

①—Front, 1⁷/₈"; Rear, 1³/₈".
②—Front, 2½"; Rear, 1⁵⁷/₆₄".
③—Front, 2.1"; Rear, 1.6".

④—If equipped with rear disk brakes, rear disc brake caliper bore, 2.6".

⑤—Rear disc brake caliper bore, 2.1".
⑥—Front, 2.5"; Rear, 1.89".

DRUM BRAKES

See Car Chapters For Brake Adjustments

APPLICATION INDEX

①—Exc. sta. wag. with 6 cyl. engine.
②—With 4 cyl. engine.
③—Exc. 4 cyl. engine.
④—Exc. Spirit GT models with rally tuned suspension.
⑤—Exc. models with V8 engine.
⑥—Sta. wag. with 6 cyl. engine.
⑦—Models with V8 engine.
⑧—Spirit GT with rally tuned suspension.
⑨—Exc. sta. wag.
⑩—Sta. wag.
⑪—2 & 3 door hatchback.
⑫—Exc. 2 & 3 door hatchback.

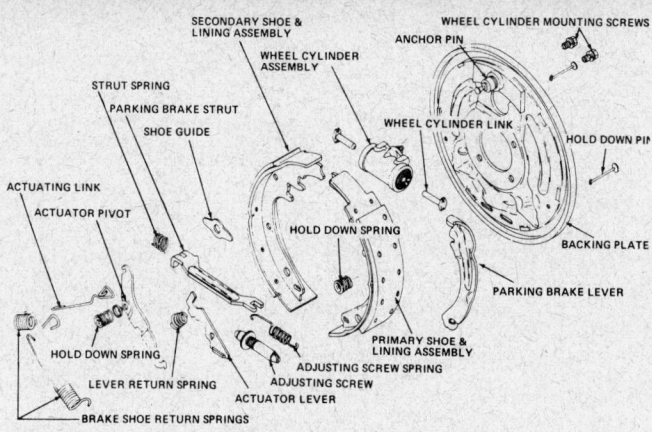

Fig. 1 Drum brake assembly. Type 1

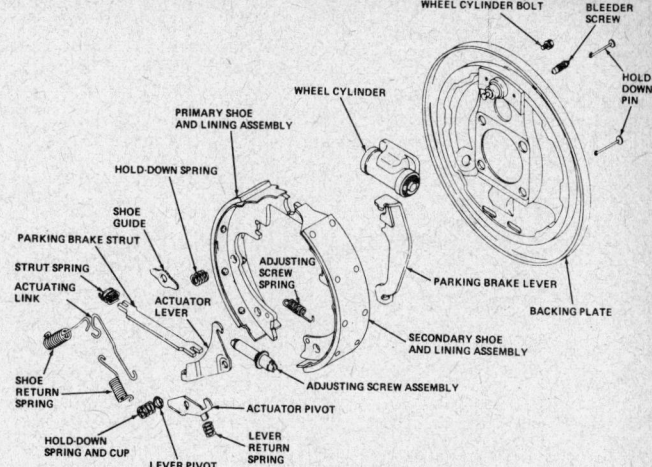

Fig. 2 Drum brake assembly. Type 2

SERVICE PRECAUTIONS

When working on or around brake assemblies, care must be taken to prevent breathing asbestos dust, as many manufacturers incorporate asbestos fibers in the production of brake linings. During routine service operations the amount of asbestos dust from brake lining wear is at a low level, due to a chemical breakdown during use and a few precautions will minimize exposure.

CAUTION: Do not sand or grind brake linings unless suitable local exhaust ventilation equipment is used to prevent excessive asbestos exposure.

1. Wear a suitable respirator approved for asbestos dust use during all repair procedures.
2. When cleaning brake dust from brake parts, use a vacuum cleaner with a highly efficient filter system. If a suitable vacuum cleaner is not available, use a water soaked rag.

NOTE: Do not use compressed air or dry brush to clean brake parts.

3. Keep work area clean using same equipment as for cleaning brake parts.
4. Properly dispose of rags and vacuum cleaner bags by placing them in plastic bags.
5. Do not smoke or eat while working on brake systems.

GENERAL INSPECTION
Brake Drums

Any time the brake drums are removed for brake service, the braking surface diameter should be checked with a suitable brake drum micrometer at several points to determine if they are within the safe oversize limit stamped on the brake drum outer surface. If the braking surface diameter exceeds specifications, the drum must be replaced. If the braking surface diameter is within specifications, drums should be cleaned and inspected for cracks, scores, deep grooves, taper, out of round and heat spotting. If drums are cracked

or heat spotted, they must be replaced. Minor scores should be removed with sandpaper. Grooves and large scores can only be removed by machining with special equipment, as long as the braking surface is within specifications stamped on brake drum outer surface. Any brake drum sufficiently out of round to cause vehicle vibration or noise while braking or showing taper should also be machined, removing only enough stock to true up the brake drum.

After a brake drum is machined, wipe the braking surface diameter with a denatured alcohol soaked cloth. If one brake drum is machined, the other should also be machined to the same diameter to maintain equal braking forces.

Brake Linings & Springs

Inspect brake linings for excessive wear, damage, oil, grease or brake fluid contaminated. If any of the above conditions exists, brake linings should be replaced. Do not attempt to replace only one set of brake shoes; they should be replaced as an axle set only to maintain equal braking forces. Examine brake shoe webbing, hold down and return springs for signs of overheating indicated by a slight blue color. If any component exhibits overheating signs, replace hold down and return springs with new ones. Overheated springs lose their pull and could cause brake linings to wear out prematurely. Inspect all springs for sags, bends and external damage and replace as necessary.

Inspect hold down retainers and pins for bends, rust and corrosion. If any of the above is found, replace.

Backing Plate

Inspect backing plate shoe contact surface for grooves that may restrict shoe movement and cannot be removed by lightly sanding with emery cloth or other suitable abrasive. If backing plate exhibits above condition, it should be replaced. Also inspect for signs of cracks, warpage and excessive rust, indicating need for replacement.

Adjuster Mechanism

Inspect all components for rust, corrosion, bends and fatigue. Replace as necessary. On adjuster mechanism equipped with adjuster

cable, inspect cable for kinks, fraying or elongation of eyelet and replace as necessary.

Parking Brake Cable

Inspect parking brake cable end for kinks, fraying and elongation and replace as necessary. Use a small hose clamp to compress clamp where it enters backing plate to remove.

TYPES 1, 2 & 3
Removal

1. Raise and support rear of vehicle, then remove tire and wheel assembly.
2. Remove brake drum. If brake lining is dragging on brake drum, back off brake adjustment by rotating adjustment screw. Refer to individual car chapter for procedure.

NOTE: If brake drum is rusted or corroded to axle flange and cannot be removed, lightly tap axle flange to drum mounting surface with a suitable hammer.

3. Using brake spring pliers or equivalent, unhook primary and secondary return springs, Figs. 1, 2 and 3.

NOTE: Observe location of brake parts being removed to aid during installation.

4. Remove brake hold down springs with suitable tool.
5. Lift actuating lever, then unhook actuating link from anchor pin and remove.
6. Remove actuating lever(s) and return spring.
7. Spread shoes apart and remove parking brake strut and spring.
8. Disconnect parking brake cable from lever, then remove brake shoes from backing plate.
9. Separate brake shoes by removing adjusting screw and spring, then unhook parking brake lever from shoe assembly.
10. Clean dirt from brake drum, backing plate and all other components.

CAUTION: Do not use compressed air or dry

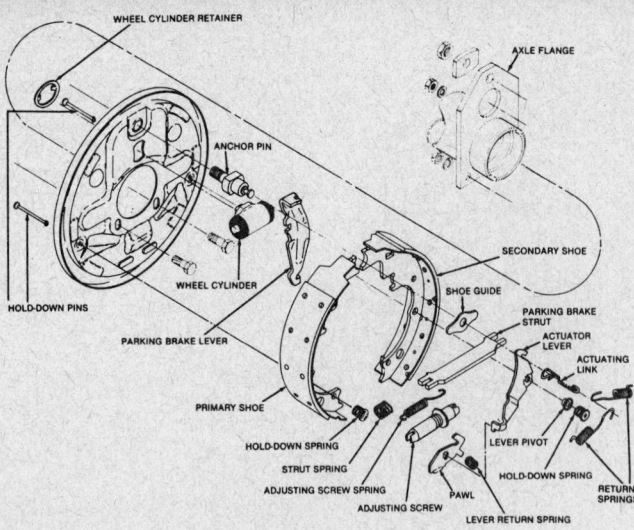

Fig. 3   Drum brake assembly. Type 3

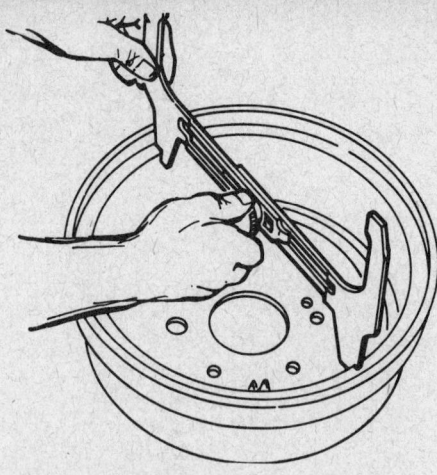

Fig. 4   Measuring brake drum inside diameter

brush to clean brake parts. Many brake parts contain asbestos fibers which, if inhaled, can cause serious injury. Clean brake parts with a water soaked rag or a suitable vacuum cleaner to minimize airborne dust.

Inspection

1. Inspect components for damage and unusual wear. Replace as necessary.
2. Inspect wheel cylinders. Boots which are torn, cut or heat damaged indicate need for wheel cylinder replacement. On type 1 brakes, remove wheel cylinder links. Fluid spill from boot center hole indicates cup leakage and need for wheel cylinder replacement. On type 2 and 3 brakes, use a small screwdriver to pry center hole of boot away from piston. If fluid spills from center hole, cup leakage is indicated and wheel cylinder should be replaced. On all types, light fluid coatings on piston within cylinder is considered normal.
3. Inspect backing plate for evidence of axle seal leakage. If leakage exists, refer to individual car chapters for axle seal replacement procedures.
4. Inspect backing plate attaching bolts, and ensure they are tight.
5. Using fine emery cloth or other suitable abrasive, clean rust and dirt from shoe contact surface on backing plate.

Installation

1. Lubricate parking brake lever fulcrum with suitable brake lube, then attach lever to brake shoe. Ensure lever operates smoothly.
2. Connect brake shoes with adjusting screw spring, then position adjusting screw.

NOTE: Ensure adjusting screw star wheel does not contact adjusting screw spring after installation and also ensure right hand thread adjusting screw is installed on left side of vehicle and left hand thread adjusting screw is installed on right side of vehicle. When brake shoe installation is completed, ensure starwheel lines up with adjusting hole in backing plate.

3. Lightly lubricate backing plate shoe contact surfaces with suitable brake lube,

then the area where parking brake cable contacts backing plate.
4. Install brake shoes on backing plate while engaging wheel cylinder links (if equipped) with shoe webbing. Connect parking brake cable to parking brake lever.

NOTE: The primary shoe (short lining) faces towards front of vehicle.

5. Install actuating levers, actuating link and return spring, Figs. 1, 2 and 3.
6. Install hold down springs with suitable tool.
7. Install primary and secondary shoe return springs using brake spring pliers or equivalent.
8. Using suitable brake drum to shoe gauge, Fig. 4, measure brake drum inside diameter. Adjust brake shoes to dimension obtained on outside portion of gauge, Fig. 5.
9. Install brake drum, wheel and tire assembly.
10. If any hydraulic connections have been opened, bleed brake system.
11. Adjust parking brake. Refer to individual car chapters for procedures.
12. Inspect all hydraulic lines and connections for leakage and repair as necessary.
13. Check master cylinder fluid level and replenish as necessary.
14. Check brake pedal for proper feel and return.
15. Lower vehicle and road test.

NOTE: Do not severely apply brakes immediately after installation of new brake linings or permanent damage may occur to linings, and/or brake drums may become scored. Brakes must be used moderately during first several hundred miles of operation to ensure proper burnishing of linings.

TYPE 4
Removal

1. Raise and support rear of vehicle, then remove tire and wheel assembly.
2. Remove brake drum. If brake drums are

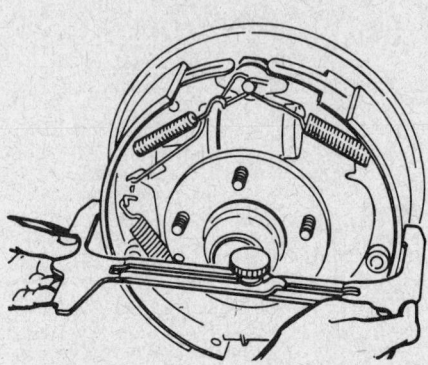

Fig. 5   Adjusting brake shoes to brake drum inside diameter

severely worn, it may be necessary to retract brake shoes, refer to individual car chapter for procedure.
3. Loosen parking brake cable equalizer nut to release all tension on cable.
4. Remove parking brake cable from parking brake lever.
5. Using a suitable pair of pliers, remove pull-back spring, Fig. 6.
6. Remove brake hold down springs and retainers using suitable tool.
7. Remove brake shoes, parking brake lever and strut and shoe retaining spring from backing plate as a unit.
8. Separate parking brake lever and strut, retaining spring and shoe assemblies.

NOTE: If brake shoes are to be reused, mark shoe positions for identification during installation.

9. Clean dirt from brake drum, backing plate and all other components.

CAUTION: Do not use compressed air or dry brush to clean brake parts. Many brake parts contain asbestos fibers which, if inhaled, can cause serious injury. Clean brake parts with a water soaked rag or a suitable vacuum cleaner to minimize airborne dust.

Inspection

1. Inspect components for damage and unusual wear. Replace as necessary.

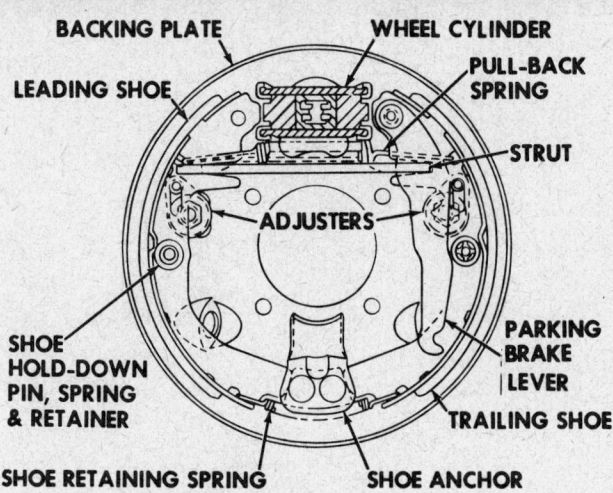

Fig. 6 Drum brake assembly. Type 4

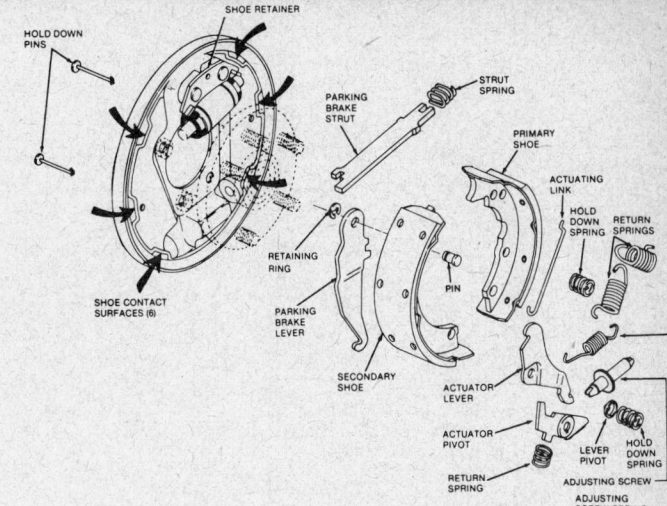

Fig. 7 Drum brake assembly. Type 5

2. Inspect backing plate for evidence of axle seal leakage. If leakage exists, refer to individual car chapter for axle seal replacement procedure.
3. Inspect backing plate attaching bolts, and ensure they are tight.
4. Inspect wheel cylinders. Pull lower edge of boot away from cylinder and inspect for evidence of brake fluid. Excessive fluid indicates cup leakage and need for wheel cylinder replacement.

NOTE: A slight amount of fluid is always present and is considered normal, acting as a lubricant for the cylinder pistons.

5. Check adjuster operation. If adjusters are frozen, worn or loose, replace adjuster and backing plate assembly.

NOTE: Torque required to turn new adjusters at initial assembly is 29–44 ft. lbs. On used assemblies, it will probably be greater.

6. Using fine emery cloth or other suitable abrasive, clean rust and dirt from shoe contact surface on backing plate.

Installation

1. Lubricate parking brake cable and lever fulcrum with suitable brake lube.
2. Attach parking brake lever to trailing shoe, Fig. 6. Ensure lever operates smoothly.
3. Lightly lubricate backing plate shoe contact surfaces with suitable brake lube.
4. Connect brake shoes with retaining spring, then position assembly over axle flange on to backing plate. Secure leading brake shoe with hold down spring and retainer.

NOTE: Ensure leading shoe webbing is engaged with adjuster peg.

5. Position parking brake strut, then secure trailing shoe with hold down spring and retainer.

NOTE: Ensure trailing shoe webbing is

engaged with adjuster peg.

6. Ensure parking brake strut is properly positioned, then install pull-back spring with suitable pliers.
7. Install parking brake cable on parking brake lever.
8. Install brake drum, then tire and wheel assembly.
9. If any hydraulic connections have been opened, bleed brake system.
10. Adjust service brake by applying service brake several times until a firm brake pedal is obtained. Check brake fluid level and replenish as necessary.
11. Adjust parking brake. Refer to individual car chapter for procedure.
12. Lower vehicle and road test.

NOTE: Do not severely apply brakes immediately after installation of new brake linings or permanent damage may occur to linings, and/or brake drums may become scored. Brakes must be used moderately during first several hundred miles of operation to ensure proper burnishing of linings.

TYPE 5
Removal

1. Raise and support rear of vehicle, then remove tire and wheel assembly.
2. Remove brake drum. If brake lining is dragging on brake drum, back off brake adjustment by rotating adjustment screw.

NOTE: If brake drum is rusted or corroded to axle flange and cannot be removed, lightly tap axle flange to drum mounting surface with a suitable hammer.

3. Using brake spring pliers or equivalent, unhook primary and secondary return springs, Fig. 7.
4. Remove hold down springs with suitable tool, then lift off lever pivot.
5. Remove hold down pins, then lift actuator lever and remove actuator link.
6. Remove actuator lever, pivot and return spring.

7. Spread shoes apart and remove parking brake strut and spring.
8. With brake shoes spread, disconnect parking brake spring from lever, then lift brake shoes, adjusting screw and spring from backing plate.
9. Note position of adjusting screw and spring, then remove from shoe assemblies.
10. Remove parking brake lever from secondary shoe.
11. Clean dirt from brake drum, backing plate and all other components.

CAUTION: Do not use compressed air or dry brush to clean brake parts. Many brake parts contain asbestos fibers which, if inhaled, can cause serious injury. Clean brake parts with a water soaked rag or a suitable vacuum cleaner to minimize airborne dust.

Inspection

1. Inspect components for damage or unusual wear. Replace as necessary.
2. On Chevette and 1000 models, inspect backing plate for evidence of axle seal leakage. If leakage exists, refer to individual car chapter for axle seal replacement procedure.
3. Inspect backing plate attaching bolts, and ensure they are tight.
4. Inspect wheel cylinders. Excessive fluid indicates cup leakage and need for wheel cylinder replacement.

NOTE: A slight amount of fluid is always present and is considered normal, acting as a lubricant for the cylinder pistons.

5. Check adjuster screw operation. If satisfactory, lightly lubricate adjusting screw and washer with suitable brake lube. If operation is unsatisfactory, replace.
6. Using fine emery cloth or other suitable abrasive, clean rust and dirt from shoe contact surfaces on backing plate, Fig. 7.

Installation

1. Lightly lubricate backing plate shoe contact surfaces with suitable brake lube.

DRUM BRAKES

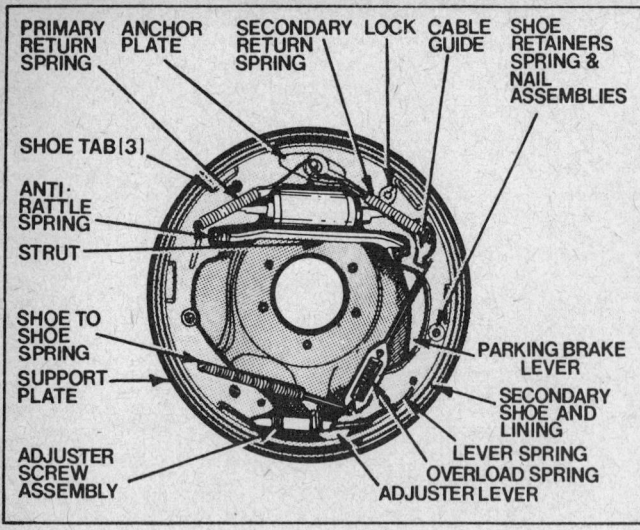

Fig. 8 Drum brake assembly. Type 6

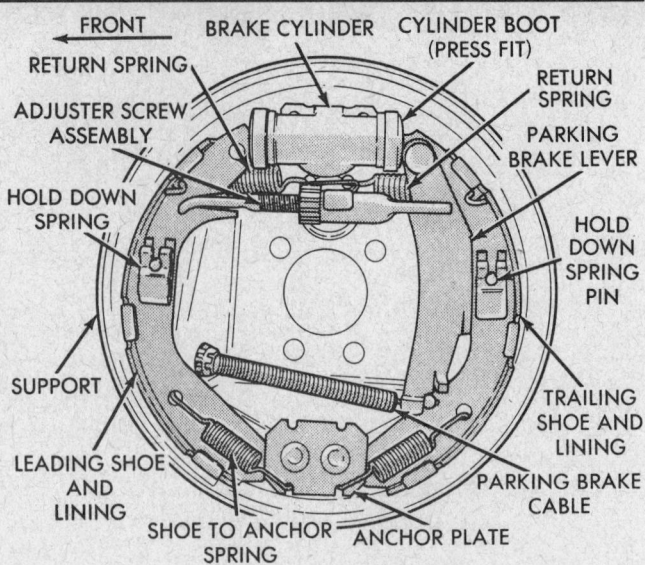

Fig. 9 Drum brake assembly. Type 7

2. Install parking brake lever on secondary shoe.
3. Connect primary and secondary brake shoes with adjusting screw spring, then position adjusting screw in same position from which it was removed.

NOTE: Ensure adjusting screw spring starwheel does not contact adjusting screw spring after installation, and also ensure right hand thread adjusting screw is installed on left side of vehicle and left hand thread adjusting screw is installed on right side of vehicle.

4. Spread brake shoes apart to clear axle flange, then install parking brake cable on lever. Position brake assembly on backing plate.
5. Spread brake shoes slightly, then install parking brake strut and spring. Spring end of strut engages the primary shoe, while the other end engages the parking brake lever and secondary shoe.
6. Install actuator lever, pivot and return spring, then hook actuating link in shoe retainer.
7. Lift actuator lever and hook actuating link to lever.
8. Install hold down pins, lever pivot and hold down springs.
9. Install primary and secondary return springs using suitable brake spring pliers.
10. Using suitable brake drum to shoe gauge, Fig. 4, measure brake drum inside diameter. Adjust brake shoes to dimension obtained on outside portion of gauge, Fig. 5.
11. Install brake drum, tire and wheel assembly.
12. If any hydraulic connections have been opened, bleed brake system.
13. Adjust parking brake. Refer to individual car chapters for procedures.
14. Inspect all hydraulic lines and connections for leakage, and repair as necessary.
15. Check master cylinder fluid level, and replenish as necessary.
16. Check brake pedal for proper feel and return.
17. Lower vehicle and road test.

NOTE: Do not severely apply brakes immediately after installation of new brake linings or permanent damage may occur to linings, and/or brake drums may become scored. Brakes must be used moderately during first several hundred miles of operation to ensure proper burnishing of linings.

TYPE 6

Removal

1. Raise and support rear of vehicle, then remove tire and wheel assembly.
2. Remove brake drum. If brake lining is dragging on brake drum, back off brake adjustment by rotating adjustment screw.

NOTE: If brake drum is rusted or corroded to axle flange and cannot be removed, lightly tap axle flange to drum mounting surface with a suitable hammer.

3. Using brake spring pliers or equivalent, remove primary and secondary shoe return springs, Fig. 8.
4. Remove automatic adjuster cable from anchor plate, then unhook from adjuster lever.
5. Remove adjuster cable, overload spring, cable guide and anchor plate.
6. Unhook adjuster lever spring from lever, then remove spring and lever.
7. Remove shoe to shoe spring from secondary shoe web, then primary shoe.
8. Spread shoes apart and remove parking brake strut and spring.
9. Using suitable tool, remove shoe retainers, then springs and nails.
10. Disconnect parking brake cable from lever, then remove brake shoes.
11. Remove parking brake lever from secondary shoe.
12. Clean dirt from brake drum, backing plate and all other components.

CAUTION: Do not use compressed air or dry brush to clean brake parts. Many brake parts

contain asbestos fibers which, if inhaled, can cause serious injury. To clean brake parts, use a water soaked rag or a suitable vacuum cleaner to minimize airborne dust.

Inspection

1. Inspect components for damage and unusual wear. Replace as necessary.
2. Inspect wheel cylinders. Boots which are torn, cut or heat damaged indicate need for wheel cylinder replacement. Peel back lower edge of boot. If fluid spills out, cup leakage is indicated and wheel cylinder should be replaced.

NOTE: A slight amount of fluid is always present and considered normal, acting as a lubricant for the cylinder pistons.

3. Inspect backing plate for evidence of seal leakage. If leakage exists, refer to individual car chapter for axle seal replacement procedure.
4. Inspect backing plate attaching bolts, and ensure they are tight.
5. Inspect adjuster screw operation. If satisfactory, lightly lubricate adjusting screw and washer with suitable brake lube. If operation is unsatisfactory, replace.
6. Using fine emery cloth or other suitable abrasive, clean rust and dirt from shoe contact surfaces on backing plate.

Installation

1. Lubricate parking brake lever fulcrum with suitable brake lube, then attach lever to secondary brake shoe. Ensure lever operates smoothly.
2. Lightly lubricate backing plate shoe contact surfaces with suitable brake lube.
3. Connect parking brake lever to cable, then slide secondary brake shoe into position.
4. Connect wheel cylinder link to brake shoe (if equipped).
5. Slide parking brake lever strut behind axle flange and into parking brake lever slot, then place parking brake anti-rattle spring over strut.

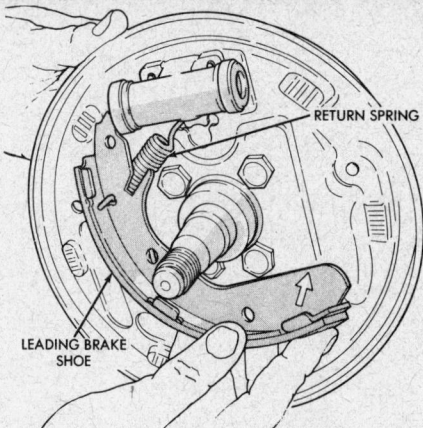

Fig. 10   Installing leading brake shoe. Type 7

NOTE: Do not severely apply brakes immediately after installation of new brake linings or permanent damage may occur to linings, and/or brake drums may become scored. Brakes must be used moderately during first several hundred miles of operation to ensure proper burnishing of linings.

TYPE 7

Removal

1. Raise and support rear of vehicle, then remove tire and wheel assembly.
2. Remove brake drum. If brake lining is dragging on brake drum, back off brake adjustment by rotating adjustment screw.
3. Disconnect parking brake cable from parking brake lever, Fig. 9.
4. Using suitable pliers, remove brake shoe to anchor springs and hold down springs.
5. Fully seat adjuster nut, then spread shoes apart and remove adjuster screw assembly.
6. Raise parking brake lever, then pull trailing shoe away from support to ease return spring tension and disengage spring end from support. Remove trailing shoe.
7. Pull leading shoe away from support to ease return spring tension and disengage spring end from support. Remove leading shoe.
8. Remove parking brake lever from trailing shoe.
9. Clean dirt from brake drum, support plate and all other components.

CAUTION: Do not use compressed air or dry brush to clean brake parts. Many brake parts contain asbestos fibers which, if inhaled, can cause serious injury. To clean brake parts, use a water soaked rag or a suitable vacuum cleaner to minimize airborne dust.

Inspection

1. Inspect components for damage and unusual wear. Replace as necessary.
2. Inspect wheel cylinders. Any torn, cut or heat damaged boots indicates need for wheel cylinder replacement. Peel back lower edge of boot. If fluid spills out, cup leakage is indicated and wheel cylinder should be replaced.

NOTE: A slight amount of fluid is always present and is considered normal. Fluid acts as a lubricant for the cylinder pistons.

3. Inspect support plate attaching bolts, and ensure they are tight.
4. Inspect adjuster screw assembly operation. If satisfactory, lightly lubricate threads with suitable brake lube. If operation is unsatisfactory, replace.
5. Using fine emery cloth or other suitable abrasive, clean rust and dirt from shoe contact surfaces on support plate.

Installation

1. Lightly lubricate support plate shoe contact surfaces with suitable brake lube.

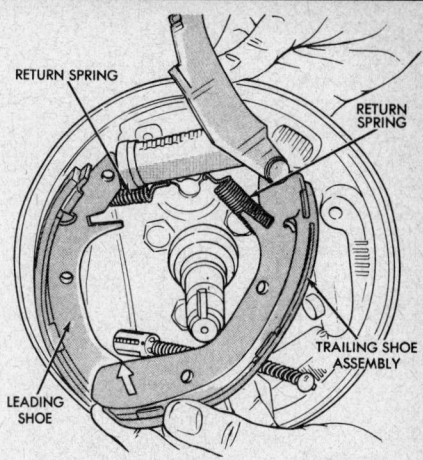

Fig. 11   Installing trailing brake shoe. Type 7

2. Remove brake drum hub grease seal and bearings, then clean and repack bearings and reinstall. Install new grease seal.
3. Position leading shoe return spring on shoe, then while holding shoe away from support, engage return spring in support plate, Fig. 10, and swing shoe end into position under anchor.
4. Install parking brake lever on trailing shoe.
5. Install trailing shoe return spring on shoe, then while holding shoe away from support, engage return spring in support plate, Fig. 11, and swing shoe end into position under anchor.
6. Spread shoes apart and install adjuster screw assembly. Ensure forked end enters the leading shoe with curved tines facing down, Fig. 9.
7. Using a suitable pair of pliers, install hold down springs and shoe to anchor springs.
8. Pull back parking brake cable return spring slightly to expose cable, then slide parking brake cable into parking brake lever and release spring.
9. Install brake drum and bearings. Refer to individual car chapter for wheel bearing adjustment procedure.
10. Adjust brakes. Refer to individual car chapter for procedure.
11. Install tire and wheel assembly.
12. If any hydraulic connections have been opened, bleed brake system.
13. Check master cylinder level, replenish as necessary.
14. Check brake pedal for proper feel and return.
15. Lower vehicle and road test.

NOTE: Do not severely apply brakes immediately after installation of new brake linings or permanent damage may occur to linings and/or brake drums may become scored. Brakes must be used moderately during first several hundred miles of operation to ensure proper burnishing of linings.

TYPE 8

Removal

1. Raise and support rear of vehicle, then remove tire and wheel assembly.

6. Position primary brake shoe on backing plate, then connect wheel cylinder link (if equipped) and parking brake strut.
7. Install anchor plate, then position adjuster cable eye over anchor pin.
8. Install primary shoe return spring using brake spring pliers or equivalent.
9. Place protruding hole rim of cable guide in secondary shoe web hole, then holding guide in position, install secondary shoe return spring through cable guide and secondary shoe. Install spring on anchor pin using brake spring pliers or equivalent.

NOTE: Ensure cable guide remains flat against secondary shoe web during and after return spring installation. Also ensure secondary spring end overlaps primary spring end on anchor pin.

10. Using suitable pliers, squeeze spring ends around anchor pin until parallel.
11. Install adjuster screw assembly between primary and secondary brake shoes with star wheel on secondary shoe side.

NOTE: The left side adjuster assembly stud is stamped "L" and is cadmium-plated. The right side adjuster assembly is not stamped and is colored black.

12. Install shoe to shoe spring, then position adjusting lever spring over pivot pin on shoe web.
13. Install adjusting lever under spring and over pivot pin, then slide lever slightly rearward.
14. Install nails, springs and retainers.
15. Thread adjuster cable over guide and hook end of overload spring in lever. Ensure eye of cable is pulled tight against anchor and in a straight line with guide.
16. Install brake drum, tire and wheel assembly.
17. Adjust brakes. Refer to individual car chapters for procedure.
18. If any hydraulic connections have been opened, bleed brake system.
19. Check master cylinder fluid level, and replenish as necessary.
20. Check brake pedal for proper feel and return.
21. Lower vehicle and road test.

DRUM BRAKES

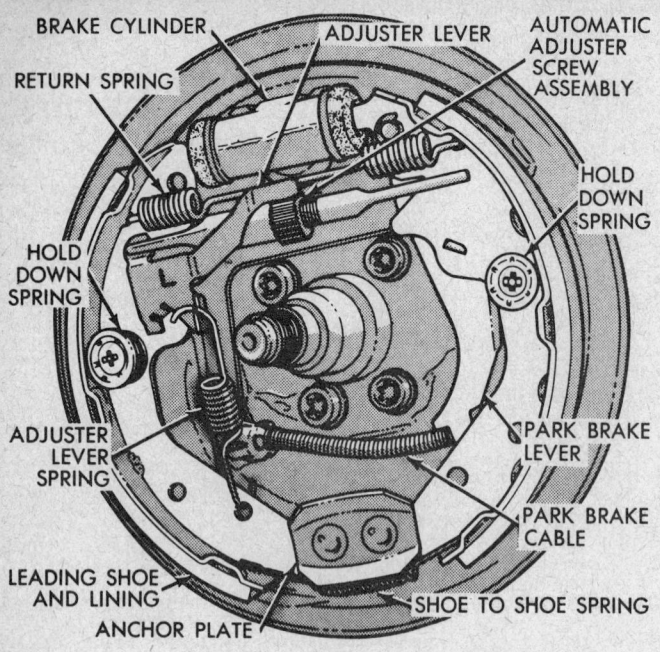

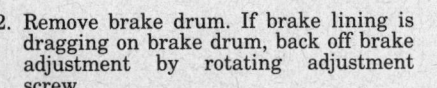

Fig. 12 Drum brake assembly. Type 8

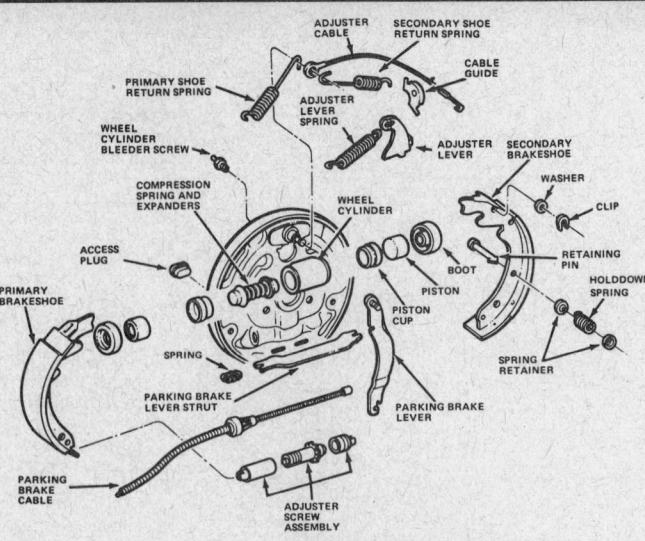

Fig. 12 Drum brake assembly. Type 9

2. Remove brake drum. If brake lining is dragging on brake drum, back off brake adjustment by rotating adjustment screw.
3. Using suitable pliers, remove adjuster lever spring, Fig. 12.
4. Remove adjuster lever.
5. Turn automatic adjuster screw out to expand shoes past wheel cylinder boot.
6. Using suitable tool, remove hold down springs.
7. Pull brake shoe assembly down and away from anchor plate.
8. Remove "C" clip retaining parking brake lever to trailing brake shoe webbing.
9. Disassemble shoe assembly.
10. Clean dirt from brake drum, anchor plate and all other components.

CAUTION: Do not use compressed air or dry brush to clean brake parts. Many brake parts contain asbestos fibers, which, if inhaled, can cause serious injury. To clean brake parts, use a water soaked rag or a suitable vacuum cleaner to minimize airborne dust.

Inspection

1. Inspect components for damage and unusual wear. Replace as necessary.
2. Inspect wheel cylinders. Any torn, cut or heat damaged boot indicates need of wheel cylinder replacement. Peel back lower edge of boot. If fluid spills out, cup leakage is indicated and wheel cylinder should be replaced.

NOTE: A slight amount of fluid is always present and is considered normal. Fluid acts as a lubricant for the cylinder pistons.

3. Inspect anchor plate attaching bolts, and ensure they are tight.
4. Inspect automatic adjuster screw assembly operation. If satisfactory, lightly

lubricate threads with suitable brake lube. If operation is unsatisfactory, replace.
5. Using fine emery cloth or other suitable abrasive, clean rust and dirt from shoe contact surfaces on anchor plate.

Installation

1. Lightly lubricate anchor plate shoe contact surfaces with suitable brake lube.
2. Remove brake drum hub grease seal and bearings, then clean and repack bearings and reinstall. Install new grease seal.
3. Assemble automatic adjuster screw assembly, return spring and shoe-to-shoe spring to brake shoe assembly.
4. Position lining assembly near anchor plate, then assemble parking brake lever to trailing shoe webbing. Secure with "C" clip.
5. Install lining assembly onto anchor plate. When positioned, back off adjuster nut to seat brake shoe ends in wheel cylinder.
6. Install hold down springs.
7. Position adjuster lever, then using suitable pliers, install adjuster lever spring.
8. Install brake drum and bearings. Refer to individual car chapter for wheel bearing adjustment procedure.
9. Adjust brakes. Refer to individual car chapter for procedure.
10. Install tire and wheel assembly.
11. If any hydraulic connections have been opened, bleed brake system.
12. Check master cylinder level, and replenish as necessary.
13. Check brake pedal for proper feel and return.
14. Lower vehicle and road test.

NOTE: Do not severely apply brakes immediately after installation of new brake linings or permanent damage may occur to linings and/or brake drums may become scored. Brakes must be used moderately during first several hundred miles of operation to ensure proper burnishing.

TYPES 9, 10 & 11

Removal

1. Raise and support rear of vehicle, then remove tire and wheel assembly.
2. Remove brake drum. If brake lining is dragging on brake drum, back off brake adjustment by rotating adjustment screw. Refer to individual car chapter for procedure.

NOTE: If brake drum is rusted or corroded to axle flange and cannot be removed, lightly tap axle flange to drum mounting surface with a suitable hammer.

3. Install suitable wheel cylinder clamp over ends of wheel cylinder to retain pistons in bore.
4. On types 9 and 10, Figs. 13 and 14, remove parking brake lever retaining clip.
5. On types 10 and 11, Figs. 14 and 15, remove adjuster lever spring, primary and secondary shoe return springs using a suitable pair of brake spring pliers. On type 9, Fig. 13, remove adjuster lever spring, secondary shoe return spring, adjuster cable eyelet and primary shoe return spring.
6. On all types, remove shoe guide plate (if equipped), and adjuster cable and guide plate.
7. Using suitable tool, compress hold down springs, then remove spring retainers, hold down springs and pins.
8. Separate springs and remove from backing plate.
9. On type 11 brake, disengage parking brake lever from secondary shoe.
10. On all types, remove parking brake lever from cable.
11. Separate all components from brake shoes.
12. Clean dirt from brake drum, backing plate and all other components.

CAUTION: Do not use compressed air or dry brush to clean brake parts. Many brake parts contain asbestos fibers which, if inhaled, can cause serious injury. Clean brake parts with a water soaked rag or a suitable vacuum cleaner to minimize airborne dust.

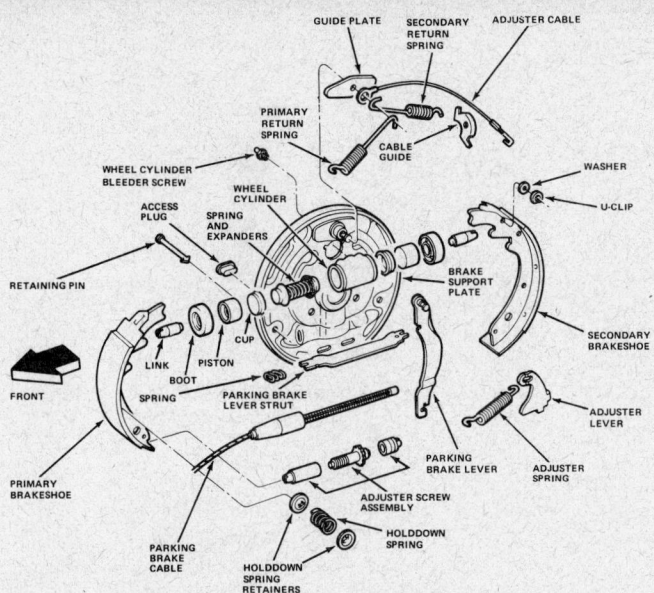

Fig. 14 Drum brake assembly. Type 10

Fig. 15 Drum brake assembly. Type 11

Inspection

1. Inspect components for damage and unusual wear. Replace as necessary.
2. Inspect wheel cylinders. Boots which are torn, cut, or heat damaged indicate need for wheel cylinder replacement. Fluid spilling from boot center hole, or wetness around wheel cylinder ends indicates cup leakage and need for wheel cylinder replacement.

NOTE: A small amount of fluid is always present and is considered normal, acting as a lubricant for the cylinder pistons.

3. Inspect backing plate for evidence of seal leakage. If leakage exists, refer to individual car chapters for axle seal replacement procedure.
4. Inspect backing plate attaching bolts and ensure they are tight.
5. Check adjuster screw operation. If satisfactory, lightly lubricate adjusting screw and washer with suitable brake lube. If operation is unsatisfactory, replace.
6. Using fine emery cloth or other suitable abrasive, clean rust and dirt from shoe contact surfaces on backing plate.

Installation

1. Lightly lubricate backing plate shoe contact surfaces with suitable brake lube.
2. On types 9 and 10, assemble parking brake lever to secondary shoe and secure with spring washer and retaining clip. Crimp ends of clip with suitable pliers. On type 11, engage parking brake lever tang with secondary shoe.
3. Position brake shoes on backing plate, primary (short lining) shoe facing front of vehicle and secondary (long lining) facing rear. Secure brake shoes with hold down springs, pins and retainers.
4. Install parking brake link and spring between shoes.
5. Loosen parking brake adjustment nut, then install parking brake cable on parking brake lever.
6. On type 9, proceed as follows:
   a. Using suitable brake spring pliers, install primary return spring from brake shoe to anchor.
   b. Install adjuster cable eyelet on anchor pin with crimp facing out.
   c. Position adjuster cable guide on secondary shoe, then using suitable brake spring pliers, install secondary return spring from brake shoe to anchor.
7. On types 10 and 11, proceed as follows:
   a. Install shoe guide plate and adjuster cable eyelet on anchor. Ensure adjuster cable crimp faces out.
   b. Ensure parking brake link is properly positioned between brake shoes and wheel cylinder links are engaged in shoe web.
   c. Using suitable brake spring pliers, install primary return spring from brake shoe to anchor, then secondary return spring from brake shoe to anchor.
8. On all types, remove wheel cylinder clamp installed during removal of brake shoes.
9. Tighten adjuster screw assembly to thread limit and back off one-half turn.
10. Install adjuster screw assembly between shoes. Ensure toothed wheel is on secondary shoe side.

NOTE: Adjuster screw assemblies are stamped R (right) and L (left). To ensure proper adjuster operation, they must be installed on their respective sides.

11. Hook adjuster cable hook into adjuster lever hole, then position adjuster spring hook in large hole in primary shoe web. Using suitable brake spring pliers, install adjuster spring in adjuster lever hole.
12. Ensure adjuster cable is properly seated in cable guide, then pull adjuster lever, cable and adjuster spring down and towards the rear, engaging lever pivot hook in the large hole of secondary shoe web.
13. After installation, check adjuster operation by pulling adjuster cable between cable guide and adjuster lever towards secondary shoe sufficiently to lift adjuster lever past one tooth on adjuster screw assembly. The adjuster lever should snap into position behind the next tooth, then upon release of adjuster cable, rotate toothed wheel one notch. If operation is not satisfactory, recheck installation.
14. Ensure brake shoe upper ends are seated against anchor pin and shoe assemblies are centered on backing plate. If not, back off parking brake adjustment.
15. Using suitable brake drum to shoe gauge, Fig. 4, measure brake drum inside diameter. Adjust brake shoes to dimension obtained on outside portion of gauge using adjuster screw.
16. Install brake drum, wheel and tire assembly.
17. If any hydraulic brake connections have been opened, bleed brake system.
18. Adjust parking brake. Refer to individual car chapter for procedures.
19. Inspect all hydraulic lines and connections for leakage and repair as necessary.
20. Check master cylinder fluid level and replenish as necessary.
21. Check brake pedal for proper feel and return.
22. Lower vehicle and road test.

NOTE: Do not severely apply brakes immediately after installation of new brake linings or permanent damage may occur to linings, and/or brake drums may become scored. Brakes must be used moderately during first several hundred miles of operation to ensure proper burnishing of linings.

TYPE 12

Removal

1. Raise and support rear of vehicle, then remove tire and wheel assembly.

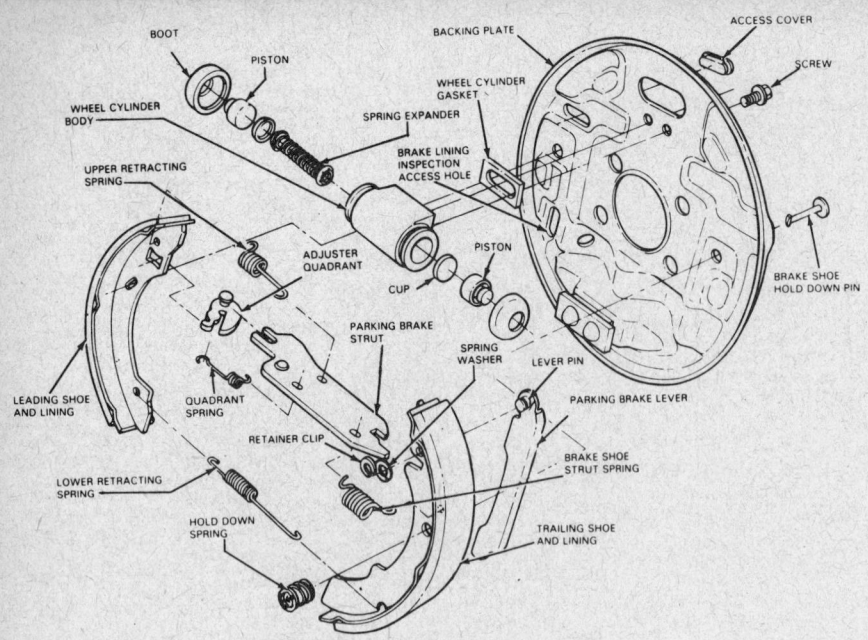

Fig. 16 Drum brake assembly. Type 12

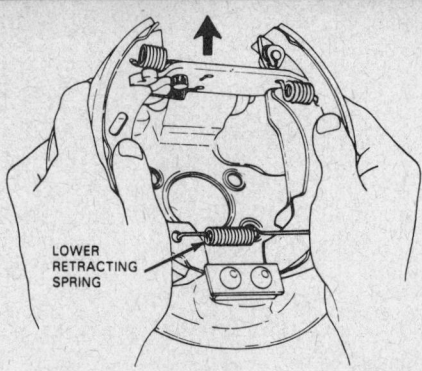

Fig. 17 Removing brake shoe and adjuster assemblies. Type 12

2. Remove brake drum. If brake lining is dragging on brake drum, back off brake adjustment. Refer to individual car chapters for procedure.
3. Using suitable tool, remove hold down retainers, springs and pins, Fig. 16.
4. Remove brake shoe and adjuster assemblies from backing plate by lifting up and away from anchor block and shoe guide, Fig. 17.

NOTE: When removing brake shoe and adjuster assemblies, use care not to damage wheel cylinder boots.

5. Remove parking brake cable from parking brake lever.
6. Remove lower retracting spring from leading and trailing shoes.
7. While holding brake shoe and adjuster assemblies, remove leading shoe upper retracting spring by rotating leading shoe over adjuster quadrant until spring is slack, then remove spring. Remove leading shoe from adjuster assembly.
8. Remove parking brake strut from trailing shoe by pulling strut outward from shoe assembly, then twisting strut downwards until spring tension is released. Unhook brake shoe strut spring, then remove parking brake strut and adjuster assembly from trailing shoe.
9. If adjuster disassembly is required, pull adjuster quadrant away from knurled pin in parking brake strut and rotate quadrant in either direction until quadrant teeth are disengaged from strut pin. Remove spring and slide quadrant out of strut.

NOTE: Do not overstress quadrant spring during removal.

10. Remove parking brake lever retaining clip and spring washer, then the parking brake lever.
11. Clean dirt from brake drum, backing plate and all other components.

CAUTION: Do not use compressed air or dry brush to clean brake parts. Many brake parts contain asbestos fibers which, if inhaled, can cause serious injury. Clean brake parts with a water soaked rag or a suitable vacuum cleaner to minimize airborne dust.

Inspection

1. Inspect components for damage and unusual wear. Replace as necessary.
2. Inspect wheel cylinders. Boots which are torn, cut or heat damaged indicate need for wheel cylinder replacement. Peel back lower edge of boot. If fluid spills out, cup leakage is indicated and wheel cylinder should be replaced.

NOTE: A slight amount of fluid is always present and is considered normal, acting as a lubricant for the cylinder pistons.

3. Inspect backing plate attaching bolts and ensure they are tight.
4. Using fine emery cloth or other suitable abrasive, clean rust and dirt from shoe contact surfaces on backing plate.

Installation

1. Lightly lubricate backing plate shoe contact surfaces with suitable brake lube.
2. Remove brake drum hub grease seal and bearings, then clean and repack bearings and reinstall. Install new grease seal.
3. Lightly lubricate strut to adjuster quadrant contact surfaces with suitable brake lube.
4. Position adjuster quadrant pin in strut slot and install quadrant spring, then pivot quadrant until it engages with strut knurled pin in third or fourth notch of outboard end of quadrant.
5. Assemble parking brake lever to trailing shoe, then install spring washer and retaining clip. Using suitable pliers,

crimp retaining clip until securely fastened.
6. Assemble parking brake strut to trailing shoe by attaching brake shoe strut spring to slots in shoe web and strut, and pivoting strut into position, tensioning spring and holding assembly in place.

NOTE: Ensure end of spring with hook parallel to the center line of spring coils is installed in shoe web hole. Installed spring should be flat against shoe web and parallel to parking brake strut.

7. Install lower retracting spring between shoes. Ensure spring hook with longest straight piece fits into trailing shoe hole, Fig. 16.
8. Install upper retracting spring by installing hooks in leading shoe web and other end in parking brake strut, then pivot leading shoe over adjuster quadrant and into position.
9. Spread shoe and strut assemblies sufficiently to fit over anchor plate and wheel cylinder piston inserts, and install onto backing plate.

NOTE: When installing brake shoe and adjuster assemblies, use care not to damage wheel cylinder boots.

10. Connect parking brake cable to parking brake lever.
11. Using suitable tool, install hold down springs, retainers and pins.
12. Using suitable brake drum to shoe gauge, Fig. 4, measure brake drum inside diameter. Adjust brake shoes to dimension obtained on outside portion of gauge, Fig. 5.
13. Install brake drum. Refer to individual car chapters for wheel bearing adjustment procedure.
14. Install tire and wheel assembly.
15. If any hydraulic connections have been opened, bleed brake system.
16. Adjust parking brake. Refer to individual car chapters for procedure.
17. Inspect all hydraulic lines and connections for leakage and repair as necessary.
18. Check master cylinder fluid level and replenish as necessary.
19. Check brake pedal for proper feel and return.
20. Lower vehicle and road test.

NOTE: Do not severely apply brakes immedi-

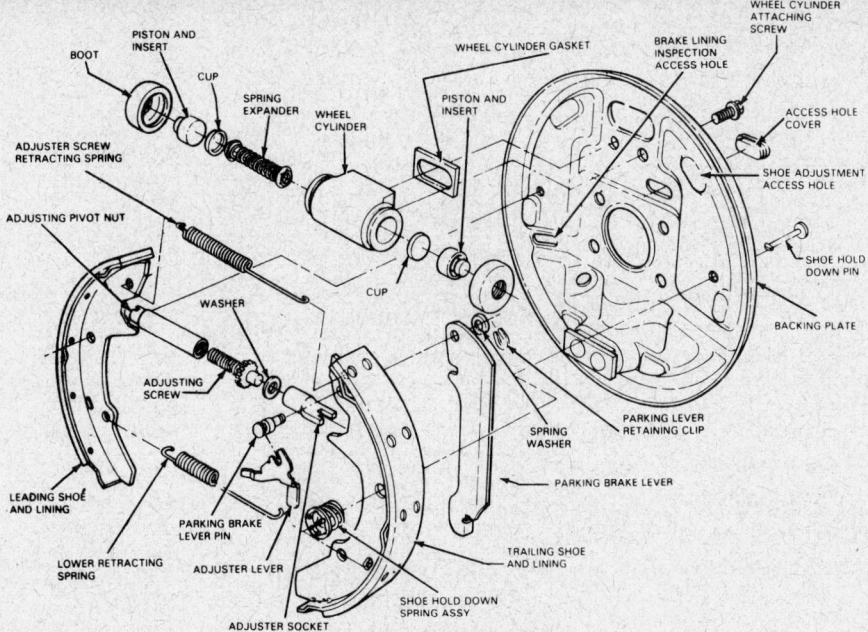

1. Lightly lubricate backing plate shoe contact surfaces with suitable brake lube.
2. Remove brake drum hub grease seal and bearings, then clean and repack bearings and reinstall. Install new grease seal.
3. Assemble parking brake lever to trailing shoe, then install spring washer and retaining clip. Using suitable pliers, crimp retaining clip until securely fastened.
4. Attach parking brake cable to parking brake lever.
5. Assemble lower retracting spring to leading and trailing shoe assemblies, then spread lower part of shoes and install on backing plate.
6. Using suitable tool, install hold down springs.
7. Tighten adjuster assembly, then back off one-half turn. Install adjuster assembly between leading shoe slot and trailing shoe/parking brake lever slot. The adjuster socket end slot must fit into trailing shoe/parking brake lever.

NOTE: Adjuster assemblies are stamped R (right) and L (left). To ensure proper adjuster operation, they must be installed on their respective sides. The letter must be installed in the upright position, facing wheel cylinder to ensure the deeper of the two slots in the adjuster socket fits in the parking brake lever.

8. Install adjuster lever in the parking brake lever groove and into the adjuster socket slot.
9. Using suitable brake spring pliers, install adjusting screw retracting spring from leading shoe slot to adjuster lever notch.
10. Using suitable brake drum to shoe gauge, Fig. 4, measure brake drum inside diameter. Adjust brake shoes to dimension obtained on outside portion of gauge, Fig. 5.
11. Install brake drum. Refer to individual car chapters for wheel bearing adjustment procedure.
12. Install tire and wheel assembly.
13. If any hydraulic connections have been opened, bleed brake system.
14. Adjust parking brake. Refer to individual car chapters for procedure.
15. Inspect all hydraulic lines and connection for leakage, and repair as necessary.
16. Check master cylinder fluid level and replenish as necessary.
17. Check brake pedal for proper feel and return.
18. Lower vehicle and road test.

NOTE: Do not severely apply brakes immediately after installation of new brake linings or permanent damage may occur to linings, and/or brake drums may become scored. Brakes must be used moderately during first several hundred miles of operation to ensure proper burnishing of linings.

Fig. 18 Drum brake assembly. Type 13

ately after installation of new brake linings or permanent damage may occur to lining, and/or brake drums may become scored. Brakes must be used moderately during first several hundred miles of operation to ensure proper burnishing of linings.

TYPE 13

Removal

1. Raise and support rear of vehicle, then remove tire and wheel assembly.
2. Remove brake drum. If brake lining is dragging on brake drum, back off brake adjustment. Refer to individual car chapters for procedure.
3. Using suitable tool, remove hold down retainers, springs and pins, Fig. 18.
4. Remove brake shoes and adjuster assemblies from backing plate by lifting up and away from wheel cylinder assembly.

NOTE: When removing brake shoe and adjuster assemblies, use care not to bend adjusting lever.

5. Remove parking brake cable from parking brake lever.
6. Remove lower retracting spring, adjuster screw retracting spring and adjuster lever.
7. Separate brake shoes, then remove parking brake lever retaining clip and spring washer and slide lever off parking brake lever pin on the trailing shoe.

8. Clean dirt from brake drum, backing plate and all other components.

CAUTION: Do not use compressed air or dry brush to clean brake parts. Many brake parts contain asbestos fibers which, if inhaled, can cause serious injury. Clean brake parts with a water soaked rag or a suitable vacuum cleaner to minimize airborne dust.

Inspection

1. Inspect components for damage and unusual wear. Replace as necessary.
2. Inspect wheel cylinders. Boots which are torn, cut or heat damaged indicate need for wheel cylinder replacement. Peel back lower edge of boot. If fluid spills out, cup leakage is indicated and wheel cylinder should be replaced.

NOTE: A small amount of fluid is always present and is considered normal, acting as a lubricant for the cylinder pistons.

3. Inspect backing plate attaching bolts and ensure they are tight.
4. Using fine emery cloth or other suitable abrasive, clean rust and dirt from shoe contact surfaces on backing plate.
5. Check adjuster screw operation. If satisfactory, lightly lubricate adjusting screw and washer with suitable brake lube. If operation is unsatisfactory, replace.

Brake Drum Specifications

Year	Model	Brake Drum Inside Dia. In.
AMERICAN MOTORS		
1977–78	Exc. Gremlin	10
	Gremlin	①
1979	Exc. Spirit	10
	Spirit	①
1980–83	Exc. Concord & Spirit	10
	Concord	9②
	Spirit	9③
BUICK (EXC. SKYHAWK, 1980–83 SKYLARK & 1982–83 CENTURY)		
1977	Century, Regal	10.997–11.007
	Electra, Riviera, Estate Wagon	10.997–11.007
	LeSabre	9.5
	Skylark	9.5
1978	Skylark	9.5
	Century, Regal	9.45
	Electra, Riviera, Estate Wagon	10.997–11.007
	LeSabre	9.5
1979	Skylark	9.5
	Century, Regal	9.45
	LeSabre	9.5
	Electra, Estate Wagon	11
	Riviera	9.45
1980	Century, Regal	9.45
	LeSabre④	9.5
	LeSabre, LeSabre Estate Wagon⑤	11
	Electra, Electra Estate Wagon	11
	Riviera	9.45
1981	Century, Regal	9.5
	LeSabre④	9.5
	LeSabre, LeSabre Estate Wagon⑤	11
	Electra, Electra Estate Wagon	11
	Riviera	9.5
1982	Regal, LeSabre	9.5
	LeSabre Estate Wagon	11
	Electra	11
	Riviera	9.5
1983	Regal & LeSabre	9.5
	LeSabre Estate Wagon	11
	Electra	11
	Riviera	9.5
CADILLAC (EXC. CIMMARON)		
1977–79	Exc. DeVille & Fleetwood	⑥
	DeVille	11
	Fleetwood	12
1980–83	Seville & Eldorado	⑥
	Brougham & DeVille	11

Year	Model	Brake Drum Inside Dia. In.
CHEVROLET (CAMARO, CHEVROLET, CORVETTE, MALIBU, MONTE CARLO & NOVA)		
1977	Exc. Chevelle & Monte Carlo	9½⑦
	Chevelle & Monte Carlo	11
1978–82	Exc. Corvette	9½⑦
	Corvette	⑥
1983	All	9½⑦
1982–83 CHEV. CAVALIER • BUICK SKYHAWK • CAD. CIMARRON • OLDS. FIRENZA • PONT. 2000		
1982–83	All	7.87
CHEVROLET CHEVETTE • PONTIAC 1000		
1977–83	All	7.88
1980–83 CHEV. CITATION, BUICK SKYLARK, OLDS. OMEGA, PONT. PHOENIX • 1982–83 CHEV. CELEBRITY, BUICK CENTURY, OLDS CUTLASS CIERA & PONT. 6000		
1980–81	All	7.874
1982–83	All	7.87
1977–80 CHEV. MONZA • BUICK SKYHAWK • OLDS. STARFIRE • PONT. SUNBIRD		
1977	All	9½
1978–79	All	⑧
1980	All	9½
CHEVROLET VEGA • PONTIAC ASTRE		
1977	All	9½
CHRYSLER CORP. FRONT WHEEL DRIVE		
1978–82	All	7.87
1983	Exc. E-Class, New Yorker & 600	7.87
	E-Class, New Yorker & 600	8.66
CHRYSLER CORP. REAR WHEEL DRIVE		
1977	LeBaron & Diplomat	10
	Aspen & Volaré	10⑨
	Chrysler, Cordoba, Charger, Monaco, Royal Monaco, Fury & Gran Fury	11
1978	Chrysler	11
	LeBaron & Diplomat	10
	Aspen & Volaré	⑩
	Cordoba & Charger	⑪
	Monaco & Fury	⑩⑪
1979	LeBaron & Diplomat	10
	Aspen & Volaré	⑩
	Chrysler, Cordoba Magnum XE & St. Regis	⑪
1980	Exc. LeBaron	⑩
	LeBaron	10

Continued

BRAKE DRUM SPECIFICATIONS—Continued

Year	Model	Brake Drum Inside Dia. In.
1981	Cordoba, Imperial, Mirada	10
	Chrysler, St. Regis, Gran Fury	10 [12]
	Diplomat & LeBaron	10 [9] [12]
1982–83	All	10 [12]

FORD & MERCURY—Full Size Models

Year	Model	Brake Drum Inside Dia. In.
1977–78	All	11.03
1979–83	All [14]	10.00
	All [15]	11.03

FORD & MERCURY—Compact & Intermediate Models

Year	Model	Brake Drum Inside Dia. In.
1977	Mercury, Comet, Granada & Monarch	10.00
	Cougar, LTD II & Thunderbird	11.03
1978–79	Cougar, LTD II & Thunderbird	11.03
	Fairmont & Zephyr	[16]
	Granada & Monarch	10.00
1980	Cougar XR-7 & Thunderbird	9.00
	Fairmont & Zephyr	[16]
	Granada & Monarch	10.00
1981	Cougar & Granada	[17]
	Cougar XR-7 & Thunderbird	9.00
	Fairmont & Zephyr	[16]
1982	Cougar & Granada	[16]
	Cougar XR-7 & Thunderbird	[15]
	Fairmont & Zephyr	9
1983	Cougar & Thunderbird	9
	Fairmont & Zephyr	9
	LTD & Marquis	[16]

FORD MUSTANG & PINTO • MERCURY BOBCAT & CAPRI

Year	Model	Brake Drum Inside Dia. In.
1977–83	All	9.0

FORD ESCORT, EXP & TEMPO • MERCURY LN7, LYNX & TOPAZ

Year	Model	Brake Drum Inside Dia. In.
1981	All	[18]
1982–83	Escort & Lynx	[18]
	EXP & LN7	8
1984	Tempo & Topaz	8

LINCOLN

Year	Model	Brake Drum Inside Dia. In.
1977–79	All	11.030
1980	Lincoln & Mark VI	[19]
1981–83	All	10.00

OLDSMOBILE (EXC. FIRENZA, STARFIRE, 1980–83 OMEGA & 1982–83 CUTLASS CIERA)

Year	Model	Brake Drum Inside Dia. In.
1977	Exc. Omega	11
	Omega	9½ [20]
1978–79	Omega	9½ [20]
	Cutlass, 98, Custom Cruiser & Toronado	11
	88	[21]
1980–83	Exc. 98 & Custom Cruiser	9½
	98 & Custom Cruiser	11

PONTIAC (EXC. ASTRE, SUNBIRD, 1000 & FRONT WHEEL DRIVE)

Year	Model	Brake Drum Inside Dia. In.
1977	Exc. Firebird & Ventura	11
	Firebird & Ventura	9.5
1978	Exc. Pontiac	9.5
	Pontiac	11
1979–81	Exc. Pontiac	9.5
	Pontiac	[22]
1982–83	Exc. Bonneville	9.5
	Bonneville	[22]

①—With 4 cyl. engine, 9"; exc. 4 cyl. engine, 10".
②—Concord sta. wag. w/6 cyl. engine, 10".
③—Spirit GT models w/rally tuned suspension, 10".
④—Models w/V6 engine.
⑤—Models w/V8 engine.
⑥—Rear disc brake.
⑦—On Chevrolet sta. wagon, 11".
⑧—Exc. Monza, 9⅞"; Monza, 9½".
⑨—Wagon, 11".
⑩—Exc. taxi & police, 10"; taxi & police, 11".
⑪—Exc. 9¼" axle, 10"; 9¼" axle, 11".
⑫—Heavy duty, 11".
⑬—Sedan exc. police, taxi & trailer tow.
⑭—Station wagon, police, taxi & trailer tow.
⑮—With 6 cyl. engine, 9"; w/V8 engine, 10".
⑯—Exc. sta. wag., 9"; sta. wag., 10".
⑰—Models w/4 or 6 cyl. engine, 9"; models w/V8 engine, 10".
⑱—Exc. 2 & 3 door hatchback, 8"; 2 & 3 door hatchback, 7".
⑲—V8-302, 10"; V8-351W, 11.03".
⑳—With 5 speed trans., 11".
㉑—Exc. models w/V8-403, 9½"; models w/V8-403, 11".
㉒—With 4¾" bolt circle, 9.5"; w/5" bolt circle, 11".

CARBURETORS

INDEX

CARBURETION

Since carburetion is dependent in several ways on both compression and ignition, it should always be checked last when tuning an engine.

Before adjusting the carburetor, consider the factors outlined below and which definitely affect engine performance.

Performance Complaints

Flooding, flat spots or other performance complaints are often caused by dirt, or water in the carburetor. To aid in diagnosing the complaint, the carburetor should be carefully removed from the engine without draining the fuel from the bowl. The contents of the fuel bowl can then be examined for contamination as the carburetor is disassembled. A magnet moved through the fuel in the bowl will pick up any iron oxide dust that may have caused needle valve leakage.

Check float setting carefully. Too high a level will cause flooding while too low a level

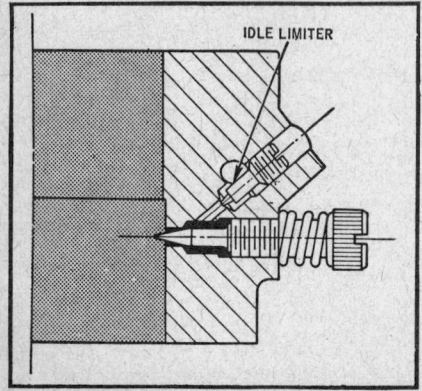

Internal idle mixture limiter

will starve the engine.

Before installing carburetor, fill the bowl with clean fuel and operate the throttle by hand several times to visually check the discharge from pump jets.

Inspect gasketed surfaces between body and air horn. Small nicks or burrs should be smoothed down to eliminate air or fuel leakage. On carburetors having a vacuum piston, be especially particular when inspecting the top surface of the inner wall of the bowl around the vacuum piston passage. A poor seal at this location may contribute to a "cutting out" on turns complaint.

Dirty or Rusty Choke Housing

In cases where it is found that the interior of the choke housing is dirty, gummed or rusty while the carburetor itself is comparatively clean, look for a punctured or eroded manifold heat tube (if one is used).

Manifold Heat Control Valve

An engine equipped with a manifold heat control valve can operate with the valve stuck in either the open or closed position. Because of this, an inoperative valve is frequently overlooked at vehicle lubrication or tune-up.

A valve stuck in the "heat-off" position can result in slow warm up, deposits in combustion chamber, carburetor icing, flat spots during acceleration, low gas mileage and spark plug fouling.

A valve stuck in the "heat-on" position can result in power loss, engine knocking, sticking or burned valves and spark plug burning.

To prevent the possibility of a stuck valve, check and lubricate the valve each time the vehicle is lubricated or tuned-up. Check the operation of the valve manually. To lubricate the valve, place a few drops of penetratng oil on the valve shaft where it passes through the manifold. Then move the valve up and down a few times to work the oil in. *Do not use engine oil to lubricate the valve as it will leave a resi-*

due which hampers valve operation.

Carburetor Flange

Check the flange for looseness on the manifold. If one of the flange nuts is loose as little as one-half turn, a sufficient amount of air will enter the intake manifold below the throttle plate to destroy engine idle and all engine performance.

If a tight fit cannot be obtained by tightening the nuts, install a new gasket but be sure that all the old gasket material has been removed.

Throttle Linkage

If the throttle linkage is adjusted so that the accelerator pedal will strike the floor board before the throttle plate is wide open, it will result in low top speed.

Fuel Lines

A restriction of the fuel line will result in an apparent vapor lock action or a definite cut-off of gasoline. This can generally be corrected by

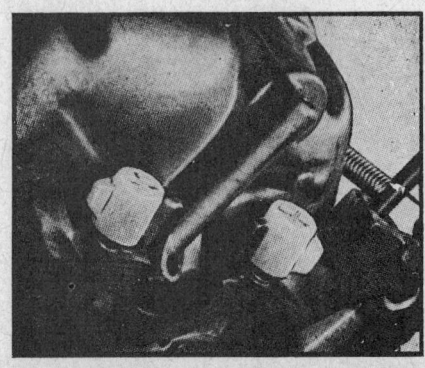

External idle mixture limiter

blowing out the line with compressed air. In some cases, it may be necessary to replace the line.

Fuel Pump

The pump should be tested to make sure that it will draw an adequate supply of fuel from the tank and deliver it to the carburetor under all conditions of operation. If the pump functions inefficiently, proper adjustment and operation of the carburetor is impossible because the fuel will not be maintained at the prescribed level in the idle passages and main discharge jet (or jets) of the carburetor under all operating conditions.

Fuel Tank

The fuel tank should not be overlooked as a possible source of trouble with carburetion. A shortage of fuel at the fuel pump or carburetor may be caused by material obstructing the mouth of the feed pipe in the tank, or by a restriction of the air vents in the filler cap and neck.

An unusual amount of dirt, water or gum in the fuel filter indicates that the tank is contaminated with these substances, which should be cleaned out to prevent future failure of the pump or carburetor.

Intake Manifold Leaks

Leakage of air into the intake manifold at any point will affect carburetion and general engine performance. Air may leak into the manifold through the joints at the carburetor or cylinder head, cracks in the manifold, cracks or poor connections in the vacuum hoses or lines, or the connections of any accessories which may be connected to the manifold. All such joints should be tested for leaks.

To test the intake manifold for leaks, apply oil from an oil can along the gasket joints with the engine idling. An air leak is indicated when oil is drawn past the gaskets by the suction of the engine. Tighten the nuts or cap screws holding the manifold to the engine and retest for leaks. If tightening fails to stop the leaks, replace the manifold gaskets. If the new gaskets fail to stop the leaks, carefully inspect the manifold for cracks and test any suspicious area with oil.

Air Cleaner

An air cleaner with a dirty element, will restrict the air flow through the carburetor and cause a rich mixture at high speeds. In such a condition the air cleaner likewise will not properly remove dirt from the air, and the dirt entering the engine will cause rapid formation of carbon, sticking valves, and wear of piston rings and cylinder bores.

Automatic Choke

The choke mechanism must be inspected and cleaned to make sure it is operating freely. Sluggish action or sticking of the choke will cause excessive fuel consumption, poor performance during warm-up, and possibly hard starting.

Choke Thermostat

If necessary to adjust the choke more than two marks from the specified setting, either rich or lean, it indicates that the thermostat spring may be bent or has lost its tension.

Carburetor Ball Checks

Whenever it becomes necessary to dismantle a carburetor be sure to account for the ball checks that may be found under pump plungers and compensating or power valves.

CARBURETOR IDLE ADJUST

The slow idle adjustment method, referred to as "Lean Roll" method, insures proper idle, ignition timing and mixture settings for greatest possible exhaust emission reduction and proper engine operation. It should be noted here that smooth idle is extremely sensitive to vacuum leaks. If rough idle is noted, check for vacuum leaks at the carburetor, manifold, etc.

Carburetor Idle Limiters

Some carburetors are equipped with idle adjustment limiters which restrict the maximum idle richness of the air/fuel mixture and prevents overly rich adjustments. There are two types of idle limiters: internal and external (see illustrations). The internal needle limiter is located in the idle channel and is not visible externally. This limiter is set and sealed at the factory and, under no circumstances, during normal service or during overhaul, should the seal be removed and adjustments made to this needle.

The other type of idle limiter is an external idle limiter cap installed on the knurled head of the idle mixture adjusting screw. Any adjustment to the idle fuel mixture on carburetors with this type of limiter must be made within the range of the limiter cap.

Under no circumstances may the limiter cap, the stop boss or the power valve cover, which the limiter caps stop against, be mutilated or deformed in any way to render the limiter inoperative. A satisfactory idle is obtainable within the range of the limiter cap.

The addition of idle limiters does not eliminate the need for adjusting idle speed and mixture. All the limiters do is prevent overly rich mixtures, which increase the amount of hydro-carbons emitted into the atmosphere.

1. With engine at operating temperature, set parking brake and block drive wheels.
2. Make sure choke valve is wide open.
3. Ensure that the air cleaner thermostatic valve is open.
4. On carburetors so equipped, hold hot idle compensator hole closed with eraser on pencil.
5. Turn air conditioner off or on according to directions given in *Tune Up Charts* in car chapters.
6. Set idle mixture screw for maximum idle rpm.
7. Adjust speed screw or solenoid to obtain the specified rpm in Drive or Neutral as specified.
8. Set ignition timing according to specifications with vacuum advance line disconnected and hole in manifold plugged.
9. Adjust mixture screw IN to obtain a 20 rpm drop (lean roll).
10. Adjust mixture screw OUT ¼ turn.
11. Repeat Steps 9 and 10 for second mixture screw (2 and 4 barrel carbs).
12. Readjust speed screw (or solenoid screw) if necessary to obtain specified rpm.
13. On model S with solenoid on carburetor, electrically disconnect solenoid and adjust carburetor idle speed screw to obtain 400 rpm in neutral, then reconnect wire to solenoid.

SERVICE BULLETINS

Carter Thermo-Quad

When installing the bowl cover on Carter TQ carburetors, it is important that the float lever pins are correctly positioned (centered in their supports). If the pins are not properly placed, they may be trapped between the gasket surfaces. When the bowl cover screws are tightened, the bowl will crack, Fig. 1.

Rochester Quadrajet

Delco/Rochester advises the possibility exists that the wrong throttle body to float bowl gaskets are being used by servicemen on Quadrajet carburetors. When this wrong substitution is made, vacuum leaks occur and cause rough idle due to air bypassing the primary throttle valves through the canister purge passage in the throttle body because the gasket will not seal this passage.

The difference between the throttle body to bowl gaskets is shown in Fig. 2.

Carter Thermo-Quad

The metering rods are preset to specifications by the manufacturer. No additional adjustment should be attempted since an accurate adjustment cannot be made in the field. An improper adjustment may result in the exhaust emissions exceeding specifications. Also, maladjustment of the metering rods may prevent the carburetor from returning to the idle position from wide open throttle (WOT) due to throttle shaft binding, resulting in poor fuel economy.

Holley 2245

Some difficulty may be encountered when adjusting curb idle speed on these carburetors. This condition may be caused by the side of the carburetor interfering with the throttle lever. To correct this condition, the throttle lever may be filed to remove excess metal causing the interference, Fig. 3.

Holley 5210-C

A possible cause of hard cold starting on vehicles equipped with this model carburetor may be binding choke linkage, preventing proper choke operation. To determine if binding choke linkage is the cause of hard starting, remove air cleaner with engine cold, then

CARBURETORS

FLOAT PIN TRAPPED BETWEEN GASKET SURFACES

Fig. 1   Carter Thermo-quad float lever pins improperly placed

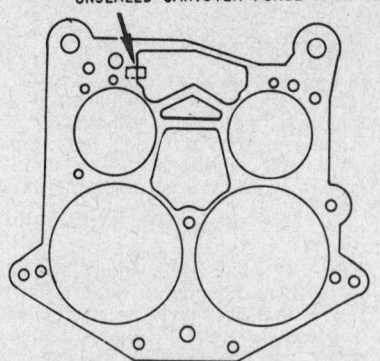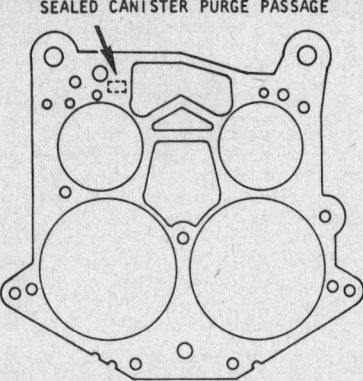

Fig. 2   Delco/Rochester Quadrajet throttle body to float bowl gaskets

REMOVE SHADED AREA FROM THROTTLE LEVER

Fig. 3   Removing excess metal from throttle lever. Holley 2245 carburetors

fully depress and release the accelerator pedal once. If choke blade does not fully close, the linkage is binding. This binding condition may occur at the contact point between the fast idle lever and fast idle cam. To correct this condition, proceed as follows:

1. Lubricate contact surface of fast idle lever tang with Lubriplate 1050520 or equivalent.
2. Reset dechoke adjustment to .300 inch instead of the production specification of .375 inch, listed in the Holley 5210 Specification Chart.
3. Bend tang at existing bend so tang slopes toward the choke housing, Fig. 4.

NOTE: Do not bend tang at tip since this will not achieve the desired results.

Motorcraft 2150

On some applications, the clearance between the carburetor choke pulldown vacuum hose and the EGR spacer may be less than 1/4 inch. If improper clearance exists, cut 1/2 inch off hose and recheck clearance.

1980 Rochester 2SE & E2SE

When servicing these units, care should be taken not to disturb the special friction reducing coating applied to the primary and secondary throttle shafts, the secondary actuating lever and lockout lever. On units for V6 engine, the secondary throttle bore and valve are also coated with a special graphite compound.

1982 Rochester E2SE

In vehicles equipped with this model carburetor, the instrument panel choke light may remain on for some time after the engine is started. This problem may be traced to a choke heater relay that has too low a shut-off

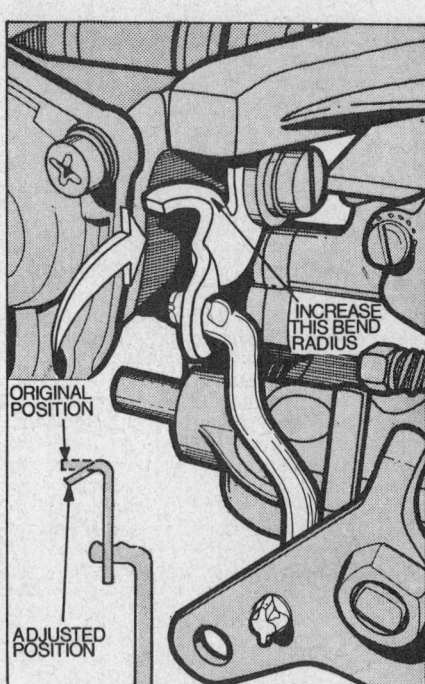

INCREASE THIS BEND RADIUS

ORIGINAL POSITION

ADJUSTED POSITION

Fig. 4   Revised unloader (Dechoke) adjustment. Holley 5210

voltage and remains energized, causing the light to stay on. This can be corrected by replacing the existing relay with relay part No. 14039662.

Carter Carburetor Section

CARTER YF SERIES ADJUSTMENT SPECIFICATIONS

See Tune Up Chart in car chapter for curb and fast idle speeds.

Year	Carb. Model	Float Level	Float Drop	Fast Idle Cam Setting	Dechoke or Unloader Setting	Pulldown Setting	Choke Setting
AMERICAN MOTORS							
1977	7111	15/32	1 3/8	.201 ①	.275	.221	2 Rich
	7151	15/32	1 3/8	.195 ①	.275	.215	1 Rich
	7152	15/32	1 3/8	.195 ②	.275	.215	1 Rich
	7153	15/32	1 3/8	.195 ①	.275	.215	Index
	7189	15/32	1 3/8	.201 ②	.275	.215	1 Rich
	7195	15/32	1 3/8	.195 ①	.275	.221	1 Rich
	7223	15/32	1 3/8	.195 ②	.275	.215	Index
1978	7201	15/32	1 3/8	.195 ①	.275	.215	Index
	7232	15/32	1 3/8	.201 ①	.275	.221	2 Rich
	7233	15/32	1 3/8	.201 ②	.275	.221	1 Rich
	7235	15/32	1 3/8	.195 ②	.275	.215	Index
	7267	15/32	1 3/8	.195 ②	.275	.215	1 Rich
1978–79	7228	15/32	1 3/8	.195 ①	.275	.215	1 Rich
	7229	15/32	1 3/8	.195 ②	.275	.215	1 Rich

①—1600 RPM hot on 2nd step of cam with TCS solenoid & EGR disconnected.
②—1500 RPM hot on 2nd step of cam with TCS solenoid & EGR disconnected.

Year	Carb. Model	Float Level	Float Drop	Fast Idle Cam Setting	Dechoke or Unloader Setting	Pulldown Setting	Choke Setting
FORD MOTOR CO.							
1977	B7DF-ABA	25/32	1 19/32	.140	.250	.260	Index
	D7BE-BA	25/32	1 19/32	.140	.250	.260	1 Rich
	D7BE-BC	25/32	1 19/32	.140	.250	.260	1 Rich
	DDE-DA	25/32	1 19/32	.140	.250	.260	1 Rich
	D7DE-DD	25/32	1 19/32	.140	.250	.260	1 Rich
1978	D8DE-BA	25/32	1 19/32	.140	.250	.230	2 Rich
	D8DE-DA	25/32	1 19/32	.140	.250	.230	2 Rich
	D8DE-EA	25/32	1 19/32	.140	.250	.200	2 Rich
	D8KE-AA	25/32	1 19/32	.140	.250	.230	2 Rich
1979	D9BE-RA	25/32	—	.140	.250	.180	1 Rich
	D9BE-UA①	25/32	—	.140	.250	.180	1 Rich
	D9BE-UA②	25/32	—	.140	.250	.200	2 Rich
	D9DE-AA	25/32	—	.140	.250	.230	1 Rich
	D9DE-AB	25/32	—	.140	.250	.230	2 Rich
	D9DE-BA	25/32	—	.140	.250	.230	1 Rich
	D9DE-BB	25/32	—	.140	.250	.230	2 Rich
	D9DE-CA	25/32	—	.140	.250	.260	1 Rich
	D9DE-CB	25/32	—	.140	.250	.260	1 Rich
	D9DE-CC	25/32	—	.140	.250	.260	2 Rich
	D9DE-CD	25/32	—	.140	.250	.260	2 Rich
	D9DE-DA	25/32	—	.140	.250	.260	1 Rich
	D9DE-DB	25/32	—	.140	.250	.260	1 Rich
	D9DE-DC	25/32	—	.140	.250	.260	2 Rich
	D9DE-DD	25/32	—	.140	.250	.260	2 Rich
	D9DE-EA	25/32	—	.140	.250	.230	1 Rich

Continued

See Tune Up Chart in car chapter for curb and fast idle speeds.

Year	Carb. Model	Float Level	Float Drop	Fast Idle Cam Setting	Dechoke or Unloader Setting	Pulldown Setting	Choke Setting
FORD MOTOR CO.—Continued							
	D9DE-EB	25/32	—	.140	.250	.230	2 Rich
	D9DE-UA	25/32	—	.140	.250	.200	2 Rich
	D9DE-VA	25/32	—	.140	.250	.200	2 Rich
1980	DEDE-GA	25/32	—	.140	.250	.260	—
	DEDE-HA	25/32	—	.140	.250	.260	—
	EODE-GA	25/32	1½	.140	.250	.260	2 Rich
	EODE-HA	25/32	1½	.140	.250	.260	2 Rich
	EODE-JA	25/32	1½	.140	.250	.260	2 Rich
	EODE-LA	25/32	1½	.140	.250	.250	2 Rich
	EODE-MA	25/32	1½	.140	.250	.250	2 Rich
	EODE-NA	25/32	1½	.140	.250	.260	2 Rich
1983	E3ZE-ABA	21/32	—	.140	.220	.260	③
	E3ZE-ACA	21/32	—	.140	.220	.260	③
	E3ZE-ADA	21/32	—	.140	.220	.260	③
	E3ZE-AEA	21/32	—	.140	.220	.260	③
	E3ZE-ASA	21/32	—	.160	.220	.260	③
	E3ZE-ATA	21/32	—	.160	.220	.260	③
	E3ZE-LA	21/32	—	.140	.220	.260	③
	E3ZE-MA	21/32	—	.140	.220	.260	③
	E3ZE-TB	21/32	—	.140	.220	.260	③
	E3ZE-TC	21/32	—	.140	.220	.240	③
	E3ZE-UA	21/32	—	.140	.220	.260	③
	E3ZE-UB	21/32	—	.140	.220	.240	③
	E3ZE-VA	21/32	—	.140	.220	.260	③
	E3ZE-YA	21/32	—	.140	.220	.260	③

①—6-200 engine.   ②—6-250 engine.   ③—Tamper-resistant.

MODEL YF SERIES ADJUSTMENTS

The YF Series carburetor, Figs. 1, thru 7, is a single-barrel, downdraft unit combining the fundamental features of other Carter carburetors. In addition, it features a diaphragm-type accelerating pump. It also has a diaphragm-operated metering rod, both vacuum and mechanically controlled.

Float Adjustment

Fig. 8—Invert the air horn assembly, and check the clearance from the top of the float to the bottom of the air horn with the float level gauge. Hold the air horn at eye level when gauging the float level. The float arm (lever) should be resting on the needle pin. Do not load the needle when adjusting the float. Bend the float arm as necessary to adjust the float level (clearance). Do not bend the tab at the end of the float arm. It prevents the float from striking the bottom of the fuel bowl when empty.

Float Drop Adjustment

Fig. 9—Hold air horn upright and measure maximum clearance from top of float to bottom of air horn with float drop gauge. Bend tab at end of float arm to obtain specified setting listed under YF Adjustment Specifications.

Metering Rod Adjustment

Fig. 10—If equipped, cut off the tamperproof cup covering the adjusting screw. Back out the idle speed adjusting screw until the throttle plate is closed tight in the throttle bore. Press down on upper end of diaphragm shaft until diaphragm bottoms in vacuum chamber. Metering rod should contact bottom of metering rod well, and metering rod should contact lifter link at the outer end nearest the springs and at supporting lug. For models not equipped with metering rod adjusting screw, adjust by bending lip of metering rod arm to which metering rod is attached, up or down as required. For models equipped with a metering rod adjusting screw, turn the adjusting screw until metering rod just bottoms in the body casting. For final adjustments turn metering rod adjusting screw in (clockwise) one additional turn.

Fast Idle Cam Linkage Adjustment

Position fast idle screw on second step of fast idle cam and against shoulder of highest step, Fig. 11. Using a drill of specified size, check clearance between lower edge of choke plate and bore, Refer to YF Specifications Chart. To adjust, bend choke connector rod as required.

Choke Plate Pulldown Adjustment

Bend a 0.026 in. diameter wire gauge at a 90 degree angle approximately ⅛-inch from one end. Insert the bent end of the gauge between the choke piston slot and the right hand slot in choke housing. Rotate the choke piston lever counterclockwise until gauge is snug in the piston slot. Exert a light pressure on choke piston lever to hold the gauge in place, then use a drill with a diameter equal to the specified pulldown clearance between the lower edge of choke plate and carburetor bore to check clearance, Fig. 12.

To adjust the choke plate pulldown clearance, bend the choke piston lever as required to obtain specified setting.

NOTE: When bending the lever, be careful not to distort the piston link. Install the choke thermostatic spring housing and gasket. Set the housing to specifications.

Dechoke Adjustment

Hold the throttle plate fully open and close the choke plate as far as possible without forcing it. Use a drill of specified diameter to

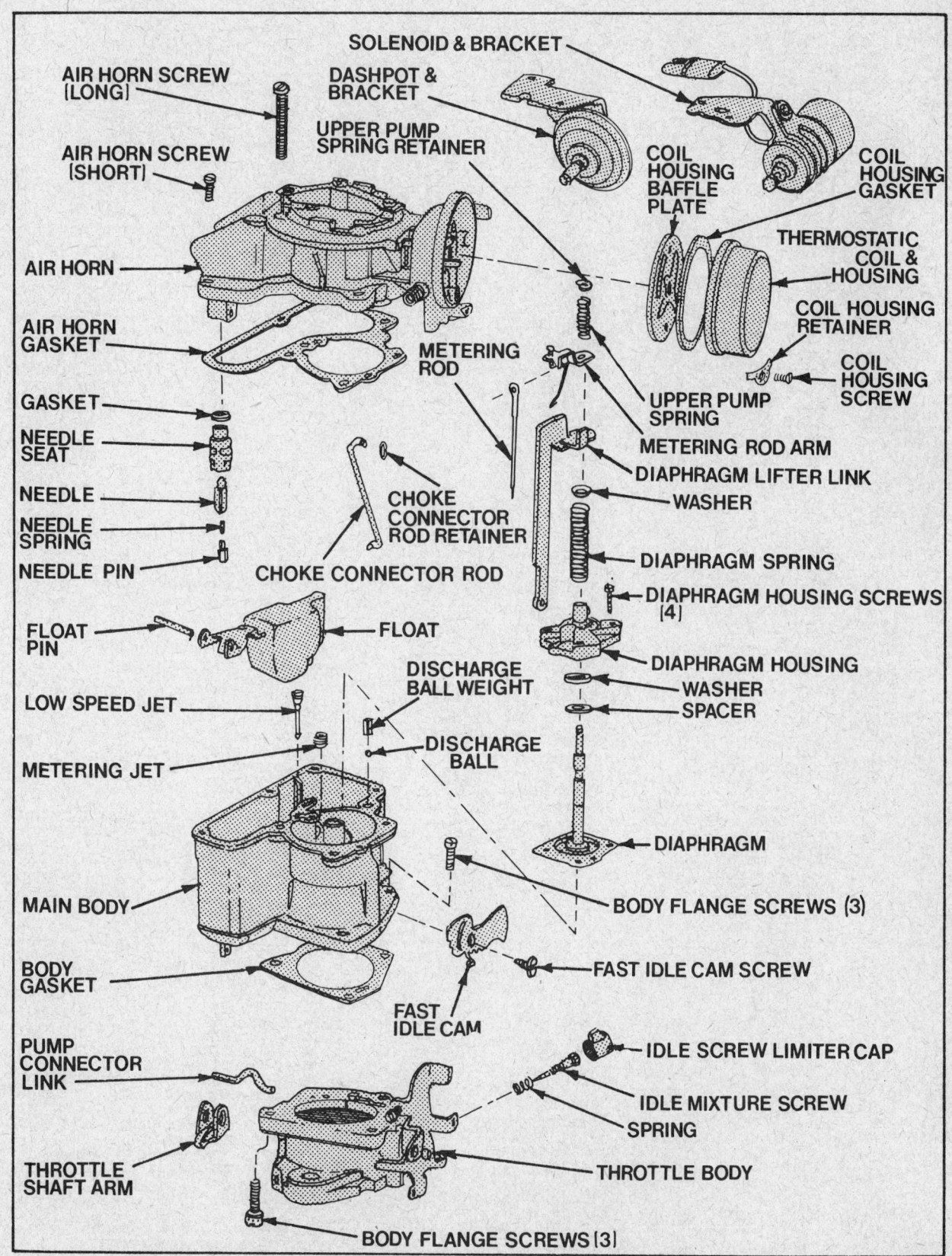

Fig. 1 Carter Model YF Series carburetor. 1977–78 American Motors less altitude compensation

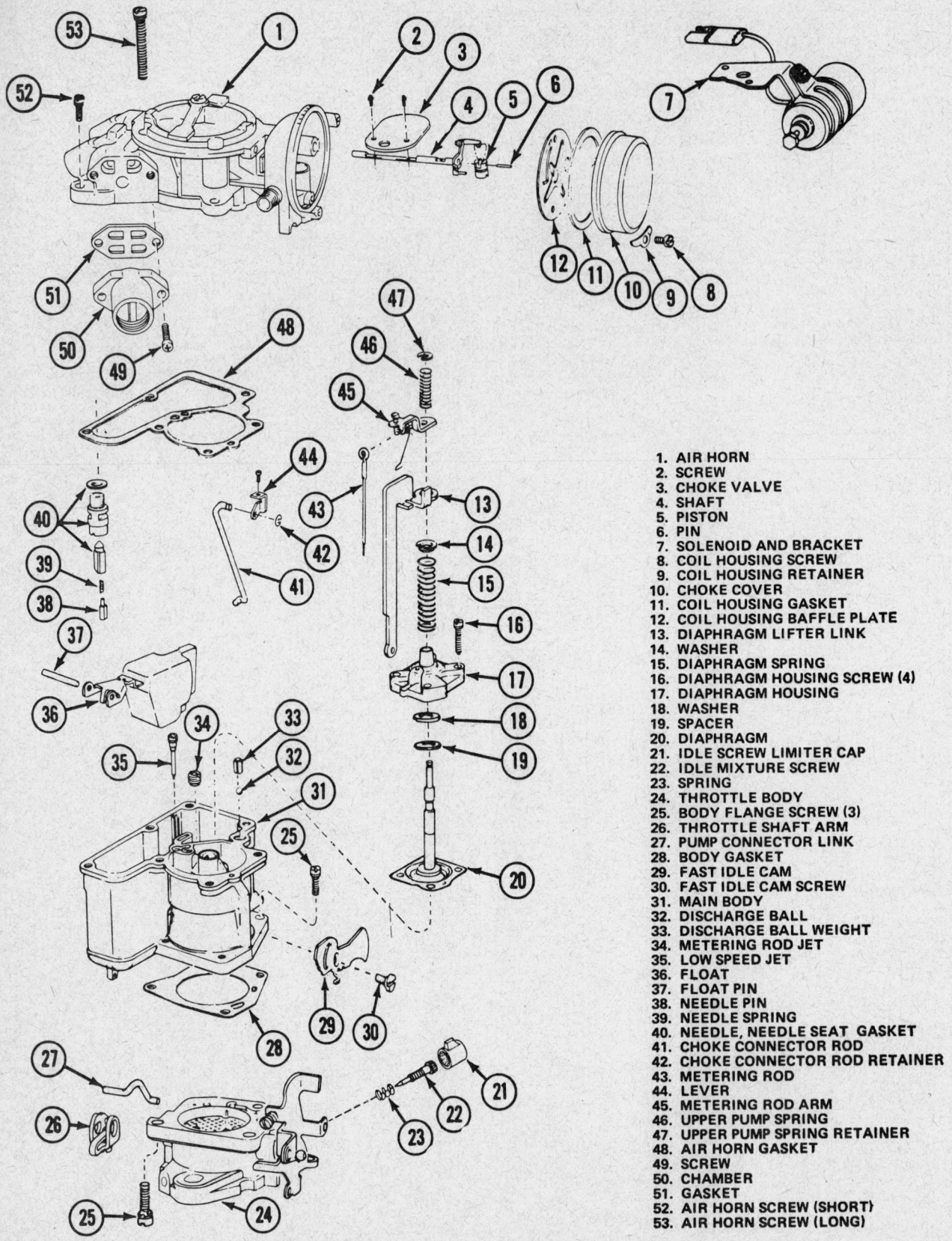

1. AIR HORN
2. SCREW
3. CHOKE VALVE
4. SHAFT
5. PISTON
6. PIN
7. SOLENOID AND BRACKET
8. COIL HOUSING SCREW
9. COIL HOUSING RETAINER
10. CHOKE COVER
11. COIL HOUSING GASKET
12. COIL HOUSING BAFFLE PLATE
13. DIAPHRAGM LIFTER LINK
14. WASHER
15. DIAPHRAGM SPRING
16. DIAPHRAGM HOUSING SCREW (4)
17. DIAPHRAGM HOUSING
18. WASHER
19. SPACER
20. DIAPHRAGM
21. IDLE SCREW LIMITER CAP
22. IDLE MIXTURE SCREW
23. SPRING
24. THROTTLE BODY
25. BODY FLANGE SCREW (3)
26. THROTTLE SHAFT ARM
27. PUMP CONNECTOR LINK
28. BODY GASKET
29. FAST IDLE CAM
30. FAST IDLE CAM SCREW
31. MAIN BODY
32. DISCHARGE BALL
33. DISCHARGE BALL WEIGHT
34. METERING ROD JET
35. LOW SPEED JET
36. FLOAT
37. FLOAT PIN
38. NEEDLE PIN
39. NEEDLE SPRING
40. NEEDLE, NEEDLE SEAT GASKET
41. CHOKE CONNECTOR ROD
42. CHOKE CONNECTOR ROD RETAINER
43. METERING ROD
44. LEVER
45. METERING ROD ARM
46. UPPER PUMP SPRING
47. UPPER PUMP SPRING RETAINER
48. AIR HORN GASKET
49. SCREW
50. CHAMBER
51. GASKET
52. AIR HORN SCREW (SHORT)
53. AIR HORN SCREW (LONG)

Fig. 2 Carter Model YF Series carburetor. 1977–78 American Motors with altitude compensation

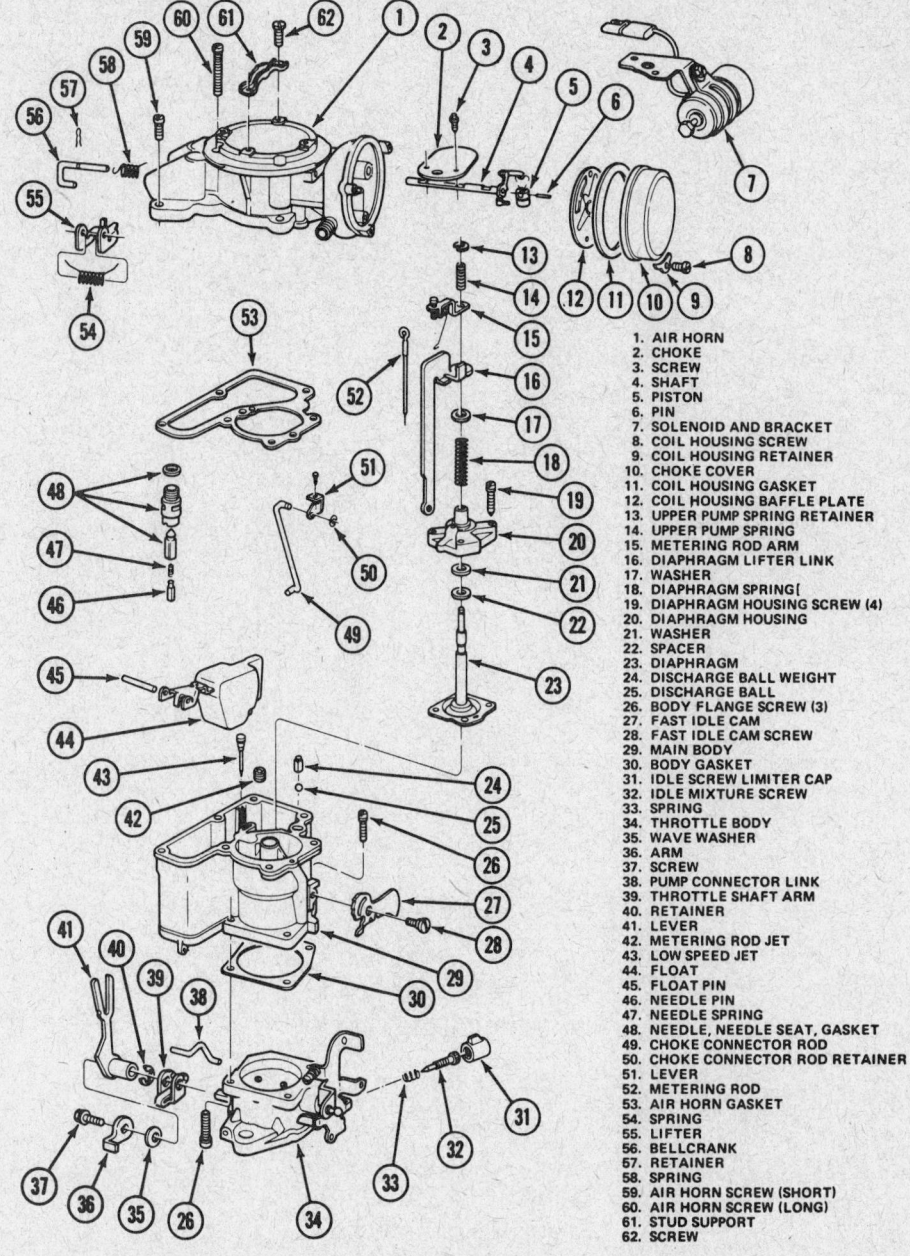

1. AIR HORN
2. CHOKE
3. SCREW
4. SHAFT
5. PISTON
6. PIN
7. SOLENOID AND BRACKET
8. COIL HOUSING SCREW
9. COIL HOUSING RETAINER
10. CHOKE COVER
11. COIL HOUSING GASKET
12. COIL HOUSING BAFFLE PLATE
13. UPPER PUMP SPRING RETAINER
14. UPPER PUMP SPRING
15. METERING ROD ARM
16. DIAPHRAGM LIFTER LINK
17. WASHER
18. DIAPHRAGM SPRING
19. DIAPHRAGM HOUSING SCREW (4)
20. DIAPHRAGM HOUSING
21. WASHER
22. SPACER
23. DIAPHRAGM
24. DISCHARGE BALL WEIGHT
25. DISCHARGE BALL
26. BODY FLANGE SCREW (3)
27. FAST IDLE CAM
28. FAST IDLE CAM SCREW
29. MAIN BODY
30. BODY GASKET
31. IDLE SCREW LIMITER CAP
32. IDLE MIXTURE SCREW
33. SPRING
34. THROTTLE BODY
35. WAVE WASHER
36. ARM
37. SCREW
38. PUMP CONNECTOR LINK
39. THROTTLE SHAFT ARM
40. RETAINER
41. LEVER
42. METERING ROD JET
43. LOW SPEED JET
44. FLOAT
45. FLOAT PIN
46. NEEDLE PIN
47. NEEDLE SPRING
48. NEEDLE, NEEDLE SEAT, GASKET
49. CHOKE CONNECTOR ROD
50. CHOKE CONNECTOR ROD RETAINER
51. LEVER
52. METERING ROD
53. AIR HORN GASKET
54. SPRING
55. LIFTER
56. BELLCRANK
57. RETAINER
58. SPRING
59. AIR HORN SCREW (SHORT)
60. AIR HORN SCREW (LONG)
61. STUD SUPPORT
62. SCREW

Fig. 3 Carter Model YF Series carburetor. 1979 American Motors

check the clearance between choke plate and air horn, Fig. 13. If clearance is not within specification, adjust by bending arm on choke trip lever of the throttle lever. Bending the arm downward will decrease the clearance, bending it upward will increase the clearance.

If the choke plate clearance and fast idle cam linkage adjustment was performed with the carburetor on the engine, adjust the engine idle speed and fuel mixture. Adjust dashpot (if so equipped).

Altitude Compensator Adjustment

1977–78 American Motors
For operation on vehicle above 4000 feet in altitude, rotate plug fully counterclockwise, Fig. 14. For operation on vehicles below 400 feet in altitude, rotate plug fully clockwise, Fig. 14.

NOTE: Whenever the position of the altitude compensator plug is changed, the ignition timing must also be corrected. Refer to the "Tune-up Specifications" in the individual car chapter.

Dashpot Adjustment

With the engine idle speed and mixture properly adjusted, and the engine at normal operating temperature, loosen the antistall dashpot lock nut, Fig. 15. Hold the throttle in the curb idle position and depress the dashpot plunger. Measure the clearance between the throttle lever and plunger tip. Turn the antistall dashpot to provide 7/64" ± 1/64" clearance between the tip of the plunger and the throttle lever. Tighten the locknut to secure the adjustment.

1983 Ford

NOTE: To perform this adjustment, engine

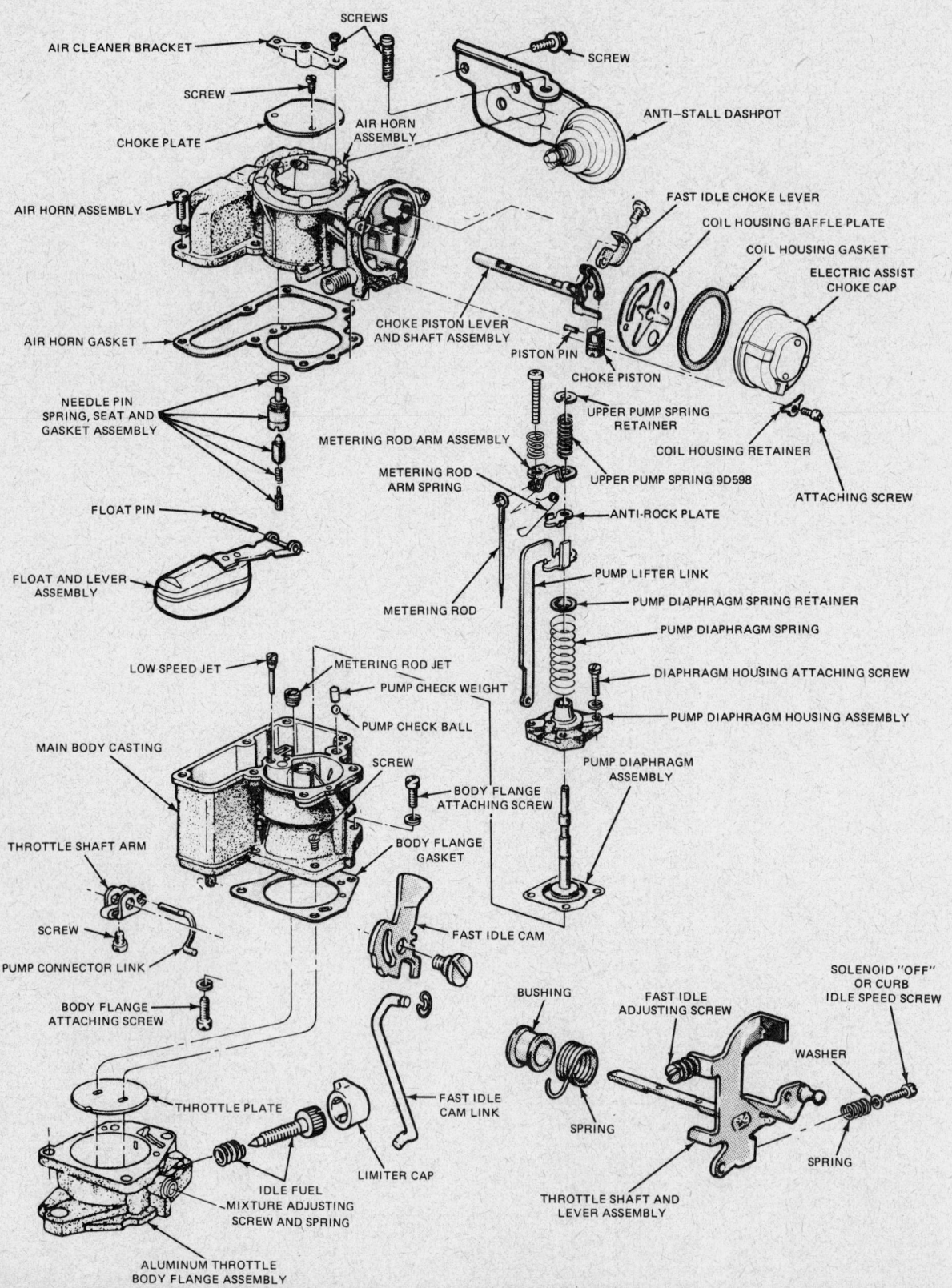

Fig. 4 Carter Model YF Series carburetor. 1977 Ford

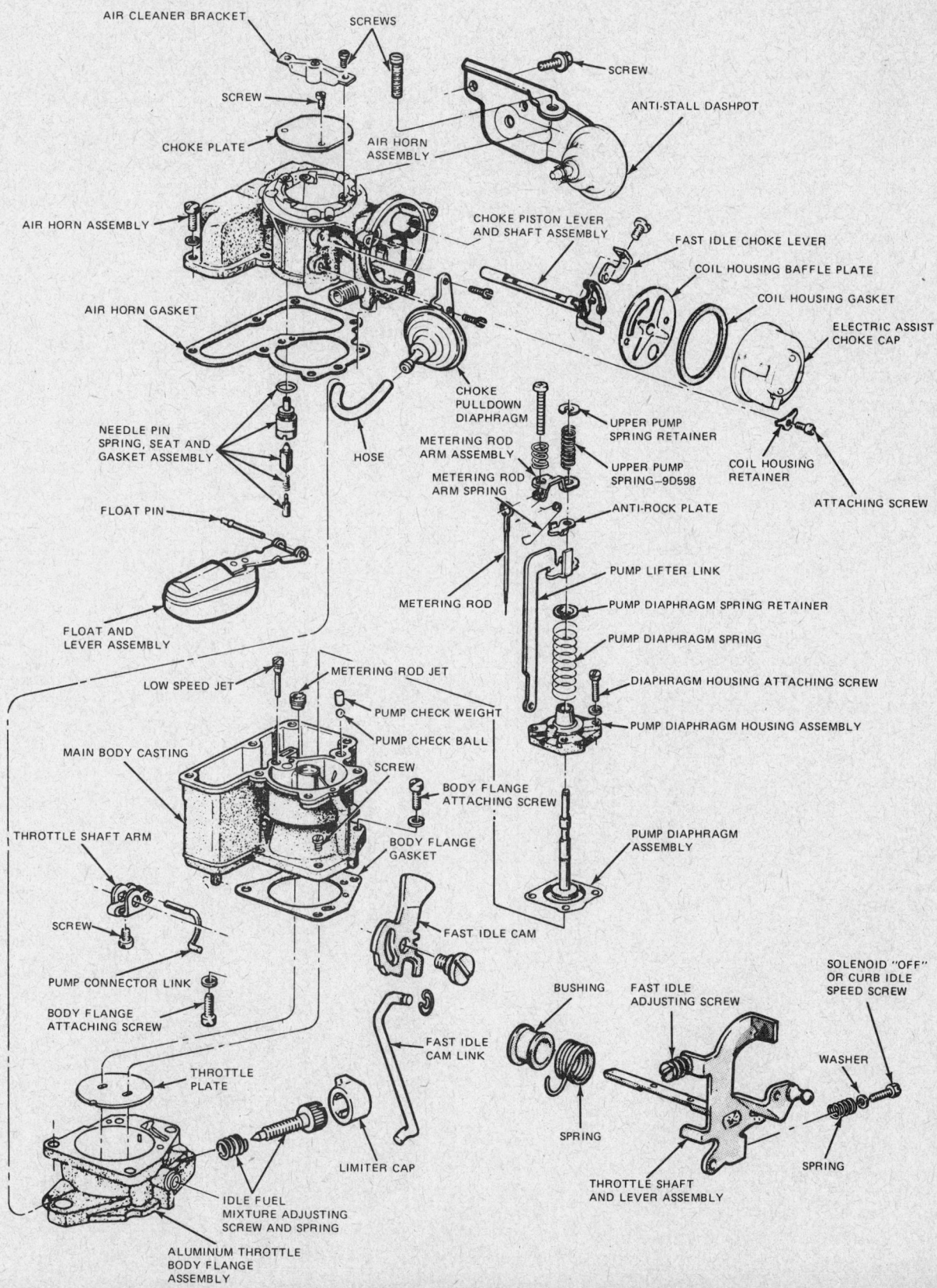

Fig. 5 Carter Model YF Series carburetor. 1978–80 Ford

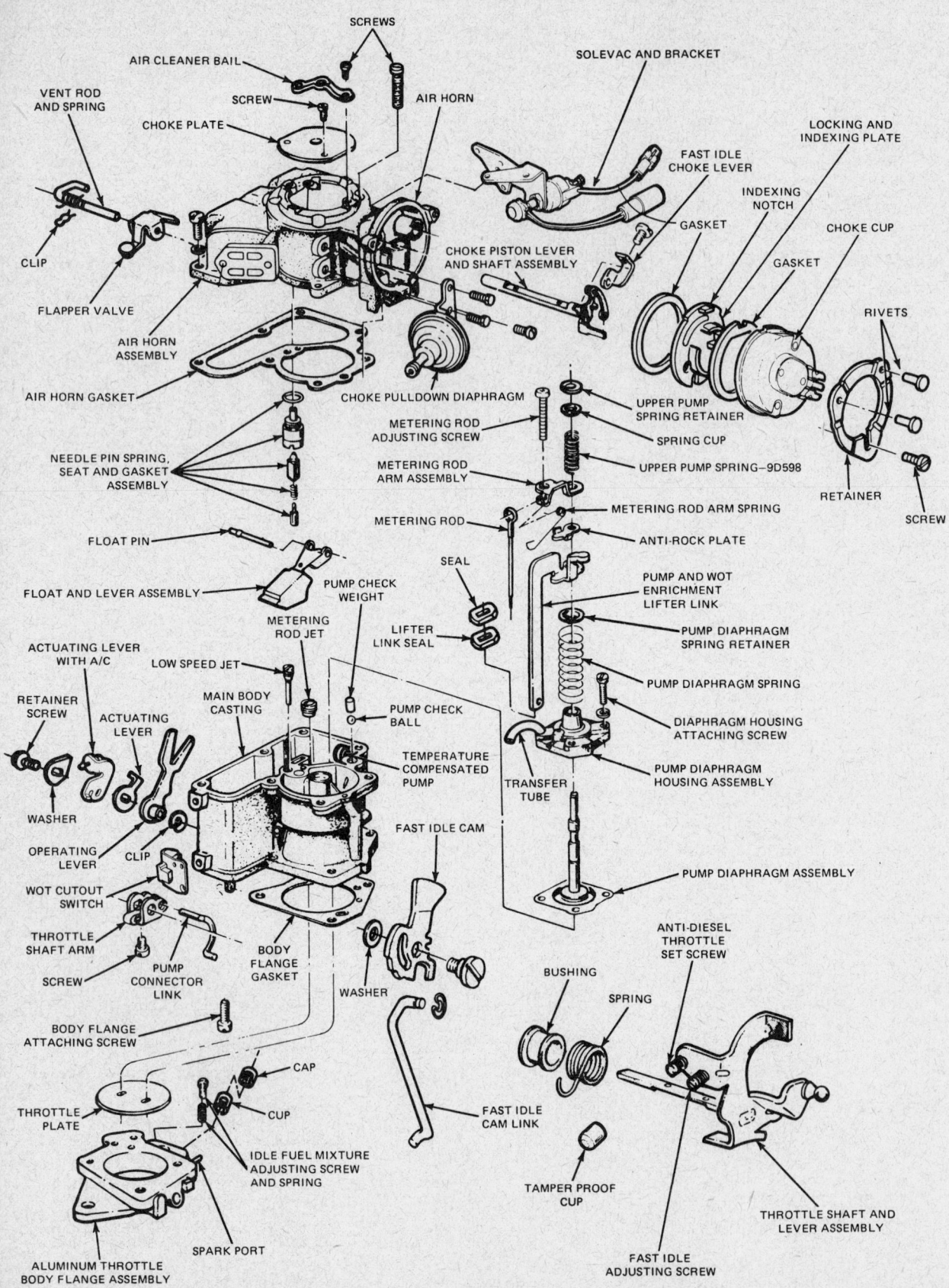

Fig. 6 Exploded view of Carter Model YF series carburetor. 1983 Ford less feedback solenoid

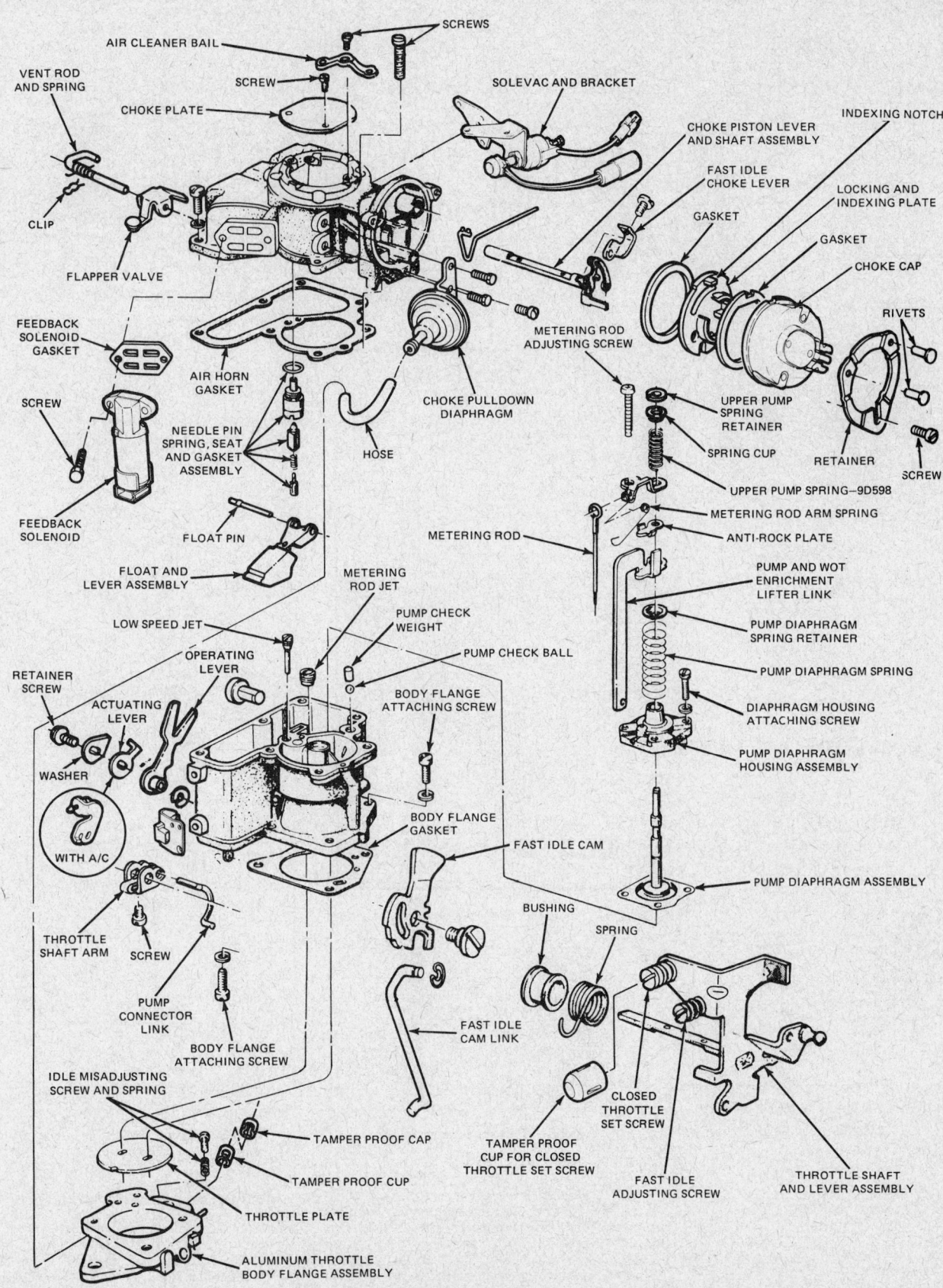

Fig. 7 Exploded view of Carter Model YF series carburetor. 1983 Ford with feedback solenoid

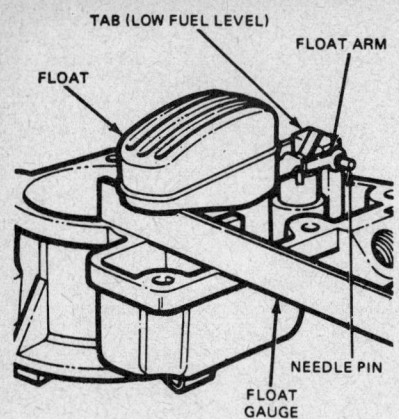

Fig. 8   YF float level adjustment

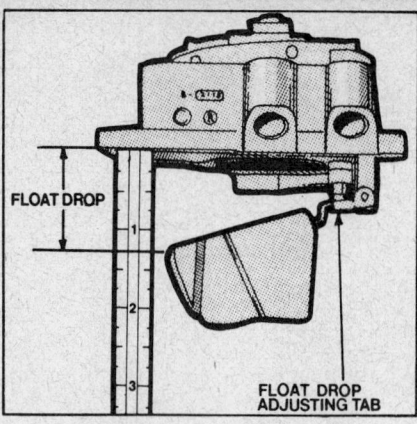

Fig. 9   YF float drop adjustment

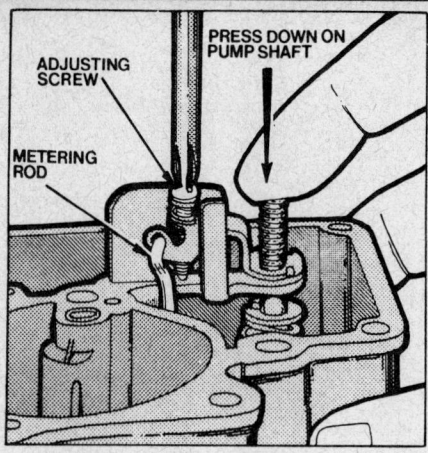

Fig. 10   YF metering rod adjustment

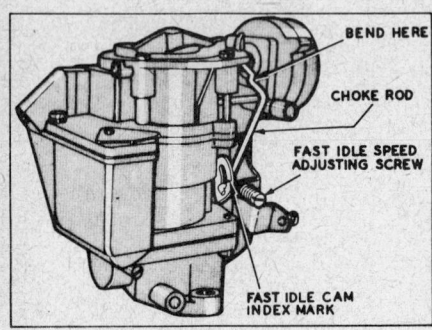

Fig. 11   YF fast idle cam linkage adjustment

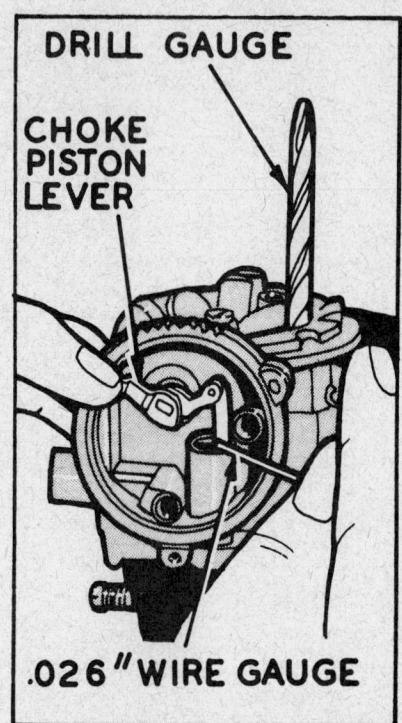

Fig. 12   YF choke plate pulldown adjustment

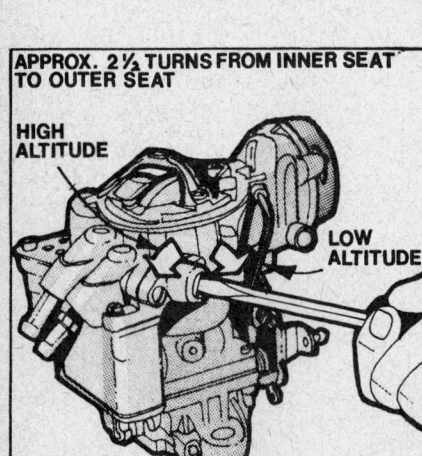

Fig. 14   Altitude compensator adjustment. 1977–78 American Motors

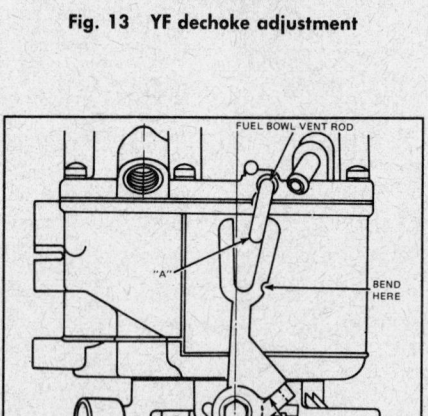

Fig. 13   YF dechoke adjustment

Fig. 15   YF dashpot adjustment

Fig. 16   YF mechanical fuel bowl vent adjustment

idle must be set to specifications and must be at normal operating temperature.

Open throttle lever so actuating lever does not make contact with fuel bowl vent rod, Fig. 16. Close throttle lever to idle set position and measure travel of fuel bowl vent rod at point "A," Fig. 16. This distance represents vent rod travel from point where there is no contact with actuating lever to point where actuating lever moves vent rod to idle set position. Bend throttle actuating lever as needed until travel measures .100–.150 inch.

Automatic Choke Adjustment

Loosen choke cover retaining screws and turn choke cover so that line or Index mark on cover lines up with the specified mark listed in *YF Specifications Chart* on choke housing.

CARTER BBD ADJUSTMENT SPECIFICATIONS
See Tune Up Chart in car chapter for curb and fast idle speeds.

Year	Carb. Model	Float Level	Pump Travel Inch	Bowl Vent Clearance	Choke Unloader Clearance	Initial Choke Valve Clearance	Choke Vacuum Kick Clearance	Fast Idle Cam Position Clearance	Automatic Choke Setting
AMERICAN MOTORS									
1977	8103	1/4	.496	—	.280	.150	—	.120	1 Rich
	8104	1/4	.520	—	.280	.128	—	.095	1 Rich
	8117	1/4	.480	—	.280	.152	—	.112	1 Rich
1978	8128	1/4	.496	①	.280	.150	—	.110	Index
	8129	1/4	.520	①	.280	.128	—	.095	1 Rich
1979	8185	1/4	.470	①	.280	.140	—	.110	1 Rich
	8186	1/4	.520	①	.280	.150	—	.110	1 Rich
	8187	1/4	.470	①	.280	.140	—	.110	1 Rich
	8221	1/4	.530	①	.280	.150	—	.110	1 Rich
1980	8216	1/4	.520	①	.280	.140	—	.090	2 Rich
	8246	1/4	.520	①	.280	.140	—	.095	2 Rich
	8247	1/4	.520	①	.280	.150	—	.095	1 Rich
	8248	1/4	.520	①	.280	.150	—	.095	1 Rich
	8253	1/4	.470	①	.280	.128	—	.095	2 Rich
	8256	1/4	.470	①	.280	.128	—	.093	2 Rich
	8278	1/4	.542	①	.280	.140	—	.093	Index
	8313	1/4	.520	①	.280	.140	—	.095	1 Rich
1981	8302	1/4	.500	①	.280	.128	—	.095	1 Rich
	8303	1/4	.500	①	.280	.128	—	.090	1 Rich
	8306	1/4	.500	①	.280	.128	—	.095	1 Rich
	8307	1/4	.500	①	.280	.128	—	.095	1 Rich
	8308	1/4	.500	①	.280	.128	—	.095	2 Rich
	8309	1/4	.520	①	.280	.128	—	.093	2 Rich
	8310	1/4	.525	①	.280	.140	—	.095	Index
1982	8338	1/4	.520	①	.280	.140	—	.095	②
	8339	1/4	.520	①	.280	.140	—	.095	②
1983	8360	1/4	.520	①	.280	.140	—	.095	②
	8362	1/4	.520	①	.280	.140	—	.095	②
	8364	1/4	.520	①	.280	.140	—	.095	②
	8367	1/4	.520	①	.280	.140	—	.095	②
CHRYSLER CORP.									
1977	8087S	1/4	15/32③	—	.280	—	.100	.070	⑤
	8089S	1/4	15/32③	—	.280	—	.130	.070	⑤
	8090S	1/4	15/32③	—	.280	—	.130	.070	⑤
	8093S	1/4	15/32③	—	.310	—	.130	.070	⑤
	8094S	1/4	15/32③	—	.310	—	.070	.070	⑤
	8096S	1/4	15/32③	—	.310	—	.110	.070	⑤
	8126S	1/4	④	—	.310	—	.110	.070	⑤
	8127S	1/4	15/32③	—	.280	—	.110	.070	⑤
	8135S	1/4	15/32③	—	.310	—	.070	.070	⑤
	8145S	1/4	15/32③	—	.310	—	.110	.070	⑤
	8170S	1/4	1/2③	.080③	.310	—	.110	.070	⑤
	8171S	1/4	1/2③	.080③	.310	—	.110	.070	⑤
	8172S	1/4	1/2③	.080③	.310	—	.110	.070	⑤
1978	8136S	1/4	1/2③	.080③	.280	—	.110	.070	⑤
	8137S	1/4	1/2③	.080③	.280	—	.100	.070	⑤
	8143S	1/4	1/2③	.080③	.280	—	.150	.070	⑤
	8175S	1/4	1/2③	.080③	.280	—	.160	.070	⑤
	8177S	1/4	1/2③	.080③	.280	—	.100	.070	⑤
1979	8198S	1/4	1/2③	.080③	.280	—	.100	.070	⑤
	8199S	1/4	1/2③	.080③	.280	—	.100	.070	⑤

Continued

CARTER BBD ADJUSTMENT SPECIFICATIONS—Continued

See Tune Up Chart in car chapter for curb and fast idle speeds.

Year	Carb. Model	Float Level	Pump Travel Inch	Bowl Vent Clearance	Choke Unloader Clearance	Initial Choke Valve Clearance	Choke Vacuum Kick Clearance	Fast Idle Cam Position Clearance	Automatic Choke Setting
CHRYSLER CORP.—Continued									
1980	8233S	1/4	1/2③	.080③	.280	—	.130	.070	③
	8237S	1/4	1/2③	.080③	.280	—	.110	.070	③
1981	8291S	1/4	1/2③	—	.280	—	.130	.070	③
1982	8291S	1/4	1/2①	.080①	.280	—	.130	.070	③
1983	8291S	1/4	15/32①	.080①	.280	—	.130	.070	③

①—Bowl vent should begin to open with fast idle cam on second step of cam.
②—Gold index key, O; red index key, 1NR; green index key, 2NR.
③—At idle.
④—Model less red tag, 15/32 inch at idle; model with red tag, 1/2 inch at idle.
⑤—Tamper-resistant.

MODEL BBD ADJUSTMENTS

Fig. 1 is an exploded view of a typical BBD two barrel carburetor. Note that American Motors units are equipped with an automatic choke coil. Fig. 2 is an external view of a typical 1977–78 unit used on Chrysler Corp. vehicles equipped with Lean Burn System. Fig. 3 is a typical view of 1977–78 units less Lean Burn and all 1979 Chrysler Corp. vehicles. Fig. 4 is an external view of units used on 1980–83 Chrysler Corp. vehicles less Electronic Feedback Carburetor System. Fig. 4A is an external view of units used on 1981–83 Chrysler Corp. vehicles equipped with Electronic Feedback Carburetor System. On some Chrysler vehicles equipped with a manual transmission, a dashpot is mounted on the carburetor. On some Chrysler vehicles equipped with an automatic transmission, an idle enrichment system is used to reduce cold engine stalling by the use of an additional metering system which enriches the mixture in the off idle position. This system is controlled by a vacuum diaphragm mounted near the top of the carburetor.

Float Level Adjustment

Fig. 5—With carburetor body inverted so that weight of floats ONLY is forcing needle against its seat, use a T-scale or the tool shown, and check the float level from surface of fuel bowl to crown of each float at center.

If an adjustment is necessary, hold floats on bottom of bowl and bend float lip as required to give the specified dimension.

CAUTION: When bending the float lip, do not allow the lip to push against the needle as the synthetic rubber tip (if used) can be compressed sufficiently to cause a false setting which will affect correct level of fuel in bowl. After being compressed, the tip is very slow to recover its original shape.

Accelerator Pump

1¼″ Bore Units, Fig. 6
1. Back off curb idle adjusting screw, completely closing throttle valve, then open choke valve, allowing throttle valves to seat in bores. Ensure accelerator pump "S" link is located in outer hole or pump arm.

2. Turn curb idle adjusting screw until screw contacts, stop, then rotate screw two additional turns.
3. Measure distance between air horn surface and top of accelerator pump shaft. Refer to BBD Specifications Chart.
4. Adjust by loosening pump arm adjusting screw and rotating sleeve until proper dimension is obtained. Tighten adjusting screw.

Bowl Vent Valve

Chrysler, Fig. 7

NOTE: The accelerator pump stroke and curb idle speed must be properly adjusted before making this adjustment.

1. Remove step-up piston cover plate and gasket.
2. Insert specified gauge between top of bowl vent valve and seat. Refer to the BBD Specifications Chart.
3. Adjust by bending bowl vent lever tab while supporting bowl vent lever assembly.
4. Install step-up piston cover gasket and cover.

American Motors

NOTE: This adjustment is not precise and is only necessary to ensure that the mechanical fuel bowl vent is open at idle and closed at greater throttle openings.

1. Remove rollover check valve from air horn to provide access to metering rod area.
2. Open throttle and place fast idle speed screw on high step of cam.
3. Move cam manually until fast idle speed screw drops into second step of fast idle cam. Observe the bowl vent which should just begin to open at this time.
4. If valve is not closed on high, fourth or third steps of cam, bend valve tab until it is closed.
5. If valve does not begin to open with fast idle speed screw on second step of cam, bend tab until it is just off its seat.

Choke Unloader Adjustment

Fig. 8—The choke unloader is a mechanical device to partially open the choke valve at wide open throttle. It is used to eliminate choke enrichment during engine cranking. Engines that have been flooded or stalled by excessive choke enrichment can be cleared by the use of the unloader. Adjust as follows:
1. Hold throttle valve in wide open position. Insert the specified drill size between upper edge of choke valve and inner wall of air horn.
2. With a finger lightly pressing against choke valve, a slight drag should be felt as the drill is being withdrawn.
3. If an adjustment is necessary, bend unloader tang on throttle lever until specified opening has been obtained.

Fast Idle Cam Position

Chrysler, Fig. 9
1. With fast idle adjusting screw contacting second highest step on fast idle cam, move choke valve toward closed position with light pressure on choke shaft lever.
2. Insert the specified size drill between top of choke valve and air horn wall. An adjustment will be necessary if a slight drag is not obtained as drill is being removed.
3. Adjust by bending fast idle connector rod at angle.

American Motors
1. On 1977–80 units, loosen choke cover and rotate 1/4 turn rich, then tighten one retaining screw.
2. On 1981 units, grind heads off choke housing cover breakaway screws, then remove remaining portion of screws. On 1982–83 units, grind off rivet heads, then remove retainer, choke cover and coil, gasket, baffle and remaining portion of rivets.
3. On 1982–83 units, install baffle, gasket, choke cover, coil and retainer.
4. On 1981–83 units, rotate cover 1/4 turn rich, then install and tighten one retaining straight slot type screw.

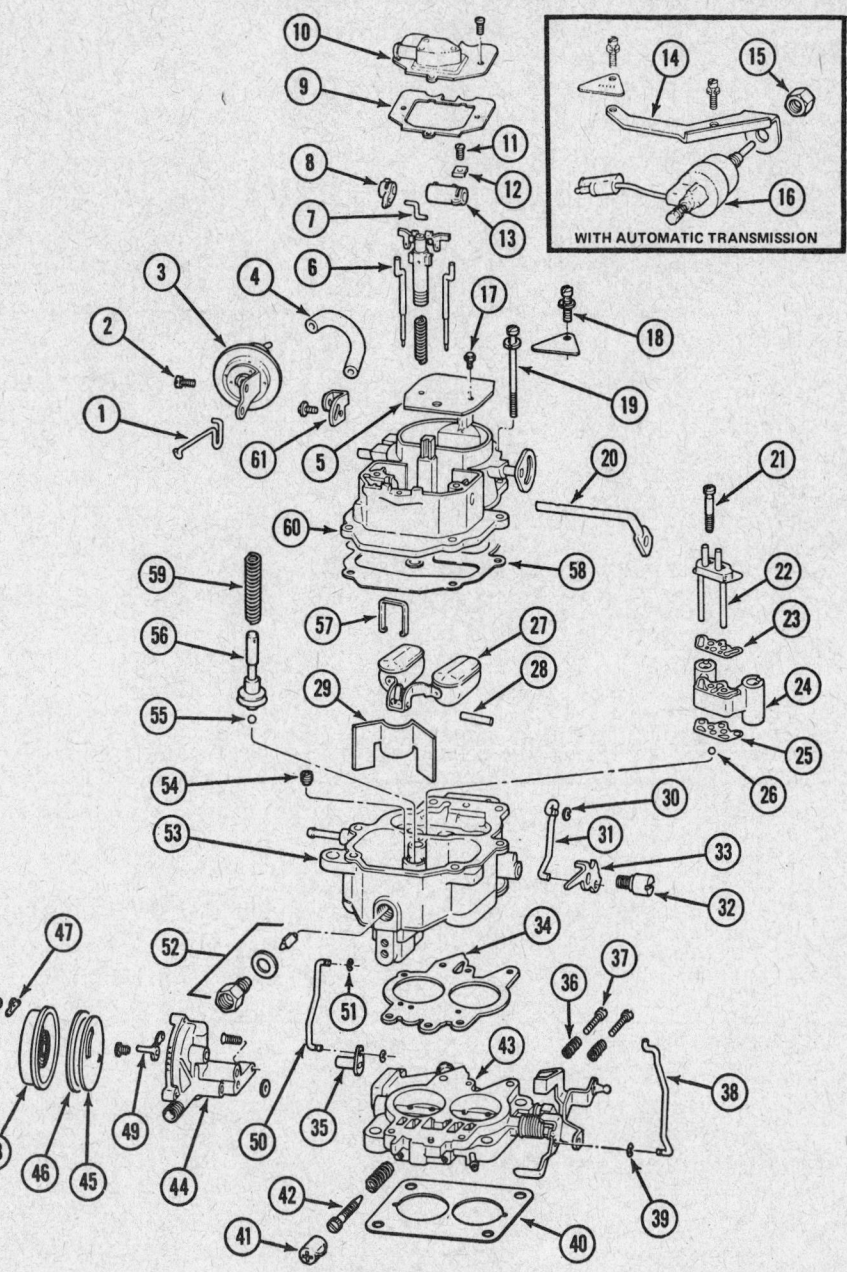

WITH AUTOMATIC TRANSMISSION

1. DIAPHRAGM CONNECTOR LINK
2. SCREW
3. CHOKE VACUUM DIAPHRAGM
4. HOSE
5. VALVE
6. METERING ROD
7. S-LINK
8. PUMP ARM
9. GASKET
10. ROLLOVER CHECK VALVE
11. SCREW
12. LOCK
13. ROD LIFTER
14. BRACKET
15. NUT
16. SOLENOID
17. SCREW
18. AIR HORN RETAINING SCREW (SHORT)
19. AIR HORN RETAINING SCREW (LONG)
20. PUMP LEVER
21. VENTURI CLUSTER SCREW

22. IDLE FUEL PICK-UP TUBE
23. GASKET
24. VENTURI CLUSTER
25. GASKET
26. CHECK BALL (SMALL)
27. FLOAT
28. FULCRUM PIN
29. BAFFLE
30. CLIP
31. CHOKE LINK
32. SCREW
33. FAST IDLE CAM
34. GASKET
35. THERMOSTATIC CHOKE SHAFT
36. SPRING
37. SCREW
38. PUMP LINK
39. CLIP
40. GASKET
41. LIMITER CAP
42. SCREW

43. THROTTLE BODY
44. CHOKE HOUSING
45. BAFFLE
46. GASKET
47. RETAINER
48. CHOKE COIL
49. LEVER
50. CHOKE ROD
51. CLIP
52. NEEDLE AND SEAT ASSEMBLY
53. MAIN BODY
54. MAIN METERING JET
55. CHECK BALL (LARGE)
56. ACCELERATOR PUMP PLUNGER
57. FULCRUM PIN RETAINER
58. GASKET
59. SPRING
60. AIR HORN
61. LEVER

Fig. 1   Exploded view of Carter model BBD 1¼" two barrel carburetor. Typical

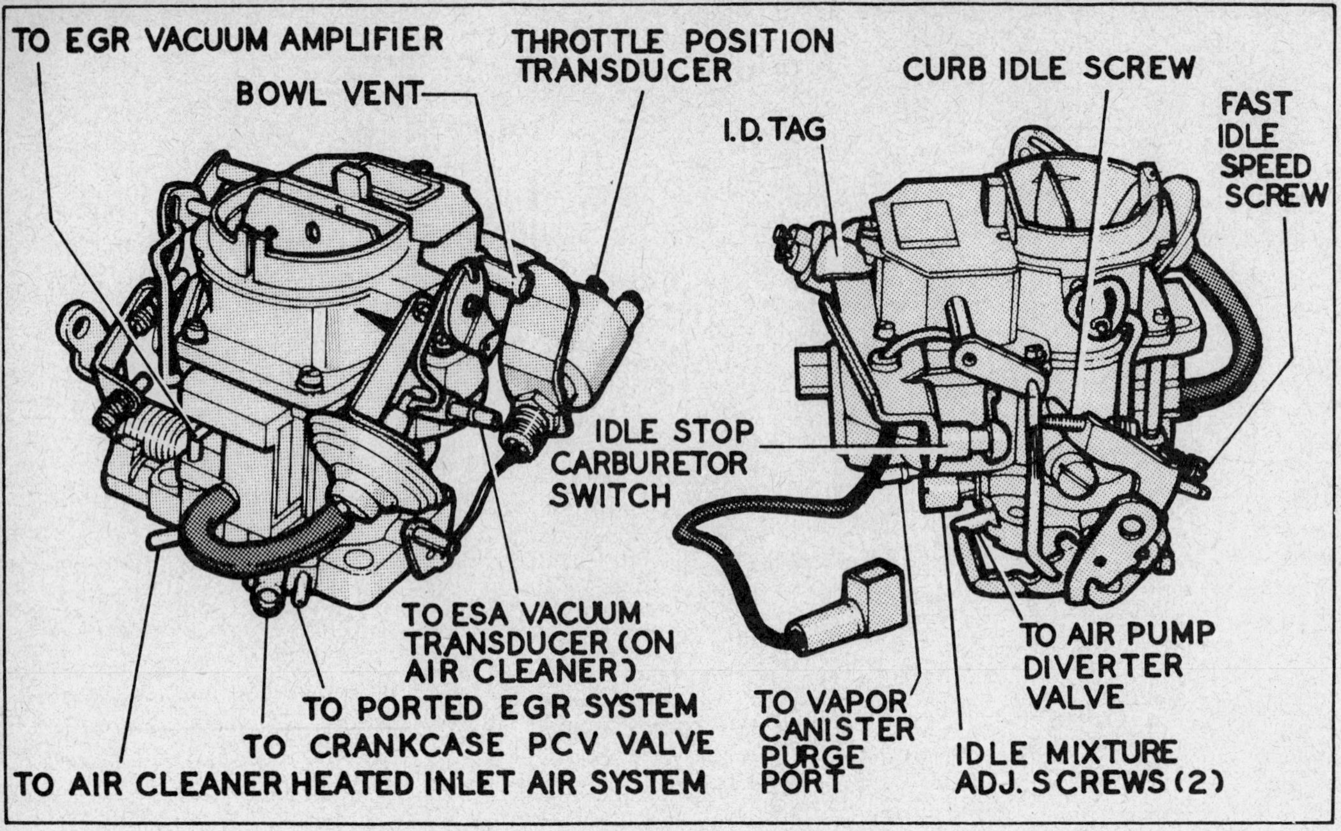

CARBURETORS

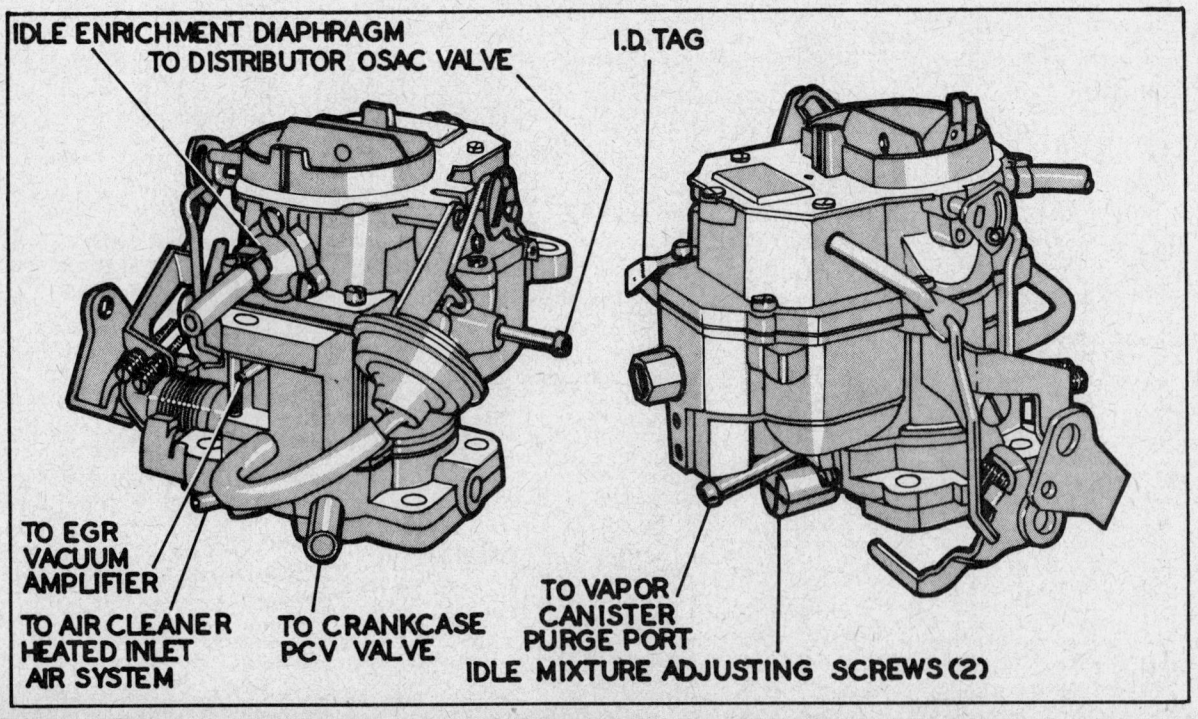

TO EGR VACUUM AMPLIFIER

BOWL VENT

THROTTLE POSITION TRANSDUCER

I.D. TAG

CURB IDLE SCREW

FAST IDLE SPEED SCREW

IDLE STOP CARBURETOR SWITCH

TO ESA VACUUM TRANSDUCER (ON AIR CLEANER)

TO PORTED EGR SYSTEM

TO CRANKCASE PCV VALVE

TO AIR CLEANER HEATED INLET AIR SYSTEM

TO VAPOR CANISTER PURGE PORT

TO AIR PUMP DIVERTER VALVE

IDLE MIXTURE ADJ. SCREWS (2)

Fig. 2 BBD 1¼" carburetor assembly. 1977–78 with Lean Burn (Typical)

IDLE ENRICHMENT DIAPHRAGM

TO DISTRIBUTOR OSAC VALVE

I.D. TAG

TO EGR VACUUM AMPLIFIER

TO AIR CLEANER HEATED INLET AIR SYSTEM

TO CRANKCASE PCV VALVE

TO VAPOR CANISTER PURGE PORT

IDLE MIXTURE ADJUSTING SCREWS (2)

Fig. 3 BBD 1¼" carburetor assembly. 1977–79 less Lean Burn & 1979 All (Typical)

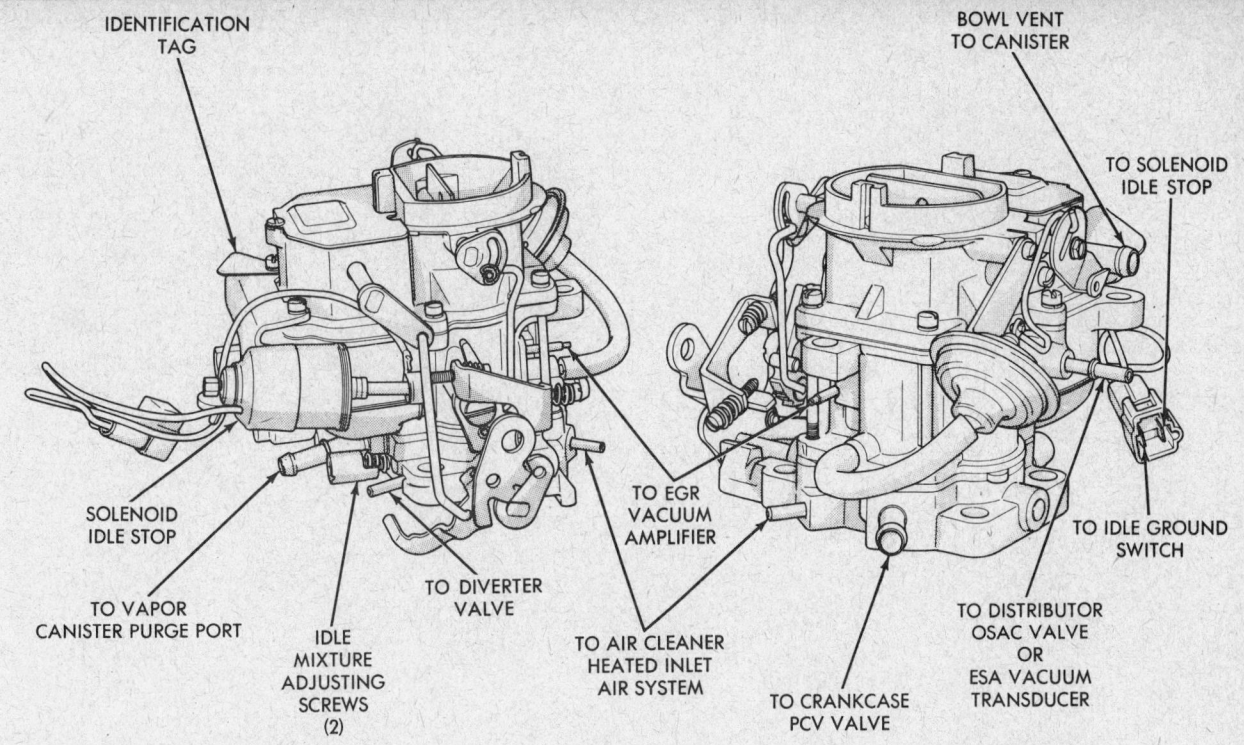

Fig. 4   BBD 1¼" carburetor assembly. 1980—83 units less Electronic Feedback Carburetor System (Typical)

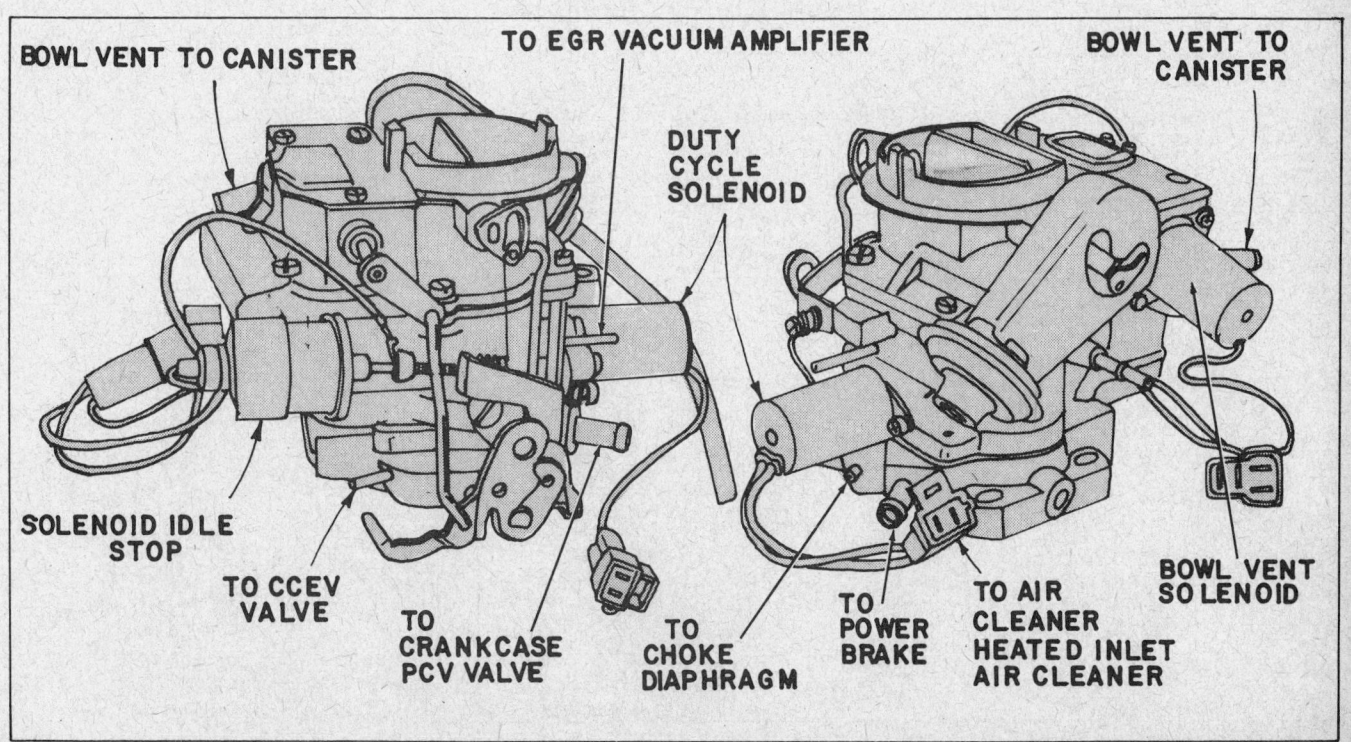

Fig. 4A   BBD 1¼" carburetor assembly. 1981—83 units with Electronic Feedback Carburetor System (Typical)

CARBURETORS

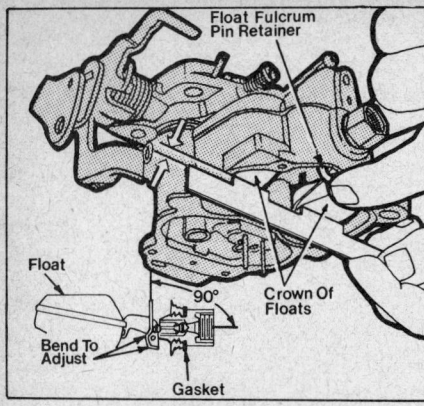

Fig. 5   Checking float level. BBD carburetors

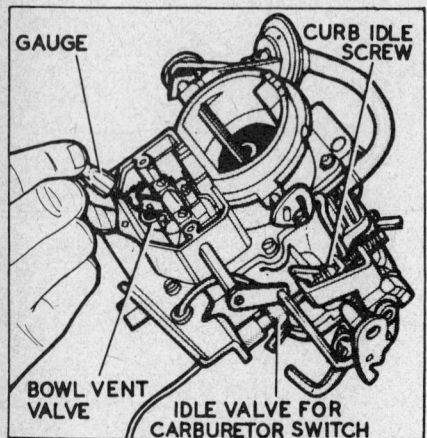

Fig. 7   Bowl vent valve adjustment. 1978–80 & 1982–83 Chrysler BBD carburetor

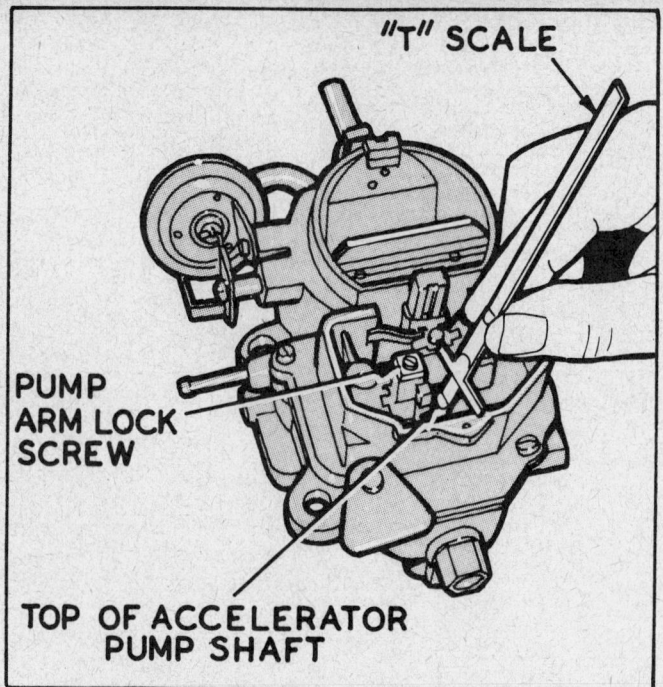

Fig. 6   Accelerator pump setting, BBD 1¼" bore carburetors

5. On all units, open throttle slightly and position fast idle speed adjustment screw on second step of cam.
6. Insert specified gauge between choke valve and air horn wall.
7. Adjust as necessary by bending fast idle cam link down to increase resistance, or up to decrease resistance.
8. On 1977–80 units, loosen choke cover

retaining screw and adjust cover index to specifications, then tighten all cover screws.
9. On 1981–83 units, remove screw retaining cover and adjust cover index to specifications, then install and tighten breakaway screws on 1981 models or standard replacement screws on 1982–83 models. On 1981 models, note drive portion of screws will break off and leave rivet-type heads to retain cover.

Initial Choke Valve Clearance

American Motors
Fig. 10—Loosen choke cover and rotate ¼ turn rich, then tighten one screw. On 1981–83 units, rivets or screws must be drilled off to loosen cover. Refer to "Fast Idle Cam Position" adjustment for procedure. Open throttle valve slightly to place fast idle screw on high step of cam. Using, an external vacuum

source, apply at least 19 inches of vacuum to pull diaphragm against stop. Measure clearance between choke plate and air horn wall. Adjust by bending diaphragm connector link.

Choke Vacuum Kick Adjustment

1978–83 Chrysler
Fig. 11—Open throttle and close choke, then close throttle to trap fast idle cam at closed choke position. Using an external vacuum source, apply 15 or more inches of vacuum to diaphragm. Apply a closing force on choke lever to completely compress spring in diaphragm stem without distorting linkage. Note that the solid rod stem of diaphragm extends to an internal stop as spring compresses. Measure clearance between top of choke valve and air horn wall at throttle lever side. Adjust clearance by bending diaphragm link at "U" bend. Remove external vacuum source and linkage for free movement.

1977 Chrysler
Fig. 11—The choke diaphragm adjustment controls the fuel delivery while the engine is

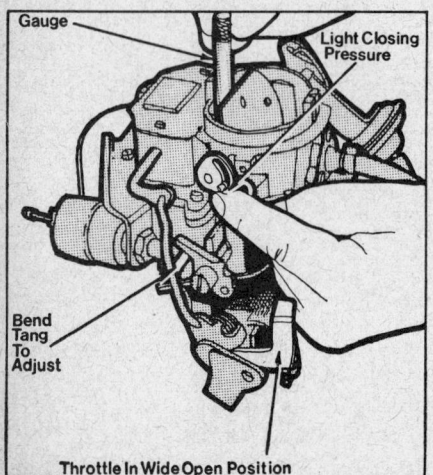

Fig. 8   Choke unloader setting. BBD carburetors

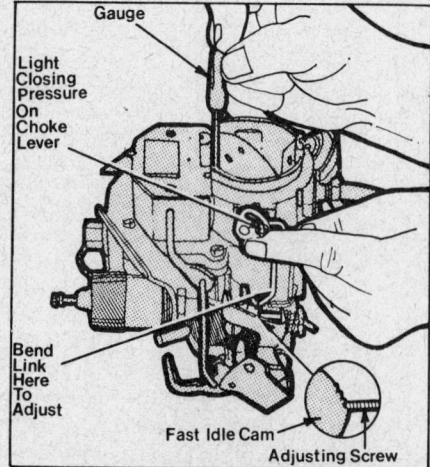

Fig. 9   Fast idle cam position adjustment. Chrysler BBD 1¼" bore carburetors

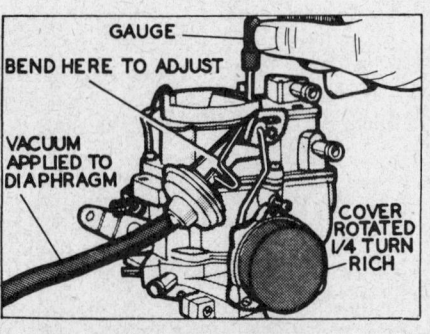

Fig. 10   Initial choke valve clearance adjustment. American Motors BBD unit

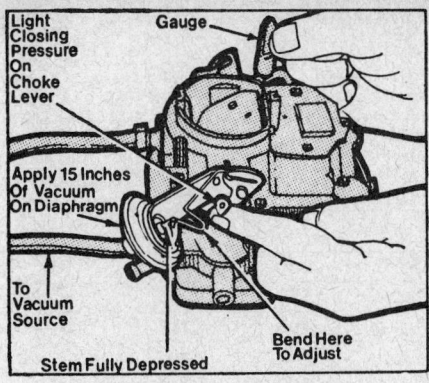

Fig. 11 Choke vacuum kick setting.
BBD 1¼" bore carburetors

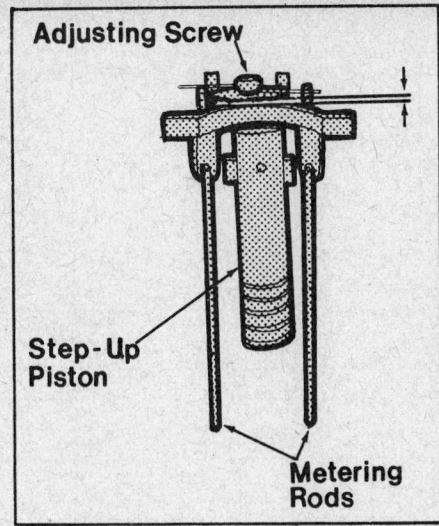

Fig. 12 Step-up piston adjustment

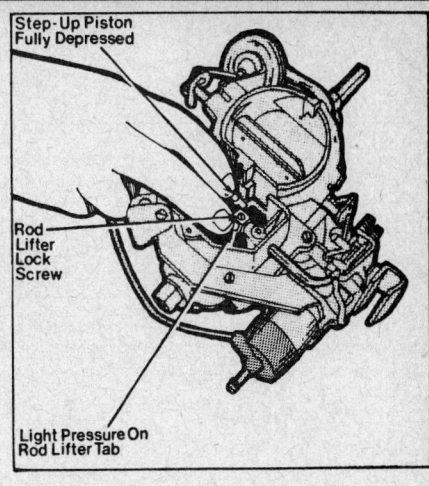

Fig. 13 Step-up piston adjustment.
BBD 1¼" carburetors

running. It positions the choke valve within the air horn by action of the linkage between choke shaft and diaphragm. The diaphragm must be energized to measure the vacuum kick adjustment. Use either a distributor test machine with a vacuum source, or vacuum supplied by another vehicle.

1. If adjustment is to be made with engine running, disconnect fast idle linkage to allow choke to close to kick position with engine at curb idle. If an auxiliary vacuum source is to be used, open throttle valves (engine not running) and move choke to closed position. Release throttle first, then release choke.
2. When using an auxiliary vacuum source, disconnect vacuum hose from carburetor and connect it to hose from vacuum supply with a small length of tube to act as a fitting. Removal of hose from diaphragm may require forces which damage the system. Apply a vacuum of 15 or more inches of mercury.
3. Insert the specified drill size between choke valve and wall of air horn. Apply sufficient closing pressure on lever to which choke rod attaches to provide a minimum choke valve opening without distortion of diaphragm link. Note that the cylindrical stem of diaphragm will extend as internal spring is compressed. This spring must be fully compressed for proper measurement of vacuum kick adjustment.
4. An adjustment will be necessary if a slight drag is not obtained as drill is being

removed. Shorten or lengthen diaphragm link to obtain correct choke opening. Length changes should be made carefully by bending (opening or closing) the bend provided in the diaphragm link. *Do not apply twisting or bending force to diaphragm.*
5. Reinstall vacuum hose on correct carburetor fitting. Return fast idel linkage to its original condition if it has been disturbed as in Step 1.
6. Check as follows: With no vacuum applied to diaphragm, choke valve should move freely between open and closed positions. If movement is not free, examine linkage for misalignment or interferences caused by bending operation. Repeat adjustment if necessary.

Step-up Piston Adjustment

1¼" BBD Units, Figs. 12 & 13
1. On 1978–83 Chrysler units and 1977 and 1979–83 American Motors units, adjust vacuum piston gap to .035 inch. On 1978 American Motors units, adjust vacuum piston gap to .040 inch. Rotate allen head screw on top of piston to adjust gap.
2. On all units, install step-up piston assembly into air horn bore, ensuring metering

rods are positioned in the metering jets.
3. Back off curb idle screw until throttle valves are completely closed. Count number of turns so that screw can be returned to its original setting.
4. Fully depress piston and while applying moderate pressure on rod lifter, tighten rod lifter screw.
5. Release piston and rod lifter and reset curb idle screw.

Dashpot Adjustment

American Motors
With curb idle speed properly adjusted, hold dashpot plunger firmly against stop. Measure clearance between plunger and throttle lever with throttle in idle position. Clearance should be .104 inch. To adjust, loosen locknut and rotate dashpot.

Chrysler
To adjust the dashpot, have the curb idle speed and mixture properly adjusted, and install a tachometer. Position throttle lever so that actuating tab on lever is contacting stem of dashpot but not depressing it. Engine RPM should be 2500 RPM. If not correct, screw dashpot in or out as required, then tighten lock nut on dashpot against the bracket.

CARTER TQ ADJUSTMENT SPECIFICATIONS

See Tune Up Chart in car chapters for curb and fast idle speeds.

Year	Carb. Model	Float Setting	Secondary Throttle Linkage	Secondary Air Valve Opening	Secondary Air Valve Spring	Pump Travel	Choke Control Lever (Off Car)	Choke Vacuum Kick	Choke Unloader	Choke Setting
CHRYSLER CORP.										
1977	9076S	27/32	①	1/2	④	⑤	3⅜	.100	.310	⑧
	9077S	27/32	①	31/64	1½ Turn	33/64 ②	3⅜	.100	.310	⑧
	9078S	27/32	①	1/2	1¼ Turn	33/64 ②	3⅜	.100	.310	⑧
	9080S	27/32	①	1/2	1¼ Turn	33/64 ③	3⅜	.100	.310	⑧
	9081S	27/32	①	1/2	1¼ Turn	33/64 ②	3⅜	.100	.310	⑧
	9093S	27/32	①	17/32	1¼ Turn	33/64 ③	3⅜	.100	.310	⑧
	9101S	27/32	①	1/2	1¼ Turn	33/64 ②	3⅜	.100	.310	⑧
	9102S	27/32	①	31/64	1½ Turn	33/64 ②	3⅜	.100	.310	⑧

Continued

CARBURETORS

See Tune Up Chart in car chapters for curb and fast idle speeds.

Year	Carb. Model	Float Setting	Secondary Throttle Linkage	Secondary Air Valve Opening	Secondary Air Valve Spring	Pump Travel	Choke Control Lever (Off Car)	Choke Vacuum Kick	Choke Unloader	Choke Setting
CHRYSLER CORP.—Continued										
	9103S	27/32	①	31/64	1½ Turn	33/64②	3⅜	.100	.310	⑧
	9115S	27/32	①	1/2	2¼ Turn	31/64②	3⅜	.150	.310	⑧
	9119S	27/32	①	1/2	1¼ Turn	33/64②	3⅜	.100	.310	⑧
1978	9104S	29/32	①	1/2	1½ Turn	31/64②	3⅜	.150	.310	⑧
	9109S	27/32	①	1/2	1½ Turn	33/64②	3⅜	.100	.310	⑧
	9110S	27/32	①	1/2	1½ Turn	33/64②	3⅜	.100	.310	⑧
	9112S	29/32	①	1/2	1½ Turn	33/64②	3⅜	.100	.310	⑧
	9134S	29/32	①	1/2	1½ Turn	31/64③	3⅜	.100	.310	⑧
	9140S	29/32	①	1/2	1½ Turn	33/64②	3⅜	.150	.310	⑧
	9147S	29/32	①	1/2	1½ Turn	31/64③	3⅜	.100	.310	⑧
	9148S	29/32	①	1/2	1½ Turn	33/64②	3⅜	.100	.310	⑧
1979	9195S	29/32	①	3/8	2 Turns	33/64②	3⅜	.100	.310	⑧
	9196S	29/32	①	1/2	2 Turns	33/64②	3⅜	.100	.310	⑧
	9198S	29/32	①	1/2	2 Turns	33/64②	3⅜	.100	.310	⑧
	9202S	29/32	①	1/2	2 Turns	33/64②	3⅜	.100	.310	⑧
	9245S	29/32	①	3/8	2 Turns	33/64②	3⅜	.100	.310	⑧
	9246S	29/32	①	1/2	2 Turns	33/64②	3⅜	.100	.310	⑧
1980	9244S	29/32	①	1/2	2½ Turns	11/32⑥	3⅜	.100	.310	⑧
	9234A	29/32	①	1/2	2¼ Turns	33/64⑥⑦	3.30	.110	.310	⑧
	9320S	29/32	①	3/8	2¼ Turns	33/64⑥⑦	3.30	.110	.310	⑧
1981	9372S	29/32	①	13/32	1¾ Turns	33/64⑥⑦	3⅜	.130	.312	⑧
	9373S	29/32	①	13/32	1¾ Turns	33/64⑥⑦	3⅜	.130	.312	⑧
	9381S	29/32	①	13/32	1¾ Turns	33/64⑥⑦	3⅜	.130	.312	⑧
1982	9337S	29/32	①	13/32	1¾ Turns	33/64⑥⑦	3⅜	.130	.312	⑧
	9372S	29/32	①	13/32	1¾ Turns	33/64⑥⑦	3⅜	.130	.312	⑧
	9385S	29/32	①	13/32	1¾ Turns	33/64⑥⑦	3⅜	.130	.312	⑧
1983	9374S	29/32	①	13/32	1¾ Turns	33/64⑥⑦	3⅜	.130	.310	⑧
	9385S	29/32	①	13/32	1¾ Turns	33/64⑥⑦	3⅜	.130	.310	⑧

①—Adjust link so primary and secondary stops both contact at same time.
②—Secondary stage pick/up adjustment 5/16 inch.
③—Secondary stage pick/up adjustment 22/64 inch.
④—Models less red tag. 1½ turns; models with red tag, 2¼ turns.
⑤—Models less red tag, 33/64 inch, refer to note ②.
Models with red tag, 31/64 inch, refer to note ③.
⑥—Slot No. 2.
⑦—Secondary stage pick/up adjustment 25/64 inch.
⑧—Tamper-resistant.

MODEL TQ ADJUSTMENTS

The TQ (Thermo-Quad) carburetor, Figs. 1 through 4, is unique in design in that it has a black main body or fuel bowl of molded phenolic resin. This acts as an effective heat insulator. Fuel is kept cooler by about 20 degrees Fahrenheit than in carburetors of all metal design. Another reason for the lower operating temperatures is its suspended design metering system. All calibration points with the exception of the idle adjusting screws, are in the upper aluminum casting or air horn and are in effect suspended in cavities in the plastic main body.

On 1977–79 vehicles with automatic transmissions, an idle enrichment system is used to reduce cold engine stalling by the use of an additional metering system, which enriches the mixture in the off idle position. This system is controlled by a vacuum diaphragm mounted near the top of the carburetor.

Float Setting

Fig. 5—With bowl cover inverted, gasket installed and floats resting on seated needle, the dimension of each float from bowl cover gasket to bottom side of float should be as shown in *TQ Specifications Chart*. To adjust, bend float lever.

NOTE: When adjusting, do not allow lip of float lever to be pressed against needle.

Secondary Throttle Linkage

Fig. 6—Hold fast idle lever in curb idle position and invert carburetor. Open primary throttle valve until the primary and secondary stops contact simultaneously. To adjust, bend secondary throttle operating rod at angle until correct adjustment is obtained.

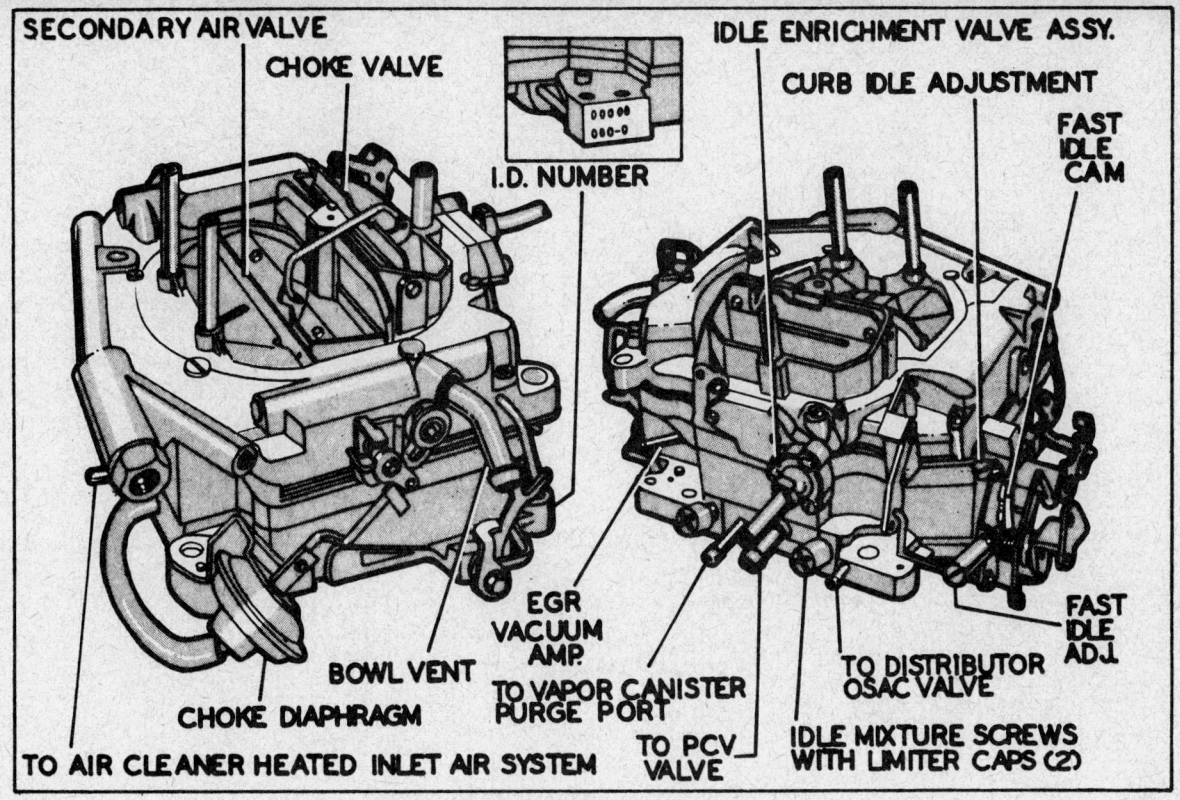

SECONDARY AIR VALVE

CHOKE VALVE

I.D. NUMBER

IDLE ENRICHMENT VALVE ASSY.

CURB IDLE ADJUSTMENT

FAST IDLE CAM

EGR VACUUM AMP.

TO VAPOR CANISTER PURGE PORT

BOWL VENT

CHOKE DIAPHRAGM

TO AIR CLEANER HEATED INLET AIR SYSTEM

TO PCV VALVE

TO DISTRIBUTOR OSAC VALVE

IDLE MIXTURE SCREWS WITH LIMITER CAPS (2)

FAST IDLE ADJ.

Fig. 1   TQ carburetor assembly. 1977 (Typical)

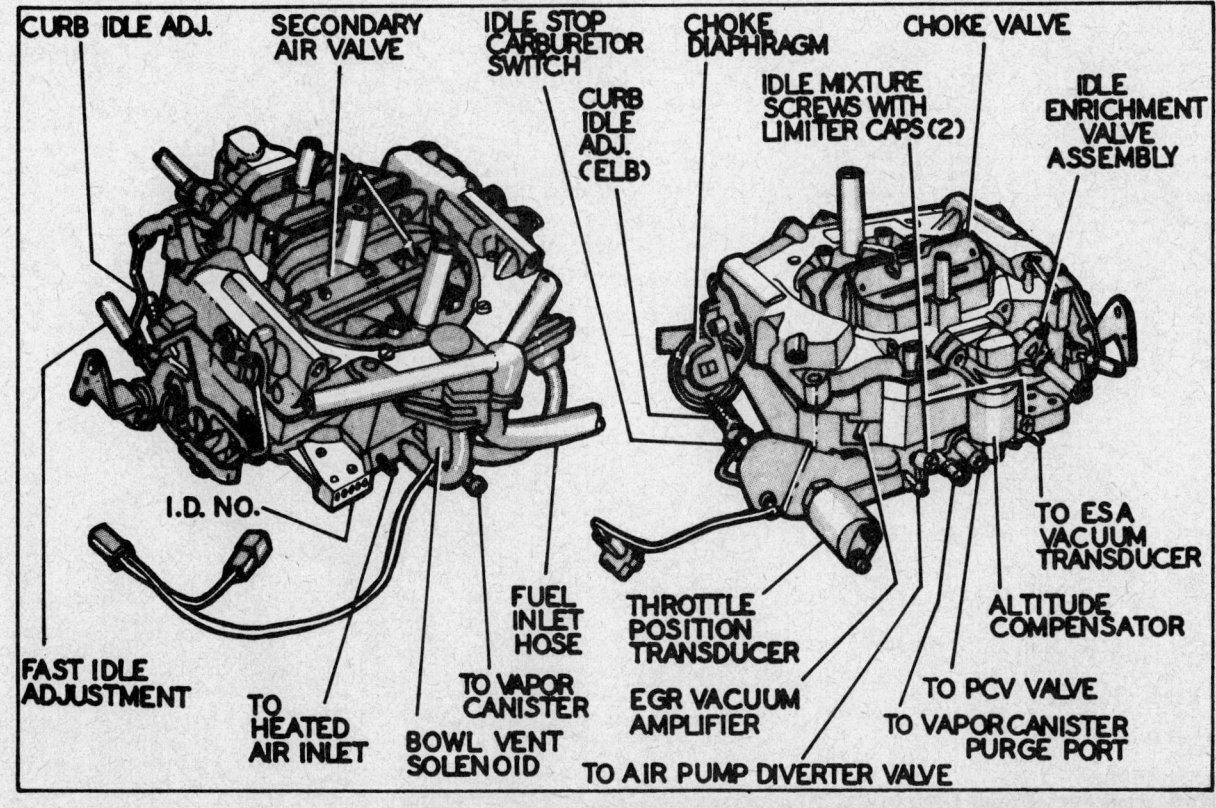

CURB IDLE ADJ.

SECONDARY AIR VALVE

IDLE STOP CARBURETOR SWITCH

CURB IDLE ADJ. (ELB)

CHOKE DIAPHRAGM

IDLE MIXTURE SCREWS WITH LIMITER CAPS (2)

CHOKE VALVE

IDLE ENRICHMENT VALVE ASSEMBLY

I.D. NO.

FAST IDLE ADJUSTMENT

TO HEATED AIR INLET

BOWL VENT SOLENOID

TO VAPOR CANISTER

FUEL INLET HOSE

THROTTLE POSITION TRANSDUCER

EGR VACUUM AMPLIFIER

TO AIR PUMP DIVERTER VALVE

TO PCV VALVE

TO VAPOR CANISTER PURGE PORT

ALTITUDE COMPENSATOR

TO ESA VACUUM TRANSDUCER

Fig. 2   TQ carburetor assembly. 1978-79 (Typical)

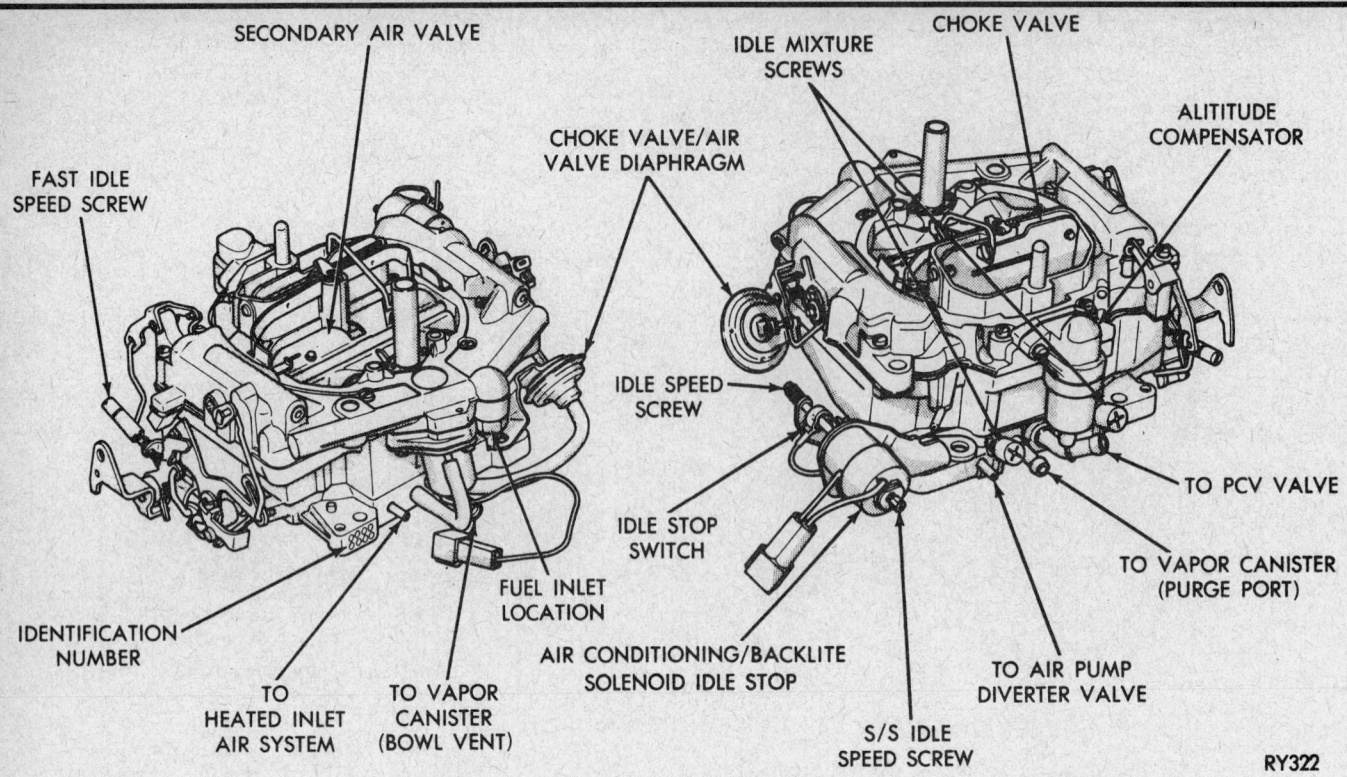

FAST IDLE
SPEED SCREW

SECONDARY AIR VALVE

CHOKE VALVE/AIR
VALVE DIAPHRAGM

IDLE MIXTURE
SCREWS

CHOKE VALVE

ALITITUDE
COMPENSATOR

IDLE SPEED
SCREW

IDLE STOP
SWITCH

IDENTIFICATION
NUMBER

FUEL INLET
LOCATION

TO
HEATED INLET
AIR SYSTEM

TO VAPOR
CANISTER
(BOWL VENT)

AIR CONDITIONING/BACKLITE
SOLENOID IDLE STOP

S/S IDLE
SPEED SCREW

TO AIR PUMP
DIVERTER VALVE

TO VAPOR CANISTER
(PURGE PORT)

TO PCV VALVE

RY322

Fig. 3 TQ carburetor assembly. 1980—83 (Typical)

Secondary Air Valve Opening

Fig. 7
1. With air valve in closed position, the opening along air valve at its long side must be at its maximum and parallel with air horn gasket surface.
2. With air valve wide open, the opening of the air valve at the short side and air horn must be as shown in *TQ Specifications Chart*. The corner of air valve is notched for adjustment. Bend the corner with a pair of pliers to give proper opening.

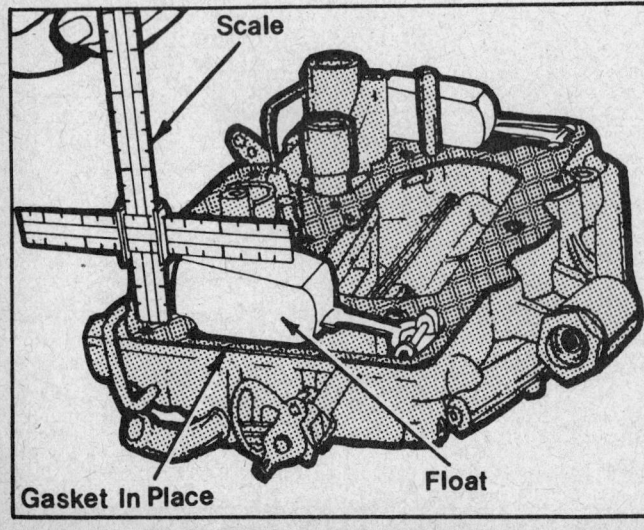

Scale

Gasket In Place

Float

Fig. 5 TQ float setting

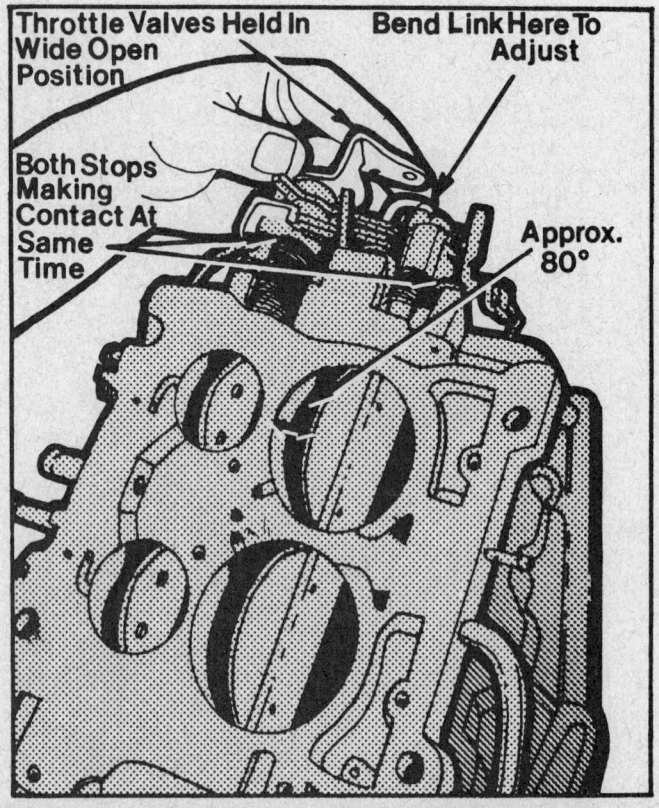

Throttle Valves Held In
Wide Open
Position

Bend Link Here To
Adjust

Both Stops
Making
Contact At
Same
Time

Approx.
80°

Fig. 6 TQ secondary throttle adjustment

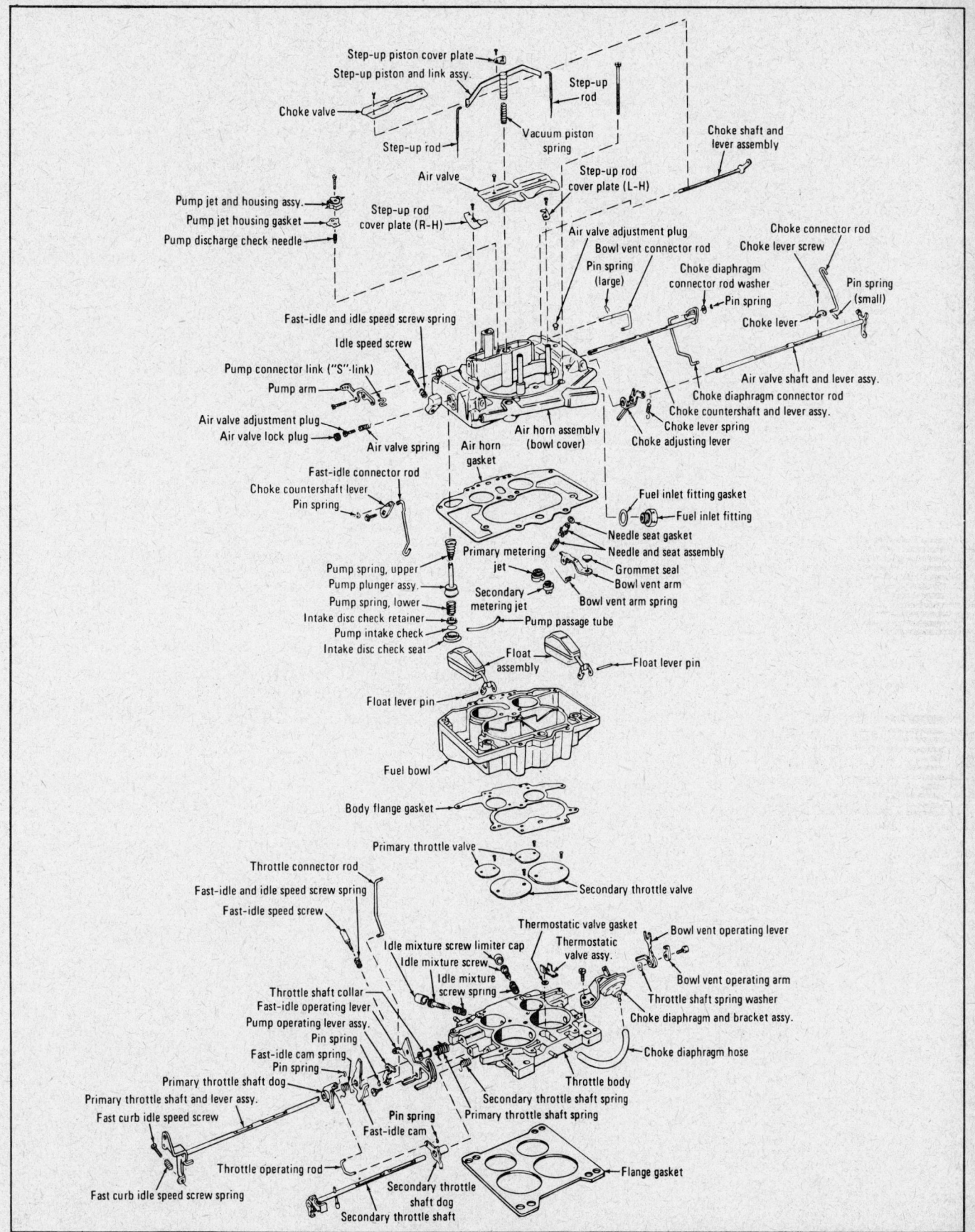

Fig. 4 Carter TQ model exploded view (Typical)

CARBURETORS

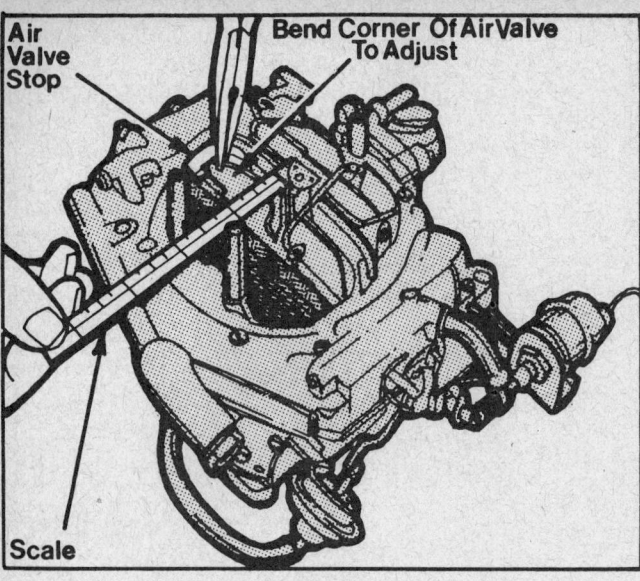

Fig. 7 TQ secondary air valve opening

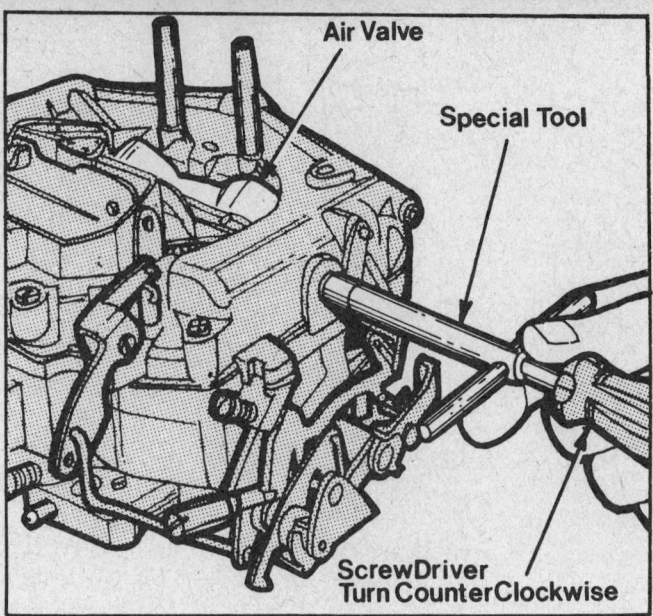

Fig. 8 TQ secondary air valve spring tension

Secondary Air Valve Spring Tension

Fig. 8—Loosen air valve lock plug and allow air valve to position itself wide open. With a long screwdriver that will enter center of tool C-4152 positioned on air valve adjustment plug, turn plug counter-clockwise until air valve contacts stop lightly, then turn additional turn as specified in *TQ Specifications Chart*. Hold plug with screwdriver and tighten lock plug securely with tool C-4152.

Accelerator Pump Stroke

1977–79 & 1983 Units
Fig. 9—First Stage. Ensure throttle connector rod is in center hole on three hold pump arm or inner hole on two hole pump arm. With idle adjusting screw adjusted to the specified curb idle speed, measure distance from air horn surface to top of accelerator pump plunger. If equipped with an idle stop solenoid the ignition switch must be in the on position. Dimensions should be as shown in the *TQ Specifications Chart*. Bend throttle connector rod at lower angle to adjust.

Second Stage. With choke in the open position, open throttle until secondary lockout latch is just applied. Plunger downward travel stops at this point. Measure distance from air horn surface to top of accelerator pump plunger. Dimension should be shown in the *TQ Specifications Chart*. Bend tang on throttle to adjust.

1980–82 Units
Fig. 10—Ensure that throttle connector rod is in the specified hole of the pump arm. With idle adjusting screw adjusted to the specified curb idle speed, measure distance from air horn surface to top of accelerator pump plunger. Dimensions should be as shown in the TQ Specification Chart. Adjust plunger height by bending throttle connector rod in area indicated in Fig. 10.

Choke Control Lever

Fig. 11—Place carburetor on a flat surface. Close choke by pushing on choke lever with throttle partly open. Measure vertical distance between top of rod hole in control lever and base of carburetor (flat surface). Dimension should be as shown in TQ Specifications Chart. Adjust by bending link connecting the two choke shafts.

Choke Diaphragm Connector Rod

Fig. 12—Apply a vacuum of 15 inches Hg or more to fully depress diaphragm. An auxilliary source like a distributor test machine can be used for this purpose. With air valve closed, adjust connector rod to give .040″ clearance between air valve and stop.

Fig. 9 TQ accelerator pump stroke adjustment, with staged pump system. 1977–79 & 1983 units

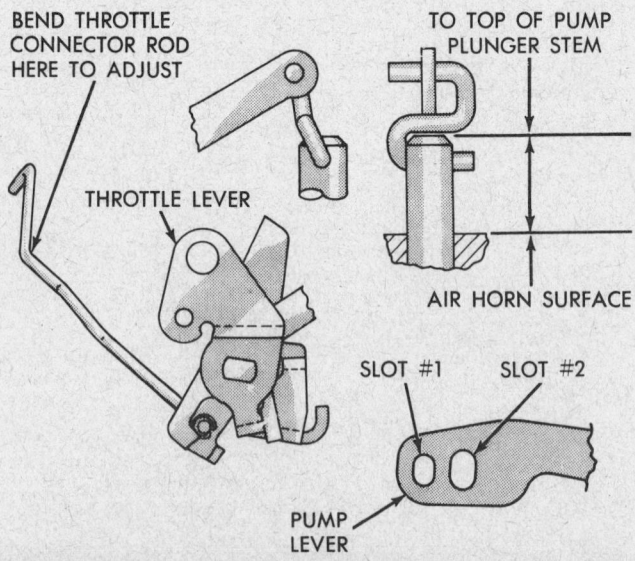

Fig. 10 TQ accelerator pump stroke adjustment. 1980–82 units

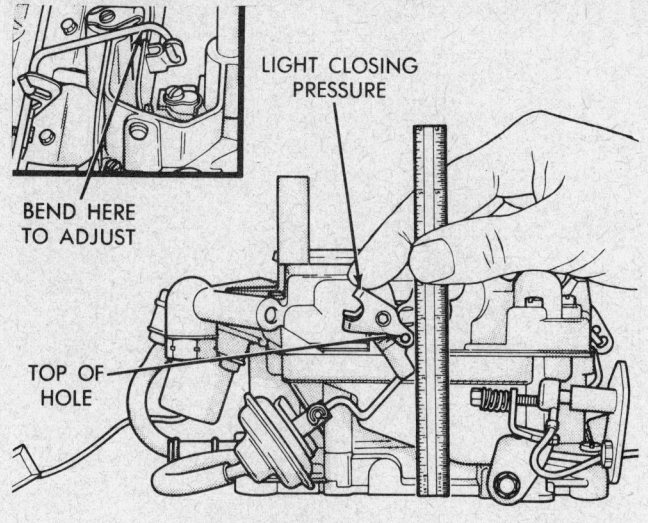

Fig. 11 TQ choke control lever adjustment

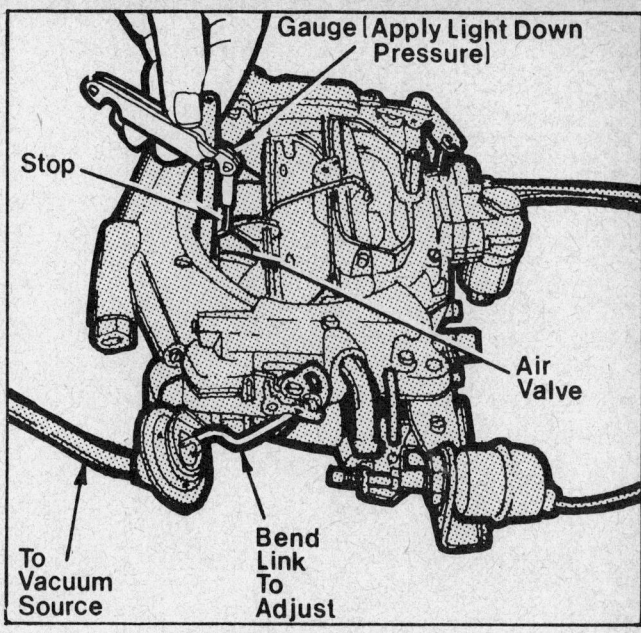

Fig. 12 TQ choke diaphragm connector rod

Vacuum Kick Adjustment

Fig. 13—With engine running, back off fast idle speed screw until choke can be closed to kick position at idle. Note number of screw turns so fast idle can be turned back to original adjustment. Insert a gauge or drill of specified size between long side (lower edge) of choke valve and air horn wall. Apply sufficient pressure on choke control lever to provide a minimum choke valve opening. The spring connecting the control lever to the adjustment lever must be fully extended for proper adjustment. Bend tang as shown to change contact with end of diaphragm rod. Do not adjust diaphragm rod. A slight drag should be felt as drill is being removed.

Fast Idle Cam & Linkage

Fig. 14—With fast idle adjusting screw on second step of fast idle cam, move choke valve toward closed position with light pressure on choke control lever. Clearance between choke valve lower edge and air horn wall should be .100 inch. Adjust by bending fast idle connector rod at angle.

Choke Unloader Adjustment

Fig. 15—Hold throttle valves in wide open position and insert specified drill between long side (lower edge) of choke valve and inner wall of air horn. With finger lightly pressing against choke valve control lever, a slight drag should be felt as drill is withdrawn. Refer to TQ Specification Chart for proper drill size or dimension. Adjust by bending tang on fast idle control lever.

Secondary Throttle Lockout

Fig. 16—Move choke control lever to open choke position. Measure clearance between lockout lever and stop. Clearance should be .060–.090 inch on 1977 and 1980–83 units and .075 inch on 1978–79 units. Adjust by bending tang on fast idle control lever.

Bowl Vent Valve Adjustment

1977–78 Units
Fig. 17—Remove bowl vent valve checking hole plug in bowl cover. With throttle valves at curb idle, insert a narrow ruler down through hole. Allow ruler to rest lightly on top

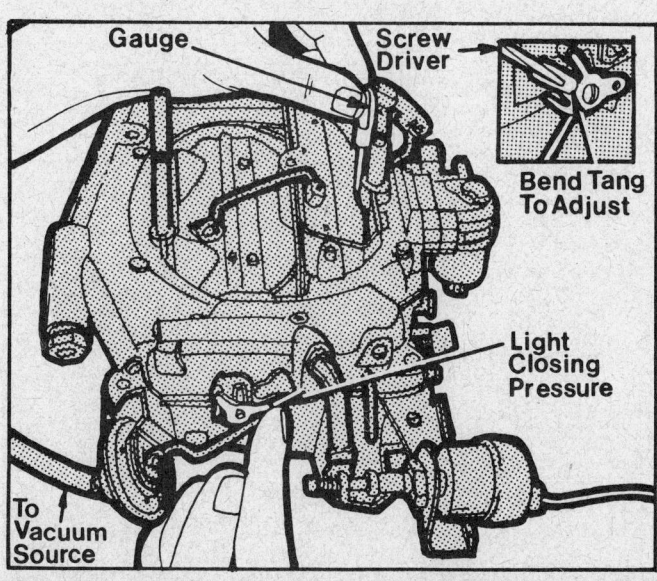

Fig. 13 TQ vacuum kick adjustment

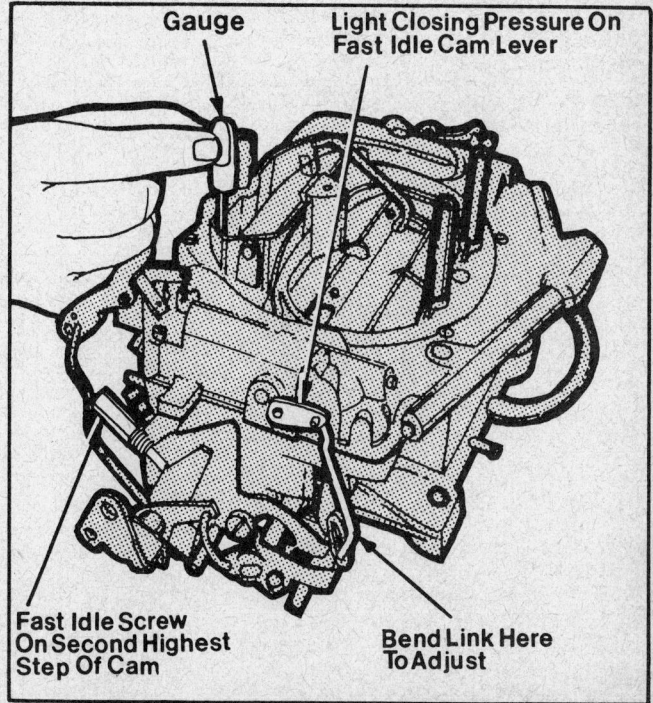

Fig. 14 TQ fast idle cam & linkage adjustment

CARBURETORS

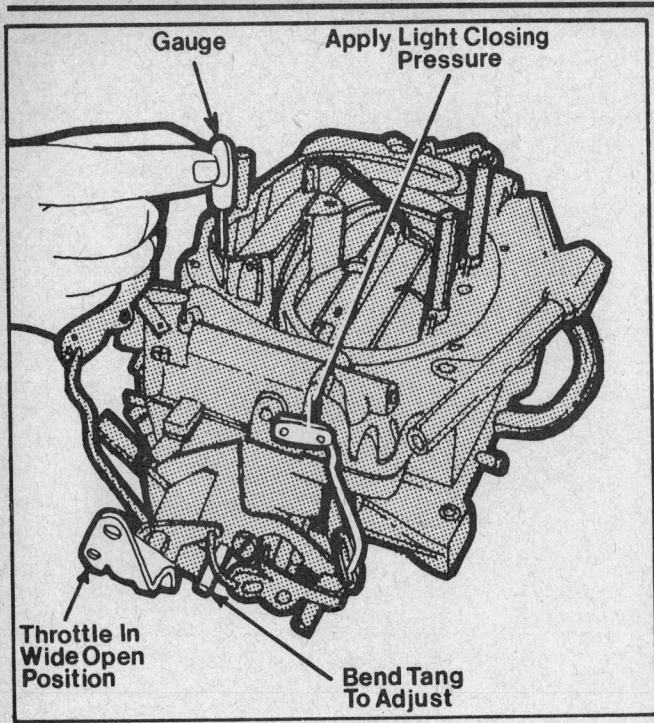

Fig. 15 TQ choke unloader adjustment

Fig. 16 TQ secondary throttle lockout

of valve. Dimension should be .812 inch. Adjust by bending bowl vent operating lever at notch. Install a new plug.

Solenoid Bowl Vent Valve Check

Fig. 18, 1978–83
1. Remove air cleaner.
2. Disconnect vacuum hose from solenoid bowl vent diaphragm.
3. Connect an external vacuum source and apply 15 inches of vacuum to the diaphragm.
4. Observe valve movement through air horn vent tube. Valve should move when vacuum is applied.
5. Turn ignition switch "On" and disconnect external vacuum source. The valve should remain in the downward position until the ignition switch is turned "Off".
6. If the valve does not move when vacuum

is applied, the diaphragm is defective and requires replacement. If the valve does not remain in the downward position when the ignition switch is turned "On" and the vacuum source removed, the solenoid or wiring is defective.
7. Install air cleaner.

Fast Idle Speed

NOTE: On 1977 Chrysler models without Electronic Lean Burn system, remove air cleaner and plug vacuum fittings to heated air control and OSAC valves. On 1978–79 Chrysler models without Electronic Lean Burn system, remove air cleaner and eliminate vacuum ignition advance and EGR signals, then cap or plug disconnected vacuum lines. On Chrysler models with Electronic Lean Burn system, remove top of air cleaner

and lift air cleaner for access to carburetor. Also, use a jumper wire to ground carburetor idle stop switch, then disconnect and plug vacuum hose to EGR valve.

CAUTION: On 1983 units, disconnect engine harness lead from the oxygen sensor and ground the engine harness lead. Do not exert any pulling force on the wire attached to the sensor. Allow the engine to run for approximately two minutes to allow the effect of disconnecting the sensor to take place.

Fig. 19—With engine off and transmission in Park or Neutral, open throttle slightly. Close choke valve until fast idle screw is positioned on second step of cam against shoulder of first step. Start engine and stabilize RPM, then adjust fast idle speed. Refer to Tune Up Chart located in car chapter.

NOTE: On models with Electronic Lean Burn system, if speed continues to rise slowly, the carburetor idle stop switch has not been properly grounded.

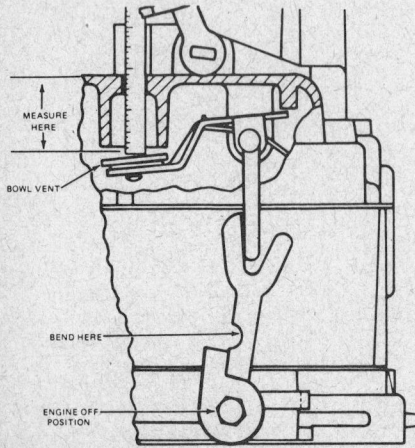

Fig. 17 TQ bowl vent valve adjustment, 1977–78

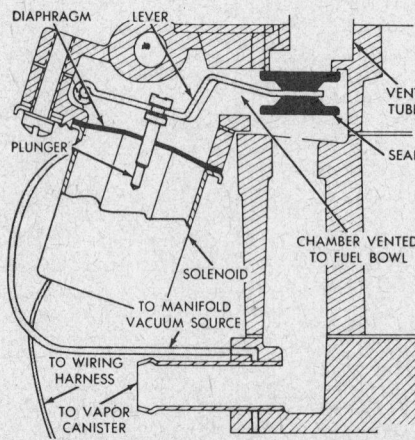

Fig. 18 TQ solenoid bowl vent check. 1978–83 units

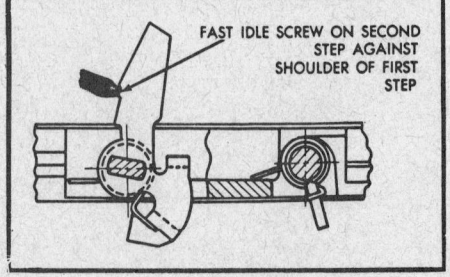

Fig. 19 TQ fast idle speed cam position

Motorcraft Carburetor Section

MODEL 740 CARBURETOR ADJUSTMENT SPECIFICATIONS

See Tune Up Chart in car chapters for curb and fast idle speeds.

Year	Carb. Model ①	Float Level (Dry)	Float Drop	Choke Pulldown Clearance	Fast Idle Cam Clearance	Dechoke Clearance	Dashpot Clearance	Choke Setting ②
1981	E1EE-AAA	.250	1.693	.118	.079	.138	.138	Index
	E1EE-ACA	.250	1.693	.157	.079	.138	.157	1 Lean
	E1EE-ADA	.250	1.693	.118	.079	.138	.138	Index
	E1EE-AEA	.250	1.693	.118	.079	.138	.138	Index
	E1EE-AFA	.250	1.693	.118	.079	.138	.138	Index
	E1EE-AHA	.250	1.693	.098	.079	.138	.157	Index
	E1EE-AMA	.250	—	.157	.079	.138	.157	1 Lean
	E1EE-AVA	.250	1.693	.098	.079	.138	.157	Index
	E1EE-LA	.250	1.693	.118	.079	.138	.138	Index
	E1EE-MA	.250	1.693	.157	.079	.138	.157	1 Lean
	E1EE-PA	.250	1.693	.157	.079	.138	.157	1 Lean
	E1EE-RA	.250	1.693	.157	.079	.138	.157	1 Lean
	E1EE-SA	.250	1.693	.118	.079	.138	.138	Index
	E1EE-TA	.250	1.693	.118	.079	.138	.138	Index
1981–82	E1EE-ALA	.250	—	.157	.079	.138	.157	1 Lean
	E1EE-APA	.250	—	.157	.079	.138	.157	1 Lean
	E1EE-NA	.250	—	.157	.079	.138	.157	1 Lean
	E1EE-ZA	.250	—	.157	.079	.138	.157	1 Lean
1982	E1GE-CA	.250	—	.118	.079	.138	.138	Index
	E1GE-DA	.250	—	.118	.079	.138	.138	Index
	E1GE-EA	.250	—	.157	.079	.138	.157	1 Lean
	E1GE-GA	.250	—	.157	.079	.138	.157	1 Lean
	E2EE-AGA, AHA	.250	—	.138	.079	.138	.157	Index
	E2EE-JA	.250	—	.138	.079	.138	.059	Index
	E2EE-JC	.295	—	.256	.079	.138	.157	Index
	E2EE-GA	.250	—	.138	.079	.138	.059	Index
	E2EE-GC	.250	—	.138	.079	.138	.138	Index
	E2EE-LA	.250	—	.138	.079	.138	.157	Index
	E2EE-LC	.250	—	.177	.079	.138	.157	Index
	E2EE-MA	.250	—	.138	.079	.138	.157	Index
	E2EE-MC	.250	—	.177	.079	.138	.157	Index
	E2EE-NA	.250	—	.138	.079	.138	.157	Index
	E2EE-NC	.250	—	.177	.079	.138	—	Index
	E2EE-PA	.250	—	.138	.079	.138	.157	Index
	E2EE-PC	.250	—	.177	.079	.138	—	Index
	E2EE-SA	.250	—	.138	.079	.138	.059	Index
	E2EE-VA	.250	—	.138	.079	.138	.157	1 Lean
	E2EE-YA	.250	—	.138	.079	.138	.157	1 Lean
	E2EE-ZA	.250	—	.156	.079	.138	.157	1 Lean
	E2GE-AA	.250	—	.167	.079	.138	.157	Index
1983	E3EE-AA	.295	1.693	.138	.079	.138	—	—
	E3EE-BA	.295	1.693	.138	.079	.138	—	—
	E3EE-CA	.295	1.693	.315	.079	.138	.098	—
	E3EE-DA	.295	1.693	.335	.079	.138	.079	—
	E3EE-EA	.295	1.693	.315	.079	.138	.098	—
	E3EE-GB	.295	1.693	.256	.079	.138	.138	—
	E3EE-JA	.295	1.693	.138	.079	.138	.157	—
	E3EE-KA	.295	1.693	.138	.079	.138	.157	—
	E3EE-NA	.295	1.693	.138	.079	.138	—	—
	E3EE-PA	.295	1.693	.138	.079	.138	.157	—
	E3GE-DA	.295	1.693	.167	.079	.138	—	—
	E3GE-DC	.295	1.693	.167	.079	.138	—	—

CARBURETORS

See Tune Up Chart in car chapters for curb and fast idle speeds.

Year	Carb. Model ①	Float Level (Dry)	Float Drop	Choke Pulldown Clearance	Fast Idle Cam Clearance	Dechoke Clearance	Dashpot Clearance	Choke Setting ②
	E3GE-FA	.295	1.693	.167	.079	.138	—	—
	E3GE-FC	.295	1.693	.167	.079	.138	—	—
	E3GE-HA	.295	1.693	.167	.079	.138	.157	—
	E3GE-HC	.295	1.693	.167	.079	.138	—	—
	E3GE-JA	.295	1.693	.167	.079	.138	.157	—
	E3GE-JC	.295	1.693	.167	.079	.138	—	—
	E3GE-KB	.295	1.693	.295	.079	.138	.157	—
	E3GE-KD	.295	1.693	.295	.079	.138	.157	—
	E3GE-LA	.295	1.693	.295	.079	.138	.157	—
	E3GE-LC	.295	1.693	.295	.079	.138	.157	—
	E3GE-MA	.295	1.693	.276	.098	.138	.157	—
	E3GE-NA	.295	1.693	.276	.098	.138	.157	—
	E3GE-PA	.295	1.693	.256	.079	.138	.157	—
	E3GE-RA	.295	1.693	.256	.079	.138	.157	—
	E3GE-SA	.295	1.693	.256	.079	.138	.157	—
	E3GE-UA	.295	1.693	.276	.098	.138	.157	—

①—Stamped on tag attached to bowl cover.　②—Tamper-resistant.

MODEL 740 ADJUSTMENTS

Description

The Motorcraft Model 740 carburetor, Figs. 1 and 2, consists of five basic systems: choke system, idle system, main metering system, acceleration system and power enrichment system.

The choke system is used for cold engine starting and consists of a bi-metallic spring and an electric heater. The idle system is adjustable and provides for the proper air/fuel ratio for both idle and low speed operation. The main metering system provides the correct air/fuel ratio for normal cruising speeds. A main metering system is used for primary and secondary stage operation. The acceleration system consists of a diaphragm type pump that is mechanically operated by the primary throttle linkage. This system provides fuel to the primary stage during acceleration. The power enrichment system consists of a vacuum operated power valve and a secondary stage pull over system that is regulated by airflow. This system is used together with the main metering system to provide proper vehicle operation during periods of moderate to heavy acceleration. The distributor and EGR vacuum ports are located in the primary venturi area of the carburetor.

Fuel Inlet System

The fuel inlet system maintains a specified fuel level in the fuel bowl, allowing the fuel metering system to deliver the correct air/fuel mixture to the engine. The fuel inlet needle position is controlled by a float and lever assembly hinged on the float pin. The amount of fuel entering the bowl is regulated by the distance the inlet needle is moved off its seat. When the float drops, it causes the inlet needle to drop and this allows additional fuel to enter the bowl. As the fuel level reaches a specified level, the inlet needle is raised to a position that will allow only enough fuel to enter to replace that being used by the me-

tering systems. The float bowl uses a solenoid valve to operate the dual venting system, Fig. 3. When the ignition is On, the bowl is vented internally to the air cleaner. This balances the bowl with carburetor inlet air. When the ignition is Off, the bowl is vented externally, and fuel vapors are stored in the carbon canister to be drawn into the engine when the engine is started.

Idle System

Fuel for idle and off idle operation flows from the bowl through the primary main metering jet into the main well. Fuel then flows through an idle fuel restriction and is mixed with air entering through the primary idle air bleed. This air/fuel mixture travels past the idle transfer holes which serve as additional air bleeds during curb idle. The air/fuel mixture then moves past the idle mixture screw tip which controls the amount of mixture discharged into the engine from below the throttle plate. At speeds slightly above idle, the idle transfer holes begin discharging additional air/fuel mixture. This occurs because the increased opening of the throttle plates exposes the idle transfer holes to intake manifold vacuum. As the throttle opening and engine speed increase, airflow through the carburetor is increased. This creates a vacuum in the venturi causing the main metering system to begin operation.

Fuel Shut-Off System

When the ignition switch is in the On position, the fuel shut off system solenoid is in the operational position. This allows fuel to flow through the idle system of the carburetor. When the ignition switch is in the Off position, the solenoid releases, stopping the flow of fuel to the carburetor idle system. On 1982–83 units, fuel flow through the idle system is shut off during deceleration as vehicle and engine sensors provide a signal to de-energize the idle fuel solenoid. The sole-

noid is automatically energized by the sensors to allow the engine to idle when necessary.

Main Metering System

As engine speed increases, air velocity through the booster venturi creates a vacuum in the venturi. Fuel begins to flow through the main metering system due to high pressure in the bowl and low pressure at the main discharge nozzle. Fuel flows from the fuel bowl through the main jet and into the main well. Then the fuel travels up the main well tube where it is mixed with air. Air, supplied through the high speed air bleed, mixes with the fuel through small holes in the sides of the main well tubes. The proper air fuel ratio is maintained because the high speed air bleed meters an increased amount of air whenever venturi vacuum increases. As the air/fuel mixture moves to the discharge port, it is discharged into the booster venturi.

Secondary Progression

When the primary throttle plate is opened approximately 45°, the secondary throttle plate begins to open, Fig. 4. The air/fuel mixture begins flowing from the secondary transfer holes as they are exposed to manifold vacuum. As the throttle plates are opened further, the secondary main metering system begins to operate. This system is similar to the primary main metering system.

Accelerator Pump System

When the throttle plates are opened quickly, air flows through the carburetor almost immediately. Because fuel is heavier than air, there is a brief time lag before fuel flow can gain enough speed to maintain proper air/fuel ratio. During this lag, the accelerator pump system supplies the necessary extra fuel to maintain correct air/fuel ratio until the other metering systems can respond. When the throttle plates are opened, the diaphragm rod

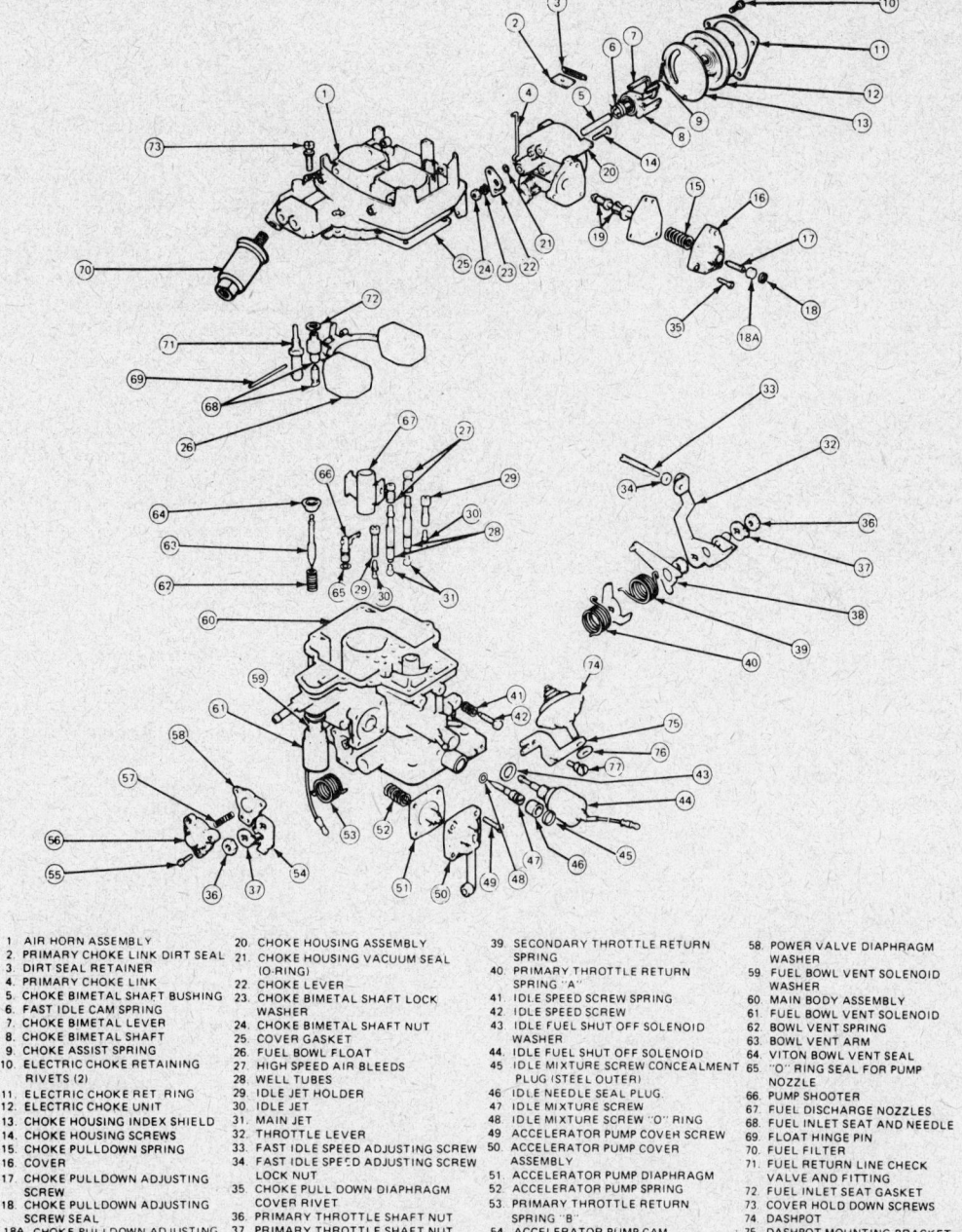

1. AIR HORN ASSEMBLY	20. CHOKE HOUSING ASSEMBLY	39. SECONDARY THROTTLE RETURN SPRING
2. PRIMARY CHOKE LINK DIRT SEAL	21. CHOKE HOUSING VACUUM SEAL (O-RING)	40. PRIMARY THROTTLE RETURN SPRING "A"
3. DIRT SEAL RETAINER	22. CHOKE LEVER	41. IDLE SPEED SCREW SPRING
4. PRIMARY CHOKE LINK	23. CHOKE BIMETAL SHAFT LOCK WASHER	42. IDLE SPEED SCREW
5. CHOKE BIMETAL SHAFT BUSHING	24. CHOKE BIMETAL SHAFT NUT	43. IDLE FUEL SHUT OFF SOLENOID WASHER
6. FAST IDLE CAM SPRING	25. COVER GASKET	44. IDLE FUEL SHUT OFF SOLENOID
7. CHOKE BIMETAL LEVER	26. FUEL BOWL FLOAT	45. IDLE MIXTURE SCREW CONCEALMENT PLUG (STEEL OUTER)
8. CHOKE BIMETAL SHAFT	27. HIGH SPEED AIR BLEEDS	46. IDLE NEEDLE SEAL PLUG.
9. CHOKE ASSIST SPRING	28. WELL TUBES	47. IDLE MIXTURE SCREW
10. ELECTRIC CHOKE RETAINING RIVETS (2)	29. IDLE JET HOLDER	48. IDLE MIXTURE SCREW "O" RING
11. ELECTRIC CHOKE RET. RING	30. IDLE JET	49. ACCELERATOR PUMP COVER SCREW
12. ELECTRIC CHOKE UNIT	31. MAIN JET	50. ACCELERATOR PUMP COVER ASSEMBLY
13. CHOKE HOUSING INDEX SHIELD	32. THROTTLE LEVER	51. ACCELERATOR PUMP DIAPHRAGM
14. CHOKE HOUSING SCREWS	33. FAST IDLE SPEED ADJUSTING SCREW	52. ACCELERATOR PUMP SPRING
15. CHOKE PULLDOWN SPRING	34. FAST IDLE SPEED ADJUSTING SCREW LOCK NUT	53. PRIMARY THROTTLE RETURN SPRING "B"
16. COVER	35. CHOKE PULL DOWN DIAPHRAGM COVER RIVET.	54. ACCELERATOR PUMP CAM
17. CHOKE PULLDOWN ADJUSTING SCREW	36. PRIMARY THROTTLE SHAFT NUT	55. POWER VALVE COVER SCREW
18. CHOKE PULLDOWN ADJUSTING SCREW SEAL	37. PRIMARY THROTTLE SHAFT NUT LOCKING TAB	56. POWER VALVE COVER
18A. CHOKE PULLDOWN ADJUSTING CONCEALMENT PLUG	38. SECONDARY THROTTLE OPERATING LEVER	57. POWER VALVE SPRING
19. CHOKE PULLDOWN DIAPHRAGM ASSEMBLY		

58. POWER VALVE DIAPHRAGM WASHER	68. FUEL INLET SEAT AND NEEDLE
59. FUEL BOWL VENT SOLENOID WASHER	69. FLOAT HINGE PIN
60. MAIN BODY ASSEMBLY	70. FUEL FILTER
61. FUEL BOWL VENT SOLENOID	71. FUEL RETURN LINE CHECK VALVE AND FITTING
62. BOWL VENT SPRING	72. FUEL INLET SEAT GASKET
63. BOWL VENT ARM	73. COVER HOLD DOWN SCREWS
64. VITON BOWL VENT SEAL	74. DASHPOT
65. "O" RING SEAL FOR PUMP NOZZLE	75. DASHPOT MOUNTING BRACKET
66. PUMP SHOOTER	76. DASHPOT ADJUSTING LOCK NUT
67. FUEL DISCHARGE NOZZLES	77. DASHPOT MOUNTING BRACKET SCREW

Fig. 1   Disassembled view of Motorcraft Model 740 carburetor. 1981

is pushed upward, forcing fuel from the pump chamber into the discharge passage. Fuel under pressure moves the discharge check ball off its seat. This fuel then travels through the pump discharge valve where it enters the primary venturi through the pump discharge nozzle.

Primary Power Enrichment System

The air/fuel ratio must be increased during periods of heavy acceleration or high speed operation. The power enrichment system, controlled by intake manifold vacuum, supplies extra fuel during these operating conditions. Manifold vacuum is applied to the power valve diaphragm from an opening in the carburetor base where it is connected by passages in the main body to the diaphragm. During idle and light load conditions, high manifold vacuum overcomes the force of the power valve spring and the valve is held closed. When the throttle opening is increased and intake manifold vacuum drops, the valve opens and fuel flows from the bowl through the power valve into the primary main well. This extra fuel is then added to the main metering system fuel to provide the increased air/fuel ratio necessary for high speed or heavy load operation.

Secondary Power Enrichment System

The secondary system is provided with an air velocity operated power system for fuel enrichment, Fig. 5. As the secondary throttle plate nears wide open position, air velocity through the secondary venturi creates a low pressure area at the discharge opening in the air horn. Fuel flows from the bowl through a vertical channel. During this time, air enters through a calibrated air bleed and mixes with the fuel, and this mixture is discharged through the opening.

Choke Plate Pulldown Adjustment

NOTE: On these units, it is necessary to remove the carburetor to remove the three rivets retaining the choke housing cover. Using a 1/8 inch or No. 30 drill bit, remove rivet head, then drive rivet out using a 1/8 inch

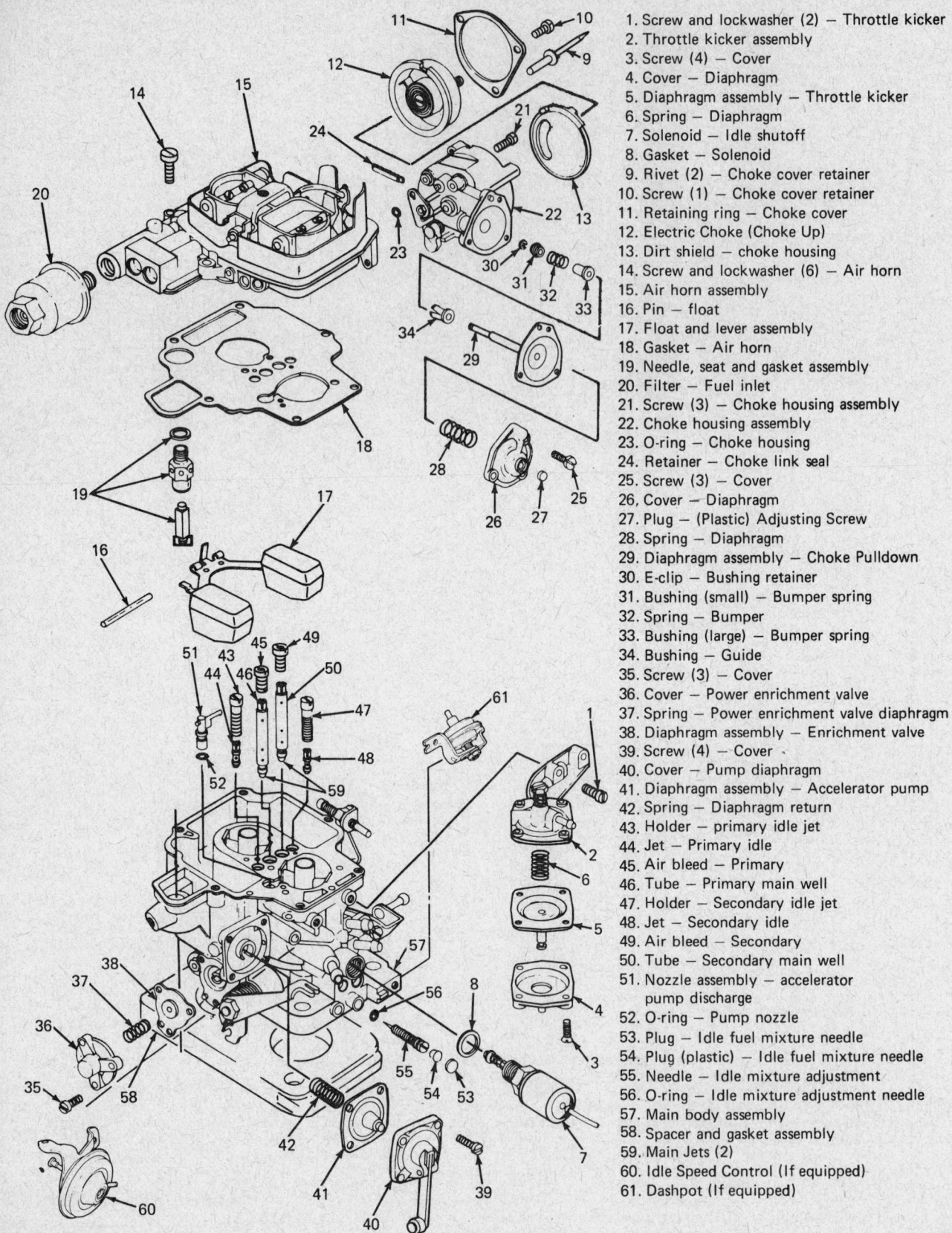

1. Screw and lockwasher (2) — Throttle kicker
2. Throttle kicker assembly
3. Screw (4) — Cover
4. Cover — Diaphragm
5. Diaphragm assembly — Throttle kicker
6. Spring — Diaphragm
7. Solenoid — Idle shutoff
8. Gasket — Solenoid
9. Rivet (2) — Choke cover retainer
10. Screw (1) — Choke cover retainer
11. Retaining ring — Choke cover
12. Electric Choke (Choke Up)
13. Dirt shield — choke housing
14. Screw and lockwasher (6) — Air horn
15. Air horn assembly
16. Pin — float
17. Float and lever assembly
18. Gasket — Air horn
19. Needle, seat and gasket assembly
20. Filter — Fuel inlet
21. Screw (3) — Choke housing assembly
22. Choke housing assembly
23. O-ring — Choke housing
24. Retainer — Choke link seal
25. Screw (3) — Cover
26. Cover — Diaphragm
27. Plug — (Plastic) Adjusting Screw
28. Spring — Diaphragm
29. Diaphragm assembly — Choke Pulldown
30. E-clip — Bushing retainer
31. Bushing (small) — Bumper spring
32. Spring — Bumper
33. Bushing (large) — Bumper spring
34. Bushing — Guide
35. Screw (3) — Cover
36. Cover — Power enrichment valve
37. Spring — Power enrichment valve diaphragm
38. Diaphragm assembly — Enrichment valve
39. Screw (4) — Cover
40. Cover — Pump diaphragm
41. Diaphragm assembly — Accelerator pump
42. Spring — Diaphragm return
43. Holder — primary idle jet
44. Jet — Primary idle
45. Air bleed — Primary
46. Tube — Primary main well
47. Holder — Secondary idle jet
48. Jet — Secondary idle
49. Air bleed — Secondary
50. Tube — Secondary main well
51. Nozzle assembly — accelerator pump discharge
52. O-ring — Pump nozzle
53. Plug — Idle fuel mixture needle
54. Plug (plastic) — Idle fuel mixture needle
55. Needle — Idle mixture adjustment
56. O-ring — Idle mixture adjustment needle
57. Main body assembly
58. Spacer and gasket assembly
59. Main Jets (2)
60. Idle Speed Control (If equipped)
61. Dashpot (If equipped)

Fig. 2 Exploded view of Motorcraft Model 740 carburetor. 1982–83

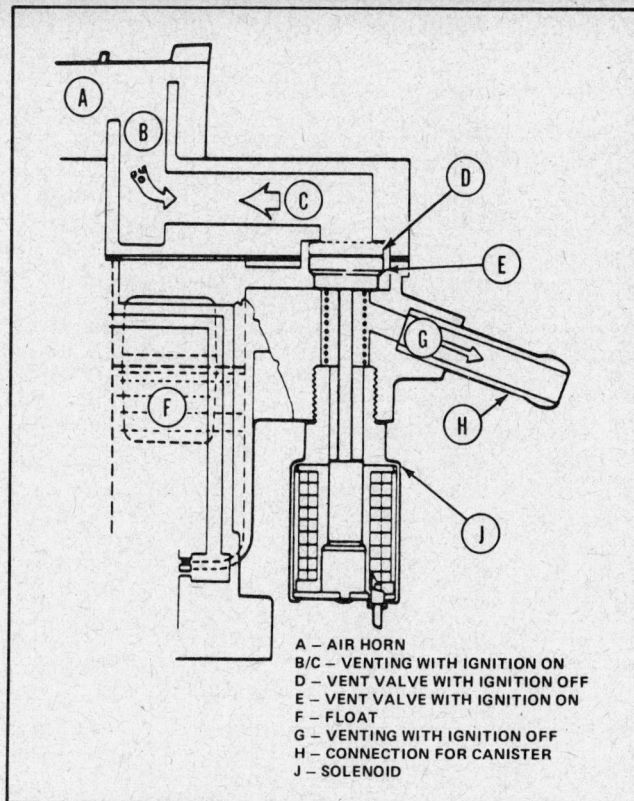

A – AIR HORN
B/C – VENTING WITH IGNITION ON
D – VENT VALVE WITH IGNITION OFF
E – VENT VALVE WITH IGNITION ON
F – FLOAT
G – VENTING WITH IGNITION OFF
H – CONNECTION FOR CANISTER
J – SOLENOID

Fig. 3 Carburetor fuel bowl vent system

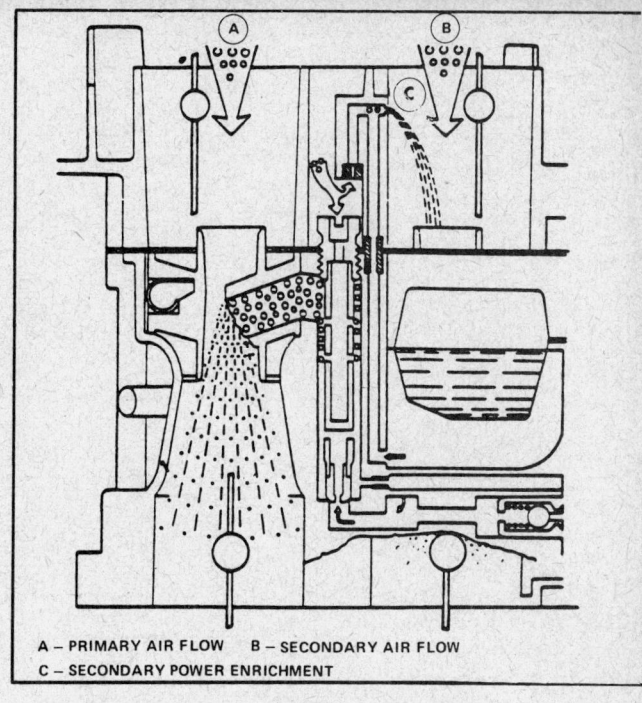

A – PRIMARY AIR FLOW   B – SECONDARY AIR FLOW
C – SECONDARY POWER ENRICHMENT

Fig. 5 Carburetor secondary power enrichment system

diameter punch.

Position fast idle adjusting screw on high step of fast idle cam. Using an external vacuum source, apply 17 inches Hg. of vacuum to vacuum channel adjacent to the primary bore on the base of the carburetor. The modulator spring should not be compressed. Using the specified drill, check clearance between choke plate and air horn wall. If clearance is not within limits as listed in the Model 740 Carburetor Adjustment Specifications, remove choke pulldown motor adjusting screw cover

and adjust as required.

Fast Idle Cam Kickdown Adjustment

Position fast idle screw on kickdown of fast idle cam against shoulder of top step. Manually close the primary choke plate and measure distance between choke plate and air horn wall. To obtain specified clearance, adjust right fork of choke bimetal shaft, which engages the fast idle cam, by bending upward or downward.

Float Level Adjustment

1982–83
Invert air horn with gasket in place and hold at a 45° angle so that the float tang rests lightly on inlet needle. Measure clearance at end of float. Adjust to specifications by removing float and bending float level adjusting tang as needed.

Float Drop Adjustment

1983
Hold air horn in normal position with gasket in place. Measure distance from air horn gasket to bottom of float. Adjust to specifications by removing float and bending float drop tang as needed, Fig. 6.

Dashpot Adjustment

1983
Depress dashpot into dashpot assembly. Measure distance between accelerator lever pad and dashpot. Adjust to specifications by loosening dashpot adjusting screw on end of dashpot and rotating dashpot as needed. Torque adjusting screw to 53 inch lbs. and recheck clearance.

Fig. 4 Carburetor secondary progression system

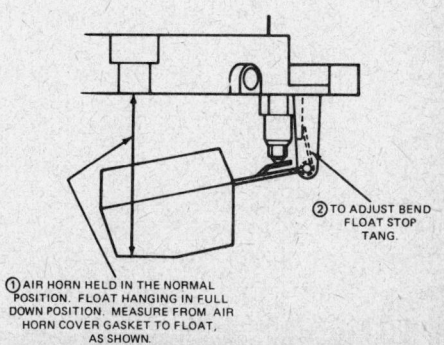

① AIR HORN HELD IN THE NORMAL POSITION. FLOAT HANGING IN FULL DOWN POSITION. MEASURE FROM AIR HORN COVER GASKET TO FLOAT, AS SHOWN.

② TO ADJUST BEND FLOAT STOP TANG.

Fig. 6 Float drop adjustment

CARBURETORS

MODEL 2100, 2150-2V CARB. ADJUSTMENT SPECIFICATIONS

See Tune Up Chart in car chapters for curb and fast idle speeds.

Year	Carb. Model ①	Float Level (Dry)	Fuel Level (Wet)	Pump Setting Hole No.②	Choke Plate Clearance (Pull down)	Fast Idle Cam Linkage Clearance	Dechoke Clearance ③	Dashpot Setting	Choke Setting
AMERICAN MOTORS									
1977	7RA2	5/16	25/32	No. 3	.136	.126	.250	—	1 Rich
	7RA2A	5/16	25/32	No. 3	.104	.089	.250	—	1 Rich
	7RA2C	5/16	25/32	No. 3	.130	.120	.250	—	1 Rich
	7RA2CP	5/16	25/32	No. 3	.136	.126	.250	—	1 Rich
	7DA2	5/16	25/32	No. 3	.136	.126	.250	—	Index
1978	8DA2	35/64	25/32	No. 3	.136	.126	.250	—	Index
	8DA2A	35/64	15/16	No. 3	.089	.078	.170	—	2 Rich
	8RA2	35/64	25/32	No. 3	.136	.126	.250	—	1 Rich
	8RA2A	35/64	25/32	No. 3	.089	.078	.170	—	2 Rich
	8RA2C	35/64	25/32	No. 3	.136	.120	.250	—	1 Rich
1979	9DA2	5/16	25/32	No. 3	.125	.113	.300	—	1 Rich
FORD MOTOR CO.									
1977	D7AE-ACA	7/16	13/16	No. 2	.156	.170	—	—	Index
	D7AE-AHA	7/16	13/16	No. 3	.179	.189	—	—	Index
	D7AE-AKA	7/16	13/16	No. 3	.179	.189	—	—	Index
	D7BE-YA	7/16	13/16	No. 2	.147	.167	—	—	1 Rich
	D7OE-LA	7/16	13/16	No. 4	.169	.189	—	—	3 Rich
	D7OE-RA	3/4	3/4	No. 3	.167	.187	—	—	2 Rich
	D7OE-TA	7/16	13/16	No. 3	.185	.205	—	—	2 Rich
	D7YE-EA	3/8	3/4	No. 3	.122	.142	—	—	2 Rich
1978	D8AE-JA	3/8	3/4	No. 3	.167	—	—	—	3 Rich
	D8BE-ACA	7/16	3/4	No. 4	.155	—	—	—	2 Rich
	D8BE-ADA	7/16	13/16	No. 2	.110	—	—	—	3 Rich
	D8BE-AEA	7/16	13/16	No. 2	.110	—	—	—	4 Rich
	D8BE-AFA	7/16	13/16	No. 2	.110	—	—	—	4 Rich
	D8BE-MB	3/8	13/16	No. 3	.122	—	—	—	Index
	D8DE-HA	7/16	13/16	No. 3	.157	—	—	—	Index
	D8KE-EA	7/16	13/16	No. 2	.135	—	—	—	3 Rich
	D8OE-BA	3/8	3/4	No. 3	.167	—	—	—	3 Rich
	D8OE-EA	7/16	13/16	No. 2	.136	—	—	—	Index
	D8OE-HA	7/16	13/16	No. 3	.180	—	—	—	2 Rich
	D8SE-CA	7/16	13/16	No. 3	.150	—	—	—	2 Rich
	D8SE-DA	7/16	13/16	No. 3	.147	—	—	—	3 Rich
	D8SE-EA	7/16	13/16	No. 3	.147	—	—	—	3 Rich
	D8SE-FA	3/8	13/16	No. 3	.147	—	—	—	3 Rich
	D8SE-GA	3/8	13/16	No. 3	.147	—	—	—	3 Rich
	D8WE-DA	7/16	13/16	No. 4	.143	—	—	—	1 Rich
	D8YE-AB	3/8	13/16	No. 3	.122	—	—	—	Index
	D8ZE-TA	3/8	3/4	No. 4	.122	—	—	—	Index
	D8ZE-UA	3/8	3/4	No. 4	.135	—	—	—	Index
	D84E-EA	7/16	13/16	No. 2	.110	—	—	—	3 Rich
1979	D9AE-AHA	7/16	13/16	No. 3	.147	—	.250	—	3 Rich
	D9AE-AJA	7/16	13/16	No. 3	.147	—	.250	—	3 Rich
	D9AE-ANB	7/16	13/16	No. 3	.129	—	—	—	1 Rich
	D9AE-APB	7/16	13/16	No. 3	.129	—	—	—	1 Rich
	D9AE-AVB	7/16	13/16	No. 3	.129	—	—	—	1 Rich
	D9AE-AYA	7/16	13/16	No. 3	.129	—	—	—	1 Rich
	D9AE-AYB	7/16	13/16	No. 3	.129	—	—	—	1 Rich
	D9AE-TB	7/16	13/16	No. 3	.129	—	—	—	2 Rich
	D9AE-UB	7/16	13/16	No. 3	.129	—	—	—	2 Rich

Continued

MODEL 2100, 2150-2V CARB. ADJUSTMENT SPECIFICATIONS—Continued

See Tune Up Chart in car chapters for curb and fast idle speeds.

Year	Carb. Model ①	Float Level (Dry)	Fuel Level (Wet)	Pump Setting Hole No.②	Choke Plate Clearance (Pull down)	Fast Idle Cam Linkage Clearance	Dechoke Clearance ③	Dashpot Setting	Choke Setting
FORD MOTOR CO.—Continued									
	D9BE-VB	7/16	13/16	No. 3	.153	—	.250	—	2 Rich
	D9BE-YB	7/16	13/16	No. 3	.153	—	—	—	2 Rich
	D9DE-NB	7/16	13/16	No. 3	.153	—	.250	—	2 Rich
	D9DE-RA	7/16	13/16	No. 2	.125	—	.115	—	3 Rich
	D9DE-RB	7/16	13/16	No. 2	.125	—	.115	—	3 Rich
	D9DE-RD	7/16	13/16	No. 2	.125	—	—	—	3 Rich
	D9DE-SA	7/16	13/16	No. 2	.125	—	.250	—	3 Rich
	D9DE-SC	7/16	13/16	No. 2	.125	—	—	—	3 Rich
	D9ME-BA	7/16	13/16	No. 2	.136	—	.115	—	Index
	D9ME-CA	7/16	13/16	No. 2	.136	—	.115	—	Index
	D9OE-CB	7/16	13/16	No. 3	.132	—	.115	—	3 Rich
	D9OE-DB	7/16	13/16	No. 3	.132	—	—	—	3 Rich
	D9OE-EA	7/16	13/16	No. 3	.132	—	.115	—	2 Rich
	D9OE-FA	7/16	13/16	No. 3	.132	—	.115	—	2 Rich
	D9SE-GA	7/16	13/16	No. 3	.150	—	.250	—	2 Rich
	D9VE-LC	3/8	3/4	No. 3	.145	—	.250	—	3 Rich
	D9VE-SA	7/16	13/16	No. 3	.147	—	—	—	3 Rich
	D9VE-UB	7/16	13/16	No. 3	.155	—	.250	—	3 Rich
	D9VE-VA	3/8	3/4	No. 3	.145	—	—	—	3 Rich
	D9VE-YB	3/8	3/4	No. 2	.145	—	.250	—	3 Rich
	D9WE-CB	7/16	13/16	No. 3	.132	—	—	—	3 Rich
	D9WE-DB	7/16	13/16	No. 3	.132	—	—	—	3 Rich
	D9WE-EB	7/16	13/16	No. 3	.132	—	—	—	2 Rich
	D9WE-FB	7/16	13/16	No. 3	.132	—	—	—	2 Rich
	D9WE-JA	7/16	13/16	No. 3	.150	—	.250	—	2 Rich
	D9WE-MB	7/16	13/16	No. 3	.132	—	—	—	1 Rich
	D9WE-NB	7/16	13/16	No. 3	.132	—	—	—	1 Rich
	D9YE-EA	7/16	13/16	No. 3	.118	—	.115	—	1 Rich
	D9YE-FA	7/16	13/16	No. 3	.118	—	.115	—	1 Rich
	D9YE-AB	7/16	13/16	No. 3	.118	—	.115	—	Index
	D9YE-BB	7/16	13/16	No. 3	.118	—	.115	—	Index
	D9YE-CA	7/16	13/16	No. 2	.118	—	.115	—	Index
	D9YE-DA	7/16	13/16	No. 2	.118	—	.115	—	Index
	D9ZE-AYA	7/16	13/16	No. 3	.138	—	.115	—	Index
	D9ZE-BFB	7/16	13/16	No. 2	.125	—	—	—	3 Rich
	D9ZE-BGB	7/16	13/16	No. 2	.125	—	—	—	3 Rich
	D9ZE-BHB	7/16	13/16	No. 2	.125	—	.250	—	3 Rich
	D9ZE-BJB	7/16	13/16	No. 2	.125	—	—	—	3 Rich
1980	D84E-TA	—	13/16	No. 2	.125	—	.250	—	3 Rich
	D84E-UA	—	13/16	No. 2	.125	—	.250	—	3 Rich
	D9AE-ANA	—	13/16	No. 3	.129	—	.250	—	1 Rich
	D9AE-APA	—	13/16	No. 3	.129	—	.250	—	1 Rich
	D9AE-AVA	—	13/16	No. 3	.129	—	.250	—	1 Rich
	D9AE-AYA	—	13/16	No. 3	.129	—	.250	—	1 Rich
	E0AE-AGA	—	13/16	No. 3	.159	—	.250	—	—
	E0BE-ASA	—	13/16	No. 2	.104	—	.250	—	3 Rich
	E0BE-ATA	—	13/16	No. 3	.116	—	.250	—	4 Rich
	E0BE-AUA	—	13/16	No. 3	.116	—	.250	—	4 Rich
	E0DE-SA	—	13/16	No. 2	.104	—	.250	—	3 Rich
	E0DE-TA	—	13/16	No. 2	.104	—	.250	—	3 Rich
	E0DE-VA	—	13/16	No. 2	.104	—	.250	—	—

Continued

CARBURETORS

See Tune Up Chart in car chapters for curb and fast idle speeds.

Year	Carb. Model ①	Float Level (Dry)	Fuel Level (Wet)	Pump Setting Hole No.②	Choke Plate Clearance (Pull down)	Fast Idle Cam Linkage Clearance	Dechoke Clearance ③	Dashpot Setting	Choke Setting
FORD MOTOR CO.—Continued									
	E0KE-CA	—	13/16	No. 3	.116	—	.250	—	3 Rich
	E0KE-DA	—	13/16	No. 3	.116	—	.250	—	3 Rich
	E0KE-GA	—	13/16	No. 3	.116	—	.250	—	4 Rich
	E0KE-HA	—	13/16	No. 3	.116	—	.250	—	4 Rich
	E0KE-JA	—	13/16	No. 3	.116	—	.250	—	4 Rich
	E0KE-KA	—	13/16	No. 3	.116	—	.250	—	4 Rich
	E0SE-GA	—	13/16	No. 2	.104	—	.250	—	3 Rich
	E0SE-HA	—	13/16	No. 2	.104	—	.250	—	3 Rich
	E0SE-LA	—	13/16	No. 2	.104	—	.250	—	3 Rich
	E0SE-MA	—	13/16	No. 2	.104	—	.250	—	3 Rich
	E0SE-NA	—	13/16	No. 2	.104	—	.250	—	3 Rich
	E0SE-PA	—	13/16	No. 2	.137	—	.250	—	3 Rich
	E0VE-FA	—	13/16	No. 2	.104	—	.250	—	—
	E0WE-BA	—	13/16	No. 2	.137	—	.250	—	3 Rich
	E0WE-CA	—	13/16	No. 2	.137	—	.250	—	3 Rich
	E04E-AAA	—	13/16	No. 2	.104	—	.250	—	4 Rich
	E04E-ABA	—	13/16	No. 2	.104	—	.250	—	4 Rich
	E04E-ACA	—	13/16	No. 2	.104	—	.250	—	4 Rich
	E04E-ADA	—	13/16	No. 2	.104	—	.250	—	4 Rich
	E04E-AEA	—	13/16	No. 2	.104	—	.250	—	4 Rich
	E04E-CA	—	13/16	No. 2	.104	—	.250	—	3 Rich
	E04E-EA	—	13/16	No. 2	.104	—	.250	—	3 Rich
	E04E-FA	—	13/16	No. 2	.104	—	.250	—	3 Rich
	E04E-KA	—	13/16	No. 2	.137	—	.250	—	3 Rich
	E04E-PA	—	13/16	No. 2	.104	—	.250	—	3 Rich
	E04E-RA	—	13/16	No. 2	.104	—	.250	—	3 Rich
	E04E-SA	—	13/16	No. 2	.104	—	.250	—	3 Rich
	E04E-VA	—	13/16	No. 2	.104	—	.250	—	3 Rich
	E04E-YA	—	13/16	No. 2	.104	—	.250	—	3 Rich
	E04E-ZA	—	13/16	No. 2	.104	—	.250	—	4 Rich
1981	E1AE-ADA	7/16	13/16	No. 3	.124	—	.250	—	V Notch
	E1AE-AEA	7/16	13/16	No. 3	.124	—	.250	—	V Notch
	E1AE-TA	—	13/16	No. 2	.104	—	.250	—	④
	E1AE-UA	—	13/16	No. 2	.104	—	.250	—	④
	E1AE-YA	Float	13/16	No. 3	.124	—	.250	—	④
	E1AE-ZA	—	13/16	No. 3	.124	—	.250	—	④
	E1KE-AA	7/16	13/16	No. 3	.120	—	.250	—	V Notch
	E1KE-BA	7/16	13/16	No. 3	.120	—	.250	—	V Notch
	E1KE-CA	7/16	13/16	No. 3	.124	—	.250	—	V Notch
	E1KE-DA	7/16	13/16	No. 3	.124	—	.250	—	V Notch
	E1KE-EA	7/16	13/16	No. 3	.124	—	.250	—	V Notch
	E1KE-FA	7/16	13/16	No. 3	.124	—	.250	—	V Notch
	E1KE-GA	7/16	13/16	No. 3	.120	—	.250	—	V Notch
	E1KE-HA	7/16	13/16	No. 3	.120	—	.250	—	V Notch
	E1KE-RA	7/16	13/16	No. 3	.124	—	.250	—	V Notch
	E1KE-SA	7/16	13/16	No. 3	.124	—	.250	—	V Notch
	E1WE-CA	7/16	13/16	No. 2	.120	—	.250	—	V Notch
	E1WE-DA	7/16	13/16	No. 2	.120	—	.250	—	V Notch
	E1WE-EA	7/16	13/16	No. 2	.120	—	.250	—	V Notch
	E1WE-FA	7/16	13/16	No. 2	.120	—	.250	—	V Notch
1982	E2AE-SA	7/16	13/16	No. 2	.172	—	.250	—	V-Notch
	E2BE-AAA, ABA	7/16	13/16	No. 2	.110	—	.250	.0045	V-Notch

Continued

MODEL 2100, 2150-2V CARB. ADJUSTMENT SPECIFICATIONS—Continued

See Tune Up Chart in car chapters for curb and fast idle speeds.

Year	Carb. Model ①	Float Level (Dry)	Fuel Level (Wet)	Pump Setting Hole No.②	Choke Plate Clearance (Pull down)	Fast Idle Cam Linkage Clearance	Dechoke Clearance ③	Dashpot Setting	Choke Setting
FORD MOTOR CO.—Continued									
	E2BE-ACA, ADA	7/16	13/16	No. 2	.113	—	.250	—	V-Notch
	E2BE-AGA, AHA	7/16	13/16	No. 2	.113	—	.250	.0041	V-Notch
	E2BE-AJA, AKA	7/16	13/16	No. 2	.110	—	.250	.0045	V-Notch
	E2BE-ALA, AMA	7/16	13/16	No. 2	.113	—	.250	—	V-Notch
	E2BE-UA	7/16	13/16	No. 2	.110	—	.250	.0045	V-Notch
	E2BE-VA	7/16	13/16	No. 2	.113	—	.250	.0045	V-Notch
	E2DE-JA	7/16	13/16	No. 2	.137	—	.250	.0045	V-Notch
	E2DE-KA	7/16	13/16	No. 2	.137	—	.250	.0045	V-Notch
	E2DE-LA	7/16	13/16	No. 2	.137	—	.250	.0045	V-Notch
	E2DE-MA	7/16	13/16	No. 2	.137	—	.250	.0045	V-Notch
	E2KE-AA, BA	7/16	13/16	No. 2	.140	—	.250	.0045	V-Notch
	E2KE-CA, DA	7/16	13/16	No. 2	.140	—	.250	.0045	V-Notch
	E2VE-CA	7/16	13/16	No. 2	.113	—	.250	.0045	V-Notch
	E2WE-EA	7/16	13/16	No. 2	.137	—	.250	.0045	V-Notch
	E2WE-FA	7/16	13/16	No. 2	.137	—	.250	.0045	V-Notch
	E2ZE-BAA, BBA	13/32	25/32	No. 2	.172	—	.250	.0045	V-Notch
	E2ZE-BCA, BDA	13/32	25/32	No. 2	.172	—	.250	.0045	V-Notch
	E2ZE-BGA, BHA	13/32	25/32	No. 2	.190	—	.250	.0045	V-Notch
	E24E-AA, BA	7/16	13/16	No. 2	.110	—	.250	.0045	V-Notch
	E24E-CA, DA	7/16	13/16	No. 2	.110	—	.250	.0045	V-Notch
	E24E-EA, FA	7/16	13/16	No. 2	.110	—	.250	.0045	V-Notch
	E24E-GA, HA	7/16	13/16	No. 2	.110	—	.250	—	V-Notch
	E24E-JA, KA	7/16	13/16	No. 2	.110	—	.250	—	V-Notch
	E25E-CA	7/16	13/16	No. 2	.137	—	.250	—	V-Notch
	E25E-DA	7/16	13/16	No. 2	.144	—	.250	.0045	V-Notch
1983	E3AE-ABA, ACA	7/16	13/16	No. 3	.103	—	.250	—	V-Notch
	E3AE-ADA, AEA	7/16	13/16	No. 3	.103	—	.250	—	V-Notch
	E3AE-AFA, AGA	7/16	13/16	No. 3	.103	—	.250	—	V-Notch
	E3AE-AKA, ALA	7/16	13/16	No. 3	.103	—	.250	—	V-Notch
	E3AE-EA	7/16	13/16	No. 2	—	—	.250	—	V-Notch
	E3AE-RA, SA	7/16	13/16	No. 3	.103	—	.250	—	V-Notch
	E3AE-TA, UA	7/16	13/16	No. 3	.103	—	.250	—	V-Notch
	E3CE-AA, BA	7/16	13/16	No. 3	.103	—	.250	.0045	V-Notch
	E3CE-EA, FA	7/16	13/16	No. 3	.113	—	.250	—	V-Notch
	E3CE-GA, HA	7/16	13/16	No. 3	.103	—	.250	—	V-Notch
	E3CE-JA, KA	7/16	13/16	No. 3	.103	—	.250	—	V-Notch
	E3CE-LA, MA	7/16	13/16	No. 3	.103	—	.250	—	V-Notch
	E3CE-NA, PA	7/16	13/16	No. 3	.120	—	.250	—	V-Notch
	E3SE-ALA, AMA	7/16	13/16	No. 3	.107	—	.250	—	V-Notch
	E3SE-ANA, APA	7/16	13/16	No. 3	.101	—	.250	—	V-Notch
	E3SE-ATA, AA	7/16	13/16	No. 3	.113	—	.250	—	V-Notch
	E3SE-BDA, BEA	7/16	13/16	No. 3	.107	—	.250	—	V-Notch
	E3SE-BFA, BGA	7/16	13/16	No. 3	.107	—	.250	—	V-Notch
	E3SE-EA, FA	7/16	13/16	No. 3	.113	—	.250	—	V-Notch
	E3SE-GA, HA	7/16	13/16	No. 3	.120	—	.250	—	V-Notch
	E3SE-JA, KA	7/16	13/16	No. 3	.101	—	.250	—	V-Notch
	E3SE-LA, MA	7/16	13/16	No. 3	.107	—	.250	—	V-Notch
	E3SE-NA, PA	7/16	13/16	No. 3	.107	—	.250	—	V-Notch

①—Stamped on left side of fuel bowl or on tag attached to bowl cover.
②—With link in inboard hole in pump lever.
③—Minimum clearance between choke plate and air horn wall with throttle plates wide open.
④—3 Rich or V Notch.

CARBURETORS

MODEL 2100, 2150-2V ADJUSTMENTS

Models 2100, 2150-2V, Figs. 1 Thru 3

These carburetors have two main bodies—the air horn and throttle body. The air horn assembly, which serves as a cover for the throttle body, contains the choke plate and vents for the fuel bowl. On 1977 Ford units and 1978–79 American Motors 2100 units, an external bowl vent valve is used. On 2150 units installed on V-6 engines, the air horn assembly contains a fuel deceleration system which consists of a metered pickup orifice in the fuel bowl and air/fuel mixing orifices and bleeds.

A choke modulator assembly is incorporated in 2100 units, Fig. 4. This system, through the use of a bimetal sensor and a series of diaphragms, pulls open the choke plate within 15–60 seconds. The system operates only during times when underhood temperatures are above 60 degrees F. On Ford units, an electric choke system is incorporated which opens choke plate within 1–1½ minutes when underhood temperatures are above approximately 55° to 60°. On 1977–78 Ford units, the electric choke system is supplied current to open the choke plate when underhood temperatures are between 80° and 110°F. On 1979–83 Ford units, the electric choke system is supplied current to open the choke when underhood temperatures are between 54 and 74°F.

Some 2150 units are equipped with an altitude compensation aneroid to improve high altitude emission control and driveability. Intake air entering the bypass valve is metered into the air flow above the throttle plates, leaning the mixture for high altitude operation. Air flow is controlled by a valve activated by an aneroid attached to the rear of the carburetor main body. Also, these units are equipped with a choke in the bypass air intake, linked to the main choke.

The throttle plate, accelerating pump, power (enrichment) valve and fuel bowl are in the throttle body. The choke housing is attached to the throttle body.

The two bodies each contain a main and booster venturi, main fuel discharge, accelerating pump discharge, idle fuel discharge, and a throttle plate. On some units, an antistall dashpot is attached to the carburetor when the vehicle is equipped with an automatic transmission.

Float Level (Dry) Adjustment

NOTE: 1983 units used on Thunderbird and XR-7 car models incorporate a spring loaded fuel inlet needle. The ball must not be compressed when checking float level. Seat the needle by raising the float with light finger pressure applied to the float tab, then lower the float until a light step is felt, and check the setting. Repeat this procedure several times before making final adjustment.

Fig. 5—This is a preliminary adjustment; the final adjustment must be made after the carburetor is mounted on the engine.

With air horn removed, float raised and fuel inlet needle seated, measure distance between top surface of throttle body and top surface of float. Take measurement near center of float at a point ⅛″ from free end of float.

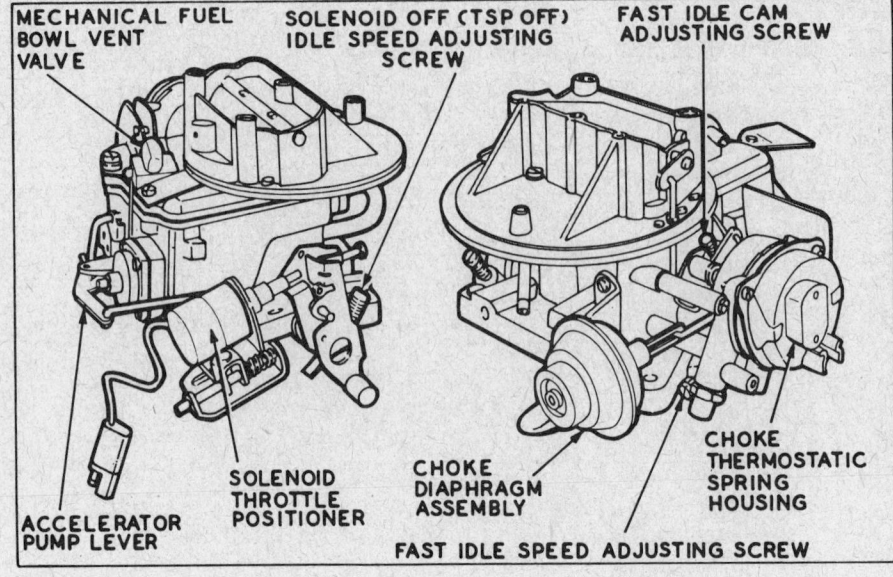

Fig. 1 Typical Motorcraft 2150 carburetor

If a cardboard float gauge is used, place the gauge in the corner of the enlarged end section of the fuel bowl as shown. The gauge should touch the float near the end but not on the end radius.

Depress the float tab to seat the fuel inlet needle. The float height is measured from the gasket surface of the throttle body with gasket removed. If the float height is not as listed in the *Ford Specifications Chart*, bend tab on float as required to achieve the desired setting.

Fuel Level (Wet) Adjustment

Fig. 6—With vehicle on a level surface, operate engine until normal temperature is reached, then stop engine and check fuel level as follows:
1. Remove carburetor air cleaner.
2. Remove air horn retaining screws and carburetor identification tag.
3. Temporarily leave air horn and gasket in position on throttle body and start engine.
4. Allow engine to idle for several minutes, then rotate air horn and remove air horn gasket to gain access to float or floats.
5. While engine is idling, use a standard depth gauge to measure vertical distance from top machined surface of throttle body to level of fuel in bowl. The measurement must be made at least ¼″ away from any vertical surface to assure an accurate reading.
6. If the fuel level is not as listed in the Specifications chart, stop the engine to avoid any fire hazard due to fuel spray when float setting is disturbed.
7. To adjust fuel level, bend float tab (contacting fuel inlet needle) upward in relation to original position to raise the fuel level, and downward to lower it.

8. Each time an adjustment is made to the float tab to alter the fuel level, the engine must be started and permitted to idle for at least three minutes to stabilize the fuel level. Check fuel level after each adjustment until the specified level is achieved.
9. Assemble carburetor with a new air horn gasket. Then adjust idle speed and mixture, and anti-stall dashpot, if so equipped.

Accelerating Pump Adjustment

Fig. 7
The primary throttle shaft lever (Overtravel lever) has four holes on most units. However, some units have three holes. On units with three holes in the overtravel lever, the holes are numbered as shown in Fig. 7 with the No. 1 hole omitted. The accelerator pump hole has two holes, inboard and outboard.

NOTE: The stroke should not be changed from the specified setting.

1977–79 Units
1. To release rod from retainer clip, press tab end of clip toward rod. Then, at the same time, press rod away from clip until it is disengaged.
2. Position clip over specified hole in overtravel lever. Press ends of clip together and insert operating rod through clip and lever. Release clip to engage rod.

1980 Units
1. Using a suitable punch, tap retainer pin from accelerator pump cover, then rotate pump link and rod assembly until key on rod end is aligned with key hole in pump overtravel lever.

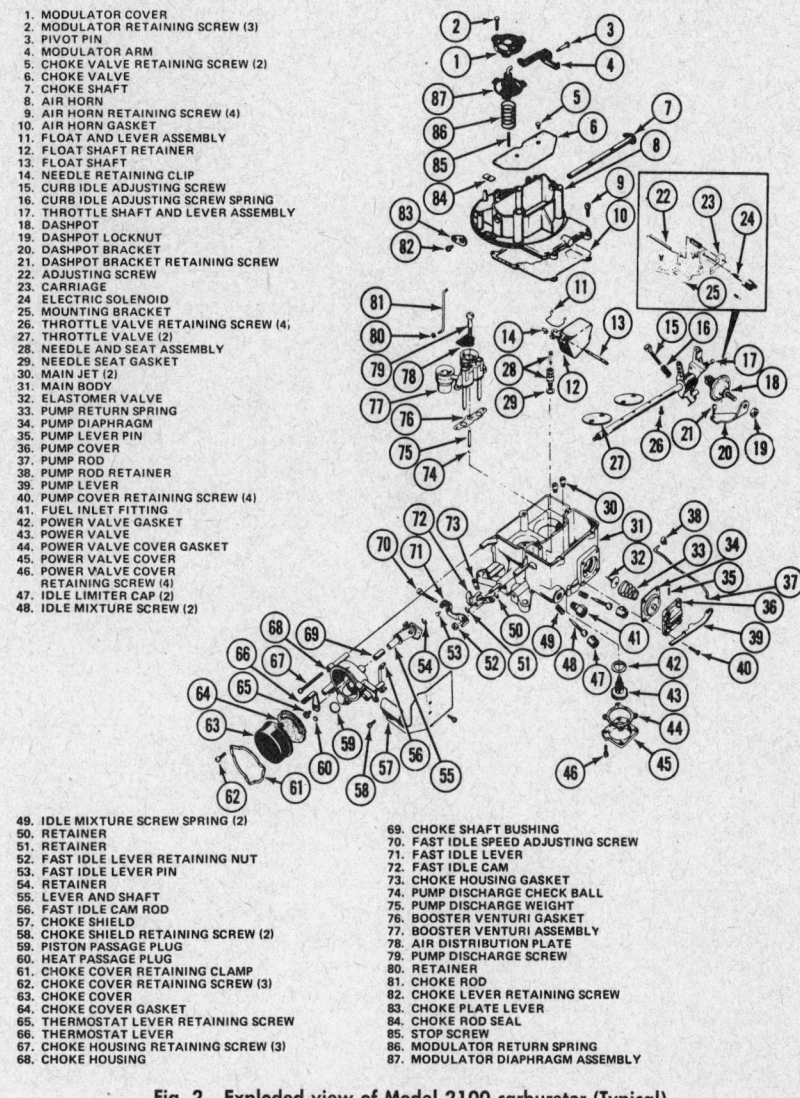

1. MODULATOR COVER
2. MODULATOR RETAINING SCREW (3)
3. PIVOT PIN
4. MODULATOR ARM
5. CHOKE VALVE RETAINING SCREW (2)
6. CHOKE VALVE
7. CHOKE SHAFT
8. AIR HORN
9. AIR HORN RETAINING SCREW (4)
10. AIR HORN GASKET
11. FLOAT AND LEVER ASSEMBLY
12. FLOAT SHAFT RETAINER
13. FLOAT SHAFT
14. NEEDLE RETAINING CLIP
15. CURB IDLE ADJUSTING SCREW
16. CURB IDLE ADJUSTING SCREW SPRING
17. THROTTLE SHAFT AND LEVER ASSEMBLY
18. DASHPOT
19. DASHPOT LOCKNUT
20. DASHPOT BRACKET
21. DASHPOT BRACKET RETAINING SCREW
22. ADJUSTING SCREW
23. CARRIAGE
24. ELECTRIC SOLENOID
25. MOUNTING BRACKET
26. THROTTLE VALVE RETAINING SCREW (4)
27. THROTTLE VALVE (2)
28. NEEDLE AND SEAT ASSEMBLY
29. NEEDLE SEAT GASKET
30. MAIN JET (2)
31. MAIN BODY
32. ELASTOMER VALVE
33. PUMP RETURN SPRING
34. PUMP DIAPHRAGM
35. PUMP LEVER PIN
36. PUMP COVER
37. PUMP ROD
38. PUMP ROD RETAINER
39. PUMP LEVER
40. PUMP COVER RETAINING SCREW (4)
41. FUEL INLET FITTING
42. POWER VALVE GASKET
43. POWER VALVE
44. POWER VALVE COVER GASKET
45. POWER VALVE COVER
46. POWER VALVE COVER
    RETAINING SCREW (4)
47. IDLE LIMITER CAP (2)
48. IDLE MIXTURE SCREW (2)

49. IDLE MIXTURE SCREW SPRING (2)
50. RETAINER
51. RETAINER
52. FAST IDLE LEVER RETAINING NUT
53. FAST IDLE LEVER PIN
54. RETAINER
55. LEVER AND SHAFT
56. FAST IDLE CAM ROD
57. CHOKE SHIELD
58. CHOKE SHIELD RETAINING SCREW (2)
59. PISTON PASSAGE PLUG
60. HEAT PASSAGE PLUG
61. CHOKE COVER RETAINING CLAMP
62. CHOKE COVER RETAINING SCREW (3)
63. CHOKE COVER
64. CHOKE COVER GASKET
65. THERMOSTAT LEVER RETAINING SCREW
66. THERMOSTAT LEVER
67. CHOKE HOUSING RETAINING SCREW (3)
68. CHOKE HOUSING

69. CHOKE SHAFT BUSHING
70. FAST IDLE SPEED ADJUSTING SCREW
71. FAST IDLE LEVER
72. FAST IDLE CAM
73. CHOKE HOUSING GASKET
74. PUMP DISCHARGE CHECK BALL
75. PUMP DISCHARGE WEIGHT
76. BOOSTER VENTURI GASKET
77. BOOSTER VENTURI ASSEMBLY
78. AIR DISTRIBUTION PLATE
79. PUMP DISCHARGE SCREW
80. RETAINER
81. CHOKE ROD
82. CHOKE LEVER RETAINING SCREW
83. CHOKE PLATE LEVER
84. CHOKE ROD SEAL
85. STOP SCREW
86. MODULATOR RETURN SPRING
87. MODULATOR DIAPHRAGM ASSEMBLY

Fig. 2   Exploded view of Model 2100 carburetor (Typical)

2. Position rod in specified hole in over-travel lever, then reassemble pump link and rod assembly.

1981-83 Units
1. Support accelerator pump housing at roll pin connection.
2. Using a suitable punch, tap retainer pin from accelerator pump cover and lever.
3. Rotate lever and rod assembly upward until key on rod end is aligned with key hole on pump overtravel lever.
4. Remove rod, clip and pin assembly from overtravel lever.
5. Position rod, clip and pin assembly in the specified hole, then reassemble pump link and rod assembly.

Choke Plate Clearance (Pulldown) Adjustment

2100 UNITS
1977 American Motors
1. Loosen the choke over retaining screws.

Rotate the choke cover ¼ turn counter-clockwise (rich) from index and tighten the retaining screws. Disconnect the choke heat inlet tube.
2. Align the fast idle speed adjusting screw with the second step of the fast idle cam, Fig. 8
3. Start the engine without moving the accelerator linkage. Turn the fast idle cam lever adjusting screw out counter-clockwise 3 full turns.
4. Measure the clearance between the lower edge of the choke valve and the air horn wall. Refer to *2100 Specifications Chart* for the correct setting. Adjust by grasping the modulator arm securely with a pair of pliers at point "A" and twisting the arm at point "B" with a second pair of pliers. Twist toward the front of the carburetor to increase clearance and toward the rear to decrease clearance, Fig. 9

CAUTION: Use extreme care while twisting

the modulator arm to avoid damaging the nylon piston rod of the modulator assembly.

NOTE: Connect the choke heat tube. Turn the fast idle cam lever adjusting screw in (clockwise) 3 full turns. Do not reset the choke cover until the fast idle cam linkage adjustment has been performed.

1978-79 American Motors
1. Loosen choke cover retaining screws and rotate cover ¼ turn counterclockwise, then tighten one screw.
2. Disconnect choke heat inlet tube. Align fast idle speed adjusting screw with second step of fast idle cam.
3. Start engine without moving accelerator linkage. Turn fast idle cam lever adjust-

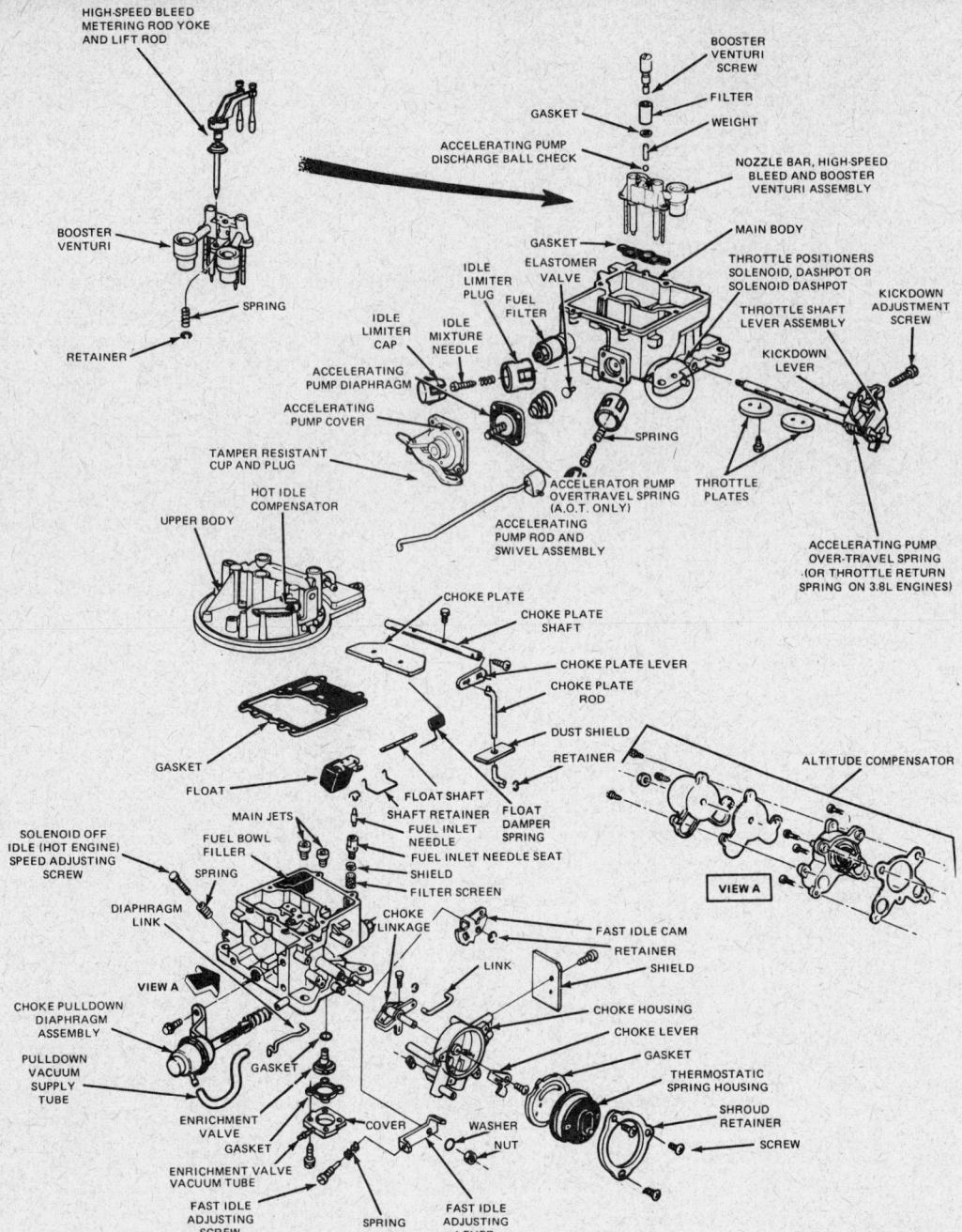

Fig. 3 Exploded view of Model 2150 carburetor (Typical)

ing screw counterclockwise three turns. Measure clearance between upper edge of choke valve and air horn wall, Fig. 10. Refer to 2100, 2150 Specification Chart.
4. Adjust by turning set screw on bottom of modulator.
5. Stop engine and connect choke heat tube. Adjust fast idle cam clearance.

2150 UNITS

CAUTION: Do not attempt to turn the diaphragm adjusting screw without first loosening the Loctite which has been applied to the threads of the screw. The Loctite can be softened by heating the area around the screw

with an electric soldering gun or by applying Loctite to the screw. When the Loctite has softened enough, the screw can be turned without causing any damage.

1977–78 American Motors & 1977–80 Ford
1. Set throttle on fast idle cam top step, Fig. 8, then loosen choke thermostatic housing retaining screws and set housing 90° in rich direction.
2. Activate pulldown motor by manually forcing pulldown control diaphragm link in direction of applied vacuum or by applying vacuum to external vacuum tube.

3. Check clearance between lower edge of choke plate and center of carburetor air horn wall nearest fuel bowl Fig. 11. Refer to 2150 Specifications Chart. If clearance is not as specified, reset by adjusting diaphragm stop on end of choke pull-down diaphragm.

NOTE: After completing choke plate clearance adjustment, leave choke thermostatic housing in the full rich position and check fast idle cam setting as described under Fast Idle Cam Position Adjustment.

1981–83 Ford
1. Remove carburetor from engine, then us-

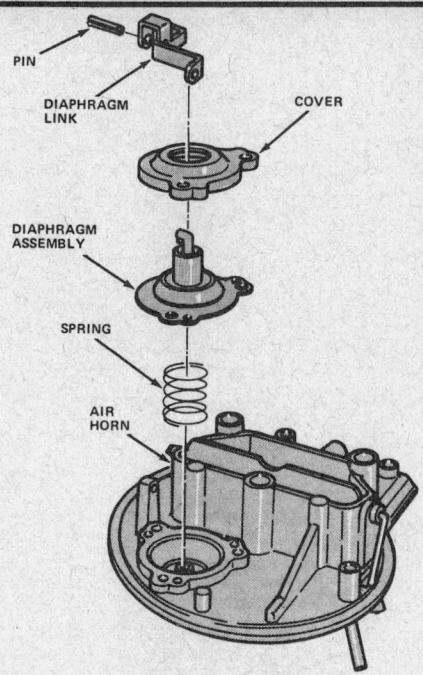

Fig. 4 Motorcraft 2100 choke diaphragm assembly

ing a suitable punch, center punch choke retaining cap screw heads.

2. Using a ¼ inch drill bit, drill screw heads deep enough to remove retainer from cap, then remove choke cap by inserting a flat chisel between cap and gasket.

3. Remove remaining portion of choke cap retaining screws using pliers. Also clean epoxy sealer and gasket from choke cap and housing mating surfaces.

4. Rotate choke thermostatic housing to lightly close choke plate, then rotate housing an additional 90°.

5. Using the edge of a file, file a ⅛ inch deep groove on pulldown motor tamper resistance cover ¼ inch from rear edge of pulldown motor.

NOTE: On 1982–83 models, a tamper resistance cover is not used on the pulldown motor.

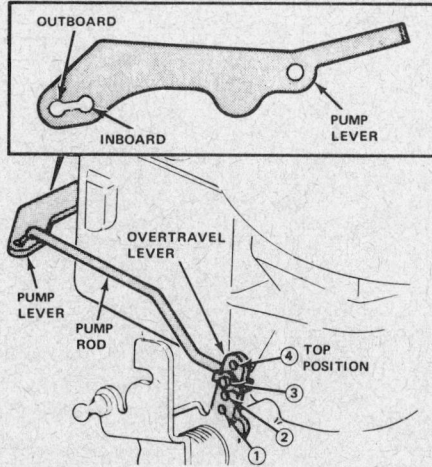

Fig. 7 Pump stroke adjusting points, 2100, 2150

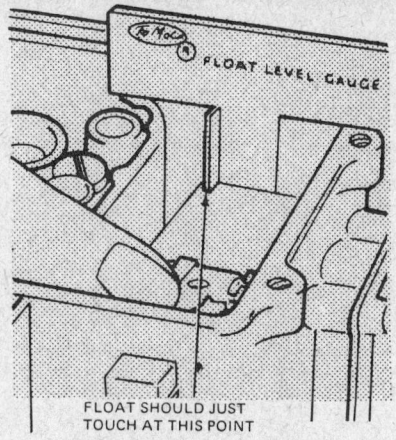

FLOAT SHOULD JUST TOUCH AT THIS POINT

Fig. 5 Float level adjustment.

6. Using a suitable awl inserted in filed groove, carefully tap plug from pulldown motor.

7. Activate pulldown motor using an external vacuum source or by manually forcing the diaphragm to the retracted position.

8. Using a drill bit of the specified size, measure clearance between choke plate and carburetor air horn wall, Fig. 11.

9. Loosen pulldown motor adjusting screw as described in Caution above, then remove adjusting screw and clean remaining thread locking compound.

10. Reinstall adjusting screw and adjust. Rotate adjusting screw clockwise to decrease pulldown and counter-clockwise to increase pulldown.

11. After completing adjustment, use Loctite 240 or equivalent to lock adjusting screw

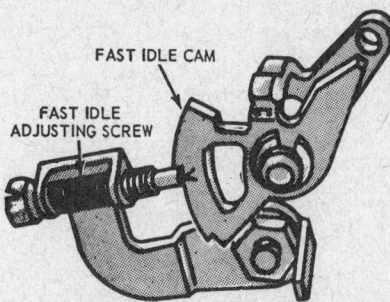

FAST IDLE CAM

FAST IDLE ADJUSTING SCREW

CONVENTIONAL ONE - PIECE FAST IDLE LEVER

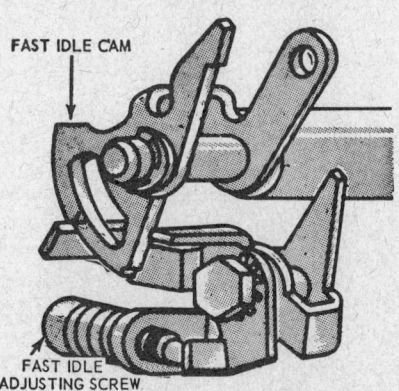

FAST IDLE CAM

FAST IDLE ADJUSTING SCREW

TWO - PIECE FAST IDLE LEVER

Fig. 8 Motorcraft fast idle adjustment 2100, 2150

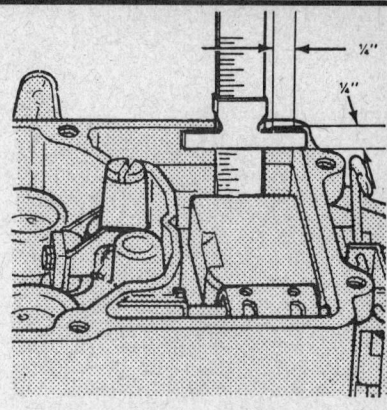

Fig. 6 Fuel level adjustment.

in position, then tap tamper resistance cover into place on pulldown motor. Apply epoxy sealer MT13 or equivalent to edge and groove on cover.

NOTE: After completing choke plate clearance adjustment, leave choke thermostatic housing in the full rich position and check fast idle cam setting as described under Fast Idle Cam

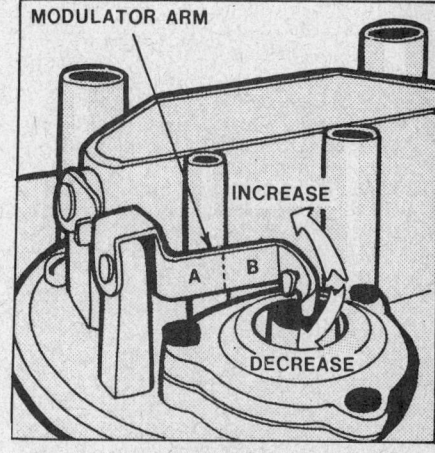

MODULATOR ARM

INCREASE

A B

DECREASE

Fig. 9 Choke plate pulldown clearance 2100. 1977 American Motors.

GAUGE

DECREASE

INCREASE

Fig. 10 Choke plate pulldown clearance adjust. 1978–79 American Motors 2100 units

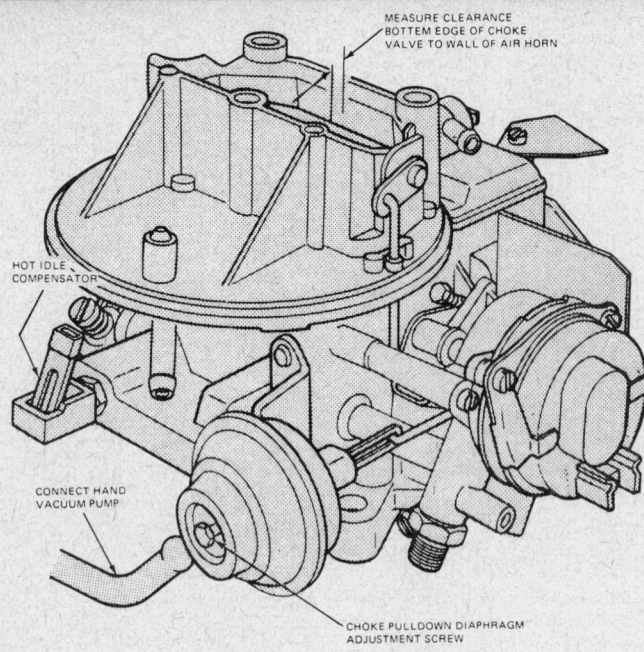

MEASURE CLEARANCE BOTTOM EDGE OF CHOKE VALVE TO WALL OF AIR HORN

HOT IDLE COMPENSATOR

CONNECT HAND VACUUM PUMP

CHOKE PULLDOWN DIAPHRAGM ADJUSTMENT SCREW

Fig. 11 Choke plate pulldown adjustment, 2150 (Typical). 1977–82 Ford

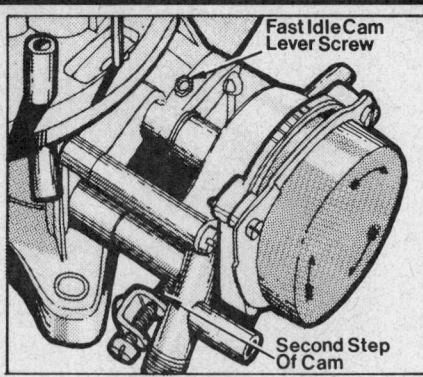

Fast Idle Cam Lever Screw

Second Step Of Cam

Fig. 12 Fast idle cam clearance adjustment 2100. 1977–79 American Motors

Choke Unloader Tang

Bend Tang

Fast Idle Cam

Fig. 13 Choke unloader adjustment 1977–79 American Motors

Position Adjustment.

1977–79 American Motors Units
1. Push downward on fast idle cam lever until fast idle speed adjusting screw contacts the second step of cam and is against the high step shoulder.
2. Measure clearance between lower edge of choke valve and air horn wall. Refer to the 2100, 2150 Specifications Chart.
3. Adjust by turning fast idle cam lever screw, Fig. 12.
4. Set choke cover housing to specifications.

FAST IDLE CAM POSITION ADJUSTMENT

1977–83 Ford Units
1. With choke thermostatic housing in the rich position, cycle throttle to set fast idle cam.
2. Activate pull down by applying an external vacuum source.
3. Cycle throttle and observe fast idle cam. Fast idle cam should drop to the kickdown step and fast idle speed screw should be opposite the V notch on the cam.
4. Align screw with notch on fast idle cam by rotating screw on fast idle cam lever.
5. Reconnect vacuum hose to choke pulldown motor.
6. Reset choke thermostatic housing to specification listed in Model 2100, 2150 Carburetor Adjustment Specifications.

NOTE: On 1981–83 units, apply three ½ inch beads of MT-13 sealant to each side of choke cap gasket adjacent to choke housing screw bosses, then position gasket to housing. Position choke cap and retainer to housing, then install break-away screws finger tight. Tighten each screw until head breaks off, then reinstall carburetor.

Dechoke (Choke Unloader) Clearance

1977–79 American Motors Units
1. Hold throttle fully open and apply pressure on choke valve toward the closed position.
2. Measure clearance between lower edge of choke valve and air horn wall. Refer to the 2100, 2150 Specifications Chart.
3. Adjust by bending the unloader tang contacting fast idle cam, Fig. 13. Bending the tang toward the cam increases the clearance and bending the tang away from the cam decreases the clearance.

NOTE: Do not bend unloader tang downward from a horizontal plane.

4. After making adjustment, open the throttle until the unloader tang is directly below the fast idle cam pivot. A clearance of .070 inch must be obtained between the unloader tang and the edge of the fast idle cam, Fig. 14.

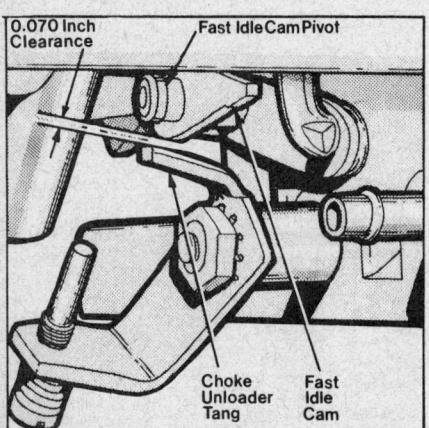

0.070 Inch Clearance

Fast Idle Cam Pivot

Choke Unloader Tang

Fast Idle Cam

Fig. 14 Choke unloader to fast idle cam clearance. 1977–79 American Motors

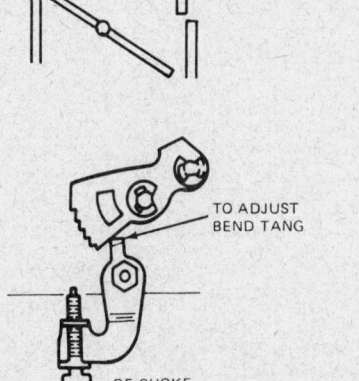

MEASURE HERE

TO ADJUST BEND TANG

DE-CHOKE

Fig. 15 Dechoke clearance adjustment. 1977–83 Ford 2150 units

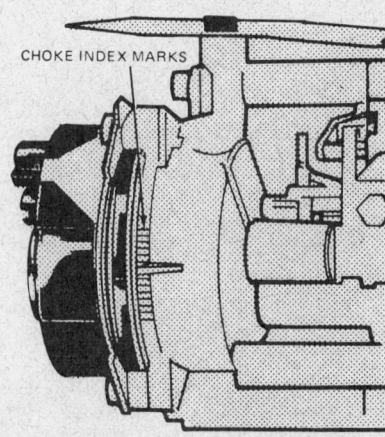

CHOKE INDEX MARKS

Fig. 16 Automatic choke adjustment. 2100, 2150

1977–83 Ford Units

1. Hold throttle in the wide open position and measure clearance between lower edge of choke plate and air horn wall using the specified size drill. Refer to Models 2100 and 2150 Carburetor Specifica-

tions.
2. To adjust clearance, bend metal tang on fast idle speed lever attached to throttle shaft, Fig. 15.
3. Rotate throttle lever to ensure minimum throttle effort during dechoke tang engagement.

Automatic Choke Valve Tension

Turn thermostatic spring cover against spring tension until index mark on cover is aligned with mark specified in the *Ford Specifications Chart* on choke housing, Fig. 16.

MODEL 2700 & 7200 VV CARB. ADJUSTMENT SPECIFICATIONS

See Tune Up Chart for Curb and Fast idle speeds.

Year	Carb Model (Code 9510)	Float Level (Dry)	Float Drop	Internal Vent	Venturi Valve Limiter	Fast Idle Cam	Control Vacuum Regulator	Choke Setting
1977	D7Z3-AC	13/64	1 15/32	.010	61/64	①	⑲	Index
	D7Z3-BD	13/64	1 15/32	.010	13/32	②	⑲	Index
	D7ZE-GD, GE	13/64	1 15/32	.010	61/64	①	⑲	Index
	D7Z3-GE	13/64	1 15/32	.010	61/64	①	⑲	Index
	77TF-MA, NA	13/64	1 15/32	.010	61/64	①	⑲	Index
1978	D8BE-EB	13/64	1 15/32	.010	3/4	①	—	Index
	D84E-DB	13/64	1 15/32	.010	61/64	①	—	Index
1979	D84E-KA	13/64	1 15/32	.010	61/64	①	.225–.235	Index
	D84E-VA	13/64	1 15/32	.010	③	①	.225–.235	Index
	D9AE-ACA	13/64	1 15/32	.010	3/4	①	.245–.255	Index
	D9AE-CB	13/64	1 15/32	.010	③	④	.085–.095	Index
	D9AE-JB	13/64	1 15/32	.010	③	①	.085–.095	Index
	D9AE-YB	13/64	1 15/32	.010	③	①	.085–.095	Index
	D9AE-ZB	13/64	1 15/32	.010	③	④	.085–.095	Index
	D9BE-AFA	13/64	1 15/32	.010	③	④	.225–.235	Index
	D9DE-HB	13/64	1 15/32	.010	③	⑤	.225–.235	Index
	D9ME-AA	13/64	1 15/32	—	3/4	①	.245–.255	Index
	D9ME-ACA	13/64	1 15/32	.010	⑥	①	.245–.255	Index
	D9ZE-AZB	13/64	1 15/32	.010	③	④	.225–.235	Index
	D9ZE-BEA	13/64	1 15/32	.010	③	④	.225–.235	Index
	D9ZE-LB	13/64	1 15/32	.010	13/32	①	.225–.235	Index
	D9ZE-LC	13/64	1 15/32	.010	⑦	⑧	.225–.235	Index
	D94E-EB	13/64	1 15/32	.010	③	④	.225–.235	Index
	D94E-GA	13/64	1 15/32	.010	③	④	.225–.235	Index
	D94E-JA	13/64	1 15/32	.010	③	④	.225–.235	Index
	D945-FA	13/64	1 15/32	.010	③	④	.225–.235	Index
1980	E0AE-AAA	13/64	1 15/32	—	③	⑨	.070–.080	1 Rich
	E0AE-ACA	13/64	1 15/32	—	③	⑨	.070–.080	1 Rich
	E0AE-ADA	13/64	1 15/32	—	⑩	①	.270–.280	Index
	E0AE-AHA	13/64	1 15/32	—	⑩	⑪	—	—
	E0AE-APA	13/64	1 15/32	—	③	⑨	.070–.080	1 Rich
	E0AE-ATA	13/64	1 15/32	—	⑩	①	.270–.280	—
	E0AE-AVA	13/64	1 15/32	—	③	⑨	.070–.080	—
	E0AE-BA	13/64	1 15/32	—	⑩	⑫	.245–.255	Index
	E0AE-LA ⑬⑭	13/64	1 15/32	—	⑩	⑫	.245–.255	Index
	E0AE-LA ⑬⑮	13/64	1 15/32	—	⑩	①	.245–.255	—
	E0AE-PA	13/64	1 15/32	—	⑩	⑫	.245–.255	Index
	E0AE-ZA	13/64	1 15/32	—	③	⑨	.070–.080	1 Rich
1981	D9AE-AZA	13/64	1 15/32	—	③	①	.245–.255	Index
	E1AE-AAA	13/64	1 15/32	—	③	⑨	.070–.080	Index
	E1AE-ACA	13/64	1 15/32	—	⑯	⑰	.245–.255	Index
	E1AE-AGA	13/64	1 15/32	—	⑩	⑰	.245–.255	Index
	E1AE-KA	13/64	1 15/32	—	⑩	①	.245–.255	Index
	E1AE-LA	13/64	1 15/32	—	⑱	⑰	.245–.255	Index
	E1AE-MA	13/64	1 15/32	—	⑩	⑰	.245–.255	Index
	E1AE-SA	13/64	1 15/32	—	⑱	⑰	.245–.255	Index
	E1DE-AA	13/64	1 15/32	—	⑯	⑰	.245–.255	Index
	E1SE-EA	13/64	1 15/32	—	⑩	⑰	.245–.255	Index

Continued

CARBURETORS

MODEL 2700 & 7200 VV CARB. ADJUSTMENT SPECIFICATIONS—Continued

See Tune Up Chart for Curb and Fast idle speeds.

Year	Carb Model (Code 9510)	Float Level (Dry)	Float Drop	Internal Vent	Venturi Valve Limiter	Fast Idle Cam	Control Vacuum Regulator	Choke Setting
	E1SE-VA	13/64	1 15/32	—	⑩	⑫	.245–.255	Index
	E1VE-AA	13/64	1 15/32	—	⑩	⑰	.245–.255	Index
1982	E1AE-ACA	13/64	1 15/32	—	⑩	⑰	.245–.255	Index
	E1AE-AGA	13/64	1 15/32	—	⑩	⑰	.245–.255	Index
	E1AE-SA	13/64	1 15/32	—	⑱	⑰	.245–.255	1 Rich
	E2AE-ABA, RA	13/64	1 15/32	—	⑩	⑰	.245–.255	Index
	E2AE-AGA, AHA	13/64	1 15/32	—	⑱	⑰	.245–.255	1 Rich
	E2AE-LB	13/64	1 15/32	—	⑩	⑰	.295–.305	Index
	E2AE-LC	13/64	1 15/32	—	⑩	⑰	.295–.305	Index
	E2AE-MA	13/64	1 15/32	—	⑱	⑰	.245–.255	1 Rich
	E2AE-MB	13/64	1 15/32	—	⑱	⑰	.245–.255	1 Rich
	E2AE-TA	13/64	1 15/32	—	⑱	⑰	.245–.255	Index
	E2AE-TB	13/64	1 15/32	—	⑱	⑰	.245–.255	Index
	E2DE-NA, SA, TA, UA	13/64	1 15/32	—	⑩	⑰	.295–.305	Index
	E2SE-DA, FA	13/64	1 15/32	—	⑩	⑰	.070–.080	Index
	E2SE-DB	13/64	1 15/32	—	⑩	⑰	.070–.080	Index
	E25E-ABA	13/64	1 15/32	—	⑩	⑰	.245–.255	Index
	E25E-AC, YA	13/64	1 15/32	—	⑩	⑰	.070–.080	Index
	E25E-FA	13/64	1 15/32	—	⑩	⑰	.245–.255	Index
	E25E-GA, SA, UA	13/64	1 15/32	—	⑩	⑰	.245–.255	Index
	E25E-GB, TA	13/64	1 15/32	—	⑩	⑰	.245–.255	Index

①—1 Notch rich on third step.
②—Bobcat and Pinto, 4 Notches rich on second step. Except Bobcat and Pinto, 1 notch rich on third step.
③—Limiter adjusting screw setting, .94–.98 inch; limiter stop screw setting, .99–1.01 inch.
④—5 notches rich on second highest step.
⑤—5 notches rich on highest step.
⑥—Limiter adjusting screw setting, .73–.77 inch; limiter stop screw setting, .99–1.01 inch.
⑦—Limiter adjusting screw setting, .38–.42

inch; limiter stop screw setting, .73–.77 inch.
⑧—1 notch rich on second step.
⑨—1 notch rich on forth step.
⑩—Limiter adjusting screw setting, .39–.41 inch; limiter stop screw setting, .99–1.01 inch.
⑪—.13/.14 on third highest step.
⑫—.14/.15 on third highest step.
⑬—Refer to engine calibration code on engine identification lable located at rear of left valve cover. The calibration code is located on the label after the engine code number

and is preceded by the letter C and the revision code is located below the calibration code and is preceded by the letter R.
⑭—Except Calibration code 012C-R5.
⑮—Calibration code 012C-R5.
⑯—Limiter adjusting screw setting, .48–.52 inch; limiter stop screw setting .99–1.01 inch.
⑰—.355–.365 inch on second step.
⑱—Limiter adjusting screw setting, .74–.76 inch; limiter stop screw setting, .99–1.01 inch.
⑲—See text.

MODEL 2700 & 7200 VV ADJUSTMENTS

The Motorcraft model 2700 and carburetors, Figs. 1 through 4 are two bore, variable venturi units. The model 7200 carburetor is used in conjunction with EEC system. The variable venturis, located at the top of the throttle bores, are small oblong castings that slide across the throttle bores. The venturis are positioned by a spring loaded diaphragm valve regulated by a vacuum signal obtained below the venturis in the throttle bores. As the throttle is opened, the vacuum signal increases, thereby, opening the venturis and permitting more air to enter the carburetor while maintaining approximately the same venturi air velocity.

Tapered metering rods are attached to the venturi valves and fit into the metering jets. As the venturis are positioned in response to air demand, the metering rods slide in the jets to provide the proper air-fuel mixture during all modes of engine operation. By the use of the variable venturi principle, the only auxiliary fuel metering systems required are the accelerator pump, idle trim, starting enrichment and cold running enrichment.

Some 1978 2700 units are equipped with an altitude compensation feature which provides improved emission control and driveability at

high altitude. This compensation is accomplished through the use of a bellows and pintle valve unit, Fig. 5. The bellows senses barometric pressure and opens the pintle valve accordingly. Opening the valve allows control vacuum to lower the pressure in the fuel bowl area, causing the fuel mixture to be leaner.

Fuel Level Adjustment

Fig. 6—Remove upper body assembly and replace the upper body gasket. With the upper body inverted, measure vertical distance from the upper body cast surface and the bottom of float. To adjust, bend float operating lever away from the fuel inlet needle to decrease the setting or toward the needle to increase the setting. After adjustment, the float pontoon must be parallel with the gasket surface. Check and adjust float drop, if necessary.

Float Drop Adjustment

Fig. 7—With upper body held in upright position, measure verticle distance between the cast surface of the upper body and the bottom of float. To adjust, bend stop tab on float lever away from hinge pin to increase setting or toward the hinge pin to decrease setting.

Cold Enrichment Metering Rod Adjustment

NOTE: On some 1979–82 vehicles, it is necessary to remove the carburetor to remove the rivets on the choke housing. Remove the top two rivets with a 1/8 inch diameter twist drill. The third bottom rivet is located in a "Blind" hole and is removed by lightly tapping the rear of the retainer ring using a punch and hammer. The rivet, retainer ring, choke housing and gasket can then be removed.

1977–79 Units

Fig. 8—Remove choke cap and install stator cap, tool T77L-9848-A as a weight to seat the cold enrichment rod. Install dial indicator with plunger contacting the top of the cold enrichment rod and zero the indicator. Remove the stator cap and reinstall at the index position. The dial indicator should read .125 inch. If rod height is not within specifications, turn adjusting nut clockwise to increase height or counterclockwise to decrease height. Reinstall choke cap and position at proper setting.

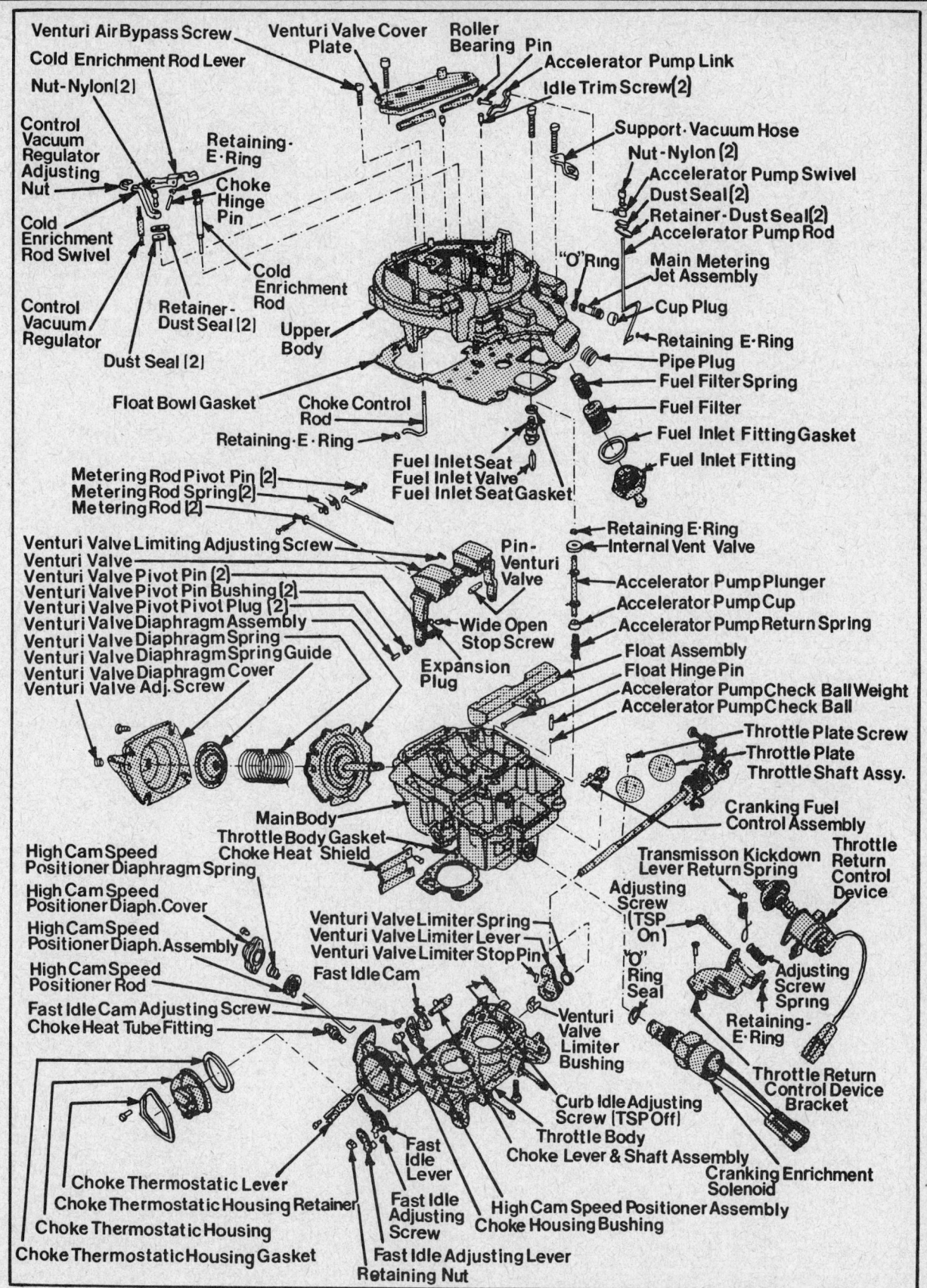

Fig. 1 Motorcraft model 2700 variable venturi carburetor, disassembled

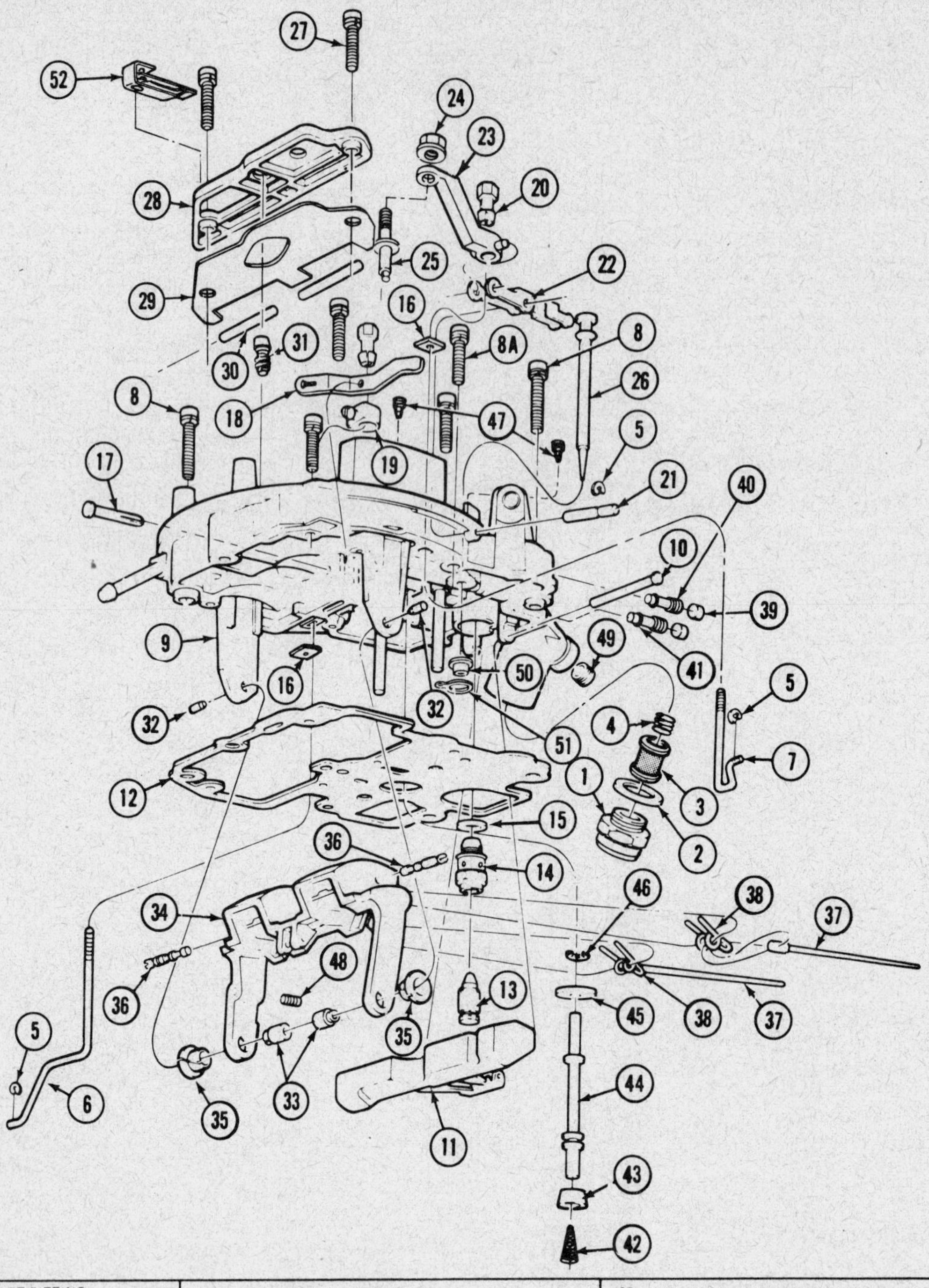

CARBURETORS

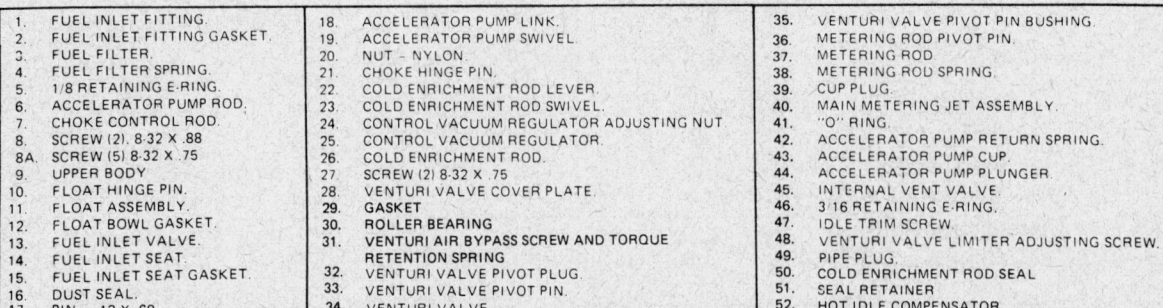

1. FUEL INLET FITTING.	18. ACCELERATOR PUMP LINK.	35. VENTURI VALVE PIVOT PIN BUSHING.
2. FUEL INLET FITTING GASKET.	19. ACCELERATOR PUMP SWIVEL.	36. METERING ROD PIVOT PIN.
3. FUEL FILTER.	20. NUT – NYLON.	37. METERING ROD.
4. FUEL FILTER SPRING.	21. CHOKE HINGE PIN.	38. METERING ROD SPRING.
5. 1/8 RETAINING E-RING.	22. COLD ENRICHMENT ROD LEVER.	39. CUP PLUG.
6. ACCELERATOR PUMP ROD.	23. COLD ENRICHMENT ROD SWIVEL.	40. MAIN METERING JET ASSEMBLY.
7. CHOKE CONTROL ROD.	24. CONTROL VACUUM REGULATOR ADJUSTING NUT.	41. "O" RING.
8. SCREW (2) 8-32 X .88	25. CONTROL VACUUM REGULATOR.	42. ACCELERATOR PUMP RETURN SPRING.
8A. SCREW (5) 8-32 X .75	26. COLD ENRICHMENT ROD.	43. ACCELERATOR PUMP CUP.
9. UPPER BODY	27. SCREW (2) 8-32 X .75	44. ACCELERATOR PUMP PLUNGER.
10. FLOAT HINGE PIN.	28. VENTURI VALVE COVER PLATE.	45. INTERNAL VENT VALVE.
11. FLOAT ASSEMBLY.	29. GASKET.	46. 3-16 RETAINING E-RING.
12. FLOAT BOWL GASKET.	30. ROLLER BEARING.	47. IDLE TRIM SCREW.
13. FUEL INLET VALVE.	31. VENTURI AIR BYPASS SCREW AND TORQUE	48. VENTURI VALVE LIMITER ADJUSTING SCREW.
14. FUEL INLET SEAT.	RETENTION SPRING	49. PIPE PLUG.
15. FUEL INLET SEAT GASKET.	32. VENTURI VALVE PIVOT PLUG.	50. COLD ENRICHMENT ROD SEAL
16. DUST SEAL.	33. VENTURI VALVE PIVOT PIN.	51. SEAL RETAINER
17. PIN ...12 X .69	34. VENTURI VALVE	52. HOT IDLE COMPENSATOR

Fig. 2 Upper body exploded view. Model 7200

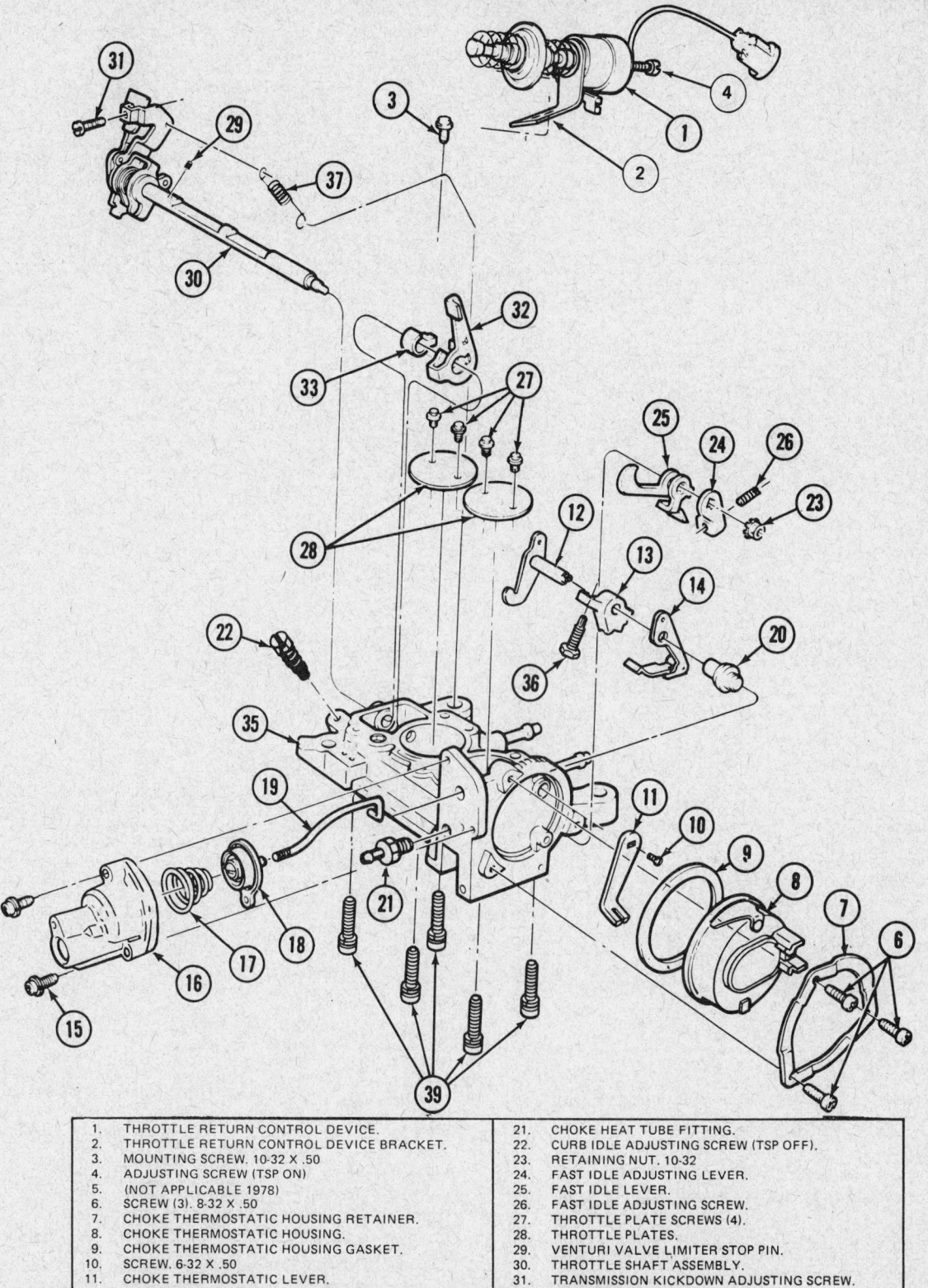

Fig. 3   Lower body exploded view. Model 7200

1. THROTTLE RETURN CONTROL DEVICE.	21. CHOKE HEAT TUBE FITTING.
2. THROTTLE RETURN CONTROL DEVICE BRACKET.	22. CURB IDLE ADJUSTING SCREW (TSP OFF).
3. MOUNTING SCREW. 10-32 X .50	23. RETAINING NUT. 10-32
4. ADJUSTING SCREW (TSP ON)	24. FAST IDLE ADJUSTING LEVER.
5. (NOT APPLICABLE 1978)	25. FAST IDLE LEVER.
6. SCREW (3). 8-32 X .50	26. FAST IDLE ADJUSTING SCREW.
7. CHOKE THERMOSTATIC HOUSING RETAINER.	27. THROTTLE PLATE SCREWS (4).
8. CHOKE THERMOSTATIC HOUSING.	28. THROTTLE PLATES.
9. CHOKE THERMOSTATIC HOUSING GASKET.	29. VENTURI VALVE LIMITER STOP PIN.
10. SCREW. 6-32 X .50	30. THROTTLE SHAFT ASSEMBLY.
11. CHOKE THERMOSTATIC LEVER.	31. TRANSMISSION KICKDOWN ADJUSTING SCREW.
12. CHOKE LEVER AND SHAFT ASSEMBLY.	32. VENTURI VALVE LIMITER LEVER.
13. FAST IDLE CAM.	33. VENTURI VALVE LIMITER BUSHING.
14. HIGH CAM SPEED POSITIONER ASSEMBLY.	34. (NOT APPLICABLE 1978)
15. SCREW (2). 8-32 X .75	35. THROTTLE BODY.
16. HIGH CAM SPEED POSITIONER DIAPHRAGM COVER.	36. FAST IDLE CAM ADJUSTING SCREW.
17. HIGH CAM SPEED POSITIONER DIAPHRAGM SPRING.	37. TRANSMISSION KICKDOWN LEVER RETURN SPRING.
18. HIGH CAM SPEED POSITIONER DIAPHRAGM ASSEMBLY.	38. (NOT APPLICABLE 1978)
19. HIGH CAM SPEED POSITIONER ROD.	39. SCREW (5) 8-32 X .75
20. CHOKE HOUSING BUSHING.	

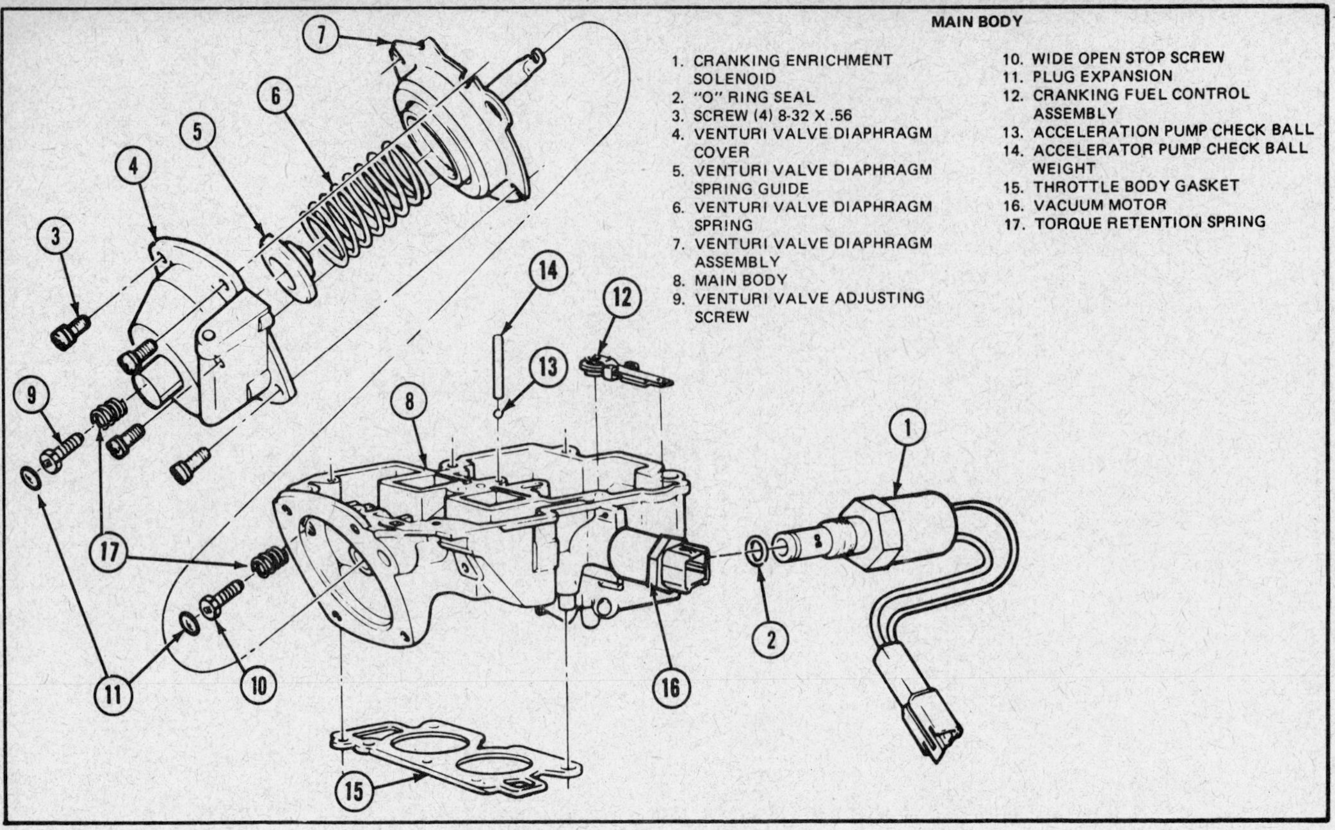

MAIN BODY

1. CRANKING ENRICHMENT SOLENOID
2. "O" RING SEAL
3. SCREW (4) 8-32 X .56
4. VENTURI VALVE DIAPHRAGM COVER
5. VENTURI VALVE DIAPHRAGM SPRING GUIDE
6. VENTURI VALVE DIAPHRAGM SPRING
7. VENTURI VALVE DIAPHRAGM ASSEMBLY
8. MAIN BODY
9. VENTURI VALVE ADJUSTING SCREW
10. WIDE OPEN STOP SCREW
11. PLUG EXPANSION
12. CRANKING FUEL CONTROL ASSEMBLY
13. ACCELERATION PUMP CHECK BALL
14. ACCELERATOR PUMP CHECK BALL WEIGHT
15. THROTTLE BODY GASKET
16. VACUUM MOTOR
17. TORQUE RETENTION SPRING

Fig. 4   Main body exploded view. Model 7200

1980–82 Units

Fig. 8—Remove carburetor from vehicle, then remove choke cap. Install choke weight tool T77L-9848-A7 on choke bimetal lever, then install dial indicator with contact positioned on top of cold enrichment metering rod and zero indicator. Install stator cap and rotate to index, then note indicator reading. Reading should be between as indicated in Fig. 9, under the run position 75°F column. If reading is not within limits, adjust by turning the choke enrichment adjusting nut until reading is within limits. Do not remove or reset dial indicator to check the start position 0°F adjustment. To check this adjustment, rotate thermostat lever clockwise until cold enrichment metering rod travel stop screw is bottomed against the upper body and note indicator reading. If reading is not within limits listed in Fig. 9, under start position 0°F column, adjust by turning the travel stop screw. Without removing or resetting dial indicator, perform control vacuum regulator adjustment as described under Control Vacuum-Regulator (CVR) Adjustment, then recheck cold enrichment metering rod run position 75°F adjustment. Remove adjustment limiting diaphragm cover, then seat diaphragm using finger and note dial indicator reading, Fig. 10. If reading is not within limits listed in Fig. 9, under start position 75°F column, rotate diaphragm until dial indicator reads within specifications. Align holes on diaphragm and casting, then install diaphragm cover. Push inward on diaphragm rod until diaphragm is seated, then rotate thermostat lever clockwise until choke shaft lever pin touches fast idle intermediate lever and note indicator reading, Fig. 11. If reading is not within limits listed in Fig. 9, under run position 0°F column, remove lead ball from choke diaphragm cover and rotate adjusting screw clockwise to increase or counter-clockwise to decrease height, Fig. 11. After completing adjustment, install lead ball and choke cover.

Control Vacuum Adjustment

1977–79 All & 1980 2700 Units

Fig. 12—Install tachometer to engine, then start engine at set idle speed to specifications. With a 5/32 inch allen wrench, rotate venturi valve diaphram clockwise until the valve firmly closes. Connect a vacuum gauge to the vacuum tap on the venturi valve cover. With engine at curb idle, use a 1/8 inch allen wrench to rotate the venturi bypass adjusting screw to obtain the specified setting, Fig. 13. It may be necessary to readjust the idle speed at this time. Rotate the venturi valve diaphram adjusting screw until vacuum drops to the specified level, Fig. 13, however, it is necessary to open and close the throttle to obtain the vacuum drop. Check and adjust curb idle, if necessary.

Internal Vent Adjustment

1977–79 2700 Units

NOTE: This adjustment must be checked and adjusted, if necessary, whenever the curb idle is adjusted.

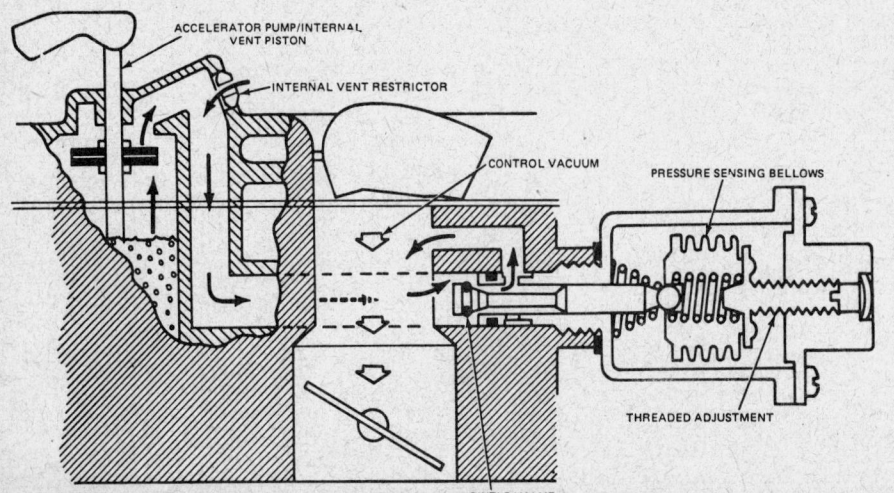

ACCELERATOR PUMP/INTERNAL VENT PISTON

INTERNAL VENT RESTRICTOR

CONTROL VACUUM

PRESSURE SENSING BELLOWS

THREADED ADJUSTMENT

PINTLE VALVE

Fig. 5   Altitude compensator. 1978 2700 units

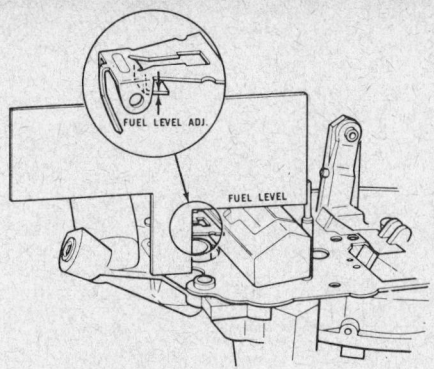

Fig. 6   Fuel level adjustment

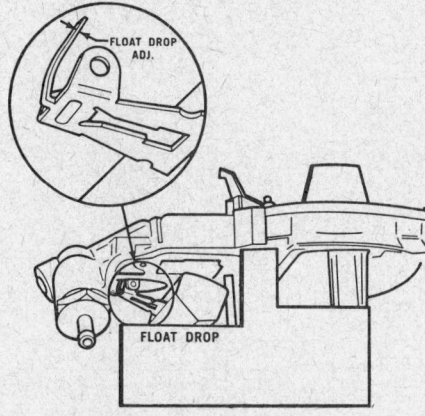

Fig. 7   Float drop adjustment

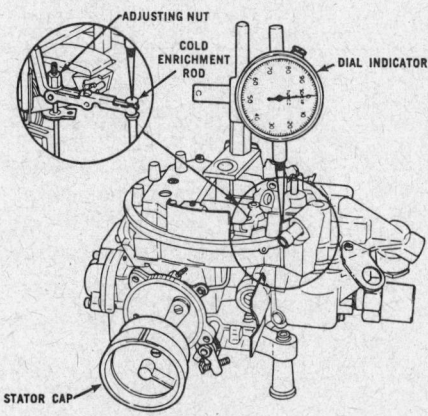

Fig. 8   Cold enrichment metering rod adjustment

| Year | Carb. Ident. No. | Carb. Model | Cold Enrichment Metering Rod Adjustment | | | |
| | | | Run Position | | Start Position | |
			0°F	75°F	0°F	75°F
1980	E0AE-AAA	2700	.295–.305	.115–.135	.520–.530	.460–.490
	E0AE-ACA, APA, AVA, ZA	2700	.315–.325	.115–.135	.520–.530	.460–.490
	E0AE-ADA, ATA	7200	.345–.355	.115–.135	.520–.530	.420–.450
	E0AE-BA, LA, PA, VA	7200	.345–.355	.115–.135	.520–.530	.460–.490
1981	E1AE-AAA	2700	.295–.305	.115–.135	.485–.495	.460–.490
	D9AE-AZA	7200	—	.120–.130	—	—
	E1AE-ACA, AGA, EA, LA, MA, SA	7200	.345–.355	.115–.135	.485–.495	.460–.490
	E1AE-KA, VA	7200	.345–.355	.115–.135	.520–.530	.460–.490
	E1DE-AA, E1VE-AA	7200	.345–.355	.115–.135	.485–.495	.460–.490
1982	E1AE-ACA	7200	.345–.355	.115–.135	.485–.495	.430–.460
	E1AE-AGA	7200	.345–.355	.115–.135	.485–.495	.440–.480
	E1AE-SA	7200	.345–.355	.115–.135	.485–.495	.440–.480
	E2AE-ABA, RA	7200	.345–.355	.115–.135	.485–.495	.430–.460
	E2AE-AGA, AHA	7200	.345–.355	.115–.135	.485–.495	.440–.480
	E2AE-LB	7200	.345–.355	.115–.135	.520–.530	.430–.460
	E2AE-LC	7200	.345–.355	.115–.135	.520–.530	.430–.460
	E2AE-MA	7200	.345–.355	.115–.135	.485–.495	.440–.480
	E2AE-MB	7200	.345–.355	.115–.135	.485–.495	.440–.480
	E2AE-NA, SA	7200	.345–.355	.115–.135	.520–.530	.430–.460
	E2AE-TA	7200	.345–.355	.115–.135	.485–.495	.430–.460
	E2AE-TB	7200	.345–.355	.115–.135	.485–.495	.430–.460
	E2DE-NA, SA, TA, UA	7200	.345–.355	.115–.135	.485–.495	.440–.480
	E2SE-DA, FA	7200	.345–.355	.115–.135	.520–.530	.460–.490
	E2SE-DB	7200	.345–.355	.115–.135	.520–.530	.460–.490
	E25E-ABA	7200	.345–.355	.115–.135	.485–.495	.430–.460
	E25E-AC, YA	7200	.345–.355	.115–.135	.520–.530	.460–.490
	E25E-FA	7200	.345–.355	.115–.135	.520–.530	.430–.460
	E25E-GA, SA, UA	7200	.345–.355	.115–.135	.520–.530	.430–.460
	E25E-GB, TA	7200	.345–.355	.115–.135	.520–.530	.430–.460

Fig. 9   Cold enrichment metering rod adjustment specification chart. 1980–82 Units

Fig. 14—With curb idle adjusted to specifications, place a .010 inch feeler gauge between the accelerator pump stem and the pump operating link. Rotate the nylon adjusting nut until a slight drag on the feeler gauge is obtained when removed.

Fast Idle Cam Adjustment

NOTE: On some 1979–82 California vehicles, it is necessary to remove the carburetor to remove the rivets on the choke housing. Remove the top two rivets with a 1/8 inch diameter twist drill. The third bottom rivet is located in a "Blind" hole and is removed by lightly tapping the rear of the retainer ring using a punch and hammer. The rivet, retainer ring, choke housing and gasket can then be removed.

Fig. 15—Remove choke cap and place the fast idle lever in the corner of the specified step of the fast idle cam with the high cam speed positioner retracted. If adjustment is performed on the bench, hold throttle closed with a rubber band to maintain cam position. Install stator cap, tool T77L-9848-A, and rotate clockwise until lever contacts adjusting screw. Rotate adjusting screw until index mark on stator cap aligns with the specified notch on the choke casting. Remove stator cap and reinstall choke cap.

Venturi Valve Limiter Adjustment

Fig. 16—Remove venturi valve cover and roller bearings, then the expansion plug located at rear of main body on the throttle side of carburetor. With an allen wrench, remove venturi valve wide open stop screw. Block the throttle wide open, then apply light closing pressure on the venturi valve and check gap between the valve and the air horn wall. If gap is not within specifications, adjust as follows: manually open the venturi valve to the wide open position and insert appropriate allen wrench into the hole from which the stop screw was removed. Rotate limiter adjusting screw clockwise to increase gap or counterclockwise to decrease gap. Remove allen wrench, apply light closing pressure to valve and recheck gap. If gap is within specifications, reinstall venturi valve wide open stop screw and rotate screw clockwise until screw contacts valve. Push venturi valve to wide open position and check gap between the valve and air horn wall, then rotate stop screw until gap is within specifications. Install new expansion plug in access hole. Reinstall venturi valve cover and roller bearings.

Control Vacuum Regulator (CVR) Adjustment

1977

NOTE: The cold enrichment metering rod adjustment must be performed before making this adjustment.

CARBURETORS

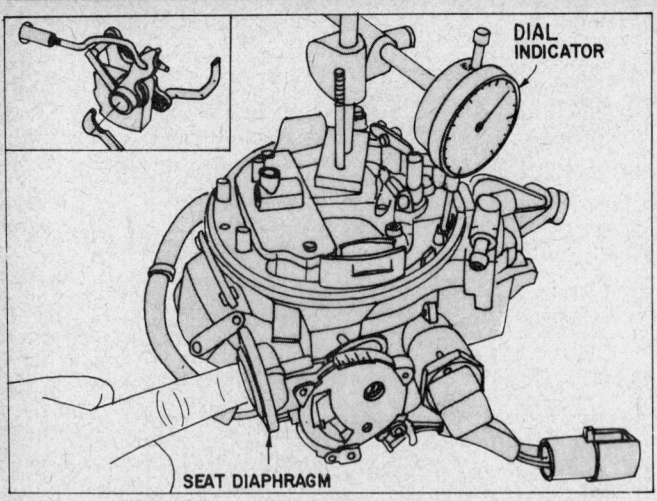

Fig. 10 Checking cold enrichment metering rod Start 75°F position adjustment. 1980–82 Units

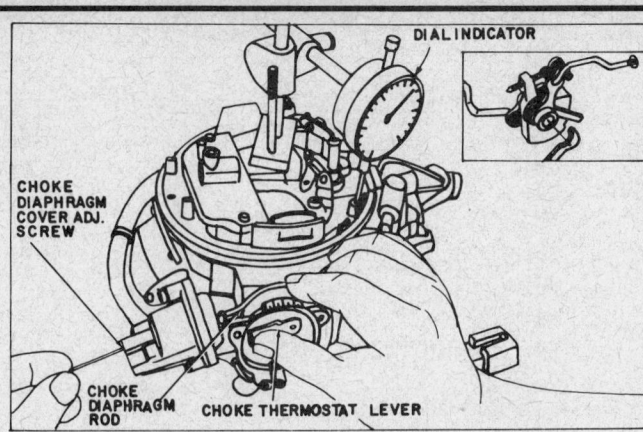

Fig. 11 Adjusting cold enrichment metering rod Run 0°F position. 1980–82

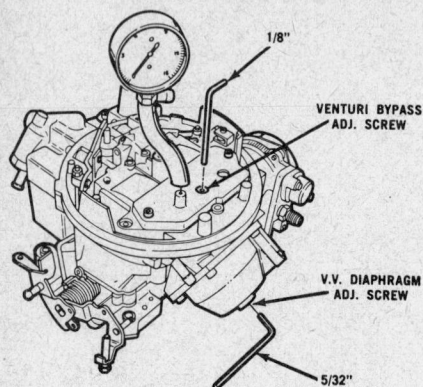

Fig. 12 Control vacuum adjustment. 1977–79 All & 1980 2700 Units

| Year | Carb. Ident. No. | Carb. Model | Control Vacuum Adjustment | |
			Venturi Air Bypass (Inches H₂O)	Venturi Valve Diaphragm (Inches H₂O)
1977–78	All	2700	—	4.5–6.5
1979	D84E-KA	2700	—	4.5–6.5
	D84E-VA	2700	4.9–5.6	4.6–5.1
	D9AE-CB, JB, YB, ZB	2700	6.8–7.3	4.6–5.1
	D9BE-AFA	2700	4.9–5.6	4.6–5.1
	D9DE-HB	2700	4.9–5.6	4.6–5.1
	D9ZE-AZB, BEA	2700	4.9–5.6	4.6–5.1
	D9ZE-ZC	2700	6.8–7.3	4.6–5.1
	D94E-EB, GA	2700	6.8–7.3	4.6–5.1
	D94E-JA	2700	4.9–5.6	4.6–5.1
	D945-FA	2700	4.9–5.6	4.6–5.1
	D9ME-AA	7200	7.3–7.8	4.6–5.1
1980	All	2700	8	6

Fig. 13 Control vacuum adjustment specification chart. 1977–79 All & 1980 2700 Units

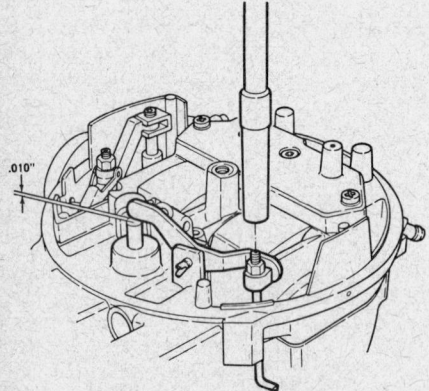

Fig. 14 Internal vent adjustment. 1977–79 2700 Units

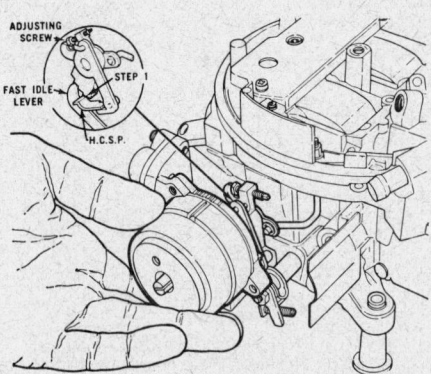

Fig. 15 Fast idle cam adjustment

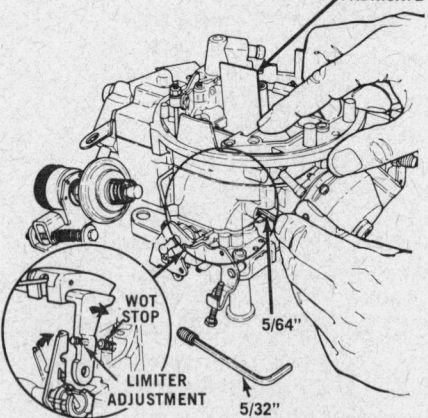

Fig. 16 Venturi valve limiter adjustment

Fig. 17—Rotate choke cap 180 degrees clockwise from index position and open and close the throttle to position the cam. Lightly apply pressure on the CVR rod and, if any downward travel is present, the valve is not seated and requires adjustment. If no downward travel is noted, rotate adjusting screw counter-clockwise until some downward travel is present. Rotate CVR rod clockwise until the adjusting nut starts to travel upward. Then, lightly apply pressure on the CVR rod and if any downward travel occurs, rotate adjusting screw clockwise in ¼ turn increments until no

downward travel occurs. Reset choke cap to specified setting.

1978-82

Fig. 18—With the dial indicator installed, remove the stator cap with tool T77L-9848-A. Press downward on CVR rod until bottomed on seat. Note the dial indicator reading. If not within specifications, place a ⅜ inch box end wrench over CVR adjusting nut and, using a

³⁄₃₂ inch allen wrench, turn CVR rod to adjust the travel.

High Cam Speed Positioner Adjustment

Fig. 19—Place high cam speed positioner in the corner of the specified cam step. Then,

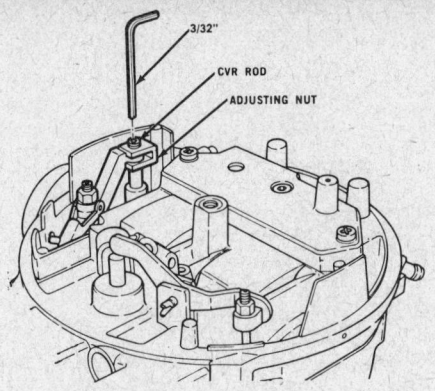

Fig. 17 Control vacuum regulator (CVR) adjustment. 1977 units

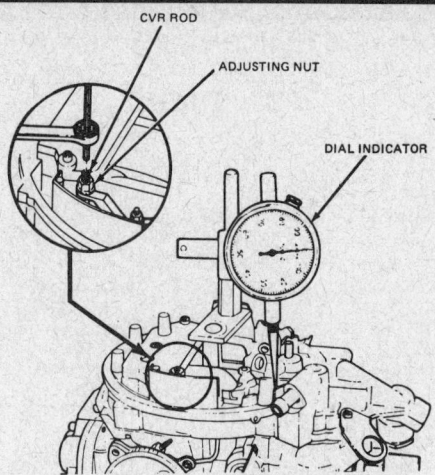

Fig. 18 Control vacuum regulator (CVR) adjustment. 1978–82 units

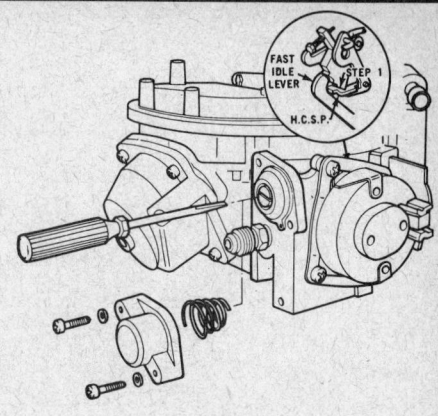

Fig. 19 High cam speed positioner adjustment

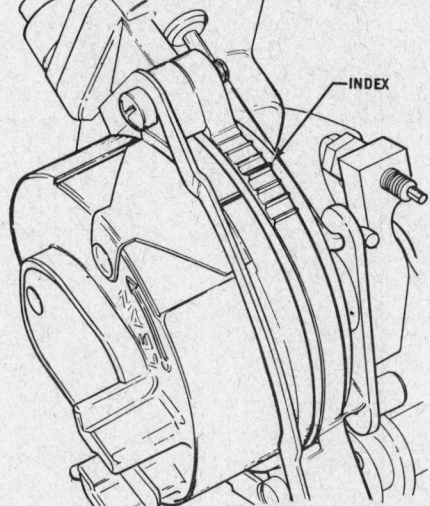

Fig. 20 Choke cap adjustment

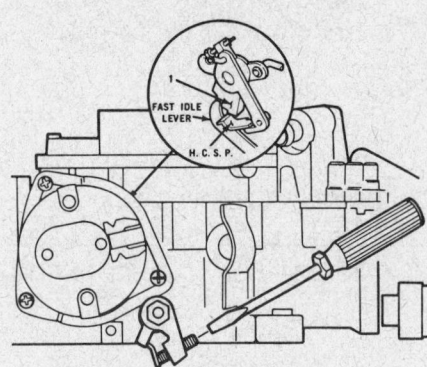

Fig. 21 Fast idle speed adjustment

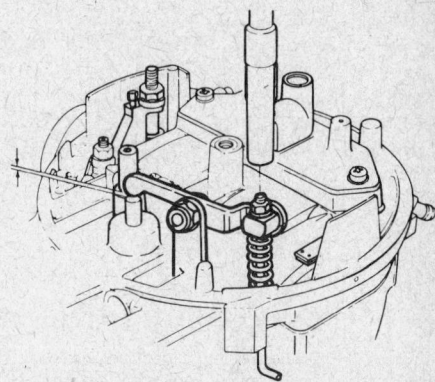

Fig. 22 Checking accelerator pump stem clearance. 1977–81 Units

Year	Carb. Model	Accelerator Pump Stem Clearance
1979	2700	.005–.015
	7200	.010–.030
1980–81	All	.010①

① —Plus one turn counter-clockwise.

Fig. 23 Accelerator pump stem clearance specification chart. 1979–81 Units

place the fast idle lever in the corner of the high cam speed positioner and hold throttle firmly closed. Remove diaphragm cover and rotate diaphragm assembly clockwise until lightly bottomed on casting, then rotate assembly counterclockwise ½ to 1½ turns, until the vacuum port and diaphragm hole align. Reinstall diaphragm cover.

Choke Cap Adjustment

Fig. 20—With choke cap installed, rotate choke cap clockwise until notch on cap is aligned with specified notch on housing.

Fast Idle Speed Adjustment

Fig. 21—Disconnect and plug the EGR vacuum line. With engine at curb idle and at normal operating temperature, place fast idle lever on specified step of fast idle cam. Ensure that the high cam speed positioner lever is disengaged, then rotate fast idle adjusting screw clockwise to increase speed or counterclockwise to decrease speed.

Accelerator Pump Stem Clearance

1979–81 Units
Fig. 22—After setting curb idle speed to specification, apply a slight downward pressure on

top of nylon nut located on accelerator pump stem and check clearance between pump stem and accelerator pump lever using a feeler gauge. Clearance should be as listed in Fig. 23. To adjust clearance, rotate nylon adjusting nut on top of accelerator pump stem clockwise to decrease clearance or counter-clockwise to increase clearance.

MODEL 4350-4V ADJUSTMENT SPECIFICATIONS

See Tune Up Chart in car chapters for curb and fast idle speeds.

Year	Carb. Model	Float Level (Dry)	Pump Setting (Hole No.)	Choke Plate Clearance (Pulldown)	Fast Idle Cam Linkage Setting	Auxiliary Inlet Valve Setting	Dechoke Clearance	Choke Setting
1977	D7VE-SA	1.00	#1	②	.140	.030	.300	Index
1978	D8VE-FA	1.00	#1	.160	.170	.030	.300	Index
	D8VE-GA	1.00	#1	.160	.170	.030	.300	Index

① —Initial setting; .160". Delayed setting; .210". ② —Initial setting; .140". Delayed setting; .190".

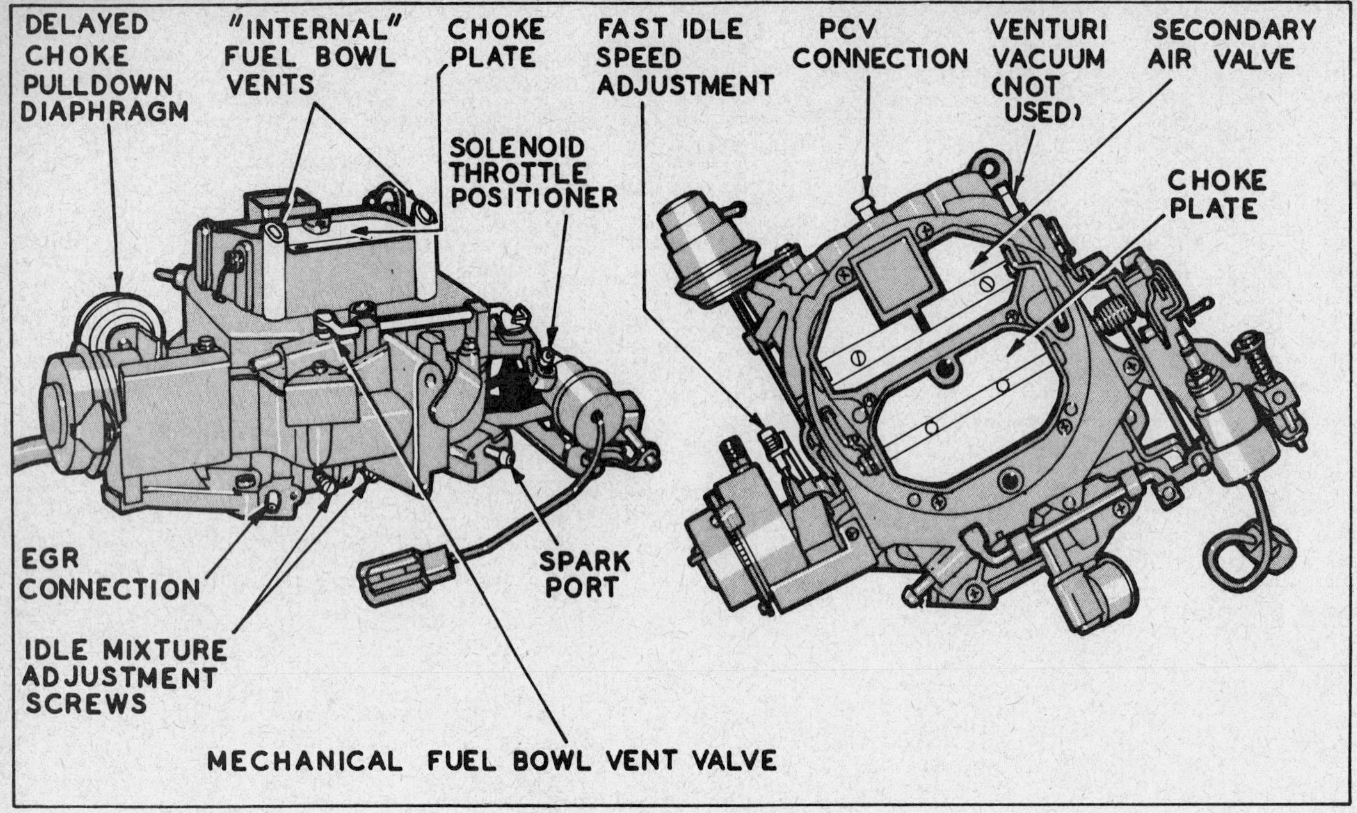

CARBURETORS

DELAYED CHOKE PULLDOWN DIAPHRAGM

"INTERNAL" FUEL BOWL VENTS

CHOKE PLATE

FAST IDLE SPEED ADJUSTMENT

PCV CONNECTION

VENTURI VACUUM (NOT USED)

SECONDARY AIR VALVE

SOLENOID THROTTLE POSITIONER

CHOKE PLATE

EGR CONNECTION

IDLE MIXTURE ADJUSTMENT SCREWS

SPARK PORT

MECHANICAL FUEL BOWL VENT VALVE

Fig. 1   Motorcraft 4350 4V carburetor assembly

MODEL 4350-4V ADJUSTMENTS

The model 4350, Figs. 1, 2 and 2A, is a four barrel, three piece, separately cast design consisting of an upper body, main body and throttle body. The fuel bowl is vented by a mechanical fuel bowl vent valve to the carbon canister which opens when the engine is off and closes when the engine is running.

The upper main body consists of the choke plate, boost venturi assembly, secondary air valve, acceleration pump plunger, mechanical fuel vent valve and fuel inlet and float system.

The main body consists of the fuel bowl, primary fuel metering system vacuum piston and rods.

The throttle body consists of the primary and secondary throttle plates. The primary throttle is actuated by the accelerator linkage and the secondary throttle is actuated by a linkage from the primary throttle lever. A lockout tang coupled to the automatic choke linkage, prevents operation until choke is fully off. The secondary throttle shaft is split and loosely coupled in the center to permit tighter secondary plate seating.

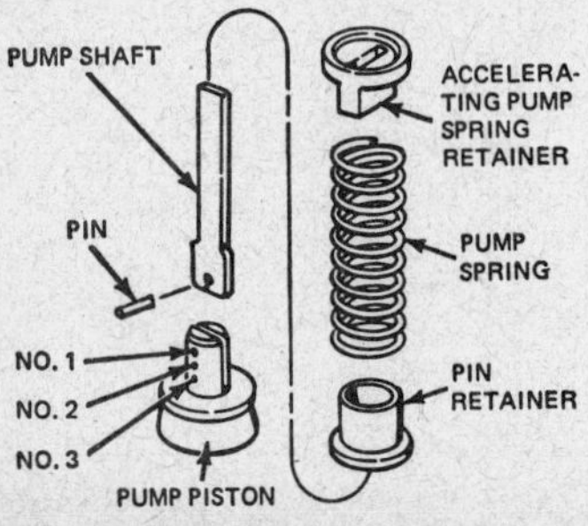

Primary fuel metering is accomplished by tapered metering rods that are raised or lowered according to engine vacuum and are limited by a mechanical system and throttle plate opening.

Fuel inlet is controlled by twin floats on either side of the carburetor. The piston type accelerator pump is suspended into the pump well by a linkage and operating rod which are part of upper body.

The choke system consists of a bimetallic thermostatic choke system which operates when underhood temperatures are below 60°F and an electric assist choke system which operates when underhood temperatures are above 60°F. On Ford models, this carburetor is equipped with a vacuum operated delayed choke system, Fig. 6, which operates in addition to the usual pulldown system. On American Motors models, a thermostatic bypass valve, which is integral with the choke heat tube, helps prevent premature choke valve opening. For service information on the choke system, refer to the "Emission Control System" chapter.

Some carburetors are equipped with high altitude compensation to provide improved high altitude emission control and driveabil- ity. Air passing the bypass intake is metered into the air flow below the primary, thus providing the leaner air fuel mixture required at high altitudes. Air flow is controlled by a valve controlled by an aneroid attached to the rear of the carburetor. To provide improved cold engine starts at high altitudes, the bypass is equipped with a choke plate connected to the main choke system.

Accelerator Pump Adjustment

The piston-to-shaft pin position which is the only adjustment, is pre-set to deliver the cor-

PUMP SHAFT

PIN

NO. 1
NO. 2
NO. 3

PUMP PISTON

ACCELERATING PUMP SPRING RETAINER

PUMP SPRING

PIN RETAINER

Fig. 3   Accelerator pump stroke adjustment

ADJUST

Fig. 4   Mechanical fuel vent valve adjustment

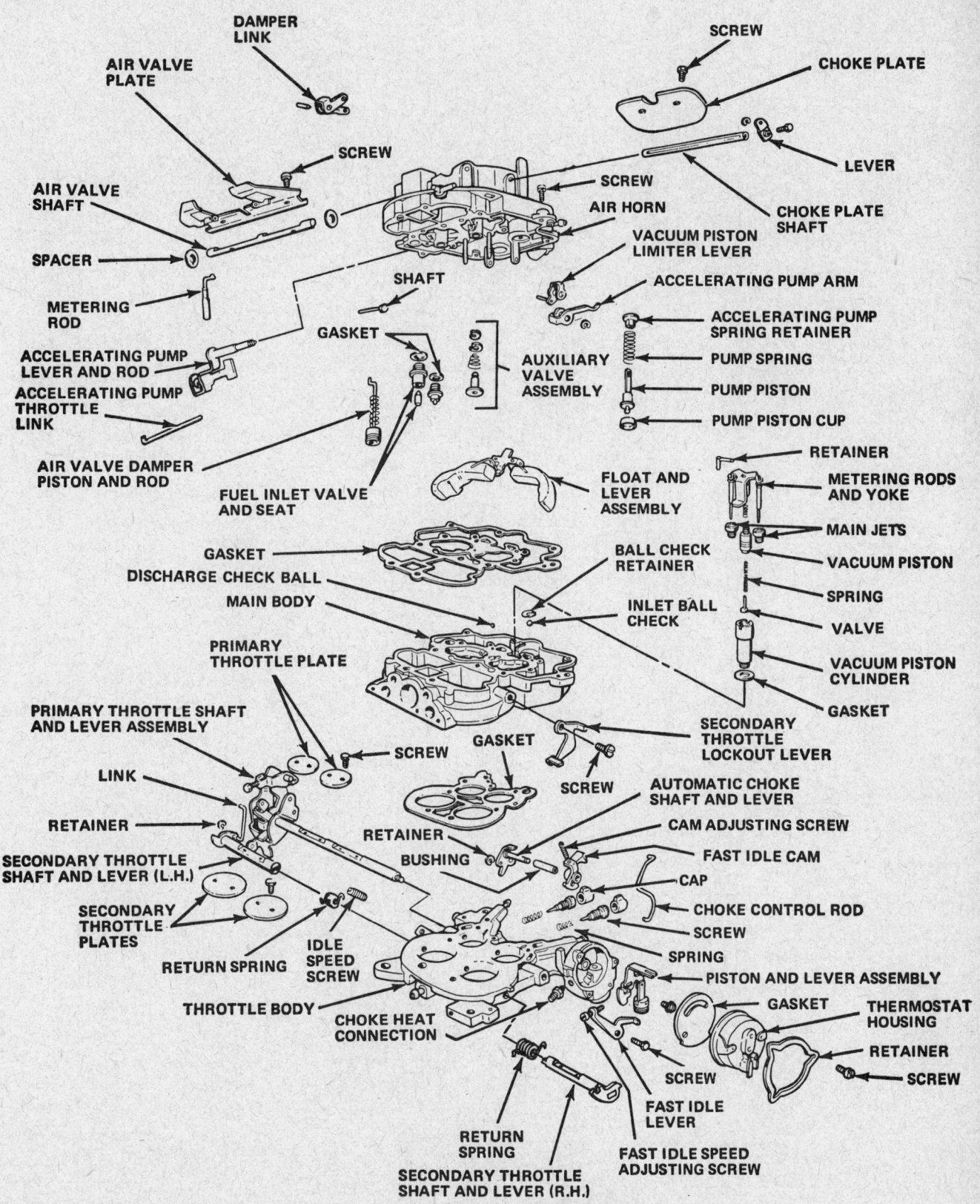

Fig. 2 Exploded view of 4350 4V carburetor without altitude compensation

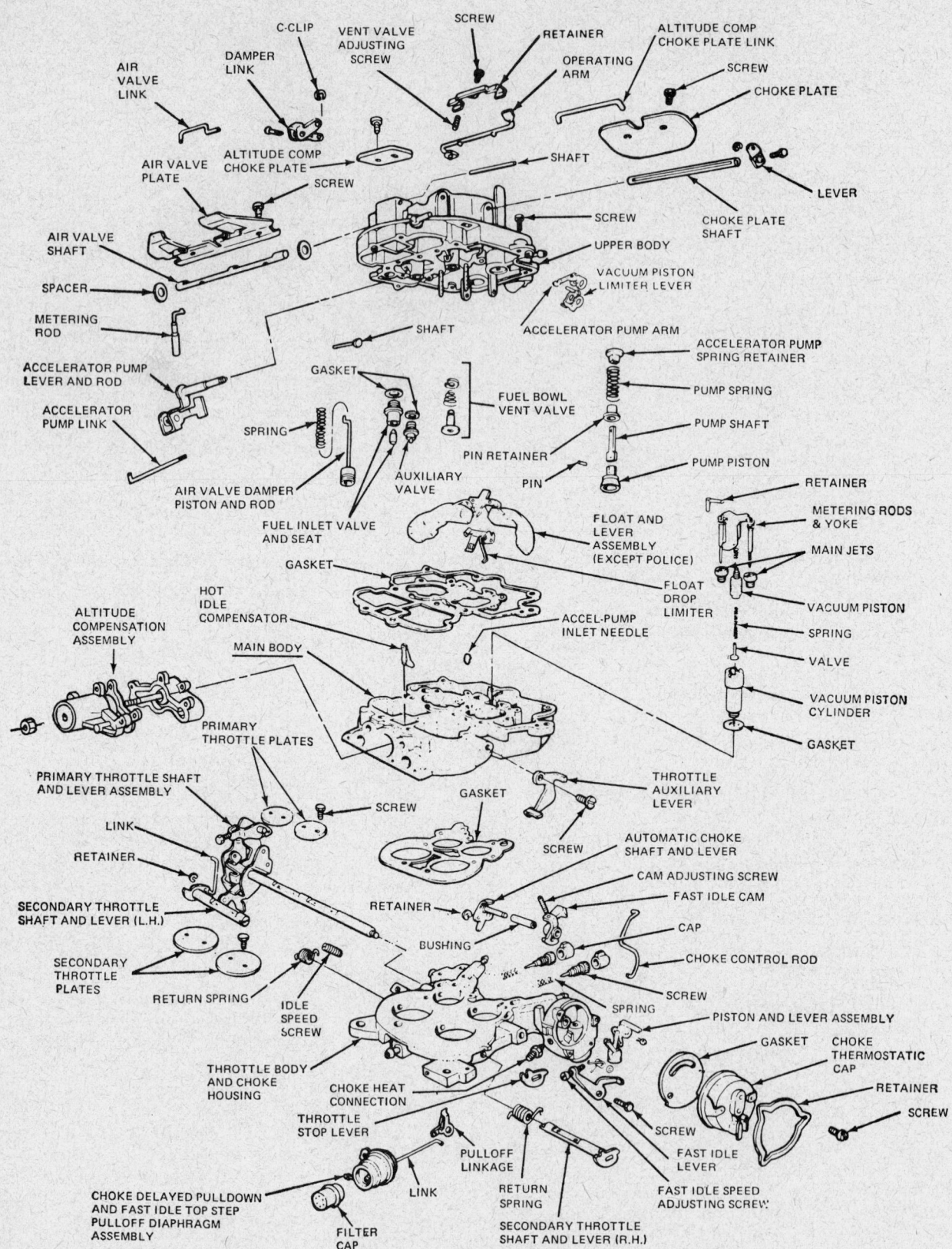

Fig. 2A Exploded view of 4350 4V carburetor with high altitude compensation.

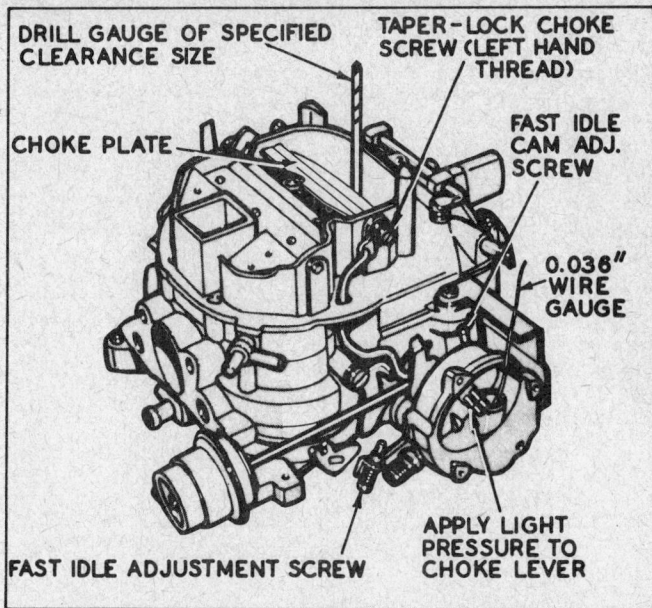

Fig. 5   Initial choke plate pulldown adjustment

Fig. 6   Choke plate delayed pulldown adjustment

rect amount of fuel for the engine on which it is installed and should not be changed from the specified setting. Do not attempt to adjust the accelerator pump stroke by turning the vacuum limiter level adjusting nut. This adjustment is pre-set and changing it could affect driveability.

1. Remove air horn assembly, then disconnect accelerator pump from operating lever by depressing spring and sliding arm out of pump shaft slot.
2. Disassemble spring and nylon keeper retaining adjustment pin. Refer to 4350 specifications chart. If pin is not in specified hole, remove it, reposition shaft in specified hole and reinstall pin, Fig. 3.
3. Slide nylon retainer over pin and position spring on shaft, then compress spring on shaft and install pump on arm.

Vent Valve Adjustment

1. With engine at curb idle speed and the solenoid throttle positioner de-energized (if used), adjust the vent valve so the adjusting screw just contacts the drive tab on the accelerator pump lever, Fig. 4. Turn adjusting screw one additional turn after screw contacts drive tab.
2. With engine off, observe that vent operating linkage pushes down on vent valve stem.

Initial Choke Pulldown

1. Remove choke housing assembly, then open throttle about half-way and position fast idle adjusting screw on high step of fast idle cam.
2. Bend a .036″ wire gauge at 90° angle, about ⅛″ from end, then insert bent end of gauge between choke piston slot and upper edge of right hand slot in choke housing, Fig. 5.
3. Rotate choke lever counterclockwise until gauge is snug in piston slot, then apply light force to lever to hold gauge and move top of choke rod away from carburetor while moving bottom of rod toward carburetor to remove end play from linkage.
4. Using a drill gauge or pin of specified size, check clearance between lower edge of choke plate and wall, Fig. 5. Refer to 4350 specifications chart.
5. Adjust clearance to specifications, by turning lock screw on choke plate shaft 3 full turns in a clockwise direction. Pry choke lever from shaft to break taper lock. Choke lever should rotate freely on choke shaft.
6. With drill gauge and .036″ wire gauge positioned as above, tighten, screw on choke shaft.
7. Install choke housing assembly.

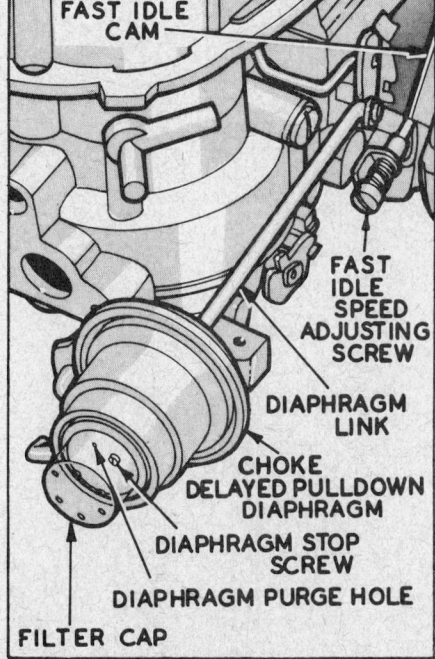

Fig. 7   Choke plate delayed pulldown stop screw adjustment

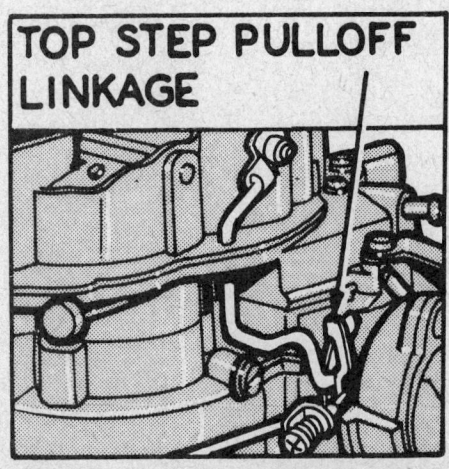

Fig. 8   Fast idle top step pulloff adjustment

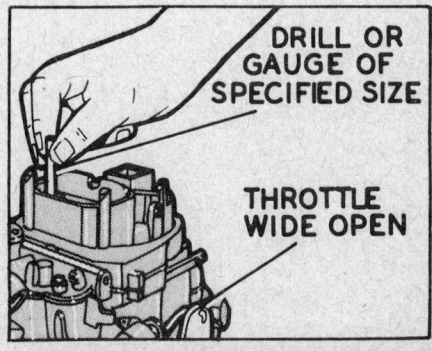

Fig. 9   Dechoke clearance adjustment

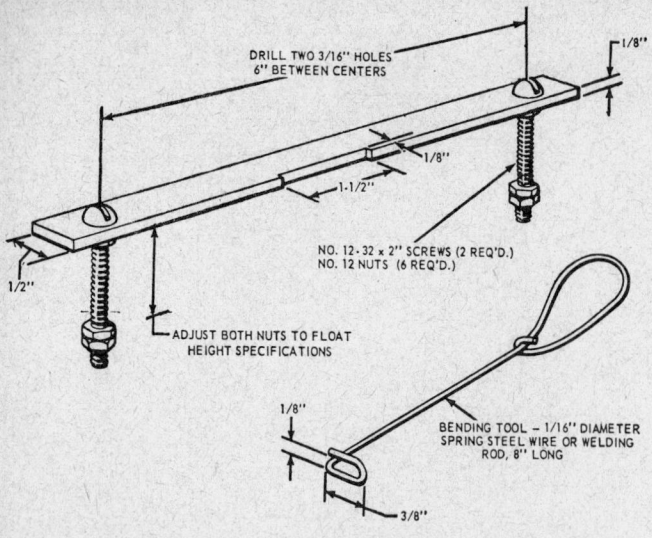

Fig. 10 Float setting gauge and bending tool

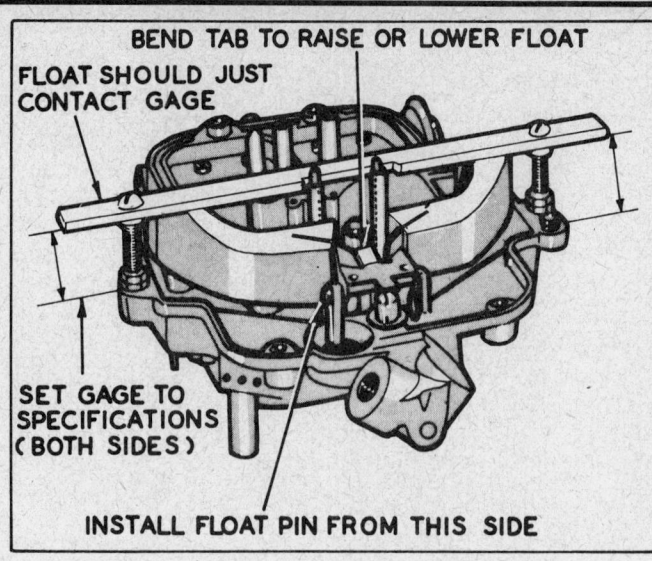

Fig. 11 Float setting

Delayed Choke Pulldown

The delayed choke pulldown opens the choke to a wider setting about 6 to 18 seconds after the engine is started.

1. With throttle set on fast idle cam, note position of index marks on choke housing, loosen retaining screws and rotate cap 90° in closing (rich) direction.
2. Connect a vacuum source of 14–18 inches Hg. to vacuum supply port of delayed choke pulldown diaphragm and check clearance between lower edge of choke plate and wall, Fig. 6. Refer to 4350 specifications chart.
3. Adjust clearance to specifications by turning stop screw on delayed choke pulldown diaphragm, Fig. 7.

Fast Idle Top Step Pulloff

1. Operate delayed pulldown diaphragm manually or by applying 14 to 18 inches Hg.
2. Position fast idle speed screw on top step fast idle cam with choke plate closed. If necessary, rotate choke housing cap to close choke plate.

3. Observe that fast idle speed adjusting screw drops to second step of cam as delayed choke pulldown diaphragm is operated, Fig. 8.

Dechoke (Unloader) Clearance

1. Hold throttle plate fully open and apply pressure on choke valve toward close position.
2. Measure clearance between lower edge of choke valve and air horn wall. Fig. 9. Refer to 4350 Specifications Chart.
3. Adjust clearance to specifications by bending unloader tang which contacts fast idle cam forward to increase or rearward to decrease clearance.

NOTE: Do not bend tang downward from a horizontal plane. After adjustment, make certain that there is at least .070 inch clearance between unloader tang and choke housing with throttle fully open.

Float Setting

To simplify float setting, refer to Fig. 10 for construction of an adjustable float gauge and float tab bending tool.

1. Adjust gauge to specified height and insert gauge into air horn, Fig. 11.
2. Check clearance and alignment of floats to gauge. Refer to 4350 Specifications Chart. Both floats should just touch gauge. If necessary, align floats by twisting floats slightly.
3. To raise float setting, insert open end of bending tool to right side of float lever tab between needle and float hinge. Raise float lever off needle and bend tap downward.
4. To lower float setting, insert open end of bending tool to left side of float lever tab between needle and float hinge. Support float lever and bend tap upward.
5. If above gauge is not available, invert upper body and measure distance from top of float to gasket surface of upper body. Adjust alignment and height of floats with bending tool as described previously.

Auxiliary Valve Setting

Check auxiliary valve clearance as shown in Fig. 12. If necessary to adjust clearance, use bending tool, Fig. 10.

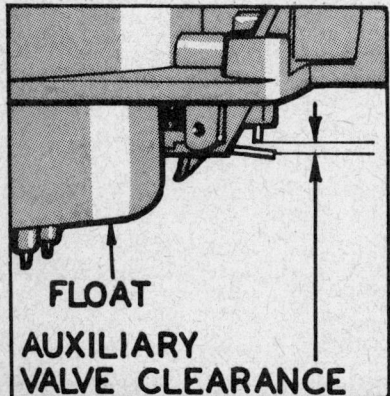

Fig. 12 Auxiliary inlet valve adjustment

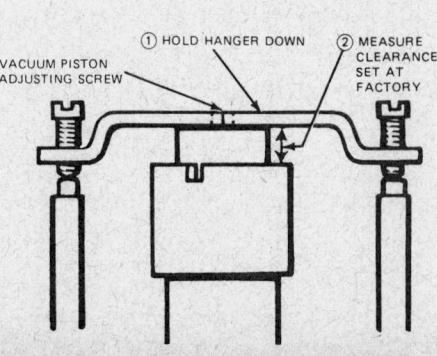

Fig. 13 Measuring vacuum piston setting

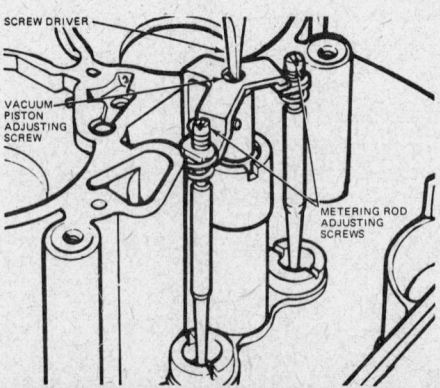

Fig. 14 Vacuum piston & metering rod adjusting screws

Vacuum Piston & Metering Rods Adjustment

The metering rod adjustment is set at the factory and no attempt should be made to alter this adjustment. Prior to removing metering rod and vacuum piston during carburetor disassembly, depress metering rod hanger, then measure and note clearance between top of vacuum piston and bottom edge of metering rod hanger for use during carburetor assembly, Fig. 13.

If metering rod adjustment has been disturbed, manually depress metering rod hanger. Using a screwdriver with a blade width of less than 3/32 inch, carefully turn vacuum piston and metering rod adjusting screws counterclockwise until metering rod hanger is fully seated against top of vacuum piston, Fig. 14. While holding metering rod hanger lightly in the full downward position, turn each metering rod adjusting screw clockwise until metering rod hanger just starts to rise. Metering rods are now set in proper relation to vacuum piston. Turn vacuum piston adjusting screw clockwise until clearance noted during disassembly is obtained between top of vacuum piston and bottom of metering rod hanger.

Fast Idle Cam

1. Loosen choke cover screws and rotate cover to align index marks on cover and housing. Then, rotate cover an additional 90° counterclockwise and tighten attaching screws.
2. Place fast idle speed adjusting screw on kickdown (center) step of fast idle cam. Fully close choke plate and check clearance between air horn and lower edge of choke plate. Adjust by turning fast idle cam adjusting screw, ensuring adjusting screw remains on kickdown step during

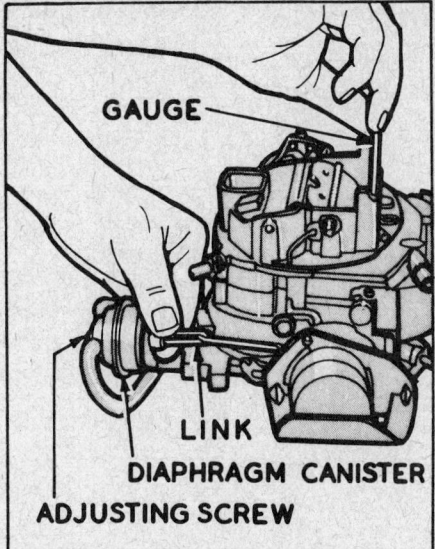

Fig. 15   Initial choke valve clearance adjustment. American Motors units with vacuum diaphragm

adjustment.
3. Loosen choke cove screws and rotate cover to specified index mark and tighten cover screws.

American Motors Units With Vacuum Diaphragm

Initial Choke Valve Clearance

1. Loosen choke cover screws, open throttle and rotate choke cover until choke valve closes. Then, tighten one cover screw to hold cover in place.
2. Close throttle. The fast idle screw should be on top step of cam.
3. Bottom choke diaphragm on setscrew, however, do not press on links, Fig. 15.
4. Measure clearance between air horn and lower edge of choke valve, Fig. 15. Adjust by turning adjusting screw at rear of diaphragm housing.
5. Adjust fast idle cam linkage.
6. Loosen choke cover screw and set choke cover to specifications.

Choke Plate Indexing

1. Loosen choke lever attaching screw and pry lever from choke shaft to permit choke valve rotation.

NOTE: The choke lever attaching screw has a left hand thread.

2. Loosen choke cover screws and rotate cover 90° counterclockwise so the choke shaft lever contracts cam adjusting screw.
3. Position fast idle screw on top step of fast idle cam. Then, back off cam adjusting screw until clearance is obtained between screw and choke shaft lever.
4. Turn cam adjusting screw until it contacts choke shaft lever, then turn 6–7 additional turns.
5. Manually close choke plate and tighten choke shaft lever attaching screw.
6. Adjust initial choke valve clearance and fast idle cam linkage.
7. Set choke cover and tighten cover screws.

MODEL 5200 ADJUSTMENT SPECIFICATIONS

See Tune Up Chart in car chapters for curb and fast idle speeds.

Year	Carb. Model (9510) ①	Float Level	Pump Setting (Hole)	Choke Pulldown	Dechoke Clearance	Fast Idle Cam Clearance	Choke Setting
1977	D7EE-BGA	29/64	#2	.24	.24	.12	Index
	D7EE-BHA	29/64	#2	.24	.24	.12	Index
	D7EE-BLA	29/64	#2	.24	.24	.12	1 Rich
	D7EE-BMA	29/64	#2	.24	.24	.12	1 Rich
1978	D8BE-AKA	29/64	#2	.24	.24	.12	2 Rich
	D8EE-ANA	29/64	#2	.24	.24	.12	2 Rich
	D8BE-FA	29/64	#2	.24	.24	.12	2 Rich
	D8BE-HA	29/64	#2	.24	.24	.12	1 Rich
	D8EE-ATA	29/64	#2	.20	.24	.12	2 Rich
	D8EE-AUA	29/64	#2	.24	.24	.12	2 Rich
	D8EE-AVA	29/64	#2	.24	.24	.12	2 Rich
	D8EE-CA	29/64	#2	.24	.24	.12	1 Rich
	D8EE-DA	29/64	#2	.24	.24	.12	2 Rich
	D8EE-JA	29/64	#2	.24	.24	.12	2 Rich
	D8EE-KA	29/64	#2	.24	.24	.12	1 Rich
	D8ZE-RA	29/64	#2	.24	.24	.12	1 Rich

Continued

CARBURETORS

See Tune Up Chart in car chapters for curb and fast idle speeds.

Year	Carb. Model (9510) ①	Float Level	Pump Setting (Hole)	Choke Pulldown	Dechoke Clearance	Fast Idle Cam Clearance	Choke Setting
	D8ZE-SA	29/64	#2	.24	.24	.12	1 Rich
1979	D9BE-AAA	29/64	#2	.24	.24	.12	2 Rich
	D9BE-ABA	29/64	#2	.24	.24	.12	2 Rich
	D9BE-ACA	29/64	#2	.24	.24	.12	2 Rich
	D9BE-ADA	29/64	#2	.24	.24	.12	2 Rich
	D9BE-AGA	29/64	#2	.24	.24	.12	2 Rich
	D9EE-ALA	29/64	#2	.24	.24	.12	2 Rich
	D9EE-AMA	29/64	#2	.24	.24	.12	2 Rich
	D9EE-ANA	29/64	#2	.24	.24	.12	1 Rich
	D9EE-APA	29/64	#2	.24	.24	.12	1 Rich
	D9EE-ARA	29/64	#2	.24	.24	.12	1 Rich
	D9EE-ASA	29/64	#2	.24	.24	.12	1 Rich
	D9EE-ATA	29/64	#2	.24	.24	.12	1 Rich
	D9EE-AUA	29/64	#2	.24	.24	.12	1 Rich
	D9EE-AVA	29/64	#2	.24	.24	.12	1 Rich
	D9EE-AYA	29/64	#2	.24	.24	.12	1 Rich
	D9ZE-BCA	29/64	#2	.24	.24	.12	1 Rich
	D9ZE-BDA	29/64	#2	.24	.24	.12	1 Rich
	D9ZE-MD	29/64	#3②	.24	.24	.12	2 Rich
	D9ZE-ND	29/64	#3	.24	.24	.12	2 Rich
1980	D9EE-ANA	29/64	#2	.24	.24	.12	1 Rich
	D9EE-APA	29/64	#2	.24	.24	.12	1 Rich
	E0EE-AEA	29/64	#2	.20	.20	.08	1 Lean
	E0EE-AEB	29/64	#2	.24	.20	.06	1 Rich
	E0EE-AFA	29/64	#2	.20	.20	.08	1 Lean
	E0EE-AFB	29/64	#2	.24	.20	.06	1 Rich
	E0EE-GA	29/64	#2	.24	.20	.08	2 Rich
	E0EE-JA	29/64	#2	.20	.20	.08	1 Lean
	E0EE-JC	29/64	—	.20	.20	.08	2 Rich
	E0EE-JD	29/64	#2	.20	.20	.08	2 Rich
	E0EE-RA	29/64	#2	.24	.20	.08	2 Rich
	E0EE-TA	29/64	#2	.20	.20	.08	1 Lean
	E0EE-TC	29/64	—	.20	.20	.08	2 Rich
	E0EE-TD	29/64	#2	.20	.20	.08	2 Rich
	E0ZE-AAA	29/64	#3	.28	.24	.16	2 Rich
	E0ZE-ACA	29/64	#2	.28	.24	.16	Index
	E0ZE-ACB	29/64	—	.28	.24	.12	Index
	E0ZE-ACC	29/64	—	.28	.24	.16	Index
	E0ZE-AMA	29/64	—	.28	.24	.16	Index
	E0ZE-ATA	29/64	#2	.28	.24	.12	Index
	E0ZE-ATB	29/64	#2	.28	.24	.12	Index
	E0ZE-AZA	29/64	#3	.28	.39	.16	Index
1981	D9EE-ANA	29/64	#2	.24	.20	.12	—
	D9EE-APA	29/64	#2	.24	.20	.12	—
	E0EE-GA	29/64	#2	.20	.20	.08	—
	E0EE-RB	29/64	#2	.20	.20	.08	—
	E1ZE-VA	29/64	#2	.20	.20	.08	—
	E1ZE-YA	29/64	#2	.20	.20	.08	—
1982	E1BE-RA	15/32	#2	.197	.197	.079	—
	E1ZE-ACA	15/32	#2	.197	.197	.079	—
	E1ZE-ADB	15/32	#3	.276	.394	.236	—
	E1ZE-VA	15/32	#2	.197	.197	.079	—
	E1ZE-YA	15/32	#2	.197	.197	.079	—

Continued

MODEL 5200 ADJUSTMENT SPECIFICATIONS—Continued

See Tune Up Chart in car chapters for curb and fast idle speeds.

Year	Carb. Model (9510) ①	Float Level	Pump Setting (Hole)	Choke Pulldown	Dechoke Clearance	Fast Idle Cam Clearance	Choke Setting
	E2ZE-AAA	15/32	#2	.236	.236	.118	—
	E2ZE-ABA	15/32	#2	.236	.236	.118	—
	E2ZE-AFA	15/32	#2	.236	.236	.118	—
	E2ZE-AGA	15/32	#2	.236	.236	.118	—
	E2ZE-AHA	15/32	#2	.236	.236	.118	—

①—Tag attached to carburetor
②—Bottom.

MODEL 5200 ADJUSTMENTS

This carburetor is a two stage, two venturi carburetor, Figs. 1 and 2. The primary stage or venturi is smaller than the secondary venturi. The secondary is operated by mechanical linkage.

The primary stage includes a curb idle system, accelerator pump system, idle transfer system, main metering system and power enrichment system.

The secondary stage includes a transfer system, main metering system, and power system. Both the primary and secondary systems draw fuel from a common fuel bowl.

On 1977–80 models, the automatic choke is equipped with only the electric heater assist.

Some 1977 units are equipped with an altitude compensation feature which is controlled by the driver. This is a two piece manual system that utilizes the carburetor supplemental metering system when the dash panel control is placed in the "Sea Level" position and the normal fuel metering system when the control is in the "Altitude" position.

1978–82 units are equipped with a vacuum operated, solenoid assisted fuel bowl vent which is called a "Switching Bowl Vent". With the engine "Off", a spring holds the external vent open, closing the internal vent passage. In this position, the fuel bowl vapors pass to the evaporative emission canister. When the engine is started, manifold vacuum acting on the diaphragm overcomes the spring pressure and pulls the external vent to the seated position, uncovering the internal vent passage. A holding solenoid, connected to the ignition circuit, holding the vent closed to prevent the vent opening under low vacuum conditions. The vent will close only when the ignition is turned "Off".

Dry Float Setting

Fig. 3—With the bowl cover held in an inverted position and the float tang resting lightly on the spring loaded fuel inlet needle, measure the clearance between the edge of the float and the bowl cover. Adjust clearance by bending the float tang up or down as required, Fig. 4.

NOTE: Do not scratch or damage the tang. Adjust both floats equally.

Float Drop

1981 Units
Fig. 4A—Invert float cover and measure float drop using a suitable gauge. Float drop should be 1 inch ± 1/8 inch. If float drop is not within specifications, adjust by bending float drop tang, Fig. 4.

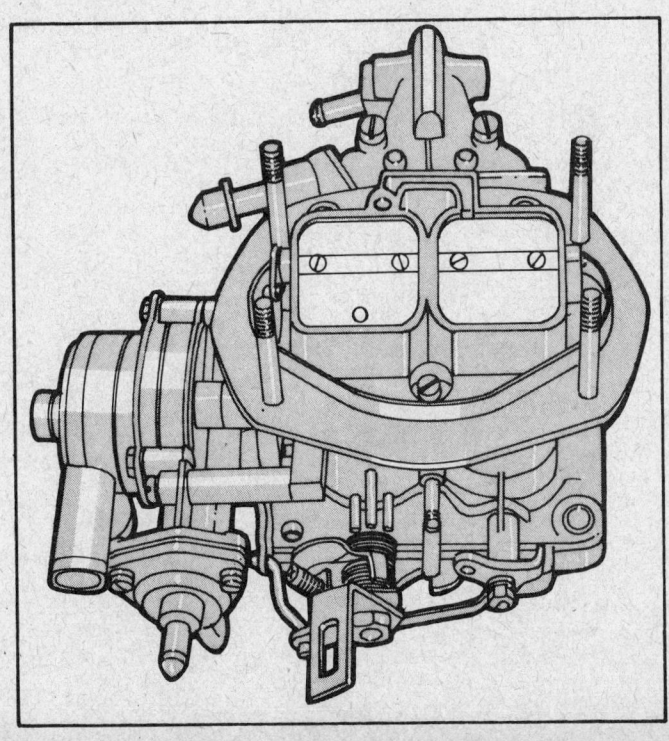

Fig. 1   Model 5200-2V carburetor

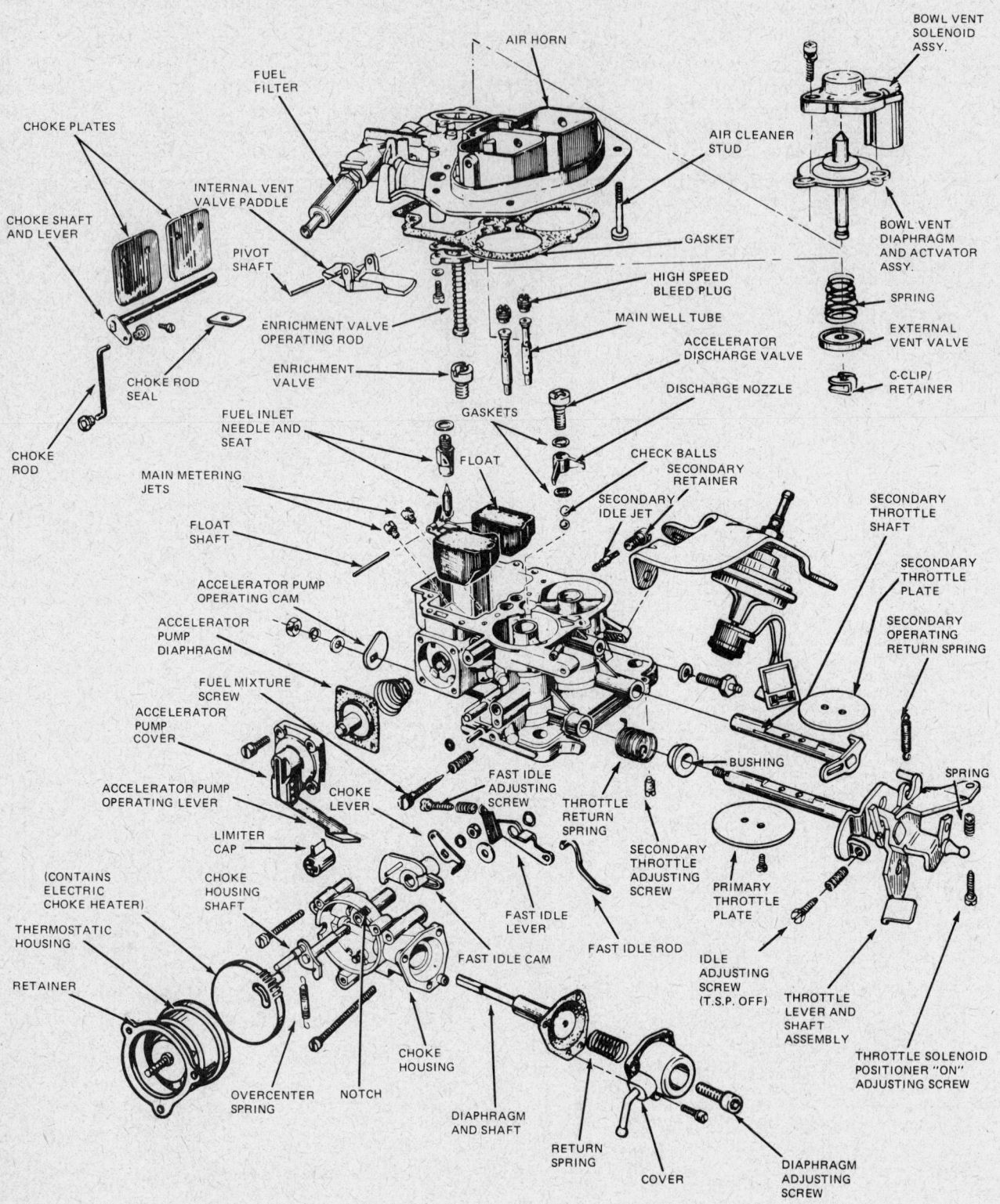

Fig. 2 Exploded view of model 5200 carburetor (Typical)

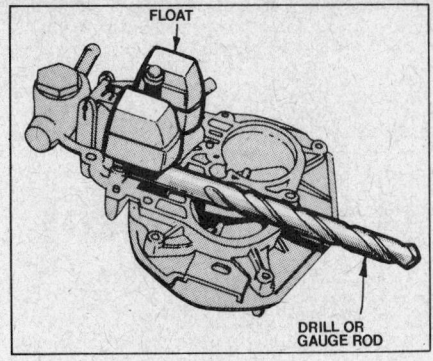

Fig. 3 Dry float setting

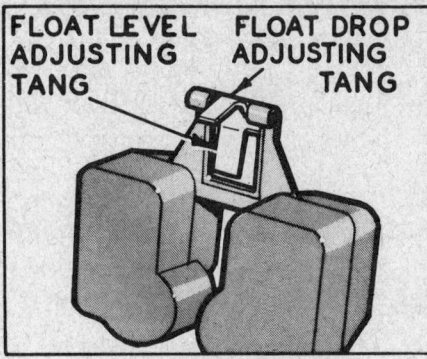

Fig. 4 Float adjusting point

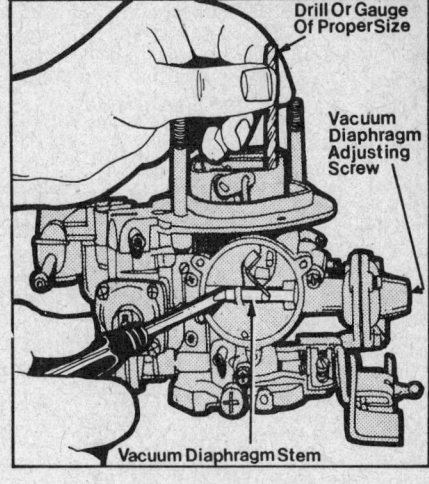

Fig. 6 Choke plate pull-down

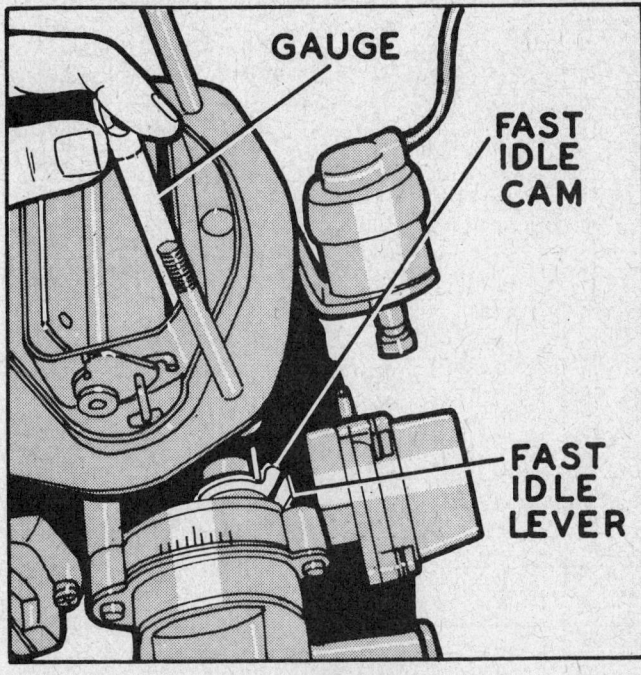

Fig. 5 De-choke adjustment

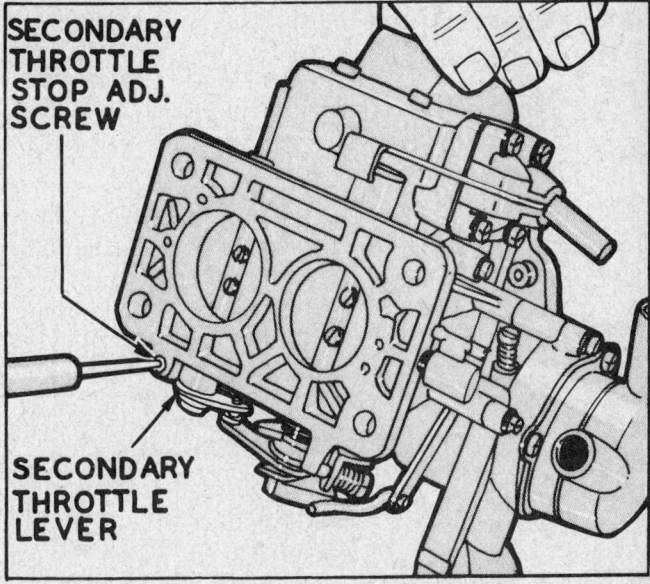

Fig. 8 Secondary throttle stop adjustment

Dechoke Clearance

Fig. 5—Hold throttle lever in wide open position and take slack out of choke linkage by applying finger pressure to top edge of choke plate. Measure clearance between lower edge of choke plate and air horn wall. Adjust by bending tab on fast idle lever where it touches the fast idle cam.

Choke Plate Vacuum Pull-Down

NOTE: On 1981–82 vehicles, it is necessary to remove the carburetor to remove rivets retaining choke cover to choke housing. Using a ⅛ inch or No. 30 drill bit, remove rivet heads, then drive rivet out using a ⅛ inch diameter punch.

Fig. 6—Remove the three screws and ring retaining choke spring cover and pull the water cover and/or choke spring cover from carburetor. On 1977 and 1981–82 units, place fast idle cam on high step. On 1978–80 units, place fast idle cam on second step. Push the diaphragm stem back against its stop. Place gauge rod or drill between the lower edge of the choke plate and the air horn wall. Remove the slack from the choke linkage by applying finger pressure to the top edge of the choke plate. Adjust the choke plate-to-air horn clearance by removing the plug from the diaphragm and turning the adjusting screw in or out as required.

Fast Idle Cam Clearance

Fig. 7—Insert specified drill or gauge between the lower edge of the choke plate and the air horn wall. With the fast idle screw held

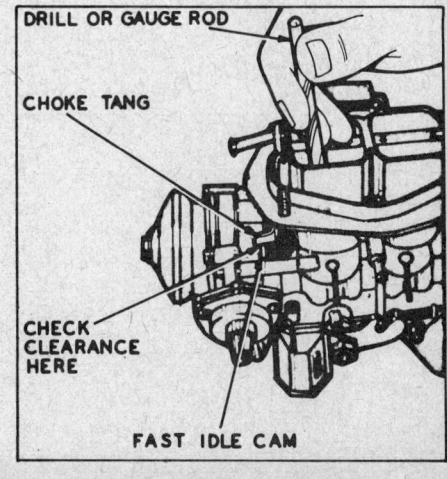

Fig. 7 Fast idle cam clearance

CARBURETORS

on the second step of the fast idle cam, measure the clearance between the tang of the choke lever and the arm on the fast idle cam. Adjust clearance by bending choke lever tang up or down as required. Refer to *5200 Specifications Chart.*

Secondary Throttle Stop Screw Adjustment

Fig. 8—Back off the secondary throttle stop screw until the secondary throttle plate seats in its bore. Turn the screw in until it touches the tab on the secondary throttle lever. On all units except when used on 2800 cc engines, turn the screw inward an additional 1/4 turn. On units used on 2800 cc engines, turn screw inward an additional 3/4 turn.

GM Delco/Rochester Carburetor Section

MODEL 2GC & 2GE CARBURETOR ADJUSTMENT SPECIFICATIONS

See Tune Up Chart in car chapters for curb and fast idle speeds.

Year	Carb. Production No.	Float Level	Float Drop	Pump Rod	Idle Vent	Intermediate Choke Rod	Vacuum Break		Choke Setting	Choke Rod	Choke Unloader
							Throttle Lever Side	Choke Side			
1977	17057104, 105	7/16	19/32	1 21/32	—	.120	—	②	Index	.260	.325
	17057107, 109	7/16	19/32	1 17/32	—	.120	—	②	Index	.260	.325
	17057108, 110	19/32	19/32	1 21/32	—	.120	—	②	Index	.260	.325
	17057111, 113	19/32	19/32	1 17/32	—	.120	—	②	Index	.260	.325
	17057112	19/32	19/32	1 21/32	—	.120	—	②	Index	.260	.325
	17057114	19/32	19/32	1 17/32	—	.120	—	②	Index	.260	.325
	17057121, 123	19/32	19/32	1 17/32	—	.120	—	②	Index	.260	.325
	17057140	15/32	15/32	1 9/32	—	.120	.140	.100	1 Rich	.080	.180
	17057141, 145	7/16	15/32	1 1/2	—	.120	.110	.040	1 Rich	.080	.140
	17057143, 144	7/16	15/32	1 17/32	—	.120	.130	.100	1 Rich	.080	.140
	17057146, 148	7/16	15/32	1 17/32	—	.120	.100	.040	3 Rich	.080	.140
	17057147	7/16	15/32	1 1/2	—	.120	.110	.040	1 Rich	.080	.140
	17057149	7/16	15/32	1 9/16	—	.120	.110	.040	1 Lean	.080	.140
	17057180, 182	7/16	15/32	1 17/32	—	.120	.110	.060	1 Rich	.080	.140
	17057188, 190	19/32	19/32	1 21/32	—	.120	—	②	Index	.260	.325
	17057192, 194	19/32	19/32	1 21/32	—	.120	—	②	Index	.260	.325
	17057404	1/2	19/32	1 21/32	—	.120	—	③	1/2 Lean	.260	.325
	17057405	1/2	19/32	1 5/8	—	.120	—	③	1/2 Lean	.260	.325
	17057408, 410	21/32	19/32	1 5/8	—	.120	—	③	1 Lean	.260	.325
	17057412	21/32	19/32	1 5/8	—	.120	—	③	1 Lean	.260	.325
	17057414	21/32	19/32	1 21/32	—	.120	—	③	1 Lean	.260	.325
	17057445	7/16	15/32	1 1/2	—	.120	.140	.110	1 Lean	.080	.140
	17057446, 447	7/16	15/32	1 1/2	—	.120	.130	.110	1 Rich	.080	.140
	17057448	7/16	15/32	1 1/2	—	.120	.130	.110	1 Rich	.080	.140
1978	17058102, 103	15/32	19/32	1 17/32	—	.120	—	④	Index	.260	.325
	17058104, 105	15/32	19/32	1 21/32	—	.120	—	②	Index	.260	.325
	17058107, 109	15/32	19/32	1 17/32	—	.120	—	②	Index	.260	.325
	17058108, 110	19/32	19/32	1 21/32	—	.120	—	④	Index	.260	.325
	17058111	15/32	19/32	1 17/32	—	.120	—	②	Index	.260	.325
	17058112, 114	19/32	19/32	1 21/32	—	.120	—	④	Index	.260	.325
	17058113	19/32	19/32	1 17/32	—	.120	—	②	Index	.260	.325
	17058121, 123	19/32	19/32	1 17/32	—	.120	—	②	Index	.260	.325
	17058126, 128	19/32	19/32	1 17/32	—	.120	—	.130	Index	.260	.325
	17058140	7/16	15/32	1 19/32	—	.120	.110	.070	1 Rich	.080	.140
	17058141	7/16	15/32	1 19/32	①	.120	.140	.100	1 Rich	.080	.140
	17058143	7/16	15/32	1 9/16	①	.120	.110	.080	1 Rich	.080	.140
	17058144	7/16	15/32	1 5/8	①	.120	.110	.060	1 Rich	.080	.140
	17058145	7/16	15/32	1 19/32	①	.120	.110	.060	1 Rich	.080	.140
	17058147	7/16	15/32	1 19/32	①	.120	.140	.100	1 Rich	.080	.140
	17058148, 149	7/16	15/32	1 19/32	①	.120	.110	.080	1 Rich	.080	.140
	17058182, 183	7/16	15/32	1 19/32	①	.120	.110	.080	1 Rich	.080	.140
	17058185	7/16	15/32	1 19/32	①	.120	.110	.050	1 Rich	.080	.140
	17058187, 189	7/16	15/32	1 19/32	①	.120	.110	.080	1 Rich	.080	.140

Continued

MODEL 2GC & 2GE CARBURETOR ADJUSTMENT SPECIFICATIONS—Continued

See Tune Up Chart in car chapters for curb and fast idle speeds.

Year	Carb. Production No.	Float Level	Float Drop	Pump Rod	Idle Vent	Intermediate Choke Rod	Vacuum Break		Choke Setting	Choke Rod	Choke Unloader
							Throttle Lever Side	Choke Side			
	17058188	7/16	1 5/32	1 19/32	①	.120	.120	.050	1 Rich	.080	.140
	17058404, 405	1/2	19/32	1 21/32	—	.120	—	③	1/2 Lean	.260	.325
	17058408, 410	21/32	19/32	1 21/32	—	.120	—	③	1/2 Lean	.260	.325
	17058412, 414	21/32	19/32	1 21/32	—	.120	—	③	1/2 Lean	.260	.325
	17058444	7/16	1 5/32	1 19/32	①	.120	.140	.100	1 Rich	.080	.140
	17058446	7/16	1 5/32	1 19/32	①	.120	.130	.110	1 Rich	.080	.140
	17058447	7/16	1 5/32	1 19/32	①	.120	.150	.110	1 Rich	.080	.140
	17058448	7/16	1 5/32	1 19/32	①	.120	.140	.110	1 Rich	.080	.140

①—With idle speed properly adjusted, the vent valve should be just closed at idle.
②—.130 inch before first scheduled tune-up; .160 inch after first scheduled tune-up.
③—.140 inch before first scheduled tune-up; .160 inch after first scheduled tune-up.
④—.130 inch before first scheduled tune-up; .150 inch after first scheduled tune-up.

MODEL 2GC & 2GE ADJUSTMENTS

The Model 2GC and 2GE carburetors use a carburetor mounted choke coil, Figs. 1 and 2. The choke coil on the Model 2GE is electrically assisted.

Float Level Adjustment

Figs. 3 & 4—Adjust float level as directed for the type of float shown in the specification listed in the *Rochester Specifications Chart.*

Float Drop Adjustment

Figs. 5 & 6—Adjust float drop as directed for the type of float shown in the specification listed in the *Rochester Specifications Chart.*

Pump Rod Adjustment

Fig. 7—Back out idle stop screw and completely close throttle valves in bore. Place proper size gauge listed in the *Rochester Specifications Chart* on top of air horn ring. Bend pump rod at lower angle to obtain specified dimension to top of pump rod.

Idle Vent Adjustment

Fig. 8—Open throttle until vent valve just closes. Place proper size gauge on top of air horn ring. Dimension to top of pump rod should be as specified in the *Rochester Specifications Chart.* Adjust by bending tang on pump lever.

Bowl Vent Adjustment

Fig. 9—Set idle speed to specifications, then with the idle screw on second step of fast idle cam, vent valve should just be closed. To adjust, turn vent valve screw.

Intermediate Choke Rod Adjustment

2GC & 2GE Models, Fig. 10—Remove thermostat cover and coil assembly, then with fast idle screw on high step of cam and choke valve closed, the edge of choke lever must align with edge of .120" plug gauge as shown. To adjust, bend choke rod at point shown.

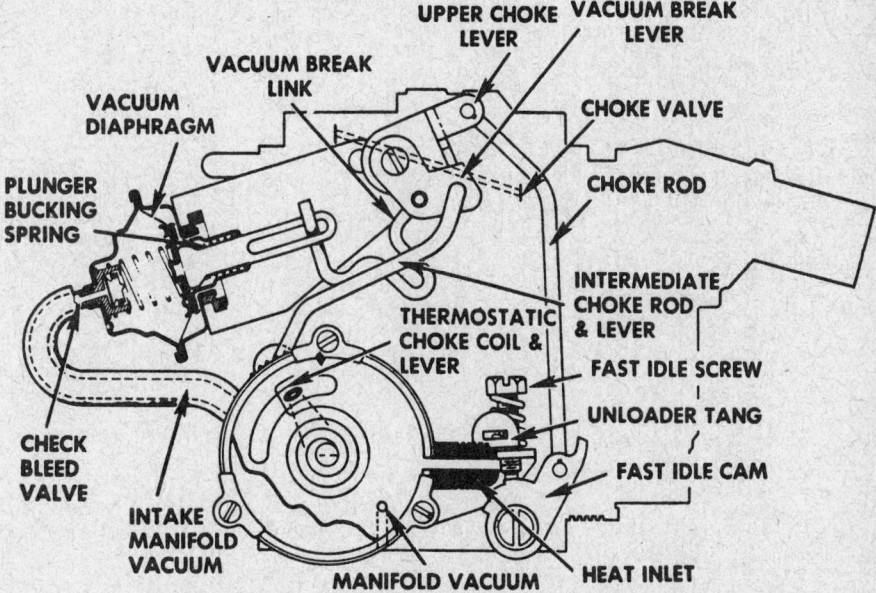

Fig. 2 Carburetor mounted automatic choke

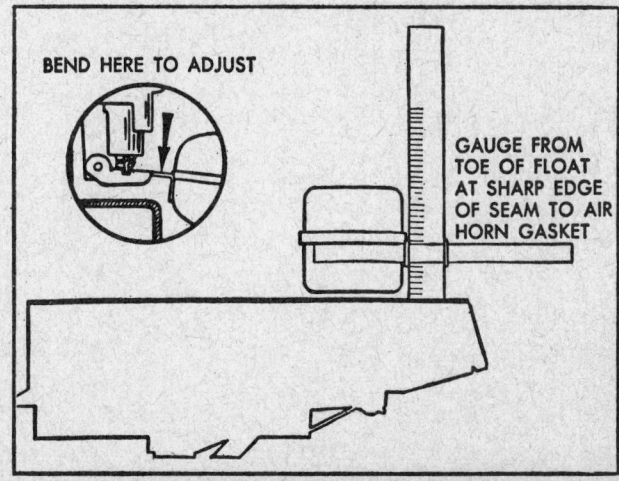

Fig. 3 Float level adjustment (brass float)

CARBURETORS

1. **HORN ASM,** Carb Air
2. **SCREW,** Air Horn (Short)
3. **SCREW,** Air Horn (Long)
4. **VALVE KIT,** Idle Vent
5. **SCREW,** Vent Valve Cover
6. **COVER,** Vent Valve
7. **GASKET,** Vent Valve
8. **BREAK & BRACKET ASM,** Auxiliary Vacuum
9. **SCREW,** Control Attaching
10. **VALVE,** Choke
11. **LINK,** Auxiliary Vacuum Break
12. **LEVER,** Choke Shaft

20. **WASHER,** Pump Lever
21. **SPRING,** Fuel Filter
22. **FILTER,** Fuel Inlet
23. **GASKET,** Filter Nut
24. **NUT,** Fuel Inlet Filter
25. **WASHER,** Lock
26. **SCREW,** Venturi Cluster-Outer
27. **SCREW,** Venturi Cluster-Center
28. **GASKET,** Center Screw
29. **CLUSTER ASM,** Venturi
30. **INSERT,** Main Well
31. **GASKET,** Venturi Cluster
32. **VALVE ASM,** Auxiliary Power
33. **SPRING,** Pump Return
34. **GASKET,** Aux Power Valve
35. **BALL,** Pump Inlet Check
36. **SCREW,** Fast Idle Cam
37. **CAM,** Fast Idle
38. **BOWL ASM,** Float
39. **SCREW,** Idle Stop
40. **SPRING,** Idle Stop Screw
41. **ROD,** Pump
42. **ROD,** Choke Intermediate
43. **CLIP,** Pump Rod
44. **BODY ASM,** Throttle
45. **SPRING,** Idle Needle
46. **NEEDLE,** Idle
47. **SCREW,** Throttle Body
48. **SEAL,** Inter Choke Shaft Dust
49. **GASKET,** Choke Housing
50. **HOUSING,** Choke
51. **SCREW,** Choke Housing
52. **GASKET,** Thermostat Cover
53. **COIL & GASKET,** Thermostat Cover
54. **SCREW,** Thermostat Cover
55. **RETAINER,** Thermostat Cover
56. **SHAFT,** Intermediate Choke
57. **SCREW,** Choke Lever
58. **LEVER,** Intermediate Choke
59. **ROD,** Auxiliary Choke
60. **HOSE,** Vacuum
61. **GASKET,** Throttle Body
62. **BAFFLE,** Fuel
63. **PIN,** Float Lever Hinge
64. **FLOAT ASM,** Carb
65. **GASKET,** Power Valve
66. **VALVE ASM,** Power
67. **JET,** Standard
68. **BALL,** Pump Discharge
69. **SPRING,** Pump Return
70. **GUIDE,** Pump Discharge
71. **GASKET,** Air Horn
72. **CLIP,** Float Needle Pull
73. **NEEDLE & SEAT ASM,** Carb
74. **GASKET,** Needle Seat
75. **PISTON ASM,** Power
76. **LINK,** Vacuum Break
77. **SCREW,** Choke Lever
78. **LEVER,** Choke
79. **SCREW,** Control Attaching
80. **CONTROL & BRACKET ASM,** Vacuum Break
81. **SCREW,** Solenoid Mtg Bracket

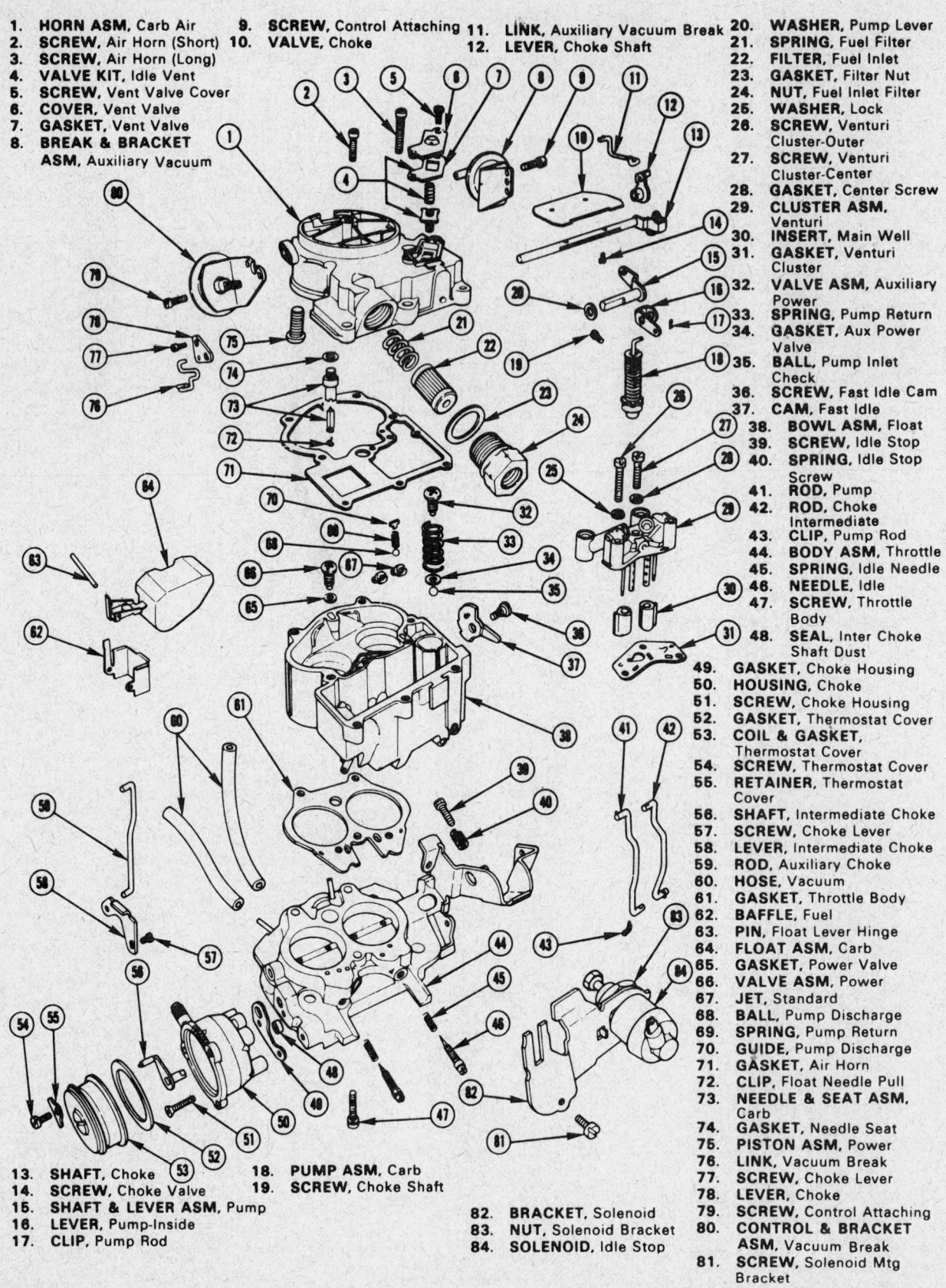

13. **SHAFT,** Choke
14. **SCREW,** Choke Valve
15. **SHAFT & LEVER ASM,** Pump
16. **LEVER,** Pump-Inside
17. **CLIP,** Pump Rod

18. **PUMP ASM,** Carb
19. **SCREW,** Choke Shaft

82. **BRACKET,** Solenoid
83. **NUT,** Solenoid Bracket
84. **SOLENOID,** Idle Stop

Fig. 1   Exploded view of Rochester model 2GC carburetor (Typical of model 2GE)

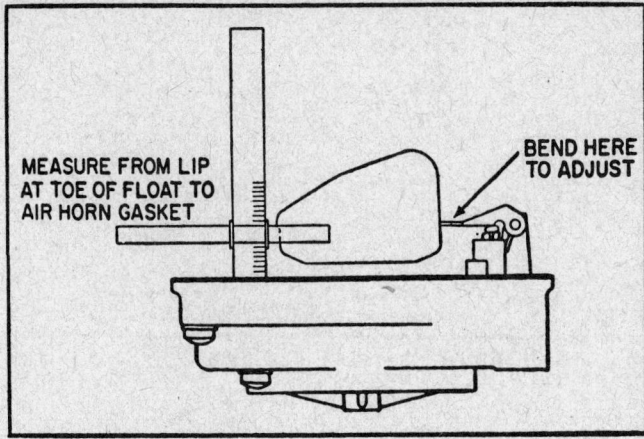

Fig. 4   Float level adjustment (nitrophyl float)

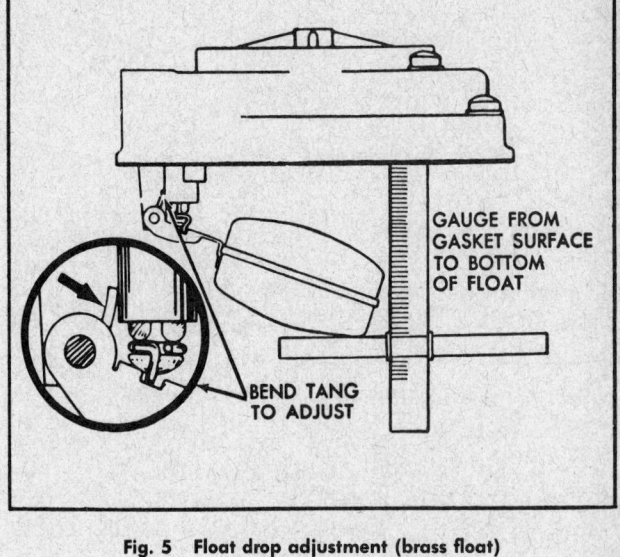

Fig. 5   Float drop adjustment (brass float)

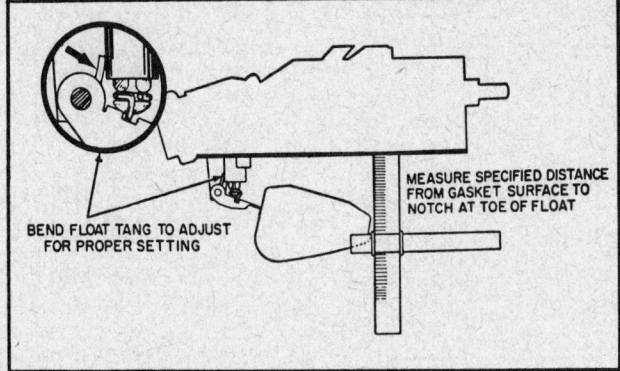

Fig. 6   Float drop adjustment (nitrophyl float)

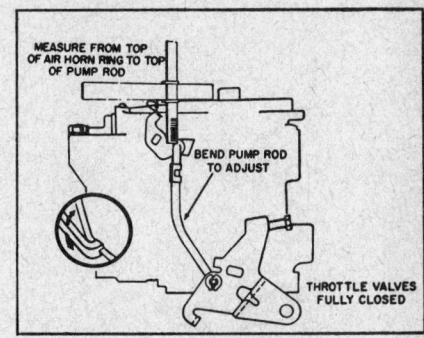

Fig. 7   Pump rod adjustment

Vacuum Break Adjustment

Figs. 11 & 12—Place fast idle screw on high step of cam, then using an outside vacuum source, seat vacuum diaphragm. On purge type vacuum diaphragms, cover bleed hole so that diaphragm will not bleed down. Hold choke towards closed position, then with vacuum diaphragm seated and rod in end of slot in plunger, check clearance between upper edge of choke valve and air horn wall. Refer to *Rochester Specifications Chart*. To adjust, bend vacuum break rod at point shown.

Automatic Choke Setting

Carburetor Mounted Choke, Fig. 13—Place idle screw on high step of fast idle cam, then loosen three retaining screws and rotate choke cover against coil tension until index mark is in line with specified point on choke housing (see *Rochester Specifications Chart*).

Choke Rod Adjustment

Fig. 14—It is important to position both slow idle and fast idle screws as follows before making choke rod adjustment.

1. On models using a single idle stop screw, turn stop screw in until it just contacts bottom step of fast idle cam. Then turn screw in one full turn farther.

2. On models using both a slow idle and a fast idle screw, turn slow idle stop screw in until it just contacts stop. Then turn this screw in one full turn from this point. Next turn the fast idle screw in until it touches bottom step of fast idle cam.

3. On all models, place idle screw on second

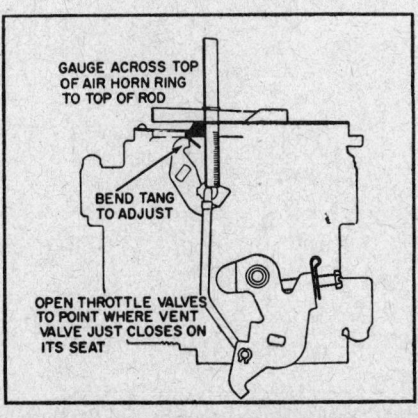

Fig. 8   Idle vent adjustment for 2GC carburetors

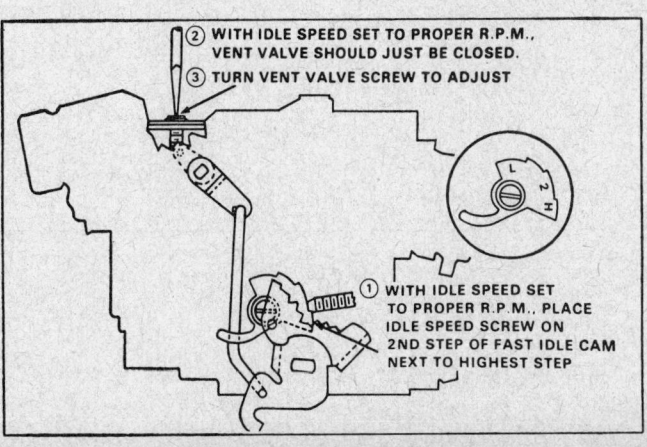

Fig. 9   Bowl vent adjustment

CARBURETORS

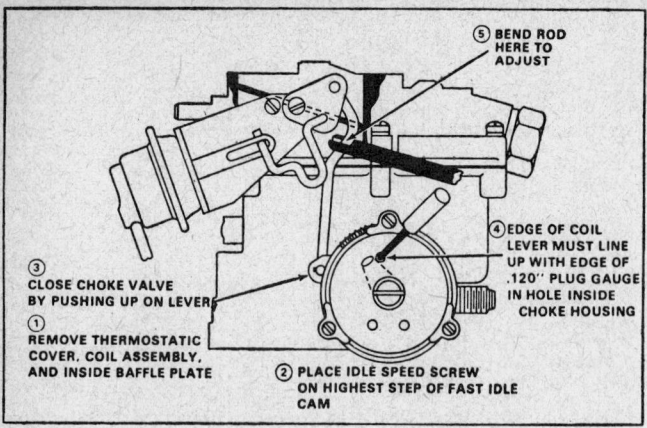

Fig. 10 Intermediate choke rod adjustment

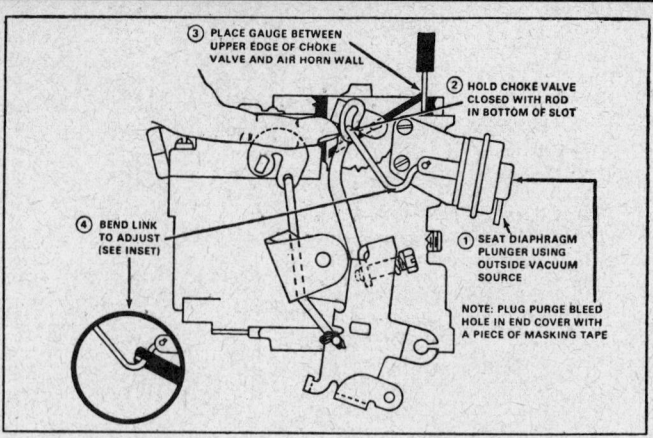

Fig. 11 Primary (throttle lever side) vacuum break adjustment

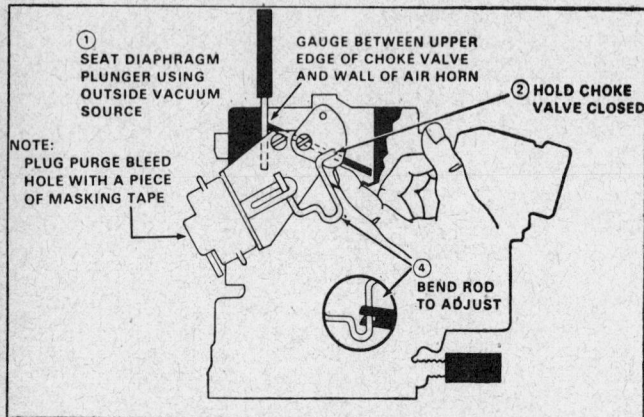

Fig. 12 Auxiliary (choke side) vacuum break adjustment

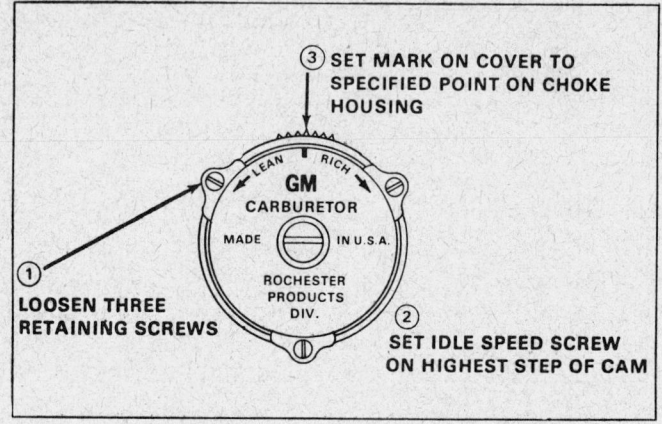

Fig. 13 Automatic choke adjustment for 2GC, 2GE carburetors

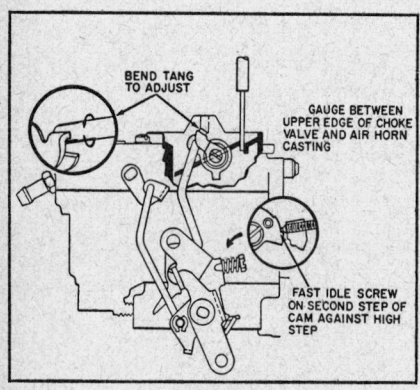

Fig. 14 Choke rod adjustment

step of fast idle cam against shoulder of high step. While holding screw in this position, check clearance between upper edge of choke valve and air horn wall as shown. Adjust to specified dimension by bending tang on choke lever and collar assembly (see *Rochester Specifications Chart*).

Choke Unloader Adjustment

Fig. 15—With throttle valves held wide open, the choke valve should be open just enough to admit the specified gauge between upper edge of choke valve and air horn wall (see *Rochester Specifications Chart*). To adjust, bend tang on throttle lever.

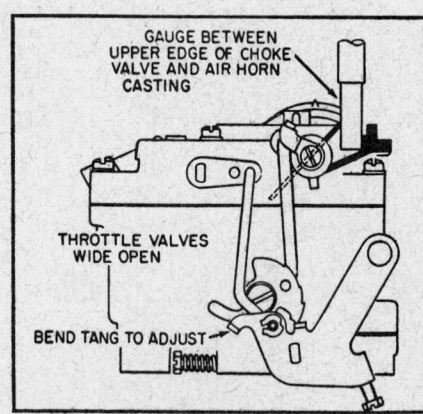

Fig. 15 Choke unloader adjustment for 2GC & 2GE carburetors

QUADRAJET E4M & M4M SERIES ADJUSTMENT SPECIFICATIONS

See Tune Up Chart in car chapters for curb and fast idle speeds.

Year	Carb. Production No.	Float Level	Pump Rod Hole	Pump Rod Adj.	Fast Idle (Bench) Turns	Choke Coil Lever	Choke Rod	Vacuum Break Front	Vacuum Break Rear	Air-Valve Dash-pot	Choke Setting	Choke Unleader	Air-Valve Valve Spring Wind-Up
1977	17057202, 204	15/32	Inner	9/32	3	.120	.325	②	—	.015	2 Lean	.280	7/8
	17057203	15/32	Inner	9/32	3	.120	.325	②	—	.015	3 Lean	.280	7/8
	17057210	15/32	Inner	9/32	3	.120	.325	③	—	.015	2 Lean	.280	1
	17057211	15/32	Inner	9/32	3	.120	.325	③	—	.015	3 Lean	.280	1
	17057226	15/32	Inner	9/32	3	.120	.325	.180	—	.015	2 Lean	.285	1
	17057228	13/32	Inner	9/32	3	.120	.325	③	—	.015	2 Lean	.280	1
	17057230	13/32	Inner	3/8	2	.120	.080	.140	.120	.030	2 Rich	.230	1/2
	17057231	17/32	Inner	3/8	2	.120	.080	.140	.140	.030	2 Rich	.230	3/4
	17057232	13/32	Outer	3/8	2	.120	.080	.140	.120	.030	2 Rich	.230	1/2
	17057233	13/32	Inner	3/8	2	.120	.080	.140	.140	.030	2 Rich	.230	3/4
	17057234	13/32	Inner	9/32	2	.120	.080	.140	.120	.030	2 Rich	.230	3/4
	17057235	17/32	Inner	9/32	2	.120	.080	.140	.120	.030	2 Rich	.230	3/4
	17057236	13/32	Inner	9/32	2	.120	.080	.140	.140	.030	2 Rich	.230	3/4
	17057241, 242	5/16	Outer	3/8	2	.120	.095	.120	.105	.015	1 Rich	.240	3/4
	17057248	5/16	Outer	3/8	3	.120	.095	.130	.110	.015	Index	.240	3/4
	17057250, 252	13/32	Inner	9/32	3	.120	.100	.135	.180	.030	2 Rich	.220	1/2
	17057253, 255	13/32	Inner	9/32	3	.120	.100	.135	.180	.030	2 Rich	.220	1/2
	17057256	13/32	Inner	9/32	3	.120	.100	.135	.180	.030	2 Rich	.220	1/2
	17057257, 258	15/32	Inner	9/32	3	.120	.100	.135	.225	.030	3 Rich	.220	1/2
	17057262, 266	17/32	Outer	3/8	3	.120	.130	.150	.240	.030	1 Rich	.220	1/2
	17057263	17/32	Outer	3/8	3	.120	.130	.165	.240	.030	1 Rich	.220	5/8
	17057274	17/32	Outer	3/8	3	.120	.130	.150	.240	.030	1 Rich	.220	1/2
	17057502, 504	15/32	Inner	9/32	3	.120	.325	④	—	.015	2 Lean	.280	7/8
	17057510, 528	15/32	Inner	9/32	3	.120	.325	.180	—	.015	2 Lean	.280	1
	17057530, 533	13/32	Outer	7/16	2	.120	.080	.150	.150	.030	2 Rich	.230	1/2
	17057550, 553	13/32	Inner	9/32	3	.120	.100	.135	.225	.030	2 Rich	.220	1/2
	17057552	15/32	Inner	9/32	3	.120	.100	.135	.225	.030	3 Rich	.220	1/2
	17057582, 584	15/32	Outer	3/8	3	.120	.325	③	—	.015	2 Lean	.280	7/8
1978	17058202, 204	15/32	Inner	9/32	3	.120	46°	⑤	—	.015	2 Lean	42°	7/8
	17058203	15/32	Inner	9/32	3	.120	46°	⑤	—	.015	3 Lean	42°	7/8
	17058210, 228	15/32	Inner	9/32	3	.120	46°	⑥	—	.015	2 Lean	42°	1
	17058211	15/32	Inner	9/32	3	.120	46°	⑥	—	.015	3 Lean	42°	1
	17058230	13/32	Inner	9/32	3	.120	16°	25°	39°	.030	2 Rich	35°	1/2
	17058232	13/32	Inner	9/32	2	.120	16°	26°	28°	.030	2 Rich	35°	3/4
	17058233	13/32	Inner	9/32	2	.120	16°	26°	28°	.030	2 Rich	35°	1/2
	17058240	7/32	Inner	9/32	3	.120	14 1/2°	21°	23°	.015	Index	38°	3/4
	17058241	5/16	Outer	3/8	3	.120	18°	21 1/2°	19°	.015	1 Rich	38°	3/4
	17058246	7/32	Outer	3/8	3	.120	14 1/2°	23°	23°	.015	Index	38°	3/4
	17058250, 253	13/32	Inner	9/32	3	.120	18°	23°	30 1/2°	.030	2 Rich	35°	1/2
	17058254	15/32	Inner	9/32	3	.120	19°	24°	—	.030	3 Rich	35°	1/2
	17058257, 258	13/32	Inner	9/32	3	.120	19°	24°	36 1/2°	.030	2 Rich	35°	1/2
	17058259	13/32	Inner	9/32	3	.120	19°	24°	30 1/2°	.030	2 Rich	35°	1/2
	17058263	17/32	Outer	3/8	3	.120	23°	28°	40°	.030	Index	35°	5/8
	17058264, 278	17/32	Outer	3/8	3	.120	23 1/2°	26°	40°	.030	1 Rich	35°	1/2
	17058266, 274	17/32	Outer	3/8	3	.120	23 1/2°	26°	40°	.030	Index	35°	1/2
	17058272	15/32	Outer	3/8	3	.120	14 1/2°	24°	32°	.030	2 Rich	36°	5/8
	17058276	17/32	Outer	3/8	3	.120	23 1/2°	26°	40°	.030	Index	35°	1/2
	17058282, 284	15/32	Inner	9/32	3	.120	46°	27°	—	.015	Index	42°	7/8
	17058502, 504	15/32	Inner	9/32	3	.120	46°	①	—	.015	2 Lean	42°	7/8
	17058530, 531	13/32	Inner	9/32	2	.120	16°	26°	28°	.030	2 Rich	35°	1/2
	17058532, 533	13/32	Inner	9/32	2	.120	16°	26°	28°	.030	2 Rich	35°	1/2
	17058540	7/32	Inner	9/32	3	.120	14 1/2°	21°	23°	.015	Index	38°	3/4

Continued

CARBURETORS

QUADRAJET E4M & M4M SERIES ADJUSTMENT SPECIFICATIONS—Continued

See Tune Up Chart in car chapters for curb and fast idle speeds.

Year	Carb. Production No.	Float Level	Pump Rod Hole	Pump Rod Adj.	Fast Idle (Bench) Turns	Choke Coil Lever	Choke Rod	Vacuum Break Front	Vacuum Break Rear	Air-Valve Dash-pot	Choke Setting	Choke Unleader	Air-Valve Valve Spring Wind-Up
	17058550, 553	13/32	Inner	9/32	3	.120	19°	24°	36½°	.030	2 Rich	35°	1/2
	17058555	13/32	Inner	9/32	3	.120	19°	24°	36½°	.030	2 Rich	35°	1/2
	17058559	15/32	Inner	9/32	3	.120	19°	24°	—	.030	3 Rich	36½°	1/2
	17058582, 584	15/32	Inner	9/32	3	.120	46°	⑥	—	.015	2 Lean	42°	7/8
1979	17059202, 204	15/32	Inner	1/4	2	.120	38°	28°	—	.015	1 Lean	38°	7/8
	17059203, 207	15/32	Inner	1/4	2	.120	38°	27°	—	.015	2 Lean	38°	7/8
	17059210	15/32	Inner	9/32	2	.120	38°	27°	—	.015	1 Lean	38°	1
	17059211	15/32	Inner	9/32	2	.120	38°	27°	—	.015	2 Lean	38°	1
	17059216, 217	15/32	Inner	1/4	2	.120	38°	27°	—	.015	1 Lean	38°	7/8
	17059218, 222	15/32	Inner	9/32	2	.120	38°	28°	—	.015	2 Lean	38°	7/8
	17059228	15/32	Inner	9/32	2	.120	38°	27°	—	.015	1 Lean	38°	1
	17059230	13/32	Inner	9/32	1½	.120	16°	25°	37°	.030	2 Rich	25°	1/2
	17059232	13/32	Inner	9/32	2¼	.120	16°	26°	28°	.030	2 Rich	25°	1/2
	17059240, 243	7/32	Inner	9/32	2	.120	14.5°	21°	21°	.015	1 Rich	30°	3/4
	17059241	5/16	Inner	3/8	2	.120	18°	20°	20.5°	.015	1 Rich	38°	3/4
	17059242	7/32	Inner	9/32	2	.120	14.5°	15°	13°	.015	2 Rich	30°	3/4
	17059247, 249	5/16	Outer	3/8	2	.120	18°	20°	19°	.015	1 Rich	38°	3/4
	17059250, 251	13/32	Inner	9/32	2	.120	18°	23°	30.5°	.030	2 Rich	35°	1/2
	17059253	13/32	Inner	9/32	2	.120	18°	23	30.5	.030	2 Rich	35°	1/2
	17059256, 258	13/32	Inner	9/32	2	.120	19°	24°	32°	.030	2 Rich	35°	1/2
	17059259	13/32	Inner	9/32	2	.120	18°	23°	30.5°	.030	2 Rich	35°	1/2
	17059263	17/32	Outer	3/8	2	.120	23°	28°	38°	.030	Index	35°	5/8
	17059271	7/16	Outer	3/8	2	.120	20°	25°	34°	.030	1 Rich	33°	5/8
	17059272	15/32	Outer	3/8	2	.120	14.5°	23°	29.5°	.030	2 Rich	33°	5/8
	17059282, 284	15/32	Inner	1/4	2	.120	38°	27°	—	.015	1 Lean	38°	7/8
	17059502, 504	15/32	Inner	1/4	2	.120	38°	28°	—	.015	2 Lean	38°	7/8
	17059505, 507	15/32	Inner	1/4	2	.120	38°	28°	—	.015	1 Lean	38°	7/8
	17059530, 532	13/32	Inner	9/32	2¼	.120	16°	26°	28°	.030	2 Rich	25°	1/2
	17059540, 543	7/32	Inner	9/32	2	.120	14.5°	21°	23°	.015	1 Rich	38°	3/4
	17059544	7/32	Inner	9/32	2	.120	14.5°	21°	21°	.015	1 Rich	30°	3/4
	17059546	7/32	Inner	9/32	2	.120	14.5°	21°	21°	.015	Index	30°	3/4
	17059547	7/32	Inner	9/32	2	.120	14.5°	21°	18°	.015	1 Rich	30°	3/4
	17059548	7/32	Inner	9/32	2	.120	14.5°	21°	15°	.015	1 Rich	30°	3/4
	17059553, 554	13/32	Inner	9/32	2	.120	19°	24°	36.5°	.030	2 Rich	35°	1/2
	17059555	13/32	Inner	9/32	2	.120	19°	26°	36.5°	.030	2 Rich	35°	1/2
	17059582, 584	15/32	Outer	11/32	2	.120	38°	33°	—	.015	1 Lean	46°	7/8
1980	17080202, 204	7/16	Inner	1/4	4	.120	20°	27°	—	.025	⑦	38°	7/8
	17080207	7/16	Inner	1/4	4	.120	20°	27°	—	.025	⑦	38°	7/8
	17080228	7/16	Inner	9/32	4	.120	20°	30°	—	.025	⑦	38°	7/8
	17080230	7/16	Inner	9/32	—	.120	16°	26°	24°	.025	⑦	35°	1/2
	17080240	3/16	Inner	9/32	—	.120	14.5°	16°	16°	.025	⑦	30°	9/16
	17080241	7/16	Inner	7/16	—	.120	18°	23°	20.5°	.025	⑦	38°	3/4
	17080242	13/32	Inner	9/32	—	.120	14.5°	15°	18°	.025	⑦	35°	9/16
	17080243	3/16	Inner	9/32	—	.120	14.5°	16°	16°	.025	⑦	30°	9/16
	17080244	5/16	Inner	9/32	—	.120	24.5°	18°	14°	.025	⑦	38°	5/8
	17080249	7/16	Inner	9/32	1½	.120	18°	23°	20.5°	.025	⑦	38°	3/4
	17080250, 251	13/32	Inner	9/32	3	.120	17°	26°	34°	.025	⑦	35°	1/2
	17080252, 253	13/32	Inner	9/32	3	.120	17°	26°	34°	.025	⑦	35°	1/2
	17080259, 260	13/32	Inner	9/32	3	.120	17°	26°	34°	.025	⑦	35°	1/2
	17080270	15/32	Outer	3/8	1½	.120	14.5°	26°	34°	.025	⑦	35°	5/8
	17080271	15/32	Outer	3/8	—	.120	20°	25°	34°	.025	⑦	33°	5/8

Continued

QUADRAJET E4M & M4M SERIES ADJUSTMENT SPECIFICATIONS—Continued

See Tune Up Chart in car chapters for curb and fast idle speeds.

Year	Carb. Production No.	Float Level	Pump Rod		Fast Idle (Bench) Turns	Choke Coil Lever	Choke Rod	Vacuum Break		Air-Valve Dash-pot	Choke Setting	Choke Unleader	Air-Valve Valve Spring Wind-Up
			Hole	Adj.				Front	Rear				
	17080272	15/32	Outer	3/8	1½	.120	14.5°	23°	29.5°	.025	⑦	33°	5/8
	17080274	15/32	Outer	5/16	1½	.120	16°	20°	28°	.025	⑦	33°	5/8
	17080282, 284	7/16	Outer	11/32	4	.120	20°	25°	—	.025	⑦	38°	7/8
	17080502, 504	1/2	—	—	4	.120	20°	24°	30°	.025	⑦	38°	7/8
	17080530	17/32	—	9/32	—	.120	16°	25°	47°	.025	⑦	40°	1/2
	17080540, 543	3/8	—	—	—	.120	14.5°	19°	23°	.025	⑦	38°	9/16
	17080542	3/8	—	—	4	.120	14.5°	19°	13°	.025	⑦	38°	9/16
	17080546	—	—	—	—	—	—	—	—	—	—	—	—
	17080547	—	—	—	—	—	—	—	—	—	—	—	—
	17080548	—	—	—	—	—	—	—	—	—	—	—	—
	17080553	15/32	—	9/32	3	.120	17°	25°	35°	.025	⑦	35°	1/2
	17080554	15/32	—	9/32	3	.120	17°	25°	34°	.025	⑦	35°	1/2
1981	17081202	11/32	—	—	4½	.120	20°	26°	—	.025	⑦	38°	7/8
	17081203	11/32	—	—	4½	.120	20°	26°	—	.025	⑦	38°	7/8
	17081204	11/32	—	—	4½	.120	20°	26°	—	.025	⑦	38°	7/8
	17081207	11/32	—	—	4½	.120	20°	26°	—	.025	⑦	38°	7/8
	17081216	11/32	—	—	4½	.120	20°	26°	—	.025	⑦	38°	7/8
	17081217	11/32	—	—	4½	.120	20°	26°	—	.025	⑦	38°	7/8
	17081218	11/32	—	—	4½	.120	20°	26°	—	.025	⑦	38°	7/8
	17081242	5/16	—	—	4½	.120	24.5°	17°	15°	.025	⑦	38°	9/16
	17081243	1/4	—	—	4½	.120	24.5°	19°	17°	.025	⑦	38°	9/16
	17081245	3/8	—	—	3	.120	24.5°	28°	24°	.025	⑦	38°	5/8
	17081247	3/8	—	—	3	.120	24.5°	28°	24°	.025	⑦	38°	5/8
	17081248	3/8	—	—	2	.120	24.5°	28°	24°	.025	⑦	38°	5/8
	17081249	3/8	—	—	3	.120	24.5°	28°	24°	.025	⑦	38°	5/8
	17081253	15/32	—	—	3	.120	14°	25°	36°	.025	⑦	35°	5/8
	17081254	15/32	—	—	3	.120	14°	25°	36°	.025	⑦	35°	1/2
	17081270	7/16	—	—	4½	.120	14.5°	24°	34°	.025	⑦	35°	5/8
	17081272	7/16	—	—	4½	.120	14.5°	24°	40°	.025	⑦	35°	5/8
	17081274	7/16	—	—	4½	.120	16°	24°	35°	.025	⑦	35°	5/8
	17081289	13/32	—	—	2	.120	24.5°	28°	24°	.025	⑦	38°	5/8
1982	17082202	11/32	—	—	3	.120	20°	27°	—	.025	⑦	38°	7/8
	17082203	11/32	—	—	3	.120	38°	27°	—	.025	⑦	38°	7/8
	17082204	11/32	—	—	3	.120	20°	27°	—	.025	⑦	38°	7/8
	17082207	11/32	—	—	3	.120	38°	27°	—	.025	⑦	38°	7/8
	17082244	7/16	—	—	3	.120	24.5°	21°	16°	.025	⑦	32°	9/16
	17082245	3/8	—	—	3	.120	24.5°	26°	26°	.025	⑦	32°	5/8
	17082246	3/8	—	—	3	.120	24.5°	26°	26°	.025	⑦	32°	5/8
	17082247	3/8	—	—	3	.120	18°	26°	26°	.025	⑦	32°	5/8
	17082248	13/32	—	—	3	.120	24.5°	28°	24°	.025	⑦	38°	5/8
	17082251	15/32	—	—	3	.120	14°	25°	45°	.025	⑦	35°	1/2
	17082253	15/32	—	—	3	.120	14°	25°	36°	.025	⑦	35°	1/2
	17082264	7/16	—	—	3	.120	24.5°	21°	16°	.025	⑦	32°	9/16
	17082265	3/8	—	—	3	.120	24.5°	26°	26°	.025	⑦	32°	5/8
	17082266	3/8	—	—	3	.120	24.5°	26°	26°	.025	⑦	32°	5/8
	17082267	3/8	—	—	3	.120	24.5°	28°	24°	.025	⑦	38°	5/8
	17082268	13/32	—	—	3	.120	24.5°	28°	24°	.025	⑦	38°	5/8
1983	17082265	3/8	—	—	3	.120	24.5°	26°	26°	.025	⑦	32°	5/8
	17082266	3/8	—	—	3	.120	24.5°	26°	26°	.025	⑦	32°	5/8
	17082267	3/8	—	—	3	.120	18°	26°	26°	.025	⑦	32°	5/8
	17082268	3/8	—	—	3	.120	18°	26°	26°	.025	⑦	32°	5/8
	17083202	11/32	—	—	3⅜	.120	20°	—	27°	.025	⑦	38°	7/8
	17083203	11/32	—	—	3⅜	.120	38°	—	27°	.025	⑦	38°	7/8

Continued

QUADRAJET E4M & M4M SERIES ADJUSTMENT SPECIFICATIONS—Continued

See Tune Up Chart in car chapters for curb and fast idle speeds.

Year	Carb. Production No.	Float Level	Pump Rod		Fast Idle (Bench) Turns	Choke Coil Lever	Choke Rod	Vacuum Break		Air-Valve Dash-pot	Choke Setting	Choke Unleader	Air-Valve Valve Spring Wind-Up
			Hole	Adj.				Front	Rear				
	17083204	11/32	—	—	3 3/8	.120	20°	—	27°	.025	⑦	38°	7/8
	17083206	11/32	—	—	3 3/8	.120	20°	—	27°	.025	⑦	38°	7/8
	17083207	11/32	—	—	3 3/8	.120	38°	—	27°	.025	⑦	38°	7/8
	17083216	11/32	—	—	3 3/8	.120	20°	—	27°	.025	⑦	38°	7/8
	17083218	11/32	—	—	3 3/8	.120	20°	—	27°	.025	⑦	38°	7/8
	17083236	11/32	—	—	3	.120	20°	—	27°	.025	⑦	38°	7/8
	17083242	9/32	—	—	3	.120	24.5°	20°	—	.025	⑦	38°	9/16
	17083244	1/4	—	—	3	.120	24.5°	21°	16°	.025	⑦	32°	9/16
	17083248	3/8	—	—	3	.120	24.5°	26°	26°	.025	⑦	32°	5/8
	17083250	7/16	—	—	3	.120	14°	27°	42°	.025	⑦	35°	1/2
	17083253	7/16	—	—	3	.120	14°	27°	41°	.025	⑦	35°	1/2
	17083506	7/16	—	—	3	.120	20°	27°	36°	.025	⑦	36°	7/8
	17083508	7/16	—	—	3	.120	20°	27°	36°	.025	⑦	36°	7/8
	17083524	7/16	—	—	3	.120	20°	25°	36°	.025	⑦	36°	7/8
	17083526	7/16	—	—	3	.120	20°	25°	36°	.025	⑦	36°	7/8
	17083553	7/16	—	—	3	.120	14°	27°	41°	.025	⑦	35°	1/2

①—28° before first scheduled tune-up; 31° after first scheduled tune-up.
②—.160 inch before first scheduled tune-up; .245 inch after first scheduled tune-up.
③—.180 inch before first scheduled tune-up; .275 inch after first scheduled tune-up.
④—.165 inch before first scheduled tune-up; .260 inch after first scheduled tune-up.
⑤—27° before first scheduled tune-up; 30° after first scheduled tune-up.
⑥—30° before first scheduled tune-up; 33° after first scheduled tune-up.
⑦—Tamper-resistant

QUADRAJET E4M & M4M SERIES CARBURETOR ADJUSTMENTS

The M4M Series (M4MC, M4MCA and M4MEA) Quadrajet carburetor, Fig. 1, are two stage, downdraft carburetors. These units are similar in design to the previously used Quadrajet carburetors. A triple venturi system, with 1 7/32 inch venturi, is used on the primary side of the carburetor with 1 3/8 inch primary throttle bores. The secondary side has two 2 1/4 inch bores.

The primary side of the carburetor has six systems of operation: float, idle, main metering, power, pump and choke. The secondary side has one metering system which supplements the primary main metering system and receives fuel from a common float chamber.

An Adjustable Part Throttle (A.P.T.) feature incorporates an adjustable metering rod assembly operating in a fixed jet. On some models, a barometric pressure-sensitive aneroid (Bellows) is an integral part of the A.P.T. metering rod assembly. This provides a close tolerance control of fuel flow to the main metering system, thereby controlling air/fuel ratios during part throttle operation.

Some units use a multiple stage power enrichment system with two power pistons. One piston is an auxiliary power piston with a single metering rod operating in a fixed jet. The primary power piston with two metering rods operates in replaceable metering jets. This system provides sensitive control of the air/fuel ratio during light engine power requirements while providing richer mixtures during moderate to heavy engine loads.

All units use a bowl mounted choke housing with a thermostatic coil assembly. Also, a dual vacuum break system is used to improve cold engine warm-up and drive-away performance. Cadillac units use a three stage electric choke with a ceramic resistor for precise timing of the choke valve opening to improve engine warm-up performance.

The E4M series (E4MC and E4ME) carburetors are used on vehicles equipped with the C4 (Computor Controlled Catalytic Converter) System or Computer Control Command System, Fig. 2. An electrically operated mixture control solenoid is mounted in the float bowl and is used to control air and fuel metered to idle and main metering systems of the carburetor. Fuel metering is controlled by two special stepped primary metering rods, operating in removable jets and positioned by a plunger in the solenoid which is controlled by an electrical signal from the Electronic Control Module. Air metering to the idle system is controlled by an idle air bleed valve located in the air horn, which follows movement of the mixture control solenoid plunger to control the amount of bleed air into the idle system. A throttle position sensor mounted in the float bowl, is used to electrically signal the Electronic Control module of various throttle position changes.

On some 1981–83 units, an idle speed control mounted on the float bowl is used to control idle speed. On these units, the curb idle speed is programmed into the Electronic Control Module and no attempt should be made to adjust idle speed. On some 1981–83 models an idle load compensator mounted on the float bowl is used to control idle speed. The compensator uses manifold vacuum to sense changes in engine load and compensates by adjusting curb idle speed. This unit should not be adjusted, unless if during diagnosis, curb idle speed is not within specifications.

NOTE: On 1980–83 units the choke cover is retained to the choke housing by three pop rivets. With float bowl and throttle body properly supported, carefully align a No. 21 drill on pop rivet head. Drill only enough to remove the rivet heads, then using a small hammer and drift, drive remainder of rivet from choke housing. A service kit is available for choke cover installation. The choke cover should be removed only during major carburetor overhaul or if the choke coil is damaged.

Float Level Adjustment

Fig. 3—With an adjustable T-scale, measure distance from top of float bowl gasket surface, with gasket removed, to top of float at a point 3/16 inch back from toe. Dimension should be as specified in the Specification Chart. To adjust, bend float arm.

NOTE: On units equipped with Computer Controlled Catalytic Converter (C-4) System

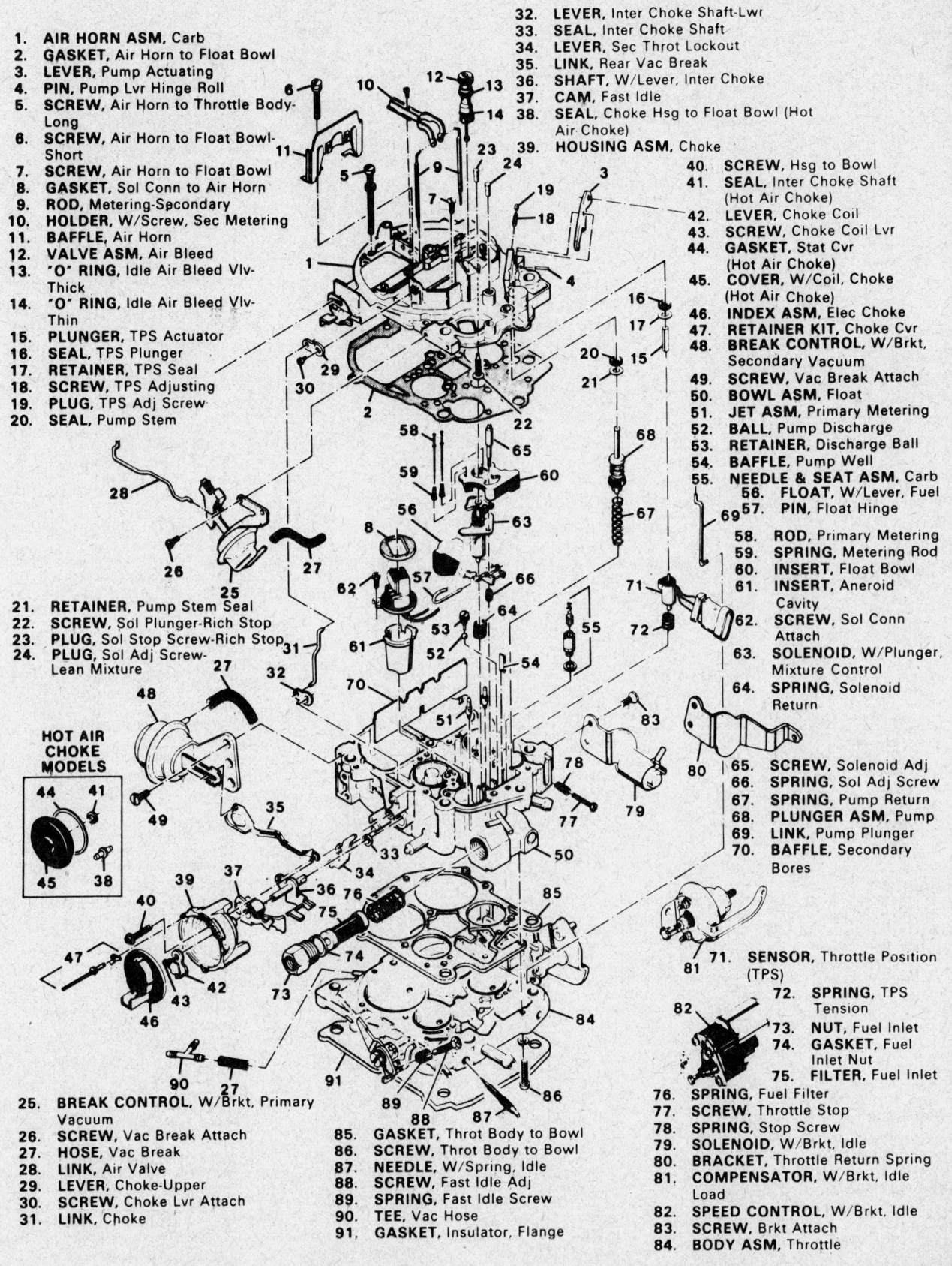

1. **AIR HORN ASM,** Carb
2. **GASKET,** Air Horn to Float Bowl
3. **LEVER,** Pump Actuating
4. **PIN,** Pump Lvr Hinge Roll
5. **SCREW,** Air Horn to Throttle Body-Long
6. **SCREW,** Air Horn to Float Bowl-Short
7. **SCREW,** Air Horn to Float Bowl
8. **GASKET,** Sol Conn to Air Horn
9. **ROD,** Metering-Secondary
10. **HOLDER,** W/Screw, Sec Metering
11. **BAFFLE,** Air Horn
12. **VALVE ASM,** Air Bleed
13. **"O" RING,** Idle Air Bleed Vlv-Thick
14. **"O" RING,** Idle Air Bleed Vlv-Thin
15. **PLUNGER,** TPS Actuator
16. **SEAL,** TPS Plunger
17. **RETAINER,** TPS Seal
18. **SCREW,** TPS Adjusting
19. **PLUG,** TPS Adj Screw
20. **SEAL,** Pump Stem

21. **RETAINER,** Pump Stem Seal
22. **SCREW,** Sol Plunger-Rich Stop
23. **PLUG,** Sol Stop Screw-Rich Stop
24. **PLUG,** Sol Adj Screw-Lean Mixture

HOT AIR CHOKE MODELS

25. **BREAK CONTROL,** W/Brkt, Primary Vacuum
26. **SCREW,** Vac Break Attach
27. **HOSE,** Vac Break
28. **LINK,** Air Valve
29. **LEVER,** Choke-Upper
30. **SCREW,** Choke Lvr Attach
31. **LINK,** Choke

32. **LEVER,** Inter Choke Shaft-Lwr
33. **SEAL,** Inter Choke Shaft
34. **LEVER,** Sec Throt Lockout
35. **LINK,** Rear Vac Break
36. **SHAFT,** W/Lever, Inter Choke
37. **CAM,** Fast Idle
38. **SEAL,** Choke Hsg to Float Bowl (Hot Air Choke)
39. **HOUSING ASM,** Choke
40. **SCREW,** Hsg to Bowl
41. **SEAL,** Inter Choke Shaft (Hot Air Choke)
42. **LEVER,** Choke Coil
43. **SCREW,** Choke Coil Lvr
44. **GASKET,** Stat Cvr (Hot Air Choke)
45. **COVER,** W/Coil, Choke (Hot Air Choke)
46. **INDEX ASM,** Elec Choke
47. **RETAINER KIT,** Choke Cvr
48. **BREAK CONTROL,** W/Brkt, Secondary Vacuum
49. **SCREW,** Vac Break Attach
50. **BOWL ASM,** Float
51. **JET ASM,** Primary Metering
52. **BALL,** Pump Discharge
53. **RETAINER,** Discharge Ball
54. **BAFFLE,** Pump Well
55. **NEEDLE & SEAT ASM,** Carb
56. **FLOAT,** W/Lever, Fuel
57. **PIN,** Float Hinge

58. **ROD,** Primary Metering
59. **SPRING,** Metering Rod
60. **INSERT,** Float Bowl
61. **INSERT,** Aneroid Cavity
62. **SCREW,** Sol Conn Attach
63. **SOLENOID,** W/Plunger, Mixture Control
64. **SPRING,** Solenoid Return
65. **SCREW,** Solenoid Adj
66. **SPRING,** Sol Adj Screw
67. **SPRING,** Pump Return
68. **PLUNGER ASM,** Pump
69. **LINK,** Pump Plunger
70. **BAFFLE,** Secondary Bores

71. **SENSOR,** Throttle Position (TPS)
72. **SPRING,** TPS Tension
73. **NUT,** Fuel Inlet
74. **GASKET,** Fuel Inlet Nut
75. **FILTER,** Fuel Inlet
76. **SPRING,** Fuel Filter
77. **SCREW,** Throttle Stop
78. **SPRING,** Stop Screw
79. **SOLENOID,** W/Brkt, Idle
80. **BRACKET,** Throttle Return Spring
81. **COMPENSATOR,** W/Brkt, Idle Load
82. **SPEED CONTROL,** W/Brkt, Idle
83. **SCREW,** Brkt Attach
84. **BODY ASM,** Throttle
85. **GASKET,** Throt Body to Bowl
86. **SCREW,** Throt Body to Bowl
87. **NEEDLE,** W/Spring, Idle
88. **SCREW,** Fast Idle Adj
89. **SPRING,** Fast Idle Screw
90. **TEE,** Vac Hose
91. **GASKET,** Insulator, Flange

Exploded view of Rochester model E4M carburetor

CARBURETORS

1. **HORN ASM**, Air
2. **SCREW**, Air Horn
3. **SCREW**, Air Horn
4. **PIN**, Lever Roll
5. **CAM**, Secondary Air Valve
6. **LEVER**, Secondary Metering Rod
7. **HOLDER KIT**, Metering Rod Secondary
8. **SCREW**, Metering Rod Holder

15. **PISTON ASM**, Power
16. **SPRING**, Power Piston
17. **ROD**, Carb Metering
19. **BALL**, Pump Discharge
20. **JET**, Main Metering
21. **INSERT**, Float Bowl
22. **FLOAT ASM**, Carb
23. **PIN**, Float Hinge
24. **PUMP ASM**, Carb
25. **SPRING**, Pump Piston
26. **ROD**, W/Spring Auxiliary Metering
27. **PISTON ASM**, Auxiliary Power
28. **SCREW**, Aneroid Attaching
29. **ROD ASM**, APT
30. **CLIP**, Float Needle Pull
31. **NEEDLE**, W/Seat Carb
32. **GASKET**, Needle Seat
33. **SPRING**, Idle Stop Screw
34. **SCREW**, Idle Stop
35. **SOLENOID**, W/Bracket Idle Stop
36. **SCREW**, Throttle Return Bracket
37. **SPRING**, Fuel Filter
38. **FILTER**, Fuel Inlet
39. **GASKET**, Filter Nut
40. **NUT**, Fuel Inlet Filter
41. **ROD**, Pump
42. **SPRING**, Idle Needle
43. **NEEDLE**, Idle
44. **SCREW**, Throttle Body
45. **SCREW**, Fast Idle Adjust
46. **SPRING**, Fast Idle Screw
47. **SCREW**, Fast Idle Lever Attaching
48. **SPRING**, Cam Lever
49. **LEVER**, Fast Idle
50. **LEVER**, Cam Follower
51. **BODY ASM**, Throttle
52. **HOSE**, Vacuum
53. **GASKET**, Throttle Body
54. **COVER ASM**, Thermostat

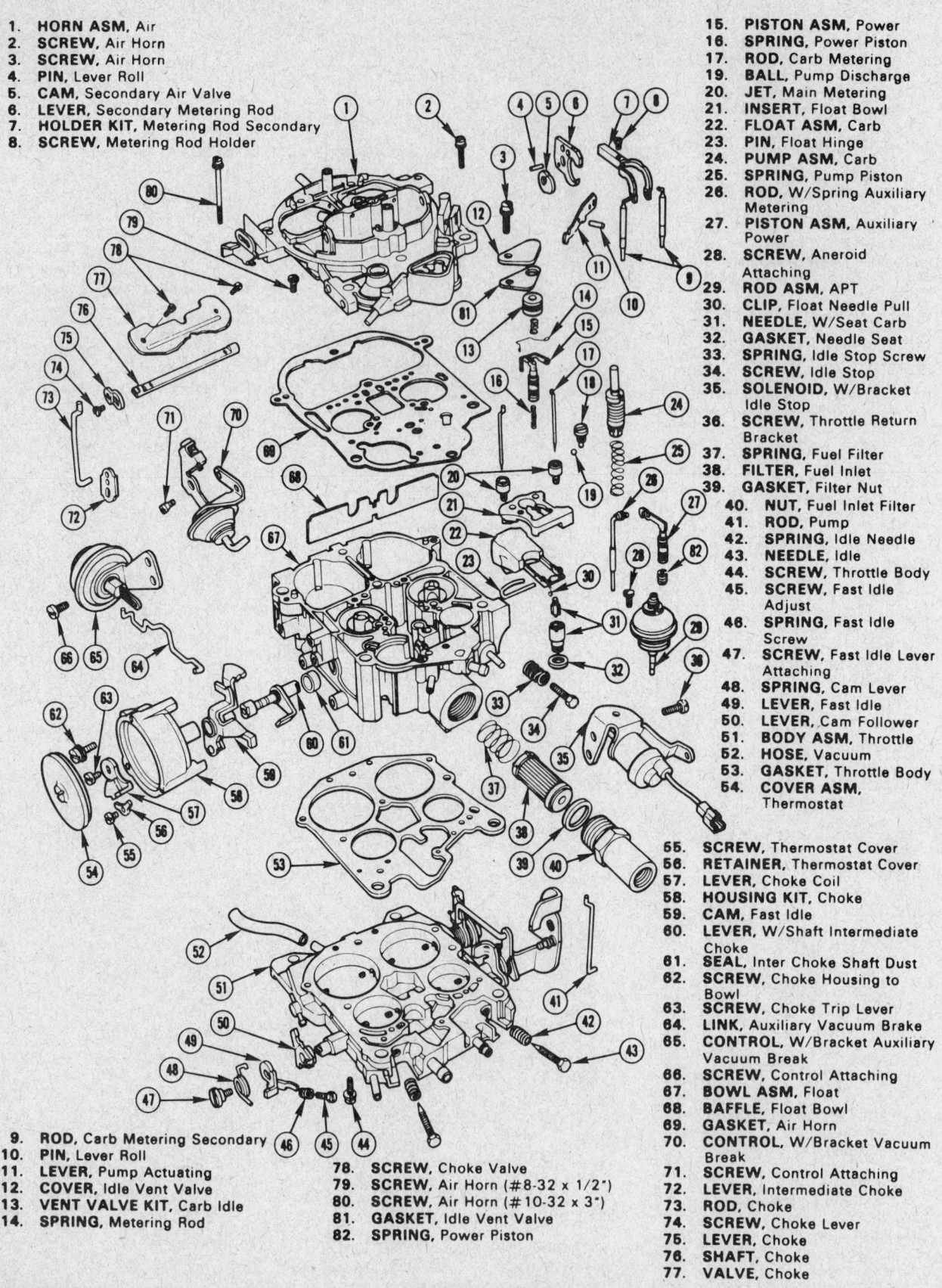

55. **SCREW**, Thermostat Cover
56. **RETAINER**, Thermostat Cover
57. **LEVER**, Choke Coil
58. **HOUSING KIT**, Choke
59. **CAM**, Fast Idle
60. **LEVER**, W/Shaft Intermediate Choke
61. **SEAL**, Inter Choke Shaft Dust
62. **SCREW**, Choke Housing to Bowl
63. **SCREW**, Choke Trip Lever
64. **LINK**, Auxiliary Vacuum Brake
65. **CONTROL**, W/Bracket Auxiliary Vacuum Break
66. **SCREW**, Control Attaching
67. **BOWL ASM**, Float
68. **BAFFLE**, Float Bowl
69. **GASKET**, Air Horn
70. **CONTROL**, W/Bracket Vacuum Break
71. **SCREW**, Control Attaching
72. **LEVER**, Intermediate Choke
73. **ROD**, Choke
74. **SCREW**, Choke Lever
75. **LEVER**, Choke
76. **SHAFT**, Choke
77. **VALVE**, Choke

9. **ROD**, Carb Metering Secondary
10. **PIN**, Lever Roll
11. **LEVER**, Pump Actuating
12. **COVER**, Idle Vent Valve
13. **VENT VALVE KIT**, Carb Idle
14. **SPRING**, Metering Rod

78. **SCREW**, Choke Valve
79. **SCREW**, Air Horn (#8-32 x 1/2")
80. **SCREW**, Air Horn (#10-32 x 3")
81. **GASKET**, Idle Vent Valve
82. **SPRING**, Power Piston

Exploded view of Rochester model M4M carburetor

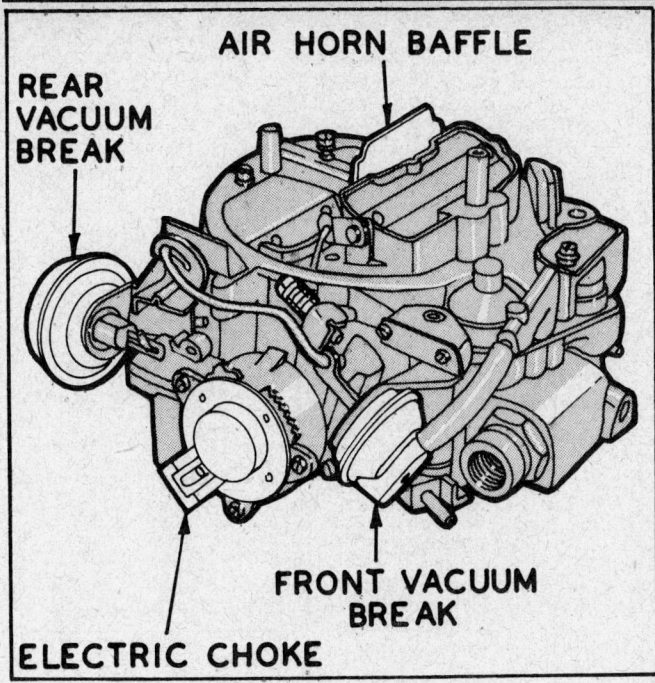

Fig. 1 Quadrajet M4M series carburetor (Typical)

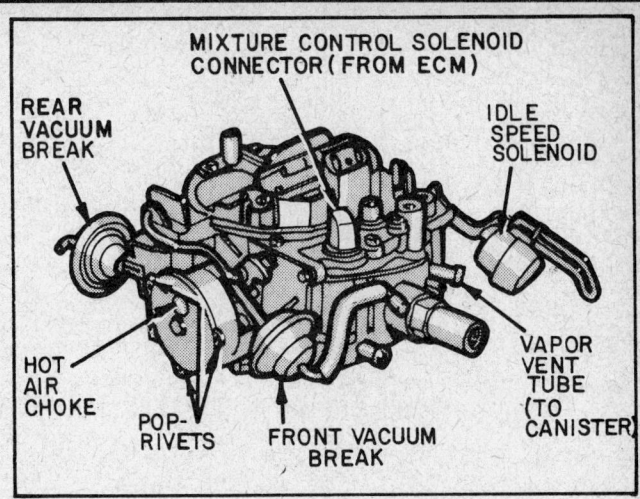

Fig. 2 Quadrajet E4M series carburetor (Typical)

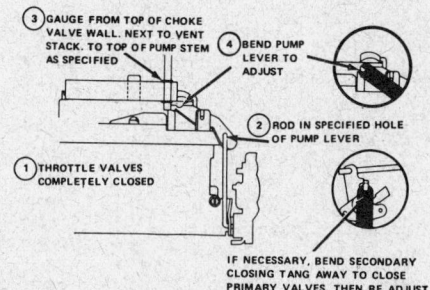

Fig. 4 Quadrajet M4M series pump rod adjustment. 1977-80 Less C-4 System

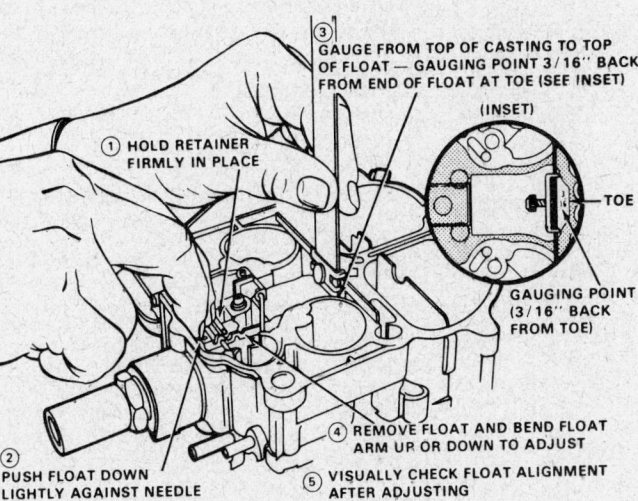

Fig. 3 Quadrajet E4M & M4M series float level adjustment

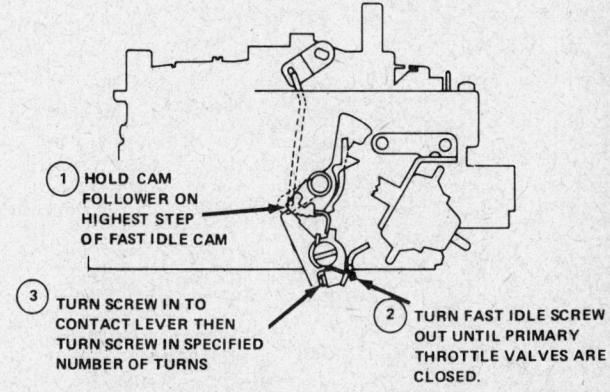

Fig. 5 Quadrajet E4M & M4M series fast idle adjustment (Bench)

or Computer Command Control System, adjust float if level varies more than 1/16 inch from specified setting as follows:

a. If float level is too high, hold retainer firmly in place and push downward on center of float pontoon to obtain correct setting.

b. If float level is too low, lift out metering rods, then remove solenoid connector attaching screws. Turn lean mixture solenoid screw clockwise, noting number of turns, until screw is lightly bottomed in float bowl. Turn screw counter-clockwise and remove screw, then lift solenoid and connector from float bowl. Remove float and bend float arm to adjust. After adjusting, check float alignment. Reverse procedure to install components removed. When installing lean mix-

ture screw, ensure that screw is backed out of float bowl the exact number of turns as noted during removal.

Pump Rod Adjustment

1977-80 M4M Units
Fig. 4—With throttle valves completely closed and pump rod in specified hole, measure distance from top of choke valve wall (next to vent stack) to top of pump stem. Dimension should be as specified in the Specification Chart. To adjust, bend pump lever.

Fast Idle Adjustment

Fig. 5—With cam follower on highest step of

cam, turn fast idle screw out until primary throttle valve is completely closed. Turn screw in to contact lever, then turn screw in the additional turns listed in the Specification Chart.

Choke Coil Lever Adjustment

Fig. 6—With thermostatic coil assembly removed from choke housing, push upward on coil tang to close choke valve. Insert gauge specified in the Specification Chart into hole in choke housing. The choke coil lever should contact the gauge. If not, bend choke rod to adjust.

Choke Rod Adjustment

Plug Gauge Method
Fig. 7—With the fast idle adjustment per-

CARBURETORS

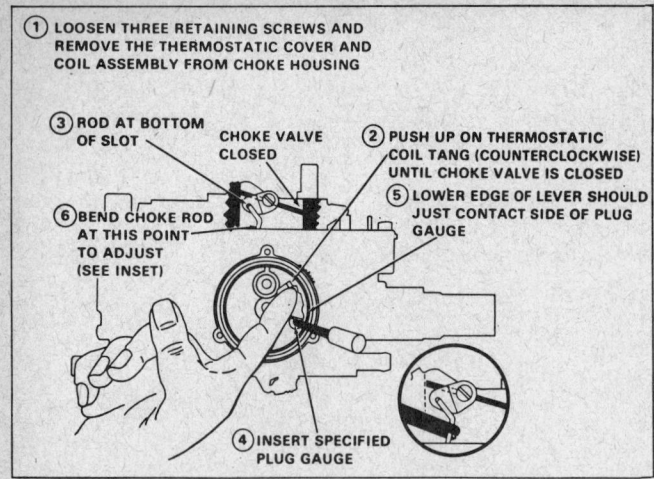

Fig. 6 Quadrajet E4M & M4M series choke coil lever adjustment

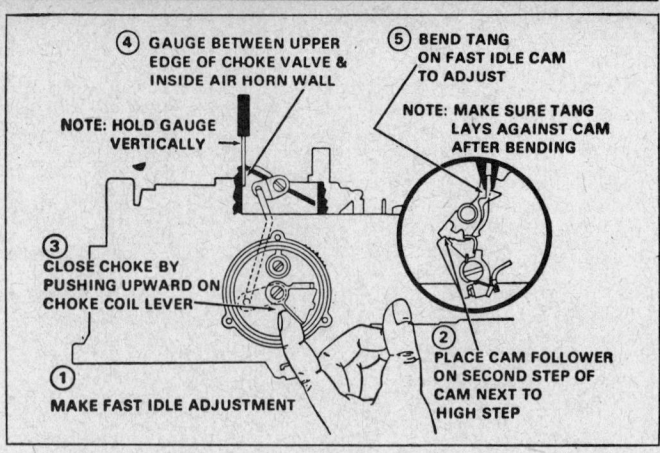

Fig. 7 Quadrajet M4M series choke rod adjustment. Plug gauge method

formed, and the cam follower on the second step of the fast idle cam, next to high step, close choke valve by pushing upward on choke lever. Measure dimension between the upper edge of the choke valve and air horn wall. Dimension should be as specified in the Specification Chart. To adjust, bend fast idle cam tang.

Angle Gauge Method

NOTE: On 1980–83 units, do not remove rivets and choke cover to perform this adjustment. Use a rubber band on the vacuum break lever tang to hold the choke valve in the closed position.

Fig. 8—Perform fast idle adjustment before making this adjustment. Rotate degree scale until zero is opposite pointer, then with choke valve completely closed, place magnet squarely on top of choke valve and rotate bubble until centered. Refer to Specification Chart for proper setting. Rotate scale so the specified degree for adjustment is opposite pointer. Place cam follower on second step of cam next to high step. Close choke by pushing

upward on choke coil lever. To adjust, bend tang on fast idle cam until bubble is centered. Remove gauge.

Front Vacuum Adjustment

Plug Gauge Method
Fig. 9—Place cam follower on highest step of fast idle cam, then using an external vacuum source, seat diaphragm. Push choke coil lever upward until vacuum break lever tang contacts vacuum break plunger stem tang. Measure dimension between upper edge of choke valve and air horn wall. Dimension should be as specified in the M4M Series Specification Chart. To adjust, turn vacuum break plunger adjusting screw.

Angle Gauge Method

NOTE: On 1980–83 units, do not remove rivets or choke cover to place choke valve in the closed position. Use a rubber band on vacuum break lever tang to hold choke valve in the closed position. On 1981–82 units, remove vacuum break from carburetor and position bracket in a vise, then grind off weld holding

adjusting screw cover. Remove adjusting screw cover, then reinstall vacuum break.

Fig. 10—Rotate degree scale until zero is opposite pointer, then with choke valve completely closed, place magnet squarely on top of choke valve and rotate bubble until centered. Refer to Specification Chart to obtain proper setting for adjustment. Rotate scale so the specified degree for adjustment is opposite pointer. Seat choke diaphragm using an external vacuum source. On some models, it will be necessary to plug air bleed with a piece of masking tape. Hold choke valve toward closed position, pushing counter-clockwise on inside coil lever. To adjust, rotate screw until bubble is centered. Remove gauge.

Rear Vacuum Break Adjustment

Plug Gauge Method
Fig. 11—Place cam follower on highest step of fast idle cam, then using an external vacuum source, seat diaphragm. Push upward on choke coil lever toward closed choke position until stem is seated. With choke rod in bottom of slot, insert gauge specified in the Specification Chart between upper edge of choke valve and air horn wall. To adjust, bend vacuum break rod.

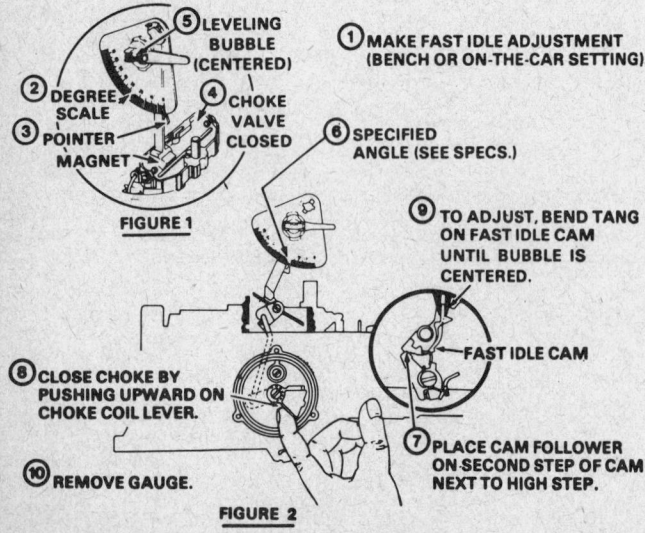

Fig. 8 Quadrajet E4M & M4M series choke rod adjustment. Angle gauge method

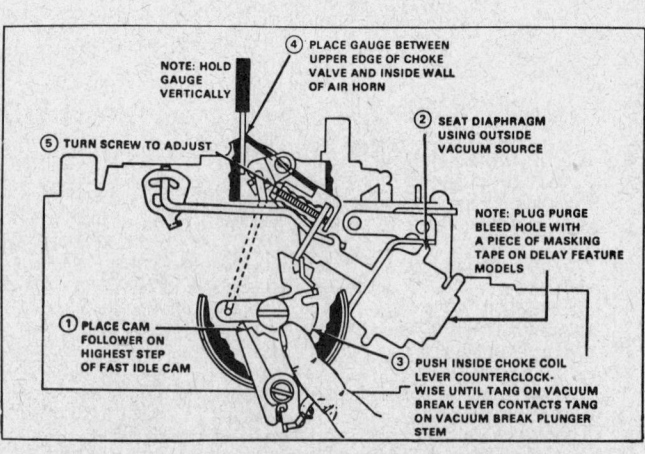

Fig. 9 Quadrajet M4M series front vacuum break adjustment. Plug gauge method

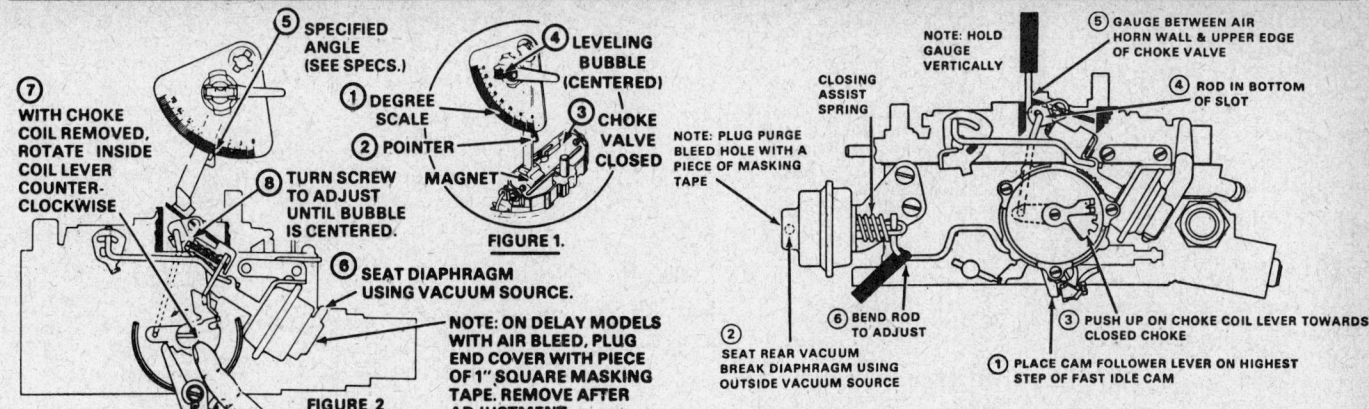

Fig. 10 Quadrajet E4M & M4M series front vacuum break adjustment. Angle gauge method

Fig. 11 Quadrajet M4M series rear vacuum break adjustment. Plug gauge method

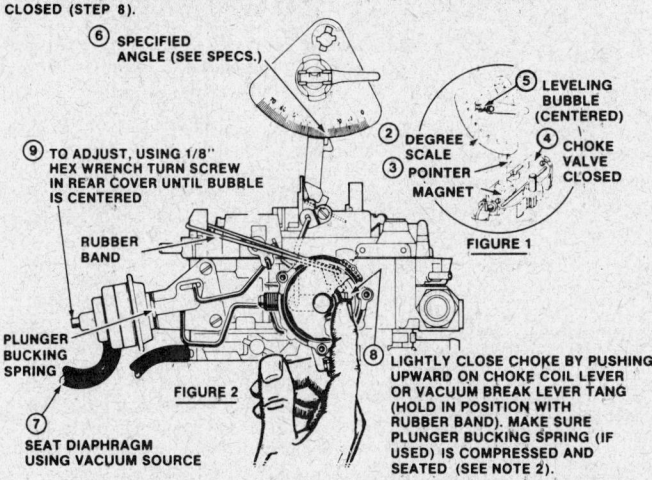

① MAKE CHOKE COIL LEVER AND FAST IDLE ADJUSTMENT (BENCH OR ON-THE-CAR SETTING).
NOTE 1: DO NOT REMOVE RIVETS AND CHOKE COVER TO PERFORM THIS ADJUSTMENT. USE RUBBER BAND ON VACUUM BREAK LEVER TANG TO HOLD CHOKE VALVE CLOSED (STEP 8).

NOTE 2: ON DELAY MODELS, PLUG END COVER WITH A 2GC TYPE ACCELERATOR PUMP PLUNGER CUP. REMOVE CUP AFTER ADJUSTMENT.

Fig. 12 Quadrajet E4M & M4M series rear vacuum break adjustment (units w/ adjusting screw). Angle gauge method

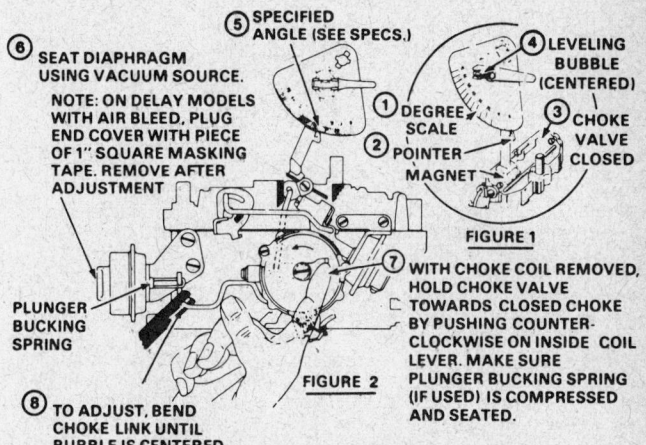

Fig. 13 Quadrajet E4M & M4M series vacuum break adjustment (units less adjusting screw). Angle gauge method

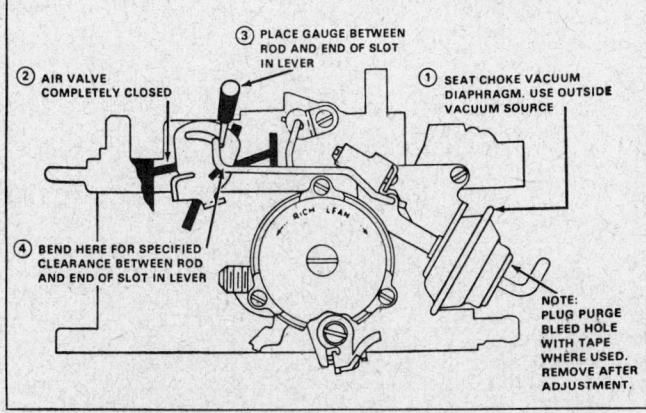

Fig. 14 Quadrajet M4M series air-valve dashpot adjustment

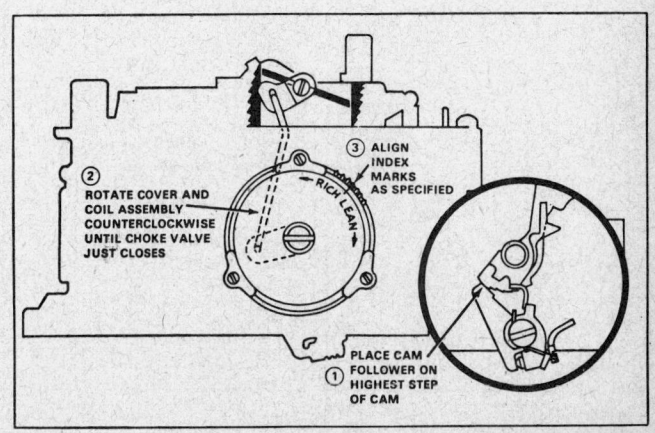

Fig. 15 Quadrajet M4M series automatic choke coil adjustment

CARBURETORS

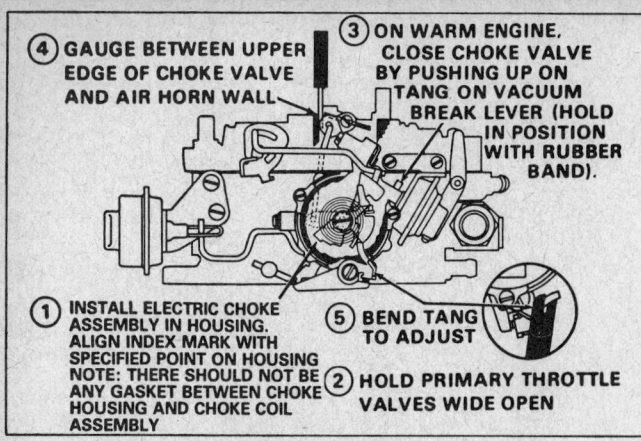

Fig. 16 Quadrajet M4M series choke unloader adjustment. Plug gauge method

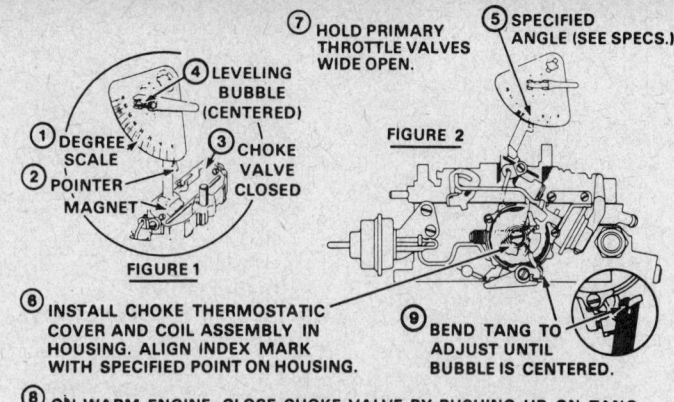

Fig. 17 Quadrajet E4M & M4M series choke unloader adjustment. Angle gauge method

Angle Gauge Method

NOTE: On 1981, remove vacuum break from carburetor and position in a vise, then grind off adjusting screw cap and reinstall vacuum break. After completing adjustment, apply a suitable sealer over adjusting screw head.

Fig. 12 & 13—Rotate degree scale until zero is opposite pointer, then with choke valve completely closed, place magnet squarely on top of choke valve and rotate bubble until centered. Refer to Specification Chart for proper setting for adjustment. Rotate scale so specified degree for adjustment is opposite pointer. Seat choke diaphragm using an external vacuum source. On some models, it will be necessary to plug air bleed with a piece of masking tape. Hold choke valve toward closed position, pushing counter-clockwise on inside coil lever. On units equipped with an adjusting screw, using a 1/8 in. hex wrench, turn adjust-

ing screw in rear cover until bubble is centered, Fig. 12. On units less adjusting screw, bend choke link until bubble is centered, Fig. 13. Remove gauge.

Air Valve Dashpot Adjustment

Fig. 14—Using an external vacuum source, seat choke vacuum diaphragm. Then, with the air valve completely closed, place gauge specified in the Specification Chart between air valve rod and end of slot in air valve lever. To adjust, bend rod at air valve end.

Choke Coil Adjustment

Fig. 15—Install choke coil and cover assembly. On Cadillac units, do not install a gasket between the choke housing and electric choke assembly. Place fast idle cam follower on highest step of fast idle cam. Rotate coil and cover assembly counter-clockwise until choke just closes, then align index mark on choke

cover with the specified index mark on choke housing. Refer to the Specification Chart.

Choke Unloader Adjustment

Plug Gauge Method
Fig. 16—With the choke coil adjustment performed, close choke, valve and open throttle valve. To close choke valve on a warm engine, push upward on tang of intermediate choke lever that contacts the fast idle cam and hold in place with a rubber band. Measure dimension between upper edge of choke valve and air horn wall. To adjust, bend tang on fast idle lever.

Angle Gauge Method
Fig. 17—Rotate degree scale until zero is opposite pointer, then with choke valve completely closed, place magnet squarely on top of choke valve and rotate bubble until centered. Refer to Specification Chart for proper setting for adjustment. Rotate scale so specified degree for adjustment is opposite pointer. Install choke cover and coil assembly and align index mark with specified point on housing. Hold primary throttle valve wide open and close choke valve by pushing upward on vacuum break lever tang. Hold in position with a rubber band. To adjust, bend tang on fast idle lever until bubble is centered. Remove gauge.

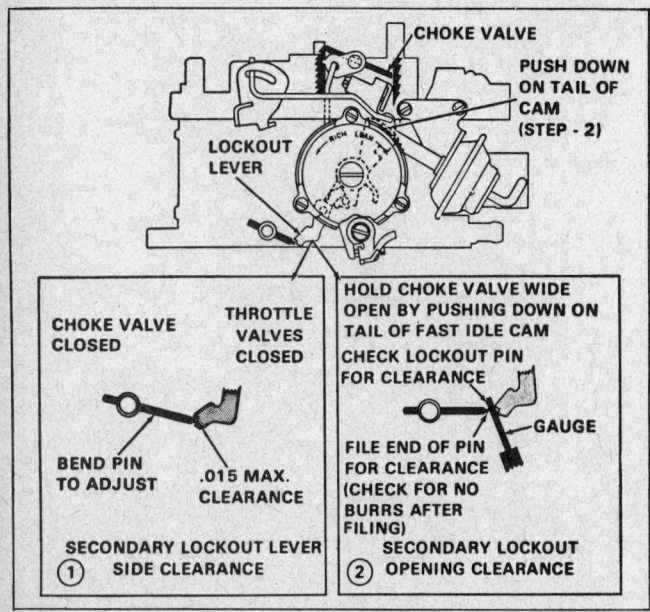

Fig. 18 Quadrajet E4M & M4M series secondary throttle valve lockout adjustment

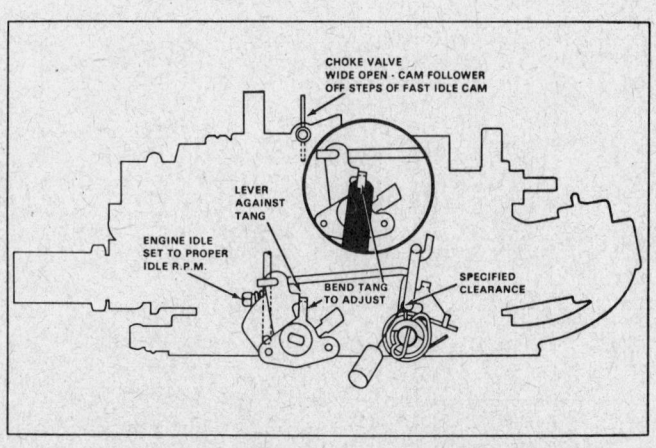

Fig. 19 Quadrajet E4M & M4M series secondary throttle valve closing adjustment. 1977–82 units

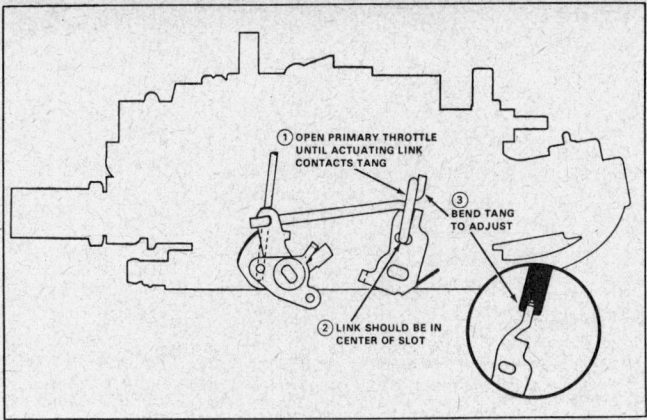

Fig. 20 Quadrajet E4M & M4M series secondary throttle valve opening adjustment. 1977–82 units

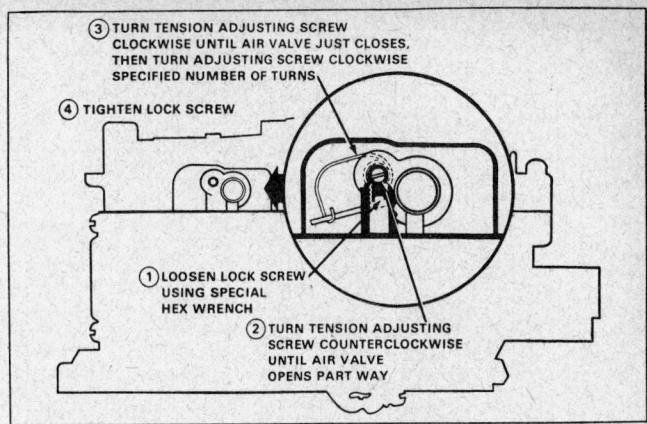

Fig. 21 Quadrajet E4M & M4M series air-valve spring wind-up adjustment

Secondary Throttle Valve Lockout Adjustment

Lockout-Pin Clearance
Fig. 18—With choke and throttle valves fully closed, measure clearance between lockout-pin and lockout lever. Maximum clearance should not exceed .015 inch. To adjust, bend lockout-pin.

Opening Clearance
Fig. 18—Push downward on fast idle cam tail to open choke valve, then push lockout lever counter-clockwise so upper end of lever contacts the round pin in fast idle cam. Measure clearance between lockout-pin and lockout lever toe. Clearance should be .015 inch. To obtain proper clearance, file metal from end of lockout-pin.

Secondary Throttle Valves Adjustment

1977–82 UNITS
Throttle Closing
Fig. 19—With curb idle speed set, hold choke valve open with cam follower lever off fast idle cam steps. Measure clearance between forward edge of slot in the secondary throttle valve pick-up lever and the secondary actuating rod. On 1977 units except Pontiac and all 1978-82 units, clearance should be .020 inch. On 1977 Pontiac, clearance should be .030 in. To adjust, bend secondary closing tang on primary throttle lever.

Throttle Opening
Fig. 20—Open primary throttle lever until link lightly contacts secondary lever tang.

The bottom end of the link should be in the center of the slot in secondary lever. To adjust, bend tang on secondary lever.

Air Valve Spring Wind-Up Adjustment

Fig. 21—Remove front vacuum break diaphragm unit and air valve dashpot rod. Loosen lock screw and rotate spring adjusting screw counter-clockwise until air valve is partially open. Hold air valve closed, then rotate adjusting screw clockwise specified number of turns after the spring contacts pin. Refer to the Specification Chart. Tighten lock screw and install air valve dashpot rod and the front vacuum break diaphragm unit.

Idle Load Compensator Adjustment

1981 V8-307 & 1982–83 Models w/E4MC Carb.

NOTE: On some 1981 models with V8-307 engine, and 1982–83 models with E4MC, an idle load compensator mounted on the float bowl is used to control idle speed. This unit should not be adjusted, unless if during diagnosis, curb idle speed is not within specifications. This adjustment should be performed with engine at operating temperature and choke and A/C off.

1. Remove air cleaner assembly and plug vacuum hose to thermal vacuum valve.
2. Disconnect and plug hoses to EGR valve, canister purge port and idle load compensator.
3. Apply parking brake and block wheels, then back throttle stop screw out 3 turns.
4. With engine operating, place transmission selector lever in drive position, adjust plunger to obtain 725 RPM. The jam nut on the plunger must be held in position to prevent damage to guide tabs. If a replacement idle load compensator is being installed, the plunger should be set to obtain a clearance of $61/64$ inch from jam nut to tip of plunger.
5. Connect vacuum hose to idle load compensator and note idle speed. If idle speed requires adjustment, stop engine and remove idle load compensator.
6. With idle load compensator removed, remove rubber and metal plug from center outlet tube.
7. Using a .090 inch allen wrench, rotate center outlet tube adjusting screw to obtain 550 RPM on 1981 models, or 500 RPM on 1982–83 models. Each turn of the adjusting screw will change idle speed approximately 75 to 100 RPM. Rotate adjusting screw counter-clockwise to increase engine speed and clockwise to decrease engine speed.
8. Reinstall rubber plug on center outlet tube, then install idle load compensator on carburetor. If a final adjustment is necessary it will be necessary to repeat steps 6, 7 and 8.
9. Apply a suitable vacuum source to idle load compensator to fully retract plunger.
10. Adjust throttle body idle stop screw to obtain 550 RPM on 1981 models, or 500 RPM on 1982–83 models, then reconnect all vacuum hoses and install air cleaner.

DUAL-JET 2MC, M2MC, M2ME 200, 210 & E2ME ADJUSTMENT SPECIFICATIONS

See Tune Up Chart in car chapters for curb and fast idle speeds.

Year	Carb. Production No.	Float Level	Pump Rod		Choke Coil Lever	Choke Rod	Vacuum Break				Choke Un-loader	Choke Setting
			Hole	Adj.			Rich	Lean	Front	Rear		
1977	17057150, 151	1/8	Outer	11/32	.120	.085	.090	.160	—	—	.190	2 Rich
	17057156, 158	1/8	Outer	11/32	.120	.085	.090	.160	—	—	.190	1 Rich
	17057157	1/8	Outer	3/8	.120	.090	.100	.190	—	—	.190	1 Rich
	17057172, 176	11/32	Inner	1/4	.120	.075	—	—	①	②	.240	2 Rich
	17057173, 177	11/32	Outer	5/16	.120	.075	—	—	③	②	.240	2 Rich

Continued

CARBURETORS

See Tune Up Chart in car chapters for curb and fast idle speeds.

Year	Carb. Production No.	Float Level	Pump Rod		Choke Coil Lever	Choke Rod	Vacuum Break				Choke Un-loader	Choke Setting
			Hole	Adj.			Rich	Lean	Front	Rear		
1978	17058130, 131	1/4	Inner	1/4	.120	46°	—	—	24°	—	46°	Index
	17058132, 133	1/4	Inner	1/4	.120	46°	—	—	24°	—	46°	Index
	17058150, 152	3/8	Inner	1/4	.120	14°	—	—	35°	25°	35°	2 Rich
	17058151, 156	3/8	Outer	11/32	.120	14°	—	—	38°	25°	35°	2 Rich
	17058154, 155	3/8	Outer	11/32	.120	14°	—	—	27°	40°	35°	2 Rich
	17058158	3/8	Outer	11/32	.120	14°	—	—	38°	25°	35°	2 Rich
	17058160	11/32	Inner	1/4	.120	22.5°	—	—	25°	32°	33°	2 Rich
	17058192	5/16	Inner	9/32	.120	14.5°	—	—	21°	19°	50°	2 Rich
	17058450	3/8	Outer	11/32	.120	14°	—	—	27°	45°	35°	2 Rich
	17058496	1/4	Outer	3/8	.120	15°	—	—	24°	34°	38°	1 Rich
1979	17059104, 106	15/32	Inner	1/4	.120	38°	—	—	27°	—	38°	④
	17059108, 110	1/4	Inner	1/4	.120	38°	—	—	28°	—	38°	2 Lean
	17059130, 132	1/4	Inner	9/32	.120	38°	—	—	27°	—	38°	Index
	17059131	1/4	Inner	3/8	.120	38°	—	—	27°	—	38°	1 Lean
	17059133	1/4	Inner	9/32	.120	38°	—	—	27°	—	38°	1 Lean
	17059134, 135	15/32	Inner	1/4	.120	38°	—	—	27°	—	38°	1 Lean
	17059136, 137	15/32	Inner	1/4	.120	38°	—	—	27°	—	38°	1 Lean
	17059138, 139	1/4	Inner	1/4	.120	38°	—	—	28°	—	38°	1 Lean
	17059140, 141	1/4	Inner	1/4	.120	38°	—	—	28°	—	38°	1 Lean
	17059150, 152	3/8	Inner	1/4	.120	14°	—	—	32°	23°	35°	2 Rich
	17059151	3/8	Outer	11/32	.120	14°	—	—	38°	25°	35°	2 Rich
	17059154	3/8	Outer	11/32	.120	14°	—	—	27°	40°	35°	2 Rich
	17059160	11/32	Inner	1/4	.120	20°	—	—	23°	31°	32°	2 Rich
	17059170, 171	1/4	Inner	9/32	.120	38°	—	—	27°	—	38°	Index
	17059180, 190	11/32	Inner	1/4	.120	24.5°	—	—	19°	17°	38°	2 Rich
	17059184	11/32	Inner	1/4	.120	24.5°	—	—	19°	17°	35°	2 Rich
	17059191	11/32	Inner	9/32	.120	24.5°	—	—	19°	17°	38°	2 Rich
	17059193	13/32	Inner	1/4	.120	24.5°	—	—	19°	17°	35°	2 Rich
	17059194	11/32	Inner	1/4	.120	24.5°	—	—	19°	17°	35°	2 Rich
	17059196	11/32	Inner	1/4	.120	24.5°	—	—	23°	21°	42°	1 Rich
	17059430, 432	9/32	Inner	9/32	.120	38°	—	—	27°	—	38°	1 Lean
	17059434, 436	15/32	Inner	1/4	.10	38°	—	—	29°	—	38°	1 Lean
	17059450	3/8	Outer	11/32	.120	14°	—	—	27°	45°	35°	2 Rich
	17059491, 492	11/32	Inner	9/32	.120	24.5°	—	—	23°	21°	42°	1 Rich
	17059496	5/16	Inner	3/8	.120	24.5°	—	—	21°	30°	38°	2 Rich
	17059498	11/32	Inner	9/32	.120	24.5°	—	—	23°	21°	42°	2 Rich
1980	17080108, 110	3/8	Inner	5/16	.120	20°	—	—	25°	—	38°	⑧
	17080130, 131	5/16	Inner	5/16	.120	20°	—	—	25°	—	38°	⑧
	17080132, 133	5/16	Inner	5/16	.120	20°	—	—	25°	—	38°	⑧
	17080138, 140	3/8	Inner	5/16	.120	20°	—	—	25°	—	38°	⑧
	17080146, 147	11/32	Inner	1/4	.120	20°	—	—	25°	—	38°	⑧
	17080148, 149	11/32	Inner	1/4	.120	20°	—	—	25°	—	38°	⑧
	17080150, 152	3/8	Outer	11/32	.120	14°	—	—	38°	27°	35°	⑧
	17080153	3/8	Outer	11/32	.120	14°	—	—	38°	27°	35°	⑧
	17080160	5/16	Inner	1/4	.120	14.5°	—	—	28.5°	33.5°	37.5°	⑧
	17080185, 187	9/32	Inner	1/4	.120	24.5°	—	—	19°	14°	38°	⑧
	17080190	9/32	Inner	1/4	.120	24.5°	—	—	22°	20°	38°	⑧
	17080191	11/32	Inner	1/4	.120	24.5°	—	—	18°	18°	38°	⑧
	17080192	9/32	Inner	1/4	.120	24.5°	—	—	22°	20°	38°	⑧
	17080195, 197	9/32	Inner	1/4	.120	24.5°	—	—	19°	14°	38°	⑧
	17080490, 492	5/16	—	3/8	.120	24.5°	—	—	21°	33°	38°	⑧
	17080491	5/16	—	3/8	.120	24.5°	—	—	21°	35°	38°	⑧
	17080493, 495	5/16	—	3/8	.120	24.5°	—	—	21°	30°	38°	⑧
	17080496, 498	5/16	—	3/8	.120	24.5°	—	—	21°	30°	38°	⑧

Continued

DUAL-JET 2MC, M2MC, M2ME 200, 210 & E2ME ADJUSTMENT SPECIFICATIONS—Continued
See Tune Up Chart in car chapters for curb and fast idle speeds.

Year	Carb. Production No.	Float Level	Pump Rod		Choke Coil Lever	Choke Rod	Vacuum Break				Choke Unloader	Choke Setting
			Hole	Adj.			Rich	Lean	Front	Rear		
1981	17080185, 187	9/32	Inner	1/4	.120	24.5°	—	—	19°	14°	38°	⑧
	17080191	11/32	Inner	1/4	.120	24.5°	—	—	18°	18°	38°	⑧
	17080491	5/16	—	—	.120	24.5°	—	—	21°	35°	38°	⑧
	17080496, 498	5/16	—	—	.120	24.5°	—	—	21°	35°	38°	⑧
	17081130, 132	13/32	Inner	—	.120	20°	—	—	25°	—	38°	⑧
	17081131, 133	13/32	Inner	—	.120	20°	—	—	25°	—	38°	⑧
	17081138, 140	13/32	Inner	—	.120	20°	—	—	25°	—	40°	⑧
	17081150, 152	13/32	—	—	.120	14°	—	—	24°	36°	35°	⑧
	17081160	11/32	—	—	.120	14.5°	—	—	24°	37°	35°	⑧
	17081191, 196	5/16	—	—	.120	24.5°	—	—	28°	24°	38°	⑧
	17081192, 197	3/8	—	—	.120	24.5°	—	—	28°	24°	38°	⑧
	17081194	5/16	—	—	.120	24.5°	—	—	21°	30°	38°	⑧
	17081198	3/8	—	—	.120	24.5°	—	—	28°	24°	38°	⑧
	17081199	3/8	—	—	.120	18°	—	—	28°	24°	38°	⑧
1982	17082130	3/8	—	—	.120	20°	—	—	27°	—	38°	⑧
	17082132	3/8	—	—	.120	20°	—	—	27°	—	38°	⑧
	17082138	3/8	—	—	.120	20°	—	—	27°	—	38°	⑧
	17082140	3/8	—	—	.120	20°	—	—	27°	—	38°	⑧
	17082150	13/32	—	—	.120	14°	—	—	24°	38°	35°	⑧
	17082150⑤	13/32	—	—	.120	14°	—	—	24°	40°	35°	⑧
	17082182	5/16	—	—	.120	18°	—	—	28°	24°	32°	⑧
	17082184	5/16	—	—	.120	18°	—	—	28°	24°	32°	⑧
	17082186	5/16	—	—	.120	18°	—	—	21°	19°	27°	⑧
	17082192	5/16	—	—	.120	18°	—	—	28°	24°	32°	⑧
	17082194	5/16	—	—	.120	18°	—	—	28°	24°	32°	⑧
	17082196	5/16	—	—	.120	18°	—	—	21°	19°	27°	⑧
	17082497	5/16	—	—	.120	24.5°	—	—	28°	24°	32°	⑧
	17082916	5/16	—	—	—	25°	—	—	21°	19°	27°	⑧
1983	17082130	3/8	—	—	.120	20°	—	—	27°	—	38°	⑧
	17082132	3/8	—	—	.120	20°	—	—	27°	—	38°	⑧
	17083130	3/8	—	—	.120	20°	—	—	27°	—	38°	⑧
	17083132	3/8	—	—	.120	20°	—	—	27°	—	38°	⑧
	17083190	5/16	—	—	.120	18°	—	—	28°	24°	32°	⑧
	17083192	5/16	—	—	.120	18°	—	—	28°	24°	32°	⑧
	17083193	5/16	—	—	.120	⑥	—	—	⑦	28°	27°	⑧
	17083194	5/16	—	—	.120	17°	—	—	27°	25°	35°	⑧
	17084195	5/16	—	—	.120	17°	—	—	23°	28°	27°	⑧

①—With angle gauge, 24°; with plug gauge, .135 inch.

②—Before first scheduled tune up—with angle gauge, 36°; with plug gauge, .225 inch. After first scheduled tune up—with angle gauge, 38°; with plug gauge, .240 inch.

③—With angle gauge, 28°; with plug gauge, .165 inch.

④—2 notches clockwise

⑤—High Altitude

⑥—Chevrolet models and Oldsmobile F.W.D. models, 17°; all others, 18°.

⑦—Chevrolet models and Oldsmobile F.W.D. models, 23°; all others, 24°.

⑧—Tamper-resistant.

DUAL-JET 2MC, M2MC, M2ME 200, 210, E2MC & E2ME ADJUSTMENTS

The Dual Jet carburetor, Figs. 1, 2 and 3, is a two barrel, single stage unit, incorporating the design features of the primary side of the Quadrajet (four barrel) carburetor. The E2M model is used with the Computer Controlled Catalytic Converter System (C-4 System) or Computer Control Command System. The triple venturi stack up, plus the smaller 1³/₈ inch bores result in good fuel metering control during all phases of operation.

The main metering system has a separate main well for each main nozzle for good fuel flow through the venturi.

On models except E2M models, an adjustable part throttle screw is used in the float bowl to aid in controlling fuel mixtures for good emission control. This screw is factory preset and should not be adjusted in service. However, if it becomes necessary to replace the float bowl, the new service float bowl will include the adjustable part throttle screw which has been preset.

On E2M models, an electrically operated mixture control solenoid, mounted in the fuel bowl, is used to control the fuel-air mixture metered to the idle and main metering systems. Fuel metering is controlled by two stepped metering rods positioned by a plunger in the mixture control solenoid. The solenoid plunger is controlled or "Pulsed" by an electrical output signal from the Electronic Control Module (ECM). The ECM, responding from a signal from the oxygen sensor, energizes the solenoid, to move the plunger and metering rods to control fuel delivery to the idle and main metering systems. At the same time, air metering to the idle system is controlled by an idle air bleed valve, located in the air horn, which follows movement of the mixture control solenoid plunger to control the amount of air bleed into the idle system to lean or richen the mixture. The movement or "Cycling" of the solenoid plunger occurs approximately 10 times per second, thereby controlling the fuel-air mixture to achieve optimum mixture ratios. The positioning of the mixture control solenoid in the float bowl, rich stop setting and idle air bleed valve in the air horn are factory adjusted and no attempt should be made to alter these settings except during major carburetor overhaul or when air horn or float bowl replacement is necessary.

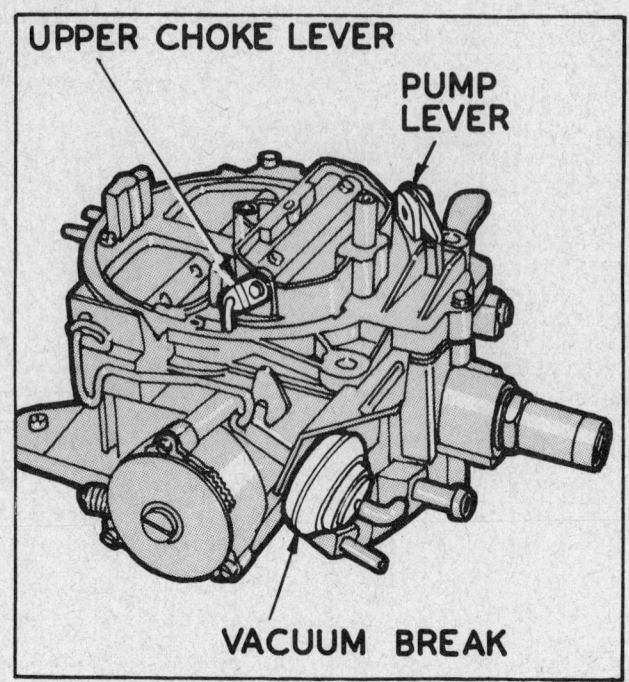

Fig. 1   Rochester Dual-Jet 2MC & M2MC 200 carburetor (typical)

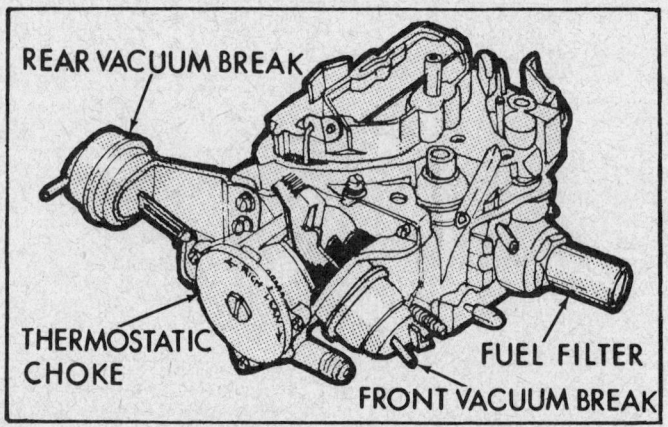

Fig. 2   Rochester Dual-Jet M2MC 210 carburetor

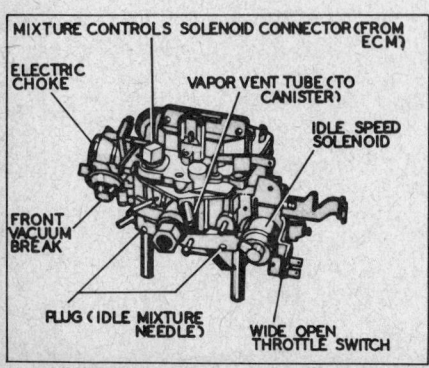

Fig. 3   Rochester Dual-Jet model E2ME

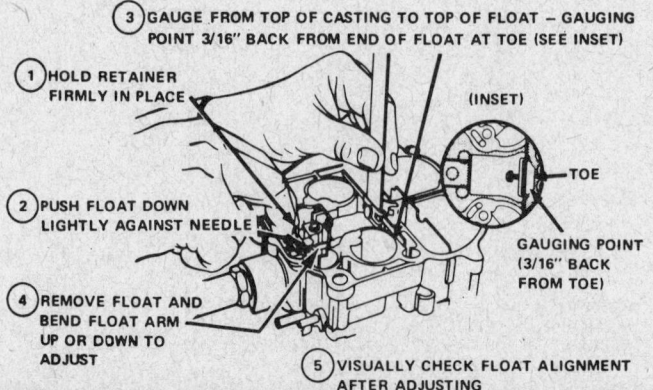

Fig. 4   Float level adjustment Exc. E2M units

1. **HORN ASM**, Air
2. **SCREW**, Air Horn (Short)
3. **LEVER**, Pump Actuating
4. **PIN**, Lever Roll
5. **GASKET**, Air Horn
6. **SPRING**, Metering Rod-Primary
7. **PISTON ASM**, Power
8. **ROD**, Metering Primary
9. **PLUG**, Pump Discharge
10. **BALL**, Pump Discharge

21. **SOLENOID**, Idle Stop (W/Bracket)
22. **SPRING**, Idle Stop Screw
23. **SCREW**, Idle Stop
24. **SCREW**, Solenoid Mtg Bracket
25. **SPRING**, Fuel Filter
26. **FILTER**, Fuel Inlet
27. **GASKET**, Fuel Filter Nut
28. **NUT**, Fuel Inlet Filler
29. **ROD**, Pump
30. **SPRING**, Idle Needle
31. **NEEDLE**, Idle
32. **BODY ASM**, Throttle
33. **SCREW**, Throttle Body
34. **SCREW**, Fast Idle Adjust
35. **SPRING**, Fast Idle Screw
36. **LEVER**, Fast Idle
37. **SPRING**, Fast Idle
38. **SCREW**, Fast Idle
39. **LEVER**, Cam Follower
40. **HOSE**, Vacuum
41. **GASKET**, Throttle Body
42. **INSERT**, Aneroid Cavity
43. **SCREW**, Choke Lever
44. **SCREW**, Thermostat Cover
45. **RETAINER**, Thermostat Cover
46. **LEVER**, Thermostat Coil
47. **SHAFT**, Intermediate Choke
48. **SEAL**, Intermediate Choke Shaft
49. **COIL & GASKET**, Thermostat Cover
50. **SCREW**, Choke Housing
51. **SEAL**, Inter Choke Shaft Dust
52. **HOUSING**, Choke
53. **CAM**, Fast Idle

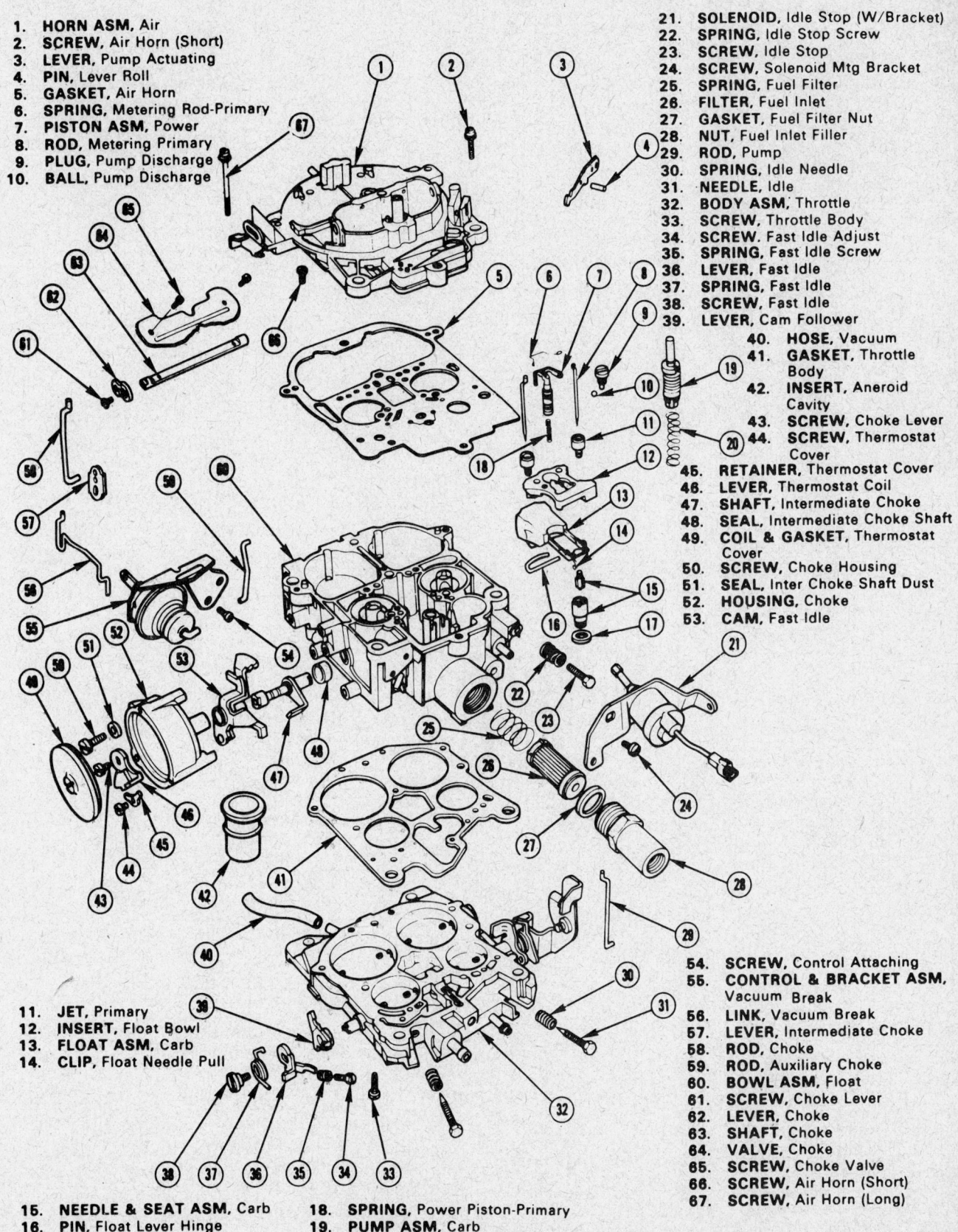

11. **JET**, Primary
12. **INSERT**, Float Bowl
13. **FLOAT ASM**, Carb
14. **CLIP**, Float Needle Pull

54. **SCREW**, Control Attaching
55. **CONTROL & BRACKET ASM**, Vacuum Break
56. **LINK**, Vacuum Break
57. **LEVER**, Intermediate Choke
58. **ROD**, Choke
59. **ROD**, Auxiliary Choke
60. **BOWL ASM**, Float
61. **SCREW**, Choke Lever
62. **LEVER**, Choke
63. **SHAFT**, Choke
64. **VALVE**, Choke
65. **SCREW**, Choke Valve
66. **SCREW**, Air Horn (Short)
67. **SCREW**, Air Horn (Long)

15. **NEEDLE & SEAT ASM**, Carb
16. **PIN**, Float Lever Hinge
17. **GASKET**, Needle Seat

18. **SPRING**, Power Piston-Primary
19. **PUMP ASM**, Carb
20. **SPRING**, Pump Return

Exploded view of Rochester model 2MC carburetor

CARBURETORS

1. **AIR HORN**
2. **SCREW**, Air Horn (Short)
3. **SCREW**, Air Horn (Long)
4. **VALVE**, Choke
5. **SCREW**, Choke Valve
6. **LEVER**, Pump Actuating
7. **PIN**, Pump Lever
8. **GASKET**, Air Horn
9. **INSERT**, Float Bowl
10. **PIN**, Float Hinge
11. **FLOAT ASM.**

24. **SPRING**, Idle Stop Screw
25. **SCREW**, Idle Stop
26. **FILTER NUT**, Fuel Inlet
27. **GASKET**, Filter Nut

34. **GASKET**, Flange
35. **SCREW**, Fast Idle Adj
36. **SPRING**, Fast Idle Adj Screw
37. **SCREW**, Fast Idle Lever
38. **SPRING**, Cam Lever
39. **LEVER**, Fast Idle
40. **LEVER**, Cam Follower
41. **GASKET**, Throttle Body
42. **ROD**, Pump
43. **BOWL ASM**, Float
44. **SEAL**, Choke Housing to Bowl
45. **SHAFT & LEVER ASM.**, Intermediate Choke
46. **CAM**, Fast Idle
47. **CHOKE HOUSING KIT**
48. **SEAL**, Inter Choke Shaft (Dust)
49. **RETAINER**, Stat Cover
50. **SCREW**, Stat Cover
51. **LEVER**, Stat Coil
52. **STATOR COVER**, Coil & Gasket
53. **GASKET**, Stat Cover
54. **SCREW**, Coil Lever
55. **SCREW**, Choke Housing to Bowl
56. **LINK**, Auxiliary Vacuum Break
57. **SCREW**, Auxiliary Vacuum Break
58. **VACUUM BREAK & BRACKET**, Choke Side (Auxiliary)

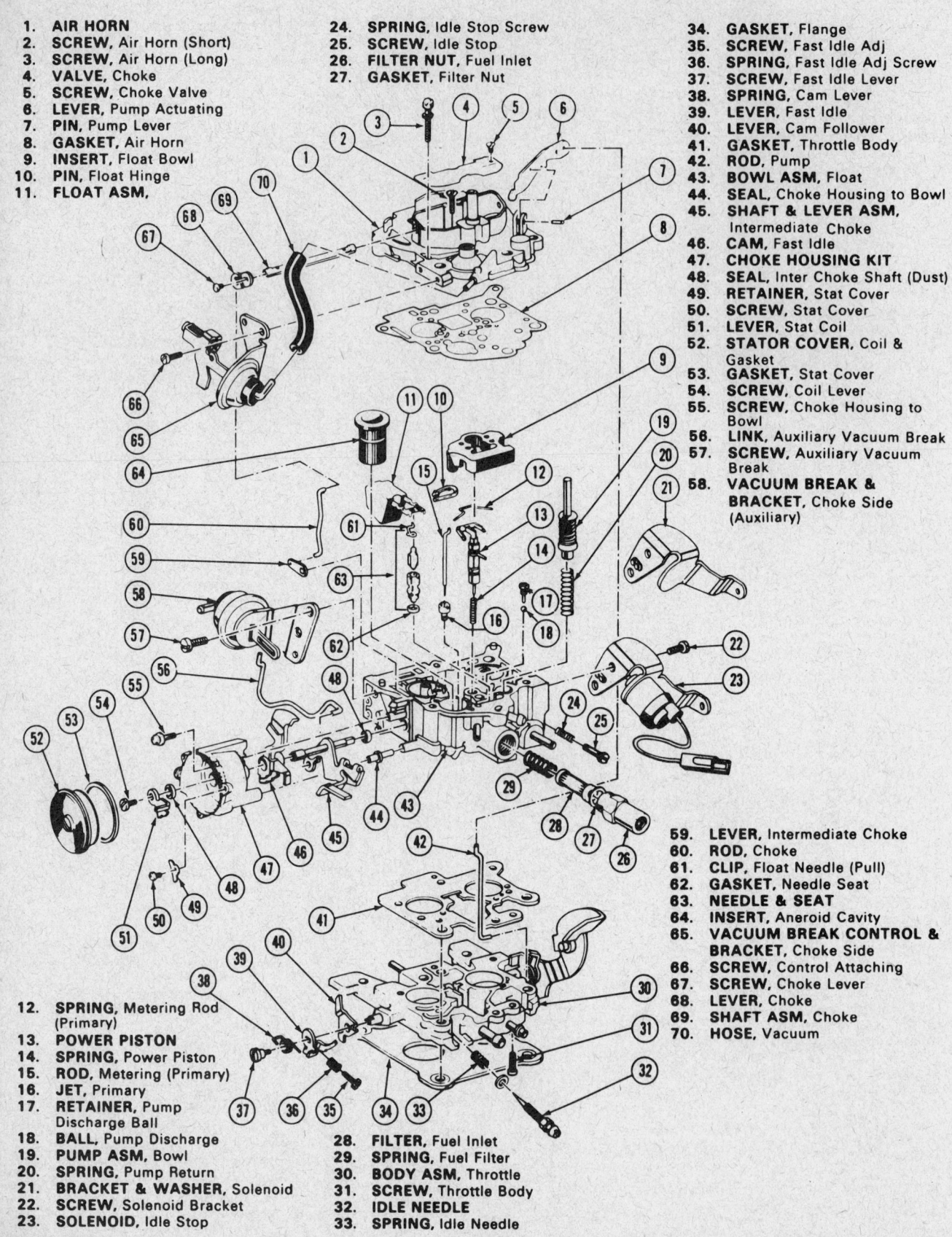

12. **SPRING**, Metering Rod (Primary)
13. **POWER PISTON**
14. **SPRING**, Power Piston
15. **ROD**, Metering (Primary)
16. **JET**, Primary
17. **RETAINER**, Pump Discharge Ball
18. **BALL**, Pump Discharge
19. **PUMP ASM**, Bowl
20. **SPRING**, Pump Return
21. **BRACKET & WASHER**, Solenoid
22. **SCREW**, Solenoid Bracket
23. **SOLENOID**, Idle Stop

28. **FILTER**, Fuel Inlet
29. **SPRING**, Fuel Filter
30. **BODY ASM**, Throttle
31. **SCREW**, Throttle Body
32. **IDLE NEEDLE**
33. **SPRING**, Idle Needle

59. **LEVER**, Intermediate Choke
60. **ROD**, Choke
61. **CLIP**, Float Needle (Pull)
62. **GASKET**, Needle Seat
63. **NEEDLE & SEAT**
64. **INSERT**, Aneroid Cavity
65. **VACUUM BREAK CONTROL & BRACKET**, Choke Side
66. **SCREW**, Control Attaching
67. **SCREW**, Choke Lever
68. **LEVER**, Choke
69. **SHAFT ASM**, Choke
70. **HOSE**, Vacuum

Exploded view of Rochester model M2M carburetor

1. AIR HORN ASSEMBLY
2. AIR HORN GASKET
3. PUMP ACTUATING LEVER
4. PUMP LEVER HINGE ROLL PIN
5. AIR HORN SCREW (SHORT)
6. AIR HORN SCREW (COUNTERSUNK)
7. SOLENOID CONNECTOR TO AIR HORN GASKET
8. IDLE AIR BLEED VALVE
9. IDLE AIR BLEED VALVE "O" RING (THICK)
10. IDLE AIR BLEED VALVE "O" RING (THIN)
11. TPS ACTUATOR PLUNGER
12. TPS PLUNGER SEAL
13. TPS SEAL RETAINER
14. TPS ADJUSTING SCREW
15. TPS SCREW PLUG
16. PUMP PLUNGER SEAL
17. PUMP SEAL RETAINER
18. SOLENOID PLUNGER STOP SCREW (RICH MIXTURE STOP)
19. PLUNGER STOP SCREW PLUG (RICH MIXTURE STOP)
20. SOLENOID ADJUSTING SCREW PLUG (LEAN MIXTURE)
21. FRONT VACUUM BREAK & BRACKET
22. VACUUM BREAK ATTACHING SCREW
23. VACUUM HOSE
24. UPPER CHOKE ROD LEVER
25. CHOKE LEVER SCREW
26. CHOKE ROD
27. LOWER CHOKE ROD LEVER
28. INTERMEDIATE CHOKE SHAFT SEAL
29. REAR VACUUM BREAK LINK
30. INTERMEDIATE CHOKE SHAFT & LEVER
31. FAST IDLE CAM
32. CHOKE HOUSING TO BOWL SEAL (HOT AIR CHOKE)
33. CHOKE HOUSING

34. CHOKE HOUSING TO BOWL SCREW
35. INTERMEDIATE CHOKE SHAFT SEAL (HOT AIR CHOKE)
36. CHOKE COIL LEVER
37. CHOKE COIL LEVER SCREW

38. STAT COVER GASKET (HOT AIR CHOKE)
39. STAT COVER & COIL ASSEMBLY (HOT AIR CHOKE)
40. STAT COVER & COIL ASSEMBLY (ELECTRIC CHOKE)
41. STAT COVER ATTACHING KIT
42. REAR VACUUM BREAK ASSEMBLY
43. VACUUM BREAK ATTACHING SCREW
44. FLOAT BOWL ASSEMBLY
45. PRIMARY METERING JETS
46. PUMP DISCHARGE BALL
47. PUMP DISCHARGE BALL RETAINER
48. PUMP WELL BAFFLE
49. NEEDLE & SEAT ASSEMBLY
50. FLOAT ASSEMBLY
51. FLOAT ASSEMBLY HINGE PAN
52. PRIMARY METERING RODS
53. PRIMARY METERING ROD SPRINGS
54. FLOAT BOWL INSERT
55. BOWL CAVITY INSERT
56. CONNECTOR ATTACHING SCREW
57. MIXTURE CONTROL SOLENOID & PLUNGER
58. SOLENOID TENSION SPRING
59. SOLENOID ADJUSTING SCREW (LEAN MIXTURE)
60. SOLENOID ADJUSTING SCREW SPRING
61. PUMP RETURN SPRING
62. PUMP ASSEMBLY
63. PUMP LINK
64. THROTTLE POSITION SENSOR (TPS)
65. TPS TENSION SPRING
66. FUEL INLET FILTER NUT
67. FILTER NUT GASKET
68. FUEL INLET FILTER
69. FUEL FILTER SPRING
70. IDLE STOP SCREW
71. IDLE STOP SCREW SPRING
72. IDLE SPEED SOLENOID & BRACKET
73. THROTTLE RETURN SPRING BRACKET
74. IDLE LOAD COMPENSATOR & BRACKET
75. IDLE SPEED CONTROL & BRACKET
76. BRACKET ATTACHING SCREW
77. THROTTLE BODY
78. THROTTLE BODY GASKET
79. THROTTLE BODY SCREW
80. IDLE NEEDLE & SPRING ASSEMBLIES
81. FAST IDLE ADJUSTING SCREW
82. FAST IDLE SCREW SPRING
83. VACUUM HOSE TEE
84. FLANGE GASKET

HOT AIR CHOKE MODELS

Exploded view of Rochester model E2M carburetor

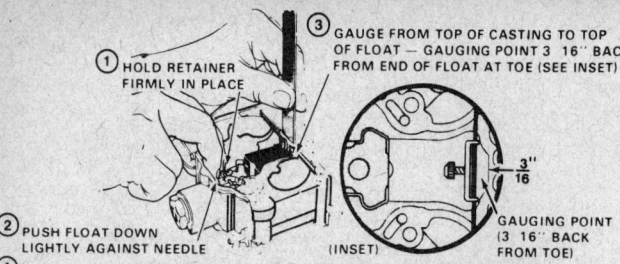

① HOLD RETAINER FIRMLY IN PLACE

③ GAUGE FROM TOP OF CASTING TO TOP OF FLOAT — GAUGING POINT 3 16" BACK FROM END OF FLOAT AT TOE (SEE INSET)

3"/16

(INSET)

GAUGING POINT (3 16" BACK FROM TOE)

② PUSH FLOAT DOWN LIGHTLY AGAINST NEEDLE

④ IF FLOAT LEVEL VARIES OVER ±1/16" FROM SPECIFICATIONS, ADJUST FLOAT AS FOLLOWS:

LEVEL TOO HIGH — HOLD RETAINER FIRMLY IN PLACE (① AND ②) AND PUSH DOWN ON CENTER OF FLOAT PONTOON TO OBTAIN CORRECT SETTING.

LEVEL TOO LOW — LIFT OUT METERING RODS. REMOVE SOLENOID CONNECTOR SCREWS. TURN LEAN MIXTURE SOLENOID SCREW CLOCKWISE COUNTING NUMBER OF TURNS UNTIL SCREW IS BOTTOMED LIGHTLY IN FLOAT BOWL. RECORD NUMBER OF TURNS COUNTED. TURN SCREW COUNTERCLOCKWISE AND REMOVE SCREW. LIFT SOLENOID AND CONNECTOR FROM FLOAT BOWL. REMOVE FLOAT AND BEND FLOAT ARM UP TO ADJUST. VISUALLY CHECK FLOAT ALIGNMENT AFTER ADJUSTING. REVERSE PROCEDURE TO RE-INSTALL PARTS REMOVED, MAKING SURE SOLENOID LEAN MIXTURE SCREW IS BACKED OUT OF FLOAT BOWL EXACTLY THE SAME NUMBER OF TURNS COUNTED AT DISASSEMBLY.

Fig. 5   Float level adjustment. E2M units

On some 1981–83 E2M units, an idle speed control mounted on the float bowl is used to control idle speed. On these units, the curb idle speed is programmed into the Electronic Control Module and no attempt should be made to adjust idle speed. On some 1981–82 models with V8 engine, an idle load compensator mounted on the float bowl is used to control idle speed. The compensator uses manifold vacuum to sense changes in engine load and compensates by adjusting curb idle speed. This unit should not be adjusted, unless if during diagnosis, curb idle speed is not within specifications.

NOTE: On 1980-83 units, the cover is retained to the choke housing by three pop rivets. With float bowl and throttle body properly supported, carefully align a No. 21 drill on pop rivet head. Drill only deep enough to remove rivet head, then using a small hammer and drift, drive remainder of rivet from choke housing. A service kit is available for choke cover installation. The choke cover should be removed only during major carburetor overhaul or if the choke coil is damaged.

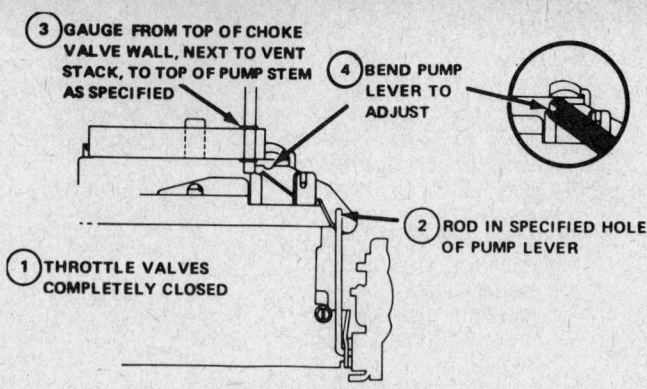

③ GAUGE FROM TOP OF CHOKE VALVE WALL, NEXT TO VENT STACK, TO TOP OF PUMP STEM AS SPECIFIED

④ BEND PUMP LEVER TO ADJUST

② ROD IN SPECIFIED HOLE OF PUMP LEVER

① THROTTLE VALVES COMPLETELY CLOSED

Fig. 6   Pump rod adjustment. 1977–80

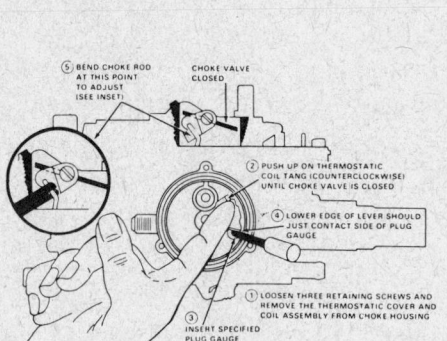

⑤ BEND CHOKE ROD AT THIS POINT TO ADJUST (SEE INSET)

CHOKE VALVE CLOSED

② PUSH UP ON THERMOSTATIC COIL TANG (COUNTERCLOCKWISE) UNTIL CHOKE VALVE IS CLOSED

④ LOWER EDGE OF LEVER SHOULD JUST CONTACT SIDE OF PLUG GAUGE

① LOOSEN THREE RETAINING SCREWS AND REMOVE THE THERMOSTATIC COVER AND COIL ASSEMBLY FROM CHOKE HOUSING

③ INSERT SPECIFIED PLUG GAUGE

Fig. 7   Choke coil lever adjustment

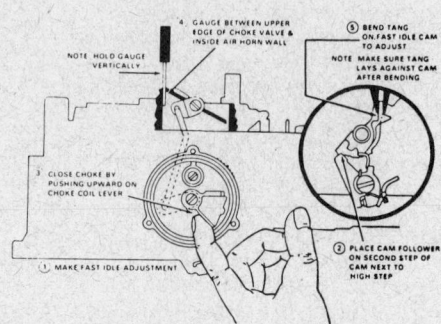

④ GAUGE BETWEEN UPPER EDGE OF CHOKE VALVE & INSIDE AIR HORN WALL

NOTE: HOLD GAUGE VERTICALLY

⑤ BEND TANG ON FAST IDLE CAM TO ADJUST. NOTE: MAKE SURE TANG LAYS AGAINST CAM AFTER BENDING

③ CLOSE CHOKE BY PUSHING UPWARD ON CHOKE COIL LEVER

② PLACE CAM FOLLOWER ON SECOND STEP OF CAM NEXT TO HIGH STEP

① MAKE FAST IDLE ADJUSTMENT

Fig. 8   Choke rod adjustment. Plug Gauge Method

Float Level Adjustment

Exc. E2M Units
Fig. 4—With adjustable T-scale, measure from top of float bowl gasket surface (gasket removed) to top of float at toe (locate gauging point 3/16" back from toe). Adjust as directed in the illustration to the dimension listed in the *Specifications Chart*. Make sure retaining pin is held firmly in place and tang of float is seated on float needle.

E2M Units
Fig. 5—With an adjustable T-scale, measure from top of float bowl gasket surface (gasket removed) to top of float at toe (locate gauging point 3/16 inch back from toe). If float level is

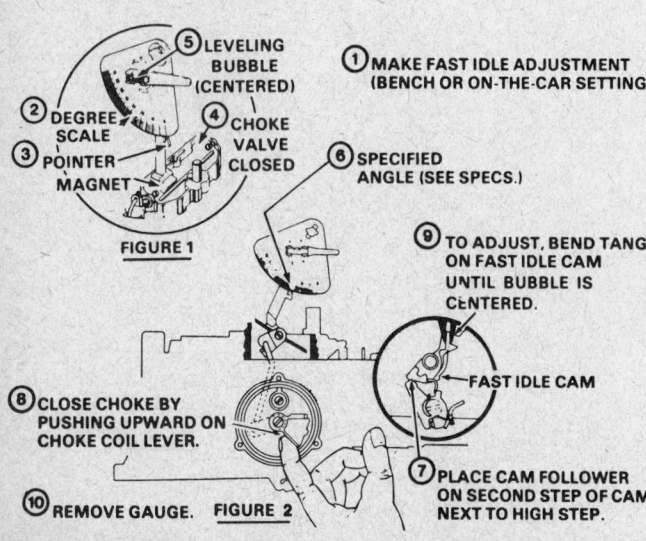

⑤ LEVELING BUBBLE (CENTERED)

② DEGREE SCALE

③ POINTER MAGNET

④ CHOKE VALVE CLOSED

FIGURE 1

① MAKE FAST IDLE ADJUSTMENT (BENCH OR ON-THE-CAR SETTING).

⑥ SPECIFIED ANGLE (SEE SPECS.)

⑨ TO ADJUST, BEND TANG ON FAST IDLE CAM UNTIL BUBBLE IS CENTERED.

FAST IDLE CAM

⑧ CLOSE CHOKE BY PUSHING UPWARD ON CHOKE COIL LEVER.

⑩ REMOVE GAUGE.   FIGURE 2

⑦ PLACE CAM FOLLOWER ON SECOND STEP OF CAM NEXT TO HIGH STEP.

Fig. 9   Choke rod adjustment. Angle gauge method

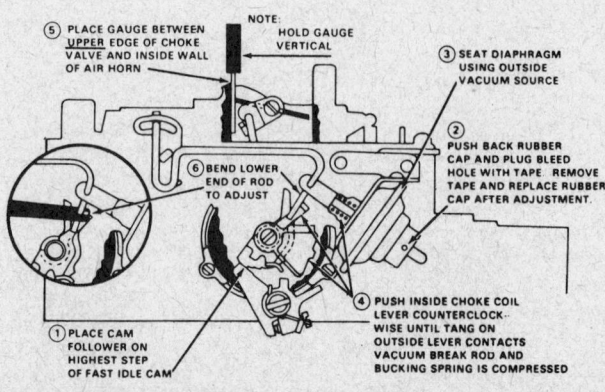

⑤ PLACE GAUGE BETWEEN UPPER EDGE OF CHOKE VALVE AND INSIDE WALL OF AIR HORN

NOTE: HOLD GAUGE VERTICAL

③ SEAT DIAPHRAGM USING OUTSIDE VACUUM SOURCE

② PUSH BACK RUBBER CAP AND PLUG BLEED HOLE WITH TAPE. REMOVE TAPE AND REPLACE RUBBER CAP AFTER ADJUSTMENT.

⑥ BEND LOWER END OF ROD TO ADJUST

① PLACE CAM FOLLOWER ON HIGHEST STEP OF FAST IDLE CAM

④ PUSH INSIDE CHOKE COIL LEVER COUNTERCLOCKWISE UNTIL TANG ON OUTSIDE LEVER CONTACTS VACUUM BREAK ROD AND BUCKING SPRING IS COMPRESSED

Fig. 10   Vacuum break adjustment, rich setting. 2MC units

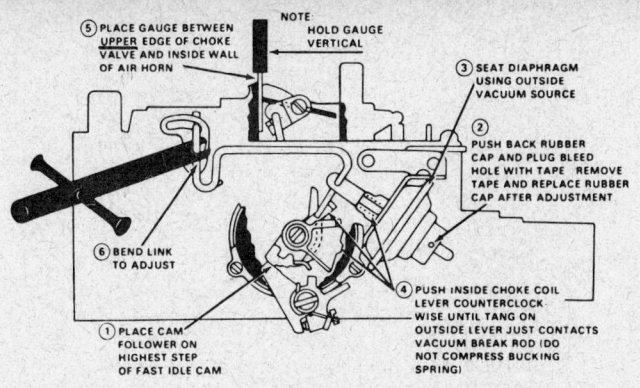

Fig. 11 Vacuum break adjustment, lean setting. 2MC units

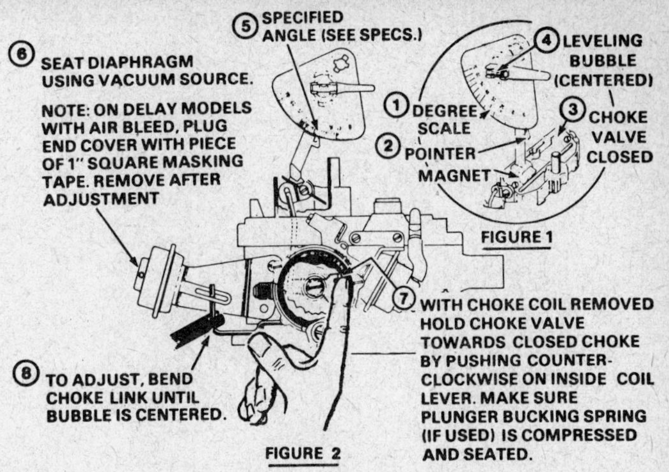

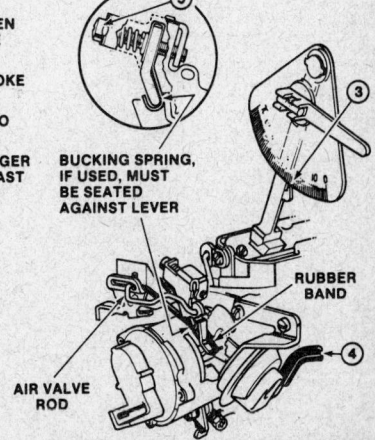

Fig. 12 Vacuum break adjustment, rear setting (angle gauge method). 1977-82 units

too high, hold retainer firmly in plate and lightly push down float against needle, then push downward on center of float to obtain correct setting. If float level is too low, remove metering rods and the solenoid connector screws. Turn lean mixture solenoid screw clockwise, counting the number of turns until lightly bottomed in the float bowl. Then, turn screw counterclockwise and remove screw. Remove float and bend arm upward to adjust. Check float alignment. Install lean mixture solenoid screw until lightly bottomed, then back out screw exactly the same number of turns previously noted. Install solenoid connector screws and the metering rods.

Pump Rod Adjustment

1977-80 Units, Fig. 6
With throttle valves completely closed and pump rod in specified hole in pump lever, measure from top of choke valve wall (next to vent stack) to top of pump stem. Dimension should be as listed in the *Specifications Chart*. To adjust, bend pump lever as required.

NOTE: Support lever with a screwdriver while bending lever.

Choke Coil Lever Adjustment

Fig. 7—With thermostatic coil assembly re-

moved, push upward on coil tang until choke valve closes. Insert gauge specified in the Specifications Chart into choke housing hole. The lower edge of choke coil lever should just contact gauge. To adjust, bend choke rod as required.

Choke Rod Adjustment

Plug Gauge Method
Fig. 8—With fast idle adjustment made, and cam follower on second step of fast idle cam and against the high step, push upward on choke coil lever until choke valve closes. Dimension between upper edge of choke valve and air horn wall should be as specified in the Specifications Chart. Adjust by bending tang on intermediate choke lever.

Angle Gauge Method

NOTE: On 1980-83 units, do not remove rivets or choke cover to place choke valve in the closed position. Use a rubber band on vacuum break lever tang to hold choke valve closed.

Fig. 9—Rotate degree scale until the zero is opposite pointer, then with choke valve com-

pletely closed, place magnet squarely on top of choke valve and rotate bubble until centered. Refer to the Specification Chart for proper setting for adjustment. Rotate scale so specified degree setting for adjustment is opposite pointer. Place cam follower on second step of cam, next to high step. Close choke by pushing upward on choke coil lever. To adjust, bend tang on fast idle lever until the bubble is centered.

Vacuum Break Adjustment

Rich Setting, 2MC Units
Fig. 10—With cam follower on highest step of fast idle cam, plug diaphragm bleed hole with tape, then using an external vacuum source, seat the diaphragm. Push choke coil lever counter-clockwise until outside lever tang contacts vacuum break rod and the bucking spring is compressed. Insert gauge specified in the 2MC Specification Chart between the upper edge of choke valve and air horn wall. To adjust, bend lower end of rod.

Lean Setting, 2MC Units
Fig. 11—With cam follower on highest step of fast idle cam, plug diaphragm bleed hole with tape, then using an external vacuum source,

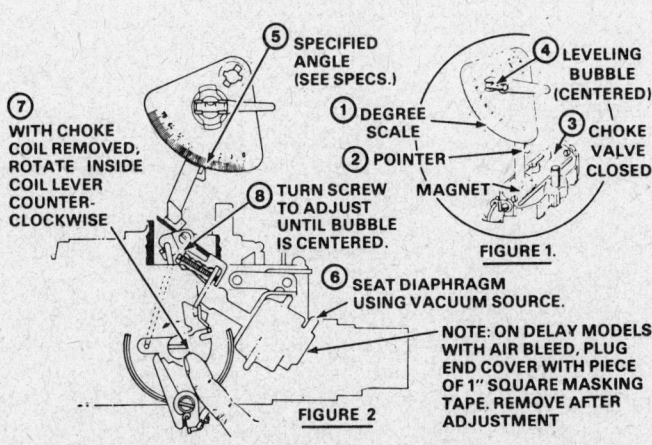

Fig. 13 Vacuum break adjustment, front setting (angle gauge method). 1977-82 units

Fig. 14 Vacuum break adjustment, rear setting (angle gauge method). 1983 units

CARBURETORS

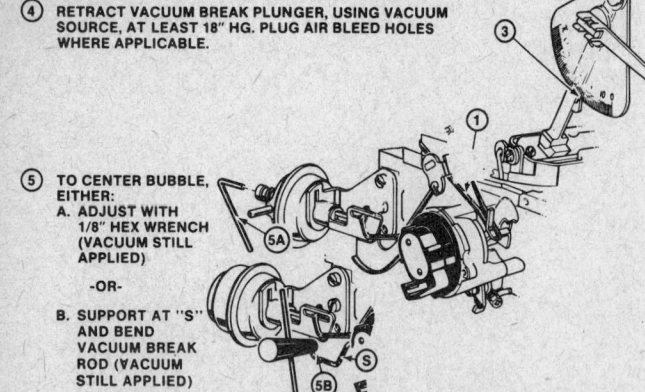

① ATTACH RUBBER BAND TO GREEN TANG OF INTERMEDIATE CHOKE SHAFT.

② OPEN THROTTLE TO ALLOW CHOKE VALVE TO CLOSE.

③ SET UP ANGLE GAGE AND SET ANGLE TO SPECIFICATION.

④ RETRACT VACUUM BREAK PLUNGER, USING VACUUM SOURCE, AT LEAST 18" HG. PLUG AIR BLEED HOLES WHERE APPLICABLE.

⑤ TO CENTER BUBBLE, EITHER:
A. ADJUST WITH 1/8" HEX WRENCH (VACUUM STILL APPLIED)
-OR-
B. SUPPORT AT "S" AND BEND VACUUM BREAK ROD (VACUUM STILL APPLIED)

Fig. 15   Vacuum break adjustment, front setting (angle gauge method). 1983 units

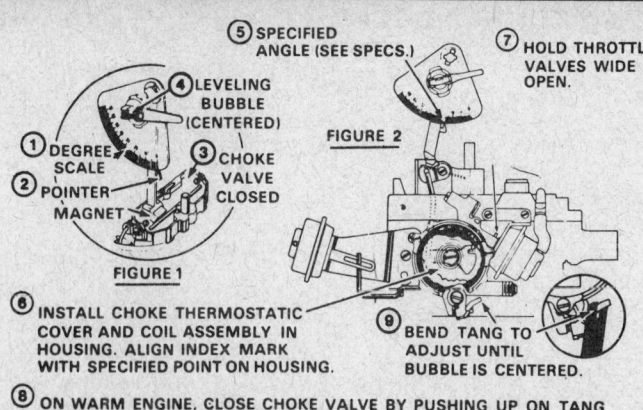

⑤ SPECIFIED ANGLE (SEE SPECS.)

④ LEVELING BUBBLE (CENTERED)

① DEGREE SCALE

② POINTER MAGNET

③ CHOKE VALVE CLOSED

FIGURE 1

FIGURE 2

⑦ HOLD THROTTLE VALVES WIDE OPEN.

⑥ INSTALL CHOKE THERMOSTATIC COVER AND COIL ASSEMBLY IN HOUSING. ALIGN INDEX MARK WITH SPECIFIED POINT ON HOUSING.

⑨ BEND TANG TO ADJUST UNTIL BUBBLE IS CENTERED.

⑧ ON WARM ENGINE, CLOSE CHOKE VALVE BY PUSHING UP ON TANG ON VACUUM BREAK LEVER (HOLD IN POSITION WITH RUBBER BAND).

Fig. 17   Choke unloader adjustment. 1978–83 units

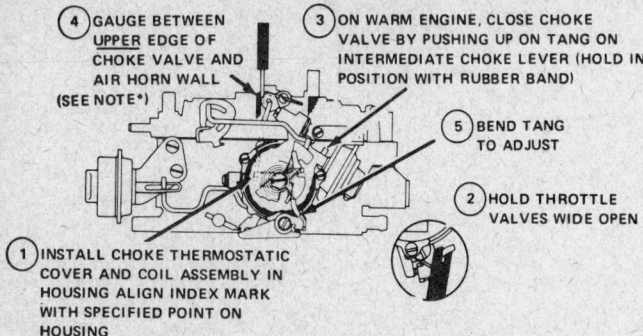

④ GAUGE BETWEEN UPPER EDGE OF CHOKE VALVE AND AIR HORN WALL (SEE NOTE*)

③ ON WARM ENGINE, CLOSE CHOKE VALVE BY PUSHING UP ON TANG ON INTERMEDIATE CHOKE LEVER (HOLD IN POSITION WITH RUBBER BAND)

⑤ BEND TANG TO ADJUST

② HOLD THROTTLE VALVES WIDE OPEN

① INSTALL CHOKE THERMOSTATIC COVER AND COIL ASSEMBLY IN HOUSING ALIGN INDEX MARK WITH SPECIFIED POINT ON HOUSING

Fig. 16   Choke unloader adjustment. 1977 units

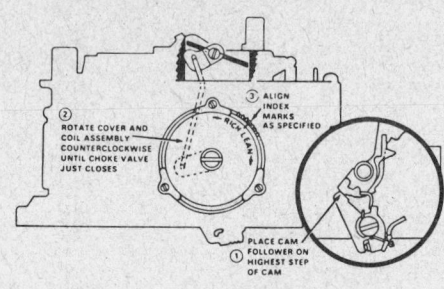

② ROTATE COVER AND COIL ASSEMBLY COUNTERCLOCKWISE UNTIL CHOKE VALVE JUST CLOSES

③ ALIGN INDEX MARKS AS SPECIFIED

① PLACE CAM FOLLOWER ON HIGHEST STEP OF CAM

Fig. 18   Choke coil adjustment

seat the diaphragm. Push choke coil lever counter-clockwise until outside lever tang lightly contacts vacuum break rod without compressing bucking spring. Insert gauge specified in the 2MC Specification Chart between upper edge of choke valve and air horn wall. To adjust, bend upper end of rod.

Rear Setting (Gauge Method), 1977–82 Exc. 2MC Units

NOTE: On 1980–82 units, do not remove rivets or choke cover to place choke valve in the closed position. Use a rubber band on vacuum break lever tang to hold choke valve closed. On 1981 units, remove vacuum break from carburetor and place bracket in a vise, then grind off weld holding adjusting screw cover. Remove adjusting screw cover, then reinstall vacuum break and proceed with adjustment.

Fig. 12—Rotate degree scale until zero is opposite pointer, then with choke valve completely closed, place magnet on top of choke valve and rotate bubble until it is centered. Refer to Specification Chart and rotate scale to degrees specified. Using an external vacuum source, seat choke diaphragm, then remove choke coil and rotate inside choke coil lever counterclockwise making sure bucking

spring is compressed and seated. To make final adjustment, bend link until bubble is centered.

Front Setting (Gauge Method), 1977–82 Exc. 2MC Units

NOTE: On 1980–82 units, do not remove rivets or choke cover to place choke valve in the closed position. Use a rubber band on vacuum break lever tang to hold choke valve closed. On 1981–82 units, remove vacuum break and place bracket in a vise, then grind off adjusting screw cover and reinstall vacuum break. After completing adjustment apply a suitable sealer to adjusting screw head.

Fig. 13—Rotate degree scale until zero is opposite pointer, then with choke valve completely closed, place gauge on top of choke valve and rotate bubble until it is centered. Refer to Specifications Chart and rotate gauge to degrees specified. Using an external vacuum source, seat choke vacuum diaphragm, then remove choke coil and rotate inside coil lever counterclockwise. To make final adjustment, turn screw in or out until bubble is centered.

Rear Setting (Gauge Method), 1983 Units
Fig. 14—Attach a rubber band to the green

tang of intermediate choke shaft to hold choke valve closed. Install angle gauge and rotate scale to specification. Refer to Specifications Chart. Using an outside vacuum source, retract the vacuum break plunger, then plug the air bleed holes, if applicable. Make final adjustment with vacuum still applied by turning adjusting screw with a 1/8 inch allen wrench or by bending vacuum break rod until bubble is centered.

Front Setting (Gauge Method), 1983 Units
Fig. 15—Attach a rubber band to the green tang of intermediate choke shaft to hold choke valve closed. Install angle gauge and rotate scale to specification. Refer to Specifications Chart. Using an outside vacuum source, retract the vacuum break plunger, then plug the air bleed holes, if applicable. Make final adjustment with vacuum still applied by turning screw in or out until bubble is centered.

Choke Unloader Adjustment

1977 Units
Fig. 16—Install choke cover and coil assembly and align index mark with specified point on housing. Hold throttle valves wide open. On a warm engine, close choke valve by pushing upward on tang on intermediate choke

lever and hold in position with a rubber band. Insert specified gauge between upper edge of choke valve and air horn wall. To adjust, bend fast idle lever tang.

1978–83 Units, Angle Gauge Method
Fig. 17—Rotate degree scale until the zero is opposite pointer, then with choke valve completely closed, place magnet squarely on top of choke valve and rotate bubble until centered. Refer to the Specification Chart for proper setting for adjustment. Rotate scale until specified degree for adjustment is opposite pointer. Install choke cover and coil assembly and align index mark with specified point on housing. Hold throttle valves wide open. On a warm engine close choke valve by pushing upward on tang on vacuum break lever and hold in position with a rubber band. To adjust, bend fast idle lever tang until the bubble is centered.

Choke Coil Adjustment

1977–79 Units
Fig. 18—Place the fast idle cam follower on the highest step of the fast idle cam. Rotate choke cover and coil assembly counter-clockwise until the choke valve just closes and the index point on cover aligns with the specified index point on the choke housing.

Idle Load Compensator Adjustment

1981–82 E2M Units

NOTE: On some 1981–82 models with V8 engine, an idle load compensator mounted on the float bowl is used to control idle speed. This unit should not be adjusted, unless if during diagnosis, curb idle speed is not within specifications. This adjustment should be performed with engine at operating temperature and choke and A/C off.

1. Remove air cleaner assembly and plug vacuum hose to thermal vacuum valve.
2. Disconnect and plug hoses to EGR valve, canister purge port and idle load compensator.
3. Apply parking brake and block wheels, then back throttle stop screw out 3 turns.
4. With engine operating, place transmission selector lever in drive position, adjust plunger to obtain 750 RPM. The jam nut on the plunger must be held in position to prevent damage to guide tabs. If a replacement idle load compensator is being installed, the plunger should be set to obtain a clearance of 61/64 inch from jam nut to tip of plunger.
5. Connect vacuum hose to idle load compensator and note idle speed. If idle speed requires adjustment, stop engine and remove idle load compensator.
6. With idle load compensator removed, remove rubber and metal plug from center outlet tube.
7. Using a .090 inch allen wrench, rotate center outlet tube adjusting screw to obtain 550 RPM on 1981 models, or 500 RPM on 1982 models. Each turn of the adjusting screw will change idle speed approximately 75 to 100 RPM. Rotate adjusting screw counter-clockwise to increase engine speed and clockwise to decrease engine speed.
8. Reinstall rubber plug on center outlet tube, then install idle load compensator on carburetor. If a final adjustment is necessary it will be necessary to repeat steps 6, 7 and 8.
9. Apply a suitable vacuum source to idle load compensator to fully retract plunger.
10. Adjust throttle body idle stop screw to obtain 550 RPM on 1981 models, or 500 RPM on 1982 models, then reconnect all vacuum hoses and install air cleaner.

MONOJET 1ME CARBURETOR ADJUSTMENT SPECIFICATIONS

See Tune Up Chart in car chapter for curb and fast idle speeds.

Year	Carb. Part No. ①	Float Level	Metering Rod	Choke Coil Lever	Choke Rod	Vacuum Break	Unloader	Choke Setting
1977	17057013	3/8	.080	.120	.100	.125	.325	1 Rich
	17057014	3/8	.090	.120	.100	.125	.325	2 Rich
	17057015	3/8	.080	.120	.100	.125	.325	1 Rich
	17057016	3/8	.080	.120	.105	.105	.325	1 Lean
	17057018	3/8	.080	.120	.085	.120	.325	2 Rich
	17057020	3/8	.090	.120	.100	.125	.325	2 Rich
	17057030	5/32	.080	.120	.050	.080	.200	2 Rich
	17057031	5/32	.080	.120	.050	.080	.200	2 Rich
	17057032	5/32	.080	.120	.050	.080	.200	2 Rich
	17057034	5/32	.080	.120	.050	.080	.200	2 Rich
	17057035	5/32	.080	.120	.050	.080	.200	2 Rich
	17057042	5/32	.080	.120	.050	.075	.200	1 Rich
	17057044	5/32	.080	.120	.050	.075	.200	1 Rich
	17057045	5/32	.080	.120	.050	.075	.200	1 Rich
	17057310	3/8	.100	.120	—	—	—	Index
	17057312	3/8	.100	.120	—	—	—	Index
	17057314	3/8	.080	.120	.100	.110	.225	Index
	17057318	3/8	.080	.120	.100	.110	.225	Index
	17057332	5/32	.080	.120	.050	.075	.200	2 Rich
	17057334	5/32	.080	.120	.050	.075	.200	2 Rich
	17057335	5/32	.080	.120	.050	.075	.200	2 Rich
1978	17058013	3/8	.080	.120	.180	.200	.500	Index
	17058014	5/16	.100	.120	.180	.200	.500	Index
	17058020	5/16	.100	.120	.180	.200	.500	Index
	17058031	5/32	.080	.120	.105	.150	.500	2 Rich
	17058032	5/32	.080	.120	.080	.130	.500	3 Rich
	17058033	5/32	.080	.120	.080	.130	.500	2 Rich
	17058034	5/32	.080	.120	.080	.130	.500	3 Rich

Continued

CARBURETORS

See Tune Up Chart in car chapter for curb and fast idle speeds.

Year	Carb. Part No. ①	Float Level	Metering Rod	Choke Coil Lever	Choke Rod	Vacuum Break	Unloader	Choke Setting
	17058035	5/32	.080	.120	.080	.130	.500	3 Rich
	17058036	5/32	.080	.120	.080	.130	.500	3 Rich
	17058037	5/32	.080	.120	.080	.130	.500	2 Rich
	17058038	5/32	.080	.120	.080	.130	.500	3 Rich
	17058042	5/32	.080	.120	.080	②	.500	2 Rich
	17058044	5/32	.080	.120	.080	②	.500	2 Rich
	17058045	5/32	.080	.120	.080	②	.500	2 Rich
	17058314	3/8	.100	.120	.190	.245	.400	Index
	17058332	5/32	.080	.120	.080	②	.500	2 Rich
	17058334	5/32	.080	.120	.080	②	.500	2 Rich
	17058335	5/32	.080	.120	.080	②	.500	2 Rich
	17058339	5/32	.080	.120	.080	②	.500	2 Rich
1979	17059012	5/16	.095	.120	.180	.200	.500	Index
	17059013	3/8	.100	.120	.180	.200	.400	Index
	17059014	3/8	.100	.120	.180	.200	.400	Index
	17059020	3/8	.100	.120	.180	.200	.400	Index
	17059023	5/16	.095	.120	.180	.200	.500	Index
	17059314	3/8	.100	.120	.190	.245	.400	Index

①—On tag attached to carburetor. ②—Below 30,000 miles, .130 inch; above 30,000 miles, .160 inch.

Monojet 1ME Adjustments

This Monojet carburetor is a single bore, downdraft carburetor incorporating a triple venturi in conjunction with a plain tube nozzle. The main metering system fuel flow is controlled by a main well air bleed and a variable orifice jet. Power enrichment is provided through a mechanically operated metering rod, connected by linkage to the throttle shaft. A fuel pull-over enrichment is used to supplement main metering mixtures at higher engine RPM.

An automatic choke system using an electrically heated choke coil is incorporated into this carburetor. The vacuum diaphragm unit, mounted externally on the air horn, is connected to the thermostatic coil lever through a connecting link. The electric choke coil is contained in a housing mounted on a bracket attached to the float bowl.

Float Level Adjustment

Fig. 1
1. Hold float retaining pin firmly in place and float arm against top of float needle by pushing downward on float arm at point between needle seat and hinge pin as shown.
2. With adjustable T-scale, measure distance from top of float at toe to float bowl gasket surface (gasket removed). Measurement should be at a point 1/16" in from end of flat surface at float toe (not on radius).
3. Bend float pontoon up or down at float arm junction to adjust.

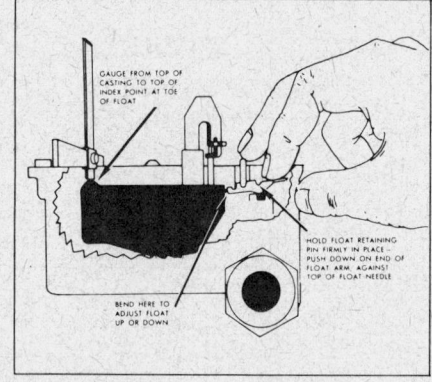

Fig. 1 Float level adjustment

Metering Rod Adjustment

Fig. 2
1. Remove metering rod by holding throttle valve wide open. Push downward on metering rod against spring tension, then slide metering rod out of slot in holder and remove from main metering jet.
2. To check adjustment, back out idle solenoid screw and rotate fast idle cam so that fast idle cam follower is not contacting steps on cam.
3. With throttle valve completely closed, apply pressure to top of power piston and hold piston down against its stop.

4. While holding downward pressure on power piston, swing metering rod holder over flat surface of bowl casting next to carburetor bore.
5. Use specified size drill and insert between bowl casting sealing bead and lower surface of metering rod holder. Drill should have a slide fit between both surfaces as shown.
6. To adjust, carefully bend metering rod holder up or down at point shown.
7. After adjustment, install metering rod.

Choke Coil Lever Adjustment

Fig. 3
1. With fast idle adjusting screw on fast idle cam high step, close choke valve.
2. Insert a .120 inch gauge pin through hole in lever and into casting. If holes do not align, bend link to adjust.

Fast Idle Adjustment

Chevette, Fig. 4
1. Adjust curb idle speed, if necessary.
2. Connect a tachometer to engine.
3. Start engine, set parking brake and place transmission in Neutral.
4. With engine at normal operating temperature, turn fast idle speed screw to adjust fast idle.
5. Stop engine and remove tachometer.

Exc. Chevette, Figs. 5 & 6
1. Set normal engine idle speed.

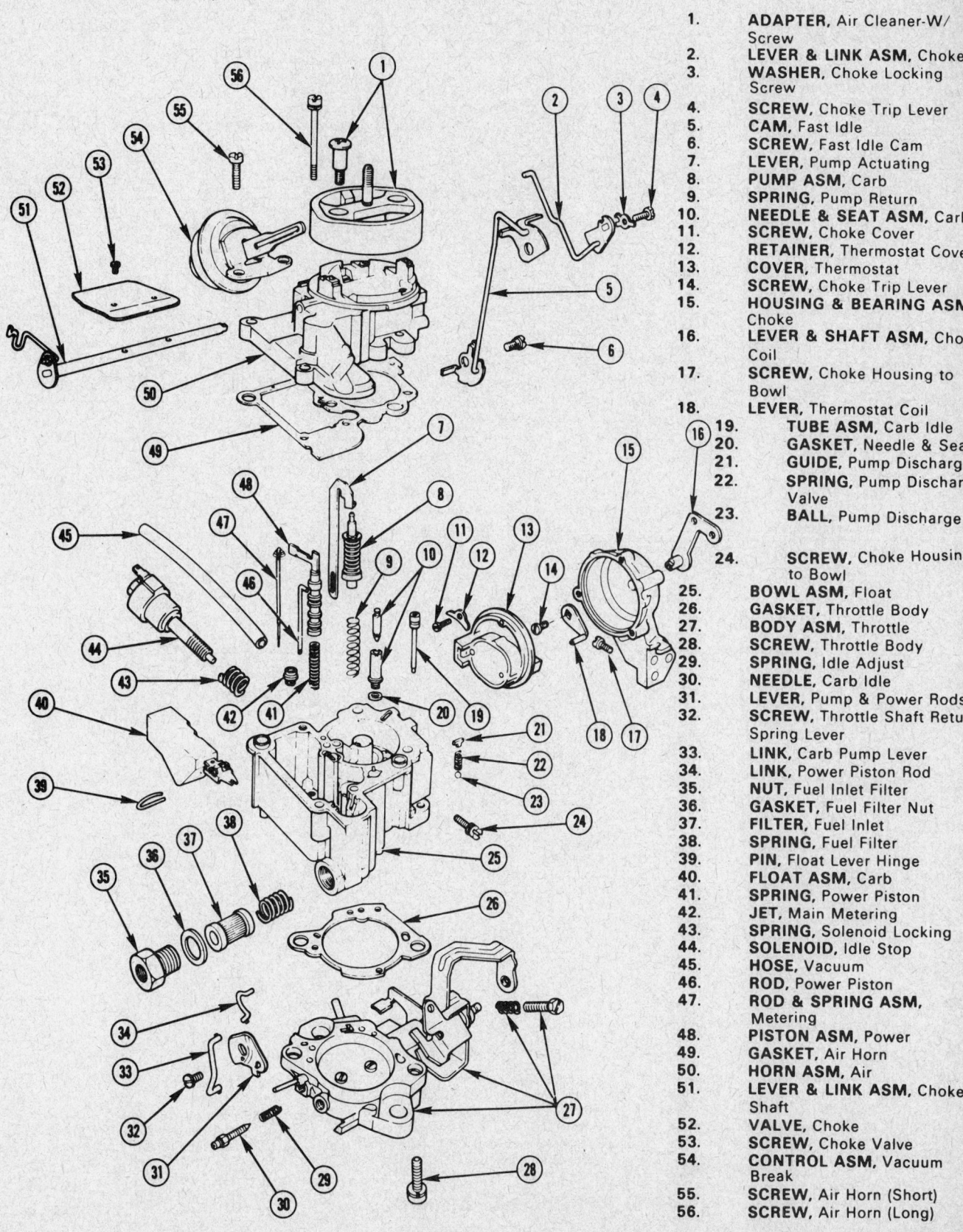

1. **ADAPTER,** Air Cleaner-W/ Screw
2. **LEVER & LINK ASM,** Choke
3. **WASHER,** Choke Locking Screw
4. **SCREW,** Choke Trip Lever
5. **CAM,** Fast Idle
6. **SCREW,** Fast Idle Cam
7. **LEVER,** Pump Actuating
8. **PUMP ASM,** Carb
9. **SPRING,** Pump Return
10. **NEEDLE & SEAT ASM,** Carb
11. **SCREW,** Choke Cover
12. **RETAINER,** Thermostat Cover
13. **COVER,** Thermostat
14. **SCREW,** Choke Trip Lever
15. **HOUSING & BEARING ASM,** Choke
16. **LEVER & SHAFT ASM,** Choke Coil
17. **SCREW,** Choke Housing to Bowl
18. **LEVER,** Thermostat Coil
19. **TUBE ASM,** Carb Idle
20. **GASKET,** Needle & Seat
21. **GUIDE,** Pump Discharge
22. **SPRING,** Pump Discharge Valve
23. **BALL,** Pump Discharge
24. **SCREW,** Choke Housing to Bowl
25. **BOWL ASM,** Float
26. **GASKET,** Throttle Body
27. **BODY ASM,** Throttle
28. **SCREW,** Throttle Body
29. **SPRING,** Idle Adjust
30. **NEEDLE,** Carb Idle
31. **LEVER,** Pump & Power Rods
32. **SCREW,** Throttle Shaft Return Spring Lever
33. **LINK,** Carb Pump Lever
34. **LINK,** Power Piston Rod
35. **NUT,** Fuel Inlet Filter
36. **GASKET,** Fuel Filter Nut
37. **FILTER,** Fuel Inlet
38. **SPRING,** Fuel Filter
39. **PIN,** Float Lever Hinge
40. **FLOAT ASM,** Carb
41. **SPRING,** Power Piston
42. **JET,** Main Metering
43. **SPRING,** Solenoid Locking
44. **SOLENOID,** Idle Stop
45. **HOSE,** Vacuum
46. **ROD,** Power Piston
47. **ROD & SPRING ASM,** Metering
48. **PISTON ASM,** Power
49. **GASKET,** Air Horn
50. **HORN ASM,** Air
51. **LEVER & LINK ASM,** Choke Shaft
52. **VALVE,** Choke
53. **SCREW,** Choke Valve
54. **CONTROL ASM,** Vacuum Break
55. **SCREW,** Air Horn (Short)
56. **SCREW,** Air Horn (Long)

Exploded view of Rochester model 1ME carburetor

CARBURETORS

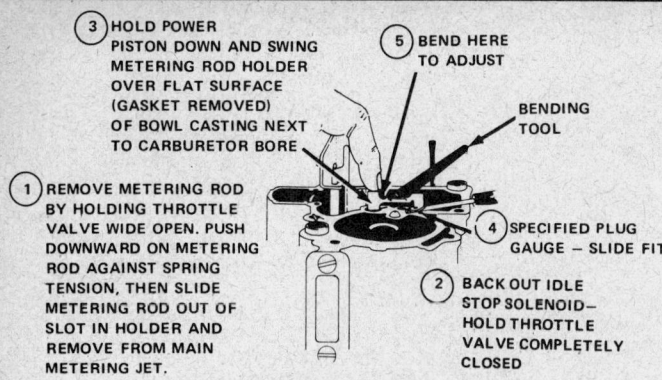

③ HOLD POWER PISTON DOWN AND SWING METERING ROD HOLDER OVER FLAT SURFACE (GASKET REMOVED) OF BOWL CASTING NEXT TO CARBURETOR BORE

⑤ BEND HERE TO ADJUST

BENDING TOOL

① REMOVE METERING ROD BY HOLDING THROTTLE VALVE WIDE OPEN. PUSH DOWNWARD ON METERING ROD AGAINST SPRING TENSION, THEN SLIDE METERING ROD OUT OF SLOT IN HOLDER AND REMOVE FROM MAIN METERING JET.

④ SPECIFIED PLUG GAUGE – SLIDE FIT

② BACK OUT IDLE STOP SOLENOID - HOLD THROTTLE VALVE COMPLETELY CLOSED

Fig. 2   Metering rod adjustment

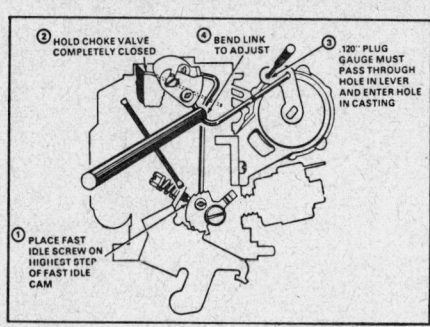

② HOLD CHOKE VALVE COMPLETELY CLOSED

④ BEND LINK TO ADJUST

③ .120" PLUG GAUGE MUST PASS THROUGH HOLE IN LEVER AND ENTER HOLE IN CASTING

① PLACE FAST IDLE SCREW ON HIGHEST STEP OF FAST IDLE CAM

Fig. 3   Choke coil lever adjustment

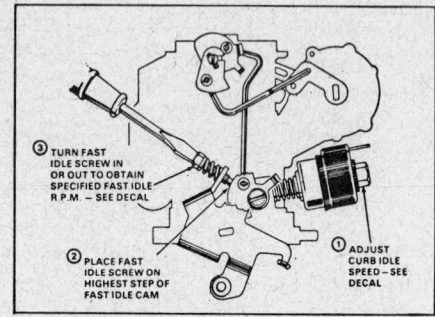

③ TURN FAST IDLE SCREW IN OR OUT TO OBTAIN SPECIFIED FAST IDLE R.P.M. – SEE DECAL

② PLACE FAST IDLE SCREW ON HIGHEST STEP OF FAST IDLE CAM

① ADJUST CURB IDLE SPEED – SEE DECAL

Fig. 4   Fast idle adjustment. Chevette

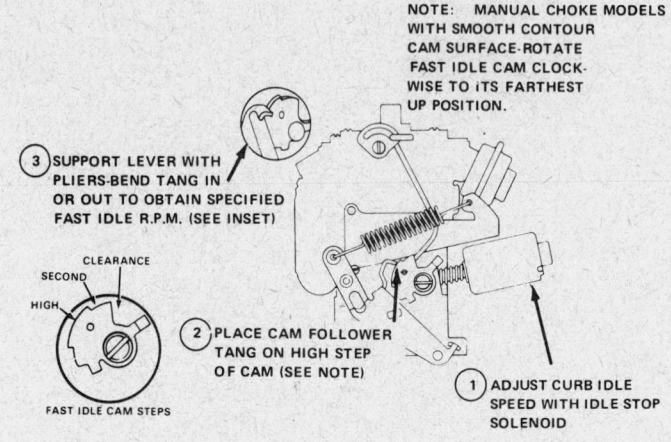

NOTE: MANUAL CHOKE MODELS WITH SMOOTH CONTOUR CAM SURFACE-ROTATE FAST IDLE CAM CLOCKWISE TO ITS FARTHEST UP POSITION.

③ SUPPORT LEVER WITH PLIERS-BEND TANG IN OR OUT TO OBTAIN SPECIFIED FAST IDLE R.P.M. (SEE INSET)

CLEARANCE
SECOND
HIGH

FAST IDLE CAM STEPS

② PLACE CAM FOLLOWER TANG ON HIGH STEP OF CAM (SEE NOTE)

① ADJUST CURB IDLE SPEED WITH IDLE STOP SOLENOID

Fig. 5   Fast idle adjustment. 1977 exc. Chevette

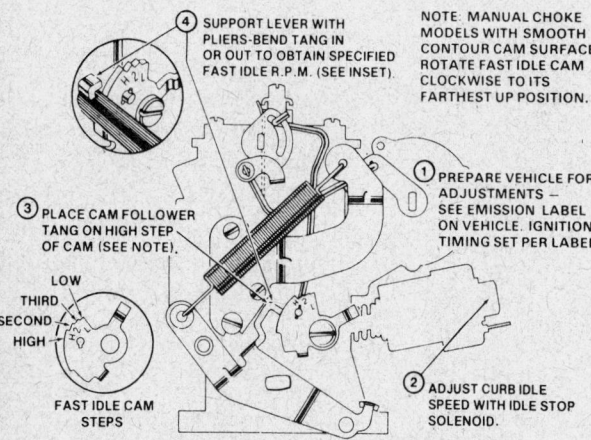

④ SUPPORT LEVER WITH PLIERS-BEND TANG IN OR OUT TO OBTAIN SPECIFIED FAST IDLE R.P.M. (SEE INSET).

NOTE: MANUAL CHOKE MODELS WITH SMOOTH CONTOUR CAM SURFACE ROTATE FAST IDLE CAM CLOCKWISE TO ITS FARTHEST UP POSITION.

③ PLACE CAM FOLLOWER TANG ON HIGH STEP OF CAM (SEE NOTE)

LOW
THIRD
SECOND
HIGH

FAST IDLE CAM STEPS

① PREPARE VEHICLE FOR ADJUSTMENTS – SEE EMISSION LABEL ON VEHICLE. IGNITION TIMING SET PER LABEL.

② ADJUST CURB IDLE SPEED WITH IDLE STOP SOLENOID.

Fig. 6   Fast idle adjustment. 1978–79 exc. Chevette

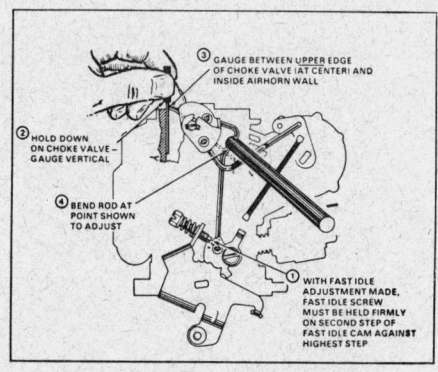

③ GAUGE BETWEEN UPPER EDGE OF CHOKE VALVE (AT CENTER) AND INSIDE AIRHORN WALL

② HOLD DOWN ON CHOKE VALVE - GAUGE VERTICAL

④ BEND ROD AT POINT SHOWN TO ADJUST

① WITH FAST IDLE ADJUSTMENT MADE, FAST IDLE SCREW MUST BE HELD FIRMLY ON SECOND STEP OF FAST IDLE CAM AGAINST HIGHEST STEP

Fig. 7   Choke rod adjustment. 1977

2. Place fast idle cam follower tang on highest step of cam.
3. To adjust, insert screwdriver in slot provided in fast idle cam follower tang and bend inwards (towards cam) or outward to obtain specified dimension.

Choke Rod Adjustment

Figs. 7 & 8
1. With fast idle adjustment made, place fast idle cam follower on second step of fast idle cam and hold firmly against the

rise to the high step.
2. Rotate choke towards direction of closed choke by applying force to choke coil lever.
3. Bend choke rod at point shown to obtain proper dimension between specified edge of choke valve and air horn wall.

Vacuum Break Adjustment

Figs. 9 & 10
1. With fast idle screw on fast idle cam high step, seat diaphragm using an outside

vacuum source. Cover purge hole with a piece of tape.
2. Close choke valve to compress plunger bucking spring and seat plunger stem.
3. Place gauge between specified edge of choke valve and air horn wall. Bend link to adjust.

Unloader Adjustment

Figs. 11 & 12
1. With choke properly indexed and throttle valve held wide open, manually close

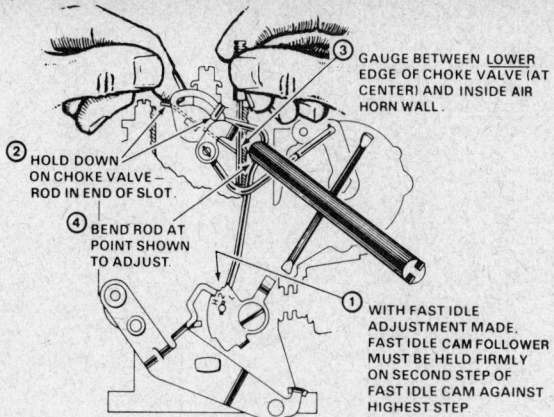

Fig. 8 Choke rod adjustment. 1978–79

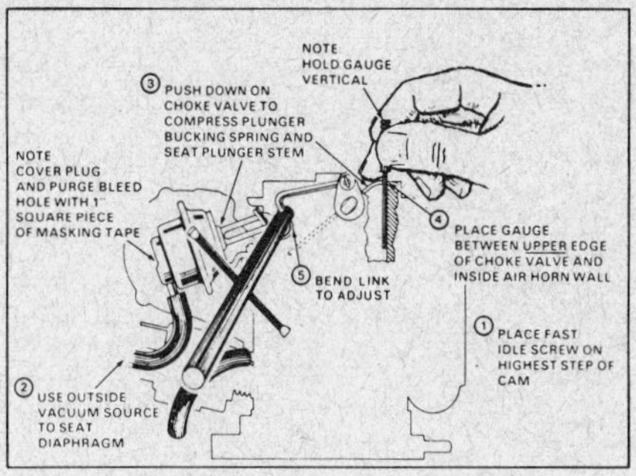

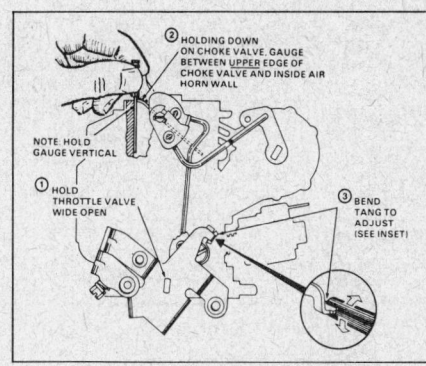

Fig. 9 Vacuum break adjustment. 1977

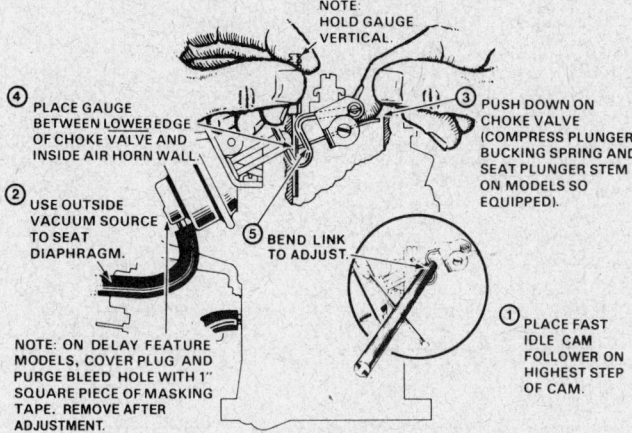

Fig. 10 Vacuum break adjustment. 1978–79

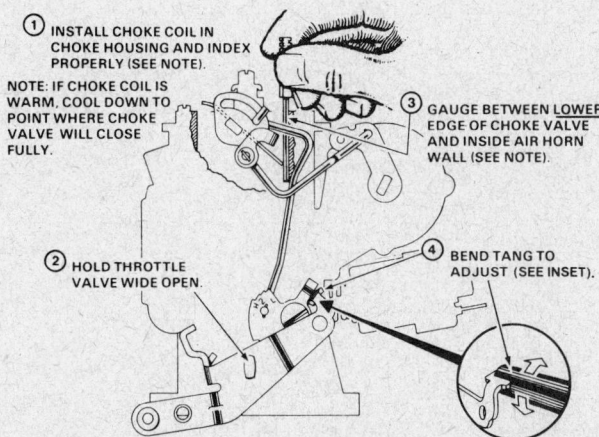

Fig. 11 Unloader adjustment. 1977

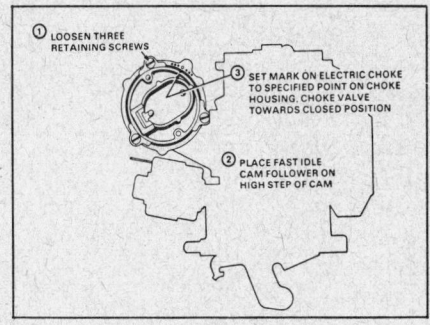

Fig. 12 Unloader adjustment. 1978–79

Fig. 13 Choke coil adjustment

choke valve with gauge between specified edge of choke valve and air horn wall.

2. If distance is not within specifications, bend unloader tang to adjust.

Choke Coil Adjustment

Fig. 13

1. Install electric choke assembly into housing, ensuring coil tang contacts lower side of coil lever pick-up arm.
2. Place fast cam follower on high step of cam.
3. Rotate cover and coil assembly counterclockwise until choke valve just closes, then align cover index point with the specified mark on housing.
4. Install and tighten cover retainers and screws.

NOTE: Do not install a choke cover gasket between the choke assembly and housing since the ground contact for the choke is provided by a metal plate at the rear of the choke assembly.

CARBURETORS

See Tune Up Chart in car chapters for curb and fast idle speeds.

Year	Carb. Production No.	Float Level	Accel. Pump	Choke Coil Lever	Choke Rod	Vacuum Break		Air Valve Rod	Choke Setting	Unloader	Secondary Lockout
						Primary	Secondary				
AMERICAN MOTORS											
1980	17080681	3/16	17/32	.085	18°	20°	—	2°	②	32°	.065
	17080683	3/16	1/2	.085	18°	20°	—	2°	②	32°	.065
	17080686, 688	3/16	1/2	.085	18°	20°	—	2°	②	32°	.065
	17080781, 782	3/16	7/32	.085	18°	20°	—	2°	②	32°	.065
1981	17081790	.256	.128	.085	—	19°	—	2°	②	32°	.065
	17081791, 796	.208	.128	.085	—	19°	—	2°	②	32°	.065
	17081792, 793	.256	.128	.085	—	19°	—	2°	②	32°	.065
	17081794, 795	.256	.128	.085	—	19°	—	2°	②	32°	.065
	17081797	.208	.128	.065	—	19°	—	2°	②	32°	.085
	17081993	.256	.128	.085	—	19°	—	2°	②	32°	.065
1982	17082380	.125	.128	.085	—	21°	—	2°	②	34°	.050—.080
	17082383	.256	.128	.085	—	21°	—	2°	②	34°	.050—.080
	17082385	.256	.128	.085	—	21°	—	2°	②	34°	.050—.080
	17082386	.125	.128	.050—.080	—	19°	—	2°	②	34°	.050—.080
	17082387	.125	.128	.085	—	19°	—	2°	②	34°	.050—.080
	17082388	.125	.128	.085	—	19°	—	2°	②	34°	.050—.080
	17082389	.125	.128	.085	—	19°	—	2°	②	34°	.050—.080
1983	17082380	①	.128	.085	—	21°	—	2°	②	34°	.050—.080
	17083384	.138	.128	.085	—	19°	—	2°	②	34°	.050—.080
	17083385	.138	.128	.085	—	19°	—	2°	②	34°	.050—.080

①—Man. trans., .216; auto. trans., .138.   ②—Tamper-resistant.

Year	Carb. Production No.	Float Level	Accel. Pump	Choke Coil Lever	Choke Rod	Vacuum Break		Air Valve Rod	Choke Setting	Unloader	Secondary Lockout
						Primary	Secondary				
GENERAL MOTORS											
1979	17059674	7/32	1/2	.085	18°	22°	—	.025	2 Rich	32°	.030
	17059675	7/32	17/32	.085	18°	22°	—	.025	1 Rich	32°	.030
	17059676	7/32	1/2	.085	18°	22°	—	.025	2 Rich	32°	.030
	17059677	7/32	17/32	.085	18°	22°	—	.025	1 Rich	32°	.030
	17059750	3/32	15/32	.085	21°	22°	35°	.040	Index	35°	.030
	17059751	3/16	15/32	.085	21°	22°	35°	.040	Index	35°	.030
	17059752	3/16	15/32	.085	21°	22°	35°	.040	Index	35°	.030
	17059753	3/16	15/32	.085	21°	22°	35°	.040	Index	35°	.030
1980	17059614, 616	3/16	1/2	.085	18°	17°	—	1°	⑤	36°	.025
	17059615, 617	3/16	17/32	.085	18°	19°	—	1°	⑤	36°	.025
	17059618, 620	3/16	1/2	.085	18°	17°	—	1°	⑤	36°	.025
	17059619, 621	3/16	17/32	.085	18°	19°	—	1°	⑤	36°	.025
	17059622, 624	5/32	17/32	.085	18°	17°	—	1°	⑤	36°	.025
	17059623, 625	5/32	17/32	.085	18°	19°	—	1°	⑤	36°	.025
	17059650, 652	1/4	17/32	.085	24°	30°	38°	1°	⑤	30°	.025
	17059651, 653	1/4	17/32	.085	24°	30°	37°	1°	⑤	30°	.025
	17059660, 662	1/4	17/32	.085	24°	30°	32°	1°	⑤	30°	.025
	17059664, 665	1/4	17/32	.085	24°	30°	32°	1°	⑤	30°	.025
	17059666, 667	1/4	17/32	.085	24°	26°	32°	1°	⑤	30°	.025
	17059714, 716	5/32	1/2	.085	18°	19°	—	1°	⑤	32°	.025
	17059715, 717	5/32	1/2	.085	18°	21°	—	1°	⑤	32°	.120
	17059718, 720	5/32	1/2	.085	18°	19°	—	1°	⑤	32°	.025
	17059721, 723	5/32	17/32	.085	①	23°	—	1°	⑤	32°	.025
	17059722, 724	5/32	15/32	.085	①	19°	—	1°	⑤	32°	.025
	17059760	1/4	—	.085	16°	24°	30°	1°	⑤	35°	.025
	17059762, 763	1/4	—	.085	16°	24°	33°	1°	⑤	35°	.025
	17059768	1/4	—	.085	16°	20°	30°	1°	⑤	35°	.025

Continued

ROCHESTER 2SE & E2SE ADJUSTMENT SPECIFICATIONS—Continued

See Tune Up Chart in car chapters for curb and fast idle speeds.

Year	Carb. Production No.	Float Level	Accel. Pump	Choke Coil Lever	Choke Rod	Vacuum Break Primary	Vacuum Break Secondary	Air Valve Rod	Choke Setting	Unloader	Secondary Lockout
GENERAL MOTORS—Continued											
	17059774, 776	5/32	1/2	.085	18°	19°	—	1°	⑤	32°	.025
	17059775, 777	5/32	17/32	.085	18°	21°	—	1°	⑤	32°	.025
	17080621, 622	1/8	9/16	—	17°	22°	35°	2°	⑤	41°	—
	17080623, 626	1/8	9/16	—	17°	22°	35°	2°	⑤	41°	—
	17080674, 676	3/16	1/2	.085	18°	19°	—	2°	⑤	32°	.025
	17080675, 677	3/16	1/2	.085	18°	21°	—	2°	⑤	32°	.025
	17080720, 722	1/8	9/16	—	17°	20°	35°	2°	⑤	41°	—
	17080721, 723	1/8	9/16	—	17°	23.5°	35°	2°	⑤	41°	—
1981	17081650, 652	1/4	—	—	17°	25°	34°	1°	⑤	35°	.012
	17081651, 653	1/4	—	—	17°	29°	35°	1°	⑤	35°	.012
	17081656, 658	1/4	—	—	25°	30°	35°	1°	⑤	33°	.012
	17081670, 672	5/32	—	—	18°	19°	—	1°	⑤	32°	.012
	17081671, 673	5/32	—	—	33.5°	21°	—	1°	⑤	32°	.012
	17081740, 742	1/4	—	—	17°	25°	34°	1°	⑤	35°	.012
	17081746, 748	1/4	—	—	25°	30°	35°	1°	⑤	33°	.012
1982	17081600, 06	5/16	—	.085	18°	23°	27°	1°	⑤	35°	.025
	17081601	5/16	—	.085	18°	21°	27°	1°	⑤	35°	.025
	17081607, 09	5/16	—	.085	18°	21°	27°	1°	⑤	35°	.025
	17082300, 04	5/16	—	.085	18°	23°	27°	1°	⑤	35°	.025
	17082301, 03	5/16	—	.085	18°	21°	27°	1°	⑤	35°	.025
	17082305	5/16	—	.085	18°	21°	27°	1°	⑤	35°	.025
	17082316	1/4	—	.085	17°	30°	34°	1°	⑤	45°	.025
	17082317	1/4	—	.085	17°	30°	35°	1°	⑤	45°	.025
	17082320, 21	1/4	—	.085	25°	30°	35°	1°	⑤	45°	.025
	17082390	13/32	—	.085	17°	30°	34°	1°	⑤	45°	.025
	17082391	13/32	—	.085	25°	30°	35°	1°	⑤	45°	.025
	17082446, 48	5/16	—	.085	18°	20°	27°	1°	⑤	35°	.025
	17082447, 49	5/16	—	.085	18°	20°	25°	1°	⑤	35°	.025
	17082490	13/32	—	.085	17°	30°	34°	1°	⑤	45°	.025
	17082491	13/32	—	.085	25°	30°	35°	1°	⑤	45°	.025
	17082630	5/16	—	.085	18°	23°	27°	1°	⑤	35°	.025
	17082631	5/16	—	.085	18°	23°	25°	1°	⑤	35°	.025
	17082632	5/16	—	.085	18°	20°	27°	1°	⑤	35°	.025
	17082640	1/4	—	.085	17°	30°	34°	1°	⑤	45°	.025
	17082641	1/4	—	.085	17°	30°	35°	1°	⑤	45°	.025
	17082642	1/4	—	.085	25°	30°	35°	1°	⑤	45°	.025
1983	17083356	13/32	—	.085	22°	25°	35°	1°	⑤	30°	—
	17083357	13/32	—	.085	22°	25°	35°	1°	⑤	30°	—
	17083358	13/32	—	.085	22°	25°	35°	1°	⑤	30°	—
	17083359	13/32	—	.085	22°	25°	35°	1°	⑤	30°	—
	17083368	②	—	.085	22°	25°	35°	1°	⑤	30°	—
	17083369	②	—	.085	22°	25°	35°	1°	⑤	30°	—
	17083370	②	—	.085	22°	25°	35°	1°	⑤	30°	—
	17083371	②	—	.085	22°	25°	35°	1°	⑤	30°	—
	17083450	③	—	.085	28°	27°	35°	1°	⑤	45°	—
	17083451	③	—	.085	28°	27°	35°	1°	⑤	45°	—
	17083452	③	—	.085	28°	27°	35°	1°	⑤	45°	—
	17083453	③	—	.085	28°	27°	35°	1°	⑤	45°	—
	17083454	③	—	.085	28°	27°	35°	1°	⑤	45°	—
	17083455	③	—	.085	28°	27°	35°	1°	⑤	45°	—
	17083456	③	—	.085	28°	27°	35°	1°	⑤	45°	—

Continued

CARBURETORS

See Tune Up charts in car chapters for curb and fast idle speeds.

Year	Carb. Production No.	Float Level	Accel. Pump	Choke Coil Lever	Choke Rod	Vacuum Break Primary	Vacuum Break Secondary	Air Valve Rod	Choke Setting	Unloader	Secondary Lockout
GENERAL MOTORS—Continued											
	17083458	1/4	—	.085	28°	27°	35°	1°	⑤	45°	—
	17083459	1/4	—	.085	28°	27°	35°	1°	⑤	45°	—
	17083630	④	—	.085	28°	27°	35°	1°	⑤	45°	—
	17083631	④	—	.085	28°	27°	35°	1°	⑤	45°	—
	17083632	④	—	.085	28°	27°	35°	1°	⑤	45°	—
	17083633	④	—	.085	28°	27°	35°	1°	⑤	45°	—
	17083634	④	—	.085	28°	27°	35°	1°	⑤	45°	—
	17083635	④	—	.085	28°	27°	35°	1°	⑤	45°	—
	17083636	④	—	.085	28°	27°	35°	1°	⑤	45°	—
	17083650	1/8	—	.085	28°	27°	35°	1°	⑤	45°	—

①—Early models with three step fast idle cam, 18°; late models with two step fast idle cam, 33°.
②—Pontiac models, 13/32"; exc. Pontiac models, 1/8".
③—Citation and Camaro, 1/8"; exc. Citation and Camaro, 1/4".
④—Pontiac and Buick models, 13/32"; exc. Pontiac and Buick models, 1/4".
⑤—Tamper-resistant.

VARAJET 2SE & E2SE ADJUSTMENTS

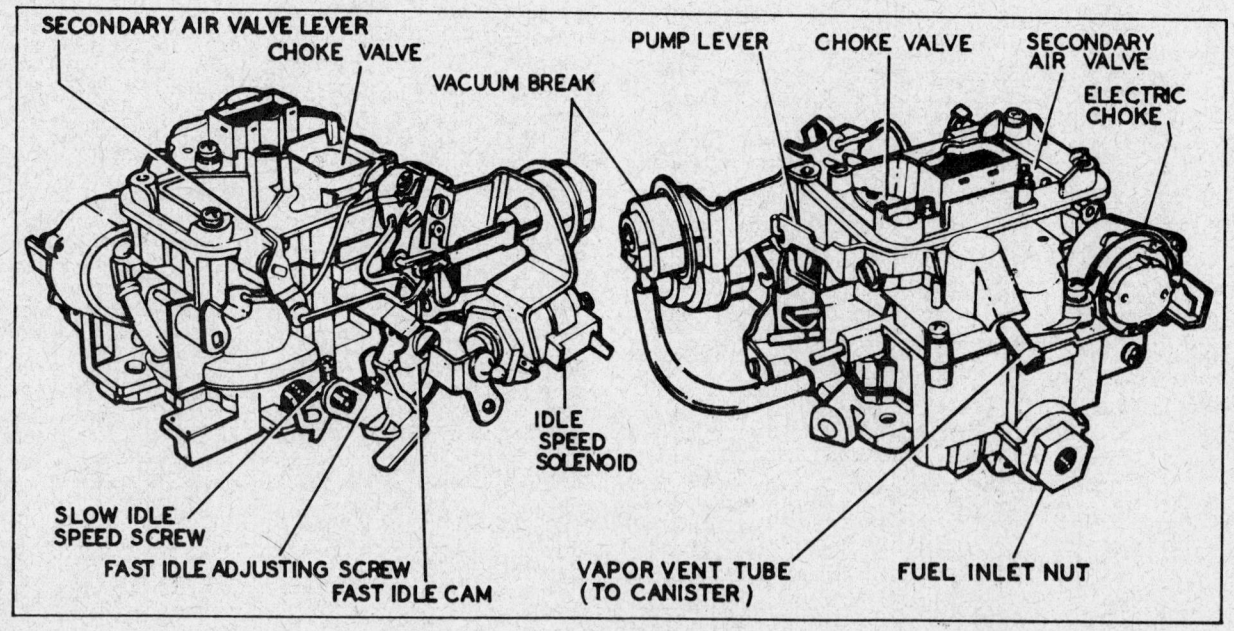

Fig. 1   Varajet 2SE Carburetor

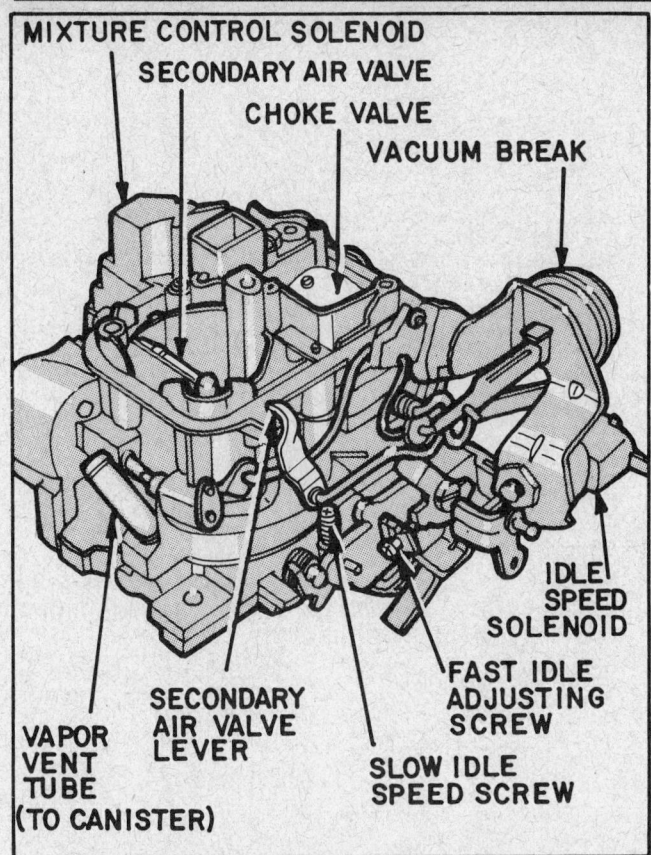

Fig. 1A   Varajet E2SE Carburetor (Typical)

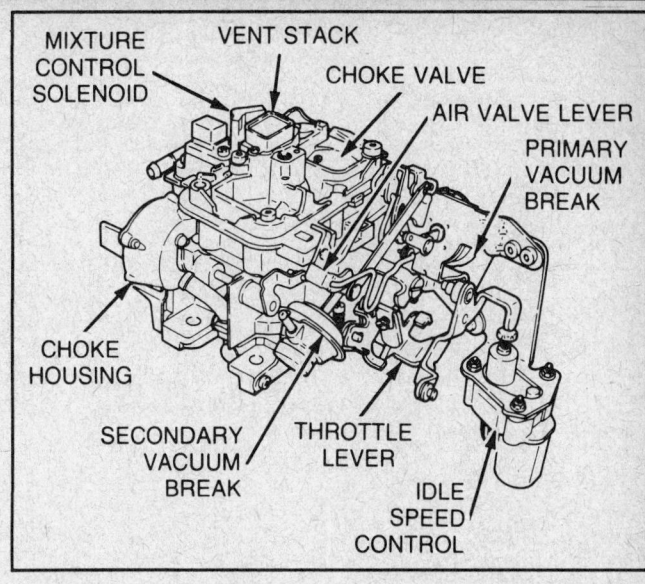

Fig. 1B   E2SE carburetor equipped with idle speed control motor

The Varajet models 2SE and E2SE, Figs. 1 and 1A, are two barrel, two stage, down draft design carburetors. Aluminum die castings are used for the air horn, float bowl and throttle body. A heat insulator gasket is used between the throttle body and float bowl to reduce heat transfer to the float bowl.

The primary stage has a triple venturi, with a small 35mm bore, resulting in good fuel metering control during idle and part throttle operation. The secondary stage has a 46mm bore, providing sufficient air capacity for engine power requirements. An air valve is used in the secondary stage with a single tapered metering rod.

The float chamber is internally vented through a vertical vent cavity in the air horn. The float chamber is also externally vented through a tube in the air horn. A hose connects this tube directly to a vacuum operated vapor vent valve located in the vapor canister. When the engine is not running, the canister vapor vent valve is open, allowing fuel vapor from the float chamber to pass into the canister where the vapor is stored until normally purged.

An adjustable part throttle screw is used in the float bowl to aid emission control. This screw is factory pre-set and a plug is installed to prevent further adjustment or fuel leakage. The plug should not be removed or the screw setting disturbed. If float bowl replacement is required, the service float bowl will include a factory pre-set and plugged adjustable part throttle screw.

A hot idle compensator is used on some models and is located in the air horn. The opening and closing of the hot idle compensator valve is controlled by a bi-metal strip that is calibrated to a specific temperature. When the valve opens, additional air is allowed to

bypass the throttle valves and enter the intake manifold to prevent rough idle during periods of hot engine operation.

The idle mixture screw is recessed in the throttle body and is sealed with a hardened steel plug to prevent alteration of the factory pre-set mixture setting. The plug should not be removed and the mixture screw readjusted unless required by major carburetor overhaul or throttle body replacement.

The E2SE carburetor, includes special design features for use with the Computor Controlled Catalytic Converter (C4) System or the Computer Command System. An electrically operated mixture control solenoid mounted in the air horn, controls air and fuel metered to the idle and main metering systems of the carburetor. The plunger located at the end of the solenoid is submerged in fuel in the fuel chamber of the float bowl. This plunger is controlled by an electrical signal from the Electronic Control Module (ECM). The Electronic Control Module responding to signals from the oxygen sensor in the exhaust and other engine operating condition signals, energizes the solenoid to move the plunger down to the lean position or de-energizes the solenoid to move the plunger up to the rich position to control fuel delivery to the idle and main metering systems. When the plunger is in the lean position, fuel metering is controlled by a lean mixture screw located in the float bowl. When the plunger is in the rich position, the additional fuel is metered to the main fuel well through a rich mixture screw located at the end of the fuel supply channel in the float bowl. Air metered to the idle system is controlled by the up and down movement of the mixture control solenoid plunger. The plunger increases or decreases air supplied to the idle system which is further metered by the

idle air bleed screw. The plunger cycles up and down approximately 10 times per second, controlling air and fuel mixtures.

On 1981 models wth 4-151 engine and air conditioning and 1982 models with 4-112 (1.8L) engine, an idle speed control motor which is controlled by the Electronic Control Module is used to control idle speed, Fig. 1B. The curb idle speed is programmed into the Electronic Control Module and no attempt should be made to adjust idle speed using the idle speed control motor.

CAUTION: On 1980–83 units, use care not to remove the special friction reducing coating applied to the primary and secondary throttle shafts, the secondary actuating lever and lockout lever. On 1980 V6 engine units and on all 1981–83 units, a special graphite compound is also applied to the secondary throttle bore and valve.

Float Level Adjustment

Fig. 2
1. Hold float retainer firmly in place and push float lightly against needle.
2. With an adjustable T-scale, measure distance between float bowl gasket surface (gasket removed) and float toe.
3. To adjust, remove float and bend float arm.

NOTE: On some 1983 units, a float stabilizing spring is used. Use care when removing this spring.

4. Check float alignment after adjustment.

Pump Adjustment

NOTE: The pump adjustment should not be altered from the specified setting.

1979–80 General Motors Units, Fig. 3
1. Close throttle valves and ensure that fast idle screw is not contacting fast idle cam steps.
2. Measure distance between air horn cast-

CARBURETORS

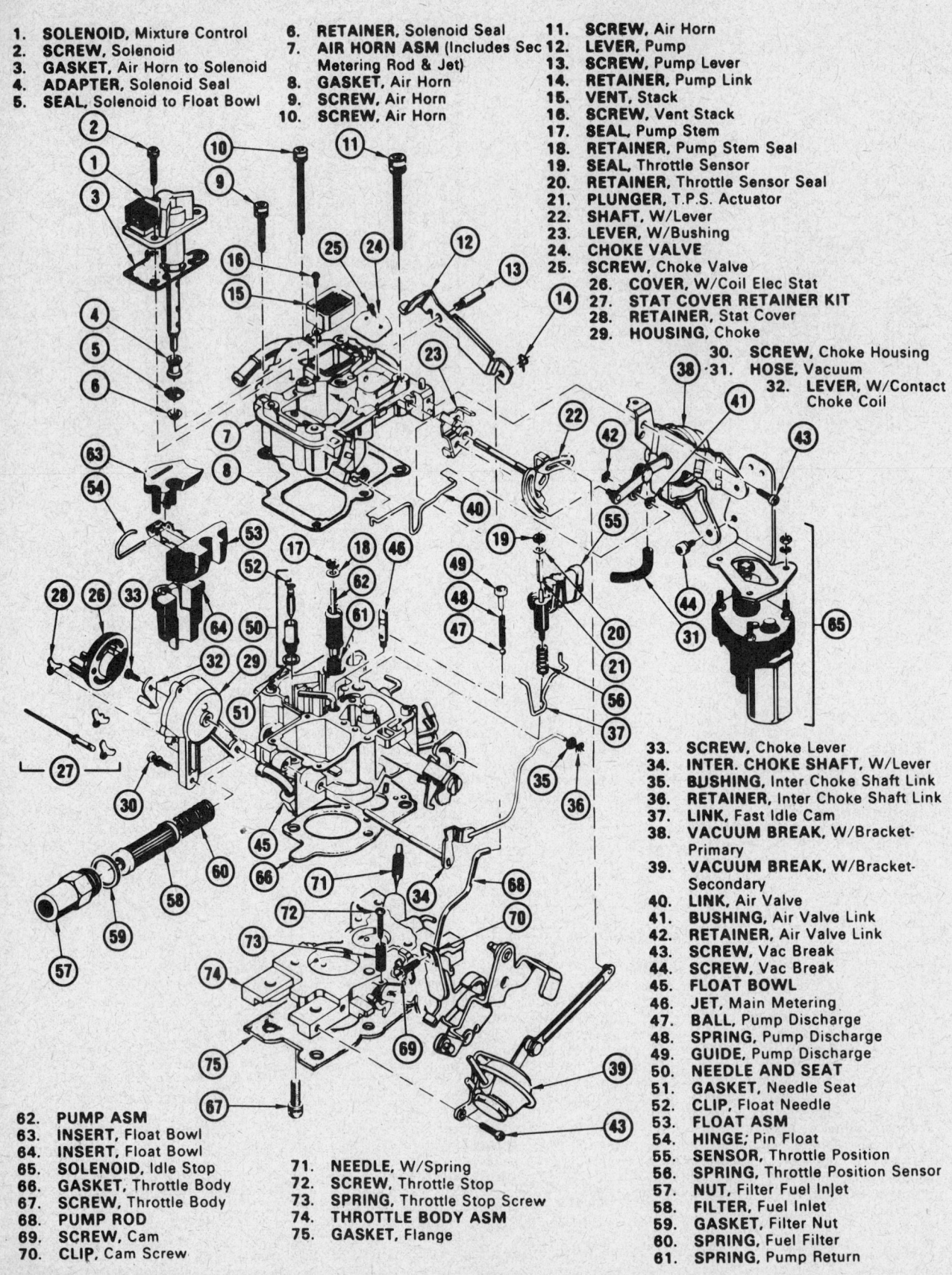

1. **SOLENOID**, Mixture Control
2. **SCREW**, Solenoid
3. **GASKET**, Air Horn to Solenoid
4. **ADAPTER**, Solenoid Seal
5. **SEAL**, Solenoid to Float Bowl

6. **RETAINER**, Solenoid Seal
7. **AIR HORN ASM** (Includes Sec Metering Rod & Jet)
8. **GASKET**, Air Horn
9. **SCREW**, Air Horn
10. **SCREW**, Air Horn

11. **SCREW**, Air Horn
12. **LEVER**, Pump
13. **SCREW**, Pump Lever
14. **RETAINER**, Pump Link
15. **VENT**, Stack
16. **SCREW**, Vent Stack
17. **SEAL**, Pump Stem
18. **RETAINER**, Pump Stem Seal
19. **SEAL**, Throttle Sensor
20. **RETAINER**, Throttle Sensor Seal
21. **PLUNGER**, T.P.S. Actuator
22. **SHAFT**, W/Lever
23. **LEVER**, W/Bushing
24. **CHOKE VALVE**
25. **SCREW**, Choke Valve
26. **COVER**, W/Coil Elec Stat
27. **STAT COVER RETAINER KIT**
28. **RETAINER**, Stat Cover
29. **HOUSING**, Choke
30. **SCREW**, Choke Housing
31. **HOSE**, Vacuum
32. **LEVER**, W/Contact Choke Coil

33. **SCREW**, Choke Lever
34. **INTER. CHOKE SHAFT**, W/Lever
35. **BUSHING**, Inter Choke Shaft Link
36. **RETAINER**, Inter Choke Shaft Link
37. **LINK**, Fast Idle Cam
38. **VACUUM BREAK**, W/Bracket-Primary
39. **VACUUM BREAK**, W/Bracket-Secondary
40. **LINK**, Air Valve
41. **BUSHING**, Air Valve Link
42. **RETAINER**, Air Valve Link
43. **SCREW**, Vac Break
44. **SCREW**, Vac Break
45. **FLOAT BOWL**
46. **JET**, Main Metering
47. **BALL**, Pump Discharge
48. **SPRING**, Pump Discharge
49. **GUIDE**, Pump Discharge
50. **NEEDLE AND SEAT**
51. **GASKET**, Needle Seat
52. **CLIP**, Float Needle
53. **FLOAT ASM**
54. **HINGE**; Pin Float
55. **SENSOR**, Throttle Position
56. **SPRING**, Throttle Position Sensor
57. **NUT**, Filter Fuel Inlet
58. **FILTER**, Fuel Inlet
59. **GASKET**, Filter Nut
60. **SPRING**, Fuel Filter
61. **SPRING**, Pump Return

62. **PUMP ASM**
63. **INSERT**, Float Bowl
64. **INSERT**, Float Bowl
65. **SOLENOID**, Idle Stop
66. **GASKET**, Throttle Body
67. **SCREW**, Throttle Body
68. **PUMP ROD**
69. **SCREW**, Cam
70. **CLIP**, Cam Screw

71. **NEEDLE**, W/Spring
72. **SCREW**, Throttle Stop
73. **SPRING**, Throttle Stop Screw
74. **THROTTLE BODY ASM**
75. **GASKET**, Flange

Exploded view of Rochester model E2SE carburetor (Typical of model 2SE)

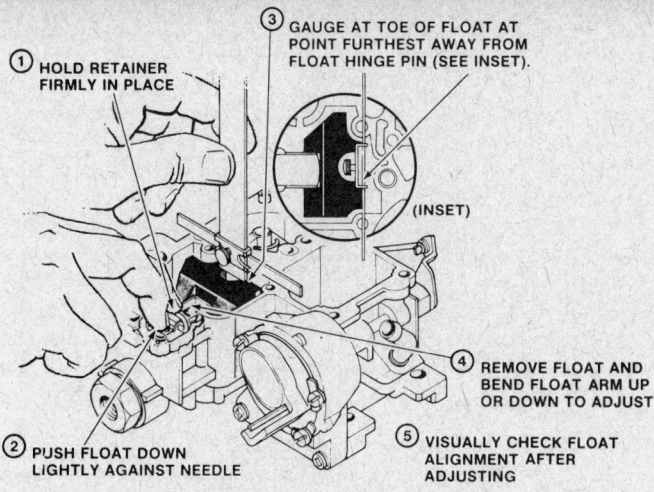

① HOLD RETAINER FIRMLY IN PLACE

③ GAUGE AT TOE OF FLOAT AT POINT FURTHEST AWAY FROM FLOAT HINGE PIN (SEE INSET).

(INSET)

④ REMOVE FLOAT AND BEND FLOAT ARM UP OR DOWN TO ADJUST

② PUSH FLOAT DOWN LIGHTLY AGAINST NEEDLE

⑤ VISUALLY CHECK FLOAT ALIGNMENT AFTER ADJUSTING

Fig. 2   Float level adjustment

① THROTTLE VALVES COMPLETELY CLOSED. MAKE SURE FAST IDLE SCREW IS OFF STEPS OF FAST IDLE CAM.

③ IF NECESSARY TO ADJUST, REMOVE PUMP LEVER RETAINING SCREW AND REMOVE PUMP LEVER BY ROTATING LEVER TO REMOVE FROM PUMP ROD. PLACE LEVER IN A VISE, PROTECTING LEVER FROM DAMAGE, AND BEND END OF LEVER (NEAREST NECKED DOWN SECTION).

NOTE: DO NOT BEND LEVER IN A SIDEWAYS OR TWISTING MOTION.

② GAUGE FROM AIR HORN CASTING SURFACE TO TOP OF PUMP STEM. DIMENSION SHOULD BE AS SPECIFIED.

⑤ OPEN AND CLOSE THROTTLE VALVES CHECKING LINKAGE FOR FREEDOM OF MOVEMENT AND OBSERVING PUMP LEVER ALIGNMENT.

④ REINSTALL PUMP LEVER AND RETAINING SCREW. RECHECK PUMP ADJUSTMENT ① AND ② TIGHTEN RETAINING SCREW SECURELY AFTER THE PUMP ADJUSTMENT IS CORRECT.

Fig. 3   Pump adjustment (Typical). 1979-80 units

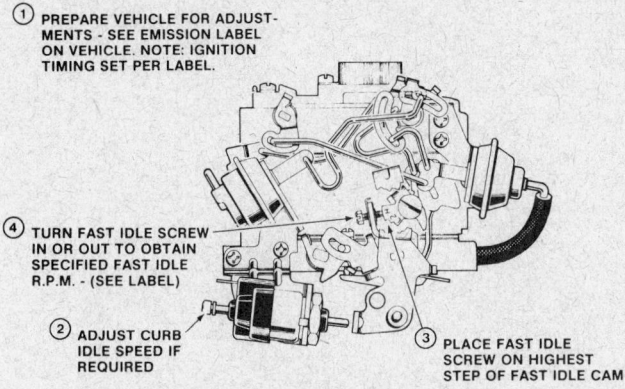

① PREPARE VEHICLE FOR ADJUSTMENTS - SEE EMISSION LABEL ON VEHICLE. NOTE: IGNITION TIMING SET PER LABEL.

④ TURN FAST IDLE SCREW IN OR OUT TO OBTAIN SPECIFIED FAST IDLE R.P.M. - (SEE LABEL)

② ADJUST CURB IDLE SPEED IF REQUIRED

③ PLACE FAST IDLE SCREW ON HIGHEST STEP OF FAST IDLE CAM

Fig. 4   Fast idle adjustment

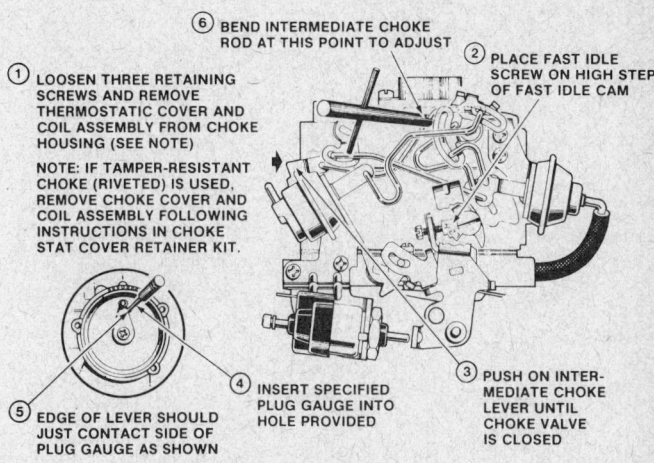

① LOOSEN THREE RETAINING SCREWS AND REMOVE THERMOSTATIC COVER AND COIL ASSEMBLY FROM CHOKE HOUSING (SEE NOTE)

NOTE: IF TAMPER-RESISTANT CHOKE (RIVETED) IS USED, REMOVE CHOKE COVER AND COIL ASSEMBLY FOLLOWING INSTRUCTIONS IN CHOKE STAT COVER RETAINER KIT.

⑥ BEND INTERMEDIATE CHOKE ROD AT THIS POINT TO ADJUST

② PLACE FAST IDLE SCREW ON HIGH STEP OF FAST IDLE CAM

③ PUSH ON INTERMEDIATE CHOKE LEVER UNTIL CHOKE VALVE IS CLOSED

④ INSERT SPECIFIED PLUG GAUGE INTO HOLE PROVIDED

⑤ EDGE OF LEVER SHOULD JUST CONTACT SIDE OF PLUG GAUGE AS SHOWN

Fig. 5   Choke coil lever adjustment (Typical)

ing surface and top of pump stem.
3. To adjust, remove pump lever retaining screw and the pump lever. Place the lever in a vise and bend lever end. Do not bend lever in a twisting motion.
4. Install pump lever and retaining screw. Recheck pump adjustment.
5. Operate throttle valves to check for freedom of movement and pump lever alignment.

1980-83 American Motors Units
1. With throttle valves in wide open position and fast idle screw off fast idle cam step, measure distance from air horn casting to top of pump stem. Refer to Specifications Chart.
2. To make adjustment, remove pump lever retaining screw and lever by rotating from pump rod. Do not twist or bend lever sideways.
3. Secure lever in a soft-jawed vise and bend end of lever as necessary, then install pump lever and retaining screw.
4. Measure distance between air horn casting and top of pump stem and tighten retaining screw if correct.
5. Open and close throttle valves several times to ensure free movement of linkage and proper alignment of pump lever.

Fast Idle Adjustment

Fig. 4
1. Adjust curb idle speed, if necessary.
2. Place fast idle screw on highest step of cam.
3. Turn fast idle screw to obtain specified fast idle speed.

Choke Coil Lever Adjustment

Fig. 5
1. Loosen choke cover retaining screws, then the cover and coil assembly from choke housing. If a riveted choke cover is used, remove choke cover and coil assembly as outlined in the choke cover retainer kit.

NOTE: On 1980-83 units with riveted choke cover, the cover should not be removed unless a major overhaul is being performed on the carburetor or the choke coil is damaged.

2. Place fast idle screw on high step of cam.
3. Push the intermediate choke lever until the choke valve closes.
4. Insert specified gauge into hole provided in choke housing. The edge of the lever

should just contact gauge.
5. To adjust, bend intermediate choke rod.

Choke Rod Adjustment

NOTE: The choke coil lever and fast idle adjustments must be made before performing this adjustment.

Fig. 6
1. Rotate degree scale until zero is opposite pointer, then with choke valve completely closed, place magnet on top of choke valve and rotate bubble until centered.
2. Rotate scale so specified degree for adjustment is opposite pointer.
3. Place fast idle screw on second step of cam against shoulder of high step.
4. Close choke by pushing intermediate choke lever.

NOTE: On 1983 units, attach rubber band to intermediate choke lever to hold choke valve closed.

5. Push vacuum break lever toward open choke position until lever contacts rear tang on choke lever.
6. To adjust, bend fast idle cam rod until bubble is centered.

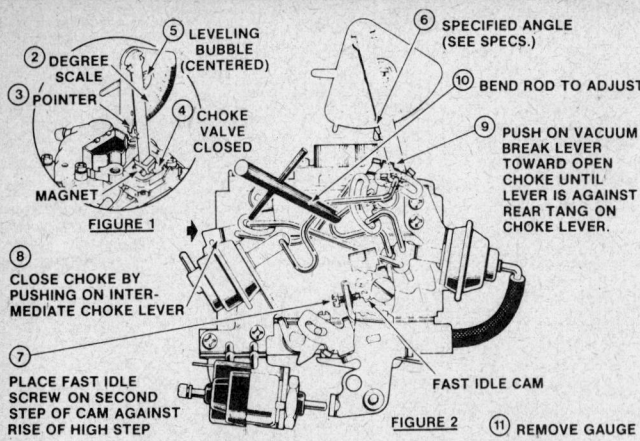

Fig. 6   Choke rod adjustment 1979–82 units. (Typical)

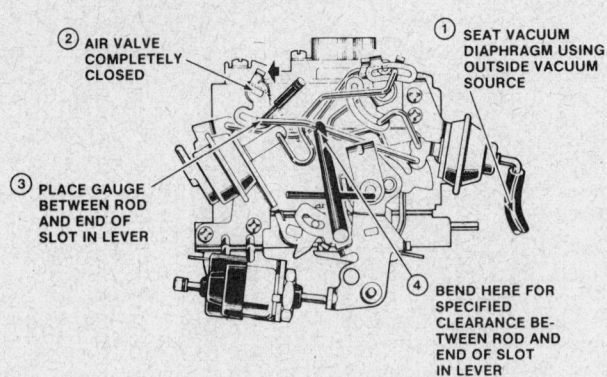

Fig. 7   Air valve rod adjustment (Plug Gauge Method). 1979 units

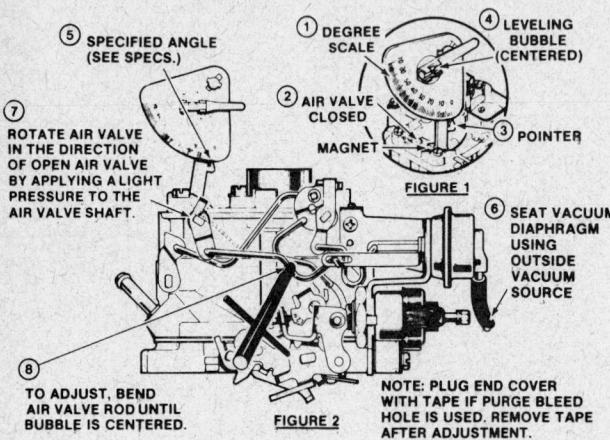

Fig. 8   Air valve rod adjustment (Angle Gauge Method). 1980–82 units

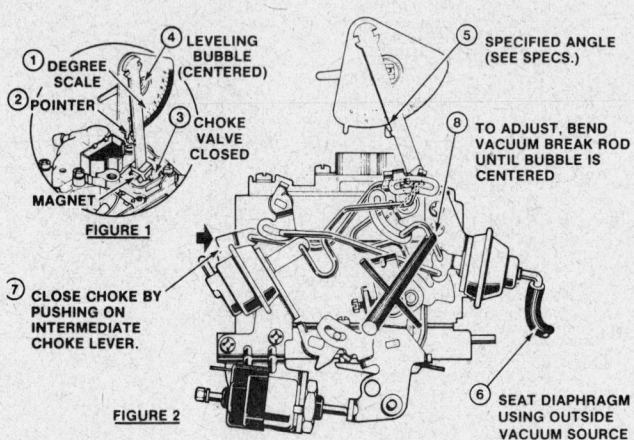

Fig. 9   Primary vacuum break adjustment (Typical). 1979–80 units

Air Valve Rod Adjustment

1979 Units (Plug Gauge Method), Fig. 7
1. Seat vacuum diaphragm with an external vacuum source.
2. Close air valve completely.
3. Place specified gauge between rod and end of lever in slot.
4. To adjust, bend air valve rod.

1980–83 Units (Angle Gauge Method), Fig. 8
1. Rotate gauge scale until pointer is opposite zero.
2. With air valve completely closed, place magnet on top of air valve and rotate bubble until centered.
3. Rotate scale so that specified degree for adjustment is opposite pointer.
4. Seat vacuum diaphragm using an external vacuum source.
5. Rotate air valve toward the open position by applying light pressure to the air valve shaft.
6. To adjust, bend air valve rod until bubble is centered.

Primary Vacuum Break Adjustment

1979–80 All Units & 1981 2SE Units, Fig. 9
1. Rotate degree scale until zero is opposite pointer, then with choke valve completely closed, place magnet on top of choke valve and rotate bubble until centered.
2. Rotate degree scale so specified degree for adjustment is opposite pointer.
3. Seat vacuum diaphragm with an external vacuum source.
4. Hold choke valve toward closed position by pushing on intermediate choke lever.
5. To adjust, bend vacuum break rod as shown until bubble is centered.

1981–82 E2SE Units, Fig. 10

NOTE: Before performing adjustment procedure, remove primary vacuum break from carburetor and position bracket in vise, then grind off adjusting screw cap and reinstall vacuum break.

1. Rotate degree scale until zero is opposite pointer, then with choke valve completely closed and fast idle screw on high step of fast idle cam, place magnet squarely on top of choke valve and rotate bubble until it is centered.
2. Rotate scale so that specified degree for adjustment is opposite pointer.
3. Seat choke vacuum diaphragm using a vacuum source with over 5 inches Hg of vacuum. Check to ensure that air valve rod is not restricting the vacuum diaphragm from being seated. It maybe necessary to bend air valve rod to obtain a slight clearance between rod and end of slot in air valve lever. If the air valve rod adjustment is disturbed, refer to the Air Valve Rod Adjustment procedure after completing the primary vacuum break adjustment.
4. Hold choke valve toward the closed position by lightly pushing on intermediate lever and note angle gauge reading.
5. If adjustment is necessary, use a 1/8 inch hex wrench to rotate adjusting screw in rear cover until bubble is centered.
6. After completing adjustment, apply a suitable sealer over adjusting screw head.

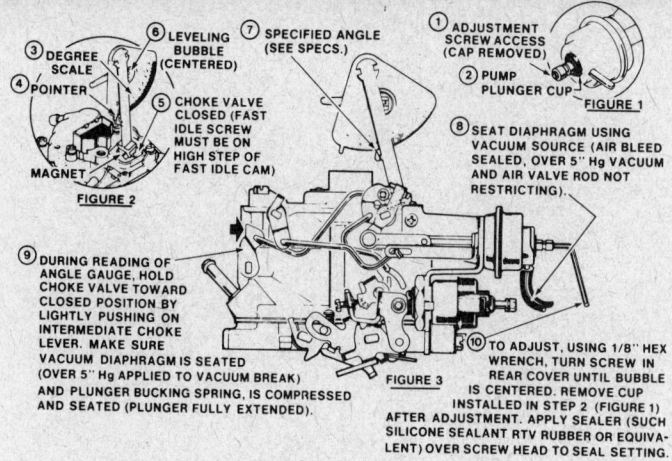

Fig. 10 Primary vacuum break adjustment (Typical). 1981–82 E2SE units

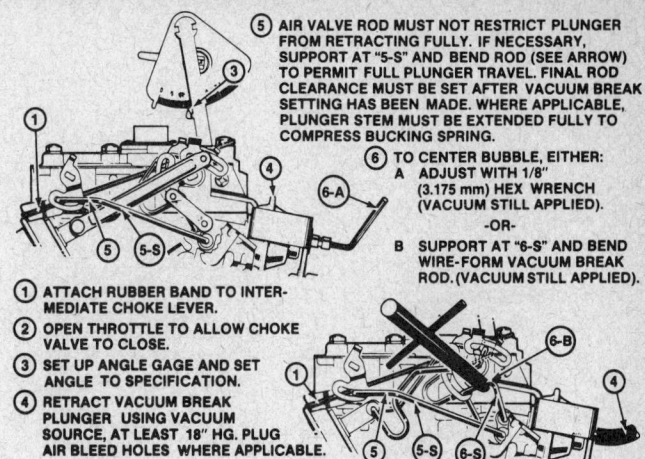

Fig. 11 Primary vacuum break adjustment. 1983 units

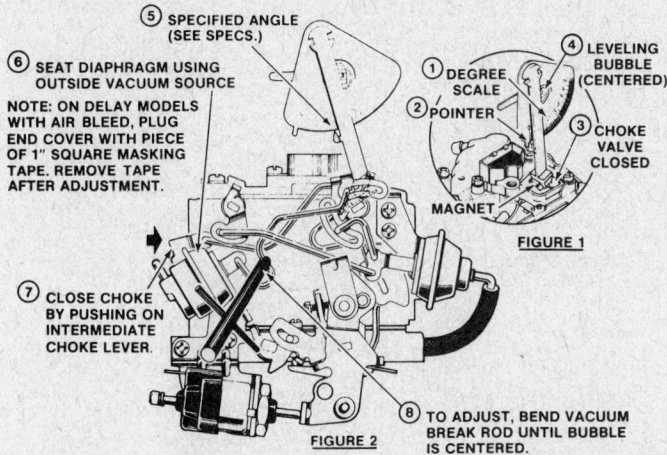

Fig. 12 Secondary vacuum break adjustment. 1979–80 units

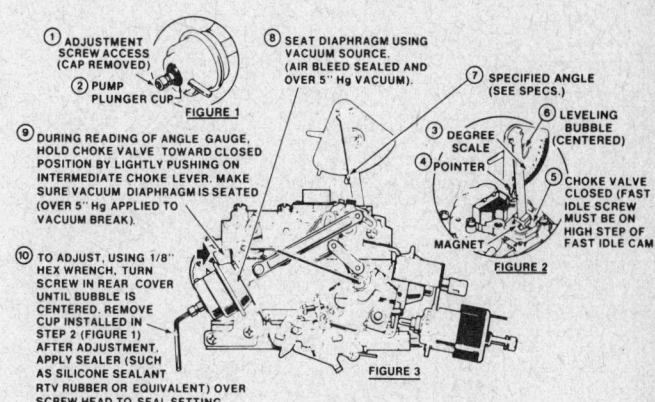

Fig. 13 Secondary vacuum break adjustment (Typical). 1981–82 units

1983 Units, Fig. 11
1. Attach rubber band to intermediate choke shaft to hold choke valve closed.
2. Install angle gauge and set angle to specifications. Refer to Specifications Chart.
3. Using outside vacuum source, retract vacuum break plunger with a minimum of 15 inches Hg of vacuum.
4. Ensure that air valve rod does not restrict plunger from full retraction. If necessary, bend rod as shown to permit full plunger travel.
5. Make adjustment with vacuum still applied, by rotating adjusting screw with a 1/8 inch Allen wrench, or bending rod as shown until bubble is centered.

Secondary Vacuum Break Adjustment

1979–80 Units, Fig. 12
1. Rotate degree scale until zero is opposite pointer, then with choke valve completely closed, place magnet on top of choke valve and rotate bubble until centered.
2. Rotate scale so specified degree for adjustment is opposite pointer.

3. Seat vacuum diaphragm with an external vacuum source.
4. Hold choke valve toward closed position by pushing on intermediate choke lever. Ensure that bucking spring, if used, is compressed and seated.
5. To adjust, bend vacuum break rod as shown until bubble is centered.

1981–82 Units, Fig. 13

NOTE: Before performing adjustment procedure, remove secondary vacuum break from carburetor and position bracket in a vise, then grind off adjusting screw cap and reinstall vacuum break. Plug vacuum break end cover using an accelerator pump plunger cup or equivalent. After completing adjustment remove pump plunger cup.

1. Rotate degree scale so that zero is opposite pointer, then with choke valve completely closed and fast idle screw on high step of fast idle cam, place magnet on top of choke valve and rotate until bubble is centered.
2. Rotate scale so that specified degree for

adjustment is opposite pointer.
3. Seat choke diaphragm using a vacuum source with over 5 inches Hg of vacuum.
4. Hold choke valve toward the closed position by lightly pushing on intermediate choke lever and note angle gauge reading. When noting reading check to ensure that vacuum diaphragm is seated.
5. Rotate adjusting screw in rear cover until bubble is centered. After completing adjustment, apply a suitable sealer over adjusting screw head.

NOTE: Remove pump plunger cup from end cover before applying sealer over adjusting screw head.

1983 Units, Fig. 14
1. Attach rubber band to intermediate choke lever to hold choke valve closed.
2. Install angle gauge and set angle to specifications. Refer to Specifications Chart.
3. Using outside vacuum source, retract vacuum break plunger with a minimum of 15 inches Hg of vacuum, then plug air bleed holes if applicable.

CARBURETORS

① **ATTACH RUBBER BAND TO INTER-MEDIATE CHOKE LEVER.**

② **OPEN THROTTLE TO ALLOW CHOKE VALVE TO CLOSE.**

③ **SET UP ANGLE GAGE AND SET ANGLE TO SPECIFICATION.**

④ **RETRACT VACUUM BREAK PLUNGER USING VACUUM SOURCE, AT LEAST 18" HG. PLUG AIR BLEED HOLES WHERE APPLICABLE.**

WHERE APPLICABLE, PLUNGER STEM MUST BE EXTENDED FULLY TO COM-PRESS PLUNGER BUCKING SPRING.

⑤ **TO CENTER BUBBLE, EITHER:**

A. ADJUST WITH 1/8" (3.175 mm) HEX WRENCH (VACUUM STILL APPLIED)
-OR-

B. SUPPORT AT "5-S", BEND WIRE-FORM VACUUM BREAK ROD (VACUUM STILL APPLIED)

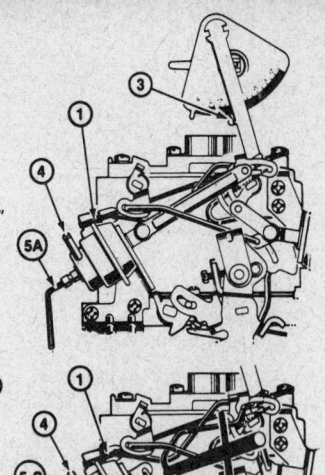

Fig. 14 Secondary vacuum break adjustment. 1983 units

② **PLACE FAST IDLE SCREW ON HIGH STEP OF CAM**

① **LOOSEN THREE RETAINING SCREWS**

③ **SET SCRIBE LINE ON ELECTRIC CHOKE TO SPECIFIED POINT ON CHOKE HOUSING - CHOKE VALVE TOWARD CLOSED POSITION**

Fig. 15 Choke setting adjustment. 1979 2SE units

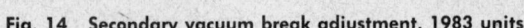

① **DEGREE SCALE**
② **POINTER**
④ **LEVELING BUBBLE (CENTERED)**
③ **CHOKE VALVE CLOSED**
MAGNET   FIGURE 1

⑤ **SPECIFIED ANGLE (SEE SPECS.)**
⑨ **BEND TANG TO ADJUST UNTIL BUBBLE IS CENTERED.**
FIGURE 2

⑧ **ON WARM ENGINE, CLOSE CHOKE VALVE BY PUSHING CLOCKWISE ON INTERMEDIATE CHOKE LEVER (HOLD IN POSITION WITH RUBBER BAND).**

⑥ **INSTALL CHOKE THERMOSTATIC COVER AND COIL ASSEMBLY IN HOUSING. ALIGN INDEX MARK WITH SPECIFIED POINT ON HOUSING.**

⑦ **HOLD PRIMARY THROTTLE VALVE WIDE OPEN**

Fig. 16 Unloader adjustment (Typical)

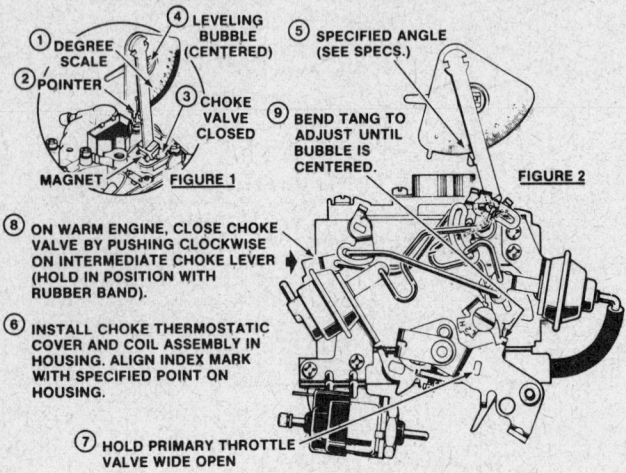

① **HOLD CHOKE VALVE WIDE OPEN BY PUSHING COUNTER-CLOCKWISE ON INTERMEDIATE CHOKE LEVER.**

④ **IF NECESSARY TO ADJUST, BEND LOCKOUT LEVER TANG CONTACTING FAST IDLE CAM.**

③ **GAUGE CLEARANCE - DIMENSION SHOULD BE AS SPECIFIED.**

② **OPEN THROTTLE LEVER UNTIL END OF SECONDARY ACTUATING LEVER IS OPPOSITE TOE OF LOCKOUT LEVER.**

Fig. 17 Secondary lockout adjustment

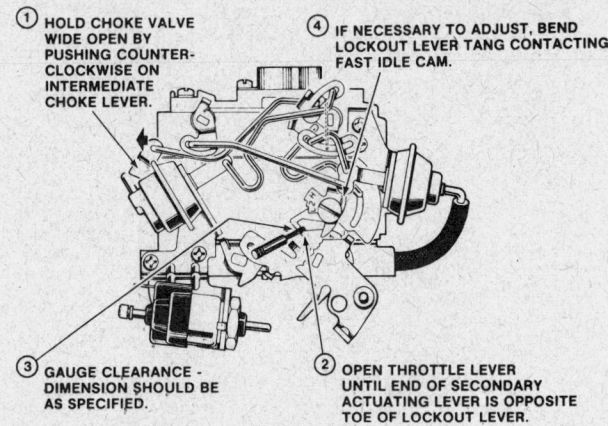

4. Make final adjustment with vacuum still applied, by rotating adjusting screw with a 1/8 inch Allen wrench, or bending rod as shown until bubble is centered.

1979 2SE Units, Fig. 15
1. Loosen choke cover retaining screws.
2. Place fast idle screw on high step of cam.
3. Align scribe line on choke cover with specified point on housing. Rotate cover toward closed choke position.
4. Tighten choke cover retaining screws.

Unloader Adjustment

Fig. 16
1. Rotate degree scale until zero is opposite pointer, then with choke valve completely closed, place magnet on top of choke valve and rotate bubble until centered.
2. Rotate degree scale so specified degree for adjustment is opposite pointer.
3. With choke setting properly adjusted, hold primary throttle valve wide open.
4. On warm engines and 1983 units, close

③ **TURN TENSION ADJUSTING SCREW COUNTERCLOCKWISE UNTIL AIR VALVE JUST CLOSES. THEN TURN ADJUSTING SCREW COUNTERCLOCKWISE SPECIFIED NUMBER OF TURNS.**

② **TURN TENSION ADJUSTING SCREW CLOCKWISE UNTIL AIR VALVE OPENS PART WAY.**

① **LOOSEN LOCK SCREW USING HEX WRENCH.**

⑤ **USE LITHIUM BASE GREASE TO LUBRICATE AIR VALVE SHAFT PIN AND CLOSING SPRING. ESPECIALLY CONTACT AREA.**

④ **TIGHTEN LOCK SCREW.**

Fig. 18 Air valve spring adjustment. 1982–83 E2SE models

choke valve by pushing on intermediate choke lever and hold in position with a rubber band.
5. To adjust, bend tang on throttle lever until bubble is centered.

Secondary Lockout Adjustment

Fig. 17
1. Hold choke valve wide open by pulling on intermediate choke lever.
2. Position throttle lever until end of secondary actuating lever is opposite toe of lockout lever.

3. Insert specified gauge between throttle lever and secondary lockout lever toe.
4. To adjust, bend lockout lever tang contacting fast idle cam.

Air Valve Spring Adjustment

1982–83 E2SE Units, Fig. 18
1. Loosen lock screw, then turn adjusting screw clockwise until air valve is partially open.

NOTE: On 1983 units, it may be necessary to remove the intermediate choke rod to

gain access to the lock screw.

2. Turn adjusting screw counterclockwise until air valve just closes, then turn screw an additional turn counterclockwise and tighten lock screw.

NOTE: On 1983 units with part no. 17083650, rotate the screw 1/2 turn only.

3. Lubricate air valve shaft pin and closing spring with lithium base grease.

Holley Carburetor Section

1000, 2000 & 6145 SERIES CARB. ADJUSTMENT SPECIFICATIONS

See Tune Up Chart in car chapter for curb and fast idle speeds.

Year	Carb. Part No. ①	Carb. Model	Float Level (Dry)	Fuel Level (Wet)	Pump Setting	Bowl Vent Clearance	Fast Idle Bench	Choke Unloader Clearance	Vacuum Kick Drill Size	Cam Position Drill Size	Choke Setting
CHRYSLER CORP.											
1977	R-7632A	1945	②	—	2⁷/₃₂ ③	1/16	.080	.250	.110	.080	⑩
	R-7633A	1945	②	—	2²¹/₆₄ ④	1/16	.080	.250	.110	.080	⑩
	R-7635A	1945	②	—	2²¹/₆₄ ④	—	.080	.250	.110	.080	⑩
	R-7671A	2245	3/16	—	5/16 ⑤	.025	.110	.170	.110	.110	⑩
	R-7744A	1945	②	—	2²¹/₆₄ ④	1/16	.080	.250	.130	.080	⑩
	R-7745A	1945	②	—	2⁷/₃₂	1/16	.080	.250	.150	.080	⑩
	R-7746A	1945	②	—	2²¹/₆₄	1/16	.080	.250	.110	.080	⑩
	R-7764A	1945	②	—	2⁷/₃₂	1/16	.080	.250	.110	.080	⑩
	R-7765A	1945	②	—	2²¹/₆₄	1/16	.080	.250	.110	.080	⑩
1978	R-7988A	1945	②	—	2⁷/₃₂	1/16	.080	.250	.110	.080	⑩
	R-7989A	1945	②	—	2²¹/₆₄	1/16	.080	.250	.110	.080	⑩
	R-7990A	2280	9/32	—	⑥	.030	.070	.310	.150	.070	⑩
	R-7991A	2245	3/16	—	17/64 ⑤	.025	.110	.170	.110	.110	⑩
	R-8008A	1945	②	—	2²¹/₆₄	1/16	.080	.250	.110	.080	⑩
	R-8010A	1945	②	—	2²¹/₆₄	1/16	.080	.250	.130	.080	⑩
1979	R-8448A	2280	9/32	—	⑥	.030	.070	.310	.150	.070	⑩
	R-8450A	2245	3/16	—	17/64 ⑤	.025	.110	.170	.110	.110	⑩
	R-8452A	1945	②	—	1⁵/₈ ③	1/16	.080	.250	.110	.080	⑩
	R-8523A	1945	②	—	1⁴⁵/₆₄ ⑤	1/16	.080	.250	.110	.080	⑩
	R-8680A	1945	②	—	1⁵/₈ ③	1/16	.080	.250	.110	.080	⑩
1980	R-8718A	1945	②	—	1⁴⁵/₆₄ ⑦	1/16	.090	.250	.150	.090	⑩
	R-8831A	1945	②	—	1⁵/₈ ⑧	1/16	.090	.250	.140	.090	⑩
	R-9179A	1945	②	—	1³/₄ ⑧	—	.090	—	.150	.090	⑩
1981	R-9687A	1945	⑨	—	1³⁹/₆₄ ⑧	—	.090	.250	.150	.090	⑩
	R-9695A	6145	⑨	—	1³⁹/₆₄ ⑧	—	.090	.250	.150	.090	⑩
1982	R-9628A	1945	⑨	—	1.615 ⑧	—	.090	.250	.150	.090	⑩
	R-9687A	1945	⑨	—	1.615 ⑧	—	.090	.250	.150	.090	⑩
	R-9695A	6145	⑨	—	1.615 ⑧	—	.090	.250	.150	.090	⑩
1983	R-4042A	6145	⑨	—	1.615 ⑧	—	.090	.250	.150	.090	⑩

①—Located on tag attached to carburetor or on casting.
②—Flush with top of bowl cover gasket with bowl inverted.
③—Slot #2
④—Slot #3
⑤—Slot #1
⑥—Flush with top of bowl vent casting.
⑦—Hole position No. 1.
⑧—Hole position No. 2.
⑨—Flush with top of bowl casting to .050 inch above with bowl inverted.
⑩—Tamper-resistant.

CARBURETORS

Year	Carb. No.	Carb. Model	Float Level	Fuel Bowl Vent Setting	Accelerator Pump		Fast Idle Cam	Choke Pulldown	Dechoke	Choke Setting
					Pump Hole No.	Pump Setting				
FORD MOTOR CO.										
1978	D8BE-AAA	1946	①	½ Turn③	2	—	—	.110	.150	Index
	D8BE-AB	1946	①	½ Turn③	—	—	—	—	—	—
	D8BE-AGA	1946	①	½ Turn③	2	—	—	.110	.150	Index
	D8BE-AHA	1946	①	½ Turn③	2	—	—	.110	.150	Index
	D8BE-RA	1946	①	½ Turn③	2	—	—	.110	.150	Index
	D8BE-UC	1946	①	½ Turn③	2	—	—	.150	.150	Index
1979	D9BE-AEA	1946	①	½ Turn③	2	2.25	.055	.080	.150	Index
	D9BE-AHA	1946	②	½ Turn③	2	2.31	.130	.150	.150	Index
	D9BE-AJA	1946	②	½ Turn③	2	2.31	.130	.150	.150	Index
	D9BE-AMA	1946	①	½ Turn③	2	2.31	.070	.095	.150	Index
	D9BE-BKA	1946	①	½ Turn③	2	2.31	.055	.080	.150	Index
	D9BE-LA	1946	①	½ Turn③	2	2.21	.055	.080	.150	Index
1980	E0BE-AAA, ZA	1946-C	②	—	1	—	.090	.115	.150	2 Rich
	E0BE-ALA, AMA	1946	①	—	2	—	.070	.100	.150	Index
	E0EE-ANA, APA	1946	①	—	2	—	.070	.100	.150	—
	E0ZE-BAA, BBA	1946	①	—	2	—	.086	.120	.150	2 Rich
	E0ZE-DA, EA	1946	①	—	2	—	.070	.110	.150	2 Rich
	E0ZE-FA, GA	1946	①	—	2	—	.070	.110	.150	2 Rich
1981	E0BE-AA, CA	1946	.690	—	2	2.15	.070	.100	.150	2 Rich
	E1BE-AFA, AKA	1946	.690	—	2	2.15	.082	.113	.150	2 Rich
	E1BE-AGA	1946	.690	—	2	2.15	.086	.120	.150	2 Rich
	E1BE-ARA, ASA	1946	—	—	—	2.15	—	—	—	—
1982	E1BE-AGA	1946	.690	—	2	—	.086	.120	.150	2 Rich
	E2BE-BA	1946	.690	—	2	—	.078	.110	.150	2 Rich
	E2BE-CA	1946	.690	—	2	—	.078	.110	.150	2 Rich
	E2BE-HA	1946	.690	—	2	—	.078	.110	.150	2 Rich
	E2BE-JA	1946	.690	—	2	—	.078	.110	.150	2 Rich
	E2BE-SA	1946	.690	—	2	—	.078	.110	.150	2 Rich
	E2BE-TA	1946	.690	—	2	—	.078	.110	.150	2 Rich
1983	E2BE-BA	1946	.690	—	2	—	.078	.110	.150	2 Rich
	E2BE-CA	1946	.690	—	2	—	.078	.110	.150	2 Rich
	E2BE-SA	1946	.690	—	2	—	.078	.110	.150	2 Rich
	E2BE-TA	1946	.690	—	2	—	.078	.110	.150	2 Rich
	E3BE-CA	1946	.690	—	2	—	.078	.100	.150	2 Rich
	E3BE-DA	1946	.690	—	2	—	.078	.100	.150	2 Rich
	E3SE-AA	1946	.690	—	2	—	.078	.095	.150	2 Rich
	E3SE-BA	1946	.690	—	2	—	.078	.095	.150	2 Rich
	E3SE-CA	1946	.690	—	2	—	.078	.105	.150	2 Rich
	E3SE-DA	1946	.690	—	2	—	.078	.105	.150	2 Rich

①—Setting at toe. Refer to text for procedure. ②—Setting at heel. Refer to text for procedure. ③—Clockwise.

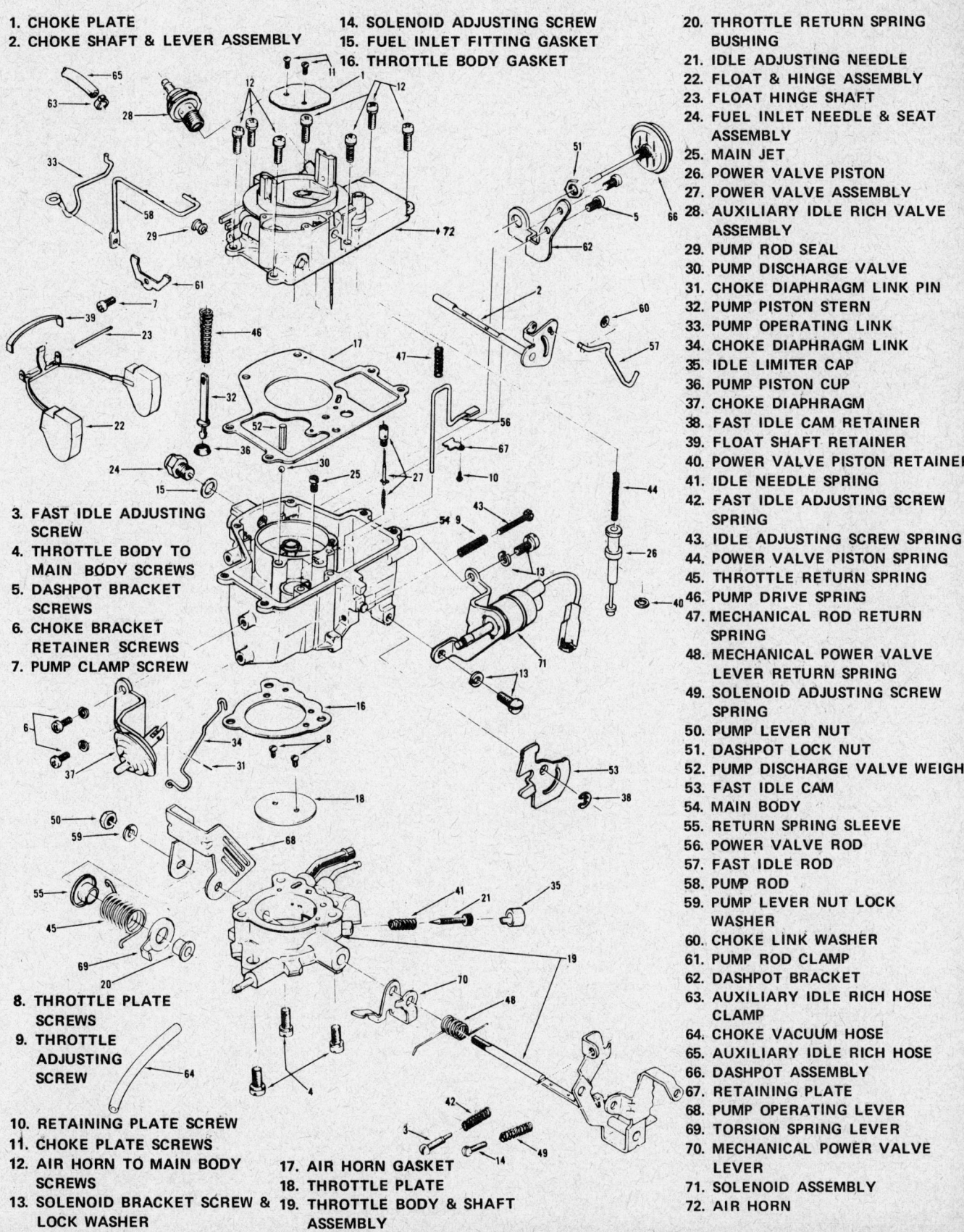

1. CHOKE PLATE
2. CHOKE SHAFT & LEVER ASSEMBLY

14. SOLENOID ADJUSTING SCREW
15. FUEL INLET FITTING GASKET
16. THROTTLE BODY GASKET

20. THROTTLE RETURN SPRING BUSHING
21. IDLE ADJUSTING NEEDLE
22. FLOAT & HINGE ASSEMBLY
23. FLOAT HINGE SHAFT
24. FUEL INLET NEEDLE & SEAT ASSEMBLY
25. MAIN JET
26. POWER VALVE PISTON
27. POWER VALVE ASSEMBLY
28. AUXILIARY IDLE RICH VALVE ASSEMBLY
29. PUMP ROD SEAL
30. PUMP DISCHARGE VALVE
31. CHOKE DIAPHRAGM LINK PIN
32. PUMP PISTON STERN
33. PUMP OPERATING LINK
34. CHOKE DIAPHRAGM LINK
35. IDLE LIMITER CAP
36. PUMP PISTON CUP
37. CHOKE DIAPHRAGM
38. FAST IDLE CAM RETAINER
39. FLOAT SHAFT RETAINER
40. POWER VALVE PISTON RETAINER
41. IDLE NEEDLE SPRING
42. FAST IDLE ADJUSTING SCREW SPRING
43. IDLE ADJUSTING SCREW SPRING
44. POWER VALVE PISTON SPRING
45. THROTTLE RETURN SPRING
46. PUMP DRIVE SPRING
47. MECHANICAL ROD RETURN SPRING
48. MECHANICAL POWER VALVE LEVER RETURN SPRING
49. SOLENOID ADJUSTING SCREW SPRING
50. PUMP LEVER NUT
51. DASHPOT LOCK NUT
52. PUMP DISCHARGE VALVE WEIGHT
53. FAST IDLE CAM
54. MAIN BODY
55. RETURN SPRING SLEEVE
56. POWER VALVE ROD
57. FAST IDLE ROD
58. PUMP ROD
59. PUMP LEVER NUT LOCK WASHER
60. CHOKE LINK WASHER
61. PUMP ROD CLAMP
62. DASHPOT BRACKET
63. AUXILIARY IDLE RICH HOSE CLAMP
64. CHOKE VACUUM HOSE
65. AUXILIARY IDLE RICH HOSE
66. DASHPOT ASSEMBLY
67. RETAINING PLATE
68. PUMP OPERATING LEVER
69. TORSION SPRING LEVER
70. MECHANICAL POWER VALVE LEVER
71. SOLENOID ASSEMBLY
72. AIR HORN

3. FAST IDLE ADJUSTING SCREW
4. THROTTLE BODY TO MAIN BODY SCREWS
5. DASHPOT BRACKET SCREWS
6. CHOKE BRACKET RETAINER SCREWS
7. PUMP CLAMP SCREW

8. THROTTLE PLATE SCREWS
9. THROTTLE ADJUSTING SCREW
10. RETAINING PLATE SCREW
11. CHOKE PLATE SCREWS
12. AIR HORN TO MAIN BODY SCREWS
13. SOLENOID BRACKET SCREW & LOCK WASHER

17. AIR HORN GASKET
18. THROTTLE PLATE
19. THROTTLE BODY & SHAFT ASSEMBLY

Exploded view of Holley model 1945 carburetor

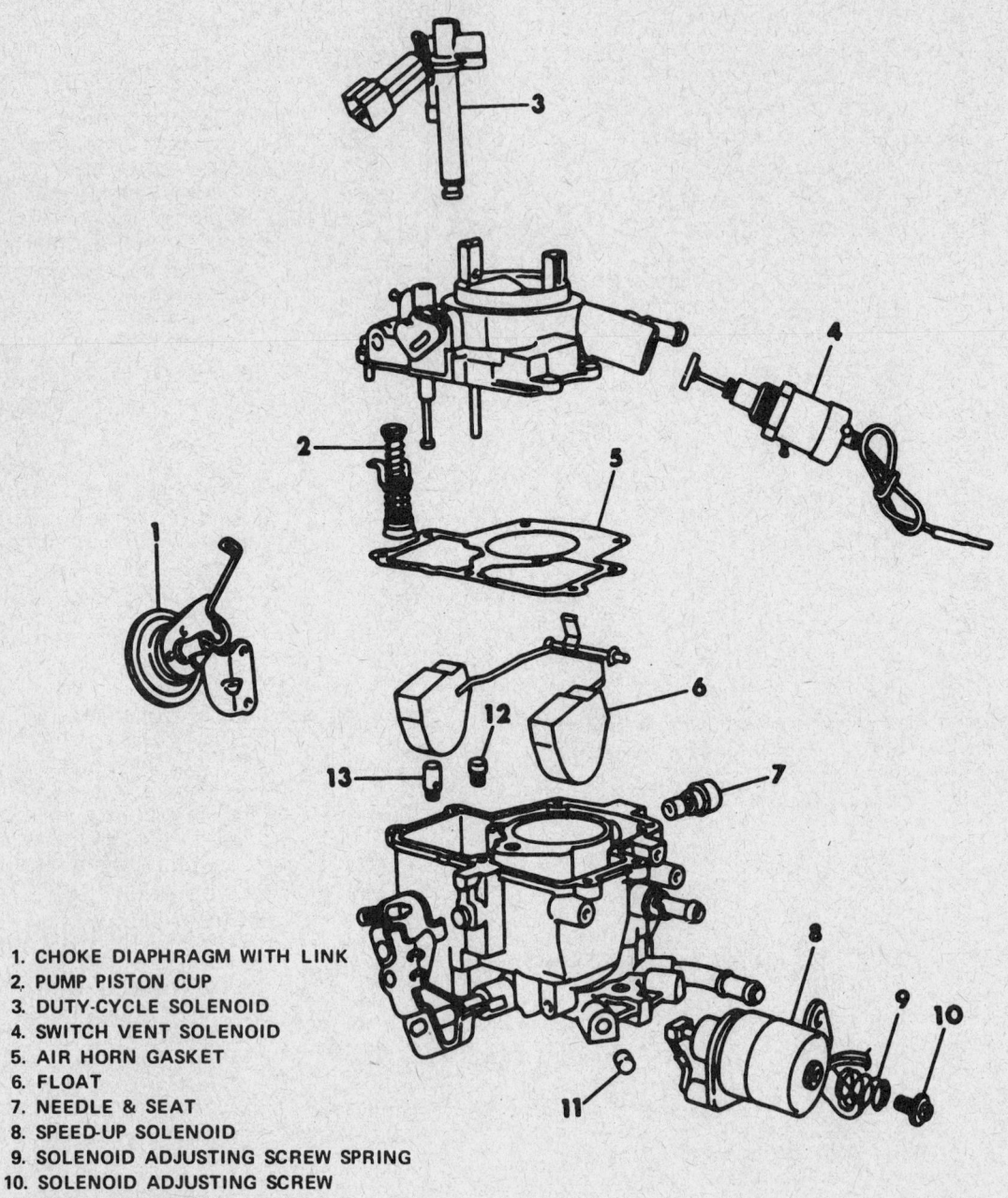

1. CHOKE DIAPHRAGM WITH LINK
2. PUMP PISTON CUP
3. DUTY-CYCLE SOLENOID
4. SWITCH VENT SOLENOID
5. AIR HORN GASKET
6. FLOAT
7. NEEDLE & SEAT
8. SPEED-UP SOLENOID
9. SOLENOID ADJUSTING SCREW SPRING
10. SOLENOID ADJUSTING SCREW
11. IDLE NEEDLE PLUG
12. MAIN JET
13. POWER VALVE

Exploded view of Holley model 6145 carburetor

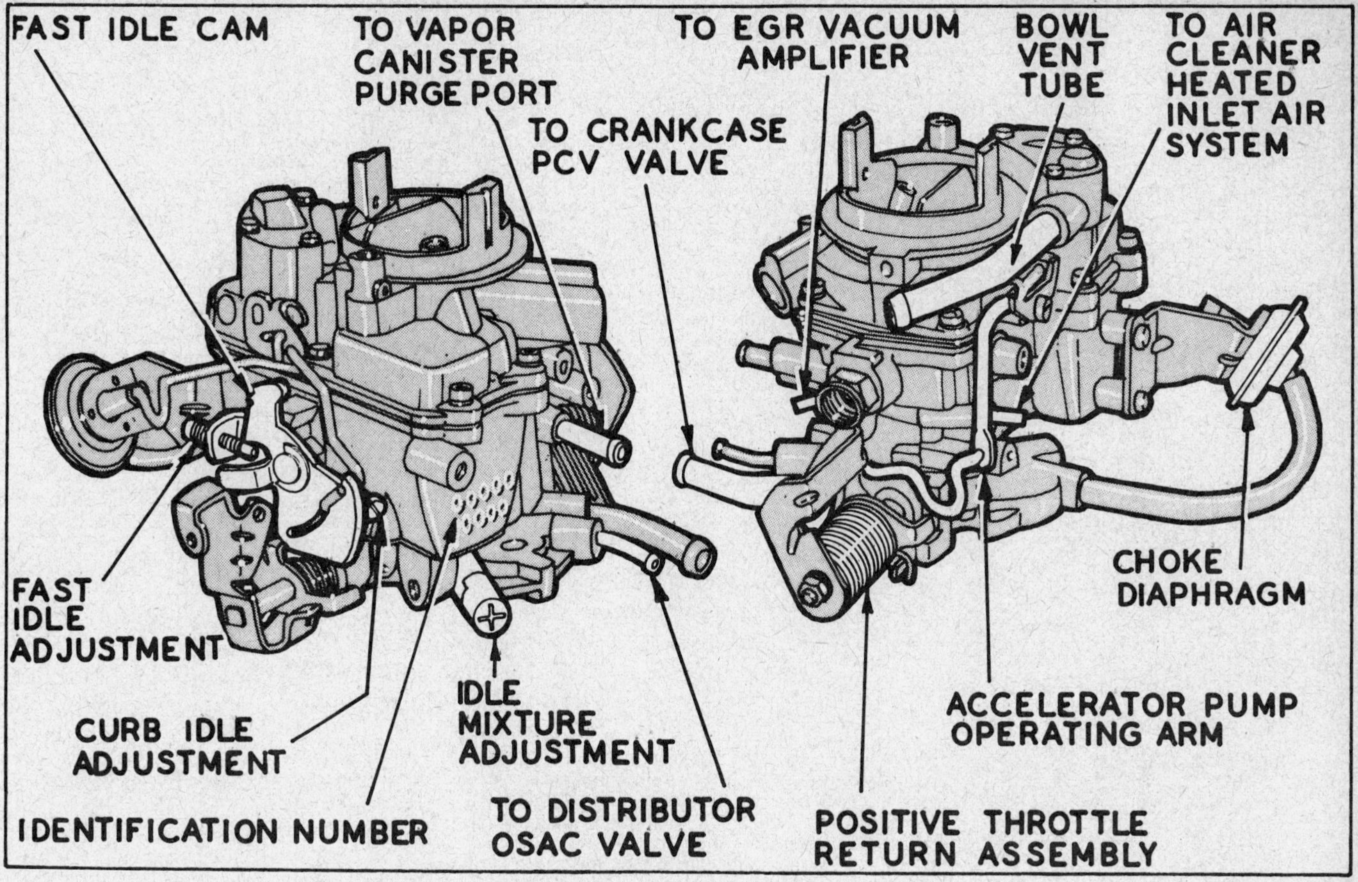

FAST IDLE CAM

TO VAPOR CANISTER PURGE PORT

TO EGR VACUUM AMPLIFIER

BOWL VENT TUBE

TO AIR CLEANER HEATED INLET AIR SYSTEM

TO CRANKCASE PCV VALVE

FAST IDLE ADJUSTMENT

CHOKE DIAPHRAGM

CURB IDLE ADJUSTMENT

IDLE MIXTURE ADJUSTMENT

ACCELERATOR PUMP OPERATING ARM

IDENTIFICATION NUMBER

TO DISTRIBUTOR OSAC VALVE

POSITIVE THROTTLE RETURN ASSEMBLY

Fig. 1 Holley model 1945 single barrel carburetor. (Typical)

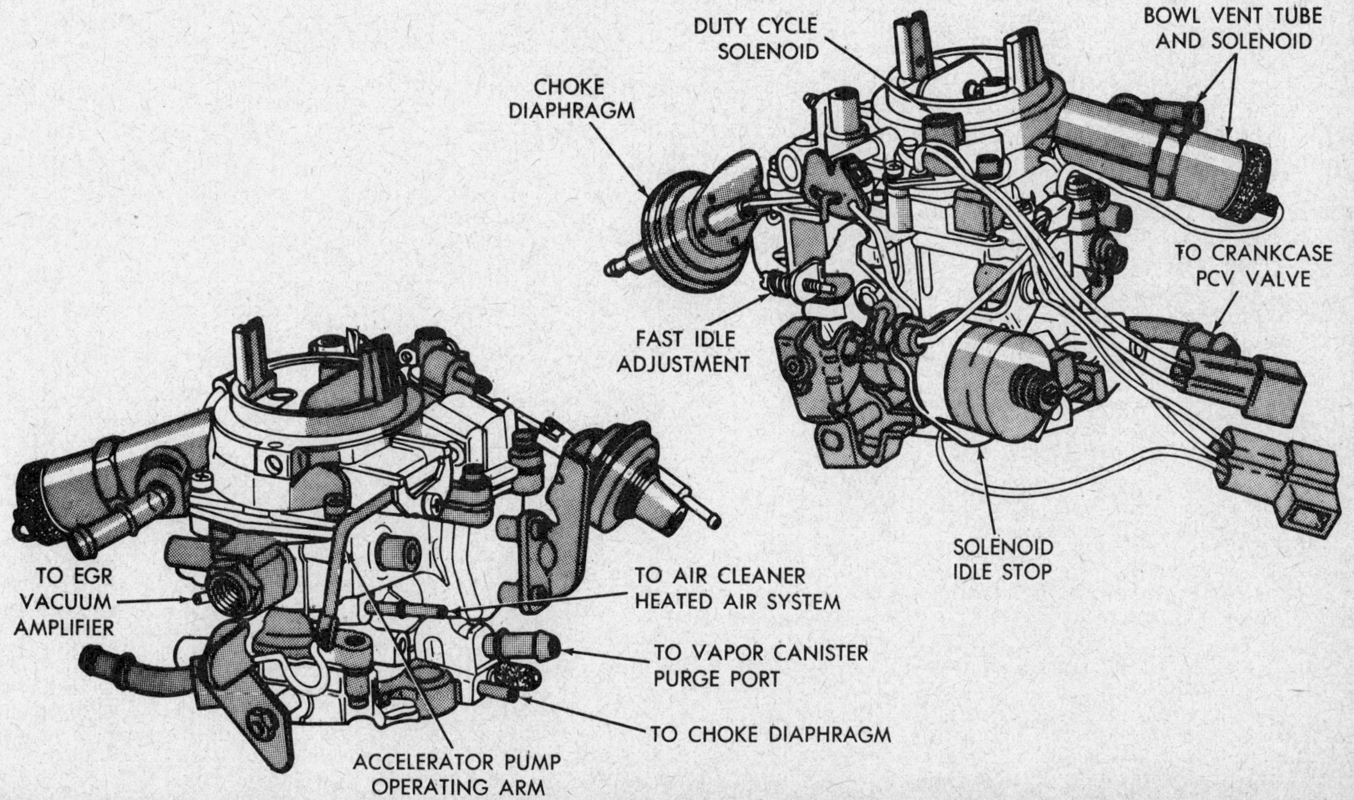

DUTY CYCLE SOLENOID

BOWL VENT TUBE AND SOLENOID

CHOKE DIAPHRAGM

TO CRANKCASE PCV VALVE

FAST IDLE ADJUSTMENT

SOLENOID IDLE STOP

TO EGR VACUUM AMPLIFIER

TO AIR CLEANER HEATED AIR SYSTEM

TO VAPOR CANISTER PURGE PORT

TO CHOKE DIAPHRAGM

ACCELERATOR PUMP OPERATING ARM

Fig. 1A Holley model 6145 electronic feedback single barrel carburetor

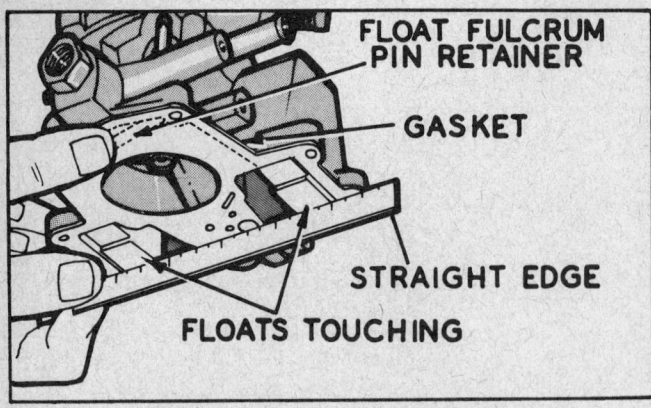

Fig. 2   Measuring float level. 1945 & 6145 carburetor

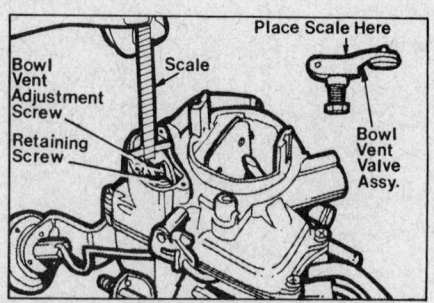

Fig. 3   Bowl vent valve adjustment.
1977–80 1945 carburetor

MODELS 1945 & 6145

These single barrel carburetors, Figs. 1 and 1A, utilize dual nitrophyl floats to control the fuel level, thus permitting high angularity operation during the most severe operating conditions. Also, the float construction eliminates the possibility of a malfunction due to a punctured float.

An electric choke system is incorporated to open the choke at approximately 60 degrees F.

The accelerator pump is of the piston type and is operated by a rod and a link connected to the throttle lever.

The power enrichment system on all units, consists of a power valve installed near the center of the carburetor body and a vacuum piston located in the bowl cover.

A spring-loaded modulated power valve is used. A vacuum passage in the throttle body transmits manifold vacuum to the vacuum piston chamber in the bowl cover. Under light throttle and load conditions, vacuum acting on the vacuum piston is sufficient to overcome the spring tension. When the throttle valve is opened to 55 degrees, vacuum acting on the vacuum piston is bled to the atmosphere and manifold vacuum is closed off. The throttle shaft is provided with a small hole which aligns with a port in the base of the carburetor when the throttle valve is opened to 55 degrees. This vents the vacuum piston chamber to the atmosphere, allowing the spring tension to open the power valve.

The 6145 electronic feedback carburetor also incorporates a duty cycle solenoid which provides a limited regulation of air-fuel ratio in response to electrical signals from the spark control computer. The solenoid meters the main fuel system and operates in parallel with a conventional fixed main metering jet.

When there is no electrical signal applied to the solenoid, the valve spring pushes upward through the main system fuel valve, fully uncovering the solenoid controlled main metering orifice so that the richest condition exists within the carburetor for any given airflow. When the electrical signal is applied to the solenoid, the field windings are energized, thus causing the armature to move the push rod and main system valve downward against the valve spring. This movement will continue until the main system valve bottoms against the main system valve seat. In this position the solenoid controlled main metering orifice is fully sealed so that the leanest condition exists within the carburetor for any given airflow. This condition will remain unchanged until the signal from the spark control computer to the solenoid is switched off. The main system fuel maybe regulated between richest and leanest limits by controlling the amount of time that the solenoid is in the power on position. Under normal operating conditions, 12 volts at a frequency of 10 Hz is applied to the field windings. By controlling the duration of the voltage signal, the power on time to total time, referred to as the duty cycle, is established.

Dry Float Setting

Fig. 2—Hold float fulcrum retaining pin in position and invert carburetor bowl. Place a straight edge across surface of bowl, contracting float toes. Remove straight edge and measure distance float dropped from surface of fuel bowl. Refer to Holley Specifications Chart. Adjust by bending float tang to obtain proper dimension.

Bowl Vent Valve Adjustment

1977–80 Fig. 3—With throttle at curb idle, measure distance between the cover support surface and the flat on the plastic bowl vent lever. The distance should be 1/16 inch. If not

within specifications, turn bowl vent lever adjusting screw to obtain specified distance.

Fast Idle Cam Position Adjustment

Fig. 4—With fast idle speed adjusting screw contacting second highest step on fast idle cam, move choke valve toward closed position with light pressure on choke shaft lever. Insert specified gauge between top of choke valve and wall of air horn. Refer to *Holley Specifications Chart*. An adjustment will be necessary if a slight drag is not obtained as drill shank is being removed. Adjust by bending fast idle link at lower angle, until correct valve opening has been obtained.

Choke Vacuum Kick Adjustment

NOTE: Test can be made on or off vehicle.

Fig. 5—If adjustment is to be made with engine running, back off fast idle speed screw until choke can be closed to the kick position with engine at curb idle. (Note number of screw turns required so that fast idle can be returned to original adjustment). If an auxiliary vacuum source is to be used, open throttle valve (engine not running) and move choke to closed position. Release throttle first, then release choke.

When using an auxiliary vacuum source, disconnect vacuum hose from carburetor and connect it to hose from vacuum supply with a small length of tube to act as a fitting. Removal of hose from diaphragm may require forces which damage the system. Apply a vacuum of 15 or more inches of mercury.

Insert gauge between top of choke valve and wall of air horn. Refer to *Holley Specifications Chart*. Apply sufficient closing pressure on lever to which choke rod attaches to provide a minimum choke valve opening without distortion of diaphragm link.

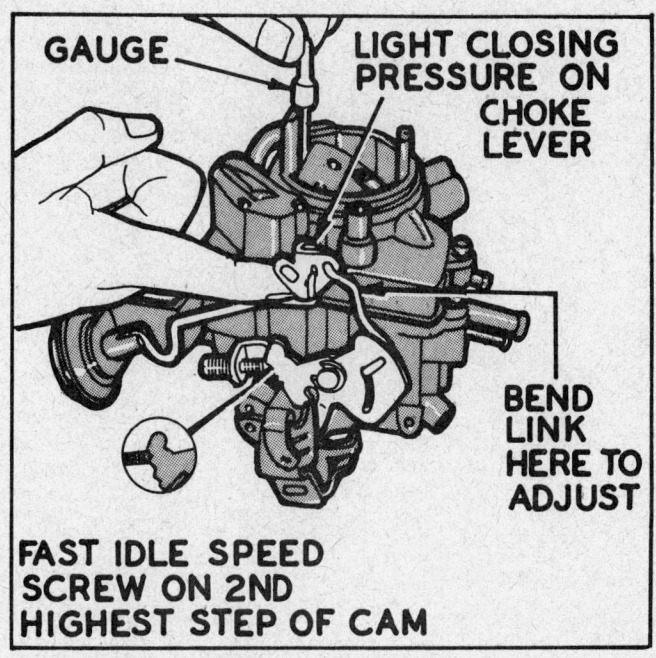

Fig. 4   Fast idle cam position adjustment. 1945 & 6145 carburetor

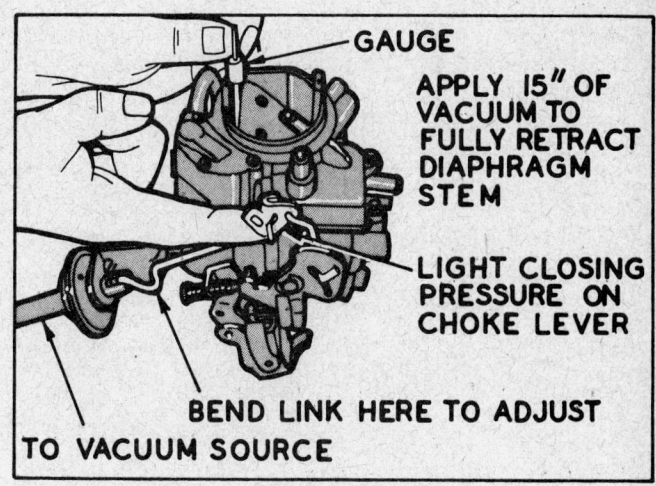

Fig. 5   Choke vacuum kick adjustment. 1977–81 1945 & 6145 carburetor. (Typical of 1982–83)

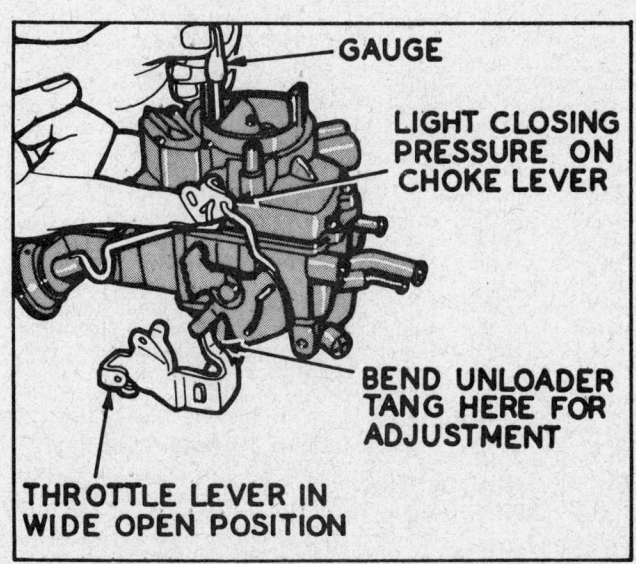

Fig. 6   Choke unloader adjustment. 1945 & 6145 carburetor

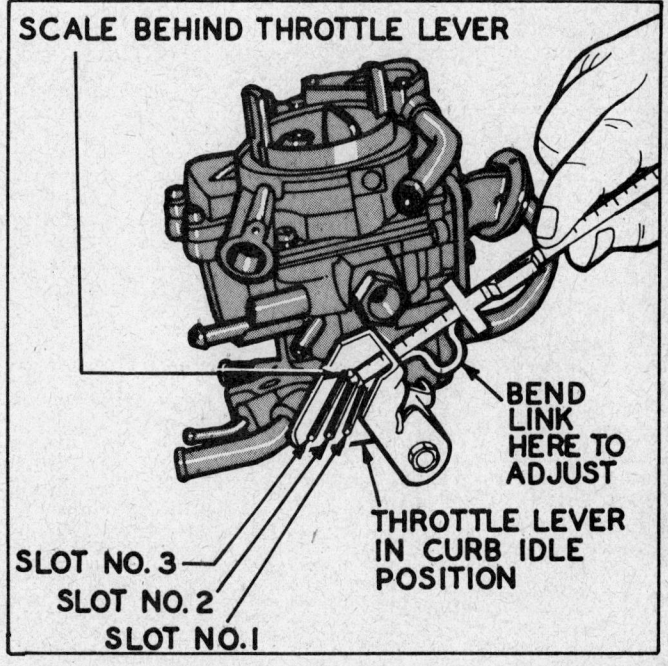

Fig. 7   Accelerator pump adjustment. 1977–79 1945 carburetor

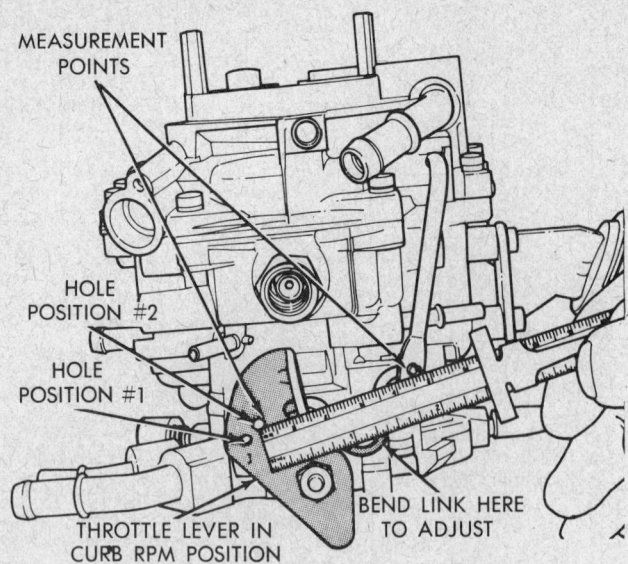

Fig. 8 Accelerator pump adjustment. 1980–83 1945 & 6145 carburetor

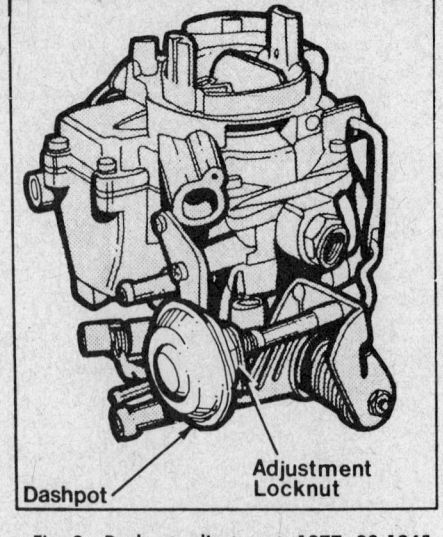

Fig. 9 Dashpot adjustment. 1977–80 1945 carburetor

NOTE: The cylindrical stem of diaphragm extends as the internal spring is compressed. This spring must be fully compressed for proper measurement of vacuum kick adjustment.

Adjustment is necessary if slight drag is not obtained when removing the gauge. Shorten or lengthen diaphragm link to obtain correct choke valve opening. Length changes should be made by carefully opening or closing the U-bend provided in the link. Improper bending causes contact between the U-section and the diaphragm assembly.

NOTE: Do not apply twisting or bending force to diaphragm.

After completion of adjustment, reinstall vacuum hose on correct carburetor fitting.

Return fast idle screw to its original location if disturbed. Make following check. With no vacuum applied to diaphragm, the choke valve should move freely between open and closed positions. If movement is not free, examine linkage for misalignment or interferences caused by bending operation.

NOTE: On 1982–83 models, adjustment is made by means of a 5/64 inch allen wrench inserted into vacuum diaphragm.

Choke Unloader (Wide Open Kick) Adjustment

Fig. 6—With throttle valves in wide open position, insert drill gauge between upper edge of choke valve and inner wall of air horn. Refer to *Holley Specifications Chart.* With a finger lightly pressing against shaft lever, a slight drag should be felt as drill is being withdrawn. Adjust by bending unloader tang on throttle lever until correct opening has been obtained.

Accelerator Pump Setting

Figs. 7 & 8—With throttle at curb idle position, measure length of pump operating link. Refer to *Holley Specification Chart.* Adjust by bending link between throttle lever and pump operating rod.

Dashpot Setting

1977–80 Fig. 9—With curb idle speed and mixture properly set, install a tachometer on engine. Start engine and position throttle lever so actuating tab on lever contacts the dashpot stem, however, not depressing the stem. Permit the engine speed to stabilize. Engine speed should be 2300 RPM on 1979–80 models or 2500 RPM on 1977–78 models. To adjust, loosen locknut and turn the dashpot to obtain proper engine RPM.

MODEL 1946

This carburetor, Figs. 1, 2, and 2A, uses seven basic systems to provide the correct air/fuel mixture under various operating conditions. The systems are as follows: fuel inlet system, idle system, main metering system, power enrichment system, accelerator pump system, external fuel bowl vent system and automatic choke system. The carburetor is divided into three main assemblies which are the air horn assembly, the main body assembly and the throttle body assembly.

The air horn assembly contains the fuel bowl vent, enrichment valve piston and the accelerator pump piston, cup, spring and operating lever. Also contained in the air horn is the choke plate, shaft, lever, housing and choke cap. The idle air bleed and the high speed bleed restrictors are also found in the air horn assembly.

The main body assembly contains the fuel inlet system including the needle and seat assembly, the float, float hinge pin and retainer. The centrally located venturi contains two venturi vacuum boosters and the main discharge passage. The accelerator pump well, passages, check ball and weight, main metering jet, enrichment valve, idle tube and hot idle compensator are also located in the main body assembly. The venturi vacuum pick-up tube, manifold vacuum and EGR port vacuum pick-up tubes are incorporated in the main body assembly.

The throttle body assembly regulates air flow through the carburetor and provides the mounting flange for the carburetor. The throttle plate, shaft lever and return spring assemblies regulate air flow. Also located in the throttle body assembly are the spark vacuum port, EGR vacuum port, idle transfer slot, curb idle discharge port and the idle mixture adjusting screw.

Float Level Adjustment

Fig. 3—With air horn removed, place a finger over float hinge pin retainer and invert main body. Do not lose accelerator pump check ball and weight. Using a straight edge, check position of floats. The floats should touch the straight edge at points shown in illustration. On all 1981–83 units, the floats should touch straightedge at the heel. To adjust, bend float tang.

Accelerator Pump Adjustment

Fig. 4—With the accelerator pump operating link in the specified slot, measure the length of the rod from inner side of tab to outer side of radius. To adjust, bend rod at U-joint.

Fast Idle Cam Position Adjustment

Fig. 5—With fast idle adjusting screw contacting second highest step of fast idle cam, move choke plate toward closed position. Insert specified gauge between upper edge of choke valve and air horn wall. To adjust, bend fast idle cam link.

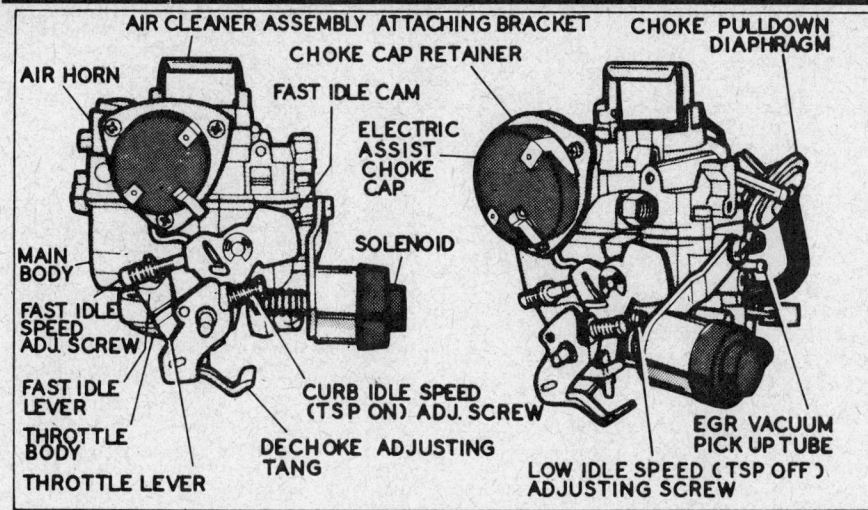

Fig. 1 Holley model 1946 one barrel carburetor (Typical)

Choke Pulldown Adjustment

NOTE: On 1981–83 units, the carburetor must be removed from the vehicle to remove the rivets retaining the choke cap to the choke housing. Using a 1/8 inch or No. 30 drill, remove rivet heads, then drive out rivet using a 1/8 inch diameter punch.

Figs. 6 & 6A—On 1980 California 1946-C units and all 1981–83 units, remove choke thermostatic housing, retainer ring and screws, then temporarily remove choke thermostatic housing index spacer. Reinstall choke thermostatic housing, retainer and screws. On all units, loosen choke cover screw, rotate housing 90 degrees in the rich direction and tighten screws. Using an external vacuum source, apply sufficient vacuum to retract vacuum diaphragm. Push on small metal plate in the bottom of the linkage slot to ensure that the diaphragm is fully retracted. Insert specified gauge between upper edge of choke valve and air horn wall. On 1977–80 units, bend diaphragm link at U-bend to adjust. On 1981–83 units, drill a 3/32 inch hole through pull down motor adjusting screw plug, then remove plug using an easy out. Turn adjusting screw inward or outward as necessary. After completing adjustment, install a replacement plug in adjusting screw access hole.

Dechoke Adjustment

Fig. 7—With throttle held in wide open position, insert specified gauge between upper edge of choke valve and air horn wall. With light pressure against choke shaft lever, a slight drag should be felt when removing the gauge. To adjust, bend unloader tang on throttle lever.

External Fuel Bowl Vent Adjustment

1977–79 All & 1980 Units Except 1946-C
Fig. 8—Disconnect canister vent hose from

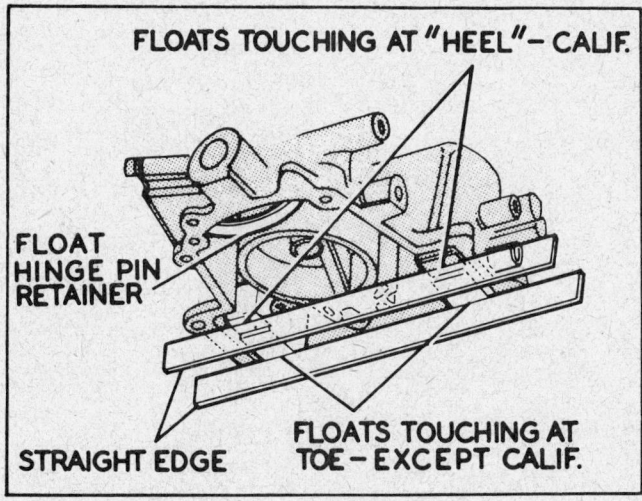

Fig. 3 Float adjustment. 1946 carburetor

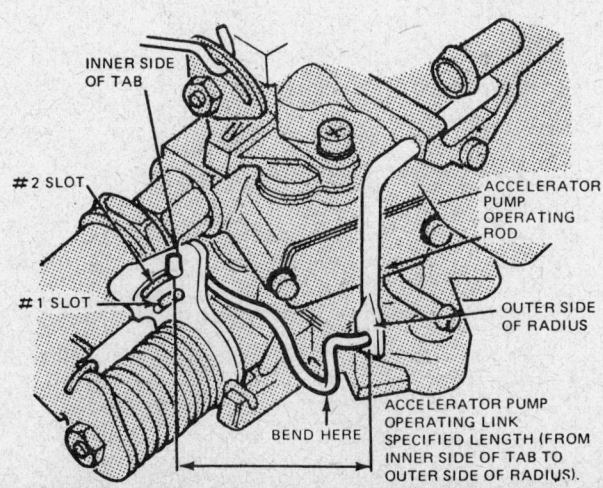

Fig. 4 Accelerator pump adjustment. 1946 carburetor

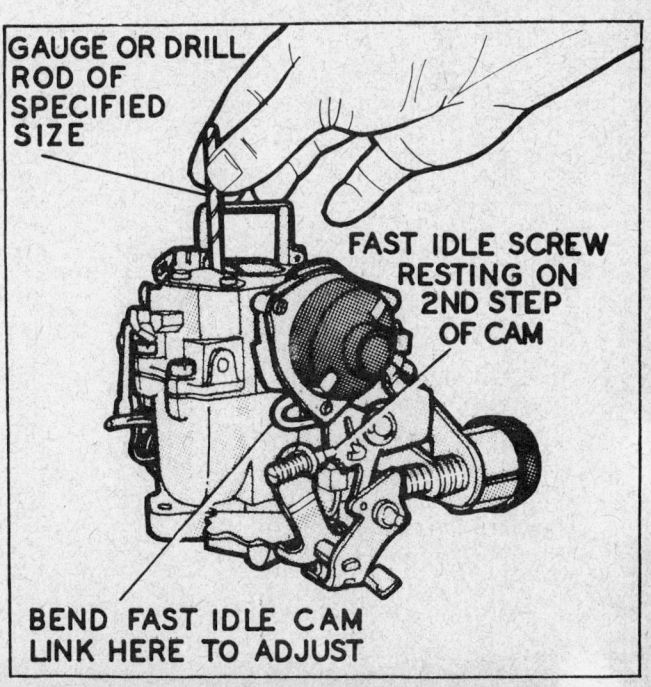

Fig. 5 Fast idle cam adjustment. 1946 carburetor

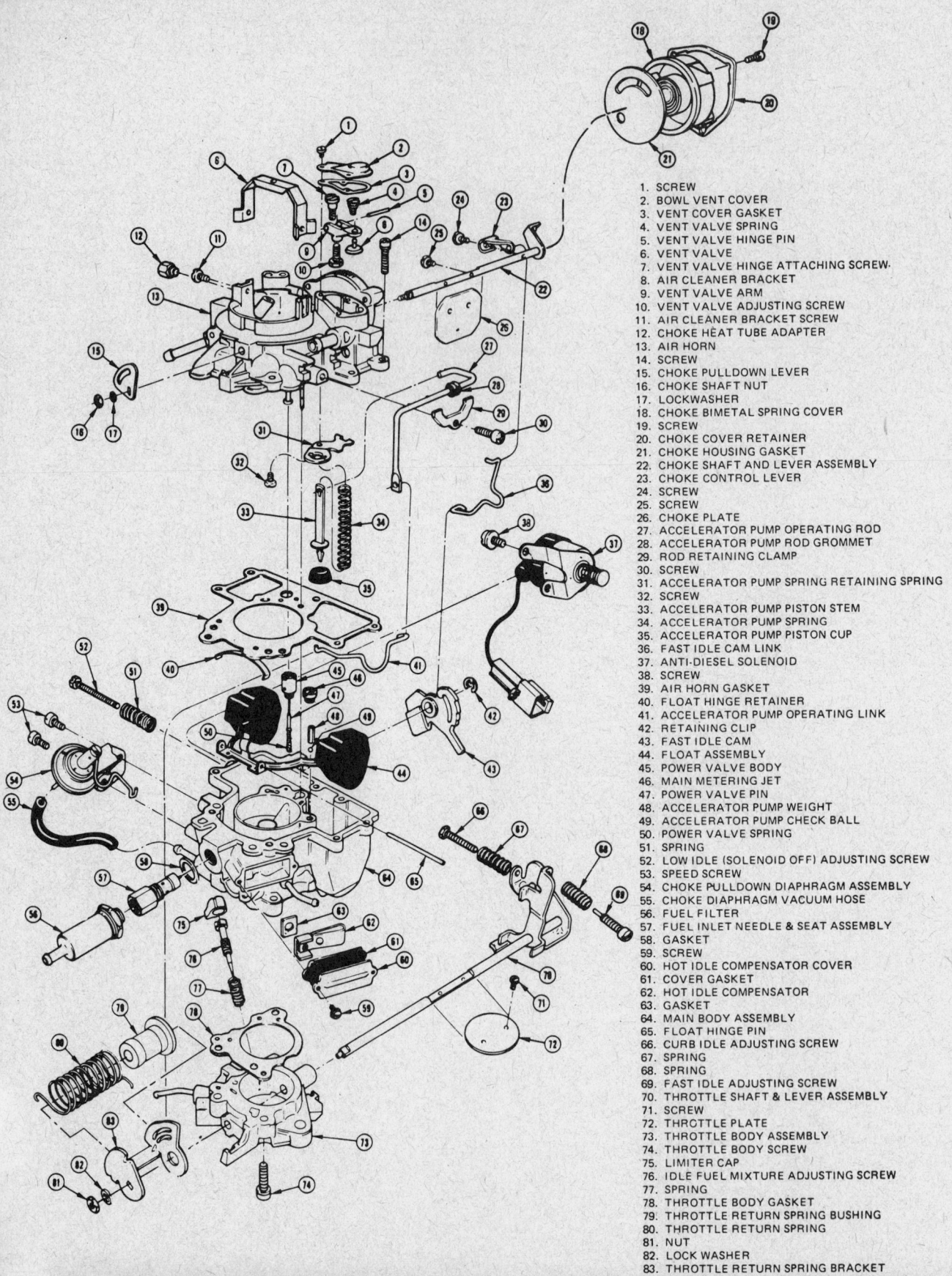

1. SCREW
2. BOWL VENT COVER
3. VENT COVER GASKET
4. VENT VALVE SPRING
5. VENT VALVE HINGE PIN
6. VENT VALVE
7. VENT VALVE HINGE ATTACHING SCREW
8. AIR CLEANER BRACKET
9. VENT VALVE ARM
10. VENT VALVE ADJUSTING SCREW
11. AIR CLEANER BRACKET SCREW
12. CHOKE HEAT TUBE ADAPTER
13. AIR HORN
14. SCREW
15. CHOKE PULLDOWN LEVER
16. CHOKE SHAFT NUT
17. LOCKWASHER
18. CHOKE BIMETAL SPRING COVER
19. SCREW
20. CHOKE COVER RETAINER
21. CHOKE HOUSING GASKET
22. CHOKE SHAFT AND LEVER ASSEMBLY
23. CHOKE CONTROL LEVER
24. SCREW
25. SCREW
26. CHOKE PLATE
27. ACCELERATOR PUMP OPERATING ROD
28. ACCELERATOR PUMP ROD GROMMET
29. ROD RETAINING CLAMP
30. SCREW
31. ACCELERATOR PUMP SPRING RETAINING SPRING
32. SCREW
33. ACCELERATOR PUMP PISTON STEM
34. ACCELERATOR PUMP SPRING
35. ACCELERATOR PUMP PISTON CUP
36. FAST IDLE CAM LINK
37. ANTI-DIESEL SOLENOID
38. SCREW
39. AIR HORN GASKET
40. FLOAT HINGE RETAINER
41. ACCELERATOR PUMP OPERATING LINK
42. RETAINING CLIP
43. FAST IDLE CAM
44. FLOAT ASSEMBLY
45. POWER VALVE BODY
46. MAIN METERING JET
47. POWER VALVE PIN
48. ACCELERATOR PUMP WEIGHT
49. ACCELERATOR PUMP CHECK BALL
50. POWER VALVE SPRING
51. SPRING
52. LOW IDLE (SOLENOID OFF) ADJUSTING SCREW
53. SPEED SCREW
54. CHOKE PULLDOWN DIAPHRAGM ASSEMBLY
55. CHOKE DIAPHRAGM VACUUM HOSE
56. FUEL FILTER
57. FUEL INLET NEEDLE & SEAT ASSEMBLY
58. GASKET
59. SCREW
60. HOT IDLE COMPENSATOR COVER
61. COVER GASKET
62. HOT IDLE COMPENSATOR
63. GASKET
64. MAIN BODY ASSEMBLY
65. FLOAT HINGE PIN
66. CURB IDLE ADJUSTING SCREW
67. SPRING
68. SPRING
69. FAST IDLE ADJUSTING SCREW
70. THROTTLE SHAFT & LEVER ASSEMBLY
71. SCREW
72. THROTTLE PLATE
73. THROTTLE BODY ASSEMBLY
74. THROTTLE BODY SCREW
75. LIMITER CAP
76. IDLE FUEL MIXTURE ADJUSTING SCREW
77. SPRING
78. THROTTLE BODY GASKET
79. THROTTLE RETURN SPRING BUSHING
80. THROTTLE RETURN SPRING
81. NUT
82. LOCK WASHER
83. THROTTLE RETURN SPRING BRACKET

Fig. 2   Disassembled view of Holley Model 1946 carburetor (Typical). 1977–80 units

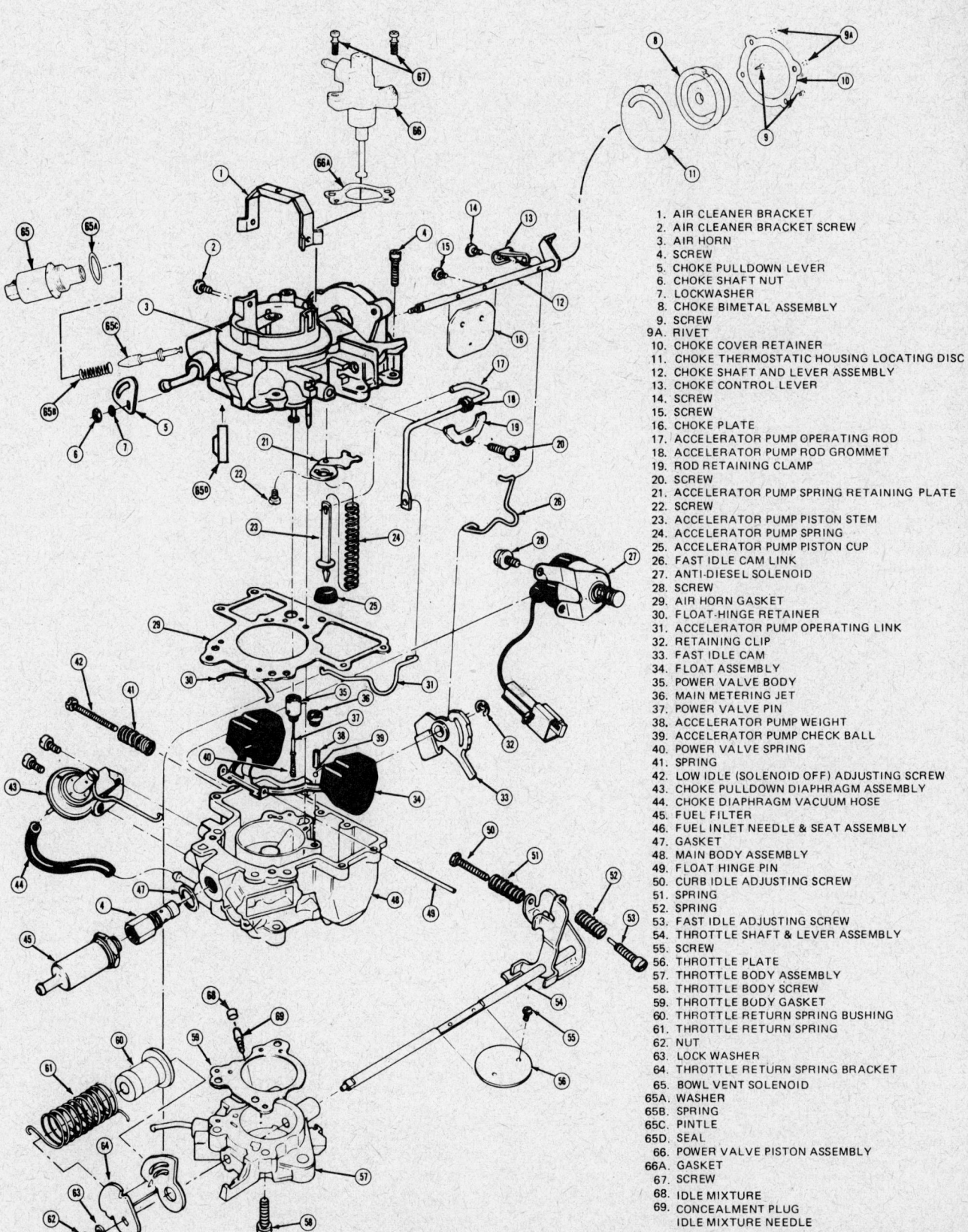

1. AIR CLEANER BRACKET
2. AIR CLEANER BRACKET SCREW
3. AIR HORN
4. SCREW
5. CHOKE PULLDOWN LEVER
6. CHOKE SHAFT NUT
7. LOCKWASHER
8. CHOKE BIMETAL ASSEMBLY
9. SCREW
9A. RIVET
10. CHOKE COVER RETAINER
11. CHOKE THERMOSTATIC HOUSING LOCATING DISC
12. CHOKE SHAFT AND LEVER ASSEMBLY
13. CHOKE CONTROL LEVER
14. SCREW
15. SCREW
16. CHOKE PLATE
17. ACCELERATOR PUMP OPERATING ROD
18. ACCELERATOR PUMP ROD GROMMET
19. ROD RETAINING CLAMP
20. SCREW
21. ACCELERATOR PUMP SPRING RETAINING PLATE
22. SCREW
23. ACCELERATOR PUMP PISTON STEM
24. ACCELERATOR PUMP SPRING
25. ACCELERATOR PUMP PISTON CUP
26. FAST IDLE CAM LINK
27. ANTI-DIESEL SOLENOID
28. SCREW
29. AIR HORN GASKET
30. FLOAT-HINGE RETAINER
31. ACCELERATOR PUMP OPERATING LINK
32. RETAINING CLIP
33. FAST IDLE CAM
34. FLOAT ASSEMBLY
35. POWER VALVE BODY
36. MAIN METERING JET
37. POWER VALVE PIN
38. ACCELERATOR PUMP WEIGHT
39. ACCELERATOR PUMP CHECK BALL
40. POWER VALVE SPRING
41. SPRING
42. LOW IDLE (SOLENOID OFF) ADJUSTING SCREW
43. CHOKE PULLDOWN DIAPHRAGM ASSEMBLY
44. CHOKE DIAPHRAGM VACUUM HOSE
45. FUEL FILTER
46. FUEL INLET NEEDLE & SEAT ASSEMBLY
47. GASKET
48. MAIN BODY ASSEMBLY
49. FLOAT HINGE PIN
50. CURB IDLE ADJUSTING SCREW
51. SPRING
52. SPRING
53. FAST IDLE ADJUSTING SCREW
54. THROTTLE SHAFT & LEVER ASSEMBLY
55. SCREW
56. THROTTLE PLATE
57. THROTTLE BODY ASSEMBLY
58. THROTTLE BODY SCREW
59. THROTTLE BODY GASKET
60. THROTTLE RETURN SPRING BUSHING
61. THROTTLE RETURN SPRING
62. NUT
63. LOCK WASHER
64. THROTTLE RETURN SPRING BRACKET
65. BOWL VENT SOLENOID
65A. WASHER
65B. SPRING
65C. PINTLE
65D. SEAL
66. POWER VALVE PISTON ASSEMBLY
66A. GASKET
67. SCREW
68. IDLE MIXTURE
69. CONCEALMENT PLUG
      IDLE MIXTURE NEEDLE

Fig. 2A   Disassembled view of Holley Model 1946 Carburetor (Typical). 1981–83 units

CARBURETORS

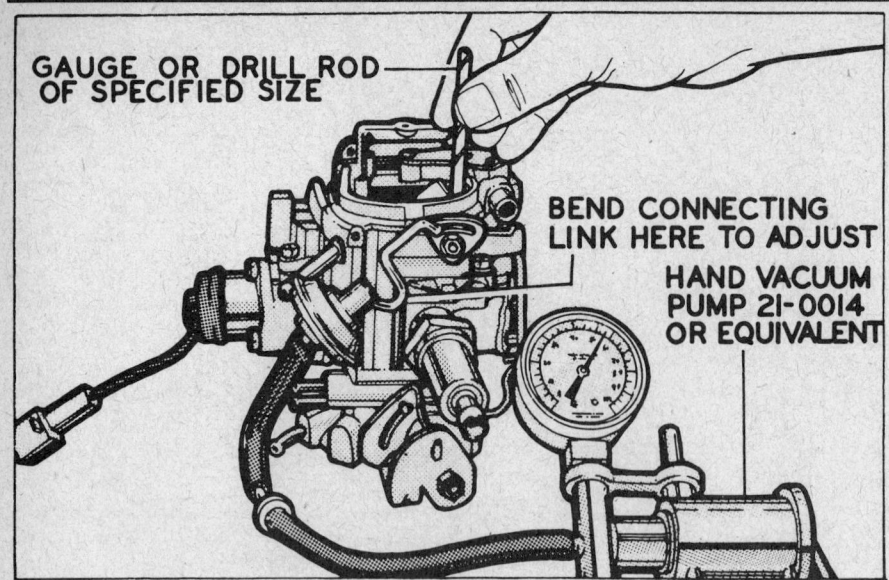

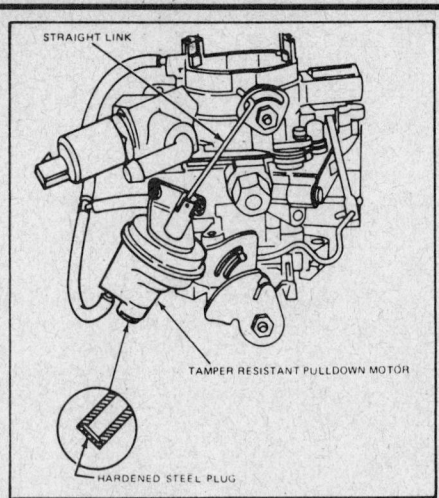

Fig. 6A Choke pulldown adjustment. 1981—83 Model 1946 carburetor

Fig. 6 Choke pulldown adjustment. 1977—80 Model 1946 carburetor

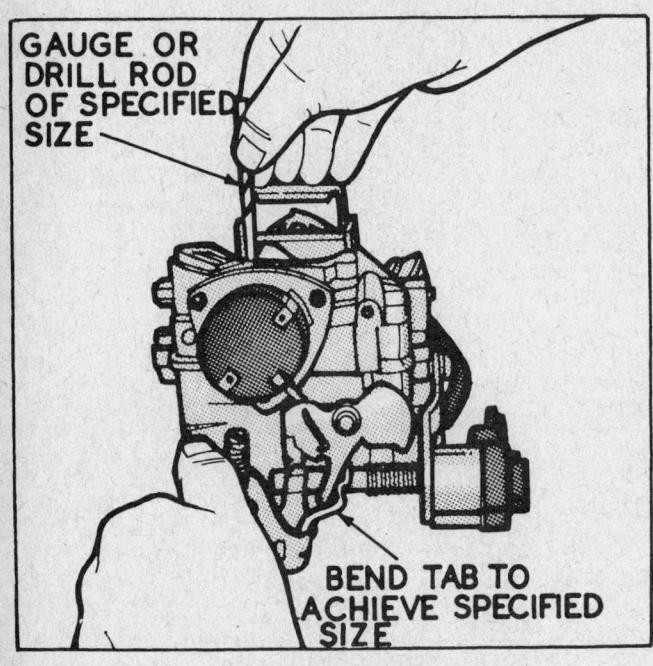

Fig. 7 Dechoke adjustment. 1946 carburetor

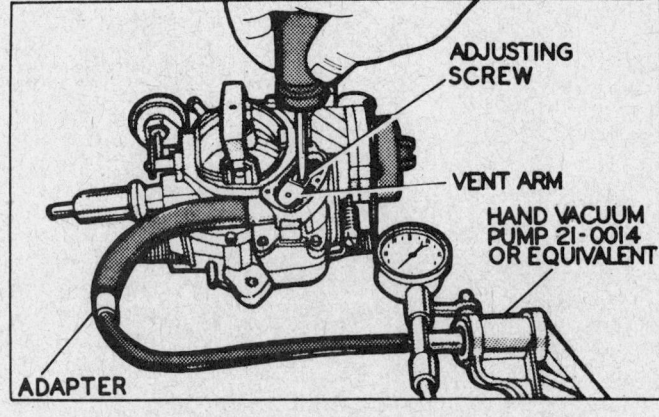

Fig. 8 External fuel bowl vent adjustment. 1946 carburetor

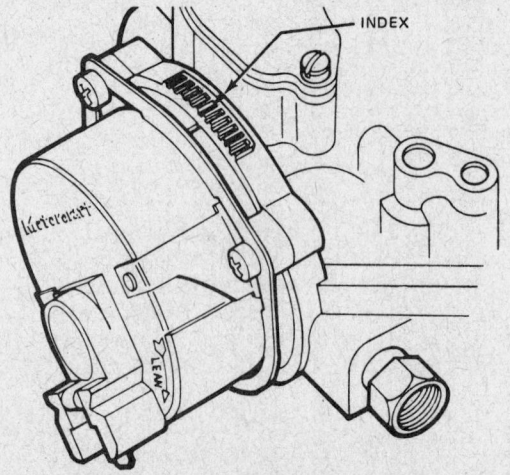

Fig. 9 Choke setting adjustment. 1946 carburetor

bowl vent tube. Connect an external vacuum source to bowl vent tube. Remove bowl vent cover, gasket and spring. Rotate vent adjusting screw clockwise until the adjusting screw protrudes 1/8 inch or less above vent arm. Apply vacuum to vent tube and slowly turn the adjusting screw counterclockwise in 1/8 turn increments until vacuum reading indicates that the valve is closed. Remove vacuum and rotate the adjusting screw 1/2 turn clockwise. Install bowl vent spring, gasket and cover. Connect canister vent hose.

Choke Setting Adjustment

Fig. 9—Loosen choke cover retaining screws and rotate cover to align mark on cover with specified mark on housing. Tighten choke cover retaining screws.

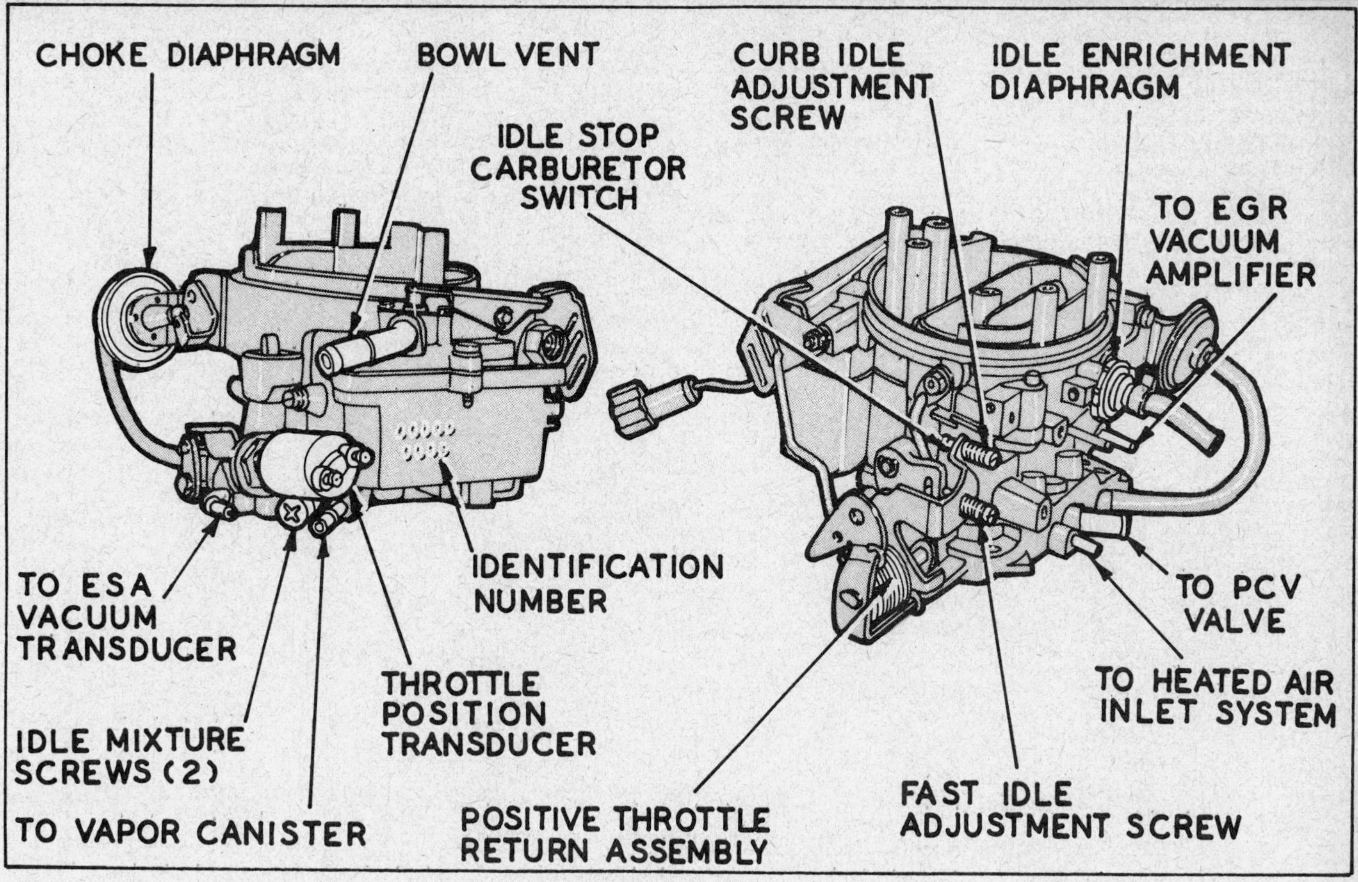

Fig. 1 Holley model 2245 two-barrel carburetor (Typical)

CHOKE DIAPHRAGM

BOWL VENT

CURB IDLE ADJUSTMENT SCREW

IDLE ENRICHMENT DIAPHRAGM

IDLE STOP CARBURETOR SWITCH

TO EGR VACUUM AMPLIFIER

TO ESA VACUUM TRANSDUCER

IDLE MIXTURE SCREWS (2)

TO VAPOR CANISTER

IDENTIFICATION NUMBER

THROTTLE POSITION TRANSDUCER

POSITIVE THROTTLE RETURN ASSEMBLY

FAST IDLE ADJUSTMENT SCREW

TO HEATED AIR INLET SYSTEM

TO PCV VALVE

MODEL 2245

This carburetor, Fig. 1, is a two-barrel unit but can be considered as two carburetors built side by side into one unit, utilizing the same fuel and air inlets. Each throat of the carburetor has its own throttle valve and main metering systems and are supplemented by the float, accelerating, idle and power systems. An electric choke system is incorporated to open choke at approximately 60° to 63°. On vehicles with automatic transmissions, an idle enrichment system is used to reduce cold engine stalling by the use of an additional metering system which enrichens the mixture in the off idle position. This system is controlled by a vacuum diaphragm mounted near the top of the carburetor.

Float Adjustment

Invert air horn so that weight of float only is forcing needle against seat. Measure the clearance between top of float and float stop, Fig. 2. Be sure drill gauge is perfectly level when measuring. Refer to *Holley Specifications Chart*. Adjust by bending float lip toward or away from needle, using a narrow blade screwdriver, Fig. 3, until correct clearance of setting has been obtained.

Float Drop Adjustment

Check float drop, by holding air horn in an upright position. The bottom edge of float should be parallel to underside surface of air horn, Fig. 4. Adjust by bending tang on float arm until parallel surfaces have been obtained.

Fast Idle Cam Position Adjustment

Fig. 5—With fast idle speed adjusting screw contacting second highest step on fast idle cam, move choke valve toward closed position with light pressure on choke shaft lever. Insert specified gauge between top of choke valve and wall of air horn. Refer to *Holley Specifications Chart*. An adjustment will be necessary if a slight drag is not obtained as drill shank is being removed. Adjust by bending fast idle link at angle, until correct valve opening has been obtained.

Choke Vacuum Kick Adjustment

NOTE: Test can be made on or off vehicle.

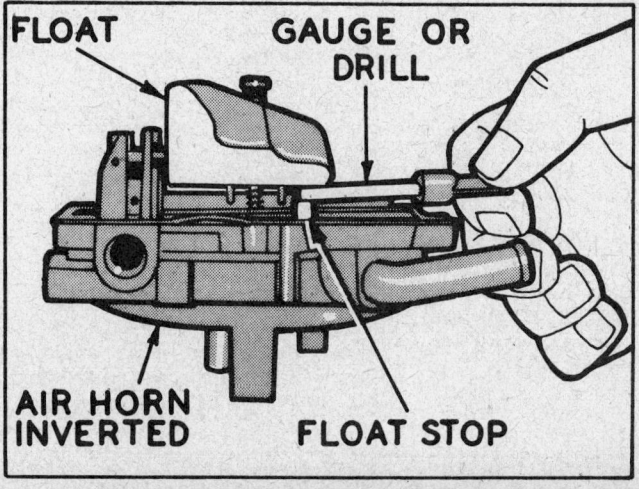

FLOAT

GAUGE OR DRILL

AIR HORN INVERTED

FLOAT STOP

Fig. 2 Checking float level on 2245 carburetor

CARBURETORS

1. CHOKE PLATE
2. CHOKE SHAFT & LEVER ASSEMBLY
3. FAST IDLE LEVER
4. CHOKE PLATE SCREW
5. FAST IDLE ADJUSTING SCREW
6. THROTTLE STOP SCREW
7. BRACKET RETAINER SCREW
8. FUEL BOWL BAFFLE SCREW
9. THROTTLE BODY TO MAIN BODY
   SCREW & LOCK WASHER

10. AIR HORN TO MAIN BODY SCREW
    & LOCK WASHER
11. AIR HORN TO MAIN BODY SCREW
    & LOCK WASHER
12. THROTTLE PLATE SCREW &
    LOCK WASHER
13. MAIN BODY GASKET
14. THROTTLE BODY GASKET
15. FUEL INLET NEEDLE SEAT
    GASKET

16. FUEL INLET FITTING GASKET
17. THROTTLE PLATE
18. THROTTLE BODY & SHAFT ASSEMBLY
19. IDLE ADJUSTING NEEDLE
20. FLOAT ASSEMBLY
21. FUEL INLET NEEDLE &
    SEAT ASSEMBLY
22. FUEL INLET FITTING
23. MAIN JET (CHOKE SIDE)
24. MAIN JET (THROTTLE SIDE)
25. PUMP DISCHARGE VALVE
26. AIR VENT VALVE
27. POWER VALVE ASSEMBLY
28. PUMP PISTON CUP
29. CHOKE DIAPHRAGM LINK
    PIN
30. FLOAT HINGE PIN
31. STOP & CABLE ASSEMBLY
    PIN
32. ACCELERATOR PUMP
    ASSEMBLY

33. PUMP STEM ASSEMBLY
34. PUMP LINK
35. CHOKE DIAPHRAGM LINK
36. IDLE ADJUSTING NEEDLE LIMITER
37. CHOKE DIAPHRAGM ASSEMBLY
38. LEVER RETAINER
39. FAST IDLE CAM RETAINER
40. FAST IDLE & THROTTLE STOP
    SCREW SPRING
41. IDLE NEEDLE SPRING
42. VENT VALVE LEVER SPRING
43. THROTTLE LEVER SPRING
44. PUMP DRIVE SPRING
45. FAST IDLE LEVER NUT
46. PUMP LEVER NUT
47. FAST IDLE CAM
48. FAST IDLE ROD
49. PUMP LEVER NUT LOCK
    WASHER
50. FAST IDLE LEVER LOCK
    WASHER
51. PUMP DRIVE SPRING WASHER
52. CHOKE VACUUM HOSE
53. FUEL BOWL BAFFLE
54. PUMP LEVER
55. AIR VENT VALVE LEVER
56. PUMP LEVER SHAFT
57. STOP & CABLE ASSEMBLY
    FLANGE GASKET

58. VENT VALVE SCREW & HOT
    IDLE COMPENSATOR COVER
    SCREWS
59. MODULATOR SCREWS
60. SOLENOID BRACKET SCREW
61. MODULATOR BRACKET SCREW
62. POWER VALVE ADJUSTING
    SCREW
63. SOLENOID ADJUSTING SCREW
64. MODULATOR ADJUSTING SCREW
65. EGR ADJUSTING NEEDLE
66. VENT VALVE BODY
67. AUXILIARY IDLE RICH VALVE
68. POWER VALVE PISTON
69. HOT IDLE COMPENSATOR SEAL
70. MODULATOR DIAPHRAGM LINK
71. HOT IDLE COMPENSATOR COVER
72. POWER VALVE PISTON RETAINER
73. VENT VALVE SPRING

74. SOLENOID ADJUSTING SCREW
    SPRING
75. POWER VALVE SPRING
76. NUT
77. MODULATOR LOCK NUT
78. LOCK WASHER
79. SPRING WASHER
80. LINK RETAINER
81. VENT VALVE CLAMP
82. AUXILIARY IDLE RICH HOSE
    CLAMP
83. HOT IDLE COMPENSATOR
    ASSEMBLY
84. MODULATOR BRACKET
85. MODULATOR ASSEMBLY (THROTTLE
    SIDE)
86. MODULATOR & BRACKET ASSEMBLY
    (DIAPHRAGM SIDE)
87. MODULATOR LEVER & BUSHING
    ASSEMBLY
88. MODULATOR PICKUP LEVER
89. SOLENOID & BRACKET ASSEMBLY
90. AUXILIARY IDLE RICH HOSE
91. AIR HORN & PLUG ASSEMBLY
92. MAIN BODY & PLUG ASSEMBLY

Exploded view of Holley model 2245 carburetor

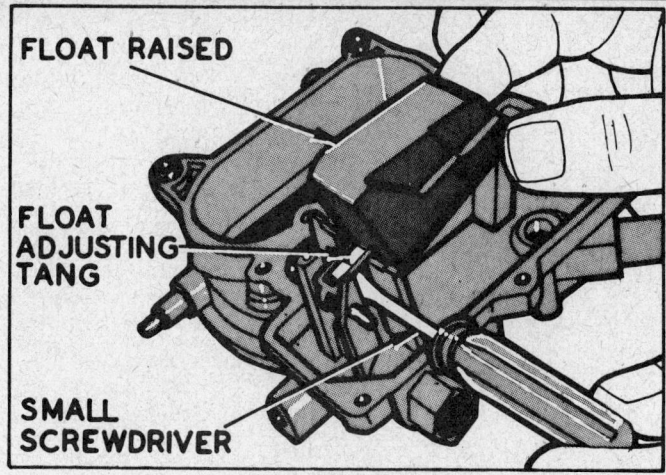

FLOAT RAISED

FLOAT ADJUSTING TANG

SMALL SCREWDRIVER

Fig. 3   Adjusting float on 2245 carburetor

UNDERSIDE SURFACE OF AIR HORN

BOTTOM EDGE OF FLOAT SHOULD BE PARALLEL

Fig. 4   Checking float drop on 2245 carburetor

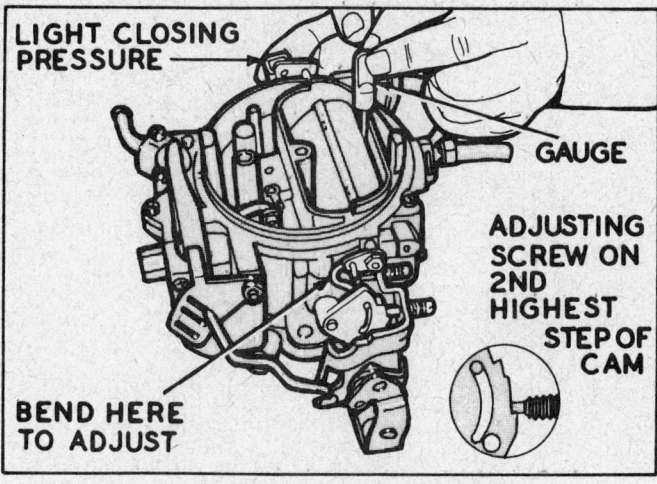

LIGHT CLOSING PRESSURE

GAUGE

ADJUSTING SCREW ON 2ND HIGHEST STEP OF CAM

BEND HERE TO ADJUST

Fig. 5   Fast idle cam position adjustment on 2245 carburetor

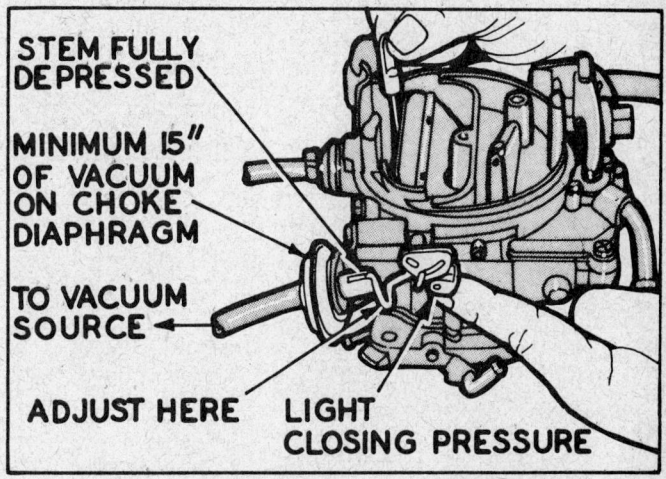

STEM FULLY DEPRESSED

MINIMUM 15" OF VACUUM ON CHOKE DIAPHRAGM

TO VACUUM SOURCE

ADJUST HERE   LIGHT CLOSING PRESSURE

Fig. 6   Vacuum kick adjustment on 2245 carburetor

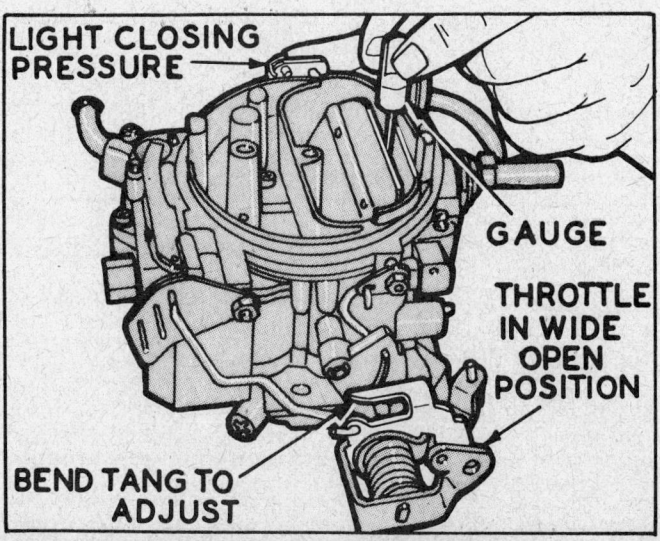

LIGHT CLOSING PRESSURE

GAUGE

THROTTLE IN WIDE OPEN POSITION

BEND TANG TO ADJUST

Fig. 7   Choke unloader adjustment on 2245 carburetor

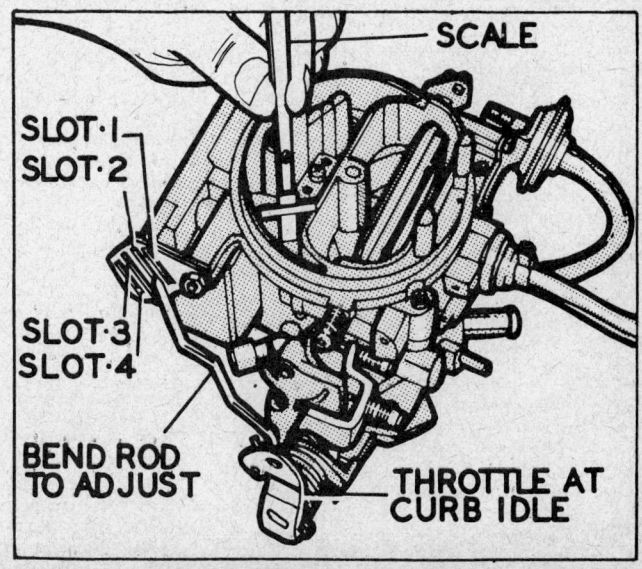

SCALE

SLOT·1
SLOT·2

SLOT·3
SLOT·4

BEND ROD TO ADJUST   THROTTLE AT CURB IDLE

Fig. 8   Accelerator pump adjustment on 2245 carburetor

CARBURETORS

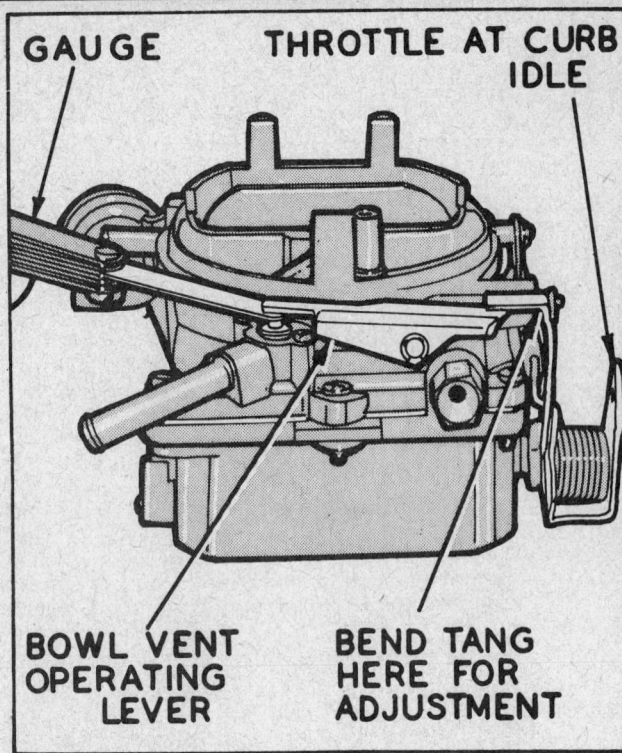

GAUGE THROTTLE AT CURB IDLE

BOWL VENT OPERATING LEVER

BEND TANG HERE FOR ADJUSTMENT

Fig. 9 Bowl vent adjustment on 2245 carburetor

Fig. 6—If adjustment is to be made with engine running, back off fast idle speed screw until choke can be closed to the kick position with engine at curb idle. (Note number of screw turns required so that fast idle can be returned to original adjustment). If an auxiliary vacuum source is to be used, open throttle valve (engine not running) and move choke to closed position. Release throttle first, then release choke.

When using an auxiliary vacuum source, disconnect vacuum hose from carburetor and connect it to hose from vacuum supply with a small length of tube to act as a fitting. Removal of hose from diaphragm may require forces which damage the system. Apply 15 or more inches of vacuum to diaphragm.

Insert gauge between top of choke valve and wall of air horn. Refer to *Holley Specifications Chart*. Apply sufficient closing pressure on lever to which choke rod attaches to provide a minimum choke valve opening without distortion of diaphragm link.

NOTE: The cylindrical stem of diaphragm extends as the internal spring is compressed. This spring must be fully compressed for proper measurement of vacuum kick adjustment.

Adjustment is necessary if slight drag is not obtained when removing the gauge. Shorten or lengthen diaphragm link to obtain correct choke valve opening. Length changes should be made by carefully opening or closing the U-bend provided in the link. Improper bending causes contact between the U-section and the diaphragm assembly.

NOTE: Do not apply twisting or bending force to diaphragm.

After completion of adjustment, reinstall vacuum hose on correct carburetor fitting. Return fast idle screw to its original location if disturbed. Make following check. With no vacuum applied to diaphragm, the choke valve should move freely between open and closed positions. If movement is not free, examine linkage for misalignment or interferences caused by bending operation.

Choke Unloader (Wide Open Kick) Adjustment

Fig. 7—With throttle valves in wide open position, insert drill gauge between upper edge of choke valve and inner wall of air horn. Refer to *Holley Specifications Chart*. With a finger lightly pressing against shaft lever, a slight drag should be felt as drill is being withdrawn. Adjust by bending unloader tang on throttle lever until correct opening has been obtained.

Accelerator Pump Adjustment

Fig. 8—Back off curb idle speed adjusting screw. Open choke valve so that fast idle cam allows throttle valves to be completely seated in bores. Be sure that pump connector rod is installed in correct slot of accelerator pump rocker arm.

Using a suitable scale, measure pump travel (drop) between curb idle and wide open throttle. To adjust, bend pump operating rod until proper setting is obtained.

Bowl Vent Valve Clearance Adjustment

Fig. 9—With the throttle valves at curb idle, it should be possible to insert the specified gauge between the bowl vent valve plunger stem and operating rod. Refer to *Holley Specifications Chart*. Adjust by bending the tang on pump lever to change arc of contact with throttle lever, until correct clearance has been obtained.

MODEL 2280

This carburetor, Fig. 1, uses four basic metering systems. The basic idle system provides the proper air/fuel mixture for idle and low speed operations. The accelerator pump system provides additional fuel during acceleration. The main metering system provides the proper air/fuel mixture during normal cruising conditions. The power enrichment system, combining a mechanical and vacuum operated power valve, provides a richer mixture when higher engine power is required.

In addition to the four basic systems, there is a fuel inlet system which supplies fuel to the four basic systems and a choke system which temporarily enriches the mixture to aid in starting and running a cold engine.

Float Adjustment

Fig. 2—Invert main body so the weight of the floats only is forcing the needle against the seat. Hold finger against hinge pin retainer to fully seat in the float hinge cradle. Using a suitable scale, measure distance between the float bowl surface and the toe of each float. To adjust, bend the float tang. If necessary, bend either float arm to equalize individual float positions.

Accelerator Pump Adjustment

Fig. 3—Remove bowl vent cover plate and vent valve spring. Do not dislodge vent valve lever retainer. Ensure that accelerator pump rod is in the inner hole of the pump operating lever and the throttle is at curb idle. Place a straight edge on bowl vent cover surface of air horn over accelerator pump lever. Adjust until lever surface is flush with air horn surface by bending the accelerator pump connector rod. Install vent valve lever spring and bowl vent cover plate.

NOTE: If this adjustment is changed, the bowl vent and mechanical power valve adjustments must be reset.

Choke Unloader Adjustment

Fig. 4—Hold throttle valves in wide open position. Lightly press finger against control lever to move choke valve toward closed position. Insert specified gauge between top of choke valve and air horn wall. To adjust, bend tang on accelerator pump lever.

Choke Vacuum Kick Adjustment

Fig. 5—Open throttle, close choke, then close throttle to trap fast idle cam at closed choke position. Apply approximately 15 inches of vacuum to diaphragm with an external vac-

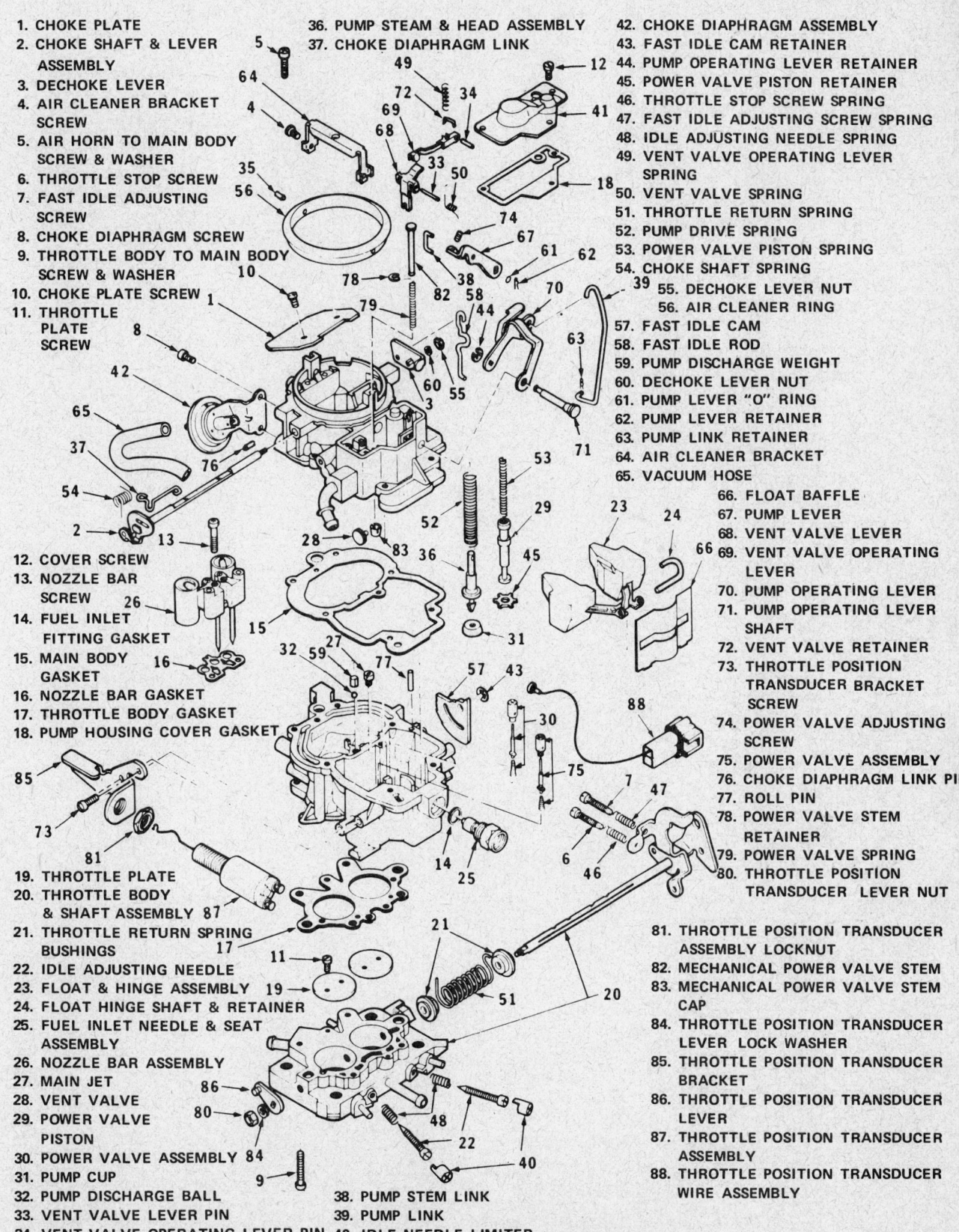

1. CHOKE PLATE
2. CHOKE SHAFT & LEVER ASSEMBLY
3. DECHOKE LEVER
4. AIR CLEANER BRACKET SCREW
5. AIR HORN TO MAIN BODY SCREW & WASHER
6. THROTTLE STOP SCREW
7. FAST IDLE ADJUSTING SCREW
8. CHOKE DIAPHRAGM SCREW
9. THROTTLE BODY TO MAIN BODY SCREW & WASHER
10. CHOKE PLATE SCREW
11. THROTTLE PLATE SCREW

36. PUMP STEAM & HEAD ASSEMBLY
37. CHOKE DIAPHRAGM LINK

42. CHOKE DIAPHRAGM ASSEMBLY
43. FAST IDLE CAM RETAINER
44. PUMP OPERATING LEVER RETAINER
45. POWER VALVE PISTON RETAINER
46. THROTTLE STOP SCREW SPRING
47. FAST IDLE ADJUSTING SCREW SPRING
48. IDLE ADJUSTING NEEDLE SPRING
49. VENT VALVE OPERATING LEVER SPRING
50. VENT VALVE SPRING
51. THROTTLE RETURN SPRING
52. PUMP DRIVE SPRING
53. POWER VALVE PISTON SPRING
54. CHOKE SHAFT SPRING
55. DECHOKE LEVER NUT
56. AIR CLEANER RING
57. FAST IDLE CAM
58. FAST IDLE ROD
59. PUMP DISCHARGE WEIGHT
60. DECHOKE LEVER NUT
61. PUMP LEVER "O" RING
62. PUMP LEVER RETAINER
63. PUMP LINK RETAINER
64. AIR CLEANER BRACKET
65. VACUUM HOSE
66. FLOAT BAFFLE
67. PUMP LEVER
68. VENT VALVE LEVER
69. VENT VALVE OPERATING LEVER
70. PUMP OPERATING LEVER
71. PUMP OPERATING LEVER SHAFT
72. VENT VALVE RETAINER
73. THROTTLE POSITION TRANSDUCER BRACKET SCREW
74. POWER VALVE ADJUSTING SCREW
75. POWER VALVE ASSEMBLY
76. CHOKE DIAPHRAGM LINK PIN
77. ROLL PIN
78. POWER VALVE STEM RETAINER
79. POWER VALVE SPRING
80. THROTTLE POSITION TRANSDUCER LEVER NUT
81. THROTTLE POSITION TRANSDUCER ASSEMBLY LOCKNUT
82. MECHANICAL POWER VALVE STEM
83. MECHANICAL POWER VALVE STEM CAP
84. THROTTLE POSITION TRANSDUCER LEVER LOCK WASHER
85. THROTTLE POSITION TRANSDUCER BRACKET
86. THROTTLE POSITION TRANSDUCER LEVER
87. THROTTLE POSITION TRANSDUCER ASSEMBLY
88. THROTTLE POSITION TRANSDUCER WIRE ASSEMBLY

12. COVER SCREW
13. NOZZLE BAR SCREW
14. FUEL INLET FITTING GASKET
15. MAIN BODY GASKET
16. NOZZLE BAR GASKET
17. THROTTLE BODY GASKET
18. PUMP HOUSING COVER GASKET
19. THROTTLE PLATE
20. THROTTLE BODY & SHAFT ASSEMBLY
21. THROTTLE RETURN SPRING BUSHINGS
22. IDLE ADJUSTING NEEDLE
23. FLOAT & HINGE ASSEMBLY
24. FLOAT HINGE SHAFT & RETAINER
25. FUEL INLET NEEDLE & SEAT ASSEMBLY
26. NOZZLE BAR ASSEMBLY
27. MAIN JET
28. VENT VALVE
29. POWER VALVE PISTON
30. POWER VALVE ASSEMBLY
31. PUMP CUP
32. PUMP DISCHARGE BALL
33. VENT VALVE LEVER PIN
34. VENT VALVE OPERATING LEVER PIN
35. AIR CLEANER RING RETAINING PIN

38. PUMP STEM LINK
39. PUMP LINK
40. IDLE NEEDLE LIMITER
41. ACCELERATOR PUMP HOUSING COVER

Exploded view of Holley model 2280 carburetor

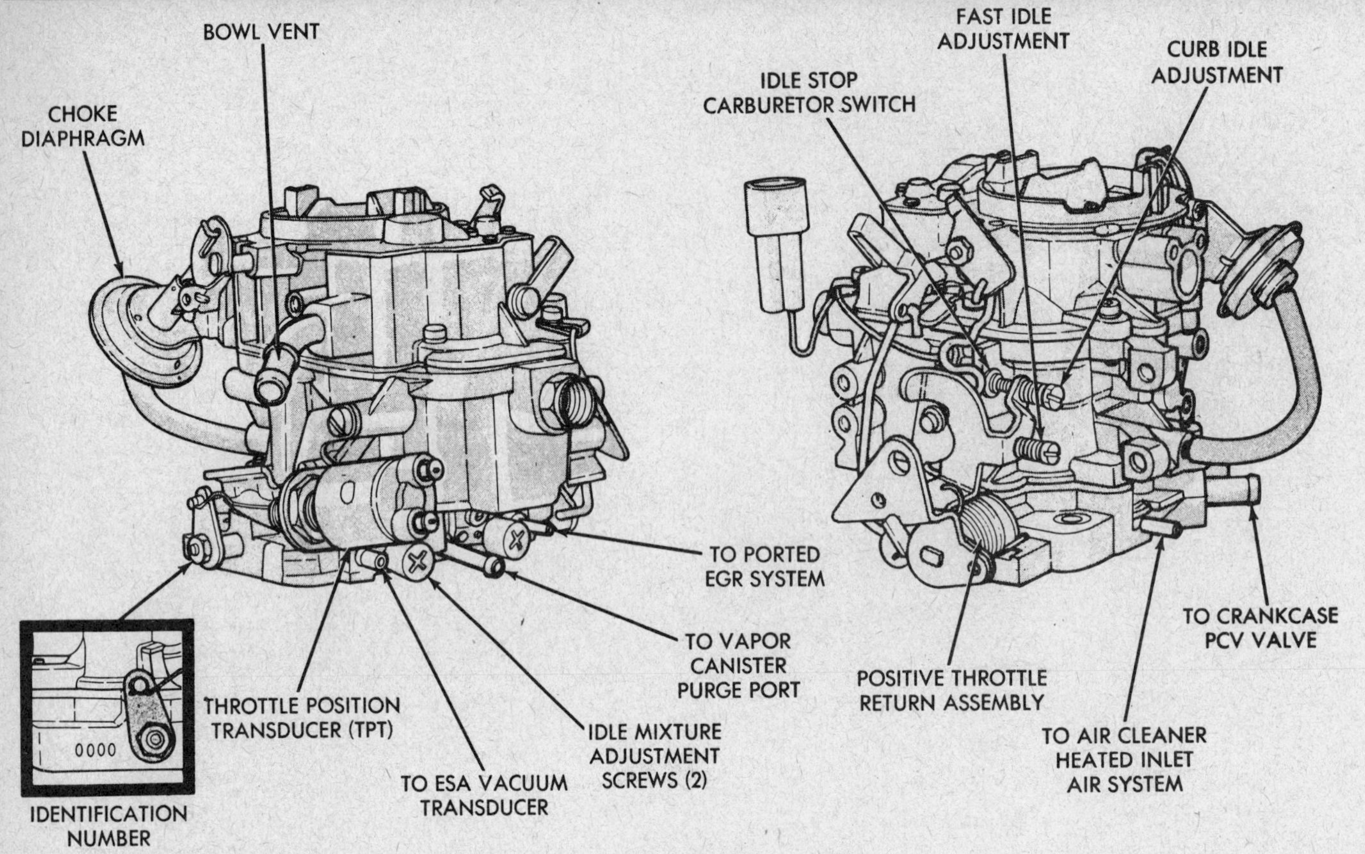

CARBURETORS

CHOKE
DIAPHRAGM

BOWL VENT

IDLE STOP
CARBURETOR SWITCH

FAST IDLE
ADJUSTMENT

CURB IDLE
ADJUSTMENT

TO PORTED
EGR SYSTEM

TO VAPOR
CANISTER
PURGE PORT

THROTTLE POSITION
TRANSDUCER (TPT)

TO ESA VACUUM
TRANSDUCER

IDLE MIXTURE
ADJUSTMENT
SCREWS (2)

IDENTIFICATION
NUMBER

0000

POSITIVE THROTTLE
RETURN ASSEMBLY

TO AIR CLEANER
HEATED INLET
AIR SYSTEM

TO CRANKCASE
PCV VALVE

Fig. 1   Holley model 2280 two barrel carburetor

uum source. Apply closing pressure on choke lever to completely compress spring in diaphragm stem without distorting linkage. The cylindrical stem of the diaphragm extends to a stop as the spring compresses. Insert specified

gauge between top of choke valve and air horn wall. Adjust by bending diaphragm link at U-bend. Check for free movement between the open and adjusted positions.

Fast Idle Cam Position Adjustment

Fig. 6—With fast idle speed adjusting screw contacting second highest step of fast idle cam, move choke valve toward closed position

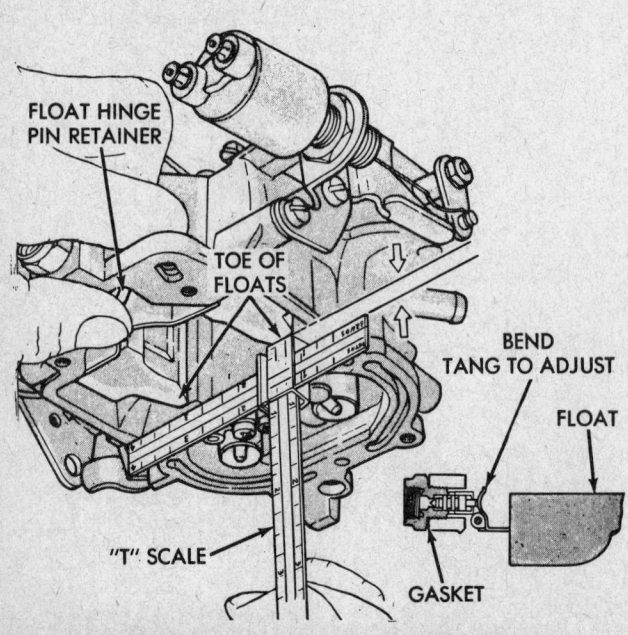

FLOAT HINGE
PIN RETAINER

TOE OF
FLOATS

BEND
TANG TO ADJUST

FLOAT

"T" SCALE

GASKET

Fig. 2   Float adjustment. 2280 carburetor

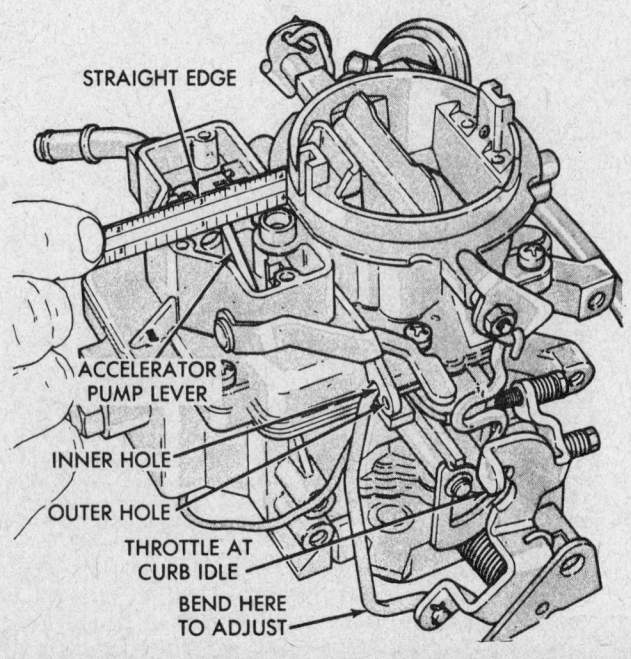

STRAIGHT EDGE

ACCELERATOR
PUMP LEVER

INNER HOLE

OUTER HOLE

THROTTLE AT
CURB IDLE

BEND HERE
TO ADJUST

Fig. 3   Accelerator pump adjustment. 2280 carburetor

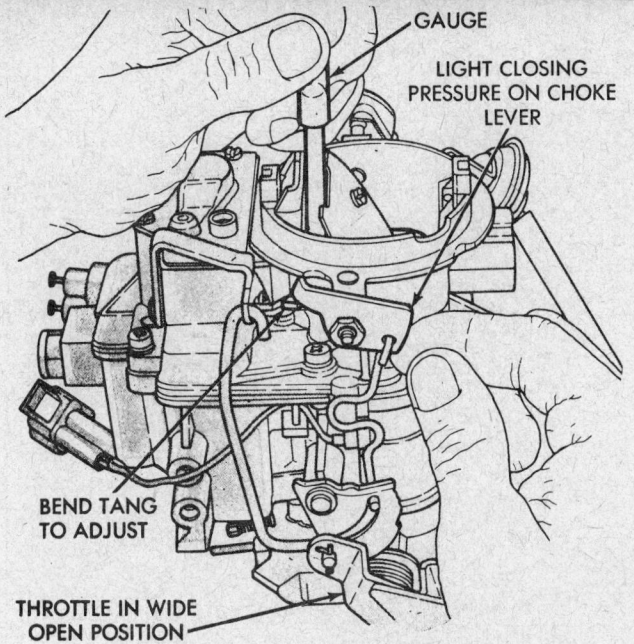

Fig. 4   Choke unloader adjustment. 2280 carburetor

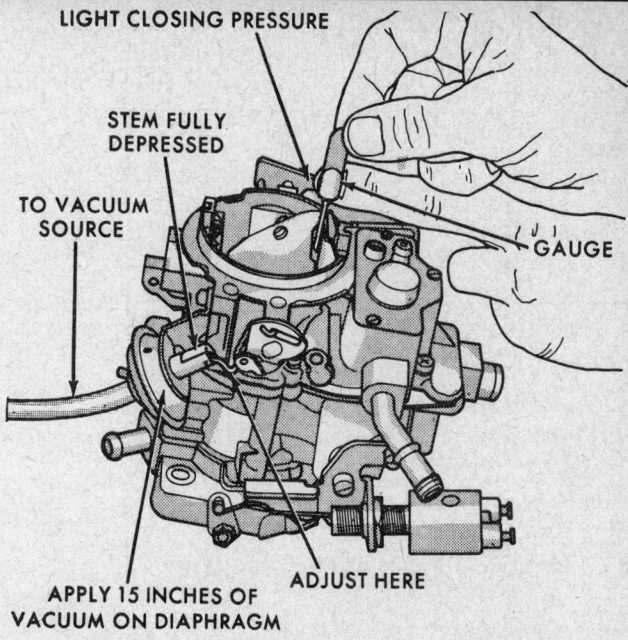

Fig. 5   Choke vacuum kick adjustment. 2280 carburetor

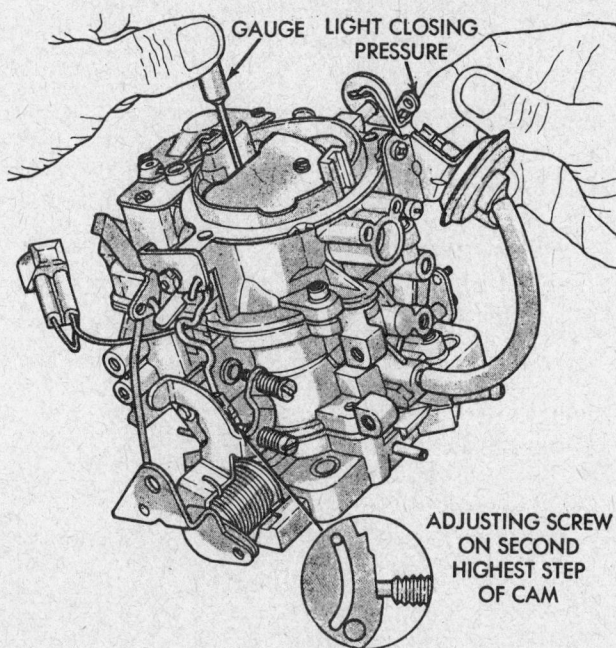

Fig. 6   Fast idle cam position adjustment. 2280 carburetor

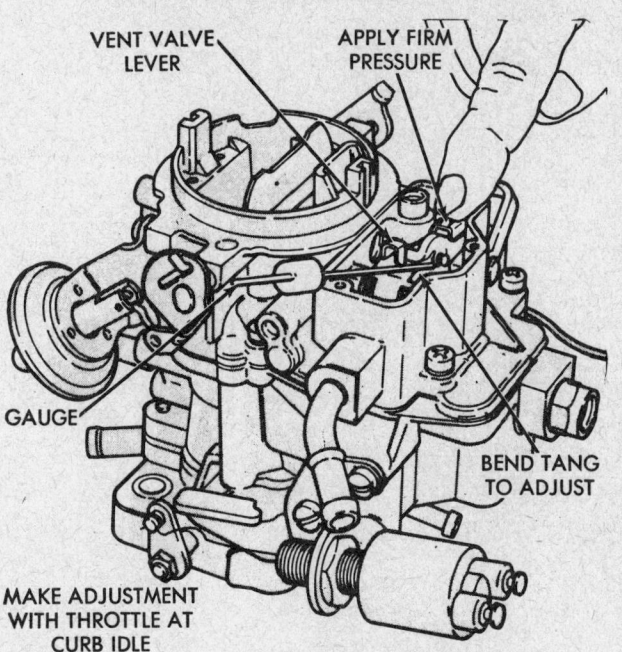

Fig. 7   Bowl vent valve adjustment. 2280 carburetor

with light pressure on choke shaft lever. Insert specified gauge between top of choke valve and air horn wall. To adjust, bend the U-bend in fast idle connector link to obtain proper setting.

Bowl Vent Valve Adjustment

Fig. 7—Remove bowl vent cover plate and vent valve lever spring. Do not dislodge vent valve lever retainer. With throttle at curb idle, press downward on vent valve lever where spring seats. Measure distance between contact surfaces of vent valve tang and vent valve lever. Adjust by bending end of vent valve lever. Install vent valve lever spring and bowl vent cover plate.

Mechanical Power Valve Adjustment

Fig. 8—Remove bowl vent cover plate, vent valve lever spring and retainer, then the vent valve lever and pivot pin. Hold throttle in wide open position. Insert a 5/64 inch allen wrench in mechanical power valve adjustment screw. Push screw downward and release to determine if clearance exists. Turn screw clockwise until zero clearance is obtained. Adjust by turning screw one turn counter-clockwise. Install vent valve lever, pivot pin and retainer, then the vent valve lever spring and bowl vent cover plate.

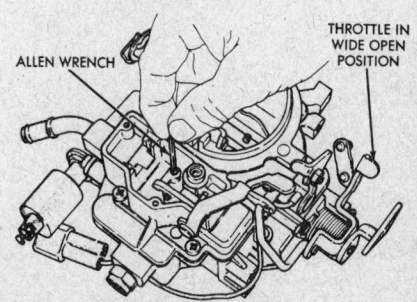

Fig. 8   Mechanical power valve adjustment. 2280 carburetor

4180-C CARB. ADJUSTMENT SPECIFICATIONS

See Tune Up Chart in car chapter for curb and fast idle speeds.

Year	Carb. Part No.	Float Level (Dry)	Fuel Level (Wet)	Accel. Pump	Dechoke Clearance	Pulldown Setting	Choke Setting
1983	E3ZE-AUA	①	②	—	.300	.205	3 Rich
	E3ZE-AUB	①	②	—	.300	.205	3 Rich
	E3ZE-BGA	①	②	—	.300	.205	3 Rich
	E3ZE-BGB	①	②	—	.300	.205	3 Rich

①—Refer to text.　②—Bottom of sight plug.

MODEL 4180-C

The Holley Model 4180-C, Figs. 1, 2 and 3, is a four barrel, downdraft, two-stage carburetor. This unit can be considered as two dual carburetors, one which supplies an air/fuel mixture throughout the entire engine operating range (primary stage), and the other which functions only when a greater quantity of air/fuel mixture is needed (secondary stage).

The primary stage contains a fuel bowl, metering block and accelerating pump assembly. Each primary barrel contains a primary and booster venturi, throttle plate, main fuel discharge nozzle and idle fuel passage.

The secondary stage contains a fuel bowl, metering body and secondary throttle operating diaphragm assembly. The secondary barrels each contain a primary and booster venturi, throttle plate, idle fuel passages, main secondary fuel discharge nozzle and a transfer system fuel passage from the primary fuel bowl.

A constant fuel supply is provided to fuel metering systems by a fuel inlet system for both primary and secondary stages. A fuel balance tube is not used.

Float Level (Dry) Adjustment

Fig. 4—This is a preliminary adjustment only, and final adjustment must be made after carburetor is installed on engine.

With float assemblies and fuel bowls removed, adjust floats so they are parallel to the fuel bowls with the tops of the fuel bowls inverted.

Fuel Level (Wet) Adjustment

1. With vehicle resting on a flat surface, operate engine until normal operating

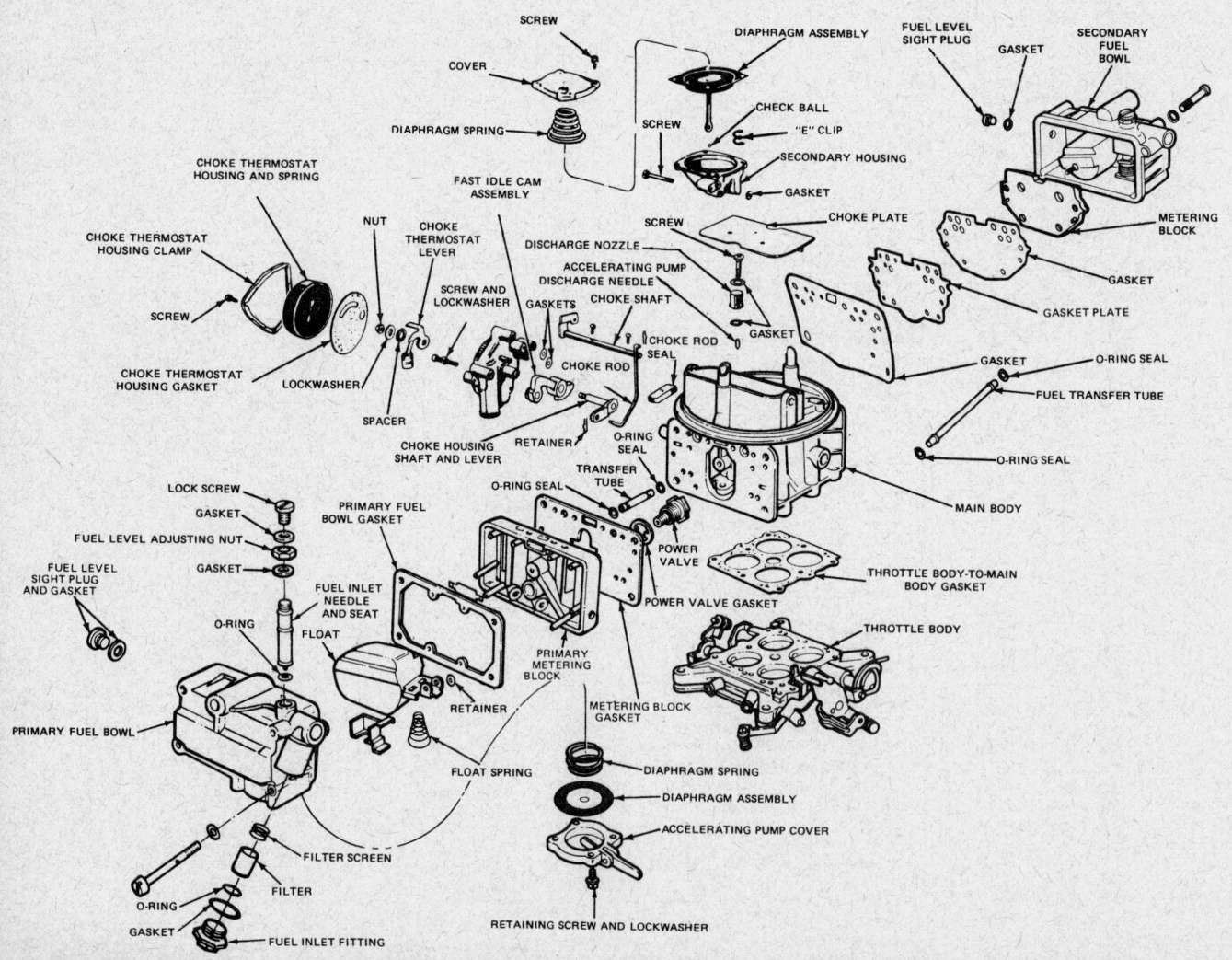

Fig. 1 Exploded view of Holley model 4180-C carburetor

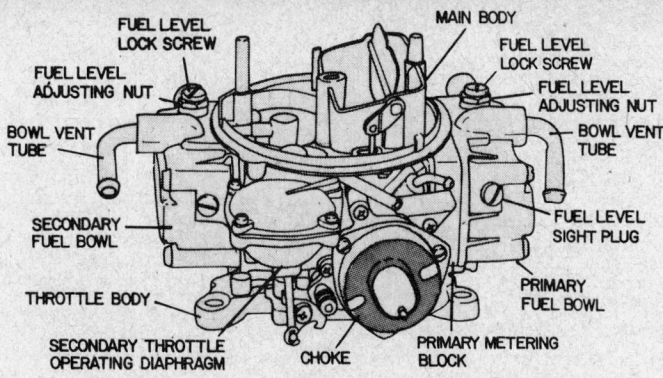

Fig. 2 Right side view of Holley model 4180-C carburetor

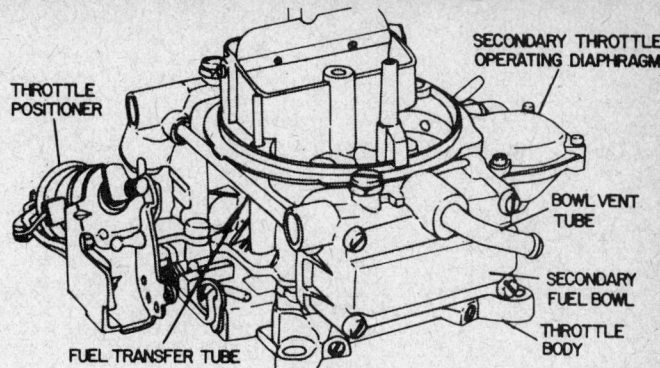

Fig. 3 Left side view of Holley model 4180-C carburetor

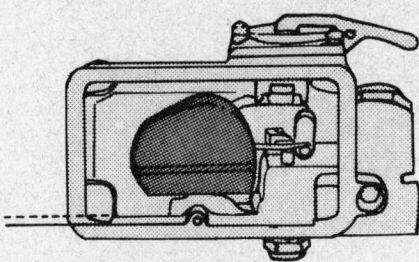

TURN ADJUSTING NUT UNTIL FLOAT IS PARALLEL WITH TOP OF BOWL (HOLDING BOWL UPSIDE DOWN)

Fig. 4 Dry float level adjustment

NOTE: Never loosen lock screw or nut or attempt to adjust fuel level with sight plug removed or engine running, as this will create a potential fire hazard.

5. Adjust fuel level as necessary by loosening lock screw, then turning adjusting nut clockwise to lower fuel level or counterclockwise to raise fuel level, Fig. 5. Tighten lock screw and install sight plug, using old gasket, then run engine at 1000 rpm for approximately 30 seconds to stabilize fuel level.

NOTE: Each 1/6 turn of the adjusting nut will change fuel level approximately 1/32 inch.

6. Stop engine, remove sight plug and recheck fuel level. Repeat step 5 until fuel level is at bottom of sight plug hole, then reinstall sight plug using a new gasket.
7. Perform steps 3 through 6 for secondary fuel bowl.

NOTE: To stabilize fuel level in the secondary fuel bowl, the secondary throttle must be used.

Accelerating Pump Lever Adjustment

Fig. 6—With throttle plates in the wide open position, and pump arm manually depressed, insert a feeler gauge of the specified thickness between operating lever adjustment screw head and pump arm. Refer to 4180-C Carburetor Adjustment Specifications Chart. Adjust clearance as necessary by loosening the lock screw, then turning the adjusting nut while holding the screw. Turn the adjusting nut in to increase clearance or out to decrease clearance. When proper clearance is obtained, hold nut and tighten screw. Note that 1/2 turn of the adjusting nut is equal to approximately .015 inch.

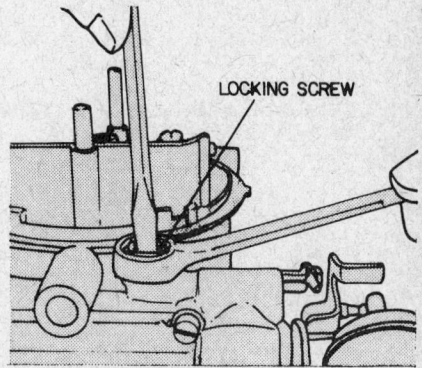

LOCKING SCREW

Fig. 5 Wet fuel level adjustment

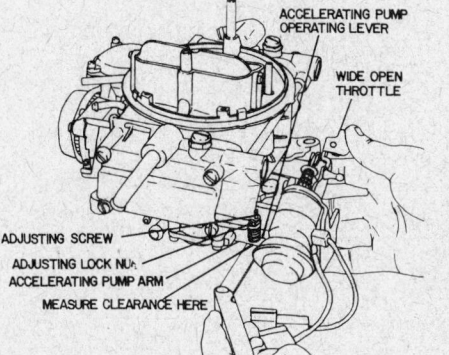

Fig. 6 Accelerating pump lever adjustment

temperature is reached.
2. Remove air cleaner, then operate engine at approximately 1000 rpm for 30 seconds to stabilize fuel level.
3. Stop engine, then remove sight plug from side of primary carburetor bowl.
4. Fuel level should be at bottom of sight plug hole. If fuel level is below sight plug hole, raise fuel level. If fuel overflows when plug is removed, lower fuel level.

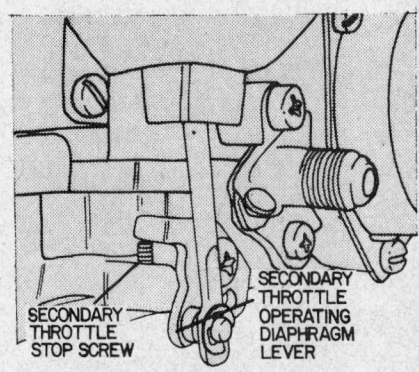

Fig. 7 Secondary throttle plate adjustment

Secondary Throttle Plate Adjustment

Fig. 7—With carburetor removed from engine, hold secondary throttle plates closed, then turn secondary throttle shaft lever adjusting screw out until throttle plates seat in throttle bores. Turn adjusting screw in until it just makes contact with secondary lever, then turn screw in an additional 1/4 turn.

CARBURETORS

5210 CARB. ADJUSTMENT SPECIFICATIONS

See Tune Up Chart in car chapter for curb and fast idle speeds.

Year	Carb. Part No.	Float Level (Dry)	Float Drop	Pump Position	Fast Idle Cam Index	Vacuum Plate Pulldown	Vacuum Break Primary	Vacuum Break Secondary	Unloader Setting	Choke Setting
AMERICAN MOTORS										
1977	7711	.420	—	—	.140	.246	—	—	.300	1 Rich
	7712	.420	—	—	.140	.246	—	—	.300	1 Rich
	7799	.420	—	—	.135	.215	—	—	.300	Index
	7846	.420	—	—	.101	.204	—	—	.300	1 Rich
1978	7846	.420	—	—	.177	.180	—	—	.300	Index
	8163	.420	—	—	.193	.191	—	—	.300	1 Rich
	8164	.420	—	—	.204	.202	—	—	.300	1 Rich
	8165	.420	—	—	.101	.284	—	—	.300	1 Rich
1979	7846	.420	—	—	.193	.191	—	—	.300	1 Rich
	8548	.420	—	—	.204	.191	—	—	.300	1 Rich
	8549	.420	—	—	.191	.266	—	—	.300	1 Rich
	8675	.420	—	—	.173	.177	—	—	.300	Index
GENERAL MOTORS										
1977	458102, 04	.420	1"	①	.120	—	.250	—	.350	3 Rich
	458103, 05	.420	1"	①	.120	—	.250	—	.350	3 Rich
	458106, 08	.420	1"	#1	.120	—	.275	—	.400	3 Rich
	458107, 09	.420	1"	#2	.160	—	.275	.400	.350	3 Rich
	458110, 12	.420	1"	#1	.160	—	.325	.400	.350	3 Rich
	527200, 02	.520	1"	#2	.150	—	.300	—	.400	4 Rich
	527201, 03	.520	1"	#2	.150	—	.325	—	.400	4 Rich
	527204, 06	.520	1"	#2	.150	—	.325	—	.400	2 Rich
1978	10001047	.520	1"	—	.150	—	.325	.400	.350	1 Rich
	10001048	.520	1"	—	.150	—	.300	.400	.350	2 Rich
	10001049	.520	1"	—	.150	—	.325	.400	.350	1 Rich
	10001050	.520	1"	—	.150	—	.300	.400	.350	2 Rich
	10001052	.520	1"	—	.150	—	.325	.400	.350	2 Rich
	10001054	.520	1"	—	.150	—	.325	.400	.350	2 Rich
	10004048	.520	1"	—	.150	—	.300	—	.350	2 Rich
	10004049	.520	1"	—	.150	—	.300	—	.350	2 Rich
1979	466361	.500	—	—	.110	—	.250	—	.350	2 Rich
	466362	.500	—	—	.110	—	.250	—	.350	2 Rich
	466363	.500	—	—	.110	—	.250	—	.350	2 Rich
	466364	.500	—	—	.110	—	.250	—	.350	2 Rich
	466365	.500	—	—	.130	—	.305	—	.350	1 Rich
	466366	.500	—	—	.130	—	.305	—	.350	1 Rich
	466367	.500	—	—	.130	—	.305	—	.350	1 Rich
	466368	.500	—	—	.130	—	.305	—	.350	1 Rich
	466369	.500	—	—	.110	—	.245	—	.350	2 Rich
	466370	.500	—	—	.110	—	.250	—	.350	2 Rich
	466371	.500	—	—	.110	—	.245	—	.350	2 Rich
	466372	.500	—	—	.110	—	.250	—	.350	2 Rich
	466373	.500	—	—	.130	—	.305	—	.350	1 Rich
	466374	.500	—	—	.130	—	.305	—	.350	1 Rich
	466375	.500	—	—	.130	—	.305	—	.350	1 Rich
	466376	.500	—	—	.130	—	.305	—	.350	1 Rich
1980	14004461	.500	—	—	.110	—	.120	—	.350	—
	14004462	.500	—	—	.110	—	.120	—	.350	—
	14004463	.500	—	—	.110	—	.120	—	.350	—
	14004464	.500	—	—	.110	—	.120	—	.350	—
	14004465	.500	—	—	.110	—	.120	—	.350	—

Continued

5210 CARB. ADJUSTMENT SPECIFICATIONS—continued

See Tune Up Chart in car chapter for curb and fast idle speeds.

Year	Carb. Part No.	Float Level (Dry)	Float Drop	Pump Position	Fast Idle Cam Index	Vacuum Plate Pulldown	Vacuum Break		Unloader Setting	Choke Setting
							Primary	Secondary		
	14004466	.500	—	—	.110	—	.120	—	.350	—
	14004467	.500	—	—	.110	—	.120	—	.350	—
	14004468	.500	—	—	.110	—	.120	—	.350	—

①—Manual trans., #2; auto. trans., #1.

MODEL 5210

The Holley 5210 two–barrel carburetor, Figs. 1 and 2, has a number of unique features. An automatic choke system activated by a water heated bi-metal thermostatic coil and a primary venturi smaller in size than the secondary venturi.

An Exhaust Gas Recirculation (EGR) system is used on all applications with the EGR valve located in the intake manifold.

Carburetors used on 1977–78 vehicles use a primary and secondary vacuum break. The secondary vacuum break is used on some vehicles.

Float Adjustment

Fig. 3—With the air horn inverted and the float tang resting lightly on the spring loaded fuel inlet needle, measure the clearance between the bowl cover and the end of each float. Refer to *Holley 5210 Specifications Chart*. Adjust by bending the float tang as required.

SOLENOID ASSISTED BOWL VENT — IDLE SOLENOID

ELECTRIC CHOKE

CHOKE VACUUM BREAK

CURB IDLE ADJUSTMENT SCREW — SOLENOID ADJUSTMENT SCREW

HOT IDLE COMPENSATOR

Fig. 1   Holley 5210 2 barrel carburetor

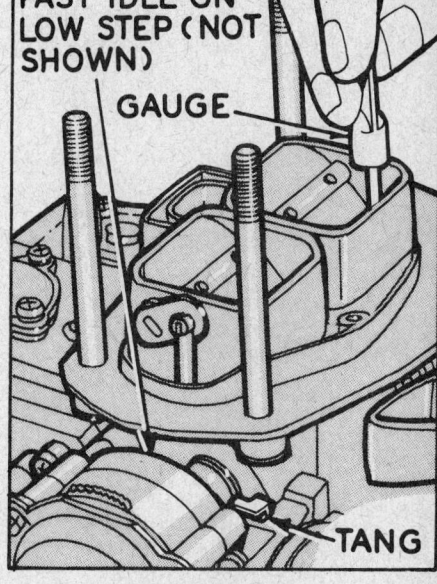

FAST IDLE ON LOW STEP (NOT SHOWN)

GAUGE

TANG

Fig. 4   Fast idle cam index adjustment 5210 Holley carburetor

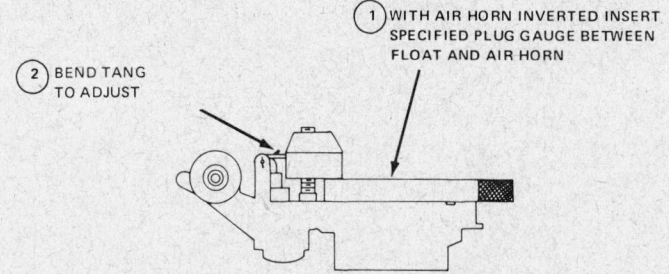

① WITH AIR HORN INVERTED INSERT SPECIFIED PLUG GAUGE BETWEEN FLOAT AND AIR HORN

② BEND TANG TO ADJUST

Fig. 3   Checking float level on 5210 carburetor

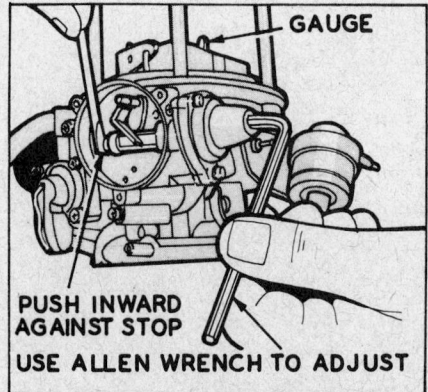

GAUGE

PUSH INWARD AGAINST STOP

USE ALLEN WRENCH TO ADJUST

Fig. 5   Vacuum pull down adjustment 5210 Holley carburetor

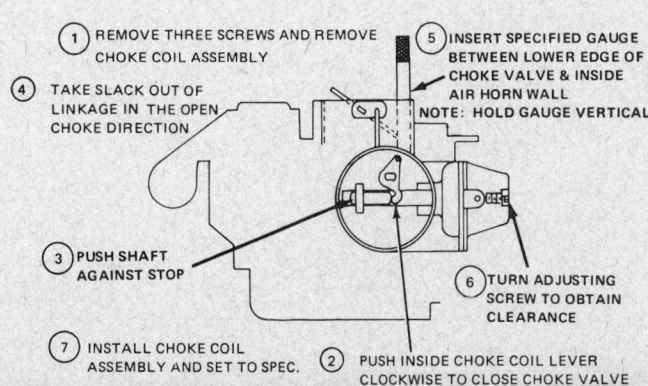

① REMOVE THREE SCREWS AND REMOVE CHOKE COIL ASSEMBLY

④ TAKE SLACK OUT OF LINKAGE IN THE OPEN CHOKE DIRECTION

③ PUSH SHAFT AGAINST STOP

⑦ INSTALL CHOKE COIL ASSEMBLY AND SET TO SPEC.

⑤ INSERT SPECIFIED GAUGE BETWEEN LOWER EDGE OF CHOKE VALVE & INSIDE AIR HORN WALL
NOTE: HOLD GAUGE VERTICAL

⑥ TURN ADJUSTING SCREW TO OBTAIN CLEARANCE

② PUSH INSIDE CHOKE COIL LEVER CLOCKWISE TO CLOSE CHOKE VALVE

Fig. 5A   Primary vacuum break adjustment 5210 Holley carburetor

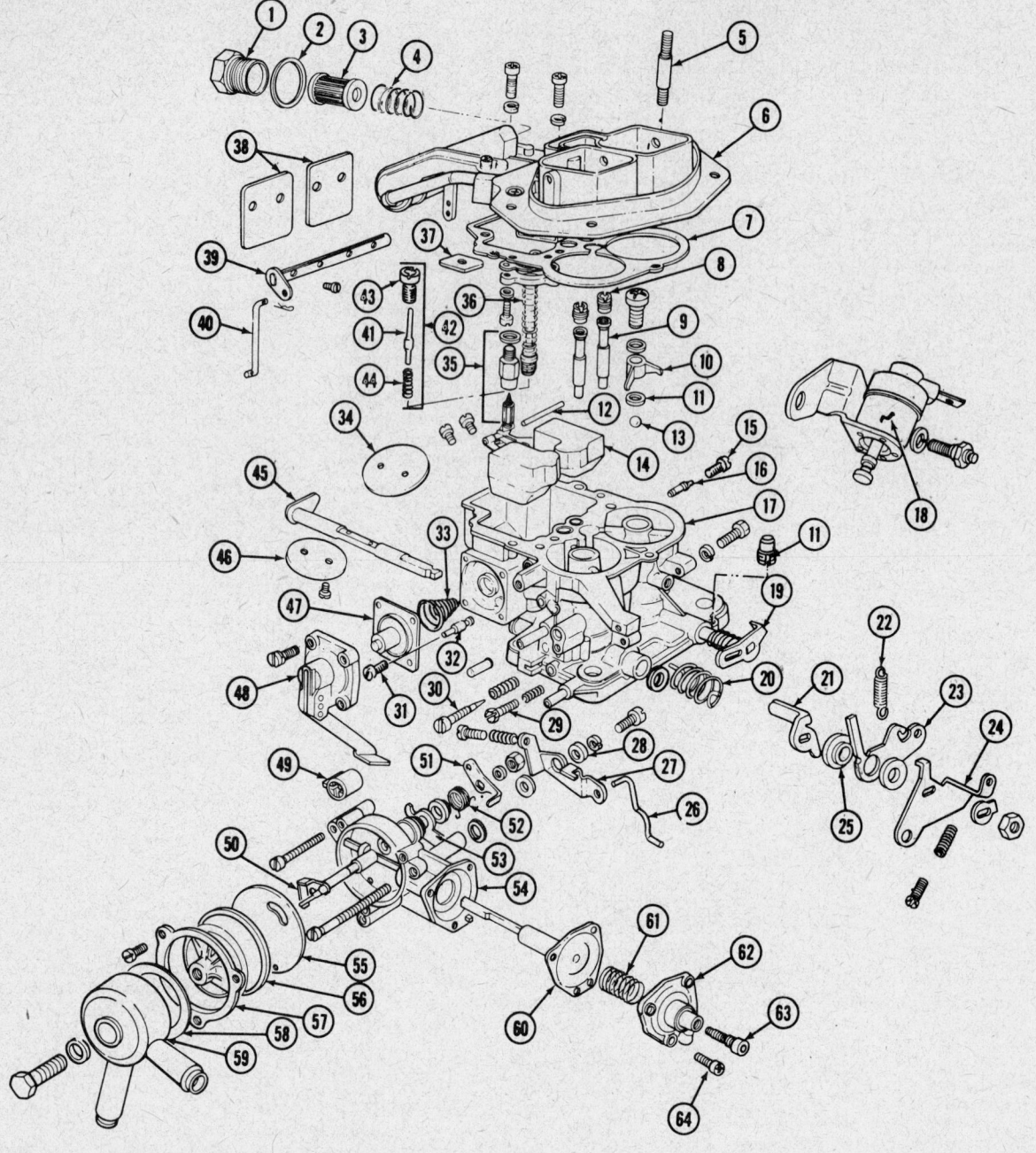

1. Fuel Inlet Nut
2. Gasket
3. Filter
4. Spring
5. Studs, Air Cleaner
   Attachment
6. Air Horn
7. Gasket
8. High Speed Bleed
9. Main Well Tube
10. Pump Discharge Nozzle
11. Gasket
12. Float Shaft
13. Discharge Check Ball
14. Float
15. Retainer
16. Secondary Idle Jet
17. Carburetor Body Assembly

18. Idle Stop Solenoid
19. Secondary Throttle Lever
20. Throttle Return Spring
21. Idle Lever
22. Secondary Operating Lever
    Return Spring
23. Secondary Operating Lever
24. Throttle Lever
25. Bushing
26. Fast Idle Rod
27. Fast Idle Lever
28. Bushing
29. Low Idle Screw
30. Fuel Mixture Screw
31. Retainer
32. Primary Idle Jet
33. Return Spring

34. Secondary Throttle Plate
35. Fuel Inlet Needle
    and Seat Assembly
36. Power Valve
    Economizer Assembly
37. Choke Rod Seal
38. Choke Plates
39. Choke Shaft and Lever
40. Choke Rod
41. Power Valve
42. Power Valve Assembly
43. Seat
44. Spring
45. Primary Throttle Shaft
    and Lever Assembly
46. Primary Throttle Plate
47. Accelerator Pump

48. Accelerator Pump Cover
49. Mixture Screw Limiter Cap
50. Choke Housing Shaft
51. Choke Lever
52. Fast Idle Cam Spring
53. Fast Idle Cam
54. Choke Housing
55. Gasket
56. Thermostatic Housing
57. Retainer
58. Gasket
59. Water Cover
60. Diaphragm and Shaft
61. Return Spring
62. Choke Diaphragm Cover
63. Hex Head Screw
64. Cover Screw

Fig. 2 Exploded view of a typical Holley 5210 carburetor

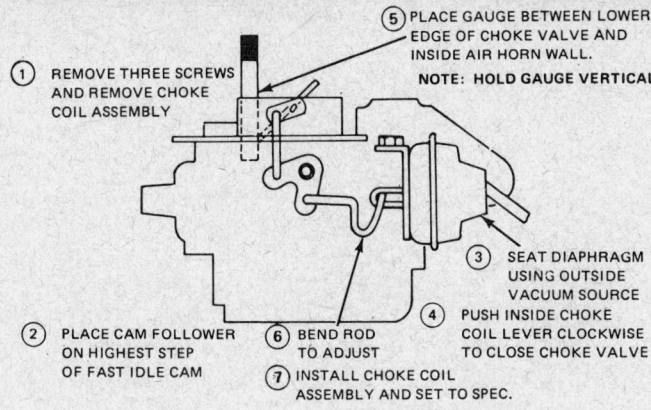

Fig. 5B Secondary vacuum break adjustment 5210 Holley carburetor

① REMOVE THREE SCREWS AND REMOVE CHOKE COIL ASSEMBLY

② PLACE CAM FOLLOWER ON HIGHEST STEP OF FAST IDLE CAM

⑤ PLACE GAUGE BETWEEN LOWER EDGE OF CHOKE VALVE AND INSIDE AIR HORN WALL.
NOTE: HOLD GAUGE VERTICAL

⑥ BEND ROD TO ADJUST

⑦ INSTALL CHOKE COIL ASSEMBLY AND SET TO SPEC.

③ SEAT DIAPHRAGM USING OUTSIDE VACUUM SOURCE

④ PUSH INSIDE CHOKE COIL LEVER CLOCKWISE TO CLOSE CHOKE VALVE

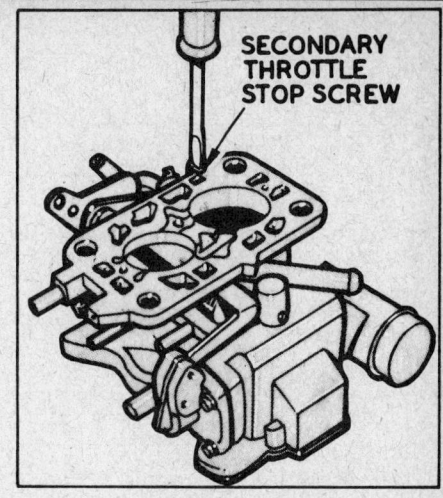

SECONDARY THROTTLE STOP SCREW

Fig. 6 Secondary throttle plate adjustment

FAST IDLE SPEED ADJUSTING SCREW

Fig. 7 Fast idle adjustment 5210 Holley carburetor

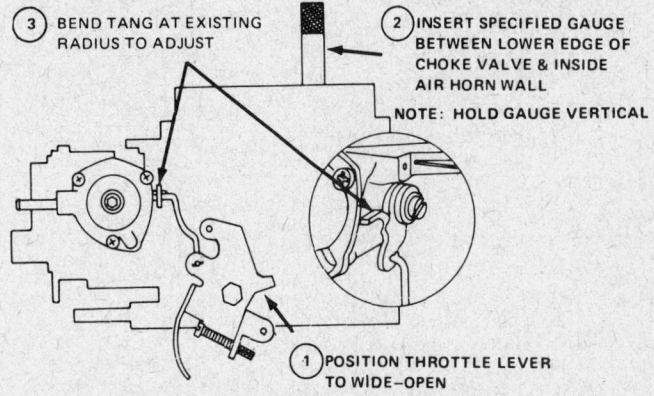

③ BEND TANG AT EXISTING RADIUS TO ADJUST

② INSERT SPECIFIED GAUGE BETWEEN LOWER EDGE OF CHOKE VALVE & INSIDE AIR HORN WALL
NOTE: HOLD GAUGE VERTICAL

① POSITION THROTTLE LEVER TO WIDE-OPEN

Fig. 8 Unloader adjustment. 1977–79 units

Fast Idle Cam Index Adjustment

Fig. 4—Place the fast idle screw on the second step of the fast idle cam and against the shoulder of the first step. Place a drill or gauge on the down stream side of the choke plate. Refer to *5210 Specifications Chart*. Adjust by bending the choke lever tang.

Vacuum Plate Pulldown Adjustment

Fig. 5—Remove the three hex headed screws and ring retaining the choke bimetal cover. Do not remove the choke water housing screw if adjusting on the car. Pull the choke water housing and bimetal cover assembly out of the way. With a screwdriver or suitable tool, push the diaphragm stem back against the stop. Place drill or gauge on the down stream side of the primary choke plate. Take all the slack out of the linkage. Refer to *5210 Specifications Chart*. Adjust by turning adjusting screw in or out with an 5/32 inch Allen wrench.

Vacuum Break

Primary, 1977–80
Fig. 5A—Remove choke coil assembly, then push inside choke coil lever clockwise to close choke valve and push shaft against stop to remove slack from linkage in open choke direction. Refer to 5210 Specifications Chart and insert specified gauge between lower edge of choke valve and inside air horn wall. Adjust by turning screw to obtain clearance.

Secondary, 1977–78
Fig. 5B—Remove choke coil assembly and place cam follower on highest step of fast idle cam. Using an outside vacuum source, seat diaphragm, then push inside choke coil lever clockwise to close choke valve. Refer to 5210 Specifications Chart and insert specified gauge between lower edge of choke valve and inside air horn wall. To adjust, bend rod.

Secondary Throttle Plate Adjustment

Fig. 6—Back out the secondary throttle stop screw, until the secondary throttle plate seats in the carburetor bore. Turn screw in until it makes contact with tab on the secondary throttle lever, then turn screw in an additional 1/4 turn.

Fast Idle Adjustment

Fig. 7—With engine at operating temperature, air cleaner off, choke off, A/C off and EGR valve free to operate, position fast idle screw on second step of fast idle cam and adjust by turning fast idle screw in or out. Refer to 5210 Specifications Chart.

Unloader (Dechoke) Adjustment

1977–80 Units
Fig. 8—Position throttle in wide open position and insert specified gauge between lower edge of choke valve and air horn wall. To adjust, bend fast idle lever tang.

CARBURETORS

MODEL 5220 ADJUSTMENT SPECIFICATIONS

See Tune Up Chart in car chapters for curb and fast idle speeds.

Year	Model No.	Float Level	Float Drop	Acc. Pump Hole No.	Choke Vacuum Kick	Choke Setting
1978	R-8376A	.480	1⅞″	2	.070	2 Rich
	R-8384A	.480	1⅞″	2	.070	2 Rich
	R-8385A	.480	1⅞″	2	.070	2 Rich
	R-8386A	.480	1⅞″	2	.070	2 Rich
	R-8387A	.480	1⅞″	2	.070	2 Rich
	R-8504A	.480	1⅞″	2	.070	2 Rich
	R-8505A	.480	1⅞″	2	.070	2 Rich
	R-8506A	.480	1⅞″	2	.070	2 Rich
	R-8507A	.480	1⅞″	2	.070	2 Rich
	R-8630A	.480	1⅞″	2	.070	2 Rich
	R-8631A	.480	1⅞″	2	.070	2 Rich
	R-8632A	.480	1⅞″	2	.070	2 Rich
1979	R-8451A	.480	1⅞″	2	.070	2 Rich
	R-8524A	.480	1⅞″	2	.040	2 Rich
	R-8525A	.480	1⅞″	2	.070	2 Rich
	R-8526A	.480	1⅞″	2	.040	2 Rich
	R-8527A	.480	1⅞″	2	.070	2 Rich
	R-8528A	.480	1⅞″	2	.040	2 Rich
	R-8529A	.480	1⅞″	2	.070	2 Rich
	R-8530A	.480	1⅞″	2	.040	2 Rich
	R-9026A	.480	1⅞″	2	.040	2 Rich
	R-9028A	.480	1⅞″	2	.040	2 Rich
1980	R-8676A	.480	1⅞″	2	.070	①
	R-8840A	.480	1⅞″	2	.070	①
	R-8841A	.480	1⅞″	2	.040	①
	R-8842A	.480	1⅞″	2	.040	①
	R-9108A	.480	1⅞″	2	.070	①
	R-9109A	.480	1⅞″	2	.100	①
	R-911A	.480	1⅞″	2	.040	①
	R-9395A	.480	1⅞″	2	.070	①
	R-9396A	.480	1⅞″	2	.070	①
	R-9397A	.480	1⅞″	2	.040	①
	R-9398A	.480	1⅞″	2	.040	①
1982	R-9582A	.480	1⅞	3	.060	①
	R-9583A	.480	1⅞	3	.060	①
	R-9584A	.480	1⅞	3	.060	①
	R-9585A	.480	1⅞	3	.060	①
1983	R-40020A	.480	1⅞	3	.055	①
	R-40022A	.480	1⅞	3	.055	①

①—Tamper-resistant.

MODEL 5220

The Holley model 5220, Figs. 1 and 2, is a staged dual venturi carburetor. The primary bore or venturi is smaller than the secondary bore. The secondary stage is mechanically operated by linkage connecting the primary and secondary throttle levers. The primary stage includes a curb idle and transfer system, diaphragm type accelerator pump system, main metering system and power enrichment system. The secondary stage includes a main metering system and power system. Both the primary and secondary venturi draw fuel from a common fuel bowl. The electric automatic choke has a bimetal two stage heating element. The carburetor also has an electronic solenoid and a vacuum operated bowl vent.

Float Level Adjustment

Figs. 3 & 4—Invert air horn and insert specified gauge between float and air horn. To adjust, use a small screwdriver to bend tang.

Float Drop Adjustment

Figs. 5 & 6—Using a suitable depth gauge, measure float drop. To adjust, use a small screwdriver to bend tang.

Choke Vacuum Kick Adjustment

Fig. 7—Open throttle, close choke, then close throttle to trap fast idle system in closed choke position. Using an external vacuum source, apply 15 inches of vacuum to choke diaphragm. Apply closing pressure to position choke at smallest opening without distorting linkage. An internal spring will compress to a stop inside choke system. Insert specified gauge between upper edge of choke valve and air horn wall at primary throttle end of carburetor. To adjust, rotate allen head screw in center of diaphragm housing.

Fast Idle Speed Adjustment

Fig. 8—Remove top of air cleaner and eliminate EGR signal. Cap or plug all disconnected vacuum fittings. Do not disconnect vacuum

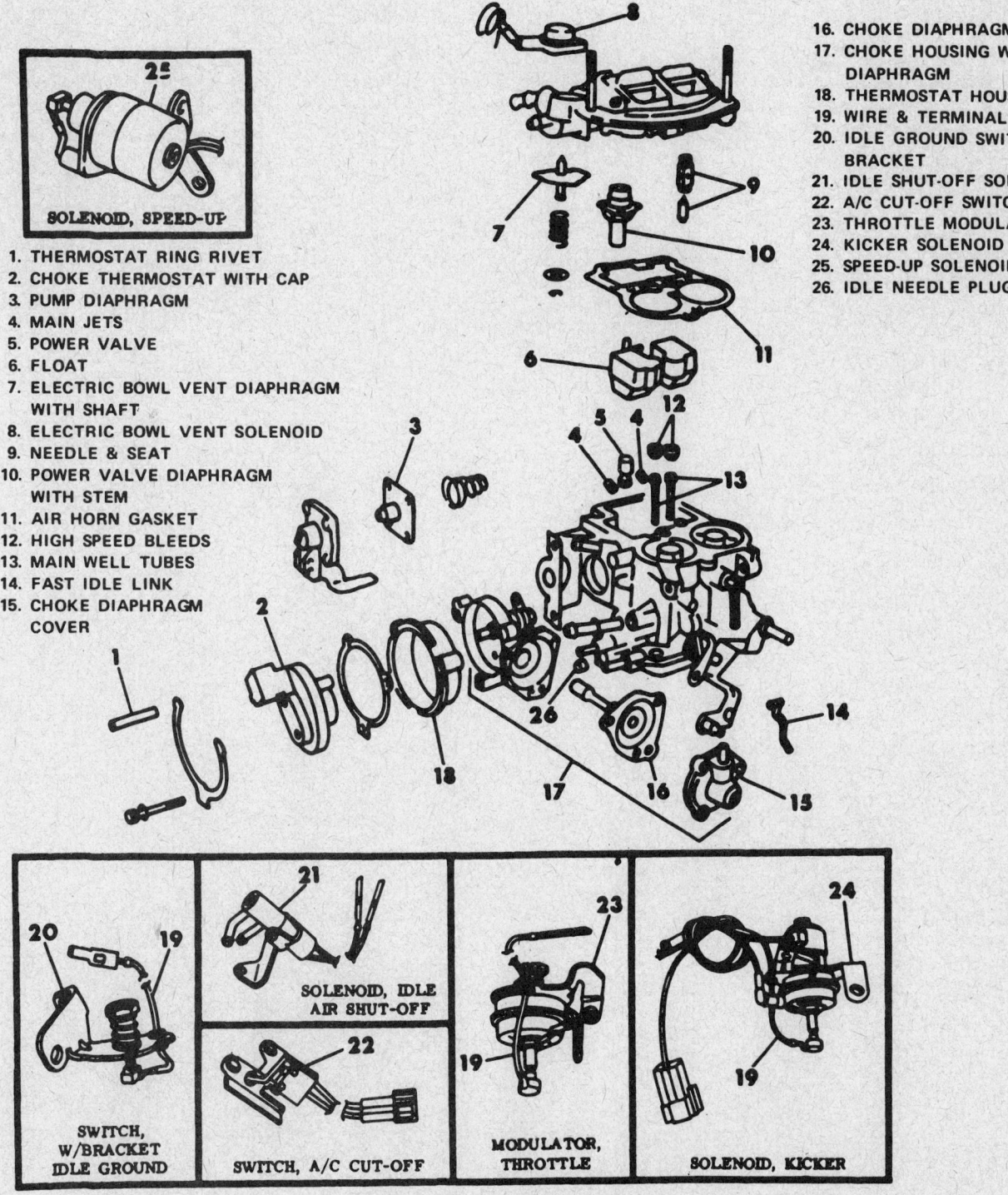

SOLENOID, SPEED-UP

1. THERMOSTAT RING RIVET
2. CHOKE THERMOSTAT WITH CAP
3. PUMP DIAPHRAGM
4. MAIN JETS
5. POWER VALVE
6. FLOAT
7. ELECTRIC BOWL VENT DIAPHRAGM WITH SHAFT
8. ELECTRIC BOWL VENT SOLENOID
9. NEEDLE & SEAT
10. POWER VALVE DIAPHRAGM WITH STEM
11. AIR HORN GASKET
12. HIGH SPEED BLEEDS
13. MAIN WELL TUBES
14. FAST IDLE LINK
15. CHOKE DIAPHRAGM COVER

16. CHOKE DIAPHRAGM
17. CHOKE HOUSING WITH DIAPHRAGM
18. THERMOSTAT HOUSING
19. WIRE & TERMINAL
20. IDLE GROUND SWITCH WITH BRACKET
21. IDLE SHUT-OFF SOLENOID
22. A/C CUT-OFF SWITCH
23. THROTTLE MODULATOR
24. KICKER SOLENOID
25. SPEED-UP SOLENOID
26. IDLE NEEDLE PLUG

SWITCH, W/BRACKET IDLE GROUND

SOLENOID, IDLE AIR SHUT-OFF

SWITCH, A/C CUT-OFF

MODULATOR, THROTTLE

SOLENOID, KICKER

Exploded view of Holley model 5220 carburetor

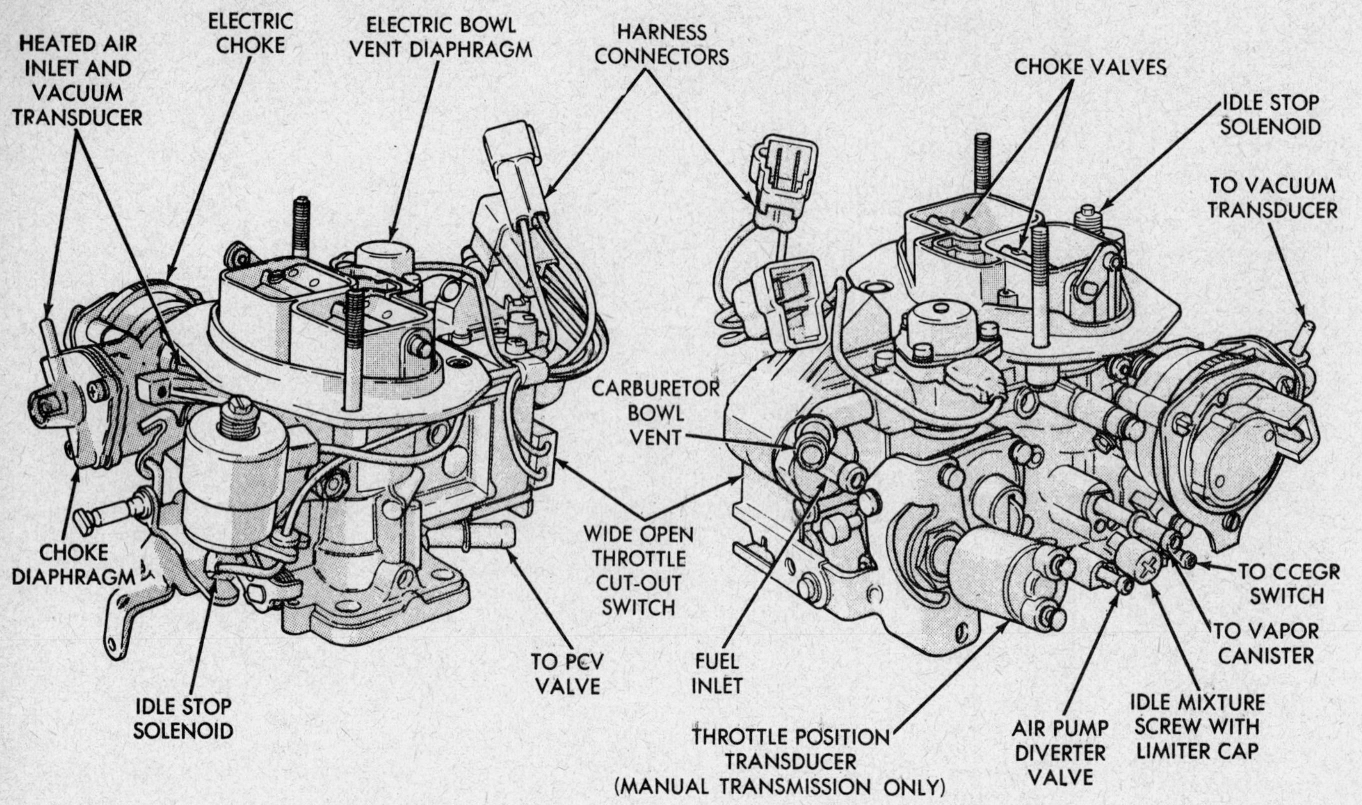

CARBURETORS

HEATED AIR INLET AND VACUUM TRANSDUCER

ELECTRIC CHOKE

ELECTRIC BOWL VENT DIAPHRAGM

HARNESS CONNECTORS

CHOKE VALVES

IDLE STOP SOLENOID

TO VACUUM TRANSDUCER

CARBURETOR BOWL VENT

WIDE OPEN THROTTLE CUT-OUT SWITCH

TO PCV VALVE

FUEL INLET

THROTTLE POSITION TRANSDUCER (MANUAL TRANSMISSION ONLY)

AIR PUMP DIVERTER VALVE

IDLE MIXTURE SCREW WITH LIMITER CAP

TO CCEGR SWITCH

TO VAPOR CANISTER

CHOKE DIAPHRAGM

IDLE STOP SOLENOID

Fig. 1 Holley model 5220 carburetor. Vehicles equipped with air conditioning (Typical)

HEATED AIR INLET AND VACUUM TRANSDUCER

ELECTRIC CHOKE

ELECTRIC BOWL VENT DIAPHRAGM

HARNESS CONNECTORS

CHOKE VALVES

IDLE STOP SOLENOID

TO VACUUM TRANSDUCER

CARBURETOR BOWL VENT

FUEL INLET

TO PCV VALVE

CHOKE DIAPHRAGM

IDLE STOP SOLENOID

THROTTLE POSITION TRANSDUCER (MANUAL TRANSMISSION ONLY)

AIR PUMP DIVERTER VALVE

IDLE MIXTURE SCREW WITH LIMITER CAP

TO CCEGR SWITCH

TO VAPOR CANISTER

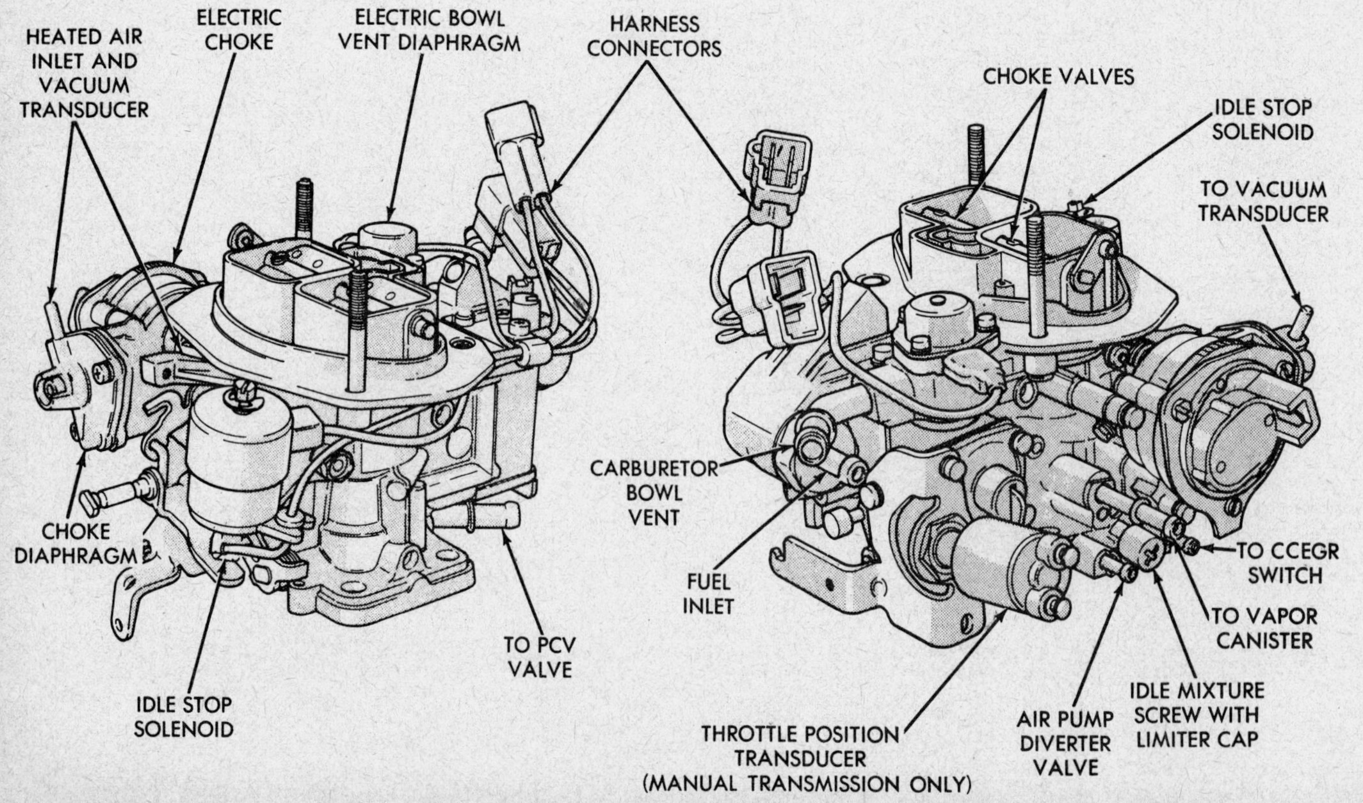

Fig. 2 Holley model 5220 carburetor. Vehicles less air conditioning (Typical)

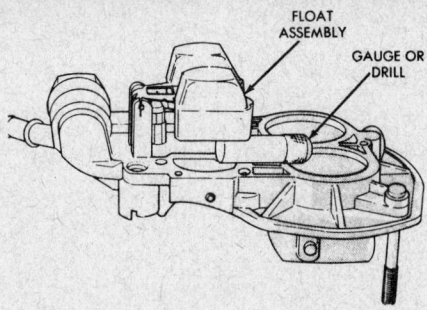

Fig. 3   Measuring float level. 5220 carburetor

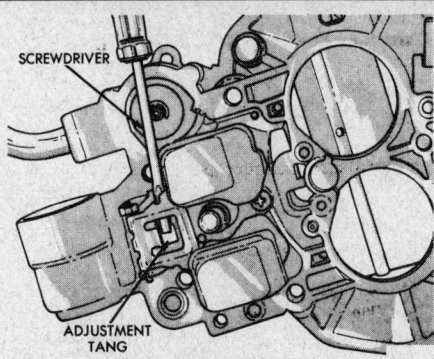

Fig. 4   Adjusting float level. 5220 carburetor

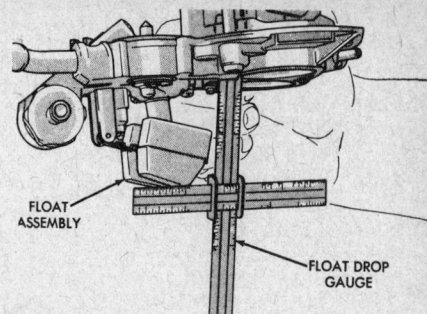

Fig. 5   Measuring float drop. 5220 carburetor

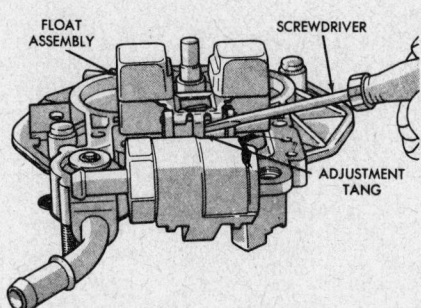

Fig. 6   Adjusting float drop. 5220 carburetor

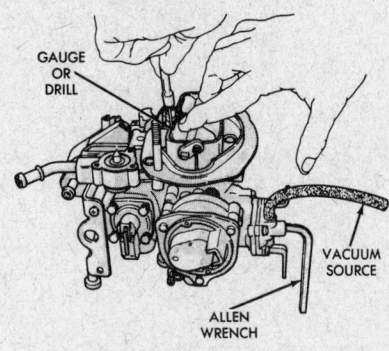

Fig. 7   Choke vacuum kick adjustment. 5220 carburetor

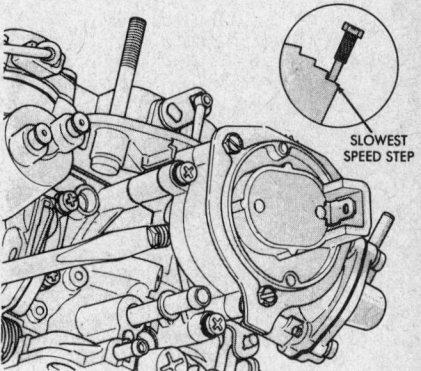

Fig. 8   Fast idle speed adjustment. 5220 carburetor (Typical)

hose to spark control computer. Use a jumper wire to ground idle stop switch. Turn A/C "Off". Disconnect engine cooling fan at radiator and complete the circuit at plug with a jumper wire to energize fan. Apply parking brake, place transmission in Neutral with engine "Off", open throttle slightly and place lowest speed step of fast idle cam under adjusting screw. Start engine and determine stabilized speed. The choke valve must be fully open. If engine continues to rise, the idle stop switch is not grounded properly. To adjust speed, turn speed screw to obtain proper RPM. Reposition screw on cam after each adjustment to provide proper throttle closing torque and screw position.

Choke Setting Adjustment

1978–79

Loosen choke coil cap retaining screws and rotate cap assembly to align mark on cap with specified mark on housing. Tighten choke coil cap retaining screws.

CARBURETORS

MODEL 6149

The model 6149 carburetor, Fig. 1, is a single barrel, booster type, feedback unit. The carburetor uses twelve basic systems to provide the correct air/fuel mixture under various operating conditions. The systems are: fuel inlet system, idle system, idle transfer system, main metering system, feedback system, auxiliary main metering system, wide open throttle (WOT) pullover enrichment system, accelerator pump system, choke system, throttle position sensor (TPS) system, hot idle compensator (HIC) valve system and mechanical fuel bowl vent system.

Float Level Adjustment

Fig. 2—With air horn removed, place a finger over float hinge pin retainer and invert main body. Use care not to lose accelerator pump check ball and weight. Using a straight edge, check position of floats. The extreme outside edge of floats should be flush with surface of main body casting without gasket. Adjust as necessary by bending float tabs to raise or lower float level. After completing adjustment, invert main body and ensure float moves freely without contacting fuel bowl walls.

Accelerator Pump Adjustment

Fig. 3—Measure length of accelerator pump operating stroke from inside edge at pump operating rod to inside edge at throttle lever hole. Adjust as necessary by bending loop in operating link.

Mechanical Fuel Bowl Vent Adjustment

Off Vehicle
Fig. 4—With choke plate secured wide open, set throttle at TSP Off position. Turn TSP Off adjustment screw counterclockwise until throttle plate is closed in throttle bore. Adjust as necessary by bending fuel bowl vent actuator lever until specified clearance is obtained. Do not bend fuel bowl vent arm and/or adjacent part of actuator lever.

On Vehicle

NOTE: Curb idle speed must be adjusted to specifications before performing this adjustment.

Fig. 4—With choke plate secured wide open, turn ignition On to activate TSP (engine not running). Open throttle to extend TSP plunger and ensure throttle is in idle set position, contacting TSP plunger. Measure clearance between fuel bowl vent arm and bowl vent actuating lever. Adjust as necessary by bending bowl vent actuator until specified clearance is obtained. Do not bend fuel bowl vent arm and/or adjacent part of actuator lever.

Auxiliary Main Jet/Pullover Valve Timing Adjustment

Fig. 5—Measure protrusion of adjustment screw at rear of throttle pick-up lever. Adjust as necessary by turning screw until protrusion measures .335–.355 inch.

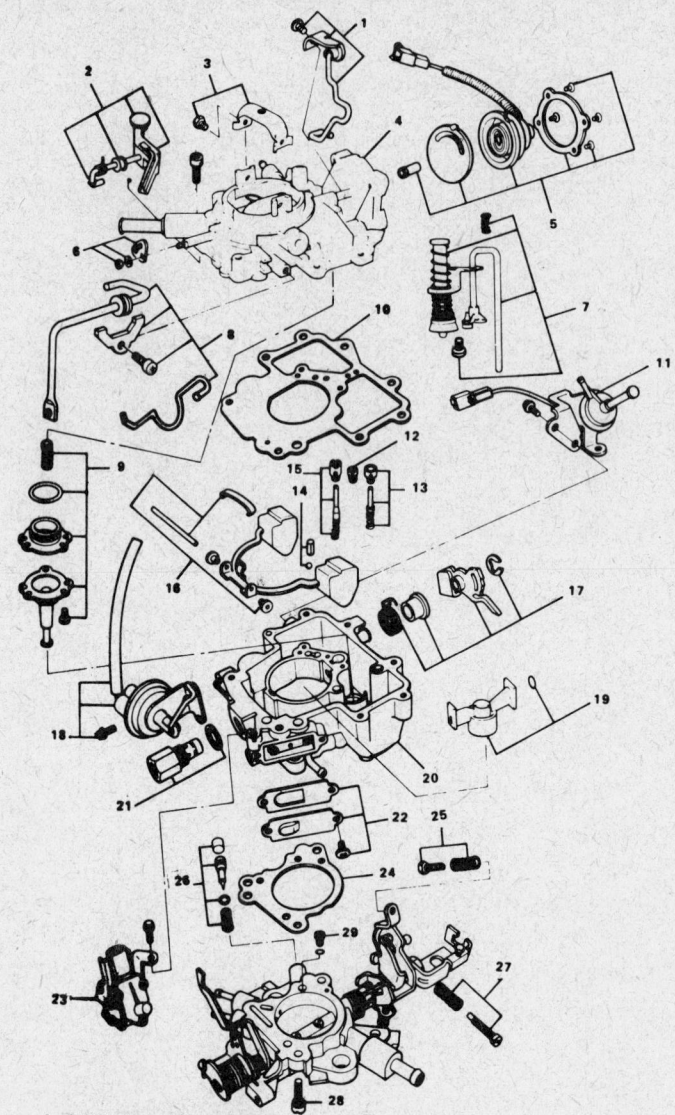

1. CHOKE LINKAGE ASSEMBLY
2. MECHANICAL FUEL BOWL VENT ASSEMBLY
3. AIR CLEANER BRACKET AND RETAINING SCREW
4. AIR HORN ASSEMBLY AND ATTACHING SCREW
5. CHOKE BIMETAL ASSEMBLY
6. CHOKE PULLDOWN LEVER, LOCK WASHER AND RETAINING NUT
7. ACCELERATOR PUMP ASSEMBLY AND AUXILIARY MAIN JET/PULLOVER VALVE ACTUATING ROD AND SEAL PUCK WITH RETAINING SCREW
8. ACCELERATOR PUMP ACTUATOR ASSEMBLY
9. MAIN FEEDBACK CONTROL ASSEMBLY
10. AIR HORN GASKET
11. SOLEKICKER AND ATTACHING SCREW
12. MAIN METERING JET
13. WOT ENRICHMENT PULLOVER VALVE
14. ACCELERATOR PUMP CHECK BALL AND WEIGHT
15. MAIN SYSTEM FEEDBACK METERING VALVE ASSEMBLY
16. FLOAT ASSEMBLY
17. FAST IDLE CAM ASSEMBLY
18. PULLDOWN DIAPHRAGM AND LINKAGE ASSEMBLY, HOSE AND RETAINING SCREW
19. DROP-IN BOOSTER VENTURI AND 'O' RING
20. MAIN BODY ASSEMBLY
21. FUEL INLET FITTING AND GASKET
22. HOT IDLE COMPENSATOR GASKET, COVER AND SCREW
23. THROTTLE POSITION SENSOR AND ATTACHING SCREW
24. THROTTLE BODY GASKET
25. CURB IDLE RPM ADJUSTING SCREW AND SPRING
26. IDLE MIXTURE COMPONENTS
27. FAST IDLE RPM ADJUSTING SCREW AND SPRING
28. THROTTLE BODY ASSEMBLY AND ATTACHING SCREW
29. IDLE CHANNEL RESTRICTOR AND 'O' RING

Fig. 1   Exploded view of Holley Model 6149 carburetor

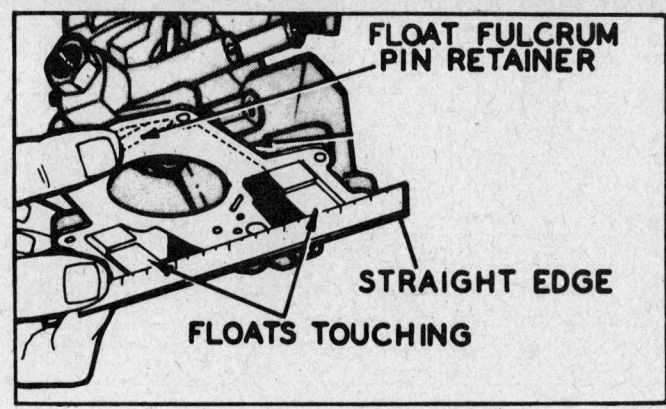

Fig. 2   Float adjustment. 6149 carburetor

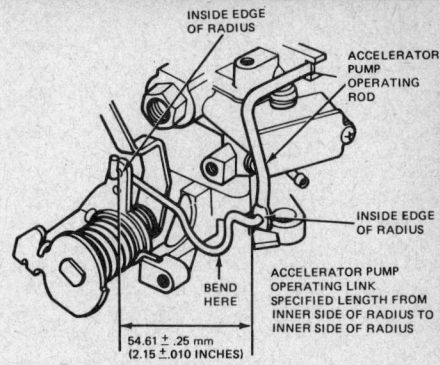

Fig. 3   Accelerator pump adjustment. 6149 carburetor

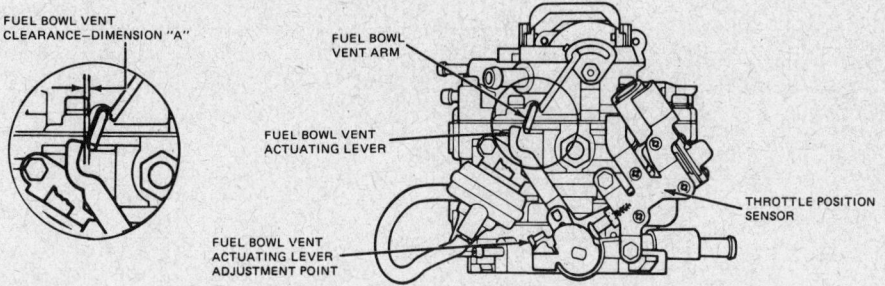

Fig. 4   Mechanical fuel bowl vent adjustment. 6149 carburetor

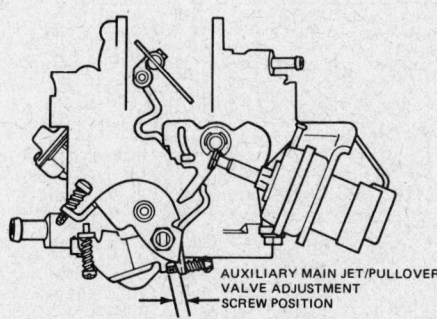

Fig. 5   Auxiliary main jet/pullover valve timing adjustment. 6149 carburetor

Feedback Controlled Main System Diaphragm Adjustment

Fig. 6—Drill a 3/32 inch hole through lead sealing disc on diaphragm adjustment screw, then pry disc off using a suitable punch. Adjust as necessary by turning adjustment screw until top of screw is .170–.190 inch below top of air horn adjustment screw boss. On carburetors with an "S" stamped on top of air horn, adjust to .240–.260 inch. Install a new lead sealing disc and secure by staking with a suitable punch. After completing adjustment, apply a maximum vacuum of 10 inches Hg and ensure diaphragm does not leak.

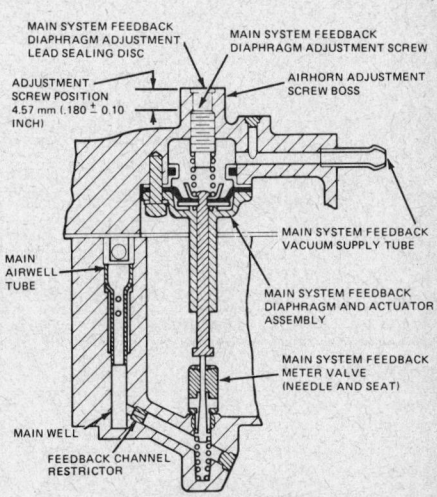

Fig. 6   Feedback controlled main system diaphragm adjustment. 6149 carburetor

CARBURETORS

HOLLEY MODEL 6500 ADJUSTMENT SPECIFICATIONS

See Tune Up Chart in car chapters for curb and fast idle speeds.

Year	Carb. Model	Float Level	Pump Level Hole No.	Choke Plate Pulldown	Fast Idle Cam Clearance	Dechoke	Choke Setting
FORD MOTOR CO.							
1979	D9EE-AEC	15/32	#2	.24	.12	.24	2 Rich
	D9EE-AFC	15/32	#2	.24	.12	.24	2 Rich
	D9EE-AGC	15/32	#2	.24	.12	.24	2 Rich
	D9EE-AHC	15/32	#2	.24	.12	.24	2 Rich
	D9EE-AJC	15/32	#2	.24	.12	.24	1 Rich
	D9EE-AKC	15/32	#2	.24	.12	.24	1 Rich
	D9EE-AZA	15/32	#2	.24	.12	.24	2 Rich
	D9EE-BAA	15/32	#2	.24	.12	.24	2 Rich
	D9EE-BBA	15/32	#2	.24	.12	.24	2 Rich
	D9EE-BCA	15/32	#2	.24	.12	.24	2 Rich
	D9ZE-SB	15/32	#2	.24	.12	.24	2 Rich
	D9ZE-TB	15/32	#2	.24	.12	.24	2 Rich
	EE0E-NA	15/32	#2	.24	.12	.24	Index
	EE0E-NC	15/32	#3	.24	.12	.39	—
	EE0E-ND	15/32	#3	.24	.12	.39	—
	EE0E-VA	15/32	#2	.24	.12	.24	—
	EE0E-VC	15/32	#3	.24	.12	.39	Index
	EE0E-VD	15/32	#3	.24	.12	.39	—
	EEZE-AFA	15/32	#2	.24	.12	.39	Index
	EEZE-AFC	15/32	—	.24	.12	.39	—
	EEZE-SA	15/32	#2	.24	.12	.39	Index
	EEZE-SC	15/32	—	.24	.12	.39	—
1981	E1DE-DA	15/32	#3	.24	.12	.39	—
	E1DE-EA	15/32	#3	.24	.12	.39	—
	E1ZE-RA	15/32	#3	.24	.12	.39	—
	E1ZE-SA	15/32	#3	.24	.12	.39	—
1982	E2ZE-ACA	15/32	#3	.276	.118	.394	—
	E2ZE-ADA	15/32	#3	.276	.118	.394	—
	E2ZE-APA	15/32	#2	.276	.118	.394	—
	E2ZE-ARA	15/32	#2	.276	.118	.394	—
	E2ZE-UA	15/32	#3	.276	.118	.394	—
	E2ZE-VA	15/32	#3	.276	.118	.394	—

MODEL 6500

The Holley Model 6500 carburetor, Fig. 1, is used with the Ford Feedback Electronic Engine Control System. This carburetor is basically the same as the Motorcraft Model 5200 as described elsewhere in this chapter. The Model 6500 is equipped with an externally variable auxiliary fuel metering system in place of the enrichment valve used on the Motorcraft Model 5200. The auxiliary system consists of a metering valve assembly, metering valve operating piston and a diaphragm.

The feedback metering valve supplements fuel entering the main well through the conventional metering jet and channel. The amount of fuel entering the main well through the metering valve depends on the position of the tapered metering rod in the orifice. The position of the metering rod depends on the metering rod operation piston assembly.

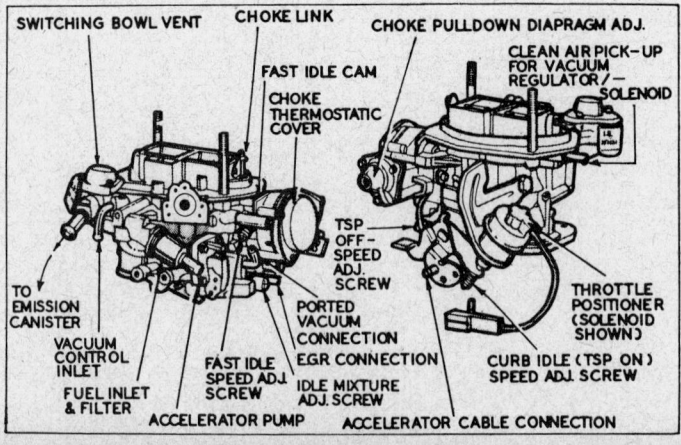

Fig. 1 Model 6500 carburetor

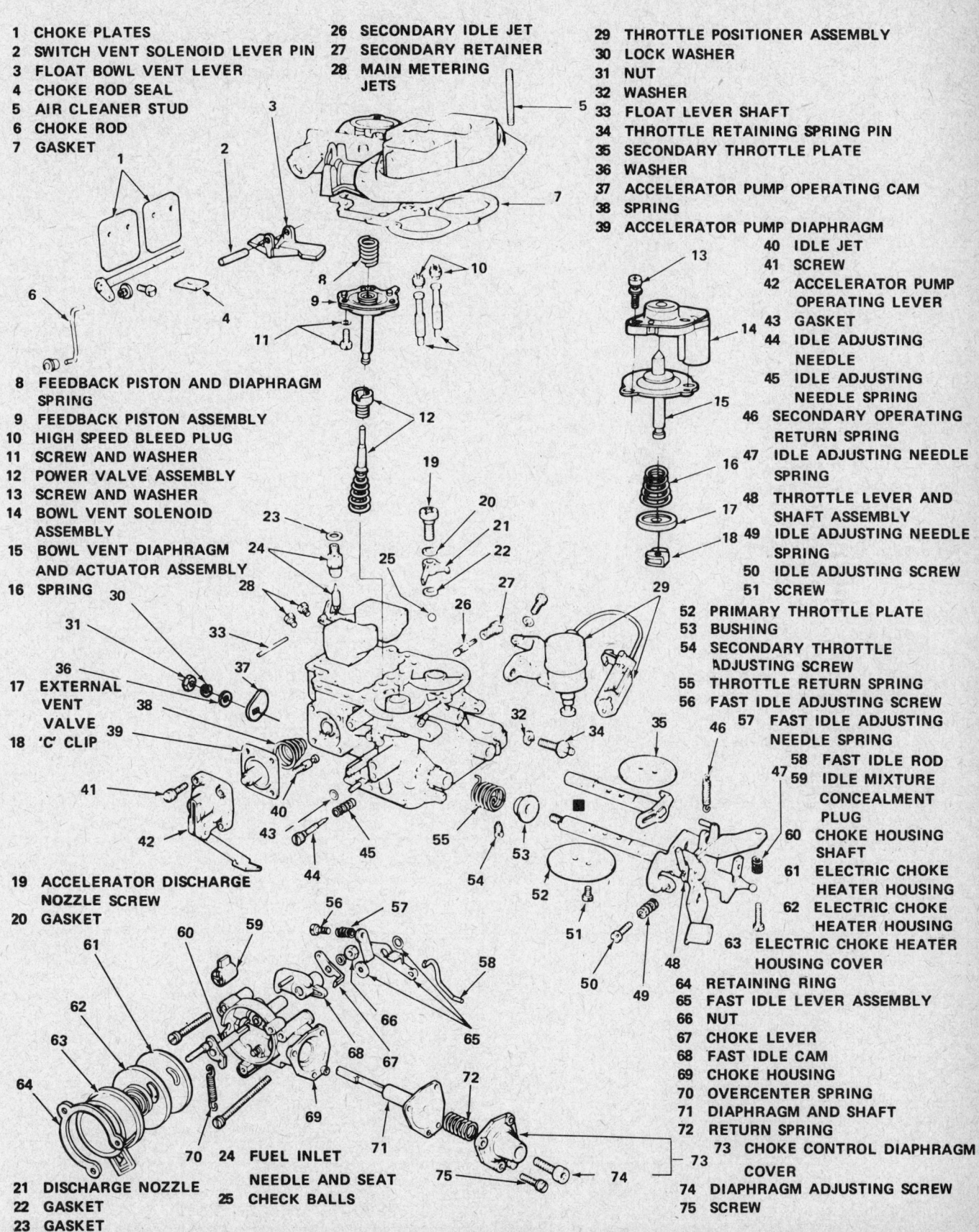

1 CHOKE PLATES
2 SWITCH VENT SOLENOID LEVER PIN
3 FLOAT BOWL VENT LEVER
4 CHOKE ROD SEAL
5 AIR CLEANER STUD
6 CHOKE ROD
7 GASKET

8 FEEDBACK PISTON AND DIAPHRAGM SPRING
9 FEEDBACK PISTON ASSEMBLY
10 HIGH SPEED BLEED PLUG
11 SCREW AND WASHER
12 POWER VALVE ASSEMBLY
13 SCREW AND WASHER
14 BOWL VENT SOLENOID ASSEMBLY
15 BOWL VENT DIAPHRAGM AND ACTUATOR ASSEMBLY
16 SPRING
17 EXTERNAL VENT VALVE
18 'C' CLIP

19 ACCELERATOR DISCHARGE NOZZLE SCREW
20 GASKET

21 DISCHARGE NOZZLE
22 GASKET
23 GASKET
24 FUEL INLET NEEDLE AND SEAT
25 CHECK BALLS

26 SECONDARY IDLE JET
27 SECONDARY RETAINER
28 MAIN METERING JETS

29 THROTTLE POSITIONER ASSEMBLY
30 LOCK WASHER
31 NUT
32 WASHER
33 FLOAT LEVER SHAFT
34 THROTTLE RETAINING SPRING PIN
35 SECONDARY THROTTLE PLATE
36 WASHER
37 ACCELERATOR PUMP OPERATING CAM
38 SPRING
39 ACCELERATOR PUMP DIAPHRAGM
40 IDLE JET
41 SCREW
42 ACCELERATOR PUMP OPERATING LEVER
43 GASKET
44 IDLE ADJUSTING NEEDLE
45 IDLE ADJUSTING NEEDLE SPRING
46 SECONDARY OPERATING RETURN SPRING
47 IDLE ADJUSTING NEEDLE SPRING
48 THROTTLE LEVER AND SHAFT ASSEMBLY
49 IDLE ADJUSTING NEEDLE SPRING
50 IDLE ADJUSTING SCREW
51 SCREW
52 PRIMARY THROTTLE PLATE
53 BUSHING
54 SECONDARY THROTTLE ADJUSTING SCREW
55 THROTTLE RETURN SPRING
56 FAST IDLE ADJUSTING SCREW
57 FAST IDLE ADJUSTING NEEDLE SPRING
58 FAST IDLE ROD
59 IDLE MIXTURE CONCEALMENT PLUG
60 CHOKE HOUSING SHAFT
61 ELECTRIC CHOKE HEATER HOUSING
62 ELECTRIC CHOKE HEATER HOUSING
63 ELECTRIC CHOKE HEATER HOUSING COVER
64 RETAINING RING
65 FAST IDLE LEVER ASSEMBLY
66 NUT
67 CHOKE LEVER
68 FAST IDLE CAM
69 CHOKE HOUSING
70 OVERCENTER SPRING
71 DIAPHRAGM AND SHAFT
72 RETURN SPRING
73 CHOKE CONTROL DIAPHRAGM COVER
74 DIAPHRAGM ADJUSTING SCREW
75 SCREW

Exploded view of Holley model 6500 carburetor

CARBURETORS

Control vacuum from the vacuum regulator solenoid is transmitted to the cavity above the metering rod diaphragm. When no vacuum is present, the valve spring causes the valve to move to the lowest (richest) position and maximum fuel can pass through the orifice. As vacuum is applied to the diaphragm, spring pressure is overcome and the metering rod rises, reducing the orifice area and less fuel passes through the orifice. The metering valve is calibrated so the maximum vacuum signal supplied by the vacuum regulator solenoid raises the rod to the highest (leanest) position.

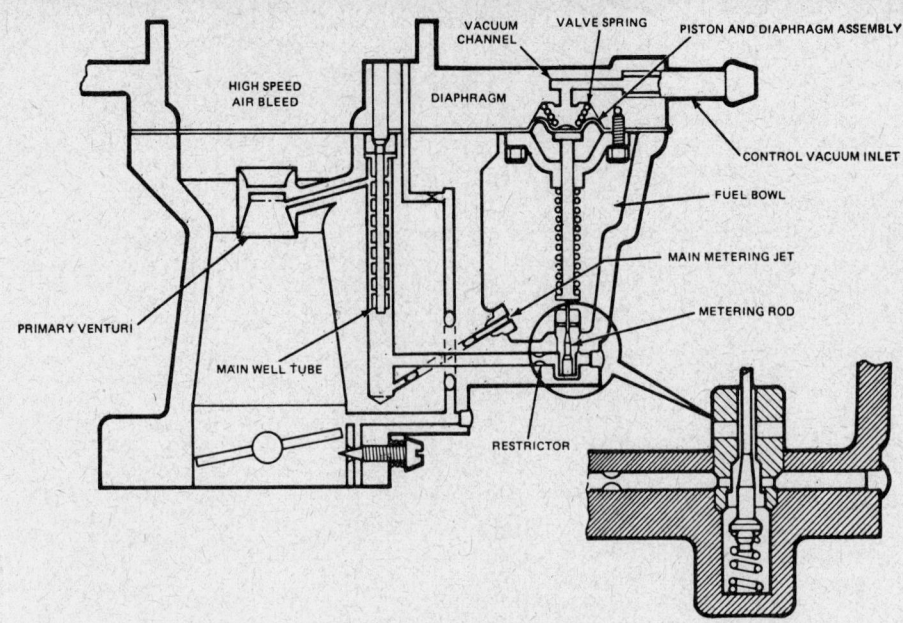

Fig. 2 Fuel metering system

Adjustments

All adjustments for the Model 6500 are the same as the Motorcraft Model 5200 as described elsewhere in this chapter, however, the choke plate vacuum pulldown adjustment is different.

Choke Plate Vacuum Pulldown Adjustment

NOTE: On 1981–82 vehicles, it is necessary to remove the carburetor from the vehicle to remove rivets retaining the choke cover to choke housing. Using a 1/8 inch or No. 30 drill bit, remove rivet heads, then drive rivets out using a 1/8 inch diameter punch.

1. Remove choke cap, bi-metal heater assembly and plastic shield.
2. Place fast idle speed adjusting screw on top step of fast idle cam.
3. Using a suitable screwdriver, push diaphragm stem back against stop and place specified gauge between lower edge of choke valve and air horn wall, Fig. 3.
4. Remove slack from choke linkage by attaching a rubber band to choke operating lever, Fig. 3.
5. To adjust, rotate vacuum diaphragm adjusting screw as required to obtain proper setting, Fig. 4.

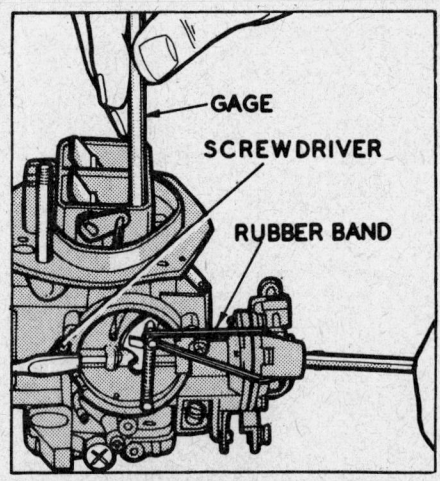

Fig. 3 Measuring choke plate vacuum pulldown

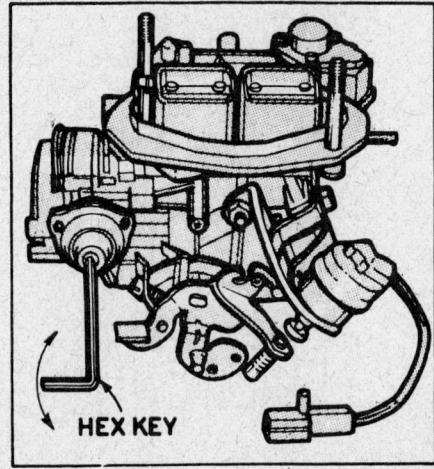

Fig. 4 Adjusting choke plate vacuum pulldown

MODEL 6510-C ADJUSTMENT SPECIFICATIONS

See Tune-Up chart in car chapter for curb and fast idle speeds.

Year	Carb. Model	Float level	Float Drop	Fast Idle Cam	Vacuum Break	Unloader	Choke Coil	Secondary Throttle Stop Screw
GENERAL MOTORS								
1978	10001056	.520	1	.150	.250	.350	1 Rich	①
	10001058	.520	1	.150	.250	.350	1 Rich	①
	10005603	.520	1	.150	.275	.350	2 Rich	①
	10005604	.520	1	.150	.275	.350	2 Rich	①
1979	10008489	.520	1	.150	.250	.350	2 Rich	①
	10008490	.520	1	.150	.250	.350	2 Rich	①
	10008491	.520	1	.150	.250	.350	2 Rich	①
	10008492	.520	1	.150	.250	.350	2 Rich	①
	10009973	.520	1	.150	.275	.350	2 Rich	①
	10009974	.520	1	.150	.275	.350	2 Rich	①

Continued

MODEL 6510-C ADJUSTMENT SPECIFICATIONS—Continued

See Tune-Up chart in car chapter for curb and fast idle speeds.

Year	Carb. Model	Float level	Float Drop	Fast Idle Cam	Vacuum Break	Unloader	Choke Coil	Secondary Throttle Stop Screw
GENERAL MOTORS								
1980	14004469	.500	—	.130	.300	.350	—	①
	14004470	.500	—	.130	.300	.350	—	①
	14004471	.500	—	.130	.300	.350	—	①
	14004472	.500	—	.130	.300	.350	—	①
1981	14004768, 769	.500	—	.130	.300	.350	—	①
	14004770, 771	.500	—	.130	.300	.350	—	①
	14004777	.500	—	.130	.300	.350	—	①
1982	14032364	.500	—	.080	.270	.350	—	①
	14032365	.500	—	.080	.270	.350	—	①
	14032366	.500	—	.080	.270	.350	—	①
	14032367	.500	—	.080	.270	.350	—	①
	14032368	.500	—	.080	.270	.350	—	①
	14032369	.500	—	.080	.270	.350	—	①
	14032370	.500	—	.080	.270	.350	—	①
	14032371	.500	—	.080	.270	.350	—	①
	14033392	.500	—	.080	.270	.350	—	①
	14033393	.500	—	.080	.270	.350	—	①
	14047072	.500	—	.080	.270	.350	—	①
1983	14048827	.500	—	.080	.270	.350	—	①
	14048828	.500	—	.080	.300	.350	—	①
	14048829	.500	—	.080	.270	.350	—	①

①—Refer to text for adjustment.

MODEL 6510-C

Description

The Holley Model 6510-C carburetor, Figs. 1 and 2, is a controlled air-fuel ratio carburetor of a staged two barrel design with the primary bore smaller in size than the secondary bore. The secondary throttle is mechanically operated through interconnected linkage. This carburetor is used with the Electronic Fuel Control (EFC) system described elsewhere in this manual.

This carburetor utilizes four basic fuel metering systems: idle system, feedback controlled main metering system, acceleration system and power enrichment system.

The idle system is a separate factory adjusted system which provides a proper air-fuel mixture for both idle and low speed operation. The main metering system provides the correct air-fuel mixture for all normal and cruising speeds and aids in power enrichment. Fuel for acceleration is provided by the mechanically operated acceleration system. The power enrichment system consists of the accelerator pump discharge nozzle pullover and a secondary stage airflow regulated pullover system. These systems are used in conjunction with the main metering systems to provide adequate performance during periods of moderate to heavy acceleration.

Located in the primary bore are one or two vacuum ports for distributor vacuum spark advance, EGR vacuum and vapor canister purge depending upon emission control system usage.

A solenoid assisted vacuum operated bowl vent is used to vent the fuel vapors to the canister and not into the engine when the engine is operating. The vent is used in conjunction with existing internal venting through the air horn.

On 1978–79 models, a hot idle compensator is used to maintain smooth engine idle during periods of excessive high temperature operation by allowing additional air to enter the primary throttle bore.

An electrically heated automatic choke system is used to provide correct air-fuel mixtures for cold start and warm-up operation. The automatic choke system is equipped with a vacuum break controlled by an external vacuum supply and a vacuum delay valve to prevent prolonged fast idle.

On 1983 models, a stepped speed control (SSC) is used. The SSC system consists of three major components: a throttle lever actuator, solenoid vacuum control and electronic speed sensor.

The throttle lever actuator is mounted on the carburetor and opens the primary throttle blades a preset amount in excess of curb idle when engine vacuum is applied to it. A solenoid control valve controls the actuating vacuum.

The solenoid vacuum control valve is mounted separately from the carburetor. When the valve is open, manifold vacuum is applied to the SSC throttle lever actuator. The valve will be energized and held open by any of the following conditions:

a. On models with manual transmission, when engine speed exceeds the calibrated value of the electronic speed sensor.

b. On models equipped with air condition-ing, during the first ten seconds of engine operation.

c. On models equipped with power steering, when power steering output pressure exceeds power steering pressure switch calibration.

d. On models equipped with air conditioning, when compressor clutch is engaged, or when the engine coolant temperature light is illuminated.

The electronic speed sensor is mounted separately from the solenoid vacuum valve. The sensor monitors engine speed at the distributor and provides the vacuum valve with a continuous electrical signal as long as the preset engine speed is exceeded.

ADJUSTMENTS

Float Level Adjustment

Fig. 3—With air horn inverted, insert specified gauge between float and air horn. Bend tang to adjust.

Float Drop Adjustment

1978–79 Units
Fig. 4—With air horn removed, measure distance between bottom of air horn and top of float. Refer to specifications chart for correct measurement. Bend tang to adjust.

Fast Idle Cam Adjustment

Fig. 5—Set fast idle cam in position so the screw contacts second high step. Insert specified gauge between lower edge of choke valve and air horn wall. Bend tang to adjust.

CARBURETORS

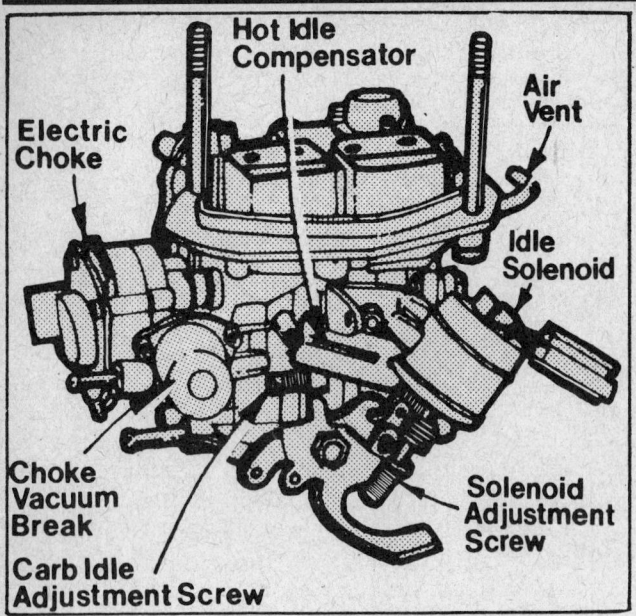

Fig. 1 Holley model 6510-C carburetor. 1978–79 (Typical of 1980–83)

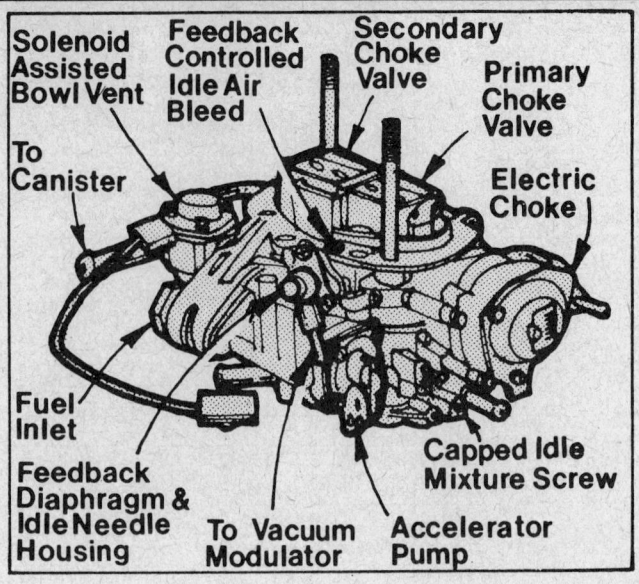

Fig. 2 Holley model 6510-C carburetor. 1978–79 (Typical of 1980–83)

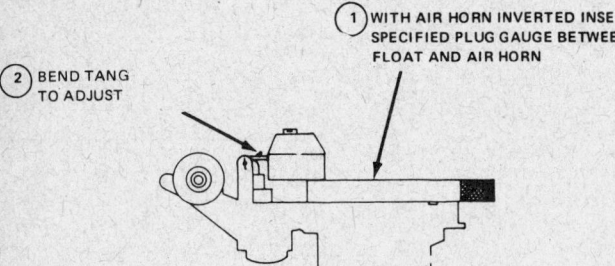

Fig. 3 Float level adjustment

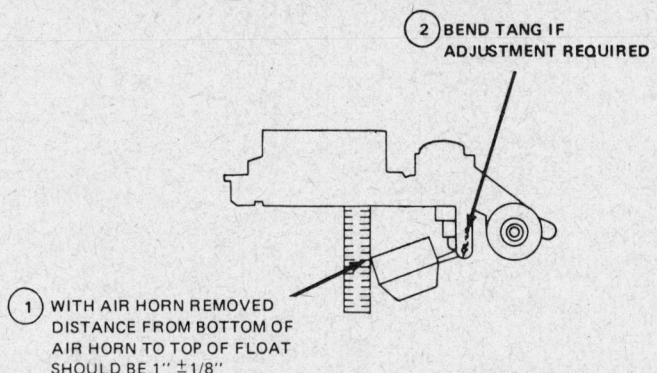

Fig. 4 Float drop adjustment. 1978–79 Units

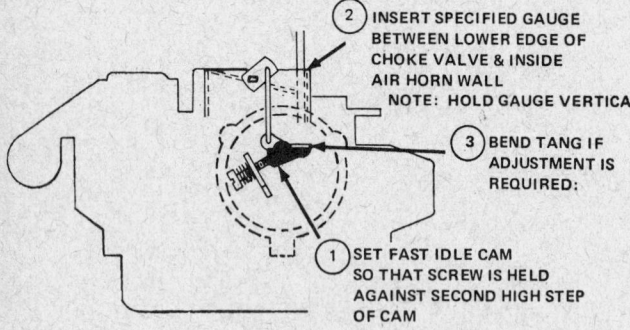

Fig. 5 Fast idle cam adjustment

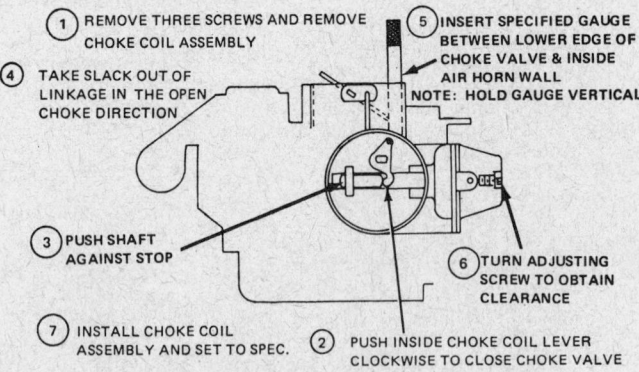

Fig. 6 Vacuum break adjustment. 1978–79 Units

Vacuum Break Adjustment

1978–79 Units

Fig. 6—Remove choke coil assembly. Push choke coil lever clockwise to close choke valve. Push vacuum break shaft against stop. Remove slack from linkage in the choke open direction. Insert specified gauge between lower edge of choke valve and air horn wall. Rotate vacuum break adjusting screw to obtain specified clearance. Install and adjust choke coil assembly.

1980–83 Units

Fig. 6A—On 1983 units, remove adjusting screw plug. On all units, apply an external vacuum source to vacuum break to seat diaphragm. Rotate fast idle cam clockwise to close choke valve. Remove slack from linkage in the choke open direction. Insert the specified gauge between choke valve and air horn wall. Turn adjusting screw to obtain clearance.

Unloader Adjustment

Fig. 7—Place throttle lever in wide open position. Insert specified gauge between lower edge of choke valve and air horn wall. Bend tang at existing radius to adjust.

Choke Coil Adjustment

1978–79 Units

Fig. 8—Loosen choke coil cover retaining screws with choke coil lever located inside tang, rotate cover to align mark on cover with

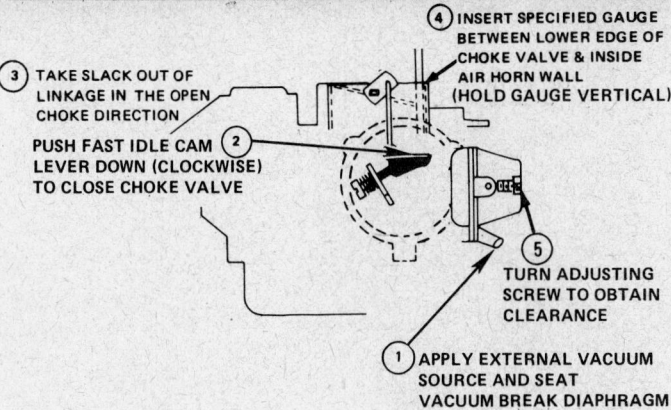

③ TAKE SLACK OUT OF LINKAGE IN THE OPEN CHOKE DIRECTION

PUSH FAST IDLE CAM LEVER DOWN (CLOCKWISE) TO CLOSE CHOKE VALVE ②

④ INSERT SPECIFIED GAUGE BETWEEN LOWER EDGE OF CHOKE VALVE & INSIDE AIR HORN WALL (HOLD GAUGE VERTICAL)

⑤ TURN ADJUSTING SCREW TO OBTAIN CLEARANCE

① APPLY EXTERNAL VACUUM SOURCE AND SEAT VACUUM BREAK DIAPHRAGM

Fig. 6A Vacuum break adjustment. 1980–82 Units (Typical of 1983)

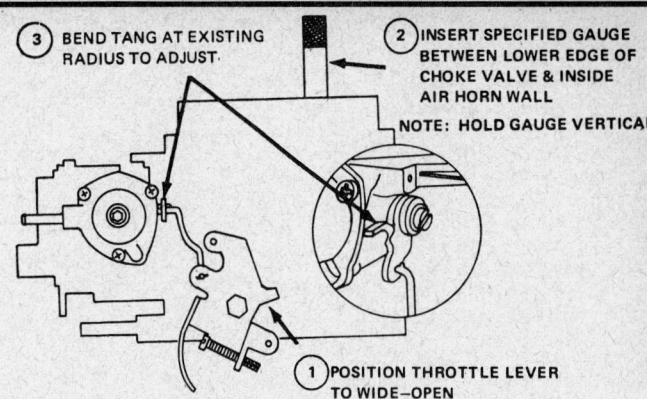

③ BEND TANG AT EXISTING RADIUS TO ADJUST

② INSERT SPECIFIED GAUGE BETWEEN LOWER EDGE OF CHOKE VALVE & INSIDE AIR HORN WALL

NOTE: HOLD GAUGE VERTICAL

① POSITION THROTTLE LEVER TO WIDE–OPEN

Fig. 7 Unloader adjustment

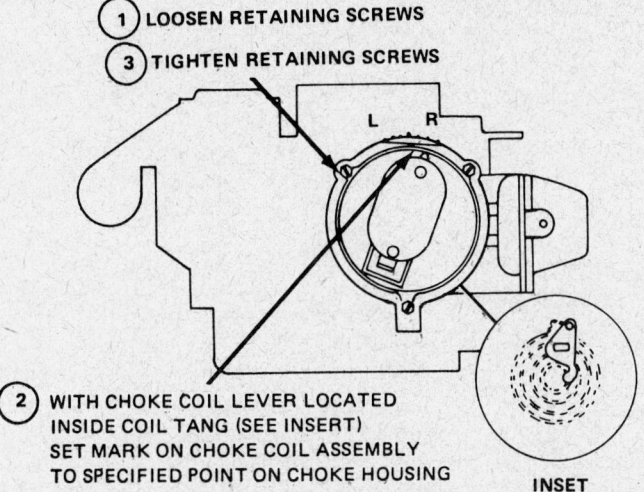

① LOOSEN RETAINING SCREWS

③ TIGHTEN RETAINING SCREWS

② WITH CHOKE COIL LEVER LOCATED INSIDE COIL TANG (SEE INSERT) SET MARK ON CHOKE COIL ASSEMBLY TO SPECIFIED POINT ON CHOKE HOUSING

INSET

Fig. 8 Choke coil adjustment. 1978–79 Units

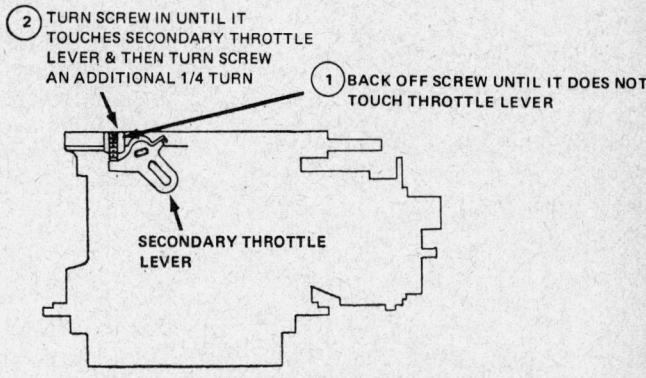

② TURN SCREW IN UNTIL IT TOUCHES SECONDARY THROTTLE LEVER & THEN TURN SCREW AN ADDITIONAL 1/4 TURN

① BACK OFF SCREW UNTIL IT DOES NOT TOUCH THROTTLE LEVER

SECONDARY THROTTLE LEVER

Fig. 9 Secondary throttle stop screw adjustment

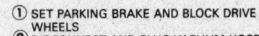

① SET PARKING BRAKE AND BLOCK DRIVE WHEELS
② DISCONNECT ELECTRICAL LEAD FROM A/C COMPRESSOR AND TURN A/C CONTROL SWITCH ON
③ WITH ENGINE RUNNING, VISUALLY CHECK TO SEE THAT ACTUATOR IS FULLY EXTENDED
④ ADJUST ACTUATOR SCREW TO OBTAIN RPM SPECIFIED ON VEHICLE EMISSION CONTROL INFORMATION LABEL
⑤ RECONNECT A/C COMPRESSOR LEAD AND TURN A/C OFF

ACTUATOR

ACTUATOR ADJUSTING SCREW

Fig. 11 Stepped Speed Control adjustment. 1983 models with air conditioning

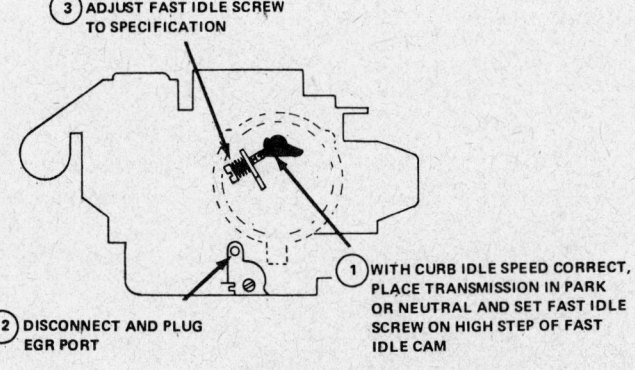

③ ADJUST FAST IDLE SCREW TO SPECIFICATION

① WITH CURB IDLE SPEED CORRECT, PLACE TRANSMISSION IN PARK OR NEUTRAL AND SET FAST IDLE SCREW ON HIGH STEP OF FAST IDLE CAM

② DISCONNECT AND PLUG EGR PORT

Fig. 10 Fast idle speed adjustment

① SET PARKING BRAKE AND BLOCK DRIVE WHEELS
② DISCONNECT AND PLUG VACUUM HOSE AT SSC ACTUATOR
③ CONNECT A VACUUM SOURCE (5 IN. HG. MIN.) TO ACTUATOR AND CHECK TO SEE THAT IT IS FULLY EXTENDED
④ WITH ENGINE RUNNING ADJUST ACTUATOR SCREW TO OBTAIN RPM SPECIFIED ON VEHICLE EMISSION CONTROL INFORMATION LABEL
⑤ UNPLUG AND RECONNECT VACUUM HOSE TO ACTUATOR

ACTUATOR

ACTUATOR ADJUSTING SCREW

CONNECT VACUUM SOURCE

Fig. 12 Stepped Speed Control adjustment. 1983 models less air conditioning

specified mark on choke coil housing. Tighten choke coil cover retaining screws.

Secondary Throttle Stop Screw Adjustment

Fig. 9—Back off secondary throttle stop screw until clear of throttle lever. Rotate screw inward until the screw contacts secondary throttle lever, then an additional 1/4 turn.

Fast Idle Speed Adjustment

Fig. 10—With curb idle speed adjusted, place transmission in neutral or park and place fast idle screw on high step of cam. Disconnect and plug EGR port, and on 1983 units, the canister purge hose and purge control hose at the canister. Rotate fast idle adjusting screw to obtain specified fast idle speed.

Stepped Speed Control Adjustment

1983 Models With Air Conditioning
Fig. 11—With parking brake applied and drive wheels blocked, disconnect electrical lead at A/C compressor and turn A/C system on. With engine running, check that actuator is fully extended. Turn actuator adjusting screw to adjust speed as necessary.

1983 Models Less Air Conditioning
Fig. 12—With parking brake applied and drive wheels blocked, disconnect and plug vacuum hose at SSC actuator. Using an outside vacuum source, apply a minimum of 5 inches Hg to the actuator and ensure that it extends fully. With engine running, turn actuator adjusting screw to adjust speed as necessary.

CARBURETORS

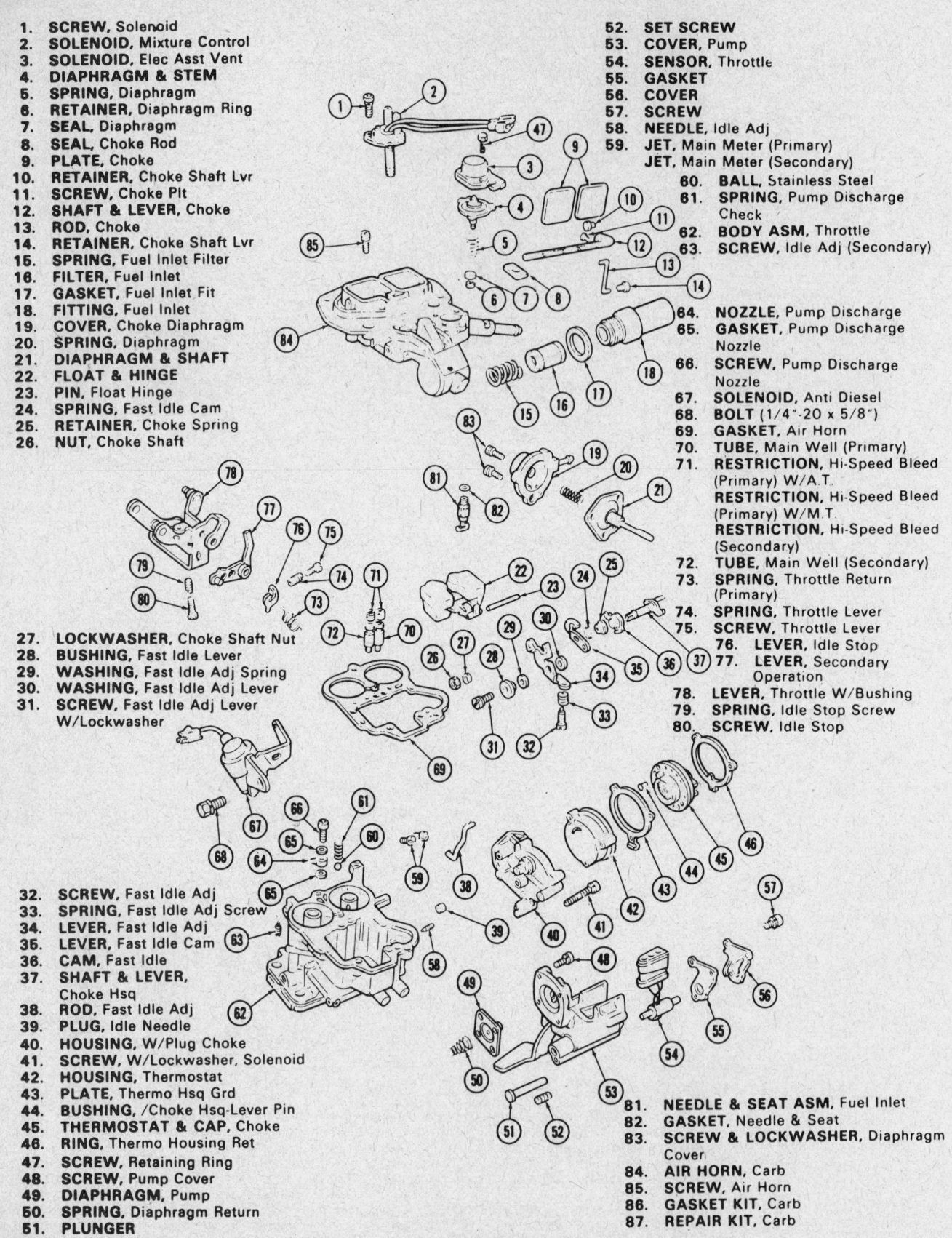

1. **SCREW**, Solenoid
2. **SOLENOID**, Mixture Control
3. **SOLENOID**, Elec Asst Vent
4. **DIAPHRAGM & STEM**
5. **SPRING**, Diaphragm
6. **RETAINER**, Diaphragm Ring
7. **SEAL**, Diaphragm
8. **SEAL**, Choke Rod
9. **PLATE**, Choke
10. **RETAINER**, Choke Shaft Lvr
11. **SCREW**, Choke Plt
12. **SHAFT & LEVER**, Choke
13. **ROD**, Choke
14. **RETAINER**, Choke Shaft Lvr
15. **SPRING**, Fuel Inlet Filter
16. **FILTER**, Fuel Inlet
17. **GASKET**, Fuel Inlet Fit
18. **FITTING**, Fuel Inlet
19. **COVER**, Choke Diaphragm
20. **SPRING**, Diaphragm
21. **DIAPHRAGM & SHAFT**
22. **FLOAT & HINGE**
23. **PIN**, Float Hinge
24. **SPRING**, Fast Idle Cam
25. **RETAINER**, Choke Spring
26. **NUT**, Choke Shaft

27. **LOCKWASHER**, Choke Shaft Nut
28. **BUSHING**, Fast Idle Lever
29. **WASHING**, Fast Idle Adj Spring
30. **WASHING**, Fast Idle Adj Lever
31. **SCREW**, Fast Idle Adj Lever
   W/Lockwasher

32. **SCREW**, Fast Idle Adj
33. **SPRING**, Fast Idle Adj Screw
34. **LEVER**, Fast Idle Adj
35. **LEVER**, Fast Idle Cam
36. **CAM**, Fast Idle
37. **SHAFT & LEVER**,
   Choke Hsq
38. **ROD**, Fast Idle Adj
39. **PLUG**, Idle Needle
40. **HOUSING**, W/Plug Choke
41. **SCREW**, W/Lockwasher, Solenoid
42. **HOUSING**, Thermostat
43. **PLATE**, Thermo Hsq Grd
44. **BUSHING**, /Choke Hsq-Lever Pin
45. **THERMOSTAT & CAP**, Choke
46. **RING**, Thermo Housing Ret
47. **SCREW**, Retaining Ring
48. **SCREW**, Pump Cover
49. **DIAPHRAGM**, Pump
50. **SPRING**, Diaphragm Return
51. **PLUNGER**

52. **SET SCREW**
53. **COVER**, Pump
54. **SENSOR**, Throttle
55. **GASKET**
56. **COVER**
57. **SCREW**
58. **NEEDLE**, Idle Adj
59. **JET**, Main Meter (Primary)
   JET, Main Meter (Secondary)
60. **BALL**, Stainless Steel
61. **SPRING**, Pump Discharge
   Check
62. **BODY ASM**, Throttle
63. **SCREW**, Idle Adj (Secondary)

64. **NOZZLE**, Pump Discharge
65. **GASKET**, Pump Discharge
   Nozzle
66. **SCREW**, Pump Discharge
   Nozzle
67. **SOLENOID**, Anti Diesel
68. **BOLT** (1/4"-20 x 5/8")
69. **GASKET**, Air Horn
70. **TUBE**, Main Well (Primary)
71. **RESTRICTION**, Hi-Speed Bleed
   (Primary) W/A.T.
   RESTRICTION, Hi-Speed Bleed
   (Primary) W/M.T.
   RESTRICTION, Hi-Speed Bleed
   (Secondary)
72. **TUBE**, Main Well (Secondary)
73. **SPRING**, Throttle Return
   (Primary)
74. **SPRING**, Throttle Lever
75. **SCREW**, Throttle Lever
76. **LEVER**, Idle Stop
77. **LEVER**, Secondary
   Operation
78. **LEVER**, Throttle W/Bushing
79. **SPRING**, Idle Stop Screw
80. **SCREW**, Idle Stop

81. **NEEDLE & SEAT ASM**, Fuel Inlet
82. **GASKET**, Needle & Seat
83. **SCREW & LOCKWASHER**, Diaphragm
   Cover
84. **AIR HORN**, Carb
85. **SCREW**, Air Horn
86. **GASKET KIT**, Carb
87. **REPAIR KIT**, Carb

Exploded view of Holley model 6510-C carburetor

MODEL 6520 ADJUSTMENT SPECIFICATIONS

See Tune Up Chart in car chapter for curb and fast idle speeds.

Year	Model No.	Float Level	Float Drop	Acc. Pump Hole No.	Choke Vacuum Kick	Choke Setting
1981	R-9052A	.480	1⅞	2	.070	—
	R-9053A	.480	1⅞	2	.070	—
	R-9054A	.480	1⅞	2	.040	—
	R-9055A	.480	1⅞	2	.040	—
	R-9060A	.480	1⅞	2	.030	—
	R-9061A	.480	1⅞	2	.030	—
	R-9125A	.480	1⅞	2	.030	—
	R-9126A	.480	1⅞	2	.030	—
	R-9602A	.480	1⅞	2	.065	—
	R-9603A	.480	1⅞	2	.065	—
	R-9604A	.480	1⅞	2	.065	—
	R-9605A	.480	1⅞	2	.065	—
1982	R-9503A	.480	1⅞	3	.060	—
	R-9504A	.480	1⅞	3	.070	—
	R-9505A	.480	1⅞	3	.070	—
	R-9506A	.480	1⅞	3	.070	—
	R-9507A	.480	1⅞	3	.085	—
	R-9508A	.480	1⅞	3	.085	—
	R-9509A	.480	1⅞	3	.085	—
	R-9510A	.480	1⅞	3	.085	—
	R-9750A	.480	1⅞	3	.060	—
	R-9751A	.480	1⅞	3	.060	—
	R-9752A	.480	1⅞	3	.070	—
	R-9753A	.480	1⅞	3	.070	—
	R-9822A	.480	1⅞	2	.047	—
	R-9823A	.480	1⅞	2	.047	—
	R-9824A	.480	1⅞	2	.040	—
	R-9940A	.480	1⅞	3	.050	—
	R-9941A	.480	1⅞	3	.050	—
	R-9942A	.480	1⅞	3	.050	—
	R-9943A	.480	1⅞	3	.050	—
1983	R-40003A	.480	1⅞	3	.070	—
	R-40004A	.480	1⅞	3	.065	—
	R-40006A	.480	1⅞	3	.080	—
	R-40007A	.480	1⅞	3	.070	—
	R-40008A	.480	1⅞	3	.070	—
	R-40010A	.480	1⅞	3	.065	—
	R-40012A	.480	1⅞	3	.070	—
	R-40014A	.480	1⅞	3	.080	—
	R-40080A	.480	1⅞	2	.045	—
	R-40081A	.480	1⅞	2	.045	—

MODEL 6520

The Holley model 6520, Fig. 1, is a staged dual venturi electronic feedback carburetor. The primary bore is smaller than the secondary bore. The secondary stage is mechanically operated by linkage connecting the primary and secondary throttle levers. The primary stage includes a curb idle and transfer system, diaphragm type accelerator pump system, main metering system and a fuel regulator solenoid responsive to oxygen sensor. The secondary stage includes a main metering sys-

tem and power system. Both the primary and secondary venturi draw fuel from a common fuel bowl. The electric automatic choke incorporates a two stage heating element. On manual transmission carburetors, only one choke valve is used, while on automatic transmission carburetors, two choke valves are used.

The 6520 electronic feedback carburetor also incorporates a duty cycle solenoid which provides a limited regulation of air-fuel ratio in response to electrical signals from the spark control computer. The solenoid meters the main fuel system and operates in parallel with a conventional fixed main metering jet.

When there is no electrical signal applied to the solenoid, the valve spring pushes upward through the main system fuel valve, fully uncovering the solenoid controlled main metering orifice so that the richest condition exists within the carburetor for any given airflow. When the electrical signal is applied to the solenoid, the field windings are energized, thus causing the armature to move the push rod and main system valve downward against the valve spring. This movement will continue until the main system valve bottoms against the main system valve seat. In this position the solenoid controlled main metering orifice is fully sealed so that the leanest condition exists within the carburetor for any given airflow. This condition will remain unchanged until the signal from the spark control computer to the solenoid is switched off. The main system fuel maybe regulated between richest and leanest limits by controlling the amount of time that the solenoid is in the power on position. Under normal operating conditions, 12 volts at a frequency of 10 Hz is applied to the field windings. By controlling the duration of the voltage signal, the power on time to total time, referred to as the duty cycle, is established.

1983 units incorporate a deceleration fuel shut off system which provides a very lean air-fuel mixture during deceleration. This is accomplished by opening a solenoid controlled idle air bleed. This system also prevents engine dieseling by making the air-fuel mixture too lean to support combustion when the engine is turned off. The fuel shut off solenoid opens the additional idle air bleed when the throttle is closed and engine RPM is above a preset speed.

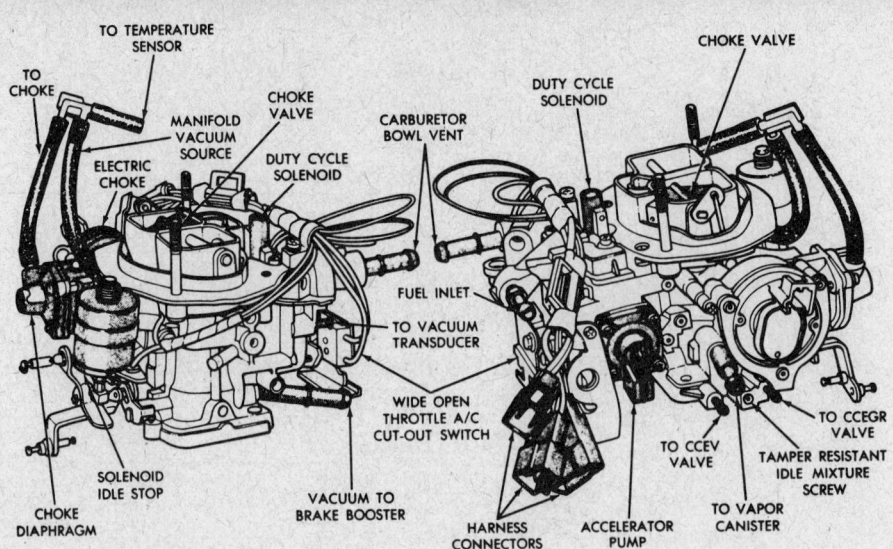

Fig. 1 Holley Model 6520 Carburetor. 1981–82 (Typical of 1983)

Float Level Adjustment

Figs. 2 & 3—Invert air horn and insert specified gauge between float and air horn. To adjust, use a small screwdriver to bend tang.

Float Drop Adjustment

Figs. 4 & 5—Using a suitable depth gauge measure float drop. To adjust, use a small screwdriver to bend tang.

Choke Vacuum Kick Adjustment

Fig. 6—Open throttle and close choke valve, then close throttle to retain choke valve in the closed position. Disconnect vacuum hose from carburetor and connect an external vacuum source. Apply 15 inches Hg. of vacuum or more. Apply sufficient closing pressure to choke valve, using care not to distort linkage. Note that an internal spring will compress to a stop within the choke system. Insert the specified gauge in center area between top of choke valve and air horn wall at primary throttle end of carburetor. Adjust clearance by rotating the allen head screw in center of diaphragm housing.

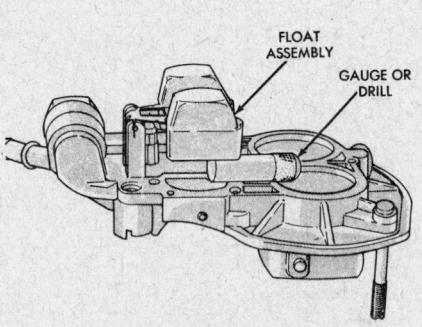

Fig. 2 Measuring float level. 6520 carburetor

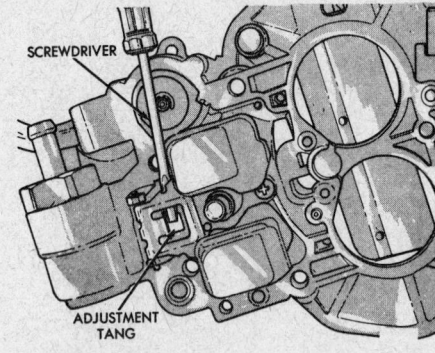

Fig. 3 Adjusting float level. 6520 carburetor

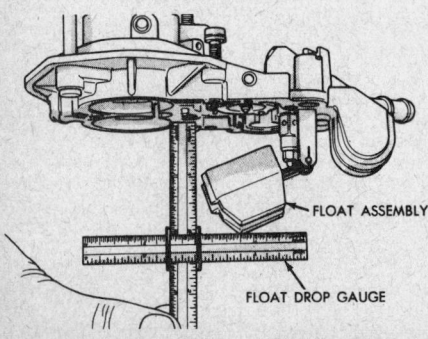

Fig. 4 Measuring float drop. 6520 carburetor

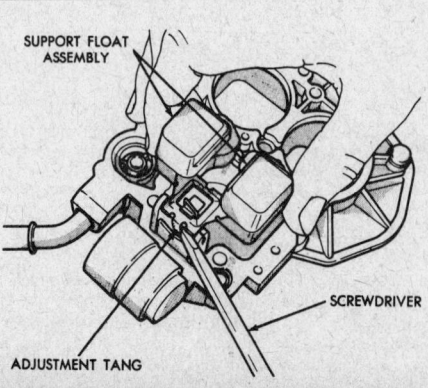

Fig. 5 Adjusting float drop. 6520 carburetor

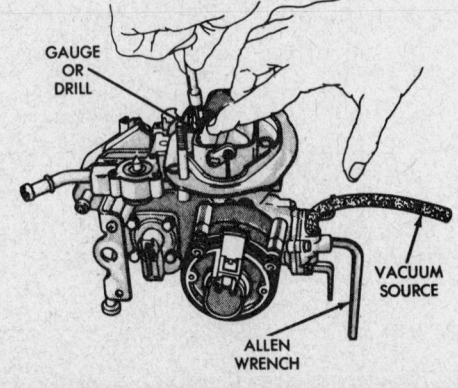

Fig. 6 Adjusting choke vacuum kick. 6520 carburetor

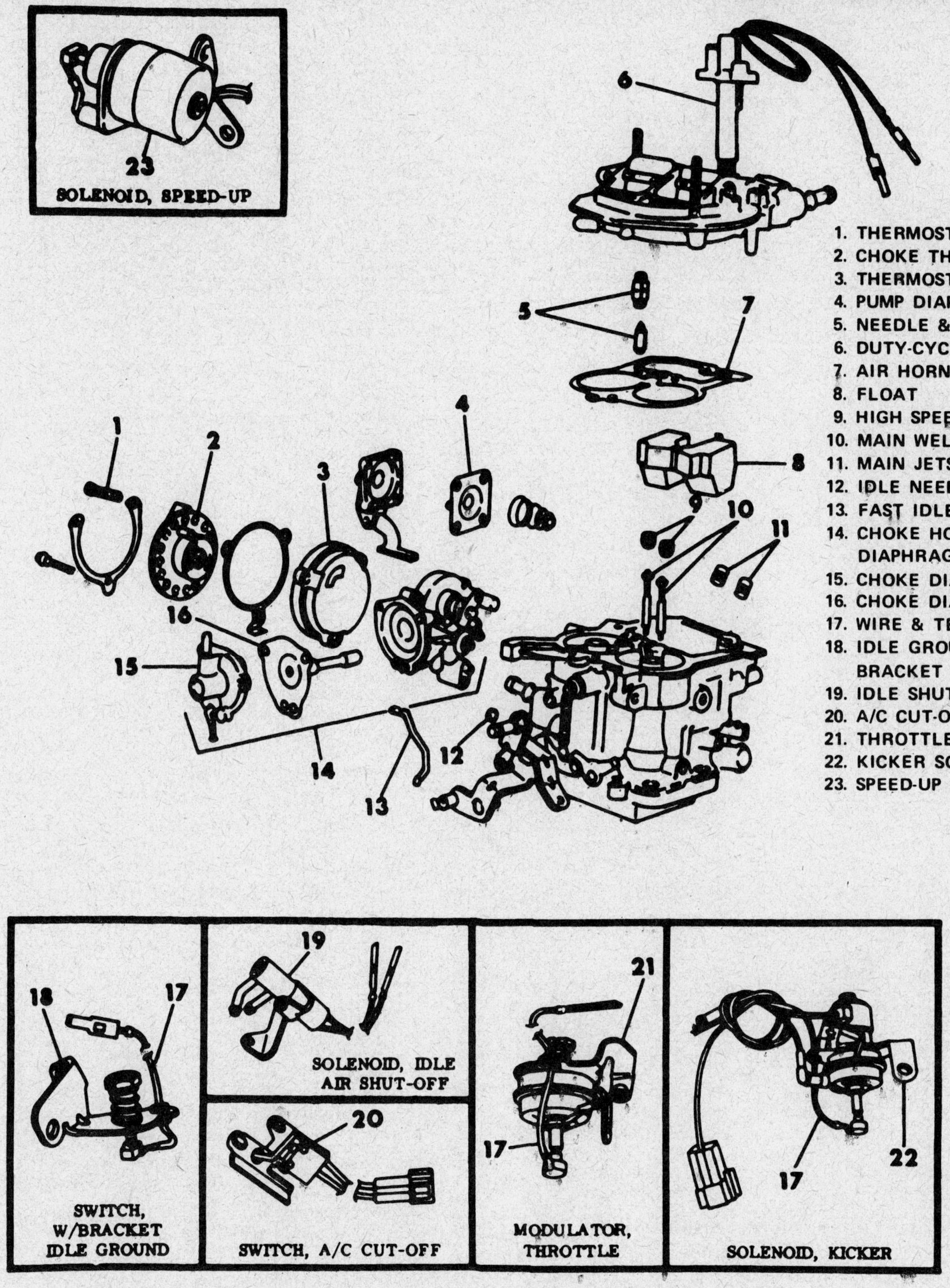

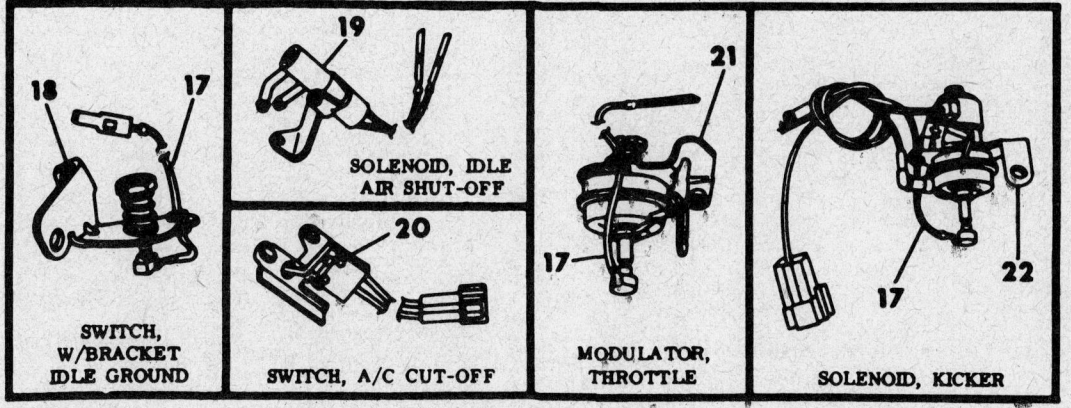

SOLENOID, SPEED-UP

23

1. THERMOSTAT RING RIVET
2. CHOKE THERMOSTAT WITH CAP
3. THERMOSTAT HOUSING
4. PUMP DIAPHRAGM
5. NEEDLE & SEAT
6. DUTY-CYCLE SOLENOID
7. AIR HORN GASKET
8. FLOAT
9. HIGH SPEED BLEEDS
10. MAIN WELL TUBES
11. MAIN JETS
12. IDLE NEEDLE PLUG
13. FAST IDLE LINK
14. CHOKE HOUSING WITH DIAPHRAGM
15. CHOKE DIAPHRAGM COVER
16. CHOKE DIAPHRAGM WITH SHAFT
17. WIRE & TERMINAL
18. IDLE GROUND SWITCH WITH BRACKET
19. IDLE SHUT-OFF SOLENOID
20. A/C CUT-OFF SWITCH
21. THROTTLE MODULATOR
22. KICKER SOLENOID
23. SPEED-UP SOLENOID

SWITCH, W/BRACKET IDLE GROUND

SOLENOID, IDLE AIR SHUT-OFF

SWITCH, A/C CUT-OFF

MODULATOR, THROTTLE

SOLENOID, KICKER

Exploded view of Holley model 6520 carburetor

CARBURETORS

MIKUNI CARBURETOR ADJUSTMENT SPECIFICATIONS

See Tune Up Chart in Car Chapter for curb and fast idle speeds.

Year	Model No.	Float Level	Fast Idle Opening At 68°F	Choke Breaker Opening At 14°F	Unloader Opening At 32°F
1981–82	MD025430	.779	14.5°	.067	.051
	MD025432	.779	14.5°	.067	.051
1983	MD017066	.779	14.5°	.067	.051
	MD017306	.779	14.5°	.067	.051
	MD017307	.779	14.5°	.067	.051

MIKUNI MODELS

The Mikuni carburetor, Fig. 1, is a conventional downdraft two barrel compound type carburetor. The automatic choke on these units is of the thermo-wax type which is controlled by engine coolant temperature. The main body on these units consists of a black resin compound. Other features of these units include a diaphragm type accelerator pump, bowl vent, fuel cut-off solenoid, air switching valve, sub EGR valve, coasting air valve, jet air control valve. California units also incorporate a high altitude compensation system.

Float Level Adjustment

Fig. 2—Invert air horn, with gasket removed, and measure distance from bottom of float to surface of air horn, using a suitable depth gauge. If reading is not within limits, the shim located under needle seat must be changed. Use shim kit MD606952 or equivalent, which has three shims with thicknesses of .0118 inch, .0157 inch and .0196 inch. Adding or removing a shim will change float level by three times the thickness of the shim.

COASTING AIR VALVE (CAV)

TO CANISTER

FUEL INLET

VACUUM HOSE CONNECTOR

ENRICHMENT VALVE

IDLE VACUUM UNIT

ACCELERATOR PUMP

AIR SWITCHING VALVE (ASV)

SUB EGR CONTROL VALVE

FUEL CUT-OFF SOLENOID

TAMPER RESISTANT IDLE MIXTURE SCREW

HARNESS CONNECTORS

VACUUM DIAPHRAGM

JET AIR CONTROL VALVE (JACV)

BOWL VENT VALVE

Fig. 1 Mikuni carburetor assembly

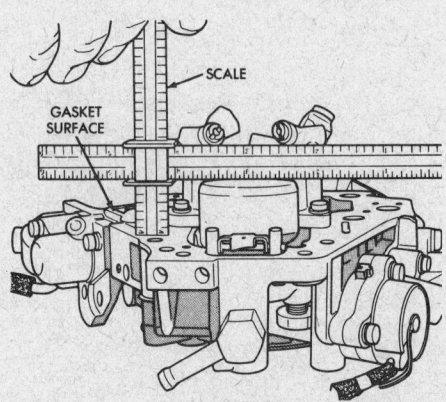

SCALE

GASKET SURFACE

Fig. 2 Float level adjustment. Mikuni carburetor

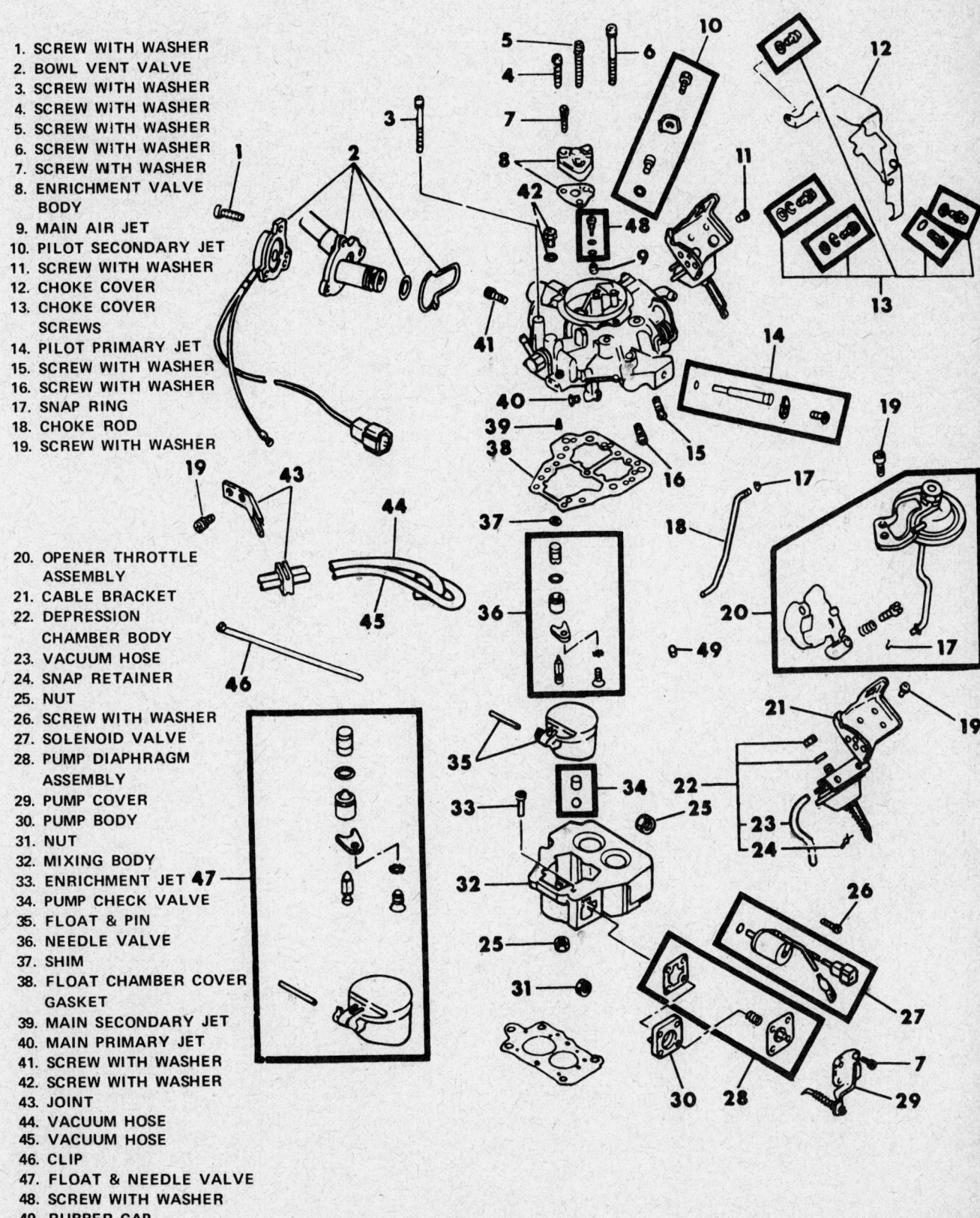

1. SCREW WITH WASHER
2. BOWL VENT VALVE
3. SCREW WITH WASHER
4. SCREW WITH WASHER
5. SCREW WITH WASHER
6. SCREW WITH WASHER
7. SCREW WITH WASHER
8. ENRICHMENT VALVE BODY
9. MAIN AIR JET
10. PILOT SECONDARY JET
11. SCREW WITH WASHER
12. CHOKE COVER
13. CHOKE COVER SCREWS
14. PILOT PRIMARY JET
15. SCREW WITH WASHER
16. SCREW WITH WASHER
17. SNAP RING
18. CHOKE ROD
19. SCREW WITH WASHER
20. OPENER THROTTLE ASSEMBLY
21. CABLE BRACKET
22. DEPRESSION CHAMBER BODY
23. VACUUM HOSE
24. SNAP RETAINER
25. NUT
26. SCREW WITH WASHER
27. SOLENOID VALVE
28. PUMP DIAPHRAGM ASSEMBLY
29. PUMP COVER
30. PUMP BODY
31. NUT
32. MIXING BODY
33. ENRICHMENT JET
34. PUMP CHECK VALVE
35. FLOAT & PIN
36. NEEDLE VALVE
37. SHIM
38. FLOAT CHAMBER COVER GASKET
39. MAIN SECONDARY JET
40. MAIN PRIMARY JET
41. SCREW WITH WASHER
42. SCREW WITH WASHER
43. JOINT
44. VACUUM HOSE
45. VACUUM HOSE
46. CLIP
47. FLOAT & NEEDLE VALVE
48. SCREW WITH WASHER
49. RUBBER CAP

Exploded view of Mikuni carburetor

TUNE UP SERVICE

CONTENTS

Tune up service has become increasingly important to the modern automotive engine with its vastly improved power and performance. With improved fuel and electrical systems and exhaust emission controls with their inherently critical settings, engines have become more sensitive to usage and operating conditions, which have a decided effect on power and performance. It is important, therefore, that this service be performed on the engine according to the recommendations of the vehicle manufacturer.

In addition to the servicing of spark plugs, ignition points and condenser, if equipped, a proper tune up includes a number of tests to check the condition of the engine and its related systems and uncover sources of future problems.

TUNE UP PROCEDURE

Since a quality tune up is dependent upon the proper operation of a number of systems, we have listed here in a logical sequence, the steps to be followed:

1. Diagnosis. This is to consist of a compression test, cylinder balance test, oscilloscope check, manifold vacuum test, charging circuit and cranking voltage test.
2. Service spark plugs.
3. Service ignition system, secondary wiring, distributor and coil.
4. Check and service battery and charging system.
5. Service manifold heat valve, if used.
6. Service carburetor, linkage, fuel and air filters and crankcase filter (if equipped).
7. Check operation of various emission control devices.

Once these mechanical checks have been performed the tune up can be finalized. The final steps are:

1. Setting the dwell on 1977–79 American Motors 4-121 engines with standard ignition distributors.
2. Setting slow idle, idle fuel mixture, choke and ignition timing if adjustments are possible and within federal and state laws.
3. Adjusting the fast idle.
4. Checking ignition output and secondary resistance.
5. Road test.

DIAGNOSIS & TESTING

Before a satisfactory tune up can be performed, the existing condition of the engine and its related systems must be determined. A tune up should not be attempted if tests indicate internal engine problems such as burnt valves, worn rings, blown head gasket, etc., until such conditions have been corrected.

Oscilloscope Test

Although oscilloscopes differ in many ways, they all display a light or "trace" on a screen which measures the voltage present at a given point and time. As the ignition system operates, its voltage creates a pattern on the screen. This pattern, when read in accordance with the manufacturer's instructions for the particular unit, indicates the condition of the entire ignition system.

Compression Test

An engine cannot be tuned to develop maximum power and smooth performance unless the proper compression is obtained in each cylinder.

CAUTION: Before cranking engine for a compression test, the ignition system should be disabled. On all ignition systems except American Motors and General Motors H.E.I. with internal ignition coil, disconnect coil wire from distributor cap and ground wire to engine block. On American Motors and General Motors H.E.I. with internal ignition coils disconnect B+ lead from distributor cap.

1. Remove any foreign matter from around spark plugs by blowing out plug area with compressed air. Then remove plugs.
2. Remove air cleaner and block throttle and choke in wide open position.
3. Insert compression gauge firmly in spark plug opening and crank engine through at least four compression strokes to obtain highest possible reading.
4. Test and record compression of each cylinder. Refer to chart, Fig. 1, for minimum compression pressures as indicated by percentages.
5. If one or more cylinders read low, inject about a tablespoon of engine oil on top of pistons in the low reading cylinders. Crank engine several times and recheck compression.
6. If compression is higher, it indicates worn piston rings. If compression does not improve, valves are sticking or seating poorly. If two adjacent cylinders show low compression and injecting oil does not improve the condition, the cause may be a head gasket leak between cylinders.

Manifold Vacuum Test

Manifold vacuum is affected by carburetor adjustment, valve timing, ignition timing, valve condition, cylinder compression, condition of positive crankcase ventilation system

MAXIMUM PSI	MINIMUM PSI		MAXIMUM PSI	MINIMUM PSI		MAXIMUM PSI	MINIMUM PSI	
	75%	80%		75%	80%		75%	80%
134	101	107	174	131	139	214	160	171
136	102	109	176	132	141	216	162	173
138	104	110	178	133	142	218	163	174
140	105	112	180	135	144	220	165	176
142	107	114	182	136	146	222	166	178
144	108	115	184	138	147	224	168	179
146	110	117	186	140	149	226	169	181
148	111	118	188	141	150	228	171	182
150	113	120	190	142	152	230	172	184
152	114	122	192	144	154	232	174	186
154	115	123	194	145	155	234	175	187
156	117	125	196	147	157	236	177	189
158	118	126	198	148	158	238	178	190
160	120	128	200	150	160	240	180	192
162	121	130	202	151	162	242	181	194
164	123	131	204	153	163	244	183	195
166	124	133	206	154	165	246	184	197
168	126	134	208	156	166	248	186	198
170	127	136	210	157	168	250	187	200
172	129	138	212	158	170			

Fig. 1 Compression pressure limit chart

Fig. 2   Checking ignition timing with timing light

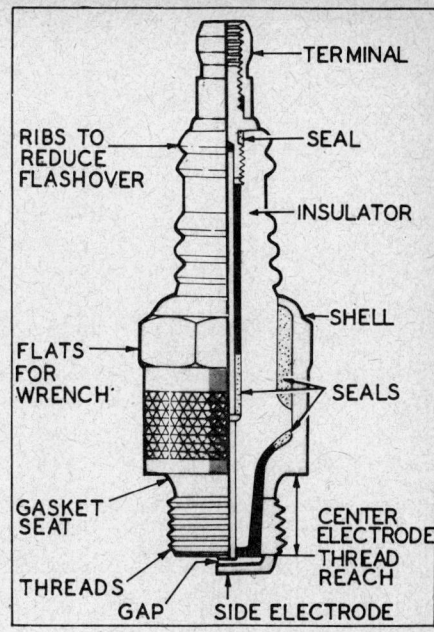

Fig. 3   Spark plug details

and leakage of manifold, carburetor, carburetor spacer or cylinder head gaskets.

Because abnormal gauge readings may indicate that more than one of the above factors is at fault, use care in analyzing an abnormal reading. For example, if the vacuum is low, the correction of one item may increase the vacuum enough to indicate that the trouble has been corrected. It is important, therefore, that each cause of an abnormal reading be investigated and further tests conducted, where necessary, to arrive at the correct diagnosis of the trouble. To check manifold vacuum, proceed as follows:

1. Bring engine to operating temperature.
2. Connect an accurate vacuum gauge to the intake manifold.
3. Operate engine at recommended idle speed.
4. Check vacuum reading on gauge.

Test Conclusions

NORMAL READING: 18 inches or more. Allowance should be made for the effect of altitude on gauge reading.
LOW & STEADY: Loss of power in all cylinders possibly caused by late ignition or valve timing, or loss of compression.
VERY LOW: Intake manifold, carburetor spacer or head gasket leak.
NEEDLE FLUCTUATES STEADILY AS SPEED INCREASES: Partial or complete loss of power in one or more cylinders caused by a leaky head or manifold gasket, burnt valve, weak valve spring or a defect in the ignition system.
GRADUAL DROP IN READING AT IDLE SPEED: Excessive back pressure in exhaust system.
INTERMITTENT FLUCTUATION: Defect in ignition system or sticking valve.
SLOW FLUCTUATION OR DRIFTING OF NEEDLE: Improper idle mixture, carburetor, carburetor spacer, intake manifold gasket leak or restricted crankcase ventilation system.

Cranking Voltage Test

The condition of the starting circuit can be checked by connecting a voltmeter across the battery posts, grounding the coil so the engine will not fire and cranking the engine. If, during cranking, the voltage reading drops below 9.6 volts, there is high resistance in the circuit.

Charging Circuit Test

The performance of the charging circuit should be checked during any tuneup. See specific unit section of this manual for test procedures.

Ignition Timing

The use of a timing light, Fig. 2, is recommended for checking and setting ignition timing.

NOTE: The use of an inductive type timing light is recommended when checking and setting ignition timing on electronic ignition systems.

Some engines have a provision for monolithic method of ignition timing utlizing a timing receptacle designed to accept an electronic probe. The receptacle is usually mounted at the front of the engine and the electronic probe is connected to electronic equipment which reads out the engine timing. These engines can also be timed using a timing light.

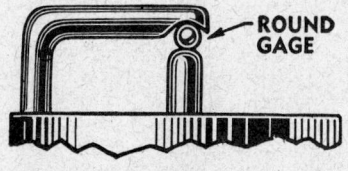

RIGHT

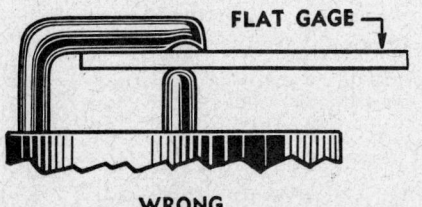

WRONG

Fig. 4   Correct and incorrect spark plug gauges

NOTE: The timing light should be connected to the number 1 spark plug lead by the use of an adapter. The boots around the connections should not be pierced to connect the light as this can cause spark arcing and misfiring.

Combustion Efficiency Test

This test checks the carburetor air/fuel mixture by measuring the amount of various chemicals present in the engine exhaust under different conditions. By following the manufacturer's instructions for the specific unit, the carburetor idle, intermediate, high speed and accelerator pump circuits can be checked for proper operation.

This test is especially important when working on engines equipped with exhaust emission controls because of the more critical mixture adjustments on such units.

SERVICE

Spark Plugs

1. Examine firing ends of plugs for evidence of oil fouling gas fouling, burned or overheated condition. *Oil fouling is usually identified by wet, sludgy deposits caused by excessive oil consumption. Gas fouling is identified by dry, black, fluffy deposits caused by incomplete combustion. Burned or overheated spark plugs are identified by white, burned or blistered insulator nose and badly burned electrodes. Improper fuel, insufficient cooling or improper ignition timing normally are the cause. Normal conditions are usually identified by white powdery deposits or rusty-brown to grayish-tan powdery deposits.*

2. Clean plugs with a suitable sand blast cleaner following the manufacturers instructions.
3. Remove carbon and other deposits from threads with a stiff wire brush.

NOTE: Do not use brush to clean electrodes as small pieces of wire can stick inside plug and later cause misfiring.

4. Using a small file, dress center and side electrodes to obtain flat parallel surfaces, Fig. 3.
5. If flat surfaces were obtained on used spark plugs or when installing new spark plugs, use a flat-bladed spark plug gage to check the gap. If a flat surface was not obtained due to erosion, use a wire-type spark plug gage to check the gap, Fig. 4. Refer to the Tune Up Specifications in the car chapters for spark plug gap specifications.
6. Adjust the gap to specification by bending the side electrode, never the center electrode.
7. Be sure to install gaskets, if used. Install and torque spark plugs to specifications. Refer to the Engine Tightening Torque Specifications in the car chapters for torque specifications.

NOTE: Several fuel refiners in areas of the United States have introduced a manganese compound fuel additive (MMT) for use in unleaded fuel. Fuel treated with MMT causes the entire tip of the spark plug to be coated with a rust colored deposit as a result of the combustion process. This rust colored deposit may be diagnosed incorrectly as being coolant in the combustion chamber. Spark plug performance is not affected by MMT deposits.

SERVICE NOTE

Improper installation of spark plugs is one of the greatest single causes of unsatisfactory spark plug performance. Improper installation is the result of one or more of the following practices: 1) Installation of plugs with insufficient torque to fully seat the gasket; 2) excessive torque which changes gap settings; 3) installation of plugs on dirty gasket seal; 4) installation of plugs to corroded spark plug hole threads.

Failure to install plugs properly will cause them to operate at excessively high temperatures and result in reduced operating life under mild operation or complete destruction under severe operation where the intense heat cannot be dissipated rapidly enough.

Always remove carbon deposits in hole threads before installing plugs. When corrosion is present in threads, normal torque is not sufficent to compress the plug gasket (if used) and early failure from overheating will result.

Always use a new gasket (if required) and wipe seats in head clean. The gasket must be fully compressed on clean seats to complete heat transfer and provide a gas tight seal in the cylinder. For this reason as well as the necessity of maintaining correct plug gap, the use of correct torque is extremely important during installation.

Ignition System

1. Check to be sure all connections are clean and tight. Repair or replace any wires that are frayed, loose, or damaged. Replace brittle or damaged spark plug wires.
2. Remove distributor cap, clean and inspect for cracks, carbon tracks and burned or corroded terminals. Replace cap if necessary.
3. Clean rotor and inspect for damage or deterioration. Replace rotor if necessary.
4. Check distributor centrifugal advance mechanism (if used) by turning distributor rotor in direction of running rotation as far as possible, then release rotor to see if springs return it to its retarded position. If rotor does not return readily, the distributor must be disassembled and cause of trouble corrected.
5. Using a suitable hand operated vacuum pump, check distributor vacuum advance mechanism diaphragm for free operation.
6. On 1977–79 American Motors 4-121 engine with standard ignition distributor, examine distributor points and clean or replace if necessary. Points with an overall gray color and only slight roughness or pitting need not be replaced.
7. On 1977–79 American Motors 4-121 engine with standard ignition distributor, clean dirty points with a clean point file. Use only a few strokes of the file. The file should not be used on other metals and should not be allowed to become dirty or greasy. *Never use emery cloth or sandpaper to clean points since particles will embed and cause arcing and rapid burning of points.* Do not attempt to remove all roughness nor dress the point surfaces down smooth. Merely remove scale or dirt.
8. On 1977–79 American Motors 4-121 engine with standard ignition distributors, replace points that are badly burned or pitted. Where burned or badly pitted points are encountered, the ignition system and engine should be checked to determine the cause of the trouble so it can be eliminated. Unless the condition causing point burning is corrected, new points will provide no better service than the old points. See "Standard Ignition Distributors" chapter for an analysis of point burning or pitting, and for proper installation of points and condensor.

Battery & Cables

Inspect for signs of corrosion on battery, cables and surrounding area, loose or broken carriers, cracked or bulged cases, dirt and acid, electrolyte leakage and low electrolyte level. Fill cells to proper level with distilled water or water passed through a "demineralizer."

The top of the battery should be clean and the battery hold-down bolts properly tightened.

For best results when cleaning batteries, wash first with a dilute ammonia or soda solution to neutralize any acid present and then flush off with clean water. Care must be taken to keep vent plugs tight so that the neutralizing solution does not enter the battery.

To insure good contact, the battery cables should be tight on the battery posts. Oil battery terminal felt washer. If the battery posts or cables terminals are corroded, the cables should be cleaned separately with a soda solution and a wire brush.

If the battery has remained undercharged, check for a loose alternator belt, defective alternator, high resistance in charging circuit, oxidized voltage regulator contact points, or a low voltage setting.

If the battery has been using too much water, the voltage regulator setting may be too high.

Fuel System

All fuel filters and the air cleaner element should be serviced during a tune up.

Since carburetion is dependent in several ways on both compression and ignition, it should always be checked last when tuning an engine. Refer to the Carburetor Chapter for pertinent data on specific units.

Service Bulletins

Chevrolet Monza 2 + 2 Spark Plug Replacement

When replacing spark plugs on V8 engines equipped with air conditioning and power steering, it is not necessary to release the engine mounts. The following procedure should be used: Have available a 1", 1½" and a 3" extension which are customarily used in spark plug servicing. Also needed are a 5/8" spark plug socket and a flex handle. Obtain a 5" to 6" length of windshield wiper hose which should be attached to a No. 3 spark plug end to facilitate installation, Fig. 1.

Insert a ¼" × 1½" stud or rod into the windshield wiper hose to achieve some rigidity in the windshield wiper hose structure as shown in Fig. 1. Then insert a ¼" × 1" bolt into other end of hose to allow for easier rotation. Now proceed to install No. 3 spark plug. Once the spark plug is started in the threads of the cylinder head, you may then remove the hose and proceed to tighten the spark plug with the appropriate tools. All other spark plugs can be replaced in the conventional manner using an applicable extension.

1981 Cadillac 4.1L V-6 Rough Engine Operation

If conditions of rough engine operation or poor driveability are encountered at speeds of approximately 50 mph, the distributor main-shaft washer could be faulty, Fig. 2.

To diagnose this condition, connect an ignition scope to engine, then operate engine at approximately 1900 RPM and observe scope pattern. Using a suitable timing light, check ignition timing. If the scope pattern is erratic or indicates as high as ten ignition pulses, or ignition timing is retarded −10 degrees at 1800 RPM, check distributor date code. If date code is between 1A06 and 1D29, the existing wave washer should be removed and the replacement wave washer, part # 1984360 should be installed, Fig. 2. If the distributor date code does not fall within the limits, do not replace the wave washer as the condition is probably related to the fuel or ignition system.

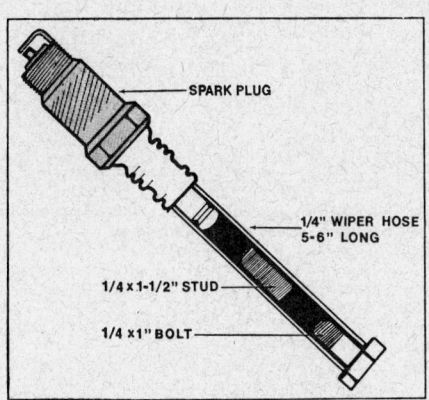

Fig. 1   Monza 2 + 2 spark plug replacement tool

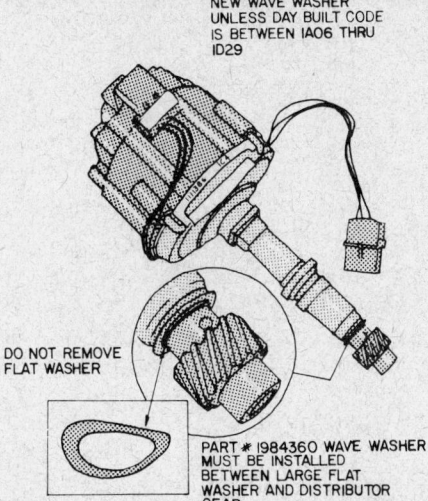

DO NOT ADD OR REPLACE NEW WAVE WASHER UNLESS DAY BUILT CODE IS BETWEEN 1A06 THRU 1D29

DO NOT REMOVE FLAT WASHER

PART # 1984360 WAVE WASHER MUST BE INSTALLED BETWEEN LARGE FLAT WASHER AND DISTRIBUTOR GEAR

Fig. 2   Correct wave washer installation

Ignition Coils & Resistors

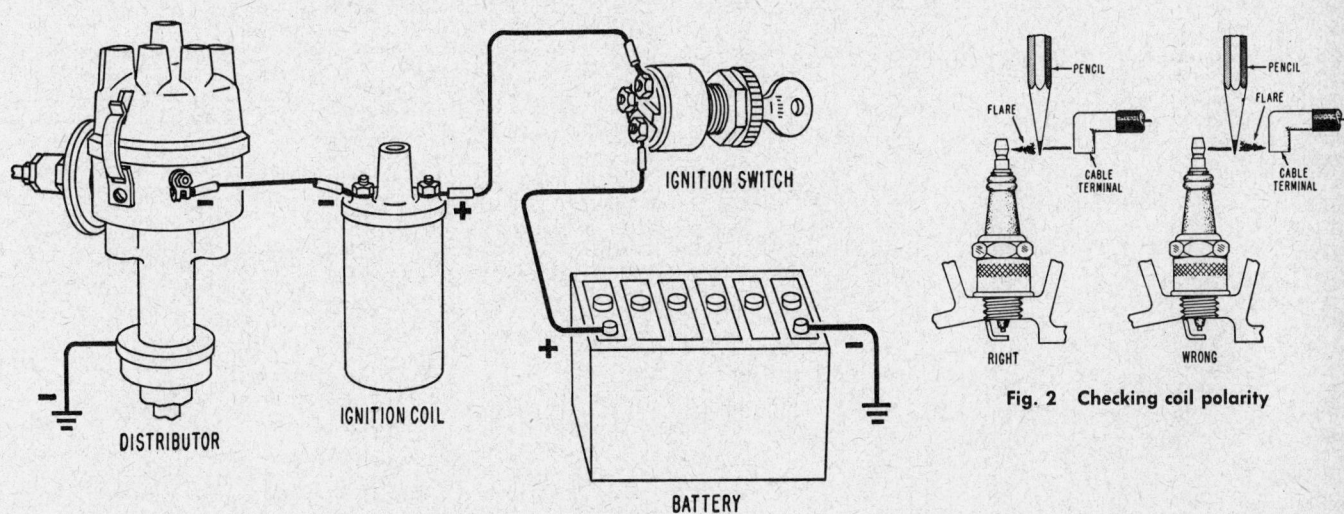

IGNITION SWITCH

DISTRIBUTOR

IGNITION COIL

BATTERY

Fig. 1   Wiring connections for coil with negative ground system

PENCIL

FLARE

CABLE TERMINAL

RIGHT

PENCIL

FLARE

CABLE TERMINAL

WRONG

Fig. 2   Checking coil polarity

IGNITION COILS

1977—79 American Motors 4-121 Engine with Standard Ignition Distributor

If poor ignition performance is obtained and the coil is suspected, it may be tested on the car or it may be removed for the test.

Ignition coils are often condemned when the trouble is actually in the ignition switch. A completely defective ignition switch will produce an open primary circuit, giving the same indications as if the coil were completely dead. A partly defective ignition switch will cause a weak spark.

By cutting the ignition switch out of the circuit, it can easily be determined whether the coil is defective or the fault lies in the ignition switch.

In the absence of any testing equipment a simple check of an ignition coil can be made as follows: Turn on ignition switch with breaker points closed. Remove the high tension cable from the center socket of the distributor cap and hold it 1/4″ to 1/2″ away from a clean spot on the engine. If the coil and other units connected to it are in good condition a spark should jump from the wire to the engine as the points are opened. If not, use a jumper wire from the distributor terminal to the engine; if the primary is in good condition a spark will occur.

All ignition coils with metal containers can be tested for grounded windings by placing one test clip on a clean part of the metal container and touching the other clip to the primary and high tension terminals. If the lamp lights or tiny sparks appear at the points of contact, the windings are grounded and the coil should be replaced.

Coil Polarity

Most coils are marked positive and negative at the primary terminals. When installing or connecting a coil be sure to make the connections as shown in Fig. 1. A reversal of this polarity may affect the performance of the engine (or the radio).

If the coil is not marked as to its polarity, it can be checked by holding any high tension wire about 1/4″ away from its spark plug terminal with the engine running. Insert the point of a wooden lead pencil between the spark plug and the wire, Fig. 2. If the spark flares and has a slight orange tinge on the spark plug side of the pencil, polarity is correct. If the spark flares on the cable side, coil connections should be reversed.

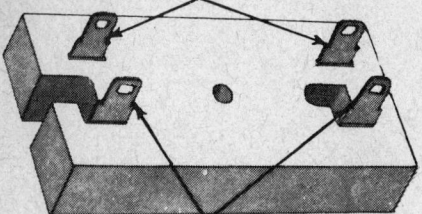

AUXILIARY BALLAST RESISTOR

NORMAL BALLAST RESISTOR

Fig. 3   Dual ballast resistor, Chrysler Corp. electronic ignition system 1977–80. All exc. 1978–79 Omni & Horizon

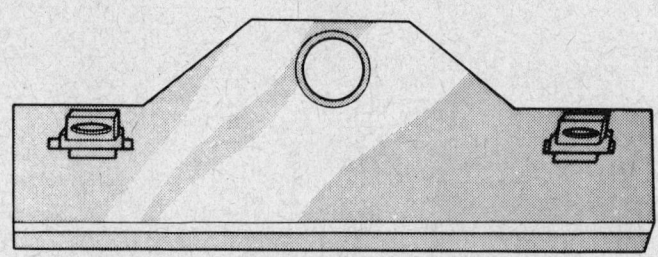

Fig. 4   Ballast resistor. 1978–79 Omni, Horizon & 1981–83 Chrysler Corp. exc. 1980–83 front wheel drive models

IGNITION RESISTORS

Block Type Ballast Resistors

SERVICE NOTE: If the engine fires when the ignition switch is turned on but quits when the switch is released to its running position, it indicates that the resistor is defective and must be replaced.

A dual ballast resistor is used on all 1977–80 Chrysler Corp. vehicles equipped with electronic ignition, except 1978–79 Omni and Horizon, Fig. 3. The normal side of the resistor is a compensating resistance in the primary circuit. At low engine speeds, current is maintained for a longer period of time in this side of the resistor, causing the unit to heat up, in turn increasing resistance. This increased resistance reduces the primary circuit voltage, protecting the ignition coil from high voltage at low engine speeds.

As engine speed increases, the period of time in which current is maintained in the normal side of the resistor is shorter, causing the unit to cool, in turn decreasing resistance.

This decreased resistance permits the primary circuit voltage to increase for high speed operation.

During engine start, the normal side of the ballast resistor is by-passed, allowing full battery voltage to be applied to the primary circuit.

The auxiliary side of the ballast resistor limits voltage to the control unit, thereby protecting the unit.

A single ballast resistor, Fig. 4, is used on 1978–79 Omni, Horizon and 1980–83 Chrysler Corp. except 1980–83 front wheel drive models. This resistor is bypassed during the engine starting procedure to allow full battery voltage to reach the ignition coil.

Wire Type Resistors

The special resistance wires used with 12-volt systems are five to six feet long and contained in the regular wiring harness. The wire is made of stainless steel or special alloy, plastic-coated and covered with a glass braid. There is a relatively small temperature rise and the resistance wire is switched out of the circuit for starting and back in again for running.

On Bosch and Ford systems, Fig. 5 and 6, the resistor is by-passed through a terminal on the starter relay which is connected directly to the positive terminal of the coil.

Service Note

If the engine fires when the ignition switch is turned on but quits when the switch is released to the "run" position, it indicates that the resistance wire has lost its continuity or there is a bad connection at the resistor terminals. If the wire is defective, it must be replaced.

CAUTION: Do not attempt to operate the engine for an extended length of time with the resistor by-passed by means of a jumper wire as the breaker points will burn.

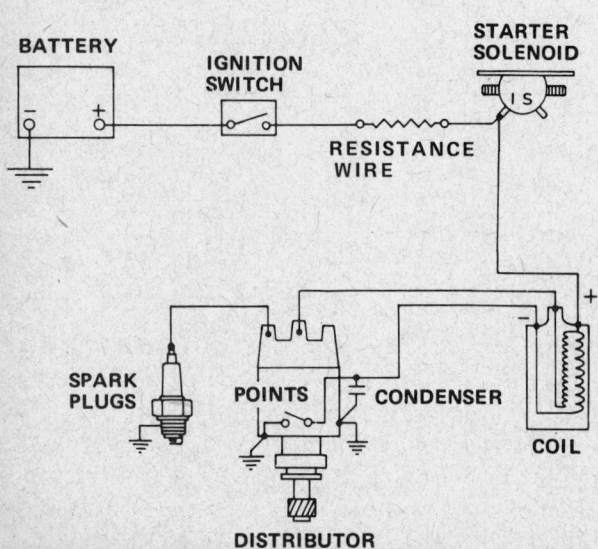

Fig. 5   Bosch ignition circuit diagram

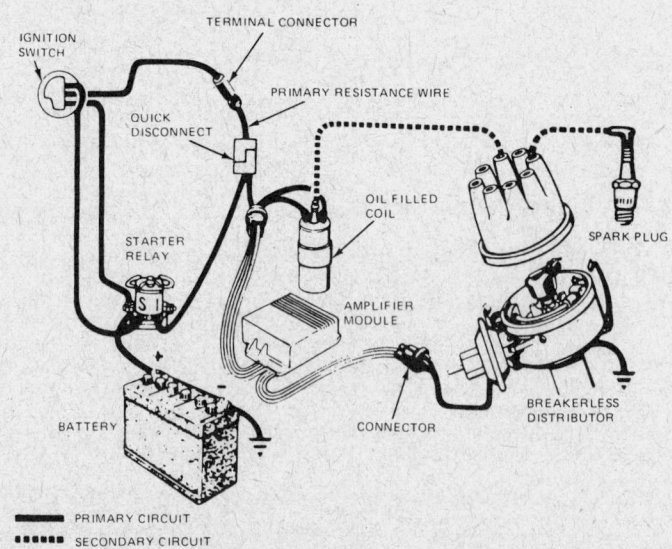

Fig. 6   Ford ignition circuit diagram with a resistance wire connected to a three-terminal ignition switch

IGNITION COIL & RESISTOR SPECIFICATIONS

Year	Model	Coil Draw, Amps.		Coil Resistance, Ohms		Ignition Resistor Ohms @ 75°F.
		Engine Stopped	Engine Idling	Primary @ 75°F.	Secondary @ 75°F.	
AMERICAN MOTORS—All Models						
1977	4 Cyl.	4.0	2.0	1.60–1.80	9400–11700	1.8
	6 Cyl. & V8 B.I.D.①	4.0	2.0	1.25–1.40	9000–15000	—
1978–79	4 Cyl.	4.0	2.0	1.60–1.80	9400–11700	2.0
	6 Cyl. & V8 Breakerless	4.0	2.0–2.4	1.13–1.23	7700–9300	1.35
1980–83	Exc. H.E.I.	4.0	2.0–2.4	1.13–1.23	7700–9300	1.35
1981–83	H.E.I.	—	—	0	②	—

①—Breakerless Inductive Discharge.
②—Reading should be less than infinity with ohmmeter set on highest scale.

Year	Model	Coil Draw, Amps.		Coil Resistance, Ohms		Ignition Resistor Ohms @ 75°F.
		Engine Stopped	Engine Idling	Primary @ 75°F.	Secondary @ 75°F.	
CHRYSLER CORP.—All Models						
1977	①	—	—	1.60–1.79	9400–11700	.50–.60③
	②	—	—	1.41–1.62	8000–11200	.50–.60③
1978–79	All Models①	—	—	1.60–1.79	9400–11700	.50–.60③
	All Models Exc. Front Wheel Drive②	—	—	1.34–1.55	9000–12200	.50–.60③
	Front Wheel Drive②	—	—	1.41–1.62	8000–11200	.50–.60③
1980	All Models①	—	—	1.60–1.79	9400–11700	④
	All Models Exc. Front Wheel Drive②	—	—	1.34–1.55	9000–12200	1.12–1.38
	Front Wheel Drive②	—	—	1.41–1.62	8000–11200	—
1981–83	All Models①	—	—	1.60–1.79	9400–11700	④
	All Models Exc. Front Wheel Drive②	—	—	1.34–1.55	9000–12200	1.12–1.38
	Front Wheel Drive②	—	—	1.41–1.62	9000–12200	—
	Front Wheel Drive⑤	—	—	0.7–0.85	9000–11000	—

①—Prestolite coils.
②—Essex or Echlin coils.
③—Auxiliary (control unit side) 4.75–5.75.
④—Except front wheel drive, 1.12–1.38; Front wheel drive, no resistor used.
⑤—Mitsubishi coils.

Year	Model	Coil Draw, Amps.		Coil Resistance, Ohms		Ignition Resistor Ohms @ 75°F.
		Engine Stopped	Engine Idling	Primary @ 75°F.	Secondary @ 75°F.	
FORD MOTOR CO.—All Models						
1977	Breakerless	—	—	1.0–2.0	7000–13000	1.30–1.40
1978–83	Dura Spark I	—	—	.71–.77	7350–8250	—
	Dura Spark II & III	—	—	1.13–1.23	7700–9300	1.05–1.15
1982–83	T.F.I.①	—	—	.3–1.0	8000–11500	—

①—Escort, EXP, LN7 & Lynx with auto. trans. and Thick Film Integrated Ignition & all Tempo & Topaz

Year	Model	Coil Draw, Amps.		Coil Resistance, Ohms		Ignition Resistor Ohms @ 75°F.
		Engine Stopped	Engine Idling	Primary @ 75°F.	Secondary @ 75°F.	
GENERAL MOTORS—All Models						
1977–80	H.E.I.①	—	—	0–1.0	6000–30000	—
1981–83	H.E.I.①	—	—	0	②	—

①—High Energy Ignition.
②—Reading should be less than infinity with ohmmeter set on highest scale.

STANDARD IGNITION DISTRIBUTORS

CONTENTS

BREAKER CONTACT POINTS

Contact Analysis

The normal color of points should be a light gray. If the contact surfaces are black it is usually caused by oil vapor or grease from the cam. If they are blue, the cause is usually excessive heating due to improper alignment, high resistance or open condenser circuit.

If the contacts develop a crater or depression on one point and a high spot of metal on the other, the cause is an electrolytic action transferring metal from one contact to the other, Fig. 1, due to an unbalanced ignition system, which can sometimes be improved by a slight change in condenser capacity. If the mound is on the positive point, Fig. 2, install a condenser of greater capacity; if on the negative point, Fig. 3, use a condenser of lesser capacity.

One of the most common causes of point failure is the presence of oil or grease on the contact surfaces, usually from over-lubrication of the wick at the top of the cam or too much grease on the rubbing block of the breaker arm.

Breaker Point Gap

If points are set too close, arcing and burning will occur, causing hard starting and poor low speed performance. If points are set too wide, the cam angle or dwell will be too small

to allow saturation of the coil at high engine speeds, resulting in weak spark.

Contact point opening has a direct bearing on cam angle or dwell which is the number of degrees that the breaker cam rotates from the time the points close until they open again, Fig. 4. The cam angle or dwell increases as point opening is decreased and vice versa. If point gap is set with a feeler gauge, the cam angle or dwell should be checked either with a portable dwell meter or by installing the distributor in a distributor tester.

Breaker Arm Spring Tension

Breaker arm spring tension is important. If the tension is too great the arm will bounce, causing an interruption of the current in the coil and misfiring. If the spring tension is too little, the rubbing block will not follow the cam, causing a variation in cam dwell. The spring tension should always be set at the high limit as given in the *Distributor Specifications* chart in the car chapter, as it will be reduced as the rubbing block wears.

Hook a spring scale on the breaker arm and pull in a straight line as shown in Fig. 5. Take a reading as the points start to separate under the slow and steady pull of the scale. If the tension is not within specifications, loosen the screw that holds the end of the point spring and slide the end of the spring in or out as necessary. Tighten the screw and recheck the spring tension.

Breaker Point Alignment

Check alignment of points with points closed, Fig. 6. Align new points where necessary but do not attempt to align used points. Instead, replace used points where serious misalignment is observed. After aligning points, adjust point gap.

Adjusting Breaker Gap

Specifications for breaker gap, *as measured with a feeler gauge*, are listed in the *Tune Up Specifications* in the car chapters. However, if at all possible, this should be set on a distributor tester, with a dial indicator, Fig. 7, or by hooking up a portable dwell meter with the distributor cap and rotor removed and, while cranking the engine, setting the dwell.

NOTE: When setting the dwell with the engine cranking, be sure to ground the coil secondary lead and do not operate the starter for sustained periods at a time.

This eliminates the possibility of an incorrect gap because of rough points, Fig. 8.

The advantage of a distributor testing machine is that it not only measures cam angle or dwell but it also uncovers irregularities between cam lobes, point bounce, alignment of rubbing block with cam, alignment of contacts and breaker arm spring tension.

CONDENSER

A condenser should not be condemned because the points are burned or oxidized. Oil vapor, or grease from the cam, or high resistance may be the cause of such a condition.

Fig. 1   Showing how metal from one contact transfers to the other

Condensers should be tested with a good condenser tester for leakage, break-down, capacity, and resistance in series in the condenser circuit. Manufacturers of condenser testers furnish complete instructions as to their use.

CENTRIFUGAL ADVANCE

When engine speed increases, the spark must be introduced in the cylinder earlier in the cycle in order that the fuel charge can be ignited and will have time to burn and deliver its power to the piston. To provide this spark advance based on engine speed, the centrifugal advance mechanism is used.

This mechanism, Fig. 9, consists of centrifugal advance weights which throw out against spring tension as the engine speed increases. This movement imparts, through a toggle arrangement, rotational motion to the breaker cam or plate, depending on the model, causing it to rotate a number of degrees with respect to the distributor drive shaft. This

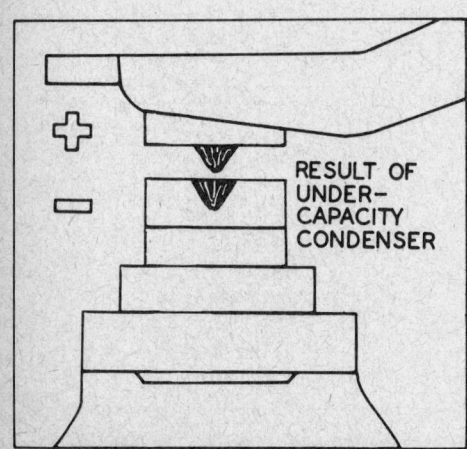

Fig. 2   Mound on positive point

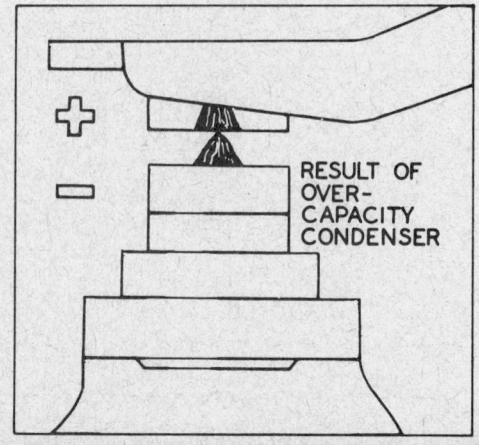

Fig. 3   Mound on negative point

Fig. 4   Cam angle or dwell

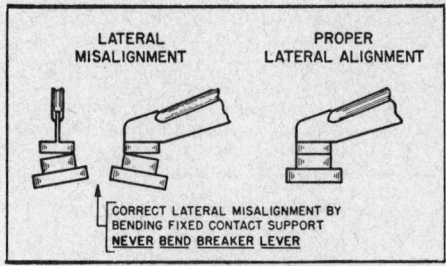

Fig. 6   Breaker point alignment

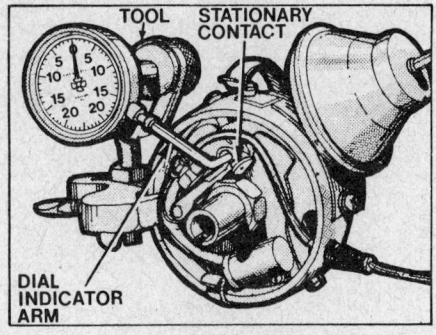

Fig. 7   Dial indicator for measuring breaker gap

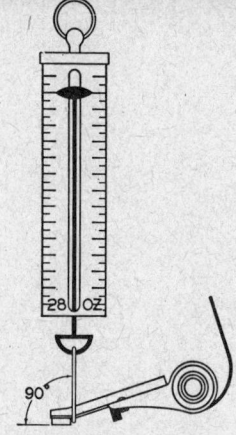

Fig. 5   Measuring breaker spring tension

causes the points to be opened and closed earlier in the cycle so the spark is delivered to the cylinder earlier.

In servicing the distributor, all weights should be removed from the hinge pins, cleaned and checked for excessive wear, either in the weights or pins, or the plate which is slotted for the movement of the pins on top of the governor weights. Replacement should be made if there is any appreciable wear in the slots, as any wear at this point would change the characteristic of the spark advance.

If these parts are in good condition, the hinge pins should be lubricated before being reassembled, by greasing the hinge pins and filling the pockets in the governor weights with grease. Do not use vaseline for this purpose as its melting point is comparatively low.

When installing new centrifugal advance assemblies, it is important that the spacer washers between the housing and shaft be installed correctly. If incorrectly installed, the advance assembly will be too high, causing it to rub against the bottom of the breaker plate.

On some distributors, both springs are alike, while on others there is one heavy and one light spring.

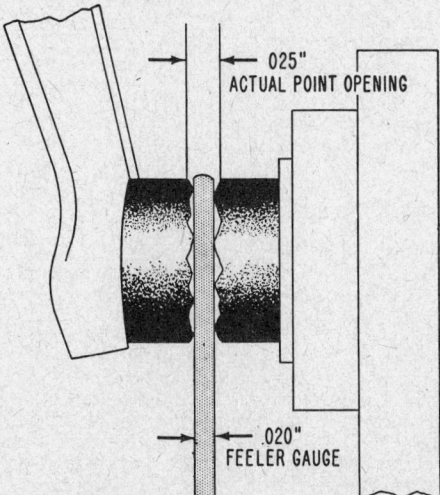

Fig. 8   Why flat feeler gauge will not provide accurate point spacing if points are rough

VACUUM ADVANCE

The vacuum advance unit consists of a spring loaded diaphragm, which is connected through linkage to the distributor breaker plate. The spring loaded side of the diaphragm is connected through a vacuum line to the carburetor or intake manifold. As vacuum increases, the diaphragm is drawn toward the source of vacuum, the diaphragm linkage is pulled with it and the breaker plate, attached to the linkage, is turned to advance the timing.

BOSCH DISTRIBUTOR SERVICE
Distributor, Replace

Removal
1. Remove air cleaner, then the distributor water shield.
2. Remove distributor cap with wires attached and position aside.
3. Disconnect vacuum hose from vacuum advance unit.
4. Disconnect distributor primary wiring connector.
5. Scribe a mark on distributor housing aligned with tip of distributor rotor.
6. Scribe a mark between distributor housing and engine block.
7. Remove distributor holddown nut and clamp.
8. Remove distributor from engine.

Installation
1. Clean distributor mounting pad on engine.
2. Install new distributor mounting gasket.
3. If engine was not cranked after distributor was removed, proceed as follows:
   a. Align rotor tip with mark scribed on housing.
   b. Slide distributor into engine, aligning the mark on distributor housing with mark on engine. It may be necessary to move distributor rotor and shaft slightly to mesh distributor gear with camshaft gear. The rotor should align with the scribe mark on housing when the distributor is fully installed into engine.
   c. Install distributor holddown clamp

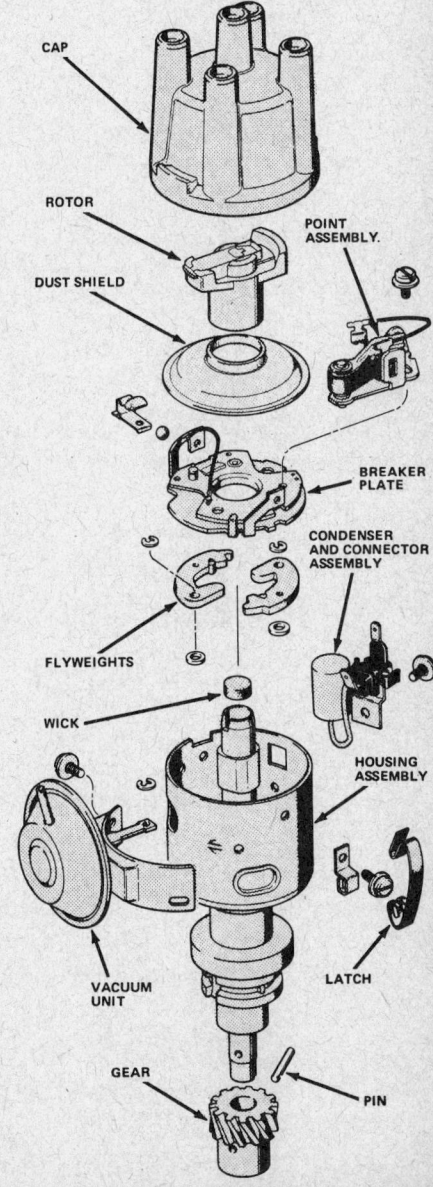

Fig. 9   Exploded view of Bosch distributor. American Motors 4-121 engine

and nut.
4. If the engine was cranked after the distributor was removed, proceed as follows.
   a. Remove No. 1 spark plug.
   b. Place finger over spark plug hole and crank engine until compression pressure is felt. Then, continue to crank engine until timing mark on crankshaft pulley is aligned with "0" mark, top dead center on timing plate.
   c. Position distributor rotor tip to align with the No. 1 cylinder firing position in distributor cap. This is indicated by a manufactured mark on the edge of the distributor housing, Then, turn rotor 1/8 turn clockwise past the No. 1 firing position mark.

   d. Install distributor into engine and align scribe mark made between distributor housing and engine.
   e. Install distributor holddown clamp and nut.
5. Install distributor cap.
6. Connect vacuum hose to vacuum advance unit and the distributor primary wiring.
7. Adjust ignition timing to specifications. Refer to the individual car chapters.

Distributor Service

NOTE: Replacement parts for servicing the distributor shaft, drive gear, bushing and cam are not available. In addition, the advance weights, advance springs and breaker plate are not serviceable since the breaker plate is permanently staked into the housing.

If distributor has been disassembled, refer to Fig. 9 at reassembly.

1. Lubricate pivot pins and install advance weights. Lubricate shaft and install cam assembly.
2. Install advance springs and advance plate, securing plate with clip and screws.
3. Insert grommet and condenser wire through hole in housing and install condenser and contact points.
4. Install vacuum advance unit. Hook vacuum advance rod over pin in advance plate and install snap ring.

ELECTRONIC IGNITION SYSTEMS

INDEX

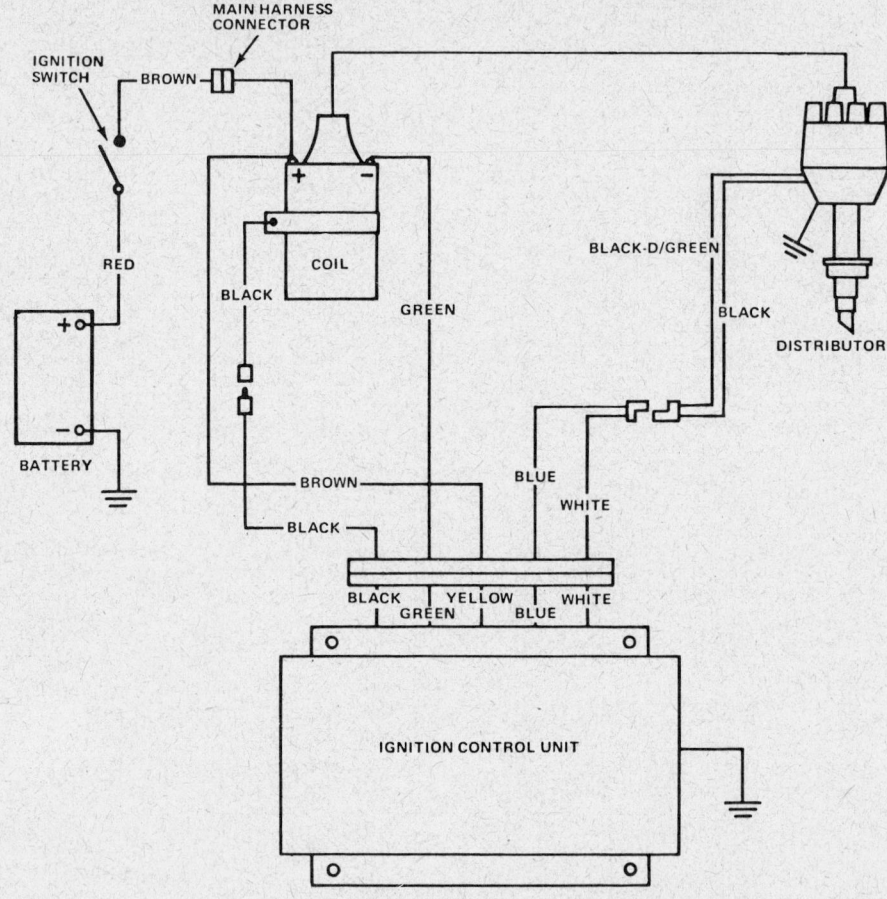

Fig. 1 BID ignition system wiring

AMERICAN MOTORS BREAKERLESS INDUCTIVE DISCHARGE (BID) IGNITION SYSTEM

Description

The BID ignition system incorporates four major units; an electronic control unit, ignition coil, distributor and high tension wires, Fig. 1. The electronic control unit is a solid-state, moisture resistant module with the components sealed in a potting compound to resist vibration and environmental conditions. Since the control unit has an internal current regulator, a resistance wire or ballast resistor is not necessary in the primary circuit. Battery voltage is applied to the ignition coil positive terminal when the ignition switch is in the "On" or "Start" position, therefore, an ignition system bypass is not required in this system. The primary coil circuit is electronically regulated by this unit.

The ignition coil is of standard construction and requires no special service.

The distributor is conventional except the contact points, condenser and cam are replaced by a sensor and trigger wheel, and since no wearing occurs between the trigger wheel and sensor, dwell angle remains constant. The sensor receives an alternating current signal from the electronic control unit. The sensor develops an electro-magnetic field used to detect the presence of metal which are the leading edges of the trigger wheel teeth.

Operation

When the ignition switch is placed in the

"Start" or "Run" position, the control unit is activated. An oscillator within the control unit excites the sensor coil, in turn developing the electromagnetic field. When a leading edge of a trigger wheel tooth enters the electromagneticic field, the tooth reduces the sensor oscillation strength to a predetermined level, in turn activating the demodulator circuit. The demodulator circuit controls a power transistor located in series with the coil primary circuit. The power transistor switches the coil primary circuit off, thereby inducing a high voltage in the coil secondary winding. The high voltage is then delivered to the spark plugs through the distributor rotor, cap and high tension wires.

System Quick Test, Fig. 2

The BID system may be tested quickly on the vehicle using No. 57 bulb and a jumper wire. Refer to Fig. 2 for procedure.

Comprehensive testing may be performed as outlined under "Troubleshooting".

Troubleshooting, Fig. 3

1. Disconnect Electronic Control Unit (ECU) ground wire and the 4-wire connector. Using a small wire brush and solvent, clean the terminals. Leave connectors disconnected.
2. Disconnect battery cables, then momentarily move ignition switch to START and allow it to move to ON.
3. Measure resistance of entire ignition feed circuit by connecting an ohmmeter to battery positive B1 and F3 terminal in the 4-wire connector.
4. If resistance is less than 1 ohm, tighten main harness connector attaching screw to fully seat connector. If resistance is 1 ohm or more, isolate trouble area by connecting the ohmmeter and measuring the resistance of each portion of the ignition feed circuit between the following terminals: B1 and B2, B2 and A1, A1 and H1, F3 and C1, C1 and H2, H1 and H2, AV and DV. Clean, tighten or reposition connectors as needed.
5. Inspect coil primary connections for looseness and proper assembly. Wire terminals must be between channel washer and nut, channel washer tabs must be facing up. Reposition and tighten as needed.
6. Connect an ohmmeter between F3 and F4 terminals to measure coil primary circuit resistance. If resistance is 1–2 ohms, proceed to step 7. If resistance is less than 1 ohm, replace coil and proceed to step 8. If resistance is more than 2 ohms, isolate trouble and insure that the resistance between the following terminals is as follows: C1 and C2, 1–2 ohms; F3 and C1, O ohms; F4 and C2, O ohms. Replace coil or repair troubled area and proceed to step 7. If coil was replaced, proceed to step 8.
7. Measure coil secondary resistance by removing coil secondary wire from coil and connecting ohmmeter between C1 and C3.

NOTE: Set ohmmeter to the 1,000 ohm scale before testing secondary resistance.

If resistance is 9,000–15,000 ohms, reconnect coil secondary wire and proceed to step 8. If resistance is less than 9,000 ohms or more than 15,000 ohms, replace coil and reconnect coil secondary wire and proceed to Step 8.

8. Remove distributor cap, rotor and dust cover and check for 1.6–2.4 ohms resistance between F1 and F2 terminals.

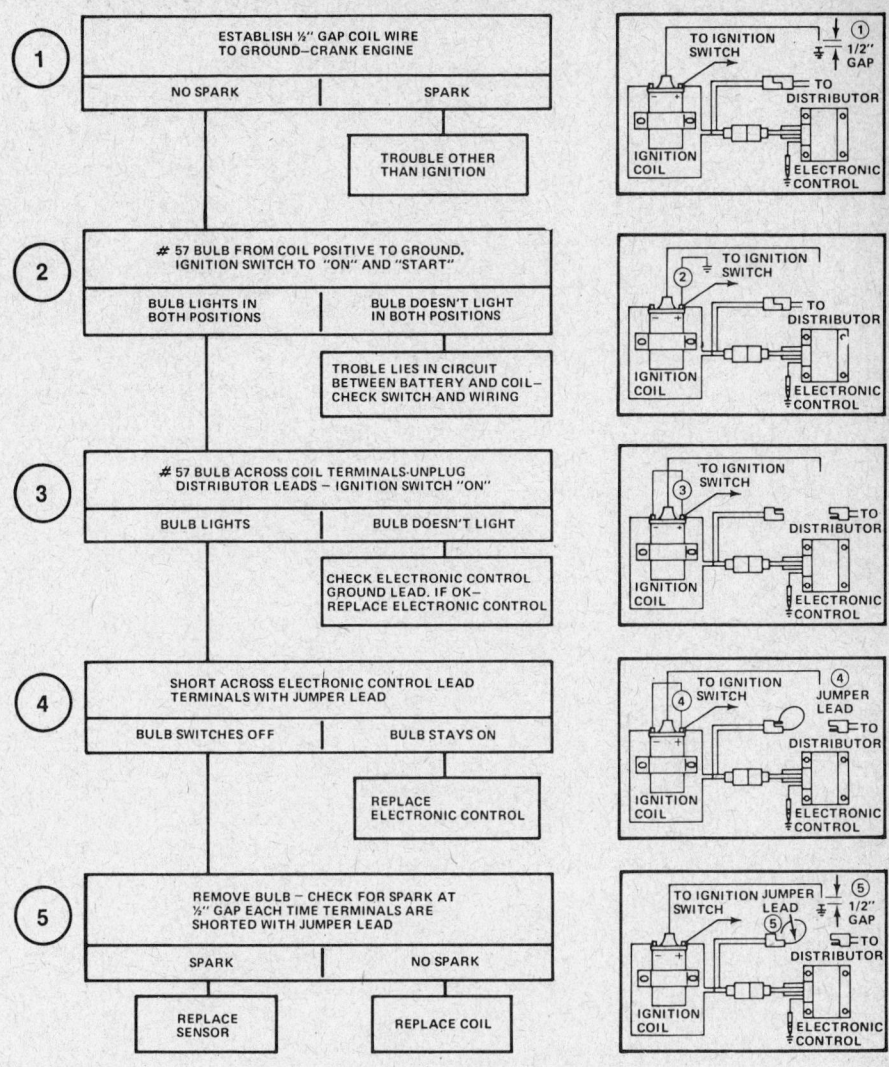

Fig. 2   American Motors BID system quick test

NOTE: Pull and flex sensor wires, firmly squeeze molded sensor grommet at distributor, and apply firm side to side pressure on sensor post while checking resistance.

If resistance is as specified and steady, proceed to step 10. If resistance is too high or low, or if needle fluctuates or wavers, proceed to step 9.

9. Disconnect 2-wire connector and check for 1.6–2.4 ohms resistance between S1 and S2 terminals.

NOTE: Pull and flex sensor wires, firmly squeeze molded sensor wire grommet at distributor, and apply firm side to side pressure on sensor post.

If resistance is as specified and steady, proceed to step 10. If resistance is too high or too low, or if needle fluctuates or wavers, replace sensor and proceed to step 10.

10. Using a small wire brush and solvent, clean terminals S1, S2, S3 and S4.
11. Measure resistance of ECU ground circuit by connecting an ohmmeter between

terminal G2 and battery negative cable G4. Resistance should be 0 ohms. Clean and tighten connections as needed.
12. Using pliers, squeeze terminals E1, E2, E3, E4 and G1 until terminals have a distinct oval shape, thereby assuring a tight fit when terminals are connected.
13. Using petroleum jelly, coat the male terminals in the 4-wire connector and ground connectors and around the outer edge of the terminal end of the ECU 4-wire connector.
14. Connect the 4-wire and ground connectors.
15. Connect Pulse Simulator J-25331 to the S3 and S4 terminals and reconnect battery cables. Remove coil secondary wire from distributor and place end of wire 1/2 inch from ground, then with ignition switch ON, operate simulator and observe for spark across the 1/2 inch gap. If spark jumps gap, proceed to step 17. If spark does not jump gap, proceed to step 16.
16. Disconnect wire from coil negative terminal, then connect one pulse simulator clip to the coil negative terminal and connect the remaining clip to the ground. With ignition switch ON, operate pulse simulator and observe for spark across the 1/2

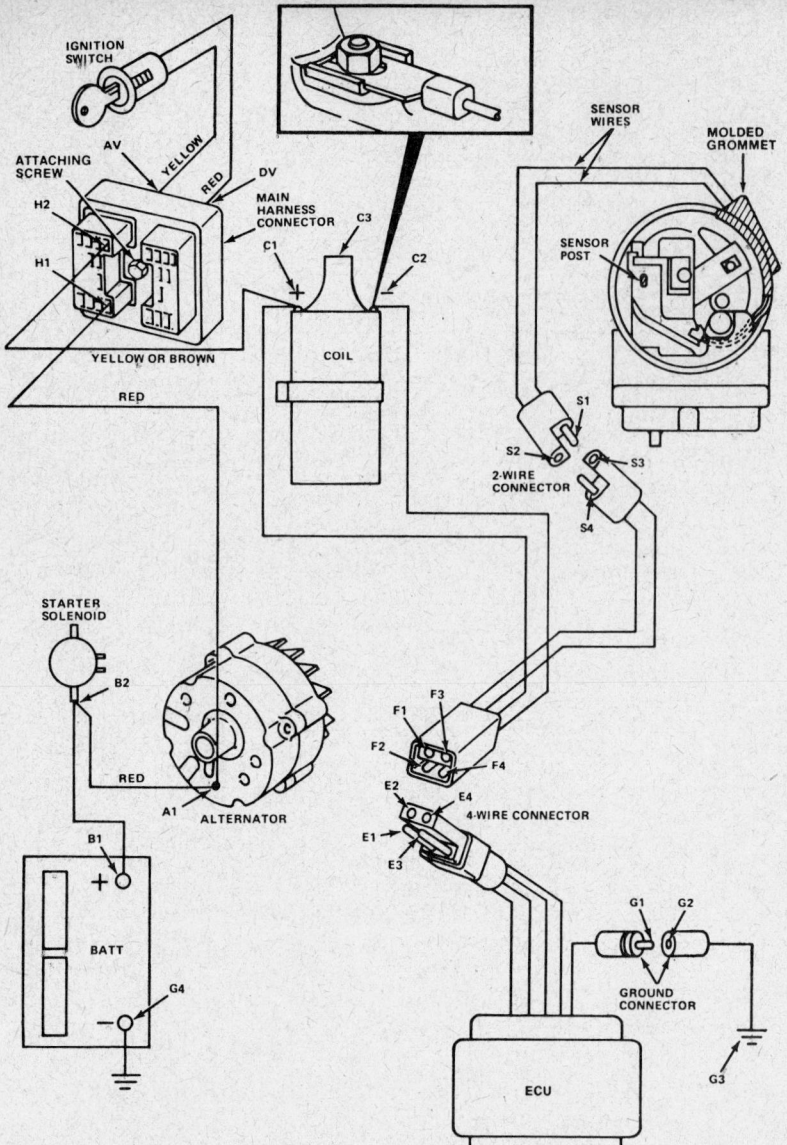

Fig. 3 BID ignition system checkpoints

inch gap when button is released. If spark jumps the gap, replace ECU unit and proceed to step 17. If spark does not jump gap, replace coil before proceeding to step 17.

NOTE: If ECU unit is replaced, squeeze and lubricate the connectors as described in steps 12 and 13.

17. Disconnect pulse simulator. Before connecting 2-wire connector, squeeze and lubricate terminals as described in steps 12 and 13. Connect coil negative wire.
18. Inspect distributor cap for cracks and carbon tracks. Replace as necessary. Install dust cover, rotor, distributor cap and coil secondary wire.

NOTE: If the malfunction still exists after performing the above procedure, connect an engine oscillosocope and measure the ignition dwell. A scope must be used because a dwell meter will not accurately measure the dwell

on this system. Start the engine and observe the dwell readings, then lower the hood being careful not to squeeze the oscillosocope leads between the fender and hood and allow the engine and wiring harness to warm up for 10 minutes. Prior to, during and after the engine warm up period, the dwell must be 23° on V8 engines and 32° for 6 cylinder engines and the dwell must not vary more than 3° at any time. If the dwell readings are as specified at all times, the malfunction may be caused by the fuel system. If the fuel system checks out OK and the malfunction still exists, replace the ECU unit and recheck the dwell. If the dwell readings are still not as specified above, replace the ignition wiring harness and recheck the dwell as above. If the dwell is below specifications, disconnect the 4-wire connector and measure the sensor circuit resistance and integrity as described in step 8. If sensor circuit resistance and integrity are within specifications, replace ECU unit. If sensor circuit resistance is too high or too low, or if needle fluctuates, replace the sensor. Be sure to squeeze and lubricate the terminals as described in steps 12 and 13.

Distributor, Replace

Removal

1. Remove distributor cap with wires and position aside.
2. Disconnect vacuum advance hose and distributor primary wiring.
3. Mark position of rotor tip on distributor housing, then mark relative position of housing to engine.
4. Remove distributor holddown bolt and clamp, then remove distributor.

Installation

1. Clean distributor mounting pad on engine and install a new distributor mounting gasket.
2. Turn rotor about 1/8 of a turn counterclockwise past the mark first placed on the distributor housing.
3. Install distributor, aligning the second mark placed on the housing with the one placed on the engine. It may be necessary to move the rotor slightly or rotate the oil pump shaft with a long, flat blade screwdriver to start gear into mesh with camshaft gear, but rotor should line up with first housing mark when distributor is down in place.
4. Install distributor holddown clamp, screw and lockwasher, but do not tighten screw until ignition timing has been set. Connect vacuum line, primary wiring and install cap.

NOTE: If the engine was cranked after the distributor was removed from the engine, crank the engine to bring No. 1 piston up on its compression stroke and align the timing mark with TDC on the timing plate. Then turn rotor until it is in position to fire No. 1 cylinder. Install distributor as outlined above and adjust ignition timing to specifications. Refer to the individual car chapters.

Component Replacement

1. Place distributor in a suitable holding fixture and remove cap, rotor and dust shield, Fig. 4.
2. Using a small gear puller, remove trigger wheel. Ensure puller jaws are gripping trigger wheel inner shoulder to prevent trigger wheel damage. Also, use a thick flat washer or nut as a spacer and do not press against small center shaft.
3. Loosen sensor locking screw approximately three turns, lift sensor lead grommet from distributor bowl and pull sensor leads from slot around sensor spring pivot pin. Release sensor spring, ensure spring clears sensor leads and slide sensor from bracket.

NOTE: The sensor locking screw utilizes a tamper proof head design and requires tool J-25097 for removal. However, if special tool is not available, use a small needlenose plier to remove screw. The service (replacement) sensor has a standard slotted head screw.

4. If vacuum control unit is to be replaced, remove retaining screw and vacuum unit.
5. Install new vacuum control unit and assemble sensor, sensor guide, flat washer and retaining screw.

NOTE: Install retaining screw far enough to hold assembly together and ensure it does not protrude past bottom of sensor.

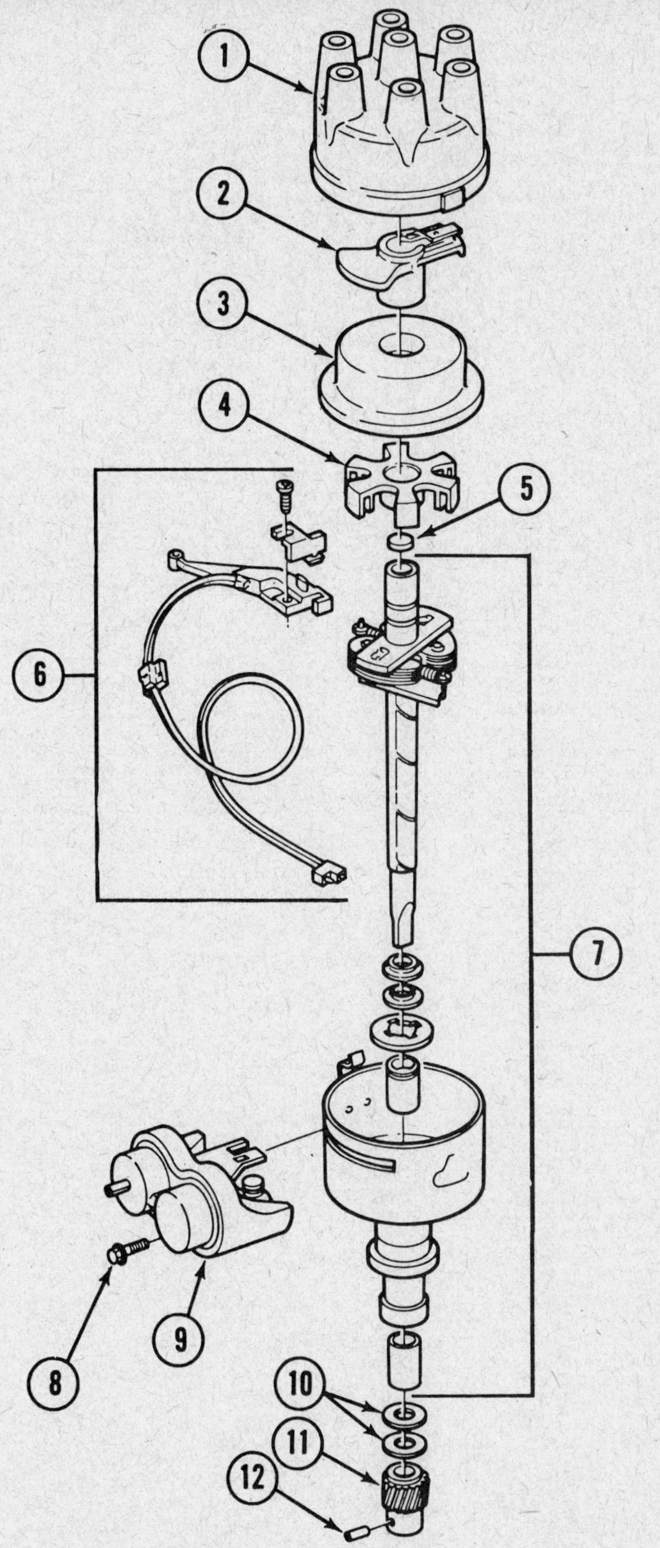

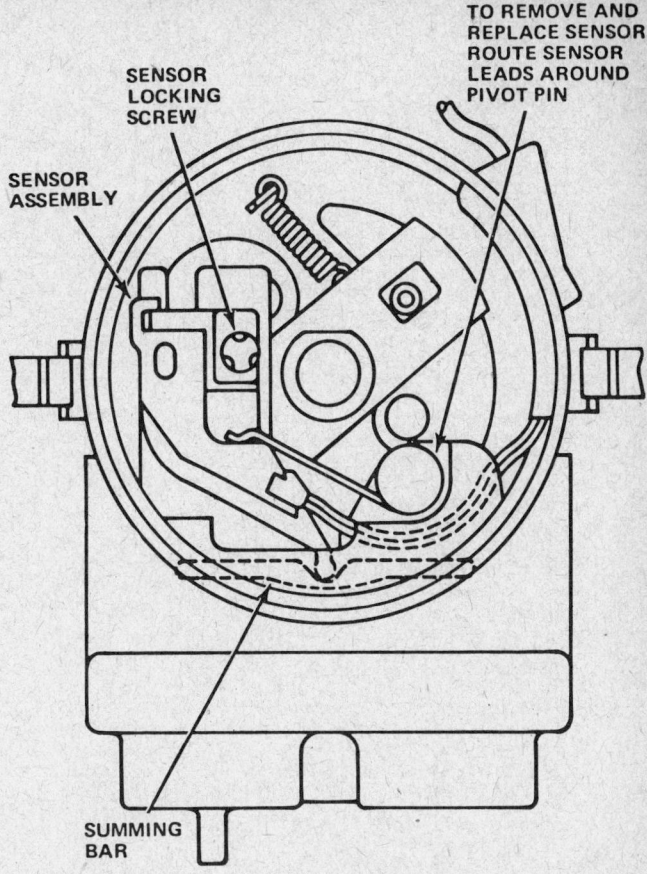

1
2
3
4
5
6
7
8
9
10
11
12

1. DISTRIBUTOR CAP
2. ROTOR
3. DUST SHIELD
4. TRIGGER WHEEL
5. FELT
6. SENSOR ASSEMBLY
7. HOUSING
8. VACUUM CONTROL SCREW
9. VACUUM CONTROL
10. SHIM
11. DRIVE GEAR
12. PIN

Fig. 4 BID distributor exploded view

TO REMOVE AND REPLACE SENSOR ROUTE SENSOR LEADS AROUND PIVOT PIN
SENSOR LOCKING SCREW
SENSOR ASSEMBLY
SUMMING BAR

Fig. 5 Sensor installation

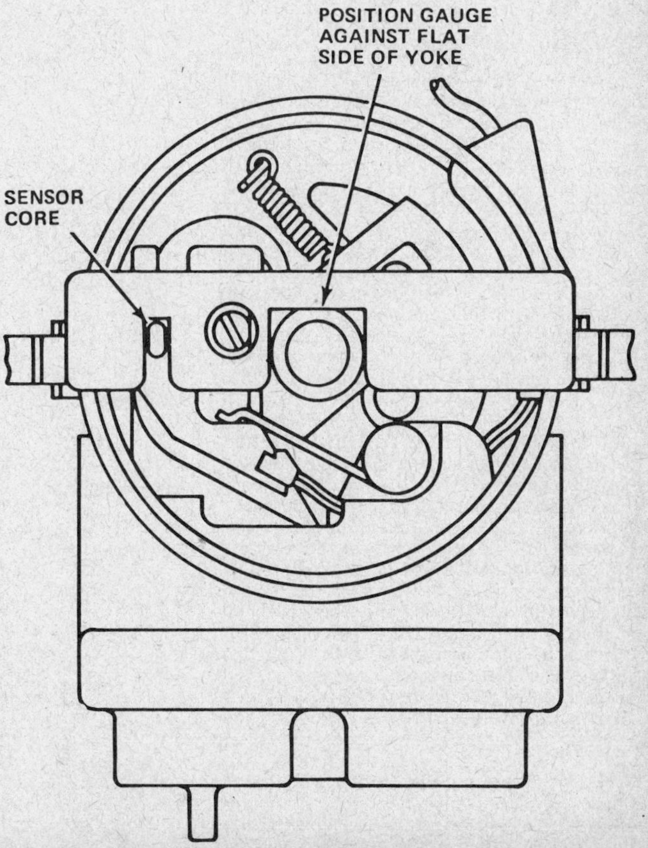

POSITION GAUGE AGAINST FLAT SIDE OF YOKE
SENSOR CORE

Fig. 6 Positioning sensor

6. If vacuum control has been replaced and original sensor is being used, replace special head screw with standard slotted head screw.

7. Install sensor assembly on vacuum chamber bracket, ensuring tip of sensor is located properly in summing bar. Place sensor spring on sensor and route sensor leads around spring pivot pin, Fig. 5. Install sensor lead grommet and position leads away from trigger wheel.

8. Install sensor positioning gauge over yoke, ensure gauge is against flat of shaft, and move sensor sideways until gauge can be positioned. Snug retaining screw and check sensor position by removing and installing gauge, Fig. 6. When gauge can be removed and replaced without sensor side movement, sensor is positioned properly. Tighten retaining screw and check sensor position.

9. Place trigger wheel on yoke and check if sensor core is positioned approximately in center of trigger wheel legs. Bend a .050 inch gauge wire to dimension specified in Fig. 7, and place between trigger wheel legs and sensor base. Press trigger wheel onto yoke until legs contact gauge wire.

10. Apply 3 to 5 drops of light engine oil to felt wick in top of yoke, then install dust shield, rotor and cap.

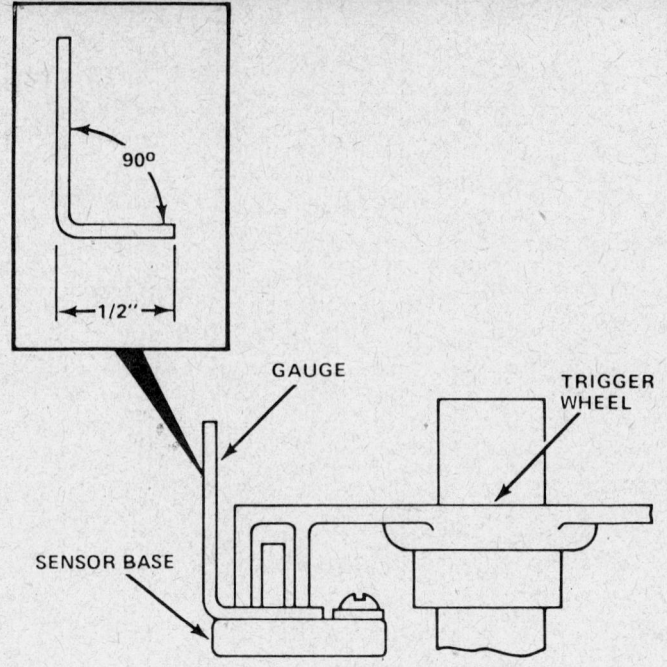

Fig. 7 Trigger wheel installation

AMERICAN MOTORS SOLID STATE IGNITION SYSTEM

This ignition system, Figs. 8, 9 and 10 is used on 1978–83 vehicles except those equipped with the four cylinder engine. The solid state ignition system consists of the ignition switch, electronic ignition control unit, ignition coil, primary resistance wire and bypass, distributor, spark plugs and on 1983 models, a knock sensor and a MCU unit.

The electronic ignition control unit is a solid state, moisture resistant module. The component parts are sealed in a potting material to resist vibration and environmental conditions. The control unit is incorporated with reverse polarity protection and transient voltage protection.

The distributor incorporates a sensor and trigger wheel. Current flowing through the ignition coil creates a magnetic field in the primary windings. When the circuit is opened, the magnetic field collapses and induces a high voltage in the coil secondary windings. This circuit is electronically controlled by the electronic ignition control unit. The distributor sensor and trigger wheel provide the signal to operate the control unit. The trigger wheel is mounted on the distributor shaft and has one tooth for each cylinder. The sensor, a coil of fine wire mounted to a permanent magnet, develops an electromagnetic force that is sensitive to the presence of ferrous metal. The sensor detects the trigger wheel teeth as the teeth pass the sensor. When a trigger wheel tooth approaches the pole piece of the sensor, it reduces the reluctance of the magnetic field, increasing field strength. Field strength decreases as the tooth moves away from the pole piece. This increase and decrease of field strength generates an alternating current which is interpreted by the electronic ignition control unit. The control unit then opens and closes the ignition coil primary circuit.

Since there are no contacting surfaces and no wear occurs, the dwell angle requires no adjustment. The dwell angle is electronically controlled by the electronic ignition control unit. When the coil circuit is switched open,

an electronic timer in the control unit keeps the circuit open only long enough for the spark to discharge. Then, it automatically closes the ignition coil primary circuit.

On 1983 models, the knock sensor detects audible spark knock about to occur, then sends a signal to the MCU unit to retard ignition timing.

NOTE: Due to design characteristics of the knock sensor system, occasional audible spark knock of low intensity and short duration is considered normal. Do not attempt to correct audible spark knock unless duration is lengthy or constant and occurs primarily above 3000 RPM.

Trouble Shooting
Secondary Circuit Test
1. Disconnect coil wire from distributor cap and, using insulated pliers, hold wire approximately ½ inch from a good engine ground.
2. Crank engine and observe wire for spark.

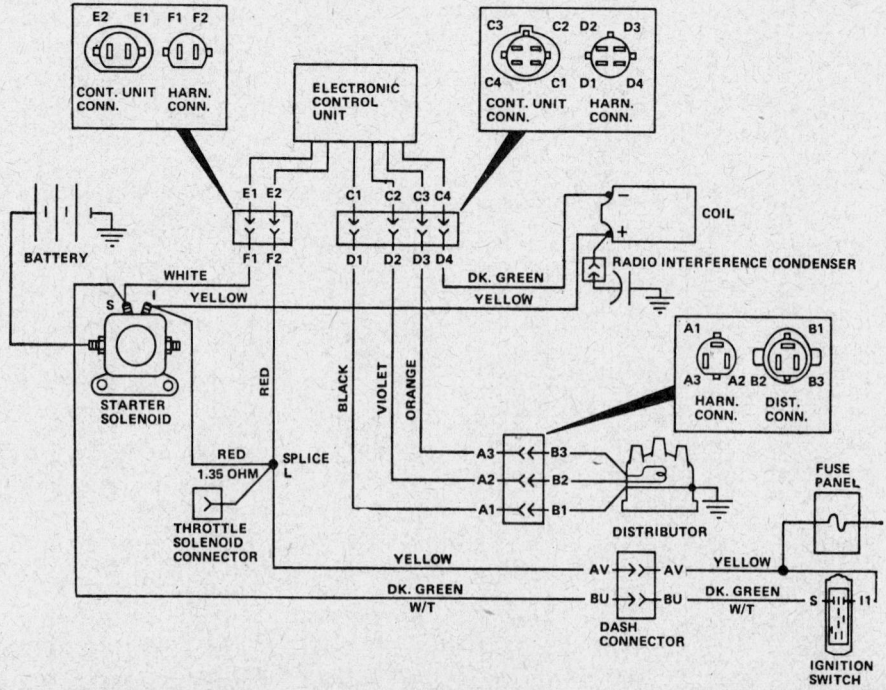

Fig. 8 1978–81 American Motors solid state ignition system schematic

If no spark occurs, proceed to Step 5. If spark occurs, proceed to Step 3.

3. Reconnect coil wire to distributor cap. Remove wire from one spark plug.

CAUTION: On 1980–83 models, do not remove ignition secondary cables from spark plugs on cylinders 1 or 5 (six cylinder engines). On 1977–79 models, do not remove ignition secondary cables on cylinders 3 or 5 on six cylinder or cylinders 3 or 4 on V8 engines while performing this test since the sensor may be damaged.

4. Using insulated pliers, hold wire approximately ½ inch from a good engine ground. Crank engine and observe wire for spark. If spark occurs, check for fuel system problems or incorrect ignition timing. If no spark occurs, check for defective distributor cap, rotor or spark plug wires.

5. If no spark occurs at coil wire, measure coil wire resistance. If resistance is greater than 10,000 ohms on 1977–80 models or greater than 7700–9300 ohms at 75° F. or 12,000 ohms at 200° F. on 1981–83 models, replace wire.

6. If malfunction still exists, proceed to the following tests or diagnosis procedures.

Intermittent Failure Diagnosis

Since intermittent failure may be caused by loose or corroded terminals, defective components, poor ground connections or defective wiring, it is necessary to check all wiring connections in the ignition system. Also, refer to Fig. 11 for further diagnosis.

Ignition Coil Primary Circuit Test

1. Turn ignition switch "On" and connect a voltmeter between ignition coil positive terminal and the ground. If voltage is 5.5–6.5 volts, proceed to Step 2. If battery voltage is noted, proceed to Step 4. If voltage is below 5.5 volts, disconnect condenser lead. If voltage is now 5.5–6.5 volts, replace condenser. If voltage is still not within specifications, proceed to Step 6.

2. Turn ignition switch to "Start" and measure voltage at coil positive terminal while cranking engine. If battery voltage is present while cranking engine, the ignition coil primary circuit is satisfactory. If voltage present is less than battery voltage, proceed to Step 3.

3. Check for shorted or open circuit in wire attached to starter solenoid "I" terminal. Check for defective starter solenoid. Repair as necessary.

4. Place ignition switch in "On" position, disconnect wire from starter solenoid "I" terminal and measure voltage at ignition coil positive terminal. If voltage drops to 5.5–6.5 volts, replace starter solenoid. If voltage remains constant at battery voltage, connect a jumper wire between ignition coil negative terminal and the ground. If voltage drops to 5.5–6.5 volts, proceed to Step 5. If not, repair defective resistance wire and repeat Step 2.

5. Check continuity between ignition coil negative terminal and terminal "D4", Figs. 8, 9 and 10. Also, check continuity between terminal "D1" and the ground. If continuity is present, replace electronic ignition control unit. If continuity is not present, locate and repair open circuit.

6. Turn ignition switch "Off" and measure resistance between ignition coil positive terminal and the dash connector "AV" on 1977–81 models, Fig. 8, or dash connector "FW" on 1982–83 models, Figs. 9 and 10. If resistance is greater than 1.40 ohms,

repair or replace resistance wire. If resistance is 1.30–1.40 ohms, proceed to Step 7.

7. On 1977–81 models, with ignition "Off", measure resistance between dash connector "AV" and ignition switch terminal "I1", Fig. 8. On 1982–83 models, with ignition "Off", measure resistance between dash connector "FW" and ignition switch terminal "I1", Figs. 9 and 10. If resistance is less than .1 ohm, replace ignition switch or repair switch feed wire. If resistance is greater than .1 ohm, check

and repair terminal connections at dash connector or defective wiring.

Coil Test

1. Inspect ignition coil for oil leaks, exterior damage and carbon tracks. If satisfactory, proceed to Step 2. If not, replace ignition coil.

2. Disconnect ignition coil connector and connect ohmmeter between coil terminals. If resistance is 1.13–1.23 ohms at 75° F. or 1.5 ohms at 200° F., proceed to

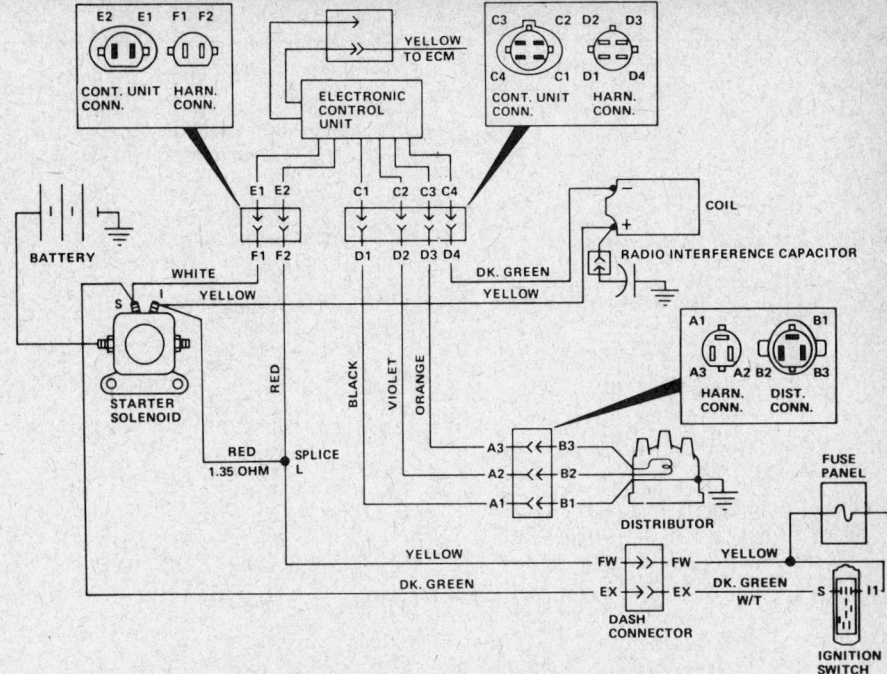

Fig. 9   1982 American Motors solid state ignition system schematic

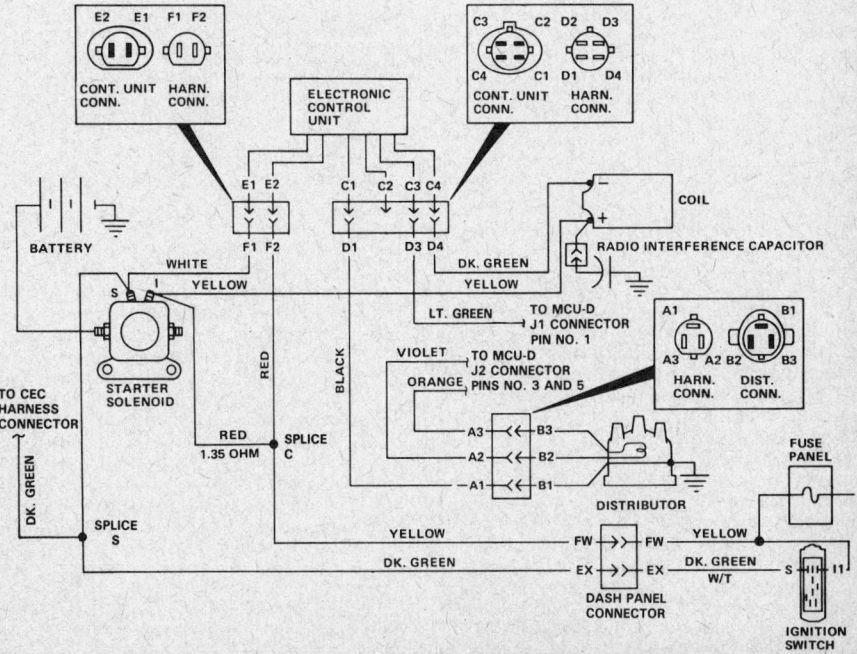

Fig. 10   1983 American Motors solid state ignition system schematic

ELECTRONIC IGNITION SYSTEMS

Condition	Possible Cause	Correction
ENGINE FAILS TO START (No spark at plugs)	1. No voltage to ignition system.	1. Check battery, ignition switch and wiring. Repair as required.
	2. Electronic Control Unit ground lead inside distributor open, loose or corroded.	2. Clean, tighten or repair as required.
	3. Primary wiring connectors not fully engaged.	3. Clean and fully engage connectors.
	4. Coil open or shorted.	4. Test coil. Replace if faulty.
	5. Electronic Control Unit defective.	5. Replace Electronic Control Unit.
	6. Cracked distributor cap.	6. Replace cap.
	7. Defective rotor.	7. Replace rotor.
ENGINE BACKFIRES BUT FAILS TO START	1. Incorrect ignition timing.	1. Check timing. Adjust as required.
	2. Moisture in distributor.	2. Dry cap and rotor.
	3. Distributor cap faulty.	3. Check cap for loose terminals, cracks and dirt. Clean or replace as required.
	4. Ignition wires not in correct firing order.	4. Install in correct order.
ENGINE RUNS ONLY WITH KEY IN START POSITION	1. Open in resistance wire or excessive resistance.	1. Repair resistance wire.
ENGINE CONTINUES TO RUN WITH KEY OFF	1. Defective starter solenoid.	1. Replace solenoid.
	2. Shorted diode in alternator indicator lamp circuit.	2. Replace diode.
ENGINE DOES NOT OPERATE SMOOTHLY AND/OR ENGINE MISFIRES AT HIGH SPEED	1. Spark plugs fouled or faulty.	1. Clean and gap plugs. Replace as required.
	2. Ignition cables faulty.	2. Check cables. Replace as required.
	3. Spark advance system(s) faulty.	3. Check operation. Repair as required.
	4. "I" terminal shorted to starter terminal in solenoid.	4. Replace solenoid.
	5. Trigger wheel pin missing.	5. Install pin.
	6. Distributor wires installed in wrong firing order.	6. Install wires correctly.
	7. Two plug wires of consecutive firing cylinders routed next to each other.	7. Re-route plug wires away from each other.
EXCESSIVE FUEL CONSUMPTION	1. Incorrect ignition timing.	1. Check timing. Adjust as required.
	2. Spark advance system(s) faulty.	2. Check operation. Repair as required.
	3. MCU (micro processor) faulty	3. Test system. Repair as required.
ERRATIC TIMING ADVANCE	1. Faulty vacuum advance assembly.	1. Check operation. Replace if required.
	2. Centrifugal weights sticking.	2. Remove dirt, corrosion.
TIMING NOT AFFECTED BY VACUUM	1. Defective vacuum advance unit.	1. Replace vacuum advance unit.
	2. Advance unit adjusting screw too far counterclockwise.	2. Turn screw clockwise to bring advance curve within specifications.
	3. Sensor pivot corroded.	3. Clean pivot.
INTERMITTENT OPERATION	1. Loose or corroded terminals.	1. Tighten terminals, remove corrosion, apply electrical grease.
	2. Defective pick-up coil.	2. Perform pick-up coil test.
	3. Defective control unit.	3. Perform control unit tests.
	4. Loose ground connector in distributor.	4. Clean and tighten ground connection.
	5. Wires to distributor shorted together or to ground.	5. Check for frayed, pinched, or burned wires.
	6. Trigger wheel pin missing.	6. Install new pin.

Fig. 11 American Motors solid state ignition system service diagnosis chart

Step 3. If not, replace ignition coil.
3. Connect ohmmeter between ignition coil center tower and the plus or minus terminal. Resistance should be 7700–9300 ohms at 75° F or 12000 ohms at 200° F. If not replace ignition coil.

Sensor & Control Unit Test
1. Disconnect the four wire connector at the control unit, Figs. 8, 9 and 10. Disconnect coil wire from center tower of distributor and hold wire approximately ½ inch from a good engine ground with insulated pliers, then turn ignition "On". If spark is observed at coil wire, proceed to next step. If not, proceed to Step 5.
2. On 1978–82 models, use a suitable ohmmeter to measure resistance between terminals "D2" and "D3" of the harness connector, Figs. 8 and 9. On 1983 models,

disconnect "J2" connector from MCU-D, Fig. 10, then using a suitable ohmmeter, measure resistance between pins 3 and 5 of MCU-D "J2" connector. On all models, if resistance is 400–800 ohms, proceed to step 6. If resistance is not 400–800 ohms, proceed to next step.
3. Disconnect and connect the three-wire connector at distributor while measuring resistance between terminals "D2" and "D3" of the harness connector on 1978–82 models. Figs. 8 and 9, or between pins 3 and 5 of MCU-D "J2" connector on 1983 models, Fig. 10. On all models, if resistance is now 400–800 ohms, proceed to step 6. If resistance is not 400–800 ohms, disconnect distributor three-wire connector and proceed to next step.
4. Measure resistance between terminals "B2" and "B3" of the distributor connec-

tor, Figs. 8, 9 and 10. If resistance is 400–800 ohms, repair or replace harness between distributor three-wire connector and control unit four-wire connector on 1978–82 models. On 1983 models, repair or replace harness between distributor three-wire connector and MCU-D "J2" connector.
5. Connect an ohmmeter between terminal "D1" of the harness connector, Figs. 8, 9 and 10, and the battery negative terminal. If reading is below .002 ohm, repeat Step 2. If not, check for an improper ground. Check ground cable resistance, distributor to engine block resistance and distributor ground screw to terminal "D1" resistance, Figs. 8, 9 and 10.
6. Using a suitable voltmeter connected between terminals "D2" and "D3" of the harness connector on 1978–82 models, or

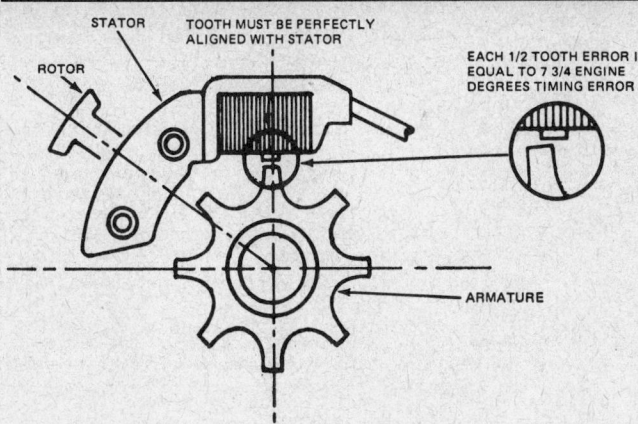

Fig. 12 Distributor stator & armature segment alignment

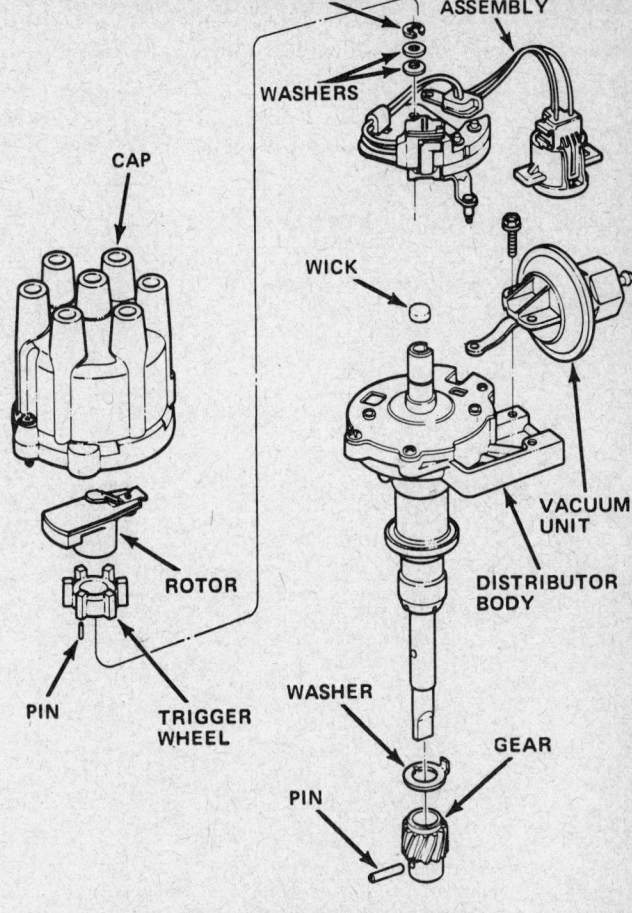

Fig. 13 American Motors distributor used with solid state ignition system (Typical)

between pins 3 and 5 of MCU-D "J2" connector on 1983 models, Figs. 8, 9 and 10, observe reading while cranking engine. If voltmeter reading fluctuates, it indicates proper sensor and trigger wheel operation. If not, the trigger wheel is defective or the distributor is not rotating.

Ignition Feed to Control Unit Test

NOTE: Perform the "Ignition Coil Primary Circuit Test" before performing this test.

1. Disconnect two wire connector from control unit and connect a voltmeter between terminal "F2" and the ground, Figs. 8, 9 and 10. Turn ignition "On". If voltmeter reading is within .2 volts of battery voltage, replace control unit and proceed to Step 3. If voltmeter reading is not within .2 volt of battery voltage, proceed to next step.
2. Locate and repair cause of voltage reduction as noted in Step 1. Check for a corroded dash connector or defective ignition switch. Then, check for spark at coil wire. Spark should be present at coil wire. If not, replace control unit.
3. Connect the two wire connector at control unit and disconnect the four wire connector from control unit. Connect an ammeter between terminal "C1" and the ground, Figs. 8, 9 and 10. If ammeter reading is 1 ±.1 amp., the system is satisfactory. If ammeter reading is higher or lower, replace module.

Current Flow Test
1. Remove connector from coil.
2. Depress plastic barb and remove positive wire from connector. Remove negative wire in same manner.
3. Connect an ammeter between coil positive terminal and the disconnected positive wire.
4. Connect a jumper wire between coil negative terminal and the engine ground.
5. Turn ignition "On" and note ammeter reading. Reading should be approximately 7 amps. and not exceeding 7.6 amps. If reading exceeds 7.6 amps., replace ignition coil.
6. Remove jumper wire from coil negative terminal and connect the coil green wire to negative terminal. Ammeter reading should be approximately 4 amps. If reading is less than 3.5 amps., check for poor connections at the three wire and four wire connectors or a poor ground at dis-

tributor ground screw. If reading is greater than 5 amps., the control unit is defective, requiring replacement.
7. Start and run engine. Ammeter reading should be 2–2.4 amps. If not, replace control unit.

Distributor, Replace

Removal
1. Remove No. 1 spark plug and crank engine until compression pressure is felt. Slowly rotate engine in direction of normal rotation until timing mark on crankshaft pulley aligns with proper timing mark on timing plate. Refer to the individual car chapters for timing specifications. Remove distributor cap and ensure alignment of rotor and armature with index mark on top of magnetic pickup and mark on distributor housing, Fig. 12.
2. Disconnect vacuum advance hose and distributor primary wiring.
3. Remove distributor holddown bolt and clamp, then remove distributor.

Installation
1. Clean distributor mounting pad on engine and install a new distributor mounting gasket.
2. Ensure engine is still aligned with the proper timing marks. Align the rotor with the marks on the distributor housing and the armature with the mark on top of the magnetic pickup. It may be necessary to move the rotor slightly or rotate the oil pump shaft with a long, flat

bladed screwdriver to mesh distributor gear with camshaft gear. The rotor should align with the housing mark when distributor is installed properly, Fig. 12.
3. Install distributor holddown clamp, bolt and lockwasher, but do not tighten bolt until ignition timing has been set. Connect vacuum line, primary wiring and install distributor cap. Adjust ignition timing to specifications found in the individual car chapters.

NOTE: If the engine was cranked after the distributor was removed from the engine, refer to step 1 of removal procedure to properly position crankshaft before installing distributor.

Distributor Service

Trigger Wheel & Sensor, Replace
1. Remove distributor cap and rotor, Fig. 13.
2. Remove trigger wheel with a suitable gear puller. Use a flat washer to prevent gear puller from contacting inner shaft. The trigger wheel may also be removed by using two screwdrivers to pry trigger wheel upward. Remove pin.
3. On six cylinder distributors, remove sensor retainers and washers from pivot pin on base plate.
4. On V8 distributors, remove sensor snap ring from shaft, then the retainer from vacuum unit to sensor drive pin and posi-

tion vacuum unit lever aside.

5. On all distributors, remove ground screw from harness tab.
6. Remove sensor assembly from distributor housing.
7. Reverse procedure to assemble.

Vacuum Unit, Replace
1. Disconnect vacuum hose.
2. On six cylinder distributors, remove vacuum unit attaching screws and the vac-

uum unit, Fig. 13. It is necessary to tilt the vacuum unit to disengage the link from the sensor pin and also loosen the base plate screws for clearance.
3. On V8 distributors, remove distributor cap and the retainer from the sensor pin. Remove vacuum unit attaching screws and the vacuum unit, Fig. 13.
4. Reverse procedure to install. If a new vacuum unit is installed, it must be calibrated as follows:
   a. Insert an appropriate size allen

wrench into vacuum hose tube of original vacuum unit. Rotate allen wrench clockwise and note the number of turns required to bottom the adjusting screw.
   b. Insert allen wrench into vacuum hose tube of replacement vacuum unit. Turn the allen wrench clockwise until the adjusting screw is bottomed, then rotate allen wrench counterclockwise the number of turns noted in the previous step.

Chrysler Corp. Rear Wheel Drive Models W/Electronic Ignition System

DESCRIPTION

This system, Figs. 1 through 3, is composed of a magnetic distributor, an electronic control unit, a wiring harness, a production coil and a single or dual ballast resistor.

The distributor is essentially the same as the conventional type except the contacts have been replaced by a pickup coil or coils and the cam by a reluctor. With a conventional contact type system, the voltage necessary to fire the spark plugs is developed by interrupting the current flowing through the primary of the ignition coil by opening a set of contacts. With the Electronic System, the voltage is produced the same way except that the current is interrupted by a transistor in the electronic control unit. This happens each time the control unit receives a "timing" pulse from the distributor magnetic pickup(s).

Since the magnetic pickup(s), reluctor and the control unit, which replace the contact points and cam, do not normally change or wear out with service, engine timing and dwell do not require periodic adjusting. This minimizes regular ignition maintenance of cleaning and replacing the spark plugs.

TROUBLE SHOOTING

Engine Will Not Start—Fuel System OK

1. Wiring harness electrical terminals covered with grease.
2. Faulty ballast resistor.
3. Faulty ignition coil.
4. Faulty pickup(s) or improper pickup air gap(s).
5. Faulty wiring.
6. Faulty control unit.

Engine Surges Severely—Not Lean Carburetor

1. Wiring.
2. Faulty pickup leads.
3. Ignition coil.

Engine Misses—Carburetion Good

1. Spark plugs.
2. Secondary cables.
3. Ignition coil.
4. Wiring.
5. Control unit.

SYSTEM TESTING

NOTE: To completely test components and circuits of the electronic ignition system, special testers should be used. However, in event the testers are not available, the following procedures may be utilized. A voltmeter with a 20,000 ohm/volt rating, and an ohmmeter with a 1.5 volt battery for 1977–80 models and a 9.0 volt battery for 1981–83 models should be used for testing. Before performing any electrical tests, ensure all wiring is properly connected.

1977–80 Models
Harness Wiring Test
1. Check battery voltage and note reading.
2. Disconnect harness connector from control unit.

CAUTION: Before disconnecting or connecting harness connector, ensure ignition switch is in the "Off" position.

3. Turn ignition switch to "On" position.
4. Connect the voltmeter between harness

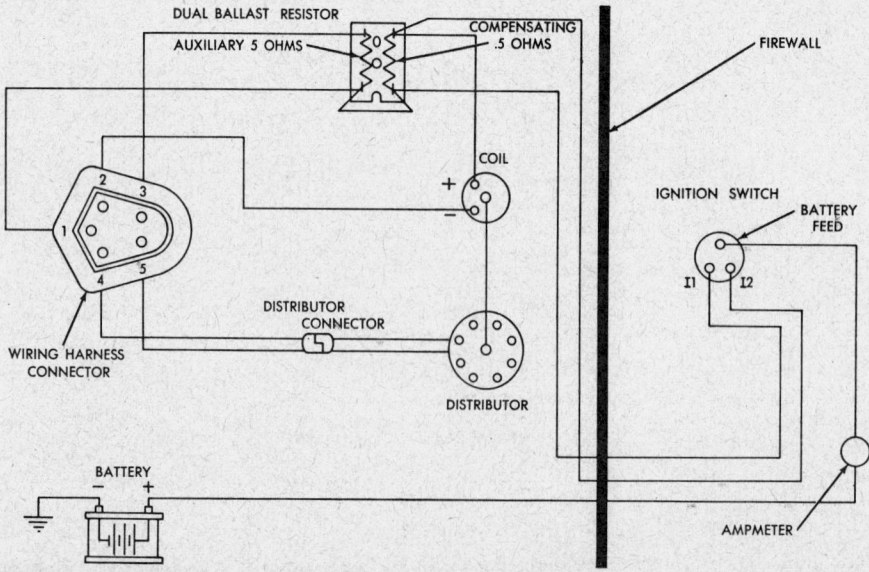

Fig. 1 Chrysler electronic ignition wiring. 1977–79

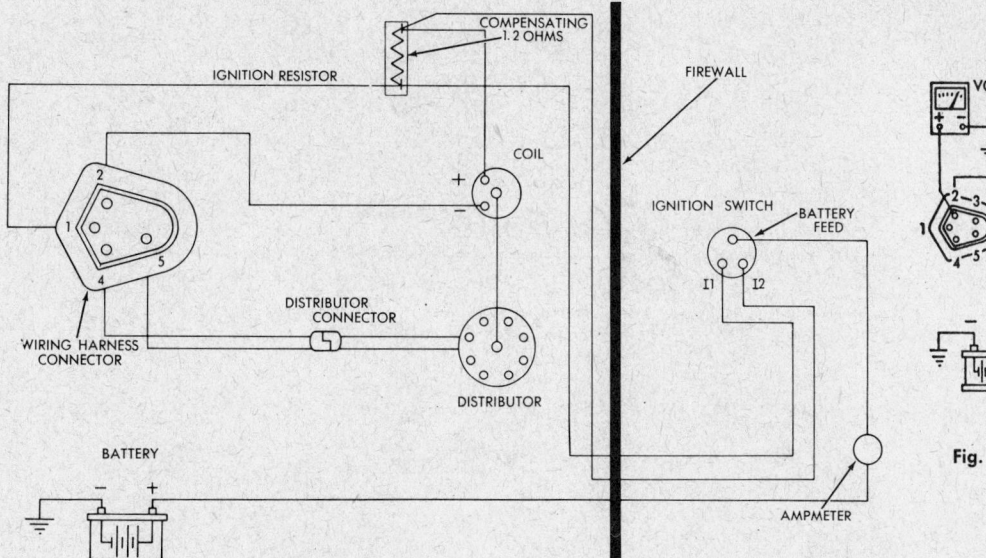

Fig. 2 Chrysler electronic ignition wiring. 1980

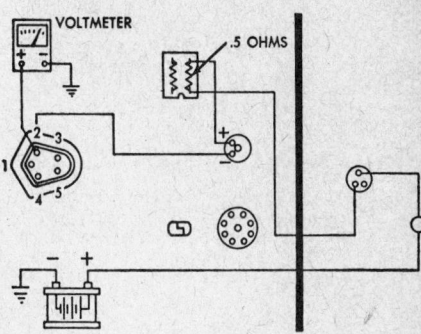

Fig. 5 Harness wiring test, No. 2 cavity. 1977—80 (Typical)

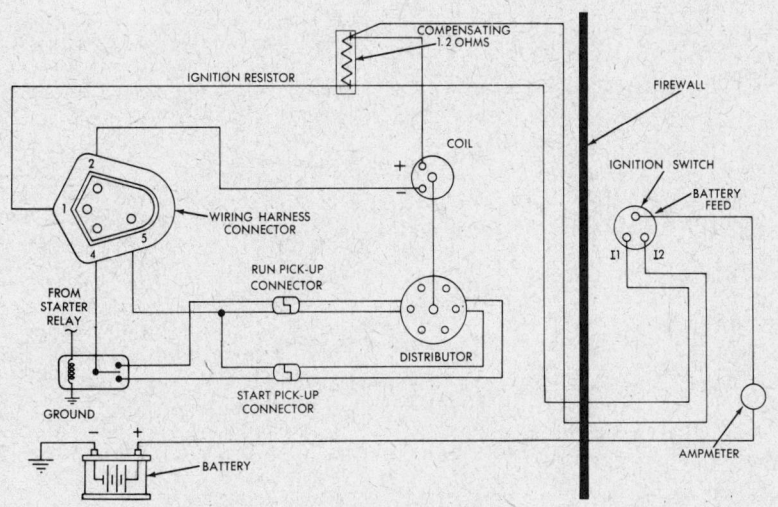

Fig. 3 Chrysler electronic ignition wiring. 1981—83

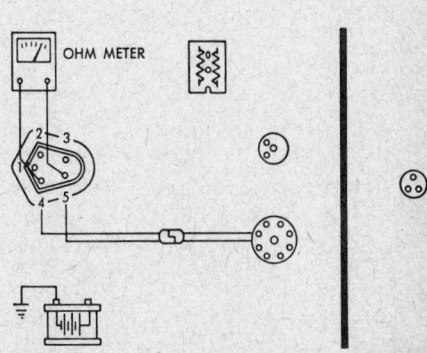

Fig. 6 Harness wiring test, No. 3 cavity. 1977—79 (Typical)

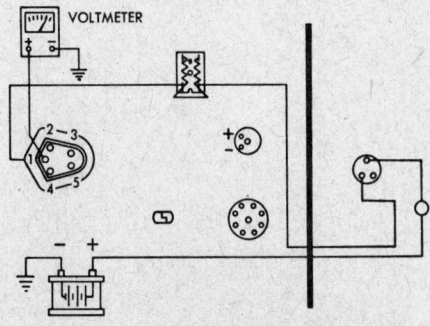

Fig. 4 Harness wiring test, No. 1 cavity. 1977—80 (Typical)

Fig. 7 Pick-up coil test, cavity Nos. 4 & 5. 1977—80 (Typical)

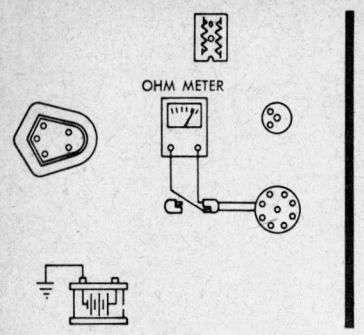

Fig. 8 Pick-up coil test, distributor lead connector. 1977–80 (Typical)

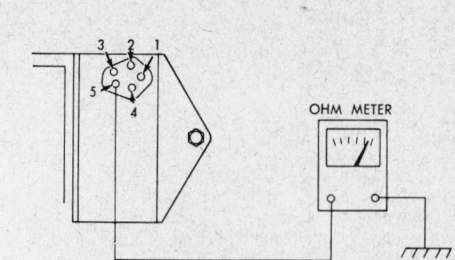

Fig. 9 Control unit ground circuit test. 1977–80 (Typical)

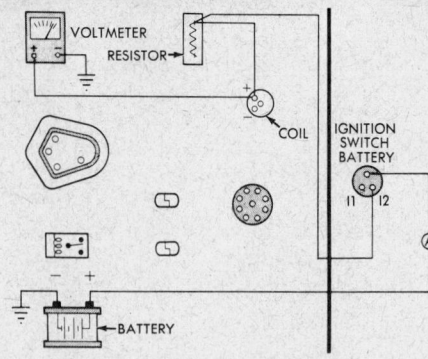

Fig. 10 Checking battery voltage at coil positive terminal. 1981–83

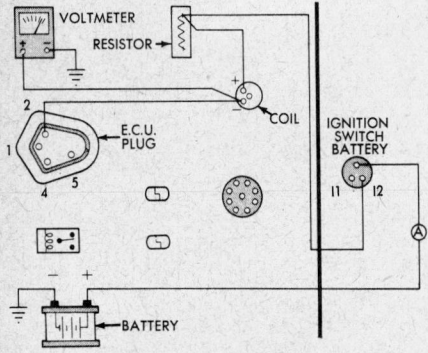

Fig. 11 Checking battery voltage at coil negative terminal. 1981–83

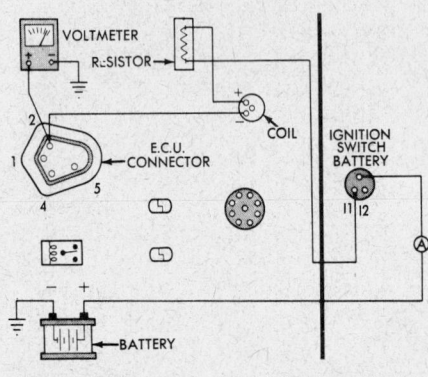

Fig. 12 Checking battery voltage at No. 2 cavity. 1981–83

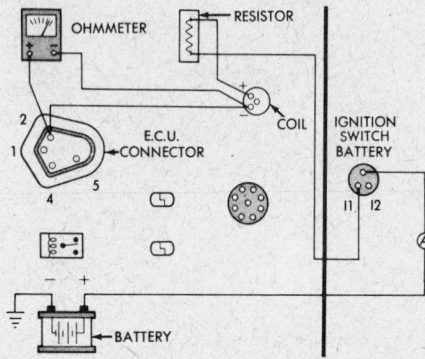

Fig. 13 Checking continuity between coil negative terminal and No. 2 cavity. 1981–83

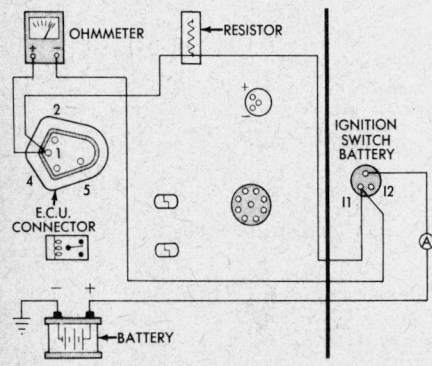

Fig. 14 Checking continuity between ignition switch and No. 1 cavity. 1981–83

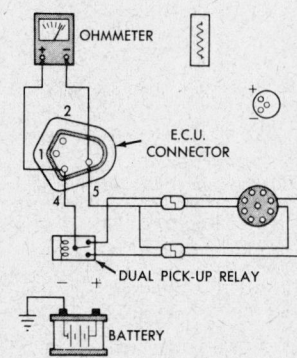

Fig. 15 Checking resistance between cavities No. 4 & 5. 1981–83

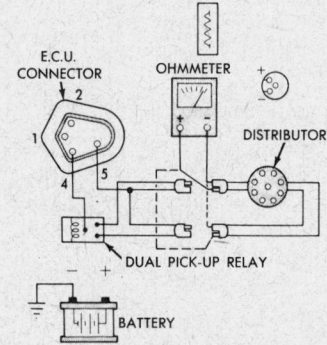

Fig. 16 Testing pick up coil resistance. 1981–83

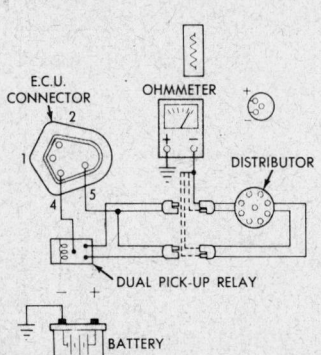

Fig. 17 Checking for short circuit at pick up coil terminal. 1981–83

connector cavity No. 1 and the ground. Voltage reading should be within 1 volt of battery voltage earlier noted. If not, check circuit between cavity No. 1 and the battery, Fig. 4.

5. Connect voltmeter between harness connector cavity No. 2 and ground. Voltage reading should be within 1 volt of battery voltage noted in step 1. If not, check circuit between cavity No. 2 and battery, Fig. 5.

6. On 1977–79, connect voltmeter between harness connector cavity No. 3 and ground. Voltage reading should be within 1 volt of battery voltage noted in step 1. If not, check circuit between cavity No. 3 and battery, Fig. 6.

7. Turn ignition switch to off position.

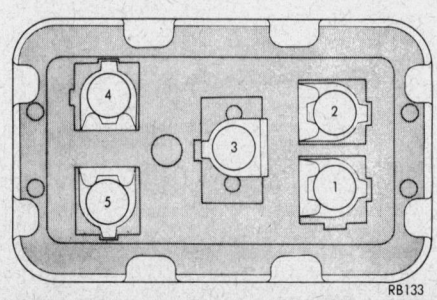

Fig. 18 Dual Pick up start-run relay. 1981–83

Distributor Pick-up Coil Test

1. Connect an ohmmeter between harness connector cavities numbers 4 and 5, Fig. 7. Resistance reading should be 150 to 900 ohms.
2. If reading is not as specified in above step, disconnect distributor dual lead connector and connect ohmmeter between the two leads on distributor side of connector, Fig. 8. If resistance is not between 150 and 900 ohms, replace pick-up coil.
3. Connect one ohmmeter lead to a good ground and the other lead to either connector of the distributor. If ohmmeter shows a reading, the pickup coil must be replaced.

Control Unit Ground Circuit Test

Connect an ohmmeter between control unit connector pin No. 5 and the ground, Fig. 9. If ohmmeter indicates infinite resistance, tighten bolts securing control unit to firewall and recheck resistance. If reading is still infinite, replace control unit.

1981–83 Models

1. Visually check all spark plug cables and spark plugs for proper installation or damage.
2. Check for proper installation of primary ignition coil wire at coil terminals and at ballast resistor.
3. If above checks are satisfactory, check and record battery voltage.
4. Disconnect coil secondary lead from distributor cap. Turn ignition On, then momentarily ground negative terminal of coil using suitable jumper wire while holding coil secondary lead 1/4 inch from good ground. If no spark is observed, turn ignition Off, then disconnect four-wire electrical connector at electronic control unit. If spark is observed, proceed to step 10.

NOTE: Before connecting or disconnecting the harness connector from the control unit, check to ensure that the ignition switch is in the Off position.

5. Repeat step 4. If spark is observed, replace electronic control unit.
6. If no spark is observed, measure voltage at coil positive terminal. Reading obtained should be within one volt of previously recorded battery voltage.
7. If voltage reading is zero, replace starter relay and check wiring between battery positive terminal and coil, Fig. 10.
8. If voltage reading obtained in step 6 is not continuous, replace ignition resistor and repeat step 6.
9. Check battery voltage at coil negative terminal, Fig. 11. Reading obtained should be within one volt of battery voltage. If voltage reading is satisfactory, but no spark is observed when coil negative terminal is grounded, replace coil.
10. If spark was obtained in step 4 or step 9, but engine will not start, check to ensure that four-wire connector is disconnected from electronic control unit, then with ignition On, check for battery voltage at cavity 2 of ECU harness connector. Reading obtained should be within one volt of battery voltage, Fig. 12.
11. If voltage reading is not satisfactory, turn ignition Off, and check for continuity between cavity 2 and coil negative terminal using suitable ohmmeter, Fig. 13. If continuity is not present, check for damaged wiring or loose connections and repair as necessary.
12. If voltage reading in step 10 is satisfactory, check for battery voltage at cavity 2 of ECU connector. If battery voltage is not obtained, turn ignition Off and check for continuity between cavity 1 and ignition switch using suitable ohmmeter, Fig. 14. If continuity is not present, check for damaged wiring or loose connections and repair as necessary.
13. If battery voltage is obtained at cavity 2 of ECU connector, turn ignition Off and check resistance between cavities 4 and 5 of ECU harness connector using suitable ohmmeter, Fig. 15. Reading of 150–900 ohms should be obtained.
14. If reading is satisfactory, check wiring between cavities 4 and 5 for open or short circuit and repair as necessary. If wiring is satisfactory, check for proper operation of dual pick up start-run relay as described under "Dual Pick Up Start-Run Relay Test".
15. If ohmmeter reading obtained in step 13 is not between 150–900 ohms, disconnect pick up leads and measure resistance at distributor side of pick up lead, Fig. 16. If reading obtained is not between 150–900 ohms, replace pick up coils as necessary.
16. Check for short circuit at each distributor side of pick up lead by connecting ohmmeter as indicated in Fig. 17. If ohmmeter indicates pick up is shorted, replace pick up coil.
17. If pick up coil is satisfactory, check for proper ECU ground contact by connecting ohmmeter between pin 5 of ECU and ground. If ohmmeter indicates poor ECU ground contact, check for proper ECU installation or poor ECU electrical connections.
18. If ECU is properly grounded, reconnect all electrical connections and check again for spark. If no spark is available, replace ECU.

Dual Pick up Start-Run Relay Test, 1981–83 Models

1. Disconnect two-way connector from pins 5 and 4 of dual pick up start-run relay, Fig. 18.
2. Connect suitable ohmmeter between pins 4 and 5 of relay.
3. If ohmmeter reading of 20–30 ohms cannot be obtained, replace relay.

DISTRIBUTOR SERVICE

Distributor, Replace

Removal

1. Disconnect vacuum line at distributor.
2. Disconnect distributor pickup lead(s) at wiring harness connector, then remove distributor cap.
3. Mark position of rotor on distributor body and engine block surface so that distributor can be installed in the same position.
4. Remove holddown and/or bolt and lift distributor from engine.

Installation

1. If engine was cranked after distributor was removed from engine, rotate crankshaft to bring No. 1 piston up on its compression stroke and align timing mark on crankshaft pulley with "O" (TDC) mark on timing cover.
2. With distributor gasket or O-ring in place, hold distributor over mounting pad.
3. Turn rotor to a position just ahead of the No. 1 distributor cap terminal.
4. Install distributor, engaging distributor gear with camshaft drive gear on 6 cylinder engines. On V-8 engines, engage tang of distributor shaft with slot in oil pump drive gear. With distributor fully seated on engine, rotor should be under No. 1 cap terminal.
5. Install distributor holddown and/or bolt, distributor cap, pick-up lead(s) and vacuum line.
6. Adjust ignition timing to specifications found in the individual car chapters.

Distributor Shaft & Bushing Wear Test

1. Remove distributor from vehicle and clamp distributor in a vise. Use extreme caution not to damage distributor.
2. Attach a dial indicator to housing so plunger rests against reluctor sleeve.
3. Place a wire loop around reluctor sleeve and hook a spring scale on the other end of the loop. Apply a one pound pull in line with indicator plunger and read movement on indicator. Movement must not exceed .006 inch. If movement exceeds limit, replace either housing or shaft to bring movement back within tolerance.

Distributor Disassemble

1. Remove rotor and vacuum advance unit, Figs. 19 thru 21.
2. Remove reluctor by prying up from bottom of reluctor using two screwdrivers with a maximum blade width of 7/16 in. Use care not to damage or distort reluctor teeth.
3. Remove two screws and lockwashers attaching lower plate to distributor housing, then lift out lower plate, upper plate and pick-up coil as an assembly. Do not remove distributor cap clamp springs.
4. On six cylinder units, if distributor housing, or shaft and governor assembly are to be replaced, proceed as follows:
   a. If gear is worn or damaged, scribe a line on end of shaft from center to edge, so that line is centered between two gear teeth, Fig. 22. Do not scribe line completely across shaft. Remove distributor drive gear retaining pin and slide gear off end of shaft.

NOTE: Support hub of gear so that pin can be driven out without damaging shaft.

   b. If necessary use a file to clean burrs from around pin hole area on shaft, then remove lower thrust washer.
   c. Push shaft upward and remove from distributor body.
5. On eight cylinder units, if distributor housing, shaft, reluctor sleeve or governor weights are to replace, proceed as follows:
   a. Remove distributor shaft retaining

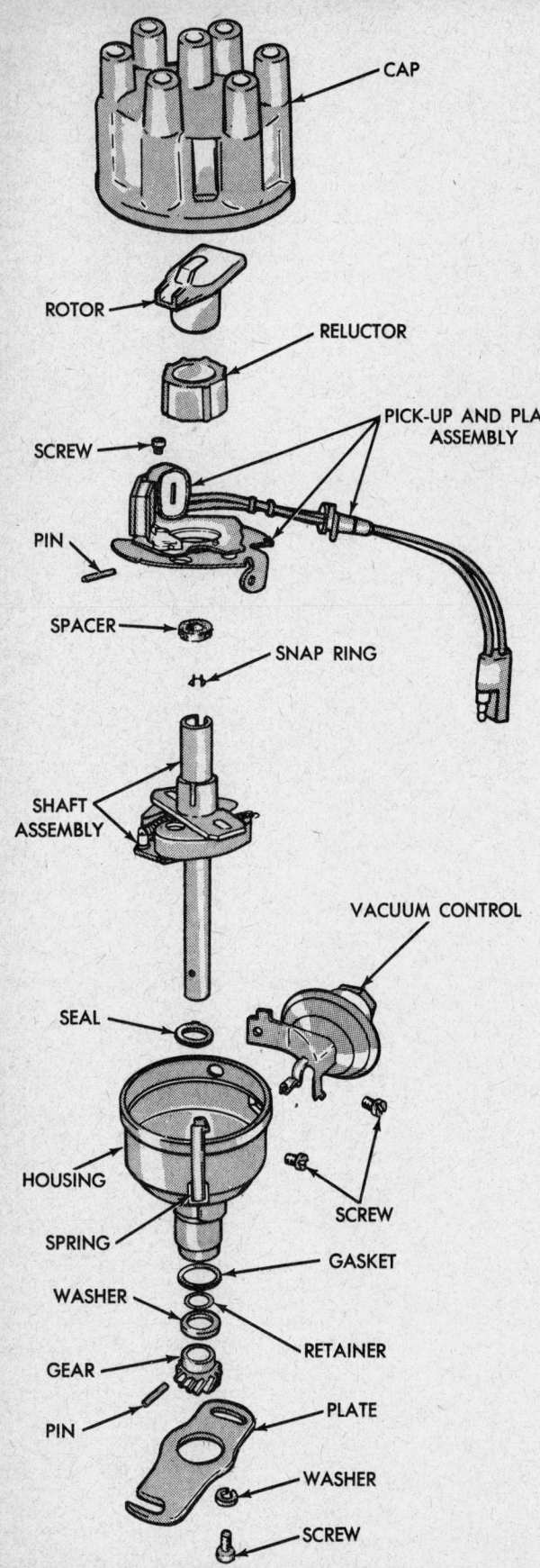

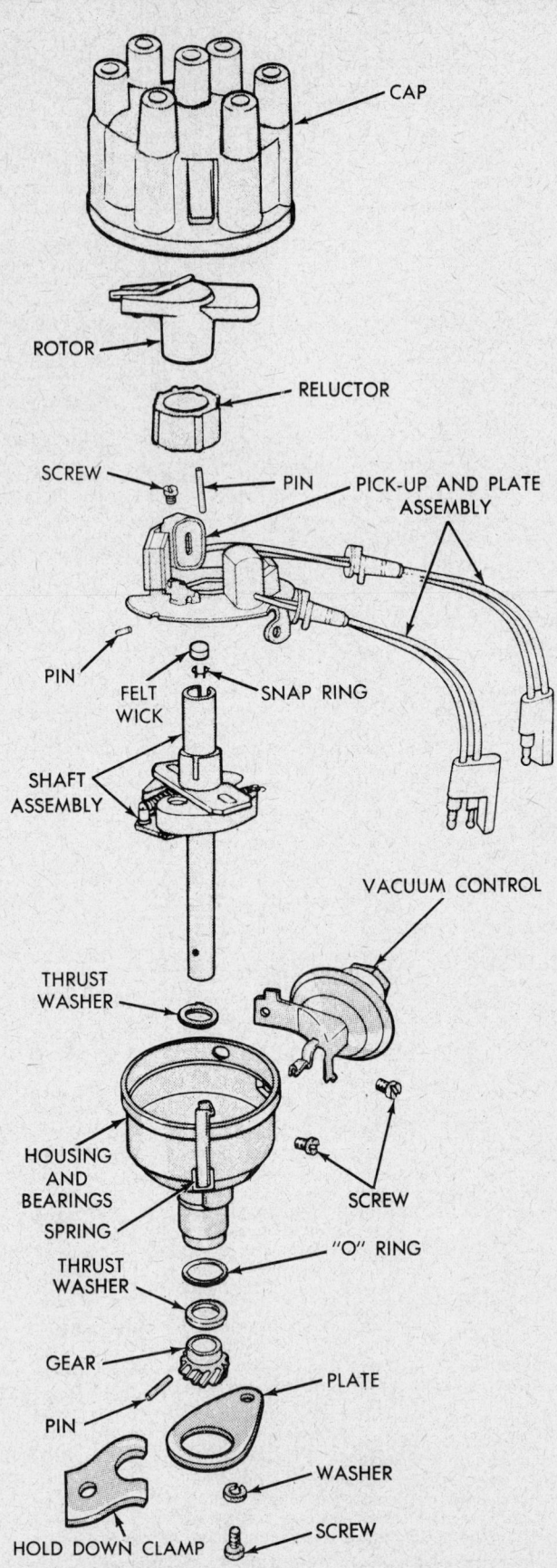

Fig. 19 Disassembled view of Chrysler 6 cylinder engine electronic distributor with single pick up.

Fig. 20 Disassembled view of Chrysler 6 cylinder engine electronic distributor with dual pick up.

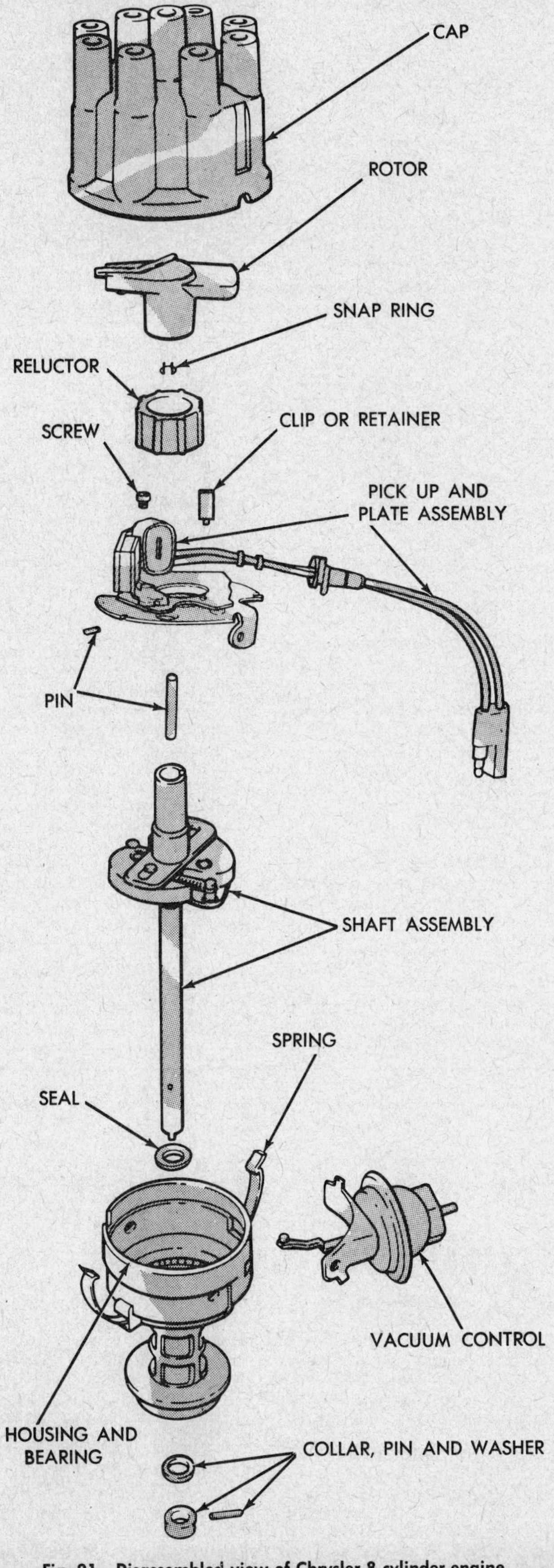

CAP

ROTOR

SNAP RING

RELUCTOR

SCREW

CLIP OR RETAINER

PICK UP AND
PLATE ASSEMBLY

PIN

SHAFT ASSEMBLY

SPRING

SEAL

VACUUM CONTROL

HOUSING AND
BEARING

COLLAR, PIN AND WASHER

Fig. 21   Disassembled view of Chrysler 8 cylinder engine
electronic distributor.

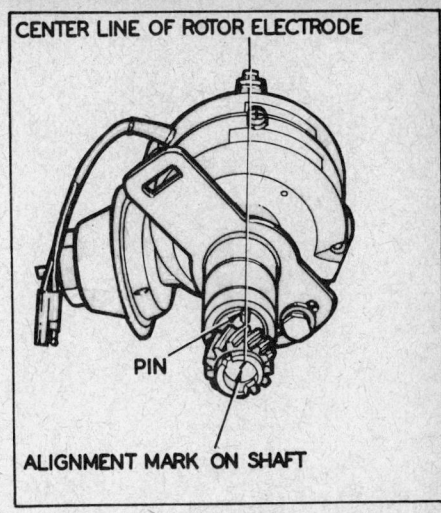

Fig. 22   Scribe line on distributor shaft. 6
cylinder units

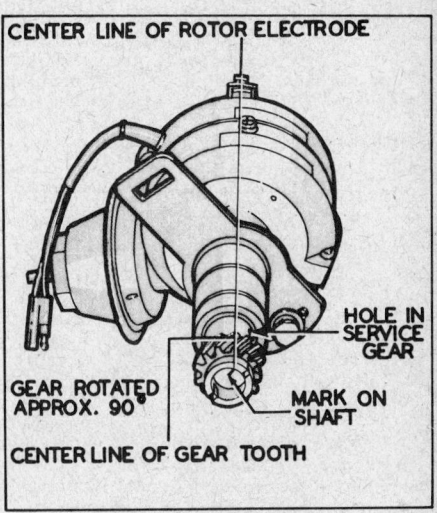

Fig. 23   Aligning gear teeth with center line of
rotor electrode. 6 cylinder units

pin and slide retainer off end of
shaft.
b. If necessary, use a file to clean burrs
from around pin hole area on shaft,
then remove lower thrust washer.
c. Push shaft upward and remove from
distributor housing.

Distributor Assemble

1. Lubricate and test operation of governor
weights. Inspect weight springs for distortion and bearing surfaces and pins for
damage.
2. Lubricate upper thrust washer and install onto shaft. Install shaft into housing, Figs. 19 through 21.
3. On 6 cylinder units, install lower thrust
washer and distributor gear and roll pin.
If a replacement distributor gear is to be
installed, proceed as follows:
a. Install thrust washer and replacement
gear on rotor shaft. Position pin hole
in replacement gear approximately 90
degrees from hole in distributor shaft,
with scribed line made during disassembly between gear teeth, Fig. 22.

NOTE: On replacement distributor

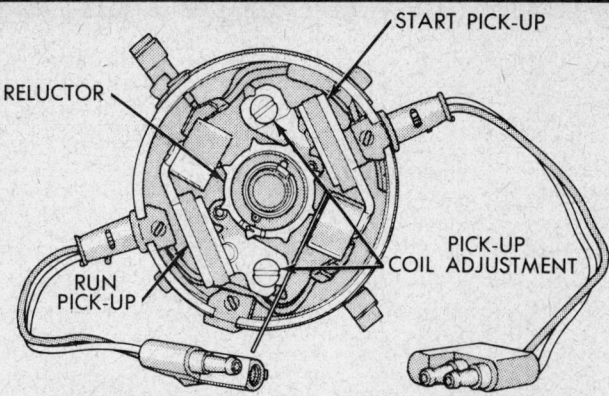

Fig. 24 Air gap adjustment. Distributors equipped with dual pick up

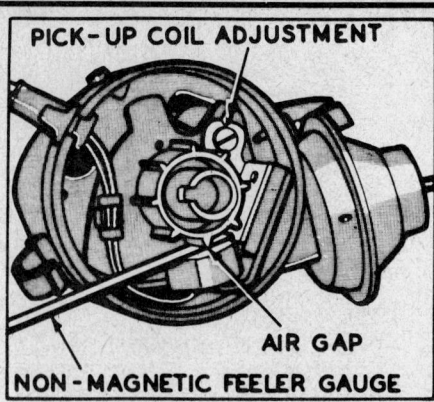

Fig. 25 Air gap adjustment. Distributors equipped with single pick up

gears, the roll pin hole is located higher than the original gear roll pin hole, so that distributor shaft will not be weakened when the shaft is rotated 90 degrees and drilled to accommodate the replacement gear.

b. Before drilling through shaft and gear, place a .007 in. feeler gauge between gear and thrust washer and observe that centerline between two gear teeth is in line with centerline of rotor electrode, Fig. 23. Drill a .124 to .129 in. hole and install roll pin.

NOTE: Support gear hub when installing roll pin so gear teeth will not be damaged.

4. On eight cylinder units, install distributor shaft retainer and pin, Fig. 21.
5. On all units, install lower plate, upper plate and pick-up coil assembly, Figs. 19 through 21.
6. Attach vacuum advance unit to pick-up plate, then install vacuum advance unit attaching screws and washers.
7. Position reluctor keeper pin into place on reluctor sleeve, then slide reluctor down reluctor sleeve and press firmly into position. Install keeper pin.
8. Lubricate felt pad located in top of reluctor sleeve with one drop of light engine oil, then install rotor.

Pick-up Replacement & Air Gap Adjustment

1. With distributor removed from vehicle, perform Steps 1 to 3 as outlined in Distributor Disassemble.
2. Remove pick-up coil and upper plate by depressing retainer clip and moving it away from mounting stud. Pick-up coil cannot be removed from upper plate.
3. Lightly lubricate upper plate pivot pin and lower plate support pins with distributor lubricant. Install upper plate pivot pin through smallest hole in lower plate and install retainer clip.

NOTE: The upper plate must ride on the support pins on the lower plate.

4. Install lower and upper plates and pick-up coil as an assembly and install distributor into vehicle.

NOTE: On dual pick up distributors, the start pick up may be identified by a two prong male connector and the run pick up may be identified by a male-female plug, Fig. 24.

5. To set air gap on all single pick up distributors and on start pick up of dual pick up distributors, align one reluctor tooth with pick up pole and install a .006

inch non-magnetic feeler gauge between reluctor tooth and pick up pole, Figs. 24 and 25. Rotate pick up coil until contact is made between reluctor tooth, feeler gauge and pick up pole. Tighten pick up coil hold down screw and remove feeler gauge. The feeler gauge should be removed without force. If it cannot, readjust gap.
6. To set air gap on run pick up of dual pick up distributors, first adjust start pick up as described in step 5, then adjust run pick up as described in step 5. Use a .012 inch non-magnetic feeler gauge to adjust run pick up air gap.
7. Perform a second gap check using a .008 inch feeler gauge on all single pick up distributors and on start pick up of dual pick up distributor or a .014 inch feeler gauge on run pick up of dual pick up distributors. Do not force feeler gauge between reluctor tooth and pick up pole as it is possible to do so. The feeler gauge should not be able to fit between the reluctor tooth and pick up pole if air gap is correctly set. Apply vacuum to vacuum control unit. Pick up should not contact reluctor tooth. Readjust air gap if contact occurs.

NOTE: If pick up contacts reluctor teeth on one side of shaft only, the distributor shaft is most likely bent and shaft replacement required.

1981–83 Chrysler Corp. Front Wheel Drive Models W/4-156 (2.6L) Engine Electronic Ignition System

DESCRIPTION

This system consists of the distributor, Fig. 1, ignition switch, ignition coil, ECU igniter and spark plugs. Primary circuit current is controlled by the ECU igniter in response to timing signals produced by the distributor pick up. The distributor consists of the power distribution section, signal generator, ECU igniter, advance mechanism and drive gear section. The signal generator is a small magneto which produces a signal that is processed by the ECU to determine the exact time to open the primary circuit and fire the spark plugs.

SYSTEM TESTING

1. Disconnect high tension lead from distributor and hold end of cable 3/16–3/8 inch from good engine ground. Crank engine and check for spark at end of high tension lead.
2. If spark is present, continue cranking engine while slowly moving coil high tension lead away from engine ground. If arcing occurs at coil tower, replace coil. If no spark is present at coil high tension lead or spark is weak, turn ignition On and check voltage at coil negative terminal using suitable voltmeter.

3. If voltage reading obtained is the same as battery voltage, system is operating satisfactorily. If reading is three volts or less, the distributor is defective and must be checked further. If zero reading is obtained, check for open circuit in ignition wiring and repair as necessary.
4. Connect special jumper wire, Fig. 2, to coil negative terminal. Turn ignition On, position coil high tension lead as described in step 1, then momentarily touch other end of jumper wire to a good ground.
5. If no spark is observed at coil high tension lead, check for presence of voltage at coil positive terminal. If battery voltage read-

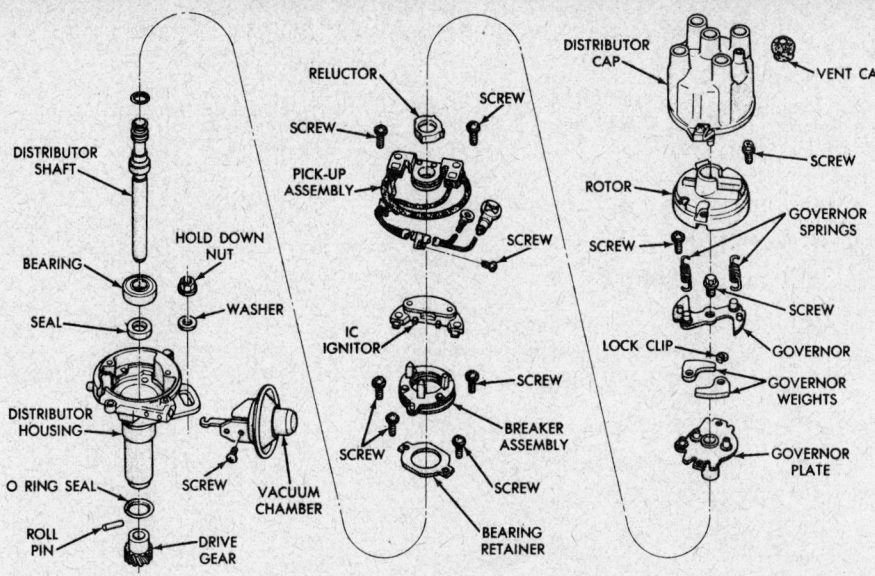

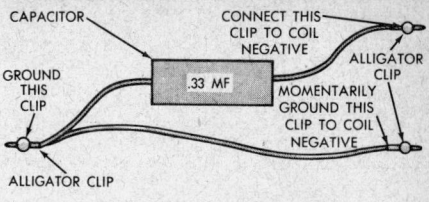

Fig. 2 Coil negative terminal jumper wire

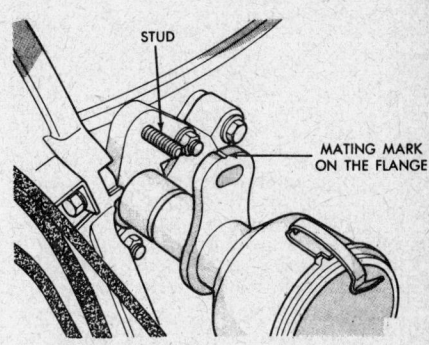

Fig. 3 Aligning distributor and engine mating marks

Fig. 1 Disassembled view of electronic ignition distributor. 1981—83 Chrysler front wheel drive models w/4-156 (1.6L) engine

ing is obtained at coil positive terminal, replace coil. If proper voltage cannot be obtained, check for loose connections or damaged wiring and repair as necessary.

DISTRIBUTOR SERVICE

Distributor, Replace

Removal
1. Rotate engine until No. 1 cylinder is at TDC on compression stroke.
2. Disconnect battery ground cable.
3. Remove distributor cap and mark relationship of rotor to distributor housing.
4. Remove distributor wiring harness.
5. Disconnect vacuum hose from distributor.
6. Remove distributor retaining nut, then the distributor.

Installation
1. Align mating mark on distributor housing with rotor.
2. Install distributor into engine aligning mating mark on distributor mounting flange with center of distributor retaining stud, Fig. 3.
3. Install retaining nut, vacuum hose, secondary ignition cables and distributor wiring harness.
4. Connect battery ground cable, start engine and adjust ignition timing.

Disassembly

1. Remove distributor rotor.
2. Remove governor assembly retaining screw, Fig. 1 and governor assembly.

NOTE: Governor springs are not interchangeable and must be installed in their original positions. Note position of each spring during disassembly for reference during assembly.

---

3. Remove wire retaining clamp from side of distributor.
4. Remove pick up coil and ECU igniter retaining screws, then remove pick up coil and ECU igniter as an assembly.
5. Remove vacuum chamber retaining screws, then the vacuum chamber assembly.
6. Remove breaker assembly retaining screws, then the breaker assembly.
7. Remove bearing retainer plate screws, then the bearing retainer plate.
8. Mark relationship of distributor drive gear to distributor shaft, then punch out distributor drive gear retaining pin and remove gear from shaft.
9. Remove distributor shaft and bearing assembly from housing.
10. Remove distributor housing seal.

Assembly

1. Lubricate distributor housing seal with suitable grease and install into distributor housing.
2. Install distributor shaft and bearing assembly into distributor housing.
3. Install distributor drive gear onto shaft and align marks made during disassembly.
4. Install drive gear roll pin, then install bearing retainer and retaining screws.
5. Install breaker assembly and retaining screws.
6. Install vacuum chamber onto distributor housing and secure with retaining screws.
7. Install pick up coil and ECU igniter as an assembly into housing, then install retaining screws.
8. Install wire retaining clamp and governor assembly. If governor assembly was disassembled, check to ensure that governor springs are installed in original positions.
9. Install governor assembly retaining screw and rotor.

Pick Up Assembly, Replace

1. Remove distributor as described under "Distributor Service" under "Distributor, Replace".
2. Perform steps 1 through 4 as described under "Distributor Service" under "Disassembly".
3. Reverse procedure to install.

1980 Chrysler Corp. Horizon & Omni W/Electronic Ignition System

DESCRIPTION

This system consists primarily of the battery, ignition switch, control unit, coil, distributor and spark plugs, Fig. 1.

There are two basic circuits in this system; the primary and secondary. The primary circuit consists of the battery, ignition switch, primary windings of the ignition coil, power switching transistor of the control unit and the ground circuit. The secondary circuit consists of the coil secondary circuit, distributor rotor and cap, spark plugs, wires and ground circuit.

The compensating resistance of the circuit maintains consistant current in variation to engine speed. During starting, this resistance is by-passed and full battery voltage is supplied to the ignition coil.

In addition to the two basic circuits, there is the pick coil circuit and control unit feed circuit.

The pick up circuit senses the proper timing for the control unit switching transistor. The reluctor rotates with the distributor shaft and produces a voltage pulse in the magnetic pick up coil each time a spark plug is to fire. This pulse is transmitted through the pick up coil to the power switching transistor in the control unit causing the transistor to interrupt the current flow through the primary circuit. This interruption induces a high voltage in the secondary coil circuit and fires a spark plug. The length of time that the switching transistor allows the flow of current in the primary circuit is determined by the electronic circuitry in the control unit.

SYSTEM TESTING

Harness & Connections Test

1. Check battery voltage using a voltmeter. Battery voltage should be at least 12 volts.
2. Disconnect connector from control unit.

CAUTION: The ignition switch must be in the "Off" position whenever any connector is disconnected or connected.

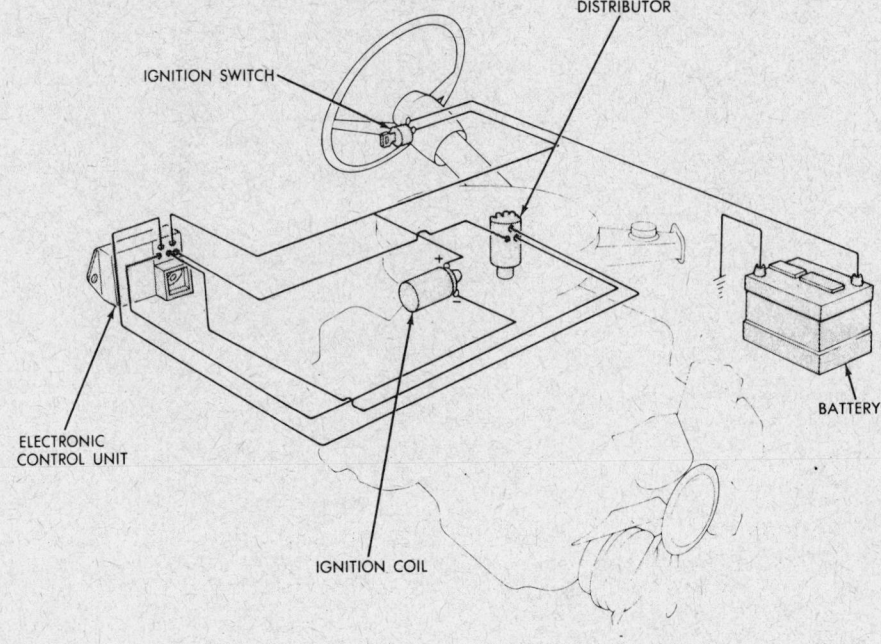

Fig. 1   Electronic Ignition System. 1980 Horizon & Omni

3. Turn ignition switch "On" and connect negative lead of voltmeter to ground.
4. Connect positive lead of voltmeter to connector cavity No. 2, Fig. 2 Voltage reading should be within 1 volt of reading taken in Step 1 with all accessories off. If there is more than 1 volt difference, check circuit shown in Fig. 2.
5. Connect positive lead of voltmeter to connector cavity No. 5, Fig. 3. Voltage reading should be within 1 volt of reading taken in Step 1 with all accessories off. If there is more than 1 volt difference, check circuit shown in Fig. 3.
6. Turn ignition switch "Off" and reconnect wiring harness to control unit.
7. Disconnect wiring harness connector from distributor and turn ignition switch to "On".

8. Connect positive lead to voltmeter to connector cavity No. 1, Fig. 4. Voltage reading should be within 1 volt of reading taken in Step 1 with all accessories off. If there is more than 1 volt difference, turn ignition switch "Off" and disconnect control unit connection. Connect an ohmmeter from distributor connector cavity No. 1 to control unit connector cavity No. 1, Fig. 5. If there is no continuity, replace wiring harness.
9. Make sure that ignition switch is "Off"

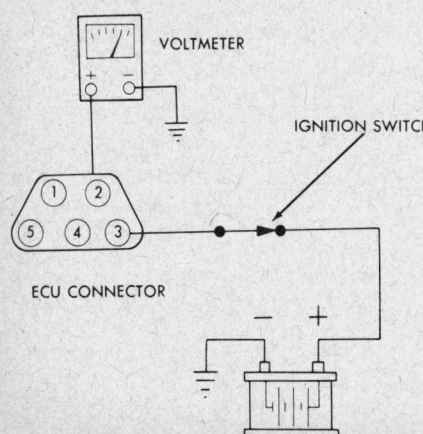

Fig. 2   Cavity No. 2 and related circuitry test

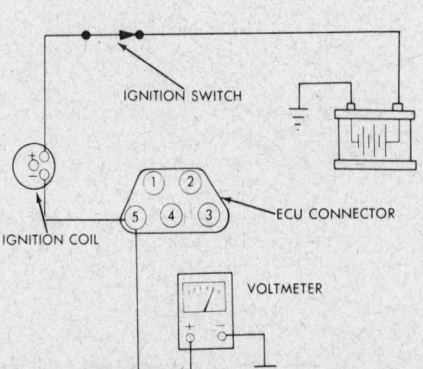

Fig. 3   Cavity No. 5 and related circuitry test

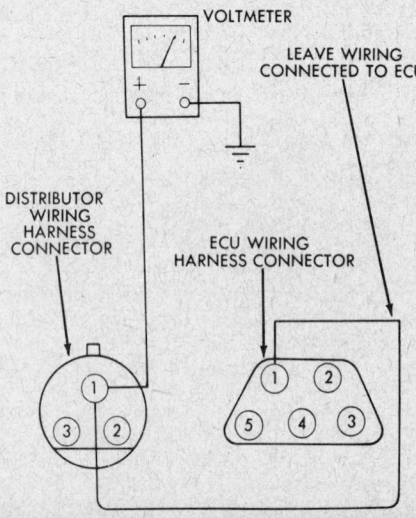

Fig. 4   Cavity No. 1 and related circuitry test

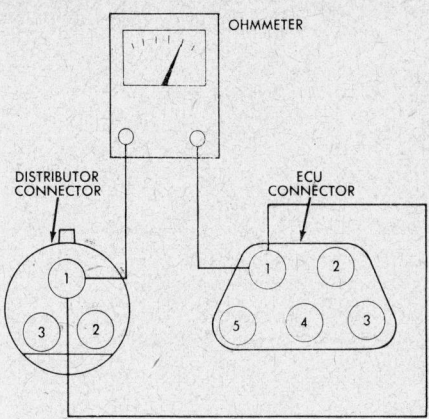

Fig. 5   Cavity No. 1 continuity test

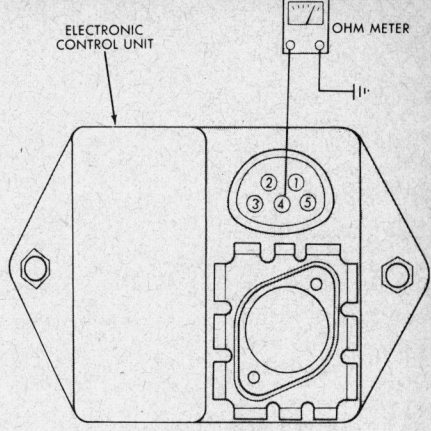

Fig. 7   Pin No. 4 continuity test

(Fig. 6 — Cavity No. 2 continuity test)

and reconnect wiring harness to control unit.

10. Connect one ohmmeter lead to a good ground and the other lead to distributor wiring harness connector No. 2, Fig. 6. If ohmmeter does not indicate continuity, disconnect connector from control unit and connect ungrounded ohmmeter lead to control unit connector pin No. 4, Fig. 7. If ohmmeter does not indicate continuity, remove control unit mounting bolts, clean control unit surface area which comes in contact with bolts, reinstall and tighten bolts and recheck for continuity. If continuity still does not exist, replace control unit.

Ignition Secondary System Test

1. Disconnect cable from center tower of distributor and hold cable about 3/16 inch from engine.

CAUTION: Make sure that there are no fuel leaks before performing this test.

---

2. If arcing does not occur while cranking engine, remove wire harness connector from distributor and connect a jumper wire to wiring harness connector cavity

No. 3, Fig. 8. Intermittently short the other end of jumper wire to ground. If there is a spark at cable, replace distributor pick up.

NOTE: When replacing pick up, check to make sure that rotor vanes are grounded, Fig. 9. Connect one lead of an ohmmeter to a good ground and the other lead to a shutterblade. If there is no continuity, push rotor down on shaft. If still there is no continuity, remove rotor, clean top of shaft and replace rotor. If still there is no continuity, replace rotor with one of the correct type (do not substitute rotor from previous year vehicles). Do not start engine until continuity has been obtained.

3. Crank engine again. If there is still no spark, replace control unit and recheck. If still there is no spark, replace ignition coil.

DISTRIBUTOR SERVICE
Spark Plug Wires, Replace

NOTE: The coil wire and spark plug end of

the spark plug wires are replaced in a conventional manner. To replace the distributor end of the spark plug wires, use the following procedure.

1. Remove distributor cap.
2. Using a pair of suitable long nosed pliers, remove spark plug wires from distributor cap by squeezing wire clips and pushing out, Fig. 10.

NOTE: Do not remove spark plug wires from distributor cap unless nipples are damaged or cable testing indicates high resistance or broken insulation.

---

3. Refer to Fig. 11 for proper installation of spark plug wires. Ensure positive locking terminal electrode is fully seated in cap.

Distributor, Replace

Removal
1. Disconnect distributor pickup lead wire at harness connector.

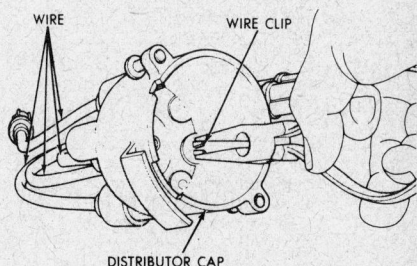

Fig. 10   Spark plug wire removal

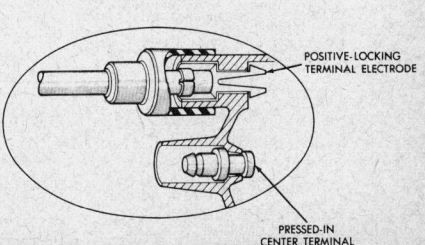

Fig. 11   Spark plug wire installation

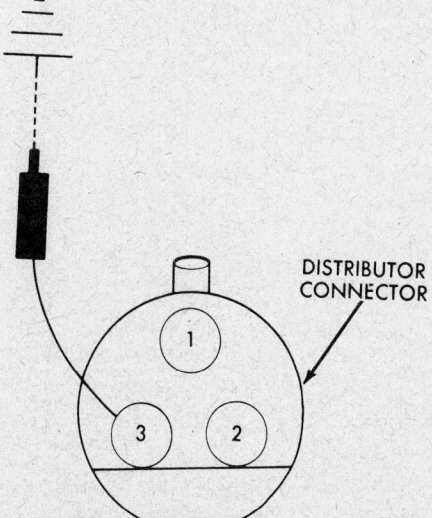

Fig. 8   Grounding cavity No. 3 to ground with jumper wire

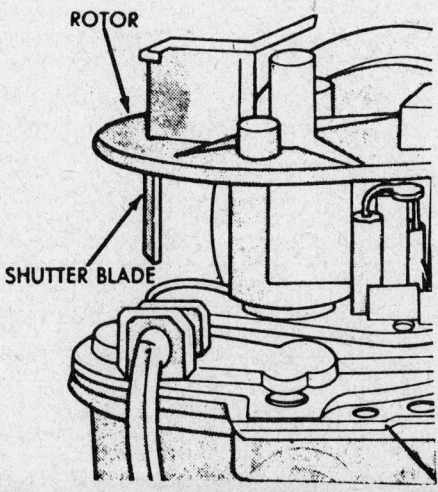

Fig. 9   Rotor vanes

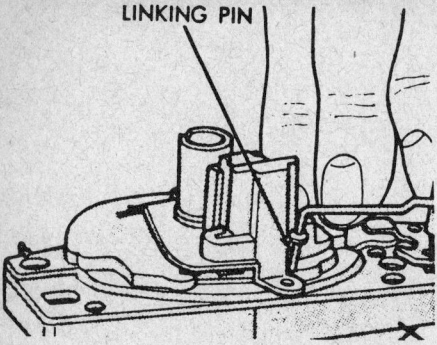

LINKING PIN

Fig. 12   Replacing vacuum chamber

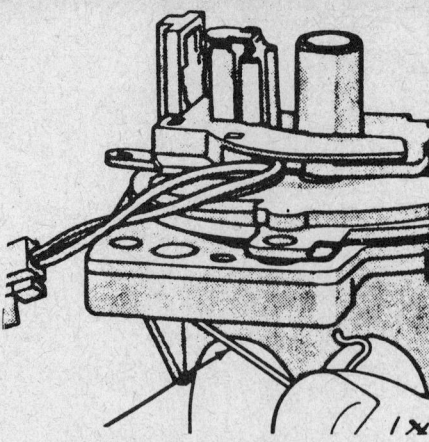

Fig. 13   Replacing retaining clips

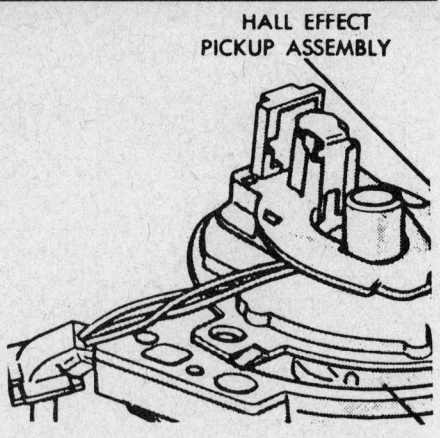

HALL EFFECT PICKUP ASSEMBLY

Fig. 14   Replacing pick up assembly

2. Remove distributor cap.
3. Rotate engine until distributor rotor faces toward cylinder block then scribe a mark on the block to indicate rotor position.
4. Remove distributor hold down screw.
5. Remove distributor from engine.

NOTE: Do not crank engine while distributor is removed.

Installation
1. Position distributor in engine.
2. Engage distributor drive gear with camshaft drive gear so the distributor rotor will align with the scribe mark on cylinder block.
3. If the engine was cranked while the distributor was removed, proceed as follows:
   a. Rotate crankshaft until No. 1 piston is at top dead center, compression stroke. The pointer on clutch housing should align with the "0" mark on the flywheel.
   b. Rotate distributor rotor to a position ahead of the No. 1 distributor cap terminal.
   c. Install distributor into engine, engaging distributor drive gear with camshaft drive gear. The rotor should be properly positioned under the distributor cap No. 1 terminal.
4. Install distributor cap.

5. Install distributor hold down screw finger tight.
6. Connect distributor pickup lead wire.
7. Adjust ignition timing. Refer to the "Tune Up Specifications" found in the individual car chapters.

Disassembly
1. Place distributor in a short jawed vise, then remove distributor cap and rotor.
2. Remove vacuum chamber retaining screws, then lift up to disengage linking pin and remove vacuum chamber, Fig. 12.
3. Remove pick up assembly retaining clips, Fig. 13, and pick up assembly, Fig. 14.
4. Place drive gear on vise so that roll pin can be removed, then remove drive pin using a punch.
5. Remove drive gear and drive shaft from housing.
6. If necessary remove wires from distributor cap by pinching wire clips with pliers and pushing out.

Assembly
1. Clean and inspect all parts. Lubricate housing bushings with engine oil.

2. Install drive shaft into housing, then install drive gear onto shaft and retain with roll pin.
3. Install pick up assembly, Fig. 14.

NOTE: Pick up assembly leads may be damaged if not properly installed. Make sure lead retainer is in locating hole properly before installing distributor cap. "T" shaped attachment on retainer must slip into locating hole. When distributor is installed, leads are behind distributor housing and cannot be easily checked for proper positioning.

4. Install pick up assembly retaining clips, Fig. 13.
5. Connect vacuum chamber linking pin and install vacuum chamber and retaining screws, Fig. 12.
6. Install rotor and distributor rotor.

Pick Up Assembly, Replace
1. Remove distributor cap and rotor.
2. Remove vacuum chamber retaining screws and vacuum chamber, Fig. 12.
3. Remove retaining clips, Fig. 13, and pick up assembly, Fig. 14.

Chrysler Corp. Rear Wheel Drive Models W/ Electronic Spark Control (Lean Burn) System

SERVICE NOTE
Ignition Timing, Adjust

1977-81
1. Connect a tachometer to engine and a suitable timing light to No. 1 cylinder.

NOTE: Do not puncture ignition cables or boots with test probes.

2. Start engine, then apply parking brake and place transmission in Neutral. Allow

engine to reach operating temperature.
3. Disconnect and plug EGR vacuum hose at EGR valve and vacuum hose to Electronic Spark Control computor, then connect a jumper wire from carburetor switch to ground.
4. Disconnect PCV valve and vapor canister purge hose from carburetor. Do not plug hoses.
5. Check idle speed and adjust as necessary, then reconnect PCV valve vacuum hose and vapor canister purge hose.
6. Loosen distributor hold down bracket screw just enough so that distributor housing can be rotated.

7. Check and adjust ignition timing as necessary.
8. Tighten distributor hold down screw, then recheck idle speed and ignition timing.
9. Remove test equipment and connect vacuum hoses.

1982-83
1. Connect a suitable tachometer to engine and a suitable adjustable timing light to No. 1 cylinder secondary cable.

NOTE: Do not puncture ignition second-

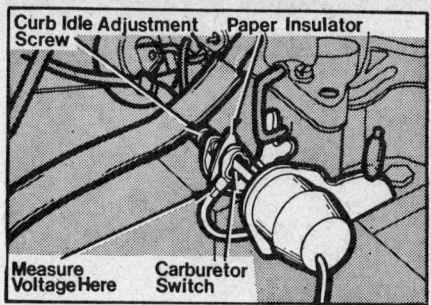

Fig. 1   Power & vacuum transducer tests

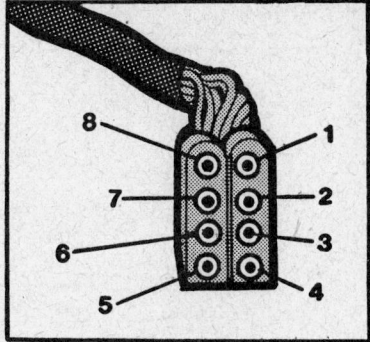

Fig. 2   Dual connector. 1977 Exc. Diplomat & LaBaron

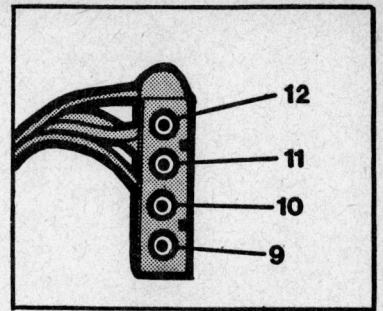

Fig. 3   Single connector. 1977 Exc. Diplomat & LaBaron

ary cables or boots with test probes.

2. Set parking brake, start engine and place gear selector in neutral. Run engine until warm.
3. On vehicles equipped with carburetor switch, connect a jumper wire between carburetor switch and a known good ground.
4. Ensure curb idle speed is set at or below specifications. Adjust as necessary.
5. Check ignition timing. If within ± 2° of specifications, shut engine "Off" and remove timing light, tachometer and carburetor ground wire. If outside of tolerance, proceed to step 6.
6. Loosen distributor hold down arm screw, rotate distributor housing until correct timing marks are lined up, ensuring idle speed is still at or below specified curb idle speed.
7. Tighten distributor hold down screw, then recheck idle speed and ignition timing.
8. Turn engine "Off" and remove timing light, tachometer and carburetor ground wire.

Ignition System Starting Test

1. Remove the coil wire from distributor cap and hold end of wire about ¼ in. from a good engine ground. On 1977–81 models, have assistant crank engine while observing spark at coil wire. On 1981–83 models, turn ignition "On," then intermittently jump coil negative terminal to a good ground while observing coil wire.
2. The spark at the coil wire must be constant and bright blue. If spark is satisfactory, on 1977–80 models continue to crank engine, and on 1981–83 models intermittently jump coil negative terminal while slowly moving. If arcing occurs at the coil tower, replace coil. If spark is weak or not constant or there is no spark, proceed to the "Failure To Start Test."

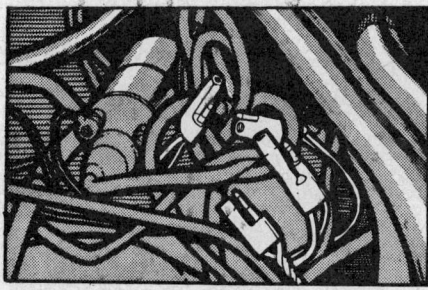

Fig. 4   Distributor heads. 1977 Exc. Diplomat & LeBaron

3. If spark is satisfactory and no arcing occurs at coil tower, the ignition system is producing the necessary high secondary voltage. However, ensure this voltage is transmitted to the spark plugs by checking the distributor rotor, cap, spark plug wires, and spark plugs. If satisfactory, the ignition system is not faulty. It will be necessary to check the fuel system and engine mechanical components.

Failure To Start Test

NOTE: Before proceeding with this test, perform "Ignition System Starting Test". Failure to do so may lead to unnecessary diagnostic time and incorrect test results.

1977 Exc. Diplomat & LeBaron

1. With a voltmeter, measure and note voltage at battery. Battery specific gravity must be at least 1.220, temperature corrected, to deliver the necessary voltage to operate the cranking and ignition systems properly.
2. Disconnect wiring harness connector from "Coolant Switch."
3. Place a piece of paper between curb idle adjusting screw and carburetor switch, Fig. 1, or ensure curb idle adjusting screw is not contacting switch.
4. Connect negative lead of voltmeter to an engine ground.
5. Turn ignition switch to "Run" position and measure voltage at carburetor switch terminal, Fig. 1. If voltage is greater than 5 volts but less than 10 volts, proceed to Step 7. If voltage is greater than 10 volts, check continuity between terminal 2 of the dual connector and the ground with ignition switch in "Off" position. Continuity should be noted. If continuity does not exist, check for poor ground connection. If voltage is less than 5 volts, turn ignition switch to "OFF" and disconnect dual connector from bottom of "Spark Control Computer". Turn ignition switch to "Run" and measure voltage at terminal 4 of dual connector, Fig. 2. Voltage should be within 1 volt of battery voltage. If voltage is satisfactory, proceed to Step 6. If not, check wiring between terminal 4 of dual connector, Fig. 2, and ignition switch for opens, shorts or improper connections.
6. Turn ignition switch to "OFF" and disconnect single connector from bottom of "Spark Control Computer." Check continuity between terminal 11 of single connector, Fig. 3, and carburetor switch terminal. There should be continuity be-

tween these two points. If not, check wiring for opens, shorts or improper connections. If continuity is noted, check continuity between terminal 2 of dual connector, Fig. 2, and the ground. If continuity is noted, replace "Spark Control Computer". If not, check wiring for opens or improper connections and only proceed to Step 7 if engine still fails to start.
7. Turn ignition switch to "Run" and with positive lead of voltmeter, measure voltage at terminals 7 and 8 of disconnected leads from computer, Fig. 2. Voltage should be within 1 volt of battery voltage. If so, proceed to step 8. If not, proceed as follows:
Terminal 7—Check wiring and connections between connector and ignition switch. Also, check 5 ohm side of ballast resistor.
Terminal 8—Check wiring and connections between connector and ignition switch. Also, check primary windings of coil and ½ ohm side of ballast resistor.
8. Turn ignition switch to "OFF" position and measure resistance between terminals 5 and 6 of dual connector Fig. 2. Resistance should be between 150 and 900 ohms. If resistance is satisfactory, proceed to Step 9. If not, disconnect "Start Pick Up" coil leads from distributor and measure resistance at distributor leads, Fig. 4. If resistance is between 150 and 900 ohms, there is an open, shorted, or improper connection between distributor connector and terminals 5 and 6 of dual connector, Fig. 2. If resistance is not within specifications, the "Start Pick Up" coil

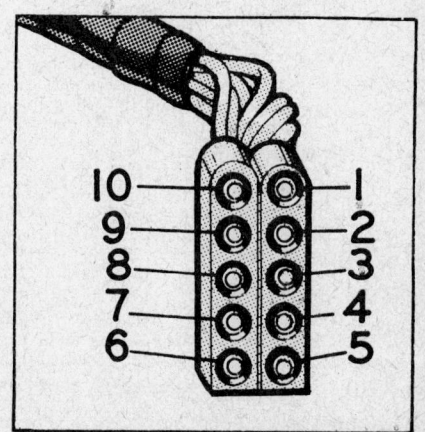

Fig. 5   Dual Connector. 1977 Diplomat & LeBaron; 1978–83 All

Fig. 6 Transducer terminal resistance & idle stop solenoid checks

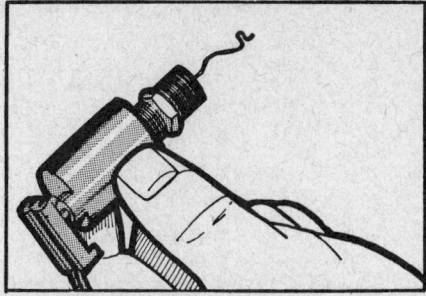

Fig. 7 Throttle transducer

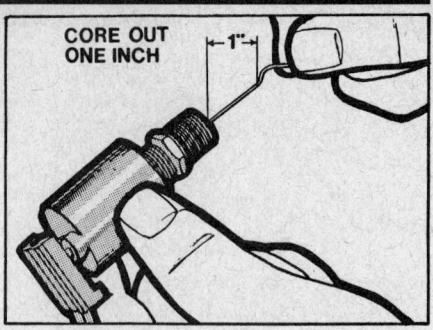

Fig. 8 Checking with test transducer

is faulty.

9. Connect one lead of ohmmeter to engine ground and with other lead, check for continuity at each terminal of distributor leads, Fig. 4. There should be no continuity. Reconnect distributor leads and proceed to Step 10. If there is continuity, replace "Start Pick Up" coil.

10. Remove distributor cap and check and adjust air gap of "Start Pick Up" coil outlined under "Pick-up Replacement & Air Gap Adjustment", Chrysler Corp. Rear Wheel Drive Models, Less Electronic Spark Control (Lean Burn) System. Refer to the Pick-up Air Gap Specification Chart for air gap dimensions.

11. Install distributor cap, reconnect all wiring and start engine. If engine still fails to start, replace "Spark Control Computer"

12. After installing new computer and engine still fails to start, reinstall original one and repeat test procedure, since one of the test procedures may not have been performed correctly.

1977 Diplomat & LeBaron; 1978–79 All

1. With a voltmeter, measure and note battery voltage. Battery specific gravity must be at least 1.220, temperature corrected, to deliver the necessary voltage to operate the cranking and ignition systems properly.

2. Disconnect wiring harness connector from coolant switch.

3. Place a piece of paper between curb idle adjusting screw and carburetor switch, Fig. 1, or ensure curb idle adjusting screw is not contacting carburetor switch.

4. Connect negative lead of voltmeter to an engine ground.

5. Turn ignition switch to "Run" position and measure voltage at carburetor switch, Fig. 1. If voltage is greater than 5 volts but less than 10 volts, proceed to Step 7. If voltage is greater than 10 volts, turn ignition switch to "Off" position and disconnect dual connector from bottom of "Spark Control Computer", Fig. 5, then check continuity between terminal 10 and the ground. If voltage is less than 5 volts, turn ignition switch to "Run" position and measure voltage at terminal 2 of the dual connector, Fig. 5. Voltage should be within one volt of battery voltage. If voltage is satisfactory, proceed to Step 6. If not, check wiring between terminal 2, Fig. 5, and the ignition switch for opens, shorts or improper connections.

6. With ignition switch in "Off" position, check continuity between terminal 7 of dual connector, Fig. 5, and the carburetor switch terminal. There should be continuity between these two points. If not, check wiring for opens, shorts or improper connections. If continuity is noted, check continuity between terminal 10 of dual connector, Fig. 5, and the ground. If continuity is noted, replace "Spark Control Computer". If not, check wiring for opens or

improper connections and only proceed to Step 7 if engine still fails to start.

7. Turn ignition switch to "Run" position and measure the voltage between terminal 1, Fig. 5, and the ground. Voltage should be within one volt of battery voltage. If so, proceed to Step 8. If not, proceed as follows:

    Terminal 1—Check wiring and connections between dual connector and ignition switch.

8. Turn ignition switch to "Off" position and measure resistance between terminals 5 and 9 of dual connector, Fig. 5. Resistance should be between 150 and 900 ohms. If so, proceed to Step 9. If not, disconnect "Pick-Up Coil" lead from distributor and measure resistance between terminals at distributor side of connector. If resistance is between 150 and 900 ohms, there is an open, shorted or improper connection between the distributor connector and terminals 5 and 9 of the dual connector. If resistance is still not within specifications, the "Pick-Up Coil" is faulty.

9. Check for continuity between each terminal on distributor side of distributor connector and the engine ground. There should be no continuity. Reconnect distributor connector and proceed to Step 10. If continuity is present, replace "Pick-Up Coil".

10. Remove distributor cap and air gap of "Pick-Up Coil". Refer to "Pick-Up Replacement & Air Gap Adjustment", Chrysler Corp. Rear Wheel Drive Models, Less Electronic Spark Control (Lean Burn) System. Adjust air gap if necessary.

11. Install distributor cap, reconnect all wiring and start engine. If engine still fails to start, replace "Spark Control Computer".

12. After installing new computer and engine still fails to start, reinstall original computer and repeat test procedure since one of the test procedures may not have been performed correctly.

1980 All Models

1. With a voltmeter, measure and note battery voltage. Battery specific gravity must be at least 1.220, temperature corrected, to deliver voltage to operate cranking and ignition system properly.

2. Place a piece of paper between curb idle adjusting screw and carb switch, Fig. 1, or ensure that carburetor idle adjusting screw is not touching carb switch.

3. Connect negative lead of voltmeter to a good engine ground.

4. Rotate ignition switch to Run position and measure voltage at carburetor switch terminal. If voltage is approximately 5 volts, proceed to step 6. If voltage is not at least 5 volts, place ignition switch in Off position and disconnect wire connector from bottom of Spark Control Computer,

Fig. 5. Rotate ignition switch back to the Run position and measure voltage at wire connector terminal 2, Fig. 5. Voltage should be within one volt of battery voltage noted previously. If voltage is correct proceed to step 5. If voltage is incorrect, check wiring between wire terminal 2 and ignition switch for open or short circuits or improper connections.

5. With ignition switch in the Off position, disconnect wire connector from Spark Control Computer. Using an ohmmeter, check for continuity between connector terminal 7, Fig. 5, and carburetor switch terminal. Continuity should exist between these two points. If not, check wiring for open or short circuit or improper connections. If continuity is noted, check for continuity between connector terminal 10 and engine ground. If continuity exist, replace Spark Control Computer. If not, check wiring for open circuit or improper connections and proceed to step 6 only if engine still fails to start.

6. Place ignition switch in the Run position and with positive lead of voltmeter, measure voltage from computer connector terminal 1 to ground Fig. 5. Voltage reading should be within one volt of battery voltage noted previously. If proper voltage reading is indicated, proceed to step 7. If improper voltage reading is indicated, check wiring and connection between connector terminal No. 1 and ignition switch.

7. Place ignition switch in the off position, then using an ohmmeter, measure resistance between terminals No. 5 and 9 for run pickup coil and terminals 3 and 9 for start pickup coil Fig. 5. Resistance should be between 150 and 900 ohms. If not, disconnect pickup coil leads from distributor and measure resistance at lead going into distributor. If resistance is now between 150 and 900 ohms, this would indicate an open or short circuit or improper connection between distributor connector and terminals 5 and 9 or terminals 3 and 9 of dual connector. If resistance is not within specifications, pickup coil is defective.

8. Connect one ohmmeter lead to engine ground and with the other lead check for continuity at each terminal going to the distributor. There should be no continuity. Reconnect distributor lead and proceed to step 9. If there is continuity, replace pickup coil.

9. Remove distributor cap and check air gap of pickup coil. Refer to Pickup Coil Replacement and Air Gap Adjustment and adjust gap as necessary.

10. Install distributor cap and reconnect all wiring, then start engine. If engine fails to start, replace spark control computer.

11. After installing new computer and engine

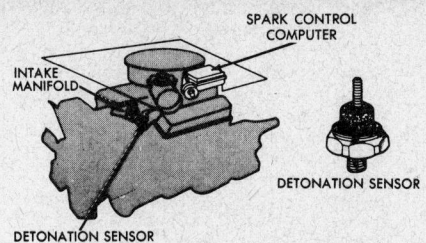

Fig. 8A Detonation sensor location

still fails to start, reinstall original computer and repeat test procedure since one of the test procedures may have been performed incorrectly.

1981-83 All Models

1. Turn ignition "Off". Remove 10 way connector from base of Spark Control Computer. Turn ignition "On", then holding end of coil wire about ¼" away from a ground, momentarily short coil negative wire to ground. If a spark is obtained, replace Spark Control Computer. If no spark is obtained, proceed to step 2.
2. Using a voltmeter, check for battery voltage at coil positive terminal with the ignition "On". If voltage is within 1 volt of battery voltage, proceed to step 4. If not, proceed to step 3.
3. Using an ohmmeter, check continuity of wiring between battery and coil positive, repair as necessary and repeat step 2.
4. Using a voltmeter, check for battery voltage at coil negative. If within 1 volt of battery voltage, proceed to step 5. If not, replace coil.
5. If voltage is correct, but no spark is obtained when grounding coil negative, replace coil.
6. If spark is obtained, but engine will not start, place ignition switch in "On" position. Using a suitable voltmeter, measure voltage of disconnected 10 way connector cavity 1, Fig. 5 to ground. Voltage should be within 1 volt of battery voltage. If voltage is within 1 volt of battery voltage, proceed to step 8. If not, proceed to step 7.
7. Using an ohmmeter, check continuity of wire for opens and repair as necessary (no power between coil negative and 10 way connector). Repeat step 6.
8. Place a piece of paper between curb idle adjusting screw and carburetor switch, Fig. 1, or ensure curb idle adjusting screw is not contacting carburetor switch.
9. Connect negative lead of voltmeter to a good engine ground.
10. Rotate ignition switch to "On" position and measure voltage at carburetor switch terminal. If voltage is approximately 5 volts, proceed to step 12. If voltage is not at least 5 volts, place ignition switch in "Off" position and disconnect wire connector from bottom of Spark Control Computer, Fig. 5. Rotate ignition switch back to the "On" position and measure voltage at wire connector terminal 2, Fig. 5. Voltage should be within one volt of battery voltage noted previously. If voltage is correct proceed to step 11. If voltage is incorrect check wiring between wire terminal 2 and ignition switch for open or short circuits or improper connections.
11. With ignition switch in the "Off" position, disconnect wire connector from Spark Control Computer. Using an ohmmeter, check for continuity between connector terminal 7, Fig. 5, and carburetor switch

terminal. Continuity should exist between these two points. If not, check wiring for open or short circuit or improper connections. If continuity is noted, check for continuity between connector terminal 10 and engine ground. If continuity exists, replace Spark Control Computer. If not, check wiring for open circuit or improper connections and proceed to step 12 only if engine still fails to start.
12. Place ignition switch in the "Off" position, then using an ohmmeter, measure resistance between terminals No. 5 and 9 for run pickup coil and terminals 3 and 9 for start pickup coil Fig. 5. Resistance should be between 150 and 900 ohms. If not, disconnect pickup coil leads from distributor and measure resistance at lead going into distributor. If resistance is now between 150 and 900 ohms, this would indicate an open or short circuit or improper connection between distributor connector and terminals 5 and 9 or terminals 3 and 9 of dual connector. If resistance is not within specifications, pickup coil is defective.
13. Connect one ohmmeter lead to engine ground and with the other lead check for continuity at each terminal going to the distributor. There should be no continuity. Reconnect distributor lead and proceed to step 14. If there is continuity, replace pickup coil.
14. Remove distributor cap and check air gap of pickup coil. Refer to Pickup Coil Replacement and Air Gap Adjustment and adjust gap as necessary.
15. Install distributor cap and reconnect all wiring, then start engine. If engine fails to start, replace spark control computer.
16. After installing new computer and engine still fails to start, reinstall original computer and repeat test procedure since one of the test procedures may have been performed incorrectly.

Poor Performance Tests

Run Pick-Up Function Test, 1977 Exc. Diplomat & LeBaron

1. Start and run engine for about 1½ minutes. Then, disconnect "Start Pick Up" lead from distributor. If engine continues to run, reconnect "Start Pick Up" lead and proceed to "Start Timer Advance Schedule Test." If engine stopped proceed to Step 2.
2. Reconnect "Start Pick Up" lead at distributor, turn ignition switch to "OFF" and disconnect dual connector from bottom of "Spark Control Computer." Measure resistance between terminals 3 and 5 of dual connector, Fig. 2. Resistance should be between 150 and 900 ohms. If so, proceed to Step 3. If not, disconnect "Run Pick Up" coil leads from distributor and measure resistance at distributor leads. If resistance is now between 150 and 900 ohms, check for open, shorted or improper connections of the wiring between distributor connector and terminals 3 and 5 of dual connector, Fig. 2. If resistance is not within specifications, the "Run Pick Up" coil is faulty. Replace "Run Pick Up" coil and repeat Step 1. If engine still fails to run, proceed to Step 3.
3. Disconnect "Run Pick Up" coil from distributor. Connect one lead of ohmmeter to an engine ground and, with other lead, check for continuity at each terminal of distributor leads. There should be no continuity. If not, reconnect distributor leads and proceed to Step 4. If continuity is noted, replace "Run Pick Up" coil and

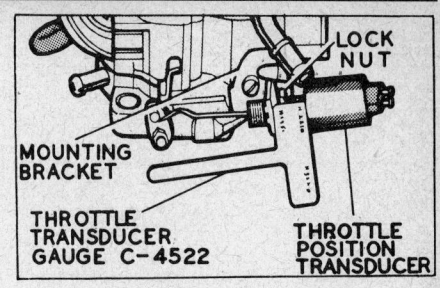

Fig. 9 Throttle position transducer adjustment. 1978-79

repeat Step 1. If engine still fails to run, proceed to Step 4.
4. Remove distributor cap and check and adjust air gap of "Run Pick Up" coil as outlined under "Pick-up Replacement & Air Gap Adjustment", Chrysler Corp. Rear Wheel Drive Models, Less Electronic Spark Control (Lean Burn) System. Refer to the Pick-up Air Gap Specification Chart for air gap dimensions.
5. If engine still fails to run, replace "Spark Control Computer" and repeat Step 1. If engine again fails to run, reinstall original computer and repeat complete test since one of the test procedures may not have been performed correctly.

Start Timer Advance Schedule Test, 1977-79

1. Connect an adjustable timing light to engine so total timing advance at crankshaft can be checked.
2. Start engine, snap throttle open and close and immediately place gear selector in drive.

NOTE: Fully apply service brakes before placing vehicle in drive.

Observe timing mark on crankshaft damper immediately after vehicle is in drive and adjust timing light so basic timing signal is observed at timing plate. The meter on the timing light should indicate amount of advance as indicated under specifications. Continue to observe timing for 90 seconds while adjusting timing light to maintain basic timing signal. The additional advance should slowly reduce to the basic timing signal after approximately one minute. If timing did not increase and/or did not return to basic, replace "Spark Control Computer." If checked satisfactory, proceed to "Throttle Advance Schedule Test."

NOTE: Do not remove timing light since it is needed for further testing.

Speed Advance Schedule Test, 1977-80

NOTE: Before performing this test, ensure the basic timing signal and hot curb idle are within specifications. Disconnect wiring harness connector from throttle position transducer.

Start and run engine for two minutes. Increase engine speed to specified test level and adjust timing light so that basic timing is observed at timing indicator. The additional advance observed on the timing light meter should be as specified. Refer to the Chrysler Lean Burn Specification Charts. If advance is not within specifications, replace "Spark Control Computer" and repeat test.

Throttle Advance Schedule Test, 1977 Exc. Diplomat & LeBaron

NOTE: Before proceeding with test, ensure "Throttle Position Transducer" is adjusted properly.

1. Place ignition switch in the "OFF" position and disconnect single connector from bottom of "Spark Control Computer."
2. Measure resistance between terminals 9 and 10 of single connector, Fig. 3. Resistance should be between 50 and 90 ohms. If so, reconnect single connector and proceed to Step 3. If not, remove connector from "Throttle Position Transducer" and measure resistance at transducer terminals, Fig. 5. If resistance is between 50 and 90 ohms, there is an open, short, or improper connection of wiring between terminals 9 and 10 of single connector, Fig. 3, and the terminals connecting to the transducer. If resistance is not within specifications, replace "Throttle Position transducer" and proceed to Step 3.
3. Reconnect all wiring and turn ignition switch to the "Run" position but do not start engine. Connect negative lead of a voltmeter to an engine ground. With positive lead of voltmeter, touch one terminal of "Throttle Position Transducer", Fig. 6, while fully opening throttle of carburetor and closing. Observe voltmeter reading. Repeat procedure with other terminal of transducer. Either of the terminals should show approximately a 2 volt change on voltmeter when throttle is opened and closed. If 2 volt change is noted, proceed to Step 4. If not, do not replace transducer since the "Spark Control Computer" can cause transducer to function improperly. It will be necessary to proceed to Step 4 to check malfunction.
4. Position throttle linkage on fast idle cam, ground carburetor switch with a jumper wire, disconnect wiring harness connector from "Throttle Position Transducer", and connect harness connector to a known good transducer of the same type suitable for testing.
5. Move core of test transducer inward to fully bottom out, start engine, wait 90 seconds, then move core outward about 1 inch, Fig. 8.
6. Adjust timing light so basic timing signal is observed at timing plate. The meter on the timing light should indicate additional amount of advance as listed under specifications. If advance is within specifications, move core back into transducer and timing should return to basic setting. If timing advanced and returned, proceed to Step 7. If timing did not advance and/or did not return, replace "Spark Control Computer." Also, after replacing computer, recheck "Throttle Position Transducer" as described in Step 3, to ensure transducer is satisfactory. If not, replace transducer.
7. Return timing light meter to zero and move core of test transducer inward and outward about 1 inch, Fig. 8, 5 or 6 times very quickly and observe timing marks. There should be additional advance as listed under specifications for about one second and then return to basic setting. If not, replace "Spark Control Computer". Also, if "Throttle Position Transducer" failed in Step 3, replace transducer since "Spark Control Computer" is not causing it to check unsatisfactory.
8. Remove test transducer and reconnect all wiring.

Throttle Advance Schedule Test, 1977 Diplomat & LeBaron; 1978–79 All

NOTE: Before performing this test, ensure "Throttle Position Transducer" is adjusted properly.

1. With ignition switch in "Off" position, disconnect dual connector from "Spark Control Computer".
2. Measure of resistance between terminals 8 and 9 of dual connector. Resistance should be between 50 and 90 ohms. If resistance is within specifications, reconnect connector and proceed to Step 3. If not, disconnect connector from "Throttle Position Transducer" and measure resistance between transducer terminals. If resistance is between 50 and 90 ohms, there is an open, short or improper connection between terminals 8 and 9 of dual connector and the "Throttle Position Transducer". If resistance is not within specifications, replace "Throttle Position Transducer".
3. Position throttle linkage on fast idle cam, ground carburetor switch with a jumper wire, disconnect "Throttle Position Transducer" connector and connect connector to a known good transducer of the same type suitable for testing.
4. Move core of test transducer inward to fully bottom out, start engine, wait 90 seconds and move core outward approximately one inch.
5. Adjust timing light so basic timing signal is observed at timing plate. The timing light meter should indicate additional amount of advance as indicated in the Chrysler Lean Burn Specification Charts. If within specifications, move core back into transducer and timing should return to basic setting. If timing did not advance and/or did not return to basic setting, replace "Spark Control Computer". Retest "Throttle Position Transducer" after replacing "Spark Control Computer".

Poor Fuel Economy, Performance & Unusually High Idle Speed Tests

1. On 1977–80 models, connect suitable ohmmeter between black wire with tracer terminal of coolant switch and ground.
2. On 1981–83 models, turn ignition Off, then connect suitable ohmmeter between center terminal of temperature switch and ground for coolant temperature switch or between center terminal and ground terminal of charge temperature switch.

For Engine Cold

1. On 1977–80 models, continuity should be present at terminal. If not, replace coolant switch.

NOTE: Disregard terminal of coolant switch with orange wire connected since this wire has no function in system.

2. On 1981–83 models, continuity should be present with resistance less than 100 ohms. If not, replace switch. Charge temperature switch must be cooler than 60°F in order to perform test properly.

For Engine Hot

1. Terminal reading should show no continuity. If continuity is present, replace coolant switch.

Detonation Sensor Test, 1980–83 Models

1. Connect a suitable timing light to engine.
2. Set parking brake. Start engine and position throttle on second step of fast idle cam (at least 1200 RPM).
3. Using a suitable hand operated vacuum pump, apply 16″ of vacuum to Spark Control Computer transducer.
4. Using a small metal object, tap lightly on the intake manifold near the detonation sensor, Fig. 8A. At the same time, using the timing light, look for a decrease in spark advance at the timing marks. The decrease is proportional to the strength and frequency of the tapping. 11° is the maximum timing decrease.
5. Kick engine down to normal idle speed and turn ignition "Off". Remove timing light and vacuum pump.

Coolant Sensor Test, 1981–83 Models

1. Connect ohmmeter to terminals of coolant sensor.
2. With engine cold and ambient temperature less than 90°F., resistance should be 500–1000 ohms.
3. With engine at normal operating temperature, resistance should be greater than 1300 ohms.
4. If resistance is not as specified, replace sensor.

Vacuum Advance Schedule Test, 1977 Exc. Diplomat & LeBaron

1. Connect and adjust timing light to engine so total timing advance at crankshaft can be checked.
2. Check "Idle Stop Solenoid" by turning ignition key to "Run" position, but do not start engine. Disconnect solenoid lead wire, push plunger inward until bottomed out, and while holding throttle linkage open, reconnect solenoid lead wire, Fig. 5. The solenoid plunger should extend and remain extended. Release throttle linkage and plunger should hold throttle linkage. If not, replace "Idle Stop Solenoid". Start and run engine to reach operating temperature.
3. Ensure the transmission is in neutral and the parking brake is applied.
4. Place a piece of paper between carburetor switch and curb idle adjustment screw, Fig. 1. If curb idle adjustment screw is not contacting carburetor switch, ensure fast idle cam is not in fast idle position or is binding, linkage is not binding, or throttle stop screw is not over adjusted. Adjust timing light so basic timing signal can be observed at timing plate. The meter on the timing light should indicate additional amount of advance as listed under the specifications. If advance is not within specifications, replace "Spark Control Computer". If advance is within specifications, run engine for approximately 6 to 9 minutes and ensure a minimum of 16 inches of vacuum is available at the transducer.
5. After 6 to 9 minutes, adjust timing light so basic timing signal can be observed at timing plate. The timing light meter should indicate additional amount of advance as listed under specifications. If advance is not within specifications, replace spark control computer. If advance is within specifications, proceed to next step.
6. Remove paper installed between carburetor switch and curb idle adjustment screw. The timing should return to the

basic setting. If timing does not return to basic setting, ensure the curb idle adjustment screw is contacting carburetor switch. Then, turn engine off and check wire between Terminal 11 of single connector, Fig. 3, at bottom of computer for opens, shorts and improper connections. If wiring is satisfactory, repeat test. If timing will not return to basic setting, replace "Spark Control Computer".

Vacuum Advance Schedule Test, 1977 Diplomat & LeBaron; 1978 All

1. Connect and adjust timing light so that total timing advance at crankshaft can be checked.
2. Start engine, place transmission in neutral and apply parking brake.
3. With engine at normal operating temperature, place a piece of paper between carburetor switch and curb idle adjusting screw, Fig. 1. If curb idle adjusting screw is not contacting carburetor switch, ensure that fast idle cam is not on or is binding, linkage is not binding or throttle stop screw is not over adjusted. Adjust timing light so basic timing is observed at timing plate. Run engine for nine minutes and ensure there is a minimum of 16 inches of vacuum at the transducer. The timing light meter should indicate the additional amount of advance as listed in the Chrysler Lean Burn Specification Chart. If advance is not within specifications, replace "Spark Control Computer."
4. Remove piece of paper between carburetor switch and curb idle adjusting screw. Timing should return to basic setting. If timing does not return to basic setting, ensure that curb idle adjusting screw is not contacting carburetor switch. Then, turn engine "Off" and check wire between terminal 7 of the dual connector and carburetor switch terminal for opens, shorts or improper connections. If check is satisfactory and if timing still will not return to basic setting, replace "Spark Control Computer".

Vacuum Advance Schedule Test, 1979–80

NOTE: If computer fails to obtain specified settings, replace computer.

1. Connect timing light and tachometer to engine.
2. Start engine and allow to reach operating temperature. If engine is at operating temperature, wait at least one minute for start up advance to return to basic timing. Place transmission in Neutral and apply parking brake.
3. Check basic timing and adjust as necessary.
4. Remove vacuum line at transducer and plug line.
5. Ground carburetor switch and remove connector on throttle position transducer, if equipped.
6. Increase engine speed to 1100 rpm and check speed advance timing. Timing should be as listed in Chrysler Lean Burn Specification Charts.
7. With engine operating at 1100 rpm, remove carburetor switch ground and connect vacuum line to vacuum transducer.
8. Check zero time offset. Timing should be as listed in Chrysler Lean Burn Specification Chart.
9. Allow accumulator to clock-up, refer to Chrysler Lean Burn Specification Chart. Operate engine at 1100 rpm and check

vacuum advance. Refer to Chrysler Lean Burn Specification Chart.
10. Disconnect and plug vacuum line at vacuum transducer and operate engine at 1500 rpm.
11. Note speed advance timing.
12. Reconnect vacuum line to vacuum transducer and recheck vacuum advance.
13. Return engine to idle speed, then connect wire to carburetor switch if equipped, and install connector on throttle position transducer.

Spark Advance Of Spark Control Computer Test, 1981–83 Models

1. Ensure engine is fully warmed up and the temperature sensor is connected and operating properly.
2. Set ignition timing to specifications.
3. Place a piece of paper between curb idle adjusting screw and carburetor switch, Fig. 1, or ensure curb idle adjusting screw is not contacting carburetor switch.
4. Remove and plug vacuum transducer line.
5. Using a suitable hand operated vacuum pump, apply 16″ of vacuum to Spark Control Computer transducer on all 8 cylinder models. On all 6 cylinder models, apply 10″ of vacuum to Spark Control Computer transducer.
6. Increase engine speed to 2000 RPM on all 1981–82 models, or 1500 RPM on 1983 models, wait 1 minute (or specified clock up time, see specifications). Advance specifications are in addition to basic timing advance. On systems equipped with an accumulator the specified time must be reached with the carburetor switch ungrounded before checking the specified spark advance schedule (see specifications).
7. If the computer fails to obtain specified settings, replace computer.

Carburetor Switch Test, 1981–83 Models

NOTE: On most systems, grounding the carburetor switch eliminates all spark advance.

1. Turn ignition Off, then disconnect 10-way connector from computer.
2. Check to ensure throttle is fully closed, then check continuity between pin 7 of harness connector and ground using suitable ohmmeter, Fig. 5.
3. If continuity is not present, check for open circuit in carburetor switch wiring circuit and repair as necessary.
4. Open throttle and check continuity between pin 7 of harness connector and ground. Continuity should not be present.

EGR System Test, 1981–83 Models

NOTE: The electronic EGR control is incorporated into the Spark Control Computer on all models. On 1981–82 6 cylinder non-California models, the EGR time delay is located in a cowl mounted timer. On 1981–83 8 cylinder models, 1981–82 6 cylinder California models and all 1983 6 cylinder models, the time delay is integral with the Spark Control Computer. Before proceeding with test, ensure engine temperature sensors are operating properly.

1. With engine cold and ignition Off, connect one lead of suitable voltmeter to gray wire terminal on EGR solenoid. Connect second voltmeter lead to ground.
2. Start engine and check voltmeter read-

ing. Reading should be less than one volt. Reading will remain at this value until engine reaches normal operating temperature and electronic EGR schedule has timed out. EGR Solenoid will then de-energize and voltmeter will indicate charging system voltage.
3. If system does not de-energize in specified amount of time, replace solenoid.
4. If voltmeter indicates charging system voltage before EGR schedule is complete, replace Spark Control Computer or cowl mounted timer as necessary.

NOTE: All 1981 V8-318 and 1982–83 V8-318 non-California models equipped with 2 barrel carburetors have no thermal delay at ambient temperatures below 60°F. This engine will operate according to EGR time delay schedule only. Refer to Chrysler Electronic Spark Control (Lean Burn) Specification Chart for delay schedules.

5. If an engine is started warm, the EGR solenoid will be energized for the duration of time delay schedule only. It will then de-energize.

Electronic Throttle Control Test, 1981–83 Models

NOTE: The electronic throttle control system is incorporated in the Spark Control Computer on 8 cylinder models and all 6 cylinder California models. On 1981–82 6 cylinder models except California and all 1983 6 cylinder models, the electronic throttle control utilizes two cowl mounted timers. A carburetor mounted solenoid is energized whenever the air conditioner, heater, electronic heated backlite or electronic timers are activated. The timers operate with a two second delay after the throttle is closed or with an EGR time delay after an engine start condition.

1. Connect tachometer to engine, then start engine and run until operating temperature is reached.
2. Depress accelerator, then release. Curb idle speed should increase for length of time of EGR schedule.
3. Curb idle speed should increase when air conditioner, heater and/or electronic heated backlite are operated and return to normal when components are turned Off.

NOTE: Air conditioner clutch will cycle on and off as air conditioner operates and should not be mistaken as part of electronic control system operation.

4. If curb idle speed does not increase and decrease as described above, disconnect three-way electrical connector from carburetor.
5. Connect ohmmeter between carburetor solenoid black wire terminal and ground. Resistance should be 15–35 ohms. If not, replace solenoid.
6. Start engine and measure voltage between black wire of three-way connector and ground before EGR time delay has timed out. Voltmeter reading should indicate charging system voltage. If not, replace Spark Control Computer or cowl mounted gray start timer as necessary.
7. With engine operating and voltmeter connected as described in step 6, turn on air conditioner, heater and/or electronic heated backlite. Voltmeter should read

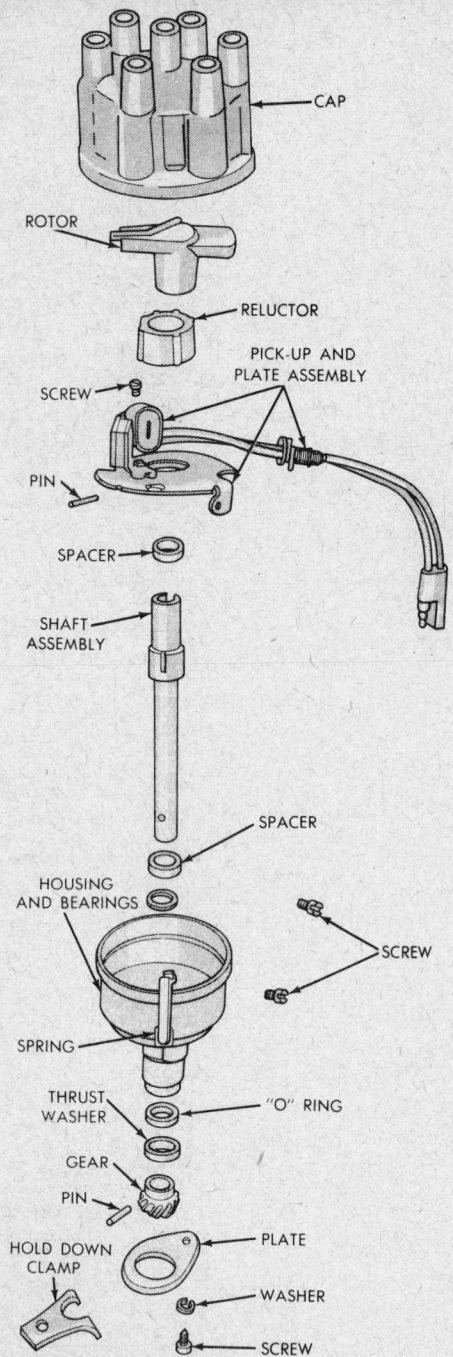

Fig. 10 Electronic spark control (Lean Burn) distributor with single pick up exploded view. 6 cylinder

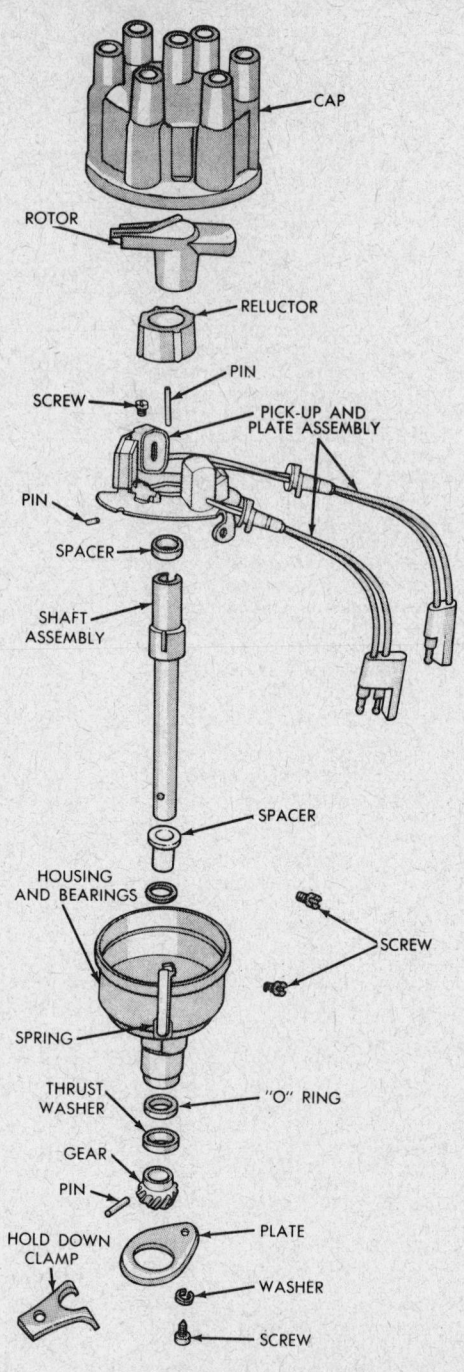

Fig. 10A Electronic spark control (Lean Burn) distributor with dual pick up exploded view. 6 cylinder

charging system voltage after time delay has timed out. If not, check wiring between three-way harness connector and instrument panel for damage and repair as necessary.

Throttle Position Transducer Adjustment

1977

This adjustment can only be performed when the "Air Temperature Sensor", located inside the computer, is below 135° F. If necessary to adjust the transducer when the engine is at operating temperature, it is necessary to cool the "Air Temperature Sensor".

NOTE: The "Air Temperature Sensor" may be cooled with a suitable cooling agent to rapidly lower the temperature of the sensor. To cool the sensor, remove the air cleaner top, insert the spray nozzle of the cooling agent into the computer and direct the spray over the sensor for approximately 15 seconds or until it is frosted.

If adjustment procedure takes longer than 3 or 4 minutes, turn engine off and re-cool "Air Temperature Sensor".

1. Start engine and wait at least 1½ minutes before proceeding with procedure.
2. Connect a jumper wire between carburetor switch terminal and the ground.
3. Disconnect electrical connector from transducer.
4. Check and adjust timing at crankshaft, if

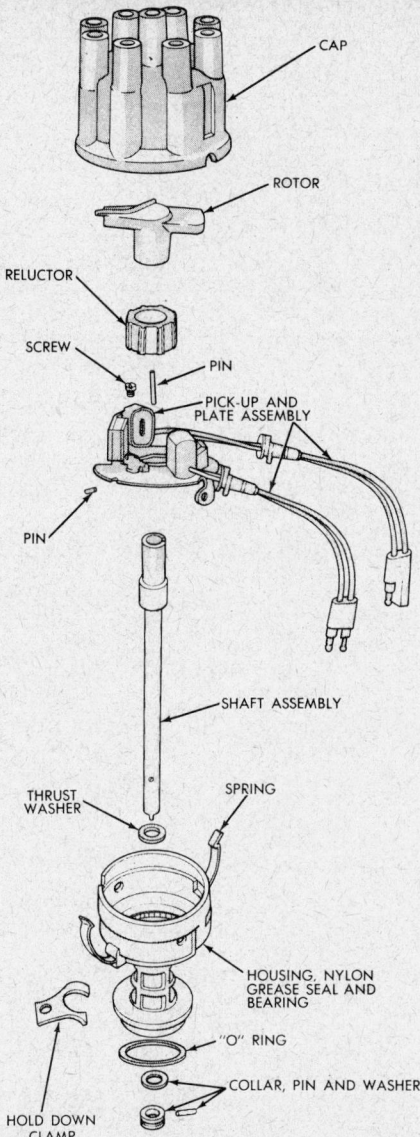

Fig. 11 Electronic spark control (Lean Burn) distributor with dual pick up exploded view. 8 cylinder

necessary.
5. Reconnect transducer electrical connector and recheck timing at crankshaft.
6. If timing is greater than specified, loosen transducer locknut and rotate transducer clockwise until timing returns to specified limits. Then, turn transducer an additional ½ turn clockwise and tighten locknut. If timing is at the specified limits, loosen transducer locknut and rotate transducer counter-clockwise until tim-

ing just starts to advance from specified limit. At that point, turn transducer an additional ½ turn and tighten locknut.

1978–79
1. Disconnect connector from transducer.
2. Loosen locknut.
3. Place special tool C-4522 between outer portion of transducer and transducer mounting bracket, Fig. 9.
4. Adjust transducer by rotating transducer until a clearance fit is obtained.
5. Tighten locknut and reconnect connector.

Distributor, Replace

Refer to "Chrysler Corp. Rear Wheel Drive Models W/Electronic Ignition System" for distributor replacement procedure.

Distributor Service

Disassembly, Figs. 10 thru 11A
1. Remove rotor. If necessary, use two screwdrivers under upper part of rotor to pry off.
2. Remove reluctor by prying up from bottom of reluctor with two screwdrivers (7/16 inch maximum width of screwdrivers). Use care not to distort or damage reluctor teeth.
3. Remove the two screws retaining plate to housing and lift out the plate and pick up coil as an assembly.

NOTE: The distributor clamp springs are held in place by peened metal around the openings and should not be removed.

4. On 6 cylinder distributors, refer to "Chrysler Corp. Rear Wheel Drive Models W/Electronic Ignition System" for procedures.
5. On V8 distributors, refer to "Chrysler Corp. Rear Wheel Drive Models W/Electronic Ignition System" and perform the "Distributor Shaft & Bushing Wear Test". If side play exceeds .006 inch, replace housing shaft and reluctor sleeve as follows:
   a. Remove distributor shaft retaining pin and slide retainer off end of shaft.
   b. Using a file, clean burrs from around pin hole in shaft and remove lower thrust washer.
   c. Push shaft up and remove through top of distributor body.

Assembly, Figs. 10 thru 11A
1. Lubricate and install upper thrust washer(s) on shaft and slide shaft into distributor body.
2. Install distributor shaft retainer and pin.
3. Install plate and pick up coil assembly and retaining screws.
4. Position reluctor keeper pin into position on reluctor sleeve.
5. Slide reluctor down reluctor sleeve and

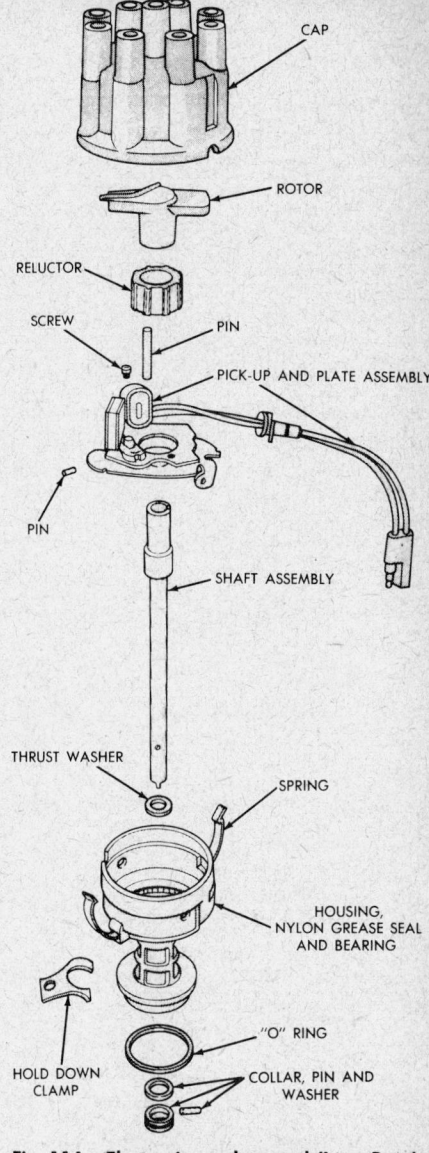

Fig. 11A Electronic spark control (Lean Burn) distributor exploded view. Electronic Fuel Injection

press firmly into place, then install keeper pin.

Pick Up Replacement & Air Gap Adjustment

NOTE: For pick up replacement and/or pick up air gap adjustment, refer to "Chrysler Corp. Rear Wheel Drive Models W/Electronic Ignition System" for procedures.

ELECTRONIC IGNITION SYSTEMS

1977 CHRYSLER ELECTRONIC SPARK CONTROL (LEAN BURN) SPECIFICATION CHART

Spark Control Computer	4091072 ①	4091073 ①	4091074 ①	4091195 ①
	(4094022) ②	(4094008) ②	(4094023) ②	(4106056) ②
Start Timer Advance Schedule	5°–9°	5°–9°	5°–9°	8°
Delay Time In Seconds	90	90	90	90
Throttle Advance Schedule	10° ③			
a. Test Transducer Core Out 1 inch	6°–10° @ 75°F 3°–6° @ 105°F	8°–12°	3°–5° @ 75°F 2°–3° @ 105°F	8°–12°
b. Test transducer Core Moved Quickly In and Out	10°	10°	5°	—
Vacuum Advance Schedule				
a. Operating Vacuum Range	0 to 16 Inches Hg	0 to 16 Inches Hg	0 to 12 Inches Hg	0 to 14 Inches Hg
b. Advance Off Idle (Carb. Switch Isolated With Paper)	3°–5°	6°–8°	None	13°–15°
c. Accumulation Time in Minutes	7–9	7–9	7–9	8
d. Advance After Accumulation Time	34°	34°	28°	32°–36°
Speed Advance				
Ground Carb. Switch and Disconnect Throttle Transducer Before Checking	3°–5° @ 2000 rpm	1°–3° @ 2000 rpm	7°–9° @ 1200 rpm	1°–3° @ 2000 rpm 3°–7° @ 4000 rpm

Spark Control Computer	4091421 ①	4091440 ①	4091468 ①	4091476 ①
	(4094021) ②	(4094022) ②	(4057923) ②	(4094026) ②
Start Timer Advance Schedule	5°–9°	5°–9°	8°	5°–9°
Delay Time In Seconds	90	90	90	90
Throttle Advance Schedule				
a. Test Transducer Core Out 1 inch	7°–9° @ 75°F 5°–7° @ 105°F	8°–12°	8°–12°	7°–9° @ 75°F 5°–7° @ 105°F
b. Test Transducer Core Moved Quickly In and Out	8°	10°	—	8°
Vacuum Advance Schedule				
a. Operating Vacuum Range	0 to 12 Inches Hg	0 to 16 Inches Hg	0 to 14 Inches Hg	0 to 12 Inches Hg
b. Advance Off Idle (Carb. Switch Isolated With Paper)	None	3°–5°	None	None
c. Accumulation Time in Minutes	7–9	7–9	8	7–9
d. Advance After Accumulation Time	30°	34°	32°–36°	28°
Speed Advance				
Ground Carb. Switch and Disconnect Throttle Transducer Before Checking	5°–7° @ 2000 rpm	2°–4° @ 2000 rpm	1°–3° @ 2000 rpm 3°–7° @ 4000 rpm	0°–2° @ 2000 rpm

Spark Control Computer	4091477 ①	4091946 ①	4091447 ①	4091448 ①
	(4094023) ②	(4106057) ②	(4106055) ②	(4106056) ②
Start Timer Advance Schedule	5°–9°	8°	8°	8°
Delay Time In Seconds	90	90	90	90
Throttle Advance Schedule				
a. Test Transducer Core Out 1 inch	4°–6°	3°–5°	3°–5°	3°–5°
b. Test Transducer Core Moved Quickly In and Out	5°	—	—	—
Vacuum Advance Schedule				
a. Operating Vacuum Range	0 to 12 Inches Hg	0 to 14 Inches Hg	0 to 14 Inches Hg	0 to 14 Inches Hg
b. Advance Off Idle (Carb. Switch Isolated With Paper)	None	4°–8°	None	10°–14°
c. Accumulation Time in Minutes	7–9	8	8	8
d. Advance After Accumulation Time	28°	26°–30°	32°–36°	26°–30°
Speed Advance				
Ground Carb. Switch and Disconnect Throttle Transducer Before Checking	7°–11° @ 2000 rpm	0°–3° @ 2000 rpm 1°–5° @ 4000 rpm	0°–3° @ 2000 rpm 1°–5° @ 4000 rpm	0°–3° @ 2000 rpm 1°–5° @ 4000 rpm

① —Production part number.
② —Remanufactured part number.
③ —If equipped with remanufactured spark control computer, disregard temperature specifications since there is no air temperature sensor.

1978 CHRYSLER ELECTRONIC SPARK CONTROL (LEAN BURN) SPECIFICATION CHART

Spark Control Computer	4091730①	4091731①	4091732①	4091786①
	(4106061)②	(4106067)②	(4106068)②	(4106069)②
Start Timer Advance Schedule	8°	8°	8°	8°
Delay Time In Seconds	60	60	60	60
Throttle Advance Schedule				
Test Transducer Core Out 1 Inch	7°–9° @ 100°F 3°–6° @ 140°F	4°–6° @ 100°F 2°–4° @ 140°F	5°–7° @ 100°F 2°–5° @ 140°F	5°–7° @ 100°F 2°–4° @ 140°F
Vacuum Advance Schedule				
a. Operating Vacuum Range	0 to 12 Inches Hg	0 to 14 Inches Hg	0 to 14 Inches Hg	0 to 15.5 Inches Hg
b. Advance Off Idle (Carb. Switch Isolated With Paper)	None	7°–11°	None	5°–9°
c. Accumulation Time In Minutes	8	8	8	7
d. Advance After Accumulation Time	28°–32°	23°–27°	26°–30°	18°–22°
Speed Advance				
Ground Carb. Switch and Disconnect Throttle Transducer Before Checking	4°–8° @ 2000 rpm 8°–12° @ 4000 rpm	4°–8° @ 2000 rpm 10°–14° @ 4000 rpm	0°–3° @ 2000 rpm 2°–6° @ 4000 rpm	0°–1° @ 2000 rpm 0°–2° @ 4000 rpm

Spark Control Computer	4091787①	4091788①	4091791①	4091923①
	(4106070)②	(4106071)②	(4106073)②	
Start Timer Advance Schedule	8°	8°	8°	8°
Delay Time In Seconds	60	60	60	60
Throttle Advance Schedule				
Test Transducer Core Out 1 Inch	5°–7° @ 100°F 2°–4° @ 140°F	7°–9° @ 100°F 4°–6° @ 140°F	4°–6° @ 100°F 1°–4° @ 140°F	5°–7° @ 100°F 2°–5° @ 140°F
Vacuum Advance Schedule				
a. Operating Vacuum Range	0 to 14 Inches Hg	0 to 14 Inches Hg	0 to 12 Inches Hg	0 to 14 Inches Hg
b. Advance Off Idle (Carb. Switch Isolated With Paper)	None	7°–11°	None	8°–12°
c. Accumulation Time In Minutes	8	8	8	8
d. Advance After Accumulation Time	23°–27°	20°–24°	20°–24°	24°–28°
Speed Advance				
Ground Carb. Switch and Disconnect Throttle Transducer Before Checking	2°–5° @ 2000 rpm 7°–11° @ 4000 rpm	1°–5° @ 2000 rpm 4°–8° @ 4000 rpm	7°–11° @ 2000 rpm 8°–12° @ 4000 rpm	1°–4° @ 2000 rpm 6°–10° @ 4000 rpm

Spark Control Computer	4091924①	4091954①	4091955①	4111012①
	(4106075)②	(4106076)②	(4106077)②	(4106079)②
Start Timer Advance Schedule	8°	8°	8°	8°
Delay Time In Seconds	60	60	60	60
Throttle Advance Schedule				
Test Transducer Core Out 1 Inch	9°–11° @ 100°F 5°–8° @ 140°F	5°–7° @ 100°F 2°–5° @ 140°F	7°–9° @ 100°F 4°–6° @ 140°F	0°
Vacuum Advance Schedule				
a. Operating Vacuum Range	0 to 14 Inches Hg	0 to 15.5 Inches Hg	0 to 14 Inches Hg	0 to 15.5 Inches Hg
b. Advance Off Idle (Carb. Switch Isolated With Paper)	None	None	7°–11°	None
c. Accumulation Time In Minutes	8	8	7	8
d. Advance After Accumulation Time	21°–25°	18°–22°	20°–24°	18°–22°
Speed Advance				
Ground Carb. Switch and Disconnect Throttle Transducer Before Checking	10°–15° @ 2000 rpm 16°–21° @ 4000 rpm	0°–1° @ 2000 rpm 0°–2° @ 4000 rpm	1°–5° @ 2000 rpm 4°–8° @ 4000 rpm	4°–8° @ 2000 rpm 6°–10° @ 4000 rpm

Continued

ELECTRONIC IGNITION SYSTEMS

1978 CHRYSLER ELECTRONIC SPARK CONTROL (LEAN BURN) SPECIFICATION CHART—Continued

Spark Control Computer	4111013①	4111014①	4111015①	4111159①
	(4106080)②	(4106081)②	(4106082)②	(4106085)②
Start Timer Advance Schedule	8°	8°	8°	8°
Delay Time In Seconds	60	60	60	60
Throttle Advance Schedule				
Test Transducer Core Out 1 Inch	9°–11° @ 100°F 5°–8° @ 140°F	5°–7° @ 100°F 2°–5° @ 140°F	5°–7° @ 100°F 2°–5° @ 140°F	5°–7° @ 100°F 2°–5° @ 140°F
Vacuum Advance Schedule				
a. Operating Vacuum Range	0 to 14 Inches Hg	0 to 12 Inches Hg	0 to 12 Inches Hg	0 to 15.5 Inches Hg
b. Advance Off Idle (Carb. Switch Isolated With Paper)	None	2°–6°	2°–6°	None
c. Accumulation Time In Minutes	8	8	8	8
d. Advance After Accumulation Time	21°–25°	18°–22°	18°–22°	18°–22°
Speed Advance				

Ground Carb. Switch and
  Disconnect Throttle Transducer
  Before Checking
	10°–14° @ 2000 rpm
	16°–21° @ 4000 rpm
		8°–12° @ 2000 rpm
		12°–16° @ 4000 rpm
			8°–12° @ 2000 rpm
			12°–16° @ 4000 rpm
				0–1° @ 2000 rpm
				0–2° @ 4000 rpm

Spark Control Computer	4111169①	4111170①	4111172①	4111217①
	(4106086)②	(4106087)②	(4106088)②	(4106089)②
Start Timer Advance Schedule	None	None	None	8°
Delay Time In Seconds	None	None	None	60
Throttle Advance Schedule				
Test Transducer Core Out 1 Inch	5°–7° @ 100°F 2°–5° @ 140°F	5°–7° @ 100°F 2°–5° @ 140°F	5°–7° @ 100°F 2°–7° @ 140°F	0°
Vacuum Advance Schedule				
a. Operating Vacuum Range	0 to 10 Inches Hg	0 to 10 Inches Hg	0 to 10 Inches Hg	4–14 Inches Hg
b. Advance Off Idle (Carb. Switch Isolated With Paper)	5°–9°	5°–9°	5°–9°	6°–10°
c. Accumulation Time In Minutes	8	8	8	7
d. Advance After Accumulation Time	16°–20°	16°–20°	16°–20°	18°–22°
Speed Advance				

Ground Carb. Switch and
  Disconnect Throttle Transducer
  Before Checking
	1°–5° @ 2000 rpm
	4°–8° @ 4000 rpm
		1°–5° @ 2000 rpm
		4°–8° @ 4000 rpm
			1°–5° @ 2000 rpm
			4°–8° @ 4000 rpm
				8°–12° @ 2000 rpm
				12°–16° @ 4000 rpm

Spark Control Computer	4111218①	4111222①	4111253①	4111278①
Start Timer Advance Schedule	8°	8°	8°	8°
Delay Time In Seconds	60	60	60	60
Throttle Advance Scedule				
Test Transducer Core Out 1 Inch	0°	0°	5°–7° @ 100°F 2°–5° @ 140°F	7°–9° @ 100°F 4°–6° @ 140°F
Vacuum Advance Schedule				
a. Operating Vacuum Range	4–14 Inches Hg	4–14 Inches Hg	0–10 Inches Hg	0–12 Inches Hg
b. Advance Off Idle (Carb. Switch Isolated With Paper)	2°–6°	2°–6°	None	None
c. Accumulation Time In Minutes	8	8	8	8
d. Advance After Accumulation Time	18°–22°	18°–22°	23°–27°	26°–30°
Speed Advance				

Ground Carb. Switch and
  Disconnect Throttle Transducer
  Before Checking
	8°–2° @ 2000 rpm
	12°–16° @ 4000 rpm
		8°–12° @ 2000 rpm
		12°–16° @ 4000 rpm
			6°–11° @ 2000 rpm
			11°–16° @ 4000 rpm
				0°–3° @ 2000 rpm
				2°–6° @ 4000 rpm

Continued

1978 CHRYSLER ELECTRONIC SPARK CONTROL (LEAN BURN)
SPECIFICATION CHART—Continued

Spark Control Computer	4111283①	4145237①
Start Timer Advance Schedule	8°	8°
Delay Time In Seconds	60	60
Throttle Advance Schedule		
Test Transducer Core	7°–9° @ 100°F.	9°–11° @ 100°F.
Out 1 Inch	4°–6° @ 140°F.	5°–8° @ 140°F.
Vacuum Advance Schedule		
a. Operating Vacuum Range	0–12 Inches Hg	0–14 Inches Hg
b. Advance Off Idle (Carb. Switch Isolated With Paper)	None	None
c. Accumulation Time In Minutes	8	8
d. Advance After Accumulation Time	26°–30°	26°–30°
Speed Advance		
Ground Carb. Switch and Disconnect Throttle Transducer Before Checking	0°–3° @ 2000 rpm 2°–6° @ 4000 rpm	10°–14° @ 2000 rpm 16°–21° @ 4000 rpm

①—Production part number.
②—Remanufactured part number.

1979 CHRYSLER ELECTRONIC SPARK CONTROL (LEAN BURN)
SPECIFICATION CHART

Spark Control Computer	4111373① 4111697②	4111392① 4111676②	4111439① 4111677②	4111440① 4111678②	4111441① 4111679②	4111442① 4111680②
Start Up Advance (60 Seconds)	5°	5°	5°	5°	5°	5°
Crank + Electrical (Basic Timing)	10° + 5°	10° + 6°	10° + 6°	10° + 6°	12° + 0°	10° + 6°
Vacuum Advance Range (In. Hg.)	5–11	4–13	4–12	4–12	4–12	4–12
Zero Time Offset	0°–3°	8°–12°	0°–3°	8°–12°	6°–10°	6°–10°
Accumulator Time In Minutes	8	8	8	8	8	8
Vacuum Adv.—Full Accumulator						
@ 1100 rpm	11°–15°	16°–20°	8°–12°	12°–16°	11°–17°	8°–12°
@ 1500 rpm	18°–22°	23°–27°	18°–22°	18°–22°	18°–22°	18°–22°
Throttle Max. Advance (Throttle Open 20°)	6°–10°	3°–7°	6°–10°	3°–7°	0°	6°–10°
Speed Advance						
@ 1100 rpm	0°–2°	0°–1°	2°–6°	0°–1°	3°–7°	2°–6°
@ 2000 rpm	1°–4°	1°–5°	6°–10°	1°–5°	8°–12°	6°–10°
@ 4000 rpm	3°–5°	10°–14°	10°–14°	10°–14°	12°–16°	10°–14°

Spark Control Computer	4111492① 4111681②	4111540① 4111682②	4111574① 4111683②	4111575① 4111684②	4111674① 4111685②
Start Up Advance (60 Seconds)	5°	5°	5°	5°	5°
Crank + Electrical (Basic Timing)	10° + 6°	10° + 6°	10° + 6°	10° + 6°	10° + 6°
Vacuum Advance Range (In. Hg.)	4–13	4–12	4–13	4–10	4–13
Zero Time Offset	8°–12°	8°–12°	0°–3°	2°–6°	0°–3°
Accumulator Time In Minutes	8	8	8	8	8
Vacuum Adv.—Full Accumulator					
@ 1100 rpm	16°–20°	12°–16°	16°–20°	11°–15°	16°–22°
@ 1500 rpm	23°–27°	16°–22°	23°–27°	18°–22°	23°–27°
Throttle Max. Advance (Throttle Open 20°)	3°–7°	3°–7°	3°–7°	6°–10°	3°–7°
Speed Advance					
@ 1100 rpm	0°–1°	0°–1°	0°–1°	2°–6°	0°–1°
@ 2000 rpm	1°–5°	1°–5°	1°–5°	6°–10°	1°–5°
@ 4000 rpm	10°–14°	10°–14°	10°–14°	10°–14°	10°–14°

①—Production part number.
②—Remanufactured part number.

1980 CHRYSLER ELECTRONIC SPARK CONTROL (LEAN BURN) SPECIFICATION CHART

Spark Control Computer	4105007	414500	4145003	4145004	4145087
Crank + Run (Basic Timing)	12° + 0°	8° + 8°	8° + 8°	12° + 0°	8° + 8°
Vacuum Advance (Range)	0–10	4–14	4–14	4–14	4–14
Zero Time Advance	0°–2°	23°–27°	28°–32°	23°–27°	21°–25°
Accumulator Time In Minutes	1	0	0	0	0
Vacuum Adv.—Full Accumulator @ 1100 rpm	0°–2°	10°–14°	14°–18°	0°–2°	0°–2°
@ 2500 rpm	20°–24°	23°–27°	28°–32°	23°–27°	21°–25°
Speed Advance @ 1100 rpm	0°–2°	1°–4°	0°–2°	0°–4°	0°–2°
@ 2000 rpm	1°–5°	4°–8°	1°–5°	4°–8°	4°–8°
@ 4800 rpm	1°–5°	12°–16°	12°–16°	16°–20°	12°–16°
Warm Up Schedule In Seconds	100	—	25	—	—

1981 CHRYSLER ELECTRONIC SPARK CONTROL (LEAN BURN) SPECIFICATION CHART

Spark Control Computer	4145431	4145457	4145466	4145725
Basic Timing	16°	16°	16°	12°
Vacuum Advance (Range)	3–10	4–14	1–14	2–12
Accumulator Time In Minutes	.5	0	0	0
Spark Advance Test @ 2000 RPM	20 ± 4	34 ± 4	34 ± 4	29 ± 4
Electronic EGR Time Delay	60 sec.	60 sec.	20 sec.	—
Electronic Throttle Control Time Delay	90 sec.	60 sec.	20 sec.	AIS①
Oxygen Feedback Electronic Air Switching Time	65 sec.	30 sec.	90 sec.	70 sec.

Spark Control Computer	4145726	4145788	4145817	4145850
Basic Timing	12°	16°	16°	16°
Vacuum Advance (Range)	2–12	4–14	3–10	4–14
Accumulator Time In Minutes	0	0	.5	0
Spark Advance Test @ 2000 RPM	23 ± 4	34 ± 4	20 ± 4	34 ± 4
Electronic EGR Time Delay	—	60 sec.	90 sec.	60 sec.
Electronic Throttle Control Time Delay	AIS①	60 sec.	90 sec.	60 sec.
Oxygen Feedback Electronic Air Switching Time	70 sec.	20 sec.	65 sec.	20 sec.

①—Automatic idle speed motor.

1982 CHRYSLER ELECTRONIC SPARK CONTROL (LEAN BURN) SPECIFICATION CHART

Spark Control Computer	4145452	4145701	4145726	4145907
Basic Timing	16°	12°	12°	12°
Vacuum Advance (Range)	4–14	2–12	2–12	1–14
Accumulator Time In Minutes	0	0	0	0
Spark Advance Test @ 2000 RPM	29 ± 4	23 ± 4	23 ± 4	34 ± 4
Electronic EGR Time Delay	35 sec.	—	—	20 sec.
Electronic Throttle Control Time Delay	—	AIS①	AIS①	20 sec.
Oxygen Feedback Electronic Air Switching Time	—	70 sec.	70 sec.	90 sec.

Continued

1982 CHRYSLER ELECTRONIC SPARK CONTROL (LEAN BURN)
SPECIFICATION CHART—Continued

Spark Control Computer	4145980	4145996	4145998	4289034
Basic Timing	16°	16°	16°	12°
Vacuum Advance (Range)	1—14	4—14	4—14	3—10
Accumulator Time In Minutes	0	0	0	0.5
Spark Advance Test @ 2000 RPM	34 ± 4	34 ± 4	34 ± 4	20 ± 4
Electronic EGR Time Delay	20 sec.	60 sec.	60 sec.	60 sec.
Electronic Throttle Control Time Delay	—	60 sec.	60 sec.	60 sec.
Oxygen Feedback Electronic Air Switching Time	90 sec.	20 sec.	20 sec.	65 sec.

①—Automatic idle speed motor.

1983 CHRYSLER ELECTRONIC SPARK CONTROL (LEAN BURN)
SPECIFICATION CHART

Spark Control Computer	4145726	4145996	4289058	4289061
Basic Timing	12°	16°	16°	16°
Vacuum Advance (Range)	2—12	4—14	3—10	3—10
Accumulator Time In Minutes	0	0	60 sec.	60 sec.
Spark Advance Test @ 1500 RPM	23 ± 4	18 ± 4	14 ± 4	8 ± 4②
Electronic EGR Time Delay	—	60 sec.	65 sec.	65 sec.
Electronic Throttle Control Time Delay	①	—	—	—
Oxygen Feedback Electronic Air Switching Time	70 sec.	—	—	—

Spark Control Computer	4289063	4289065	4289104
Basic Timing	16°	16°	12°
Vacuum Advance (Range)	2—14	2—14	2—12
Accumulator Time In Minutes	0	0	0
Spark Advance Test @ 1500 RPM	30 ± 4	30 ± 4	20 ± 4
Electronic EGR Time Delay	60 sec.	60 sec.	—
Electronic Throttle Control Time Delay	—	—	①
Oxygen Feedback Electronic Air Switching Time	—	—	70 sec.

①—Automatic idle speed motor. ②—At 2000 RPM.

Chrysler Corp. Front Wheel Drive Models W/ Electronic Spark Control (Lean Burn) System

SYSTEM TESTING

Ignition System Starting Test

1. Remove coil wire from distributor cap and hold end of wire approximately 1/4 inch from a good engine ground. Crank engine and observe spark at coil wire.
2. The spark at the coil wire must be constant and bright blue in color. If so, continue to crank engine and slowly move coil wire away from the ground. If arcing occurs at the coil tower, replace coil. If spark is weak, not constant or there is no spark, proceed to the "Failure To Start Test".
3. If spark is satisfactory and no arcing occurs at the coil tower, the ignition system is producing the necessary high secondary voltage. However, this voltage is transmitted to the spark plugs by the distributor rotor, cap, spark plug wires and spark plugs and must also be checked. If satisfactory, the ignition system is not at fault. It will be necessary to check the fuel system and engine mechanical components.

Failure To Start Test

NOTE: Before performing this test, perform the "Ignition System Starting Test". Failure

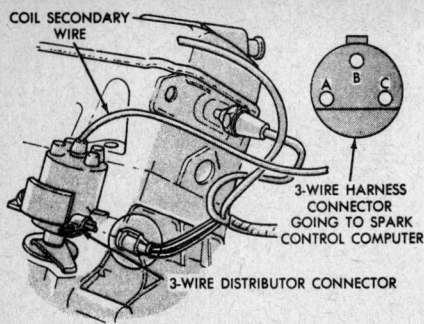

Fig. 1   Distributor 3-wire harness connector 4-105 (1.7L). Typical of 4-97 (1.6L) & 4-135 (2.2L)

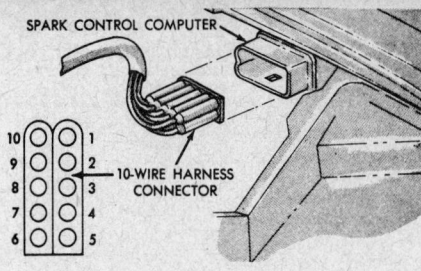

Fig. 2   Spark control computer 10-wire connector

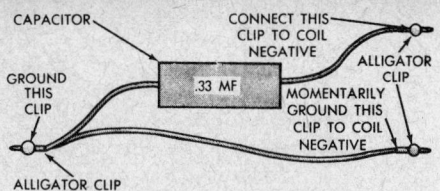

Fig. 3   Coil negative terminal jumper wire. 1981—83 models

to do so may lead to unnecessary diagnostic time and incorrect test results.

1978—80

1. With a voltmeter, measure and note battery voltage. Battery specific gravity must be at least 1.220, temperature corrected, to deliver the necessary voltage to operate the cranking and ignition systems properly.
2. Disconnect wire from ignition coil negative terminal.
3. Remove coil wire from distributor cap.
4. With ignition switch in "On" position and using a jumper wire, momentarily ground the ignition coil negative terminal while holding the coil wire ¼ inch from a good engine ground. A spark should be obtained.
5. If no spark was obtained in Step 4, measure voltage at ignition coil positive terminal. Voltage should be at least 9 volts. If specified voltage is noted, the ignition coil is defective, requiring replacement. If specified voltage is not noted, check ballast resistor, wiring and connections. If engine still does not start, proceed to Step 6.
6. If spark was obtained in Step 4, turn ignition switch to "Off" position, reconnect ignition coil negative terminal wire and disconnect the distributor 3-wire harness, Fig. 1.
7. Turn ignition switch to "On" position and measure voltage between pin "B" on harness connector and the engine ground, Fig. 1. Voltage obtained should be battery voltage. If battery voltage is obtained, proceed to Step 11. If not, proceed to Step 8.
8. Turn ignition switch to "Off" position and disconnect the 10-wire harness connector from "Spark Control Computer", Fig. 2.

NOTE: Do not remove grease from harness connector or connector cavity since the grease is used to prevent moisture from corroding the terminals. There must be at least ¼ inch of grease on the bottom of the computer connector cavity. If not, apply a liberal amount of Mopar Multipurpose grease, part number 2932524, or equivalent over end of connector plug before reinstallation.

9. Check continuity between pin "B" of the distributor connector, Fig. 1, and terminal 3 of the "Spark Control Computer" connector, Fig. 2. If continuity is not noted, repair wire. If continuity exists, proceed to Step 10.

10. Turn ignition switch to "On" position and measure voltage between terminals 2 and 10 of the "Spark Control Computer" connector. Battery voltage should be obtained. If not, check wiring and connections. If battery voltage is obtained, the "Spark Control Computer" is defective, requiring replacement.
11. Connect "Spark Control Computer" 10-wire harness connector, turn ignition switch to "On" position and hold coil wire ¼ inch from a good ground. Using a jumper wire, momentarily connect pins "A" and "C" of the distributor connector, Fig. 1. A spark should be obtained. If not, proceed to Step 12. If a spark is obtained, the Hall Effect Pick-up assembly is defective, requiring replacement.
12. Turn ignition to "Off" position and disconnect "Spark Control Computer" 10-wire harness connector, Fig. 2.
13. Check continuity between pin "C" of the 3-wire distributor connector, Fig. 1, and terminal 9 of the "Spark Control Computer" connector, Fig. 2. Also check continuity between pin "A" of distributor connector, Fig. 1, and terminal 5 of the "Spark Control Computer" connector, Fig. 2. If continuity exists, the "Spark Control Computer" is defective, requiring replacement. If no continuity exists, repair wiring and repeat Step 11.

1981—83

1. Perform steps 1 thru 4 as described under "Failure To Start Test" under "1978—80". Use jumper wires shown in Fig. 3, when performing tests on 1981—83 models.
2. If spark was obtained, proceed to step 5. If not, turn ignition Off, then disconnect 10-wire electrical connector at Spark Control Computer.

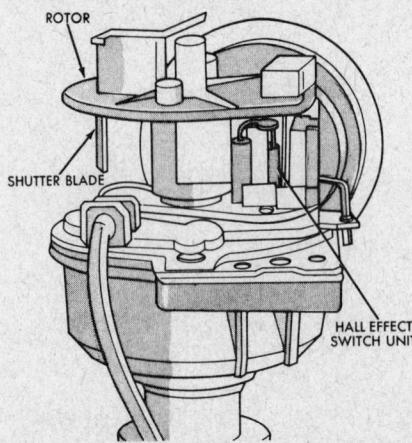

Fig. 4   Rotor shutter blades. 1981—83 models

NOTE: Do not remove grease from harness connector or connector cavity since grease is used to prevent moisture from corroding the terminals. There must be at least ⅛ inch of grease on bottom of computer connector cavity. If not, apply a liberal amount of Mopar Multi-purpose grease, part number 2932524 or equivalent over end of connector plug before installation.

3. Turn ignition On, hold coil wire ¼ inch from ground and momentarily ground coil negative terminal using jumper wire, Fig. 3. If spark is present, replace Spark Control Computer. If spark is not present, measure voltage at coil positive terminal using suitable voltmeter. Voltage reading should be within one volt of battery voltage.
4. If no voltage was obtained at coil positive terminal, check for open circuit between battery and coil and repair as necessary. If voltage was obtained, measure voltage at coil negative terminal. Reading should be within one volt of battery voltage. If no voltage is present or voltage is present but spark is not, replace coil.
5. If spark was obtained in step 2, but engine will not start, hold open carburetor switch with thin piece of paper and measure voltage at carburetor switch. Reading obtained should be at least five volts. If voltage reading is satisfactory, proceed to step 9. If no voltage is present, turn ignition Off, then disconnect 10-wire connector from Spark Control Computer.
6. Turn ignition On and measure voltage between connector cavity 2 and ground, Fig. 2. Reading should be within one volt of battery voltage. If not, check for continuity between battery and cavity 2 using ohmmeter. If continuity is not present, check for open circuit between battery and cavity 2 and repair as necessary.
7. If battery voltage is present in step 6, turn ignition Off and check continuity between carburetor switch and cavity 7 of 10 way connector. If continuity is not present, check for open circuit between cavity 7 and carburetor switch and repair as necessary.
8. If continuity is present in step 7, check continuity between cavity 10 and ground. If continuity is present, replace Spark Control Computer. If continuity is not present between cavity 10 and ground, check for damaged wiring or an open circuit and repair as necessary. If wiring is satisfactory, but engine will not start, proceed to step 9.
9. Reconnect 10-wire connector into Spark Control Computer, turn ignition On and hold coil wire ¼ inch from ground. Disconnect distributor electrical connector and connect jumper wire between terminals A and C of connector, Fig. 1. Spark should be observed at coil wire.
10. If spark is present at coil wire, but engine

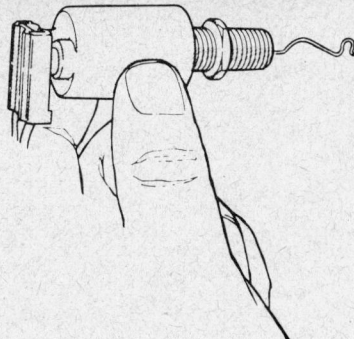

Fig. 5 Throttle position transducer

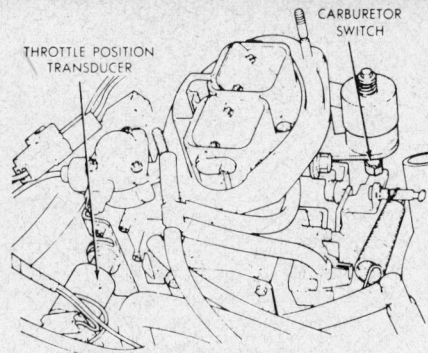

Fig. 6 Carburetor switch & throttle position transducer

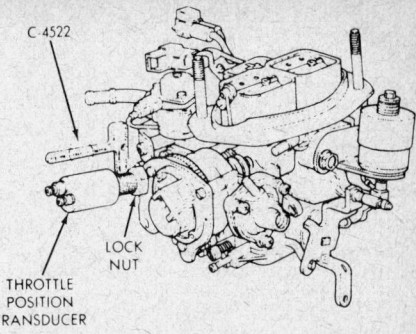

Fig. 7 Throttle position transducer adjustment

will not start, replace pick up assembly and perform rotor test as described in step 16.

NOTE: When replacing Hall effect pick up assembly, check to ensure rotor shutter blades are grounded, Fig. 4. Connect one lead of suitable ohmmeter to shutter blade and other lead to ground. If continuity is not present, press downward on rotor shaft and recheck continuity. If continuity is still not present, replace rotor. Check to ensure that new rotor is marked ESA on top. Do not start engine until continuity has been obtained.

11. If no spark is present at coil wire check voltage between cavity B of distributor connector and ground, Fig. 1. Reading obtained should be within one volt of battery voltage. If battery voltage is not present, proceed to step 13. If battery voltage is present, turn ignition off and disconnect 10-way connector from Spark Advance Computer. Check for continuity between cavity C of distributor connector, Fig. 1, and cavity 9 of 10-way connector. Repeat procedure between cavity A of distributor connector and cavity 5 of 10-way connector.
12. If continuity is not present, open circuit exists in harness wiring. Repair as necessary. If continuity is present, replace Spark Advance Computer.
13. If no battery voltage is present at cavity A of distributor connector, turn ignition Off, then disconnect 10-wire connector from Spark Control Computer.
14. Check for continuity between cavity A of distributor connector and cavity 3 of 10-wire connector. If continuity is not present, repair open circuit in wire between cavities as necessary.
15. If continuity is present, turn ignition On and check for voltage between cavity 2 and 10 of 10-wire connector. If battery voltage is present, replace Spark Control Computer. If battery voltage is not present, check for proper computer ground circuit connection and repair as necessary.
16. To perform rotor test, check to ensure that rotor is stamped ESA on top. Turn ignition Off, then using suitable ohmmeter, check for good rotor ground contact at distributor shaft. If continuity is indicated, rotor is satisfactory. If continuity is not indicated, check to ensure that rotor is properly seated on shaft.

Poor Performance Tests

Carburetor Switch Test

NOTE: On 1980–83 models, grounding the carburetor switch eliminates spark advance on most models. On models with feedback carburetor it also provides a fixed fuel/air ratio.

1. With ignition switch in "Off" position, disconnect 10-wire harness connector from "Spark Control Computer."
2. With throttle completely closed, check continuity between terminal 7 and the engine ground, Fig. 2. Continuity should exist. If not, check wiring and carburetor switch.
3. With throttle opened, check continuity between terminal 7 and the engine ground, Fig. 2. Continuity should not exist.

Coolant Switch Test, All Exc. 1981 2.2 L

1. With ignition switch in "Off" position, disconnect wire from coolant switch.
2. Check continuity between coolant switch terminal and the engine ground. The ohmmeter readings should be as follows: Engine cold, below 150°—Continuity should exist. If not, replace coolant switch. Engine hot, above 150°—No continuity should exist. If continuity exists, replace coolant switch.

Coolant Sensor Test, 1981 2.2 L

1. With ignition Off, disconnect coolant sensor electrical connector.
2. Connect ohmmeter leads to terminals of sensor.
3. Resistance should be 500–1000 ohms with engine cold and ambient temperature less than 90°F.
4. With engine at normal operating temperature, resistance should be 1300 ohms.
5. Replace coolant sensor if specifications cannot be obtained.

Spark Advance Test, 1981–83 Units

1. Run engine until normal operating temperature is reached, then disconnect carburetor switch electrical connector. Check to ensure that coolant sensor is operating as described in "Poor Performance Tests" under "Coolant Sensor Test".
2. Disconnect and plug vacuum transducer vacuum hose.
3. Apply 16 inches Hg. vacuum from outside vacuum source to vacuum transducer.
4. Increase engine speed to 2000 RPM, wait

one minute, then check amount of advance timing. Refer to "Chrysler Front Wheel Drive Electronic Spark Control (Lean Burn) Specification Chart" for specification.

NOTE: On certain models equipped with an accumulator, the accumulator must be allowed to time out with the carburetor switch disconnected before checking spark advance.

5. If spark advance specifications cannot be obtained, replace Spark Control Computer.

Start Advance Timing Test, 1978–79 Models

1. Connect an adjustable timing light to engine so total timing advance can be checked.
2. Connect a jumper wire between carburetor switch and the engine ground.
3. Start engine and adjust timing light to align specified timing marks. The timing light meter should indicate the amount of advance listed in the "Chrysler Front Wheel Drive Electronic Spark Control (Lean Burn) Specification Chart." Continue to observe timing for 90 seconds while adjusting timing light to maintain basic timing signal. If timing did not increase and/or did not return to basic setting, replace "Spark Control Computer".

Speed Advance Test, 1978–80 Models

1. Disconnect connector from "Throttle Position Transducer", 1978 manual transmission model. On 1980 models, remove vacuum line from vacuum transducer.
2. Start and run engine for two minutes. Increase engine speed to specified test level and adjust timing light so basic timing setting can be observed at timing indicator. The timing light meter should indicate additional advance as listed in the "Chrysler Front Wheel Drive Electronic Spark Control (Lean Burn) Specification Chart". If not, replace "Spark Control Computer" and repeat test.

Throttle Advance Test, 1978 Manual Trans. models

NOTE: Before performing this test, ensure the "Throttle Position Transducer" is properly adjusted.

1. With ignition switch in "Off" position, disconnect 10-wire harness connector from "Spark Control Computer", Fig. 2.
2. Measure resistance between terminals 8 and 9 of connector, Fig. 2. Resistance

should be 50 to 90 ohms. If resistance is within specifications, connect connector and proceed to Step 3. If resistance is not within specifications, disconnect connector from "Throttle Position Transducer" and measure resistance between transducer terminals. If resistance is between 50 and 90 ohms, there is an open, short or improper connection between terminals 8 and 9 of "Spark Control Computer" connector and the "Throttle Position Transducer" connector. If resistance is not within specifications, replace "Throttle Position Transducer".

3. Place throttle linkage on fast idle cam, ground carburetor switch with a jumper wire, disconnect connector from "Throttle Position Transducer" and connect connector to a known good transducer of the same type suitable for testing.
4. Move core of test transducer inward until fully bottomed, Fig. 5.
5. Start engine, wait 90 seconds and move transducer core outward approximately one inch, Fig. 5.
6. Adjust timing light so timing marks are aligned. The timing light meter should indicate additional amount of advance as listed in the "Chrysler Front Wheel Drive Electronic Spark Control (Lean Burn) Specification Chart". If within specifications, move transducer core inward and timing should return to basic setting. If timing does not advance and/or did not return to basic setting, replace Spark Control Computer. After computer replacement, repeat test.

Vacuum Advance Test, 1978 Units
1. Connect and adjust timing light to engine so total timing advance can be checked.
2. Start and run engine to obtain normal operating temperature with transmission in neutral and parking brake applied.
3. Place a piece of paper between carburetor switch and throttle lever, Fig. 6. If curb idle adjusting screw is not contacting carburetor switch, ensure fast idle cam is not on or binding, or throttle stop screw is not over adjusted. Adjust timing light so basic timing signal can be observed. Run engine for 9 minutes and ensure that a minimum of 16 inches of vacuum is present at transducer. The timing light meter should indicate additional amount of advance as listed in the "Chrysler Front Wheel Drive Electronic Spark Control (Lean Burn) Specification Chart". If not, replace Spark Control Computer.

Vacuum Advance Test, 1979–80 Units

NOTE: If computer fails to obtain specified settings, replace computer.

1. Connect timing light and tachometer to engine.
2. Start engine and allow to reach operating temperature. If engine is at operating temperature, wait for at least one minute for start advance to return to basic timing. Place transmission Neutral and apply parking brake.
3. Check basic timing and adjust as necessary. Refer to "Chrysler Front Wheel Drive Electronic Spark Control (Lean Burn) Specification Chart".
4. Remove and plug vacuum line at vacuum transducer.
5. Ground carburetor switch, then increase engine speed to 1100 rpm and check speed advance timing. Refer to "Chrysler Front Wheel Drive Electronic Spark Control (Lean Burn) Specification Chart".

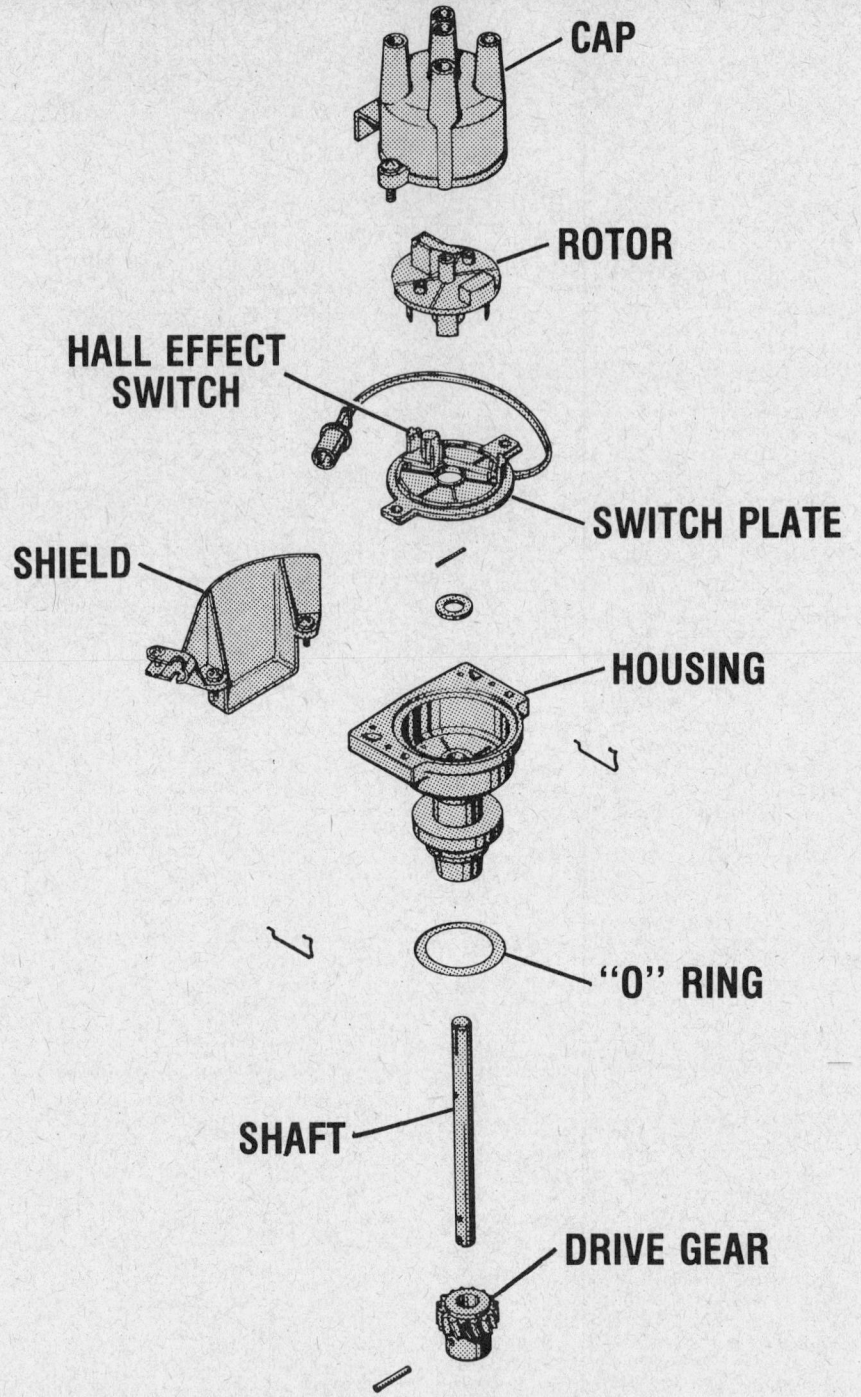

Fig. 8   Hall Effect electronic ignition distributor, typical

6. Operate engine at 2000 rpm and remove carburetor switch ground and connect vacuum line to vacuum transducer. Check zero timing, refer to "Chrysler Front Wheel Drive Specification Chart".
7. Allow accumulator to clock-up, refer to "Chrysler Front Wheel Drive Electronic Spark Control (Lean Burn) Specification Chart". Operate engine at 1100 rpm, then check vacuum advance. Vacuum advance should be as listed in "Chrysler Front Wheel Drive Electronic Spark Control (Lean Burn) Specification Chart".
8. Disconnect and plug vacuum line at

transducer and increase engine speed to 3000 rpm. Note advance speed timing.
9. Reconnect vacuum line to vacuum transducer and check vacuum advance. Refer to "Chrysler Front Wheel Drive Electronic Spark Control (Lean Burn) Specification Chart".
10. Return engine to curb idle speed. Then connect wire to carburetor switch.

Basic Advance Timing Test, 1981–83 Models
1. Connect a suitable tachometer and adjustable timing light to engine.

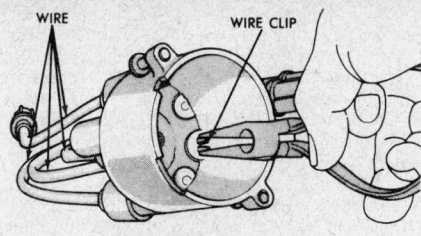

Fig. 9 Spark plug wire removal

2. Connect a jumper wire from carburetor switch to ground.
3. Set parking brake and start vehicle, then using the timing light adjustment feature, adjust timing light so specified timing mark is lined up with pointer.
4. The adjustable timing light meter should show amount of advance as shown in "Chrysler Front Wheel Drive Electronic Spark Control (Lean Burn) Specification Chart".

Throttle Position Transducer Adjustment, 1978 Units

1. Disconnect connector from transducer.
2. Loosen lock nut.
3. Place special tool C-4522 between outer portion of transducer and transducer mounting bracket, Fig. 7.
4. Adjust transducer until a clearance fit is obtained.
5. Tighten lock nut and reconnect connector.

DISTRIBUTOR SERVICE
Removal

1.6 Liter Engines
1. Disconnect primary wiring connector at distributor, then remove splash shield from distributor.
2. Loosen distributor cap retaining screws, then remove distributor cap.
3. Rotate crankshaft until rotor is pointing in direction of engine block, then scribe a line on block to indicate rotor position during installation.
4. Remove distributor hold down bolt, then carefully lift distributor from engine.

1.7 & 2.2 Liter Engines
1. Disconnect primary wiring connector at distributor, then on 1982–83 models, remove pick-up coil retaining screw.
2. On all 1982–83 models, remove splash shield from retaining screws, then remove shield.
3. On all models, loosen distributor cap retaining screws, then remove distributor cap.
4. Rotate crankshaft until rotor is pointing in direction of engine block, then scribe a line on block to indicate rotor position during installation.
5. Remove distributor hold down bolt, then carefully lift distributor from engine.

Installation

1.6 Liter Engine
1. With gasket installed on base of distributor, position distributor in engine.
2. Engage distributor drive with camshaft

offset drive tang so distributor rotor will align with scribe mark made during removal.
3. If engine was cranked while distributor was removed, proceed as follows:
   a. Rotate crankshaft until No. 1 piston is at top dead center of compression stroke. The mark on crankshaft pulley should be aligned with "0" mark on timing cover.
   b. Rotate distributor rotor to a position ahead of No. 1 distributor cap terminal.
   c. Install distributor into engine, engaging distributor drive with camshaft offset drive tang. The rotor should be properly positioned under distributor cap No. 1 terminal.
4. Install distributor cap.
5. Install distributor hold down screw finger tight.
6. Install splash shield, then connect primary wiring connector at distributor.
7. Adjust ignition timing. Refer to "Tune Up Specifications" in individual car chapters.

1.7 & 2.2 Liter Engines
1. With gasket installed on base of distributor, position distributor into engine.
2. Engage distributor drive gear with camshaft drive gear so distributor rotor will align with scribe mark made during removal.
3. If engine was cranked while distributor was removed, proceed as follows:
   a. Rotate crankshaft until No. 1 piston is at top dead center of compression stroke. The pointer on clutch housing or bell housing should align with "0" mark on flywheel.
   b. Rotate distributor rotor to a position ahead of No. 1 distributor cap terminal.
   c. Install distributor into engine, engaging distributor drive with camshaft drive gear. The rotor should be properly positioned under distributor cap No. 1 terminal.
4. Install distributor cap, then the distributor hold down screw finger tight.
5. On 1982–83 models, install splash shield.
6. Connect primary wiring connector to distributor.
7. On 1982–83 models, install pick-up coil retaining screw.
8. Adjust ignition timing. Refer to "Tune Up Specifications" in individual car chapters.

Disassembly

1.6 & 1.7 Liter Engines
1. Remove rotor from shaft, Fig. 8.
2. On 1978–81 models, remove screw holding pick-up lead.
3. Remove Hall Effect Pick-up Assembly lock springs and the pick-up assembly.
4. On 1978–81 models, remove two screws securing shield to distributor and the shield.
5. Mark position of drive gear on distributor shaft.
6. Remove roll pin with a suitable punch.
7. Remove drive gear, then the distributor shaft from housing.
8. Remove nylon spacer from shaft.

2.2 Liter Engine
1. Remove rotor from shaft and disconnect pick up electrical connector.
2. Remove Hall Effect Pick-up Assembly retaining clips.
3. On 1981 models, remove splash shield

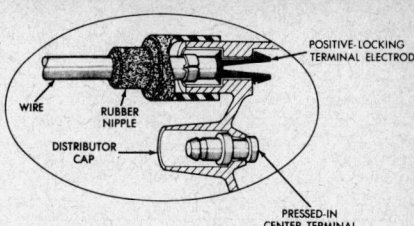

Fig. 10 Spark plug wire installation

screws, then the splash shield.
4. Remove Hall Effect Pick-up Assembly.
5. Remove distributor drive gear roll pin using punch, then remove drive gear, Fig. 8.
6. Remove drive gear thrust washer and distributor shaft.
7. Remove distributor to block seal.

Assembly

1.6 & 1.7 Liter Engines
1. Lightly lubricate housing bushings with engine oil.
2. Install shaft into housing, ensuring nylon spacer is resting on housing bushing.
3. Install drive gear onto distributor shaft in original position, aligning mating marks.
4. Drive in roll pin.
5. On 1978–81 models, install shield onto housing.
6. Place Hall Effect Pick-up Assembly into housing and secure with lock springs.
7. On 1978–81 models, secure Hall Effect Pick-up Assembly lead.
8. Install rotor onto shaft.

2.2 Liter Engine
1. Lubricate distributor housing bushings with engine oil, then install engine seal onto distributor housing.
2. Install distributor shaft thrust washer onto distributor shaft, then install shaft into distributor housing.
3. Install distributor drive gear thrust washer, then install distributor drive gear onto distributor shaft.
4. Install drive gear roll pin using punch.
5. Install Hall Effect Pick-up Assembly, then on 1981 models, install splash shield.
6. Install Hall Effect Pick-up Assembly retaining clips, then install rotor.

Spark Plug Wires, Replace

NOTE: The coil wire and spark plug end of spark plug wires are replaced in a conventional manner. To replace distributor end of spark plug wires, use the following procedure.

1. Remove distributor cap.
2. Using a pair of suitable long nosed piers, remove spark plug wires from distributor cap by squeezing wire clips and pushing out, Fig. 9.

NOTE: Do not remove spark plug wires from distributor cap unless nipples are damaged or cable testing indicates high resistance or broken insulation.

3. Refer to Fig. 10 for proper installation of spark plug wires. Ensure positive locking terminal electrode is fully seated in cap.

ELECTRONIC IGNITION SYSTEMS

SERVICE NOTE
Ignition Timing, Adjust

1977–81

1. Connect a tachometer to engine and a suitable timing light to No. 1 cylinder.

NOTE: Do not puncture ignition cables or boots with test probes.

---

2. Start engine, then apply parking brake and place transmission in Neutral. Allow engine to reach operating temperature.
3. Disconnect and plug EGR vacuum hose at EGR valve and vacuum hose to Electronic Spark Control computor, then connect a jumper wire from carburetor switch to ground.
4. Disconnect PCV valve and vapor canister purge hose from carburetor. Do not plug hoses.
5. Check idle speed and adjust as necessary, then reconnect PCV valve vacuum hose and vapor canister purge hose.
6. Loosen distributor hold down bracket screw just enough so that distributor housing can be rotated.
7. Check and adjust ignition timing as necessary.
8. Tighten distributor hold down screw, then recheck idle speed and ignition timing.
9. Remove test equipment and connect vacuum hoses.

1982–83

1. Connect a suitable tachometer to engine and a suitable adjustable timing light to No. 1 cylinder secondary cable.

NOTE: Do not puncture ignition secondary cables or boots with test probes.

---

2. Set parking brake, start engine and place gear selector in neutral. Run engine until warm.
3. On vehicles equipped with carburetor switch, connect a jumper wire between carburetor switch and a known good ground. Disconnect and plug vacuum line from transducer.
4. Ensure curb idle speed is set at or below specifications. Adjust as necessary.
5. Check ignition timing. If within ±2° of specifications, shut engine "Off" and remove timing light, tachometer and carburetor ground wire. If outside of tolerance, proceed to step 6.
6. Loosen distributor hold down arm screw, rotate distributor housing until correct timing marks are lined up, ensuring idle speed is still at or below specified curb idle speed.
7. Tighten distributor hold down screw, then recheck idle speed and ignition timing.
8. Turn engine "Off" and remove timing light, tachometer and carburetor ground wire.
9. Reconnect vacuum hose.

1978 CHRYSLER FRONT WHEEL DRIVE ELECTRONIC SPARK CONTROL (LEAN BURN) SPECIFICATION CHART

Spark Control Computer	5206467①	5206501①	5206516①	5206525①
	(4106062)②	(4106063)②	—	(4106065)②
Start Timer Advance Schedule	8°	8°	8°	8°
Delay Time In Seconds	60	60	60	60
Throttle Advance Schedule	—	—	—	—
Test Transducer Core Out 1 Inch	0°	0°	4°–6° @ 100°F 4°–6° @ 140°F	4°–6° @ 100°F 4°–6° @ 140°F
Vacuum Advance Schedule	—	—	—	—
a. Operating Vacuum Range	0 to 14 Inches Hg	0 to 14 Inches Hg	0 to 14 Inches Hg	0 to 14 Inches Hg
b. Advance Off Idle (Carb. Switch Isolated With Paper)	None	6°–10°	2°–6°	2°–6°
c. Accumulation Time in Minutes	8	7	8	8
d. Advance After Accumulation Time	18°–22°	18°–22°	18°–22°	18°–22°
Speed Advance	—	—	—	—
Ground Carb. Switch and Disconnect Throttle Transducer Before Checking	6°–10° @ 2000 rpm 18°–22° @ 6000 rpm	6°–10° @ 2000 rpm 18°–22° @ 6000 rpm	6°–10° @ 2000 rpm 18°–22° @ 6000 rpm	5°–9° @ 2000 rpm 13°–17° @ 6000 rpm

1978 CHRYSLER FRONT WHEEL DRIVE ELECTRONIC SPARK CONTROL (LEAN BURN) SPECIFICATION CHART—Continued

Spark Control Computer	5206526①	5206666①
	(4106066)②	(4106112)②
Start Timer Advance Schedule	8°	8°
Delay Time In Seconds	60	60
Throttle Advance Schedule	—	—
Test Transducer Core Out 1 Inch	0°	4°–6° @ 100°F 4°–6° @ 140°F
Vacuum Advance Schedule	—	—
a. Operating Vacuum Range	0 to 14 Inches Hg	0 to 14 Inches Hg
b. Advance Off Idle (Carb. Switch Isolated With Paper)	2°–6°	6°–10°
c. Accumulation Time in Minutes	8	7
d. Advance After Accumulation Time	18°–22°	18°–22°
Speed Advance	—	—
Ground Carb. Switch and Disconnect Throttle Transducer Before Checking	6°–10° @ 2000 rpm 18°–22° @ 6000 rpm	5°–9° @ 2000 rpm 13°–17° @ 6000 rpm

1979 CHRYSLER FRONT WHEEL DRIVE ELECTRONIC SPARK CONTROL (LEAN BURN) SPECIFICATION CHART

Spark Control Computer	5206721①	5206784①	5206785①	5206790①
	4111686②	4111687②	4111688②	4111689②
Start Up Advance (60 Seconds)	5°	5°	5°	5°
Crank + Electrical (Basic Timing)	10° + 5°	10° + 5°	10° + 5°	10° + 5°
Vacuum Advance Range (In. Hg.)	0–10	0–10	0–10	0–10
Zero Time Offset	6°–10°	2°–6°	3°–7°	0°–3°
Accumulator Time In Minutes	8	8	8	8
Vacuum Adv.—Full Accumulator				
@ 1100 rpm	18°–22°	18°–22°	18°–22°	18°–22°
@ 1500 rpm	23°–27°	23°–27°	28°–32°	28°–32°
Throttle Max. Advance (Throttle Open 20°)	0°	0°	0°	0°
Speed Advance				
@ 1100 rpm	0°–3°	0°–3°	0°–3°	0°–3°
@ 2000 rpm	8°–12°	8°–12°	8°–12°	8°–12°
@ 4000 rpm	18°–22°	18°–22°	16°–22°	18°–22°

①—Production part number.   ②—Remanufactured part number.

1980 CHRYSLER FRONT WHEEL DRIVE ELECTRONIC SPARK CONTROL (LEAN BURN) SPECIFICATION CHART

Spark Control Computer	5213008	5213012
Crank + Run = (Basic Timing)	10° + 0°	10° + 0°
Vacuum Advance (Range)	0" to 10"	0" to 10"
Zero Time Advance	18° to 22°	23° to 27°
Accumulator Time (In Minutes)	0	0
Vacuum Adv.—Full Accumulator		
@ 2000 RPM	5° to 9°	5° to 9°
@ 3000 RPM	18° to 22°	23° to 27°
Speed Adv. (Ground Carb. Switch)		
@ 1100 RPM	0° to 3°	0° to 3°
@ 2000 RPM	8° to 12°	13° to 17°
@ 4800 RPM	18° to 22°	20° to 24°
Warm Up Schedule (In Seconds)	25	25
Throttle Maximum Advance (Throttle Open 20°)	0°	0°

1981 CHRYSLER FRONT WHEEL DRIVE ELECTRONIC SPARK CONTROL (LEAN BURN) SPECIFICATION CHART

Spark Control Computer	5213101	5213111	5213128	5213133
Basic Timing	12°	10°	10°	10°
Vacuum Advance (Range)	0–10"	0–10"	0–10"	0–10"
Accumulator Time (In Minutes)	0	0	0	0
Spark Advance Test @ 2000 RPM	38° ± 4°	35° ± 4°	28° ± 4°	23° ± 4°

Spark Control Computer	5213138	5213143	5213148	5213268
Basic Timing	10°	10°	10°	12°
Vacuum Advance (Range)	0–10"	0–10"	0–10"	0–10"
Accumulator Time (In Minutes)	0	0	7	0
Spark Advance Test @ 2000 RPM	23° ± 4°	25° ± 4°	33° ± 4°	43° ± 4°

Spark Control Computer	5213249	5213343	5213345
Basic Timing	10°	10°	10°
Vacuum Advance (Range)	0–10"	0–10"	0–10"
Accumulator Time (In Minutes)	0	0	0
Spark Advance Test @ 2000 RPM	33° ± 4°	25° ± 4°	25° ± 4°

1982 CHRYSLER FRONT WHEEL DRIVE ELECTRONIC SPARK CONTROL (LEAN BURN) SPECIFICATION CHART

Spark Control Computer	5213437	5213438	5213480	5213481
Basic Timing	12°	20°	12°	12°
Vacuum Advance (Range)	0–10″	0–12″	0–12″	0–12″
Accumulator Time (In Minutes)	0	0	0	0
Spark Advance Test @ 2000 RPM	55° ± 4°	50° ± 4°	45° ± 4°	47° ± 4°

Spark Control Computer	5213482	5213483	5213542	5213544
Basic Timing	12°	12°	12°	12°
Vacuum Advance (Range)	0–12″	0–12″	0–10″	0–10″
Accumulator Time (In Minutes)	0	0	0	0
Spark Advance Test @ 2000 RPM	45° ± 4°	45° ± 4°	55° ± 4°	50° ± 4°

Spark Control Computer	5213546	5213546①	5213594	
Basic Timing	12°	12°	12°	
Vacuum Advance (Range)	0–10″	0–12″	0–10″	
Accumulator Time (In Minutes)	0	0	0	
Spark Advance Test @ 2000 RPM	43° ± 4°	31° ± 4°	37° ± 4°	

①—High Altitude

1983 CHRYSLER FRONT WHEEL DRIVE ELECTRONIC SPARK CONTROL (LEAN BURN) SPECIFICATION CHART

Spark Control Computer	5213438	5213641	5213691	5213832
Basic Timing	20°	12°	10°	10°
Vacuum Advance (Range)	0–12″	0–12″	2–12″	2–12″
Accumulator Time (In Minutes)	0	0	0	0
Spark Advance Test @ 2000 RPM	30° ± 4°	23° ± 4°	28° ± 4°	28° ± 4°

Spark Control Computer	5213834	5213836	5213838	5213840①
Basic Timing	10°	10°	10°	6°
Vacuum Advance (Range)	2–12″	2–12″	2–12″	2–21″
Accumulator Time (In Minutes)	0	0	0	0
Spark Advance Test @ 2000 RPM	28° ± 4°	34° ± 4°	31° ± 4°	34° ± 4°

①—High Altitude

Misar Electronic Spark Timing (E.S.T.) System

DESCRIPTION

1977 Toronado

This system uses the basic H.E.I. distributor. However, the pick-up coil, pole piece and advance mechanisms have been deleted and the rotor has been redesigned, Fig. 1. This system incorporates a crankshaft sensor, engine coolant temperature sensor and a controller unit.

The engine coolant temperature sensor resistance changes with changes in coolant temperature.

The electronic controller unit is mounted under the glove compartment and receives signals from the crankshaft sensor (crankshaft position and speed), engine coolant temperature sensor, engine vacuum and atmospheric pressure. The controller unit selects the most efficient advance as determined by the input signals and sends a signal to the distributor module to fire the spark plugs.

The electrical harness which connects these units together and to the vehicle harness, contains two vacuum hoses which are both connected to the controller unit. The white hose is connected to engine vacuum, while the black one is vented to atmospheric pressure outside of the vehicle.

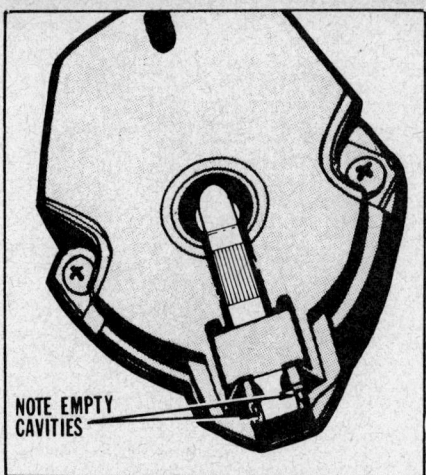

Fig. 1   Redesigned rotor used on E.S.T. system. 1977 Tornado

The crankshaft sensor is mounted at the front of the engine with a disc located between the harmonic balancer and pulley.

A "Check Ignition" light, located in the instrument panel will go on under the following conditions:
1. Ignition switch is in start position. This mode provides a bulb check.
2. If system voltage is low and there is a heavy electrical load such as operation of power windows or other electrical accessories. Under this condition, the "check ignition" light will go off when the electrical load is removed, providing system voltage returns to normal. The alternator warning light may also go on under these conditions.
3. When checking reference timing and controller circuit is grounded.
4. If controller fails to advance spark timing.

1978 Toronado

This system is similar to the system used on the 1977 Toronado, except that the crankshaft sensor and pulse generator disc have been eliminated. The functions of the crankshaft sensor and pulse generator disc are performed by the pick-up coil and timer core which are located in the distributor, Fig. 2. The electronic circuitry has also been redesigned, Fig. 3. The rotor mounting plate, Fig. 2, is constructed of brass, which is a non-magnetic metal. The reason for this is so that the brass mounting plate will prevent the signal produced by the pickup coil from being affected by magnetic attraction.

With these modifications, the ignition timing can be set by turning the distributor, however the reference timing connector must be grounded with a jumper wire.

1977 TORONADO SYSTEM SERVICE & DIAGNOSIS

Adjusting Distributor Position

1. Disconnect ignition feed wire and remove distributor cap.
2. Crank engine until rotor points toward rear of engine and number one piston is

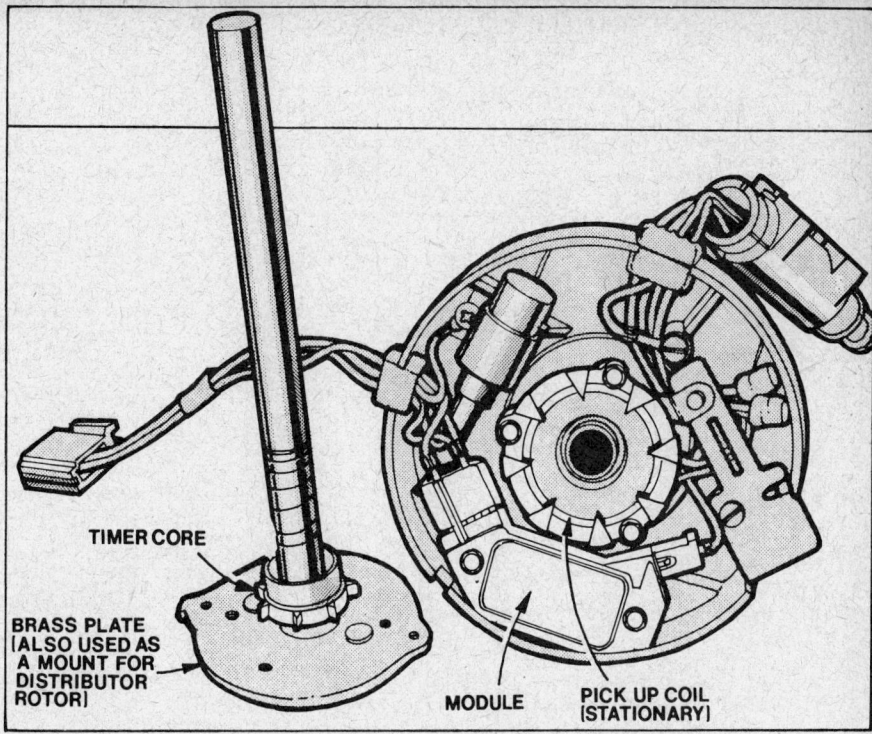

Fig. 2   Electronic Spark Timing (E.S.T.) distributor. 1978 Toronado

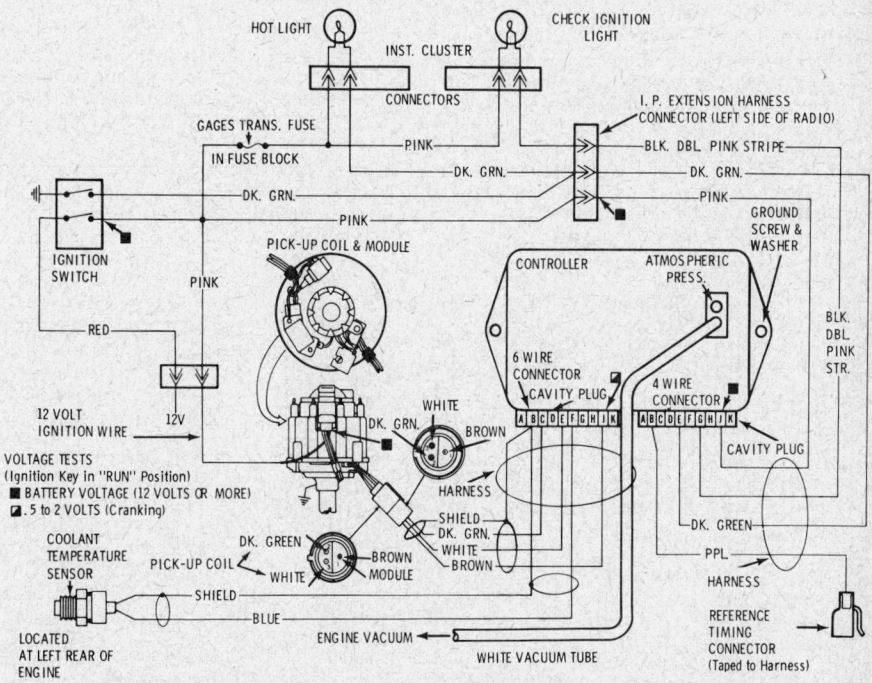

Fig. 3   Electronic Spark Timing (E.S.T.) wiring circuit. 1978 Toronado

almost on TDC (0 degrees on timing indicator).
3. Using a socket on crankshaft bolt, turn crankshaft to 0 degrees.
4. White mark on rotor should be aligned with white mark on distributor housing, Fig. 4. If not, loosen distributor clamp bolt

and turn distributor to align.

NOTE: This is the final distributor position.

5. Tighten distributor clamp bolt.

ELECTRONIC IGNITION SYSTEMS

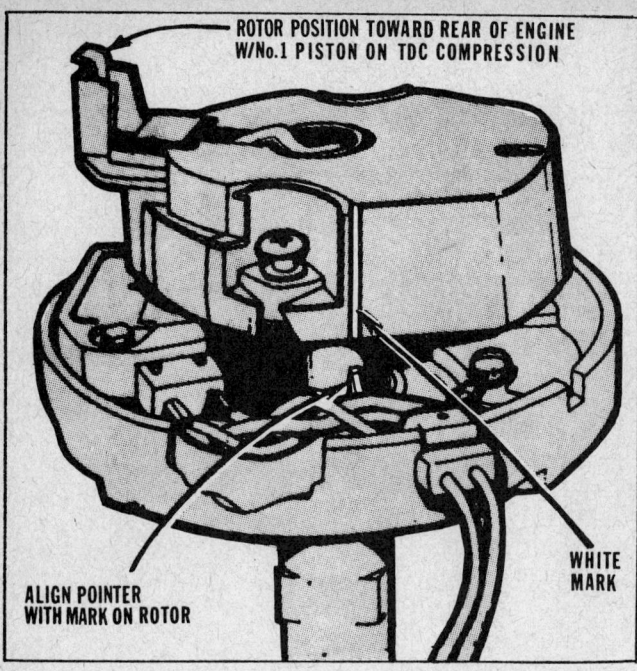

Fig. 4 Rotor and distributor alignment mark. 1977 Toronado

ROTOR POSITION TOWARD REAR OF ENGINE
W/No.1 PISTON ON TDC COMPRESSION

WHITE MARK

ALIGN POINTER WITH MARK ON ROTOR

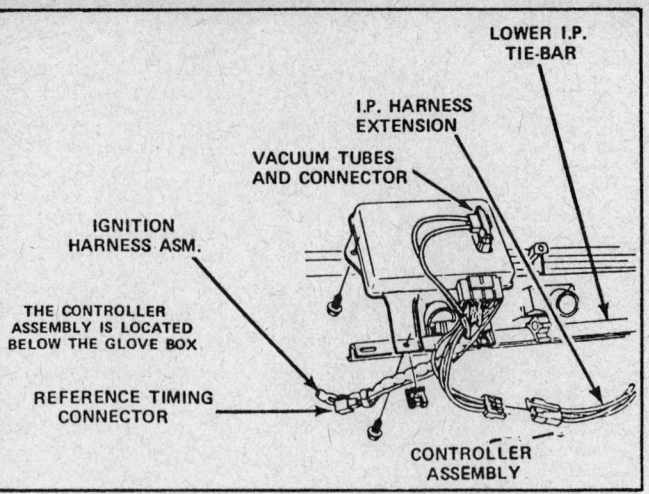

Fig. 5 Reference timing connector. 1977 Toronado

Adjusting Reference Timing

NOTE: Timing should be checked with a magnetic probe timing meter.

1. With distributor postion correctly adjusted, connect the open reference timing connector (taped to harness), Fig. 5, to ground using a jumper wire.
2. With transmission in PARK, drive wheels blocked and parking brake applied, start engine and run at low idle. Timing should be at 20 degrees.

NOTE: Engine speed will not affect timing. Also, the "check timing" light should be on.

3. If timing is incorrect, stop engine, then loosen timing adjuster clamp bolts and rotate timing adjuster bolt, Fig. 6, clockwise to retard timing. One complete turn equals about one degree.

NOTE: Do not rotate distributor in an attempt to adjust ignition timing.

4. Recheck timing. If correct, stop engine, then tighten adjuster bolt clamp bolts and disconnect jumper wire.

Crankshaft Sensor, Replace & Align

1. Turn ignition OFF and mark sensor position on mounting surfaces so that sensor can be installed in original position.
2. Disconnect sensor harness connector, then remove crankshaft sensor timing adjuster clamp bolts and sensor.
3. Install crankshaft sensor in original position and leave adjuster clamp bolts slightly loose until after checking reference timing.
4. Check clearance between disc and crankshaft sensor, Fig. 7. To adjust, loosen clearance adjustment bolts, Fig. 6.
5. Reconnect harness connector.
6. Check reference timing.

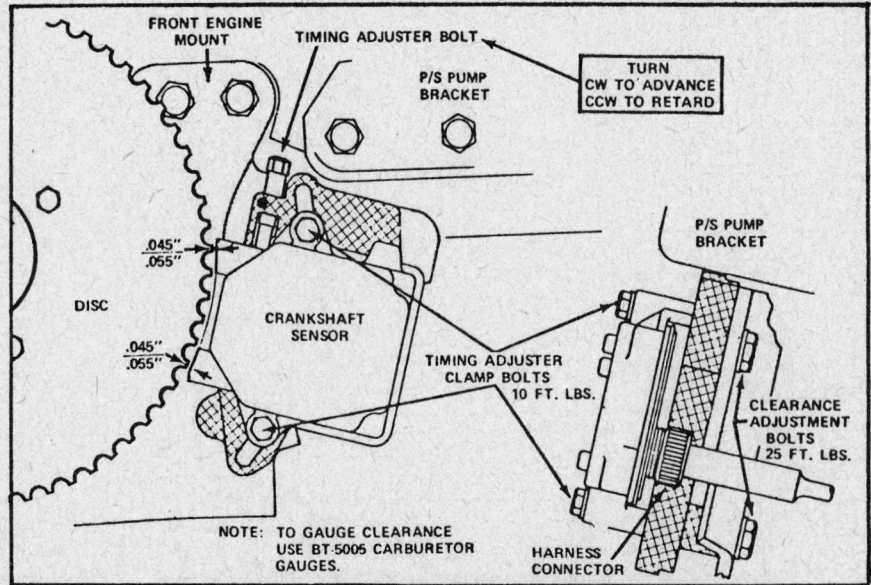

Fig. 6 Crankshaft sensor to disc clearance. 1977 Toronado

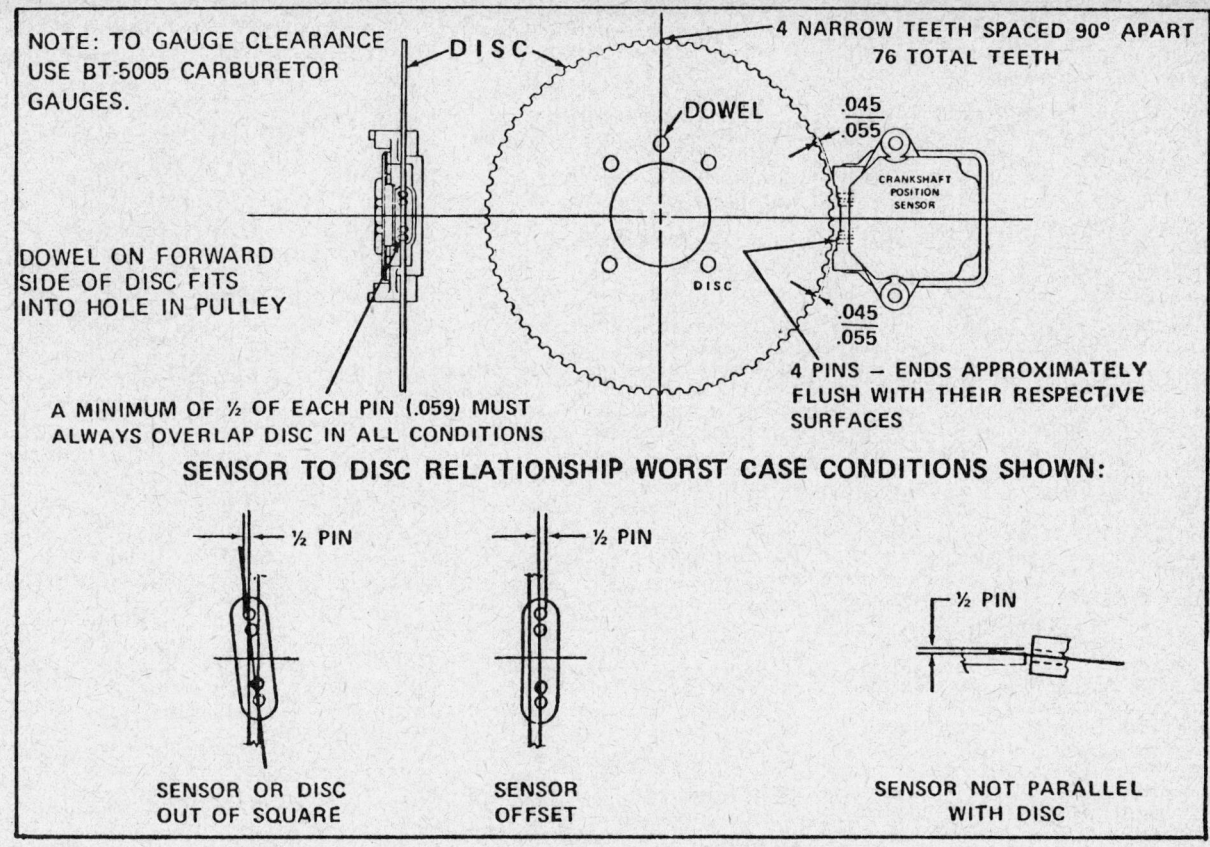

Fig. 7   Crankshaft sensor alignment. 1977 Toronado

ENGINE TIMING ADVANCE IN CRANKSHAFT DEGREES

1. Engine **MUST BE** at operating temperature.

2. Connect tachometer and timing meter.

3. Disconnect controller assembly vacuum tube (white) from manifold vacuum "T". Plug "T" and connect vacuum pump and gauge to white tube. Use pump to get vacuum readings shown.

NOTE: 1400 RPM at 15" of vacuum gives maximum advance. If advance is less than specification, slowly increase vacuum to get maximum advance. If advance is now within specification, instruments/gauges used are inaccurate. If not within specification, replace controller assembly.

EXCEPT CALIFORNIA			CALIFORNIA		
ENGINE RPM	VACUUM (INCHES)	*CRANKSHAFT DEGREES	ENGINE RPM	VACUUM (INCHES)	*CRANKSHAFT DEGREES
600	16.5	29 to 34	600	13.5	17 to 20
600	15	27 to 31	600	12	17 to 20
1000	12	29 to 37	1000	12	19 to 22
1400	15	44 to 61	1400	15	44 to 61
1400	10.5	37 to 41	2000	18	31 to 49
1400	6	25 to 35	2000	0	31 to 34
2000	18	44 to 53			
2000	0	28 to 31			

* Advance specifications are approximate depending upon accuracy of tachometer, vacuum gauge and timing meter.

Fig. 9   Engine timing advance specifications. 1977 Toronado

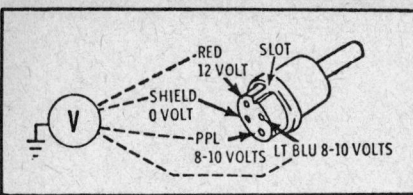

Fig. 8 Crankshaft sensor connector test connections

System Diagnosis

Engine Will Not Start (Engine Cranks Normally, Battery fully Charged)

1. Check EST fuse in fuse panel. If fuse is blown, proceed to step 2. If fuse is not blown, proceed to step 3.
2. Disconnect 3-wire connector near controller unit, then replace fuse and turn ignition ON. If fuse does not blow, locate and repair short in red wire from connector on controller unit to crankshaft sensor. If fuse blows again, locate and repair short circuit in pink wire with double-black stripes from 3-wire connector through instrument panel harness to fuse panel.
3. Check for spark at the spark plugs. If there is no spark, proceed to step 4. If there is spark, check distributor position and reference timing. If correct, trouble is not in ignition. Check fuel system and spark plugs.
4. Inspect crankshaft sensor, disc and harness for damage. Check sensor alignment and clearance at disc. Check black ground wire and screw in distributor. If connection is good, turn ignition key to RUN position and check voltage as follows:
   a. Ignition wire (black with pink stripe) at connector on distributor. If voltage is less than 12 volts, check wire from distributor to ignition switch for loose connections or open circuit. Also check ignition switch.
   b. Terminal J (pink and red) wires in connector at controller unit. If voltage is less than 12 volts, check pink wire for loose connection or open circuit from connector at controller unit to 3-wire connector near controller, then the pink wire with double-black stripes through instrument panel harness to fuse panel.
   c. Tan wire in 2-wire connector near distributor. Do not disconnect wire. Voltage should be .5–2 volts while cranking the engine. If voltage is not as specified, proceed to step 5. If voltage is as specified, check distributor, coil, and module. Replace defective parts.
5. Check voltage at terminal C (tan wire) in connector at controller unit. Voltage should be .5–2 volts. If voltage is not as specified, proceed to step 6. If voltage is as specified, check tan wire from controller to 2-wire connector near distributor for loose connection or open circuit. Replace or repair as necessary.
6. Check voltage at terminal D (light blue wire) in connector at controller unit while cranking engine. Record reading, then check voltage again with crankshaft sensor disconnected and placed aside so as not to damage it. If voltages are the same, proceed to step 7. If voltages are not the same, replace controller unit.
7. Turn ignition key to RUN position and check voltage at crankshaft sensor harness connector, Fig. 8. If voltages are as

specified, proceed to step 8. If voltages are not as specified, replace harness.
8. Turn ignition key to RUN position and check voltage at both 8–10 volt terminals. If voltage is not 8–10 volts at both terminals, proceed to step 9. If voltage is as specified, replace crankshaft sensor.
9. Turn ignition key to RUN position and check voltage at controller unit. Voltage at terminals D (light blue) and E (purple) should be 8–10 volts. If voltage is as specified, replace harness. If voltage is not as specified, replace controller unit.

Engine Detonates (Recommended Octane Rating Fuel Used)

1. Check white vacuum hose from intake manifold to controller unit for kinks, obstructions, leakage or heat damage.

NOTE: A partially obstructed hose would prevent fast drop of vacuum on acceleration.

If hose is in good condition and not leaking, disconnect coolant temperature sensor and check resistance. At engine operating temperature, the resistance should be 500 to 2,000 ohms. At 70° F., the resistance should be 25,000 to 55,000 ohms. If resistance is as specified, proceed to step 2. If resistance is not as specified or if there is an open circuit in the sensor, replace sensor.
2. With ignition off, disconnect controller unit connector and connect a jumper wire between terminals B (black wire) and F (white wire) in connector. Connect an ohmmeter to the 2 terminals in coolant temperature harness connector.
3. If ohmmeter reading is less than 1 ohm, check crankshaft sensor alignment and disc for damage, Fig. 5. Check reference timing. If no damage is found and sensor alignment and reference timing are correct, replace controller unit.
4. If ohmmeter reading is more than 1 ohm or indicates an open circuit, check for open circuit in black and white wires. Repair or replace harness as necessary.

Engine Starts Then Stops When Key Is Turned to "RUN" Position

1. Turn ignition key to RUN, then disconnect crankshaft sensor connector and check voltages as shown in Fig. 8.
2. If voltage reading at 12 volt terminal or shield terminal are not as specified, repair or replace harness.
3. If voltage reading at either 8–10 volt terminal are not as specified, check voltage at controller unit connector from ground to terminal D (light blue) and E (purple). Reading should be 8–10 volts at both terminals. If both readings are as specified, replace harness. If readings are not as specified, replace controller unit.
4. If all voltage readings are as specified in Fig. 8, reconnect crankshaft sensor connector and connect jumper wire to reference timing connector (purple wire) near controller and connect jumper wire to ground.
5. Start engine and run at idle. Check voltage at controller unit connector terminal E (purple). Voltage reading should be 3–5 volts. If voltage is as specified, replace controller unit. If voltage is not as specified, check disc alignment, Fig. 7. If alignment is correct, replace crankshaft sensor.

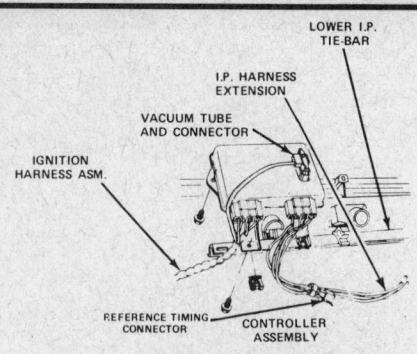

Fig. 10 Electronic Spark Timing (E.S.T.) reference timing connector. 1978 Toronado

Hard Starting, Rough Idle, Poor Performance (Battery Fully Charged)

1. Check fuel system, choke, spark plugs and cables.
2. Make sure harness connections to distributor, coolant temperature sensor and controller unit are good.
3. Inspect crankshaft sensor for alignment. Make sure clearance between sensor and disc is .045–.055 inches, Fig. 7. Also make sure harness and connector are in good condition.
4. Check all vacuum hoses for kinks, obstructions, leakage or heat damage. Repair or replace as necessary.
5. Check distributor cap and rotor for signs of arcing. Check ground wire and screw in distributor. Check module with tester J-24624.
6. Check distributor position and reference timing.
7. With engine idling, transmission in PARK and parking brakes applied, connect voltmeter to ground and touch other probe to ignition wire (black with pink stripe) in connector on distributor. If voltage is less than 12 volts, check for loose connection between distributor connector and ignition switch.
8. Connect voltmeter to ground and J terminal (pink and red wires) in controller unit. If less than 12 volts, check for loose connection through instrument panel harness connector to fuse panel.
9. If problem has not been located, proceed as follows:
10. Turn ignition key to RUN position, then disconnect crankshaft sensor connector and check voltage at 12 volt terminal and at shield terminal, Fig. 8. If voltages are as specified, proceed to step 11. If voltages are not as specified, repair or replace harness.
11. Turn ignition key to RUN position and check voltage at both 8–10 volt terminals. If voltages are as specified, proceed to step 12. If voltages are not as specified, with crankshaft sensor disconnected, check for 8–10 volts at both terminals D (light blue) and E (purple) of controller unit. If voltages are as specified, replace harness, if not, replace controller unit.
12. Reconnect crankshaft sensor connector, then with key in RUN position and engine stopped, check reference voltage at controller unit connector terminal D (light blue). Record voltage, then check voltage again with engine at idle speed. If voltage readings are different, proceed to step 13. If voltage readings are the same, replace crankshaft sensor.
13. With engine idling, check for 3–5 volts at

1. Engine **MUST BE** at operating temperature and timing set to specification.

2. Connect tachometer and timing meter. Do not ground reference timing connector.

3. Disconnect controller assembly vacuum tube (white) from manifold vacuum "T". Plug "T" and connect vacuum pump and gage to white tube. Use pump such as BT-7517 to get vacuum readings shown.

NOTE: 1400 RPM at 15" of vacuum gives maximum advance. If advance is less than specification, slowly increase vacuum to get maximum advance. If advance is now within specification, instruments/gages used are inaccurate. If not within specification, replace controller.

EXCEPT CALIFORNIA CARS			CALIFORNIA CARS		
ENGINE RPM	VACUUM (INCHES)	*CRANKSHAFT DEGREES	ENGINE RPM	VACUUM (INCHES)	*CRANKSHAFT DEGREES
600	16.5	29 to 34	600	13.5	15 to 22
600	15	27 to 31	600	12	15 to 22
1000	12	32 to 35	1000	12	17 to 25
1400	15	49 to 62	1400	15	39 to 65
1400	10.5	38 to 40	2000	18	24 to 33
1400	6	27 to 35	2000	0	23 to 32
2000	18	44 to 47			
2000	0	29 to 31			

* Advance specifications are approximate depending upon accuracy of tachometer, vacuum gage and timing meter.

Fig. 11   Electronic Spark Timing (E.S.T.) engine timing advance specifications. 1978

controller unit connector terminal E (purple). If voltage is as specified, proceed to step 14. If voltage is not as specified, replace crankshaft sensor.
14. With engine idling, check for 1–4 volts at tan wire in 2-wire connector near distributor. If voltage is as specified, proceed to step 15. If voltage is not as specified, replace controller unit assembly.
15. Check engine advance. Refer to chart in Fig. 9. If advance is not as specified, proceed to step 16. If advance is as specified, problem is not in ignition. Recheck steps 1, 3, 4, 5, and 6.
16. Disconnect coolant temperature sensor and check resistance of sensor at sensor terminals. At engine operating temperature, resistance should be 500 to 2,000 ohms. At 70° F., resistance should be 25,000 to 55,000 ohms. If resistance is as specified, proceed to step 17. If resistance is not as specified, replace coolant sensor.
17. With ignition OFF, disconnect controller unit connector and connect a jumper wire between terminals B (black wire) and F (white wire) in connector. Connect an ohmmeter to the 2 terminals in temperature sensor harness connector. If ohmmeter reads less than 1 ohm resistance, replace controller unit. If ohmmeter reads more than 1 ohm or indicates an open circuit, check for open circuit in black and white wires and repair or replace harness as necessary.

Hot Light ON (Ignition Key In "RUN" Position)
1. Check usual causes of "Hot Light On" condition. Correct as required.
2. Disconnect 2-wire connector at coolant temperature sensor and turn ignition to RUN position. If hot light remains on,

proceed to step 3. If hot light goes off, replace coolant temperature sensor.
3. Turn ignition switch OFF, then disconnect 3-wire connector near controller unit and turn ignition switch to RUN. If hot light goes off, proceed to step 4. If hot light remains on, locate and repair short in dark green wire circuit from 3-wire connector to instrument cluster and to ignition switch.
4. Disconnect controller unit connector and connect an ohmmeter to the 2 terminals in coolant temperature sensor connector. Ohmmeter should indicate an open circuit. Connect ohmmeter to ground and connector terminals. White wire terminal should indicate an open circuit. If all readings are as specified, replace controller unit. If all readings are not as specified, black and white wires are shorted together. Repair or replace harness as required.

"Check Ignition" Light "On" (Engine Running, Battery Fully Charged)
1. Check reference timing wire (purple) connector at controller unit, Fig. 3. The connector should be disconnected and not grounded.
2. With engine running, transmission in PARK and parking brakes applied, check voltage at controller unit terminal J (pink and red wires). If voltage is less than 11 volts, proceed to step 3. If voltage is above 11 volts, turn ignition key to RUN position (engine off) and disconnect 3-wire connector near controller unit. If light goes out, replace controller unit. If light remains on, circuit between H terminal and light is grounded. Repair or replace harness as required.
3. With all accessories turned off and engine running at fast idle, connect a voltmeter

to battery. If voltmeter reading is more than 12 volts, proceed to step 4. If voltmeter reading is less than 12 volts, check fan belt tension and charging system.
4. Check for loose connection from terminal J in controller unit through instrument panel harness connectors to fuse panel. Repair as required.

1978 TORONADO SYSTEM SERVICE
Adjusting Reference Timing

1. Connect reference timing connector (taped to harness), Fig. 10, to ground using a suitable jumper wire.
2. Connect timing light or magnetic probe timing meter and start engine.

NOTE: The "Check Ignition" should be on if reference timing connector is properly connected.

3. Check timing. If timing is not to specifications, loosen distributor clamp bolt and turn distributor as necessary, then tighten clamp bolt.
4. Disconnect jumper wire from reference timing connector. The "Check Ignition" light should go out.

System Diagnosis

Refer to Fig. 11 for engine timing advance specifications, and to Figs. 12 thru 15 for system diagnosis.

NOTE: Make sure controller case is grounded at all times while performing diagnosis.

ELECTRONIC IGNITION SYSTEMS

IGNITION SYSTEM DIAGNOSIS - TORONADO

(MAKE SURE CONTROLLER CASE IS GROUNDED)

ENGINE DOES NOT START. CRANKS OK,
BATTERY FULLY CHARGED.

Check for spark at plug with AC/ST-125 or J-26792

SPARK OK

Trouble is not ignition.
Check spark plugs, cables
and fuel system.

NO SPARK

Turn ignition key to "run" and check voltage at the following locations. (Look at circuit diagram for wire connections.)
1. Ignition wire to distributor. 12 volts or more is ok. Less than 12 volts, check ignition wire from distributor to ignition switch for loose or open connections. Also check ignition switch. (Should be 12 volts or more at ignition No. 1 terminal.)
2. Make sure controller case is grounded.
3. Check voltage at terminal J (PNK wire) in 4 wire connector at controller. 12 volts or more is ok. Less than 12 volts, check PNK wire from controller to ignition switch for loose or open connections.
4. Check voltage at terminal J (Brn wire) in 6 wire connector at controller. Should be .5 to 2 volts while cranking.

VOLTAGE OK

Check distributor cap, rotor
ignition coil and module. (pickup
coil is ok). Check wiring from
controller to distributor for
open circuit (see circuit diagram)
Replace part that checks bad.

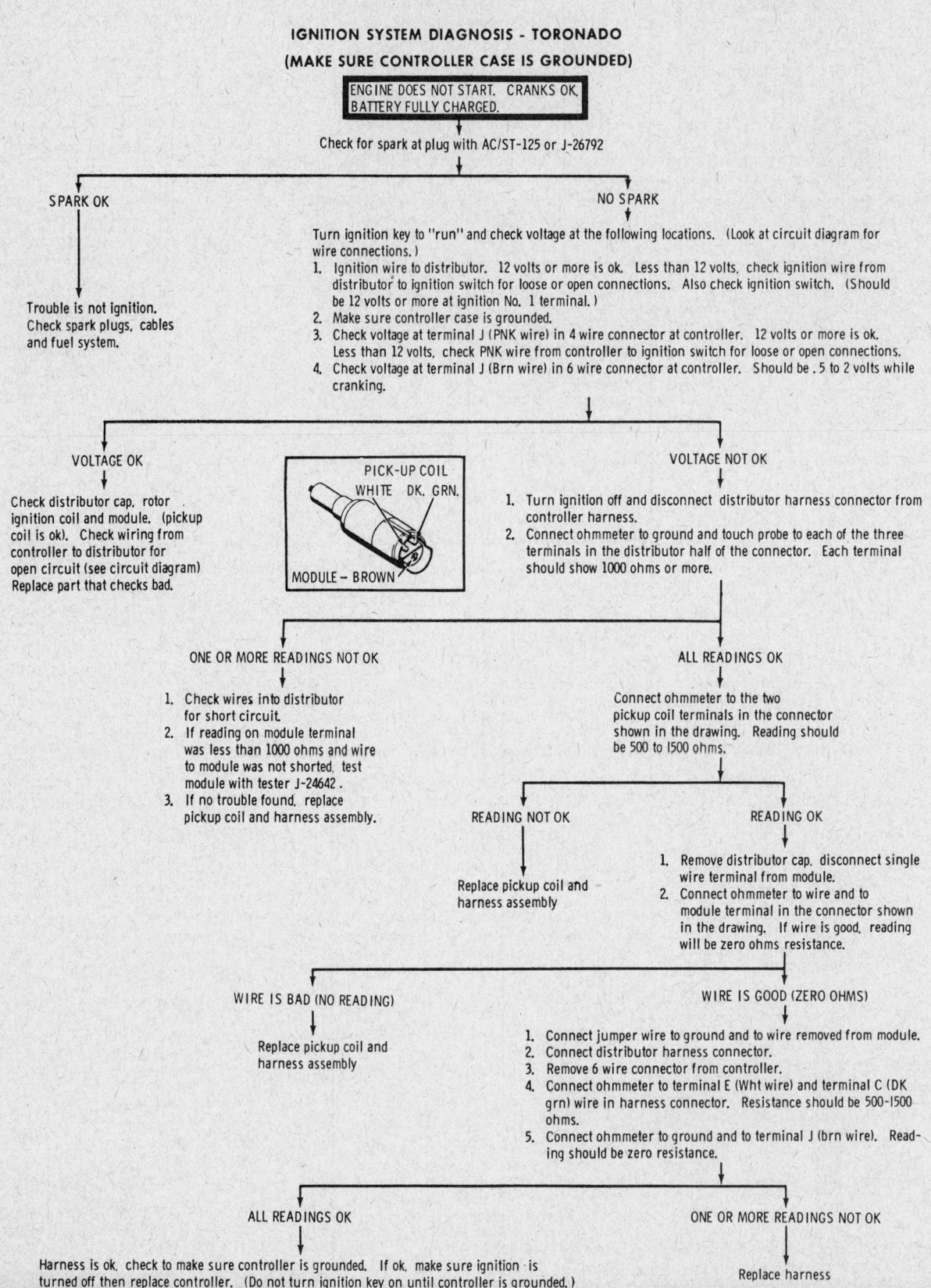

PICK-UP COIL
WHITE   DK. GRN.

MODULE – BROWN

VOLTAGE NOT OK

1. Turn ignition off and disconnect distributor harness connector from controller harness.
2. Connect ohmmeter to ground and touch probe to each of the three terminals in the distributor half of the connector. Each terminal should show 1000 ohms or more.

ONE OR MORE READINGS NOT OK

1. Check wires into distributor
for short circuit.
2. If reading on module terminal
was less than 1000 ohms and wire
to module was not shorted, test
module with tester J-24642.
3. If no trouble found, replace
pickup coil and harness assembly.

ALL READINGS OK

Connect ohmmeter to the two
pickup coil terminals in the connector
shown in the drawing. Reading should
be 500 to 1500 ohms.

READING NOT OK

Replace pickup coil and
harness assembly

READING OK

1. Remove distributor cap, disconnect single
wire terminal from module.
2. Connect ohmmeter to wire and to
module terminal in the connector shown
in the drawing. If wire is good, reading
will be zero ohms resistance.

WIRE IS BAD (NO READING)

Replace pickup coil and
harness assembly

WIRE IS GOOD (ZERO OHMS)

1. Connect jumper wire to ground and to wire removed from module.
2. Connect distributor harness connector.
3. Remove 6 wire connector from controller.
4. Connect ohmmeter to terminal E (Wht wire) and terminal C (DK grn) wire in harness connector. Resistance should be 500-1500 ohms.
5. Connect ohmmeter to ground and to terminal J (brn wire). Reading should be zero resistance.

ALL READINGS OK

Harness is ok, check to make sure controller is grounded. If ok, make sure ignition is
turned off then replace controller. (Do not turn ignition key on until controller is grounded.)

ONE OR MORE READINGS NOT OK

Replace harness

Fig. 12 Electronic Spark Timing (E.S.T.) system diagnosis chart (part 1 of 4). 1978 Toronado

IGNITION SYSTEM DIAGNOSIS - TORONADO CONTINUED
(MAKE SURE CONTROLLER CASE IS GROUNDED)

HARD STARTING, ROUGH ENGINE, POOR PERFORMANCE
(Battery fully charged - 12 Volts or more)

---

1. If CHECK IGNITION light is on (engine running), use diagnosis chart CHECK IGNITION LIGHT ON - ENGINE RUNNING.
2. If CHECK IGNITION light is off, check fuel system, choke, spark plugs and cables.
3. Check all vacuum hoses and white vacuum tube to controller for pinches or leaks.
4. Make sure harness connections to distributor, coolant sensor and controller are good and controller is grounded.

5. Connect voltmeter to ground and touch probe to ignition wire at distributor 12 volts or more is ok. If less, check ignition wire from distributor to ignition switch. Also check ignition switch. Refer to circuit diagram.
6. Connect voltmeter to ground and touch probe to terminal J (PNK wire) in 4 wire connector at controller. Should be 12 volts or more. If less, check PNK wire from controller to ignition switch for loose connections. Also check ignition switch.
7. Remove distributor cap, check rotor and cap for signs of arcing. Check module with J-24642.
8. Check reference timing.
9. Check engine timing advance. See ENGINE TIMING ADVANCE IN CRANKSHAFT DEGREES chart.

ENGINE TIMING ADVANCE IS OK

Problem is not ignition. Recheck steps 2, 3 and 5.

ENGINE TIMING ADVANCE IS NOT OK

Turn ignition off and disconnect coolant temperature sensor and check resistance of sensor at sensor terminals. Resistance should be about 500 to 2,000 ohms. Engine at operating temperature. (25,000 to 55,000 ohms at room temperature.) 70°F. (21°C).

INCORRECT RESISTANCE

Replace coolant temperature sensor.

CORRECT RESISTANCE

1. Disconnect 6 wire connector at controller and connect terminal B (shield wire) to terminal F (blue wire) with a short jumper wire pushed into wire side of connector.
2. Check resistance by connecting ohmmeter to the two terminals in the temperature sensor connector. Resistance should be 1 ohm or less.

RESISTANCE OK

Make sure ignition is turned off then replace controller. (Do not turn ignition key on until controller is grounded.

METER READS OPEN CIRCUIT OR MORE THAN 1 OHM

Replace 6 wire connector harness.

Fig. 13   Electronic Spark Timing (E.S.T.) system diagnosis chart (part 2 of 4), 1978 Toronado

ELECTRONIC IGNITION SYSTEMS

IGNITION SYSTEM DIAGNOSIS - TORONADO CONTINUED
(MAKE SURE CONTROLLER CASE IS GROUNDED)

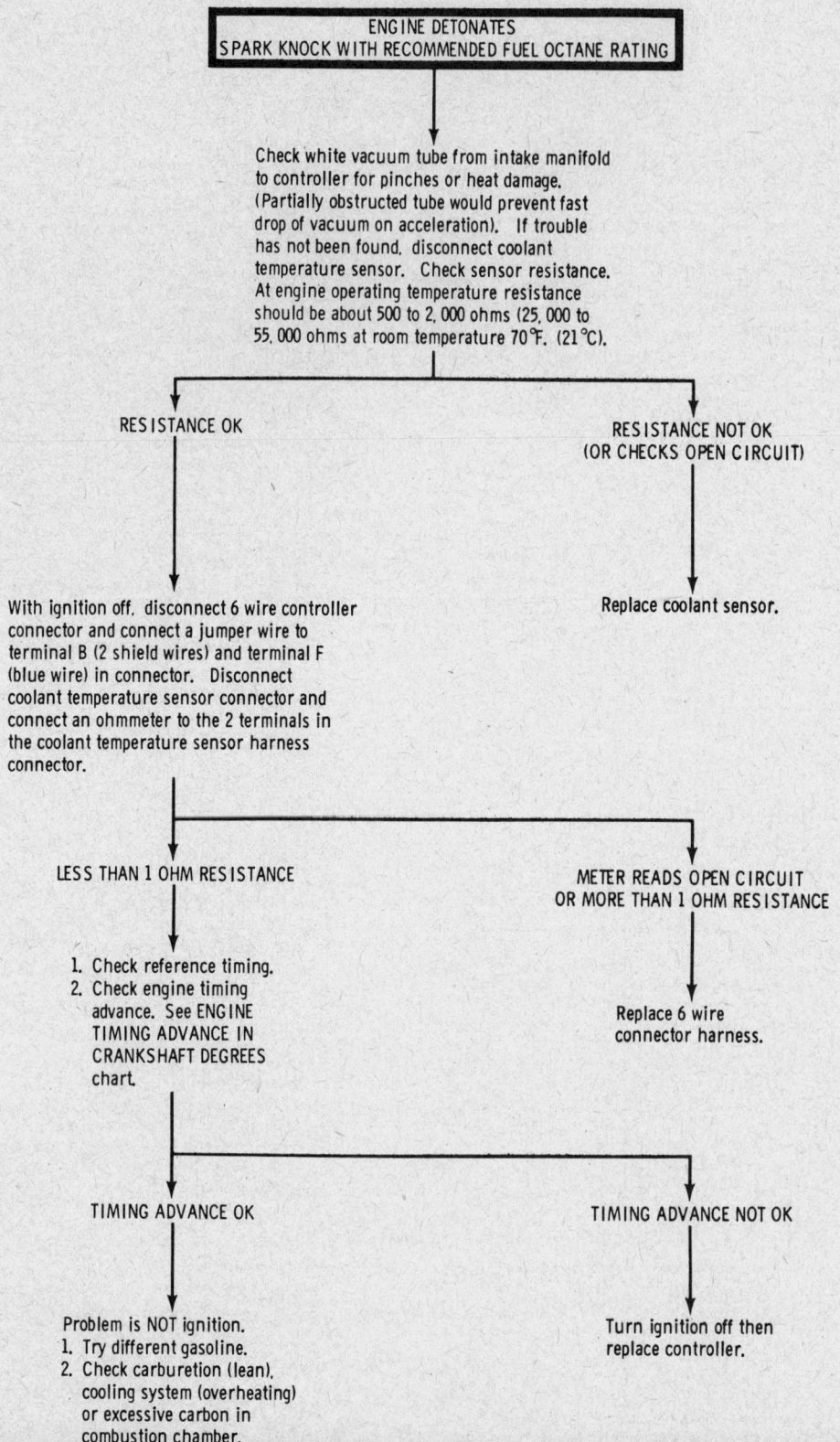

Fig. 14 Electronic Spark Timing (E.S.T.) system diagnosis chart (part 3 of 4). 1978 Toronado

**IGNITION SYSTEM DIAGNOSIS-TORONADO CONTINUED
(MAKE SURE CONTROLLER CASE IS GROUNDED)**

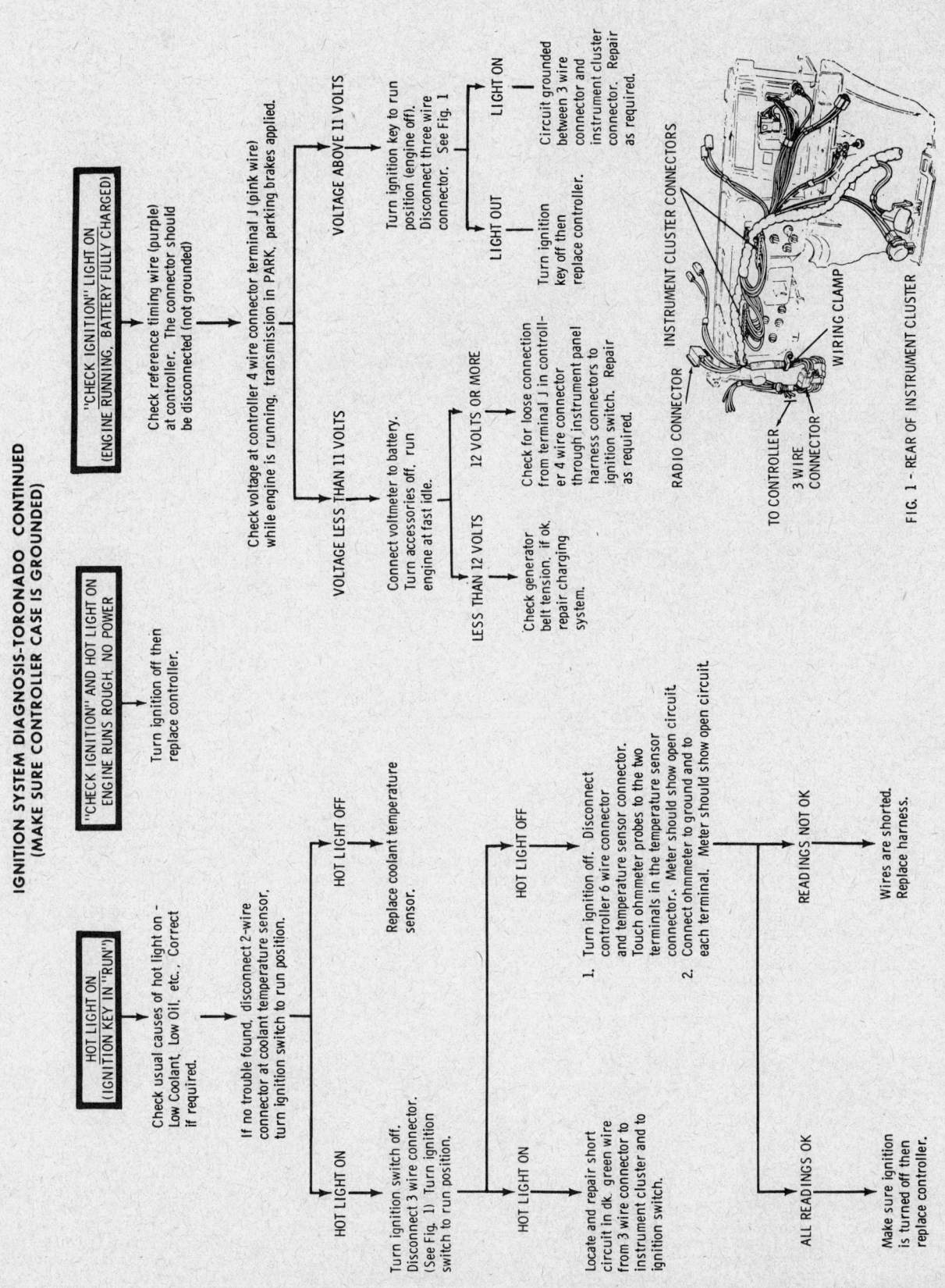

**"CHECK IGNITION" LIGHT ON
(ENGINE RUNNING, BATTERY FULLY CHARGED)**

Check reference timing wire (purple) at controller. The connector should be disconnected (not grounded)

Check voltage at controller 4 wire connector terminal J (pink wire) while engine is running, transmission in PARK, parking brakes applied.

VOLTAGE ABOVE 11 VOLTS

Turn ignition key to run position (engine off). Disconnect three wire connector. See Fig. 1

LIGHT ON

Circuit grounded between 3 wire connector and instrument cluster connector. Repair as required.

LIGHT OUT

Turn ignition key off then replace controller.

VOLTAGE LESS THAN 11 VOLTS

Connect voltmeter to battery. Turn accessories off. run engine at fast idle.

12 VOLTS OR MORE

Check for loose connection from terminal J in controller 4 wire connector through instrument panel harness connectors to ignition switch. Repair as required.

LESS THAN 12 VOLTS

Check generator belt tension. if ok. repair charging system.

**"CHECK IGNITION" AND HOT LIGHT ON
ENGINE RUNS ROUGH. NO POWER**

Turn ignition off then replace controller.

**HOT LIGHT ON
(IGNITION KEY IN "RUN")**

Check usual causes of hot light on - Low Coolant, Low Oil, etc.. Correct if required.

If no trouble found, disconnect 2-wire connector at coolant temperature sensor, turn ignition switch to run position.

HOT LIGHT OFF

Replace coolant temperature sensor.

HOT LIGHT ON

Turn ignition switch off. Disconnect 3 wire connector. (See Fig. 1) Turn ignition switch to run position.

HOT LIGHT OFF

1. Turn ignition off. Disconnect controller 6 wire connector and temperature sensor connector. Touch ohmmeter probes to the two terminals in the temperature sensor connector.. Meter should show open circuit.
2. Connect ohmmeter to ground and to each terminal. Meter should show open circuit.

READINGS NOT OK

Wires are shorted. Replace harness.

ALL READINGS OK

Make sure ignition is turned off then replace controller.

HOT LIGHT ON

Locate and repair short circuit in dk. green wire from 3 wire connector to instrument cluster and to ignition switch.

RADIO CONNECTOR

INSTRUMENT CLUSTER CONNECTORS

WIRING CLAMP

TO CONTROLLER 3 WIRE CONNECTOR

FIG. 1 - REAR OF INSTRUMENT CLUSTER

Fig. 15 Electronic Spark Timing (E.S.T.) system diagnosis chart (part 4 of 4). 1978 Toronado

Electronic Spark Selection (ESS) System

The Electronic Spark Selection (ESS) System is standard on all 1978–80 Seville, 1979–80 Eldorado, 1979 Brougham and DeVille California models less electronic fuel injection and all 1980 Brougham and DeVille. This system is able to advance or retard the entire spark curve under certain operating conditions. This improves fuel economy at cruising speeds, reduces exhaust emissions and improves hot engine restarting.

The system used on Eldorado is similar to the system used on Seville. The system used on Brougham and DeVille models less electronic fuel injection do not have EGR solenoids; a three-way coolant temperature switch is needed to signal the ESS decoder for spark retard during cold weather operation and to prevent over advance during hot engine operation.

Spark advance is retarded from normal engine timing during cranking, Fig. 1. Spark retard improved hot restarting by lessening the demand on the starting system since the spark is delivered to the cylinder when the piston is closer to top dead center. Ignition and the associated start of combustion pressure build-up in the cylinder occur closer to the point where the piston starts the downward motion at the beginning of the power stroke. This reduces demand on the starting system since the starter is not required to crank the engine a longer period of time against a high combustion pressure during engine starting.

Spark advance is also retarded from normal engine timing when coolant temperature is below approximately 130° F. (54° C.) on 1978–79 California vehicles and all 1980 vehicles. This shortens the catalytic converter warm-up time thereby reducing exhaust gas hydrocarbon emissions. The catalytic converter is brought up to operating temperature faster since higher exhaust gas temperature is obtained when the spark is retarded.

There is no modification to normal ignition timing during normal city operation when outside of the cruise mode at normal operating temperature. Cruise conditions are identified by high manifold vacuums and high engine speeds. Normal spark advance occurs any time below the cruise mode and/or manifold vacuum points. California vehicles have retarded spark when the engine is cold as described previously. All other vehicles have normal spark advance at this time.

Spark timing is advanced over normal engine timing during cruise conditions to improve fuel economy, Fig. 1. Ignition occurs earlier in the compression stroke giving the

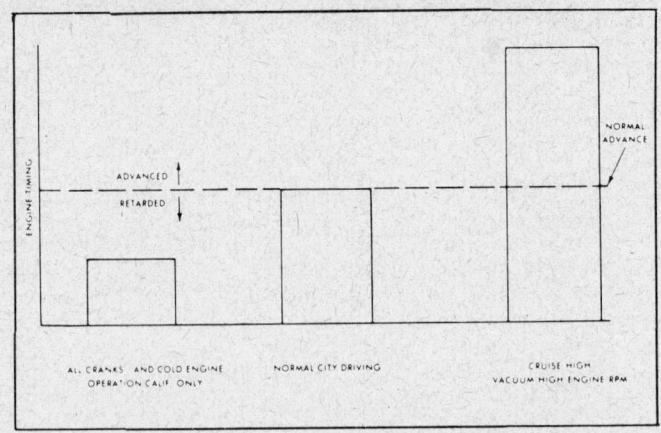

Fig. 1   Electronic Spark Selection (ESS) system operating modes

fuel-air mixture more time to burn which increases efficiency and improves fuel economy.

This system includes an electronic decoder and a H.E.I. distributor which has been modified for the ESS system. The pick-up coil signal is sent to the electronic decoder to provide engine speed and ignition timing information. This signal is from the speed of the timer core and the relationship to the pole piece. The ESS system distributor has a five pin module in place of the 4 pin module used in conventional H.E.I. units. The electronic decoder output signal is sent to this new additional pin on the module. At this point, the decoder signal either delays or does not delay the shutting-off current in the primary winding in the ignition coil.

The spark is retarded from normal engine timing when current shut-off in the primary winding is delayed. Ignition then takes place at a later time when the piston is closer to top dead center.

Maximum delay of the primary winding current shut-off occurs when the engine is cranking and during cold engine operation on California vehicles only. This is also the point of maximum spark retard from normal ignition timing. During normal city operation, the delay is less which results in normal advance during the normal city operation mode. Spark timing advanced over normal ignition timing occurs when there is no delay in shutting-off the primary current.

Existing components are utilized to provide input to the electronic decoder to further identify engine operating conditions which influence timing for any operating mode.

Engine coolant temperature is sensed indirectly at the EGR on/off solenoid. This solenoid valve is controlled by the electronic fuel injection system electronic control unit (ECU). Engine coolant temperature is an input to the ECU on all EFI equipped vehicles. On California vehicles, the ESS circuit to the EGR solenoid activates before the solenoid. On all except California vehicles, the ESS circuit to the EGR solenoid is activated after the solenoid.

The EFI ECU sends a signal to the EGR solenoid when the engine is cold through the solenoid windings to ground and closing the valve and shutting off EGR. There are approximately 12 volts across the solenoid when the engine is cold. On California vehicles, there are approximately 12 volts at the decoder when the engine is cold. On all except California vehicles, there is a ground potential at the decoder on cold engines. The decoder recognizes the difference in voltage and processes it as an input to retard the spark from normal ignition timing on California vehicles. Spark is not retarded on cold engine on all except California vehicles.

When the engine warms up, the ECU signal to the EGR solenoid is terminated to open the EGR valve. There is now a ground potential on warm engine on all vehicles, just like there was on all vehicles except California models. Therefore, the spark is not retarded from normal spark timing.

Diagnosis of the Electronic Spark Selection (ESS) system must be accomplished through the use of a special tester, tool No. J-24642.

1977–83 High Energy Ignition System (H.E.I.)

DESCRIPTION

NOTE: On Buick and Pontiac Turbo models and 1980 Pontiac 301 4 Bbl. E/C engine H.E.I. service procedures, refer to this section for diagnosis. For Electronic Spark Control (ESC)

diagnosis, refer to Buick car chapter Turbocharger Section.

The H.E.I. system, Figs. 1, 2 and 3, utilizes an all-electronic module, pickup coil and timer core in place of the conventional ignition points and condenser (the condenser is used for noise suppression only). Point pitting and

rubbing block wear resulting in retarded ignition timing, are eliminated.

The magnetic pickup consists of a rotating timer core attached to the distributor shaft, a stationary pole piece, permanent magnet and pickup coil.

When the distributor shaft rotates, the teeth of the timer core line up and pass the teeth of the pole piece inducing voltage in the

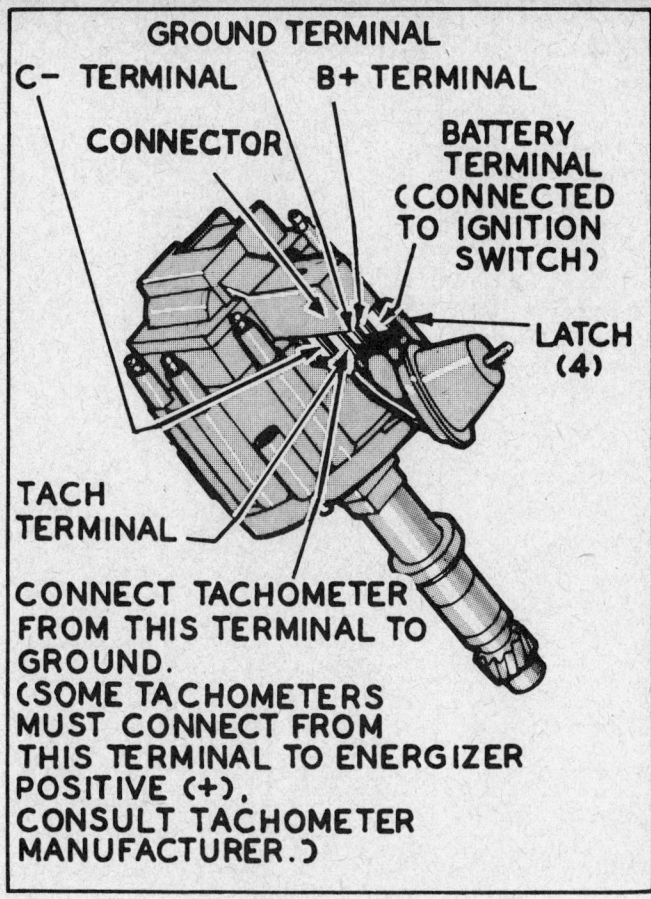

Fig. 1 H.E.I. distributor external components. Except units with external coil

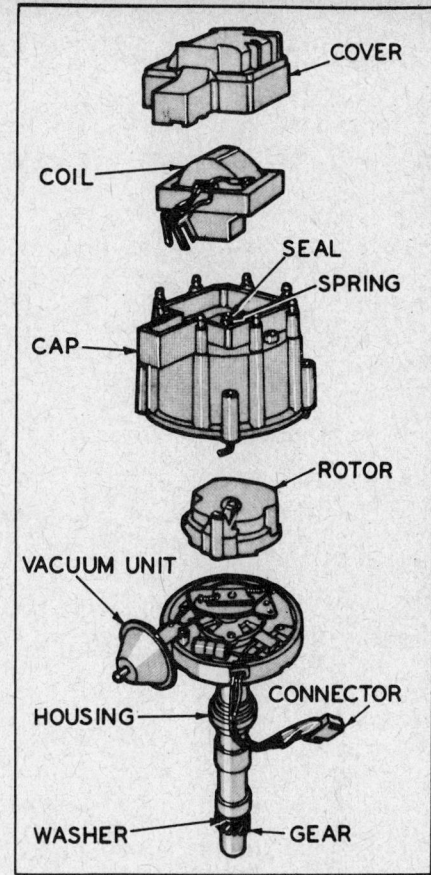

Fig. 2 H.E.I. distributor internal components. Except units with external coil

pickup coil which signals the all-electronic module to open the ignition coil primary circuit. Maximum inductance occurs at the moment the timer core teeth are lined up with the teeth on the pole piece. At the instant the timer core teeth start to pass the pole teeth, the primary current decreases and a high voltage is induced in the ignition coil secondary winding and is directed through the rotor and high voltage leads to fire the spark plugs.

NOTE: Since this is a full 12 volt system it does not require a resistance wire.

The vacuum diaphragm is connected by linkage to the pole piece. When the diaphragm moves against spring pressure it rotates the pole piece allowing the poles to advance relative to the timer core. The timer core is rotated about the shaft by conventional advance weights, thus providing centrifugal advance.

CAUTION: Never connect a wire directly between the "Tach" terminal, Figs. 1 and 3 of the distributor connector and the ground since this will damage the electronic circuitry of the module.

A convenient tachometer connection is incorporated in the wiring connector on the side of the distributor, Figs. 1 and 3. However due to its transistorized design, the high energy ignition system will not trigger some models of engine tachometers.

NOTE: A diagnostic connector is used on some 1977–80 vehicles. This connector is located in the engine compartment on the left front fender or skirt and can be identified by its bright orange color. On vehicles equipped with this connector, a tachometer may be connected between terminals 6 and G.

CAUTION: When using a timing light to adjust ignition timing, the connection should be made at the No. 1 spark plug. Forcing foreign objects through the boot at the No. 1 terminal of the distributor cap will damage the boot and could cause engine misfiring.

The spark plug boot has been designed to form a tight seal around the spark plug and should be twisted ½ turn before removal.

Electronic Spark Timing (EST) System

This system is used on some 1980 GM models and can be identified by the addition of a four-wire distributor connector. The H.E.I. distributor used in this system is a modified unit and does not have a vacuum advance unit or centrifugal weights. The electronic module has seven pins. A spark shield is used under the rotor to protect the electronic circuits from false impulses.

The EST system consists of a digital computer (ECM) and engine sensors. EST controls the ignition timing in relation to crankshaft position and spark dwell. Crankshaft position is determined by distributor reference pulses received from the pick-up coil. Engine timing advance is determined by the engine speed and its load. This advance is then modified by the engine coolant temperature during starting, the actual engine coolant temperature, the barometric pressure, manifold pressure and throttle switch.

The following input signals determine the spark advance signal to the distributor:
a. System power.
b. Ignition on signal.
c. Engine crank signal.
d. Throttle switch.
e. Distributor references pulses.
f. Manifold absolute pressure (MAP).
g. Ambient pressure.
h. Engine coolant temperature.

SYSTEM DIAGNOSIS

1980 Units with EST

NOTE: For ignition system diagnosis, refer to "1981–83 High Energy Ignition With Electronic Spark Timing (HEI-EST) System" under System Diagnosis. For EST diagnosis, use the following procedure.

1. With engine idling, check voltage output terminal of MAP sensor as vacuum hose is disconnected and reconnected several times.
2. If no sensor output change is indicated, inspect MAP hose for leakage or obstructions.
3. If output sensor change is indicated:
   a. Disconnect 4-terminal connector at distributor. Do not ground "Test" lead.
   b. With engine idling, connect a jumper wire between teminals "A" and "B" in distributor side of EST connector.
   c. Connect a test light from B+ supply to terminal "C" in distributor side of EST connector.
4. If engine stops running, check for an open or grounded lead to terminal "A" in distributor side of EST connector. If lead is OK, replace EST (HEI) module.
5. If engine continues running and test light is on, check for ground in lead to terminal "C" in distributor side of EST connector.
6. If engine continues running and test light is off, remove jumper wire between terminals "A" and "B" in distributor side of EST connector:
   a. If engine continues running, check for open circuit to terminal "C", or short between terminals "A" and "B" in distributor side of EST connector.
   b. If engine stops running, check for open or short circuits or grounding on each of the leads from the ECM to the 4-terminal EST connector. Also check EST lead to ESC control, is used. If harness is OK, replace ECM.

1977–83 Units With Internal Coil Exc. 1980 Units with EST

Refer to H.E.I. diagnosis charts, Figs. 4 and 5, for diagnosis procedures.

1977–83 Units with External Coil

With the wiring connector properly attached to connector at side of distributor cap and all the spark plug leads properly connected at plugs and at distributor terminals. Proceed as follows:

Engine Will Not Start

1. Connect voltmeter between "BAT" terminal lead on distributor connector and ground and turn on ignition switch.
2. If voltage is zero, there is an open circuit between the distributor and the bulkhead connector; or between the bulkhead connector and the ignition switch; or between the ignition switch and the starter solenoid. Repair as required.
3. If reading is battery voltage, hold one spark plug lead with insulated pliers approximately 1/4 inch away from a dry area of engine block and crank engine. If a spark is visible, the distributor has been eliminated as source of trouble. Check spark plugs and fuel system.
4. If there is no visible spark, perform the "Component Checkout" and proceed as described further on.

Engine Starts But Runs Rough

1. Check for proper fuel delivery to carburetor.
2. Check all vacuum hoses for leakage.
3. Visually inspect and listen for sparks jumping to ground.
4. Check ignition timing.
5. Check centrifugal advance mechanism for proper operation.
6. Remove spark plugs and check for un-

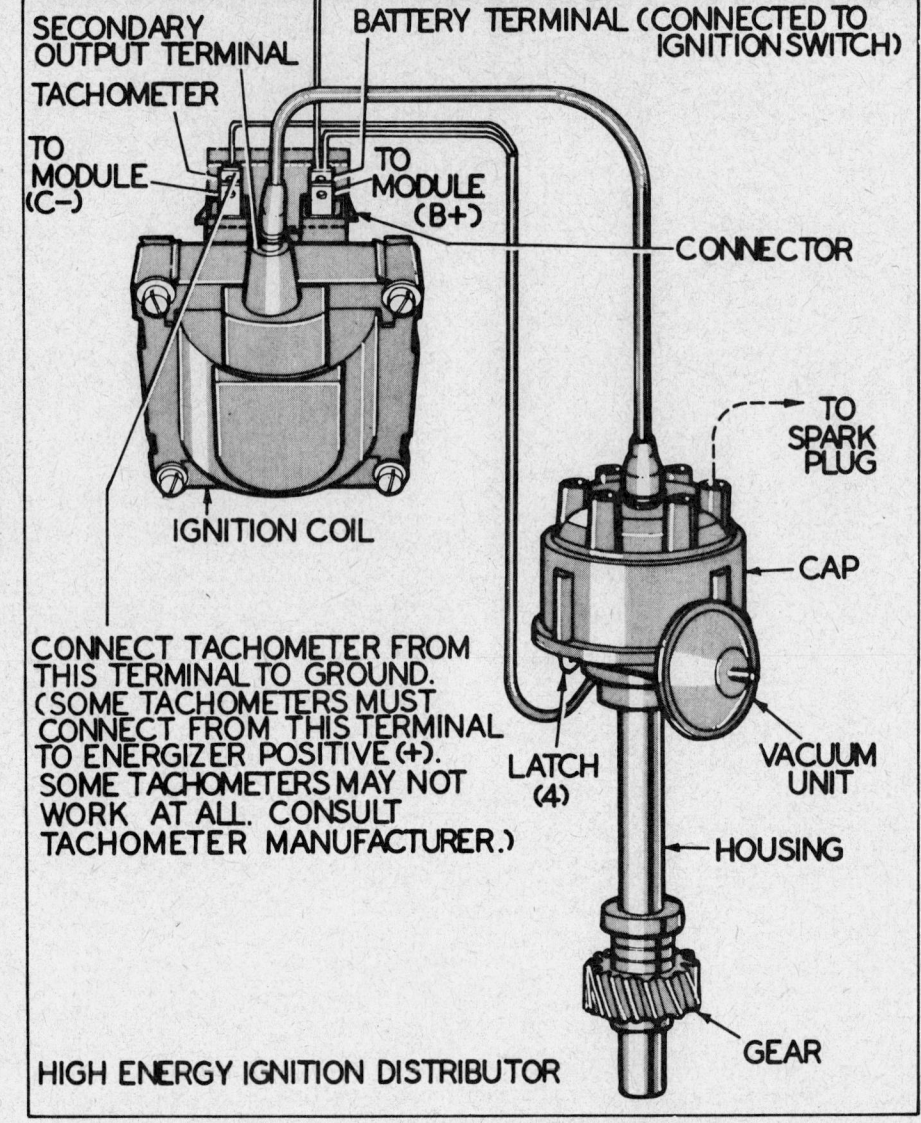

CONNECT TACHOMETER FROM THIS TERMINAL TO GROUND. (SOME TACHOMETERS MUST CONNECT FROM THIS TERMINAL TO ENERGIZER POSITIVE (+). SOME TACHOMETERS MAY NOT WORK AT ALL. CONSULT TACHOMETER MANUFACTURER.)

HIGH ENERGY IGNITION DISTRIBUTOR

Fig. 3 H.E.I. distributor components. 1977–83 Inline 4 & 6 cyl. units with external coil

usual defects, such as very wide gap, abnormal fouling, cracked insulators (inside and out), etc.
7. If no defects are found, perform the "Component Checkout" procedure as described below.

Component Checkout

1. Remove cap and coil assembly.
2. Inspect cap, coil and rotor for spark arcover.
3. On V6 and V8 engines:
   a. Connect ohmmeter, Fig. 6, step 1. If ohmmeter reading is other than zero or very near to zero, the ignition coil must be replaced.
   b. If no ohmmeter reading was observed in step 1, reconnect ohmmeter both ways, Fig. 6, step 2. If both ohmmeter readings are infinite on high scale, replace ignition coil.
4. On inline 4 and 6 cylinder engines:
   a. Connect ohmmeter, Fig. 7, step 1. If reading is not infinite, replace coil.
   b. Connect ohmmeter, Fig. 7, step 2. If reading is not zero or near zero, replace coil.
   c. Connect ohmmeter, Fig. 7, step 3. If reading is infinite, replace coil.

5. Connect an external vacuum source to the vacuum advance unit. Replace vacuum unit if inoperative.
6. If vacuum unit is operating properly, connect ohmmeter, Fig. 8, step 1. If ohmmeter reading on middle scale is not infinite at all times, pick-up coil must be replaced.
7. With ohmmeter connected, Fig. 8, step 2, reading should be within 500 to 1500 ohms.

NOTE: Tester J-24624 is required to test the module. If this tester is not available, and malfunction still exists after performing the above checks, replace module.

DISTRIBUTOR, REPLACE

Except Chevette

Removal

1. Disconnect electrical connectors from distributor cap. On Cadillac models with fuel injection, disconnect speed sensor connector at distributor trigger. Remove

ENGINE CRANKS, BUT WILL NOT START

NOTE: IF A TACHOMETER IS CONNECTED TO THE TACHOMETER TERMINAL, DISCONNECT IT BEFORE PROCEEDING WITH THE TEST.

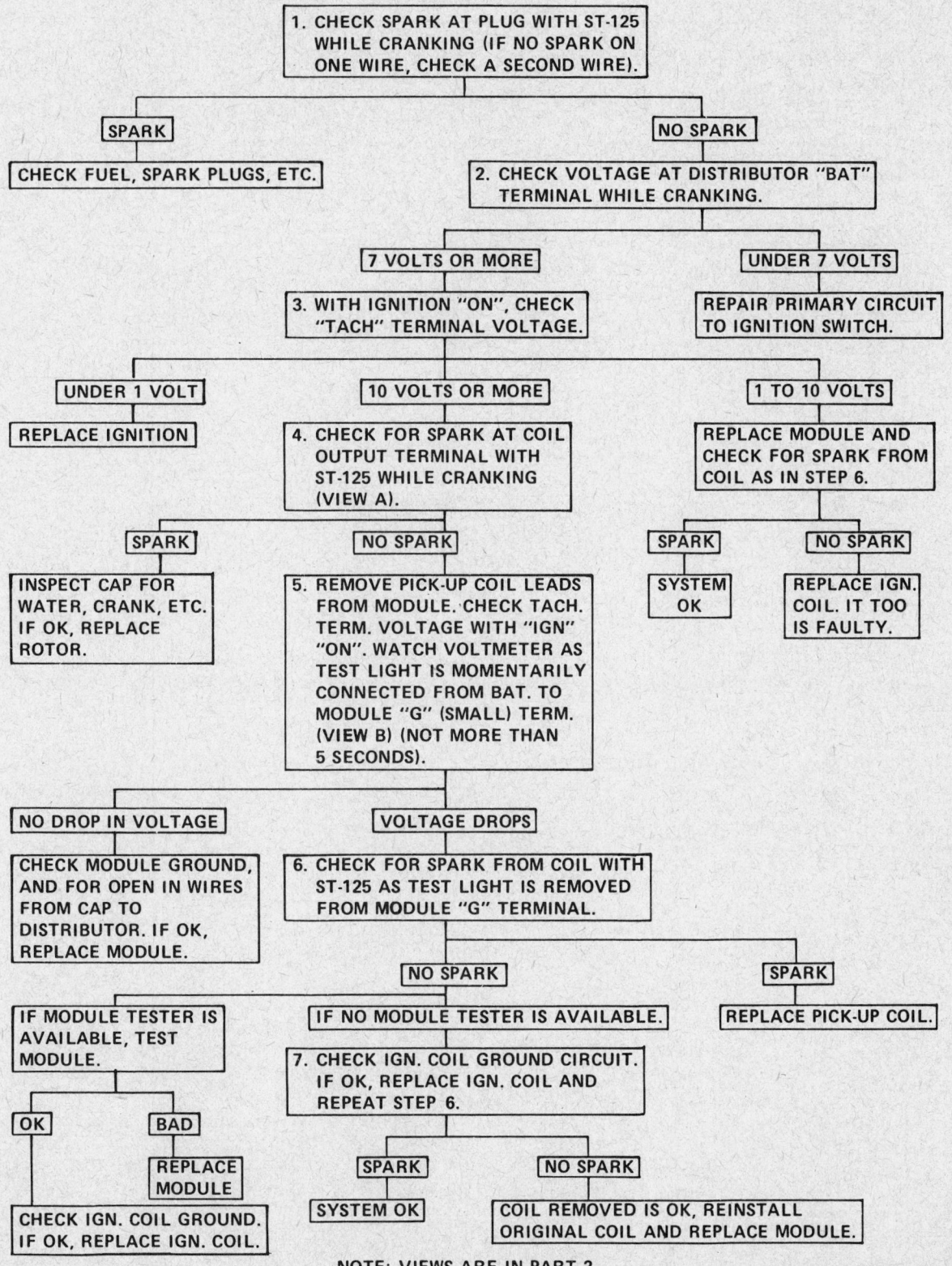

NOTE: VIEWS ARE IN PART 2.

Fig. 4   H.E.I. ignition system diagnosis chart (part 1 of 2). 1977–83 except units with external coil or 1980 units with EST

ELECTRONIC IGNITION SYSTEMS

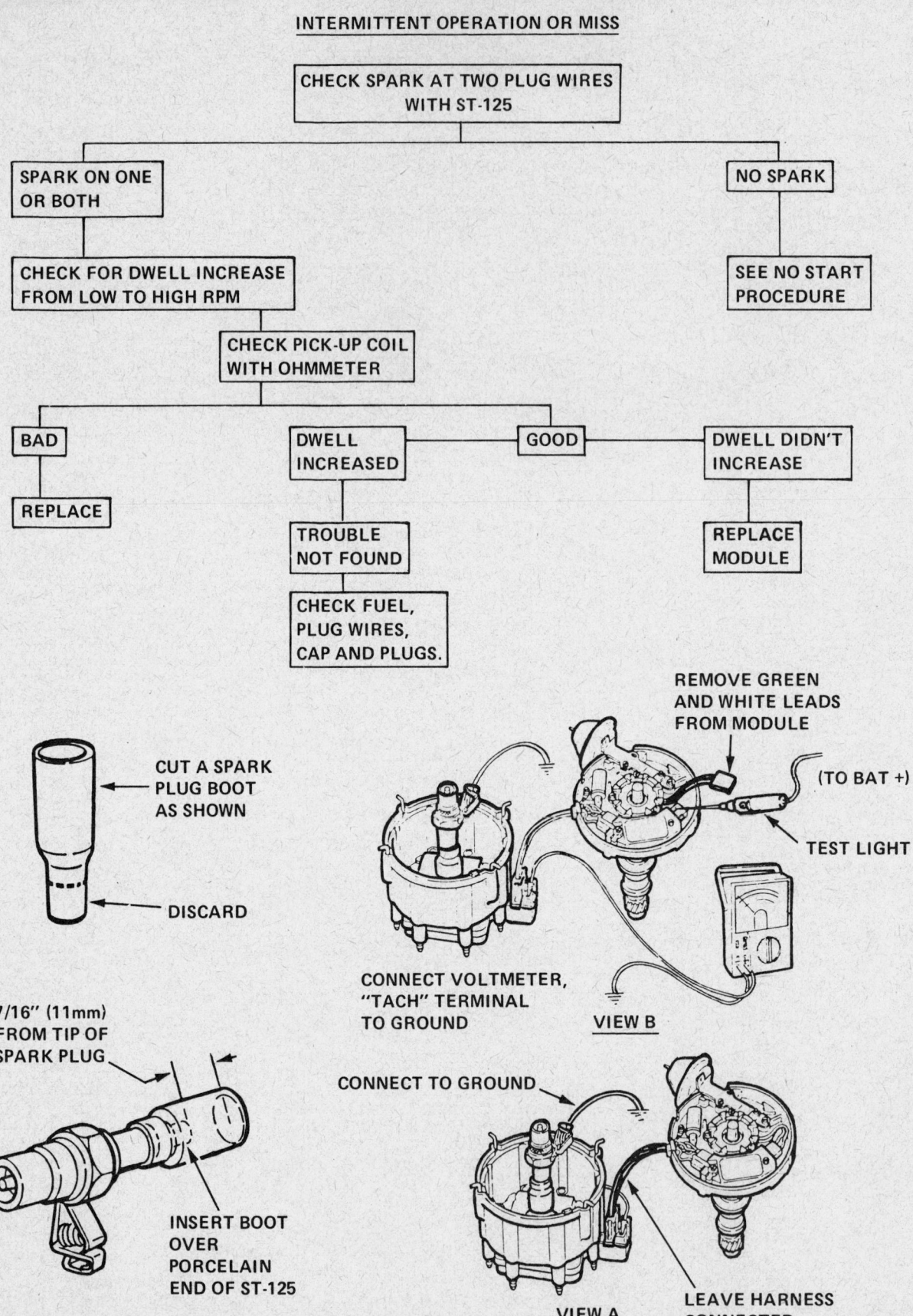

INTERMITTENT OPERATION OR MISS

CHECK SPARK AT TWO PLUG WIRES WITH ST-125

SPARK ON ONE OR BOTH

NO SPARK

CHECK FOR DWELL INCREASE FROM LOW TO HIGH RPM

SEE NO START PROCEDURE

CHECK PICK-UP COIL WITH OHMMETER

BAD

REPLACE

DWELL INCREASED

GOOD

DWELL DIDN'T INCREASE

REPLACE MODULE

TROUBLE NOT FOUND

CHECK FUEL, PLUG WIRES, CAP AND PLUGS.

CUT A SPARK PLUG BOOT AS SHOWN

DISCARD

7/16" (11mm) FROM TIP OF SPARK PLUG

INSERT BOOT OVER PORCELAIN END OF ST-125

REMOVE GREEN AND WHITE LEADS FROM MODULE

(TO BAT +)

TEST LIGHT

CONNECT VOLTMETER, "TACH" TERMINAL TO GROUND

VIEW B

CONNECT TO GROUND

VIEW A

LEAVE HARNESS CONNECTED

Fig. 5 H.E.I. ignition system diagnosis chart (part 2 of 2). 1977–83 except units with external coil or 1980 units with EST

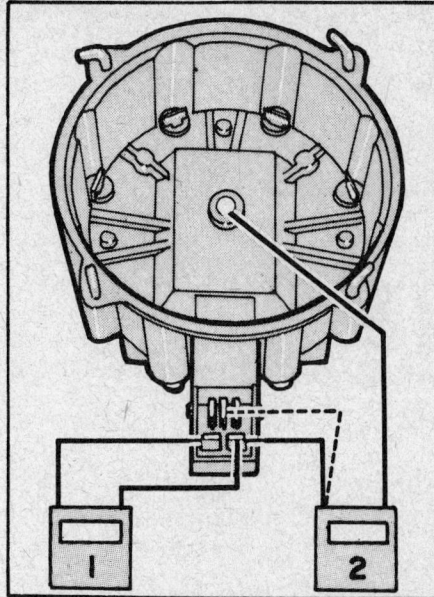

Fig. 6 H.E.I. distributor ignition coil ohmmeter test. Except units with external coil

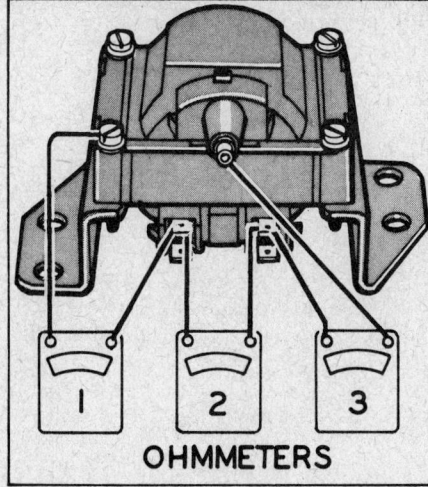

OHMMETERS

Fig. 7 H.E.I. distributor ignition coil ohmmeter test. 1977–83 Inline 4 & 6 cyl. units with external coil

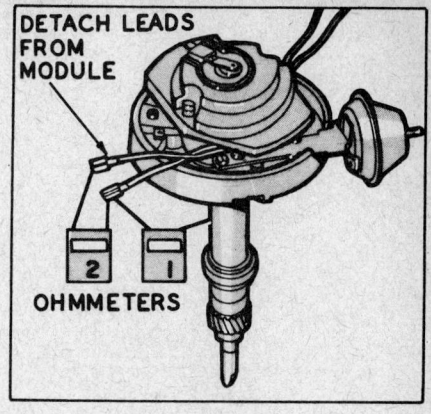

OHMMETERS

Fig. 8 Distributor pickup coil ohmmeter test

cap and position aside.
2. Remove vacuum advance hose and mark position of distributor in engine.
3. Mark position of rotor on distributor housing, then remove distributor hold-down bolt and clamp.
4. Pull distributor up until rotor just stops turning and mark this position on housing. Remove distributor from engine.

Installation

1. If engine was not cranked after distributor was removed from engine, proceed as follows:
   a. Position rotor to align with mark made on housing in step 4 of Removal procedure.
   b. Slide distributor into engine, aligning distributor housing to engine mark made in step 2 of Removal procedure. With distributor fully seated, rotor should align with mark made on housing in step 3 of Removal procedure.

c. Install distributor cap, connect electrical connectors and attach vacuum advance hose.
   d. Adjust ignition timing to specifications found in the individual car chapters.
2. If engine was cranked after distributor was removed from engine, proceed as follows:
   a. Remove No. 1 spark plug and crank engine until compression pressure is felt in No. 1 cylinder. Slowly rotate engine until Top Dead Center (TDC) is indicated.
   b. Turn rotor to a position just ahead of the No. 1 distributor cap terminal.
   c. Slide distributor into engine. Install distributor cap, connect electrical connectors and attach vacuum advance hose.
   d. Adjust ignition timing to specifications found in the individual car chapters.

NOTE: When using a timing light to adjust ignition timing, the connection should be

made at the No. 1 spark plug. Forcing foreign objects through the boot at the No. 1 terminal of the distributor cap will damage the boot and could cause engine misfiring.

Chevette

1. On models equipped with A/C, disconnect wire connector from compressor, then remove through bolt, two adjusting bolts, and upper compressor mounting bracket.
2. Raise vehicle, then remove two retaining bolts and position lower compressor bracket outward for clearance.
3. On all models, remove air cleaner and distributor cap, position distributor cap out of way.
4. Remove ignition coil cover and mounting bracket bolts.
5. Disconnect distributor primary lead from coil terminal.
6. Remove fuel pump and push rod.

NOTE: Push rod must be installed in same direction as removed.

7. Scribe a mark on engine in line with rotor, noting approximate position of distributor housing in relation to engine.
8. Remove distributor hold down bolt and clamp and remove distributor.

NOTE: Avoid rotating engine while distributor is removed.

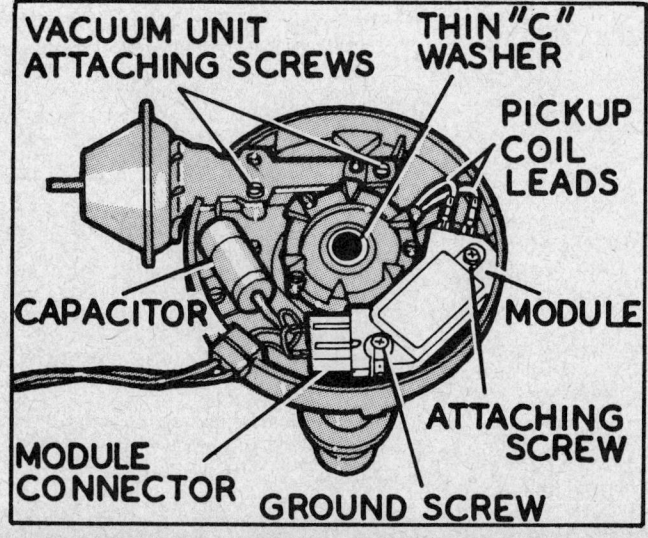

VACUUM UNIT ATTACHING SCREWS
THIN "C" WASHER
PICKUP COIL LEADS
CAPACITOR
MODULE
MODULE CONNECTOR
ATTACHING SCREW
GROUND SCREW

Fig. 9 H.E.I. distributor component replacement

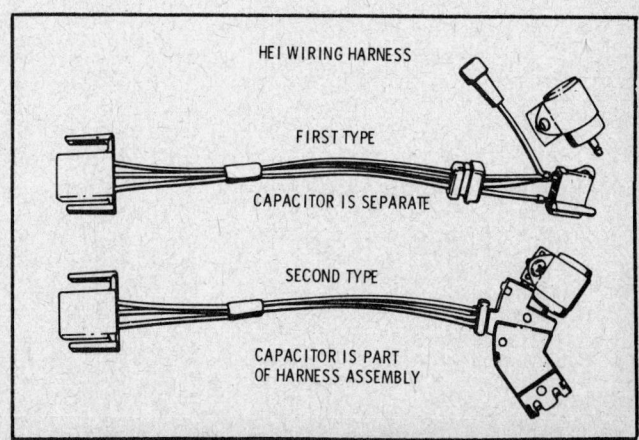

HEI WIRING HARNESS
FIRST TYPE
CAPACITOR IS SEPARATE
SECOND TYPE
CAPACITOR IS PART OF HARNESS ASSEMBLY

Fig. 10 H.E.I. wiring harness indentification

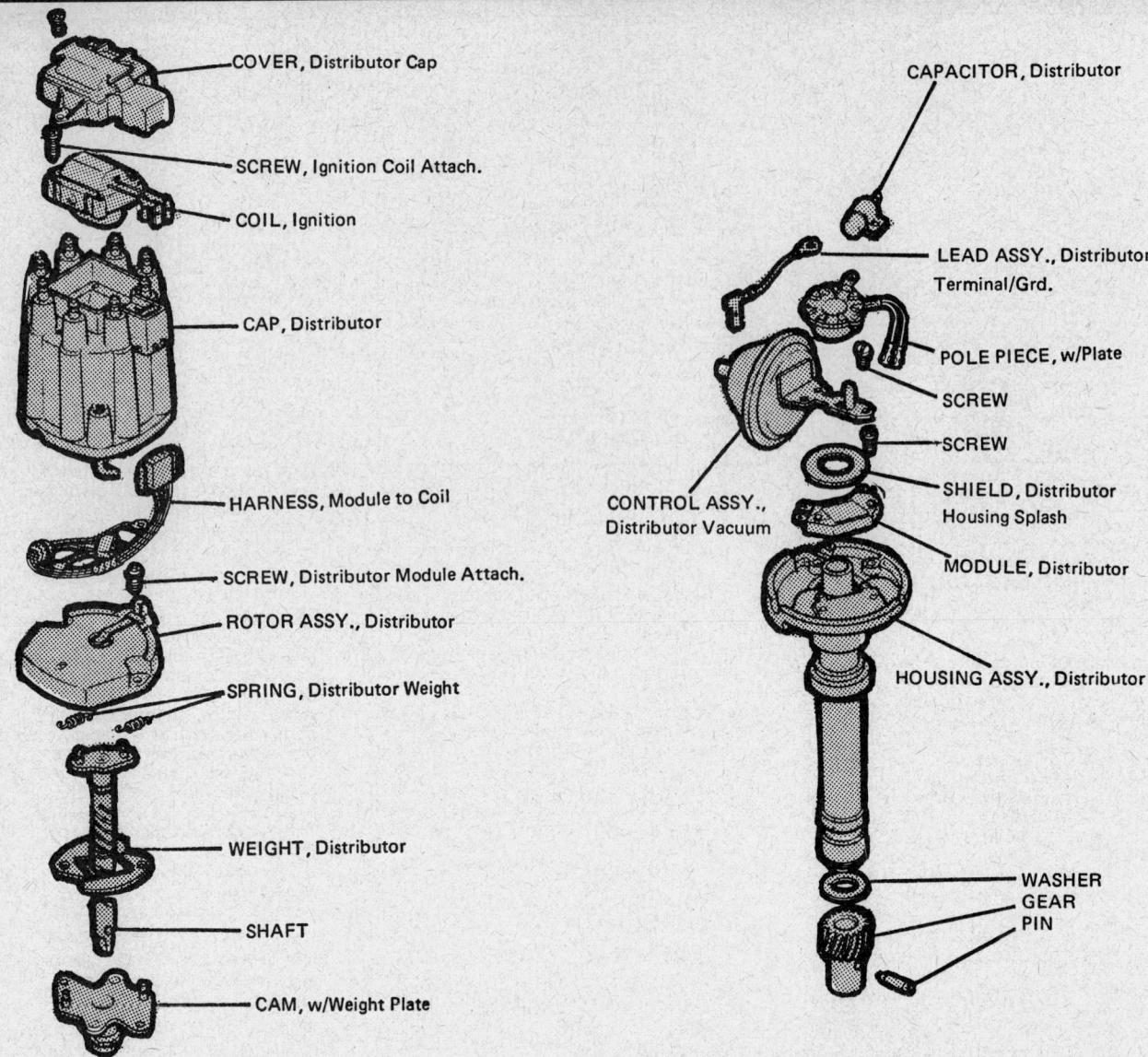

Fig. 11 Exploded view of H.E.I. distributor (Typical). All except Cadillac with fuel injecction

9. Reverse procedure to install, then adjust ignition timing.

NOTE: When using a timing light to adjust ignition timing, the connection should be made at the No. 1 spark plug. Forcing foreign objects through the boot at the No. 1 terminal of the distributor cap will damage the boot and could cause engine misfiring.

COMPONENTS, REPLACE

Ignition Coil Replacement, Fig. 2

Except Units With External Coil
1. Remove screws holding distributor cover to distributor cap and remove distributor cover.
2. Remove four screws holding coil to cap.
3. Remove harness connector and battery wire from side of distributor cap.
4. Push coil leads out of position in cap and remove coil.
5. Reverse procedure to install.

1977 Inline 4 & 6 Cyl. Unit With External Coil
1. Disconnect ignition switch to coil lead from coil.
2. Disconnect coil to distributor leads from coil.
3. Remove coil to engine retaining screws and remove coil.
4. Reverse procedure to install.

Module Replacement, Fig. 9

1. Disconnect wiring harness connector at side of distributor cap and remove distributor cap.
2. Remove rotor and disconnect wires from module terminals.
3. Remove two mounting screws and remove module.

NOTE: Two types of H.E.I. wiring harness are used, Fig. 10. The second type is a wiring harness, connector and capacitor which is serviced as an assembly.

4. Reverse procedure to install.

CAUTION: At installation, coat bottom of new module with dielectric lubricant (furnished with new module) to aid in heat transfer into distributor housing. Failure to apply lubricant will cause excessive heat at module and premature module failure.

Pole Piece, Magnet or Pick-Up Coil Replacement, Fig. 9

Removal
1. With distributor removed, disconnect wires at module terminals.
2. Remove roll pin from drive gear by driving out with 1/8 inch diameter drift punch.
3. Remove gear, shim and the tanged washer from distributor shaft. Remove any burrs that may have been caused by removal of pin.
4. Remove distributor shaft from housing.
5. Remove washer from upper end of distributor housing.

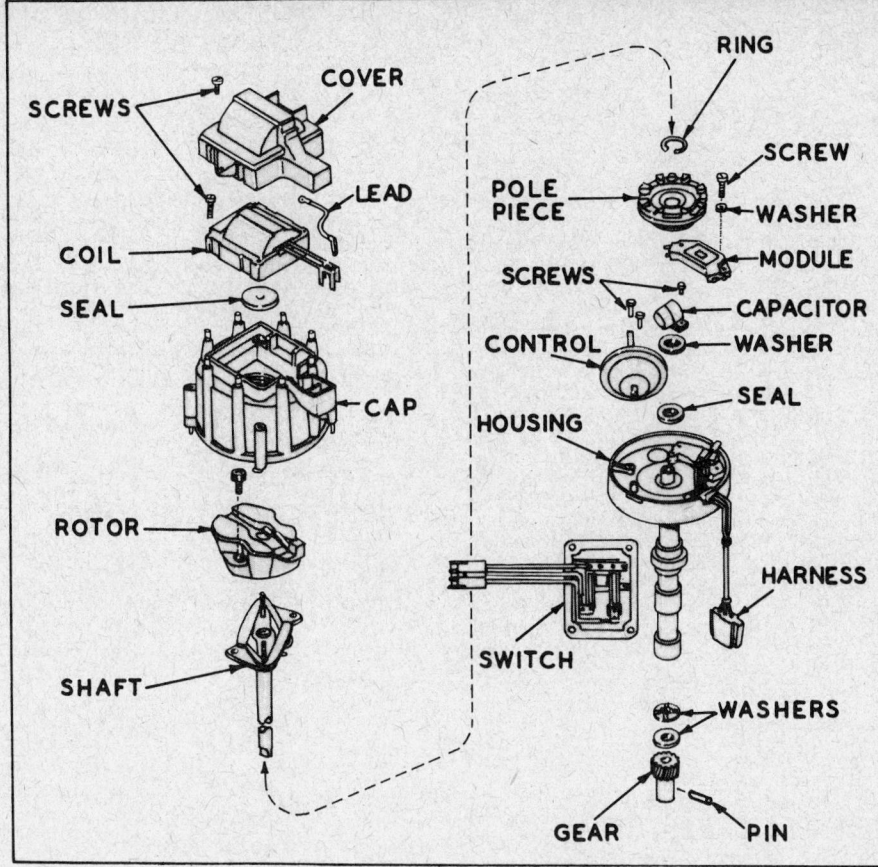

Fig. 12 Exploded view of H.E.I. distributor. Cadillac with fuel injection

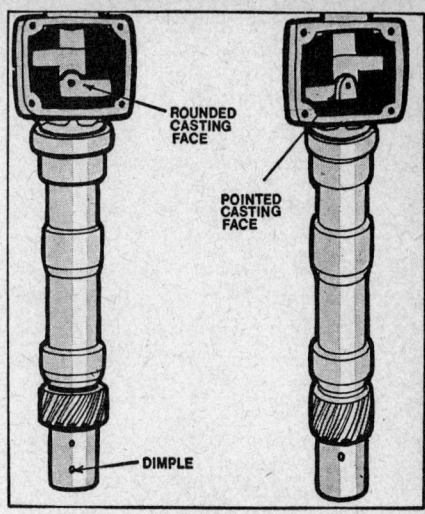

Fig. 13 Speed sensor location

NOTE: Bushings in the housing are not serviceable.

6. Remove three screws securing pole piece to housing and remove pole piece, magnet and pick-up coil.

Installation
1. Install pick-up coil, magnet and pole piece and loosely install three screws holding pole piece.
2. With washer installed at top of housing, install distributor shaft and rotate to check for proper clearance between pole piece teeth and timer core teeth.
3. If necessary, realign pole piece to provide adequate clearance and secure properly.
4. Install tanged washer, shim and drive gear (teeth up) to bottom of shaft. Align drive gear and install new roll pin.

DISTRIBUTOR SERVICE

Disassembly, Figs. 11 & 12

NOTE: Some of the following steps do not apply to the Toronado MISAR system or Cadillac DEFI or units with EST systems.

1. Remove distributor.
2. Remove rotor.
3. Remove advance springs and weights (if equipped).
4. Remove module retaining screws and move module to a position where connector may be removed.

5. Remove wires from module terminals.
6. Support distributor gear so that distributor shaft will not be damaged, then remove roll pin by driving it out with a punch.
7. Remove gear, shim and tanged washer from shaft. Remove any burrs that may have been caused by removal of roll pin.

NOTE: Some distributors do not use a shim or tanged washer.

8. On Cadillac models with EFI:
   a. Remove the four screws retaining speed sensor, then remove speed sensor and gasket, Fig. 13.
   b. Remove plug from opposite side of sensor housing on distributor.
   c. Remove roll pin from magnet assembly.
9. Remove distributor shaft and magnet assembly.
10. Remove pole piece retaining screws, pole piece, magnet and pick-up coil.
11. Remove lock ring from top of housing, pick-up coil retainer and felt washer.
12. Remove vacuum advance unit (if equipped).
13. Remove capacitor and wiring harness from distributor housing.

Assembly, Figs. 11 & 12
1. Install vacuum advance unit (if used) and secure with two screws.
2. Place felt washer over lubricant reservoir at top of housing.
3. Position pick up coil retainer onto housing with vacuum advance arm over actu-

ating pin of vacuum advance mechanism and secure with lock ring.
4. Install pick up coil magnet and pole piece. Loosely install the three retaining screws.
5. Install distributor shaft and rotate to check for even clearance all around between pole piece and shaft projections.
6. Move pole piece to provide even clearance and secure with three retaining screws.
7. On Cadillac models with EFI:
   a. Position distributor shaft so speed sensor rotating magnet can be installed in distributor housing, Fig. 13.
   b. Engage speed sensor rotating magnet on distributor shaft and install shaft into position. Do not install roll pin.
8. Install drive with teeth up onto shaft.

NOTE: Drive gear has a dimple on one side next to drive pin hole. Align drive gear so that dimple is on same side of shaft as the rotor pointer. Temporarily install rotor to ensure correct alignment.

9. Install tanged washer, shim and drive gear, then retain with a new roll pin.
10. On Cadillac models with EFI:
    a. Install speed sensor rotating magnet and retain with new roll pin.
    b. Using a new gasket, position speed sensor onto distributor housing with wiring harness coming out of top of sensor (directly below distributor housing) and retain with four screws.
11. Install capacitor and loosely install retaining screw.
12. Install connector on module with tab on top, then liberally apply silicone grease to bottom of module and install screws.

CAUTION: Failure to apply silicone grease to module will cause excessive heat build-up of module and premature failure.

13. Position wiring harness with grommet in housing notch, then connect pink wire to capacitor stud and black wire to capacitor retaining screw. Tighten screw.
14. Reconnect wires to module, then install centrifugal advance weights and springs.

1980–81 Electronic Module Retard System (EMR)

DESCRIPTION

NOTE: For distributor component diagnosis, distributor replacement, component replacement and distributor service, refer to "1981–83 High Energy Ignition with Electronic Spark Timing (HEI-EST) System" for procedures.

This system is used on early 1980 Oldsmobile models with V8-260 (V.I.N. code F) and V8-307 (V.I.N. code Y), also on Oldsmobile and Pontiac models with V8-350 (V.I.N. code R) and on 1981 Chevrolet V6-229 (V.I.N. code K).

The Electronic Module Retard System (EMR) is comprised of a five terminal ignition module located in the distributor, an EMR vacuum switch and six port Thermal Vacuum Switch (TVS) on Oldsmobile except V8-350 California models and a vacuum operated electrical switch on Chevrolet models. On Oldsmobile and Pontiac V8-350 California models, the EMR function is controlled by the C-4 system Electronic Control Module (ECM).

On Oldsmobile except V8-350 California models, during engine operation below 120° F. the six port TVS directs engine vacuum to the EMR switch, closing the switch contacts. With the EMR vacuum switch contacts closed, the EMR module is grounded and timing is retarded 10° ± 2°. During periods of cold engine operation when engine vacuum drops below 4 in. Hg., the EMR vacuum switch contacts will open, allowing normal timing advance. When engine is operating at normal temperature the TVS is closed, therefore no vacuum reaches the EMR vacuum valve and the engine operates with normal timing advance.

On Chevrolet models, a vacuum operated vacuum switch controls EMR module grounding. When the EMR module is grounded, the timing is retarded a calibrated number of crankshaft degrees. When the retard circuit is opened, the distributor operates in a conventional manner, using vacuum and centrifugal advance mechanisms to control ignition timing.

NOTE: If the EMR module is removed or replaced for any reason, the ignition timing must be checked and reset to specifications as necessary.

SYSTEM DIAGNOSIS

For EMR diagnosis, refer to Figs. 1, 2 and 3. For ignition system diagnosis, refer to "1981–83 High Energy Ignition With Electronic Spark Timing (HEI-EST) System" under System Diagnosis.

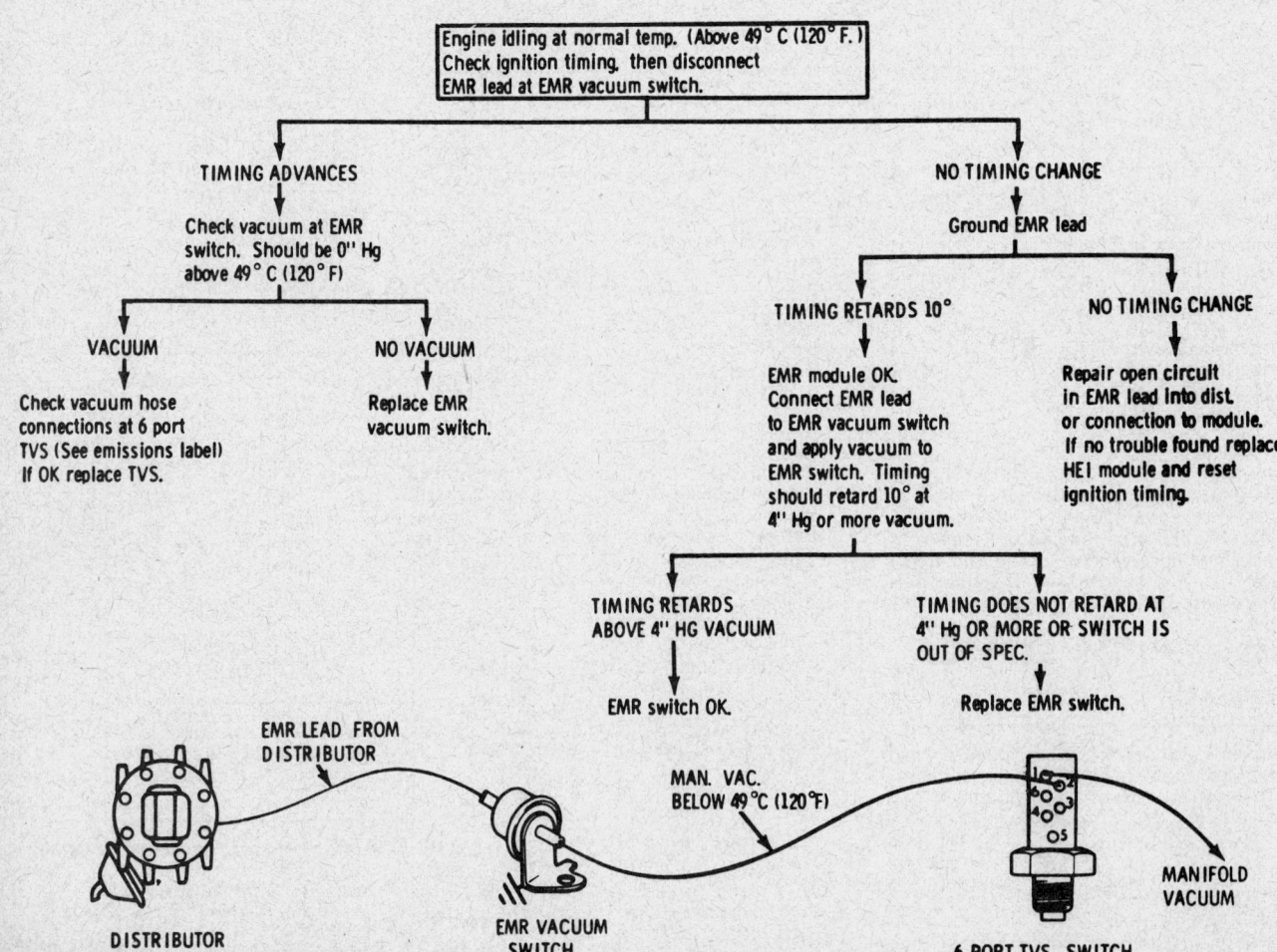

Fig. 1 EMR system diagnosis. 1980 Oldsmobile models exc. V8-350 Calif.

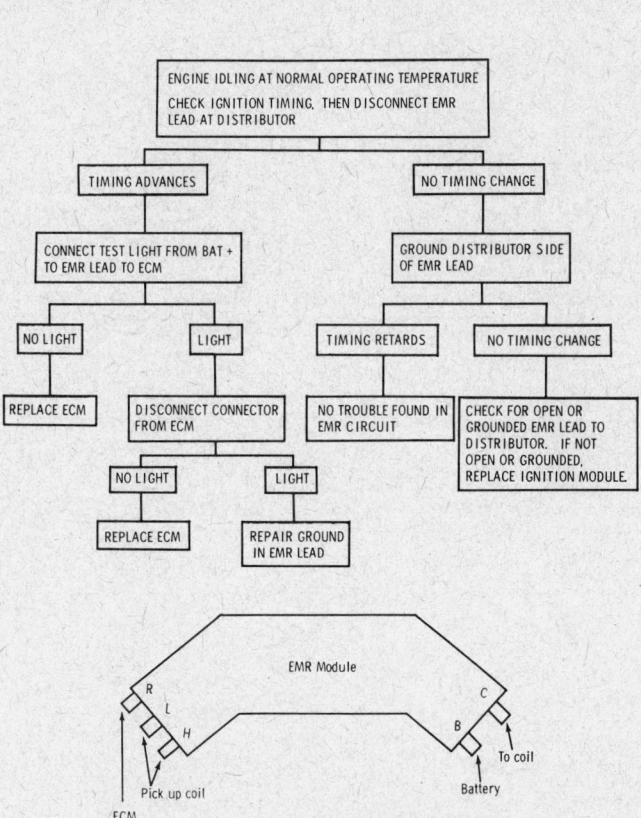

Fig. 2   EMR system diagnosis. 1980 Oldsmobile & Pontiac V8-350 Calif. models

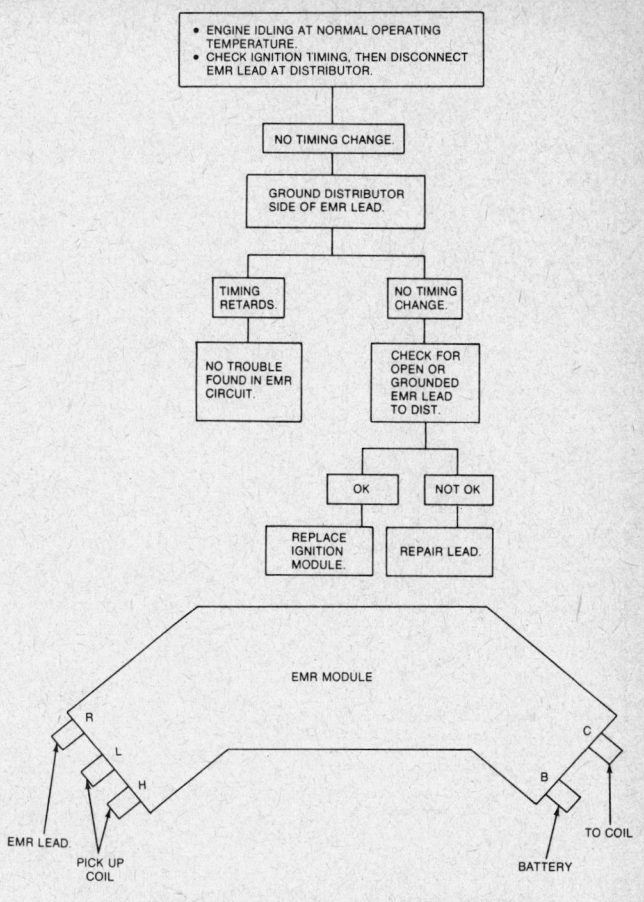

Fig. 3   EMR system diagnosis. 1981 Chevrolet V6-229

1981—83 High Energy Ignition W/ Electronic Spark Timing (HEI-EST) System

DESCRIPTION

The High Energy Ignition System with Electronic Spark Timing (HEI-EST) is used on all 1981–83 GM models except 1981 Chevrolet V6-229 (V.I.N. code K), which uses Electronic Module Retard (EMR).

The HEI-EST system consists of an electronic distributor, Figs. 1 and 2, with the ignition coil mounted on the distributor cap on 6 and 8 cylinder models, or with an externally mounted coil on 4 cylinder models. All spark timing changes in the HEI-EST system are performed electronically by the Electronic Control Module (ECM). The ECM monitors information from various engine sensors, determines the correct spark timing and signals the distributor to change timing as necessary. A secondary spark advance system is incorporated into the system to signal the ignition module in case of ECM failure. The HEI-EST system does not use vacuum or mechanical advance.

On some HEI-EST systems, Electronic Spark Control (ESC) is used to retard spark advance when detonation occurs. The spark is retarded for 20 seconds, then the spark control returns to EST.

The ESC system consists of three basic components: sensor, distributor and controller. The ESC sensor is an accelerometer or magneto-strictive device, mounted on the engine block. It detects presence, or absence, and intensity of detonation by vibration characteristics of the engine. The sensor's output is an electrical signal which is sent to the controller. A failure of the sensor would allow no retard.

The distributor is an HEI-EST unit with an electronic module modified so that it can respond to ESC controller signal. The command is delayed when detonation is detected, providing the level of retard required. The amount of retard is determined by the severity of detonation.

The ESC controller processes the sensor signal into a command signal to the distributor to adjust spark timing. This is a continuous process monitoring and controlling detonation. The controller is a hard-wired signal processor and amplifier which operates from 6 to 16 volts. Controller failure would be indicated by no ignition, no retard of full retard.

NOTE: Since this is a full 12 volt system, no resistance wire is used. Also, a diagnostic connector is used on some models. This connector is located in the engine compartment on the left side front fender skirt. On vehicles equipped with this connector, a tachometer may be connected between terminals 6 and G.

A tachometer connection is incorporated in the wiring connector on the side of the distributor on 6 and 8 cylinder models, next to the coil battery terminal on Chevette and 1000 models, at the coil brown wire connector on Century, Citation, Cutlass Ciera, Omega,

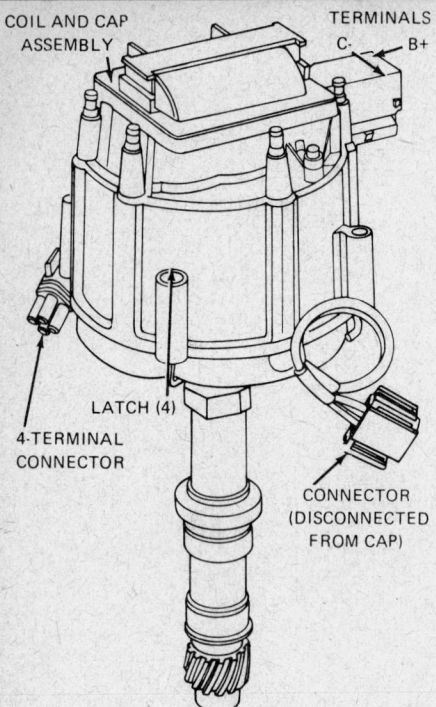

Fig. 1 HEI-EST Distributor with internal coil. 1981–83 models with 6 & 8 cylinder engine

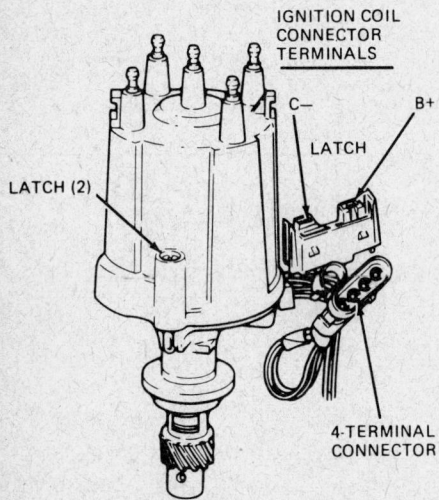

Fig. 2 HEI-EST distributor with external coil. 1981–83 models with 4 cylinder engine

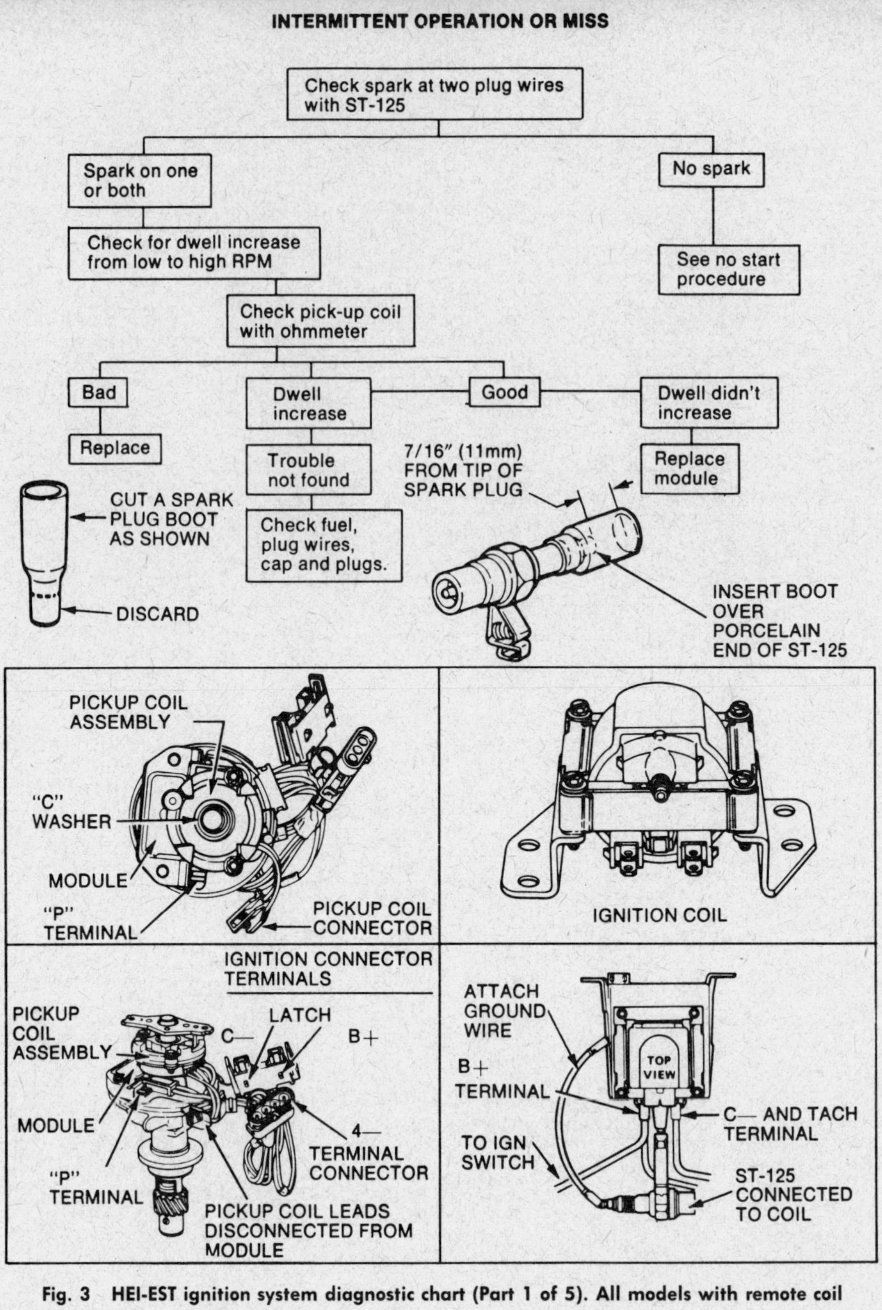

INTERMITTENT OPERATION OR MISS

Check spark at two plug wires with ST-125

- Spark on one or both
  - Check for dwell increase from low to high RPM
    - Check pick-up coil with ohmmeter
      - Bad → Replace
      - Dwell increase → Trouble not found → Check fuel, plug wires, cap and plugs.
      - Good
      - Dwell didn't increase → Replace module
- No spark → See no start procedure

CUT A SPARK PLUG BOOT AS SHOWN — DISCARD

7/16" (11mm) FROM TIP OF SPARK PLUG

INSERT BOOT OVER PORCELAIN END OF ST-125

PICKUP COIL ASSEMBLY
"C" WASHER
MODULE
"P" TERMINAL
PICKUP COIL CONNECTOR

IGNITION COIL

IGNITION CONNECTOR TERMINALS
PICKUP COIL ASSEMBLY
LATCH
C—
B+
MODULE
"P" TERMINAL
PICKUP COIL LEADS DISCONNECTED FROM MODULE
4 TERMINAL CONNECTOR

ATTACH GROUND WIRE
B+ TERMINAL
TOP VIEW
C— AND TACH TERMINAL
TO IGN SWITCH
ST-125 CONNECTED TO COIL

Fig. 3 HEI-EST ignition system diagnostic chart (Part 1 of 5). All models with remote coil

Phoenix, Skylark and 6000 models or at the tach connector taped to the engine wiring harness at the engine compartment side of the firewall on Cavalier, Cimarron, Firenza, 2000 and Skyhawk models. On AMC vehicles with HEI, the tach terminal is located opposite the positive terminal on the ignition coil. If vehicle is not equipped with a tachometer, there is a remote tach terminal located above the heater fan motor housing also.

CAUTION: Never connect a wire directly between the Tach terminal of the distributor connector and ground as this will damage the electronic circuitry of the module. When using a timing light to adjust ignition timing, the

connection should be made at the No. 1 spark plug. Forcing foreign objects through the boot at the No. 1 spark plug terminal will damage the boot and cause engine misfire.

SYSTEM DIAGNOSIS

Refer to HEI diagnosis charts, Figs. 3 thru 22 for diagnosis procedures.

DISTRIBUTOR COMPONENT DIAGNOSIS

Units With Remote Coil

Testing Ignition Coil
1. Connect a suitable ohmmeter as shown in

Fig. 23, step 1, Using the high scale, read ohmmeter. Should read very high or infinite. If not, replace coil.
2. Connect ohmmeter as shown in Fig. 23, step 2. Using the low scale, read ohmmeter. Should read very low or zero. If not, replace coil.
3. Connect ohmmeter as shown in Fig. 23, step 3. Using the high scale, read ohmmeter. Should not read infinite. If it does, replace coil.

Testing Pickup Coil
1. Remove distributor rotor, then disconnect pickup coil leads from module.
2. Connect ohmmeter as shown in Figs. 24 and 25, step 1. Connect a suitable vacuum source to vacuum advance chamber (if equipped) and note ohmmeter reading

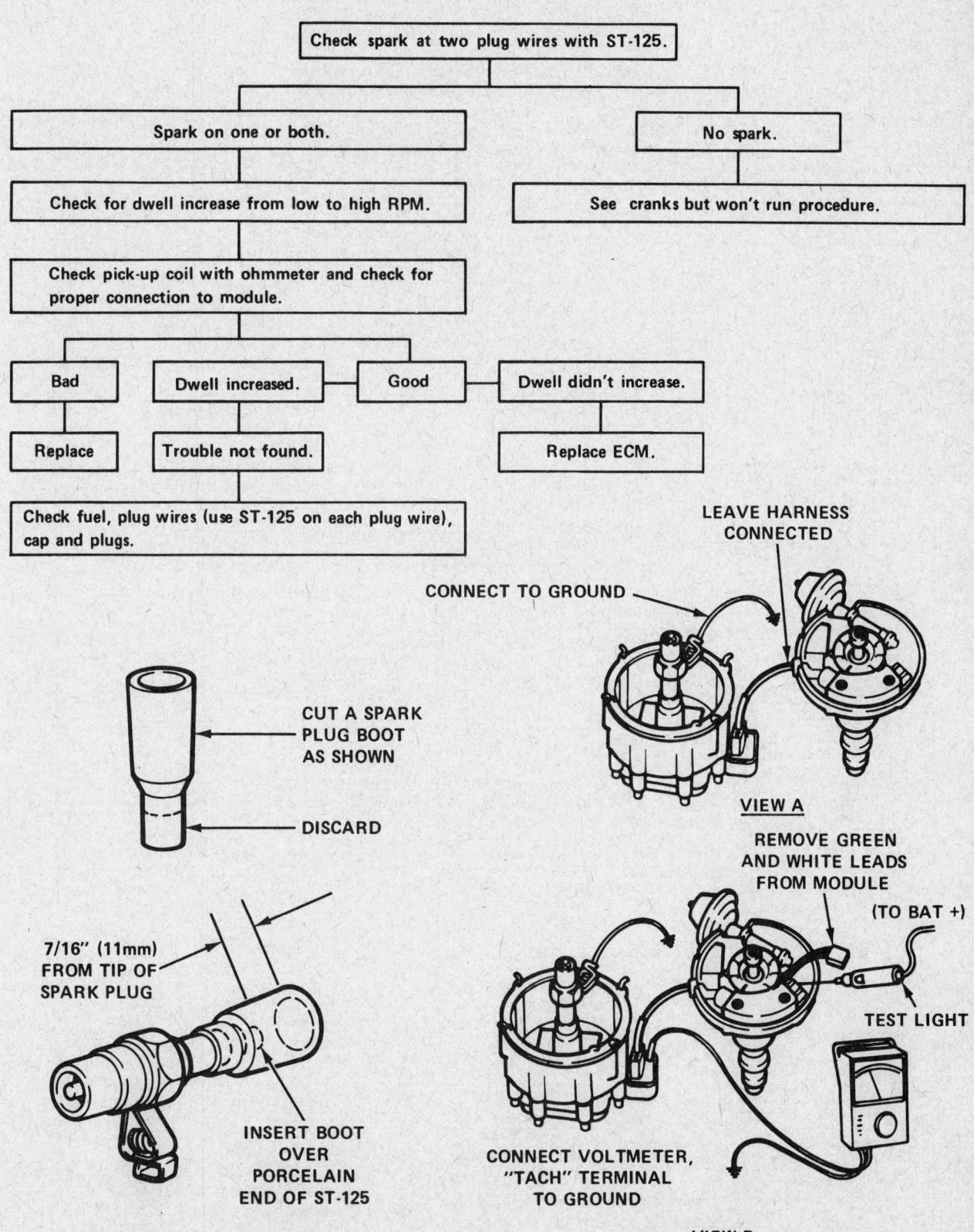

INTERMITTENT OPERATION OR MISS

Check spark at two plug wires with ST-125.

Spark on one or both.

No spark.

Check for dwell increase from low to high RPM.

See cranks but won't run procedure.

Check pick-up coil with ohmmeter and check for proper connection to module.

Bad → Replace

Dwell increased. → Trouble not found.

Good

Dwell didn't increase. → Replace ECM.

Check fuel, plug wires (use ST-125 on each plug wire), cap and plugs.

CUT A SPARK PLUG BOOT AS SHOWN

DISCARD

7/16" (11mm) FROM TIP OF SPARK PLUG

INSERT BOOT OVER PORCELAIN END OF ST-125

LEAVE HARNESS CONNECTED

CONNECT TO GROUND

VIEW A

REMOVE GREEN AND WHITE LEADS FROM MODULE

(TO BAT +)

TEST LIGHT

CONNECT VOLTMETER, "TACH" TERMINAL TO GROUND

VIEW B

Fig. 4   HEI-EST ignition system diagnostic chart (Part 1 of 5). All models with integral coil

ELECTRONIC IGNITION SYSTEMS

ENGINE CRANKS, BUT WILL NOT RUN

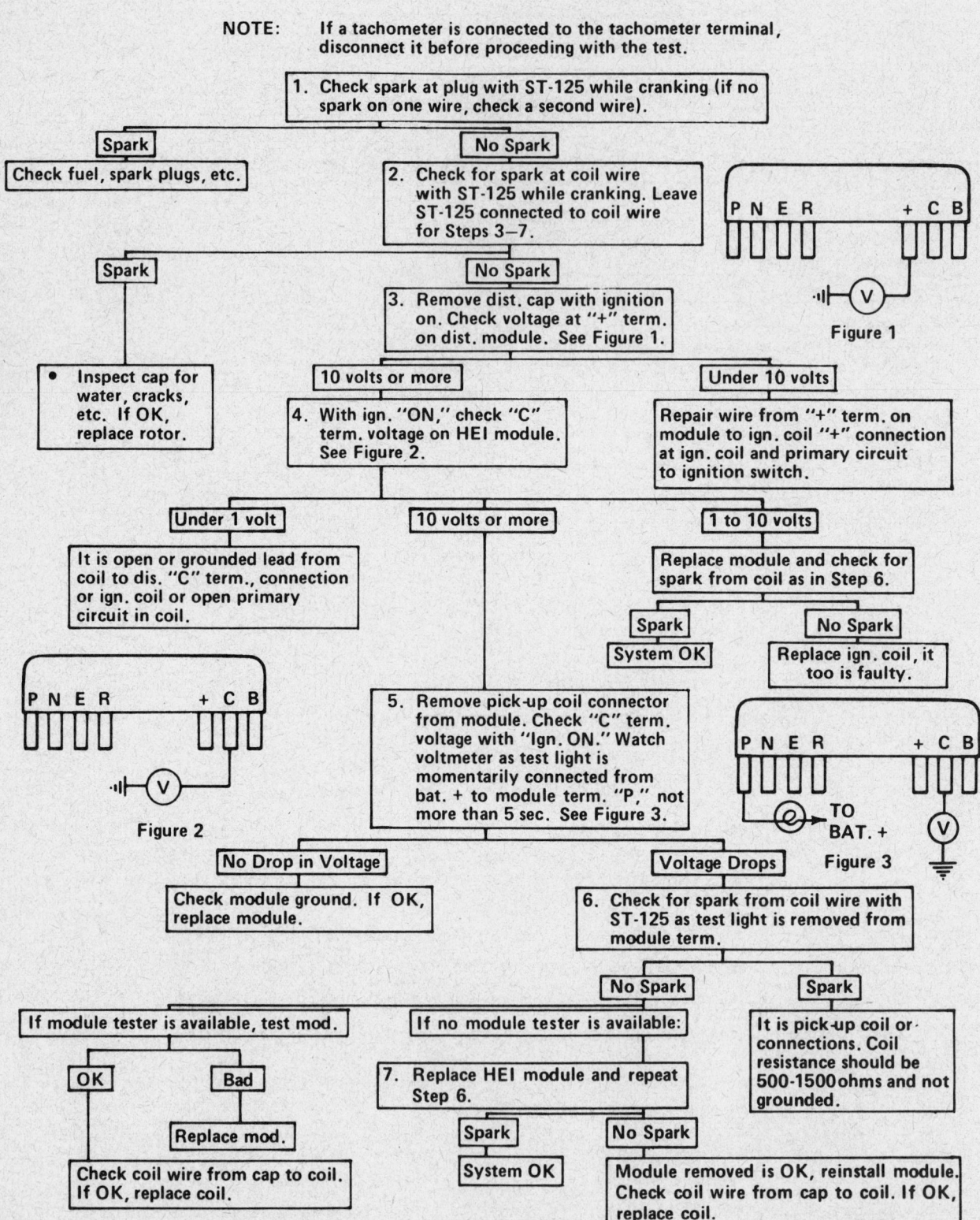

NOTE: If a tachometer is connected to the tachometer terminal, disconnect it before proceeding with the test.

1. Check spark at plug with ST-125 while cranking (if no spark on one wire, check a second wire).

Spark — Check fuel, spark plugs, etc.

No Spark

2. Check for spark at coil wire with ST-125 while cranking. Leave ST-125 connected to coil wire for Steps 3—7.

Figure 1

Spark

No Spark

3. Remove dist. cap with ignition on. Check voltage at "+" term. on dist. module. See Figure 1.

• Inspect cap for water, cracks, etc. If OK, replace rotor.

10 volts or more

4. With ign. "ON," check "C" term. voltage on HEI module. See Figure 2.

Under 10 volts — Repair wire from "+" term. on module to ign. coil "+" connection at ign. coil and primary circuit to ignition switch.

Under 1 volt — It is open or grounded lead from coil to dis. "C" term., connection or ign. coil or open primary circuit in coil.

Figure 2

10 volts or more

1 to 10 volts — Replace module and check for spark from coil as in Step 6.

Spark — System OK

No Spark — Replace ign. coil, it too is faulty.

5. Remove pick-up coil connector from module. Check "C" term. voltage with "Ign. ON." Watch voltmeter as test light is momentarily connected from bat. + to module term. "P," not more than 5 sec. See Figure 3.

Figure 3 — TO BAT. +

No Drop in Voltage — Check module ground. If OK, replace module.

Voltage Drops

6. Check for spark from coil wire with ST-125 as test light is removed from module term.

No Spark

Spark — It is pick-up coil or connections. Coil resistance should be 500-1500 ohms and not grounded.

If module tester is available, test mod.

OK

Bad — Replace mod.

Check coil wire from cap to coil. If OK, replace coil.

If no module tester is available:

7. Replace HEI module and repeat Step 6.

Spark — System OK

No Spark — Module removed is OK, reinstall module. Check coil wire from cap to coil. If OK, replace coil.

Fig. 5   HEI-EST ignition system diagnostic chart (Part 2 of 5). 1981 models with remote coil

ENGINE CRANKS, BUT WILL NOT RUN

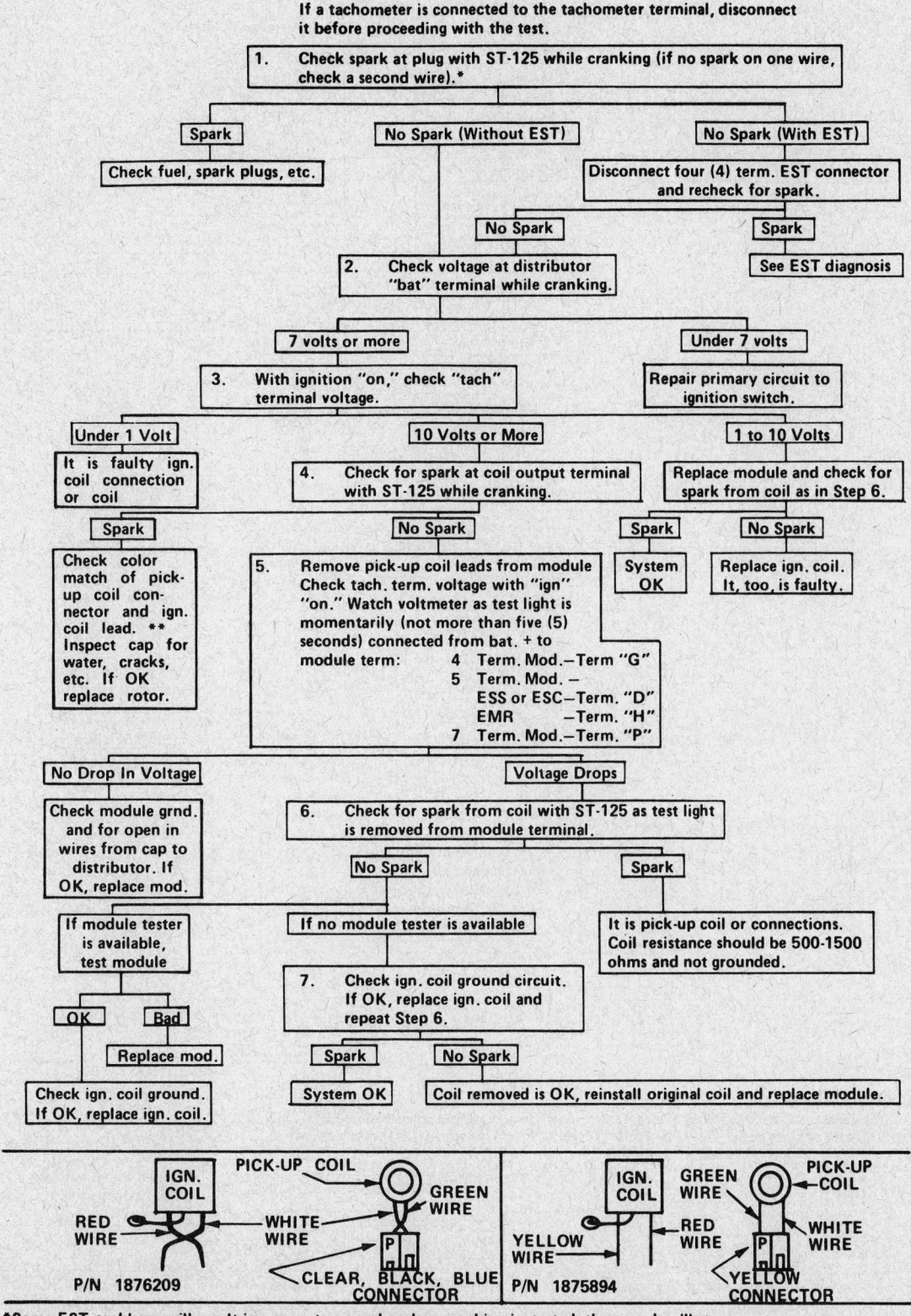

If a tachometer is connected to the tachometer terminal, disconnect it before proceeding with the test.

1. Check spark at plug with ST-125 while cranking (if no spark on one wire, check a second wire).*

Spark → Check fuel, spark plugs, etc.

No Spark (Without EST)

No Spark (With EST) → Disconnect four (4) term. EST connector and recheck for spark.

No Spark

Spark → See EST diagnosis

2. Check voltage at distributor "bat" terminal while cranking.

7 volts or more

3. With ignition "on," check "tach" terminal voltage.

Under 7 volts → Repair primary circuit to ignition switch.

Under 1 Volt → It is faulty ign. coil connection or coil

Spark → Check color match of pick-up coil connector and ign. coil lead. ** Inspect cap for water, cracks, etc. If OK replace rotor.

10 Volts or More

4. Check for spark at coil output terminal with ST-125 while cranking.

No Spark

5. Remove pick-up coil leads from module Check tach. term. voltage with "ign" "on." Watch voltmeter as test light is momentarily (not more than five (5) seconds) connected from bat. + to module term:
  4 Term. Mod.—Term "G"
  5 Term. Mod.—
     ESS or ESC—Term. "D"
     EMR   —Term. "H"
  7 Term. Mod.—Term. "P"

1 to 10 Volts → Replace module and check for spark from coil as in Step 6.

Spark → System OK

No Spark → Replace ign. coil. It, too, is faulty.

No Drop In Voltage → Check module grnd. and for open in wires from cap to distributor. If OK, replace mod.

Voltage Drops

6. Check for spark from coil with ST-125 as test light is removed from module terminal.

No Spark

Spark → It is pick-up coil or connections. Coil resistance should be 500-1500 ohms and not grounded.

If module tester is available, test module

OK / **Bad** → Replace mod.

Check ign. coil ground. If OK, replace ign. coil.

If no module tester is available

7. Check ign. coil ground circuit. If OK, replace ign. coil and repeat Step 6.

Spark → System OK

No Spark → Coil removed is OK, reinstall original coil and replace module.

IGN. COIL — PICK-UP COIL — GREEN WIRE — WHITE WIRE — RED WIRE — CLEAR, BLACK, BLUE CONNECTOR — P/N 1876209

IGN. COIL — GREEN WIRE — PICK-UP COIL — RED WIRE — WHITE WIRE — YELLOW WIRE — YELLOW CONNECTOR — P/N 1875894

*Some EST problems will result in one or two sparks when cranking is started, then spark will stop. This is considered a "no spark" condition.

Fig. 6 HEI-EST ignition system diagnostic chart (Part 2 of 5). 1981 models with integral coil

ENGINE CRANKS, BUT WILL NOT RUN

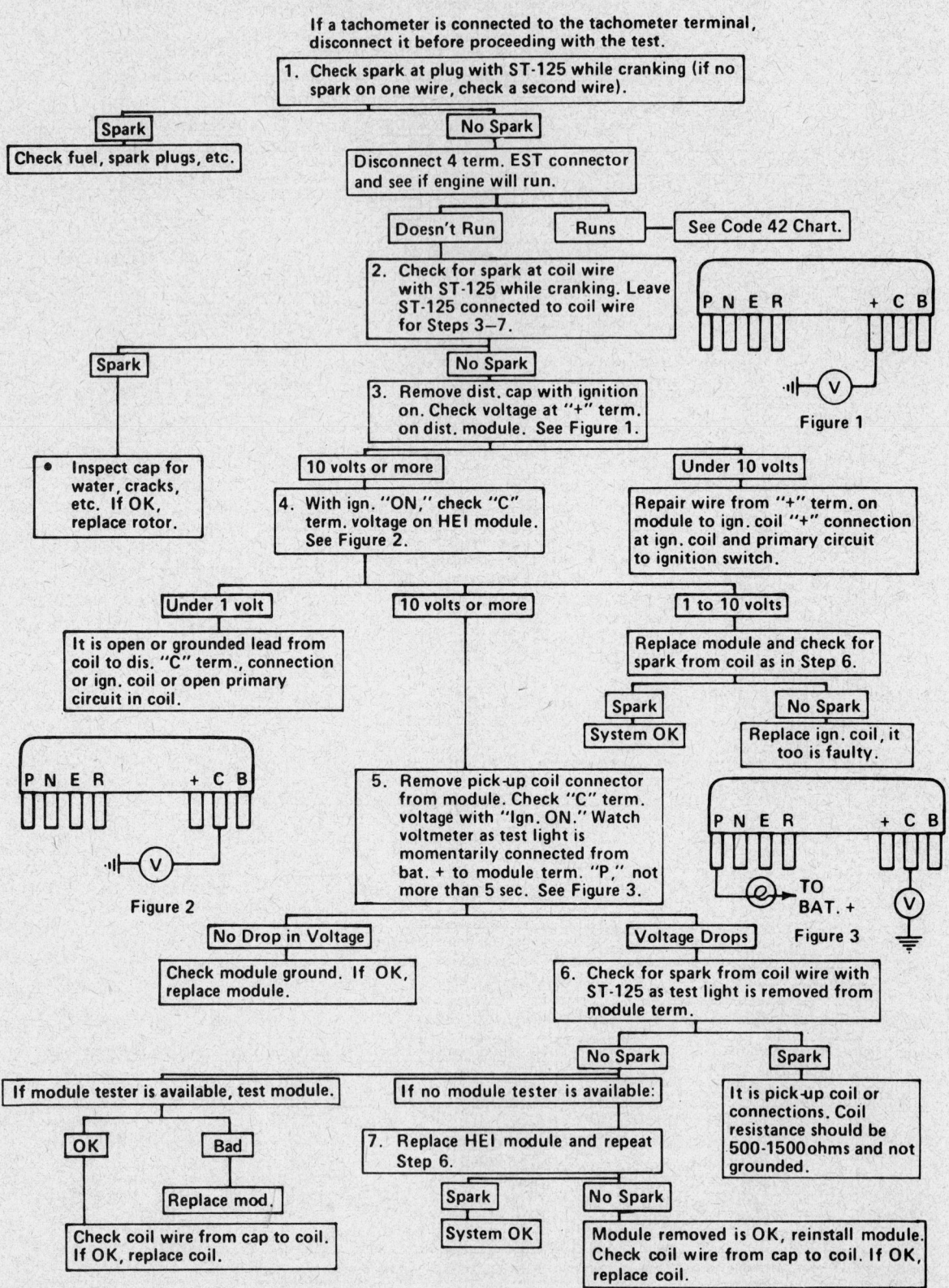

If a tachometer is connected to the tachometer terminal, disconnect it before proceeding with the test.

1. Check spark at plug with ST-125 while cranking (if no spark on one wire, check a second wire).

Spark

Check fuel, spark plugs, etc.

No Spark

Disconnect 4 term. EST connector and see if engine will run.

Doesn't Run | **Runs** — See Code 42 Chart.

2. Check for spark at coil wire with ST-125 while cranking. Leave ST-125 connected to coil wire for Steps 3–7.

Spark

• Inspect cap for water, cracks, etc. If OK, replace rotor.

No Spark

3. Remove dist. cap with ignition on. Check voltage at "+" term. on dist. module. See Figure 1.

P N E R   + C B

Figure 1

10 volts or more

4. With ign. "ON," check "C" term. voltage on HEI module. See Figure 2.

Under 10 volts

Repair wire from "+" term. on module to ign. coil "+" connection at ign. coil and primary circuit to ignition switch.

Under 1 volt

It is open or grounded lead from coil to dis. "C" term., connection or ign. coil or open primary circuit in coil.

P N E R   + C B

Figure 2

10 volts or more

5. Remove pick-up coil connector from module. Check "C" term. voltage with "Ign. ON." Watch voltmeter as test light is momentarily connected from bat. + to module term. "P," not more than 5 sec. See Figure 3.

1 to 10 volts

Replace module and check for spark from coil as in Step 6.

Spark

System OK

No Spark

Replace ign. coil, it too is faulty.

P N E R   + C B

TO BAT. +

Figure 3

No Drop in Voltage

Check module ground. If OK, replace module.

Voltage Drops

6. Check for spark from coil wire with ST-125 as test light is removed from module term.

No Spark

If module tester is available, test module.

OK | **Bad**

Replace mod.

Check coil wire from cap to coil. If OK, replace coil.

If no module tester is available:

7. Replace HEI module and repeat Step 6.

Spark

System OK

No Spark

Module removed is OK, reinstall module. Check coil wire from cap to coil. If OK, replace coil.

Spark

It is pick-up coil or connections. Coil resistance should be 500-1500 ohms and not grounded.

Fig. 7 HEI-EST ignition system diagnostic chart (Part 2 of 5). 1982–83 models w/ remote coil exc. 1983 Chevette & 1000

ENGINE CRANKS, BUT WILL NOT RUN

If a tachometer is connected to the tachometer terminal, disconnect it before proceeding with the test.
Intermittent no start may be caused by wrong pick-up or ignition coil.

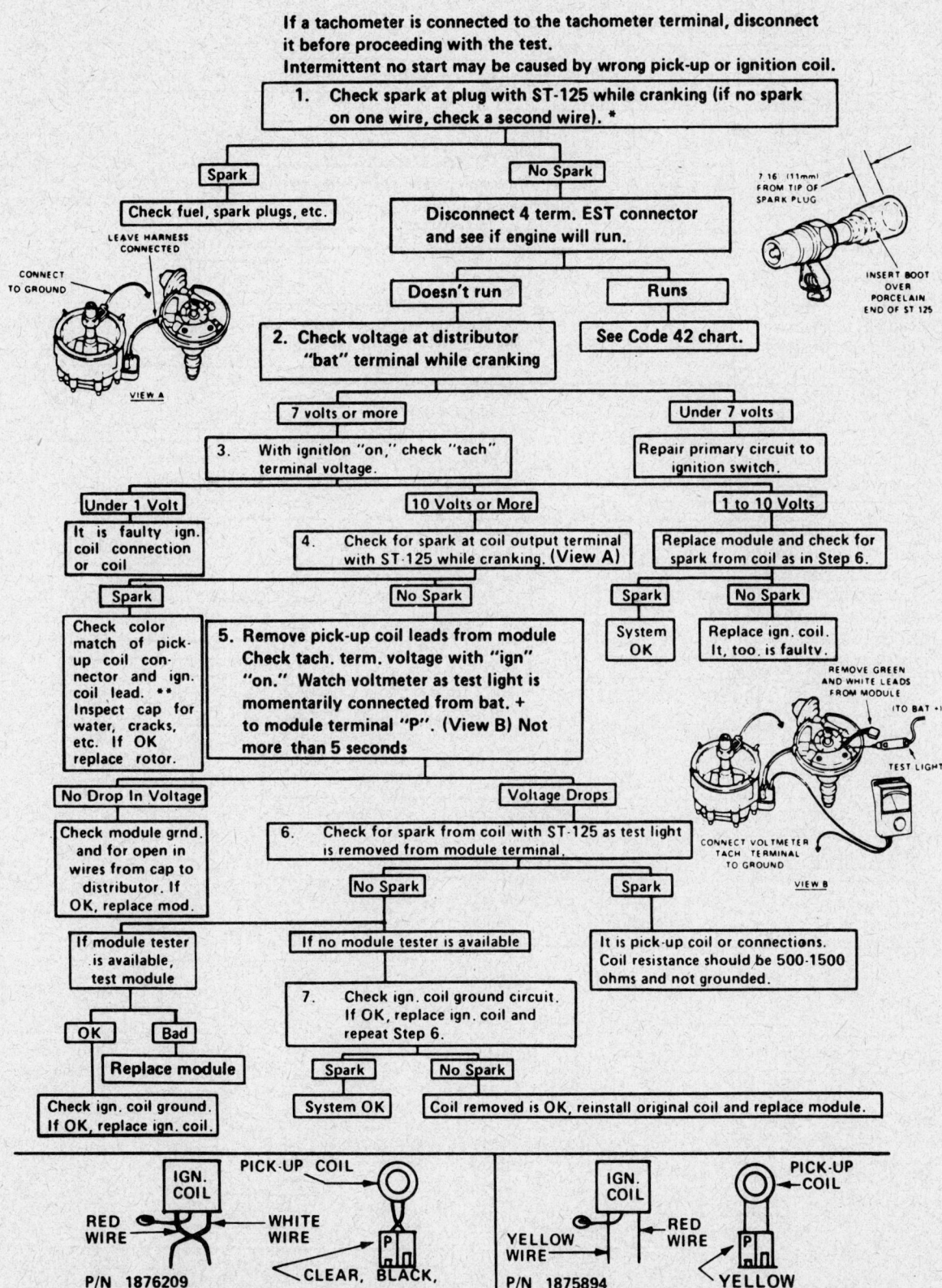

* A few sparks and then nothing, is considered no spark.

Fig. 8   HEI-EST ignition system diagnostic chart (Part 2 of 5). 1982–83 models w/ integral coil

ELECTRONIC IGNITION SYSTEMS

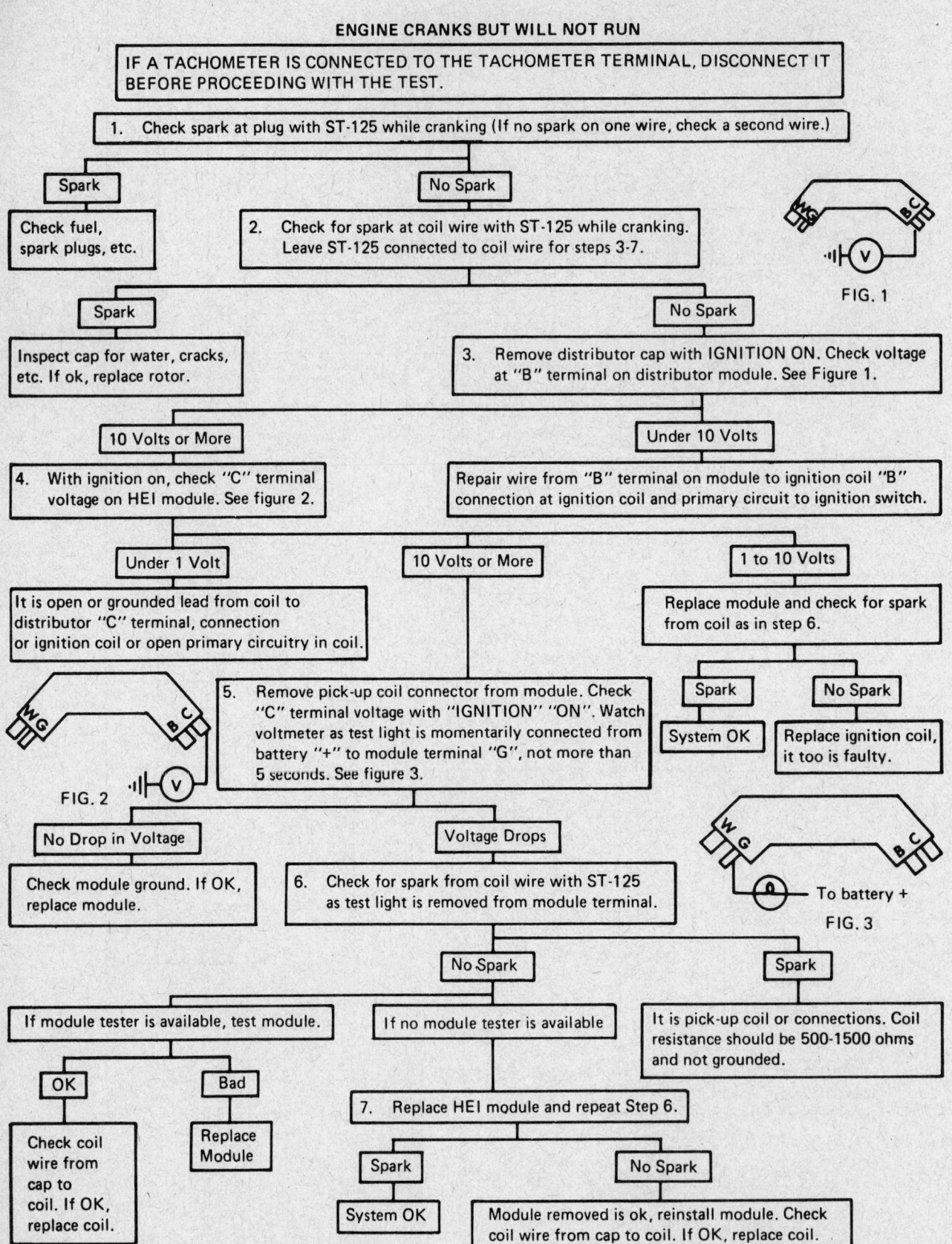

ENGINE CRANKS BUT WILL NOT RUN

IF A TACHOMETER IS CONNECTED TO THE TACHOMETER TERMINAL, DISCONNECT IT BEFORE PROCEEDING WITH THE TEST.

1. Check spark at plug with ST-125 while cranking (If no spark on one wire, check a second wire.)

Spark

Check fuel, spark plugs, etc.

No Spark

2. Check for spark at coil wire with ST-125 while cranking. Leave ST-125 connected to coil wire for steps 3-7.

FIG. 1

Spark

Inspect cap for water, cracks, etc. If ok, replace rotor.

No Spark

3. Remove distributor cap with IGNITION ON. Check voltage at "B" terminal on distributor module. See Figure 1.

10 Volts or More

4. With ignition on, check "C" terminal voltage on HEI module. See figure 2.

Under 10 Volts

Repair wire from "B" terminal on module to ignition coil "B" connection at ignition coil and primary circuit to ignition switch.

Under 1 Volt

It is open or grounded lead from coil to distributor "C" terminal, connection or ignition coil or open primary circuitry in coil.

10 Volts or More

1 to 10 Volts

Replace module and check for spark from coil as in step 6.

Spark

System OK

No Spark

Replace ignition coil, it too is faulty.

FIG. 2

5. Remove pick-up coil connector from module. Check "C" terminal voltage with "IGNITION" "ON". Watch voltmeter as test light is momentarily connected from battery "+" to module terminal "G", not more than 5 seconds. See figure 3.

No Drop in Voltage

Check module ground. If OK, replace module.

Voltage Drops

6. Check for spark from coil wire with ST-125 as test light is removed from module terminal.

To battery +

FIG. 3

No Spark

If module tester is available, test module.

OK

Check coil wire from cap to coil. If OK, replace coil.

Bad

Replace Module

If no module tester is available

7. Replace HEI module and repeat Step 6.

Spark

System OK

No Spark

Module removed is ok, reinstall module. Check coil wire from cap to coil. If OK, replace coil.

Spark

It is pick-up coil or connections. Coil resistance should be 500-1500 ohms and not grounded.

Fig. 9 HEI-EST ignition system diagnostic chart (Part 2 of 5). 1983 Chevette & 1000

BYPASS OR EST PROBLEM

If vehicle will not start and run, check for grounded EST wire to ECM terminal "12." (Grounded and open EST circuit on 5.0L VIN "Y".)

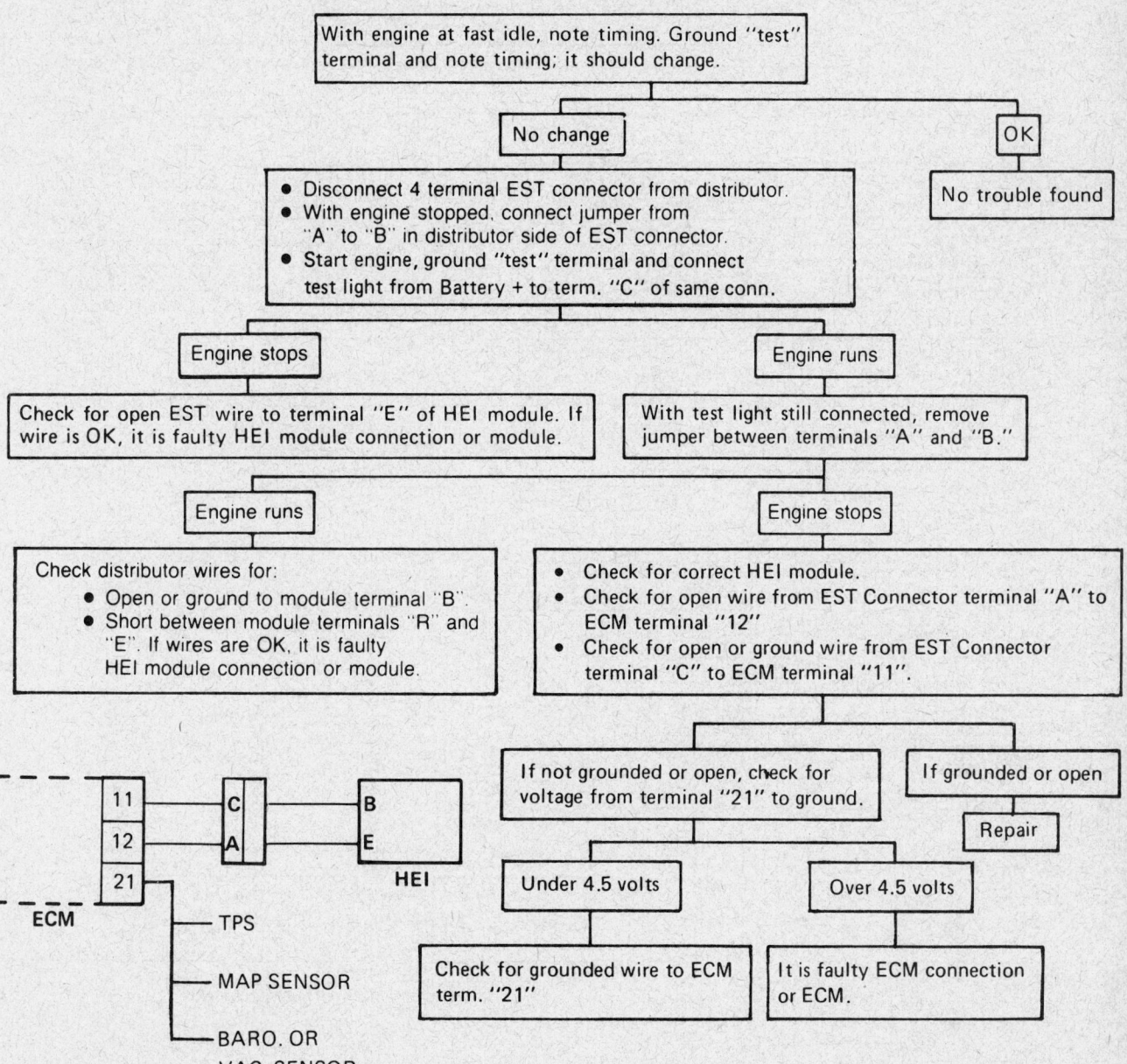

Fig. 10   HEI-EST ignition system code 24 chart (Part 2 of 5). 1982—83 models (Use this chart with 1982—83 HEI-EST ignition system diagnostic charts)

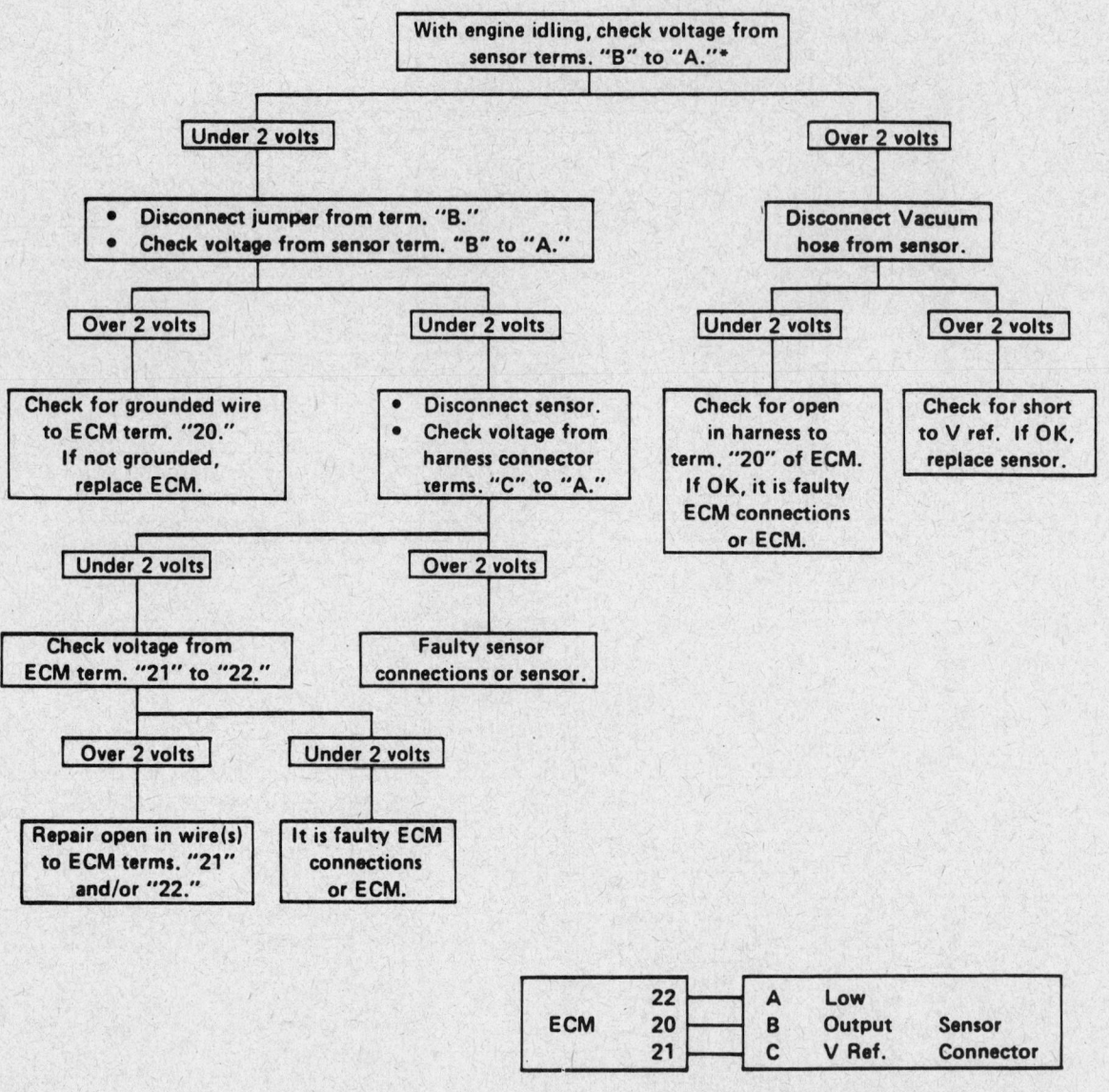

VACUUM SENSOR CIRCUIT

Check for over 34kPa (10 inches) of vacuum at sensor with engine idling. If not OK, repair.

With engine idling, check voltage from sensor terms. "B" to "A."*

Under 2 volts

Over 2 volts

- Disconnect jumper from term. "B."
- Check voltage from sensor term. "B" to "A."

Disconnect Vacuum hose from sensor.

Over 2 volts

Under 2 volts

Check for grounded wire to ECM term. "20." If not grounded, replace ECM.

- Disconnect sensor.
- Check voltage from harness connector terms. "C" to "A."

Under 2 volts

Over 2 volts

Check for open in harness to term. "20" of ECM. If OK, it is faulty ECM connections or ECM.

Check for short to V ref. If OK, replace sensor.

Under 2 volts

Over 2 volts

Check voltage from ECM term. "21" to "22."

Faulty sensor connections or sensor.

Over 2 volts

Under 2 volts

Repair open in wire(s) to ECM terms. "21" and/or "22."

It is faulty ECM connections or ECM.

ECM	22	A	Low	
	20	B	Output	Sensor
	21	C	V Ref.	Connector

High Vacuum = High Output

*This requires use of three jumpers between the sensor and the connector. They can be made using terminals 12014836 and 12014837.

Fig. 11 Vacuum sensor diagnostic chart (Part 3 of 5). All models with vacuum sensor.

MAP SENSOR CIRCUIT

Check for over 34 kPa (10 inches) vacuum at MAP sensor with engine idling.
If not OK, repair hoses or connections.

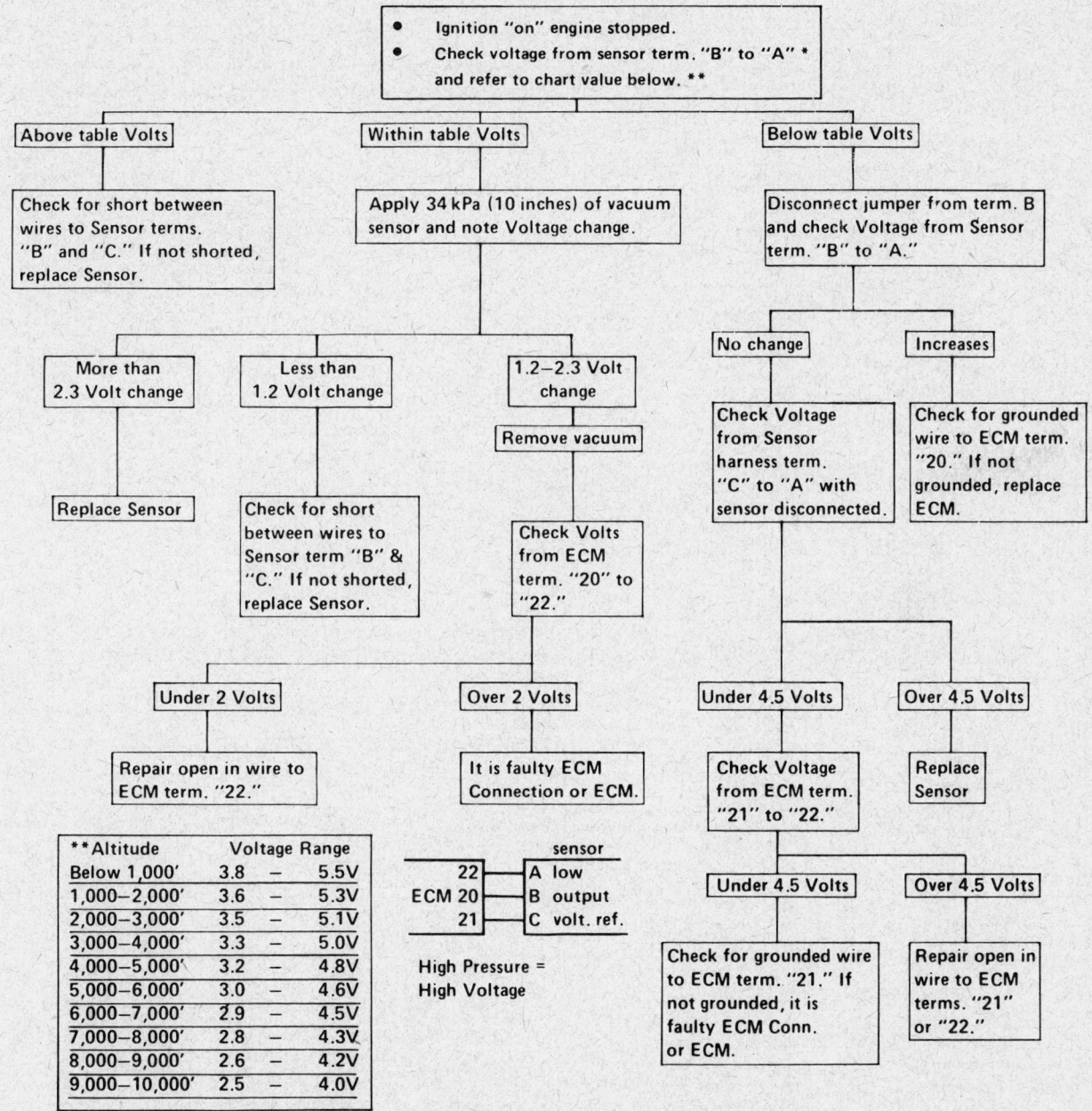

- Ignition "on" engine stopped.
- Check voltage from sensor term. "B" to "A" *
  and refer to chart value below. **

Above table Volts

Check for short between wires to Sensor terms. "B" and "C." If not shorted, replace Sensor.

Within table Volts

Apply 34 kPa (10 inches) of vacuum sensor and note Voltage change.

Below table Volts

Disconnect jumper from term. B and check Voltage from Sensor term. "B" to "A."

More than 2.3 Volt change

Replace Sensor

Less than 1.2 Volt change

Check for short between wires to Sensor term "B" & "C." If not shorted, replace Sensor.

1.2–2.3 Volt change

Remove vacuum

Check Volts from ECM term. "20" to "22."

No change

Check Voltage from Sensor harness term. "C" to "A" with sensor disconnected.

Increases

Check for grounded wire to ECM term. "20." If not grounded, replace ECM.

Under 2 Volts

Repair open in wire to ECM term. "22."

Over 2 Volts

It is faulty ECM Connection or ECM.

Under 4.5 Volts

Check Voltage from ECM term. "21" to "22."

Over 4.5 Volts

Replace Sensor

Under 4.5 Volts

Check for grounded wire to ECM term. "21." If not grounded, it is faulty ECM Conn. or ECM.

Over 4.5 Volts

Repair open in wire to ECM terms. "21" or "22."

**Altitude	Voltage Range	
Below 1,000'	3.8 –	5.5V
1,000–2,000'	3.6 –	5.3V
2,000–3,000'	3.5 –	5.1V
3,000–4,000'	3.3 –	5.0V
4,000–5,000'	3.2 –	4.8V
5,000–6,000'	3.0 –	4.6V
6,000–7,000'	2.9 –	4.5V
7,000–8,000'	2.8 –	4.3V
8,000–9,000'	2.6 –	4.2V
9,000–10,000'	2.5 –	4.0V

sensor

```
        22 ─── A low
ECM  20 ─── B output
        21 ─── C volt. ref.
```

High Pressure =
High Voltage

*This requires use of three jumpers which can be made using terms. part numbers 12014836 and 12014837.

Fig. 12 MAP sensor diagnostic chart (Part 3 of 5). All models with MAP sensor

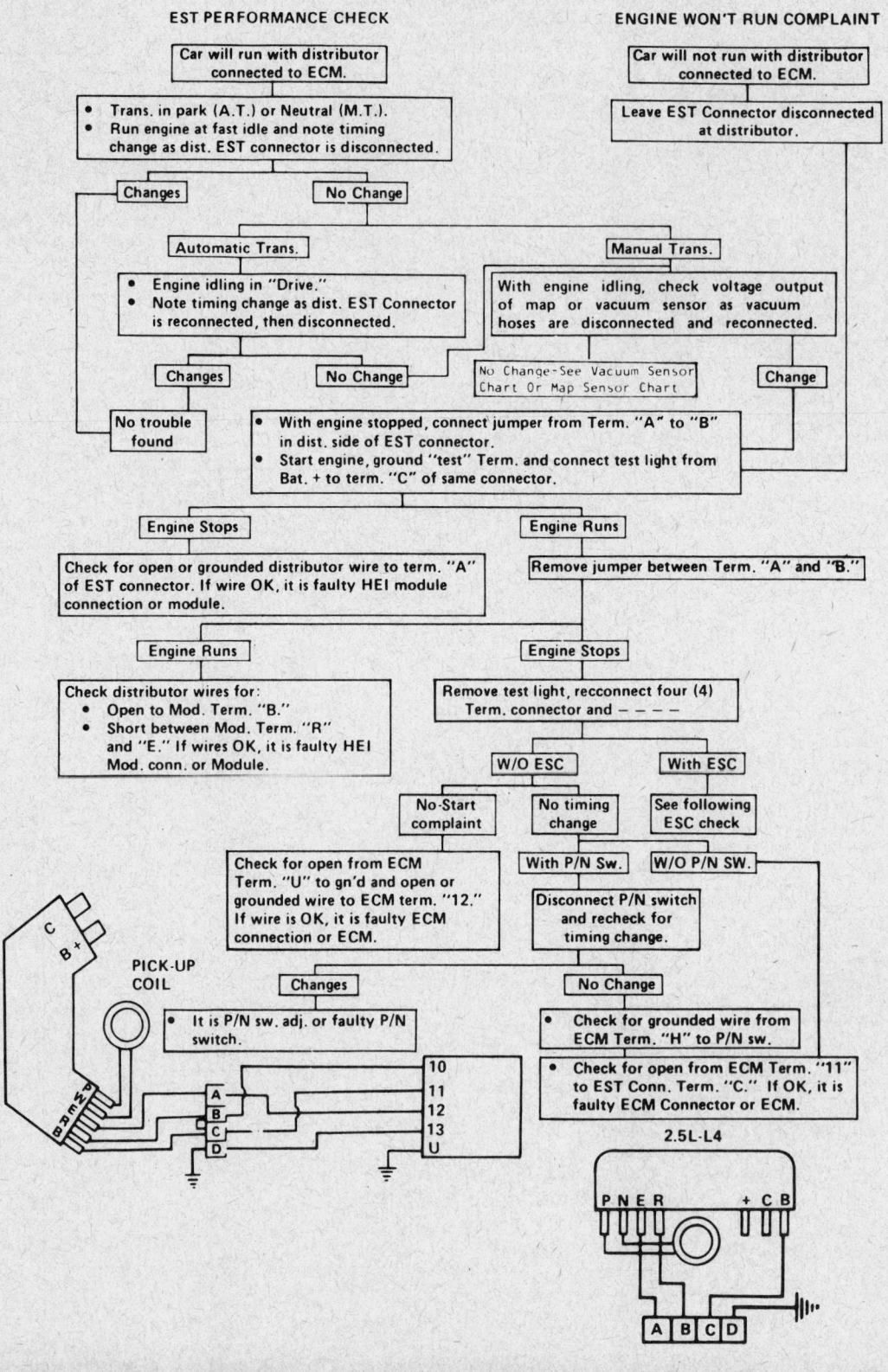

EST DIAGNOSIS

Fig. 13 EST diagnostic chart (Part 4 of 5). All 1981 models & 1982 Chevette & 1000

EST PERFORMANCE CHECK

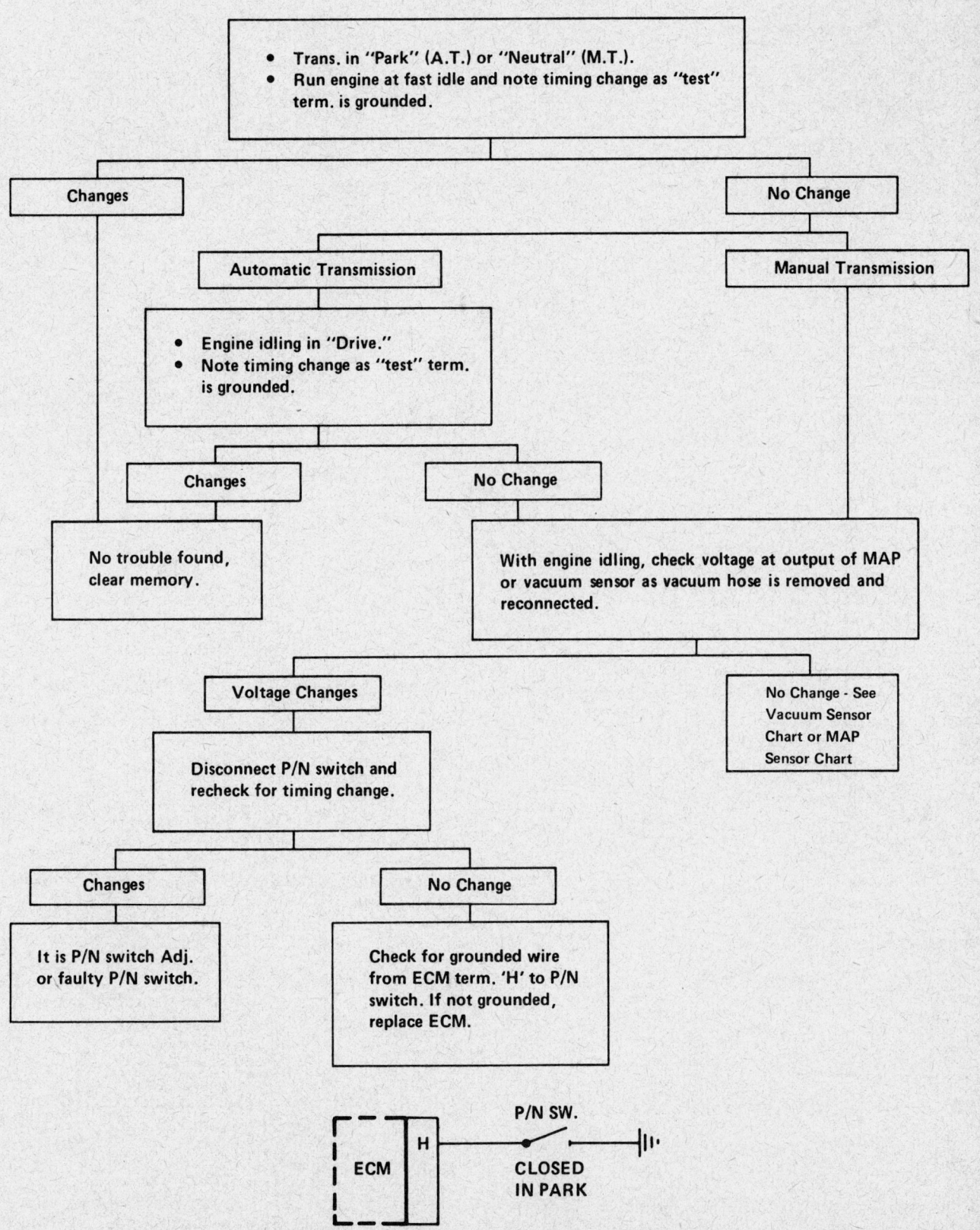

Fig. 14   EST performance check (Part 4 of 5). All 1982–83 models exc. 1982–83 Chevette, 1000, 1982 Corvette & 1982–83 Oldsmobile w/V8-307 (V.I.N. codes Y & 9)

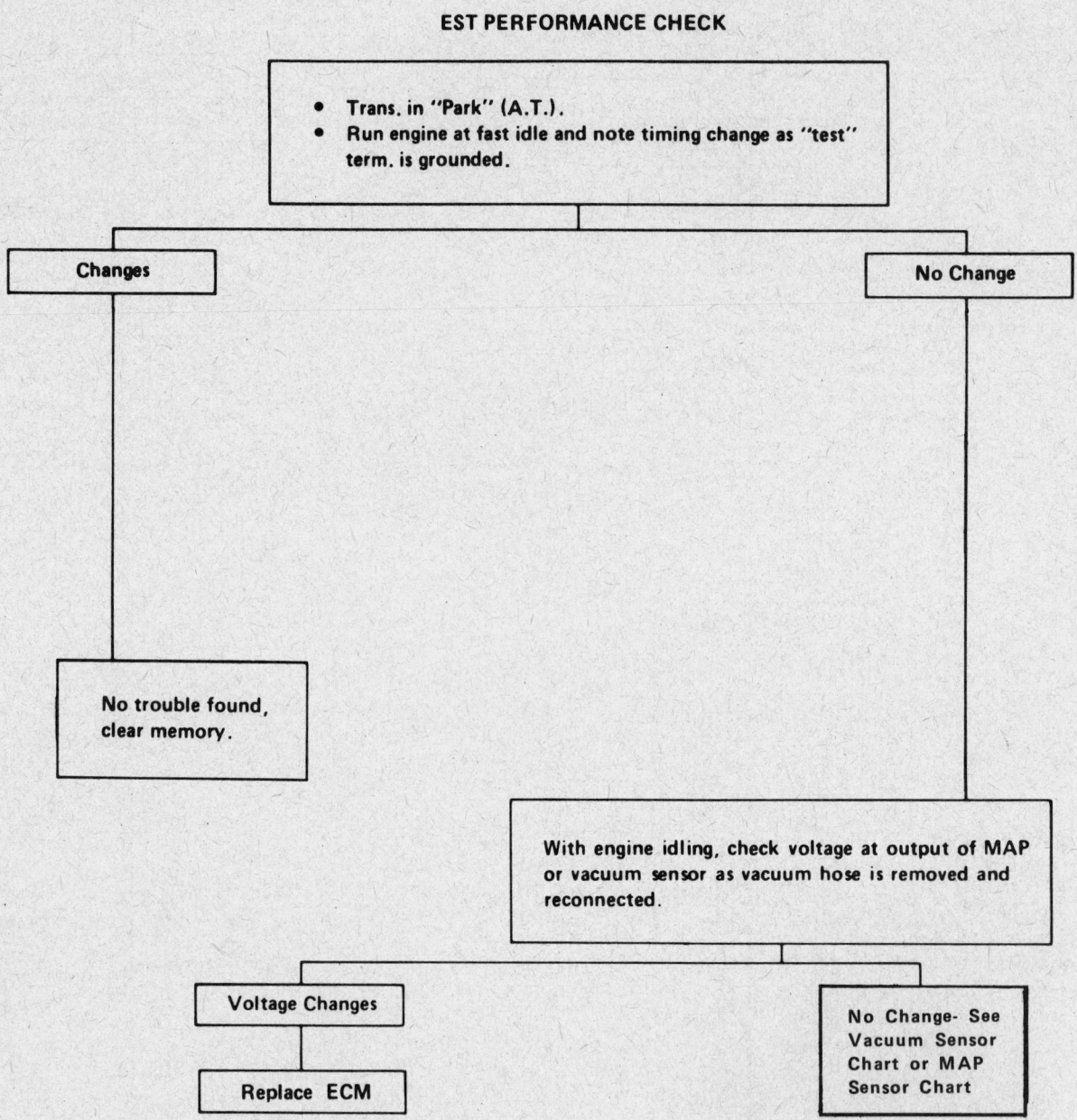

EST PERFORMANCE CHECK

- Trans. in "Park" (A.T.).
- Run engine at fast idle and note timing change as "test" term. is grounded.

Changes → No trouble found, clear memory.

No Change → With engine idling, check voltage at output of MAP or vacuum sensor as vacuum hose is removed and reconnected.

Voltage Changes → Replace ECM

No Change- See Vacuum Sensor Chart or MAP Sensor Chart

Fig. 15   EST performance check (Part 4 of 5). 1982—83 Oldsmobile models w/ V8-307 (V.I.N. codes Y & 9)

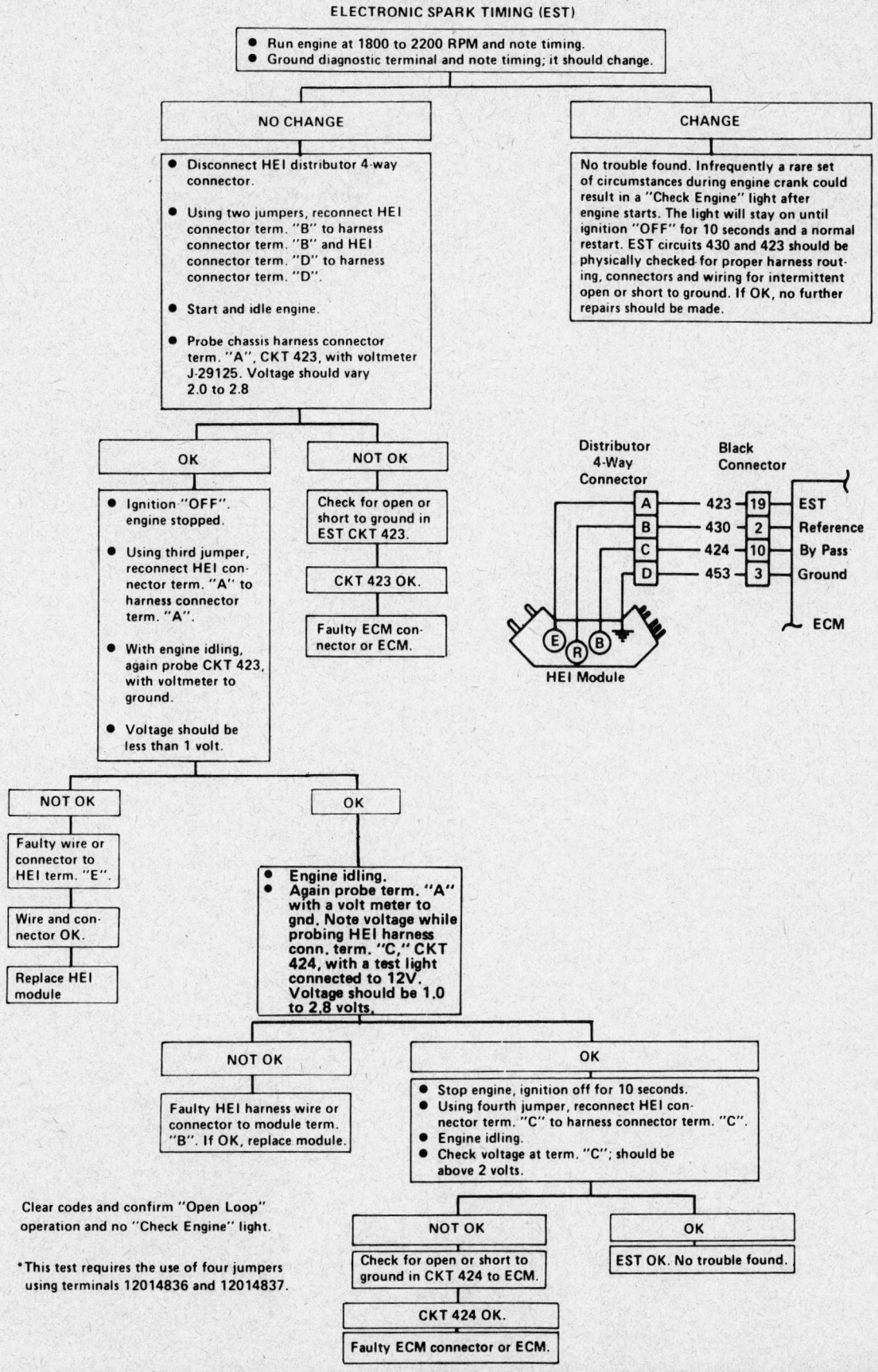

FUEL INJECTION
ELECTRONIC SPARK TIMING (EST)

- Run engine at 1800 to 2200 RPM and note timing.
- Ground diagnostic terminal and note timing; it should change.

NO CHANGE

- Disconnect HEI distributor 4-way connector.
- Using two jumpers, reconnect HEI connector term. "B" to harness connector term. "B" and HEI connector term. "D" to harness connector term. "D".
- Start and idle engine.
- Probe chassis harness connector term. "A", CKT 423, with voltmeter J-29125. Voltage should vary 2.0 to 2.8

CHANGE

No trouble found. Infrequently a rare set of circumstances during engine crank could result in a "Check Engine" light after engine starts. The light will stay on until ignition "OFF" for 10 seconds and a normal restart. EST circuits 430 and 423 should be physically checked for proper harness routing, connectors and wiring for intermittent open or short to ground. If OK, no further repairs should be made.

OK

- Ignition "OFF", engine stopped.
- Using third jumper, reconnect HEI connector term. "A" to harness connector term. "A".
- With engine idling, again probe CKT 423, with voltmeter to ground.
- Voltage should be less than 1 volt.

NOT OK

Check for open or short to ground in EST CKT 423.

CKT 423 OK.

Faulty ECM connector or ECM.

Distributor 4-Way Connector — **Black Connector**

A	423 – 19	EST
B	430 – 2	Reference
C	424 – 10	By Pass
D	453 – 3	Ground

ECM

HEI Module

NOT OK

Faulty wire or connector to HEI term. "E".

Wire and connector OK.

Replace HEI module

OK

- Engine idling.
- Again probe term. "A" with a volt meter to gnd. Note voltage while probing HEI harness conn. term. "C," CKT 424, with a test light connected to 12V. Voltage should be 1.0 to 2.8 volts.

NOT OK

Faulty HEI harness wire or connector to module term. "B". If OK, replace module.

OK

- Stop engine, ignition off for 10 seconds.
- Using fourth jumper, reconnect HEI connector term. "C" to harness connector term. "C".
- Engine idling.
- Check voltage at term. "C"; should be above 2 volts.

Clear codes and confirm "Open Loop" operation and no "Check Engine" light.

*This test requires the use of four jumpers using terminals 12014836 and 12014837.

NOT OK

Check for open or short to ground in CKT 424 to ECM.

CKT 424 OK.

Faulty ECM connector or ECM.

OK

EST OK. No trouble found.

Fig. 16 EST diagnostic chart (Part 4 of 5). All 1982 Corvette

ELECTRONIC IGNITION SYSTEMS

ESC CHECK

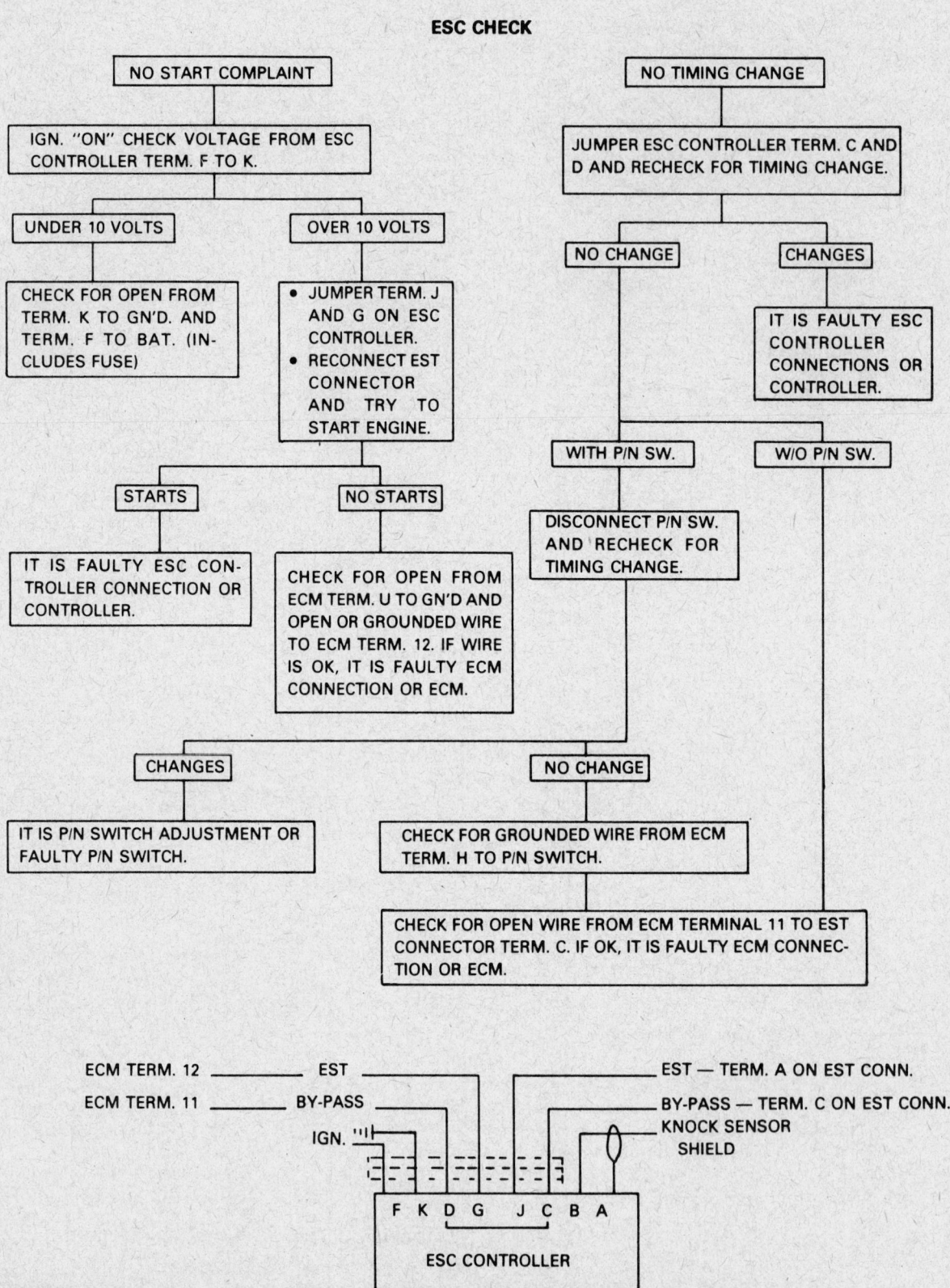

Fig. 17 ESC diagnostic chart (Part 5 of 5). 1981 models (if equipped)

ESC PERFORMANCE DIAGNOSTIC

This chart should only be used after other causes of knock have been checked, i.e., timing, lack of EGR, engine temp., etc.

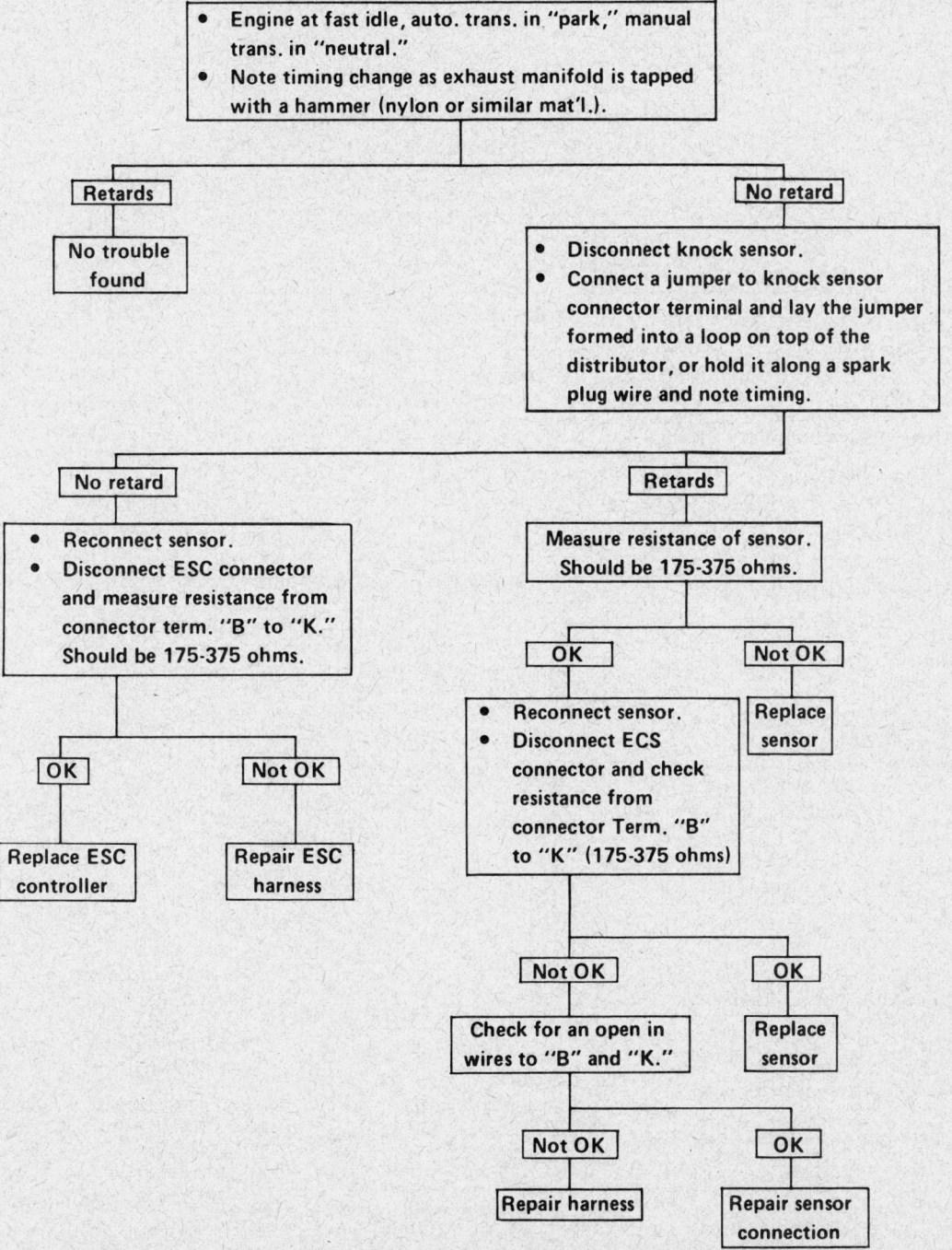

Fig. 18 ESC performance problem diagnosis (Part 5 of 5). 1981 models (if equipped)

ENGINE CRANKS BUT DOES NOT START

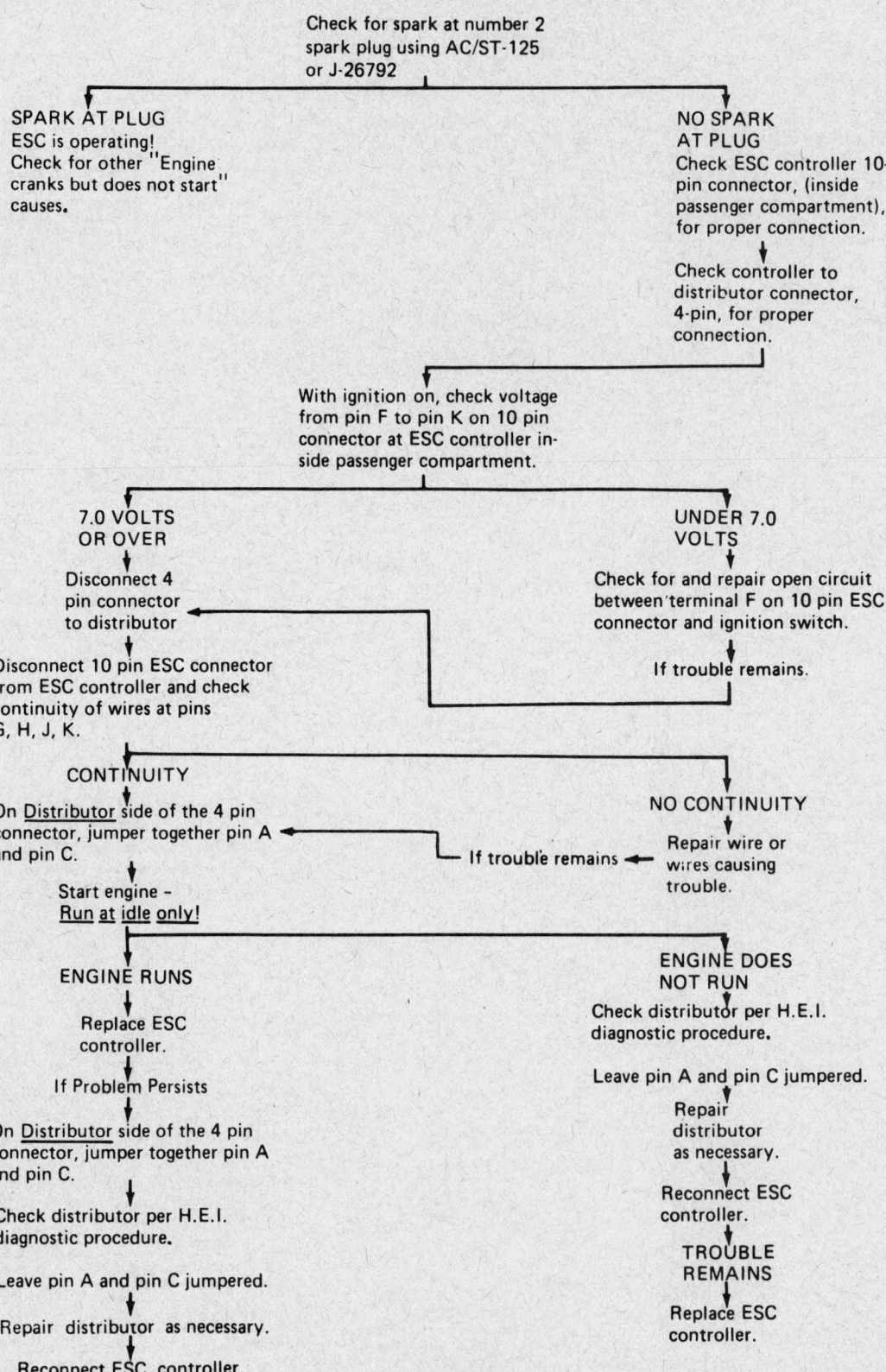

Check for spark at number 2 spark plug using AC/ST-125 or J-26792

SPARK AT PLUG
ESC is operating!
Check for other "Engine cranks but does not start" causes.

NO SPARK AT PLUG
Check ESC controller 10-pin connector, (inside passenger compartment), for proper connection.

Check controller to distributor connector, 4-pin, for proper connection.

With ignition on, check voltage from pin F to pin K on 10 pin connector at ESC controller inside passenger compartment.

7.0 VOLTS OR OVER
Disconnect 4 pin connector to distributor

Disconnect 10 pin ESC connector from ESC controller and check continuity of wires at pins G, H, J, K.

UNDER 7.0 VOLTS
Check for and repair open circuit between terminal F on 10 pin ESC connector and ignition switch.

If trouble remains.

CONTINUITY
On Distributor side of the 4 pin connector, jumper together pin A and pin C.

NO CONTINUITY
Repair wire or wires causing trouble.

If trouble remains

Start engine – Run at idle only!

ENGINE RUNS
Replace ESC controller.

If Problem Persists

On Distributor side of the 4 pin connector, jumper together pin A and pin C.

Check distributor per H.E.I. diagnostic procedure.

Leave pin A and pin C jumpered.

Repair distributor as necessary.

Reconnect ESC controller.

ENGINE DOES NOT RUN
Check distributor per H.E.I. diagnostic procedure.

Leave pin A and pin C jumpered.

Repair distributor as necessary.

Reconnect ESC controller.

TROUBLE REMAINS
Replace ESC controller.

Fig. 19 ESC diagnostic chart (Part 5 of 5). 1982–83 models (if equipped)

ESC DIAGNOSTIC PROCEDURES

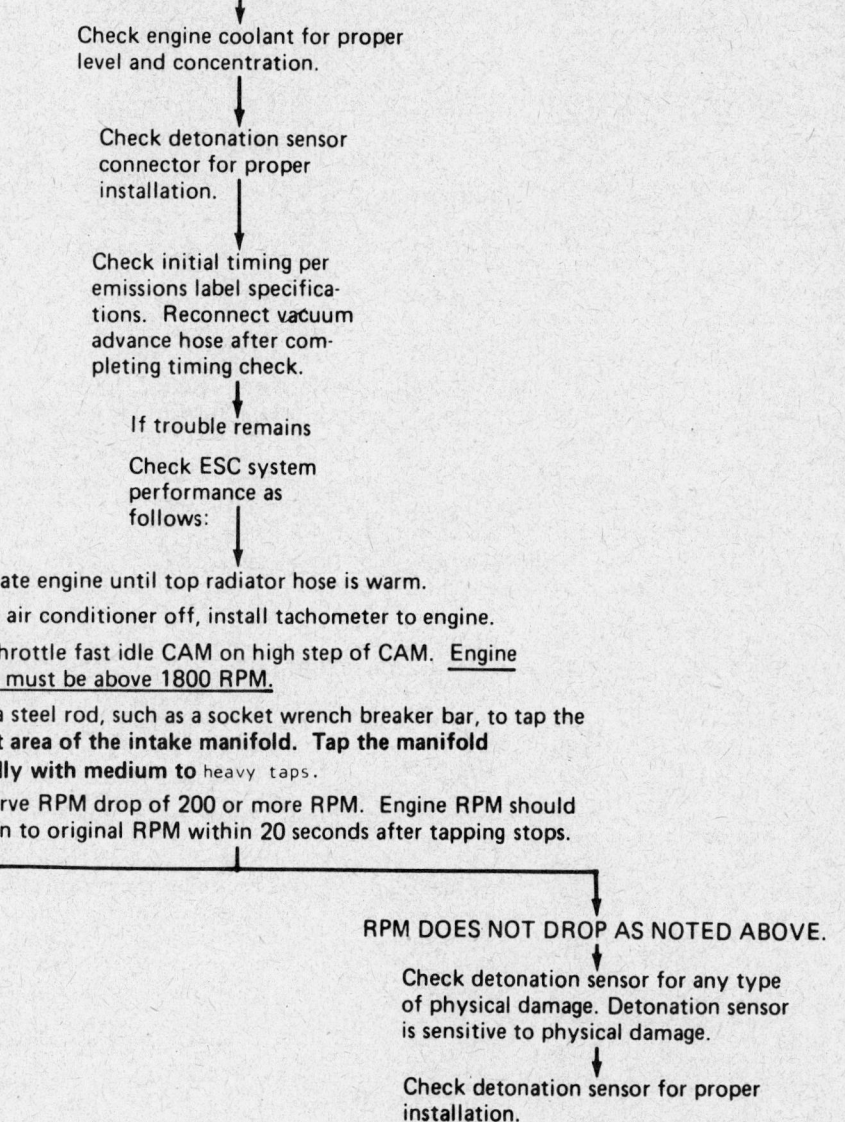

ENGINE DETONATION

Check engine coolant for proper level and concentration.

Check detonation sensor connector for proper installation.

Check initial timing per emissions label specifications. Reconnect vacuum advance hose after completing timing check.

If trouble remains

Check ESC system performance as follows:

Operate engine until top radiator hose is warm.

Turn air conditioner off, install tachometer to engine.

Set throttle fast idle CAM on high step of CAM. Engine RPM must be above 1800 RPM.

Use a steel rod, such as a socket wrench breaker bar, to tap the front area of the intake manifold. Tap the manifold rapidly with medium to heavy taps.

Observe RPM drop of 200 or more RPM. Engine RPM should return to original RPM within 20 seconds after tapping stops.

RPM DROPS AS NOTED ABOVE.

Disconnect 4 pin connector to distributor.

On the distributor side of the connector, jumper together pin A and pin C.

Check distributor per H.E.I. diagnostic procedure.

Distributor checks OK.

Reconnect distributor to ESC controller.

Check carburetor, turbocharger (if equipped) and other sources of engine detonation

RPM DOES NOT DROP AS NOTED ABOVE.

Check detonation sensor for any type of physical damage. Detonation sensor is sensitive to physical damage.

Check detonation sensor for proper installation.

Check polarity of ohmmeter leads before proceeding

Disconnect detonation sensor connector at cowl. On the sensor side of the harness, connect the positive lead of the ohmmeter to the connector terminal attached to the center conductor of the sensor lead. Connect the negative lead to ground. Resistance: 175 to 375 OHMS.

CONTINUED ON NEXT PAGE

Fig. 20   ESC diagnostic chart (Part 5 of 5). 1982–83 models (if equipped)

ELECTRONIC IGNITION SYSTEMS

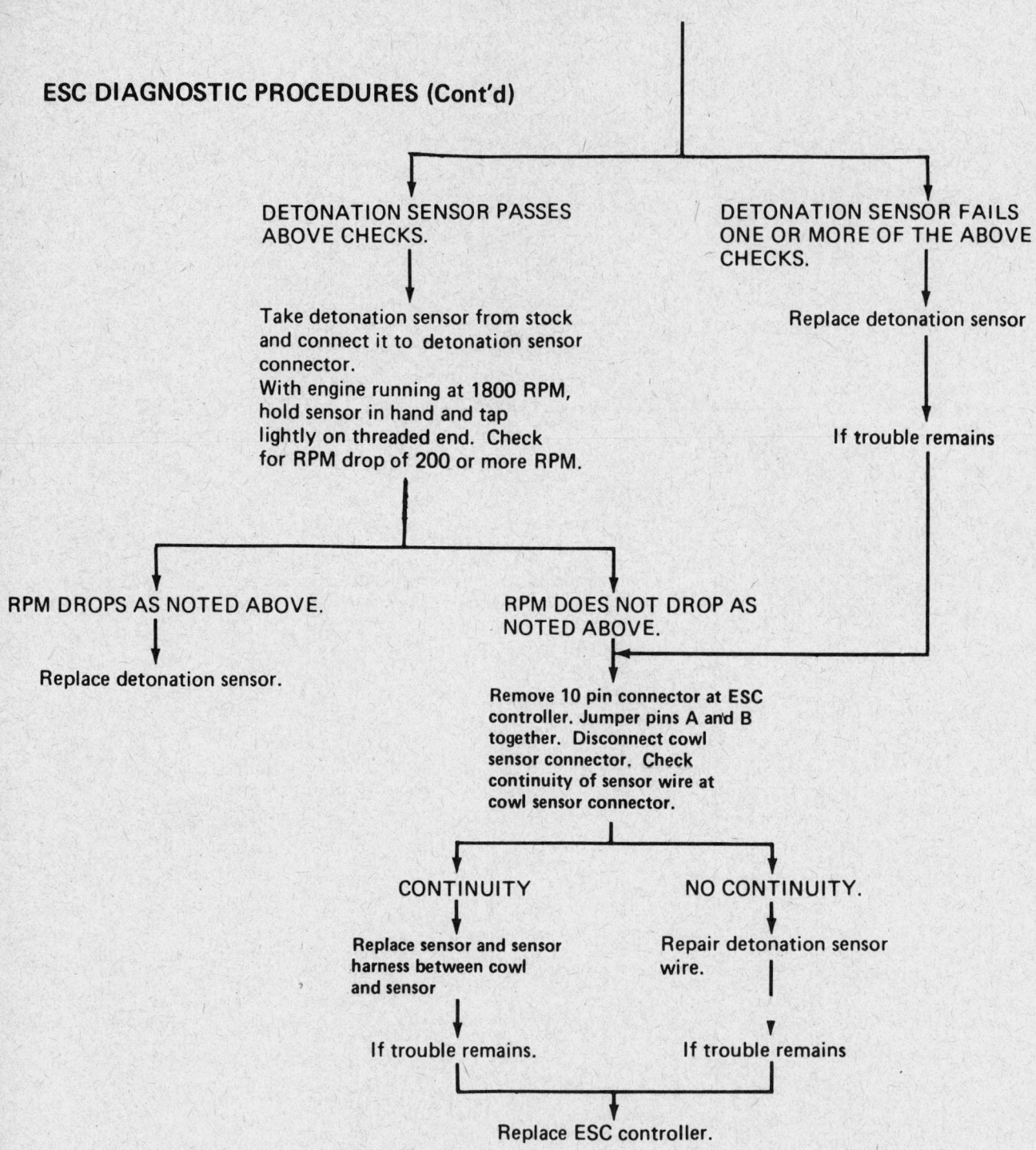

ESC DIAGNOSTIC PROCEDURES (Cont'd)

DETONATION SENSOR PASSES ABOVE CHECKS.

Take detonation sensor from stock and connect it to detonation sensor connector.
With engine running at 1800 RPM, hold sensor in hand and tap lightly on threaded end. Check for RPM drop of 200 or more RPM.

DETONATION SENSOR FAILS ONE OR MORE OF THE ABOVE CHECKS.

Replace detonation sensor

If trouble remains

RPM DROPS AS NOTED ABOVE.

Replace detonation sensor.

RPM DOES NOT DROP AS NOTED ABOVE.

Remove 10 pin connector at ESC controller. Jumper pins A and B together. Disconnect cowl sensor connector. Check continuity of sensor wire at cowl sensor connector.

CONTINUITY

Replace sensor and sensor harness between cowl and sensor

If trouble remains.

NO CONTINUITY.

Repair detonation sensor wire.

If trouble remains

Replace ESC controller.

Fig. 21 ESC diagnostic chart (Part 5 of 5). 1982–83 models (if equipped)

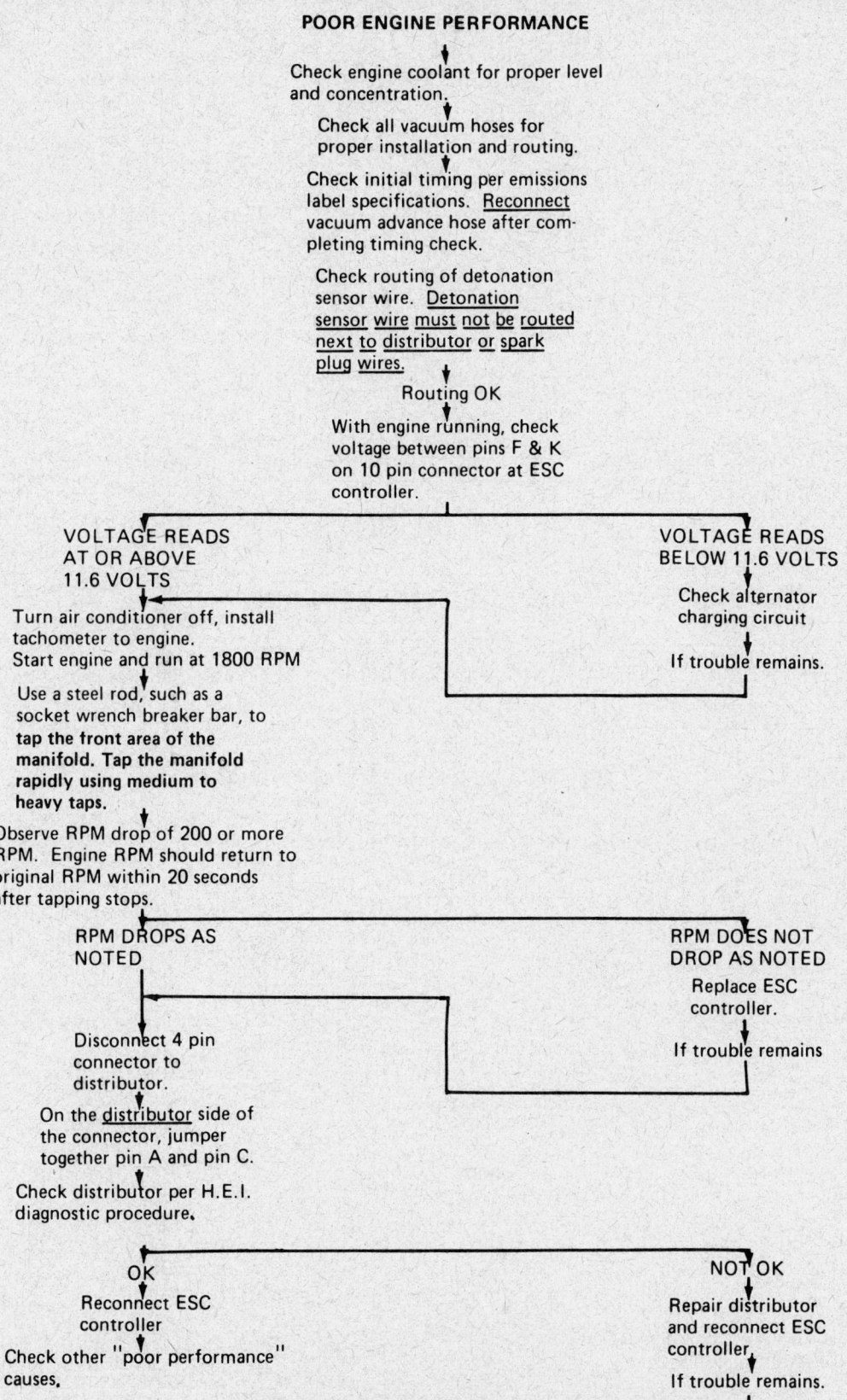

POOR ENGINE PERFORMANCE

Check engine coolant for proper level and concentration.

Check all vacuum hoses for proper installation and routing.

Check initial timing per emissions label specifications. Reconnect vacuum advance hose after completing timing check.

Check routing of detonation sensor wire. Detonation sensor wire must not be routed next to distributor or spark plug wires.

Routing OK

With engine running, check voltage between pins F & K on 10 pin connector at ESC controller.

VOLTAGE READS AT OR ABOVE 11.6 VOLTS

Turn air conditioner off, install tachometer to engine. Start engine and run at 1800 RPM

Use a steel rod, such as a socket wrench breaker bar, to tap the front area of the manifold. Tap the manifold rapidly using medium to heavy taps.

Observe RPM drop of 200 or more RPM. Engine RPM should return to original RPM within 20 seconds after tapping stops.

RPM DROPS AS NOTED

Disconnect 4 pin connector to distributor.

On the distributor side of the connector, jumper together pin A and pin C.

Check distributor per H.E.I. diagnostic procedure.

OK

Reconnect ESC controller

Check other "poor performance" causes.

VOLTAGE READS BELOW 11.6 VOLTS

Check alternator charging circuit

If trouble remains.

RPM DOES NOT DROP AS NOTED

Replace ESC controller.

If trouble remains

NOT OK

Repair distributor and reconnect ESC controller.

If trouble remains.

Fig. 22 ESC performance problem diagnosis (Part 5 of 5). 1982–83 models (if equipped)

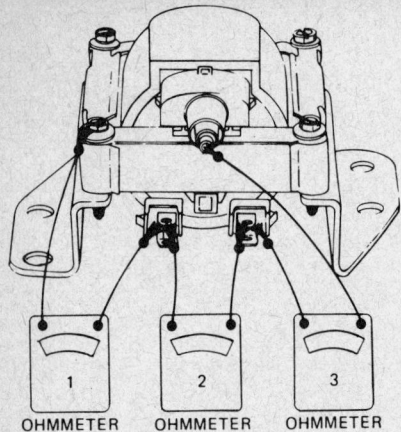

Fig. 23   Testing remote ignition coil

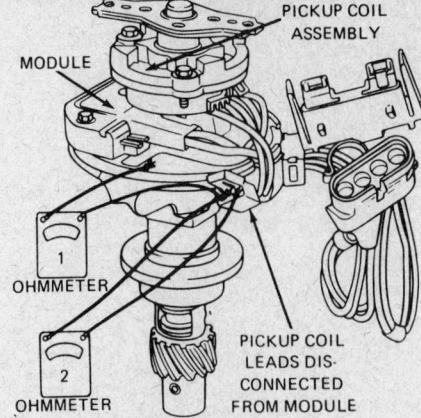

Fig. 24   Testing remote coil distributor pickup coil less Hall Effect switch

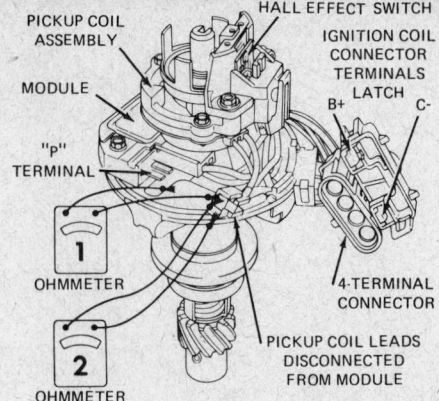

Fig. 25   Testing remote coil distributor pickup coil w/ Hall Effect switch

throughout entire vacuum advance range. If no vacuum advance is used, flex leads by hand to check for opens. Ohmmeter should read infinite at all times. If not, pickup coil is defective and must be replaced.

3. Connect ohmmeter as shown in Figs. 24 and 25, step 2. Repeat step 2. Ohmmeter should read one steady value between 500–1500 ohms. If not, pickup coil is defective and must be replaced.

NOTE: Ohmmeter may deflect if vacuum advance range causes timing core teeth to align. This is not to be considered a defect.

Testing Hall Effect Switch (If Equipped), Fig. 25
1. Carefully noting polarity, connect battery and suitable voltmeter as shown in Fig. 26.
2. Voltmeter should read less than 0.5 volts. If not, replace Hall Effect switch.
3. Insert knife blade as shown in Fig. 26. Voltmeter should read within 0.5 volts of battery voltage. If not, replace Hall Effect switch.

Units With Integral Coil

Testing Ignition Coil
1. Connect a suitable ohmmeter as shown in Fig. 27, step 1. Using the low scale, read ohmmeter. Should be near zero or zero. If not, replace coil.
2. Connect ohmmeter both ways as shown in Fig. 27, step 2. Using the high scale, read ohmmeter. If both readings are infinite, replace coil.

Testing Pickup Coil
1. Remove distributor rotor, then disconnect pickup coil leads from module.
2. Connect ohmmeter as shown in Fig. 28, step 1. Connect a suitable vacuum source to vacuum advance chamber (if equipped) and note ohmmeter reading throughout entire vacuum advance range. If no vacuum advance is used, flex leads by hand to check for opens. Ohmmeter should read infinite at all times. If not, pickup coil is defective and must be replaced.
3. Connect ohmmeter as shown in Fig. 28, step 2. Repeat step 2. Ohmmeter should read one steady value between 500–1500 ohms. If not, pickup coil is defective and must be replaced.

NOTE: Ohmmeter may deflect if vacuum

advance range causes timing core teeth to align. This is not to be considered a defect.

Testing Hall Effect Switch (If Equipped)
Refer to "Units With Remote Coil".

DISTRIBUTOR, REPLACE

Models Equipped With Integral Coil Distributor

1. Disconnect battery and tachometer lead from distributor cap.
2. Disconnect coil connectors from distributor cap and 4 terminal connector (if equipped).

NOTE: Do not use a tool of any kind to release coil connectors or damage to lock tabs will result.

3. Remove distributor cap with ignition high tension wires connected and position aside. Remove vacuum hose (if equipped).
4. Remove distributor clamp screw and hold down clamp.
5. Mark relationship of rotor to distributor housing, then lift distributor from engine slightly until rotor stops turning. Mark relationship of new rotor position on distributor housing, then remove distributor from engine.
6. If engine was not cranked after distributor was removed from engine, proceed as follows:
   a. Position rotor to align with second

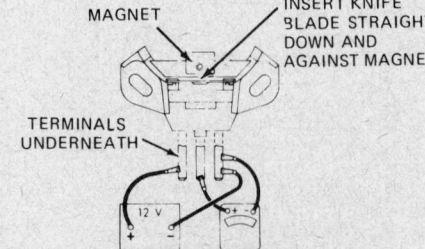

Fig. 26   Testing Hall Effect switch

mark made on distributor housing prior to removing distributor.
   b. Install distributor into engine and align rotor with first mark made on distributor housing prior to removing distributor.
   c. Install distributor cap and connect all electrical connectors.
   d. Adjust ignition timing as specified in individual car chapters.
7. If engine was cranked after distributor was removed from engine, proceed as follows:
   a. Remove No. 1 spark plug and crank engine until compression pressure is felt in No. 1 cylinder. Slowly rotate engine until top dead center is indicated.
   b. Turn rotor to a position just ahead of No. 1 spark plug tower on distributor cap.
   c. Install distributor. Connect 4 terminal connector (if equipped).
   d. Install distributor cap, coil connectors, tachometer lead and battery feed wire.
   e. Adjust ignition timing to specifications in individual car chapters.

Models Equipped With Remote Coil Distributor

Chevette
1. Disconnect battery ground cable, then disconnect wiring harness from distributor.
2. Remove distributor cap with ignition cables connected and position aside.
3. Remove ignition coil as described under "Ignition Coil, Replace".
4. Remove air cleaner and disconnect fuel pump hoses at fuel pump.
5. Remove fuel pump and push rod.
6. Mark relationship of rotor to distributor housing and distributor housing to engine, then remove distributor hold down clamp and remove distributor from engine.
7. Install distributor checking to ensure that marks made during removal align.
8. Install hold down clamp and distributor cap.
9. Connect distributor wiring harness electrical connector.
10. Install fuel pump, air cleaner and ignition coil.
11. Adjust ignition timing as specified in individual car chapter.

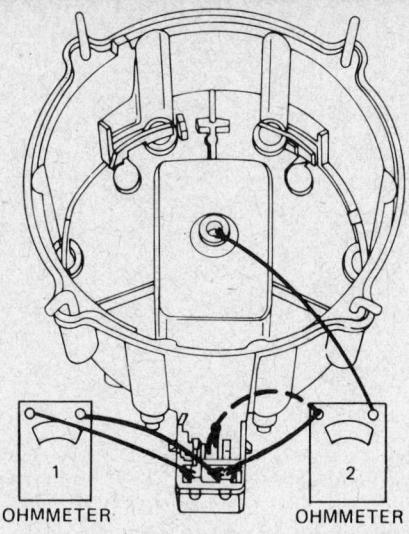

Fig. 27 Testing integral ignition coil

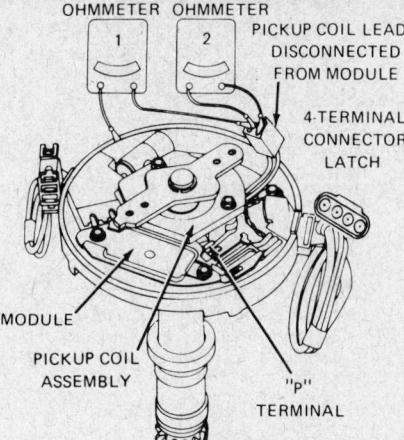

Fig. 28 Testing integral coil distributor pickup coil

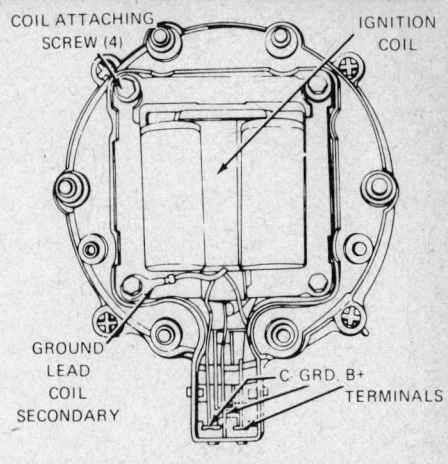

Fig. 29 Removing ignition coil cover. 1981–83 models with internal coil

1981 Citation, Omega, Phoenix & Skylark

1. Disconnect distributor harness electrical connector.
2. Loosen distributor clamp screw, then rotate distributor to gain access to distributor cap retaining latches.
3. Release latches, then remove distributor cap and position aside.
4. Remove distributor hold down clamp, then mark position of rotor in relation to distributor housing.
5. Slowly lift distributor from engine until rotor stops rotating and mark relationship of rotor to distributor housing.
6. Remove distributor from engine.
7. Reverse procedure to install. When installing distributor, align rotor with second mark made on distributor housing prior to removal. Install distributor into engine and check to ensure that rotor aligns with first mark made on distributor housing prior to removal.

1982–83 Celebrity, Century, Citation, Cutlass Ciera, Omega, Phoenix, Skylark & 6000

1. Raise and support vehicle.
2. Remove two bolts securing rear engine cradle.
3. Lower cradle enough to allow for access to distributor.
4. Remove five brake line support to floorpan retaining screws.
5. Remove coil wire and distributor cap and position aside.
6. Mark relationship of rotor to distributor housing and distributor housing to engine block, then remove distributor hold down clamp and remove distributor from engine.
7. Reverse procedure to install. Ensure marks made during disassembly are correctly lined up during distributor installation.
8. Adjust ignition timing as specified in individual car chapter.

Cavalier, Cimarron, Firenza, 2000 & Skyhawk Exc. 1982–83 Firenza, Skyhawk & 2000 with 1.8L OHC Engine

1. Disconnect battery ground cable and remove air cleaner.
2. Release distributor cap latches, then remove distributor cap and position aside.

---

3. Disconnect AIR pipe to exhaust manifold hose at AIR Management valve.
4. Remove rear engine lift bracket bolt and nut from stud, then position assembly aside.
5. Mark relationship of rotor to distributor housing and distributor housing to block.
6. Remove distributor hold down clamp, then remove distributor from engine.
7. Reverse procedure to install. Check to ensure that marks made during removal align after distributor is installed.

1982–83 Firenza, Skyhawk & 2000 with 1.8L OHC Engine

1. Disconnect battery ground cable.
2. Remove spark plug wires and ignition coil.
3. Disconnect distributor wiring.
4. Remove two nuts securing distributor body to cylinder head and remove distributor.
5. Reverse procedure to install. Adjust ignition timing to specifications in individual car chapters. Torque nuts 9–15 ft. lbs.

NOTE: No gear is used to drive the distributor. A lug at the distributor base engages a slot on camshaft end.

1982–83 AMC

1. Disconnect distributor wire connector from coil.
2. Remove distributor cap and position aside.
3. Remove vacuum advance hose.
4. Remove distributor hold down bolt and clamp.
5. Mark relationship of rotor to distributor housing and distributor housing to engine block, then pull distributor up until rotor stops turning and mark relationship of rotor to distributor housing again.
6. Remove distributor.
7. If engine was not cranked after distributor was removed from engine, proceed as follows;
   a. Position rotor to align with second mark made on distributor housing prior to removing distributor.
   b. Install distributor into engine and align rotor with first mark made on distributor housing prior to removing distributor.

---

   c. Install distributor cap and connect all electrical and vacuum connections.
   d. Adjust ignition timing as specified in individual car chapter.
8. If engine was cranked after distributor was removed from engine, proceed as follows;
   a. Remove No. 1 spark plug and crank engine until compression pressure is felt in No. 1 cylinder. Slowly rotate engine until top dead center is indicated.
   b. Turn rotor to a position just ahead of No. 1 spark plug tower on distributor cap.
   c. Install distributor. Connect vacuum hose.
   d. Install distributor cap and connect all electrical connectors.
   e. Adjust ignition timing as specified in individual car chapter.

COMPONENTS, REPLACE

Ignition Coil Replacement

Units With Internal Coil
1. Remove electrical connector from distributor cap by lifting retaining tabs.
2. Remove three coil cover attaching screws, then remove cover, Fig. 29.
3. Remove coil attaching screws, then remove ignition coil with leads from distributor cap.
4. Remove coil arc seal.
5. Reverse procedure to install.

Units With External Coil
1. On 1981–83 Citation, Omega, Phoenix & Skylark & 1982–83 Celebrity, Century, Cutlass Ciera & 6000, proceed as follows:
   a. Remove bolt securing radio capacitor to coil.
   b. Disconnect coil electrical connector and high tension lead.
   c. Remove three coil mounting bolts, then remove coil.
   d. Reverse procedure to install.
2. On Chevette models, proceed as follows:
   a. Remove coil cover, then disconnect ignition switch to coil lead at coil.
   b. Disconnect coil high tension lead, then remove coil retaining bolts and the coil.
   c. Reverse procedure to install.
3. On Cavalier, Cimarron, Firenza, 2000 & Skyhawk models, proceed as follows:

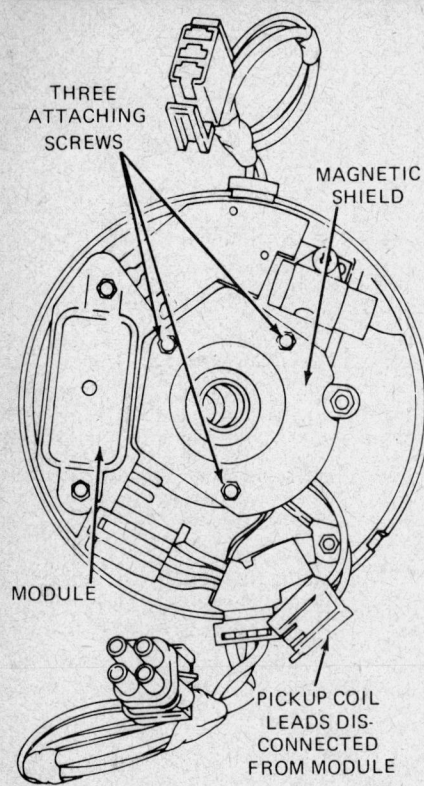

Fig. 30 Removing distributor shield. 1981–83 models equipped with 6 & 8 cylinder engines

NOTE: On 1982–83 Firenza, Skyhawk and 2000 with 1.8L OHC engine, the coil is located at the rear of the engine near the end of the cam cover.

a. Disconnect battery ground cable, then raise and support vehicle.
b. Disconnect fuel pump lines at fuel pump, then remove vacuum pipe retaining bracket nut at coil and position pipe aside.
c. Remove fuel pump, then remove coil mounting bolts.
4. On 1982–83 AMC models, proceed as follows:
   a. Disconnect distributor wire connector from coil
   b. Disconnect coil high tension lead.

NOTE: When removing coil high tension lead, twist boot one half turn and pull on boot only to prevent damage to coil high tension lead.

c. Remove coil attaching screws and coil.
d. Reverse procedure to install.

Module Replacement

1. Remove distributor cap and rotor.
2. Remove module retaining screws, then lift module upward.
3. Disconnect module electrical connector. Note position of electrical connector prior to disconnecting. Remove module from distributor.
4. Reverse procedure to install. Check to ensure that module electrical connector is installed in proper position. If module is not being replaced, do not wipe grease from module or distributor base. If new module is to be installed, coat module and distributor base with pack of grease supplied with replacement module.

Pick Up Coil, Replace

1. Remove distributor from engine.
2. Mark relationship of distributor shaft and driven gear for reference during assembly.
3. Remove roll pin and driven gear from shaft.
4. Remove distributor cap, magnetic shield (if equipped), shaft and rotor.
5. Remove C washer on top of pick up coil assembly, then disconnect pick up coil leads from module and remove pick up coil assembly.
6. Reverse procedure to install.

Hall Effect Switch (If Equipped), Replace

1. Remove distributor cap and rotor.
2. Remove switch retaining screws, then while pulling switch away, remove wiring connector. Remove switch.
3. Reverse procedure to install.

NOTE: After Hall Effect switch is installed, spin distributor shaft to ensure teeth do not touch. If necessary loosen, then re-tighten pick up coil teeth and Hall Effect switch to eliminate contact.

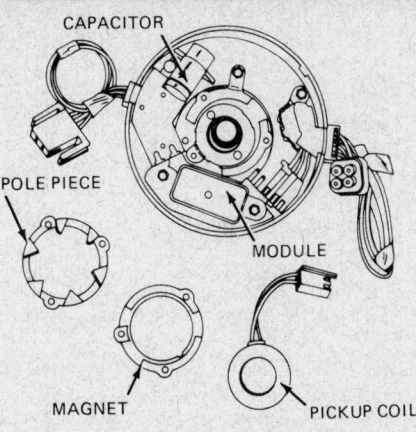

Fig. 31 Pick up coil disassembled. 1981–83 models equipped with 6 & 8 cylinder engines

DISTRIBUTOR SERVICE

6 & V8 Engines
1. Remove cap and coil as an assembly.
2. Remove rotor and pick up coil leads from module.
3. Mark relationship of distributor shaft and driven gear for reference during assembly.
4. Remove roll pin and driven gear.
5. Remove distributor shaft assembly.
6. Remove shield, Fig. 30.
7. Remove retaining ring, pick up coil, magnet and pole piece, Fig. 31.
8. Remove module retaining screws and capacitor screw, then remove module, capacitor and harness assembly from distributor.
9. Disconnect wiring harness from module. Reverse procedure to assemble.

4 Cylinder Engine
1. Remove rotor, then disconnect pick up coil leads from module.
2. Mark relationship of distributor shaft and driven gear for reference during assembly.
3. Remove roll pin and driven gear from distributor shaft.
4. Remove C washer retaining ring, then remove pick up coil assembly.
5. Disconnect module electrical connectors, then remove module retaining screws and the module.
6. Clean distributor base, then apply suitable silicone lubricant between module and base.
7. Reverse procedure to assemble.

Ford Solid State Ignition Systems

INTERMITTENT VEHICLE OPERATION DIAGNOSTIC PROCEDURE

1. With engine running at idle, move all primary wires, connectors and battery cables shown in Fig. 1 by pushing, pulling and twisting by hand. If vehicle stalls, make necessary repairs to wire or connector.
2. Remove fuel filter and check fuel pump pressure using a suitable pressure gauge. If fuel pump pressure is not within specifications listed in the individual car chapters of this manual, check fuel system for proper operation and repair as necessary.

NOTE: On models equipped with 4-98 and 4-140 engines, the fuel return line must be pinched off when checking fuel pump pressure.

3. Examine a sample of fuel from the fuel tank for contaminants. If fuel is contaminated, clean the fuel system and replace fuel filter.
4. With engine off, disconnect secondary wire from ignition coil. Inspect coil for cracks or carbon tracings, and the wires for cracks. If any damage is found, replace components as needed.
5. Inspect distributor cap for damage or carbon tracings. If any damage is found, replace cap and/or rotor as needed.
6. On models equipped with stator, remove distributor cap and position a 250 watt heat lamp 1 to 2 inches away from stator for 5 to 10 minutes. Measure resistance between orange and purple wires located at inner left hand fender apron. Lightly tap pick-up coil with a screwdriver. If resistance is less than 400 ohms or greater than 1000 ohms, replace stator.
7. On Escort/EXP and Lynx/LN7 models except those equipped with T.F.I., perform the following test:
   a. Connect suitable voltmeter to terminals of four-wire electrical connector that mate with orange and purple connector wires at inner left hand fender apron.

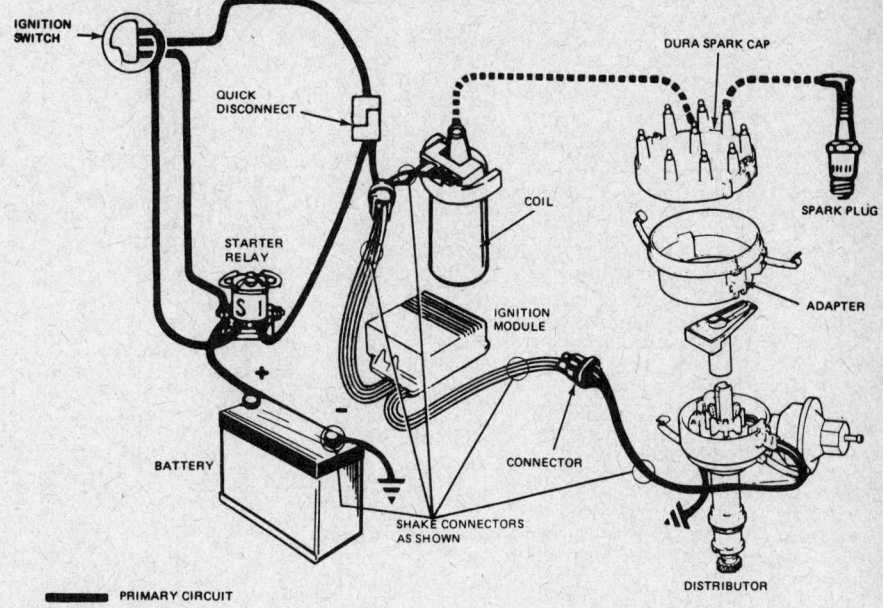

PRIMARY CIRCUIT
SECONDARY CIRCUIT

Fig. 1 Ignition wire inspection

   b. Set voltmeter at a 2 volt DC scale, then crank engine and reconnect the four-wire electrical connector.
   c. If voltmeter needle does not oscillate, replace distributor assembly.
8. On non-T.F.I. models, with engine running at idle, heat ignition module with a 250 watt heat lamp positioned 1 to 2 inches from module. If engine stalls, replace module with a known good unit. If this corrects the malfunction, recheck original module by reconnecting it to circuit.

NOTE: Do not allow module temperature to exceed 212° F. This can be checked after the first 10 minutes by applying drops of water to module housing. Repeat every two minutes thereafter until water droplets begin to boil.

9. Measure primary circuit ground resistance at ignition module connector black wire. If resistance is not zero ohms, remove distributor cap and inspect retaining screw at rubber plug where wires enter distributor. If screw or connection is loose or corroded, an intermittent high resistance or complete loss of ground may be causing ignition problem.

NOTE: If ignition malfunction occurs only under extreme low ambient temperature conditions, check for an open in feed to white lead to module.

10. Start engine several times and jiggle ignition switch with engine idling. If engine stalls, repair or replace ignition switch and/or connectors as needed. If engine does not stall, replace ignition module.

Ford 1977–80 Dura Spark I & II Solid State Ignition Systems

The Dura Spark ignition systems are controlled by an electronic module. The Dura Spark systems produce higher spark plug voltages, permitting the use of wider spark plug gaps required to ignite the leaner air/fuel mixtures.

There are three variations of this ignition system as shown in Figs. 1 through 3.

The distributor shaft and armature rotation, Fig. 4, causes the armature poles to pass by the core of the magnetic pick-up assembly. As an armature tooth approaches the pole piece, it reduces the reluctance of the magnetic circuit, thus increasing the field strength. The resulting alternating voltage is applied to the ignition module at a rate proportional to engine speed. The ignition module shuts off the primary circuit each time it receives a pulse from the magnetic pick-up. The timing circuitry in the module leaves the circuit "Off" just long enough for the coil to discharge into the secondary circuit then turns the primary circuit "On" again. Maximum time is allowed for the coil to discharge.

Special low resistance ignition coils are used, therefore conventional ignition coils are not to be used on these systems. The ignition coil can be identified by its blue color and the terminals are marked differently, Fig. 5.

The electronic module, Fig. 6, is the brain of this system and is well protected from outside elements such as heat and shock. The heat sink containing all the electronic devices is sealed in a mixture of epoxy and sand. This module can not be disassembled and must be replaced if malfunctioning.

The ignition system is protected against electrical current produced during normal vehicle operation and against reverse polarity or high voltage accidentally applied if vehicle is jump started.

CAUTION: The ignition system will be damaged if other than volt-ohm test procedures are used to check alternator output. This alternator test procedure is outlined in the "Ford Motorcraft Alternator" section, under "Voltmeter Test."

Do not use the volt-amp test procedure or any other test that utilizes a knife switch on the battery terminal.

SYSTEM DIAGNOSIS

NOTE: When performing diagnostic or service procedures on models equipped with Dura-Spark II, the ignition switch should remain in the "Off" position unless otherwise stated in the procedure. On these units, a spark will be generated when the ignition switch is placed from the "On" position to "Off", which may inadvertently cause the engine to rotate, resulting in personal injury.

Secondary Circuit Test
Rotor Air Gap
1. Connect an oscilloscope with voltage pick-up on coil to distributor cable. Set

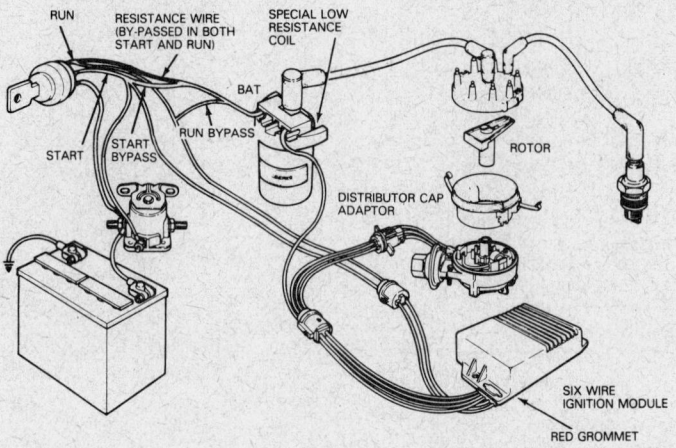

Fig. 1   Dura Spark Ignition system. 1977–79 California

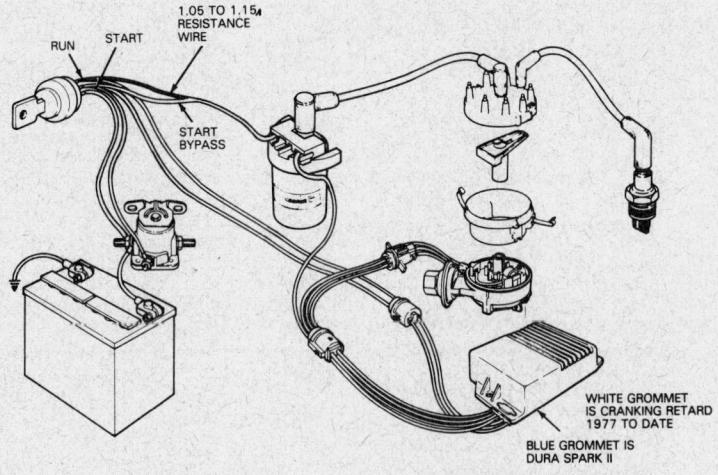

Fig. 2   Dura Spark II ignition system. 1977–80

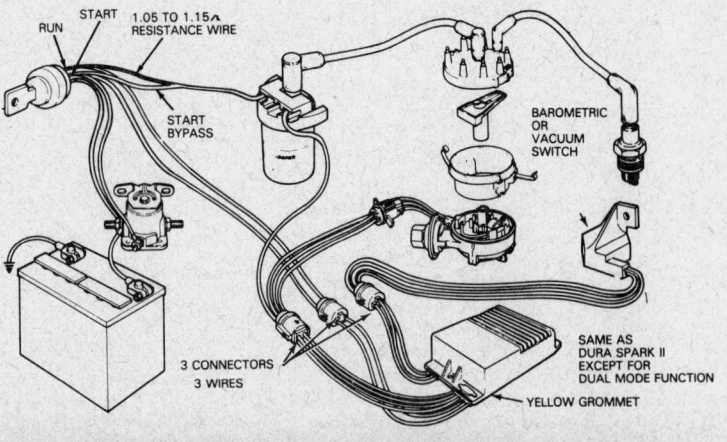

Fig. 3   Dura Spark II with dual mode ignition system. 1978–80

oscilloscope to 30KV parade pattern.
2. Disconnect any spark plug wire (except no. 1) and ground it firmly to engine block.

CAUTION: While engine is running, do not disconnect spark plug wires 1 or 3 on 4 cylinder engine, 1, 3, or 5 on inline 6 cylinder engine, 1 or 4 on V6 engine or 1 or 8 on V8 engine. These contacts in the distributor cap are above the stator and arcing may result when the circuit is open.

3. Run engine at 1000 rpm and observe height of firing spike of disconnected cylinder. Firing spike should be 8 KV or less.
4. If firing spike is 8000 volts or less, air gap resistance is within acceptable limits. If firing spike is greater than 8000 volts, replace rotor and repeat test. If still too high, replace distributor cap.

NOTE: White deposits on rotor tip are normal and should not be removed. If rotor is replaced, coat new rotor tip with silicone grease.

Spark Plug Firing Voltage Test

1. Reconnect spark plug lead, then run engine at 2000 rpm and set oscilloscope to 30 KV parade pattern.
2. Check for firing spikes which are appreciably lower or higher (5 KV) than the other cylinders.
3. Normal firing spikes should be approximately 15 KV.
4. Expand pattern to inspect individual firing spikes. If all spikes are below or above specifications, check rotor, distributor cap or coil to distributor cable.
5. To check low firing voltage, disconnect spark plug wire from spark plug and hold it so that spark cannot arc to ground:
   a. If spike does not increase to 28,000 volts or more (coil output), check for a cracked distributor cap with a grounded terminal.
   b. If spike does not rise, replace affected spark plug.
6. To check high firing voltage, disconnect spark plug wire from spark plug and ground the wire:
   a. If high spike drops, replace spark plug.
   b. If high spike remains, check spark plug wire and its connection at distributor cap.

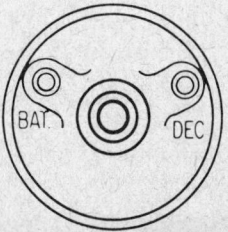

Fig. 5   Ignition coil identification

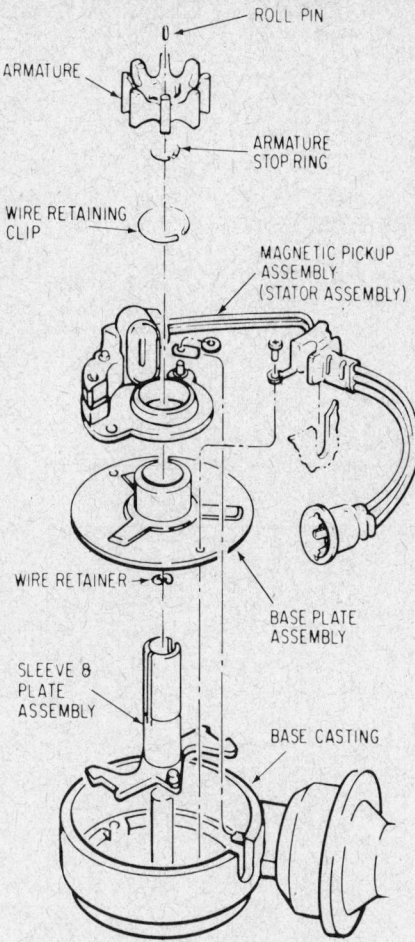

Fig. 4   Breakerless distributor (typical)

Spark Plug Wires Continuity Test
1. Remove distributor cap and disconnect suspected wire from spark plug or coil.
2. Using an ohmmeter, check wire resistance through distributor cap. Resistance should be 5000 ohms per inch or less.
3. If resistance of wire is greater than 5000 ohms per inch, replace wire.

Spark Plug Wire Inspection
1. Clean off any deposits of road salt, dirt etc. from wires, boots, distributor cap and coil using water and a mild soap solution.
2. Inspect wires and boots for cuts, punctures, scrapes and burns. Replace as required.
3. Inspect wire terminals for corrosion. Remove corrosion with fine sandpaper.
4. Coat inside of all boots with silicone grease before reinstalling.

Primary Circuit Test

NOTE: The flow chart in Fig. 7, and test procedures provide a sequence for testing which should locate most problems in the primary ignition circuit. It is important to perform these tests in the exact order listed to check all portions of the system. A volt-ohmmeter, 15 inch jumper wire, straight pin, modified spark plug and ballast resistor, Fig. 8, are required to check the system.

Test 1, Tap Test
1. Remove distributor cap and rotor. Crank engine to align one tooth of armature with magnet in pick-up coil, Fig. 9.
2. On Dura Spark I system, install ballast resistor Motorcraft DY-36 in series with primary circuit at BAT terminal of ignition coil, Fig. 10. Using a straight pin, pierce both red and white leads of module to short these two leads together, Fig. 10.

CAUTION: Never install bypass until after the ballast resistor is in place or permanent damage to module or coil may result.

3. Remove coil wire from distributor cap and connect to a well grounded modified spark plug, Fig. 8, or hold wire 1/4" from engine. Turn ignition switch to Run and tap distributor body with a screwdriver handle.
4. If there are sparks, proceed to test 2. If ther are no sparks, proceed to Test 4.

Test 2, Voltage Drop On Module White Wire
1. On Dura Spark I, remove pin from red wire only, leaving pin to make contact with white wire only, Fig. 11.
2. Connect positive lead of voltmeter to positive battery terminal and negative lead of voltmeter to pin in white wire. Crank engine and observe voltmeter reading. Reading should not exceed 1 volt.
3. If reading is above 1 volt, repair circuit feeding white wire, then repeat Test 1. If reading is less than 1 volt, perform Test 3.

Test 3, Crank Test
1. Crank engine while checking for sparks.
2. If there are no sparks, perform Test 6. If there are sparks, ignition system is functioning properly. Remove pin and ballast resistor. Check fuel system and refer to "Testing for Intermittent Conditions".

Test 4, Voltage Drop On Module Red Wire

1. On Dura Spark I, remove pin from white wire only, leaving pin to make contact with red wire, Fig. 12.
2. On Dura Spark II, insert pin into red wire to make contact, Fig. 12.
3. Measure voltage drop on red wire of ignition module with key in On position. Connect positive lead of voltmeter to positive terminal and negative lead to red wire.

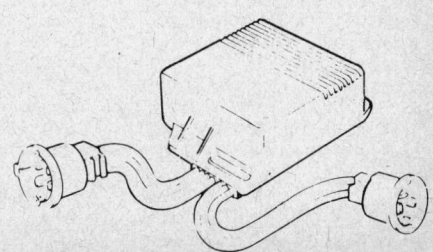

Fig. 6   Electronic control module (typical)

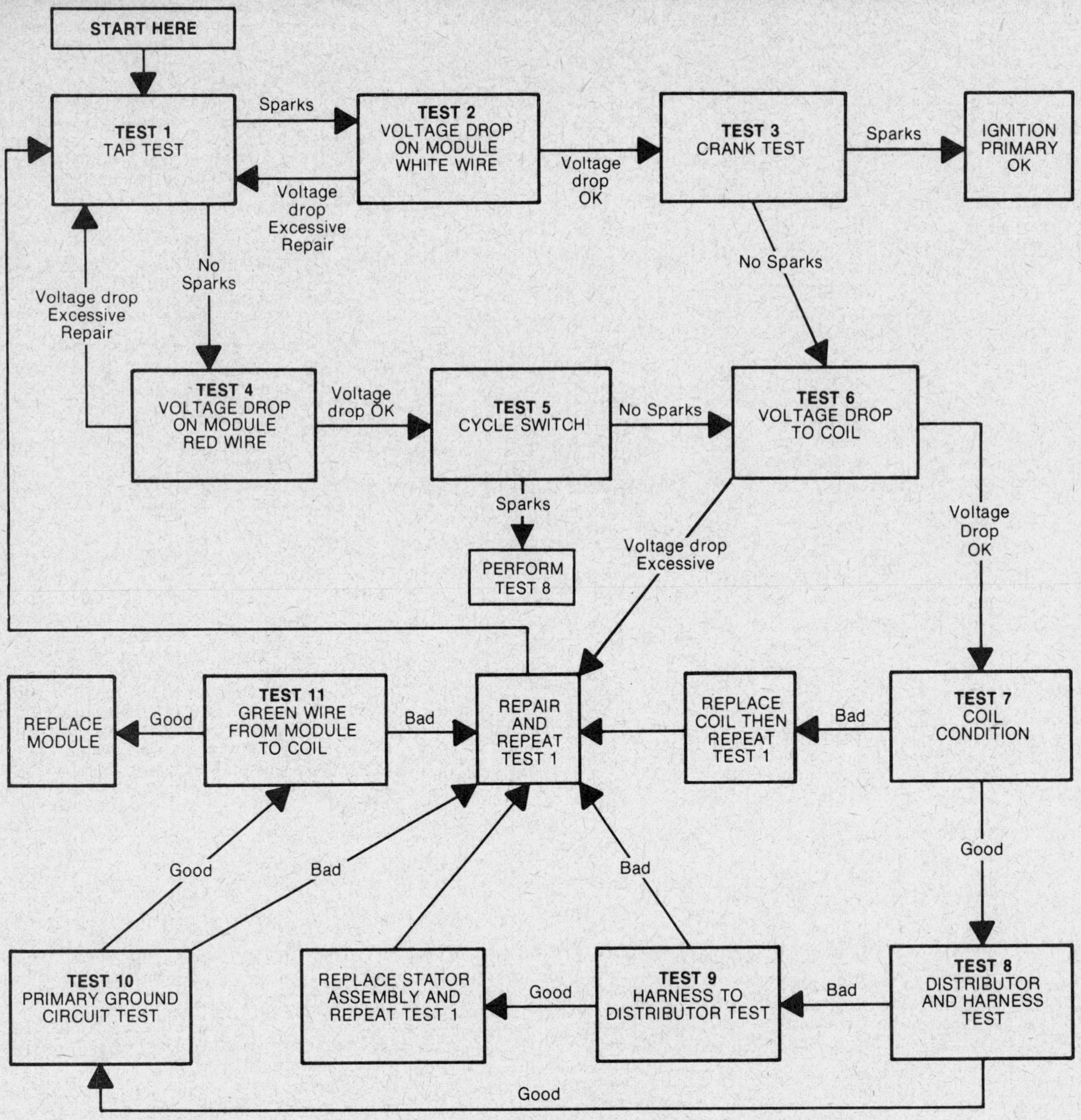

ELECTRONIC IGNITION SYSTEMS

```
START HERE
   │
   ▼
┌──────────────┐  Sparks   ┌──────────────────┐  Voltage    ┌──────────────┐  Sparks   ┌──────────────┐
│   TEST 1     │─────────▶ │     TEST 2       │  drop       │    TEST 3    │─────────▶ │  IGNITION    │
│   TAP TEST   │           │  VOLTAGE DROP    │  OK         │  CRANK TEST  │           │  PRIMARY     │
│              │◀───────── │  ON MODULE       │ ──────────▶ │              │           │    OK        │
└──────────────┘ Voltage   │  WHITE WIRE      │             └──────────────┘           └──────────────┘
                  drop     └──────────────────┘
                Excessive                                         │ No Sparks
                 Repair                                           │
   │ No Sparks                                                    ▼
   ▼
┌──────────────┐  Voltage  ┌──────────────┐  No Sparks  ┌──────────────────┐
│   TEST 4     │  drop OK  │   TEST 5     │ ──────────▶ │     TEST 6       │
│ VOLTAGE DROP │─────────▶ │ CYCLE SWITCH │             │  VOLTAGE DROP    │
│ ON MODULE    │           │              │             │   TO COIL        │
│  RED WIRE    │           └──────────────┘             └──────────────────┘
└──────────────┘                 │ Sparks                    │          │ Voltage
                                 ▼                           │          │  Drop OK
Voltage drop              ┌──────────────┐    Voltage drop   │          ▼
Excessive Repair          │   PERFORM    │    Excessive      │
                          │   TEST 8     │                   │
                          └──────────────┘                   │
```

Fig. 7 System diagnosis flow chart

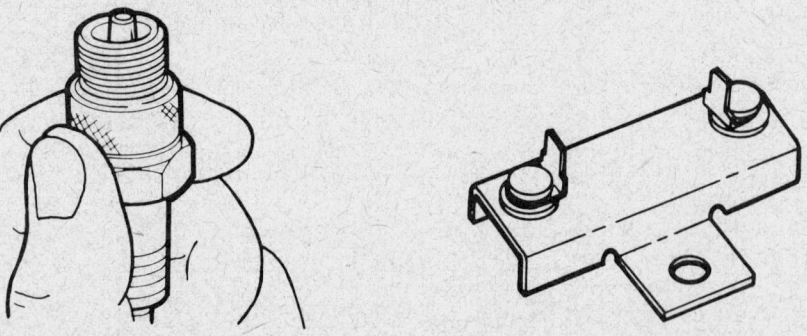

MODIFIED SPARK PLUG WITH THE SIDE
ELECTRODE REMOVED

BALLAST RESISTOR
MOTORCRAFT PART NO DY-36

Fig. 8 Test equipment

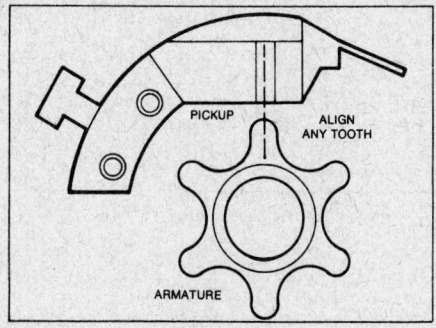

Fig. 9 Aligning armature with magnet in pick-up coil

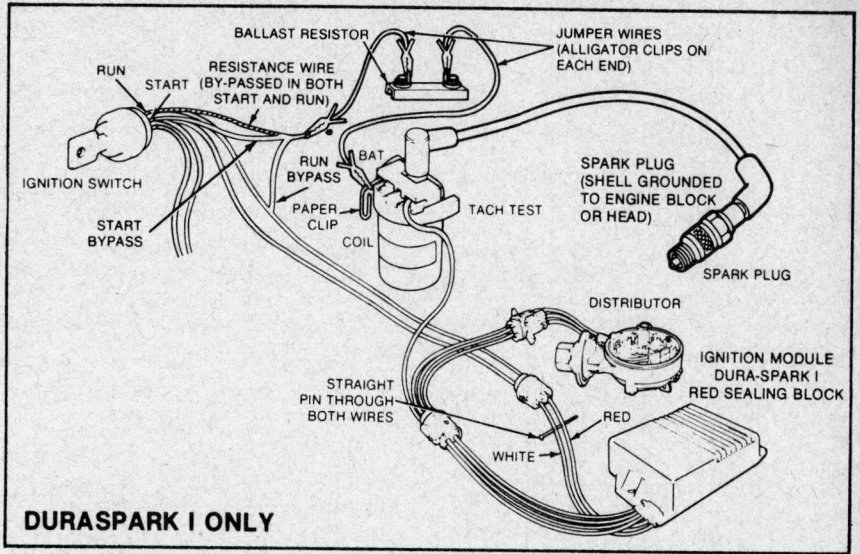

Fig. 10 Ballast resistor installed in primary circuit. Dura Spark I system

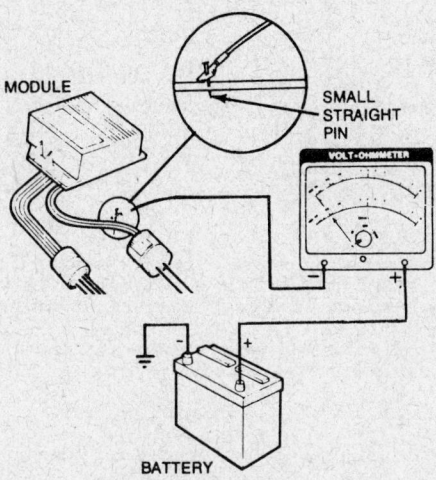

Fig. 11 Checking voltage drop on module white wire

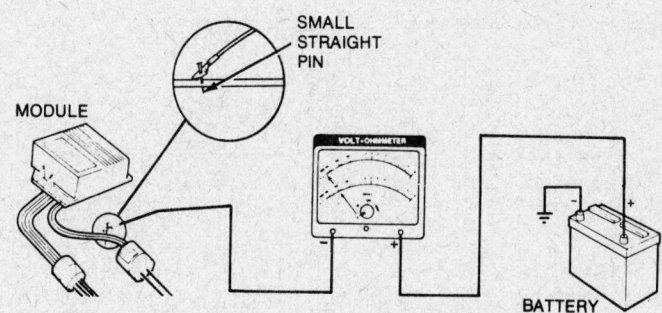

Fig. 12 Checking voltage drop on module red wire

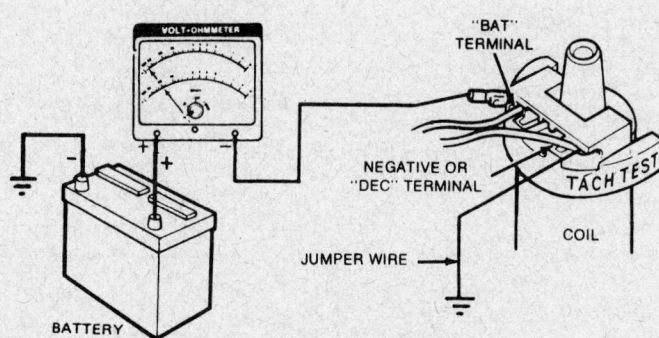

Fig. 13 Checking voltage drop to coil

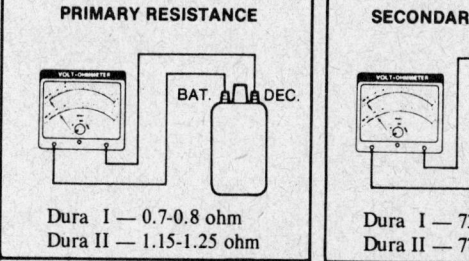

Fig. 14 Checking coil condition

4. If reading is above 1 volt, repair circuit feeding red wire, then repeat Test 1. If reading is below 1 volt, perform Test 5.

Test 5, Cycle Switch
1. On Dura Spark I, pierce both red and white wires of module to short these two leads using a straight pin.

NOTE: On Dura Spark II, do not install straight pin.

2. Cycle ignition switch On and Off or turn ignition switch On and disconnect and reconnect distributor connector. A spark should be seen at the modified spark plug each time the ignition switch is cycled, or each time the connector is disconnected.
3. If there are no sparks, perform Test 6. If there are sparks, perform Test 8.

Test 6, Voltage Drop to Coil, Fig. 13.
1. Connect jumper wire from "DEC" termi-

nal to ground. Turn ignition switch to Start and then Run positions.
2. Measure voltage drop to "BAT" terminal of coil:
   a. While cranking engine, voltage drop should be no more than 1 volt.
   b. With ignition switch at Run, voltage drop should be less than 1 volt on Duraspark I, and less than 6.5 volts on Duraspark II.
3. If voltage drop is within specifications,

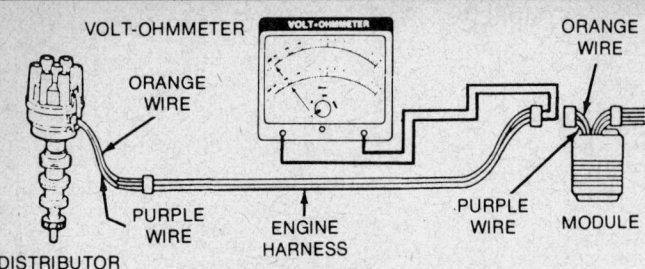

Fig. 15   Distributor and harness test

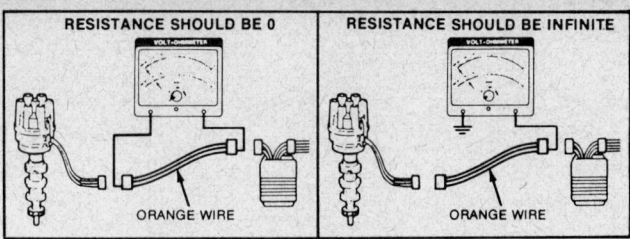

Fig. 16   Harness to distributor test

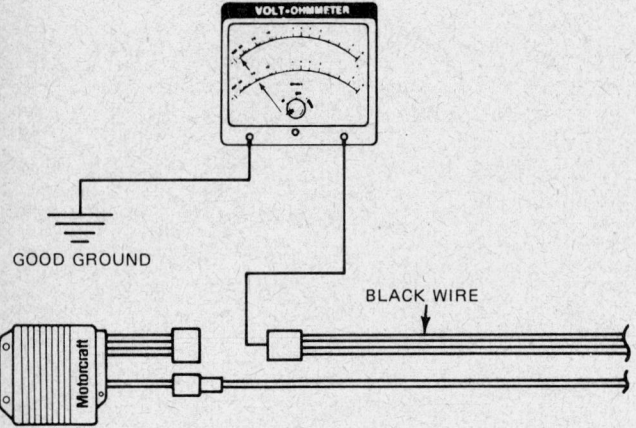

Fig. 17   Primary ground circuit test

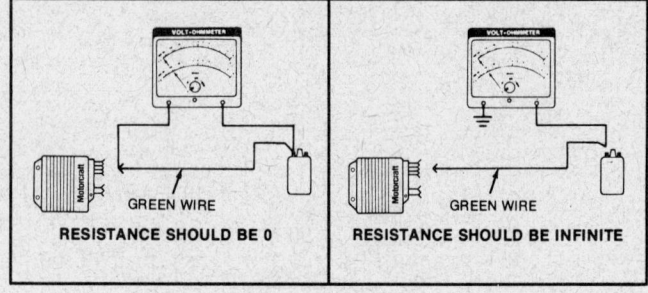

Fig. 18   Checking green wire from module to coil

perform Test 7. If voltage drop is not within specifications, perform repairs as necessary and repeat test.

Test 7, Coil Condition

Refer to Fig. 14, for ohmmeter connections to check coil primary and secondary resistance. Resistance values should be as specified. If resistance values are within specifications, perform Test 8. If not, replace coil and repeat Test 1.

Test 8, Distributor & Harness Test, Fig. 15

1. Disconnect module connector with purple and orange wires. Test distributor by connecting a voltmeter to orange and purple wires at harness side of male connector.

NOTE: Do not use a voltmeter combined with a dwell-meter, as slight needle oscillations of ½ volt may not be detectable on this type of test equipment. Also, a digital volt-ohmmeter will not function on this test.

CAUTION: If vehicle is equipped with a catalytic converter, disconnect air supply line between by-pass valve and manifold before cranking engine with ignition off. This will prevent damage to the catalytic converter. Also, after testing, run engine for at least three minutes before reconnecting air supply line, to clear excess fuel from exhaust system.

2. Set voltmeter to its lowest scale and

crank engine. Meter needle should oscillate slightly (about ½ volt). Refer to "Distributor Testing" for additional information.

3. If voltmeter indications are as specified, perform Test 10. If not, perform Test 9.

Test 9, Harness To Distributor Test, Fig. 16

1. Check for open or shorted condition in orange and purple wires from module connector (harness side) to distributor connector (harness side).

2. If wires are not open or shorted, replace stator assembly and repeat test. If a shorted or open condition exists, make necessary repairs and repeat test.

Test 10, Primary Ground Circuit Test, Fig. 17

1. Connect an ohmmeter to black lead at harness side of module connector and a good ground.

2. With ohmmeter at its lowest scale, there should be no measurable resistance.

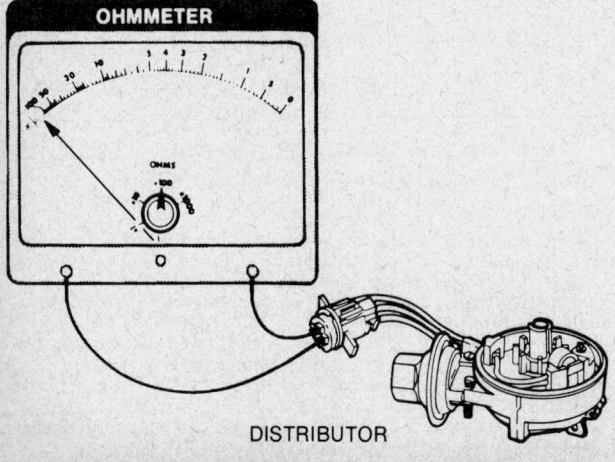

Fig. 19   Checking pick-up coil in distributor

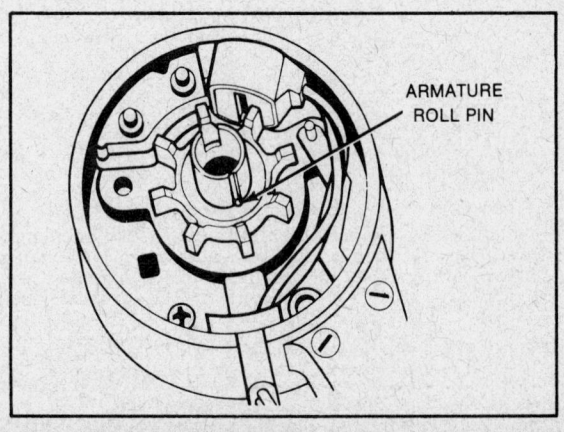

Fig. 20   Armature roll pin

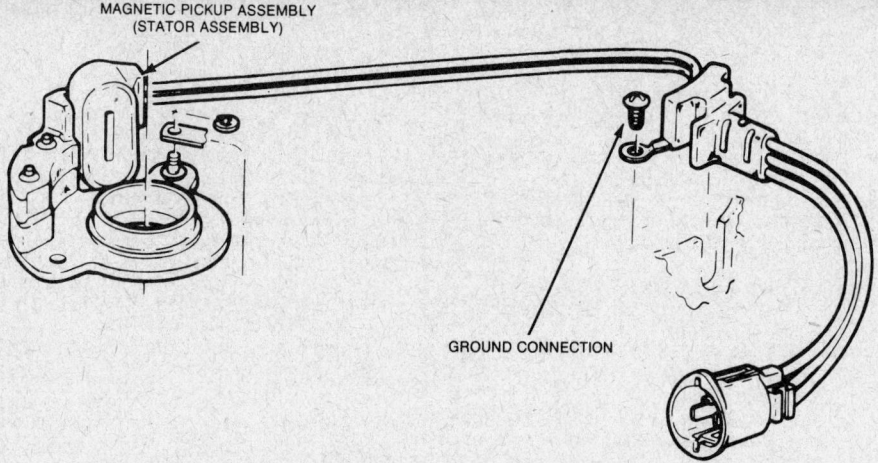

MAGNETIC PICKUP ASSEMBLY
(STATOR ASSEMBLY)

GROUND CONNECTION

Fig. 21   Magnetic pick-up assembly and lead

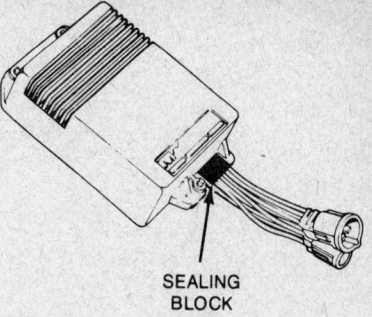

SEALING
BLOCK

Fig. 22   Module identification

3. If there is no measurable resistance, perform Test 11. If resistance can be measured, check ground in distributor and wire from module to distributor. Repair or replace as necessary and repeat test.

Test 11, Green Wire From Module To Coil, Fig. 18

1. Check green wire from module to coil for open or shorted condition.
2. If wires are open or shorted, repair or replace as necessary and repeat test. If shorted or open condition does not exist, refer to "Testing For Intermittent Conditions". If problem cannot be found, replace module.

Coil Testing

If an oscilloscope is available, connect oscilloscope and disconnect one spark plug wire not allowing it to arc to ground. Crank engine while observing coil reserve voltage. Voltage spike should be 28 KV or more.

Distributor Testing

Test 1, Fig. 19

Connect an ohmmeter between parallel blades of distributor connector. Resistance should be 400–1000 ohms. A reading of less than 400 ohms indicates a short while an infinity reading indicates an open. With ignition switch off, check resistance between orange wire and ground and purple wire and ground. Reading at each wire should be greater than 70,000 ohms.

Test 2, Fig. 20

Remove distributor cap and check that roll pin retaining armature on distributor shaft is in place. If roll pin is missing, armature can rotate in relation to distributor shaft causing timing to be out of specifications. Check for correct connection of orange and purple wires between distributor and module. If wires are reversed, distributor timing will be 22½ degrees out of phase.

Test 3

If a known good distributor is available, connect it to harness, turn ignition switch "On" and spin distributor by hand while checking for sparks.

Engine Starts Normally At Moderate Temperature But Starts Hard Or Will Not Start In Extremely Cold Temperature

1. Check for open in feed to white lead to module.

Engine Quits Intermittently With Complete Loss Of Ignition

1. Check primary circuit ground resistance at ignition module connector black wire. Resistance should be zero ohms.
2. If resistance is not zero ohms, remove distributor cap and inspect retaining screw at rubber plug where wires enter distributor, Fig. 21. A loose or cross threaded screw or a dirty or corroded connection at this screw can cause an intermittent high resistance or a complete loss of ground.

Module Idenitification

The ignition module can be identified as to type of ignition system by the color of the sealing block, Fig. 22.

Sealing Block Color	Type Of Ignition System
Red	Dura Spark I
White	Dura Spark II (With Cranking Retard)
Blue	Dura Spark II
Yellow	Dura Spark II (Dual Mode)
Green Or Black	Early Solid State Ignition
Brown	EEC System

DISTRIBUTOR, REPLACE
Removal

NOTE: On some 4 and 6 cylinder models, it may be necessary to position thermactor air pump aside to gain access to distributor. It may also be necessary to disconnect the thermactor air filter.

1. Disconnect distributor wiring connector from the engine wiring harness.
2. Disconnect vacuum advance hose, then remove distributor cap and position aside.
3. Remove rotor and adapter, then reinstall rotor.
4. Mark position of distributor in engine and position of rotor on the distributor housing to aid installation.
5. Remove distributor hold-down and clamp, then lift distributor out of engine.

CAUTION: Do not crank engine after the distributor has been removed.

Installation

1. If engine was not cranked after distributor was removed from engine, proceed as follows:
   a. Position the distributor in the engine, aligning the housing to block marks

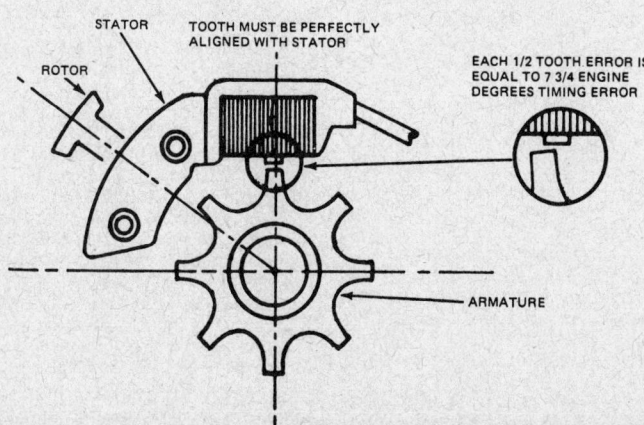

STATOR

TOOTH MUST BE PERFECTLY
ALIGNED WITH STATOR

ROTOR

EACH 1/2 TOOTH ERROR IS
EQUAL TO 7 3/4 ENGINE
DEGREES TIMING ERROR

ARMATURE

Fig. 23   Armature tooth and stator alignment

and rotor to housing marks made before removal.

b. Install the distributor hold-down and clamp but do not tighten bolt until timing has been adjusted.

c. Install distributor cap and wires, then connect distributor wiring connector to engine wiring harness and attach vacuum advance hose.

d. Adjust ignition timing to specifications found in the individual car chapters.

2. If engine was cranked after distributor was removed from engine, proceed as follows:

a. Remove No. 1 spark plug and crank engine until compression pressure is felt in No. 1 cylinder. Slowly rotate engine until the correct initial timing mark on the crankshaft damper aligns with the timing pointer.

b. Position the distributor in the engine with rotor at number one firing position and armature tooth aligned with stator as shown in Fig. 23.

NOTE: Ensure oil pump intermediate shaft properly engages the distributor shaft. It may be necessary to crank the engine with the starter after the distributor drive gear is partially engaged in order to engage the oil pump intermediate shaft.

c. Install distributor hold-down bolt and clamp but do not tighten bolt until timing has been adjusted.

d. Install distributor cap and wires, then connect distributor wiring connector to engine wiring harness and attach vacuum advance hose.

3. Adjust ignition timing to specifications found in the individual car chapters.

CAUTION: Due to higher ignition system voltage, a timing light specifically designed for this system should be used when checking ignition timing. If a timing light designed for this system is not available, an inductive pickup type timing light may operate satisfactorily if a piece of split vacuum hose is first placed around the spark plug wire.

COMPONENT REPLACEMENT

Magnetic Pickup Assembly

Removal

1. Remove distributor cap and rotor, then disconnect distributor wiring harness plug, Fig. 4.
2. Using two screw drivers, pry armature from advance plate sleeve and remove roll pin.
3. Remove snap ring securing pickup assembly to base plate. On 4 and 6 cylinder models, remove washer and wave washer.
4. On all models, remove snap ring securing vacuum advance link to pickup assembly.
5. Remove pickup assembly ground screw and lift assembly from distributor.
6. Disconnect vacuum advance link from pickup assembly post.

Installation

1. Position pickup assembly over base plate and slide wiring harness into slot on side of distributor housing, Fig. 4.

2. On 4 and 6 cylinder models, install washers. On all models, install snap ring securing pickup assembly to base plate.
3. Position vacuum advance link on pickup assembly post and install snap ring.
4. Insert ground screw through wiring harness tab and install on base plate.
5. Install armature on advance plate sleeve, ensure roll pin is engaged in slot.
6. Install distributor rotor and cap, then connect distributor wiring harness plug to vehicle wiring harness.

Vacuum Advance Unit, Replace

1. Remove distributor cap and rotor.
2. Disconnect vacuum lines, then remove snap ring that secures vacuum advance link to pickup assembly.
3. Remove vacuum advance attaching screws, then tilt unit downward to disconnect link.
4. Carefully remove unit from distributor.
5. Reverse procedure to install.

Fixed Base Plate, Replace

1. Remove distributor cap and rotor.
2. Remove vacuum advance unit and magnetic pickup assembly.
3. Remove attaching screws and lift base plate from distributor.
4. Reverse procedure to install.

RESISTANCE WIRE, REPLACE

NOTE: The special resistance wire, must be of a specified length and diameter to reduce operating voltage of the ignition system. Under no circumstances should the resistance wire be replaced by any other wire but the correct service resistance wire. When a replacement resistance wire is installed, the damaged resistance wire should be isolated from the system.

1977–78 Bobcat & Pinto, Fig. 24

1. Disconnect battery ground cable.
2. From under instrument panel, detach fuse panel mounted on bracket on right hand side of steering column.
3. Pull fuse panel and wiring downward to expose damaged resistor wire.
4. From back of fuse panel, cut damaged resistor wire (single strand steel wire) close to the panel and the wiring, and insulate cuts ends with D6AZ-19627-A tape, Fig. 24.
5. From same terminal (second wire), cut the circuit No. 16A red light green stripe (multiple strand copper) wire about 2 inches from fuse panel and install a C5AZ-14294-B bullet terminal on each cut end, Fig. 24.
6. Reconnect the No. 16A circuit with a B6A-14487-A double connector.
7. Connect one end of replacement D7AZ-12250-A resistor wire into the double connector and route and loop the excess length along the harness to the ignition switch. Secure resistor wire to wiring harness with tape or a strap.
8. Disconnect multiple connector from ignition switch and cut circuit no. 262 brown pink stripe wire about 2 inches from the connector.

9. Install a C5AZ-14294-B bullet terminal on each cut end, then reconnect the No. 262 circuit with a B6A-14487-A double connector.
10. Connect the remaining end of the new resistor wire into the double connector.
11. Reconnect all disassembled components and reconnect battery ground cable.
12. Turn ignition key to "Start" position and check if engine continues to run when key is released to "Run" position. If engine does not continue to run, use a voltohmmeter and check for proper voltage and or/resistance at ignition coil. With new D7AZ-12250-A resistor wire installed, the resistance should be 1.05 to 1.15 ohms at 75° F, and voltage should be 6.4 volts at the coil.

NOTE: Inspect all wiring adjacent to the resistor wire for damage, and repair as necessary.

1977–78 Mustang, Fig. 25

1. Disconnect battery ground cable.
2. From engine side of dash panel, release wiring harness connector from fuse panel.
3. From under left side of instrument panel, release connector and fuse panel from dash and pull downward to facilitate releasing multiple connector from fuse panel.
4. From multiple connector disconnected from fuse panel and dash panel, cut and remove No. 16 red-light green stripe single strand wire resistance wire close to connector and harness.
5. Insulate cut ends of wire using tape D6AZ-19627-A or equivalent.
6. From the same terminal in connector that the resistance wire was removed, cut the No. 262 brown-pink stripe wire about 2 inches from the connector.
7. On each cut end, install bullet terminal C5AZ-14294-B or equivalent.
8. Reconnect No. 262 wire using double connector B6A-14487-A or equivalent.
9. Install one end of replacement resistance wire into the double connector, then route and loop excess length along harness to ignition switch.
10. Secure resistance wire along wiring harness using adjustable strap or suitable tape.
11. Disconnect multiple connector from ignition switch and cut red-light green stripe wire about 2 inches from ignition switch connector.
12. Install bullet terminal C5AZ-14294-B or equivalent at each cut end.
13. Reconnect cut No. 16A circuit using double connector B6A-14487-A double connector or equivalent.
14. Connect remaining end of replacement resistance wire to double connector.
15. Reconnect all disassembled components and battery ground cable.
16. Rotate ignition switch to start position and check to ensure that engine will continue to operate when ignition switch is returned to the run position. If engine will not continue to operate, check for proper voltage and resistance at ignition coil. Resistance should be 1.05 to 1.15 ohms at 75° F. Voltage should be approximately 6.4 volts at the coil.

NOTE: Inspect all wiring adjacent to resistor wire for damage and repair as necessary.

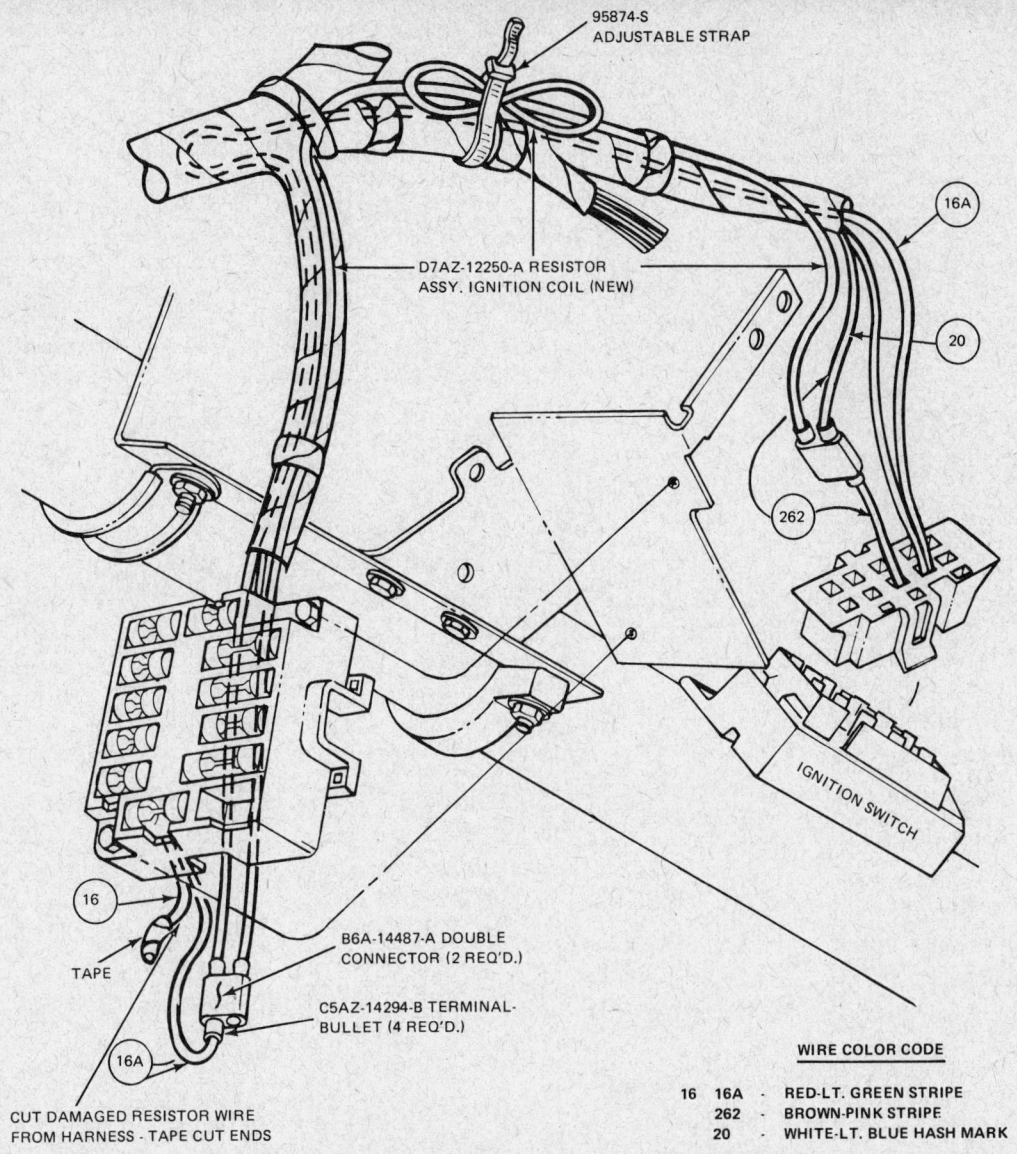

95874-S
ADJUSTABLE STRAP

D7AZ-12250-A RESISTOR
ASSY. IGNITION COIL (NEW)

16A

20

262

IGNITION SWITCH

16

TAPE

B6A-14487-A DOUBLE
CONNECTOR (2 REQ'D.)

C5AZ-14294-B TERMINAL-
BULLET (4 REQ'D.)

16A

CUT DAMAGED RESISTOR WIRE
FROM HARNESS - TAPE CUT ENDS

WIRE COLOR CODE

16 16A - RED-LT. GREEN STRIPE
262 - BROWN-PINK STRIPE
20 - WHITE-LT. BLUE HASH MARK

Fig. 24   Resistance wire installation. 1977–78 Bobcat & Pinto

1977–78 Granada, Monarch & Versailles, Fig. 26

1. Disconnect battery ground cable.
2. From inside vehicle, remove fuse panel cover, then remove two screws attaching fuse panel to instrument panel.
3. Pull fuse panel below instrument panel, then at back of fuse panel, cut No. 16A single strand resistance wire close to panel and insulate cut ends with tap D6AZ-19627-A or equivalent.
4. From same terminal, cut No. 16 red-light green stripe multiple strand copper wire about 2 inches from fuse panel and install C5AZ-14294-B bullet terminal or equivalent on each cut end.
5. Install one end of replacement resistance wire into double connector, then route and loop excessive length of resistance wire along wiring harness to half moon shaped multiple connector that connects with harness above parking brake assembly. Secure replacement resistance wire

along wiring harness using adjustable strap or suitable tape.
6. Disconnect half moon shaped connector from wiring harness above parking brake assembly, then pull wire connector downward to facilitate cutting and removal of No. 16A red-light green stripe single strand resistance wire.
7. Insulate ends of resistance wire with tape D6AZ-19627-A or equivalent.
8. From same terminal as resistance wire was cut, cut No. 262 brown-pink strip wire about 2 inches from connector and install bullet terminal C5AZ-12294-B or equivalent on each cut end.
9. Reconnect circuit No. 262 with double connector B6A-14487-A or equivalent.
10. Install remaining end of replacement resistance wire into double connector.
11. Reconnect all disassembled components and battery ground cable.
12. Rotate ignition key to start position and check to ensure that engine will continue to operate after ignition switch is returned to run position. If engine will not

continue to operate, check voltage and resistance at ignition coil. Resistance should be 1.05 to 1.15 ohms at 75° F. Voltage should be approximately 6.4 volts at coil.

NOTE: Inspect all wiring adjacent to resistor wire for damage and repairs as necessary.

1977–78 Cougar, LTD II & Thunderbird, Fig. 27

1. Disconnect battery ground cable.
2. From engine compartment, disconnect wiring connector at dash panel.
3. From inside vehicle, remove release wire connector from dash panel and disconnect from fuse panel.
4. Pull connector disconnected from fuse panel downward below instrument panel to facilitate removal of No. 16B red-light green single strand resistance wire.
5. Cut resistance wire close to fuse panel

ELECTRONIC IGNITION SYSTEMS

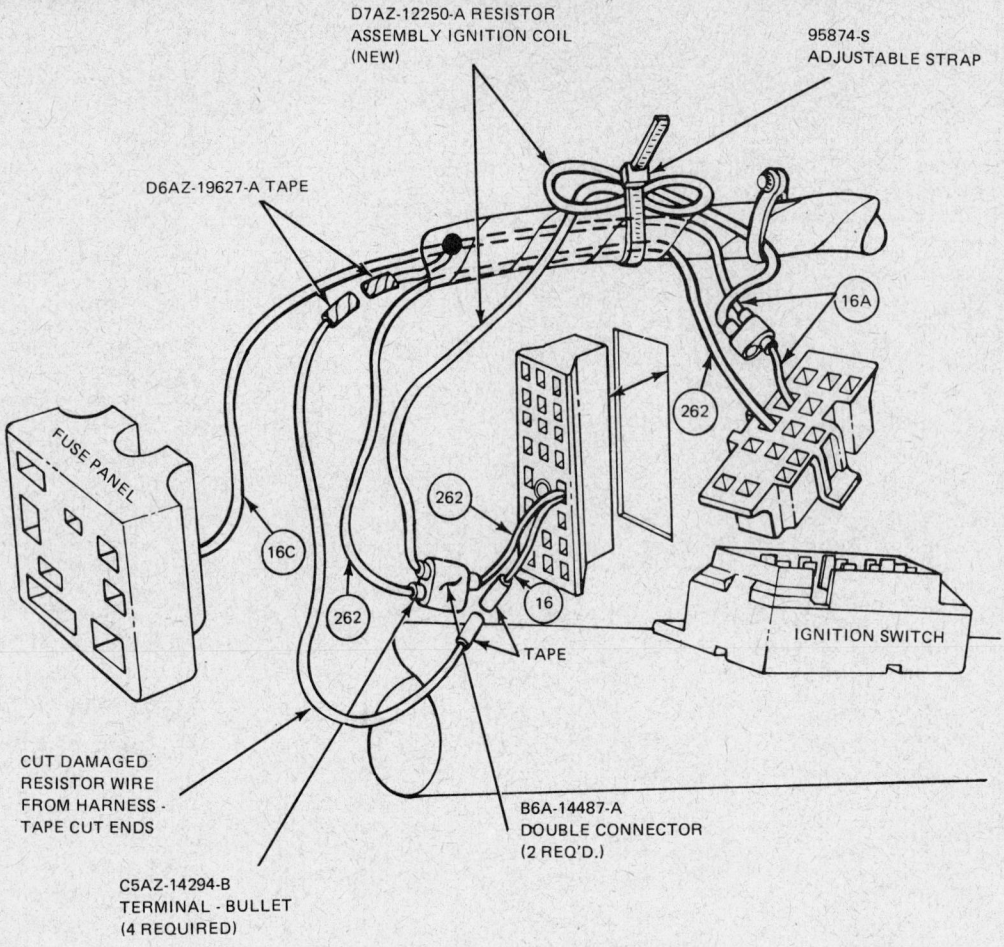

D7AZ-12250-A RESISTOR
ASSEMBLY IGNITION COIL
(NEW)

95874-S
ADJUSTABLE STRAP

D6AZ-19627-A TAPE

FUSE PANEL

16C

262

262

16

16A

262

TAPE

IGNITION SWITCH

CUT DAMAGED
RESISTOR WIRE
FROM HARNESS -
TAPE CUT ENDS

C5AZ-14294-B
TERMINAL - BULLET
(4 REQUIRED)

B6A-14487-A
DOUBLE CONNECTOR
(2 REQ'D.)

WIRE COLOR CODE

16 16A 16C - RED-LT. GREEN STRIPE

262 - BROWN-PINK STRIPE

Fig. 25   Resistance wire installation. 1977–78 Mustang

and insulate tape D6AZ-19627-A or equivalent.

6. From the same terminal as resistance wire was removed, cut No. 262 brown pink stripe multiple strand wire about 2 inches from connector and install bullet terminals C5AZ-142924-B or equivalent on each cut end.

7. Reconnect circuit No. 262 using double connector B6A-14487-A or equivalent.

8. Install one end of replacement resistance wire into double connector, then route and loop excessive length along wiring harness to ignition switch. Secure resistance wire using an adjustable strap or suitable tape.

9. Remove instrument cluster as described in car chapter under Instrument Cluster, Replace.

10. Disconnect wire connector from ignition switch to facilitate removal of No. 16B red-light green single strand resistance wire. Insulate cut ends with tape D6AZ-19627-A or equivalent.

11. From the same terminal as resistance wire was removed, cut No. 16 red-light green multiple strand wire about 2 inches from connector and install bullet-connector C5AZ-14294-B or equivalent on cut ends.

12. Reconnect circuit No. 16 using double connector B6A-14487-A or equivalent.

13. Connect remaining end of replacement resistance wire into double connector.

14. Reconnect all disassembled components and battery ground cable.

15. Rotate ignition switch to start position, then check to ensure that engine will run when ignition switch is returned to the run position. If engine fails to operate check voltage and resistance at ignition coil. Resistance should be 1.05 to 1.15 ohms at 75°F. Voltage should be approximately 6.4 volts at coil.

NOTE: Inspect all wiring adjacent to the resistor wire for damage and repair as necessary.

1977–78 Mark V, Fig. 28

1. Disconnect battery ground cable.

2. Disconnect multiple wire connector at dash panel.

3. From under left side of instrument panel, release connector and fuse panel from dash panel, then pull downward to facilitate releasing fuse panel from multiple connector.

4. After releasing fuse panel from multiple connector, cut No. 16A red-light green stripe single strand wire close to fuse panel. Insulate both cut ends with tape D6AZ-19627-A or equivalent.

5. From the same terminal that the resistance wire was removed, cut No. 16 red-light green wire approximately 2 inches from fuse panel, then install bullet terminal C5AZ-14294-B or equivalent on cut ends.

6. Reconnect red-light green wire No. 16 using double connector B6A-14487-A or equivalent.

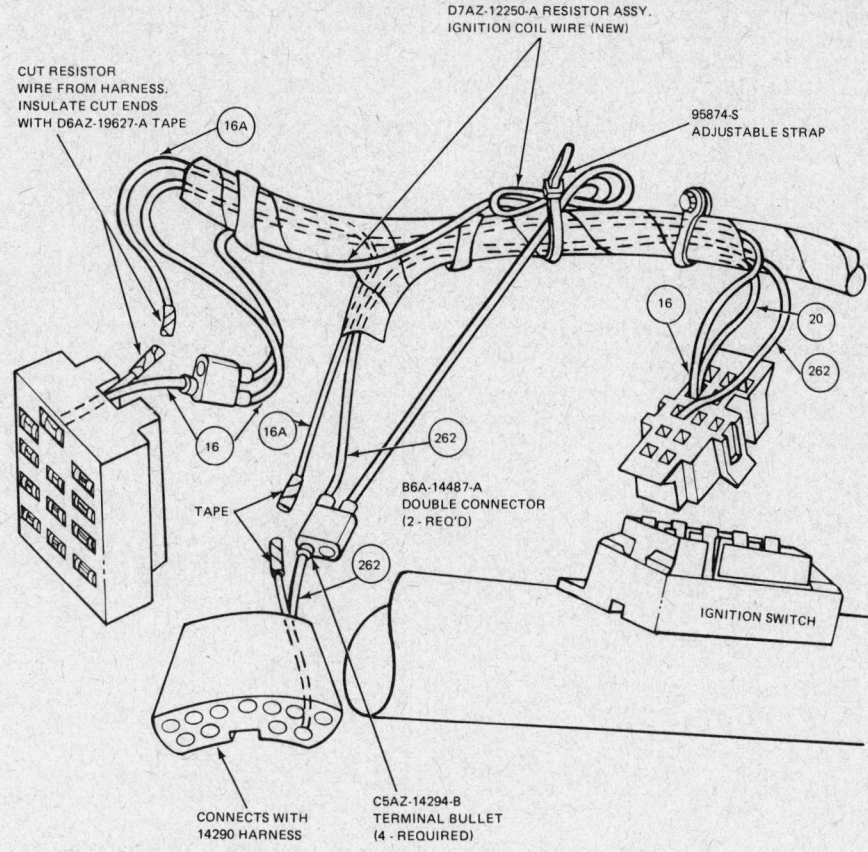

CUT RESISTOR
WIRE FROM HARNESS.
INSULATE CUT ENDS
WITH D6AZ-19627-A TAPE

D7AZ-12250-A RESISTOR ASSY.
IGNITION COIL WIRE (NEW)

95874-S
ADJUSTABLE STRAP

16A

16

16A

262

20

262

TAPE

B6A-14487-A
DOUBLE CONNECTOR
(2 - REQ'D)

262

IGNITION SWITCH

CONNECTS WITH
14290 HARNESS

C5AZ-14294-B
TERMINAL BULLET
(4 - REQUIRED)

WIRE COLOR CODE

16 - RED-LT. GREEN STRIPE
262 - BROWN-PINK STRIPE
20 - WHITE-LT. BLUE HASH MARK

Fig. 26 Resistance wire installation. 1977—78 Granada, Monarch & Versailles

7. Install one end of replacement resistance wire into double connector and route resistance wire along wiring harness toward ignition switch. Loop excessive length of resistance wire and route back toward multiple connector. Secure resistance wire to wiring harness using adjustable strap or suitable tape.
8. At multiple connector, cut No. 16A red-light green stripe single strand resistance wire close to connector and insulate both cut ends with tape D6AZ-19627 B or equivalent.
9. From the same terminal that the resistance wire was removed, cut wire No. 262 brown-pink strip wire approximately 2 inches from the connector. On each cut end install bullet terminal C5AZ-14294-A or equivalent.
10. Reconnect circuit No. 262 brown-pink strip wire, using double connector B6A-14487-A or equivalent.
11. Install remaining end of resistance wire into double connector.
12. Reconnect all disassembled components and battery ground cable.
13. Start engine, then check to ensure that engine will continue to operate when ignition switch is returned to the run position. If engine will not continue to operate, check voltage and resistance at ignition coil. Resistance should be 1.05 to 1.15 at 75° F. Voltage should be approxi-

mately 6.4 volts at coil.

NOTE: Inspect all wiring adjacent to resistor wire for damage and repair as necessary.

1977—78 Lincoln Continental, Fig. 29

1. Disconnect battery ground cable.
2. Disconnect the 14398 and 14290 wiring connector from the 14401 wiring at the dash panel, Fig. 29.
3. From inside vehicle, release the 14401 wiring connector from the dash panel and fuse panel, Fig. 29.
4. Pull connector disconnected from fuse panel downward and disconnect circuit No. 16A resistor wire (red-light green stripe).
5. Release resistor wire and terminal from connector cavity, then cut resistor wire and terminal (single wire) close to harness and insulate exposed end with tape.
6. Fabricate a 4 inch long 16 GA. jumper wire, then install a D20Z-14474-C terminal wire snap-on on one end and a C5AZ-14294-B bullet terminal on the other end,

Fig. 28.

7. Connect the jumper wire with the D20Z-14474-C terminal into the vacated cavity of the connector at the firewall and install a B7A-14487-A single connector on remaining bullet terminal of the jumper wire.
8. Install replacement D7AZ-12250-A resistor wire into single connector of jumper wire and route and loop the excess as shown in Fig. 29. Secure resistor wire to harness using tape or a strap.
9. Disconnect the 14401 connector from ignition switch connector and pull down ward, then cut either the No. 16 or 16C red-light green stripe wire, about 2 inches from connector.
10. Install a C5AZ-14294-B bullet terminal on each cut end, then reconnect the No. 16 circuit with a B6A-14487-A double connector, and install the remaining end of the new resistor wire into the double connector.
11. Reconnect all disassembled parts and reconnect the battery ground cable.
12. Start engine, then check if engine continues to run when key is released to "Run" position. If engine does not continue to run, use a volt-ohm-meter and check for proper voltage and/or resistance at ignition coil. With new D7AZ-12250-A resistor wire installed, the resistance should be 1.05 to 1.15 ohms at 75° and voltage

ELECTRONIC IGNITION SYSTEMS

should be 6.4 volts at the coil.

NOTE: Inspect all wiring adjacent to the resistor wire for damage, and repair as necessary.

1979 Ford, Lincoln Continental & Mercury, Fig. 30

1. Disconnect battery ground cable.
2. From engine compartment, disconnect wire connector from fuse panel connector at left side of dash panel.
3. Remove steering column lower panel, then detach steering column from instrument panel.
4. From inside vehicle, detach wire connector that mates with connector located at rear of fuse panel.
5. Pull wire connector disconnected from fuse panel below instrument panel to facilitate removal of resistance wire.
6. Locate No. 16A red-light green stripe resistance wire in connector and retract terminal retaining tab using a small screwdriver or large paper clip, then pull terminal from connector.
7. Cut resistance wire as close to the harness as possible and insulate exposed ends with suitable electrical tape.
8. Locate ignition switch wire connector and about three inches from connector, unwrap tape to expose circuits welded to harness.
9. Cut No. 16A red-light green stripe resistance wire from wiring harness at weld. Approximately 1-1/2 inches from the wire connector, cut No. 16 red-light green stripe wire and install C5AZ-14294-B or equivalent to each cut end. Reconnect No. 16 red-light green stripe wiring circuit using double connector B6A-14487-A or equivalent.
10. Install one end of replacement resistance wire into remaining opening of double connector. Rewrap exposed welded circuits using suitable tape.
11. Route replacement resistance wire to connector behind fuse panel. Use suitable tape to support resistance wire when routing along harness.

NOTE: Do not fold, loop or overlap resistance wire onto itself under the harness covering.

12. Using a 4 inch length 16 gauge wire, strip 3/8 inch of insulation from each end, then install a D02B-14474-CB on one end and a C5AZ-14294-B bullet connector on the other end. Install female connector into vacated cavity of fuse panel connector, where damaged resistance wire was removed. Push terminal firmly into position until lock snaps into place.
13. Connect free end of replacement wire to free end of jumper wire, using single connector B7A-14487-A.
14. Reconnect wire connector to back of fuse panel and connect with wiring harness at dash panel.
15. Reconnect battery ground cable.
16. Start vehicle and check to ensure that engine will operate when ignition switch is returned to the run position. If engine does not continue to operate, check voltage and resistance at ignition coil IGN terminal. Resistance should be 1.05 to 1.15 ohms at 75° F. Voltage should be approximately 6.4 volts.

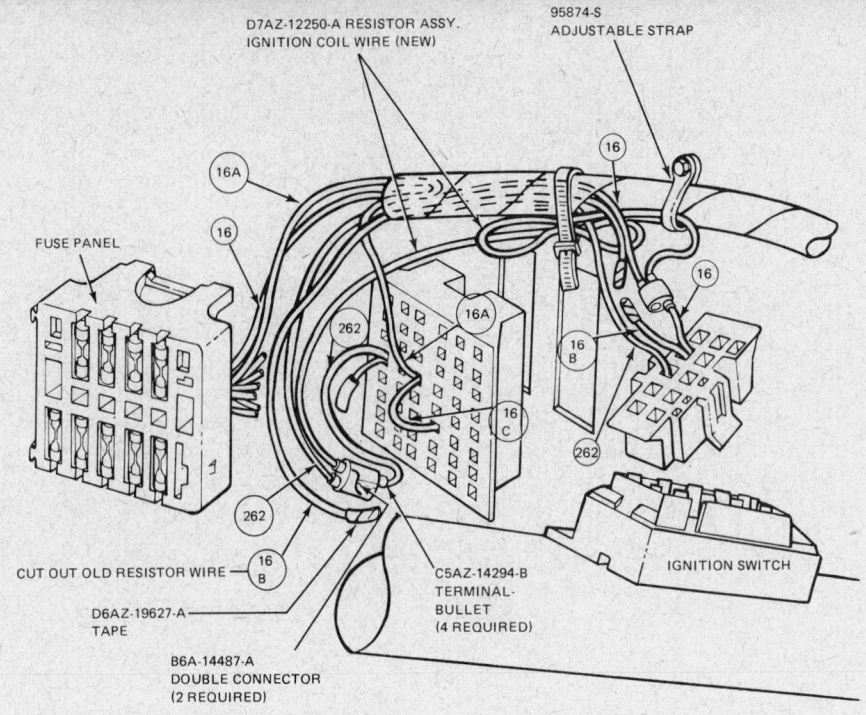

WIRE COLOR CODE

16-16A-16B-16C - RED-LT. GREEN STRIPE
262 - BROWN-PINK STRIPE

Fig. 27   Resistance wire installation. 1977—78 Cougar, LTD II & Thunderbird

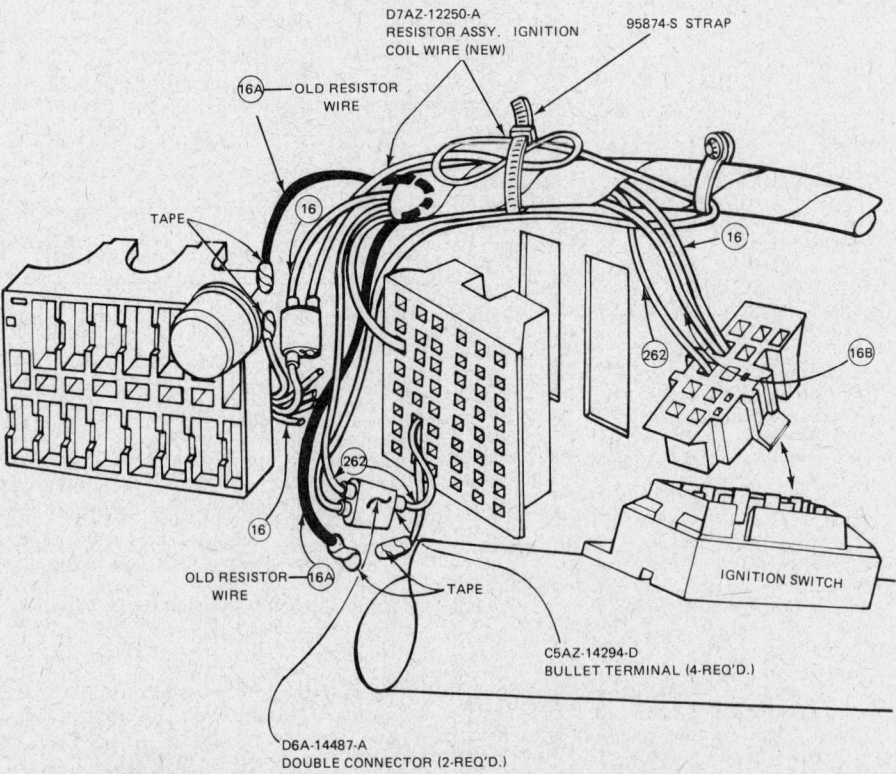

WIRE COLOR CODE

16, 16A, 16B - RED-LIGHT GREEN STRIPE
262 - BROWN-PINK STRIPE

Fig. 28   Resistance wire installation. 1977—78 Mark V

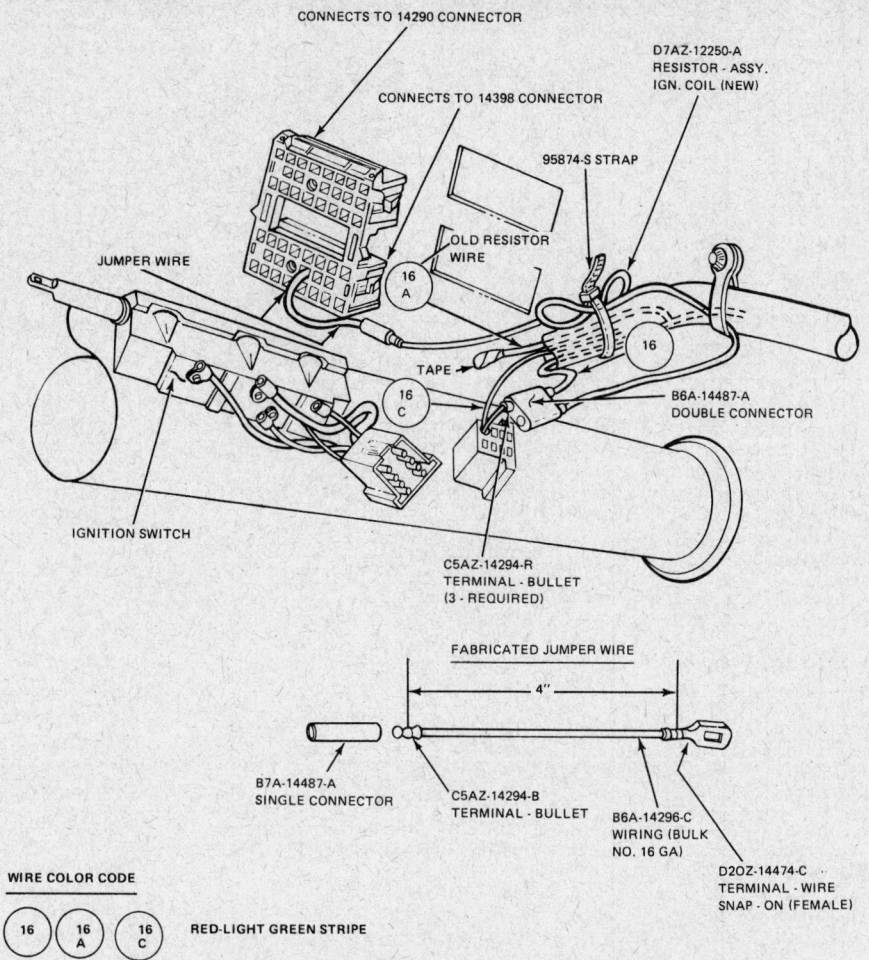

Fig. 29   Resistance wire installation. 1977—78 Lincoln Continental

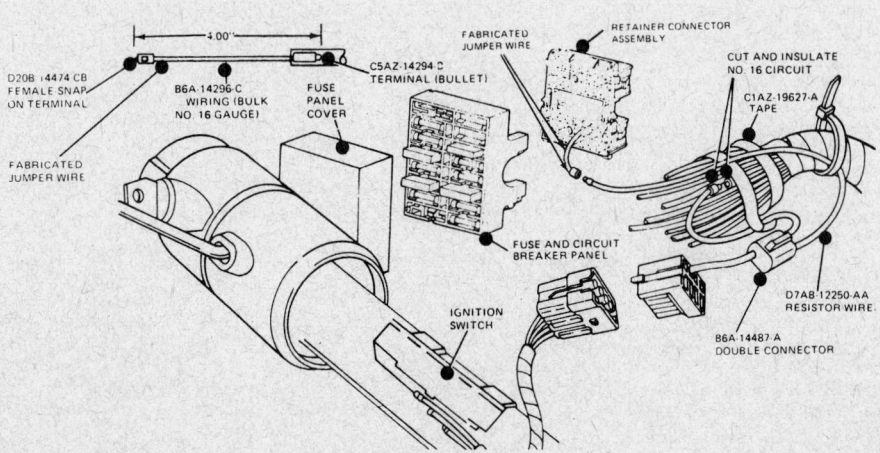

Fig. 30   Resistance wire installation. 1979 Ford, Lincoln Continental & Mercury

Ford 1981–83 Dura Spark II Solid State Ignition System

DESCRIPTION

This system, Figs. 1 and 2, is described under "Ford 1977–80 Dura Spark I & II Solid State Ignition Systems".

SYSTEM DIAGNOSIS

NOTE: When performing diagnostic or service procedures on models equipped with Dura-Spark II, the ignition switch should remain in the "Off" position unless otherwise stated in the procedure. On these units, a spark will be generated when the ignition switch is placed from the "On" position to "Off", which may inadvertently cause the engine to rotate, resulting in personal injury.

Spark Plug Firing Voltage Test

1. Connect an oscilloscope with voltage pick up on coil to distributor cable.
2. Refer to "Ford 1977–80 Dura Spark I & II Solid State Ignition System" under "Spark Plug Firing Voltage Test" and perform steps 2 thru 4.

Spark Plug Wire Continuity Test

1. Remove distributor cap and disconnect suspected wire from spark plug or coil.

2. Using an ohmmeter, check wire resistance through distributor cap. Resistance should be 5000 ohms per inch. If reading is greater than as specified, replace wire.

Spark Plug Wire Inspection

1. Clean off any deposits of dirt from wires, boots, distributor cap and coil using mild soap and water solution.
2. Inspect wires and boots for cuts, punctures or other damage.
3. Inspect wire terminals for corrosion and clean with fine sandpaper.
4. Coat all boots with silicone grease before installing.

Test 1, Start Circuit

1. Connect a suitable spark tester between coil wire and a suitable ground, Fig. 3.
2. While cranking engine, check for sparks.
3. If spark is observed, start circuit is satisfactory. If spark does not occur, measure coil wire resistance. If resistance exceeds 5000 ohms per inch, replace wire.
4. If coil wire is satisfactory, inspect coil for signs of carbon tracking or external damage and inspect distributor shaft with engine cranking to ensure distributor shaft rotation. Proceed to test 5.

Test 2, Run Circuit

1. While observing spark tester, cycle igni-

tion switch from "Off" to "Run" position several times (a spark should be generated at the spark tester each time the ignition switch is turned "Off").
2. If spark is observed;
   a. Inspect distributor cap, rotor and adapter for signs of carbon tracking and cracks, replace as necessary.
   b. Ensure armature to sleeve roll pin is correctly installed, repair as necessary.
   c. Ensure orange and purple wires are not crossed between distributor and ignition module.
   d. Check ignition timing, adjust as necessary.
3. If spark does not occur, proceed to test 3.

Test 3, Module Voltage

1. With ignition "Off", install a straight pin into module red wire, Fig. 4. Connect a suitable voltmeter positive lead to straight pin and ground negative lead to distributor base. Turn ignition "On" and measure voltage.

NOTE: Do not allow straight pin to contact engine ground.

2. If reading obtained is 90% of battery voltage or greater, module voltage is satisfactory. Proceed to test 4.
3. If reading obtained is less than 90% of

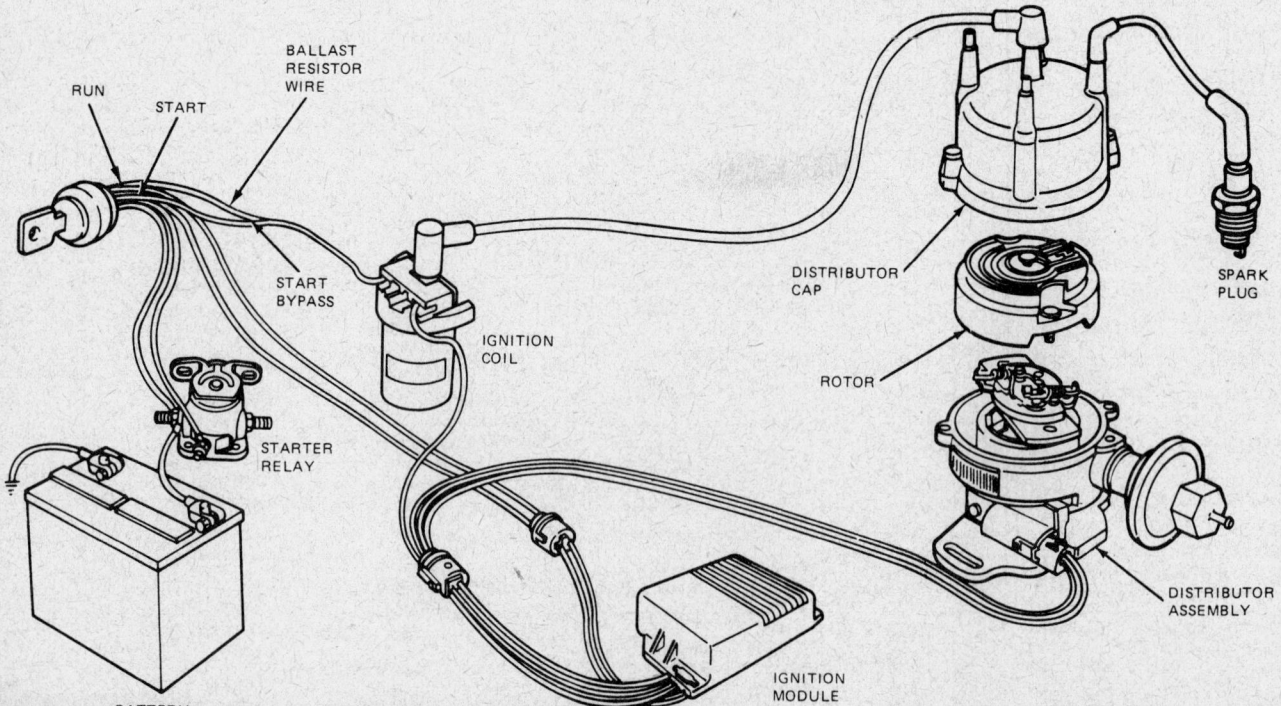

Fig. 1 Dura Spark II ignition systems. 1981–83 Escort, EXP, LN7 & Lynx

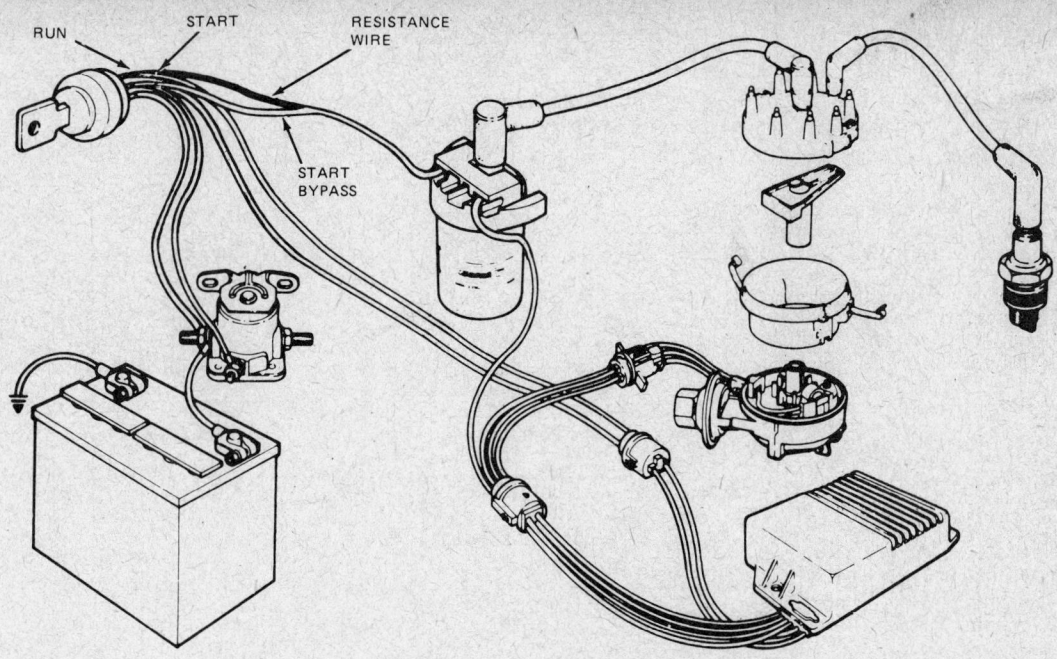

Fig. 2   Dura Spark II ignition system. 1981–83 Exc. Escort, EXP, LN7 & Lynx

battery voltage, inspect ignition switch and wiring between ignition switch and module, repair as necessary.

Test 4, Ballast Resistor

1. Disconnect module connector with red and white wires then, ignition coil connector.
2. Using a suitable ohmmeter, measure resistance between Batt. terminal of ignition coil connector and wiring harness connector wire that joins red wire in module connector.
3. If resistance is 0.8–1.6 ohms, ballast resistor is satisfactory. If resistance is less than 0.8 ohms or greater than 1.6 ohms, replace ballast resistor.

Test 5, Supply Voltage Circuit

1. Reconnect coil wire to distributor cap (if still removed).
   a. If starter relay is equipped with a I

terminal, disconnect starter cable from starter relay.
   b. If starter relay is equipped with a S terminal, disconnect S wire from relay.
2. With ignition "Off", install straight pins into module red and white wires.

NOTE: Do not allow straight pins to contact engine ground.

3. Using a suitable voltmeter, connect negative lead to ground at distributor base.
   a. With ignition in "On" position, measure voltage at red wire pin.
   b. Place ignition in "Start" position, measure voltage at white wire pin and at coil Batt. terminal.

NOTE: When measuring voltages, wiggle wires to simulate any open circuits that might exist.

4. If readings obtained are 90% of battery voltage or greater, supply circuits are satisfactory. Proceed to test 6.
5. If readings obtained are less than 90% of battery voltage;
   a. Defective wiring harness or connectors in supply voltage circuits.
   b. Defective ignition switch.
   c. Defective ignition coil or radio interference capacitor.

Test 6, Ignition Coil Supply Voltage

1. Connect positive lead of voltmeter to coil

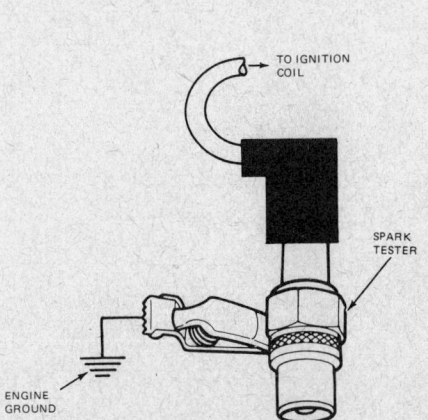

Fig. 3   Spark plug tester

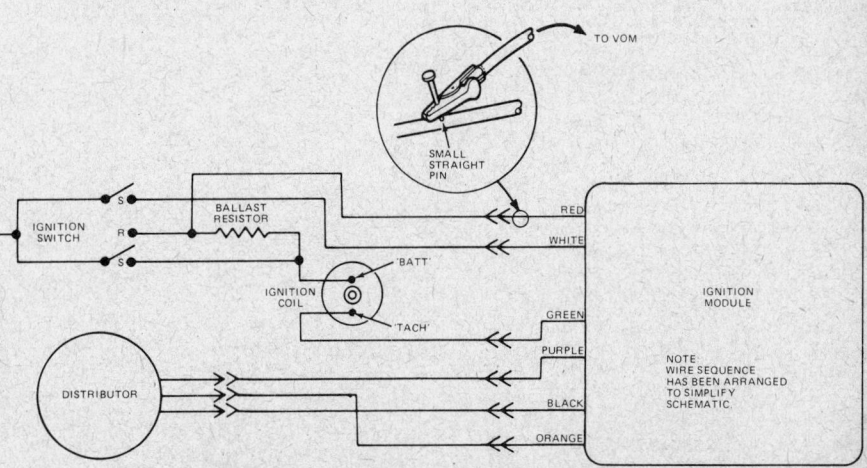

Fig. 4   Dura Spark II ignition system module voltage test connections

Batt. terminal and negative lead to ground at distributor base.

2. Turn ignition switch to "On" position.
3. Observe voltmeter reading. If 6–8 volts, proceed to test 7. If less than 6 volts or more than 8 volts, proceed to test 12.

Test 7, Distributor Stator Assembly & Wiring Harness

1. Disconnect module 4 wire connector. Inspect connectors for dirt and corrosion.
2. Using a suitable ohmmeter, measure resistance of stator and wiring harness between wiring harness terminals joining orange and purple wires of module connector, Fig. 5.

NOTE: When measuring resistance, wiggle wires to simulate any open circuits that might exist.

3. If resistance is 400–1300 ohms, test results are satisfactory. Proceed to test 8. If resistance is less than 400 ohms or more than 1300 ohms, proceed to test 11.

Test 8, Ignition Module to Distributor Stator Assembly Wiring Harness

1. Disconnect module 4 wire connector. Inspect connectors for dirt and corrosion.
2. Using a suitable ohmmeter, connect one lead to ground at distributor base. Using other lead, alternately measure resistance of harness wiring which connects to orange and purple wires of module connector to ground, Fig. 6.
3. If test results are greater than 70,000 ohms, circuits are satisfactory. If test results are less than 70,000 ohms, inspect and repair as necessary wiring harness between module connector and distributor. Also inspect distributor grommet.

Test 9, Ignition Coil Secondary Resistance

1. Disconnect and inspect ignition coil electrical connector.
2. Using a suitable ohmmeter, measure resistance between coil Batt. terminal and high tension lead terminal.
3. If resistance is between 7700–10,500 ohms, coil is satisfactory. If not between limits, replace coil.

Test 10, Coil Tach Terminal to Module Connector Circuit

1. Disconnect module 4 wire connector. Inspect connectors for dirt and corrosion.
2. Using a suitable ohmmeter, measure resistance between coil connector tach wire and the terminal in the wiring harness connector that joins the green wire of the module connector, Fig. 7.
3. If resistance is less than 1 ohm, circuit is satisfactory. If resistance is over 1 ohm, inspect and repair wiring harness as necessary.

Test 11, Distributor Stator Assembly

Escort, EXP, LN7 & Lynx

1. Disconnect distributor electrical connec-

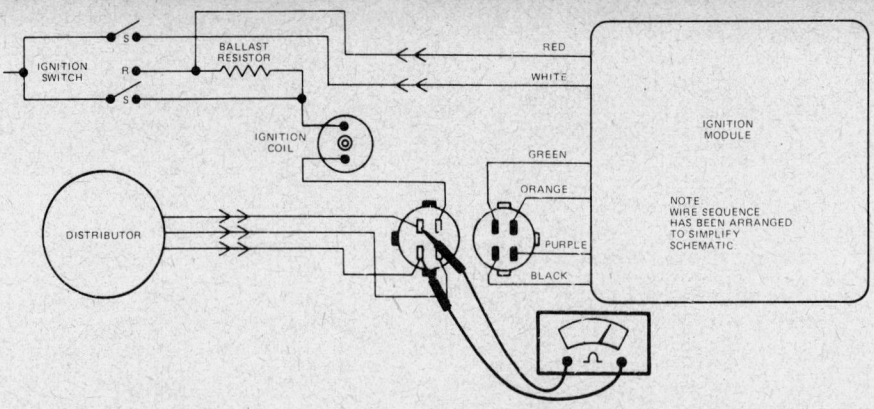

Fig. 5 Dura Spark II ignition system stator assembly & wiring harness test connections

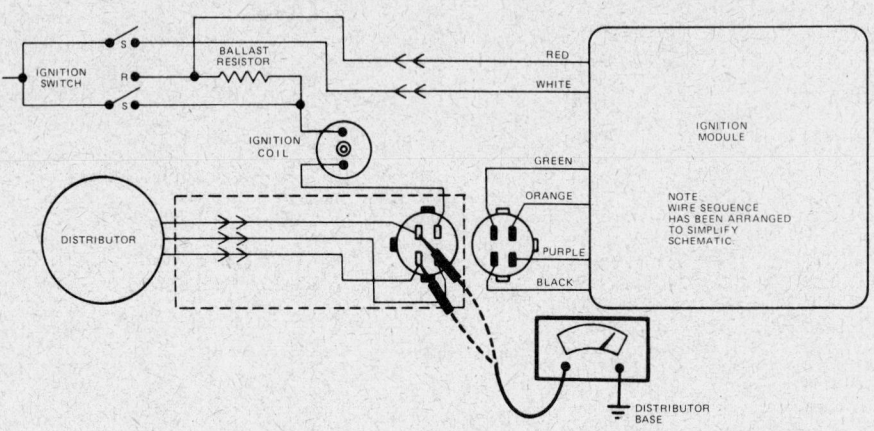

Fig. 6 Dura Spark II ignition system module to stator wiring harness test connections

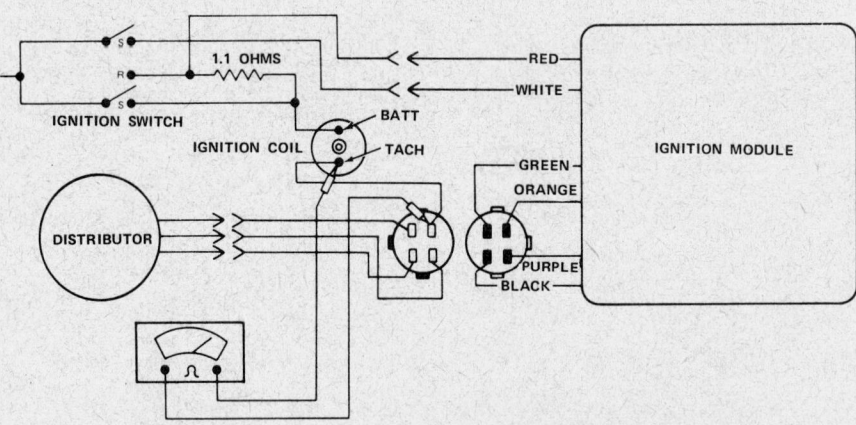

Fig. 7 Dura Spark II ignition system coil tach terminal to module connector circuit test connections

tor. Inspect connectors for dirt and corrosion.
2. Using a suitable ohmmeter, measure resistance across black/orange stripe wire and black/purple stripe wire in distributor connector, Fig. 8.

NOTE: The distributor stator assembly

wire connector wire colors cannot be seen without removal of connector holddown plate or distributor cap.

3. If readings obtained are within 650–1300 ohms, circuit is satisfactory. If readings are less than 650 or more than 1300 ohms, replace stator assembly.

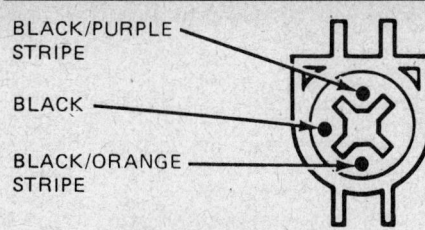

Fig. 8 Distributor electrical connector. 1981–83 Dura Spark II ignition system. Escort, EXP, LN7 & Lynx

BLACK/PURPLE STRIPE

BLACK

BLACK/ORANGE STRIPE

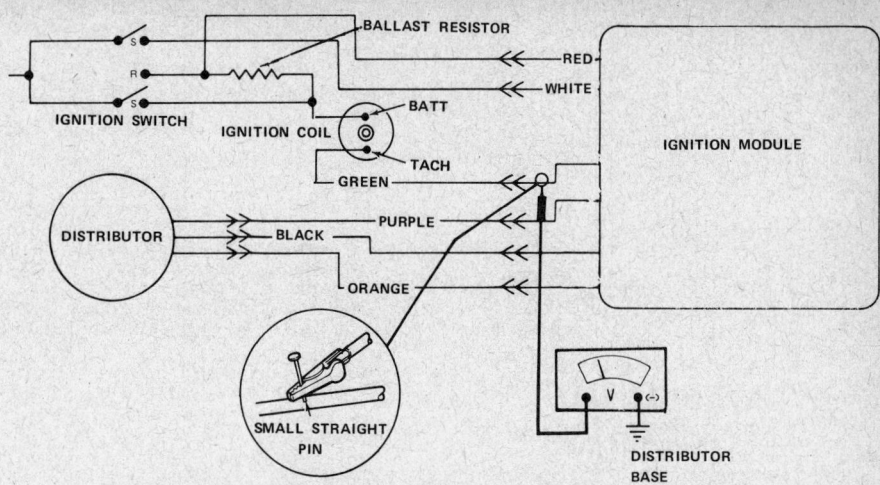

Fig. 9 Dura Spark II ignition system coil primary circuit test connections

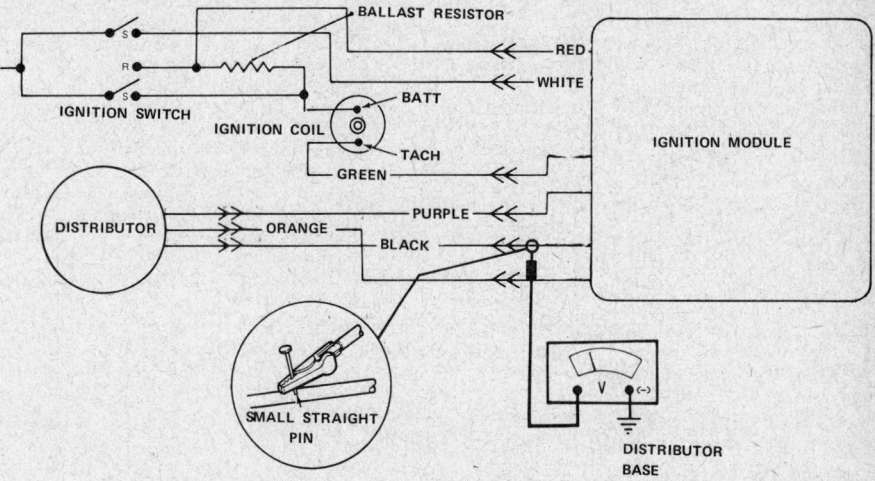

Fig. 10 Dura Spark II ignition system ground circuit test connections

Exc. Escort, EXP, LN7 & Lynx

1. Disconnect distributor electrical connector. Inspect connections for dirt or corrosion.
2. Using a suitable ohmmeter, measure resistance across orange and purple wires in distributor connector.
3. If readings obtained are within 400–1000 ohms, circuit is satisfactory. If readings are less than 400 or more than 1000 ohms, replace stator assembly.

Test 12, Ignition Coil Primary Resistance

1. Disconnect ignition coil electrical connector.
2. Using a suitable ohmmeter, measure resistance between coil Batt. terminal and Tach terminal.
3. If reading obtained is 0.8–1.6 ohms, coil is satisfactory. If not, replace coil.

Test 13, Primary Circuit

1. With ignition "Off", install a straight pin into module green wire, Fig. 9. Connect a suitable voltmeter positive lead to straight pin and ground negative lead to distributor base. Turn ignition "On" and measure voltage.

NOTE: Do not allow straight pin to contact engine ground.

2. If voltage obtained is more than 1.5 volts, circuit is satisfactory. Proceed to test 14.
3. If voltage obtained is less than 1.5 volts, inspect wiring harness and connectors between ignition coil and module. Repair as necessary.

Test 14, Ground Circuit

1. With ignition "Off", install a straight pin into module black wire, Fig. 10. Connect a suitable voltmeter positive lead to straight pin and ground negative lead to distributor base. Turn ignition "On" and measure voltage.
2. If voltage obtained is more than 0.5 volts, circuit is satisfactory. Proceed to test 15.
3. If voltage obtained is less than 0.5 volts, replace ignition module.

Test 15, Distributor Ground Circuit

Escort, EXP, LN7 & Lynx

1. Disconnect distributor electrical connec-tor. Inspect connections for dirt and corrosion.
2. Using a suitable ohmmeter, measure resistance between distributor base and black wire in distributor connector, Fig. 8.

NOTE: The distributor stator assembly wire connector wire colors cannot be seen without removal of connector holddown or distributor cap.

3. If reading obtained is less than 1 ohm, circuit is satisfactory. If reading is more than 1 ohm, inspect and repair distributor ground screw.

Exc. Escort, EXP, LN7 & Lynx

1. Disconnect distributor electrical connector. Inspect connections for dirt or corrosion.
2. Using a suitable ohmmeter, measure resistance between distributor base and black wire in distributor connector.

NOTE: When measuring resistance, wiggle wires to simulate any open circuits which might exist.

3. If reading obtained is less than 1 ohm, circuit is satisfactory. If reading is more than 1 ohm, inspect and repair distributor ground screw.

DISTRIBUTOR, REPLACE

Escort, EXP, LN7 & Lynx

Removal
1. Disconnect primary circuit connector from distributor.
2. Disconnect vacuum hose from distributor vacuum advance.
3. Remove distributor cap, then mark relationship of rotor to distributor housing and relationship of distributor housing to engine for reference during installation.
4. Remove rotor, then remove distributor retaining bolts and the distributor.

Installation
1. Check to ensure that distributor base O ring is in place.

2. Install distributor into engine checking to ensure that marks made during removal align. Also check that offset tang of drive coupling seats into camshaft groove.
3. Install retaining bolts, rotor, vacuum and electrical connectors and cap.
4. Start engine and adjust ignition timing as specified in the individual car chapters.

Exc. Escort, EXP, LN7 & Lynx

Refer to "Distributor, Replace" procedure in "Ford 1977–80 Dura Spark I and II Solid State Ignition Systems."

COMPONENT REPLACEMENT

Escort, EXP, LN7 & Lynx

Vacuum Advance Unit, Replace
1. Remove distributor cap and position aside with ignition wires attached.
2. Disconnect vacuum advance vacuum hose.
3. Remove diaphragm retaining screws, then partially remove diaphragm assembly until it clears distributor base.
4. Tilt diaphragm assembly to disconnect rod from stator pivot pin, then remove vacuum advance assembly.
5. Check diaphragm O ring for damage, then align threaded hole in advance assembly housing with screw hole in base.
6. Rotate stator assembly clockwise to position stator pivot pin.
7. Insert vacuum advance assembly through base until rod engages stator pivot pin.

8. Continue seating advance assembly into base until threaded hole in diaphragm casting aligns with hole in base.
9. Install diaphragm retaining screw, connect vacuum hose and install distributor cap.

Stator Assembly, Replace
1. Remove distributor and vacuum advance assembly.
2. Using a small screwdriver or other suitable tool, remove drive coupling spring. Use care not to damage parts.
3. Clean distributor drive end then, using paint, make reference marks on distributor drive coupling and shaft to aid in reassembly.
4. Position distributor in a suitable holding device. Using a suitable drift and hammer, drive pin out of shaft and remove coupling.
5. Inspect end of shaft assembly and in area of drive pin hole for burrs. If necessary, use fine emery paper to polish shaft. Wipe shaft clean prior to removal to prevent damage to seal and bushing in distributor base.
6. Remove shaft assembly by gently pulling out of distributor base.
7. Inspect distributor shaft and centrifugal advance assembly. Centrifugal advance assembly should advance freely and return to original position. If binding occurs, the entire distributor should be replaced.
8. Remove screws securing stator connector to distributor housing then screws securing the stator retainer in distributor housing.
9. Gently lift stator assembly out of distributor housing.
10. Pull stator retainer assembly from stator.

11. Inspect distributor O-rings, replace as necessary.
12. Inspect distributor base bushing for signs of wear and heat damage. if bushing is damaged, replace complete distributor.
13. Inspect distributor shaft oil seal. If oil seal is damaged, replace complete distributor.

NOTE: If seal spring retainer (inside seal) is missing or damaged, it can be replaced.

14. Inspect distributor base casting for cracks and wear. If base is cracked or worn, replace complete distributor.
15. Assemble stator retainer to stator. Position retainer so horseshoe opening of retainer is at the vacuum advance diaphragm rod pivot point.
16. Install stator assembly in distributor base with vacuum advance diaphragm pivot point positioned approximately in front of diaphragm mounting hole.
17. Install stator securing screws, ensure stator is free to rotate. If not, disassemble and check parts. Position wire connector and install securing screws.
18. Lightly lubricate distributor shaft and install.

NOTE: Do not over lubricate.

19. Reverse steps 1 through 4 to complete assembly.

Exc. Escort, EXP, LN7 & Lynx

Refer to "Component Replacement" procedure in "Ford 1977–80 Dura Spark I and II Solid State Ignition Systems."

Ford 1982–83 Thick Film Integrated (TFI) Ignition System Escort, EXP, LN7 & Lynx

DESCRIPTION

On this system the ignition module is mounted on a mounting pad located on the distributor bowl, Figs. 1 and 2. The ignition coil is potted in plastic and has external laminations similar to a transformer.

NOTE: On these units, do not reapply or remove any of the silicone coating from the distributor cap electrodes. Also when installing a replacement distributor rotor, apply a coating approximately 1/32 inch thick, of silicone dielectric compound D7AZ-19A331-A or equivalent to the brass rotor electrode.

SYSTEM DIAGNOSIS

Spark Plug Firing Voltage Test

1. Connect an oscilloscope with voltage pick up on coil to distributor cable.

2. Refer to "Ford 1977–80 Dura Spark I & II Solid State Ignition System" under "Spark Plug Firing Voltage Test" and perform steps 2 thru 4.

Spark Plug Wire Continuity Test

1. Remove distributor cap and disconnect suspected wire from spark plug or coil.
2. Using an ohmmeter, check wire resistance through distributor cap. Resistance should be 5000 ohms per inch. If reading is greater than as specified, replace wire.

Spark Plug Wire Inspection

1. Clean off any deposits of dirt from wires, boots, distributor cap and coil using mild soap and water solution.
2. Inspect wires and boots for cuts, punctures or other damage.
3. Inspect wire terminals for corrosion and clean with fine sandpaper.
4. Coat all boots with silicone grease before installing.

Circuit Tests

Test 1, Start Circuit
1. Connect a suitable spark tester between coil wire and a suitable ground, Fig. 3.
2. While cranking engine, check for sparks.
3. If spark is observed, start circuit is satisfactory. If spark does not occur, measure coil wire resistance. If resistance exceeds 5000 ohms per inch, replace wire.
4. If coil wire is satisfactory, inspect coil for signs of carbon tracking or external damage and inspect distributor shaft with engine cranking to ensure distributor shaft rotation. Proceed to test 2.

Test 2, Ignition Coil Primary Circuit Switching
1. With ignition "Off", install a straight pin in ignition coil negative wire 1 inch from connector, Fig. 4.

NOTE: Do not allow straight pin to contact engine ground.

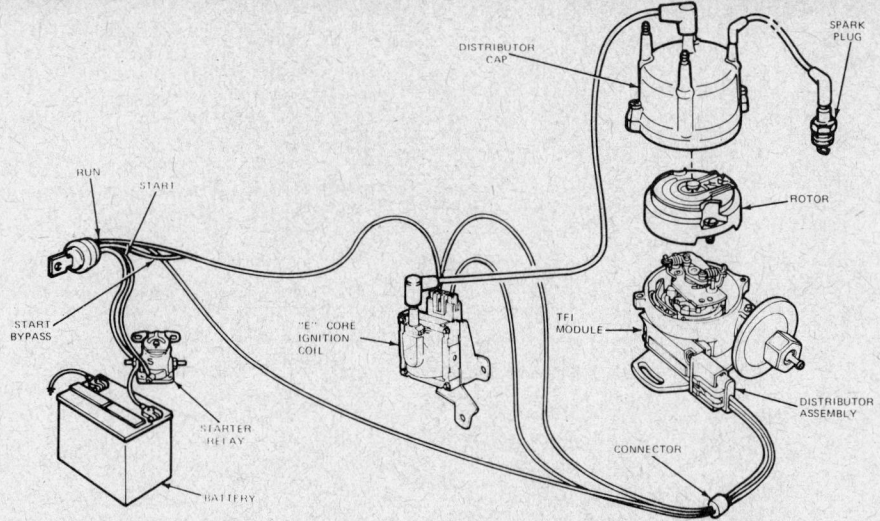

Fig. 1 Thick Film Integrated (TFI) Ignition System. 1982–83 Escort, EXP, LN7 & Lynx

2. Connect a suitable 12 volt test light between ground and straight pin. While observing test light, crank engine.
3. If test light flashes, circuit is satisfactory. Proceed to test 3. If test light glows but does not flash, proceed to test 5. If light does not glow or flash, proceed to test 7.

Test 3, Ignition Coil Primary Resistance
1. With ignition "Off", disconnect ignition coil connector. Inspect connector for dirt and corrosion.
2. Using a suitable ohmmeter, measure resistance between coil positive to negative terminals.
3. If reading is 0.3–1.0 ohm, coil is satisfactory. Proceed to test 4. If reading is less than 0.3 ohm or more than 1.0 ohm, replace coil.

Test 4, Ignition Coil Secondary Resistance
1. Disconnect and inspect ignition coil electrical connector.
2. Using a suitable ohmmeter, measure resistance between coil negative terminal and high tension lead terminal.
3. If resistance is between 8000–11,500 ohms, coil is satisfactory. If not between limits, replace coil.

Test 5, Wiring Harness
1. Disconnect wiring harness connector from distributor ignition module. Inspect connector for dirt and corrosion.

NOTE: To remove distributor connector, push connector tabs.

2. Disconnect wire at "S" terminal of starter relay.
3. Connect the negative lead of a suitable voltmeter to distributor base. Connect positive lead to a straight pin to serve as a probe.
4. Turn ignition "On", probe terminals 1 and 2, Fig. 5, and record voltages.
5. Turn ignition to "Start" position and probe terminals 2 and 3, Fig. 5. Record voltage.
6. If voltages obtained are 90% of battery voltage, circuit is satisfactory. If obtained voltages are less than 90% of battery voltage, a defective wiring harness or ignition switch is indicated.

Test 6, Stator Assembly & Module
1. Remove distributor, then remove ignition module.
2. Inspect stator wiring, wire connections and ground screw

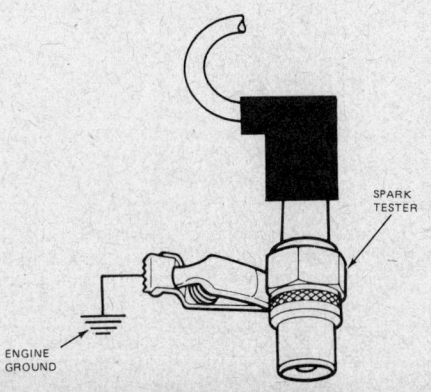

Fig. 2 Exploded view of TFI ignition system distributor. 1982–83 Escort, EXP, LN7 & Lynx

3. Using a suitable ohmmeter, measure stator resistance, Fig. 6
4. If resistance is 650–1300 ohms, stator is satisfactory. Replace ignition module. If readings are out of specifications, ignition module is satisfactory. Replace stator assembly.

Test 7, Primary Circuit
1. Disconnect wiring harness connector from distributor ignition module. Inspect connector for dirt and corrosion.

NOTE: To remove distributor connector, push connector tabs.

2. Connect the negative lead of a suitable voltmeter to distributor base. Connect positive lead to a straight pin to serve as a probe.
3. Turn ignition "On" and note voltage at

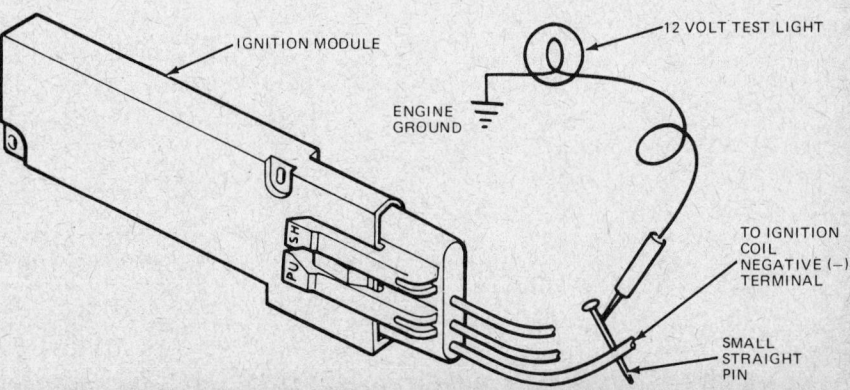

Fig. 3 Spark plug tester

Fig. 4 TFI ignition system ignition coil primary circuit switching test connections

terminal 1 of connector, Fig. 7.

4. If reading is within 90% of battery voltage, circuit is satisfactory. If reading is not within 90% of battery voltage, proceed to test 8.

Test 8, Ignition Coil Primary Voltage

1. Connect the negative lead of a suitable voltmeter to distributor base. Connect positive lead to ignition coil negative terminal.
2. Turn ignition "On" and note voltage.
3. If reading is within 90% of battery voltage, circuit is satisfactory. If reading is not within 90% of battery voltage, a defective wiring harness between ignition module and ignition coil negative terminal is indicated.

Test 9, Ignition Coil Supply Voltage

1. Connect the negative lead of a suitable voltmeter to distributor base. Connect positive lead to ignition coil positive terminal.
2. Turn ignition "On" and note voltage.
3. If reading is within 90% of battery voltage, circuit is satisfactory. If reading is not within 90% of battery voltage, a defective wiring harness or ignition switch is indicated.

DISTRIBUTOR, REPLACE

Removal

1. Disconnect primary wire connector from distributor and vacuum hose from vacuum advance unit.
2. Using a screwdriver, remove distributor cap and position aside with wires attached.

NOTE: Mark position of rotor to distributor housing and position of distributor housing to engine for reference during installation.

---

3. Remove rotor attaching screws, then remove rotor.
4. Remove distributor hold down bolts, then remove distributor.

NOTE: Some models use special distributor hold down bolts. To remove these bolts, tool No. T82L-12270-A or equivalent must be used.

Installation

1. Check to ensure that distributor base O-ring is in position.
2. Install distributor into engine, checking to ensure that marks made during removal are aligned. Also check to ensure that offset tang of drive coupling is seated in camshaft groove.
3. Install retaining bolts, rotor, vacuum advance hose, primary wire connector and distributor cap.
4. Start engine and adjust ignition timing.

COMPONENT REPLACEMENT, FIG. 2

Vacuum Advance Unit, Replace

1. Remove distributor cap and position aside with ignition wires attached.
2. Disconnect vacuum advance vacuum

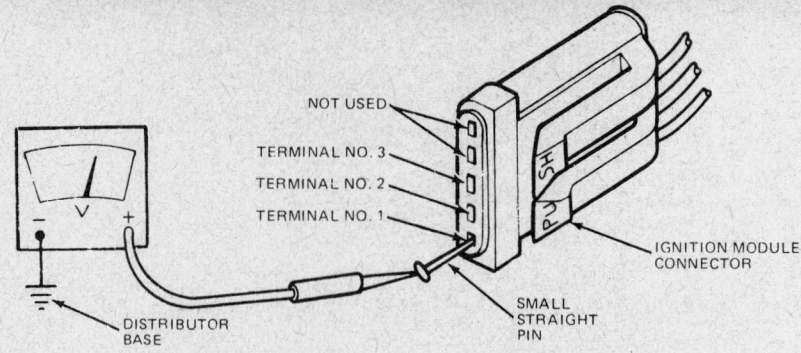

Fig. 5 TFI ignition system wiring harness test connections

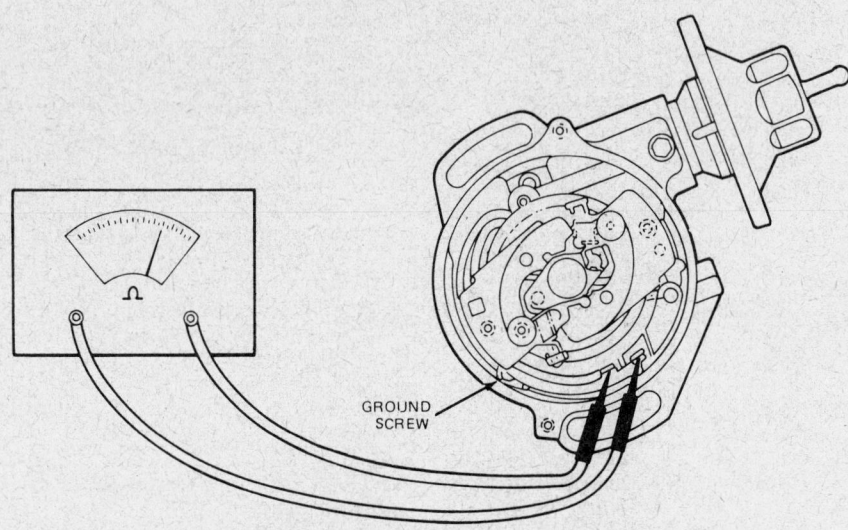

Fig. 6 TFI ignition system stator assembly test connections

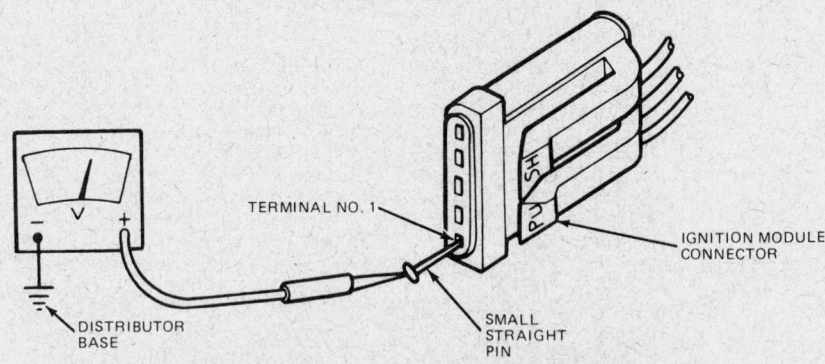

Fig. 7 TFI ignition system primary system test connections

hose.

3. Remove diaphragm retaining screw, then partially remove diaphragm assembly until it clears distributor base.
4. Tilt diaphragm assembly to disconnect rod from stator pivot pin, then remove vacuum advance assembly.
5. Check diaphragm O ring for damage, then align threaded hole in advance assembly housing with screw hole in base.
6. Rotate stator assembly clockwise to position stator pivot pin.
7. Insert vacuum advance assembly through base until rod engages stator pivot pin.
8. Continue seating advance assembly into base until threaded hole in diaphragm casting aligns with hole in base.
9. Install diaphragm retaining screw, con-

nect vacuum hose and install distributor cap.

TFI Ignition Module

Removal
1. Remove distributor as described under Distributor, Replace.
2. Remove two screws attaching TFI module to distributor housing.
3. Pull right hand side of module downward toward distributor mounting flange, then up to disengage module terminals from connector in distributor base. Pull toward flange and away from distributor.

Installation
1. Apply a 1/32 inch thick coating of silicone grease D7A2-19A331-A or equivalent to metal base of TFI module.
2. Position TFI module on distributor mounting flange.
3. Carefully position TFI module toward distributor base to securely engage the three distributor connector pins.
4. Install two TFI module attaching screws and torque to 9 to 16 inch lbs.
5. Install distributor as described under Distributor, Replace.

Stator Assembly, Replace

1. Remove distributor and vacuum advance assembly, Fig. 2.
2. Using a small screwdriver or other suitable tool, remove drive coupling spring.

Use care not to damage parts.
3. Clean distributor drive and then, using paint, make reference marks on distributor drive coupling and shaft to aid in reassembly.
4. Position distributor in a suitable holding device. Using a suitable drift and hammer, drive pin out of shaft and remove coupling.
5. Inspect end of shaft assembly and in area of drive pin hole for burrs. If necessary use fine emery paper to polish shaft. Wipe shaft clean prior to removal to prevent damage to seal and bushing in distributor base.
6. Remove shaft assembly by gently pulling out of distributor base.
7. Inspect distributor shaft and centrifugal advance assembly. Centrifugal advance assembly should advance freely and return to original position. If binding occurs, the entire distributor should be replaced.
8. Remove screws securing stator connector to distributor housing then screws securing the stator retainer in distributor housing. Remove connector from top of module.
9. Gently lift stator assembly out of distributor housing.
10. Pull stator retainer assembly from stator.
11. Inspect distributor O-rings, replace as necessary.
12. Inspect distributor base bushing for signs of wear and heat damage. If bushing is

damaged, replace complete distributor.
13. Inspect distributor shaft oil seal. If oil seal is damaged, replace complete distributor.

NOTE: If seal spring retainer (inside seal) is missing or damaged, it can be replaced.

14. Inspect distributor base casting for cracks and wear. If base is cracked or worn, replace complete distributor.
15. Assemble stator retainer to stator. Position retainer so horseshoe opening of retainer is at the vacuum advance diaphragm rod pivot point.
16. Install stator assembly in distributor base with vacuum advance diaphragm pivot point positioned approximately in front of diaphragm mounting hole.
17. Install stator securing screws, ensure stator is free to rotate. If not, disassemble and check parts. Install wire connector securing screws.
18. Position module connector on top of three pins and press down to seat the connector.
19. Lightly lubricate distributor shaft and install.

NOTE: Do not over lubricate.

20. Reverse steps 1 through 4 to complete assembly.

Ford 1983–84 Thick Film Integrated (TFI) IV Ignition System Escort, EXP, LN7, Lynx, Tempo & Topaz

DESCRIPTION

On this system, the ignition module is attached to a mounting pad located on the distributor bowl, Fig. 1. The ignition coil is potted in plastic and has external laminations similar to a transformer.

NOTE: On these units, do not reapply or remove any of the silicone coating from the distributor cap electrodes.

SYSTEM DIAGNOSIS

Spark Plug Firing Voltage Test

1. Connect an oscilloscope with voltage pick up on coil to distributor cable.
2. Refer to "Ford 1977–80 Dura Spark I & II Solid State Ignition System" under "Spark Plug Firing Voltage Test" and perform steps 2 through 4.

Spark Plug Wire Continuity Test

1. Remove distributor cap and disconnect suspected wire from spark plug or coil.
2. Measure wire resistance through distributor cap using a suitable ohmmeter. Resistance should measure 5000 ohms per inch. If resistance is greater than 5000 ohms per inch, replace wire.

Spark Plug Wire Inspection

1. Clean off any dirt deposits from wires, boots, distributor cap and coil using mild soap and water solution.
2. Inspect wires and boots for cuts, punctures, or other damage.
3. Inspect wire terminals for corrosion, and clean with fine sandpaper.
4. Coat all boots with silicone grease before reinstalling.

Circuit Tests

Test 1, Ignition Coil Secondary Voltage
1. Connect a suitable spark plug tester

between coil wire and engine ground, Fig. 2.
2. Crank engine and check for sparks.
3. If no sparks occur, proceed to step 4. If sparks are observed, coil secondary voltage is satisfactory. Proceed to step 5.
4. Measure coil wire resistance using a suitable ohmmeter. If resistance exceeds 5000 ohms per foot, replace wire. If resistance is less than 5000 ohms per foot, inspect coil for damage or signs of carbon tracking, and replace as needed. If coil is satisfactory, check distributor shaft rotation while cranking engine. If shaft rotates properly, proceed to "Test 2."
5. Inspect distributor cap and rotor for damage or signs of carbon tracking, and service as needed. If engine still will not start, proceed to "Test 5."

Test 2, Ignition Coil Primary Circuit Switching
1. Disconnect electrical connector from ignition module by depressing tabs.
2. Clean any corrosion or dirt buildup on

ELECTRONIC IGNITION SYSTEMS

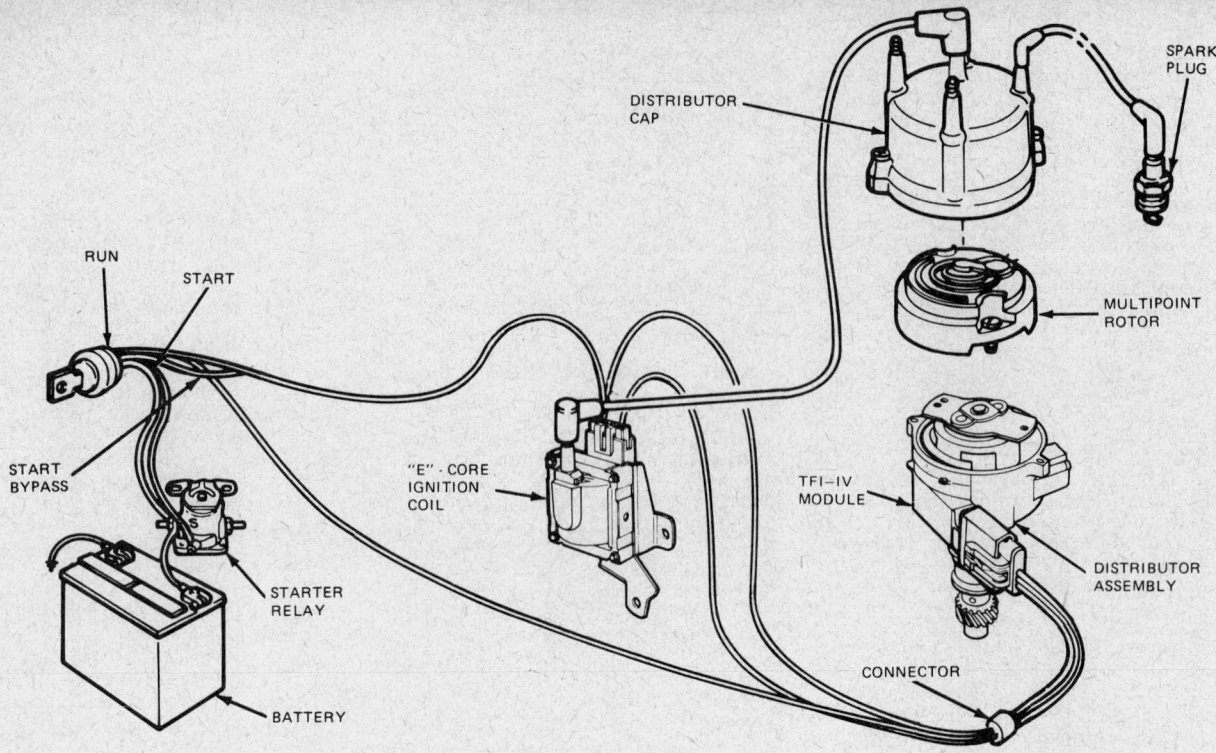

Fig. 1   Thick film integrated (TFI) IV ignition system. 1983 Escort, EXP, LN7 & Lynx W/EFI & 1984 Tempo & Topaz

connector, then reconnect to module.

3. Connect a suitable 12 volt test lamp between coil tach terminal and ground, Fig. 3. Observe test lamp while cranking engine.

4. If test lamp flashes, proceed to "Test 3." If test lamp lights continuously, proceed to "Test 5." If test lamp does not light or lights dimly, proceed to "Test 8."

Test 3, Ignition Coil Primary Resistance

1. Turn ignition off, then disconnect ignition coil electrical connector.
2. Inspect connector for dirt and corrosion, and clean as necessary.
3. Measure resistance between ignition coil positive and negative terminals, Fig. 4.
4. If resistance is .3–1 ohm, coil is satisfactory. Proceed to "Test 4."
5. If resistance is greater than 1 ohm or less

than .3 ohm, replace ignition coil.

Test 4, Ignition Coil Secondary Resistance

1. Measure resistance between ignition coil negative and high voltage terminals, Fig. 5.
2. If resistance is 8,000–11,500 ohms, coil is satisfactory. Proceed to "Test 5."
3. If resistance is less than 8,000 ohms or greater than 11,500 ohms, replace ignition coil.

Test 5, Wiring Harness

1. Disconnect electrical connector from ignition module by depressing tabs.
2. Inspect connector for dirt or corrosion and clean as necessary.
3. Disconnect electrical connector at starter relay "S" terminal.

4. Connect negative lead of a suitable voltmeter to distributor base. Connect positive lead to a straight pin to serve as a probe, Fig. 6.
5. Measure and record voltage at terminal No. 2 with ignition in Run position.
6. Measure and record voltage at terminal No. 3 with ignition in Run and Start positions.
7. Measure and record voltage at terminal No. 4 with ignition in Start position.
8. If all voltage readings are 90% or more of battery voltage, wiring harness is satisfactory. Proceed to "Test 6."
9. If any or all voltage readings are less than 90% of battery voltage, inspect harness and electrical connectors, and repair or replace as necessary.

Test 6, Circuit Continuity

1. Disconnect electrical connector from ignition module by depressing tabs.
2. Inspect connector for dirt or corrosion and

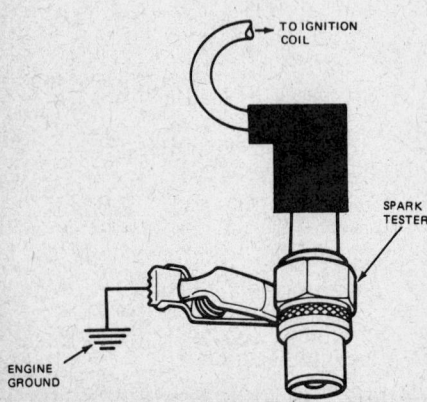

Fig. 2   Spark plug tester

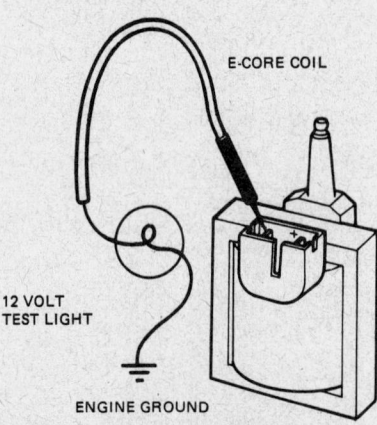

Fig. 3   TFI IV ignition system ignition coil primary circuit switching test connections

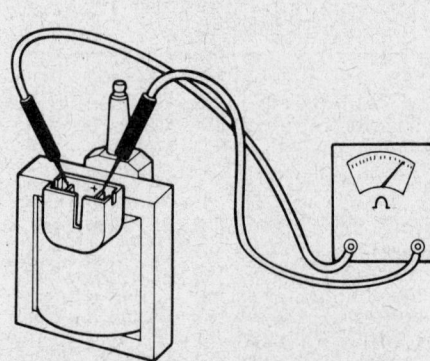

Fig. 4   TFI IV ignition system ignition coil primary resistance test connections

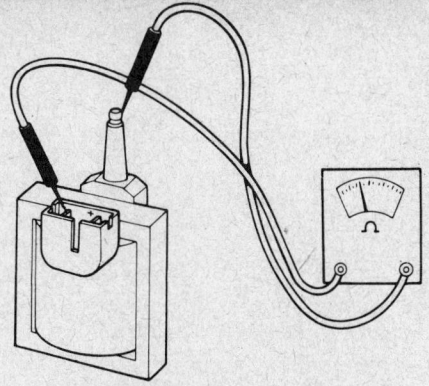

Fig. 5 TFI IV ignition system ignition coil secondary resistance test connections

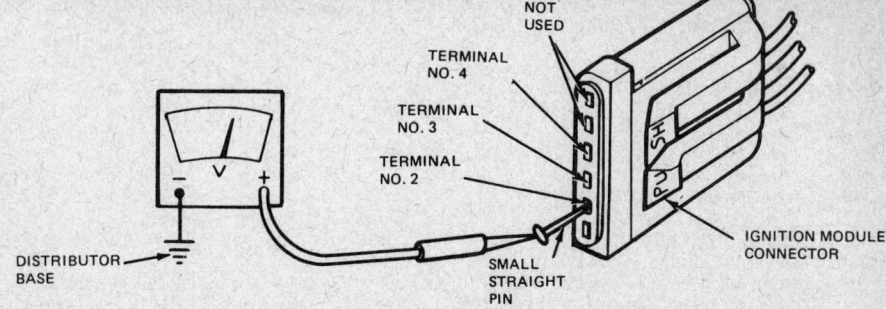

Fig. 6 TFI IV ignition system wiring harness & primary circuit continuity test connections

clean as necessary, then reconnect to module.

3. Disconnect pin in-line connector, then check for spark.
4. If no sparks occur, proceed to "Test 7."
5. If sparks are observed, check IMS wire for continuity. If wire is satisfactory, problem is not in ignition system.

Test 7, Distributor & TFI-IV Module

1. Remove distributor and ignition module assembly from vehicle.
2. Install a new ignition module on distributor.
3. Connect electrical connector to module. Ground unit with a jumper wire from distributor to ground.
4. Rotate distributor by hand and check for sparks using a suitable spark tester.
5. If sparks are observed, reinstall original distributor with new ignition module.
6. If no sparks occur, sensor is faulty. Replace distributor with original ignition module.

Test 8, Primary Circuit Continuity

1. Disconnect electrical connector from ignition module by depressing tabs.
2. Inspect connector for dirt or corrosion, and clean as necessary.
3. Connect negative lead of a suitable voltmeter to distributor base. Connect positive lead to a straight pin inserted into connector terminal No. 2, Fig. 6.
4. Measure and record voltage at terminal No. 2 with ignition in Run position.
5. If voltage reading is at least 90% of battery voltage, refer to "Test 5."
6. If voltage reading is less than 90% of battery voltage, proceed to "Test 9."

Test 9, Ignition Coil Primary Voltage

1. Connect negative lead of a suitable voltmeter to distributor base, Fig. 7.
2. Measure and record voltage at ignition coil negative terminal with ignition in Run position.

3. If voltage reading is at least 90% of battery voltage, inspect wiring harness between ignition module and coil negative terminal, and repair as necessary.
4. If voltage reading is less than 90% of battery voltage, inspect wiring harness between ignition module and coil negative terminal. If wiring is satisfactory, proceed to "Test 10."

Test 10, Ignition Coil Supply Voltage

1. Disconnect electrical connector from ignition coil.
2. Connect negative lead of a suitable voltmeter to distributor base, Fig. 8.
3. Measure and record voltage at ignition coil positive terminal with ignition in Run position.
4. If voltage reading is at least 90% of battery voltage, inspect ignition coil terminals and electrical connectors for dirt, corrosion and damage. If satisfactory, replace coil.
5. If voltage reading is less than 90% of battery voltage, repair circuit between ignition coil and ignition switch.

DISTRIBUTOR, REPLACE

Removal

1. Disconnect primary wire connector from distributor.
2. Using a screwdriver, remove distributor cap and position aside with wires attached.

NOTE: Before removing distributor cap, mark position of No. 1 tower on distributor base for assembly reference.

3. Remove distributor rotor, then disconnect ignition module electrical connector.
4. Remove distributor hold down bolt(s) and clamp, and the distributor.

NOTE: Some models use special distributor

hold down bolts. To remove these bolts, use tool No. T82L-12270-A or equivalent.

Installation

1. Rotate engine until No. 1 piston is on compression stroke.
2. Align timing marks for correct initial timing.
3. Rotate distributor shaft until center rod on rotor is pointing toward mark made on distributor base during removal. Continue to rotate shaft slightly until leading edge of vane is centered in vane switch stator assembly.
4. Rotate distributor in block until leading edge and vane stator switch assembly are aligned, and rotor is pointing to No. 1 cap terminal.

NOTE: If vane and switch stator cannot be aligned by rotating distributor in block, slide distributor out of block just enough to disengage distributor gear. Rotate distributor shaft to engage a different gear tooth, then repeat steps 1 through 4 as needed.

5. Install distributor clamp and hold down bolt. Do not tighten bolt at this time.
6. Connect distributor to wiring harness.
7. Install distributor cap, rotor and ignition wires. Ensure ignition wires are attached securely to distributor cap and spark plugs.
8. Torque distributor attaching screws to 18–23 inch lbs. and the rotor screws to 23–25 inch lbs.
9. Adjust ignition timing to specifications found in the individual car chapters.
10. Torque distributor hold down bolt to 17–25 ft. lbs.

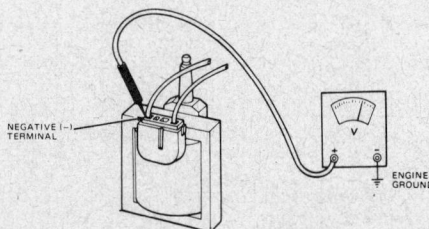

Fig. 7 TFI IV ignition system ignition coil primary voltage test connections

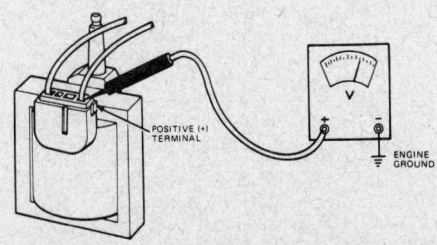

Fig. 8 TFI IV ignition system ignition coil supply voltage test connections

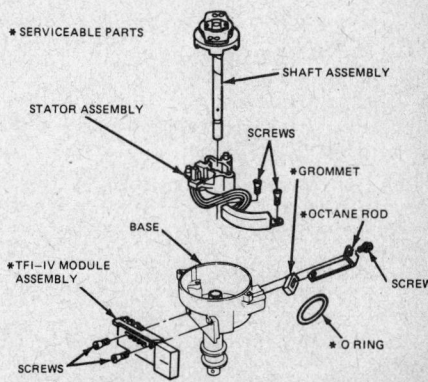

Fig. 9 Exploded view of TFI IV ignition system distributor

COMPONENT REPLACEMENT

TFI-IV Ignition Module

Removal
1. Remove distributor as described under "Distributor, Replace."
2. Remove 2 module attaching screws, Fig. 9.
3. Slide right side of module down distributor mounting flange, then back up to disengage module terminals from connector in distributor base. Remove module from distributor.

NOTE: Do not attempt to remove module before moving toward distributor flange, as connector pins will be damaged.

Installation
1. Apply a 1/32 inch coating of silicone grease D7A2-19A331-A or equivalent to metal base of module.
2. Position module on distributor mounting flange.
3. Carefully position module toward distributor base to securely engage the 3 distributor connector pins.
4. Install 2 module attaching screws and torque to 9–16 inch lbs.
5. Install distributor as described under "Distributor, Replace."

Octane Rod, Replace

1. Remove distributor cap and rotor.
2. Remove octane rod attaching screw from octane adjustment boss.
3. Slide octane rod and grommet out and disengage from stator retaining post, Fig. 9.
4. Reverse procedure to install. Torque attaching screw to 15–35 inch lbs.

Ford 1978–83 Dura Spark III Solid State Ignition System

DESCRIPTION

The Dura Spark III system, Fig. 1, is used on engines equipped with Electronic Engine Control (EEC). The system primary side consists of the battery, ignition switch, primary wiring, EEC system input and an ignition module. The secondary side consists of a distributor, distributor cap, adapter and rotor, spark plug cables and spark plugs. When the ignition switch is in the On position, the primary circuit and the ignition coil are energized. The EEC system provides a signal which tells the ignition module to turn off the coil primary circuit. The off and on times of the primary circuit are controlled by the EEC computer. When the circuit is turned Off, the magnetic field built up in the ignition coil collapses, inducing a high voltage into the coil secondary windings. This high voltage is then delivered to the spark plugs by the rotor and secondary ignition wires.

SYSTEM DIAGNOSIS

NOTE: Before proceeding with system diagnosis, ensure battery is fully charged and all accessories are "Off". Inspect all vacuum hoses and spark plug wires for proper routing and secure connections. Inspect engine compartment ignition wiring harness and connectors for signs of insulation damage, burning, overheating and loose or broken connections. repair as necessary.

Secondary Circuit Tests

Spark Plug Firing Voltage Test, 1978–81 Models
1. Connect an oscilloscope with voltage pick up on coil to distributor cable. Set oscilloscope to 30 KV parade pattern.
2. Connect timing light to No. 1 spark plug, then start engine and operate at 2000 RPM.
3. Apply 25 inches Hg. of vacuum from outside source to BP port of MAP sensor.
4. Check oscilloscope for highest firing spikes. If highest spikes are between 6 and 20 KV, system is operating properly.
5. If reading is greater than 20 KV or highest spike is 50% greater than lowest, refer to "Primary Circuit Test" under "Test 3, Ignition Coil Primary Voltage."
6. If voltage reading is less than 6 KV, refer to "Spark Plug Wires Continuity Test."
7. Check ignition timing at 2000 RPM. If reading is not between 27 and 30° BTDC, EEC system is malfunctioning and must be repaired.

Spark Plug Firing Voltage Test, 1982–83 Models
1. Connect an oscilloscope with voltage pick-up on coil to distributor wire. Set oscilloscope to parade pattern.
2. Start engine, then while slowly increasing engine RPM from idle to 2000 RPM, observe scope pattern. If the average spark plug firing voltage is 15 KV and the spark plug firing voltages do not vary more than 5 KV, the system is operating properly.
3. If the spark plug firing voltages do not vary more than 5 KV and the average spark plug firing voltage is more than 15 KV, check;
   a. Ignition coil wire for proper installation and resistance. Resistance should be less than 5000 ohms per inch. If more, replace.
   b. Spark plugs for wide gaps.
   c. Distributor cap and rotor for excessive clearance.
   d. Distributor cap and rotor for lack of silicone compound on rotor.
   e. Distributor rotor alignment. See Distributor Rotor, Replace.
4. If the spark plug firing voltages vary more than 5 KV, check;
   a. Spark plug gap(s) or worn electrodes.
   b. Correct distributor cap, adapter and rotor installation.
   c. Distributor rotor alignment. See Distributor Rotor, Replace.
5. If one or more spark plug firing voltages are unusually high, check;
   a. Disconnected spark plug wire(s).
   b. Spark plug gap(s) or open plug wire(s).
6. If one or more spark plug firing voltages are unusually low, check;
   a. Spark plug(s) for fouling or narrow gap(s).
   b. Spark plug wires for grounding.
   c. Distributor cap and adapter for tracking.
7. If spark plug firing voltages are inverted, check;
   a. Ignition coil primary connector for improper installation. If installation is satisfactory, replace coil.

Spark Plug Wire Continuity Test, All Models
1. Remove distributor cap and disconnect suspected wire from spark plug or coil.
2. Using an ohmmeter, check wire resistance through distributor cap.
3. Resistance should be 5000 ohms per inch. If reading is greater than specified, replace wire.

Spark Plug Wire Inspection, All Models
1. Clean off any deposits of dirt from wires, boots, distributor cap and coil using mild soap and water solution.
2. Inspect wires, boots for cuts, punctures or other damage.
3. Inspect wire terminals for corrosion and clean with fine sandpaper.
4. Coat all boots with silicone grease before installing.

Secondary Circuit Voltage Drop, 1978–81 Models
1. Connect an oscilloscope with voltage pick up on coil to distributor cable.
2. Disconnect a spark plug wire and ground firmly to engine block.
3. Start engine and operate at idle speed.
4. If oscilloscope indicates reading of 8 KV, distributor cap voltage drop is satisfactory.
5. If reading is greater than 8 KV, check for damaged cap or rotor and replace.
6. If an abnormal scope pattern is obtained, check for worn or damaged distributor parts.

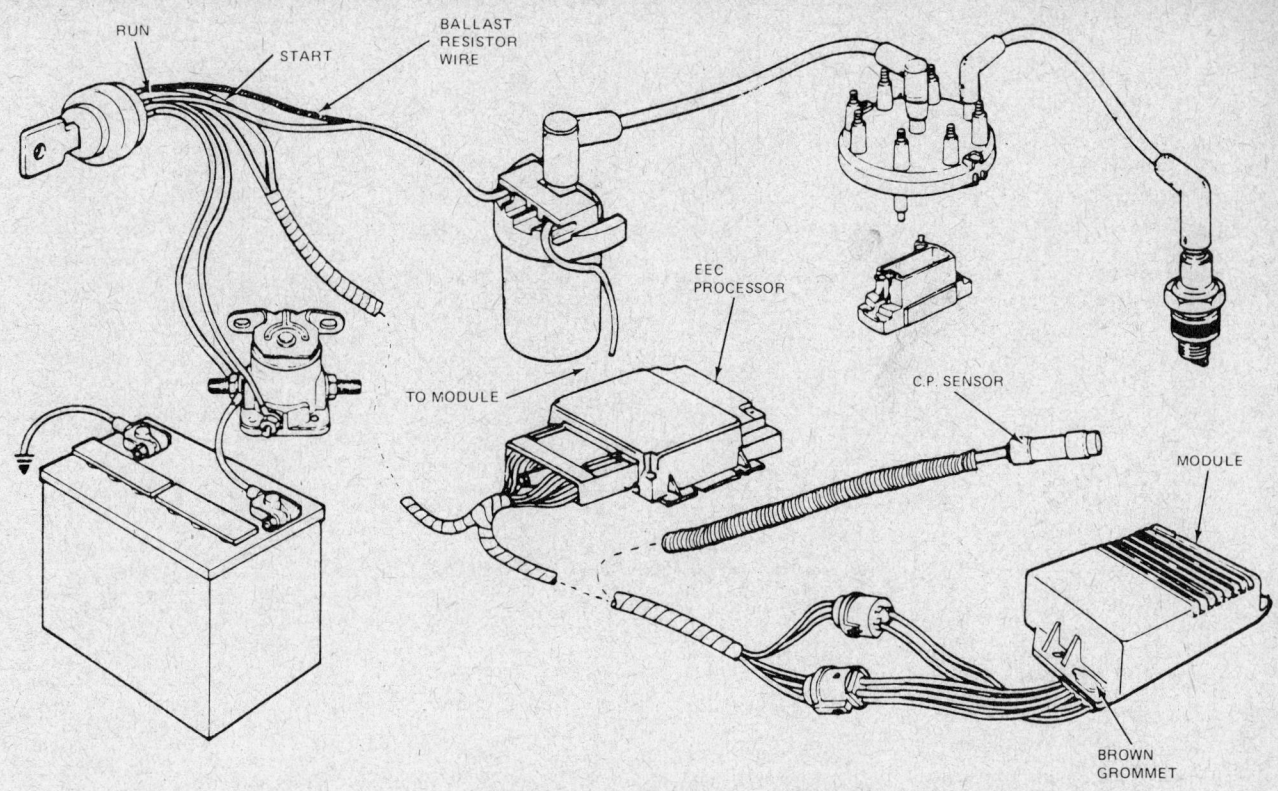

RUN
START
BALLAST RESISTOR WIRE
EEC PROCESSOR
TO MODULE
C.P. SENSOR
MODULE
BROWN GROMMET

Fig. 1   Dura Spark III ignition system, typical. 1978—83

Primary Circuit Tests, 1978—81 Models

Test 1, Ignition Coil Output
1. Disconnect spark plug wire and ground firmly to engine block.
2. Crank engine while checking for spark.
3. If spark is observed, system is operating properly.
4. If no spark is observed, remove cap and crank engine to verify rotor movement.
5. If rotor does not move when engine is cranked, repair distributor as necessary.

Test 2, Trigger Test
1. Disconnect ignition module connector and install ignition diagnostic test adapter into wiring circuit, Fig. 2.
2. Disconnect ignition coil secondary wire from distributor cap and attach to spark tester, Fig. 3. Connect spark tester to suitable ground, then turn ignition to Run position.
3. On Dura Spark III systems used on 1978—79 Lincoln Versailles, momentarily touch diagnostic adapter lead to negative battery terminal. A spark should occur at the spark tester whenever lead is removed from negative terminal. On Dura Spark III systems used on other models, momentarily touch diagnostic adapter lead to positive battery terminal. Spark should occur whenever lead touches battery terminal.
4. If spark occurs, system is operating properly. If not, refer to "Test 3, Ignition Coil Primary Voltage".

Test 3, Ignition Coil Primary Voltage
1. Turn ignition to Run position. Connect voltmeter between BATT terminal of ignition coil and ground.
2. If reading is between 5 and 8 volts, ignition system is satisfactory. If reading is greater than 8 volts, refer to "Test 7, Ground Circuit Check". If reading is less than 6 volts, refer to "Test 6, Wiring Harness Short Circuit" and to "Test 8, Ignition Coil Circuit".
3. In addition, check for open circuit in power supply circuit such as battery lead to ignition coil.

Test 4, Module Run Circuit
1. Turn ignition key to Run position.
2. Measure voltage between red module wire and engine ground by connecting straight pin to voltmeter positive lead and inserting into red wire.

NOTE: Do not allow straight pin to contact ground.

3. If reading is within 90% of battery voltage, system is operating properly.
4. If not, check for open circuit in run circuit wiring harness and repair as necessary.

Test 5, Start Circuit Voltage
1. On starter relays equipped with I terminal, disconnect cable between starter relay and starter motor.
2. On starter relays without I terminal, disconnect electrical connector at relay S terminal.
3. Hold ignition switch in Start position and measure voltage between coil BATT terminal and ground and between white module wire and ground. Connect straight pin to voltmeter lead and insert into white wire to perform test.

4. If reading is greater than 90% of battery voltage, system is satisfactory.
5. If reading is less than 90% of battery voltage, check for open circuit in ballast resistor bypass wire or module start wire and repair as necessary. Also check for defective ignition switch.

Test 6, Wiring Harness Short Circuit
1. Disconnect ignition module, ignition coil and EEC computer connectors and inspect for damage.
2. Check for damaged primary circuit wiring and repair as necessary.
3. Place transmission in Park and set parking brake. Check resistance between module connector orange wire terminal and ground, Fig. 3.
4. Measure resistance between the following connector wire terminals:
   a. Red to white wire terminals.
   b. Red to green wire terminals.
   c. Red to orange wire terminals.
   d. White to green wire terminals.
   e. White to orange wire terminals.
5. If any resistance reading obtained is less than 70,000 ohms, repair damaged wire in that circuit as necessary.

Test 7, Ground Circuit Check
1. Disconnect ignition module connector containing black wire and check for damage.
2. Check resistance between black wire terminal in module connector and ground.
3. If resistance is less than one ohm, system is satisfactory.
4. If resistance is greater than one ohm, check for open circuit at battery ground strap connection and repair as necessary.

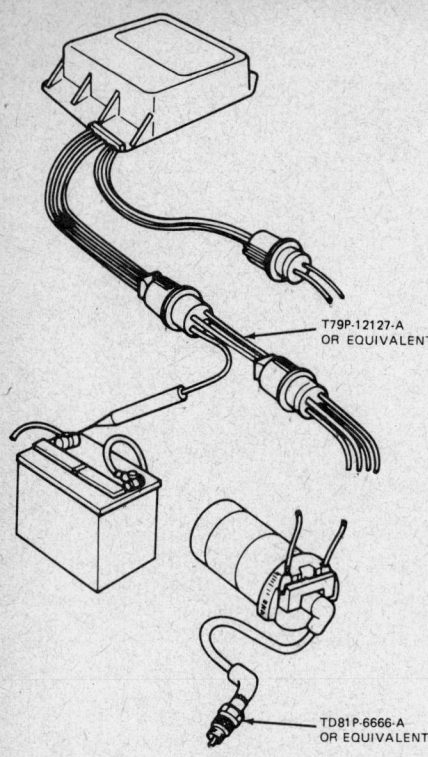

Fig. 2 Installing ignition diagnostic test adapter. 1978–83 Dura Spark III ignition system

Test 8, Ignition Coil Circuit

1. Disconnect ignition coil and module connectors and inspect for damage.
2. Measure resistance between green wire terminal of module connector and TACH terminal on ignition coil connector.
3. If resistance is less than 2 ohms, circuit is satisfactory. If resistance is greater than 2 ohms, check for open circuit in TACH terminal and repair as necessary.
4. Measure resistance between red wire terminal of module connector and BATT terminal on ignition connector.
5. If resistance is less than 2 ohms, circuit is satisfactory. If resistance is greater than 2 ohms, inspect primary wiring and ignition resistor for opens or corrosion and repair as necessary.

Test 9, Module Output Check

1. Connect any connectors that were previously disconnected.
2. Connect voltmeter between coil TACH terminal and ground.
3. Set voltmeter on highest scale, then firmly ground ignition coil high tension lead to engine block.
4. Crank engine, then switch voltmeter to lowest scale.
5. If meter needle fluctuates, module is operating satisfactorily. If not, refer to "Test 10, Module Check".

NOTE: If difficulty is encountered in performing this test using a voltmeter, a test light may be substituted in its place. The light flashing would correspond to the voltmeter needle fluctuating.

Test 10, Module Check

1. Disconnect module connector containing green wire.
2. Connect voltmeter between green wire terminal of module connector and ground.
3. Turn ignition to Run position and check voltage.
4. If reading is more than 90% of battery voltage, replace ignition module.
5. If reading is less than 90% of battery voltage, refer to "Test 11, Continuity Check".

Test 11, Continuity Check

1. Check resistance between green wire terminal in harness side module connector and coil TACH terminal.
2. If ohmmeter indicates less than one ohm, system is operating satisfactorily.
3. If reading is greater than one ohm, check for open circuit in wire between coil TACH terminal and ignition module and repair as necessary.

Test 12, Coil Primary Circuit Check

1. Disconnect ignition coil electrical connector.
2. Measure resistance between coil BATT and TACH terminals.
3. If reading is between 1 and 2 ohms, primary circuit is satisfactory.
4. If not, replace coil.

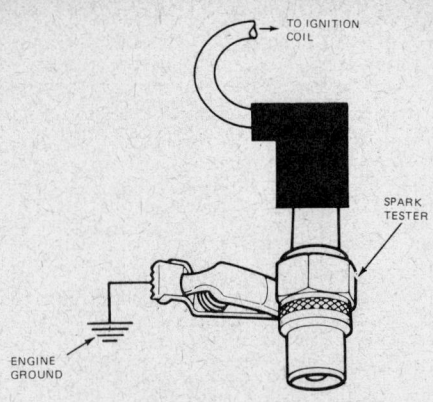

Fig. 3 Spark tester

Test 13, Coil Secondary Circuit Check

1. Check resistance between coil TACH terminal and high tension lead terminal.
2. If reading is between 7700 and 9600 ohms, secondary circuit is satisfactory.
3. If not, replace ignition coil.

Primary Circuit Tests, 1982–83 Models

Test 1, Run Circuit

1. Disconnect ignition module three wire-connector and install ignition diagnostic test adapter into wiring circuit, Fig. 2.
2. Connect spark tester, Fig. 4, between ignition coil and ground.
3. Turn ignition "On", then while observing spark tester, touch diagnostic test lead to battery positive terminal. Spark should occur every time lead touches battery.
4. If spark occurs, circuit is satisfactory. If not, proceed to test 2.

Test 2, Start Circuit

1. Remove diagnostic test adapter installed in test 1 but, leave spark tester attached.
2. While cranking over engine with ignition switch, observe spark tester for sparks.
3. If sparks occur, circuit is satisfactory. If not, proceed to test 3.

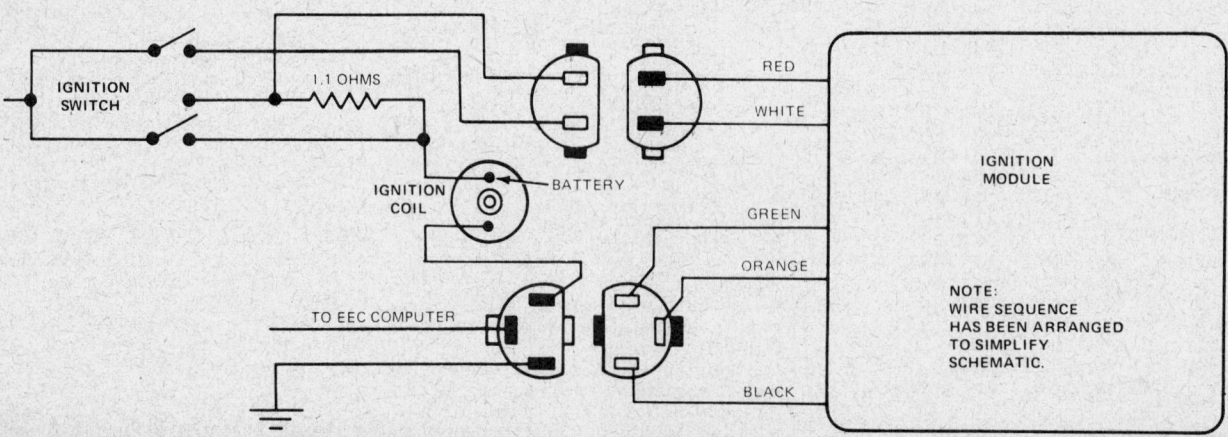

Fig. 4 Electrical schematic. 1978–83 Dura Spark III ignition system

Test 3, Start Voltage

1. Reconnect coil wire to distributor cap.
   a. If starter relay is equipped with a I terminal, disconnect starter cable from starter relay.
   b. If starter relay is equipped with S terminal, disconnect S wire from relay.
2. With ignition "Off", install straight pin into module white wire, Fig. 5.
3. Connect a suitable voltmeter between ground and straight pin.
4. Turn ignition switch to "Start" position and note voltage.
5. Move voltmeter positive lead to coil Batt. connector and note voltage with ignition switch in start "position".
6. If voltage obtained is 90% of battery voltage, circuit is satisfactory. If voltage obtained is less than 90% of battery voltage, a defective ignition switch or wiring harness is indicated.

Test 4, Ignition Coil Primary Circuit Switching

1. Disconnect ignition module three wire connector and install ignition diagnostic test adapter into wiring circuit, Fig. 2.
2. Connect a suitable test light between coil Tach terminal and engine ground.
3. Turn ignition "On", then while observing test light, touch diagnostic test lead to battery positive terminal. Test light should flash every time lead touches battery.
4. If test light flashes, circuit is satisfactory. If not, Proceed to test 6.

Test 5, Ignition Coil Secondary Resistance

1. Disconnect and inspect ignition coil electrical connector.
2. Using a suitable ohmmeter, measure resistance between coil Batt. terminal and high tension lead terminal.
3. If resistance is between 7700–10,500 ohms, coil is satisfactory. If not between limits, replace coil.

Test 6, Supply Voltage Circuits

1. Remove diagnostic test adapter installed in test 4 and test light, then;
   a. If starter relay is equipped with a I terminal, disconnect starter cable from starter relay.
   b. If starter relay is equipped with S terminal, disconnect S wire from relay.
2. With ignition "Off", install straight pins into module red and white wires, Fig. 6.

NOTE: Do not allow straight pins to contact engine ground.

3. Using a suitable voltmeter, connect negative lead to ground.
   a. With ignition in "On" position, measure voltage at red wire pin.
   b. Place ignition in "Start" position, measure voltage at white wire pin and at coil Batt. terminal.

NOTE: When measuring voltages, wiggle wires to simulate any open circuits that might exist.

4. If readings obtained are 90% of battery voltage, supply circuits are satisfactory. Proceed to test 7.
5. If readings obtained are less than 90% of battery voltage;

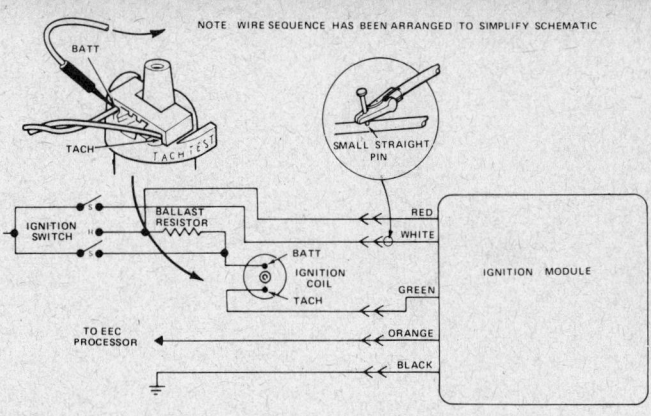

Fig. 5 Dura Spark III ignition system start voltage test connections. 1982–83 models

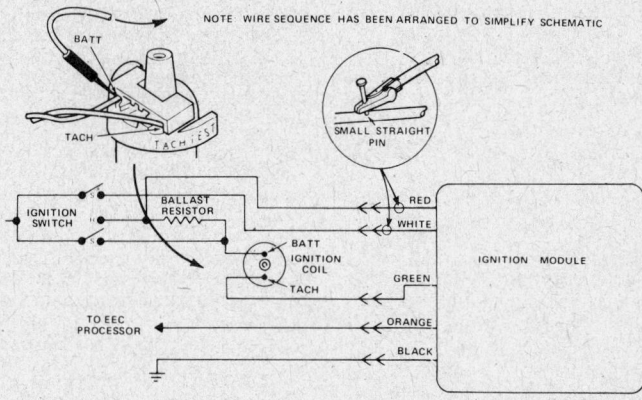

Fig. 6 Dura Spark III ignition system supply voltage test connections. 1982–83 models

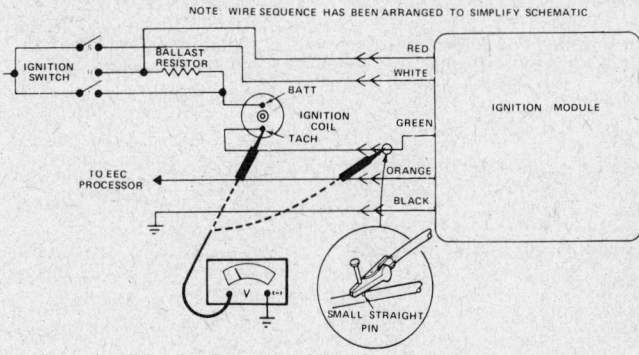

Fig. 7 Dura Spark III ignition system module to coil wire test connections. 1982–83 models

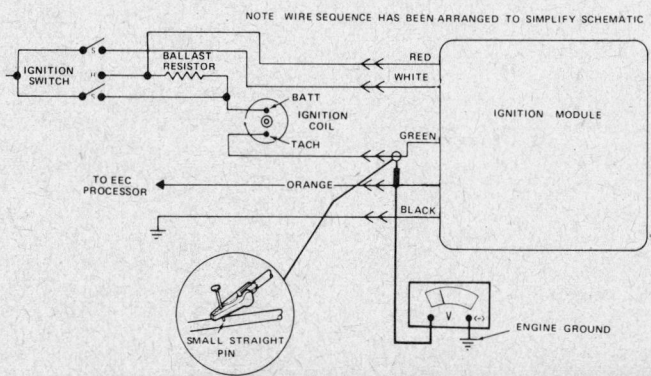

Fig. 8 Dura Spark III ignition system primary circuit continuity test connections. 1982–83 models

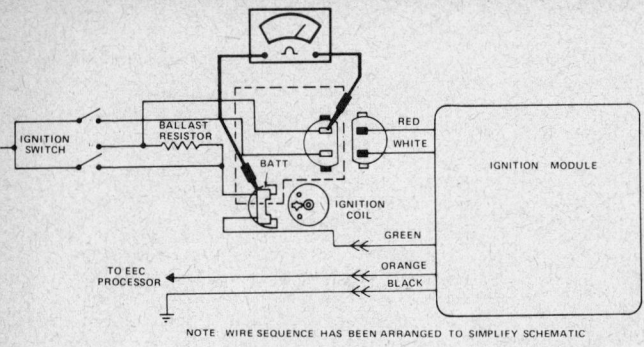

Fig. 9 Dura Spark III ignition system ballast resistor test connections. 1982—83 models

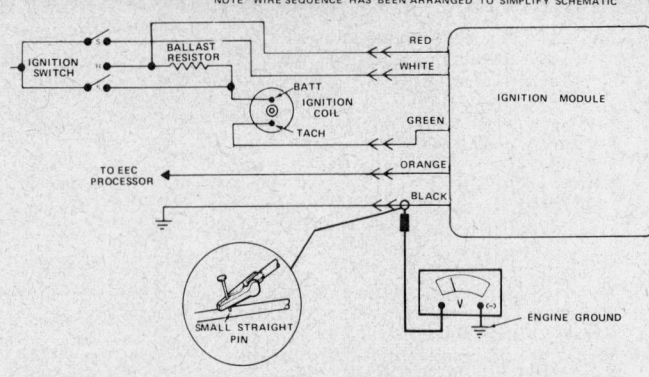

Fig. 10 Dura Spark III ignition system ground circuit test connections. 1982—83 models

a. Defective wiring harness or connectors in supply voltage circuits.
b. Defective ignition switch.
c. Defective ignition coil or radio interference capacitor.

Test 7, Ignition Coil Supply Voltage

1. Connect positive lead of voltmeter to coil Batt. terminal and negative lead to ground.
2. Turn ignition switch to "On" position.
3. Observe voltmeter reading. If 6–8 volts, circuit is satisfactory. If less than 6 volts or more than 8 volts, proceed to test 9.

Test 8, Testing Tach Wire

1. Disconnect and inspect module three wire connector and coil connector.
2. Using a suitable ohmmeter, connect one lead to ground and the other to the coil connector Tach. terminal. Measure resistance.
3. If readings obtained are one ohm or less, circuit is satisfactory. If readings are more than one ohm, repair short in tach wire.

Test 9, Ignition Coil Primary Resistance

1. Disconnect and inspect ignition coil connector.
2. Using a suitable tachometer, measure resistance between coil Batt. and Tach. terminals.
3. If readings are 0.8–1.6 ohms, circuit is satisfactory. If readings are out of specifications, replace coil.

Test 10, Module to Coil Wire

1. With ignition "Off", insert straight pin in module green wire, Fig. 7.

NOTE: Do not allow straight pin to contact engine ground.

2. Using a suitable voltmeter, connect negative lead to ground.
3. Turn ignition "On", then measure voltage at green wire pin and Tach. terminal of ignition coil, Fig. 7.
4. If voltmeter shows less than 1/2 volt difference, circuit is satisfactory. If more than 1/2 volt difference, inspect and repair wiring harness between coil and module.

Test 11, Primary Circuit Continuity

1. Leave straight pin in green wire as outlined in test 10.
2. Turn ignition "On", then using a suitable

voltmeter connected to ground, measure voltage at green wire pin, Fig. 8.
3. If voltage exceeds 1 1/2 volts, proceed to test 13. If voltage obtained is 1 1/2 volts or less, proceed to test 12.

Test 12, Ballast Resistor

1. Disconnect and inspect module two wire connector and ignition coil connector, Fig. 9.
2. Using a suitable ohmmeter, measure resistance between coil connector Batt. terminal and wiring harness connector which mates with module red wire, Fig. 9.
3. If reading is 0.8–1.6 ohms, circuit is satisfactory. If reading is less than 0.8 ohms or more than 1.6 ohms, replace ballast resistor.

Test 13, Ground Circuit

1. With ignition "Off", install straight pin in module black wire, Fig. 10.

NOTE: Do not allow straight pin to touch engine ground.

2. Using a suitable ohmmeter, connect negative lead to engine ground and positive lead to black wire pin.
3. Turn ignition "On", measure voltage.
4. If voltage obtained was more than 1 1/2 volts, proceed to test 14. If voltage obtained was less than 1 1/2 volts, replace ignition module.

Test 14, Wiring Harness Ground Circuit

1. Disconnect module three wire connector, inspect connector for dirt and corrosion.
2. Using a suitable ohmmeter, connect one lead to engine ground. Connect other lead to wiring harness terminal which mates with black module wire terminal. Measure resistance.

NOTE: When measuring resistances, wiggle wires to simulate any open circuits that might exist.

3. If resistance is less than one ohm, inspect wiring harness connector and module black wire. If no problem is found, it is either intermittent or not in ignition system.
4. If resistance is greater than one ohm, inspect and repair wiring harness between ignition module and ground connection.

DISTRIBUTOR, REPLACE

Early Models, Fig. 11

1. Remove distributor cap. Install rotor alignment tool T78P-12200-A and remove rotor. Refer to Distributor Rotor, Replace.
2. With rotor alignment tool in position, remove distributor hold down bolt and clamp. Remove alignment tool.
3. Carefully remove distributor from engine block, noting position of rotor blades in relation to distributor housing as distributor drive gear is felt to disengage with cam gear.

NOTE: Do not rotate engine after distributor has been removed.

4. Install distributor in engine block. Ensure the distributor hold down flange slot is aligned with the clamp bolt hole and rotor upper blade slot is aligned with the slot in the distributor cap adapter.
5. Install distributor hold down bolt and clamp. Torque to 17 ft. lbs.
6. Align rotor and install distributor cap. Refer to Distributor Rotor, Replace.

Late Models, Fig. 12

1. Remove distributor cap and rotor. Position crankshaft as outlined in Distributor Rotor, Replace.

NOTE: The alignment slot in the adapter should be aligned with the alignment slot in the sleeve assembly.

2. Remove distributor hold down bolt and clamp.
3. Carefully remove distributor from engine block, noting position of the large slot in the sleeve in relation to the adapter alignment slot as distributor drive gear is felt to disengage with cam gear.

NOTE: Do not rotate engine after distributor has been removed.

4. Install distributor in engine block. Ensure the distributor hold down flange slot is aligned with the clamp bolt hole and adapter alignment slot is aligned with the large sleeve alignment slot.

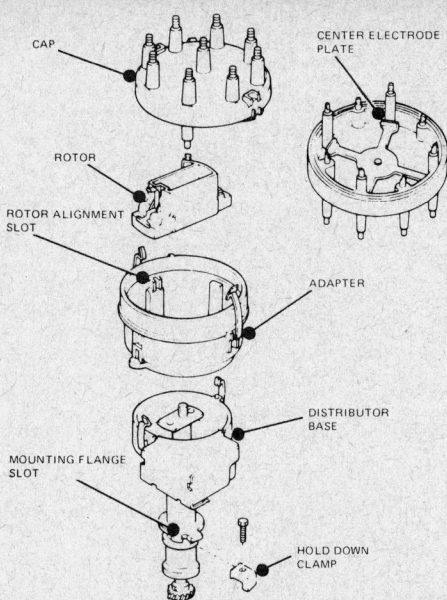

Fig. 11 Early model Dura Spark III distributor

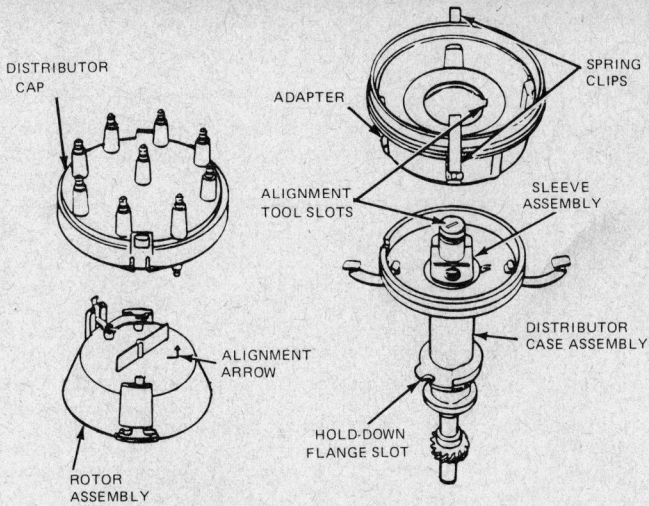

Fig. 12 Late model Dura Spark III distributor

5. Install distributor hold down bolt and clamp. Torque to 17 ft. lbs.

DISTRIBUTOR ROTOR, REPLACE

Early Models, Fig. 11

1. Remove distributor cap.
2. Position the crankshaft to align the rotor upper blade slot with the distributor cap adapter slot to enable the rotor alignment tool T78P-12200-A to fall into place, Fig. 13.

NOTE: If alignment is not possible of rotor and adapter due to damage, position No. 1 cylinder at TDC on compression stroke with timing marks aligned at O.

3. Remove rotor alignment tool, then remove rotor retaining screws and rotor.
4. Position rotor on distributor shaft with upper rotor blade slot facing adapter slot. Install, but do not tighten rotor retaining screws.
5. Position rotor alignment tool as shown in Fig. 13, then tighten rotor retaining screws to 15–20 in. lbs.
6. Remove rotor alignment tool and install distributor cap.

Late Models, Fig. 12

NOTE: Beginning in 1983, the Dura Spark III ignition system rotor was changed to a conventional design. This rotor has no adjustment facilities, therefore no replacement procedure is necessary.

1. Remove distributor cap and rotor.
2. Position No. 1 piston on compression stroke, then rotate crankshaft until rotor alignment tool, T79P-12200-A or equivalent, can be inserted into alignment slots, Fig. 14.
3. Check vibration damper and timing pointer alignment marks. If timing point-

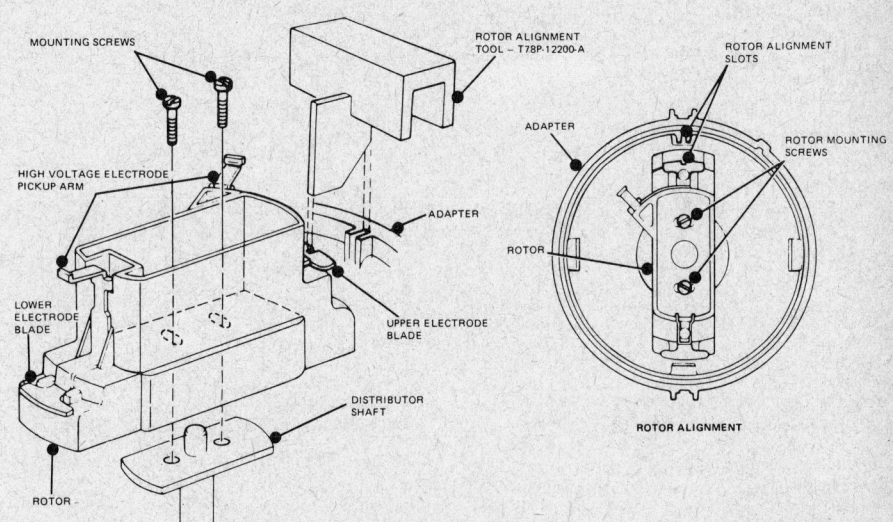

Fig. 13 Early model rotor alignment

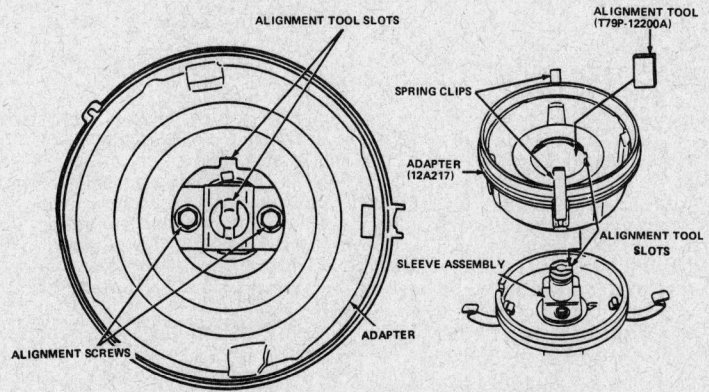

Fig. 14 Late model rotor alignment

er is within ± 4° of TDC, alignment is satisfactory. If alignment is out of specifications, position vibration damper at TDC with cylinder No. 1 at TDC. Loosen sleeve assembly adjustment screws and rotate sleeve until rotor alignment tool can be inserted into alignment slots, Fig. 14. Torque adjustment screws to 25–35 in. lbs. and remove tool.

4. Replace rotor and distributor cap.

AUTOMATIC TRANSMISSIONS/TRANSAXLES

> **NOTE:** This chapter deals only with maintenance, adjustments and "in car" repairs. For major service work, Motor's Automatic Transmission Manual is available.

INDEX

GM Turbo Hydra-Matic 125, 125C Automatic Transaxle

IDENTIFICATION

These transaxles may be identified by a model tag attached to the oil pan flange pad to the right of the oil dipstick at the rear of the transaxle.

Citation, Omega, Phoenix & Skylark
1980 .... CV, PZ
1981 .... CD, CT, CV, PZ
1982 ...... CE, CL, CT, CV, PI, PK, PL, PZ
1983 .... CE, CL, CT, PD, PW
Cavalier, Cimarron Firenza, 2000 & Skyhawk
1982 .... CI, CJ, PE
1983 .... CA, CB, CF, P3, PG
Celebrity, Century, Cutlass Ciera & 6000
1982 .... BF, BL, CL, OP, PI, PL
1983 .... BF, BL, CL, OP, PD, PW

DESCRIPTION

1980–81 Citation, Omega, Phoenix & Skylark models are equipped with the 125 automatic transaxle, Fig. 1. 1982–83 Cavalier, Celebrity, Century, Cimarron, Citation, Cutlass Ciera, Firenza, 2000, Omega, Phoenix, Skyhawk, Skylark & 6000 models use the 125C automatic transaxle, Figs. 1 and 1A.

NOTE: The 125 and 125C automatic transaxles are identical, except the 125C incorporates a pressure plate and damper assembly. Refer to the 125 automatic transaxle for service procedures.

These automatic transaxles are designed for use as a transverse mounted front wheel drive unit. The unit consists primarily of a 3 element torque converter, compound plane-

tary gear set and dual sprocket and drive link assembly. A differential and final drive gear set is also incorporated in the transaxle case. Three multiple disc clutches, a roller clutch and a band provide the friction elements required to obtain the desired functions of the planetary gearset. Hydraulic pressure required to operate the friction elements and automatic control is provided by a vane type pump.

TROUBLE SHOOTING

No Drive In D Range

1. Low fluid level.
2. Manual linkage improperly adjusted.
3. Restricted or plugged screen or damaged screen O-ring.
4. Pressure regulator valve sticking.
5. Damaged pump rotor splines.
6. Manual valve disconnected.
7. Case cover gaskets mispositioned.
8. Forward clutch worn or damaged.
9. Roller clutch worn or damaged.

1–2 Upshift At Full Throttle Only

1. Throttle valve cable improperly adjusted, binding or damaged.
2. Throttle lever and bracket assembly mispositioned, binding or disconnected.
3. Throttle valve and plunger binding.
4. Pump and control valve assembly gaskets or spacer plate leaking or damaged.

No 1–2 Upshift, 1st Speed Only

1. Governor assembly damaged.

2. Governor fluid passages leaking or blocked.
3. Governor cover leaking.
4. 1–2 shift valve or 1–2 throttle valve sticking in downshift position.
5. Excessive leakage between intermediate band apply pin and case bore.
6. Damaged or worn band.
7. Intermediate servo assembly damaged, worn or leaking.

No 2–3 Upshift, 1st & 2nd Speed Only

1. Pump and control valve assembly damaged.
2. 2–3 shift valve or 2–3 throttle valve sticking in downshift position.
3. Drive sprocket oil seals damaged or feed passages blocked.
4. Intermediate servo piston seal ring damaged.
5. Governor assembly shaft seal ring damaged.

3rd Speed Only

1. 2–3 shift valve stuck in upshift position.
2. Governor assembly feed passages plugged.

Drive In Neutral Position

1. Manual linkage improperly adjusted.
2. Forward clutch does not release.
3. Cross leakage to forward clutch passage.

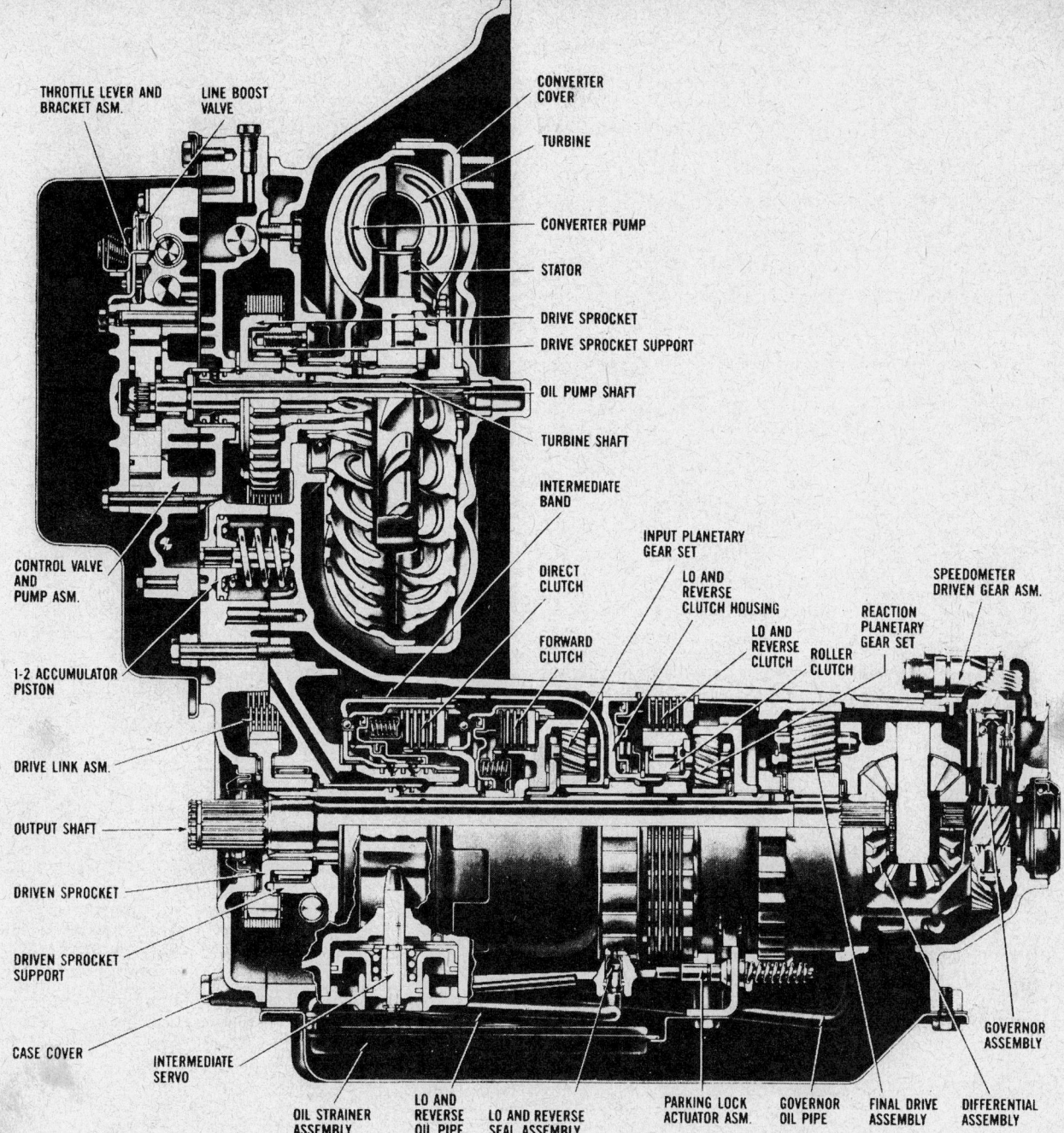

Fig. 1 Sectional view of Turbo Hydra-Matic 125 automatic transaxle

No Drive or Slips In Reverse

1. Throttle valve cable improperly adjusted or binding.
2. Manual linkage improperly adjusted.
3. Throttle valve binding.
4. Shift valve binding.
5. Reverse boost valve binding.
6. Low and reverse clutch damaged or worn.
7. Direct clutch damaged or worn.

Slips On 1–2 Upshift

1. Low fluid level.

2. Separator plate and gaskets damaged or mispositioned.
3. 1–2 accumulator valve sticking.
4. 1–2 accumulator piston seal leaking.
5. Excessive leaking between intermediate band apply pin and case bore.
6. Intermediate Servo assembly damaged or worn.
7. Throttle valve improperly adjusted.
8. Throttle valve binding.
9. Shift throttle valve binding.

Rough 1–2 Upshift

1. Throttle valve cable improperly adjusted

or binding.
2. Throttle valve and plunger binding.
3. Shift throttle valve binding.
4. 1–2 accumulator valve binding.
5. 1–2 accumulator damaged.
6. Intermediate servo assembly damaged or worn.

Slips 2–3 Upshift

1. Low fluid level.
2. Throttle valve cable improperly adjusted.
3. Throttle valve binding.
4. Spacer plates and gaskets damaged or

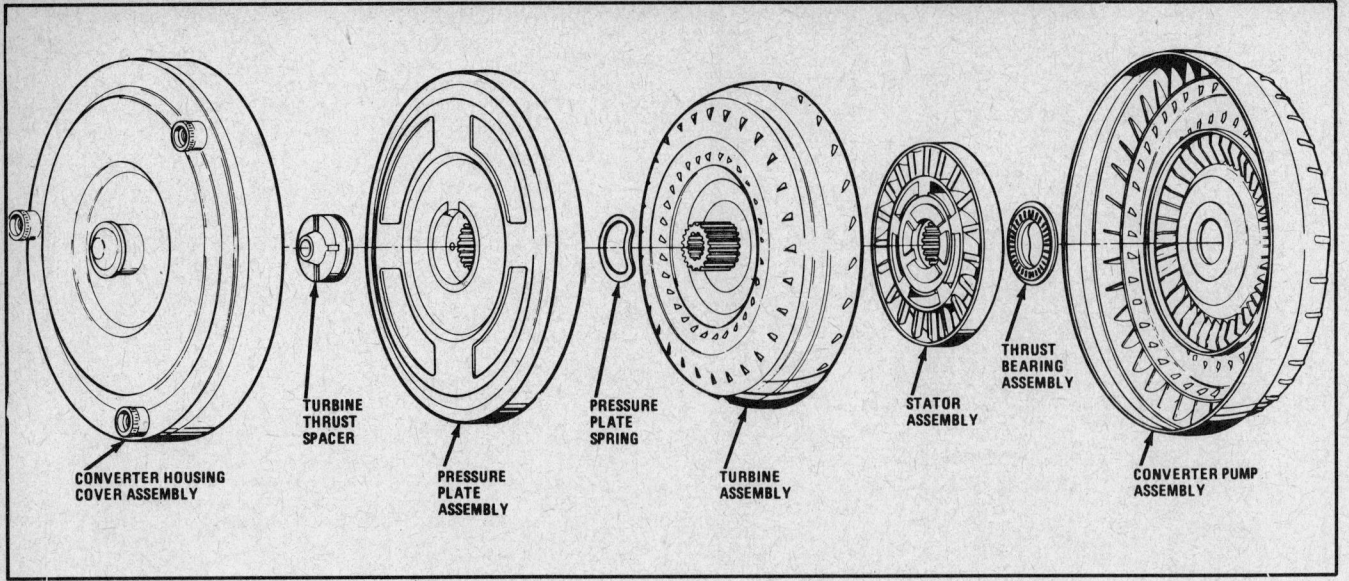

Fig. 1A   Torque converter clutch exploded view. 125C transaxle

mispositioned.
5. Intermediate servo assembly damaged.
6. Direct clutch damaged or worn.

Rough 2–3 Upshift

1. Throttle valve cable improperly adjusted.
2. Throttle valve and plunger binding.
3. Shift throttle valve binding.

No Engine Braking In Intermediate Range

1. Intermediate servo assembly damaged or worn.
2. Intermediate band damaged or worn.

No Engine Braking In Low Range

1. Low and reverse clutch assembly damaged or worn.

No Part Throttle or Detent Downshifts

1. Throttle valve bushing passages blocked.
2. 2–3 throttle valve bushing passages blocked.
3. Valve body gaskets damaged or mispositioned.
4. Spacer plate hole plugged.
5. Throttle valve cable improperly adjusted.
6. Shift throttle valve binding.
7. Throttle valve binding.

Low or High Shift Points

1. Throttle valve cable improperly adjusted.
2. Throttle valve binding.
3. Shift throttle valve binding.
4. Line boost valve binding.
5. Throttle valve plunger binding.
6. 1–2 or 2–3 throttle valve binding.
7. Valve body spacer plate or gaskets damaged or mispositioned.
8. Throttle lever and bracket assembly binding or disconnected.
9. Governor shaft seal ring damaged.
10. Governor cover O-ring damaged.

Will Not Hold In Park Position

1. Manual linkage improperly adjusted.
2. Parking pawl binding or broken.
3. Parking brake loose or damaged.
4. Actuator rod or plunger damaged.
5. Inside detent lever and pin assembly damaged.
6. Manual detent roller and spring assembly damaged.

Transaxle Noisy

1. Low fluid level.
2. Screen plugged or screen O-ring damaged.
3. Coolant in fluid.
4. Transaxle grounded to body.
5. Roller bearing damaged or worn.
6. If noisy in 3rd gear or on turns only, check differential and final drive unit.

High or Low Fluid Pressure

1. Throttle valve cable improperly adjusted or binding.
2. Throttle lever and bracket assembly binding or damaged.
3. Throttle valve or plunger binding.
4. Shift throttle valve binding.
5. Line boost valve binding.
6. Throttle valve boost valve or reverse boost valve binding.
7. Pressure regulator valve and spring binding.
8. Pressure relief valve damaged.
9. Manual valve disconnected.
10. Pump damaged.

MAINTENANCE

To check fluid, drive vehicle for at least 15 minutes to bring fluid to operating temperature (200° F). With vehicle on a level surface and engine idling in Park and parking brake applied, the level on the dipstick should be at the "Full" mark. To bring the fluid level from the ADD mark to the FULL mark requires one pint of fluid. If vehicle cannot be driven sufficiently to bring fluid to operating temperature, the level on the dipstick should be between the two dimples on the dipstick with

fluid temperature at 70° F. Note that the two dimples are located above the FULL mark.

If additional fluid is required, use only Dexron II automatic transmission fluid.

NOTE: An early change to a darker color from the usual red color and or a strong odor that is usually associated with overheated fluid is normal and should not be considered as a positive sign of required maintenance or unit failure.

CAUTION: When adding fluid, do not over fill, as foaming and loss of fluid through the vent may occur as the fluid heats up. Also, if fluid level is too low, complete loss of drive may occur especially when cold, which can cause transmission failure.

Every 100,000 miles, the oil should be drained, the oil pan removed, the screen cleaned and fresh fluid added. For vehicles subjected to more severe use such as heavy city traffic especially in hot weather, prolonged periods of idling or towing, this maintenance should be performed every 15,000 miles.

Changing Fluid

1. Raise and support vehicle, then position drain pan under oil pan.
2. Remove front and side oil pan attaching bolts, then loosen rear pan attaching bolts.
3. Carefully pry oil pan loose from transaxle case and allow fluid to drain.
4. Remove remaining attaching bolt, oil pan and gasket. Thoroughly clean pan before reinstalling.
5. Remove and discard screen and O-ring seal.
6. Install replacement screen and O-ring seal, locating screen against dipstick stop.
7. Install gasket on oil pan, then install pan and torque attaching bolts to 12 ft. lbs.
8. Lower vehicle and add approximately 4 qts. of fluid.
9. With selector in park, parking brake applied and engine at idle speed and operating temperature, check fluid level and

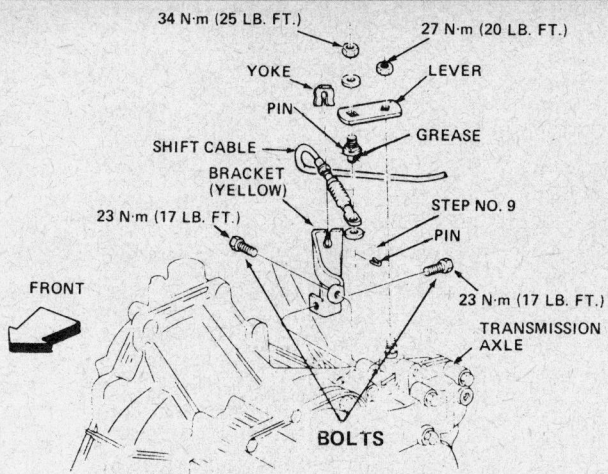

Fig. 2 Manual cable mounting. 1980–81 models

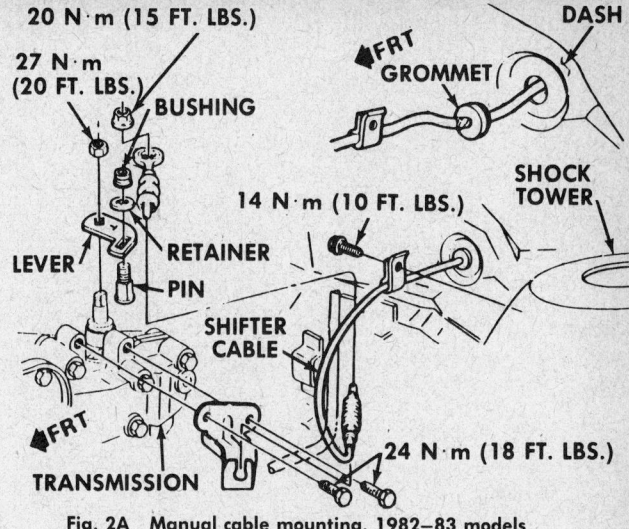

Fig. 2A Manual cable mounting. 1982–83 models

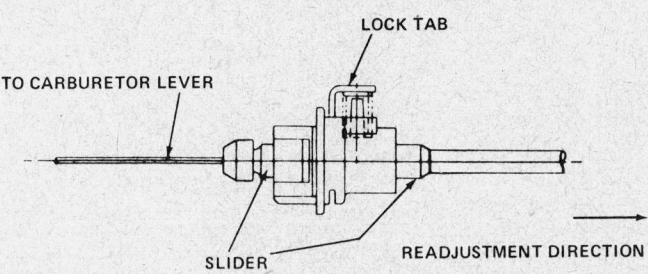

Fig. 3 Downshift cable adjustment

add fluid as necessary.

NOTE: Do not race engine or move shift lever through ranges.

Fig. 4 Pump cover & valve body assembly attaching bolts. THM 125

IN-VEHICLE ADJUSTMENTS

Manual Linkage, Adjust

1. Place transaxle shift lever in "Neutral" position.
2. Place transaxle lever in "Neutral" position by moving transaxle lever clockwise to the "L" detent, then move lever counter clockwise through three detent positions to "Neutral".
3. On 1980–81 vehicles, attach shift cable to pin, Fig. 2, then torque attaching nut to specifications.
4. On 1982–83 vehicles, loosely assemble retainer, bushing and shift cable to pin, Fig. 2A, then torque attaching nut to specifications.

T.V. or Downshift Cable, Adjust

4-151
1. Disengage snap lock so that cable is free to slide, Fig. 3.
2. Ensure cable housing is fully seated into control cable bracket and is secured to the transmission. Also ensure cable is attached to the carburetor idler lever.
3. Rotate carburetor idler lever to its full travel stop and hold in this position.

4. Keeping idler lever firmly against stop, push snap lock until it is flush with downshift cable fitting.
5. Release carburetor idler lever.

V6-173
1. Disengage snap lock so that cable is free to slide, Fig. 3.
2. Ensure cable is installed in the support and attached to transmission and carburetor lever, then open carburetor lever to wide-open throttle position.
3. Keeping carburetor lever in the wide-open throttle position, push snap lock downward until top is flush with rest of cable.

IN-VEHICLE, REPAIRS

Valve Body, Replace

1. Remove valve body cover and gasket.
2. On THM 125C transaxles, remove solenoid retaining bolt and the solenoid, then disconnect converter clutch wires from 3rd gear pressure switch.
3. Remove screws attaching throttle lever and bracket assembly, then remove throt-

tle lever and bracket assembly with T.V. cable link.
4. On THM 125 transaxles, remove pump cover screws except for one screw shown in Fig. 4. Loosen, but do not remove this screw.
5. On THM 125C transaxles, remove the auxiliary valve body screws except for the one screw shown in Fig. 4A. Loosen, but do not remove, this screw.
6. Remove remaining valve body retaining screws, then the valve body and pump assembly.
7. On THM 125C transaxles, separate valve body from auxiliary valve body.
8. Reverse procedure to install. On THM 125 transaxles, torque 1 x 25mm., 1 x 45mm., and 1 x 65mm. valve body attaching bolts to 8 ft. lbs. Torque 1.25 x 65mm. and 1.25 x 85mm. bolts to 18 ft. lbs. On THM 125C transaxles, torque 1 x 20mm., 1 x 45mm., 1 x 65mm., and 1 x 90mm. valve body attaching bolts to 8 ft. lbs. Torque 1.25 x 85mm. and 1.25 x 130mm. bolts to 18 ft. lbs.
9. Using new gasket, install valve body cover to transaxle and torque bolts to 12 ft. lbs.

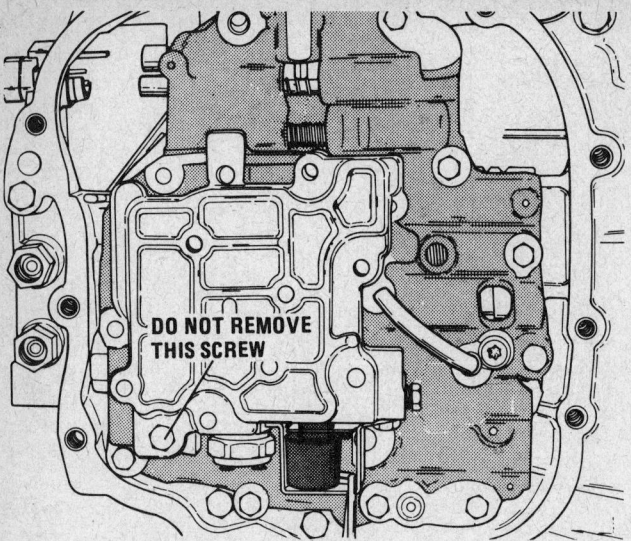

Fig. 4A Valve body & auxiliary valve body retaining screws. THM 125C

Fig. 5 Removing & installing governor assembly

NOTE: THM 125C transaxle valve body covers and oil pans can have a raised rib, depressed rib or flat sealing flange. RTV sealant should be used on all oil pans and valve body covers that have a flat sealing flange. Gaskets should be used on all oil pans and valve body covers that have either depressed or raised rib sealing flanges.

Intermediate Servo, Replace

1. Remove oil pan and gasket, then remove screen and O-ring.
2. Remove reverse oil pipe retaining brackets, intermediate servo cover and gasket.
3. Remove intermediate servo assembly.
4. Reverse procedure to install. Torque intermediate servo cover screws to 8 ft. lbs.

Governor, Replace

1. Remove speedometer driven gear and sleeve.
2. Remove governor cover and O-ring.
3. Remove speedometer drive gear thrust washer and gear, then remove governor assembly, Fig. 5.
4. Reverse procedure to install. Torque governor cover attaching bolts to 9 ft. lbs.

TRANSAXLE, REPLACE

1980–81 Citation, Omega, Phoenix & Skylark

1. Disconnect battery ground cable at transaxle and attach cable to upper radiator hose with tape.
2. Disconnect detent cable at carburetor, then remove detent cable attaching screw at transaxle. Pull up on detent cable cover at transaxle, until cable is exposed, then disconnect cable from rod.
3. Remove two transaxle strut bracket bolts at transaxle, if equipped.
4. Remove all engine to transaxle bolts except the one bolt near the starter motor. The bolt nearest the cowl is installed from the engine side.

5. Loosen the engine to transaxle bolt nearest the starter, but do not remove bolt.
6. Disconnect speedometer cable at upper and lower cable coupling. On models equipped with cruise control, disconnect speedometer cable at transducer.
7. Remove clip and washer and disconnect transaxle linkage at transaxle, then remove two shift linkage bracket bolts.
8. Disconnect transaxle oil cooler lines at transaxle.
9. Install engine holding fixture J-22825-1 and J-22825-20 and raise engine slightly to relieve weight from engine mounts.
10. Unlock steering column, then raise and support vehicle.
11. Remove two nuts attaching stabilizer bar left hand side lower control arm.
12. Remove four bolts attaching the plate that retains stabilizer to left hand side of cradle.
13. Loosen four bolts attaching stabilizer bar bracket to right hand side of cradle, then pull stabilizer bar down from left hand side of vehicle.
14. Disconnect front and rear transaxle mounts at cradle.
15. Remove two rear center crossmember bolts.
16. Remove right hand side front cradle attaching bolts. To gain access to attaching nuts, pull back on splash shield next to frame rail.
17. Remove upper bolt from lower front transaxle damper, if equipped.
18. Remove left hand side front and rear cradle to body attaching bolts.
19. Remove left front wheel and tire assembly.
20. Place tool No. J-28468 behind axle shaft cones and pull cones out away from transaxle. Position axle shafts out of way and plug bores to prevent fluid leakage.
21. Swing partial cradle toward left hand side of vehicle and secure to fender well with wire.
22. Remove four converter shield attaching bolts and shield.
23. Remove two transaxle extension bolts from engine to transaxle bracket.
24. Secure a suitable transaxle jack to transaxle case, then remove three converter to flywheel attaching bolts.
25. Remove the remaining transaxle to engine bolt located near starter motor.

26. Remove transaxle by sliding toward left hand side of vehicle away from engine.
27. Reverse procedure to install. Note the following when installing transaxle:
    a. Slide right axle shaft into case as transaxle is being installed.
    b. Install cradle to body bolts before installing stabilizer bar attachments.
    c. Use pry hole located on cradle to aid in stabilizer bar installation.

1982–83 Celebrity, Century, Cutlass Ciera, Citation, Omega, Phoenix, Skylark & 6000

1. Disconnect battery ground cable, then remove air cleaner.
2. Disconnect T.V. cable from transaxle and carburetor, then remove strut shock bracket bolts from transaxle.
3. Remove oil cooler lines from strut bracket.
4. Remove all transaxle to engine attaching bolts except the one nearest the starter. Loosen, but do not remove this bolt.
5. Disconnect speedometer cable at upper and lower couplings, then remove shift linkage retaining clip, washer and bracket bolts.
6. Disconnect oil cooler lines at transaxle.
7. Remove front and left sections of cradle as follows:
    a. Install engine support fixture J-22825-1 and J-22825-45 and torque fasteners to 30 ft. lbs.
    b. Position support hook into lifting bracket and tighten coupling nut only enough to remove slack from hook.

CAUTION: Engine support fixture must be located in center of cowl for 4 cylinder engines and on strut towers for 6 cylinder engines. Support fixture is not designed to support entire weight of engine and transaxle. Improper use may result in vehicle damage and/or personal injury.

    c. Remove intermediate shaft to steering gear stub shaft attaching bolt, then raise and support vehicle.
    d. Support engine with suitable jack, then remove left front wheel/tire assembly.
    e. Remove power steering line brackets and steering gear mounting bolts.
    f. Disconnect drive line vibration absorber, if equipped.
    g. Disconnect left lower ball joint at steering knuckle, then remove both front stabilizer bar reinforcements and bushings.

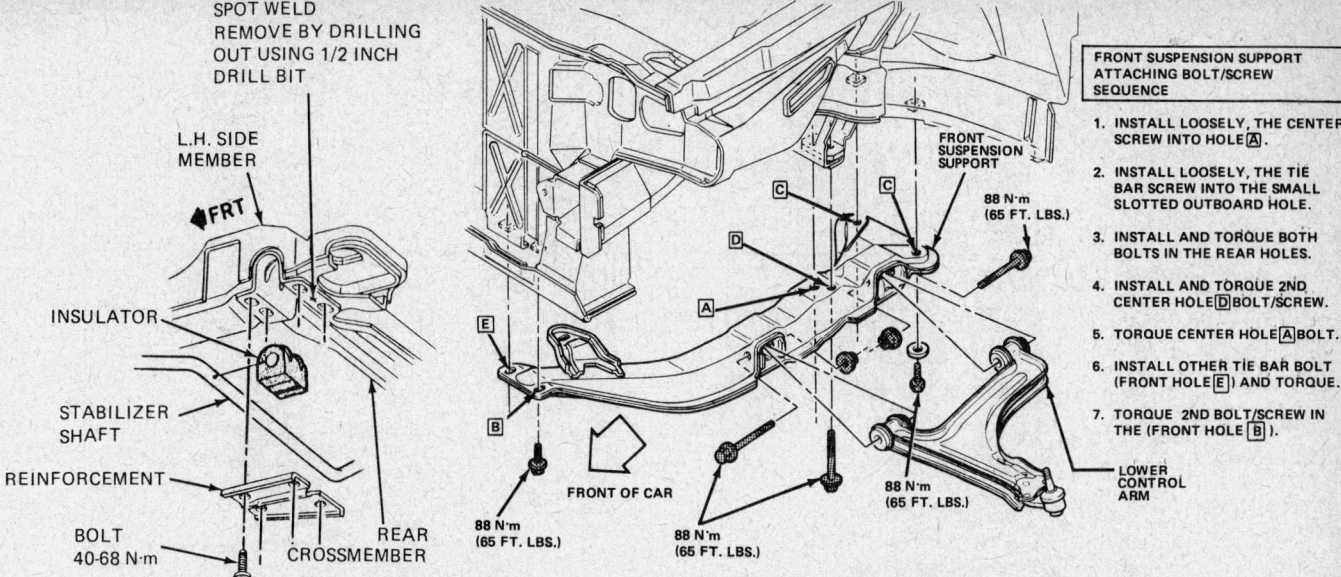

SPOT WELD
REMOVE BY DRILLING
OUT USING 1/2 INCH
DRILL BIT

L.H. SIDE
MEMBER

FRT

INSULATOR

STABILIZER
SHAFT

REINFORCEMENT

BOLT
40-68 N·m

REAR
CROSSMEMBER

Fig. 6 Drilling cradle spot weld

FRONT SUSPENSION SUPPORT
ATTACHING BOLT/SCREW
SEQUENCE

1. INSTALL LOOSELY, THE CENTER SCREW INTO HOLE A.
2. INSTALL LOOSELY, THE TIE BAR SCREW INTO THE SMALL SLOTTED OUTBOARD HOLE.
3. INSTALL AND TORQUE BOTH BOLTS IN THE REAR HOLES.
4. INSTALL AND TORQUE 2ND CENTER HOLE D BOLT/SCREW.
5. TORQUE CENTER HOLE A BOLT.
6. INSTALL OTHER TIE BAR BOLT (FRONT HOLE E) AND TORQUE.
7. TORQUE 2ND BOLT/SCREW IN THE (FRONT HOLE B).

FRONT SUSPENSION SUPPORT

88 N·m (65 FT. LBS.)

LOWER CONTROL ARM

FRONT OF CAR

88 N·m (65 FT. LBS.)

88 N·m (65 FT. LBS.)

88 N·m (65 FT. LBS.)

Fig. 7 Front suspension support attaching bolt sequence

h. Using a ½ inch drill bit, drill through spot weld located between rear holes of left stabilizer bar mounting, Fig. 6.
i. Disconnect engine and transaxle mounts from cradle, then remove side crossmember bolts.
j. Remove left side body mount bolts, then the left and front cradle assembly.
8. Install axle shaft boot protectors, then position axle shaft puller behind axle shaft cones and pull cones away from transaxle.
9. Remove left axle shaft and plug bore in transaxle to avoid fluid leakage.
10. Remove starter, then the converter shield.
11. Remove the three flywheel to converter attaching bolts.
12. Remove engine to transaxle bracket extension bolts, then the rear transaxle mount bracket assembly. Raise transaxle if necessary.
13. Remove the one remaining engine to transaxle bolt located near the starter.
14. Slide transaxle towards drivers side and remove from vehicle.
15. Reverse procedure to install. Note the following when installing transaxle:
   a. Position a ½ inch drill bit into drilled hole, Fig. 6, before tightening cradle bolts.
   b. Slide right axle shaft into case as transaxle is being installed.
   c. Check front suspension alignment after transaxle installation.

d. Check and adjust T. V. cable if necessary.

1982–83 Cavalier, Cimarron, Firenza, 2000 & Skyhawk

1. Disconnect battery ground cable from transaxle.
2. Insert a ¼ x 2 inch bolt into hole in right front motor mount to prevent mislocation of mount during transaxle removal.
3. Remove air cleaner, then disconnect T.V. cable from carburetor.
4. Remove T.V. cable retaining bolt from transaxle, pull up cable cover and disconnect cable from transaxle rod.
5. Remove engine wire harness retaining bolt, disconnect air management hose, then position harness aside.
6. Raise and support engine with a suitable lifting device so that weight is taken off motor mounts.
7. Remove top transaxle mount and bracket assembly, then disconnect shift control linkage from transaxle.
8. Remove top engine to transaxle attaching bolts and loosen, but do not remove, the bolt nearest the starter.
9. Raise and support vehicle, unlock steering column and remove both front wheel/tire assemblies.
10. Remove cotter pin and ball joint retaining nut, then separate ball joint from control arm. Repeat procedure for other side.
11. Remove stabilizer bar to left lower control arm attaching bolt.

12. Remove the six left front suspension support to body attaching bolts, then position axle shaft removal tools J-28468 and J-23907 behind axle shaft cones and pull cones away from transaxle.
13. Remove axle shafts and plug transaxle bores to prevent fluid leakage.
14. Remove transaxle control cable bracket retaining nut, then the transaxle to engine attaching stud.
15. Disconnect speedometer cable and transaxle mounting strut.
16. Remove the four torque converter shield to transaxle attaching bolts, then the shield.
17. Remove the torque converter to flex plate retaining bolts, then disconnect and plug the transaxle cooler lines.
18. Remove starter.
19. Remove brake and fuel line brackets from left side of underbody and position aside.
20. Remove the last engine to transaxle attaching bolt, separate transaxle from engine by sliding away from engine and remove transaxle from vehicle.
21. Reverse procedure to install, making sure:
   a. Axle shafts are installed after transaxle is in place.
   b. To follow the tightening sequence shown in Fig. 7 when installing the front suspension support assembly.
   c. To readjust throttle valve (T.V.) cable.
   d. To check front suspension alignment.

Turbo Hydra-Matic 180, 180C Automatic Transmission

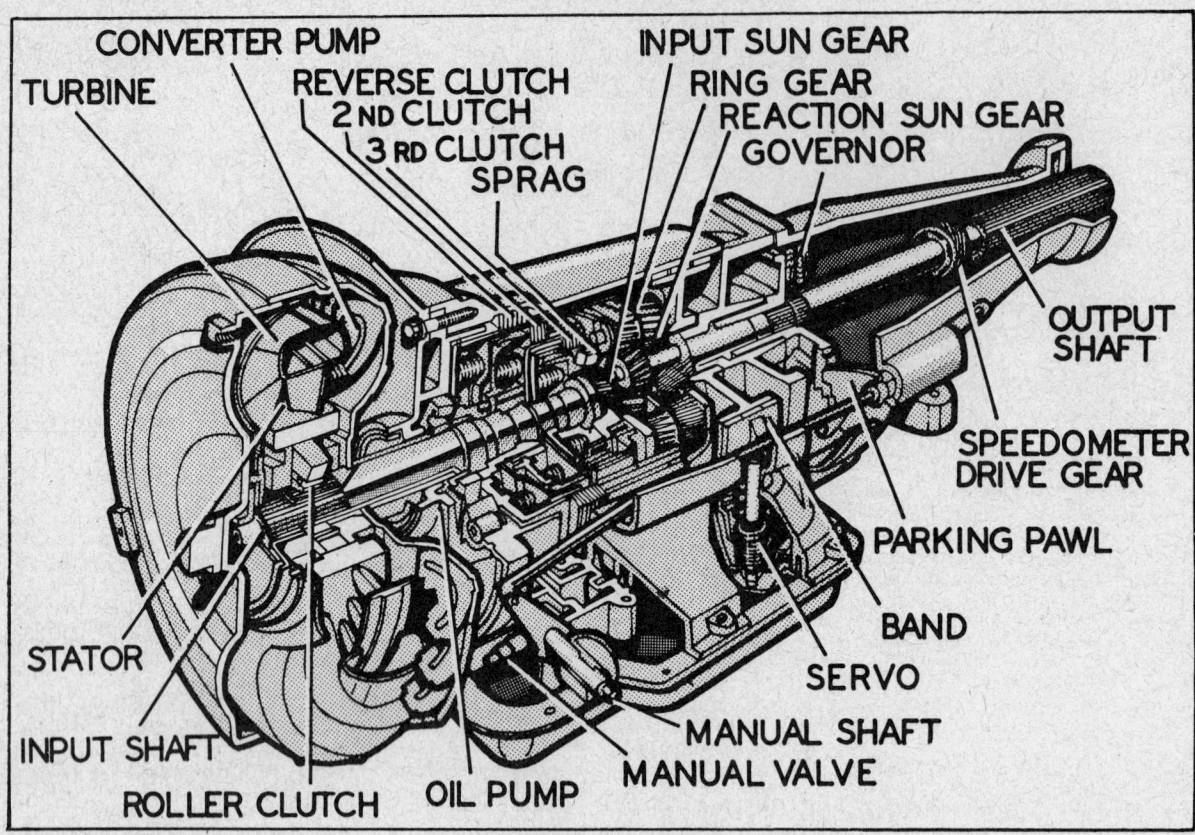

CONVERTER PUMP
TURBINE
REVERSE CLUTCH
2 ND CLUTCH
3 RD CLUTCH
SPRAG
INPUT SUN GEAR
RING GEAR
REACTION SUN GEAR
GOVERNOR
OUTPUT SHAFT
SPEEDOMETER DRIVE GEAR
PARKING PAWL
BAND
SERVO
MANUAL SHAFT
MANUAL VALVE
STATOR
INPUT SHAFT
ROLLER CLUTCH
OIL PUMP

Fig. 1 Turbo Hydra-Matic 180 transmission

TRANSMISSION IDENTIFICATION

This transmission may be identified by the following codes located on the tag attached to the right side of the transmission.

CHEVETTE & 1000
1977–78 4-98	ND
1979 4-98	NS
1980 4-98	MD
1981 4-98	ST
1982 4-98	VQ
1983 4-98	TN

GENERAL DESCRIPTION

This transmission is a fully automatic unit consisting of a three-element hydraulic torque converter on the 180 series or a four-element hydraulic torque converter on the 180C series, and a planetary gear set, Fig. 1. Three multiple disc clutches, a roller clutch and a band provide the friction elements required to obtain the desired function of the compound planetary gear set. The compound planetary gear set provides three forward speeds and reverse.

The torque converter couples the engine to the planetary gears through oil and provides torque multiplication. It consists of s pump or driving member, a turbine or driven member and a stator assembly. The stator is mounted on a one-way roller clutch which allows the stator to turn clockwise but not counterclockwise.

The torque converter housing is filled with oil and rotates at engine speed. The converter pump is an integral part of the converter housing, therefore the pump blades rotating at engine speed set the oil within the converter into motion and direct it to the turbine causing the turbine to rotate. As the oil passes through the turbine it travels in such a direction that if it were not redirected by the stator it would strike the rear of the converter pump blades and impede its pumping action. Therefore at low turbine speeds, the oil is redirected by the stator to the converter pump in such a manner that it actually assists the converter pump to deliver power or multiply engine torque. As turbine speed increases, the direction of the oil leaving the turbine changes and flows against the rear side of the stator vanes in a clockwise direction. Since the stator is now impeding the smooth flow of oil, its roller clutch releases and it revolves freely on its

shaft. Once the stator becomes inactive, there is no further multiplication of torque within the converter. At this point the converter is acting as a fluid coupling since the converter pump and turbine are being driven at about the same speed, or at a one-to-one ratio.

The hydraulic system in this transmission is pressurized by a gear type pump to provide the working pressures required to operate the friction elements and automatic controls.

TROUBLESHOOTING
Low Fluid Level

1. Fluid coming out of filler tube.
2. External fluid leak.
3. Defective vacuum modulator.

Fluid Coming Out of Filler Tube

1. High fluid level.
2. Engine coolant in transmission fluid.
3. Clogged external vent.
4. Leak in pump suction circuit.

Torque Converter Housing Leak

1. Converter housing seal.

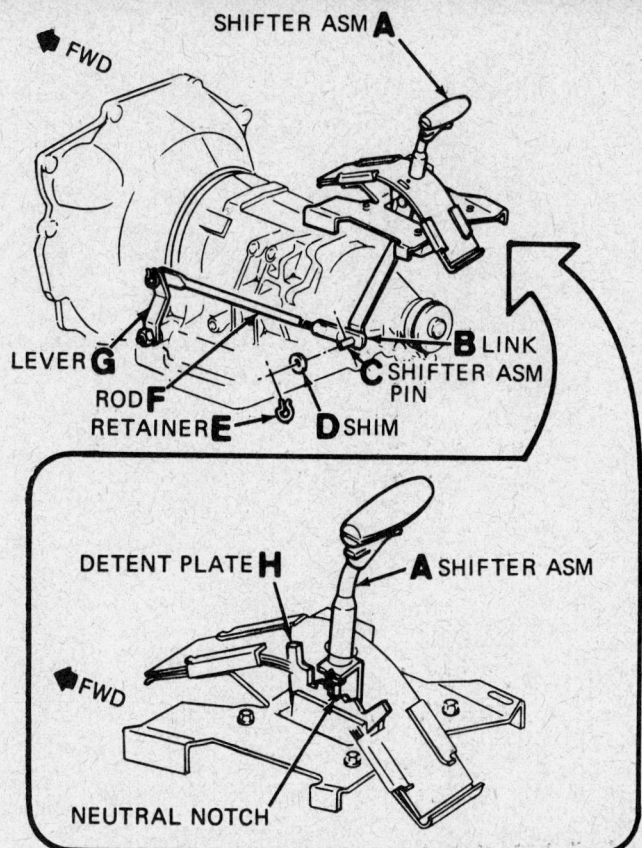

Fig. 2   Manual linkage adjustment. 1977–82 Turbo Hydra-Matic 180

2. Converter to case seal.
3. Loose transmission attaching bolts.

Transmission Case External Leak

1. Shifter shaft seal.
2. Extension seal.
3. Oil pan gasket.
4. Extension to case gasket.
5. Vacuum modulator gasket.
6. Drain plug gasket.
7. Cooler line fittings.
8. Fluid tube seal ring.
9. Detent cable seal ring.
10. Pressure gauge fitting.
11. Electrical connector seal.

Low Fluid Pressure

1. Low fluid level.
2. Clogged screen.
3. Leak in oil pump suction or pressure circuit.
4. Stuck priming valve.
5. Faulty pressure regulator valve.
6. Missing sealing ball in valve body.

High Fluid Pressure

1. Modulator vacuum line leaking.
2. Defective vacuum modulator.
3. Leak in vacuum system.
4. Defective pressure regulator valve.

No Drive

1. Low fluid level.

2. Clogged screen.
3. Manual valve linkage or inner transmission selector lever disconnected.
4. Broken input shaft.
5. Pressure regulator valve stuck in open position.
6. Defective oil pump.

Delayed Engagement

1. Manual valve position does not coincide with valve body channels.
   a. Missing selector lever shaft retaining pin.
   b. Loose connecting rod to manual valve connection.
   c. Loose selector lever shaft nut.

No Drive When Shifting From P to D, L2 Or L1

1. Parking pawl does not engage.

Harsh Engagement

1. Band servo piston jamming.
2. Low fluid level.
3. Defective oil pump.
4. Missing screen.
5. Missing sealing ball in valve body.

Shudder on Acceleration

1. Low fluid pressure.
2. Wrong modulator valve installed.
3. Stuck pressure regulator valve.
4. Missing sealing ball in valve body.

Drive in L1 & R But Not In D Or L2

1. Input sprag installed backwards.
2. Failed input sprag.

Drive in R But Not In D, L2 Or L1

1. Worn band, slipping.
2. Band servo piston jamming.
3. Excessive leak in band servo.
4. Parking pawl does not disengage.

Drive In D, L2 & L1 But Not In R

1. Failed reverse clutch.

Drive In Neutral Position

1. Linkage improperly adjusted.
2. Broken planetary gear set.
3. Band improperly adjusted.

No 1-2 Upshift In D & L2

1. Stuck governor valves.
2. 1-2 shift valve stuck in first gear position.
3. Leaking seal rings in oil pump hub.
4. Excessive leak in governor pressure circuit.
5. Clogged governor screen.

No 2-3 Upshift In D

1. 2-3 shift valve stuck.
2. Excessive leak in governor pressure circuit.

Upshifts In D & L2 Only At Full Throttle

1. Faulty vacuum modulator.
2. Modulator vacuum line leaking.
3. Leak in vacuum system.
4. Stuck detent valve or cable.

Upshifts In D Or L2 Only At Part Throttle No Detent Upshift

1. Stuck detent regulator valve.
2. Detent cable broken or adjusted improperly.

Drive In 1st. Gear of D Or L2

1. L1 and R control valve stuck in L1 or R position.

No Part Throttle 3-2 Downshift At Low Speeds

1. Stuck 3-2 downshift control valve.

No Forced Downshifts

1. Detent cable broken or improperly adjusted.
2. Stuck detent pressure regulator valve.

Immediate Downshift After Full Throttle Upshift & Releasing Accelerator

1. Detent valve stuck in open position.
2. Detent cable stuck.
3. Clogged or leaking vacuum modulator line.

Transmission Downshifts At High Vehicle Speeds

1. Missing selector lever shaft retaining pin.
2. Loose selector lever linkage to manual valve connection.
3. Pressure leak at governor.

Hard Disengagement From Park Position

1. Missing steel guide bushing from parking pawl actuating rod.
2. Stuck manual valve selector lever.

Slipping 1-2 Shift

1. Low fluid pressure.
2. Missing sealing ball in valve body.
3. Leaking second clutch piston seals.
4. Second clutch piston centrifugal ball stuck open.
5. Second clutch piston cracked or broken.
6. Second clutch plates worn.
7. Leaking oil pump hub sealing rings.

Slipping 2-3 Shift

1. Low fluid pressure.
2. Improper band adjustment.
3. Third clutch piston seals leaking.
4. Third clutch piston centrifugal ball stuck open.
5. Third clutch piston cracked or broken.
6. Worn input shaft bushing.
7. Missing sealing ball in valve body.

Harsh 1-2 Shift

1. High fluid pressure.
2. 1-2 accumulator valve stuck.
3. Second clutch spring cushion broken.
4. Second gear ball valve missing.

Harsh 2-3 Shift

1. High fluid pressure.
2. Improper band adjustment.

Harsh 3-2 Detent Downshift At High Vehicle Speeds

1. High speed downshift valve stuck open.
2. Improper band adjustment.

Harsh 3-2 Coast Downshift

1. Low speed downshift timing valve stuck open.

Engine Flare On High Speed Forced Downshift

1. Low fluid pressure.
2. Loose band adjustment.

Engine Flare On Low Speed Forced Downshift

1. Low fluid pressure.
2. Loose band adjustment.
3. High speed downshift timing valve stuck in closed position.
4. Sprag race does not engage on 3-1 downshift.

No Engine Braking In L1

1. Selector level linkage improperly adjusted.
2. Stuck low manual control valve.

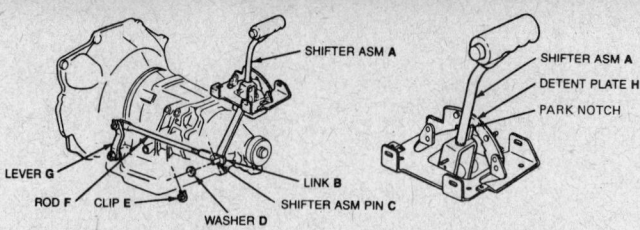

Fig. 3 Manual linkage adjustment. 1983 Turbo Hydra-Matic 180

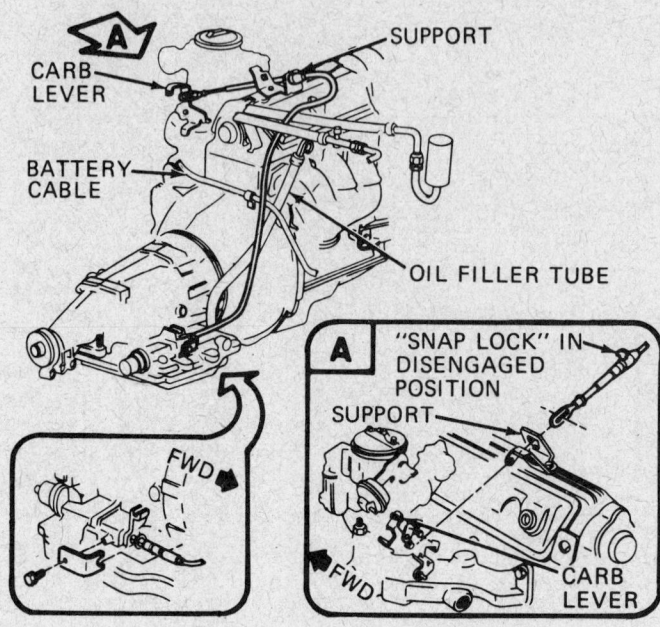

Fig. 4 Detent cable adjustment.
1977–81 Turbo Hydra-Matic 180

No Engine Braking In L2

1. Selector lever linkage improperly adjusted.

No Park

1. Selector lever linkage improperly adjusted.
2. Parking lock actuator spring broken.
3. Parking pawl.
4. Governor hub.

Excessive Noises In All Drive Ranges

1. Excessive backlash between sun gear and planetary gears.
2. Lock plate on planetary carrier loose.
3. Defective thrust bearing.
4. Worn bearing bushings.
5. Excessive transmission axial play.
6. Unhooked parking pawl spring contacting governor hub.
7. Converter balancing weights loose.
8. Converter housing attaching bolts loose and contacting converter.

Screeching Noise On Acceleration

1. Converter failure.

Short Vibrating Hissing Noise Before 1-2 Upshift

1. Reverse clutch dampening cushion wearing into transmission case.

MAINTENANCE

To check fluid, drive vehicle for at least 15 minutes to bring fluid to operating temperature (200° F). With vehicle on a level surface and engine idling in Park and parking brake applied, the level on the dipstick should be at the "F" mark. To bring the fluid level from the ADD mark to the FULL mark requires one pint of fluid. If vehicle cannot be driven sufficiently to bring fluid to operating temperature, the level on the dipstick should be between the two dimples on the dipstick with fluid temperature at 70° F.

If additional fluid is required, use only Dexron II automatic transmission fluid.

NOTE: An early change to a darker color from the usual red color and or a strong odor that is usually associated with overheated fluid is normal and should not be considered as a positive sign of required maintenance or unit failure.

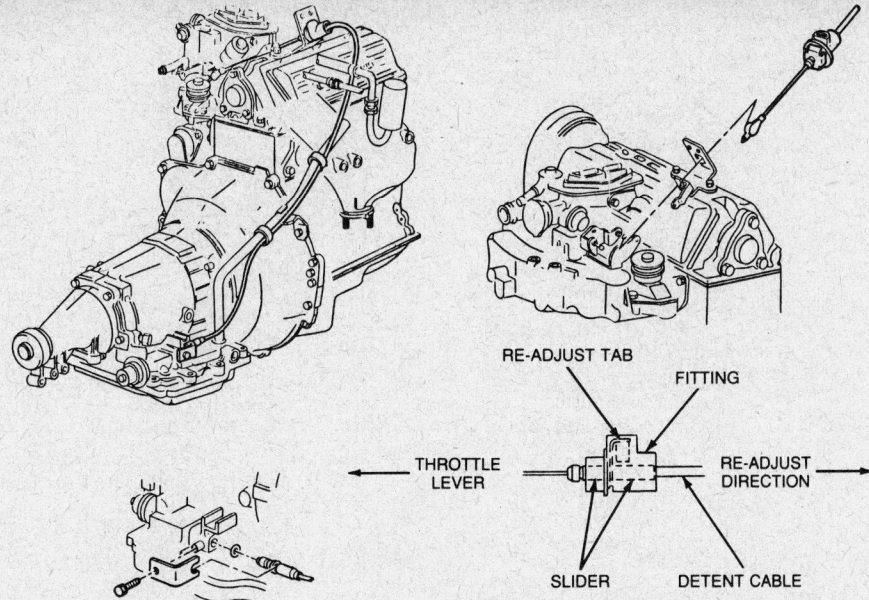

Fig. 5 Detent cable adjustment. 1982–83 Turbo Hydra-Matic 180. Gasoline engine

CAUTION: When adding fluid, do not over fill, as foaming and loss of fluid through the vent may occur as the fluid heats up. Also, if fluid level is too low, complete loss of drive may occur especially when cold, which can cause transmission failure.

Every 60,000 miles on 1976–79 vehicles, or every 100,000 miles on 1980–83 vehicles, the oil should be drained, the oil pan removed, the screen cleaned and fresh fluid added. For vehicles subjected to more severe use such as heavy city traffic especially in hot weather, prolonged periods of idling or towing, this maintenance should be performed every 15,000 miles.

Draining Bottom Pan

1. Raise vehicle, then remove drain plug and allow fluid to drain for at least 5 minutes.
2. If oil screen is to be serviced, remove oil pan bolts, oil pan and gasket.
3. Remove oil screen to valve body bolts, screen and gasket.
4. Thoroughly clean oil screen and oil pan with solvent.
5. Install oil screen using a new gasket and torque attaching bolts to 13–15 ft. lbs., then install oil pan using a new gasket and torque attaching bolts to 13–15 ft. lbs.
6. Add three quarts of fluid, then with engine idling and parking brake applied, move selector lever through each range and return selector lever to PARK.
7. Check fluid level and add fluid as required to bring level between the two dimples on the dipstick.

Adding Fluid To Dry Transmission

1. Add 4.9 quarts of fluid.
2. With transmission in PARK and parking brake applied, start engine and place carburetor on fast idle cam.

3. Move shifter lever through each range then with transmission in PARK, add additional fluid as required to bring the level between the two dimples on the dipstick.

IN-VEHICLE ADJUSTMENTS

Manual Linkage, Adjust

1977–82
1. Place shifter assembly (A) in Neutral position, Fig. 2.
2. With link (B) loosely assembled to rod (F) and rod (F) attached to lever (G), place lever (G) in Neutral position. To obtain Neutral position, move lever (G) clockwise to maximum detent poition (Park), then counterclockwise two detents to Neutral position.
3. While holding lever (G) in Neutral position, adjust link (B) until hole aligns with shifter assembly pin (C), then install link onto pin.
4. Install shim (D) and retainer (E).

CAUTION: The above procedure must be followed exactly, since any inaccuracies may result in premature failure of the transmission due to operation without controls in full detent.

1983
1. Place shifter assembly (A) in Park position, Fig. 3.
2. With link (B) loosely attached to lever (G), place lever (G) in Park position. To obtain Park position, move lever (G) clockwise to maximum detent position (Park).
3. Maintain lever (G) in Park position and adjust link (B) until hole aligns with shifter assembly pin (C), then install link onto pin.
4. Install washer (D) and retainer (E).

CAUTION: The above procedure must be followed exactly, as any inaccuracies may result in premature failure of the transmission due to operation without controls in full detent.

T.V. or Detent Cable, Adjust

1977–1981
1. Disengage cable "Snap Lock" from support, Fig 4.

NOTE: Cable should be free to slide through "Snap Lock".

2. With cable installed in support and attached to transmission and carburetor lever, move carburetor lever to wide open throttle position.
3. Push "Snap Lock" flush and return carburetor lever to closed position.

1982–83
1. Depress re-adjust tab and move slider back through fitting away from throttle body until slider stops against fitting, Figs. 5 and 6.
2. Release re-adjust tab and open carburetor or pump lever to "full throttle stop" position to automatically adjust cable. Release carburetor or pump lever.
3. Check cable for sticking or binding and road test vehicle. If delayed or only full throttle shifts still occur, proceed as follows:
   a. Remove oil pan and inspect throttle lever and bracket assembly, Fig. 7.
   b. Check T.V. exhaust valve lifter rod for distortion or binding in control valve assembly or spacer plate.
   c. Check that the lifter spring holds lifter rod up against bottom of control valve assembly.
   d. Check that T.V. plunger is not binding, and inspect transmission for proper throttle lever to cable link.

IN-VEHICLE REPAIRS

Valve Body, Replace

1. Drain transmission and remove oil pan and screen.
2. Remove screw and retainer securing detent cable to transmission, then disconnect detent cable.
3. Remove throttle lever and bracket assembly. Use caution not to bend the throttle lever link.
4. Remove manual detent roller and spring assembly
5. Remove transfer plate reinforcement attaching bolts and the reinforcement.
6. Remove servo cover and gasket.
7. Remove valve body attaching bolts, then the valve body and transfer plate.

NOTE: The two check balls in the case may fall out when removing the valve body.

8. Remove transfer plate to valve body bolts, then the plate from valve body.
9. Reverse procedure to install.

Servo Assembly, Replace

1. Remove valve body from transmission as

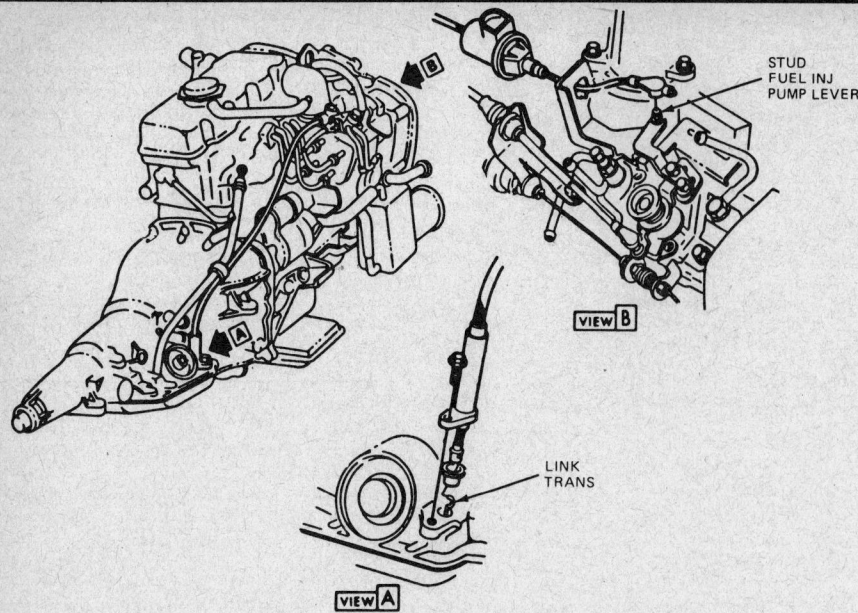

LINK TRANS

Fig. 6 Detent cable adjustment. 1982—83 Turbo Hydra-Matic 180. Diesel engine

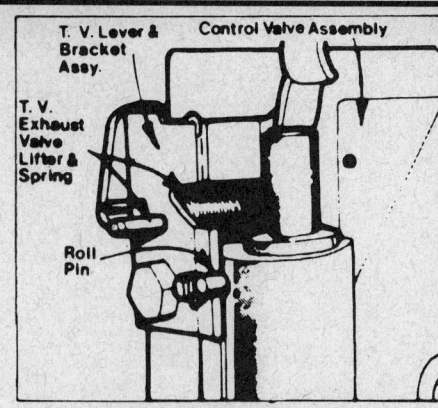

Fig. 7 Throttle lever and bracket assembly. 1982—83 Turbo Hydra-Matic 180

outlined previously.

2. Compress servo piston with tool J-23075.
3. With suitable pliers, remove servo piston snap ring and slowly loosen the tool. Remove tool, servo piston return spring and apply rod from transmission.
4. Install apply rod, return spring and piston into case.
5. Use tool J-23075 to compress spring and install snap ring. Remove tool.
6. With a 3/16 inch wrench on servo adjusting bolt, adjust apply rod by torquing bolt to 40 inch lbs, then back off bolt exactly 5 turns. Tighten lock nut while holding apply rod in position.
7. Install valve body.

Speedometer Driven Gear, Replace

1. Remove bolt securing driven gear housing retainer, then the retainer.
2. Pull speedometer driven gear from housing.
3. Install speedometer driven gear into housing, then the retainer into slot of driven gear housing.

4. Install retainer attaching bolt

Rear Extension Oil Seal

1. Remove propeller shaft.
2. Remove oil seal with a screwdriver or suitable tool.
3. Lubricate new seal lip with transmission fluid and install seal into extension housing with tool J-21426.
4. Install propeller shaft.

TRANSMISSION, REPLACE

1. Disconnect battery ground cable then disconnect detent downshift cable from bracket.
2. Remove air cleaner and dipstick, then on vehicles with air conditioning remove the 5 heater core retaining screws, disconnect connector and place heater core assembly aside.
3. Raise and support vehicle and remove propeller shaft.
4. Disconnect speedometer cable, electrical lead, oil cooler lines, and shift control linkage.

5. Support transmission with suitable jack and remove the crossmember retaining bolts.
6. Remove converter to bracket retaining nuts, then disconnect exhaust pipes from rear of catalytic converter and from exhaust manifolds and remove catalytic converter and converter bracket as an assembly.
7. Remove converter dust shield and remove converter to flywheel bolts.
8. Lower transmission until it is barely supported by jack and remove transmission to engine bolts.
9. Raise transmission to its normal position, then support engine with jack and lower and remove transmission from vehicle.

NOTE: Use converter holding tool J-5384, or keep rear of transmission lower than the front to prevent the converter from sliding out.

10. Before installing transmission, place two inch blocks between rack and pinion housing assembly and oil pan to permit correct alignment of engine and transmission. Before installing flexplate to converter bolts, make sure than converter pilot hub is installed in crankshaft and that welded brackets on converter are flush with flexplate and converter rotates freely in this position.
11. Reverse the remaining procedure to install and torque converter to flexplate bolts to 20-30 ft. lbs. (27—41 Nm).

Turbo Hydra-Matic 200, 200C Automatic Transmission

TRANSMISSION IDENTIFICATION

This transmission may be identified by the following codes located on the serial number plate attached to the right side of the transmission.

BUICK

	Code
1977 V6-231 Skyhawk Except Calif.	BH
V6-231 Skylark Calif.	BL
V6-231 Skylark Except Calif.	BZ
V8-350 LeSabre & Riviera	OS
V8-301 LeSabre & Riviera	PZ

BUICK—Cont'd

	Code
1978 V6-231 Century Sta. Wag. & LeSabre	5BZ
V8-305 Century	5CO
V8-350 LeSabre	5BA, 50S, 5PZ
1979 V6-231 Century & Regal	BZ
V8-301 Century & Regal	PG, PH
V8-305 Century & Regal	CR
1980 V8-265 Century & Regal	PG, PW, BZ
V8-350 Electra & LeSabre	BA, OT
1981 Century & Regal V6-231	BZ
Electra & LeSabre V6-252	BM, BY
Century & Regal V8-265	PG
Electra & LeSabre V8-307	OG
Century & Regal V8-350	OT
Electra & LeSabre V8-350	OT
1982—83 V6-262 Regal (Diesel)	OR

CADILLAC

	Code
1978 Seville (Diesel)	OT, OX
1979 Seville (Diesel)	AH, AX
1980 DeVille & Brougham (Diesel)	AS, AX

CHEVROLET

	Code
1977 V8-305 Nova	CE
V8-305 Monza	CD, CK
4-97 Chevette Less A/C	CN
V8-305 Full Size	CO, CR
4-85 Chevette	CU
V8-350 Full Size	CY

CHEVROLET—Cont'd

	Code
4-97 Chevette With A/C	CZ
1978 Chevrolet	CO,CY
Malibu	BZ, CD, CS
Monza	CA
1979 Chevette	CN
Chevrolet	CU, CV
Malibu &	
Monte Carlo	BZ, CA, CR, CS
Monza	PA, PC
1980 Camaro	CK
Chevette	CN
Chevrolet	CE, CK
Malibu & Monte Carlo	CA, CC, CK
Monza	PA, PB, PC, PY
1981 Chevette 4-98	CN
Chevette 4-110 (Diesel)	CY
Malibu & Monte Carlo	
V6-231	BZ
Chevrolet V8-267	CE
Malibu & Monte Carlo	
V8-267	CE
Chevrolet V8-305	CU
Malibu & Monte Carlo	
V8-305	CC
Chevrolet V8-350	OT
1982 Chevette	CY
Camaro 4-151	PS
Camaro V6-173	CN
Malibu & Monte Carlo	
V6-262 (Diesel)	OR
Chevrolet V8-267	CQ
Camaro V8-305	CK, CO
1983 Chevette 4-110 (Diesel)	JY
Camaro 4-151	HB

CHEVROLET—Cont'd

	Code
Malibu & Monte Carlo V6-262 (Diesel)	OR
Camaro V8-305	PS

OLDSMOBILE

	Code
1977 V6-231 Starfire Except Calif.	BH
V6-231 Omega Calif.	BL
V6-231 Omega Except Calif.	BZ
V8-305 Starfire	CD
V8-350 Full Size	OS
V8-260 Omega	OZ
1978 Cutlass	BZ, CO, CR, OW
Full Size	BZ, OS, OT, OW
Starfire	PY
1979 Cutlass V6-231	BZ
Cutlass V8-260 (Exc. Diesel)	OW①, OR②
Cutlass V8-260 (Diesel)	OZ
Cutlass V8-305	CR
Full Size V8-350 (Diesel)	OT①, OX②
Starfire	PB, PY
1980 Cutlass V6-231	BD, EZ
Cutlass V8-260	OZ
Cutlass V8-305	CC
Cutlass V8-350 (Diesel)	OT
Full Size V8-265	PG
Full Size V8-350 (Diesel)	OT
Full Size V8-350 (Exc. Diesel)	OS
Starfire 4-151 Exc. Calif.	PY
Starfire 4-151 Calif.	PB
1981 Cutlass V6-231	BZ
Cutlass V8-260	OW
Cutlass V8-350	OT
88 V8-260	OW

OLDSMOBILE—Cont'd

	Code
88 V8-307	OG
88 V8-350	OT
98 V6-252	BY
98 V8-307	OG
98 V8-350	OT
1982–83 V6-262 Cutlass (Diesel)	OR

PONTIAC

	Code
1977 V6-231 Sunbird Except Calif.	BH
V6-231 Phoenix & Ventura Calif.	BL
V6-231 Sunbird Calif.	BU
V6-231 Phoenix & Ventura Except Calif	BZ
4-151 Sunbird	PY
4-151 Phoenix & Ventura Except Calif	PY
V8-301 Full Size Except Calif	PZ
V8-350 Full Size	OS
1978 4-151 Phoenix & Sunbird	PY
V6-231 LeMans Exc. Sta. Wag.	BZ
V6-231 Full Size	BZ
V8-301 LeMans & Grand Prix	PG, PH
V8-301 Full Size	PH
V8-305 LeMans	CO, CR
V8-305 Grand Prix	CO
1979 4-151 Sunbird	PB, PY
V6-231 LeMans Sta. Wag.	BZ
V8-301 Grand Prix & LeMans Exc. Sta. Wag.	PG, PH, PL
V8-305 Grand Prix & LeMans Exc. Sta. Wag.	CC, CR

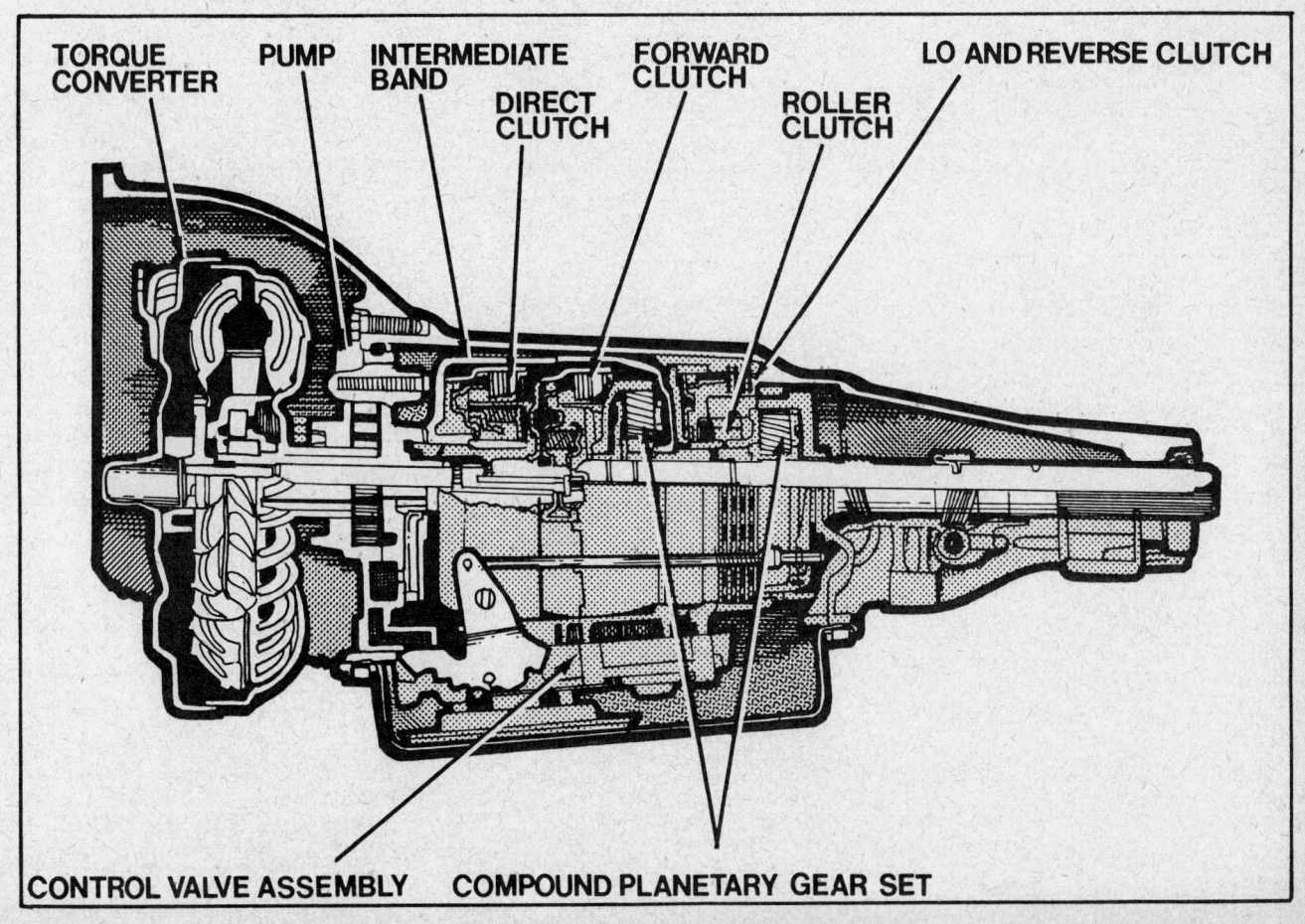

Fig. 1 Turbo Hydra-Matic 200 transmission

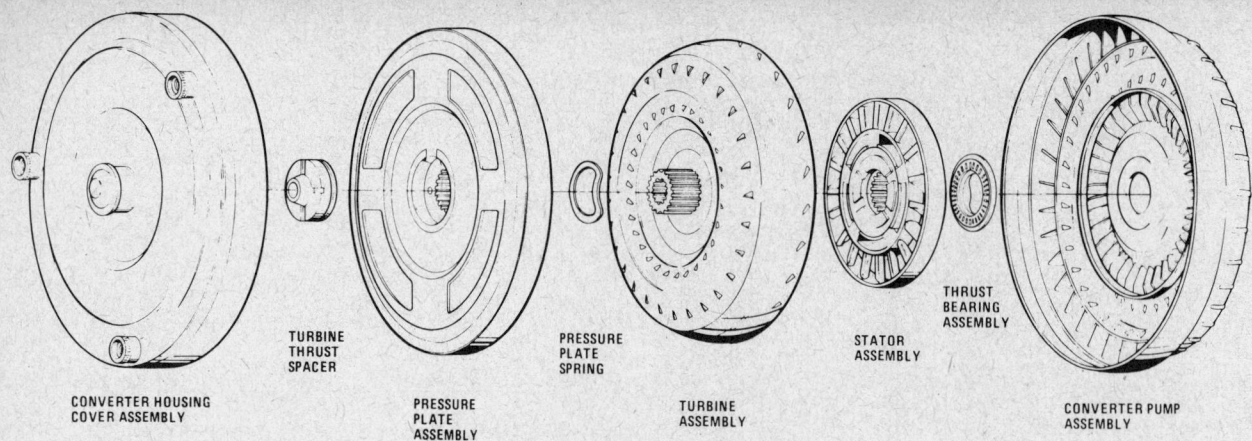

CONVERTER HOUSING COVER ASSEMBLY — TURBINE THRUST SPACER — PRESSURE PLATE ASSEMBLY — PRESSURE PLATE SPRING — TURBINE ASSEMBLY — STATOR ASSEMBLY — THRUST BEARING ASSEMBLY — CONVERTER PUMP ASSEMBLY

Fig. 1A   Torque converter clutch, 200C transmission

PONTIAC—Cont'd.

	Code
1980 4-151 Sunbird	PB, PY
LeMans & Grand Prix	BZ, PG, PW
LeMans	CA, CK, CM
Firebird	PD
Full Size (Diesel)	OT
Full Size	BA, PG
1981 1000 4-98	CN
LeMans V6-231	BZ
LeMans & Grand Prix V8-265	PG
LeMans V8-350 (Diesel)	OT
Full Size V8-265	PG
Full Size V8-307	OG
Full Size V8-350 (Diesel)	OT
1982 Firebird 4-151	PS
Firebird V6-173	CN
Firebird V8-305	CK, CO
1983 Firebird 4-151	HB
Firebird V8-305	PS

①—Exc. high altitude.
②—High altitude.
③—High output.

DESCRIPTION

The Turbo Hydra-Matic 200 and 200C transmissions, Figs. 1 and 1A, are fully automatic and consist of a three element torque converter and a compound planetary gear set. Three multiple disc clutches, a roller clutch and a band provide the required friction elements to obtain the desired function of the planetary gear set. In addition, the 200C transmission is equipped with a locking torque converter. The converter clutch assembly consists of a three element torque converter with a converter clutch. The converter clutch is splined to the turbine assembly and, when operated, applies against the converter cover, providing a mechanical direct drive coupling of the engine to the planetary gears. When the converter clutch is released the assembly operates as a normal torque converter.

TROUBLE SHOOTING GUIDE

No Drive in Drive Range

1. Low oil level.
2. Manual linkage maladjusted.
3. Low oil pressure due to:

a. Restricted or plugged oil screen.
b. Oil screen gasket improperly installed.
c. Oil pump pressure regulator.
d. Pump drive gear tangs damaged by converter.
e. Case porosity in intake bore
4. Forward clutch malfunctioning due to:
a. Forward clutch not applying due to cracked piston, damaged or missing seals, burned clutch plates, snap ring not in groove.
b. Forward clutch seal rings damaged or missing on turbine shaft, leaking feed circuits due to damaged or mispositioned gasket.
c. Clutch housing check ball stuck or missing
d. Cup plug leaking or missing from rear of turbine shaft in clutch apply passage.
e. Incorrect forward clutch piston assembly or incorrect number of clutch plates.
5. Roller clutch malfunctioning due to missing rollers or springs or possibly galled rollers.

Oil Pressure High Or Low

1. Throttle valve cable maladjusted, binding, disconnected or broken.
2. Throttle lever and bracket improperly installed, disconnected or binding.
3. Throttle valve shift valve, throttle valve or plunger binding.
4. Pressure regulator valve and spring malfunctioning due to:
a. Binding valve.
b. Incorrect spring.
c. Oil pressure control orifice in pump cover plugged, causing high oil pressure.
d. Pressure regulator bore plug leaking.
5. Manual valve disconnected.
6. Intermediate boost valve binding, causing oil pressures to be incorrect in 2nd and low ranges.
7. Orifice in spacer plate at end of intermediate boost valve plugged.
8. Reverse boost valve binding, causing pressure to be incorrect in reverse only.
9. Orifice in spacer plate at end of reverse boost valve plugged.

1-2 Shift At Full Throttle Only

1. Throttle valve cable maladjusted, binding, disconnected or broken.

2. Throttle lever and bracket assembly binding or disconnected.
3. Throttle valve exhaust ball lifter or number 5 check ball binding, mispositioned or disconnected.

NOTE: If number 5 ball is fully seated, it will cause full throttle valve pressure regardless of throttle valve position.

4. Throttle valve and plunger binding.
5. Valve body gaskets leaking, damaged or incorrectly installed.
6. Porous control valve assembly.

First Speed Only, No 1-2 Shift

1. Due to governor and governor feed passages:
a. Plugged governor oil feed orifice in spacer plate.
b. Plugged orifice in spacer plate that feeds governor oil to the shift valves.
c. Balls missing in governor assembly
d. Governor cover O-ring missing or leaking. If governor cover O-ring leaks, an external oil leak will be present and there will be no upshift.
e. Governor shaft seal missing or damaged.
f. Governor driven gear stripped.
g. Governor weights binding.
h. Governor assembly missing.
2. Control valve assembly 1-2 shift valve or 1-2 throttle valve stuck in downshift position.
3. Porosity in case channels or undrilled 2nd speed feed holes.
4. Excessive leakage between case bore and intermediate band apply ring.
5. Intermediate band anchor pin missing or disconnected from band.
6. Missing or broken intermediate band.
7. Due to intermediate servo assembly:
a. Servo to cover oil seal ring damaged or missing.
b. Porous servo cover or piston.
c. Incorrect intermediate band apply pin.
d. Incorrect cover and piston.

1st & 2nd Only, No 2-3 Shift

1. 2-3 shift valve or 2-3 throttle valve stuck in downshift position.
2. Direct clutch feed orifice in spacer plate plugged.

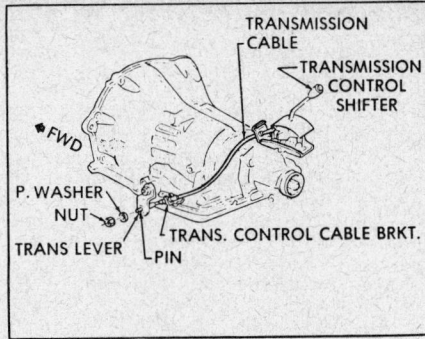

Fig. 2 Console shift manual linkage adjustment. Monza, Skyhawk, Starfire & Sunbird

3. Valve body gaskets leaking, damaged or incorrectly installed.
4. Porosity between case passages.
5. Pump passages plugged or leaking.
6. Pump gasket incorrectly installed.
7. Rear seal on pump cover leaking or missing.
8. Direct clutch oil seals missing or damaged.
9. Direct clutch piston or housing cracked.
10. Direct clutch plates damaged or missing.
11. Direct clutch backing plate snap ring out of groove.
12. Intermediate servo to case oil seal broken or missing on intermediate servo piston.
13. Intermediate servo exhaust hole in case between servo piston seals plugged or undrilled.

Moves Forward In Neutral

1. Manual linkage maladjusted.
2. Forward clutch does not release.
3. Cross leakage between pump passages.
4. Cross leakage to forward clutch through clutch passages.

No Drive in Reverse or Slips in Reverse

1. Throttle valve cable binding or maladjusted.
2. Manual linkage maladjusted.
3. Throttle valve binding.
4. Reverse boost valve binding in bore.
5. Low overrun clutch valve binding in bore.
6. Reverse clutch piston cracked, broken or has missing seals.
7. Reverse clutch plates burned.
8. Reverse clutch has incorrect selective spacer ring.
9. Porosity in passages to direct clutch.
10. Pump to case gasket improperly installed or missing.
11. Pump passages cross leaking or restricted.
12. Pump cover seals damaged or missing.
13. Direct clutch piston or housing cracked.
14. Direct clutch piston seals cut or missing.
15. Direct clutch housing ball check, stuck, leaking or missing.
16. Direct clutch plates burned.
17. Incorrect direct clutch piston.
18. Direct clutch orifices plugged in spacer plate.
19. Intermediate servo to case seal cut or missing.

Slips 1-2 Shift

1. Aerated oil due to low level.
2. 2nd speed feed orifice in spacer plate partially blocked.
3. Improperly installed or missing spacer plate gasket.
4. 1-2 accumulator valve stuck, causing low 1-2 accumulator pressure.
5. Weak or missing 1-2 accumulator valve spring.
6. 1-2 accumulator piston seal leaking or spring missing or broken.
7. Leakage between 1-2 accumulator piston and pin.
8. Incorrect intermediate band apply pin.
9. Excessive leakage between intermediate band apply pin and case.
10. Porous intermediate servo piston.
11. Servo cover to servo seal damaged or missing.
12. Incorrect servo and cover.
13. Throttle valve cable improperly adjusted.
14. Shift throttle valve or throttle valve binding.
15. Intermediate band worn or burned.
16. Case porosity in 2nd clutch passages.

Rough 1-2 Shift

1. Throttle valve cable improperly adjusted or binding.
2. Throttle valve or plunger binding.
3. Shift throttle or 1-2 accumulator valve binding.
4. Incorrect intermediate servo pin.
5. Intermediate servo piston to case seal damaged or missing.
6. 1-2 accumulator oil ring damaged, piston stuck, bore damaged or spring broken or missing.

Slips 2-3 Shift

1. Low oil level.
2. Throttle valve cable improperly adjusted.
3. Throttle valve binding.
4. Direct clutch orifice in spacer plate partially blocked.
5. Spacer plate gaskets improperly installed or missing.
6. Intermediate servo to case seal damaged.
7. Porous direct clutch feed passages in case.
8. Pump to case gasket improperly installed or missing.
9. Pump passages cross feeding, leaking or restricted.
10. Pump cover oil seal rings damaged or missing.
11. Direct clutch piston or housing cracked.
12. Direct clutch piston seals cut or missing.
13. Direct clutch plates burned.

Rough 2-3 Shift

1. Throttle valve cable improperly installed or missing.
2. Throttle valve or throttle valve plunger binding.
3. Shift throttle valve binding.
4. Intermediate servo exhaust hole undrilled or plugged between intermediate servo piston seals.
5. Direct clutch exhaust valve number 4

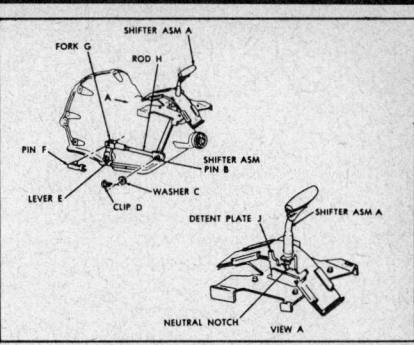

Fig. 3 Console shift manual linkage adjustment. Chevette & 1000

check ball missing or improperly installed.

No Engine Braking In 2nd Speed

1. Intermediate boost valve binding in valve body.
2. Intermediate-Reverse number 3 check ball improperly installed or missing.
3. Shift throttle valve number 3 check ball improperly installed or missing.
4. Intermediate servo to cover seal missing or damaged.
5. Intermediate band off anchor pin, broken or burned.

No Engine Braking In 1st Speed

1. Low overrun clutch valve binding in valve body.

NOTE: The following conditions will also cause no reverse.

2. Low-reverse clutch piston seals broken or missing.
3. Porosity in low-reverse piston or housing.
4. Low-reverse clutch housing snap ring out of case.
5. Cup plug or rubber seal missing or damaged between case and low-reverse clutch housing.

No Part Throttle Downshift

1. Throttle plunger bushing passages obstructed.
2. 2-3 throttle valve bushing passages obstructed.
3. Valve body gaskets improperly installed or damaged.
4. Spacer plate hole obstructed or undrilled.
5. Throttle valve cable maladjusted.
6. Throttle valve or shift throttle valve binding.

Low or High Shift Points

1. Throttle valve cable binding or disconnected.
2. Throttle valve or shift throttle valve binding.
3. Number 1 throttle shift check ball improperly installed or missing.
4. Throttle valve plunger, 1-2 or 2-3 throttle valves binding.
5. Valve body gaskets improperly installed or missing.
6. Pressure regulator valve binding.

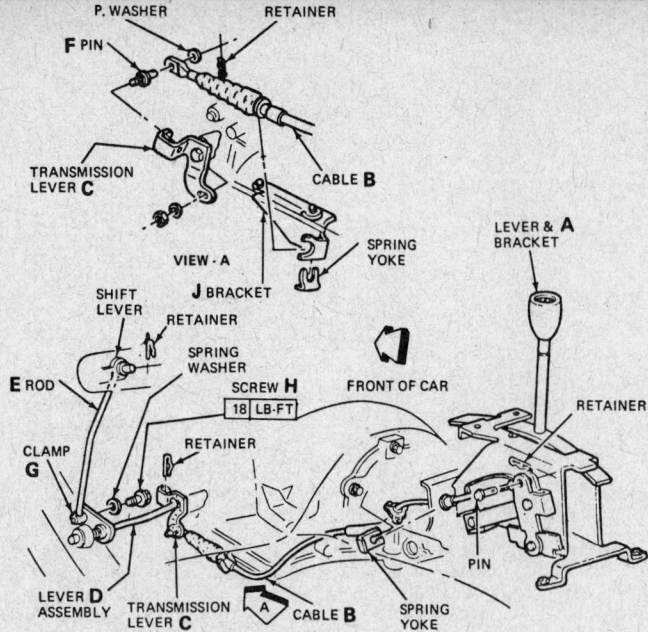

Fig. 4 Console shift manual linkage adjustment. 1976–79 Nova, Omega, Phoenix, Skylark & Ventura

7. Throttle valve exhaust number 5 check ball and lifter, improperly installed, disconnected or missing.
8. Throttle lever binding, disconnected or loose at valve body mounting bolt or not positioned at the throttle valve plunger bushing pin locator.
9. Governor shaft to cover seal broken or missing.
10. Governor cover O-rings broken or missing.

NOTE: Outer ring will leak externally and the inner ring will leak internally.

---

11. Case porosity.

Will Not Hold In Park

1. Manual linkage maladjusted.
2. Parking pawl binding in case.
3. Actuator rod or plunger damaged.
4. Parking pawl damaged.
5. Parking bracket loose or damaged.
6. Detent lever nut loose.
7. Detent lever hole worn or damaged.
8. Detent roller to valve body bolt loose.
9. Detent roller or pin damaged, incorrectly installed or missing.

Converter Clutch Applied in All Ranges, Engine Stalls When Transmission Put in Gear

1. Converter clutch valve stuck in apply position.

Converter Clutch Applies Erratically

1. Vacuum hose leak.
2. Vacuum switch malfunction.
3. Release oil exhaust orifice at pump blocked or restricted.
4. Turbine shaft "O" ring damaged.

5. Converter malfunction, clutch pressure plate warped.
6. "O" ring damaged at solenoid.
7. Solenoid bolts loose.
8. Governor pressure switch malfunction.

MAINTENANCE

To check fluid, drive vehicle for at least 15 minutes to bring fluid to operating temperature (200° F.). With vehicle on a level surface and engine idling in Park and parking brake applied, the level on the dipstick should be at the "F" mark. To bring the fluid level from the ADD mark to the FULL mark requires 1 pint of fluid. If vehicle cannot be driven sufficiently to bring fluid to operating temperature, the level on the dipstick should be between the two dimples on the dipstick with fluid temperature at 70° F.

If additional fluid is required, use only Dexron or Dexron II automatic transmission fluid.

NOTE: An early change to a darker color from the usual red color and or a strong odor that is usually associated with overheated fluid is normal and should not be considered as a positive sign of required maintenance or unit failure.

CAUTION: When adding fluid, do not overfill, as foaming and loss of fluid through the vent may occur as the fluid heats up. Also, if fluid level is too low, complete loss of drive may occur especially when cold, which can cause transmission failure.

Every 60,000 miles, on 1977–79 vehicles, or 100,000 miles on 1980–83 vehicles, the oil should be drained, the oil pan removed, the screen cleaned and fresh fluid added. For vehicles subjected to more severe use such as heavy city traffic, especially in hot weather, and prolonged periods of idling or towing, this maintenance should be performed every 15,000 miles.

Draining Bottom Pan

1. Remove front and side oil pan attaching bolts, then loosen the rear oil pan attaching bolts.
2. Carefully pry oil pan loose and allow fluid to drain into a suitable container.
3. Remove the oil pan and gasket, then remove the screen attaching bolts and remove screen.
4. Thoroughly clean oil screen and oil pan with solvent.
5. Install oil screen using a new gasket and torque attaching bolts to 6–10 ft. lbs., then install oil pan using a new gasket and torque attaching bolts to 10–13 ft. lbs.
6. Add 3 quarts of fluid, then with engine idling and parking brake applied, move selector lever through each range and return selector lever to PARK.
7. Check fluid level and add fluid as required to bring level between the two dimples on the dipstick.

Adding Fluid To Dry Transmission and Converter

1. Add 4½ quarts of fluid.
2. With transmission in PARK and parking brake applied, start engine and place carburetor on fast idle cam.
3. Move shifter lever through each range, then with transmission in PARK, add additional fluid as required to bring the level between the two dimples on the dipstick.

MANUAL LINKAGE, ADJUST
Console Shift

Monza, Skyhawk, Starfire & Sunbird
1. Loosen nut on transmission lever, Fig. 2.
2. Place transmission control shifter in Neutral position.
3. Place transmission lever in Neutral position.
4. Torque transmission lever nut to 20 ft. lbs.
5. Check for proper operation.

Chevette & 1000
1. Place shift lever (A) in neutral position, Fig. 3.
2. Move lever (E) clockwise to maximum detent to PARK, then move lever counterclockwise two detent positions to NEUTRAL.
3. With lever (E) in NEUTRAL, insert pin (F) on fork (G). Adjust rod (H) until hole in rod aligns with shifter assembly pin (B) and install rod on pin.

1977–79 Nova, Omega, Phoenix, Skylark & Ventura, Fig. 4
1. Attach cable (B) to transmission lever (A) with pin, retainer and spring, yoke, then place transmission lever (A) in Drive position.
2. Install lever assembly (D), then place lever (D) in Drive position by turning lever (C) counterclockwise to Low and then clockwise three detent positions to Drive.
3. Install cable (B) to lever (C) with pin (F) and retainer and bracket (J) with spring yoke.
4. Place transmission lever (A) in Park position and turn ignition switch to Lock position.

5. Install rod (E) to shift lever with retainer; then slide clamp (G) onto rod (E) and loosely assemble clamp, spring washer and screw (H) to lever (D).

6. Remove column lash by rotating shift lever downward and retain rod (E) with screw (H).

1977 Century, Chevelle, Cutlass, Grand Prix, LeMans, Malibu, Monte Carlo & Regal, Fig. 5

1. Place shift lever in Park position and transmission lever in Park position.
2. Move pin to obtain a "free pin" fit in transmission lever and torque retaining nut to 20 ft. lbs.

1978–79 Chevelle, 1978–81 Century, Grand Prix, LeMans, 1978–83 Cutlass, Malibu, Monte Carlo & Regal, Figs. 5A & 5B

1. Loosen shift rod clamp screw, then the pin in transmission manual lever.
2. Place shift lever and manual lever in Park position and ignition key in Lock position.
3. Torque cable pin nut to 20 ft. lbs., then rotate manual lever fully against Park stop and release lever.
4. Pull shift rod downward against lock stop, then torque clamp screw to 20 ft. lbs.

Column Shift

Intermediate Models Figs. 6, 7, 7A & 7B

1. Place shift lever and transmission lever in Neutral position.
2. Assemble clamp, spring washer and screw to equalizer lever and control rod.
3. Hold clamp flush against equalizer lever and lightly tighten clamping screw against rod.
4. On all models except 1978–79 Cadillac Seville and 1980–81 DeVille and Brougham with diesel engine, torque clamp screw to 20 ft. lbs. On 1978–79 Cadillac Seville and 1980–81 DeVille and Brougham with diesel engine, torque clamp screw to 23 ft. lbs.

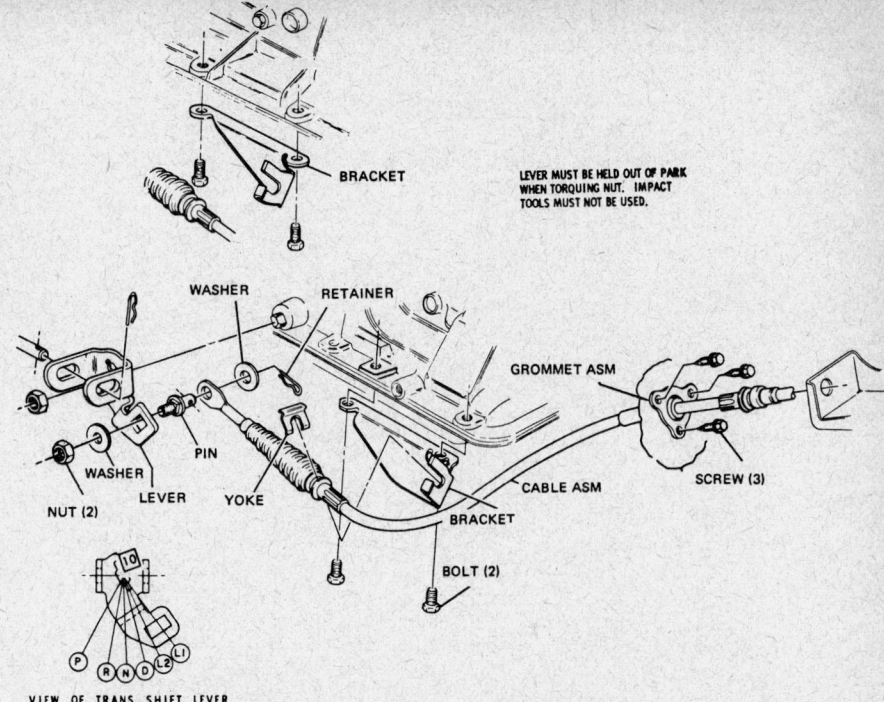

LEVER MUST BE HELD OUT OF PARK WHEN TORQUING NUT. IMPACT TOOLS MUST NOT BE USED.

VIEW OF TRANS SHIFT LEVER

Fig. 5 Console shift manual linkage adjustment. 1977 Century, Chevelle, Cutlass, Grand Prix, LeMans, Malibu, Monte Carlo & Regal

NOTE: Do not exert force in either direction on rod or equalizer rod while tightening screw.

All Full Size Models Except Grand Prix, Fig. 8

1. Position shift lever and transmission lever in Neutral position.

2. Hold clamp flush against equalizer lever and lightly tighten.
3. Torque bolt to 20 ft. lbs.

NOTE: Do not exert force in either direction on rod or equalizer rod while tightening screw.

T.V. or Detent Cable Adjustment

Exc. 1977–81 Chevette, 1981 1000 & All 1982–83 Models

1. Disengage snap lock. Cable should be free to slide through snap lock.

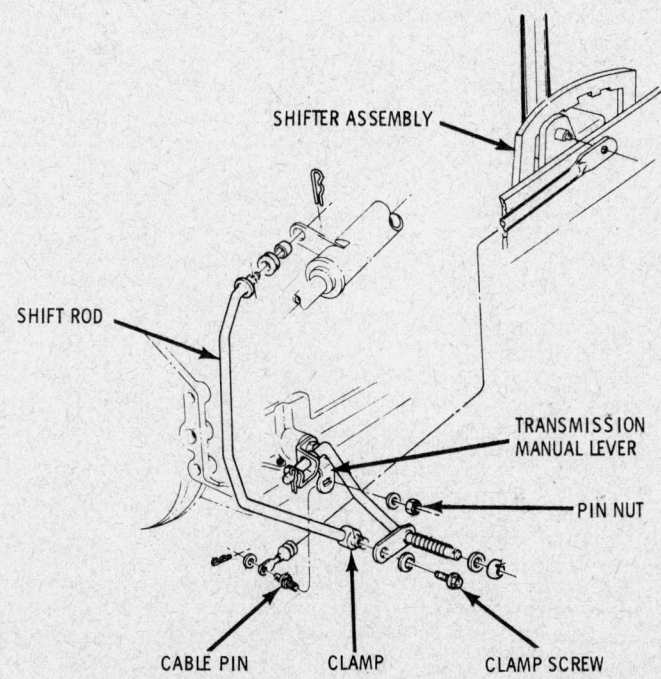

Fig. 5A Console shift manual linkage adjustment. 1978–79 Chevelle, 1978–80 Century, Cutlass, Grand Prix, LeMans, Malibu, Monte Carlo & Regal

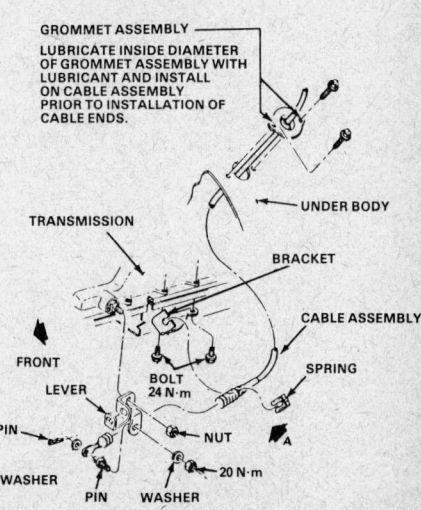

GROMMET ASSEMBLY
LUBRICATE INSIDE DIAMETER OF GROMMET ASSEMBLY WITH LUBRICANT AND INSTALL ON CABLE ASSEMBLY PRIOR TO INSTALLATION OF CABLE ENDS.

Fig. 5B Console shift manual linkage adjustment. 1981 Century, Grand Prix, LeMans, 1981–83 Cutlass, Malibu, Monte Carlo & Regal

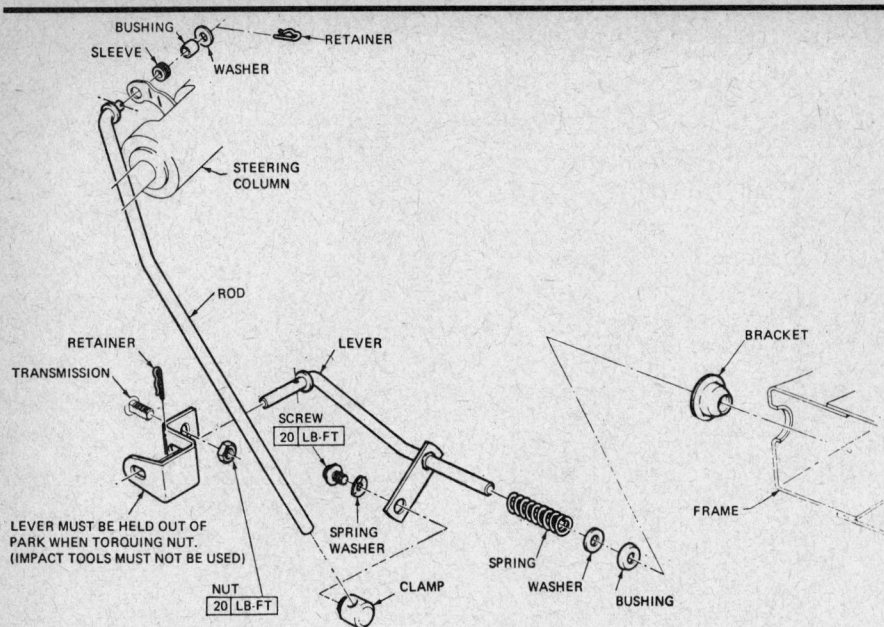

Fig. 6 Column shift manual linkage adjustment. Nova, Omega, Phoenix, Skylark & Ventura

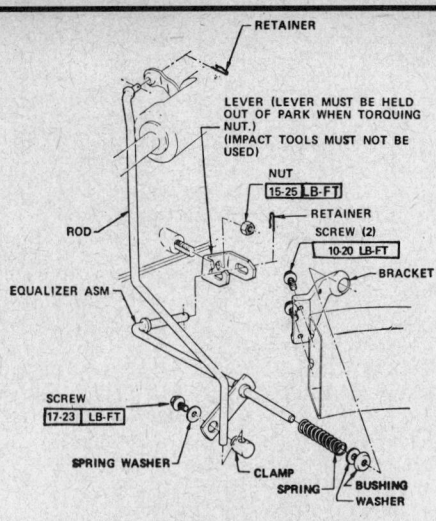

Fig. 7 Column shift manual linkage adjustments. 1978–79 Chevelle, 1978–80 Century, Cutlass, Grand Prix, LeMans, Monte Carlo & Regal

2. Place carburetor in the wide open position.
3. Engage snap lock and position flush with cable fitting.

1977–81 Chevette & 1981 1000
1. Disconnect cable from support, Fig. 9. and check that cable is free to slide through snap lock.
2. With cable installed in support and connected to transmission and carburetor lever, move throttle valve to wide open position.
3. Push snap lock until flush with support and throttle valve.

1982–83 Chevette Equipped With Diesel Engine
1. Remove cruise control rod on vehicles equipped with cruise control.
2. Disconnect throttle valve linkage from throttle assembly.

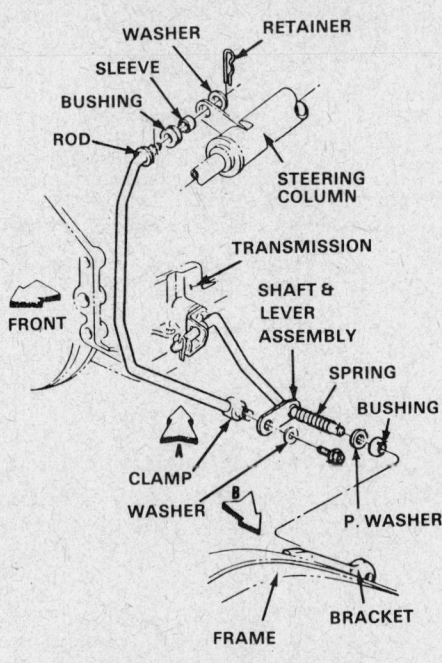

Fig. 7B Column shift manual linkage adjustment. 1981–83 intermediate models (typical)

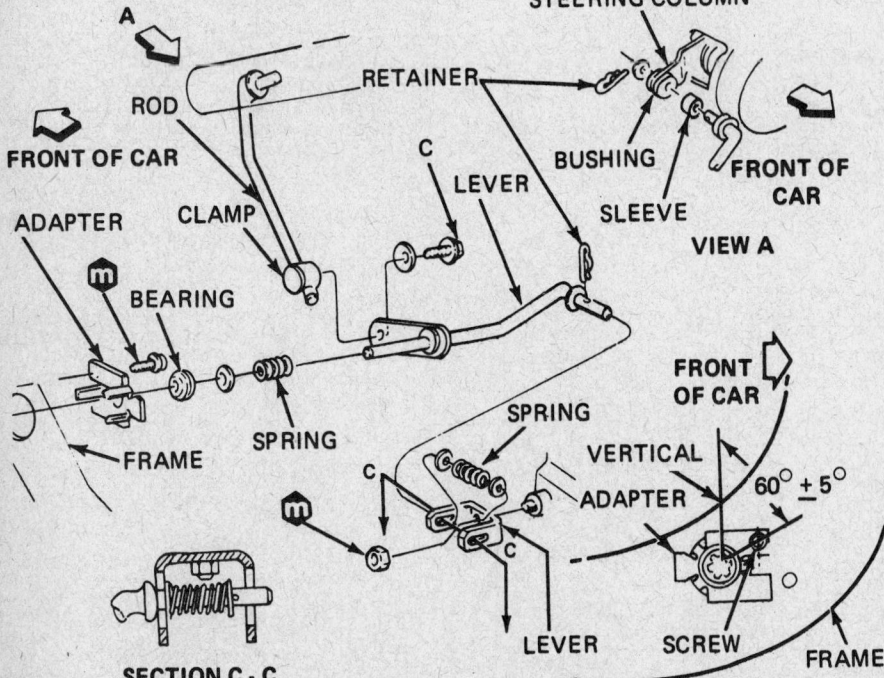

Fig. 7A Column shift manual linkage adjustment. 1978–79 Cadillac Seville & 1980–81 DeVille & Brougham with diesel engine

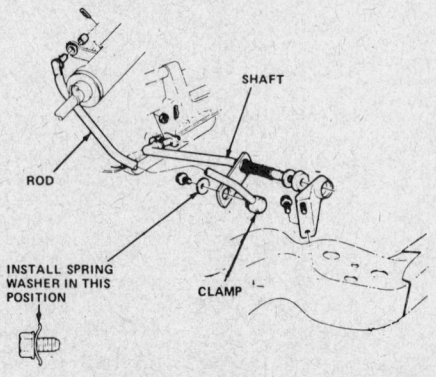

Fig. 8 Column shift linkage adjustment. All full size models except Grand Prix

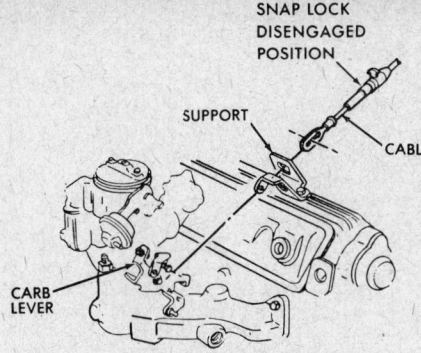

Fig. 9 Detent downshift cable adjust. 1977–81 Chevette & 1981 1000

T.H.M. 200C TORQUE CONVERTER CLUTCH SWITCH ADJUSTMENTS

Low Vacuum Switch

1. Disconnect vacuum and electrical connectors from low vacuum switch, Fig. 10.
2. Connect a suitable test light to either terminal of vacuum switch. Connect a suitable jumper cable from the other terminal to a good ground.
3. Connect remaining lead of test light to power side of removed vacuum switch connector.
4. Attach suitable vacuum pump to vacuum port of switch.
5. Turn ignition on, then actuate vacuum pump. On V6-231 and 252 engines, test light should remain off until vacuum pump gauge reads 5.5–6.5 in. Hg. On V8-265 and 301 engines the test light should remain off until vacuum gauge reads 6.5–7.5 in. Hg. On V8-307 engines, the test light should remain off until vacuum gauge reads 8 in. Hg. On V8-350 gas engines, light should remain off until vacuum gauge reads 7.5–8.5 in. Hg. On V8-350 diesel engines, test light should remain off until vacuum reads 5–6 in. Hg.
6. Decrease vacuum slowly. Light should remain on until vacuum drops to .3–1.3 in. Hg. on V6-231 and 252 engines, 1.2–2.2 in. on V8-265 and 301 engines, 1.5–2.5 in. Hg. on V8-307 and 350 gas engines and 3.5–4.5 in. Hg. on V8-350 diesel engines. Decreasing vacuum beyond above values should cause light to go out.
7. If above results cannot be obtained, switch is defective and must be replaced.
8. The point at which light comes on and the point at which light goes out must have at least 4 in. of vacuum difference.

High Vacuum Switch

NOTE: The high vacuum switch must be adjusted anytime the throttle rod, transmis-

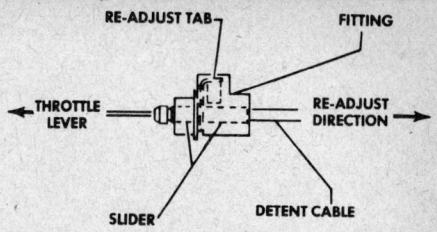

Fig. 9A Self-adjusting throttle valve cable

sion vacuum valve and high idle speed adjustments are changed.

1. Disconnect high vacuum switch electrical connector, Fig. 10.
2. Connect the leads of a suitable test light across the terminals of the high vacuum switch.
3. Energize fast idle solenoid by disconnecting pink and green wire from coolant switch and operate engine at high idle speed, then remove cap from back of high vacuum switch.
4. Before adjustment is performed, the test light must be on, indicating that the switch contacts are closed. If test light is off, close the switch contacts by turning switch adjusting screw clockwise until contacts close.
5. Adjust vacuum switch by turning adjusting screw counterclockwise until switch contact just opens and test light goes off. Turn adjusting screw counterclockwise an additional 1/8–3/16 turn.
6. Reinstall cap on back of vacuum switch and reconnect high vacuum switch and coolant switch electrical connectors.

IN VEHICLE REPAIRS

Valve Body Assembly

1. Drain transmission fluid, then remove oil pan and screen.
2. Remove detent cable retaining bolt and disconnect cable.
3. Remove throttle lever and bracket assembly. Use care to avoid bending throttle lever link.
4. Remove detent roller and spring assembly.

---

3. Loosen lock nut on pump rod, then shorten rod by rotating several turns.
4. Rotate throttle lever assembly to full throttle position and secure in this position.
5. Lengthen pump rod by rotating in opposite direction as described in step 3 until injection pump lever contacts full throttle stop.
6. Release throttle lever assembly and tighten pump rod lock nut.
7. Disconnect pump rod from throttle lever assembly.
8. Connect throttle valve linkage to throttle assembly.
9. Depress metal locking tab on upper end of cable and hold in this position.
10. Position slider through fitting and away from lever assembly until slider contacts metal fitting.
11. Release metal tab, then rotate throttle lever assembly to full throttle position and release.
12. Connect pump rod to lever assembly, then connect cruise control throttle rod, if equipped.
13. On models equipped with cruise control, adjust servo throttle rod until minimum amount of slack is present. Install clip into first hole closest to bellcrank that is within servo bail.

All 1982–83 Models Equipped With Gasoline Engine

1. With engine off, depress locking tab and move slider rearward through fitting until slider contacts fitting, Fig. 9A.
2. Release locking tab, then move carburetor throttle lever to wide open position and release.
3. On 1982–83 Camaro and Firebird with 4-151 engine, rotate idler lever to the maximum travel stop position. The cable will ratchet through its slider and automatically adjust itself. Release throttle idler lever. Do not adjust using the TBI or carburetor lever.
4. Check cable for sticking or binding, then test vehicle for proper operation.
5. If transmission does not shift properly, raise and support vehicle and remove transmission oil pan. Inspect throttle lever and bracket assembly on valve body for damage. Check to ensure that throttle valve exhaust valve rod is not worn or damaged. Check to ensure that lifter spring holds lifter rod against bottom of valve body and that throttle valve plunger is not sticking.

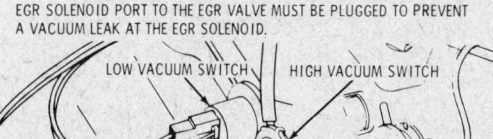

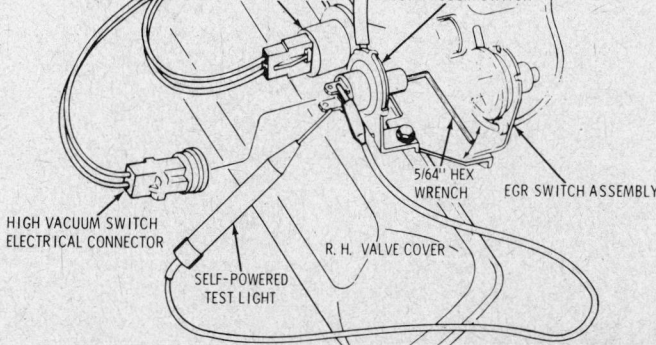

Fig. 10 Vacuum switch location

5. Support valve body and remove retaining bolts, then while holding manual valve, remove valve assembly, spacer plate and gaskets as an assembly to prevent dropping the five check balls.

NOTE: After removing valve body assembly, the intermediate band anchor band pin, and reverse cup plug may be removed.

6. To install control valve, reverse removal procedure and torque all valve body bolts to 8 ft. lbs.

CAUTION: Ensure that intermediate band anchor pin is located on intermediate band prior to installation of valve body, as damage will result.

Governor

Exc. 1982–83 Camaro & Firebird
1. Disconnect battery ground cable and remove air cleaner.
2. On Chevrolet models with air conditioning, remove the five heater core cover screws, then disconnect the electrical connectors and position heater core cover aside.
3. Disconnect exhaust pipe and allow to hang down.
4. Support transmission, then remove transmission rear support bolts and propeller shaft and lower transmission until enough clearance is obtained to remove governor.
5. Remove governor retainer ring and cover, then remove governor and washer.

NOTE: If governor to case washer falls into transmission, use a small magnet to remove it. If it cannot be easily removed, replace the washer with a new one.

6. To install governor, reverse removal procedure.

CAUTION: Do not attempt to hammer governor assembly into case, as damage to governor, case or cover may result.

1982–83 Camaro & Firebird
1. Raise and support vehicle.
2. Remove governor retaining ring and cover and the two seal rings.
3. Remove governor from case.
4. Reverse procedure to install.

Pressure Regulator Valve

1. Drain transmission fluid, then remove oil pan and screen.
2. Using a small screwdriver or tool J-24684, Fig. 11, compress regulator spring.
3. Remove retaining ring and slowly release spring tension.
4. Remove pressure regulator bore plug, valve, spring and guide.
5. To assemble, install pressure regulator spring, guide and valve with stem end first and bore plug with hole side out.
6. Using a small screwdriver or tool J-24684, Fig. 11, compress regulator spring and install retaining ring.

Fig. 11 Removing or installing pressure regulator

Governor Pressure Switch

1. Drain transmission fluid from pan, then remove pan.
2. Disconnect electrical connector from switch, then remove switch using suitable socket.
3. Reverse procedure to install.

TRANSMISSION REPLACE

Buick

1. Disconnect battery ground cable.
2. Remove oil lever dipstick and bolt from upper end of oil filler tube.
3. Raise and properly support vehicle.
4. Remove detent cable retaining bolt from transmission, then disconnect detent cable from link (T.V. cable on 200C transmission). Plug hole to avoid entry of dirt or loss of fluid.
5. Disconnect transmission cooler lines, and remove catalytic converter bracket, if necessary.
6. Remove flywheel inspection cover, then the flywheel to converter bolts.
7. If equipped with console shift, disconnect shift control cable from transmission. If equipped with column shift, remove cotter pin and disconnect manual shift linkage.
8. Disconnect speedometer cable and remove propeller shaft.
9. Remove transmission support to mount bolts, and transmission support to frame bolts. Support engine, then raise transmission with a jack and remove support.
10. Lower transmission slightly and remove the engine to transmission bolts.
11. Carefully lower transmission using care to avoid damaging the detent cable and shift linkage.
12. Reverse procedure to install.

1978–79 Cadillac Seville & 1980–81 DeVille & Brougham with Diesel Engine

1. From inside vehicle, hold sleeve and pull cable outward, then lift snap lock.
2. Remove transmission oil level dipstick and upper dipstick tube retaining bolt.
3. Raise vehicle, then remove detent cable (T.V. cable on 200C transmission) retaining bolt.
4. Remove detent cable from link and plug hole.
5. Disconnect transmission cooler line at transmission.
6. Remove catalytic converter support bracket.

7. Support engine, then remove flywheel cover and three bolts attaching converter to flywheel.

NOTE: Mark flywheel and converter so they can be installed in the same position.

8. Disconnect speedometer cable, then remove cotter pin from shift linkage.
9. Remove propeller shaft.
10. Remove transmission support attaching bolts, then raise transmission using a suitable jack and remove support.
11. Lower transmission slightly and remove transmission to engine attaching bolts.
12. Move transmission rearward and carefully lower from vehicle.

NOTE: Use tool No. J-21366 to hold converter in position.

13. Reverse procedure to install.

Chevrolet

Exc. Chevette & 1982–83 Camaro
1. Disconnect battery ground cable and the detent cable from carburetor (T.V. cable on 200C transmission). Remove filler tube and air cleaner.
2. On vehicles with air conditioning, remove five heater core cover screws from heater assembly. Disconnect electrical connector and, with hoses attached, place heater core cover aside.
3. Raise vehicle and remove propeller shaft.
4. Disconnect speedometer cable, electrical lead to case, oil cooler pipes and the shift linkage.
5. Support transmission with a suitable jack and remove the four rear transmission support bolts.
6. Remove nuts securing catalytic converter bracket to support.
7. On Monza and Vega models, disconnect torque arm from transmission and push toward left side of vehicle.
8. On all models, disconnect exhaust pipe at rear of catalytic converter, then at the manifold. Remove exhaust pipe catalytic converter and converter bracket as an assembly.
9. On all models, remove torque converter under pan.
10. Remove converter to flywheel bolts.
11. Lower transmission slightly and remove engine to transmission bolts.
12. Raise transmission and move rearward, then lower from vehicle.
13. Reverse procedure to install.

Chevette
1. Disconnect battery ground cable then disconnect detent downshift cable from bracket (T.V. cable on 200C transmission).
2. Remove air cleaner and dipstick, then on vehicles with air conditioning, remove the 5 heater core cover retaining screws, disconnect connector and place heater core cover assembly aside.
3. Raise and support vehicle and remove propeller shaft.
4. Disconnect speedometer cable, electrical lead, oil cooler lines, and shift control linkage.
5. Support transmission with suitable jack and remove the crossmember retaining bolts.

6. Remove converter to bracket retaining nuts, then disconnect exhaust pipes from rear of catalytic converter and from exhaust manifolds and remove catalytic converter and converter bracket as an assembly.
7. Remove converter dust shield and remove converter to flywheel bolts.
8. Lower transmission until it is barely supported by jack and remove transmission to engine bolts.
9. Raise transmission to its normal position, then support engine with jack and lower and remove transmission from vehicle.

NOTE: Use converter holding tool J-5384, or keep rear of transmission lower than the front to prevent the converter from sliding out.

10. Before installing transmission, place two inch blocks between rack and pinion housing assembly and oil pan to permit correct alignment of engine and transmission.
11. Reverse removal procedure to install and torque converter to flywheel bolts to 30–40 ft. lbs. (40–54 N-m).

1982–83 Camaro
1. Disconnect battery ground cable, then remove air cleaner.
2. Disconnect T.V. cable from carburetor, then remove filler tube.
3. Raise and support vehicle.
4. Remove propeller shaft and disconnect catalytic converter to transmission bracket.
5. Disconnect speedometer cable and T.C.C. electrical connector.
6. Remove torque arm to transmission bolts.

NOTE: When arm is disconnected from

transmission, rear spring force will cause torque arm to move toward the floor pan. When disconnecting the arm, carefully place a piece of wood between the floor pan and torque arm to avoid personal injury and damage to the floor pan.

7. Remove flywheel cover and converter to flywheel attaching bolts. Mark flywheel and converter for reference during reassembly.
8. Support transmission with a suitable jack, then remove transmission rear mount bolt and crossmember.
9. Lower transmission slightly and remove T.V. cable and oil cooler lines.
10. Support engine using tool BT-6424 or equivalent and remove transmission to engine bolts.
11. Remove transmission from vehicle.
12. Reverse procedure to install.

Oldsmobile
1. Disconnect battery ground cable and the detent cable (T.V. cable on 200C transmission). from carburetor or accelerator lever. Remove filler tube.
2. Raise vehicle and disconnect detent cable, shift linkage and oil cooler pipes.
3. Remove catalytic converter support bracket and flywheel cover pan.
4. Remove flywheel to converter bolts.
5. Disconnect speedometer cable and remove propeller shaft.
6. On Starfire, disconnect torque arm from transmission.
7. On all models, remove transmission support to transmission bolts and the transmission support to frame bolts.
8. Support and raise transmission with a suitable jack, then remove support.
9. Lower transmission slightly and remove engine to transmission bolts.
10. Move transmission rearward and lower

from vehicle.
11. Reverse procedure to install.

Pontiac

Exc. 1000 & 1982–83 Firebird
1. Disconnect battery ground cable.
2. Disconnect detent cable (T.V. cable on 200C transmission) from carburetor, then remove dipstick and oil filler tube from transmission.
3. Raise and support vehicle.
4. Remove detent cable retaining bolt and cable. Plug opening to prevent entry of dirt.
5. Disconnect transmission cooler lines and speedometer cable from transmission.
6. Disconnect shift linkage from selector lever. If equipped with console, remove spring clip and detent cable from transmission bracket.
7. Remove catalytic converter support bracket.
8. Remove flywheel cover and then the flywheel to converter bolts.
9. Remove propeller shaft.
10. Remove transmission support to transmission mount bolts and transmission support to mount bolts.
11. Raise transmission with a suitable jack and remove support, then lower transmission and remove transmission to engine bolts.
12. Remove transmission being careful not to damage oil cooler lines and detent cable.
13. Reverse procedure to install.

1000
Refer to "Transmission, Replace" under "Chevette" for procedure.

1982–83 Firebird
Refer to "Transmission Replace" under "1982–83 Camaro" for procedure.

Turbo Hydra-Matic 200-4R Automatic Transmission

TRANSMISSION IDENTIFICATION

The transmission identification number is stamped on the left hand side of the transmission.

BUICK

		Code
1981	V6-252 Electra & LeSabre①	BY
	V6-252 Electra & LeSabre②	BM
	V6-307 Electra	OG
1982	V6-252 Electra & Le Sabre	BY
	V8-307 Electra & Le Sabre	OG
	V8-350 Diesel Electra & Le Sabre	OM
1983	V6-231③ Regal	BR
	V6-252 Electra & LeSabre	BY
	V8-307 Electra & LeSabre	OG
	V8-350 Diesel Electra, LeSabre & Regal	OM

CADILLAC

		Code
1981	V6-252 Brougham & DeVille	BY
1982	V6-252 Brougham & DeVille	BY

CADILLAC—Cont'd

		Code
	V8-250④ Brougham & DeVille	AA
	V8-250⑤ Brougham & DeVille	AP
	V8-350 Diesel Brougham & DeVille	OM
1983	V6-252 Brougham & DeVille	BY
	V8-250④ Brougham & DeVille	AA
	V8-250⑤ Brougham & DeVille	AP
	V8-350 Diesel Brougham & DeVille	OM

CHEVROLET

		Code
1981	V8-305 Impala & Caprice	CU
1982	V8-267 Caprice & Impala	CQ
	V8-305 Caprice & Impala	CR
	V8-350 Diesel Caprice & Impala	OM
1983	V8-350 Diesel Caprice & Impala	OM

OLDSMOBILE

		Code
1981	V8-252 88	BY
	V8-307 98	OG
1982	V6-252 98	BY

OLDSMOBILE—Cont'd

		Code
	V8-307 88 & 98	OG
	V8-350 Diesel 88 & 98	OM
1983	V6-252 98	BY
	V8-307 88 & 98	OG
	V8-307 Hurst/Olds	OZ
	V8-350 Diesel 88 & 98	OM

PONTIAC

		Code
1981	V8-307 Catalina & Bonneville	OG
1983	V8-350 Diesel Parisienne	OM

① —With 3.23 axle ratio.
② —With 2.93 axle ratio.
③ —Turbocharged engine.
④ —Except high altitude.
⑤ —High altitude.

DESCRIPTION

This transmission is a fully automatic unit consisting primarily of a three-element hy-

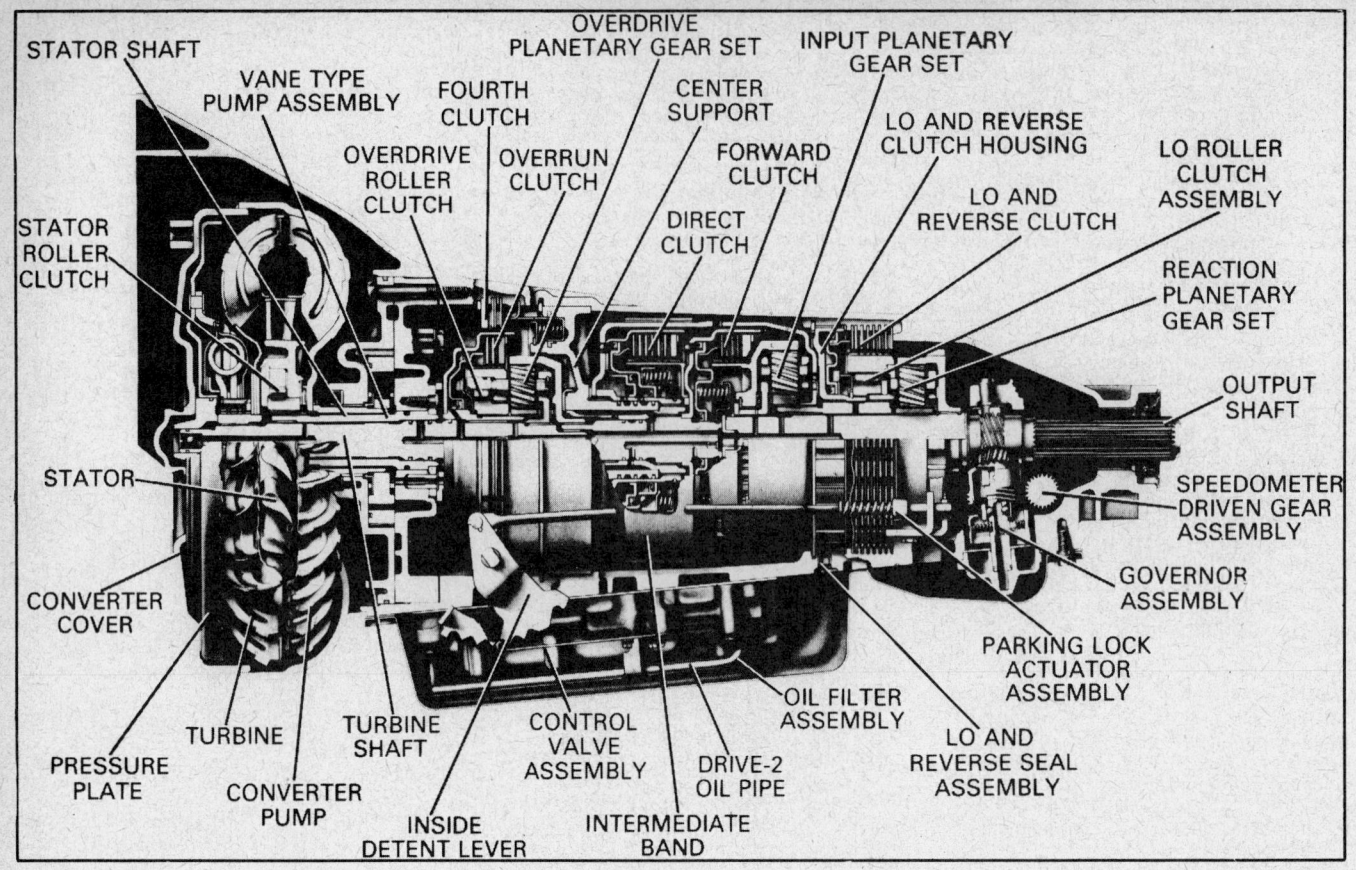

Fig. 1 THM 200-4R crossectional view. 1981—83

draulic torque converter with a converter clutch, a compound planetary gear set and an overdrive unit, Fig. 1. Five multiple-disc clutches and a band provide the friction elements required to obtain the desired function of the compound planetary gear set and the overdrive unit.

The torque converter couples the engine to the overdrive unit and planetary gears through oil and provides torque multiplication. The combination of the compound planetary gear set and the overdrive unit provides four forward ratios and one reverse. Fully automatic changing of the gear ratios is determined by vehicle speed and engine torque.

The hydraulic system in this transmission is pressurized by a variable capacity vane type pump to provide the working pressure required to operate the friction elements and automatic controls.

TROUBLE-SHOOTING

No Drive

1. Low fluid level.
2. Manual linkage maladjusted.
3. Low fluid pressure.
   a. Plugged or restricted oil filter.
   b. Cut or missing oil filter O-ring seals.
   c. Faulty pressure regulator valve.
   d. Damaged pump rotor tangs.
   e. Porosity in oil filter to pump intake bore.
4. Springs missing in overdrive unit roller clutch.
5. Overdrive unit rollers galled or missing.
6. Forward Clutch.
   a. Forward clutch does not apply—piston cracked, seals missing, damaged;

clutch plates burned; snap ring out of groove.
   b. Missing or damaged forward clutch oil seal rings; leak in feed circuits; pump to case gasket improperly positioned or damaged.
   c. Stuck or missing clutch housing ball check.
   d. Cup plug leaking or missing in the rear of the forward clutch shaft in the clutch apply passage.
7. Lo and reverse roller clutch springs missing.
8. Lo and reverse roller clutch rollers galled or missing.

High Or Low Oil Pressure

1. Throttle valve cable misadjusted, binding, unhooked, broken, or wrong link.
2. Damaged or leaking throttle valve assembly.
   a. Throttle lever and bracket assembly binding, unhooked or improperly positioned.
   b. Binding throttle valve or plunger valve.
3. Pressure regulator valve binding.
4. Throttle valve boost valve
   a. Valve binding.
   b. Wrong valve (causing low oil pressure only)
5. Reverse boost valve binding.
6. Manual valve unhooked or improperly positioned.
7. Pressure relief valve ball missing or spring damaged.
8. Pump.
   a. Slide stuck.
   b. Slide seal damaged or missing.

   c. Decrease air bleed orifice missing or damaged causing high oil pressure.
   d. Decrease air bleed orifice plugged causing low oil pressure.
9. Throttle valve limit valve binding.
10. Line bias valve binding in open position causing high oil pressure.
11. Line bias valve binding in closed position causing low oil pressure.
12. Incorrect orifices or passages in control valve assembly spacer plate or case.

1-2 Shift Only At Full Throttle

1. Throttle valve cable binding, unhooked, broken, or improperly adjusted.
2. Throttle lever and bracket assembly binding or unhooked.
3. Throttle valve exhaust ball lifter or #5 ball binding, improperly positioned, or unhooked.
4. #5 ball sealed causing full throttle valve pressure regardless of throttle valve position.
5. Throttle valve and plunger binding.
6. Control valve body gaskets leaking, damaged, or incorrectly installed.
7. Porous case assembly.

No 1-2 Shift

1. Governor and governor feed passages.
   a. Plugged governor oil feed orifice in spacer plate.
   b. Check balls missing in governor assembly.
   c. Missing or leaking inner governor cover rubber O-ring seal.
   d. Governor shaft seal missing or dam-

aged.
  e. Stripped governor driven gear.
  f. Governor weights binding on pin.
  g. Governor driven gear not engaged with governor shaft.
2. Control valve assembly
  a. 1-2 shift, Lo 1st/Detent, or 1-2 throttle valve stuck in downshift position.
  b. Spacer plate gaskets improperly positioned.
3. Case
  a. Case channels porous or 2nd oil feed hole undrilled.
  b. Excessive leakage between case bore and intermediate band apply rings.
  c. Intermediate band anchor pin missing or unhooked from band.
  d. Broken or missing band.
4. Intermediate servo assembly.
  a. Missing servo cover oil seal.
  b. Porosity in serve; cover, inner piston, or outer piston.
  c. Incorrect intermediate band apply pin.
  d. Incorrect usage of cover and piston.
5. 1-2 accumulator.
  a. Loose 1-2 accumulator housing bolts.
  b. Damaged 1-2 accumulator housing face.
  c. Missing or damaged accumulator plate.

No 2-3 Shift

1. Control valve assembly and spacer plate.
  a. 2-3 shift valve or 2-3 throttle valve stuck in the downshift position.
  b. Leaking, damaged or incorrectly installed valve body gaskets.
  c. Reverse/3rd check ball not seating, damaged or missing.
2. Case channels porous.
3. Center support.
  a. Plugged or undrilled center support direct clutch feed passage.
  b. Damaged steel oil seal rings on center support.
4. Direct clutch.
  a. Inner oil seal ring on piston damaged or missing.
  b. Center oil seal ring on direct clutch hub damaged or missing.
  c. Check ball and/or retainer damaged or missing from direct clutch piston.
  d. Damaged or missing direct clutch piston or housing.
  e. Damaged or missing direct clutch plates.
  f. Direct clutch backing plate snap ring not in groove.
  g. Release spring guide improperly located, preventing piston check ball from seating in retainer.
5. Intermediate servo assembly (third clutch accumulator oil passages).
  a. Broken or missing servo to case oil seal ring on intermediate servo piston.
  b. Intermediate servo and/or capsule missing or damaged.
  c. Plugged or undrilled exhaust hole in case between servo piston seal rings.
  d. Bleed orifice cup plug missing from intermediate servo pocket in case.

No Drive In R Or Slips In R

1. Binding or improperly adjusted throttle valve cable.
2. Improperly adjusted manual linkage.
3. Binding throttle valve.
4. Throttle valve limit valve binding.
5. Binding line bias valve.
6. Reverse boost valve binding in pressure regulator bore.

7. Reverse/3rd or Lo/Reverse check ball missing or seat in spacer plate damaged.
8. Reverse clutch.
  a. Cracked piston, or missing inner or outer seals.
  b. Clutch plates burned.
  c. Missing or damaged reverse oil seal in case.
  d. Missing clutch plate or wave plate.
9. Center support.
  a. Loose or missing center support attaching bolts.
  b. Blocked or undrilled passages.
  c. Porosity.
10. Direct clutch housing.
  a. Cracked housing or piston.
  b. Missing or damaged inner or outer piston seal.
  c. Missing or damaged check ball in either the direct clutch housing or the piston.
  d. Plates burned.
11. Plugged Lo/Reverse overrun clutch orifice in spacer plate.

Drive In Neutral

1. Manual linkage improperly adjusted or disconnected.
2. Forward clutch.
  a. Clutch does not release.
  b. Sticking exhaust check ball.
  c. Plates burned together.
3. Case cross leaking to forward clutch passage (D4).

Slipping 1-2 Shift

1. Low fluid level.
2. Spacer plate gaskets damaged or incorrectly installed.
3. Accumulator valve.
  a. Valve sticking in valve body causing low 1-2 accumulator pressure.
  b. Weak or missing spring.
4. 1-2 accumulator piston.
  a. Leaking seal, broken or missing spring.
  b. Leak between piston and pin.
  c. Binding 1-2 accumulator piston.
  d. Damaged 1-2 accumulator piston bore.
5. Intermediate band apply pin.
  a. Incorrect selection of apply pin.
  b. Excessive leakage between apply pin and case.
  c. Apply pin feed hole not completely drilled.
6. Intermediate servo assembly.
  a. Porosity in piston.
  b. Damaged or missing cover to servo oil seal ring.
  c. Leak between servo apply pin and case.
7. Improperly adjusted throttle valve cable.
8. Throttle valve binding, causing low throttle valve pressure.
9. Binding throttle valve limit valve.
10. Line bias valve sticking, causing low line pressure.
11. Worn or burned intermediate band.
12. Case porosity in 2nd clutch passage.

Rough 1-2 Shift

1. Throttle valve cable binding or improperly adjusted.
2. Binding throttle valve to throttle valve plunger.
3. Binding throttle valve limit valve.
4. Binding accumulator valve.
5. Binding line bias valve.
6. Intermediate servo assembly.
  a. Incorrect selection apply pin.

  b. Damaged or missing servo piston to case oil seal ring.
  c. Bleed cup plug missing in case.
7. 1-2 accumulator.
  a. Oil ring damaged.
  b. Piston stuck.
  c. Broken or missing spring.
  d. Damaged bore.
8. 1-2 shift check ball #8 missing or sticking.

Slipping 2-3 Shift

1. Low fluid level.
2. Improperly adjusted throttle valve cable.
3. Binding throttle valve.
4. Spacer plate and gaskets.
  a. Direct clutch orifice partially blocked in spacer plate.
  b. Gaskets out of position or damaged.
5. Intermediate servo assembly.
  a. Damaged or missing servo to case oil seal ring.
  b. Damaged piston or servo bore.
  c. Intermediate servo orifice bleed cup plug in case missing.
  d. Case porous in the servo bore area.
6. Direct clutch feed.
  a. Direct clutch feed channels porous.
  b. Loose case to support bolts causing leakage.
  c. Cracked direct clutch piston or housing.
  d. Cut or missing piston seals.
  e. Burned direct clutch plates.
  f. Check ball in piston and/or housing missing, damaged, or leaking.
  g. Check ball capsule damaged.
  h. Release spring guide improperly located preventing check ball from seating in piston.
7. Center support.
  a. Channels cross feeding, leaking, or restricted.
  b. Damaged or missing oil seal rings.

Rough 2-3 Shift

1. Missing or improperly positioned throttle valve cable.
2. Throttle valve and plunger.
  a. Throttle valve plunger binding.
  b. Throttle valve binding.
3. Throttle valve limit valve binding.
4. Intermediate servo assembly exhaust hole undrilled or plugged between intermediate servo piston seals, preventing intermediate servo piston from completing its stroke.
5. 3-2 exhaust check ball #4 missing or improperly positioned.
6. 3rd accumulator check ball #2 missing or improperly positioned.

Slipping 3-4 Shift

1. Low fluid level.
2. Control valve assembly and spacer plate.
  a. Gaskets of space plate damaged or incorrectly installed.
  b. Accumulator valve sticking causing low 3-4 accumulator pressure.
  c. Weak or missing accumulator valve spring.
3. 3-4 accumulator.
  a. Piston stuck.
  b. Damaged bore or oil ring.
4. Center support porosity.
5. Loose center support attaching bolts.
6. Fourth clutch piston surface or seals damaged.
7. Improper clutch plate usage.
8. Burned fourth clutch plates.
9. Case

a. Porosity.
b. 1-2 accumulator housing bolts loose.
c. 3-4 accumulator piston seal damaged.
d. 3-4 accumulator leaking between the piston and pin.
e. 3-4 accumulator bore damaged.

Rough 3-4 Shift

1. Throttle valve cable improperly positioned or missing.
2. Throttle valve and plunger.
   a. Throttle valve plunger binding.
   b. Throttle valve binding.
3. Throttle valve limit valve binding.
4. 3-4 accumulator.
   a. Piston stuck.
   b. Bore damaged.
5. Fourth clutch piston binding.

No Converter Clutch Application

1. Electrical problem.
   a. 12 volts not being supplied to clutch solenoid.
   b. Defective solenoid.
   c. Damaged electrical connector.
   d. Defective pressure switch.
   e. Wire grounded.
2. Converter clutch shift valve or throttle valve stuck.
3. Pump Assembly.
   a. Plugged converter signal oil orifice in pump.
   b. Damaged or missing solenoid O-ring.
   c. Orificed cup plug missing in oil cooler passage in pump.
   d. Damaged or improperly positioned pump to case gasket.
   e. Converter clutch application valve stuck.
   f. Cup plug missing from application passage.

Rough Converter Clutch Application

1. Damaged converter clutch pressure plate.
2. Damaged or missing check ball in end of turbine shaft.

Converter Clutch Does Not Release

1. Converter clutch apply valve stuck.
2. Damaged converter.
3. Missing cup plug in pump release passage.
4. Missing or damaged turbine shaft end seal.
5. Hole not drilled through turbine shaft.

First, Second and Third Speed Only, No 3-4 Shift

1. Control valve assembly and spacer plate.
   a. 3-4 shift valve or 3-4 throttle valve stuck.
   b. Plugged spacer plate orifice.
2. Center support.
   a. Plugged or undrilled oil passages.
   b. Loose or missing center support attaching bolts.
   c. Cracked or damaged fourth clutch piston.
   d. Damaged, missing or improperly assembled fourth clutch piston seals.
   e. Improper plate usage.
   f. Burned fourth clutch plates.
   g. Binding overrun clutch plates.
3. Case porosity.
4. Orificed cup plug missing in 3-4 accumu-

lator passage in case.
5. Leakage between accumulator piston and pin.
6. 3-4 accumulator bore damaged.

No Engine Braking In L1

1. Improperly adjusted manual linkage.
2. D-3 orifice in spacer plate plugged.
3. Control valve body gaskets leaking, damaged, or incorrectly installed.
4. D-2 oil pipe leaking or out of position.
5. L1 overrun clutch valve binding in valve body.
6. L1/Reverse check ball #10 improperly positioned or missing.
7. L1/Detent check ball #9 improperly positioned or missing.
8. PT/D-3 check ball #3 improperly positioned or missing.
9. Turbine shaft and overrun clutch. No manual 3rd or 2nd should also be a complaint with the following:
   a. Plugged or undrilled D-3 oil passage in turbine shaft.
   b. D-3 oil passage not drilled through in overrun clutch hub.
   c. Missing or damaged oil seals in the overrun clutch piston.
   d. Burned overrun clutches.
   e. Overrun clutch backing plate snap ring out of groove.
10. Case porosity.
11. L1/Reverse clutch assembly. No reverse should also be a complaint with any of the following conditions:
    a. Broken or missing piston seals.
    b. Clutch housing snap ring out of case.
    c. Cracked/porous piston or housing.
    d. Missing or damaged cup plug or rubber seal between case and L1/Reverse clutch housing.

No Engine Braking In L2

1. Manual linkage improperly adjusted.
2. Valve body gaskets leaking, damaged, or improperly installed.
3. Leaking or out of position D-2 oil pipe.
4. Plugged D-3 orifice in spacer plate.
5. PT/D-3 check ball #3 improperly positioned or missing.
6. Porous case.
7. Missing or damaged intermediate servo cover to case oil seal ring.
8. Intermediate band off anchor pin.
9. Broken or burned intermediate band.
10. D-3 oil passage not drilled through in overrun clutch hub.
11. Missing or damaged oil seals in the overrun clutch piston.
12. Undrilled or plugged D-3 oil hole in turbine shaft.
13. Burned overrun clutches.
14. Overrun clutch backing plate snap ring out of groove.

No Engine Braking In D

1. Manual linkage improperly adjusted.
2. Plugged D-3 orifice in spacer plate.
3. Leaking, damaged, or incorrectly installed valve body gaskets.
4. PT/D-3 check ball #3 improperly positioned or missing.
5. Undrilled or plugged D-3 oil passage in turbine shaft.
6. D-3 oil hole not drilled through in overrun clutch hub.
7. Missing or damaged oil seals in the overrun clutch piston.
8. Burned overrun clutches.
9. Overrun clutch backing plate snap ring out of groove.

Will Not Hold In Park

1. Manual linkage improperly adjusted.
2. Internal linkage.
   a. Parking pawl binding in case.
   b. Damaged actuator rod, spring, or plunger.
   c. Broken parking pawl.
   d. Loose or damaged parking bracket.
   e. Missing or improperly positioned manual shaft to case pin.
3. Inside detent lever and pin assembly.
   a. Loose nut.
   b. Worn or damaged hole in lever.
4. Manual detent roller and spring assembly.
   a. Roller assembly to valve body bolt loose.
   b. Pin or roller damaged, improperly positioned, or missing.

No Part Throttle Downshifts

1. Binding throttle valve.
2. Throttle valve limit valve binding.
3. Plugged or undrilled spacer plate hole.
4. Improperly positioned or damaged valve body gaskets.
5. Throttle valve modulator downshift valve stuck.
6. Improperly set throttle valve cable.

No Part Throttle 4-3 Downshift

On selected models with a part throttle passage in the throttle plunger bushing.
1. Throttle plunger bushing passages not open.
2. 3-4 throttle valve bushing passages not open.
3. PT/D-3 check ball #3 incorrectly positioned or missing.
4. Improperly positioned or damaged valve body gaskets.
5. Improperly set throttle valve cable.
6. Throttle valve limit valve binding.

Low Or High Shift Point

1. Binding or improperly adjusted throttle valve cable.
2. Throttle valve limit valve binding.
3. Throttle valve binding.
4. Throttle valve modulator upshift valve binding.
5. Throttle valve modulator downshift valve binding.
6. Improperly positioned, leaking, or damaged valve body gaskets.
7. Throttle valve plunger binding.
8. 1-2, 2-3, or 3-4 throttle valves binding in bushings.
9. Pressure regulator valve binding.
10. Throttle valve exhaust ball #5 and lifter improperly positioned, unhooked, or missing.
11. Throttle lever and bracket assembly.
    a. Binding, unhooked, or loose at mounting valve body bolt.
    b. Not positioned at the throttle valve plunger bushing pin locator.
12. Broken or missing governor shaft to cover seal ring.
13. Broken or missing governor cover gasket.
14. Porous case.

MAINTENANCE

To check fluid, drive vehicle for at least 15 minutes to bring fluid to operating temperature (200° F.). With vehicle on a level surface and engine idling in Park and parking brake applied, the level on the dipstick should be at the "F" mark. To bring the fluid level from the

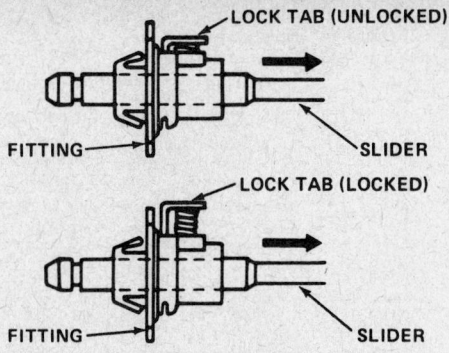

Fig. 2 Self adjusting throttle valve linkage

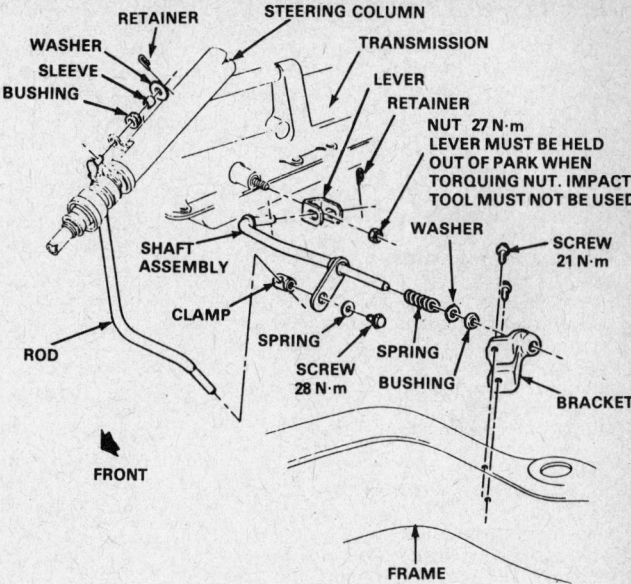

Fig. 3 Column mounted shift linkage adjustment

ADD mark to the FULL mark requires 1 pint of fluid. If vehicle cannot be driven sufficiently to bring fluid to operating temperature, the level on the dipstick should be between the two dimples on the dipstick with fluid temperature at 70° F.

If additional fluid is required, use only Dexron II automatic transmission fluid.

NOTE: An early change to a darker color from the usual red color and or a strong odor that is usually associated with overheated fluid is normal and should not be considered as a positive sign of required maintenance of unit failure.

CAUTION: When adding fluid, do not overfill, as foaming and loss of fluid through the vent may occur as the fluid heats up. Also, if fluid level is too low, complete loss of drive may occur especially when cold, which can cause transmission failure.

Every 100,000 miles, the oil should be drained, the oil pan removed, the screen cleaned and fresh fluid added. For vehicles subjected to more severe use such as heavy city traffic especially in hot weather, prolonged periods of idling or towing, this maintenance should be performed every 15,000 miles.

Draining Bottom Pan

1. Remove front and side oil pan attaching bolts, then loosen the rear oil pan attaching bolts.
2. Carefully pry oil pan loose and allow fluid to drain into a suitable container.
3. Remove the oil pan and gasket, then remove the screen attaching bolts and remove screen.
4. Thoroughly clean oil screen and oil pan with solvent.
5. Install oil screen using a new gasket, then install oil pan using a new gasket and torque attaching bolts to 10–13 ft. lbs.
6. Add approximately 3 quarts of fluid, then with engine idling and parking brake applied, move selector lever through each range and return selector lever to PARK.
7. Check fluid level and add fluid as required to bring level between the two dimples on the dipstick.

ADJUSTMENTS

Throttle Valve Linkage

Models Equipped With Diesel Engine

1. Remove cruise control rod on vehicles equipped with cruise control.

2. Disconnect throttle valve linkage from throttle assembly.
3. Loosen lock nut on pump rod, then shorten rod by rotating several turns.
4. Rotate throttle lever assembly to full throttle position and secure in this position.
5. Lengthen pump rod by rotating in opposite direction as described in step 3 until injection pump lever contacts full throttle stop.
6. Release throttle lever assembly and tighten pump rod lock nut.
7. Disconnect pump rod from throttle lever assembly.
8. Connect throttle valve linkage to throttle assembly.
9. Depress metal locking tab on upper end of cable and hold in this position.
10. Position slider through fitting and away from lever assembly until slider contacts metal fitting.
11. Release metal tab, then rotate throttle lever assembly to full throttle position

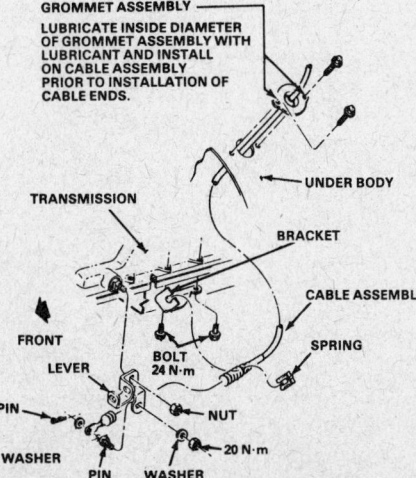

Fig. 4 Console mounted shift linkage adjustment

and release.
12. Connect pump rod to lever assembly, then connect cruise control throttle rod, if equipped.
13. On models equipped with cruise control, adjust servo throttle rod until minimum amount of slack is present. Install clip into first hole closest to bellcrank that is within servo bail.

Models Equipped With Gasoline Engine, Manual Type Linkage

1. With engine off, disconnect throttle valve linkage retaining lock.
2. Rotate throttle lever to wide open position and hold in this position.
3. Connect throttle valve linkage retaining lock.

Self Adjusting Linkage, All Models

1. With engine off, depress locking tab and move slider rearward through fitting until slider contacts fitting, Fig. 2.
2. Release locking tab, then move carburetor throttle lever to wide open position and release.
3. Check cable for sticking or binding, then test vehicle for proper operation.
4. If transmission does not shift properly, raise and support vehicle and remove transmission oil pan. Inspect throttle lever and bracket assembly on valve body for damage. Check to ensure that throttle valve exhaust valve rod is not worn or damaged. Check to ensure that lifter spring holds lifter rod against bottom of valve body and that throttle valve plunger is not sticking.

Manual Linkage

Column Mounted

1. Position transmission shift lever in Neutral.
2. Position transmission manual valve lever in Neutral detent.
3. With clamp spring washer and screw assembled onto equalizer lever and control rod, hold clamp against equalizer lever, then snug tighten clampscrew against control rod, Fig. 3.

Console Mounted

1. Position console shift lever in Park position.
2. Position transmission manual valve lever in Park detent.
3. Position pin, Fig. 4, until pin fits loosely in transmission lever, then tighten attaching nut.

IN-VEHICLE REPAIRS

Intermediate Servo, Replace

1. Remove intermediate servo cover retaining ring, using a small screwdriver.
2. Remove servo cover and discard seal ring.
3. Remove servo piston and band apply pin assembly.
4. Reverse procedure to install.

Speedometer Driven Gear, Replace

1. Disconnect speedometer cable.
2. Remove bolt, retainer, speedometer driven gear and the O-ring seal.
3. Reverse procedure to install.

Rear Oil Seal, Replace

1. Remove propeller shaft.
2. Pry seal from extension housing with a suitable tool.
3. Drive new oil seal into extension housing, using a suitable tool.
4. Install propeller shaft.

Valve Body, Replace

1. Drain transmission oil pan.
2. Remove oil pan and filter.
3. Remove screw and washer securing T.V. cable to transmission and disconnect the cable.
4. Remove throttle lever and bracket assembly. Use caution not to bend throttle lever link.
5. Disconnect electrical connectors at the 4-3 pressure switch and the 4th clutch pressure switch.
6. Remove solenoid attaching bolts, clips and solenoid assembly.
7. Remove manual detent roller and spring assembly.
8. Remove valve body retaining bolts while supporting valve body. Secure manual valve and remove valve body. Use caution not to lose the three check balls.
9. Reverse procedure to install. Torque valve body bolts to 12 ft. lbs.

1-2 & 3-4 Accumulator, Replace

1. Remove valve body.
2. While supporting 1-2 accumulator housing, remove housing retaining bolts. Then, remove housing and gasket.
3. Support valve body spacer plate, gaskets and accumulator plate to prevent loss of the eight check balls and the 3-4 accumulator spring piston and pin located in the case. Remove remaining retaining bolt on accumulator plate.

NOTE: The intermediate band anchor pin may become dislodged after removing spacer plate and gaskets.

4. Reverse procedure to install.

Governor, Replace

1. Drain transmission oil pan.
2. Remove oil pan and filter.
3. Remove governor attaching bolts, cover and gasket. The governor may come out with the cover. Also, it may be necessary to rotate output shaft counterclockwise while removing governor.
4. Reverse procedure to install.

TRANSMISSION, REPLACE

1981 Cadillac

1. Disconnect battery ground cable.
2. Remove transmission oil level dipstick. Remove upper bolt on dipstick tube.
3. Raise and support vehicle.
4. Disconnect throttle valve cable from retainer.
5. Disconnect transmission cooler lines from transmission.
6. Remove flywheel under cover. Remove three flywheel to converter attaching bolts. It may be necessary to remove catalytic converter support bracket to gain access to bolts. Mark flywheel and converter for reference during installation.
7. Support engine with suitable jack, then disconnect speedometer cable.
8. Disconnect manual shift linkage from transmission.
9. Mark driveshaft and companion flange for reference during installation, then remove driveshaft.
10. Remove transmission crossmember to transmission mount bolts. Remove transmission crossmember to frame bolts.
11. Raise transmission with suitable jack and remove crossmember.
12. Lower transmission slightly, then remove transmission to engine mounting bolts.
13. Lower transmission and remove from vehicle. Use caution not to drop torque converter as transmission is being removed. Install suitable converter holding tool to secure converter.
14. Reverse procedure to install.

All 1981–83 Models Except 1981 Cadillac

1. Disconnect battery ground cable and remove air cleaner.
2. Disconnect throttle valve cable from carburetor.
3. Remove transmission oil level dipstick. Remove upper bolt on dipstick tube.
4. Raise and support vehicle.
5. Mark driveshaft and companion flange for reference during installation, then remove driveshaft.
6. Disconnect speedometer cable and manual shift linkage from transmission.
7. Disconnect torque converter clutch solenoid electrical connector.
8. Remove flywheel under cover. Mark flywheel and converter for reference during installation. Remove three flywheel to converter attaching bolts.
9. Remove catalytic converter support bracket bolts and the tunnel strap.
10. Remove transmission crossmember to transmission mount bolts. Remove transmission crossmember to frame bolts.
11. Support transmission with suitable jack, then move crossmember rearward.
12. Lower transmission slightly and disconnect throttle valve cable and oil cooler lines.
13. Support engine with suitable jack, then remove engine to transmission mounting bolts.
14. Lower jack and remove transmission from vehicle. Use caution not to drop torque converter as transmission is removed. Install suitable converter holding tool to secure converter.
15. Reverse procedure to install.

Turbo Hydra-Matic 250, 250C, 350, 350C Automatic Transmission

TRANSMISSION IDENTIFICATION

A production day and shift built number, transmission model and model year are stamped on the 1-2 accumulator cover, which is located on the middle lower right side of the transmission case.

BUICK	Code
1977 V6-231 Skyhawk	KD
V6-231 Skylark	KK
V6-231 Skylark	KS
V6-231 Century	KE
V6-231 Century	KW
V6-231 LeSabre, Estate Wag. & Riviera	KW
V8-301 Skylark	KC
V8-305 Skylark	KJ
V8-350 Skylark	KX
V8-350 Century	KA
V8-350 Century	LE

BUICK—Cont'd	Code
V8-350 LeSabre, Estate Wag. & Riviera	JB
V8-350 Electra	JB
V8-350 Riviera & Electra	LT
V8-350 Estate Wag. & Skylark	LC
V8-403 Century	LM
V8-403 LeSabre & Estate Wagon	LA
1978 V6-196 Century	5KD
V6-231 Skyhawk	5KA
V6-231 Century, LeSabre & Skylark	5KE
V6-231 Century & LeSabre	5KJ

BUICK—Cont'd

	Code
V6-231 Skyhawk	5KL
V8-301 LeSabre	5MO
V8-305 Century, LeSabre & Skylark	5JC
V8-305 Century & Skylark	5KC
V8-350 LeSabre	5KH, 5LA, 5LH
V8-350 Century, LeSabre & Skylark	5JD
V8-403 Century, LeSabre & Skylark	5JD
V8-403 LeSabre	5LC, 5LE, 5LK
1979 V6-196 Century & Regal	6KD
V6-231 Century & Regal	6KE, 6KJ
V6-231 LeSabre	6KC
V6-231 Skyhawk	6KA, 6KL
V6-231 Skylark	6KX
V8-301 Century & Regal	6MA, 6MP
V8-301 LeSabre	6MD
V8-305 Century & Regal	6JC
V8-305 Skylark	6JC, 6TA
V8-350 Century & Regal	6JD
V8-350 LeSabre	6LA, 6LH
V8-350 LeSabre	6KH
V8-350 Skylark	6JD, 6TR
V8-403 LeSabre	6LC, 6LE, 6LK
1980 Century & Regal	7JE, 7KC, 7KH, 7KJ, 7KS, 7KT, 7KV, 7TB, 7KH
Electra & LeSabre	7KD, 7KJ, 7KN, 7LA, 7TB, 7WB, 7WC, TW6
Skyhawk	7KA
1981 V6-231 Century & Regal	KD, KT, WK
V6-231 LeSabre & Estate Wag.	KD
V6-252 LeSabre, Estate Wag. & Electra	KK
V6-307 LeSabre & Estate Wag.	LB, XA, XL
V6-350 LeSabre & Estate Wag.	LA, LD
1982 V6-231 Estate Wagon, LeSabre & Regal	KA
V6-231 Regal Turbo	KL
V6-231 Regal	WK
V6-252 Regal 4 Barrel Carb.	KE
V6-252 Estate Wagon & LeSabre 4 Barrel Carb.	KK
V8-307 Estate Wagon & LeSabre	XL
V8-350 Regal Diesel	LB, WX
V8-350 Estate Wagon & LeSabre Diesel	LD
V8-350 Estate Wagon & LeSabre Diesel	WT
1983 V6-231 LeSabre & Regal	KA
V6-231 Regal	WK
V6-252 Regal	KE
V8-350 Estate Wagon & LeSabre (Diesel)	LJ
V8-350 Regal (Diesel)	LB

CADILLAC

	Code
1982 V8-350 Brougham & DeVille Diesel	WT

CHEVROLET

	Code
1977 4-140 Monza & Vega Exc. Calif.	AP
4-140 Monza & Vega Calif.	AO
6-250 Chevelle & Monte Carlo Exc. Calif.	AD
6-250 Chevrolet Exc. Calif.	AD
6-250 Nova & Camaro Exc. Calif.	WK
6-250 Nova & Camaro Calif.	AN
V8-305 Chevelle & Monte Carlo	AF
V8-305 Chevrolet	AF
V8-305 Nova & Camaro	AG

CHEVROLET—Cont'd

	Code
V8-350 Chevelle & Monte Carlo	AH
V8-350 Chevrolet	AH
V8-350 Nova & Camaro Exc. Z-28	AJ
V8-350 Z-28 & Corvette	AM
1978 Monza	KK, KL, WC
Camaro & Nova	AG, AJ
Camaro	AN, WB, WK
Nova	AH, WL, WZ
Malibu & Monte Carlo	AG, AJ, AN
Malibu & Monte Carlo	KE, TE
Chevrolet	AG, AJ, AN
Chevrolet	KE, WK
Corvette	TL, WB
1979 V6-200 Malibu & Monte Carlo	WA
V6-231 Monza	KA
6-250 Exc. Nova, Calif.	TT
6-250 Exc. Nova & Calif.	TP
6-250 Nova, Calif.	TS
6-250 Nova, Exc. Calif.	TC
V8-305 Exc. Monza	TA
V8-305 Monza	WD
V8-350 Exc. Full Size Exc. Calif., Camaro Z-28 or Corvette	TR
V8-350 Full Size Calif.	XA
V8-350 Camaro Z-28	WF
V8-350 Corvette	TB, WB
1980 Chevrolet, Malibu & Monte Carlo	7KD, 7JE, 7JS, 7WD, 7WL
Malibu & Monte Carlo	7JJ, 7JK, 7JN, 7KC, 7KJ
Camaro	7JD, 7JJ, 7JK, 7JL, 7KF
Chevrolet	7JE, 7KH, 7TZ, 7WC, 7WH
Corvette	7JC, 7TW
Monza	7KA
1981 V6-229 Malibu & Monte Carlo	WP
V6-229 Camaro	JC, XP
V6-229 Chevrolet, Malibu & Monte Carlo	XP
V6-231 Malibu & Monte Carlo	KD, KT, WK, XX
V6-231 Chevrolet	KD
V8-267 Malibu, Monte Carlo & Chevrolet	XS
V8-267 Camaro, Chevrolet, Malibu & Monte Carlo	WC
V8-305 Malibu & Monte Carlo	WD, XK
V8-305 Camaro, Chevrolet	WD
V8-350 Malibu & Monte Carlo	WE
V8-350 Chevrolet	LA, LD, WS, WW
V8-350 Corvette	JD
1982 V6-229 Caprice, Impala, Malibu & Monte Carlo	WD, XP
V6-231 Caprice, Impala, Malibu & Monte Carlo	KA
V6-231 Malibu & Monte Carlo	WK
V8-267 Caprice, Impala, Malibu & Monte Carlo	WC
V8-267 Caprice & Impala, Malibu & Monte Carlo	XS
V8-305 Malibu & Monte Carlo	WD, XK
V8-305 Malibu & Monte Carlo (Diesel)	LB, WX
V8-350 Caprice & Impala Diesel	LD, WT
1983 V6-229 Caprice & Impala	XP
V6-231 Caprice & Impala	KA
V6-231 Malibu & Monte Carlo	WK
V8-305 Caprice & Impala	XK
V8-305 Malibu & Monte Carlo	WD, WE
V8-350 Caprice & Impala (Diesel)	LD, LJ
V8-350 Malibu & Monte Carlo (Diesel)	LB

OLDSMOBILE

	Code
1977 4-140 Starfire Exc. Calif.	AP
4-140 Starfire	AO
V6-231 Omega	KK
V6-231 Cutlass & 88	KE
V8-260 Cutlass	LH
V8-305 Omega	KJ
V8-350 Omega	KX
V8-350 Omega Hi Alt.	LK
V8-350 Omega Calif.	LL
V8-350 Cutlass Exc. Hi Alt. & Calif.	LX
V8-350 Cutlass Exc. Hi Alt.	LE
V8-350 Cutlass Hi Alt.	LD
V8-350 88 Exc. Hi Alt.	LC
V8-350 88 Wagon	LZ
V8-350 88 Wagon Hi Alt.	LK
V8-350 98	LC
V8-350 98 Exc. Hi Alt.	LT
V8-350 98 Hi Alt.	LK
V8-403 Cutlass Exc. Hi Alt.	LM
V8-403 Cutlass Hi Alt.	LP
V8-403 88 Exc. Hi Alt.	LA
V8-403 88 Hi Alt.	LJ
V8-403 98	LA
V8-403 98 Hi Alt.	LS
V8-403 98 Hi Alt.	LJ
1978 V6-231 Starfire	KA, KL
V6-231 Omega	KC
V6-231 Cutlass & 88	KE
V8-260 Cutlass & 88	LD
V8-305 Starfire	WC
V8-305 Omega & Cutlass	JC
V8-350 Omega & Cutlass	JD
V8-350 88	LA, LH
V8-350 Diesel Custom Cruiser	LJ
V8-403 88	LC, LE, LK
1979 V6-231 Cutlass	KE
V6-231 Omega, Calif.	KX
V6-231 Omega, Exc. Calif.	KE
V6-231 88 Exc. Sta. Wag.	KC
V6-231 Starfire (2.56 Axle)	KA
V6-231 Starfire (2.93 Axle)	KL
V8-260 Cutlass & 88 Exc. Sta. Wag.	LD
V8-301 88 Exc. Sta. Wag.	MA
V8-305 Cutlass	JC
V8-305 Omega, Exc. Calif. & Hi Alt.	JC
V8-305 Starfire	WC
V8-350 (Chev. Built) Cutlass & Omega	JD
V8-350 (Olds. Built) Cutlass Exc. Hi Alt.	LA
V8-350 (Olds. Built) 88 Exc. Sta. Wag. Exc. Hi Alt.	LA
V8-350 (Olds. Built) 88 Exc. Sta. Wag., Hi Alt.	LH
V8-350 (Olds. Built) 88 Sta. Wag., Exc. Hi Alt. & Calif.	LH
V8-350 (Diesel) Cutlass Sta. Wag. Exc. Calif. & Hi Alt.	LS
V8-350 (Diesel) Cutlass Sta. Wag., 88 Exc. Sta. Wag. & 98 Exc. Hi Alt.	LJ
V8-403 88 Sta. Wag. (2.41 or 3.08 Axle)	LC
V8-403 88 Sta. Wag. Hi Alt.	LE
V8-403 88 Sta. Wag. (3.23 Axle) Exc. Hi Alt.	LK
V8-403 88 Sta. Wag., Exc. Calif. & Hi Alt.	LW
1980 V6-231 Cutlass & 88 Exc. Sta. Wagon	KH, KS
V6-231 Cutlass	KC
V6-231 Starfire	KA
V8-260 Cutlass	LC, LD
V8-305 Cutlass	JE, JK, WD, WL
V8-305 88 Exc. Sta. Wagon	TT
V8-305 88 Sta. Wagon	WA
V8-350 Cutlass	LJ
V8-350 88	LA
V8-350 88 Wagon, Exc. Diesel	TY

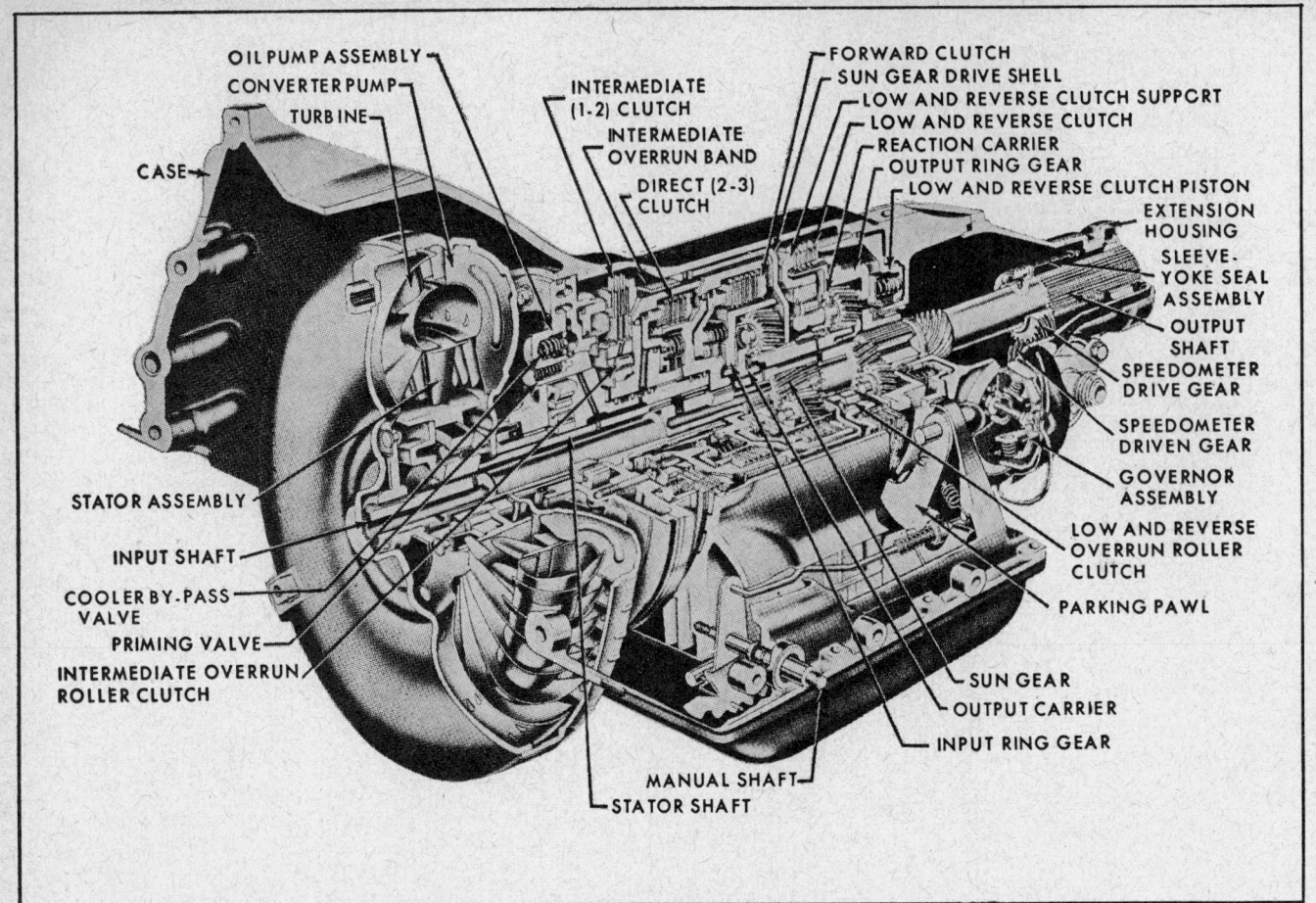

Fig. 1 Cutaway view of Turbo Hydra-Matic 350 transmission

OLDSMOBILE—Cont'd

	Code
V8-350 88 Wagon, Diesel	WC
1981 V6-231 Cutlass	WK, XX
V6-231 88 & 98	KD
V8-260 Cutlass	LC
V8-267 Cutlass	WC
V8-307 Cutlass & 88 & 98	XL
V8-350 88 & 98	LA, LD
1982 V6-231 Cutlass	WK
V6-231 Cutlass & 88	KA
V8-260 Cutlass & 88	LA
V8-307 Cutlass	C3
V8-307 Cutlass & 88	XL
V8-350 Cutlass (Diesel)	LB
V8-350 88 (Diesel)	LD
V8-350 88 & 98 (Diesel)	WT
1983 V6-231 Cutlass	WK
V6-231 Cutlass & 88	KA
V8-307 Cutlass & 88	XL
V8-350 Cutlass (Diesel)	LB
V8-350 88 (Diesel)	LJ

PONTIAC

	Code
1977 4-140 Astre & Sunbird Exc. Calif. & Hi Alt.	AO
4-140 Astre & Sunbird Calif. & Hi Alt.	AP
V6-231 Astre & Sunbird	KD
V6-231 Astre & Sunbird (2.56 Ratio)	KL

PONTIAC—Cont'd.

	Code
V6-231 Astre & Sunbird (2.93 Ratio)	KP
V6-231 Firebird	MC
V6-231 LeMans	JB
V6-231 LeMans, Catalina & Bonneville	MD
V8-301 Ventura & Firebird	MX
V8-301 LeMans, Catalina & Bonneville	MM
V8-350 Firebird	MA
V8-350 LeMans, Catalina & Bonneville	ME
V8-350 LeMans & Grand Prix	LE
V8-350 LeMans & Grand Prix Alt. Perf. Pkg.	LD
V8-350 Catalina & Bonneville	ML
V8-350 Catalina, Bonneville & Ventura	LL
V8-400 Firebird	MG
V8-400 LeMans, Catalina & Bonneville Exc. Police & Trailer	MR
V8-400 Catalina & Bonneville Police & Trailer	MP
V8-403 Firebird	MZ
V8-403 LeMans & Grand Prix	LM
V8-403 Catalina & Bonneville Exc. Police & Trailer	LA
1978 V6-231 Sunbird	KA, KL
V6-231 Firebird & Phoenix	KC
V6-231 Grand Prix & LeMans	KE
V6-231 Catalina & Bonneville	KE
V8-301 Grand Prix & LeMans	MP

PONTIAC—Cont'd.

	Code
V8-301 Catalina & Bonneville	MD, MH, MP
V8-305 Firebird & Phoenix	JC
V8-305 Grand Prix & LeMans	JC
V8-350 Firebird, Phoenix & LeMans	JD
V8-350 Catalina & Bonneville	KH, LA, LH
V8-400 Firebird Exc. Trans Am	MC
V8-400 Firebird Trans Am	MK
V8-400 Catalina & Bonneville	ME, MJ
V8-403 Firebird	LP
V8-403 Catalina & Bonneville	LC, LE
1979 V6-231 Bonneville & Catalina, Exc. Hi Alt.	KC
V6-231 Firebird & Phoenix, Exc. Hi Alt.	KX
V6-231 LeMans, Exc. Sta. Wagon & Grand Prix	KE
V6-231 Sunbird, Exc. Calif.	KL
V6-231 Sunbird, Exc. Hi Alt.	KA
V8-301 Firebird, Exc. Calif. & Hi Alt.	ME, MJ
V8-301 Bonneville, Catalina & LeMans, Exc. Sta. Wagon, Calif. or Hi Alt.	MA, MP
V8-305 Firebird, Calif. & Phoenix, Exc. Hi Alt.	JC
V8-305 Phoenix (with Opt. Axle), Exc. Hi Alt.	TA
V8-305 Sunbird, Exc. Hi Alt.	WD

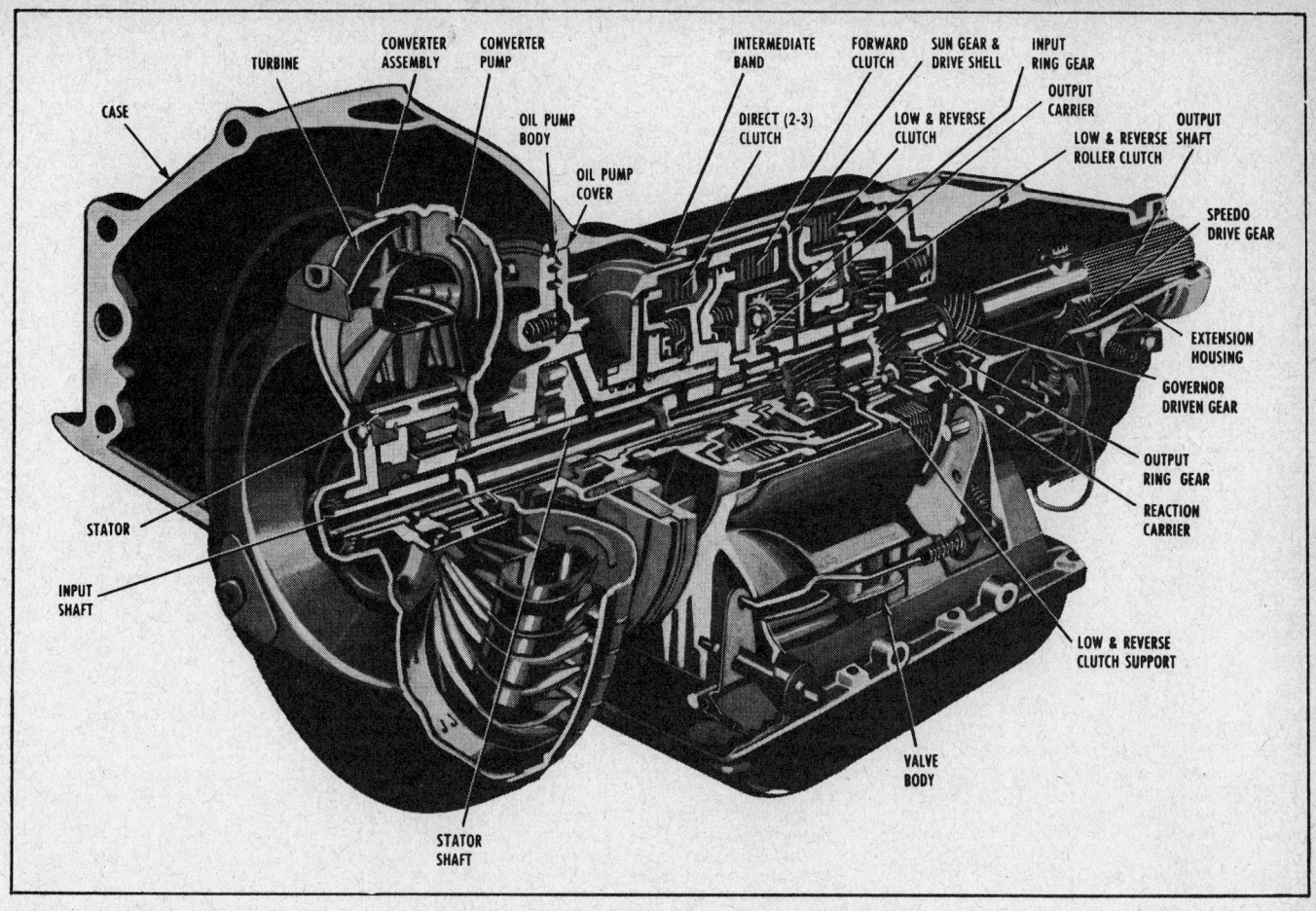

Fig. 2 Cutaway view of Turbo Hydra-Matic 250 transmission

PONTIAC—Cont'd.   Code

V8-350 Bonneville & Catalina, Hi
Alt. .... LH
V8-350 Firebird & LeMans Sta.
Wag., Hi Alt. Phoenix, Calif. &
Hi Alt. .... JD
V8-350 Bonneville & Catalina,
Calif. .... LA
V8-350 Bonneville & Catalina,
Exc. Calif. & Hi Alt. .... KH
V8-350 Phoenix (with Opt. Axle),
Calif. & Hi Alt. .... TR
V8-403 Bonneville & Catalina,
Calif. .... LC, LK
V8-403 Bonneville & Catalina,
Hi Alt. .... LE
1980 Firebird .... MC
Full Size .... TB
Grand Prix .... MD, TB
LeMans, Grand Am ...... HD, MD, TB
1981 V6-231 LeMans & Grand
Prix .... WK, XX
V6-231 LeMans, Bonneville &
Catalina..................... KD
V6-231 Firebird .... KY
V6-265 LeMans & Grand Prix LC
V8-301 LeMans .... MA
V8-350 Bonneville &
Catalina.................. LA, LD
1982 V6-231 Bonneville & Grand
Prix .... KA, WK
V6-252 Bonneville & Grand Prix
4 Barrel Carb. .... KE
V8-350 Bonneville & Grand Prix
Diesel Exc. Calif. .... LB, WX

PONTIAC—Cont'd.   Code

1983 V6-229 Parisienne .... XD, XH
V6-231 Bonneville & Grand
Prix .... KA, KC, WK
V8-305 Parisienne .... XD, XH
V8-305 Bonneville & Grand
Prix .... WD, XK
V8-350 Parisienne (Diesel) ...... WH
V8-350 Bonneville & Grand Prix
(Diesel) .... LB

DESCRIPTION

The 1977–82 Turbo Hydra-Matic 250, 250C, 350 & 350C, Figs. 1, 2 and 2A, are fully automatic three-speed transmissions consisting of a three-element torque converter and a compound planetary gear set. The 1983 series Turbo Hydra-Matic 250C & 350C transmissions have a four-element hydraulic torque converter and a planetary gear set. The Turbo Hydra-Matic 350 transmission has four multiple-disc clutches, two roller clutches and a band to provide the required friction elements to obtain the desired function of the planetary gear set. The Turbo Hydra-Matic 250 transmission uses an adjustable intermediate band in place of the intermediate clutch found in the Turbo Hydra-Matic 350. Also, the Turbo Hydra-Matic 250 has three multiple-disc

clutches and one roller clutch.

The friction elements couple the engine to the planetary gears through oil pressure, providing three forward speeds and one reverse.

The three element torque converter is of welded construction and is serviced as an assembly. The unit consists of a pump or driving member, a turbine or driven member and a stator assembly. When required, the torque converter supplements the gears by multiplying engine torque. In addition, the 250C and 350C transmissions are equipped with a locking torque converter. The converter clutch assembly consists of a three element torque converter with a converter clutch. The converter clutch is splined to the turbine assembly and, when operated, applies against the converter cover, providing a mechanical direct drive coupling of the engine to the planetary gears. When the converter clutch is released the assembly operates as a normal torque converter.

TROUBLE SHOOTING GUIDE

No Drive In Drive Range

1. Low oil level (check for leaks).
2. Manual control linkage improperly adjusted.
3. Low oil pressure due to blocked strainer,

defective pressure regulator, pump assembly or pump drive gear. See that tangs have not been damaged by converter. Check case for porosity in intake bore.
4. Check control valve assembly to be sure manual valve has not been disconnected from inner lever.
5. Forward clutch may be stuck or damaged. Check pump feed circuits to forward clutch, including clutch drum ball check.
6. Roller clutch assembly broken or damaged.

Oil Pressure High or Low

High Pressure
1. Vacuum line or fittings leaking.
2. Vacuum modulator.
3. Modulator valve.
4. Pressure regulator.
5. Oil pump.

Low Pressure
1. Vacuum line or fittings obstructed.
2. Vacuum modulator.
3. Modulator valve.
4. Pressure regulator.
5. Governor.
6. Oil pump.

1-2 Shift At Full Throttle Only

1. Detent valve may be sticking or linkage may be misadjusted.
2. Vacuum line or fittings leaking.
3. Control valve body gaskets leaking, damaged or incorrectly installed. Detent valve train or 1-2 valve stuck.
4. Check case for porosity.

First Speed Only, No 1-2 Shift

T.H.M. 250 & 350
1. Governor valve may be sticking.
2. Driven gear in governor assembly loose, worn or damaged. If driven gear shows damage, check output shaft drive gear for nicks or rough finish.
3. Control valve governor feed channel blocked or gaskets leaking. 1-2 shift valve train stuck closed.
4. Check case for blocked govenor feed channels or for scored governor bore which will allow cross pressure leak. Check case for porosity.
5. Intermediate clutch or seals damaged.
6. Intermediate roller clutch damaged.

T.H.M. 250
1. Intermediate servo piston seals damaged, missing or installed improperly.
2. Intermediate band improperly adjusted.
3. Intermediate servo apply rod broken.

1st & 2nd Only, No 2-3 Shift

1. Control valve 2-3 shift train stuck. Valve body gaskets leaking, damaged or improperly installed.
2. Pump hub-to-direct clutch oil seal rings broken or missing.
3. Direct clutch piston seals damaged. Piston ball check stuck or missing.

No First Speed

T.H.M. 250
1. Intermediate band adjusted too tightly.
2. 1-2 shift valve stuck in upshift position.

T.H.M. 350
1. Excessive number of clutch plates in intermediate clutch pack.
2. Incorrect intermediate clutch piston.

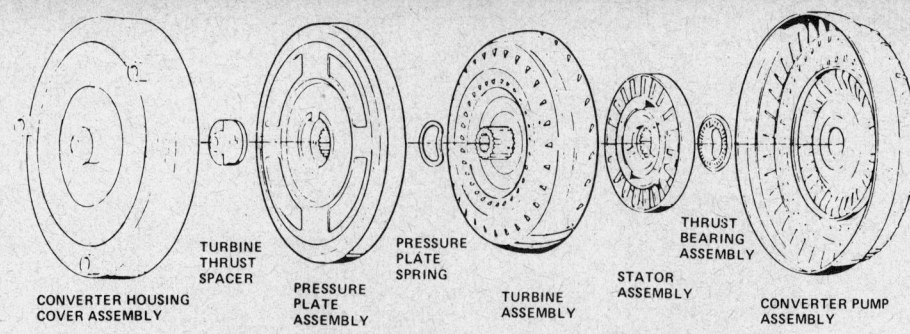

Fig. 2A Torque converter clutch 250C & 350C transmission

Moves Forward In Neutral

1. Manual linkage misadjusted.
2. Forward clutch not releasing.

No Forward or Reverse Operation

1. Fatigue failure of forward clutch housing due to excessive pinion pin runout in output carrier.

No Drive In Reverse or Slips In Reverse

1. Low oil level.
2. Manual linkage misadjusted.
3. Modulator valve stuck.
4. Modulator and reverse boost valve stuck.
5. Pump hub-to-direct clutch oil seal rings broken or missing.
6. Direct clutch piston seal cut or missing.
7. Low and reverse clutch piston seal cut or missing.
8. Number 1 check ball missing.
9. Control valve body gaskets leaking or damaged.
10. 2-3 valve train stuck in upshifted position.
11. 1-2 valve train stuck in upshifted position.
12. Intermediate servo piston or pin stuck so intermediate band is applied.
13. Low and reverse clutch piston out or seal damaged.
14. Direct clutch plates burned—may be caused by stuck ball check in piston.
15. Forward clutch not releasing.

Slips In All Ranges

1. Low oil level.
2. Vacuum modulator valve defective or sticking.
3. Filter assembly plugged or leaking.
4. Pressure regulator valve stuck.
5. Pump to case gasket damaged.
6. Check case for cross leaks or porosity.
7. Forward clutch slipping.

Slips 1-2 Shift

T.H.M. 250 & 350
1. Low oil level.
2. Vacuum modulator assembly defective.
3. Modulator valve sticking.
4. Pump pressure regulator valve defective.
5. 1-2 accumulator oil ring damaged or missing. Case bore damaged.
6. Pump to case gasket mispositioned or damaged.
7. Check for case porosity.
8. Intermediate clutch piston seals damaged. Clutch plates burned.

T.H.M. 250
1. Intermediate servo piston seals damaged or missing.
2. Burned intermediate band.

T.H.M. 350
1. 2-3 accumulator oil ring damaged or missing.

Rough 1-2 Shift

T.H.M. 250 & 350
1. Vacuum modulator, check for loose fittings, restrictions in line or defective modulator assembly.
2. Modulator valve stuck.
3. Valve body regulator or boost valve stuck.
4. Pump to case gasket mispositioned or damaged.
5. Check case for porosity.
6. Check 1-2 accumulator assembly for damaged oil rings, stuck piston, broken or missing spring, or damaged case bore.

T.H.M. 250
1. Intermediate band improperly adjusted.
2. Improper or broken servo spring.

T.H.M. 350
1. Burned intermediate clutch plates.
2. Improper number of intermediate clutch plates.

Slips 2-3 Shift

1. Low oil level.
2. Modulator valve or vacuum modulator assembly defective.
3. Pump pressure regulator valve or boost valve; pump to case gasket mispositioned.
4. Check case for porosity.
5. Direct clutch piston seals or ball check leaking.

Rough 2-3 Shift

1. High oil pressure. Vacuum leak, modulator valve sticking or pressure regulator or boost valve inoperative.
2. 2-3 accumulator piston stuck, spring broken or missing.

No Engine Braking In Second Speed

1. Intermediate servo or 2-3 accumulator oil rings or bores leaking or accumulator piston stuck.
2. Intermediate band burned or broken.
3. Low oil pressure: Pressure regulator and/or boost valve stuck.

No Engine Braking In 1st Speed

1. Manual low control valve assembly

stuck.
2. Low oil pressure: Pressure regulator and/or boost valve stuck.
3. Low and reverse clutch piston inner seal damaged.

No Part Throttle Downshift

1. Oil pressure: Vacuum modulator assembly, modulator valve or pressure regulator valve train malfunctioning.
2. Detent valve and linkage sticking, disconnected or broken.
3. 2-3 shift valve stuck.

No Detent Downshifts

1. 2-3 valve stuck.
2. Detent valve and linkage sticking, disconnected or broken.

Low or High Shift Points

1. Oil pressure: Check engine vacuum at transmission end of modulator pipe.
2. Vacuum modulator assembly, vacuum line connections at engine and transmission, modulator valve, pressure regulator valve train.
3. Check governor for sticking valve, restricted or leaking feed holes, damaged pipes or plugged feed line.
4. Detent valve stuck open.
5. 1-2 or 2-3 valve train sticking.
6. Check case for porosity.

Won't Hold In Park

1. Manual linkage misadjusted.
2. Parking brake lever and actuator assembly defective.
3. Parking pawl broken or inoper'tive.
4. Defective or improperly installed inner lever and actuating rod assembly.
5. Parking lock bracket loose, burred or rough edges, or improperly installed.
6. Parking pawl disengaging spring missing, broken or installed improperly.

Burned Forward Clutch Plates

1. Check ball in clutch drum damaged, stuck or missing.
2. Clutch piston cracked, seals damaged or missing.
3. Low line pressure.
4. Pump cover oil seal rings missing, broken or undersize; ring groove oversize.
5. Transmission case valve body face not flat or porosity between channels.

Burned Intermediate Clutch Plates

T.H.M. 350
1. Intermediate clutch piston seals damaged or missing.
2. Low line pressure.
3. Transmission case valve body face not flat or porosity between channels.

Burned Intermediate Band

T.H.M. 250
1. Intermediate servo piston seals damaged or missing.
2. Low line pressure.
3. Transmission case valve body face not flat or porosity between channels.

Burned Direct Clutch Plates

1. Restricted orifice in vacuum line to modulator.

---

2. Check ball in clutch drum damaged, stuck or missing.
3. Defective modulator.
4. Clutch piston cracked, seals damaged or missing.
5. Transmission case valve body face not flat or porosity between channels.

Noisy Transmission

NOTE: Before checking transmission for noise, ensure noise is not coming from water pump, alternator or any belt driven accessory.

Park, Neutral & All Driving Ranges
1. Low fluid level.
2. Plugged or restricted screen.
3. Damaged screen to valve body gasket.
4. Porosity in valve body intake area.
5. Transmission fluid contaminated with water.
6. Porosity at transmission case intake port.
7. Improperly installed case to pump gasket.
8. Pump gears damaged.
9. Driving gear assembled backwards.
10. Crescent interference in pump.
11. Damaged or worn pump oil seals.
12. Loose converter to flywheel bolts.
13. Damaged converter.

1st, 2nd And/Or Reverse Gear
1. Planetary gears or thrust bearings damaged.
2. Damaged input or output ring gear.

Acceleration In Any Gear
1. Transmission case or transmission oil cooler lines contacting underbody.
2. Broken or loose engine mounts.

Squeal At Low Vehicle Speed
1. Speedometer driven gear shaft seal requires lubrication or replacement.

Converter Clutch Applied in All Ranges, Engine Stalls When Transmission Put in Gear

1. Converter clutch apply valve in auxiliary valve body stuck in apply position.

Converter Clutch Applies Erratically

1. Vacuum hose leak.
2. Vacuum switch malfunction.
3. Release oil orifice at pump blocked or restricted.
4. Turbine shaft "O" ring damaged or missing.
5. Converter malfunction, clutch pressure plate warped, etc.
6. "O" ring at solenoid damaged or missing.
7. Solenoid bolts loose.

Converter Clutch Applies at Very Low or Very High 3rd Gear Speeds

1. Governor switch malfunction.
2. Governor malfunction.
3. High line pressures.
4. Converter clutch valve sticking or binding.
5. Solenoid malfunction.

Converter Clutch Applied at All Times in 3rd Gear

1. Governor pressure switch shorted to ground.
2. Ground wire from solenoid shorted to case.

MAINTENANCE

Fluid should be checked every 6,000 miles with engine idling, selector lever in neutral position, parking brake set and transmission at operating temperature. Use only General Motors Dexron transmission fluid when adding oil. Do not overfill.

Every 24,000 miles, except on 1980-83 models, remove drain plug in transmission oil pan and drain transmission oil sump. Add 1½ quarts after replacing plug, check fluid and add enough fluid to bring level to Full mark. On 1980-83 models drain transmission oil sump every 100,000 miles. Add 2½ quarts on vehicles equipped with THM 250 units and 3 quarts on vehicles equipped with THM 350 units after replacing plug, check fluid and add enough fluid to bring level to ½ inch below Add mark.

NOTE: A revised type Dexron fluid is used in these transmissions. An early change to a darker color from the usual red color and or a strong odor that is usually associated with overheated fluid is normal, and should not be treated as a positive sign of needed maintenance or failure.

The normal maintenance schedule for drain and refill of this type fluid, except on 1980 models, remains unchanged at 24,000 miles under normal service and 12,000 miles under severe operating conditions, such as trailer towing. On 1980-83 models, drain and refill transmission every 100,000 miles under normal service and every 15,000 miles under severe operating conditions.

MANUAL LINKAGE, ADJUST

Buick Exc. Skyhawk

Console Shift, 1977-81 Century, 1977-83 Electra, LeSabre & Regal
1. Place selector lever in Park position.
2. Place transmission lever in Park position.
3. Position pin to obtain a free pin fit in the transmission lever and torque nut to 15-25 ft. lbs.
4. Check for proper operation.

Console Shift, 1977-79 Skylark
Refer to Chevrolet for adjustment procedure.

Column Shift 1977-83
1. Loosen adjusting clamp bolt.
2. Place selector lever against Neutral stop.
3. Place transmission in Neutral.
4. Tighten clamp bolt to 17-23 ft. lbs.

Chevrolet Exc. Monza & Vega

Console Shift 1977-81 Camaro, Malibu & Monte Carlo, 1977-79 Nova & Buick Skylark
1. Loosen swivel screw so rod is free to move

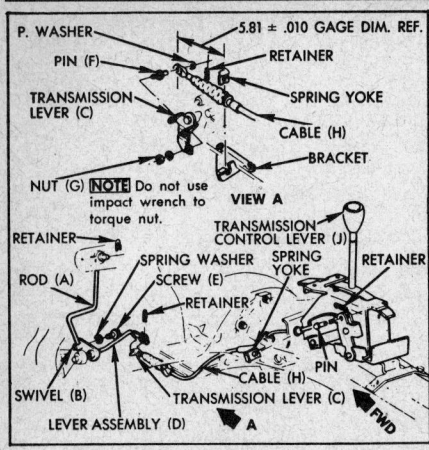

Fig. 3 Manual linkage adjustment. Camaro, Malibu & Monte Carlo, Nova & Buick Skylark

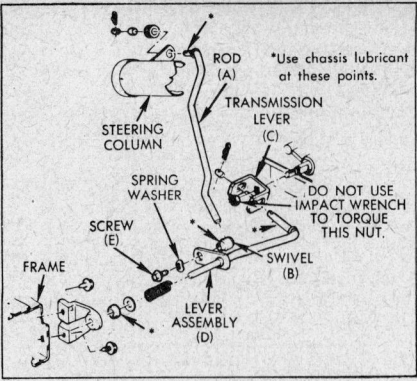

Fig. 4 Column shift linkage. 1977–79 All (Typical)

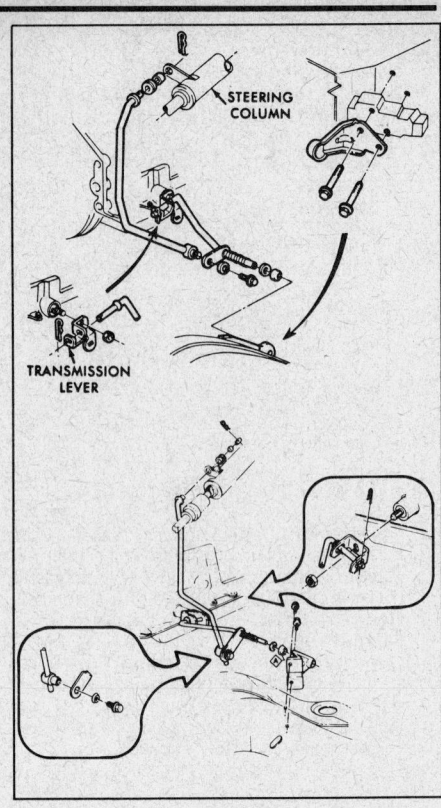

Fig. 5 Column shift linkage, 1980–83 intermediates (top) & full size (bottom)

in swivel, Fig. 3.

2. Place transmission control lever in Drive and loosen pin in transmission lever, so it moves in the slot.
3. Move transmission lever counterclockwise to L1 detent and then three detents clockwise to Drive position. Tighten nut on transmission lever to 20 ft. lbs.
4. Place transmission control lever in Park and ignition switch in the Lock position and pull lightly against lock stop, then tighten swivel screw to 20 ft. lbs. Check for proper operation.

Column Shift, 1977–83 All

1. Place transmission lever in Neutral by moving lever counter-clockwise to L1 detent then clockwise three detent positions to Neutral.
2. Place selector lever in Neutral as determined by mechanical stop on steering column. Do not use indicator as reference.
3. Assemble swivel, spring washer and screw to lever assembly then tighten screw to 20 ft. lbs., Figs. 4 and 5.

Astre & Vega, 1977–80 Monza, Skyhawk, Starfire & Sunbird

1. Loosen nut on transmission lever, Fig. 6.
2. Place transmission control shifter in Neutral position.
3. Place transmission lever in Neutral position.
4. Torque transmission lever nut to 20 ft. lbs.
5. Check for proper operation.

Oldsmobile Exc. Starfire

Console Shift

1. Loosen shift rod clamp screw and pin in transmission manual lever. Place shift handle and transmission manual lever in Park position.
2. With rod held lightly against Park stop, tighten screw in clamp at lower end of shift rod.
3. Move pin to give "free pin" fit in manual lever and tighten nut.

Column Shift

1. Loosen shift rod clamp screw and place outer lever in the Neutral position. Hold

column shift lever in Neutral position and tighten clamp. Check operation.

Pontiac Exc. Astre & Sunbird

Console Shift

1. Disconnect shift cable at transmission lever.
2. Adjust back drive, as outlined under "Back Drive, Adjust" procedure.
3. Unlock ignition switch, move transmission lever two detents counterclockwise, then place transmission shift lever against Neutral stop.
4. Assemble cable to transmission lever, torque nut to 20 ft. lbs.

Column Shift

With shift rod clamp and screw loosely assembled to shift rod, set transmission outer lever in Park position. Check to see that steering column lever is in Park position and tighten clamp on shift rod.

BACK DRIVE, ADJUST

1. Disconnect lower rod at transmission lever.
2. Move transmission lever to Park position.
3. Place transmission selector lever in Park position.
4. Attach lower rod to transmission lever and check for proper operation.

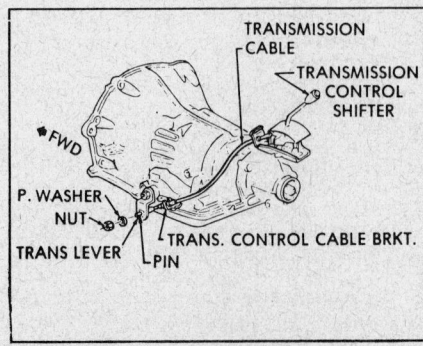

Fig. 6 Manual linkage adjustment. 1977–80 Astre, Monza, Skyhawk, Starfire, Sunbird & Vega

NOTE: Any inaccuracies in the above adjustments may result in premature failure of the transmission due to operation without the controls in full detent. Such operation results in reduced oil pressure and in turn partial engagement of the affected clutches.

T.V. OR DETENT CABLE, ADJUST

Models Equipped With Diesel Engine

1. Remove cruise control rod on vehicles equipped with cruise control.
2. Disconnect throttle valve linkage from throttle assembly.
3. Loosen lock nut on pump rod, then shorten rod by rotating several turns.
4. Rotate throttle lever assembly to full throttle position and secure in this position.
5. Lengthen pump rod by rotating in opposite direction as described in step 3 until injection pump lever contacts full throttle stop.
6. Release throttle lever assembly and tighten pump rod lock nut.
7. Disconnect pump rod from throttle lever assembly.
8. Connect throttle valve linkage to throttle assembly.
9. Depress metal locking tab on upper end of cable and hold in this position.
10. Position slider through fitting and away from lever assembly until slider contacts metal fitting.

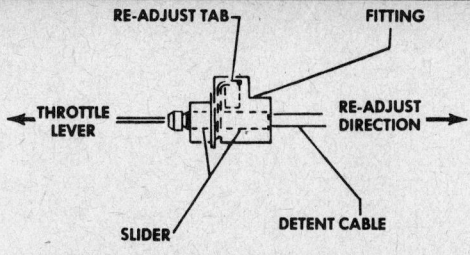

Fig. 6A Self adjusting throttle valve cable

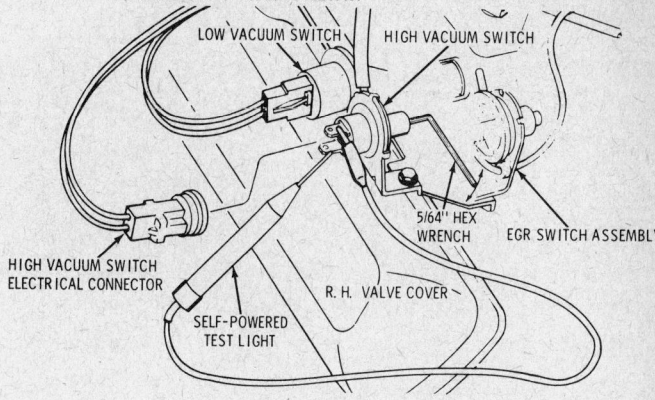

Fig. 7 Vacuum switch location.

11. Release metal tab, then rotate throttle lever assembly to full throttle position and release.
12. Connect pump rod to lever assembly, then connect cruise control throttle rod, if equipped.
13. On models equipped with cruise control, adjust servo throttle rod until minimum amount of slack is present. Install clip into first hole closest to bellcrank that is within servo bail.

Models Equipped With Gasoline Engine

1. With engine off, depress locking tab and move slider rearward through fitting until slider contacts fitting, Fig. 6A.
2. Release locking tab, then move carburetor throttle lever to wide open position and release.
3. Check cable for sticking or binding, then test vehicle for proper operation.
4. If transmission does not shift properly, raise and support vehicle and remove transmission oil pan. Inspect throttle lever and bracket assembly on valve body for damage. Check to ensure that throttle valve exhaust valve rod is not worn or damaged. Check to ensure that lifter spring holds lifter rod against bottom of valve body and that throttle valve plunger is not sticking.

INTERMEDIATE BAND, ADJUST

Turbo Hydra-Matic 250

Since the Turbo Hydra-Matic 250 transmission uses an intermediate band instead of a clutch (used in the Turbo Hydra-Matic 350 transmission) to control the operation of the planetary gear sets, it is necessary to adjust the intermediate band as follows:

1. Loosen adjusting screw lock nut, located on case right side, 1/2 turn.
2. Torque adjusting screw to 30 inch pounds, then back off screw 3 turns.
3. Torque adjusting screw lock nut to 15 foot pounds while holding adjusting screw in position.

T.H.M. 250C & 350C TORQUE CONVERTER CLUTCH SWITCH ADJUSTMENTS

Low Vacuum Switch

1. Disconnect vacuum and electrical connectors from low vacuum switch, Fig. 7.
2. Connect a suitable test light to either terminal of vacuum switch. Connect a suitable jumper cable from the other terminal to a good ground.
3. Connect remaining lead of test light to

power side of removed vacuum switch connector.
4. Attach suitable vacuum pump to vacuum port of switch.
5. Turn ignition on, then actuate vacuum pump. On V6-231, 252 engines, test light should remain off until vacuum pump gauge reads 5.5–6.5 in. Hg. On V8-265, 301 engines the test light should remain off until vacuum gauge reads 6.5–7.5 in. Hg. On V8-350 gas engines, test light should remain off until vacuum gauge reads 7.5–8.5 in. Hg. On V8-350 diesel engines, test light should remain off until vacuum gauge reads 5–6 in. Hg.
6. Decrease vacuum slowly. Light should remain on until vacuum drops to .3–1.3 in. Hg. on V6-231, 252 engines, 1.2–2.2 in. Hg. on V8-265, 301 engines, 1.5–2.5 in. Hg. on V8-350 gas engines and 3.5–4.5 in. Hg. on V8-350 diesel engines. Decreasing vacuum beyond above values should cause light to go out.
7. If above results cannot be obtained, switch is defective and must be replaced.
8. The point at which light comes on and the point at which light goes out must have at least 4 in. of vacuum difference.

High Vacuum Switch

NOTE: The high vacuum switch must be adjusted anytime the throttle rod, transmission vacuum valve and high idle speed adjustments are changed.

1. Disconnect high vacuum switch electrical connector, Fig. 7.
2. Connect the leads of a suitable test light across the terminals of the high vacuum switch.
3. Energize fast idle solenoid by disconnecting pink and green wire from coolant switch and operate engine at high idle speed, then remove cap from back of high vacuum switch.
4. Before adjustment is performed, the test lght must be on, indicating that the switch contacts are closed. If test light is off, close the switch contacts by turning switch adjusting screw clockwise until contacts close.
5. Adjust vacuum switch by turning adjusting screw counterclockwise until switch

contact just opens and test light goes off. Turn adjusting screw counterclockwise an additional 1/8–3/16 turn.
6. Reinstall cap on back of vacuum switch and reconnect high vacuum switch and coolant switch electrical connectors.

IN CAR REPAIRS
Valve Body Assembly

Without Locking Clutch
1. Remove oil pan and strainer.
2. Remove retaining pin to disconnect downshift actuating lever bracket, remove valve body attaching bolts and detent roller and spring assembly.
3. Remove valve body assembly while disconnecting manual control valve link from range selector inner lever.

CAUTION: Do not drop valve.

4. Remove manual valve and link from valve body assembly.
5. Reverse procedure to install.

With Locking Clutch
1. Remove oil pan and filter.
2. Remove detent roller spring assembly from valve body, then disconnect solenoid wires from governor pressure switch and case electrical connector.
3. Remove solenoid attaching bolts, then the solenoid.
4. Remove manual shaft retaining clip and slide manual shaft outward.
5. Remove valve body attaching bolts, then the valve body.
6. Remove auxiliary valve body attaching bolts, then the auxiliary valve body from the valve body.
7. Reverse procedure to install.

Auxiliary Valve Body Solenoid

1. Remove oil pan and filter.
2. Remove solenoid wire clip, then disconnect solenoid electrical connectors.
3. Remove two solenoid attaching bolts, then the solenoid, Fig. 8.
4. Reverse procedure to install.

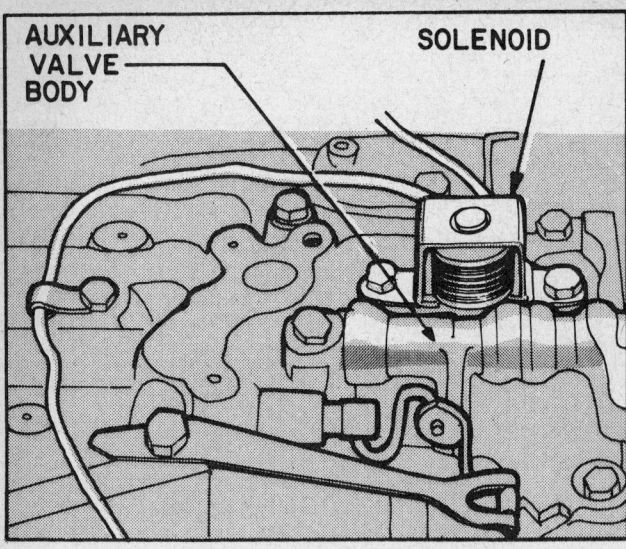

Fig. 8 Auxiliary valve body solenoid

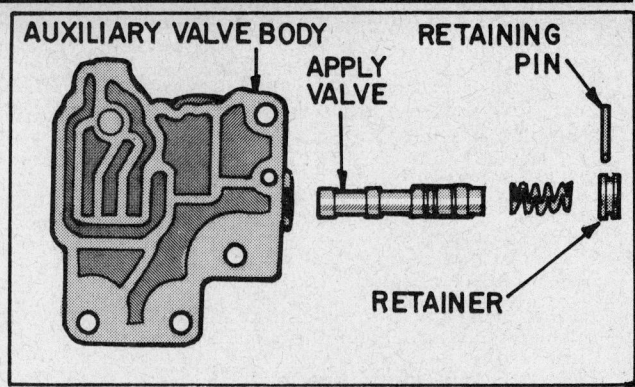

Fig. 9 Auxiliary valve body & valve

Auxiliary Valve Body and Valve

1. Remove solenoid as outlined above.
2. Remove retaining bolts, then the auxiliary valve body.
3. Remove apply valve retaining pin, retainer, spring, then the apply valve, Fig. 9.
4. Reverse procedure to install.

Governor Pressure Switch

1. Drain transmission fluid from pan, then remove pan.
2. Disconnect electrical connector from switch, then remove switch using suitable socket.
3. Reverse procedure to install.

Governor

1. Remove governor cover retainer and cover.
2. Remove governor.

Intermediate Clutch Accumulator Piston Assembly

1. Remove two oil pan bolts adjacent to accumulator piston cover, install compressor on pan lip and retain with these two bolts, Fig. 10.
2. Compress intermediate clutch accumulator piston cover and remove retaining ring piston cover and O ring from case.
3. Remove spring and intermediate clutch accumulator piston.

Vacuum Modulator & Modulator Valve Assembly

1. Disconnect vacuum hose from modulator stem and remove vacuum modulator screw and retainer.
2. Remove modulator and its O ring.
3. Remove modulator valve from case.

Extension Housing Oil Seal

1. Remove propeller shaft.
2. Pry out lip seal with screwdriver or small chisel.

Manual Shaft, Range Selector Inner Lever & Parking Linkage Assemblies

1. Remove oil pan and strainer.
2. Remove manual shaft to case retainer and unthread jam nut holding range selector inner lever to manual shaft.
3. Remove jam nut and remove manual shaft from range selector inner lever and case. *Do not remove manual shaft lip seal unless replacement is required.*
4. Disconnect parking pawl actuating rod from range selector inner lever and remove bolt from case.
5. Remove bolts and parking lock bracket.
6. Remove pawl disengaging spring.
7. If necessary to replace pawl or shaft, clean up bore in case and remove shaft retaining plug, shaft and pawl.

TRANSMISSION, REPLACE

Buick Exc. Skyhawk

1. Disconnect battery ground cable.
2. Raise car and remove propeller shaft. If necessary, disconnect exhaust crossover

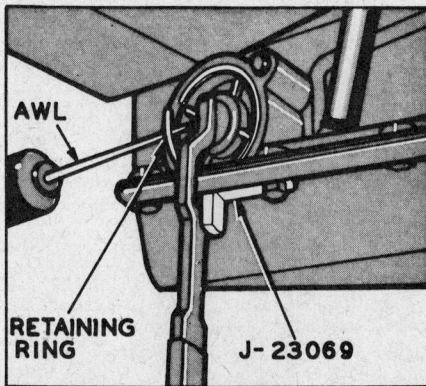

Fig. 10 Intermediate clutch accumulator piston removal

pipe. On Turbo 350 units, remove catalytic converter support bracket, if equipped.
3. Place suitable jack under transmission and fasten transmission securely to jack.
4. Remove vacuum line from vacuum modulator.
5. Loosen cooler line nuts and separate cooler lines from transmission.
6. Remove detent cable from accelerator or carburetor lever assembly. *Do not bend cable.* Remove plastic guide from bracket and slide cable out through slot.
7. Remove detent cable from detent valve link.
8. Remove crossmember.
9. Disconnect speedometer cable, shift linkage and filler pipe. Remove filler pipe.
10. Support engine at oil pan.
11. Remove transmission flywheel cover pan.
12. Mark flywheel and converter for reassembly and remove three flywheel to converter bolts.
13. Be sure transmission is supported by transmission jack and remove transmission case to engine block bolts.
14. Move transmission rearward to provide clearance between converter and crankshaft. Install converter holding tool, lower transmission and remove.

1982–83 Cadillac

1. Disconnect negative battery cable and disconnect detent cable at upper end, then remove top two transmission to engine bolts.
2. Raise and support vehicle.
3. Disconnect transmission linkage and remove speedometer drive cable at transmission, then, using suitable tools, disconnect oil coooler lines at transmission and cap lines and plug connector holes. Move oil cooler lines aside.
4. Disconnect vacuum pipe hose from modulator and position out of way, then remove propeller shaft and lower flexplate inspection cover.
5. Remove the three converter to flexplate attaching bolts, rotating converter and flexplate for bolt accessibility. Do not pry on flexplate ring gear or transmission case.
6. Place suitable jack under rear of engine, then remove four bolts from tunnel strap and remove strap.
7. Remove two rear engine mount to extension housing bolts, then position suitable jack under transmission and raise it sufficiently to take load off rear engine support and remove converter bracket.

8. Remove one bolt from strut support to crossmember, then remove two bolts from each side of rear engine support and slide support back out of position. Support will hang from parking brake cable and exhaust pipe.
9. Remove rear engine support crossmember and remove four remaining transmission housing to engine attaching bolts, lowering engine and transmission, if necessary, to gain access.
10. Disengaging transmission case from locating dowels on engine, move transmission toward rear of car.
11. Install converter holding clamp, J-21366, or equivilant, on front of transmission case and lower transmission from car.
12. Reverse procedure to install.

Chevrolet Exc. Monza & Vega

1. Disconnect negative battery cable and raise car.
2. Remove propeller shaft, disconnect speedometer cable, detent cable, modulator vacuum line and oil cooler lines. Disconnect catalytic converter support bracket from transmission.
3. Disconnect shift linkage.
4. Support transmission with suitable jack and remove crossmember.
5. Remove converter under pan.
6. Remove converter to flywheel bolts.
7. On all models except Nova, loosen exhaust pipe to manifold bolts approximately 1/4 inch. Lower transmission until jack is barely supporting transmission.

NOTE: On V8 engines, care must be taken not to lower the rear of the transmission too far as the distributor housing may be forced against firewall causing damage to the distributor.

8. Remove transmission to engine mounting bolts and remove oil filler tube at transmission.
9. Raise transmission to its normal position, support engine with jack and slide transmission rearward from engine and lower it away from vehicle.
10. Reverse procedure to install.

Oldsmobile Exc. Starfire

1. Disconnect battery ground cable.
2. Disconnect detent cable from accelerator or carburetor lever assembly.
3. Remove transmission oil level dipstick. Remove catalytic converter support bracket, if equipped.
4. Raise car and remove detent cable from link. Plug hole.
5. Disconnect oil cooler lines at transmission.
6. Remove flywheel cover pan and mark converter and flywheel for reassembly. Remove three flywheel to converter bolts.
7. Disconnect vacuum modulator line. Remove speedometer clip and driven gear. Plug hole.
8. Disconnect shift linkage.
9. Remove propeller shaft.
10. Support transmission with a suitable jack and remove crossmember.
11. Lower transmission slightly and remove transmission to engine bolts.
12. Remove oil level indicator tube and clip holding detent cable to tube.
13. Lower transmission being careful not to damage cooler lines, detent cable, modulator line and shift linkage.
14. Reverse procedure to install.

Pontiac Exc. Astre & Sunbird

1. Disconnect battery ground cable and release parking brake.
2. Raise car and remove propeller shaft. Remove catalytic converter support bracket, if equipped.
3. Disconnect speedometer cable, vacuum hose at modulator, detent cable at transmission and shift linkage.

NOTE: When removing detent cable, be careful not to bend it.

4. Support transmission with a suitable jack and remove crossmember.
5. Remove converter dust pan, mark flywheel and converter for reassembly and remove flywheel to converter bolts. Make sure converter hub is free of converter.

6. Disconnect transmission filler pipe at engine and remove pipe from transmission.
7. Lower transmission and engine to gain access to cooler line fitting nuts and disconnect cooler lines. On some models it may be necessary to loosen the exhaust system.
8. With transmission in lowered position, remove the transmission to engine bolts.
9. Raise transmission to its normal position, support engine and slide transmission rearward and lower it away from car.

NOTE: When lowering transmission, keep rear of transmission lower than the front so as not to lose the converter.

10. Reverse procedure to install.

Astre & Vega, Monza, Skyhawk, Starfire & Sunbird

1. Disconnect battery ground cable.
2. Remove air cleaner and disconnect downshift cable from carburetor. Release parking brake.
3. Raise vehicle and remove propeller shaft. Disconnect torque arm from transmission, if equipped.
4. Remove catalytic converter bracket from transmission and disconnect exhaust pipe and converter.
5. Disconnect speedo cable, modulator vacuum line, shift linkage and downshift cable from transmission.
6. Support transmission with a suitable jack and disconnect transmission rear mount from crossmember, then remove crossmember.
7. Remove converter cover, then converter to flywheel bolts.
8. Lower transmission until it is barely supported and remove transmission to engine bolts.
9. Remove oil filter tube and on V8 models, disconnect oil cooler lines.
10. Raise transmission, support engine with a suitable jack and slide transmission rearward and lower unit from vehicle.
11. Reverse procedure to install.

Turbo Hydra-Matic 325-4L Automatic Transmission

TRANSMISSION IDENTIFICATION

This transmission may be identified by a model tag attached to the transmission on the left side of the converter housing.

Eldorado, Riviera, Seville & Toronado
1982–83   AB, AJ, AL, AM,
BJ, BE, OE, OK

DESCRIPTION

The Turbo Hydra-Matic 325-4L transmission, Fig. 1, is a fully automatic front wheel drive unit consisting of a four-element torque converter with converter clutch, three compound planetary gear sets and an overdrive unit. Five multiple disc clutches, two roller clutches and a band provide the friction elements required to obtain the desired function of the compound planetary gear sets and the overdrive unit. The combination of the compound planetary gear sets and the overdrive unit provides four forward ratios and one reverse. Changing of the gear ratios is fully automatic in relation to vehicle speed and engine torque.

The torque converter couples the engine to the overdrive unit and planetary gears through oil and hydraulically provides torque multiplication. It consists of a pump or driven member, a turbine or driven member and a stator assembly. With the engine running, the converter pump acts as a centrifugal pump, picking up oil at its center and discharging it at the rim located between the blades. The shape of the converter pump blades causes the oil to leave the pump spinning in a clockwise direction towards the turbine blades. As the oil strikes the turbine blades, it creates a force which enables the turbine to turn. After the oil has imparted its force to the turbine, it follows the contour of the turbine shell and blades and leaves the turbine in a counterclockwise direction, or opposite engine rotation. If this oil is allowed to enter the inner section of the converter pump, it will hinder the ability of the pump to deliver oil with any force due to the opposing rotation of pump blades to oil flow. To prevent this from happening, a stator assembly is added to redirect the oil returning from the turbine and change its rotation back to that of the converter pump blades. The stator is located between the pump and turbine and is mounted on a one-way roller clutch which allows it to rotate clockwise, but not counterclockwise. The clockwise flow of oil is used to assist the engine in turning the converter pump. This increases the force of the oil driving the turbine and results in the multiplication of torque from the engine. As turbine and vehicle speed increase, the stator becomes inactive

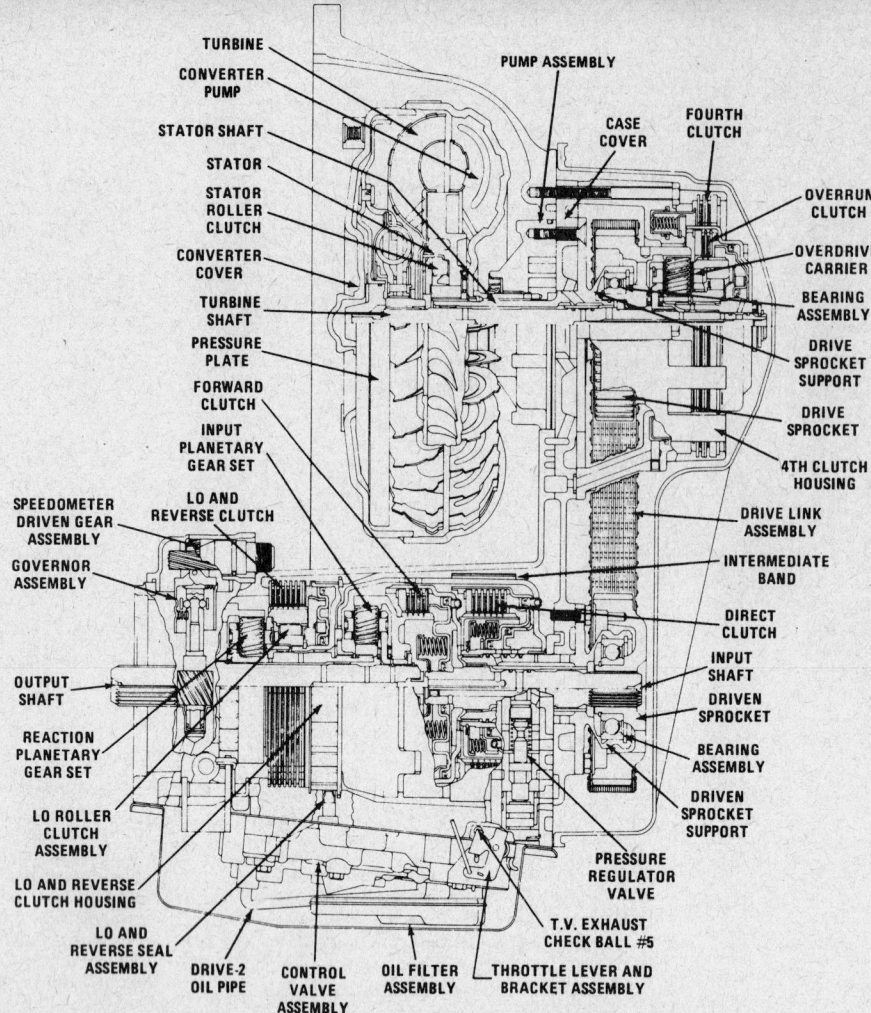

Fig. 1   Sectional view of Turbo Hydra-Matic 325-4L transmission

and torque multiplication ceases. At this point, the converter is acting as a fluid coupling, since the converter pump and turbine are turning at approximately the same speed.

The converter clutch provides a direct mechanical coupling of the engine to the transmission. This mechanical coupling prevents the slippage that occurs in conventional torque converters and results in improved fuel economy. The application and release of the converter clutch is determined by a series of controls and by drive range selection.

The hydraulic system in this transmission is pressurized by a gear-type pump to provide the working pressures required to operate the friction elements and automatic controls.

MAINTENANCE

Checking Fluid Level

To check fluid level, drive vehicle at least 15 miles to allow fluid to reach normal operating temperature (190°–200 °F). With vehicle on level surface, parking brake applied and engine running at slow idle, move selector lever through each range, then into Park position. The level on the dipstick should be at the Full Hot mark. To bring fluid level from the Add to Full mark requires only one pint of fluid. If vehicle cannot be driven sufficiently to bring fluid to normal operating temperature, the level on the dipstick should be

approximately ½ inch above the Full mark with fluid temperature at 65–85°F, Fig. 2.

If additional fluid is required, use Dexron II, or equivalent, automatic transmission fluid.

NOTE: The transmission fluid now being used may appear to be darker or have a stronger odor. This is normal and not a positive sign of required transmission maintenance or transmission failure.

CAUTION: An overfilled transmission can cause foaming and loss of fluid through the vent, resulting in slippage and/or transmission failure. A low fluid level can also cause slippage, particularly when the transmission is cold or the vehicle is driven on a steep hill.

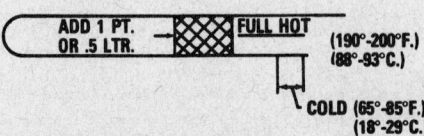

'COLD' READING IS ABOVE 'FULL' MARK

Fig. 2   Transmission oil dipstick level

Every 100,000 miles, the transmission fluid should be drained, the oil pan removed, the screen cleaned and fresh fluid added. For vehicles subjected to more severe use such as heavy city traffic, where temperatures reach 90°F, or prolonged periods of idle or towing, this maintenance should be performed every 15,000 miles.

Changing Fluid

1. Raise and support vehicle, then position drain pan under transmission oil pan.
2. Remove front and side oil pan attaching bolts, then loosen rear bolts approximately four turns.
3. Carefully pry transmission oil pan loose with screwdriver and allow fluid to drain.
4. Remove remaining bolts, pan and gasket.
5. Drain remaining fluid from pan, clean with solvent and dry with compressed air.
6. Remove transmission screen, clean thoroughly with solvent and dry with compressed air.

NOTE: Paper or felt type filters should be replaced.

7. Install new gasket and "O"-ring onto screen assembly. Lubricate "O"-ring with petroleum jelly.

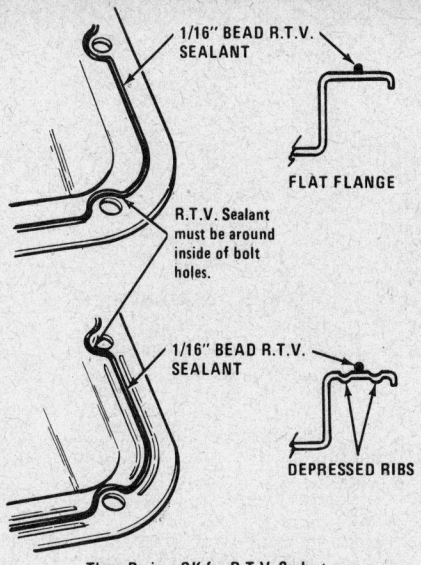

1/16" BEAD R.T.V. SEALANT

FLAT FLANGE

R.T.V. Sealant must be around inside of bolt holes.

1/16" BEAD R.T.V. SEALANT

DEPRESSED RIBS

These Designs OK for R.T.V. Sealant
Typical Oil Pan – Cutaway Section

Fig. 3   Flat or depressed rib sealing flange

8. Install transmission screen, then position new gasket onto pan and install pan. Torque pan attaching bolts to 12 ft. lbs.

NOTE: Some THM 325-4L transmissions may be built using R.T.V. (Room Temperature Vulcanizing) silicone sealant in place of standard gaskets. If oil pan or side cover is equipped with flat or depressed rib flanges, Fig. 3, use, a 1/16 inch bead of R.T.V. sealant to seal surfaces. If pan or side cover is equipped with a raised rib flange, Fig. 4, conventional gaskets must be used.

9. Lower vehicle and add approximately 5 qts. of Dexron II type transmission fluid through filler tube.
10. Apply parking brake, start engine and allow to idle. Do not race engine.
11. Move selector lever through each range, then position lever in Park and check fluid level.

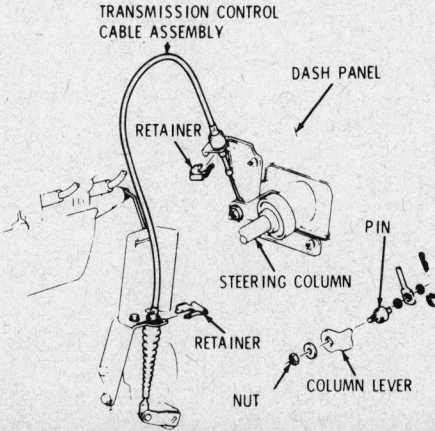

TRANSMISSION CONTROL CABLE ASSEMBLY

DASH PANEL

RETAINER

PIN

STEERING COLUMN

RETAINER

NUT

COLUMN LEVER

Fig. 5   Shift control cable adjustment

IN-VEHICLE ADJUSTMENTS

Shift Control Cable, Adjust

1. Position steering column shift lever in neutral gate notch, then loosen attaching nut at column lever, Fig. 5.
2. Set transmission lever in neutral detent, then move pin to give "free pin" fit in column lever and torque attaching nut two to 20 ft. lbs.
3. Check that starter will not crank in any position except Neutral or Park. Adjust neutral start switch, if necessary.

Throttle Valve (T.V.) Cable, Adjust

Self-Adjusting Type
1. Depress lock tab, then move slider in direction away from carburetor throttle body, Fig. 6.
2. Release lock tab and open carburetor lever to full throttle stop position to automatically adjust T.V. cable.

Manual Type, With Gasoline Engine
1. Pushing upward, unlock T.V. cable snap-lock button, Fig. 7.
2. Rotate carburetor lever to wide open throttle position and hold.
3. Pushing downward, lock T.V. cable snap lock-button, then release carburetor throttle lever.

Manual Type, With Diesel Engine
1. Remove cruise control rod from bell-crank, if equipped.
2. Unlock T.V. cable snap-lock button, then disconnect T.V. cable and throttle rod from bell crank, Fig. 8.
3. Rotate bell crank to full throttle stop and hold in this position.
4. Pull throttle rod and pump lever to full throttle stop position, Fig. 9, then adjust throttle rod to meet bell crank. Do not connect throttle rod to bell crank at this time.
5. Release bell crank, then reconnect T.V. cable.
6. Rotate and hold bell crank to full throttle stop, then lock T.V. cable snap-lock button.
7. Reconnect throttle and cruise control rods.

NOTE: If bell crank full throttle stop is not obtained when accelerator pedal is completely depressed, all full throttle adjustments must be made by completely depressing the accelerator pedal instead of rotating the bell crank by hand.

IN-VEHICLE REPAIRS

Valve Body, Replace

1. Drain transmission fluid and remove oil pan and screen.
2. Remove screw and disconnect T.V. cable from transmission.
3. Remove throttle lever and bracket assembly, then disconnect converter clutch wiring connections.
4. Remove oil transfer pipes and hold-down brackets.
5. Support valve body and remove retaining bolts.
6. Remove valve body, noting location of check ball.

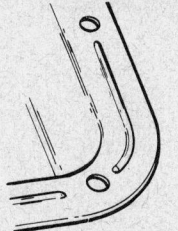

RAISED RIB

Typical Oil Pan – Cutaway Section

Fig. 4   Raised rib sealing flange

NOTE: If accumulator housing is removed, support spacer plate during removal and note location of check balls in spacer plate and accumulator housing.

7. Reverse procedure to install. Torque valve body retaining bolts to 10 ft. lbs.

NOTE: Intermediate band anchor pin must locate on intermediate band, or damage to transmission may result.

Intermediate Servo, Replace

1. Install tool No. J-28493 on transmission case and tighten bolt to depress servo cover.
2. Using a small screwdriver, remove servo cover retaining ring, then remove tool.
3. Remove servo cover, then remove servo piston and band apply pin assembly.
4. Reverse procedure to install.

Speedometer Gears, Replace

1. Disconnect speedometer cable, then remove driven gear attaching bolt, retainer and driven gear.
2. Remove governor cover attaching screws and governor cover.
3. Remove governor and speedometer drive gear assembly.
4. Remove speedometer drive gear from governor assembly.
5. Reverse procedure to install.

Pressure Regulator Valve, Replace

1. Drain transmission fluid and remove oil pan and screen.

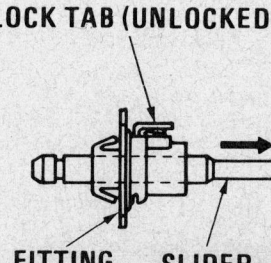

LOCK TAB (UNLOCKED)

FITTING   SLIDER

Fig. 6   Adjusting T.V. cable. Self-adjusting type

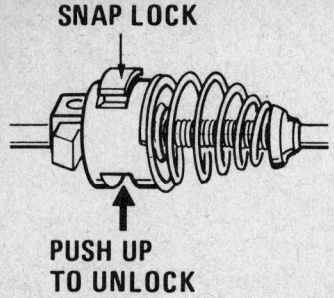

SNAP LOCK

PUSH UP TO UNLOCK

Fig. 7   Adjusting T.V. cable. Manual type (gasoline engine)

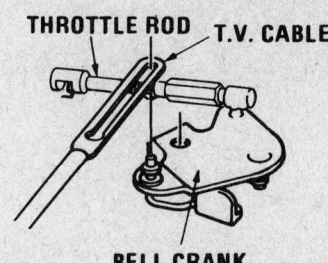

THROTTLE ROD   **T.V. CABLE**

BELL CRANK

Fig. 8   Disconnecting T.V. cable & throttle rod

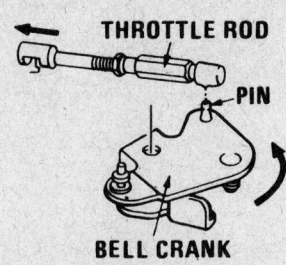

THROTTLE ROD

PIN

BELL CRANK

Fig. 9   Adjusting throttle rod

2. Push in on pressure regulator valve, and compress valve spring with a small screwdriver.
3. Remove retaining ring, then slowly release spring tension and remove pressure regulator valve.

TRANSMISSION, REPLACE

Exc. Models With Turbocharged Engine

1. Disconnect battery ground cable, then the speedometer cable.
2. Remove air cleaner assembly, then disconnect T.V. cable from bellcrank (diesel engine) or carburetor throttle lever (gasoline engine).
3. Support engine with suitable engine holding fixture.
4. Remove top and the two left upper final drive-to-transmission attaching bolts.
5. Remove remaining accessible engine-to-transmission bolts.
6. Raise and support vehicle, then remove starter.
7. Disconnect converter clutch electrical connections from transmission.
8. Disconnect and plug transmission cooler lines, then remove flywheel inspection cover.
9. On vehicles equipped with V-8 engines, disconnect "Y" pipe from left exhaust pipe.
10. Disconnect right exhaust pipe from exhaust manifold.
11. On all gasoline engine equipped vehicles, disconnect catalytic converter hanger bolts.
12. Lower and support exhaust system approximately five inches, then remove crossmember attaching bolts and the

crossmember.
13. Position a suitable transmission jack under transmission, then remove the three remaining final drive-to-transmission bolts.
14. Remove torque converter-to-flywheel attaching bolts, then disconnect shift linkage from transmission.
15. Remove final drive-support bracket bolt and the right transmission mount-through, and bracket bolts.
16. Remove left transmission mount-through bolt, then the lower support bracket-to-transmission bolt.
17. Raise transmission about two inches and remove remaining upper bracket-to-transmission bolts and the last engine-to-transmission bolt.
18. Carefully lower transmission while disengaging the final drive.
19. Install torque converter holding fixture and remove transmission from vehicle.
20. Reverse procedure to install. Torque starter mounting bolts to 30 ft. lbs., transmission mount-to-frame nut to 40 ft. lbs., transmission-to-engine attaching bolts to 35 ft. lbs., flywheel-to-converter bolts to 35 ft. lbs., final drive-to-transmission bolts to 30 ft. lbs. and final drive-support bracket bolt to 35 ft. lbs.

Models With Turbocharged Engine

1. Disconnect battery ground cable, then the speedometer cable.
2. Remove heated air pipe.
3. Remove turbocharger assembly, then the four top engine-to-transmission attaching bolts.
4. Remove top final drive-to-transmission bolt and two final drive-to-engine attaching bolts, then loosen retaining bracket at engine.

5. Support engine with a suitable engine holding fixture, then raise and support vehicle.
6. Disconnect shift linkage from transmission.
7. Disconnect and cap transmission cooler lines, then remove remaining final drive-to-transmission bolts.
8. Remove final drive cover, then disconnect right output shaft bearing support from engine.
9. Turn wheels to gain clearance between final drive and steering linkage, then separate final drive from transmission. Support final drive unit.
10. Remove outlet pipe/converter assembly which was disconnected when turbocharger was removed.
11. Remove starter and the two remaining transmission-to-engine attaching bolts.
12. Disconnect converter cover and position aside.
13. Remove flex plate-to-converter attaching bolts, then position transmission jack under transmission.
14. Remove both transmission mount-through bolts, then the right-mount bracket from transmission.
15. Remove left-mount brackets from both frame and transmission by pulling out inner fender liner and removing attaching bolts through access holes in frame.
16. Separate transmission from engine, then carefully lower and remove from vehicle.
17. Reverse procedure to install. Torque starter mounting bolts to 30 ft. lbs., transmission mount-to-frame nut to 40 ft. lbs., transmission-to-engine attaching bolts to 35 ft. lbs., flywheel-to-converter bolts to 35 ft. lbs., final drive-to-transmission bolts to 30 ft. lbs. and final drive-support bracket bolt to 35 ft. lbs.

Turbo Hydra-Matic 400 Automatic Transmission

TRANSMISSION IDENTIFICATION

An identification plate is attached to the transmission. The plate indicates year of production, code letters, and serial number.

	Code
BUICK	
1977–78 V8-350	BB
V8-350	OB
V8-403	OD
1979 V8-350	BB, OB
V8-403	OC, OD
1980 LeSabre	BB
Electra	BB, OB

	Code
CADILLAC	
1977–78 Fleetwood & DeVille Exc. E.F.I. & Hi. Alt.	AD
Fleetwood & DeVille E.F.I. Exc. Calif. Emiss.	AB
Fleetwood & DeVille Calif. Emiss. Exc. E.F.I.	AE
Fleetwood & DeVille Exc. E.F.I.,	

	Code
CADILLAC—Cont'd	
Hi. Alt. & Calif. Emiss.	AA
Fleetwood & DeVille Hi. Alt.	AL
Seville (2.56 Axle)	AC
Seville (3.08 Axle)	AH
1978 Seville V8-350 Diesel	AT
1979 Fleetwood & DeVille Exc. E.F.I. & Hi Alt.	AD

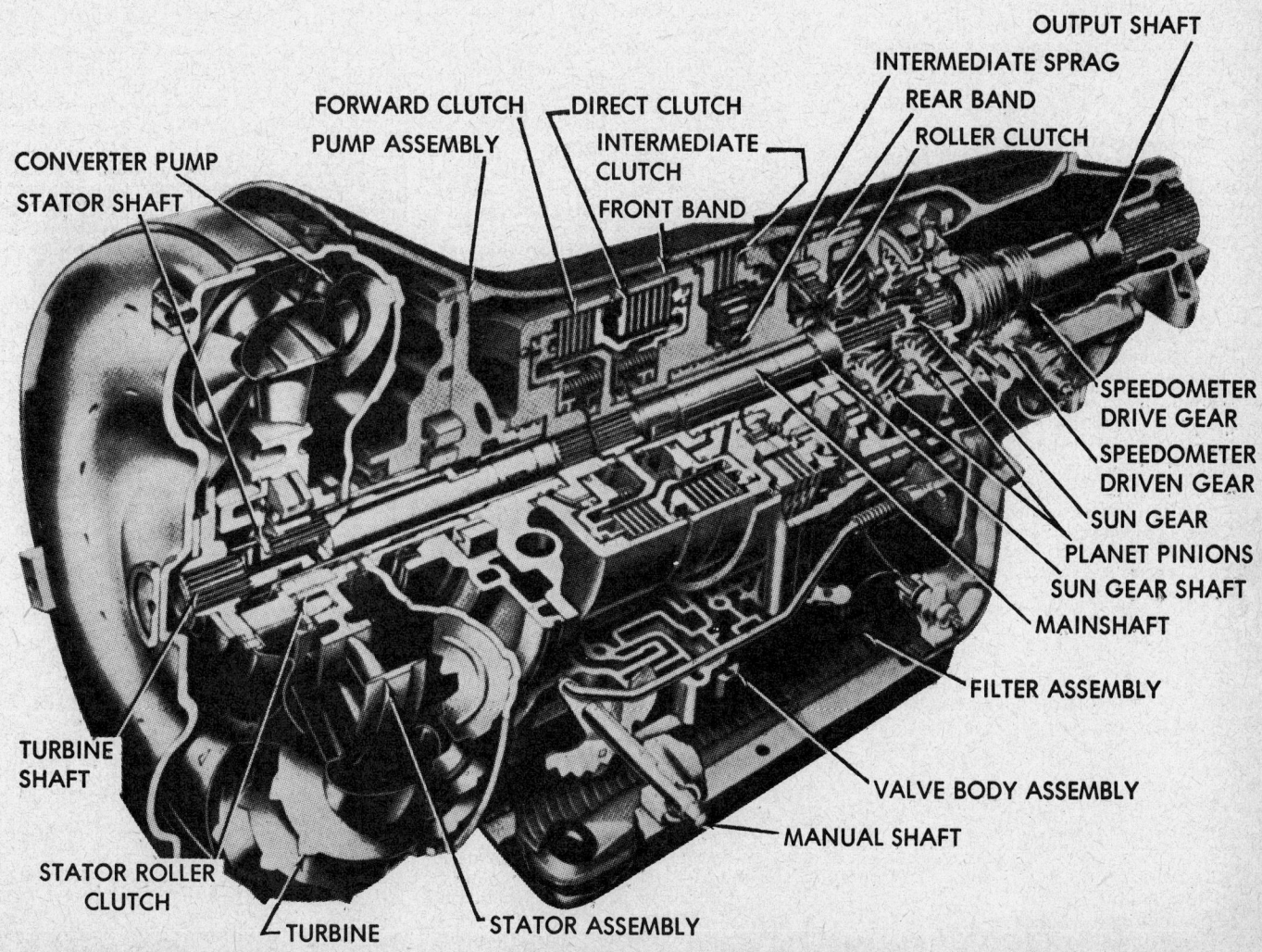

Fig. 1 Cutaway view of transmission assembly

	Code		Code		Code

CADILLAC—Cont'd

Fleetwood & DeVille Exc. Calif. . . . AB
Fleetwood & DeVille Calif. Exc.
 E.F.I. . . . . AE
Seville, Calif. . . . . AC
Seville, Hi Alt. . . . . AH
Seville, Exc. Calif. & Hi Alt. . . . . . . AA
1980 Fleetwood Coupe, Fleetwood
 Brougham, DeVille . . . . AB, AD, AE
1981 DeVille & Brougham①③ . . . . AE
 DeVille & Brougham②③ . . . . AD
 DeVille & Brougham④ . . . . AB

CHEVROLET

1977 V8-350 Corvette . . . . CB

OLDSMOBILE

1977–78 V8-350 Cutlass Wag. & 98 . . . . OB
 V8-403 Cutlass Wag. . . . . OC
 V8-403 98 . . . . OD
1979 V8-350 98 . . . . OB
 V8-403 98 (3.08, 3.23 axle) . . . . OC
 V8-403 98 (2.41, 2.56 axle) . . . . OD
1980 V8-305 98 . . . . OA
 V8-350 98 . . . . OB

PONTIAC

1977 V8-301 LeMans & Grand Prix . . . . PA
 V8-350 4 Bar. Carb. (LeMans Sta.
 Wag.) . . . . OB
 V8-350 Grand Prix . . . . PB

PONTIAC—Cont'd.

V8-400 LeMans & Grand Prix
 Police & Trailer . . . . PD
V8-400 LeMans Sta. Wag. Exc.
 Trailer . . . . PC
V8-400 Grand Prix Exc.
 Trailer . . . . PC
V8-403 LeMans Sta. Wag. Exc.
 Trailer . . . . OC

①—With 2.28 axle ratio.
②—With 2.73 axle ratio.
③—Except California.
④—California.

GENERAL DESCRIPTION

This transmission, Fig. 1, is a fully automatic unit consisting of a three-element hydraulic torque converter and a compound planetary gear set. Three multiple-disc clutches, two one-way clutches, and two bands provide the friction elements required to obtain the desired functions of the planetary gear set.

The torque converter, the multiple-disc clutches and the one-way clutches couple the engine to the planetary gears through oil pressure, providing three forward speeds and reverse. The torque converter, when required, supplements the gears by multiplying engine torque.

Torque Converter

The torque converter is of welded construction and is serviced as an assembly. The unit is made up of two vaned sections, or halves, that face each other in an oil-filled housing. The pump half of the converter is connected to the engine and the turbine half is connected to the transmission.

When the engine makes the converter pump revolve, it sends oil against the turbine, making it revolve also. The oil then returns in a circular flow back to the converter pump, continuing this flow as long as the engine is running.

Stator

The converter also has a smaller vaned section, called a stator, that funnels the oil back to the converter pump through smaller openings, at increased speed. The speeded up oil directs additional force to the engine-driven converter pump, thereby multiplying engine torque. In other words, without the stator, the unit is nothing more than a fluid coupling.

External Controls

The external control connections to the transmission are:
1. Manual linkage to select the desired operating range.
2. Engine vacuum to operate the vacuum modulator unit.
3. An electrical signal to operate an electric detent solenoid.

Vacuum Modulator

A vacuum modulator is used to sense engine torque input to the transmission automatically. The vacuum modulator transmits this signal to the pressure regulator, which controls line pressure, so that all torque requirements of the transmission are met and proper shift spacing is obtained at all throttle openings.

Detent Solenoid

The detent solenoid is activated by an electric switch at the carburetor. When the throttle is opened sufficiently to close this switch, the solenoid in the transmission is activated, causing a downshift at speeds below 70 mph. At lower speeds, downshifts will occur at lesser throttle openings without use of the electric switch.

TROUBLE SHOOTING GUIDE

Oil Pressure High or Low

1. Vacuum line or fittings clogged or leaking.
2. Vacuum modulator.
3. Modulator valve.
4. Pressure regulator.
5. Oil pump.
6. Governor.

No Drive In Drive Range

1. Low oil level (check for leaks).
2. Manual control linkage not adjusted properly.
3. Low oil pressure. Check for blocked strainer, defective pressure regulator, pump assembly or pump drive gear. See that tangs have not been damaged by converter.
4. Check control valve assembly to see if manual valve has been disconnected from manual lever pin.
5. Forward clutch may be struck or damaged. Check pump feed circuits to forward clutch including clutch drum ball check.
6. Sprag or roller clutch assembled incorrectly.

1–2 Shift At Full Throttle Only

1. Detent switch may be sticking or defective.
2. Detent solenoid may be stuck open, loose or have leaking gasket.
3. Control valve assembly may be leaking, damaged or incorrectly installed.
4. Porous transmission case.

1st Speed Only—No 1–2 Shift

1. Governor valve may be sticking.
2. Driven gear in governor assembly loose, worn or damaged.
3. The 1–2 shift valve in control valve assembly stuck closed. Check governor feed channels for blocks, leaks, and position. Also check control valve body gaskets for leaks and damage.
4. Intermediate clutch plug in case may be leaking or blown out.
5. Check for porosity between channels and for blocked governor feed channels in case.
6. Check intermediate clutch for proper operation.

No 2–3 Shift—1st & 2nd Only

1. Detent solenoid may be stuck open.
2. Detent switch may not be properly adjusted.
3. Control valve assembly may be stuck, leaking, damaged, or incorrectly installed.
4. Check direct clutch case center support for broken, leaking or missing oil rings.
5. Check clutch piston seals and piston ball check in clutch assembly.

Moves Forward In Neutral

1. Manual control linkage improperly adjusted.
2. Forward clutch does not release.
3. Oil pump.
4. Internal linkage.

No Drive In Reverse or Slips In Reverse

1. Check oil level.
2. Manual control linkage improperly adjusted.
3. Vacuum modulator assembly may be defective.
4. Vacuum modulator valve sticking.
5. Strainer may be restricted or leaking at intake.
6. Regulator or boost valve in pump assembly may be sticking.
7. Control valve assembly may be stuck, leaking or damaged.
8. Rear servo and accumulator may have damaged or missing servo piston seal ring.
9. Reverse band burned out or damaged. Determine that apply pin or anchor pins engage properly.

10. Direct clutch may be damaged or may have stuck ball check in piston.
11. Forward clutch does not release.
12. Low—reverse ball check missing from case.

Slips In All Ranges & On Starts

1. Check oil level.
2. Vacuum modulator defective.
3. Modulator valve sticking.
4. Strainer assembly plugged or leaking at neck.
5. Pump assembly regulator or boost valve sticking.
6. Leaks from damaged gaskets or cross leaks from porosity of case.
7. Forward and direct clutches burned.

Slips 1—2 Shift

1. Incorrect oil level.
2. Vacuum modulator valve sticking.
3. Vacuum modulator defective.
4. Pump pressure regulator valve defective.
5. Porosity between channels in case.
6. Control valve assembly.
7. Pump—to—case gasket may be mispositioned.
8. Intermediate clutch plug in case may be missing or leaking excessively.
9. Intermediate clutch piston seal missing or damaged.
10. Intermediate clutch plates burned.
11. Front or rear accumulator oil ring may be damaged.

Slips 2—3 Shift

1. Items 1 through 6 under Slips 1—2 Shift will also cause 2—3 shift slips.
2. Direct clutch plates burned.
3. Oil seal rings on direct clutch may be damaged permitting excessive leaking between tower and bushing.

Rough 1—2 Shift

1. Modulator valve sticking.
2. Modulator assembly defective.
3. Pump pressure regulator or boost valve stuck or inoperative.
4. Control valve assembly loosened from case, damaged or mounted with wrong gaskets.
5. Intermediate clutch ball missing or not sealing.
6. Porosity between channels in case.
7. Rear servo accumulator assembly may have oil rings damaged, stuck piston, broken or missing spring or damaged bore.

Rough 2—3 Shift

1. Items 1, 2 and 3 under Rough 1—2 Shift will also cause rough 2—3 shift.
2. Front servo accumulator spring broken or missing. Accumulator piston may be sticking.

No Engine Braking in Second Speed

1. Front servo or accumulator oil rings may be leaking.
2. Front band may be broken or burned out.

---

3. Front bank not engaged on anchor pin and/or servo pin.

No Engine Braking In Low Range

1. Low—reverse check ball may be missing from control valve assembly.
2. Rear servo may have damaged oil seal ring, bore or piston.
3. Rear servo apply pressure, leaking.
4. Rear band broken, burned out or not engaged on anchor pins or servo pin.

No Part Throttle Downshifts

1. Vacuum modulator assembly.
2. Modulator valve.
3. Regulator valve train.
4. Control valve assembly has stuck 3—2 valve or broken spring.

No Detent Downshifts

1. Detent switch needs fuse, connections tightened or adjustment.
2. Detent solenoid may be inoperative.
3. Detent valve train in control valve assembly malfunctioning.

Low or High Shift Points

1. Oil pressure. Check vacuum modulator assembly, vacuum line connections, modulator valve, and pressure regulator valve train.
2. Governor may have sticking valve or feed holes that are leaking, plugged or damaged.
3. Detent solenoid may be stuck open or loose.
4. Control valve assembly. Check detent, 3—2, and 1—2 shift valve trains, and check spacer plate gaskets for positioning.
5. Check case for porosity, missing or leaking intermediate plug.

Won't Hold In Park

1. Manual control linkage improperly adjusted.
2. Internal linkage defective; check for chamfer on actuator rod sleeve.
3. Parking pawl broken or inoperative

Noisy Transmission

1. Pump noises caused by high or low oil level.
2. Cavitation due to plugged strainer, porosity in intake circuit or water in oil.
3. Pump gears may be damaged.
4. Gear noise in low gear of Drive Range.
5. Transmission contacting body.
6. Defective planetary gear set.
7. Clutch noises during application can be worn or burned clutch plates.

Forward Clutch Plates Burned

1. Check ball in clutch housing damaged, stuck or missing.
2. Clutch piston cracked, seals damaged or missing.
3. Low line pressure.
4. Manual valve mispositioned.
5. Restricted oil feed to forward clutch.
6. Pump cover oil seal rings missing, broken or undersize; ring groove oversize.
7. Case valve body face not flat or porosity between channels.

---

8. Manual valve bent and center land not properly ground.

Intermediate Clutch Plates Burned

1. Constant bleed orifice in center support missing.
2. Rear accumulator piston oil ring damaged or missing.
3. 1-2 accumulator valve stuck in control valve assembly.
4. Intermediate clutch piston seal damaged or missing.
5. Center support bolt loose.
6. Low line pressure.
7. Intermediate clutch plug in case missing.
8. Case valve body face not flat or porosity between channels.
9. Manual valve bent and center land not ground properly.

Direct Clutch Plates Burned

1. Restricted orifice in vacuum line to modulator.
2. Check ball in direct clutch piston damaged, stuck or missing.
3. Defective modulator bellows.
4. Center support bolt loose.
5. Center support oil rings or grooves damaged or missing.
6. Clutch piston seals damaged or missing.
7. Front and rear servo pistons and seals damaged.
8. Manual valve bent and center land not cleaned up.
9. Case valve body face not flat or porosity between channels.
10. Intermediate sprag clutch installed backwards.
11. 3-2 valve, 3-2 spring or 3-2 spacer pin installed in wrong location in 3-2 valve bore.

MAINTENANCE

Checking & Adding Fluid

Fluid level should be checked at every engine oil change. The full ("F") and "ADD" marks on the transmission dipstick are one pint apart and determine the correct fluid level at normal operating temperature (170° F.). *Careful attention to transmission oil temperature is necessary as proper fluid level at low operating temperatures will be below the "ADD" mark on the dipstick. Proper fluid level at higher operating temperatures will rise above the "F" mark.*

Fluid level must always be checked with the car on a level surface, and with the engine running to make certain the converter is full. To determine proper fluid level, proceed as follows:

1. Operate engine at a fast idle for about 1½ minutes with selector lever in park ("P") position.
2. Reduce engine speed to slow idle and check fluid level.
3. With engine running add Dexron fluid as required.

NOTE: Cadillac uses an extended-life Dexron transmission fluid. With this new fluid, strainer replacement and fluid change is now recommended at 100,000 miles under normal operating conditions and 50,000 miles under severe or abnormal service such as trailer towing.

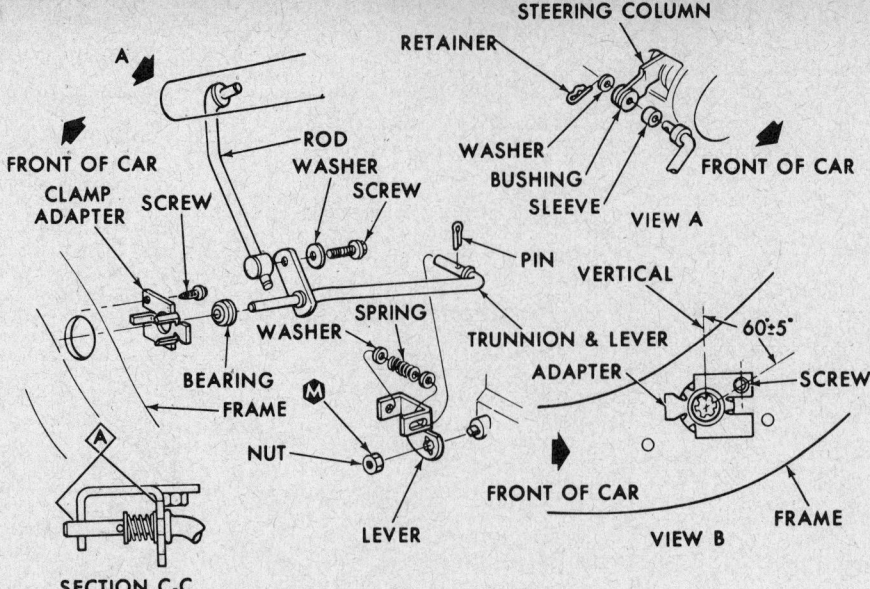

Fig. 2 Manual linkage adjustment. 1977–79 Seville

This recommendation applies only to the improved fluid and its availability for service. If the new fluid is not available, the former fluid can be used but then the 24,000 mile maintenance rule will apply.

Buick, Oldsmobile and Pontiac models: a revised type Dexron fluid is used in these transmissions. An early change to a darker color from the usual red color and or a strong odor that is usually associated with overheated fluid is normal, and should not be treated as a positive sign of needed maintenance or unit failure.

The normal maintenance schedule for drain and refill of this type fluid remains unchanged at 24,000 miles under normal service and 12,000 miles under severe operating conditions, such as trailer towing.

CAUTION: *Do not overfill as foaming might occur when the fluid heats up. If fluid level is too low, especially when cold, complete loss of drive may result after quick stops. Extremely low fluid level will result in damage to transmission.*

Draining Bottom Pan Only

1. Disconnect filler tube at bottom pan and allow fluid to drain. Remove and discard filler tube O-ring.
2. Use a new O-ring on filler tube and install tube on pan.
3. Lower car and add three quarts of Dexron transmission fluid through filler tube when replacing intake pipe and strainer assembly. When just draining bottom pan, add only two quarts.
4. Operate engine at a fast idle for about 1½ minutes with selector lever in park ("P") position.
5. Reduce engine speed to slow idle and check fluid level. Then add fluid as required to bring it to the proper level.

Adding Fluid to Fill Dry Transmission and Converter

1. Add seven quarts of fluid through filler tube.
2. Operate engine at a fast idle for about 1½ minutes with selector lever in park ("P") position.
3. Reduce engine speed to slow idle and add three more quarts of fluid.
4. Check fluid level and add as required to bring it to the proper level.

BACK DRIVE LINKAGE, ADJUST

Adjust back drive at trunnion so that:
1. Transmission is in full detent in each selector position.
2. With key in Run position and transmission in Reverse, key cannot be removed and steering wheel is not locked.
3. With key in Lock position and transmission in Park, key can be removed and steering wheel is locked.

MANUAL LINKAGE, ADJUST

Buick Column Shift

1977-80
1. Loosen shift rod adjusting clamp bolts.
2. Place selector lever against Neutral stop.
3. Place transmission lever in Neutral.
4. Tighten clamp bolt to 17-23 ft. lbs.

Buick Console Shift

1977-80
1. Place selector lever and transmission lever in Park position.
2. Position pin to obtain "Free pin" fit in transmission lever and torque nut to 15-25 ft. lbs.

3. Adjust back drive as outlined previously.

Cadillac

1977-81
1. Loosen nut or screw on shift rod trunnion, Figs. 2 and 3.
2. Pull trunnion lever upward to Park position, then downward to the third (Neutral) step.
3. Place steering column selector lever in Neutral position.
4. Tighten the shift rod trunnion nut or screw.
5. Check for proper operation.

Chevrolet Corvette

1977
1. Loosen transmission lever nut.
2. Move transmission lever counterclockwise to its maximum position, then clockwise 5 detent positions to Park.
3. Place shift lever in Park and insert a .040" spacer forward of pawl as shown in Fig. 4 and tighten nut to 20 ft. lbs.

Oldsmobile

Column Shift, 1977-80
1. Loosen shift rod clamp bolt and place transmission outer lever in Neutral position, Figs. 5 and 6.
2. Push on shift rod until selector lever is against Neutral position stop in upper steering column.
3. Tighten bolt in clamp on lower end of shift rod to 20 ft. lbs.
4. Check for proper operation.

Console Shift, 1977
1. Loosen shift rod clamp bolt. Fig. 7.
2. Place selector lever in Park position. Place transmission lever in Park position with ignition key in Lock position.
3. Hold shift rod against Lock stop and tighten clamp screw.

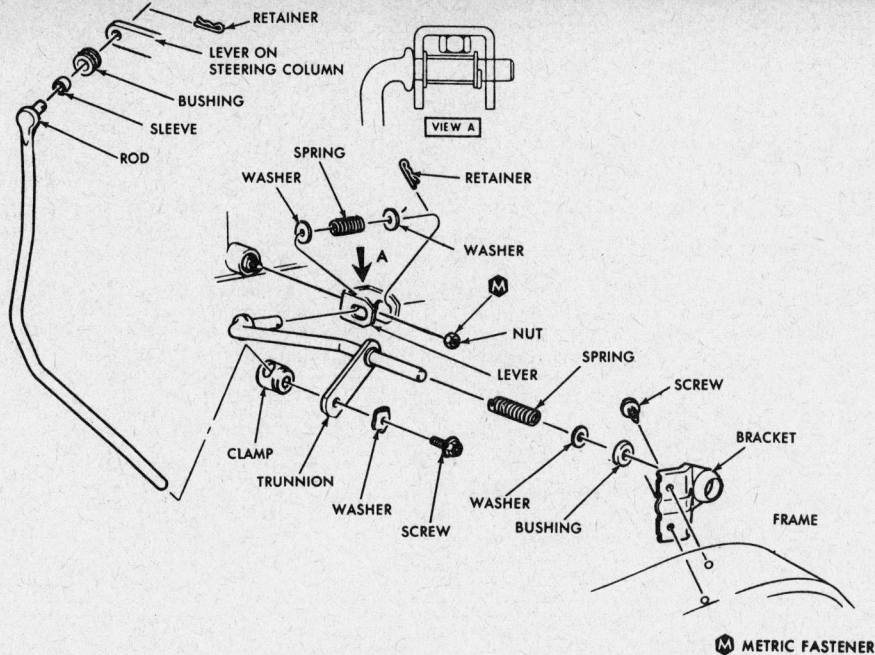

Fig. 3   Manual linkage adjustment. 1977–81 Cadillac except Seville

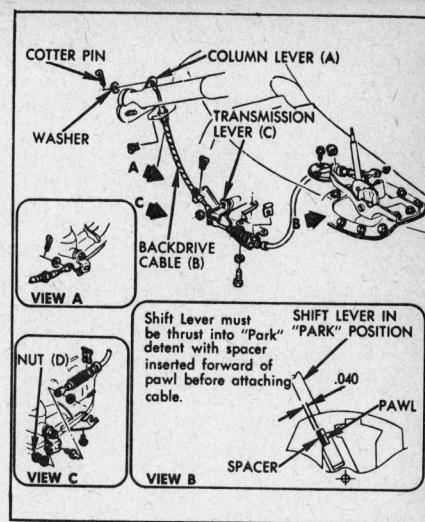

Fig. 4   Floor shift adjustment. 1977 Corvette

4. Set pin to give free pin fit and tighten nut.
5. Check for proper operation.

Pontiac

Column Shift, 1977
1. Place column shift lever in neutral gate notch, then loosen swivel clamp screw.
2. Place transmission shift lever in neutral detent.
3. Torque swivel clamp screw to 20 ft. lbs.
4. Check for proper operation.

Console Shift, 1977
1. Disconnect shift cable from transmission, Fig. 8.
2. Adjust back drive linkage as outlined at the front of this section.
3. After adjusting back drive, unlock ignition and set transmission and gear selector in Neutral position.
4. Install cable and tighten nut to 20 ft. lbs.

DOWNSHIFT SWITCHES
Buick

1977-80
Push switch lever all the way towards dash.

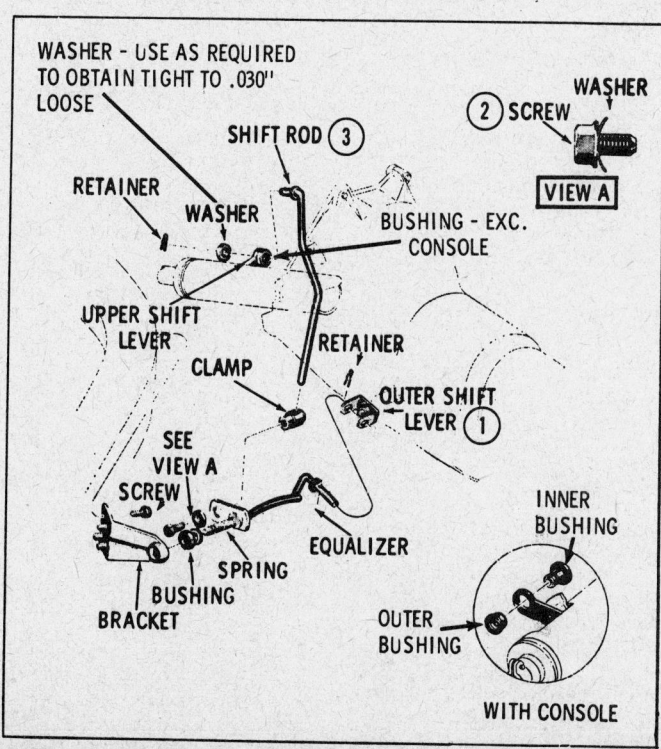

Fig. 5   Shift linkage adjustment. Oldsmobile full size (typical)

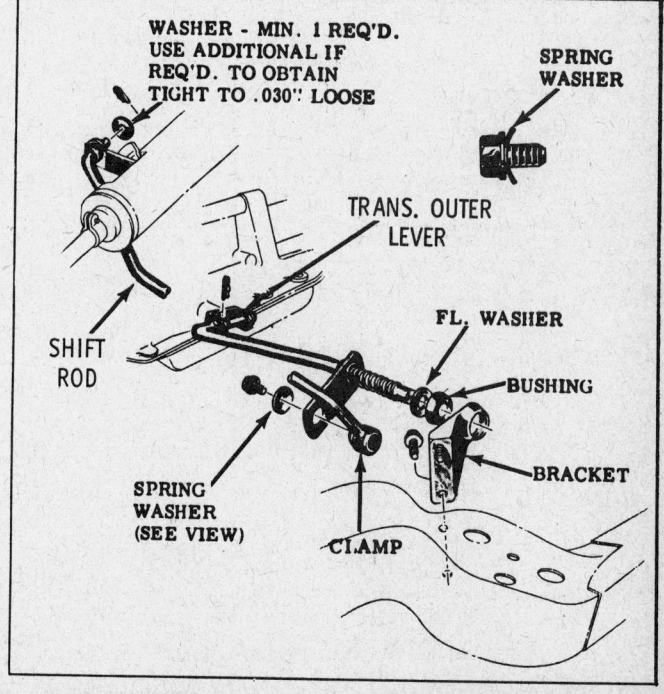

Fig. 6   Shift linkage. Oldsmobile intermediates (typical)

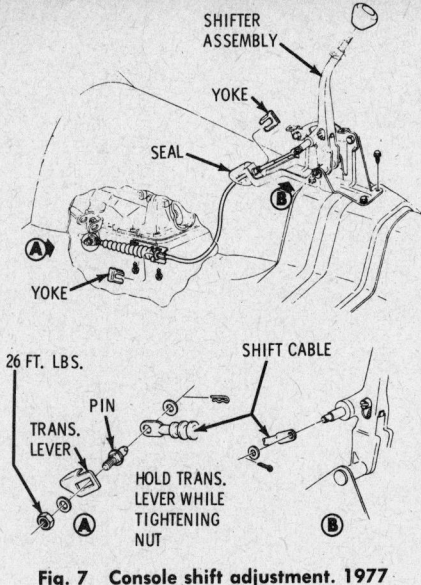

Fig. 7 Console shift adjustment. 1977 Oldsmobile

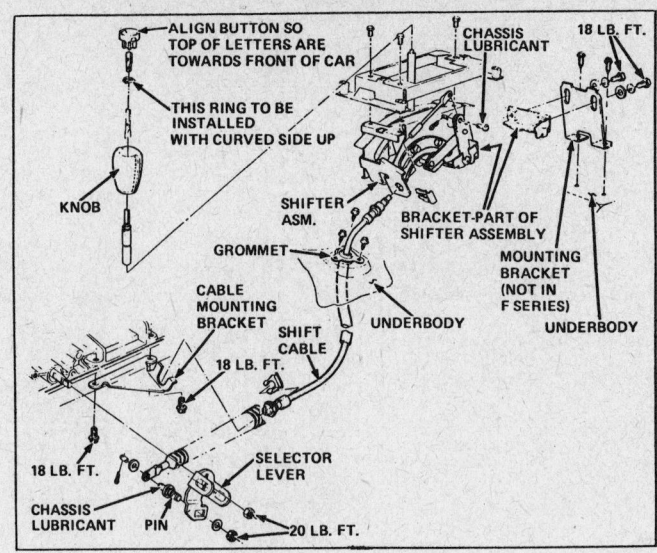

Fig. 8 Console shift adjustment. 1977 Pontiac (Typical)

Final adjustment is made automatically the first time accelerator pedal is depressed to floor.

Cadillac

1977-81

1. Remove air cleaner.
2. Make certain carburetor is adjusted to specification and that linkage is at low speed idle setting.
3. Loosen two mounting screws and insert a #42 drill through calibrating hole below lower wire terminal extending through to carburetor side of switch, Fig. 9. Adjust position of switch so that lever just touches the carburetor adapter plate arm.

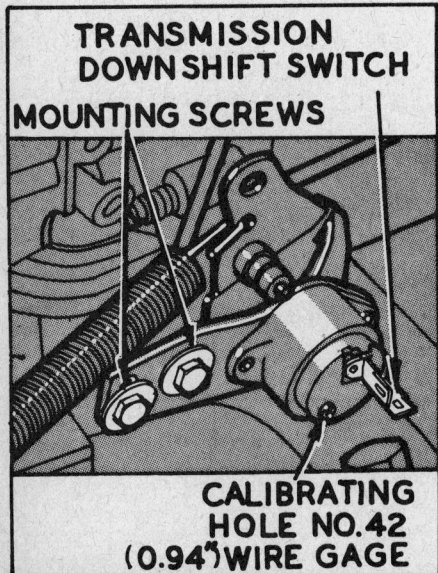

Fig. 9 Detent switch adjustment. 1977-81 Cadillac

4. Tighten mounting screws and remove drill.
5. Install air cleaner.

Chevrolet

1977

Install switch as shown in Fig. 10. After installing, press switch plunger as far forward as possible. This switch will then adjust itself the first time the accelerator pedal is pushed to floor.

Oldsmobile

1977-80

1. Push plunger of switch forward until flush with switch housing.
2. Push accelerator pedal to wide open position to set switch.
3. Energizing of switch can be checked with a test light.

Pontiac

1977

After installing switch, fully bottom plunger to insure proper setting then fully depress accelerator pedal, Fig. 11.

IN CAR REPAIRS

Services outlined in this section can be performed without removing the transmission from the vehicle.

Pressure Regulator Valve

NOTE: A solid type pressure regulator valve must be used only in a pump cover with a "Squared Off" (machined) pressure regulator boss, Fig. 12. A pressure regulator valve with

oil holes and an orifice cup plug may be used with either type pump.

1. Remove bottom pan and strainer.
2. Using a screwdriver or steel rod, compress regulator boost valve bushing against pressure regulator spring, Fig. 13.

CAUTION: Pressure regulator spring is under extreme pressure and will force valve bushing out of bore when snap ring is removed if valve bushing is not held securely.

3. Continue to exert pressure on valve bush-

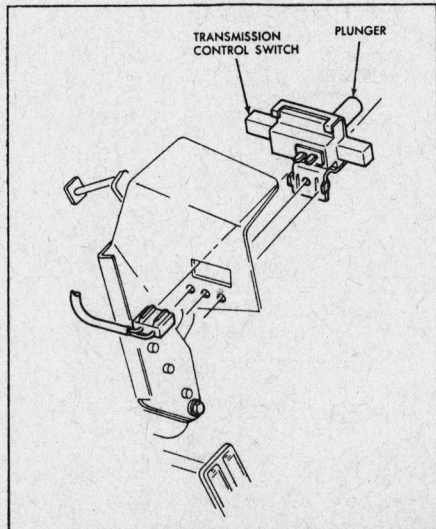

Fig. 10 Detent switch adjustment. 1977 Chevrolet models

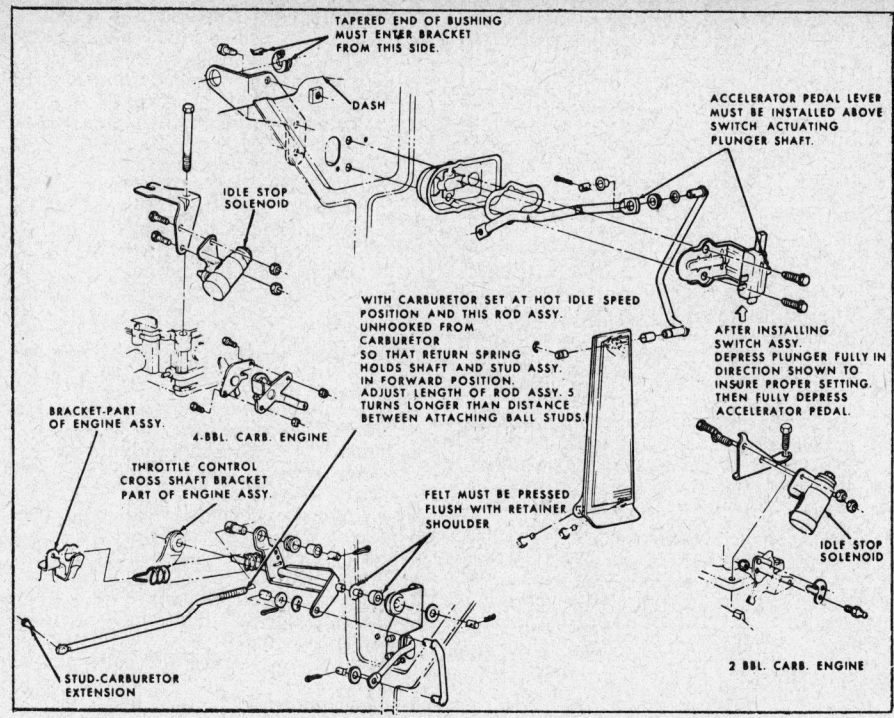

Fig. 11 Detent switch adjustment. 1977 Pontiac (Typical)

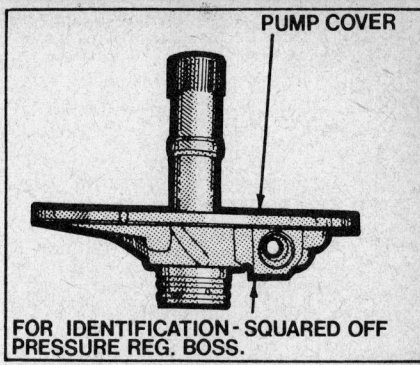

FOR IDENTIFICATION – SQUARED OFF PRESSURE REG. BOSS.

Fig. 12 Pressure regulator identification

2. Pry out seal with screwdriver.
3. Install new seal with a suitable seal driver.
4. Install propeller shaft.

TRANSMISSION, REPLACE

Buick

1. Raise and support front and rear of car. Remove propeller shaft.
2. Disconnect exhaust crossover pipe, if necessary, and on 1977-79 models remove catalytic converter support bracket from transmission.
3. Place suitable jack under transmission.
4. Remove vacuum line from vacuum modulator.
5. Separate cooler lines from transmission.
6. Remove transmission crossmember.
7. Remove detent electrical connector from transmission case.
8. Disconnect speedometer cable.
9. Disconnect shift linkage from transmission.
10. Remove transmission filler pipe.
11. Support engine at oil pan.
12. Remove flywheel cover pan.
13. Mark flywheel and converter pump for reassembly in same position, then remove three converter pump-to-flywheel bolts.
14. Remove transmission-to-engine bolts.
15. Move transmission rearward to provide clearance between converter pump and crankshaft. Install a suitable holding tool to secure converter. Then lower and remove transmission.
16. Reverse above procedure to install.

Cadillac

1. Disconnect battery ground cable and raise vehicle.
2. Disconnect transmission shift linkage, speedometer cable, downshift connector, and the Track Master electrical connector, if equipped.
3. Disconnect and plug oil cooler lines from transmission and position aside. Also, plug transmission ports.
4. Disconnect vacuum line from vacuum modulator and position aside.
5. Remove propeller shaft.
6. Remove lower flywheel housing cover and the three converter to flywheel attaching bolts.

NOTE: This is accomplished by inserting a heavy screwdriver in open slot under one of the converter weld nuts and rotating the converter with a 1¼ inch deep

---

ing and remove snap ring. Gradually release pressure on valve bushing until spring force is exhausted.

4. Carefully remove regulator boose valve bushing and valve, and pressure regulator spring. Be careful not to drop parts as they will fall out if they are not held.
5. Remove pressure regulator valve and spring retainer. Remove spacers if present.
6. Reverse procedure to install.

Control Valve Body

1. Remove bottom pan and strainer.
2. Disconnect pressure switch lead wire.
3. Remove control valve body attaching screws and detent roller spring assembly. *Do not remove solenoid attaching screws.*
4. Remove control valve body and governor pipes. If care is used in removing control valve body, the six check balls will stay in place above spacer plate.
5. Remove governor pipes and manual valve from control valve body.
6. Reverse procedure to install.

Governor

1. Remove governor cover and discard gasket.
2. Withdraw governor from case.
3. Reverse procedure to install, using a new gasket.

Modulator & Modulator Valve

1. Remove modulator attaching screw and retainer.
2. Remove modulator assembly from case and discard O-ring seal.
3. Remove modulator valve from case.
4. Reverse procedure to install, using a new O-ring seal.

Parking Linkage

1. Remove bottom pan and oil strainer.
2. Unthread jam nut holding detent lever to manual shaft.
3. Remove manual shaft retaining pin from case.
4. Remove manual shaft and jam nut from case.
5. Remove O-ring seal from manual shaft.
6. Remove parking actuator rod and detent lever assembly.
7. Remove parking pawl bracket, pawl return spring and pawl shaft retainer.
8. Remove parking pawl shaft, O-ring seal and parking pawl.
9. Reverse procedure to install, using new seals and gasket.

Rear Seal

1. Remove propeller shaft.

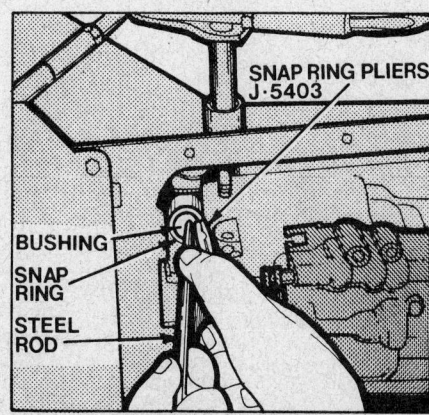

SNAP RING PLIERS J-5403

BUSHING
SNAP RING
STEEL ROD

Fig. 13 Removing and installing Pressure regulator valve

socket until the bolts are accessible. Do not pry on ring gear or transmission case to rotate converter as damage may result.

7. Support rear of engine with a suitable jack.
8. On Seville, remove lateral strut-rod from rear engine mount and cross-member. Also remove two nuts from tunnel strap, then the strap.
9. Remove two nuts from tunnel strap, then the strap.
10. Remove two rear engine mounts to extension housing screws.
11. Support transmission with a suitable jack and raise transmission slightly, releasing load from rear engine support crossmember, and remove shim.
12. Remove rear engine support crossmember bolts, then the space from crossmember right side.
13. Disconnect exhaust pipe from manifold and remove rear engine support crossmember.
14. Remove engine to transmission bolts.

NOTE: It may be necessary to slightly lower the engine and transmission to gain access to the upper attaching bolts.

15. Move transmission rearward, disengaging transmission case from engine locating dowels, and install a suitable converter holding tool.
16. Lower transmission from vehicle.
17. Reverse procedure to install. Torque engine to transmission case bolts to 35 ft. lbs. and the converter to flywheel bolts to 30 ft. lbs.

Chevrolet

Before raising car, disconnect negative battery cable and release the parking brake.
1. Raise vehicle, remove propeller shaft and catalytic converter support bracket from transmission.

2. Disconnect speedometer cable, electrical lead to case connector, vacuum modulator line and cooler lines.
3. Disconnect shift control linkage.
4. Support transmission with suitable jack.
5. Disconnect rear mount from frame crossmember.
6. Remove two bolts at each end of frame crossmember (plus through bolt at inside of frame and parking brake pulley on Corvette). Remove crossmember.
7. Remove converter underpan.
8. Remove converter to flywheel bolts.
9. On Chevrolet and Chevelle, loosen exhaust pipe to manifold bolts about 1/4".
10. Lower transmission until jack is barely supporting it.
11. Remove transmission to engine mounting bolts and remove oil filler tube.
12. Raise transmission to its normal position, support engine with jack and slide transmission rearward from engine and lower it away from car.

NOTE: Use converter holding tool when lowering transmission or keep rear of transmission lower than front so as not to lose converter.

13. Reverse removal procedure to install transmission.

Oldsmobile

1. Remove flywheel cover and torque converter attaching bolts.
2. Mark flywheel and converter so they can be installed in same position.
3. Support engine at rear.
4. Disconnect solenoid wires and manual shift linkage at side of transmission.
5. Disconnect oil cooler lines, vacuum modulator line and oil filler pipe.
6. Disconnect parking brake cable.
7. Before removing propeller shaft, scribe marks on drive shaft and companion

flange for correct assembly.
8. Disconnect exhaust pipe bracket from rear of crossmember and catalytic converter support bracket from transmission, if necessary.
9. Support transmission, then remove crossmember.
10. Unfasten transmission from engine.
11. Move transmission away from engine, then, before removing transmission, fasten a suitable piece of strap iron to housing to prevent converter from falling out as transmission is removed.

Pontiac

1. Disconnect battery and release parking brake. Then raise car.
2. Remove propeller shaft and catalytic converter support bracket from transmission.
3. Disconnect speedometer cable, electrical lead to case connector, vacuum line at modulator, and oil cooler pipes.
4. Disconnect shift control linkage.
5. Support transmission with jack.
6. Disconnect rear mount from transmission and crossmember.
7. Remove crossmember (2 bolts at each end).
8. Remove converter dust shield.
9. Remove converter-to-flex plate bolts.
10. Loosen exhaust pipe to manifold about 1/4", and lower transmission until jack is barely supporting it.
11. Remove transmission-to-engine mount bolts.
12. Raise transmission to its normal position, slide it rearward and lower it away from vehicle.

NOTE: When lowering transmission, keep rear of unit lower than front so as not to drop converter.

13. Reverse procedure to install.

GM Front Wheel Drive Turbo Hydra-matic 325 Automatic Transmission

TRANSMISSION IDENTIFICATION

This transmission may be identified by the following codes located on the serial number plate attached to the left side of the converter housing.

Buick

1979	Riviera V6-231	6BJ
	Riviera V8-350	6OJ
1980	Riviera	BJ, OJ, OK, OL, OM
1981	Riviera V6-231	BJ
	Riviera V6-252	BE
	Riviera V8-307	OH
	Riviera V8-350 Diesel	OK

Cadillac

1979	Eldorado	AJ
1980	Eldorado & Seville	AF, AJ, AK
1981	Eldorado & Seville	AG, OK

Oldsmobile

1979	Toronado V8-350①	OJ
	Toronado V8-350②	OK
1980	Toronado V8-305	OH
	Toronado V8-350①	OJ
	Toronado V8-350②	OK
1981	Toronado V6-252	BE
	Toronado V8-307	OH
	Toronado V8-350 Diesel	OK

①—Except diesel engine
②—Diesel engine

GENERAL DESCRIPTION

This transmission is a fully automatic front wheel drive unit consisting primarily of a three-element hydraulic torque converter and a compound planetary gear set, Fig. 1. Three multiple disc clutches, a roller clutch and a band provide the friction elements required to obtain the desired function of the compound planetary gear set. The compound planetary gear set provides three forward speeds and reverse.

The torque converter couples the engine to the planetary gears through oil and provides torque multiplication. It consists of a pump or driving member, a turbine or driven member and a stator assembly. The stator is mounted on a one-way roller clutch which allows the stator to turn clockwise but not counterclockwise.

The torque converter housing is filled with oil and rotates at engine speed. The converter pump is an integral part of the converter housing, therefore the pump blades rotating at engine speed set the oil within the converter into motion and direct it to the turbine causing the turbine to rotate. As the oil passes through the turbine it travels in such a direction that if it were not redirected by the stator it would strike the rear of the converter pump blades and impede its pumping action. Therefore at low turbine speeds, the oil is redirected

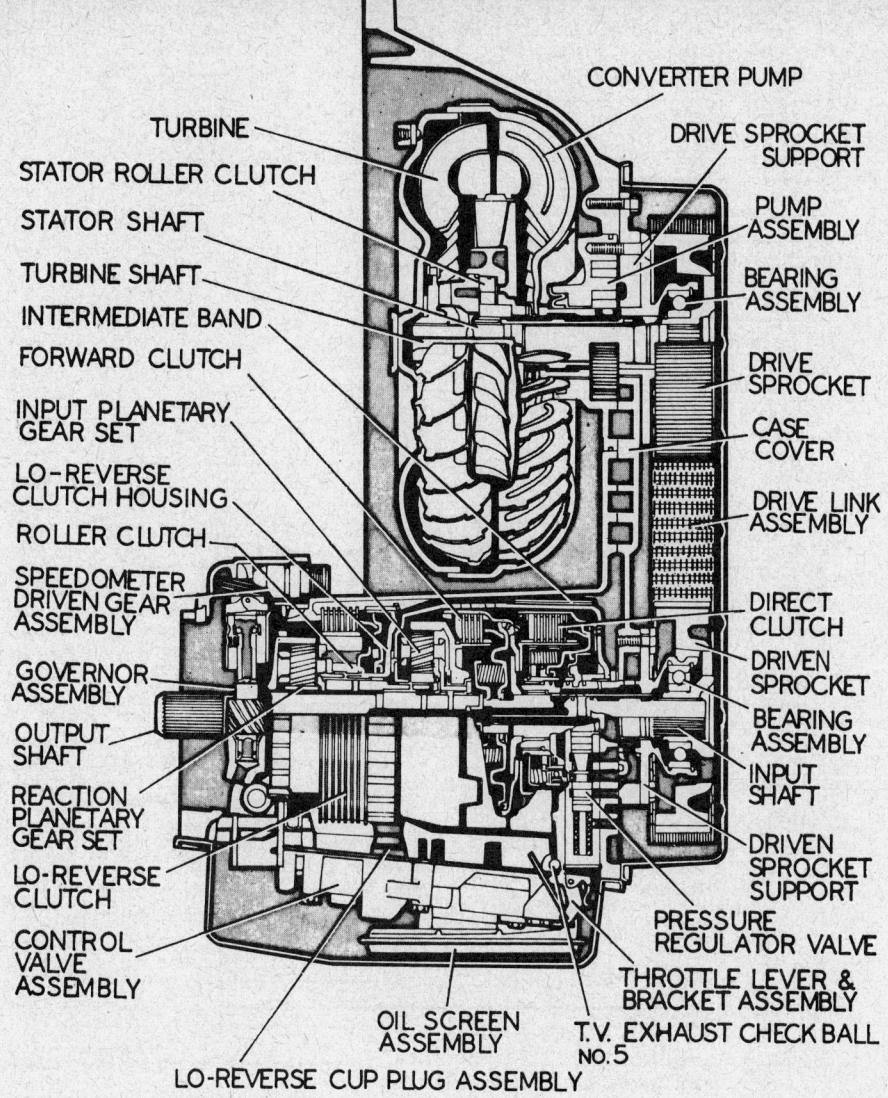

Fig. 1 Sectional view of Turbo Hydra-Matic 325 automatic transmission

Labels on figure:
- TURBINE
- STATOR ROLLER CLUTCH
- STATOR SHAFT
- TURBINE SHAFT
- INTERMEDIATE BAND
- FORWARD CLUTCH
- INPUT PLANETARY GEAR SET
- LO-REVERSE CLUTCH HOUSING
- ROLLER CLUTCH
- SPEEDOMETER DRIVEN GEAR ASSEMBLY
- GOVERNOR ASSEMBLY
- OUTPUT SHAFT
- REACTION PLANETARY GEAR SET
- LO-REVERSE CLUTCH
- CONTROL VALVE ASSEMBLY
- OIL SCREEN ASSEMBLY
- LO-REVERSE CUP PLUG ASSEMBLY
- CONVERTER PUMP
- DRIVE SPROCKET SUPPORT
- PUMP ASSEMBLY
- BEARING ASSEMBLY
- DRIVE SPROCKET
- CASE COVER
- DRIVE LINK ASSEMBLY
- DIRECT CLUTCH
- DRIVEN SPROCKET
- BEARING ASSEMBLY
- INPUT SHAFT
- DRIVEN SPROCKET SUPPORT
- PRESSURE REGULATOR VALVE
- THROTTLE LEVER & BRACKET ASSEMBLY
- T.V. EXHAUST CHECK BALL NO. 5

by the stator to the converter pump in such a manner that it actually assists the converter pump to deliver power or multiply engine torque. As turbine speed increases, the direction of the oil leaving the turbine changes and flows against the rear side of the stator vanes in a clockwise direction. Since the stator is now impeding the smooth flow of oil, its roller clutch releases and it revolves freely on its shaft. Once the stator becomes inactive, there is no further multiplication of torque within the converter. At this point the converter is acting as a fluid coupling since the converter pump and turbine are being driven at about the same speed, or at a one-to-one ratio.

The hydraulic system in this transmission is pressurized by a gear type pump to provide the working pressures required to operate the friction elements and automatic controls.

TROUBLE-SHOOTING

Refer to Figs. 2 through 9 for transmission trouble. Also, refer to the following for causes of low oil pressure, high oil pressure, burned direct clutch, burned forward clutch, burned lo-reverse clutch and burned intermediate band.

Causes of Low Oil Pressure

1. Low oil level.
2. Throttle valve system (pressure low in neutral and drive, low to normal in intermediate and reverse):
   a. Throttle valve cable sticking or incorrectly adjusted.
   b. Incorrect cable or link being used.
   c. Throttle valve stuck.
   d. Throttle valve shift valve stuck.
3. Clogged oil screen or O-ring seal missing, leaking or damaged.
4. Control valve assembly bolts loose.
5. Pressure regulator stuck or wrong size.
6. Control valve assembly:
   a. Check balls no. 1 and/or no. 3 missing or out of place.
   b. Control valves stuck.
   c. 1-2 accumulator piston missing, seal damaged, leaking or missing.
   d. Internal leaks.
7. Damaged pump gears.
8. Line boost passage blocked.
9. Lo-Reverse clutch housing to case seal cup plug leaking (low oil pressure in reverse).

Causes of High Oil Pressure

1. Throttle valve system (pressure high in neutral and drive, normal to high in intermediate and reverse):
   a. Throttle valve cable misadjusted or sticking.
   b. Incorrect link or cable being used.
   c. Throttle valve stuck.
   d. Throttle valve shift valve stuck.
2. Pressure regulator valve stuck or wrong size.
3. Control valve assembly valves stuck.
4. Reverse boost orifice in spacer plate plugged (high pressure in reverse only).
5. Line pressure control orifice in pump cover restricted or not drilled.
6. Internal pump or case leaks.

Causes of Burned Direct Clutch

1. Case and cover assembly:
   a. Leaking or damaged seal rings on drive sprocket support.
   b. Driven sprocket support sleeve loose or mispositioned.
   c. Cup plug leaking or missing.
   d. No. 6 check ball missing or mispositioned.
   e. Low oil pressure. Refer to "Causes of Low Oil Pressure."
   f. Channels blocked or interconnected.
   g. No. 7 check ball missing from case cover.
2. Direct clutch assembly:
   a. Seals cut, missing or rolled out of groove.
   b. Apply ring missing, incorrect apply ring, or incorrect number of clutch plates used.
   c. Exhaust ball capsule in piston or housing damaged and not sealing. Refer to "Causes of Low Oil Pressure".
   d. Spring guide located over check ball preventing ball from seating.
3. Intermediate servo assembly:
   a. Incorrect servo piston or cover used.
   b. Servo bore scored or damaged.
   c. Servo orifice bleed plug missing.
4. Control valve assembly:
   a. Control valve assembly to case bolts loose.
   b. Sealing surface on control valve assembly, spacer place, case and/or gasket damaged and leaking.
   c. Porosity in control valve assembly and/or case channels.

Causes of Burned Forward Clutch

1. Case and case cover assembly:
   a. Pump to case cover face damaged.
   b. Leaking or damaged seal rings on driven sprocket support.
   c. Driven sprocket support sleeve loose or mispositioned.
   d. Cup plugs leaking or missing.
   e. No. 6 check ball missing or mispositioned.
   f. Low oil pressure. Refer to "Causes of Low Oil Pressure."
   g. Channels blocked or interconnected.
2. Forward clutch assembly:
   a. Seal rings on input shaft damaged or missing.
   b. Cup plug in input shaft damaged or missing.
   c. Input shaft feed passage or orifice restricted.
   d. Housing exhaust ball capsule damaged or missing.
   e. Input shaft passages interconnected.
   f. Housing or shaft seal surface damaged.

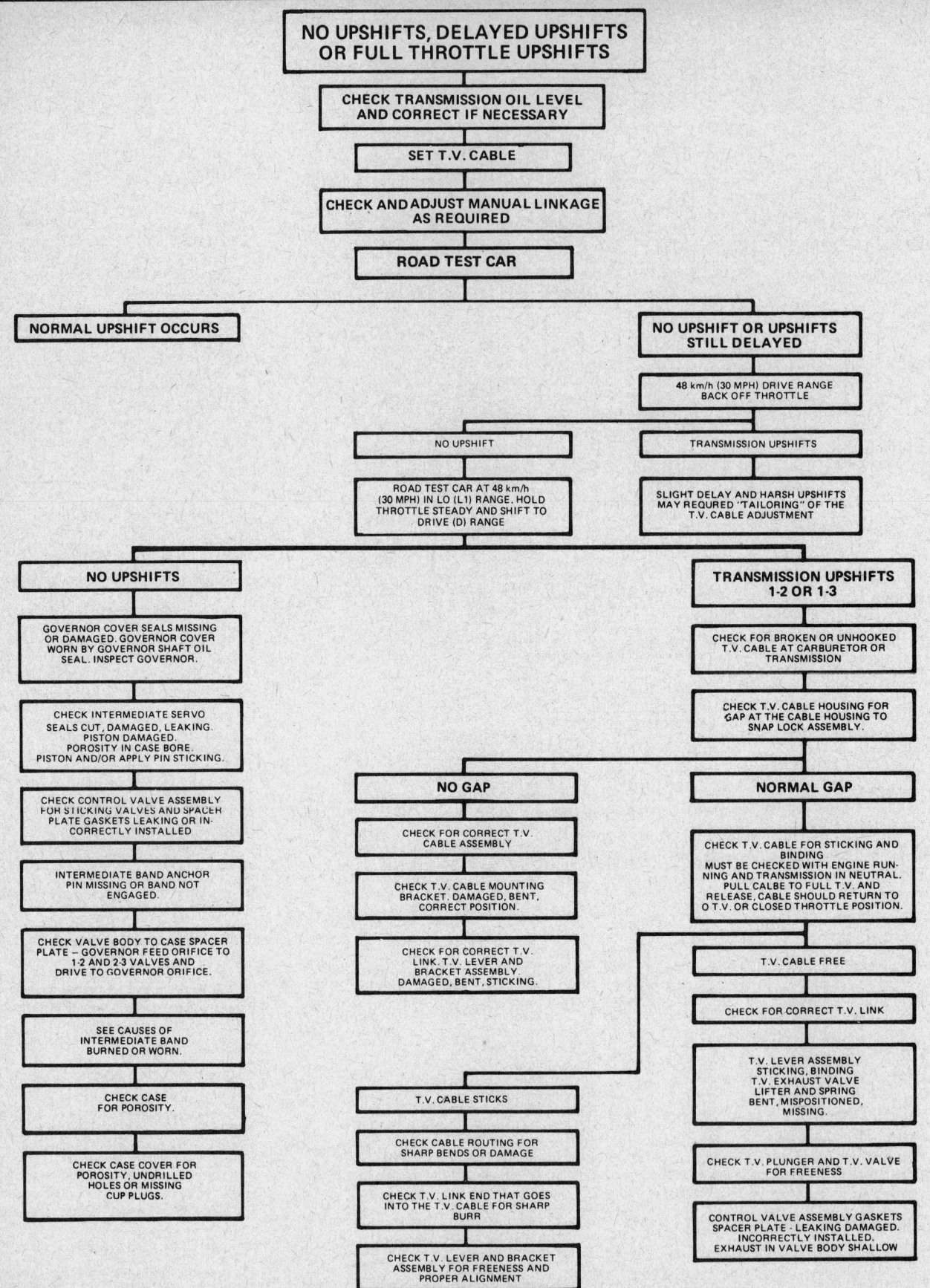

Fig. 2   THM 325 Trouble-shooting chart, Part 1 of 8

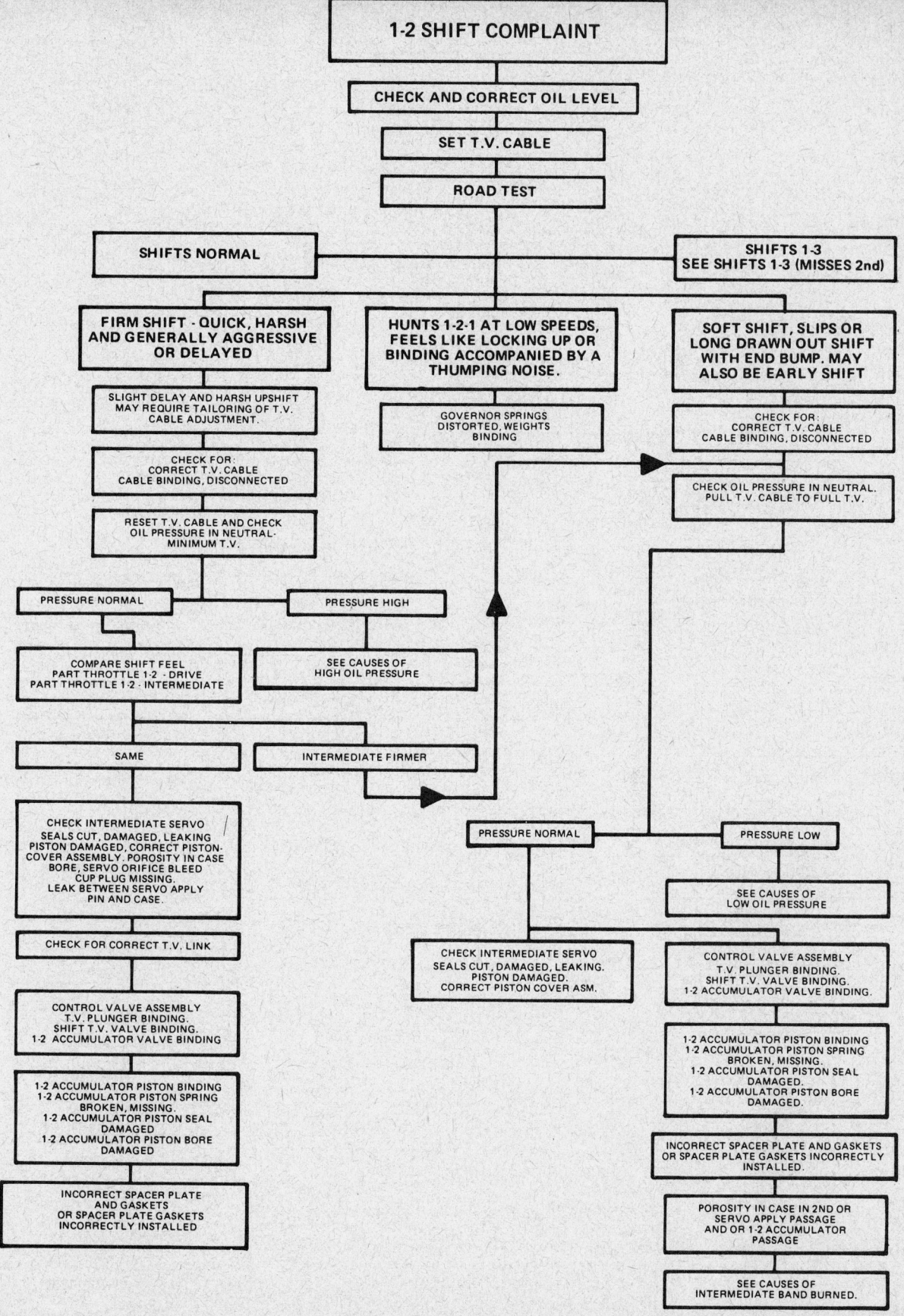

Fig. 3 THM 325 Trouble-shooting chart, Part 2 of 8

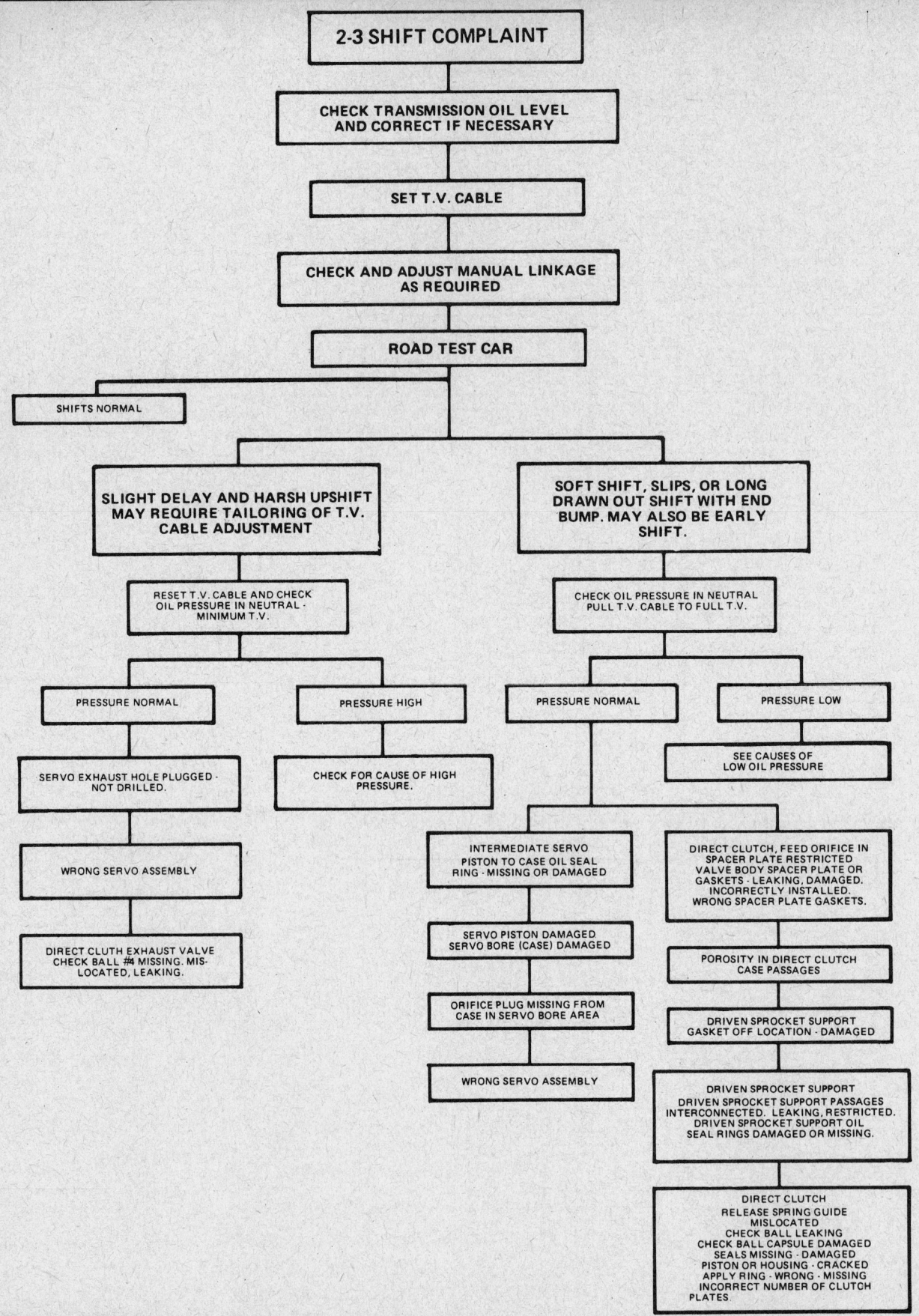

2-3 SHIFT COMPLAINT

CHECK TRANSMISSION OIL LEVEL AND CORRECT IF NECESSARY

SET T.V. CABLE

CHECK AND ADJUST MANUAL LINKAGE AS REQUIRED

ROAD TEST CAR

SHIFTS NORMAL

SLIGHT DELAY AND HARSH UPSHIFT MAY REQUIRE TAILORING OF T.V. CABLE ADJUSTMENT

SOFT SHIFT, SLIPS, OR LONG DRAWN OUT SHIFT WITH END BUMP. MAY ALSO BE EARLY SHIFT.

RESET T.V. CABLE AND CHECK OIL PRESSURE IN NEUTRAL - MINIMUM T.V.

CHECK OIL PRESSURE IN NEUTRAL PULL T.V. CABLE TO FULL T.V.

PRESSURE NORMAL

PRESSURE HIGH

PRESSURE NORMAL

PRESSURE LOW

SERVO EXHAUST HOLE PLUGGED - NOT DRILLED.

CHECK FOR CAUSE OF HIGH PRESSURE.

SEE CAUSES OF LOW OIL PRESSURE

WRONG SERVO ASSEMBLY

INTERMEDIATE SERVO PISTON TO CASE OIL SEAL RING - MISSING OR DAMAGED

DIRECT CLUTCH, FEED ORIFICE IN SPACER PLATE RESTRICTED VALVE BODY SPACER PLATE OR GASKETS - LEAKING, DAMAGED. INCORRECTLY INSTALLED. WRONG SPACER PLATE GASKETS.

DIRECT CLUTH EXHAUST VALVE CHECK BALL #4 MISSING. MIS-LOCATED, LEAKING.

SERVO PISTON DAMAGED SERVO BORE (CASE) DAMAGED

POROSITY IN DIRECT CLUTCH CASE PASSAGES

ORIFICE PLUG MISSING FROM CASE IN SERVO BORE AREA

DRIVEN SPROCKET SUPPORT GASKET OFF LOCATION - DAMAGED

WRONG SERVO ASSEMBLY

DRIVEN SPROCKET SUPPORT DRIVEN SPROCKET SUPPORT PASSAGES INTERCONNECTED. LEAKING, RESTRICTED. DRIVEN SPROCKET SUPPORT OIL SEAL RINGS DAMAGED OR MISSING.

DIRECT CLUTCH RELEASE SPRING GUIDE MISLOCATED CHECK BALL LEAKING CHECK BALL CAPSULE DAMAGED SEALS MISSING - DAMAGED PISTON OR HOUSING - CRACKED APPLY RING - WRONG - MISSING INCORRECT NUMBER OF CLUTCH PLATES.

Fig. 4 THM 325 Trouble-shooting chart, Part 3 of 8

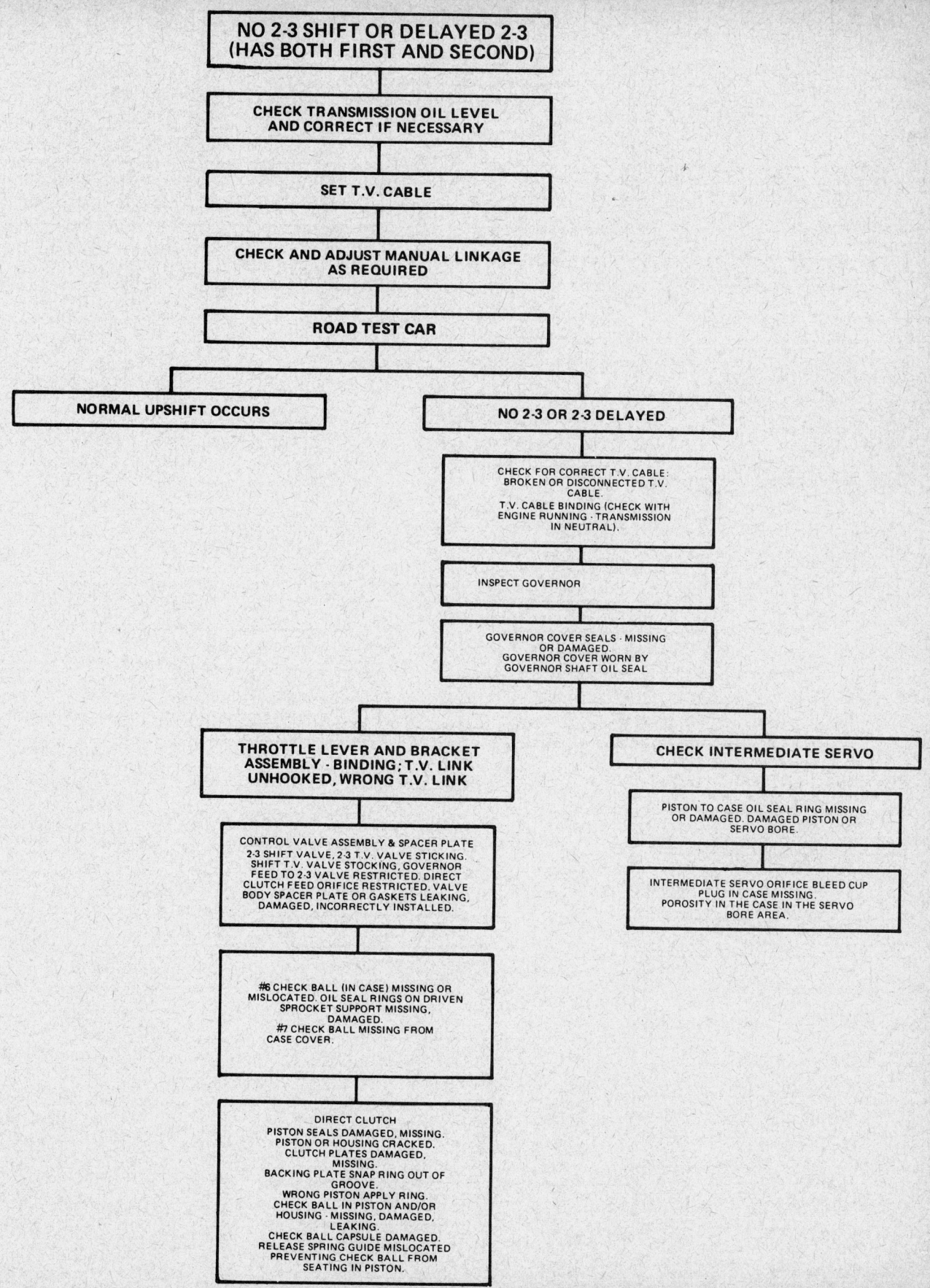

Fig. 5 THM 325 Trouble-shooting chart, Part 4 of 8

NO DRIVE

A "NO DRIVE" COMPLAINT CAN BE REPORTED UNDER SEVERAL
CONDITIONS OR IN DIFFERENT OPERATING RANGES. SELECT
FROM THE FOLLOWING CONDITIONS THE ONE THAT
BEST REPRESENTS THE PROBLEM:

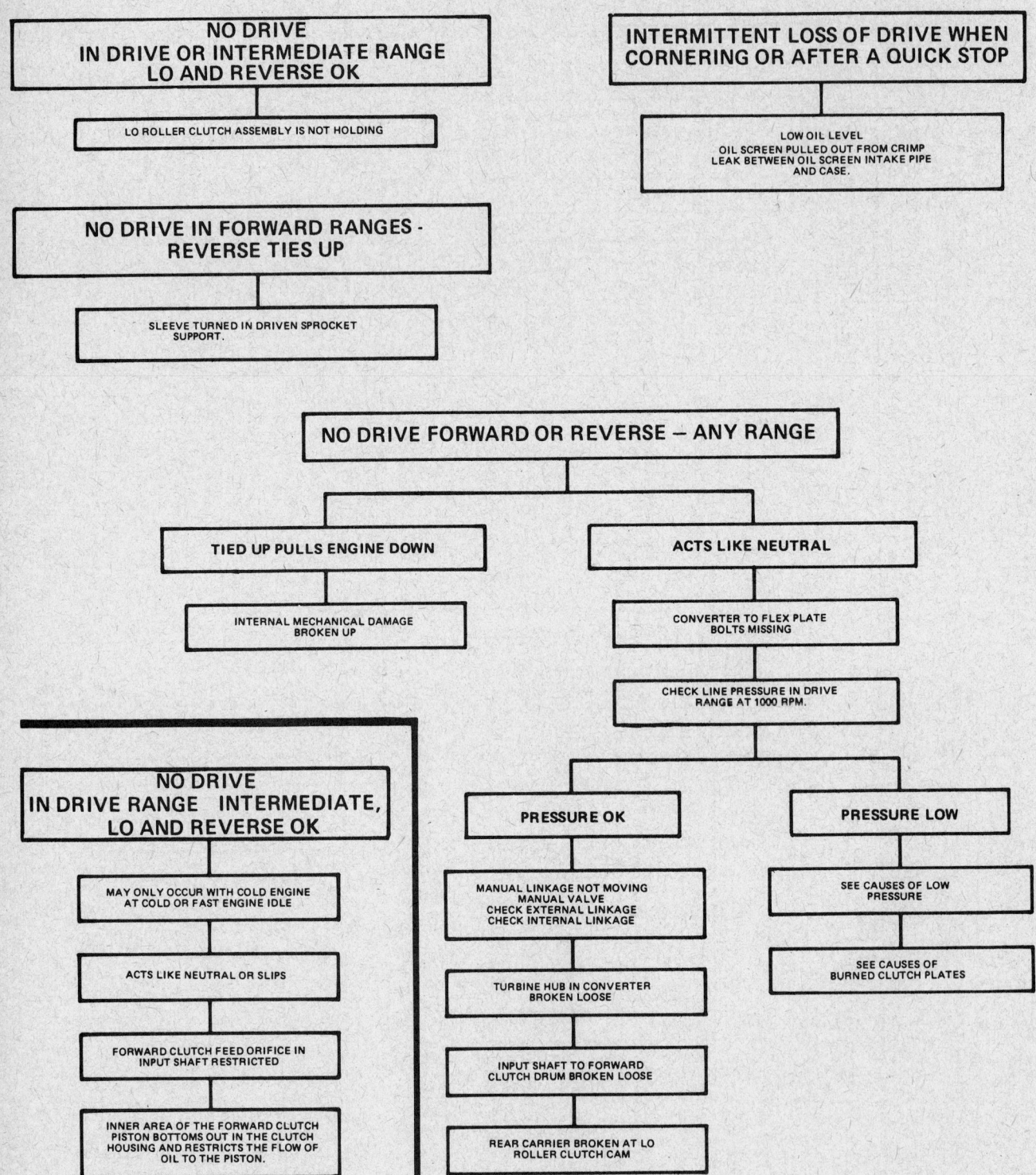

Fig. 6   THM 325 Trouble-shooting chart, Part 5 of 8

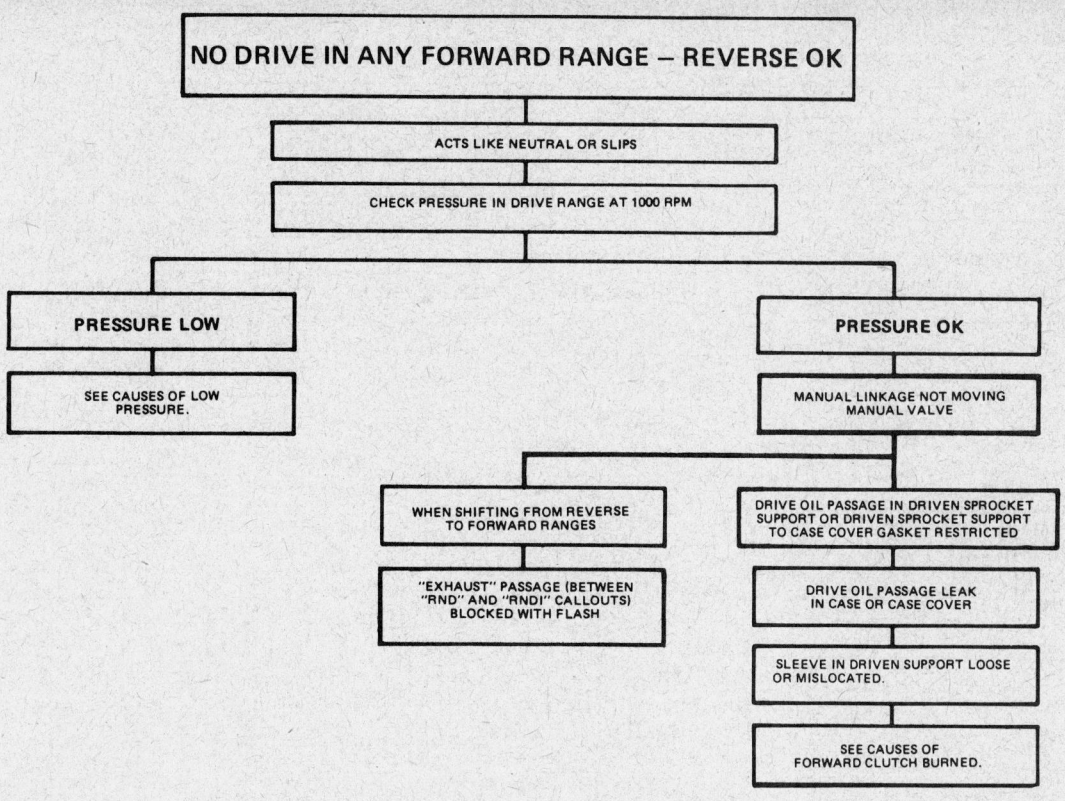

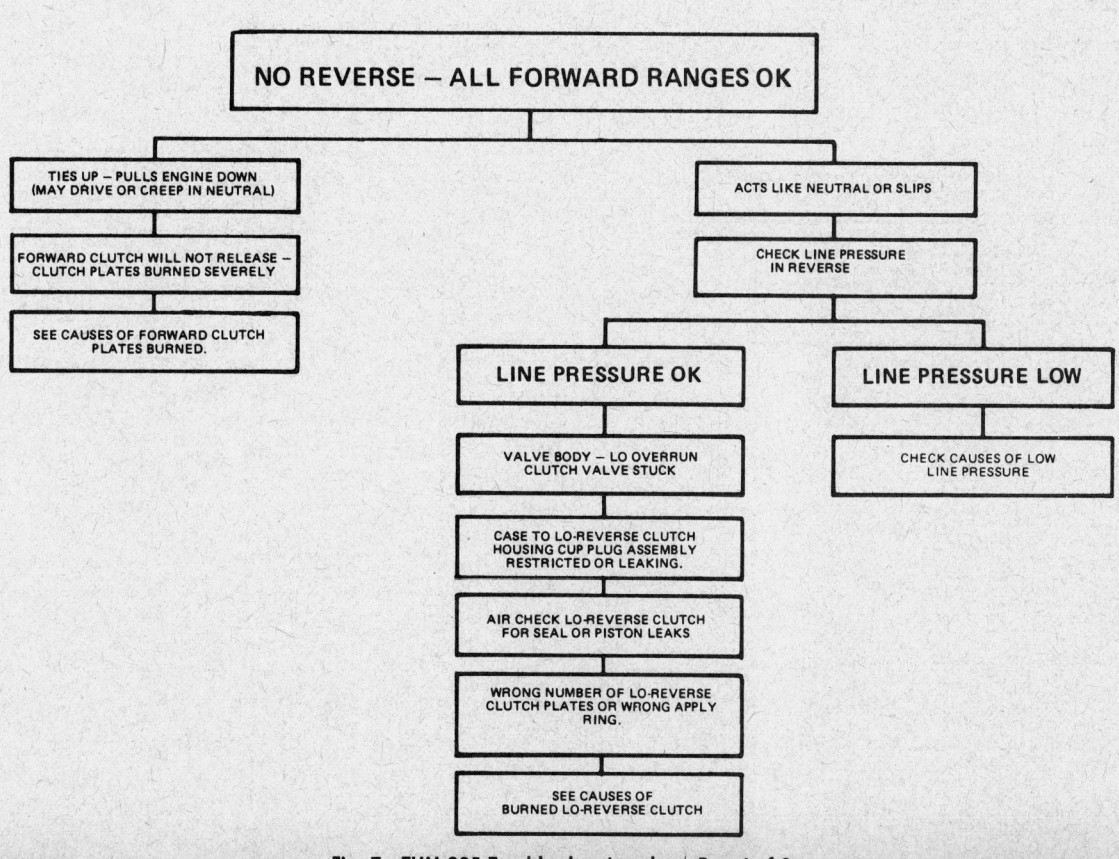

Fig. 7   THM 325 Trouble-shooting chart, Part 6 of 8

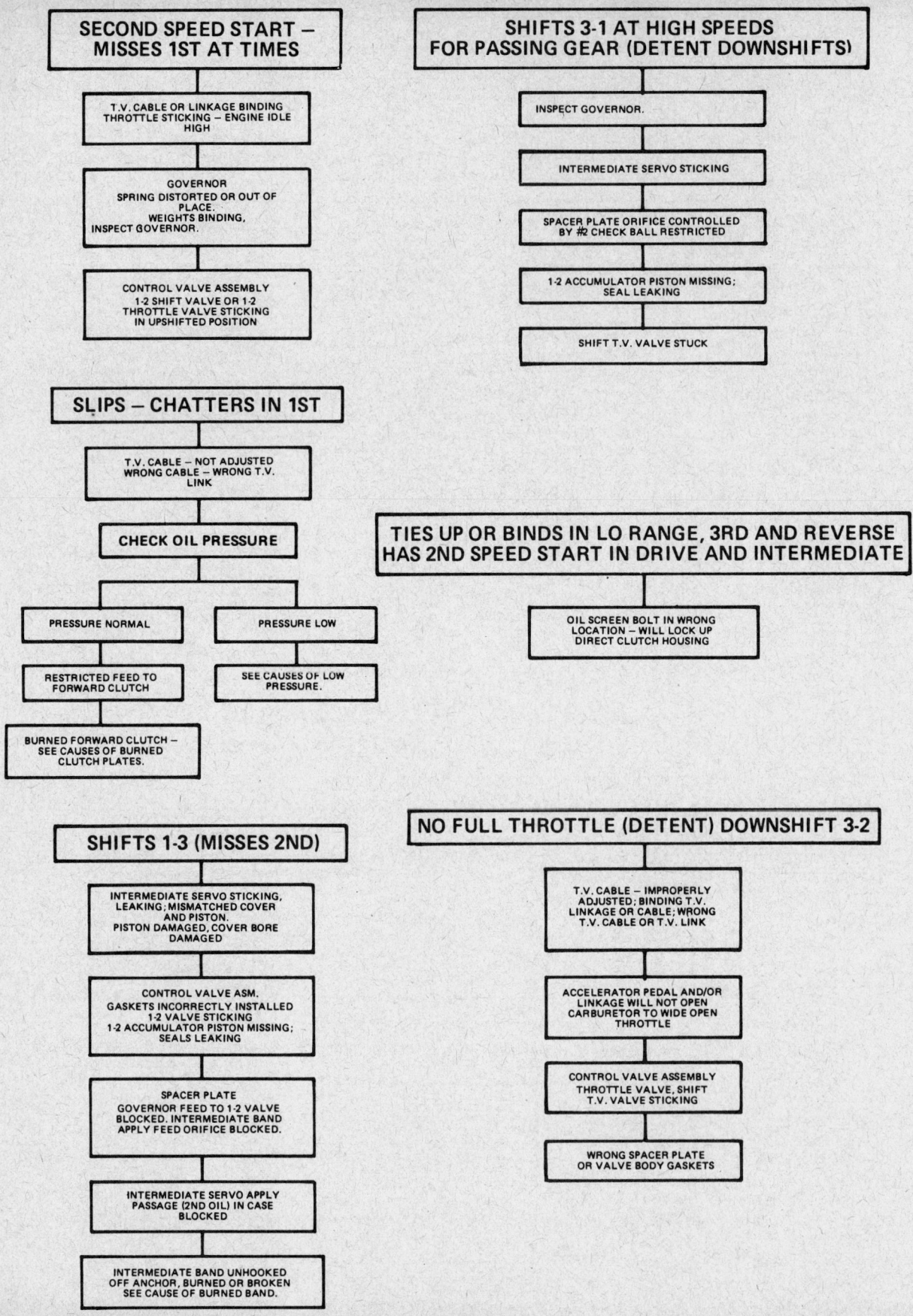

SECOND SPEED START — MISSES 1ST AT TIMES

- T.V. CABLE OR LINKAGE BINDING THROTTLE STICKING — ENGINE IDLE HIGH
- GOVERNOR SPRING DISTORTED OR OUT OF PLACE. WEIGHTS BINDING, INSPECT GOVERNOR.
- CONTROL VALVE ASSEMBLY 1-2 SHIFT VALVE OR 1-2 THROTTLE VALVE STICKING IN UPSHIFTED POSITION

SLIPS — CHATTERS IN 1ST

- T.V. CABLE — NOT ADJUSTED WRONG CABLE — WRONG T.V. LINK
- CHECK OIL PRESSURE
  - PRESSURE NORMAL
    - RESTRICTED FEED TO FORWARD CLUTCH
    - BURNED FORWARD CLUTCH — SEE CAUSES OF BURNED CLUTCH PLATES.
  - PRESSURE LOW
    - SEE CAUSES OF LOW PRESSURE.

SHIFTS 1-3 (MISSES 2ND)

- INTERMEDIATE SERVO STICKING, LEAKING; MISMATCHED COVER AND PISTON. PISTON DAMAGED, COVER BORE DAMAGED
- CONTROL VALVE ASM. GASKETS INCORRECTLY INSTALLED 1-2 VALVE STICKING 1-2 ACCUMULATOR PISTON MISSING; SEALS LEAKING
- SPACER PLATE GOVERNOR FEED TO 1-2 VALVE BLOCKED. INTERMEDIATE BAND APPLY FEED ORIFICE BLOCKED.
- INTERMEDIATE SERVO APPLY PASSAGE (2ND OIL) IN CASE BLOCKED
- INTERMEDIATE BAND UNHOOKED OFF ANCHOR, BURNED OR BROKEN SEE CAUSE OF BURNED BAND.

SHIFTS 3-1 AT HIGH SPEEDS FOR PASSING GEAR (DETENT DOWNSHIFTS)

- INSPECT GOVERNOR.
- INTERMEDIATE SERVO STICKING
- SPACER PLATE ORIFICE CONTROLLED BY #2 CHECK BALL RESTRICTED
- 1-2 ACCUMULATOR PISTON MISSING; SEAL LEAKING
- SHIFT T.V. VALVE STUCK

TIES UP OR BINDS IN LO RANGE, 3RD AND REVERSE HAS 2ND SPEED START IN DRIVE AND INTERMEDIATE

- OIL SCREEN BOLT IN WRONG LOCATION — WILL LOCK UP DIRECT CLUTCH HOUSING

NO FULL THROTTLE (DETENT) DOWNSHIFT 3-2

- T.V. CABLE — IMPROPERLY ADJUSTED; BINDING T.V. LINKAGE OR CABLE; WRONG T.V. CABLE OR T.V. LINK
- ACCELERATOR PEDAL AND/OR LINKAGE WILL NOT OPEN CARBURETOR TO WIDE OPEN THROTTLE
- CONTROL VALVE ASSEMBLY THROTTLE VALVE, SHIFT T.V. VALVE STICKING
- WRONG SPACER PLATE OR VALVE BODY GASKETS

Fig. 8   THM 325 Trouble-shooting chart, Part 7 of 8

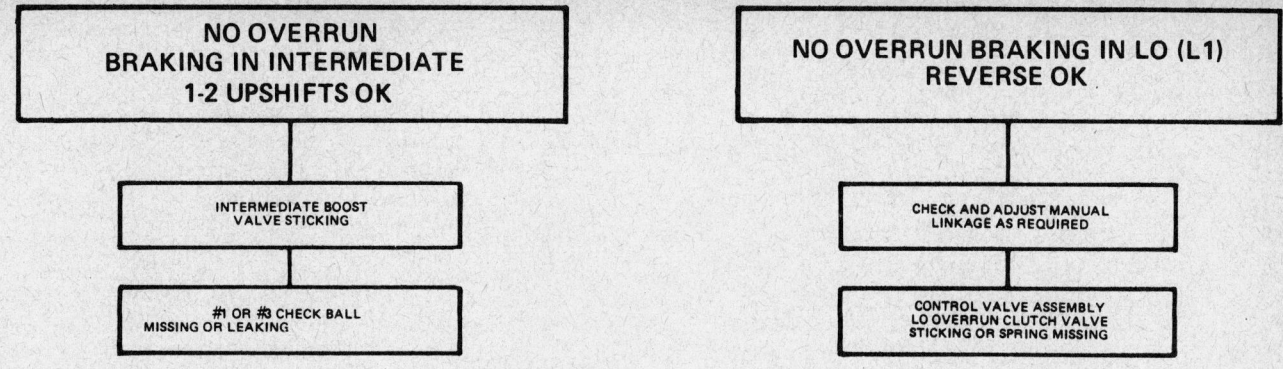

NO OVERRUN
BRAKING IN INTERMEDIATE
1-2 UPSHIFTS OK

NO OVERRUN BRAKING IN LO (L1)
REVERSE OK

INTERMEDIATE BOOST
VALVE STICKING

CHECK AND ADJUST MANUAL
LINKAGE AS REQUIRED

#1 OR #3 CHECK BALL
MISSING OR LEAKING

CONTROL VALVE ASSEMBLY
LO OVERRUN CLUTCH VALVE
STICKING OR SPRING MISSING

CAUTION: BEFORE CHECKING TRANSMISSION FOR WHAT IS BELIEVED TO BE "TRANS. NOISE,"
MAKE CERTAIN THE NOISE IS NOT FROM THE WATER PUMP, ALTERNATOR, AIR CONDITIONER,
POWER STEERING, ETC. THESE COMPONENTS CAN BE ISOLATED BY REMOVING THE PROPER BELT
AND RUNNING THE ENGINE NOT MORE THAN TWO MINUTES AT ONE TIME.

TRANSMISSION NOISY

PARK, NEUTRAL & ALL DRIVING RANGES

DURING ACCELERATION —
ANY GEAR

PUMP CAVITATION
OIL LEVEL LOW
PLUGGED OR RESTRICTED SCREEN
DAMAGED SCREEN "O" RING SEAL
POROSITY IN CASE INTAKE AREA
WATER IN OIL.
POROSITY OR VOIDS AT TRANS.
INTAKE PORT.

TRANSMISSION OR COOLER LINES
GROUNDED TO UNDERBODY.
MOTOR MOUNTS LOSE OR BROKEN

325 MODEL ONLY—DRIVE LINK ASSEMBLY,
WORN OR DAMAGED, MAY SOUND
LIKE POPCORN POPPING.

PUMP ASSEMBLY
GEARS DAMAGED
DRIVING GEAR ASSEMBLED
BACKWARDS
CRESCENT INTERFERENCE.

SQUEAL AT LOW CAR
SPEED, ESPECIALLY HOT

SPEEDOMETER DRIVEN GEAR SHAFT
SEAL —
SEAL REQUIRES LUBRICATION OR
REPLACEMENT

CONVERTER
LOOSE BOLTS (CONVERTER TO
FLEX PLATE)
CONVERTER DAMAGE
CRACKED OR BROKEN FLEX PLATE

IF SPEEDOMETER DRIVEN GEAR
SHAFT APPEARS TWISTED, CHECK
FOR PRESENCE OF ENGINE COOLANT
IN TRANSMISSION.

FIRST, SECOND AND/OR
REVERSE

PLANETARY GEAR SET
1. THOROUGHLY CLEAN, DRY & INSPECT CLOSELY. THE ROLLER THRUST
   BEARINGS AND THRUST RACES FOR A PITTING OR ROUGH CONDITION.
2. INSPECT GEARS FOR DAMAGE, WEAR, PITTING AND PINIONS FOR TILT.

Fig. 9 THM 325 Trouble-shooting chart, Part 8 of 8

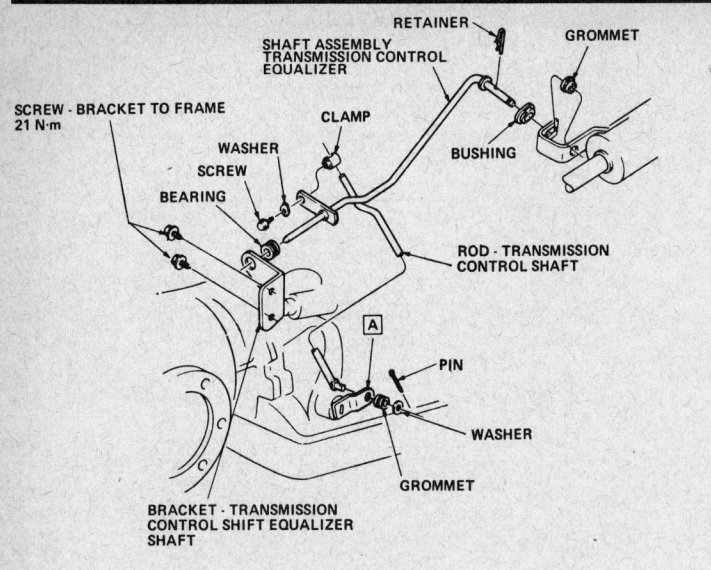

RETAINER

SHAFT ASSEMBLY
TRANSMISSION CONTROL
EQUALIZER

GROMMET

THROTTLE CONTROL CABLE

THROTTLE CONTROL
BRACKET

SCREW - BRACKET TO FRAME
21 N·m

CLAMP

WASHER
SCREW

BEARING

BUSHING

ROD - TRANSMISSION
CONTROL SHAFT

A

PIN

WASHER

GROMMET

BRACKET - TRANSMISSION
CONTROL SHIFT EQUALIZER
SHAFT

Fig. 10 Manual linkage

VIEW-A

READJUSTMENT
LOCK TAB
FITTING
CARB LEVER
SLIDER - READJUST DIRECTION

VIEW-B

Fig. 11 Downshift linkage adjustment

g. Piston seals missing or damaged.
h. Apply ring missing, wrong apply ring or incorrect number of clutch plates used.
i. Piston damaged or leaking.
3. Control valve assembly and case:
a. Control valve assembly to case bolts loose.
b. Sealing surface on control valve assembly, spacer plate, case or gaskets damaged or leaking.
c. Porosity between channels in control valve or case.

Causes of Burned Lo-Reverse Clutch

1. Pump assembly:
a. Leaking seal rings on drive sprocket support
b. Driven sprocket sleeve loose or mispositioned.
c. Cup plug leaking or missing.
d. No. 6 check ball missing or mispositioned in case.
e. Reverse feed passage restricted or leaking.
f. Low oil pressure. Refer to "Causes of Low Oil Pressure".
2. Lo-reverse clutch assembly:
a. Housing seal area damaged.
b. Piston or seals damaged.
c. Apply ring missing, wrong apply ring used, or incorrect number of clutch plates used.
3. Control valve assembly:
a. Reverse boost valve sticking.
b. Check balls missing or mispositioned.
4. Case assembly;
a. Lo-reverse clutch housing to case plug assembly hole restricted, damaged or not seated properly.

Causes of Burned Intermediate Band

1. Band anchor pin missing or not engaged in band.
2. Band not properly aligned or apply pin not engaged.
3. Intermediate servo assembly:
a. Incorrect size piston or cover.
b. Seals missing or damaged.
c. Incorrect band apply pin.

4. Leak in clutch apply system.
5. Control valve assembly:
a. 1-2 accumulator piston missing or seal leaking.
b. 1-2 accumulator valve sticking.
6. Case cover no. 7 check ball missing or not seating properly.

MAINTENANCE

Adding Oil

To check fluid, drive vehicle for at least 15 minutes to bring fluid to operating temperature (190°–200° F.). With vehicle on a level surface and engine idling in Park and parking brake applied, the level on the dipstick should be at the Full Hot mark. To bring the fluid level from the ADD mark to the FULL mark requires one pint of fluid. If vehicle cannot be driven sufficiently to bring fluid to operating temperature, the level on the dipstick should be between the two dimples on the dipstick with fluid temperature at 65°–85° F.

If additional fluid is required, use only Dexron II automatic transmission fluid.

NOTE: An early change to a darker color from the usual red color and or a strong odor that is usually associated with overheated fluid is normal and should not be considered as a positive sign of required maintenance or unit failure.

CAUTION: When adding fluid, do not over fill, as foaming and loss of fluid through the vent may occur as the fluid heats up. Also, if fluid level is too low, complete loss of drive may occur especially when cold, which can cause transmission failure.

Every 100,000 miles, the oil should be drained, the oil pan removed, the screen cleaned and fresh fluid added. For vehicles subjected to more severe use such as heavy city traffic especially in hot weather, prolonged periods of idling or towing, this maintenance should be performed every 15,000 miles.

Changing Oil

1. Raise vehicle and position drain pan under transmission pan.
2. Loosen rear pan attaching bolts approximately four turns.
3. Carefully pry transmission pan loose with a screwdriver and allow fluid to drain.
4. Remove pan attaching bolts, pan and pan gasket.
5. Drain remaining fluid from pan, then clean pan with solvent and dry with compressed air.
6. Remove transmission screen. Remove O-ring seal from intake pipe or case bore.
7. Thoroughly clean screen assembly with solvent and dry with compressed air.
8. Install O-ring on intake pipe, then install screen retainer.
9. Install gasket on pan, then install pan and torque attaching bolts to 12 ft. lbs.
10. Lower vehicle and add approximately 5 qts. of Dexron II type transmission fluid through filler tube.
11. Start engine and operate at idle speed, then move selector lever through each range.
12. Place transmission in Park position and check fluid level.

MANUAL LINKAGE, ADJUST

1. Loosen transmission control shaft rod

clamp, Fig. 10.
2. Place shift lever in Neutral position.
3. Place transmission lever in Neutral position.
4. While holding clamp flush against control equalizer shaft assembly, tighten screw against rod finger tight.
5. Tighten clamp screw to 20 ft. lbs. No force should be exerted on in either direction on the rod or equalizer shaft assembly when tighten clamp screw.
6. Check neutral start switch adjustment and adjust as necessary.

DOWNSHIFT CABLE, ADJUST

1. After assembling cable to transmission install cable fitting into engine bracket.
2. Install cable terminal on carburetor lever.
3. Open carburetor lever to full throttle stop position to automatically adjust slider on cable to the correct setting, Fig. 11.
4. Release carburetor lever.
5. If cable readjustment is necessary, depress and hold metal tab and move slider back through fitting in direction away from carburetor lever until slider stops against fitting, Fig. 11. Release metal lock tab and repeat steps 3. and 4.

IN-VEHICLE REPAIRS
Valve Body, Replace

1. Drain transmission fluid and remove oil pan and screen.
2. Remove screw and disconnect downshift cable.
3. Remove throttle lever and bracket assembly. Use care not to bend throttle lever link.
4. Remove manual detent roller and spring assembly.
5. Support valve body and remove attaching bolts.
6. While holding manual valve with fingers, remove valve body spacer plate and gaskets together to prevent dropping of four check balls located in valve body and fifth check ball located on spacer plate.

NOTE: After removing valve body, intermediate band anchor pin and reverse

clutch cup plug may come out.

7. Place valve body on bench with spacer plate side facing upward and remove check ball from spacer plate.
8. Reverse procedure to install. Torque valve body attaching bolts to 8 ft. lbs.

NOTE: Intermediate band anchor pin must locate on intermediate band or damage to transmission may result.

Intermediate Servo, Replace

1. Install tool No. J-28493 on transmission case and tighten bolt to depress servo cover.
2. Using a small screwdriver, remove servo cover retaining ring, then remove tool.
3. Remove servo cover, then remove servo piston and band apply pin assembly.
4. Reverse procedure to install.

Speedometer Gears, Replace

1. Disconnect speedometer cable, then remove driven gear attaching bolt, retainer and driven gear.
2. Remove governor cover attaching screws and governor cover.
3. Remove governor and speedometer drive gear assembly.
4. Remove speedometer drive gear from governor assembly.
5. Reverse procedure to install.

Pressure Regulator Valve, Replace

1. Drain transmission fluid and remove oil pan and screen.
2. Push in on pressure regulator valve, compress valve spring with a small screwdriver.
3. Remove retaining ring, then slowly release spring tension and remove pressure regulator guide.

DRIVE LINK BELT OR SPROCKETS

Refer to Cadillac Section, Eldorado and Seville Drive Link Belt, for removal and installation procedures.

TRANSMISSION, REPLACE

1. Disconnect battery ground cable.
2. Disconnect speedometer cable and downshift cable from transmission.
3. Support engine with a suitable holding fixture.
4. Remove three upper final drive to transmission attaching bolts.
5. Remove five transmission to engine mounting bolts and the dipstick tube assembly.
6. Raise and support vehicle.
7. Remove splash shield.
8. Disconnect starter wiring and remove the starter.
9. Disconnect transmission oil cooler lines from transmission.
10. Loosen but do not remove torque converter cover screw nearest dipstick tube brace and remove all other screws and cover.
11. Remove the two nuts and bolts securing left hand exhaust pipe to the crossover pipe, then slide the flanges apart for clearance.
12. Support transmission with a suitable jack.
13. Remove the three remaining final drive to the transmission bolts.
14. Remove the remaining transmission to engine bolt and loosen the final drive support bracket.
15. Remove three flywheel to converter bolts.
16. Disconnect shift control linkage at transmission.
17. Remove left and right hand transmission mounts.
18. Slowly lower transmission and move rearward to disengage splines from final drive unit. With transmission lowered install a suitable converter holding tool.
19. Reverse procedure to install. Torque bolts as follows:

	Ft. Lbs.
Starter mounting bolts	30
Transmission mount to frame nut	40
Transmission to engine bolts	35
Flywheel to converter bolts	35
Final drive to transmission bolts	30

GM Front Wheel Drive
Turbo Hydra-Matic 425 Automatic
Transmission

TRANSMISSION IDENTIFICATION

CADILLAC ELDORADO

1977–78 Exc. Electronic Fuel Injection . . AJ
1977–78 Electronic Fuel Injection . . . . . AK

OLDSMOBILE TORONADO

1977–78 Exc. Below . . . . OJ
1977 California . . . . OM

DESCRIPTION

This transmission is a fully automatic unit used for front wheel drive applications, Fig. 1. It consists primarily of a three-element hydraulic torque converter, dual sprocket and chain link assembly, compound planetary gear set, three multiple disc clutches, a sprag clutch, a roller clutch, two band assemblies, and a hydraulic control system.

Torque Converter

The torque converter consists of a pump or driving member, a turbine or driver member and a stator or reaction member.

The stator is mounted on a one-way roller clutch which allows it to overrun when not used as a reaction member.

The torque converter couples the engine to the planetary gear set through the use of a drive sprocket, a chain link assembly, and a driven sprocket. Clockwise engine torque turns the drive sprocket clockwise. This, in turn, drives the driven sprocket in a clockwise

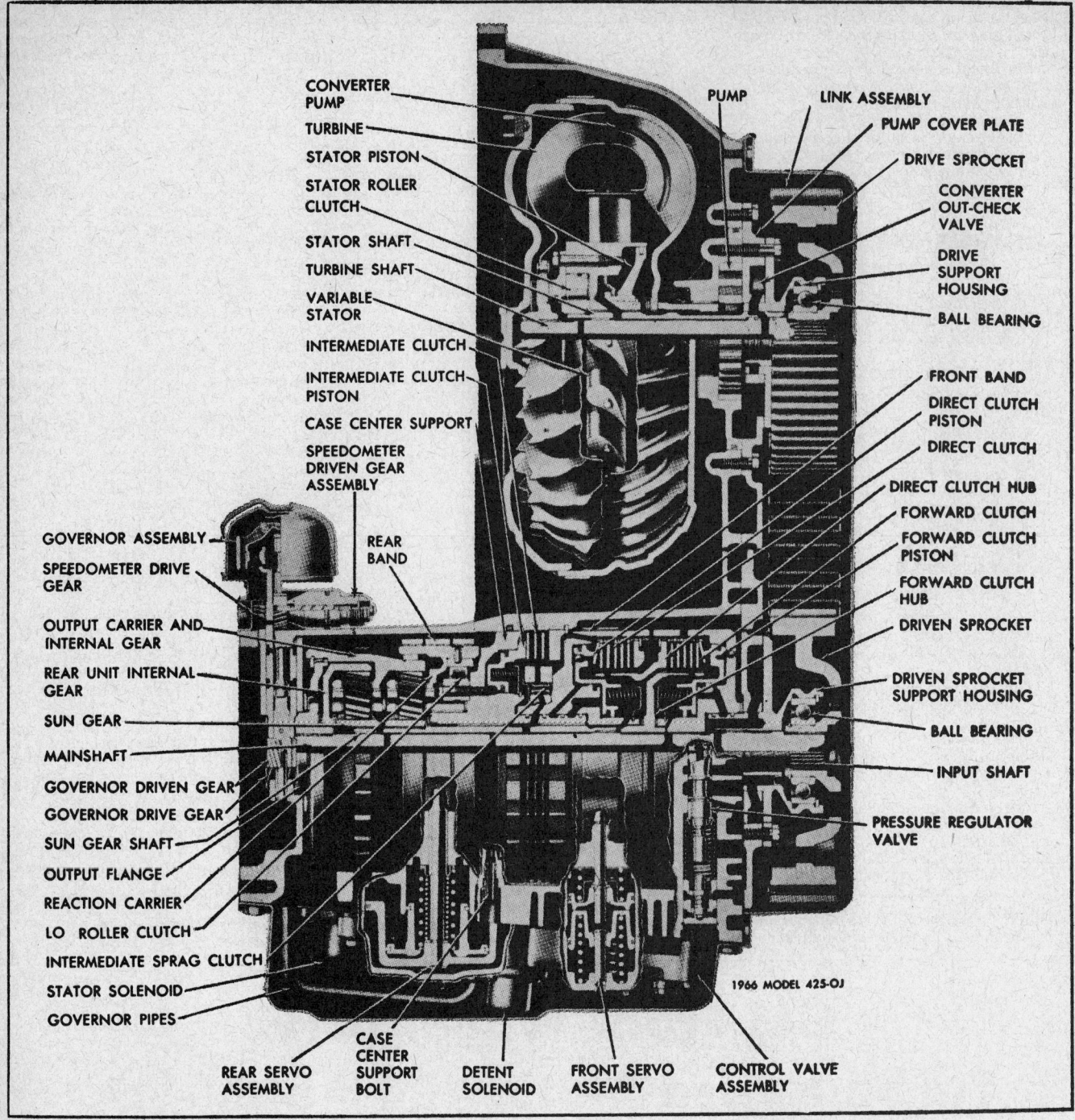

Fig. 1 General Motors Turbo Hydra-Matic 425

Labels (clockwise from top left):
CONVERTER PUMP · TURBINE · STATOR PISTON · STATOR ROLLER CLUTCH · STATOR SHAFT · TURBINE SHAFT · VARIABLE STATOR · INTERMEDIATE CLUTCH · INTERMEDIATE CLUTCH PISTON · CASE CENTER SUPPORT · SPEEDOMETER DRIVEN GEAR ASSEMBLY · GOVERNOR ASSEMBLY · SPEEDOMETER DRIVE GEAR · OUTPUT CARRIER AND INTERNAL GEAR · REAR UNIT INTERNAL GEAR · SUN GEAR · MAINSHAFT · GOVERNOR DRIVEN GEAR · GOVERNOR DRIVE GEAR · SUN GEAR SHAFT · OUTPUT FLANGE · REACTION CARRIER · LO ROLLER CLUTCH · INTERMEDIATE SPRAG CLUTCH · STATOR SOLENOID · GOVERNOR PIPES · REAR BAND · REAR SERVO ASSEMBLY · CASE CENTER SUPPORT BOLT · DETENT SOLENOID · FRONT SERVO ASSEMBLY · CONTROL VALVE ASSEMBLY · PUMP · LINK ASSEMBLY · PUMP COVER PLATE · DRIVE SPROCKET · CONVERTER OUT-CHECK VALVE · DRIVE SUPPORT HOUSING · BALL BEARING · FRONT BAND · DIRECT CLUTCH PISTON · DIRECT CLUTCH · DIRECT CLUTCH HUB · FORWARD CLUTCH · FORWARD CLUTCH PISTON · FORWARD CLUTCH HUB · DRIVEN SPROCKET · DRIVEN SPROCKET SUPPORT HOUSING · BALL BEARING · INPUT SHAFT · PRESSURE REGULATOR VALVE · 1966 MODEL 425-OJ

direction. This in effect is a reverse in the direction of engine torque due to the side mounting of the gear unit.

Planetary Gear Set

The gear set provides three forward ratios and reverse. The approximate gear ratios are: First 2½ to 1, second 1½ to 1, third 1.1 to 1, reverse 2.1 to 1. Second and third are also multiplied by a lesser degree.

Converter stall ratio, first gear (2½ × 2) equals 5 to 1. Converter stall ratio, reverse (2.1 × 2) equals 4.2 to 1.

External Controls

External control connections to the transmission are: a) engine vacuum, b) 12-volt electrical signals, c) manual linkage control.

Engine vacuum is used to operate the vacuum modulator assembly. The vacuum modulator automatically senses any change in torque input to the transmission that the driver induces through a change in accelerator position.

On all models an electrical signal is used to operate an electrical solenoid. The solenoid is activated by a switch at the carburetor. When the throttle is opened sufficiently to close this switch, the solenoid in the transmission is activated, causing a downshift at speeds below approximately 70 mph. At lower speeds, downshifts will occur at lesser speeds without use of the switch.

TROUBLE SHOOTING GUIDE

NOTE: In many of the following diagnosis procedures, it is recommended that air pressure be applied to help in determining if the seal, rings or pistons are stuck, missing or damaged. Therefore, when air is applied, listen carefully for escaping air and piston action as air is applied to a particular area.

No Drive In "D" Range

1. Low oil level. Check for external leaks or vacuum modulator diaphragm leaking.
2. Manual linkage maladjusted. Correct alignment in manual lever shift quadrant.
3. Low oil pressure.
4. Oil strainer O-ring seal missing or damaged, neck weld leaking, strainer blocked.
5. Oil pump pressure regulator stuck or inoperative. Pump drive gear tangs damaged by converter.
6. Case porosity in intake bore.
7. Control valve. Manual valve disconnected from manual lever pin. (Other shift lever positions would also be affected.)
8. Forward clutch does not apply. Piston cracked; seals missing or damaged. These defects can be checked by removing the valve body and applying air pressure to the drive cavity in the case valve body face. Missing, damaged or worn oil rings on driven support housing can also be checked in this manner at the same time because they can also cause the forward clutch not to apply. Clutch plates burned.
9. Roller clutch inoperative. Rollers worn, damaged springs, or damaged races. May be checked by placing selector lever in "L" range.

No Drive In "R" or Slips In Reverse

1. Low oil level.
2. Manual linkage.
3. Oil pressure. Vacuum modulator defective, modulator valve sticking.
4. Restricted strainer, leak at intake pipe or O-ring seal. Pressure regulator or boost valve sticking.
5. Control valve body gaskets leaking or damaged (other malfunctions may also be indicated). Low-reverse check ball missing from case (this will cause no overrun braking in low range). The 2–3 valve train stuck open (this will also cause 1–3 upshifts in drive range). Reverse feed passage not drilled; also check case passages. Apply air to reverse passage in case valve body face.
6. Rear servo and accumulator. Servo piston seal ring broken or missing. Apply air pressure to drilled hole in intermediate clutch passage of case valve body face to check for piston operation and excessive leakage. Band apply pin too short (this may also cause no overrun braking or slip in overrun braking in low range).
7. Rear band burned, loose lining, apply pin or anchor pin not engaged; band broken.
8. Direct clutch outer seal damaged or missing. Clutch plates burned (may be caused by stuck ball check in piston).
9. Forward clutch does not release (will also cause drive in neutral range).

Drive In Neutral

1. Manual linkage maladjusted.
2. Forward clutch does not release (this condition will also cause no reverse).

1st Speed Only—No 1–2 Upshift

1. Governor valve sticking; driven gear loose, damaged or worn. If driven gear shows signs of wear or damage, check output flange drive gear for nicks or rough finish.
2. Control valve. The 1–2 shift valve train stuck closed. Dirt, chips or damaged valve in 1–2 shift valve train. Governor feed channels blocked or leaking; pipes out of position. Valve body gaskets leaking or damaged. Case porosity between oil channels. Governor feed passage blocked.
3. Intermediate clutch. Case center support oil rings missing, broken or defective. Clutch piston seals missing, improperly assembled, cut or damaged. Apply air to intermediate clutch passage located in case valve body face to check for these defects.

1–2 Shift Obtained Only At Full Throttle

1. Detent switch sticking or defective.
2. Detent solenoid loose, gasket leaking, sticks open, electrical wire pinched between cover and casting.
3. Control valve body gasket leaking or damaged. Detent valve train stuck.

1st & 2nd Speeds Only No 2–3 Shift

1. Detent solenoid stuck open (the 2–3 shift would occur at very high speeds) may be diagnosed as no 2–3 shift.
2. Detent switch sticking or defective.
3. Control valve body. The 2–3 valve train stuck with dirt or foreign material. Valve body gaskets leaking or damaged.
4. Direct clutch. Case center support oil rings missing or broken. Clutch piston seals missing, improperly assembled, cut or damaged; piston ball check stuck or missing. Apply air to direct clutch passage in case valve body face to check these conditions.

Slips In All Ranges

1. Oil level incorrect.
2. Low oil pressure. Vacuum modulator defective or valve sticking. Oil strainer plugged or leaks at neck; O-ring (case to strainer) missing or damaged. Pressure regulator or boost valve sticking.
3. Case cross channel leaks; porosity.
4. Forward, intermediate and direct clutches slipping. Clutch plates burned. Always look for a primary defect that would cause clutch plates to burn. (Missing feed holes, seals and oil rings, etc., are primary defects).
5. Roller clutch rollers worn; springs or cage damaged, and worn or damaged races (operates normally in low and reverse ranges).

Slips 1–2 Shift

1. Oil level incorrect.
2. Low oil pressure. Look for defective vacuum modulator or valve sticking. Pump pressure regulator valve stuck.
3. Front servo accumulator piston cracked or porous, oil ring damaged or missing.
4. Control valve. The 1–2 accumulator valve train (may cause a slip-bump shift). Porous valve body or case valve body face.
5. Rear servo accumulator oil ring missing or damaged; case bore damaged; piston cracked or damaged.
6. Case porous between oil passages.

7. Intermediate clutch lip seals missing, cut or damaged. Apply air pressure to intermediate clutch passage in case valve body face to check. Clutch plates burned. Case center support leaks in feed circuits (oil rings damaged or grooves damaged) or excessive leak between tower and bushing.

Rough 1–2 Shift

1. Oil pressure. Check vacuum modulator for loose fittings, restrictions in line; defective vacuum modulator. Modulator valve stuck. Pressure regulator boost valve stuck.
2. Control valve. 1–2 accumulator valve train; valve body-to-case bolts loose; gaskets inverted, off location, or damaged.
3. Case. Intermediate clutch passage check ball missing or not seating. Case porous between channels.
4. Rear servo accumulator piston stuck. Apply air pressure to 1–2 accumulator passage in case valve body face (you should hear the servo piston move). Broken or missing spring; bore scored or damaged.

Slips 2–3 Shift

1. Oil level high or low.
2. Low oil pressure. Modulator defective or valve sticking. Pump pressure regulator valve or boost valve sticking.
3. Control valve. Accumulator piston pin leak at valve body end.
4. Direct clutch piston seals leaking. Case center support oil seal rings damaged or excessive leak between tower and bushing. Apply air to direct clutch passage in case valve body face. If air comes out intermediate passage, center support is defective.

Rough 2–3 Shift

1. Oil pressure high. Vacuum modulator defective or valve sticking. Pump pressure regulator valve or boost valve stuck or inoperative.
2. Front servo accumulator spring missing or broken; accumulator piston stuck.

Shifts Occur at too High or too Low Car Speed

1. Oil pressure. Vacuum modulator defective or valve sticking. Leak in vacuum line (engine to transmission). Vacuum modulator line fitting on carburetor blocked. Pump pressure regulator valve or boost valve train stuck.
2. Governor valve stuck or sticking. Feed holes restricted or leaking; pipes damaged or mispositioned.
3. Detent solenoid stuck open or loose on valve body (will cause late shifts).
4. Control valve. Detent valve train sticking; 3–2 valve train sticking; 1–2 shift valve stuck; 1–2 detent valve sticking open (will probably cause early 2–3 shift).
5. Spacer plate gaskets inverted or mispositioned; orifice holes missing or blocked; check balls missing or mislocated.
6. Case porous in channels or foreign material blocking channels.

No Detent Downshift

1. Detent switch mispositioned or electrical connections loose.
2. Solenoid defective or electrical connections loose.
3. Control valve detent valve train stuck.

No Engine Braking—Super Range 2nd Speed

1. Front servo or accumulator piston rings broken or missing. Case or valve body bores worn oversize, causing excessive leakage.
2. Front band worn or burned (check for cause); band end lugs broken or damaged; band lugs not engaged on anchor pins or servo apply pin (check for cause).

No Engine Braking—Low Range 1st Speed

1. Control valve low-reverse check ball missing from case.
2. Rear servo oil ring damaged or missing; piston damaged or porous, causing a leak in apply pressure.
3. Rear band lining worn or burned (check for cause); band end lugs broken; band ends not engaged on anchor pin or servo apply pin. These items will also cause slip in reverse or no reverse.

Will Not Hold Car In Park Position

1. Manual linkage maladjusted (external).
2. Parking brake lever and actuator rod assembly defective (check for proper actuator spring action). Parking pawl broken or inoperative.

Poor Performance or Rough Idle

1. Stator switch defective or maladjusted.
2. Stator solenoid defective or wire ground to solenoid housing; electrical connection loose; stator valve train stuck (located in valve body); oil feed circuit to stator restricted or blocked (check feed hole in stator shaft); converter-out check valve broken or missing (reed valve located in cover plate under drive support housing).
3. Turbine shaft converter return passage not drilled; oil seal rings broken, worn or missing.
4. Case porous in feed circuit channels or foreign material blocking feed circuit.
5. Converter assembly defective.

Transmission Noise

1. Pump noise. Oil level high or low; water in oil, driving gear assembled upside down; driving or driven gear teeth damaged.
2. Gear noise (1st gear drive range). Check planetary pinions for tooth damage. Check sun gear and front and rear internal gears for tooth finish or damage.
3. Clutch noise during application. Check clutch plates.
4. Sprocket and chain link assembly. Chain link too long (sounds similar to popcorn popping). There will be a rough burr along teeth of drive sprocket if chain link is too long; replace chain link and drive sprocket. Drive or driven sprocket teeth damaged. Engine mounts worn or damaged.

Burned Forward Clutch Plates

1. Check ball in clutch housing damaged, stuck or missing.
2. Clutch piston cracked, seals damaged or missing.
3. Low line pressure.

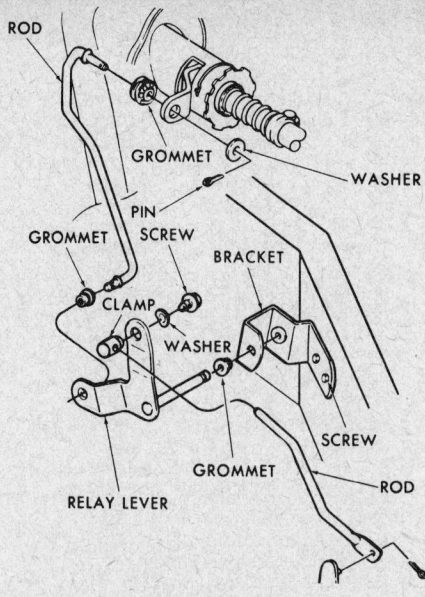

Fig. 2 Manual control linkage adjustment. Cadillac Eldorado (typical)

4. Manual valve mispositioned.
5. Restricted oil feed to forward clutch.
6. Pump cover oil seal rings missing, broken or undersize or ring groove oversize.
7. Case valve body face not flat or porosity between channels.
8. Manual valve bent and center land not ground properly.

Burned Intermediate Clutch Plates

1. Rear accumulator piston oil ring damaged or missing.
2. 1-2 accumulator valve stuck in control valve stuck in control valve assembly.
3. Intermediate clutch piston seals damaged or missing.
4. Center support bolt loose.
5. Low line pressure.
6. Intermediate clutch plug in case missing.
7. Case valve body face not flat or porosity between channels.
8. Manual valve bent and center land not ground properly.

Burned Direct Clutch Plates

1. Restricted orifice in vacuum line to modulator.
2. Check ball in direct clutch piston damaged, stuck or missing.
3. Defective modulator bellows.
4. Center support bolt loose.
5. Center support oil rings or grooves damaged or missing.
6. Clutch piston seals damaged or missing.
7. Front and rear servo pistons and seals damaged.
8. Manual valve bent and center land not cleaned up.
9. Case valve body face not flat or porosity between channels.
10. Intermediate sprag clutch installed backwards.

MAINTENANCE

Adding Oil

The fluid level should be checked at every engine oil change interval, and should be changed at 24,000 mile intervals. The fluid level should be checked with the selector lever in PARK position, engine running at idle speed and car on a level surface. The oil indicator and filler tube are located under the hood at the left front corner of the engine. *The filler tube comes out from the final drive housing but it is for the transmission.*

NOTE: If any work is performed on the transmission, it will require the following amounts of oil to bring the oil to the correct level:
1. Pan removed 5½ qts.
2. Drive cover sprocket housing ½ qt.
3. Converter changed 3½ qts.
4. Total overhaul (total capacity) 13 qts.

Changing Oil

When changing transmission oil, first add 4 quarts, start the engine, and add oil to bring the fluid level to the FULL mark on the dipstick. Use only Dexron automatic transmission oil.

NOTE: Cadillac uses an extended-life Dexron transmission fluid. With this new fluid, strainer replacement and fluid change is now recommended at 100,000 miles under normal operating conditions and 50,000 miles under severe or abnormal service such as trailer towing.

This recommendation applies only to the improved fluid and its availability for service. If the new fluid is not available, the former fluid can be used but then the 24,000 mile maintenance rule will apply.

Oldsmobile is using a revised type Dexron fluid. An early change to a darker color from the usual red color and or a strong odor that is usually associated with overheated fluid is normal, and should not be treated as a positive sign of needed maintenance or unit failure.

The normal maintenance schedule for drain and refill of this type fluid remains unchanged at 24,000 miles under normal service and 12,000 miles under severe operating conditions, such as trailer towing. Also on Olds Toronado, the normal maintenance schedule for drain and refill is 60,000 miles.

MANUAL LINKAGE, ADJUST

Cadillac Eldorado

1. Referring to Fig. 2, loosen adjusting screw on relay lever.
2. Pull relay rod up to position transmission shift valve in Park, then push rod down to the third (Neutral) step. Make sure rod is centered in this detent position.
3. Position selector lever in Neutral against quadrant stop in steering column.
4. Tighten relay rod adjusting screw, making sure shift lever is held against Neutral stop while this operation is being performed.

Olds Toronado

Make the adjustment as directed in Fig. 3.

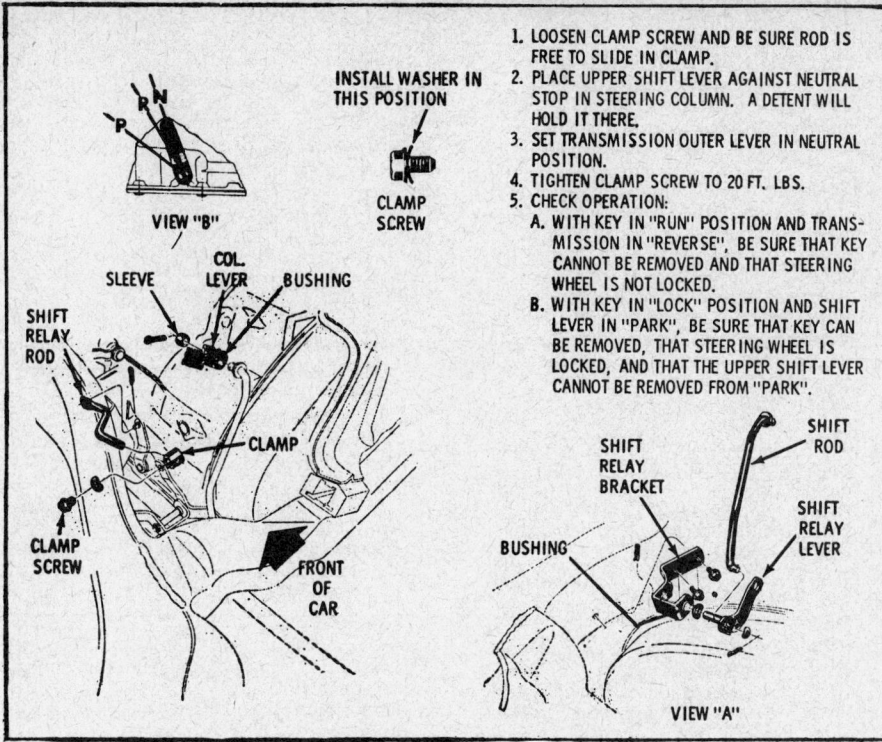

1. LOOSEN CLAMP SCREW AND BE SURE ROD IS FREE TO SLIDE IN CLAMP.
2. PLACE UPPER SHIFT LEVER AGAINST NEUTRAL STOP IN STEERING COLUMN. A DETENT WILL HOLD IT THERE.
3. SET TRANSMISSION OUTER LEVER IN NEUTRAL POSITION.
4. TIGHTEN CLAMP SCREW TO 20 FT. LBS.
5. CHECK OPERATION:
   A. WITH KEY IN "RUN" POSITION AND TRANSMISSION IN "REVERSE", BE SURE THAT KEY CANNOT BE REMOVED AND THAT STEERING WHEEL IS NOT LOCKED.
   B. WITH KEY IN "LOCK" POSITION AND SHIFT LEVER IN "PARK", BE SURE THAT KEY CAN BE REMOVED, THAT STEERING WHEEL IS LOCKED, AND THAT THE UPPER SHIFT LEVER CANNOT BE REMOVED FROM "PARK".

Fig. 3   Shift linkage adjustment. Toronado column shift, 1977–78

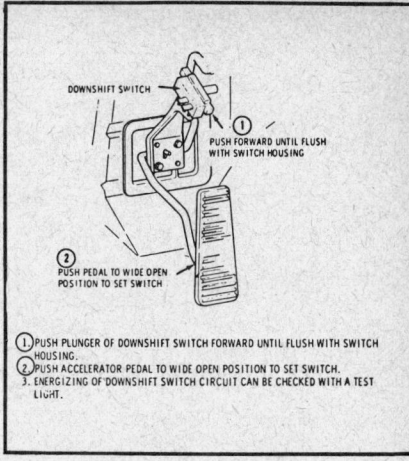

Fig. 4   Downshift switch adjustment. Oldsmobile Toronado

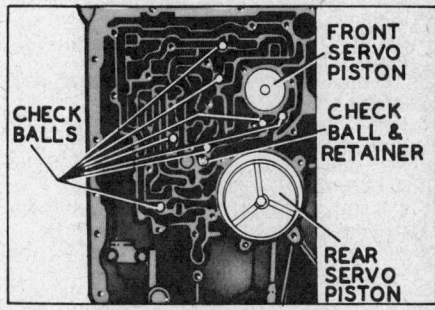

Fig. 5   Location of check balls

DOWNSHIFT SWITCH, ADJUST

Cadillac Eldorado

1. Remove carburetor air cleaner.
2. Make sure that carburetor is properly adjusted and that throttle linkage is at low speed idle setting.
3. If the downshift switch is properly adjusted, a #42 (wire gauge size) drill can be inserted in the calibrating hole below lower wire terminal extending through to carburetor side of switch.
4. If adjustment is necessary, loosen the two switch mounting screws and position the switch for proper alignment.
5. With switch positioned, tighten mounting screws, remove drill gauge and install air cleaner.

Olds Toronado

Adjust detent downshift switch as described in Fig. 4

NOTE: Trailer Hauling Switch (Y-73 option) is bronze colored. When checking the special throttle switches with a test lamp, the test lamp *should light only* when the throttle valves are at idle or at wide open throttle position. The test lamp *will not light* at the 40° throttle opening as it does when checking a regular switch.

IN CAR REPAIRS

Operations Not Requiring Transmission Removal

1. Oil cooler fitting replacement or adjustment.
2. Governor assembly service.

3. Vacuum modulator, bushing and valve service.
4. Speedometer drive gear service.
5. Cruise Control service.
6. Oil level check.
7. Oil pressure check with oil pressure gauge.

Units That Can Be Serviced After Oil Pan Removal

1. Oil pan and pan-to-case gasket.
2. Pressure regulator valve assembly.
3. Valve body assembly.
4. Rear servo and accumulator assembly.
5. Front servo and accumulator assembly.
6. Governor pipes.
7. Detent solenoid.
8. Stator solenoid.
9. Solenoid connector.
10. Manual linkage.
11. Parking linkage.
12. Valve body-to-case spacers and gaskets.
13. Check balls for proper location (7 balls), Fig. 5.
14. Detent roller and spring assembly.

TRANS., REPLACE

1977–78 Olds Toronado

Removal
1. Disconnect battery.
2. Disconnect oil cooler lines at transmission and speedometer cable at governor. Remove governor and cover opening to prevent entry of dirt.
3. Install a suitable engine support bar, such as shown in Fig. 6.
4. Remove three upper final drive to transmission attaching bolts, Fig. 7.
5. Remove bolts A, B, C, D, Fig. 8.
6. Remove flywheel cover plate bolt, A, Fig. 9.

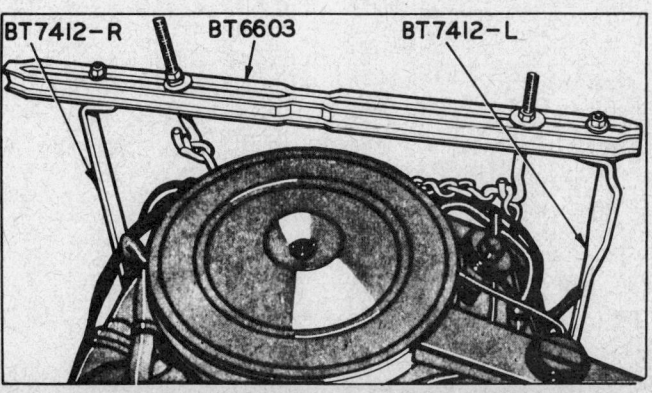

Fig. 6   Installing support bar. Olds Toronado

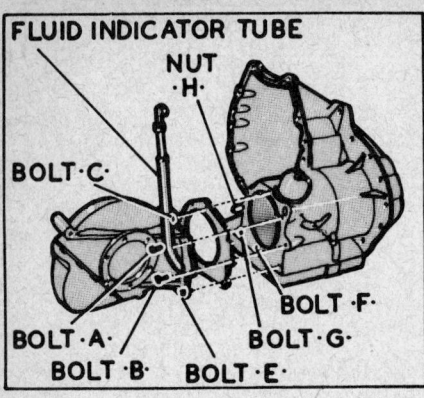

FLUID INDICATOR TUBE
NUT H
BOLT C
BOLT A
BOLT B
BOLT F
BOLT G
BOLT E

Fig. 7 Transmission attachment. 1977–78 Oldsmobile Toronado

7. Hoist car and remove starter.
8. Remove bolts B, C, and D from flywheel cover plate, Fig. 9.
9. Remove flywheel to converter bolt E, Fig. 9. Rotate flywheel until bolts are removed.
10. Disconnect vacuum modulator line and stator wiring.
11. Install transmission lift.
12. Remove shift linkage.
13. Remove bolts E, F, G and nut H, Fig. 7.
14. Remove bolts A and B, Fig. 10.
15. Remove two upper engine mount bracket-to-transmission bolts.
16. Remove four bracket-to-engine mount bolts.
17. Slide transmission rearward and down.
18. Attach converter holding strap to housing to prevent converter from falling out when transmission is being removed.
19. After transmission is removed from vehicle, the link assembly cover insulator can be removed or installed.

Installation

When installing the transmission the engine mount bracket must be positioned loosely on the link assembly cover until the transmission is in place. Then reverse removal procedure and torque bolts to ft-lb values as follows:

Engine to converter housing 30
Engine bracket to transmission—
1977–78 60
Engine bracket to rubber mount—
1977–78 60
Oil cooler lines to transmission—
1977–78 12
Final drive to transmission—
1977–78 30

1977–78 Cadillac Eldorado

Removal—Figs. 11 and 12
1. Disconnect ground cable at battery.
2. Remove transmission dipstick.
3. Remove filler tube.
4. Remove bolts at locations A, B and C, securing final drive case to transmission.
5. Disconnect speedometer cable from governor and detent solenoid connector from transmission case.
6. Disconnect oil cooler pipes from transmission.
7. Cap pipes and plug connector holes in transmission and radiator.
8. Remove bolt securing cooler pipe bracket to final drive bracket and position pipes away from governor.
9. Remove nut at location H, securing final drive case to transmission.
10. Remove bolts at locations I, J, K and L, securing transmission to engine and adapter plate.
11. Remove upper left bolt securing rear engine mount bracket to transmission.
12. Remove ground strap from cowl.
13. Remove upper left nut securing converter cover plate to transmission.

NOTE: Use a 7/16" universal socket and extension and reach underneath left exhaust manifold. Removal of this screw can be facilitated by having a helper under the car, verbally guiding socket onto nut.

14. Position safety chain over top of transmission.
15. Raise vehicle and place on jack stands.
16. Disconnect leads from starter motor.
17. Remove bolt at location O, securing starter motor to transmission case and remove ground strap from bolt.
18. Remove bolt at location P and remove starter.
19. Remove three remaining screws securing converter cover plate to transmission and remove cover plate.
20. Position transmission jack.
21. Disconnect electrical connector from transmission connector.
22. Remove pipe from vacuum modulator.
23. Secure transmission to transmission jack adapter plate with safety chain.
24. Remove three flex plate-to-converter attaching bolts.

NOTE: This can be done by installing a 9/16-18 bolt and washer into end of crankshaft at vibration damper, after removing cork plug, and rotating converter and flex plate until bolts are accessible for re-

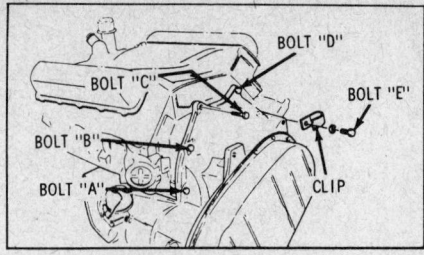

BOLT "D"
BOLT "C"
BOLT "E"
BOLT "B"
BOLT "A"
CLIP

Fig. 8 Transmission to engine attachment

moval. Do not pry on flex plate ring gear to rotate flex plate and converter as flex plate may be damaged.

25. Remove bolts at locations M and N securing transmission to engine and adapter plate.
26. On left side of transmission, separate relay rod from manual yoke.
27. Remove bolts at locations D, E and F, and nut at location G, securing final drive to transmission.

NOTE: Position drain pan under point where transmission and final drive meet as approximately 1½ quarts of transmission fluid will be lost when transmission and final drive are separated.

28. Remove five bolts and washers securing rear of acromat (cushion) to front cross bar and frame horns and allow acromat to hang free.
29. Through access holes in bottom of front cross bar, remove left bolt and loosen right bolt securing front engine mount to front cross bar. Turn wheels all the way to the left to provide maximum clearance.
30. Have a helper, using a large pry bar, shift engine forward, while you use a small pry bar to help separate transmission from engine and final drive. *Select pry points*

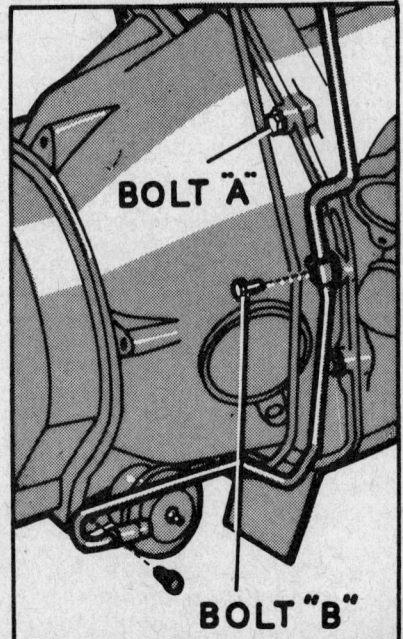

BOLT "A"
BOLT "B"

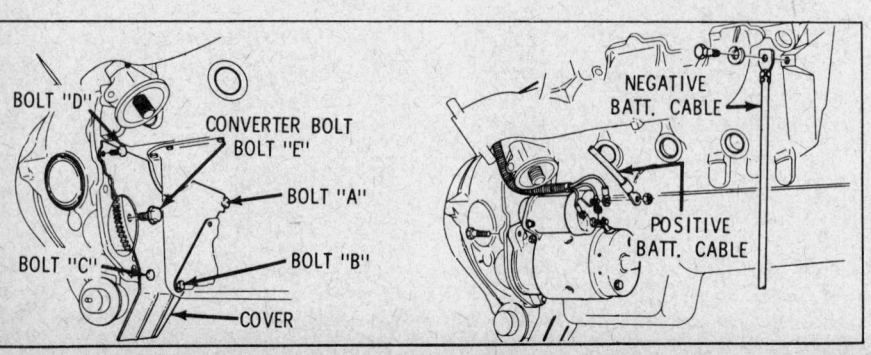

BOLT "D"
CONVERTER BOLT
BOLT "E"
BOLT "A"
BOLT "C"
BOLT "B"
COVER
NEGATIVE BATT. CABLE
POSITIVE BATT. CABLE

Fig. 9 Converter attachment

Fig. 10 Transmission to engine attachment

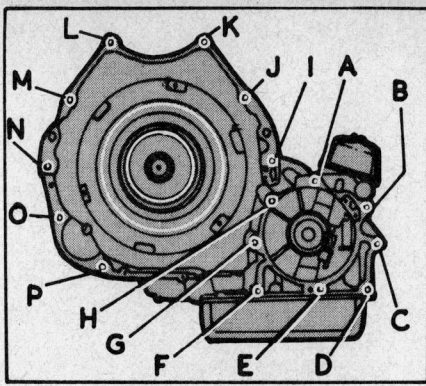

Fig. 11 Transmission attaching bolt locations. Cadillac Eldorado

with care to avoid damaging any components.

31. After initial separation has been made, allow transmission oil to drain at final drive junction.
32. Remove two bolts on right side securing rear engine mount bracket to transmission.
33. Through access hole in bottom of transmission support bar, remove two bolts, one each side, securing rear mounts to transmission support bar, and position mounts and bracket rearward to underbody.
34. While a helper pries and holds engine forward, move transmission rearward to disengage transmission case from dowels on engine adapter and to disengage final drive from studs on transmission case. Top of transmission should be tilted slightly rearward.
35. Slowly lower transmission, making certain top of transmission case clears flex plate ring gear and splined input shaft of final drive, until converter is approximately half-way exposed from flex plate.
36. Install a suitable clamp to transmission case at location N to avoid possibility of converter becoming disengaged when transmission is removed.
37. Lower transmission from car.

CAUTION: Rear engine mount bracket will follow transmission from car; to avoid damage or injury, remove bracket as soon as there is sufficient clearance.

38. Remove and discard final drive gasket and clean mounting surface of final drive.

Installation

1. Position transmission, on jack, under car.
2. Install new gasket on final drive, after first soaking gasket with transmission fluid.
3. Position rear engine mount bracket on top of transmission support bar against underbody.
4. Raise transmission in place until converter is approximately half-way covered by flex plate, then remove converter holding clamp.
5. While a helper assists in holding engine forward with pry bar, continue raising transmission, making certain top of

transmission case clears splined input shaft of final drive, and position to engine.
6. Position transmission to engine and final drive by aligning following points in the order listed, while a helper assists:
   a. Studs on transmission case to mounting holes in final drive.
   b. Guide holes in transmission case to dowels on adapter.
   c. Internal flange on final drive to transmission.

NOTE: As engagement of splined final drive input shaft to transmission is hidden, extreme care must be taken to avoid damaging transmission and final drive.

To facilitate engagement of final drive splines, rotate one front wheel while a helper holds the other. When alignment is complete and proper, gap between final drive case and transmission should not exceed ¼″.

7. Loosely install bolts (⅜ × 1¼) at locations D and F attaching transmission to final drive and bolt (⅜ × 2½) at location N attaching transmission to engine adapter, alternately tightening bolts to avoid cocking transmission. *Do not torque bolts at this time.*
8. Working in engine compartment, loosely install bolt (⅜ × 1⅜) at location J attaching transmission to adapter. *Do not torque bolt at this time.*
9. Install bolt (⅜ × 1⅜) at location M attaching transmission to adapter plate. *Do not torque bolt at this time.*
10. Position rear engine mount bracket to transmission and loosely install bolts at locations K and L.
11. Position rear engine mounts and bracket to transmission support bar and loosely install bolts through access holes in bottom of bar, attaching mounts to bar.
12. Reposition engine if necessary and install left bolt securing front engine mount to front cross bar. Tighten both front mount bolts to 30-ft-lbs.
13. Remove transmission jack.
14. Torque rear engine mounts to transmission support bar bolts to 55 ft-lbs. Torque rear engine mount to bracket bolts to 25 ft. lbs. Torque transmission to adapter to engine bolts (located N) to 30 ft-lbs. Torque transmission to adapter bolts (location M) to 30 ft-lbs.

NOTE: The procedure for securing the converter to the flex plate outlined in steps 15 through 17 must be strictly followed, otherwise damage to the flex plate and transmission will result from improper installation.

15. Rotate converter until two of the three weld nuts on converter line up with two of the three bolt holes in flex plate. Position converter so that weld nuts are flush with flex plate, making certain converter is not cocked and that pilot in center of converter is properly seated in crankshaft.
16. Loosely install two flex plate to converter bolts through accessible holes in flex plate.
17. Rotate flex plate and converter by rotating bolt previously installed in forward end of crankshaft until third bolt hole is

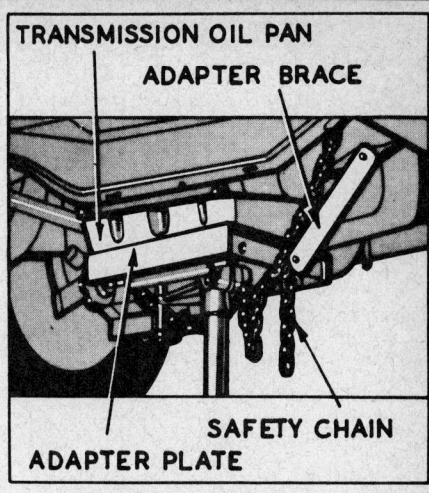

Fig. 12 Positioning transmission jack to transmission. Cadillac Eldorado

accessible. Install the third flex plate to converter bolt and torque all three bolts to 30 foot pounds. Remove bolt from crankshaft and install cork plug.

18. Install hose on vacuum modulator.
19. Install electrical connector to transmission connector.
20. Position converter cover plate to transmission case and install two lower and one upper right bolts securing cover plate to transmission, tightening to 5 ft-lbs.
21. Position starter to transmission case and install bolt at location P.
22. Position ground strap to transmission and install bolt securing ground strap and starter to transmission at location O. Tighten bolts at locations O and P to 25 ft-lbs.
23. Install leads on starter motor.
24. Install bolts at locations C and E and nut at location G, securing transmission to final drive.
25. Torque bolts at locations C through F to 35 foot pounds.
26. On all models, connect relay rod to manual yoke with a cotter pin.
27. Check operation of manual linkage and adjust.
28. Lower vehicle.
29. Install bolts at locations A and B and the nut at location H. Torque bolts to 35 foot pounds.
30. Install upper left bolt securing converter cover plate to transmission in the manner described for removing it in Step 13.
31. Install bolt at location I and torque bolts at locations I, J, K, and L to 25 foot pounds.
32. Torque oil cooler pipe connectors at transmission case to 20 foot pounds. Clean cooler pipe ends with a suitable solvent, connect pipes to transmission and torque pipe fittings to 20 foot pounds.
33. On all models, connect speedometer to governor and detent solenoid connector to transmission case.
34. Install new O-ring seal on transmission oil filler tube through hole in final drive case. Fasten filler tube bracket to exhaust manifold.
35. Install body ground strap to firewall.
36. Connect battery cable, fill transmission with fluid and install hood if previously removed.

Turbo Hydra-Matic 700-R4 Automatic Transmission

TRANSMISSION IDENTIFICATION

CHEVROLET
1982 Corvette .... YA
1983 Camaro V8-305 W/TBI .... PQ
  Caprice & Impala V8-305 .... YK

PONTIAC
1983 Firebird V8-305 W/TBI .... PQ

DESCRIPTION

The model 700-R4, Fig. 1, is a fully automatic transmission consisting of a 3-element hydraulic torque converter with the addition of a converter clutch.

Also two planetary gear sets, five multiple-disc type clutches, two roller or one-way clutches and a band are used which provide the friction elements to produce four forward speeds, the last of which is overdrive.

The torque converter, through oil, couples the engine power to the gear sets and hydraulically provides additional torque multiplication when required. Also, through the converter clutch, the converter drive and driven members operate as one unit when applied, providing mechanical drive from the engine through the transmission.

The gear ratio changes are fully automatic in relation to the vehicle speed and engine torque. Vehicle speed and engine torque are directed to the transmission providing the proper gear ratio for maximum efficiency and performance at all throttle openings.

A hydraulic system pressurized by a variable capacity vane-type pump, provides the operating pressure required for the operation of the friction elements and automatic controls.

TROUBLE SHOOTING GUIDE

Oil Pressure High or Low

1. Pump assembly pressure regulator valve binding, dirty or damaged spring.
2. T.V. and reverse boost plug and bushing are dirty, sticking, damaged or incorrectly assembled.
3. Pump assembly pressure relief ball not seated or damaged.
4. Pump assembly slide sticking.
5. Pump assembly not regulating.
6. Excess rotor clearance in pump assembly.
7. Manual valve not engaged or damaged.
8. T.V. exhaust valve binding or damaged.
9. Throttle lever and bracket assembly, misassembled, binding, damaged or check valve missing.
10. Valve body throttle valve or plunger sticking.
11. Valve body T.V. limit valve sticking.
12. Throttle link, not engaged, damaged, incorrect, burr on upper end or hanging on T.V. sleeve.
13. Filter, restricted has missing "O"-ring or hole in intake pipe.

High or Low Shift Points

1. T.V. cable binding or not set.
2. Improper external linkage travel.
3. Binding throttle valve or plunger.
4. T.V. modulator up or down valve sticking.
5. Valve body gaskets or spacer plate mispositioned or damaged.
6. T.V. limit valve sticking.
7. Pump assembly, sticking pressure regulator valve, T.V. boost valve.
8. Pump slide sticking.

First Speed Only—No Upshift

1. Sticking governor valve.
2. Governor driven gear is damaged.
3. Governor driven gear retainer pin missing.
4. Nicks or burrs on output shaft.
5. Correct governor retainer pin in case (longer or shorter).
6. Burrs on governor sleeve.
7. Burrs on governor case.

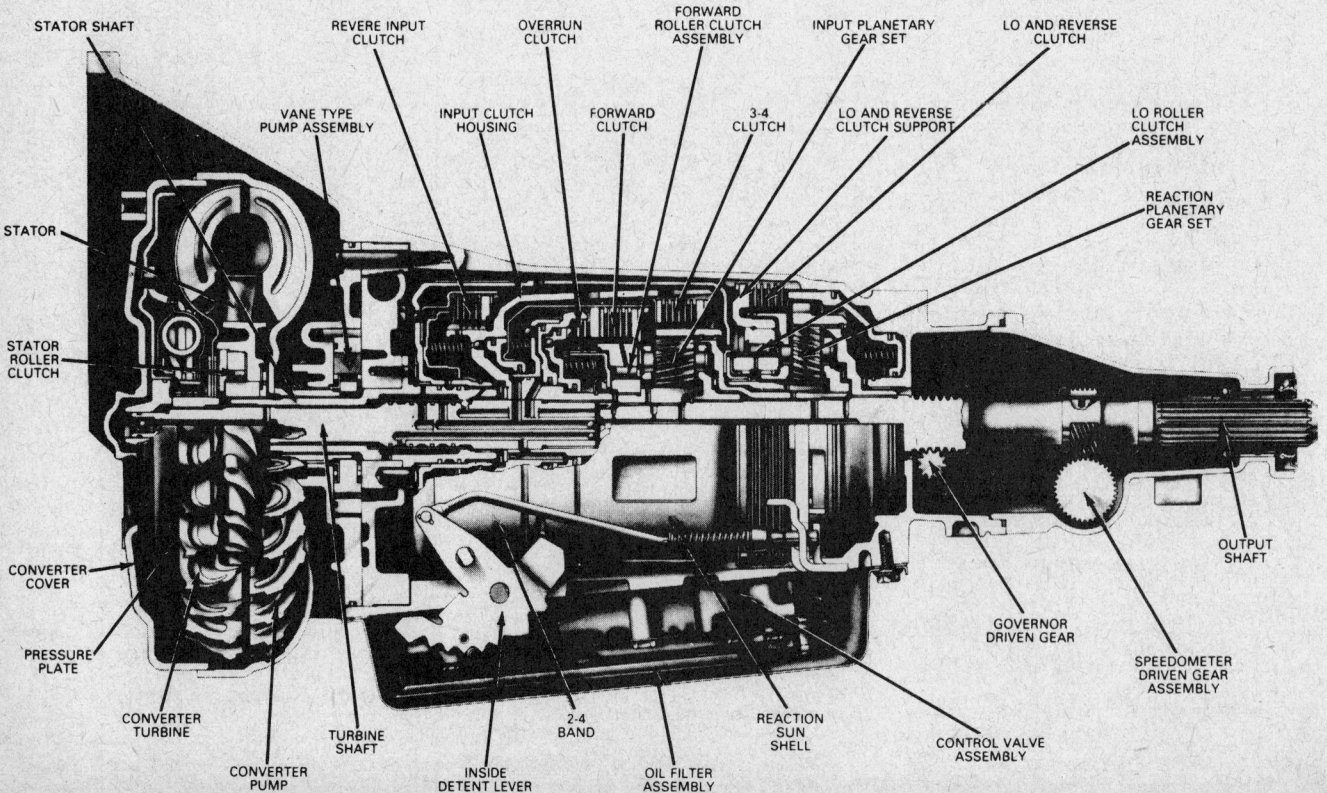

Fig. 1 700-R4 automatic transmission

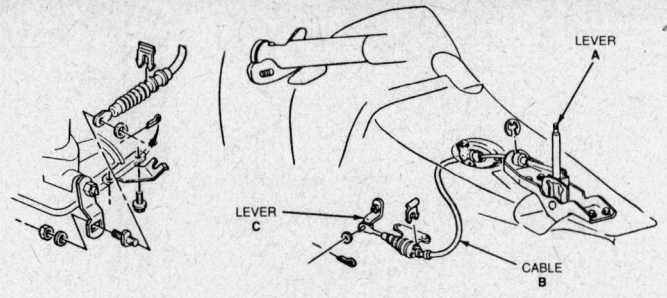

Fig. 2   Manual linkage. 1982 Corvette

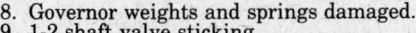

Fig. 3   Column shift manual linkage. Exc. 1982 Corvette

8. Governor weights and springs damaged.
9. 1-2 shaft valve sticking.
10. Valve body gaskets or spacer plate are mispositioned.
11. Valve body pad—porosity and/or damaged lands.
12. Restricted or damaged governor screen.
13. 2-4 servo apply passages, servo apply pin and pin hole in case, restricted or damaged.
14. Damaged or missing servo piston seals.
15. 2-4 band assembly burned, band anchor pin not engaged.
16. 2-4 band assembly apply end broken.

Slips In First Gear

1. Forward clutch plates burned.
2. Porosity—forward clutch piston.
3. Forward clutch seals cut or damaged.
4. Damaged forward clutch housing.
5. Forward clutch internal leak.
6. Forward clutch housing check ball damage.
7. Low oil or oil pressure.
8. Accumulator valve sticking.
9. Valve body lands or interconnected passages damaged.
10. Valve body gasket, spacer plate damaged or mispositioned.
11. Binding internal T.V. linkage.
12. 1-2 accumulator piston assembly, piston or bore porous.
13. 1-2 accumulator piston assembly seals cut or damaged.
14. Leak between piston and pin.
15. Missing or broken accumulator spring.

1-2 Full Throttle Shifts Only

1. T.V. cable not connected.
2. T.V. cable too long or short.
3. Throttle lever bracket assembly misassembled or binding.
4. Missing exhaust check valve.
5. Throttle link not connected, burr on upper end or hanging on T.V. sleeve.
6. Throttle valve or plunger hanging or sticking in full open position.
7. Inter-connected passages-pump, case or valve body restricted or damaged.

1-2 Slip Or Rough

1. Throttle lever and bracket assembly damaged or incorrectly installed.
2. Throttle valve or bushing sticking.
3. Sticking 1-2 shift valve train.
4. Valve body gasket or spacer plate mispositioned.
5. Sticking line bias valve.
6. Sticking accumulator valve.
7. Sticking T.V. limit valve.
8. Incorrect 2-4 servo apply pin.
9. 2-4 servo oil seal rings or seals dam-

aged.
10. 2-4 servo bores, damaged.
11. 2-4 servo oil passages, restricted or missing.
12. 2nd accumulator piston seal damaged.
13. Accumulator spring, missing.
14. 2nd accumulator bores, damaged.
15. 2nd accumulator piston, porous.
16. 2nd accumulator oil passages, restricted or missing.
17. Burned 2-4 band.

2-3 Slip Or Rough

1. 2-3 shift valve train, sticking.
2. Accumulator valve sticking.
3. Valve body gasket or spacer plate mispositioned.
4. Throttle valve sticking.
5. T.V. limit valve sticking.
6. 3-4 clutch plates burned or excessive clutch plate travel.
7. 3-4 piston seals cut or damaged.
8. 3-4 piston porosity.
9. 3-4 piston exhaust ball open.
10. Apply passages restricted.
11. 3-4 clutch check ball capsule damaged or misassembled.

3-4 Slip Or Rough

1. 3-4 accumulator spring missing.
2. 3-4 piston porosity.
3. Accumulator feed passages restricted.
4. 3-4 accumulator piston oil seal ring broken.
5. Accumulator case bore damaged.
6. Servo band apply incorrect.
7. Servo piston seals damaged or missing.
8. Servo piston bores damaged.
9. Servo piston porosity.
10. 3-4 clutch burned. (Refer to 2-3 slip for other clutch diagnosis.)
11. 2-4 band burned.
12. Valve body 2-3 shift valve train sticking.
13. Accumulator valve sticking.
14. Valve body gaskets or spacer plate mispositioned.
15. Valve body throttle valve sticking.
16. T.V. limit valve sticking.

No Reverse Or Slips In Reverse

1. Forward clutch will not release.
2. Manual linkage improperly adjusted.

3. Pump assembly reverse boost plug sticking.
4. Valve body gaskets or spacer plate mispositioned.
5. Lo reverse clutch piston seals cut or damaged.
6. Low reverse clutch apply passages restricted or missing.
7. Lo reverse clutch plates burned.
8. Lo reverse clutch cover plate loose or cover plate gasket damaged.
9. Reverse input clutch plates burned.
10. Reverse input clutch piston seals cut or damaged.
11. Reverse input clutch apply passage restricted or missing.
12. Reverse input clutch housing exhaust ball and capsule damaged.

No Part Throttle Downshift

1. Binding external or internal linkage.
2. Valve body T.V. modulator downshift valve binding.
3. Valve body throttle valve binding.
4. Valve body throttle valve bushing. Feed hole restricted or missing.
5. Valve body check ball #3 mispositioned.

No Overrun Braking Manual 3-2-1

1. External manual linkage not properly adjusted.
2. Overrun clutch plates burned.
3. Overrun clutch inner or outer piston seals damaged.
4. Overrun clutch piston exhaust ball sticking or missing.
5. Overrun clutch piston porosity.
6. Valve body gaskets or spacer plate mispositioned or orifice holes plugged.
7. Valve body 4-3 sequence valve sticking.
8. Valve body check balls 3, 9 or 10 mispositioned.
9. Turbine shaft oil feed passages restricted or missing.
10. Turbine shaft oil seal ring damaged.
11. Turbine shaft plug missing.

No Converter Clutch Apply

1. 12 volts not being supplied to the transmission.
2. Defective transmission outside electrical connector.
3. Defective inside electrical connectors,

AUTOMATIC TRANSMISSIONS/TRANSAXLES

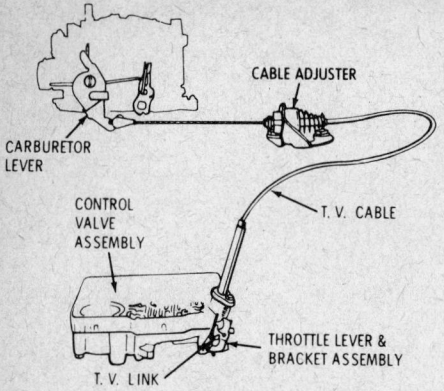

Fig. 4   T.V. cable & linkage

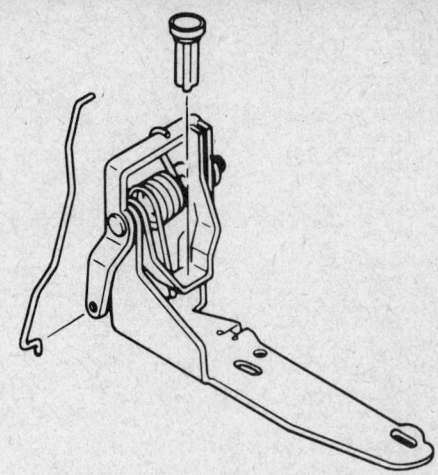

Fig. 5   Throttle lever & bracket assembly

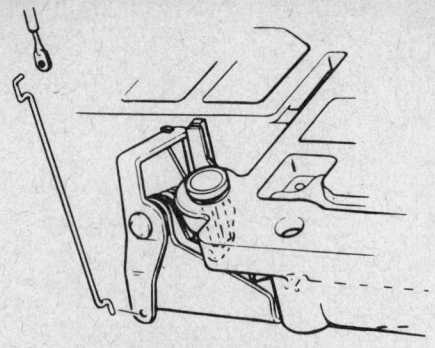

Fig. 6   Throttle lever & bracket assembly alignment

Fig. 7   Throttle lever to cable link

wiring harness, solenoid.
4. Defective electrical ground inside transmission.
5. Defective pressure switch or improper connection.
6. Solenoid not grounded.
7. Valve body converter clutch shift or throttle valve sticking.
8. Valve body casting or spacer plate in converter clutch valve area is mispositioned or damaged.
9. Converter clutch apply valve stuck or installed backwards.
10. Pump assembly signal oil orifice restricted or missing.
11. Pump assembly "O"-ring on solenoid damaged or missing.
12. Pump-to-case gasket damaged or mispositioned.
13. Pump assembly cup plug missing from apply passage.
14. Pump assembly orifice plug missing from cooler input passage.
15. High or uneven bolt torque on cover to body.
16. Converter clutch stop valve or retainer ring not installed properly.

Converter Shudder

1. Converter clutch pressure plate damaged.
2. Check ball on end of turbine shaft damaged.
3. Sticking converter clutch shift valve in valve body.
4. Sticking converter clutch apply valve in valve body.
5. Restricted converter clutch apply passage.
6. Low oil or oil pressure.
7. Engine not tuned properly.

No Converter Release

1. Converter clutch apply valve stuck in open position.
2. "O"-ring or check ball in end of turbine shaft damaged.
3. Internal converter damaged.

Drives In Neutral

1. Forward clutch burned or not releasing.
2. Manual linkage or manual valve incorrectly set, or disconnected internal linkage.
3. Interconnected case passages.

No Park Or Will Not Hold In Park

1. Actuator rod assembly bent or damaged.

2. Actuator rod spring binding, or improper crimp.
3. Parking lock pawl return spring damaged, or not assembled properly.
4. Actuator rod is not attached to inside detent lever.
5. Parking brake bracket damaged or bolts not torqued.
6. Inside detent lever nut not torqued.
7. Detent roller improperly installed or damaged.
8. Parking lock pawl binding or damaged.
9. Parking lock pawl interference with lo reverse piston.

NOTE: Be careful to always check oil level, T.V. cable and oil pressure following each troubleshooting procedure.

MAINTENANCE

Fluid level should be checked at every engine oil change. Frequency of change for transmission fluid is dependent on the type of driving conditions in which the vehicle is used. If the transmission is subjected to severe service such as: use in heavy city traffic when the outside temperature regularly reaches 90° F., use in very hilly or mountainous areas, commercial use such as taxi or delivery service, the fluid should be changed every 15,000 miles. Otherwise, change the fluid every 100,000 miles, using Dexron II or equivalent automatic transmission fluid. To check fluid at operating temperature (190°–200°F.), which is obtained only after 15 miles of highway-type driving:
1. Apply parking brake and block wheels.
2. Place selector lever in park and start but do not race, engine. Move selector lever through each range.
3. Check fluid immediately with selector lever in park, engine running at slow idle, and vehicle on level surface. Fluid level should be at full hot mark.

Changing Fluid

1. Raise and support vehicle.
2. Place drain pan under transmission oil pan, loosen pan bolts on front of pan, pry carefully with screwdriver to loosen oil pan, and allow fluid to drain.
3. Remove remaining oil pan bolts, oil pan, and gasket.
4. Drain fluid from pan, then clean pan and

dry thoroughly with compressed air.
5. Remove oil filter to valve body bolt, then remove filter and gasket, replace with new filter and gasket and install filter attaching bolt. Torque to specification.
6. Install new gasket on oil pan, then install oil pan and torque bolts to 8 ft. lbs.
7. Lower vehicle and add five quarts of automatic transmission fluid through filler tube.
8. With selector lever in park and parking brake applied, start engine and let idle. Do not race engine.
9. Move selector lever through each range, return to park position, check fluid, and add additional fluid to bring level between dimples on dipstick.

Adding Fluid to Fill Dry Transmission and Converter

1. Add 11½ quarts of transmission fluid through filler tube.
2. Place selector lever in park, depress accelerator to place carburetor on fast idle cam, and move selector lever through each range. Do not race engine.
3. With selector lever in park, engine running at idle (1–3 minutes), and vehicle on level surface, check fluid level and add additional fluid to bring level between dimples on dipstick.

MANUAL LINKAGE, ADJUST

1982 Corvette

1. Place selector lever (A) in "PARK" position, Fig. 2.
2. Place transmission lever (C) in "PARK" position by rotating lever clockwise to last detent position.
3. Connect cable (B) to levers (A) and (C).

Exc. 1982 Corvette

1. Loosen swivel clamp screw.
2. Position shift lever in neutral gate.
3. Position transmission lever in neutral detent.
4. While holding swivel clamp flush against equalizer lever, tighten swivel clamp screw, Fig. 3.

NOTE: Do not exert force in either direction on rod or equalizer lever while tightening swivel clamp screw.

T.V. CABLE, ADJUST

The T.V. cable should not be thought of as an automatic downshift cable. It controls line pressures, shift points, shift feel, part throttle downshifts, and detent downshifts. The function of the cable is similar to the combined functions of a vacuum modulator and detent downshift cable. The T.V. cable operates the throttle lever and bracket assembly, Figs. 4 and 5.

1. Stop engine.
2. Depress re-adjust tab and move slider through fitting, away from lever assembly, until slider stops against fitting. Release re-adjust tab.
3. Open carburetor lever to full throttle stop position to automatically adjust cable, then release carburetor lever and check cable for sticking or binding.
4. Road test vehicle. If delayed or only full throttle shifts still occur, proceed as follows:
   a. Remove oil pan and inspect throttle lever and bracket assembly, Fig. 6.
   b. Check T.V. exhaust valve lifter rod for distortion, or binding in control valve assembly or spacer plate.
   c. Make sure T.V. exhaust check ball moves up and down in conjunction with lifter.
   d. Make sure lifter spring holds lifter rod up against control valve assembly.
   e. Make sure T.V. plunger is not stuck.
   f. Inspect transmission for correct throttle lever to cable link, Fig. 7.

SERVO ASSEMBLY, REPLACE

1. Remove two oil pan bolts and install tool J-29714 or equivalent, on oil pan flange to depress servo cover.
2. Remove servo cover retaining ring, then remove tool.
3. Remove cover, and seal ring which may be in case.
4. Remove servo piston and bore-apply pin assembly.
5. Reverse procedure to install.

SPEEDOMETER DRIVEN GEAR, REPLACE

1. Disconnect speedometer cable.
2. Remove retainer bolt, retainer, speedometer driven gear, and "O"-ring seal.
3. Reverse procedure to install, using new "O"-ring and adjusting fluid level.

REAR OIL SEAL, REPLACE

1. Remove drive shaft, and tunnel strap, if equipped.
2. Using suitable tool, pry out lip oil seal.
3. Coat outer casting of new oil seal with suitable sealer and drive into place with installer J-21426.
4. Install tunnel strap if used, then install driveshaft.

GOVERNOR, REPLACE

1. Raise and support vehicle.
2. Remove governor cover from case using extreme care not to damage cover. If cover is damaged, it must be replaced.
3. Remove governor.
4. Reverse procedure to install and check fluid level.

CONTROL VALVE ASSEMBLY, REPLACE

1. Drain and remove oil pan and remove filter and gasket.
2. Disconnect electrical connectors at valve body.
3. Remove detent spring and roller assembly from valve body and remove valve body to case bolts.
4. Remove valve body assembly while disconnecting manual control valve link from range selector inner lever and removing throttle lever bracket from T.V. link.
5. Reverse procedure to install. Torque bolts to 8 ft. lbs. and replenish fluid.

TRANSMISSION, REPLACE

1. Remove air cleaner assembly, then, disconnect T.V. cable at its upper end. Remove transmission oil dipstick and bolt holding dipstick tube, if accessible.
2. Raise and support vehicle and remove driveshaft.
3. Disconnect speedometer cable, shift linkage, and all electrical leads at transmission as well as any clips that retain the leads to the transmission case.
4. Remove flywheel cover, mark flywheel and torque converter to maintain original balance. Remove torque converter to flywheel bolts and/or nuts.
5. Disconnect catalytic converter support bracket.
6. Remove transmission support to transmission mount bolt and transmission support to frame bolts and insulators, if used.
7. Position a suitable jack under transmission, raise transmission slightly, and slide transmission support rearward.
8. Lower transmission to gain access to oil cooler lines and T.V. cable attachments, disconnect oil cooler lines and T.V. cable, and cap all openings.
9. Support engine with suitable tool, remove transmission to engine bolts, and disconnect transmission assembly.
10. Install torque converter holding tool J-21366 or equivalent, and remove transmission assembly from vehicle.
11. Reverse procedure to install.

Chrysler Torqueflite Automatic Transaxle

IDENTIFICATION

A seven digit part number is stamped on a pad located at the rear of the transaxle on the transmission oil pan flange. This number must be referred to when servicing the transmission due to differences in some internal components.

CHRYSLER CORP. FRONT WHEEL DRIVE

1978–80 4-105 . . . . A-404
1981–82 4-105, 4-135 &
    4-156 . . . . A-404, A-413, & A-470
1983 4-97, 4-105, 4-135 &
    4-156 . . . . . . A-404, A-413, A-415 & A-470

DESCRIPTION

These transaxles combine a torque converter, automatic 3 speed transmission, final drive gearing and differential combined into one unit. The torque converter, transaxle and differential assemblies are housed in an integral aluminum die cast housing, Fig. 1.

NOTE: The differential oil sump is separate from the transaxle pump. Ensure differential oil lever is 1/8 to 3/8 inch below the oil filler hole on the differential cover.

The torque converter is connected to the crankshaft through a flexible drive plate. Converter cooling is accomplished by an oil to water type cooler, located in the radiator side tank. The torque converter cannot be disassembled.

The transaxle consists of two multiple disc clutches, an overrunning clutch, two servos, a hydraulic accumulator, two bands and two planetary gear assemblies to provide three forward and one reverse gear. The sun gear is connected to the front clutch retainer. The hydraulic system consists of an oil pump, and a single valve body which contains all of the valves except the governor valves. Output torque from the main drive gears is transferred through helical gears to the transfer shaft. An integral ring gear on the transfer shaft drives the differential ring gear.

TROUBLE SHOOTING GUIDE

Harsh Engagement From N to D Or R

1. High idle speed.
2. Defective or leaking valve body.
3. High hydraulic pressure.
4. Worn or damaged rear clutch.

Delayed Engagement From N to D Or R

1. Low hydraulic pressure.
2. Defective or leaking valve body.
3. Low-reverse servo, band or linkage malfunction.
4. Low fluid level.

5. Incorrect gearshift linkage adjustment.
6. Clogged transmission oil filter.
7. Faulty oil pump.
8. Worn or damaged input shaft seal rings.
9. Aerated fluid.
10. Low idle speed.
11. Worn or damaged reaction shaft support seal rings.
12. Worn or defective front clutch.
13. Worn or defective rear clutch.

Runaway Upshifts

1. Low hydraulic pressure.
2. Defective or leaking valve body.
3. Low fluid level.
4. Clogged transmission oil filter.
5. Aerated fluid.
6. Incorrect throttle linkage adjustment.
7. Worn or damaged reaction shaft support seal rings.
8. Kickdown servo, band or linkage malfunction.
9. Worn or faulty front clutch.

No Upshift

1. Low hydraulic pressure.
2. Defective or leaking valve body.
3. Low fluid level.
4. Incorrect gearshift linkage adjustment.
5. Incorrect throttle linkage adjustment.
6. Worn or damaged governor support seal rings.
8. Faulty governor.
9. Kickdown servo, band or linkage malfunction.
10. Worn or faulty front clutch.

3-2 Kickdown Runaway

1. Low hydraulic pressure.
2. Defective or leaking valve body.
3. Low fluid level.
4. Aerated fluid.
5. Incorrect throttle linkage adjustment.
6. Kickdown band adjustment.
7. Worn or damaged reaction shaft support seal rings.
8. Kickdown servo, band or linkage malfunction.
9. Worn or faulty from clutch.

No Kickdown Or Normal Downshift

1. Defective or leaking valve body.
2. Incorrect throttle linkage adjustment.
3. Faulty governor.
4. Kickdown servo, band or linkage malfunction.

Erratic Shifts

1. Low hydraulic pressure.
2. Defective or leaking valve body.
3. Low fluid level.
4. Incorrect gearshift linkage adjustment.
5. Clogged transmission oil filter.
6. Faulty oil pump.
7. Aerated fluid.
8. Incorrect throttle linkage adjustment.
9. Worn or damaged governor support seal rings.
10. Worn or damaged reaction shaft support seal rings.
11. Faulty governor.
12. Kickdown servo, band or linkage malfunction.
13. Worn or faulty front clutch.

Slips In 1, 2 Or D

1. Low hydraulic pressure.
2. Defective or leaking valve body.
3. Low fluid level.

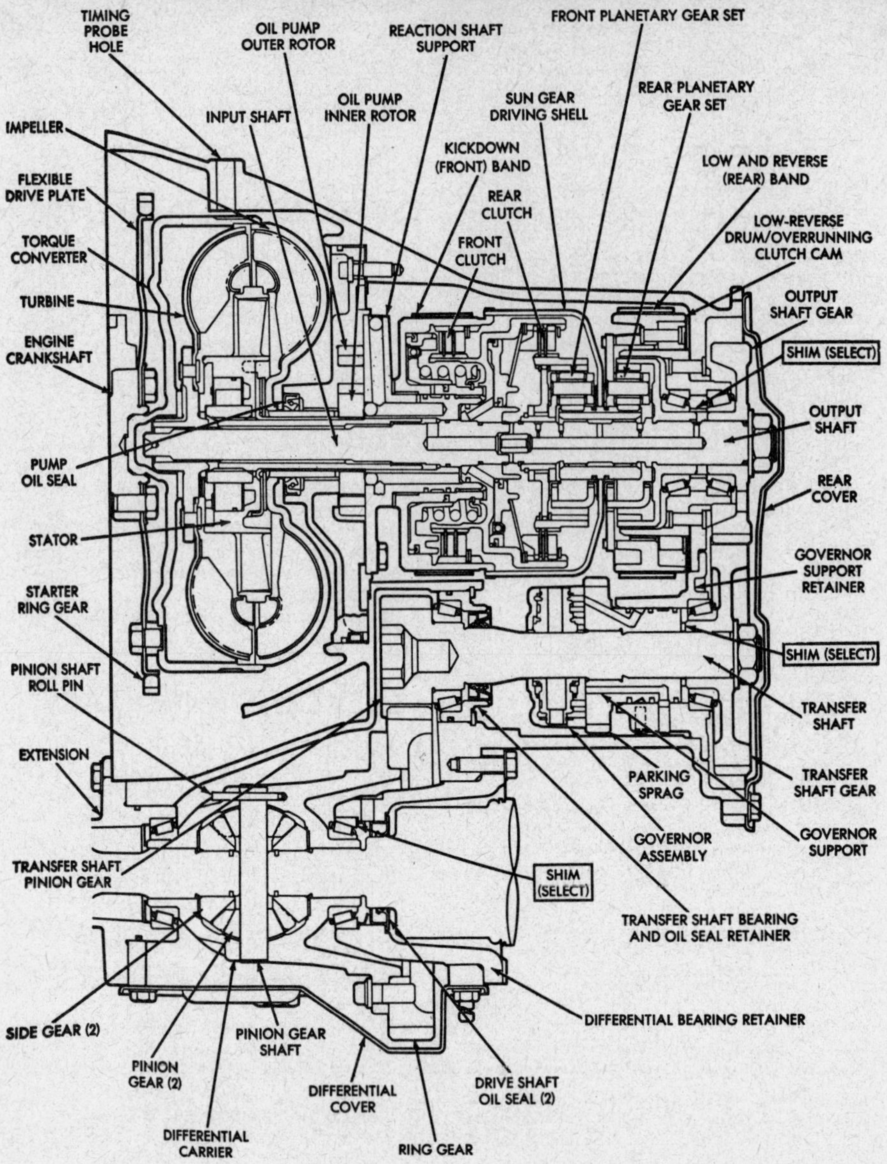

Fig. 1 Sectional view of automatic transaxle. Typical

4. Incorrect gearshift linkage adjustment.
5. Clogged transmission oil filter.
6. Faulty oil pump.
7. Worn or damaged input shaft seal rings.
8. Aerated fluid.
9. Incorrect throttle linkage adjustment.
10. Overrunning clutch not holding.
11. Worn or faulty rear clutch.
12. Overrunning clutch worn damaged or seized.

Slips In R Only

1. Low hydraulic pressure.
1. Low-reverse band adjustment.
3. Defective or leaking valve body.
4. Low-reverse servo, band or linkage malfunction.
5. Low fluid level.
6. Incorrect gearshift linkage adjustment.
7. Faulty oil pump.
8. Aerated fluid.
9. Worn or damaged reaction shaft seal rings.
10. Worn or faulty front clutch.

Slips In All Ranges

1. Low hydraulic pressure.
2. Defective or leaking valve body.
3. Low fluid level.
4. Clogged transmission oil filter.
5. Faulty oil pump.
6. Worn or damaged input shaft seal rings.
7. Aerated fluid.

No Drive In Any Range

1. Low hydraulic pressure.
2. Defective or leaking valve body.
3. Low fluid level.
4. Clogged transmission oil filter.
5. Faulty oil pump.
6. Planetary gear sets damaged or seized.

No Drive In 1, 2 or D

1. Low hydraulic pressure.
2. Defective or leaking valve body.
3. Low fluid level.

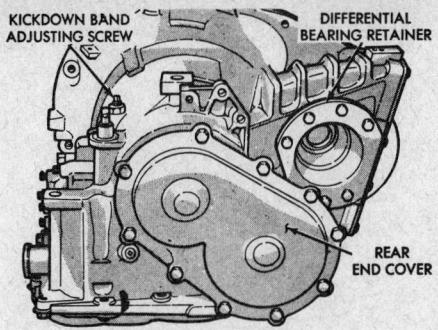

Fig. 2 Kickdown band adjusting screw location

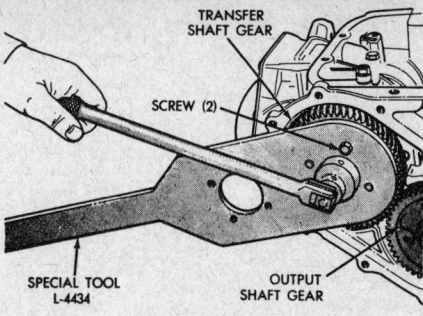

Fig. 3 Loosening transfer shaft gear retaining nut

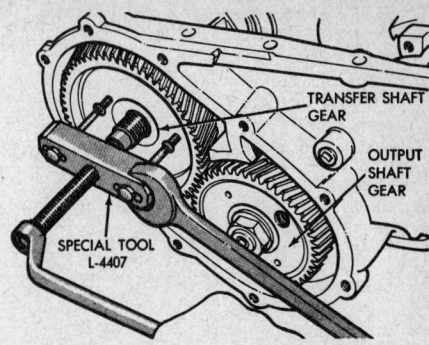

Fig. 4 Removing transfer shaft gear

4. Worn or damaged input shaft seal rings.
5. Overrunning clutch not holding.
6. Worn or faulty rear clutch.
7. Planetary gear sets damaged or seized.
8. Overrunning clutch worn, damaged or seized.

No Drive In R

1. Low hydraulic pressure.
2. Low-reverse band adjustment.
3. Defective or leaking valve body.
4. Low-reverse servo, band or linkage malfunction.
5. Incorrect gearshift linkage adjustment.
6. Worn or damaged reaction shaft support seal rings.
7. Worn or faulty front clutch.
8. Worn or faulty rear clutch.
9. Planetary gear sets damaged or seized.

Drive In Neutral

1. Defective or leaking valve body.
2. Incorrect gearshift linkage adjustment.
3. Insufficient clutch plate clearance.
4. Worn or faulty rear clutch.
5. Rear clutch dragging.

Drags or Locks

1. Low-reverse band adjustment.
2. Kickdown band adjustment.
3. Planetary gear sets damaged or seized.
4. Overrunning clutch worn, damaged or seized.

Hard To Fill (Oil Blows Out Filler Tube)

1. Clogged transmission oil filter.
2. Aerated fluid.
3. High fluid level.
4. Breather clogged.

Transmission Overheats

1. Stuck switch valve.
2. High idle speed.
3. Low hydraulic pressure.
4. Low fluid level.
5. Incorrect gearshift adjustment.
6. Faulty oil pump.
7. Kickdown band adjustment too tight.
8. Faulty cooling system.
9. Insufficient clutch plate clearance.

Harsh Upshifts

1. Low hydraulic pressure.
2. Incorrect throttle linkage adjustment.
3. Kickdown band adjustment.
4. High hydraulic pressure.

Delayed Upshift

1. Incorrect throttle linkage adjustment.

2. Kickdown band adjustment.
3. Worn or damaged governor support seal rings.
4. Worn or damaged reaction shaft support seal rings.
5. Faulty governor.
6. Kickdown servo, band or linkage malfunction.
7. Worn or faulty front clutch.

Grating, Scraping Or Growling Noise

1. Low-reverse band out of adjustment.
2. Kickdown band adjustment.
3. Output shaft bearing or bushing damaged.
4. Planetary gear sets damaged or seized.
5. Overrunning clutch worn, damaged or seized.

Buzzing Noise

1. Defective or leaking valve body.
2. Low fluid level.
3. Aerated fluid.
4. Overrunning clutch inner race damaged.

MAINTENANCE

Adding Oil

To check fluid level, apply the parking brake and operate engine at idle speed with transmission in Neutral or Park position. Add fluid as necessary.

Changing Oil

Fluid and filter changes are not required for average passenger car use. Severe usage such as commercial type usage or prolonged operation in city traffic, requires that fluid be changed and bands adjusted every 15,000 miles.

Whenever factory fill fluid is changed, only fluid of the type labeled Dexron should be used.

1. Raise vehicle and place a suitable drain pan under transmission oil pan.
2. Loosen transmission oil pan attaching bolts and allow fluid to drain, then remove oil pan.
3. Replace oil filter and adjust bands if necessary, then install oil pan and gasket.
4. Add four quarts of approved automatic transmission fluid through the filler tube.
5. Start engine and allow to idle for at least two minutes, then with parking brake applied move selector lever momentarily to each position. Place selector lever in

Neutral or Park and check fluid level. Add fluid to bring level to Add mark.
6. Recheck fluid level after transmission has reached operating temperature. The level should be between Add and Full marks.

BANDS, ADJUST

Kickdown Band

1. Loosen lock nut and back off nut approximately five turns, Fig. 2.
2. Using tool No. C-3380-A and adapter C-3705, tighten band adjusting screw to 47 to 50 inch lbs. If adapter C-3705 is not used, tighten adjusting screw to 72 inch lbs.
3. Back off adjusting screw 2½ turns on all 1978–80 models and 1981 404 models, 3 turns on 1981 413 and 470 models, 1982–83 404 models and 1983 415 models, or 2¾ turns on 1982–83 413 and 470 models. Torque lock nut to 35 ft. lbs. while preventing adjusting screw from turning.

Low Reverse Band, Adjust

The low reverse band is adjustable on 413 and 470 models only.
1. Loosen locknut and back off nut approximately five turns.
2. Torque adjusting nut to 41 inch lbs.
3. Back off adjusting nut 3½ turns, then torque locknut to 20 ft. lbs.

GEARSHIFT LINKAGE, ADJUST

1. Place selector lever in Park position.
2. Raise vehicle, then loosen swivel lock bolt.
3. Move transmission lever to PARK position.
4. Torque swivel lock bolt to 90 inch lbs., then check adjustment.

NOTE: On 1981–83 models with column shift, apply a 10 pound forward load on the cable housing insulator while torquing swivel lock bolt. On models with console shift, apply a minimum forward load of 10 pounds on the console shift lever knob while torquing swivel lock bolt. On some models, it may be necessary to apply the forward load to the transaxle lever while tightening lock bolt.

THROTTLE CABLE, ADJUST

1. Perform adjustment with engine at oper-

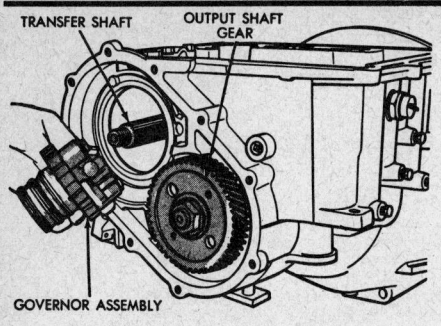

Fig. 5 Removing governor assembly

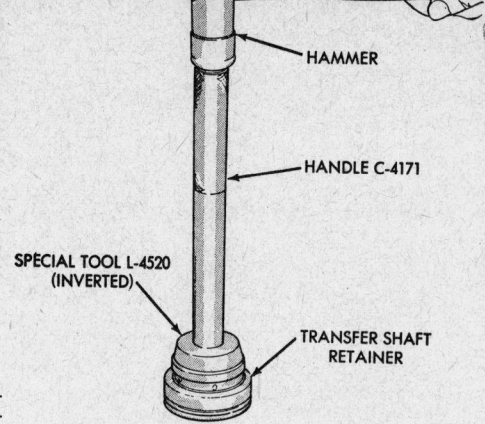

Fig. 6 Installing transfer shaft oil seal

ating temperature, otherwise ensure carburetor is not on fast idle cam by disconnecting choke.
2. Loosen adjusting bracket lock screw.
3. Hold transmission lever rearward against internal stop and tighten adjusting bracket lock screw to 105 inch lbs.

VALVE BODY, REPLACE

1. Loosen transmission oil pan attaching bolts and allow transmission to drain, then remove oil pan.
2. Remove oil filter attaching screws and oil filter.
3. Using a screwdriver, remove E–clip, then remove parking rod.
4. Remove seven valve body attaching bolts, then remove valve body and governor oil tubes.

GOVERNOR & TRANSFER SHAFT OIL SEAL, REPLACE

1. Remove rear cover attaching bolts and rear cover.
2. Using tool No. L-4434, remove transfer shaft gear retaining nut, Fig. 3.
3. Using tool No. L-4407, remove transfer shaft gear and shim, Fig. 4.
4. Remove governor support retainer, then remove low-reverse band anchor pin.
5. Remove governor assembly, Fig. 5.

6. Remove transfer shaft retainer snap ring, then using tool No. L-4512 and a suitable puller, remove transfer shaft and retainer assembly.
7. Remove transfer shaft retainer from shaft.
8. Using a screwdriver, remove oil seal from transfer shaft retainer.
9. Using tool No. L-4520 and C-4171, tap oil seal into shaft retainer, Fig. 6.
10. Reverse procedure to install. Torque transfer shaft gear retaining nut to 200 ft. lbs.

TRANSMISSION, REPLACE

NOTE: The transaxle and converter must be removed as an assembly.

1. Disconnect battery cables.
2. Disconnect transaxle shift control and throttle cables from transaxle and position aside.
3. Remove upper cooler tube, then support engine with suitable engine lifting equipment.
4. Remove three upper bell housing bolts.
5. Remove wheel hub nut and left splash shield.
6. Drain fluid from differential, then re-

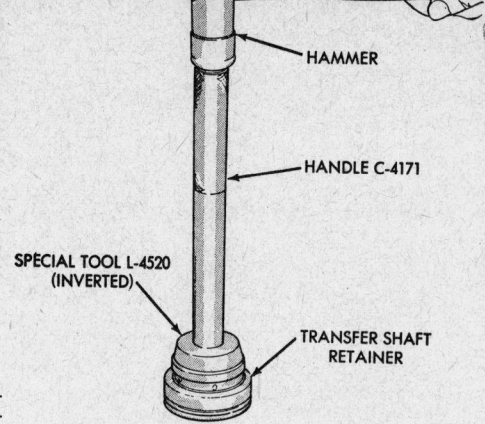

Fig. 7 Prying drive shaft out of side gear

move cover.
7. Remove speedometer adapter, cable and pinion as an assembly.
8. Remove sway bar and both lower ball joint to steering knuckle bolts.
9. Pry lower ball joint from steering knuckle, then remove drive shaft from hub.
10. Rotate both drive shafts until circlip ends are visible in the opening, then while squeezing circlip ends together, remove drive shaft from side gear, Fig. 7.
11. Mark position of torque converter to drive plate and remove torque converter retaining bolts.
12. Remove access plug in right splash shield to rotate engine.
13. Remove lower cooler tube and neutral/park safety switch wire.
14. Remove engine mount bracket from front crossmember.
15. Remove front engine mount insulator through bolt and bell housing bolts.
16. Support transaxle with a suitable jack.
17. Remove left engine mount and long through bolt.
18. Remove lower bell housing bolts.
19. Move transaxle away from engine and lower from vehicle.

NOTE: It may be necessary to pry transaxle away from vehicle between the extension housing and engine block for proper clearance.

20. Reverse procedure to install. Use RTV sealant when installing differential cover.

Chrysler Torqueflite & American Motors Torque-Command Automatic Transmission

IDENTIFICATION

Transmission Identification markings shown in the following application chart are cast in raised letters and numerals on the lower left side of the bell housing.
NOTE: There are sufficient variations within each of the main categories listed below to make it necessary to service them by serial number—a stamped 7-digit number appearing on the oil pan side rail.

CHRYSLER CORPORATION

1981–83 6-225 .... A-904, A-904 HD①
V8-318 Federal &
California .... A-904 LA
V8-318 Federal &
California .... A-727 HD①
1977–80 6-225 .... A-904
6-225 Police & Taxi A-904-HD
V8-318 Aspen, Volare, Diplomat &
LeBaron A-904-LA

CHRYSLER CORPORATION—Cont'd.

V8-318 Exc. Aspen &
Volare A-727
V8-360 Aspen & Volare A-904-LA
V8-360 Exc. Aspen &
Volare A-727
V8-360 H.P. A-727
1977–79 V8-400, 440 .... A-727

AMERICAN MOTORS

1977–79 6-232, 258 engines 904
6-258, V8-304, 360
Heavy Duty 727
V8-304 engine 998
V8-360, engine 727
1977–79 4-121 904
1980–83 4-151 904
6-258 .... 904, 998
①—HD-Heavy duty

DESCRIPTION

These transmissions, Figs. 1 and 2, combine a torque converter with a fully automatic three speed gear system. The converter housing and transmission case are an integral aluminum casting. The transmission consists of two multiple disc clutches, an overrunning (one-way) clutch, two servos and bands and two planetary gear sets to provide three forward speeds and reverse.

The common sun gear of the planetary gear sets is connected to the front clutch by a driving shell that is splined to the sun gear and to the front clutch retainer.

The hydraulic system consists of a single oil pump and a valve body that contains all the valves except the governor valve.

Venting of the transmission is accomplished by a drilled passage through the upper part of the front pump housing.

The torque converter is attached to the engine crankshaft through a flexible driving plate. The converter is cooled by circulating the transmission fluid through an oil-to-water type cooler located in the radiator lower tank. The converter is a sealed assembly that cannot be disassembled. On 1978–83 Chrysler Corp., the lock-up torque converter is used on all vehicles except 6-225 California, and heavy duty applications. On 1979 American Motors vehicles with V8 engine, and 1980–83 models with 6 cyl. engine, the lock-up torque converter is used.

TROUBLE SHOOTING GUIDE

Harsh Engagement in D-1-2-R

1. Engine idle speed too high.
2. Hydraulic pressures too high or too low.
3. Low-reverse band out of adjustment.
4. Accumulator sticking, broken rings or spring.
5. Low-reverse servo, band or linkage malfunction.
6. Worn or faulty front and/or rear clutch.
7. Valve body malfunction or leakage.
8. Throttle linkage sticking or incorrect adjustment.
9. Accumulator broken seal rings, scratched bore, broken or collapsed spring, cracked piston.

Delayed Engagement in D-1-2-R

1. Low fluid level.
2. Incorrect manual linkage adjustment.
3. Oil filter clogged.
4. Hydraulic pressures too high or low.
5. Valve body malfunction or leakage.
6. Accumulator sticking, broken rings or spring.
7. Clutches or servos sticking or not operating.
8. Faulty front oil pump.
9. Worn or faulty front and/or rear clutch.
10. Worn or broken input shaft and/or reaction shaft support seal rings.
11. Aerated fluid.
12. Incorrect idle adjustment.
13. Incorrect low and reverse band adjustment.

Runaway or Harsh Upshift and 3-2 Kickdown

1. Low fluid level.
2. Incorrect throttle linkage adjustment.
3. Hydraulic pressures too high or low.
4. Kickdown band out of adjustment.
5. Valve body malfunction or leakage.
6. Governor malfunction.

7. Accumulator sticking, broken rings or spring.
8. Clutches or servos sticking or not operating.
9. Kickdown servo, band or linkage malfunction.
10. Worn or faulty front clutch.
11. Worn or broken input shaft and/or reaction shaft support seal rings.
12. Aerated oil.
13. Clogged oil filter.

No Upshift

1. Low fluid level.
2. Incorrect throttle linkage adjustment.
3. Kickdown band out of adjustment.
4. Hydraulic pressures too high or low.
5. Governor sticking.
6. Valve body malfunction or leakage.
7. Accumulator sticking, broken rings or spring.
8. Clutches or servos sticking or not operating.
9. Faulty oil pump.
10. Kickdown servo, band or linkage malfunction.
11. Worn or faulty front clutch.
12. Worn or broken input shaft and/or reaction shaft support seal rings.
13. Incorrect gearshift linkage adjustment.
14. Governor support seal rings broken or worn.

Delayed Upshift

1. Incorrect throttle linkage adjustment.
2. Kickdown band out of adjustment.
3. Governor support seal rings broken or worn.
4. Worn or broken reaction shaft support seal rings.
5. Governor malfunction.

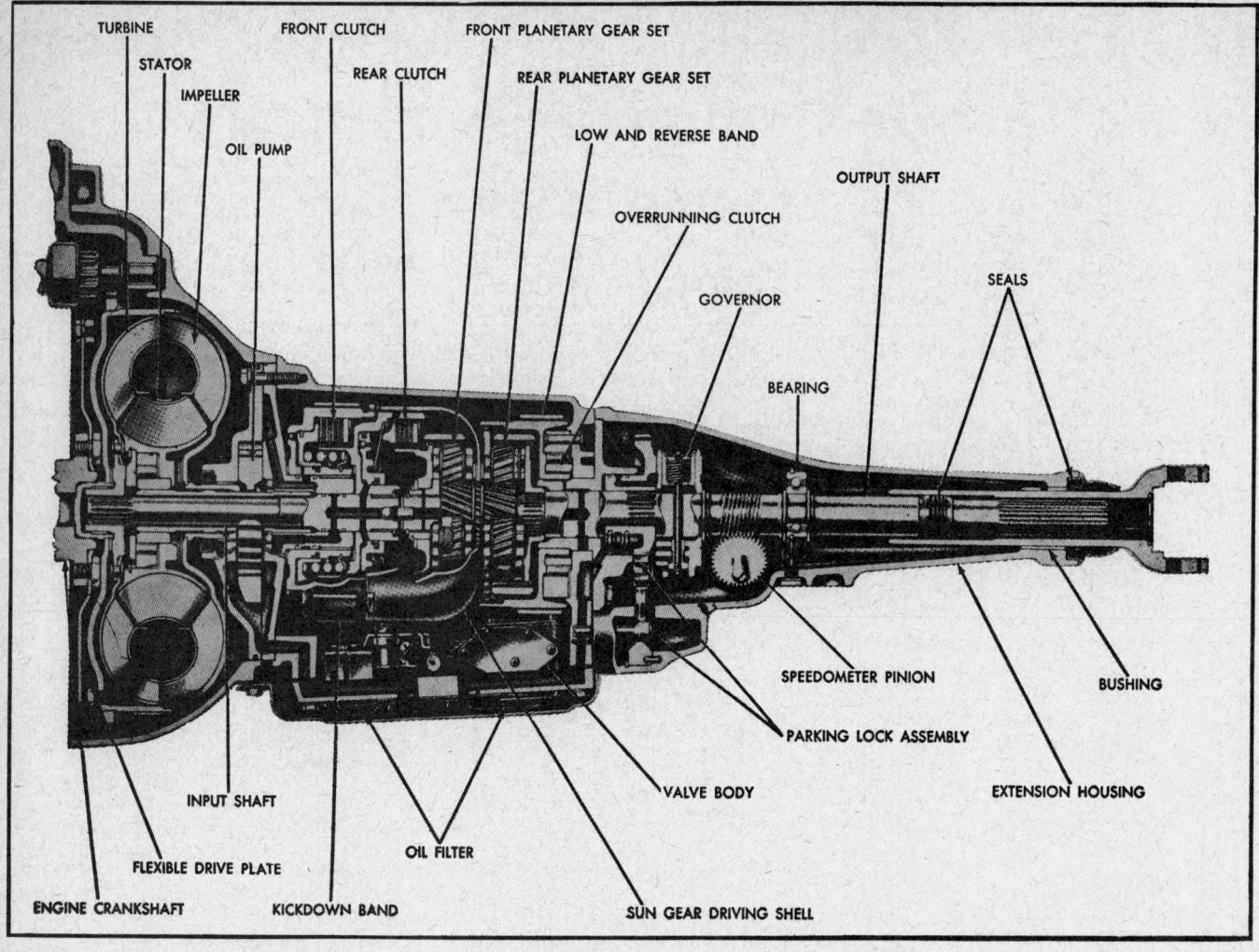

Fig. 1 Series 904 Torqueflite transmission used on 1977–83 (typical). 998 model is similar

6. Kickdown servo band or linkage malfunction.
7. Worn or faulty front clutch.

No Kickdown or Normal Downshift

1. Incorrect throttle linkage adjustment.
2. Incorrect gearshift linkage adjustment.
3. Kickdown band out of adjustment.
4. Hydraulic pressure too high or low.
5. Governor sticking.
6. Valve body malfunction or leakage.
7. Accumulator sticking, broken rings or spring.
8. Clutches or servos sticking or not operating.
9. Kickdown servo, band or linkage malfunction.
10. Overrunning clutch not holding.
11. Low fluid level.

Erratic Shifts

1. Low fluid level.
2. Aerated fluid.
3. Incorrect throttle linkage adjustment.
4. Incorrect gearshift control linkage adjustment.
5. Hydraulic pressures too high or low.
6. Governor sticking.
7. Oil filter clogged.
8. Valve body malfunction or leakage.

9. Clutches or servos sticking or not operating.
10. Faulty oil pump.
11. Worn or broken input shaft and/or reaction shaft support rings.
12. Governor support seal rings broken or worn.
13. Kickdown servo band or linkage malfunction.
14. Worn or faulty front clutch.

Slips In Forward Drive Positions

1. Low oil level.
2. Aerated fluid.
3. Incorrect throttle linkage adjustment.
4. Incorrect gearshift control linkage adjustment.
5. Hydraulic pressures too low.
6. Valve body malfunction or leakage.
7. Accumulator sticking, broken rings or springs.
8. Clutches or servos sticking or not operating.
9. Worn or faulty front and/or rear clutch.
10. Overrunning clutch not holding.
11. Worn or broken input shaft and/or reaction shaft support seal rings.
12. Clogged oil filter.
13. Faulty oil pump.
14. Overrunning clutch worn, broken or seized.

15. Incorrect kickdown band adjustment.

Slips In Reverse Only

1. Low fluid level.
2. Aerated fluid.
3. Incorrect gearshift control linkage adjustment.
4. Hydraulic pressures too high or low.
5. Low-reverse band out of adjustment.
6. Valve body malfunction or leakage.
7. Front clutch or rear servo sticking or not operating.
8. Low-reverse servo, band or linkage malfunction.
9. Faulty oil pump.
10. Worn or broken reaction shaft support seal rings.
11. Worn or faulty front clutch.

Slips In All Positions

1. Low fluid level.
2. Hydraulic pressures too low.
3. Valve body malfunction or leakage.
4. Faulty oil pump.
5. Clutches or servos sticking or not operating.
6. Worn or broken input shaft and/or reaction shaft support seal rings.
7. Oil filter clogged.
8. Aerated oil.

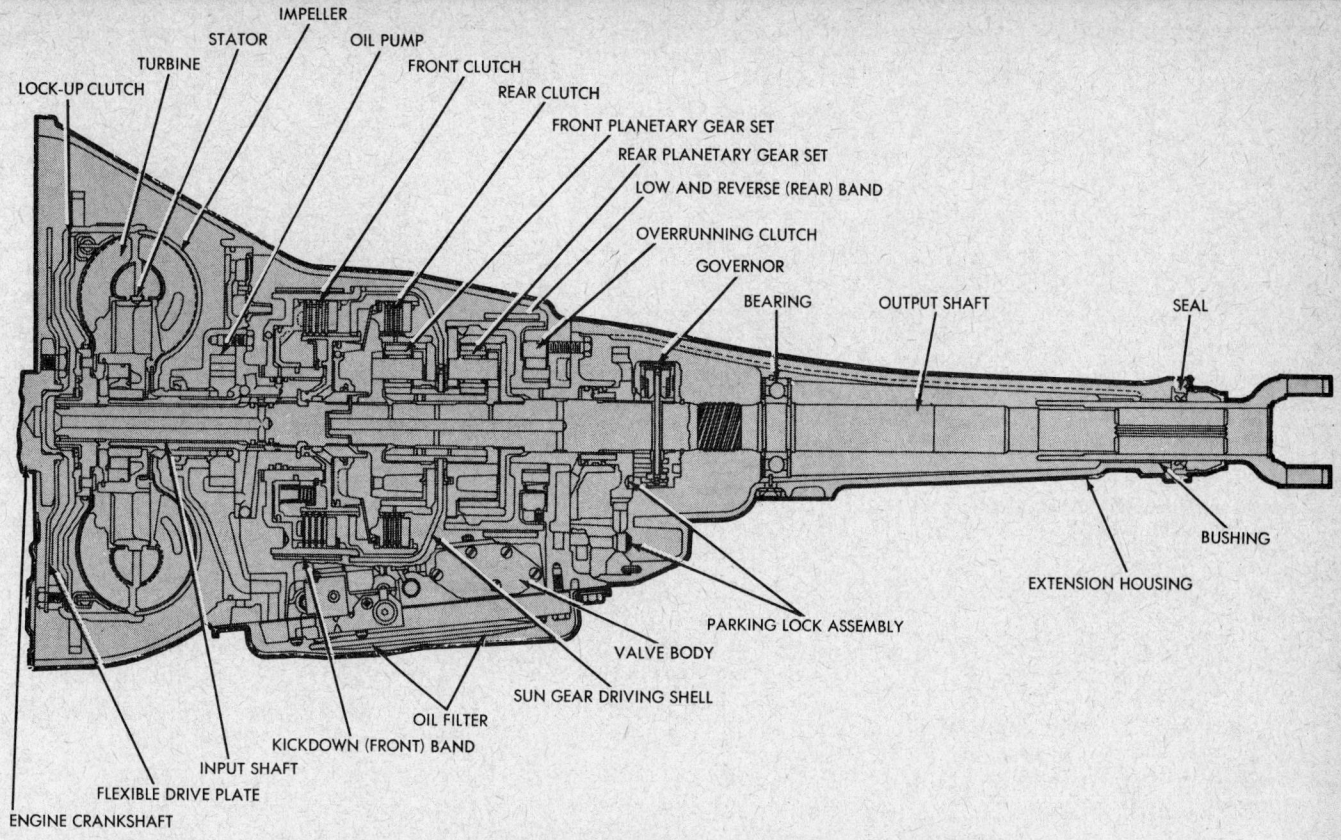

LOCK-UP CLUTCH
TURBINE
STATOR
IMPELLER
OIL PUMP
FRONT CLUTCH
REAR CLUTCH
FRONT PLANETARY GEAR SET
REAR PLANETARY GEAR SET
LOW AND REVERSE (REAR) BAND
OVERRUNNING CLUTCH
GOVERNOR
BEARING
OUTPUT SHAFT
SEAL
BUSHING
EXTENSION HOUSING
PARKING LOCK ASSEMBLY
VALVE BODY
SUN GEAR DRIVING SHELL
OIL FILTER
KICKDOWN (FRONT) BAND
INPUT SHAFT
FLEXIBLE DRIVE PLATE
ENGINE CRANKSHAFT

Fig. 2 Series 727 Torqueflite transmission used on 1977–83 (typical)

No Drive In Any Position

1. Low fluid level.
2. Hydraulic pressures too low.
3. Oil filter clogged.
4. Valve body malfunction or leakage.
5. Faulty oil pump.
6. Clutches or servos sticking or not operating.
7. Planetary gear sets broken or seized.
8. Torque converter failure.
9. Incorrect gearshift linkage adjustment.

No Drive In Forward Drive Positions

1. Hydraulic pressures too low.
2. Valve body malfunction or leakage.
3. Accumulator sticking, broken rings or spring.
4. Clutches or servos sticking or not operating.
5. Worn or faulty rear clutch.
6. Overrunning clutch not holding.
7. Worn or broken input shaft and/or reaction shaft support seal rings.
8. Low fluid level.
9. Planetary gear sets broken or seized.
10. Overrunning clutch worn, broken or seized.
11. Incorrect gearshift linkage adjustment.

No Drive In Reverse

1. Incorrect gearshift control linkage adjustment.
2. Hydraulic pressures too low.
3. Low-reverse band out of adjustment.
4. Valve body malfunction or leakage.
5. Front clutch or rear servo sticking or not operating.

6. Low-reverse servo, band or linkage malfunction.
7. Worn or faulty front and/or rear clutch.
8. Worn or broken reaction shaft support seal rings.
9. Planetary gear sets broken or seized.

Drives In Neutral

1. Incorrect gearshift control linkage adjustment.
2. Valve body malfunction or leakage.
3. Rear clutch worn, faulty, dragging or inoperative.
4. Insufficient clutch plate clearance.

Drags or Locks

1. Kickdown band out of adjustment.
2. Low-reverse band out of adjustment.
3. Kickdown and/or low-reverse servo, band or linkage malfunction.
4. Front and/or rear clutch faulty.
5. Planetary gear sets broken or seized.
6. Overrunning clutch worn, broken or seized.
7. Hydraulic pressure too low.
8. Valve body: nicks, scratches and burrs on valve and plugs. Rounded edges on valve lands. Scratches on bores, collapsed springs. Nicked or warped mating surfaces.
9. Accumulator, broken seal rings, scratched bore, broken or collapsed spring, cracked piston.

Grating, Scraping or Growling Noise

1. Kickdown band out of adjustment.
2. Low-reverse band out of adjustment.
3. Output shaft bearing and/or bushing

damaged.
4. Governor support binding or broken seal rings.
5. Oil pump scored or binding.
6. Front and/or rear clutch faulty.
7. Planetary gear sets broken or seized.
8. Overrunning clutch worn, broken or seized.
9. Low fluid level.
10. Clogged oil filter.

Buzzing Noise

1. Low fluid level.
2. Pump sucking air.
3. Valve body malfunction.
4. Overrunning clutch inner race damaged.
5. Aerated oil.
6. Governor valve: burrs, nicks, scores or binding on weights, shaft and valve.
7. Collapsed or distorted springs or distorted snap ring. Cracked or warped body. Dirty filter.

Hard to Fill, Oil Flows Out Filler Tube

1. High fluid level.
2. Breather clogged.
3. Oil filter clogged.
4. Aerated fluid.
5. Clogged lines to cooler.

Transmission Overheats

1. Low fluid level.
2. Kickdown band adjustment too tight.
3. Low-reverse band adjustment too tight.
4. Faulty cooling system.
5. Cracked or restricted oil cooler line or fitting.
6. Faulty oil pump.

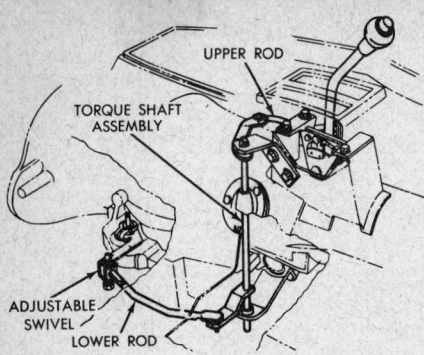

Fig. 3 Console gearshift linkage. 1977–78 Charger. 1977–79 Aspen, Cordoba, Fury & Volare, 1977–79 Diplomat, LeBaron & Monaco, 1979 Magnum & 1980–83 All

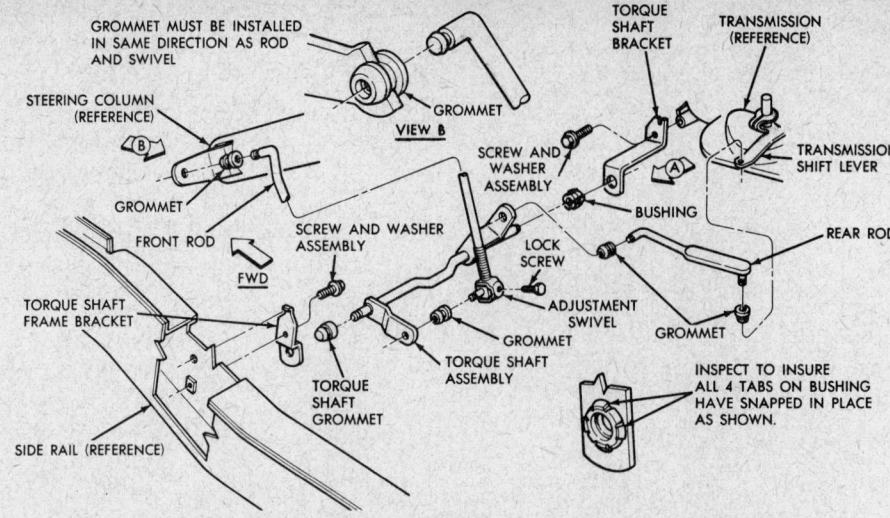

Fig. 4 Column gearshift linkage. 1977–81 except Aspen, Diplomat, LeBaron & Volare, 1980–81 Cordoba & Mirada & 1981 Imperial

7. Insufficient clutch plate clearance in front and/or rear clutches.
8. Engine idle too low.
9. Hydraulic pressures too low.
10. Incorrect gearshift linkage adjustment.
11. Kickdown band adjustment too tight.
12. Clogged oil filter.
13. Valve body: Nicks, scratches and burrs on valve and plugs. Rounded edges on valve lands. Scratches on bores, collapsed springs. Nicked or warped mating surfaces.

Starter Will Not Energize in Neutral or Park

1. Incorrect gearshift control linkage adjustment.
2. Faulty or incorrectly adjusted neutral starting switch.
3. Broken lead to neutral switch.

Sluggish Acceleration, Excessive Throttle Needed To Maintain Speed

1. Low fluid level.
2. Sticking or incorrect throttle linkage adjustment.
3. Faulty torque converter or clutches.
4. Incorrect hydraulic pressures.

No Lock-Up

1. Faulty input shaft, seal ring, locking clutch or torque converter.
2. Sticking failsafe switch, lock-up valve or switch valve.
3. Faulty oil pump.

Will Not Unlock

1. Sticking failsafe valve, lock-up valve, switch valve or governor valve.
2. Valve body malfunctioning.

Remains Locked-Up At Too Low A Speed In Drive

1. Sticking failsafe valve, lock-up valve or governor valve.

Locks Up Or Drags In Low Or Second

1. Sticking failsafe valve.
2. Faulty oil pump.

Engine Stalls Or Is Sluggish In Reverse

1. Plugged cooler lines or fittings.

2. Valve body malfunctioning or, faulty oil pump.

Loud Chatter While Locking-Up When Cold

1. Leaking turbine hub seal.
2. Faulty torque converter.

Vibrations After Lock-Up

1. Throttle linkage misadjusted, or sticking governor valve.
2. Engine requires tune-up, or otherwise not performing properly.
3. Exhaust system contacting vehicle.

Vibration When Vehicle Is Accelerated In Neutral

1. Unbalanced torque converter.

Overheating (Oil Blowing Out Of Dipstick Or Pump Seal)

1. Sticking switch valve.

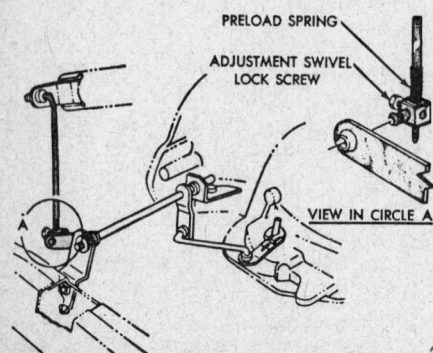

Fig. 5 Column gearshift linkage. 1977–79 Aspen & Volare, 1977–79 Diplomat & LeBaron

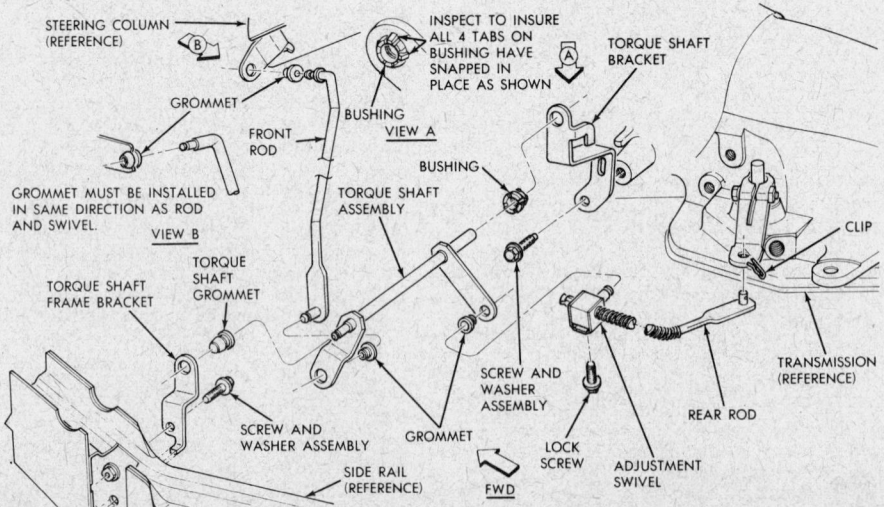

Fig. 6 Column gearshift linkage. 1980 Aspen, & Volare, 1980–81 Cordoba, Diplomat, LeBaron & Mirada, 1981 Imperial & all 1982–83 models

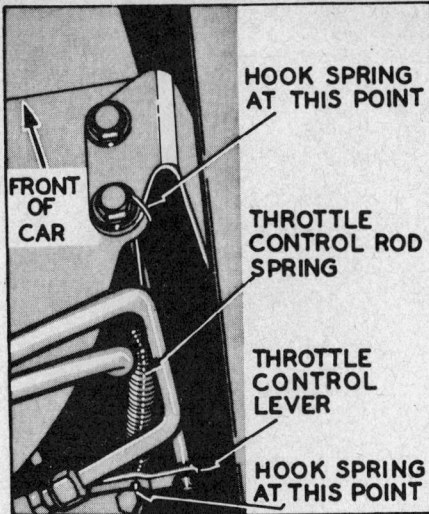

Fig. 7 Install spring on lever.
1977–83 American Motors

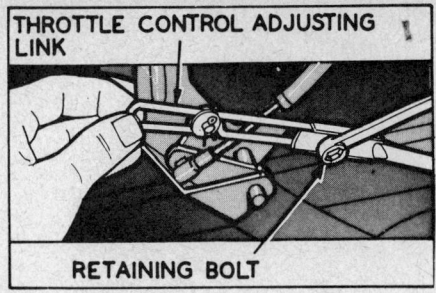

Fig. 8 Six cylinder throttle linkage.
1978–83 American Motors (Typical)

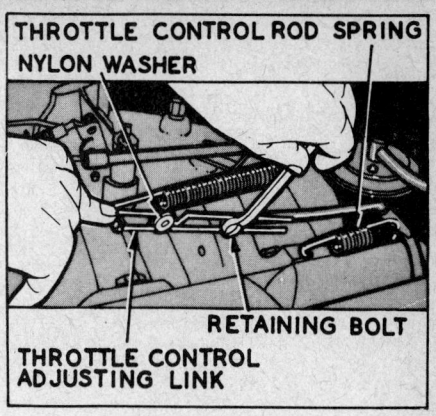

Fig. 9 V8 throttle linkage.
1977–79 American Motors

2. Plugged cooler lines or fittings.

MAINTENANCE
Checking Oil Level

To check the oil level, apply the parking brake and operate the engine at idle speed with the transmission in Neutral position.

Changing Oil

Fluid and filter changes or band adjustments are not required for average passenger car use. Severe usage such as police, taxi, trailer towing or prolonged operation in city traffic, requires that fluid and filter be changed and bands adjusted every 24,000 miles on 1977 models, and every 15,000 miles on 1978–83 models.

Whenever the factory fill fluid is changed, only fluids of the type labeled DEXRON should be used.

1. Remove drain plug (if equipped) from transmission oil pan and drain oil.

NOTE: *If the oil pan does not have a drain plug, loosen pan bolts and tap pan with a soft mallet to break it loose, permitting fluid to drain.*

2. On 1977 models, remove flywheel access plate, remove torque converter drain plug and allow to drain. Replace plug.
3. Remove transmission oil pan, replace filter or clean intake screen and pan, adjust bands and reinstall.
4. Add 6 quarts on 1977 or 4 quarts on 1978–83 units, of automatic transmission fluid through filler tube.
5. Start engine.
6. Allow engine to idle for about two minutes. With parking brake applied, move selector lever momentarily to each position and place in neutral.

BANDS, ADJUST
Kickdown Band

The kickdown band adjusting screw is located on the left side of the transmission case

near the throttle lever shaft.
1. Loosen lock nut and back off approximately five turns. Check adjusting screw for free turning in transmission case.
2. Using an inch-pound torque wrench, tighten the band adjusting screw to a reading of 72 inch lbs.
3. Back off adjusting screw the number of turns indicated:

Chrysler Corp.
1977–79
  A-904, A-904LA & V8-440
    dual exhaust w/A-727 . . . . 2 turns
  A-727 Exc. 440 dual
    exhaust . . . . 2½ turns
1980–83
  All units . . . . 2½ turns

American Motors
1977–81
  904 & 998 model trans. . . . . . . 2 turns
1977–79
  727 model trans. . . . . 2½ turns
1982–83
  904 model trans. with
    4 Cyl. engine . . . . 2½ turns
  904 model trans. with
    6 Cyl. engine . . . . 2 turns
  998 model trans. . . . . 3 turns

Hold adjusting screw in this position and tighten locknut.

Low and Reverse Band

1. Raise vehicle, drain transmission and remove oil pan.
2. Inspect fluid for friction material or metal particles which indicate damaged or worn parts.
3. Loosen adjusting screw lock nut and back off nut approximately five turns. Check adjusting screw for free turning in lever.
4. Using an inch pound torque wrench, tighten band adjusting screw to 72 in. lbs. on all except 904 and 1978–81 998 series transmissions. On 904 and 1978–81 998 series transmissions, tighten adjusting screw to 41 in. lbs.
5. Back off adjusting screw the number of turns indicated:

American Motors
904 Series . . . . 7 turns
998 Series . . . . 4 turns
727 Series . . . . 2 turns

Chrysler Corp.
A-904 . . . . 7 turns
A-904-LA . . . . 4 turns
A-727 . . . . 2 turns

6. Hold adjusting screw and tighten lock nut to 35 ft. lbs., then install oil pan and refill transmission.

GEARSHIFT CONTROL LINKAGE, ADJUST

1977–83 Chrysler Corp.

1. Referring to Figs. 3 to 6, place selector lever in Park and loosen control rod swivel clamp screw a few turns.
2. Move transmission control lever all the way to rear (in Park detent).
3. With both levers still in Park position, tighten swivel clamp screw securely. On all 1981–83 models, torque swivel clamp screw to 90 inch lbs.

1977–83 American Motors

Place the selector lever in the Park position and place the transmission shift lever in the Park detent. Adjust the shift rod to obtain a "free pin" fit. Check steering column lock for ease of operation. Move selector lever to Neutral position and check safety switch operation.

THROTTLE LINKAGE, ADJUST

1977–83 American Motors

1. Disconnect throttle control spring, then use spring to hold transmission throttle control lever forward against stop, Fig. 7.
2. Block choke open and set throttle off fast idle.

NOTE: On carburetors equipped with a throttle solenoid, energize solenoid and open throttle part way to allow solenoid to lock and return carburetor to idle.

3. Loosen retaining bolt on throttle control adjusting link. On 6 cylinder engines, do not remove spring clip and nylon washer. On V8 engines, remove spring clip and nylon washer from link.
4. On 6 cylinder engines, pull on end of link to eliminate lash and tighten retaining bolt, Fig. 8. On V8 engines, push on end of link to eliminate lash and tighten link retaining bolt, Fig. 9, then install nylon washer and spring clip.
5. Reconnect throttle control rod spring.

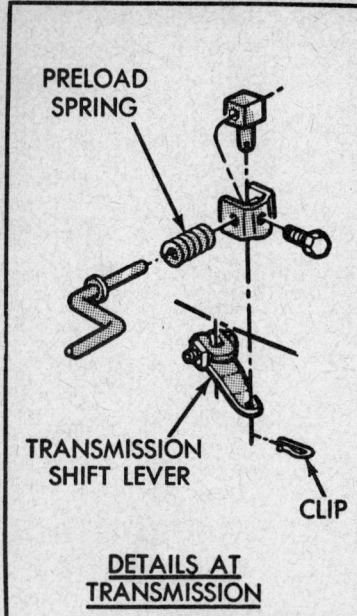

PRELOAD SPRING

TRANSMISSION SHIFT LEVER

CLIP

DETAILS AT TRANSMISSION

Fig. 10 Throttle linkage adjustment. All 1977–79 Chrysler Corp. models

1977–83 Chrysler Corp.

NOTE: Before proceeding with the adjustment, disconnect the choke rod at the carburetor or block the choke valve wide open. Open the throttle slightly to release the fast idle cam, then return carburetor to the hot idle position.

Hold or fasten the transmission lever firmly forward against the stop while performing the adjustment to insure a proper adjustment.

1. Support vehicle on hoist and loosen swivel lock screw, Figs. 10 and 10A.

NOTE: To insure correct adjustment, swivel must be free to slide along flat end of throttle rod so that preload spring action is not restricted. If necessary, disassemble and clean or repair parts to assure free action.

2. Hold transmission lever firmly forward against its internal stop and tighten swivel lock screw to 100 inch lbs.

NOTE: Adjustment is now finished. Linkage backlash was automatically removed by the preload spring.

3. Lower vehicle and test linkage operation by moving throttle rod rearward and slowly releasing it making certain that it returns fully.

EXTENSION HOUSING & PARKING LOCK CONTROL ROD

NOTE: On models except Aspen, Volare, Diplomat, LeBaron and all 1982–83 models, unload both torsion bars, then remove the left torsion bar and lower one side of the torsion

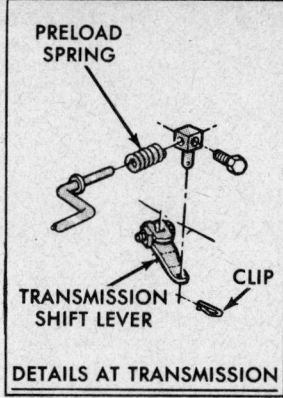

PRELOAD SPRING

TRANSMISSION SHIFT LEVER

CLIP

DETAILS AT TRANSMISSION

Fig. 10A Throttle linkage adjustment. All 1980–83 Chrysler Corp. models

bar crossmember for clearance.

1. Mark parts for reassembly and remove propeller shaft.
2. Remove speedometer pinion and adapter assembly, then drain about two quarts of fluid from transmission.
3. Remove extension housing to crossmember bolts, then raise transmission with jack and remove crossmember.
4. Remove extension housing to transmission bolts. On console shift models, remove torque shaft lower bracket to extension housing bolts.

NOTE: In the following step, the gearshift must be in "low" therefore positioning the parking lock control rod rearward so it can be disengaged or engaged with the parking lock sprag.

5. Remove two screws, plate and gasket from bottom of extension housing mounting pad, then spread snap ring from output shaft bearing, Fig. 11, and carefully tap extension housing off output shaft bearing.
6. Slide extension housing off shaft to remove parking sprag and spring, then remove snap ring and slide reaction plug and pin assembly out of housing, Fig. 12.
7. To replace parking lock control rod, refer to "Valve Body".

OUTPUT SHAFT OIL SEAL

1. Mark propeller shaft to aid in reassembly and remove propeller shaft being careful not to scratch or nick surface on sliding spline yoke.
2. Using a screwdriver and hammer, drive between extension housing and seal and remove seal.
3. Position new seal and drive it into extension housing using tool C-3995 or C-3972.
4. Carefully install yoke into housing, then align marks made at removal and install propeller shaft.

GOVERNOR

1. Remove extension housing, then remove output shaft bearing rear snap ring and remove bearing. On 727 Series, remove remaining snap ring from shaft.

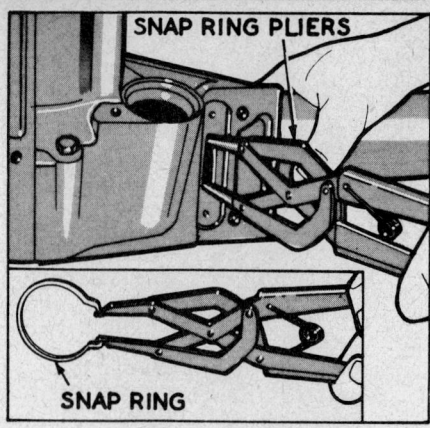

SNAP RING PLIERS

SNAP RING

Fig. 11 Removing or installing extension housing snap ring

2. Remove snap ring, Fig. 13, from weight end of governor valve shaft and remove valve shaft from governor body.
3. Remove large snap ring from weight end of governor housing, and lift out weight assembly.
4. Remove snap ring from inside governor weight and remove inner weight and spring from outer weight.
5. Remove snap ring from behind governor housing, then slide governor housing and parking brake sprag assembly off output shaft. If necessary, separate governor housing from sprag (4 screws).
6. The primary cause of governor operating failure is due to a sticking governor valve or weights. Rough surfaces may be removed with crocus cloth. Thoroughly clean all parts and check for free movement before assembly.
7. Reverse above operations to assemble and install governor.

VALVE BODY

1. Drain transmission and remove oil pan.
2. Loosen clamp bolts and remove throttle and gear selector levers from manual lever, Fig. 14.
3. Remove neutral safety switch and oil filter.
4. Place a drain pan under transmission and remove the ten valve body to transmission bolts. Hold valve body in place while removing bolts.
5. Carefully lower valve body while pulling it forward to disengage parking control rod.

NOTE: It may be necessary to rotate output shaft to permit parking control rod to clear sprag.

6. Remove accumulator piston and spring from transmission case. Inspect piston for nicks, scores and wear. Inspect spring for distortion. Inspect rings for freedom in piston grooves and wear or breakage. Replace parts as necessary.

TRANSMISSION, REPLACE
American Motors 1977–83

CAUTION: The hood must be open to prevent

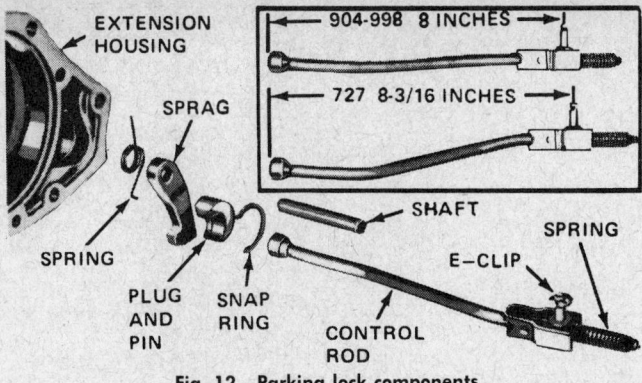

Fig. 12 Parking lock components

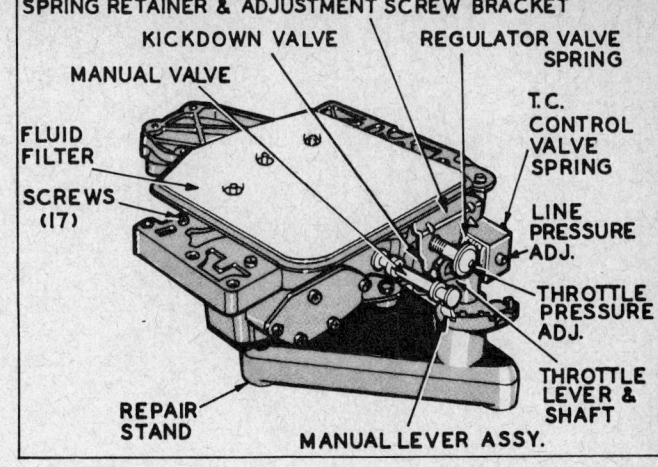

Fig. 14 Valve body external parts

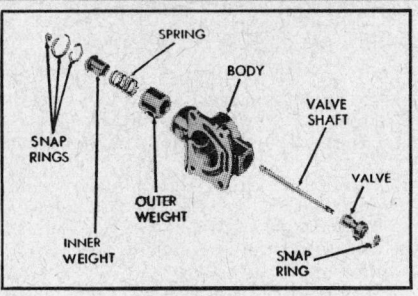

Fig. 13 Governor disassembled

damage to hood and air cleaner when removing rear crossmember.

1. Disconnect fan shroud. Remove front cover from bell housing.
2. Drain fluid from transmission as described in "Changing Oil". Remove filler tube and starter.
3. Mark rear universal joint and yoke for alignment purposes during installation. Then remove propeller shaft.

NOTE: Disconnect catalytic converter, if equipped, and front exhaust pipes for clearance.

4. Disconnect speedometer cable, throttle and shift linkages, neutral safety switch and transmission controlled spark switch wires. Remove transmission oil cooler lines.
5. Mark converter and drive plate for alignment purposes during installation. Remove converter to drive plate bolts.
6. Install a suitable jack under transmission and remove crossmember from side sill and rear support cushion.
7. Remove support cushion and adapter from extension housing.
8. Remove transmission to engine attaching bolts and move transmission an adequate distance to the rear to clear crankshaft.
9. Lower transmission, maintaining pressure against converter, until transmission clears engine.
10. Reverse procedure to install.

Chrysler Corp. 1977–83

CAUTION: The transmission and converter

must be removed as an assembly, otherwise, the converter drive plate, front pump bushing and oil seal will be damaged. The drive plate will not support the load; therefore, none of the weight of the transmission should be allowed to rest on the plate during removal.

NOTE: Some V8-400 and 440 engines were built with a forged crankshaft requiring a different torque converter and damper than the engines using the cast crankshaft.

This forged crankshaft is normally only used in the 400-4-BBL, HP engine with manual transmission.

If replacement of the crankshaft, torque converter, crankshaft damper or short engine is required, it is important that matching parts are used otherwise severe engine vibration will result, (Consult Chrysler Parts Dept.).

The cast crankshaft engine can be easily identified since it has the letter "E" stamped on the engine numbering pad following the built date.

1. Disconnect battery ground cable.

NOTE: Some models will require that the exhaust system be lowered for clearance.

2. Remove engine to transmission struts (if equipped), then disconnect transmission cooler lines and remove starter motor, cooler line bracket and converter access cover.
3. Drain fluid from transmission as described in "Changing Oil".
4. Mark converter and drive plate to aid in reassembly. The crankshaft flange bolt circle, inner and outer circle of holes in the drive plate, and the four tapped holes in front face of converter all have one hole offset so these parts will be installed in the original position. This maintains balance of the engine and converter.
5. Remove converter to drive plate bolts. Rotate engine clockwise using socket wrench to gain access to all bolts.

CAUTION: Do not rotate converter or

drive plate by prying with a screwdriver or similar tool as the drive plate might become distorted. Also, the starter should never be engaged if the drive plate is not attached to the converter with at least one bolt or if the transmission case-to-engine bolts have been loosened.

6. Mark drive shaft to aid in reassembly and remove drive shaft.
7. Disconnect neutral and back-up light switch and gearshift and torque shaft assembly from transmission.

NOTE: When disassembling linkage rods from levers which use plastic grommets as retainers, the grommets should be replaced with new ones.

8. Disconnect throttle rod from lever at left side of transmission, then remove linkage bellcrank from transmission, if so equipped.
9. Install a suitable fixture or jack that will support engine, then raise transmission slightly with a jack to relieve the load on the supports, and remove the crossmember.

NOTE: Some models have a torsion bar anchor crossmember that remains in place and requires a careful downward tilt on front of transmission as it is being lowered. If these models have a vibration dampening weight bolted to rear of extension housing, it must be removed.

10. Remove transmission to engine bolts and carefully work transmission and converter assembly rearward off engine block dowels and disengage converter hub from end of crankshaft. Using a small C-clamp on edge of bell housing, hold converter in place during transmission removal.
11. Remove transmission assembly from under vehicle.
12. Reverse procedure to install.

Ford Automatic Transaxle

DESCRIPTION

The transaxle combines an automatic transmission and differential into a front drive unit, Fig. 1. The components are housed in a one piece case and when bolted to the engine and installed in the vehicle, the engine/transaxle assembly is mounted transversely with the transaxle on the left side of the engine compartment. The transaxle consists of three friction clutches, one band and a single one way clutch. When applied as necessary, these components transmit engine torque through a compound planetary gearset which provides three forward and one reverse gear ratios. The planetary transmits engine torque to the input gear which meshes with the differential idler gear. The differential gear, riveted to the differential case, is in mesh with the idler gear. When the powerflow reaches the differential, engine torque flows outward to the wheels through the differential gears.

TROUBLESHOOTING GUIDE

Slow Initial Engagement

1. Improper fluid level.
2. Damaged or improperly adjusted manual linkage.
3. Incorrect throttle valve linkage adjustment.
4. Contaminated fluid.
5. Improper clutch or band application or oil control pressure.
6. Dirt in valve body.

Rough Initial Engagement In Forward Or Reverse

1. Improper fluid level.
2. Engine idle too high.
3. Automatic choke closed on warm engine.
4. Play in halfshafts, constant velocity joints or engine mounts.
5. Improper clutch or band application or oil control pressure.
6. Incorrect throttle valve linkage adjustment.
7. Dirt in valve body.

No Drive, Any Gear

1. Improper fluid level.
2. Damaged or improperly adjusted manual linkage.
3. Improper clutch or band application or oil control pressure.
4. Internal leak.
5. Loose valve body.
6. Damaged or worn clutches or bands.
7. Valve body sticking or dirty.

No Drive In 1, 2 or D

1. Improper fluid level.
2. Damaged or improperly adjusted manual linkage.
3. Improper one way clutch or band application.
4. Incorrect oil pressure.
5. Damaged or worn band, servo or clutches.

6. Loose valve body.
7. Valve body sticking or dirty.

No Reverse or Slips In Reverse

1. Improper fluid level.
2. Damaged or improperly adjusted manual linkage.
3. Play in halfshafts, constant velocity joints or engine mounts.
4. Improper oil pressure control.
5. Damaged or worn reverse clutch.
6. Loose valve body.
7. Valve body sticking or dirty.

No Start In Park Or Neutral

1. Neutral start switch improperly adjusted.
2. Neutral start wire damaged.
3. Manual linkage improperly adjusted.

No Drive or Slips In D

1. Damaged or worn one way clutch.
2. Improper fluid level.
3. Damaged or worn band.
4. Incorrect throttle valve linkage adjustment.

No Drive or Slips In 2

1. Improper fluid level.
2. Incorrect throttle valve linkage adjustment.
3. Damaged or worn intermediate friction clutch.
4. Improper clutch application.
5. Internal leakage.
6. Valve body dirty or sticking.
7. Band or drum glazed.

Take Off In 2nd or 3rd

1. Improper fluid level.
2. Damaged or improperly adjusted manual linkage.
3. Improper band or clutch application.
4. Damaged or worn governor.
5. Loose valve body.
6. Valve body sticking or dirty.
7. Leaks between valve body and case mating surface.

Incorrect Shift Points

1. Improper fluid level.
2. Throttle valve linkage improperly adjusted.
3. Improper clutch or band application.
4. Improper oil control pressure.
5. Damaged or worn governor.
6. Valve body dirty or sticking.

No Upshift In D

1. Improper fluid level.
2. Throttle valve linkage improperly adjusted.
3. Improper band or clutch application.
4. Improper oil control pressure.
5. Damaged or worn governor.
6. Valve body sticking or dirty.

Shift 1-3 In D

1. Improper fluid level.

2. Damaged or worn intermediate friction clutch.
3. Improper clutch application.
4. Improper oil control pressure.
5. Valve body sticking or dirty.

Runaway Upshifts

1. Improper fluid level.
2. Improper band or clutch application.
3. Improper oil pressure.
4. Damaged or worn direct clutch or servo.
5. Valve body sticking or dirty.

Delayed 1-2 Shift

1. Improper fluid level.
2. Improper engine performance.
3. Improper throttle valve linkage adjustment.
4. Improper intermediate clutch application.
5. Improper oil control pressure.
6. Damaged intermediate clutch.
7. Valve body sticking or dirty.

Rough 1-2 Upshift

1. Improper fluid level.
2. Improper throttle valve linkage adjustment.
3. Incorrect engine idle or performance.
4. Improper intermediate clutch application.
5. Improper oil control pressure.
6. Valve body sticking or dirty.

Rough 2-3 Upshift

1. Improper fluid level.
2. Incorrect engine performance.
3. Improper band release or direct clutch application.
4. Improper oil control pressure.
5. Valve body sticking or dirty.
6. Damaged or worn servo release and direct clutch piston check ball.
7. Improper throttle valve linkage adjustment.

Rough 3-2 Downshift At Closed Throttle In D

1. Improper fluid level.
2. Incorrect engine idle or performance.
3. Improper throttle valve linkage adjustment.
4. Improper band or clutch application.
5. Improper oil control pressure.
6. Improper governor operation.
7. Valve body sticking or dirty.

No Forced Downshifts

1. Improper fluid level.
2. Improper clutch or band application.
3. Improper oil control pressure.
4. Damaged internal kickdown linkage.
5. Throttle valve linkage improperly adjusted.
6. Valve body sticking or dirty.
7. Dirty or sticking governor.

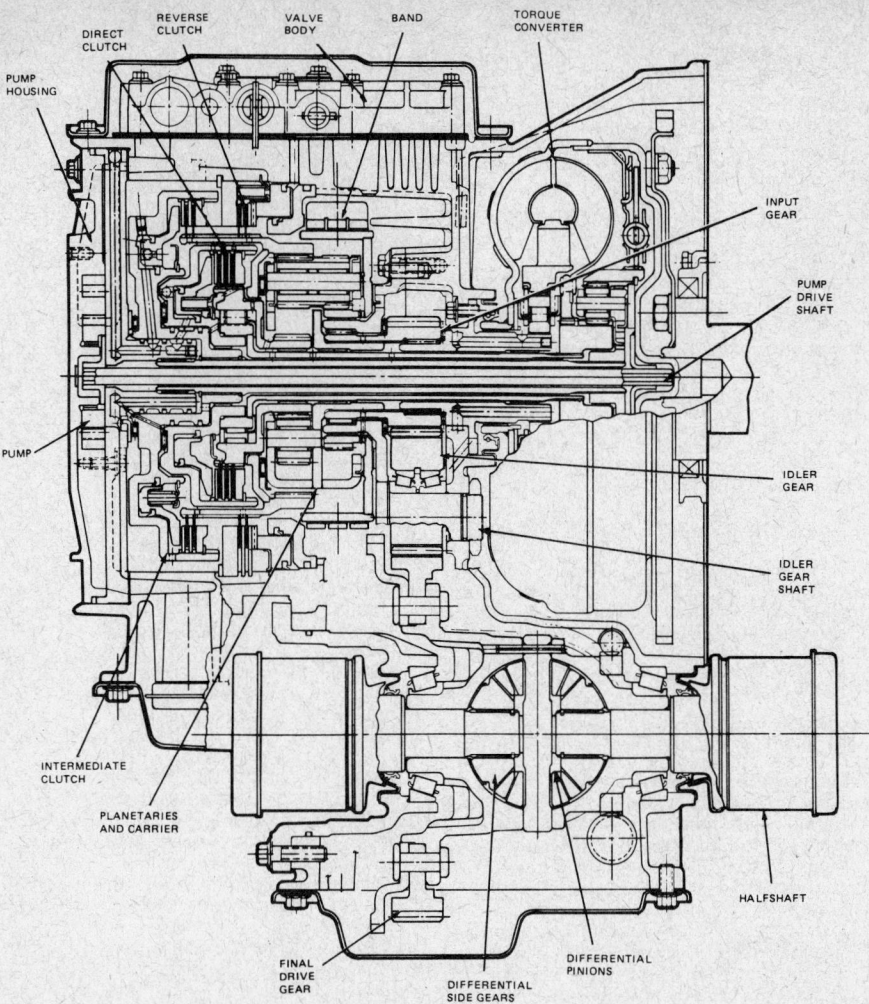

Fig. 1 Automatic transaxle. Sectional view

position. Place lever in Park position and check fluid level with engine at operating temperature. Add fluid as necessary.

IN-VEHICLE ADJUSTMENTS

Gearshift Linkage

1. Position selector lever in Drive position against rearward stop.
2. Raise and support vehicle, then loosen manual lever to control cable retaining nut.
3. Position transmission manual lever at second detent from most rearward position. This is Drive position.
4. Torque attaching nut to 10–15 ft. lbs. (14–20 Nm).
5. Lower vehicle and check for proper operation of transmission in each selector lever position.

Throttle Valve Linkage

1981–82
1. Operate engine at curb idle speed, then turn engine Off. Ensure that carburetor throttle lever is against hot engine curb idle stop with choke off.

NOTE: Ensure throttle lever is not on choke fast idle cam.

2. Position coupling lever adjustment screw at its midpoint, then ensure throttle valve linkage shaft assembly is seated fully upward into coupling lever, Fig. 2.
3. Loosen sliding trunnion block bolt on throttle valve control rod assembly at least one turn.
4. Rotate transaxle throttle valve control lever upward to ensure throttle valve lever is against its internal idle stop. Maintain force on throttle control lever, then torque bolt on trunnion block to 24–36 in. lbs. (2.7–4.1 Nm).
5. Check that carburetor throttle lever is still against hot engine curb idle stop. If not, repeat steps 1 through 6.

1983
1. Operate engine until normal operating temperature is reached, then turn engine off. Ensure carburetor throttle lever is against hot engine curb idle stop with choke off.

NOTE: Ensure throttle lever is not on choke fast idle cam.

2. Loosen sliding trunnion block bolt on throttle valve control rod assembly at least one turn. Ensure control rod is corrosion free so trunnion block is free to slide.
3. Idle engine in park. With light force, rotate throttle valve control lever upward against its internal idle stop. Maintain about a 1 lb. force on throttle control lever and torque bolt on trunnion block to 24–36 in. lbs.

IN-VEHICLE REPAIRS

Valve Body, Replace

1. Remove battery and battery tray.
2. Remove ignition coil and transaxle dipstick.
3. Disconnect all hoses and lines from air

Downshift Runaway

1. Improper fluid level.
2. Throttle valve linkage improperly adjusted.
3. Band improperly adjusted.
4. Improper band or clutch application.
5. Improper oil control pressure.
6. Damaged or worn servo.
7. Glazed band or drum.
8. Valve body sticking or dirty.

No Engine Braking In 1

1. Improper fluid level.
2. Throttle valve linkage improperly adjusted.
3. Damaged or improperly adjusted manual linkage.
4. Improperly adjusted band or clutch.
5. Improper oil control pressure.
6. Glazed band or drum.
7. Valve body sticking or dirty.

No Engine Braking In 2

1. Improper fluid level.
2. Throttle valve linkage improperly adjusted.
3. Manual linkage improperly adjusted.
4. Improper band or clutch application.

5. Improper oil control system.
6. Leaking servo.
7. Glazed band or drum.

MAINTENANCE

Adding Oil

To check fluid level, apply parking brake, operate engine at idle speed with vehicle on level surface and transmission in Park position. Add fluid as necessary to bring mark on dipstick between "Add" and "Full" marks.

Changing Oil

Fluid and filter changes are not required for average passenger car use. Severe usage such as commercial use or prolonged periods of idling require fluid and filter be changed every 20,000 miles. Whenever fluid is changed only fluid labeled Dexron II should be used.
1. Raise and support vehicle.
2. Loosen transaxle oil pan attaching bolts and allow fluid to drain.
3. Remove oil pan and clean thoroughly.
4. Install new gasket onto pan, then the pan onto transaxle.
5. Fill transaxle to correct fluid level, then operate engine at idle. With parking brake applied, move selector lever to each

management valve, then remove valve from transaxle valve body cover.

4. Disconnect neutral safety switch electrical connector, and the fuel evaporator hose from frame rail.
5. Disconnect electrical connectors from fan motor and temperature sending unit.
6. Remove valve body cover bolts, then the valve body cover and gasket.
7. Remove valve body bolts, then the valve body and gasket.
8. Reverse procedure to install. Install guide pins to properly align valve body before tightening attaching bolts. One alignment pin may have to be temporarily removed to allow attachment of manual valve. Ensure roller on end of throttle valve plunger engages cam on end of throttle lever shaft. Torque valve body bolts to 6–8 ft. lbs. (8–11 Nm) and valve body cover bolts to 7–9 ft. lbs. (9–12 Nm).

Governor

1. Disconnect battery ground cable, and all hoses and lines from air management valve.
2. Remove managed air valve supply hose band to intermediate shift control bracket attaching screw.
3. Remove air cleaner, then using a long screwdriver, remove governor cover retaining clip.
4. Remove governor cover, then the governor.
5. Reverse procedure to install.

Servo

1. Disconnect battery ground cable.
2. Disconnect electrical connectors from fan motor and temperature sending unit.
3. Disconnect FM capacitor wiring, if equipped.
4. Remove two fan shroud to radiator attaching nuts, then the fan and fan shroud.
5. Remove filler tube to case attaching bolt, then the filler tube and dipstick.
6. Remove lower left side mount to case attaching bolt from the left side front mount.
7. Remove servo cap and snap ring using tool T81P-70027A or equivalent.
8. Reverse procedure to install.

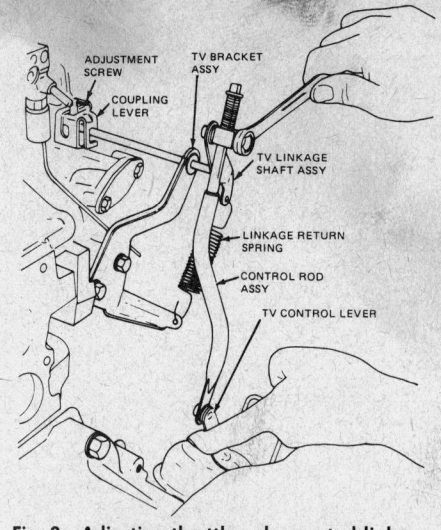

ADJUSTMENT SCREW
TV BRACKET ASSY
COUPLING LEVER
TV LINKAGE SHAFT ASSY
LINKAGE RETURN SPRING
CONTROL ROD ASSY
TV CONTROL LEVER

Fig. 2   Adjusting throttle valve control linkage

Transaxle, Replace

1. Disconnect battery ground cable, then raise and support vehicle.
2. Remove bolts attaching managed air valve to valve body cover.
3. Disconnect electrical connector from neutral safety switch.
4. Disconnect throttle valve linkage and manual cable at their levers.
5. Remove two transaxle to engine upper attaching bolts.
6. Remove nut from control arm to steering knuckle attaching bolt, then remove bolt using suitable punch and hammer. Repeat procedure on other side of vehicle. Nuts and bolts must be discarded.
7. Using a pry bar, disengage control arms from steering knuckles.

NOTE: Do not hammer on knuckles. Plastic shield installed behind rotor contains a molded pocket which accepts lower control arm ball joint. When separating control arm from knuckle, clearance for ball joint may be obtained by bending shield backwards towards rotor. Failure to provide clearance for the ball joint may result in damage to the shield.

8. Remove bolts attaching stabilizer bar brackets to frame rails and discard bolts.
9. Remove stabilizer bar to control arm attaching nuts and washers. Remove stabilizer bar. Discard nut.
10. Remove bolts securing brake hose routing clips to suspension strut brackets.
11. Remove steering gear tie rods from steering knuckles.
12. Remove halfshaft from right side of transaxle, then position halfshaft on transaxle housing.
13. Disengage left side halfshaft from differential side gear by inserting tool T81P-4026A or equivalent into right side halfshaft opening and driving out inner constant velocity joint.
14. Pull left side halfshaft from transaxle and wire to underbody. Do not allow shaft to hang unsupported.
15. Install seal plugs T81P-1177B or equivalent into differential seals.
16. Remove starter support bracket, then disconnect starter cable from starter.
17. Remove starter, then the transaxle support bracket.
18. Remove dust cover from torque converter housing. Remove torque converter to flywheel attaching nuts.
19. Remove left side front mounts to body bracket attaching nut. Remove bracket to body attaching bolts and remove bracket.
20. Remove left rear insulator attaching nut, and disconnect oil cooler lines.
21. Remove manual lever bracket to transaxle case attaching bolts.
22. Support transaxle with suitable jack, then remove four remaining transaxle to engine attaching bolts.
23. Using a screwdriver inserted between flywheel and torque converter, position transaxle and converter away from engine until torque converter studs clear flywheel.
24. Lower transaxle two to three inches and disconnect speedometer cable.
25. Lower transaxle and remove from vehicle.
26. Reverse procedure to install. Before installing halfshafts, replace circlip on constant velocity joint stub shaft. When installing halfshafts, ensure splines of constant velocity joint align with splines in differential.

FORD C3 & C4 Automatic Transmission

TRANSMISSION IDENTIFICATION

Each transmission may be identified by the tag attached to the low-reverse servo cover bolt. The tag includes the model prefix and suffix, a service identification number and a build date code. The service identification number indicates changes to service details which affect interchangeability when the transmission model is not changed. For interpretation of this number the Ford Master Parts Catalog should be consulted.

Year	Car Model	Trans. Code	Engine Model	Year	Car Model	Trans. Code	Engine Model
C3 Transmission				**C3 Transmission—Cont'd.**			
1977	Bobcat	77DT-BA, CA	4-140		Mustang II	77DT-DA, EA	4-140
	Bobcat	77DT-GA	V6-171		Mustang II	77DT-FA, GA	V6-171
	Mustang II	77DT-BA, CA	4-140		Pinto	77DT-BA, CA	4-140

C3 Transmission—Cont'd.

Year	Car Model	Trans. Code	Engine Model
	Pinto	77DT-FA, GA	V6-171
1978	Bobcat	78DT-ACA, ADA	4-140
	Bobcat	78DT-AGA	V6-171
	Fairmont	78DT-SA	4-140
	Fairmont	78DT-BAA, BCA	6-200
	Fairmont①	78DT-BJA	6-200
	Mustang II	78DT-ACA, ADA	4-140
	Mustang II	78DT-AGA	V6-171
	Pinto	78DT-ACA, ADA	4-140
	Pinto	78DT-AGA	V6-171
	Zephyr	78DT-SA	4-140
	Zephyr	78DT-BAA, BCA	6-200
	Zephyr①	78DT-BJA	6-200
1979	Bobcat	79DT-AA	4-140
	Bobcat	79DT-DA	V6-171
	Capri	79DT-EA, GA	4-140
	Capri	79DT-HA	V6-171
	Fairmont	79DT-KA, MA	4-140
	Fairmont	79DT-NA	6-200
	Mustang	79DT-EA, GA	4-140
	Mustang	79DT-HA	V6-171
	Pinto	79DT-AA	4-140
	Pinto	79DT-DA	V6-171
	Zephyr	79DT-KA, MA	4-140
	Zephyr	79DT-NA	6-200
1980	Bobcat	80DT-AA, AB	4-140
	Capri②	80DT-CA, CB	4-140
	Capri③	80DT-CDA, CDB	4-140
	Capri	80DT-EA, EB	6-200
	Cougar	80DT-LB	6-200
	Fairmont②	80DT-CA, CB, HA, HB	4-140
	Fairmont③	80DT-CDA, CDB	4-140
	Fairmont	80DT-EA, EB, LA, LB, CEB	6-200
	Mustang②	80DT-CA, CB	4-140
	Mustang③	80DT-CDA, CDB	4-140
	Mustang	80DT-EA, EB	6-200
	Pinto	80DT-AA, AB	4-140
	Thunderbird	80DT-LB	6-200
	Zephyr②	80DT-CA, CB, HA, HB	4-140
	Zephyr③	80DT-CDA, CDB	4-140
	Zephyr	80DT-EA, EB, LA, LB, CEB	6-200
1981	Capri	81DT-CFA, HA	4-140
	Capri	81DT-DAA, AB, EA, EB	6-200
	Cougar & XR7	81DT-CFA, HA, KA, MA	4-140
	Cougar & XR7	81DT-DAA, AB, DA, DB	6-200
	Cougar & XR7	81DT-DEA, EB, GA, GB	6-200
	Fairmont	81DT-CFA, HA, KA, MA	4-140
	Fairmont	81DT-DAA, AB, DA, DB, EA, EB, GA, GB	6-200
	Granada	81DT-CFA, HA, KA, MA	4-140
	Granada	81DT-DAA, AB, DA, DB, EA, EB, GA, GB	6-200
	Mustang	81DT-CFA, HA	4-140
	Mustang	81DT-DAA, AB, EA, EB	6-200
	Thunderbird	81DT-DDA, DB, GA, GB	6-200
	Zephyr	81DT-CFA, HA, KA, MA	4-140
	Zephyr	81DT-DAA, AB, DA, DB, EA, EB, GA, GB	6-200
1982	Capri	82DT-AAA, ACA	4-140

C3 Transmission—Cont'd.

Year	Car Model	Trans. Code	Engine Model
	Capri	82DT-BBA	6-200
	Cougar	82DT-AAA, ABA	4-140
	Cougar	82DT-AAA, ADA	4-140
	Fairmont	82DT-AAA, ABA	4-140
	Fairmont	82DT-ACA, ADA	4-140
	Fairmont	82DT-BAA, BBA	6-200
	Granada	82DT-AAA, ADA	4-140
	Granada	82DT-ACA, ADA	4-140
	Mustang	82DT-AAA, ACA	4-140
	Mustang	82DT-BBA	6-200
	Zephyr	82DT-AAA, ABA	4-140
	Zephyr	82DT-ACA, ADA	4-140
	Zephyr	82DT-BAA, BBA	6-200
1983	Capri	83DT-AAB	4-140
	Fairmont	83DT-AAB, ABB	4-140
	Fairmont	82DT-BAA	6-200
	LTD/Marquis	83DT-AAB, ABB, AGB, AHB	4-140
	Mustang	83DT-AAB	4-140
	Zephyr	83DT-AAB, ABB	4-140
	Zephyr	82DT-BAA, BBA	6-200

C4 Transmission

Year	Car Model	Trans. Code	Engine Model
1977	Bobcat	PEJ-P	4-140
	Bobcat	PEJ-L	6-171
	Bobcat	PEJ-M2	6-171
	Comet	PEB-N1	6-200
	Comet	PEE-CJ2	6-250
	Comet	PEE-CS1	V8-302
	Comet	PEE-CZ	V8-302
	Cougar	PEE-V8	V8-302
	Cougar	PEF-AA2	V8-351M
	Cougar	PEF-AB2	V8-351M
	Cougar	PEF-K	V8-351W
	Ford	PEA-CH	V8-302
	Ford	PEF-AP1	V8-351W
	Granada	PEE-BU	6-250
	Granada	PEE-CK2	6-250
	Granada	PEE-CD1	6-250
	Granada	PEE-CP1	6-250
	Granada	PEE-CA4	V8-302
	Granada	PEE-CE2	V8-302
	Granada	PEE-CB2	V8-302
	Granada	PEE-DN	V8-302
	Granada	PEE-CW	V8-302
	Granada	PEF-AE1	V8-351W
	Granada	PEF-AE2	V8-351W
	Granada	PEF-AF1	V8-351W
	Granada	PEF-AF2	V8-351W
	LTD II	PEE-M9	V8-302
	LTD II	PEE-V8	V8-302
	LTD II	PEF-AA2, 3	V8-351M
	LTD II	PEF-AB2, 3	V8-351M
	LTD II	PEF-K, 1	V8-351W
	Maverick	PEB-N1	6-250
	Maverick	PEE-CJ2	6-250
	Maverick	PEE-CS1	V8-302
	Maverick	PEE-CZ	V8-302
	Monarch	PEE-BU	6-250
	Monarch	PEE-CD1	6-250
	Monarch	PEE-CK2	6-250
	Monarch	PEE-CP1	6-250
	Monarch	PEE-CA4	V8-302
	Monarch	PEE-CB2	V8-302
	Monarch	PEE-CE2	V8-302
	Monarch	PEE-CW	V8-302
	Monarch	PEE-DN	V8-302
	Monarch	PEF-AE1	V8-351W
	Monarch	PEF-AF1	V8-351W
	Mustang II	PEH-H	4-140
	Mustang II	PEJ-M2	6-171
	Mustang II	PEE-BY	V8-302
	Mustang II	PEE-CC1	V8-302

C4 Transmission—Cont'd.

Year	Car Model	Trans. Code	Engine Model
	Pinto	PEJ-P	4-140
	Pinto	PEJ-L	6-171
	Pinto	PEJ-M2	6-171
	Thunderbird	PEE-M9	V8-302
	Thunderbird	PEE-V8	V8-302
	Thunderbird	PEF-AA2	V8-351M
	Thunderbird	PEF-AB2	V8-351M
	Thunderbird	PEF-K, 1	V8-351M
	Versailles	PEE-DH	V8-302
	Versailles	PEE-DJ	V8-302
	Versailles	PEE-DV	V8-302
	Versailles	PEE-DW	V8-302
	Versailles	PEF-AM	V8-351W
	Versailles	PEF-AN	V8-351W
1978	Bobcat	PEJ-P2	4-140
	Bobcat	PEJ-M4	V6-231
	Cougar	PEE-M11, M12	V8-302
	Cougar	PEE-V10, V11	V8-302
	Cougar	PEE-DY	V8-302
	Cougar	PEF-K3	V8-351W
	Cougar	PEF-AA5, AB5	V8-351M
	Fairmont	PEB-N3, P1, R	6-200
	Fairmont①	PEB-S	6-200
	Fairmont	PEE-CS3, CS4	V8-302
	Fairmont	PEE-CT1, CT2	V8-302
	Fairmont	PEE-DA, ED	V8-302
	Ford	PEA-CH2, CL	V8-302
	Ford	PEF-AP3	V8-351W
	Granada	PEE-CD3, CP3	6-250
	Granada	PEE-CA6, CE4	V8-302
	Granada	PEE-CW2	V8-302
	LTD II	PEE-M11, M12	V8-302
	LTD II	PEE-V10, V11	V8-302
	LTD II	PEE-DY	V8-302
	LTD II	PEF-K3	V8-351W
	LTD II	PEF-AA5, AB5	V8-351M
	Monarch	PEE-CD3, CP3	6-250
	Monarch	PEE-CA6, CE4	V8-302
	Monarch	PEE-CW2	V8-302
	Mustang II	PEJ-P2	4-140
	Mustang II	PEJ-M4	V6-171
	Mustang II	PEE-BY2, CC3	V8-302
	Pinto	PEJ-P2	4-140
	Pinto	PEJ-M4	V6-231
	Thunderbird	PEE-M11, M12	V8-302
	Thunderbird	PEE-V10, V11	V8-302
	Thunderbird	PEF-K3	V8-351W
	Thunderbird	PEF-AA5, AB5	V8-351M
	Versailles	PEE-DH3, DJ3	V8-302
	Versailles	PEE-EF, EG	V8-302
	Versailles	PEE-EH, EJ	V8-302
	Zephyr	PEB-N3, P1, R	6-200
	Zephyr①	PEB-S	6-200
	Zephyr	PEE-CS3, CS4	V8-302
	Zephyr	PEE-CT1, CT2	V8-302
	Zephyr	PEE-DA, ED	V8-302
1979	Bobcat	PEJ-Y	4-140
	Bobcat	PEJ-M6, V	V6-171
	Capri	PEJ-S, S1	V6-171
	Capri	PEJ-W, W1	V6-171
	Capri	PEE-BY4	V8-302
	Cougar	PEE-M14, V13	V8-302
	Cougar	PEF-AA7, AB7	V8-351
	Fairmont	PEB-N5, P3	6-200
	Fairmont	PEB-R2, S2	6-200
	Fairmont	PEB-T	6-200
	Fairmont	PEE-CS6, CT4	V8-302
	Fairmont	PEE-DA2, ED2	V8-302
	Fairmont	PEE-ES, ET	V8-302
	Fairmont	PEE-EU, EV	V8-302
	Fairmont	PEE-FD	V8-302
	Ford	PEE-DZ1, DZ	V8-302
	Ford	PEE-EA, EA1	V8-302
	Ford	PEE-EM1, EM	V8-302
	Ford	PEE-FB, FB1	V8-302

AUTOMATIC TRANSMISSIONS/TRANSAXLES

C4 Transmission—Cont'd.

Year	Car Model	Trans. Code	Engine Model
	Ford	PEE-FC, FE	V8-302
	Ford	PEF-AT, AT1	V8-351
	Ford	PEF-AU, AU1	V8-351
	Ford	PEF-AZ, AZ1	V8-351
	Granada	PEE-CD5, CP5	6-250
	Granada	PEE-CA8, CE6	V8-302
	Granada	PEE-CW4	V8-302
	LTD II	PEE-M14, V13	V8-302
	LTD II	PEF-AA7, AB7	V8-351
	Mercury	PEE-DZ, DZ1	V8-302
	Mercury	PEE-EA, EA1	V8-302
	Mercury	PEE-EM, EM1	V8-302
	Mercury	PEE-FB, FB1	V8-302
	Mercury	PEE-FC, FE	V8-302
	Mercury	PEF-AT, AT1	V8-351
	Mercury	PEF-AU, AU1	V8-351
	Mercury	PEF-AZ, AZ1	V8-351
	Monarch	PEE-CD5, CP5	6-250
	Monarch	PEE-CA8, CE6	V8-302
	Monarch	PEE-CW4	V8-302
	Mustang	PEJ-S, S1	V6-171
	Mustang	PEJ-W, W1	V6-171
	Mustang	PEE-BY4	V8-302
	Pinto	PEJ-Y	4-140
	Pinto	PEJ-M6, V	V6-171
	Thunderbird	PEE-M14, V13	V8-302
	Thunderbird	PEF-AA7, AB7	V8-351
	Versailles	PEE-DH5, DJ5	V8-302
	Versailles	PEE-EW, EW1	V8-302
	Versailles	PEE-EY, EY1	V8-302
	Versailles	PEE-EZ, FA	V8-302
	Zephyr	PEB-N5, P3	6-200
	Zephyr	PEB-R2, S2	6-200
	Zephyr	PEB-T	6-200
	Zephyr	PEE-CS6, CT4	V8-302
	Zephyr	PEE-DA2, ED2	V8-302
	Zephyr	PEE-ES, ET	V8-302
	Zephyr	PEE-EU, EV	V8-302
	Zephyr	PEE-FD, DH5	V8-302
	Zephyr	PEE-DJ5, EW	V8-302
	Zephyr	PEE-EW1, EY	V8-302
	Zephyr	PEE-EY1, EZ	V8-302
	Zephyr	PEE-FA	V8-302
1980	Bobcat	PEJ-Z, 1,2	4-140
	Capri	PEJ-AC, 1, 2	4-140
	Capri	PEB-P, 4, 5, 6	6-200
	Capri	PEM-B, E, N, 1, 2	V8-255
	Cougar	PEB-T3	6-200
	Cougar	PEM-D, L	V8-255
	Cougar	PEE-FL, FN	V8-302
	Fairmont	PEJ-AC, AD, 1	4-140
	Fairmont	PEB-N, 6, 7, 8	6-200
	Fairmont	PEB-P, 4, 5, 6	6-200
	Fairmont	PEB-S, 3, 4	6-200
	Fairmont	PEB-T, 1, 2, 3	6-200
	Fairmont	PEB-U, 1, 2	6-200
	Fairmont	PEM-C, 1, 2, D, 1, 2, E, 1, 2	V8-255
	Fairmont	PEM-G, 1, H, 1, 2, M, 1, 2	V8-255
	Fairmont	PEM-L, 1, 2, N, 1, 2	V8-255
	Ford	PEE-D, Z, 3, 4, 5	V8-302
	Ford	PEE-FA, 3, 4, 5	V8-302
	Ford	PEE-EM, 3, 4	V8-302
	Ford	PEE-FC1, 2	V8-302
	Ford	PEE-FE1, 2, 3	V8-302
	Granada	PEL-A1, 2, B1, 2, C1	6-250
	Granada	PEL-D1	6-250
	Granada	PEM-J1, K1, P, R	V8-255
	Granada	PEE-CW5, 6, 7	V8-302
	Granada	PEE-FP, 1, 2	V8-302
	Granada	PEE-FR1, 2	V8-302
	Mercury	PEE-DZ3, 4, 5	V8-302
	Mercury	PEE-EA3, 4, 5	V8-302
	Mercury	PEE-EM3, 4	V8-302

C4 Transmission—Cont'd.

Year	Car Model	Trans. Code	Engine Model
	Mercury	PEE-FC1, 2	V8-302
	Mercury	PEE-FE1, 2, 3	V8-302
	Monarch	PEL-A1, 2, B1, 2, C1, D1	6-250
	Monarch	PEL, J1, K1, P, R	V8-255
	Mustang	PEJ-AC1	4-140
	Mustang	PEB-P4, 5, 6	6-200
	Mustang	PEM-B1, 2, E1, 2, N1, 2	V8-255
	Pinto	PEJ-Z1, 2	4-140
	Thunderbird	PEB-T3	6-200
	Thunderbird	PEM-D1, 2, L1, 2	V8-255
	Thunderbird	PEE-FL, FN1, 2	V8-302
	Versailles	PEE-EY2	V8-302
	Versailles	PEE-FV1, 2	V8-302
	Zephyr	PEJ-AC1, 2, AD1, 2	4-140
	Zephyr	PEB-N6, 7, 8	6-200
	Zephyr	PEB-P4, 5, 6	6-200
	Zephyr	PEB-S3, 4	6-200
	Zephyr	PEB-T1, 2, 3, U1, 2	6-200
	Zephyr	PEM-C1, 2, D1, 2, E1, 2	V8-255
	Zephyr	PEM-G1, H1, 2, L1, 2	V8-255
	Zephyr	PEM-M1, 2, N1, 2	V8-255
1981	Capri	PEB-P8, P9	6-200
	Capri	PEJ-AC3	4-140
	Capri	PEJ-AC4	4-140
	Capri	PEM-E5, E6, W, W1	V8-255
	Capri	PEM-AD, D1, AK	V8-255
	Capri	PEM-A1, B1	6-200
	Cougar & XR7	PEB-N10, 11, P8, P9	6-200
	Cougar & XR7	PEB-Z, Z1	6-200
	Cougar & XR7	PEJ-AC3	4-140
	Cougar & XR7	PEJ-AC4	4-140
	Cougar & XR7	PEJ-AD3, D4	4-140
	Cougar & XR7	PEM-C5, C6, D5, D6, E5, E6, AC, AC1	V8-255
	Cougar & XR7	PEM-AD, AD1, AE, AE1, AL, AL1	V8-255
	Cougar & XR7	PEM-AM, AM1, AN, AN1	V8-255
	Cougar & XR7	PEN-A, A1, B, B1	6-200
	Fairmont	PEB-N10, N11	6-200
	Fairmont	PEB-P8, P9, U4, U5, Z, Z1	6-200
	Fairmont	PEJ-AC3, AC4, AD3, AD4	4-140
	Fairmont	PEM-C5, C6, D5, D6, E5, E6	V8-255
	Fairmont	PEM-AC, AC1, AD, AD1	V8-255
	Fairmont	PEM-AL, AL1, AM, AM1, AN, AN1	V8-255
	Fairmont	PEN-A, A1, B, B1	6-200
	Granada	PEB-N10, N11	6-200
	Granada	PEB-P8, P9	6-200
	Granada	PEJ-AC3, AC4, AD3, AD4	4-140
	Granada	PEN-A, A1, B, B1	6-200
	Granada	PEM-C5, C6, E5, E6	V8-255
	Granada	PEM-AC, AC1, AD, AD1	V8-255
	Granada	PEM-AL, AL1, AM, AM1, AN, AN1	V8-255
	Mustang	PEB-P8, P9	6-200
	Mustang	PEJ-AC3, AC4	4-140
	Mustang	PEM-E5, E6, W, W1, AD, AD1, AK, AK1	V8-255
	Thunderbird	PEB-Z, Z1	6-200

C4 Transmission—Cont'd.

Year	Car Model	Trans. Code	Engine Model
	Thunderbird	PEM-D5, D6, AC, AC1, AE, AE1	V8-255
	Zephyr	PEB-N10, N11, P8, P9, U4, U5	6-200
	Zephyr	PEB-Z, Z1	6-200
	Zephyr	PEJ-AC3, D3, D4	4-140
	Zephyr	PEM-C5, C6, D5, D6, E5, E6	V8-255
	Zephyr	PEM-AC, C1, AD, D1	V8-255
	Zephyr	PEM-AL, L1, AM, M1, AN, N1	V8-255
	Zephyr	PEN-A, A1, B, B1	6-200

①—Police & taxi.
②—Without turbocharger.
③—With turbocharger.

DESCRIPTION

The main control incorporates a manually selective first and second gear range. The transmission features a drive range that provides for fully automatic upshifts and downshifts, and manually selected low and second gears.

The transmission consists essentially of a torque converter, a compound planetary gear train, two multiple disc clutches, a one-way clutch and a hydraulic control system, Figs. 1 and 2.

For all normal driving the selector lever is moved to the green dot under "Drive" on the selector quadrant on the steering column or on the floor console. As the throttle is advanced from the idle position, the transmission will upshift automatically to intermediate gear and then to high.

The driver can force downshift the transmission from high to intermediate at speeds up to 65 mph. A detent on the downshift linkage warns the driver when the carburetor is wide open. Accelerator pedal depression through the detent will bring in the downshift.

With the throttle closed the transmission will downshift automatically as the car speed drops to about 10 mph. With the throttle open at any position up to the detent, the downshifts will come in automatically at speeds above 10 mph and in proportion to throttle opening. This prevents engine lugging on steep hill climbing, for example.

When the selector lever is moved to "L" with the transmission in high, the transmission will downshift to intermediate or to low depending on the road speed. At speed above 25 mph, the downshift will be from high to intermediate. At speeds below 25 mph, the downshift will be from high to low. With the selector lever in the "L" position the transmission cannot upshift.

TROUBLE SHOOTING GUIDE

Rough Initial Engagement In D1 or D2

1. Engine idle speed.
2. Vacuum diaphragm unit or tubes re-

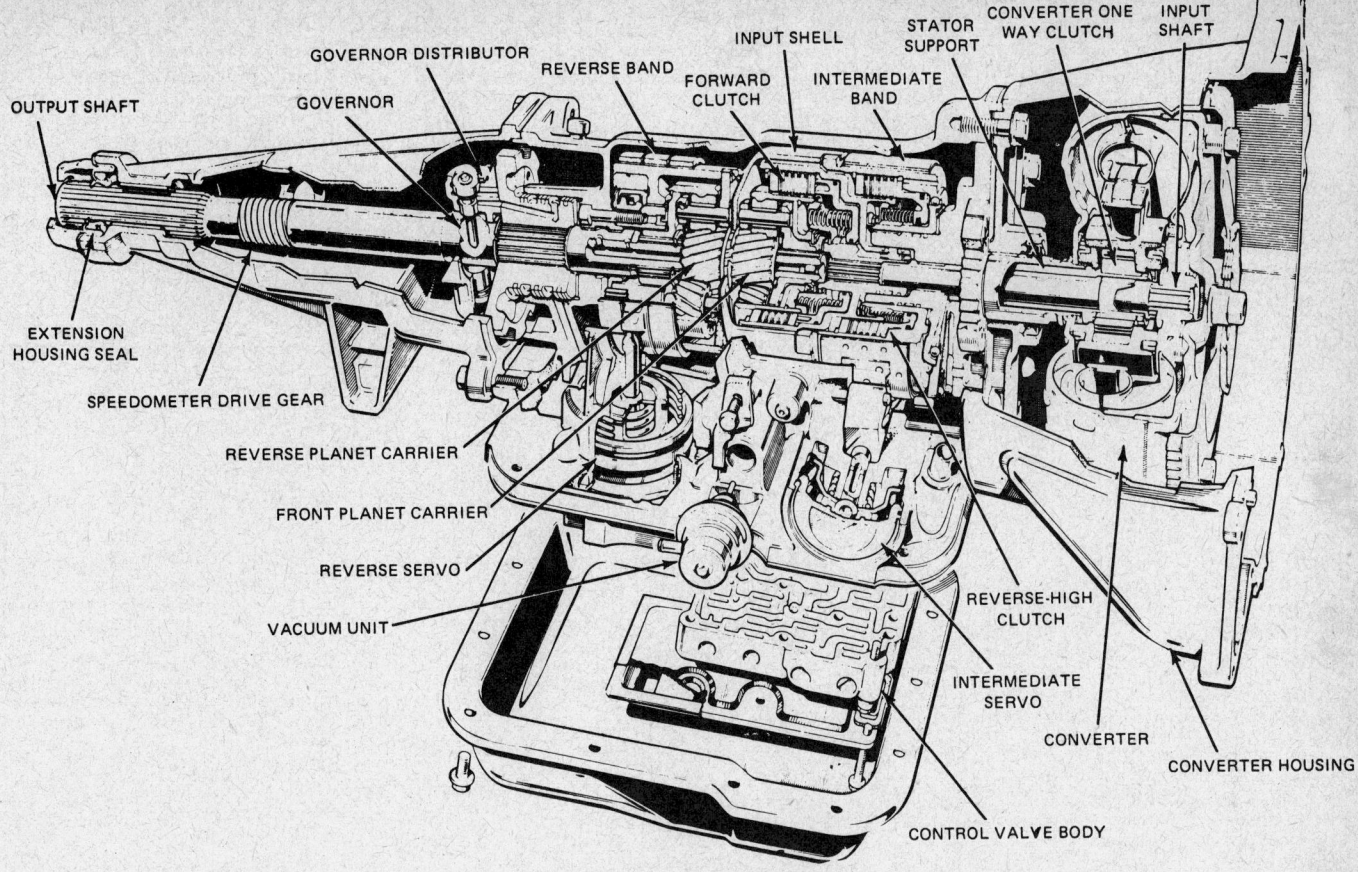

Fig. 1 C3 Dual Range Automatic

stricted, leaking or maladjusted.
3. Check control pressure.
4. Pressure regulator.
5. Valve body.
6. Forward clutch.

1-2 or 2-3 Shift Points Erratic

1. Check fluid level.
2. Vacuum diaphragm unit or tubes restricted, leaking or maladjusted.
3. Immediate servo.
4. Manual linkage adjustment.
5. Governor.
6. Check control pressure.
7. Valve body.
8. Make air pressure check.

Rough 1-2 Upshifts

1. Vacuum diaphragm unit or tubes restricted, leaking or maladjusted.
2. Intermediate servo.
3. Intermediate band.
4. Check control pressure.
5. Valve body.
6. Pressure regulator.

Rough 2-3 Upshifts

1. Vacuum diaphragm unit or tubes restricted, leaking or maladjusted.
2. Intermediate servo.
3. Check control pressure.
4. Pressure regulator.
5. Intermediate band.
6. Valve body.
7. Make air pressure check.
8. Reverse-high clutch.

9. Reverse-high clutch piston air bleed valve.

Dragged Out 1-2 Shift

1. Check fluid level.
2. Vacuum diaphragm unit or tubes restricted, leaking or maladjusted.
3. Intermediate servo.
4. Check control pressure.
5. Intermediate band.
6. Valve body.
7. Pressure regulator.
8. Make air pressure check.
9. Leakage in hydraulic system.

Engine Overspeeds on 2-3 Shift

1. Manual linkage.
2. Check fluid level.
3. Vacuum diaphragm unit or tubes restricted, leaking or maladjusted.
4. Reverse servo.
5. Check control pressure.
6. Valve body.
7. Pressure regulator.
8. Intermediate band.
9. Reverse-high clutch.
10. Reverse-high clutch piston air bleed valve.

No 1-2 or 2-3 Shift

1. Manual linkage.
2. Downshift linkage, including inner lever position.
3. Vacuum diaphragm unit or tubes restricted, leaking or maladjusted.

4. Governor.
5. Check control pressure.
6. Valve body.
7. Intermediate band.
8. Intermediate servo.
9. Reverse-high clutch.
10. Reverse-high clutch piston air bleed valve.

No 3-1 Shift in D1 or 3-2 Shift in D2

1. Governor.
2. Valve body.

No Forced Downshifts

1. Downshift linkage, including inner lever position.
2. Valve body.
3. Vacuum diaphragm unit or tubes restricted, leaking or maladjusted.

Runaway Engine on Forced 3-2 Downshift

1. Check control pressure.
2. Intermediate servo.
3. Intermediate band.
4. Pressure regulator.
5. Valve body.
6. Vacuum diaphragm unit or tubes restricted, leaking or maladjusted.
7. Leakage in hydraulic system.

Rough 3-2 or 3-1 Shift at Closed Throttle

1. Engine idle speed.

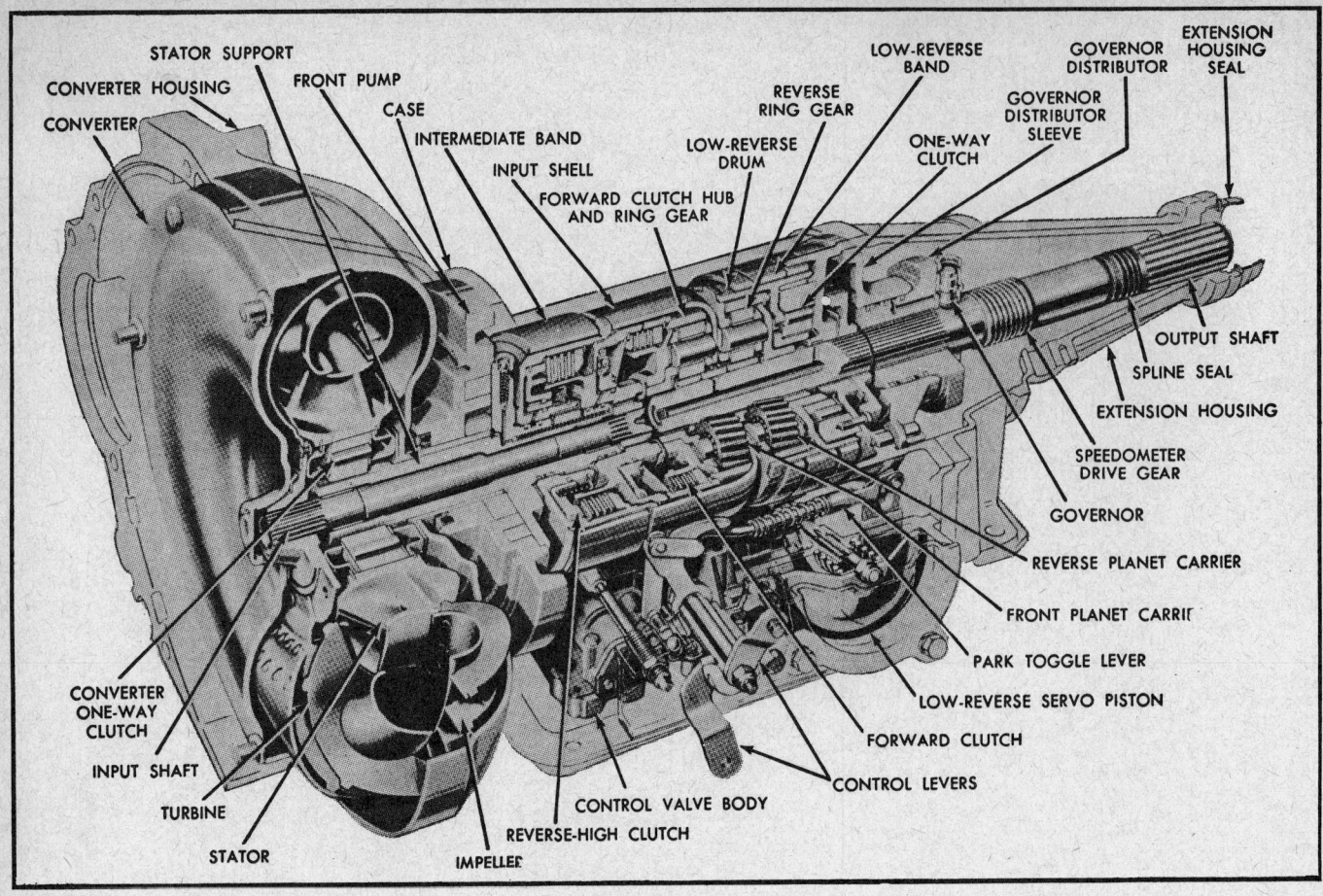

STATOR SUPPORT
CONVERTER HOUSING
FRONT PUMP
CONVERTER
CASE
INTERMEDIATE BAND
INPUT SHELL
FORWARD CLUTCH HUB
AND RING GEAR
LOW-REVERSE
BAND
REVERSE
RING GEAR
LOW-REVERSE
DRUM
ONE-WAY
CLUTCH
GOVERNOR
DISTRIBUTOR
GOVERNOR
DISTRIBUTOR
SLEEVE
EXTENSION
HOUSING
SEAL
OUTPUT SHAFT
SPLINE SEAL
EXTENSION HOUSING
SPEEDOMETER
DRIVE GEAR
GOVERNOR
REVERSE PLANET CARRIER
FRONT PLANET CARRIER
PARK TOGGLE LEVER
LOW-REVERSE SERVO PISTON
FORWARD CLUTCH
CONTROL LEVERS
CONTROL VALVE BODY
REVERSE-HIGH CLUTCH
IMPELLER
STATOR
TURBINE
INPUT SHAFT
CONVERTER
ONE-WAY
CLUTCH

Fig. 2 C4 Dual Range Automatic

2. Vacuum diaphragm unit or tubes restricted, leaking or maladjusted.
3. Intermediate servo.
4. Valve body.
5. Pressure regulator.

Shifts 1-3 in D1 and D2

1. Intermediate band.
2. Intermediate servo.
3. Vacuum diaphragm unit or tubes restricted, leaking or maladjusted.
4. Valve body.
5. Governor.
6. Make air pressure check.

No Engine Braking In 1st Gear —Manual Low

1. Manual linkage.
2. Reverse band.
3. Reverse servo.
4. Valve body.
5. Governor.
6. Make air pressure check.

Slips or Chatters in 1st Gear—D1

1. Check fluid level.
2. Vacuum diaphragm unit or tubes restricted, leaking or maladjusted.
3. Check control pressure.
4. Pressure regulator.
5. Valve body.
6. Forward clutch.
7. Leakage in hydraulic system.
8. Planetary one-way clutch.

Slips or Chatters in 2nd Gear

1. Check fluid level.
2. Vacuum diaphragm unit or tubes restricted, leaking or maladjusted.
3. Intermediate servo.
4. Intermediate band.
5. Check control pressure.
6. Pressure regulator.
7. Valve body.
8. Make air pressure check.
9. Forward clutch.
10. Leakage in hydraulic system.

Slips or Chatters in R

1. Check fluid level.
2. Vacuum diaphragm unit or tubes restricted, leaking or maladjusted.
3. Reverse band.
4. Check control pressure.
5. Reverse servo.
6. Pressure regulator.
7. Valve body.
8. Make air pressure check.
9. Reverse-high clutch.
10. Leakage in hydraulic system.
11. Reverse-high piston air bleed valve.

No Drive in D1 Only

1. Check fluid level.
2. Manual linkage.
3. Check control pressure.
4. Valve body.
5. Make air pressure check.
6. Planetary one-way clutch.

No Drive in D2 Only

1. Check fluid level.
2. Manual linkage.
3. Check control pressure.
4. Intermediate servo.
5. Valve body.
6. Make air pressure check.
7. Leakage in hydraulic system.
8. Planetary one-way clutch.

No Drive in L Only

1. Check fluid level.
2. Manual linkage.
3. Check control pressure.
4. Valve body.
5. Reverse servo.
6. Make air pressure check.
7. Leakage in hydraulic system.
8. Planetary one-way clutch

No Drive in R Only

1. Check fluid level.
2. Manual linkage.
3. Reverse band.
4. Check control pressure.
5. Reverse servo.
6. Valve body.
7. Make air pressure check.
8. Reverse-high clutch.
9. Leakage in hydraulic system.
10. Reverse-high clutch piston air bleed valve.

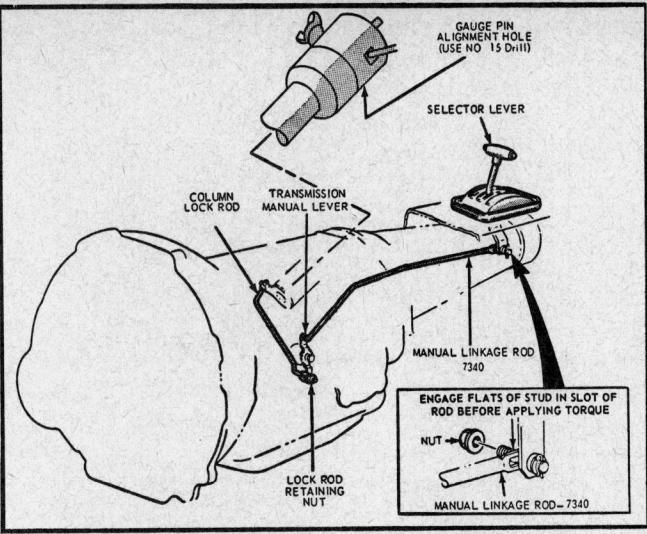

Fig. 3   Floorshift linkage adjustment. Rod type (Typical).
Column lock rod is used on some models

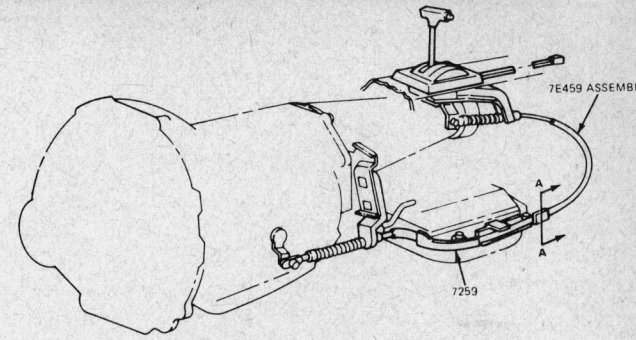

Fig. 3A   Floorshift linkage adjustment. Cable type

No Drive in Any Selector Position

1. Check fluid level.
2. Manual linkage.
3. Check control pressure.
4. Pressure regulator.
5. Valve body.
6. Make air pressure check.
7. Leakage in hydraulic system.
8. Front pump.

Lockup in D1 Only

1. Reverse-high clutch.
2. Parking linkage.
3. Leakage in hydraulic system.

Lockup in D2 Only

1. Reverse band.
2. Reverse servo.
3. Reverse-high clutch.
4. Parking linkage.
5. Leakage in hydraulic system.
6. Planetary one-way clutch.

Lockup in L Only

1. Intermediate band.
2. Intermediate servo.
3. Reverse-high clutch.
4. Parking linkage.
5. Leakage in hydraulic system.

Lockup in R Only

1. Intermediate band.
2. Intermediate servo.
3. Forward clutch.
4. Parking linkage.
5. Leakage in hydraulic system.

Parking Lock Binds or Won't Hold

1. Manual linkage.
2. Parking linkage.

Maximum Speed Too Low, Poor Acceleration

1. Engine performance.
2. Brakes bind.
3. Converter one-way clutch.

Noisy in N or P

1. Check fluid level.
2. Pressure regulator.
3. Front pump.
4. Planetary assembly.

Noisy in All Gears

1. Check fluid level.
2. Pressure regulator.
3. Planetary assembly.
4. Forward clutch.
5. Front pump.
6. Planetary one-way clutch.

Car Moves Forward in N

1. Manual linkage.
2. Forward clutch.

MAINTENANCE

NOTE: Ford Motor Company recommends the use of an automatic transmission fluid with the specification No. ESW-M2C33-F (Type F) for 1977–80 C3 and 1977–79 C4 units. On 1980–81 C4 and 1981–83 C3 units, it is recommended that an automatic transmission fluid meeting specification No. ESP-MC138-CJ or Dextron II series D be used. Use of a fluid other than specified above may result in transmission malfunction or failure.

Checking Oil Level

1. With transmission at operating temperature, park vehicle on a level surface.
2. Run engine at idle speed with service and parking brakes applied and move selector lever through each range. Return selector lever to Park.
3. With engine idling, remove dipstick and check fluid level. Fluid level should be between the Add and Full marks.
4. Add specified fluid as required to bring the fluid to the proper level.

Drain & Refill

NOTE: *Normal maintenance and lubrication requirements do not necessitate periodic fluid changes. If a major failure has occurred in the transmission, it will have to be removed for service. At this time the converter must be thoroughly flushed to remove any foreign matter.*

When filling a dry transmission and converter, install five quarts of specified fluid. Start engine, shift the selector lever through all ranges and place it at P position. Check fluid level and add enough to raise the level in the transmission to the "F" (full) mark on the dipstick.

When a partial drain and refill is required due to front band adjustment or minor repair, proceed as follows:

1. Loosen and remove all but two oil pan bolts and drop one edge of the pan to drain the oil.

NOTE: Some models of the C4 transmission can be drained by removing the filler tube from the pan.

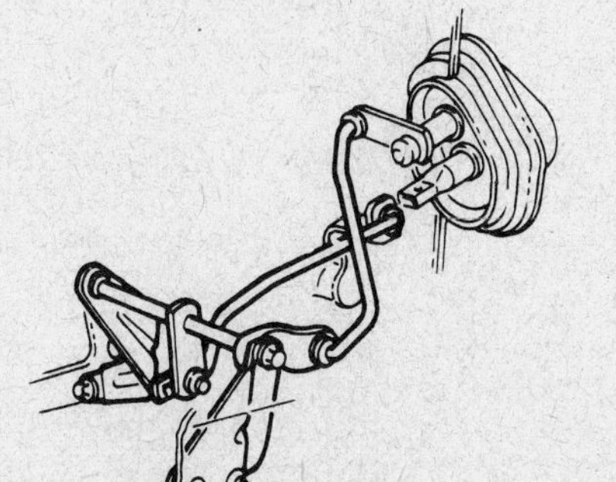

Fig. 4   1980–81 Cougar XR-7 & Thunderbird manual linkage, adjust.

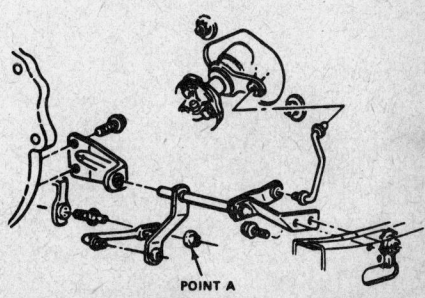

Fig. 5   Manual linkage (typical)
1977–78 Ford & Mercury column shift

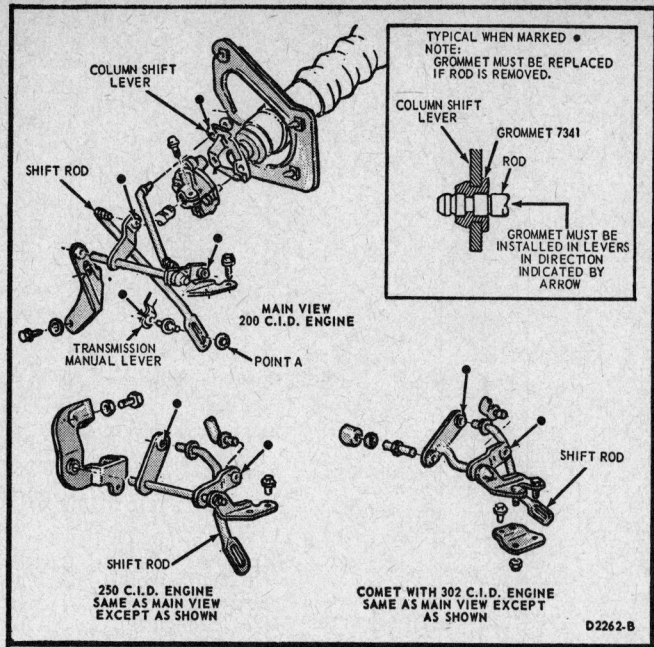

Fig. 6 Manual linkage. Maverick & Comet column shift

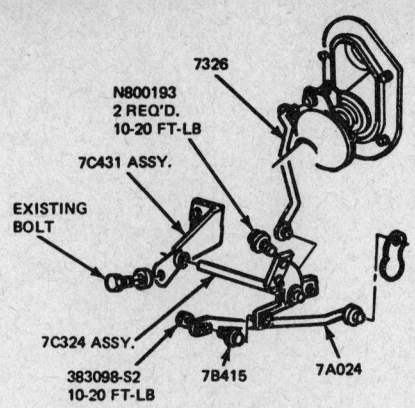

Fig. 7 Manual linkage (typical) 1978 Fairmont & Zephyr column shift

2. Remove and clean pan and screen.
3. Place a new gasket on pan and install pan and screen.
4. Add three quarts of specified fluid to transmission.
5. Run engine at idle speed for about two minutes.
6. Check oil level and add oil as necessary.
7. Run engine at a fast idle until it reaches normal operating temperature.
8. Shift selector lever through all ranges and then place it in P position.
9. Add fluid as required to bring the level to the full mark.

MANUAL LINKAGE, ADJUST

Floor Shift
1. Place transmission selector lever in D position.
2. Raise vehicle and loosen shift rod retaining nut, Figs. 3 and 3A.

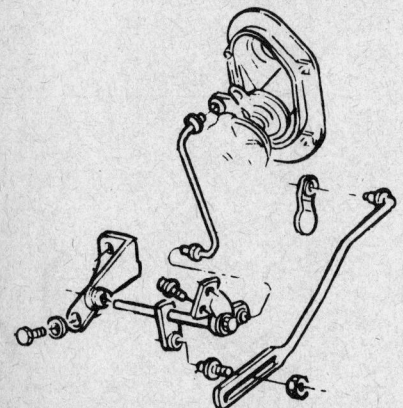

Fig. 7A Column shift linkage adjustment. 1979–81 Fairmont & Zephyr & 1981 Cougar & Granada

NOTE: On some models, shift linkage adjustment is done at the transmission end of shift rod.

3. Move transmission manual lever to D position.
4. Torque attaching nut to 10 to 20 ft. lbs. on 1977 models. On 1979–83 models, torque attaching nut to 10 to 15 ft. lbs.

Column Shift
1. Place selector lever in "D" position. Use suitable force on the lever to keep it against the "D" stop during adjustment.
2. Raise vehicle and loosen shift rod adjusting nut at point A, Figs. 4 through 9A. On models with shift cable, remove nut at point A and remove cable from transmission manual lever stud, Fig. 8.
3. Shift transmission manual lever into drive position, second detent from the full counter clockwise position.
4. On models equipped with shift cable, place cable end on transmission manual lever stud. Align flats on stud with flats on cable, then install adjustment nut.
5. On all models, tighten adjustment at point A. Ensure selector lever is against D stop when tightening adjustment nut.
6. Check transmission for proper operation in all selector lever detent positions.

THROTTLE & DOWNSHIFT LINKAGE, ADJUST

Figs. 10 through 13A
1. Disconnect downshift lever return spring and hold throttle lever in wide open position.
2. Hold downshift rod against the through detent stop with suitable force.
3. On all models except Versailles, adjust downshift screw to provide 0.01–0.08 inch clearance between screw and throttle arm. On Versailles models, adjust screw to provide 0.01–0.03 inch clearance.
4. Reconnect downshift lever return spring.

BANDS, ADJUST

NOTE: The intermediate and low-reverse bands adjusting screw locknut must be discarded and a new one installed each time a band is adjusted.

Intermediate Band

C3 & C4
1. On C3 units, disconnect downshift linkage from transmission lever.
2. On all units, discard adjusting screw locknut and install a new locknut.
3. With tools shown in Figs. 14 and 15, tighten adjusting screw until tool handle clicks. *This tool is a pre-set torque wrench which clicks and overruns when the torque on the adjusting screw reaches 10 ft-lbs.*
4. On 1977–80 C3 units, back off adjusting screw 1½ turns or 2 turns on 1981–83 units. On C4 units back screw off 1¾ turns for coarse pitch threads or 3 turns for fine pitch threads. Torque locknut to 35–45 ft. lbs.
5. Hold adjusting screw from turning and tighten locknut.
6. On C3 units, connect downshift linkage to transmission lever.

C4 Low-Reverse Band
1. Loosen lock nut several turns.
2. Tighten adjusting screw until tool handle clicks, Fig. 16. *Tool shown is a pre-set*

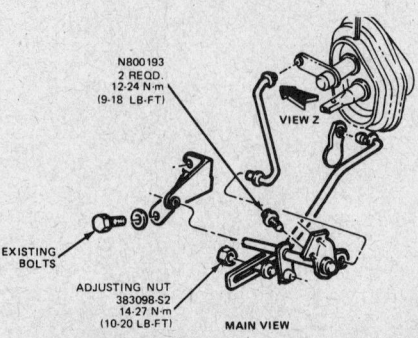

Fig. 7B Column shift manual linkage. 1982 Cougar & Granada, 1982–83 Fairmont & Zephyr, 1983 LTD & Marquis

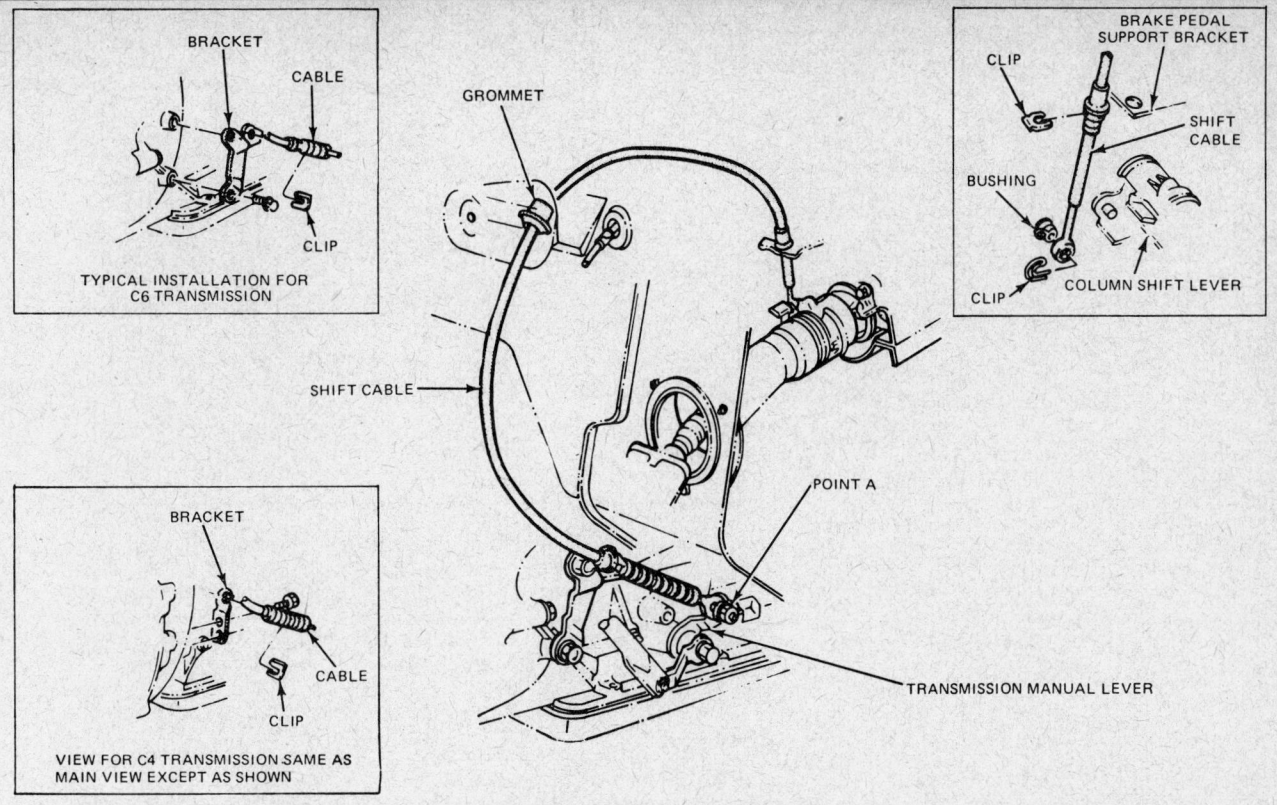

Fig. 8 Manual linkage. 1977–80 Granada & Monarch; 1977–79 Cougar, LTD II & Thunderbird & 1977–80 Versailles column shift

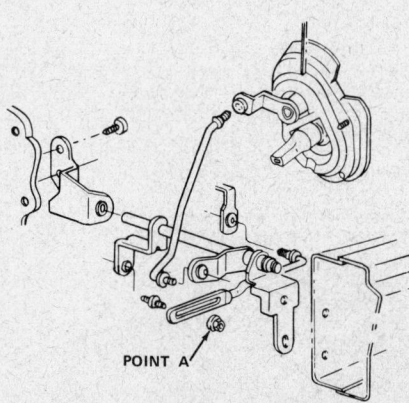

Fig. 9 Manual linkage, column shift. 1979 Ford & Mercury

torque wrench which clicks and overruns when the torque on the adjusting screw reaches 10 ft-lbs.

3. Back off adjusting screw exactly 3 full turns.
4. Hold adjusting screw from turning and tighten lock nut.

CONTROL VALVE

NOTE: All fasteners used on C3 transmissions are designed to metric specifications.

1. Support vehicle on jack stands.
2. Drain transmission fluid, then remove oil pan, fluid screen, gasket and on early C3

units, remove three spacers.

NOTE: If fluid is to be reused, filter it through a 100 mesh screen.

3. On C3 units:
   a. Remove control valve attaching bolts. Note the different length and location of each bolt.
   b. Carefully remove control valve while unlocking and detaching selector lever connecting rod.
4. On C4 units:
   a. Shift selector lever into PARK and remove the two detent spring to control valve and case bolts.
   b. Remove remaining control valve to

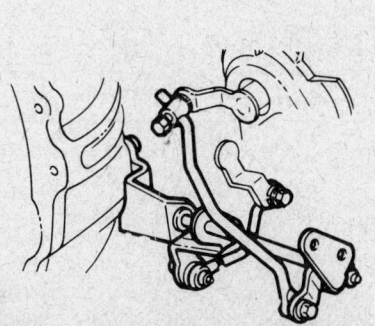

Fig. 9A Manual linkage, column shift. 1980 Ford & Mercury

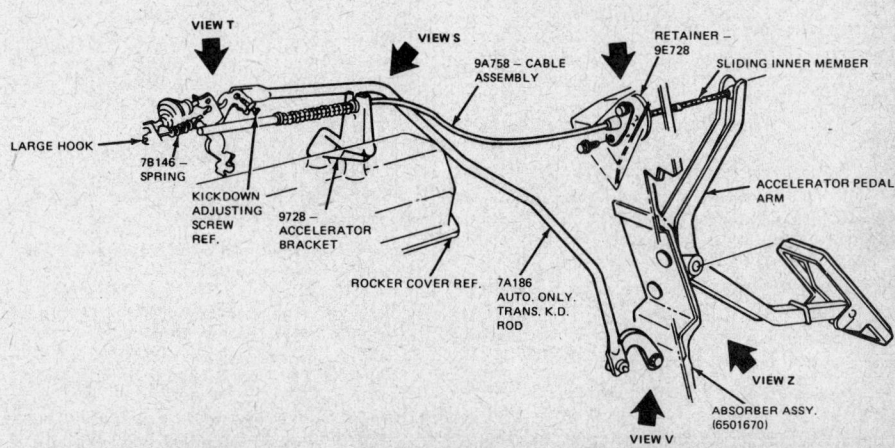

Fig. 10 Downshift & throttle linkage. Ford & Mercury

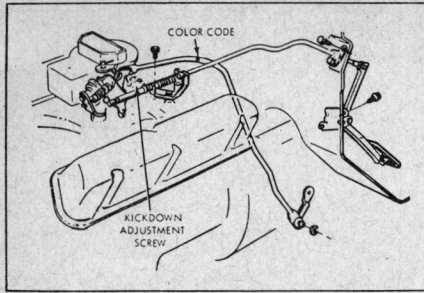

Fig. 11 Throttle and downshift linkage. (Typical). V6 & V8 engines except Ford & Mercury

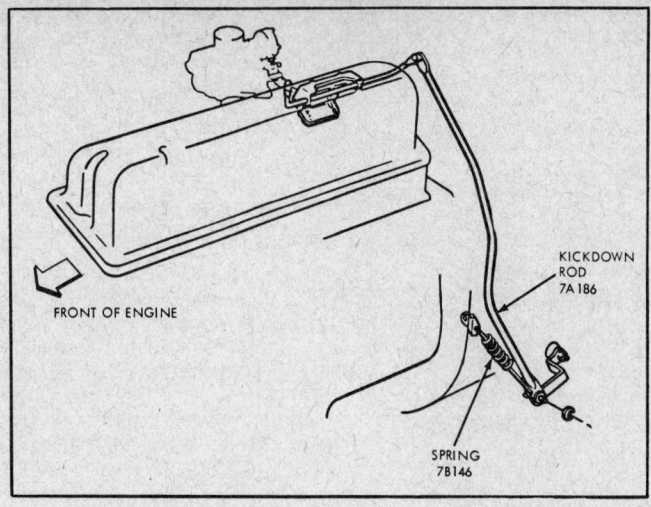

Fig. 12 Downshift linkage (Typical). 6-200, 250

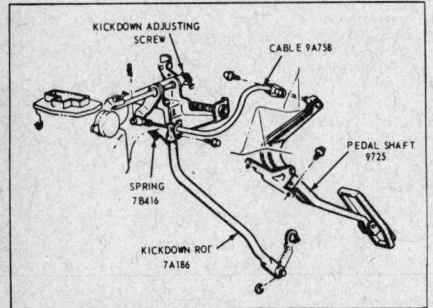

Fig. 13 Throttle & downshift linkage. (Typical). 1977-79 4-140

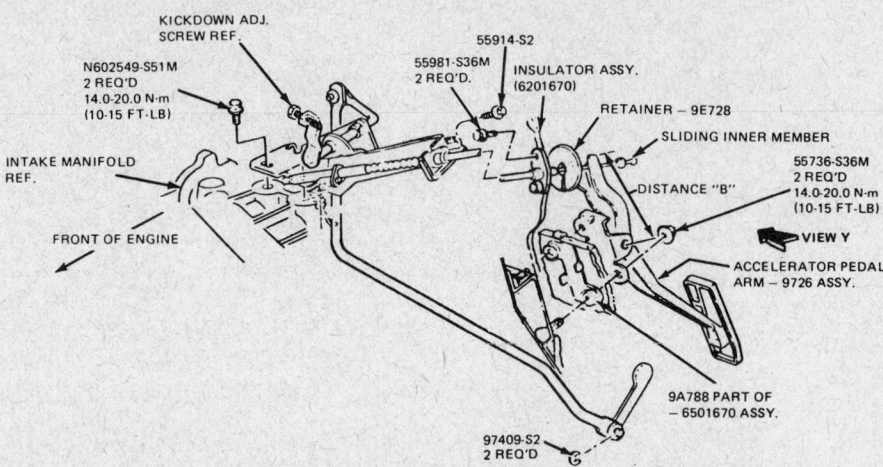

Fig. 13A Throttle & downshift linkage (Typical). 1980-83 4-140

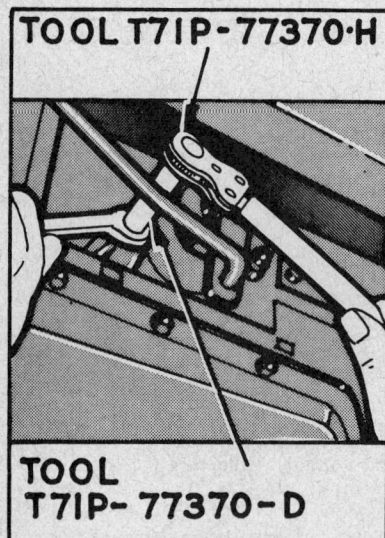

Fig. 14 Intermediate band adjustment. C4

case bolts, then while holding manual valve inward, remove control valve.

NOTE: Failure to hold manual valve inward, while removing control valve, could cause manual valve to become damaged.

5. After installing valve, torque attaching bolts to 84–108 in. lbs. on C3 units and 80–120 in. lbs. on C4 units.

SERVO REPAIR

C4 Intermediate Servo

1. Support vehicle on jack stands.

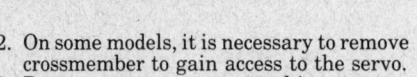

Fig. 15 Intermediate band adjustment. C3

2. On some models, it is necessary to remove crossmember to gain access to the servo.
3. Remove servo cover attaching screws, servo cover, gasket, piston and piston return spring.
4. Replace piston seals. Lubricate new seals with transmission fluid before installation.
5. Reverse procedure to install.

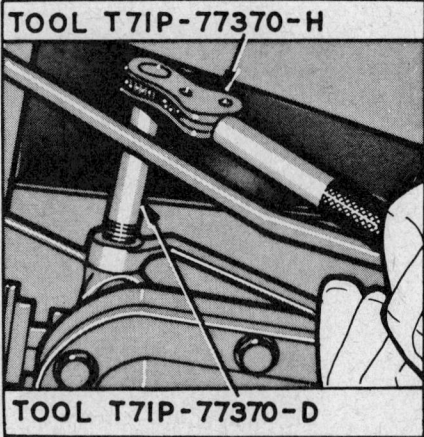

Fig. 16 Low-reverse band adjustment. C4

C4 Low-Reverse Servo

1. Support vehicle on jack stands.
2. Loosen reverse band adjusting screw locknut and torque adjusting screw to 10 ft. lbs. With adjusting screw torqued, the band strut is forced against case, preventing the strut from falling out of position when removing servo piston.

Fig. 17   Rear servo removal C3

3. Remove servo cover retaining bolts, servo cover, seal and servo piston from case.
4. On some models, the piston seal is bonded to the piston, requiring piston replacement. To remove piston from stem, insert a small screwdriver through hole in stem and remove piston from stem, insert a small screwdriver through hole in stem and remove piston retaining nut, piston, accumulator spring and spacer.
5. On all other models, replace piston seals. Lubricate new seals with transmission fluid before installation.
6. Reverse procedure to install making sure to readjust low-reverse band.

NOTE: If the band cannot be adjusted, the low-reverse band struts are not in position. Remove the fluid pan and valve body to install the struts into position. Adjust the band.

C3 Rear Servo

1. Support vehicle on jack stands, then drain transmission.
2. Remove oil filter screws, gasket and on early models, three spacers.
3. Remove servo cover retaining screws, servo cover, piston and spring, Fig. 17.
4. Reverse procedure to install.

EXTENSION HOUSING

1. Support vehicle on jack stands and remove driveshaft.

NOTE: Scribe marks on driveshaft yoke and companion flange, to insure proper positioning of driveshaft during assembly.

2. Support transmission with suitable jack and disconnect speedometer cable.

NOTE: On some models, it will be necessary to disconnect the exhaust system from the exhaust manifolds to perform the following step.

3. Remove engine rear support to crossmember attaching bolts or nuts, then raise transmission slightly and remove rear support from extension housing.

NOTE: On some models, it will be necessary to remove crossmember in order to remove rear support from extension housing.

4. Loosen extension housing bolts and allow transmission fluid to drain and remove extension housing.

GOVERNOR

1. Remove extension housing as described previously.
2. On 1977 C3 units, remove governor retaining pin snap ring, then the retaining pin, Fig. 18.
3. On all other units, remove governor to governor housing retaining bolts and slide governor off output shaft.
4. Reverse procedure to install. Torque governor retaining bolts to 7 to 10 ft. lbs.

TRANSMISSION, REPLACE

All Models

1. Support vehicle on jack stands and remove converter housing lower cover.
2. Drain transmission oil pan and the converter. Use a wrench on crankshaft pulley nut to rotate crankshaft and converter to gain access to drain plug.

NOTE: Do not rotate overhead camshaft engines in opposite direction of normal rotation.

3. Remove converter to flywheel bolts or nuts.
4. Remove propeller shaft.
5. Remove vacuum line hose from transmission vacuum unit. Disconnect vacuum

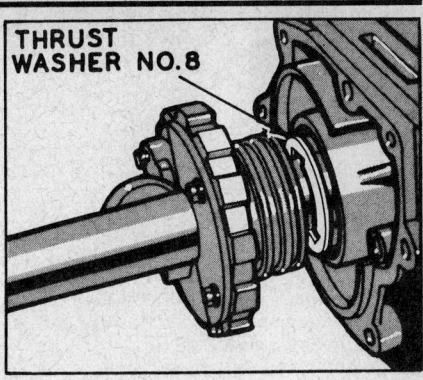

Fig. 18   Governor removal. C3

line from clip.
6. If equipped, disconnect TRS switch wire.
7. Remove two extension housing to crossmember bolts.
8. Remove speedometer cable from extension housing.
9. Disconnect exhaust system if necessary.

NOTE: On some models with C3 transmission, remove rear engine support.

10. On all models, disconnect oil cooler lines from transmission.
11. Remove the manual and kickdown linkage rods from transmission shift levers.
12. Where necessary disconnect the neutral start switch wires.
13. Remove starter.
14. Remove transmission fluid filler tube.
15. Support transmission with suitable jack and remove cross-member.
16. Remove converter housing to engine bolts and lower transmission from vehicle.
17. Reverse procedure to install.

NOTE: Flywheel assemblies used with C3 transmissions have a pilot hole to ensure proper flywheel to converter alignment. During installation, the flywheel must be indexed with the pilot hole in the six o'clock position. Because the flywheel has only one converter drain plug access hole, it is necessary to rotate the converter so the drain plug is located at 4 o'clock position with a 2.3 Litre engine, and 8 o'clock position with a 2.8 Litre engine. On some models with C4 transmission, align dyed converter drive stud into painted flywheel hole to maintain initial engine to transmission balance.

FORD C5 Automatic Transmission

TRANSMISSION IDENTIFICATION

Each transmission is identified by a tag, Fig. 1, located under the lower front intermediate servo cover bolt. The tag indicates model prefix and suffix, assembly part numbers, and the build date code. The service identification number indicates changes to service details which affect interchangeability within the same transmission model line.

Year	Car Model	Trans. Model	Engine Model	Year	Car Model	Trans. Model	Engine Model
1982	Mustang/Capri	PEN-G	6-200		Granada/Cougar & XR7	PEN-K	6-200
	Mustang/Capri	PEM-AM3	V8-255		Granada/Cougar & XR7	PEN-P	6-200
	Fairmont/Zephyr	PEN-C	6-200		Granada/Cougar & XR7	PEP-B	V6-232
	Fairmont/Zephyr	PEN-G	6-200		Granada/Cougar & XR7	PEP-D	V6-232
	Zephyr	PEN-P	6-200		Granada/Cougar & XR7	PEP-E	V6-232
	Fairmont/Zephyr	PEM-AL3	V8-255		Granada/Cougar & XR7	PEP-F	V6-232
	Granada/Cougar & XR7	PEN-C	6-200		Granada/Cougar & XR7	PEP-G	V6-232
	Granada/Cougar & XR7	PEN-G	6-200		Granada/Cougar & XR7	PEP-H	V6-232
	Granada/Cougar & XR7	PEN-J	6-200		Granada/Cougar & XR7	PEP-N	V6-232

AUTOMATIC TRANSMISSIONS/TRANSAXLES

Year	Car Model	Trans. Model	Engine Model
	Granada/Cougar & XR7	PEP-P	V6-232
	Thunderbird	PEN-K	6-200
	Thunderbird	PEB-Z2	6-200
	Thunderbird	PEN-S	6-200
1983	Mustang/Capri	PEP-B1	V6-232
	Mustang/Capri	PEP-R	V6-232
	Fairmont/Zephyr	PEN-G1	6-200
	Fairmont/Zephyr	PEN-P1	6-200
	Fairmont/Zephyr	PEN-AA	6-200
	Fairmont/Zephyr	PEN-AB	6-200
	Fairmont/Zephyr	PEN-BA	6-200
	Fairmont/Zephyr	PEN-CA	6-200
	LTD/Marquis	PEN-S1	6-200
	LTD/Marquis	PEN-U	6-200
	LTD/Marquis	PEN-Y	6-200
	LTD/Marquis	PEN-Z	6-200
	LTD/Marquis	PEP-R	V6-232
	LTD/Marquis	PEP-W	V6-232
	Thunderbird/Cougar	PEP-V	V6-232
	Thunderbird/Cougar	PEP-W	V6-232

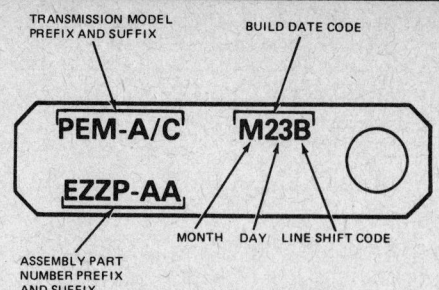

Fig. 1 C5 identification tag

DESCRIPTION

The C5 transmission, Fig. 2, is a three-speed fully automatic unit. First and second gear can be selected manually. The transmission consists of a welded torque converter assembly, a two-unit planetary gear train, and a hydraulic system which controls gear selection and automatic shifts. Larger displacement engines use a 12-inch torque converter which has a converter clutch. The planetary gear train, which is the same as that used in the C4 with minor changes, is a Simpson design with two gear sets in series and common sun gear. Gear operation is controlled by two friction clutches and two bands.

In spite of some similarities to the C4, the C5 incorporates major differences in the hydraulic system. The valve body is different and the converter relief valve has been moved from the reactor support in the pump assembly to the timing valve body. As a result C4 oil pump assemblies cannot be used when servicing the C5.

With the selector in P (Park) position the transmission is in neutral and the output shaft is locked to the case by the parking pawl. In R (Reverse) the transmission is in reverse gear. In N (Neutral) the engine is in neutral and the output shaft is not locked to the case. D (Drive) is the normal driving range in which the vehicle starts in low with automatic upshifts to second (intermediate) and high (direct drive). With throttle closed, the transmission downshifts from high to low, when vehicle speed drops to 10 mph. In 2 (intermediate), the transmission shifts to second gear and remains there regardless of speed. In 1 (low), the transmission stays in low and does not upshift. If placed in 1 above 25 mph, the transmission will shift to second and downshift to low, once vehicle speed has dropped below 25 mph. At speeds below 25 mph, the transmission shifts to low immediately.

TROUBLE SHOOTING GUIDE

Slow Initial Engagement

1. Improper fluid level.
2. Damaged or improperly adjusted linkage.
3. Contaminated fluid.
4. Improper clutch and band application or low main control pressure.

Rough Initial Engagements in Either Forward or Reverse

1. Improper fluid level.
2. High engine idle.
3. Automatic choke on (warm temp.).
4. Looseness in the driveshaft U-joint or engine mount.
5. Incorrect linkage adjustment.
6. Improper clutch or band application, or oil control pressure.

No or Delayed Forward Engagement

1. Improper fluid level.
2. Manual linkage, misadjusted or damaged.
3. Low main control pressure.
4. Valve body bolts, loose or too tight.
5. Valve body, dirty or sticking valve.
6. Forward clutch assembly burnt or damaged.
7. Forward clutch assembly piston seals worn or cut.
8. Forward clutch assembly cylinder ball check not seating.

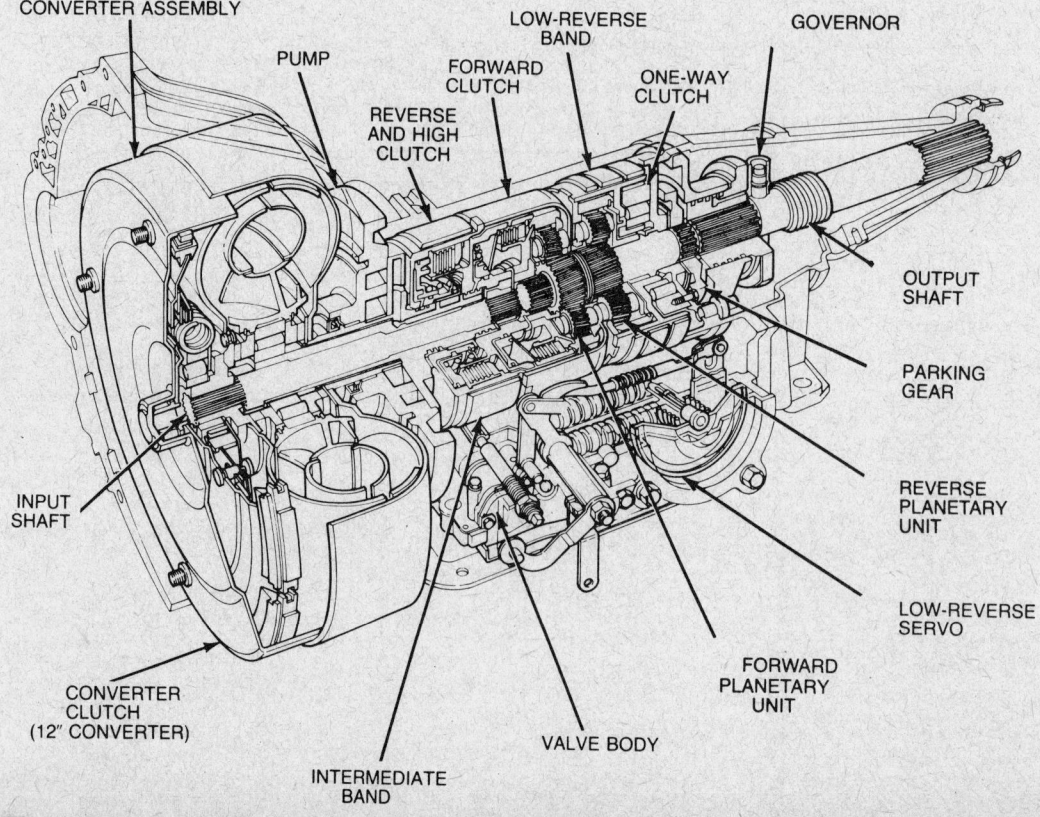

Fig. 2 Ford C5 transmission

9. Forward clutch assembly stator support seal ring grooves, damaged or worn.

No or Delayed Reverse Engagement

1. Improper fluid level.
2. Low main control pressure in reverse.
3. Manual linkage misadjusted or damaged.
4. Valve body, dirty or sticking valve.
5. Valve body bolts loose or too tight.
6. Reverse clutch assembly, burnt or worn.
7. Reverse clutch assembly piston seals, worn or cut.
8. Reverse clutch assembly piston ball not seating.
9. Reverse clutch assembly stator support seal rings or ring grooves, worn or damaged.

No or Delayed Reverse Engagement and/or No Engine Braking in Manual Low (1)

1. Low reverse band or servo piston burnt or worn.
2. Low reverse servo seal worn or cut.
3. Low reverse servo bore damaged.
4. Low reverse servo piston sticking in bore.
5. Low reverse band, line pressure low.
6. Low reverse bands out of adjustment.
7. Polished or glazed band or drum.

No Engine Braking in Manual Second Gear

1. Improper fluid level.
2. Linkage out of adjustment.
3. Intermediate band out of adjustment.
4. Improper band or clutch application, or oil pressure control system.
5. Intermediate servo leaking.
6. Polished or glazed band or drum.

No Engagement Forward and Reverse

1. Pump gear damaged.
2. Output shaft broken.
3. Turbine shaft or input shaft broken.

Forward Engagement Slip, Shudders or Chatters

1. Improper fluid level.
2. Manual linkage misadjusted or damaged.
3. Low main control pressure.
4. Valve body bolts, loose or too tight.
5. Valve body dirty or sticking valve.
6. Forward clutch piston ball check not sealing.
7. Forward clutch piston seal cut or worn.
8. Contamination blocking forward clutch feed hole.
9. Low (planetary) one way clutch damaged.

Reverse Engagement Slip, Shudders or Chatters

1. Improper fluid level.
2. Low main control pressure in reverse.
3. Reverse servo or servo bore damaged.
4. Low (planetary) one-way clutch damaged.
5. Reverse clutch drum bushing damaged.
6. Reverse clutch stator support seal rings

or ring grooves worn or damaged.
7. Reverse clutch piston seal cut or worn.
8. Reverse band out of adjustment or damaged.
9. Looseness in the driveshaft U-joints or engine mounts.

No Drive, Slips or Chatters in First Gear "D"

1. Damaged or worn one-way clutch.

No Drive, Slips or Chatters in Second

1. Improper fluid level.
2. Damaged or improperly adjusted linkage.
3. Intermediate band out of adjustment.
4. Improper band or clutch application, or oil pressure control.
5. Damaged or worn servo and/or internal leaks.
6. Dirty or sticking valve body.
7. Polished or glazed intermediate band or drum.

Start Up in Second or Third

1. Improper fluid level.
2. Damaged or improperly adjusted linkage.
3. Improper band and/or clutch application, or oil pressure control system.
4. Damaged or worn governor, governor sticking.
5. Valve body loose.
6. Dirty or sticking valve body.
7. Cross leaks between valve body and case mating surface.

Shift Points Incorrect

1. Improper fluid level.
2. Improper vacuum hose routing or leaks.
3. Improper operation of EGR system.
4. Throttle out of adjustment.
5. Improper clutch or band application, or oil pressure control system.
6. Damaged or worn governor.
7. Dirty or sticking valve body.

All Upshifts Harsh, Delayed or No Upshifts

1. Improper fluid level.
2. Manual linkage misadjusted or damaged.
3. Governor sticking.
4. Main control pressure too high.
5. Valve body bolts loose or too tight.
6. Valve body dirty or valves sticking.
7. Vacuum leak to diaphragm unit.

All Upshifts Early or Sluggish

1. Improper fluid level.
2. Low main control pressure.
3. Valve body loose or too tight.
4. Valve body valve sticking.
5. Governor valve sticking.

No Low to Second Upshift

1. Improper fluid level.
2. Manual linkage misadjusted or damaged.
3. Governor valve sticking.
4. Valve body bolts loose or too tight.
5. Valve body dirty or sticking valves.

6. Intermediate clutch or band and/or servo assembly burnt.
7. Intermediate piston seals worn or cut.
8. Intermediate piston not positioned properly.
9. Intermediate clutch in improper stack up.
10. Low line pressure in intermediate clutch or band.

Rough, Harsh, or Delayed Upshift Low to Second

1. Governor valve sticking.
2. Improper fluid level.
3. Poor engine performance.
4. Main control pressure too high.
5. Valve body bolts loose or too tight.
6. Valve body dirty or valves sticking.
7. Intermediate band out of adjustment.
8. Damaged intermediate servo.
9. Engine vacuum leak.

Early, Soft or Slipping Low to Second Upshift

1. Improper fluid level.
2. Low main control.
3. Valve body bolts loose or too tight.
4. Valve body dirty or valves sticking.
5. Governor valve sticking.
6. Incorrect engine performance.
7. Intermediate band out of adjustment.
8. Damaged intermediate servo or band.
9. Polished or glazed band or drum.

No Second to Third Upshift

1. Low fluid level.
2. Low main control pressure to direct clutch.
3. Valve body bolts too loose or too tight.
4. Valve body dirty or valves sticking.
5. Converter damper hub weld broken.

Harsh or Delayed Second to Third Upshift

1. Low fluid level.
2. Valve body bolts loose or too tight.
3. Valve body dirty or valves sticking.
4. Damaged or worn intermediate servo release and high clutch piston check ball.
5. Incorrect engine performance.
6. Engine vacuum leak.

Early or Soft Second to Third Upshift

1. Improper fluid level.
2. Valve body bolts loose or too tight.
3. Valve body dirty or valves sticking.

Erratic Shifts

1. Improper fluid level.
2. Throttle linkage binding or sticking.
3. Valve body bolts loose or too tight.
4. Valve body dirty or valves sticking.
5. Governor valve sticking.
6. Output shaft collector body seal rings (large cast iron) worn or cut.

Shifts From Low to Third in "D"

1. Improper fluid level.
2. Intermediate band out of adjustment.
3. Damaged intermediate servo and/or

internal leaks.
4. Polished or glazed band or drum.
5. Improper band or clutch application, or oil pressure control system.
6. Valve body dirty or valves sticking.

Engine Over Speeds on Second to Third Upshift

1. Improper fluid level.
2. Linkage out of adjustment.
3. Improper band or clutch application, or oil pressure control system.
4. Damaged or worn high clutch and/or intermediate servo.
5. Valve body dirty or valves sticking.

Rough or Shudder Third to Low Shift at Closed Throttle

1. Improper fluid level.
2. Incorrect engine idle or performance.
3. Improper linkage adjustment.
4. Improper clutch or band application, or oil pressure control system.
5. Improper governor operation.
6. Valve body dirty or valves sticking.

No Forced Downshift

1. Improper fluid level.
2. Kickdown linkage out of adjustment.
3. Damaged internal kickdown linkage.
4. Damaged or misadjusted (short) throttle linkage.

5. Valve body dirty or valves sticking.
6. Dirty or sticking governor.

Engine Runaway on Third to Second Shift

1. Improper fluid level.
2. Linkage out of adjustment.
3. Intermediate band out of adjustment.
4. Improper band or clutch application, or oil pressure control system.
5. Damaged or worn intermediate servo.
6. Polished or glazed band or drum.
7. Valve body dirty or valves sticking.

Shift Efforts High

1. Manual shift linkage damaged or misadjusted.
2. Inner manual lever nut loose.
3. Manual level retainer pin damaged.

No Start in "P"

1. Manual linkage misadjusted.
2. Plug connector for the neutral start switch does not fit properly.
3. Neutral start switch plunger travel, inadequate.

No Start in "P" and "N"

1. Plug connector for the neutral start switch does not fit properly.

Transmission Overheats

1. Improper fluid level.
2. Incorrect engine idle or performance.
3. Improper band or clutch application, or oil pressure control system.
4. Restriction in cooler or lines.
5. Seized converter one-way clutch.
6. Valve body dirty or valves sticking.

MAINTENANCE

Checking Oil Level

1. With engine idling, foot brake applied and vehicle on level surface, move selector lever through each range, pausing in each position.
2. Place selector in Park and apply parking brake. Leave engine running during fluid level check.
3. Clean dirt from transmission fluid dipstick cap and remove dipstick. Wipe dipstick and push back into tube making sure it is fully seated.
4. Pull dipstick out and check fluid level. With transmission at operating temperature, fluid level should be between arrows. With transmission cool, fluid level should read between inner holes. Use only Type H fluid, Ford spec. ESP M2C166-H. Do not overfill.
5. Insert dipstick, making sure it is fully seated.

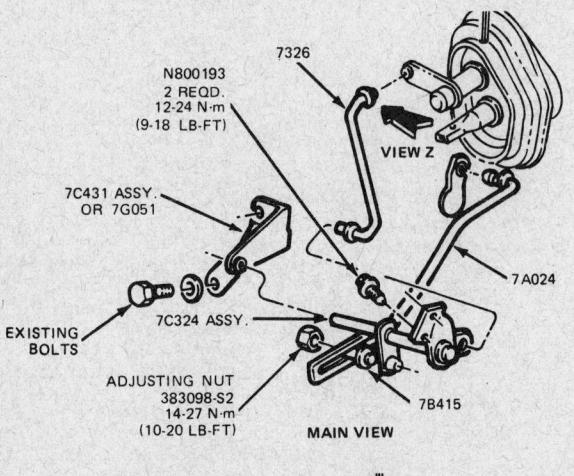

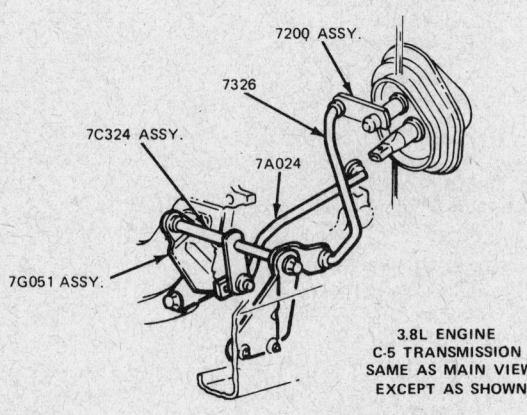

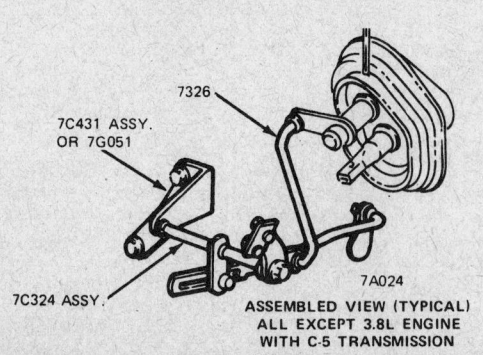

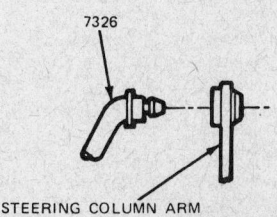

Fig. 3 Column shift manual linkage. 1982 Cougar & Granada, 1982–83 Fairmont & Zephyr, 1983 Cougar, LTD, Marquis & Thunderbird

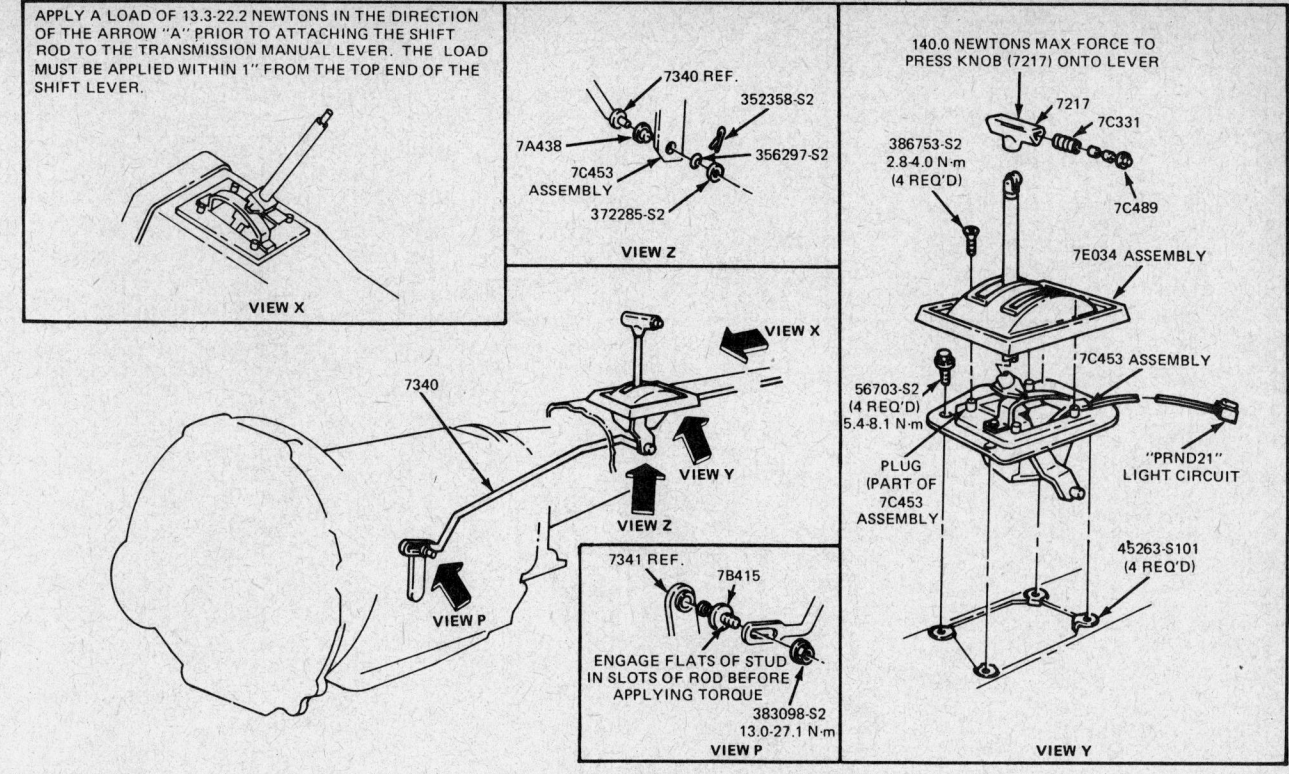

APPLY A LOAD OF 13.3-22.2 NEWTONS IN THE DIRECTION OF THE ARROW "A" PRIOR TO ATTACHING THE SHIFT ROD TO THE TRANSMISSION MANUAL LEVER. THE LOAD MUST BE APPLIED WITHIN 1" FROM THE TOP END OF THE SHIFT LEVER.

VIEW X

7340 REF.
352358-S2
7A438
356297-S2
7C453 ASSEMBLY
372285-S2
VIEW Z

140.0 NEWTONS MAX FORCE TO PRESS KNOB (7217) ONTO LEVER
7217
7C331
386753-S2 2.8-4.0 N·m (4 REQ'D)
7C489
7E034 ASSEMBLY
7C453 ASSEMBLY
56703-S2 (4 REQ'D) 5.4-8.1 N·m
"PRND21" LIGHT CIRCUIT
PLUG (PART OF 7C453 ASSEMBLY)
45263-S101 (4 REQ'D)
VIEW Y

7340
VIEW X
VIEW Y
VIEW Z
VIEW P

7341 REF.
7B415
ENGAGE FLATS OF STUD IN SLOTS OF ROD BEFORE APPLYING TORQUE
383098-S2 13.0-27.1 N·m
VIEW P

Fig. 4 Floor shift manual linkage. Exc. V8-255

MANUAL LINKAGE, ADJUST

1. Locate slotted rod in linkage and loosen nut or screw, Figs. 3, 4 & 5.
2. Place selector in "D" firmly against gate stop.
3. Move manual shift lever on transmission to "D" position, three detents away from Park.
4. Tighten nut securely.
5. Move shift lever through all ranges. Check to see that detents agree with markings on shift lever. Make sure that lever cannot be moved from "D" position to 2, without ungating lever.

DOWNSHIFT LINKAGE, ADJUST

1. Hold throttle lever wide open against stop.
2. Push rod down so down shift valve is forced to bottom in valve body.
3. Measure clearance between tip of adjusting screw and throttle lever, Fig. 6. Clearance should be .050–.070 inch.
4. Turn screw, if necessary, to obtain this clearance.

BANDS, ADJUST

To determine the need for adjustments, the bands can be checked as follows:

Make sure oil level is correct. Then shift selector to "R" and 2, checking for firm engagement. If engagement in "R" is delayed or mushy, adjust rear band, Fig. 7. If engagement in 2 is delayed or mushy, adjust front band, Fig. 8. Adjust bands as follows:

1. Loosen adjuster stop, remove and discard locknut. Install new locknut loosely.
2. Torque screw to 10 ft. lbs.
3. Back screw off exactly 4¼ turns for the front (intermediate) band; 3 turns for the rear (low-reverse) band.
4. Hold adjustment and torque new locknut to 35–45 ft. lbs.

VALVE BODY, REPLACE

1. Raise vehicle.
2. Loosen pan bolts and drain transmission fluid.
3. Remove oil pan bolts, pan, and gasket.
4. Shift transmission lever to Park, and remove two bolts attaching detent spring to valve body and case.
5. Remove filter.
6. Remove remaining valve body bolts. Hold manual valve in valve body and remove valve body from case. Manual valve must be held to prevent it from being bent or damaged.
7. Clean and remove all gasket material from pan and pan mounting face. Remove and discard nylon shipping plug, if found in pan.
8. Position valve body in case. Make sure inner downshift lever is between downshift lever stop and downshift valve. The two lands on end of manual valve must engage actuating pin on manual detect lever. Install seven valve body bolts.
9. Position detent spring on lower valve body and install spring-to-case bolt.
10. Hold detent spring roller in center of manual detent lever and install detent spring-to-lower valve body bolt. Torque bolt to 80–120 inch lbs.
11. Torque valve body bolts to 80–120 inch lbs.
12. Position filter and torque bolt to 30 inch lbs.
13. Install pan using new gasket and torque bolts to 12–16 ft. lbs.
14. Lower vehicle and fill transmission with fluid. Check pan area for leakage.

EXTENSION HOUSING, REPLACE

1. Raise vehicle and remove driveshaft.
2. Using suitable jack, support transmission.
3. Remove speedometer cable from extension housing.
4. Remove engine rear support to crossmember nuts.
5. Raise transmission and remove rear support bolts. Remove crossmember.
6. Loosen extension housing bolts and let transmission drain.
7. Remove the six extension housing bolts and vacuum tube clip and remove extension housing.
8. Reverse procedure to install, noting the following torques: extension housing bolts, 28–40 ft. lbs; crossmember nuts, 35–50 ft. lbs.; rear support bolts, 25–35 ft. lbs.

GOVERNOR, REPLACE

1. Refer to "Extension Housing, Replace"

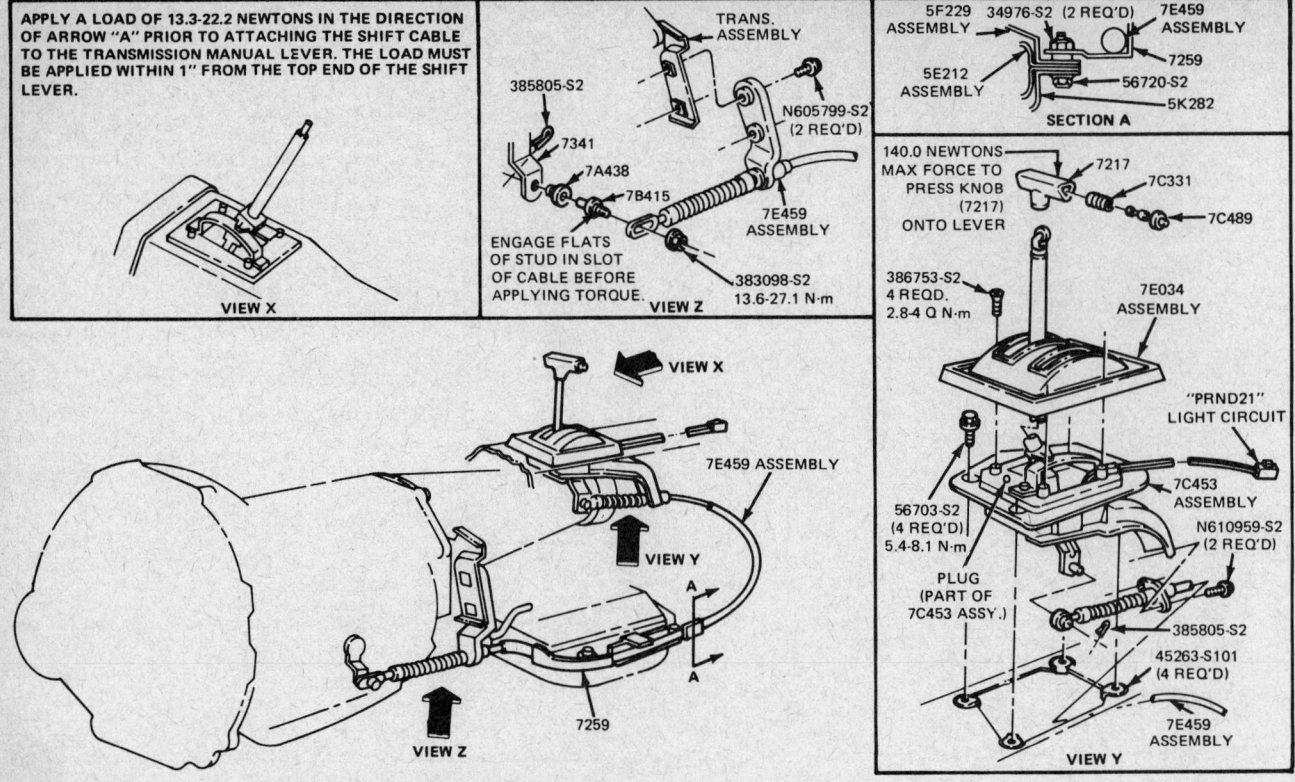

Fig. 5 Floor shift manual linkage. V8-255

and remove extension housing.

2. Remove bolts holding governor housing to governor distributor.
3. Slide governor away from distributor body and off output shaft.
4. Reverse procedure to install. Torque governor bolts to 80–120 inch lbs.

LOW-REVERSE SERVO, REPLACE

Exc. Mustang & Capri With V8-255 Engine

1. Raise and support vehicle.
2. Loosen low-reverse band adjusting screw lock nut. Torque band adjusting screw to 10 ft. lbs. to prevent band strut from falling when reverse servo piston assembly is removed.
3. Disengage neutral switch harness from clips on servo cover.

4. Remove servo cover bolts, servo cover, and seal from case.
5. Remove servo piston from case. If seal is bad, piston must be replaced.
6. Install piston in case. Install cover with new seal. Use two 5/16-18×1¼ bolts to position cover against case. Install two cover bolts, remove two locating bolts and install remaining bolts. Torque to 12–20 ft. lbs.
7. Position neutral switch harness in clips.
8. Adjust low-reverse band. Refer to "Bands, Adjust" procedure.

NOTE: If band cannot be adjusted properly, low-reverse band struts are not in position. Remove oil pan and valve body. Position struts and install valve body and pan. Adjust band.

9. Lower vehicle and check transmission fluid level.

Mustang & Capri With V8-255 Engine

1. Disconnect fan shroud and position against engine.
2. Raise vehicle and position suitable transmission jack under transmission.

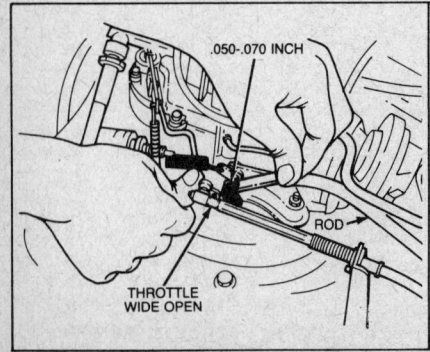

Fig. 6 Downshift rod adjustment

Fig. 7 Low-Reverse band adjustment

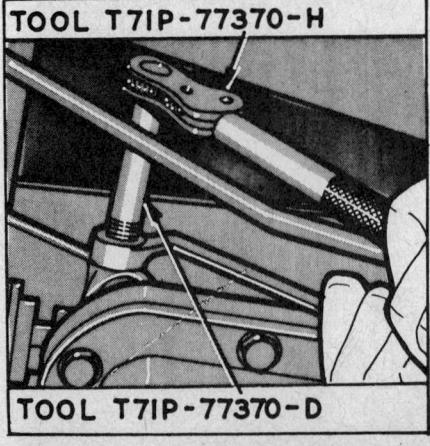

Fig. 8 Intermediate band adjustment

3. Remove transmission crossmember bolts.
4. Lower transmission.
5. Loosen low-reverse band adjusting screw lock nut. Torque band adjusting screw to 10 ft. lbs. to prevent band strut from falling down.
6. Disengage neutral switch wiring harness from clips on servo cover.
7. Remove servo cover bolts, servo cover, and seal from case.
8. Remove servo piston and spring from case. If piston seal is bad, piston must be replaced.
9. Install piston and return spring in case. Install cover with new seal. Use two 5/16-18×1 1/4 bolts to position cover. Install two cover bolts, remove two locating bolts and install remaining two cover bolts. Torque bolts to 12–20 ft. lbs.
10. Position neutral start switch wiring harness in clips.
11. Refer to "Bands, Adjust" procedure to adjust low-reverse band.

NOTE: If band cannot be adjusted properly, low-reverse band struts are not in position. Remove oil pan and valve body. Position struts and install valve body and pan. Adjust band.

12. Raise transmission into position and install crossmember bolts. Torque nuts to 35–50 ft. lbs.
13. Remove transmission jack and lower vehicle.
14. Install fan shroud and check transmission fluid.

INTERMEDIATE SERVO, REPLACE

1. Disconnect fan shroud from radiator and push shroud back against engine.
2. Raise vehicle.
3. Support transmission with suitbable jack

and remove crossmember bolts.
4. Lower transmission.
5. On Granada and Cougar models with V6-232 engine, disconnect oil cooler line.
6. On all models, remove servo cover bolts.
7. Remove servo cover/piston assembly and return spring from case.
8. Remove and discard servo cover gasket.
9. Position new gasket on servo cover so notch aligns with fluid passage in case.
10. Install piston return spring and servo cover/piston assembly in case. Use two 5/16-18×1 1/4 bolts to position cover against case. Install two cover bolts, remove locating bolts and install remaining cover bolts. Torque bolts to 12–20 ft. lbs.
11. Refer to "Bands, Adjust" and adjust intermediate band.

NOTE: If band cannot be adjusted properly, intermediate band strut is not in position. Remove oil pan and valve body. Position struts and install valve body and oil pan. Adjust band.

12. On Granada and Cougar models with V6-232 engine, connect transmission oil cooler line.
13. On all models, raise transmission into position and install crossmember bolts. Torque nuts to 35–50 ft. lbs.
14. Remove jack and lower vehicle.
15. Position fan shroud bolt to radiator. Check transmission fluid level.

TRANSMISSION, REPLACE

1. Disconnect battery ground cable.
2. On Granada and Cougar models with V6-232 engine, remove air cleaner assembly.
3. On all models, remove fan shroud bolts and position shroud back over fan.
4. On Granada and Cougar models with V6-232 and Mustang and Capri models with V8-255, loosen clamp and disconnect thermactor air injection hose at catalytic

converter check valve.
5. On Granada and Cougar models with V6-232 engine, remove the top two engine-to-transmission bolts.
6. On all models, remove driveshaft after raising vehicle.
7. Disconnect muffler inlet pipe from catalytic converter outlet pipe. Support muffler pipe assembly.
8. Disconnect exhaust pipes from exhaust manifolds.
9. Release catalytic converter hangers from bracket by pulling back on converter.
10. Remove speedometer cable clamp bolt and pull cable out of extension housing.
11. Disconnect neutral start switch harness connector.
12. Disconnect kick down rod at transmission lever.
13. Disconnect shift linkage at bellcrank. On vehicles with floor shifts, remove shift cable routing bracket bolts and disconnect cable at transmission lever.
14. Remove converter dust shield.
15. Remove torque converter drive plate nuts. Crankshaft can be turned by using socket and ratchet handle on crankshaft pulley bolt.
16. Remove starter.
17. Loosen nuts attaching rear support to No. 3 crossmember.
18. Position suitable jack under transmission oil pan.
19. Remove bolt attaching No. 3 crossmember to body brackets.
20. Lower transmission enough to allow access to cooler line fittings. Disconnect cooler lines.
21. Remove all transmission-to-engine bolts.
22. Pull transmission back to clear converter studs. Lower transmission.
23. Reverse procedure to install. Note the following torque values: engine-to-transmission bolts, 40–50 ft. lbs.; no. 3 crossmember bolts, 20–30 ft. lbs.; rear support nuts, 30–50 ft. lbs.; torque converter-to-drive-plate nuts, 20–30 ft. lbs.; linkage bellcrank bracket, 12–16 ft. lbs.; speedometer cable clamp, 36–54 inch lbs.

FORD C6 Automatic Transmission

TRANSMISSION IDENTIFICATION

An identification tag attached to the servo cover bolt, includes the model prefix and suffix

Year	Car Model	Trans. Code	Engine Model
1977	Cougar	PJA-AT, AU	V8-351M
	Cougar	PJA-G11, 13	V8-400
	Cougar	PJA-H12, 13	V8-400
	Cougar	PJA-R4, 5	V8-400
	Cougar	PJA-S4, 5	V8-400
	Cougar	PJA-BJ	V8-400
	Ford	PJA-PU, 1	V8-351M
	Ford	PJA-BH, 1	V8-400
	Ford	PJA-BV, 1	V8-400
	Ford	PJA-C13, 14, 15	V8-400
	Ford	PJD-G10, 11 12	V8-460
	Ford	PJD-AH2, 3	V8-460

Year	Car Model	Trans. Code	Engine Model
	Ford	PJD-AP, 1	V8-460
	Ford	PJD-AR, 1	V8-460
	Ford	PJC-H13, 14	V8-460
	Lincoln	PJA-BL	V8-400
	Lincoln	PJD-F12, 13	V8-460
	Lincoln	PJD-AG2	V8-460
	Lincoln	PJD-AN	V8-460
	LTD II	PJA-AU1	V8-351M
	LTD II	PJA-C11, 12, 13	V8-400
	LTD II	PJA-R4, 5, 6	V8-400
	LTD II	PJA-SR4, 5, 6	V8-400
	LTD II	PJA-H12, 13, 14	V8-400
	LTD II	PJA-BJ1	V8-400
	Mark V	PJA-BK, 1	V8-400
	Mark V	PJA-BW	V8-400
	Mark V	PJD-E12, 13	V8-460
	Mark V	PJD-AF2	V8-460
	Mark V	PJD-AM	V8-460
	Mercury	PJA-BU	V8-351M
	Mercury	PJA-C13, 14	V8-400
	Mercury	PJA-BH	V8-400
	Mercury	PJA-BV	V8-400

Year	Car Model	Trans. Code	Engine Model
	Mercury	PJC-H13	V8-460
	Mercury	PJC-M	V8-460
	Mercury	PJD-G10, 11	V8-460
	Mercury	PJD-AH2	V8-460
	Mercury	PJD-AP	V8-460
	Mercury	PJD-AR	V8-460
	Thunderbird	PJA-AU, 1	V8-351M
	Thunderbird	PJA-G11, 12, 13	V8-400
	Thunderbird	PJA-R4, 5, 6	V8-400
	Thunderbird	PJA-S4, 5, 6	V8-400
	Thunderbird	PJA-H12, 13, 14	V8-400
	Thunderbird	PJA-BJ, 1	V8-400
1978	Cougar	PJA-BJ3, 4	V8-351
	Cougar	PJA-G15, 16	V8-400
	Cougar	PJA-H16, 17	V8-400
	Ford	PJA-BU3, 4	V8-351M
	Ford	PJA-C17, 18	V8-400
	Ford	PJA-BH3, 4	V8-400
	Ford	PJD-AP3, 4	V8-400
	Ford ①	PJC-H16, 17	V8-460
	Lincoln	PJA-CA3, 4	V8-400
	Lincoln	PJA-CC, 1	V8-400

Year	Car Model	Trans. Code	Engine Model
	Lincoln	PJA-CZ	V8-400
	Lincoln	PJD-AN3, 4	V8-460
	LTD II	PJA-BJ3, 4	V8-351, 400
	LTD II	PJA-G15, 16	V8-400
	LTD II	PJA-H16, 17	V8-400
	Mark V	PJA-BW3, 4	V8-400
	Mark V	PJA-CY	V8-400
	Mark V	PJA-CB, 1	V8-400
	Mark V	PJD-AM3, 4	V8-460
	Mercury	PJA-BU3, 4	V8-351M
	Mercury	PJA-C17, 18	V8-400
	Mercury	PJA-BH3, 4	V8-400
	Mercury	PJC-M3, 4	V8-460
	Mercury	PJD-AP3, 4	V8-460
	Thunderbird	PJA-BJ3, 4	V8-351, 400
	Thunderbird	PJA-G15	V8-400
	Thunderbird	PJA-H16, 17	V8-400
1979	Cougar	PJA-DK	V8-351
	Ford	PGD-BZ, BH	V8-351
	Ford	PGD-CF, CH	V8-351
	Ford	PGD-CR, CT	V8-351
	Ford	PGD-CU	V8-351
	Lincoln	PJA-CA6, DB	V8-400
	Lincoln	PJA-DD	V8-400
	LTD II	PJA-DK	V8-351
	Mark V	PJA-BW6, DA	V8-400
	Mark V	PJA-DC	V8-400
	Mercury	PGD-BH, BZ	V8-351
	Mercury	PGD-CF, CH	V8-351
	Mercury	PGD-CR, CT	V8-351
	Mercury	PGD-CU	V8-351

Year	Car Model	Trans. Code	Engine Model
	Thunderbird	PJA-DK	V8-351
1980	Ford	PGD-BH5, CU5	V8-302
	Ford	PGD-DD, DE, DG	V8-351
	Mercury	PGD-BH5, CU5	V8-302
	Mercury	PGD-DD, DE, DG	V8-351

①—Police or fleet

DESCRIPTION

As shown in Fig. 1, the transmission consists essentially of a torque converter, a compound planetary gear train controlled by one band, three disc clutches and a one-way clutch, and a hydraulic control system.

The transmission is made so that a system of manual and automatic shifting is provided.

Automatic & Manual Shifting

This unit has a shift pattern which is indicated on the selector as P-R-N-D-2-1. This refers respectively to Park, Reverse, Neutral, Full Automatic, Second Gear (manual), Low Gear (manual).

In this unit an overriding control is provided which enables the driver to exercise his own judgement with regard to the gear ratios to be selected and an understanding of what is possible greatly enhances the pleasure to be derived from driving the car. No automatic mechanism has the power of anticipation, but the driver can see ahead and has the means for over-riding the automatic mechanism.

Automatic Shift

In "D" position the shift sequence is fully automatic in that the transmission starts in low gear and upshifts through second gear to third or high gear.

Manual Shifting

The shift to 2 or 1 is done manually by shifting the lever from neutral to either position. In "1" position, the transmission starts in 1st (low gear) and is retained. In "2" position it starts in 2nd gear and remains in 2nd gear, regardless of road speed.

Manual Shift To "1"

Manual shifting from "D" to "1" can also be accomplished any time. Here the transmission immediately shifts to second and remains in second until the predetermined governor control speed allows it to shift down to low gear where it remains. The governor speed control at this point eliminates the possibility of a direct down shift to low gear until the road speed is reduced.

Shift Lever Controls

A shift lever button control is used to shift from neutral to reverse or park, also when shifting from "D" to "2" or "1" position. However, the button control function is not required when shifting from neutral to "D", or to shift forward from "1" to "2" position.

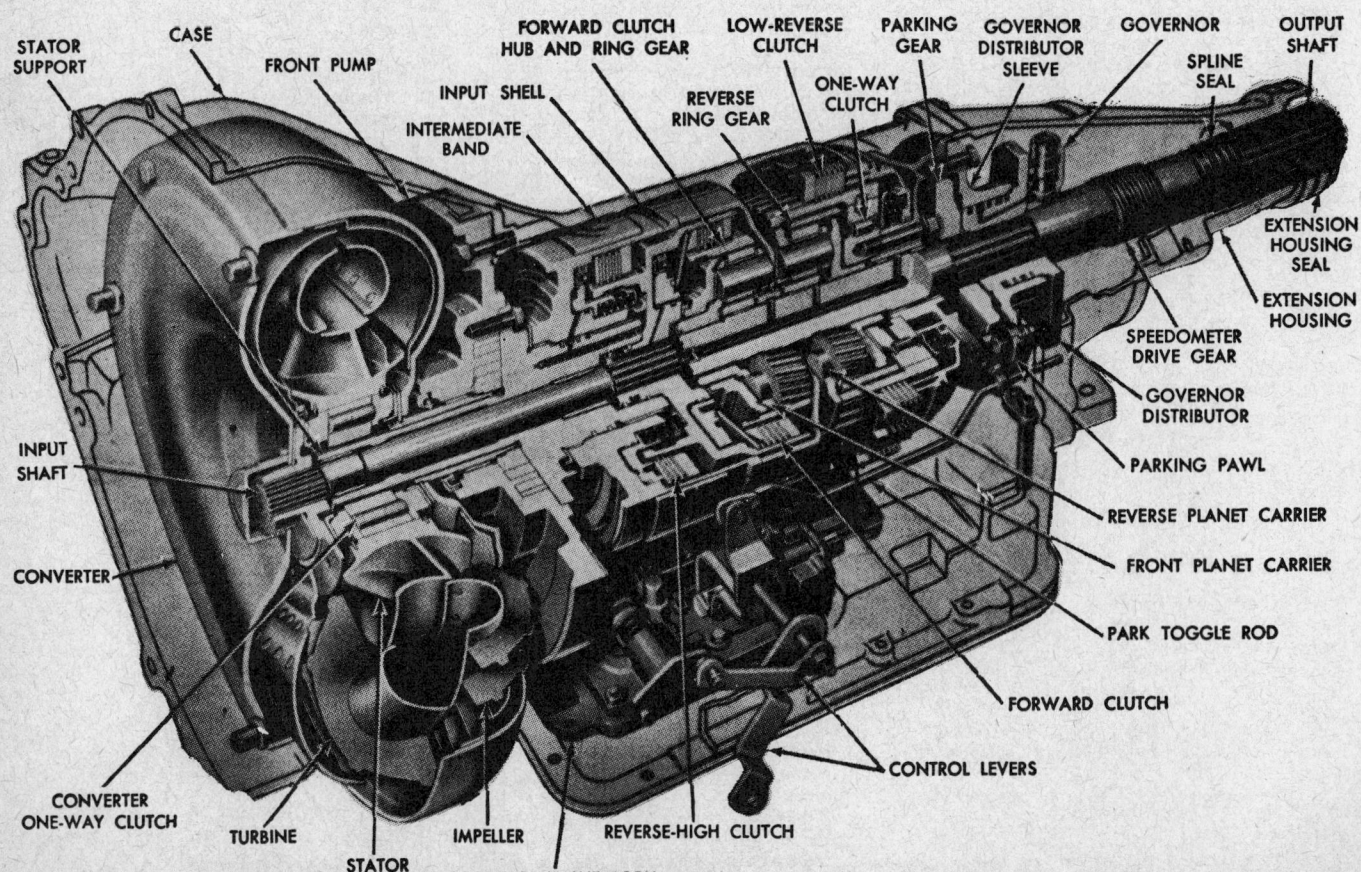

Fig. 1 Sectional view of C6 transmission

Parking Pawl

The transmission gear train is in neutral in both P and N positions. There is no pressure to any clutch and only the transmission input shaft turns. In park, a pawl engages a parking gear which is splined to the transmission output shaft, Fig. 1, to lock the rear wheels to the transmission main case.

A neutral start switch, mounted on the transmission and operated by the selector linkage, completes the engine cranking circuit in P and N only so that the engine cannot be started in any drive gear.

Forced Downshifts

Forced downshifts (kickdown shifts) from high to second gear are possible at speeds as high as 65 mph. In D1 it is possible to force a downshift to 1st gear up to 30 mph.

The carburetor is at full throttle before the accelerator is floored. Up to full throttle, a "torque demand" downshift to 2nd is possible up to 40 mph. "Kickdown" shifts require depressing the accelerator to the floor to actuate the downshift valve in the transmission.

TROUBLE SHOOTING GUIDE

No Drive In Forward Speeds

1. Manual linkage adjustment.
2. Check control pressure.
3. Valve body.
4. Make air pressure check.
5. Forward clutch.
6. Leakage in hydraulic system.

Rough Initial Engagement in D, D1, D2 or 2

1. Engine idle speed too high.
2. Vacuum diaphragm unit or tubes restricted, leaking or maladjusted.
3. Check control pressure.
4. Valve body.
5. Forward clutch.

1–2 or 2–3 Shift Points Incorrect or Erratic

1. Check fluid level.
2. Vacuum diaphragm unit or tubes restricted, leaking or maladjusted.
3. Downshift linkage, including inner lever position.
4. Manual linkage adjustment.
5. Governor defective.
6. Check control pressure.
7. Valve body.
8. Make air pressure check.

Rough 1–2 Upshifts

1. Vacuum diaphragm unit or tubes restricted, leaking or maladjusted.
2. Intermediate servo.
3. Intermediate band
4. Check control pressure.
5. Valve body.

Rough 2–3 Shifts

1. Vacuum diaphragm or tubes restricted, leaking or maladjusted.
2. Intermediate servo.
3. Check control pressure.
4. Intermediate band.
5. Valve body.
6. Make air pressure check.

7. Reverse–high clutch.
8. Reverse–high clutch piston air bleed valve.

Dragged Out 1–2 Shift

1. Check fluid level.
2. Vacuum diaphragm unit or tubes restricted, leaking or maladjusted.
3. Intermediate servo.
4. Check control pressure.
5. Intermediate band.
6. Valve body.
7. Make air pressure check.
8. Leakage in hydraulic system.

Engine Overspeeds on 2–3 Shift

1. Manual linkage adjustment.
2. Check fluid level.
3. Vacuum diaphragm unit or tubes restricted, leaking or maladjusted.
4. Intermediate servo.
5. Check control pressure.
6. Valve body.
7. Intermediate band.
8. Reverse–high clutch.
9. Reverse–high clutch piston air bleed valve.

No 1–2 or 2–3 Shift

1. Manual linkage adjustment.
2. Downshift linkage including inner lever position.
3. Vacuum diaphragm unit or tubes restricted, leaking or maladjusted.
4. Governor.
5. Check control pressure.
6. Valve body.
7. Intermediate band.
8. Intermediate servo.
9. Reverse–high clutch.
10. Leakage in hydraulic system.

No 3–1 Shift In D1, 2 or 3–2 Shift In D2 or D

1. Governor.
2. Valve body.

No Forced Downshifts

1. Downshift linkage, including inner lever position.
2. Check control pressure.
3. Valve body.

Runaway Engine on Forced 3–2 Shift

1. Check control pressure.
2. Intermediate servo.
3. Intermediate band.
4. Valve body.
5. Vacuum diaphragm unit or tubes restricted, leaking or maladjusted.
6. Leakage in hydraulic system.

Rough 3–2 Shift or 3–1 Shift at Closed Throttle

1. Engine idle speed.
2. Vacuum diaphragm unit or tubes restricted, leaking or maladjusted.
3. Intermediate servo.
4. Check control pressure.
5. Valve body.

Shifts 1–3 In D, D1, 2, D2

1. Intermediate band.
2. Intermediate servo.
3. Valve body.
4. Governor.
5. Make air pressure check.

No Engine Braking in 1st Gear—Manual Low Range

1. Manual linkage adjustment.
2. Low–reverse clutch.
3. Valve body.
4. Governor.
5. Make air pressure check.
6. Leakage in hydraulic system.

Creeps Excessively

1. Engine idle speed too high.

Slips or Chatters In 1st Gear, D1

1. Check fluid level.
2. Vacuum diaphragm unit or tubes restricted, leaking or maladjusted.
3. Check control pressure.
4. Valve body.
5. Forward clutch.
6. Leakage in hydraulic system.
7. Planetary one–way clutch.

Slips or Chatters In 2nd Gear

1. Check fluid level.
2. Vacuum diaphragm unit or tubes restricted, leaking or maladjusted.
3. Intermediate servo.
4. Intermediate band.
5. Check control pressure.
6. Valve body.
7. Make air pressure check.
8. Forward clutch.
9. Leakage in hydraulic system.

Slips or Chatters In Reverse

1. Check fluid level.
2. Vacuum diaphragm unit or tubes restricted, leaking or maladjusted.
3. Manual linkage adjustment.
4. Low–reverse clutch.
5. Check control pressure.
6. Valve body.
7. Make air pressure check.
8. Reverse–high clutch.
9. Leakage in hydraulic system.
10. Reverse–high clutch piston air bleed valve.

No Drive In D1 or 2

1. Manual linkage adjustment.
2. Check control pressure.
3. Valve body.
4. Planetary one–way clutch.

No Drive In D, D2

1. Check fluid level.
2. Manual linkage adjustment.
3. Check control pressure.
4. Intermediate servo.
5. Valve body.
6. Make air pressure check.
7. Leakage in hydraulic system.

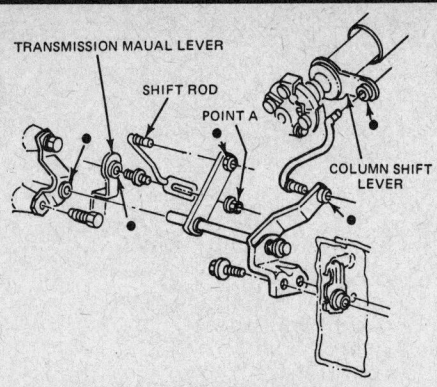

**Fig. 2 Column shift linkage.
1977–79 Lincoln Continental (Typical)**

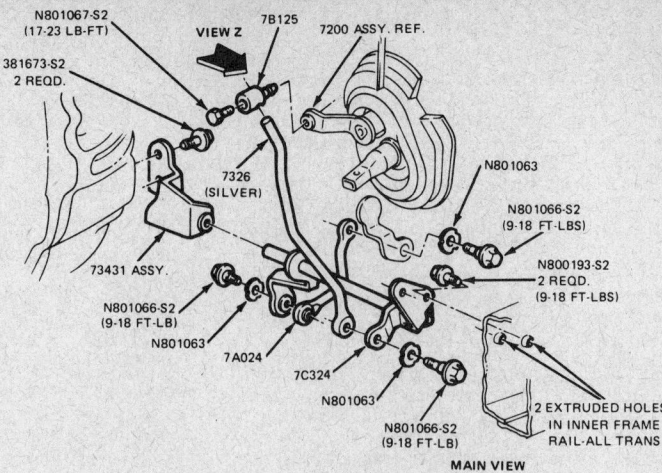

Fig. 3 Column shift linkage. 1980 Ford & Mercury

No Drive In L or 1

1. Check fluid level.
2. Check control pressure.
3. Valve body.
4. Make air pressure check.
5. Leakage in hydraulic system.

No Drive In R Only

1. Check fluid level.
2. Manual linkage adjustment.
3. Low–reverse clutch.
4. Check control pressure.
5. Valve body.
6. Make air pressure check.
7. Reverse–high clutch.
8. Leakage in hydraulic system.
9. Reverse–high clutch piston air bleed valve.

No Drive In Any Selector Position

1. Check fluid level.
2. Manual linkage adjustment.
3. Check control pressure.
4. Valve body.
5. Make air pressure check.
6. Leakage in hydraulic system.
7. Front pump.

Lockup In D1 or 2

1. Valve body.
2. Parking linkage.
3. Leakage in hydraulic system.

Lockup In D2 or D

1. Low–reverse clutch.
2. Valve body.
3. Reverse–high clutch.
4. Parking linkage.
5. Leakage in hydraulic system.
6. Planetary one–way clutch.

Lockup In L or 1

1. Valve body.
2. Parking linkage.
3. Leakage in hydraulic system.

Lockup In R only

1. Valve body.
2. Forward clutch.
3. Parking linkage.
4. Leakage in hydraulic system.

Parking Lock Binds or Does Not Hold

1. Manual linkage adjustment.
2. Parking linkage.

Transmission Overheats

1. Oil cooler and connections.
2. Valve body.
3. Vacuum diaphragm unit or tubes restricted, leaking or maladjusted.
4. Check control pressure.
5. Converter one–way clutch.
6. Converter pressure check valves.

Maximum Speed Too Low, Poor Acceleration

1. Engine performance.
2. Car brakes.
3. Forward clutch.

Transmission Noisy In N and P

1. Check fluid level.
2. Valve body.
3. Front pump.

Noisy In 1st, 2nd, 3rd or Reverse

1. Check fluid level.
2. Valve body.
3. Planetary assembly.
4. Forward clutch.
5. Reverse–high clutch.
6. Planetary one–way clutch.

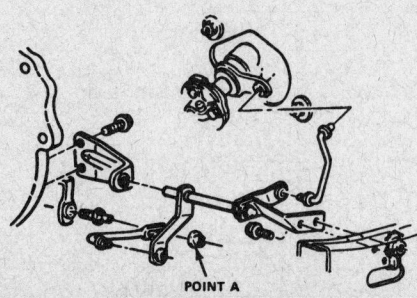

**Fig. 4 Manual linkage (Typical).
1977–78 Ford & Mercury column shift**

Car Moves Forward In N

1. Manual linkage adjustment.
2. Forward clutch.

Fluid Leak

1. Check fluid level.
2. Converter drain plugs.
3. Oil pan gasket, filler tube or seal.
4. Oil cooler and connections.
5. Manual or downshift lever shaft seal.
6. ⅛" pipe plugs in case.
7. Extension housing–to–case gasket.
8. Extension housing rear oil seal.
9. Speedometer driven gear adapter seal.
10. Vacuum diaphragm unit or tubes.
11. Intermediate servo.
12. Engine rear oil seal.

MAINTENANCE

Checking Oil Level

1. Make sure car is on a level floor.
2. Apply parking brake firmly.
3. Run engine at normal idle speed. If transmission fluid is cold, run engine at a fast idle until fluid reaches normal operating temperature. When fluid is warm, slow engine to normal idle speed.
4. Shift selector lever through all positions, then place lever at "P". Do not shut down engine during fluid level checks.
5. Clean all dirt from dipstick cap before removing dipstick from filler tube.
6. Pull dipstick out of tube, wipe it clean and push it all the way back in tube.
7. Pull dipstick out of tube again and check fluid level. If necessary, add enough fluid to raise the level to the "F" mark on dipstick. Do not overfill.

Drain & Refill

NOTE: The Ford Motor Company recommends the use of an automatic transmission fluid with Qualification No. M2C-138-CJ for 1977–80 models. The recommended fluid is said to have a greater coefficient of friction and greater ability to handle maximum engine torques without band or clutch slippage.

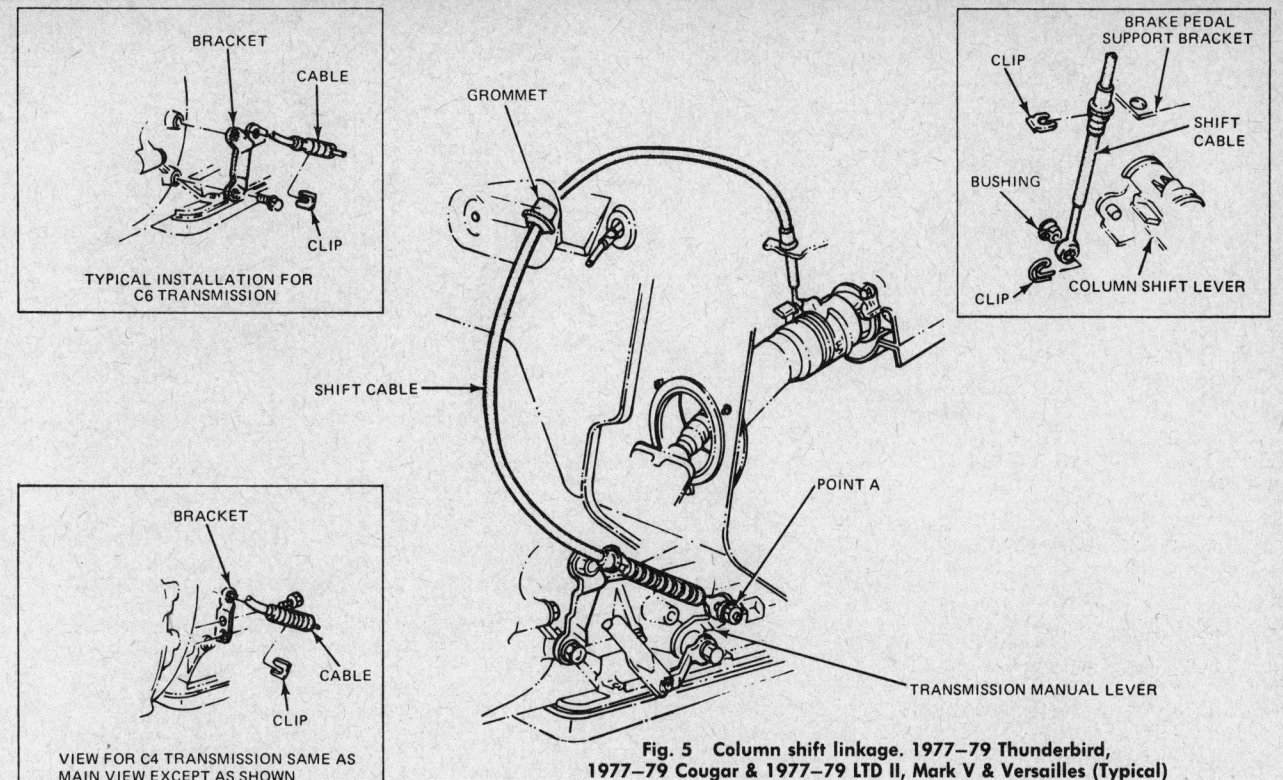

Fig. 5   Column shift linkage. 1977–79 Thunderbird, 1977–79 Cougar & 1977–79 LTD II, Mark V & Versailles (Typical)

Normal maintenance and lubrication requirements do not necessitate periodic fluid changes. If a major failure has occurred in the transmission, it will have to be removed for service. At this time the converter and transmission cooler must be thoroughly flushed to remove any foreign matter.

1. To drain the fluid, loosen pan attaching bolts and allow fluid to drain.
2. After fluid has drained to the level of the pan flange, remove pan bolts working from rear and both sides of pan to allow it to drop and drain slowly.
3. When fluid has stopped draining, remove and clean pan and screen. Discard pan gasket.
4. Using a new gasket, install pan.
5. Add 3 quarts of recommended fluid to transmission through filler tube.
6. Run engine at idle speed for 2 minutes, and then run it at a fast idle until it reaches normal operating temperature.
7. Shift selector lever through all positions, place it at "P" and check fluid level.
8. If necessary, add enough fluid to transmission to bring it to the "F" mark on the dipstick.

MANUAL LINKAGE, ADJUST

All Models

Column Shift

1. Place selector lever into "D" position using suitable force to hold it tight against the stop.
2. Loosen shift rod adjusting nut, point A in Figs. 2 through 6.
3. Shift transmission manual lever to D.
4. Make sure selector lever has not moved from D position then tighten adjusting nut to 10–20 ft. lbs.

Floor Shift

1. Place transmission selector lever in D position.
2. Raise car and loosen shift rod retaining nut, Fig. 7.
3. Move transmission manual lever to D position.

Fig. 6   Manual linkage, column shift. 1979 Ford & Mercury

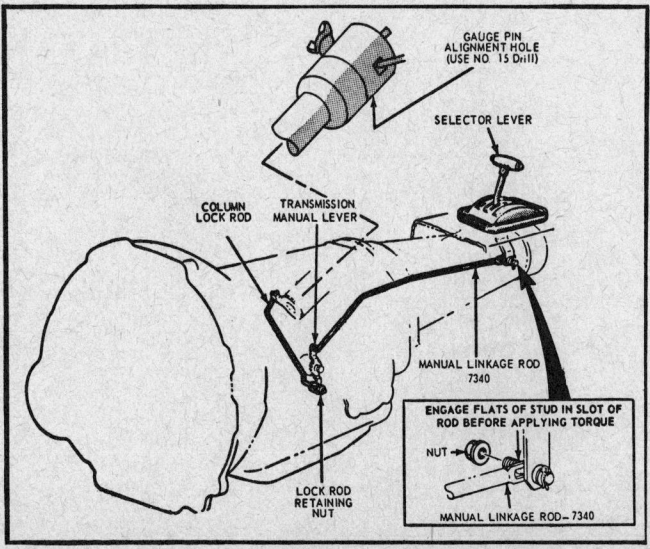

Fig. 7   Manual linkage, floor shift. Typical. Column lock rod is used on some models

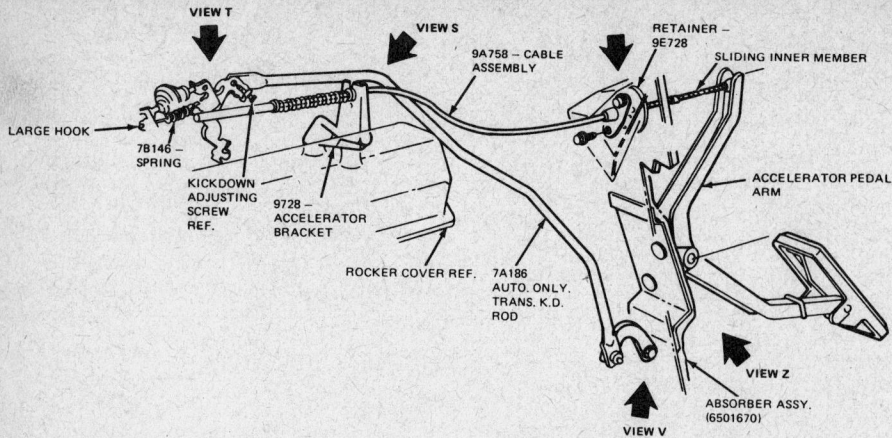

Fig. 8 Throttle & downshift linkage. 1977–80 Ford, Mercury & Lincoln Continental (typical)

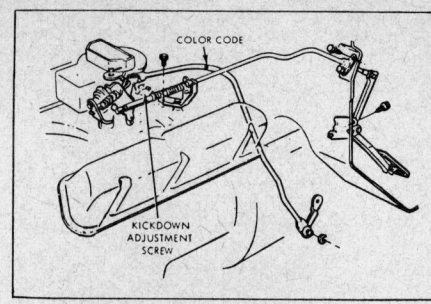

Fig. 9 Throttle & downshift linkage. 1977 Cougar, LTD II & Thunderbird

3. Lower car and fill transmission to the correct level with specified fluid.

4. Tighten retaining nut to 10–20 ft. lbs.

THROTTLE & DOWNSHIFT LINKAGE

Adjusting the throttle linkage is important to be certain the throttle and kickdown systems are properly adjusted. The kickdown system should come in when the accelerator is pressed through detent, and not before detent. See Figs. 8 and 9.

All Models

1. Hold carburetor lever in the wide open throttle position.
2. Hold downshift rod against through detent stop.
3. On all models except Versailles, adjust downshift screw to provide 0.01–0.08 inch clearance between throttle arm and screw. On Versailles models, adjust screw for 0.01–0.03 inch clearance.
4. Connect downshift lever return spring.

BAND ADJUSTMENT

NOTE: When making the intermediate band adjustment, the lock nut must be discarded and a new one installed each time the band is adjusted.

1. Loosen the locknut on the adjusting screw several turns, Fig. 10.
2. Torque the screw to 10 ft. lbs, or until the adjuster wrench overruns.
3. Back the screw off exactly 1½ turns.
4. Hold the adjustment and torque the locknut to the 35–45 ft. lbs.

OIL PAN & CONTROL VALVE

Removal
1. Raise car on hoist or jack stands.
2. Loosen and remove all but two oil pan bolts from front of case and drop rear edge of pan to drain fluid. Remove and clean pan and screen.
3. Unfasten and remove valve body.

Installation
1. Position valve body to case, making sure that selector and downshift levers are engaged, then install and torque attaching bolts to specifications.
2. Using a new pan gasket, secure pan to case and torque bolts to specifications.

INTERMEDIATE SERVO

Removal, Exc. Continental
1. Raise car and remove engine rear support-to-extension housing bolts.
2. Raise transmission high enough to relieve weight from support.
3. Remove support (1 bolt).
4. Lower transmission.
5. Place drain pan beneath servo.
6. Remove servo cover-to-case bolts.
7. Loosen band adjusting screw locknut.
8. Remove servo cover, piston, spring and gasket from case, *screwing band adjusting screw inward as piston is removed. This insures that there will be enough tension on the band to keep the struts properly engaged in the band end notches while the piston is removed.*

Removal, Continental
1. Raise vehicle and remove servo cover retaining bolts.
2. Remove manual and downshift control rod splash shield from frame side rail and reinforcement plate from beneath transmission oil pan.
3. Loosen band adjusting screw locknut.
4. Remove engine rear mount to crossmember nuts and with a suitable jack, raise transmission to remove weight from crossmember.
5. Remove engine rear support to extension housing bolts, then the support.

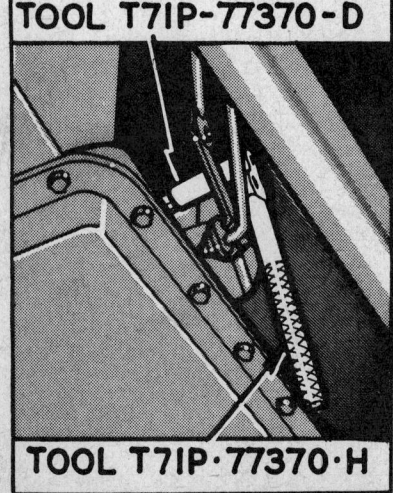

TOOL T7IP-77370-D

TOOL T7IP-77370-H

Fig. 10 Band adjustment

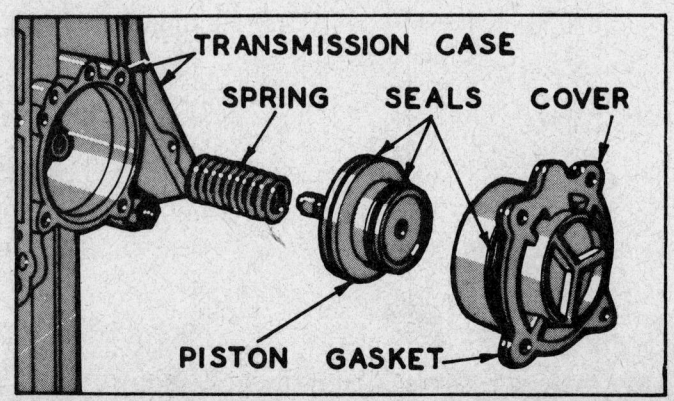

TRANSMISSION CASE
SPRING SEALS COVER
PISTON GASKET

Fig. 11 Intermediate servo disassembled

6. Remove servo cover, piston, spring and gasket from case, turning adjusting screw inward as piston is removed. This places enough tension on the band to keep struts properly engaged in band end notches as piston is withdrawn.

Installation, All

NOTE: If piston or piston sealing lips are damaged, replace complete piston and rod assembly, Fig. 11.

1. Coat piston and servo cover seal with transmission fluid. Coat a new servo cover gasket with petroleum jelly and install on cover.
2. Install piston into servo cover and spring onto piston stem.
3. Insert piston stem in case. Secure cover with bolts, taking care to back off band adjusting screw while tightening cover bolts. Make sure that vent tube retaining clip is in place.
4. Raise transmission high enough to install engine rear support. Secure support to extension housing. Lower transmission as required to install support-to-crossmember bolt.
5. On Continental models, secure manual and downshift rod splash shield to frame side rail.
6. Remove jack supporting transmission and adjust the band as outlined previously.
7. Lower car and replenish fluid as required.

EXTENSION HOUSING & GOVERNOR

Removal
1. Raise vehicle and disconnect parking brake cable from equalizer and on Continental models, remove the equalizer.
2. Disconnect drive shaft from rear axle flange and remove from transmission.
3. Disconnect speedometer cable from extension housing.

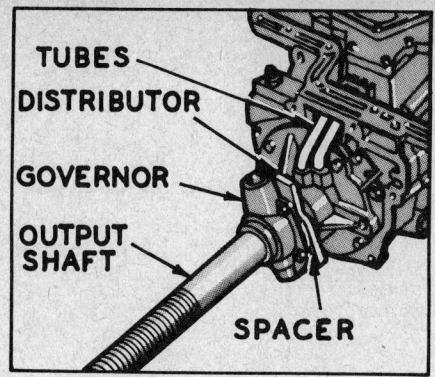

Fig. 12 Governor installed

4. Remove engine rear support to extension housing bolts and on Continental models, remove reinforcement plate from beneath oil pan.
5. Raise transmission slightly with a suitable jack to remove weight from engine rear support.
6. Remove engine rear support to crossmember bolt and the support.
7. Lower transmission to permit access to extension housing bolts. Remove bolts and slide housing off output shaft.
8. Disconnect governor from distributor (4 bolts) and slide governor off output shaft.

Installation, Fig. 12
1. Secure governor to distributor flange.
2. Position new gasket on transmission.
3. Secure extension housing to case.
4. Raise transmission to position engine rear support on crossmember and install the support attaching bolt.
5. Lower transmission and remove jack. Install engine rear support to extension housing bolts and on Continental models, oil pan reinforcement plate.
6. Install speedometer cable.
7. On Continental models, install parking brake cable equalizer and on all models, connect parking brake cable to equalizer. Adjust parking brake.

8. Install drive shaft.
9. Correct transmission fluid level.

TRANSMISSION, REPLACE

NOTE: On models with the neutral safety switch wire harness connected at the dash panel, disconnect the harness before raising the vehicle.

NOTE: On Mark V models, disconnect fan shroud from radiator.

1. Raise vehicle and drain transmission and converter.

NOTE: On Continental models, disconnect idler arm from frame side rail.

2. Remove drive shaft and starter.
3. Remove four converter to flywheel attaching bolts.
4. Disconnect parking brake front cable from equalizer.
5. Disconnect speedometer cable and transmission linkage.
6. Disconnect TRS switch wire, if equipped.
7. On 1977–79 Continental, remove lower shift rod bellcrank and pry upper shift rod bellcrank from converter housing and allow bellcrank to hang free.
8. Where necessary, disconnect muffler inlet pipes from exhaust manifold.
9. Support the transmission with a suitable jack, remove parking brake rear cables from the equalizer and remove the crossmember.
10. Lower transmission and remove oil cooler lines, vacuum line and transmission oil filler tube.
11. Secure the transmission to the jack with the chain, remove the converter housing to cylinder block bolts and carefully move the transmission away from the engine, at the same time lowering it to clear the underside of the vehicle.
12. Reverse procedure to install.

FORD FMX Automatic Transmission

TRANSMISSION IDENTIFICATION

The identification tag on 1977–80 FMX units is on the lower right hand extension housing-to-case bolt.

Year	Engine	Trans. Code
FORD MODELS		
1977	8-351M②	PHB-AW
	8-400	PHB-AW
	8-400	PHB-AC4
1978	8-351M	PHB-BB
	8-400	PHB-BC, 1
1979	8-302	PHB-PH
1980	8-351	PHB-BK, 1
	8-351	PHB-BP, 1
	8-351	PHB-BT, 1
	8-351	PHB-BU, 1

Year	Engine	Trans. Code
LTD II MODELS		
1977	8-351W①	PHB-Z8
	8-351M②	PHB-AT1
	8-351M②	PHB-AY
	8-351M②	PHB-AL2
	8-400	PHB-AL2
1978	8-351W	PHB-Z9
	8-351M	PHB-AT2
	8-400	PHB-BD, BE
1979	8-302	PHB-BG
	8-351M	PHB-AT2, AT3
	8-351W	PHB-Z9
MERCURY MODELS		
1977	8-351M②	PHB-AW
	8-400	PHB-AW
	8-400	PHB-AC4

Year	Engine	Trans. Code
MERCURY MODELS—Cont'd		
1978	8-351M	PHB-BB
	8-400	PHB-BC, 1
1979	8-302	PHB-PH
1980	8-302	PHB-BH2, 3
	8-351	PHB-BK, 1
	8-351	PHB-BP, 1
	8-351	PHB-BT, 1
	8-351	PHB-BT, 1
COUGAR MODELS		
1977	8-351W①	PHB-Z8
	8-351M②	PHB-AT1
	8-351M②	PHB-AY
	8-351M②	PHB-AL2
	8-400	PHB-AL2
1978	8-351W	PHB-Z9

Year	Engine	Trans. Code

COUGAR MODELS—Cont'd

	8-351M	PHB-AT2
	8-400	PHB-BD, BE
1979	8-302	PHB-BG
	8-351M	PHB-AT2, AT3
	8-351W	PHB-Z9

THUNDERBIRD MODELS

1977	8-351W①	PHB-Z8
	8-351M②	PHB-AT1
	8-351M②	PHB-AY
	8-351M②	PHB-AL2
	8-400	PHB-AL4
1978	8-351W	PHB-Z9
	8-351M	PHB-AT2
	8-400	PHB-BD, BE
1979	8-302	PHB-BG
	8-351W	PHB-Z9
	8-351M	PHB-AT3

①—Windsor engine.
②—Modified engine.

DESCRIPTION

Operation

This transmission, Fig. 1, features a drive range that provides for fully automatic upshifts and downshifts, and manually selected low and second gears. The six selector lever positions provided are P (park), R (reverse), N (neutral), D (automatic drive range), 2 (second gear hold) and 1 (low gear hold).

D is a fully automatic range providing for a first gear start with automatic upshifts to second and high gear occurring at appropriate intervals.

Second gear (2) is a manually selected second gear hold. When the selector lever is moved to 2, the transmission will engage and remain in second gear, regardless of throttle opening or road speed.

Low gear (1) is a manually selected first gear hold. When the selector lever is moved to this position the transmission will remain in first gear. To provide engine braking, moving the lever to this position will cause the transmission to downshift from 2nd when the car speed reaches about 22 to 39 mph depending on axle ratio and tire size.

D—Drive

The normal automatic driving range is indicated by D. In this range the car starts off in first gear and gives the best combination of automatic gear shifts to provide for economy and full power starts. As the accelerator is depressed and the car picks up speed, automatic shifts to second and high gears will occur. The transmission will automatically downshift as speed decreases. Forced downshifts in D are made by pressing the accelerator pedal all the way to the floor.

2—Second Gear Hold

When the car is started and the shift lever is moved to 2, the car will start off and remain in second gear, regardless of throttle opening or road speed. This range is especially useful for starting the car on icy pavements or other slippery surfaces. Similarly, when engine braking is required and the shift lever is moved from D to 2, the transmission will engage and remain in second gear.

Selector lever position 2 is not a cruising range in the usual sense of the term. While the transmission is capable of limited cruising in second gear, maximum fuel economy and best all-around performance are realized in D range.

1—Low Gear Hold

This range is identical in operation to manual low range except that when the shift lever is moved to 1 to provide engine braking, the automatic shift from second to low gear will occur between 22 and 39 mph (exact shift point will vary with axle ratio and tire size).

TROUBLE SHOOTING GUIDE

Rough Initial Engagement

1. Idle speed.
2. Vacuum unit or tubes.
3. Front band.

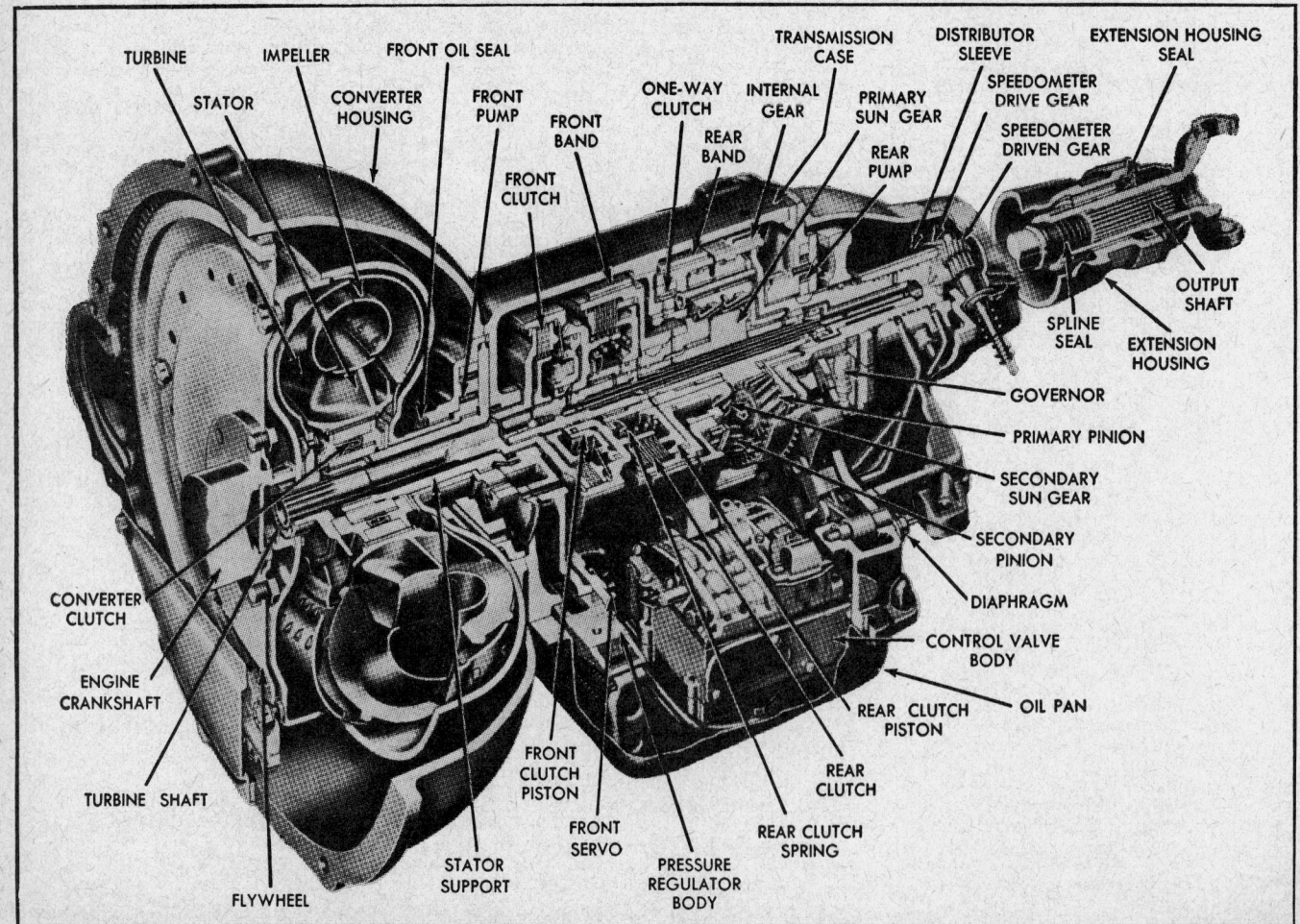

Fig. 1 FMX three speed dual range unit with cast iron case

4. Check control pressure.
5. Pressure regulator.
6. Valve body.

Shift Points High, Low or Erratic

1. Fluid level.
2. Vacuum unit or tubes.
3. Manual linkage.
4. Governor.
5. Check control pressure.
6. Valve body.
7. Downshift linkage.

Rough 2—3 Shift

1. Manual linkage.
2. Front band.
3. Vacuum unit or tubes.
4. Pressure regulator.
5. Valve body.
6. Front servo.

Engine Overspeeds, 2—3 Shift

1. Vacuum unit or tubes.
2. Front band.
3. Valve body.
4. Pressure regulator.

No 1—2 or 2—3 Shifts

1. Governor.
2. Valve body.
3. Manual linkage.
4. Rear clutch.
5. Front band.
6. Front servo.
7. Leakage in hydraulic system.
8. Pressure regulator.

No Forced Downshifts

1. Downshift linkage.
2. Check control pressure.
3. Valve body.

Rough 3—2 or 3—1 Shifts

1. Engine idle speed.
2. Vacuum unit or tubes.
3. Valve body.

Slips or Chatters in 2nd

1. Fluid level.
2. Vacuum unit or tubes.
3. Front band.
4. Check control pressure.
5. Pressure regulator.
6. Valve body.
7. Front servo.
8. Front clutch.
9. Leakage in hydraulic system.

Slips or Chatters in 1st

1. Fluid level.
2. Vacuum unit or tubes.
3. Check control pressure.
4. Pressure regulator.
5. Valve body.
6. Front clutch.
7. Leakage in hydraulic system.
8. Fluid distributor sleeve in output shaft.
9. Planetary one-way clutch.

Slips or Chatters in Reverse

1. Fluid level.
2. Rear band.
3. Check control pressure.

4. Pressure regulator.
5. Valve body.
6. Rear servo.
7. Rear clutch.
8. Vacuum unit or tubes.
9. Leakage in hydraulic system.
10. Fluid distributor sleeve in output shaft.

No Drive in D or D2

1. Valve body.
2. Make air pressure check.
3. Manual linkage.
4. Front clutch.
5. Leak in hydraulic system.
6. Fluid distributor sleeve in output shaft.

No Drive in D1

1. Manual linkage.
2. Valve body.
3. Planetary one-way clutch.

No Drive in L

1. Manual linkage.
2. Front clutch.
3. Valve body.
4. Make air pressure check.
5. Leak in hydraulic system.
6. Fluid distributor sleeve in output shaft.

No Drive in D1

1. Manual linkage.
2. Valve body.
3. Planetary one-way clutch.

No Drive in L

1. Manual linkage.
2. Front clutch.
3. Valve body.
4. Make air pressure check.
5. Leak in hydraulic system.
6. Fluid distributor sleeve in output shaft.

No Drive in R

1. Rear band.
2. Rear servo.
3. Valve body.
4. Make air pressure check.
5. Rear clutch.
6. Leak in hydraulic system.
7. Fluid distributor sleeve in output shaft.

No Drive in Any Range

1. Fluid level.
2. Manual linkage.
3. Check control pressure.
4. Pressure regulator.
5. Valve body.
6. Make air pressure check.
7. Leak in hydraulic system.

Lockup in D or D1

1. Manual linkage.
2. Rear servo.
3. Front servo.
4. Rear clutch.
5. Parking linkage.
6. Leak in hydraulic system.

Lockup in D2

1. Manual linkage.
2. Rear band.
3. Rear servo.
4. Rear clutch.
5. Parking linkage.

6. Leak in hydraulic system.
7. Planetary one-way clutch.

Lockup in R

1. Front band.
2. Front servo.
3. Front clutch.
4. Parking linkage.
5. Leak in hydraulic system.

Lockup in L

1. Front band.
2. Pressure regulator.
3. Valve body.
4. Rear clutch.
5. Parking linkage.
6. Leak in hydraulic system.

Parking Lock Binds or Won't Hold

1. Manual linkage.
2. Parking linkage.

Transmission Overheats

1. Oil cooler and connections.
2. Pressure regulator.
3. Converter one-way clutch.

Engine Runaway on Forced Downshift

1. Front band.
2. Pressure regulator.
3. Valve body.
4. Front servo.
5. Vacuum unit or tubes.
6. Leak in hydraulic system.

Maximum Speed Below Normal, Acceleration Poor

1. Converter one-way clutch.

No 3—1 Downshift

1. Engine idle speed.
2. Vacuum unit or tubes.
3. Valve body.

Noise in Neutral

1. Pressure regulator.
2. Front clutch.
3. Front pump.

Noise in 1—2—3 or R

1. Pressure regulator.
2. Planetary assembly.
3. Front clutch.
4. Rear clutch.
5. Front pump.

Noise in Reverse

1. Pressure regulator.
2. Front pump.

Noise on Coast in Neutral

1. Rear pump.

MAINTENANCE

Adding Fluid

The fluid level in the transmission should be checked at 1000-mile intervals. Make sure that the car is standing level, and firmly apply the parking brake.

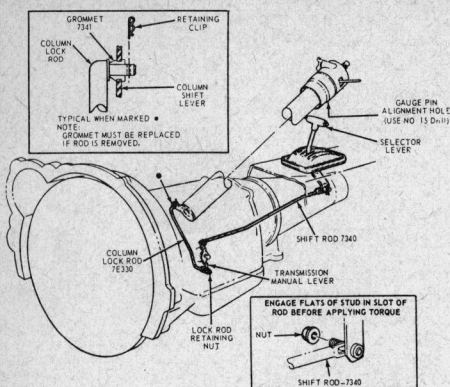

Fig. 2 Manual linkage. Floor shift (typical)

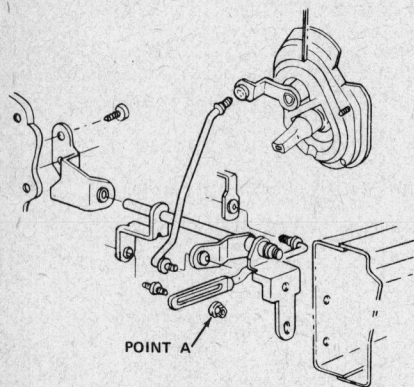

Fig. 5 Manual linkage, column shift. 1979 Ford & Mercury

Run the engine at normal idle speed. If the transmission fluid is cold, run the engine at fast idle speed until the fluid reaches normal operating temperature. When the fluid is warm, slow the engine down to normal idle speed, shift the transmission through all ranges and then place the lever at P.

Clean all dirt from the transmission fluid dipstick cap before removing the dipstick from the filler tube. Pull the dipstick out of the tube, wipe it clean and push it all the way back into the tube.

Pull the dipstick out again and check the fluid level. If necessary, add enough Type F Automatic Transmission Fluid to the transmission to raise the fluid level to the F (full mark) on the dipstick.

Changing Fluid

NOTE: Normal maintenance and lubrication does not require periodic transmission fluid changes. However, a major transmission repair will require that the fluid be drained and be replaced with type F "lifetime" fluid.

1. Raise and support vehicle on hoist, then place a drain pan under transmission.
2. Loosen pan bolts and drain fluid until it has reached level of pan flange, then remove bolts working from rear and both sides of pan allowing to drop and drain slowly.
3. When fluid has completely drained, remove and thoroughly clean pan and filter.
4. Install filter, then using a new gasket install oil pan and add three quarts of fluid.

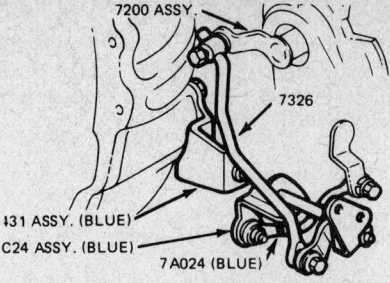

Fig. 3 Manual linkage. 1980 Ford & Mercury column shift

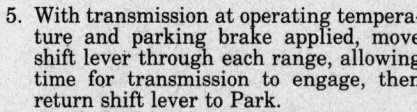

5. With transmission at operating temperature and parking brake applied, move shift lever through each range, allowing time for transmission to engage, then return shift lever to Park.
6. Check fluid level and add fluid as necessary to bring level between ADD and FULL mark.

MANUAL LINKAGE, ADJUST

Cougar, Ford, LTD II, Mercury, & 1977–79 Thunderbird

Floor Shift, Fig. 2
1. Place selector lever in D.
2. Raise vehicle and loosen manual shift rod retaining nut.

NOTE: On 1977–78 Cougar and LTD II, the shift rod retaining nut is located at the transmission end of the shift rod.

3. Move transmission manual lever to D position.
4. Torque nut to 10–20 ft-lbs.

Column Shift
1. Place selector lever in D position.
2. Raise vehicle and loosen shift rod adjusting nut at point A, Figs. 3 through 5. On models with shift cable, remove nut at point A and remove cable from transmission manual lever stud, Fig. 6.
3. Shift transmission manual lever into drive position, second detent from the full counter clockwise position.
4. On models equipped with shift cable, place cable end on transmission manual

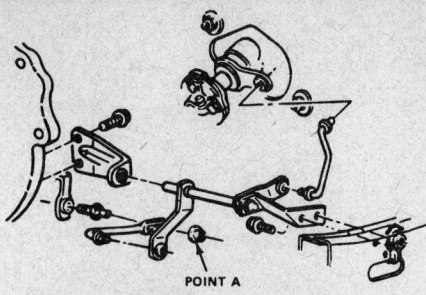

Fig. 4 Manual linkage (Typical). 1977–78 Ford & Mercury column shift

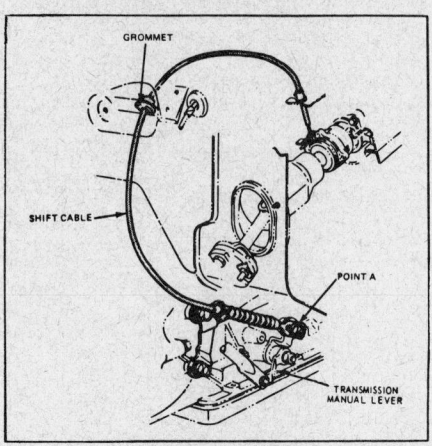

Fig. 6 Manual linkage. 1977–79 Cougar; 1977–79 LTD II & Thunderbird column shift.

lever stud. Align flats on stud with flats on cable, then install adjustment nut.
5. On all models, tighten adjustment at point A. Ensure selector lever is against D stop when tightening adjustment nut.
6. Check transmission for proper operation in all selector lever detent positions.

THROTTLE LINKAGE, ADJUST

All Models, Figs. 7 & 8

1. Disconnect downshift lever return spring and hold throttle lever in wide open position and the downshift rod against the through detent stop.
2. Hold downshift rod against the through

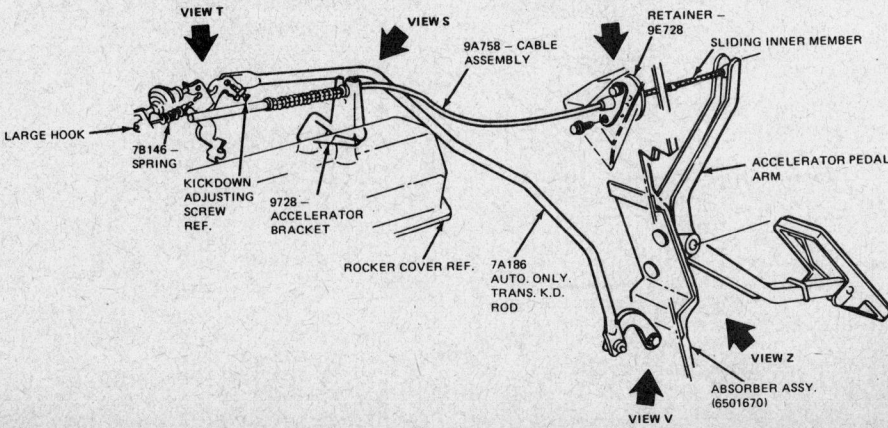

Fig. 7 Throttle & Downshift linkage. 1977-80 Ford & Mercury (typical)

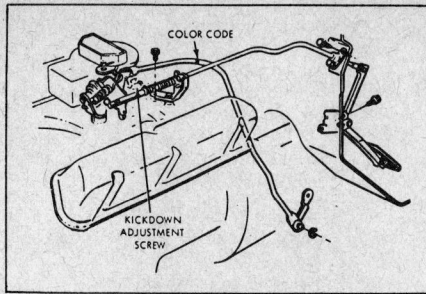

Fig. 8 Throttle & downshift linkage. 1977–79 Cougar; 1977–79 LTD II & Thunderbird

detent stop.
3. Adjust downshift screw to provide .01 to .08 inch clearance between screw.
4. Connect downshift lever return spring and throttle arm.

BAND ADJUSTMENTS

Front Band

1. Drain fluid from transmission, remove and clean oil pan and screen.
2. Loosen front servo adjusting screw locknut.
3. Pull back on actuating rod and insert a 1/4 inch spacer between adjusting screw and servo piston stem, Fig. 9.
4. Tighten adjusting screw to 10 inch-lbs. torque. Remove spacer and tighten adjusting screw an additional 3/4 turn. Hold adjusting screw stationary and tighten locknut securely.
5. Install oil pan with new gasket and add fluid to transmission.

Rear Band

NOTE: There is no access hole in the floor pan to adjust the rear band. With the use of special tools this band can be adjusted externally as follows, Fig. 10, 11.

1. Loosen rear band adjusting screw locknut. A special tool is required to gain access in limited space.
2. Tighten adjusting screw until special tool clicks. It is preset to overrun when torque reaches 10 ft. lbs.

NOTE: If screw is found to be tighter than

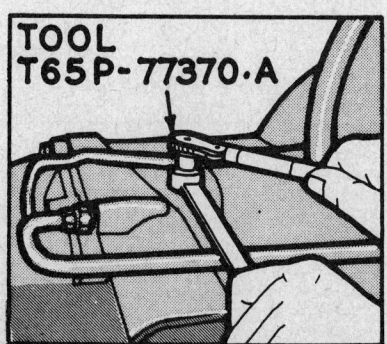

Fig. 10 Rear band adjustment. 1977–79 Ford & Mercury full size

10 ft. lbs., loosen screw and tighten until wrench clicks and overruns.

3. Back off adjusting screw 1 1/2 turns.

NOTE: Severe damage may result if adjusting screw is not backed off the exact amount of turns indicated.

4. Hold adjusting screw stationary and tighten locknut securely.

CONTROL VALVE BODY

1. Support vehicle on hoist, then drain transmission fluid and remove pan.

NOTE: If fluid is to be reused, filter it through a 100-mesh screen before replacing it in transmission.

2. Disconnect hoses from vacuum diaphragm unit, then using Snap-On tool S8696-A, remove vacuum diaphragm and push rod.
3. Remove fluid screen retaining clip and small compensator pressure tube.
4. Remove main pressure oil tube, by gently prying up end that connects to main control valve, then remove other end of tube from pressure regulator.

NOTE: Tube must be removed in this manner. Failure to do so, could kink or bend tube causing excessive internal transmission leakage.

5. Loosen front servo bolts three turns, then remove the three control valve body screws, and lower valve body while pulling it off front servo tubes, being careful not to damage valve body or tubes.
6. Before installing control valve, check for bent manual valve by rolling it on a flat surface.

NOTE: Before torquing control valve attaching bolts, move valve toward center of case until clearance is less than .050 inch between manual valve and actuating pin.

7. After installing control valve, torque control valve attaching bolts to 8–10 ft. lbs., front servo bolts to 30–35 ft. lbs. and vacuum diaphragm to 15–23 ft. lbs.
8. After completing assembly, adjust front and rear bands. If valve body was replaced, adjust control linkage.

FRONT & REAR SERVOS

1. Drain transmission fluid and remove oil pan and screen.
2. Remove vacuum diaphragm, then loosen control valve body attaching bolts.
3. Remove retaining bolts from servo, then hold actuating strut and remove servo.
4. After installation, if front servo was serviced, torque front servo attaching bolts to 30–35 ft. lbs. and adjust front band. If rear servo was serviced, torque rear servo attaching bolts to 40–45 ft. lbs., adjust rear bands and check for less than .050 inch clearance between manual lever actuating pin and manual lever as outlined under "Control Valve."

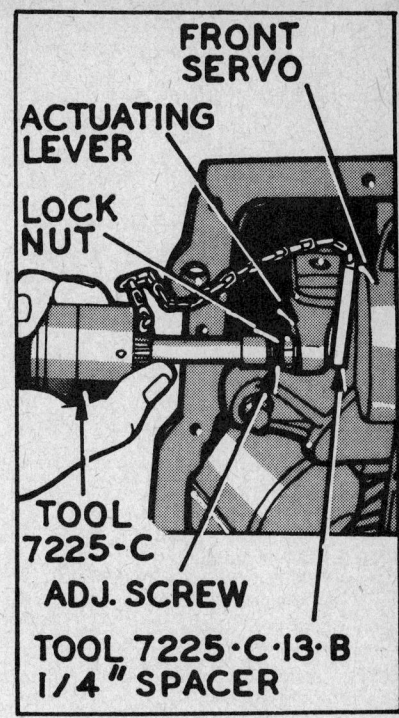

Fig. 9 Front band adjustment. Ford, Mercury and Thunderbird

EXTENSION HOUSING BUSHING & REAR SEAL

Proper removal and installation of extension housing bushing and rear seal will necessitate the use of five specialty tools. When removing bushing and rear seal, the vehicle will have to be raised and driveshaft removed.

EXTENSION HOUSING

1. Drain transmission fluid and remove driveshaft.
2. Disconnect speedometer cable from housing and remove engine rear supports to crossmember nuts.

Fig. 11 Rear band adjustment. 1977–79 Cougar; 1977–79 LTD II & Thunderbird

3. Raise transmission slightly with suitable jack, then remove crossmember to side rail bolts and position the crossmember out of way.
4. Remove the two engine rear support-to-extension housing bolts and remove support.
5. Remove extension housing attaching bolts, then slide housing off output shaft and remove gasket.

NOTE: Hold output shaft and rear support from moving rearward to prevent needle bearing and race from dropping out.

GOVERNOR

1. Remove extension housing as outlined previously.
2. Remove governor to counterweight screws and lift governor from counterweight.

NOTE: When removing governor, hold output shaft and rear support from moving rearward to prevent needle bearing and race from dropping out.

3. When installing governor torque attaching bolts to 50–60 in. lbs.

PRESSURE REGULATOR

1. Drain transmission fluid and remove oil pan and fluid screen.
2. Remove small compensator pressure tube from control valve body and pressure regulator.
3. Remove main pressure oil tube by gently prying up end that connects to main control valve assembly, then remove other end of tube from pressure regulator.

NOTE: Tube must be removed in this manner. Failure to do so, could kink or bend tube, causing excessive internal transmission leakage.

4. Remove pressure regulator spring retainer, springs and spacer.

NOTE: Maintain pressure on retainer to prevent springs from falling out.

5. Remove regulator attaching bolts and remove regulator.
6. After installing regulator, torque attaching bolts to 17–22 ft. lbs.

PARKING PAWL

1. Drain transmission fluid and remove driveshaft.
2. Support rear of transmission and remove crossmember, then remove the two engine rear support-to-extension housing bolts and remove support.
3. Disconnect speedometer cable and remove oil pan and screen.
4. Loosen rear band adjusting screw locknut and tighten adjusting screw to 24 in. lbs.

NOTE: This will hold planetary carrier and clutch assemblies in place during parking pawl removal.

5. Remove small compensator pressure tube from pressure regulator and control valve body.
6. Remove main pressure oil tube by gently prying up end that connects to main valve body assembly, then remove other end of tube from pressure regulator.

NOTE: Tube must be removed in this manner. Failure to do so could kink or bend tube, causing excessive internal transmission leakage.

7. Remove vacuum diaphragm and loosen front servo attaching bolts, then remove valve body attaching bolts and lower valve body while pulling it off servo tubes, being careful not to damage valve body or tubes.
8. Remove rear servo bolts and remove servo and struts.
9. Remove extension housing and output shaft rear support.
10. Using a magnet, remove parking pawl pin from case, then working from inside of case, drive on shoulder of toggle lever pin with a small punch to move retaining plug part way out of case. Using a pair of pliers, remove plug.
11. Slide toggle lever toward front of case. Cock lever to one side to apply pressure on pin, then move toggle to rear of case to move pin outward.
12. Remove pawl and toggle lever as an assembly.
13. During assembly refer to "Control Valve Body" and "Front & Rear Servos" for installation. After assembly, adjust front and rear bands as outlined previously.

TRANSMISSION, REPLACE

NOTE: On some models, it is necessary to remove the two upper converter housing to engine bolts before raising vehicle.

1. Raise vehicle and place on jack stands, then drain transmission oil pan.
2. Remove converter access cover and remove converter drain plug.
3. Remove converter to flywheel attaching nuts, reinstall converter drain plugs and converter housing access cover to hold converter in place when transmission is removed.
4. Remove starter and propeller shaft.
5. Where necessary, disconnect exhaust pipes from manifold.
6. Disconnect oil cooler lines, speedometer cable, vacuum hose and manual downshift linkage.
7. Disconnect TRS switch wire, if equipped.
8. Support transmission with suitable jack and remove crossmember.

NOTE: On some models, it is necessary to remove the engine rear support to transmission bolts before crossmember removal.

9. Lower transmission and remove filler tube and dipstick.
10. Remove converter housing-to-engine bolts. Move transmission and jack rearward and lower away from vehicle.
11. Reverse procedure to install.

Ford (Jatco) Automatic Transmission

TRANSMISSION IDENTIFICATION

Granada & Monarch

1977–80 6-250 . . . . PLA

DESCRIPTION

The Jatco transmission, Fig. 1, is a three speed unit capable of providing automatic upshifts and downshifts through the three forward gear ranges, also manual selection of first and second gears. This transmission consists of a torque converter, planetary gear train, two multiple disc clutches, one multiple disc brake, a one-way clutch and a hydraulic control system.

MAINTENANCE

NOTE: Use only fluid that meets Ford Motor Company specification ESP-M2C138-CJ. Use of a fluid other than specified may result in transmission malfunction or failure.

Checking Oil Level

1. With transmission at operating temperature, park vehicle on level surface.
2. Run engine at idle speed with service and parking brakes applied and move selector lever through all ranges and return to Park position.
3. With engine idling, remove dipstick and check fluid level. Fluid level should be between Add and Full marks.
4. Add specified fluid to bring fluid to proper level.

Drain & Refill

NOTE: Normal maintenance and lubrication requirements do not necessitate periodic fluid changes.

When filling a dry transmission and converter, add five quarts of specified fluid. Start engine, move selector lever through all ranges and return to Park position. Check fluid level and add fluid to bring level to Full mark.

When a partial drain and refill is required due to a minor repair, proceed as follows:
1. Loosen and remove all but two oil pan

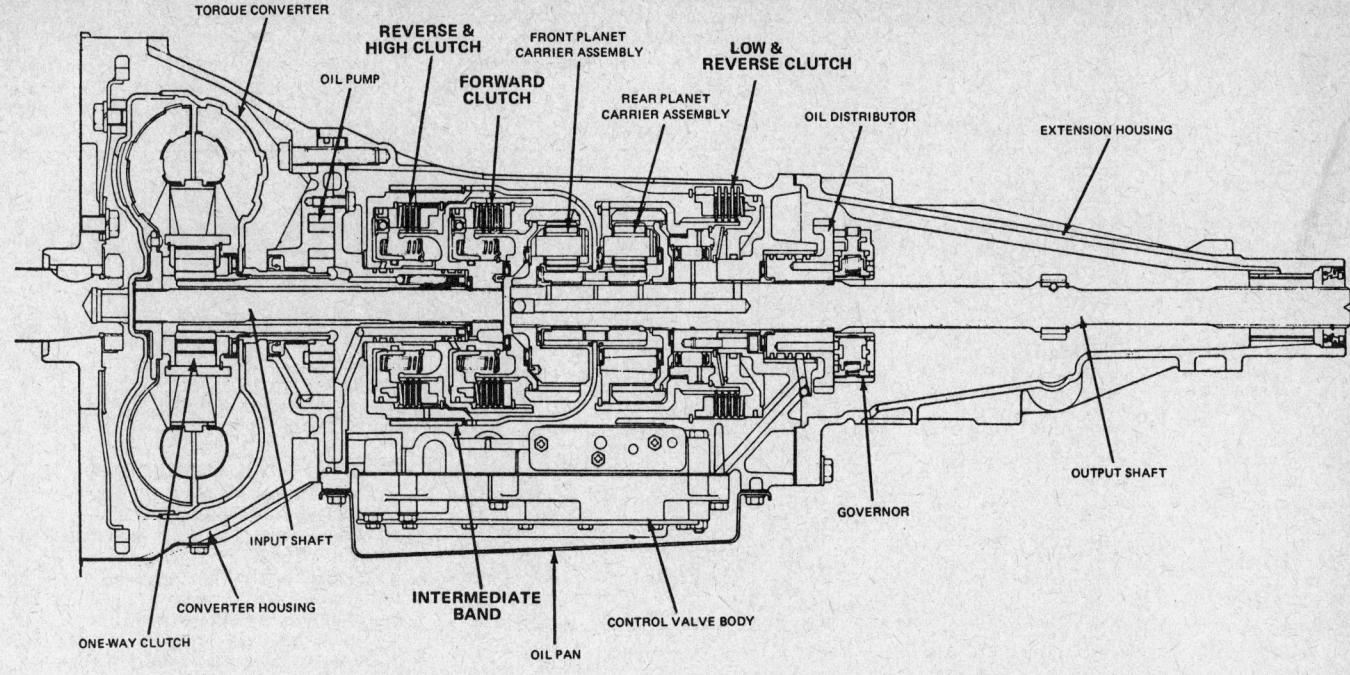

Fig. 1 Ford (Jatco) transmission

bolts and drop one edge of the pan to drain oil.
2. Remove and clean oil pan and screen.
3. Place a new gasket on pan and install pan and screen.
4. Add three quarts of specified fluid to transmission.
5. Operate engine at idle speed for approximately two minutes, then run at fast idle until transmission reaches operating temperature.
6. Move selector lever through all ranges and return to Park position, recheck oil level and add fluid, if necessary, to bring level to between Add and Full marks.

INTERMEDIATE BAND, ADJUST

1. Raise and support vehicle.
2. Remove servo cover retaining bolts and cover, Fig. 2.
3. Loosen adjusting screw locknut and torque adjusting screw to 10 ft. lbs.
4. Back off adjusting screw two turns, then while holding adjusting screw stationary, torque adjusting screw locknut to 22–29 ft. lbs.
5. Install servo cover, gasket and bolts. Torque servo cover bolts to 5 ft. lbs.

IN VEHICLE REPAIRS

Control Valve Body

1. Raise vehicle, drain transmission and remove oil pan.
2. Remove downshift solenoid, vacuum diaphragm, vacuum diaphragm rod and O-rings.
3. Remove valve body to case attaching bolts. Hold manual valve to keep it from sliding out of the valve body, then remove valve body from the case.

NOTE: Failure to hold the manual valve while removing control assembly may result in valve damage.

4. Reverse procedure to install.

Servo

1. Raise and support vehicle.
2. Drain transmission fluid and remove oil pan.
3. Remove control valve body.
4. Remove servo cover bolts and cover.
5. Remove servo retainer to case bolts and remove retainer and servo piston as an assembly.
6. Remove return spring and apply strut.
7. Reverse procedure to install. Make sure to torque control valve body bolts to 5 ft. lbs.

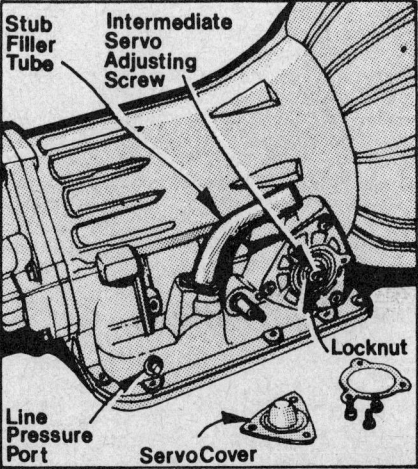

Fig. 2 Intermediate band adjustment

8. Adjust intermediate band as described previously.

Extension Housing Seal

1. Raise vehicle and disconnect drive shaft.
2. Using a sharp chisel, remove seal from extension housing.
3. Install seal with a suitable tool.
4. Connect drive shaft.

Extension Housing

1. Raise vehicle and disconnect drive shaft from rear axle.
2. Disconnect speedometer cable from extension housing.
3. Remove transmission rear support to crossmember bolts, raise transmission slightly with a suitable jack and loosen extension housing bolts to drain transmission fluid.
4. Remove extension housing to case bolts, then the extension housing.

CAUTION: On 1979–80 models, do not lose washer from parking panel shaft.

5. Reverse procedure to install.

Governor

1. Remove the extension housing as outlined previously.
2. Remove governor housing to oil distributor bolts, then the governor housing from distributor.
3. Reverse procedure to install.

TRANSMISSION, REPLACE

1. Disconnect battery ground cable.
2. Raise and support vehicle.
3. Drain transmission fluid and remove driveshaft.

4. Disconnect speedometer cable, shift cable, vacuum diaphragm line, downshift solenoid wire and oil cooler lines.
5. Remove converter housing cover, then the converter to flywheel nuts.
6. Remove transmission rear support to crossmember nuts.
7. Support transmission with a suitable jack and remove crossmember.
8. Secure transmission to jack with a safety chain, then lower transmission and remove starter motor.
9. Remove transmission to engine bolts and oil filler tube.
10. Using a pry bar, exert pressure between flex plate and converter to prevent converter from disengaging transmission when assembly is removed.
11. Lower transmission and converter as an assembly and remove from vehicle.
12. Reverse procedure to install.

Ford Automatic Overdrive Transmission

TRANSMISSION IDENTIFICATION

Year	Car Model	Trans. Code	Engine Model
1980	Cougar	PKA-Y, 1, 2, 3	V8-302
	Ford	PKA-E, 1, 2, 3	V8-302
	Ford	PKA-C, 1, 2, 3	V8-351
	Ford	PKA-R, 1, 2, 3	V8-351
	Ford	PKA-T, 1, 2, 3	V8-351
	Ford	PKA-Z, 1, 2, 3	V8-351
	Lincoln	PKA-M, 1, 2, 3	V8-302
	Lincoln	PKA-D, 1, 2, 3	V8-351
	Lincoln	PKA-U, 1, 2, 3	V8-351
	Mercury	PKA-W, 1, 2, 3	V8-302
	Mercury	PKA-C, 1, 2, 3	V8-351
	Mercury	PKA-R, 1, 2, 3	V8-351
	Mercury	PKA-T, 1, 2, 3	V8-351
	Mercury	PKA-Z, 1, 2, 3	V8-351
	Mark VI	PKA-M, 1, 2, 3	V8-302
	Mark VI	PKA-D, 1, 2, 3	V8-351
	Mark VI	PKA-U, 1, 2, 3	V8-351
	Thunderbird	PKA-Y, 1, 2, 3	V8-302
1981	Cougar & XR-7	PKA-AH	V8-255
		PKA-Y8	V8-302
	Ford & Mercury	PKA-AF, AT	V8-255
		PKA-E6, AG, AL	V8-302
		PKA-C6, C8, R8, T8, Z8, AR, AS	V8-351
	Lincoln	PKA-M8	V8-302
	Mark VI	PKA-M8	V8-302
	Thunderbird	PKA-AH	V8-255
		PKA-Y8	V8-302
1982	Continental	PKA-BF, 1, 2	V6-232
	Continental	PKA-BD, 1, 2	V8-302
	Cougar & XR7	PKA-BH, 1	6-232
	Cougar & XR7	PKA-BH, 1	V6-232
	Ford	PKA-AT5	V8-255
	Ford	PKA-AG5, AU5	V8-302
	Ford	PKA-AY, BB	V8-302
	Ford	PKA-C13, AS5	V8-351
	Mark VI	PKA-M13, BC	V8-302
	Mercury	PKA-AF5, 6	V8-255
	Mercury	PKA-AT5, 6	V8-255
	Mercury	PKA-AG	V8-302
	Mercury	PKA-AG5, 6	V8-302
	Mercury	PKA-AU5, 6	V8-302
	Mercury	PKA-AY1	V8-302
	Mercury	PKA-BB, 1	V8-302
	Mercury	PKA-C13, 14	V8-351
	Mercury	PKA-AS5, 6	V8-351
	Thunderbird	PKA-BH	V6-232
	Thunderbird	PKA-AH5	V8-255
	Town Car	PKA-M13, 14, 15	V8-302
	Town Car	PKA-BC, 1, 2	V8-302
1983	Continental	PKA-BD12	V8-302
	Cougar/Thunderbird	PKA-BR, BT	V6-232
	Cougar/Thunderbird	PKA-K	V8-302
	Ford/Mercury	PKA-AU17	V8-302
	Ford/Mercury	PKA-AG17	V8-302
	Ford/Mercury	PKA-AY12	V8-302
	Ford/Mercury	PKA-BB12	V8-302
	Ford/Mercury	PKA-C25	V8-351
	Ford/Mercury	PKA-AS17	V8-351
	LTD/Marquis	PKA-BR, BT	V6-232
	Mark VI	PKA-M25	V8-302
	Mark VI	PKA-BC5	V8-302

DESCRIPTION

This unit is a 4 speed automatic transmission incorporating an integral overdrive feature. With selector lever in 1 position, the transmission will start and remain in first gear until the selector lever is moved to another position. In 3 position, the transmission will automatically shift through 1-2-3 range, but will not engage overdrive. In D position, the transmission will automatically select the appropriate time to shift into overdrive (4th gear). The design of the transmission features a split torque path in third gear, where 40% of the engine torque is transmitted hydraulically through the torque converter and 60% is transmitted mechanically through solid connections (direct drive input shaft) to the driveshaft. When transmission is in overdrive (4th gear), 100% of engine torque is transmitted through the direct drive input shaft.

The transmission consists essentially of a torque converter assembly, compound planetary gear train and a hydraulic control system, Fig. 1. For gear control the transmission has four friction clutches, two one-way roller clutches and two bands. Overdrive is accomplished by the addition of a band to lock the reverse sun gear while driving the planet carrier. The torque converter operation is similar to other types of automatic transmission, but has an added damper assembly and input shaft for 3rd gear and overdrive. The direct drive input shaft couples the engine directly to the direct clutch. This shaft is driven by the torque converter cover through the damper assembly which cushions engine shock to the transmission.

TROUBLE SHOOTING GUIDE

Rough Initial Engagement in Forward or Reverse

1. Improper fluid level.
2. High engine idle.
3. Loose driveshaft, engine mounts or U-joints.
4. Sticking or dirty valve body.
5. Improper clutch or band application, or low oil control pressure.

Slow Initial Engagement

1. Improper fluid level.
2. Damaged or improperly adjusted linkage.
3. Contaminated fluid.
4. Low main control pressure or improper clutch and band application.

Harsh Engagements With Warm Engine

1. Improper fluid level.
2. Damaged or improperly adjusted linkage.
3. High engine idle.
4. Sticking or dirty valve body.

Slow Forward Engagement

1. Improper fluid level.
2. Damaged or improperly adjusted linkage.
3. Low main control pressure.
4. Sticking or dirty valve body.
5. Blocked filter.
6. Damaged pump.

Slow Reverse Engagement

1. Improper fluid level.
2. Damaged or improperly adjusted linkage.
3. Low main control pressure.
4. Damaged forward clutch assembly.
5. Sticking or dirty valve body.
6. Blocked filter.
7. Damaged pump.

No Engine Braking In Manual Low

1. Improper fluid level.
2. Damaged or improperly adjusted linkage.
3. Damaged low reverse servo piston band.
4. Damaged planetary low one-way clutch.

No Engine Braking In Manual 2nd

1. Improper fluid level.
2. Damaged or improperly adjusted linkage.
3. Improper clutch or band application.
4. Improper control system pressure.
5. Leaking intermediate servo.
6. Damaged intermediate one-way clutch.

Slips Or Chatters In Drive

1. Improper fluid level.
2. Improper throttle valve rod adjustment.
3. Damaged or improperly adjusted link-

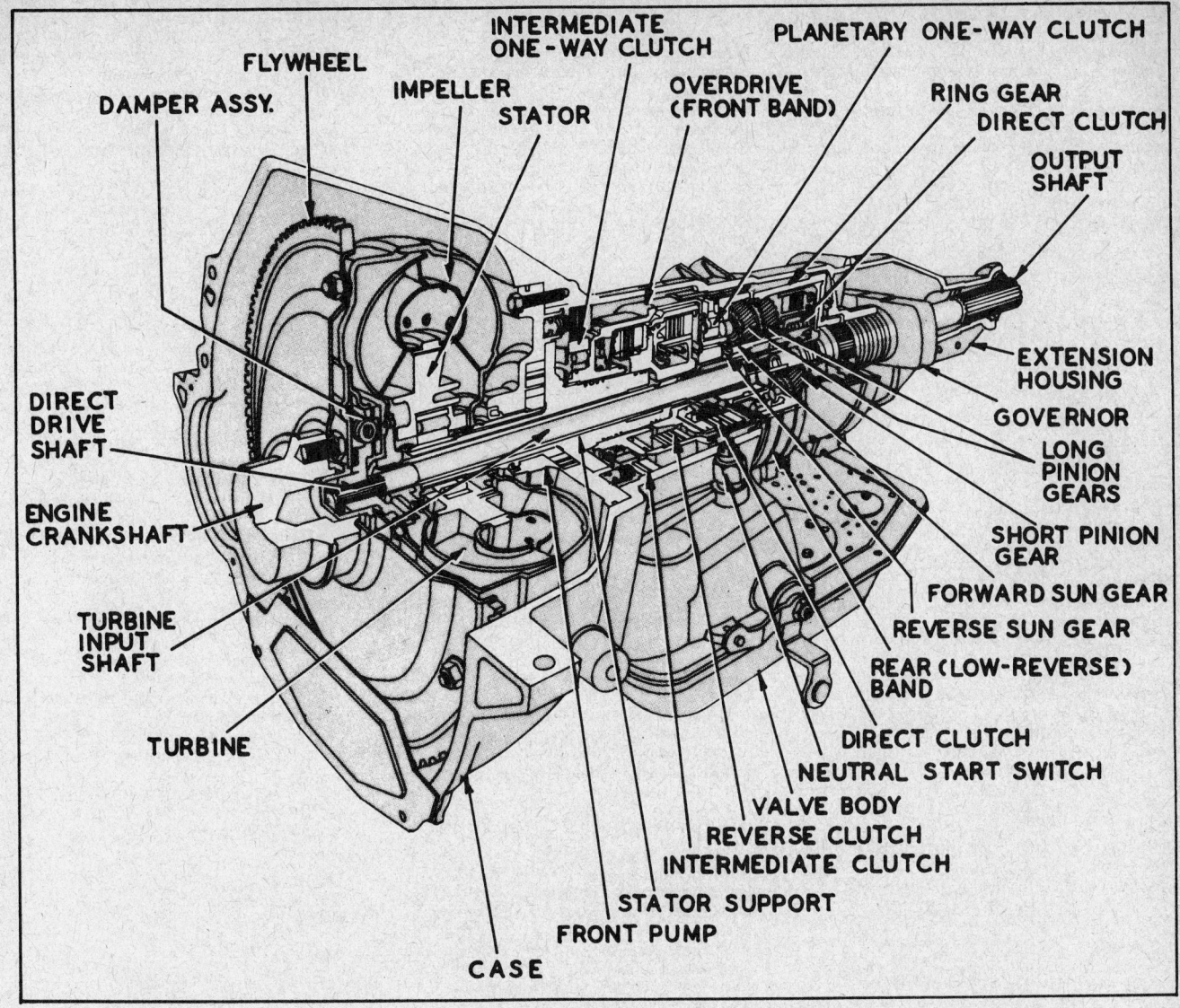

Fig. 1   Sectional view of Ford Automatic Overdrive Transmission

age.
4. Low main control pressure.
5. Sticking or dirty valve body.
6. Open forward clutch check valve.
7. Damaged forward clutch piston seal.
8. Blocked forward clutch feed hole.
9. Damaged planetary low one-way clutch.

Slips Or Chatters In Reverse

1. Improper fluid level.
2. Low main control pressure in reverse.
3. Damaged reverse servo bore.
4. Damaged planetary low one-way clutch.
5. Damaged reverse clutch drum bushing.
6. Worn reverse clutch stator support seal rings or grooves.
7. Reverse clutch piston seal.
8. Reverse band adjustment.
9. Loosen driveshaft, engine mounts or U-joints.

No Drive Or Slips Or Chatters In D2

1. Improper fluid level.

2. Damaged or improperly adjusted linkage.
3. Intermediate friction or one-way clutch.
4. Blocked intermediate bleed hole or bleed hole not at 12 o'clock position.
5. Sticking or dirty valve body.
6. Damaged or worn servo.

No Drive Or Slips Or Chatters In D1

1. Damaged planetary low one-way clutch.

Starts In 2nd Or 3rd

1. Improper fluid level.
2. Damaged or improperly adjusted linkage.
3. Improper clutch or band application.
4. Improper control system pressure.
5. Sticking governor valve.
6. Sticking or dirty valve body.
7. Leaking valve body mating surface.

Improper Shift Points

1. Improper fluid level.

2. Damaged or improperly adjusted linkage.
3. Improper speedometer gear installed.
4. Improper clutch or band application.
5. Improper control system pressure.
6. Damaged or worn governor.
7. Sticking or dirty valve body.

Harsh, Delayed or No Upshifts

1. Improper fluid level.
2. Damaged or improperly adjusted linkage.
3. Governor sticking.
4. High main control pressure.
5. Sticking or dirty valve body.

All Upshifts Early

1. Improper fluid level.
2. Damaged or improperly adjusted linkage.
3. Low main control pressure.
4. Sticking throttle control valve or valve body.
5. Sticking governor valve.

AUTOMATIC TRANSMISSIONS/TRANSAXLES

No 1-2 Upshifts

1. Improper fluid level.
2. Damaged or improperly adjusted linkage.
3. Low main control pressure to intermediate friction clutch.
4. Sticking, leaking or bent diaphragm unit.
5. Sticking or dirty valve body.
6. Burnt intermediate clutch, band or servo.

Early or Slipping Upshift In 1-2

1. Improper fluid level.
2. Improperly tuned engine.
3. Damaged or improperly adjusted linkage.
4. High main control pressure.
5. Sticking governor valve.

No 2-3 Upshift

1. Improper fluid level.
2. Damaged or improperly adjusted linkage.
3. Low main control pressure to direct clutch.
4. Sticking or dirty valve body.
5. Burnt or worn direct clutch.
6. Broken weld on converter damper hub.

Early Or Slipping 2-3 Upshift

1. Improper fluid level.
2. Improperly tuned engine.
3. Damaged or improperly adjusted linkage.
4. Cut or worn 2-3 accumulator piston seals.
5. Plugged 2-3 accumulator piston drain hole.
6. Damaged accumulator.
7. Dirty or sticking valve body.
8. Leaking vacuum diaphragm.

No 3-4 Upshift

1. Low fluid level.
2. Damaged or improperly adjusted linkage.
3. Low pressure to overdrive band servo.
4. Sticking or dirty valve body.
5. Burnt or worn overdrive band assembly.
6. Blocked case passage.
7. Broken converter damper hub.

Early or Slipping 3-4

1. Improper fluid level.
2. Damaged or improperly adjusted linkage.
3. Low main control pressure to overdrive band servo.
4. Sticking or dirty valve body.
5. Burnt overdrive band assembly.
6. Damaged or glazed reverse clutch drum or overdrive band.

Erratic Shifts

1. Improper fluid level.
2. Improperly tuned engine.
3. Damaged or improperly adjusted linkage.
4. Dirty or sticking valve body.
5. Sticking governor valve.
6. Damaged output shaft collector body seal rings.

Shifts 1-3 In D

1. Improper fluid level.
2. Damaged or burnt intermediate friction clutch.
3. Damaged intermediate one-way clutch.
4. Improper control system pressure or clutch application.
5. Sticking or dirty valve body.
6. Sticking governor valve.

Late 2-3 Shifting

1. Improper fluid level.
2. Damaged or improperly adjusted linkage.
3. Improper control system pressure or clutch application.
4. Damaged or worn high clutch or intermediate servo.
5. Sticking or dirty valve body.
6. Broken converter damper hub.

Shift Hunting 3-4 or 4-3

1. Improperly tuned engine.
2. Damaged or improperly adjusted linkage.

No Forced Downshifts

1. Improper fluid level.
2. Damaged or improperly adjusted linkage.
3. Improper control system pressure or clutch application.
4. Sticking or dirty valve body.
5. Sticking or dirty governor.

3-1 Shift At Closed Throttle In D

1. Improper fluid level.
2. Improperly tuned engine.
3. Damaged or improperly adjusted linkage.
4. Improper control system pressure or clutch application.
5. Improper governor operation.
6. Sticking or dirty valve body.

Harsh Or Slipping 4-2 Or 3-1 Shift

1. Improper fluid level.
2. Improperly tuned engine.
3. Damaged or improperly adjusted linkage.
4. Improper application of intermediate friction and one-way clutch.
5. Sticking or dirty valve body.

High Shift Effort

1. Damaged or improperly adjusted linkage.
2. Loose manual lever nut.
3. Damaged manual lever retainer pin.

Transmission Overheats

1. Improper fluid level.
2. Improperly tuned engine.
3. Improper control system pressure or clutch application.
4. Restricted cooler or lines.
5. Seized converter one-way clutch.
6. Sticking or dirty valve body.

Clunk Or Squawk In 1-2 Or 2-3

1. Blocked intermediate bleed hole or bleed hole not at 12 o'clock position.
2. Misaligned anti-clunk spring.

Harsh Downshift Coasting Clunk

1. Improperly seated anti-clunk spring.
2. Damaged or improperly adjusted linkage.

Poor Vehicle Acceleration

1. Improperly tuned engine.
2. Seized torque converter one-way clutch.

Slipping Shift Followed By Sudden Engagement

1. Throttle valve linkage set too short.

Transmission Noisy (Valve Resonance)

1. Improper fluid level.
2. Damaged or improperly adjusted linkage.
3. Improper control system pressure or clutch application.
4. Cooler lines contacting frame, floor pan or other components.
5. Sticking or dirty valve body.
6. Internal leakage or pump cavitation.

Transmission Noisy (Other Than Valve Resonance)

1. Improper fluid level.
2. Damaged or improperly adjusted linkage.
3. Contaminated fluid.
4. Loose converter to flywheel housing bolts or nuts.
5. Loose or worn speedometer driven gear.
6. Damaged or worn extension housing bushing seal or driveshaft.
7. Damaged or worn front or rear planetary and/or one-way clutch.

THROTTLE VALVE LINKAGE DIAGNOSIS

Refer to the following for TV linkage conditions and subsequent shift troubles.

TV Control Linkage Adjusted Too Short

1. Early or soft up-shifts.
2. Harsh light throttle shift into and out of overdrive.
3. No forced downshift at proper speeds.

TV Linkage Adjusted Too Long

1. Harsh idle engagement after engine warm up.
2. Clunking when throttle is released after heavy acceleration.
3. Harsh coasting downshifts out of overdrive.

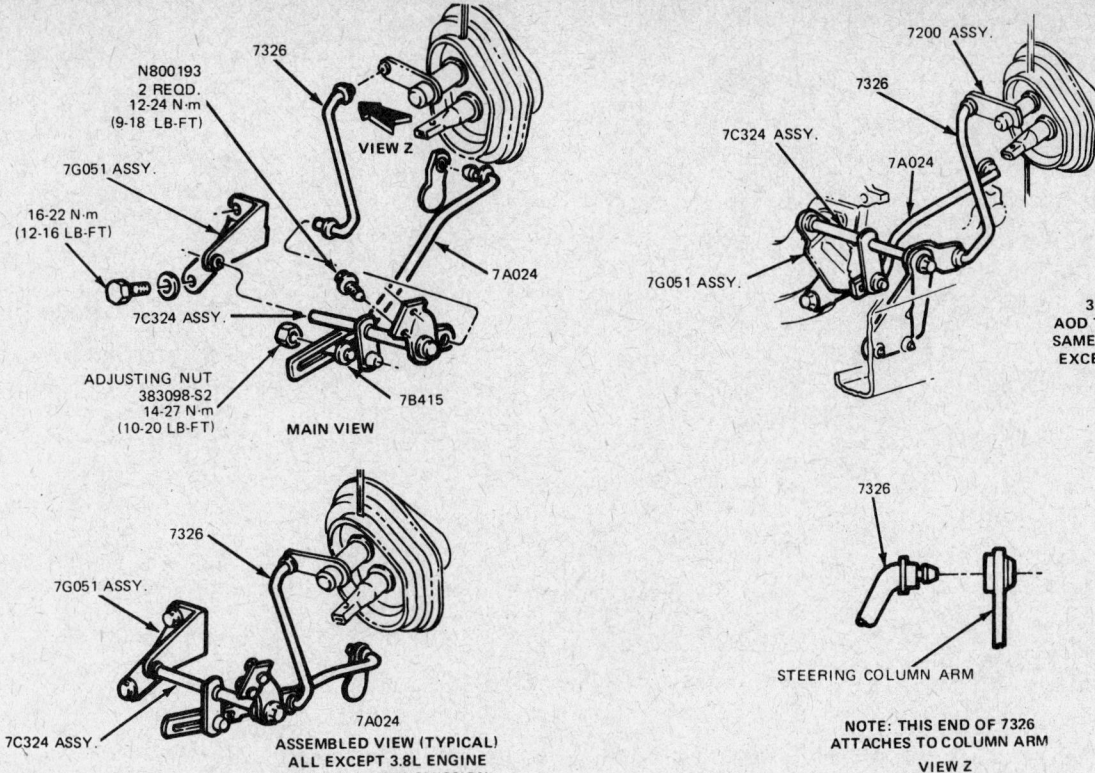

Fig. 2 Manual linkage. 1980—82 Cougar, XR-7, 1980—83 Thunderbird, 1982—83 Continental, 1983 Cougar, LTD & Marquis

Interference Preventing Return of TV Control Rod

1. Delayed or harsh upshifts.
2. Harsh idle engagement.

Binding Grommets Preventing TV Linkage Return

1. Delayed or harsh upshifts.
2. Harsh idle engagement.

TV Control Rod Disconnected

1. Delayed or harsh upshifts.
2. Harsh idle engagement.

Clamping Bolt on Trunnion at Lower End of TV Control Rod Loose.

1. Delayed or harsh upshifts.
2. Harsh idle engagement.

Linkage Lever Return Spring Broken or Disconnected.

1. Delayed or harsh upshifts.
2. Harsh idle engagements.

MAINTENANCE

Checking Oil Level

1. With transmission at operating tempera-

ture, park vehicle on level surface.
2. Operate engine at idle speed with parking brake applied and move selector lever through each detent position. Return selector lever to Park.
3. With engine idling, remove dipstick and check fluid level. Fluid level should be between arrows on dipstick.
4. Add fluid as necessary to bring fluid to proper level. Use only fluid meeting Ford Qualification No. M2C-138-CJ or Dexron II.

MANUAL LINKAGE, ADJUST

1. Position selector lever against D detent stop. It is recommended that an 8 pound weight be suspended from the selector lever to hold the lever against the D stop.
2. Position transmission lever in D detent. The D detent is the third detent from the front of the transmission.
3. Tighten adjusting nut, Figs. 2, 3 and 3A, and check transmission for proper operation.

THROTTLE VALVE LINKAGE, ADJUST

At Transmission

1. Position screw at linkage lever at midpoint, ensure that throttle is against idle stop. Set parking brake and place transmission lever in Neutral.
2. Loosen bolt on control rod trunnion block, Fig. 4. Clean rod and trunnion so that

trunnion slides freely on rod.
3. Push up on lower end of rod to ensure that carburetor linkage lever is held firmly against throttle lever.
4. Release rod and check to ensure that rod stays in position.
5. Push transmission lever against its internal stop and tighten bolt on trunnion.
6. Check to ensure throttle lever is against idle stop.

At Carburetor

1. Position throttle lever at idle stop, place shift lever in neutral and set parking brake (engine off).
2. Turn linkage lever adjusting screw counterclockwise until end of screw is flush with throttle lever face.
3. Turn adjusting screw clockwise to provide .005 inch clearance between end of screw and throttle lever. Continue turning adjusting screw an additional three turns. If screw travel is limited, one turn is acceptable.
4. If adjusting screw cannot be turned at least one turn, refer to the "At Transmission" procedure.

NOTE: Whenever idle speed is adjusted by more than 50 RPM, the adjustment screw on the linkage lever at the carburetor should also be adjusted as listed in the "Idle Speed/Throttle Valve Linkage Adjustment Chart", Fig. 2A. If idle speed was adjusted, ensure that .005 inch clearance exists between linkage lever adjusting screw and the throttle lever. The throttle lever should be at the idle stop and the shift lever in Neutral.

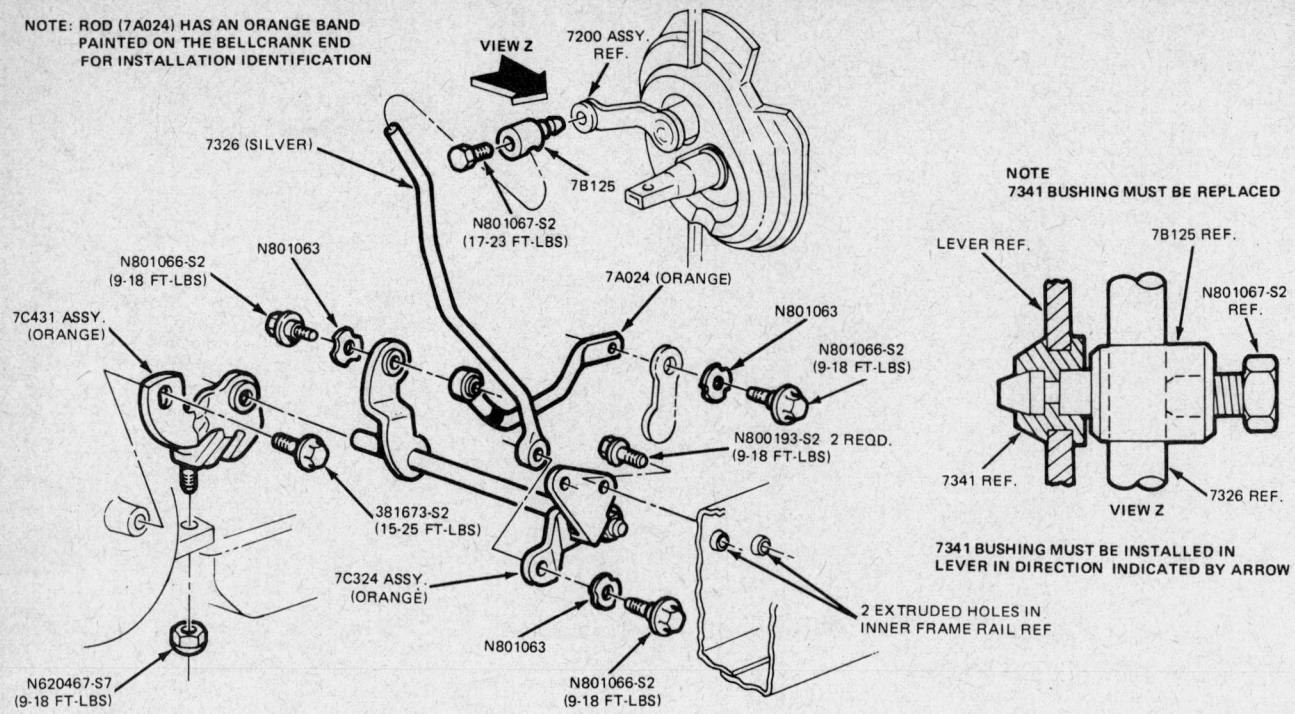

NOTE: ROD (7A024) HAS AN ORANGE BAND PAINTED ON THE BELLCRANK END FOR INSTALLATION IDENTIFICATION

NOTE
7341 BUSHING MUST BE REPLACED

7341 BUSHING MUST BE INSTALLED IN LEVER IN DIRECTION INDICATED BY ARROW

Fig. 3   Manual linkage. 1980 Lincoln Continental & 1980–81 Ford, Mercury, & Mark VI

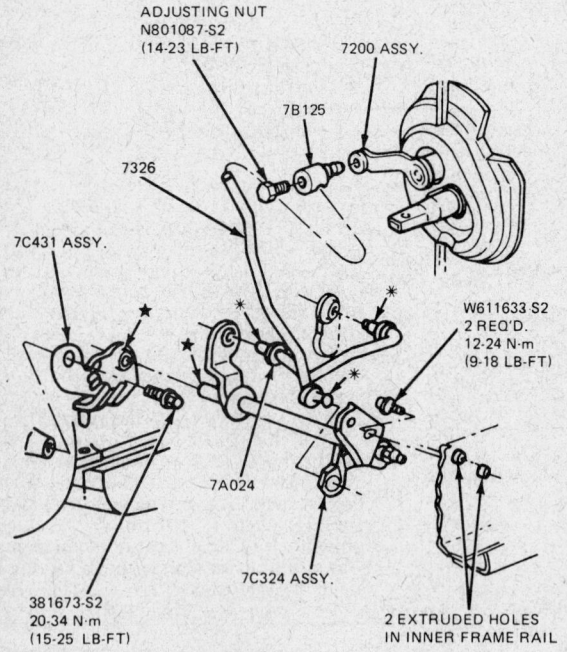

* LUBRICATE WITH ESE-M2C96-E ENGINE OIL
★ LUBRICATE I.D. OF BEARING LIBERALLY WITH ESA-MIC75-B

Fig. 3A   Manual Linkage. 1982–83 Ford, Lincoln Town Car, Mark VI & Mercury

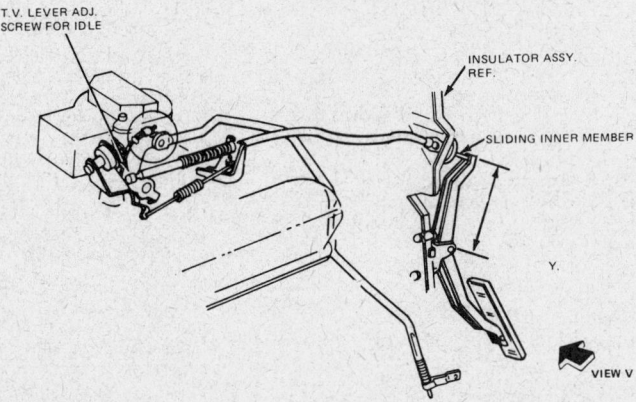

Fig. 4   Throttle valve linkage adjustment

Change on Linkage Lever Adj. Screw	Idle Speed Change
No change.	Less than 50 RPM
1½ turns counterclockwise	50–100 RPM increase
1½ turns clockwise	50–100 RPM decrease
2½ turns counterclockwise	100–150 RPM increase
2½ turns clockwise	100–150 RPM decrease

Fig. 4A   Idle Speed/Throttle Valve Linkage Adjustment Chart

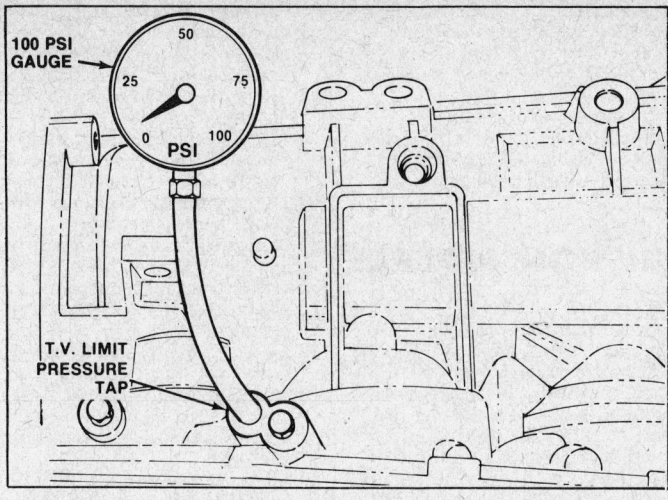

Fig. 5   Gauge connections to throttle valve pressure tap

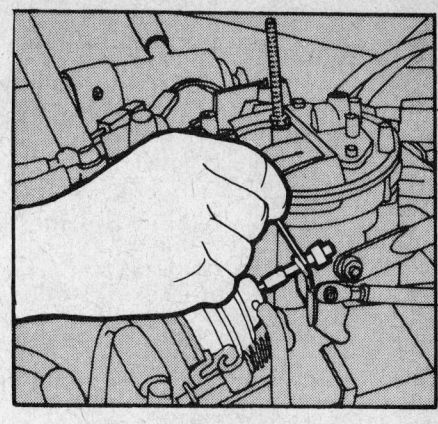

Fig. 6   Positioning throttle lever

THROTTLE VALVE PRESSURE ADJUSTMENT

1. Connect an 0-100 psi pressure gauge to throttle valve limit pressure tap, Fig. 5. Use a gauge hose long enough so that gauge can be viewed from under hood.
2. Check to ensure that throttle lever is against idle stop. Operate engine at idle speed in Neutral with parking brake applied.
3. Place a 1/16 inch drill between linkage lever adjusting screw and throttle lever, Fig. 6. Pressure gauge reading should be 5 psi or lower. If pressure gauge reading is above 5 psi linkage is set too long. Back linkage lever adjusting screw out as necessary to reduce pressure.
4. Remove 1/16 inch drill and insert a 5/16 inch drill. With engine idling in Neutral, pressure gauge reading should be at least 22 psi. If pressure gauge reading is below 22 psi, linkage is set too short. Turn linkage lever adjusting screw as necessary to bring pressure to 22 psi.

NOTE: If correct pressure cannot be obtained by turning linkage lever adjusting screw, it may be necessary to adjust control rod length at transmission.

IN-VEHICLE REPAIRS

Control Valve Body

1. Raise and support vehicle, drain transmission fluid, then remove transmission pan, gasket and filter.
2. Remove detent spring attaching bolt, then the spring.
3. Remove valve body to case attaching bolts, then the valve body.
4. Reverse procedure to install. Use suitable guide pins to align valve body to case.

Overdrive Servo Assembly

1. Remove valve body as previously described.
2. Compress overdrive servo piston cover with a suitable tool, then remove snap ring retainer.
3. Apply compressed air to servo piston release passage and remove the overdrive servo piston cover and spring. Remove piston from cover, then the rubber seal from piston and cover.
4. Install new servo piston and cover seals on the servo piston and cover.
5. Lubricate all seals, piston and piston bore with transmission fluid.
6. Install servo piston into cover, then the return spring into servo piston.
7. Install overdrive piston assembly into overdrive servo bore.
8. Compress overdrive piston using suitable tool, then install snap ring retainer.
9. Install valve body, filter, pan and gasket. Refill transmission to proper fluid level.

Reverse Servo Assembly

1. Refer to "Overdrive Servo Assembly" procedure for replacement. Apply compressed air to the servo piston release passage to remove servo piston from case.

NOTE: Reverse servo piston is under spring pressure. Use caution when removing servo piston cover.

3-4 Accumulator Piston

1. Remove valve body as previously described.
2. Compress 3-4 accumulator piston cover, then remove snap ring retainer.
3. Release cover slowly, then remove piston cover, return spring and piston. Some models do not use a spring.
4. Remove seal from 3-4 accumulator cover and piston and inspect for damage and wear.

5. Install new seals on 3-4 accumulator cover, if necessary. Lubricate cover pocket of case with transmission fluid.
6. Install 3-4 accumulator piston and return spring into case, then the cover.
7. Compress cover using suitable tool, then install snap ring. Ensure cover is reseated snugly against snap ring.
8. Install valve body, filter, pan and gasket. Refill transmission pan to proper fluid level.

2-3 Accumulator Piston

1. Refer to "3-4 Accumulator Piston" procedure for replacement.

Extension Housing

1. Raise and support vehicle.
2. Disconnect parking brake cable from equalizer, if necessary. On Lincoln Continental remove equalizer.
3. Disconnect drive shaft from rear axle flange, then remove drive shaft from transmission.
4. Disconnect speedometer cable from extension housing.
5. Remove engine rear support to extension housing attaching bolts. On Lincoln Continental, remove reinforcement plate.
6. Support transmission with suitable jack and raise transmission enough to remove weight from rear engine support.
7. Remove engine rear support from crossmember, then lower transmission and remove extension housing attaching bolts. Slide extension housing from output shaft and allow fluid to drain.
8. Reverse procedure to install.

Governor

1. Remove extension housing as described above.

NOTE: If governor body only is being removed, proceed to step 4.

2. Remove governor to output shaft retaining snap ring.
3. Remove governor assembly from output shaft using suitable tool. Remove governor driveball.
4. Remove governor to counterweight attaching screws. Remove governor from counterweight.
5. Reverse procedure to install.

Internal & External Shift Linkage

1. Raise and support vehicle.
2. Drain transmission fluid from pan, then remove pan and gasket.
3. Disconnect shift rod at transmission manual lever, then the throttle valve linkage at transmission, Figs. 3 and 4.
4. Disconnect inner throttle lever spring. Remove detent spring.
5. Hold outer throttle lever, then loosen outer throttle lever attaching nut. Remove attaching nut and lock washer.
6. Remove outer throttle lever seal, then the manual lever roll pin.

7. Remove outer manual lever attaching bolt, then the outer manual lever.
8. Remove inner throttle lever and spring.
9. Remove inner manual lever and park pawl actuating rod.
10. Remove manual lever oil seal.
11. Reverse procedure to install. Adjust transmission manual linkage and throttle linkage as outlined previously.

TRANSMISSION, REPLACE

1. Raise and support vehicle.
2. Drain transmission fluid from pan. After fluid is drained, install pan.
3. Remove converter access cover from lower end of converter housing. Rotate engine to gain access to converter drain plug. Remove drain plug, drain fluid from converter, then replace drain plug.
4. Remove converter to flywheel attaching nuts, then the driveshaft from vehicle.
5. Disconnect battery cable from starter motor, then remove starter motor. Disconnect neutral start switch electrical connector.
6. Remove rear mount to crossmember bolts and crossmember to frame bolts.
7. Remove engine rear support to extension housing bolts.
8. Disconnect manual linkage from transmission, then remove bolts securing bellcrank bracket to convertor housing.
9. Raise transmission with suitable jack and remove crossmember.
10. Lower transmission slightly and disconnect oil cooler lines and speedometer cable from transmission.
11. Remove filler tube and dipstick from transmission.
12. With transmission secured to jack, remove converter housing to cylinder block attaching bolts. Move transmission and converter assembly rearward, then lower transmission and remove from under vehicle.
13. Reverse procedure to install. On Lincoln Continental and Mark VI, align yellow balancing marks on converter and flywheel. Lubricate pilot.